Professional
ASP.NET 3.5
In C# and VB

Bill Evjen
Scott Hanselman
Devin Rader

Wiley Publishing, Inc.

Professional ASP.NET 3.5
In C# and VB

Published by
Wiley Publishing, Inc.
10475 Crosspoint Boulevard
Indianapolis, IN 46256
www.wiley.com

Published simultaneously in Canada

ISBN: 978-0-470-18757-9

Manufactured in the United States of America

10 9 8 7 6 5 4 3 2

Library of Congress Cataloging-in-Publication Data is available from the publisher.

For general information on our other products and services please contact our Customer Care Department within the United States at (800) 762-2974, outside the United States at (317) 572-3993 or fax (317) 572-4002.

Wiley also publishes its books in a variety of electronic formats. Some content that appears in print may not be available in electronic books.

Professional
ASP.NET 3.5
In C# and VB

Chapter 1: Application and Page Frameworks 1
Chapter 2: ASP.NET Server Controls and Client-Side Scripts 61
Chapter 3: ASP.NET Web Server Controls 103
Chapter 4: Validation Server Controls 185
Chapter 5: Working with Master Pages 219
Chapter 6: Themes and Skins 253
Chapter 7: Data Binding in ASP.NET 3.5 275
Chapter 8: Data Management with ADO.NET 361
Chapter 9: Querying with LINQ 437
Chapter 10: Working with XML and LINQ to XML 477
Chapter 11: IIS7 537
Chapter 12: Introduction to the Provider Model 567
Chapter 13: Extending the Provider Model 605
Chapter 14: Site Navigation 639
Chapter 15: Personalization 699
Chapter 16: Membership and Role Management 733
Chapter 17: Portal Frameworks and Web Parts 787
Chapter 18: HTML and CSS Design with ASP.NET 835
Chapter 19: ASP.NET AJAX 867
Chapter 20: ASP.NET AJAX Control Toolkit 901
Chapter 21: Security 965
Chapter 22: State Management 1003
Chapter 23: Caching 1039
Chapter 24: Debugging and Error Handling 1071
Chapter 25: File I/O and Streams 1107
Chapter 26: User and Server Controls 1159
Chapter 27: Modules and Handlers 1241
Chapter 28: Using Business Objects 1263
Chapter 29: Building and Consuming Services 1291
Chapter 30: Localization 1347
Chapter 31: Configuration 1373
Chapter 32: Instrumentation 1425
Chapter 33: Administration and Management 1463
Chapter 34: Packaging and Deploying ASP.NET Applications 1491
Appendix A: Migrating Older ASP.NET Projects 1525
Appendix B: ASP.NET Ultimate Tools 1541
Appendix C: Silverlight 1565
Appendix D: ASP.NET Online Resources 1585
Index 1587

About the Authors

Bill Evjen is an active proponent of .NET technologies and community-based learning initiatives for .NET. He has been actively involved with .NET since the first bits were released in 2000. In the same year, Bill founded the St. Louis .NET User Group (www.stlnet.org), one of the world's first such groups. Bill is also the founder and former executive director of the International .NET Association (www.ineta.org), which represents more than 500,000 members worldwide.

Based in St. Louis, Missouri, USA, Bill is an acclaimed author and speaker on ASP.NET and XML Web Services. He has authored or co-authored more than fifteen books including *Professional C# 2008, Professional VB 2008, ASP.NET Professional Secrets, XML Web Services for ASP.NET*, and *Web Services Enhancements: Understanding the WSE for Enterprise Applications* (all published by Wiley Publishing, Inc.). In addition to writing, Bill is a speaker at numerous conferences, including DevConnections, VSLive, and TechEd. Along with these items, Bill works closely with Microsoft as a Microsoft Regional Director and an MVP.

Bill is the Technical Architect for Lipper (www.lipperweb.com), a wholly-owned subsidiary of Reuters, the international news and financial services company. He graduated from Western Washington University in Bellingham, Washington, with a Russian language degree. When he isn't tinkering on the computer, he can usually be found at his summer house in Toivakka, Finland. You can reach Bill at evjen@yahoo.com.

Scott Hanselman works for Microsoft as a Senior Program Manager in the Developer Division, aiming to spread the good word about developing software, most often on the Microsoft stack. Before this he worked in eFinance for 6+ years and before that he was a Principal Consultant at a Microsoft Partner for nearly 7 years. He was also involved in a few things like the MVP and RD programs and will speak about computers (and other passions) whenever someone will listen to him. He blogs at http://www.hanselman.com and podcasts at http://www.hanselminutes.com and contributes to http://www.asp.net, http://www.windowsclient.net, and http://www.silverlight.net.

Devin Rader is a Product Manager on the Infragistics Web Client team, responsible for leading the creation of Infragistics ASP.NET and Silverlight products. Devin is also an active proponent and member of the .NET developer community, being a co-founder of the St. Louis .NET User Group, an active member of the New Jersey .NET User Group, a former board member of the International .NET Association (INETA), and a regular speaker at user groups. He is also a contributing author on the Wrox title *Silverlight* 1.0 and a technical editor for several other Wrox publications, and has written columns for ASP.NET Pro magazine, as well as .NET technology articles for MSDN Online. You can find more of Devin's musings at www.geekswithblogs.com/devin.

Credits

Acquisitions Director
Jim Minatel

Development Editors
Adaobi Obi Tulton
Sydney Jones

Technical Editors
Eric Engler
Alexei Gorkov
Doug Holland
Darren Kindberg
Mark Strawmeyr

Production Editor
Angela Smith

Copy Editors
Nancy Rapoport
Sydney Jones

Editorial Manager
Mary Beth Wakefield

Production Manager
Tim Tate

Vice President and Executive Group Publisher
Richard Swadley

Vice President and Executive Publisher
Joseph B. Wikert

Project Coordinator, Cover
Lynsey Stanford

Proofreader
Sossity Smith

Indexer
J & J Indexing

Acknowledgments

I have said it before, and I will say it again: Writing a book may seem like the greatest of solo endeavors, but it requires a large team of people working together to get technical books out the door-and this book is no exception. First and foremost, I would like to thank Jim Minatel of Wrox for giving me the opportunity to write the original ASP.NET book, which then led to this special edition. There is nothing better than getting the opportunity to write about your favorite topic for the world's best publisher!

Besides Jim, I worked with the book's development editor, Adaobi Obi Tulton. Adaobi kept the book moving along even with all the interruptions coming our way. Without Adaobi's efforts, this book would not have happened.

I worked closely with both Scott Hanselman and Devin Rader on this book, and these guys deserve a lot of thanks. I appreciate your help and advice throughout the process. Thanks guys!

I would also like to thank the various editors who worked on this book: Alexei Gorkov, Mark Strawmeyr, Darren Kindberg, Eric Engler, and Doug Holland. Big and ongoing thanks go to the Wrox/Wiley gang including Joe Wikert (publisher), Katie Mohr (acquisitions editor), and David Mayhew (marketing).

Finally, thanks to my entire family. Book writing is a devil in disguise as it is something that I love to do but at the same time, takes way too much time away from my family. Thanks to my family for putting up with this and for helping me get these books out the door. I love you all.

— Bill Evjen

Contents

Introduction xxxi

Chapter 1: Application and Page Frameworks 1

Application Location Options 1
Built-In Web Server 2
IIS 3
FTP 3
Web Site Requiring FrontPage Extensions 5
The ASP.NET Page Structure Options 5
Inline Coding 7
Code-Behind Model 9
ASP.NET 3.5 Page Directives 11
@Page 12
@Master 15
@Control 17
@Import 18
@Implements 20
@Register 20
@Assembly 21
@PreviousPageType 21
@MasterType 21
@OutputCache 22
@Reference 22
ASP.NET Page Events 23
Dealing with PostBacks 24
Cross-Page Posting 25
ASP.NET Application Folders 32
\App_Code Folder 32
\App_Data Folder 37
\App_Themes Folder 37
\App_GlobalResources Folder 38
\App_LocalResources 38
\App_WebReferences 38
\App_Browsers 38

Compilation **39**
Build Providers **43**
Using the Built-in Build Providers 44
Using Your Own Build Providers 45
Global.asax **50**
Working with Classes Through VS2008 **53**
Summary **59**

Chapter 2: ASP.NET Server Controls and Client-Side Scripts **61**

ASP.NET Server Controls **61**
Types of Server Controls 62
Building with Server Controls 63
Working with Server Control Events 65
Applying Styles to Server Controls **68**
Examining the Controls' Common Properties 68
Changing Styles Using Cascading Style Sheets 70
HTML Server Controls **73**
Looking at the HtmlControl Base Class 76
Looking at the HtmlContainerControl Class 77
Looking at All the HTML Classes 78
Using the HtmlGenericControl Class 79
Manipulating Pages and Server Controls with JavaScript **80**
Using Page.ClientScript.RegisterClientScriptBlock 82
Using Page.ClientScript.RegisterStartupScript 83
Using Page.ClientScript.RegisterClientScriptInclude 85
Client-Side Callback **86**
Comparing a Typical Postback to a Callback 86
Using the Callback Feature — A Simple Approach 87
Using the Callback Feature with a Single Parameter 92
Using the Callback Feature — A More Complex Example 95
Summary **101**

Chapter 3: ASP.NET Web Server Controls **103**

An Overview of Web Server Controls **103**
The Label Server Control **104**
The Literal Server Control **106**
The TextBox Server Control **107**
Using the Focus() Method 108
Using AutoPostBack 108
Using AutoCompleteType 110

The Button Server Control **111**
The CausesValidation Property 111
The CommandName Property 111
Buttons That Work with Client-Side JavaScript 112
The LinkButton Server Control **114**
The ImageButton Server Control **115**
The HyperLink Server Control **116**
The DropDownList Server Control **117**
Visually Removing Items from a Collection **119**
The ListBox Server Control **121**
Allowing Users to Select Multiple Items 121
An Example of Using the ListBox Control 122
Adding Items to a Collection 124
The CheckBox Server Control **124**
How to Determine Whether Check Boxes Are Checked 126
Assigning a Value to a Check Box 126
Aligning Text Around the Check Box 126
The CheckBoxList Server Control **127**
The RadioButton Server Control **129**
The RadioButtonList Server Control **131**
Image Server Control **132**
Table Server Control **134**
The Calendar Server Control **136**
Making a Date Selection from the Calendar Control 137
Choosing a Date Format to Output from the Calendar 138
Making Day, Week, or Month Selections 139
Working with Date Ranges 139
Modifying the Style and Behavior of Your Calendar 141
AdRotator Server Control **145**
The Xml Server Control **146**
Panel Server Control **147**
The PlaceHolder Server Control **150**
BulletedList Server Control **150**
HiddenField Server Control **155**
FileUpload Server Control **156**
Uploading Files Using the FileUpload Control 157
Giving ASP.NET Proper Permissions to Upload Files 160
Understanding File Size Limitations 161
Uploading Multiple Files from the Same Page 162
Placing the Uploaded File into a Stream Object 164
Moving File Contents from a Stream Object to a Byte Array 165

MultiView and View Server Controls **166**
Wizard Server Control **170**
Customizing the Side Navigation 171
Examining the AllowReturn Attribute 172
Working with the StepType Attribute 172
Adding a Header to the Wizard Control 173
Working with the Wizard's Navigation System 173
Utilizing Wizard Control Events 174
Using the Wizard Control to Show Form Elements 176
ImageMap Server Control **180**
Summary **182**

Chapter 4: Validation Server Controls **185**

Understanding Validation **185**
Client-Side versus Server-Side Validation **186**
ASP.NET Validation Server Controls **187**
Validation Causes 188
The RequiredFieldValidator Server Control 189
The CompareValidator Server Control 194
The RangeValidator Server Control 198
The RegularExpressionValidator Server Control 201
The CustomValidator Server Control 202
The ValidationSummary Server Control 208
Turning Off Client-Side Validation **211**
Using Images and Sounds for Error Notifications **212**
Working with Validation Groups **213**
Summary **217**

Chapter 5: Working with Master Pages **219**

Why Do You Need Master Pages? **219**
The Basics of Master Pages **221**
Coding a Master Page **223**
Coding a Content Page **225**
Mixing Page Types and Languages 229
Specifying Which Master Page to Use 231
Working with the Page Title 232
Working with Controls and Properties from the Master Page 233
Specifying Default Content in the Master Page **240**
Programmatically Assigning the Master Page **241**
Nesting Master Pages **243**
Container-Specific Master Pages **246**

Event Ordering **248**
Caching with Master Pages **248**
ASP.NET AJAX and Master Pages **249**
Summary **252**

Chapter 6: Themes and Skins 253

Using ASP.NET Themes **253**
Applying a Theme to a Single ASP.NET Page 253
Applying a Theme to an Entire Application 255
Removing Themes from Server Controls 256
Removing Themes from Web Pages 257
Understanding Themes When Using Master Pages 257
Understanding the StyleSheetTheme Attribute 258
Creating Your Own Themes **258**
Creating the Proper Folder Structure 258
Creating a Skin 259
Including CSS Files in Your Themes 261
Having Your Themes Include Images 264
Defining Multiple Skin Options **267**
Programmatically Working with Themes **269**
Assigning the Page's Theme Programmatically 269
Assigning a Control's SkinID Programmatically 270
Themes, Skins, and Custom Controls **270**
Summary **274**

Chapter 7: Data Binding in ASP.NET 3.5 275

Data Source Controls **275**
SqlDataSource Control 277
LINQ Data Source Control 289
AccessDataSource Control 294
XmlDataSource Control 294
ObjectDataSource Control 295
SiteMapDataSource Control 300
Configuring Data Source Control Caching **300**
Storing Connection Information **301**
Using Bound List Controls with Data Source Controls **304**
GridView 304
Editing GridView Row Data 320
Deleting GridView Data 327
DetailsView 330
Inserting, Updating, and Deleting Data Using DetailsView 335

ListView 336
FormView 345
Other Databound Controls 350
DropDownList, ListBox, RadioButtonList, and CheckBoxList 350
TreeView 350
Ad Rotator 351
Menu 351
Inline Data-Binding Syntax 352
Data-Binding Syntax Changes 353
XML Data Binding 353
Expressions and Expression Builders 354
Summary 359

Chapter 8: Data Management with ADO.NET 361

Basic ADO.NET Features 362
Common ADO.NET Tasks 362
Basic ADO.NET Namespaces and Classes 367
Using the Connection Object 368
Using the Command Object 370
Using the DataReader Object 371
Using Data Adapter 373
Using Parameters 376
Understanding DataSet and DataTable 379
Using Oracle as Your Database with ASP.NET 3.5 384
The DataList Server Control 387
Looking at the Available Templates 387
Working with ItemTemplate 388
Working with Other Layout Templates 390
Working with Multiple Columns 392
The ListView Server Control 393
Looking at the Available Templates 394
Using the Templates 394
Creating the Layout Template 396
Creating the ItemTemplate 398
Creating the EditItemTemplate 398
Creating the EmptyItemTemplate 399
Creating the InsertItemTemplate 399
The Results 400
Using Visual Studio for ADO.NET Tasks 402
Creating a Connection to the Data Source 402
Working with a Dataset Designer 404
Using the CustomerOrders DataSet 409

Asynchronous Command Execution **414**
Asynchronous Connections 435
Summary **435**

Chapter 9: Querying with LINQ **437**

LINQ to Objects **437**
Traditional Query Methods 437
Replacing Traditional Queries with LINQ 446
Data Grouping 453
Other LINQ Operators 454
LINQ Joins 455
Paging Using LINQ 457
LINQ to XML **458**
Joining XML Data 461
LINQ to SQL **462**
Insert, Update, and Delete Queries through LINQ 471
Extending LINQ 475
Summary **475**

Chapter 10: Working with XML and LINQ to XML **477**

The Basics of XML **478**
The XML InfoSet 480
XSD–XML Schema Definition 481
Editing XML and XML Schema in Visual Studio 2008 483
XmlReader and XmlWriter **486**
Using XDocument Rather Than XmlReader 488
Using Schema with XmlTextReader 489
Validating Against a Schema Using an XDocument 491
Including NameTable Optimization 493
Retrieving .NET CLR Types from XML 495
ReadSubtree and XmlSerialization 497
Creating CLR Objects from XML with LINQ to XML 498
Creating XML with XmlWriter 499
Creating XML with LINQ for XML 502
Improvements for XmlReader and XmlWriter in 2.0 504
XmlDocument and XPathDocument **505**
Problems with the DOM 505
XPath, the XPathDocument, and XmlDocument 505
DataSets **510**
Persisting DataSets to XML 510
XmlDataDocument 511

The XmlDataSource Control **513**
XSLT **517**
XslCompiledTransform 518
XSLT Debugging 523
Databases and XML **524**
FOR XML AUTO 524
SQL Server 2005 and the XML Data Type 528
Summary **535**

Chapter 11: IIS7 **537**

Modular Architecture of IIS7 **537**
IIS-WebServer 538
IIS-WebServerManagementTools 541
IIS-FTPPublishingService 542
Extensible Architecture of IIS7 **542**
IIS7 and ASP.NET Integrated Pipeline **542**
Building a Customized Web Server **544**
Update Dependencies 545
Installing IIS7 on Windows Vista 545
Installing IIS7 on Windows Server 2008 545
Command-Line Setup Options 546
Unattended Setup Option 548
Upgrade 548
Internet Information Services (IIS) Manager **549**
Application Pools 550
Web Sites 554
Hierarchical Configuration 555
Delegation 561
Moving an Application from IIS6 to IIS7 **564**
Summary **566**

Chapter 12: Introduction to the Provider Model **567**

Understanding the Provider **568**
The Provider Model in ASP.NET 3.5 **569**
Setting Up Your Provider to Work with Microsoft SQL Server 7.0, 2000, 2005, or 2008 571
Membership Providers 577
Role Providers 581
The Personalization Provider 585
The SiteMap Provider 586

SessionState Providers 588
Web Event Providers 590
Configuration Providers 598
The WebParts Provider 601
Configuring Providers **603**
Summary **604**

Chapter 13: Extending the Provider Model **605**

Providers Are One Tier in a Larger Architecture **605**
Modifying Through Attribute-Based Programming **606**
Simpler Password Structures Through the SqlMembershipProvider 607
Stronger Password Structures Through the SqlMembershipProvider 610
Examining ProviderBase **611**
Building Your Own Providers **613**
Creating the CustomProviders Application 613
Constructing the Class Skeleton Required 614
Creating the XML User Data Store 617
Defining the Provider Instance in the web.config File 618
Not Implementing Methods and Properties of the MembershipProvider Class 619
Implementing Methods and Properties of the MembershipProvider Class 620
Using the XmlMembershipProvider for User Login 628
Extending Pre-Existing Providers **629**
Limiting Role Capabilities with a New LimitedSqlRoleProvider Provider 630
Using the New LimitedSqlRoleProvider Provider 634
Summary **638**

Chapter 14: Site Navigation **639**

XML-Based Site Maps **640**
SiteMapPath Server Control **642**
The PathSeparator Property 644
The PathDirection Property 646
The ParentLevelsDisplayed Property 646
The ShowToolTips Property 647
The SiteMapPath Control's Child Elements 648
TreeView Server Control **648**
Identifying the TreeView Control's Built-In Styles 652
Examining the Parts of the TreeView Control 653
Binding the TreeView Control to an XML File 654
Selecting Multiple Options in a TreeView 656

Specifying Custom Icons in the TreeView Control 659
Specifying Lines Used to Connect Nodes 661
Working with the TreeView Control Programmatically 663

Menu Server Control **669**
Applying Different Styles to the Menu Control 670
Menu Events 675
Binding the Menu Control to an XML File 676

SiteMap Data Provider **678**
ShowStartingNode 678
StartFromCurrentNode 679
StartingNodeOffset 680
StartingNodeUrl 681

SiteMap API **681**
URL Mapping **684**
Sitemap Localization **685**
Structuring the Web.sitemap File for Localization 685
Making Modifications to the Web.config File 686
Creating Assembly Resource (.resx) Files 687
Testing the Results 687

Security Trimming **689**
Setting Up Role Management for Administrators 690
Setting Up the Administrators' Section 691
Enabling Security Trimming 692

Nesting SiteMap Files **694**
Summary **696**

Chapter 15: Personalization **699**

The Personalization Model **699**
Creating Personalization Properties **700**
Adding a Simple Personalization Property 701
Using Personalization Properties 702
Adding a Group of Personalization Properties 706
Using Grouped Personalization Properties 707
Defining Types for Personalization Properties 707
Using Custom Types 708
Providing Default Values 711
Making Personalization Properties Read-Only 711

Anonymous Personalization **711**
Enabling Anonymous Identification of the End User 711
Working with Anonymous Identification 714
Anonymous Options for Personalization Properties 715
Warnings about Anonymous User Profile Storage 716

Programmatic Access to Personalization **717**
Migrating Anonymous Users 717
Personalizing Profiles 718
Determining Whether to Continue with Automatic Saves 719
Personalization Providers **721**
Working with SQL Server Express Edition 721
Working with Microsoft's SQL Server 7.0/2000/2005/2008 722
Using Multiple Providers 724
Managing Application Profiles **725**
Properties of the ProfileManager Class 725
Methods of the ProfileManager Class 726
Building the ProfileManager.aspx Page 726
Examining the Code of ProfileManager.aspx Page 730
Running the ProfileManager.aspx Page 731
Summary **732**

Chapter 16: Membership and Role Management **733**

Authentication **734**
Authorization **734**
ASP.NET 3.5 Authentication **734**
Setting Up Your Web Site for Membership 734
Adding Users 737
Asking for Credentials 752
Working with Authenticated Users 760
Showing the Number of Users Online 762
Dealing with Passwords 764
ASP.NET 3.5 Authorization **769**
Using the LoginView Server Control 769
Setting Up Your Web Site for Role Management 771
Adding and Retrieving Application Roles 775
Deleting Roles 777
Adding Users to Roles 778
Getting All the Users of a Particular Role 779
Getting All the Roles of a Particular User 781
Removing Users from Roles 781
Checking Users in Roles 782
Understanding How Roles Are Cached 783
Using the Web Site Administration Tool **784**
Public Methods of the Membership API **784**
Public Methods of the Roles API **786**
Summary **786**

Chapter 17: Portal Frameworks and Web Parts 787

Introducing Web Parts 787
Building Dynamic and Modular Web Sites 789
Introducing the WebPartManager Control 789
Working with Zone Layouts 790
Understanding the WebPartZone Control 794
Allowing the User to Change the Mode of the Page 797
Modifying Zones 808
Working with Classes in the Portal Framework 814
Creating Custom Web Parts 818
Connecting Web Parts 824
Building the Provider Web Part 825
Building the Consumer Web Part 828
Connecting Web Parts on an ASP.NET Page 830
Understanding the Difficulties in Dealing with Master Pages When Connecting Web Parts 833
Summary 834

Chapter 18: HTML and CSS Design with ASP.NET 835

Caveats 836
HTML and CSS Overview 836
Introducing CSS 837
Creating Style Sheets 837
CSS Rules 840
CSS Inheritance 849
Element Layout and Positioning 850
Working with HTML and CSS in Visual Studio 857
ASP.NET 2.0 CSS–Friendly Control Adapters 864
Summary 865

Chapter 19: ASP.NET AJAX 867

Understanding the Need for AJAX 867
Before AJAX 868
AJAX Changes the Story 869
ASP.NET AJAX and Visual Studio 2008 871
Client-Side Technologies 872
Server-Side Technologies 873
Developing with ASP.NET AJAX 874
ASP.NET AJAX Applications 874
Building a Simple ASP.NET Page Without AJAX 876
Building a Simple ASP.NET Page with AJAX 877

ASP.NET AJAX's Server-Side Controls **883**
The ScriptManager Control 884
The ScriptManagerProxy Control 886
The Timer Control 887
The UpdatePanel Control 888
The UpdateProgress Control 892
Using Multiple UpdatePanel Controls **896**
Summary **899**

Chapter 20: ASP.NET AJAX Control Toolkit **901**

Downloading and Installing **901**
New Visual Studio Templates 902
Adding the New Controls to the VS2008 Toolbox 904
The ASP.NET AJAX Controls **904**
ASP.NET AJAX Control Toolkit Extenders 907
AlwaysVisibleControlExtender 908
AnimationExtender 910
AutoCompleteExtender 912
CalendarExtender 915
CollapsiblePanelExtender 916
ConfirmButtonExtender and ModalPopupExtender 918
DragPanelExtender 920
DropDownExtender 922
DropShadowExtender 924
DynamicPopulateExtender 926
FilteredTextBoxExtender 930
HoverMenuExtender 931
ListSearchExtender 933
MaskedEditExtender and MaskedEditValidator 934
MutuallyExclusiveCheckBoxExtender 937
NumericUpDownExtender 938
PagingBulletedListExtender 939
PopupControlExtender 941
ResizableControlExtender 942
RoundedCornersExtender 944
SliderExtender 946
SlideShowExtender 947
TextBoxWatermarkExtender 950
ToggleButtonExtender 951
UpdatePanelAnimationExtender 953
ValidatorCalloutExtender 954

ASP.NET AJAX Control Toolkit Server Controls **955**
Accordion Control 955
NoBot Control 958
PasswordStrength Control 960
Rating Control 961
TabContainer Control 962
Summary **963**

Chapter 21: Security **965**

Authentication and Authorization **966**
Applying Authentication Measures **966**
The <authentication> Node 967
Windows-Based Authentication 968
Forms-Based Authentication 976
Passport Authentication 986
Authenticating Specific Files and Folders **986**
Programmatic Authorization **987**
Working with User.Identity 988
Working with User.IsInRole() 989
Pulling More Information with WindowsIdentity 990
Identity and Impersonation **993**
Securing Through IIS **995**
IP Address and Domain Name Restrictions 995
Working with File Extensions 996
Using the ASP.NET MMC Snap-In 999
Using the IIS 7.0 Manager 1000
Summary **1001**

Chapter 22: State Management **1003**

What Are Your Choices? **1004**
Understanding the Session Object in ASP.NET **1006**
Sessions and the Event Model 1006
Configuring Session State Management 1008
In-Process Session State 1008
Out-of-Process Session State 1016
SQL-Backed Session State 1022
Extending Session State with Other Providers 1024
Cookieless Session State 1026
Choosing the Correct Way to Maintain State 1028
The Application Object **1028**
QueryStrings **1029**

Cookies **1029**
PostBacks and Cross-Page PostBacks **1030**
Hidden Fields, ViewState, and ControlState **1032**
Using HttpContext.Current.Items for Very Short-Term Storage **1037**
Summary **1038**

Chapter 23: Caching **1039**

Caching **1039**
Output Caching 1039
Partial Page (UserControl) Caching 1042
Post-Cache Substitution 1043
HttpCachePolicy and Client-Side Caching 1046
Caching Programmatically **1048**
Data Caching Using the Cache Object 1048
Controlling the ASP.NET Cache 1049
Cache Dependencies 1049
Using the SQL Server Cache Dependency **1055**
Enabling Databases for SQL Server Cache Invalidation 1056
Enabling Tables for SQL Server Cache Invalidation 1056
Looking at SQL Server 2000 1057
Looking at the Tables That Are Enabled 1058
Disabling a Table for SQL Server Cache Invalidation 1058
Disabling a Database for SQL Server Cache Invalidation 1059
SQL Server 2005 Cache Invalidation 1059
Configuring Your ASP.NET Application **1060**
Testing SQL Server Cache Invalidation **1062**
Adding More Than One Table to a Page 1064
Attaching SQL Server Cache Dependencies to the Request Object 1064
Attaching SQL Server Cache Dependencies to the Cache Object 1065
Summary **1069**

Chapter 24: Debugging and Error Handling **1071**

Design-Time Support **1071**
Syntax Notifications 1072
Immediate and Command Window 1074
Task List 1074
Tracing **1075**
System.Diagnostics.Trace and ASP.NET's Page.Trace 1076
Page-Level Tracing 1076
Application Tracing 1076
Viewing Trace Data 1077

Tracing from Components 1080
Trace Forwarding 1082
TraceListeners 1082
Diagnostic Switches 1087
Web Events 1088
Debugging 1090
What's Required 1090
IIS versus ASP.NET Development Server 1091
Starting a Debugging Session 1092
New Tools to Help You with Debugging 1096
Client-side Javascript Debugging 1098
SQL Stored Proc Debugging 1101
Exception and Error Handling 1101
Handling Exceptions on a Page 1102
Handling Application Exceptions 1103
Http Status Codes 1104
Summary 1105

Chapter 25: File I/O and Streams 1107

Working with Drives, Directories, and Files 1108
The DriveInfo Class 1108
The Directory and DirectoryInfo Classes 1111
File and FileInfo 1117
Working with Paths 1122
File and Directory Properties, Attributes, and Access Control Lists 1126
Reading and Writing Files 1133
Streams 1134
Readers and Writers 1138
Compressing Streams 1143
Working with Serial Ports 1148
Network Communications 1149
WebRequest and WebResponse 1149
Sending Mail 1156
Summary 1156

Chapter 26: User and Server Controls 1159

User Controls 1160
Creating User Controls 1160
Interacting with User Controls 1162
Loading User Controls Dynamically 1164

Server Controls **1169**
WebControl Project Setup 1170
Control Attributes 1175
Control Rendering 1176
Adding Tag Attributes 1181
Styling HTML 1183
Themes and Skins 1186
Adding Client-Side Features 1187
Detecting and Reacting to Browser Capabilities 1196
Using ViewState 1199
Raising PostBack Events 1203
Handling PostBack Data 1207
Composite Controls 1209
Templated Controls 1212
Creating Control Design-Time Experiences 1219
Summary **1239**

Chapter 27: Modules and Handlers 1241

Processing HTTP Requests **1241**
IIS 5/6 and ASP.NET 1241
IIS 7 and ASP.NET 1242
ASP.NET Request Processing 1243
HttpModules **1244**
HttpHandlers 1254
Summary **1261**

Chapter 28: Using Business Objects 1263

Using Business Objects in ASP.NET 3.5 **1263**
Creating Precompiled .NET Business Objects 1264
Using Precompiled Business Objects in Your ASP.NET Applications 1266
COM Interop: Using COM Within .NET **1268**
The Runtime Callable Wrapper 1268
Using COM Objects in ASP.NET Code 1269
Error Handling 1274
Deploying COM Components with .NET Applications 1277
Using .NET from Unmanaged Code **1279**
The COM-Callable Wrapper 1279
Using .NET Components Within COM Objects 1281
Early versus Late Binding 1285

Error Handling 1285
Deploying .NET Components with COM Applications 1287
Summary **1289**

Chapter 29: Building and Consuming Services **1291**

Communication Between Disparate Systems **1291**
Building a Simple XML Web Service **1293**
The WebService Page Directive 1294
Looking at the Base Web Service Class File 1295
Exposing Custom Datasets as SOAP 1296
The XML Web Service Interface 1299
Consuming a Simple XML Web Service **1302**
Adding a Web Reference 1302
Invoking the Web Service from the Client Application 1304
Transport Protocols for Web Services **1307**
HTTP-GET 1308
HTTP-POST 1311
SOAP 1311
Overloading WebMethods **1312**
Caching Web Service Responses **1315**
SOAP Headers **1316**
Building a Web Service with SOAP Headers 1317
Consuming a Web Service Using SOAP Headers 1319
Requesting Web Services Using SOAP 1.2 1321
Consuming Web Services Asynchronously **1323**
Windows Communication Foundation **1326**
The Larger Move to SOA 1326
WCF Overview 1327
Building a WCF Service 1327
Building the WCF Consumer **1335**
Adding a Service Reference 1336
Working with Data Contracts 1339
Namespaces 1344
Summary **1344**

Chapter 30: Localization **1347**

Cultures and Regions **1347**
Understanding Culture Types 1348
The ASP.NET Threads 1349
Server-Side Culture Declarations 1352
Client-Side Culture Declarations 1353
Translating Values and Behaviors 1355

ASP.NET 3.5 Resource Files **1362**
Making Use of Local Resources 1362
Making Use of Global Resources 1369
Looking at the Resource Editor **1370**
Summary **1372**

Chapter 31: Configuration **1373**

Configuration Overview **1374**
Server Configuration Files 1375
Application Configuration File 1377
How Configuration Settings Are Applied 1378
Detecting Configuration File Changes 1379
Configuration File Format 1379
Common Configuration Settings **1380**
Connecting Strings 1380
Configuring Session State 1381
Compilation Configuration 1385
Browser Capabilities 1387
Custom Errors 1389
Authentication 1390
Anonymous Identity 1393
Authorization 1394
Locking-Down Configuration Settings 1396
ASP.NET Page Configuration 1397
Include Files 1399
Configuring ASP.NET Runtime Settings 1399
Configuring the ASP.NET Worker Process 1402
Storing Application-Specific Settings 1404
Programming Configuration Files 1405
Protecting Configuration Settings 1412
Editing Configuration Files 1416
Creating Custom Sections **1417**
Using the NameValueFileSectionHandler Object 1418
Using the DictionarySectionHandler Object 1420
Using the SingleTagSectionHandler Object 1421
Using Your Own Custom Configuration Handler 1422
Summary **1424**

Chapter 32: Instrumentation **1425**

Working with the Event Log **1425**
Reading from the Event Log 1426
Writing to the Event Logs 1428

Using Performance Counters **1430**
Viewing Performance Counters Through an Administration Tool 1431
Building a Browser-Based Administrative Tool 1434
Application Tracing **1439**
Understanding Health Monitoring **1439**
The Health Monitoring Provider Model 1441
Health Monitoring Configuration 1442
Writing Events via Configuration: Running the Example 1449
Routing Events to SQL Server 1450
Buffering Web Events 1453
E-mailing Web Events 1456
Summary **1461**

Chapter 33: Administration and Management **1463**

The ASP.NET Web Site Administration Tool **1463**
The Home Tab 1465
The Security Tab 1465
The Application Tab 1474
The Provider Tab 1477
Configuring ASP.NET in IIS on Vista **1479**
.NET Compilation 1481
.NET Globalization 1482
.NET Profile 1482
.NET Roles 1483
.NET Trust Levels 1484
.NET Users 1484
Application Settings 1485
Connection Strings 1486
Pages and Controls 1486
Providers 1487
Session State 1487
SMTP E-mail 1489
Summary **1489**

Chapter 34: Packaging and Deploying ASP.NET Applications **1491**

Deployment Pieces **1492**
Steps to Take before Deploying **1492**
Methods of Deploying Web Applications **1493**
Using XCopy 1493
Using the VS Copy Web Site Option 1496

Deploying a Precompiled Web Application 1499
Building an Installer Program 1501
Looking More Closely at Installer Options 1510
Working with the Deployment Project Properties 1510
The File System Editor 1514
The Registry Editor 1518
The File Types Editor 1519
The User Interface Editor 1520
The Custom Actions Editor 1522
The Launch Conditions Editor 1523
Summary 1524

Appendix A: Migrating Older ASP.NET Projects 1525

Migrating Is Not Difficult 1525
Running Multiple Versions of the Framework Side by Side 1526
Upgrading Your ASP.NET Applications 1526
When Mixing Versions — Forms Authentication 1528
Upgrading — ASP.NET Reserved Folders 1529
ASP.NET 3.5 Pages Come as XHTML 1529
No Hard-Coded .js Files in ASP.NET 3.5 1531
Converting ASP.NET 1.x Applications in Visual Studio 2008 1532
Migrating from ASP.NET 2.0 to 3.5 1537

Appendix B: ASP.NET Ultimate Tools 1541

Debugging Made Easier 1541
Firebug 1542
YSlow 1543
IE WebDeveloper Toolbar and Firefox WebDeveloper 1544
Aptana Studio — Javascript IDE 1545
Profilers: dotTrace or ANTS 1546
References 1548
PositionIsEverything.net, QuirksMode.org, and HTMLDog.com 1548
Visibone 1549
www.asp.net 1549
Tidying Up Your Code 1550
Refactor! for ASP.NET from Devexpress 1550
Code Style Enforcer 1551
Packer for .NET — Javascript Minimizer 1552
Visual Studio Add-ins 1553
ASPX Edit Helper Add-In for Visual Studio 1553
Power Toys Pack Installer 1554

Extending ASP.NET **1555**
ASP.NET AJAX Control Toolkit 1555
Atif Aziz's ELMAH — Error Logging Modules and Handlers 1556
Helicon's ISAPI_Rewrite 1557
General Purpose Developer Tools **1558**
Telerik's Online Code Converter 1558
WinMerge and Differencing Tools 1559
Reflector 1560
CR_Documentor 1561
Process Explorer 1562
Summary **1563**

Appendix C: Silverlight **1565**

Extending ASP.NET Apps with Silverlight **1565**
Step 1: A Basic ASP.NET Application 1566
Finding Vector-Based Content 1568
Converting Vector Content to XAML 1569
Tools for Viewing and Editing XAML 1571
Integrating with Your Existing ASP.NET Site 1578
Receiving Silverlight Events in JavaScript 1581
Accessing Silverlight Elements from JavaScript Events 1583
Summary **1584**

Appendix D: ASP.NET Online Resources **1585**

Author Blogs **1585**
ASP.NET Influential Blogs **1585**
Web Sites **1586**

Index **1587**

Introduction

Simply put, you will find that ASP.NET 3.5 is an amazing technology to use to build your Web solutions! When ASP.NET 1.0 was introduced in 2000, many considered it a revolutionary leap forward in the area of Web application development. ASP.NET 2.0 was just as exciting and revolutionary and ASP.NET 3.5 is continuing a forward march in providing the best framework today in building applications for the Web. Although the foundation of ASP.NET was laid with the release of ASP.NET 1.0, ASP.NET 3.5 continues to build on this foundation by focusing on the area of developer productivity.

This book covers the whole of ASP.NET. It not only introduces new topics, it also shows you examples of these new technologies in action. So sit back, pull up that keyboard, and let's have some fun!

A Little Bit of History

Before organizations were even thinking about developing applications for the Internet, much of the application development focused on thick desktop applications. These thick-client applications were used for everything from home computing and gaming to office productivity and more. No end was in sight for the popularity of this application model.

During that time, Microsoft developers developed its thick-client applications using mainly Visual Basic (VB).

Visual Basic was not only a programming language; it was tied to an IDE that allowed for easy thick-client application development. In the Visual Basic model, developers could drop controls onto a form, set properties for these controls, and provide code behind them to manipulate the events of the control. For example, when an end user clicked a button on one of the Visual Basic forms, the code behind the form handled the event.

Then, in the mid-1990s, the Internet arrived on the scene. Microsoft was unable to move the Visual Basic model to the development of Internet-based applications. The Internet definitely had a lot of power, and right away, the problems facing the thick-client application model were revealed. Internet-based applications created a single instance of the application that everyone could access. Having one instance of an application meant that when the application was upgraded or patched, the changes made to this single instance were immediately available to each and every user visiting the application through a browser.

To participate in the Web application world, Microsoft developed Active Server Pages (ASP). ASP was a quick and easy way to develop Web pages. ASP pages consisted of a single page that contained a mix of markup and languages. The power of ASP was that you could include VBScript or JScript code instructions in the page executed on the Web server before the page was sent to the end user's Web browser. This was an easy way to create dynamic Web pages customized based on instructions dictated by the developer.

ASP used script between brackets and percentage signs — <% %> — to control server-side behaviors. A developer could then build an ASP page by starting with a set of static HTML. Any dynamic element needed by the page was defined using a scripting language (such as VBScript or JScript). When a user requested the page from the server by using a browser, the `asp.dll` (an ISAPI application that provided a bridge between the scripting language and the Web server) would take hold of the page and define all the dynamic aspects of the page on-the-fly based on the programming logic specified in the script. After all the dynamic aspects of the page were defined, the result was an HTML page output to the browser of the requesting client.

As the Web application model developed, more and more languages mixed in with the static HTML to help manipulate the behavior and look of the output page. Over time, such a large number of languages, scripts, and plain text could be placed in a typical ASP page that developers began to refer to pages that utilized these features as *spaghetti code*. For example, it was quite possible to have a page that used HTML, VBScript, JavaScript, Cascading Style Sheets, T-SQL, and more. In certain instances, it became a manageability nightmare.

ASP evolved and new versions were released. ASP 2.0 and 3.0 were popular because the technology made it relatively straightforward and easy to create Web pages. Their popularity was enhanced because they appeared in the late 1990s, just as the dotcom era was born. During this time, a mountain of new Web pages and portals were developed, and ASP was one of the leading technologies individuals and companies used to build them. Even today, you can still find a lot of `.asp` pages on the Internet — including some of Microsoft's own Web pages.

However, even at the time of the final release of Active Server Pages in late 1998, Microsoft employees Marc Anders and Scott Guthrie had other ideas. Their ideas generated what they called XSP (an abbreviation with no meaning) — a new way of creating Web applications in an object-oriented manner instead of the procedural manner of ASP 3.0. They showed their idea to many different groups within Microsoft, and they were well received. In the summer of 2000, the beta of what was then called ASP+ was released at Microsoft's Professional Developers Conference. The attendees eagerly started working with it. When the technology became available (with the final release of the .NET Framework 1.0), it was renamed ASP.NET — receiving the .NET moniker that most of Microsoft's new products were receiving at that time.

Before the introduction of .NET, the model that classic ASP provided and what developed in Visual Basic were so different that few VB developers also developed Web applications-and few Web application developers also developed the thick-client applications of the VB world. There was a great divide. ASP.NET bridged this gap. ASP.NET brought a Visual Basic–style eventing model to Web application development, providing much-needed state management techniques over stateless HTTP. Its model is much like the earlier Visual Basic model in that a developer can drag and drop a control onto a design surface or form, manipulate the control's properties, and even work with the code behind these controls to act on certain events that occur during their lifecycles. What ASP.NET created is really the best of both models, as you will see throughout this book.

I know you will enjoy working with this latest release of ASP.NET 3.5. Nothing is better than getting your hands on a new technology and seeing what is possible. The following section discusses the goals of ASP.NET so you can find out what to expect from this new offering!

The Goals of ASP.NET

ASP.NET 3.5 is another major release of the product and builds upon the core .NET Framework 2.0 with additional classes and capabilities. This release of the Framework was code-named *Orcas* internally at Microsoft. You might hear others referring to this release of ASP.NET as *ASP.NET Orcas*. ASP.NET 3.5 continues on a path to make ASP.NET developers the most productive developers in the Web space.

Ever since the release of ASP.NET 2.0, the Microsoft team has had goals focused around developer productivity, administration, and management, as well as performance and scalability.

Developer Productivity

Much of the focus of ASP.NET 3.5 is on productivity. Huge productivity gains were made with the release of ASP.NET 1.*x*; could it be possible to expand further on those gains?

One goal the development team had for ASP.NET was to eliminate much of the tedious coding that ASP.NET originally required and to make common ASP.NET tasks easier. The developer productivity capabilities are presented throughout this book. Before venturing into these capabilities, this introduction will first start by taking a look at the older ASP.NET 1.0 technology in order to make a comparison to ASP.NET 3.5. Listing I-1 provides an example of using ASP.NET 1.0 to build a table in a Web page that includes the capability to perform simple paging of the data provided.

Listing I-1: Showing data in a DataGrid server control with paging enabled (VB only)

```
<%@ Page Language="VB" AutoEventWireup="True" %>
<%@ Import Namespace="System.Data" %>
<%@ Import Namespace="System.Data.SqlClient" %>

<script runat="server">

    Private Sub Page_Load(ByVal sender As System.Object, _
      ByVal e As System.EventArgs)
        If Not Page.IsPostBack Then
            BindData()
        End If
    End Sub

    Private Sub BindData()
        Dim conn As SqlConnection = New SqlConnection("server='localhost';
           trusted_connection=true; Database='Northwind'")
        Dim cmd As SqlCommand = New SqlCommand("Select * From Customers", conn)
        conn.Open()

        Dim da As SqlDataAdapter = New SqlDataAdapter(cmd)
        Dim ds As New DataSet

        da.Fill(ds, "Customers")

        DataGrid1.DataSource = ds
        DataGrid1.DataBind()
    End Sub

    Private Sub DataGrid1_PageIndexChanged(ByVal source As Object, _
      ByVal e As System.Web.UI.WebControls.DataGridPageChangedEventArgs)
        DataGrid1.CurrentPageIndex = e.NewPageIndex
        BindData()
    End Sub

</script>
<html>
```

```
<head>
</head>
<body>
    <form runat="server">
        <asp:DataGrid id="DataGrid1" runat="server" AllowPaging="True"
         OnPageIndexChanged="DataGrid1_PageIndexChanged"></asp:DataGrid>
    </form>
</body>
</html>
```

Although quite a bit of code is used here, this is a dramatic improvement over the amount of code required to accomplish this task using classic Active Server Pages 3.0. We will not go into the details of this older code; we just want to demonstrate that in order to add any additional common functionality (such as paging) for the data shown in a table, the developer had to create custom code.

This is one area where the developer productivity gains are most evident. ASP.NET 3.5 provides a control called the GridView server control. This control is much like the DataGrid server control, but the GridView server control (besides offering many other additional features) contains the built-in capability to apply paging, sorting, and editing of data with relatively little work on your part. Listing I-2 shows you an example of the GridView server control. This example builds a table of data from the Customers table in the Northwind database that includes paging.

Listing I-2: Viewing a paged dataset with the new GridView server control

```
<%@ Page Language="VB" %>

<script runat="server">

</script>

<html xmlns=http://www.w3.org/1999/xhtml>
<head runat="server">
    <title>GridView Demo</title>
</head>
<body>
    <form runat="server">
        <asp:GridView ID="GridView1" Runat="server" AllowPaging="True"
         DataSourceId="Sqldatasource1" />
        <asp:SqlDataSource ID="SqlDataSource1" Runat="server"
         SelectCommand="Select * From Customers"
         ProviderName="System.Data.OleDb"
         ConnectionString="Provider=SQLOLEDB;Server=localhost;uid=sa;
         pwd=password;database=Northwind" />
    </form>
</body>
</html>
```

That's it! You can apply paging by using a couple of new server controls. You turn on this capability using a server control attribute, the `AllowPaging` attribute of the GridView control:

```
<asp:GridView ID="GridView1" Runat="server" AllowPaging="True"
DataSourceId="SqlDataSource1" />
```

The other interesting event occurs in the code section of the document:

```
<script runat="server">

</script>
```

These two lines of code are not actually needed to run the file. They are included here to make a point — *you don't need to write any server-side code to make this all work!* You have to include only some server controls: one control to get the data and one control to display the data. Then the controls are wired together.

Performance and Scalability

One of the highlights for ASP.NET that was set by the Microsoft team was to provide the world's fastest Web application server. This book also addresses a number of performance tactics available in ASP.NET 3.5.

One of the most exciting performance capabilities is the caching capability aimed at exploiting Microsoft's SQL Server. ASP.NET 3.5 includes a feature called *SQL cache invalidation*. Before ASP.NET 2.0, it was possible to cache the results that came from SQL Server and to update the cache based on a time interval — for example, every 15 seconds or so. This meant that the end user might see stale data if the result set changed sometime during that 15-second period.

In some cases, this time interval result set is unacceptable. In an ideal situation, the result set stored in the cache is destroyed if any underlying change occurs in the source from which the result set is retrieve — in this case, SQL Server. With ASP.NET 3.5, you can make this happen with the use of SQL cache invalidation. This means that when the result set from SQL Server changes, the output cache is triggered to change, and the end user always sees the latest result set. The data presented is never stale.

ASP.NET 3.5 provides 64-bit support. This means that you can run your ASP.NET applications on 64-bit Intel or AMD processors.

Because ASP.NET 3.5 is fully backward compatible with ASP.NET 1.0, 1.1 and 2.0, you can now take any former ASP.NET application, recompile the application on the .NET Framework 3.5, and run it on a 64-bit processor.

Additional Features of ASP.NET 3.5

You just learned some of the main goals of the ASP.NET team that built ASP.NET. To achieve these goals, the team built a mountain of features into each and every release of ASP.NET. A few of these features are described in the following sections.

New Developer Infrastructures

An exciting aspect of ASP.NET 3.5 is that there are infrastructures are in place for you to use in your applications. The ASP.NET team selected some of the most common programming operations performed with Web applications to be built directly into ASP.NET. This saves you considerable time and coding.

Membership and Role Management

Prior to ASP.NET 2.0, if you were developing a portal that required users to log in to the application to gain privileged access, invariably you had to create it yourself. It can be tricky to create applications with areas that are accessible only to select individuals.

You will find with ASP.NET 3.5, this capability is built in. You can validate users as shown in Listing I-3.

Listing I-3: Validating a user in code

VB

```
If (Membership.ValidateUser (Username.Text, Password.Text)) Then
   ' Allow access code here
End If
```

C#

```
if (Membership.ValidateUser (Username.Text, Password.Text)) {
   // Allow access code here
}
```

A series of APIs, controls, and providers in ASP.NET 3.5 enable you to control an application's user membership and role management. Using these APIs, you can easily manage users and their complex roles — creating, deleting, and editing them. You get all this capability by using the APIs or a built-in Web tool called the Web Site Administration Tool.

As far as storing users and their roles, ASP.NET 3.5 uses an `.mdf` file (the file type for the SQL Server Express Edition) for storing all users and roles. You are in no way limited to just this data store, however. You can expand everything offered to you by ASP.NET and build your own providers using whatever you fancy as a data store. For example, if you want to build your user store in LDAP or within an Oracle database, you can do so quite easily.

Personalization

One advanced feature that portals love to offer their membership base is the capability to personalize their offerings so that end users can make the site look and function however they want. The capability to personalize an application and store the personalization settings is completely built into the ASP.NET Framework.

Because personalization usually revolves around a user and possibly a role that this user participates in, the personalization architecture can be closely tied to the membership and role infrastructures. You have a couple of options for storing the created personalization settings. The capability to store these settings in either Microsoft Access or in SQL Server is built into ASP.NET 3.5. As with the capabilities of the membership and role APIs, you can use the flexible provider model, and then either change how the built-in provider uses the available data store or build your own custom data provider to work with a completely new data store. The personalization API also supports a union of data stores, meaning that you can use more than one data store if you want.

Because it is so easy to create a site for customization using these new APIs, this feature is quite a value-add for any application you build.

The ASP.NET Portal Framework

During the days of ASP.NET 1.0, developers could go to the ASP.NET team's site (found at `asp.net`) and download some Web application demos such as IBuySpy. These demos are known as Developer Solution

Kits and are used as the basis for many of the Web sites on the Internet today. Some were even extended into opensource frameworks such as DotNetNuke.

The nice thing about IBuySpy was that you could use the code it provided as a basis to build either a Web store or a portal. You simply took the base code as a starting point and extended it. For example, you could change the look and feel of the presentation part of the code or introduce advanced functionality into its modular architecture. Developer Solution Kits are quite popular because they make performing these types of operations so easy.

Because of the popularity of frameworks such as IBuySpy, ASP.NET 3.5 offers built-in capability for using Web Parts to easily build portals. The possibilities for what you can build using the Portal Framework is astounding. The power of building using Web Parts is that it easily enables end users to completely customize the portal for their own preferences.

Site Navigation

The ASP.NET team members realize that end users want to navigate through applications with ease. The mechanics to make this work in a logical manner are sometimes hard to code. The team solved the problem in ASP.NET with a series of navigation-based server controls.

First, you can build a site map for your application in an XML file that specific controls can inherently work from. Listing I-4 shows a sample site map file.

Listing I-4: An example of a site map file

```
<?xml version="1.0" encoding="utf-8" ?>

<siteMap xmlns="http://schemas.microsoft.com/AspNet/SiteMap-File-1.0">
   <siteMapNode title="Home" description="Home Page" url="default.aspx">
      <siteMapNode title="News" description="The Latest News" url="News.aspx">
         <siteMapNode title="U.S." description="U.S. News"
          url="News.aspx?cat=us" />
         <siteMapNode title="World" description="World News"
          url="News.aspx?cat=world" />
         <siteMapNode title="Technology" description="Technology News"
          url="News.aspx?cat=tech" />
         <siteMapNode title="Sports" description="Sports News"
          url="News.aspx?cat=sport" />
      </siteMapNode>
      <siteMapNode title="Finance" description="The Latest Financial Information"
        url="Finance.aspx">
         <siteMapNode title="Quotes" description="Get the Latest Quotes"
          url="Quotes.aspx" />
         <siteMapNode title="Markets" description="The Latest Market Information"
          url="Markets.aspx">
            <siteMapNode title="U.S. Market Report"
             description="Looking at the U.S. Market" url="MarketsUS.aspx" />
            <siteMapNode title="NYSE"
             description="The New York Stock Exchange" url="NYSE.aspx" />
         </siteMapNode>
         <siteMapNode title="Funds" description="Mutual Funds"
          url="Funds.aspx" />
```

```
        </siteMapNode>
        <siteMapNode title="Weather" description="The Latest Weather"
         url="Weather.aspx" />
    </siteMapNode>
</siteMap>
```

After you have a site map in place, you can use this file as the data source behind a couple of site navigation server controls, such as the TreeView and the SiteMapPath server controls. The TreeView server control enables you to place an expandable site navigation system in your application. Figure I-1 shows you an example of one of the many looks you can give the TreeView server control.

```
⊟ Home
   ⊟ News
         U.S.
         World
         Technology
         Sports
   ⊟ Finance
         Quotes
      ⊟ Markets
            U.S. Market Report
            NYSE
         Funds
      Weather
```

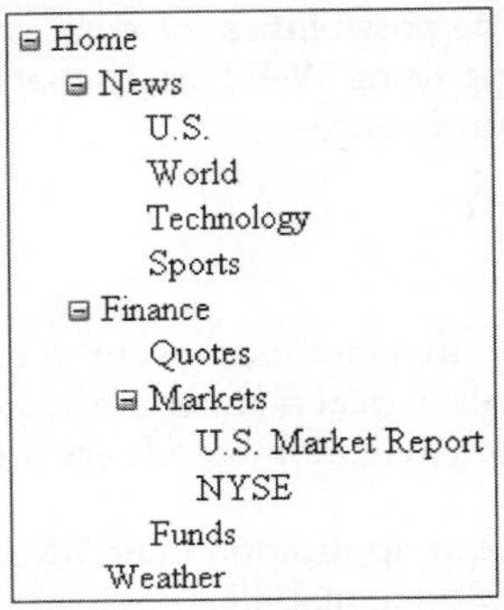

Figure I-1

SiteMapPath is a control that provides the capability to place what some call *breadcrumb navigation* in your application so that the end user can see the path that he has taken in the application and can easily navigate to higher levels in the tree. Figure I-2 shows you an example of the SiteMapPath server control at work.

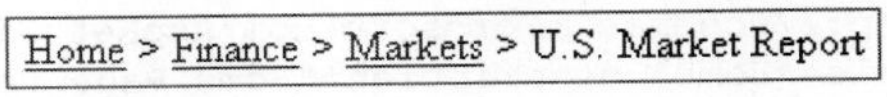

Home > Finance > Markets > U.S. Market Report

Figure I-2

These site navigation capabilities provide a great way to get programmatic access to the site layout and even to take into account things like end-user roles to determine which parts of the site to show.

The ASP.NET Compilation System

Compilation in ASP.NET 1.0 was always a tricky scenario. With ASP.NET 1.0, you could build an application's code-behind files using ASP.NET and Visual Studio, deploy it, and then watch as the `.aspx` files were compiled page by page as each page was requested. If you made any changes to the code-behind file in ASP.NET 1.0, it was not reflected in your application until the entire application was rebuilt. That meant that the same page-by-page request had to be done again before the entire application was recompiled.

Everything about how ASP.NET 1.0 worked with classes and compilation is different from how it is in ASP.NET 3.5. The mechanics of the compilation system actually begin with how a page is structured in ASP.NET 3.5. In ASP.NET 1.0, either you constructed your pages using the code-behind model or by placing all the server code inline between `<script>` tags on your `.aspx` page. Most pages were constructed using the code-behind model because this was the default when using Visual Studio .NET 2002 or 2003. It was quite difficult to create your page using the inline style in these IDEs. If you did, you were deprived of the use of IntelliSense, which can be quite the lifesaver when working with the tremendously large collection of classes that the .NET Framework offers.

ASP.NET 3.5 offers a different code-behind model than the 1.0/1.1 days because the .NET Framework 3.5 has the capability to work with *partial classes* (also called partial types). Upon compilation, the separate files are combined into a single offering. This gives you much cleaner code-behind pages. The code that was part of the `Web Form Designer Generated` section of your classes is separated from the code-behind classes that you create yourself. Contrast this with the ASP.NET 1.0 `.aspx` file's need to derive from its own code-behind file to represent a single logical page.

ASP.NET 3.5 applications can include a `\App_Code` directory where you place your class's source. Any class placed here is dynamically compiled and reflected in the application. You do not use a separate build process when you make changes as you did with ASP.NET 1.0. This is a *just save and hit* deployment model like the one in classic ASP 3.0. Visual Studio 2008 also automatically provides IntelliSense for any objects that are placed in the `\App_Code` directory, whether you are working with the code-behind model or are coding inline.

ASP.NET 3.5 also provides you with tools that enable you to precompile your ASP.NET applications — both `.aspx` pages and code behind — so that no page within your application has latency when it is retrieved for the first time. Doing this is also a great way to discover any errors in the pages without invoking every page. Precompiling your ASP.NET 2.0 applications is as simple as using `aspnet_compiler.exe` and employing some of the available flags. As you precompile your entire application, you also receive error notifications if any errors are found anywhere within it. Precompilation also enables you to deliver only the created assembly to the deployment server, thereby protecting your code from snooping, unwanted changes, and tampering after deployment. You see examples of these scenarios later in this book.

Health Monitoring for Your ASP.NET Applications

The built-in health monitoring capabilities are rather significant features designed to make it easier to manage a deployed ASP.NET application. Health monitoring provides what the term implies — the capability to monitor the health and performance of your deployed ASP.NET applications.

ASP.NET health monitoring is built around various health monitoring events (which are referred to as *Web events*) occurring in your application. Using the health monitoring system enables you to perform event logging for Web events such as failed logins, application starts and stops, or any unhandled exceptions. The event logging can occur in more than one place; therefore, you can log to the event log or even back to a database. In addition to performing this disk-based logging, you can also use the system to e-mail health-monitoring information.

Besides working with specific events in your application, you can also use the health monitoring system to take health snapshots of a running application. As you can with most systems that are built into ASP.NET 3.5, you are able to extend the health monitoring system and create your own events for recording application information.

Health monitoring is already enabled by default in the system `.config` files. The default setup for health monitoring logs all errors and failure audits to the event log. For instance, throwing an error in your application results in an error notification in the Application log.

You can change the default event logging behaviors simply by making some minor changes to your application's `web.config` file. For instance, suppose that you want to store this error event information in a SQL Express file contained within the application. This change can be made by adding a `<healthMonitoring>` node to your `web.config` file as presented in Listing I-5.

Listing I-5: Defining health monitoring in the web.config file

```
<healthMonitoring enabled="true">
   <providers>
      <clear />
      <add name="SqlWebEventProvider" connectionStringName="LocalSqlServer"
       maxEventDetailsLength="1073741823" buffer="false" bufferMode="Notification"
       type="System.Web.Management.SqlWebEventProvider,
          System.Web,Version=2.0.0.0,Culture=neutral,
          PublicKeyToken=b03f5f7f11d50a3a"/>
   </providers>
   <rules>
      <clear />
      <add name="All Errors Default" eventName="All Errors"
       provider="SqlWebEventProvider"
       profile="Default" minInstances="1" maxLimit="Infinite"
       minInterval="00:01:00" custom="" />
      <add name="Failure Audits Default" eventName="Failure Audits"
       provider="SqlWebEventProvider" profile="Default" minInstances="1"
       maxLimit="Infinite" minInterval="00:01:00" custom="" />
   </rules>
</healthMonitoring>
```

After this change, events are logged in the `ASPNETDB.MDF` file that is automatically created on your behalf if it does not already exist in your project.

Opening up this SQL Express file, you will find an `aspnet_WebEvent_Events` table where all this information is stored.

You will learn much more about the health monitoring capabilities provided with ASP.NET 3.5 in Chapter 32.

Reading and Writing Configuration Settings

Using the `WebConfigurationManager` class, you have the capability to read and write to the server or application configuration files. This means that you can write and read settings in the `machine.config` or the `web.config` files that your application uses.

The capability to read and write to configuration files is not limited to working with the local machine in which your application resides. You can also perform these operations on remote servers and applications.

Of course, a GUI-way exists in which you can perform these read or change operations on the configuration files at your disposal. The exciting thing, however, is that the built-in GUI tools that provide this functionality (such as the ASP.NET MMC snap-in when using Windows XP, or the new IIS interface if you are using Windows Vista) use the `WebConfigurationManager` class that is also available for building custom administration tools.

Listing I-6 shows an example of reading a connection string from an application's `Web.config` file.

Listing I-6: Reading a connection string from the application's Web.config file

VB

```
Protected Sub Page_Load(ByVal sender As Object, ByVal e As System.EventArgs)
   Try
      Dim connectionString As String = _
         ConfigurationManager.ConnectionStrings("Northwind").
            ConnectionString.ToString()
      Label1.Text = connectionString
   Catch ex As Exception
      Label1.Text = "No connection string found."
   End Try
End Sub
```

C#

```
protected void Page_Load(object sender, EventArgs e)
{
   try
   {
      string connectionString =
         ConfigurationManager.ConnectionStrings["Northwind"].
            ConnectionString.ToString();
      Label1.Text = connectionString;
   }
   catch (Exception)
   {
      Label1.Text = "No connection string found.";
   }
}
```

This little bit of code writes the Northwind connection string found in the `web.config` file to the screen using a Label control. As you can see, it is rather simple to grab items from the configuration file.

Localization

ASP.NET is making it easier to localize applications than ever before. In addition to using Visual Studio, you can create resource files (`.resx`) that allow you to dynamically change the pages you create based upon the culture settings of the requestor.

ASP.NET 3.5 provides the capability to provide resources application-wide or just to particular pages in your application through the use of two new application folders — `App_GlobalResources` and `App_LocalResources`.

The items defined in any `.resx` files you create are then accessible directly in the ASP.NET server controls or programmatically using expressions such as:

```
<%= Resources.Resource.Question %>
```

This system is straightforward and simple to implement. This topic is covered in greater detail in Chapter 30

Expanding on the Page Framework

ASP.NET pages can be built based upon visual inheritance. This was possible in the Windows Forms world, but it is something that is relatively new with ASP.NET. You also gain the capability to easily apply a consistent look and feel to the pages of your application by using themes. Many of the difficulties in working with ADO.NET is made easier through a series of data source controls that take care of accessing and retrieving data from a large collection of data stores.

Master Pages

With the capability of *master pages* in ASP.NET, you can use visual inheritance within your ASP.NET applications. Because many ASP.NET applications have a similar structure throughout their pages, it is logical to build a page template once and use that same template throughout the application.

In ASP.NET, you do this by creating a `.master` page, as shown in Figure I-3.

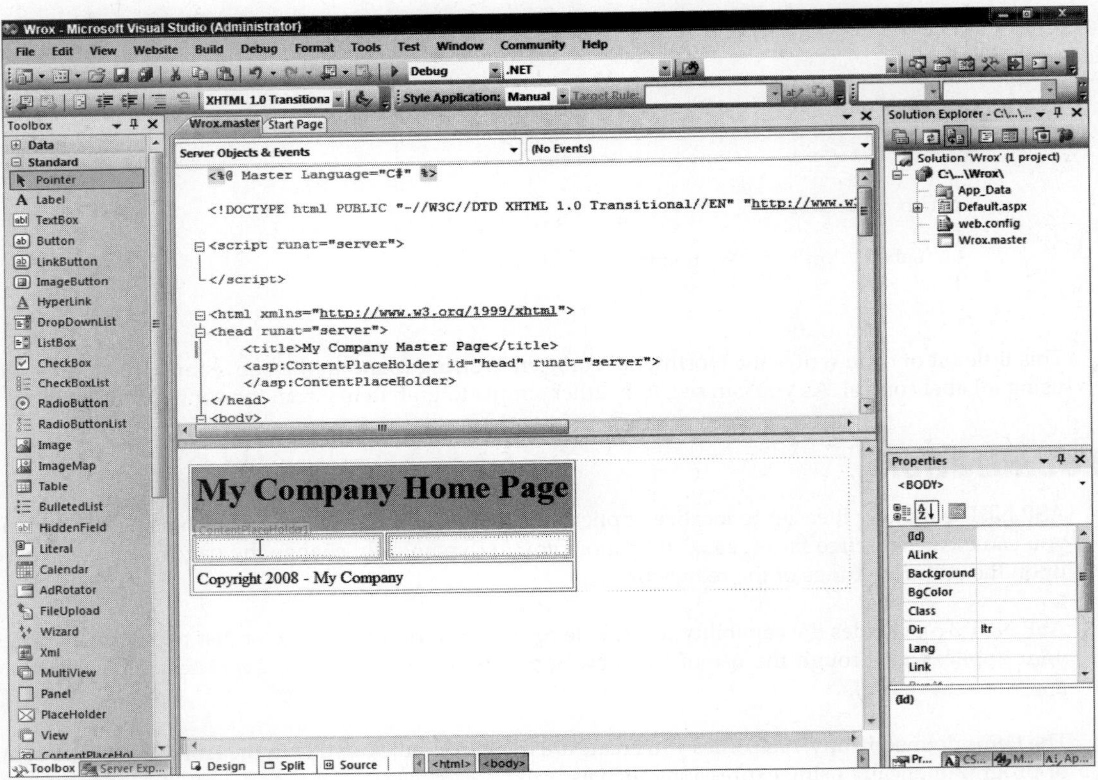

Figure I-3

An example master page might include a header, footer, and any other elements that all the pages can share. Besides these core elements, which you might want on every page that inherits and uses this template, you can place `<asp:ContentPlaceHolder>` server controls within the master page itself for the subpages (or content pages) to use in order to change specific regions of the master page template. The editing of the subpage is shown in Figure I-4.

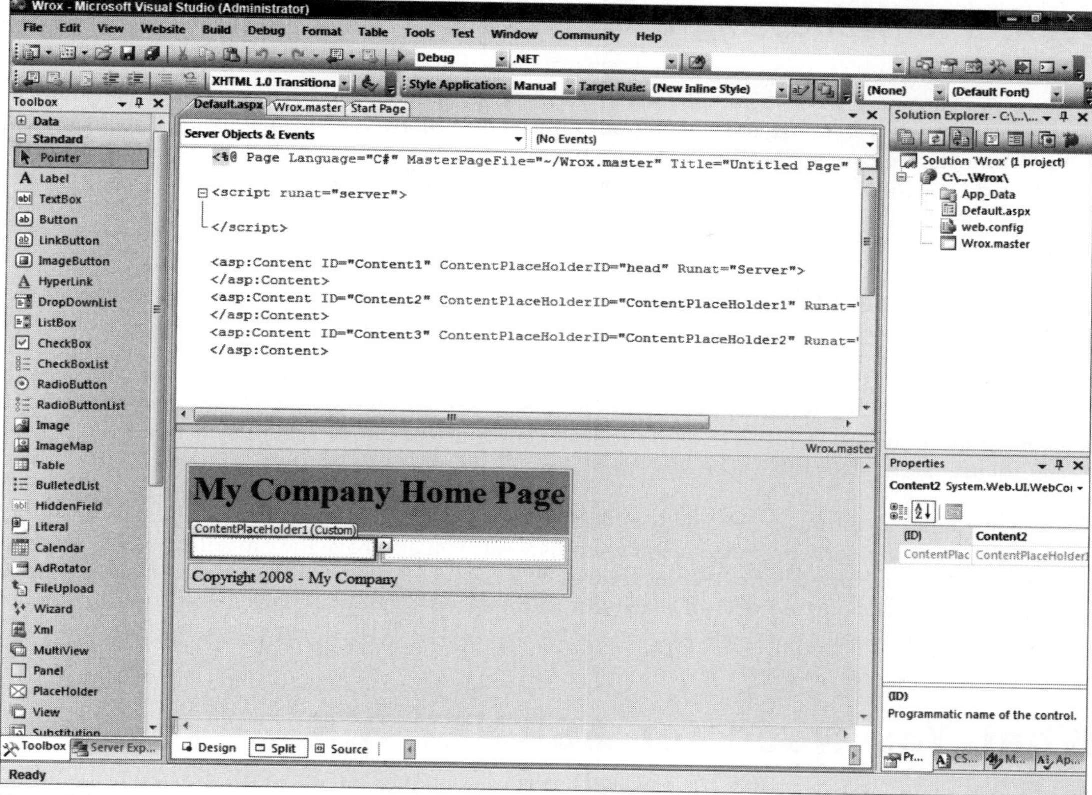

Figure I-4

When an end user invokes one of the subpages, he is actually looking at a single page compiled from both the subpage and the master page that the particular subpage inherited from. This also means that the server and client code from both pages are enabled on the new single page.

The nice thing about master pages is that you have a single place to make any changes that affect the entire site. This eliminates making changes to each and every page within an application.

Themes

The inclusion of themes in ASP.NET has made it quite simple to provide a consistent look and feel across your entire site. Themes are simple text files where you define the appearance of server controls that can be applied across the site, to a single page, or to a specific server control. You can also easily incorporate graphics and Cascading Style Sheets, in addition to server control definitions.

Themes are stored in the `/App_Theme` directory within the application root for use within that particular application. One cool capability of themes is that you can dynamically apply them based on settings that use the personalization service provided by ASP.NET. Each unique user of your portal or application can have her own personalized look and feel that she has chosen from your offerings.

Objects for Accessing Data

One of the more code-intensive tasks in ASP.NET 1.0 was the retrieval of data. In many cases, this meant working with a number of objects. If you have been working with ASP.NET for a while, you know that it was an involved process to display data from a Microsoft SQL Server table within a DataGrid server control. For instance, you first had to create a number of new objects. They included a `SqlConnection` object followed by a `SqlCommand` object. When those objects were in place, you then created a `SqlDataReader` to populate your DataGrid by binding the result to the DataGrid. In the end, a table appeared containing the contents of the data you were retrieving (such as the Customers table from the Northwind database).

ASP.NET today eliminates this intensive procedure with the introduction of a set of objects that work specifically with data access and retrieval. These new data controls are so easy to use that you access and retrieve data to populate your ASP.NET server controls without writing any code. You saw an example of this in Listing I-2, where an `<asp:SqlDataSource>` server control retrieved rows of data from the Customers table in the Northwind database from SQL Server. This SqlDataSource server control was then bound to the new GridView server control via the use of simple attributes within the GridView control itself. It really could not be any easier!

The great news about this functionality is that it is not limited to just Microsoft's SQL Server. In fact, several data source server controls are at your disposal. You also have the capability to create your own. In addition to the SqlDataSource server control, ASP.NET 3.5 includes the AccessDataSource, XmlDataSource, ObjectDataSource, SiteMapDataSource, and the new LinqDataSource server control. You use all these data controls later in this book.

What You Need for ASP.NET 3.5

You might find it best to install Visual Studio 2008 to work through the examples in this book; you can, however, just use Microsoft's Notepad and the command-line compilers that come with the .NET Framework 3.5. To work through *every* example in this book, you need the following:

- Windows Server 2003, Windows Server 2008, Windows 2000, Windows XP, or Windows Vista
- Visual Studio 2008 (this will install the .NET Framework 3.5)
- SQL Server 2000, 2005, or 2008
- Microsoft Access or SQL Server Express Edition

The nice thing is that you are not required to have Microsoft Internet Information Services (IIS) to work with ASP.NET 3.5 because ASP.NET includes a built-in Web server based on the previously released Microsoft Cassini technology. Moreover, if you do not have a full blown version of SQL Server, don't be alarmed. Many examples that use this database can be altered to work with Microsoft's SQL Server Express Edition, which you will find free on the Internet.

Who Should Read This Book?

This book was written to introduce you to the features and capabilities that ASP.NET 3.5 offers, as well as to give you an explanation of the foundation that ASP.NET provides. We assume you have a general understanding of Web technologies, such as previous versions of ASP.NET, Active Server Pages 2.0/3.0, or JavaServer Pages. If you understand the basics of Web programming, you should not have much trouble following along with this book's content.

If you are brand new to ASP.NET, be sure to check out *Beginning ASP.NET 3.5: In C# and VB* by Imar Spaanjaars (Wiley Publishing, Inc., 2008) to help you understand the basics.

In addition to working with Web technologies, we also assume that you understand basic programming constructs, such as variables, `For Each` loops, and object-oriented programming.

You may also be wondering whether this book is for the Visual Basic developer or the C# developer. We are happy to say that it is for both! When the code differs substantially, this book provides examples in both VB and C#.

What This Book Covers

This book spends its time reviewing the 3.5 release of ASP.NET. Each major new feature included in ASP.NET 3.5 is covered in detail. The following list tells you something about the content of each chapter.

- **Chapter 1, "Application and Page Frameworks."** The first chapter covers the frameworks of ASP.NET applications as well as the structure and frameworks provided for single ASP.NET pages. This chapter shows you how to build ASP.NET applications using IIS or the built-in Web server that comes with Visual Studio 2008. This chapter also shows you the folders and files that are part of ASP.NET. It discusses ways to compile code and shows you how to perform cross-page posting. This chapter ends by showing you easy ways to deal with your classes from within Visual Studio 2008.
- **Chapters 2, 3, and 4:** These three chapters are grouped here because they all deal with server controls. This batch of chapters starts by examining the idea of the server control and its pivotal role in ASP.NET development. In addition to looking at the server control framework, these chapters delve into the plethora of server controls that are at your disposal for ASP.NET development projects. Chapter 2, "ASP.NET Server Controls and Client-Side Scripts," looks at the basics of working with server controls. Chapter 3, "ASP.NET Web Server Controls," covers the controls that have been part of the ASP.NET technology since its initial release and the controls that have been added in each of the ASP.NET releases. Chapter 4, "Validation Server Controls," describes a special group of server controls: those for validation. You can use these controls to create beginning-to-advanced form validations.
- **Chapter 5, "Working with Master Pages."** Master pages are a great capability found in ASP.NET. They provide a means of creating templated pages that enable you to work with the entire application, as opposed to single pages. This chapter examines the creation of these templates and how to apply them to your content pages throughout an ASP.NET application.
- **Chapter 6, "Themes and Skins."** The Cascading Style Sheet files you are allowed to use in ASP.NET 1.0/1.1 are simply not adequate in many regards, especially in the area of server controls. When using these early versions, the developer can never be sure of the HTML output these files might generate. This chapter looks at how to deal with the styles that your applications require and shows you how to create a centrally managed look-and-feel for all the pages of your application by using themes and the skin files that are part of a theme.
- **Chapters 7, "Data Binding in ASP.NET 3.5."** One of the more important tasks of ASP.NET is presenting data, and this chapter shows you how to do that. ASP.NET provides a number of

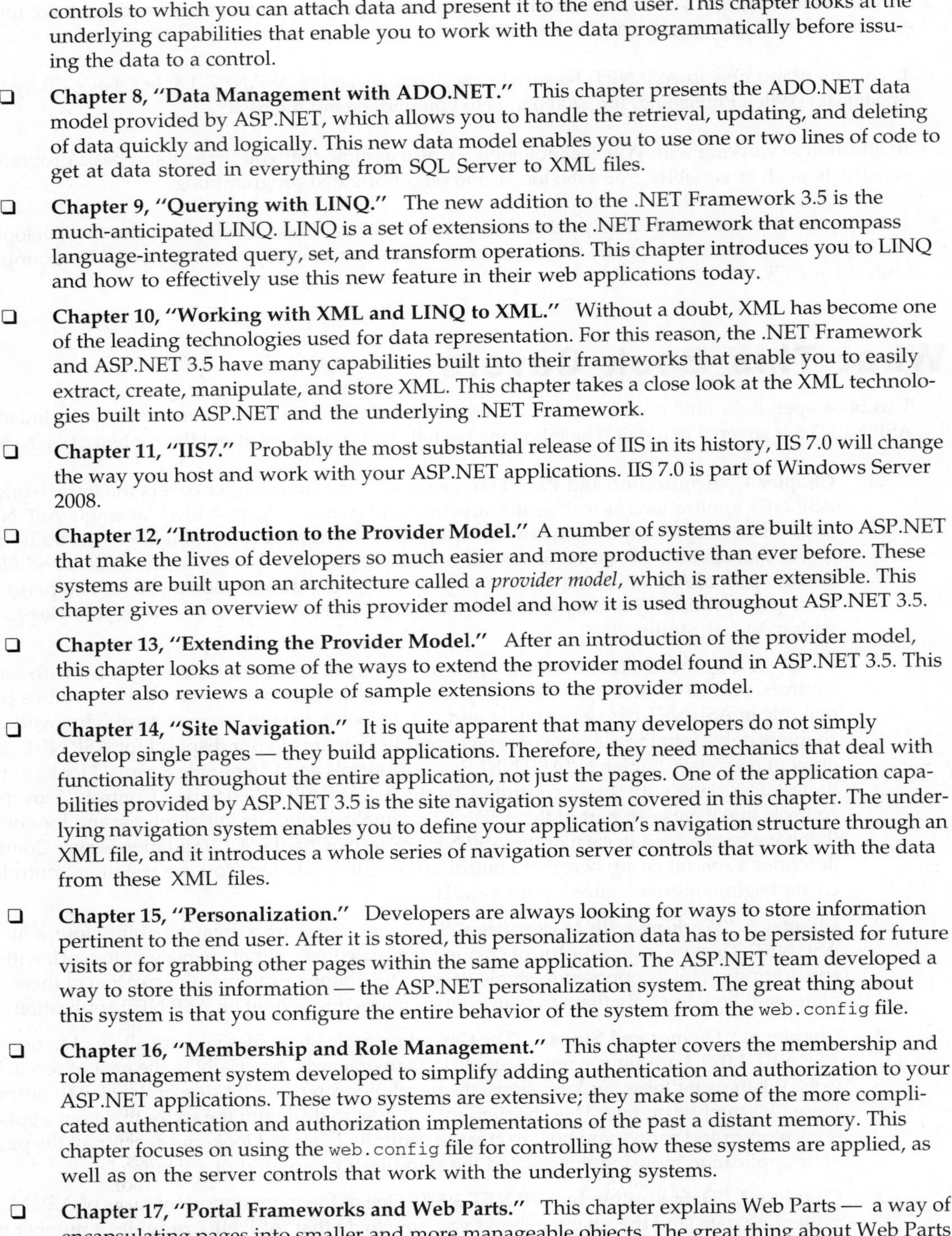

controls to which you can attach data and present it to the end user. This chapter looks at the underlying capabilities that enable you to work with the data programmatically before issuing the data to a control.

- **Chapter 8, "Data Management with ADO.NET."** This chapter presents the ADO.NET data model provided by ASP.NET, which allows you to handle the retrieval, updating, and deleting of data quickly and logically. This new data model enables you to use one or two lines of code to get at data stored in everything from SQL Server to XML files.
- **Chapter 9, "Querying with LINQ."** The new addition to the .NET Framework 3.5 is the much-anticipated LINQ. LINQ is a set of extensions to the .NET Framework that encompass language-integrated query, set, and transform operations. This chapter introduces you to LINQ and how to effectively use this new feature in their web applications today.
- **Chapter 10, "Working with XML and LINQ to XML."** Without a doubt, XML has become one of the leading technologies used for data representation. For this reason, the .NET Framework and ASP.NET 3.5 have many capabilities built into their frameworks that enable you to easily extract, create, manipulate, and store XML. This chapter takes a close look at the XML technologies built into ASP.NET and the underlying .NET Framework.
- **Chapter 11, "IIS7."** Probably the most substantial release of IIS in its history, IIS 7.0 will change the way you host and work with your ASP.NET applications. IIS 7.0 is part of Windows Server 2008.
- **Chapter 12, "Introduction to the Provider Model."** A number of systems are built into ASP.NET that make the lives of developers so much easier and more productive than ever before. These systems are built upon an architecture called a *provider model*, which is rather extensible. This chapter gives an overview of this provider model and how it is used throughout ASP.NET 3.5.
- **Chapter 13, "Extending the Provider Model."** After an introduction of the provider model, this chapter looks at some of the ways to extend the provider model found in ASP.NET 3.5. This chapter also reviews a couple of sample extensions to the provider model.
- **Chapter 14, "Site Navigation."** It is quite apparent that many developers do not simply develop single pages — they build applications. Therefore, they need mechanics that deal with functionality throughout the entire application, not just the pages. One of the application capabilities provided by ASP.NET 3.5 is the site navigation system covered in this chapter. The underlying navigation system enables you to define your application's navigation structure through an XML file, and it introduces a whole series of navigation server controls that work with the data from these XML files.
- **Chapter 15, "Personalization."** Developers are always looking for ways to store information pertinent to the end user. After it is stored, this personalization data has to be persisted for future visits or for grabbing other pages within the same application. The ASP.NET team developed a way to store this information — the ASP.NET personalization system. The great thing about this system is that you configure the entire behavior of the system from the `web.config` file.
- **Chapter 16, "Membership and Role Management."** This chapter covers the membership and role management system developed to simplify adding authentication and authorization to your ASP.NET applications. These two systems are extensive; they make some of the more complicated authentication and authorization implementations of the past a distant memory. This chapter focuses on using the `web.config` file for controlling how these systems are applied, as well as on the server controls that work with the underlying systems.
- **Chapter 17, "Portal Frameworks and Web Parts."** This chapter explains Web Parts — a way of encapsulating pages into smaller and more manageable objects. The great thing about Web Parts

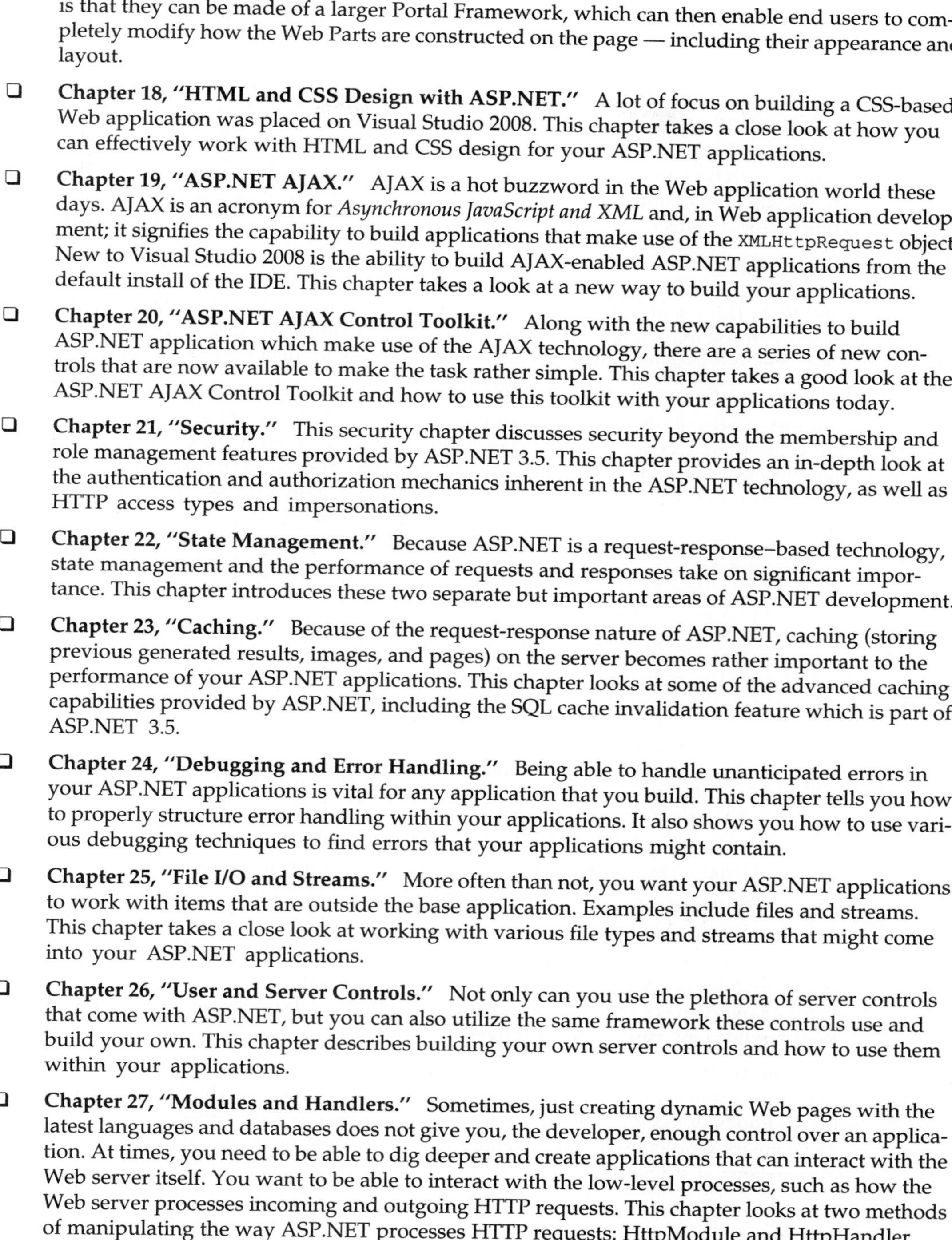

is that they can be made of a larger Portal Framework, which can then enable end users to completely modify how the Web Parts are constructed on the page — including their appearance and layout.

- **Chapter 18, "HTML and CSS Design with ASP.NET."** A lot of focus on building a CSS-based Web application was placed on Visual Studio 2008. This chapter takes a close look at how you can effectively work with HTML and CSS design for your ASP.NET applications.
- **Chapter 19, "ASP.NET AJAX."** AJAX is a hot buzzword in the Web application world these days. AJAX is an acronym for *Asynchronous JavaScript and XML* and, in Web application development; it signifies the capability to build applications that make use of the `XMLHttpRequest` object. New to Visual Studio 2008 is the ability to build AJAX-enabled ASP.NET applications from the default install of the IDE. This chapter takes a look at a new way to build your applications.
- **Chapter 20, "ASP.NET AJAX Control Toolkit."** Along with the new capabilities to build ASP.NET application which make use of the AJAX technology, there are a series of new controls that are now available to make the task rather simple. This chapter takes a good look at the ASP.NET AJAX Control Toolkit and how to use this toolkit with your applications today.
- **Chapter 21, "Security."** This security chapter discusses security beyond the membership and role management features provided by ASP.NET 3.5. This chapter provides an in-depth look at the authentication and authorization mechanics inherent in the ASP.NET technology, as well as HTTP access types and impersonations.
- **Chapter 22, "State Management."** Because ASP.NET is a request-response–based technology, state management and the performance of requests and responses take on significant importance. This chapter introduces these two separate but important areas of ASP.NET development.
- **Chapter 23, "Caching."** Because of the request-response nature of ASP.NET, caching (storing previous generated results, images, and pages) on the server becomes rather important to the performance of your ASP.NET applications. This chapter looks at some of the advanced caching capabilities provided by ASP.NET, including the SQL cache invalidation feature which is part of ASP.NET 3.5.
- **Chapter 24, "Debugging and Error Handling."** Being able to handle unanticipated errors in your ASP.NET applications is vital for any application that you build. This chapter tells you how to properly structure error handling within your applications. It also shows you how to use various debugging techniques to find errors that your applications might contain.
- **Chapter 25, "File I/O and Streams."** More often than not, you want your ASP.NET applications to work with items that are outside the base application. Examples include files and streams. This chapter takes a close look at working with various file types and streams that might come into your ASP.NET applications.
- **Chapter 26, "User and Server Controls."** Not only can you use the plethora of server controls that come with ASP.NET, but you can also utilize the same framework these controls use and build your own. This chapter describes building your own server controls and how to use them within your applications.
- **Chapter 27, "Modules and Handlers."** Sometimes, just creating dynamic Web pages with the latest languages and databases does not give you, the developer, enough control over an application. At times, you need to be able to dig deeper and create applications that can interact with the Web server itself. You want to be able to interact with the low-level processes, such as how the Web server processes incoming and outgoing HTTP requests. This chapter looks at two methods of manipulating the way ASP.NET processes HTTP requests: HttpModule and HttpHandler.

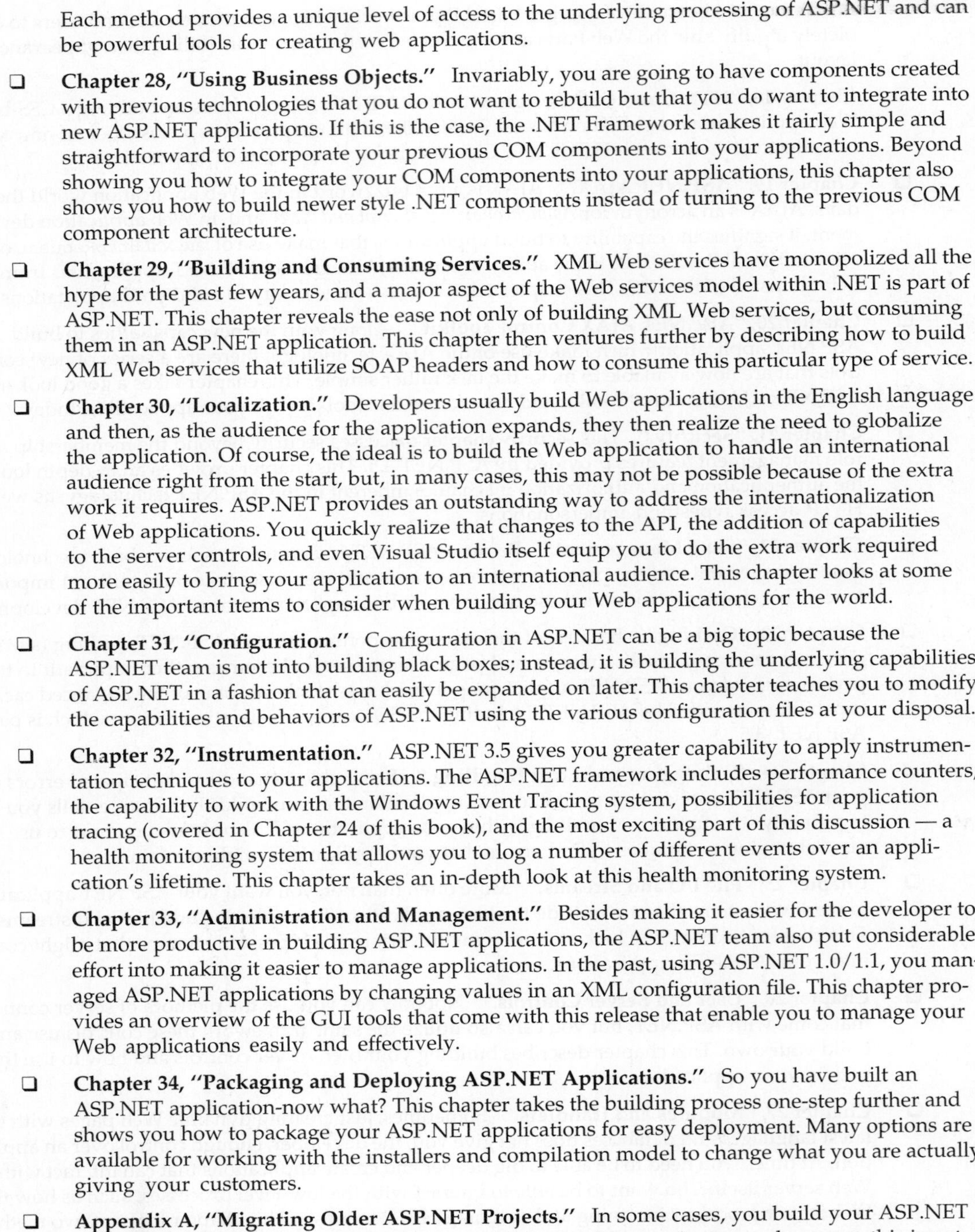

Each method provides a unique level of access to the underlying processing of ASP.NET and can be powerful tools for creating web applications.

- **Chapter 28, "Using Business Objects."** Invariably, you are going to have components created with previous technologies that you do not want to rebuild but that you do want to integrate into new ASP.NET applications. If this is the case, the .NET Framework makes it fairly simple and straightforward to incorporate your previous COM components into your applications. Beyond showing you how to integrate your COM components into your applications, this chapter also shows you how to build newer style .NET components instead of turning to the previous COM component architecture.
- **Chapter 29, "Building and Consuming Services."** XML Web services have monopolized all the hype for the past few years, and a major aspect of the Web services model within .NET is part of ASP.NET. This chapter reveals the ease not only of building XML Web services, but consuming them in an ASP.NET application. This chapter then ventures further by describing how to build XML Web services that utilize SOAP headers and how to consume this particular type of service.
- **Chapter 30, "Localization."** Developers usually build Web applications in the English language and then, as the audience for the application expands, they then realize the need to globalize the application. Of course, the ideal is to build the Web application to handle an international audience right from the start, but, in many cases, this may not be possible because of the extra work it requires. ASP.NET provides an outstanding way to address the internationalization of Web applications. You quickly realize that changes to the API, the addition of capabilities to the server controls, and even Visual Studio itself equip you to do the extra work required more easily to bring your application to an international audience. This chapter looks at some of the important items to consider when building your Web applications for the world.
- **Chapter 31, "Configuration."** Configuration in ASP.NET can be a big topic because the ASP.NET team is not into building black boxes; instead, it is building the underlying capabilities of ASP.NET in a fashion that can easily be expanded on later. This chapter teaches you to modify the capabilities and behaviors of ASP.NET using the various configuration files at your disposal.
- **Chapter 32, "Instrumentation."** ASP.NET 3.5 gives you greater capability to apply instrumentation techniques to your applications. The ASP.NET framework includes performance counters, the capability to work with the Windows Event Tracing system, possibilities for application tracing (covered in Chapter 24 of this book), and the most exciting part of this discussion — a health monitoring system that allows you to log a number of different events over an application's lifetime. This chapter takes an in-depth look at this health monitoring system.
- **Chapter 33, "Administration and Management."** Besides making it easier for the developer to be more productive in building ASP.NET applications, the ASP.NET team also put considerable effort into making it easier to manage applications. In the past, using ASP.NET 1.0/1.1, you managed ASP.NET applications by changing values in an XML configuration file. This chapter provides an overview of the GUI tools that come with this release that enable you to manage your Web applications easily and effectively.
- **Chapter 34, "Packaging and Deploying ASP.NET Applications."** So you have built an ASP.NET application-now what? This chapter takes the building process one-step further and shows you how to package your ASP.NET applications for easy deployment. Many options are available for working with the installers and compilation model to change what you are actually giving your customers.
- **Appendix A, "Migrating Older ASP.NET Projects."** In some cases, you build your ASP.NET 3.5 applications from scratch, starting everything new. In many instances, however, this is not

an option. You need to take an ASP.NET application that was previously built on the 1.0, 1.1, or 2.0 versions of the .NET Framework and migrate the application so that it can run on the .NET Framework 3.5. This appendix focuses on migrating ASP.NET 1.x, or 2.0 applications to the 3.5 framework.

- **Appendix B, "ASP.NET Ultimate Tools."** This chapter takes a look at the tools avilalable to you as an ASP.NET developer. Many of the tools here will help you to expedite your development process and in many cases, make you a better developer.
- **Appendix C, "Silverlight."** Called WPF/E during its development days and now called Silverlight, this is a means to build fluid applications using XAML. This new technology enables developers with really rich vector-based applications.
- **Appendix D, "ASP.NET Online Resources."** This small appendix points you to some of the more valuable online resources for enhancing your understanding of ASP.NET.

Conventions

This book uses a number of different styles of text and layout to help differentiate among various types of information. Here are examples of the styles used and an explanation of what they mean:

- New words being defined are shown in *italics*.
- Keys that you press on the keyboard, such as Ctrl and Enter, are shown in initial caps and spelled as they appear on the keyboard.
- File and folder names, file extensions, URLs, and code that appears in regular paragraph text are shown in a `monospaced` typeface.

When we show a block of code that you can type as a program and run, it's shown on separate lines, like this:

```
public static void Main()
{
   AFunc(1,2,"abc");
}
```

or like this:

```
public static void Main()
{
   AFunc(1,2,"abc");
}
```

Sometimes you see code in a mixture of styles, like this:

```
// If we haven't reached the end, return true, otherwise
// set the position to invalid, and return false.
pos++;

if (pos < 4)
   return true;

else {
```

```
        pos = -1;
        return false;
    }
```

When mixed code is shown like this, the code with the gray background is what you should focus on in the current example.

We demonstrate the syntactical usage of methods, properties, and so on using the following format:

```
SqlDependency="database:table"
```

Here, the italicized parts indicate *placeholder text:* object references, variables, or parameter values that you need to insert.

Most of the code examples throughout the book are presented as numbered listings that have descriptive titles, like this:

Listing I-7: Targeting WML devices in your ASP.NET pages

Each listing is numbered (for example: *1-3*) where the first number represents the chapter number and the number following the hyphen represents a sequential number that indicates where that listing falls within the chapter. Downloadable code from the Wrox Web site (`www.wrox.com`) also uses this numbering system so that you can easily locate the examples you are looking for.

All code is shown in both VB and C#, when warranted. The exception is for code in which the only difference is, for example, the value given to the `Language` attribute in the `Page` directive. In such situations, we don't repeat the code for the C# version; the code is shown only once, as in the following example:

```
<%@ Page Language="VB"%>

<html xmlns="http://www.w3.org/1999/xhtml">
<head runat="server">
    <title>DataSetDataSource</title>
</head>
<body>
    <form id="form1" runat="server">
        <asp:DropDownList ID="Dropdownlist1" Runat="server" DataTextField="name"
         DataSourceID="XmlDataSource1">
        </asp:DropDownList>

        <asp:XmlDataSource ID="XmlDataSource1" Runat="server"
         DataFile="~/Painters.xml">
        </asp:DataSetDataSource>
    </form>
</body>
</html>
```

Source Code

As you work through the examples in this book, you may choose either to type all the code manually or to use the source code files that accompany the book. All the source code used in this book is available for download at www.wrox.com. When you get to the site, simply locate the book's title (either by using the Search box or one of the topic lists) and click the Download Code link. You can then choose to download all the code from the book in one large zip file or download just the code you need for a particular chapter.

Because many books have similar titles, you may find it easiest to search by ISBN; this book's ISBN is 978-0-470-18757-9.

After you download the code, just decompress it with your favorite compression tool. Alternatively, you can go to the main Wrox code download page at www.wrox.com/dynamic/books/download.aspx to see the code available for this book and all other Wrox books. Remember, you can easily find the code you are looking for by referencing the listing number of the code example from the book, such as "Listing I-7." We used these listing numbers when naming the downloadable code files.

Errata

We make every effort to ensure that there are no errors in the text or in the code. However, no one is perfect, and mistakes do occur. If you find an error in one of our books, such as a spelling mistake or faulty piece of code, we would be very grateful if you'd tell us about it. By sending in errata, you may spare another reader hours of frustration; at the same time, you are helping us provide even higher-quality information.

To find the errata page for this book, go to www.wrox.com and locate the title using the Search box or one of the title lists. Then, on the book details page, click the Book Errata link. On this page, you can view all errata that have been submitted for this book and posted by Wrox editors. A complete book list including links to each book's errata is also available at www.wrox.com/misc-pages/booklist.shtml.

If you don't spot "your" error already on the Book Errata page, go to www.wrox.com/contact/techsupport.shtml and complete the form there to send us the error you have found. We'll check the information and, if appropriate, post a message to the book's errata page and fix the problem in subsequent editions of the book.

p2p.wrox.com

For author and peer discussion, join the P2P forums at p2p.wrox.com. The forums are a Web-based system for you to post messages relating to Wrox books and technologies and to interact with other readers and technology users. The forums offer a subscription feature that enables you to receive e-mail on topics of interest when new posts are made to the forums. Wrox authors, editors, other industry experts, and your fellow readers are represented in these forums.

At http://p2p.wrox.com you will find a number of different forums that will help you not only as you read this book but also as you develop your own applications. To join the forums, just follow these steps:

1. Go to p2p.wrox.com and click the Register link.
2. Read the terms of use and click Agree.
3. Supply the information required to join, as well as any optional information you want to provide, and click Submit.

You will receive an e-mail with information describing how to verify your account and complete the joining process.

You can read messages in the forums without joining P2P, but you must join in order to post messages.

After you join, you can post new messages and respond to other users' posts. You can read messages at any time on the Web. If you would like to have new messages from a particular forum e-mailed to you, click the Subscribe to this Forum icon by the forum name in the forum listing.

For more information about how the forum software works, as well as answers to many common questions specific to P2P and Wrox books, be sure to read the P2P FAQs. Simply click the FAQ link on any P2P page.

1

Application and Page Frameworks

The evolution of ASP.NET continues! The progression from Active Server Pages 3.0 to ASP.NET 1.0 was revolutionary, to say the least. And now the revolution continues with the latest release of ASP.NET — version 3.5. The original introduction of ASP.NET 1.0 fundamentally changed the Web programming model. ASP.NET 3.5 is just as revolutionary in the way it will increase your productivity. As of late, the primary goal of ASP.NET is to enable you to build powerful, secure, dynamic applications using the least possible amount of code. Although this book covers the new features provided by ASP.NET 3.5, it also covers all the offerings of ASP.NET technology.

If you are new to ASP.NET and building your first set of applications in ASP.NET 3.5, you may be amazed by the vast amount of wonderful server controls it provides. You may marvel at how it enables you to work with data more effectively using a series of data providers. You may be impressed at how easily you can build in security and personalization.

The outstanding capabilities of ASP.NET 3.5 do not end there, however. This chapter looks at many exciting options that facilitate working with ASP.NET pages and applications. One of the first steps you, the developer, should take when starting a project is to become familiar with the foundation you are building on and the options available for customizing that foundation.

Application Location Options

With ASP.NET 3.5, you have the option — using Visual Studio 2008 — to create an application with a virtual directory mapped to IIS or a standalone application outside the confines of IIS. Whereas the early Visual Studio .NET 2002/2003 IDEs forced developers to use IIS for all Web applications, Visual Studio 2008 (and Visual Web Developer 2008 Express Edition, for that matter) includes a built-in Web server that you can use for development, much like the one used in the past with the ASP.NET Web Matrix.

This built-in Web server was previously presented to developers as a code sample called Cassini. In fact, the code for this mini Web server is freely downloadable from the ASP.NET team Web site found at `www.asp.net`.

The following section shows you how to use the built-in Web server that comes with Visual Studio 2008.

Built-In Web Server

By default, Visual Studio 2008 builds applications without the use of IIS. You can see this when you select New ➪ Web Site in the IDE. By default, the location provided for your application is in `C:\Users\Bill\Documents\Visual Studio 2008\WebSites` if you are using Windows Vista (shown in Figure 1-1). It is not `C:\Inetpub\wwwroot\` as it would have been in Visual Studio .NET 2002/2003. By default, any site that you build and host inside `C:\Users\Bill\Documents\Visual Studio 2008\WebSites` (or any other folder you create) uses the built-in Web server that is part of Visual Studio 2008. If you use the built-in Web server from Visual Studio 2008, you are not locked into the `WebSites` folder; you can create any folder you want in your system.

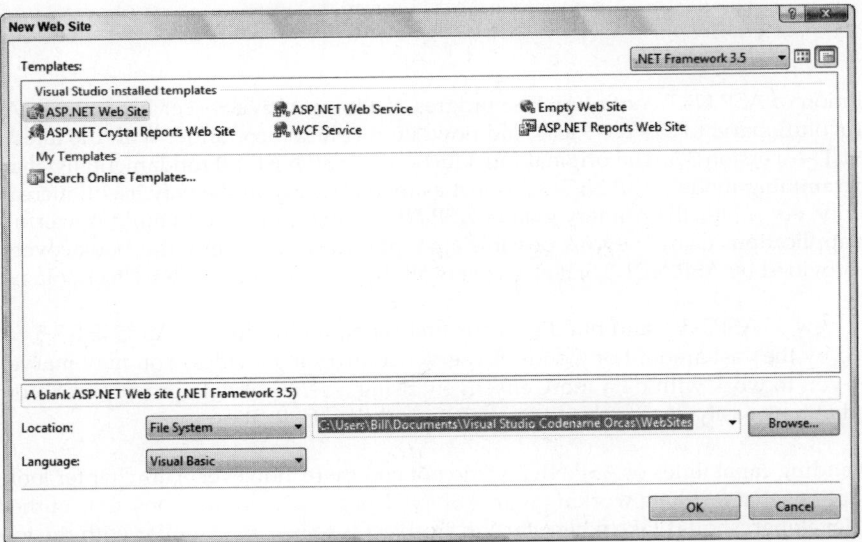

Figure 1-1

To change from this default, you have a handful of options. Click the Browse button in the New Web Site dialog. This brings up the Choose Location dialog, shown in Figure 1-2.

If you continue to use the built-in Web server that Visual Studio 2008 provides, you can choose a new location for your Web application from this dialog. To choose a new location, select a new folder and save your `.aspx` pages and any other associated files to this directory. When using Visual Studio 2008, you can run your application completely from this location. This way of working with the ASP.NET pages you create is ideal if you do not have access to a Web server because it enables you to build applications that do not reside on a machine with IIS. This means that you can even develop ASP.NET applications on operating systems such as Windows XP Home Edition.

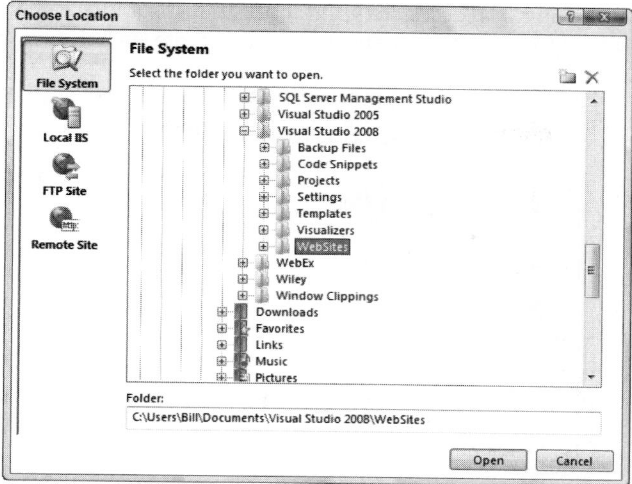

Figure 1-2

IIS

From the Choose Location dialog, you can also change where your application is saved and which type of Web server your application employs. To use IIS (as you probably did when you used Visual Studio .NET 2002/2003), select the Local IIS button in the dialog. This changes the results in the text area to show you a list of all the virtual application roots on your machine. You are required to run Visual Studio as an administrator user if you want to see your local IIS instance.

To create a new virtual root for your application, highlight Default Web Site. Two accessible buttons appear at the top of the dialog box (see Figure 1-3). When you look from left to right, the first button in the upper-right corner of the dialog box is for creating a new Web application — or a virtual root. This button is shown as a globe inside a box. The second button enables you to create virtual directories for any of the virtual roots you created. The third button is a Delete button, which allows you to delete any selected virtual directories or virtual roots on the server.

After you have created the virtual directory you want, click the Open button. Visual Studio 2008 then goes through the standard process to create your application. Now, however, instead of depending on the built-in Web server from ASP.NET 3.5, your application will use IIS. When you invoke your application, the URL now consists of something like `http://localhost/MyWeb/Default.aspx`, which means it is using IIS.

FTP

Not only can you decide on the type of Web server for your Web application when you create it using the Choose Location dialog, but you can also decide where your application is going to be located. With the previous options, you built applications that resided on your local server. The FTP option enables you to actually store and even code your applications while they reside on a server somewhere else in your enterprise — or on the other side of the planet. You can also use the FTP capabilities to work on different locations within the same server. Using this new capability provides a wide range of possible options.

The built-in capability giving FTP access to your applications is a major enhancement to the IDE. Although formerly difficult to accomplish, this task is now quite simple, as you can see from Figure 1-4.

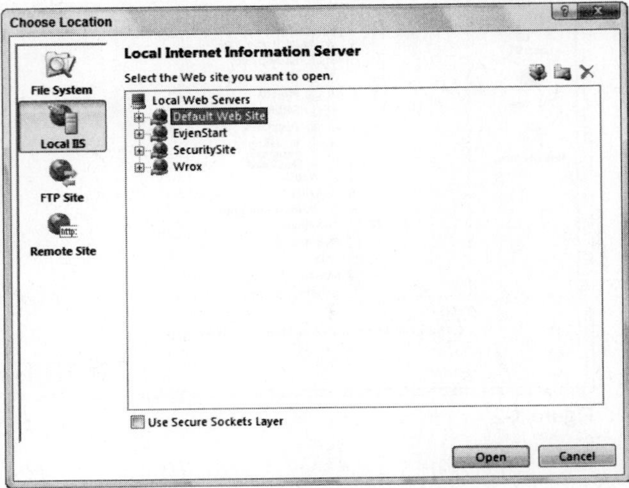

Figure 1-3

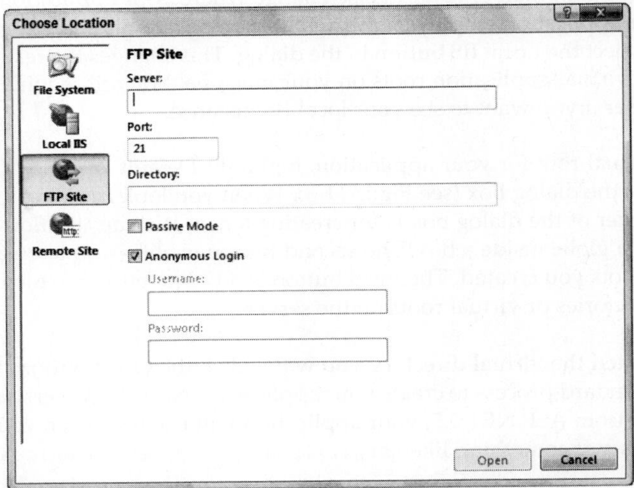

Figure 1-4

To create your application on a remote server using FTP, simply provide the server name, the port to use, and the directory — as well as any required credentials. If the correct information is provided, Visual Studio 2008 reaches out to the remote server and creates the appropriate files for the start of your application, just as if it were doing the job locally. From this point on, you can open your project and connect to the remote server using FTP.

Web Site Requiring FrontPage Extensions

The last option in the Choose Location dialog is the Remote Sites option. Clicking this button provides a dialog that enables you to connect to a remote or local server that utilizes FrontPage Extensions. This option is displayed in Figure 1-5.

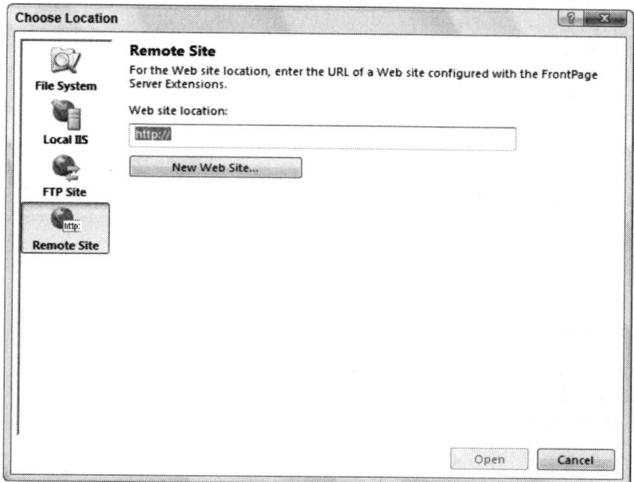

Figure 1-5

The ASP.NET Page Structure Options

ASP.NET 3.5 provides two paths for structuring the code of your ASP.NET pages. The first path utilizes the code-inline model. This model should be familiar to classic ASP 2.0/3.0 developers because all the code is contained within a single `.aspx` page. The second path uses ASP.NET's code-behind model, which allows for code separation of the page's business logic from its presentation logic. In this model, the presentation logic for the page is stored in an `.aspx` page, whereas the logic piece is stored in a separate class file: `.aspx.vb` or `.aspx.cs`. It is considered best practice to use the code-behind model as it provides a clean model in separation of pure UI elements from code that manipulates these elements. It is also seen as a better means in maintaining code.

One of the major complaints about Visual Studio .NET 2002 and 2003 is that it forced you to use the code-behind model when developing your ASP.NET pages because it did not understand the code-inline model. The code-behind model in ASP.NET was introduced as a new way to separate the presentation code and business logic. Listing 1-1 shows a typical `.aspx` page generated using Visual Studio .NET 2002 or 2003.

Listing 1-1: A typical .aspx page from ASP.NET 1.0/1.1

```
<%@ Page Language="vb" AutoEventWireup="false" Codebehind="WebForm1.aspx.vb"
    Inherits="WebApplication.WebForm1"%>
<!DOCTYPE HTML PUBLIC "-//W3C//DTD HTML 4.0 Transitional//EN">
<HTML>
 <HEAD>
    <title>WebForm1</title>
    <meta name="GENERATOR" content="Microsoft Visual Studio .NET 7.1">
    <meta name="CODE_LANGUAGE" content="Visual Basic .NET 7.1">
    <meta name="vs_defaultClientScript" content="JavaScript">
    <meta name="vs_targetSchema"
      content="http://schemas.microsoft.com/intellisense/ie5">
 </HEAD>
 <body>
    <form id="Form1" method="post" runat="server">
       <P>What is your name?<br>
       <asp:TextBox id="TextBox1" runat="server"></asp:TextBox><BR>
       <asp:Button id="Button1" runat="server" Text="Submit"></asp:Button></P>
       <P><asp:Label id="Label1" runat="server"></asp:Label></P>
    </form>
 </body>
</HTML>
```

The code-behind file created within Visual Studio .NET 2002/2003 for the `.aspx` page is shown in Listing 1-2.

Listing 1-2: A typical .aspx.vb/.aspx.cs page from ASP.NET 1.0/1.1

```
Public Class WebForm1
    Inherits System.Web.UI.Page

#Region " Web Form Designer Generated Code "

    'This call is required by the Web Form Designer.
    <System.Diagnostics.DebuggerStepThrough()> Private Sub InitializeComponent()

    End Sub
    Protected WithEvents TextBox1 As System.Web.UI.WebControls.TextBox
    Protected WithEvents Button1 As System.Web.UI.WebControls.Button
    Protected WithEvents Label1 As System.Web.UI.WebControls.Label

    'NOTE: The following placeholder declaration is required by the Web Form
        Designer.
    'Do not delete or move it.
    Private designerPlaceholderDeclaration As System.Object

    Private Sub Page_Init(ByVal sender As System.Object, ByVal e As
      System.EventArgs) Handles MyBase.Init
        'CODEGEN: This method call is required by the Web Form Designer
        'Do not modify it using the code editor.
        InitializeComponent()
    End Sub
```

```
#End Region

    Private Sub Page_Load(ByVal sender As System.Object, ByVal e As
      System.EventArgs) Handles MyBase.Load
        'Put user code to initialize the page here
    End Sub

    Private Sub Button1_Click(ByVal sender As System.Object, ByVal e As
      System.EventArgs) Handles Button1.Click
        Label1.Text = "Hello " & TextBox1.Text
    End Sub
End Class
```

In this code-behind page from ASP.NET 1.0/1.1, you can see that a lot of the code that developers never have to deal with is hidden in the `#Region` section of the page. Because ASP.NET 3.5 is built on top of .NET 3.5, which in turn is utilizing the core .NET 2.0 Framework, it can take advantage of the .NET Framework capability of partial classes. Partial classes enable you to separate your classes into multiple class files, which are then combined into a single class when the application is compiled. Because ASP.NET 3.5 combines all this page code for you behind the scenes when the application is compiled, the code-behind files you work with in ASP.NET 3.5 are simpler in appearance and the model is easier to use. You are presented with only the pieces of the class that you need. Next, we will look at both the inline and code-behind models from ASP.NET 3.5.

Inline Coding

With the .NET Framework 1.0/1.1, developers went out of their way (and outside Visual Studio .NET) to build their ASP.NET pages inline and avoid the code-behind model that was so heavily promoted by Microsoft and others. Visual Studio 2008 (as well as Visual Web Developer 2008 Express Edition) allows you to build your pages easily using this coding style. To build an ASP.NET page inline instead of using the code-behind model, you simply select the page type from the Add New Item dialog and make sure that the Place Code in Separate File check box is unchecked. You can get at this dialog by right clicking the project or the solution in the Solution Explorer and selecting Add New Item (see Figure 1-6).

From here, you can see the check box you need to unselect if you want to build your ASP.NET pages inline. In fact, many page types have options for both inline and code-behind styles. The following table shows your inline options when selecting files from this dialog.

File Options Using Inline Coding	File Created
Web Form	`.aspx` file
AJAX Web Form	`.aspx` file
Master Page	`.master` file
AJAX Master Page	`.master` file
Web User Control	`.ascx` file
Web Service	`.asmx` file

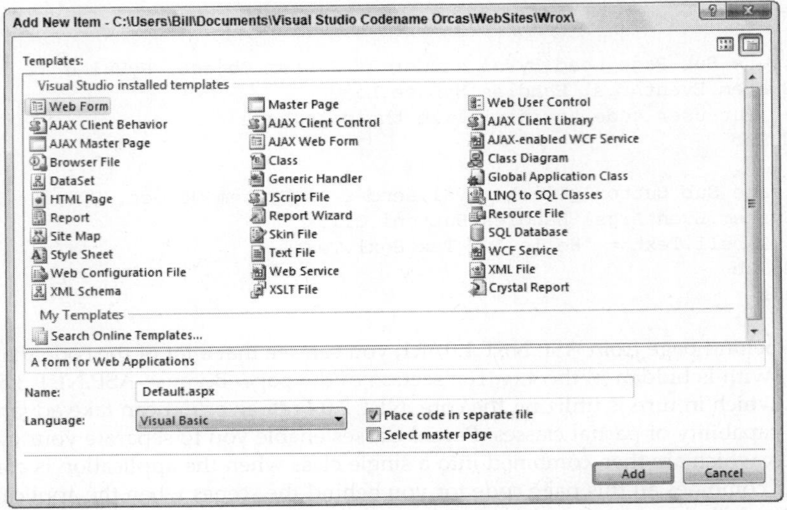

Figure 1-6

By using the Web Form option with a few controls, you get a page that encapsulates not only the presentation logic, but the business logic as well. This is illustrated in Listing 1-3.

Listing 1-3: A simple page that uses the inline coding model

VB

```
<%@ Page Language="VB" %>

<!DOCTYPE html PUBLIC "-//W3C//DTD XHTML 1.1//EN"
 "http://www.w3.org/TR/xhtml11/DTD/xhtml11.dtd">

<script runat="server">
    Protected Sub Button1_Click(ByVal sender As Object, _
       ByVal e As System.EventArgs)

        Label1.Text = "Hello " & Textbox1.Text
    End Sub
</script>

<html xmlns="http://www.w3.org/1999/xhtml" >
<head runat="server">
    <title>Simple Page</title>
</head>
<body>
    <form id="form1" runat="server">
        What is your name?<br />
        <asp:Textbox ID="Textbox1" Runat="server"></asp:Textbox><br />
        <asp:Button ID="Button1" Runat="server" Text="Submit"
         OnClick="Button1_Click" />
        <p><asp:Label ID="Label1" Runat="server"></asp:Label></p>
    </form>
</body>
</html>
```

C#

```
<%@ Page Language="C#" %>

<!DOCTYPE html PUBLIC "-//W3C//DTD XHTML 1.1//EN"
 "http://www.w3.org/TR/xhtml11/DTD/xhtml11.dtd">

<script runat="server">
    protected void Button1_Click(object sender, System.EventArgs e)
    {
        Label1.Text = "Hello " + Textbox1.Text;
    }
</script>
```

From this example, you can see that all the business logic is encapsulated in between `<script>` tags. The nice feature of the inline model is that the business logic and the presentation logic are contained within the same file. Some developers find that having everything in a single viewable instance makes working with the ASP.NET page easier. Another great thing is that Visual Studio 2008 provides IntelliSense when working with the inline coding model and ASP.NET 3.5. Before Visual Studio 2005, this capability did not exist. Visual Studio .NET 2002/2003 forced you to use the code-behind model and, even if you rigged it so your pages were using the inline model, you lost all IntelliSense capabilities.

Code-Behind Model

The other option for constructing your ASP.NET 3.5 pages is to build your files using the code-behind model.

It is important to note that the more preferred method is the code-behind model rather than the inline model. This method employs the proper segmentation between presentation and business logic in many cases. You will find that many of the examples in this book use an inline coding model because it works well in showing an example in one listing. Even though the example is using an inline coding style, it is my recommendation that you move the code to employ the code-behind model.

To create a new page in your ASP.NET solution that uses the code-behind model, select the page type you want from the New File dialog. To build a page that uses the code-behind model, you first select the page in the Add New Item dialog and make sure the Place Code in Separate File check box is checked. The following table shows you the options for pages that use the code-behind model.

File Options Using Code-Behind	File Created
Web Form	`.aspx` file `.aspx.vb` or `.aspx.cs` file
AJAX Web Form	`.aspx` file `.aspx.vb` or `.aspx.cs` file
Master Page	`.master` file `.master.vb` or `.master.cs` file
AJAX Master Page	`.master.vb` or `.master.cs` file
Web User Control	`.ascx` file `.ascx.vb` or `.ascx.cs` file
Web Service	`.asmx` file `.vb` or `.cs` file

The idea of using the code-behind model is to separate the business logic and presentation logic into separate files. Doing this makes it easier to work with your pages, especially if you are working in a team environment where visual designers work on the UI of the page and coders work on the business logic that sits behind the presentation pieces. In the earlier Listings 1-1 and 1-2, you saw how pages using the code-behind model in ASP.NET 1.0/1.1 were constructed. To see the difference in ASP.NET 3.5, look at how its code-behind pages are constructed. This is illustrated in Listing 1-4 for the presentation piece and Listing 1-5 for the code-behind piece.

Listing 1-4: An .aspx page that uses the ASP.NET 3.5 code-behind model

VB

```
<%@ Page Language="VB" AutoEventWireup="false" CodeFile="Default.aspx.vb"
    Inherits="_Default" %>

<!DOCTYPE html PUBLIC "-//W3C//DTD XHTML 1.1//EN"
 "http://www.w3.org/TR/xhtml11/DTD/xhtml11.dtd">

<html xmlns="http://www.w3.org/1999/xhtml">
<head runat="server">
    <title>Simple Page</title>
</head>
<body>
    <form id="form1" runat="server">
        What is your name?<br />
        <asp:Textbox ID="Textbox1" Runat="server"></asp:Textbox><br />
        <asp:Button ID="Button1" Runat="server" Text="Submit"
         OnClick="Button1_Click" />
        <p><asp:Label ID="Label1" Runat="server"></asp:Label></p>
    </form>
</body>
</html>
```

C#

```
<%@ Page Language="C#" CodeFile="Default.aspx.cs" Inherits="_Default" %>
```

Listing 1-5: A code-behind page

VB

```
Partial Class _Default
    Inherits System.Web.UI.Page

    Protected Sub Button1_Click(ByVal sender As Object, _
       ByVal e As System.EventArgs) Handles Button1.Click

        Label1.Text = "Hello " & TextBox1.Text
    End Sub
End Class
```

C#

```
using System;
using System.Data;
using System.Configuration;
```

```
using System.Linq;
using System.Web;
using System.Web.Security;
using System.Web.UI;
using System.Web.UI.WebControls;
using System.Web.UI.WebControls.WebParts;
using System.Web.UI.HtmlControls;
using System.Xml.Linq;

public partial class _Default : System.Web.UI.Page
{
    protected void Button1_Click(object sender, EventArgs e)
    {
        Label1.Text = "Hello " + Textbox1.Text;
    }
}
```

The `.aspx` page using this ASP.NET 3.5 code-behind model has some attributes in the `Page` directive that you should pay attention to when working in this mode. The first is the `CodeFile` attribute. This is an attribute in the `Page` directive and is meant to point to the code-behind page that is used with this presentation page. In this case, the value assigned is `Default.aspx.vb` or `Default.aspx.cs`. The second attribute needed is the `Inherits` attribute. This attribute was available in previous versions of ASP.NET, but was little used before ASP.NET 2.0. This attribute specifies the name of the class that is bound to the page when the page is compiled. The directives are simple enough in ASP.NET 3.5. Look at the code-behind page from Listing 1-5.

The code-behind page is rather simple in appearance because of the partial class capabilities that .NET 3.5 provides. You can see that the class created in the code-behind file uses partial classes, employing the `Partial` keyword in Visual Basic 2008 and the `partial` keyword from C# 2008. This enables you to simply place the methods that you need in your page class. In this case, you have a button-click event and nothing else.

Later in this chapter, we look at the compilation process for both of these models.

ASP.NET 3.5 Page Directives

ASP.NET directives are something that is a part of every ASP.NET page. You can control the behavior of your ASP.NET pages by using these directives. Here is an example of the `Page` directive:

```
<%@ Page Language="VB" AutoEventWireup="false" CodeFile="Default.aspx.vb"
    Inherits="_Default" %>
```

Eleven directives are at your disposal in your ASP.NET pages or user controls. You use these directives in your applications whether the page uses the code-behind model or the inline coding model.

Basically, these directives are commands that the compiler uses when the page is compiled. Directives are simple to incorporate into your pages. A directive is written in the following format:

```
<%@ [Directive] [Attribute=Value] %>
```

From this, you can see that a directive is opened with a `<%@` and closed with a `%>`. It is best to put these directives at the top of your pages or controls because this is traditionally where developers expect to see them (although the page still compiles if the directives are located at a different place). Of course, you can also add more than a single attribute to your directive statements, as shown in the following:

```
<%@ [Directive] [Attribute=Value] [Attribute=Value] %>
```

The following table describes the directives at your disposal in ASP.NET 3.5.

Directive	Description
`Assembly`	Links an assembly to the Page or user control for which it is associated.
`Control`	Page directive meant for use with user controls (`.ascx`).
`Implements`	Implements a specified .NET Framework interface.
`Import`	Imports specified namespaces into the Page or user control.
`Master`	Enables you to specify master page–specific attributes and values to use when the page parses or compiles. This directive can be used only with master pages (`.master`).
`MasterType`	Associates a class name to a Page in order to get at strongly typed references or members contained within the specified master page.
`OutputCache`	Controls the output caching policies of a Page or user control.
`Page`	Enables you to specify page specific attributes and values to use when the page parses or compiles. This directive can be used only with ASP.NET pages (`.aspx`).
`PreviousPageType`	Enables an ASP.NET page to work with a postback from another page in the application.
`Reference`	Links a Page or user control to the current Page or user control.
`Register`	Associates aliases with namespaces and class names for notation in custom server control syntax.

The following sections provide a quick review of each of these directives.

@Page

The `@Page` directive enables you to specify attributes and values for an ASP.NET page (`.aspx`) to be used when the page is parsed or compiled. This is the most frequently used directive of the bunch. Because the ASP.NET page is such an important part of ASP.NET, you have quite a few attributes at your disposal. The following table summarizes the attributes available through the `@Page` directive.

Attribute	Description
AspCompat	Permits the page to be executed on a single-threaded apartment thread when given a value of True. The default setting for this attribute is False.
Async	Specifies whether the ASP.NET page is processed synchronously or asynchronously.
AsyncTimeout	Specifies the amount of time in seconds to wait for the asynchronous task to complete. The default setting is 45 seconds. This is a new attribute of ASP.NET 3.5.
AutoEventWireup	Specifies whether the page events are autowired when set to True. The default setting for this attribute is True.
Buffer	Enables HTTP response buffering when set to True. The default setting for this attribute is True.
ClassName	Specifies the name of the class that is bound to the page when the page is compiled.
ClientTarget	Specifies the target user agent a control should render content for. This attribute needs to be tied to an alias defined in the <clientTarget> section of the web.config.
CodeFile	References the code-behind file with which the page is associated.
CodeFileBaseClass	Specifies the type name of the base class to use with the code-behind class, which is used by the CodeFile attribute.
CodePage	Indicates the code page value for the response.
CompilationMode	Specifies whether ASP.NET should compile the page or not. The available options include Always (the default), Auto, or Never. A setting of Auto means that if possible, ASP.NET will not compile the page.
CompilerOptions	Compiler string that indicates compilation options for the page.
CompileWith	Takes a String value that points to the code-behind file used.
ContentType	Defines the HTTP content type of the response as a standard MIME type.
Culture	Specifies the culture setting of the page. ASP.NET 3.5 includes the capability to give the Culture attribute a value of Auto to enable automatic detection of the culture required.
Debug	Compiles the page with debug symbols in place when set to True.
Description	Provides a text description of the page. The ASP.NET parser ignores this attribute and its assigned value.
EnableEventValidation	Specifies whether to enable validation of events in postback and callback scenarios. The default setting of True means that events will be validated.

Attribute	Description
`EnableSessionState`	Session state for the page is enabled when set to `True`. The default setting is `True`.
`EnableTheming`	Page is enabled to use theming when set to `True`. The default setting for this attribute is `True`.
`EnableViewState`	View state is maintained across the page when set to `True`. The default value is `True`.
`EnableViewStateMac`	Page runs a machine-authentication check on the page's view state when the page is posted back from the user when set to `True`. The default value is `False`.
`ErrorPage`	Specifies a URL to post to for all unhandled page exceptions.
`Explicit`	Visual Basic `Explicit` option is enabled when set to `True`. The default setting is `False`.
`Language`	Defines the language being used for any inline rendering and script blocks.
`LCID`	Defines the locale identifier for the Web Form's page.
`LinePragmas`	`Boolean` value that specifies whether line pragmas are used with the resulting assembly.
`MasterPageFile`	Takes a `String` value that points to the location of the master page used with the page. This attribute is used with content pages.
`MaintainScrollPositionOnPostback`	Takes a `Boolean` value, which indicates whether the page should be positioned exactly in the same scroll position or if the page should be regenerated in the uppermost position for when the page is posted back to itself.
`ResponseEncoding`	Specifies the response encoding of the page content.
`SmartNavigation`	Specifies whether to activate the ASP.NET Smart Navigation feature for richer browsers. This returns the postback to the current position on the page. The default value is `False`.
`Src`	Points to the source file of the class used for the code behind of the page being rendered.
`Strict`	Compiles the page using the Visual Basic `Strict` mode when set to `True`. The default setting is `False`.
`StylesheetTheme`	Applies the specified theme to the page using the ASP.NET 3.5 themes feature. The difference between the `StylesheetTheme` and `Theme` attributes is that `StylesheetTheme` will not override preexisting style settings in the controls, whereas `Theme` will remove these settings.

Attribute	Description
Theme	Applies the specified theme to the page using the ASP.NET 3.5 themes feature.
Title	Applies a page's title. This is an attribute mainly meant for content pages that must apply a page title other than what is specified in the master page.
Trace	Page tracing is enabled when set to True. The default setting is False.
TraceMode	Specifies how the trace messages are displayed when tracing is enabled. The settings for this attribute include SortByTime or SortByCategory. The default setting is SortByTime.
Transaction	Specifies whether transactions are supported on the page. The settings for this attribute are Disabled, NotSupported, Supported, Required, and RequiresNew. The default setting is Disabled.
UICulture	The value of the UICulture attribute specifies what UI Culture to use for the ASP.NET page. ASP.NET 3.5 includes the capability to give the UICulture attribute a value of Auto to enable automatic detection of the UICulture.
ValidateRequest	When this attribute is set to True, the form input values are checked against a list of potentially dangerous values. This helps protect your Web application from harmful attacks such as JavaScript attacks. The default value is True.
ViewStateEncryptionMode	Specifies how the ViewState is encrypted on the page. The options include Auto, Always, and Never. The default is Auto.
WarningLevel	Specifies the compiler warning level at which to stop compilation of the page. Possible values are 0 through 4.

Here is an example of how to use the @Page directive:

```
<%@ Page Language="VB" AutoEventWireup="false" CodeFile="Default.aspx.vb"
    Inherits="_Default" %>
```

@Master

The @Master directive is quite similar to the @Page directive except that the @Master directive is meant for master pages (.master). In using the @Master directive, you specify properties of the templated page that you will be using in conjunction with any number of content pages on your site. Any content pages (built using the @Page directive) can then inherit from the master page all the master content (defined in the master page using the @Master directive). Although they are similar, the @Master directive has fewer attributes available to it than does the @Page directive. The available attributes for the @Master directive are shown in the following table.

Attribute	Description
AutoEventWireup	Specifies whether the master page's events are autowired when set to True. Default setting is True.
ClassName	Specifies the name of the class that is bound to the master page when compiled.
CodeFile	References the code-behind file with which the page is associated.
CompilationMode	Specifies whether ASP.NET should compile the page or not. The available options include Always (the default), Auto, or Never. A setting of Auto means that if possible, ASP.NET will not compile the page.
CompilerOptions	Compiler string that indicates compilation options for the master page.
CompileWith	Takes a String value that points to the code-behind file used for the master page.
Debug	Compiles the master page with debug symbols in place when set to True.
Description	Provides a text description of the master page. The ASP.NET parser ignores this attribute and its assigned value.
EnableTheming	Indicates the master page is enabled to use theming when set to True. The default setting for this attribute is True.
EnableViewState	Maintains view state for the master page when set to True. The default value is True.
Explicit	Indicates that the Visual Basic Explicit option is enabled when set to True. The default setting is False.
Inherits	Specifies the CodeBehind class for the master page to inherit.
Language	Defines the language that is being used for any inline rendering and script blocks.
LinePragmas	Boolean value that specifies whether line pragmas are used with the resulting assembly.
MasterPageFile	Takes a String value that points to the location of the master page used with the master page. It is possible to have a master page use another master page, which creates a nested master page.
Src	Points to the source file of the class used for the code behind of the master page being rendered.
Strict	Compiles the master page using the Visual Basic Strict mode when set to True. The default setting is False.
WarningLevel	Specifies the compiler warning level at which you want to abort compilation of the page. Possible values are from 0 to 4.

Here is an example of how to use the @Master directive:

```
<%@ Master Language="VB" CodeFile="MasterPage1.master.vb"
    AutoEventWireup="false" Inherits="MasterPage" %>
```

@Control

The @Control directive is similar to the @Page directive except that @Control is used when you build an ASP.NET user control. The @Control directive allows you to define the properties to be inherited by the user control. These values are assigned to the user control as the page is parsed and compiled. The available attributes are fewer than those of the @Page directive, but quite a few of them allow for the modifications you need when building user controls. The following table details the available attributes.

Attribute	Description
AutoEventWireup	Specifies whether the user control's events are autowired when set to True. Default setting is True.
ClassName	Specifies the name of the class that is bound to the user control when the page is compiled.
CodeFileBaseClass	Specifies the type name of the base class to use with the code-behind class, which is used by the CodeFile attribute.
CodeFile	References the code-behind file with which the user control is associated.
CompilerOptions	Compiler string that indicates compilation options for the user control.
CompileWith	Takes a String value that points to the code-behind file used for the user control.
Debug	Compiles the user control with debug symbols in place when set to True.
Description	Provides a text description of the user control. The ASP.NET parser ignores this attribute and its assigned value.
EnableTheming	User control is enabled to use theming when set to True. The default setting for this attribute is True.
EnableViewState	View state is maintained for the user control when set to True. The default value is True.
Explicit	Visual Basic Explicit option is enabled when set to True. The default setting is False.
Inherits	Specifies the CodeBehind class for the user control to inherit.
Language	Defines the language used for any inline rendering and script blocks.

Attribute	Description
LinePragmas	Boolean value that specifies whether line pragmas are used with the resulting assembly.
Src	Points to the source file of the class used for the code behind of the user control being rendered.
Strict	Compiles the user control using the Visual Basic Strict mode when set to True. The default setting is False.
WarningLevel	Specifies the compiler warning level at which to stop compilation of the user control. Possible values are 0 through 4.

The @Control directive is meant to be used with an ASP.NET user control. The following is an example of how to use the directive:

```
<%@ Control Language="VB" Explicit="True"
    CodeFile="WebUserControl.ascx.vb" Inherits="WebUserControl"
    Description="This is the registration user control." %>
```

@Import

The @Import directive allows you to specify a namespace to be imported into the ASP.NET page or user control. By importing, all the classes and interfaces of the namespace are made available to the page or user control. This directive supports only a single attribute: Namespace.

The Namespace attribute takes a String value that specifies the namespace to be imported. The @Import directive cannot contain more than one attribute/value pair. Because of this, you must place multiple namespace imports in multiple lines as shown in the following example:

```
<%@ Import Namespace="System.Data" %>
<%@ Import Namespace="System.Data.SqlClient" %>
```

Several assemblies are already being referenced by your application. You can find a list of these imported namespaces by looking in the root web.config file found at C:\Windows\Microsoft.NET\Framework\v2.0.50727\CONFIG. You can find this list of assemblies being referenced from the <assemblies> child element of the <compilation> element. The settings in the root web.config file are as follows:

```
<assemblies>
   <add assembly="mscorlib"/>
   <add assembly="System, Version=2.0.0.0, Culture=neutral,
       PublicKeyToken=b77a5c561934e089"/>
   <add assembly="System.Configuration, Version=2.0.0.0, Culture=neutral,
       PublicKeyToken=b03f5f7f11d50a3a"/>
   <add assembly="System.Web, Version=2.0.0.0, Culture=neutral,
       PublicKeyToken=b03f5f7f11d50a3a"/>
   <add assembly="System.Data, Version=2.0.0.0, Culture=neutral,
       PublicKeyToken=b77a5c561934e089"/>
   <add assembly="System.Web.Services, Version=2.0.0.0, Culture=neutral,
       PublicKeyToken=b03f5f7f11d50a3a"/>
```

```
    <add assembly="System.Xml, Version=2.0.0.0, Culture=neutral,
        PublicKeyToken=b77a5c561934e089"/>
    <add assembly="System.Drawing, Version=2.0.0.0, Culture=neutral,
        PublicKeyToken=b03f5f7f11d50a3a"/>
    <add assembly="System.EnterpriseServices, Version=2.0.0.0, Culture=neutral,
        PublicKeyToken=b03f5f7f11d50a3a"/>
    <add assembly="System.Web.Mobile, Version=2.0.0.0, Culture=neutral,
        PublicKeyToken=b03f5f7f11d50a3a"/>
    <add assembly="*"/>
    <add assembly="System.Runtime.Serialization, Version=3.0.0.0, Culture=neutral,
        PublicKeyToken=b77a5c561934e089, processorArchitecture=MSIL"/>
    <add assembly="System.IdentityModel, Version=3.0.0.0, Culture=neutral,
        PublicKeyToken=b77a5c561934e089, processorArchitecture=MSIL"/>
    <add assembly="System.ServiceModel, Version=3.0.0.0, Culture=neutral,
        PublicKeyToken=b77a5c561934e089"/>
    <add assembly="System.ServiceModel.Web, Version=3.5.0.0, Culture=neutral,
        PublicKeyToken=31bf3856ad364e35"/>
    <add assembly="System.WorkflowServices, Version=3.5.0.0, Culture=neutral,
        PublicKeyToken=31bf3856ad364e35"/>
</assemblies>
```

Because of this reference in the root `web.config` file, these assemblies need not be referenced in a References folder, as you would have done in ASP.NET 1.0/1.1. You can actually add or delete assemblies that are referenced from this list. For example, if you have a custom assembly referenced continuously by each and every application on the server, you can simply add a similar reference to your custom assembly next to these others. Note that you can perform this same task through the application-specific `web.config` file of your application as well.

Even though assemblies might be referenced, you must still import the namespaces of these assemblies into your pages. The same root `web.config` file contains a list of namespaces automatically imported into each and every page of your application. This is specified through the `<namespaces>` child element of the `<pages>` element.

```
<namespaces>
   <add namespace="System" />
   <add namespace="System.Collections" />
   <add namespace="System.Collections.Specialized" />
   <add namespace="System.Configuration" />
   <add namespace="System.Text" />
   <add namespace="System.Text.RegularExpressions" />
   <add namespace="System.Web" />
   <add namespace="System.Web.Caching" />
   <add namespace="System.Web.SessionState" />
   <add namespace="System.Web.Security" />
   <add namespace="System.Web.Profile" />
   <add namespace="System.Web.UI" />
   <add namespace="System.Web.UI.WebControls" />
   <add namespace="System.Web.UI.WebControls.WebParts" />
   <add namespace="System.Web.UI.HtmlControls" />
</namespaces>
```

From this XML list, you can see that quite a number of namespaces are imported into each and every one of your ASP.NET pages. Again, you can feel free to modify this selection in the root `web.config` file or even make a similar selection of namespaces from within your application's `web.config` file.

For instance, you can import your own namespace in the `web.config` file of your application in order to make the namespace available on every page where it is utilized.

```
<?xml version="1.0"?>
<configuration>
   <system.web>
      <pages>
         <namespaces>
            <add namespace="MyCompany.Utilities" />
         </namespaces>
      </pages>
   </system.web>
</configuration>
```

Remember that importing a namespace into your ASP.NET page or user control gives you the opportunity to use the classes without fully identifying the class name. For example, by importing the namespace `System.Data.OleDb` into the ASP.NET page, you can refer to classes within this namespace by using the singular class name (`OleDbConnection` instead of `System.Data.OleDb.OleDbConnection`).

@Implements

The `@Implements` directive gets the ASP.NET page to implement a specified .NET Framework interface. This directive supports only a single attribute: `Interface`.

The `Interface` attribute directly specifies the .NET Framework interface. When the ASP.NET page or user control implements an interface, it has direct access to all its events, methods, and properties.

Here is an example of the `@Implements` directive:

```
<%@ Implements Interface="System.Web.UI.IValidator" %>
```

@Register

The `@Register` directive associates aliases with namespaces and class names for notation in custom server control syntax. You can see the use of the `@Register` directive when you drag and drop a user control onto any of your `.aspx` pages. Dragging a user control onto the `.aspx` page causes Visual Studio 2008 to create an `@Register` directive at the top of the page. This registers your user control on the page so that the control can then be accessed on the `.aspx` page by a specific name.

The `@Register` directive supports five attributes, as described in the following table.

Attribute	Description
`Assembly`	The assembly you are associating with the `TagPrefix`.
`Namespace`	The namespace to relate with `TagPrefix`.
`Src`	The location of the user control.
`TagName`	The alias to relate to the class name.
`TagPrefix`	The alias to relate to the namespace.

Here is an example of how to use the @Register directive to import a user control to an ASP.NET page:

```
<%@ Register TagPrefix="MyTag" Namespace="MyName.MyNamespace"
    Assembly="MyAssembly" %>
```

@Assembly

The @Assembly directive attaches assemblies, the building blocks of .NET applications, to an ASP.NET page or user control as it compiles, thereby making all the assembly's classes and interfaces available to the page. This directive supports two attributes: Name and Src.

- Name: Enables you to specify the name of an assembly used to attach to the page files. The name of the assembly should include the file name only, not the file's extension. For instance, if the file is MyAssembly.vb, the value of the name attribute should be MyAssembly.
- Src: Enables you to specify the source of the assembly file to use in compilation.

The following provides some examples of how to use the @Assembly directive:

```
<%@ Assembly Name="MyAssembly" %>
<%@ Assembly Src="MyAssembly.vb" %>
```

@PreviousPageType

This directive is used to specify the page from which any cross-page postings originate. Cross-page posting between ASP.NET pages is explained later in the section "Cross-Page Posting" and again in Chapter 17.

The @PreviousPageType directive is a new directive that works with the new cross-page posting capability that ASP.NET 3.5 provides. This simple directive contains only two possible attributes: TypeName and VirtualPath:

- TypeName: Sets the name of the derived class from which the postback will occur.
- VirtualPath: Sets the location of the posting page from which the postback will occur.

@MasterType

The @MasterType directive associates a class name to an ASP.NET page in order to get at strongly typed references or members contained within the specified master page. This directive supports two attributes:

- TypeName: Sets the name of the derived class from which to get strongly typed references or members.
- VirtualPath: Sets the location of the page from which these strongly typed references and members will be retrieved.

Details of how to use the @MasterType directive are shown in Chapter 8. Here is an example of its use:

```
<%@ MasterType VirtualPath="~/Wrox.master" %>
```

@OutputCache

The @OutputCache directive controls the output caching policies of an ASP.NET page or user control. This directive supports the ten attributes described in the following table.

Attribute	Description
CacheProfile	Allows for a central way to manage an application's cache profile. Use the CacheProfile attribute to specify the name of the cache profile detailed in the web.config.
Duration	The duration of time in seconds that the ASP.NET page or user control is cached.
Location	Location enumeration value. The default is Any. This is valid for .aspx pages only and does not work with user controls (.ascx). Other possible values include Client, Downstream, None, Server, and ServerAndClient.
NoStore	Specifies whether to send a no-store header with the page.
Shared	Specifies whether a user control's output can be shared across multiple pages. This attribute takes a Boolean value and the default setting is false.
SqlDependency	Enables a particular page to use SQL Server cache invalidation.
VaryByControl	Semicolon-separated list of strings used to vary the output cache of a user control.
VaryByCustom	String specifying the custom output caching requirements.
VaryByHeader	Semicolon-separated list of HTTP headers used to vary the output cache.
VaryByParam	Semicolon-separated list of strings used to vary the output cache.

Here is an example of how to use the @OutputCache directive:

```
<%@ OutputCache Duration="180" VaryByParam="None" %>
```

Remember that the Duration attribute specifies the amount of time in *seconds* during which this page is to be stored in the system cache.

@Reference

The @Reference directive declares that another ASP.NET page or user control should be compiled along with the active page or control. This directive supports just a single attribute:

- VirtualPath: Sets the location of the page or user control from which the active page will be referenced.

Here is an example of how to use the @Reference directive:

```
<%@ Reference VirtualPath="~/MyControl.ascx" %>
```

ASP.NET Page Events

ASP.NET developers consistently work with various events in their server-side code. Many of the events that they work with pertain to specific server controls. For instance, if you want to initiate some action when the end user clicks a button on your Web page, you create a button-click event in your server-side code, as shown in Listing 1-6.

Listing 1-6: A sample button-click event shown in VB

```
Protected Sub Button1_Click(sender As Object, e As EventArgs) Handles Button1.Click
   Label1.Text = TextBox1.Text
End Sub
```

In addition to the server controls, developers also want to initiate actions at specific moments when the ASP.NET page is being either created or destroyed. The ASP.NET page itself has always had a number of events for these instances. The following list shows you all the page events you could use in ASP.NET 1.0/1.1:

- `AbortTransaction`
- `CommitTransaction`
- `DataBinding`
- `Disposed`
- `Error`
- `Init`
- `Load`
- `PreRender`
- `Unload`

One of the more popular page events from this list is the `Load` event, which is used in VB as shown in Listing 1-7.

Listing 1-7: Using the Page_Load event

```
Protected Sub Page_Load(ByVal sender As Object, ByVal e As System.EventArgs)
   Handles Me.Load

   Response.Write("This is the Page_Load event")
End Sub
```

Besides the page events just shown, ASP.NET 3.5 has the following events:

- `InitComplete`: Indicates the initialization of the page is completed.
- `LoadComplete`: Indicates the page has been completely loaded into memory.
- `PreInit`: Indicates the moment immediately before a page is initialized.

- `PreLoad`: Indicates the moment before a page has been loaded into memory.
- `PreRenderComplete`: Indicates the moment directly before a page has been rendered in the browser.

An example of using any of these events, such as the `PreInit` event, is shown in Listing 1-8.

Listing 1-8: Using the new page events

VB

```
<script runat="server" language="vb">
    Protected Sub Page_PreInit(ByVal sender As Object, ByVal e As System.EventArgs)
        Page.Theme = Request.QueryString("ThemeChange")
    End Sub
</script>
```

C#

```
<script runat="server">
    protected void Page_PreInit(object sender, System.EventArgs e)
    {
        Page.Theme = Request.QueryString["ThemeChange"];
    }
</script>
```

If you create an ASP.NET 3.5 page and turn on tracing, you can see the order in which the main page events are initiated. They are fired in the following order:

1. `PreInit`
2. `Init`
3. `InitComplete`
4. `PreLoad`
5. `Load`
6. `LoadComplete`
7. `PreRender`
8. `PreRenderComplete`
9. `Unload`

With the addition of these choices, you can now work with the page and the controls on the page at many different points in the page-compilation process. You see these useful new page events in code examples throughout the book.

Dealing with PostBacks

When you are working with ASP.NET pages, be sure you understand the page events just listed. They are important because you place a lot of your page behavior inside these events at specific points in a page lifecycle.

In Active Server Pages 3.0, developers had their pages post to other pages within the application. ASP.NET pages typically post back to themselves in order to process events (such as a button-click event).

For this reason, you must differentiate between posts for the first time a page is loaded by the end user and *postbacks*. A postback is just that — a posting back to the same page. The postback contains all the form information collected on the initial page for processing if required.

Because of all the postbacks that can occur with an ASP.NET page, you want to know whether a request is the first instance for a particular page or is a postback from the same page. You can make this check by using the `IsPostBack` property of the `Page` class, as shown in the following example:

VB

```
If Page.IsPostBack = True Then
   ' Do processing
End If
```

C#

```
if (Page.IsPostBack == true) {
   // Do processing
}
```

In addition to checking against a `True` or `False` value, you can also find out if the request is not a postback in the following manner:

VB

```
If Not Page.IsPostBack Then
   ' Do processing
End If
```

C#

```
if (!Page.IsPostBack) {
   // Do processing
}
```

Cross-Page Posting

One common feature in ASP 3.0 that is difficult to achieve in ASP.NET 1.0/1.1 is the capability to do cross-page posting. Cross-page posting enables you to submit a form (say, `Page1.aspx`) and have this form and all the control values post themselves to another page (`Page2.aspx`).

Traditionally, any page created in ASP.NET 1.0/1.1 simply posted to itself, and you handled the control values within this page instance. You could differentiate between the page's first request and any postbacks by using the `Page.IsPostBack` property, as shown here:

```
If Page.IsPostBack Then
   ' deal with control values
End If
```

Even with this capability, many developers still wanted to be able to post to another page and deal with the first page's control values on that page. This is something that is possible in ASP.NET 3.5, and it is quite a simple process.

For an example, create a page called `Page1.aspx` that contains a simple form. This page is shown in Listing 1-9.

Listing 1-9: Page1.aspx

VB

```
<%@ Page Language="VB" %>

<!DOCTYPE html PUBLIC "-//W3C//DTD XHTML 1.1//EN"
 "http://www.w3.org/TR/xhtml11/DTD/xhtml11.dtd">

<script runat="server">
    Protected Sub Button1_Click(ByVal sender As Object, _
       ByVal e As System.EventArgs)

        Label1.Text = "Hello " & TextBox1.Text & "<br />" & _
            "Date Selected: " & Calendar1.SelectedDate.ToShortDateString()

    End Sub
</script>

<html xmlns="http://www.w3.org/1999/xhtml">
<head runat="server">
    <title>First Page</title>
</head>
<body>
    <form id="form1" runat="server">
        Enter your name:<br />
        <asp:Textbox ID="TextBox1" Runat="server">
        </asp:Textbox>
        <p>
        When do you want to fly?<br />
        <asp:Calendar ID="Calendar1" Runat="server"></asp:Calendar></p>
        <br />
        <asp:Button ID="Button1" Runat="server" Text="Submit page to itself"
         OnClick="Button1_Click" />
        <asp:Button ID="Button2" Runat="server" Text="Submit page to Page2.aspx"
         PostBackUrl="~/Page2.aspx" />
        <p>
        <asp:Label ID="Label1" Runat="server"></asp:Label></p>
    </form>
</body>
</html>
```

C#

```
<%@ Page Language="C#" %>

<script runat="server">
```

```
    protected void Button1_Click (object sender, System.EventArgs e)
    {
        Label1.Text = "Hello " + TextBox1.Text + "<br />" +
            "Date Selected: " + Calendar1.SelectedDate.ToShortDateString();
    }
</script>
```

The code from `Page1.aspx`, as shown in Listing 1-9, is quite interesting. First, two buttons are shown on the page. Both buttons submit the form, but each submits the form to a different location. The first button submits the form to itself. This is the behavior that has been the default for ASP.NET 1.0/1.1. In fact, nothing is different about `Button1`. It submits to `Page1.aspx` as a postback because of the use of the `OnClick` property in the button control. A `Button1_Click` method on `Page1.aspx` handles the values that are contained within the server controls on the page.

The second button, `Button2`, works quite differently. This button does not contain an `OnClick` method as the first button did. Instead, it uses the `PostBackUrl` property. This property takes a string value that points to the location of the file to which this page should post. In this case, it is `Page2.aspx`. This means that `Page2.aspx` now receives the postback and all the values contained in the `Page1.aspx` controls. Look at the code for `Page2.aspx`, shown in Listing 1-10.

Listing 1-10: Page2.aspx

VB

```
<%@ Page Language="VB" %>

<!DOCTYPE html PUBLIC "-//W3C//DTD XHTML 1.1//EN"
 "http://www.w3.org/TR/xhtml11/DTD/xhtml11.dtd">

<script runat="server">
    Protected Sub Page_Load(ByVal sender As Object, ByVal e As System.EventArgs)
        Dim pp_Textbox1 As TextBox
        Dim pp_Calendar1 As Calendar

        pp_Textbox1 = CType(PreviousPage.FindControl("Textbox1"), TextBox)
        pp_Calendar1 = CType(PreviousPage.FindControl("Calendar1"), Calendar)

        Label1.Text = "Hello " & pp_Textbox1.Text & "<br />" & _
            "Date Selected: " & pp_Calendar1.SelectedDate.ToShortDateString()
    End Sub
</script>

<html xmlns="http://www.w3.org/1999/xhtml" >
<head runat="server">
    <title>Second Page</title>
</head>
<body>
    <form id="form1" runat="server">
        <asp:Label ID="Label1" Runat="server"></asp:Label>
    </form>
</body>
</html>
```

Continued

C#

```
<%@ Page Language="C#" %>

<!DOCTYPE html PUBLIC "-//W3C//DTD XHTML 1.1//EN"
 "http://www.w3.org/TR/xhtml11/DTD/xhtml11.dtd">

<script runat="server">
    protected void Page_Load(object sender, System.EventArgs e)
    {
        TextBox pp_Textbox1;
        Calendar pp_Calendar1;

        pp_Textbox1 = (TextBox)PreviousPage.FindControl("Textbox1");
        pp_Calendar1 = (Calendar)PreviousPage.FindControl("Calendar1");

        Label1.Text = "Hello " + pp_Textbox1.Text + "<br />" + "Date Selected: " +
           pp_Calendar1.SelectedDate.ToShortDateString();
    }
</script>
```

You have a couple of ways of getting at the values of the controls that are exposed from `Page1.aspx` from the second page. The first option is displayed in Listing 1-10. To get at a particular control's value that is carried over from the previous page, you simply create an instance of that control type and populate this instance using the `FindControl()` method from the `PreviousPage` property. The `String` value assigned to the `FindControl()` method is the `Id` value, which is used for the server control from the previous page. After this is assigned, you can work with the server control and its carried-over values just as if it had originally resided on the current page. You can see from the example that you can extract the `Text` and `SelectedDate` properties from the controls without any problem.

Another way of exposing the control values from the first page (`Page1.aspx`) is to create a `Property` for the control. This is shown in Listing 1-11.

Listing 1-11: Exposing the values of the control from a Property

VB

```
<%@ Page Language="VB" %>

<!DOCTYPE html PUBLIC "-//W3C//DTD XHTML 1.1//EN"
 "http://www.w3.org/TR/xhtml11/DTD/xhtml11.dtd">

<script runat="server">
   Public ReadOnly Property pp_TextBox1() As TextBox
       Get
           Return TextBox1
       End Get
   End Property

   Public ReadOnly Property pp_Calendar1() As Calendar
```

```
        Get
            Return Calendar1
        End Get
    End Property

    Protected Sub Button1_Click(ByVal sender As Object, ByVal e As System.EventArgs)
        Label1.Text = "Hello " & TextBox1.Text & "<br />" & _
            "Date Selected: " & Calendar1.SelectedDate.ToShortDateString()
    End Sub
</script>
```

C#

```
<%@ Page Language="C#" %>

<!DOCTYPE html PUBLIC "-//W3C//DTD XHTML 1.1//EN"
 "http://www.w3.org/TR/xhtml11/DTD/xhtml11.dtd">

<script runat="server">
    public TextBox pp_TextBox1
    {
        get
        {
            return TextBox1;
        }
    }

    public Calendar pp_Calendar1
    {
        get
        {
            return Calendar1;
        }
    }

    protected void Button1_Click (object sender, System.EventArgs e)
    {
        Label1.Text = "Hello " + TextBox1.Text + "<br />" +
            "Date Selected: " + Calendar1.SelectedDate.ToShortDateString();
    }
</script>
```

Now that these properties are exposed on the posting page, the second page (`Page2.aspx`) can more easily work with the server control properties that are exposed from the first page. Listing 1-12 shows you how `Page2.aspx` works with these exposed properties.

Listing 1-12: Consuming the exposed properties from the first page

VB

```
<%@ Page Language="VB" %>
<%@ PreviousPageType VirtualPath="Page1.aspx" %>
```

Continued

```
<!DOCTYPE html PUBLIC "-//W3C//DTD XHTML 1.1//EN"
 "http://www.w3.org/TR/xhtml11/DTD/xhtml11.dtd">

<script runat="server">
    Protected Sub Page_Load(ByVal sender As Object, ByVal e As System.EventArgs)
        Label1.Text = "Hello " & PreviousPage.pp_Textbox1.Text & "<br />" & _
            "Date Selected: " & _
            PreviousPage.pp_Calendar1.SelectedDate.ToShortDateString()
    End Sub
</script>
```

C#

```
<%@ Page Language="C#" %>
<%@ PreviousPageType VirtualPath="Page1.aspx" %>

<!DOCTYPE html PUBLIC "-//W3C//DTD XHTML 1.1//EN"
 "http://www.w3.org/TR/xhtml11/DTD/xhtml11.dtd">

<script runat="server">
    protected void Page_Load(object sender, System.EventArgs e)
    {
        Label1.Text = "Hello " + PreviousPage.pp_TextBox1.Text + "<br />" +
            "Date Selected: " +
            PreviousPage.pp_Calendar1.SelectedDate.ToShortDateString();
    }
</script>
```

In order to be able to work with the properties that `Page1.aspx` exposes, you have to strongly type the `PreviousPage` property to `Page1.aspx`. To do this, you use the `PreviousPageType` directive. This new directive allows you to specifically point to `Page1.aspx` with the use of the `VirtualPath` attribute. When that is in place, notice that you can see the properties that `Page1.aspx` exposes through IntelliSense from the `PreviousPage` property. This is illustrated in Figure 1-7.

As you can see, working with cross-page posting is straightforward. Notice that, when you are cross posting from one page to another, you are not restricted to working only with the postback on the second page. In fact, you can still create methods on `Page1.aspx` that work with the postback before moving onto `Page2.aspx`. To do this, you simply add an `OnClick` event for the button in `Page1.aspx` and a method. You also assign a value for the `PostBackUrl` property. You can then work with the postback on `Page1.aspx` and then again on `Page2.aspx`.

What happens if someone requests `Page2.aspx` before she works her way through `Page1.aspx`? It is actually quite easy to determine if the request is coming from `Page1.aspx` or if someone just hit `Page2.aspx` directly. You can work with the request through the use of the `IsCrossPagePostBack` property that is quite similar to the `IsPostBack` property from ASP.NET 1.0/1.1. The `IsCrossPagePostBack` property enables you to check whether the request is from `Page1.aspx`. Listing 1-13 shows an example of this.

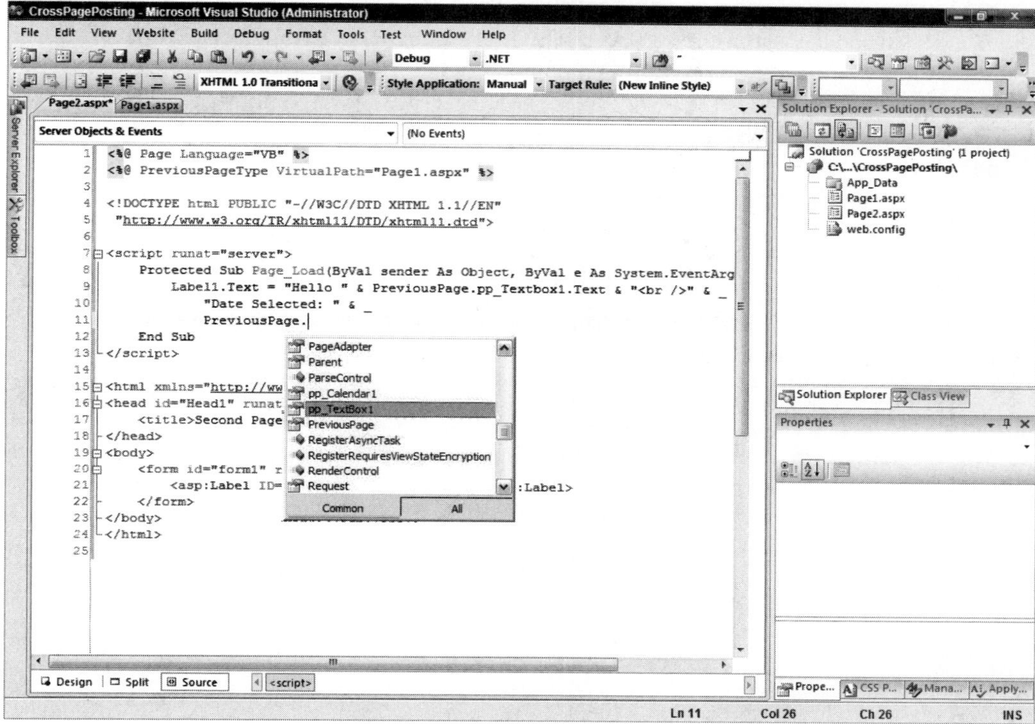

Figure 1-7

Listing 1-13: Using the IsCrossPagePostBack property

VB

```
<%@ Page Language="VB" %>
<%@ PreviousPageType VirtualPath="Page1.aspx" %>

<!DOCTYPE html PUBLIC "-//W3C//DTD XHTML 1.1//EN"
 "http://www.w3.org/TR/xhtml11/DTD/xhtml11.dtd">

<script runat="server">
    Protected Sub Page_Load(ByVal sender As Object, ByVal e As System.EventArgs)
      If Not PreviousPage Is Nothing And PreviousPage.IsCrossPagePostBack Then
        Label1.Text = "Hello " & PreviousPage.pp_Textbox1.Text & "<br />" & _
            "Date Selected: " & _
            PreviousPage.pp_Calendar1.SelectedDate.ToShortDateString()
```

Continued

```
        Else
            Response.Redirect("Page1.aspx")
        End If
    End Sub
</script>
```

C#

```
<%@ Page Language="C#" %>
<%@ PreviousPageType VirtualPath="Page1.aspx" %>

<!DOCTYPE html PUBLIC "-//W3C//DTD XHTML 1.1//EN"
 "http://www.w3.org/TR/xhtml11/DTD/xhtml11.dtd">

<script runat="server">
    protected void Page_Load(object sender, System.EventArgs e)
    {
      if (PreviousPage != null && PreviousPage.IsCrossPagePostBack) {
        Label1.Text = "Hello " + PreviousPage.pp_TextBox1.Text + "<br />" +
            "Date Selected: " +
            PreviousPage.pp_Calendar1.SelectedDate.ToShortDateString();
      }
      else
      {
         Response.Redirect("Page1.aspx");
      }
    }
</script>
```

ASP.NET Application Folders

When you create ASP.NET applications, notice that ASP.NET 3.5 uses a file-based approach. When working with ASP.NET, you can add as many files and folders as you want within your application without recompiling each and every time a new file is added to the overall solution. ASP.NET 3.5 includes the capability to automatically precompile your ASP.NET applications dynamically.

ASP.NET 1.0/1.1 compiled everything in your solution into a DLL. This is no longer necessary because ASP.NET applications now have a defined folder structure. By using the ASP.NET defined folders, you can have your code automatically compiled for you, your application themes accessible throughout your application, and your globalization resources available whenever you need them. Look at each of these defined folders to see how they work. The first folder reviewed is the `\App_Code` folder.

\App_Code Folder

The `\App_Code` folder is meant to store your classes, `.wsdl` files, and typed datasets. Any of these items stored in this folder are then automatically available to all the pages within your solution. The nice thing about the `\App_Code` folder is that when you place something inside this folder, Visual Studio 2008 automatically detects this and compiles it if it is a class (`.vb` or `.cs`), automatically creates your XML Web service proxy class (from the `.wsdl` file), or automatically creates a typed dataset for you from your `.xsd` files. After the files are automatically compiled, these items are then instantaneously available to any of your ASP.NET pages that are in the same solution. Look at how to employ a simple class in your solution using the `\App_Code` folder.

The first step is to create an `\App_Code` folder. To do this, simply right-click the solution and choose Add ASP.NET Folder ➪ App_Code. Right away you will notice that Visual Studio 2008 treats this folder differently than the other folders in your solution. The `\App_Code` folder is shown in a different color (gray) with a document pictured next to the folder icon. See Figure 1-8.

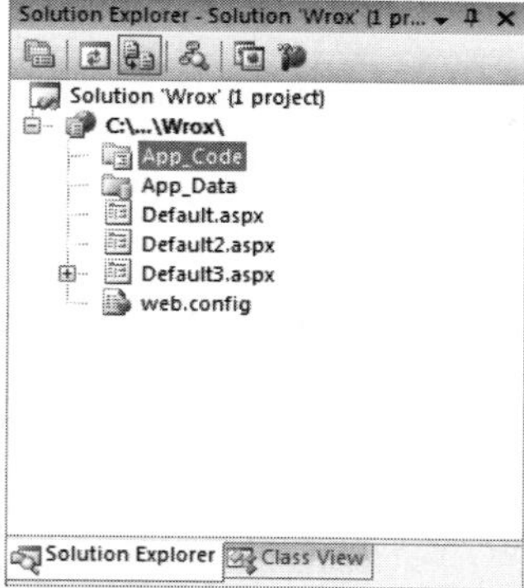

Figure 1-8

After the `\App_Code` folder is in place, right-click the folder and select Add New Item. The Add New Item dialog that appears gives you a few options for the types of files that you can place within this folder. The available options include an AJAX-enabled WCF Service, a Class file, a LINQ to SQL Class, a Text file, a DataSet, a Report, and a Class Diagram if you are using Visual Studio 2008. Visual Web Developer 2008 Express Edition offers only the Class file, Text file, and DataSet file. For the first example, select the file of type Class and name the class `Calculator.vb` or `Calculator.cs`. Listing 1-14 shows how the `Calculator` class should appear.

Listing 1-14: The Calculator class

VB

```
Imports Microsoft.VisualBasic

Public Class Calculator
    Public Function Add(ByVal a As Integer, ByVal b As Integer) As Integer
        Return (a + b)
    End Function
End Class
```

C#

```
using System;

public class Calculator
{
    public int Add(int a, int b)
        {
            return (a + b);
    }
}
```

What's next? Just save this file, and it is now available to use in any pages that are in your solution. To see this in action, create a simple .aspx page that has just a single Label server control. Listing 1-15 shows you the code to place within the Page_Load event to make this new class available to the page.

Listing 1-15: An .aspx page that uses the Calculator class

VB

```
<%@ Page Language="VB" %>

<!DOCTYPE html PUBLIC "-//W3C//DTD XHTML 1.1//EN"
 "http://www.w3.org/TR/xhtml11/DTD/xhtml11.dtd">

<script runat="server">
    Protected Sub Page_Load(ByVal sender As Object, ByVal e As System.EventArgs)
        Dim myCalc As New Calculator
        Label1.Text = myCalc.Add(12, 12)
    End Sub
</script>
```

C#

```
<%@ Page Language="C#" %>

<!DOCTYPE html PUBLIC "-//W3C//DTD XHTML 1.1//EN"
 "http://www.w3.org/TR/xhtml11/DTD/xhtml11.dtd">

<script runat="server">
    protected void Page_Load(object sender, System.EventArgs e)
    {
        Calculator myCalc = new Calculator();
        Label1.Text = myCalc.Add(12, 12).ToString();
    }
</script>
```

When you run this .aspx page, notice that it utilizes the Calculator class without any problem, with no need to compile the class before use. In fact, right after saving the Calculator class in your solution or moving the class to the \App_Code folder, you also instantaneously receive IntelliSense capability on the methods that the class exposes (as illustrated in Figure 1-9).

To see how Visual Studio 2008 works with the \App_Code folder, open the Calculator class again in the IDE and add a Subtract method. Your class should now appear as shown in Listing 1-16.

Listing 1-16: Adding a Subtract method to the Calculator class

VB

```
Imports Microsoft.VisualBasic

Public Class Calculator
    Public Function Add(ByVal a As Integer, ByVal b As Integer) As Integer
        Return (a + b)
    End Function

    Public Function Subtract(ByVal a As Integer, ByVal b As Integer) As Integer
        Return (a - b)
```

```
    End Function
End Class
```

C#

```
using System;

public class Calculator
{
    public int Add(int a, int b)
    {
            return (a + b);
    }

    public int Subtract(int a, int b)
    {
            return (a - b);
    }
}
```

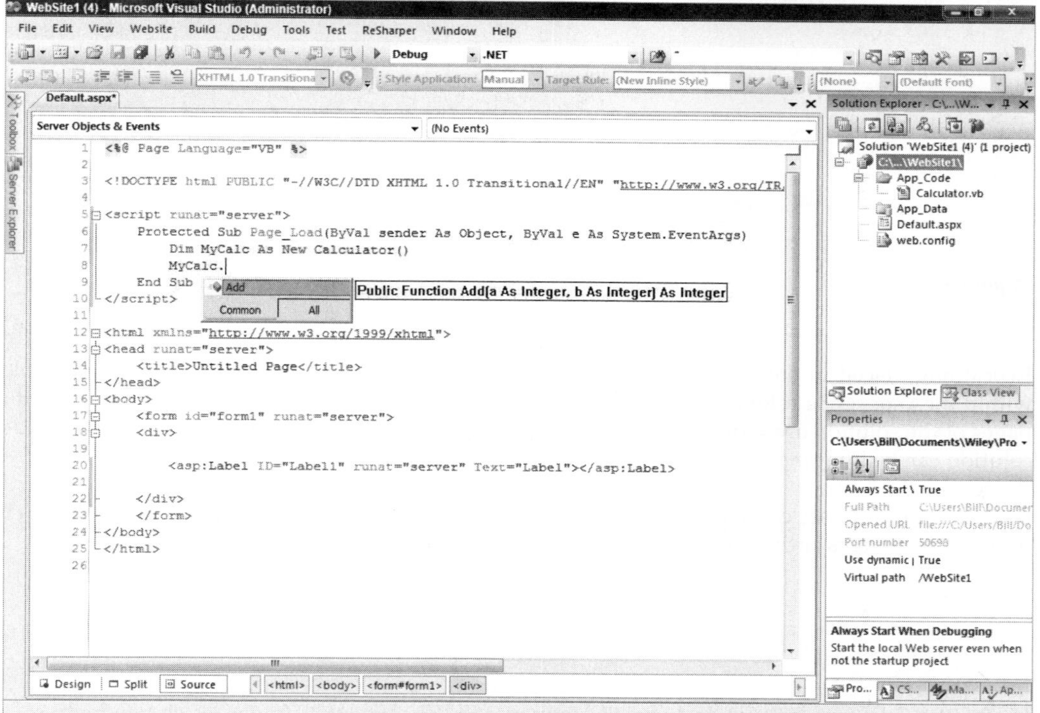

Figure 1-9

After you have added the `Subtract` method to the `Calculator` class, save the file and go back to your `.aspx` page. Notice that the class has been recompiled by the IDE, and the new method is now available to your page. You see this directly in IntelliSense. Figure 1-10 shows this in action.

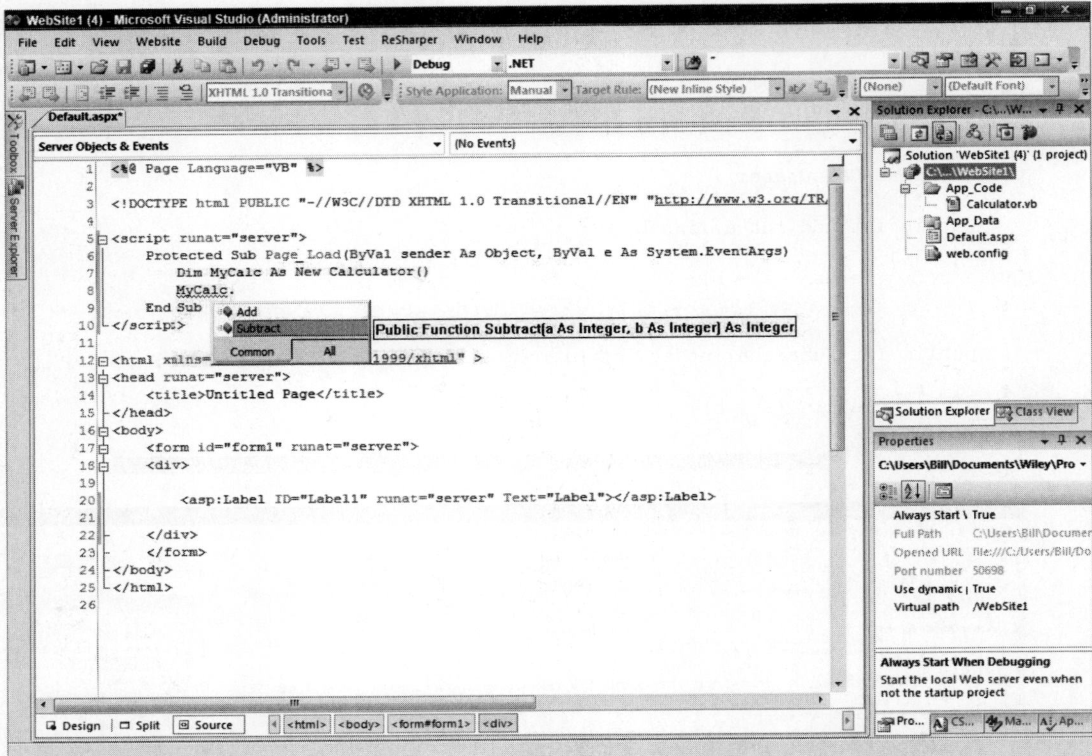

Figure 1-10

Everything placed in the \App_Code folder is compiled into a single assembly. The class files placed within the \App_Code folder are not required to use a specific language. This means that even if all the pages of the solution are written in Visual Basic 2008, the `Calculator` class in the \App_Code folder of the solution can be built in C# (`Calculator.cs`).

Because all the classes contained in this folder are built into a single assembly, you *cannot* have classes of different languages sitting in the root \App_Code folder, as in the following example:

```
\App_Code
    Calculator.cs
    AdvancedMath.vb
```

Having two classes made up of different languages in the \App_Code folder (as shown here) causes an error to be thrown. It is impossible for the assigned compiler to work with two different languages. Therefore, in order to be able to work with multiple languages in your \App_Code folder, you must make some changes to the folder structure and to the `web.config` file.

The first step is to add two new subfolders to the \App_Code folder — a \VB folder and a \CS folder. This gives you the following folder structure:

```
\App_Code
   \VB
      Add.vb
   \CS
      Subtract.cs
```

This still will not correctly compile these class files into separate assemblies, at least not until you make some additions to the web.config file. Most likely, you do not have a web.config file in your solution at this moment, so add one through the Solution Explorer. After it is added, change the <compilation> node so that it is structured as shown in Listing 1-17.

Listing 1-17: Structuring the web.config file so that classes in the \App_Code folder can use different languages

```
<compilation>
   <codeSubDirectories>
      <add directoryName="VB"></add>
      <add directoryName="CS"></add>
   </codeSubDirectories>
</compilation>
```

Now that this is in place in your web.config file, you can work with each of the classes in your ASP.NET pages. In addition, any C# class placed in the CS folder is now automatically compiled just like any of the classes placed in the VB folder. Because you can add these directories in the web.config file, you are not required to name them VB and CS as we did; you can use whatever name tickles your fancy.

\App_Data Folder

The \App_Data folder holds the data stores utilized by the application. It is a good spot to centrally store all the data stores your application might use. The \App_Data folder can contain Microsoft SQL Express files (.mdf files), Microsoft Access files (.mdb files), XML files, and more.

The user account utilized by your application will have read and write access to any of the files contained within the \App_Data folder. By default, this is the ASPNET account. Another reason for storing all your data files in this folder is that much of the ASP.NET system — from the membership and role management systems to the GUI tools, such as the ASP.NET MMC snap-in and ASP.NET Web Site Administration Tool — is built to work with the \App_Data folder.

\App_Themes Folder

Themes are a new way of providing a common look-and-feel to your site across every page. You implement a theme by using a .skin file, CSS files, and images used by the server controls of your site. All these elements can make a *theme*, which is then stored in the \App_Themes folder of your solution. By storing these elements within the \App_Themes folder, you ensure that all the pages within the solution can take advantage of the theme and easily apply its elements to the controls and markup of the page. Themes are discussed in great detail in Chapter 6 of this book.

\App_GlobalResources Folder

Resource files are string tables that can serve as data dictionaries for your applications when these applications require changes to content based on things such as changes in culture. You can add Assembly Resource Files (`.resx`) to the `\App_GlobalResources` folder, and they are dynamically compiled and made part of the solution for use by all your `.aspx` pages in the application. When using ASP.NET 1.0/1.1, you had to use the `resgen.exe` tool and had to compile your resource files to a `.dll` or `.exe` for use within your solution. It is considerably easier to deal with resource files in ASP.NET 3.5. Simply placing your application-wide resources in this folder makes them instantly accessible. Localization is covered in detail in Chapter 31.

\App_LocalResources

Even if you are not interested in constructing application-wide resources using the `\App_GlobalResources` folder, you may want resources that can be used for a single `.aspx` page. You can do this very simply by using the `\App_LocalResources` folder.

You can add resource files that are page-specific to the `\App_LocalResources` folder by constructing the name of the `.resx` file in the following manner:

- `Default.aspx.resx`
- `Default.aspx.fi.resx`
- `Default.aspx.ja.resx`
- `Default.aspx.en-gb.resx`

Now, the resource declarations used on the `Default.aspx` page are retrieved from the appropriate file in the `\App_LocalResources` folder. By default, the `Default.aspx.resx` resource file is used if another match is not found. If the client is using a culture specification of `fi-FI` (Finnish), however, the `Default.aspx.fi.resx` file is used instead. Localization of local resources is covered in detail in Chapter 30.

\App_WebReferences

The `\App_WebReferences`folder is a new name for the previous `Web References` folder used in previous versions of ASP.NET. Now you can use the `\App_WebReferences` folder and have automatic access to the remote Web services referenced from your application. Web services in ASP.NET are covered in Chapter 30.

\App_Browsers

The `\App_Browsers` folder holds `.browser` files, which are XML files used to identity the browsers making requests to the application and understanding the capabilities these browsers have. You can find a list of globally accessible .browser files at C:\Windows\Microsoft.NET\Framework\v2.0.50727\CONFIG\Browsers. In addition, if you want to change any part of these default browser definition files, just copy the appropriate .browser file from the Browsers folder to your application's \App_Browsers folder and change the definition.

Compilation

You already saw how Visual Studio 2008 compiles pieces of your application as you work with them (for instance, by placing a class in the \App_Code folder). The other parts of the application, such as the .aspx pages, can be compiled just as they were in earlier versions of ASP.NET by referencing the pages in the browser.

When an ASP.NET page is referenced in the browser for the first time, the request is passed to the ASP.NET parser that creates the class file in the language of the page. It is passed to the ASP.NET parser based on the file's extension (.aspx) because ASP.NET realizes that this file extension type is meant for its handling and processing. After the class file has been created, the class file is compiled into a DLL and then written to the disk of the Web server. At this point, the DLL is instantiated and processed, and an output is generated for the initial requester of the ASP.NET page. This is detailed in Figure 1-11.

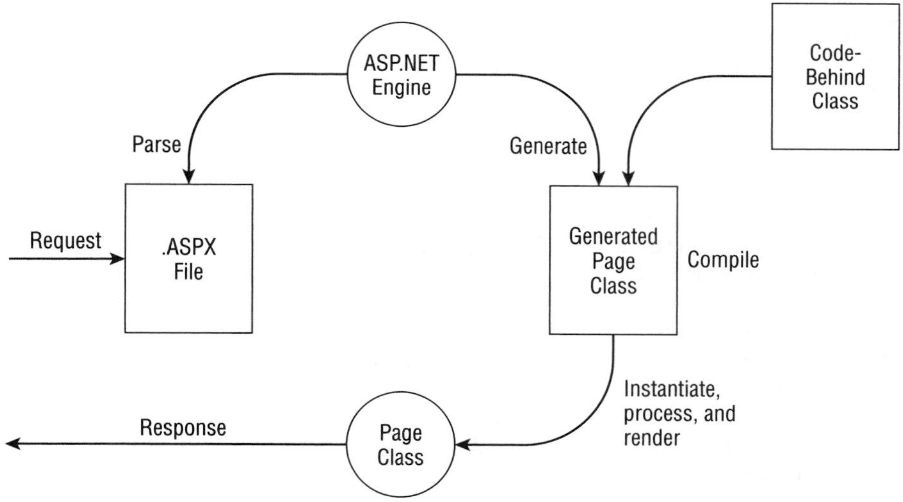

Figure 1-11

On the next request, great things happen. Instead of going through the entire process again for the second and respective requests, the request simply causes an instantiation of the already-created DLL, which sends out a response to the requester. This is illustrated in Figure 1-12.

Because of the mechanics of this process, if you made changes to your .aspx code-behind pages, you found it necessary to recompile your application. This was quite a pain if you had a larger site and did not want your end users to experience the extreme lag that occurs when an `.aspx` page is referenced for the first time after compilation. Many developers, consequently, began to develop their own tools that automatically go out and hit every single page within their application to remove this first-time lag hit from the end user's browsing experience.

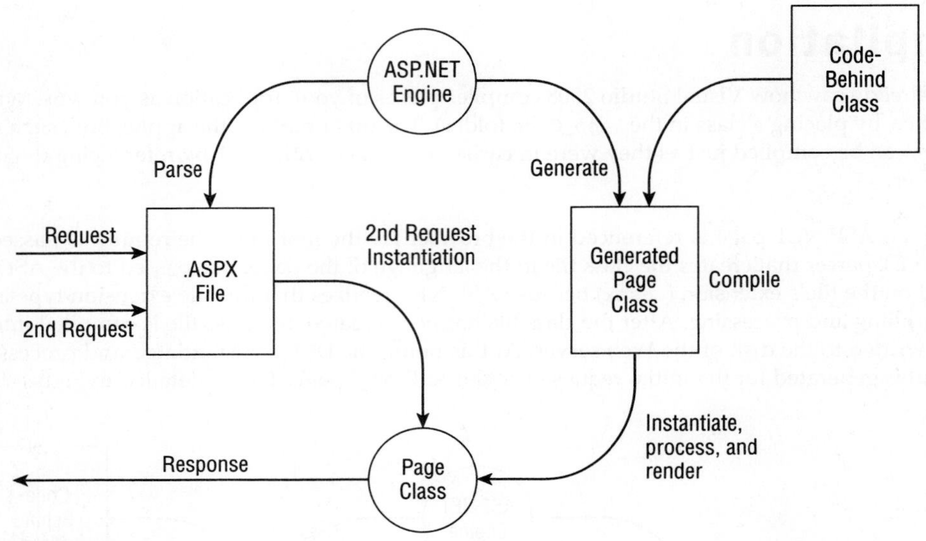

Figure 1-12

ASP.NET 3.5 provides a few ways to precompile your entire application with a single command that you can issue through a command line. One type of compilation is referred to as *in-place precompilation*. In order to precompile your entire ASP.NET application, you must use the `aspnet_compiler.exe` tool that now comes with ASP.NET 3.5. You navigate to the tool using the Command window. Open the Command window and navigate to `C:\Windows\Microsoft.NET\Framework\v2.0.50727\`. When you are there, you can work with the `aspnet_compiler` tool. You can also get to this tool directly by pulling up the Visual Studio 2008 Command Prompt. Choose Start⇨All Programs⇨Microsoft Visual Studio 2008⇨Visual Studio Tools⇨Visual Studio 2008 Command Prompt.

After you get the command prompt, you use the aspnet_compiler.exe tool to perform an in-place precompilation using the following command:

```
aspnet_compiler -p "C:\Inetpub\wwwroot\WROX" -v none
```

You then get a message stating that the precompilation is successful. The other great thing about this precompilation capability is that you can also use it to find errors on any of the ASP.NET pages in your application. Because it hits each and every page, if one of the pages contains an error that won't be triggered until runtime, you get notification of the error immediately as you employ this precompilation method.

The next precompilation option is commonly referred to as *precompilation for deployment*. This is an outstanding capability of ASP.NET that enables you to compile your application down to some DLLs, which can then be deployed to customers, partners, or elsewhere for your own use. Not only are minimal steps required to do this, but also after your application is compiled, you simply have to move around the DLL and some placeholder files for the site to work. This means that your Web site code is completely removed and placed in the DLL when deployed.

However, before you take these precompilation steps, create a folder in your root drive called, for example, `Wrox`. This folder is the one to which you will direct the compiler output. When it is in place, you can return to the compiler tool and give the following command:

```
aspnet_compiler -v [Application Name] -p [Physical Location] [Target]
```

Therefore, if you have an application called `INETA` located at `C:\Websites\INETA`, you use the following commands:

```
aspnet_compiler -v /INETA -p C:\Websites\INETA C:\Wrox
```

Press the Enter key, and the compiler either tells you that it has a problem with one of the command parameters or that it was successful (shown in Figure 1-13). If it was successful, you can see the output placed in the target directory.

Figure 1-13

In the example just shown, `-v` is a command for the virtual path of the application, which is provided by using `/INETA`. The next command is `-p`, which is pointing to the physical path of the application. In this case, it is `C:\Websites\INETA`. Finally, the last bit, `C:\Wrox`, is the location of the compiler output. The following table describes some of the possible commands for the `aspnet_compiler.exe` tool.

Command	Description
`-m`	Specifies the full IIS metabase path of the application. If you use the `-m` command, you cannot use the `-v` or `-p` command.
`-v`	Specifies the virtual path of the application to be compiled. If you also use the `-p` command, the physical path is used to find the location of the application.

Command	Description
`-p`	Specifies the physical path of the application to be compiled. If this is not specified, the IIS metabase is used to find the application.
`-u`	If this command is utilized, it specifies that the application is updatable.
`-f`	Specifies to overwrite the target directory if it already exists.
`-d`	Specifies that the debug information should be excluded from the compilation process.
`[targetDir]`	Specifies the target directory where the compiled files should be placed. If this is not specified, the output files are placed in the application directory.

After compiling the application, you can go to `C:\Wrox` to see the output. Here you see all the files and the file structures that were in the original application. However, if you look at the content of one of the files, notice that the file is simply a placeholder. In the actual file, you find the following comment:

```
This is a marker file generated by the precompilation tool
and should not be deleted!
```

In fact, you find a `Code.dll` file in the `bin` folder where all the page code is located. Because it is in a DLL file, it provides great code obfuscation as well. From here on, all you do is move these files to another server using FTP or Windows Explorer, and you can run the entire Web application from these files. When you have an update to the application, you simply provide a new set of compiled files. A sample output is displayed in Figure 1-14.

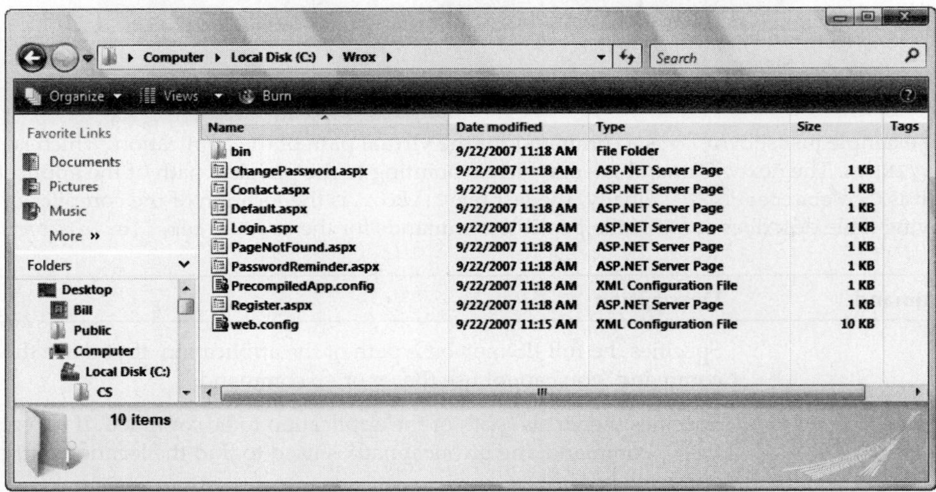

Figure 1-14

Note that this compilation process does not compile *every* type of Web file. In fact, it compiles only the ASP.NET-specific file types and leaves out of the compilation process the following types of files:

- HTML files
- XML files
- XSD files
- `web.config` files
- Text files

You cannot do much to get around this, except in the case of the HTML files and the text files. For these file types, just change the file extensions of these file types to `.aspx`; they are then compiled into the `Code.dll` like all the other ASP.NET files.

Build Providers

As you review the various ASP.NET folders, note that one of the more interesting folders is the \App_Code folder. You can simply drop code files, XSD files, and even WSDL files directly into the folder for automatic compilation. When you drop a class file into the \App_Code folder, the class can automatically be utilized by a running application. In the early days of ASP.NET, if you wanted to deploy a custom component, you had to precompile the component before being able to utilize it within your application. Now ASP.NET simply takes care of all the work that you once had to do. You do not need to perform any compilation routine.

Which file types are compiled in the App_Code folder? As with most things in ASP.NET, this is determined through settings applied in a configuration file. Listing 1-18 shows a snippet of configuration code taken from the master `Web.config` file found in ASP.NET 3.5.

Listing 1-18: Reviewing the list of build providers

```
<compilation>
   <buildProviders>
      <add extension=".aspx" type="System.Web.Compilation.PageBuildProvider" />
      <add extension=".ascx"
       type="System.Web.Compilation.UserControlBuildProvider" />
      <add extension=".master"
       type="System.Web.Compilation.MasterPageBuildProvider" />
      <add extension=".asmx"
       type="System.Web.Compilation.WebServiceBuildProvider" />
      <add extension=".ashx"
       type="System.Web.Compilation.WebHandlerBuildProvider" />
      <add extension=".soap"
       type="System.Web.Compilation.WebServiceBuildProvider" />
      <add extension=".resx" type="System.Web.Compilation.ResXBuildProvider" />
      <add extension=".resources"
```

Continued

```
type="System.Web.Compilation.ResourcesBuildProvider" />
      <add extension=".wsdl" type="System.Web.Compilation.WsdlBuildProvider" />
      <add extension=".xsd" type="System.Web.Compilation.XsdBuildProvider" />
      <add extension=".js" type="System.Web.Compilation.ForceCopyBuildProvider" />
      <add extension=".lic"
       type="System.Web.Compilation.IgnoreFileBuildProvider" />
      <add extension=".licx"
       type="System.Web.Compilation.IgnoreFileBuildProvider" />
      <add extension=".exclude"
       type="System.Web.Compilation.IgnoreFileBuildProvider" />
      <add extension=".refresh"
       type="System.Web.Compilation.IgnoreFileBuildProvider" />
   </buildProviders>
</compilation>
```

This section contains a list of build providers that can be used by two entities in your development cycle. The build provider is first used is during development when you are building your solution in Visual Studio 2008. For instance, placing a `.wsdl` file in the App_Code folder during development in Visual Studio causes the IDE to give you automatic access to the dynamically compiled proxy class that comes from this `.wsdl` file. The other entity that uses the build providers is ASP.NET itself. As stated, simply dragging and dropping a `.wsdl` file in the App_Code folder of a deployed application automatically gives the ASP.NET application access to the created proxy class.

A build provider is simply a class that inherits from `System.Web.Compilation.BuildProvider`. The `<buildProviders>` section in the `Web.config` allows you to list the build provider classes that will be utilized. The capability to dynamically compile any WSDL file is defined by the following line in the configuration file.

```
<add extension=".wsdl" type="System.Web.Compilation.WsdlBuildProvider" />
```

This means that any file utilizing the `.wsdl` file extension is compiled using the `WsdlBuildProvider`, a class that inherits from `BuildProvider`. Microsoft provides a set number of build providers out of the box for you to use. As you can see from the set in Listing 1-18, a number of providers are available in addition to the `WsdlBuildProvider`, including providers such as the `XsdBuildProvider`, `PageBuildProvider`, `UserControlBuildProvider`, `MasterPageBuildProvider`, and more. Just by looking at the names of some of these providers you can pretty much understand what they are about. The next section, however, reviews some other providers whose names might not ring a bell right away.

Using the Built-in Build Providers

Two of the providers that this section covers are the `ForceCopyBuildProvider` and the `IgnoreFile-BuildProvider`, both of which are included in the default list of providers.

The `ForceCopyBuildProvider` is basically a provider that copies only those files for deployment that use the defined extension. (These files are not included in the compilation process.) An extension that utilizes the `ForceCopyBuildProvider` is shown in the predefined list in Listing 1-18. This is the `.js` file type (a JavaScript file extension). Any `.js` files are simply copied and not included in the compilation process (which makes sense for JavaScript files). You can add other file types that you want to be a part of this copy process with the command shown here:

```
<add extension=".chm" type="System.Web.Compilation.ForceCopyBuildProvider" />
```

In addition to the `ForceCopyBuildProvider`, you should also be aware of the `IgnoreFileBuildProvider` class. This provider causes the defined file type to be ignored in the deployment or compilation process. This means that any file type defined with `IgnoreFileBuildProvider` is simply ignored. Visual Studio will not copy, compile, or deploy any file of that type. So, if you are including Visio diagrams in your project, you can simply add the following `<add>` element to the `web.config` file to have this file type ignored. An example is presented here:

```
<add extension=".vsd" type="System.Web.Compilation.IgnoreFileBuildProvider" />
```

With this in place, all `.vsd` files are ignored.

Using Your Own Build Providers

In addition to using the predefined build providers out of the box, you can also take this build provider stuff one-step further and construct your own custom build providers to use within your applications.

For example, suppose you wanted to construct a `Car` class dynamically based upon settings applied in a custom `.car` file that you have defined. You might do this because you are using this `.car` definition file in multiple projects or many times within the same project. Using a build provider makes it simpler to define these multiple instances of the `Car` class.

An example of the `.car` file type is presented in Listing 1-19.

Listing 1-19: An example of a .car file

```
<?xml version="1.0" encoding="utf-8" ?>
<car name="EvjenCar">
  <color>Blue</color>
  <door>4</door>
  <speed>150</speed>
</car>
```

In the end, this XML declaration specifies the name of the class to compile as well as some values for various properties and a method. These elements make up the class. Now that you understand the structure of the `.car` file type, the next step is to construct the build provider. To accomplish this task, create a new Class Library project in the language of your choice within Visual Studio. Name the project `CarBuildProvider`. The `CarBuildProvider` contains a single class — `Car.vb` or `Car.cs`. This class inherits from the base class `BuildProvider` and overrides the `GenerateCode()` method of the `BuildProvider` class. This class is presented in Listing 1-20.

Listing 1-20: The CarBuildProvider

VB

```
Imports System.IO
Imports System.Web.Compilation
Imports System.Xml
Imports System.CodeDom

Public Class Car
```

Continued

```
    Inherits BuildProvider

    Public Overrides Sub GenerateCode(ByVal myAb As AssemblyBuilder)
        Dim carXmlDoc As XmlDocument = New XmlDocument()

        Using passedFile As Stream = Me.OpenStream()
            carXmlDoc.Load(passedFile)
        End Using

        Dim mainNode As XmlNode = carXmlDoc.SelectSingleNode("/car")
        Dim selectionMainNode As String = mainNode.Attributes("name").Value

        Dim colorNode As XmlNode = carXmlDoc.SelectSingleNode("/car/color")
        Dim selectionColorNode As String = colorNode.InnerText

        Dim doorNode As XmlNode = carXmlDoc.SelectSingleNode("/car/door")
        Dim selectionDoorNode As String = doorNode.InnerText

        Dim speedNode As XmlNode = carXmlDoc.SelectSingleNode("/car/speed")
        Dim selectionSpeedNode As String = speedNode.InnerText

        Dim ccu As CodeCompileUnit = New CodeCompileUnit()
        Dim cn As CodeNamespace = New CodeNamespace()
        Dim cmp1 As CodeMemberProperty = New CodeMemberProperty()
        Dim cmp2 As CodeMemberProperty = New CodeMemberProperty()
        Dim cmm1 As CodeMemberMethod = New CodeMemberMethod()

        cn.Imports.Add(New CodeNamespaceImport("System"))

        cmp1.Name = "Color"
        cmp1.Type = New CodeTypeReference(GetType(System.String))
        cmp1.Attributes = MemberAttributes.Public
        cmp1.GetStatements.Add(New CodeSnippetExpression("return """ & _
           selectionColorNode & """"))

        cmp2.Name = "Doors"
        cmp2.Type = New CodeTypeReference(GetType(System.Int32))
        cmp2.Attributes = MemberAttributes.Public
        cmp2.GetStatements.Add(New CodeSnippetExpression("return " & _
           selectionDoorNode))

        cmm1.Name = "Go"
        cmm1.ReturnType = New CodeTypeReference(GetType(System.Int32))
        cmm1.Attributes = MemberAttributes.Public
        cmm1.Statements.Add(New CodeSnippetExpression("return " & _
           selectionSpeedNode))

        Dim ctd As CodeTypeDeclaration = New CodeTypeDeclaration(selectionMainNode)
        ctd.Members.Add(cmp1)
        ctd.Members.Add(cmp2)
        ctd.Members.Add(cmm1)

        cn.Types.Add(ctd)
        ccu.Namespaces.Add(cn)
```

```
        myAb.AddCodeCompileUnit(Me, ccu)
    End Sub

End Class
```

C#

```
using System.IO;
using System.Web.Compilation;
using System.Xml;
using System.CodeDom;

namespace CarBuildProvider
{
    class Car : BuildProvider
    {
        public override void GenerateCode(AssemblyBuilder myAb)
        {
            XmlDocument carXmlDoc = new XmlDocument();

            using (Stream passedFile = OpenStream())
            {
                carXmlDoc.Load(passedFile);
            }
            XmlNode mainNode = carXmlDoc.SelectSingleNode("/car");
            string selectionMainNode = mainNode.Attributes["name"].Value;

            XmlNode colorNode = carXmlDoc.SelectSingleNode("/car/color");
            string selectionColorNode = colorNode.InnerText;

            XmlNode doorNode = carXmlDoc.SelectSingleNode("/car/door");
            string selectionDoorNode = doorNode.InnerText;

            XmlNode speedNode = carXmlDoc.SelectSingleNode("/car/speed");
            string selectionSpeedNode = speedNode.InnerText;

            CodeCompileUnit ccu = new CodeCompileUnit();
            CodeNamespace cn = new CodeNamespace();
            CodeMemberProperty cmp1 = new CodeMemberProperty();
            CodeMemberProperty cmp2 = new CodeMemberProperty();
            CodeMemberMethod cmm1 = new CodeMemberMethod();

            cn.Imports.Add(new CodeNamespaceImport("System"));

            cmp1.Name = "Color";
            cmp1.Type = new CodeTypeReference(typeof(string));
            cmp1.Attributes = MemberAttributes.Public;
            cmp1.GetStatements.Add(new CodeSnippetExpression("return \"" +
               selectionColorNode + "\""));

            cmp2.Name = "Doors";
            cmp2.Type = new CodeTypeReference(typeof(int));
            cmp2.Attributes = MemberAttributes.Public;
            cmp2.GetStatements.Add(new CodeSnippetExpression("return " +
```

```
                    selectionDoorNode));

                cmm1.Name = "Go";
                cmm1.ReturnType = new CodeTypeReference(typeof(int));
                cmm1.Attributes = MemberAttributes.Public;
                cmm1.Statements.Add(new CodeSnippetExpression("return " +
                    selectionSpeedNode));

                CodeTypeDeclaration ctd = new CodeTypeDeclaration(selectionMainNode);
                ctd.Members.Add(cmp1);
                ctd.Members.Add(cmp2);
                ctd.Members.Add(cmm1);

                cn.Types.Add(ctd);
                ccu.Namespaces.Add(cn);

                myAb.AddCodeCompileUnit(this, ccu);
            }
        }
    }
```

As you look over the `GenerateCode()` method, you can see that it takes an instance of `AssemblyBuilder`. This `AssemblyBuilder` object is from the `System.Web.Compilation` namespace and, because of this, your Class Library project needs to have a reference to the `System.Web` assembly. With all the various objects used in this `Car` class, you also have to import in the following namespaces:

```
Imports System.IO
Imports System.Web.Compilation
Imports System.Xml
Imports System.CodeDom
```

When you have done this, one of the tasks remaining in the `GenerateCode()` method is loading the `.car` file. Because the .car file is using XML for its form, you are able to load the document easily using the `XmlDocument` object. From there, by using the CodeDom, you can create a class that contains two properties and a single method dynamically. The class that is generated is an abstract representation of what is defined in the provided `.car` file. On top of that, the name of the class is also dynamically driven from the value provided via the name attribute used in the main `<Car>` node of the `.car` file.

The `AssemblyBuilder` instance that is used as the input object then compiles the generated code along with everything else into an assembly.

What does it mean that your ASP.NET project has a reference to the `CarBuildProvider` assembly in its project? It means that you can create a `.car` file of your own definition and drop this file into the App_Code folder. The second you drop the file into the App_Code folder, you have instant programmatic access to the definition specified in the file.

To see this in action, you first need a reference to the build provider in either the server's `machine.config` or your application's `web.config` file. A reference is shown in Listing 1-21.

Listing 1-21: Making a reference to the build provider in the web.config file

```
<configuration>
   <system.web>
      <compilation debug="false">
```

```
        <buildProviders>
          <add extension=".car" type="CarBuildProvider.Car"/>
        </buildProviders>
      </compilation>
    </system.web>
</configuration>
```

The `<buildProviders>` element is a child element of the `<compilation>` element. The `<buildProviders>` element takes a couple of child elements to add or remove providers. In this case, because you want to add a reference to the custom `CarBuildProvider` object, you use the `<add>` element. The `<add>` element can take two possible attributes — `extension` and `type`. You must use both of these attributes. In `extension` attribute, you define the file extension that this build provider will be associated with. In this case, you use the `.car` file extension. This means that any file using this file extension is associated with the class defined in the `type` attribute. The `type` attribute then takes a reference to the `CarBuildProvider` class that you built — `CarBuildProvider.Car`.

With this reference in place, you can create the `.car` file that was shown earlier in Listing 1-19. Place the created .car file in the App_Code folder. You instantly have access to a dynamically generated class that comes from the definition provided via the file. For example, because I used `EvjenCar` as the value of the name attribute in the `<Car>` element, this will be the name of the class generated, and I will find this exact name in IntelliSense as I type in Visual Studio.

If you create an instance of the `EvjenCar` class, you also find that you have access to the properties and the method that this class exposes. This is shown in Figure 1-15.

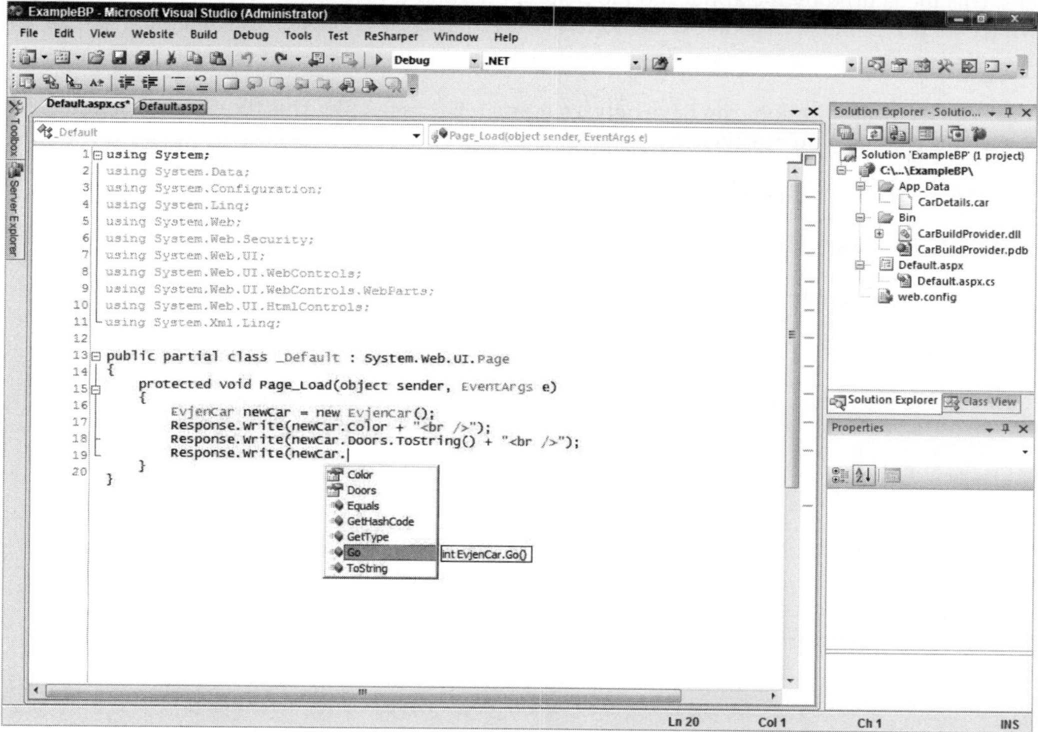

Figure 1-15

In addition to getting access to the properties and methods of the class, you also gain access to the values that are defined in the `.car` file. This is shown in Figure 1-16. The simple code example shown in Figure 1-15 is used for this browser output.

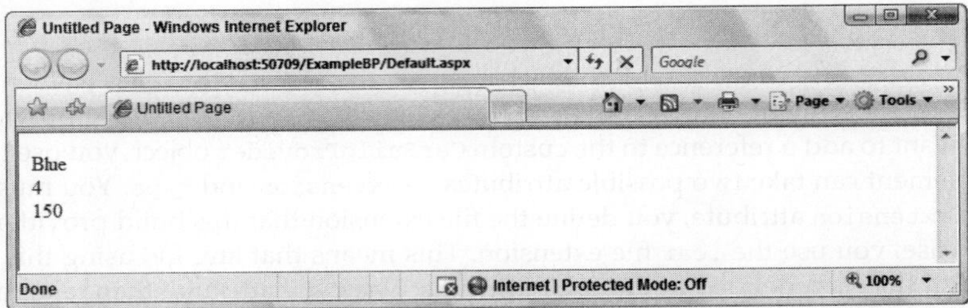

Figure 1-16

Although a car class is not the most useful thing in the world, this example shows you how to take the build provider mechanics into your own hands to extend your application's capabilities.

Global.asax

If you add a new item to your ASP.NET application, you get the Add New Item dialog. From here, you can see that you can add a Global Application Class to your applications. This adds a `Global.asax` file. This file is used by the application to hold application-level events, objects, and variables — all of which are accessible application-wide. Active Server Pages developers had something similar with the `Global.asa` file.

Your ASP.NET applications can have only a single `Global.asax` file. This file supports a number of items. When it is created, you are given the following template:

```
<%@ Application Language="VB" %>

<script runat="server">

    Sub Application_Start(ByVal sender As Object, ByVal e As EventArgs)
        ' Code that runs on application startup
    End Sub

    Sub Application_End(ByVal sender As Object, ByVal e As EventArgs)
        ' Code that runs on application shutdown
    End Sub

    Sub Application_Error(ByVal sender As Object, ByVal e As EventArgs)
        ' Code that runs when an unhandled error occurs
    End Sub

    Sub Session_Start(ByVal sender As Object, ByVal e As EventArgs)
        ' Code that runs when a new session is started
    End Sub

    Sub Session_End(ByVal sender As Object, ByVal e As EventArgs)
```

```
        ' Code that runs when a session ends.
        ' Note: The Session_End event is raised only when the sessionstate mode
        ' is set to InProc in the Web.config file. If session mode is
        ' set to StateServer
        ' or SQLServer, the event is not raised.
    End Sub

</script>
```

Just as you can work with page-level events in your .aspx pages, you can work with overall application events from the Global.asax file. In addition to the events listed in this code example, the following list details some of the events you can structure inside this file:

- Application_Start: Called when the application receives its very first request. It is an ideal spot in your application to assign any application-level variables or state that must be maintained across all users.
- Session_Start: Similar to the Application_Start event except that this event is fired when an individual user accesses the application for the first time. For instance, the Application_Start event fires once when the first request comes in, which gets the application going, but the Session_Start is invoked for each end user who requests something from the application for the first time.
- Application_BeginRequest: Although it not listed in the preceding template provided by Visual Studio 2008, the Application_BeginRequest event is triggered before each and every request that comes its way. This means that when a request comes into the server, before this request is processed, the Application_BeginRequest is triggered and dealt with before any processing of the request occurs.
- Application_AuthenticateRequest: Triggered for each request and enables you to set up custom authentications for a request.
- Application_Error: Triggered when an error is thrown anywhere in the application by any user of the application. This is an ideal spot to provide application-wide error handling or an event recording the errors to the server's event logs.
- Session_End: When running in InProc mode, this event is triggered when an end user leaves the application.
- Application_End: Triggered when the application comes to an end. This is an event that most ASP.NET developers won't use that often because ASP.NET does such a good job of closing and cleaning up any objects that are left around.

In addition to the global application events that the Global.asax file provides access to, you can also use directives in this file as you can with other ASP.NET pages. The Global.asax file allows for the following directives:

- @Application
- @Assembly
- @Import

These directives perform in the same way when they are used with other ASP.NET page types.

An example of using the Global.asax file is shown in Listing 1-22. It demonstrates how to log when the ASP.NET application domain shuts down. When the ASP.NET application domain shuts down, the ASP.NET application abruptly comes to an end. Therefore, you should place any logging code in the Application_End method of the Global.asax file.

Listing 1-22: Using the Application_End event in the Global.asax file

VB

```
<%@ Application Language="VB" %>
<%@ Import Namespace="System.Reflection" %>
<%@ Import Namespace="System.Diagnostics" %>

<script runat="server">

    Sub Application_End(ByVal sender As Object, ByVal e As EventArgs)
        Dim MyRuntime As HttpRuntime = _
           GetType(System.Web.HttpRuntime).InvokeMember("_theRuntime", _
           BindingFlags.NonPublic Or BindingFlags.Static Or _
           BindingFlags.GetField, _
           Nothing, Nothing, Nothing)

        If (MyRuntime Is Nothing) Then
            Return
        End If

        Dim shutDownMessage As String = _
           CType(MyRuntime.GetType().InvokeMember("_shutDownMessage", _
           BindingFlags.NonPublic Or BindingFlags.Instance Or
           BindingFlags.GetField, _
           Nothing, MyRuntime, Nothing), System.String)

        Dim shutDownStack As String = _
           CType(MyRuntime.GetType().InvokeMember("_shutDownStack", _
           BindingFlags.NonPublic Or BindingFlags.Instance Or
           BindingFlags.GetField, _
           Nothing, MyRuntime, Nothing), System.String)

        If (Not EventLog.SourceExists(".NET Runtime")) Then
            EventLog.CreateEventSource(".NET Runtime", "Application")
        End If

        Dim logEntry As EventLog = New EventLog()
        logEntry.Source = ".NET Runtime"
        logEntry.WriteEntry(String.Format(_
            "shutDownMessage={0}\r\n\r\n_shutDownStack={1}", _
            shutDownMessage, shutDownStack), EventLogEntryType.Error)
    End Sub

</script>
```

C#

```
<%@ Application Language="C#" %>
<%@ Import Namespace="System.Reflection" %>
<%@ Import Namespace="System.Diagnostics" %>
```

```
<script runat="server">

    void Application_End(object sender, EventArgs e)
    {
        HttpRuntime runtime =
           (HttpRuntime)typeof(System.Web.HttpRuntime).InvokeMember("_theRuntime",
           BindingFlags.NonPublic | BindingFlags.Static | BindingFlags.GetField,
           null, null, null);

        if (runtime == null)
        {
            return;
        }

        string shutDownMessage =
           (string)runtime.GetType().InvokeMember("_shutDownMessage",
           BindingFlags.NonPublic | BindingFlags.Instance | BindingFlags.GetField,
           null, runtime, null);

        string shutDownStack =
           (string)runtime.GetType().InvokeMember("_shutDownStack",
           BindingFlags.NonPublic | BindingFlags.Instance | BindingFlags.GetField,
           null, runtime, null);

        if (!EventLog.SourceExists(".NET Runtime"))
        {
            EventLog.CreateEventSource(".NET Runtime", "Application");
        }

        EventLog logEntry = new EventLog();
        logEntry.Source = ".NET Runtime";
        logEntry.WriteEntry(String.Format("\r\n\r\n_" +
           "shutDownMessage={0}\r\n\r\n_shutDownStack={1}",
           shutDownMessage, shutDownStack), EventLogEntryType.Error);
    }

</script>
```

With this code in place in your `Global.asax` file, start your ASP.NET application. Next, do something to cause the application to restart. You could, for example, make a change to the `web.config` file while the application is running. This triggers the `Application_End` event, and you see the following addition (shown in Figure 1-17) to the event log.

Working with Classes Through VS2008

This chapter showed you how to work with classes within your ASP.NET projects. In constructing and working with classes, you will find that Visual Studio 2008 is quite helpful. Two particularly useful items are a class designer file and an Object Test Bench. The class designer file has an extension of `.cd` and gives you a visual way to view your class, as well as all the available methods, properties, and other class items it contains. The Object Test Bench built into Visual Studio gives you a way to instantiate your classes and test them without creating a test application, a task which can be quite time consuming.

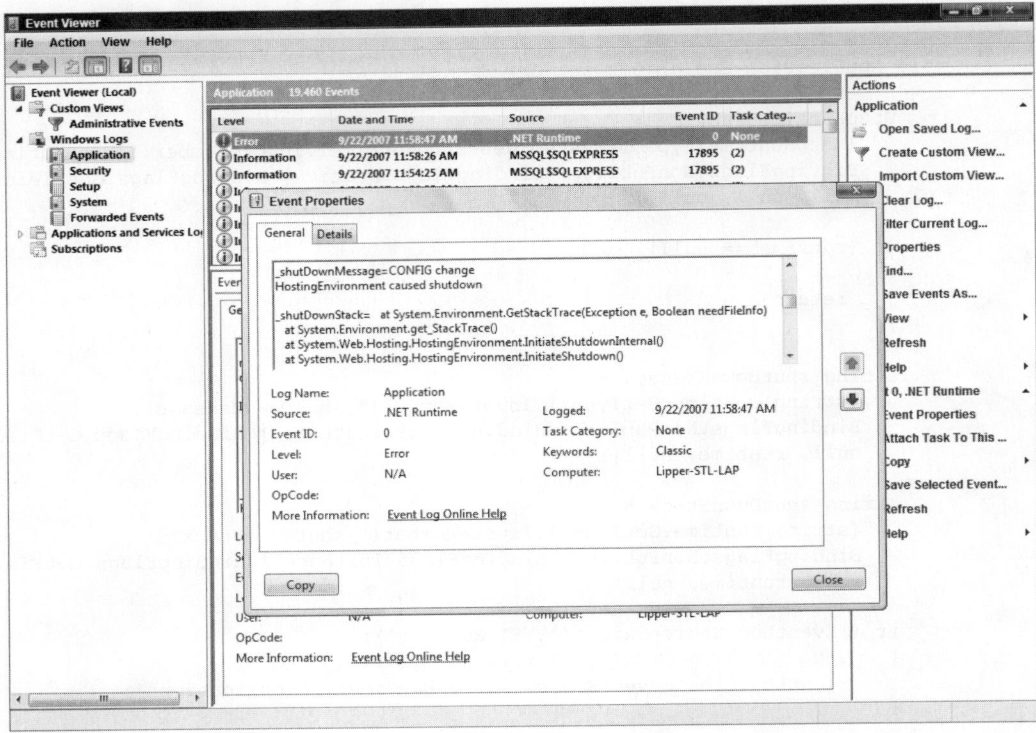

Figure 1-17

To see these items in action, create a new Class Library project in the language of your choice. This project has a single class file, `Class1.vb` or `.cs`. Delete this file and create a new class file called `Calculator.vb` or `.cs`, depending on the language you are using. From here, complete the class by creating a simple `Add()` and `Subtract()` method. Each of these methods takes in two parameters (of type `Integer`) and returns a single Integer with the appropriate calculation performed.

After you have the `Calculator` class in place, the easiest way to create your class designer file for this particular class is to right-click on the `Calculator.vb` file directly in the Solution Explorer and select View Class Diagram from the menu. This creates a `ClassDiagram1.cd` file in your solution.

The visual file, `ClassDiagram1.cd`, is presented in Figure 1-18.

The new class designer file gives you a design view of your class. In the Document Window of Visual Studio, you see a visual representation of the `Calculator` class. The class is represented in a box and provides the name of the class, as well as two available methods that are exposed by the class. Because of the simplicity of this class, the details provided in the visual view are limited.

You can add additional classes to this diagram simply by dragging and dropping class files onto the design surface. You can then arrange the class files on the design surface as you wish. A connection is in place for classes that are inherited from other class files or classes that derive from an interface or abstract class. In fact, you can extract an interface from the class you just created directly in the class designer by right-clicking on the Calculator class box and selecting Refactor ➪ Extract Interface from the provided menu. This launches the Extract Interface dialog that enables you to customize the interface creation. This dialog box is presented in Figure 1-19.

After you click OK, the `ICalculator` interface is created and is then visually represented in the class diagram file, as illustrated in Figure 1-20.

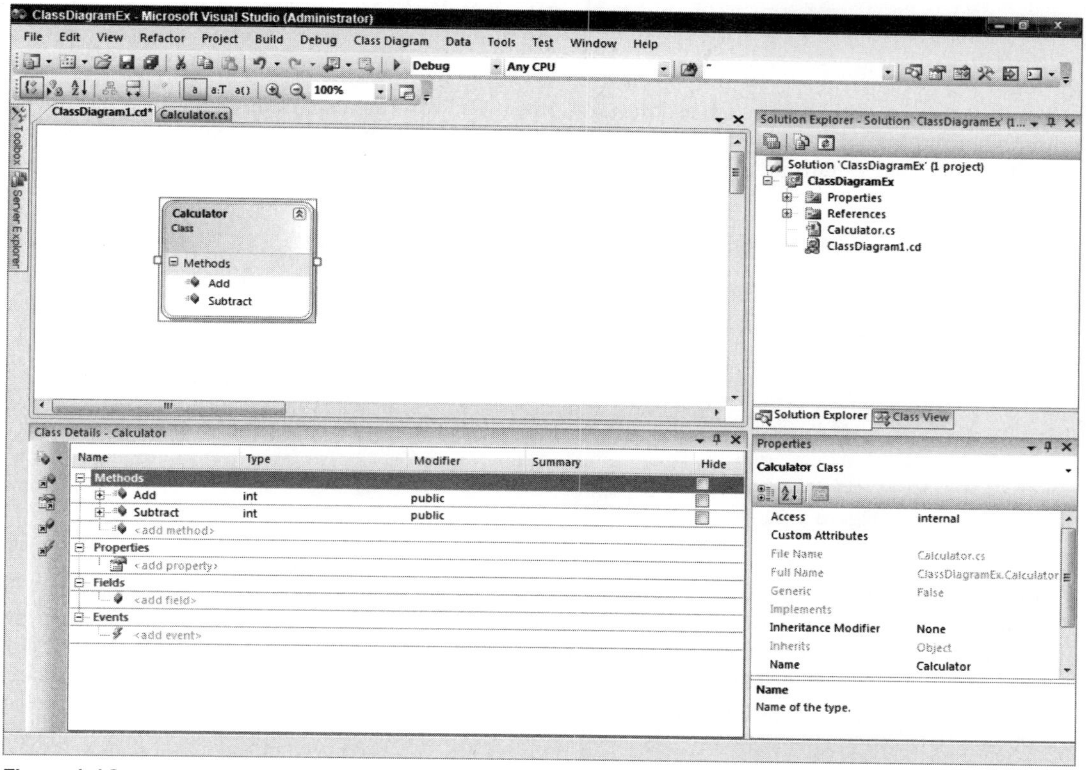

Figure 1-18

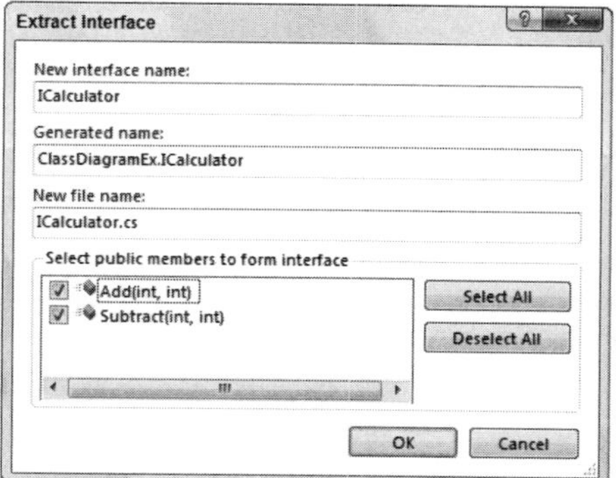

Figure 1-19

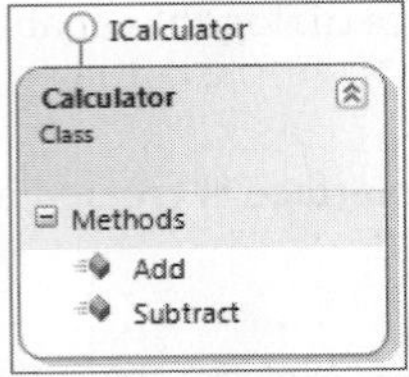

Figure 1-20

In addition to creating items such as interfaces on-the-fly, you can also modify your `Calculator` class by adding additional methods, properties, events, and more through the Class Details pane found in Visual Studio. The Class Details pane is presented in Figure 1-21.

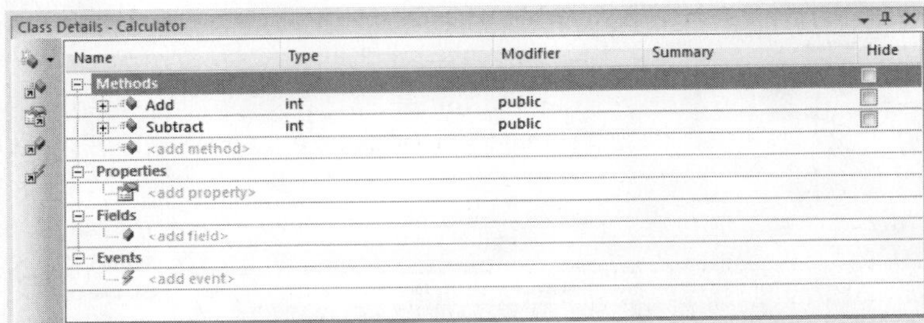

Figure 1-21

From this view of the class, you can directly add any additional methods, properties, fields, or events without directly typing code in your class file. When you enter these items in the Class Details view, Visual Studio generates the code for you on your behalf. For an example of this, add the additional `Multiply()` and `Divide()` methods that the `Calculator` class needs. Expanding the plus sign next to these methods shows the parameters needed in the signature. This is where you add the required `a` and `b` parameters. When you have finished, your Class Details screen should appear as shown in Figure 1-22.

Class Details - Calculator

Name	Type	Modifier	Summary	Hide
Methods				
Add	int	public		
Subtract	int	public		
Multiply	int	public		
(a	int	None		
, b	int	None		
) <add parameter>				
Divide	int	public		
(a	int	None		
, b	int	None		
) <add parameter>				
<add method>				

Figure 1-22

After you have added new `Multiply()` and `Divide()` methods and the required parameters, you see that the code in the `Calculator` class has changed to indicate these new methods are present. When the framework of the method is in place, you also see that the class has not been implemented in any fashion. The C# version of the `Multply()` and `Divide()` methods created by Visual Studio is presented in Listing 1-23.

Listing 1-23: The framework provided by Visual Studio's class designer

```
public int Multiply(int a, int b)
{
   throw new System.NotImplementedException();
}

public int Divide(int a, int b)
{
   throw new System.NotImplementedException();
}
```

The new class designer files give you a powerful way to view and understand your classes better — sometimes a picture really is worth a thousand words. One interesting last point on the `.cd` file is that Visual Studio is really doing all the work with this file. If you open the `ClassDesigner1.cd` file in Notepad, you see the results presented in Listing 1-24.

Listing 1-24: The real ClassDesigner1.cd file as seen in Notepad

```
<?xml version="1.0" encoding="utf-8"?>
<ClassDiagram MajorVersion="1" MinorVersion="1">
  <Class Name="ClassDiagramEx.Calculator">
    <Position X="1.25" Y="0.75" Width="1.5" />
    <TypeIdentifier>
      <HashCode>AAIAAAAAQAAAAAAAAADAAAAAAAAAAAAAAAAAAAAAAA=</HashCode>
      <FileName>Calculator.cs</FileName>
    </TypeIdentifier>
    <Lollipop Position="0.2" />
  </Class>
  <Font Name="Segoe UI" Size="8.25" />
</ClassDiagram>
```

As you can see, it is a rather simple XML file that defines the locations of the class and the items connected to the class.

In addition to using the new class designer to provide a visual representation of your classes, you can also use it to instantiate and test your new objects. To do this, right-click on the `Calculator` class file in the `ClassDiagram1.cd` file and select Create Instance⇨Calculator() from the provided menu.

This launches the Create Instance dialog that simply asks you to create a new name for your class instantiation. This dialog is illustrated in Figure 1-23.

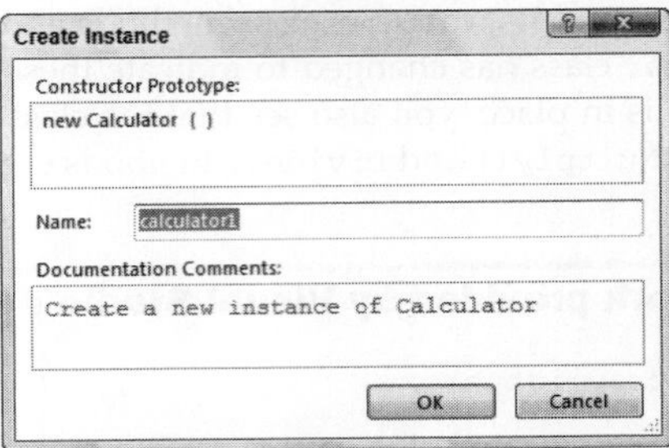

Figure 1-23

From here, click OK and you see a visual representation of this instantiation in the new Object Test Bench directly in Visual Studio. The Object Test Bench now contains only a single gray box classed calculator1. Right-click on this object directly in the Object Test Bench, and select Invoke Method⇨Add(int, int) from the provided menu. This is illustrated in Figure 1-24.

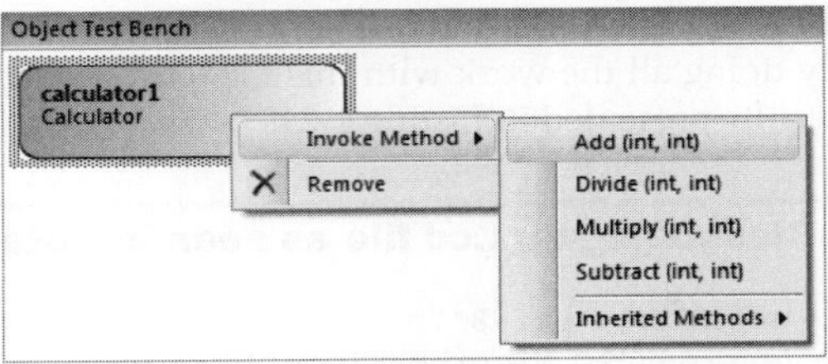

Figure 1-24

Selecting the Add method launches another dialog — the Invoke Method dialog. This dialog enables you to enter values for the required parameters, as shown in Figure 1-25.

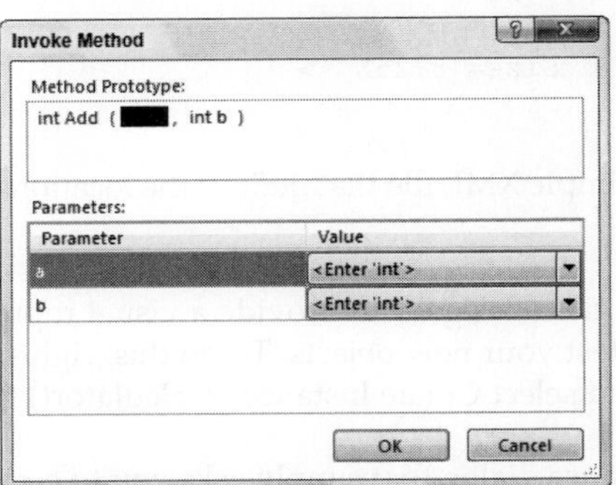

Figure 1-25

After providing values and clicking OK, you see another dialog that provides you with the calculated result, as shown in Figure 1-26.

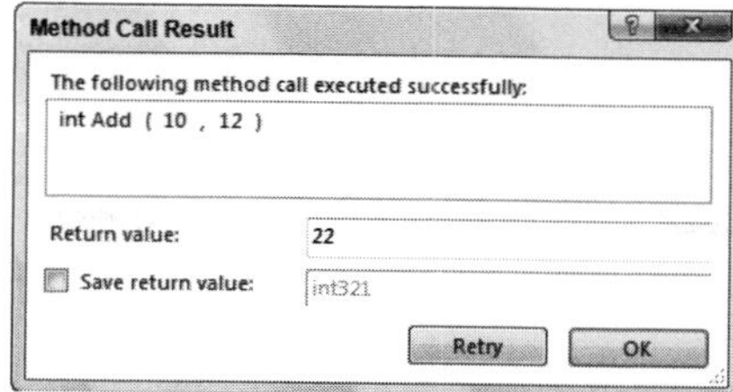

Figure 1-26

This is a simple example. When you start working with more complex objects and collections, however, this feature is even more amazing because the designer enables you to work through the entire returned result visually directly in the IDE.

Summary

This chapter covered a lot of ground. It discussed some of the issues concerning ASP.NET applications as a whole and the choices you have when building and deploying these new applications. With the help of Visual Studio 2008, you now have options about which Web server to use when building your application and whether to work locally or remotely through the new built-in FTP capabilities.

ASP.NET 3.5 and Visual Studio 2008 make it easy to build your pages using an inline coding model or to select a new and better code-behind model that is simpler to use and easier to deploy. You also learned about the new cross-posting capabilities and the new fixed folders that ASP.NET 3.5 has incorporated to make your life easier. These folders make their resources available dynamically with no work on your part. You saw some of the outstanding new compilation options that you have at your disposal. Finally, you looked at ways in which Visual Studio 2008 makes it easy to work with the classes of your project.

As you worked through some of the examples, you may have been thinking, ''WOW!'' But wait . . . there's plenty more to come!

2

ASP.NET Server Controls and Client-Side Scripts

As discussed in the previous chapter, ASP.NET evolved from Microsoft's earlier Web technology called Active Server Pages (referred to as *ASP* then and *classic ASP* today). This model was completely different from today's ASP.NET. Classic ASP used interpreted languages to accomplish the construction of the final HTML document before it was sent to the browser. ASP.NET, on the other hand, uses true compiled languages to accomplish the same task. The idea of building Web pages based on objects in a compiled environment is one of the main focuses of this chapter.

This chapter looks at how to use a particular type of object in ASP.NET pages called a *server control*, and how you can profit from using this control. We also introduce a particular type of server control — the HTML server control. The chapter also demonstrates how you can use JavaScript in ASP.NET pages to modify the behavior of server controls.

The rest of this chapter shows you how to use and manipulate server controls, both visually and programmatically, to help with the creation of your ASP.NET pages.

ASP.NET Server Controls

In the past, one of the difficulties of working with classic ASP was that you were completely in charge of the entire HTML output from the browser by virtue of the server-side code you wrote. Although this might seem ideal, it created a problem because each browser interpreted the HTML given to it in a slightly different manner.

The two main browsers out there at the time were Microsoft's Internet Explorer and Netscape Navigator. This meant that not only did developers have to be cognizant of the browser type to which they were outputting HTML, but they also had to take into account which versions of those particular browsers might be making a request to their application. Some developers resolved the issue by creating two separate applications. When an end user made an initial request to the application, the code made a browser check to see what browser type was making the request. Then, the ASP page would redirect the request down one path for an IE user, or down another path for a Netscape user.

Because requests came from so many different versions of the same browser, the developer often designed for the lowest possible version that might be used to visit the site. Essentially, everyone lost out by using the lowest common denominator as the target. This technique ensured that the page was rendered properly in most browsers making a request, but it also forced the developer to dumb-down his application. If applications were always built for the lowest common denominator, the developer could never take advantage of some of the more advanced features offered by newer browser versions.

ASP.NET server controls overcome these obstacles. When using the server controls provided by ASP.NET, you are not specifying the HTML to be output from your server-side code. Rather, you are specifying the functionality you want to see in the browser and letting the ASP.NET decide for you on the output to be sent to the browser.

When a request comes in, ASP.NET examines the request to see which browser type is making the request, as well as the version of the browser, and then it produces HTML output specific to that browser. This process is accomplished by processing a User Agent header retrieved from the HTTP Request to *sniff* the browser. This means that you can now build for the best browsers out there without worrying about whether features will work in the browsers making requests to your applications. Because of the previously described capabilities, you will often hear these controls referred to as *smart controls*.

Types of Server Controls

ASP.NET provides two distinct types of server controls — HTML server controls and Web server controls. Each type of control is quite different and, as you work with ASP.NET, you will see that much of the focus is on the Web server controls. This does not mean that HTML server controls have no value. They do provide you with many capabilities — some that Web server controls do not give you.

You might be asking yourself which is the better control type to use. The answer is that it really depends on what you are trying to achieve. HTML server controls map to specific HTML elements. You can place an `HtmlTable` server control on your ASP.NET page that works dynamically with a `<table>` element. On the other hand, Web server controls map to specific functionality that you want on your ASP.NET pages. This means an `<asp:Panel>` control might use a `<table>` or an another element altogether — it really depends on the capability of the browser making the request.

The following table provides a summary of information on when to use HTML server controls and when to use Web server controls.

Control Type	When to Use This Control Type
HTML Server	When converting traditional ASP 3.0 Web pages to ASP.NET Web pages and speed of completion is a concern. It is a lot easier to change your HTML elements to HTML server controls than it is to change them to Web server controls. When you prefer a more HTML-type programming model. When you want to explicitly control the code that is generated for the browser.
Web Server	When you require a richer set of functionality to perform complicated page requirements. When you are developing Web pages that will be viewed by a multitude of browser types and that require different code based upon these types. When you prefer a more Visual Basic–type programming model that is based on the use of controls and control properties.

Of course, some developers like to separate certain controls from the rest and place them in their own categories. For instance, you may see references to the following types of controls:

- **List controls:** These control types allow data to be bound to them for display purposes of some kind.
- **Rich controls:** Controls, such as the Calendar control, that display richer content and capabilities than other controls.
- **Validation controls:** Controls that interact with other form controls to validate the data that they contain.
- **Mobile controls:** Controls that are specific for output to devices such as mobile phones, PDAs, and more.
- **User controls:** These are not really controls, but page templates that you can work with as you would a control on your ASP.NET page.
- **Custom controls:** Controls that you build yourself and use in the same manner as the supplied ASP.NET server controls that come with the default install of ASP.NET 3.5.

When you are deciding between HTML server controls and Web server controls, remember that no hard and fast rules exist about which type to use. You might find yourself working with one control type more than another, but certain features are available in one control type that might not be available in the other. If you are trying to accomplish a specific task and you do not see a solution with the control type you are using, take a look at the other control type because it may very well hold the answer. Also, realize that you can mix and match these control types. Nothing says that you cannot use both HTML server controls and Web server controls on the same page or within the same application.

Building with Server Controls

You have a couple of ways to use server controls to construct your ASP.NET pages. You can actually use tools that are specifically designed to work with ASP.NET 3.5 that enable you to visually drag and drop controls onto a design surface and manipulate the behavior of the control. You can also work with server controls directly through code input.

Working with Server Controls on a Design Surface

Visual Studio 2008 enables you to visually create an ASP.NET page by dragging and dropping visual controls onto a design surface. You can get to this visual design option by clicking the Design tab at the bottom of the IDE when viewing your ASP.NET page. You can also show the Design view and the Source code view in the same document window. This is a new feature available in Visual Studio 2008. When the Design view is present, you can place the cursor on the page in the location where you want the control to appear and then double-click the control you want in the Toolbox window of Visual Studio. Unlike the 2002 and 2003 versions of Visual Studio, Visual Studio 2008 does a really good job (as does the previous Visual Studio 2005) of not touching your code when switching between the Design and Source tabs.

In the Design view of your page, you can highlight a control and the properties for the control appear in the Properties window. For example, Figure 2-1 shows a Button control selected in the design panel, and its properties are displayed in the Properties window on the lower right.

Changing the properties in the window changes the appearance or behavior of the highlighted control. Because all controls inherit from a specific base class (`WebControl`), you can also highlight multiple controls at the same time and change the base properties of all the controls at once. You do this by holding down the Ctrl key as you make your control selections.

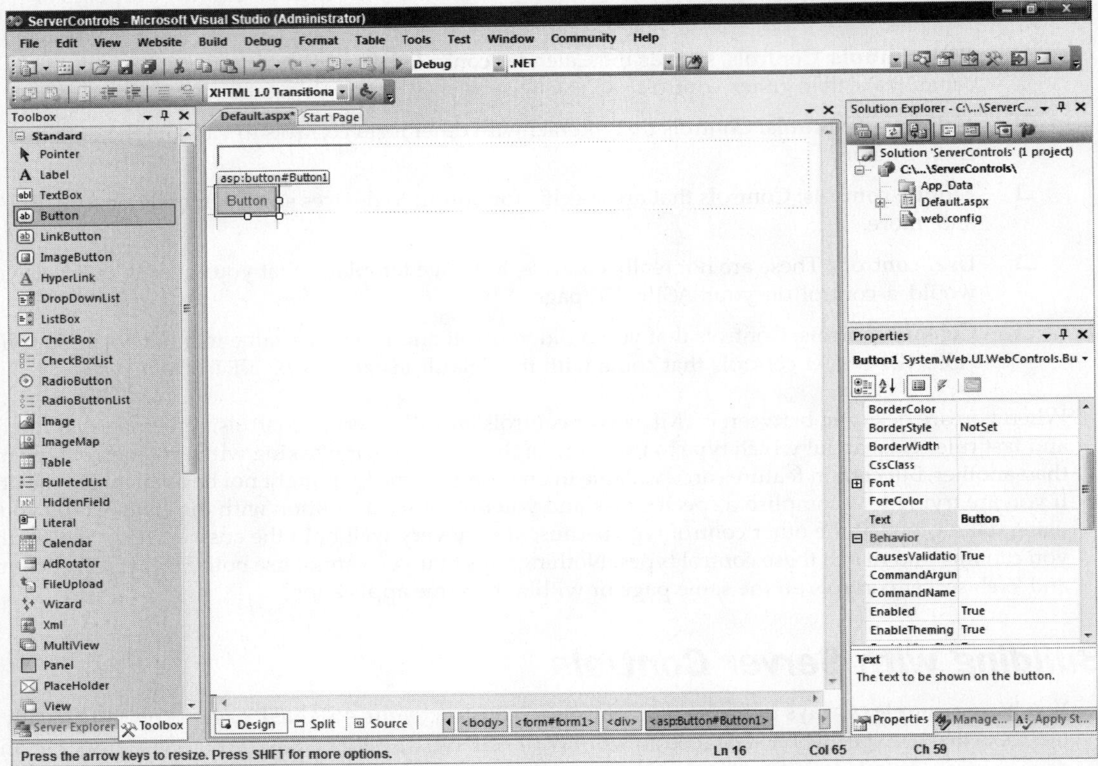

Figure 2-1

Coding Server Controls

You also can work from the code page directly. Because many developers prefer this, it is the default when you first create your ASP.NET page. Hand-coding your own ASP.NET pages may seem to be a slower approach than simply dragging and dropping controls onto a design surface, but it isn't as slow as you might think. You get plenty of assistance in coding your applications from Visual Studio 2008. As you start typing in Visual Studio, the IntelliSense features kick in and help you with code auto-completion. Figure 2-2, for example, shows an IntelliSense drop-down list of possible code completion statements that appeared as the code was typed.

The IntelliSense focus is on the most commonly used attribute or statement for the control or piece of code that you are working with. Using IntelliSense effectively as you work is a great way to code with great speed.

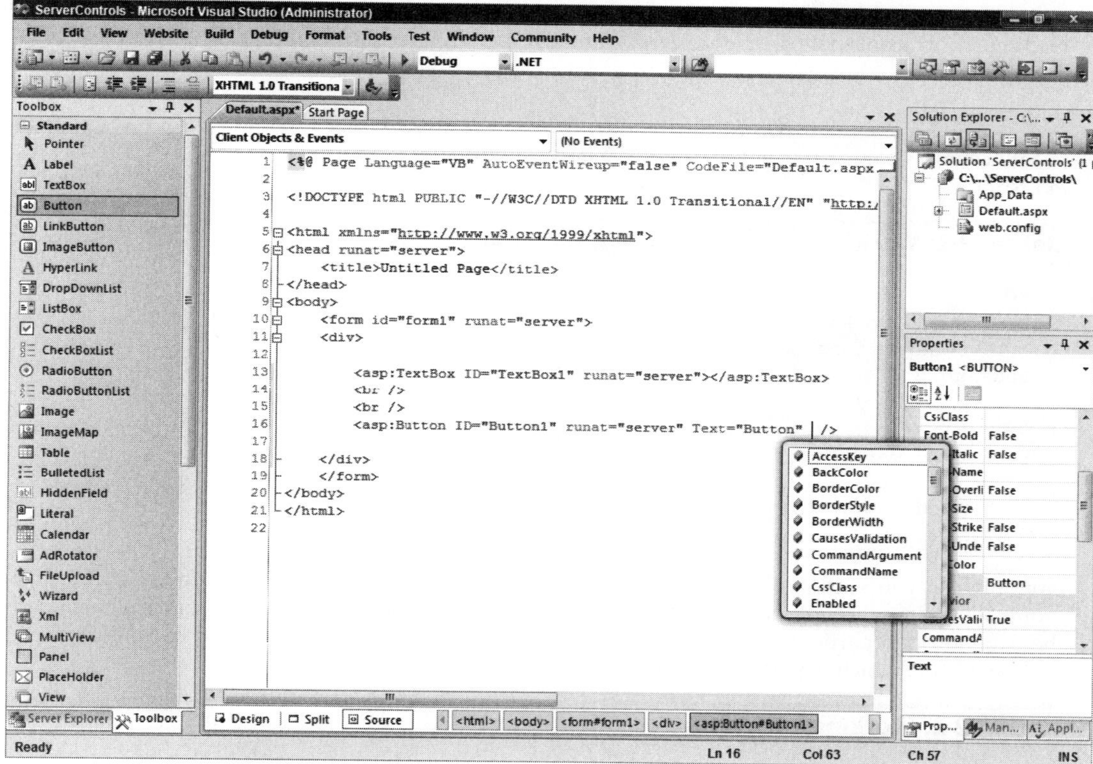

Figure 2-2

As with Design view, the Source view of your page lets you drag and drop controls from the Toolbox onto the code page itself. For example, dragging and dropping a TextBox control onto the code page produces the same results as dropping it on the design page:

```
<asp:TextBox ID="TextBox1" Runat="server"></asp:TextBox>
```

You can also highlight a control in Source view or simply place your cursor in the code statement of the control, and the Properties window displays the properties of the control. Now, you can apply properties directly in the Properties window of Visual Studio, and these properties are dynamically added to the code of your control.

Working with Server Control Events

As discussed in Chapter 1, ASP.NET uses more of a traditional Visual Basic event model than classic ASP. Instead of working with interpreted code, you are actually coding an event-based structure for your pages. Classic ASP used an interpreted model — when the server processed the Web page, the code of the page was interpreted line-by-line in a linear fashion where the only "event" implied was the page loading. This meant that occurrences you wanted to get initiated early in the process were placed at the top of the page.

Today, ASP.NET uses an event-driven model. Items or coding tasks get initiated only when a particular event occurs. A common event in the ASP.NET programming model is `Page_Load`, which is illustrated in Listing 2-1.

Listing 2-1: Working with specific page events

VB

```
Protected Sub Page_Load(ByVal sender As Object, ByVal e As System.EventArgs)
   ' Code actions here
End Sub
```

C#

```
protected void Page_Load(object sender, EventArgs e)
{
   // Code actions here
}
```

Not only can you work with the overall page — as well as its properties and methods at particular moments in time through page events — but you can also work with the server controls contained on the page through particular control events. For example, one common event for a button on a form is `Button_Click`, which is illustrated in Listing 2-2.

Listing 2-2: Working with a Button Click event

VB

```
Protected Sub Button1_Click(ByVal sender As Object, ByVal e As System.EventArgs)
   ' Code actions here
End Sub
```

C#

```
protected void Button1_Click(object sender, EventArgs e)
{
   // Code actions here
}
```

The event shown in Listing 2-2 is fired only when the end user actually clicks the button on the form that has an `OnClick` attribute value of `Button1_Click`. Therefore, not only does the event handler exist in the server-side code of the ASP.NET page, but that handler is also hooked up using the `OnClick` property of the server control in the associated ASP.NET page markup, as illustrated in the following code:

```
<asp:Button ID="Button1" Runat="server" Text="Button" OnClick="Button1_Click" />
```

How do you fire these events for server controls? You have a couple of ways to go about it. The first way is to pull up your ASP.NET page in the Design view and double-click the control for which you want to create a server-side event. For instance, double-clicking a Button server control in Design view creates the structure of the `Button1_Click` event within your server-side code, whether the code is in a code-behind file or inline. This creates a stub handler for that server control's most popular event.

With that said, be aware that a considerable number of additional events are available to the Button control that you cannot get at by double-clicking the control. To access them, pull up the page that contains the server-side code, select the control from the first drop-down list at the top of the IDE, and then choose the particular event you want for that control in the second drop-down list. Figure 2-3 shows the event drop-down list displayed. You might, for example, want to work with the Button control's `PreRender` event rather than its `Click` event. The handler for the event you choose is placed in your server-side code.

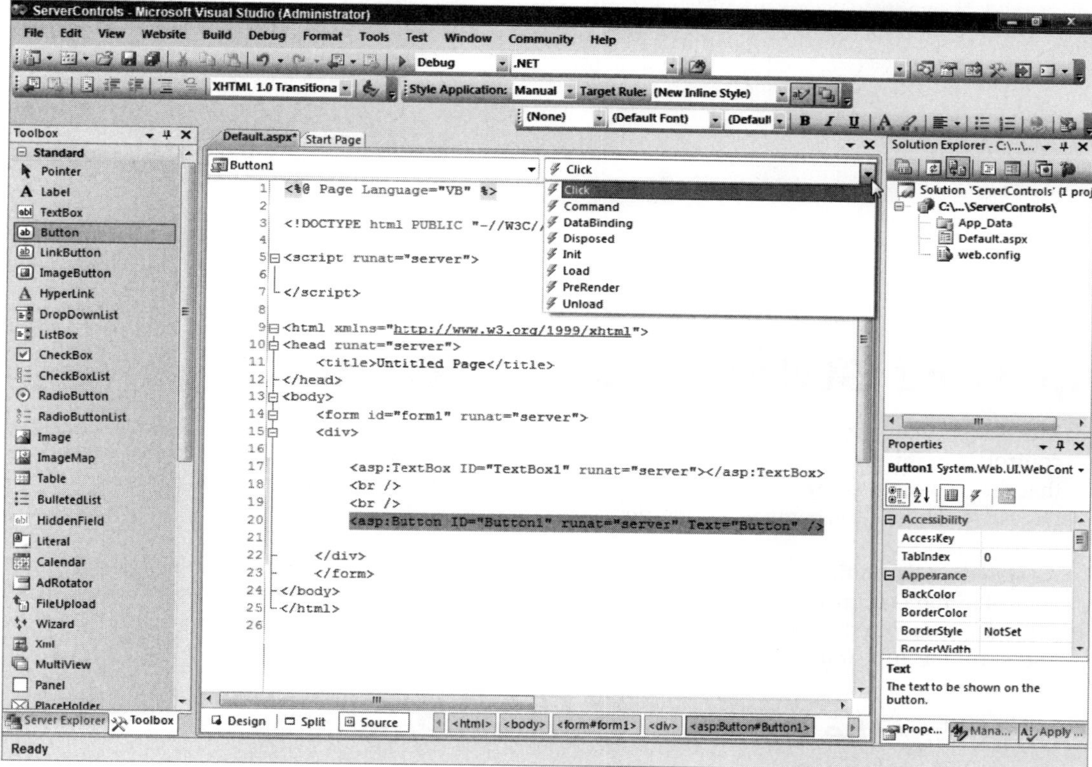

Figure 2-3

The second way is to bind to server-side events for your server controls from the Properties window of Visual Studio. This works only from Design view of the page. In Design view, highlight the server control that you want to work with. The properties for the control then appear in the Properties window, along with an icon menu. One of the icons, the Events icon, is represented by a lightning bolt (shown in Figure 2-4).

Clicking the Events icon pulls up a list of events available for the control. You simply double-click one of the events to get that event structure created in your server-side code.

After you have an event structure in place, you can program specific actions that you want to occur when the event is fired.

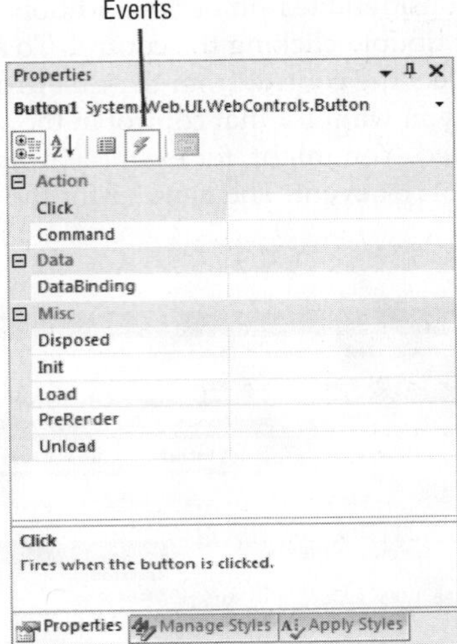

Figure 2-4

Applying Styles to Server Controls

More often than not, you want to change the default style (which is basically no style) to the server controls you implement in your applications. You most likely want to build your Web applications so that they reflect your own look-and-feel. One way to customize the appearance of the controls in your pages is to change the controls' properties.

As stated earlier in this chapter, to get at the properties of a particular control you simply highlight the control in the Design view of the page from Visual Studio. If you are working from the Source view, place the cursor in the code of the control. The properties presented in the Properties window allow you to control the appearance and behavior of the selected control.

Examining the Controls' Common Properties

Many of the default server controls that come with ASP.NET 3.5 are derived from the `WebControl` class and share similar properties that enable you to alter their appearance and behavior. Not all the derived controls use all the available properties (although many are implemented). Another important point is that not all server controls are implemented from the `WebControl` class. For instance, the Literal, PlaceHolder, Repeater, and XML server controls do not derive from the `WebControl` base class, but instead the `Control` class.

HTML server controls also do not derive from the `WebControl` base class because they are more focused on the set attributes of particular HTML elements. The following table lists the common properties the server controls share.

Property	Description
`AccessKey`	Enables you to assign a character to be associated with the Alt key so that the end user can activate the control using quick-keys on the keyboard. For instance, you can assign a Button control an `AccessKey` property value of `K`. Now, instead of clicking the button on the ASP.NET page (using a pointer controlled by the mouse), the end user can simply press Alt + K.
`Attributes`	Enables you to define additional attributes for a Web server control that are not defined by a public property.
`BackColor`	Controls the color shown behind the control's layout on the ASP.NET page.
`BorderColor`	Assigns a color that is shown around the physical edge of the server control.
`BorderWidth`	Assigns a value to the width of the line that makes up the border of the control. Placing a number as the value assigns the number as a pixel-width of the border. The default border color is black if the `BorderColor` property is not used in conjunction with the `BorderWidth` property setting.
`BorderStyle`	Enables you to assign the design of the border that is placed around the server control. By default, the border is created as a straight line, but a number of different styles can be used for your borders. Other possible values for the `BorderStyle` property include `Dotted`, `Dashed`, `Solid`, `Double`, `Groove`, `Ridge`, `Inset`, and `Outset`.
`CssClass`	Assigns a custom CSS (Cascading Style Sheet) class to the control.
`Enabled`	Enables you to turn off the functionality of the control by setting the value of this property to `False`. By default, the `Enabled` property is set to `True`.
`EnableTheming`	Enables you to turn on theming capabilities for the selected server control. The default value is `True`.
`Font`	Sets the font for all the text that appears anywhere in the control.
`ForeColor`	Sets the color of all the text that appears anywhere in the control.
`Height`	Sets the height of the control.
`SkinID`	Sets the skin to use when theming the control.
`Style`	Enables you to apply CSS styles to the control.
`TabIndex`	Sets the control's tab position in the ASP.NET page. This property works in conjunction with other controls on the page.
`ToolTip`	Assigns text that appears in a yellow box in the browser when a mouse pointer is held over the control for a short length of time. This can be used to add more instructions for the end user.
`Width`	Sets the width of the control.

You can see these common properties in many of the server controls you work with. Some of the properties of the `WebControl` class presented here work directly with the themeing system built into ASP.NET such as the `EnableTheming` and `SkinID` properties. These properties are covered in more detail in Chapter 6. You also see additional properties that are specific to the control you are viewing. Learning about the properties from the preceding table enables you to quickly work with Web server controls and to modify them to your needs.

Next take a look at some additional methods of customizing the look-and-feel of your server controls.

Changing Styles Using Cascading Style Sheets

One method of changing the look-and-feel of specific elements on your ASP.NET page is to apply a *style* to the element. The most rudimentary method of applying a defined look-and-feel to your page elements is to use various style-changing HTML elements such as `<font>`, `<b>`, and `<i>` directly.

All ASP.NET developers should have a good understanding of HTML. For more information on HTML, please read Wrox's Beginning Web Programming with HTML, XHTML, and CSS (Wiley Publishing, Inc.; ISBN 978-0470-25931-3). You can also learn more about HTML and CSS design in ASP.NET by looking at Chapter 18 of this book.

Using various HTML elements, you can change the appearance of many items contained on your pages. For instance, you can change a string's style as follows:

```
<font face="verdana"><b><i>Pork chops and applesauce</i></b></font>
```

You can go through an entire application and change the style of page elements using any of the appropriate HTML elements. You'll quickly find that this method works, but it is tough to maintain. To make any global style changes to your application, this method requires that you go through your application line-by-line to change each item individually. This can get cumbersome very fast!

Besides applying HTML elements to items to change their style, you can use another method known as *Cascading Style Sheets* (CSS). This alternative, but greatly preferred, styling technique allows you to assign formatting properties to HTML tags throughout your document in a couple of different ways. One way is to apply these styles directly to the HTML elements in your pages using *inline styles*. The other way involves placing these styles in an external stylesheet that can be placed either directly in an ASP.NET page or kept in a separate document that is simply referenced in the ASP.NET page. You explore these methods in the following sections.

Applying Styles Directly to HTML Elements

The first method of using CSS is to apply the styles directly to the tags contained in your ASP.NET pages. For instance, you apply a style to a string, as shown in Listing 2-3.

Listing 2-3: Applying CSS styles directly to HTML elements

```
<p style="color:blue; font-weight:bold">
   Pork chops and applesauce
</p>
```

This text string is changed by the CSS included in the <p> element so that the string appears bold and blue. Using the style attribute of the <p> element, you can change everything that appears between the opening and closing <p> elements. When the page is generated, the first style change applied is to the text between the <p> elements. In this example, the text has changed to the color blue because of the `color:blue` declaration, and then the `font-weight:bold` declaration is applied. You can separate the styling declarations using semicolons, and you can apply as many styles as you want to your elements.

Applying CSS styles in this manner presents the same problem as simply applying various HTML style elements — this is a tough structure to maintain. If styles are scattered throughout your pages, making global style changes can be rather time consuming. Putting all the styles together in a stylesheet is the best approach. A couple of methods can be used to build your stylesheets.

Working with the Visual Studio Style Builder

Visual Studio 2008 includes Style Builder, a tool that makes the building of CSS styles fairly simple. It can be quite a time saver because so many possible CSS definitions are available to you. If you are new to CSS, this tool can make all the difference.

The Visual Studio Style Builder enables you to apply CSS styles to individual elements or to construct your own stylesheets. To access the New Style tool when applying a style to a single page element, highlight the page element and then right-click it. From the menu that appears, select Style. Style Builder is shown in Figure 2-5.

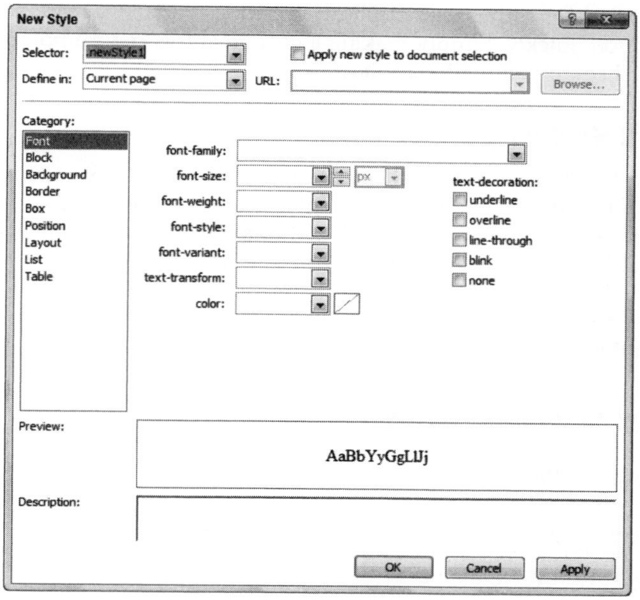

Figure 2-5

You can use the Visual Studio Style Builder to change quite a bit about your selected item. After making all the changes you want and clicking OK, you see the styles you chose applied to the selected element.

Creating External StyleSheets

You can use a couple of different methods to create stylesheets. The most common method is to create an *external* stylesheet — a separate stylesheet file that is referenced in the pages that employ the defined styles. To begin the creation of your external stylesheet, add a new item to your project. From the Add New Item dialog box, create a stylesheet called `StyleSheet.css`. Add the file to your project by pressing the Add button. Figure 2-6 shows the result.

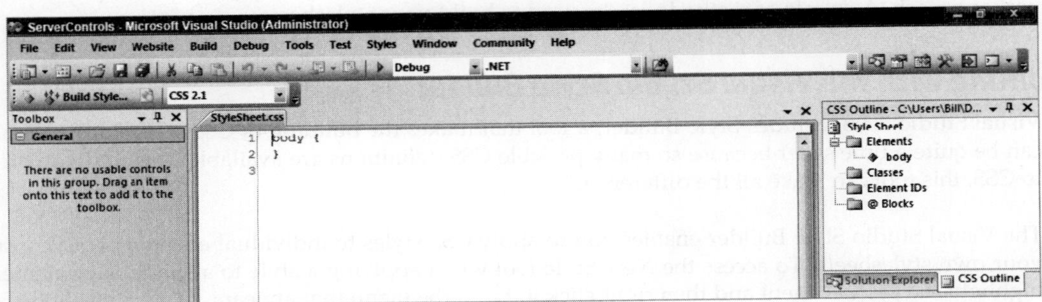

Figure 2-6

Using an external stylesheet within your application enables you to make global changes to the look-and-feel of your application quickly. Simply making a change at this central point cascades the change as defined by the stylesheet to your entire application.

Creating Internal Stylesheets

The second method for applying a stylesheet to a particular ASP.NET page is to bring the defined stylesheet into the actual document by creating an *internal* stylesheet. Instead of making a reference to an external stylesheet file, you bring the style definitions into the document. Note, however, that it is considered best practice to use external, rather than internal, stylesheets.

Consider using an internal stylesheet only if you are applying certain styles to a small number of pages within your application. Listing 2-4 shows the use of an internal stylesheet.

Listing 2-4: Using an internal stylesheet

```
<%@ Page Language="VB" %>

<html xmlns="http://www.w3.org/1999/xhtml" >
<head runat="server">
    <title>My ASP.NET Page</title>

    <style type="text/css">
        <!--
```

```
            body {
               font-family: Verdana;
            }

            a:link {
               text-decoration: none;
               color: blue;
            }

            a:visited {
               text-decoration: none;
               color: blue;
            }

            a:hover {
               text-decoration: underline;
               color: red;
            }

        -->
    </style>

</head>
<body>
    <form id="form1" runat="server">
    <div>
        <a href="Default.aspx"<Home</a>
    </div>
    </form>
</body>
</html>
```

In this document, the internal stylesheet is set inside the opening and closing `<head>` elements. Although this is not a requirement, it is considered best practice. The stylesheet itself is placed between `<style>` tags with a type attribute defined as `text/css`.

HTML comment tags are included because not all browsers support internal stylesheets (it is generally the older browsers that do not accept them). Putting HTML comments around the style definitions hides these definitions from very old browsers. Except for the comment tags, the style definitions are handled in the same way they are done in an external stylesheet.

HTML Server Controls

ASP.NET enables you to take HTML elements and, with relatively little work on your part, turn them into server-side controls. Afterward, you can use them to control the behavior and actions of elements implemented in your ASP.NET pages.

Of course, you can place any HTML you want in your pages. You have the option of using the HTML placed in the page as a server-side control. You can also find a list of HTML elements contained in the Toolbox of Visual Studio (shown in Figure 2-7).

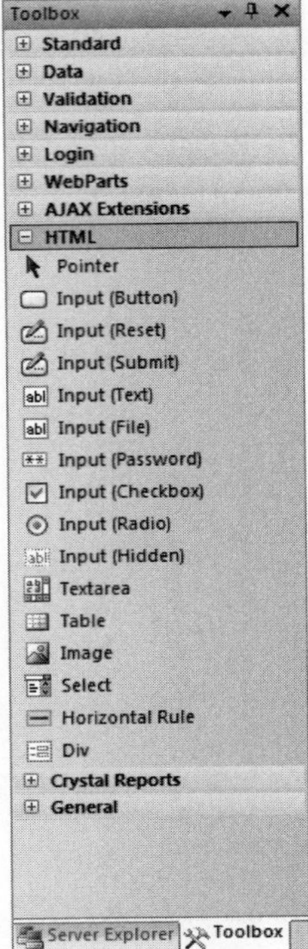

Figure 2-7

Dragging and dropping any of these HTML elements from the Toolbox to the Design or Source view of your ASP.NET page in the Document window simply produces the appropriate HTML element. For instance, placing an HTML Button control on your page produces the following results in your code:

```
<input id="Button1" type="button" value="button" />
```

In this state, the Button control is not a server-side control. It is simply an HTML element and nothing more. You can turn this into an HTML server control in a couple of different ways. First let's take a look at how you would approach this if you were using Visual Studio 2005. From VS2005, in Design view, you can right-click the element and select Run As Server Control from the menu. This causes a few things to happen. The first thing is that a small green triangle appears on the visual element. The Button element, after it has been turned into an HTML server control, looks like Figure 2-8.

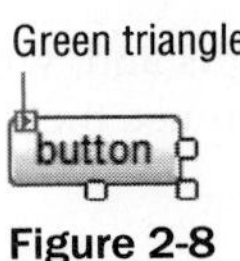

Figure 2-8

In Source view, you simply change the HTML element by adding a `runat="server"` to the control:

```
<input id="Button1" type="button" value="button" runat="server" />
```

Using Visual Studio 2008, you won't find the Run As Server Control option in the menu. Therefore, in the Source view of the page, select the `Button1` option in the Object drop-down list on the page. At first, you will see only that `Button1` is available only in the client-side objects, as illustrated in Figure 2-9.

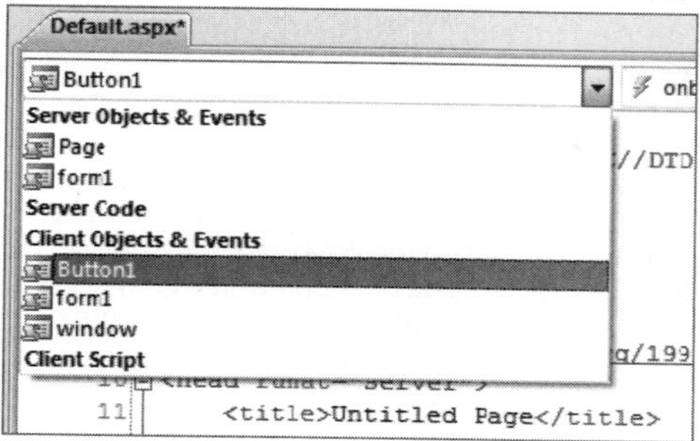

Figure 2-9

By adding the `runat="server"` to the element yourself, going back to this drop-down list, you will notice that the `Button1` object is now presented in the Server Objects & Events section in addition to the Client Objects & Events section, as shown in Figure 2-10.

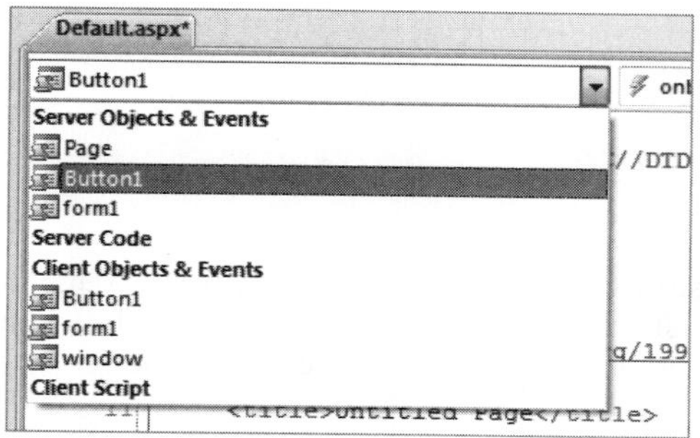

Figure 2-10

After the element is converted to a server control (through the addition of the `runat="server"` attribute and value), you can work with the selected element as you would work with any of the Web server controls. For instance, selecting `Button1` from the Source view of the page in the Server Objects & Events section and then selecting the `ServerClick` option from the list of server-side events generates a button-click event for the control. Listing 2-5 shows an example of some HTML server controls.

Listing 2-5: Working with HTML server controls

VB

```
<%@ Page Language="VB" %>

<script runat="server">
    Protected Sub Button1_ServerClick(ByVal sender As Object, _
       ByVal e As System.EventArgs)
```

Continued

```
        Response.Write("Hello " & Text1.Value)
    End Sub
</script>

<html xmlns="http://www.w3.org/1999/xhtml">
<head runat="server">
    <title>Using HTML Server Controls</title>
</head>
<body>
    <form id="form1" runat="server">
    <div>
        What is your name?<br />
        <input id="Text1" type="text" runat="server" />
        <input id="Button1" type="button" value="Submit" runat="server"
         onserverclick="Button1_ServerClick" />
    </div>
    </form>
</body>
</html>
```

C#

```
<%@ Page Language="C#" %>

<script runat="server">
    protected void Button1_ServerClick(object sender, EventArgs e)
    {
        Response.Write("Hello " + Text1.Value);
    }
</script>
```

In this example, you can see two HTML server controls on the page. Both are simply typical HTML elements with the additional `runat="server"` attribute added. If you are working with HTML elements as server controls, you must include an `id` attribute so that the server control can be identified in the server-side code.

The Button control includes a reference to a server-side event using the `OnServerClick` attribute. This attribute points to the server-side event that is triggered when an end user clicks the button — in this case, `Button1_ServerClick`. Within the `Button1_ServerClick` event, the value placed in the text box is output by using the `Value` property.

Looking at the HtmlControl Base Class

All the HTML server controls use a class that is derived from the `HtmlControl` base class (fully qualified as `System.Web.UI.HtmlControls.HtmlControl`). These classes expose many properties from the control's derived class. The following table details some of the properties available from this base class. Some of these items are themselves derived from the base `Control` class.

Method or Property	Description
Attributes	Provides a collection of name/value of all the available attributes specified in the control, including custom attributes.
Disabled	Allows you to get or set whether the control is disabled using a Boolean value.
EnableTheming	Enables you, using a Boolean value, to get or set whether the control takes part in the page theming capabilities.
EnableViewState	Allows you to get or set a Boolean value that indicates whether the control participates in the page's view state capabilities.
ID	Allows you to get or set the unique identifier for the control.
Page	Allows you to get a reference to the Page object that contains the specified server control.
Parent	Gets a reference to the parent control in the page control hierarchy.
Site	Provides information about the container for which the server control belongs.
SkinID	When the EnableTheming property is set to True, the SkinID property specifies the named skin that should be used in setting a theme.
Style	Makes references to the CSS style collection that applies to the specified control.
TagName	Provides the name of the element that is generated from the specified control.
Visible	Specifies whether the control is visible (rendered) on the generated page.

You can find a more comprehensive list in the SDK.

Looking at the HtmlContainerControl Class

The HtmlControl base class is used for those HTML classes that are focused on HTML elements that can be contained within a single node. For instance, the <img>, <input>, and <link> elements work from classes derived from the HtmlControl class.

Other HTML elements such as <a>, <form>, and <select>, require an opening and closing set of tags. These elements use classes that are derived from the HtmlContainerControl class — a class specifically designed to work with HTML elements that require a closing tag.

Because the HtmlContainerControl class is derived from the HtmlControl class, you have all the Html-Control class's properties and methods available to you as well as some new items that have been declared in the `HtmlContainerControl` class itself. The most important of these are the `InnerText` and `InnerHtml` properties:

- `InnerHtml`: Enables you to specify content that can include HTML elements to be placed between the opening and closing tags of the specified control.
- `InnerText`: Enables you to specify raw text to be placed between the opening and closing tags of the specified control.

Looking at All the HTML Classes

It is quite possible to work with every HTML element because a corresponding class is available for each one of them. The .NET Framework documentation shows the following classes for working with your HTML server controls:

- `HtmlAnchor` controls the `<a>` element.
- `HtmlButton` controls the `<button>` element.
- `HtmlForm` controls the `<form>` element.
- `HtmlHead` controls the `<head>` element.
- `HtmlImage` controls the `<img>` element.
- `HtmlInputButton` controls the `<input type="button">` element.
- `HtmlInputCheckBox` controls the `<input type="checkbox">` element.
- `HtmlInputFile` controls the `<input type="file">`element.
- `HtmlInputHidden` controls the `<input type="hidden">` element.
- `HtmlInputImage` controls the `<input type="image">` element.
- `HtmlInputPassword` controls the `<input type="password">` element.
- `HtmlInputRadioButton` controls the `<input type="radio">` element.
- `HtmlInputReset` controls the `<input type="reset">` element.
- `HtmlInputSubmit` controls the `<input type="submit">` element.
- `HtmlInputText` controls the `<input type="text">` element.
- `HtmlLink` controls the `<link>`element.
- `HtmlMeta` controls the `<meta>` element.
- `HtmlSelect` controls the `<select>` element.
- `HtmlTable` controls the `<table>` element.
- `HtmlTableCell` controls the `<td>` element.
- `HtmlTableRow` controls the `<tr>` element.
- `HtmlTextArea` controls the `<textarea>` element.
- `HtmlTitle` controls the `<title>` element.

You gain access to one of these classes when you convert an HTML element to an HTML server control. For example, convert the `<title>` element to a server control this way:

```
<title id="Title1" runat="Server"/>
```

That gives you access to the `HtmlTitle` class for this particular HTML element. Using this class instance, you can perform a number of tasks including providing a text value for the page title dynamically:

VB

```
Title1.Text = DateTime.Now.ToString()
```

C#

```
Title1.Text = DateTime.Now.ToString();
```

You can get most of the HTML elements you need by using these classes, but a considerable number of other HTML elements are at your disposal that are not explicitly covered by one of these HTML classes. For example, the `HtmlGenericControl` class provides server-side access to any HTML element you want.

Using the HtmlGenericControl Class

You should be aware of the importance of the `HtmlGenericControl` class; it gives you some capabilities that you do not get from any other server control offered by ASP.NET. For instance, using the `HtmlGenericControl` class, you can get server-side access to the `<meta>`, `<p>`, `<span>`, or other elements that would otherwise be unreachable.

Listing 2-6 shows you how to change the `<meta>` element in your page using the `HtmlGenericControl` class.

Listing 2-6: Changing the <meta> element using the HtmlGenericControl class

VB

```
<%@ Page Language="VB" %>

<script runat="server">
    Protected Sub Page_Load(ByVal sender As Object, ByVal e As System.EventArgs)
        Meta1.Attributes("Name") = "description"
        Meta1.Attributes("CONTENT") = "Generated on: " & DateTime.Now.ToString()
    End Sub
</script>

<html xmlns="http://www.w3.org/1999/xhtml">
<head runat="server">
    <title>Using the HtmlGenericControl class</title>
    <meta id="Meta1" runat="server" />
</head>
<body>
    <form id="form1" runat="server">
    <div>
        The rain in Spain stays mainly in the plains.
```

Continued

```
        </div>
    </form>
</body>
</html>
```

C#

```
<%@ Page Language="C#" %>

<script runat="server">
    protected void Page_Load(object sender, EventArgs e)
    {
        Meta1.Attributes["Name"] = "description";
        Meta1.Attributes["CONTENT"] = "Generated on: " + DateTime.Now.ToString();
    }
</script>
```

In this example, the page's `<meta>` element is turned into an HTML server control with the addition of the `id` and `runat` attributes. Because the `HtmlGenericControl` class (which inherits from `HtmlControl`) can work with a wide range of HTML elements, you cannot assign values to HTML attributes in the same manner as you do when working with the other HTML classes (such as `HtmlInputButton`). You assign values to the attributes of an HTML element through the use of the `HtmlGenericControl` class's `Attributes` property, specifying the attribute you are working with as a string value.

The following is a partial result of running the example page:

```
<html xmlns="http://www.w3.org/1999/xhtml">
<head>
    <meta id="Meta1" Name="description"
     CONTENT="Generated on: 2/5/2008 2:42:52 PM"></meta>
    <title>Using the HtmlGenericControl class</title>
</head>
```

By using the `HtmlGenericControl` class, along with the other HTML classes, you can manipulate every element of your ASP.NET pages from your server-side code.

Manipulating Pages and Server Controls with JavaScript

Developers generally like to include some of their own custom JavaScript functions in their ASP.NET pages. You have a couple of ways to do this. The first is to apply JavaScript directly to the controls on your ASP.NET pages. For example, look at a simple Label server control, shown in Listing 2-7, which displays the current date and time.

Listing 2-7: Showing the current date and time

VB

```
Protected Sub Page_Load(ByVal sender As Object, ByVal e As System.EventArgs)
   TextBox1.Text = DateTime.Now.ToString()
End Sub
```

C#

```
protected void Page_Load(object sender, EventArgs e) {
   TextBox1.Text = DateTime.Now.ToString();
}
```

This little bit of code displays the current date and time on the page of the end user. The problem is that the date and time displayed are correct for the Web server that generated the page. If someone sits in the Pacific time zone (PST), and the Web server is in the Eastern time zone (EST), the page won't be correct for that viewer. If you want the time to be correct for anyone visiting the site, regardless of where they reside in the world, you can employ JavaScript to work with the TextBox control, as illustrated in Listing 2-8.

Listing 2-8: Using JavaScript to show the current time for the end user

```
<%@ Page Language="VB" %>

<html xmlns="http://www.w3.org/1999/xhtml" >
<head runat="server">
    <title>Using JavaScript</title>
</head>
<body onload="javascript:document.forms[0]['TextBox1'].value=Date();">
    <form id="form1" runat="server">
    <div>
        <asp:TextBox ID="TextBox1" Runat="server" Width="300"></asp:TextBox>
    </div>
    </form>
</body>
</html>
```

In this example, even though you are using a standard TextBox server control from the Web server control family, you can get at this control using JavaScript that is planted in the `onload` attribute of the <body> element. The value of the `onload` attribute actually points to the specific server control via an anonymous function by using the value of the `ID` attribute from the server control: `TextBox1`. You can get at other server controls on your page by employing the same methods. This bit of code produces the result illustrated in Figure 2-11.

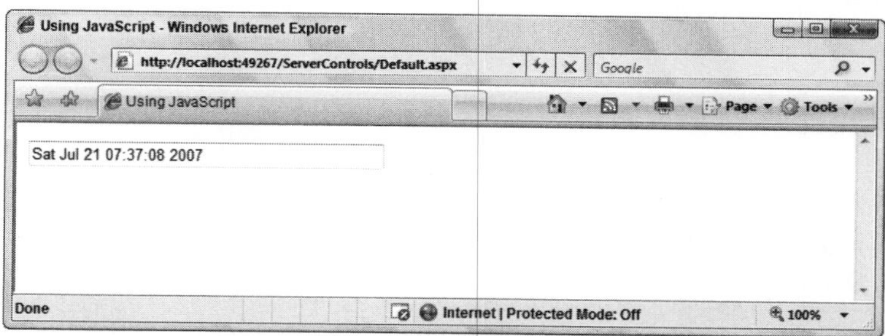

Figure 2-11

ASP.NET uses the `Page.ClientScript` property to register and place JavaScript functions on your ASP .NET pages. Three of these methods are reviewed here. More methods and properties than just these two are available through the `ClientScript` object (which references an instance of `System.Web.UI`

`.ClientScriptManager`), but these are the more useful ones. You can find the rest in the SDK documentation.

The `Page.RegisterStartupScript` *and the* `Page.RegisterClientScriptBlock` *methods from the .NET Framework 1.0/1.1 are now considered obsolete. Both of these possibilities for registering scripts required a key/script set of parameters. Because two separate methods were involved, there was an extreme possibility that some key name collisions would occur. The* `Page.ClientScript` *property is meant to bring all the script registrations under one umbrella, making your code less error prone.*

Using Page.ClientScript.RegisterClientScriptBlock

The `RegisterClientScriptBlock` method allows you to place a JavaScript function at the top of the page. This means that the script is in place for the startup of the page in the browser. Its use is illustrated in Listing 2-9.

Listing 2-9: Using the RegisterClientScriptBlock method

VB

```
<%@ Page Language="VB" %>

<script runat="server">
    Protected Sub Page_Load(ByVal sender As Object, ByVal e As System.EventArgs)
      Dim myScript As String = "function AlertHello() { alert('Hello ASP.NET'); }"
      Page.ClientScript.RegisterClientScriptBlock(Me.GetType(), "MyScript", _
         myScript, True)
    End Sub
</script>

<html xmlns="http://www.w3.org/1999/xhtml">
<head runat="server">
    <title>Adding JavaScript</title>
</head>
<body>
    <form id="form1" runat="server">
    <div>
        <asp:Button ID="Button1" Runat="server" Text="Button"
         OnClientClick="AlertHello()" />
    </div>
    </form>
</body>
</html>
```

C#

```
<%@ Page Language="C#" %>

<script runat="server">
    protected void Page_Load(object sender, EventArgs e)
    {
      string myScript = @"function AlertHello() { alert('Hello ASP.NET'); }";
      Page.ClientScript.RegisterClientScriptBlock(this.GetType(),
         "MyScript", myScript, true);
    }
</script>
```

From this example, you can see that you create the JavaScript function `AlertHello()` as a string called `myScript`. Then using the `Page.ClientScript.RegisterClientScriptBlock` method, you program the script to be placed on the page. The two possible constructions of the `RegisterClientScriptBlock` method are the following:

- `RegisterClientScriptBlock` (*type, key, script*)
- `RegisterClientScriptBlock` (*type, key, script, script tag specification*)

In the example from Listing 2-9, you are specifying the type as `Me.GetType()`, the key, the script to include, and then a `Boolean` value setting of `True` so that .NET places the script on the ASP.NET page with `<script>` tags automatically. When running the page, you can view the source code for the page to see the results:

```
<html xmlns="http://www.w3.org/1999/xhtml">
<head><title>
    Adding JavaScript
</title></head>
<body>
    <form method="post" action="JavaScriptPage.aspx" id="form1">
<div>
<input type="hidden" name="__VIEWSTATE"
 value="/wEPDwUKMTY3NzE5MjIyMGRkiyYSRMg+bcXi9DiawYlbxndiTDo=" />
</div>


<script type="text/javascript">
<!--
function AlertHello() { alert('Hello ASP.NET'); }// -->
</script>

    <div>
        <input type="submit" name="Button1" value="Button" onclick="AlertHello();"
         id="Button1" />
    </div>
    </form>
</body>
</html>
```

From this, you can see that the script specified was indeed included on the ASP.NET page before the page code. Not only were the `<script>` tags included, but the proper comment tags were added around the script (so older browsers will not break).

Using Page.ClientScript.RegisterStartupScript

The `RegisterStartupScript` method is not too much different from the `RegisterClientScriptBlock` method. The big difference is that the `RegisterStartupScript` places the script at the bottom of the ASP.NET page instead of at the top. In fact, the `RegisterStartupScript` method even takes the same constructors as the `RegisterClientScriptBlock` method:

- `RegisterStartupScript` (*type, key, script*)
- `RegisterStartupScript` (type, key, script, script tag specification)

So what difference does it make where the script is registered on the page? A lot, actually!

If you have a bit of JavaScript that is working with one of the controls on your page, in most cases you want to use the `RegisterStartupScript` method instead of `RegisterClientScriptBlock`. For example, you'd use the following code to create a page that includes a simple `<asp:TextBox>` control that contains a default value of `Hello ASP.NET`.

```
<asp:TextBox ID="TextBox1" Runat="server">Hello ASP.NET</asp:TextBox>
```

Then use the `RegisterClientScriptBlock` method to place a script on the page that utilizes the value in the `TextBox1` control, as illustrated in Listing 2-10.

Listing 2-10: Improperly using the RegisterClientScriptBlock method

VB

```
Protected Sub Page_Load(ByVal sender As Object, ByVal e As System.EventArgs)
   Dim myScript As String = "alert(document.forms[0]['TextBox1'].value);"
   Page.ClientScript.RegisterClientScriptBlock(Me.GetType(), "myKey", myScript, _
      True)
End Sub
```

C#

```
protected void Page_Load(object sender, EventArgs e)
{
   string myScript = @"alert(document.forms[0]['TextBox1'].value);";
   Page.ClientScript.RegisterClientScriptBlock(this.GetType(),
      "MyScript", myScript, true);
}
```

Running this page (depending on the version of IE your are using) gives you a JavaScript error, as shown in Figure 2-12.

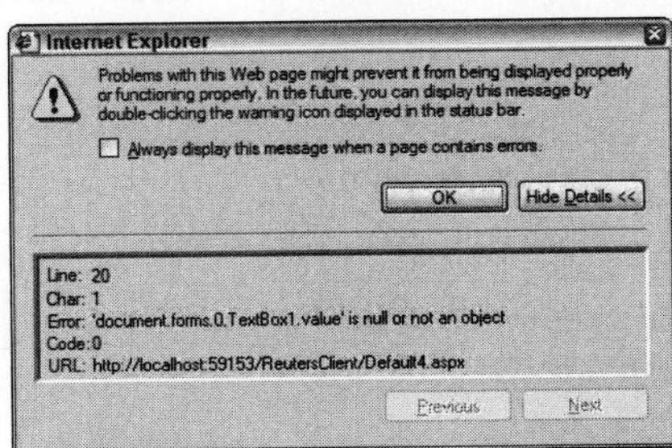

Figure 2-12

The reason for the error is that the JavaScript function fired before the text box was even placed on the screen. Therefore, the JavaScript function did not find `TextBox1`, and that caused an error to be thrown by the page. Now try the `RegisterStartupScript` method shown in Listing 2-11.

Listing 2-11: Using the RegisterStartupScript method

VB

```
Protected Sub Page_Load(ByVal sender As Object, ByVal e As System.EventArgs)
   Dim myScript As String = "alert(document.forms[0]['TextBox1'].value);"
```

```
    Page.ClientScript.RegisterStartupScript(Me.GetType(), "myKey", myScript, _
      True)
End Sub
```

C#

```
protected void Page_Load(object sender, EventArgs e)
{
   string myScript = @"alert(document.forms[0]['TextBox1'].value);";
   Page.ClientScript.RegisterStartupScript(this.GetType(),
      "MyScript", myScript, true);
}
```

This approach puts the JavaScript function at the bottom of the ASP.NET page, so when the JavaScript actually starts, it finds the `TextBox1` element and works as planned. The result is shown in Figure 2-13.

Figure 2-13

Using Page.ClientScript.RegisterClientScriptInclude

The final method is `RegisterClientScriptInclude`. Many developers place their JavaScript inside a `.js` file, which is considered a best practice because it makes it very easy to make global JavaScript changes to the application. You can register the script files on your ASP.NET pages using the `RegisterClientScriptInclude` method illustrated in Listing 2-12.

Listing 2-12: Using the RegisterClientScriptInclude method

VB

```
Dim myScript As String = "myJavaScriptCode.js"
Page.ClientScript.RegisterClientScriptInclude("myKey", myScript)
```

C#

```
string myScript = "myJavaScriptCode.js";
Page.ClientScript.RegisterClientScriptInclude("myKey", myScript);
```

This creates the following construction on the ASP.NET page:

```
<script src="myJavaScriptCode.js" type="text/javascript"></script>
```

Client-Side Callback

ASP.NET 3.5 includes a client callback feature that enables you to retrieve page values and populate them to an already-generated page without regenerating the page. This was introduced with ASP.NET 2.0. This capability makes it possible to change values on a page without going through the entire postback cycle; that means you can update your pages without completely redrawing the page. End users will not see the page flicker and reposition, and the pages will have a flow more like the flow of a thick-client application.

To work with the new callback capability, you have to know a little about working with JavaScript. This book does not attempt to teach you JavaScript. If you need to get up to speed on this rather large topic, check out Wrox's *Beginning JavaScript, Third Edition*, by Paul Wilton and Jeremy McPeak (Wiley Publishing, Inc., ISBN: 978-0-470-05151-1).

You can also accomplish client callbacks in a different manner using ASP.NET AJAX. You will find more information on this in Chapters 19 and 20.

Comparing a Typical Postback to a Callback

Before you jump into some examples of the new callback feature, first look at a comparison to the current postback feature of a typical ASP.NET page.

When a page event is triggered on an ASP.NET page that is working with a typical postback scenario, a lot is going on. The diagram in Figure 2-14 illustrates the process.

In a normal postback situation, an event of some kind triggers an HTTP Post request to be sent to the Web server. An example of such an event might be the end user clicking a button on the form. This sends the HTTP Post request to the Web server, which then processes the request with the `IPostbackEventHandler` and runs the request through a series of page events. These events include loading the state (as found in the view state of the page), processing data, processing postback events, and finally rendering the page to be interpreted by the consuming browser once again. The process completely reloads the page in the browser, which is what causes the flicker and the realignment to the top of the page.

On the other hand, you have the alternative of using the callback capabilities, as shown in the diagram in Figure 2-15.

In this case, an event (again, such as a button click) causes the event to be posted to a script event handler (a JavaScript function) that sends off an asynchronous request to the Web server for processing. `ICallbackEventHandler` runs the request through a pipeline similar to what is used with the postback — but you notice that some of the larger steps (such as rendering the page) are excluded from the process chain. After the information is loaded, the result is returned to the script callback object. The script code then

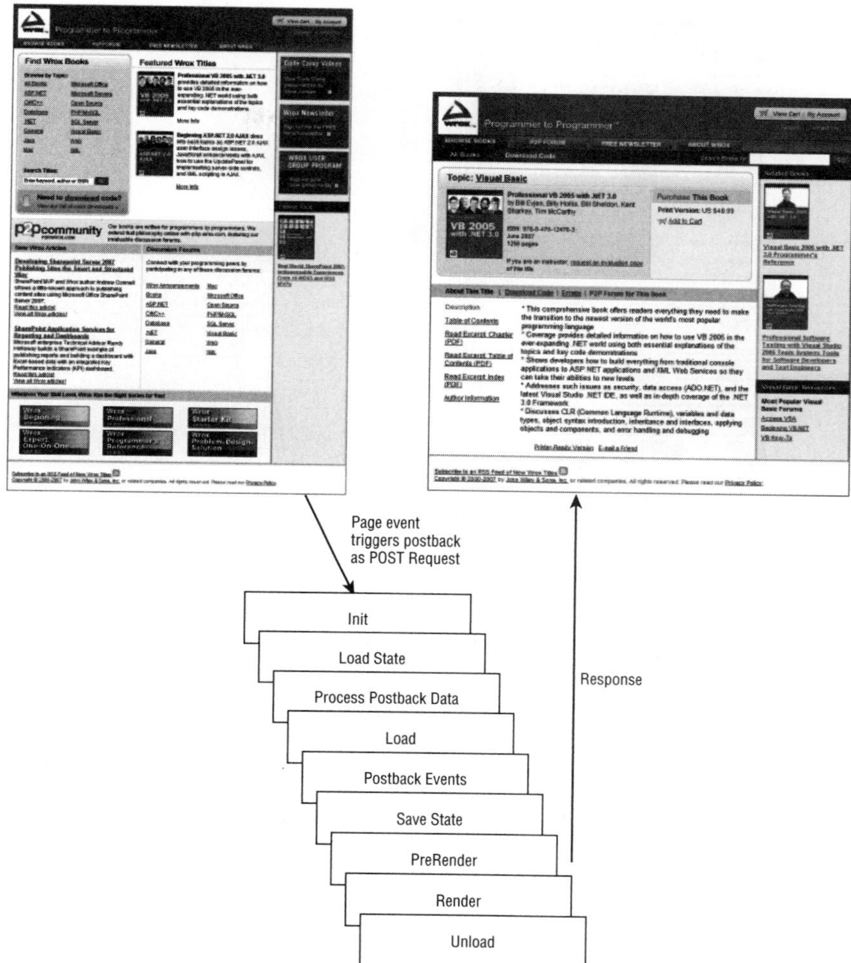

Figure 2-14

pushes this data into the Web page using JavaScript's capabilities to do this without refreshing the page. To understand how this all works, look at the simple example in the following section.

Using the Callback Feature — A Simple Approach

Begin examining the callback feature by looking at how a simple ASP.NET page uses it. For this example, you have only an HTML button control and a TextBox server control (the Web server control version). The idea is that when the end user clicks the button on the form, the callback service is initiated and a random number is populated into the text box. Listing 2-13 shows an example of this in action.

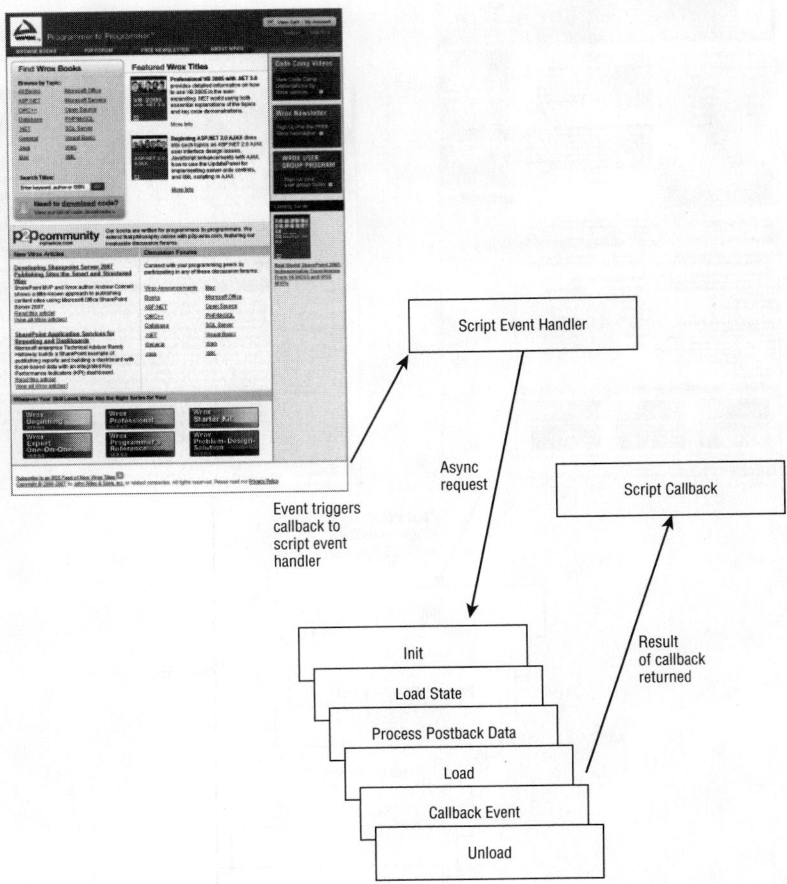

Figure 2-15

Listing 2-13: Using the callback feature to populate a random value to a Web page

.aspx page (VB version)

```
<%@ Page Language="VB" AutoEventWireup="false" CodeFile="RandomNumber.aspx.vb"
    Inherits="RandomNumber" %>

<html xmlns="http://www.w3.org/1999/xhtml">
<head runat="server"<
    <title>Callback Page</title>

    <script type="text/javascript">
        function GetNumber(){
            UseCallback();
        }

        function GetRandomNumberFromServer(TextBox1, context){
```

```
            document.forms[0].TextBox1.value = TextBox1;
        }
    </script>

</head>
<body>
    <form id="form1" runat="server">
    <div>
        <input id="Button1" type="button" value="Get Random Number"
         onclick="GetNumber()" />
        <br />
        <br />
        <asp:TextBox ID="TextBox1" Runat="server"></asp:TextBox>
    </div>
    </form>
</body>
</html>
```

VB (code-behind)

```
Partial Class RandomNumber
    Inherits System.Web.UI.Page
    Implements System.Web.UI.ICallbackEventHandler

    Dim _callbackResult As String = Nothing

    Protected Sub Page_Load(ByVal sender As Object, ByVal e As System.EventArgs) _
       Handles Me.Load

        Dim cbReference As String = Page.ClientScript.GetCallbackEventReference( _
           Me, "arg", "GetRandomNumberFromServer", "context")
        Dim cbScript As String = "function UseCallback(arg, context)" & _
           "{" & cbReference & ";" & "}"

        Page.ClientScript.RegisterClientScriptBlock(Me.GetType(), _
           "UseCallback", cbScript, True)
    End Sub

    Public Sub RaiseCallbackEvent(ByVal eventArgument As String) _
       Implements System.Web.UI.ICallbackEventHandler.RaiseCallbackEvent

       _callbackResult = Rnd().ToString()
    End Sub

    Public Function GetCallbackResult() As String _
       Implements System.Web.UI.ICallbackEventHandler.GetCallbackResult

        Return _callbackResult
    End Function
End Class
```

C# (code-behind)

```
using System;
using System.Data;
using System.Configuration;
```

Continued

```
using System.Collections;
using System.Web;
using System.Web.Security;
using System.Web.UI;
using System.Web.UI.WebControls;
using System.Web.UI.WebControls.WebParts;
using System.Web.UI.HtmlControls;

public partial class RandomNumber : System.Web.UI.Page,
   System.Web.UI.ICallbackEventHandler
{
    private string _callbackResult = null;

    protected void Page_Load(object sender, EventArgs e)
    {
        string cbReference = Page.ClientScript.GetCallbackEventReference(this,
           "arg", "GetRandomNumberFromServer", "context");
        string cbScript = "function UseCallback(arg, context)" +
           "{" + cbReference + ";" + "}";

        Page.ClientScript.RegisterClientScriptBlock(this.GetType(),
           "UseCallback", cbScript, true);
    }

    public void RaiseCallbackEvent(string eventArg)
    {
        Random rnd = new Random();
        _callbackResult = rnd.Next().ToString();
    }

    public string GetCallbackResult()
    {
        return _callbackResult;
    }
}
```

When this page is built and run in the browser, you get the results shown in Figure 2-16.

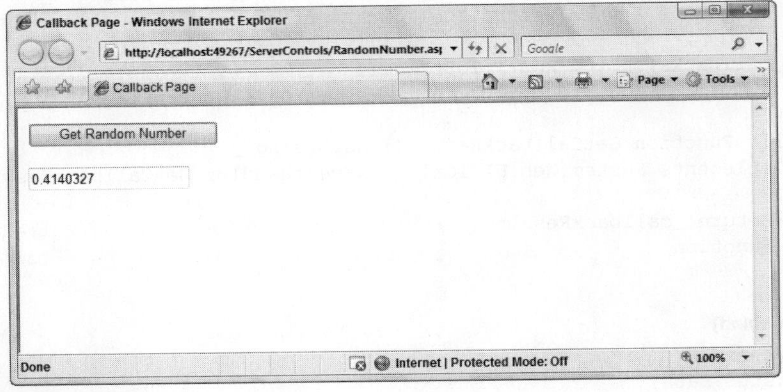

Figure 2-16

Clicking the button on the page invokes the client callback capabilities of the page, and the page then makes an asynchronous request to the code behind of the same page. After getting a response from this part of the page, the client script takes the retrieved value and places it inside the text box — all without doing a page refresh!

Now take a look at the .aspx page, which simply contains an HTML button control and a TextBox server control. Notice that a standard HTML button control is used because a typical <asp:button> control does not work here. No worries. When you work with the HTML button control, just be sure to include an onclick event to point to the JavaScript function that initiates this entire process:

```
<input id="Button1" type="button" value="Get Random Number"
 onclick="GetNumber()" />
```

You do not have to do anything else with the controls themselves. The final thing to include in the page is the client-side JavaScript functions to take care of the callback to the server-side functions. GetNumber() is the first JavaScript function that's instantiated. It starts the entire process by calling the name of the client script handler that is defined in the page's code behind. A string type result from GetNumber() is retrieved using the GetRandomNumberFromServer() function. GetRandomNumberFromServer() simply populates the string value retrieved and makes that the value of the Textbox control — specified by the value of the ID attribute of the server control (TextBox1):

```
<script type="text/javascript">
   function GetNumber(){
      UseCallback();
   }

   function GetRandomNumberFromServer(TextBox1, context){
      document.forms[0].TextBox1.value = TextBox1;
   }
</script>
```

Now turn your attention to the code behind.

The Page class of the Web page implements the System.Web.UI.ICallbackEventHandler interface:

```
Partial Class RandomNumber
    Inherits System.Web.UI.Page
    Implements System.Web.UI.ICallbackEventHandler

    ' Code here

End Class
```

This interface requires you to implement a couple of methods — the RaiseCallbackEvent and the Get-CallbackResult methods, both of which work with the client script request. RaiseCallbackEvent enables you to do the work of retrieving the value from the page, but the value can be only of type string:

```
Public Sub RaiseCallbackEvent(ByVal eventArgument As String) _
   Implements System.Web.UI.ICallbackEventHandler.RaiseCallbackEvent

   _callbackResult = Rnd().ToString()
End Sub
```

The `GetCallbackResult` is the method that actually grabs the returned value to be used:

```
Public Function GetCallbackResult() As String _
    Implements System.Web.UI.ICallbackEventHandler.GetCallbackResult

        Return _callbackResult
End Function
```

In addition, the `Page_Load` event includes the creation and placement of the client callback script manager (the function that will manage requests and responses) on the client:

```
Dim cbReference As String = Page.GetCallbackEventReference(Me, "arg", _
    "GetRandomNumberFromServer", "context")
Dim cbScript As String = "function UseCallback(arg, context)" & _
    "{" & cbReference & ";" & "}"

Page.ClientScript.RegisterClientScriptBlock(Me.GetType(), _
    "UseCallback", cbScript, True)
```

The function placed on the client for the callback capabilities is called `UseCallback()`. This `string` is then populated to the Web page itself using the `Page.ClientScript.RegisterClientScripBlock` that also puts `<script>` tags around the function on the page. Make sure that the name you use here is the same name you use in the client-side JavaScript function presented earlier.

In the end, you have a page that refreshes content without refreshing the overall page. This opens the door to a completely new area of possibilities. One caveat is that the callback capabilities described here use XmlHTTP and, therefore, the client browser needs to support XmlHTTP (Microsoft's Internet Explorer and FireFox do support this feature). Because of this, .NET Framework 2.0 and 3.5 have the `SupportsCallBack` and the `SupportsXmlHttp` properties. To ensure this support, you could put a check in the page's code behind when the initial page is being generated. It might look similar to the following:

VB

```
If (Page.Request.Browser.SupportsXmlHTTP) Then

End If
```

C#

```
if (Page.Request.Browser.SupportsXmlHTTP == true) {

}
```

Using the Callback Feature with a Single Parameter

Now you will build a Web page that utilizes the callback feature but requires a parameter to retrieve a returned value. At the top of the page, place a text box that gathers input from the end user, a button, and another text box to populate the page with the result from the callback.

The page asks for a ZIP Code from the user and then uses the callback feature to instantiate an XML Web service request on the server. The Web service returns the latest weather for that particular ZIP Code in a string format. Listing 2-14 shows an example of the page.

Listing 2-14: Using the callback feature with a Web service

.aspx page (VB version)

```
<%@ Page Language="VB" AutoEventWireup="false" CodeFile="WSCallback.aspx.vb"
    Inherits="WSCallback" %>

<html xmlns="http://www.w3.org/1999/xhtml">
<head runat="server">
    <title>Web Service Callback</title>

    <script type="text/javascript">
        function GetTemp(){
            var zipcode = document.forms[0].TextBox1.value;
            UseCallback(zipcode, "");
        }

        function GetTempFromServer(TextBox2, context){
            document.forms[0].TextBox2.value = "Zipcode: " +
            document.forms[0].TextBox1.value + " | Temp: " + TextBox2;
        }
    </script>
</head>
<body>
    <form id="form1" runat="server">
    <div>
        <asp:TextBox ID="TextBox1" Runat="server"></asp:TextBox>
        <br />
        <input id="Button1" type="button" value="Get Temp" onclick="GetTemp()" />
        <br />
        <asp:TextBox ID="TextBox2" Runat="server" Width="400px">
        </asp:TextBox>
        <br />
        <br />
    </div>
    </form>
</body>
</html>
```

VB (code-behind)

```
Partial Class WSCallback
    Inherits System.Web.UI.Page
    Implements System.Web.UI.IcallbackEventHandler

    Dim _callbackResult As String = Nothing

    Protected Sub Page_Load(ByVal sender As Object, ByVal e As System.EventArgs) _
       Handles Me.Load

        Dim cbReference As String = Page.ClientScript.GetCallbackEventReference( _
           Me, "arg", "GetTempFromServer", "context")
```

Continued

```
        Dim cbScript As String = "function UseCallback(arg, context)" & _
           "{" & cbReference & ";" & "}"

        Page.ClientScript.RegisterClientScriptBlock(Me.GetType(), _
           "UseCallback", cbScript, True)
    End Sub

    Public Sub RaiseCallbackEvent(ByVal eventArgument As String) _
       Implements System.Web.UI.ICallbackEventHandler.RaiseCallbackEvent

        Dim ws As New Weather.TemperatureService
        _callbackResult = ws.getTemp(eventArgument).ToString()
    End Sub
    Public Function GetCallbackResult() As String _
       Implements System.Web.UI.ICallbackEventHandler.GetCallbackResult

        Return _callbackResult
    End Function
End Class
```

C# (code-behind)

```
using System;
using System.Data;
using System.Configuration;
using System.Collections;
using System.Web;
using System.Web.Security;
using System.Web.UI;
using System.Web.UI.WebControls;
using System.Web.UI.WebControls.WebParts;
using System.Web.UI.HtmlControls;

public partial class WSCallback : System.Web.UI.Page,
   System.Web.UI.ICallbackEventHandler
{
    private string _callbackResult = null;

    protected void Page_Load(object sender, EventArgs e)
    {
        string cbReference = Page.ClientScript.GetCallbackEventReference(this,
           "arg", "GetTempFromServer", "context");
        string cbScript = "function UseCallback(arg, context)" +
           "{" + cbReference + ";" + "}";

        Page.ClientScript.RegisterClientScriptBlock(this.GetType(),
           "UseCallback", cbScript, true);
    }

    public void RaiseCallbackEvent(string eventArg)
    {
        Weather.TemperatureService ws = new Weather.TemperatureService();
        _callbackResult = ws.getTemp(eventArg).ToString();
    }
```

```
        public string GetCallbackResult()
        {
            return _callbackResult;
        }
    }
```

What you do not see on this page from the listing is that a Web reference has been made to a remote Web service that returns the latest weather to the application based on a ZIP Code the user supplied.

To get at the Web service used in this demo, the location of the WSDL file at the time of this writing is `http://ws.strikeiron.com/InnerGears/ForecastByZip2?WSDL`. *For more information on working with Web services in your ASP.NET applications, check out Chapter 30.*

After building and running this page, you get the results illustrated in Figure 2-17.

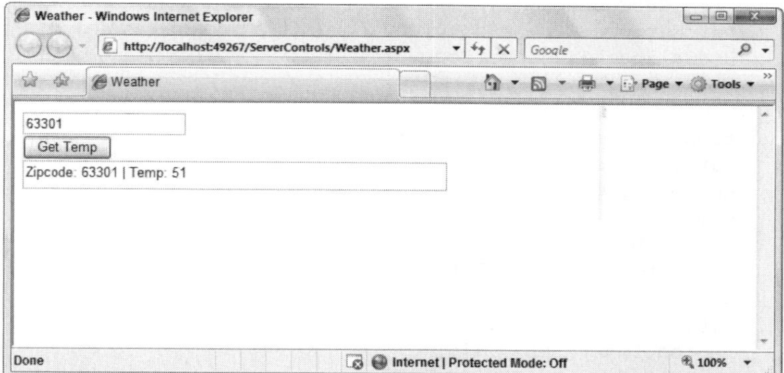

Figure 2-17

The big difference with the client callback feature is that this example sends in a required parameter. That is done in the `GetTemp()` JavaScript function on the `.aspx` part of the page:

```
function GetTemp(){
   var zipcode = document.forms[0].TextBox1.value;
   UseCallback(zipcode, "");
}
```

The JavaScript function shows the population that the end user input into `TextBox1` and places its value in a variable called `zipcode` that is sent as a parameter in the `UseCallback()` method.

This example, like the previous one, updates the page without doing a complete page refresh.

Using the Callback Feature — A More Complex Example

So far, you have seen an example of using the callback feature to pull back a single item as well as to pull back a string whose output is based on a single parameter that was passed to the engine. The next example takes this operation one step further and pulls back a collection of results based upon a parameter provided.

This example works with an instance of the Northwind database found in SQL Server. For this example, create a single page that includes a TextBox server control and a button. Below that, place a table that will be populated with the customer details from the customer ID provided in the text box. The .aspx page for this example is provided in Listing 2-15.

Listing 2-15: An ASP.NET page to collect the CustomerID from the end user

.aspx Page

```
<%@ Page Language="VB" AutoEventWireup="false"
    CodeFile="Default.aspx.vb" Inherits="_Default" %>

<html xmlns="http://www.w3.org/1999/xhtml">
<head runat="server">
    <title>Customer Details</title>

    <script type="text/javascript">
        function GetCustomer(){
            var customerCode = document.forms[0].TextBox1.value;
            UseCallback(customerCode, "");
        }

        function GetCustDetailsFromServer(result, context){
            var i = result.split("|");
            customerID.innerHTML = i[0];
            companyName.innerHTML = i[1];
            contactName.innerHTML = i[2];
            contactTitle.innerHTML = i[3];
            address.innerHTML = i[4];
            city.innerHTML = i[5];
            region.innerHTML = i[6];
            postalCode.innerHTML = i[7];
            country.innerHTML = i[8];
            phone.innerHTML = i[9];
            fax.innerHTML = i[10];
        }
    </script>
</head>
<body>
    <form id="form1" runat="server">
    <div>
        <asp:TextBox ID="TextBox1" runat="server"></asp:TextBox> 
        <input id="Button1" type="button" value="Get Customer Details"
         onclick="GetCustomer()" /><br />
        <br />
      <table cellspacing="0" cellpadding="4" rules="all" border="1"
       id="DetailsView1"
       style="background-color:White;border-color:#3366CC;border-width:1px;
          border-style:None;height:50px;width:400px;border-collapse:collapse;">
        <tr style="color:#003399;background-color:White;">
           <td>CustomerID</td><td><span id="customerID" /></td>
        </tr><tr style="color:#003399;background-color:White;">
            <td>CompanyName</td><td><span id="companyName" /></td>
        </tr><tr style="color:#003399;background-color:White;">
```

```
            <td>ContactName</td><td><span id="contactName" /></td>
         </tr><tr style="color:#003399;background-color:White;">
            <td>ContactTitle</td><td><span id="contactTitle" /></td>
         </tr><tr style="color:#003399;background-color:White;">
            <td>Address</td><td><span id="address" /></td>
         </tr><tr style="color:#003399;background-color:White;">
            <td>City</td><td><span id="city" /></td>
         </tr><tr style="color:#003399;background-color:White;">
            <td>Region</td><td><span id="region" /></td>
         </tr><tr style="color:#003399;background-color:White;">
            <td>PostalCode</td><td><span id="postalCode" /></td>
         </tr><tr style="color:#003399;background-color:White;">
            <td>Country</td><td><span id="country" /></td>
         </tr><tr style="color:#003399;background-color:White;">
            <td>Phone</td><td><span id="phone" /></td>
         </tr><tr style="color:#003399;background-color:White;">
            <td>Fax</td><td><span id="fax" /></td>
         </tr>
      </table>
   </div>
   </form>
</body>
</html>
```

As in the previous examples, two JavaScript functions are contained in the page. The first, `GetCustomer()`, is the function that passes in the parameter to be processed by the code-behind file on the application server. This is quite similar to what appeared in the previous example.

The second JavaScript function, however, is different. Looking over this function, you can see that it is expecting a long string of multiple values:

```
function GetCustDetailsFromServer(result, context){
   var i = result.split("|");
   customerID.innerHTML = i[0];
   companyName.innerHTML = i[1];
   contactName.innerHTML = i[2];
   contactTitle.innerHTML = i[3];
   address.innerHTML = i[4];
   city.innerHTML = i[5];
   region.innerHTML = i[6];
   postalCode.innerHTML = i[7];
   country.innerHTML = i[8];
   phone.innerHTML = i[9];
   fax.innerHTML = i[10];
}
```

The multiple results expected are constructed in a pipe-delimited string, and each of the values is placed into an array. Then each string item in the array is assigned to a particular `<span>` tag in the ASP.NET page. For instance, take a look at the following bit of code:

```
customerID.innerHTML = i[0];
```

The `i[0]` variable is the first item found in the pipe-delimited string, and it is assigned to the `customerID` item on the page. This `customerID` identifier comes from the following `<span>` tag found in the table:

```
<span id="customerID" />
```

Now, turn your attention to the code-behind file for this page, as shown in Listing 2-16.

Listing 2-16: The code-behind file for the Customer Details page

VB

```
Imports System.Data
Imports System.Data.SqlClient

Partial Class _Default
    Inherits System.Web.UI.Page
    Implements System.Web.UI.ICallbackEventHandler

    Dim _callbackResult As String = Nothing

    Public Function GetCallbackResult() As String _
       Implements System.Web.UI.ICallbackEventHandler.GetCallbackResult
        Return _callbackResult
    End Function

    Public Sub RaiseCallbackEvent(ByVal eventArgument As String) _
       Implements System.Web.UI.ICallbackEventHandler.RaiseCallbackEvent
        Dim conn As SqlConnection = New _
           SqlConnection("Data Source=.;Initial Catalog=Northwind;User ID=sa")
        Dim cmd As SqlCommand = New _
           SqlCommand("Select * From Customers Where CustomerID = '" & _
           eventArgument & "'", conn)

        conn.Open()

        Dim MyReader As SqlDataReader
        MyReader = cmd.ExecuteReader(CommandBehavior.CloseConnection)

        Dim MyValues(10) As String

        While MyReader.Read()
            MyValues(0) = MyReader("CustomerID").ToString()
            MyValues(1) = MyReader("CompanyName").ToString()
            MyValues(2) = MyReader("ContactName").ToString()
            MyValues(3) = MyReader("ContactTitle").ToString()
            MyValues(4) = MyReader("Address").ToString()
            MyValues(5) = MyReader("City").ToString()
            MyValues(6) = MyReader("Region").ToString()
            MyValues(7) = MyReader("PostalCode").ToString()
            MyValues(8) = MyReader("Country").ToString()
            MyValues(9) = MyReader("Phone").ToString()
            MyValues(10) = MyReader("Fax").ToString()
```

```
        End While

        Conn.Close()

        _callbackResult = String.Join("|", MyValues)
    End Sub

    Protected Sub Page_Load(ByVal sender As Object, _
       ByVal e As System.EventArgs) Handles Me.Load
        Dim cbReference As String = _
           Page.ClientScript.GetCallbackEventReference(Me, "arg", _
              "GetCustDetailsFromServer", "context")
        Dim cbScript As String = "function UseCallback(arg, context)" & _
           "{" & cbReference & ";" & "}"

        Page.ClientScript.RegisterClientScriptBlock(Me.GetType(), _
           "UseCallback", cbScript, True)
    End Sub
End Class
```

C#

```
using System;
using System.Data;
using System.Configuration;
using System.Collections;
using System.Web;
using System.Web.Security;
using System.Web.UI;
using System.Web.UI.WebControls;
using System.Web.UI.WebControls.WebParts;
using System.Web.UI.HtmlControls;
using System.Data.SqlClient;

public partial class Default2 : System.Web.UI.Page,
   System.Web.UI.ICallbackEventHandler
{
    private string _callbackResult = null;

    protected void Page_Load(object sender, EventArgs e)
    {
        string cbReference = Page.ClientScript.GetCallbackEventReference(this,
           "arg", "GetCustDetailsFromServer", "context");
        string cbScript = "function UseCallback(arg, context)" +
           "{" + cbReference + ";" + "}";

        Page.ClientScript.RegisterClientScriptBlock(this.GetType(),
           "UseCallback", cbScript, true);
    }

    #region ICallbackEventHandler Members
```

Continued

```
    public string GetCallbackResult()
    {
        return _callbackResult;
    }

    public void RaiseCallbackEvent(string eventArgument)
    {
        SqlConnection conn = new
           SqlConnection("Data Source=.;Initial Catalog=Northwind;User ID=sa");
        SqlCommand cmd = new
           SqlCommand("Select * From Customers Where CustomerID = '" +
           eventArgument + "'", conn);

        conn.Open();

        SqlDataReader MyReader;
        MyReader = cmd.ExecuteReader(CommandBehavior.CloseConnection);

        string[] MyValues = new string[11];

        while (MyReader.Read())
        {
            MyValues[0] = MyReader["CustomerID"].ToString();
            MyValues[1] = MyReader["CompanyName"].ToString();
            MyValues[2] = MyReader["ContactName"].ToString();
            MyValues[3] = MyReader["ContactTitle"].ToString();
            MyValues[4] = MyReader["Address"].ToString();
            MyValues[5] = MyReader["City"].ToString();
            MyValues[6] = MyReader["Region"].ToString();
            MyValues[7] = MyReader["PostalCode"].ToString();
            MyValues[8] = MyReader["Country"].ToString();
            MyValues[9] = MyReader["Phone"].ToString();
            MyValues[10] = MyReader["Fax"].ToString();
        }

        _callbackResult = String.Join("|", MyValues);
    }

    #endregion
}
```

Much of this document is quite similar to the document in the previous example using the callback feature. The big difference comes in the `RaiseCallbackEvent()` method. This method first performs a `SELECT` statement on the Customers database based upon the `CustomerID` passed in via the `eventArgument` variable. The result retrieved from this `SELECT` statement is then made part of a string array, which is finally concatenated using the `String.Join()` method before being passed back as the value of the `_callbackResult` object.

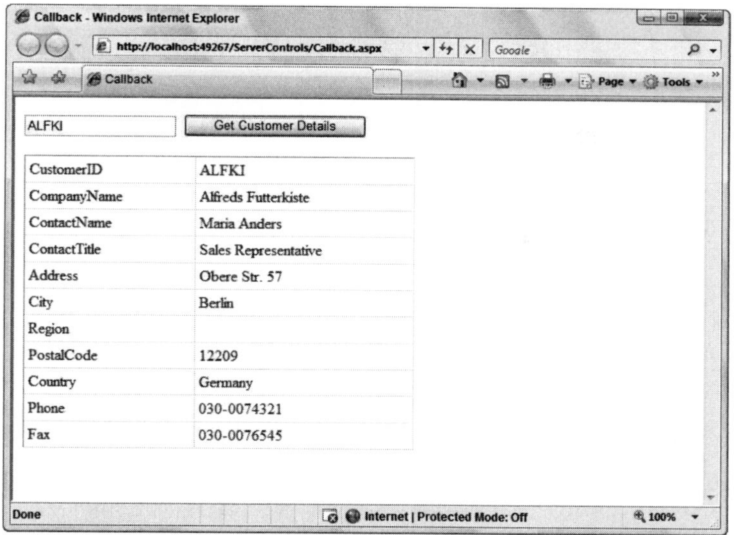

Figure 2-18

With this code in place, you can now populate an entire table of data using the callback feature. This means that the table is populated with no need to refresh the page. The results from this code operation are presented in Figure 2-18.

Summary

This chapter gave you one of the core building blocks of an ASP.NET page — the server control. The server control is an object-oriented approach to page development that encapsulates page elements into modifiable and expandable components.

The chapter also introduced you to how to customize the look-and-feel of your server controls using Cascading Style Sheets (CSS). Working with CSS in ASP.NET 3.5 is easy and quick, especially if you have Visual Studio 2008 to assist you. Finally, this chapter looked at both using HTML server controls and adding JavaScript to your pages to modify the behaviors of your controls.

3

ASP.NET Web Server Controls

Of the two types of server controls, HTML server controls and Web server controls, the latter is considered the more powerful and flexible. The previous chapter looked at how to use HTML server controls in applications. HTML server controls enable you to manipulate HTML elements from your server-side code. On the other hand, Web server controls are powerful because they are not explicitly tied to specific HTML elements; rather, they are more closely aligned to the specific functionality that you want to generate. As you will see throughout this chapter, Web server controls can be very simple or rather complex depending on the control you are working with.

The purpose of the large collection of controls is to make you more productive. These controls give you advanced functionality that, in the past, you would have had to laboriously program or simply omit. In the classic ASP days, for example, few calendars were used on Internet Web sites. With the introduction of the Calendar server control in ASP.NET 1.0, calendar creation on a site became a trivial task. Building an image map on top of an image was another task that was difficult to achieve in ASP.NET 1.*x*, but this capability was introduced as a new server control in ASP.NET 2.0.

This chapter introduces some of the available Web server controls. The first part of the chapter focuses on the Web server controls that were around during the ASP.NET 1.0/1.1 days. Then the chapter explores the server controls that were introduced back in ASP.NET 2.0. This chapter does not discuss every possible control because some server controls are introduced and covered in other chapters throughout the book.

An Overview of Web Server Controls

The Web server control is ASP.NET's most-used component. Although you may have been pretty excited by the HTML server controls shown in the previous chapter, Web server controls are definitely a notch higher in capability. They allow for a higher level of functionality that becomes more apparent as you work with them.

The HTML server controls provided by ASP.NET work in that they map to specific HTML elements. You control the output by working with the HTML attributes that the HTML element provides. The attributes can be changed dynamically on the server side before they are finally output to the client. There is a lot of power in this, and you have some HTML server control capabilities that you simply do not have when you work with Web server controls.

Web server controls work differently. They do not map to specific HTML elements, but instead enable you to define functionality, capability, and appearance without the attributes that are available to you through a collection of HTML elements. When constructing a Web page that is made up of Web server controls, you are describing the functionality, the look-and-feel, and the behavior of your page elements. You then let ASP.NET decide how to output this construction. The output, of course, is based on the capabilities of the container that is making the request. This means that each requestor might see a different HTML output because each is requesting the same page with a different browser type or version. ASP.NET takes care of all the browser detection and the work associated with it on your behalf.

Unlike HTML server controls, Web server controls are not only available for working with common Web page form elements (such as text boxes and buttons), but they can also bring some advanced capabilities and functionality to your Web pages. For instance, one common feature of many Web applications is a calendar. No HTML form element places a calendar on your Web forms, but a Web server control from ASP.NET can provide your application with a full-fledged calendar, including some advanced capabilities. In the past, adding calendars to your Web pages was not a small programming task. Today, adding calendars with ASP.NET is rather simple and is achieved with a single line of code!

Remember that when you are constructing your Web server controls, you are actually constructing a control — *a set of instructions* — that is meant for the server (not the client). By default, all Web server controls provided by ASP.NET use an `asp:` at the beginning of the control declaration. The following is a typical Web server control:

```
<asp:Label ID="Label1" runat="server" Text="Hello World"></asp:Label>
```

Like HTML server controls, Web server controls require an `ID` attribute to reference the control in the server-side code, as well as a `runat="server"` attribute declaration. As you do for other XML-based elements, you need to properly open and close Web server controls using XML syntax rules. In the preceding example, you can see the `<asp:Label>` control has a closing `</asp:Label>` element associated with it. You could have also closed this element using the following syntax:

```
<asp:Label ID="Label1" Runat="server" Text="Hello World" />
```

The rest of this chapter examines some of the Web server controls available to you in ASP.NET.

The Label Server Control

The Label server control is used to display text in the browser. Because this is a server control, you can dynamically alter the text from your server-side code. As you saw from the preceding examples of using the `<asp:Label>` control, the control uses the `Text` attribute to assign the content of the control as shown here:

```
<asp:Label ID="Label1" runat="server" Text="Hello World" />
```

Instead of using the `Text` attribute, however, you can place the content to be displayed between the `<asp:Label>` elements like this:

```
<asp:Label ID="Label1" runat="server">Hello World</asp:Label>
```

You can also provide content for the control through programmatic means, as illustrated in Listing 3-1.

Listing 3-1: Programmatically providing text to the Label control

VB

```
Label1.Text = "Hello ASP.NET"
```

C#

```
Label1.Text = "Hello ASP.NET";
```

The Label server control has always been a control that simply showed text. Ever since ASP.NET 2.0, it has a little bit of extra functionality. The big change since this release of the framework is that you can now give items in your form hot-key functionality (also known as *accelerator* keys). This causes the page to focus on a particular server control that you declaratively assign to a specific hot-key press (for example, using Alt+N to focus on the first text box on the form).

A hot key is a quick way for the end user to initiate an action on the page. For instance, if you use Microsoft Internet Explorer, you can press Ctrl+N to open a new instance of IE. Hot keys have always been quite common in thick-client applications (Windows Forms), and now you can use them in ASP.NET. Listing 3-2 shows an example of how to give hot-key functionality to two text boxes on a form.

Listing 3-2: Using the Label server control to provide hot-key functionality

```
<%@ Page Language="VB" %>

<html xmlns="http://www.w3.org/1999/xhtml">
<head runat="server">
    <title>Label Server Control</title>
</head>
<body>
    <form id="form1" runat="server">
        <p>
            <asp:Label ID="Label1" runat="server" AccessKey="N"
             AssociatedControlID="Textbox1">User<u>n</u>ame</asp:Label>
            <asp:TextBox ID="TextBox1" runat="server"></asp:TextBox></p>
        <p>
            <asp:Label ID="Label2" runat="server" AccessKey="P"
             AssociatedControlID="Textbox2"><u>P</u>assword</asp:Label>
            <asp:TextBox ID="TextBox2" Runat="server"></asp:TextBox></p>
        <p>
            <asp:Button ID="Button1" runat="server" Text="Submit" />
        </p>
    </form>
</body>
</html>
```

Hot keys are assigned with the `AccessKey` attribute. In this case, `Label1` uses `N`, and `Label2` uses `P`. The second new attribute for the Label control is the `AssociatedControlID` attribute. The `String` value placed here associates the Label control with another server control on the form. The value must be one of the other server controls on the form. If not, the page gives you an error when invoked.

With these two controls in place, when the page is called in the browser, you can press Alt+N or Alt+P to automatically focus on a particular text box in the form. In Figure 3-1, HTML-declared underlines indicate the letters to be pressed along with the Alt key to create focus on the control adjoining the text. This is not required, but we highly recommend it because it is what the end user expects when working with hot keys. In this example, the letter `n` in `Username` and the letter `P` in `Password` are underlined.

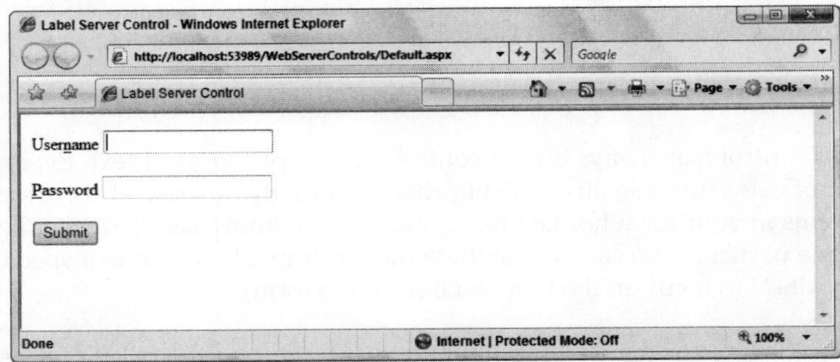

Figure 3-1

When working with hot keys, be aware that not all letters are available to use with the Alt key. Microsoft Internet Explorer already uses Alt+F, E, V, I, O, T, A, W, and H. If you use any of these letters, IE actions supersede any actions you place on the page.

The Literal Server Control

The Literal server control works very much like the Label server control does. This control was always used in the past for text that you wanted to push out to the browser, but keep unchanged in the process (a literal state). A Label control alters the output by placing `<span>` elements around the text as shown:

```
<span id="Label1">Here is some text</span>
```

The Literal control just outputs the text without the `<span>` elements. One feature found in this server control is the attribute `Mode`. This attribute enables you to dictate how the text assigned to the control is interpreted by the ASP.NET engine.

If you place some HTML code in the string that is output (for instance, `<b>Here is some text</b>`), the Literal control outputs just that and the consuming browser shows the text as bold:

```
Here is some text
```

Try using the `Mode` attribute as illustrated here:

```
<asp:Literal ID="Literal1" runat="server" Mode="Encode"
 Text="<b>Here is some text</b>"></asp:Literal>
```

Adding `Mode="Encode"` encodes the output before it is received by the consuming application:

```
&lt;b&gt;Label&lt;/b&gt;
```

Now, instead of the text being converted to a bold font, the <b> elements are displayed:

```
<b>Here is some text</b>
```

This is ideal if you want to display code in your application. Other values for the `Mode` attribute include `Transform` and `PassThrough`. `Transform` looks at the consumer and includes or removes elements as needed. For instance, not all devices accept HTML elements so, if the value of the `Mode` attribute is set to `Transform`, these elements are removed from the string before it is sent to the consuming application. A value of `PassThrough` for the `Mode` property means that the text is sent to the consuming application without any changes being made to the string.

The TextBox Server Control

One of the main features of Web pages is to offer forms that end users can use to submit their information for collection. The TextBox server control is one of the most used controls in this space. As its name suggests, the control provides a text box on the form that enables the end user to input text. You can map the TextBox control to three different HTML elements used in your forms.

First, the TextBox control can be used as a standard HTML text box, as shown in the following code snippet:

```
<asp:TextBox ID="TextBox1" runat="server"></asp:TextBox>
```

This code creates a text box on the form that looks like the one shown in Figure 3-2.

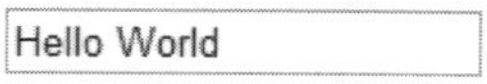

Hello World

Figure 3-2

Second, the TextBox control can allow end users to input their passwords into a form. This is done by changing the `TextMode` attribute of the TextBox control to `Password`, as illustrated here:

```
<asp:TextBox ID="TextBox1" runat="server" TextMode="Password"></asp:TextBox>
```

When asking end users for their passwords through the browser, it is best practice to provide a text box that encodes the content placed in this form element. Using an attribute and value of `TextMode="Password"` ensures that the text is encoded with either a star (*) or a dot, as shown in Figure 3-3.

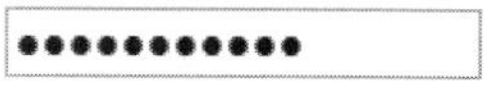

●●●●●●●●●●●

Figure 3-3

Third, the TextBox server control can be used as a multiline text box. The code for accomplishing this task is as follows:

```
<asp:TextBox ID="TextBox1" runat="server" TextMode="MultiLine"
 Width="300px" Height="150px"></asp:TextBox>
```

Giving the `TextMode` attribute a value of `MultiLine` creates a multilined text box in which the end user can enter a larger amount of text in the form. The `Width` and `Height` attributes set the size of the text area, but these are optional attributes — without them, the text area is produced in its smallest size. Figure 3-4 shows the use of the preceding code after adding some text.

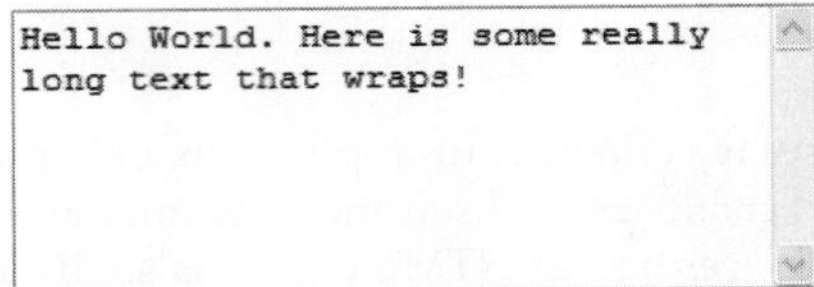

Figure 3-4

When working with a multilined text box, be aware of the `Wrap` attribute. When set to `True` (which is the default), the text entered into the text area wraps to the next line if needed. When set to `False`, the end user can type continuously in a single line until she presses the Enter key, which brings the cursor down to the next line.

Using the Focus() Method

Because the TextBox server control is derived from the base class of `WebControl`, one of the methods available to it is `Focus()`. The `Focus()` method enables you to dynamically place the end user's cursor in an appointed form element (not just the TextBox control, but in any of the server controls derived from the `WebControl` class). With that said, it is probably most often used with the TextBox control, as illustrated in Listing 3-3.

Listing 3-3: Using the Focus() method with the TextBox control

VB

```
Protected Sub Page_Load(ByVal sender As Object, ByVal e As System.EventArgs)
   TextBox1.Focus()
End Sub
```

C#

```
protected void Page_Load(object sender, EventArgs e)
{
   TextBox1.Focus();
}
```

When the page using this method is loaded in the browser, the cursor is already placed inside of the text box, ready for you to start typing. There is no need to move your mouse to get the cursor in place so you can start entering information in the form. This is ideal for those folks who take a keyboard approach to working with forms.

Using AutoPostBack

ASP.NET pages work in an event-driven way. When an action on a Web page triggers an event, server-side code is initiated. One of the more common events is an end user clicking a button on the form. If you double-click the button in Design view of Visual Studio 2008, you can see the code page with the structure of the `Button1_Click` event already in place. This is because `OnClick` is the most common event of the Button control. Double-clicking the TextBox control constructs an `OnTextChanged` event. This event is triggered when the end user moves the cursor focus outside the text box, either by clicking another element on the page after entering something into a text box, or by simply tabbing out of the text box. The use of this event is shown in Listing 3-4.

Listing 3-4: Triggering an event when a TextBox change occurs

VB

```
<%@ Page Language="VB" %>

<script runat="server">
    Protected Sub TextBox1_TextChanged(ByVal sender As Object, _
       ByVal e As System.EventArgs)

        Response.Write("OnTextChanged event triggered")
    End Sub

    Protected Sub Button1_Click(ByVal sender As Object, _
       ByVal e As System.EventArgs)

        Response.Write("OnClick event triggered")
    End Sub
</script>

<html xmlns="http://www.w3.org/1999/xhtml">
<head runat="server">
    <title>OnTextChanged Page</title>
</head>
<body>
    <form id="form1" runat="server">
    <div>
        <asp:TextBox ID="TextBox1" runat="server" AutoPostBack="True"
         OnTextChanged="TextBox1_TextChanged"></asp:TextBox>
        <asp:Button ID="Button1" runat="server" Text="Button"
         OnClick="Button1_Click" />
    </div>
    </form>
</body>
</html>
```

C#

```
<%@ Page Language="C#" %>

<script runat="server">
    protected void TextBox1_TextChanged(object sender, EventArgs e)
    {
        Response.Write("OnTextChanged event triggered");
    }

    protected void Button1_Click(object sender, EventArgs e)
    {
        Response.Write("OnClick event triggered");
    }
</script>
```

As you build and run this page, notice that you can type something in the text box, but once you tab out of it, the `OnTextChanged` event is triggered and the code contained in the `TextBox1_TextChanged` event runs. To make this work, you must add the `AutoPostBack` attribute to the TextBox control and set it to `True`. This causes the Web page to look for any text changes prior to an actual page postback. For the `AutoPostBack` feature to work, the browser viewing the page must support ECMAScript.

Using AutoCompleteType

You want the forms you build for your Web applications to be as simple to use as possible. You want to make them easy and quick for the end user to fill out the information and proceed. If you make a form too onerous, the people who come to your site may leave without completing it.

One of the great capabilities for any Web form is smart auto-completion. You may have seen this yourself when you visited a site for the first time. As you start to fill out information in a form, a drop-down list appears below the text box as you type, showing you a value that you have typed in a previous form. The plain text box you were working with has become a smart text box. Figure 3-5 shows an example of this feature.

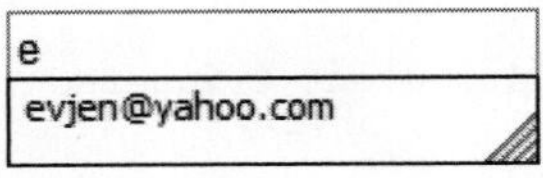

Figure 3-5

A great new aspect of the TextBox control is the `AutoCompleteType` attribute, which enables you to apply the auto-completion feature to your own forms. You have to help the text boxes on your form to recognize the type of information that they should be looking for. What does that mean? Well, first look at the possible values of the `AutoCompleteType` attribute:

```
BusinessCity            Disabled              HomeStreetAddress
BusinessCountryRegion   DisplayName           HomeZipCode
BusinessFax             Email                 JobTitle
BusinessPhone           FirstName             LastName
BusinessState           Gender                MiddleName
BusinessStateAddress    HomeCity              None
BusinessUrl             HomeCountryRegion     Notes
BusinessZipCode         HomeFax               Office
Cellular                Homepage              Pager
Company                 HomePhone             Search
Department              HomeState
```

From this list, you can see that if your text box is asking for the end user's home street address, you want to use the following in your TextBox control:

```
<asp:TextBox ID="TextBox1" runat="server"
 AutoCompleteType="HomeStreetAddress"></asp:TextBox>
```

As you view the source of the text box you created, you can see that the following construction has occurred:

```
<input name="TextBox1" type="text" vcard_name="vCard.Home.StreetAddress"
 id="TextBox1" />
```

This feature makes your forms easier to work with. Yes, it is a simple thing, but sometimes it is the little things that keep the viewers coming back again and again to your Web site.

The Button Server Control

Another common control for your Web forms is a button that can be constructed using the Button server control. Buttons are the usual element used to submit forms. Most of the time you are simply dealing with items contained in your forms through the Button control's `OnClick` event, as illustrated in Listing 3-5.

Listing 3-5: The Button control's OnClick event

VB

```
Protected Sub Button1_Click(ByVal sender As Object, ByVal e As System.EventArgs)
    ' Code here
End Sub
```

C#

```
protected void Button1_Click(object sender, EventArgs e)
{
    // Code here
}
```

The Button control is one of the easier controls to use, but there are a couple of properties of which you must be aware: `CausesValidation` and `CommandName`. They are discussed in the following sections.

The CausesValidation Property

If you have more than one button on your Web page and you are working with the validation server controls, you may not want to fire the validation for each button on the form. Setting the `CausesValidation` property to `False` is a way to use a button that will not fire the validation process. This is explained in more detail in Chapter 4.

The CommandName Property

You can have multiple buttons on your form all working from a single event. The nice thing is that you can also tag the buttons so that the code can make logical decisions based on which button on the form was clicked. You must construct your Button controls in the manner illustrated in Listing 3-6 to take advantage of this behavior.

Listing 3-6: Constructing multiple Button controls to work from a single function

```
<asp:Button ID="Button1" runat="server" Text="Button 1"
 OnCommand="Button_Command" CommandName="DoSomething1" />
<asp:Button ID="Button2" runat="server" Text="Button 2"
 OnCommand="Button_Command" CommandName="DoSomething2" />
```

Looking at these two instances of the Button control, you should pay attention to several things. The first thing to notice is what is not present — any attribute mention of an `OnClick` event. Instead, you use the `OnCommand` event, which points to an event called `Button_Command`. You can see that both Button controls are working from the same event. How does the event differentiate between the two buttons being clicked? Through the value placed in the CommandName property. In this case, they are indeed separate values — DoSomething1 and DoSomething2.

The next step is to create the Button_Command event to deal with both these buttons by simply typing one out or by selecting the Command event from the drop-down list of available events for the Button control from the code view of Visual Studio. In either case, you should end up with an event like the one shown in Listing 3-7.

Listing 3-7: The Button_Command event

VB

```
Protected Sub Button_Command(ByVal sender As Object, _
  ByVal e As System.Web.UI.WebControls.CommandEventArgs)

   Select Case e.CommandName
      Case "DoSomething1"
         Response.Write("Button 1 was selected")
      Case "DoSomething2"
         Response.Write("Button 2 was selected")
   End Select

End Sub
```

C#

```
protected void Button_Command(Object sender,
   System.Web.UI.WebControls.CommandEventArgs e)
{
   switch (e.CommandName)
   {
      case("DoSomething1"):
         Response.Write("Button 1 was selected");
         break;
      case("DoSomething2"):
         Response.Write("Button 2 was selected");
         break;
   }
}
```

Notice that this method uses System.Web.UI.WebControls.CommandEventArgs instead of the typical System.EventArgs. This gives you access to the member CommandName used in the Select Case (switch) statement as e.CommandName. Using this object, you can check for the value of the CommandName property used by the button that was clicked on the form and take a specific action based upon the value passed.

You can add some parameters to be passed in to the Command event beyond what is defined in the CommandName property. You do this by using the Button control's CommandArgument property. Adding values to the property enables you to define items a bit more granularly if you want. You can get at this value via server-side code using e.CommandArgument from the CommandEventArgs object.

Buttons That Work with Client-Side JavaScript

Buttons are frequently used for submitting information and causing actions to occur on a Web page. Before ASP.NET 1.0/1.1, people intermingled quite a bit of JavaScript in their pages to fire JavaScript events when a button was clicked. The process became more cumbersome in ASP.NET 1.0/1.1, but ever since ASP.NET 2.0, it is much easier.

You can create a page that has a JavaScript event, as well as a server-side event, triggered when the button is clicked, as illustrated in Listing 3-8.

Listing 3-8: Two types of events for the button

VB

```
<%@ Page Language="VB" %>

<script runat="server">
    Protected Sub Button1_Click(ByVal sender As Object, _
       ByVal e As System.EventArgs)

        Response.Write("Postback!")
    End Sub
</script>

<script language="javascript">
   function AlertHello()
   {
      alert('Hello ASP.NET');
   }
</script>

<html xmlns="http://www.w3.org/1999/xhtml">
<head runat="server">
    <title>Button Server Control</title>
</head>
<body>
    <form id="form1" runat="server">
        <asp:Button ID="Button1" runat="server" Text="Button"
         OnClientClick="AlertHello()" OnClick="Button1_Click" />
    </form>
</body>
</html>
```

C#

```
<%@ Page Language="C#" %>

<script runat="server">
    protected void Button1_Click(object sender, EventArgs e)
    {
        Response.Write("Postback!");
    }
</script>
```

The first thing to notice is the new attribute for the Button server control: `OnClientClick`. It points to the client-side function, unlike the `OnClick` attribute that points to the server-side event. This example uses a JavaScript function called `AlertHello()`.

One cool thing about Visual Studio 2008 is that it can work with server-side script tags that are right alongside client-side script tags. It all works together seamlessly. In the example, after the JavaScript alert dialog is issued (see Figure 3-6) and the end user clicks OK, the page posts back as the server-side event is triggered.

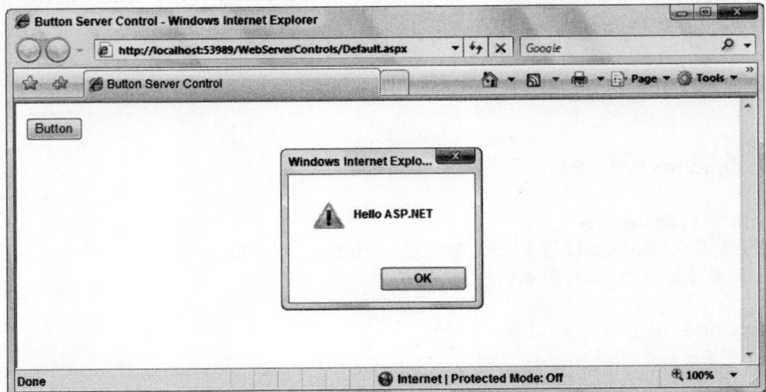

Figure 3-6

Another interesting attribute for the button controls is `PostBackUrl`. It enables you to perform cross-page posting, instead of simply posting your ASP.NET pages back to the same page, as shown in the following example:

```
<asp:Button ID="Button2" runat="server" Text="Submit page to Page2.aspx"
 PostBackUrl="Page2.aspx" />
```

Cross-page posting is covered in greater detail in Chapter 1.

The LinkButton Server Control

The LinkButton server control is a variation of the Button control. It is the same except that the LinkButton control takes the form of a hyperlink. Nevertheless, it is not a typical hyperlink. When the end user clicks the link, it behaves like a button. This is an ideal control to use if you have a large number of buttons on your Web form.

A LinkButton server control is constructed as follows:

```
<asp:LinkButton ID="LinkButton1" Runat="server" OnClick="LinkButton1_Click">
   Submit your name to our database
</asp:LinkButton>
```

Using the LinkButton control gives you the results shown in Figure 3-7.

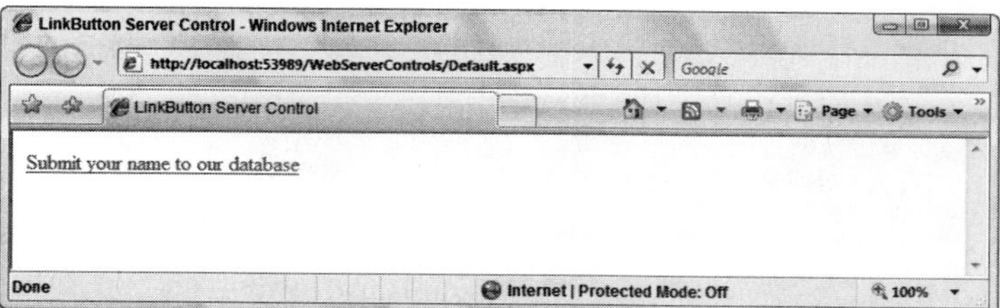

Figure 3-7

The ImageButton Server Control

The ImageButton control is also a variation of the Button control. It is almost exactly the same as the Button control except that it enables you to use a custom image as the form's button instead of the typical buttons used on most forms. This means that you can create your own buttons as images and the end users can click the images to submit form data. A typical construction of the ImageButton is as follows:

```
<asp:ImageButton ID="ImageButton1" runat="server"
 OnClick="ImageButton1_Click" ImageUrl="MyButton.jpg" />
```

The ImageButton control specifies the location of the image used by using the `ImageUrl` property. From this example, you can see that the `ImageUrl` points to `MyButton.jpg`. The big difference between the ImageButton control and the LinkButton or Button controls is that ImageButton takes a different construction for the `OnClick` event. It is shown in Listing 3-9.

Listing 3-9: The Click event for the ImageButton control

VB

```
Protected Sub ImageButton1_Click(ByVal sender As Object, _
   ByVal e As System.Web.UI.WebControls.ImageClickEventArgs)
   ' Code here
End Sub
```

C#

```
protected void ImageButton1_Click(object sender,
   System.Web.UI.WebControls.ImageClickEventArgs e)
{
   // Code here
}
```

The construction uses the `ImageClickEventArgs` object instead of the `System.EventArgs` object usually used with the LinkButton and Button controls. You can use this object to determine where in the image the end user clicked by using both `e.X` and `e.Y` coordinates.

The Search and Play Video buttons on the page shown in Figure 3-8 are image buttons.

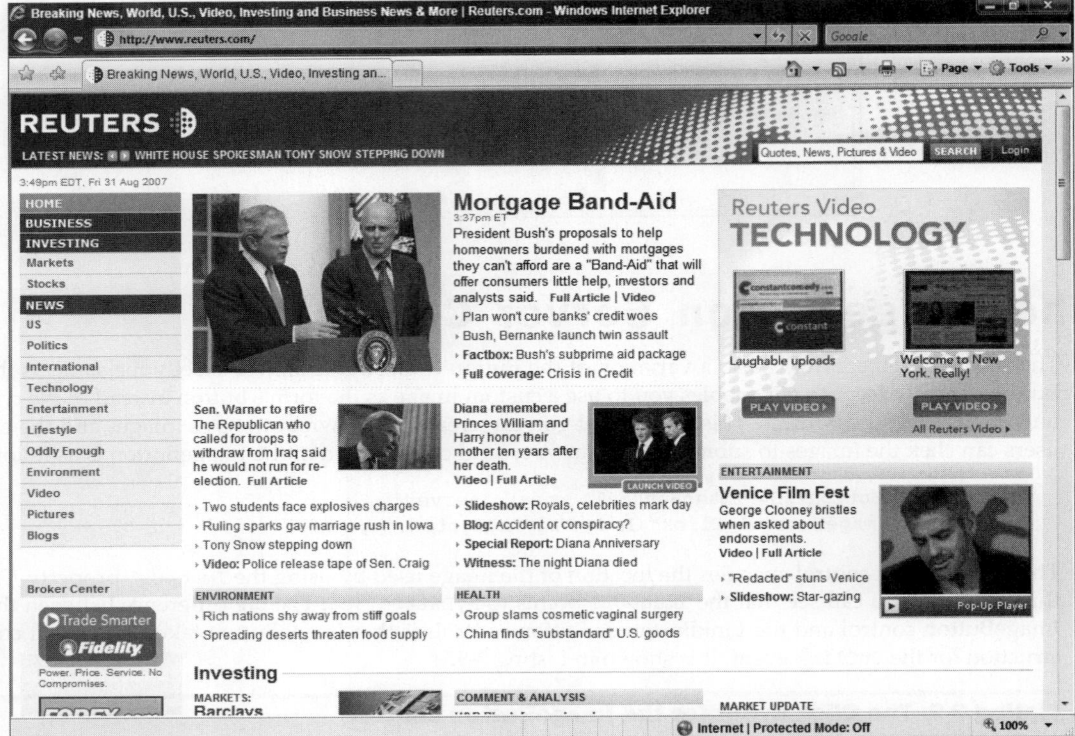

Figure 3-8

The HyperLink Server Control

The HyperLink server control enables you to programmatically work with any hyperlinks on your Web pages. Hyperlinks are links that allow end users to transfer from one page to another. You can set the text of a hyperlink using the control's `Text` attribute:

```
<asp:HyperLink ID="HyperLink1" runat="server" Text="Go to this page here"
 NavigateUrl="~/Default2.aspx"></asp:HyperLink>
```

This server control creates a hyperlink on your page with the text `Go to this page here`. When the link is clicked, the user is redirected to the value that is placed in the `NavigateUrl` property (in this case, the `Default2.aspx` page).

The interesting thing about the HyperLink server control is that it can be used for images as well as text. Instead of using the `Text` attribute, it uses the `ImageUrl` property:

```
<asp:HyperLink ID="HyperLink1" runat="server" ImageUrl="~/MyLinkImage.gif"
 NavigateUrl="~/Default2.aspx"></asp:HyperLink>
```

The HyperLink control is a great way to dynamically place hyperlinks on a Web page based either upon user input in a form or on database values that are retrieved when the page is loaded.

The DropDownList Server Control

The DropDownList server control enables you to place an HTML select box on your Web page and program against it. It is ideal when you have a large collection of items from which you want the end user to select a single item. It is usually used for a medium- to large-sized collection. If the collection size is relatively small, consider using the RadioButtonList server control (described later in this chapter).

The select box generated by the DropDownList control displays a single item and allows the end user to make a selection from a larger list of items. Depending on the number of choices available in the select box, the end user may have to scroll through a list of items. Note that the appearance of the scroll bar in the drop-down list is automatically created by the browser depending on the browser version and the number of items contained in the list.

Here is the code for DropDownList control:

```
<asp:DropDownList ID="DropDownList1" runat="server">
   <asp:ListItem>Car</asp:ListItem>
   <asp:ListItem>Airplane</asp:ListItem>
   <asp:ListItem>Train</asp:ListItem>
</asp:DropDownList>
```

This code generates a drop-down list in the browser, as shown in Figure 3-9.

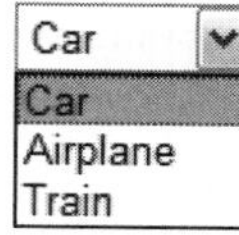

Figure 3-9

The DropDownList control comes in handy when you start binding it to various data stores. The data stores can either be arrays, database values, XML file values, or values found elsewhere. For an example of binding the DropDownList control, this next example looks at dynamically generating a DropDown-List control from one of three available arrays, as shown in Listing 3-10.

Listing 3-10: Dynamically generating a DropDownList control from an array

VB

```
<%@ Page Language="VB" %>

<script runat="server">
    Protected Sub DropDownList1_SelectedIndexChanged(ByVal sender As Object, _
      ByVal e As System.EventArgs)
        Dim CarArray() As String = {"Ford", "Honda", "BMW", "Dodge"}
        Dim AirplaneArray() As String = {"Boeing 777", "Boeing 747", "Boeing 737"}
        Dim TrainArray() As String = {"Bullet Train", "Amtrack", "Tram"}

        If DropDownList1.SelectedValue = "Car" Then
            DropDownList2.DataSource = CarArray
        ElseIf DropDownList1.SelectedValue = "Airplane" Then
            DropDownList2.DataSource = AirplaneArray
        Else
```

Continued

```
            DropDownList2.DataSource = TrainArray
        End If

        DropDownList2.DataBind()
        DropDownList2.Visible = True
    End Sub

    Protected Sub Button1_Click(ByVal sender As Object, _
      ByVal e As System.EventArgs)

        Response.Write("You selected <b>" & _
           DropDownList1.SelectedValue.ToString() & ": " & _
           DropDownList2.SelectedValue.ToString() & "</b>")

    End Sub
</script>

<html xmlns="http://www.w3.org/1999/xhtml">
<head runat="server">
    <title>DropDownList Page</title>
</head>
<body>
    <form id="form1" runat="server">
    <div>
        Select transportation type:<br />
        <asp:DropDownList ID="DropDownList1" runat="server"
         OnSelectedIndexChanged="DropDownList1_SelectedIndexChanged"
         AutoPostBack="true">
            <asp:ListItem>Select an Item</asp:ListItem>
            <asp:ListItem>Car</asp:ListItem>
            <asp:ListItem>Airplane</asp:ListItem>
            <asp:ListItem>Train</asp:ListItem>
        </asp:DropDownList> 
        <asp:DropDownList ID="DropDownList2" runat="server" Visible="false">
        </asp:DropDownList>
        <asp:Button ID="Button1" runat="server" Text="Select Options"
         OnClick="Button1_Click" />
    </div>
    </form>
</body>
</html>
```

C#

```
<%@ Page Language="C#" %>

<script runat="server">
    protected void DropDownList1_SelectedIndexChanged(object sender, EventArgs e)
    {
        string[] CarArray = new string[4] {"Ford", "Honda", "BMW", "Dodge"};
        string[] AirplaneArray = new string[3] {"Boeing 777", "Boeing 747",
           "Boeing 737"};
        string[] TrainArray = new string[3] {"Bullet Train", "Amtrack", "Tram"};

        if (DropDownList1.SelectedValue == "Car") {
            DropDownList2.DataSource = CarArray; }
```

```
            else if (DropDownList1.SelectedValue == "Airplane") {
                DropDownList2.DataSource = AirplaneArray; }
            else {
                DropDownList2.DataSource = TrainArray;
            }

            DropDownList2.DataBind();
            DropDownList2.Visible = true;
        }

        protected void Button1_Click(object sender, EventArgs e)
        {
            Response.Write("You selected <b>" +
               DropDownList1.SelectedValue.ToString() + ": " +
               DropDownList2.SelectedValue.ToString() + "</b>");
        }
    </script>
```

In this example, the second drop-down list is dynamically generated based upon the value selected from the first drop-down list. For instance, selecting `Car` from the first drop-down list dynamically creates a second drop-down list on the form that includes a list of available car selections.

This is possible because of the use of the `AutoPostBack` feature of the `DropDownList` control. When the `AutoPostBack` property is set to `True`, the method provided through the `OnSelectedIndexChanged` event is fired when a selection is made. In the example, the `DropDownList1_SelectedIndexChanged` event is fired, dynamically creating the second drop-down list.

In this method, the content of the second drop-down list is created in a string array and then bound to the second DropDownList control through the use of the `DataSource` property and the `DataBind()` method.

When built and run, this page looks like the one shown in Figure 3-10.

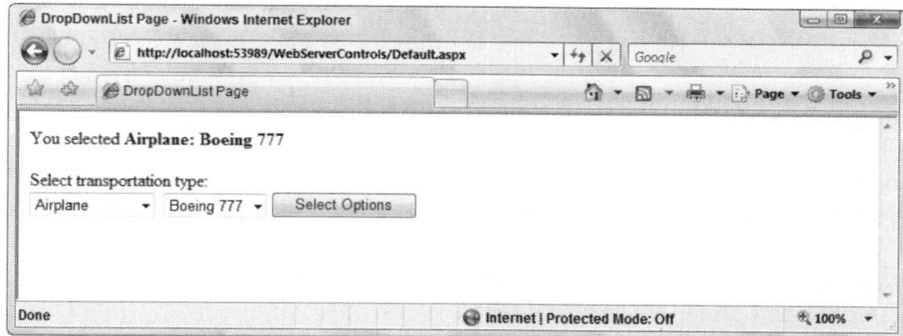

Figure 3-10

Visually Removing Items from a Collection

The DropDownList, ListBox, CheckBoxList, and RadioButtonList server controls give you the capability to visually remove items from the collection displayed in the control, although you can still work with the items that are not displayed in your server-side code.

The ListBox, CheckBoxList, and RadioButtonList controls are discussed shortly in this chapter.

For a quick example of removing items, create a drop-down list with three items, including one that you will not display. On the postback, however, you can still work with the ListItem's `Value` or `Text` property, as illustrated in Listing 3-11.

Listing 3-11: Disabling certain ListItems from a collection

VB

```
<%@ page language="VB" %>

<script runat="server">
   Protected Sub DropDownList1_SelectedIndexChanged(ByVal sender As Object, _
      ByVal e As System.EventArgs)
        Response.Write("You selected item number " & _
          DropDownList1.SelectedValue & "<br>")
        Response.Write("You didn't select item number " & _
          DropDownList1.Items(1).Value)
   End Sub
</script>

<html>
<head runat="server">
   <title>DropDownList Server Control</title>
</head>
<body>
   <form id="form1" runat="server">
      <asp:DropDownList ID="DropDownList1" Runat="server" AutoPostBack="True"
       OnSelectedIndexChanged="DropDownList1_SelectedIndexChanged">
          <asp:ListItem Value="1">First Choice</asp:ListItem>
          <asp:ListItem Value="2" Enabled="False">Second Choice</asp:ListItem>
          <asp:ListItem Value="3">Third Choice</asp:ListItem>
      </asp:DropDownList>
   </form>
</body>
</html>
```

C#

```
<%@ Page Language="C#" %>

<script runat="server">
    protected void DropDownList1_SelectedIndexChanged(object sender, EventArgs e)
    {
         Response.Write("You selected item number " +
           DropDownList1.SelectedValue + "<br>");
         Response.Write("You didn't select item number " +
           DropDownList1.Items[1].Value);
    }
</script>
```

From the code, you can see that the `<asp:ListItem>` element has an attribute: `Enabled`. The Boolean value given to this element dictates whether an item in the collection is displayed. If you use `Enabled="False"`, the item is not displayed, but you still have the capability to work with the item in the server-side code displayed in the `DropDownList1_SelectedIndexChanged` event. The result of the output from these `Response.Write` statements is shown in Figure 3-11.

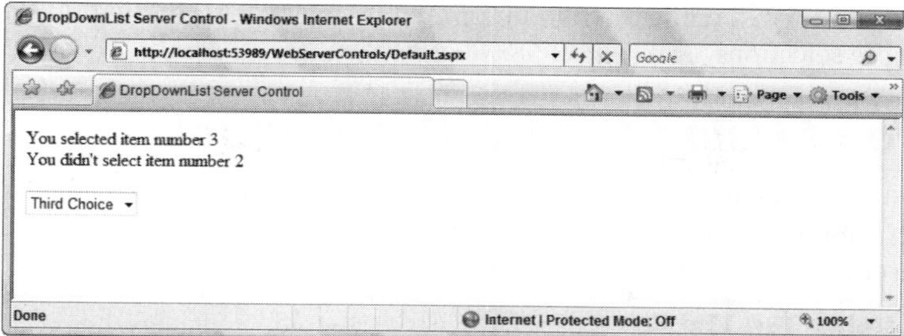

Figure 3-11

The ListBox Server Control

The ListBox server control has a function similar to the DropDownList control. It displays a collection of items. The ListBox control behaves differently from the DropDownList control in that it displays more of the collection to the end user, and it enables the end user to make multiple selections from the collection — something that is not possible with the DropDownList control.

A typical ListBox control appears in code as follows:

```
<asp:ListBox ID="ListBox1" runat="server">
   <asp:ListItem>Hematite</asp:ListItem>
   <asp:ListItem>Halite</asp:ListItem>
   <asp:ListItem>Limonite</asp:ListItem>
   <asp:ListItem>Magnetite</asp:ListItem>
</asp:ListBox>
```

This generates the browser display illustrated in Figure 3-12.

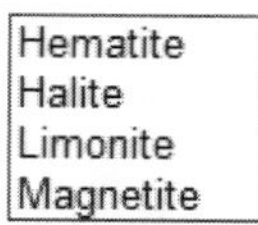

Figure 3-12

Allowing Users to Select Multiple Items

You can use the `SelectionMode` attribute to let your end users make multiple selections from what is displayed by the ListBox control. Here's an example:

```
<asp:ListBox ID="ListBox1" runat="server" SelectionMode="Multiple">
   <asp:ListItem>Hematite</asp:ListItem>
   <asp:ListItem>Halite</asp:ListItem>
   <asp:ListItem>Limonite</asp:ListItem>
   <asp:ListItem>Magnetite</asp:ListItem>
</asp:ListBox>
```

The possible values of the `SelectionMode` property include `Single` and `Multiple`. Setting the value to `Multiple` allows the end user to make multiple selections in the list box. The user must hold down either the Ctrl or Shift keys while making selections. Holding down the Ctrl key enables the user to make a single selection from the list while maintaining previous selections. Holding down the Shift key enables a range of multiple selections.

An Example of Using the ListBox Control

The ListBox control shown in Listing 3-12 allows multiple selections to be displayed in the browser when a user clicks the Submit button. The form should also have an additional text box and button at the top that enables the end user to add additional items to the ListBox.

Listing 3-12: Using the ListBox control

VB

```
<%@ Page Language="VB" %>

<script runat="server">
    Protected Sub Button1_Click(ByVal sender As Object, _
       ByVal e As System.EventArgs)

        ListBox1.Items.Add(TextBox1.Text.ToString())
    End Sub

    Protected Sub Button2_Click(ByVal sender As Object, _
       ByVal e As System.EventArgs)

        Label1.Text = "You selected from the ListBox:<br>"
        For Each li As ListItem In ListBox1.Items
            If li.Selected = True Then
                label1.Text += li.Text & "<br>"
            End If
        Next
    End Sub
</script>

<html xmlns="http://www.w3.org/1999/xhtml">
<head runat="server">
    <title>Using the ListBox</title>
</head>
<body>
    <form id="form1" runat="server">
    <div>
        <asp:TextBox ID="TextBox1" runat="server"></asp:TextBox>
        <asp:Button ID="Button1" runat="server" Text="Add an additional item"
         OnClick="Button1_Click" /><br /><br />

        <asp:ListBox ID="ListBox1" runat="server" SelectionMode="multiple">
           <asp:ListItem>Hematite</asp:ListItem>
           <asp:ListItem>Halite</asp:ListItem>
           <asp:ListItem>Limonite</asp:ListItem>
           <asp:ListItem>Magnetite</asp:ListItem>
        </asp:ListBox><br /><br />

        <asp:Button ID="Button2" runat="server" Text="Submit"
         OnClick="Button2_Click" /><br /><br />
        <asp:Label ID="Label1" runat="server"></asp:Label>
    </div>
```

```
    </form>
</body>
</html>
```

C#

```
<%@ Page Language="C#" %>

<script runat="server">
    protected void Button1_Click(object sender, EventArgs e)
    {
       ListBox1.Items.Add(TextBox1.Text.ToString());
    }

    protected void Button2_Click(object sender, EventArgs e)
    {
       Label1.Text = "You selected from the ListBox:<br>";
       foreach (ListItem li in ListBox1.Items) {
           if (li.Selected) {
               Label1.Text += li.Text + "<br>";
           }
       }
    }
</script>
```

This is an interesting example. First, some default items (four common minerals) are already placed inside the ListBox control. However, the text box and button at the top of the form allow the end user to add additional minerals to the list. Users can then make one or more selections from the ListBox, including selections from the items that they dynamically added to the collection. After a user makes his selection and clicks the button, the `Button2_Click` event iterates through the `ListItem` instances in the collection and displays only the items that have been selected.

This control works by creating an instance of a `ListItem` object and using its `Selected` property to see if a particular item in the collection has been selected. The use of the `ListItem` object is not limited to the ListBox control (although that is what is used here). You can dynamically add or remove items from a collection and get at items and their values using the `ListItem` object in the DropDownList, CheckBoxList, and RadioButtonList controls as well. It is a list-control feature. When this page is built and run, you get the results presented in Figure 3-13.

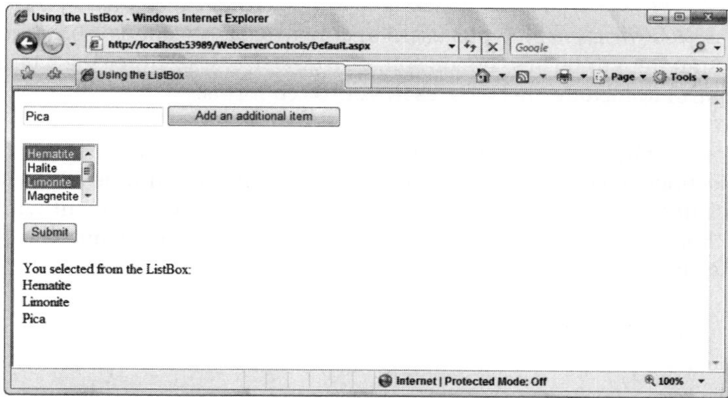

Figure 3-13

Adding Items to a Collection

To add items to the collection, you can use the following short syntax:

```
ListBox1.Items.Add(TextBox1.Text)
```

Look at the source code created in the browser, and you should see something similar to the following generated dynamically:

```
<select size="4" name="ListBox1" multiple="multiple" id="ListBox1">
     <option value="Hematite">Hematite</option>
     <option value="Halite">Halite</option>
     <option value="Limonite">Limonite</option>
     <option value="Magnetite">Magnetite</option>
     <option value="Olivine">Olivine</option>
</select>
```

You can see that the dynamically added value is a text item, and you can see its value. You can also add instances of the ListItem object to get different values for the item name and value:

VB

```
ListBox1.Items.Add(New ListItem("Olivine", "MG2SIO4"))
```

C#

```
ListBox1.Items.Add(new ListItem("Olivine", "MG2SIO4"));
```

This example adds a new instance of the `ListItem` object — adding not only the textual name of the item, but also the value of the item (its chemical formula). It produces the following results in the browser:

```
<option value="MG2SIO4">Olivine</option>
```

The CheckBox Server Control

Check boxes on a Web form enable your users to either make selections from a collection of items or specify a value of an item to be yes/no, on/off, or true/false. Use either the CheckBox control or the CheckBoxList control to include check boxes in your Web forms.

The CheckBox control allows you to place single check boxes on a form; the CheckBoxList control allows you to place collections of check boxes on the form. You can use multiple CheckBox controls on your ASP.NET pages, but then you are treating each check box as its own element with its own associated events. On the other hand, the CheckBoxList control allows you to take multiple check boxes and create specific events for the entire group.

Listing 3-13 shows an example of using the CheckBox control.

Listing 3-13: Using a single instance of the CheckBox control

VB

```
<%@ Page Language="VB" %>
<script runat="server">
    Protected Sub CheckBox1_CheckedChanged(ByVal sender As Object, _
      ByVal e As System.EventArgs)
        Response.Write("Thanks for your donation!")
    End Sub
</script>

<html xmlns="http://www.w3.org/1999/xhtml">
<head runat="server">
    <title>CheckBox control</title>
</head>
<body>
    <form id="form1" runat="server">
    <div>
        <asp:CheckBox ID="CheckBox1" runat="server" Text="Donate $10 to our cause!"
         OnCheckedChanged="CheckBox1_CheckedChanged" AutoPostBack="true" />
    </div>
    </form>
</body>
</html>
```

C#

```
<%@ Page Language="C#" %>

<script runat="server">
    protected void CheckBox1_CheckedChanged(object sender, EventArgs e)
    {
        Response.Write("Thanks for your donation!");
    }
</script>
```

This produces a page that contains a single check box asking for a monetary donation. Using the `CheckedChanged` event, `OnCheckedChanged` is used within the CheckBox control. The attribute's value points to the `CheckBox1_CheckedChanged` event, which fires when the user checks the check box. It occurs only if the `AutoPostBack` property is set to `True` (this property is set to `False` by default). Running this page produces the results shown in Figure 3-14.

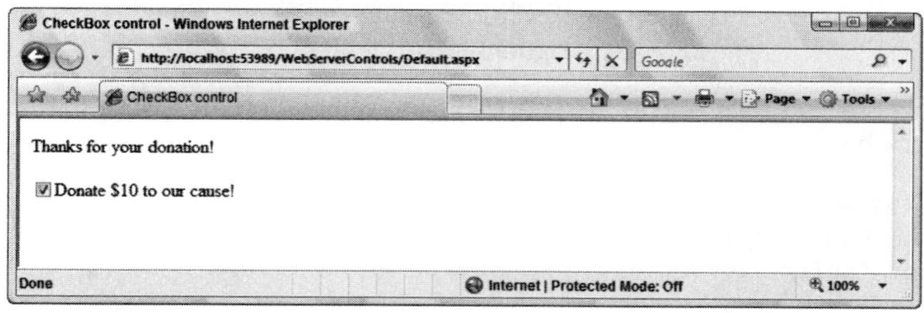

Figure 3-14

How to Determine Whether Check Boxes Are Checked

You might not want to use the `AutoPostBack` feature of the check box, but instead want to determine if the check box is checked after the form is posted back to the server. You can make this check through an `If Then` statement, as illustrated in the following example:

VB

```
If (CheckBox1.Checked = True) Then
   Response.Write("CheckBox is checked!")
End If
```

C#

```
if (CheckBox1.Checked == true) {
   Response.Write("Checkbox is checked!");
}
```

This check is done on the CheckBox value using the control's `Checked` property. The property's value is a Boolean value, so it is either `True` (checked) or `False` (not checked).

Assigning a Value to a Check Box

You can also use the `Checked` property to make sure a check box is checked based on other dynamic values:

VB

```
If (Member = True) Then
   CheckBox1.Checked = True
End If
```

C#

```
if (Member == true) {
   CheckBox1.Checked = true;
}
```

Aligning Text Around the Check Box

In the previous check box example, the text appears to the right of the actual check box, as shown in Figure 3-15.

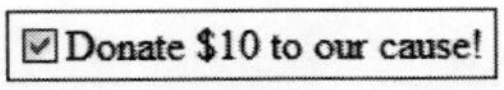

Figure 3-15

Using the CheckBox control's `TextAlign` property, you can realign the text so that it appears on the other side of the check box:

```
<asp:CheckBox ID="CheckBox1" runat="server" Text="Donate $10 to our cause!"
 OnCheckedChanged="CheckBox1_CheckedChanged" AutoPostBack="true"
 TextAlign="Left" />
```

The possible values of the `TextAlign` property are either `Right` (the default setting) or `Left`. This property is also available to the CheckBoxList, RadioButton, and RadioButtonList controls. Assigning the value `Left` produces the result shown in Figure 3-16.

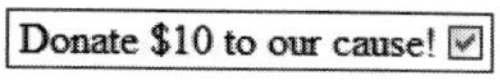

Donate $10 to our cause! ☑

Figure 3-16

The CheckBoxList Server Control

The CheckBoxList server control is quite similar to the CheckBox control, except that the former enables you to work with a collection of items rather than a single item. The idea is that a CheckBoxList server control instance is a collection of related items, each being a check box unto itself.

To see the CheckBoxList control in action, you can build an example that uses Microsoft's SQL Server to pull information from the Customers table of the Northwind example database. An example is presented in Listing 3-14.

Listing 3-14: Dynamically populating a CheckBoxList

VB

```
<%@ Page Language="VB" %>

<script runat="server">
    Protected Sub Button1_Click(ByVal sender As Object, _
       ByVal e As System.EventArgs)

        Label1.Text = "You selected:<br>"
        For Each li As ListItem In CheckBoxList1.Items
            If li.Selected = True Then
                Label1.Text += li.Text & "<br>"
            End If
        Next
    End Sub
</script>

<html xmlns="http://www.w3.org/1999/xhtml">
<head runat="server">
    <title>CheckBoxList control</title>
</head>
<body>
    <form id="form1" runat="server">
    <div>
        <asp:Button ID="Button1" runat="server" Text="Submit Choices"
         OnClick="Button1_Click" /><br /><br />
        <asp:Label ID="Label1" runat="server"></asp:Label>
        <br />
        <asp:CheckBoxList ID="CheckBoxList1" runat="server"
         DataSourceID="SqlDataSource1" DataTextField="CompanyName"
         RepeatColumns="3" BorderColor="Black"
         BorderStyle="Solid" BorderWidth="1px">
        </asp:CheckBoxList>
        <asp:SqlDataSource ID="SqlDataSource1" runat="server"
         SelectCommand="SELECT [CompanyName] FROM [Customers]"
            ConnectionString="<%$ ConnectionStrings:AppConnectionString1 %>">
        </asp:SqlDataSource>
```

Continued

```
    </div>
    </form>
</body>
</html>
```

C#

```
<%@ Page Language="C#" %>
<script runat="server">
    protected void Button1_Click(object sender, EventArgs e)
    {
        Label1.Text = "You selected:<br>";
        foreach (ListItem li in CheckBoxList1.Items) {
            if (li.Selected == true) {
                Label1.Text += li.Text + "<br>";
            }
        }
    }
</script>
```

This ASP.NET page has a SqlDataSource control on the page that pulls the information you need from the Northwind database. From the `SELECT` statement used in this control, you can see that you are retrieving the `CompanyName` field from each of the listings in the Customers table.

The CheckBoxList control binds itself to the SqlDataSource control using a few properties:

```
<asp:CheckBoxList ID="CheckBoxList1" runat="server"
 DataSourceID="SqlDataSource1" DataTextField="CompanyName"
 RepeatColumns="3" BorderColor="Black"
 BorderStyle="Solid" BorderWidth="1px">
</asp:CheckBoxList>
```

The `DataSourceID` property is used to associate the CheckBoxList control with the results that come back from the SqlDataSource control. Then the `DataTextField` property is used to retrieve the name of the field you want to work with from the results. In this example, it is the only one that is available: the `CompanyName`. That's it! CheckBoxList generates the results you want.

The remaining code consists of styling properties, which are pretty interesting. The `BorderColor`, `BorderStyle`, and `BorderWidth` properties enable you to put a border around the entire check box list. The most interesting property is the `RepeatColumns` property, which specifies how many columns (three in this example) can be used to display the results.

When you run the page, you get the results shown in Figure 3-17.

The `RepeatDirection` property instructs the CheckBoxList control about how to lay out the items bound to the control on the Web page. Possible values include `Vertical` and `Horizontal`. The default value is `Vertical`. Setting it to `Vertical` with a `RepeatColumn` setting of `3` gives the following results:

```
CheckBox1    CheckBox5    CheckBox9
CheckBox2    CheckBox6    CheckBox10
CheckBox3    CheckBox7    CheckBox11
CheckBox4    CheckBox8    CheckBox12
```

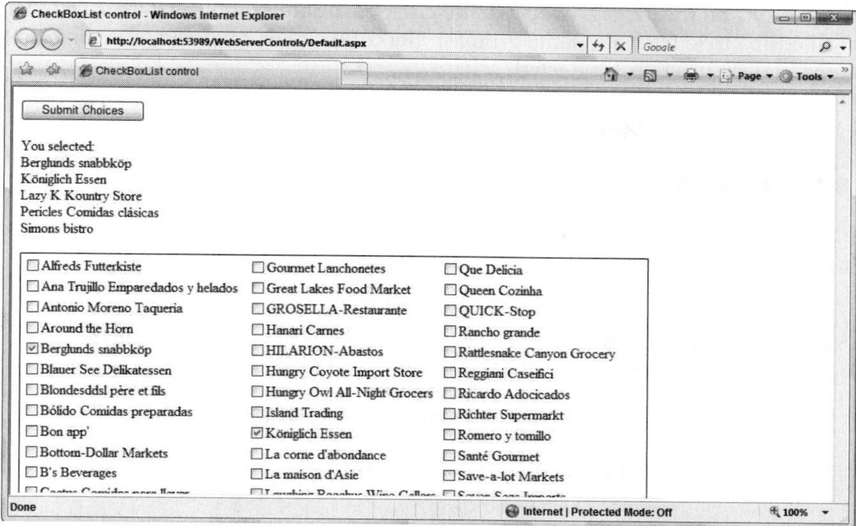

Figure 3-17

When the `RepeatDirection` property is set to `Horizontal`, you get the check box items laid out in a horizontal fashion:

```
CheckBox1     CheckBox2     CheckBox3
CheckBox4     CheckBox5     CheckBox6
CheckBox7     CheckBox8     CheckBox9
CheckBox10    CheckBox11    CheckBox12
```

The RadioButton Server Control

The RadioButton server control is quite similar to the CheckBox server control. It places a radio button on your Web page. Unlike a check box, however, a single radio button on a form does not make much sense. Radio buttons are generally form elements that require at least two options. A typical set of RadioButton controls on a page takes the following construction:

```
<asp:RadioButton ID="RadioButton1" runat="server" Text="Yes" GroupName="Set1" />
<asp:RadioButton ID="RadioButton2" runat="server" Text="No" GroupName="Set1"/>
```

Figure 3-18 shows the result.

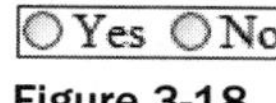

Figure 3-18

When you look at the code for the RadioButton control, note the standard `Text` property that places the text next to the radio button on the Web form. The more important property here is `GroupName`, which can be set in one of the RadioButton controls to match what it is set to in the other. This enables the radio buttons on the Web form to work together for the end user. How do they work together? Well, when one of the radio buttons on the form is checked, the circle associated with the item selected appears filled in. Any other filled-in circle from the same group in the collection is removed, ensuring that only one of the radio buttons in the collection is selected.

Listing 3-15 shows an example of using the RadioButton control.

Listing 3-15: Using the RadioButton server control

VB

```
<%@ Page Language="VB" %>

<script runat="server">
    Protected Sub RadioButton_CheckedChanged(ByVal sender As Object, _
      ByVal e As System.EventArgs)
        If RadioButton1.Checked = True Then
            Response.Write("You selected Visual Basic")
        Else
            Response.Write("You selected C#")
        End If
    End Sub
</script>

<html xmlns="http://www.w3.org/1999/xhtml">
<head runat="server">
    <title>RadioButton control</title>
</head>
<body>
    <form id="form1" runat="server">
    <div>
        <asp:RadioButton ID="RadioButton1" runat="server" Text="Visual Basic"
         GroupName="LanguageChoice" OnCheckedChanged="RadioButton_CheckedChanged"
         AutoPostBack="True" />
        <asp:RadioButton ID="RadioButton2" runat="server" Text="C#"
         GroupName="LanguageChoice" OnCheckedChanged="RadioButton_CheckedChanged"
         AutoPostBack="True" />
    </div>
    </form>
</body>
</html>
```

C#

```
<%@ Page Language="C#" %>

<script runat="server">
    protected void RadioButton_CheckedChanged(object sender, EventArgs e)
    {
        if (RadioButton1.Checked == true) {
           Response.Write("You selected Visual Basic");
        }
        else {
           Response.Write("You selected C#");
        }
    }
</script>
```

Like the CheckBox, the RadioButton control has a `CheckedChanged` event that puts an `OnCheckedChanged` attribute in the control. The attribute's value points to the server-side event that is fired when a selection is made using one of the two radio buttons on the form. Remember that the `AutoPostBack` property needs to be set to `True` for this to work correctly.

Figure 3-19 shows the results.

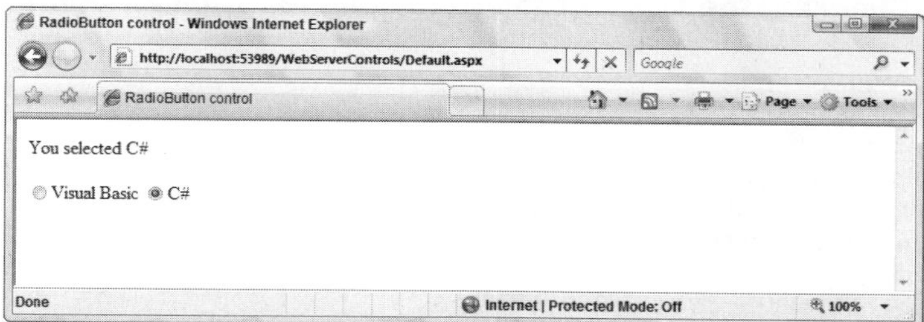

Figure 3-19

One advantage that the RadioButton control has over a RadioButtonList control (which is discussed next) is that it enables you to place other items (text, controls, or images) between the RadioButton controls themselves. RadioButtonList, however, is always a straight list of radio buttons on your Web page.

The RadioButtonList Server Control

The RadioButtonList server control lets you display a collection of radio buttons on a Web page. The RadioButtonList control is quite similar to the CheckBoxList and other list controls in that it allows you to iterate through to see what the user selected, to make counts, or to perform other actions.

A typical RadioButtonList control is written to the page in the following manner:

```
<asp:RadioButtonList ID="RadioButtonList1" runat="server">
   <asp:ListItem Selected="True">English</asp:ListItem>
   <asp:ListItem>Russian</asp:ListItem>
   <asp:ListItem>Finnish</asp:ListItem>
   <asp:ListItem>Swedish</asp:ListItem>
</asp:RadioButtonList>
```

Like the other list controls, this one uses instances of the `ListItem` object for each of the items contained in the collection. From the example, you can see that if the `Selected` property is set to `True`, one of the `ListItem` objects is selected by default when the page is generated for the first time. This produces the results shown in Figure 3-20.

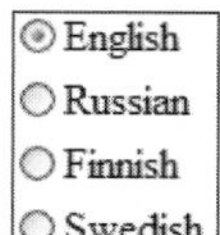

Figure 3-20

The `Selected` property is not required, but it is a good idea if you want the end user to make some sort of selection from this collection. Using it makes it impossible to leave the collection blank.

You can use the RadioButtonList control to check for the value selected by the end user in any of your page methods. Listing 3-16 shows a `Button1_Click` event that pushes out the value selected in the RadioButtonList collection.

Listing 3-16: Checking the value of the item selected from a RadioButtonList control

VB

```
<%@ Page Language="VB" %>

<script runat="server">
    Protected Sub Button1_Click(ByVal sender As Object, _
       ByVal e As System.EventArgs)

        Label1.Text = "You selected: " & _
           RadioButtonList1.SelectedItem.ToString()
    End Sub
</script>
```

C#

```
<%@ Page Language="C#" %>

<script runat="server">
    protected void Button1_Click(object sender, EventArgs e)
    {
       Label1.Text = "You selected: " +
          RadioButtonList1.SelectedItem.ToString();
    }
</script>
```

This bit of code gets at the item selected from the RadioButtonList collection of `ListItem` objects. It is how you work with other list controls that are provided in ASP.NET. The RadioButtonList also affords you access to the `RepeatColumns` and `RepeatDirection` properties (these were explained in the CheckBoxList section). You can bind this control to items that come from any of the data source controls so that you can dynamically create radio button lists on your Web pages.

Image Server Control

The Image server control enables you to work with the images that appear on your Web page from the server-side code. It is a simple server control, but it can give you the power to determine how your images are displayed on the browser screen. A typical Image control is constructed in the following manner:

```
<asp:Image ID="Image1" runat="server" ImageUrl="~/MyImage1.gif" />
```

The important property here is `ImageUrl`. It points to the file location of the image. In this case, the location is specified as the `MyImage.gif` file.

Listing 3-17 shows an example of how to dynamically change the `ImageUrl` property.

Listing 3-17: Changing the ImageUrl property dynamically

VB

```
<%@ Page Language="VB" %>

<script runat="server">
   Protected Sub Button1_Click(ByVal sender As Object, ByVal e As System.EventArgs)
        Image1.ImageUrl = "~/MyImage2.gif"
   End Sub
</script>

<html xmlns="http://www.w3.org/1999/xhtml">
<head runat="server">
    <title>Image control</title>
</head>
<body>
    <form id="form1" runat="server">
    <div>
        <asp:Image ID="Image1" runat="server" ImageUrl="~/MyImage1.gif" /><br />
        <br />
        <asp:Button ID="Button1" runat="server" Text="Change Image"
         OnClick="Button1_Click" />
    </div>
    </form>
</body>
</html>
```

C#

```
<%@ Page Language="C#" %>

<script runat="server">
    protected void Button1_Click(object sender, EventArgs e)
    {
       Image1.ImageUrl = "~/MyImage2.gif";
    }
</script>
```

In this example, an image (`MyImage1.gif`) is shown in the browser when the page is loaded for the first time. When the end user clicks the button on the page, a new image (`MyImage2.gif`) is loaded in the postback process.

Special circumstances can prevent end users from viewing an image that is part of your Web page. They might be physically unable to see the image, or they might be using a text-only browser. In these cases, their browsers look for the `<img>` element's `longdesc` attribute that points to a file containing a long description of the image that is displayed.

For these cases, the Image server control includes a `DescriptionUrl` attribute. The value assigned to it is a text file that contains a thorough description of the image with which it is associated. Here is how to use it:

```
<asp:Image ID="Image1" runat="server" DescriptionUrl="~/Image01.txt"  />
```

This code produces the following results in the browser:

```
<img id="Image1" src="INETA.jpg" longdesc="Image01.txt" alt="" />
```

Remember that the image does not support the user clicking the image. If you want to program events based on button clicks, use the ImageButton server control discussed earlier in this chapter.

Table Server Control

Tables are one of the Web page's more common elements because the HTML `<table>` element is one possible format utilized for controlling the layout of your Web page (CSS being the other). The typical construction of the Table server control is as follows:

```
<asp:Table ID="Table1" runat="server">
   <asp:TableRow Runat="server" Font-Bold="True"
    ForeColor="Black" BackColor="Silver">
      <asp:TableHeaderCell>First Name</asp:TableHeaderCell>
      <asp:TableHeaderCell>Last Name</asp:TableHeaderCell>
   </asp:TableRow>
   <asp:TableRow>
      <asp:TableCell>Bill</asp:TableCell>
      <asp:TableCell>Evjen</asp:TableCell>
   </asp:TableRow>
  <asp:TableRow>
      <asp:TableCell>Devin</asp:TableCell>
      <asp:TableCell>Rader</asp:TableCell>
   </asp:TableRow>
</asp:Table>
```

This produces the simple three-rowed table shown in Figure 3-21.

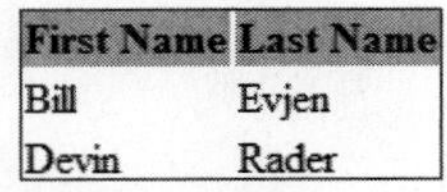

First Name	Last Name
Bill	Evjen
Devin	Rader

Figure 3-21

You can do a lot with the Table server control. For example, you can dynamically add rows to the table, as illustrated in Listing 3-18.

Listing 3-18: Dynamically adding rows to the table

VB

```
Protected Sub Page_Load(ByVal sender As Object, ByVal e As System.EventArgs)
   Dim tr As New TableRow()

   Dim fname As New TableCell()
   fname.Text = "Scott"
   tr.Cells.Add(fname)

   Dim lname As New TableCell()
```

```
        lname.Text = "Hanselman"
        tr.Cells.Add(lname)

        Table1.Rows.Add(tr)
    End Sub
```

C#

```
protected void Page_Load(object sender, EventArgs e)
{
    TableRow tr = new TableRow();

    TableCell fname = new TableCell();
    fname.Text = "Scott";
    tr.Cells.Add(fname);

    TableCell lname = new TableCell();
    lname.Text = "Hanselman";
    tr.Cells.Add(lname);

    Table1.Rows.Add(tr);
}
```

To add a single row to a Table control, you have to create new instances of the `TableRow` and `TableCell` objects. You create the `TableCell` objects first and then place them within a `TableRow` object that is added to a `Table` object.

The Table server control is enhanced with some extra features. One of the simpler new features is the capability to add captions to the tables on Web pages. Figure 3-22 shows a table with a caption.

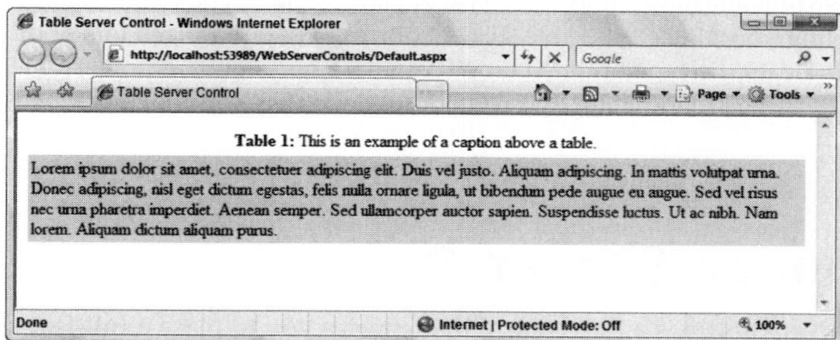

Figure 3-22

To give your table a caption, simply use the new `Caption` attribute in the Table control, as illustrated in Listing 3-19.

Listing 3-19: Using the new Caption attribute

```
<%@ Page Language="VB" %>

<html xmlns="http://www.w3.org/1999/xhtml">
```

Continued

```
<head runat="server">
    <title>Table Server Control</title>
</head>
<body>
    <form id="form1" runat="server">
        <asp:Table ID="Table1" runat="server"
         Caption="<b>Table 1:</b> This is an example of a caption above a table."
         BackColor="Gainsboro">
            <asp:TableRow ID="Tablerow1" Runat=server>
                <asp:TableCell ID="Tablecell1" Runat="server">Lorem ipsum dolor sit
                 amet, consectetuer adipiscing elit. Duis vel justo. Aliquam
                 adipiscing. In mattis volutpat urna. Donec adipiscing, nisl eget
                 dictum egestas, felis nulla ornare ligula, ut bibendum pede augue
                 eu augue. Sed vel risus nec urna pharetra imperdiet. Aenean
                 semper. Sed ullamcorper auctor sapien. Suspendisse luctus. Ut ac
                 nibh. Nam lorem. Aliquam dictum aliquam purus.</asp:TableCell>
            </asp:TableRow>
        </asp:Table>
    </form>
</body>
</html>
```

By default, the caption is placed at the top center of the table, but you can control where it is placed by using another new attribute — `CaptionAlign`. Its possible settings include `Bottom`, `Left`, `NotSet`, `Right`, and `Top`.

In the past, an `<asp:Table>` element contained any number of `<asp:TableRow>` elements. Now you have some additional elements that can be nested within the `<asp:Table>` element. These new elements include `<asp:TableHeaderRow>` and `<asp:TableFooterRow>`. They add either a header or footer to your table, enabling you to use the Table server control to page through lots of data but still retain some text in place to indicate the type of data being handled. This is quite a powerful feature when you work with mobile applications that dictate that sometimes end users can move through only a few records at a time.

The Calendar Server Control

The Calendar server control is a rich control that enables you to place a full-featured calendar directly on your Web pages. It allows for a high degree of customization to ensure that it looks and behaves in a unique manner. The Calendar control, in its simplest form, is coded in the following manner:

```
<asp:Calendar ID="Calendar1" runat="server">
</asp:Calendar>
```

This code produces a calendar on your Web page without any styles added, as shown in Figure 3-23.

<			June 2008			>
Sun	Mon	Tue	Wed	Thu	Fri	Sat
25	26	27	28	29	30	31
1	2	3	4	5	6	7
8	9	10	11	12	13	14
15	16	17	18	19	20	21
22	23	24	25	26	27	28
29	30	1	2	3	4	5

Figure 3-23

Making a Date Selection from the Calendar Control

The calendar allows you to navigate through the months of the year and to select specific days in the exposed month. A simple application that enables the user to select a day of the month is shown in Listing 3-20.

Listing 3-20: Selecting a single day in the Calendar control

VB

```
<%@ Page Language="VB" %>

<script runat="server">
    Protected Sub Calendar1_SelectionChanged(ByVal sender As Object, _
      ByVal e As System.EventArgs)
        Response.Write("You selected: " & _
          Calendar1.SelectedDate.ToShortDateString())
    End Sub
</script>

<html xmlns="http://www.w3.org/1999/xhtml">
<head id="Head1" runat="server">
    <title>Using the Calendar Control</title>
</head>
<body>
    <form id="form1" runat="server">
    <div>
        <asp:Calendar ID="Calendar1" runat="server"
         OnSelectionChanged="Calendar1_SelectionChanged">
        </asp:Calendar>
    </div>
    </form>
</body>
</html>
```

C#

```
<%@ Page Language="C#" %>

<script runat="server">
    protected void Calendar1_SelectionChanged(object sender, EventArgs e)
```

Continued

```
    {
        Response.Write("You selected: " +
          Calendar1.SelectedDate.ToShortDateString());
    }
</script>
```

Running this application pulls up the calendar in the browser. The end user can then select a single date in it. After a date is selected, the `Calendar1_SelectionChanged` event is triggered and makes use of the `OnSelectionChange` attribute. This event writes the value of the selected date to the screen. The result is shown in Figure 3-24.

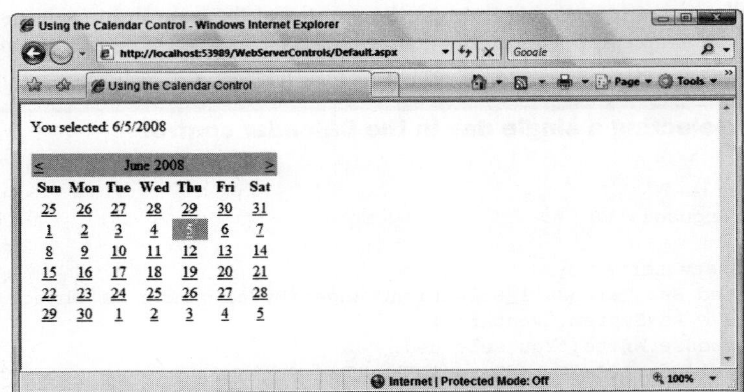

Figure 3-24

Choosing a Date Format to Output from the Calendar

When you use the `Calendar1_SelectionChanged` event, the selected date is written out using the `ToShortDateString()` method. The Calendar control also allows you to write out the date in a number of other formats, as detailed in the following list:

- `ToFileTime`: Converts the selection to the local operating system file time: `128571156000000000`.
- `ToFileTimeUtc`: Converts the selection to the operating system file time, but instead of using the local time zone, the UTC time is used: `128570976000000000`.
- `ToLocalTime`: Converts the current coordinated universal time (UTC) to local time: `6/4/2008 7:00:00 PM`.
- `ToLongDateString`: Converts the selection to a human-readable string in a long format: `Thursday, June 05, 2008`.
- `ToLongTimeString`: Converts the selection to a time value (no date is included) of a long format: `12:00:00 AM`.
- `ToOADate`: Converts the selection to an OLE Automation date equivalent: `39604`.

- `ToShortDateString`: Converts the selection to a human-readable string in a short format: `6/4/2008`.
- `ToShortTimeString`: Converts the selection to a time value (no date is included) in a short format: `12:00 AM`.
- `ToString`: Converts the selection to the following: `6/4/2008 12:00:00 AM`.
- `ToUniversalTime`: Converts the selection to universal time (UTC): `6/4/2008 6:00:00 AM`.

Making Day, Week, or Month Selections

By default, the Calendar control enables you to make single day selections. You can use the `SelectionMode` property to change this behavior to allow your users to make week or month selections from the calendar instead. The possible values of this property include `Day`, `DayWeek`, `DayWeekMonth`, and `None`.

The `Day` setting enables you to click a specific day in the calendar to highlight it (this is the default). When you use the setting of `DayWeek`, you can still make individual day selections, but you can also click the arrow next to the week (see Figure 3-25) to make selections that consist of an entire week. Using the setting of `DayWeekMonth` lets users make individual day selections or week selections. A new arrow appears in the upper-left corner of the calendar that enables users to select an entire month (also shown in Figure 3-25). A setting of `None` means that it is impossible for the end user to make any selections, which is useful for calendars on your site that are informational only.

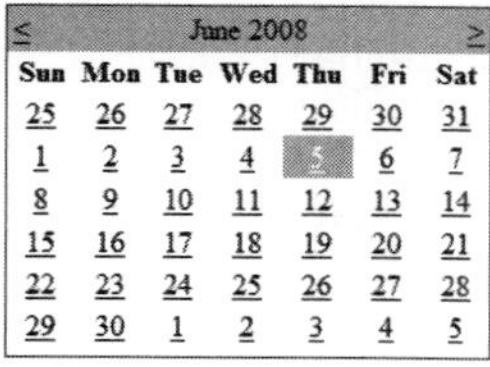

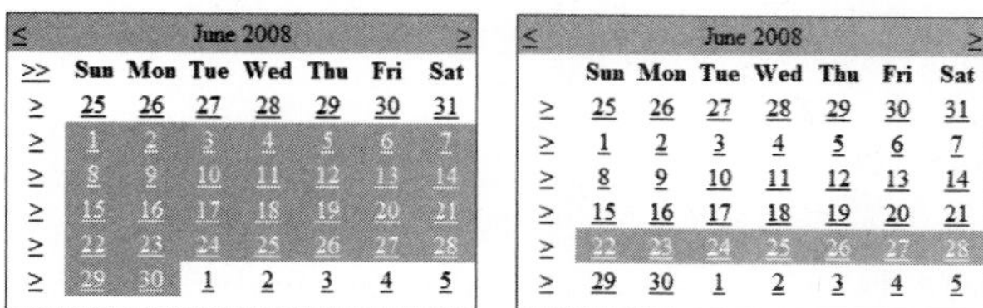

Figure 3-25

Working with Date Ranges

Even if an end user makes a selection that encompasses an entire week or an entire month, you get back from the selection only the first date of this range. If, for example, you allow users to select an entire month and one selects July 2008, what you get back (using `ToShortDateString()`) is `7/1/2008` — the first date in the date range of the selection. That might work for you, but if you require all the dates in the selected range, Listing 3-21 shows you how to get them.

Listing 3-21: Retrieving a range of dates from a selection

VB

```
<%@ Page Language="VB" %>

<script runat="server">
    Protected Sub Calendar1_SelectionChanged(ByVal sender As Object, _
      ByVal e As System.EventArgs)
        Label1.Text = "<b><u>You selected the following date/dates:</u></b><br>"

        For i As Integer = 0 To (Calendar1.SelectedDates.Count - 1)
            Label1.Text += Calendar1.SelectedDates.Item(i).ToShortDateString() & _
              "<br>"
        Next
    End Sub
</script>

<html xmlns="http://www.w3.org/1999/xhtml">
<head id="Head1" runat="server">
    <title>Using the Calendar Control</title>
</head>
<body>
    <form id="form1" runat="server">
    <div>
        <asp:Calendar ID="Calendar1" runat="server"
         OnSelectionChanged="Calendar1_SelectionChanged"
         SelectionMode="DayWeekMonth">
        </asp:Calendar><p>
        <asp:Label ID="Label1" runat="server"></asp:Label></p>
    </div>
    </form>
</body>
</html>
```

C#

```
<%@ Page Language="C#" %>

<script runat="server">
    protected void Calendar1_SelectionChanged(object sender, EventArgs e)
    {
        Label1.Text = "<b><u>You selected the following date/dates:</u></b><br>";

        for (int i=0; i<Calendar1.SelectedDates.Count; i++) {
            Label1.Text += Calendar1.SelectedDates[i].ToShortDateString() +
              "<br>";
        }
    }
</script>
```

In this example, the Calendar control lets users make selections that can be an individual day, a week, or even a month. Using a `For Next` loop, you iterate through a selection by using the `SelectedDates.Count` property. The code produces the results shown in Figure 3-26.

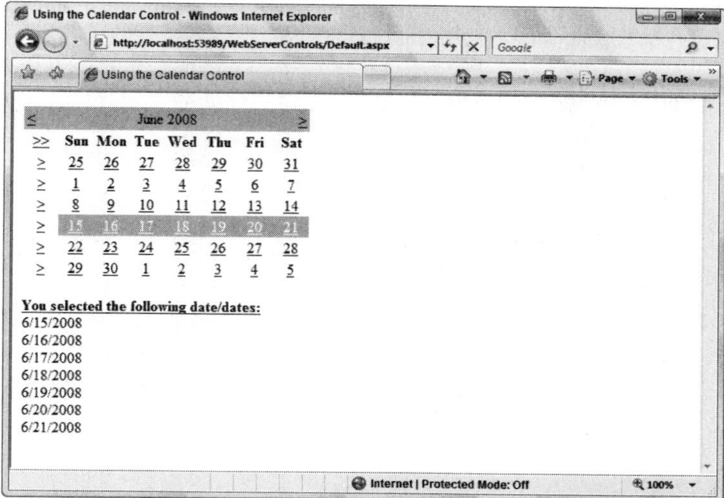

Figure 3-26

You can get just the first day of the selection by using the following:

VB

```
Calendar1.SelectedDates.Item(0).ToShortDateString()
```

C#

```
Calendar1.SelectedDates[0].ToShortDateString();
```

And you can get the last date in the selected range by using:

VB

```
Calendar1.SelectedDates.Item(Calendar1.SelectedDates.Count-1).ToShortDateString()
```

C#

```
Calendar1.SelectedDates[Calendar1.SelectedDates.Count-1].ToShortDateString();
```

As you can see, this is possible using the `Count` property of the `SelectedDates` object.

Modifying the Style and Behavior of Your Calendar

There is a lot to the Calendar control — definitely more than can be covered in this chapter. One nice thing about the Calendar control is the ease of extensibility that it offers. Begin exploring new ways to customize this control further by looking at one of the easiest ways to change it — applying a style to the control.

Using Visual Studio, you can give the controls a new look-and-feel from the Design view of the page you are working with. Highlight the Calendar control and open the control's smart tag to see the Auto Format link. That gives you a list of available styles that can be applied to your Calendar control.

The Calendar control is not alone in this capability. Many other rich controls offer a list of styles. You can always find this capability in the control's smart tag.

Some of the styles are shown in Figure 3-27.

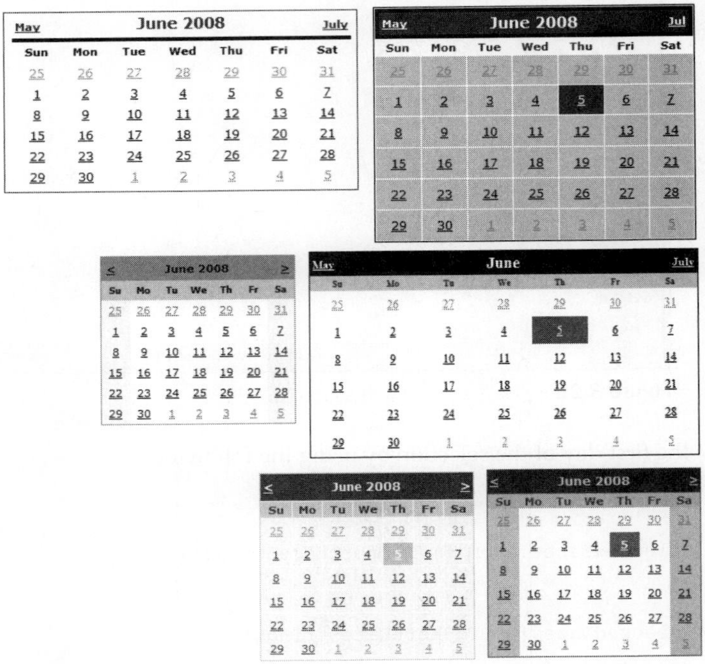

Figure 3-27

In addition to changing the style of the Calendar control, you can work with the control during its rendering process. The Calendar control includes an event called `DayRender` that allows you to control how a single date or all the dates in the calendar are rendered. Listing 3-22 shows an example of how to change one of the dates being rendered in the calendar.

Listing 3-22: Controlling how a day is rendered in the Calendar

VB

```
<%@ Page Language="VB" %>

<script runat="server">
    Protected Sub Calendar1_DayRender(ByVal sender As Object, _
      ByVal e As System.Web.UI.WebControls.DayRenderEventArgs)
        e.Cell.VerticalAlign = VerticalAlign.Top

        If (e.Day.DayNumberText = "25") Then
            e.Cell.Controls.Add(New LiteralControl("<p>User Group Meeting!</p>"))
            e.Cell.BorderColor = Drawing.Color.Black
            e.Cell.BorderWidth = 1
            e.Cell.BorderStyle = BorderStyle.Solid
```

```
            e.Cell.BackColor = Drawing.Color.LightGray
        End If
    End Sub
</script>

<html xmlns="http://www.w3.org/1999/xhtml">
<head id="Head1" runat="server">
    <title>Using the Calendar Control</title>
</head>
<body>
    <form id="form1" runat="server">
    <div>
        <asp:Calendar ID="Calendar1" runat="server"
         OnDayRender="Calendar1_DayRender" Height="190px" BorderColor="White"
         Width="350px" ForeColor="Black" BackColor="White" BorderWidth="1px"
         NextPrevFormat="FullMonth" Font-Names="Verdana" Font-Size="9pt">
            <SelectedDayStyle ForeColor="White"
             BackColor="#333399"></SelectedDayStyle>
            <OtherMonthDayStyle ForeColor="#999999"></OtherMonthDayStyle>
            <TodayDayStyle BackColor="#CCCCCC"></TodayDayStyle>
            <NextPrevStyle ForeColor="#333333" VerticalAlign="Bottom"
             Font-Size="8pt" Font-Bold="True"></NextPrevStyle>
            <DayHeaderStyle Font-Size="8pt" Font-Bold="True"></DayHeaderStyle>
            <TitleStyle ForeColor="#333399" BorderColor="Black" Font-Size="12pt"
                Font-Bold="True" BackColor="White" BorderWidth="4px">
            </TitleStyle>
        </asp:Calendar>
    </div>
    </form>
</body>
</html>
```

C#

```
<%@ Page Language="C#" %>

<script runat="server">
    protected void Calendar1_DayRender(object sender, DayRenderEventArgs e)
    {
        e.Cell.VerticalAlign = VerticalAlign.Top;

        if (e.Day.DayNumberText == "25")
        {
            e.Cell.Controls.Add(new LiteralControl("<p>User Group Meeting!</p>"));
            e.Cell.BorderColor = System.Drawing.Color.Black;
            e.Cell.BorderWidth = 1;
            e.Cell.BorderStyle = BorderStyle.Solid;
            e.Cell.BackColor = System.Drawing.Color.LightGray;
        }

    }
</script>
```

In this example, you use a Calendar control with a little style to it. When the page is built and run in the browser, you can see that the 25th of every month in the calendar has been changed by the code in the `Calendar1_DayRender` event. The calendar is shown in Figure 3-28.

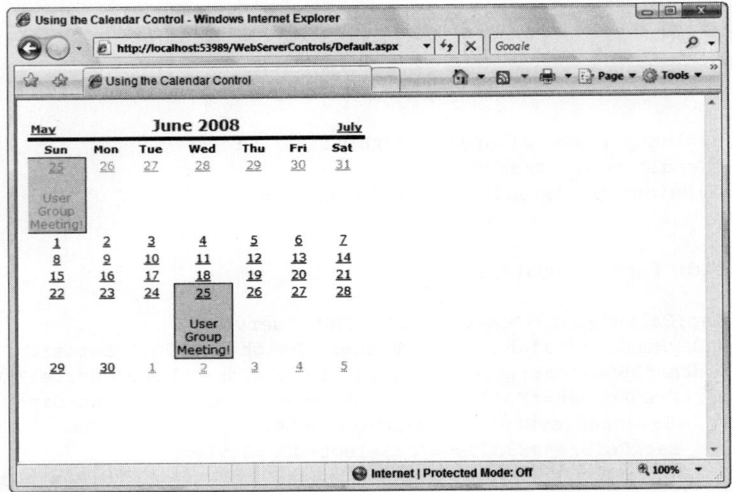

Figure 3-28

The Calendar control in this example adds an `OnDayRender` attribute that points to the `Calendar1_DayRender` event. The method is run for each of the days rendered in the calendar. The class constructor shows that you are not working with the typical `System.EventArgs` class, but instead with the `DayRenderEventArgs` class. It gives you access to each of the days rendered in the calendar.

The two main properties from the `DayRenderEventArgs` class are `Cell` and `Day`. The `Cell` property gives you access to the space in which the day is being rendered, and the `Day` property gives you access to the specific date being rendered in the cell.

From the actions being taken in the `Calendar1_DayRender` event, you can see that both properties are used. First, the `Cell` property sets the vertical alignment of the cell to `Top`. If it didn't, the table might look a little strange when one of the cells has content. Next, a check is made to see if the day being rendered (checked with the `Day` property) is the 25th of the month. If it is, the `If Then` statement runs using the `Cell` property to change the styling of just that cell. The styling change adds a control, as well as makes changes to the border and color of the cell.

As you can see, working with individual dates in the calendar is fairly straightforward. You can easily give them the content and appearance you want.

A nice feature of the `Day` property is that you can turn off the option to select a particular date or range of dates by setting the `Day` property's `IsSelectable` property to `False`:

VB

```
If (e.Day.Date < DateTime.Now) Then
   e.Day.IsSelectable = False
End If
```

C#

```
if (e.Day.Date < DateTime.Now) {
   e.Day.IsSelectable = false;
}
```

AdRotator Server Control

Although Web users find ads rather annoying, advertising continues to be prevalent everywhere on the Web. With the AdRotator control, you can configure your application to show a series of advertisements to the end users. With this control, you can use advertisement data from sources other than the standard XML file that was used with the previous versions of this control.

If you are using an XML source for the ad information, first create an XML advertisement file. The advertisement file allows you to incorporate some new elements that give you even more control over the appearance and behavior of your ads. Listing 3-23 shows an example of an XML advertisement file.

Listing 3-23: The XML advertisement file

```
<?xml version="1.0" encoding="utf-8" ?>
<Advertisements
 xmlns="http://schemas.microsoft.com/AspNet/AdRotator-Schedule-File">
 <Ad>
    <ImageUrl>book1.gif</ImageUrl>
    <NavigateUrl>http://www.wrox.com</NavigateUrl>
    <AlternateText>Visit Wrox Today!</AlternateText>
    <Impressions>50</Impressions>
    <Keyword>VB.NET</Keyword>
 </Ad>
 <Ad>
    <ImageUrl>book2.gif</ImageUrl>
    <NavigateUrl>http://www.wrox.com</NavigateUrl>
    <AlternateText>Visit Wrox Today!</AlternateText>
    <Impressions>50</Impressions>
    <Keyword>XML</Keyword>
 </Ad>
</Advertisements>
```

This XML file, used for storing information about the advertisements that appear in your application, has just a few elements detailed in the following table. Remember that all elements are optional.

Element	Description
`ImageUrl`	Takes a string value that indicates the location of the image to use.
`NavigateUrl`	Takes a string value that indicates the URL to post to when the image is clicked.
`AlternateText`	Takes a string value that is used for display either if images are turned off in the client's browser or if the image is not found.
`Impressions`	Takes a numerical value that indicates the likelihood of the image being selected for display.
`Keyword`	Takes a string value that sets the category of the image in order to allow for the filtering of ads.

Now that the XML advertisement file is in place, you can simply use the AdRotator control to read from this file. Listing 3-24 shows an example of this in action.

Listing 3-24: Using the AdRotator control as a banner ad

```
<%@ Page Language="VB" %>

<html xmlns="http://www.w3.org/1999/xhtml" >
<head runat="server">
    <title>AdRotator Page</title>
</head>
<body>
    <form id="form1" runat="server">
        <asp:AdRotator ID="AdRotator1" runat="server"
         AdvertisementFile="MyAds.xml" />
        <p>Lorem ipsum dolor sit
        amet, consectetuer adipiscing elit. Duis vel justo. Aliquam
        adipiscing. In mattis volutpat urna. Donec adipiscing, nisl eget
        dictum egestas, felis nulla ornare ligula, ut bibendum pede augue
        eu augue. Sed vel risus nec urna pharetra imperdiet. Aenean
        semper. Sed ullamcorper auctor sapien. Suspendisse luctus. Ut ac
        nibh. Nam lorem. Aliquam dictum aliquam purus.</p>
    </form>
</body>
</html>
```

The example shows the ad specified in the XML advertisement file as a banner ad at the top of the page.

You are not required to place all your ad information in the XML advertisement file. Instead, you can use another data source to which you bind the AdRotator. For instance, you bind the AdRotator to a `SqlDataSource` object that is retrieving the ad information from SQL Server in the following fashion:

```
<asp:AdRotator ID="AdRotator1" runat="server"
 DataSourceId="SqlDataSource1" AlternateTextField="AlternateTF"
 ImageUrlField="Image" NavigateUrlField="NavigateUrl" />
```

The `AlternateTextField`, `ImageUrlField`, and `NavigateUrlField` properties point to the column names that are used in SQL Server for those items.

The Xml Server Control

The Xml server control provides a means of getting XML and transforming it using an XSL style sheet. The Xml control can work with your XML in a couple of different ways. The simplest method is by using the construction shown in Listing 3-25. This control is covered in more detail in Chapter 10.

Listing 3-25: Displaying an XML document

```
<asp:Xml ID="Xml1" runat="server" DocumentSource="~/MyXMLFile.xml"
 TransformSource="MyXSLFile.xslt"></asp:Xml>
```

This method takes only a couple of attributes to make it work: `DocumentSource`, which points to the path of the XML file, and `TransformSource`, which provides the XSLT file to use in transforming the XML document.

The other way to use the Xml server control is to load the XML into an object and then pass the object to the Xml control, as illustrated in Listing 3-26.

Listing 3-26: Loading the XML file to an object before providing it to the Xml control

VB

```
Dim MyXmlDoc as XmlDocument = New XmlDocument()
MyXmlDoc.Load(Server.MapPath("Customers.xml"))

Dim MyXslDoc As XslCompiledTransform = New XslCompiledTransform()
MyXslDoc.Load(Server.MapPath("CustomersSchema.xslt"))

Xml1.Document = MyXmlDoc
Xml1.Transform = MyXslDoc
```

C#

```
XmlDocument MyXmlDoc = new XmlDocument();
MyXmlDoc.Load(Server.MapPath("Customers.xml"));

XslCompiledTransform MyXsltDoc = new XslCompiledTransform();
MyXsltDoc.Load(Server.MapPath("CustomersSchema.xslt"));

Xml1.Document = MyXmlDoc;
Xml1.Transform = MyXslDoc;
```

To make this work, you have to ensure that the `System.Xml` and `System.Xml.Xsl` namespaces are imported into your page. The example loads both the XML and XSL files and then assigns these files as the values of the `Document` and `Transform` properties.

Panel Server Control

The Panel server control encapsulates a set of controls you can use to manipulate or lay out your ASP.NET pages. It is basically a wrapper for other controls, enabling you to take a group of server controls along with other elements (such as HTML and images) and turn them into a single unit.

The advantage of using the Panel control to encapsulate a set of other elements is that you can manipulate these elements as a single unit using one attribute set in the Panel control itself. For example, setting the `Font-Bold` attribute to `True` causes each item within the Panel control to adopt this attribute.

The new addition to the Panel control is the capability to scroll with scrollbars that appear automatically depending on the amount of information that Panel control holds. You can even specify how the scrollbars should appear.

For an example of using scrollbars, look at a long version of the Lorem Ipsum text (found at `www.lipsum.com`) and place that text within the Panel control, as shown in Listing 3-27.

Listing 3-27: Using the new scrollbar feature with the Panel server control

```
<%@ Page Language="VB" %>

<html>
<head runat="server">
    <title>Panel Server Control Page</title>
</head>
<body>
    <form id="form1" runat="server">
        <asp:Panel ID="Panel1" runat="server" Height="300" Width="300"
         ScrollBars="auto">
            <p>Lorem ipsum dolor sit amet...</p>
        </asp:Panel>
    </form>
</body>
</html>
```

By assigning values to the `Height` and `Width` attributes of the Panel server control and using the `ScrollBars` attribute (in this case, set to `Auto`), you can display the information it contains within the defined area using scrollbars (see Figure 3-29).

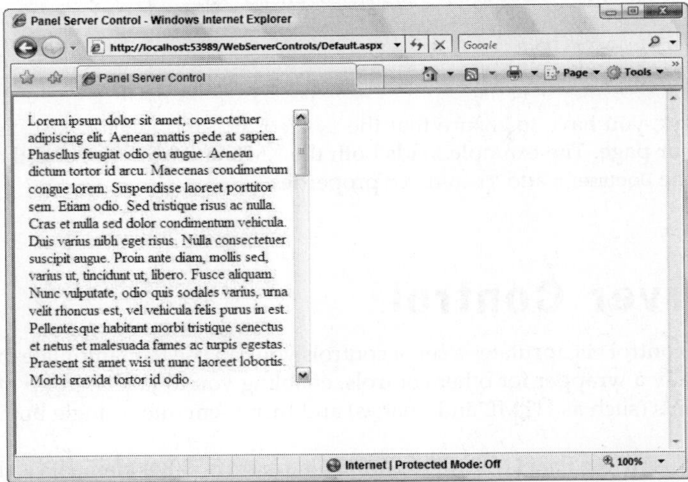

Figure 3-29

As you can see, a single vertical scrollbar has been added to the set area of 300 × 300 pixels. The Panel control wraps the text by default as required. To change this behavior, use the new `Wrap` attribute, which takes a `Boolean` value:

```
<asp:Panel ID="Panel1" runat="server"
 Height="300" Width="300" ScrollBars="Auto"
 Wrap="False" />
```

Turning off wrapping may cause the horizontal scrollbar to turn on (depending on what is contained in the panel section).

If you do not want to let the ASP.NET engine choose which scrollbars to activate, you can actually make that decision by using the `ScrollBars` attribute. In addition to `Auto`, its values include `None`, `Horizontal`, `Vertical`, and `Both`.

Another interesting attribute that enables you to change the behavior of the Panel control is `HorizontalAlign`. It enables you to set how the content in the Panel control is horizontally aligned. The possible values of this attribute include `NotSet`, `Center`, `Justify`, `Left`, and `Right`. Figure 3-30 shows a collection of Panel controls with different horizontal alignments.

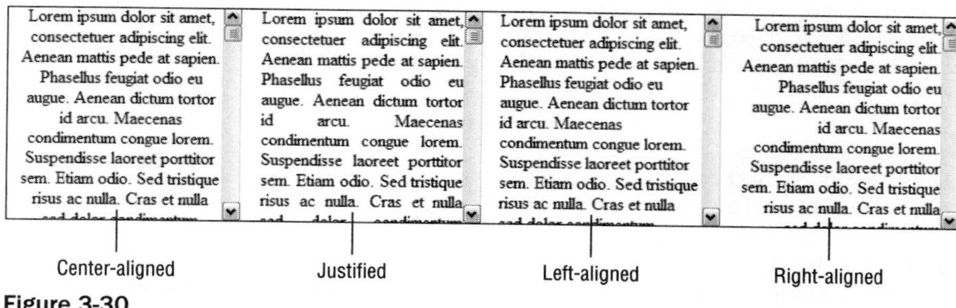

Figure 3-30

It is also possible to move the vertical scrollbar to the left side of the Panel control by using the `Direction` attribute. `Direction` can be set to `NotSet`, `LeftToRight`, and `RightToLeft`. A setting of `RightToLeft` is ideal when you are dealing with languages that are written from right to left (some Asian languages, for example). However, that setting also moves the scrollbar to the left side of the Panel control. If the scrollbar is moved to the left side and the `HorizontalAlign` attribute is set to `Left`, your content resembles Figure 3-31.

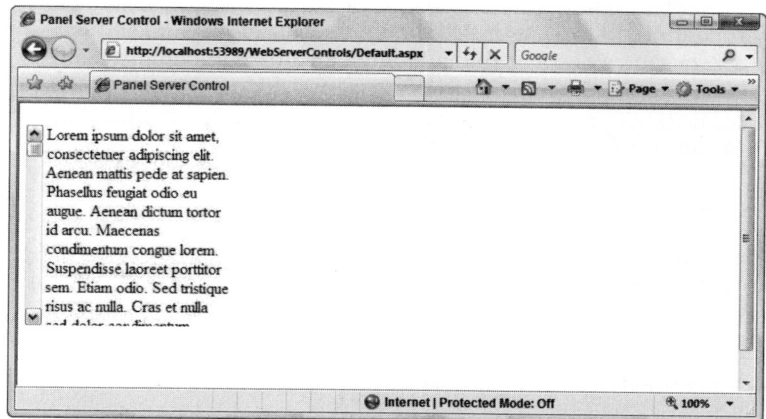

Figure 3-31

The PlaceHolder Server Control

The PlaceHolder server control works just as its name implies — it is a placeholder for you to interject objects dynamically into your page. Think of it as a marker with which you can add other controls. The capability to add controls to a page at a specific point also works with the Panel control.

To see how it works, insert a PlaceHolder control into your page and then add controls to it from your server-side code in the manner shown in Listing 3-28.

Listing 3-28: Using PlaceHolder to add controls to a page dynamically

VB

```
Dim NewLabelControl As New Label()
NewLabelControl.Text = "Hello there"
PlaceHolder1.Controls.Add(NewLabelControl)
```

C#

```
Label NewLabelControl = new Label();
NewLabelControl.Text = "Hello there";
PlaceHolder1.Controls.Add(NewLabelControl);
```

This example creates a new instance of a Label control and populates it with a value before it is added to the PlaceHolder control. You can add more than one control to a single instance of a PlaceHolder control.

BulletedList Server Control

One common HTML Web page element is a collection of items in a bulleted list. The BulletedList server control is meant to display a bulleted list of items easily in an ordered (using the HTML <ol> element) or unordered (using the HTML <ul> element) fashion. In addition, the control can determine the style used for displaying the list.

The BulletedList control can be constructed of any number of <asp:ListItem> controls or can be data-bound to a data source of some kind and populated based upon the contents retrieved. Listing 3-29 shows a bulleted list in its simplest form.

Listing 3-29: A simple BulletedList control

```
<%@ Page Language="VB" %>

<html xmlns="http://www.w3.org/1999/xhtml">
<head runat="server">
    <title>BulletedList Server Control</title>
</head>
<body>
    <form id="form1" runat="server">
        <asp:BulletedList ID="Bulletedlist1" runat="server">
            <asp:ListItem>United States</asp:ListItem>
            <asp:ListItem>United Kingdom</asp:ListItem>
            <asp:ListItem>Finland</asp:ListItem>
            <asp:ListItem>Russia</asp:ListItem>
```

```
            <asp:ListItem>Sweden</asp:ListItem>
            <asp:ListItem>Estonia</asp:ListItem>
        </asp:BulletedList>
    </form>
</body>
</html>
```

The use of the `<asp:BulletedList>` element, along with `<asp:ListItem>` elements, produces a simple bulleted list output like the one shown in Figure 3-32.

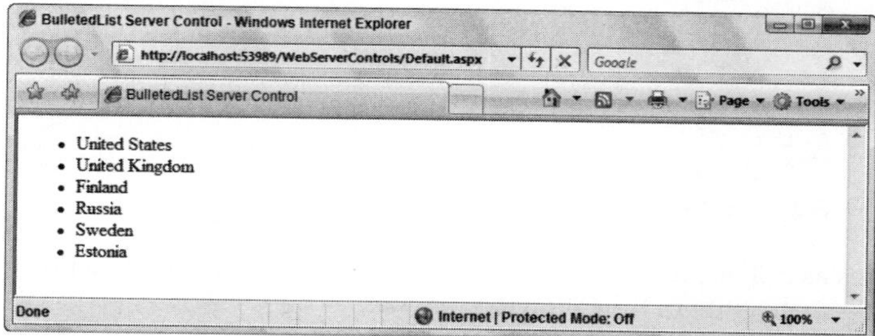

Figure 3-32

The BulletedList control also enables you to easily change the style of the list with just one or two attributes. The `BulletStyle` attribute changes the style of the bullet that precedes each line of the list. It has possible values of `Numbered`, `LowerAlpha`, `UpperAlpha`, `LowerRoman`, `UpperRoman`, `Disc`, `Circle`, `Square`, `NotSet`, and `CustomImage`. Figure 3-33 shows examples of these styles (minus the `CustomImage` setting that enables you to use any image of your choice).

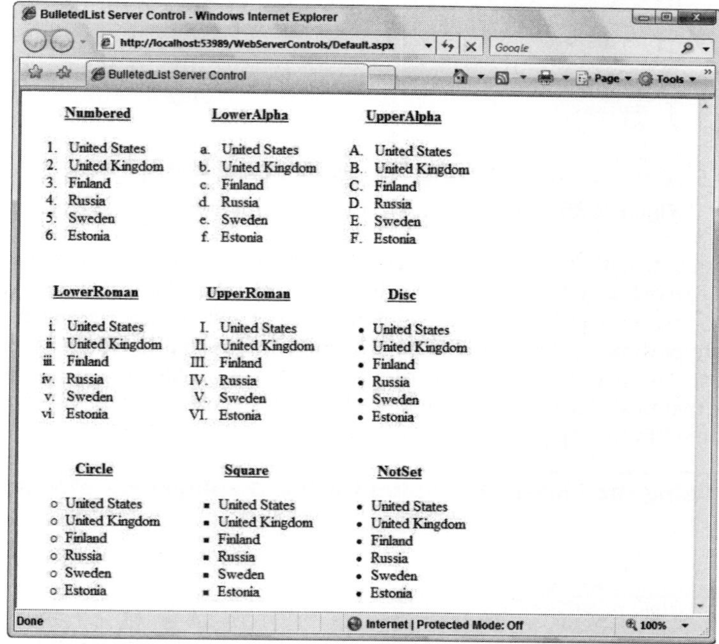

Figure 3-33

You can change the starting value of the first item in any of the numbered styles (`Numbered`, `LowerAlpha`, `UpperAlpha`, `LowerRoman`, `UpperRoman`) by using the `FirstBulletNumber` attribute. If you set the attribute's value to `5` when you use the `UpperRoman` setting, for example, you get the format illustrated in Figure 3-34.

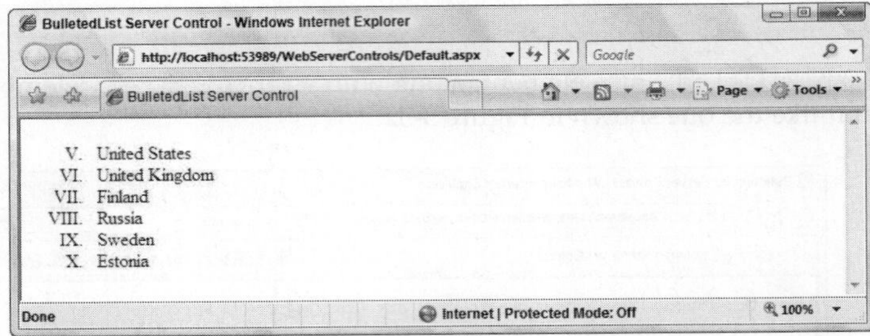

Figure 3-34

To employ images as bullets, use the `CustomImage` setting in the BulletedList control. You must also use the `BulletImageUrl` attribute in the following manner:

```
<asp:BulletedList ID="Bulletedlist1" runat="server"
 BulletStyle="CustomImage" BulletImageUrl="~/myImage.gif">
```

Figure 3-35 shows an example of image bullets.

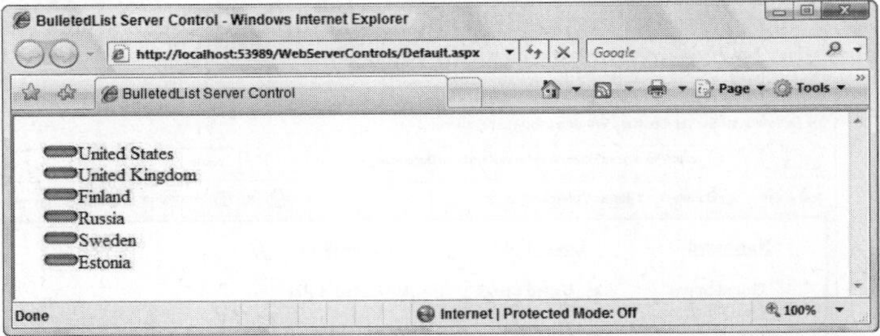

Figure 3-35

The BulletedList control has an attribute called `DisplayMode`, which has three possible values: `Text`, `HyperLink`, and `LinkButton`. `Text` is the default and has been used so far in the examples. Using `Text` means that the items in the bulleted list are laid out only as text. `HyperLink` means that each of the items is turned into a hyperlink — any user clicking the link is redirected to another page, which is specified by the `<asp:ListItem>` control's `Value` attribute. A value of `LinkButton` turns each bulleted list item into a hyperlink that posts back to the same page. It enables you to retrieve the selection that the end user makes, as illustrated in Listing 3-30.

Listing 3-30: Using the LinkButton value for the DisplayMode attribute

VB

```
<%@ Page Language="VB"%>

<script runat="server">
    Protected Sub BulletedList1_Click(ByVal sender As Object, _
```

```
        ByVal e As System.Web.UI.WebControls.BulletedListEventArgs)

         Label1.Text = "The index of item you selected: " & e.Index & _
            "<br>The value of the item selected: " & _
            BulletedList1.Items(e.Index).Text
    End Sub
</script>

<html xmlns="http://www.w3.org/1999/xhtml" >
<head runat="server">
    <title>BulletedList Server Control</title>
</head>
<body>
    <form id="form1" runat="server">
        <asp:BulletedList ID="BulletedList1" runat="server"
         OnClick="BulletedList1_Click" DisplayMode="LinkButton">
            <asp:ListItem>United States</asp:ListItem>
            <asp:ListItem>United Kingdom</asp:ListItem>
            <asp:ListItem>Finland</asp:ListItem>
            <asp:ListItem>Russia</asp:ListItem>
            <asp:ListItem>Sweden</asp:ListItem>
            <asp:ListItem>Estonia</asp:ListItem>
        </asp:BulletedList>
        <asp:Label ID="Label1" runat="server">
        </asp:Label>
    </form>
</body>
</html>
```

C#

```
<%@ Page Language="C#"%>

<script runat="server">
    protected void BulletedList1_Click(object sender,
       System.Web.UI.WebControls.BulletedListEventArgs e)
    {
         Label1.Text = "The index of item you selected: " + e.Index +
            "<br>The value of the item selected: " +
            BulletedList1.Items[e.Index].Text;
    }
</script>
```

In this example, the `DisplayMode` attribute is set to `LinkButton`, and the `OnClick` attribute is used to point to the `BulletedList1_Click` event. `BulletedList1_Click` uses the `BulletedListEventArgs` object, which only exposes the `Index` property. Using that, you can determine the index number of the item selected.

You can directly access the `Text` value of a selected item by using the `Items` property, or you can use the same property to populate an instance of the `ListItem` object, as shown here:

VB

```
Dim blSelectedValue As ListItem = BulletedList1.Items(e.Index)
```

C#

```
ListItem blSelectedValue = BulletedList1.Items[e.Index];
```

Now that you have seen how to create bulleted lists with items that you declaratively place in the code, look at how to create dynamic bulleted lists from items that are stored in a data store. The following example shows how to use the BulletedList control to data-bind to results coming from a data store; in it, all information is retrieved from an XML file.

The first step is to create the XML in Listing 3-31.

Listing 3-31: FilmChoices.xml

```
<?xml version="1.0" encoding="utf-8"?>
<FilmChoices>
   <Film
     Title="Close Encounters of the Third Kind"
     Year="1977"
     Director="Steven Spielberg" />
   <Film
     Title="Grease"
     Year="1978"
     Director="Randal Kleiser" />
   <Film
     Title="Lawrence of Arabia"
     Year="1962"
     Director="David Lean" />
</FilmChoices>
```

To populate the BulletedList server control with the `Title` attribute from the `FilmChoices.xml` file, use an XmlDataSource control to access the file, as illustrated in Listing 3-32.

Listing 3-32: Dynamically populating a BulletedList server control

```
<%@ Page Language="VB" %>

<html xmlns="http://www.w3.org/1999/xhtml" >
<head runat="server">
    <title>BulletedList Server Control</title>
</head>
<body>
    <form id="form1" runat="server">
        <asp:BulletedList ID="BulletedList1" runat="server"
          DataSourceID="XmlDataSource1" DataTextField="Title">
        </asp:BulletedList>
        <asp:XmlDataSource ID="XmlDataSource1" runat="server"
          DataFile="~/FilmChoices.xml" XPath="FilmChoices/Film">
        </asp:XmlDataSource>
    </form>
</body>
</html>
```

In this example, you use the `DataSourceID` attribute to point to the XmlDataSource control (as you would with any control that can be bound to one of the data source controls). After you are connected to the data source control, you specifically point to the `Title` attribute using the `DataTextField` attribute. After the two server controls are connected and the page is run, you get a bulleted list that is completely generated from the contents of the XML file. Figure 3-36 shows the result.

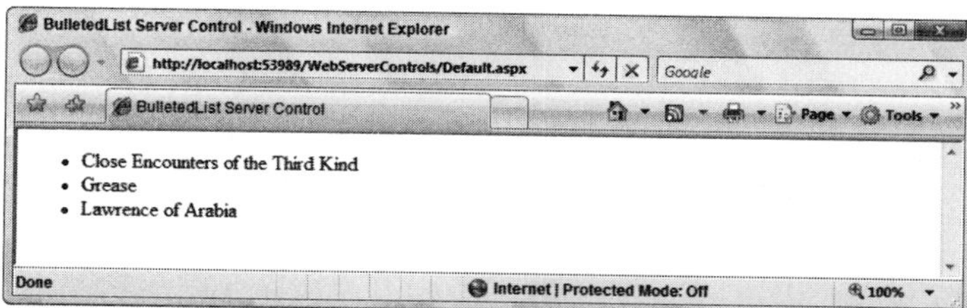

Figure 3-36

The XmlDataSource server control has some limitations in that the binding to the BulletedList server control worked in the previous example only because the `Title` *value was an XML attribute and not a subelement. The XmlDataSource control exposes XML attributes as properties only when databinding. If you are going to want to work with subelements, then you are going to have to perform an XSLT transform using the XmlDataSource control's* `TransformFile` *attribute to turn elements into attributes.*

HiddenField Server Control

For many years now, developers have been using hidden fields in their Web pages to work with state management. The `<input type="hidden">` element is ideal for storing items that have no security context to them. These items are simply placeholders for data points that you want to store in the page itself instead of using the `Session` object or intermingling the data with the view state of the page. View state is another great way to store information in a page, but many developers turn off this feature to avoid corruption of the view state or possible degradation of page performance.

Any time a hidden field is placed within a Web page, it is not interpreted in the browser in any fashion, although it is completely viewable by end users if they look at the source of the HTML page.

Listing 3-33 is an example of using the HiddenField server control to hold a GUID that can be used from page to page simply by carrying over its value as the end user navigates through your application.

Listing 3-33: Working with the HiddenField server control

VB

```
<%@ Page Language="VB" %>

<script runat="server" language="vb">
    Protected Sub Page_Load(ByVal sender As Object, ByVal e As System.EventArgs)
       HiddenField1.Value = System.Guid.NewGuid().ToString()
    End Sub
</script>

<html xmlns="http://www.w3.org/1999/xhtml" >
<head runat="server">
    <title>HiddenField Server Control</title>
</head>
<body>
    <form id="form1" runat="server">
```

Continued

```
        <asp:HiddenField ID="HiddenField1" runat="Server" />
    </form>
</body>
</html>
```

C#

```
<%@ Page Language="C#"%>

<script runat="server">
    protected void Page_Load(object sender, EventArgs e)
    {
        HiddenField1.Value = System.Guid.NewGuid().ToString();
    }
</script>
```

In this example, the `Page_Load` event populates the `HiddenField1` control with a GUID. You can see the hidden field and its value by looking at the source of the blank HTML page that is created. You should see a result similar to the following (the GUID will have a different value, of course):

```
<input type="hidden" name="HiddenField1" id="HiddenField1"
value="a031e77c-379b-4b4a-887c-244ee69584d5" />
```

On the page postback, ASP.NET can detect whether the HiddenField server control has changed its value since the last post. This enables you to change the HiddenField value with client-side script and then work with the changes in a page event.

The HiddenField server control has an event called `ValueChanged` that you can use when the value is changed:

VB

```
Protected Sub HiddenField1_ValueChanged(ByVal sender As Object, _
    ByVal e As System.EventArgs)
       ' Handle event here
End Sub
```

C#

```
protected void HiddenField1_ValueChanged(object sender, EventArgs e)
{
    // Handle event here
}
```

The `ValueChanged` event is triggered when the ASP.NET page is posted back to the server if the value of the HiddenField server control has changed since the last time the page was drawn. If the value has not changed, the method is never triggered. Therefore, the method is useful to act upon any changes to the HiddenField control — such as recording a value to the database or changing a value in the user's profile.

FileUpload Server Control

In ASP.NET 1.0/1.1, you could upload files using the HTML FileUpload server control. This control put an `<input type="file">` element on your Web page to enable the end user to upload files to the server.

To use the file, however, you had to make a couple of modifications to the page. For example, you were required to add `enctype="multipart/form-data"` to the page's `<form>` element.

ASP.NET 2.0 introduced a new FileUpload server control that makes the process of uploading files to a server even simpler. When giving a page the capability to upload files, you simply include the new `<asp:FileUpload>` control and ASP.NET takes care of the rest, including adding the `enctype` attribute to the page's `<form>` element.

Uploading Files Using the FileUpload Control

After the file is uploaded to the server, you can also take hold of the uploaded file's properties and either display them to the end user or use these values yourself in your page's code behind. Listing 3-34 shows an example of using the new FileUpload control. The page contains a single FileUpload control, plus a Button and a Label control.

Listing 3-34: Uploading files using the new FileUpload control

VB

```
<%@ Page Language="VB"%>

<script runat="server">
   Protected Sub Button1_Click(ByVal sender As Object, ByVal e As System.EventArgs)
        If FileUpload1.HasFile Then
            Try
                FileUpload1.SaveAs("C:\Uploads\" & _
                   FileUpload1.FileName)
                Label1.Text = "File name: " & _
                   FileUpload1.PostedFile.FileName & "<br>" & _
                   "File Size: " & _
                   FileUpload1.PostedFile.ContentLength & " kb<br>" & _
                   "Content type: " & _
                   FileUpload1.PostedFile.ContentType
            Catch ex As Exception
                Label1.Text = "ERROR: " & ex.Message.ToString()
            End Try
        Else
            Label1.Text = "You have not specified a file."
        End If
   End Sub
</script>

<html xmlns="http://www.w3.org/1999/xhtml" >
<head runat="server">
    <title>FileUpload Server Control</title>
</head>
<body>
    <form id="form1" runat="server">
        <asp:FileUpload ID="FileUpload1" runat="server" />
        <p>
        <asp:Button ID="Button1" runat="server" Text="Upload"
         OnClick="Button1_Click" /></p>
```

Continued

```
        <p>
        <asp:Label ID="Label1" runat="server"></asp:Label></p>
    </form>
</body>
</html>
```

C#

```
<%@ Page Language="C#"%>

<script runat="server">
    protected void Button1_Click(object sender, EventArgs e)
    {
        if (FileUpload1.HasFile)
            try {
                FileUpload1.SaveAs("C:\\Uploads\\" + FileUpload1.FileName);
                Label1.Text = "File name: " +
                     FileUpload1.PostedFile.FileName + "<br>" +
                     FileUpload1.PostedFile.ContentLength + " kb<br>" +
                     "Content type: " +
                     FileUpload1.PostedFile.ContentType;
            }
             catch (Exception ex) {
                Label1.Text = "ERROR: " + ex.Message.ToString();
             }
        else
        {
            Label1.Text = "You have not specified a file.";
        }
    }
</script>
```

From this example, you can see that the entire process is rather simple. The single button on the page initiates the upload process. The FileUpload control itself does not initiate the uploading process. You must initiate it through another event such as `Button_Click`.

When compiling and running this page, you may notice a few things in the generated source code of the page. An example of the generated source code is presented here:

```
<html xmlns="http://www.w3.org/1999/xhtml" >
<head id="Head1"><title>
 FileUpload Server Control
</title></head>
<body>
    <form name="form1" method="post" action="FileUpload.aspx" id="form1"
     enctype="multipart/form-data">
<div>
<input type="hidden" name="__VIEWSTATE" id="__VIEWSTATE"
 value="/wEPDwUKMTI3ODM5MzQ0Mg9kFgICAw8WAh4HZW5jdHlwZQUTbXVsdGlwYXJ0L2Zvcm
 0tZGF0YWRkrSpgAFaEKed5+5/8+zKglFfVLCE=" />
</div>

        <input type="file" name="FileUpload1" id="FileUpload1" />
        <p>
        <input type="submit" name="Button1" value="Upload" id="Button1" /></p>
```

```
        <p>
        <span id="Label1"></span></p>

    <div>

    <input type="hidden" name="__EVENTVALIDATION" id="__EVENTVALIDATION"
      value="/wEWAgL1wLWICAKM54rGBqfR8MhZIDWVowox+TUvybG5Xj0y" />
    </div></form>
    </body>
    </html>
```

The first thing to notice is that because the FileUpload control is on the page, ASP.NET 3.5 modified the page's `<form>` element on your behalf by adding the appropriate `enctype` attribute. Also notice that the FileUpload control was converted to an HTML `<input type="file">` element.

After the file is uploaded, the first check (done in the file's `Button1_Click` event handler) examines whether a file reference was actually placed within the `<input type="file">` element. If a file was specified, an attempt is made to upload the referenced file to the server using the `SaveAs()` method of the FileUpload control. That method takes a single `String` parameter, which should include the location where you want to save the file. In the `String` parameter used in Listing 3-34, you can see that the file is being saved to a folder called `Uploads`, which is located in the `C:\` drive.

The `PostedFile.FileName` attribute is used to give the saved file the same name as the file it was copied from. If you want to name the file something else, simply use the `SaveAs()` method in the following manner:

```
FileUpload1.SaveAs("C:\Uploads\UploadedFile.txt")
```

You could also give the file a name that specifies the time it was uploaded:

```
FileUpload1.SaveAs("C:\Uploads\" & System.DateTime.Now.ToFileTimeUtc() & ".txt")
```

After the upload is successfully completed, the Label control on the page is populated with metadata of the uploaded file. In the example, the file's name, size, and content type are retrieved and displayed on the page for the end user. When the file is uploaded to the server, the page generated is similar to that shown in Figure 3-37.

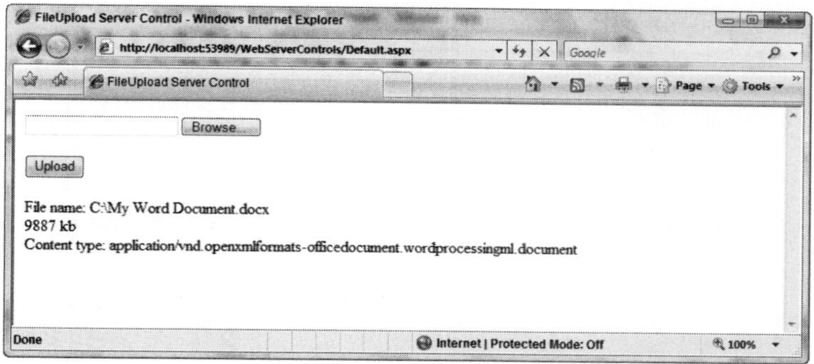

Figure 3-37

Uploading files to another server can be an error-prone affair. It is vital to upload files in your code using proper exception handling. That is why the file in the example is uploaded using a `Try Catch` statement.

Giving ASP.NET Proper Permissions to Upload Files

You might receive errors when your end users upload files to your Web server through the FileUpload control in your application. These might occur because the destination folder on the server is not writable for the account used by ASP.NET. If ASP.NET is not enabled to write to the folder you want, you can enable it using the folder's properties.

First, right-click on the folder where the ASP.NET files should be uploaded and select Properties from the provided menu. The Properties dialog for the selected folder opens. Click the Security tab to make sure the ASP.NET Machine Account is included in the list and has the proper permissions to write to disk. If it is enabled, you see something similar to what is presented in Figure 3-38.

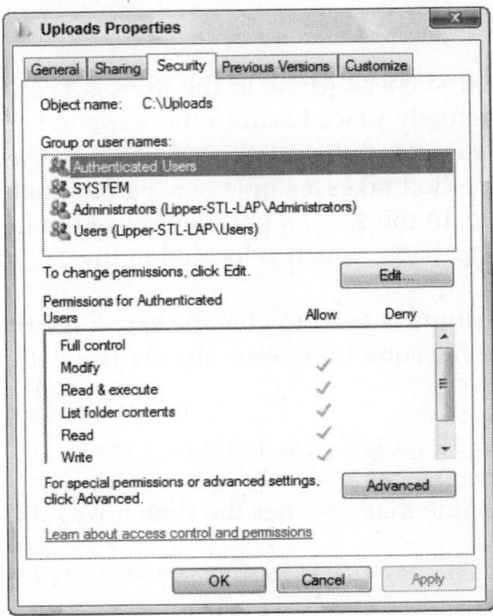

Figure 3-38

If you do not see the ASP.NET Machine Account in the list of users allowed to access the folder, add ASP.NET by clicking the Add button and entering ASPNET (without the period) in the text area provided (see Figure 3-39).

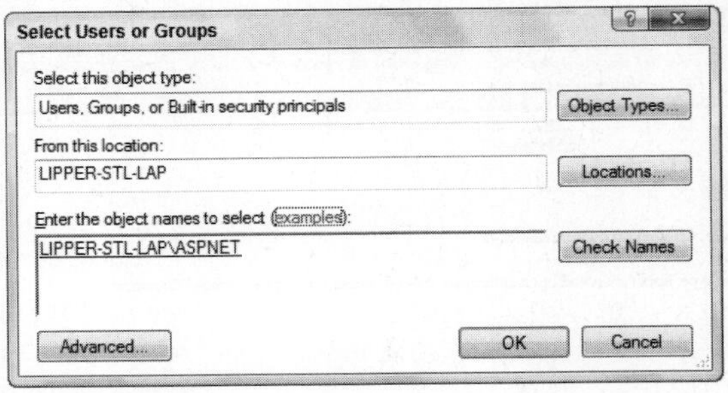

Select Users or Groups
Select this object type:
Users, Groups, or Built-in security principals
Object Types...
From this location:
LIPPER-STL-LAP
Locations...
Enter the object names to select (examples):
LIPPER-STL-LAP\ASPNET
Check Names
Advanced...
OK
Cancel

Figure 3-39

Click OK, and you can then click the appropriate check boxes to provide the permissions needed for your application.

Understanding File Size Limitations

Your end users might never encounter an issue with the file upload process in your application, but you should be aware that some limitations exist. When users work through the process of uploading files, a size restriction is actually sent to the server for uploading. The default size limitation is 4 MB (4096 KB); the transfer fails if a user tries to upload a file that is larger than 4096 KB.

A size restriction protects your application. You want to prevent malicious users from uploading numerous large files to your Web server in an attempt to tie up all the available processes on the server. Such an occurrence is called a *denial of service attack*. It ties up the Web server's resources so that legitimate users are denied responses from the server.

One of the great things about .NET, however, is that it usually provides a way around limitations. You can usually change the default settings that are in place. To change the limit on the allowable upload file size, you make some changes in either the root `web.config` file (found in the ASP.NET 2.0 configuration folder at `C:\WINDOWS\Microsoft.NET\Framework\v2.0.50727\CONFIG`) or in your application's `web.config` file.

In the `web.config` file, you can create a node called `<httpRuntime>`. In this file, you apply the settings so that the default allowable file size is dictated by the actual request size permitted to the Web server (4096 KB). The `<httpRuntime>` section of the `web.config.comments` file is shown in Listing 3-35.

Listing 3-35: Changing the file-size limitation setting in the web.config file

```
<httpRuntime
 executionTimeout="110"
 maxRequestLength="4096"
 requestLengthDiskThreshold="80"
 useFullyQualifiedRedirectUrl="false"
 minFreeThreads="8"
 minLocalRequestFreeThreads="4"
 appRequestQueueLimit="5000"
 enableKernelOutputCache="true"
 enableVersionHeader="true"
 requireRootedSaveAsPath="true"
 enable="true"
 shutdownTimeout="90"
 delayNotificationTimeout="5"
 waitChangeNotification="0"
 maxWaitChangeNotification="0"
 enableHeaderChecking="true"
 sendCacheControlHeader="true"
 apartmentThreading="false" />
```

You can do a lot with the `<httpRuntime>` section of the `web.config` file, but two properties — the `maxRequestLength` and `executionTimeout` properties — are especially interesting.

The `maxRequestLength` property is the setting that dictates the size of the request made to the Web server. When you upload files, the file is included in the request; you alter the size allowed to be uploaded by changing the value of this property. The value presented is in kilobytes. To allow files larger than the default of 4 MB, change the `maxRequestLength` property as follows:

```
maxRequestLength="11000"
```

This example changes the `maxRequestLength` property's value to 11,000 KB (around 10 MB). With this setting in place, your end users can upload 10 MB files to the server. When changing the `maxRequestLength` property, be aware of the setting provided for the `executionTimeout` property. This property sets the time (in seconds) for a request to attempt to execute to the server before ASP.NET shuts down the request (whether or not it is finished). The default setting is `90` seconds. The end user receives a timeout error notification in the browser if the time limit is exceeded. If you are going to permit larger requests, remember that they take longer to execute than smaller ones. If you increase the size of the `maxRequestLength` property, you should examine whether to increase the `executionTimeout` property as well.

If you are working with smaller files, it is advisable to reduce the size allotted for the request to the Web server by decreasing the value of the `maxRequestLength` *property. This helps safeguard your application from a denial of service attack.*

Making these changes in the `web.config` file applies this setting to all the applications that are on the server. If you want to apply this only to the application you are working with, apply the `<httpRuntime>` node to the `web.config` file of your application, overriding any setting that is in the root `web.config` file. Make sure this node resides between the `<system.web>` nodes in the configuration file.

Uploading Multiple Files from the Same Page

So far, you have seen some good examples of how to upload a file to the server without much hassle. Now, look at how to upload multiple files to the server from a single page.

No built-in capabilities in the Microsoft .NET Framework enable you to upload multiple files from a single ASP.NET page. With a little work, however, you can easily accomplish this task just as you would have in the past using .NET 1.*x*.

The trick is to import the `System.IO` class into your ASP.NET page and then to use the `HttpFileCollection` class to capture all the files that are sent in with the `Request` object. This approach enables you to upload as many files as you want from a single page.

If you wanted to, you could simply handle each and every FileUpload control on the page individually, as shown in Listing 3-36.

Listing 3-36: Handling each FileUpload control individually

VB

```
If FileUpload1.HasFile Then
    ' Handle file
End If

If FileUpload2.HasFile Then
    ' Handle file
End If
```

C#

```
if (FileUpload1.HasFile) {
   // Handle file
}
```

```
if (FileUpload2.HasFile) {
   // Handle file
}
```

If you are working with a limited number of file upload boxes, this approach works; but at the same time you may, in certain cases, want to handle the files using the `HttpFileCollection` class. This is especially true if you are working with a dynamically generated list of server controls on your ASP .NET page.

For an example of this, you can build an ASP.NET page that has three FileUpload controls and one Submit button (using the Button control). After the user clicks the Submit button and the files are posted to the server, the code behind takes the files and saves them to a specific location on the server. After the files are saved, the file information that was posted is displayed in the ASP.NET page (see Listing 3-37).

Listing 3-37: Uploading multiple files to the server

VB

```
Protected Sub Button1_Click(ByVal sender As Object, _
   ByVal e As System.EventArgs)

   Dim filepath As String = "C:\Uploads"
   Dim uploadedFiles As HttpFileCollection = Request.Files
   Dim i As Integer = 0

   Do Until i = uploadedFiles.Count
     Dim userPostedFile As HttpPostedFile = uploadedFiles(i)

     Try
        If (userPostedFile.ContentLength > 0) Then
           Label1.Text += "<u>File #" & (i + 1) & "</u><br>"
           Label1.Text += "File Content Type: " & _
              userPostedFile.ContentType & "<br>"
           Label1.Text += "File Size: " & _
              userPostedFile.ContentLength & "kb<br>"
           Label1.Text += "File Name: " & _
              userPostedFile.FileName & "<br>"

           userPostedFile.SaveAs(filepath & "\" & _
              System.IO.Path.GetFileName(userPostedFile.FileName))

           Label1.Text += "Location where saved: " & _
              filepath & "\" & _
              System.IO.Path.GetFileName(userPostedFile.FileName) & _
              "<p>"
        End If
     Catch ex As Exception
        Label1.Text += "Error:<br>" & ex.Message
     End Try
     i += 1
   Loop
End Sub
```

Continued

C#

```
protected void Button1_Click(object sender, EventArgs e)
{
   string filepath = "C:\\Uploads";
   HttpFileCollection uploadedFiles = Request.Files;

   for (int i = 0; i < uploadedFiles.Count; i++)
   {
      HttpPostedFile userPostedFile = uploadedFiles[i];

      try
      {
         if (userPostedFile.ContentLength > 0 )
         {
            Label1.Text += "<u>File #" + (i+1) +
               "</u><br>";
            Label1.Text += "File Content Type: " +
               userPostedFile.ContentType + "<br>";
            Label1.Text += "File Size: " +
               userPostedFile.ContentLength + "kb<br>";
            Label1.Text += "File Name: " +
               userPostedFile.FileName + "<br>";

            userPostedFile.SaveAs(filepath + "\\" +
               System.IO.Path.GetFileName(userPostedFile.FileName));

            Label1.Text += "Location where saved: " +
               filepath + "\\" +
               System.IO.Path.GetFileName(userPostedFile.FileName) +
               "<p>";
         }
      }
      catch (Exception Ex)
      {
         Label1.Text += "Error: <br>" + Ex.Message;
      }
   }
}
```

This ASP.NET page enables the end user to select up to three files and click the Upload Files button, which initializes the `Button1_Click` event. Using the `HttpFileCollection` class with the `Request.Files` property lets you gain control over all the files that are uploaded from the page. When the files are in this state, you can do whatever you want with them. In this case, the files' properties are examined and written to the screen. In the end, the files are saved to the Uploads folder in the root directory of the server. The result of this action is illustrated in Figure 3-40.

Placing the Uploaded File into a Stream Object

One nice feature of the FileUpload control is that it not only gives you the capability to save the file to disk, but it also lets you place the contents of the file into a `Stream` object. You do this by using the `FileContent` property, as demonstrated in Listing 3-38.

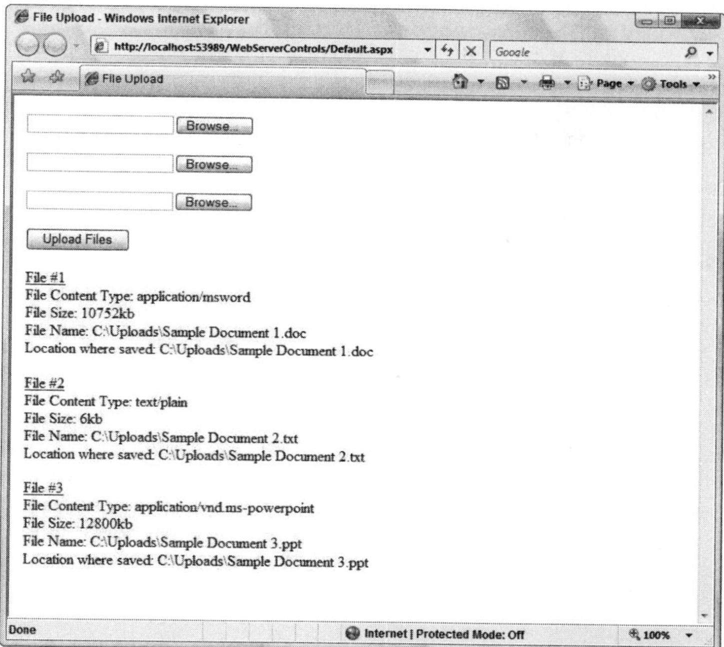

Figure 3-40

Listing 3-38: Uploading the file contents into a Stream object

VB

```
Dim myStream As System.IO.Stream
myStream = FileUpload1.FileContent
```

C#

```
System.IO.Stream myStream;
myStream = FileUpload1.FileContent;
```

In this short example, an instance of the `Stream` object is created. Then, using the FileUpload control's `FileContent` property, the content of the uploaded file is placed into the object. This is possible because the `FileContent` property returns a `Stream` object.

Moving File Contents from a Stream Object to a Byte Array

Because you have the capability to move the file contents to a `Stream` object of some kind, it is also fairly simple to move the contents of the file to a `Byte` array (useful for such operations as placing files in a database of some kind). To do so, first move the file contents to a `MemoryStream` object and then convert the object to the necessary `Byte` array object. Listing 3-39 shows the process.

Listing 3-39: Uploading the file contents into a Byte array

VB

```
Dim myByteArray() As Byte
Dim myStream As System.IO.MemoryStream

myStream = FileUpload1.FileContent
myByteArray = myStream.ToArray()
```

C#

```
Byte myByteArray[];
System.IO.Stream myStream;

myStream = FileUpload1.FileContent;
myByteArray = myStream.ToArray();
```

In this example, instances of a `Byte` array and a `MemoryStream` object are created. First, the `MemoryStream` object is created using the FileUpload control's `FileContent` property as you did previously. Then it's fairly simple to use the `MemoryStream` object's `ToArray()` method to populate the `myByteArray()` instance. After the file is placed into a `Byte` array, you can work with the file contents as necessary.

MultiView and View Server Controls

The MultiView and View server controls work together to give you the capability to turn on/off sections of an ASP.NET page. Turning sections on and off, which means activating or deactivating a series of View controls within a MultiView control, is similar to changing the visibility of Panel controls. For certain operations, however, you may find that the MultiView control is easier to manage and work with.

The sections, or views, do not change on the client-side; rather, they change with a postback to the server. You can put any number of elements and controls in each view, and the end user can work through the views based upon the sequence numbers that you assign to the views.

You can build these controls (like all server controls) from the source view or design view. If working with Visual Studio 2008, you can drag and drop a MultiView control onto the design surface and then drag and drop any number of View controls inside the MultiView control. Place the elements you want within the View controls. When you are finished, you have something like the view shown in Figure 3-41.

You also can create your controls directly in the code, as shown in Listing 3-40.

Listing 3-40: Using the MultiView and View server controls

VB

```
<%@ Page Language="VB"%>

<script runat="server">
    Protected Sub Page_Load(ByVal sender As Object, ByVal e As System.EventArgs)
        If Not Page.IsPostBack Then
            MultiView1.ActiveViewIndex = 0
        End If
```

```
    End Sub
    Sub NextView(ByVal sender As Object, ByVal e As System.EventArgs)
        MultiView1.ActiveViewIndex += 1
    End Sub
</script>

<html xmlns="http://www.w3.org/1999/xhtml" >
<head runat="server">
    <title>MultiView Server Control</title>
</head>
<body>
    <form id="form1" runat="server">
        <asp:MultiView ID="MultiView1" runat="server">
            <asp:View ID="View1" runat="server">
                Billy's Famous Pan Pancakes<p />
                <i>Heat 1/2 tsp of butter in cast iron pan.<br />
                   Heat oven to 450 degrees Fahrenheit.<br />
                </i><p />
                <asp:Button ID="Button1" runat="server" Text="Next Step"
                 OnClick="NextView" />
            </asp:View>
            <asp:View ID="View2" runat="server">
                Billy's Famous Pan Pancakes<p />
                <i>Mix 1/2 cup flour, 1/2 cup milk and 2 eggs in bowl.<br />
                   Pour in cast iron pan. Place in oven.</i><p />
                <asp:Button ID="Button2" runat="server" Text="Next Step"
                 OnClick="NextView" />
            </asp:View>
            <asp:View ID="View3" runat="server">
                Billy's Famous Pan Pancakes<p />
                <i>Cook for 20 minutes and enjoy!<br />
                </i><p />
            </asp:View>
        </asp:MultiView>
    </form>
</body>
</html>
```

C#

```
<%@ Page Language="C#"%>

<script runat="server">
    protected void Page_Load(object sender, EventArgs e)
    {
        if (!Page.IsPostBack)
        {
            MultiView1.ActiveViewIndex = 0;
        }
    }

    void NextView(object sender, EventArgs e)
    {
        MultiView1.ActiveViewIndex += 1;
    }
</script>
```

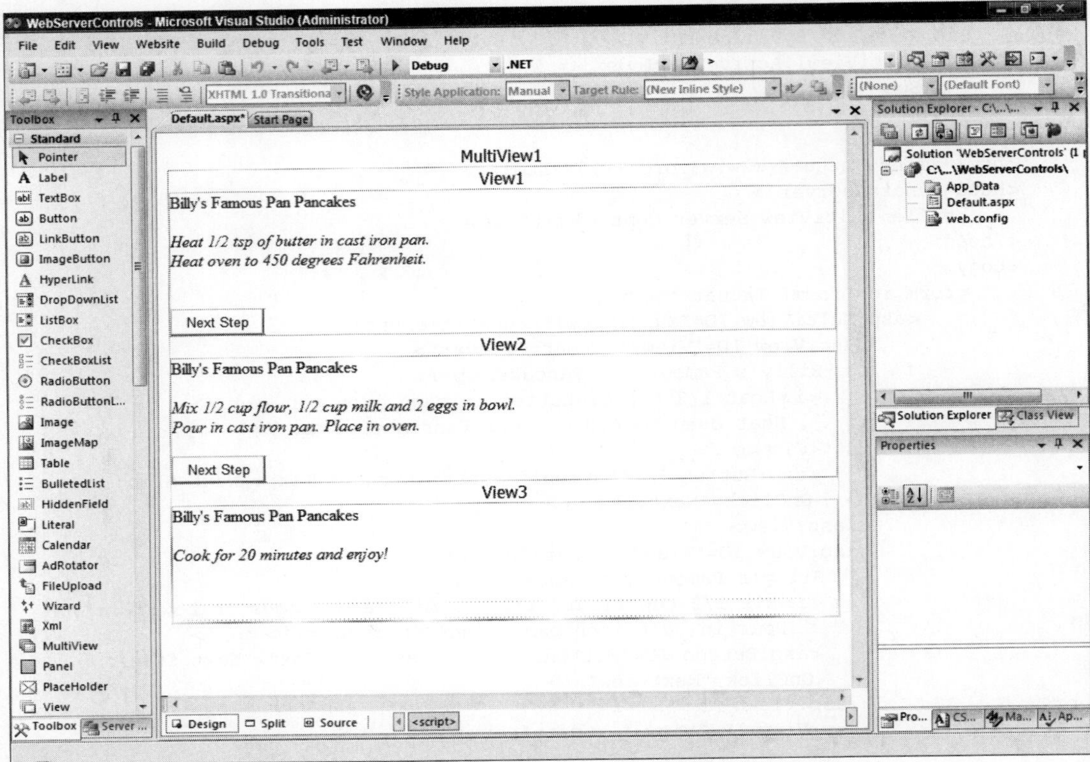

Figure 3-41

This example shows three views expressed in the MultiView control. Each view is constructed with an `<asp:View>` server control that also needs `ID` and `Runat` attributes. A button is added to each of the first two views (`View1` and `View2`) of the MultiView control. The buttons point to a server-side event that triggers the MultiView control to progress onto the next view within the series of views.

Before either of the buttons can be clicked, the MultiView control's `ActiveViewIndex` attribute is assigned a value. By default, the `ActiveViewIndex`, which describes the view that should be showing, is set to `-1`. This means that no view shows when the page is generated. To start on the first view when the page is drawn, set the `ActiveViewIndex` property to `0`, which is the first view because this is a zero-based index. Therefore, the code from Listing 3-40 first checks to see if the page is in a postback situation and if not, the `ActiveViewIndex` is assigned to the first View control.

Each of the buttons in the MultiView control triggers the `NextView` method. `NextView` simply adds one to the `ActiveViewIndex` value, thereby showing the next view in the series until the last view is shown. The view series is illustrated in Figure 3-42.

In addition to the Next Step button on the first and second views, you could place a button in the second and third views to enable the user to navigate backward through the views. To do this, create two

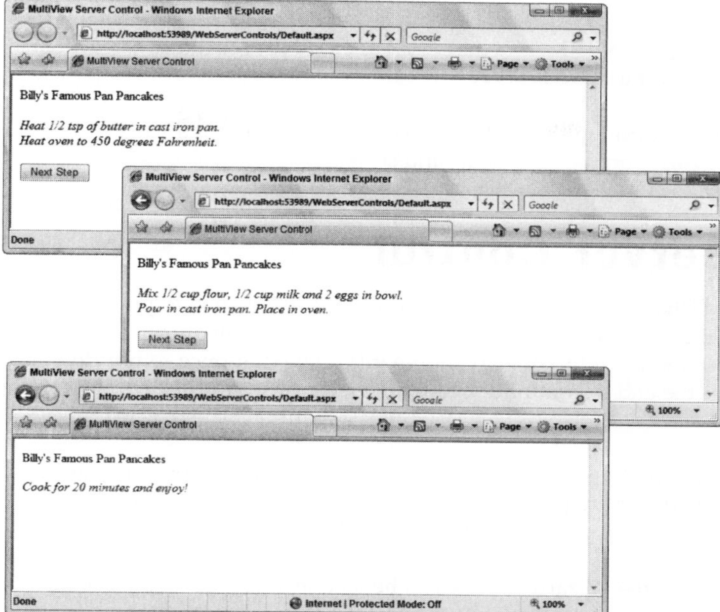

Figure 3-42

buttons titled Previous Step in the last two views and point them to the following method in their `OnClick` events:

VB

```
Sub PreviousView(ByVal sender As Object, ByVal e As System.EventArgs)
    MultiView1.ActiveViewIndex -= 1
End Sub
```

C#

```
void PreviousView(object sender, EventArgs e)
{
    MultiView1.ActiveViewIndex -= 1;
}
```

Here, the `PreviousView` method subtracts one from the `ActiveViewIndex` value, thereby showing the previous view in the view series.

Another option is to spice up the MultiView control by adding a step counter that displays (to a Label control) which step in the series the end user is currently performing. In the `Page_PreRender` event, you add the following line:

VB

```
Label1.Text = "Step " & (MultiView1.ActiveViewIndex + 1).ToString() & _
   " of " & MultiView1.Views.Count.ToString()
```

C#

```
Label1.Text = "Step " + (MultiView1.ActiveViewIndex + 1).ToString() +
   " of " + MultiView1.Views.Count.ToString();
```

Now when working through the MultiView control, the end user sees `Step 1 of 3` on the first view, which changes to `Step 2 of 3` on the next view, and so on.

Wizard Server Control

Much like the MultiView control, the Wizard server control enables you to build a sequence of steps that is displayed to the end user. Web pages are all about either displaying or gathering information and, in many cases, you don't want to display all the information at once — nor do you always want to gather everything from the end user at once. Sometimes, you want to trickle the information in from or out to the end user.

When you are constructing a step-by-step process that includes logic on the steps taken, use the Wizard control to manage the entire process. The first time you use the Wizard control, notice that it allows for a far greater degree of customization than does the MultiView control.

In its simplest form, the Wizard control can be just an `<asp:Wizard>` element with any number of `<asp:WizardStep>` elements. Listing 3-41 creates a Wizard control that works through three steps.

Listing 3-41: A simple Wizard control

```
<%@ Page Language="VB"%>

<html xmlns="http://www.w3.org/1999/xhtml" >
<head runat="server">
    <title>Wizard server control</title>
</head>
<body>
    <form id="form1" runat="server">
        <asp:Wizard ID="Wizard1" runat="server" DisplaySideBar="True"
         ActiveStepIndex="0">
            <WizardSteps>
                <asp:WizardStep runat="server" Title="Step 1">
                    This is the first step.</asp:WizardStep>
                <asp:WizardStep runat="server" Title="Step 2">
                    This is the second step.</asp:WizardStep>
                <asp:WizardStep runat="server" Title="Step 3">
                    This is the third and final step.</asp:WizardStep>
            </WizardSteps>
        </asp:Wizard>
    </form>
</body>
</html>
```

In this example, three steps are defined with the `<asp:WizardSteps>` control. Each step contains content — simply text in this case, although you can put in anything you want, such as other Web server controls or even user controls. The order in which the `WizardSteps` are defined is based completely on the order in which they appear within the `<WizardSteps>` element.

The `<asp:Wizard>` element itself contains a couple of important attributes. The first is `DisplaySideBar`. In this example, it is set to `True` by default — meaning that a side navigation system in the displayed control enables the end user to quickly navigate to other steps in the process. The `ActiveStepIndex` attribute of the Wizard control defines the first wizard step. In this case, it is the first step — `0`.

The three steps of the example Wizard control are shown in Figure 3-43.

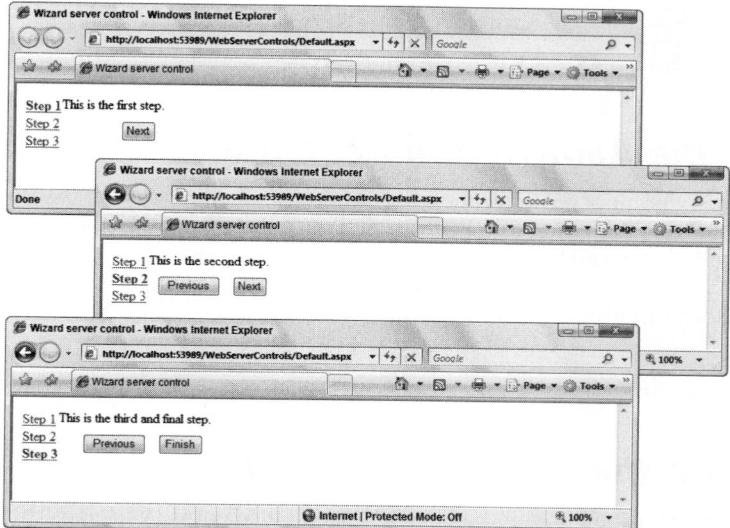

Figure 3-43

The side navigation allows for easy access to the defined steps. The Wizard control adds appropriate buttons to the steps in the process. The first step has simply a Next button, the middle step has Previous and Next buttons, and the final step has Previous and Finish buttons. The user can navigate through the steps using either the side navigation or the buttons on each of the steps. You can customize the Wizard control in so many ways that it tends to remind me of the other rich Web server controls from ASP.NET, such as the Calendar control. Because so much is possible, only a few of the basics are covered — the ones you are most likely to employ in some of the Wizard controls you build.

Customizing the Side Navigation

The steps in the Figure 3-43 example are defined as Step 1, Step 2, and Step 3. The links are created based on the `Title` property's value that you give to each of the `<asp:WizardStep>` elements in the Wizard control:

```
<asp:WizardStep runat="server" Title="Step 1">
 This is the first step.</asp:WizardStep>
```

By default, each wizard step created in Design view is titled `Step X` (with `X` being the number in the sequence). You can easily change the value of the `Title` attributes of each of the wizard steps to define the steps as you see fit. Figure 3-44 shows the side navigation of the Wizard control with renamed titles.

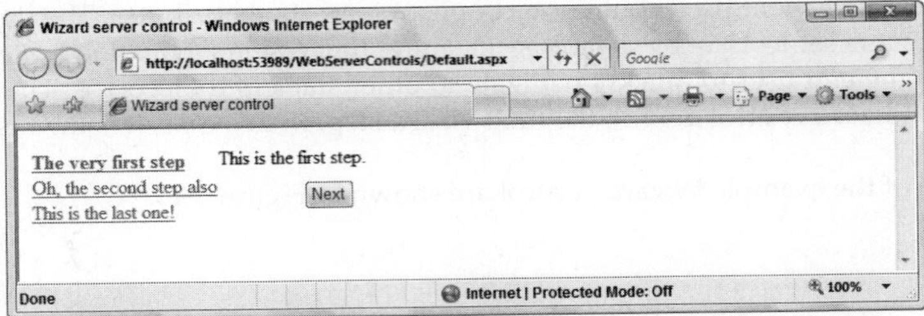

Figure 3-44

Examining the AllowReturn Attribute

Another interesting point of customization for the side navigation piece of the Wizard control is the `AllowReturn` attribute. By setting this attribute on one of the wizard steps to `False`, you can remove the capability for end users to go back to this step after they have viewed it. The end user cannot navigate backward to any viewed steps that contain the attribute, but he would be able to return to any steps that do not contain the attribute or that have it set to `True`:

```
<asp:WizardStep runat="server" Title="Step 1" AllowReturn="False">
 This is the first step.</asp:WizardStep>
```

Working with the StepType Attribute

Another interesting attribute in the `<asp:WizardStep>` element is `StepType`. The `StepType` attribute defines the structure of the buttons used on the steps. By default, the Wizard control places only a Next button on the first step. It understands that you do not need the Previous button there. It also knows to use a Next and Previous button on the middle step, and it uses Previous and Finish buttons on the last step. It draws the buttons in this fashion because, by default, the `StepType` attribute is set to `Auto`, meaning that the Wizard control determines the placement of buttons. You can, however, take control of the `StepType` attribute in the `<asp:WizardStep>` element to make your own determination about which buttons are used for which steps.

In addition to `Auto`, `StepType` value options include `Start`, `Step`, `Finish`, and `Complete`. `Start` means that the step defined has only a Next button. It simply allows the user to proceed to the next step in the series. A value of `Step` means that the wizard step has Next and Previous buttons. A value of `Finish` means that the step includes a Previous and a Finish button. `Complete` enables you to give some final message to the end user who is working through the steps of your Wizard control. In the Wizard control shown in Listing 3-42, for example, when the end user gets to the last step and clicks the Finish button, nothing happens and the user just stays on the last page. You can add a final step to give an ending message, as shown in Listing 3-42.

Listing 3-42: Having a complete step in the wizard step collection

```
<WizardSteps>
   <asp:WizardStep runat="server" Title="Step 1">
    This is the first step.</asp:WizardStep>
   <asp:WizardStep runat="server" Title="Step 2">
    This is the second step.</asp:WizardStep>
```

```
        <asp:WizardStep runat="server" Title="Step 3">
         This is the third and final step.</asp:WizardStep>
        <asp:WizardStep runat="server" Title="Final Step" StepType="Complete">
         Thanks for working through the steps.</asp:WizardStep>
    </WizardSteps>
```

When you run this Wizard control in a page, you still see only the first three steps in the side navigation. Because the last step has a `StepType` set to `Complete`, it does not appear in the side navigation list. When the end user clicks the Finish button in Step 3, the last step — `Final Step` — is shown and no buttons appear with it.

Adding a Header to the Wizard Control

The Wizard control enables you to place a header at the top of the control by means of the `HeaderText` attribute in the main `<asp:Wizard>` element. Listing 3-43 provides an example.

Listing 3-43: Working with the HeaderText attribute

```
<asp:Wizard ID="Wizard1" runat="server" ActiveStepIndex="0"
 HeaderText=" Step by Step with the Wizard control "
 HeaderStyle-BackColor="DarkGray" HeaderStyle-Font-Bold="true"
 HeaderStyle-Font-Size="20">

    ...

</asp:Wizard>
```

This code creates a header that appears on each of the steps in the wizard. The result of this snippet is shown in Figure 3-45.

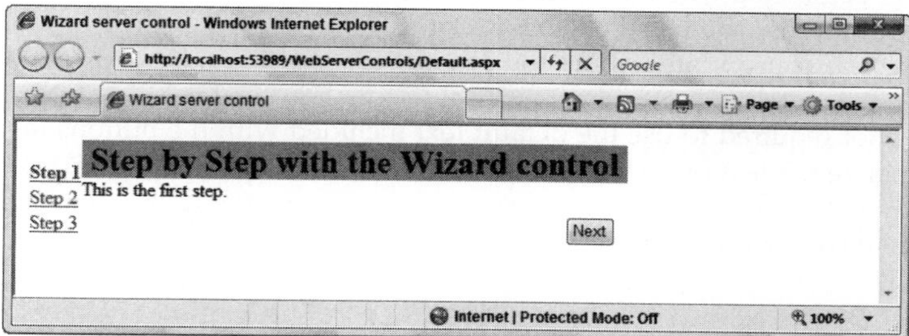

Figure 3-45

Working with the Wizard's Navigation System

As stated earlier, the Wizard control allows for a very high degree of customization — especially in the area of style. You can customize every single aspect of the process, as well as how every element appears to the end user.

Pay particular attention to the options that are available for customization of the navigation buttons. By default, the wizard steps use Next, Previous, and Finish buttons throughout the entire series of steps. From the main `<asp:Wizard>` element, you can change everything about these buttons and how they work.

First, if you look through the long list of attributes available for this element, notice that one available button is not shown by default: the Cancel button. Set the value of the `DisplayCancelButton` attribute to `True`, and a Cancel button appears within the navigation created for each and every step, including the final step in the series. Figure 3-46 shows a Cancel button in a step.

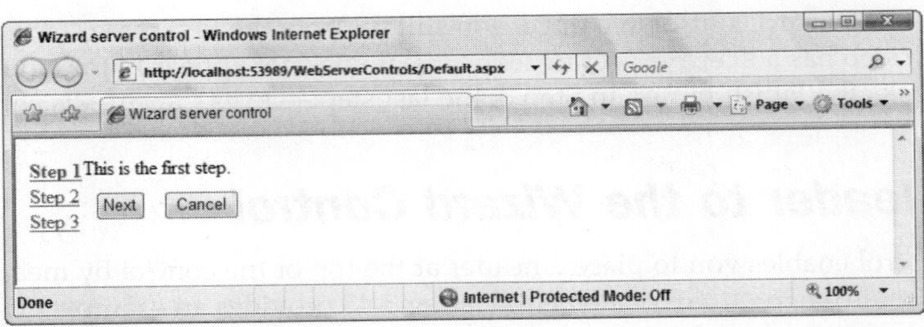

Figure 3-46

After you decide which buttons to use within the Wizard navigation, you can choose their style. By default, regular buttons appear; you can change the button style with the `CancelButtonType`, `FinishStepButtonType`, `FinishStepPreviousButtonType`, `NextStepButtonType`, `PreviousStepButtonType`, and `StartStepNextButtonType` attributes. If you use any of these button types and want all the buttons consistently styled, you must change each attribute to the same value. The possible values of these button-specific elements include `Button`, `Image`, and `Link`. `Button` is the default and means that the navigation system uses buttons. A value of `Image` enables you to use image buttons, and `Link` turns a selected item in the navigation system into a hyperlink.

In addition to these button-specific attributes of the `<asp:Wizard>` element, you can also specify a URL to which the user is directed when the user clicks either the Cancel or Finish buttons. To redirect the user with one of these buttons, you use the `CancelDestinationPageUrl` or the `FinishDestinationPageUrl` attributes and set the appropriate URL as the destination.

Finally, you are not required to use the default text included with the buttons in the navigation system. You can change the text of each of the buttons with the use of the `CancelButtonText`, `FinishStepButtonText`, `FinishStepPreviousButtonText`, `NextStepButtonText`, `PreviousStepButtonText`, and the `StartStepNextButtonText` attributes.

Utilizing Wizard Control Events

One of the most convenient capabilities of the Wizard control is that it enables you to divide large forms into logical pieces. The end user can then work systematically through each section of the form. The developer, dealing with the inputted values of the form, has a few options because of the various events that are available in the Wizard control.

The Wizard control exposes events for each of the possible steps that an end user might take when working with the control. The following table describes each of the available events.

Event	Description
`ActiveStepChanged`	Triggers when the end user moves from one step to the next. It does not matter if the step is the middle or final step in the series. This event simply covers each step change generically.
`CancelButtonClick`	Triggers when the end user clicks the Cancel button in the navigation system.
`FinishButtonClick`	Triggers when the end user clicks the Finish button in the navigation system.
`NextButtonClick`	Triggers when the end user clicks the Next button in the navigation system.
`PreviousButtonClick`	Triggers when the end user clicks the Previous button in the navigation system.
`SideBarButtonClick`	Triggers when the end user clicks one of the links contained within the sidebar navigation of the Wizard control.

By working with these events, you can create a multi-step form that saves all the end user's input information when he changes from one step to the next. You can also use the `FinishButtonClick` event to save everything that was stored in each of the steps at the end of the process. The Wizard control remembers all the end user's input in each of the steps by means of the view state in the page, which enables you to work with all these values in the last step. It also gives the end user the capability to go back to previous steps and change values before those values are saved to a data store.

The event appears in your code behind or inline code, as shown in Listing 3-44.

Listing 3-44: The FinishButtonClick event

VB

```
<script runat="server">
    Sub Wizard1_FinishButtonClick(ByVal sender As Object, _
       ByVal e As System.Web.UI.WebControls.WizardNavigationEventArgs)

    End Sub
</script>
```

C#

```
<script runat="server">
    void Wizard1_FinishButtonClick(object sender, WizardNavigationEventArgs e)
    {

    }
</script>
```

The `OnFinishButtonClick` attribute should be added to the main `<asp:Wizard>` element to point at the new `Wizard1_FinishButtonClick` event. Listing 3-45 shows how to do this.

Listing 3-45: The <asp:Wizard> Element Changes

```
<asp:Wizard ID="Wizard1" runat="server" ActiveStepIndex="0"
 OnFinishButtonClick="Wizard1_FinishButtonClick">
```

The Wizard control is one of the great new controls that enable you to break up longer workflows into more manageable pieces for your end users. By separating longer Web forms into various wizard steps, you can effectively make your forms easy to understand and less daunting to the end user.

Using the Wizard Control to Show Form Elements

So far, you have learned how to work with each of the Wizard control steps, including how to add steps to the process and how to work with the styling of the control. Now look at how you put form elements into the Wizard control to collect information from the end user in a stepped process. This is just as simple as the first examples of the Wizard control that used only text in each of the steps.

One nice thing about putting form elements in the Wizard step process is that the Wizard control remembers each input into the form elements from step to step, enabling you to save the results of the entire form at the last step. It also means that when the end user presses the Previous button, the data that he entered into the form previously is still there and can be changed.

Work through a stepped process that enters form information by building a registration process. The last step of the process saves the results to a database of your choice, although in this example, you just push the results to a Label control on the page. Listing 3-46 shows the first part of the process.

Listing 3-46: Building the form in the Wizard control

```
<asp:Wizard ID="Wizard1" runat="Server">
   <WizardSteps>
      <asp:WizardStep ID="WizardStep1" runat="server"
       Title="Provide Personal Info">
         First name:<br />
         <asp:TextBox ID="fnameTextBox" runat="server"></asp:TextBox><br />
         Last name:<br />
         <asp:TextBox ID="lnameTextBox" runat="server"></asp:TextBox><br />
         Email:<br />
         <asp:TextBox ID="emailTextBox" runat="server"></asp:TextBox><br />
      </asp:WizardStep>
      <asp:WizardStep ID="WizardStep2" runat="server"
       Title="Membership Information">
         Are you already a member of our group?<br />
         <asp:RadioButton ID="RadioButton1" runat="server" Text="Yes"
          GroupName="Member" />
         <asp:RadioButton ID="RadioButton2" runat="server" Text="No"
          GroupName="Member" />
      </asp:WizardStep>
      <asp:WizardStep ID="WizardStep3" runat="server" Title="Provided Information"
       StepType="Complete" OnActivate="WizardStep3_Activate">
```

```
            <asp:Label ID="Label1" runat="server" />
        </asp:WizardStep>
    </WizardSteps>
</asp:Wizard>
```

This Wizard control has three steps. The first step asks for the user's personal information, and the second asks for the user's membership information. The third step contains a Label control that pushes out all the information that was input. This is done through the `Activate` event that is specific for the `WizardStep` object on the third WizardStep control. The code for the `WizardStep3_Activate` event is shown in Listing 3-47.

Listing 3-47: Adding an Activate event to a WizardStep object

VB

```
Protected Sub WizardStep3_Activate(ByVal sender As Object, _
  ByVal e As System.EventArgs)

   ' You could save the inputted data to the database here instead
   Label1.Text = "First name: " & fnameTextBox.Text.ToString() & "<br>" & _
      "Last name: " & lnameTextBox.Text.ToString() & "<br>" & _
      "Email: " & emailTextBox.Text.ToString()
End Sub
```

C#

```
protected void WizardStep3_Activate(object sender, EventArgs e)
{
   Label1.Text = "First name: " + fnameTextBox.Text.ToString() + "<br>" +
      "Last name: " + lnameTextBox.Text.ToString() + "<br>" +
      "Email: " + emailTextBox.Text.ToString();
}
```

When the end user comes to the third step in the display, the `WizardStep3_Activate` method from Listing 3-47 is invoked. Using the `OnActivate` attribute in the third WizardStep control, the content provided by the end user in earlier steps is used to populate a Label control. The three steps are shown in Figure 3-47.

This example is simple and straightforward, but you can increase the complexity a little bit. Imagine you want to add another WizardStep control to the process, and you want to display it only if a user specifies that he is a member in `WizardStep2`. If he answers from the radio button selection that he is not a member, you have him skip the new step and go straight to the final step where the results are displayed in the Label control. First, add an additional `WizardStep` to the Wizard control, as shown in Listing 3-48.

Listing 3-48: Adding an additional WizardStep

```
<asp:Wizard ID="Wizard1" runat="Server">
   <WizardSteps>
      <asp:WizardStep ID="WizardStep1" runat="server"
       Title="Provide Personal Info">
         First name:<br />
         <asp:TextBox ID="fnameTextBox" runat="server"></asp:TextBox><br />
```

Continued

```
            Last name:<br />
            <asp:TextBox ID="lnameTextBox" runat="server"></asp:TextBox><br />
            Email:<br />
            <asp:TextBox ID="emailTextBox" runat="server"></asp:TextBox><br />
        </asp:WizardStep>
        <asp:WizardStep ID="WizardStep2" runat="server"
         Title="Membership Information">
            Are you already a member of our group?<br />
            <asp:RadioButton ID="RadioButton1" runat="server" Text="Yes"
             GroupName="Member" />
            <asp:RadioButton ID="RadioButton2" runat="server" Text="No"
             GroupName="Member" />
        </asp:WizardStep>
        <asp:WizardStep ID="MemberStep" runat="server"
         Title="Provide Membership Number">
            Membership Number:<br />
            <asp:TextBox ID="mNumberTextBox" runat="server"></asp:TextBox>
        </asp:WizardStep>
        <asp:WizardStep ID="WizardStep3" runat="server" Title="Provided Information"
         StepType="Complete" OnActivate="WizardStep3_Activate">
            <asp:Label ID="Label1" runat="server" />
        </asp:WizardStep>
    </WizardSteps>
</asp:Wizard>
```

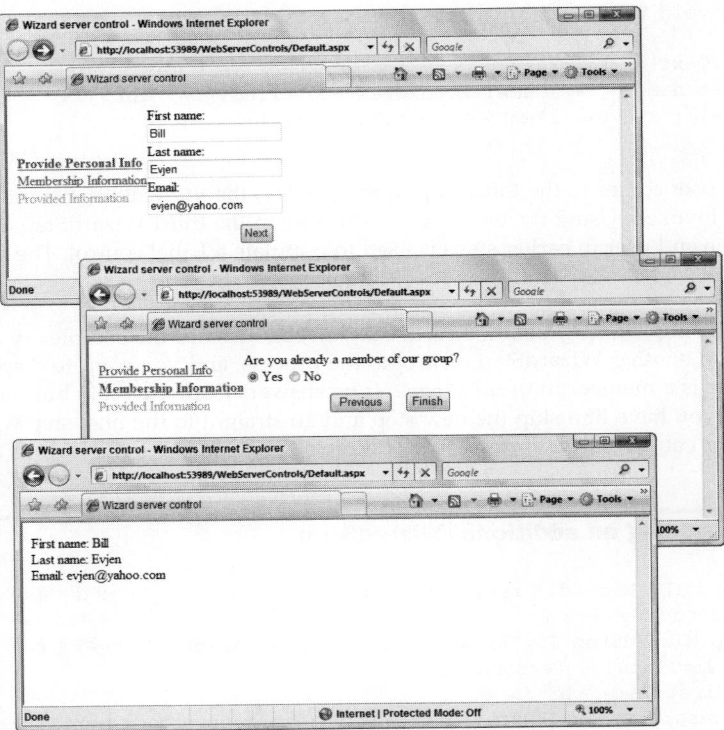

Figure 3-47

A single step was added to the workflow — one that simply asks the member for his membership number. Because you want to show this step only if the end user specifies that he is a member in `WizardStep2`, you add an event (shown in Listing 3-49) designed to check for that specification.

Listing 3-49: Applying logical checks on whether to show a step

VB

```
Sub Wizard1_NextButtonClick(ByVal sender As Object, _
  ByVal e As System.Web.UI.WebControls.WizardNavigationEventArgs)

   If e.NextStepIndex = 2 Then
      If RadioButton1.Checked = True Then
         Wizard1.ActiveStepIndex = 2
      Else
         Wizard1.ActiveStepIndex = 3
      End If
   End If
End Sub
```

C#

```
void Wizard1_NextButtonClick(object sender, WizardNavigationEventArgs e)
{
   if (e.NextStepIndex == 2) {
      if (RadioButton1.Checked == true) {
         Wizard1.ActiveStepIndex = 2; }
      else {
         Wizard1.ActiveStepIndex = 3; }
   }
}
```

To check whether you should show a specific step in the process, use the `NextButtonClick` event from the Wizard control. The event uses the `WizardNavigationEventArgs` class instead of the typical `EventArgs` class that gives you access to the `NextStepIndex` number, as well as to the `CurrentStepIndex` number.

In the example from Listing 3-49, you check whether the next step to be presented in the process is `2`. Remember that this is index `2` from a zero-based index (0, 1, 2, and so on). If it is Step `2` in the index, you check which radio button is selected from the previous WizardStep. If the `RadioButton1` control is checked (meaning that the user is a member), the next step in the process is assigned as index `2`. If the `RadioButton2` control is selected, the user is not a member, and the index is then assigned as `3` (the final step), thereby bypassing the membership step in the process.

You could also take this example and alter it a bit so that you show a WizardStep only if the user is contained within a specific role (such as Admin).

Role management is covered in Chapter 16.

Showing only a WizardStep if the user is contained within a certain role is demonstrated in Listing 3-50.

Listing 3-50: Applying logical checks on whether to show a step based upon roles

VB

```
Sub Wizard1_NextButtonClick(ByVal sender As Object, _
  ByVal e As System.Web.UI.WebControls.WizardNavigationEventArgs)
```

Continued

```
    If e.NextStepIndex = 2 Then
       If (Roles.IsUserInRole("ManagerAccess") Then
          Wizard1.ActiveStepIndex = 2
       Else
          Wizard1.ActiveStepIndex = 3
       End If
    End If
End Sub
```

C#

```
void Wizard1_NextButtonClick(object sender, WizardNavigationEventArgs e)
{
    if (e.NextStepIndex == 2) {
       if (Roles.IsUserInRole("ManagerAccess")) {
          Wizard1.ActiveStepIndex = 2; }
       else {
          Wizard1.ActiveStepIndex = 3; }
       }
    }
}
```

ImageMap Server Control

The ImageMap server control enables you to turn an image into a navigation menu. In the past, many developers would break an image into multiple pieces and put it together again in a table, reassembling the pieces into one image. When the end user clicked a particular piece of the overall image, the application picked out which piece of the image was chosen and based actions upon that particular selection.

With the new ImageMap control, you can take a single image and specify particular hotspots on the image using coordinates. An example is shown in Listing 3-51.

Listing 3-51: Specifying sections of an image that are clickable

VB

```
<%@ Page Language="VB"%>

<script runat="server">
    Protected Sub Imagemap1_Click(ByVal sender As Object, _
       ByVal e As System.Web.UI.WebControls.ImageMapEventArgs)

          Response.Write("You selected: " & e.PostBackValue)
    End Sub
</script>

<html xmlns="http://www.w3.org/1999/xhtml" >
<head runat="server">
    <title>ImageMap Control</title>
</head>
<body>
    <form id="form1" runat="server">
```

```
        <asp:ImageMap ID="Imagemap1" runat="server" ImageUrl="Kids.jpg"
         Width="300" OnClick="Imagemap1_Click" HotSpotMode="PostBack">
            <asp:RectangleHotSpot Top="0" Bottom="225" Left="0" Right="150"
             AlternateText="Sofia" PostBackValue="Sofia">
            </asp:RectangleHotSpot>
            <asp:RectangleHotSpot Top="0" Bottom="225" Left="151" Right="300"
             AlternateText="Henri" PostBackValue="Henri">
            </asp:RectangleHotSpot>
        </asp:ImageMap>
    </form>
</body>
</html>
```

C#

```
<%@ page language="C#"%>

<script runat="server">
    protected void Imagemap1_Click(object sender,
       System.Web.UI.WebControls.ImageMapEventArgs e) {

          Response.Write("You selected: " + e.PostBackValue);
    }
</script>
```

This page brings up an image of my children. If you click the left side of the image, you select Sofia, and if you click the right side of the image, you select Henri. You know which child you selected through a `Response.Write` statement, as shown in Figure 3-48.

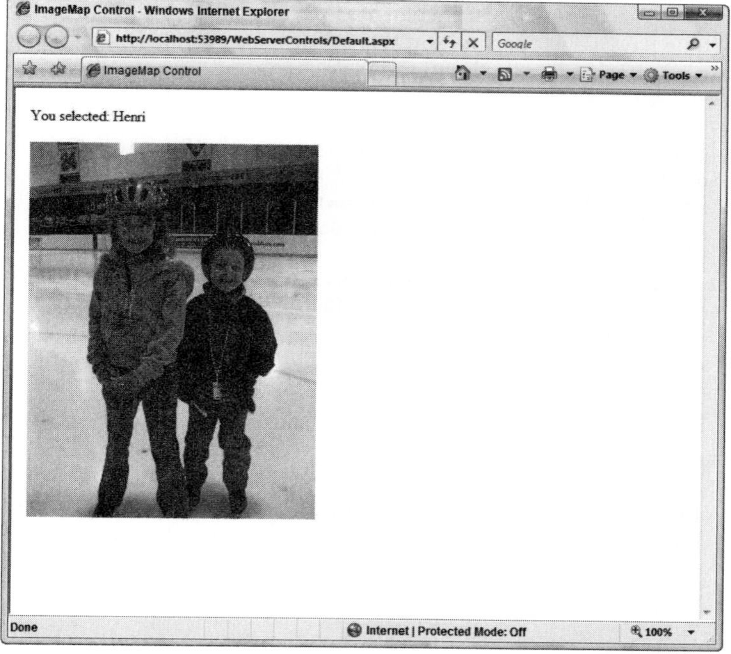

Figure 3-48

The ImageMap control enables you to specify hotspots in a couple of different ways. From the example in Listing 3-51, you can see that hotspots are placed in a rectangular fashion using the `<asp:RectangleHotSpot>` element. The control takes the `Top`, `Bottom`, `Left`, and `Right` coordinates of the rectangle that is to be the hotspot. Besides the `<asp:RectangleHotSpot>` control, you can also use the `<asp:CircleHotSpot>` and the `<asp:PolygonHotSpot>` controls. Each control takes coordinates appropriate to its shape.

After you define the hotspots on the image, you can respond to the end-user click of the hotspot in several ways. You first specify how to deal with the hotspot clicks in the root `<asp:ImageMap>` element with the use the `HotSpotMode` attribute.

The `HotSpotMode` attribute can take the values `PostBack`, `Navigate`, or `InActive`. In the previous example, the `HotSpotMode` value is set to `PostBack` — meaning that after the end user clicks the hotspot, you want to postback to the server and deal with the click at that point.

Because the `HotSpotMode` is set to `PostBack` and you have created several hotspots, you must determine which hotspot is selected. You make this determination by giving each hotspot (`<asp:RectangleHotSpot>`) a postback value with the `PostBackValue` attribute. The example uses `Sofia` as the value of the first hotspot, and `Henri` as the value for the second.

The `PostBackValue` attribute is also the helper text that appears in the browser (in the yellow box) directly below the mouse cursor when the end user hovers the mouse over the hotspot.

After the user clicks one of the hotspots, the event procedure displays the value that was selected in a `Response.Write` statement.

Instead of posting back to the server, you can also navigate to an entirely different URL when a particular hotspot is selected. To accomplish this, change the `HotSpotMode` attribute in the main `<asp:ImageMap>` element to the value `Navigate`. Then, within the `<asp:RectangleHotSpot>` elements, simply use the `NavigateUrl` attribute and assign the location to which the end user should be directed if that particular hotspot is clicked:

```
<asp:ImageMap ID="Imagemap1" runat="server" ImageUrl="kids.jpg"
 HotSpotMode="Navigate">
   <asp:RectangleHotSpot Top="0" Bottom="225" Left="0" Right="150"
    AlternateText="Sofia" NavigateUrl="SofiaPage.aspx">
   </asp:RectangleHotSpot>
   <asp:RectangleHotSpot Top="0" Bottom="225" Left="151" Right="300"
    AlternateText="Henri" NavigateUrl="HenriPage.aspx">
   </asp:RectangleHotSpot>
</asp:ImageMap>
```

Summary

This chapter explored numerous server controls, their capabilities, and the features they provide. With ASP.NET 3.5, you have more than 50 new server controls at your disposal.

Because you have so many server controls at your disposal when you are creating your ASP.NET applications, you have to think carefully about which is the best control for the task. Many controls seem similar, but they offer different features. These controls guarantee that you can build the best possible applications for all browsers.

Server controls are some of the most useful tools you will find in your ASP.NET arsenal. They are quite useful and can save you a lot of time. This chapter introduced you to some of these controls and to the different ways you might incorporate them into your next projects. All these controls are wonderful options to use on any of your ASP.NET pages and make it much easier to develop the functionality that your pages require.

4

Validation Server Controls

When you look at the Toolbox window in Visual Studio 2008 — especially if you've read Chapters 2 and 3, which cover the various server controls at your disposal — you may be struck by the number of server controls that come with ASP.NET 3.5. This chapter takes a look at a specific type of server control you find in the Toolbox window: the *validation server control.*

Validation server controls are a series of controls that enable you to work with the information your end users input into the form elements of the applications you build. These controls work to ensure the validity of the data being placed in the form.

Before you learn how to use these controls, however, this chapter will first take a look at the process of validation.

Understanding Validation

People have been constructing Web applications for a number of years. Usually the motivation is to provide or gather information. In this chapter, you focus on the information-gathering aspect of Web applications. If you collect data with your applications, collecting *valid* data should be important to you. If the information isn't valid, there really isn't much point in collecting it.

Validation comes in degrees. Validation is a set of rules that you apply to the data you collect. These rules can be many or few and enforced either strictly or in a lax manner: It really depends on you. No perfect validation process exists because some users may find a way to cheat to some degree, no matter what rules you establish. The trick is to find the right balance of the fewest rules and the proper strictness, without compromising the usability of the application.

The data you collect for validation comes from the Web forms you provide in your applications. Web forms are made up of different types of HTML elements that are constructed using raw HTML form elements, ASP.NET HTML server controls, or ASP.NET Web Form server controls. In the end, your forms are made up of many different types of HTML elements, such as text boxes, radio buttons, check boxes, drop-down lists, and more.

As you work through this chapter, you see the different types of validation rules that you can apply to your form elements. Remember that you have no way to validate the *truthfulness* of the information you collect; instead, you apply rules that respond to such questions as

- Is something entered in the text box?
- Is the data entered in the text box in the form of an e-mail address?

Notice from these questions that you can apply more than a single validation rule to an HTML form element (you'll see examples of this later in this chapter). In fact, you can apply as many rules to a single element as you want. Applying more rules to elements increases the strictness of the validation applied to the data.

Just remember that data collection on the Internet is one of the Internet's most important features, so you must make sure that the data you collect has value and meaning. You ensure this by eliminating any chance that the information collected does not abide by the rules you outline.

Client-Side versus Server-Side Validation

If you are new to Web application development, you might not be aware of the difference between client-side and server-side validation. Suppose that the end user clicks the Submit button on a form after filling out some information. What happens in ASP.NET is that this form is packaged in a *request* and sent to the server where the application resides. At this point in the request/response cycle, you can run validation checks on the information submitted. If you do this, it is called *server-side validation* because it occurs on the server.

On the other hand, it is also possible to supply a script (usually in the form of JavaScript) in the page that is posted to the end user's browser to perform validations on the data entered in the form *before* the form is posted back to the originating server. If this is the case, *client-side validation* has occurred.

Both types of validation have their pros and cons. Active Server Pages 2.0/3.0 developers (from the classic ASP days) are quite aware of these pros and cons because they have probably performed all the validation chores themselves. Many developers spent a considerable amount of their classic ASP programming days coding various validation techniques for performance and security.

Client-side validation is quick and responsive for the end user. It is something end users expect of the forms that they work with. If something is wrong with the form, using client-side validation ensures that the end user knows this as soon as possible. Client-side validation also pushes the processing power required of validation to the client meaning that you don't need to spin CPU cycles on the server to process the same information because the client can do the work for you.

With this said, client-side validation is the more insecure form of validation. When a page is generated in an end user's browser, this end user can look at the code of the page quite easily (simply by right-clicking his mouse in the browser and selecting View Code). When he does this, in addition to seeing the HTML code for the page, he can also see all the JavaScript that is associated with the page. If you are validating your form client-side, it doesn't take much for the crafty hacker to repost a form (containing the values he wants in it) to your server as valid. There are also the cases in which clients have simply disabled the client-scripting capabilities in their browsers — thereby making your validations useless.

Therefore, client-side validation should be considered a convenience and a courtesy to the end user and never as a security mechanism.

The more secure form of validation is server-side validation. Server-side validation means that the validation checks are performed on the server instead of on the client. It is more secure because these checks cannot be easily bypassed. Instead, the form data values are checked using server code (C# or VB) on the server. If the form isn't valid, the page is posted back to the client as invalid. Although it is more secure, server-side validation can be slow. It is sluggish simply because the page has to be posted to a remote location and checked. Your end user might not be the happiest surfer in the world if, after waiting 20 seconds for a form to post, he is told his e-mail address isn't in the correct format.

So what is the correct path? Well, actually, both! The best approach is always to perform client-side validation first and then, after the form passes and is posted to the server, to perform the validation checks again using server-side validation. This approach provides the best of both worlds. It is secure because hackers can't simply bypass the validation. They may bypass the client-side validation, but they quickly find that their form data is checked once again on the server after it is posted. This validation technique is also highly effective — giving you both the quickness and snappiness of client-side validation.

ASP.NET Validation Server Controls

In the classic ASP days, developers could spend a great deal of their time dealing with different form validation schemes. For this reason, with the initial release of ASP.NET, the ASP.NET team introduced a series of validation server controls meant to make it a snap to implement sound validation for forms.

ASP.NET not only introduces form validations as server controls, but it also makes these controls rather smart. As stated earlier, one of the tasks of classic ASP developers was to determine where to perform form validation — either on the client or on the server. The ASP.NET validation server controls eliminate this dilemma because ASP.NET performs browser detection when generating the ASP.NET page and makes decisions based on the information it gleans.

This means that if the browser can support the JavaScript that ASP.NET can send its way, the validation occurs on the client-side. If the client cannot support the JavaScript meant for client-side validation, this JavaScript is omitted and the validation occurs on the server.

The best part about this scenario is that even if client-side validation is initiated on a page, ASP.NET still performs the server-side validation when it receives the submitted page, thereby ensuring security won't be compromised. This decisive nature of the validation server controls means that you can build your ASP.NET Web pages to be the best they can possibly be — rather than dumbing-down your Web applications for the lowest common denominator.

Presently, six validation controls are available to you in ASP.NET 3.5. No new validation server controls have been added to ASP.NET since the initial release of the technology, but ASP.NET 2.0 introduced some new features, such as validation groups and new JavaScript capabilities. Both these features are discussed in this chapter. The available validation server controls include

- RequiredFieldValidator
- CompareValidator

- RangeValidator
- RegularExpressionValidator
- CustomValidator
- ValidationSummary

Working with ASP.NET validation server controls is no different from working with any other ASP.NET server control. Each of these controls allows you to drag and drop it onto a design surface or to work with it directly from the code of your ASP.NET page. These controls can also be modified so that they appear exactly as you wish — ensuring the visual uniqueness that your applications might require. You see some aspects of this throughout this chapter.

> **If the ASP.NET Validation controls don't meet your needs, you can certainly write your own custom validation controls. However, there are third-party controls available such as Peter Blum's Validation and More (VAM) from** `www.peterblum.com/VAM`**, which includes over 40 ASP.NET validation controls.**

The following table describes the functionality of each of the available validation server controls.

Validation Server Control	Description
RequiredFieldValidator	Ensures that the user does not skip a form entry field.
CompareValidator	Allows for comparisons between the user's input and another item using a comparison operator (equals, greater than, less than, and so on).
RangeValidator	Checks the user's input based upon a lower- and upper-level range of numbers or characters.
RegularExpressionValidator	Checks that the user's entry matches a pattern defined by a regular expression. This is a good control to use to check e-mail addresses and phone numbers.
CustomValidator	Checks the user's entry using custom-coded validation logic.
ValidationSummary	Displays all the error messages from the validators in one specific spot on the page.

Validation Causes

Validation doesn't just happen; it occurs in response to an event. In most cases, it is a button click event. The Button, LinkButton, and ImageButton server controls all have the capability to cause a page's form validation to initiate. This is the default behavior. Dragging and dropping a Button server control onto your form will give you the following initial result:

```
<asp:Button ID="Button1" Runat="server" Text="Button" />
```

If you look through the properties of the Button control, you can see that the `CausesValidation` property is set to `True`. As stated, this is the default behavior — all buttons on the page, no matter how many there are, cause the form validation to fire.

If you have multiple buttons on an ASP.NET page, and you don't want each and every button to initiate the form validation, you can set the `CausesValidation` property to `False` for all the buttons you want to ignore the validation process (for example, a form's Cancel button):

```
<asp:Button ID="Button1" Runat="server" Text="Cancel" CausesValidation="False" />
```

The RequiredFieldValidator Server Control

The RequiredFieldValidator control simply checks to see if *something* was entered into the HTML form element. It is a simple validation control, but it is one of the most frequently used. You must have a RequiredFieldValidator control for each form element on which you wish to enforce a *value-required* rule.

Listing 4-1 shows a simple use of the RequiredFieldValidator control.

Listing 4-1: A simple use of the RequiredFieldValidator server control

VB

```
<%@ Page Language="VB" %>

<script runat="server">
   Protected Sub Button1_Click(ByVal sender As Object, ByVal e As System.EventArgs)
      If Page.IsValid Then
        Label1.Text = "Page is valid!"
      End If
   End Sub
</script>

<html xmlns="http://www.w3.org/1999/xhtml">
<head runat="server">
    <title>RequiredFieldValidator</title>
</head>
<body>
    <form id="form1" runat="server">
    <div>
        <asp:TextBox ID="TextBox1" Runat="server"></asp:TextBox>
        <asp:RequiredFieldValidator ID="RequiredFieldValidator1"
         Runat="server" Text="Required!" ControlToValidate="TextBox1">
        </asp:RequiredFieldValidator>
        <br />
        <asp:Button ID="Button1" Runat="server" Text="Submit"
         OnClick="Button1_Click" />
        <br />
        <br />
        <asp:Label ID="Label1" Runat="server"></asp:Label>
```

Continued

```
        </div>
        </form>
    </body>
    </html>
```

C#

```
<%@ Page Language="C#" %>

<script runat="server">
    protected void Button1_Click(Object sender, EventArgs e) {
       if (Page.IsValid) {
        Label1.Text = "Page is valid!";
       }
    }
</script>
```

Build and run this page. You are then presented with a simple text box and button on the page. Don't enter any value inside the text box, and click the Submit button. The result is shown in Figure 4-1.

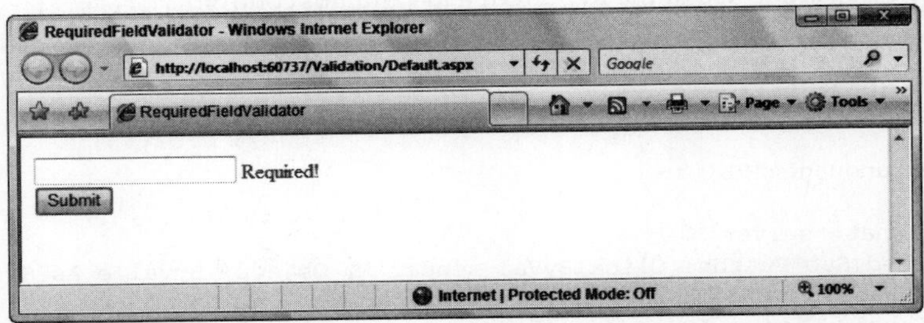

Figure 4-1

Now look at the code from this example. First, nothing is different about the TextBox, Button, or Label controls. They are constructed just as they would be if you were not using any type of form validation. This page does contain a simple RequiredFieldValidator control, however. Several properties of this control are especially notable because you will use them in most of the validation server controls you create.

The first property to look at is the `Text` property. This property is the value that is shown to the end user via the Web page if the validation fails. In this case, it is a simple `Required!` string. The second property to look at is the `ControlToValidate` property. This property is used to make an association between this validation server control and the ASP.NET form element that requires the validation. In this case, the value specifies the only element in the form — the text box.

As you can see from this example, the error message is constructed from an attribute within the `<asp:RequiredFieldValidator>` control. You can also accomplish this same task by using the `Text` attribute, as shown in Listing 4-2.

Listing 4-2: Using the Text attribute

```
<asp:RequiredFieldValidator ID="RequiredFieldValidator1"
 Runat="server" Text="Required!" ControlToValidate="TextBox1">
</asp:RequiredFieldValidator>
```

You can also express this error message between the <asp:RequiredFieldValidator> opening and closing nodes, as shown in Listing 4-3.

Listing 4-3: Placing values between nodes

```
<asp:RequiredFieldValidator ID="RequiredFieldValidator1"
 Runat="server" ControlToValidate="TextBox1">
 Required!
</asp:RequiredFieldValidator>
```

Looking at the Results Generated

Again, the RequiredFieldValidator control uses client-side validation if the browser allows for such an action. You can see the client-side validation for yourself (if your browser allows for this) by right-clicking on the page and selecting View Source from the menu. In the page code, you see the JavaScript shown in Listing 4-4.

Listing 4-4: The generated JavaScript

```
... page markup removed for clarity here ...

<script type="text/javascript">
<!--
function WebForm_OnSubmit() {
if (ValidatorOnSubmit() == false) return false;
return true;
}
// -->
</script>

... page markup removed for clarity here ...

<script type="text/javascript">
<!--
var Page_Validators =  new
Array(document.getElementById("RequiredFieldValidator1"));// -->
</script>

<script type="text/javascript">
<!--
var RequiredFieldValidator1 = document.all ?
  document.all["RequiredFieldValidator1"] :
  document.getElementById("RequiredFieldValidator1");
```

Continued

```
RequiredFieldValidator1.controltovalidate = "TextBox1";
RequiredFieldValidator1.text = "Required!";
RequiredFieldValidator1.evaluationfunction =
  "RequiredFieldValidatorEvaluateIsValid";
RequiredFieldValidator1.initialvalue = "";
// -->
</script>

... page markup removed for clarity here ...

<script type="text/javascript">
<!--
var Page_ValidationActive = false;
if (typeof(ValidatorOnLoad) == "function") {
    ValidatorOnLoad();
}

function ValidatorOnSubmit() {
    if (Page_ValidationActive) {
        return ValidatorCommonOnSubmit();
    }
    else {
        return true;
    }
}
// -->
</script>
```

In the page code, you may also notice some changes to the form elements (the former server controls) that deal with the submission of the form and the associated validation requirements.

Using the InitialValue Property

Another important property when working with the RequireFieldValidator control is the `InitialValue` property. Sometimes you have form elements that are populated with some default properties (for example, from a data store), and these form elements might present the end user with values that require changes before the form can be submitted to the server.

When using the `InitialValue` property, you specify to the RequiredFieldValidator control the initial text of the element. The end user is then required to change that text value before he can submit the form. Listing 4-5 shows an example of using this property.

Listing 4-5: Working with the InitialValue property

```
<asp:TextBox ID="TextBox1" Runat="server">My Initial Value</asp:TextBox>
  
<asp:RequiredFieldValidator ID="RequiredFieldValidator1"
 Runat="server" Text="Please change the value of the textbox!"
 ControlToValidate="TextBox1" InitialValue="My Initial Value">
</asp:RequiredFieldValidator>
```

In this case, you can see that the `InitialValue` property contains a value of `My Initial Value`. When the page is built and run, the text box contains this value as well. The RequiredFieldValidator control requires a change in this value for the page to be considered valid.

Disallowing Blank Entries and Requiring Changes at the Same Time

In the preceding example of the use of the `InitialValue` property, an interesting problem arises. First, if you run the associated example, one thing the end user can do to get past the form validation is to submit the page with no value entered in this particular text box. A blank text box does not fire a validation error because the RequiredFieldValidator control is now reconstructed to force the end user only to *change* the default value of the text box (which he did when he removed the old value). When you reconstruct the RequiredFieldValidator control in this manner, nothing in the validation rule requires that *something* be entered in the text box — just that the initial value be changed. It is possible for the user to completely bypass the form validation process by just removing anything entered in this text box.

There is a way around this, however, and it goes back to what we were saying earlier about how a form is made up of multiple validation rules — some of which are assigned to the same form element. To both require a change to the initial value of the text box and to disallow a blank entry (thereby making the element a required element), you must put an additional RequiredFieldValidator control on the page. This second RequiredFieldValidator control is associated with the same text box as the first RequiredFieldValidator control. This is illustrated in the example shown in Listing 4-6.

Listing 4-6: Using two RequiredFieldValidator controls for one form element

```
<asp:TextBox ID="TextBox1" Runat="server">My Initial Value</asp:TextBox> 

<asp:RequiredFieldValidator ID="RequiredFieldValidator1" Runat="server"
 Text="Please change value" ControlToValidate="TextBox1"
 InitialValue="My Initial Value"></asp:RequiredFieldValidator>

<asp:RequiredFieldValidator ID="RequiredFieldValidator2" Runat="server"
 Text="Do not leave empty" ControlToValidate="TextBox1">
</asp:RequiredFieldValidator>
```

In this example, you can see that the text box does indeed have two RequiredFieldValidator controls associated with it. The first, `RequiredFieldValidator1`, requires a change to the default value of the text box through the use of the `InitialValue` property. The second RequiredFieldValidator control, `RequiredFieldValidator2`, simply makes the `TextBox1` control a form element that requires a value. You get the behavior you want by applying two validation rules to a single form element.

Validating Drop-Down Lists with the RequiredFieldValidator Control

So far, you have seen a lot of examples of using the RequiredFieldValidator control with a series of text boxes, but you can just as easily use this validation control with other form elements as well.

For example, you can use the RequiredFieldValidator control with an `<asp:DropDownList>` server control. To see this, suppose that you have a drop-down list that requires the end user to select her profession from a list of items. The first line of the drop-down list includes instructions to the end user about what to select, and you want to make this a required form element as well. The code to do this is shown in Listing 4-7.

Listing 4-7: Drop-down list validations

```
<asp:DropDownList id="DropDownList1" runat="server">
   <asp:ListItem Selected="True">Select a profession</asp:ListItem>
   <asp:ListItem>Programmer</asp:ListItem>
   <asp:ListItem>Lawyer</asp:ListItem>
   <asp:ListItem>Doctor</asp:ListItem>
   <asp:ListItem>Artist</asp:ListItem>
</asp:DropDownList>
   
<asp:RequiredFieldValidator id="RequiredFieldValidator1"
  runat="server" Text="Please make a selection"
  ControlToValidate="DropDownList1"
  InitialValue="Select a profession">
</asp:RequiredFieldValidator>
```

Just as when you work with the text box, the RequiredFieldValidator control in this example associates itself with the DropDownList control using the `ControlToValidate` property. The drop-down list to which the validation control is bound has an initial value — `Select a profession`. You obviously don't want your end user to retain that value when she posts the form back to the server. So again, you use the `InitialValue` property of the RequiredFieldValidator control. The value of this property is assigned to the initial selected value of the drop-down list. This forces the end user to select one of the provided professions in the drop-down list before she is able to post the form.

The CompareValidator Server Control

The CompareValidator control allows you to make comparisons between two form elements as well as to compare values contained within form elements to constants that you specify. For instance, you can specify that a form element's value must be an integer and greater than a specified number. You can also state that values must be strings, dates, or other data types that are at your disposal.

Validating Against Other Controls

One of the more common ways of using the CompareValidator control is to make a comparison between two form elements. For example, suppose that you have an application that requires users to have passwords in order to access the site. You create one text box asking for the user's password and a second text box that asks the user to confirm the password. Because the text box is in password mode, the end user cannot see what she is typing — just the number of characters that she has typed. To reduce the chances of the end user mistyping her password and inputting this incorrect password into the system, you ask her to confirm the password. After the form is input into the system, you simply have to make a comparison between the two text boxes to see if they match. If they match, it is likely that the end user typed the password correctly, and you can input the password choice into the system. If the two text boxes do not match, you want the form to be invalid. The following example, in Listing 4-8, demonstrates this situation.

Listing 4-8: Using the CompareValidator to test values against other control values

VB

```
<%@ Page Language="VB" %>
<script runat="server">
```

```
    Protected Sub Button1_Click(sender As Object, e As EventArgs)
       If Page.IsValid Then
          Label1.Text = "Passwords match"
       End If
    End Sub

</script>

<html xmlns="http://www.w3.org/1999/xhtml">
<head runat="server">
    <title>CompareFieldValidator</title>
</head>
<body>
    <form runat="server" id="Form1">
        <p>
            Password<br>
            <asp:TextBox ID="TextBox1" Runat="server"
             TextMode="Password"></asp:TextBox>
              
            <asp:CompareValidator ID="CompareValidator1"
             Runat="server" Text="Passwords do not match!"
             ControlToValidate="TextBox2"
             ControlToCompare="TextBox1"></asp:CompareValidator>
        </p>
        <p>
            Confirm Password<br>
            <asp:TextBox ID="TextBox2" Runat="server"
             TextMode="Password"></asp:TextBox>
        </p>
        <p>
            <asp:Button ID="Button1" OnClick="Button1_Click"
             Runat="server" Text="Login"></asp:Button>
        </p>
        <p>
            <asp:Label ID="Label1" Runat="server"></asp:Label>
        </p>
    </form>
</body>
</html>
```

C#

```
<%@ Page Language="C#" %>
<script runat="server">

    protected void Button1_Click(Object sender, EventArgs e) {
       if (Page.IsValid)
          Label1.Text = "Passwords match";
    }

</script>
```

Looking at the CompareValidator control on the form, you can see that it is similar to the Required-FieldValidator control. The CompareValidator control has a property called `ControlToValidate` that associates itself with one of the form elements on the page. In this case, you need only a single CompareValidator control on the page because a single comparison is made. In this example, you are making a comparison between the value of `TextBox2` and that of `TextBox1`. Therefore, you use the `ControlToCompare` property. This specifies what value is compared to `TextBox2`. In this case, the value is `TextBox1`.

It's as simple as that. If the two text boxes do not match after the page is posted by the end user, the value of the `Text` property from the CompareValidator control is displayed in the browser. An example of this is shown in Figure 4-2.

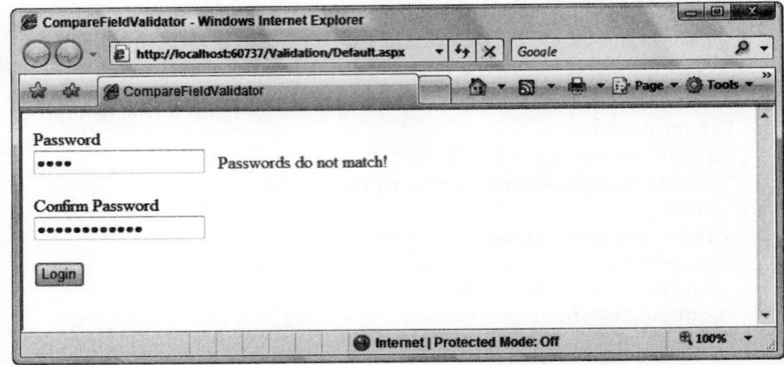

Figure 4-2

Validating Against Constants

Besides being able to validate values against values in other controls, you can also use the Compare Validator control to make comparisons against constants of specific data types. For example, suppose you have a text box on your registration form that asks for the age of the user. In most cases, you want to get back an actual number and not something such as `aa` or `bb` as a value. Listing 4-9 shows you how to ensure that you get back an actual number.

Listing 4-9: Using the CompareValidator to validate against constants

```
Age:
<asp:TextBox ID="TextBox1" Runat="server" MaxLength="3">
</asp:TextBox>
 
<asp:CompareValidator ID="CompareValidator1" Runat="server"
  Text="You must enter a number"
  ControlToValidate="TextBox1" Type="Integer"
  Operator="DataTypeCheck"></asp:CompareValidator>
```

In this example, the end user is required to enter in a number into the text box. If she attempts to bypass the validation by entering a fake value that contains anything other than a number, the page is identified as invalid, and the CompareValidator control displays the value of the `Text` property.

To specify the data types that you want to use in these comparisons, you simply use the `Type` property. The `Type` property can take the following values:

- `Currency`
- `Date`
- `Double`
- `Integer`
- `String`

Not only can you make sure that what is entered is of a specific data type, but you can also make sure that what is entered is valid when compared to specific constants. For instance, you can make sure what is entered in a form element is greater than, less than, equal to, greater than or equal to, or less than or equal to a specified value. An example of this is illustrated in Listing 4-10.

Listing 4-10: Making comparisons with the CompareValidator control

```
Age:
<asp:TextBox ID="TextBox1" Runat="server"></asp:TextBox>
   
<asp:CompareValidator ID="CompareValidator1" Runat="server"
  Operator="GreaterThan" ValueToCompare="18"
  ControlToValidate="TextBox1"
  Text="You must be older than 18 to join" Type="Integer">
</asp:CompareValidator>
```

In this case, the CompareValidator control not only associates itself with the `TextBox1` control and requires that the value must be an integer, but it also uses the `Operator` and the `ValueToCompare` properties to ensure that the number is greater than 18. Therefore, if the end user enters a value of 18 or less, the validation fails, and the page is considered invalid.

The `Operator` property can take one of the following values:

- `Equal`
- `NotEqual`
- `GreaterThan`
- `GreaterThanEqual`
- `LessThan`
- `LessThanEqual`
- `DataTypeCheck`

The `ValueToCompare` property is where you place the constant value used in the comparison. In the preceding example, it is the number `18`.

The RangeValidator Server Control

The RangeValidator control is quite similar to that of the CompareValidator control, but it makes sure that the end-user value or selection provided is between a specified range as opposed to being just greater than or less than a specified constant. For an example of this, go back to the text-box element that asks for the age of the end user and performs a validation on the value provided. This is illustrated in Listing 4-11.

Listing 4-11: Using the RangeValidator control to test an integer value

```
Age:
<asp:TextBox ID="TextBox1" Runat="server"></asp:TextBox>
  
<asp:RangeValidator ID="RangeValidator1" Runat="server"
 ControlToValidate="TextBox1" Type="Integer"
 Text="You must be between 30 and 40"
 MaximumValue="40" MinimumValue="30"></asp:RangeValidator>
```

In this example, this page consists of a text box asking for the age of the end user. The RangeValidator control makes an analysis of the value provided and makes sure the value is somewhere in the range of 30 to 40. This is done using the `MaximumValue` and `MinimumValue` properties. The RangeValidator control also makes sure what is entered is an integer data type. It uses the `Type` property, which is set to `Integer`. The collection of screenshots in Figure 4-3 shows this example in action.

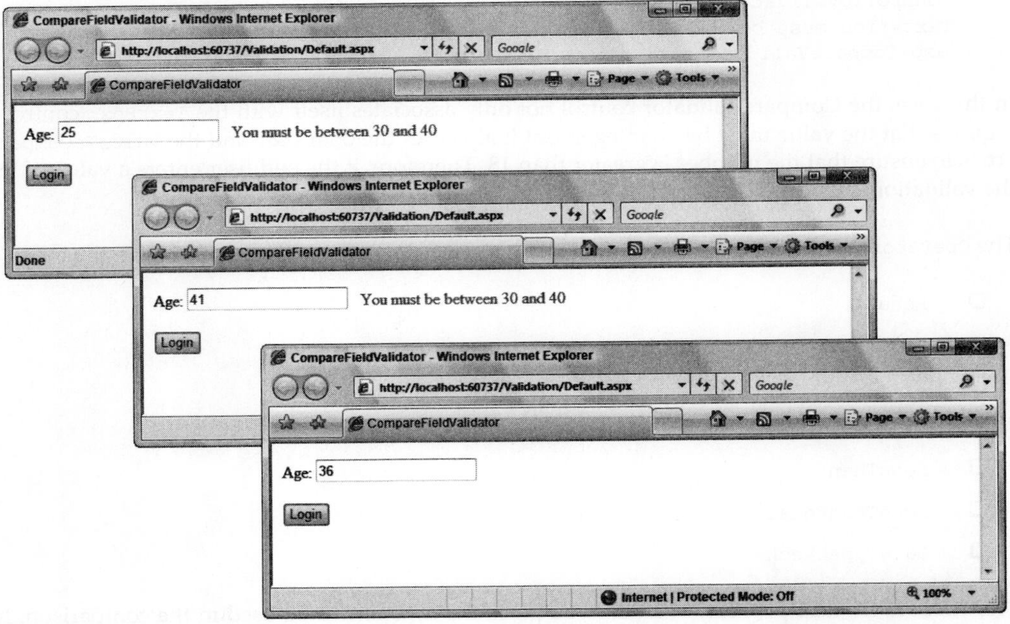

Figure 4-3

As you can see from the screenshots in Figure 4-3, a value of less than 30 causes the RangeValidator control to fire, as does a number greater than 40. A value that is somewhere between 30 and 40 (in this case 34) conforms to the validation rule of the control.

The RangeValidator control is not only about validating numbers (although it is most often used in this fashion). It can also be about validating a range of string characters as well as other items, including calendar dates. By default, the `Type` property of any of the validation controls is set to `String`. You can use the RangeValidator control to make sure what is entered in another server control (such as a calendar control) is within a certain range of dates.

For example, suppose that you are building a Web form that asks for a customer's arrival date, and the arrival date needs to be within two weeks of the current date. You can use the RangeValidator control to test for these scenarios quite easily.

Because the date range that you want to check is dynamically generated, you assign the `MaximumValue` and `MinimumValue` attribute programmatically in the `Page_Load` event. In the Designer, your sample page for this example should look like Figure 4-4.

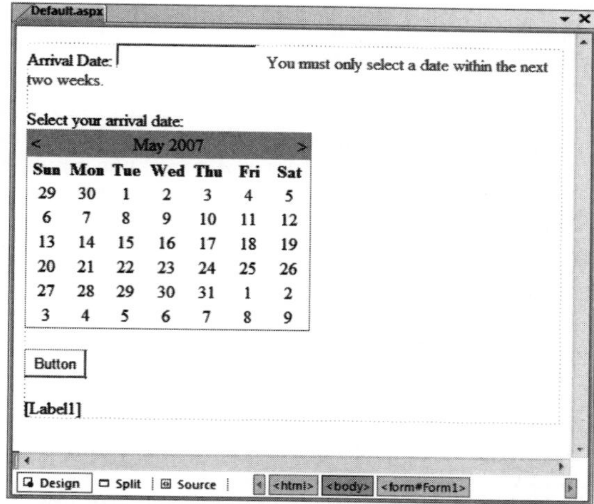

Figure 4-4

The idea is that the end user will select a date from the Calendar control, which will then populate the TextBox control. Then, when the end user clicks the form's button, he is notified if the date selected is invalid. If the date selected is valid, that date is presented through the Label control on the page. The code for this example is presented in Listing 4-12.

Listing 4-12: Using the RangeValidator control to test a string date value

VB

```
<%@ Page Language="VB" %>

<script runat="server">
    Protected Sub Page_Load(ByVal sender As Object, ByVal e As System.EventArgs)
        RangeValidator1.MinimumValue = DateTime.Now.ToShortDateString()
        RangeValidator1.MaximumValue = DateTime.Now.AddDays(14).ToShortDateString()
    End Sub

    Protected Sub Calendar1_SelectionChanged(ByVal sender As Object, _
      ByVal e As System.EventArgs)
```

Continued

```
        TextBox1.Text = Calendar1.SelectedDate.ToShortDateString()
    End Sub

    Protected Sub Button1_Click(ByVal sender As Object, _
      ByVal e As System.EventArgs)
        If Page.IsValid Then
            Label1.Text = "You are set to arrive on: " & TextBox1.Text
        End If
    End Sub
</script>

<html xmlns="http://www.w3.org/1999/xhtml">
<head runat="server">
    <title>Date Validation Check</title>
</head>
<body>
    <form id="form1" runat="server">
        Arrival Date:
        <asp:TextBox ID="TextBox1" runat="server"></asp:TextBox> 
        <asp:RangeValidator ID="RangeValidator1" runat="server"
         Text="You must only select a date within the next two weeks."
         ControlToValidate="TextBox1" Type="Date"></asp:RangeValidator><br />
        <br />
        Select your arrival date:<br />
        <asp:Calendar ID="Calendar1" runat="server"
         OnSelectionChanged="Calendar1_SelectionChanged"></asp:Calendar>
         
        <br />
        <asp:Button ID="Button1" runat="server" Text="Button"
         OnClick="Button1_Click" />
        <br />
        <br />
        <asp:Label ID="Label1" runat="server"></asp:Label>
    </form>
</body>
</html>
```

C#

```
<%@ Page Language="C#" %>

<script runat="server">
    protected void Page_Load(object sender, EventArgs e)
    {
        RangeValidator1.MinimumValue = DateTime.Now.ToShortDateString();
        RangeValidator1.MaximumValue =
           DateTime.Now.AddDays(14).ToShortDateString();
    }

    protected void Calendar1_SelectionChanged(object sender, EventArgs e)
    {
        TextBox1.Text = Calendar1.SelectedDate.ToShortDateString();
    }
```

```
        protected void Button1_Click(object sender, EventArgs e)
        {
            if (Page.IsValid)
            {
                Label1.Text = "You are set to arrive on: " + TextBox1.Text.ToString();
            }
        }
    </script>
```

From this code, you can see that when the page is loaded, the `MinimumValue` and `MaximumValue` attributes are assigned a dynamic value. In this case, the `MinimumValue` gets the `DateTime.Now.ToShortDateString()` value, while the `MaximumValue` gets a date of 14 days later.

After the end user selects a date, the selected date is populated in the `TextBox1` control using the `Calendar1_SelectionChanged` event. After a date is selected and the button on the page is clicked, the `Button1_Click` event is fired and the page is checked for form validity using the `Page.IsValid` property. An invalid page will give you the result shown in Figure 4-5.

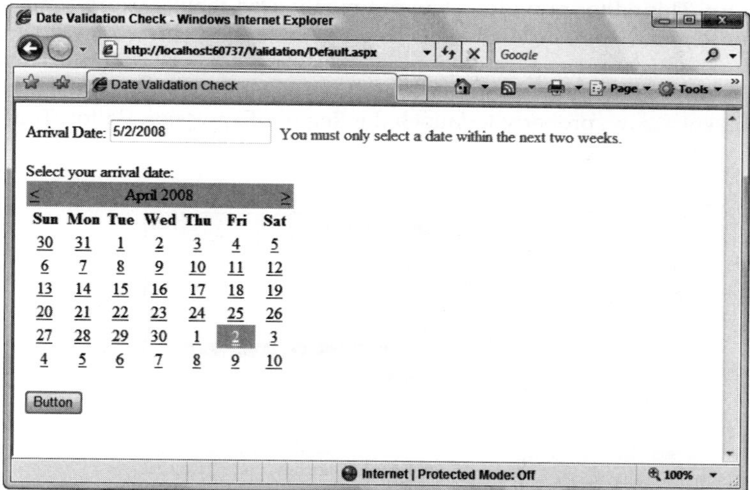

Figure 4-5

The RegularExpressionValidator Server Control

One exciting control that developers like to use is the RegularExpressionValidator control. This control offers a lot of flexibility when you apply validation rules to your Web forms. Using the RegularExpressionValidator control, you can check a user's input based on a pattern that you define using a regular expression.

This means that you can define a structure that a user's input will be applied against to see if its structure matches the one that you define. For instance, you can define that the structure of the user input must be in the form of an e-mail address or an Internet URL; if it doesn't match this definition, the page is considered invalid. Listing 4-13 shows you how to validate what is input into a text box by making sure it is in the form of an e-mail address.

Listing 4-13: Making sure the text-box value is an e-mail address

```
Email:
<asp:TextBox ID="TextBox1" Runat="server"></asp:TextBox>
   
<asp:RegularExpressionValidator ID="RegularExpressionValidator1"
  Runat="server" ControlToValidate="TextBox1"
  Text="You must enter an email address"
  ValidationExpression="\w+([-+.]\w+)*@\w+([-.]\w+)*\.\w+([-.]\w+)*">
</asp:RegularExpressionValidator>
```

Just like the other validation server controls, the RegularExpressionValidator control uses the `ControlToValidate` property to bind itself to the TextBox control, and it includes a `Text` property to push out the error message to the screen if the validation test fails. The unique property of this validation control is the `ValidationExpression` property. This property takes a string value, which is the regular expression you are going to apply to the input value.

Visual Studio 2008 makes it a little easier to use regular expressions through the use of the Regular Expression Editor. This editor provides a few commonly used regular expressions that you might want to apply to your RegularExpressionValidator. To get at this editor, you work with your page from Design view. Be sure to highlight the `RegularExpressionValidator1` server control in this Design view to see the control's properties. In the Property window of Visual Studio, click the button found next to the `ValidationExpression` property to launch the Regular Expression Editor. This editor is shown in Figure 4-6.

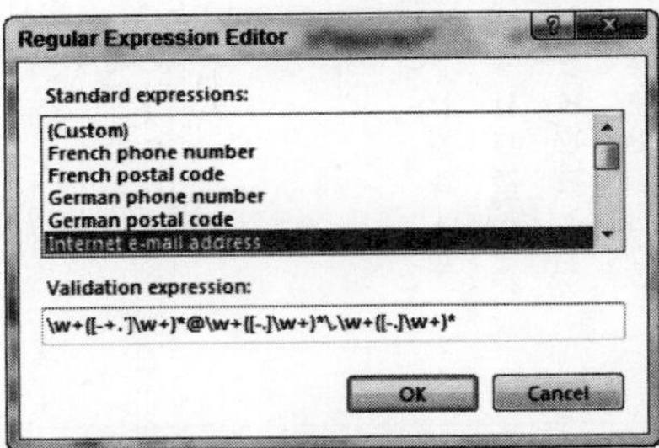

Figure 4-6

Using this editor, you can find regular expressions for things like e-mail addresses, Internet URLs, zip codes, phone numbers, and social security numbers. In addition to working with the Regular Expression Editor to help you with these sometimes complicated regular expression strings, you can also find a good-sized collection of them at an Internet site called RegExLib found at `www.regexlib.com`.

The CustomValidator Server Control

So far, you have seen a wide variety of validation controls that are at your disposal. In many cases, these validation controls address many of the validation rules that you want to apply to your Web forms.

Sometimes, however, none of these controls works for you, and you have to go beyond what they offer. This is where the CustomValidator control comes into play.

The CustomValidator control allows you to build your own client-side or server-side validations that can then be easily applied to your Web forms. Doing so allows you to make validation checks against values or calculations performed in the data tier (for example, in a database), or to make sure that the user's input validates against some arithmetic validation (for example, determining if a number is even or odd). You can do quite a bit with the CustomValidator control.

Using Client-Side Validation

One of the worthwhile functions of the CustomValidator control is its capability to easily provide custom client-side validations. Many developers have their own collections of JavaScript functions they employ in their applications, and using the CustomValidator control is one easy way of getting these functions implemented.

For example, look at a simple form that asks for a number from the end user. This form uses the CustomValidator control to perform a custom client-side validation on the user input to make sure that the number provided is divisible by 5. This is illustrated in Listing 4-14.

Listing 4-14: Using the CustomValidator control to perform client-side validations

VB

```
<%@ Page Language="VB" %>

<script runat="server">
   Protected Sub Button1_Click(ByVal sender As Object, ByVal e As System.EventArgs)
       Label1.Text = "VALID NUMBER!"
   End Sub
</script>

<html xmlns="http://www.w3.org/1999/xhtml">
<head runat="server">
    <title>CustomValidator</title>

    <script type="text/javascript">
        function validateNumber(oSrc, args) {
           args.IsValid = (args.Value % 5 == 0);
        }
    </script>

</head>
<body>
    <form id="form1" runat="server">
    <div>
        <p>
            Number:
            <asp:TextBox ID="TextBox1"
             Runat="server"></asp:TextBox>
              
            <asp:CustomValidator ID="CustomValidator1"
```

Continued

```
                Runat="server" ControlToValidate="TextBox1"
                Text="Number must be divisible by 5"
                ClientValidationFunction="validateNumber">
              </asp:CustomValidator>
        </p>
        <p>
              <asp:Button ID="Button1" OnClick="Button1_Click"
                Runat="server" Text="Button"></asp:Button>
        </p>
        <p>
              <asp:Label ID="Label1" Runat="server"></asp:Label>
        </p>
    </div>
    </form>
</body>
</html>
```

C#

```
<%@ Page Language="C#" %>
<script runat="server">

    protected void Button1_Click(Object sender, EventArgs e) {
        Label1.Text = "VALID NUMBER!";
    }

</script>
```

Looking over this Web form, you can see a couple of things happening. First, it is a simple form with only a single text box requiring user input. The user clicks the button that triggers the `Button1_Click` event, which in turn populates the `Label1` control on the page. It carries out this simple operation only if all the validation checks are performed and the user input passes these tests.

One item that is different about this page is the inclusion of the second `<script>` block found within the `<head>` section. This is the custom JavaScript. Note that Visual Studio 2008 is very friendly toward these kinds of constructions, even when you are switching between the Design and Code views of the page — something previous Visual Studio editions were rather poor at dealing with. This JavaScript function — `validateNumber` — is shown here:

```
<script type="text/javascript">
    function validateNumber(oSrc, args) {
        args.IsValid = (args.Value % 5 == 0);
    }
</script>
```

This second `<script>` section is the client-side JavaScript that you want the CustomValidator control to use when making its validation checks on the information entered into the text box. The JavaScript functions you employ are going to use the `args.IsValid` property and set this property to either `true` or `false` depending on the outcome of the validation check. In this case, the user input (`args.Value`) is checked to see if it is divisible by `5`. The Boolean value returned is then assigned to the `args.IsValid` property, which is then used by the CustomValidator control.

The CustomValidator control, like the other controls before it, uses the `ControlToValidate` property to associate itself with a particular element on the page. The property that you are interested in here is the `ClientValidationFunction` property. The string value provided to this property is the name of the client-side function that you want this validation check to employ when the CustomValidator control is triggered. In this case, it is `validateNumber`:

```
ClientValidationFunction="validateNumber"
```

If you run this page and make an invalid entry, you produce the result illustrated in Figure 4-7.

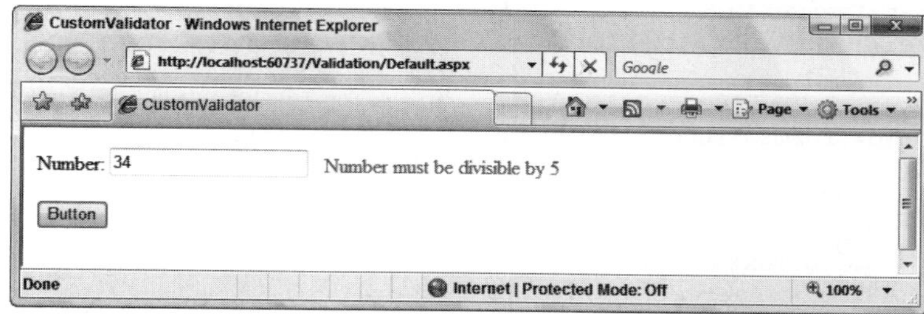

Figure 4-7

Using Server-Side Validation

Now let's move this same validation check from the client to the server. The CustomValidator control allows you to make custom server-side validations a reality as well. You will find that creating your server-side validations is just as easy as creating client-side validations.

If you create your own server-side validations, you can make them as complex as your applications require. For instance, using the CustomValidator for server-side validations is something you do if you want to check the user's input against dynamic values coming from XML files, databases, or elsewhere.

For an example of using the CustomValidator control for some custom server-side validation, you can work with the same example as you did when creating the client-side validation. Now, create a server-side check that makes sure a user-input number is divisible by 5. This is illustrated in Listing 4-15.

Listing 4-15: Using the CustomValidator control to perform server-side validations

VB

```
<%@ Page Language="VB" %>

<script runat="server">
   Protected Sub Button1_Click(ByVal sender As Object, ByVal e As System.EventArgs)
       If Page.IsValid Then
          Label1.Text = "VALID ENTRY!"
       End If
   End Sub
```

Continued

```
    Sub ValidateNumber(sender As Object, args As ServerValidateEventArgs)
       Try
          Dim num As Integer = Integer.Parse(args.Value)
          args.IsValid = ((num mod 5) = 0)
       Catch ex As Exception
          args.IsValid = False
       End Try
    End Sub
</script>

<html xmlns="http://www.w3.org/1999/xhtml">
<head runat="server">
    <title>CustomValidator</title>
</head>
<body>
    <form id="form1" runat="server">
    <div>
        <p>
           Number:
           <asp:TextBox ID="TextBox1"
            Runat="server"></asp:TextBox>
             
           <asp:CustomValidator ID="CustomValidator1"
            Runat="server" ControlToValidate="TextBox1"
            Text="Number must be divisible by 5"
            OnServerValidate="ValidateNumber"></asp:CustomValidator>
        </p>
        <p>
           <asp:Button ID="Button1" OnClick="Button1_Click"
            Runat="server" Text="Button"></asp:Button>
        </p>
        <p>
           <asp:Label ID="Label1" Runat="server"></asp:Label>
        </p>
    </div>
    </form>
</body>
</html>
```

C#

```
<%@ Page Language="C#" %>

<script runat="server">

    protected void Button1_Click(Object sender, EventArgs e) {
        if (Page.IsValid) {
           Label1.Text = "VALID ENTRY!";
        }
    }
```

```
    void ValidateNumber(object source, ServerValidateEventArgs args)
    {
       try
       {
          int num = int.Parse(args.Value);
          args.IsValid = ((num%5) == 0);
       }
       catch(Exception ex)
       {
          args.IsValid = false;
       }
    }

</script>
```

Instead of a client-side JavaScript function in the code, this example includes a server-side function — `ValidateNumber`. The `ValidateNumber` function, as well as all functions that are being constructed to work with the CustomValidator control, must use the `ServerValidateEventArgs` object as one of the parameters in order to get the data passed to the function for the validation check. The `ValidateNumber` function itself is nothing fancy. It simply checks to see if the provided number is divisible by 5.

From within your custom function, which is designed to work with the CustomValidator control, you actually get at the value coming from the form element through the `args.Value` object. Then you set the `args.IsValid` property to either `True` or `False` depending on your validation checks. From the preceding example, you can see that the `args.IsValid` is set to `False` if the number is not divisible by 5 and also that an exception is thrown (which would occur if a string value was input into the form element). After the custom function is established, the next step is to apply it to the CustomValidator control, as shown in the following example:

```
<asp:CustomValidator ID="CustomValidator1"
 Runat="server" ControlToValidate="TextBox1"
 Text="Number must be divisible by 5"
 OnServerValidate="ValidateNumber"></asp:CustomValidator>
```

To make the association between a CustomValidator control and a function that you have in your server-side code, you simply use the `OnServerValidate` attribute. The value assigned to this property is the name of the function — in this case, `ValidateNumber`.

Running this example causes the postback to come back to the server and the validation check (based on the `ValidateNumber` function) to be performed. From here, the page reloads and the `Page_Load` event is called. In the example from Listing 4-15, you can see that a check is done to see whether the page is valid. This is done using the `Page.IsValid` property:

```
If Page.IsValid Then
   Label1.Text = "VALID ENTRY!"
End If
```

Using Client-Side and Server-Side Validation Together

As stated earlier in this chapter, you have to think about the security of your forms and to ensure that the data you are collecting from the forms is valid data. For this reason, when you decide to employ client-side validations (as you did in Listing 4-14), you should take steps to also reconstruct the client-side function as a server-side function. When you have done this, you should associate the CustomValidator control to both the client-side and server-side functions. In the case of the number check validation from Listings 4-14 and 4-15, you can use both validation functions in your page and then change the CustomValidator control to point to both of these functions, as shown in Listing 4-16.

Listing 4-16: The CustomValidator control with client- and server-side validations

```
<asp:CustomValidator ID="CustomValidator1"
    Runat="server" ControlToValidate="TextBox1"
    Text="Number must be divisible by 5"
    ClientValidationFunction="validateNumber"
    OnServerValidate="ValidateNumber"></asp:CustomValidator>
```

From this example, you can see it is simply a matter of using both the `ClientValidationFunction` and the `OnServerValidate` attributes at the same time.

The ValidationSummary Server Control

The ValidationSummary control is not a control that performs validations on the content input into your Web forms. Instead, this control is the reporting control, which is used by the other validation controls on a page. You can use this validation control to consolidate error reporting for all the validation errors that occur on a page instead of leaving this up to each and every individual validation control.

You might want this capability for larger forms, which have a comprehensive form validation process. If this is the case, you may find it rather user-friendly to have all the possible validation errors reported to the end user in a single and easily identifiable manner. These error messages can be displayed in a list, bulleted list, or paragraph.

By default, the ValidationSummary control shows the list of validation errors as a bulleted list. This is illustrated in Listing 4-17.

Listing 4-17: A partial page example of the ValidationSummary control

```
<p>First name
    <asp:TextBox ID="TextBox1" Runat="server"></asp:TextBox>
      
    <asp:RequiredFieldValidator ID="RequiredFieldValidator1"
     Runat="server" ErrorMessage="You must enter your first name"
     ControlToValidate="TextBox1"></asp:RequiredFieldValidator>
</p>
<p>Last name
    <asp:TextBox ID="TextBox2" Runat="server"></asp:TextBox>
      
    <asp:RequiredFieldValidator ID="RequiredFieldValidator2"
     Runat="server" ErrorMessage="You must enter your last name"
     ControlToValidate="TextBox2"></asp:RequiredFieldValidator>
</p>
```

```
<p>
   <asp:Button ID="Button1" OnClick="Button1_Click" Runat="server"
    Text="Submit"></asp:Button>
</p>
<p>
   <asp:ValidationSummary ID="ValidationSummary1" Runat="server"
    HeaderText="You received the following errors:">
   </asp:ValidationSummary>
</p>
<p>
   <asp:Label ID="Label1" Runat="server"></asp:Label>
</p>
```

This example asks the end user for her first and last name. Each text box in the form has an associated RequiredFieldValidator control assigned to it. When the page is built and run, if the user clicks the Submit button with no values placed in either of the text boxes, it causes both validation errors to fire. This result is shown in Figure 4-8.

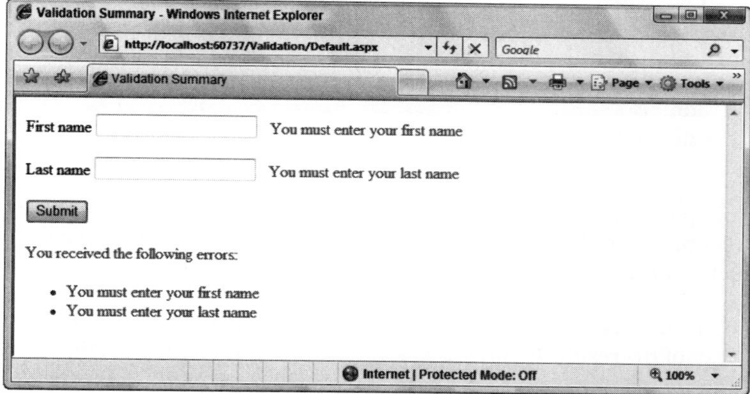

Figure 4-8

As in earlier examples of validation controls on the form, these validation errors appear next to each of the text boxes. You can see, however, that the ValidationSummary control also displays the validation errors as a bulleted list in red at the location of the control on the Web form. In most cases, you do not want these errors to appear twice on a page for the end user. You can change this behavior by using the `Text` property of the validation controls, in addition to the `ErrorMessage` property, as you have typically done throughout this chapter. This approach is shown in Listing 4-18.

Listing 4-18: Using the Text property of a validation control

```
<asp:RequiredFieldValidator ID="RequiredFieldValidator1"
 Runat="server" ErrorMessage="You must enter your first name" Text="*"
 ControlToValidate="TextBox1"></asp:RequiredFieldValidator>
or
```

Continued

```
<asp:RequiredFieldValidator ID="RequiredFieldValidator1"
 Runat="server" ErrorMessage="You must enter your first name"
 ControlToValidate="TextBox1">*</asp:RequiredFieldValidator>
```

Listing 4-18 shows two ways to accomplish the same task. The first is to use the `Text` property and the second option is to place the provided output between the tags of the `<asp:RequiredFieldValidator>` elements. Making this type of change to the validation controls produces the results shown in Figure 4-9.

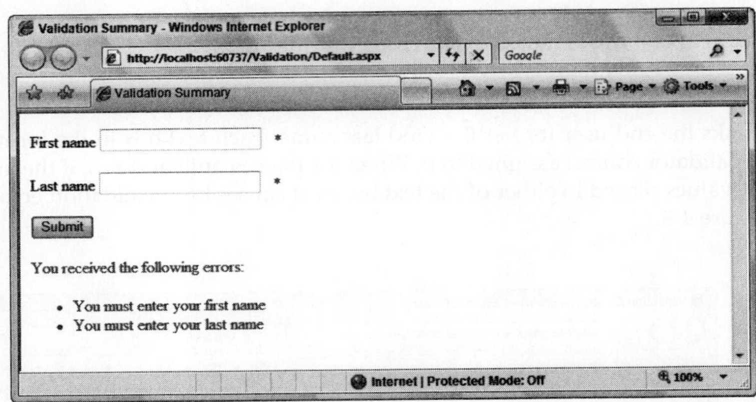

Figure 4-9

To get this result, just remember that the ValidationSummary control uses the validation control's `ErrorMessage` property for displaying the validation errors if they occur. The `Text` property is used by the validation control and is not utilized at all by the ValidationSummary control.

In addition to bulleted lists, you can use the `DisplayMode` property of the ValidationSummary control to change the display of the results to other types of formats. This control has the following possible values:

- ❑ `BulletList`
- ❑ `List`
- ❑ `SingleParagraph`

You can also utilize a dialog box instead of displaying the results to the Web page. Listing 4-19 shows an example of this behavior.

Listing 4-19: Using a dialog box to report validation errors

```
<asp:ValidationSummary ID="ValidationSummary1" Runat="server"
 ShowMessageBox="True" ShowSummary="False"></asp:ValidationSummary>
```

From this code example, you can see that the `ShowSummary` property is set to `False` — meaning that the bulleted list of validation errors are not shown on the actual Web page. However, because the `ShowMessageBox` property is set to `True`, you now get these errors reported in a message box, as illustrated in Figure 4-10.

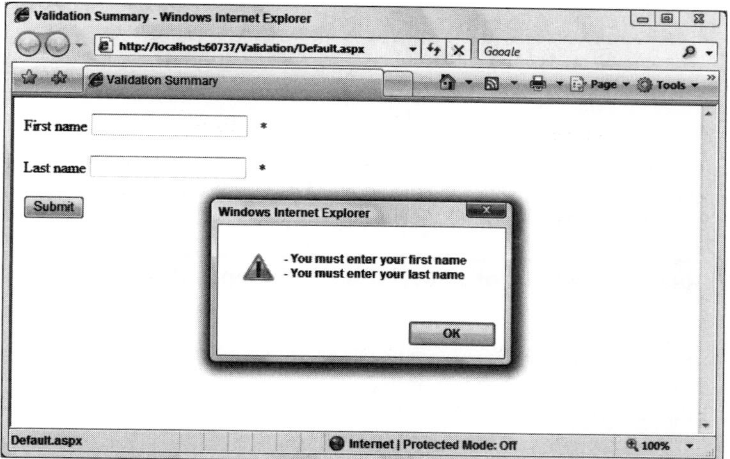

Figure 4-10

Turning Off Client-Side Validation

Because validation server controls provide clients with client-side validations automatically (if the requesting container can properly handle the JavaScript produced), you might, at times, want a way to control this behavior.

It is quite possible to turn off the client-side capabilities of these controls so that they don't independently send client-side capabilities to the requestors. For instance, you might want all validations done on the server, no matter what capabilities the requesting containers offer. You can take a couple of approaches to turning off this functionality.

The first is at the control level. Each of the validation server controls has a property called `EnableClientScript`. This property is set to `True` by default, but setting it to `False` prevents the control from sending out a JavaScript function for validation on the client. Instead, the validation check is done on the server. The use of this property is shown in Listing 4-20.

Listing 4-20: Disabling client-side validations in a validation control

```
<asp:RequiredFieldValidator ID="RequiredFieldValidator1" Runat="server"
 Text="*" ControlToValidate="TextBox1" EnableClientScript="false" />
```

You can also remove a validation control's client-side capability programmatically (shown in Listing 4-21).

Listing 4-21: Removing the client-side capabilities programmatically

VB

```
Protected Sub Page_Load(ByVal sender As Object, ByVal e As System.EventArgs)
   RequiredFieldValidator1.EnableClientScript = False
End Sub
```

Continued

C#

```
protected void Page_Load(Object sender, EventArgs e) {
   RequiredFieldValidator1.EnableClientScript = false;
}
```

Another option is to turn off the client-side script capabilities for all the validation controls on a page from within the `Page_Load` event. This can be rather helpful if you want to dynamically decide not to allow client-side validation. This is illustrated in Listing 4-22.

Listing 4-22: Disabling all client-side validations from the Page_Load event

VB

```
Protected Sub Page_Load(ByVal sender As Object, ByVal e As System.EventArgs)
   For Each bv As BaseValidator In Page.Validators
      bv.EnableClientScript = False
   Next
End Sub
```

C#

```
protected void Page_Load(Object sender, EventArgs e) {
   foreach(BaseValidator bv in Page.Validators)
   {
      bv.EnableClientScript = false;
   }
}
```

Looking for each instance of a `BaseValidator` object in the validators contained on an ASP.NET page, this `For Each` loop turns off client-side validation capabilities for each and every validation control the page contains.

Using Images and Sounds for Error Notifications

So far, we have been displaying simple textual messages for the error notifications that come from the validation server controls. In most instances, you are going to do just that — display some simple textual messages to inform end users that they input something into the form that doesn't pass your validation rules.

An interesting tip regarding the validation controls is that you are not limited to just text — you can also use images and sounds for error notifications.

To do this, you use the `Text` property of any of the validation controls. To use an image for the error, you can simply place some appropriate HTML as the value of this property. This is illustrated in Listing 4-23.

Listing 4-23: Using images for error notifications

```
<asp:RequiredFieldValidator ID="RequiredFieldValidator1"
 Runat="server" Text='<img src="error.gif">'
 ControlToValidate="TextBox1"></asp:RequiredFieldValidator>
```

As you can see from this example, instead of some text being output to the Web page, the value of the `Text` property is an HTML string. This bit of HTML is used to display an image. Be sure to notice the use of the single and double quotation marks so you won't get any errors when the page is generated in the browser. This example produces something similar to what is shown in Figure 4-11.

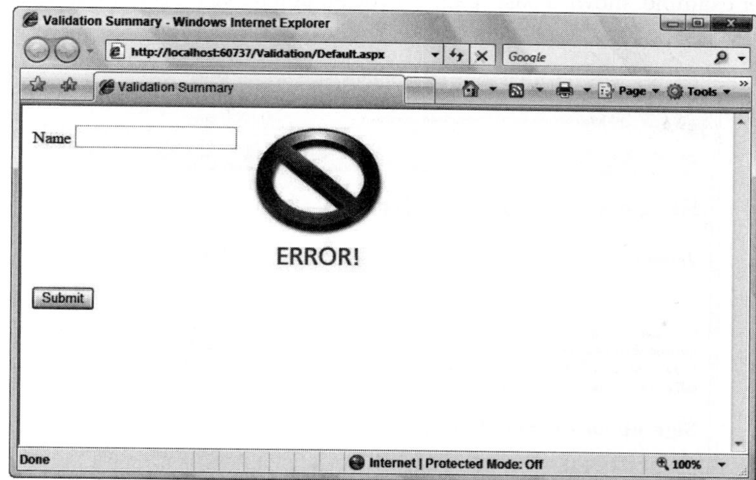

Figure 4-11

The other interesting twist you can create is to add a sound notification when the end user errs. You can do this the same way you display an image for error notifications. Listing 4-24 shows an example of this.

Listing 4-24: Using sound for error notifications

```
<asp:RequiredFieldValidator ID="RequiredFieldValidator1"
 Runat="server" Text='<bgsound src="C:\Windows\Media\tada.wav">'
 ControlToValidate="TextBox1" EnableClientScript="False">
</asp:RequiredFieldValidator>
```

You can find a lot of the Windows system sounds in the `C:\Windows\Media` directory. In this example, the `Text` uses the `<bgsound>` element to place a sound on the Web form (works only with Internet Explorer). The sound is played only when the end user triggers the validation control.

When working with sounds for error notifications, you have to disable the client-side script capability for that particular control because if you do not, the sound plays when the page is loaded in the browser, whether or not a validation error has been triggered.

Working with Validation Groups

In many instances, developers want to place more than one form on a single page. This was always possible in ASP.NET 1.0/1.1 because different button clicks could be used to perform different server-side events. Some issues related to this type of construction were problematic, however.

One of these issues was the difficulty of having validation controls for each of the forms on the page. Different validation controls were often assigned to two distinct forms on the page. When the end user submitted one form, the validation controls in the other form were fired (because the user was not working with that form), thereby stopping the first form from being submitted.

Figure 4-12, for example, shows a basic page for the St. Louis .NET User Group that includes two forms.

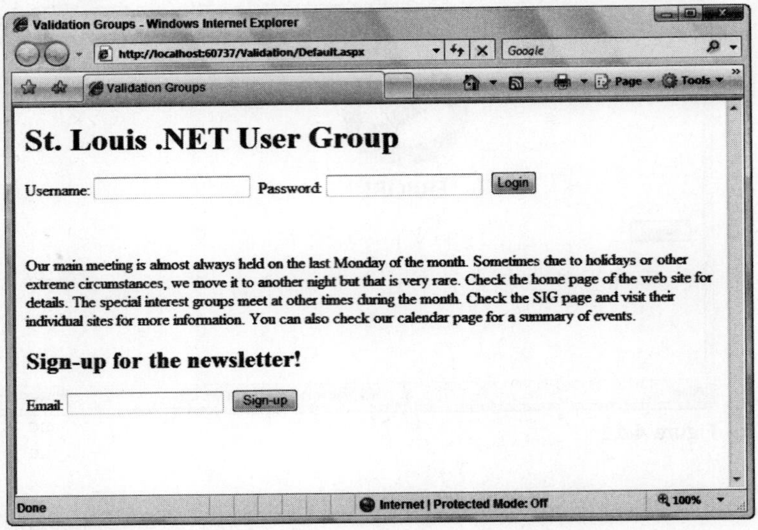

Figure 4-12

One of the forms is for members of the site to supply their usernames and passwords to log into the Members Only section of the site. The second form on the page is for anyone who wishes to sign up for the user group's newsletter. Each form has its own button and some validation controls associated with it. The problem arises when someone submits information for one of the forms. For instance, if you were a member of the group, you would supply your username and password, and click the Login button. The validation controls for the newsletter form would fire because no e-mail address was placed in that particular form. If someone interested in getting the newsletter places an e-mail address in the last text box and clicks the Sign-up button, the validation controls in the first form fire because no username and password were input in that form.

ASP.NET 3.5 provides you with a `ValidationGroup` property that enables you to separate the validation controls into separate groups. It enables you to activate only the required validation controls when an end user clicks a button on the page. Listing 4-25 shows an example of separating the validation controls on a user group page into different buckets.

Listing 4-25: Using the ValidationGroup property

```
<%@ Page Language="VB" %>

<html xmlns="http://www.w3.org/1999/xhtml">
<head runat="server">
```

```
    <title>Validation Groups</title>
</head>
<body>
    <form id="form1" runat="server">
    <div>
        <h1>St. Louis .NET User Group</h1>
        <p>Username:
        <asp:TextBox ID="TextBox1" Runat="server"></asp:TextBox>  Password:
        <asp:TextBox ID="TextBox2" Runat="server"
         TextMode="Password"></asp:TextBox> 
        <asp:Button ID="Button1" Runat="server" Text="Login"
         ValidationGroup="Login" />
            <br />
            <asp:RequiredFieldValidator ID="RequiredFieldValidator1" Runat="server"
             Text="* You must submit a username!"
             ControlToValidate="TextBox1" ValidationGroup="Login">
            </asp:RequiredFieldValidator>
            <br />
            <asp:RequiredFieldValidator ID="RequiredFieldValidator2" Runat="server"
             Text="* You must submit a password!"
             ControlToValidate="TextBox2" ValidationGroup="Login">
            </asp:RequiredFieldValidator>
        <p>
            Our main meeting is almost always held on the last Monday of the month.
            Sometimes due to holidays or other extreme circumstances,
            we move it to another night but that is very rare. Check the home page
            of the web site for details. The special
            interest groups meet at other times during the month. Check the SIG
            page and visit their individual sites for more information.
            You can also check our calendar page for a summary of events.<br />
        </p>
        <h2>Sign-up for the newsletter!</h2>
        <p>Email:
        <asp:TextBox ID="TextBox3" Runat="server"></asp:TextBox> 
        <asp:Button ID="Button2" Runat="server" Text="Sign-up"
         ValidationGroup="Newsletter" /> 
            <br />
            <asp:RegularExpressionValidator ID="RegularExpressionValidator1"
             Runat="server"
             Text="* You must submit a correctly formatted email address!"
             ControlToValidate="TextBox3" ValidationGroup="Newsletter"
             ValidationExpression="\w+([-+.]\w+)*@\w+([-.]\w+)*\.\w+([-.]\w+)*">
            </asp:RegularExpressionValidator>
            <br />
            <asp:RequiredFieldValidator ID="RequiredFieldValidator3" Runat="server"
             Text="* You forgot your email address!"
             ControlToValidate="TextBox3" ValidationGroup="Newsletter">
            </asp:RequiredFieldValidator>
        </p>
    </div>
    </form>
</body>
</html>
```

The `ValidationGroup` property on this page is shown in bold. You can see that this property takes a `String` value. Also note that not only validation controls have this new property. The core server controls also have the `ValidationGroup` property because things like button clicks must be associated with specific validation groups.

In this example, each of the buttons has a distinct validation group assignment. The first button on the form uses `Login` as a value, and the second button on the form uses `Newsletter` as a value. Then each of the validation controls is associated with one of these validation groups. Because of this, when the end user clicks the Login button on the page, ASP.NET recognizes that it should work only with the validation server controls that have the same validation group name. ASP.NET ignores the validation controls assigned to other validation groups.

Using this enhancement, you can now have multiple sets of validation rules that fire only when you want them to fire (see Figure 4-13).

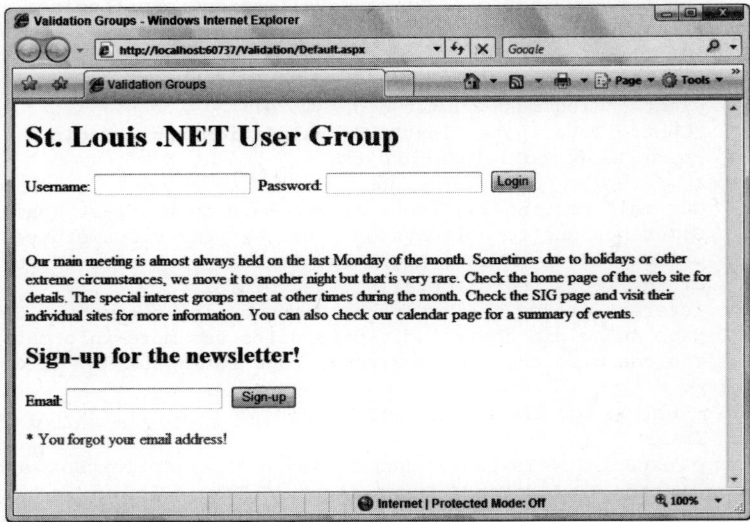

Figure 4-13

Another great feature that has been added to validation controls is a property called `SetFocusOnError`. This property takes a `Boolean` value and, if a validation error is thrown when the form is submitted, the property places the page focus on the form element that receives the error. The `SetFocusOnError` property is used in the following example:

```
<asp:RequiredFieldValidator ID="RequiredFieldValidator1" Runat="server"
 Text="* You must submit a username!"
 ControlToValidate="TextBox1" ValidationGroup="Login" SetFocusOnError="True">
</asp:RequiredFieldValidator>
```

If `RequiredFieldValidator1` throws an error because the end user didn't place a value in `TextBox1`, the page is redrawn with the focus on `TextBox1`, as shown in Figure 4-14.

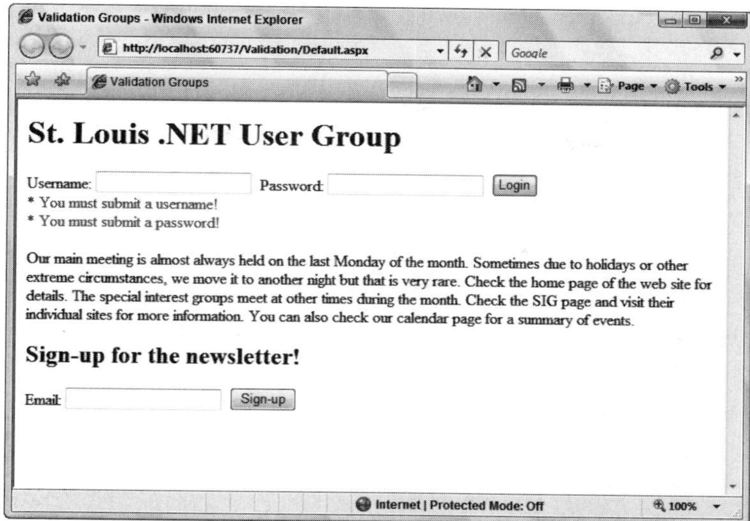

Figure 4-14

Note that if you have multiple validation controls on your page with the `SetFocusOnError` property set to `True`, and more than one validation error occurs, the uppermost form element that has a validation error gets the focus. In the previous example, if both the username text box (`TextBox1`) and the password text box (`TextBox2`) have validation errors associated with them, the page focus is assigned to the username text box because it is the first control on the form with an error.

Summary

Validation controls are a welcome addition for those developers moving from Active Server Pages to ASP.NET. They bring a lot of functionality in a simple-to-use package and, like most things in the .NET world, you can easily get them to look and behave exactly as you want them to.

Remember that the purpose of having forms in your applications is to collect data, but this data collection has no meaning if the data is not valid. This means that you must establish validation rules that can be implemented in your forms through a series of different controls — the validation server controls.

This chapter covered various validation controls in detail, including

- RequiredFieldValidator
- CompareValidator
- RangeValidator
- RegularExpressionValidator
- CustomValidator
- ValidationSummary

In addition to looking at the base validation controls, this chapter also discussed how to apply client-side and server-side validations.

5

Working with Master Pages

Visual inheritance is a great new enhancement to your Web pages provided by ASP.NET 3.5. This feature was introduced to ASP.NET in version 2.0. In effect, you can create a single template page that can be used as a foundation for any number of ASP.NET content pages in your application. These templates, called *master pages*, increase your productivity by making your applications easier to build and easier to manage after they are built. Visual Studio 2008 includes full designer support for master pages, making the developer experience richer than ever before. This chapter takes a close look at how to utilize master pages to the fullest extent in your applications and begins by explaining the advantages of master pages.

Why Do You Need Master Pages?

Most Web sites today have common elements used throughout the entire application or on a majority of the pages within the application. For instance, if you look at the main page of the Reuters News Web site (found at `www.reuters.com`), you see common elements that are used throughout the entire Web site. These common areas are labeled in Figure 5-1.

In this screen shot, notice the header section, the navigation section, and the footer section on the page. In fact, nearly every page within the entire application uses these same elements. Even before master pages, you had ways to put these elements into every page through a variety of means; but in most cases, doing so posed difficulties.

Some developers simply copy and paste the code for these common sections to each and every page that requires them. This works, but it's rather labor intensive. However, if you use the copy-and-paste method, whenever a change is required to one of these common sections of the application, you have to go into each and every page and duplicate the change. That's not much fun and an ineffective use of your time!

In the days of Classic Active Server Pages, one popular option was to put all the common sections into what was called an *include file*. You could then place this file within your page like this:

```
<!-- #include virtual="/myIncludes/header.asp" -->
```

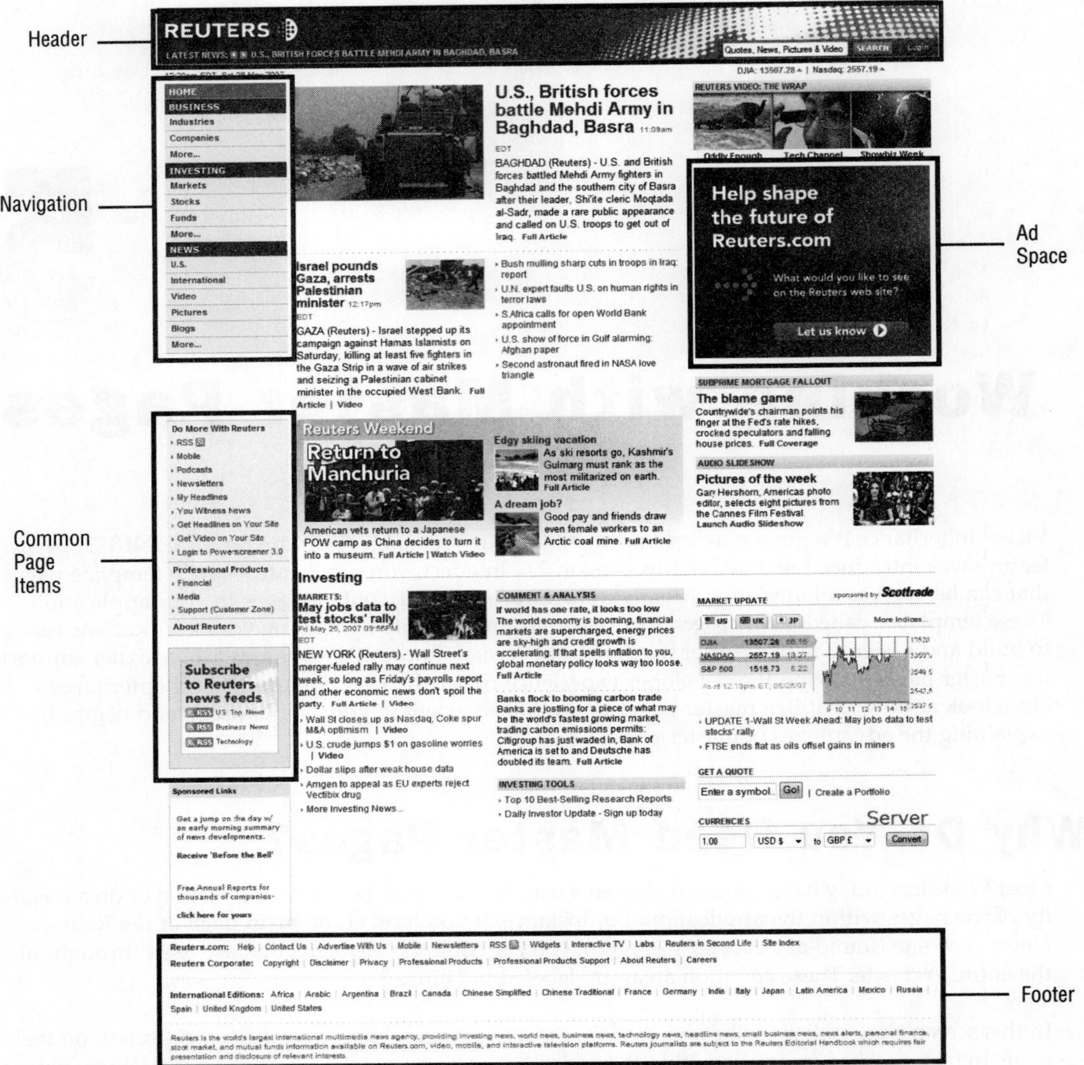

Figure 5-1

The problem with using `include` files was that you had to take into account the newly opened HTML tags in the header `include` file. These tags had to be closed in the main document or in the footer `include` file. It was usually difficult to keep all the HTML tags in order, especially if multiple people worked on a project. Web pages sometimes displayed strange results because of inappropriate or nonexistent tag closings or openings. It was also difficult to work with `include` files in a visual designer. Using `include` files didn't allow the developer to see the entire page as it would appear in a browser. The developer ended up developing the page in sections and *hoping* that the pieces would come together as planned. Many hours were wasted ''chasing tables'' opened in an include file and possibly closed later!

With the introduction of ASP.NET 1.0 in 2000, developers started using *user controls* to encapsulate common sections of their Web pages. For instance, you could build a Web page that included header, navigation, and footer sections by simply dragging and dropping these sections of code onto each page that required them.

This technique worked, but it also raised some issues. Before Visual Studio 2005 and ASP.NET 2.0, user controls caused problems similar to those related to `include` files. When you worked in the design view of your Web page, the common areas of the page displayed only as gray boxes in Visual Studio .NET 2002 and 2003. This made it harder to build a page. You could not visualize what the page you were building actually looked like until you compiled and ran the completed page in a browser. User controls also suffered from the same problem as `include` files — you had to match up the opening and closing of your HTML tags in two separate files. Personally, we prefer user controls over `include` files, but user controls aren't perfect template pieces for use throughout an application. You will find that Visual Studio corrects some of the problems by rendering user-control content in the design view. User controls are ideal if you are including only small sections on a Web page; they are still rather cumbersome, however, when working with larger page templates.

In light of the issues with `include` files and user controls, the ASP.NET team developed the idea of *master pages* — an outstanding new way of applying templates to your applications. They *inverted* the way the developer attacks the problem. Master pages live *outside* the pages you develop, while user controls live within your pages and are doomed to duplication. These master pages draw a more distinct line between the common areas that you carry over from page to page and the content areas that are unique on each page. You will find that working with master pages is easy and fun. The next section of this chapter looks at some of the basics of master pages in ASP.NET.

The Basics of Master Pages

Master pages are an easy way to provide a template that can be used by any number of ASP.NET pages in your application. In working with master pages, you create a master file that is the template referenced by a *subpage* or *content page*. Master pages use a `.master` file extension, whereas content pages use the `.aspx` file extension you're used to; but content pages are declared as such within the file's `Page` directive.

You can place anything you want to be included as part of the template in the `.master` file. This can include the header, navigation, and footer sections used across the Web application. The content page then contains all the page content except for the master page's elements. At runtime, the ASP.NET engine combines these elements into a single page for the end user. Figure 5-2 shows a diagram of how this process works.

One of the nice things about working with master pages is that you can visually see the template in the IDE when you are creating the content pages. Because you can see the entire page while you are working on it, it is much easier to develop content pages that use a template. While you are working on the content page, all the templated items are shaded gray and are not editable. The only items that are alterable are clearly shown in the template. These workable areas, called *content areas*, originally are defined in the master page itself. Within the master page, you specify the areas of the page that the content pages can use. You can have more than one content area in your master page if you want. Figure 5-3 shows the master page with a couple of content areas shown.

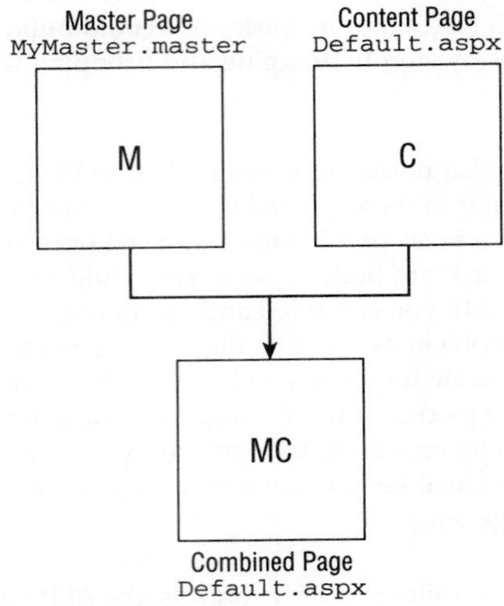

Figure 5-2

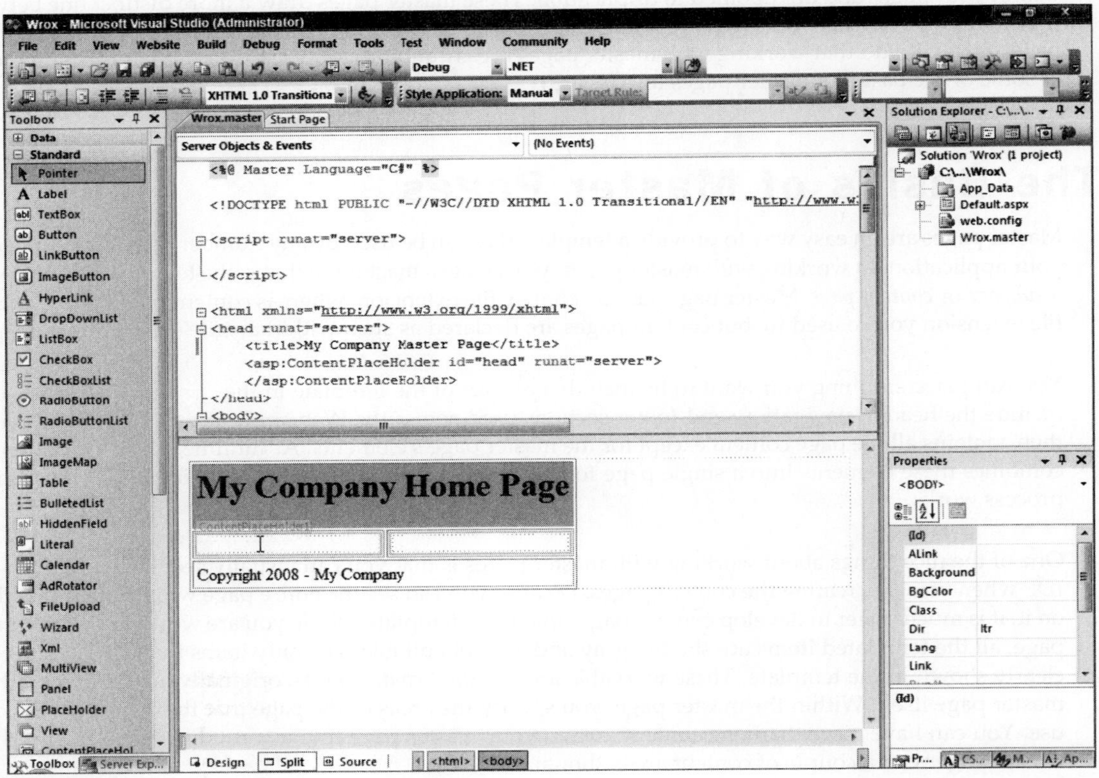

Figure 5-3

If you look at the screenshot from Figure 5-3, you can sort of see two defined areas on the page — these are content areas. The content area is represented in the design view of the page by a light dotted box that represents the ContentPlaceHolder control. Also, if you hover your mouse over the content area, you will see the name of the control appear above the control (although lightly). This hovering is also shown in action in Figure 5-3.

Companies and organizations will find using master pages ideal, as the technology closely models their typical business requirements. Many companies have a common look and feel that they apply across their intranet. They can now provide the divisions of their company with a `.master` file to use when creating a department's section of the intranet. This process makes it quite easy for the company to keep a consistent look and feel across its entire intranet.

Coding a Master Page

Now look at building the master page shown previously in Figure 5-3. You can create one in any text-based editor, such as Notepad or Visual Web Developer Express Edition, or you can use the new Visual Studio 2008. In this chapter, you see how it is done with Visual Studio 2008.

Master pages are added to your projects in the same way as regular `.aspx` pages — choose the Master Page option when you add a new file to your application, as shown in Figure 5-4.

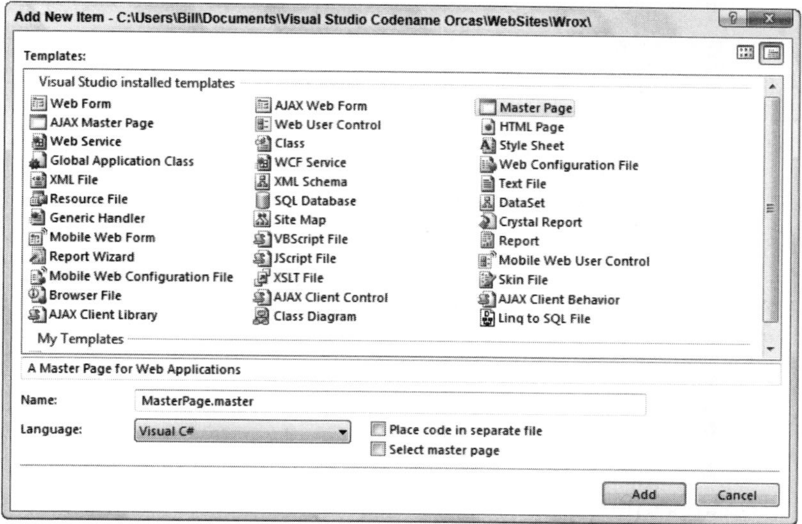

Figure 5-4

Because it's quite similar to any other `.aspx` page, the Add New Item dialog enables you to choose from a master page using the inline coding model or a master page that places its code in a separate file. Not placing your server code in a separate file means that you use the inline code model for the page you are creating. This option creates a single `.master` page. Choosing the option to place your code in a separate file means that you use the new code-behind model with the page you are creating. Selecting the check box "Place code in separate file" creates a single `.master` page, along with an associated `.master.vb` or

`.master.cs` file. You also have the option of nesting your master page within another master page by selecting the Select master page option, but this is covered later in this chapter.

A sample master page that uses the inline-coding model is shown in Listing 5-1.

Listing 5-1: A sample master page

```
<%@ Master Language="VB" %>

<script runat="server">

</script>


<html xmlns="http://www.w3.org/1999/xhtml" >
<head runat="server">
    <title>My Company Master Page</title>
    <asp:ContentPlaceHolder id="head" runat="server">
    </asp:ContentPlaceHolder>
</head>
<body>
    <form id="form1" runat="server">
        <table cellpadding="3" border="1">
            <tr bgcolor="silver">
                <td colspan="2">
                    <h1>My Company Home Page</h1>
                </td>
            </tr>
            <tr>
                <td>
                    <asp:ContentPlaceHolder ID="ContentPlaceHolder1"
                     runat="server">
                    </asp:ContentPlaceHolder>
                </td>
                <td>
                    <asp:ContentPlaceHolder ID="ContentPlaceHolder2"
                     runat="server">
                    </asp:ContentPlaceHolder>
                </td>
            </tr>
            <tr>
                <td colspan="2">
                    Copyright 2008 - My Company
                </td>
            </tr>
        </table>
    </form>
</body>
</html>
```

This is a simple master page. The great thing about creating master pages in Visual Studio 2008 is that you can work with the master page in code view, but you can also switch over to design view to create your master pages just as any other ASP.NET page.

Start by reviewing the code for the master page. The first line is the directive:

```
<%@ Master Language="VB" %>
```

Instead of using the `Page` directive, as you would with a typical `.aspx` page, you use the `Master` directive for a master page. This master page uses only a single attribute, `Language`. The `Language` attribute's value here is `VB`, but of course, you can also use `C#` if you are building a C# master page.

You code the rest of the master page just as you would any other `.aspx` page. You can use server controls, raw HTML and text, images, events, or anything else you normally would use for any `.aspx` page. This means that your master page can have a `Page_Load` event as well or any other event that you deem appropriate.

In the code shown in Listing 5-1, notice the use of a new server control — the `<asp:ContentPlaceHolder>` control. This control defines the areas of the template where the content page can place its content:

```
<tr>
   <td>
      <asp:ContentPlaceHolder ID="ContentPlaceHolder1"
       runat="server">
      </asp:ContentPlaceHolder>
   </td>
   <td>
      <asp:ContentPlaceHolder ID="ContentPlaceHolder2"
       runat="server">
      </asp:ContentPlaceHolder>
   </td>
</tr>
```

In the case of this master page, two defined areas exist where the content page can place content. Our master page contains a header and a footer area. It also defines two areas in the page where any inheriting content page can place its own content. Look at how a content page uses this master page.

Coding a Content Page

Now that you have a master page in place in your application, you can use this new template for any content pages in your application. Right-click the application in the Solution Explorer and choose Add New Item to create a new content page within your application.

To create a content page or a page that uses this master page as its template, you select a typical Web Form from the list of options in the Add New Item dialog (see Figure 5-5). Instead of creating a typical Web Form, however, you check the Select Master Page check box. This gives you the option of associating this Web Form later to some master page.

After you name your content page and click the Add button in the Add New Item dialog, you are presented with the Select a Master Page dialog, as shown in Figure 5-6.

This dialog allows you to choose the master page from which you want to build your content page. You choose from the available master pages that are contained within your application. For this example, select the new master page that you created in Listing 5-1 and click OK. This creates the content page.

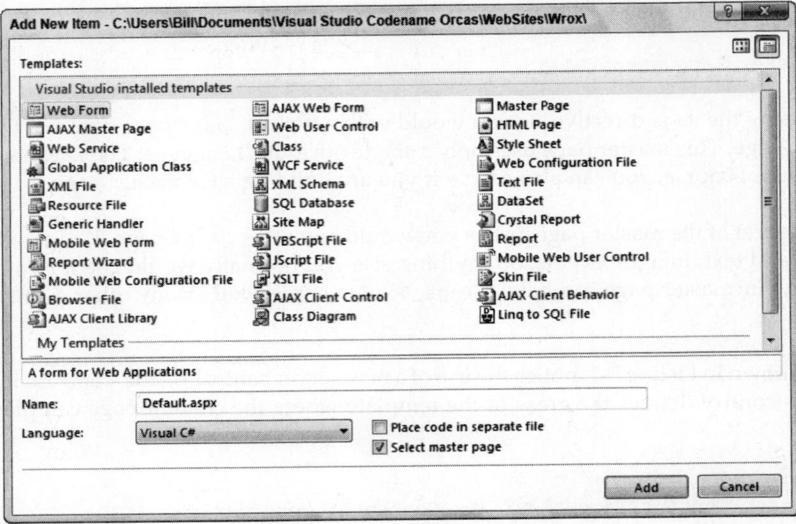

Figure 5-5

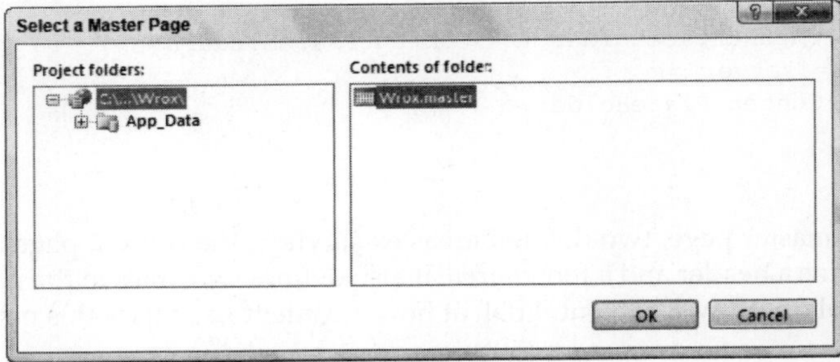

Figure 5-6

The created page is a simple .aspx page with only a couple of lines of code contained in the file, as shown in Listing 5-2.

Listing 5-2: The created content page

```
<%@ Page Language="VB" MasterPageFile="~/Wrox.master" Title="Untitled Page" %>

<script runat="server">

</script>

<asp:Content ID="Content1" ContentPlaceHolderID="head" Runat="Server">
```

```
</asp:Content>
<asp:Content ID="Content2" ContentPlaceHolderID="ContentPlaceHolder1"
 Runat="Server">
</asp:Content>
```

This content page is not much different from the typical `.aspx` page you coded in the past. The big difference is the inclusion of the `MasterPageFile` attribute within the `Page` directive. The use of this attribute indicates that this particular `.aspx` page constructs its control's based on another page. The location of the master page within the application is specified as the value of the `MasterPageFile` attribute.

The other big difference is that it contains neither the `<form id="form1" runat="server">` tag nor any opening or closing HTML tags that would normally be included in a typical `.aspx` page.

This content page may seem simple, but if you switch to the design view within Visual Studio 2008, you see the power of using content pages. What you get with visual inheritance is shown in Figure 5-7.

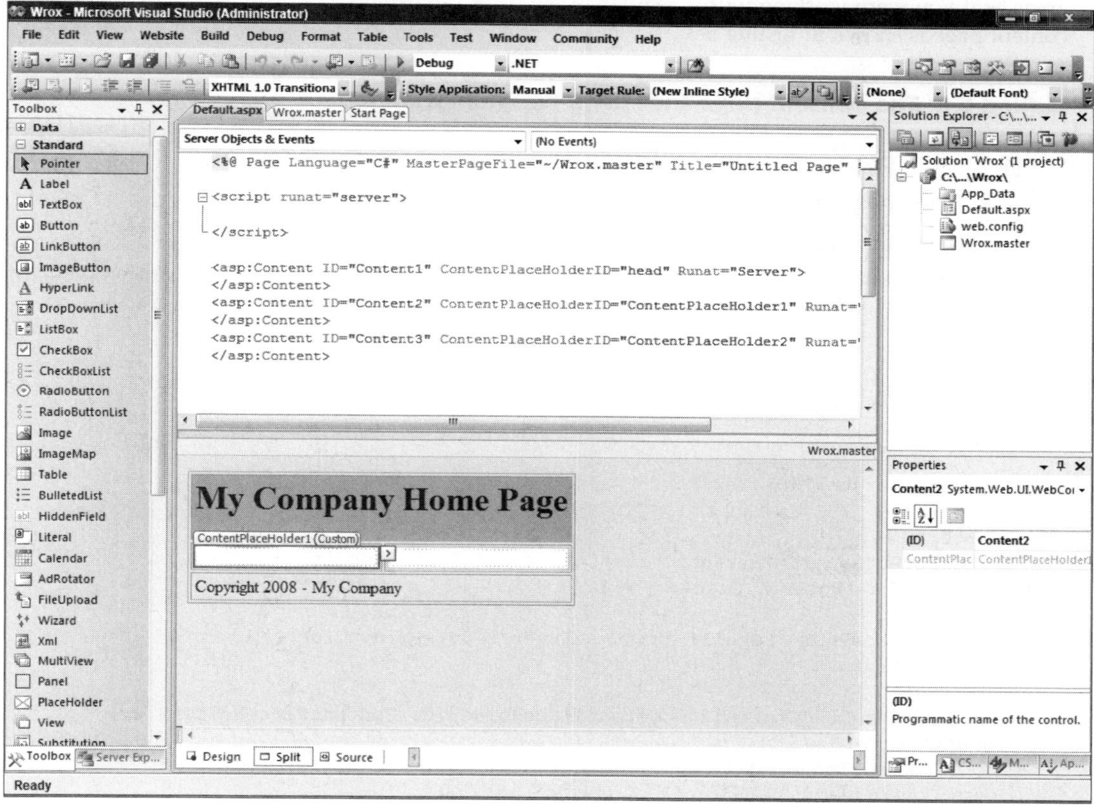

Figure 5-7

In this screenshot, you can see that just by using the `MasterPageFile` attribute in the `Page` directive, you are able to visually inherit everything that the `Wrox.master` file exposes. From the design view within Visual Studio, you can also see what master page you are working with as the name of the referenced master page is presented in the upper-right corner of the Design view page. If you try and click into the gray area that represents what is inherited from the master page, you will see that your cursor changes to show you are not allowed. This is illustrated in Figure 5-8 (the cursor is on the word Page in the title).

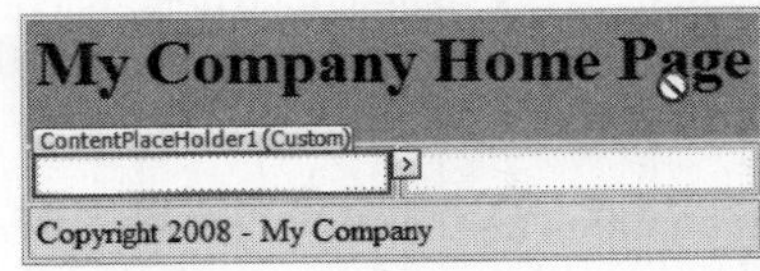

Figure 5-8

All the common areas defined in the master page are shown in gray, whereas the content areas that you specified in the master page using the `<asp:ContentPlaceHolder>` server control are shown clearly and available for additional content in the content page. You can add any content to these defined content areas as if you were working with a regular `.aspx` page. An example of using this `.master` page for a content page is shown in Listing 5-3.

Listing 5-3: The content page that uses Wrox.master

VB

```
<%@ Page Language="VB" MasterPageFile="~/Wrox.master" %>

<script runat="server">
    Protected Sub Button1_Click(ByVal sender As Object, ByVal e As System.EventArgs)
        Label1.Text = "Hello " & TextBox1.Text & "!"
    End Sub
</script>

<asp:Content ID="Content1" ContentPlaceHolderId="ContentPlaceHolder1"
 runat="server">
    <b>Enter your name:</b><br />
    <asp:Textbox ID="TextBox1" runat="server" />
    <br />
    <br />
    <asp:Button ID="Button1" runat="server" Text="Submit"
     OnClick="Button1_Click" /><br />
    <br />
    <asp:Label ID="Label1" runat="server" Font-Bold="True" />
</asp:Content>

<asp:Content ID="Content2" ContentPlaceHolderId="ContentPlaceHolder2"
 runat="server">
        <asp:Image ID="Image1" runat="server" ImageUrl="wrox.gif" />
</asp:Content>
```

C#

```
<%@ Page Language="C#" MasterPageFile="~/Wrox.master" %>
```

```
<script runat="server">
    protected void Button1_Click(object sender, System.EventArgs e)
    {
        Label1.Text = "Hello " + TextBox1.Text + "!";
    }
</script>
```

Right away you see some differences. As stated before, this page has no `<form id="form1" runat="server">` tag nor any opening or closing `<html>` tags. These tags are not included because they are located in the master page. Also notice a new server control — the `<asp:Content>` server control.

```
<asp:Content ID="Content1" ContentPlaceHolderId="ContentPlaceHolder1"
 runat="server">
   ...
</asp:Content>
```

The `<asp:Content>` server control is a defined content area that maps to a specific `<asp:ContentPlaceHolder>` server control on the master page. In this example, you can see that the `<asp:Content>` server control maps itself to the `<asp:ContentPlaceHolder>` server control in the master page that has the `ID` of `ContentPlaceHolder1`. Within the content page, you don't have to worry about specifying the location of the content because this is already defined within the master page. Therefore, your only concern is to place the appropriate content within the provided content sections, allowing the master page to do most of the work for you.

Just as when you work with any typical `.aspx` page, you can create any event handlers for your content page. In this case, you are using just a single event handler — the button click when the end user submits the form. The created `.aspx` page that includes the master page and content page material is shown in Figure 5-9.

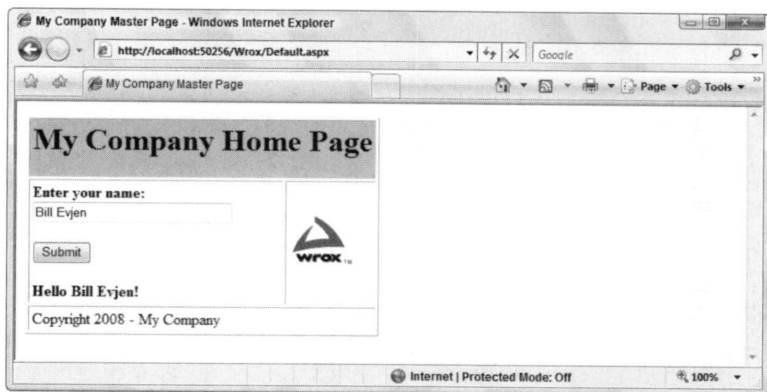

Figure 5-9

Mixing Page Types and Languages

One interesting point: When you use master pages, you are not tying yourself to a specific coding model (inline or code-behind), nor are you tying yourself to the use of a specific language. You can feel free to mix these elements within your application because they all work well.

You could use the master page created earlier, knowing that it was created using the inline-coding model, and then build your content pages using the code-behind model. Listing 5-4 shows a content page created using a Web Form that uses the code-behind option.

Listing 5-4: A content page that uses the code-behind model

.aspx (VB)

```
<%@ Page Language="VB" MasterPageFile="~/Wrox.master" AutoEventWireup="false"
    CodeFile="MyContentPage.aspx.vb" Inherits="MyContentPage" %>

<asp:Content ID="Content1" ContentPlaceHolderID="head" Runat="Server">
</asp:Content>

<asp:Content ID="Content2" ContentPlaceHolderId="ContentPlaceHolder1"
 runat="server">
    <b>Enter your name:</b><br />
    <asp:Textbox ID="TextBox1" runat="server" />
    <br />
    <br />
    <asp:Button ID="Button1" runat="server" Text="Submit" /><br />
    <br />
    <asp:Label ID="Label1" runat="server" Font-Bold="True" />
</asp:Content>

<asp:Content ID="Content3" ContentPlaceHolderId="ContentPlaceHolder2"
 runat="server">
        <asp:Image ID="Image1" runat="server" ImageUrl="ineta.JPG" />
</asp:Content>
```

VB Code-Behind

```
Partial Class MyContentPage
   Inherits System.Web.UI.Page

   Protected Sub Button1_Click(ByVal sender As Object, _
     ByVal e As System.EventArgs) Handles Button1.Click

      Label1.Text = "Hello " & TextBox1.Text & "!"
   End Sub

End Class
```

C# Code-Behind

```
public partial class MyContentPage : System.Web.UI.Page
{
    protected void Button1_Click (object sender, System.EventArgs e)
    {
        Label1.Text = "Hello " + TextBox1.Text + "!";
    }
}
```

Even though the master page is using the inline-coding model, you can easily create content pages (such as the page shown in Listing 5-4) that use the code-behind model. The pages will still work perfectly.

Not only can you mix the coding models when using master pages, you can also mix the programming languages you use for the master or content pages. Just because you build a master page in C# doesn't mean that you are required to use C# for all the content pages that use this master page. You can also build content pages in Visual Basic. For a good example, create a master page in C# that uses the `Page_Load` event handler and then create a content page in Visual Basic. Once it is complete, run the page. It works perfectly well. This means that even though you might have a master page in one of the available .NET languages, the programming teams that build applications from the master page can use whatever .NET language they want. You have to love the openness that the .NET Framework offers!

Specifying Which Master Page to Use

You just observed that it is pretty easy to specify at page level which master page to use. In the `Page` directive of the content page, you simply use the `MasterPageFile` attribute:

```
<%@ Page Language="VB" MasterPageFile="~/Wrox.master" %>
```

Besides specifying the master page that you want to use at the page level, you have a second way to specify which master page you want to use in the `web.config` file of the application. This is shown in Listing 5-5.

Listing 5-5: Specifying the master page in the web.config file

```
<configuration>
   <system.web>
      <pages masterPageFile="~/Wrox.master" />
   </system.web>
</configuration>
```

Specifying the master page in the `web.config` file causes every single content page you create in the application to inherit from the specified master page. If you declare your master page in the `web.config` file, you can create any number of content pages that use this master page. Once specified in this manner, the content page's `Page` directive can then be constructed in the following manner:

```
<%@ Page Language="VB" %>
```

You can easily override the application-wide master page specification by simply declaring a different master page within your content page:

```
<%@ Page Language="VB" MasterPageFile="~/MyOtherCompany.master" %>
```

By specifying the master page in the `web.config`, you are really not saying that you want *all* the `.aspx` pages to use this master page. If you create a normal Web Form and run it, ASP.NET will know that the page is not a content page and will run the page as a normal `.aspx` page.

If you want to apply the master page template to only a specific subset of pages (such as pages contained within a specific folder of your application), you can use the `<location>` element within the `web.config` file, as illustrated in Listing 5-6.

Listing 5-6: Specifying the master page for a specific folder in the web.config file

```
<configuration>

    <location path="AdministrationArea">
        <system.web>
            <pages masterPageFile="~/WroxAdmin.master" />
        </system.web>
    </location>

</configuration>
```

With the addition of this `<location>` section in the `web.config` file, you have now specified that a specific folder (`AdministrationArea`) will use a different master file template. This is done using the path attribute of the `<location>` element. The value of the `path` attribute can be a folder name as shown, or it can even be a specific page — such as `AdminPage.aspx`.

Working with the Page Title

When you create content pages in your application, by default all the content pages automatically use the title that is declared in the master page. For instance, you have primarily been using a master page with the title `My Company Master Page`. Every content page that is created using this particular master page also uses the same `My Company Master Page` title. You can avoid this by specifying the page's title using the `Title` attribute in the `@Page` directive in the content page. You can also work with the page title programmatically in your content pages. To accomplish this, in the code of the content page, you use the `Master` object. The `Master` object conveniently has a property called `Title`. The value of this property is the page title that is used for the content page. You code it as shown in Listing 5-7.

Listing 5-7: Coding a custom page title for the content page

VB

```
<%@ Page Language="VB" MasterPageFile="~/Wrox.master" %>

<script runat="server">
    Protected Sub Page_LoadComplete(ByVal sender As Object, _
       ByVal e As System.EventArgs)

        Master.Page.Title = "This page was generated on: " & _
           DateTime.Now.ToString()

    End Sub
</script>
```

C#

```
<%@ Page Language="C#" MasterPageFile="~/wrox.master" %>

<script runat="server">
    protected void Page_LoadComplete(object sender, EventArgs e)
    {
        Master.Page.Title = "This page was generated on: " +
           DateTime.Now.ToString();
    }
</script>
```

Working with Controls and Properties from the Master Page

When working with master pages from a content page, you actually have good access to the controls and the properties that the master page exposes. The master page, when referenced by the content page, exposes a property called `Master`. You use this property to get at control values or custom properties that are contained in the master page itself.

To see an example of this, create a GUID (unique identifier) in the master page that you can retrieve on the content page that is using the master. For this example, use the master page that was created in Listing 5-1, but add a Label server control and the `Page_Load` event (see Listing 5-8).

Listing 5-8: A master page that creates a GUID on the first request

VB

```
<%@ Master Language="VB" %>

<script runat="server">
    Protected Sub Page_Load(ByVal sender As Object, ByVal e As System.EventArgs)
        If Not Page.IsPostBack Then
            Label1.Text = System.Guid.NewGuid().ToString()
        End If
    End Sub
</script>

<html xmlns="http://www.w3.org/1999/xhtml" >
<head runat="server">
    <title>My Company Master Page</title>
    <asp:ContentPlaceHolder id="head" runat="server">
    </asp:ContentPlaceHolder>
</head>
<body>
    <form id="form1" runat="server">
        <table cellpadding="3" border="1">
            <tr bgcolor="silver">
                <td colspan="2">
                    <h1>My Company Home Page</h1>
                    <b>User's GUID:  
                        <asp:Label ID="Label1" runat="server" /></b>
                </td>
            </tr>
            <tr>
                <td>
                    <asp:ContentPlaceHolder ID="ContentPlaceHolder1"
                     runat="server">
                    </asp:ContentPlaceHolder>
                </td>
                <td>
                    <asp:ContentPlaceHolder ID="ContentPlaceHolder2"
                     runat="server">
                    </asp:ContentPlaceHolder>
```

Continued

```
                </td>
            </tr>
            <tr>
                <td colspan="2">
                    Copyright 2008 - My Company
                </td>
            </tr>
        </table>
    </form>
</body>
</html>
```

C#

```
protected void Page_Load(object sender, EventArgs e)
{
    if (!Page.IsPostBack)
    {
        Label1.Text = System.Guid.NewGuid().ToString();
    }
}
```

Now you have a Label control on the master page that you can access from the content page. You have a couple of ways to accomplish this task. The first is to use the `FindControl()` method that the master page exposes. This approach is shown in Listing 5-9.

Listing 5-9: Getting at the Label's Text value in the content page

VB

```
<%@ Page Language="VB" MasterPageFile="~/Wrox.master" %>

<script runat="server" language="vb">
    Protected Sub Page_LoadComplete(ByVal sender As Object, _
       ByVal e As System.EventArgs)

        Label1.Text = CType(Master.FindControl("Label1"), Label).Text
    End Sub

    Protected Sub Button1_Click(ByVal sender As Object, _
       ByVal e As System.EventArgs)

        Label2.Text = "Hello " & TextBox1.Text & "!"
    End Sub
</script>

<asp:Content ID="Content1" ContentPlaceHolderID="head" Runat="Server">
</asp:Content>

<asp:Content ID="Content2" ContentPlaceHolderId="ContentPlaceHolder1"
 runat="server">
    <b>Your GUID number from the master page is:<br />
```

```
        <asp:Label ID="Label1" runat="server" /></b><p>
        <b>Enter your name:</b><br />
        <asp:Textbox ID="TextBox1" runat="server" />
        <br />
        <br />
        <asp:Button ID="Button1" runat="server" Text="Submit"
         OnClick="Button1_Click" /><br />
        <br />
        <asp:Label ID="Label2" runat="server" Font-Bold="True" />
</asp:Content>

<asp:Content ID="Content3" ContentPlaceHolderId="ContentPlaceHolder2"
 runat="server">
        <asp:Image ID="Image1" runat="server" ImageUrl="Wrox.gif" />
</asp:Content>
```

C#

```
<%@ Page Language="C#" MasterPageFile="~/wrox.master" %>

<script runat="server">

    protected void Page_LoadComplete(object sender, EventArgs e)
    {
        Label1.Text = (Master.FindControl("Label1") as Label).Text;
    }

    protected void Button1_Click(object sender, EventArgs e)
    {
        Label2.Text = "<b>Hello " + TextBox1.Text + "!</b>";
    }
</script>
```

In this example, the master page in Listing 5-8 first creates a GUID that it stores as a text value in a Label server control on the master page itself. The `ID` of this Label control is `Label1`. The master page generates this GUID only on the first request for this particular content page. From here, you then populate one of the content page's controls with this value.

The interesting thing about the content page is that you put code in the `Page_LoadComplete` event handler so that you can get at the GUID value that is on the master page. This new event in ASP.NET fires immediately after the `Page_Load` event fires. Event ordering is covered later, but the `Page_Load` event in the content page always fires before the `Page_Load` event in the master page. In order to get at the newly created GUID (if it is created in the master page's `Page_Load` event), you have to get the GUID in an event that comes after the `Page_Load` event — and that is where the `Page_LoadComplete` comes into play. Therefore, within the content page's `Page_LoadComplete` event, you populate a Label server control within the content page itself. Note that the Label control in the content page has the same `ID` as the Label control in the master page, but this doesn't make a difference. You can differentiate between them with the use of the `Master` property.

Not only can you get at the server controls that are in the master page in this way, you can get at any custom properties that the master page might expose as well. Look at the master page shown in Listing 5-10; it uses a custom property for the `<h1>` section of the page.

Listing 5-10: A master page that exposes a custom property

VB

```
<%@ Master Language="VB" %>

<script runat="server">
    Protected Sub Page_Load(ByVal sender As Object, ByVal e As System.EventArgs)
        If Not Page.IsPostBack Then
            Label1.Text = Guid.NewGuid().ToString()
        End If
    End Sub

    Dim m_PageHeadingTitle As String = "My Company"

    Public Property PageHeadingTitle() As String
        Get
            Return m_PageHeadingTitle
        End Get
        Set(ByVal Value As String)
            m_PageHeadingTitle = Value
        End Set
    End Property
</script>

<html xmlns="http://www.w3.org/1999/xhtml" >
<head id="Head1" runat="server">
    <title>My Company Master Page</title>
    <asp:ContentPlaceHolder id="head" runat="server">
    </asp:ContentPlaceHolder>
</head>
<body>
    <form id="Form1" runat="server">
        <table cellpadding="3" border="1">
            <tr bgcolor="silver">
                <td colspan="2">
                    <h1><%= PageHeadingTitle %></h1>
                    <b>User's GUID:  
                        <asp:Label ID="Label1" runat="server" /></b>
                </td>
            </tr>
            <tr>
                <td>
                    <asp:ContentPlaceHolder ID="ContentPlaceHolder1"
                     runat="server">
                    </asp:ContentPlaceHolder>
                </td>
                <td>
                    <asp:ContentPlaceHolder ID="ContentPlaceHolder2"
                     runat="server">
                    </asp:ContentPlaceHolder>
                </td>
            </tr>
            <tr>
```

```
                <td colspan="2">
                    Copyright 2008 - My Company
                </td>
            </tr>
        </table>
    </form>
</body>
</html>
```

C#

```
<%@ Master Language="C#" %>

<script runat="server">
    protected void Page_Load(object sender, EventArgs e)
    {
        if (!Page.IsPostBack)
        {
            Label1.Text = System.Guid.NewGuid().ToString();
        }
    }

    string m_PageHeadingTitle = "My Company";

    public string PageHeadingTitle
    {
        get
        {
            return m_PageHeadingTitle;
        }
        set
        {
            m_PageHeadingTitle = value;
        }
    }
</script>
```

In this master page example, the master page is exposing the property you created called `PageHeadingTitle`. A default value of `"My Company"` is assigned to this property. You then place it within the HTML of the master page file between some `<h1>` elements. This makes the default value become the heading used on the page within the master page template. Although the master page already has a value it uses for the heading, any content page that is using this master page can override the `<h3>` title heading. The process is shown in Listing 5-11.

Listing 5-11: A content page that overrides the property from the master page

VB

```
<%@ Page Language="VB" MasterPageFile="~/Wrox.master" %>
<%@ MasterType VirtualPath="~/Wrox.master" %>

<script runat="server">
    Protected Sub Page_Load(ByVal sender As Object, ByVal e As System.EventArgs)
```

Continued

```
        Master.PageHeadingTitle = "My Company-Division X"
    End Sub
</script>
```

C#

```
<%@ Page Language="C#" MasterPageFile="~/Wrox.master" %>
<%@ MasterType VirtualPath="~/Wrox.master" %>

<script runat="server">
    protected void Page_Load(object sender, EventArgs e)
    {
        Master.PageHeadingTitle = "My Company-Division X";
    }
</script>
```

From the content page, you can assign a value to the property that is exposed from the master page by the use of the `Master` property. As you can see, this is quite simple to do. Remember that not only can you get at any public properties that the master page might expose, but you can also retrieve any methods that the master page contains as well.

The item that makes this all possible is the use of the `MasterType` page directive. The `MasterType` directive allows you to make a strongly typed reference to the master page and allows you to access the master page's properties via the `Master` object.

Earlier, we showed you how to get at the server controls that are on the master page by using the `FindControl()` method. The `FindControl()` method works fine, but it is a late-bound approach, and as such, the method call may fail if the control was removed from markup. Use defensive coding practices and always check for null when returning objects from `FindControl()`. Using the mechanics just illustrated (with the use of public properties shown in Listing 5-10), you can use another approach to expose any server controls on the master page. You may find this approach to be more effective.

To do this, you simply expose the server control as a public property, as shown in Listing 5-12.

Listing 5-12: Exposing a server control from a master page as a public property

VB

```
<%@ Master Language="VB" %>

<script runat="server">
    Public Property MasterPageLabel1() As Label
        Get
            Return Label1
        End Get
        Set(ByVal Value As Label)
            Label1 = Value
        End Set
    End Property
</script>
```

C#

```
<%@ Master Language="C#" %>

<script runat="server">
    public Label MasterPageLabel1
    {
        get
        {
            return Label1;
        }
        set
        {
            Label1 = value;
        }
    }
</script>
```

In this case, a public property called `MasterPageLabel1` provides access to the Label control that uses the `ID` of `Label1`. You can now create an instance of the `MasterPageLabel1` property on the content page and override any of the attributes of the Label server control. So if you want to increase the size of the GUID that the master page creates and displays in the `Label1` server control, you can simply override the `Font.Size` attribute of the Label control, as shown in Listing 5-13.

Listing 5-13: Overriding an attribute from the Label control that is on the master page

VB

```
<%@ Page Language="VB" MasterPageFile="~/Wrox.master" %>
<%@ MasterType VirtualPath="~/Wrox.master" %>

<script runat="server">
    Protected Sub Page_Load(ByVal sender As Object, ByVal e As System.EventArgs)
        Master.MasterPageLabel1.Font.Size = 25
    End Sub
</script>
```

C#

```
<%@ Page Language="C#" MasterPageFile="~/Wrox.master" %>
<%@ MasterType VirtualPath="~/Wrox.master" %>

<script runat="server">
    protected void Page_Load(object sender, EventArgs e)
    {
        Master.MasterPageLabel1.Font.Size = 25;
    }
</script>
```

This approach may be the most effective way to get at any server controls that the master page exposes to the content pages.

Specifying Default Content in the Master Page

As you have seen, the master page enables you to specify content areas that the content page can use. Master pages can consist of just one content area, or they can be made up of multiple content areas. The nice thing about content areas is that when you create a master page, you can specify default content for the content area. This default content can then be left in place and utilized by the content page if you choose not to override it. Listing 5-14 shows a master page that specifies some default content within a content area.

Listing 5-14: Specifying default content in the master page

```
<%@ Master Language="VB" %>

<html xmlns="http://www.w3.org/1999/xhtml" >
<head runat="server">
    <title>My Company</title>
    <asp:ContentPlaceHolder id="head" runat="server">
    </asp:ContentPlaceHolder>
</head>
<body>
    <form id="form1" runat="server">
        <asp:ContentPlaceHolder ID="ContentPlaceHolder1" runat="server">
        Here is some default content.
        </asp:ContentPlaceHolder><p>
        <asp:ContentPlaceHolder ID="ContentPlaceHolder2" runat="server">
        Here is some more default content.
        </asp:ContentPlaceHolder></p>
    </form>
</body>
</html>
```

To place default content within one of the content areas of the master page, you simply put it in the `ContentPlaceHolder` server control on the master page itself. Any content page that inherits this master page also inherits the default content. Listing 5-15 shows a content page that overrides just one of the content areas from this master page.

Listing 5-15: Overriding some default content in the content page

```
<%@ Page Language="VB" MasterPageFile="~/MasterPage.master" %>

<asp:Content ID="Content3" ContentPlaceHolderId="ContentPlaceHolder2"
 runat="server">
    Here is some new content.
</asp:Content>
```

This code creates a page with one content area that shows content coming from the master page itself, in addition to other content that comes from the content page (see Figure 5-10).

The other interesting point when you work with content areas in the design mode of Visual Studio 2008 is that the smart tag allows you to work easily with the default content.

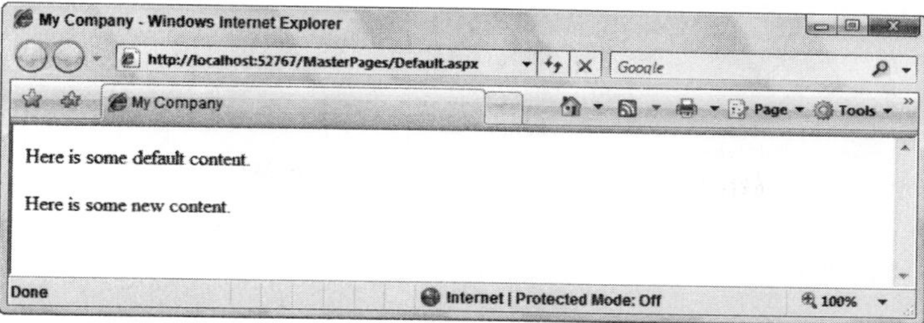

Figure 5-10

When you first start working with the content page, you will notice that all the default content is at first populated in all the Content server controls. You can change the content by clicking on the control's smart tag and selecting the Create Custom Content option from the provided menu. This option enables you to override the master page content and insert your own defined content. After you have placed some custom content inside the content area, the smart tag shows a different option — Default to Master's Content. This option enables you to return the default content that the master page exposes to the content area and to erase whatever content you have already placed in the content area — thereby simply returning to the default content. If you choose this option, you will be warned that you are about to delete any custom content you placed within the Content server control (see Figure 5-11).

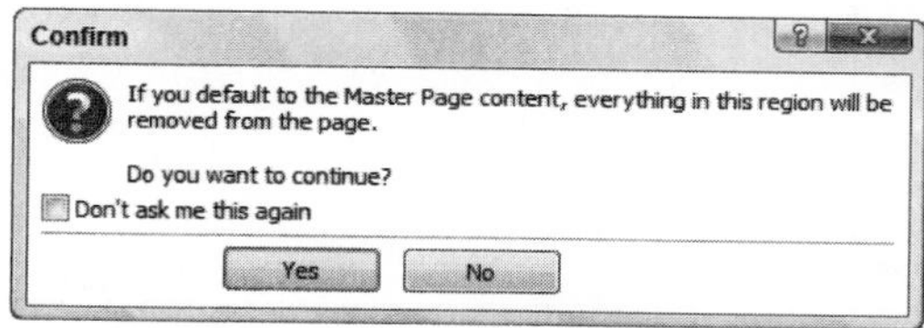

Figure 5-11

After changing one of the Content control's default content, you might be presented with something like Figure 5-12.

Programmatically Assigning the Master Page

From any content page, you can easily assign a master page programmatically. You assign the master page to the content page using the `Page.MasterPageFile` property. This can be used regardless of whether another master page is already assigned in the `@Page` directive.

To accomplish this, you use this property through the `PreInit` event. The `PreInit` event is the earliest point in which you can access the Page lifecycle. For this reason, this is where you need to assign any master page that is used by any content pages. The `PreInit` is an important event to make note of when you are working with master pages, as this is the only point where you can affect both the master and content page before they are combined into a single instance. Listing 5-16 illustrates how to assign the master page programmatically from the content page.

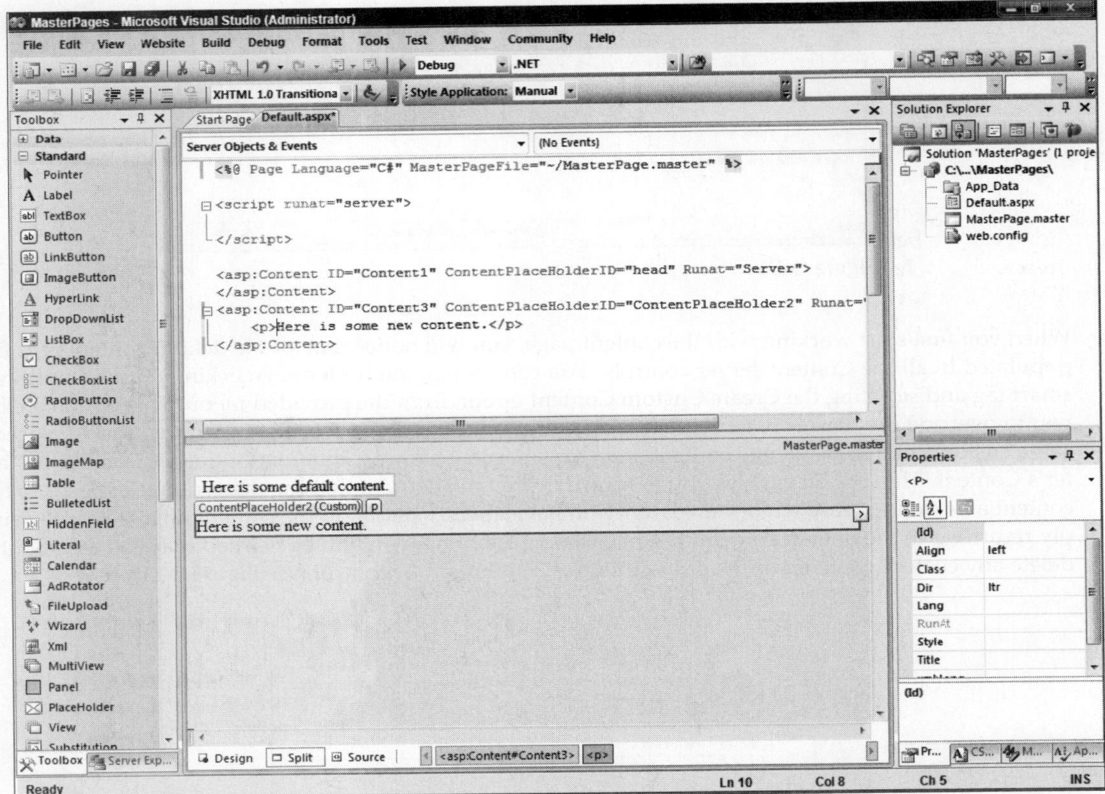

Figure 5-12

Listing 5-16: Using Page_PreInit to assign the master page programmatically

VB

```
<%@ Page Language="VB" %>

<script runat="server">
    Protected Sub Page_PreInit(ByVal sender As Object, ByVal e As System.EventArgs)
        Page.MasterPageFile = "~/MyMasterPage.master"
    End Sub
</script>
```

C#

```
<%@ Page Language="C#" %>

<script runat="server">
    protected void Page_PreInit(object sender, EventArgs e)
    {
        Page.MasterPageFile = "~/MyMasterPage.master";
    }
</script>
```

In this case, when the page is dynamically being generated, the master page is assigned to the content page in the beginning of the page construction process. It is important to note that the content page must have the expected Content controls; otherwise an error is thrown.

Nesting Master Pages

I hope you see the power that master pages provide to help you create templated Web applications. So far, you have been creating a single master page that the content page can use. Most companies and organizations, however, are not just two layers. Many divisions and groups exist within the organization that might want to use variations of the master by, in effect, having a master page within a master page. With ASP.NET, this is quite possible.

For example, imagine that Reuters is creating a master page to be used throughout the entire company intranet. Not only does the Reuters enterprise want to implement this master page company-wide, but various divisions within Reuters also want to provide templates for the subsections of the intranet directly under their control. Reuters Europe and Reuters America, for example, each wants its own unique master page, as illustrated in Figure 5-13.

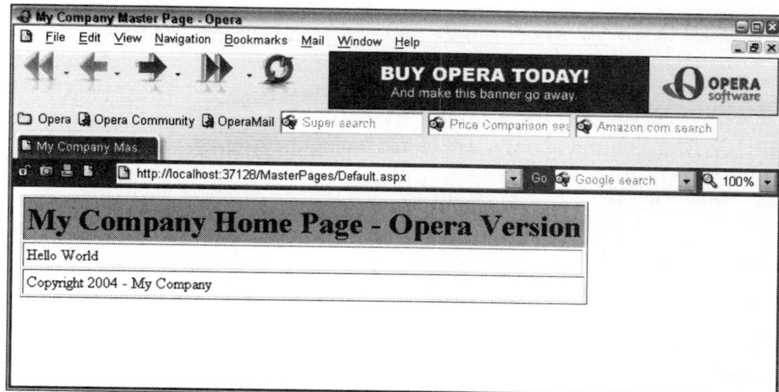

Figure 5-13

To do this, the creators of the Reuters Europe and Reuters America master pages simply create a master page that inherits from the global master page, as illustrated in Listing 5-17.

Listing 5-17: The main master page

ReutersMain.master

```
<%@ Master Language="VB" %>

<html xmlns="http://www.w3.org/1999/xhtml" >
<head runat="server">
    <title>Reuters</title>
    <asp:ContentPlaceHolder id="head" runat="server">
    </asp:ContentPlaceHolder>
</head>
```

Continued

```
    <body>
        <form id="form1" runat="server">
            <p><asp:Label ID="Label1" runat="server" BackColor="LightGray"
                BorderColor="Black" BorderWidth="1px" BorderStyle="Solid"
                Font-Size="XX-Large"> Reuters Main Master Page </asp:Label></p>
            <asp:ContentPlaceHolder ID="ContentPlaceHolder1" runat="server">
            </asp:ContentPlaceHolder>
        </form>
    </body>
    </html>
```

This is a simple master page, but excellent for showing you how this nesting capability works. The main master page is the master page used globally in the company. It has the ContentPlaceHolder server control with the `ID` of `ContentPlaceHolder1`.

When you create a submaster or nested master page, you accomplish this task in the same manner as you would when building any other master page. From the Add New Item dialog, select the Master Page option and make sure you have the Select master page option selected, as illustrated in Figure 5-14. This will take you again to the dialog that will allow you to make a master page selection.

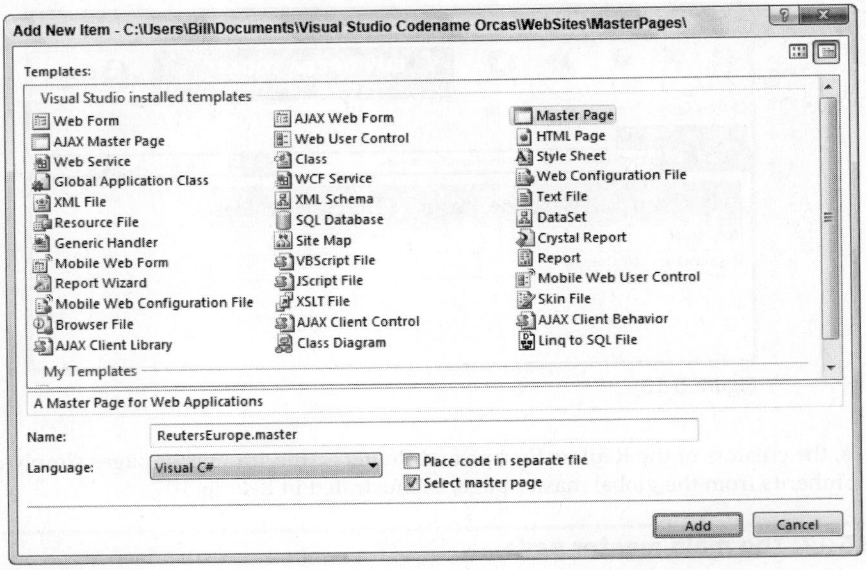

Figure 5-14

Listing 5-18 illustrates how you can work with this main master from a submaster file.

Listing 5-18: The submaster page

ReutersEurope.master

```
<%@ Master Language="VB" MasterPageFile="~/ReutersMain.master" %>

<asp:Content ID="Content1" ContentPlaceHolderID="head" Runat="Server">
</asp:Content>
```

```
<asp:Content ID="Content2" ContentPlaceHolderId="ContentPlaceHolder1"
 runat="server">
    <asp:Label ID="Label1" runat="server" BackColor="#E0E0E0" BorderColor="Black"
     BorderStyle="Dotted" BorderWidth="2px" Font-Size="Large">
     Reuters Europe </asp:Label><br /><hr />

        <asp:ContentPlaceHolder ID="ContentPlaceHolder1" runat="server">
        </asp:ContentPlaceHolder>
</asp:Content>
```

Looking this page over, you can see that it isn't much different than a typical `.aspx` page that makes use of a master page. The `MasterPageFile` attribute is used just the same, but instead of using the `@Page` directive, the `@Master` page directive is used. Then the `Content2` control also uses the `ContentPlace-HolderId` attribute of the Content control. This attribute is tying this content area to the content area `ContentPlaceHolder1`, which is defined in the main master page.

One new feature of ASP.NET 3.5 is the ability to view nested master pages directly in the Design view of Visual Studio 2008. The previous Visual Studio 2005 would actually throw an error when trying to present a nested master page. Figure 5-15 shows a nested master page in the Design view of Visual Studio 2008.

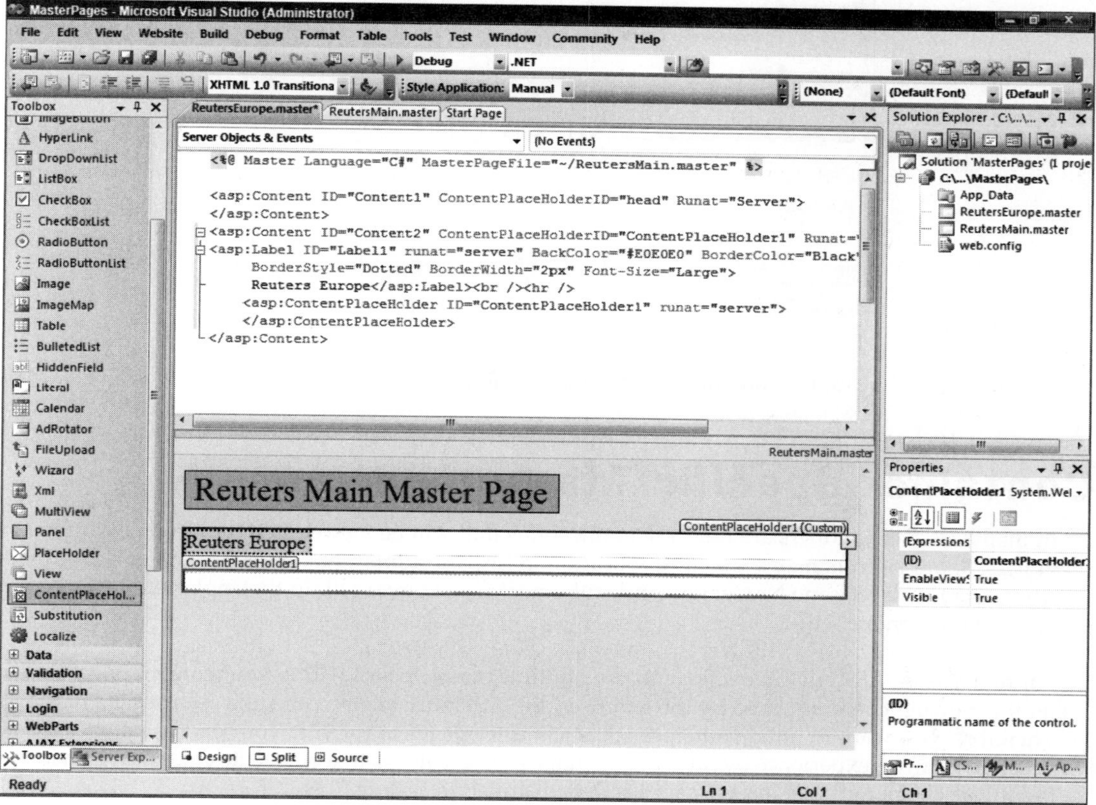

Figure 5-15

Within the submaster page presented in Listing 5-18, you can also now use as many ContentPlaceHolder server controls as you want. Any content page that uses this master can use these controls. Listing 5-19 shows a content page that uses the submaster page `ReutersEurope.master`.

Listing 5-19: The content page

Default.aspx

```
<%@ Page Language="VB" MasterPageFile="~/ReutersEurope.master" %>

<asp:Content ID="Content1" ContentPlaceHolderId="ContentPlaceHolder1"
 runat="server">
    Hello World
</asp:Content>
```

As you can see, in this content page the value of the `MasterPageFile` attribute in the `Page` directive is the submaster page that you created. Inheriting the `ReutersEurope` master page actually combines both master pages (`ReutersMain.master` and `ReutersEurope.master`) into a single master page. The Content control in this content page points to the content area defined in the submaster page as well. You can see this in the code with the use of the `ContentPlaceHolderId` attribute. In the end, you get a very non-artistic page, as shown in Figure 5-16.

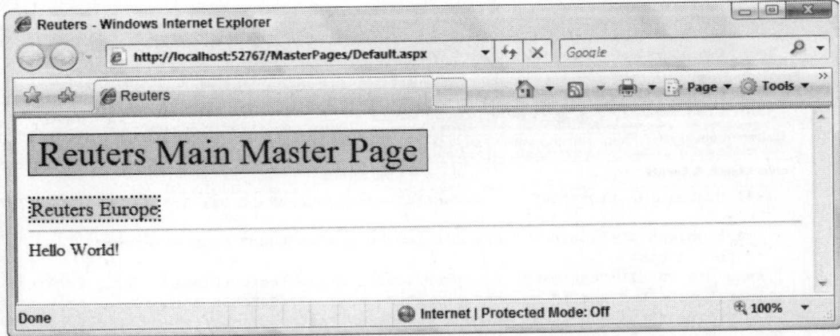

Figure 5-16

As you can see, creating a content page that uses a submaster page works pretty well.

Container-Specific Master Pages

In many cases, developers are building applications that will be viewed in a multitude of different containers. Some viewers may view the application in Microsoft Internet Explorer and some might view it using Opera or Netscape Navigator. And still other viewers may call up the application on a Pocket PC or Nokia cell phone.

For this reason, ASP.NET allows you to use multiple master pages within your content page. Depending on the viewing container used by the end user, the ASP.NET engine pulls the appropriate master file. Therefore, you want to build container-specific master pages to provide your end users with the best possible viewing experience by taking advantage of the features that a specific container provides. The capability to use multiple master pages is demonstrated in Listing 5-20.

Listing 5-20: A content page that can work with more than one master page

```
<%@ Page Language="VB" MasterPageFile="~/Wrox.master"
       Mozilla:MasterPageFile="~/WroxMozilla.master"
       Opera:MasterPageFile="~/WroxOpera.master" %>

<asp:Content ID="Content1" ContentPlaceHolderID="head" Runat="Server">
</asp:Content>

<asp:Content ID="Content2" ContentPlaceHolderId="ContentPlaceHolder1"
 runat="server">
    Hello World
</asp:Content>
```

As you can see from this example content page, it can work with three different master page files. The first one uses the attribute `MasterPageFile`. This is the default setting used for any page that doesn't fit the criteria for any of the other options. This means that if the requestor is not a Mozilla or Opera browser, the default master page, `Wrox.master`, is used. However, if the requestor is an Opera browser, `WroxOpera.master` is used instead. This is illustrated in Figure 5-17.

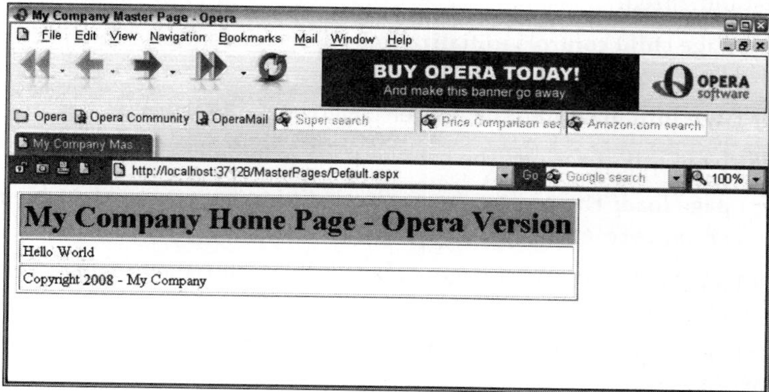

Figure 5-17

You can find a list of available browsers on the production server where the application will be hosted at `C:\Windows\Microsoft.NET\Framework\v2.0.50727\CONFIG\Browsers`. Some of the available options include the following:

- avantgo
- cassio
- Default
- docomo
- ericsson
- EZWap
- gateway
- generic
- goAmerica
- ie
- Jataayu
- jphone
- legend
- MME
- mozilla
- netscape

- nokia
- openwave
- opera
- palm
- panasonic
- pie
- webtv
- winwap
- xiino

Of course, you can also add any additional `.browser` files that you deem necessary.

Event Ordering

When you work with master pages and content pages, both can use the same events (such as the `Load` event). Be sure you know which events come before others. You are bringing two classes together to create a single page class, and a specific order is required. When an end user requests a content page in the browser, the event ordering is as follows:

- **Master page child controls initialization:** All server controls contained within the master page are first initialized.
- **Content page child controls initialization:** All server controls contained in the content page are initialized.
- **Master page initialization:** The master page itself is initialized.
- **Content page initialization:** The content page is initialized.
- **Content page load:** The content page is loaded (this is the `Page_Load` event followed by the `Page_LoadComplete` event).
- **Master page load:** The master page is loaded (this is also the `Page_Load` event followed by the `Page_LoadComplete` event).
- **Master page child controls load:** The server controls on the master page are loaded onto the page.
- **Content page child controls load:** The server controls on the content page are loaded onto the page.

Pay attention to this event ordering when building your applications. If you want to use server control values that are contained on the master page within a specific content page, for example, you can't retrieve the values of these server controls from within the content page's `Page_Load` event. This is because this event is triggered before the master page's `Page_Load` event. This problem prompted the creation of the new `Page_LoadComplete` event. The content page's `Page_LoadComplete` event follows the master page's `Page_Load` event. You can, therefore, use this ordering to get at values from the master page even though it isn't populated when the content page's `Page_Load` event is triggered.

Caching with Master Pages

When working with typical `.aspx` pages, you can apply output caching to the page by using the following construct (or variation thereof):

```
<%@ OutputCache Duration="10" Varybyparam="None" %>
```

This caches the page in the server's memory for 10 seconds. Many developers use output caching to increase the performance of their ASP.NET pages. It also makes a lot of sense for use on pages with data that doesn't become stale too quickly.

How do you go about applying output caching to ASP.NET pages when working with master pages? First, you cannot apply caching to just the master page. You cannot put the `OutputCache` directive on the master page itself. If you do so, on the page's second retrieval, you get an error because the application cannot find the cached page.

To work with output caching when using a master page, stick the `OutputCache` directive in the content page. This caches both the contents of the content page as well as the contents of the master page (remember, it is just a single page at this point). The `OutputCache` directive placed in the master page does not cause the master page to produce an error, but it will not be cached. This directive works in the content page only.

ASP.NET AJAX and Master Pages

Many of the larger ASP.NET applications today make use of master pages and the power this technology provides in the ability of building templated Web sites. ASP.NET 3.5 introduces ASP.NET AJAX as part of the default install and you will find that master pages and Ajax go together quite well.

ASP.NET AJAX is covered in Chapter 19 of this book.

Every page that is going to make use of AJAX capabilities will have to have the new ScriptManager control on the page. If the page that you want to use AJAX with is a content page making use of a master page, then you are going to have to place the ScriptManager control on the master page itself.

Note that you can only have one ScriptManager on a page.

ASP.NET 3.5 makes this process easy. Opening up the Add New Item dialog, you will notice that in addition to the Master Page option, you will also find an AJAX Master Page option as illustrated in Figure 5-18.

Selecting this option produces a page like the one presented in Listing 5-21.

Listing 5-21: The AJAX master page

```
<%@ Master Language="VB" %>

<script runat="server">

</script>

<html xmlns="http://www.w3.org/1999/xhtml">
<head runat="server">
    <title>Untitled Page</title>
    <asp:ContentPlaceHolder id="head" runat="server">
    </asp:ContentPlaceHolder>
</head>
<body>
```

Continued

```
        <form id="form1" runat="server">
        <div>
            <asp:ScriptManager ID="ScriptManager1" runat="server" />
            <asp:ContentPlaceHolder id="ContentPlaceHolder1" runat="server">

            </asp:ContentPlaceHolder>
        </div>
        </form>
    </body>
    </html>
```

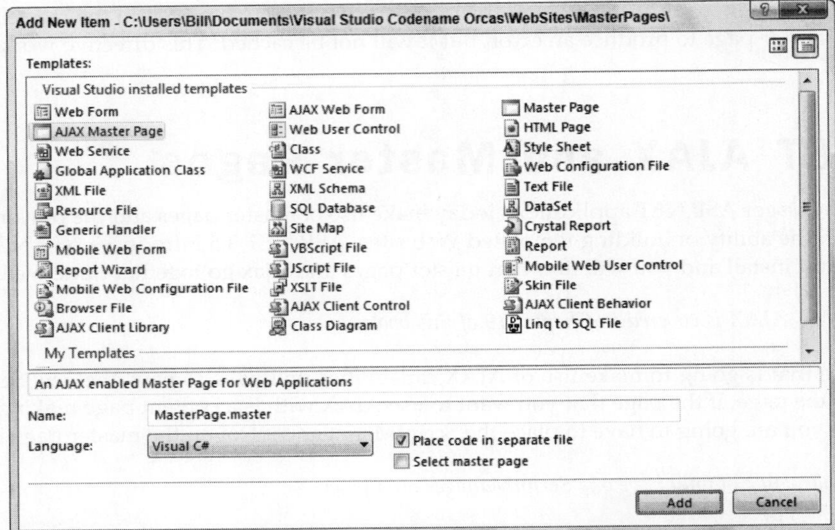

Figure 5-18

As you can see from Listing 5-21, the only real difference between this AJAX master page and the standard master page is the inclusion of the ScriptManager server control. You are going to want to use this technique if your master page includes any AJAX capabilities whatsoever, even if the content page makes no use of AJAX at all.

The ScriptManager control on the master page also is beneficial if you have common JavaScript items to place on all the pages of your Web application. For instance, Listing 5-22 shows how you could easily include JavaScript on each page through the master page.

Listing 5-22: Including scripts through your master page

```
<%@ Master Language="VB" %>

<html xmlns="http://www.w3.org/1999/xhtml">
<head runat="server">
    <title>Untitled Page</title>
```

```
        <asp:ContentPlaceHolder id="head" runat="server">
        </asp:ContentPlaceHolder>
    </head>
    <body>
        <form id="form1" runat="server">
        <div>
            <asp:ScriptManager ID="ScriptManager1" runat="server">
                <Scripts>
                    <asp:ScriptReference Path="myScript.js" />
                </Scripts>
            </asp:ScriptManager>
            <asp:ContentPlaceHolder id="ContentPlaceHolder1" runat="server">

            </asp:ContentPlaceHolder>
        </div>
        </form>
    </body>
    </html>
```

In this example, the `myScript.js` file will now be included on every content page that makes use of this AJAX master page. If your content page also needs to make use of Ajax capabilities, then you simply cannot add another ScriptManager control to the page. Instead, the content page will need to make use of the ScriptManager control that is already present on the master page.

That said, if your content page needs to add additional items to the ScriptManager control, it is able to access this control on the master page using the ScriptManagerProxy server control. Using the ScriptManagerProxy control gives you the ability to add any items to the ScriptManager that are completely specific to the instance of the content page that makes the inclusions.

For instance, Listing 5-23 shows how a content page would add additional scripts to the page through the ScriptManagerProxy control.

Listing 5-23: Adding additional items using the ScriptManagerProxy control

```
<%@ Page Language="VB" MasterPageFile="~/AjaxMaster.master" %>

<asp:Content ID="Content1" ContentPlaceHolderID="head" Runat="Server">
</asp:Content>
<asp:Content ID="Content2" ContentPlaceHolderID="ContentPlaceHolder1"
 Runat="Server">
 <asp:ScriptManagerProxy ID="ScriptManagerProxy1" runat="server">
     <Scripts>
         <asp:ScriptReference Path="myOtherScript.js" />
     </Scripts>
 </asp:ScriptManagerProxy>
</asp:Content>
```

In this case, this content page is using the ScriptManagerProxy control to add an additional script to the page. This ScriptManagerProxy control works exactly the same as the main ScriptManager control except that it is meant for content pages making use of a master page. The ScriptManagerProxy control will then interact with the page's ScriptManager control to perform the actions necessary.

Summary

When you create applications that use a common header, footer, or navigation section on pretty much every page of the application, master pages are a great solution. Master pages are easy to implement and enable you to make changes to each and every page of your application by changing a single file. Imagine how much easier this makes managing large applications that contain thousands of pages.

This chapter described master pages in ASP.NET and explained how you build and use master pages within your Web applications. In addition to the basics, the chapter covered master page event ordering, caching, and specific master pages for specific containers. In the end, when you are working with templated applications, master pages should be your first option — the power of this approach is immense.

6

Themes and Skins

When you build a Web application, it usually has a similar look-and-feel across all its pages. Not too many applications are designed with each page dramatically different from the next. Generally, for your applications, you use similar fonts, colors, and server control styles across all the pages.

You can apply these common styles individually to each and every server control or object on each page, or you can use a capability provided by ASP.NET 3.5 to centrally specify these styles. All pages or parts of pages in the application can then access them.

Themes are the text-based style definitions in ASP.NET 3.5 that are the focus of this chapter.

Using ASP.NET Themes

Themes are similar to Cascading Style Sheets (CSS) in that they enable you to define visual styles for your Web pages. Themes go further than CSS, however, in that they allow you to apply styles, graphics, and even CSS files themselves to the pages of your applications. You can apply ASP.NET themes at the application, page, or server control level.

Applying a Theme to a Single ASP.NET Page

In order to see how to use one of these themes, create a basic page, which includes some text, a text box, a button, and a calendar, as shown in Listing 6-1.

Listing 6-1: An ASP.NET page that does not use themes

```
<%@ Page Language="VB" %>

<html xmlns="http://www.w3.org/1999/xhtml">
<head runat="server">
    <title>STLNET</title>
```

```
</head>
<body>
    <form id="form1" runat="server">
        <h1>St. Louis .NET User Group</h1><br />
        <asp:Textbox ID="TextBox1" runat="server" /><br />
        <br />
        <asp:Calendar ID="Calendar1" runat="server" /><br />
        <asp:Button ID="Button1" runat="server" Text="Button" />
    </form>
</body>
</html>
```

This simple page shows some default server controls that appear just as you would expect, but that you can change with one of these new ASP.NET themes. When this theme-less page is called in the browser, it should look like Figure 6-1.

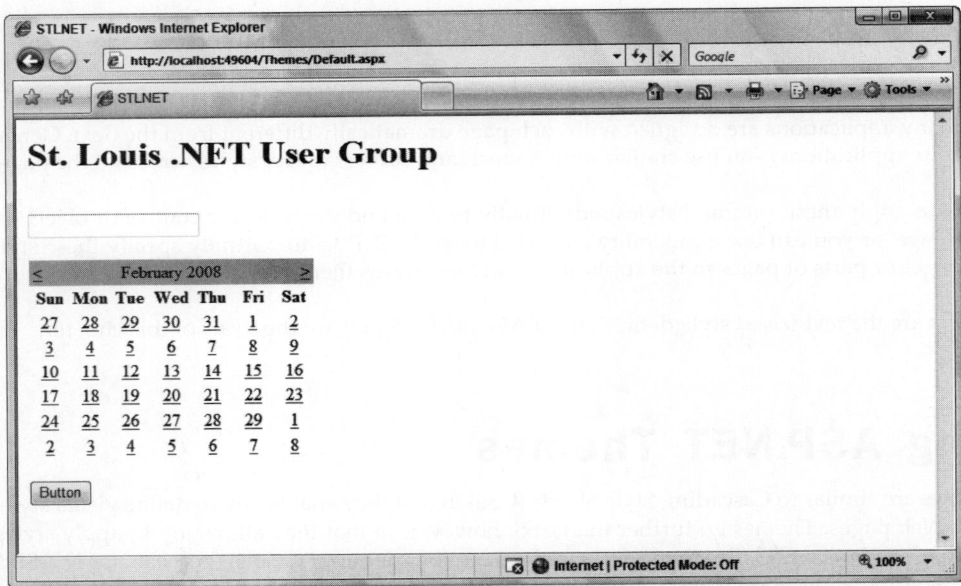

Figure 6-1

You can instantly change the appearance of this page without changing the style of each server control on the page. From within the `Page` directive, you simply apply an ASP.NET theme that you have either built (shown later in this chapter) or downloaded from the Internet:

```
<%@ Page Language="VB" Theme="SmokeAndGlass" %>
```

Adding the `Theme` attribute to the `Page` directive changes the appearance of everything on the page that is defined in an example `SmokeAndGlass` theme file. Using this theme, when we invoked the page in the browser, we got the result shown in Figure 6-2.

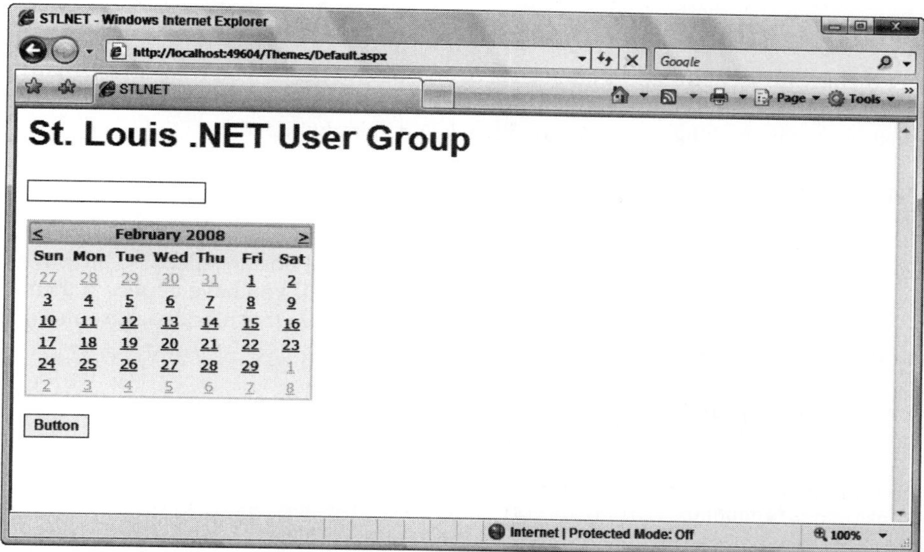

Figure 6-2

From here, you can see that everything — including the font, font color, text box, button, and more — has changed appearance. If you have multiple pages, you may find that it is nice not to have to think about applying styles to everything you do as you build because the styles are already centrally defined for you.

Applying a Theme to an Entire Application

In addition to applying an ASP.NET theme to your ASP.NET pages using the `Theme` attribute within the `Page` directive, you can also apply it at an application level from the `web.config` file. This is illustrated in Listing 6-2.

Listing 6-2: Applying a theme application-wide from the web.config file

```
<?xml version="1.0"?>

<configuration>
   <system.web>
      <pages theme="SmokeAndGlass" />
   </system.web>
</configuration>
```

If you specify the theme in the `web.config` file, you do not need to define the theme again in the `Page` directive of your ASP.NET pages. This theme is applied automatically to each and every page within your application. If you wanted to apply the theme to only a specific part of the application in this fashion, then you can do the same, but in addition, make use of the <location/> element to specify the areas of the applications for which the theme should be applied.

Removing Themes from Server Controls

Whether themes are set at the application level or on a page, at times you want an alternative to the theme that has been defined. For example, change the text box server control that you have been working with (from Listing 6-1) by making its background black and using white text:

```
<asp:Textbox ID="TextBox1" runat="server"
 BackColor="#000000" ForeColor="#ffffff" />
```

The black background color and the color of the text in the text box are specified directly in the control itself with the use of the `BackColor` and `ForeColor` attributes. If you have applied a theme to the page where this text box control is located, however, you will not see this black background or white text because these changes are overridden by the theme itself.

To apply a theme to your ASP.NET page but not to this text box control, you simply use the `Enable-Theming` property of the text box server control:

```
<asp:Textbox ID="TextBox1" runat="server"
 BackColor="#000000" ForeColor="#ffffff" EnableTheming="false" />
```

If you apply this property to the text box server control from Listing 6-1 while the `SmokeAndGlass` theme is still applied to the entire page, the theme is applied to every control on the page *except* the text box. This result is shown in Figure 6-3.

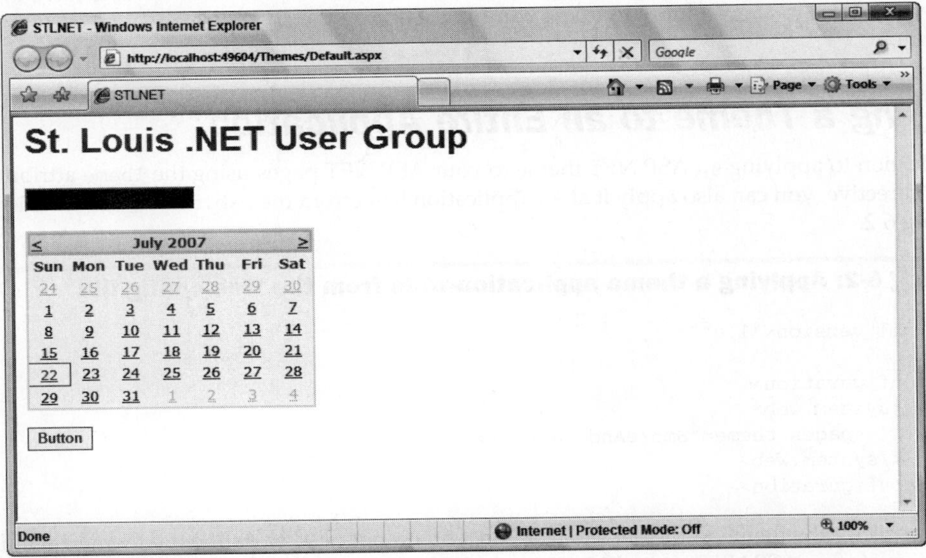

Figure 6-3

If you want to turn off theming for multiple controls within a page, consider using the Panel control (or any container control) to encapsulate a collection of controls and then set the `EnableTheming` attribute of the Panel control to `False`. This disables theming for each control contained within the Panel control.

Removing Themes from Web Pages

Now what if, when you set the theme for an entire application in the `web.config` file, you want to exclude a single ASP.NET page? It is quite possible to remove a theme setting at the page level, just as it is at the server control level.

The `Page` directive includes an `EnableTheming` attribute that can be used to remove theming from your ASP.NET pages. To remove the theme that would be applied by the theme setting in the `web.config`, you simply construct your `Page` directive in the following manner:

```
<%@ Page Language="VB" EnableTheming="False" %>
```

This construct sets the theme to nothing — thereby removing any settings that were specified in the `web.config` file. When this directive is set to `False` at the page or control level, the `Theme` directory is not searched, and no `.skin` files are applied (`.skin` files are used to define styles for ASP.NET server controls). When it is set to `True` at the page or control level, the `Theme` directory is searched and `.skin` files are applied.

If themes are disabled because the `EnableTheming` attribute is set to `False` at the page level, you can still enable theming for specific controls on this page by setting the `EnableTheming` property for the control to `True` and applying a specific theme at the same time, as illustrated here:

```
<asp:Textbox ID="TextBox1" runat="server"
 BackColor="#000000" ForeColor="#ffffff" EnableTheming="true" SkinID="mySkin" />
```

Understanding Themes When Using Master Pages

When working with ASP.NET applications that make use of master pages, notice that both the `Page` and `Master` page directives include an `EnableTheming` attribute.

Master pages are covered in Chapter 5.

If both the `Page` and `Master` page directives include the `EnableTheming` attribute, what behavior results if both are used? Suppose you have defined your theme in the `web.config` file of your ASP.NET application and you specify in the master page that theming is disabled using the `EnableTheming` attribute as shown here:

```
<%@ Master Language="VB" EnableTheming="false" %>
```

If this is the case, what is the behavior for any content pages using this master page? If the content page that is using this master page does not make any specification on theming (it does not use the `EnableTheming` attribute), what is specified in the master page naturally takes precedence and no theme is utilized as required by the `false` setting. Even if you have set the `EnableTheming` value in the content page, any value that is specified in the master page takes precedence. This means that if theming is set to `false` in the master page and set to `true` in the content page, the page is constructed with the value provided from the master page — in this case, `false`. Even if the value is set to `false` in the master page, however, you can override this setting at the control level rather than doing it in the `Page` directive of the content page.

Understanding the StyleSheetTheme Attribute

The Page directive also includes the attribute StyleSheetTheme that you can use to apply themes to a page. So, the big question is: If you have a Theme attribute and a StyleSheetTheme attribute for the Page directive, what is the difference between the two?

```
<%@ Page Language="VB" StyleSheetTheme="Summer" %>
```

The StyleSheetTheme attribute works the same as the Theme attribute in that it can be used to apply a theme to a page. The difference is that the when attributes are set locally on the page within a particular control, the attributes are overridden by the theme if you use the Theme attribute. They are kept in place, however, if you apply the page's theme using the StyleSheetTheme attribute. Suppose you have a text box control like the following:

```
<asp:Textbox ID="TextBox1" runat="server"
 BackColor="#000000" ForeColor="#ffffff" />
```

In this example, the BackColor and ForeColor settings are overridden by the theme if you have applied it using the Theme attribute in the Page directive. If, instead, you applied the theme using the StyleSheet-Theme attribute in the Page directive, the BackColor and ForeColor settings remain in place, even if they are explicitly defined in the theme.

Creating Your Own Themes

You will find that creating themes in ASP.NET is a rather simple process — although sometimes it does require some artistic capabilities. The themes you create can be applied at the application, page, or server control level. Themes are a great way to easily apply a consistent look-and-feel across your entire application.

Creating the Proper Folder Structure

In order to create your own themes for an application, you first need to create the proper folder structure in your application. To do this, right-click your project and add a new folder. Name the folder App_Themes. You can also create this folder by right-clicking on your project in Visual Studio and selecting Add ASP.NET Folder ⇨ Theme. Notice when you do this that the theme folder within the App_Themes folder does not have the typical folder icon next to it, but instead has a folder icon that includes a paintbrush. This is shown in Figure 6-4.

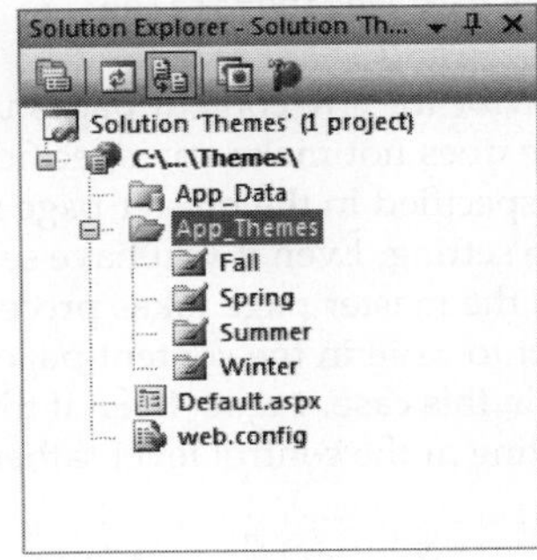

Figure 6-4

Within the App_Themes folder, you can create an additional theme folder for each and every theme that you might use in your application. For instance, if you are going to have four themes — *Summer*, *Fall*, *Winter*, and *Spring* — then you create four folders that are named appropriately.

You might use more than one theme in your application for many reasons — season changes, day/night changes, different business units, category of user, or even user preferences.

Each theme folder must contain the elements of the theme, which can include the following:

- A single skin file
- CSS files
- Images

Creating a Skin

A *skin* is a definition of styles applied to the server controls in your ASP.NET page. Skins can work in conjunction with CSS files or images. To create a theme to use in your ASP.NET applications, you use just a single skin file in the theme folder. The skin file can have any name, but it must have a .skin file extension.

Even though you have four theme folders in your application, concentrate on the creation of the Summer theme for the purposes of this chapter. Right-click the Summer folder, select Add New Item, and select Skin File from the listed options. Name the file **Summer.skin**. Then complete the skin file as shown in Listing 6-3.

Listing 6-3: The Summer.skin file

```
<asp:Label runat="server" ForeColor="#004000" Font-Names="Verdana"
           Font-Size="X-Small" />

<asp:Textbox runat="server" ForeColor="#004000" Font-Names="Verdana"
           Font-Size="X-Small" BorderStyle="Solid" BorderWidth="1px"
           BorderColor="#004000" Font-Bold="True" />

<asp:Button runat="server" ForeColor="#004000" Font-Names="Verdana"
           Font-Size="X-Small" BorderStyle="Solid" BorderWidth="1px"
           BorderColor="#004000" Font-Bold="True" BackColor="#FFE0C0" />
```

This is just a sampling of what the Summer.skin file should contain. To use it in a real application, you should actually make a definition for each and every server control option. In this case, you have a definition in place for three different types of server controls: Label, TextBox, and Button. After saving the Summer.skin file in the Summer folder, your file structure should look like Figure 6-5 from the Solution Explorer of Visual Studio 2008.

As with the regular server control definitions that you put on a typical .aspx page, these control definitions must contain the runat="server" attribute. If you specify this attribute in the skinned version of the control, you also include it in the server control you put on an .aspx page that uses this theme. Also notice that no ID attribute is specified in the skinned version of the control. If you specify an ID attribute here, you get an error when a page tries to use this theme.

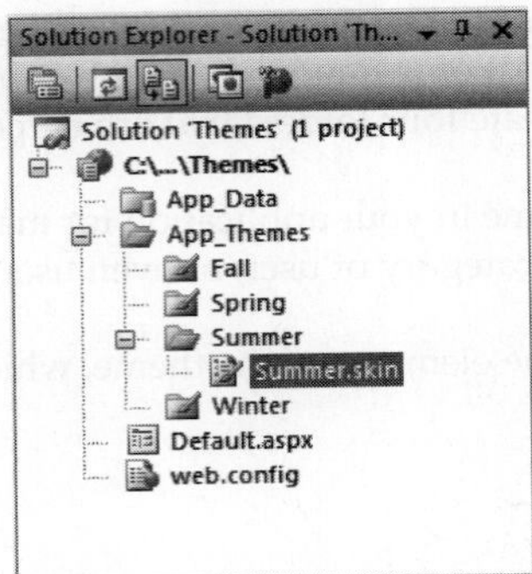

Figure 6-5

As you can see, you can supply a lot of different visual definitions to these three controls, and this should give the page a *summery* look and feel. An ASP.NET page in this project can then simply use this custom theme as was shown earlier in this chapter (see Listing 6-4).

Listing 6-4: Using the Summer theme in an ASP.NET page

VB

```
<%@ Page Language="VB" Theme="Summer" %>

<script runat="server">
   Protected Sub Button1_Click(ByVal sender As Object, ByVal e As System.EventArgs)
      Label1.Text = "Hello " & TextBox1.Text
   End Sub
</script>

<html xmlns="http://www.w3.org/1999/xhtml">
<head runat="server">
    <title>St. Louis .NET User Group</title>
</head>
<body>
    <form id="form1" runat="server">
        <asp:Textbox ID="TextBox1" runat="server">
        </asp:Textbox>
        <br />
        <br />
        <asp:Button ID="Button1" runat="server" Text="Submit Your Name"
         OnClick="Button1_Click" />
        <br />
        <br />
        <asp:Label ID="Label1" runat="server" />
    </form>
</body>
</html>
```

C#

```
<%@ Page Language="C#" Theme="Summer" %>

<script runat="server">
```

```
    protected void Button1_Click(object sender, System.EventArgs e)
    {
        Label1.Text = "Hello " + TextBox1.Text.ToString();
    }
</script>
```

Looking at the server controls on this `.aspx` page, you can see that no styles are associated with them. These are just the default server controls that you drag and drop onto the design surface of Visual Studio 2008. There is, however, the style that you defined in the `Summer.skin` file, as shown in Figure 6-6.

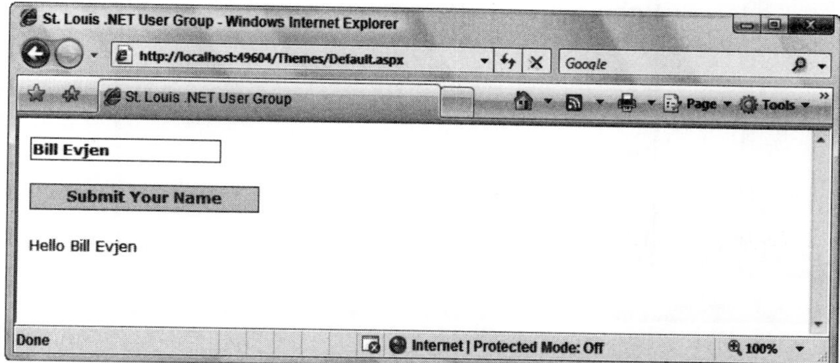

Figure 6-6

Including CSS Files in Your Themes

In addition to the server control definitions that you create from within a `.skin` file, you can make further definitions using Cascading Style Sheets (CSS). You might have noticed, when using a `.skin` file, that you could define only the styles associated with server controls and nothing else. However, developers usually use quite a bit more than server controls in their ASP.NET pages. For instance, ASP.NET pages are routinely made up of HTML server controls, raw HTML, or even raw text. At present, the *Summer* theme has only a `Summer.skin` file associated with it. Any other items have no style whatsoever applied to them.

For a theme that goes beyond the server controls, you must further define the theme style so that HTML server controls, HTML, and raw text are all changed according to the theme. You achieve this with a CSS file within your theme folder.

It is rather easy to create CSS files for your themes when using Visual Studio 2008. Right-click the `Summer` theme folder and select Add New Item. In the list of options, select the option Style Sheet and name it `Summer.css`. The `Summer.css` file should be sitting right next to your `Summer.skin` file. This creates an empty `.css` file for your theme. I will not go into the details of how to make a CSS file using Visual Studio 2008 and the CSS creation tool because this was covered earlier in Chapter 2 in this book. The process is also the same as in previous versions of Visual Studio. Just remember that the dialog that comes with Visual Studio 2008 enables you to completely define your CSS page with no need to actually code anything. A sample dialog is shown in Figure 6-7.

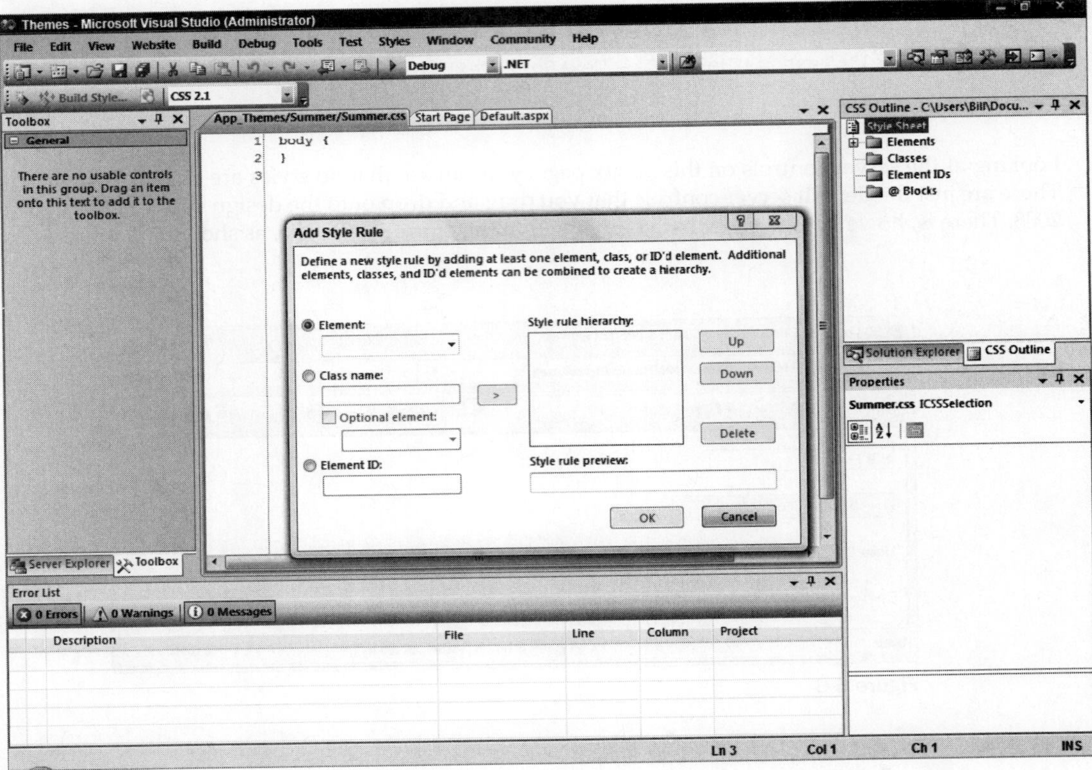

Figure 6-7

To create a comprehensive theme with this dialog, you define each HTML element that might appear in the ASP.NET page or your make use of class names or element IDs. This can be a lot of work, but it is worth it in the end. For now, create a small CSS file that changes some of the non-server control items on your ASP.NET page. This CSS file is shown in Listing 6-5.

Listing 6-5: A CSS file with some definitions

```
body
{
 font-size: x-small;
 font-family: Verdana;
 color: #004000;
}

a:link {
 color: Blue;
 text-decoration: none;
}
```

```
a:visited
{
 color: Blue;
 text-decoration: none;
}

a:hover {
 color: Red;
 text-decoration: underline overline;
}
```

In this CSS file, four things are defined. First, you define text that is found within the `<body>` tag of the page (basically all the text). Generally, plenty of text can appear in a typical ASP.NET page that is not placed inside an `<asp:Label>` or `<asp:Literal>` tag. Therefore, you can define how your text should appear in the CSS file; otherwise, your Web page may appear quite odd at times. In this case, a definition is in place for the size, the font family, and the color of the text. You make this definition the same as the one for the `<asp:Label>` server control in the `Summer.skin` file.

The next three definitions in this CSS file revolve around the `<a>` element (for hyperlinks). One cool feature that many Web pages use is responsive hyperlinks — or hyperlinks that change when you hover a mouse over them. The `A:link` definition defines what a typical link looks like on the page. The `A:visited` definition defines the look of the link if the end user has clicked on the link previously (without this definition, it is typically purple in IE). Then the `A:hover` definition defines the appearance of the hyperlink when the end user hovers the mouse over the link. You can see that not only are these three definitions changing the color of the hyperlink, but they are also changing how the underline is used. In fact, when the end user hovers the mouse over a hyperlink on a page using this CSS file, an underline and an overline appear on the link itself.

In CSS files, the order in which the style definitions appear in the `.css` file is important. This is an interpreted file — the first definition in the CSS file is applied first to the page, next the second definition is applied, and so forth. Some styles might change previous styles, so make sure your style definitions are in the proper order. For instance, if you put the `A:hover` style definition first, you would never see it. The `A:link` and `A:visited` definitions would supersede it because they are defined after it. In addition to order, other factors such as the target media type, importance (whether the declaration is specified as important or normal), and the origin of the stylesheet also play a factor in interpreting declarations.

In working with your themes that include `.css` files, you must understand what they can and cannot do for you. For instance, examine an `.aspx` file that contains two text boxes — one text box created using a server control and another text box created using a typical `<input>` HTML element:

```
<asp:Textbox ID="TextBox1" runat="server" /> 
<input type="text" />
```

Suppose you have a definition for the TextBox server control in the `.skin` file:

```
<asp:Textbox runat="server" ForeColor="#004000" Font-Names="Verdana"
 BackColor="#ffffff" Font-Size="X-Small" BorderStyle="Solid" BorderWidth="1px"
 BorderColor="#004000" Font-Bold="True" />
```

However, what if you also have a definition in your .css file for each <input> element in the ASP.NET page as shown here:

```
INPUT
{
  background-color: black;
}
```

When you run the .aspx page with these kinds of style conflicts, the .skin file takes precedence over styles applied to every HTML element that is created using ASP.NET server controls regardless of what the .css file says. In fact, this sort of scenario gives you a page in which the <input> element that is created from the server control is white, as defined in the .skin file, and the second text box is black, as defined in the .css file (see Figure 6-8).

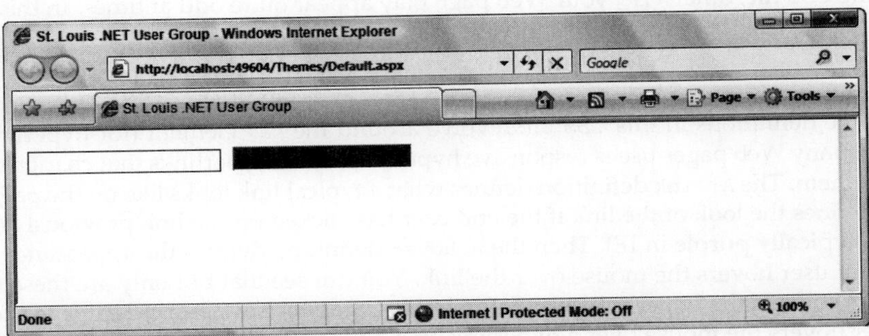

Figure 6-8

Again, other factors besides the order in which the items are defined can alter the appearance of your page. In addition to order, other factors such as the target media type, importance (whether the declaration is specified as important or normal), and the origin of the stylesheet also play a factor in interpreting declarations.

Having Your Themes Include Images

Probably one of the coolest reasons why themes, rather than CSS, are the better approach for applying a consistent style to your Web page is that themes enable you to incorporate actual images into the style definitions.

Many controls use images to create a better visual appearance. The first step in incorporating images into your server controls that consistently use themes is to create an Images folder within the theme folder itself, as illustrated in Figure 6-9.

You have a couple of easy ways to use the images that you might place in this folder. The first is to incorporate the images directly from the .skin file itself. You can do this with the TreeView server control. The TreeView control can contain images used to open and close nodes for navigation purposes. You can place images in your theme for each and every TreeView control in your application. If you do so, you can then define the TreeView server control in the .skin file, as shown in Listing 6-6.

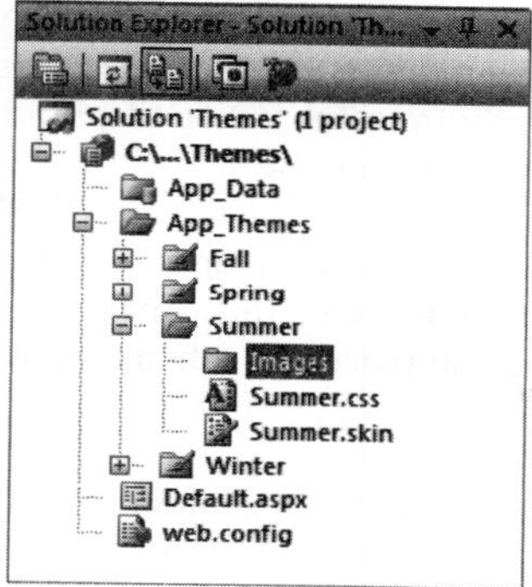

Figure 6-9

Listing 6-6: Using images from the theme folder in a TreeView server control

```
<asp:TreeView runat="server" BorderColor="#FFFFFF" BackColor="#FFFFFF"
   ForeColor="#585880" Font-Size=".9em" Font-Names="Verdana"
   LeafNodeStyle-ImageUrl="images\summer_iconlevel.gif"
   RootNodeStyle-ImageUrl="images\summer_iconmain.gif"
   ParentNodeStyle-ImageUrl="images\summer_iconmain.gif" NodeIndent="30"
   CollapseImageUrl="images\summer_minus.gif"
   ExpandImageUrl="images\summer_plus.gif">
  ...
</asp:TreeView>
```

When you run a page containing a TreeView server control, it is populated with the images held in the `Images` folder of the theme.

It is easy to incorporate images into the TreeView control. The control even specifically asks for an image location as an attribute. The new WebParts controls are used to build portals. Listing 6-7 is an example of a Web Part definition from a `.skin` file that incorporates images from the `Images` folder of the theme.

Listing 6-7: Using images from the theme folder in a WebPartZone server control

```
<asp:WebPartZone ID="WebPartZone1" runat="server"
 DragHighlightColor="#6464FE" BorderStyle="double"
 BorderColor="#E7E5DB" BorderWidth="2pt" BackColor="#F8F8FC"
 cssclass="theme_fadeblue" Font-Size=".9em" Font-Names="Verdana">
    <FooterStyle ForeColor="#585880" BackColor="#CCCCCC"></FooterStyle>
    <HelpVerb ImageURL="images/SmokeAndGlass_help.gif"
     checked="False" enabled="True" visible="True"></HelpVerb>
    <CloseVerb ImageURL="images/SmokeAndGlass_close.gif"
     checked="False" enabled="True" visible="True"></CloseVerb>
    <RestoreVerb ImageURL="images/SmokeAndGlass_restore.gif"
     checked="False" enabled="True" visible="True"></RestoreVerb>
    <MinimizeVerb ImageURL="images/SmokeAndGlass_minimize.gif"
     checked="False" enabled="True" visible="True"></MinimizeVerb>
    <EditVerb ImageURL="images/SmokeAndGlass_edit.gif"
     checked="False" enabled="True" visible="True"></EditVerb>
</asp:WebPartZone>
```

As you can see here, this series of toolbar buttons, which is contained in a WebPartZone control, now uses images that come from the aforementioned `SmokeAndGlass` theme. When this WebPartZone is then generated, the style is defined directly from the `.skin` file, but the images specified in the `.skin` file are retrieved from the `Images` folder in the theme itself.

Not all server controls enable you to work with images directly from the `Themes` folder by giving you an `image` attribute to work with. If you don't have this capability, you must work with the `.skin` file and the CSS file together. If you do, you can place your theme-based images in any element you want. Next is a good example of how to do this.

Place the image that you want to use in the `Images` folder just as you normally would. Then define the use of the images in the `.css` file. The continued `SmokeAndGlass` example in Listing 6-8 demonstrates this.

Listing 6-8: Part of the CSS file from SmokeAndGlass.css

```
.theme_header {
 background-image :url( images/smokeandglass_brownfadetop.gif);
}

.theme_highlighted {
 background-image :url( images/smokeandglass_blueandwhitef.gif);
}

.theme_fadeblue {
 background-image :url( images/smokeandglass_fadeblue.gif);
}
```

These are not styles for a specific HTML element; instead, they are CSS classes that you can put into any HTML element that you want. In this case, each CSS class mentioned here is defining a specific background image to use for the element.

After it is defined in the CSS file, you can utilize this CSS class in the `.skin` file when defining your server controls. Listing 6-9 shows you how.

Listing 6-9: Using the CSS class in one of the server controls defined in the .skin file

```
<asp:Calendar runat="server" BorderStyle="double" BorderColor="#E7E5DB"
 BorderWidth="2" BackColor="#F8F7F4" Font-Size=".9em" Font-Names="Verdana">
    <TodayDayStyle BackColor="#F8F7F4" BorderWidth="1" BorderColor="#585880"
     ForeColor="#585880" />
    <OtherMonthDayStyle BackColor="transparent" ForeColor="#CCCCCC" />
    <SelectedDayStyle ForeColor="#6464FE" BackColor="transparent"
     CssClass="theme_highlighted" />
    <TitleStyle Font-Bold="True" BackColor="#CCCCCC" ForeColor="#585880"
     BorderColor="#CCCCCC" BorderWidth="1pt" CssClass="theme_header" />
    <NextPrevStyle Font-Bold="True" ForeColor="#585880"
     BorderColor="transparent" BackColor="transparent" />
    <DayStyle ForeColor="#000000"
     BorderColor="transparent" BackColor="transparent" />
    <SelectorStyle Font-Bold="True" ForeColor="#696969" BackColor="#F8F7F4" />
    <WeekendDayStyle Font-Bold="False" ForeColor="#000000"
     BackColor="transparent" />
```

```
        <DayHeaderStyle Font-Bold="True" ForeColor="#585880"
         BackColor="Transparent" />
    </asp:Calendar>
```

This Calendar server control definition from a `.skin` file uses one of the earlier CSS classes in its definition. It actually uses an image that is specified in the CSS file in two different spots within the control (shown in bold). It is first specified in the `<SelectedDayStyle>` element. Here you see the attribute and value `CssClass="theme_highlighted"`. The other spot is within the `<TitleStyle>` element. In this case, it is using `theme_header`. When the control is rendered, these CSS classes are referenced and finally point to the images that are defined in the CSS file.

It is interesting that the images used here for the header of the Calendar control don't really have much to them. For instance, the `smokeandglass_brownfadetop.gif` image that we are using for this example is simply a thin, gray sliver, as shown in Figure 6-10.

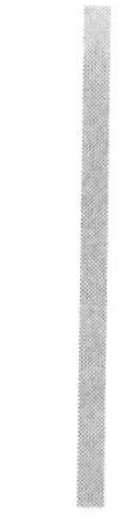

Figure 6-10

This very small image (in this case, very thin) is actually repeated as often as necessary to make it equal the length of the header in the Calendar control. The image is lighter at the top and darkens toward the bottom. Repeated horizontally, this gives a three-dimensional effect to the control. Try it out, and you can get the result shown in Figure 6-11.

<			February 2008			>
Sun	Mon	Tue	Wed	Thu	Fri	Sat
27	28	29	30	31	1	2
3	4	5	6	7	8	9
10	11	12	13	14	15	16
17	18	19	20	21	22	23
24	25	26	27	28	29	1
2	3	4	5	6	7	8

Figure 6-11

Defining Multiple Skin Options

Using the themes technology in ASP.NET, you can have a single theme; but also, within the theme's `.skin` file, you can have specific controls that are defined in multiple ways. You can frequently take advantage of this feature within your themes. For instance, you might have text box elements scattered throughout your application, but you might not want each and every text box to have the same visual appearance. In this case, you can create multiple versions of the `<asp:Textbox>` server control within your `.skin` file. In Listing 6-10 you see how to create multiple versions of the `<asp:Textbox>` control in the `.skin` file from Listing 6-3.

Listing 6-10: The Summer.skin file, which contains multiple versions of the <asp:Textbox> server control

```
<asp:Label runat="server" ForeColor="#004000" Font-Names="Verdana"
     Font-Size="X-Small" />

<asp:Textbox runat="server" ForeColor="#004000" Font-Names="Verdana"
     Font-Size="X-Small" BorderStyle="Solid" BorderWidth="1px"
     BorderColor="#004000" Font-Bold="True" />

<asp:Textbox runat="server" ForeColor="#000000" Font-Names="Verdana"
     Font-Size="X-Small" BorderStyle="Dotted" BorderWidth="5px"
     BorderColor="#000000" Font-Bold="False" SkinID="TextboxDotted" />

<asp:Textbox runat="server" ForeColor="#000000" Font-Names="Arial"
     Font-Size="X-Large" BorderStyle="Dashed" BorderWidth="3px"
     BorderColor="#000000" Font-Bold="False" SkinID="TextboxDashed" />

<asp:Button runat="server" ForeColor="#004000" Font-Names="Verdana"
     Font-Size="X-Small" BorderStyle="Solid" BorderWidth="1px"
     BorderColor="#004000" Font-Bold="True" BackColor="#FFE0C0" />
```

In this `.skin` file, you can see three definitions in place for the TextBox server control. The first one is the same as before. Although the second and third definitions have a different style, they also contain a new attribute in the definition — `SkinID`. To create multiple definitions of a single element, you use the `SkinID` attribute to differentiate among the definitions. The value used in the `SkinID` can be anything you want. In this case, it is `TextboxDotted` and `TextboxDashed`.

Note that no `SkinID` attribute is used for the first `<asp:Textbox>` definition. By not using one, you are saying that this is the default style definition to use for each `<asp:Textbox>` control on an ASP.NET page that uses this theme but has no pointer to a particular `SkinID`.

Take a look at a sample `.aspx` page that uses this `.skin` file in Listing 6-11.

Listing 6-11: A simple .aspx page that uses the Summer.skin file with multiple text-box style definitions

```
<%@ Page Language="VB" Theme="Summer" %>

<html xmlns="http://www.w3.org/1999/xhtml">
<head runat="server">
    <title>Different SkinIDs</title>
</head>
<body>
    <form id="form1" runat="server">
    <p>
        <asp:Textbox ID="TextBox1" runat="server">Textbox1</asp:Textbox>
    </p><p>
        <asp:Textbox ID="TextBox2" runat="server"
         SkinId="TextboxDotted">Textbox2</asp:Textbox>
    </p><p>
```

```
            <asp:Textbox ID="TextBox3" runat="server"
             SkinId="TextboxDashed">Textbox3</asp:Textbox>
        </p>
        </form>
    </body>
    </html>
```

This small `.aspx` page shows three text boxes, each of a different style. When you run this page, you get the results shown in Figure 6-12.

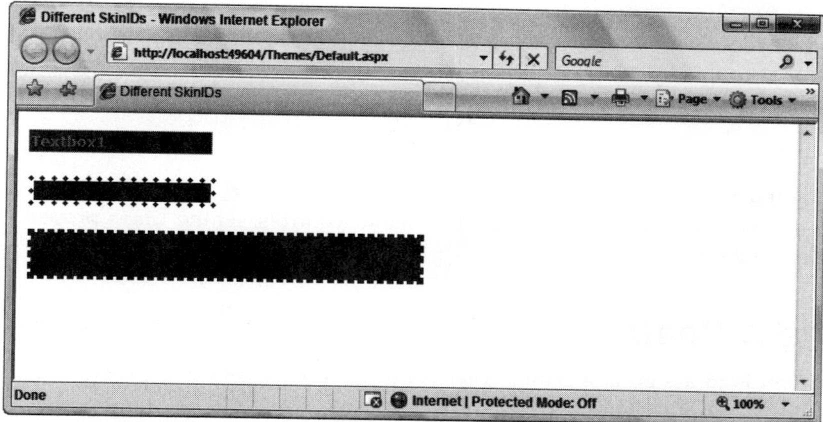

Figure 6-12

The first text box does not point to any particular `SkinID` in the `.skin` file. Therefore, the default skin is used. As stated before, the default skin is the one in the `.skin` file that does not have a `SkinID` attribute in it. The second text box then contains `SkinID="TextboxDotted"` and, therefore, inherits the style definition defined in the `TextboxDotted` skin in the `Summer.skin` file. The third text box takes the `SkinID` `TextboxDashed` and is also changed appropriately.

As you can see, it is quite simple to define multiple versions of a control that can be used throughout your entire application.

Programmatically Working with Themes

So far, you have seen examples of working with ASP.NET themes in a declarative fashion, but you can also work with themes programmatically.

Assigning the Page's Theme Programmatically

To programmatically assign the theme to the page, use the construct shown in Listing 6-12.

Listing 6-12: Assigning the theme of the page programmatically

VB

```
<script runat="server">
    Protected Sub Page_PreInit(ByVal sender As Object, ByVal e As System.EventArgs)
        Page.Theme = Request.QueryString("ThemeChange")
    End Sub
</script>
```

C#

```
<script runat="server">
    protected void Page_PreInit(object sender, System.EventArgs e)
    {
        Page.Theme = Request.QueryString["ThemeChange"];
    }
</script>
```

You must set the `Theme` of the `Page` property in or before the `Page_PreInit` event for any static controls that are on the page. If you are working with dynamic controls, set the `Theme` property before adding it to the Controls collection.

Assigning a Control's SkinID Programmatically

Another option is to assign a specific server control's `SkinID` property programmatically (see Listing 6-13).

Listing 6-13: Assigning the server control's SkinID property programmatically

VB

```
<script runat="server">
    Protected Sub Page_PreInit(ByVal sender As Object, ByVal e As System.EventArgs)
        TextBox1.SkinID = "TextboxDashed"
    End Sub
</script>
```

C#

```
<script runat="server">
    protected void Page_PreInit(object sender, System.EventArgs e)
    {
        TextBox1.SkinID = "TextboxDashed";
    }
</script>
```

Again, you assign this property before or in the `Page_PreInit` event in your code.

Themes, Skins, and Custom Controls

If you are building custom controls in an ASP.NET world, understand that end users can also apply themes to the controls that they use in their pages. By default, your custom controls are theme-enabled whether your custom control inherits from `Control` or `WebControl`.

To disable theming for your control, you can simply use the `Themeable` attribute on your class. This is illustrated in Listing 6-14.

Listing 6-14: Disabling theming for your custom controls

VB

```
Imports System
Imports System.Collections.Generic
Imports System.ComponentModel
Imports System.Text
Imports System.Web
Imports System.Web.UI
Imports System.Web.UI.WebControls

<DefaultProperty("HeaderText"), _
 ToolboxData("<{0}:WebCustomControl1 runat=server></{0}:WebCustomControl1>"), _
 Themeable(False)> _
Public Class WebCustomControl1
    Inherits WebControl

    <Bindable(True), Category("Appearance"), DefaultValue("Enter Value"), _
     Localizable(True)> Property HeaderText() As String
        Get
            Dim s As String = CStr(ViewState("HeaderText"))
            If s Is Nothing Then
                Return String.Empty
            Else
                Return s
            End If
        End Get

        Set(ByVal Value As String)
            ViewState("HeaderText") = Value
        End Set
    End Property


    Protected Overrides Sub RenderContents(ByVal output As HtmlTextWriter)
        output.Write("<h1>" & HeaderText & "<h1>")
    End Sub

End Class
```

C#

```
using System;
using System.Collections.Generic;
using System.ComponentModel;
using System.Text;
using System.Web;
using System.Web.UI;
using System.Web.UI.WebControls;

namespace ControlForThemes
```

Continued

```
{
    [DefaultProperty("HeaderText")]
    [ToolboxData("<{0}:WebCustomControl1 runat=server></{0}:WebCustomControl1>")]
    [Themeable(false)]
    public class WebCustomControl1 : WebControl
    {
        [Bindable(true)]
        [Category("Appearance")]
        [DefaultValue("Enter Value")]
        [Localizable(true)]
        public string HeaderText
        {
            get
            {
                String s = (String)ViewState["HeaderText"];
                return ((s == null) ? String.Empty : s);
            }

            set
            {
                ViewState["HeaderText"] = value;
            }
        }

        protected override void RenderContents(HtmlTextWriter output)
        {
            output.Write("<h1>" + HeaderText + "<h1>");
        }
    }
}
```

Looking over the code from the above example, you can see that theming was disabled by applying the `Themeable` attribute to the class and setting it to False.

You can use a similar approach to disable theming for the individual properties that might be in your custom controls. You do this as illustrated in Listing 6-15.

Listing 6-15: Disabling theming for properties in your custom controls

VB

```
<Bindable(True), Category("Appearance"), DefaultValue("Enter Value"), _
 Localizable(True), Themeable(False)> Property HeaderText() As String
    Get
        Dim s As String = CStr(ViewState("HeaderText"))
        If s Is Nothing Then
            Return String.Empty
        Else
            Return s
        End If
    End Get

    Set(ByVal Value As String)
```

```
            ViewState("HeaderText") = Value
        End Set
    End Property
```

C#

```
        [Bindable(true)]
        [Category("Appearance")]
        [DefaultValue("Enter Value")]
        [Themeable(false)]
        public string HeaderText
        {
            get
            {
                String s = (String)ViewState["HeaderText"];
                return ((s == null) ? String.Empty : s);
            }

            set
            {
                ViewState["HeaderText"] = value;
            }
        }
```

In this case, you set the `Themeable` attribute at the property level to `False` in the same manner as you did at the class level.

If you have enabled themes for these items, how would you go about applying a theme definition to a custom control? For this example, use the custom server control shown in Listing 6-14, but set the `Themeable` attributes to `True`. Next, create a `.skin` file in a theme and add the control to the theme as you would any other ASP.NET server control. This is illustrated in Listing 6-16.

Listing 6-16: Changing properties in a custom control in the .skin file

```
<%@ Register Assembly="ControlForThemes" Namespace="ControlForThemes"
    TagPrefix="cc1" %>
<cc1:webcustomcontrol1 runat="server" HeaderText="FROM THE SKIN FILE" />
```

When defining custom server controls in your themes, you use the same approach as you would when placing a custom server control inside of a standard ASP.NET `.aspx` page. In Listing 6-16, you can see that the custom server control is registered in the `.skin` file using the `@Register` page directive. This directive gives the custom control a `TagPrefix` value of `cc1`. Note that the `TagPrefix` values presented in this page can be different from those presented in any other `.aspx` page that uses the same custom control. The only things that have to be the same are the `Assembly` and `Namespace` attributes that point to the specific control being defined in the file. Also note the control definition in the skin file, as with other standard controls, does not require that you specify an `ID` attribute, but only the `runat` attribute along with any other property that you wish to override.

Next, create a standard `.aspx` page that uses your custom server control. Before running the page, be sure to apply the defined theme on the page using the `Theme` attribute in the `@Page` directive. With everything in place, running the page produces the following results in the browser:

```
FROM THE SKIN FILE
```

This value, which was specified in the skin file, is displayed no matter what you apply as the `HeaderText` value in the server control.

In addition to changing values of custom properties that are contained in server control, you can also change the inherited properties that come from `WebControl`. For instance, you can change settings in your skin file as shown in Listing 6-17.

Listing 6-17: Changing inherited properties in the custom control

```
<%@ Register Assembly="ControlForThemes" Namespace="ControlForThemes"
    TagPrefix="cc1" %>
<cc1:webcustomcontrol1 runat="server" BackColor="Gray" />
```

With this in place, you have changed one of the inherited properties from the skin file. This setting changes the background color of the server control to gray (even if it is set to something else in the control itself). The result is presented in Figure 6-13.

You can find more information on building your own custom server controls in Chapter 26.

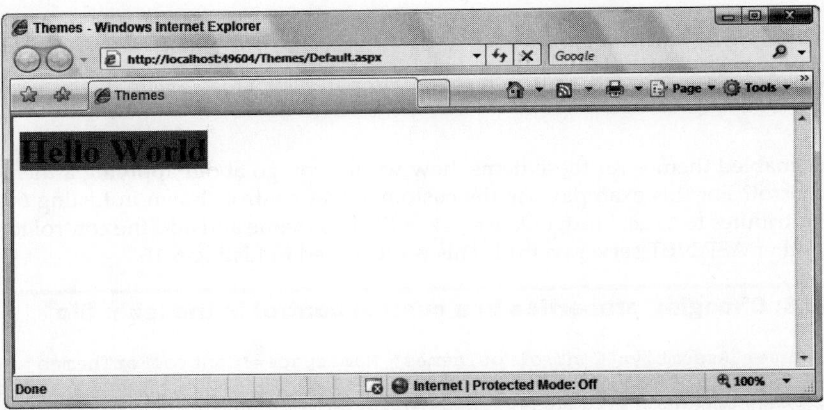

Figure 6-13

Summary

With the availability of themes and skins in ASP.NET 3.5, it is quite easy to apply a consistent look and feel across your entire application. Remember that themes can contain only simple server control definitions in a `.skin` file or elaborate style definitions, which include not only `.skin` files, but also CSS style definitions and even images!

As you will see later in the book, you can use themes in conjunction with the personalization features that ASP.NET provides. This enables your end users to customize their experiences by selecting their own themes. Your application can present a theme just for them, and it can remember their choices through the APIs that are offered in ASP.NET 3.5.

7

Data Binding in ASP.NET 3.5

One of the most exciting features of ASP.NET 1.0/1.1 was its capability to bind entire collections of data to controls at runtime without requiring you to write large amounts of code. The controls understood they were data-bound and would render the appropriate HTML for each item in the data collection. Additionally, you could bind the controls to any type of data sources, from simple arrays to complex Oracle database query results. This was a huge step forward from ASP, in which each developer was responsible for writing all the data access code, looping through a recordset, and manually rendering the appropriate HTML code for each record of data.

In ASP.NET 2.0, Microsoft took the concept of data binding and expanded it to make it even easier to understand and use by introducing a new layer of data abstraction called data source controls. It also brought into the toolbox a series of new and powerful databound controls such as the GridView, DetailsView, and FormView. ASP.NET 3.5 continues to make fetching and displaying data in ASP.NET as simple as possible by introducing the LinqDataSource control and the ListView control.

This chapter explores all the provided data source controls, and describes other data-binding features in ASP.NET. It shows how you can use the data source controls to easily and quickly bind data to data-bound controls. It also focuses on the power of the data-bound list controls included in ASP.NET 3.5, such as the GridView, DetailsView, FormView, and the new ListView control. Finally, you take a look at changes in the inline data binding syntax and inline XML data binding.

Data Source Controls

In ASP.NET 1.0/1.1, you typically performed a data-binding operation by writing some data access code to retrieve a `DataReader` or a `DataSet` object; then you bound that data object to a server control such as a DataGrid, DropDownList, or ListBox. If you wanted to update or delete the bound data, you were then responsible for writing the data access code to do that. Listing 7-1 shows a typical example of a data-binding operation in ASP.NET 1.0/1.1.

Listing 7-1: Typical data-binding operation in ASP.NET 1.0/1.1

VB

```
Dim conn As New SqlConnection()
Dim cmd As New SqlCommand("SELECT * FROM Customers", conn)

Dim da As New SqlDataAdapter(cmd)

Dim ds As New DataSet()
da.Fill(ds)

DataGrid1.DataSource = ds
DataGrid1.DataBind()
```

C#

```
SqlConnection conn = new SqlConnection();
SqlCommand cmd = new SqlCommand("SELECT * FROM Customers", conn);

SqlDataAdapter da = new SqlDataAdapter(cmd);

DataSet ds = new DataSet();
da.Fill(ds);

DataGrid1.DataSource = ds;
DataGrid1.DataBind();
```

ASP.NET 2.0 introduced an additional layer of abstraction through the use of data source controls. As shown in Figure 7-1, these controls abstract the use of an underlying data provider, such as the SQL Data Provider or the OLE DB Data Provider. This means you no longer need to concern yourself with the hows and whys of using the data providers. Instead, the data source controls do all the heavy lifting for you. You need to know only where your data is and, if necessary, how to construct a query for performing CRUD (Create, Retrieve, Update, and Delete) operations.

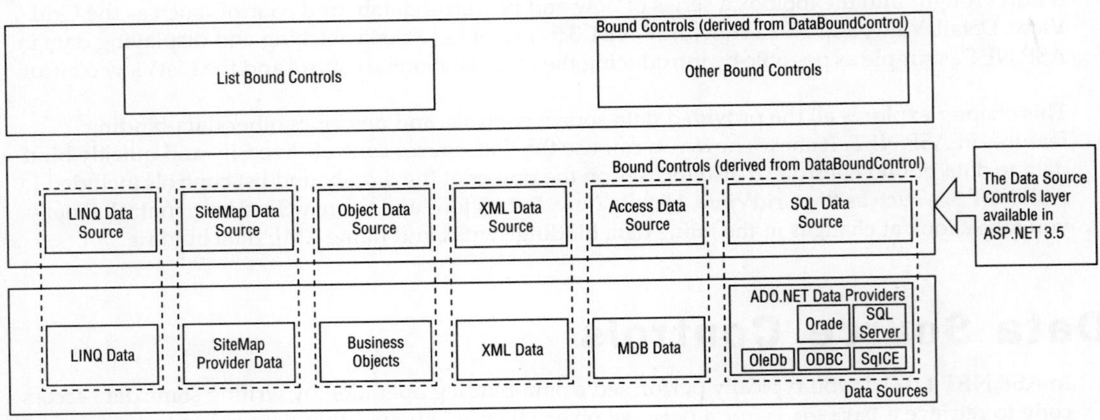

Figure 7-1

Additionally, because the data source controls all derive from the `Control` class, you can use them much as you would any other Web Server control. For instance, you can define and control the behavior of the data source control either declaratively in your HTML or programmatically. This means you can perform all manner of data access and manipulation without ever having to write one line of code. In fact, although you certainly can control the data source controls from code, the samples in this chapter show you how to perform powerful database queries using nothing more than the Visual Studio 2008 wizards and declarative syntax.

The six built-in data source controls in ASP.NET 3.5 are each used for a specific type of data access. The following table lists and describes each data source control.

Control Name	Description
SqlDataSource control	Provides access to any data source that has an ADO.NET Data Provider available; by default, the control has access to the ODBC, OLE DB, SQL Server, Oracle, and SQL Server CE providers.
LinqDataSource control	Provides access to different types of data objects using LINQ queries.
ObjectDataSource control	Provides specialized data access to business objects or other classes that return data.
XmlDataSource control	Provides specialized data access to XML documents, either physically or in-memory.
SiteMapDataSource control	Provides specialized access to site map data for a Web site that is stored by the site map provider.
AccessDataSource control	Provides specialized access to Access databases.

All the data source controls are derived from the `DataSourceControl` class, which is derived from `Control` and implements the `IDataSource` and `IListSource` interfaces. This means that although each control is designed for use with specific data sources, all data source controls share a basic set of core functionality. It also means that it is easy for you to create your own custom data source controls based on the structure of your specific data sources.

SqlDataSource Control

The SqlDataSource control is the data source control to use if your data is stored in a SQL Server, SQL Server Express, Oracle Server, ODBC data source, OLE DB data source, or Windows SQL CE Database. The control provides an easy-to-use wizard that walks you through the configuration process, or you can modify the control manually by changing the control attributes directly in Source view. In the example presented in this section, you walk through creating a SqlDataSource control and configuring it using the wizard. After you complete the configuration, you examine the source code it generates.

Begin using the control by opening an `.aspx` page inside a Visual Studio Web site project and dragging the SqlDataSource control from the toolbox onto the form. The Visual Studio toolbox has been divided into functional groups so you find all the data-related controls located under the Data section.

Configuring a Data Connection

After the control has been dropped onto the Web page, you tell it what connection it should use. The easiest way to do this is by using the Configure Data Source Wizard, shown in Figure 7-2. Launch this wizard by selecting the Configure Data Source option from the data source control's smart tag menu.

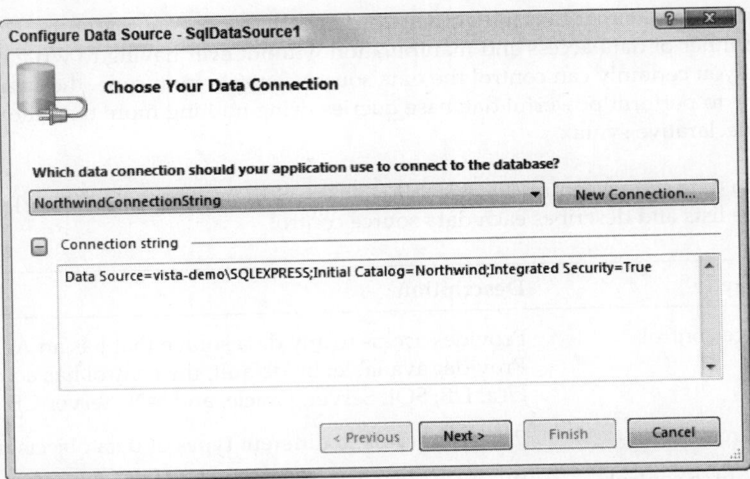

Figure 7-2

Once the wizard opens, you should create a connection to the Northwind database in SQL. You will use this connection for most of the demonstrations in this chapter.

Beginning with Microsoft SQL Server 2005, Microsoft no longer includes the Northwind sample database as part of the standard installation. You can still download the installation scripts for the sample database from the following location:

```
http://www.microsoft.com/downloads/details.aspx?FamilyId=06616212-0356-
46A0-8DA2-EEBC53A68034&displaylang=en
```

After the wizard opens, you can select an existing connection from the drop-down list or create a new connection. If you click the New Connection button, the Connection Properties dialog, shown in Figure 7-3, appears. From here, you can set all the properties of a new database connection.

Click the Change button. From here, you can choose the specific data provider you want this connection to use. By default, the control uses the ADO.NET SQL Data Provider; also available are Oracle, OLE DB, ODBC, and SQL Server Mobile Edition providers.

The list of providers is generated from the data contained in the `DbProviderFactory` *node of the* `machine.config` *file. If you have additional providers to display in the wizard you can modify your* `machine.config` *file to include specific providers' information.*

Next, simply fill in the appropriate information for your database connection. Click the Test Connection button to verify that your connection information is correct, and then click OK to return to the wizard.

After you have returned to the Data Source Configuration Wizard, notice that the connection you created is listed in the available connections drop-down list. After you select a connection string from the drop-down, the connection information shows in the Data Connection info area. This allows you to easily review the connection information for the Connection selected in the drop-down list.

Add Connection

Enter information to connect to the selected data source or click "Change" to choose a different data source and/or provider.

Data source:

Microsoft SQL Server (SqlClient) | Change...

Server name:

Refresh

Log on to the server

Use Windows Authentication

Use SQL Server Authentication

User name:

Password:

Save my password

Connect to a database

Select or enter a database name:

Attach a database file:

Browse...

Logical name:

Advanced...

Test Connection | OK | Cancel

Figure 7-3

Click the Next button to continue through the wizard. The next step allows you to choose to have the wizard save your connection information in your `web.config` file to make maintenance and deployment of your application easier. This screen allows you to specify the key under which the connection information should be stored in the configuration file. Should you choose not to store your connection information in the `web.config` file, it is stored in the actual `.aspx` page as a property of the `SqlDataSource` control named `ConnectionString`. If the provider chosen was not the SQL Data Provider, a property named `ProviderName` will be used to store that setting.

The next step in the wizard allows you to configure the `SELECT` statement your data source control will use to retrieve data from the database. This screen, shown in Figure 7-4, gives you a drop-down list of all the tables and views available in the database that you specified in your connection information. After you select a table or view, the list box allows you to select the column you want to include in the query. You can select all columns available using an asterisk (`*`), or you can choose specific columns by marking the check box located next to each column name. By clicking the WHERE or ORDER BY button, it is also possible to specify `WHERE` clause parameters for filtering and `ORDER BY` settings for sorting in your query. For now, do not enter any additional `WHERE` or `ORDER BY` settings.

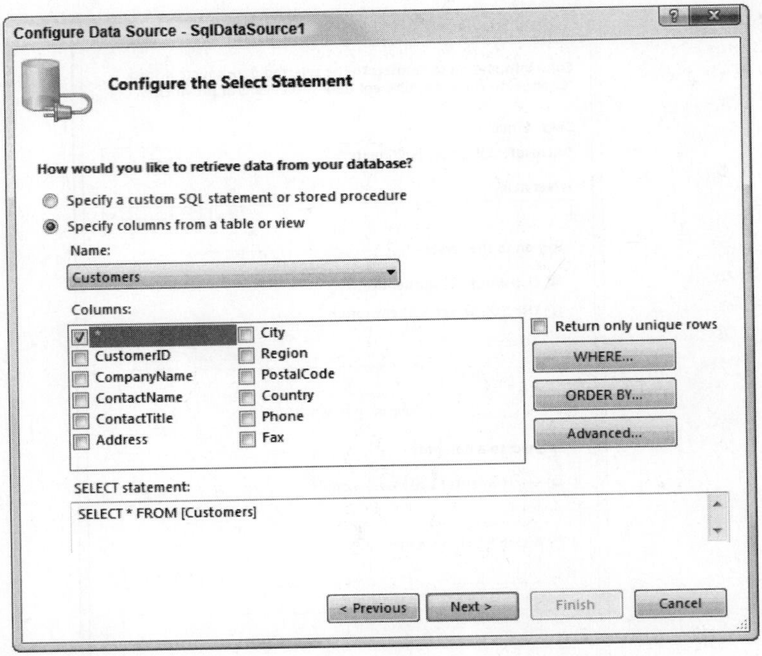

Figure 7-4

Finally, the Advanced button contains two advanced options. You can have the wizard generate `INSERT`, `UPDATE`, and `DELETE` statements for your data, based on the `SELECT` statement you created. You can also configure the data source control to use Optimistic Concurrency to prevent data concurrency issues.

Optimistic Concurrency is a database technique that can help you prevent the accidental overwriting of data. When Optimistic Concurrency is enabled, the Update and Delete SQL statements used by the SqlDataSource control are modified so that they include both the original and updated values. When the queries are executed, the data in the targeted record is compated to the SqlDataSource controls original values and if a difference is found,indicating that the data has changed since it was originally reterived by the SqlDataSource control, the Update or Delete will not occur.

The final screen of the wizard allows you to preview the data selected by your data source control to verify the query is working as you expect it to. Simply click the Finish button to complete the wizard.

When you are done configuring your data connection, you can see exactly what the configured SqlDataSource control looks like. Change to Source view in Visual Studio to see how the wizard has generated the appropriate attributes for your control. It should look something like the code in Listing 7-2.

Listing 7-2: Typical SqlDataSource control generated by Visual Studio

```
<asp:SqlDataSource ID="SqlDataSource1" Runat="server"
    SelectCommand="SELECT * FROM [Customers]"
    ConnectionString="<%$ ConnectionStrings:AppConnectionString1 %>">
</asp:SqlDataSource>
```

You can see that the control uses a declarative syntax to configure which connection it should use by creating a `ConnectionString` attribute, and what query to execute by creating a `SelectCommand` attribute. A little later in this chapter, you look at how to configure the `SqlDataSource` control to execute `INSERT`, `UPDATE`, and `DELETE` commands as this data changes.

Data Source Mode Property

One of many important properties of the SqlDataSource control is the `DataSourceMode` property. This property enables you to tell the control if it should use a `DataSet` or a `DataReader` internally when retrieving the data. This is important when you are designing data-driven ASP.NET pages. If you choose to use a `DataReader`, data is retrieved using what is commonly known as *fire hose mode*, or a forward-only, read-only cursor. This is the fastest and most efficient way to read data from your data source because a `DataReader` does not have the memory and processing overhead of a `DataSet`. But choosing to use a `DataSet` makes the data source control more powerful by enabling the control to perform other operations such as filtering, sorting, and paging. It also enables the built-in caching capabilities of the control. Each option offers distinct advantages and disadvantages, so consider this property carefully when designing your Web site. The default value for this property is to use a `DataSet` to retrieve data. The code in Listing 7-3 shows how to add the `DataSourceMode` property to your SqlDataSource control.

Listing 7-3: Adding the DataSourceMode property to a SqlDataSource control

```
<asp:SqlDataSource ID="SqlDataSource1" Runat="server"
    SelectCommand="SELECT * FROM [Customers]"
    ConnectionString="<%$ ConnectionStrings:AppConnectionString1 %>"
    DataSourceMode="DataSet">
</asp:SqlDataSource>
```

Filtering Data Using SelectParameters

Of course, when selecting data from your data source, you may not want to get every single row of data from a view or table. You want to be able to specify parameters in your query to limit the data that is returned. The data source control allows you to do this by using the `SelectParameters` collection to create parameters that it can use at runtime to alter the data that is returned from a query.

The `SelectParameters` collection consists of types that derive from the `Parameters` class. You can combine any number of parameters in the collection. The data source control then uses these to create a dynamic SQL query. The following table lists and describes the available parameter types.

Parameter	Description
`ControlParameter`	Uses the value of a property of the specified control
`CookieParameter`	Uses the key value of a cookie
`FormParameter`	Uses the key value from the Forms collection
`QuerystringParameter`	Uses a key value from the QueryString collection
`ProfileParameter`	Uses a key value from the user's profile
`SessionParameter`	Uses a key value from the current user's session

Because all the parameter controls derive from the `Parameter` class, they all contain several useful common properties. Some of these properties are shown in the following table.

Property	Description
`Type`	Allows you to strongly type the value of the parameter
`ConvertEmptyStringToNull`	Indicates the control should convert the value assigned to it to `Null` if it is equal to `System.String.Empty`
`DefaultValue`	Allows you to specify a default value for the parameter if it is evaluated as `Null`

The code in Listing 7-4 shows an example of adding a QueryStringParameter to the `SelectParameters` collection of your SqlDataSource control. As you can see, the `SelectCommand` query has been modified to include a `WHERE` clause. When you run this code, the value of the query string field `ID` is bound to the `@CustomerID` placeholder in your `SelectCommand`, allowing you to select only those customers whose `CustomerID` field matches the value of the query string field.

Listing 7-4: Filtering select data using SelectParameter controls

```
<asp:SqlDataSource ID="SqlDataSource1" Runat="server"
    SelectCommand="SELECT * FROM [Customers] WHERE ([CustomerID] = @CustomerID)"
    ConnectionString="<%$ ConnectionStrings:AppConnectionString1 %>"
    DataSourceMode="DataSet">
    <SelectParameters>
        <asp:QueryStringParameter Name="CustomerID"
            QueryStringField="ID" Type="String">
        </asp:QueryStringParameter>
    </SelectParameters>
</asp:SqlDataSource>
```

In addition to hand-coding your `SelectParameters` collection, you can create parameters using the Command and Parameter Editor dialog, which can be accessed by modifying the `SelectQuery` property of the SqlDataSource control while you are viewing the Web page in design mode. Figure 7-5 shows the Command and Parameter Editor dialog.

This dialog gives you a fast and friendly way to create `SelectParameters` for your query. Simply select the Parameter source from the drop-down list and enter the required parameter data. Figure 7-5 demonstrates how to add the `QuerystringParameter` (based on the value of the `querystring` Field ID) to your SqlDataSource control.

Conflict Detection Property

The `ConflictDetection` property allows you to tell the SqlDataSource control what style of conflict detection to use when updating the data. This determines what action should be taken if more than one user attempt to modify the same data. When the value is set to `OverwriteChanges`, the control uses a *Last in Wins* style of updating data. In this style, the control overwrites any changes to data that have been made between the time the data was retrieved by the control and the time the update is made.

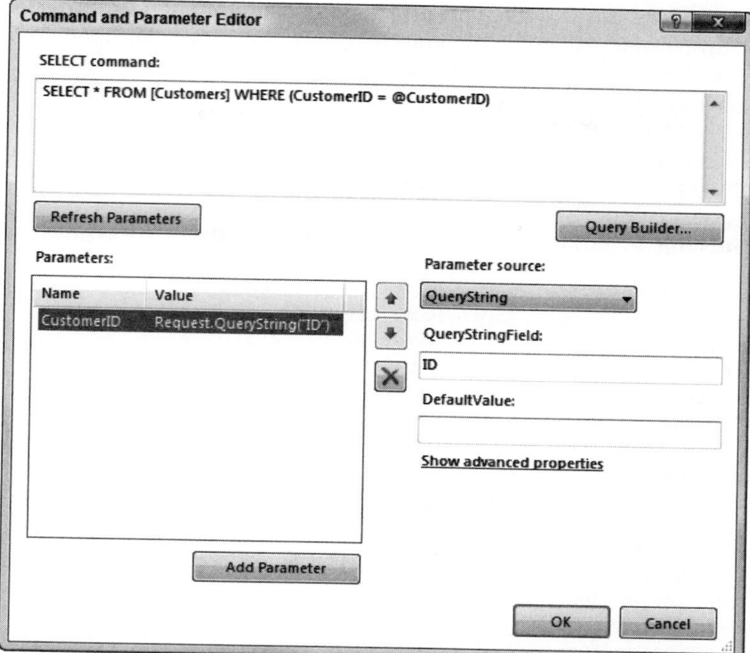

Figure 7-5

If the value is set to `CompareAllValues`, the data source control compares the original data values (what was retrieved) to the data values currently in the data store. If the data has not changed since it was retrieved, the control allows the changes to be implemented. If the control detects differences between the original data that was retrieved from the data store and what is currently in the data store, it does not allow the update to continue. This could potentially occur when you have multiple users accessing the data store and making changes to the data at the same time. In this case, another user could possibly retrieve and change the data well before you send your own changes to the data store. If you don't want to override the previous user's changes, you need to use the `CompareAllValues` value. Listing 7-5 shows how to add the `ConflictDetection` property to the SqlDataSource control.

Listing 7-5: Adding the ConflictDetection property to a SqlDataSource control

```
<asp:SqlDataSource ID="SqlDataSource1" Runat="server"
   SelectCommand="SELECT * FROM [Customers] WHERE ([CustomerID] = @CustomerID)"
    ConnectionString="<%$ ConnectionStrings:AppConnectionString1 %>"
    DataSourceMode="DataSet"
    ConflictDetection="CompareAllValues">
    <SelectParameters>
        <asp:QueryStringParameter Name="CustomerID"
            QueryStringField="id" Type="String">
        </asp:QueryStringParameter>
    </SelectParameters>
</asp:SqlDataSource>
```

As described earlier, you can also use the SqlDataSource Configuration Wizard to add optimistic concurrency to the control. Doing this causes several changes in the underlying control. First, it automatically adds the `ConflictDetection` attribute to the control and sets it to `CompareAllValues`. Second, the wizard modifies the `Update` and `Delete` parameter collections to include parameters for the original data values. It also modifies the SQL statements so that they compare the original data values to the new values. You can recognize the newly added parameters because the wizard simply prepends the prefix `original` to each data column name. Listing 7-6 shows you what the modified `UpdateParameters` looks like.

Listing 7-6: Adding original value parameters to the UpdateParameters collection

```
<UpdateParameters>
    <asp:Parameter Name="CompanyName" Type="String" />
    <asp:Parameter Name="ContactName" Type="String" />
    <asp:Parameter Name="ContactTitle" Type="String" />
    <asp:Parameter Name="Address" Type="String" />
    <asp:Parameter Name="City" Type="String" />
    <asp:Parameter Name="Region" Type="String" />
    <asp:Parameter Name="PostalCode" Type="String" />
    <asp:Parameter Name="Country" Type="String" />
    <asp:Parameter Name="Phone" Type="String" />
    <asp:Parameter Name="Fax" Type="String" />
    <asp:Parameter Name="original_CustomerID" Type="String" />
    <asp:Parameter Name="original_CompanyName" Type="String" />
    <asp:Parameter Name="original_ContactName" Type="String" />
    <asp:Parameter Name="original_ContactTitle" Type="String" />
    <asp:Parameter Name="original_Address" Type="String" />
    <asp:Parameter Name="original_City" Type="String" />
    <asp:Parameter Name="original_Region" Type="String" />
    <asp:Parameter Name="original_PostalCode" Type="String" />
    <asp:Parameter Name="original_Country" Type="String" />
    <asp:Parameter Name="original_Phone" Type="String" />
    <asp:Parameter Name="original_Fax" Type="String" />
</UpdateParameters>
```

Finally, the SqlDataSource Wizard sets an additional property called `OldValueParameterFormatString`. This attribute determines the prefix for the original data values. By default, the value is `original_0`, but you have complete control over this.

One way to determine whether your update has encountered a concurrency error is by testing the `AffectedRows` property in the SqlDataSource's `Updated` event. Listing 7-7 shows one way to do this.

Listing 7-7: Detecting concurrency errors after updating data

VB

```
Protected Sub SqlDataSource1_Updated(ByVal sender as Object, _
    ByVal e As System.Web.UI.WebControls.SqlDataSourceStatusEventArgs)

    If (e.AffectedRows > 0) Then
        Message.Text = "The record has been updated"
    Else
        Message.Text = "Possible concurrency violation"
    End If
End Sub
```

C#

```
protected void SqlDataSource1_Updated(object sender,
    SqlDataSourceStatusEventArgs e)
{
     if (e.AffectedRows > 0)
         Message.Text = "The record has been updated";
     else
         Message.Text = "Possible concurrency violation";
}
```

SqlDataSource Events

The SqlDataSource control provides a number of events that you can hook into to affect the behavior of the SqlDataSource control or to react to events that occur while the SqlDataSource control is executing. The control provides events that are raised before and after the Select, Insert, Update, and Delete commands are executed. You can use these events to alter the SQL command being sent to the data source by the control. You can cancel the operation or determine if an error has occurred while executing the SQL command.

Using the Data Source Events to Handle Database Errors

The data source control events are very useful for trapping and handling errors that occur while you are attempting to execute a SQL command against the database. For instance, Listing 7-8 demonstrates how you can use the SqlDataSource control's `Updated` event to handle a database error that has bubbled back to the application as an exception.

Listing 7-8: Using the SqlDataSource control's Updated event to handle database errors

VB

```
Protected Sub SqlDataSource1_Updated(ByVal sender As Object, _
    ByVal e As System.Web.UI.WebControls.SqlDataSourceStatusEventArgs)

    If (e.Exception IsNot Nothing) Then
        'An exception has occured executing the
        ' SQL command and needs to be handled
        lblError.Text = e.Exception.Message

        'Finally, tell ASP.NET you have handled the
        ' exception and it is to continue
        ' executing the application code
        e.ExceptionHandled = True
    End If
End Sub
```

C#

```
protected void SqlDataSource1_Updated(object sender,
    System.Web.UI.WebControls.SqlDataSourceStatusEventArgs e)
{
    if (e.Exception != null)
    {
```

Continued

```
            //An exception has occured executing the
            // SQL command and needs to be handled
            lblError.Text = e.Exception.Message;

            //Finally, tell ASP.NET you have handled the
            // exception and it is to continue
            // executing the application code
            e.ExceptionHandled = true;
        }
    }
```

Notice that the sample tests to see if the `Exception` property is `null`; if it is not (indicating an exception has occurred), the application attempts to handle the exception.

An extremely important part of this sample is the code that sets the `ExceptionHandled` property. By default, this property returns `False`. Therefore, even if you detect the `Exception` property is not null and you attempt to handle the error, the exception still bubbles out of the application. Setting the `ExceptionHandled` property to `True` tells .NET that you have successfully handled the exception and that it is safe to continue executing. Note that the `AccessDataSource` and `ObjectDataSource` controls also function in this manner.

Although the SqlDataSource control is powerful, a number of other data source controls might suit your specific data access scenario better.

Using the SqlDataSource with Oracle

Just as you would use the SqlDataSource control to connect to Microsoft's SQL Server, you can also use this same control to connect to other databases that might be contained within your enterprise, such as Oracle.

To use the SqlDataSource control with Oracle, start by dragging and dropping the SqlDataSource control onto your page's design surface. Using the SqlDataSource control's smart tag, you are then able to configure your data source by clicking the Configure Data Source link.

Within the Configure Data Source wizard, you first need to create a new connection to your Oracle database. Click on the New Connection button to open the Add Connection dialog which is shown in Figure 7-6.

By default, the Data Source is configured to work with a SQL Server database but you can change this by simply pressing the Change button. This will launch a new dialog that allows you to select Oracle. This dialog is presented here in Figure 7-7.

This discussion is for the Microsoft Oracle Provider that comes with Visual Studio. Oracle also has its own provider, named the Oracle Data Provider (ODP), and the procedures to use that would be different. Consult the ODP documentation for details.

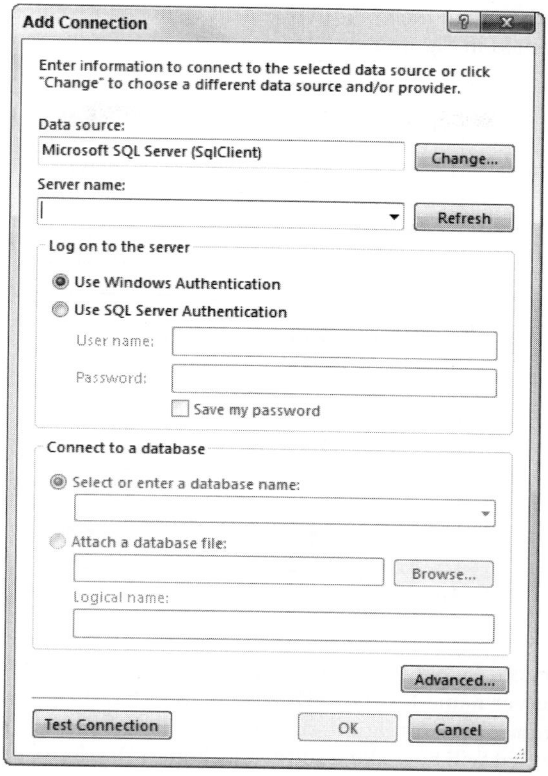

Figure 7-6

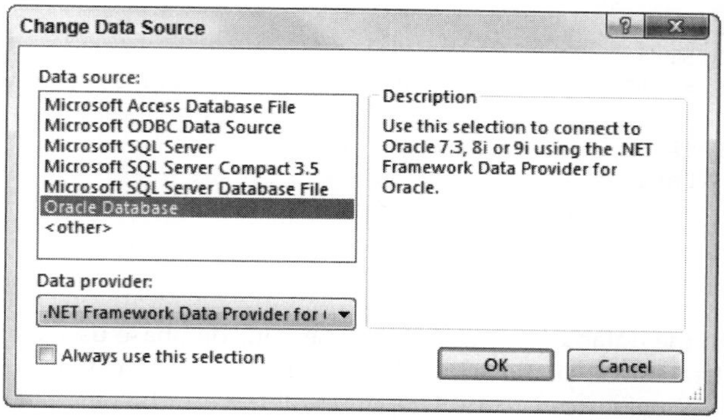

Figure 7-7

Selecting an Oracle database will then modify the Add Connection dialog so that it is more appropriate for the job. This is presented in Figure 7-8.

Figure 7-8

From the Add Connection dialog, you can add the name of the Oracle database that you are connecting to in the Server name text box. The name you place here is the name of the database that is held in the `tnsnames.ora` configuration file. This file is put into place after you install the Oracle Client on the server that will be making the connection to Oracle. You will find this file under a folder structure that is specific to the version of the Oracle client software — for example: `C:\Oracle\product\10.1.0\Client_1\NETWORK\ADMIN`. One particular database entry in this `tnsnames.ora` file is presented here:

```
MyDatabase =
  (DESCRIPTION =
    (ADDRESS_LIST =
      (ADDRESS = (PROTOCOL = TCP)(HOST = 192.168.1.101)(PORT = 1521))
    )
    (CONNECT_DATA =
      (SID = MyDatabase)
      (SERVER = DEDICATED)
    )
  )
```

After the reference to the database, you can then use your database username and password and then simply use the SqlDataSource control as you would if you were working with SQL Server. Once the configuring of the SqlDataSource is complete, you will then find a new connection to Oracle in your `<connectionStrings>` section of the `web.config` (if you chose to save the connection string there through the configuration process). An example of this is presented here:

```
<connectionStrings>
  <add name="ConnectionString"
   connectionString="Data Source=MyDatabase;User
```

```
        ID=user1;Password=admin1pass;Unicode=True"
      providerName="System.Data.OracleClient" />
  </connectionStrings>
```

LINQ Data Source Control

The LinqDataSource control is a new Data Source control introduced in ASP.NET 3.5 that allows you to use the new LINQ features of .NET 3.5 to query data objects in your application.

This chapter focuses primarily on how to use the LinqDataSource control and its design-time configuration options. If you want to learn more about LINQ, its syntax, and how it works with different object types, refer to Chapter 9 in this book.

The LinqDataSource control works much the same way as any other Data Source control, converting the properties you set on the control into queries that can be executed on the targeted data object. Much like the SqlDataSource control, which generated SQL statements based on your property settings, the LinqDataSource control converts the property settings into valid LINQ queries. When you drag the control onto the Visual Studio design surface, you can use the smart tag to configure the control. Figure 7-9 shows the initial screen of the configuration wizard.

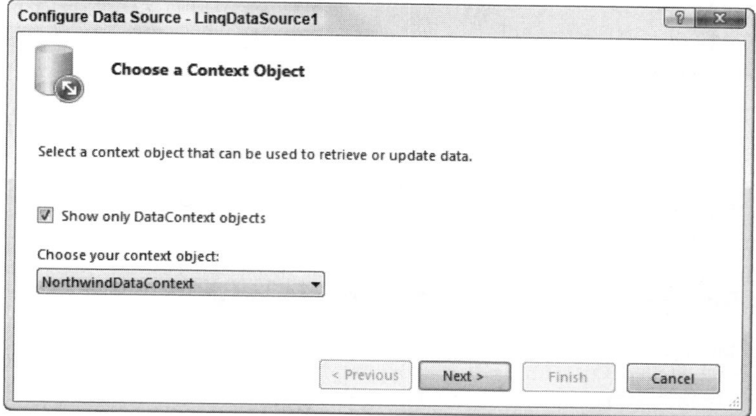

Figure 7-9

From this screen you can choose the context object you want to use as the source of your data. The context object is the base object that contains the data you want to query. By default, the wizard will show only objects that are derived from the `System.Data.Linq.DataContext` base class, which are normally data context classes created by LINQ to SQL. The wizard does give you the option of seeing all objects in your application (even those included as references in your project) and allowing you to select one of those as your context object.

Once you have selected your context object, the wizard allows you to select the specific table or property within the context object that returns the data you want to bind to, as shown in Figure 7-10. If you are binding to a class derived from `DataContext`, the table drop-down list shows all of the data tables contained in the context object. If you are binding to a standard class, then the drop-down allows you to select any enumerable property exposed by the context object.

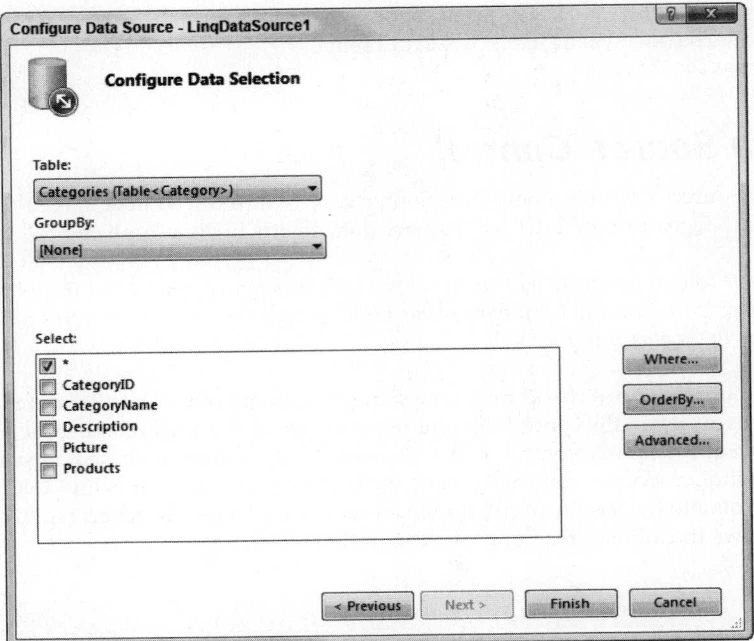

Figure 7-10

Once you have selected the table, you can click the Finish button and complete the wizard. Listing 7-9 shows the markup that is generated by the LinqDataSource Configuration Wizard after it is configured to use the Northwind database as its context object and the Customers table.

Listing 7-9: The basic LinqDataSource control markup

```
<asp:LinqDataSource ID="LinqDataSource1" runat="server"
    ContextTypeName="NorthwindDataContext" TableName="Customers"
    EnableInsert="True" EnableUpdate="True" EnableDelete="True">
</asp:LinqDataSource>
```

The LinqDataSource is now ready to be bound to a data control such as a GridView or ListView.

Notice that the markup generated by the control includes three properties: `EnableInsert`, `EnableUpdate` and `EnableDelete`. These properties allow you to configure the control to allow Insert, Update and Delete actions if the underlying data source supports them. Because the data source control knows that it is connected to a LINQ To SQL data context object, which by default supports these actions, it has automatically enabled them.

The LinqDataSource also includes a number of other basic configuration options you can use to control the selection of data from the context object. As shown in Figure 7-10, the configuration wizard also allows you to select specific fields to include in its resultset.

While this can be a convenient way to control which fields are displayed in a bound control such as the GridView, it also causes the underlying LINQ query to return a custom projection. A side effect of this is that the resulting dataset no longer supports the inserting, updating, or deletion of data. If you simply want to limit the data shown by the bound list control, you may want to consider defining the fields to display in the bound list control rather than in the data source control.

If you choose to select specific fields for the LinqDataSource control to return, the wizard adds the `Select` attribute to the markup with the appropriate LINQ projection statement. This is shown in Listing 7-10, where the control has been modified to return only the CustomerID, ContactName, ContactTitle, and Region fields.

Listing 7-10: Specifying LinqDataSource control data fields

```
<asp:LinqDataSource ID="LinqDataSource1" runat="server"
    ContextTypeName="NorthwindDataContext" TableName="Customers"
    Select="new (CustomerID, ContactName, ContactTitle, Region)">
</asp:LinqDataSource>
```

Binding the control to the GridView, you will now see that only these four specified fields are displayed. If no `Select` property is specified, the LinqDataSource control simply returns all public properties exposed by the data object.

Query Operations

The LinqDataSource control also allows you to specify different query parameters such as `Where` and `OrderBy`. Configuration of either option is available by clicking the Where or OrderBy buttons in the Controls Configuration Wizard.

Defining a Where Clause

The `Where` parameters are created using the same basic `Parameters` syntax used by other Data Source controls, which means that you can provide values from a variety of runtime sources such as Form fields, Querystring values, or even Session values. Listing 7-11 demonstrates the use of `Where` parameters.

Listing 7-11: Specifying Where clause parameters

```
<asp:LinqDataSource ID="LinqDataSource1" runat="server"
    ContextTypeName="NorthwindDataContext" TableName="Customers"
    Select="new (CustomerID, ContactName, ContactTitle, Region)"
    Where="CustomerID == @CustomerID">
    <whereparameters>
        <asp:querystringparameter DefaultValue="0" Name="CustomerID"
            QueryStringField="cid" Type="String" />
    </whereparameters>
</asp:LinqDataSource>
```

You can add multiple `Where` parameters that the control will automatically concatenate in its `Where` property using the `AND` operator. You can manually change the default value of the `Where` property if you want to have multiple `WhereParameters` defined, but only use a subset, or if you want to change which parameters are used dynamically at runtime. This is shown in Listing 7-12, where the LinqDataSource control has several `Where` parameters defined, but by default is using only one.

Listing 7-12: Using one of multiple defined WhereParameters

```
<asp:LinqDataSource ID="LinqDataSource1" runat="server"
    ContextTypeName="NorthwindDataContext" TableName="Customers"
    Select="new (CustomerID, ContactName, ContactTitle, Region)"
    Where="Country == @Country"
        OrderBy="Region, ContactTitle, ContactName">
    <whereparameters>
        <asp:querystringparameter DefaultValue="0" Name="CustomerID"
            QueryStringField="cid" Type="String" />
        <asp:querystringparameter DefaultValue="USA" Name="Country"
            QueryStringField="country" Type="String" />
        <asp:FormParameter DefaultValue="AZ" Name="Region"
            FormField="region" Type="String" />
    </whereparameters>
</asp:LinqDataSource>
```

In this case, although three `WhereParameters` are defined, the `Where` property uses only the `Country` parameter. It would be simple to change the `Where` property's value at runtime to use any of the defined parameters, based perhaps on a configuration setting set by the end user.

The LinqDataSource control also includes a property called `AutoGenerateWhereClause`, which can simplify the markup created by the control. When set to `True`, the property causes the control to ignore the value of the `Where` property and automatically use each parameter specified in the `Where` parameters collection in the query's `Where` clause.

Defining an OrderBy Clause

When defining an `OrderBy` clause, by default the wizard simply creates a comma-delimited list of fields as the value for the control's `OrderBy` property. The value of the `OrderBy` property is then appended to the control's LINQ query when it is executed.

The control also exposes an `OrderByParameters` collection, which you can also use to specify `OrderBy` values. However, in most cases using the simple `OrderBy` property will be sufficient. You would need to the use `OrderBy` parameters collection only if you need to determine the value of a variable at runtime, and then order the query results based on that value.

Grouping Query Data

The LinqDataSource control also makes it easy to specify a grouping for the resultset returned by the query. In the configuration wizard, you can select the Group By field for the query. Once a field is selected, the wizard then creates a default projection based on the groupby field. The projection includes two fields by default, the first called `key`, which represents the group objects specified in the `GroupBy` property, and the second called `it` which represents the grouped objects. You can also add your own columns to the projection and execute functions against the grouped data such as `Average`, `Min`, `Max`, and `Count`. Listing 7-13 demonstrates a very simple grouping using the LinqDataSource control.

Listing 7-13: Simple Data Grouping

```
<asp:LinqDataSource ID="LinqDataSource1" runat="server"
    ContextTypeName="NorthwindDataContext" TableName="Products"
    Select="new (key as Category, it as Products,
```

```
        Average(UnitPrice) as Average_UnitPrice)"
    GroupBy="Category">
</asp:LinqDataSource>
```

You can see in this sample that the Products table has been grouped by its `Category` property. The LinqDataSource control created a new projection containing the `key` (aliased as `Category`) and `it` (aliased as `Products`) fields. Additionally, the custom field `average_unitprice` has been added, which calculates the average unit price of the products in each category. When you execute this query and bind the results to a GridView, a simple view of the calculated average unit price is displayed. The Category and Products are not displayed because they are complex object types, and the GridView is not capable of directly displaying them.

You can access the data in either key by using the standard `ASP.NET Eval()` function. In a GridView you would do this by creating a `TemplateField`, and using `ItemTemplate` to insert the `Eval` statement as shown here:

```
<asp:TemplateField>
    <ItemTemplate>
        <%# Eval("Category.CategoryName") %>
    </ItemTemplate>
</asp:TemplateField>
```

In this case, `TemplateField` displays the `CategoryName` for each grouped category in the resultset.

Accessing the grouped items is just as easy. If, for example, you wanted to include a bullet list of each product in an individual group, you would simply add another `TemplateField`, insert a BulletList control and bind it to the Products field returned by the query, as shown next:

```
<asp:TemplateField>
    <ItemTemplate>
        <asp:BulletedList DataSource='<%# Eval("Products") %>'
            DataTextField="ProductName" runat="server" ID="BulletedList" />
    </ItemTemplate>
</asp:TemplateField>
```

Data Concurrency

Like the SqlDataSource control, the LinqDataSource control allows for data concurrency checks when updating or deleting data. As its name implies, the `StoreOriginalValuesInViewState` property indicates whether the data source control should store the original data values in ViewState. Doing this when using LINQ to SQL as the underlying data object, allows LINQ to SQL to perform data concurrency checking before submitting updates, or deleting data.

Storing the original data in ViewState, however, can cause the size of your Web page to grow significantly, affecting the performance of your Web site, so you may wish to disable the storing of data in ViewState. If you do, recognize that you are now responsible for any data concurrency checking that your application requires.

LinqDataSource Events

The LinqDataSource control also includes a number of useful events that you can use to react to actions taken by the control at runtime. Standard before and after events for Select, Insert, Update, and Delete actions are all exposed and allow you to add, remove, or modify parameters from the control's various parameter collections, or even cancel the event entirely.

Additionally, the post action events allow you to determine whether an exception has occurred while attempting to execute an Insert, Update, or Delete. If an exception has occurred, these events allow you to react to those exceptions, and either mark the exception as handled, or allow it to continue to bubble up through the application.

AccessDataSource Control

Although you can use the SqlDataSource to connect to Access databases, ASP.NET also provides a special `AccessDataSource` control. This control gives you specialized access to Access databases using the Jet Data provider, but it still uses SQL commands to perform data retrieval because it is derived from the SqlDataSource.

Despite its relative similarity to the SqlDataSource control, the AccessDataSource control has some specialized parts. First, the control does not require you to set a `ConnectionString` property. Instead, the control uses a `DataFile` property to allow you to directly specify the Access `.mdb` file you want to use for data access.

> *A side effect of not having the* `ConnectionString` *property is that the AccessDataSource cannot connect to password-protected databases. If you need to access a password-protected Access database, you can use the SqlDataSource control, which allows you to provide the username and password as part of the connection string.*

Additionally, because the AccessDataSource uses the System.Data.OleDb to perform actual data access, the order of parameters matters. You need to verify that the order of the parameters in any Select, Insert, Update, or Delete parameters collection matches the order of the parameters in the SQL statement.

XmlDataSource Control

The `XmlDataSource` control provides you with a simple way of binding XML documents, either in-memory or located on a physical drive. The control provides you with a number of properties that make it easy to specify an XML file containing data and an XSLT transform file for converting the source XML into a more suitable format. You can also provide an XPath query to select only a certain subset of data.

You can use the XmlDataSource control's Configure Data Wizard, shown in Figure 7-11, to configure the control.

Listing 7-14 shows how you might consume an RSS feed from the MSDN Web site, selecting all the item nodes within it for binding to a bound list control such as the GridView.

Listing 7-14: Using the XmlDataSource control to consume an RSS feed

```
<asp:XmlDataSource ID="XmlDataSource1" Runat="server"
    DataFile="http://msdn.microsoft.com/rss.xml"
    XPath="rss/channel/item"
</asp:XmlDataSource>
```

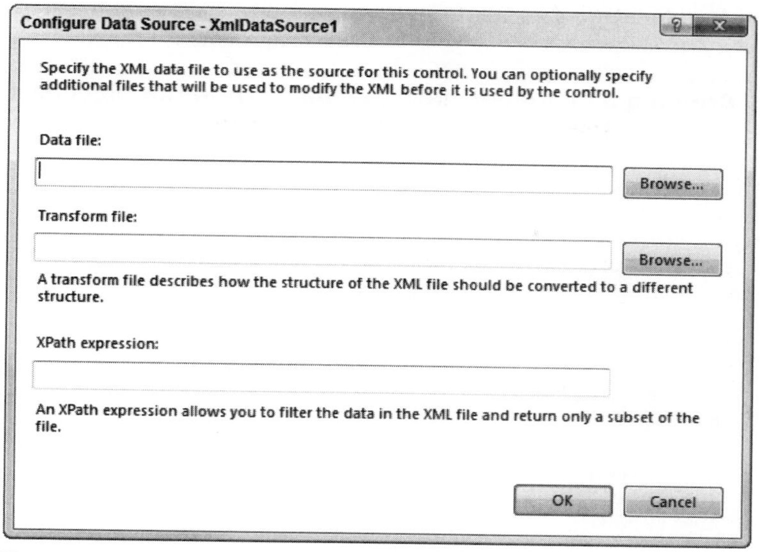

Figure 7-11

In addition to the declarative attributes you can use with the XmlDataSource, a number of other helpful properties and events are available.

Many times, your XML is not stored in a physical file, but rather is simply a string stored in your application memory or possibly in a SQL database. The control provides the `Data` property, which accepts a simple string of XML to which the control can bind. Note that if both the `Data` and `DataFile` properties are set, the `DataFile` property takes precedence over the `Data` property.

Additionally, in certain scenarios, you may want to export the bound XML out of the XmlDataSource control to other objects or even save any changes that have been made to the underlying XML if it has been bound to a control such as a GridView. The XmlDataSource control provides two methods to accommodate this. First, the `GetXmlDocument` method allows you to export the XML by returning a basic `System.Xml.XmlDocument` object that contains the XML loaded in the data source control.

Second, using the control's `Save` method, you can persist changes made to the XmlDataSource control's loaded XML back to disk. Executing this method assumes you have provided a file path in the `DataFile` property.

The XmlDataSource control also provides you with a number of specialized events. The `Transforming` event that is raised before the XSLT transform specified in the `Transform` or `TransformFile` properties is applied and allows you to supply custom arguments to the transform.

ObjectDataSource Control

The `ObjectDataSource` control is one of the most interesting data source controls in the ASP.NET toolbox. It gives you the power to bind data controls to middle-layer business objects that can be hard-coded or automatically generated from programs such as Object Relational (O/R) mappers.

To demonstrate how to use the ObjectDataSource control, create a class in the project that represents a customer. Listing 7-15 shows a class that you can use for this demonstration.

Listing 7-15: Creating a Customer class to demonstrate the ObjectDataSource control

VB

```
Public Class Customer
    Private _customerID As Integer
    Private _companyName As String
    Private _contactName As String
    Private _contactTitle As String

    Public Property CustomerID() As Integer
        Get
            Return _customerID
        End Get
        Set
            _customerID = value
        End Set
    End Property

    Public Property CompanyName() As Integer
        Get
            Return _companyName
        End Get
        Set
            _companyName = value
        End Set
    End Property

    Public Property ContactName() As Integer
        Get
            Return _contactName
        End Get
        Set
            _contactName = value
        End Set
    End Property

    Public Property ContactTitle() As Integer
        Get
            Return _contactTitle
        End Get
        Set
            _contactTitle = value
        End Set
    End Property

    Public Function [Select](ByVal customerID As Integer) As System.Data.DataSet
        ' You would implement logic here to retreive
        ' Customer data based on the customerID parameter

      Dim ds As New System.Data.DataSet()
```

```
        ds.Tables.Add(New System.Data.DataTable())
        Return ds
    End Function

    Public Sub Insert(ByVal c As Customer)
        ' Implement Insert logic
    End Sub

    Public Sub Update(ByVal c As Customer)
        ' Implement Update logic
    End Sub

    Public Sub Delete(ByVal c As Customer)
        ' Implement Delete logic
    End Sub

End Class
```

C#

```
public class Customer
{
    private int _customerID;
    private string _companyName;
    private string _contactName;
    private string _contactTitle;

    public int CustomerID
    {
        get
        {
            return _customerID;
        }

        set
        {
            _customerID = value;
        }
    }

    public string CompanyName
    {
        get
        {
            return _companyName;
        }

        set
        {
            _companyName = value;
        }
    }

    public string ContactName
    {
```

Continued

```
        get
        {
            return _contactName;
        }

        set
        {
            _contactName = value;
        }
    }

    public string ContactTitle
    {
        get
        {
            return _contactTitle;
        }

        set
        {
            _contactTitle = value;
        }
    }

    public Customer()
    {
    }

    public System.Data.DataSet Select(Int32 customerId)
    {
        // Implement logic here to retrieve the Customer
        // data based on the methods customerId parameter

        System.Data.DataSet ds = new System.Data.DataSet();
        ds.Tables.Add(new System.Data.DataTable());
        return ds;
    }

    public void Insert(Customer c)
    {
        // Implement Insert logic
    }

    public void Update(Customer c)
    {
        // Implement Update logic
    }

    public void Delete(Customer c)
    {
        // Implement Delete logic
    }

}
```

To start using the ObjectDataSource, drag the control onto the designer surface. Using the control's smart tag, load the Configuration Wizard by selecting the Configure Data Source option. After the wizard opens, it asks you to select the business object you want to use as your data source. The drop-down list shows all the classes located in the `App_Code` folder of your Web site that can be successfully compiled. In this case, you want to use the `Customer` class shown in Listing 7-8.

Click the Next button, and the wizard asks you to specify which methods it should use for the CRUD operations it can perform: SELECT, INSERT, UPDATE, and DELETE. Each tab lets you select a specific method located in your business class to perform the specific action. Figure 7-12 shows that you want the control to use a method called `Select()` to retrieve data.

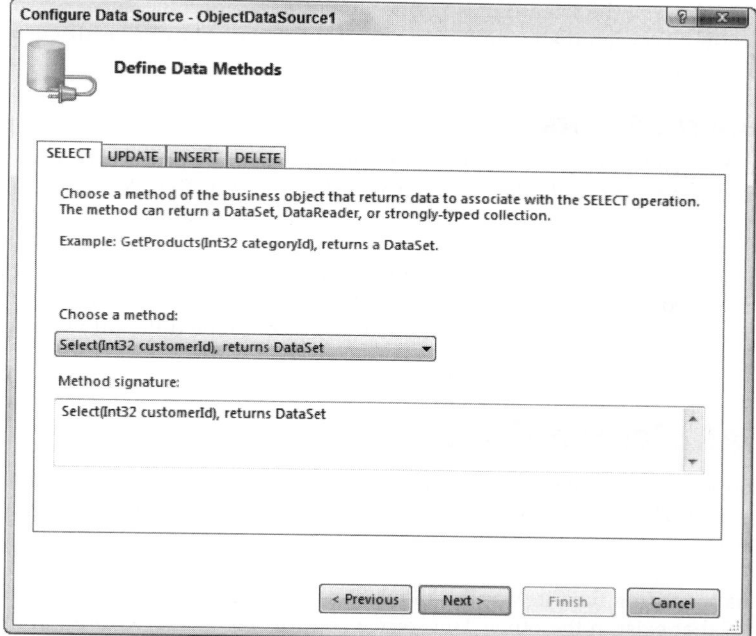

Figure 7-12

The methods the ObjectDataSource uses to perform CRUD operations must follow certain rules in order for the control to understand. For instance, the control's `SELECT` method must return a `DataSet`, `DataReader`, or a strongly typed collection. Each of the control's operation tabs explains what the control expects of the method you specify for it to use. Additionally, if a method does not conform to the rules that specific operation expects, it is not listed in the drop-down list on that tab.

Finally, if your `SELECT` method contains parameters, the wizard lets you create `SelectParameters` you can use to provide the method parameter data.

When you have completed configuring the ObjectDataSource, you should have code in your page source like that shown in Listing 7-16.

Listing 7-16: The ObjectDataSource code generated by the configuration wizard

```
<asp:ObjectDataSource ID="ObjectDataSource1" runat="server" DeleteMethod="Delete"
    InsertMethod="Insert" SelectMethod="Select" TypeName="Customer"
    UpdateMethod="Update">
    <SelectParameters>
        <asp:QueryStringParameter Name="customerID" QueryStringField="ID"
            Type="Int32" />
    </SelectParameters>
</asp:ObjectDataSource>
```

As you can see, the wizard has generated the attributes for the `SELECT`, `UPDATE`, `INSERT`, and `DELETE` methods you specified in the wizard. Also notice that it has added the `Select` parameter. Depending on your application, you could change this to any of the `Parameter` objects discussed earlier, such as a `ControlParameter` or `QuerystringParameter` object.

ObjectDataSource Events

The ObjectDataSource control exposes several useful events that you can hook into. First, it includes events that are raised before and after the control performs any of the CRUD actions, such as selecting or deleting events.

It also includes pre- and post-events that are raised when the object that is serving as the data source is created or disposed of, as well as when an event that is raised before a filter is applied to the data. All these events give you great power when you must react to the different ways the ObjectDataSource control behaves.

SiteMapDataSource Control

The `SiteMapDataSource` enables you to work with data stored in your Web site's SiteMap configuration file if you have one. This can be useful if you are changing your site map data at runtime, perhaps based on user privilege or status.

Note two items regarding the SiteMapDataSource control. First, it does not support any of the data caching options that exist in the other data source controls provided (covered in the next section), so you cannot natively cache your sitemap data. Second, the SiteMapDataSource control does not have any configuration wizards like the other data source controls. This is because the SiteMap control can be bound only to the SiteMap configuration data file of your Web site, so no other configuration is possible.

Listing 7-17 shows an example of using the SiteMap control.

Listing 7-17: Using the SiteMapDataSource control

```
<asp:SiteMapDataSource ID="SiteMapDataSource1" Runat="server" />
```

Using the SiteMapDataSource control is discussed in greater detail in Chapter 14.

Configuring Data Source Control Caching

Caching is built into all the data source controls that ship with ASP.NET except the SiteMapDataSource control. This means that you can easily configure and control data caching using the same declarative syntax. All data source controls (except the SiteMapDataSource control) enable you to create basic caching policies including a cache direction, expiration policies, and key dependencies.

Remember that the SqlDataSource control's caching features are available only if you have set the `DataSourceMode` *property to* `DataSet`. *If it is set to* `DataReader`, *the control throws a* `NotSupportedException`.

Cache duration can be set to a specific length of time, such as 3600 seconds (60 minutes), or you can set it to `Infinite` to force the cached data to never expire. Listing 7-18 shows how you can easily add caching features to a data source control.

Listing 7-18: Enabling caching on a SqlDataSource control

```
<asp:SqlDataSource ID="SqlDataSource1" Runat="server"
    SelectCommand="SELECT * FROM [Customers]"
    ConnectionString="<%$ ConnectionStrings:AppConnectionString1 %>"
    DataSourceMode="DataSet"
    ConflictDetection="CompareAllValues"
    EnableCaching="True" CacheKeyDependency="SomeKey" CacheDuration="Infinite">
    <SelectParameters>
        <asp:QueryStringParameter Name="CustomerID"
            QueryStringField="id" Type="String"></asp:QueryStringParameter>
    </SelectParameters>
</asp:SqlDataSource>
```

Some controls also extend this core set of caching features with additional caching functionality specific to their data sources. For instance, if you are using the SqlDataSource control, you can use the `SqlCacheDependency` property to create SQL dependencies. You can learn more about ASP.NET caching features in Chapter 23.

Storing Connection Information

In ASP.NET 1.0/1.1, Microsoft introduced the `web.config` file as a way of storing application configuration data in a readable and portable format. Many people quickly decided that the `web.config` file was a great place to store things like the database connection information their applications use. It was easy to access from within the application, created a single central location for the configuration data, and it was a cinch to change just by editing the XML.

Although all those advantages were great, several drawbacks existed. First, none of the information in the `web.config` file can be strongly typed. It was, therefore, difficult to find data type problems within the application until a runtime error occurred. It also meant that developers were unable to use the power of IntelliSense to facilitate development. A second problem was that although the `web.config` file was secured from access by browsers (it cannot be served up by Internet Information Server), the data within the file was clearly visible to anyone who had file access to the Web server.

Microsoft has addressed these shortcomings of the `web.config` file by adding features specifically designed to make it easier to work with and secure connection string information in the `web.config` file. Because database connection information is so frequently stored in the `web.config` file, starting with ASP.NET 2.0, a new configuration section was added in that file. The `<connectionStrings>`section is designed specifically for storing the connection string information.

If you examine your `web.config` file, you should see at least one connection string already in the `<connectionStrings>` section because our example told the Data Connection Wizard to store connections in the `web.config` file. Listing 7-19 shows how ASP.NET stores a connection string.

Listing 7-19: A typical connection string saved in the web.config file

```
<connectionStrings>
    <add name="AppConnectionString1" connectionString="Server=localhost;
        User ID=sa;Password=password;Database=Northwind;
        Persist Security Info=True" providerName="System.Data.SqlClient" />
</connectionStrings>
```

Using a separate configuration section has several advantages. First, .NET exposes the `ConnectionString` section using the `ConnectionStringSettings` class. This class contains a collection of all the connection strings entered in your `web.config` file and allows you to add, modify, or remove connection strings at runtime. Listing 7-20 shows how you can access and modify connection strings at runtime.

Listing 7-20: Modifying connection string properties at runtime

VB

```
<%@ Page Language="VB" %>

<script runat="server">

    Protected Sub Page_Load(ByVal sender As Object, ByVal e As EventArgs)
        If (Not Page.IsPostBack) Then
            ' Create a new ConnectionStringSettings object and populate it
            Dim conn As New ConnectionStringSettings()
            conn.ConnectionString = _
                 "Server=localhost;User ID=sa;Password=password" & _
                 "Database=Northwind;Persist Security Info=True"
            conn.Name = "AppConnectionString1"
            conn.ProviderName = "System.Data.SqlClient"

            ' Add the new connection string to the web.config
            ConfigurationManager.ConnectionStrings.Add(conn)
        End If

    End Sub

</script>

<html xmlns="http://www.w3.org/1999/xhtml" >
<head runat="server">
    <title>Modifying the Connection String</title>
</head>
<body>
    <form id="form1" runat="server">
    <div>
        <asp:SqlDataSource ID="SqlDataSource1" Runat="server">
        </asp:SqlDataSource>
    </div>
    </form>
```

```
</body>
</html>
```

C#

```
<%@ Page Language="C#" %>

<script runat="server">

    protected void Page_Load(object sender, EventArgs e)
    {
        if (!Page.IsPostBack)
        {
            // Create a new ConnectionStringSettings object and populate it
            ConnectionStringSettings conn = new ConnectionStringSettings();
            conn.ConnectionString =
                "Server=localhost;User ID=sa;Password=password; " +
                "Database=Northwind;Persist Security Info=True";
            conn.Name = "AppConnectionString1";
            conn.ProviderName = "System.Data.SqlClient";

            // Add the new connection string to the web.config
            ConfigurationManager.ConnectionStrings.Add(conn);
        }
    }
</script>
```

As you can see, the `ConfigurationManager` class now has a `ConnectionStrings` collection property in addition to the `AppSettings` collection used in ASP.NET 1.0. This new collection contains all the connection strings for your application.

Additionally, ASP.NET makes it much easier to build connection strings using strongly typed properties at runtime, and easier to add them to the `web.config` file. Using the new `SqlConnectionStringBuilder` class, you can build connection strings and then add them to your `ConnectionStringSettings` collection. Listing 7-21 shows how you can use the `ConnectionStringBuilder` class to dynamically assemble connection strings at runtime and save them to your `web.config` file.

Listing 7-21: Building connection strings using ConnectionStringBuilder

VB

```
' Retrieve an existing connection string into a Connection String Builder
Dim builder As New System.Data.SqlClient.SqlConnectionStringBuilder()

' Change the connection string properties
builder.DataSource = "localhost"
builder.InitialCatalog = "Northwind1"
builder.UserID = "sa"
builder.Password = "password"
builder.PersistSecurityInfo = true

' Save the connection string back to the web.config
ConfigurationManager.ConnectionStrings("AppConnectionString1").ConnectionString = _
    builder.ConnectionString
```

Continued

C#

```
// Retrieve an existing connection string into a Connection String Builder
System.Data.SqlClient.SqlConnectionStringBuilder builder = new
    System.Data.SqlClient.SqlConnectionStringBuilder();

// Change the connection string properties
builder.DataSource = "localhost";
builder.InitialCatalog = "Northwind1";
builder.UserID = "sa";
builder.Password = "password";
builder.PersistSecurityInfo = true;

// Save the connection string back to the web.config
ConfigurationManager.ConnectionStrings["AppConnectionString1"].ConnectionString =
    builder.ConnectionString;
```

Using Bound List Controls with Data Source Controls

The data source controls included in ASP.NET really shine when you combine them with the Bound List controls also included in ASP.NET. This combination allows you to declaratively bind your data source to a bound control without ever writing a single line of C# or VB code.

Fear not, those of you who like to write code. You can always use the familiar `DataBind()` *method to bind data to the list controls. In fact, that method has even been enhanced to include a Boolean overload that allows you to turn the data-binding events on or off. This enables you improve the performance of your application if you are not using any of the binding events.*

GridView

With ASP.NET 1.0/1.1, Microsoft introduced a new set of server controls designed to make developers more productive. One of the most popular controls was the DataGrid. With this one control, you could display an entire collection of data, add sorting and paging, and perform inline editing. Although this new functionality was great, many tasks still required that the developer write a significant amount of code to take advantage of this advanced functionality.

Beginning with ASP.NET 2.0, Microsoft took the basic DataGrid and enhanced it, creating a new server control called the GridView. This control makes it even easier to use those advanced DataGrid features, usually without having to write any code, and it also adds a number of new features.

Displaying Data with the GridView

Start using the GridView by dragging the control onto the designer surface of an ASP.NET Web page. You are prompted to select a data source control to bind to the grid. In this sample, you use the SqlDataSource control created earlier in the chapter.

After you assign the GridView a data source, notice a number of changes. First, the GridView changes its design-time display to reflect the data exposed by the data source control assigned to it. Should the schema of the data behind the data source control ever change, you can use the GridView's Refresh Schema option to force the grid to redraw itself based on the new data schema. Second, the GridView's smart tag has additional options for formatting, paging, sorting, and selection.

Switch the page to Source view in Visual Studio to examine GridView's code. Listing 7-22 shows the code generated by Visual Studio.

Listing 7-22: Using the GridView control in an ASP.NET Web page

```
<html>
<head runat="server">
    <title>Using the GridView server control</title>
</head>
<body>
    <form id="form1" runat="server">
    <div>
          <asp:GridView ID="GridView1" Runat="server" DataSourceID="SqlDataSource1"
              DataKeyNames="CustomerID" AutoGenerateColumns="False">
            <Columns>
                <asp:BoundField ReadOnly="True" HeaderText="CustomerID"
                     DataField="CustomerID"
                     SortExpression="CustomerID"></asp:BoundField>
                <asp:BoundField HeaderText="CompanyName" DataField="CompanyName"
                     SortExpression="CompanyName"></asp:BoundField>
                <asp:BoundField HeaderText="ContactName" DataField="ContactName"
                     SortExpression="ContactName"></asp:BoundField>
                <asp:BoundField HeaderText="ContactTitle" DataField="ContactTitle"
                     SortExpression="ContactTitle"></asp:BoundField>
                <asp:BoundField HeaderText="Address" DataField="Address"
                     SortExpression="Address"></asp:BoundField>
                <asp:BoundField HeaderText="City" DataField="City"
                     SortExpression="City"></asp:BoundField>
                <asp:BoundField HeaderText="Region" DataField="Region"
                     SortExpression="Region"></asp:BoundField>
                <asp:BoundField HeaderText="PostalCode" DataField="PostalCode"
                     SortExpression="PostalCode"></asp:BoundField>
                <asp:BoundField HeaderText="Country" DataField="Country"
                     SortExpression="Country"></asp:BoundField>
                <asp:BoundField HeaderText="Phone" DataField="Phone"
                     SortExpression="Phone"></asp:BoundField>
                <asp:BoundField HeaderText="Fax" DataField="Fax"
                     SortExpression="Fax"></asp:BoundField>
            </Columns>
        </asp:GridView>

        <asp:SqlDataSource ID="SqlDataSource1" Runat="server"
            SelectCommand="SELECT * FROM [Customers]"
            ConnectionString="<%$ ConnectionStrings:AppConnectionString1 %>"
            DataSourceMode="DataSet"
            ConflictDetection="CompareAllValues" EnableCaching="True"
```

Continued

```
            CacheKeyDependency="MyKey" CacheDuration="Infinite">
        </asp:SqlDataSource>
    </div>
    </form>
</body>
</html>
```

Figure 7-13 shows what your Web page looks like when you execute the code in the browser.

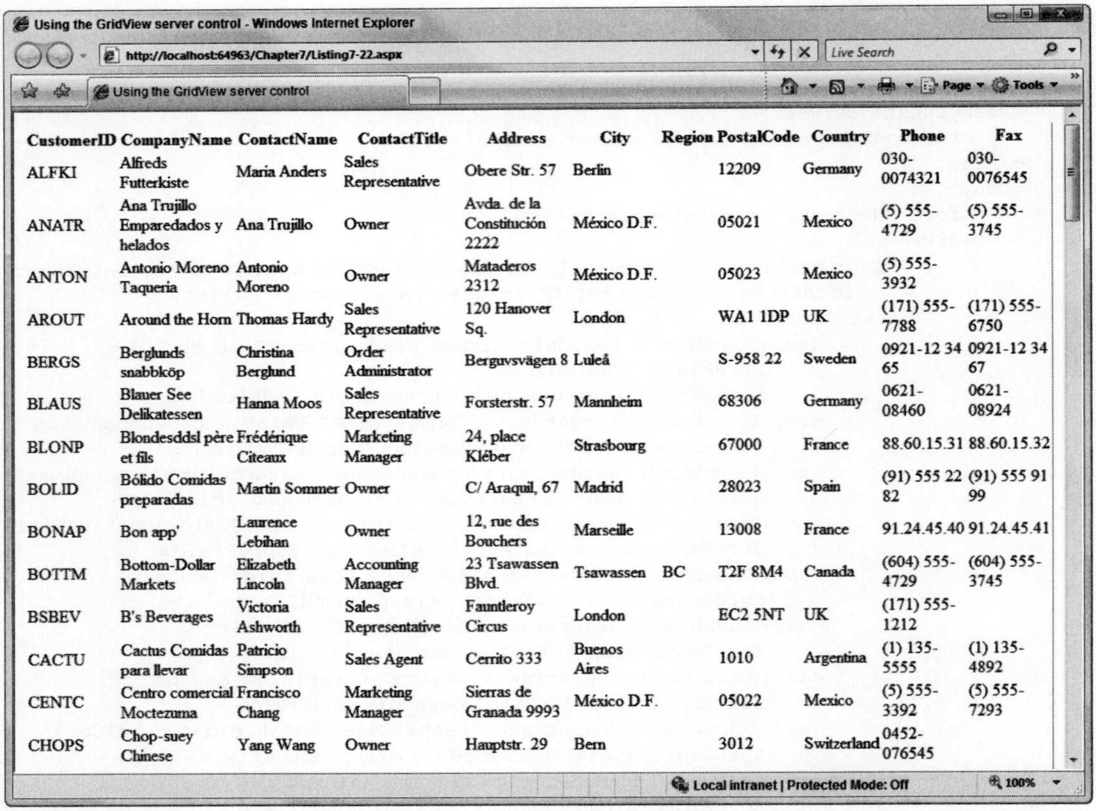

CustomerID	CompanyName	ContactName	ContactTitle	Address	City	Region	PostalCode	Country	Phone	Fax
ALFKI	Alfreds Futterkiste	Maria Anders	Sales Representative	Obere Str. 57	Berlin		12209	Germany	030-0074321	030-0076545
ANATR	Ana Trujillo Emparedados y helados	Ana Trujillo	Owner	Avda. de la Constitución 2222	México D.F.		05021	Mexico	(5) 555-4729	(5) 555-3745
ANTON	Antonio Moreno Taqueria	Antonio Moreno	Owner	Mataderos 2312	México D.F.		05023	Mexico	(5) 555-3932	
AROUT	Around the Horn	Thomas Hardy	Sales Representative	120 Hanover Sq.	London		WA1 1DP	UK	(171) 555-7788	(171) 555-6750
BERGS	Berglunds snabbköp	Christina Berglund	Order Administrator	Berguvsvägen 8	Luleå		S-958 22	Sweden	0921-12 34 65	0921-12 34 67
BLAUS	Blauer See Delikatessen	Hanna Moos	Sales Representative	Forsterstr. 57	Mannheim		68306	Germany	0621-08460	0621-08924
BLONP	Blondesddsl père et fils	Frédérique Citeaux	Marketing Manager	24, place Kléber	Strasbourg		67000	France	88.60.15.31	88.60.15.32
BOLID	Bólido Comidas preparadas	Martin Sommer	Owner	C/ Araquil, 67	Madrid		28023	Spain	(91) 555 22 82	(91) 555 91 99
BONAP	Bon app'	Laurence Lebihan	Owner	12, rue des Bouchers	Marseille		13008	France	91.24.45.40	91.24.45.41
BOTTM	Bottom-Dollar Markets	Elizabeth Lincoln	Accounting Manager	23 Tsawassen Blvd.	Tsawassen	BC	T2F 8M4	Canada	(604) 555-4729	(604) 555-3745
BSBEV	B's Beverages	Victoria Ashworth	Sales Representative	Fauntleroy Circus	London		EC2 5NT	UK	(171) 555-1212	
CACTU	Cactus Comidas para llevar	Patricio Simpson	Sales Agent	Cerrito 333	Buenos Aires		1010	Argentina	(1) 135-5555	(1) 135-4892
CENTC	Centro comercial Moctezuma	Francisco Chang	Marketing Manager	Sierras de Granada 9993	México D.F.		05022	Mexico	(5) 555-3392	(5) 555-7293
CHOPS	Chop-suey Chinese	Yang Wang	Owner	Hauptstr. 29	Bern		3012	Switzerland	0452-076545	

Figure 7-13

The GridView includes several events that are raised when the data binding occurs. These are described in the following table.

Event Name	Description
`DataBinding`	Raised as the GridViews data-binding expressions are about to be evaluated.
`RowCreated`	Raised each time a new row is created in the grid. Before the grid can be rendered, a `GridViewRow` object must be created for each row in the control. The `RowCreated` event allows you to insert custom content into the row as it is being created.

Event Name	Description
RowDataBound	Raised as each GridViewRow is bound to the corresponding data in the data source. This event allows you to evaluate the data being bound to the current row and to affect the output if you need to.
DataBound	Raised after the binding is completed and the GridView is ready to be rendered.

The RowDataBound event is especially useful, enabling you to inject logic into the binding process for each row being bound. Listing 7-23 shows how you can use the RowDataBound to examine the data being bound to the current row and to insert your own logic. The code checks to see if the databases Region column is null; if it is, the code changes the ForeColor and BackColor properties of the GridView rows.

Listing 7-23: Using the RowDataBound to examine the data being bound to the current row and to insert your own logic

VB

```
<script runat="server">
    Protected Sub GridView1_RowDataBound(ByVal sender As Object, _
        ByVal e As System.Web.UI.WebControls.GridViewRowEventArgs)

        'Test for null since gridview rows like the
        ' Header and Footer will have a null DataItem
        If (e.Row.DataItem IsNot Nothing) Then
            'Used to verify the DataItem object type
            System.Diagnostics.Debug.WriteLine(e.Row.DataItem.ToString())
            'When bound to a SqlDataSource, the DataItem
            ' is generally returned as a DataRowView object
            Dim drv As System.Data.DataRowView = _
                CType(e.Row.DataItem, System.Data.DataRowView)

            If (drv("Region") Is System.DBNull.Value) Then
                e.Row.BackColor = System.Drawing.Color.Red
                e.Row.ForeColor = System.Drawing.Color.White
            End If
        End If
    End Sub
</script>
```

C#

```
<script runat="server">
    protected void GridView1_RowDataBound(object sender, GridViewRowEventArgs e)
    {
        //Test for null since gridview rows like the
        // Header and Footer will have a null DataItem
        if (e.Row.DataItem != null)
        {
            //Used to verify the DataItem object type
    System.Diagnostics.Debug.WriteLine(e.Row.DataItem.ToString());
```

Continued

```
                //When bound to a SqlDataSource, the DataItem
                // is generally returned as a DataRowView object
                System.Data.DataRowView drv = (System.Data.DataRowView)e.Row.DataItem;

                if (drv["Region"] == System.DBNull.Value)
                {
                    e.Row.BackColor = System.Drawing.Color.Red;
                    e.Row.ForeColor = System.Drawing.Color.White;
                }
            }
        }
    </script>
```

The GridView also includes events that correspond to selecting, inserting, updating, and deleting data. You learn more about these events later in the chapter.

Using the EmptyDataText and EmptyDataTemplate Properties

In some cases, the data source bound to the GridView may not contain any data for the control to bind to. Even in these cases, you may want to provide the end user with some feedback, informing him that no data is present for the control to bind to. The GridView offers you two techniques to do this.

You first option is to use the `EmptyDataText` property. The property allows you to specify a string of text that is displayed to the user when no data is present for the GridView to bind to. When the ASP.NET page loads and the GridView determines there was no data available in its bound data source, it creates a special DataRow containing the `EmptyDataText` value and displays that to the user. Listing 7-24 shows how you can add this property to the GridView.

Listing 7-24: Adding EmptyDataText to the GridView

```
<asp:GridView ID="GridView1" Runat="server" DataSourceID="SqlDataSource1"
    DataKeyNames="CustomerID" AutoGenerateColumns="False"
    EmptyDataText="No data was found using your query">
```

The other option is to use an EmptyDataTemplate template to completely customize the special row the user sees when no data exists for the control to bind to.

A control template is simply a container that gives you the capability to add other content such as text, HTML controls, or even ASP.NET controls. The GridView control provides you with a variety of templates for various situations, including the EmptyDataTemplate template. You examine these templates throughout the rest of the GridView control section of this chapter.

You can access the template from the Visual Studio 2008 design surface in two ways. The first option is to right-click the GridView control, expand the Edit Template option in the context menu, and select the EmptyDataTemplate item from the menu. This procedure is shown in Figure 7-14.

The other option for opening the template is to select the Edit Templates option from the GridView smart tag. Selecting this option puts the GridView into template editing mode and presents you with a dialog from which you can choose the specific template you wish to edit. Simply select EmptyData-Template from the drop-down list, as shown in Figure 7-15.

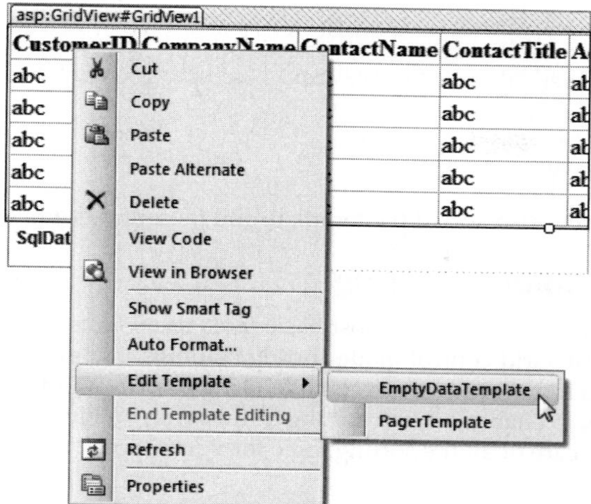

Figure 7-14

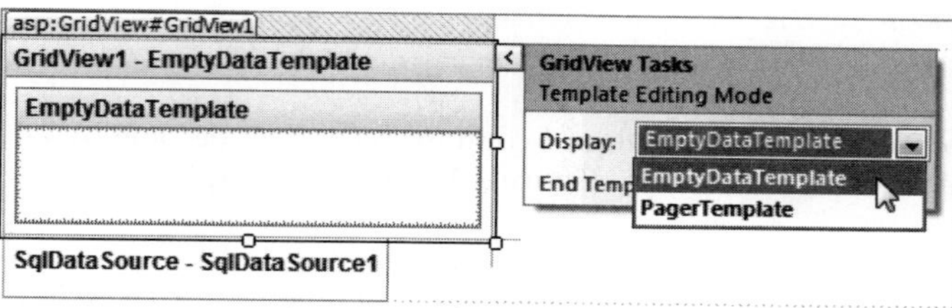

Figure 7-15

After you have entered template editing mode, you can simply add your custom text and/or controls to the template editor on the design surface. When you have finished editing the template, simply right-click, or open the GridViews smart tag and select the End Template Editing option.

Switching to Source view, you see that an `<EmptyDataTemplate>` element has been added to the GridView control. The element should contain all the controls and HTML that you added while editing the template. Listing 7-25 shows an example of an `EmptyDataTemplate`.

Listing 7-25: Using EmptyDataTemplate

```
<EmptyDataTemplate>
    <table style="width: 225px">
        <tr>
            <td colspan="2">
                No data could be found based on your query parameters.
                Please enter a new query.</td>
        </tr>
        <tr>
            <td style="width: 162px">
```

Continued

```
                <asp:TextBox ID="TextBox1" runat="server"></asp:TextBox></td>
            <td style="width: 102px">
                <asp:Button ID="Button1" runat="server" Text="Search" /></td>
        </tr>
    </table>
</EmptyDataTemplate>
```

You could, of course, have also added the template and its contents while in Source view.

Enabling GridView Column Sorting

The capability to sort data is one of the most basic tools users have to navigate through a significant amount of data. The DataGrid control made sorting columns in a grid a relatively easy task, but the GridView control takes it one step further. Unlike using the DataGrid, where you are responsible for coding the sort routine, to enable column sorting in this grid, you just set the `AllowSorting` attribute to `True`. The control takes care of all the sorting logic for you internally. Listing 7-26 shows how to add this attribute to your grid.

Listing 7-26: Adding sorting to the GridView control

```
<asp:GridView ID="GridView1" Runat="server" DataSourceID="SqlDataSource1"
    DataKeyNames="CustomerID" AutoGenerateColumns="False"
    AllowSorting="True">
```

After enabling sorting, you see that all grid columns have now become hyperlinks. Clicking a column header sorts that specific column. Figure 7-16 shows your grid after the data has been sorted by country.

GridView sorting has also been enhanced in a number of other ways. The grid can handle both ascending and descending sorting. If you repeatedly click on a column header, you cause the sort order to switch back and forth between ascending and descending. The GridView's `Sort` method can also accept multiple `SortExpressions` to enable multicolumn sorting. Listing 7-27 shows how you can use the GridView's sorting event to implement a multicolumn sort.

Listing 7-27: Adding multicolumn sorting to the GridView

VB

```
<script runat="server">
    Protected Sub GridView1_Sorting(ByVal sender As Object, _
       ByVal e As GridViewSortEventArgs)

        Dim oldExpression As String = GridView1.SortExpression
        Dim newExpression As String = e.SortExpression

        If (oldExpression.IndexOf(newExpression) < 0) Then
            If (oldExpression.Length > 0) Then
                e.SortExpression = newExpression & "," & oldExpression
            Else
                e.SortExpression = newExpression
            End If
        Else
            e.SortExpression = oldExpression
        End If
```

```
    End Sub
</script>
```

C#

```
<script runat="server">
    protected void GridView1_Sorting(object sender, GridViewSortEventArgs e)
    {
        string oldExpression = GridView1.SortExpression;
        string newExpression = e.SortExpression;

        if (oldExpression.IndexOf(newExpression) < 0)
        {
            if (oldExpression.Length > 0)
                e.SortExpression = newExpression + "," + oldExpression;
            else
                e.SortExpression = newExpression;
        }
        else
        {
            e.SortExpression = oldExpression;
        }
    }
</script>
```

Using the GridView server control - Windows Internet Explorer

http://localhost:64963/Chapter7/Listing7-26.aspx

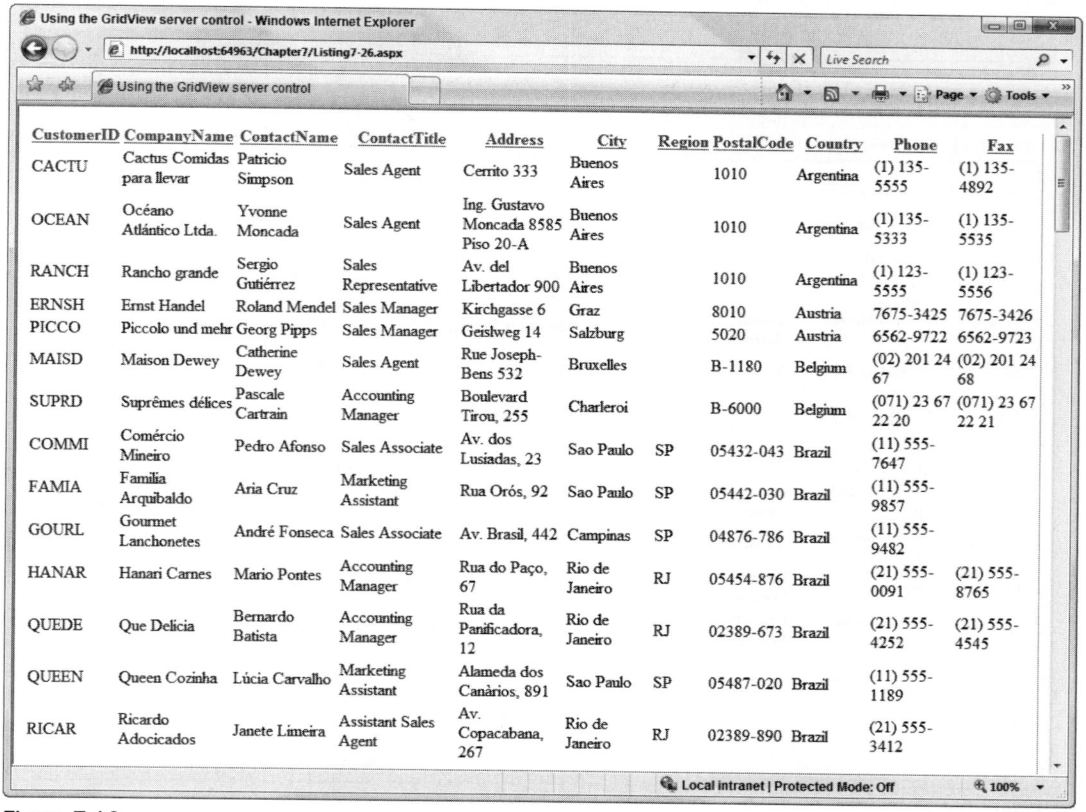

CustomerID	CompanyName	ContactName	ContactTitle	Address	City	Region	PostalCode	Country	Phone	Fax
CACTU	Cactus Comidas para llevar	Patricio Simpson	Sales Agent	Cerrito 333	Buenos Aires		1010	Argentina	(1) 135-5555	(1) 135-4892
OCEAN	Océano Atlántico Ltda.	Yvonne Moncada	Sales Agent	Ing. Gustavo Moncada 8585 Piso 20-A	Buenos Aires		1010	Argentina	(1) 135-5333	(1) 135-5535
RANCH	Rancho grande	Sergio Gutiérrez	Sales Representative	Av. del Libertador 900	Buenos Aires		1010	Argentina	(1) 123-5555	(1) 123-5556
ERNSH	Ernst Handel	Roland Mendel	Sales Manager	Kirchgasse 6	Graz		8010	Austria	7675-3425	7675-3426
PICCO	Piccolo und mehr	Georg Pipps	Sales Manager	Geislweg 14	Salzburg		5020	Austria	6562-9722	6562-9723
MAISD	Maison Dewey	Catherine Dewey	Sales Agent	Rue Joseph-Bens 532	Bruxelles		B-1180	Belgium	(02) 201 24 67	(02) 201 24 68
SUPRD	Suprêmes délices	Pascale Cartrain	Accounting Manager	Boulevard Tirou, 255	Charleroi		B-6000	Belgium	(071) 23 67 22 20	(071) 23 67 22 21
COMMI	Comércio Mineiro	Pedro Afonso	Sales Associate	Av. dos Lusíadas, 23	Sao Paulo	SP	05432-043	Brazil	(11) 555-7647	
FAMIA	Familia Arquibaldo	Aria Cruz	Marketing Assistant	Rua Orós, 92	Sao Paulo	SP	05442-030	Brazil	(11) 555-9857	
GOURL	Gourmet Lanchonetes	André Fonseca	Sales Associate	Av. Brasil, 442	Campinas	SP	04876-786	Brazil	(11) 555-9482	
HANAR	Hanari Carnes	Mario Pontes	Accounting Manager	Rua do Paço, 67	Rio de Janeiro	RJ	05454-876	Brazil	(21) 555-0091	(21) 555-8765
QUEDE	Que Delicia	Bernardo Batista	Accounting Manager	Rua da Panificadora, 12	Rio de Janeiro	RJ	02389-673	Brazil	(21) 555-4252	(21) 555-4545
QUEEN	Queen Cozinha	Lúcia Carvalho	Marketing Assistant	Alameda dos Canàrios, 891	Sao Paulo	SP	05487-020	Brazil	(11) 555-1189	
RICAR	Ricardo Adocicados	Janete Limeira	Assistant Sales Agent	Av. Copacabana, 267	Rio de Janeiro	RJ	02389-890	Brazil	(21) 555-3412	

Local intranet | Protected Mode: Off

Figure 7-16

Notice the listing uses the GridView's `Sorting` event to manipulate the value of the control's `SortExpression` property. The events parameters enable you to examine the current sort expression, direct the sort, or even cancel the sort action altogether. The GridView also offers a `Sorted` event which is raised after the sort has completed.

Enabling the GridView Pager

The GridView also greatly improves upon another common grid navigation feature — paging. Although the implementation of paging using a DataGrid greatly simplified paging (especially in comparison to paging in ASP), the GridView makes it even easier with its `AllowPaging` property. This property can be set either by adding the attribute to the GridView control in HTML mode or by checking the Enable Paging check box in the GridView's smart tag. Enabling paging in the GridView control defaults to a page size of 10 records and adds the Pager to the bottom of the grid. Listing 7-28 shows an example of modifying your grid to enable sorting and paging.

Listing 7-28: Enabling sorting and paging on the GridView control

```
<asp:GridView ID="GridView1" Runat="server" DataSourceID="SqlDataSource1"
    DataKeyNames="CustomerID" AutoGenerateColumns="False"
    AllowSorting="True" AllowPaging="True">
```

Enabling sorting and paging in your GridView creates a page that looks like Figure 7-17.

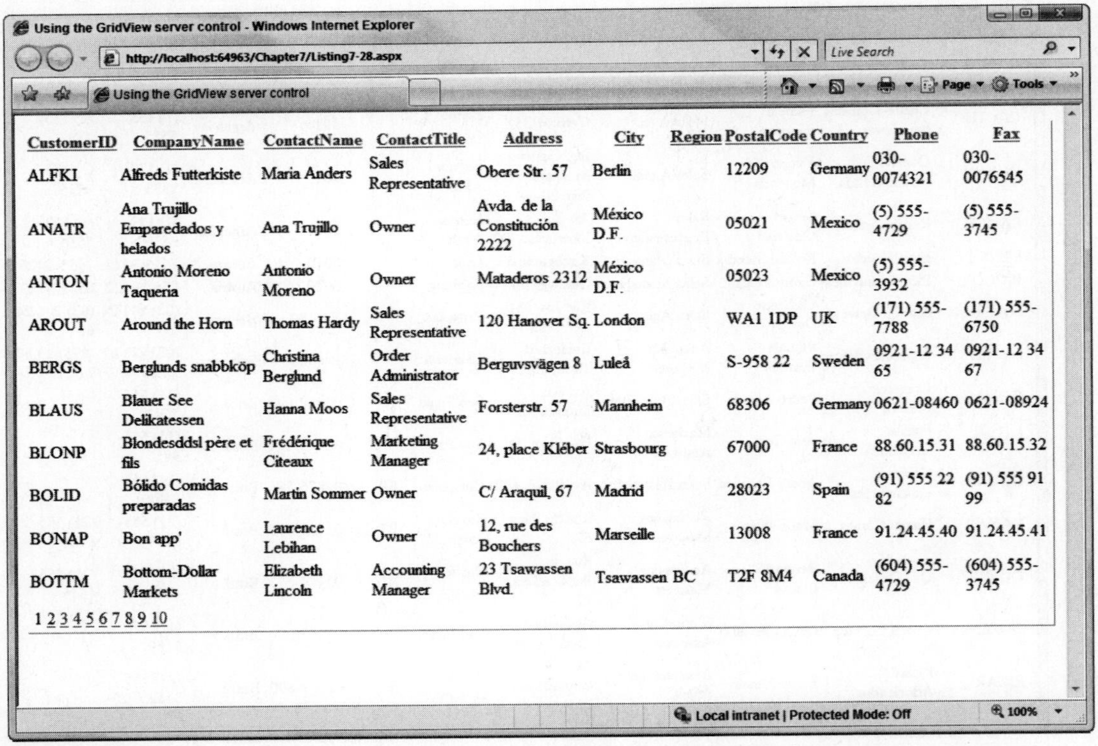

Using the GridView server control - Windows Internet Explorer

http://localhost:64963/Chapter7/Listing7-28.aspx

CustomerID	CompanyName	ContactName	ContactTitle	Address	City	Region	PostalCode	Country	Phone	Fax
ALFKI	Alfreds Futterkiste	Maria Anders	Sales Representative	Obere Str. 57	Berlin		12209	Germany	030-0074321	030-0076545
ANATR	Ana Trujillo Emparedados y helados	Ana Trujillo	Owner	Avda. de la Constitución 2222	México D.F.		05021	Mexico	(5) 555-4729	(5) 555-3745
ANTON	Antonio Moreno Taqueria	Antonio Moreno	Owner	Mataderos 2312	México D.F.		05023	Mexico	(5) 555-3932	
AROUT	Around the Horn	Thomas Hardy	Sales Representative	120 Hanover Sq.	London		WA1 1DP	UK	(171) 555-7788	(171) 555-6750
BERGS	Berglunds snabbköp	Christina Berglund	Order Administrator	Berguvsvägen 8	Luleå		S-958 22	Sweden	0921-12 34 65	0921-12 34 67
BLAUS	Blauer See Delikatessen	Hanna Moos	Sales Representative	Forsterstr. 57	Mannheim		68306	Germany	0621-08460	0621-08924
BLONP	Blondesddsl père et fils	Frédérique Citeaux	Marketing Manager	24, place Kléber	Strasbourg		67000	France	88.60.15.31	88.60.15.32
BOLID	Bólido Comidas preparadas	Martin Sommer	Owner	C/ Araquil, 67	Madrid		28023	Spain	(91) 555 22 82	(91) 555 91 99
BONAP	Bon app'	Laurence Lebihan	Owner	12, rue des Bouchers	Marseille		13008	France	91.24.45.40	91.24.45.41
BOTTM	Bottom-Dollar Markets	Elizabeth Lincoln	Accounting Manager	23 Tsawassen Blvd.	Tsawassen BC		T2F 8M4	Canada	(604) 555-4729	(604) 555-3745

1 2 3 4 5 6 7 8 9 10

Local intranet | Protected Mode: Off 100%

Figure 7-17

As with the DataGrid, the GridView allows most of the paging options to be customized. For instance, the `PagersSettings-Mode` attribute allows you to dictate how the grid's Pager is displayed using the various Pager modes including `NextPrevious`, `NextPreviousFirstLast`, `Numeric` (the default value), or `NumericFirstLast`. Additionally, by specifying the `PagerStyle` element in the GridView, you can customize how the grid displays the Pager text, including font color, size, and type, as well as text alignment and a variety of other style options. Listing 7-29 shows how you might customize your GridView control to use the `NextPrevious` mode and style the Pager text using the `PagerStyle` element. Also, you can control the number of records displayed on the page using the GridView's `PageSize` attribute.

Listing 7-29: Using the PagerStyle and PagerSettings properties in the GridView control

```
<asp:GridView ID="GridView1" Runat="server" DataSourceID="SqlDataSource1"
    DataKeyNames="CustomerID" AutoGenerateColumns="False"
    AllowSorting="True" AllowPaging="True" PageSize="10">
    <PagerStyle HorizontalAlign="Center"></PagerStyle>
    <PagerSettings Position="TopAndBottom"
        FirstPageText="Go to the first page"
        LastPageText="Go to the last page" Mode="NextPreviousFirstLast">
    </PagerSettings>
```

Figure 7-18 shows the grid after you change several style options and set the `PagerSettings-Mode` to `NextPreviousFirstLast`.

Using the GridView server control - Windows Internet Explorer

http://localhost:64963/Chapter7/Listing7-29.aspx

Go to the first page < > Go to the last page

CustomerID	CompanyName	ContactName	ContactTitle	Address	City	Region	PostalCode	Country	Phone	Fax
BSBEV	B's Beverages	Victoria Ashworth	Sales Representative	Fauntleroy Circus	London		EC2 5NT	UK	(171) 555-1212	
CACTU	Cactus Comidas para llevar	Patricio Simpson	Sales Agent	Cerrito 333	Buenos Aires		1010	Argentina	(1) 135-5555	(1) 135-4892
CENTC	Centro comercial Moctezuma	Francisco Chang	Marketing Manager	Sierras de Granada 9993	México D.F.		05022	Mexico	(5) 555-3392	(5) 555-7293
CHOPS	Chop-suey Chinese	Yang Wang	Owner	Hauptstr. 29	Bern		3012	Switzerland	0452-076545	
COMMI	Comércio Mineiro	Pedro Afonso	Sales Associate	Av. dos Lusiadas, 23	Sao Paulo	SP	05432-043	Brazil	(11) 555-7647	
CONSH	Consolidated Holdings	Elizabeth Brown	Sales Representative	Berkeley Gardens 12 Brewery	London		WX1 6LT	UK	(171) 555-2282	(171) 555-9199
DRACD	Drachenblut Delikatessen	Sven Ottlieb	Order Administrator	Walserweg 21	Aachen		52066	Germany	0241-039123	0241-059428
DUMON	Du monde entier	Janine Labrune	Owner	67, rue des Cinquante Otages	Nantes		44000	France	40.67.88.88	40.67.89.89
EASTC	Eastern Connection	Ann Devon	Sales Agent	35 King George	London		WX3 6FW	UK	(171) 555-0297	(171) 555-3373
ERNSH	Ernst Handel	Roland Mendel	Sales Manager	Kirchgasse 6	Graz		8010	Austria	7675-3425	7675-3426

Go to the first page < > Go to the last page

Local intranet | Protected Mode: Off 100%

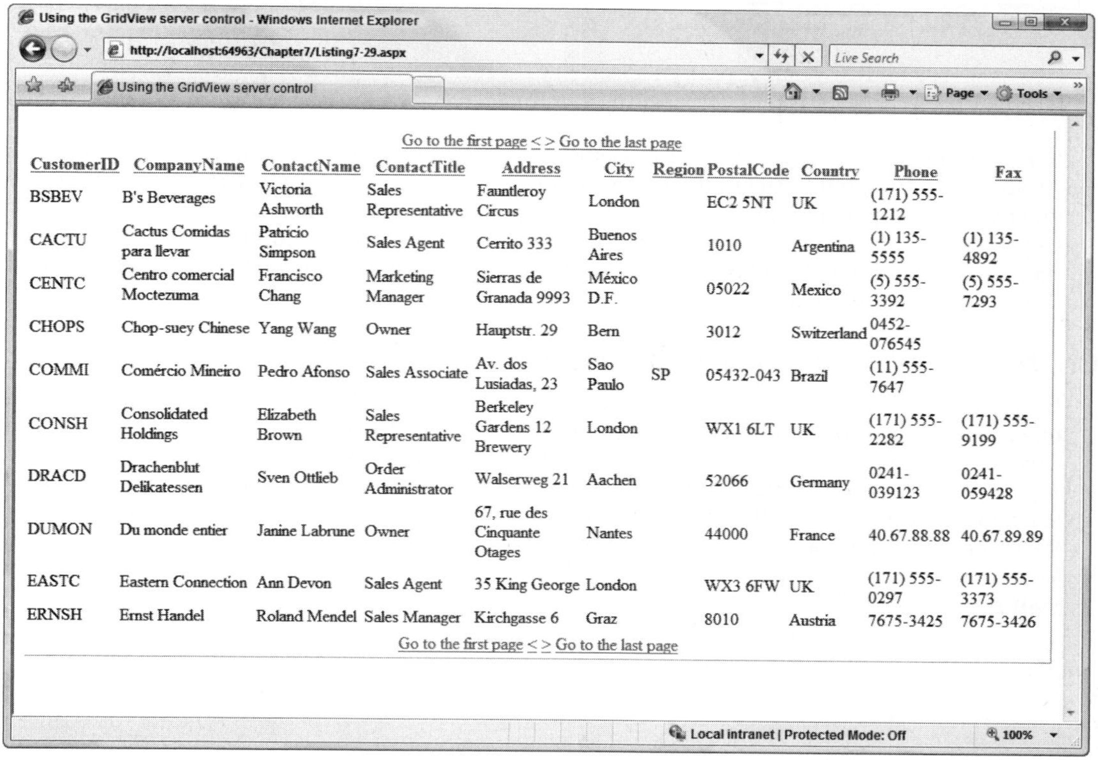

Figure 7-18

The GridView has a multitude of other Pager and Pager style options that we encourage you to experiment with. Because the list of PagerSetting and PagerStyle options is so long, all options are not listed here. You can find a full list of the options in the Visual Studio Help documents.

Additionally, the GridView control offers two events you can use to alter the standard paging behavior of the grid. The PageIndexChanging and PageIndexChangedevents are raised before and after the GridView's current page index changes. The page index changes when the user clicks the pager links in the grid. The PageIndexChanging event parameters allow you to examine the value of the new page index before it actually changes or even cancel the Paging event altogether.

The GridView also includes the EnableSortingAndPagingCallbacks property that allows you to indicate whether the control should use client callbacks to perform sorting and paging. Client callbacks can help your user avoid suffering through a complete page postback for operations such as sorting and paging the GridView. Instead of requiring a complete page postback, client callbacks use AJAX to perform the sort and page actions.

If you are interested in learning more about other ways you can integrate AJAX into your ASP.NET applications, Chapters 19 and 20 introduce you to the ASP.NET AJAX framework and how you can leverage its capabilities in your applications.

Another interesting feature of column generation is the capability to specify what the GridView should display when it encounters a Null value within the column. For an example of this, add a column using an additional <asp:BoundField> control, as shown in Listing 7-30.

Listing 7-30: Using the Null value

```
<asp:BoundField HeaderText="Region" NullDisplayText="N/A"
    DataField="Region" SortExpression="Region"></asp:BoundField>
```

In this example, the <asp:BoundField> element displays the Region column from the Customers table. As you look through the data in the Region section, notice that not every row has a value in it. If you don't want to display just a blank box to show an empty value, you can use some text in place of the empty items in the column. For this, you utilize the NullDisplayText attribute. The String value it provides is used for each and every row that doesn't have a Region value. This construct produces the results illustrated in Figure 7-19.

Customizing Columns in the GridView

Frequently, the data in your grid is not simply text data, but data that you either want to display using other types of controls or don't want to display at all. For instance, you have been retrieving the CustomerID as part of your SELECT query and displaying it in your grid. By default, the GridView control displays all columns returned as part of a query. But rather than automatically displaying the CustomerID, it might be better to hide that data from the end user. Or perhaps you are also storing the corporate URL for all your customers and want the CustomerName column to link directly to their Web sites. The GridView gives you great flexibility and power regarding how you display the data in your grid.

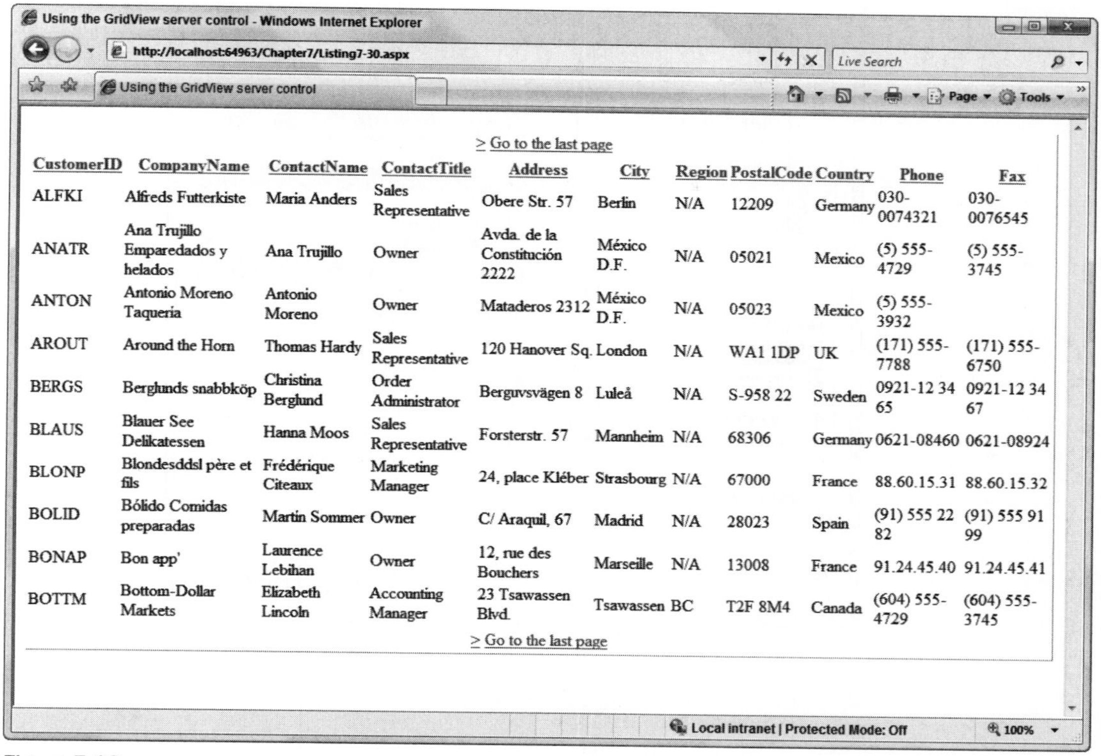

Using the GridView server control - Windows Internet Explorer

http://localhost:64963/Chapter7/Listing7-30.aspx

≥ Go to the last page

CustomerID	CompanyName	ContactName	ContactTitle	Address	City	Region	PostalCode	Country	Phone	Fax
ALFKI	Alfreds Futterkiste	Maria Anders	Sales Representative	Obere Str. 57	Berlin	N/A	12209	Germany	030-0074321	030-0076545
ANATR	Ana Trujillo Emparedados y helados	Ana Trujillo	Owner	Avda. de la Constitución 2222	México D.F.	N/A	05021	Mexico	(5) 555-4729	(5) 555-3745
ANTON	Antonio Moreno Taquería	Antonio Moreno	Owner	Mataderos 2312	México D.F.	N/A	05023	Mexico	(5) 555-3932	
AROUT	Around the Horn	Thomas Hardy	Sales Representative	120 Hanover Sq.	London	N/A	WA1 1DP	UK	(171) 555-7788	(171) 555-6750
BERGS	Berglunds snabbköp	Christina Berglund	Order Administrator	Berguvsvägen 8	Luleå	N/A	S-958 22	Sweden	0921-12 34 65	0921-12 34 67
BLAUS	Blauer See Delikatessen	Hanna Moos	Sales Representative	Forsterstr. 57	Mannheim	N/A	68306	Germany	0621-08460	0621-08924
BLONP	Blondesddsl père et fils	Frédérique Citeaux	Marketing Manager	24, place Kléber	Strasbourg	N/A	67000	France	88.60.15.31	88.60.15.32
BOLID	Bólido Comidas preparadas	Martin Sommer	Owner	C/ Araquil, 67	Madrid	N/A	28023	Spain	(91) 555 22 82	(91) 555 91 99
BONAP	Bon app'	Laurence Lebihan	Owner	12, rue des Bouchers	Marseille	N/A	13008	France	91.24.45.40	91.24.45.41
BOTTM	Bottom-Dollar Markets	Elizabeth Lincoln	Accounting Manager	23 Tsawassen Blvd.	Tsawassen	BC	T2F 8M4	Canada	(604) 555-4729	(604) 555-3745

≥ Go to the last page

Local intranet | Protected Mode: Off 100%

Figure 7-19

The GridView automatically creates a `CheckBoxField` *for columns with a data type of bit or Boolean.*

You can edit your GridView columns in two ways. You can select the Edit Columns option from the GridView smart tag. This link allows you to edit any existing columns in your grid using the Fields dialog window, shown in Figure 7-20. From here you can change a column's visibility, header text, the usual style options, and many other properties of the column.

Selecting the Add New Column link from the GridView control's smart tag displays another easy form — the Add Field dialog (shown in Figure 7-21) — with options allowing you to add completely new columns to your grid. Depending on which column field type you select from the drop-down list, the dialog presents you with the appropriate options for that column type. In this case, you want to add a hyperlink; so you select the HyperLinkField from the drop-down list. The Add Field dialog changes and lets you enter in the hyperlink information, including the URL, the data field, and a format string for the column.

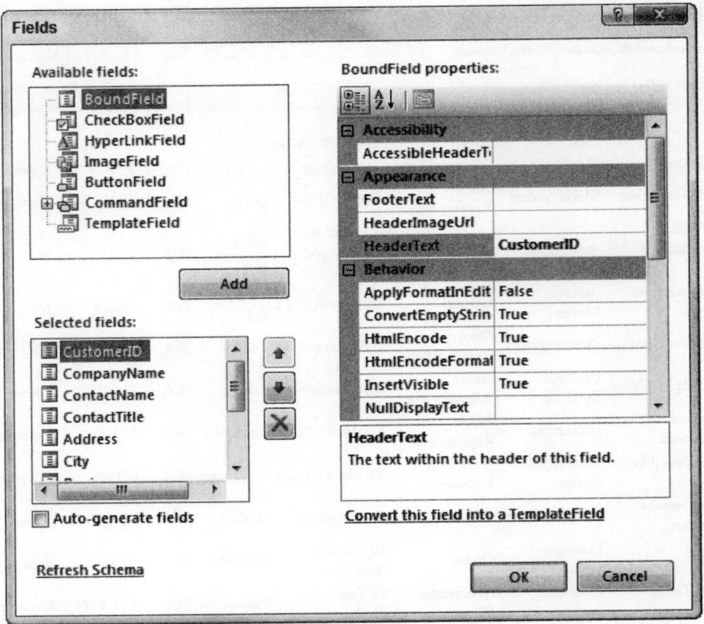

Figure 7-20

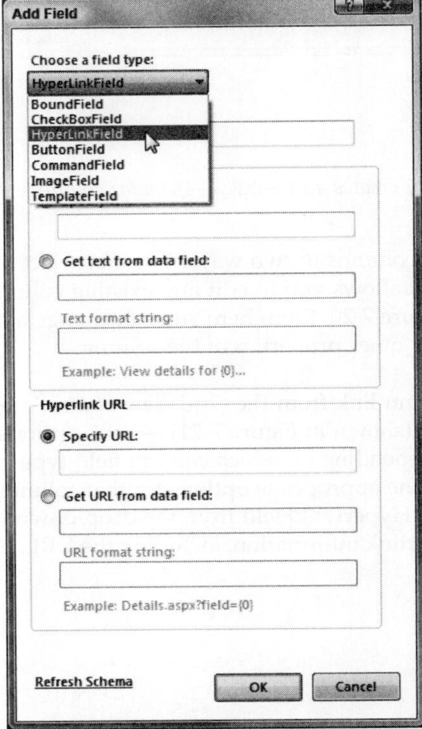

Figure 7-21

The Add Field dialog lets you select one of the field types described in the following table.

Field Control	Description
BoundField	Displays the value of a field in a data source. This is the default column type of the GridView control.
CheckBoxField	Displays a check box for each item in the GridView control. This column field type is commonly used to display fields with a Boolean value.
HyperLinkField	Displays the value of a field in a data source as a hyperlink. This column field type allows you to bind a second field to the hyperlink's URL.
ButtonField	Displays a command button for each item in the GridView control. This allows you to create a column of custom button controls, such as an Add or Remove button.
CommandField	Represents a field that displays command buttons to perform select, edit, insert, or delete operations in a data-bound control.
ImageField	Automatically displays an image when the data in the field represents an image.
TemplateField	Displays user-defined content for each item in the GridView control according to a specified template. This column field type allows you to create a customized column field.

You can also change the grid columns in the Source view. Listing 7-31 shows how you can add a HyperLinkField. Note that by providing a comma-delimited list of data field names, you can specify multiple data fields to bind to this column. You can then use these fields in your format string to pass two query string parameters.

Listing 7-31: Adding a HyperLinkField control to the GridView

```
<asp:HyperLinkField HeaderText="CompanyName"
    DataNavigateUrlFields="CustomerID,Country" SortExpression="CompanyName"
    DataNavigateUrlFormatString=
        "http://www.foo.com/Customer.aspx?id={0}&country={1}"
    DataTextField="CompanyName">
</asp:HyperLinkField>
```

Using the TemplateField Column

A key column type available in the GridView control is the TemplateField column that enables you to use templates to completely customize the contents of the column.

As described earlier in the GridView section of this chapter, a control template is simply a container to which you can add other content, such as text, HTML controls, or even ASP.NET controls.

The TemplateField provides you with six different templates that enable you to customize a specific area of the column or to create a mode that a cell in the column may enter, such as edit mode. The following table describes the available templates.

Template Name	Description
ItemTemplate	Template used for displaying an item in the TemplateField of the data-bound control
AlternatingItem-Template	Template used for displaying the alternating items of the TemplateField
EditItemTemplate	Template used for displaying a TemplateField item in edit mode
InsertItemTemplate	Template used for displaying a TemplateField item in insert mode
HeaderTemplate	Template used for displaying the header section of the TemplateField
FooterTemplate	Template used for displaying the footer section of the TemplateField

To use the TemplateField in a GridView, simply add the column type to your grid using the Add Field dialog as described in the previous section. After you have added the field, note that a new `<asp:TemplateField>` tag (like the one shown in Listing 7-32) has been added to the GridView.

Listing 7-32: The GridViews TemplateField

```
<asp:TemplateField></asp:TemplateField>
```

This element serves as the container for the various templates the column can contain. Now that you have added the column, you create your custom content. You can do this by using the template editing features of the Visual Studio 2008 design surface or by adding your own content to the TemplateField element in Source view.

You can access the template editing features from the Visual Studio design surface in two ways. The first method is to right-click the GridView and choose the Column[nn] (where *nn* is your specific column index) option from the Edit Template option in the context menu. When you use this method, each available template for the column is displayed on the Visual Studio 2008 design surface, as shown in Figure 7-22.

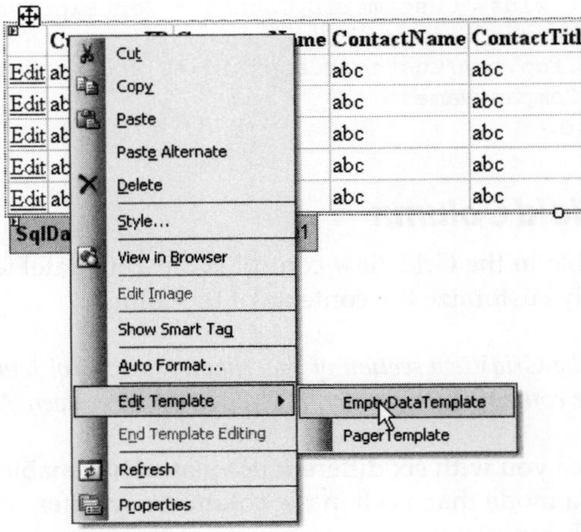

Figure 7-22

The second option is to open the GridView control's smart tag and select the Edit Template command. This opens a menu, shown in Figure 7-23, which allows you to select the column template you want to edit.

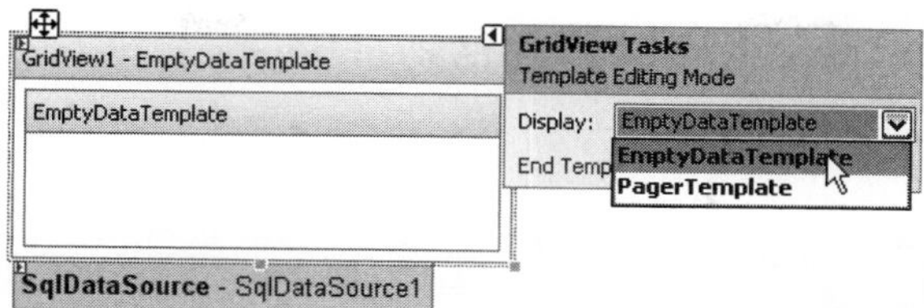

Figure 7-23

The ItemTemplate is probably the template you will use the most because it controls the default contents of each cell of the column. Listing 7-33 demonstrates how you can use the ItemTemplate to customize the contents of the column.

Listing 7-33: Using ItemTemplate

```
<asp:TemplateField HeaderText="CurrentStatus">
    <ItemTemplate>
        <table>
            <tr>
                <td align="center" style="width: 78px">
                    <asp:Button ID="Button2" runat="server" Text="Enable" /></td>
                <td align="center" style="width: 76px">
                    <asp:Button ID="Button3" runat="server" Text="Disable" /></td>
            </tr>
        </table>
    </ItemTemplate>
</asp:TemplateField>
```

Notice that, in the sample, the ItemTemplate contains a combination of HTML and ASP.NET controls. Figure 7-24 shows what the sample looks like when it is displayed in the browser.

Because the GridView control is data-bound, you can also access the data being bound to the control using data-binding expressions such as the Eval, XPath, or Bind expressions. For instance, Listing 7-34 shows how you can add a data-binding expression using the `Eval` method to set the text field of the Button control. You can read more about data-binding expressions later in this chapter.

Listing 7-34: Adding a data-binding expression

```
<asp:TemplateField HeaderText="CurrentStatus">
    <ItemTemplate>
        <table>
            <tr>
                <td align="center" style="width: 78px">
                    <asp:Button ID="Button2" runat="server"
                        Text='<%# "Enable " + Eval("CustomerID") %>' /></td>
                <td align="center" style="width: 76px">
```

Continued

```
                    <asp:Button ID="Button3" runat="server"
                        Text='<%# "Disable " + Eval("CustomerID") %>' />
                </td>
            </tr>
        </table>
    </ItemTemplate>
</asp:TemplateField>
```

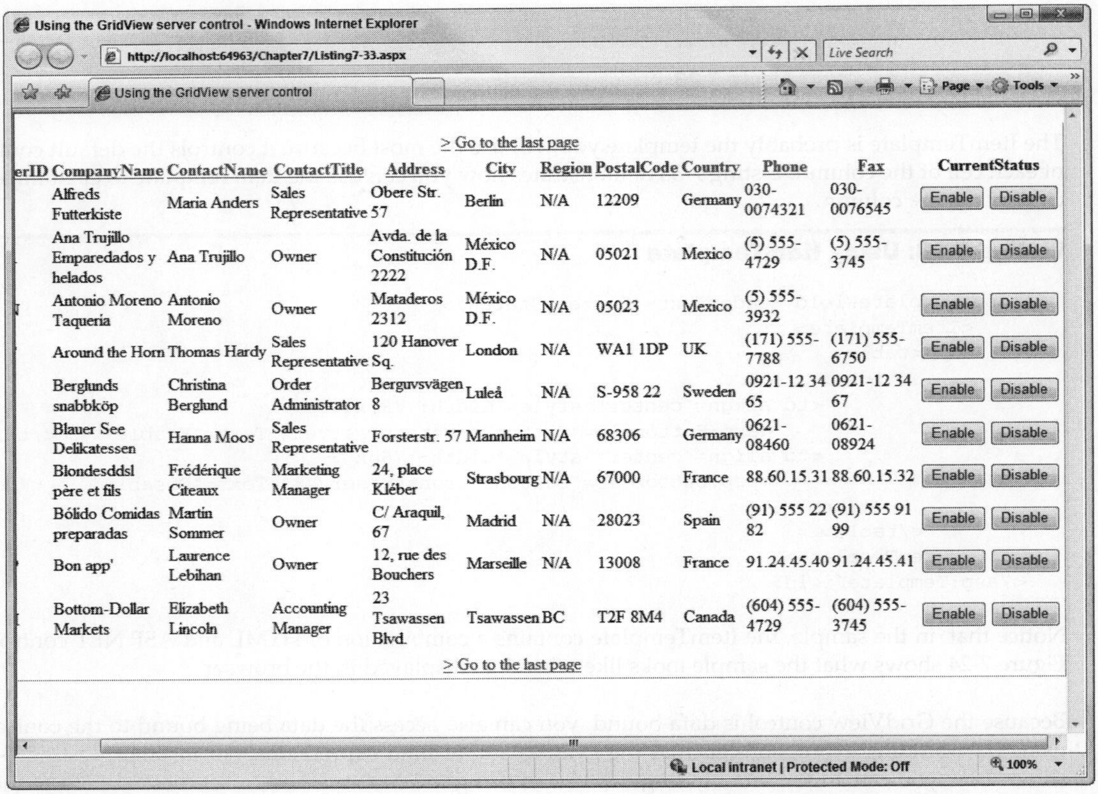

Figure 7-24

Other common templates are the InsertTemplate and EditTemplate. These templates are used by the grid when a grid row enters insert or edit mode. You examine inserting and editing data in the GridView control, including using the InsertItemTemplate and EditItemTemplate, in the next section.

Editing GridView Row Data

Not only do users want to view the data in their browser, but they also want to be able to edit the data and save changes back to the data store. Adding editing capabilities to the DataGrid was never easy, but it was important enough that developers frequently attempted to do so.

The GridView control makes it very easy to edit the data contained in the grid. To demonstrate just how easy it is, you can modify the existing grid so you can edit the customer data it contains. First, modify your existing SqlDataSource control by adding an UpdateCommand attribute. This tells the data source control what SQL it should execute when it is requested to perform an update. Listing 7-35 shows the code to add the UpdateCommand attribute.

Listing 7-35: Adding an UpdateCommand to a SqlDataSource control

```
<asp:SqlDataSource ID="SqlDataSource1" Runat="server"
    SelectCommand="SELECT * FROM [Customers]"
    ConnectionString="<%$ ConnectionStrings:AppConnectionString1 %>"
    DataSourceMode="DataSet"
    UpdateCommand="UPDATE [Customers] SET [CompanyName] = @CompanyName,
        [ContactName] = @ContactName, [ContactTitle] = @ContactTitle,
        [Address] = @Address, [City] = @City, [Region] = @Region,
        [PostalCode] = @PostalCode, [Country] = @Country, [Phone] = @Phone,
        [Fax] = @Fax WHERE [CustomerID] = @original_CustomerID">
```

Notice that the UpdateCommand includes a number of placeholders such as @CompanyName, @Country, @Region, and @CustomerID. These are placeholders for the corresponding information that will come from the selected row in GridView. In order to use the parameters, you must define them using the UpdateParameters element of the SqlDataSource control. The UpdateParameters element, shown in Listing 7-36, works much like the SelectParameters element discussed earlier in the chapter.

Listing 7-36: Adding UpdateParameters to the SqlDataSource control

```
<asp:SqlDataSource ID="SqlDataSource1" Runat="server"
    SelectCommand="SELECT * FROM [Customers]"
    ConnectionString="<%$ ConnectionStrings:AppConnectionString1 %>"
    DataSourceMode="DataSet"
    UpdateCommand="UPDATE [Customers] SET [CompanyName] = @CompanyName,
        [ContactName] = @ContactName, [ContactTitle] = @ContactTitle,
        [Address] = @Address, [City] = @City, [Region] = @Region,
        [PostalCode] = @PostalCode, [Country] = @Country, [Phone] = @Phone,
        [Fax] = @Fax WHERE [CustomerID] = @original_CustomerID">
  <UpdateParameters>
      <asp:Parameter Type="String" Name="CompanyName"></asp:Parameter>
      <asp:Parameter Type="String" Name="ContactName"></asp:Parameter>
      <asp:Parameter Type="String" Name="ContactTitle"></asp:Parameter>
      <asp:Parameter Type="String" Name="Address"></asp:Parameter>
      <asp:Parameter Type="String" Name="City"></asp:Parameter>
      <asp:Parameter Type="String" Name="Region"></asp:Parameter>
      <asp:Parameter Type="String" Name="PostalCode"></asp:Parameter>
      <asp:Parameter Type="String" Name="Country"></asp:Parameter>
      <asp:Parameter Type="String" Name="Phone"></asp:Parameter>
      <asp:Parameter Type="String" Name="Fax"></asp:Parameter>
      <asp:Parameter Type="String" Name="CustomerID"></asp:Parameter>
  </UpdateParameters>
</asp:SqlDataSource>
```

Within the UpdateParameters element, each named parameter is defined using the <asp:Parameter> element. This element uses two attributes that define the name and the data type of the parameter. In this case, all the parameters are of type String. Remember that you can also use any of the parameter types mentioned earlier in the chapter, such as the `ControlParameter` or `QueryStringParameter` in the `UpdateParameters` element.

Next, you give the grid a column it can use to trigger editing of a data row. You can do this in several ways. First, you can use the GridView's `AutoGenerateEditButton` property. When set to `True`, this property tells the grid to add to itself a `ButtonField` column with an edit button for each data row. Listing 7-37 shows how to add the `AutoGenerateEditButton` attribute to the GridView control.

Listing 7-37: Adding the AutoGenerateEditButton attribute to a SqlDataSource control

```
<asp:GridView ID="GridView1" Runat="server" DataSourceID="SqlDataSource1"
     DataKeyNames="CustomerID" AutoGenerateColumns="False"
     AllowSorting="True" AllowPaging="True"
     AutoGenerateEditButton="true">
```

The GridView control also includes `AutoGenerateSelectButton` and `AutoGenerateDeleteButton` properties, which allow you to easily add row selection and row deletion capabilities to the grid.

A second way to add an edit button is to add a `CommandField` column. This is shown in Listing 7-38.

Listing 7-38: Adding edit functionality using a CommandField

```
<asp:CommandField ShowHeader="True" HeaderText="Command"
     ShowEditButton="True"></asp:CommandField>
```

Notice that you add the `ShowEditButton` property to the `CommandField` to indicate that you want to display the edit command in this column. You can control how the command is displayed in the grid using the `ButtonType` property, which allows you to display the command as a link, a button, or even an image. Figure 7-25 shows what the grid looks like after adding the `CommandField` with the `edit` command displayed.

Now if you browse to your Web page, you see that a new edit column has been added. Clicking the Edit link allows the user to edit the contents of that particular data row.

The `CommandField` element also has attributes that allow you to control exactly what is shown in the column. You can dictate whether the column displays commands such as `Cancel`, `Delete`, `Edit`, `Insert`, and `Select`.

With the Edit `CommandField` enabled, you still have one more property to set in order to enable the grid to perform updates. You tell the grid which columns are in the table's primary key. You can accomplish this by using the `DataKeyNames` property, as illustrated in Listing 7-39.

Listing 7-39: Adding the DataKeyNames to the GridView control

```
<asp:GridView ID="GridView1" Runat="server" DataSourceID="SqlDataSource1"
     DataKeyNames="CustomerID" AutoGenerateColumns="False"
     AllowSorting="True" AllowPaging="True"
     AutoGenerateEditButton="true">
```

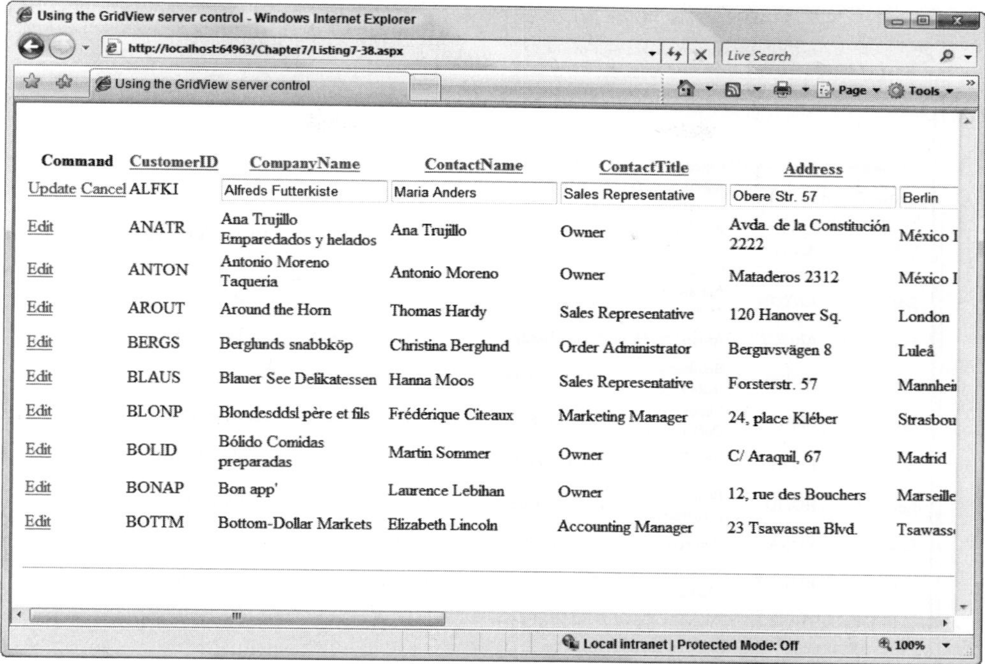

Figure 7-25

You can specify more than one column in the primary key by setting the property to a comma-delimited list.

Notice that when you add the edit capabilities to the grid, by default it allows all displayed columns to be edited. You probably won't always want this to be the case. You can control which columns the grid allows to be edited by adding the `ReadOnly` property to the columns that you do not want users to edit. Listing 7-40 shows how you can add the `ReadOnly` property to the ID column.

Listing 7-40: Adding the ReadOnly property to a BoundField

```
<asp:BoundField ReadOnly="True" HeaderText="CustomerID" DataField="CustomerID"
    SortExpression="CustomerID" Visible="False"></asp:BoundField>
```

Now if you browse to the Web page again and click the Edit button, you should see that the ID column is not editable. This is shown in Figure 7-26.

Handling Errors When Updating Data

As much as you try to prevent them, errors happen when you save data. If you allow your users to update data in your GridView control, you should implement a bit of error handling to make sure errors do not bubble up to the user.

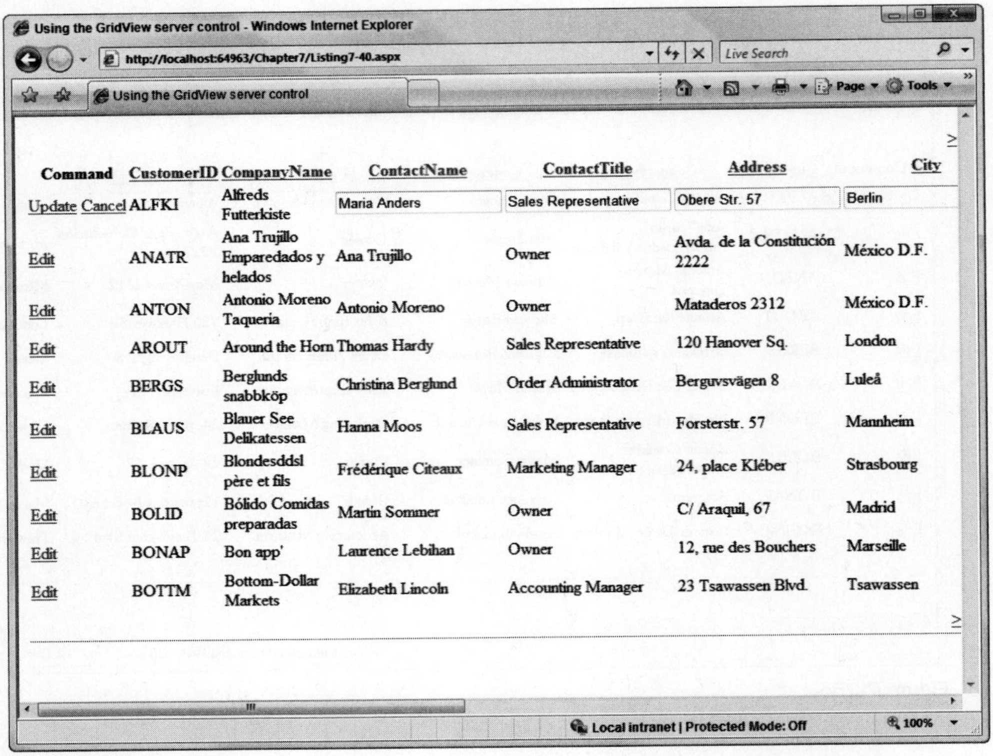
Using the GridView server control - Windows Internet Explorer
http://localhost:64963/Chapter7/Listing7-40.aspx
Using the GridView server control
Command
CustomerID
CompanyName
ContactName
ContactTitle
Address
City
Update Cancel ALFKI Alfreds Futterkiste Maria Anders Sales Representative Obere Str. 57 Berlin
Edit ANATR Ana Trujillo Emparedados y helados Ana Trujillo Owner Avda. de la Constitución 2222 México D.F.
Edit ANTON Antonio Moreno Taqueria Antonio Moreno Owner Mataderos 2312 México D.F.
Edit AROUT Around the Horn Thomas Hardy Sales Representative 120 Hanover Sq. London
Edit BERGS Berglunds snabbköp Christina Berglund Order Administrator Berguvsvägen 8 Luleå
Edit BLAUS Blauer See Delikatessen Hanna Moos Sales Representative Forsterstr. 57 Mannheim
Edit BLONP Blondesddsl père et fils Frédérique Citeaux Marketing Manager 24, place Kléber Strasbourg
Edit BOLID Bólido Comidas preparadas Martín Sommer Owner C/ Araquil, 67 Madrid
Edit BONAP Bon app' Laurence Lebihan Owner 12, rue des Bouchers Marseille
Edit BOTTM Bottom-Dollar Markets Elizabeth Lincoln Accounting Manager 23 Tsawassen Blvd. Tsawassen
Local intranet | Protected Mode: Off
100%

Figure 7-26

To check for errors when updating data through the GridView, you can use the `RowUpdated` event. Listing 7-41 shows how to check for errors after a user has attempted to update data. In this scenario, if an error does occur, you simply display a message to the user in a Label.

Listing 7-41: Checking for Update errors using the RowUpdated event

VB

```
<script runat="server">
    Protected Sub GridView1_RowUpdated(ByVal sender As Object, _
       ByVal e As System.Web.UI.WebControls.GridViewUpdatedEventArgs)

        If e.Exception IsNot Nothing Then
            Me.lblErrorMessage.Text = e.Exception.Message
        End If
    End Sub
</script>
```

C#

```
<script runat="server">
    protected void GridView1_RowUpdated(object sender, GridViewUpdatedEventArgs e)
    {
```

```
        if (e.Exception != null)
        {
            this.lblErrorMessage.Text = e.Exception.Message;
        }
    }
</script>
```

Using the TemplateField's EditItemTemplate

Earlier in the chapter, you were introduced to the TemplateField and various other available templates. One of those templates is the EditItemTemplate, which the grid uses to display the TemplateField column for a row that has entered edit mode. Although the standard BoundField allows users to edit their data only in text boxes, the TemplateField's EditItemTemplate enables you to completely customize the data editing experience of the user. For instance, the user would probably have a better editing experience if the Region column were presented as a DropDownList control during edit mode, rather than as a simple text box.

To do this, you simply change the Region column from a BoundField to a TemplateField and add an ItemTemplate and an EditItemTemplate. In the EditItemTemplate, you can add a DropDownList control and provide the proper data-binding information so that the control is bound to a unique list of Regions. Listing 7-42 shows how you can add the ItemTemplate and EditItemTemplate to the GridView.

Listing 7-42: Adding the ItemTemplate and EditItemTemplate to the GridView

```
<asp:TemplateField HeaderText="Country">
    <ItemTemplate><%# Eval("Country") %></ItemTemplate>
    <EditItemTemplate>
        <asp:DropDownList ID="DropDownList1" runat="server"
            DataSourceID="SqlDataSource2"
            DataTextField="Country" DataValueField="Country">
        </asp:DropDownList>
        <asp:SqlDataSource ID="SqlDataSource2" runat="server"
            ConnectionString="<%$ ConnectionStrings:NorthwindConnectionString %>"
            SelectCommand="SELECT DISTINCT [Country] FROM [Customers]">
        </asp:SqlDataSource>
    </EditItemTemplate>
</asp:TemplateField>
```

Notice that you use a simple Eval data-binding expression in the ItemTemplate to display the value of the column in the row's default display mode. In the EditItemTemplate, you simply include a DropDownList control and a SqlDataSource control for the drop-down list to bind to.

To select the current Country value in the DropDownList control, you use the `RowDataBound` event. Listing 7-43 shows how this is done.

Listing 7-43: Using RowDataBound

VB

```
Protected Sub GridView1_RowDataBound(ByVal sender As Object, _
    ByVal e As System.Web.UI.WebControls.GridViewRowEventArgs)

    'Check for a row in edit mode.
```

Continued

```
        If ((e.Row.RowState = DataControlRowState.Edit) Or _
            (e.Row.RowState = (DataControlRowState.Alternate Or _
            DataControlRowState.Edit))) Then

            Dim drv As System.Data.DataRowView = _
                CType(e.Row.DataItem, System.Data.DataRowView)

            Dim ddl As DropDownList = _
                CType(e.Row.Cells(8).FindControl("DropDownList1"), DropDownList)
            Dim li As ListItem = ddl.Items.FindByValue(drv("Country").ToString())
            li.Selected = True
        End If
    End Sub
```

C#

```
protected void GridView1_RowDataBound(object sender, GridViewRowEventArgs e)
{
    // Check for a row in edit mode.
    if ( (e.Row.RowState == DataControlRowState.Edit) ||
        (e.Row.RowState == (DataControlRowState.Alternate |
                            DataControlRowState.Edit)) )
    {
        System.Data.DataRowView drv = (System.Data.DataRowView)e.Row.DataItem;

        DropDownList ddl =
            (DropDownList)e.Row.Cells[8].FindControl("DropDownList1");
        ListItem li = ddl.Items.FindByValue(drv["Country"].ToString());
        li.Selected = true;
    }
}
```

As shown in the listing, to set the appropriate DropDownList value, first check that the currently bound GridViewRow is in an edit state by using the `RowState` property. The `RowState` property is a bitwise combination of DataControlRowState values. The following table shows you the possible states for a GridViewRow.

RowState	Description
Alternate	Indicates that this row is an alternate row.
Edit	Indicates the row is currently in edit mode.
Insert	Indicates the row is a new row, and is currently in insert mode.
Normal	Indicates the row is currently in a normal state.
Selected	Indicates the row is currently the selected row in the GridView.

Note that in order to determine the current RowState correctly in the previous listing, you must make multiple comparisons against the `RowState` property. The RowState can be in multiple states at once — for example, alternate and edit. Therefore, you need to use a bitwise comparison to properly determine if the GridViewRow is in an edit state. After the row is determined to be in an edit state, locate the DropDownList control in the proper GridViewRow cell by using the `FindControl` method. This method allows you to locate a server control by name. After you find the DropDownList control, locate the appropriate DropDownlist ListItem and set its `Selected` property to `True`.

You also need to use a GridView event to add the value of the DropDownList control back into the GridView after the user updates the row. For this, you can use the `RowUpdating` event as shown in Listing 7-44.

Listing 7-44: Using RowUpdating

VB

```
Protected Sub GridView1_RowUpdating(ByVal sender As Object, _
    ByVal e As System.Web.UI.WebControls.GridViewUpdateEventArgs)

    Dim gvr As GridViewRow = Me.GridView1.Rows(Me.GridView1.EditIndex)
    Dim ddl As DropDownList = _
        CType(gvr.Cells(8).FindControl("DropDownList1"), DropDownList)
    e.NewValues("Country") = ddl.SelectedValue
End Sub
```

C#

```
protected void GridView1_RowUpdating(object sender, GridViewUpdateEventArgs e)
{
    GridViewRow gvr = this.GridView1.Rows[this.GridView1.EditIndex];
    DropDownList ddl = (DropDownList)gvr.Cells[8].FindControl("DropDownList1");
    e.NewValues["Country"] = ddl.SelectedValue;
}
```

In this event, you determine GridViewRow that is currently being edited using the `EditIndex`. This property contains the index of the GridViewRow that is currently in an edit state. After you find the row, locate the DropDownList control in the proper row cell using the `FindControl` method, as in the previous listing. After you find the DropDownList control, simply add the `SelectedValue` of that control to the GridView controls `NewValues` collection.

Deleting GridView Data

Deleting data from the table produced by the GridView is even easier than editing data. Just a few additions to the code enable you to delete an entire row of data from the table. Much like with the Edit buttons you added earlier, you can easily add a Delete button to the grid by setting the `AutoGenerateDeleteButton` property to `True`. This is shown in Listing 7-45.

Listing 7-45: Adding a delete link to the GridView

```
<asp:GridView ID="GridView1" Runat="server" DataSourceID="SqlDataSource1"
    DataKeyNames="CustomerID" AutoGenerateColumns="False"
    AllowSorting="True" AllowPaging="True"
    AutoGenerateEditButton="true" AutoGenerateDeleteButton="true">
```

The addition of the `AutoGenerateDeleteButton` attribute to the GridView is the only change you make to this control. Now look at the SqlDataSource control. Listing 7-46 shows you the root element of this control.

Listing 7-46: Adding delete functionality to the SqlDataSource Control

```
<asp:SqlDataSource ID="SqlDataSource1" Runat="server"
    SelectCommand="SELECT * FROM [Customers]"
    ConnectionString="<%$ ConnectionStrings:AppConnectionString1 %>"
    DataSourceMode="DataSet"
    DeleteCommand="DELETE From Customers WHERE (CustomerID = @CustomerID)"
    UpdateCommand="UPDATE [Customers] SET [CompanyName] = @CompanyName,
        [ContactName] = @ContactName, [ContactTitle] = @ContactTitle,
        [Address] = @Address, [City] = @City, [Region] = @Region,
        [PostalCode] = @PostalCode, [Country] = @Country, [Phone] = @Phone,
        [Fax] = @Fax WHERE [CustomerID] = @original_CustomerID">
```

In addition to the `SelectCommand` and `UpdateCommand` attributes, you also add the `DeleteCommand` attribute to the SqlDataSource and provide the SQL command that deletes the specified row. Just like the `UpdateCommand` property, the `DeleteCommand` property makes use of named parameters. Because of this, you define this parameter from within the SqlDataSource control. To do this, add a `<DeleteParameters>` section to the SqlDataSource control. This is shown in Listing 7-47.

Listing 7-47: Adding a <DeleteParameters> section to the SqlDataSource control

```
<DeleteParameters>
    <asp:Parameter Name="CustomerID" Type="String">
    </asp:Parameter>
</DeleteParameters>
```

This is the only parameter definition needed for the `<DeleteParameters>` section because the SQL command for this deletion requires only the CustomerID from the row to delete the entire row.

When you run the example with this code in place, you see a Delete link next to the Edit link. Clicking the Delete link completely deletes the selected row. Remember that it is a good idea to check for database errors after you complete the deletion. Listing 7-48 shows how you can use the GridView's `RowDeleted` event and the SqlDataSources `Deleted` event to check for errors that might have occurred during the Delete.

Notice that both events provide Exception properties to you as part of the event arguments. If the properties are not empty, then an exception occurred that you can handle. If you do choose to handle the exception, then you should set the `ExceptionHandled` property to `True`; otherwise, the exception will continue to bubble up to the end user.

Listing 7-48: Using the RowDeleted event to catch SQL errors

VB

```
<script runat="server">
    Protected Sub GridView1_RowDeleted(ByVal sender As Object, _
        ByVal e As GridViewDeletedEventArgs)

        If (Not IsDBNull (e.Exception)) Then
            Me.lblErrorMessage.Text = e.Exception.Message
            e.ExceptionHandled = True
        End If
```

```
    End Sub

    Protected Sub SqlDataSource1_Deleted(ByVal sender As Object, _
        ByVal e As System.Web.UI.WebControls.SqlDataSourceStatusEventArgs)

        If (e.Exception IsNot Nothing) Then
            Me.lblErrorMessage.Text = e.Exception.Message
            e.ExceptionHandled = True
        End If
    End Sub
</script>
```

C#

```
<script runat="server">
    protected void GridView1_RowDeleted(object sender, GridViewDeletedEventArgs e)
    {
        if (e.Exception != null)
        {
            this.lblErrorMessage.Text = e.Exception.Message;
            e.ExceptionHandled = true;
        }
    }

    protected void SqlDataSource1_Deleted(object sender,
        SqlDataSourceStatusEventArgs e)
    {
        if (e.Exception != null)
        {
            this.lblErrorMessage.Text = e.Exception.Message;
            e.ExceptionHandled = true;
        }
    }
</script>
```

Other GridView Formatting Features

The GridView control includes numerous other properties that let you adjust the look and feel of the control in fine detail. The `Caption` property allows you to set a caption at the top of the grid. The `ShowHeader` and `ShowFooter` properties enable you to control whether the column headers or footers are shown. The control also includes eight different *style properties* that give you control over the look and feel of different parts of the grid. The following table describes the style properties.

Style Property	Description
`AlternatingRowStyle`	Style applied to alternating GridView rows
`EditRowStyle`	Style applied to a GridView row in edit mode
`EmptyDataRowStyle`	Style applied to the EmptyDataRow when there are datarows available for the grid to bind to
`FooterStyle`	Style applied to the footer of the GridView
`HeaderStyle`	Style applied to the header of the GridView

Style Property	Description
`PagerStyle`	Style applied to the GridView pager
`RowStyle`	Style applied to the default GridView row
`SelectedRowStyle`	Style applied to the currently selected GridView row

These style properties let you set the font, forecolor, backcolor, alignment, and many other style-related properties for these individual areas of the grid.

The GridView smart tag also includes an AutoFormat option that enables you to select from a list of predefined styles to apply to the control.

DetailsView

The DetailsView server control is a new data-bound control that enables you to view a single data record at a time. Although the GridView control is an excellent control for viewing a collection of data, many scenarios demand that you be able to drill down into an individual record. The DetailsView control allows you to do this and provides many of the same data manipulation and display capabilities as the GridView. It allows you to do things such as paging, updating, inserting, and deleting data.

To start using the DetailsView, drag the control onto the design surface. Like the GridView, you can use the DetailsView's smart tag to create and set the data source for the control. For this sample, just use the SqlDataSource control you used for the GridView. If you run the page at this point, you see that the control displays one record, the first record returned by your query. Figure 7-27 shows you what the DetailsView looks like in a Web page.

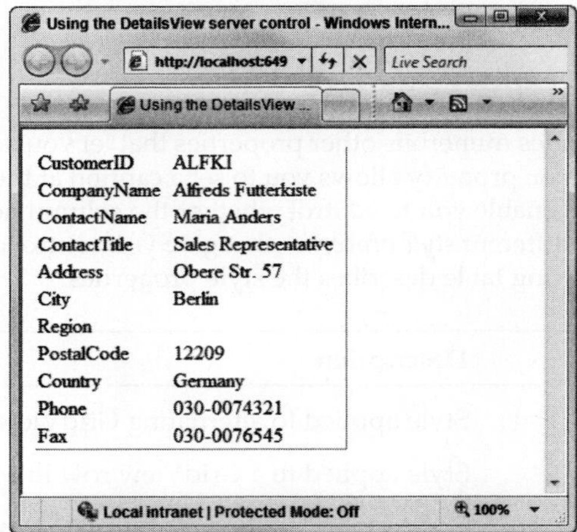

Figure 7-27

If this is all the functionality you want, you probably want to create a new SqlDataSource control and modify the `SelectCommand` so that it returns only one record, rather than returning all records as our query does. For this example, however, you want to be able to page through all the customer data returned by your query. To do this, simply turn on paging by setting the DetailsView's `AllowPaging` property to `True`. You can either check the Enable Paging check box in the DetailsView smart tag or add the attribute to the control in HTML View. Listing 7-49 shows the DetailsView code for the control.

Listing 7-49: Enabling paging on the DetailsView control

```
<asp:DetailsView ID="DetailsView1" Runat="server" DataSourceID="SqlDataSource1"
    AutoGenerateRows="False" DataKeyNames="CustomerID"></asp:DetailsView>
```

Like the GridView, the DetailsView control enables you to customize the control's Pager using the `Pager-Settings-Mode`, as well as the `Pager` style.

Customizing the DetailsView Display

You can customize the appearance of the DetailsView control by picking and choosing which fields the control displays. By default, the control displays each column from the table it is working with. Much like the GridView control, however, the DetailsView control enables you to specify that only certain selected columns be displayed, as illustrated in Listing 7-50.

Listing 7-50: Customizing the display of the DetailsView control

```
<asp:DetailsView ID="DetailsView1" Runat="server" DataSourceID="SqlDataSource1"
    AutoGenerateRows="False" DataKeyNames="CustomerID">
    <Fields>
        <asp:BoundField ReadOnly="True" HeaderText="CustomerID"
            DataField="CustomerID" SortExpression="CustomerID"
            Visible="False" />
        <asp:BoundField ReadOnly="True" HeaderText="CompanyName"
            DataField="CompanyName" SortExpression="CompanyName" />
        <asp:BoundField HeaderText="ContactName" DataField="ContactName"
            SortExpression="ContactName" />
        <asp:BoundField HeaderText="ContactTitle" DataField="ContactTitle"
            SortExpression="ContactTitle" />
    </Fields>
</asp:DetailsView>
```

Using the DetailsView and GridView Together

This section looks at a common scenario using both the GridView and the DetailsView. In this example, you use the GridView to display a master view of the data and the DetailsView to show the details of the selected GridView row. The Customers table is the data source. Listing 7-51 shows the code needed for this.

Listing 7-51: Using the GridView and DetailsView together

```
<html>
<head id="Head1" runat="server">
    <title>GridView & DetailsView Controls</title>
</head>
<body>
```

Continued

```
    <form id="form1" runat="server">
        <p>
            <asp:GridView ID="GridView1" runat="server"
                DataSourceId="SqlDataSource1" AllowPaging="True"
                BorderColor="#DEBA84" BorderStyle="None" BorderWidth="1px"
                BackColor="#DEBA84" CellSpacing="2" CellPadding="3"
                DataKeyNames="CustomerID" AutoGenerateSelectButton="True"
                AutoGenerateColumns="False" PageSize="5">
                <FooterStyle ForeColor="#8C4510"
                    BackColor="#F7DFB5"></FooterStyle>
                <PagerStyle ForeColor="#8C4510"
                    HorizontalAlign="Center"></PagerStyle>
                <HeaderStyle ForeColor="White" BackColor="#A55129"
                    Font-Bold="True"></HeaderStyle>
                <Columns>
                    <asp:BoundField ReadOnly="True" HeaderText="CustomerID"
                         DataField="CustomerID" SortExpression="CustomerID">
                    </asp:BoundField>
                    <asp:BoundField HeaderText="CompanyName"
                         DataField="CompanyName" SortExpression="CompanyName">
                    </asp:BoundField>
                    <asp:BoundField HeaderText="ContactName"
                         DataField="ContactName" SortExpression="ContactName">
                    </asp:BoundField>
                    <asp:BoundField HeaderText="ContactTitle"
                         DataField="ContactTitle" SortExpression="ContactTitle">
                    </asp:BoundField>
                    <asp:BoundField HeaderText="Address" DataField="Address"
                         SortExpression="Address"></asp:BoundField>
                    <asp:BoundField HeaderText="City" DataField="City"
                         SortExpression="City"></asp:BoundField>
                    <asp:BoundField HeaderText="Region" DataField="Region"
                         SortExpression="Region"></asp:BoundField>
                    <asp:BoundField HeaderText="PostalCode" DataField="PostalCode"
                         SortExpression="PostalCode"></asp:BoundField>
                    <asp:BoundField HeaderText="Country" DataField="Country"
                         SortExpression="Country"></asp:BoundField>
                    <asp:BoundField HeaderText="Phone" DataField="Phone"
                         SortExpression="Phone"></asp:BoundField>
                    <asp:BoundField HeaderText="Fax" DataField="Fax"
                         SortExpression="Fax"></asp:BoundField>
                </Columns>
                <SelectedRowStyle ForeColor="White" BackColor="#738A9C"
                    Font-Bold="True"></SelectedRowStyle>
                <RowStyle ForeColor="#8C4510" BackColor="#FFF7E7"></RowStyle>
            </asp:GridView>
        </p>
        <p><b>Customer Details:</b></p>
        <asp:DetailsView ID="DetailsView1" runat="server"
            DataSourceId="SqlDataSource2"
            BorderColor="#DEBA84" BorderStyle="None" BorderWidth="1px"
            BackColor="#DEBA84" CellSpacing="2" CellPadding="3"
            AutoGenerateRows="False" DataKeyNames="CustomerID">
            <FooterStyle ForeColor="#8C4510" BackColor="#F7DFB5"></FooterStyle>
```

```
            <RowStyle ForeColor="#8C4510" BackColor="#FFF7E7"></RowStyle>
            <PagerStyle ForeColor="#8C4510" HorizontalAlign="Center"></PagerStyle>
            <Fields>
                <asp:BoundField ReadOnly="True" HeaderText="CustomerID"
                      DataField="CustomerID" SortExpression="CustomerID">
                </asp:BoundField>
                <asp:BoundField HeaderText="CompanyName" DataField="CompanyName"
                     SortExpression="CompanyName"></asp:BoundField>
                <asp:BoundField HeaderText="ContactName" DataField="ContactName"
                     SortExpression="ContactName"></asp:BoundField>
                <asp:BoundField HeaderText="ContactTitle" DataField="ContactTitle"
                     SortExpression="ContactTitle"></asp:BoundField>
                <asp:BoundField HeaderText="Address" DataField="Address"
                     SortExpression="Address"></asp:BoundField>
                <asp:BoundField HeaderText="City" DataField="City"
                     SortExpression="City"></asp:BoundField>
                <asp:BoundField HeaderText="Region" DataField="Region"
                     SortExpression="Region"></asp:BoundField>
                <asp:BoundField HeaderText="PostalCode" DataField="PostalCode"
                     SortExpression="PostalCode"></asp:BoundField>
                <asp:BoundField HeaderText="Country" DataField="Country"
                     SortExpression="Country"></asp:BoundField>
                <asp:BoundField HeaderText="Phone" DataField="Phone"
                     SortExpression="Phone"></asp:BoundField>
                <asp:BoundField HeaderText="Fax" DataField="Fax"
                     SortExpression="Fax"></asp:BoundField>
            </Fields>
            <HeaderStyle ForeColor="White" BackColor="#A55129"
                Font-Bold="True"></HeaderStyle>
            <EditRowStyle ForeColor="White" BackColor="#738A9C"
                Font-Bold="True"></EditRowStyle>
        </asp:DetailsView>
        <asp:SqlDataSource ID="SqlDataSource1" runat="server"
             SelectCommand="SELECT * FROM [Customers]"
             ConnectionString="<%$ ConnectionStrings:AppConnectionString1 %>" />
        <asp:SqlDataSource ID="SqlDataSource2" runat="server"
             SelectCommand="SELECT * FROM [Customers]"
             FilterExpression="CustomerID='{0}'"
             ConnectionString="<%$ ConnectionStrings:AppConnectionString1 %>">
             <FilterParameters>
                 <asp:ControlParameter Name="CustomerID" ControlId="GridView1"
                       PropertyName="SelectedValue"></asp:ControlParameter>
             </FilterParameters>
        </asp:SqlDataSource>
    </form>
</body>
</html>
```

When this code is run in your browser, you get the results shown in Figure 7-28.

In this figure, one of the rows in the GridView has been selected (noticeable because of the gray highlighting). The details of the selected row are shown in the DetailsView control directly below the GridView control.

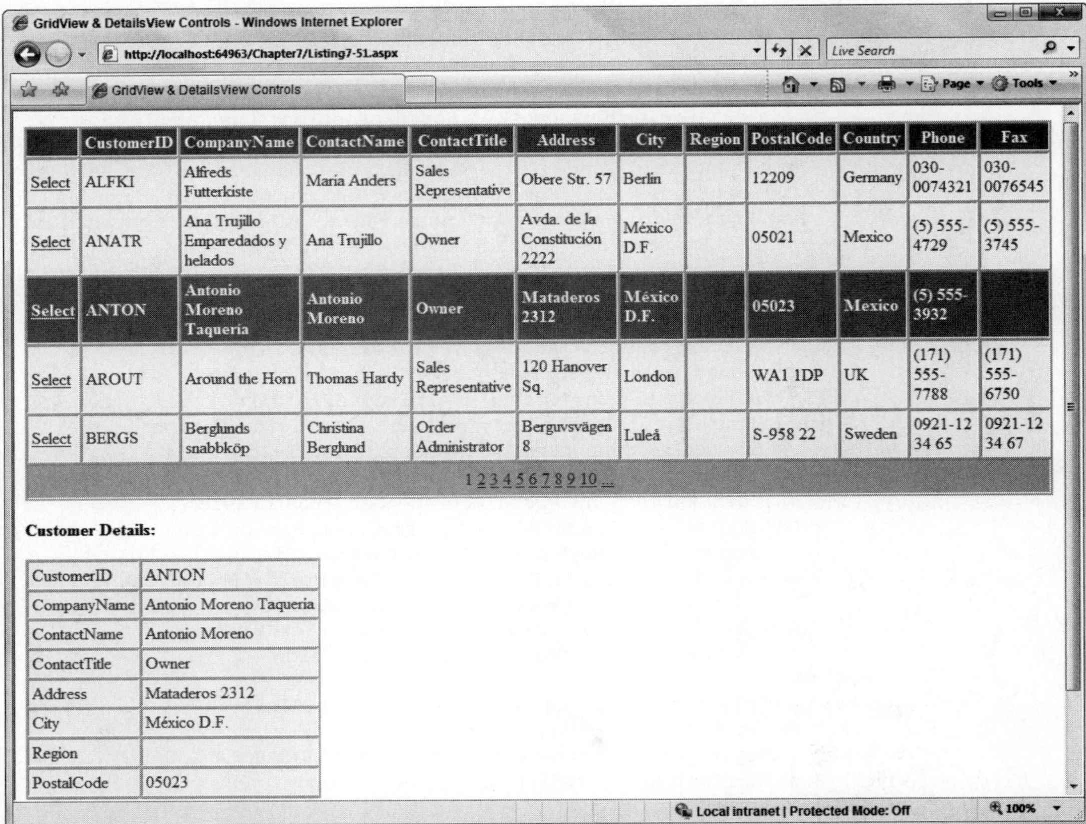

Figure 7-28

To see how this works, look at the changes that were made to the second SqlDataSource control, SqlDataSource2. Notice that a `FilterExpression` attribute has been added, which is used to filter the data reterived by the `SelectCommand`.

The value given to the `FilterExpression` attribute expresses how you want the SqlDataSource control to filter its `Select` command. In this case, the value of the `FilterExpression` is `CustomerID='0'`. This tells the SqlDataSource control to filter records that it returns by the CustomerID given to it, as shown in Listing 7-52. The `FilterExpression` attribute uses the same syntax as `String.Format`.

Listing 7-52: Filtering SqlDataSource data with a FilterExpression

```
<asp:SqlDataSource ID="SqlDataSource2" runat="server"
    SelectCommand="SELECT * FROM [Customers]"
    FilterExpression="CustomerID='{0}'"
    ConnectionString="<%$ ConnectionStrings:AppConnectionString1 %>">
    <FilterParameters>
        <asp:ControlParameter Name="CustomerID" ControlId="GridView1"
```

```
            PropertyName="SelectedValue"></asp:ControlParameter>
    </FilterParameters>
</asp:SqlDataSource>
```

The parameter specified in the `FilterExpression` attribute, `CustomerID`, is defined within the SqlDataSource control through the use of the `<FilterParameters>` element. This sample uses an `<asp:ControlParameter>` to specify the name of the parameter, the control that the parameter value is coming from (the GridView control), and the property name that is used to populate the parameter value.

Finally, be sure to include the `DataKeyNames` attribute in the GridView control. In this case supply `CustomerID` as the value. This tells the GridView which column(s) are to be used as a primary key. When a user selects a row, the value of that column is then provided to the DetailsView control via the `SelectValue` property. The procedure for adding the `DataKeyNames` attribute to the GridView is shown in Listing 7-53.

Listing 7-53: Adding the DataKeyNames attribute to the GridView

```
<asp:GridView ID="GridView1" runat="server"
            DataSourceId="SqlDataSource1" AllowPaging="True"
            BorderColor="#DEBA84" BorderStyle="None" BorderWidth="1px"
            BackColor="#DEBA84" CellSpacing="2" CellPadding="3"
            DataKeyNames="CustomerID" AutoGenerateSelectButton="True"
            AutoGenerateColumns="False" PageSize="5">
```

SelectParameters versus FilterParameters

You might have noticed in the previous example that the `FilterParameters` seem to provide the same functionality as the `SelectParameters`. Although both produce essentially the same result, they use very different methods. As you saw in the section "Filtering Data Using SelectParameters," using the `SelectParameters` allows the developer to inject values into a `WHERE` clause specified in the `SelectCommand`. This limits the rows that are returned from the SQL Server and held in memory by the data source control. The advantage is that by limiting the amount of data returned from SQL, you can make your application faster and reduce the amount of memory it consumes. The disadvantage is that you are confined to working with the limited subset of data returned by the SQL query.

`FilterParameters`, on the other hand, do not need to use a `WHERE` clause in the `SelectCommand`, requiring all the data to be returned from the SQL server to the Web server. The filter is applied to the data source control's in-memory data, rather than using a `WHERE` clause, which would have allowed SQL Server to limit the results it returns. The disadvantage of the filter method is that more data has to be transferred to the Web server. However, in some cases this is an advantage such as when you are performing many filters of one large chunk of data (for instance, to enable paging in the DetailView), you do not have to call out to SQL Server each time you need the next record. All the data is stored in cache memory by the data source control.

Inserting, Updating, and Deleting Data Using DetailsView

Inserting data using the DetailsView is similar to all the other data functions that you have performed. To insert data using the DetailsView, simply add the `AutoGenerateInsertButton` attribute to the DetailsView control as shown in Listing 7-54.

Listing 7-54: Adding an AutoGenerateInsertButton attribute to the DetailsView

```
<asp:DetailsView ID="DetailsView1" runat="server"
    DataSourceId="SqlDataSource2"
    AutoGenerateRows="False" AutoGenerateInsertButton="true"
    DataKeyNames="CustomerID">
```

Then add the `InsertCommand` and corresponding `InsertParameter` elements to the SqlDataSource control, as shown in Listing 7-55.

Listing 7-55: Adding an InsertCommand to the SqlDataSource control

```
<asp:SqlDataSource ID="sqlDataSource2" runat="server"
    SelectCommand="SELECT * FROM [Customers]"
    InsertCommand="INSERT INTO [Customers] ([CustomerID], [CompanyName],
        [ContactName], [ContactTitle], [Address], [City], [Region], [PostalCode],
        [Country], [Phone], [Fax]) VALUES (@CustomerID, @CompanyName,
        @ContactName, @ContactTitle, @Address, @City, @Region, @PostalCode,
        @Country, @Phone, @Fax)" DeleteCommand="DELETE FROM [Customers] WHERE
        [CustomerID] = @original_CustomerID"
    ConnectionString="<%$ ConnectionStrings:AppConnectionString1 %>">
    <InsertParameters>
        <asp:Parameter Type="String" Name="CustomerID"></asp:Parameter>
        <asp:Parameter Type="String" Name="CompanyName"></asp:Parameter>
        <asp:Parameter Type="String" Name="ContactName"></asp:Parameter>
        <asp:Parameter Type="String" Name="ContactTitle"></asp:Parameter>
        <asp:Parameter Type="String" Name="Address"></asp:Parameter>
        <asp:Parameter Type="String" Name="City"></asp:Parameter>
        <asp:Parameter Type="String" Name="Region"></asp:Parameter>
        <asp:Parameter Type="String" Name="PostalCode"></asp:Parameter>
        <asp:Parameter Type="String" Name="Country"></asp:Parameter>
        <asp:Parameter Type="String" Name="Phone"></asp:Parameter>
        <asp:Parameter Type="String" Name="Fax"></asp:Parameter>
    </InsertParameters>
</asp:SqlDataSource>
```

Figure 7-29 shows the DetailsView control page loaded in the browser in insert mode, ready to add a new record.

Figure 7-30 shows the DetailsView control after a new record has been inserted.

Updating and deleting data using the DetailsView control are similar to updating and deleting data from the GridView. Simply specify the `UpdateCommand` or `DeleteCommand` attributes in the DetailView control; then provide the proper `UpdateParameters` and `DeleteParameters` elements.

ListView

ASP.NET 3.5 introduces a new data-bound list control called the ListView. The idea behind the ListView control is to offer a data-bound control that bridges the gap between the highly structured GridView control introduced in ASP.NET 2.0, and the anything goes, unstructured controls DataList and Repeater.

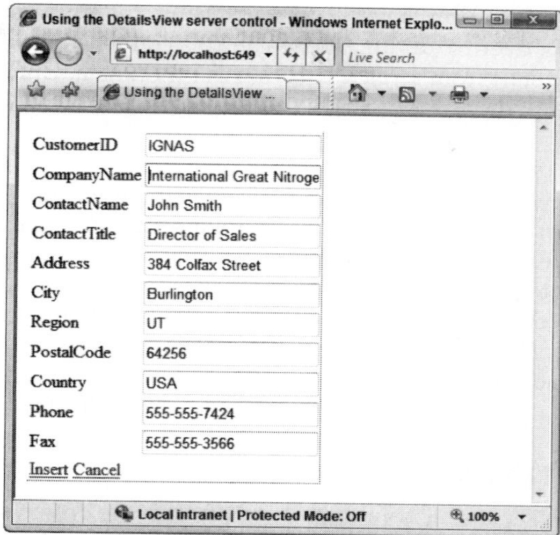

Figure 7-29

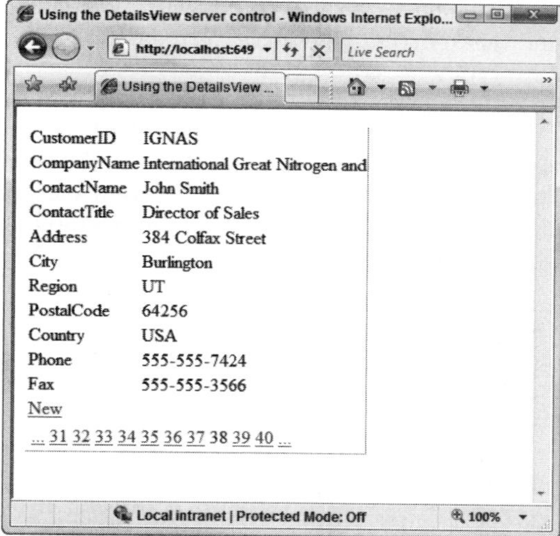

Figure 7-30

In the past, many developers who wanted a grid style data control chose the GridView because it was easy to use and offered powerful features such as data editing, paging, and sorting. Unfortunately, the more developers dug into the control, the more they found that controlling the way it rendered its HTML output was exceedingly difficult. This was problematic if you wanted to lighten the amount of markup generated by the control, or use CSS exclusively to control the control's layout and style.

On the other side of the coin, many developers were drawn the DataList or Repeater because of the enhanced control they got over rendering. These controls contained little to no notion of layout and required the developer to start from scratch in laying out their data. Unfortunately, these controls lacked some of the basic features of the GridView, such as paging and sorting, or in the case of the Repeater, any notion of data editing.

This is where the ListView attempts to fill the gap between these controls. The control itself emits no runtime generated HTML markup; instead it relies on a series of 11 different control templates that represent the different areas of the control and the possible states of those areas. Within these templates you can place markup auto-generated by the control at design-time, or markup created by the developer, but in either case the developer retains complete control over not only the markup for individual data items in the control, but of the markup for the layout of the entire control. Additionally, because the control readily understands and handles data editing and paging, you can let the control do much of the data management work, allowing you to focus primarily on the display of your data.

Getting Started with the ListView

To get started using the ListView, simply drop the control on the design surface and assign a data source to it just as you would any other data-bound list control. Once you assign the data source, however, you will see that there is no design-time layout preview available as you might expect. This is because, by default, the ListView has no layout defined and it is completely up to you to define the control's layout. In fact, the design-time rendering of the control even tells you that you need to define at least an ItemTemplate and LayoutTemplate in order to use the control. The LayoutTemplate serves as the root template for the control, and the ItemTemplate serves as the template for each individual data item in the control.

You have two options for defining the templates needed by the ListView. You can either edit the templates directly by changing the Current View option in the ListView smart tag, or you can select a predefined layout from the controls smart tag. Changing Current View allows you to see a runtime view of each of the available templates, and edit the contents of those templates directly just as you would normally edit any other control template. Figure 7-31 shows the Current View drop-down in the ListView's smart tag.

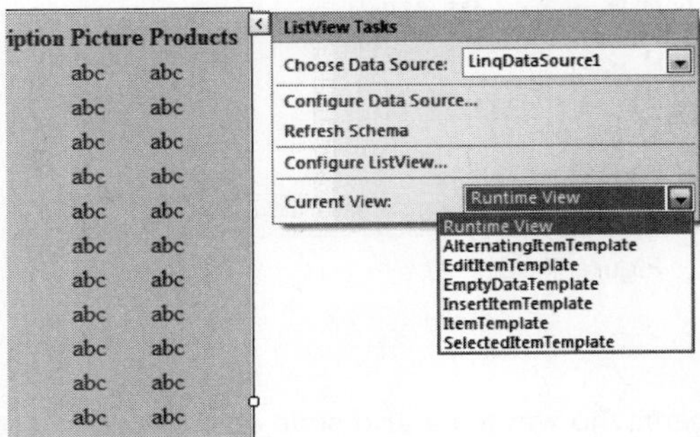

Figure 7-31

The second option and probably the easier to start with, is to choose a predefined layout template from the Configure ListView dialog. To open this dialog, simply click the ConfigureListView option from the smart tag. Once open, you are presented with a dialog that lets you select between several different pre-defined layouts, select different style options, and even configure basic behavior options such as editing and paging. This dialog is shown in Figure 7-32.

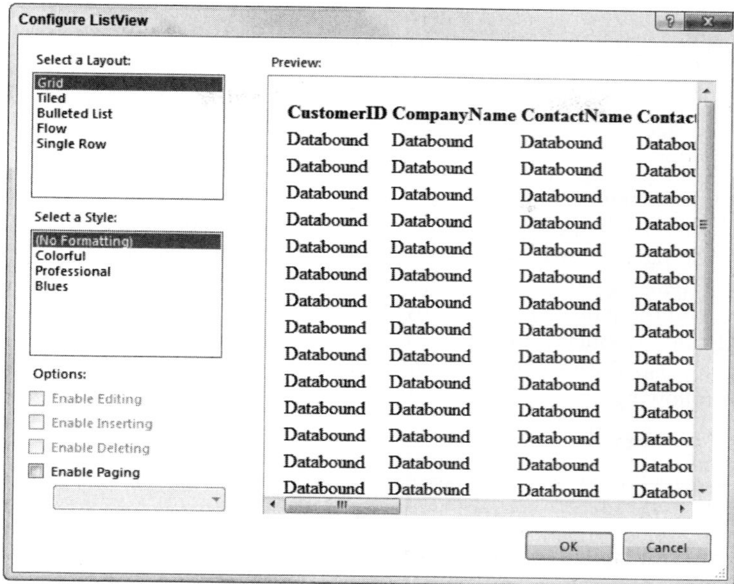

Figure 7-32

The control includes five different layout types: Grid, Tiled, Bulleted List, Flow, and Single Row and four different style options. A preview of each type is presented in the dialog, and as you change the currently selected layout and style, the preview is updated.

To see exactly how the control defines each layout option, select the Grid layout with the Colorful style and enable Inserting, Editing, Deleting, and Paging. Click OK to apply your choices and close the dialog box. When the dialog box closes, you should now see that you get a design-time preview of your layout and running the page results in the ListView generating a grid layout, as shown in Figure 7-33.

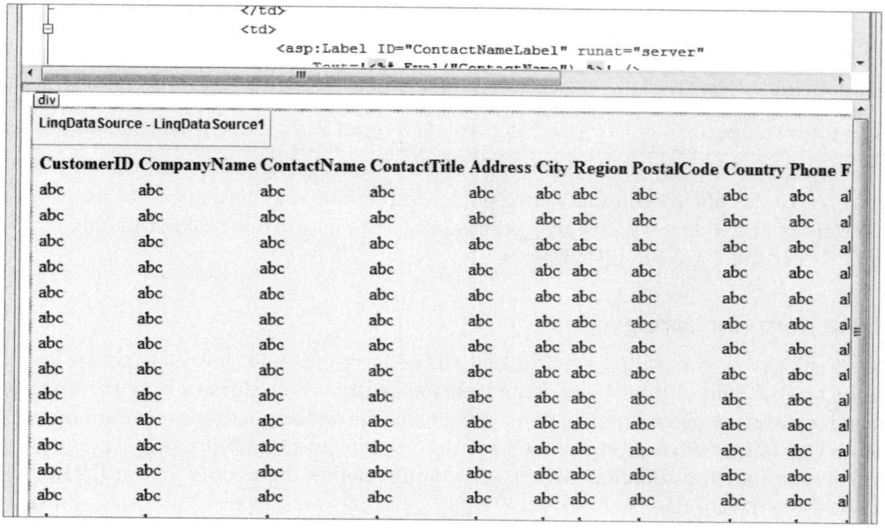

Figure 7-33

ListView Templates

Once you have applied a layout template to the ListView, if you look at the Source window in Visual Studio you can see that in order to provide the layout, the control actually generated a significant chunk of markup. This markup is generated based on the layout that you chose in the Configure ListView dialog.

If you closely examine the markup that has been generated for the Grid layout used in the previous section, you will see that, by default, the control creates markup for seven different control templates: the ItemTemplate, AlternatingItemTemplate, SelectedItemTemplate, InsertItemTemplate, EditItemTemplate, EmptyDataTemplate, and LayoutTemplate. These are just some of the 11 different templates that the control exposes, and that you can use to provide markup for the different states of the control. Choosing a different predefined layout option results in the control generating a different collection of templates. Of course, you can also always manually add or remove any of the templates yourself. All 11 templates are listed in the following table.

Template Name	Description
ItemTemplate	Provides a User Interface for each data item in the control
AlternatingItemTemplate	Provides a unique UI for alternating data items in the control
SelectedItemTemplate	Provides a unique UI for the currently selected data item
InsertItemTemplate	Provides a UI for inserting a new data item into the control
EditItemTemplate	Provides a UI for editing an existing data item in the control
EmptyItemTemplate	Provides a unique UI for rows created when there is no more data to display in the last group of the current page
EmptyDataTemplate	The template shown when the bound data object contains no data items
LayoutTemplate	The template that serves as the root container for the ListView control and is used to control the overall layout of the data items
GroupSeparatorTemplate	Used to provide a separator UI between groups
GroupTemplate	Used to provide a unique UI for grouped content
ItemSeperatorTemplate	Used to provide a separator UI between each data item

The use of templates allows the ListView control to retain a very basic level of information about the markup sections and states which can comprise the ListView, while still being able to give you almost total control over the UI of the ListView.

ListView Data Item Rendering

While the ListView is generally very flexible, allowing you almost complete control over the way it displays its bound data, it does have some basic structure which defines how the templates described in the previous section are related to one another. As described previously, at a minimum, the control requires you to define two templates, the LayoutTemplate and ItemTemplate. The LayoutTemplate is the root control template and therefore where you should define the overall layout for the collection of data items in the ListView.

For example, if you examine the template markup generated by the Grid layout, you can see the LayoutTemplate includes a `<table>` element definition, a single table row (`<tr>`) definition, and a `<td.>` element defined for each column header.

The ItemTemplate, on the other hand, is where you define the layout for an individual data item. If you again look at the markup generated for the Grid layout, its ItemTemplate is a single table row (`<tr>`) element followed by a series of table cell (`<td>`) elements that contain the actual data.

When the ListView renders itself, it knows that the ItemTemplate should be rendered within the LayoutTemplate, but what is needed is a mechanism to tell the control exactly where within the LayoutTemplate to place the ItemTemplate. The ListView control does this by looking within the LayoutTemplate for an Item Container. The Item Container is an HTML container element with the `runat = "server"` attribute set and an `id` attribute whose value is `itemContainer`. The element can be any valid HTML container element, although if you examine the default Grid LayoutTemplate you will see that it uses the `<tbody>` element.

```
<tbody id="itemContainer">
</tbody>
```

Adding to the overall flexibility of the control, even the specific Item Container element `id` that ListView looks for can be configured. While by default the control will attempt to locate an element whose `id` attribute is set to `itemContainer`, you can change the `id` value the control will look for by changing the control's `ItemContainerID` property.

If the control fails to locate an appropriate HTML element designated as the Item Container, it will throw an exception.

The ListView uses the element identified as the `itemContainer` to position not only the ItemTemplate, but any item-level template, such as the AlternativeItemTemplate, EditItemTemplate, EmptyItemTemplate, InsertItemTemplate, ItemSeperatorTemplate, and SelectedItemTemplate. During rendering, it simply places the appropriate item template into the Item Container, depending on the state of the data item (selected, editing, or alternate) for each data item it is bound to.

ListView Group Rendering

In addition to the Item Container, the ListView also supports another container type, the Group Container. The Group Container works in conjunction with the GroupTemplate to allow you to divide a large group of data items into smaller sets. The number of items in each group is set by the control's `GroupItemCount` property. This is useful is when you want to output some additional HTML after some number of item templates have been rendered. When using the GroupTemplate, the same problem exists as was discussed in the prior section. In this case, however, rather than having two templates to relate, introducing the GroupTemplate means you have three templates to relate: the ItemTemplate to the GroupTemplate, and the GroupTemplate to the LayoutTemplate.

When the ListView renders itself, it looks to see if a GroupTemplate has been defined. If the control finds a GroupTemplate, then it checks to see if a Group Container is provided in the LayoutTemplate. If you have defined the GroupTemplate, then the control requires that you define a Group Container; otherwise it throws an exception. The Group Container works the same way as the Item Container described in the previous section, except that the container element's `id` value should be `groupContainer`, rather than `itemContainer`. As with Item Container, the specific `id` value the control looks for can be changed by altering the `GroupContainerID` property of the control.

You can see an example of the Group Container being used by looking at the markup generated by the ListViews Tiled layout. The LayoutTemplate of this layout shows a table serving as the Group Container, shown here:

```
<table id="groupContainer" runat="server" border="0" style="">
</table>
```

Once a GroupContainer is defined, you need to define an Item Container, but rather than doing this in the LayoutTemplate, you need to do this in the GroupTemplate. Again, looking at the Tiled layout, you can see that within its GroupTemplate, it defined a table row which serves as the Item Container.

```
<tr id="itemContainer" runat="server">
</tr>
```

When rendering, the ListView will output its LayoutTemplate first, and then output the GroupTemplate. The ItemTemplate is then output the number of times defined by the `GroupItemCount` property. Once the group item count has been reached, the ListView outputs the GroupTemplate, then ItemTemplate again, repeating this process for each data item it is bound to.

Using the EmptyItemTemplate

When using the GroupTemplate, it is also important to keep in mind that the number of data items bound to the ListView control may not be perfectly divisible by the GroupItemCount value. This is especially important to keep in mind if you have created a ListView layout that is dependent on HTML tables for its data item arrangement because there is a chance that the last row may end up defining fewer table cells than previous table rows, making the HTML output by the control invalid, and possibly causing rendering problems. To solve this, the ListView control includes the EmptyItemTemplate. This template is rendered if you are using the GroupTemplate, and there are not enough data items remaining to reach the `GroupItemCount` value. Figure 7-34 shows an example of when the EmptyItemTemplate would be used.

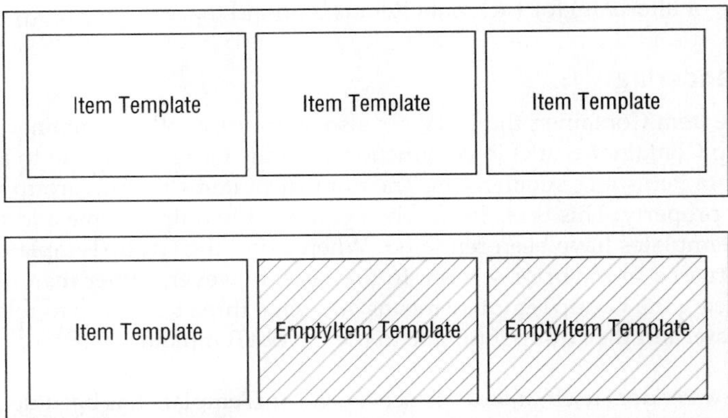

Figure 7-34

In this scenario, the data source bound to the ListView control contains four data items, but the `GroupItemCount` for the control is set to `3`, meaning there will be three ItemTemplates rendered in each group. You can see that this means for the second group rendered, there will only be a single data item remaining to render; therefore, the control will use the EmptyItemTemplate, if defined, to fill the remaining items.

You can also see another example of the use of the EmptyItemTemplate in the ListView's Tiled layout.

ListView Data Binding and Commands

Because the ListView does not generate any layout markup at runtime and does not include any of the auto field generation logic as you may be used to in the GridView, each template uses the standard ASP.NET inline data-binding syntax to position the values of each data item in the defined layout.

ASP.NET's inline data-binding syntax is covered in detail later in this chapter.

You can see this by examining the ItemTemplate of the default Grid layout created by the control. In this template, each column of the bound data source is displayed using an ASP.NET label whose text property is set to a data-binding evaluation expression:

```
<asp:Label ID="ProductNameLabel" runat="server"
    Text='<%# Eval("ProductName") %>' />
```

Because the control uses this flexible model to display the bound data, you can leverage it to place the data wherever you would like within the template, and even use the features of ASP.NET data binding to manipulate the bound data before it is displayed.

Every ListView template that displays bound data uses the same ASP.NET binding syntax, and simply provides a different template around it. For example, if you enable editing in the Grid layout you will see that the EditItemTemplate simply replaces the ASP.NET Label used by the ItemTemplate with a TextBox or Checkbox depending on the underlying data type.

```
<asp:TextBox ID="ProductNameTextBox" runat="server"
    Text='<%# Bind("ProductName") %>' />
```

Again, this flexibility allows you to choose exactly how you want to allow your end user to edit the data (if you want it to be editable). Instead of a standard ASP.NET TextBox, you could easily replace this with a DropDownList, or even a third-party editing control.

To get the ListView to show the EditItemTemplate for a data item, the control uses the same commands concept found in the GridView control. The ItemTemplate provides three commands you can use to change the state of a data item.

Command Name	Description
`Edit`	Places the specific data item into edit mode and shows the EditTemplate for the data item
`Delete`	Deletes the specific data item from the underlying data source
`Select`	Sets the ListView controls Selected index to the index of the specific data item

These commands are used in conjunction with the ASP.NET Button control's `CommandName` property. You can see these commands used in ItemTemplate of the ListViews default Grid layout by enabling

Editing and Deleting using the ListView configuration dialog. Doing this generates a new column with an Edit and Delete button, each of which specified the `CommandName` property set to Edit and Delete respectively.

```
<asp:Button ID="DeleteButton" runat="server"
    CommandName="Delete" Text="Delete" />
<asp:Button ID="EditButton" runat="server"
    CommandName="Edit" Text="Edit" />
```

Other templates in the ListView offer other commands, as shown in the table that follows.

Template	Command Name	Description
EditItemTemplate	Update	Updates the data in the ListViews data source and returns the data item to the ItemTemplate display
EditItemTemplate	Cancel	Cancels the edit and returns the data item to the ItemTemplate
InsertItemTemplate	Insert	Inserts the data into the ListViews at a source
InsertItemTemplate	Cancel	Cancels the insert and resets the InsertTemplate controls binding values

ListView Paging and the Pager Control

ASP.NET 3.5 introduced another new control called the DataPager control that the ListView uses to provide paging capabilities for itself. The DataPager control is designed to display the navigation for paging to the end user and to coordinate data paging with any data bound control that implements the `IPagableItemContainer` interface, which in ASP.NET 3.5 is the ListView control. In fact, you will notice that if you enable paging on the ListView control by checking the Paging check box in the ListView configuration dialog, the control simply inserts a new DataPager control into its LayoutTemplate. The default paging markup generated by the ListView for the Grid layout is shown here:

```
<asp:datapager ID="DataPager1" runat="server">
    <Fields>
        <asp:nextpreviouspagerfield ButtonType="Button" FirstPageText="First"
            LastPageText="Last" NextPageText="Next" PreviousPageText="Previous"
            ShowFirstPageButton="True" ShowLastPageButton="True" />
    </Fields>
</asp:datapager>
```

The markup for the control shows that within the DataPager, a `Fields` collection has been created, which contains a `NextPreviousPagerField` object. As its name implies, using the `NextPreviousPager` object results in the DataPager rendering Next and Previous buttons as its user interface. The DataPager control includes three types of `Field` objects: the `NextPreviousPagerField`, the `NumericPagerField` object, which generates a simple numeric page list, and the `TemplatePagerField`, which allows you to specify your own custom paging user interface. Each of these different `Field` types includes a variety of properties that you can use to control exactly how the DataPager displays the user interface. Additionally, because the DataPager exposes a `Fields` collection rather than a simple `Field` property, you can actually display several different `Field` objects within a single DataPager control.

The TemplatePagerField is a unique type of `Field` object that contains no User Interface itself, but simply exposes a template that you can use to completely customize the pagers user interface. Listing 7-56 demonstrates the use of the TemplatePagerField.

Listing 7-56: Creating a custom DataPager user interface

```
<asp:DataPager ID="DataPager1" runat="server">
    <Fields>
        <asp:TemplatePagerField>
            <PagerTemplate>
                Page
                <asp:Label runat="server"
                    Text="<%# (Container.StartRowIndex/Container.PageSize)+1%>" />
                of
                <asp:Label runat="server"
                    Text="<%# Container.TotalRowCount/Container.PageSize%>" />
            </PagerTemplate>
        </asp:TemplatePagerField>
    </Fields>
</asp:DataPager>
```

Notice that the sample uses ASP.NET data binding to provide the total page count, page size and the row that the page should start on; these are values exposed by the DataPager control.

If you want to use custom navigation controls in the PagerTemplate, such as a Button control to change the currently display Page, you would create standard Click an event handler for the Button. Within that event handler you can access the DataPagers StartRowIndex, TotalRowCount and PageSize properties to calculate the new StartRowIndex the ListView should use when it renders.

Unlike the paging provided by the GridView, the DataPager control, because it is a separate control, gives you total freedom over where to place it on your webpage. The samples you have seem so far have all looked at the DataPager control when it is placed directly in a ListView, but the control can be placed anywhere on the webform.

Listing 7-57: Placing the DataPager control outside of the ListView

```
<asp:DataPager ID="DataPager1" runat="server" PagedControlID="ListView1">
    <Fields>
        <asp:NumericPagerField />
    </Fields>
</asp:DataPager>
```

In Listing 7-57, the only significant change you should notice is the the use of the PagedControlID property. This property allows you to specify explicitly which control this pager should work with.

FormView

The FormView control, introduced in the ASP.NET 2.0 toolbox, functions like the DetailsView control in that it displays a single data item from a bound data source control and allows adding, editing, and deleting data. What makes it unique is that it displays the data in custom templates, which gives you much greater control over how the data is displayed and edited. Figure 7-35 shows a FormView control ItemTemplate being edited in Visual Studio. You can see that you have complete control over how your data is displayed. The FormView control also contains an EditItemTemplate and InsertItemTemplate that allows you to determine how the control displays when entering edit or insert mode.

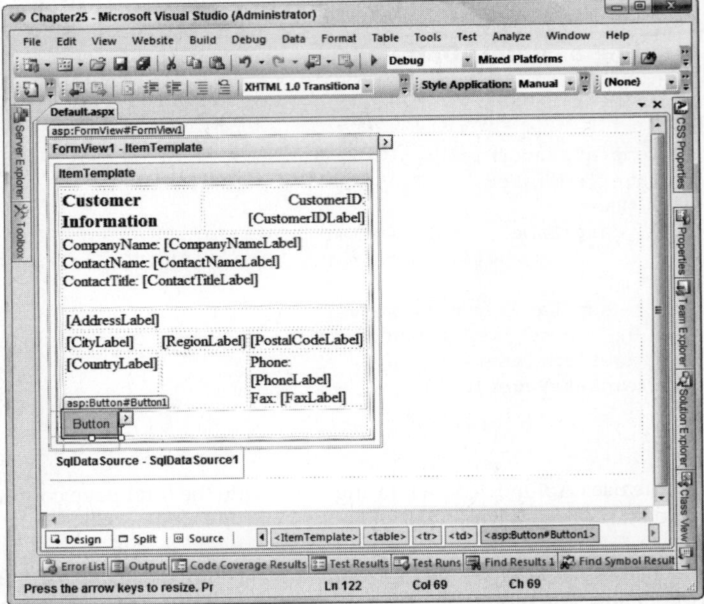

Figure 7-35

While Figure 7-35 shows the FormView control in action in Visual Studio, Figure 7-36 shows the control displaying its ItemTemplate, reflecting the custom layout that was designed in Visual Studio.

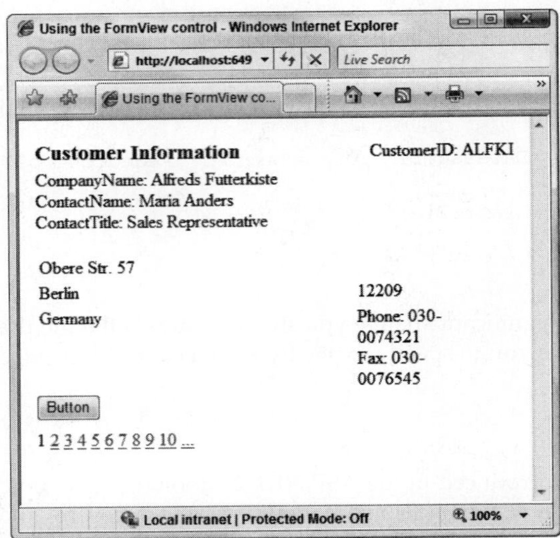

Figure 7-36

In Figure 7-37, you see the control in edit mode, showing the standard EditItemTemplate layout.

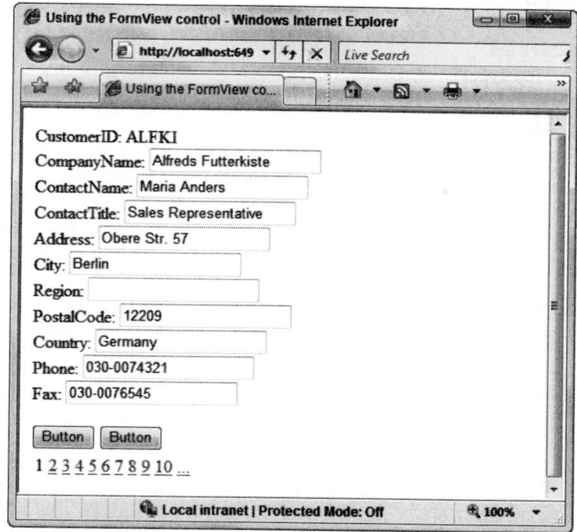

Figure 7-37

Listing 7-58 shows the code that Visual Studio generates when designing the FormView control's customized ItemTemplate.

Listing 7-58: Using a FormView control to display and edit data

```
<%@ Page Language="C#" %>

<html xmlns="http://www.w3.org/1999/xhtml" >
<head runat="server">
    <title>Using the FormView control</title>
</head>
<body>
    <form id="form1" runat="server">
    <div>
        <asp:FormView ID="FormView1" Runat="server" DataSourceID="SqlDataSource1"
             DataKeyNames="CustomerID" AllowPaging="True">
            <EditItemTemplate>
                CustomerID:
                <asp:Label Text='<%# Eval("CustomerID") %>' Runat="server"
                     ID="CustomerIDLabel1">
                </asp:Label><br />
                CompanyName:
                <asp:TextBox Text='<%# Bind("CompanyName") %>' Runat="server"
                     ID="CompanyNameTextBox"></asp:TextBox><br />
                ContactName:
                <asp:TextBox Text='<%# Bind("ContactName") %>' Runat="server"
                     ID="ContactNameTextBox"></asp:TextBox><br />
```

Continued

```
            ContactTitle:
            <asp:TextBox Text='<%# Bind("ContactTitle") %>' Runat="server"
                ID="ContactTitleTextBox"></asp:TextBox><br />
            Address:
            <asp:TextBox Text='<%# Bind("Address") %>' Runat="server"
                ID="AddressTextBox"></asp:TextBox><br />
            City:
            <asp:TextBox Text='<%# Bind("City") %>' Runat="server"
                ID="CityTextBox"></asp:TextBox><br />
            Region:
            <asp:TextBox Text='<%# Bind("Region") %>' Runat="server"
                ID="RegionTextBox"></asp:TextBox><br />
            PostalCode:
            <asp:TextBox Text='<%# Bind("PostalCode") %>' Runat="server"
                ID="PostalCodeTextBox"></asp:TextBox><br />
            Country:
            <asp:TextBox Text='<%# Bind("Country") %>' Runat="server"
                ID="CountryTextBox"></asp:TextBox><br />
            Phone:
            <asp:TextBox Text='<%# Bind("Phone") %>' Runat="server"
                ID="PhoneTextBox"></asp:TextBox><br />
            Fax:
            <asp:TextBox Text='<%# Bind("Fax") %>' Runat="server"
                ID="FaxTextBox"></asp:TextBox><br />
            <br />
            <asp:Button ID="Button2" Runat="server" Text="Button"
                CommandName="update" />
            <asp:Button ID="Button3" Runat="server" Text="Button"
                CommandName="cancel" />
        </EditItemTemplate>
        <ItemTemplate>
            <table width="100%">
                <tr>
                    <td style="width: 439px">
                    <b>
                    <span style="font-size: 14pt">Customer Information</span>
                    </b>
                    </td>
                    <td style="width: 439px" align="right">
                        CustomerID:
                        <asp:Label ID="CustomerIDLabel" Runat="server"
                            Text='<%# Bind("CustomerID") %>'>
                            </asp:Label></td>
                </tr>
                <tr>
                    <td colspan="2">
                        CompanyName:
                        <asp:Label ID="CompanyNameLabel" Runat="server"
                            Text='<%# Bind("CompanyName") %>'>
                            </asp:Label><br />
                        ContactName:
                        <asp:Label ID="ContactNameLabel" Runat="server"
                            Text='<%# Bind("ContactName") %>'>
                            </asp:Label><br />
```

```
                    ContactTitle:
                    <asp:Label ID="ContactTitleLabel" Runat="server"
                         Text='<%# Bind("ContactTitle") %>'>
                         </asp:Label><br />
                    <br />
                    <table width="100%"><tr>
                            <td colspan="3">
                                <asp:Label ID="AddressLabel" Runat="server"
                                     Text='<%# Bind("Address") %>'>
                                     </asp:Label></td>
                        </tr>
                        <tr>
                            <td style="width: 100px">
                                <asp:Label ID="CityLabel" Runat="server"
                                     Text='<%# Bind("City") %>'>
                                     </asp:Label></td>
                            <td style="width: 100px">
                                <asp:Label ID="RegionLabel" Runat="server"
                                     Text='<%# Bind("Region") %>'>
                                     </asp:Label></td>
                            <td style="width: 100px">
                                <asp:Label ID="PostalCodeLabel"
                                    Runat="server"
                                    Text='<%# Bind("PostalCode") %>'>
                                    </asp:Label>
                            </td>
                        </tr>
                        <tr>
                            <td style="width: 100px" valign="top">
                                <asp:Label ID="CountryLabel" Runat="server"
                                     Text='<%# Bind("Country") %>'>
                                     </asp:Label></td>
                            <td style="width: 100px"></td>
                            <td style="width: 100px">
                                Phone:
                                <asp:Label ID="PhoneLabel" Runat="server"
                                            Text='<%# Bind("Phone") %>'>
                                            </asp:Label><br />
                                Fax:
                                <asp:Label ID="FaxLabel" Runat="server"
                                     Text='<%# Bind("Fax") %>'>
                                     </asp:Label><br />
                            </td>
                        </tr></table>
                    <asp:Button ID="Button1" Runat="server"
                         Text="Button" CommandName="edit" />
                </td>
            </tr></table>
    </ItemTemplate>
</asp:FormView>
<asp:SqlDataSource ID="SqlDataSource1" Runat="server"
     SelectCommand="SELECT * FROM [Customers]"
     ConnectionString="<%$ ConnectionStrings:AppConnectionString1 %>">
```

Continued

```
        </asp:SqlDataSource>

    </div>
    </form>
</body>
</html>
```

Other Databound Controls

ASP.NET 1.0/1.1 contained many other controls that could be bound to data sources. ASP.NET 2.0 retained those controls, enhanced some, and added several additional bound controls to the toolbox ASP.NET 3.5 continues to include these controls in its toolbox.

DropDownList, ListBox, RadioButtonList, and CheckBoxList

Although the DropDownList, ListBox, and CheckBoxList controls largely remained the same from ASP.NET 1.0/1.1 to ASP.NET 2.0, several new properties that you might find useful were added. In addition, ASP.NET 2.0 added new RadioButtonList and BulletedList controls. All of these controls remain the same in ASP.NET 3.5.

One of the new properties available in all these controls is the `AppendDataBoundItems` property. Setting this property to `True` tells the DropDownList control to append data-bound list items to any existing statically declared items, rather then overwriting them as the ASP.NET 1.0/1.1 version would have done.

Another useful new property available to all these controls is the `DataTextFormatString`, which allows you to specify a string format for the display text of the DropDownList items.

TreeView

Another control included in the ASP.NET toolbox is the TreeView control. Because the TreeView can display only hierarchical data, it can be bound only to the XmlDataSource and the SiteMapDataSource controls. Listing 7-59 shows a sample SiteMap file you can use for your SiteMapDataSource control.

Listing 7-59: A SiteMap file for your samples

```
<siteMap>
    <siteMapNode url="page3.aspx" title="Home" description="" roles="">
        <siteMapNode url="page2.aspx" title="Content" description="" roles="" />
        <siteMapNode url="page4.aspx" title="Links" description="" roles="" />
        <siteMapNode url="page1.aspx" title="Comments" description="" roles="" />
    </siteMapNode>
</siteMap>
```

Listing 7-60 shows how you can bind a TreeView control to a SiteMapDataSource control to generate navigation for your Web site.

Listing 7-60: Using the TreeView with a SqlDataSource control

```
<%@ Page Language="C#" %>

<html xmlns="http://www.w3.org/1999/xhtml" >
<head runat="server">
    <title>Using the TreeView control</title>
</head>
<body>
    <form id="form1" runat="server">
    <div>
        <asp:TreeView ID="TreeView1" Runat="server"
             DataSourceID="SiteMapDataSource1">
        </asp:TreeView>
        <asp:SiteMapDataSource ID="SiteMapDataSource1" Runat="server" />

    </div>
    </form>
</body>
</html>
```

Ad Rotator

The familiar AdRotator control was greatly enhanced in ASP.NET 2.0. You can see the control by using the SqlDataSource or XmlDataSource controls. Listing 7-61 shows an example of binding the AdRotator to a SqlDataSource control.

Listing 7-61: Using the AdRotator with a SqlDataSource control

```
<asp:AdRotator ID="AdRotator1" runat="server"
     DataSourceId="SqlDataSource1" AlternateTextField="AlternateTF"
     ImageUrlField="Image" NavigateUrlField="NavigateUrl" />
```

For more information on the Ad Rotator control, see Chapter 5.

Menu

The last control in this section is the new Menu control. Like the TreeView control, it is capable of displaying hierarchical data in a vertical *pop-out style* menu. Also like the TreeView control, it can be bound only to the XmlDataSource and the SiteMapDataSource controls. Listing 7-62 shows how you can use the same SiteMap data used earlier in the TreeView control sample, and modify it to display using the new Menu control.

Listing 7-62: Using the Menu control with a SiteMap

```
<%@ Page Language="C#" %>

<html xmlns="http://www.w3.org/1999/xhtml" >
<head runat="server">
    <title>Using the Menu control</title>
</head>
```

Continued

```
<body>
    <form id="form1" runat="server">
    <div>
        <asp:Menu ID="Menu1" Runat="server" DataSourceID="SiteMapDataSource1">
        </asp:Menu>
        <asp:SiteMapDataSource ID="SiteMapDataSource1" Runat="server" />
    </div>
    </form>
</body>
</html>
```

For more information on using the Menu control, see Chapter 14.

Inline Data-Binding Syntax

Another feature of data binding in ASP.NET is inline data-binding syntax. Inline syntax in ASP.NET 1.0/1.1 was primarily relegated to templated controls such as the DataList or the Repeater controls, and even then it was sometimes difficult and confusing to make it work as you wanted it to. In ASP.NET 1.0/1.1, if you needed to use inline data binding, you might have created something like the procedure shown in Listing 7-63.

Listing 7-63: Using DataBinders in ASP.NET 1.0

```
<asp:Repeater id=Repeater1 runat="server">
    <HeaderTemplate>
        <table>
    </HeaderTemplate>
    <ItemTemplate>
       <tr>
          <td>
              <%# Container.DataItem("Name") %><BR/>
              <%# Container.DataItem("Department") %><BR/>
              <%# DataBinder.Eval(
                   Container.DataItem, "HireDate", "{0:mm dd yyyy}") %><BR/>
           </td>
        </tr>
    </ItemTemplate>
    <FooterTemplate>
        </table>
    </FooterTemplate>
</asp:Repeater>
```

As you can see in this sample, you are using a Repeater control to display a series of employees. Because the Repeater control is a templated control, you use data binding to output the employee-specific data in the proper location of the template. Using the `Eval` method also allows you to provide formatting information such as Date or Currency formatting at render-time.

In later versions of ASP.NET, including 3.5, the concept of inline data binding remains basically the same, but you are given a simpler syntax and several powerful new binding tools to use.

Data-Binding Syntax Changes

ASP.NET contains three different ways to perform data binding. First, you can continue to use the existing method of binding, using the `Container.DataItem` syntax:

```
<%# Container.DataItem("Name") %>
```

This is good because it means you won't have to change your existing Web pages if you are migrating from prior versions of ASP.NET. But if you are creating new Web pages, you should probably use the simplest form of binding, using the `Eval` method directly:

```
<%# Eval("Name") %>
```

You can also continue to format data using the formatter overload of the `Eval` method:

```
<%# Eval("HireDate", "{0:mm dd yyyy}" ) %>
```

In addition to these changes, ASP.NET includes a form of data binding called *two-way data binding*. In ASP.NET 1.0/1.1, using the data-binding syntax was essentially a read-only form of accessing data. Since the introduction of ASP.NET 2.0, two-way data binding has allowed you to support both read and write operations for bound data. This is done using the `Bind` method, which, other than using a different method name, works just like the `Eval` method:

```
<%# Bind("Name") %>
```

The new `Bind` method should be used in new controls such as the GridView, DetailsView, or FormView, where auto-updates to the data source are implemented.

When working with the data binding statements, remember that anything between the `<%# %>` delimiters is treated as an expression. This is important because it gives you additional functionality when data binding. For example, you could append additional data:

```
<%# "Foo " + Eval("Name") %>
```

Or you can even pass the evaluated value to a method:

```
<%# DoSomeProcess( Eval("Name") )%>
```

XML Data Binding

Because XML is becoming ever more prevalent in applications, ASP.NET also includes several ways to bind specifically to XML data sources. These new data binding expressions give you powerful ways of working with the hierarchical format of XML. Additionally, except for the different method names, these binding methods work exactly the same as the `Eval` and `Bind` methods discussed earlier. These binders should be used when you are using the XmlDataSource control. The first binding format that uses the `XPathBinder` class is shown in the following code:

```
<% XPathBinder.Eval(Container.DataItem, "employees/employee/Name") %>
```

Notice that rather than specifying a column name as in the `Eval` method, the `XPathBinder` binds the result of an XPath query. Like the standard `Eval` expression, the XPath data binding expression also has a shorthand format:

```
<% XPath("employees/employee/Name") %>
```

Also, like the `Eval` method, the XPath data binding expression supports applying formatting to the data:

```
<% XPath("employees/employee/HireDate", "{0:mm dd yyyy}") %>
```

The `XPathBinder` returns a single node using the XPath query provided. Should you want to return multiple nodes from the XmlDataSource Control, you can use the class's `Select` method. This method returns a list of nodes that match the supplied XPath query:

```
<% XPathBinder.Select(Container.DataItem,"employees/employee") %>
```

Or use the shorthand syntax:

```
<% XpathSelect("employees/employee") %>
```

Expressions and Expression Builders

Finally, ASP.NET introduces the concept of expressions and expression builders. Expressions are statements that are parsed by ASP.NET at runtime in order to return a data value. ASP.NET automatically uses expressions to do things like retrieve the database connection string when it parses the SqlDataSource control, so you may have already seen these statements in your pages. An example of the connection string Expression is shown in Listing 7-64.

Listing 7-64: A connection string Expression

```
<asp:SqlDataSource ID="SqlDataSource1" runat="server"
    ConnectionString="<%$ ConnectionStrings:NorthwindConnectionString %>"
    SelectCommand="SELECT * FROM Customers"></asp:SqlDataSource>
```

When ASP.NET is attempting to parse an ASP.NET Web page, it looks for expressions contained in the `<%$ %>`delimiters. This indicates to ASP.NET that this is an expression to be parsed. As shown in the previous listing, it attempts to locate the `NorthwindConnectionString` value from the web.config file. ASP.NET knows to do this because of the `ConnectionStrings` expression prefix, which tells ASP.NET to use the `ConnectionStringsExpressionBuilder` class to parse the expression.

ASP.NET includes several expression builders, including one for retrieving values from the AppSettings section of `web.config`: one for retrieving ConnectionStrings as shown in Listing 7-64, and one for retrieving localized resource file values. Listings 7-65 and 7-66 demonstrate using the `AppSettingsExpressionBuilder` and the `ResourceExpressionBuilder`.

Listing 7-65: Using AppSettingsExpressionBuilder

```
<asp:Label runat="server" ID="lblAppSettings"
    Text="<%$ AppSettings: LabelText %>"></asp:Label>
```

Listing 7-66: Using ResourceExpressionBuilder

```
<asp:Label runat="server" ID="lblResource"
    Text="<%$ Resources: TEST %>"></asp:Label>
```

In addition to using the expression builder classes, you can also create your own expressions by deriving a class from the `System.Web.Compilation.ExpressionBuilder` base class. This base class provides you with the overridable methods you need to implement if you want ASP.NET to parse your expression properly. Listing 7-67 shows a simple custom expression builder.

Listing 7-67: Using a simple custom expression builder

VB

```
Imports System;
Imports System.CodeDom;
Imports System.Web.Compilation;
Imports System.Web.UI;

<ExpressionPrefix("MyCustomExpression")>
<ExpressionEditor("MyCustomExpressionEditor")>
Public Class MyCustomExpression Inherits ExpressionBuilder

        Public Overrides Function
        GetCodeExpression(ByVal entry As BoundPropertyEntry,
            ByVal parsedData As object, ByVal context As ExpressionBuilderContext)
            As System.CodeDom.CodeExpression

        Return New CodeCastExpression("Int64", new CodePrimitiveExpression(1000))
    End Function
End Class
```

C#

```
using System;
using System.CodeDom;
using System.Web.Compilation;
using System.Web.UI;

[ExpressionPrefix("MyCustomExpression")]
[ExpressionEditor("MyCustomExpressionEditor")]
public class MyCustomExpression : ExpressionBuilder
{
    public override System.CodeDom.CodeExpression
        GetCodeExpression(BoundPropertyEntry entry, object parsedData,
            ExpressionBuilderContext context)
    {
        return new CodeCastExpression("Int64", new CodePrimitiveExpression(1000));
    }
}
```

In examining this sample, notice several items. First, you have derived the `MyCustomExpression` class from `ExpressionBuilder` as I discussed earlier. Second, you have overridden the `GetCodeExpression` method. This method supplies you with several parameters that can be helpful in executing this method, and it returns a `CodeExpression` object to ASP.NET that it can execute at runtime to retrieve the data value.

The `CodeExpression` class is a base class in .NET's CodeDom infrastructure. Classes that are derived from the `CodeExpression` class provide abstracted ways of generating .NET code, whether VB or C#. This CodeDom infrastructure is what helps you create and run code dynamically at runtime.

The `BoundPropertyEntry` parameter entry tells you exactly which property the expression is bound to. For example, in Listings 7-58 and 7-59, the Label's `Text` property is bound to the `AppSettings` and `Resources` expressions. The object parameter `parsedData` contains any data that was parsed and returned by the `ParseExpression` method that you see later on in the chapter. Finally, the `ExpressionBuilderContext` parameter context allows you to reference the virtual path or templated control associated with the expression.

In the body of the `GetCodeExpression` method, you are creating a new `CodeCastExpression` object, which is a class derived from the `CodeExpression` base class. The `CodeCastExpression` tells .NET to generate the appropriate code to execute a cast from one data type to another. In this case, you are casting the value 1000 to an Int64 datatype. When .NET executes the `CodeCastExpression`, it is (in a sense) writing the C# code ((long)(1000)), or (if your application was written in VB) CType(1000,Long). Note that a wide variety of classes derive from the `CodeExpression` class that you can use to generate your final code expression.

The final lines to note are the two attributes that have been added to the class. The `ExpressionPrefix` and `ExpressionEditor` attributes help .NET figure out that this class should be used as an expression, and they also help .NET locate the proper expression builder class when it comes time to parse the expression.

After you have created your expression builder class, you let .NET know about it. You do this by adding an `expressionBuilders` node to the compilation node in your `web.config` file. Notice that the value of the `ExpressionPrefix` is added to the `expressionBuilder` to help ASP.NET locate the appropriate expression builder class at runtime.

```
<compilation debug="true" strict="false" explicit="true">
    <expressionBuilders>
        <add expressionPrefix="MyCustomExpression" type="MyCustomExpression"/>
    </expressionBuilders>
</compilation>
```

The `GetCodeExpression` method is not the only member available for overriding in the `ExpressionBuilder` class. Several other useful members include the `ParseExpression`, `SupportsEvaluate`, and `EvaluateExpression` methods.

The `ParseExpression` method lets you pass parsed expression data into the `GetCodeExpression` method. For example, in Listing 7-60, the `CodeCastExpression` value 1000 was hard-coded. If, however, you want to allow a developer to pass that value in as part of the expression, you simply use the `ParseExpression` method as shown in Listing 7-68

Listing 7-68: Using ParseExpression

VB

```
Imports System;
Imports System.CodeDom;
Imports System.Web.Compilation;
Imports System.Web.UI;
```

```
<ExpressionPrefix("MyCustomExpression")>
<ExpressionEditor("MyCustomExpressionEditor")>
Public Class MyCustomExpression Inherits ExpressionBuilder

    Public Overrides Function
        GetCodeExpression(ByVal entry As BoundPropertyEntry,
            ByVal parsedData As object, ByVal context As ExpressionBuilderContext)
            As System.CodeDom.CodeExpression

        Return New CodeCastExpression("Int64",
            new CodePrimitiveExpression(passedData))
    End Function

    Public Overrides Function ParseExpression
        (ByVal expression As String, ByVal propertyType As Type,
            ByVal context As ExpressionBuilderContext) As Object

        Return expression
    End Function
End Class
```

C#

```
using System;
using System.CodeDom;
using System.Web.Compilation;
using System.Web.UI;

[ExpressionPrefix("MyCustomExpression")]
[ExpressionEditor("MyCustomExpressionEditor")]
public class MyCustomExpression : ExpressionBuilder
{
    public override System.CodeDom.CodeExpression
        GetCodeExpression(BoundPropertyEntry entry, object parsedData,
            ExpressionBuilderContext context)
    {
        return new CodeCastExpression("Int64",
            new CodePrimitiveExpression(parsedData));
    }
    public override object ParseExpression
        (string expression, Type propertyType, ExpressionBuilderContext context)
    {
        return expression;
    }
}
```

The last two `ExpressionBuilder` overrides to examine are the `SupportsEvaluate` and `Evaluate-Expression` members. You need to override these methods if you are running your Web site in a no-compile scenario (you have specified `compilationMode = "never"` in your @Page directive). The `SupportEvaluate` property returns a Boolean indicating to ASP.NET whether this expression can be evaluated while a page is executing in no-compile mode. If `True` is returned and the page is executing in no-compile mode, the `EvaluateExpression` method is used to return the data value rather than the `GetCodeExpression` method. The `EvaluateExpression` returns an object representing the data value. See Listing 7-69.

Listing 7-69: Overriding SupportsEvaluate and EvaluateExpression

VB

```
Imports System;
Imports System.CodeDom;
Imports System.Web.Compilation;
Imports System.Web.UI;

<ExpressionPrefix("MyCustomExpression")>
<ExpressionEditor("MyCustomExpressionEditor")>
Public Class MyCustomExpression Inherits ExpressionBuilder

    Public Overrides Function
        GetCodeExpression(ByVal entry As BoundPropertyEntry,
            ByVal parsedData As object, ByVal context As ExpressionBuilderContext)
            As System.CodeDom.CodeExpression

        Return New CodeCastExpression("Int64",
            new CodePrimitiveExpression(pasedData))
    End Function

    Public Overrides Function ParseExpression
        (ByVal expression As String, ByVal propertyType As Type,
            ByVal context As ExpressionBuilderContext) As Object

        Return expression
    End Function

    Public Overrides ReadOnly Property SupportsEvaluate as Boolean
        Get
            Return True
        End Get
    End Property

    Public Overrides Function EvaluateExpression(ByVal target As Object,
        ByVal Entry As BoundPropertyEntry, ByVal parsedData As Object,
        ByVal context As ExpressionBuilderContext) as Object

        Return parsedData;
    End Function

End Class
```

C#

```
using System;
using System.CodeDom;
using System.Web.Compilation;
using System.Web.UI;

[ExpressionPrefix("MyCustomExpression")]
[ExpressionEditor("MyCustomExpression123Editor")]
public class MyCustomExpression : ExpressionBuilder
{
    public override System.CodeDom.CodeExpression
```

```
        GetCodeExpression(BoundPropertyEntry entry, object parsedData,
            ExpressionBuilderContext context)
    {
        return new CodeCastExpression("Int64",
            new CodePrimitiveExpression(parsedData));
    }

    public override object ParseExpression
        (string expression, Type propertyType, ExpressionBuilderContext context)
    {
        return expression;
    }

    public override bool SupportsEvaluate
    {
        get
        {
            return true;
        }
    }

    public override object EvaluateExpression(object target,
        BoundPropertyEntry entry, object parsedData,
        ExpressionBuilderContext context)
    {
        return parsedData;
    }
}
```

As shown in Listing 7-69, you can simply return `True` from the `SupportsEvaluate` property if you want to override the `EvaluateExpression` method. Then all you do is return an object from the `Evaluate-Expression` method.

Summary

In this chapter, you examined data binding in ASP.NET. The introduction of data source controls such as the LinqDataSource control, SqlDataSource control, or the XmlDataSource control makes querying and displaying data from any number of data sources an almost trivial task. Using the data source controls' own wizards, you learned how easy it is to generate powerful data access functionality with almost no code required.

You examined how even a beginning developer can easily combine the data source controls with the GridView, ListView, and DetailsView controls to create powerful data manipulation applications with a minimal amount of coding.

You saw how ASP.NET includes a multitude of controls that can be data-bound, specifically examining how, since ASP.NET 1.0/1.1, many controls have been enhanced, and examining the features of the data bound controls that are included in the ASP.NET toolbox, such as the GridView, TreeView, ListView, and Menu controls, the new FormView control.

Finally, you looked at how the inline data-binding syntax has been improved and strengthened with the addition of the XML-specific data-binding expressions.

8

Data Management with ADO.NET

This chapter provides information on programming with the data management features that are part of ADO.NET, a key component of the .NET Framework and of your ASP.NET development. The discussion begins with the basics of ADO.NET and later dives into the ways you can use various features that make up ADO.NET to manage data contained in a relational database.

ADO.NET, first introduced in version 1.0 of the .NET Framework, provided an extensive array of features to handle live data in a connected mode or data that is disconnected from its underlying data store. ADO.NET 1.0 was primarily developed to address two specific problems in getting at data. The first had to do with the user's need to access data once and to iterate through a collection of data in a single instance. This need often arose in Web application development.

ADO.NET addresses a couple of the most common data-access strategies that are used for applications today. When classic ADO was developed, many applications could be connected to the data store almost indefinitely. Today, with the explosion of the Internet as the means of data communication, a new data technology is required to make data accessible and updateable in a disconnected architecture.

The first of these common data-access scenarios is one in which a user must locate a collection of data and iterate through this data a single time. This is a popular scenario for Web pages. When a request for data from a Web page that you have created is received, you can simply fill a table with data from a data store. In this case, you go to the data store, grab the data that you want, send the data across the wire, and then populate the table. In this scenario, the goal is to get the data in place as fast as possible.

The second way to work with data in this disconnected architecture is to grab a collection of data and use this data separately from the data store itself. This could be on the server or even on the client. Although the data is disconnected, you want the ability to keep the data (with all of its tables and relations in place) on the client side. Classic ADO data was represented by a single table that you could iterate through. ADO.NET, however, can be a reflection of the data store itself, with tables, columns, rows, and relations all in place. When you are done with the client-side copy of the data, you can persist the changes that you made in the local copy of data directly back into the data store. The technology that gives you this capability is the DataSet, which will be covered shortly.

Although classic ADO was geared for a two-tiered environment (client-server), ADO.NET addresses a multi-tiered environment. ADO.NET is easy to work with because it has a unified programming model. This unified programming model makes working with data on the server the same as working with data on the client. Because the models are the same, you find yourself more productive when working with ADO.NET.

Basic ADO.NET Features

This chapter begins with a quick look at the basics of ADO.NET and then provides an overview of basic ADO.NET capabilities, namespaces, and classes. It also reviews how to work with the `Connection`, `Command`, `DataAdapter`, `DataSet`, and `DataReader` objects.

Common ADO.NET Tasks

Before jumping into the depths of ADO.NET, step back and make sure that you understand some of the common tasks you might perform programmatically within ADO.NET. This next section looks at the process of selecting, inserting, updating, and deleting data.

The following example makes use of the `Northwind.mdf` *SQL Server Express Database file. To get this database, please search for ''Northwind and pubs Sample Databases for SQL Server 2000''. You can find this link at* `www.microsoft.com/downloads/details.aspx?familyid=06616212-0356-46a0-8da2-eebc53a68034&displaylang=en`. *Once installed, you will find the Northwind.mdf file in the C:\ SQL Server 2000 Sample Databases directory. To add this database to your ASP.NET application, create an* `App_Data` *folder within your project (if it isn't already there) and right-click on the folder and select Add Existing Item. From the provided dialog box, you are then able to browse to the location of the* `Northwind.mdf` *file that you just installed. If you are having trouble getting permissions to work with the database, make a data connection to the file from the Visual Studio Server Explorer by right-clicking on the Data Connections node and selecting Add New Connection from the provided menu. You will be asked to be made the appropriate user of the database. ThenVS will make the appropriate changes on your behalf for this to occur.*

Selecting Data

After the connection to the data source is open and ready to use, you probably want to read the data from the data source. If you do not want to manipulate the data, but simply to read it or transfer it from one spot to another, you use the `DataReader` class.

In the following example (Listing 8-1), you use the `GetCompanyNameData()` function to provide a list of company names from the SQL Northwind database.

Listing 8-1: Reading the data from a SQL database using the DataReader class

VB

```
Imports Microsoft.VisualBasic
Imports System.Collections.Generic
```

```
Imports System.Data
Imports System.Data.SqlClient

Public Class SelectingData
    Public Function GetCompanyNameData() As List(Of String)
        Dim conn As SqlConnection
        Dim cmd As SqlCommand
        Dim cmdString As String = "Select CompanyName from Customers"
        conn = New SqlConnection("Data Source=.\SQLEXPRESS;AttachDbFilename=
           |DataDirectory|\NORTHWND.MDF;Integrated Security=True;
           User Instance=True") ' Put this string on one line in your code
        cmd = New SqlCommand(cmdString, conn)
        conn.Open()

        Dim myReader As SqlDataReader
        Dim returnData As List(Of String) = New List(Of String)
        myReader = cmd.ExecuteReader(CommandBehavior.CloseConnection)

        While myReader.Read()
            returnData.Add(myReader("CompanyName").ToString())
        End While

        Return returnData
    End Function
End Class
```

C#

```
using System.Data;
using System.Data.SqlClient;
using System.Collections.Generic;

public class SelectingData
{
    public List<string> GetCompanyNameData()
    {
        SqlConnection conn;
        SqlCommand cmd;
        string cmdString = "Select CompanyName from Customers";
        conn = new
            SqlConnection(@"Data Source=.\SQLEXPRESS;AttachDbFilename=
                |DataDirectory|\NORTHWND.MDF;Integrated Security=True;
                User Instance=True");  // Put this string on one line in your code
        cmd = new SqlCommand(cmdString, conn);
        conn.Open();

        SqlDataReader myReader;
        List<string> returnData = new List<string>();

        myReader = cmd.ExecuteReader(CommandBehavior.CloseConnection);

        while (myReader.Read())
        {
            returnData.Add(myReader["CompanyName"].ToString());
```

Continued

```
            }

            return returnData;
        }
    }
```

In this example, you create an instance of both the `SqlConnection` and the `SqlCommand` classes. Then, before you open the connection, you simply pass the `SqlCommand` class a SQL command selecting specific data from the Northwind database. After your connection is opened (based upon the commands passed in), you create a `DataReader`. To read the data from the database, you iterate through the data with the `DataReader` by using the `myReader.Read()` method. After the `List(Of String)` object is built, the connection is closed, and the object is returned from the function.

Inserting Data

When working with data, you often insert the data into the data source. Listing 8-2 shows you how to do this. This data may have been passed to you by the end user through the XML Web Service, or it may be data that you generated within the logic of your class.

Listing 8-2: Inserting data into SQL Server

VB

```
Public Sub InsertData()
    Dim conn As SqlConnection
    Dim cmd As SqlCommand
    Dim cmdString As String = "Insert Customers (CustomerID, _
       CompanyName, ContactName) Values ('BILLE', 'XYZ Company', 'Bill Evjen')"
    conn = New SqlConnection("Data Source=.\SQLEXPRESS;AttachDbFilename=
           |DataDirectory|\NORTHWND.MDF;Integrated Security=True;
           User Instance=True") ' Put this string on one line in your code
    cmd = New SqlCommand(cmdString, conn)
    conn.Open()

    cmd.ExecuteNonQuery()
    conn.Close()
End Sub
```

C#

```
public void InsertData()
{
    SqlConnection conn;
    SqlCommand cmd;
    string cmdString = "Insert Customers (CustomerID, CompanyName,
       ContactName) Values ('BILLE', 'XYZ Company', 'Bill Evjen')";
    conn = new
           SqlConnection(@"Data Source=.\SQLEXPRESS;AttachDbFilename=
               |DataDirectory|\NORTHWND.MDF;Integrated Security=True;
               User Instance=True");  // Put this string on one line in your code
    cmd = new SqlCommand(cmdString, conn);
    conn.Open();

    cmd.ExecuteNonQuery();
    conn.Close();
}
```

Inserting data into SQL is pretty straightforward and simple. Using the SQL command string, you insert specific values for specific columns. The actual insertion is initiated using the `cmd.ExecuteNonQuery()` command. This executes a command on the data when you don't want anything in return.

Updating Data

In addition to inserting new records into a database, you frequently update existing rows of data in a table. Imagine a table in which you can update multiple records at once. In the example in Listing 8-3, you want to update an employee table by putting a particular value in the `emp_bonus` column if the employee has been at the company for five years or longer.

Listing 8-3: Updating data in SQL Server

VB

```
Public Function UpdateEmployeeBonus() As Integer
    Dim conn As SqlConnection
    Dim cmd As SqlCommand
    Dim RecordsAffected as Integer
    Dim cmdString As String = "UPDATE Employees SET emp_bonus=1000 WHERE " & _
       "yrs_duty>=5"
    conn = New SqlConnection("Data Source=.\SQLEXPRESS;AttachDbFilename=
           |DataDirectory|\NORTHWND.MDF;Integrated Security=True;
           User Instance=True") ' Put this string on one line in your code
    cmd = New SqlCommand(cmdString, conn)
    conn.Open()

    RecordsAffected = cmd.ExecuteNonQuery()
    conn.Close()

    Return RecordsAffected
End Function
```

C#

```
public int UpdateEmployeeBonus()
{
    SqlConnection conn;
    SqlCommand cmd;
    int RecordsAffected;
    string cmdString = "UPDATE Employees SET emp_bonus=1000 WHERE yrs_duty>=5";
    conn = new
        SqlConnection(@"Data Source=.\SQLEXPRESS;AttachDbFilename=
            |DataDirectory|\NORTHWND.MDF;Integrated Security=True;
            User Instance=True");  // Put this string on one line in your code

    cmd = new SqlCommand(cmdString, conn);
    conn.Open();

    RecordsAffected = cmd.ExecuteNonQuery();
    conn.Close();

    return RecordsAffected;
}
```

This update function iterates through all the employees in the table and changes the value of the emp_bonus field to 1000 if an employee has been with the company for more than five years. This is done with the SQL command string. The great thing about these update capabilities is that you can capture the number of records that were updated by assigning the `ExecuteNonQuery()` command to the `RecordsAffected` variable. The total number of affected records is then returned by the function.

Deleting Data

Along with reading, inserting, and updating data, you sometimes need to delete data from the data source. Deleting data is a simple process of using the SQL command string and then the `ExecuteNonQuery()` command as you did in the update example. See Listing 8-4 for an illustration of this.

Listing 8-4: Deleting data from SQL Server

VB

```
Public Function DeleteEmployee() As Integer
    Dim conn As SqlConnection
    Dim cmd As SqlCommand
    Dim RecordsAffected as Integer
    Dim cmdString As String = "DELETE Employees WHERE LastName='Evjen'"
    conn = New SqlConnection("Data Source=.\SQLEXPRESS;AttachDbFilename=
         |DataDirectory|\NORTHWND.MDF;Integrated Security=True;
         User Instance=True") ' Put this string on one line in your code
    cmd = New SqlCommand(cmdString, conn)
    conn.Open()

    RecordsAffected = cmd.ExecuteNonQuery()
    conn.Close()

    Return RecordsAffected
End Function
```

C#

```
public int DeleteEmployee()
{
    SqlConnection conn;
    SqlCommand cmd;
    int RecordsAffected;
    string cmdString = "DELETE Employees WHERE LastName='Evjen'";
    conn = new
        SqlConnection(@"Data Source=.\SQLEXPRESS;AttachDbFilename=
            |DataDirectory|\NORTHWND.MDF;Integrated Security=True;
            User Instance=True");  // Put this string on one line in your code
    cmd = new SqlCommand(cmdString, conn);
    conn.Open();

    RecordsAffected = cmd.ExecuteNonQuery();
    conn.Close();

    return RecordsAffected;
}
```

You can assign the `ExecuteNonQuery()` command to an `Integer` variable (just as you did for the update function) to return the number of records deleted.

Basic ADO.NET Namespaces and Classes

The six core ADO.NET namespaces are shown in the following table. In addition to these namespaces, each new data provider can have its own namespace. As an example, the Oracle .NET data provider adds a namespace of `System.Data.OracleClient` (for the Microsoft-built Oracle data provider).

Namespace	Description
`System.Data`	This namespace is the core of ADO.NET. It contains classes used by all data providers. It contains classes to represent tables, columns, rows, and the `DataSet` class. It also contains several useful interfaces, such as `IDbCommand`, `IDbConnection`, and `IDbDataAdapter`. These interfaces are used by all managed providers, enabling them to plug into the core of ADO.NET.
`System.Data.Common`	This namespace defines common classes that are used as base classes for data providers. All data providers share these classes. A few examples are `DbConnection` and `DbDataAdapter`.
`System.Data.OleDb`	This namespace defines classes that work with OLE-DB data sources using the .NET OleDb data provider. It contains classes such as `OleDbConnection` and `OleDbCommand`.
`System.Data.Odbc`	This namespace defines classes that work with the ODBC data sources using the .NET ODBC data provider. It contains classes such as `OdbcConnection` and `OdbcCommand`.
`System.Data.SqlClient`	This namespace defines a data provider for the SQL Server 7.0 or higher database. It contains classes such as `SqlConnection` and `SqlCommand`.
`System.Data.SqlTypes`	This namespace defines a few classes that represent specific data types for the SQL Server database.

ADO.NET has three distinct types of classes commonly referred to as `Disconnected`, `Shared`, and `Data Providers`. The `Disconnected` classes provide the basic structure for the ADO.NET framework. A good example of this type of class is the `DataTable` class. The objects of this class are capable of storing data without any dependency on a specific data provider. The `Shared` classes form the base classes for data providers and are shared among all data providers. The `Data Provider` classes are meant to work with different kinds of data sources. They are used to perform all data-management operations on specific databases. The `SqlClient` data provider, for example, works only with the SQL Server database.

A data provider contains `Connection`, `Command`, `DataAdapter`, and `DataReader` objects. Typically, in programming ADO.NET, you first create the `Connection` object and provide it with the necessary information, such as the connection string. You then create a `Command` object and provide it with the details of the SQL command that is to be executed. This command can be an inline SQL text command, a stored procedure, or direct table access. You can also provide parameters to these commands if needed. After you create the `Connection` and the `Command` objects, you must decide whether the command returns a result set. If the command doesn't return a result set, you can simply execute the command by calling one of its several `Execute` methods. On the other hand, if the command returns a result set, you must make a decision about whether you want to retain the result set for future uses without maintaining the connection to the database. If you want to retain the result set, you must create a `DataAdapter` object and use it to fill a `DataSet` or a `DataTable` object. These objects are capable of maintaining their information in a disconnected mode. However, if you don't want to retain the result set, but rather to simply process the command in a swift fashion, you can use the `Command` object to create a `DataReader` object. The `DataReader` object needs a live connection to the database, and it works as a forward-only, read-only cursor.

Using the Connection Object

The `Connection` object creates a link (or connection) to a specified data source. This object must contain the necessary information to discover the specified data source and to log in to it properly using a defined username and password combination. This information is provided via a single string called a *connection string*. You can also store this connection string in the `web.config` file of your application.

Every type of data provider has a connection object of some kind. The data provider for working with a SQL data store includes a `SqlConnection` class that performs this type of operation. The `SqlConnection` object is a class that is specific to the `SqlClient` provider. As discussed earlier in this chapter, the `SqlClient` provider is built for working with the SQL Server 7.0 and higher databases. The properties for the `SqlConnection` class are shown in the following table.

Property	Description
`ConnectionString`	This property allows you to read or provide the connection string that should be used by the `SqlConnection` object.
`Database`	This read-only property returns the name of the database to use after the connection is opened.
`Datasource`	This read-only property returns the name of the instance of the SQL Server database used by the `SqlConnection`object.
`State`	This read-only property returns the current state of the connection. The possible values are `Broken`, `Closed`, `Connecting`, `Executing`, `Fetching`, and `Open`.

Connecting to a data source is probably the most common task when you are working with data. This example and the ones that follow assume that you have a SQL Server database. In order to connect to your SQL Server database, you use the `SqlConnection` class. This is shown in Listing 8-5.

Listing 8-5: Connecting to a SQL database

VB

```
Dim conn as SqlConnection
conn = New SqlConnection("Data Source=.\SQLEXPRESS;AttachDbFilename=
          |DataDirectory|\NORTHWND.MDF;Integrated Security=True;
          User Instance=True") ' Put this string on one line in your code
conn.Open()
```

C#

```
SqlConnection conn;
conn = new
      SqlConnection(@"Data Source=.\SQLEXPRESS;AttachDbFilename=
```

```
            |DataDirectory|\NORTHWND.MDF;Integrated Security=True;
            User Instance=True");  // Put this string on one line in your code

conn.Open();
```

To make this connection work, be sure that the proper namespaces are imported before you start using any of the classes that work with SQL. The first step in making a connection is to create an instance of the `SqlConnection` class and assign it to the `conn` instance. This `SqlConnection` class is initialized after you pass in the connection string as a parameter to the class. In this case, you are connecting to the Northwind database that resides on your local machine using the system administrator's login credentials.

Another means of making a connection is to put the connection string within the application's `web.config` file and then to make a reference to the `web.config` file. With ASP.NET 3.5, you will find that there is an easy way to manage the storage of your connection strings through the use of the `web.config` file. This is actually a better way to store your connection strings rather than hard-coding them within the code of the application itself. In addition to having a single point in the application where the credentials for database access can be managed, storing credentials in the `web.config` also gives you the ability to encrypt the credentials.

To define your connection string within the `web.config` file, you are going to make use of the `<connectionStrings>` section. From this section, you can place an `<add>` element within it to define your connection. An example of this is illustrated in Listing 8-6.

Listing 8-6: Providing your connection string within the web.config file

```
<connectionStrings>
  <add name="DSN_Northwind" connectionString="Data
   Source=.\SQLEXPRESS;AttachDbFilename=|DataDirectory|\NORTHWND.MDF;Integrated
   Security=True;User Instance=True"
   providerName="System.Data.SqlClient" />
</connectionStrings>
```

In many places of this chapter, you will see that the actual connection string is broken up on multiple lines. This connection string will need to be on a single line within your code or broken up with string concatenation.

Now that you have a connection string within the `web.config` file, you can then make use of that connection string directly in your code by using the `ConnectionManager` object as illustrated here in Listing 8-7.

Listing 8-7: Using the connection string found in the web.config file

VB

```
conn = New _
   SqlConnection( _
   ConfigurationManager.ConnectionStrings("DSN_Northwind").ConnectionString)
```

C#

```
conn = new
   SqlConnection(
   ConfigurationManager.ConnectionStrings["DSN_Northwind"].ConnectionString);
```

For this line of code to work, you are going to have to make a reference to the `System.Configuration` namespace.

When you complete your connection to the data source, be sure that you close the connection by using `conn.Close()`. The .NET Framework does not implicitly release the connections when they fall out of scope.

Using the Command Object

The `Command` object uses the `Connection` object to execute SQL queries. These queries can be in the form of inline text, stored procedures, or direct table access. If the SQL query uses a `SELECT` clause, the result set it returns is usually stored in either a `DataSet` or a `DataReader` object. The `Command` object provides a number of *Execute* methods that can be used to perform various types of SQL queries.

Next, take a look at some of the more useful properties of the `SqlCommand` class, as shown in the following table.

Property	Description
`CommandText`	This read/write property allows you to set or retrieve either the T-SQL statement or the name of the stored procedure.
`CommandTimeout`	This read/write property gets or sets the number of seconds to wait while attempting to execute a particular command. The command is aborted after it times out and an exception is thrown. The default time allotted for this operation is 30 seconds.
`CommandType`	This read/write property indicates the way the `CommandText`property should be interpreted. The possible values are `StoredProcedure`, `TableDirect`, and `Text`. The value of `Text` means that your SQL statement is *inline* or contained within the code itself.
`Connection`	This read/write property gets or sets the `SqlConnection` object that should be used by this `Command` object.

Next, take a look at the various Execute methods that can be called from a `Command` object.

Property	Description
`ExecuteNonQuery`	This method executes the command specified and returns the number of rows affected.
`ExecuteReader`	This method executes the command specified and returns an instance of the `SqlDataReader` class. The DataReader object is a read-only and forward-only cursor.
`ExecuteRow`	This method executes the command and returns an instance of the `SqlRecord` class. This object contains only a single returned row.

Property	Description
ExecuteScalar	This method executes the command specified and returns the first column of the first row in the form of a generic object. The remaining rows and columns are ignored.
ExecuteXmlReader	This method executes the command specified and returns an instance of the XmlReader class. This method enables you to use a command that returns the results set in the form of an XML document.

Using the DataReader Object

The DataReader object is a simple forward-only and read-only cursor. It requires a live connection with the data source and provides a very efficient way of looping and consuming all or part of the result set. This object cannot be directly instantiated. Instead, you must call the ExecuteReader method of the Command object to obtain a valid DataReader object.

When using a DataReader object, be sure to close the connection when you are done using the data reader. If not, then the connection stays alive. The connection utilized stays alive until it is explicitly closed using the Close() method or until you have enabled your Command object to close the connection. You can close the connection after using the data reader in one of two ways. One way is to provide the CommandBehavior.CloseConnection enumeration while calling the ExecuteMethod of the Command object. This approach works only if you loop through the data reader until you reach the end of the result set, at which point the reader object automatically closes the connection for you. However, if you don't want to keep reading the data reader until the end of the result set, you can call the Close() method of the Connection object yourself.

Listing 8-8 shows the Connection, Command, and DataReader objects in action. It shows how to connect to the Northwind database (an example database found in the Microsoft's SQL Server 7.0, 2000, 2005, or 2008 database servers), read the Customers table within this database, and display the results in a GridView server control.

Listing 8-8: The SqlConnection, SqlCommand, and SqlDataReader objects in action

VB

```
<%@ Page Language="VB" %>
<%@ Import Namespace="System.Data" %>
<%@ Import Namespace="System.Data.SqlClient" %>
<%@ Import Namespace="System.Configuration" %>

<script runat="server">
    Protected Sub Page_Load(ByVal sender As Object, _
            ByVal e As System.EventArgs)

        If Not Page.IsPostBack Then
            Dim MyReader As SqlDataReader

    Dim MyConnection As SqlConnection = New SqlConnection()
```

Continued

```
            MyConnection.ConnectionString = _
        ConfigurationManager.ConnectionStrings("DSN_Northwind").ConnectionString

            Dim MyCommand As SqlCommand = New SqlCommand()
            MyCommand.CommandText = "SELECT TOP 3 * FROM CUSTOMERS"
            MyCommand.CommandType = CommandType.Text
            MyCommand.Connection = MyConnection

            MyCommand.Connection.Open()
            MyReader = MyCommand.ExecuteReader(CommandBehavior.CloseConnection)

            gvCustomers.DataSource = MyReader
            gvCustomers.DataBind()

            MyCommand.Dispose()
            MyConnection.Dispose()
        End If
    End Sub
</script>

<html>
<body>
    <form id="form1" runat="server">
    <div>
        <asp:GridView ID="gvCustomers" runat="server">
        </asp:GridView>
    </div>
    </form>
</body>
</html>
```

C#

```
<%@ Page Language="C#" %>
<%@ Import Namespace="System.Data" %>
<%@ Import Namespace="System.Data.SqlClient" %>
<%@ Import Namespace="System.Configuration" %>

<script runat="server">
    protected void Page_Load(object sender, EventArgs e)
    {
        if (!Page.IsPostBack)
        {
            SqlDataReader MyReader;
            SqlConnection MyConnection = new SqlConnection();
            MyConnection.ConnectionString =
        ConfigurationManager.ConnectionStrings["DSN_Northwind"].ConnectionString;

            SqlCommand MyCommand = new SqlCommand();
            MyCommand.CommandText = "SELECT TOP 3 * FROM CUSTOMERS";
            MyCommand.CommandType = CommandType.Text;
            MyCommand.Connection = MyConnection;

            MyCommand.Connection.Open();
```

```
            MyReader = MyCommand.ExecuteReader(CommandBehavior.CloseConnection);

            gvCustomers.DataSource = MyReader;
            gvCustomers.DataBind();

            MyCommand.Dispose();
            MyConnection.Dispose();
        }
    }
</script>
```

The code shown in Listing 8-8 uses the `SqlConnection` class to create a connection with the Northwind database using the connection string stored in the `web.config` file. This connection string is then retrieved using the `ConfigurationManager` class. It is always best to store your connection strings inside the `web.config` and to reference them in this manner. If you have a single place to work with your connection strings, any task is a lot more manageable than if you place all your connection strings in the actual code of your application.

After working with the connection string, this bit of code from Listing 8-8 creates a `Command` object using the `SqlCommand` class because you are interested in working with a SQL database. Next, the code provides the command text, command type, and connection properties. After the command and the connection are created, the code opens the connection and executes the command by calling the `ExecuteReader` method of the `MyCommand` object. After receiving the data reader from the `Command` object, you simply bind the retrieved results to an instance of the GridView control. The results are shown in Figure 8-1.

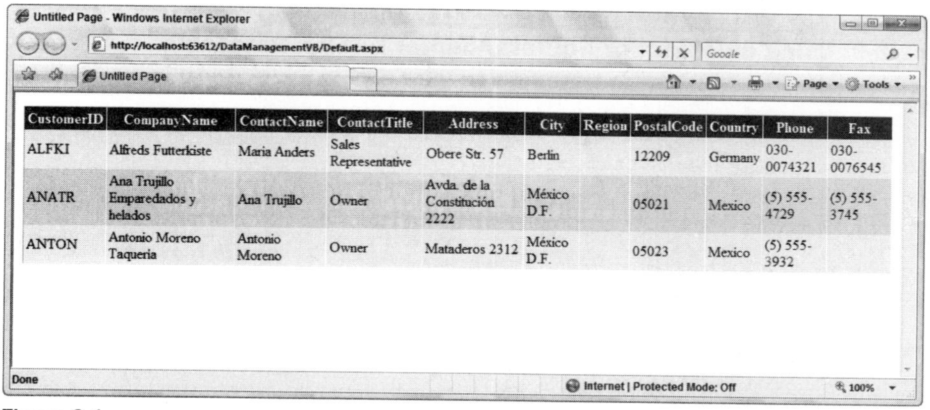
Untitled Page - Windows Internet Explorer
http://localhost:63612/DataManagementVB/Default.aspx
Untitled Page
CustomerID CompanyName ContactName ContactTitle Address City Region PostalCode Country Phone Fax
ALFKI Alfreds Futterkiste Maria Anders Sales Representative Obere Str. 57 Berlin 12209 Germany 030-0074321 030-0076545
ANATR Ana Trujillo Emparedados y helados Ana Trujillo Owner Avda. de la Constitución 2222 México D.F. 05021 Mexico (5) 555-4729 (5) 555-3745
ANTON Antonio Moreno Taquería Antonio Moreno Owner Mataderos 2312 México D.F. 05023 Mexico (5) 555-3932
Done
Internet | Protected Mode: Off
100%

Figure 8-1

Using Data Adapter

The `SqlDataAdapter` is a special class whose purpose is to bridge the gap between the disconnected `DataTable` objects and the physical data source. The `SqlDataAdapter` provides a two-way data transfer mechanism. It is capable of executing a `SELECT` statement on a data source and transferring the result set into a `DataTable` object. It is also capable of executing the standard `INSERT`, `UPDATE`, and `DELETE` statements and extracting the input data from a `DataTable` object.

The commonly used properties offered by the `SqlDataAdapter` class are shown in the following table.

Property	Description
`SelectCommand`	This read/write property sets or gets an object of type `SqlCommand`. This command is automatically executed to fill a `DataTable` with the result set.
`InsertCommand`	This read/write property sets or gets an object of type `SqlCommand`. This command is automatically executed to insert a new record to the SQL Server database.
`UpdateCommand`	This read/write property sets or gets an object of type `SqlCommand`. This command is automatically executed to update an existing record on the SQL Server database.
`DeleteCommand`	This read/write property sets or gets an object of type `SqlCommand`. This command is automatically executed to delete an existing record on the SQL Server database.

The `SqlDataAdapter` class also provides a method called `Fill()`. Calling the `Fill()` method automatically executes the command provided by the `SelectCommand` property, receives the result set, and copies it to a `DataTable` object.

The code example in Listing 8-9 illustrates how to use an object of `SqlDataAdapter` class to fill a `DataTable` object.

Listing 8-9: Using an object of SqlDataAdapter to fill a DataTable

VB

```
<%@ Page Language="VB" %>
<%@ Import Namespace="System.Data" %>
<%@ Import Namespace="System.Data.SqlClient" %>
<%@ Import Namespace="System.Configuration" %>

<script runat="server">
    Protected Sub Page_Load(ByVal sender As Object, _
            ByVal e As System.EventArgs)

        If Not Page.IsPostBack Then
            Dim MyTable As DataTable = New DataTable()

            Dim MyConnection As SqlConnection = New SqlConnection()
            MyConnection.ConnectionString = _
            ConfigurationManager.ConnectionStrings("DSN_Northwind").ConnectionString

            Dim MyCommand As SqlCommand = New SqlCommand()
            MyCommand.CommandText = "SELECT TOP 5 * FROM CUSTOMERS"
            MyCommand.CommandType = CommandType.Text
            MyCommand.Connection = MyConnection

            Dim MyAdapter As SqlDataAdapter = New SqlDataAdapter()
            MyAdapter.SelectCommand = MyCommand
```

```
            MyAdapter.Fill(MyTable)

            gvCustomers.DataSource = MyTable.DefaultView
            gvCustomers.DataBind()

            MyAdapter.Dispose()
            MyCommand.Dispose()
            MyConnection.Dispose()
        End If

    End Sub
</script>
```

C#

```
<%@ Page Language="C#" %>
<%@ Import Namespace="System.Data" %>
<%@ Import Namespace="System.Data.SqlClient" %>
<%@ Import Namespace="System.Configuration" %>

<script runat="server">
    protected void Page_Load(object sender, EventArgs e)
    {
        if (!Page.IsPostBack)
        {
            DataTable MyTable = new DataTable();

            SqlConnection MyConnection = new SqlConnection();
            MyConnection.ConnectionString =
                ConfigurationManager.
                ConnectionStrings["DSN_Northwind"].ConnectionString;

            SqlCommand MyCommand = new SqlCommand();
            MyCommand.CommandText = "SELECT TOP 5 * FROM CUSTOMERS";
            MyCommand.CommandType = CommandType.Text;
            MyCommand.Connection = MyConnection;

            SqlDataAdapter MyAdapter = new SqlDataAdapter();
            MyAdapter.SelectCommand = MyCommand;
            MyAdapter.Fill(MyTable);

            gvCustomers.DataSource = MyTable.DefaultView;
            gvCustomers.DataBind();

            MyAdapter.Dispose();
            MyCommand.Dispose();
            MyConnection.Dispose();        }
    }
</script>
```

The code shown in Listing 8-9 creates a `Connection` and `Command` object and then proceeds to create an instance of the `SqlDataAdapter` class. It then sets the `SelectCommand` property of the `DataAdapter` object to the `Command` object it had previously created. After the `DataAdapter` object is ready for executing, the code executes the `Fill()` method, passing it an instance of the `DataTable` class. The `Fill()` method populates the `DataTable` object. Figure 8-2 shows the result of executing this code.

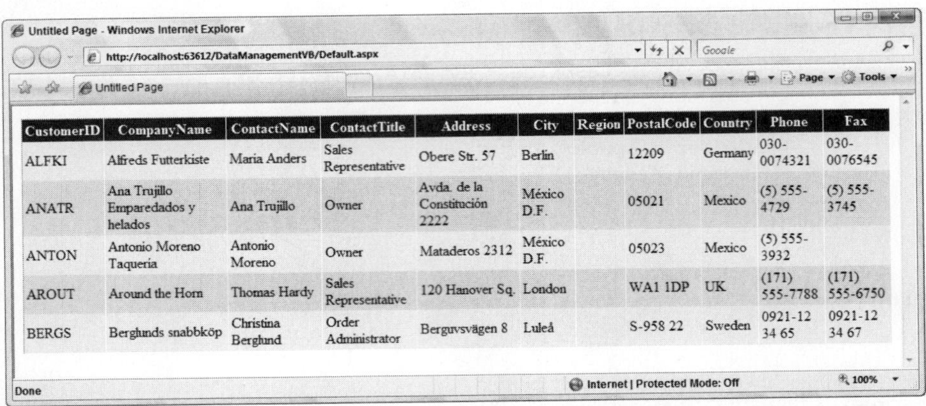

Figure 8-2

Using Parameters

Most serious database programming, regardless of how simple it might be, requires you to configure SQL statements using parameters. Using parameters helps guard against possible SQL injection attacks. Obviously, a discussion on the basics of ADO.NET programming is not complete without covering the use of parameterized SQL statements.

Creating a parameter is as simple as declaring an instance of the `SqlParameter` class and providing it the necessary information, such as parameter name, value, type, size, direction, and so on. The following table shows the properties of the `SqlParameter` class.

Property	Description
`ParameterName`	This read/write property gets or sets the name of the parameter.
`SqlDbType`	This read/write property gets or sets the SQL Server database type of the parameter value.
`Size`	This read/write property sets or gets the size of the parameter value.
`Direction`	This read/write property sets or gets the direction of the parameter, such as `Input`, `Output`, or `InputOutput`.
`SourceColumn`	This read/write property maps a column from a `DataTable` to the parameter. It enables you to execute multiple commands using the `SqlDataAdapter` object and pick the correct parameter value from a `DataTable` column during the command execution.
`Value`	This read/write property sets or gets the value provided to the parameter object. This value is passed to the parameter defined in the command during runtime.

Listing 8-10 modifies the code shown in Listing 8-5 to use two parameters while retrieving the list of customers from the database.

Listing 8-10: The use of a parameterized SQL statement

VB

```
<%@ Page Language="VB" %>
<%@ Import Namespace="System.Data" %>
<%@ Import Namespace="System.Data.SqlClient" %>
<%@ Import Namespace="System.Configuration" %>

<script runat="server">
    Protected Sub Page_Load(ByVal sender As Object, _
            ByVal e As System.EventArgs)
        If Not Page.IsPostBack Then
            Dim MyReader As SqlDataReader
            Dim CityParam As SqlParameter
            Dim ContactParam As SqlParameter

            Dim MyConnection As SqlConnection = New SqlConnection()
            MyConnection.ConnectionString = _
         ConfigurationManager.ConnectionStrings("DSN_Northwind").ConnectionString

            Dim MyCommand As SqlCommand = New SqlCommand()
            MyCommand.CommandText = _
         "SELECT * FROM CUSTOMERS WHERE CITY = @CITY AND CONTACTNAME = @CONTACT"
            MyCommand.CommandType = CommandType.Text
            MyCommand.Connection = MyConnection

            CityParam = New SqlParameter()
            CityParam.ParameterName = "@CITY"
            CityParam.SqlDbType = SqlDbType.VarChar
            CityParam.Size = 15
            CityParam.Direction = ParameterDirection.Input
            CityParam.Value = "Berlin"

            ContactParam = New SqlParameter()
            ContactParam.ParameterName = "@CONTACT"
            ContactParam.SqlDbType = SqlDbType.VarChar
            ContactParam.Size = 15
            ContactParam.Direction = ParameterDirection.Input
            ContactParam.Value = "Maria Anders"

            MyCommand.Parameters.Add(CityParam)
            MyCommand.Parameters.Add(ContactParam)

            MyCommand.Connection.Open()
            MyReader = MyCommand.ExecuteReader(CommandBehavior.CloseConnection)

            gvCustomers.DataSource = MyReader
            gvCustomers.DataBind()

            MyCommand.Dispose()
            MyConnection.Dispose()
        End If
```

Continued

```
    End Sub
</script>
```

C#

```
<%@ Page Language="C#" %>
<%@ Import Namespace="System.Data" %>
<%@ Import Namespace="System.Data.SqlClient" %>
<%@ Import Namespace="System.Configuration" %>

<script runat="server">
    protected void Page_Load(object sender, EventArgs e)
    {
        if (!Page.IsPostBack)
        {
            SqlDataReader MyReader;
            SqlParameter CityParam;
            SqlParameter ContactParam;

            SqlConnection MyConnection = new SqlConnection();
            MyConnection.ConnectionString =
        ConfigurationManager.ConnectionStrings["DSN_Northwind"].ConnectionString;

            SqlCommand MyCommand = new SqlCommand();
            MyCommand.CommandText =
        "SELECT * FROM CUSTOMERS WHERE CITY = @CITY AND CONTACTNAME = @CONTACT";
            MyCommand.CommandType = CommandType.Text;
            MyCommand.Connection = MyConnection;

            CityParam = new SqlParameter();
            CityParam.ParameterName = "@CITY";
            CityParam.SqlDbType = SqlDbType.VarChar;
            CityParam.Size = 15;
            CityParam.Direction = ParameterDirection.Input;
            CityParam.Value = "Berlin";

            ContactParam = new SqlParameter();
            ContactParam.ParameterName = "@CONTACT";
            ContactParam.SqlDbType = SqlDbType.VarChar;
            ContactParam.Size = 15;
            ContactParam.Direction = ParameterDirection.Input;
            ContactParam.Value = "Maria Anders";

            MyCommand.Parameters.Add(CityParam);
            MyCommand.Parameters.Add(ContactParam);

            MyCommand.Connection.Open();
            MyReader = MyCommand.ExecuteReader(CommandBehavior.CloseConnection);

            gvCustomers.DataSource = MyReader;
            gvCustomers.DataBind();

            MyCommand.Dispose();
```

```
                MyConnection.Dispose();
            }
        }
    </script>
```

The code shown in Listing 8-8 uses a parameterized SQL statement that receives the name of the city and the contact person to narrow the result set. These parameters are provided by instantiating a couple of instances of the `SqlParameter` class and filling in the appropriate name, type, size, direction, and value properties for each object of `SqlParameter` class. From there, you add the populated parameters to the `Command` object by invoking the `Add()` method of the `Parameters` collection. The result of executing this code is shown in Figure 8-3.

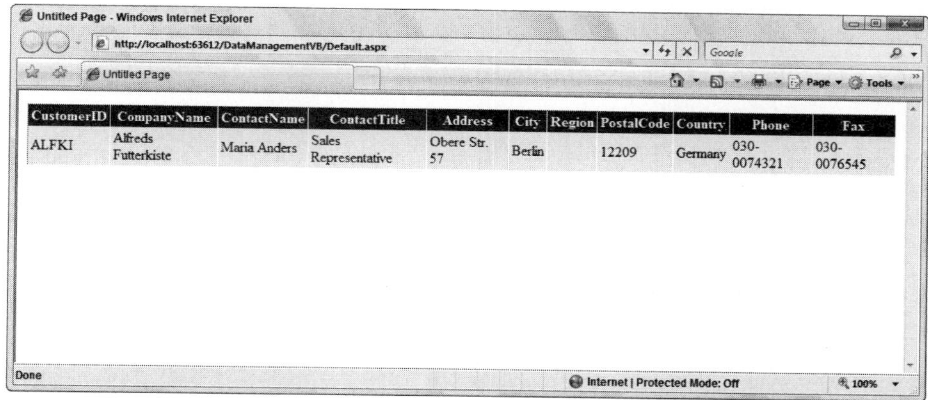

Figure 8-3

Understanding DataSet and DataTable

Most programmers agree that the `DataSet` class is the most commonly used part of ADO.NET in real-world, database-driven applications. This class provides mechanisms for managing data when it is disconnected from the data source. This capability to handle data in a disconnected state was first introduced in .NET during the 1.0 version of ADO.NET. The current 3.5 version of ADO.NET retains all the features of its predecessors and provides a few newer, much needed features.

An object created from the `DataSet` class works as a container for other objects that are created from the `DataTable` class. The `DataTable` object represents a logical table in memory. It contains rows, columns, primary keys, constraints, and relations with other `DataTable` objects. Therefore, you could have a `DataSet` that is made up of two distinct tables such as a Customers and an Orders table. Then you could use the `DataSet`, just as you would any other relational data source, to make a relation between the two tables in order to show all the orders for a particular customer.

Most of the disconnected data-driven programming is actually done using one or more `DataTable` objects within the `DataSet`. However, the previous versions of ADO.NET didn't allow you to work directly with the `DataTable` object for some very important tasks, such as reading and writing data to and from an

XML file. It didn't even allow you to serialize the DataTable object independently of the larger and encompassing DataSet object. This limitation required you to always use the DataSet object to perform any operation on a DataTable. The current version of ADO.NET removes this limitation and enables you to work directly with the DataTable for all your needs. In fact, we recommend that you don't use the DataSet object unless you need to work with multiple DataTable objects and need a container object to manage them. If you end up working with only a single table of information, then it is best to work with an instance of the DataTable object rather than a DataSet that contains only a single DataTable.

The current version of ADO.NET provides the capability to load a DataTable in memory by consuming a data source using a DataReader. In the past, you were sometimes restricted to creating multiple overloads of the same method just to work with both the DataReader and the DataTable objects. Now you have the flexibility to write the data access code one time and reuse the DataReader — either directly or to fill a DataTable, as shown in Listing 8-11.

Listing 8-11: How to load a DataTable from a DataReader

VB

```
<%@ Page Language="VB" %>
<%@ Import Namespace="System.Data" %>
<%@ Import Namespace="System.Data.SqlClient" %>
<%@ Import Namespace="System.Configuration" %>

<script runat="server">
    Protected Sub Page_Load(ByVal sender As Object, _
            ByVal e As System.EventArgs)

        If Not Page.IsPostBack Then
            Dim MyDataTable As DataTable
            Dim MyReader As SqlDataReader
            Dim CityParam As SqlParameter

            Dim MyConnection As SqlConnection = New SqlConnection()
            MyConnection.ConnectionString = _
        ConfigurationManager.ConnectionStrings("DSN_Northwind").ConnectionString

            Dim MyCommand As SqlCommand = New SqlCommand()
            MyCommand.CommandText = _
                    "SELECT * FROM CUSTOMERS WHERE CITY = @CITY"
            MyCommand.CommandType = CommandType.Text
            MyCommand.Connection = MyConnection

            CityParam = New SqlParameter()
            CityParam.ParameterName = "@CITY"
            CityParam.SqlDbType = SqlDbType.VarChar
            CityParam.Size = 15
            CityParam.Direction = ParameterDirection.Input
            CityParam.Value = "London"

            MyCommand.Parameters.Add(CityParam)

            MyCommand.Connection.Open()
            MyReader = MyCommand.ExecuteReader(CommandBehavior.CloseConnection)
```

```
            MyDataTable = New DataTable()

            ' Loading DataTable using a DataReader
            MyDataTable.Load(MyReader)

            gvCustomers.DataSource = MyDataTable
            gvCustomers.DataBind()

            MyDataTable.Dispose()
            MyCommand.Dispose()
            MyConnection.Dispose()
        End If

    End Sub

</script>
```

C#

```
<%@ Page Language="C#" %>
<%@ Import Namespace="System.Data" %>
<%@ Import Namespace="System.Data.SqlClient" %>
<%@ Import Namespace="System.Configuration" %>

<script runat="server">
    protected void Page_Load(object sender, EventArgs e)
    {
        if (!Page.IsPostBack )
        {
            DataTable MyDataTable;
            SqlDataReader MyReader;
            SqlParameter CityParam;

            SqlConnection MyConnection = new SqlConnection();
            MyConnection.ConnectionString =
        ConfigurationManager.ConnectionStrings["DSN_Northwind"].ConnectionString;

            SqlCommand MyCommand = new SqlCommand();
            MyCommand.CommandText =
               "SELECT * FROM CUSTOMERS WHERE CITY = @CITY";
            MyCommand.CommandType = CommandType.Text;
            MyCommand.Connection = MyConnection;

            CityParam = new SqlParameter();
            CityParam.ParameterName = "@CITY";
            CityParam.SqlDbType = SqlDbType.VarChar;
            CityParam.Size = 15;
            CityParam.Direction = ParameterDirection.Input;
            CityParam.Value = "London";

            MyCommand.Parameters.Add(CityParam);
            MyCommand.Connection.Open();
            MyReader = MyCommand.ExecuteReader(CommandBehavior.CloseConnection);
```

Continued

```
            MyDataTable = new DataTable();

            // Loading DataTable using a DataReader
            MyDataTable.Load(MyReader);

            gvCustomers.DataSource = MyDataTable;
            gvCustomers.DataBind();

            MyDataTable.Dispose();
            MyCommand.Dispose();
            MyConnection.Dispose();
        }
    }
</script>
```

Not only can you load a `DataTable` object from a `DataReader` object, you can also retrieve a `DataTableReader` from an existing `DataTable` object. This is accomplished by calling the `CreateDataReader` method of the `DataTable` class. This method returns an instance of the `DataTableReader` object that can be passed to any method that expects to receive a `DataReader`.

Deciding When to Use a DataSet

As revolutionary as a `DataSet` might be, it is not the best choice in every situation. Often, it may not be appropriate to use a `DataSet`; instead it might be better to use a `DataReader`.

With ADO 2.6, it was possible to perform a command upon a data store and get back a single collection of data made up of any number of rows. You could then iterate through this collection of data and use it in some fashion. Now ADO.NET can use the `DataSet` to return a collection of data that actually keeps its structure when removed from the data store. In some situations, you benefit greatly from keeping this copy in its original format. By doing so, you can keep the data disconnected in an in-memory cache in its separate tables and work with the tables individually or apply relationships between the tables. You can work with the tables in much the same manner as you do with other relational data sources — using a parent/child relationship. If it is to your advantage to work with certain data with all its relationships in place (in order to enforce a parent/child relationship upon the data); in this case, of course, it is better to use a `DataSet` as opposed to a `DataReader`.

Because the `DataSet` is a disconnected copy of the data, you can work with the same records repeatedly without having to go back to the data store. This capability can greatly increase performance and lessen the load upon the server. Having a copy of the data separate from the data store also enables you to continuously handle and shape the data locally. For instance, you might need to repeatedly filter or sort through a collection of data. In this case, it would be of great advantage to work with a `DataSet` rather than going back and forth to the data store itself.

Probably one of the greatest uses of the `DataSet` is to work with multiple data stores and come away with a single collection of data. So for instance, if you have your Customers table within SQL and the orders information for those particular customers within an Oracle database, you can very easily query each data store and create a single `DataSet` with a Customers and an Orders table in place that you can use in any fashion you choose. The DataSet is just a means of storage for data and doesn't concern itself with where the data came from. So, if you are working with data that is coming from multiple data stores, it is to your benefit to use the `DataSet`.

Because the `DataSet` is based upon XML and XML Schemas, it is quite easy to move the `DataSet` around — whether you are transporting it across tiers, processes or between disparate systems or applications. If the application or system to which you are transferring the `DataSet` doesn't understand `DataSets`, the `DataSet` represents itself as an XML file. So basically, any system or application that can interpret and understand XML can work with the `DataSet`. This makes it a very popular transport vehicle, and you see an example of it when you transport the `DataSet` from an XML Web service.

Last but not least, the `DataSet` enables you to program data with ease. It is much simpler than anything that has been provided before the .NET Framework came to the scene. Putting the data within a class object allows you to programmatically access the `DataSet`. The code example in Listing 8-12 shows you just how easy it can be.

Listing 8-12: An example of working with the DataSet object

VB

```
Dim conn As SqlConnection = New SqlConnection _
   (ConfigurationManager.ConnectionStrings("DSN_Northwind").ConnectionString)
conn.Open()
Dim da As SqlDataAdapter = New SqlDataAdapter("Select * from Customers", conn)
Dim ds As DataSet = New DataSet()
da.Fill(ds, "CustomersTable")
```

C#

```
SqlConnection conn = new SqlConnection
   (ConfigurationManager.ConnectionStrings["DSN_Northwind"].ConnectionString);
conn.Open();
SqlDataAdapter da = new SqlDataAdapter("Select * from Customers", conn);
DataSet ds = new DataSet();
da.Fill(ds, "CustomersTable");
```

Basically, when you work with data, you have to weigh when to use the `DataSet`. In some cases, you get extreme benefits from using this piece of technology that is provided with ADO.NET. Sometimes, however, you may find it is not in your best interests to use the `DataSet`. Instead, it is best to use the `DataReader`.

The `DataSet` can be used whenever you choose, but sometimes you would rather use the `DataReader` and work directly against the data store. By using the command objects, such as the `SqlCommand` and the `OleDbCommand` objects, you have a little more direct control over what is executed and what you get back as a result set. In situations where this is vital, it is to your advantage not to use the `DataSet`.

When you don't use the `DataSet`, you don't incur the cost of extra overhead because you are reading and writing directly to the data source. Performing operations in this manner means you don't have to instantiate any additional objects — avoiding unnecessary steps.

This is especially true in a situation when you work with Web Forms in ASP.NET. If you are dealing with Web Forms, the Web pages are re-created each and every time. When this happens, not only is the page re-created by the call to the data source, the `DataSet` is also re-created unless you are caching the `DataSet` in some fashion. This can be an expensive process; so, in situations such as this, you might find it to your benefit to work directly off the data source using the `DataReader`. In most situations when you are working with Web Forms, you want to work with the DataReader instead of creating a DataSet.

The Typed DataSet

As powerful as the DataSet is, it still has some limitations. The DataSet is created at runtime. It accesses particular pieces of data by making certain assumptions. Take a look at how you normally access a specific field in a DataSet that is not strongly typed (Listing 8-13).

Listing 8-13: Accessing a field in a DataSet

VB

```
ds.Tables("Customers").Rows(0).Columns("CompanyName") = "XYZ Company"
```

C#

```
ds.Tables["Customers"].Rows[0].Columns["CompanyName"] = "XYZ Company";
```

The preceding code looks at the Customers table, the first row (remember, everything is zero-based) in the column CompanyName, and assigns the value of XYZ Company to the field. This is pretty simple and straightforward, but it is based upon certain assumptions and is generated at runtime. The "Customers" and "CompanyName" words are string literals in this line of code. If they are spelled wrong or if these items aren't in the table, an error occurs at runtime.

Listing 8-14 shows you how to assign the same value to the same field by using a typed DataSet.

Listing 8-14: Accessing a field in a typed DataSet

VB

```
ds.Customers(0).CompanyName = "XYZ Company"
```

C#

```
ds.Customers[0].CompanyName = "XYZ Company";
```

Now the table name and the field to be accessed are not treated as string literals but, instead, are encased in an XML Schema and a class that is generated from the DataSet class. When you create a typed DataSet, you are creating a class that implements the tables and fields based upon the schema used to generate the class. Basically, the schema is coded into the class.

As you compare the two examples, you see that a typed DataSet is easier to read and understand. It is less error-prone, and errors are realized at compile time as opposed to runtime.

In the end, typed DataSets are optional, and you are free to use either style as you code.

Using Oracle as Your Database with ASP.NET 3.5

If you work in the enterprise space, in many cases you must work with an Oracle backend database. ADO.NET 2.0 has a built-in capability to work with Oracle using the System.Data.OracleClient namespace.

First, in order to connect ASP.NET to your Oracle database, you install the Oracle 10 g Client on your Web server. You can get this piece of software from the Oracle Web site found at `oracle.com`. If you are able to connect to your Oracle database from your Web server using SQL*Plus (an Oracle IDE for working with an Oracle database), can use the Microsoft-built Oracle data provider, `System.Data.OracleClient`.

If you are still having trouble connecting to your Oracle database, you also may try to make sure that the database connection is properly defined in your server's .ora file found at `C:\Oracle\product\10.1.0\Client_1\NETWORK\ADMIN`. *Note that the version number might be different.*

After you know you can connect to Oracle, you can make use of the Microsoft-built Oracle data provider. To utilize the built-in capabilities to connect to Oracle, your ASP.NET application must reference this DLL. To do this, right-click your project in the Visual Studio Solution Explorer and select Add Reference from the list of options presented. This gives you a long list of available .NET components. Select the `System.Data.OracleClient component`. Notice the two versions of this component (as illustrated in Figure 8-4). You select the one that is built for the .NET Framework 2.0.

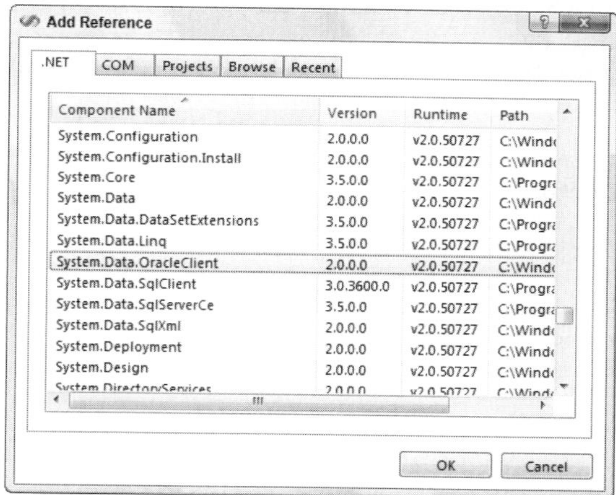

Figure 8-4

After this is added, you find the reference to this component in the `web.config` file of your ASP.NET application (as presented in Listing 8-15).

Listing 8-15: The reference to the System.Data.OracleClient DLL in the web.config

```
<configuration>
   <system.web>
      <compilation debug="true">
         <assemblies>
            <add assembly="System.Data.OracleClient,
                Version=2.0.0.0, Culture=neutral,
                PublicKeyToken=B77A5C561934E089"/>
```

Continued

```
        </assemblies>
      </compilation>
   </system.web>
</configuration>
```

With this reference in place, you also reference this available DLL in your page along with `System.Data`. This is demonstrated in Listing 8-16.

Listing 8-16: Referencing the System.Data.OracleClient DLL

VB

```
Imports System.Data
Imports System.Data.OracleClient
```

C#

```
using System.Data;
using System.Data.OracleClient;
```

With all the references in place, you are able to work with an Oracle backend in pretty much the same manner as you work with a SQL Server backend. Listing 8-17 shows you just how similar it is.

Listing 8-17: Using the OracleClient object to connect to an Oracle database

VB

```
Dim conn As OracleConnection
Dim cmd As OracleCommand

Dim cmdString As String = "Select CompanyName from Customers"
conn = New _
   OracleConnection("User Id=bevjen;Password=bevjen01;Data Source=myOracleDB")
cmd = New OracleCommand(cmdString, conn)
cmd.CommandType = CommandType.Text

conn.Open()
```

C#

```
OracleConnection conn;
OracleCommand cmd;

string cmdString = "Select CompanyName from Customers";
conn = new
   OracleConnection("User Id=bevjen;Password=bevjen01;Data Source=myOracleDB");
cmd = new OracleCommand(cmdString, conn);
cmd.CommandType = CommandType.Text;

conn.Open();
```

After you are connected and performing the PL-SQL commands you want, you can use the `OracleDataReader` object just as you would use the `SqlDataReader` object.

Notice that, in this section, I have made reference to the Microsoft-built Oracle data provider. Another option, and many developers consider this the better option, is to use the Oracle-built ODP.NET data provider instead. This data provider can be freely downloaded from the Oracle download page at `oracle.com`. *You can then reference this new DLL in your project. It is now simply a matter of importing and working with* `System.DataAccess.OracleClient` *in your applications. The Oracle-built data provider contains the capability to work with the more advanced feature provided from the Oracle 10g database.*

The DataList Server Control

The DataList control has been around since the beginning of ASP.NET. It is part of a series of controls that enable you to display your data (especially repeated types of data) using templates. Templates enable you to create more sophisticated layouts for your data and perform functionss that controls such as the GridView server control cannot.

Template-based controls like the DataList control require more work on your part. For instance, you have to build common tasks for yourself. You cannot rely on other data controls, which you might be used to, such as paging.

Looking at the Available Templates

The idea, when using template-based controls such as the DataList control, is that you put together specific templates to create your desired detailed layout. The DataList control has a number of templates that you can use to build your display. The available templates are defined here in the following table:

Template	Description
`AlternatingItemTemplate`	Works in conjunction with the `ItemTemplate` to provide a layout for all the odd rows within the layout. This is commonly used if you want to have a grid or layout where each row is distinguished in some way (such as having a different background color).
`EditItemTemplate`	Allows for a row or item to be defined on how it looks and behaves when editing.
`FooterTemplate`	Allows the last item in the template to be defined. If this is not defined, then no footer will be used.
`HeaderTemplate`	Allows the first item in the template to be defined. If this is not defined, then no header will be used.
`ItemTemplate`	The core template that is used to define a row or layout for each item in the display.
`SelectedItemTemplate`	Allows for a row or item to be defined on how it looks and behaves when selected.
`SeparatorTemplate`	The layout of any separator that is used between the items in the display.

Working with ItemTemplate

Although you have seven templates available to you for use with the DataList control, at a minimum, you are going to need the ItemTemplate. The following example, shown here in Listing 8-18, shows the company names from the Northwind database.

Listing 8-18: Showing the company names from the Northwind database using DataList

```
<%@ Page Language="VB" AutoEventWireup="false" CodeFile="DataListControl.aspx.vb"
    Inherits="DataListControl" %>

<html xmlns="http://www.w3.org/1999/xhtml">
<head runat="server">
    <title>DataList Control</title>
</head>
<body>
    <form id="form1" runat="server">
    <div>
        <asp:DataList ID="DataList1" runat="server" DataSourceID="SqlDataSource1">
            <ItemTemplate>
                Company Name:
                <asp:Label ID="CompanyNameLabel" runat="server"
                    Text='<%# Eval("CompanyName") %>' />
                <br />
                <br />
            </ItemTemplate>
        </asp:DataList>
        <asp:SqlDataSource ID="SqlDataSource1" runat="server"
            ConnectionString="<%$ ConnectionStrings:DSN_Northwind %>"
            SelectCommand="SELECT [CompanyName] FROM [Customers]">
        </asp:SqlDataSource>
    </div>
    </form>
</body>
</html>
```

As stated, the DataList control requires, at a minimum, an `ItemTemplate` element where you define the page layout for each item that is encountered from the data source. In this case, all the data is pulled from the Northwind database sample using the SqlDataSource control. The SqlDataSource control pulls only the CompanyName column from the Customers table. From there, the ItemTemplate section of the DataList control defines two items within it. The first item is a static item, "Company Name:" followed by a single ASP.NET server control, the Label server control. Second, the item is then followed by a couple of standard HTML elements. The `Text` property of the Label control uses inline data binding (as shown in the previous chapter of this book) to bind the values that are coming out of the SqlDataSource control. If there were more than one data point coming out of the SqlDataSource control, you can still specifically grab the data point that you are interested in using by specifying the item in the `Eval` statement.

```
<asp:Label ID="CompanyNameLabel" runat="server"
 Text='<%# Eval("CompanyName") %>' />
```

Using the code from Listing 8-18 gives you the following results as illustrated in Figure 8-5.

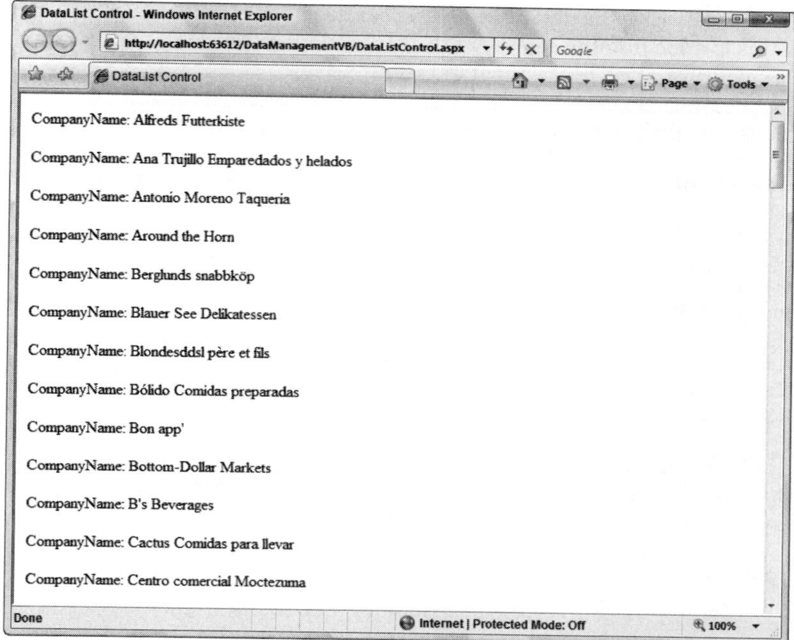

Figure 8-5

If you then look at the source of the page, you can see that the DataList control uses tables by default to lay out the elements.

```
<table id="DataList1" cellspacing="0" border="0" style="border-collapse:collapse;">
   <tr>
      <td>
         CompanyName:
         <span id="DataList1_ctl00_CompanyNameLabel">Alfreds Futterkiste</span>
         <br />
         <br />
      </td>
   </tr><tr>
      <td>
         CompanyName:
         <span id="DataList1_ctl01_CompanyNameLabel">
          Ana Trujillo Emparedados y helados</span>
         <br />
         <br />
      </td>
   </tr>

   <!-- Code removed for clarity -->

</table>
```

Although this table layout is the default, you can change this so that the DataList control outputs <span> tags instead. This is done through the use of the RepeatLayout property of the DataList control. You will need to rework your DataList, as is shown in Listing 8-19.

Listing 8-19: Changing the output style using RepeatLayout

```
<asp:DataList ID="DataList1" runat="server" DataSourceID="SqlDataSource1"
 RepeatLayout="Flow">
   <ItemTemplate>
    Company Name:
    <asp:Label ID="CompanyNameLabel" runat="server"
     Text='<%# Eval("CompanyName") %>' />
    <br />
    <br />
   </ItemTemplate>
</asp:DataList>
```

The possible options for the RepeatLayout property are either Table or Flow. Table is the default setting. The output you will get when looking at the source of the page when using the Flow setting is presented here:

```
<span id="DataList1">
   <span>
      CompanyName:
      <span id="DataList1_ctl00_CompanyNameLabel">Alfreds Futterkiste</span>
         <br />
         <br />
      </span><br />
   <span>
      CompanyName:
      <span id="DataList1_ctl01_CompanyNameLabel">
       Ana Trujillo Emparedados y helados</span>
      <br />
      <br />
   </span>

   <!-- Code removed for clarity -->

</span>
```

Working with Other Layout Templates

You will find that the other templates are just as easy to work with as the ItemTemplate. Listing 8-20 shows you how to add the AlternatingItemTemplate and the SeparatorTemplate to the company name display.

Listing 8-20: Using both the AlternatingItemTemplate and the SeparatorTemplate

```
<%@ Page Language="VB" AutoEventWireup="false" CodeFile="DataListControl.aspx.vb"
    Inherits="DataListControl" %>

<html xmlns="http://www.w3.org/1999/xhtml">
```

```
<head runat="server">
    <title>DataList Control</title>
</head>
<body>
    <form id="form1" runat="server">
    <div>
        <asp:DataList ID="DataList1" runat="server" DataSourceID="SqlDataSource1">
            <ItemTemplate>
                Company Name:
                <asp:Label ID="CompanyNameLabel" runat="server"
                    Text='<%# Eval("CompanyName") %>' />
                <br />
                <br />
            </ItemTemplate>
            <AlternatingItemTemplate>
                CompanyName:
                <asp:Label ID="CompanyNameLabel" runat="server"
                 BackColor="LightGray"
                 Text='<%# Eval("CompanyName") %>' />
                <br />
                <br />
            </AlternatingItemTemplate>
            <SeparatorTemplate>
                <hr />
            </SeparatorTemplate>
        </asp:DataList>
        <asp:SqlDataSource ID="SqlDataSource1" runat="server"
            ConnectionString="<%$ ConnectionStrings:DSN_Northwind %>"
            SelectCommand="SELECT [CompanyName] FROM [Customers]">
        </asp:SqlDataSource>
    </div>
    </form>
</body>
</html>
```

In this case, the AlternatingItemTemplate is a repeat of the ItemTemplate, but the addition of the `BackColor` property to the Label control is contained within the item. The SeparatorTemplate is used between each item, whether it is from the ItemTemplate or the AlternatingItemTemplate. In this case, a simple `<hr />` element is used to draw a line between each item. The output of this is shown here in Figure 8-6.

This process allows you to change how items are defined within the alternating rows and to put a separator between the elements. If you wanted just alternating row colors or an alternating style, it might not always be the best approach to use the `<AlternatingItemTemplate>` element, but you will find that it is better to use the `<AlternatingItemStyle>` element instead. This approach is presented here in Listing 8-21.

Listing 8-21: Using template styles

```
<asp:DataList ID="DataList1" runat="server" DataSourceID="SqlDataSource1"
 BackColor="White" BorderColor="#999999" BorderStyle="Solid" BorderWidth="1px"
 CellPadding="3" ForeColor="Black" GridLines="Vertical">
   <FooterStyle BackColor="#CCCCCC" />
```

Continued

```
        <AlternatingItemStyle BackColor="#CCCCCC" />
        <SelectedItemStyle BackColor="#000099" Font-Bold="True" ForeColor="White" />
        <HeaderStyle BackColor="Black" Font-Bold="True" ForeColor="White" />
        <ItemTemplate>
            CompanyName:
            <asp:Label ID="CompanyNameLabel" runat="server"
             Text='<%# Eval("CompanyName") %>' />
            <br />
            <br />
        </ItemTemplate>
    </asp:DataList>
```

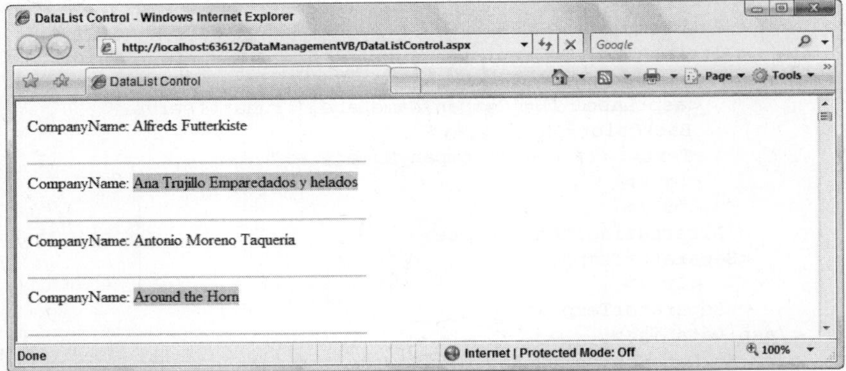

Figure 8-6

You will notice that each of the available templates also have an associated style element. Figure 8-7 shows the use of these styles.

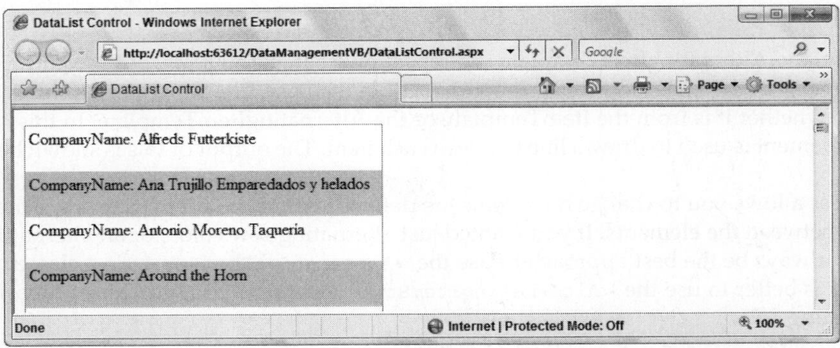

Figure 8-7

Working with Multiple Columns

Template-based controls are better at displaying items in multiple columns than other controls, such as the GridView control. The `RepeatColumns` property takes care of this. The code to make use of this property is shown in Listing 8-22.

Listing 8-22: Creating multiple columns using the RepeatColumns property

```
<asp:DataList ID="DataList1" runat="server" DataSourceID="SqlDataSource1"
 CellPadding="2" RepeatColumns="3" RepeatDirection="Horizontal">
   <ItemTemplate>
    Company Name:
    <asp:Label ID="CompanyNameLabel" runat="server"
     Text='<%# Eval("CompanyName") %>' />
    <br />
    <br />
   </ItemTemplate>
</asp:DataList>
```

Running this bit of code in your page produces the results shown in Figure 8-8.

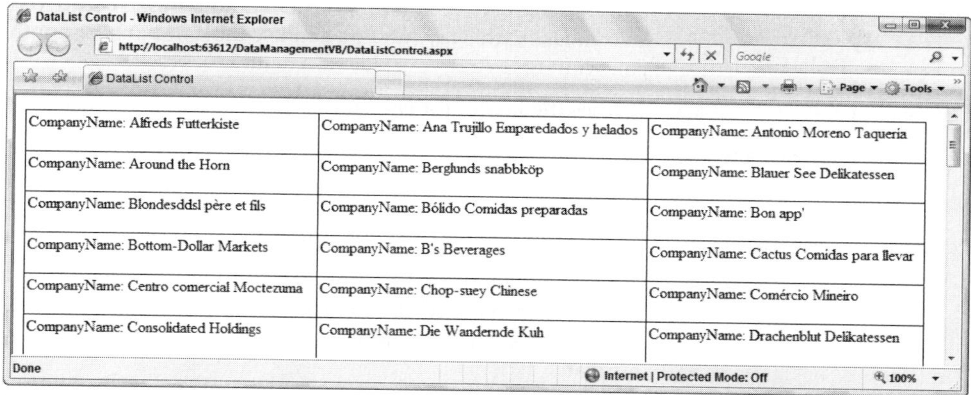

Figure 8-8

The `RepeatDirection` property instructs the DataList control about how to lay out the items bound to the control on the Web page. Possible values include `Vertical` and `Horizontal`. The default value is `Vertical`. Setting it to `Vertical` with a `RepeatColumn` setting of `3` gives the following results:

```
Item1    Item5    Item9
Item2    Item6    Item10
Item3    Item7    Item11
Item4    Item8    Item12
```

When the `RepeatDirection` property is set to `Horizontal`, you get the items laid out in a horizontal fashion:

```
Item1    Item2    Item3
Item4    Item5    Item6
Item7    Item8    Item9
Item10   Item11   Item12
```

The ListView Server Control

One of the newest template-based controls is the ListView control. This is a control that is only available in the 3.5 version of the .NET Framework. This control is considered a better alternative to the DataList control. You will find that this control gives you more control over the layout and works quite nicely in Visual Studio because it provides a set of wizards to easily set up your layout with the most common options.

Looking at the Available Templates

As with the DataList control, the ListView control has a series of available templates at your disposal. Each one of these templates controls a specific aspect of the layout. The following table defines the layout options available to this control.

Template	Description
`LayoutTemplate`	The core template that allows you to define the structure of the entire layout. Using this layout, you can use tables, spans, or anything else you want to layout your data elements.
`ItemTemplate`	Defines the layout for each individual item in the data collection.
`ItemSeparatorTemplate`	Defines the layout of any separator that is used between items.
`GroupTemplate`	A group container element that can contain any number of data items.
`GroupSeparatorTemplate`	Defines the layout of any separator that is used between groups.
`EmptyItemTemplate`	Defines the layout of the empty items that might be contained within a group. For instance, if you group by ten items and the last page contains only seven items, then the last three items will use this template.
`EmptyDataTemplate`	Defines the layout for items that do not contain data.
`SelectedItemTemplate`	Allows for a row or item to be defined on how it looks and behaves when selected.
`AlternatingItemTemplate`	Works in conjunction with the `ItemTemplate` to provide a layout for all the odd rows within the layout. This is commonly used if you want to have a grid or layout where each row is distinguished in some way (such as having a different background color).
`EditItemTemplate`	Allows for a row or item to be defined on how it looks and behaves when editing.
`InsertItemTemplate`	Allows for a row or item to be defined on how it looks and behaves when performing an insert.

Next, the following sections look at using some of these in your ASP.NET page.

Using the Templates

In creating a page that makes use of the ListView control, the first step will be to create a basic page with a ListView control on it, as illustrated here in Listing 8-23.

Listing 8-23: Creating the base page

```
<%@ Page Language="VB" AutoEventWireup="false" CodeFile="ListViewControl.aspx.vb"
    Inherits="ListViewControl" %>

<html xmlns="http://www.w3.org/1999/xhtml">
<head runat="server">
    <title>ListView Control</title>
</head>
<body>
    <form id="form1" runat="server">
    <div>

        <asp:ListView ID="ListView1" runat="server" DataKeyNames="CustomerID"
            DataSourceID="SqlDataSource1">
        </asp:ListView>

        <asp:SqlDataSource ID="SqlDataSource1" runat="server"
            ConnectionString="<%$ ConnectionStrings:DSN_Northwind %>"
            SelectCommand="SELECT * FROM [Customers] ORDER BY [CompanyName]"
            InsertCommand="INSERT INTO [Customers] ([CustomerID], [CompanyName],
               [ContactName], [ContactTitle], [Address], [City], [Region],
               [PostalCode], [Country], [Phone], [Fax]) VALUES (@CustomerID,
               @CompanyName, @ContactName, @ContactTitle, @Address, @City, @Region,
               @PostalCode, @Country, @Phone, @Fax)"
            UpdateCommand="UPDATE [Customers] SET [CompanyName] = @CompanyName,
               [ContactName] = @ContactName, [ContactTitle] = @ContactTitle,
               [Address] = @Address, [City] = @City, [Region] = @Region,
               [PostalCode] = @PostalCode, [Country] = @Country, [Phone] = @Phone,
               [Fax] = @Fax WHERE [CustomerID] = @CustomerID">
            <UpdateParameters>
                <asp:Parameter Name="CompanyName" Type="String" />
                <asp:Parameter Name="ContactName" Type="String" />
                <asp:Parameter Name="ContactTitle" Type="String" />
                <asp:Parameter Name="Address" Type="String" />
                <asp:Parameter Name="City" Type="String" />
                <asp:Parameter Name="Region" Type="String" />
                <asp:Parameter Name="PostalCode" Type="String" />
                <asp:Parameter Name="Country" Type="String" />
                <asp:Parameter Name="Phone" Type="String" />
                <asp:Parameter Name="Fax" Type="String" />
                <asp:Parameter Name="CustomerID" Type="String" />
            </UpdateParameters>
            <InsertParameters>
                <asp:Parameter Name="CustomerID" Type="String" />
                <asp:Parameter Name="CompanyName" Type="String" />
                <asp:Parameter Name="ContactName" Type="String" />
                <asp:Parameter Name="ContactTitle" Type="String" />
                <asp:Parameter Name="Address" Type="String" />
                <asp:Parameter Name="City" Type="String" />
                <asp:Parameter Name="Region" Type="String" />
                <asp:Parameter Name="PostalCode" Type="String" />
                <asp:Parameter Name="Country" Type="String" />
```

Continued

```
                <asp:Parameter Name="Phone" Type="String" />
                <asp:Parameter Name="Fax" Type="String" />
            </InsertParameters>
        </asp:SqlDataSource>
    </div>
    </form>
</body>
</html>
```

In this case, you have a base ListView control and a SqlDataSource control that has been wired up to the Northwind sample database and provided Select, Update, and Insert methods. The ListView control itself is then bound to the SqlDataSource control. It provides the primary key of the table for working with the various queries through the use of the `DataKeyNames` property.

Creating the Layout Template

The next step is to create the layout of the overall control using the LayoutTemplate. The use of this template is illustrated in Listing 8-24.

Listing 8-24: Using the LayoutTemplate element

```
<LayoutTemplate>
   <table runat="server">
      <tr runat="server">
         <td runat="server">
            <table ID="itemPlaceholderContainer" runat="server" border="1"
             style="background-color: #FFFFFF;border-collapse: collapse;
                    border-color: #999999;border-style:none;border-width:1px;
                    font-family: Verdana, Arial, Helvetica, sans-serif;">
              <tr runat="server" style="background-color:#DCDCDC;color: #000000;">
                 <th runat="server"></th>
                 <th runat="server">Customer ID</th>
                 <th runat="server">Company Name</th>
                 <th runat="server">Contact Name</th>
              </tr>
              <tr ID="itemPlaceholder" runat="server"></tr>
            </table>
         </td>
      </tr>
      <tr runat="server">
         <td runat="server" style="text-align: center;background-color: #CCCCCC;
          font-family: Verdana, Arial, Helvetica, sans-serif;color: #000000;">
            <asp:DataPager ID="DataPager1" runat="server">
               <Fields>
                  <asp:NextPreviousPagerField ButtonType="Button"
                   ShowFirstPageButton="True" ShowNextPageButton="False"
                   ShowPreviousPageButton="False" />
                  <asp:NumericPagerField />
                  <asp:NextPreviousPagerField ButtonType="Button"
                   ShowLastPageButton="True" ShowNextPageButton="False"
                   ShowPreviousPageButton="False" />
               </Fields>
```

```
            </asp:DataPager>
          </td>
        </tr>
      </table>
    </LayoutTemplate>
```

This layout template constructs the layout as a grid using tables to layout the items. A styled table is defined with a header in place. The most important part of laying out the template is that the container itself is defined using a control with the `ID` value of `itemPlaceholderContainer`. The element will also need to be made a server control by adding the `runat` property.

```
<table ID="itemPlaceholderContainer" runat="server" border="1"
 style="background-color: #FFFFFF;border-collapse: collapse;
 border-color: #999999;border-style:none;border-width:1px;
 font-family: Verdana, Arial, Helvetica, sans-serif;">

</table>
```

The placeholder for each data item needs to take the same form, but the `ID` of the server control you make needs to have a value of `itemPlaceholder`.

```
<table ID="itemPlaceholderContainer" runat="server" border="1"
 style="background-color: #FFFFFF;border-collapse: collapse;
 border-color: #999999;border-style:none;border-width:1px;
 font-family: Verdana, Arial, Helvetica, sans-serif;">
   <tr runat="server" style="background-color:#DCDCDC;color: #000000;">
      <th runat="server"></th>
      <th runat="server">Customer ID</th>
      <th runat="server">Company Name</th>
      <th runat="server">Contact Name</th>
   </tr>
   <tr ID="itemPlaceholder" runat="server"></tr>
</table>
```

It is important to keep the `itemPlaceholder` element within the itemPlaceholderContainer control, within the layout template. It cannot sit outside of the container.

The final part of this layout is the new DataPager server control. This new server control is part of ASP.NET 3.5.

```
<asp:DataPager ID="DataPager1" runat="server">
   <Fields>
      <asp:NextPreviousPagerField ButtonType="Button"
       ShowFirstPageButton="True" ShowNextPageButton="False"
       ShowPreviousPageButton="False" />
      <asp:NumericPagerField />
      <asp:NextPreviousPagerField ButtonType="Button"
       ShowLastPageButton="True" ShowNextPageButton="False"
       ShowPreviousPageButton="False" />
   </Fields>
</asp:DataPager>
```

The DataPager works with template-based data in allowing you to control how end users move across the pages of the data collection.

Now that the LayoutTemplate is in place, the next step is to create the ItemTemplate.

Creating the ItemTemplate

The ItemTemplate that you create is quite similar to the ItemTemplate that is part of the DataList control that was discussed earlier. In this case, however, the ItemTemplate is placed in the specific spot within the layout of the page where you defined the itemPlaceholder control to be. Listing 8-25 shows the ItemTemplate for this example.

Listing 8-25: Building the ItemTemplate

```
<ItemTemplate>
   <tr style="background-color:#DCDCDC;color: #000000;">
      <td>
         <asp:Button ID="EditButton" runat="server"
          CommandName="Edit" Text="Edit" />
      </td>
      <td>
         <asp:Label ID="CustomerIDLabel" runat="server"
          Text='<%# Eval("CustomerID") %>' />
      </td>
      <td>
         <asp:Label ID="CompanyNameLabel" runat="server"
          Text='<%# Eval("CompanyName") %>' />
      </td>
      <td>
         <asp:Label ID="ContactNameLabel" runat="server"
          Text='<%# Eval("ContactName") %>' />
      </td>
   </tr>
</ItemTemplate>
```

Creating the EditItemTemplate

The EditItemTemplate is the area that shows up when you decide to edit the data item (in this case, a row of data). Listing 8-26 shows the EditItemTemplate in use.

Listing 8-26: Building the EditItemTemplate

```
<EditItemTemplate>
   <tr style="background-color:#008A8C;color: #FFFFFF;">
      <td>
         <asp:Button ID="UpdateButton" runat="server"
          CommandName="Update" Text="Update" />
         <asp:Button ID="CancelButton" runat="server"
          CommandName="Cancel" Text="Cancel" />
      </td>
      <td>
         <asp:Label ID="CustomerIDLabel1" runat="server"
          Text='<%# Eval("CustomerID") %>' />
      </td>
```

```
        <td>
            <asp:TextBox ID="CompanyNameTextBox" runat="server"
             Text='<%# Bind("CompanyName") %>' />
        </td>
        <td>
            <asp:TextBox ID="ContactNameTextBox" runat="server"
             Text='<%# Bind("ContactName") %>' />
        </td>
    </tr>
</EditItemTemplate>
```

In this case, the EditItemTemplate, when shown, displays an Update and Cancel button to manipulate the editing options. When editing, the values are placed within text boxes and the values are then updated into the database through the `Update`command.

Creating the EmptyItemTemplate

If there are no values in the database, then you should prepare to gracefully show something in your layout. The `EmptyItemTemplate` is used in Listing 8-27 to perform that operation.

Listing 8-27: Building the EmptyItemTemplate

```
<EmptyDataTemplate>
    <table runat="server"
     style="background-color: #FFFFFF;border-collapse: collapse;
         border-color: #999999;border-style:none;border-width:1px;">
        <tr>
            <td>No data was returned.</td>
        </tr>
    </table>
</EmptyDataTemplate>
```

Creating the InsertItemTemplate

The last section looked at here is the `InsertItemTemplate`. This section allows you to define how a form should be laid out for inserting data, similar to that used in the `ItemTemplate`, into the data store.

Listing 8-28 shows an example of the `InsertItemTemplate`.

Listing 8-28: Building the InsertItemTemplate

```
<InsertItemTemplate>
    <tr style="">
        <td>
            <asp:Button ID="InsertButton" runat="server" CommandName="Insert"
             Text="Insert" />
            <asp:Button ID="CancelButton" runat="server" CommandName="Cancel"
             Text="Clear" />
        </td>
        <td>
            <asp:TextBox ID="CustomerIDTextBox" runat="server"
             Text='<%# Bind("CustomerID") %>' />
        </td>
```

Continued

```
            <td>
                <asp:TextBox ID="CompanyNameTextBox" runat="server"
                 Text='<%# Bind("CompanyName") %>' />
            </td>
            <td>
                <asp:TextBox ID="ContactNameTextBox" runat="server"
                 Text='<%# Bind("ContactName") %>' />
            </td>
        </tr>
    </InsertItemTemplate>
```

The Results

After you have created an additional AlternatingItemTemplate that is the same as the ItemTemplate (but styled differently), you can then run the page. Then you will be presented with your own custom grid. An example is presented in Figure 8-9.

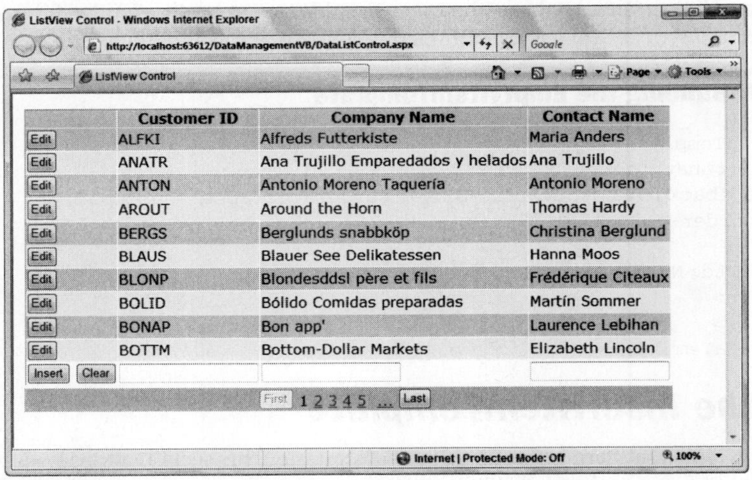

	Customer ID	Company Name	Contact Name
Edit	ALFKI	Alfreds Futterkiste	Maria Anders
Edit	ANATR	Ana Trujillo Emparedados y helados	Ana Trujillo
Edit	ANTON	Antonio Moreno Taquería	Antonio Moreno
Edit	AROUT	Around the Horn	Thomas Hardy
Edit	BERGS	Berglunds snabbköp	Christina Berglund
Edit	BLAUS	Blauer See Delikatessen	Hanna Moos
Edit	BLONP	Blondesddsl père et fils	Frédérique Citeaux
Edit	BOLID	Bólido Comidas preparadas	Martín Sommer
Edit	BONAP	Bon app'	Laurence Lebihan
Edit	BOTTM	Bottom-Dollar Markets	Elizabeth Lincoln
Insert Clear			

First 1 2 3 4 5 ... Last

Figure 8-9

From this figure, you can see that all your defined elements are in place. The header is defined through the use of the LayoutTemplate. The items in the grid are defined through the use of the ItemTemplate. The AlternatingItemTemplate, the insert form, is defined through the use of the InsertTemplate. The page navigation is defined by the new DataPager server control. Again, the DataPager control is defined within the LayoutTemplate itself.

Editing items in this template is as simple as clicking on the Edit button. This will change the view to the EditTemplate for the selected item, as illustrated in Figure 8-10.

Once you enter the edit mode here, you can change any of the values within the text boxes and then click the Update button to update the data to the new values. You can also cancel out of the operation by clicking the Cancel button.

Inserting data is as simple as filling out the form and clicking on the Insert button, as illustrated in Figure 8-11.

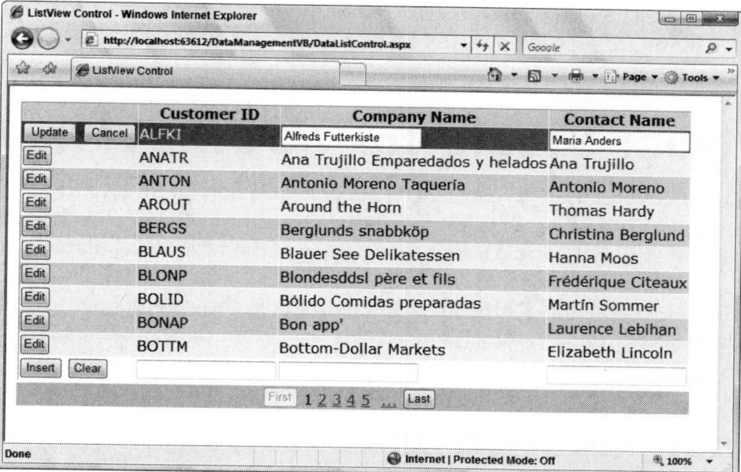

Figure 8-10

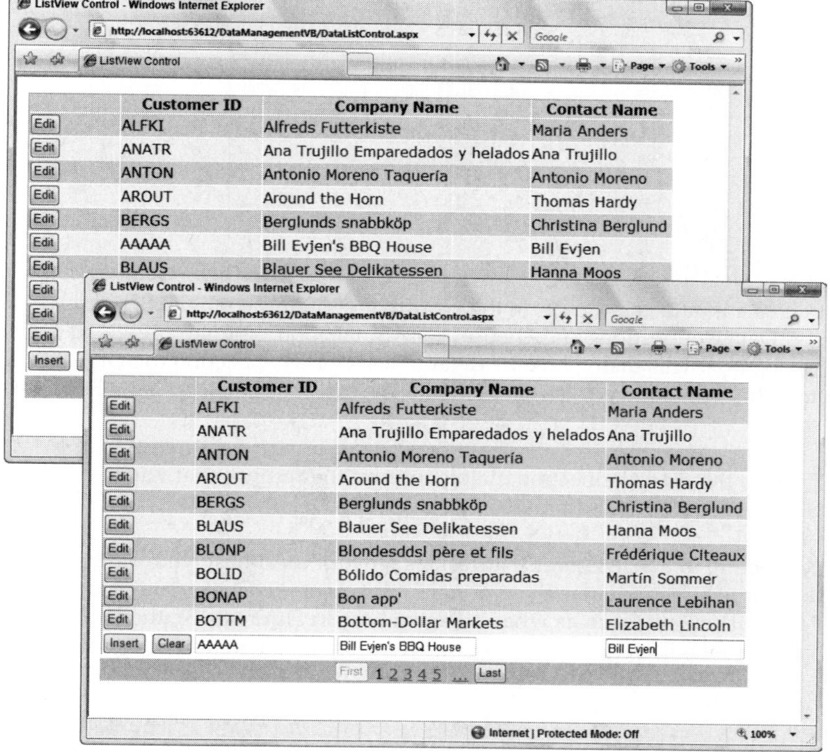

Figure 8-11

Although this example shows a grid as the output of the new ListView control, you can also structure it so that your data items are presented in any fashion you want (such as bulleted lists).

Using Visual Studio for ADO.NET Tasks

Earlier, this chapter covered how to construct a DataSet and how to fill it with data using the DataAdapter. Although you can always build this construction yourself, you also have the option of building data access into your ASP.NET applications using some of the wizards available from Visual Studio 2008.

The following example, which is a little bit of a lengthy one, shows you how to build an ASP.NET page that displays the results from a DataSet that gets its data from two separate tables. You will discover several different wizards in Visual Studio that you can work with when using ADO.NET.

Creating a Connection to the Data Source

As in code, one of the first things you do when working with data is make a connection to the data source. Visual Studio provides a visual way to make connections to your data stores. In this case, you will want to make a connection to the Northwind database in SQL Server.

When you open the Server Explorer, you will notice a section for data connections (see Figure 8-12).

Figure 8-12

The steps to create a data connection to the Northwind database in SQL Server are straightforward. Right-click on Data Connections and choose Add Connection. You are presented with the Data Link Properties dialog box. This dialog box, by default, asks for a connection to SQL Server. If you are going to connect to a different source, such as Microsoft Access, simply click on the Provider tab and change the provider.

Figure 8-13 shows the Add Connection dialog box and the settings that you need in order to connect to your local SQL Server Express Edition.

If you are connecting to a SQL Server that resides on your local host, you want to put a period (.) in the box that asks you to select or enter a server name. If you are working from a local SQL Server Express Edition file in your project (such as what is shown here in Figure 8-13), then you are going to want to use your server name with `\SQLEXPRESS`. Put in your login credentials for SQL Server and then select the database that you wish to make the connection to by using the drop-down list. The other option, if you are using a SQL Server Express Edition file, is to select the physical database file by using the Attach a Database File option.

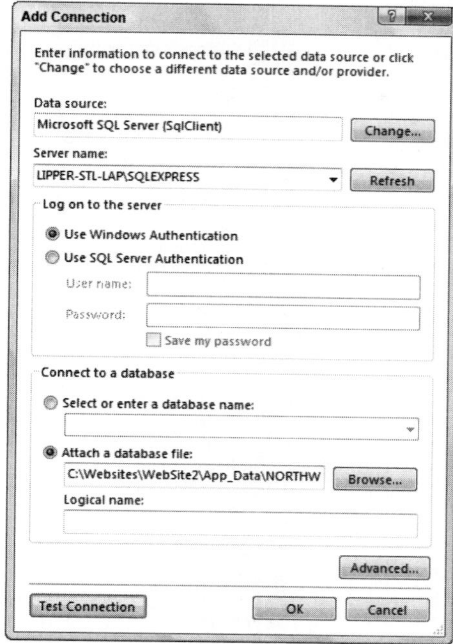

Figure 8-13

From this dialog box, you can also test the connection to ensure that everything works properly. If everything is in place, you get a confirmation stating such. Clicking OK will then cause a connection to appear in the Solution Explorer.

Expanding this connection, you find a way to access the data source just as you would by using the SQL Server Enterprise Manager (see Figure 8-14).

From here, you can work with the database and view information about all the tables and fields that are contained within the database. More specifically, you can view and work with Database Diagrams, Tables, Views, Stored Procedures, and Functions.

After you have run through this wizard, you have a connection to the Northwind database that can be used by any components that you place on any component designer that you might be working with in your application.

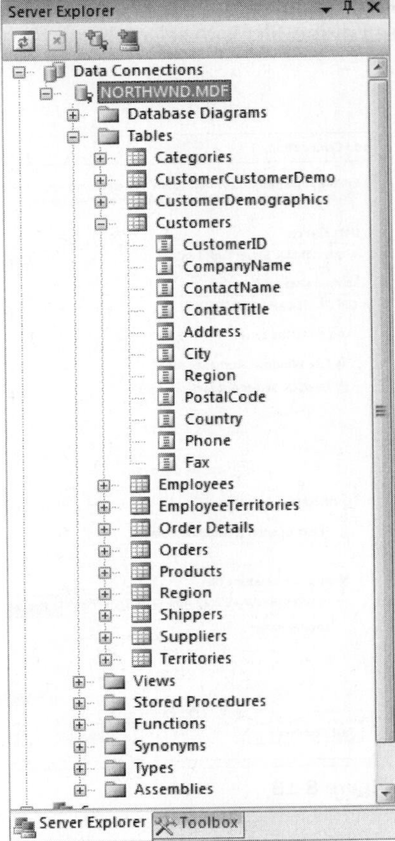

Figure 8-14

Working with a Dataset Designer

The next step is to create a typed `DataSet` object in your project that pulls its data from the Northwind database. First you need to make sure that your application has an `App_Code` folder within the solution. Right-clicking on the folder will allow you to add a new item to the folder. From the provided dialog box, add a DataSet called `CustomerOrders.xsd`. You will then be presented with the message shown in Figure 8-15.

This page is referred to as the Dataset Designer. This is the design surface for any nonvisual components that you incorporate within your `DataSet` object. Just as you can drag and drop controls onto a design surface for any Windows Forms or Web Forms application, the Dataset Designer enables you to drag and drop components onto this surface.

A component does not appear visually in your applications, but a visual representation of the component sits on the design surface. Highlighting the component allows you to modify its settings and properties in the Properties window.

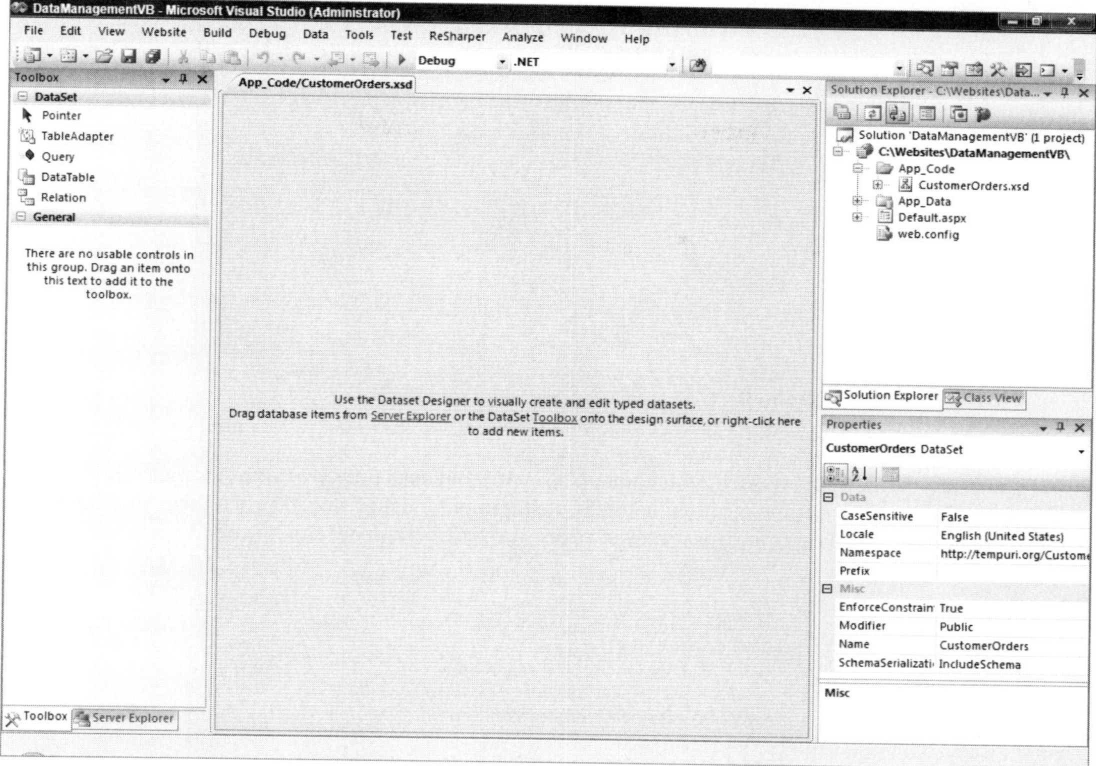

Figure 8-15

What can you drag and drop onto this surface? In the following examples, you see how to work with `TableAdapter` and `DataTable` objects on this design surface. If you open up the Toolbox window, and click the DataSet tab, you see some additional components that can be used on this design surface.

The goal of this example is to return a DataSet to the end user through an XML Web service. To accomplish this, you have to incorporate a `DataAdapter` to extract the data from the data source and to populate the `DataSet` before passing it on.

This example uses the Northwind database, and the first step you need to take is to drag and drop a `TableAdapter` onto the Dataset design surface. Dragging and dropping a `TableAdapter` onto your design surface causes a wizard to appear, as shown in Figure 8-16.

Because you want this DataSet to contain two DataTables — one for the Customers table and another for the Orders table — you have to go through this process twice.

It is important to note that the job of the `TableAdapter` object is to make the connection to the specified table as well as to perform all the select, update, insert, and delete commands that are required. For this example, you simply want the `TableAdapter` to make the select call and then later to update any changes that are made back to the SQL Server.

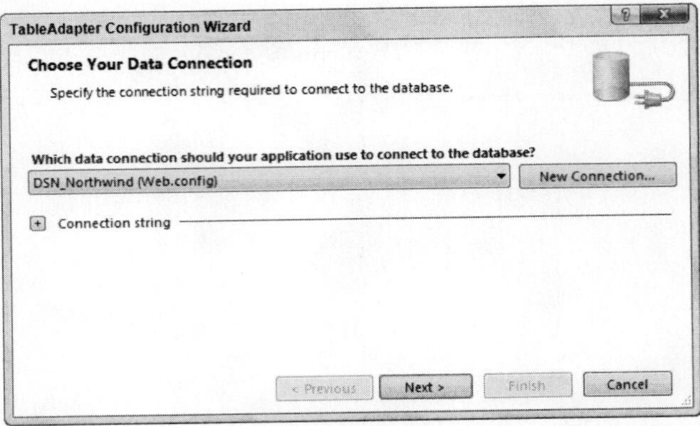

Figure 8-16

As you work through the wizard, you come to a screen that asks how you want to query the database (see Figure 8-17). You have three options: using SQL statements, using stored procedures that have already been created, or building brand-new stored procedures directly from this wizard.

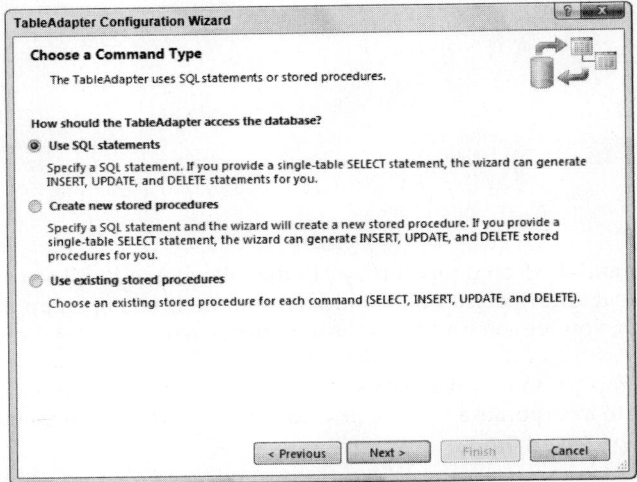

Figure 8-17

For this example, choose Use SQL statements. Selecting this option brings you to a text box where you can write your own SQL statement if you wish.

The great thing about this process is that, after you create a SQL `select` command, the TableAdapter wizard also creates the associated `insert`, `update`, and `delete` commands for you. You also have the option of building your queries using the Query Builder. This enables you to graphically design the query yourself. If this option is selected, you can choose from a list of tables in the Northwind database. For the first TableAdapter, choose Customers. For the second TableAdapter choose Orders. You make your selection by clicking the Add button and then closing the dialog box (see Figure 8-18).

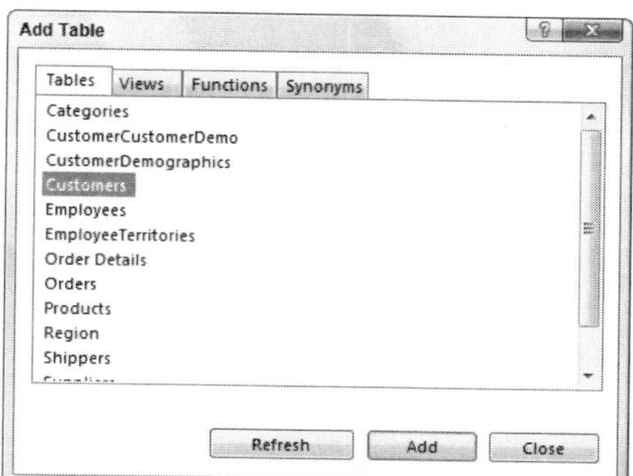

Figure 8-18

After you close the Add Table dialog box, you see a visual representation of the table that you selected in the Query Builder dialog box (see Figure 8-19). You can then select some or all the fields to be returned from the query. For this example, you want everything returned from both the Customers and the Orders table, so select the first check box with the asterisk (*). Notice that the query listed in this dialog box now says `SELECT * FROM Customers`. After the word "Customers," add text to the query so that it looks like the following:

```
SELECT Customers.* FROM Customers WHERE (CustomerID LIKE @Customer)
```

With this query, you specify that you want to return the customer information when the `CustomerID` fits the parameter that you pass into the query from your code (using `@Customer`).

After your query is in place, simply click OK and then click the Next button to have not only the `select` query, but also the `insert`, `update`, and `delete` queries generated for you.

Figure 8-20 shows you the final page after all the queries have been generated.

After you reach this point, you can either click the Previous button to return to one of the prior steps in order to change a setting or the query itself, or you can click the Finish button to apply everything to your TableAdapter. After you are finished using the wizard, notice there is a visual representation of the `CustomersTableAdapter` that you just created (see Figure 8-21). Along with that is a `DataTable` object for the Customers table. The `TableAdapter` and the `DataTable` objects that are shown on the design surface are also labeled with their IDs. Therefore, in your code, you can address this TableAdapter that you just built by referring to it as `CustomerOrdersTableAdapters.CustomersTableAdapter`. The second TableAdapter that queries the Orders table is then shown and referred to as `CustomerOrders-TableAdapters.OrdersTableAdapter`.

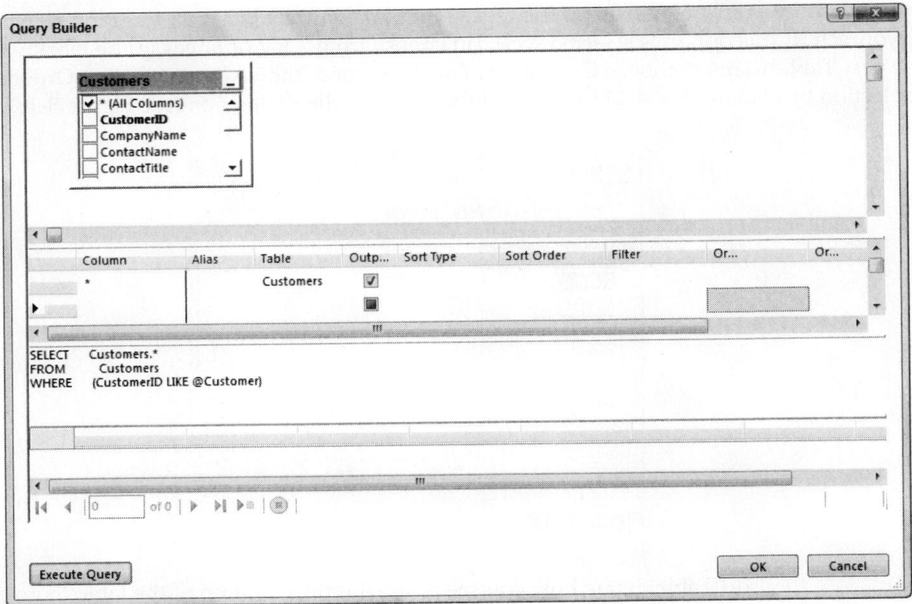

Figure 8-19

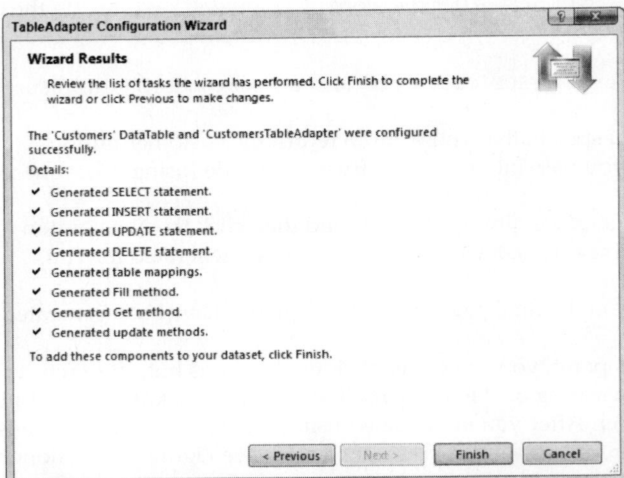

Figure 8-20

After you have the two DataAdapters in place, you will also notice that there is an automatic relation put into place for you. This is represented by the line between the two items on the page. Right-clicking on the relation, you can edit the relation with the Relation dialog box (see Figure 8-22).

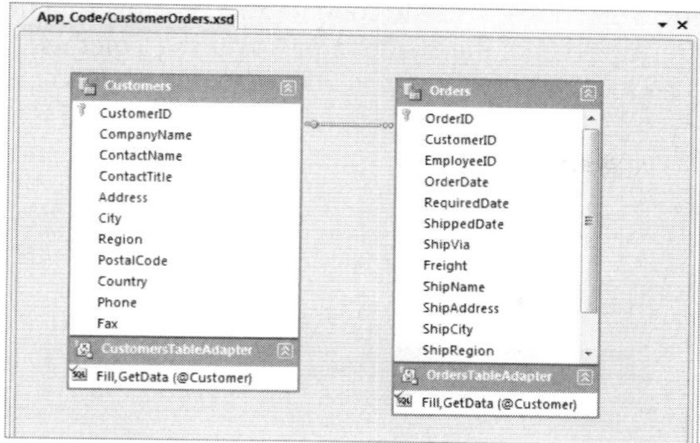

Figure 8-21

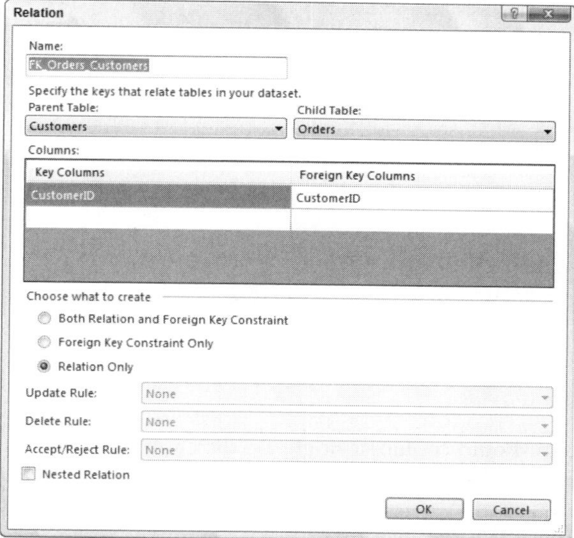

Figure 8-22

In the end, Visual Studio has taken care of a lot for you. Again, this is not the only way to complete all these tasks.

Using the CustomerOrders DataSet

Now comes the fun part — building the ASP.NET that will use all the items that were just created! The goal is to allow the end user to send in a request that contains just the CustomerID. In return, he will get back a complete DataSet containing not only the customer information, but also all the relevant order information. Listing 8-29 shows you the code to build all this functionality. You need only a single method in addition to the `Page_Load`: the `GetCustomerOrders()` method. The page should be laid out as is shown here in Figure 8-23.

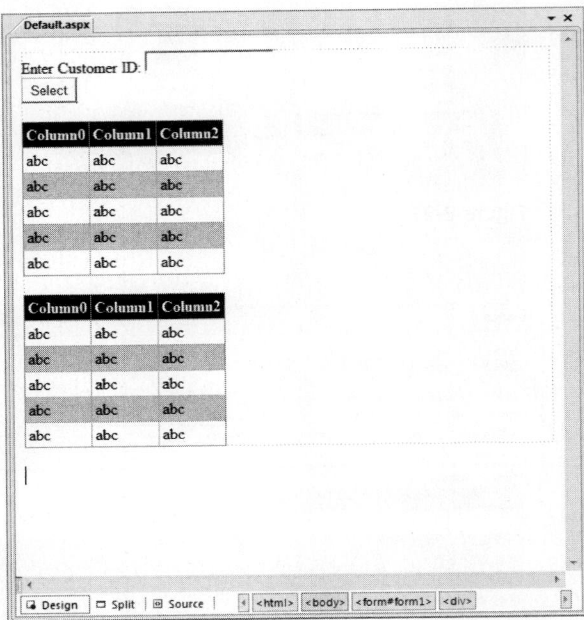

Figure 8-23

The page that you create should contain a single TextBox control, a Button control, and two GridView controls (GridView1 and GridView2). The code for the page is shown in Listing 8-29.

Listing 8-29: The .aspx page

```
<%@ Page Language="VB" AutoEventWireup="false" CodeFile="Default.aspx.vb"
    Inherits="_Default" %>

<html xmlns="http://www.w3.org/1999/xhtml">
<head runat="server">
    <title>CustomerOrders</title>
</head>
<body>
    <form id="form1" runat="server">
    <div>
```

```
        Enter Customer ID:
        <asp:TextBox ID="TextBox1" runat="server"></asp:TextBox>
        <br />


        <asp:Button ID="Button1" runat="server" Text="Select" />
        <br />
        <br />
        <asp:GridView ID="GridView1" runat="server" BackColor="White"
            BorderColor="#999999" BorderStyle="Solid" BorderWidth="1px"
            CellPadding="3" ForeColor="Black" GridLines="Vertical">
            <FooterStyle BackColor="#CCCCCC" />
            <PagerStyle BackColor="#999999" ForeColor="Black"
             HorizontalAlign="Center" />
            <SelectedRowStyle BackColor="#000099" Font-Bold="True"
             ForeColor="White" />
            <HeaderStyle BackColor="Black" Font-Bold="True" ForeColor="White" />
            <AlternatingRowStyle BackColor="#CCCCCC" />
        </asp:GridView>
        <br />
        <asp:GridView ID="GridView2" runat="server" BackColor="White"
            BorderColor="#999999" BorderStyle="Solid" BorderWidth="1px"
            CellPadding="3" ForeColor="Black" GridLines="Vertical">
            <FooterStyle BackColor="#CCCCCC" />
            <PagerStyle BackColor="#999999" ForeColor="Black"
             HorizontalAlign="Center" />
            <SelectedRowStyle BackColor="#000099" Font-Bold="True"
             ForeColor="White" />
            <HeaderStyle BackColor="Black" Font-Bold="True" ForeColor="White" />
            <AlternatingRowStyle BackColor="#CCCCCC" />
        </asp:GridView>
    </div>
    </form>
</body>
</html>
```

The code-behind for the page is presented in Listing 8-30.

Listing 8-30: The code-behind for the CustomerOrders page

VB

```
Imports System

Partial Class _Default
    Inherits System.Web.UI.Page

    Protected Sub Page_Load(ByVal sender As Object, ByVal e As System.EventArgs) _
     Handles Me.Load
```

Continued

```
        If Page.IsPostBack Then
            GetCustomerOrders(TextBox1.Text)
        End If
    End Sub

    Protected Sub GetCustomerOrders(ByVal custId As String)
        Dim myDataSet As New CustomerOrders
        Dim custDA As New CustomerOrdersTableAdapters.CustomersTableAdapter
        Dim ordersDA As New CustomerOrdersTableAdapters.OrdersTableAdapter

        custDA.Fill(myDataSet.Customers, custId)
        ordersDA.Fill(myDataSet.Orders, custId)

        myDataSet.Customers(0).Phone = "NOT AVAILABLE"
        myDataSet.Customers(0).Fax = "NOT AVAILABLE"

        GridView1.DataSource = myDataSet.Tables("Customers")
        GridView1.DataBind()

        GridView2.DataSource = myDataSet.Tables("Orders")
        GridView2.DataBind()
    End Sub
End Class
```

C#

```
using System;
using CustomerOrdersTableAdapters;

public partial class _Default : System.Web.UI.Page
{
    protected void Page_Load(object sender, EventArgs e)
    {
        if (Page.IsPostBack)
        {
            GetCustomerOrders(TextBox1.Text);
        }
    }

    protected void GetCustomerOrders(string custId)
    {
        CustomerOrders myDataSet = new CustomerOrders();
        CustomersTableAdapter custDA = new CustomersTableAdapter();
        OrdersTableAdapter ordersDA = new OrdersTableAdapter();

        custDA.Fill(myDataSet.Customers, custId);
        ordersDA.Fill(myDataSet.Orders, custId);

        myDataSet.Customers[0].Phone = "NOT AVAILABLE";
        myDataSet.Customers[0].Fax = "NOT AVAILABLE";

        GridView1.DataSource = myDataSet.Tables["Customers"];
```

```
            GridView1.DataBind();

            GridView2.DataSource = myDataSet.Tables["Orders"];
            GridView2.DataBind();
        }
    }
```

Now there is not much code here. One of the first things done in the method is to create an instance of the typed DataSet. In the next two lines of code, the `custDA` and the `ordersDA` objects are used. In this case, the only accepted parameter, `custId`, is being set for both the DataAdapters. After this parameter is passed to the TableAdapter, this TableAdapter queries the database based upon the `select` query that you programmed into it earlier using the TableAdapter wizard.

After the query, the TableAdapter is instructed to fill the instance of the DataSet. Before the DataSet is returned to the consumer, you can change how the result is output to the client. If you are passing customer information, you may want to exclude some of the information. Because the DataSet is a typed DataSet, you have programmatic access to the tables. In this example, the code specifies that in the DataSet, in the Customers table, in the first row (remember it is zero-based), make the value of the Phone and Fax fields equal to `NOT AVAILABLE`.

By compiling and running the ASP.NET page, you are able to test it from the test page using the CustomerID of ALFKI (the first record of the Customers table in the Northwind database). The results are returned to you in the browser (see Figure 8-24).

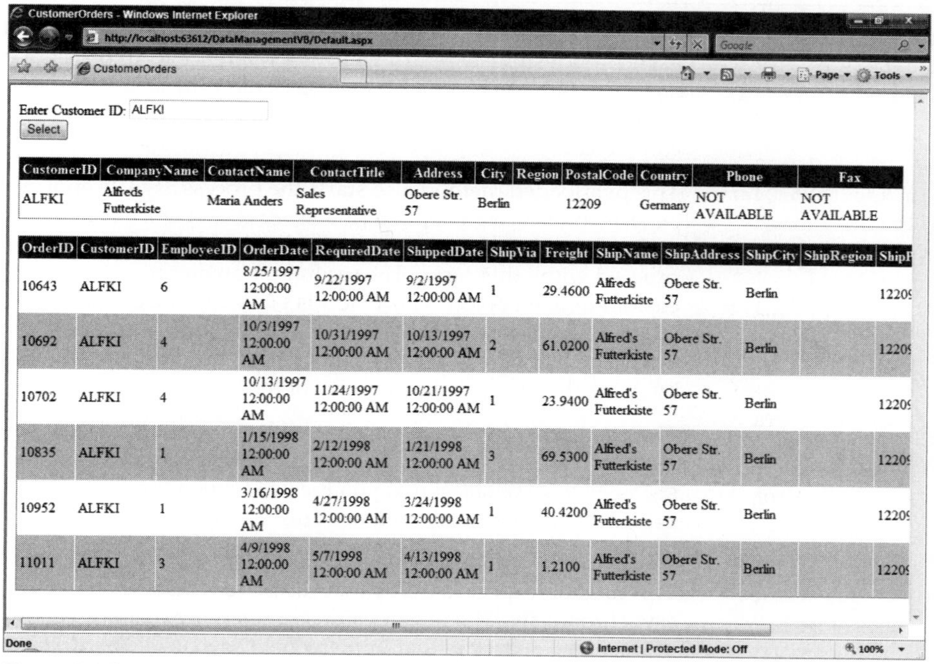

Figure 8-24

Asynchronous Command Execution

When you process data using ADO or previous versions of ADO.NET, each command is executed sequentially. The code waits for each command to complete before the next one is processed. When you use a single database, the sequential processing enables you to reuse the same connection object for all commands. However, with the introduction of MARS, you can now use a single connection for multiple, concurrent database access. Since the introduction of ADO.NET 2.0, ADO.NET has enabled users to process database commands asynchronously. This enables you to not only use the same connection, but also to use it in a parallel manner. The real advantage of asynchronous processing becomes apparent when you are accessing multiple data sources — especially when the data access queries across these databases aren't dependent on each other. You can now open a connection to the database in an asynchronous manner. When you are working with multiple databases, you can now open connections to them in a parallel fashion as well.

To make this work, be sure to add `Asynchronous Processing = true;` *to your connection string.*

Asynchronous Methods of the SqlCommand Class

The `SqlCommand` class provides a few additional methods that facilitate executing commands asynchronously. These new methods are summarized in the following table.

Method	Description
`BeginExecute-NonQuery()`	This method expects a query that doesn't return any results and starts it asynchronously. The return value is a reference to an object of the `SqlAsyncResult` class that implements the `IAsyncResult` interface. The returned object can be used to monitor the process as it runs and when it is completed.
`BeginExecuteNonQuery (callback, stateObject )`	This overloaded method also starts the process asynchronously, and it expects to receive an object of the `AsynchCallback` instance. The callback method is called after the process is finished running so that you can proceed with other tasks. The second parameter receives any custom-defined object. This object is passed to the callback automatically. It provides an excellent mechanism for passing parameters to the callback method. The callback method can retrieve the custom-defined state object by using the `AsyncState` property of the `IAsyncResult` interface.
`EndExecuteNonQuery (asyncResult)`	This method is used to access the results from the `BeginExecuteNonQuery` method. When calling this method, you are required to pass the same `SqlAsyncResult` object that you received when you called the `BeginExecuteNonQuery` method. This method returns an integer value containing the number of rows affected.
`BeginExecuteReader`	This method expects a query that returns a result set and starts it asynchronously. The return value is a reference to an object of `SqlAsyncResult` class that implements `IAsyncResult` interface. The returned object can be used to monitor the process as it runs and as it is completed.

Method	Description
`BeginExecuteReader (commandBehavior)`	This overloaded method works the same way as the one described previously. It also takes a parameter containing a command behavior enumeration just like the synchronous `ExecuteReader` method.
`BeginExecuteReader (callback, stateObject)`	This overloaded method starts the asynchronous process and it expects to receive an object of `AsyncCallback` instance. The callback method is called after the process finishes running so that you can proceed with other tasks. The second parameter receives any custom-defined object. This object is passed to the callback automatically. It provides an excellent mechanism for passing parameters to the callback method. The callback method can retrieve the custom-defined state object by using the `AsyncState` property of the `IAsyncResult` interface.
`BeginExecuteReader (callback, stateObject, commandBehavior)`	This overloaded method takes an instance of the `AsyncCallback` class and uses it to fire a callback method when the process has finished running. The second parameter receives a custom object to be passed to the callback method, and the third parameter uses the command behavior enumeration in the same way as the synchronous `ExecuteReader` method.
`EndExecuteReader`	This method is used to access the results from the `BeginExecuteReader` method. When calling this method, you are required to pass the same `SqlAsyncResult` object that you receive when you called the `BeginExecuteReader` method. This method returns a `SqlDataReader` object containing the result of the SQL query.
`BeginExecute-XmlReader`	This method expects a query that returns the result set as XML. The return value is a reference to an object of `SqlAsyncResult` class that implements `IAsyncResult` interface. The returned object can be used to monitor the process as it runs and as it is completed.
`BeginExecute-XmlReader (callback, stateObject)`	This overloaded method starts the asynchronous process, and it expects to receive an object of `AsyncCallback` instance. The callback method is called after the process has finished running so that you can proceed with other tasks. The second parameter receives any custom-defined object. This object is passed to the callback automatically. It provides an excellent mechanism for passing parameters to the callback method. The callback method can retrieve the custom-defined state object by using the `AsyncState` property of the `IAsyncResult` interface.
`EndExecuteXmlReader`	This method is used to access the results from the `BeginExecuteXmlReader` method. When calling this method, you are required to pass the same `SqlAsyncResult` object that you received when you called the `BeginExecuteXmlReader` method. This method returns an XML Reader object containing the result of the SQL query.

IAsyncResult Interface

All the asynchronous methods for the `SqlCommand` class return a reference to an object that exposes the `IAsyncResult` interface. The properties of this interface are shown in the following table.

Property	Description
`AsyncState`	This read-only property returns an object that describes the state of the process.
`AsyncWaitHandle`	This read-only property returns an instance of `WaitHandle` that can be used to set the time out, test whether the process has completed, and force the code to wait for completion.
`Completed-Synchronously`	This read-only property returns a Boolean value that indicates whether the process was executed synchronously.
`IsCompleted`	This read-only property returns a Boolean value indicating whether the process has completed.

AsyncCallback

Some of the asynchronous methods of the `SqlCommand` class receive an instance of the `AsyncCallback` class. This class is not specific to ADO.NET and is used by many objects in the .NET Framework. It is used to specify those methods that you want to execute after the asynchronous process has finished running. This class uses its constructor to receive the address of the method that you want to use for callback purposes.

WaitHandle Class

This class is an abstract class used for multiple purposes such as causing the execution to wait for any or all asynchronous processes to finish. To process more than one database command asynchronously, you can simply create an array containing wait handles for each asynchronous process. Using the static methods of the `WaitHandle` class, you can cause the execution to wait for either any or all wait handles in the array to finish processing.

The `WaitHandle` class exposes a few methods, as shown in the following table.

Method	Description
`WaitOne`	This method waits for a single asynchronous process to complete or time out. It returns a Boolean value containing `True` if the process completed successfully and `False` if it timed out.
`WaitOne (milliseconds, exitContext)`	This overloaded method receives an integer value as the first parameter. This value represents the time out in milliseconds. The second parameter receives a Boolean value specifying whether the method requires asynchronous context and should be set to `False` for asynchronous processing.
`WaitOne (timeSpan, exitContext)`	This overloaded method receives a `TimeSpan` object to represent the time-out value. The second parameter receives a Boolean value specifying whether the method requires asynchronous context and should be set to `False` for Asynchronous processing.

Method	Description
`WaitAny (waitHandles)`	This is a static method used if you are managing more than one `WaitHandle` in the form of an array. Using this method causes the execution to wait for any of the asynchronous processes that have been started and whose wait handles are in the array being passed to it. The `WaitAny` method must be called repeatedly — once for each `WaitHandle` you want to process.
`WaitAny (waitHandles, milliseconds, exitContext)`	This overloaded method receives the time-out value in the form of milliseconds and a Boolean value specifying whether the method requires asynchronous context. It should be set to `False` for asynchronous processing.
`WaitAny (waitHandles, timeSpan, exitContext`	This overloaded method receives the time-out value in the form of a `TimeSpan` object. The second parameter receives a Boolean value specifying whether the method requires asynchronous context. It should be set to `False` for asynchronous processing.
`WaitAll (waitHandles)`	This is a static method and is used to wait for all asynchronous processes to finish running.
`WaitAll (waitHandles, milliseconds, exitContext)`	This overloaded method receives the time-out value in the form of milliseconds and a Boolean value specifying whether the method requires asynchronous context. It should be set to `False` for asynchronous processing.
`WaitAll (waitHandles, timeSpan, exitContext)`	This overloaded method receives the time-out value in the form of `TimeSpan` object. The second parameter receives a Boolean value specifying whether the method requires asynchronous context. It should be set to `False` for asynchronous processing.
`Close ( )`	This method releases all wait handles and reclaims their resources.

Now that you understand asynchronous methods added to the `SqlCommand` and how to properly interact with them, you can write some code to see the asynchronous processing in action.

Approaches of Asynchronous Processing in ADO.NET

You can process asynchronous commands in three distinct ways. One approach is to start the asynchronous process and start polling the `IAsyncResult` object to see when the process has finished. The second approach is to provide a callback method while starting the asynchronous process. This approach enables you to perform other tasks in parallel. When the asynchronous process finishes, it fires the callback method that cleans up after the process and notifies other parts of the program that the asynchronous process has finished. The third and most elegant method is to associate a wait handle with the asynchronous process. Using this approach, you can start all the asynchronous processing you want and then wait for all or any of them to finish so that you can process them accordingly.

The Poll Approach

The code shown in Listing 8-31 creates an inline SQL statement to retrieve the top five records from the Orders table from the Northwind database. It starts the asynchronous process by calling the

BeginExecuteReader. After the asynchronous process has started, it uses a while loop to wait for the process to finish. While waiting, the main thread sleeps for 10 milliseconds after checking the status of the asynchronous process. After the process has finished, it retrieves the result using the EndExecuteReader method.

Listing 8-31: The Poll approach to working with asynchronous commands

VB

```
<%@ Page Language="VB" %>
<%@ Import Namespace="System.Data" %>
<%@ Import Namespace="System.Data.SqlClient" %>
<%@ Import Namespace="System.Configuration" %>

<script runat="server">
    Protected Sub Page_Load(ByVal sender As Object, ByVal e As System.EventArgs)
        Dim DBCon As SqlConnection
        Dim Command As SqlCommand = New SqlCommand()
        Dim OrdersReader As SqlDataReader
        Dim ASyncResult As IAsyncResult

        DBCon = New SqlConnection()
        DBCon.ConnectionString = _
          ConfigurationManager.ConnectionStrings("DSN_NorthWind").ConnectionString

        Command.CommandText = _
                "SELECT TOP 5 Customers.CompanyName, Customers.ContactName, " & _
                "Orders.OrderID, Orders.OrderDate, " & _
                "Orders.RequiredDate, Orders.ShippedDate " & _
                "FROM Orders, Customers " & _
                "WHERE Orders.CustomerID = Customers.CustomerID " & _
                "ORDER BY Customers.CompanyName, Customers.ContactName"
        Command.CommandType = CommandType.Text
        Command.Connection = DBCon

        DBCon.Open()

        ' Starting the asynchronous processing
        ASyncResult = Command.BeginExecuteReader()

        ' This loop with keep the main thread waiting until the
        ' asynchronous process is finished
        While Not ASyncResult.IsCompleted
            ' Sleeping current thread for 10 milliseconds
            System.Threading.Thread.Sleep(10)
        End While

        ' Retrieving result from the asynchronous process
        OrdersReader = Command.EndExecuteReader(ASyncResult)

        ' Displaying result on the screen
        gvOrders.DataSource = OrdersReader
        gvOrders.DataBind()
```

```
        ' Closing connection
        DBCon.Close()
    End Sub
</script>

<html xmlns="http://www.w3.org/1999/xhtml" >
<head id="Head1" runat="server">
    <title>The Poll Approach</title>
</head>
<body>
    <form id="form1" runat="server">
    <div>
    <asp:GridView ID="gvOrders" runat="server"
     AutoGenerateColumns="False" Width="100%">
       <Columns>
          <asp:BoundField HeaderText="Company Name"
           DataField="CompanyName"></asp:BoundField>
          <asp:BoundField HeaderText="Contact Name"
           DataField="ContactName"></asp:BoundField>
          <asp:BoundField HeaderText="Order Date"
           DataField="orderdate" DataFormatString="{0:d}"></asp:BoundField>
          <asp:BoundField HeaderText="Required Date" DataField="requireddate"
           DataFormatString="{0:d}"></asp:BoundField>
          <asp:BoundField HeaderText="Shipped Date" DataField="shippeddate"
           DataFormatString="{0:d}"></asp:BoundField>
       </Columns>
    </asp:GridView>
    </div>
    </form>
</body>
</html>
```

C#

```
<%@ Page Language="C#" %>
<%@ Import Namespace="System.Data" %>
<%@ Import Namespace="System.Data.SqlClient" %>
<%@ Import Namespace="System.Configuration" %>

<script runat="server">
    protected void Page_Load(object sender, EventArgs e)
    {
        SqlConnection DBCon;
        SqlCommand Command = new SqlCommand();
        SqlDataReader OrdersReader;
        IAsyncResult ASyncResult;

        DBCon = new SqlConnection();
        DBCon.ConnectionString =
           ConfigurationManager.ConnectionStrings["DSN_NorthWind"].ConnectionString;

        Command.CommandText =
                "SELECT TOP 5 Customers.CompanyName, Customers.ContactName, " +
                "Orders.OrderID, Orders.OrderDate, " +
                "Orders.RequiredDate, Orders.ShippedDate " +
```

Continued

```
                "FROM Orders, Customers " +
                "WHERE Orders.CustomerID = Customers.CustomerID " +
                "ORDER BY Customers.CompanyName, Customers.ContactName";

        Command.CommandType = CommandType.Text;
        Command.Connection = DBCon;

        DBCon.Open();

        // Starting the asynchronous processing
        ASyncResult = Command.BeginExecuteReader();

        // This loop with keep the main thread waiting until the
        // asynchronous process is finished
        while (!ASyncResult.IsCompleted)
        {
            // Sleeping current thread for 10 milliseconds
            System.Threading.Thread.Sleep(10);
        }

        // Retrieving result from the asynchronous process
        OrdersReader = Command.EndExecuteReader(ASyncResult);

        // Displaying result on the screen
        gvOrders.DataSource = OrdersReader;
        gvOrders.DataBind();

        // Closing connection
        DBCon.Close();
    }
</script>
```

If you set a break point at the `while` loop, you will be able to see that the code execution continues after calling the `BeginExecuteReader` method. The code then continues to loop until the asynchronous execution has finished.

The Wait Approach

The most elegant of the three approaches is neither the poll approach nor the callback approach. The approach that provides the highest level of flexibility, efficiency, and (admittedly) a bit more complexity is the wait approach. Using this approach, you can write code that starts multiple asynchronous processes and waits for any or all the processes to finish running. This approach allows you to wait for only those processes that are dependent on each other and to proceed with the ones that don't. This approach, by its design, requires you to think about asynchronous processes in great detail. You must pick a good candidate for running in parallel and, most importantly, determine how different processes depend on each other. The complexity of this approach requires you to understand its details and design the code accordingly. The end result is, typically, a very elegant code design that makes the best use of synchronous and asynchronous processing models.

The code shown in Listing 8-32 uses the `WaitOne` method of the `WaitHandle` class. This method causes the program execution to wait until the asynchronous process has finished running.

Listing 8-32: The wait approach to handling a single asynchronous process

VB

```
<%@ Page Language="VB" %>
<%@ Import Namespace="System.Data" %>
<%@ Import Namespace="System.Data.SqlClient" %>
<%@ Import Namespace="System.Configuration" %>

<script runat="server">
    Protected Sub Page_Load(ByVal sender As Object, ByVal e As System.EventArgs)
        Dim DBCon As SqlConnection
        Dim Command As SqlCommand = New SqlCommand()
        Dim OrdersReader As SqlDataReader
        Dim ASyncResult As IAsyncResult
        Dim WHandle As Threading.WaitHandle

        DBCon = New SqlConnection()
        DBCon.ConnectionString = _
           ConfigurationManager.ConnectionStrings("DSN_NorthWind").ConnectionString


        Command.CommandText = _
                "SELECT TOP 5 Customers.CompanyName, Customers.ContactName, " & _
                "Orders.OrderID, Orders.OrderDate, " & _
                "Orders.RequiredDate, Orders.ShippedDate " & _
                "FROM Orders, Customers " & _
                "WHERE Orders.CustomerID = Customers.CustomerID " & _
                "ORDER BY Customers.CompanyName, Customers.ContactName"

        Command.CommandType = CommandType.Text
        Command.Connection = DBCon

        DBCon.Open()

        ' Starting the asynchronous processing
        ASyncResult = Command.BeginExecuteReader()

        WHandle = ASyncResult.AsyncWaitHandle

        If WHandle.WaitOne = True Then
            ' Retrieving result from the asynchronous process
            OrdersReader = Command.EndExecuteReader(ASyncResult)

            ' Displaying result on the screen
            gvOrders.DataSource = OrdersReader
            gvOrders.DataBind()

            ' Closing connection
            DBCon.Close()
        Else
            ' Asynchronous process has timed out. Handle this
            ' situation here.
        End If
```

Continued

```
    End Sub
</script>

<html xmlns="http://www.w3.org/1999/xhtml" >
<head id="Head1" runat="server">
    <title>The Wait Approach</title>
</head>
<body>
    <form id="form1" runat="server">
    <div>
    <asp:GridView ID="gvOrders" runat="server"
     AutoGenerateColumns="False" Width="100%">
       <Columns>
          <asp:BoundField HeaderText="Company Name"
           DataField="CompanyName"></asp:BoundField>
          <asp:BoundField HeaderText="Contact Name"
           DataField="ContactName"></asp:BoundField>
          <asp:BoundField HeaderText="Order Date"
           DataField="orderdate" DataFormatString="{0:d}"></asp:BoundField>
          <asp:BoundField HeaderText="Required Date" DataField="requireddate"
           DataFormatString="{0:d}"></asp:BoundField>
          <asp:BoundField HeaderText="Shipped Date" DataField="shippeddate"
           DataFormatString="{0:d}"></asp:BoundField>
       </Columns>
    </asp:GridView>
    </div>
    </form>
</body>
</html>
```

C#

```
<%@ Page Language="C#" %>
<%@ Import Namespace="System.Data" %>
<%@ Import Namespace="System.Data.SqlClient" %>
<%@ Import Namespace="System.Configuration" %>

<script runat="server">
    protected void Page_Load(object sender, EventArgs e)
    {
        SqlConnection DBCon;
        SqlCommand Command = new SqlCommand();
        SqlDataReader OrdersReader;
        IAsyncResult ASyncResult;
        System.Threading.WaitHandle WHandle;

        DBCon = new SqlConnection();
        DBCon.ConnectionString =
           ConfigurationManager.ConnectionStrings["DSN_NorthWind"].ConnectionString;

        Command.CommandText =
                "SELECT TOP 5 Customers.CompanyName, Customers.ContactName, " +
                "Orders.OrderID, Orders.OrderDate, " +
                "Orders.RequiredDate, Orders.ShippedDate " +
                "FROM Orders, Customers " +
```

```
                "WHERE Orders.CustomerID = Customers.CustomerID " +
                "ORDER BY Customers.CompanyName, Customers.ContactName";

        Command.CommandType = CommandType.Text;
        Command.Connection = DBCon;

        DBCon.Open();

        // Starting the asynchronous processing
        ASyncResult = Command.BeginExecuteReader();

        WHandle = ASyncResult.AsyncWaitHandle;

        if (WHandle.WaitOne() == true)
        {
            // Retrieving result from the asynchronous process
            OrdersReader = Command.EndExecuteReader(ASyncResult);

            // Displaying result on the screen
            gvOrders.DataSource = OrdersReader;
            gvOrders.DataBind();

            // Closing connection
            DBCon.Close();
        }
        else
        {
            // Asynchronous process has timed out. Handle this
            // situation here.
        }
    }
</script>
```

If you set a break point and step through this code, you will notice that the program execution stops at the `WHandle.WaitOne` method call. The program automatically resumes when the asynchronous commands finishes its execution.

Using Multiple Wait Handles

The real power of the wait approach doesn't become apparent until you start multiple asynchronous processes. The code shown in Listing 8-33 starts two asynchronous processes. One process queries a database to get information about a specific customer and runs another query to retrieve all orders submitted by that the same customer. The code example shown in this listing creates two separate `Command` objects, Data Reader objects, and wait handles. However, it uses the same connection object for both queries to demonstrate how well Multiple Active Result Set (MARS) supports work in conjunction with the asynchronous processing.

Listing 8-33: Use of multiple wait handles in conjunction with MARS

VB

```
<%@ Page Language="VB" %>
<%@ Import Namespace="System.Data" %>
```

Continued

```
<%@ Import Namespace="System.Data.SqlClient" %>
<%@ Import Namespace="System.Configuration" %>

<script runat="server">
    Protected Sub Page_Load(ByVal sender As Object, ByVal e As System.EventArgs)
        Dim DBCon As SqlConnection
        Dim OrdersCommand As SqlCommand = New SqlCommand()
        Dim CustCommand As SqlCommand = New SqlCommand()
        Dim OrdersReader As SqlDataReader
        Dim CustReader As SqlDataReader
        Dim OrdersASyncResult As IAsyncResult
        Dim CustAsyncResult As IAsyncResult

        Dim WHandles(1) As System.Threading.WaitHandle
        Dim OrdersWHandle As System.Threading.WaitHandle
        Dim CustWHandle As System.Threading.WaitHandle

        DBCon = New SqlConnection()
        DBCon.ConnectionString = _
           ConfigurationManager.ConnectionStrings("DSN_NorthWind").ConnectionString

        CustCommand.CommandText = _
           "SELECT * FROM Customers WHERE CompanyName = 'Alfreds Futterkiste'"

        CustCommand.CommandType = CommandType.Text
        CustCommand.Connection = DBCon

        ' Selecting all orders for a specific customer
        OrdersCommand.CommandText = _
              "SELECT Customers.CompanyName, Customers.ContactName, " & _
              "Orders.OrderID, Orders.OrderDate, " & _
              "Orders.RequiredDate, Orders.ShippedDate " & _
              "FROM Orders, Customers " & _
              "WHERE Orders.CustomerID = Customers.CustomerID " & _
              "AND Customers.CompanyName = 'Alfreds Futterkiste' " & _
              "ORDER BY Customers.CompanyName, Customers.ContactName"

        OrdersCommand.CommandType = CommandType.Text
        OrdersCommand.Connection = DBCon

        DBCon.Open()

        ' Retrieving customer information asynchronously
        CustAsyncResult = CustCommand.BeginExecuteReader()

        ' Retrieving orders list asynchronously
        OrdersASyncResult = OrdersCommand.BeginExecuteReader()

        CustWHandle = CustAsyncResult.AsyncWaitHandle
        OrdersWHandle = OrdersASyncResult.AsyncWaitHandle

        ' Filling Wait Handles array with the two wait handles we
        ' are going to use in this code
        WHandles(0) = CustWHandle
```

```
        WHandles(1) = OrdersWHandle

        System.Threading.WaitHandle.WaitAll(WHandles)

        CustReader = CustCommand.EndExecuteReader(CustAsyncResult)

        OrdersReader = OrdersCommand.EndExecuteReader(OrdersASyncResult)

        gvCustomers.DataSource = CustReader
        gvCustomers.DataBind()

        gvOrders.DataSource = OrdersReader
        gvOrders.DataBind()

        DBCon.Close()
    End Sub
</script>

<html xmlns="http://www.w3.org/1999/xhtml" >
<head id="Head1" runat="server">
    <title>Wait All Approach</title>
</head>
<body>
    <form id="form1" runat="server">
    <div>
    <asp:GridView ID="gvCustomers" Width="100%" runat="server"></asp:GridView>
    <br /><br />
    <asp:GridView ID="gvOrders" Width="100%" AutoGenerateColumns="False"
     runat="server">
       <Columns>
          <asp:BoundField HeaderText="Company Name"
           DataField="CompanyName"></asp:BoundField>
          <asp:BoundField HeaderText="Contact Name"
           DataField="ContactName"></asp:BoundField>
          <asp:BoundField HeaderText="Order Date" DataField="orderdate"
           DataFormatString="{0:d}"></asp:BoundField>
          <asp:BoundField HeaderText="Required Date" DataField="requireddate"
           DataFormatString="{0:d}"></asp:BoundField>
          <asp:BoundField HeaderText="Shipped Date" DataField="shippeddate"
           DataFormatString="{0:d}"></asp:BoundField>
       </Columns>
    </asp:GridView>
    </div>
    </form>
</body>
</html>
```

C#

```
<%@ Page Language="C#" %>
<%@ Import Namespace="System.Data" %>
<%@ Import Namespace="System.Data.SqlClient" %>
<%@ Import Namespace="System.Configuration" %>

<script runat="server">
```

Continued

```
protected void Page_Load(object sender, EventArgs e)
{
    SqlConnection DBCon;
    SqlCommand OrdersCommand = new SqlCommand();
    SqlCommand CustCommand = new SqlCommand();
    SqlDataReader OrdersReader;
    SqlDataReader CustReader;
    IAsyncResult OrdersASyncResult;
    IAsyncResult CustAsyncResult;

    System.Threading.WaitHandle[] WHandles = new
       System.Threading.WaitHandle[1];
    System.Threading.WaitHandle OrdersWHandle;
    System.Threading.WaitHandle CustWHandle;

    DBCon = new SqlConnection();
    DBCon.ConnectionString =
      ConfigurationManager.ConnectionStrings["DSN_NorthWind"].ConnectionString;

    CustCommand.CommandText =
       "SELECT * FROM Customers WHERE CompanyName = 'Alfreds Futterkiste'";

    CustCommand.CommandType = CommandType.Text;
    CustCommand.Connection = DBCon;

    // Selecting all orders for a specific customer
    OrdersCommand.CommandText =
            "SELECT Customers.CompanyName, Customers.ContactName, " +
            "Orders.OrderID, Orders.OrderDate, " +
            "Orders.RequiredDate, Orders.ShippedDate " +
            "FROM Orders, Customers " +
            "WHERE Orders.CustomerID = Customers.CustomerID " +
            "AND Customers.CompanyName = 'Alfreds Futterkiste' " +
            "ORDER BY Customers.CompanyName, Customers.ContactName";

    OrdersCommand.CommandType = CommandType.Text;
    OrdersCommand.Connection = DBCon;

    DBCon.Open();

    // Retrieving customer information asynchronously
    CustAsyncResult = CustCommand.BeginExecuteReader();

    // Retrieving orders list asynchronously
    OrdersASyncResult = OrdersCommand.BeginExecuteReader();

    CustWHandle = CustAsyncResult.AsyncWaitHandle;
    OrdersWHandle = OrdersASyncResult.AsyncWaitHandle;

    // Filling Wait Handles array with the two wait handles we
    // are going to use in this code
    WHandles[0] = CustWHandle;
    WHandles[1] = OrdersWHandle;
```

```
            System.Threading.WaitHandle.WaitAll(WHandles);

            CustReader = CustCommand.EndExecuteReader(CustAsyncResult);

            OrdersReader = OrdersCommand.EndExecuteReader(OrdersASyncResult);

            gvCustomers.DataSource = CustReader;
            gvCustomers.DataBind();

            gvOrders.DataSource = OrdersReader;
            gvOrders.DataBind();

            DBCon.Close();
        }
    </script>
```

When you compile and execute the code shown in Listing 8-33, you see the result on the screen, as shown in Figure 8-25. This figure clearly shows two GridView controls that were used in the code example. The GridView control on the top shows the result of executing a query that retrieved all information related to a specific customer. The GridView control on the bottom shows the results of executing the second query that retrieved a list of all orders submitted by a specific customer.

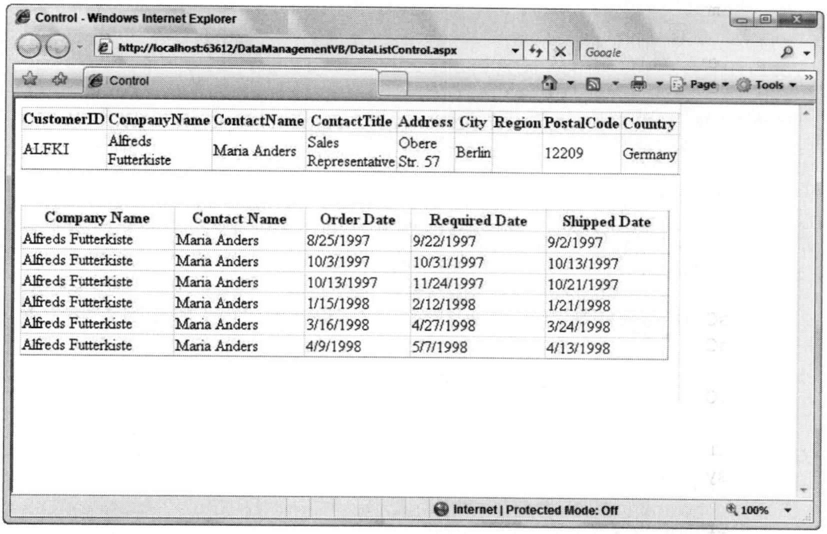
Control - Windows Internet Explorer
http://localhost:63612/DataManagementVB/DataListControl.aspx
Google
Control
Page
Tools
CustomerID CompanyName ContactName ContactTitle Address City Region PostalCode Country
ALFKI Alfreds Futterkiste Maria Anders Sales Representative Obere Str. 57 Berlin 12209 Germany
Company Name Contact Name Order Date Required Date Shipped Date
Alfreds Futterkiste Maria Anders 8/25/1997 9/22/1997 9/2/1997
Alfreds Futterkiste Maria Anders 10/3/1997 10/31/1997 10/13/1997
Alfreds Futterkiste Maria Anders 10/13/1997 11/24/1997 10/21/1997
Alfreds Futterkiste Maria Anders 1/15/1998 2/12/1998 1/21/1998
Alfreds Futterkiste Maria Anders 3/16/1998 4/27/1998 3/24/1998
Alfreds Futterkiste Maria Anders 4/9/1998 5/7/1998 4/13/1998
Internet | Protected Mode: Off
100%

Figure 8-25

The code shown in Listing 8-33 reveals some of the elegance of using the wait approach. However, it is still not the most efficient code you can write with ADO.NET 2.0. The code should allow for a wait until both asynchronous processes finish running before the data binds the result sets to the respective GridView controls.

You can change the code shown in Listing 8-33 just a little to gain even more efficiency. Replace the `WaitAll` method with the `WaitAny` method. The `WaitAny` method enables you to handle the results of each of the asynchronous processes as soon as each is completed without waiting for other processing to finish. To use the `WaitAny` method and still manage the execution of all asynchronous processes, you can also add a loop that enables you to make sure that all asynchronous processes are handled after they are completed.

The `WaitAny` method returns an Integer value that indicates an array index of the wait handle that has finished running. Using this return value, you can easily find the correct wait handle and process the result set retrieved from the query that was executed in that particular process, as shown in Listing 8-34.

Listing 8-34: Use of the WaitAny method to process multiple asynchronous processes

VB

```
<%@ Page Language="VB" %>
<%@ Import Namespace="System.Data" %>
<%@ Import Namespace="System.Data.SqlClient" %>
<%@ Import Namespace="System.Configuration" %>

<script runat="server">
    Protected Sub Page_Load(ByVal sender As Object, ByVal e As System.EventArgs)
        Dim DBCon As SqlConnection
        Dim OrdersCommand As SqlCommand = New SqlCommand()
        Dim CustCommand As SqlCommand = New SqlCommand()
        Dim OrdersReader As SqlDataReader
        Dim CustReader As SqlDataReader
        Dim OrdersASyncResult As IAsyncResult
        Dim CustAsyncResult As IAsyncResult

        Dim WHIndex As Integer
        Dim WHandles(1) As Threading.WaitHandle
        Dim OrdersWHandle As Threading.WaitHandle
        Dim CustWHandle As Threading.WaitHandle

        DBCon = New SqlConnection()
        DBCon.ConnectionString = _
           ConfigurationManager.ConnectionStrings("DSN_NorthWind").ConnectionString

        CustCommand.CommandText = _
           "SELECT * FROM Customers WHERE CompanyName = 'Alfreds Futterkiste'"

        CustCommand.CommandType = CommandType.Text
        CustCommand.Connection = DBCon

        OrdersCommand.CommandText = _
                "SELECT Customers.CompanyName, Customers.ContactName, " & _
                "Orders.OrderID, Orders.OrderDate, " & _
                "Orders.RequiredDate, Orders.ShippedDate " & _
                "FROM Orders, Customers " & _
                "WHERE Orders.CustomerID = Customers.CustomerID " & _
                "AND Customers.CompanyName = 'Alfreds Futterkiste' " & _
                "ORDER BY Customers.CompanyName, Customers.ContactName"
```

```
            OrdersCommand.CommandType = CommandType.Text
            OrdersCommand.Connection = DBCon

            ' Opening the database connection
            DBCon.Open ()

            ' Retrieving customer information asynchronously
            CustAsyncResult = CustCommand.BeginExecuteReader()

            ' Retrieving orders list asynchronously
            OrdersASyncResult = OrdersCommand.BeginExecuteReader()

            CustWHandle = CustAsyncResult.AsyncWaitHandle
            OrdersWHandle = OrdersASyncResult.AsyncWaitHandle

            ' Filling Wait Handles array with the two wait handles we
            ' are going to use in this code
            WHandles(0) = CustWHandle
            WHandles(1) = OrdersWHandle

            ' Looping 2 times because there are 2 wait handles
            ' in the array
            For Index As Integer = 0 To 1
                ' We are only waiting for any of the two
                ' asynchronous process to finish running
                WHIndex = Threading.WaitHandle.WaitAny(WHandles)

                ' The return value from the WaitAny method is
                ' the array index of the Wait Handle that just
                ' finsihed running
                Select Case WHIndex
                    Case 0
                        CustReader = CustCommand.EndExecuteReader(CustAsyncResult)

                        gvCustomers.DataSource = CustReader
                        gvCustomers.DataBind()
                    Case 1
                        OrdersReader = _
                           OrdersCommand.EndExecuteReader(OrdersASyncResult)

                        gvOrders.DataSource = OrdersReader
                        gvOrders.DataBind()

                End Select
            Next

            ' Closing connection
            DBCon.Close()
        End Sub
</script>

<html xmlns="http://www.w3.org/1999/xhtml" >
<head id="Head1" runat="server">
```

Continued

```
    <title>The Wait Any Approach</title>
</head>
<body>
    <form id="form1" runat="server">
    <div>
    <asp:GridView ID="gvCustomers" Width="100%" runat="server"></asp:GridView>
    <br /><br />
    <asp:GridView ID="gvOrders" Width="100%" AutoGenerateColumns="False"
     runat="server">
        <Columns>
            <asp:BoundField HeaderText="Company Name"
             DataField="CompanyName"></asp:BoundField>
            <asp:BoundField HeaderText="Contact Name"
             DataField="ContactName"></asp:BoundField>
            <asp:BoundField HeaderText="Order Date" DataField="orderdate"
             DataFormatString="{0:d}"></asp:BoundField>
            <asp:BoundField HeaderText="Required Date" DataField="requireddate"
             DataFormatString="{0:d}"></asp:BoundField>
            <asp:BoundField HeaderText="Shipped Date" DataField="shippeddate"
             DataFormatString="{0:d}"></asp:BoundField>
        </Columns>
    </asp:GridView>
    </div>
    </form>
</body>
</html>
```

C#

```
<%@ Page Language="C#" %>
<%@ Import Namespace="System.Data" %>
<%@ Import Namespace="System.Data.SqlClient" %>
<%@ Import Namespace="System.Configuration" %>

<script runat="server">
    protected void Page_Load(object sender, EventArgs e)
    {
        SqlConnection DBCon;
        SqlCommand OrdersCommand = new SqlCommand();
        SqlCommand CustCommand = new SqlCommand();
        SqlDataReader OrdersReader;
        SqlDataReader CustReader;
        IAsyncResult OrdersASyncResult;
        IAsyncResult CustAsyncResult;

        int WHIndex;
        System.Threading.WaitHandle[] WHandles =
           new System.Threading.WaitHandle[1];
        System.Threading.WaitHandle OrdersWHandle;
        System.Threading.WaitHandle CustWHandle;

        DBCon = new SqlConnection();
        DBCon.ConnectionString =
           ConfigurationManager.ConnectionStrings["DSN_NorthWind"].ConnectionString;
```

```
CustCommand.CommandText =
    "SELECT * FROM Customers WHERE CompanyName = 'Alfreds Futterkiste'";

CustCommand.CommandType = CommandType.Text;
CustCommand.Connection = DBCon;

OrdersCommand.CommandText =
        "SELECT Customers.CompanyName, Customers.ContactName, " +
        "Orders.OrderID, Orders.OrderDate, " +
        "Orders.RequiredDate, Orders.ShippedDate " +
        "FROM Orders, Customers " +
        "WHERE Orders.CustomerID = Customers.CustomerID " +
        "AND Customers.CompanyName = 'Alfreds Futterkiste' " +
        "ORDER BY Customers.CompanyName, Customers.ContactName";

OrdersCommand.CommandType = CommandType.Text;
OrdersCommand.Connection = DBCon;

// Opening the database connection
DBCon.Open();

// Retrieving customer information asynchronously
CustAsyncResult = CustCommand.BeginExecuteReader();

// Retrieving orders list asynchronously
OrdersASyncResult = OrdersCommand.BeginExecuteReader();

CustWHandle = CustAsyncResult.AsyncWaitHandle;
OrdersWHandle = OrdersASyncResult.AsyncWaitHandle;

// Filling Wait Handles array with the two wait handles we
// are going to use in this code
WHandles[0] = CustWHandle;
WHandles[1] = OrdersWHandle;

// Looping 2 times because there are 2 wait handles
// in the array
for (int Index = 0; Index < 2; Index++ )
{
    // We are only waiting for any of the two
    // asynchronous process to finish running
    WHIndex = System.Threading.WaitHandle.WaitAny(WHandles);

    // The return value from the WaitAny method is
    // the array index of the Wait Handle that just
    // finsihed running
    switch (WHIndex)
    {
        case 0:
            CustReader = CustCommand.EndExecuteReader(CustAsyncResult);

            gvCustomers.DataSource = CustReader;
            gvCustomers.DataBind();
```

Continued

```
                    break;
                case 1:
                    OrdersReader =
                       OrdersCommand.EndExecuteReader(OrdersASyncResult);

                    gvOrders.DataSource = OrdersReader;
                    gvOrders.DataBind();
                    break;
            }
        }
        // Closing connection
        DBCon.Close();
    }
</script>
```

Next, look at the callback approach. Using this approach, you assign a callback method to the asynchronous process and use it to display the result returned by executing the SQL query.

The Callback Approach

Listing 8-35 creates an inline SQL statement that retrieves the top five records from the database. It starts the asynchronous process by calling the `BeginExecuteReader` method and passing it the callback delegate. No further processing is needed, and the method ends after the asynchronous process has started. After the callback method is fired, it retrieves the result and displays it on the screen.

Listing 8-35: Asynchronous command processing using the callback approach

VB

```
<%@ Page Language="VB" %>
<%@ Import Namespace="System.Data" %>
<%@ Import Namespace="System.Data.SqlClient" %>
<%@ Import Namespace="System.Configuration" %>

<script runat="server">
    Private Sub Page_Load(ByVal sender As Object, ByVal e As System.EventArgs)
        Dim DBCon As SqlConnection
        Dim Command As SqlCommand = New SqlCommand()
        Dim ASyncResult As SqlAsyncResult

        DBCon = New SqlConnection()
        Command = New SqlCommand()
        DBCon.ConnectionString = _
          ConfigurationManager.ConnectionStrings("DSN_NorthWind").ConnectionString

        ' Selecting top 5 records from the Orders table
        Command.CommandText = _
                "SELECT TOP 5 Customers.CompanyName, Customers.ContactName, " & _
                "Orders.OrderID, Orders.OrderDate, " & _
                "Orders.RequiredDate, Orders.ShippedDate " & _
                "FROM Orders, Customers " & _
                "WHERE Orders.CustomerID = Customers.CustomerID " & _
                "ORDER BY Customers.CompanyName, Customers.ContactName"
```

```
        Command.CommandType = CommandType.Text
        Command.Connection = DBCon

        DBCon.Open()

        ' Starting the asynchronous processing
        AsyncResult = Command.BeginExecuteReader(New _
           AsyncCallback(AddressOf CBMethod), CommandBehavior.CloseConnection)
    End Sub

    Public Sub CBMethod(ByVal ar As SQLAsyncResult)
        Dim OrdersReader As SqlDataReader

        ' Retrieving result from the asynchronous process
        OrdersReader = ar.EndExecuteReader(ar)

        ' Displaying result on the screen
        gvOrders.DataSource = OrdersReader
        gvOrders.DataBind()
    End Sub
</script>

<html xmlns="http://www.w3.org/1999/xhtml" >
<head id="Head1" runat="server">
    <title>The Call Back Approach</title>
</head>
<body>
    <form id="form1" runat="server">
    <div>
    <asp:GridView ID="gvOrders" Width="100%" AutoGenerateColumns="False"
     runat="server">
       <Columns>
          <asp:BoundField HeaderText="Company Name"
           DataField="CompanyName"></asp:BoundField>
          <asp:BoundField HeaderText="Contact Name"
           DataField="ContactName"></asp:BoundField>
          <asp:BoundField HeaderText="Order Date" DataField="orderdate"
           DataFormatString="{0:d}"></asp:BoundField>
          <asp:BoundField HeaderText="Required Date" DataField="requireddate"
           DataFormatString="{0:d}"></asp:BoundField>
          <asp:BoundField HeaderText="Shipped Date" DataField="shippeddate"
           DataFormatString="{0:d}"></asp:BoundField>
       </Columns>
    </asp:GridView>
    </div>
    </form>
</body>
</html>
```

C#

```
<%@ Page Language="C#" %>
<%@ Import Namespace="System.Data" %>
<%@ Import Namespace="System.Data.SqlClient" %>
<%@ Import Namespace="System.Configuration" %>
```

Continued

```
<script runat="server">
    protected void Page_Load(object sender, EventArgs e)
    {
        SqlConnection DBCon;
        SqlCommand Command = new SqlCommand();
        SqlAsyncResult ASyncResult;
        DBCon = new SqlConnection();
        Command = new SqlCommand();
        DBCon.ConnectionString =
          ConfigurationManager.ConnectionStrings["DSN_NorthWind"].ConnectionString;

        // Selecting top 5 records from the Orders table
        Command.CommandText =
                "SELECT TOP 5 Customers.CompanyName, Customers.ContactName, " +
                "Orders.OrderID, Orders.OrderDate, " +
                "Orders.RequiredDate, Orders.ShippedDate " +
                "FROM Orders, Customers " +
                "WHERE Orders.CustomerID = Customers.CustomerID " +
                "ORDER BY Customers.CompanyName, Customers.ContactName";

        Command.CommandType = CommandType.Text;
        Command.Connection = DBCon;

        DBCon.Open();

        // Starting the asynchronous processing
        AsyncResult = Command.BeginExecuteReader(new AsyncCallback(CBMethod),
          CommandBehavior.CloseConnection);
    }

    public void CBMethod(SQLAsyncResult ar)
    {
        SqlDataReader OrdersReader;

        // Retrieving result from the asynchronous process
        OrdersReader = ar.EndExecuteReader(ar);

        // Displaying result on the screen
        gvOrders.DataSource = OrdersReader;
        gvOrders.DataBind();
    }
</script>
```

The callback approach enables you to handle the result of a command execution at a different part of your code. This feature is useful in cases where the command execution takes longer than usual and you want to respond to the user without waiting for the command execution to finish.

Canceling Asynchronous Processing

The asynchronous process often takes longer than expected. To alleviate this problem, you can provide an option to the user to cancel the process without waiting for the result. Canceling an asynchronous process is as easy as calling the `Cancel` method on the appropriate `Command` object. This method doesn't return any value. To roll back the work that was already completed by the `Command` object, you must provide a custom transaction to the `Command` object before executing the query. You can also handle the rollback or the commit process yourself.

Asynchronous Connections

Now that you understand how to execute multiple database queries asynchronously using the `Command` object, take a quick look at how you can open database connections asynchronously, as well. The principles of working with asynchronous connections are the same as when you work with asynchronous commands. You can still use any of the three approaches you learned previously.

In ADO.NET, the `SqlConnection` class exposes a couple of new properties needed when working asynchronously. These properties are shown in the following table.

Property	Description
`Asynchronous`	This read-only property returns a Boolean value indicating whether the connection has been opened asynchronously.
`State`	This property returns a value from `System.Data.ConnectionState` enumeration indicating the state of the connection. The possible values are as follows: ❑ `Broken` ❑ `Closed` ❑ `Connecting` ❑ `Executing` ❑ `Fetching` ❑ `Open`

Summary

In summary, ADO.NET is a powerful tool to incorporate within your ASP.NET applications. ADO.NET has a number of new technologies that provide you with data solutions that you could only dream of in the past.

Visual Studio also makes ADO.NET programming quick and easy when you use the wizards that are available. In this chapter, you saw a number of the wizards. You do not have to use these wizards in order to work with ADO.NET. On the contrary, you can use some of the wizards and create the rest of the code yourself, or you can use none of the wizards. In any case, you have complete and full access to everything that ADO.NET provides.

This chapter covered a range of advanced features of ADO.NET as well. These features are designed to give you the flexibility to handle database processing in a manner never before possible with either of the previous versions of ADO.NET or ADO.

This chapter also covered the features of Multiple Active Result Sets (MARS), which enables you to reuse a single open connection for multiple accesses to the database, even if the connection is currently processing a result set. This feature becomes even more powerful when it is used in conjunction with the asynchronous command processing.

9

Querying with LINQ

.NET 3.5 introduces a new technology called Language Integrated Query, or LINQ (pronounced "link"). LINQ is designed to fill the gap that exists between traditional .NET languages, which offer strong typing and full object-oriented development, and query languages such as SQL, with syntax specifically designed for query operations. With the introduction of LINQ into .NET, query becomes a first class concept in .NET, whether object, XML, or data queries.

LINQ includes three basic types of queries, LINQ to Objects, LINQ to XML (or XLINQ), and LINQ to SQL (or DLINQ). Each type of query offers specific capabilities and is designed to query a specific source.

In this chapter, we look at all three flavors of LINQ, and how each enables you to simplify query operations. We also look at some new language features of the .NET CLR that you will use to create LINQ queries, as well as the tooling support added to Visual Studio to support using LINQ.

LINQ to Objects

The first and most basic flavor of LINQ is LINQ to Objects. LINQ to Objects enables you to perform complex query operations against any enumerable object (any object that implements the IEnumerable interface). While the notion of creating enumerable objects that can be queried or sorted is not new to .NET, doing this in versions prior to version 3.5 usually required a significant amount of code. Often that code would end up being so complex that it would be hard for other developers to read and understand, making it difficult to maintain.

Traditional Query Methods

In order to really understand how LINQ improves your ability to query collections, you really need to understand how this is done without it. To do this, let's take a look at how you might create a simple query that includes a group and sort without using LINQ. Listing 9-1 shows a simple Movie class you can use as the basis of these examples.

Listing 9-1: A basic Movie class

VB

```
Imports Microsoft.VisualBasic

Public Class Movie
    Private _title As String
    Private _director As String
    Private _genre As Integer
    Private _runtime As Integer
    Private _releasedate As DateTime

    Public Property Title() As String
        Get
            Return _title
        End Get
        Set(ByVal value As String)
            _title = value
        End Set
    End Property

    Public Property Director() As String
        Get
            Return _director
        End Get
        Set(ByVal value As String)
            _director = value
        End Set
    End Property

    Public Property Genre() As Integer
        Get
            Return _genre
        End Get
        Set(ByVal value As Integer)
            _genre = value
        End Set
    End Property

    Public Property Runtime() As Integer
        Get
            Return _runtime
        End Get
        Set(ByVal value As Integer)
            _runtime = value
        End Set
    End Property

    Public Property ReleaseDate() As DateTime
        Get
            Return _releasedate
        End Get
        Set(ByVal value As DateTime)
```

```
            _releasedate = value
        End Set
    End Property
End Class
```

C#

```
using System;

public class Movie
{
    public string Title { get; set; }
    public string Director { get; set; }
    public int Genre { get; set; }
    public int RunTime { get; set; }
    public DateTime ReleaseDate { get; set; }
}
```

This is the basic class that is used throughout this section and the following LINQ to Object section.

Now that you have a basic class to work with, let's look at how you would normally use the class. Listing 9-2 demonstrates how to create a simple generic List of the Movie objects in an ASP.NET page, and then binding that list to a GridView control. The GridView displays the values of all public properties exposed by the Movie class.

Listing 9-2: Generating a list of Movie objects and binding to a GridView

VB

```
<%@ Page Language="VB" %>
<%@ Import Namespace="System.Collections.Generic" %>

<script runat="server">
    Protected Sub Page_Load(ByVal sender As Object, ByVal e As System.EventArgs)
        Dim movies = GetMovies()

        Me.GridView1.DataSource = movies
        Me.GridView1.DataBind()
    End Sub

    Public Function GetMovies() As List(Of Movie)
      Dim movies As Movie() = { _
          New Movie With {.Title = "Shrek", .Director = "Andrew Adamson", _
                .Genre = 0, .ReleaseDate = DateTime.Parse("5/16/2001"), _
                .Runtime = 89}, _
          New Movie With {.Title = "Fletch", .Director = "Michael Ritchie", _
                .Genre = 0, .ReleaseDate = DateTime.Parse("5/31/1985"), _
                .Runtime = 96}, _
          New Movie With {.Title = "Casablanca", .Director = "Michael Curtiz", _
                .Genre = 1, .ReleaseDate = DateTime.Parse("1/1/1942"), _
                .Runtime = 102}, _
          New Movie With {.Title = "Batman", .Director = "Tim Burton", _
                .Genre = 1, .ReleaseDate = DateTime.Parse("6/23/1989"), _
                .Runtime = 126}, _
```

Continued

```
New Movie With {.Title = "Dances with Wolves", _
    .Director = "Kevin Costner", .Genre = 1, _
    .ReleaseDate = DateTime.Parse("11/21/1990"), .Runtime = 180}, _
New Movie With {.Title = "Dirty Dancing", .Director = "Emile Ardolino", _
    .Genre = 1, .ReleaseDate = DateTime.Parse("8/21/1987"), _
    .Runtime = 100}, _
New Movie With {.Title = "The Parent Trap", .Director = "Nancy Meyers", _
    .Genre = 0, .ReleaseDate = DateTime.Parse("7/29/1998"), _
    .Runtime = 127}, _
New Movie With {.Title = "Ransom", .Director = "Ron Howard", _
    .Genre = 1, .ReleaseDate = DateTime.Parse("11/8/1996"), _
    .Runtime = 121}, _
New Movie With {.Title = "Ocean's Eleven", _
    .Director = "Steven Soderbergh", .Genre = 1, _
    .ReleaseDate = DateTime.Parse("12/7/2001"), .Runtime = 116}, _
New Movie With {.Title = "Steel Magnolias", .Director = "Herbert Ross", _
    .Genre = 1, .ReleaseDate = DateTime.Parse("11/15/1989"), _
    .Runtime = 117}, _
New Movie With {.Title = "Mystic Pizza", .Director = "Donald Petrie", _
    .Genre = 1, .ReleaseDate = DateTime.Parse("10/21/1988"), _
    .Runtime = 104}, _
New Movie With {.Title = "Pretty Woman", .Director = "Garry Marshall", _
    .Genre = 1, .ReleaseDate = DateTime.Parse("3/23/1990"), _
    .Runtime = 119}, _
New Movie With {.Title = "Interview with the Vampire", _
    .Director = "Neil Jordan", .Genre = 1, _
    .ReleaseDate = DateTime.Parse("11/11/1994"), .Runtime = 123}, _
New Movie With {.Title = "Top Gun", .Director = "Tony Scott", _
    .Genre = 2, .ReleaseDate = DateTime.Parse("5/16/1986"), _
    .Runtime = 110}, _
New Movie With {.Title = "Mission Impossible", _
    .Director = "Brian De Palma", .Genre = 2, _
    .ReleaseDate = DateTime.Parse("5/22/1996"), .Runtime = 110}, _
New Movie With {.Title = "The Godfather", _
    .Director = "Francis Ford Coppola", .Genre = 1, _
    .ReleaseDate = DateTime.Parse("3/24/1972"), .Runtime = 175}, _
New Movie With {.Title = "Carlito's Way", .Director = "Brian De Palma", _
    .Genre = 1, .ReleaseDate = DateTime.Parse("11/10/1993"), _
    .Runtime = 144}, _
New Movie With {.Title = "Robin Hood: Prince of Thieves", _
    .Director = "Kevin Reynolds", .Genre = 1, _
    .ReleaseDate = DateTime.Parse("6/14/1991"), .Runtime = 143}, _
New Movie With {.Title = "The Haunted", .Director = "Robert Mandel", _
    .Genre = 1, .ReleaseDate = DateTime.Parse("5/6/1991"), _
    .Runtime = 100}, _
New Movie With {.Title = "Old School", .Director = "Todd Phillips", _
    .Genre = 0, .ReleaseDate = DateTime.Parse("2/21/2003"), _
    .Runtime = 91}, _
New Movie With {.Title = "Anchorman: The Legend of Ron Burgundy", _
    .Director = "Adam McKay", .Genre = 0, _
    .ReleaseDate = DateTime.Parse("7/9/2004"), .Runtime = 94}, _
New Movie With {.Title = "Bruce Almighty", .Director = "Tom Shadyac", _
    .Genre = 0, .ReleaseDate = DateTime.Parse("5/23/2003"), _
    .Runtime = 101}, _
```

```
            New Movie With {.Title = "Ace Ventura: Pet Detective", _
                .Director = "Tom Shadyac", .Genre = 0, _
                .ReleaseDate = DateTime.Parse("2/4/1994"), .Runtime = 86}, _
            New Movie With {.Title = "Goonies", .Director = "Richard Donner", _
                .Genre = 0, .ReleaseDate = DateTime.Parse("6/7/1985"), _
                .Runtime = 114}, _
            New Movie With {.Title = "Sixteen Candles", .Director = "John Hughes", _
                .Genre = 1, .ReleaseDate = DateTime.Parse("5/4/1984"), _
                .Runtime = 93}, _
            New Movie With {.Title = "The Breakfast Club", _
                .Director = "John Hughes", .Genre = 1, _
                .ReleaseDate = DateTime.Parse("2/15/1985"), .Runtime = 97}, _
            New Movie With {.Title = "Pretty in Pink", .Director = "Howard Deutch", _
                .Genre = 1, .ReleaseDate = DateTime.Parse("2/28/1986"), _
                .Runtime = 96}, _
            New Movie With {.Title = "Weird Science", .Director = "John Hughes", _
                .Genre = 0, .ReleaseDate = DateTime.Parse("8/2/1985"), _
                .Runtime = 94}, _
            New Movie With {.Title = "Breakfast at Tiffany's", _
                .Director = "Blake Edwards", .Genre = 1, _
                .ReleaseDate = DateTime.Parse("10/5/1961"), .Runtime = 115}, _
            New Movie With {.Title = "The Graduate", .Director = "Mike Nichols", _
               .Genre = 1, .ReleaseDate = DateTime.Parse("4/2/1968"), _
                .Runtime = 105}, _
            New Movie With {.Title = "Dazed and Confused", _
                .Director = "Richard Linklater", .Genre = 0, _
                .ReleaseDate = DateTime.Parse("9/24/1993"), .Runtime = 103}, _
            New Movie With {.Title = "Arthur", .Director = "Steve Gordon", _
               .Genre = 1, .ReleaseDate = DateTime.Parse("9/25/1981"), _
                .Runtime = 97}, _
            New Movie With {.Title = "Monty Python and the Holy Grail", _
               .Director = "Terry Gilliam", .Genre = 0, _
               .ReleaseDate = DateTime.Parse("5/10/1975"), .Runtime = 91}, _
              New Movie With {.Title = "Dirty Harry", .Director = "Don Siegel", _
               .Genre = 2, .ReleaseDate = DateTime.Parse("12/23/1971"), _
                .Runtime = 102} _
            }

        Return New List(Of Movie)(movies)
    End Function
</script>

<html xmlns="http://www.w3.org/1999/xhtml">
<head runat="server">
    <title>My Favorite Movies</title>
</head>
<body>
    <form id="form1" runat="server">
    <div>
        <asp:GridView ID="GridView1" runat="server">
        </asp:GridView>
    </div>
    </form>
</body>
```

Continued

```
</html>
```

C#

```
<script runat="server">

    protected void Page_Load(object sender, EventArgs e)
    {
        var movies = GetMovies();

        this.GridView1.DataSource = movies;
        this.GridView1.DataBind();
    }

    public List<Movie> GetMovies()
    {
        return new List<Movie> {
            new Movie { Title="Shrek", Director="Andrew Adamson", Genre=0,
               ReleaseDate=DateTime.Parse("5/16/2001"), RunTime=89 },
            new Movie { Title="Fletch", Director="Michael Ritchie", Genre=0,
               ReleaseDate=DateTime.Parse("5/31/1985"), RunTime=96 },
            new Movie { Title="Casablanca", Director="Michael Curtiz", Genre=1,
               ReleaseDate=DateTime.Parse("1/1/1942"), RunTime=102 },
            new Movie { Title="Batman", Director="Tim Burton", Genre=1,
               ReleaseDate=DateTime.Parse("6/23/1989"), RunTime=126 },
            new Movie { Title="Dances with Wolves",
               Director="Kevin Costner",Genre=1,
               ReleaseDate=DateTime.Parse("11/21/1990"), RunTime=180 },
            new Movie { Title="Dirty Dancing", Director="Emile Ardolino", Genre=1,
               ReleaseDate=DateTime.Parse("8/21/1987"), RunTime=100 },
            new Movie { Title="The Parent Trap", Director="Nancy Meyers", Genre=0,
               ReleaseDate=DateTime.Parse("7/29/1998"), RunTime=127 },
            new Movie { Title="Ransom", Director="Ron Howard", Genre=1,
               ReleaseDate=DateTime.Parse("11/8/1996"), RunTime=121 },
            new Movie { Title="Ocean's Eleven",
               Director="Steven Soderbergh", Genre=1,
               ReleaseDate=DateTime.Parse("12/7/2001"), RunTime=116 },
            new Movie { Title="Steel Magnolias", Director="Herbert Ross", Genre=1,
               ReleaseDate=DateTime.Parse("11/15/1989"), RunTime=117 },
            new Movie { Title="Mystic Pizza", Director="Donald Petrie", Genre=1,
               ReleaseDate=DateTime.Parse("10/21/1988"), RunTime=104 },
            new Movie { Title="Pretty Woman", Director="Garry Marshall", Genre=1,
               ReleaseDate=DateTime.Parse("3/23/1990"), RunTime=119 },
            new Movie { Title="Interview with the Vampire",
               Director="Neil Jordan", Genre=1,
               ReleaseDate=DateTime.Parse("11/11/1994"), RunTime=123 },
            new Movie { Title="Top Gun", Director="Tony Scott", Genre=2,
               ReleaseDate=DateTime.Parse("5/16/1986"), RunTime=110 },
            new Movie { Title="Mission Impossible",
               Director="Brian De Palma", Genre=2,
               ReleaseDate=DateTime.Parse("5/22/1996"), RunTime=110 },
            new Movie { Title="The Godfather", Director="Francis Ford Coppola",
```

```
            Genre=1, ReleaseDate=DateTime.Parse("3/24/1972"), RunTime=175 },
        new Movie { Title="Carlito's Way", Director="Brian De Palma",
            Genre=1, ReleaseDate=DateTime.Parse("11/10/1993"), RunTime=144 },
        new Movie { Title="Robin Hood: Prince of Thieves",
            Director="Kevin Reynolds",
            Genre=1, ReleaseDate=DateTime.Parse("6/14/1991"), RunTime=143 },
        new Movie { Title="The Haunted", Director="Robert Mandel",
            Genre=1, ReleaseDate=DateTime.Parse("5/6/1991"), RunTime=100 },
        new Movie { Title="Old School", Director="Todd Phillips",
            Genre=0, ReleaseDate=DateTime.Parse("2/21/2003"), RunTime=91 },
        new Movie { Title="Anchorman: The Legend of Ron Burgundy",
            Director="Adam McKay", Genre=0,
            ReleaseDate=DateTime.Parse("7/9/2004"), RunTime=94 },
        new Movie { Title="Bruce Almighty", Director="Tom Shadyac",
            Genre=0, ReleaseDate=DateTime.Parse("5/23/2003"), RunTime=101 },
        new Movie { Title="Ace Ventura: Pet Detective", Director="Tom Shadyac",
            Genre=0, ReleaseDate=DateTime.Parse("2/4/1994"), RunTime=86 },
        new Movie { Title="Goonies", Director="Richard Donner",
            Genre=0, ReleaseDate=DateTime.Parse("6/7/1985"), RunTime=114 },
        new Movie { Title="Sixteen Candles", Director="John Hughes",
            Genre=1, ReleaseDate=DateTime.Parse("5/4/1984"), RunTime=93 },
        new Movie { Title="The Breakfast Club", Director="John Hughes",
            Genre=1, ReleaseDate=DateTime.Parse("2/15/1985"), RunTime=97 },
        new Movie { Title="Pretty in Pink", Director="Howard Deutch",
            Genre=1, ReleaseDate=DateTime.Parse("2/28/1986"), RunTime=96 },
        new Movie { Title="Weird Science", Director="John Hughes",
            Genre=0, ReleaseDate=DateTime.Parse("8/2/1985"), RunTime=94 },
        new Movie { Title="Breakfast at Tiffany's", Director="Blake Edwards",
            Genre=1, ReleaseDate=DateTime.Parse("10/5/1961"), RunTime=115 },
        new Movie { Title="The Graduate", Director="Mike Nichols",
            Genre=1, ReleaseDate=DateTime.Parse("4/2/1968"), RunTime=105 },
        new Movie { Title="Dazed and Confused", Director="Richard Linklater",
            Genre=0, ReleaseDate=DateTime.Parse("9/24/1993"), RunTime=103 },
        new Movie { Title="Arthur", Director="Steve Gordon",
            Genre=1, ReleaseDate=DateTime.Parse("9/25/1981"), RunTime=97 },
        new Movie { Title="Monty Python and the Holy Grail",
            Director="Terry Gilliam",
            Genre=0, ReleaseDate=DateTime.Parse("5/10/1975"), RunTime=91 },
        new Movie { Title="Dirty Harry", Director="Don Siegel",
            Genre=2, ReleaseDate=DateTime.Parse("12/23/1971"), RunTime=102 }
    };
  }
</script>
```

Running the sample generates a typical ASP.NET Web page that includes a simple grid showing all of the Movie data on it.

Now, what happens when you want to start performing queries on the list of movies? For example, you might want to filter this data to show only a specific genre of movie. Listing 9-3 shows a typical way you might perform this filtering.

Listing 9-3: Filtering the listing Movie objects

VB

```
Protected Sub Page_Load(ByVal sender As Object, ByVal e As System.EventArgs)
    Dim movies = GetMovies()

    Dim query As New List(Of Movie)()
    For Each m In movies
        If (m.Genre = 0) Then
            query.Add(m)
        End If
    Next

    Me.GridView1.DataSource = query
    Me.GridView1.DataBind()
End Sub
```

C#

```
protected void Page_Load(object sender, EventArgs e)
{
    var movies = GetMovies();

    var query = new List<Movie>();
    foreach (var m in movies)
    {
        if (m.Genre == 0) query.Add(m);
    }

    this.GridView1.DataSource = query;
    this.GridView1.DataBind();
}
```

As this sample shows, to filter the data so that the page displays Movies in a specific genre only requires the creation of a new temporary collection and the use of a `foreach` loop to iterate through the data.

While this technique seems easy enough, it still requires that you define what you want done (find all movies in the genre), and also that you explicitly define how it should be done (use a temporary collection and a `foreach` loop). Additionally, what happens when you need to perform more complex queries, involving grouping or sorting? Now the complexity of the code dramatically increases, as shown in Listing 9-4.

Listing 9-4: Grouping and sorting the List of Movie objects

VB

```
Public Class Grouping
    Private _genre As Integer
    Private _movieCount As Integer

    Public Property Genre() As Integer
        Get
            Return _genre
        End Get
        Set(ByVal value As Integer)
```

```
            _genre = value
        End Set
    End Property

    Public Property MovieCount() As Integer
        Get
            Return _movieCount
        End Get
        Set(ByVal value As Integer)
            _movieCount = value
        End Set
    End Property
End Class

Protected Sub Page_Load(ByVal sender As Object, ByVal e As System.EventArgs)
    Dim movies = GetMovies()

    Dim groups As New Dictionary(Of String, Grouping)

    For Each m In movies

        If (Not groups.ContainsKey(m.Genre)) Then
            groups(m.Genre) = _
                New Grouping With {.Genre = m.Genre, .MovieCount = 0}
        End If

        groups(m.Genre).MovieCount = groups(m.Genre).MovieCount + 1
    Next

    Dim results As New List(Of Grouping)(groups.Values)
    results.Sort(AddressOf MovieSort)

    Me.GridView1.DataSource = results
    Me.GridView1.DataBind()
End Sub

Private Function MovieSort(ByVal x As Grouping, ByVal y As Grouping) As Integer
    Return IIf(x.MovieCount > y.MovieCount, -1, _
        IIf(x.MovieCount < y.MovieCount, 1, 0))
End Function
```

C#

```
public class Grouping
{
    public int Genre { get; set; }
    public int MovieCount { get; set; }
}

protected void Page_Load(object sender, EventArgs e)
{
    var movies = GetMovies();

    Dictionary<int, Grouping> groups = new Dictionary<int, Grouping>();
    foreach (Movie m in movies)
```

Continued

```
    {
        if (!groups.ContainsKey(m.Genre))
        {
            groups[m.Genre] = new Grouping { Genre = m.Genre, MovieCount = 0 };
        }
        groups[m.Genre].MovieCount++;
    }

    List<Grouping> results = new List<Grouping>(groups.Values);
    results.Sort(delegate(Grouping x, Grouping y)
    {
        return
            x.MovieCount > y.MovieCount ? -1 :
            x.MovieCount < y.MovieCount ? 1 :
            0;
    });

    this.GridView1.DataSource = results;
    this.GridView1.DataBind();
}
```

To group the Movie data into genres and count how many movies are in each genre requires the addition of a new class, the creation of a Dictionary, and the implementation of a delegate, all fairly complex requirements for such a seemingly simple task, and again, not only defining very specifically what you want done, but very explicitly how it should be done.

Additionally, because the complexity of the code increases so much, it becomes quite difficult to actually determine what this code is doing. Consider this: What if you were asked to modify this code in an existing application that you were unfamiliar with? How long would it take you to figure out what it was doing?

Replacing Traditional Queries with LINQ

LINQ was created to address many of the shortcomings of querying collections of data that were discussed in the previous section. Rather than requiring you to very specifically define exactly how you want a query to execute, LINQ gives you the power to stay at a more abstract level. By simply defining what you want the query to return, you leave it up to .NET and its compilers to determine the specifics of exactly how the query will be run.

In the preceding section, you looked at the current state of object querying with today's .NET languages. In this section, let's take a look at LINQ and see how using it can greatly simplify these queries, as well as other types of queries. To do this, the samples in this section start out by simply modifying the samples from the previous section to show you how easy LINQ makes the same tasks.

Before you get started, understand that LINQ is an extension to .NET, and because of this, is isolated in its own set of assemblies. The base LINQ functionality is located in the new `System.Core.dll` assembly. This assembly does not replace any existing framework functionality, but simply augments it. Additionally, by default, projects in Visual Studio 2008 include a reference to this assembly so when starting a new ASP.NET Web project, LINQ should be readily available to you.

Basic LINQ Queries and Projections

In order to start modifying the prior sections samples to using LINQ queries, you first need to add the LINQ namespace to the Web page, as shown in Listing 9-5.

Listing 9-5: Adding the LINQ namespace

```
<%@ Import Namespace="System.Linq" %>
```

Adding this namespace gives the page access to all of the basic LINQ functionality. If you are using the code-behind development model, then the LINQ namespace should already be included in your code-behind class.

> *Note that the default web.config file included with a Visual Basic Web site already includes the System.Linq namespace declaration in it, so if you are using this type of project you do not need to manually add the namespace.*

Next, you can start by modifying code from Listing 9-2. If you remember, this basic sample simply generates a generic List of movies and binds the list to a GridView control. Listing 9-6 shows how the code can be modified to use LINQ to query the movies list and bind the resultset to the GridView.

Listing 9-6: Creating a query with LINQ

VB

```
Protected Sub Page_Load(ByVal sender As Object, ByVal e As System.EventArgs)
    Dim movies = GetMovies()

    Dim query = From m In movies _
                Select m

    Me.GridView1.DataSource = query
    Me.GridView1.DataBind()
End Sub
```

C#

```
protected void Page_Load(object sender, EventArgs e)
{
    var movies = GetMovies();

    var query = from m in movies
                select m;

    this.GridView1.DataSource = query;
    this.GridView1.DataBind();
}
```

If we deconstruct the code sample, there are three basic actions happening. First, the code uses the `GetMovies()` method to obtain the generic `List<Movie>` collection.

Next, the code uses a very simple LINQ query to select all of the Movie objects from the generic movies collection. Notice that this specific LINQ query utilizes new language keywords like `from` and `select` in the query statement. These syntax additions are first class members of the .NET languages, therefore Visual Studio 2008 can offer you development assistance such as strong type checking and IntelliSense, making it easier for you to find and fix problems in your code.

The query also defines a new variable `m`. This variable is used in two ways in the query. First, by defining it in the `from` statement from `m`, we are telling LINQ to make `m` represent the individual collection item, which in this case is a `Movie` object. Telling LINQ this enables it to understand the structure of the objects we are querying, and as you will see later, also gives us IntelliSense to help create the query.

The second use of `m` in the query is in the `select` statement. Using `m` in the `select` statement tells LINQ to output a projection that matches the structure of `m`. In this case that means LINQ creates a projection that matches the `Movie` object structure.

We could just have easily created our own custom projection by explicitly defining the fields we wanted returned from the query using the new keyword along with the select operator. This is shown below in Listing 9-7.

Listing 9-7: Creating a custom projection with LINQ

VB

```
Protected Sub Page_Load(ByVal sender As Object, ByVal e As System.EventArgs)
    Dim movies = GetMovies()

    Dim query = From m In movies _
                Select New With {m.Title, m.Genre}

    Me.GridView1.DataSource = query
    Me.GridView1.DataBind()
End Sub
```

C#

```
protected void Page_Load(object sender, EventArgs e)
{
    var movies = GetMovies();

    var query = from m in movies
                select new { m.Title, m.Genre };

    this.GridView1.DataSource = query;
    this.GridView1.DataBind();
}
```

Notice that rather than simply selecting `m`, we have defined a new projection containing only the Title and Genre values.

You can even go so far as to explicitly define the field names that the objects in the resultset will expose. For example, you may want to more explicitly name the Title and Genre fields to more fully describe their contents. Using LINQ, it's easy to do this, as shown in Listing 9-8.

Listing 9-8: Creating custom projection field names

VB

```
Protected Sub Page_Load(ByVal sender As Object, ByVal e As System.EventArgs)
    Dim movies = GetMovies()

    Dim query = From m In movies _
                Select New With {.MovieTitle = m.Title, .MovieGenre = m.Genre}

    Me.GridView1.DataSource = query
    Me.GridView1.DataBind()
End Sub
```

C#

```
protected void Page_Load(object sender, EventArgs e)
{
    var movies = GetMovies();

    var query = from m in movies
                select new { MovieTitle = m.Title, MovieGenre = m. Genre };

    this.GridView1.DataSource = query;
    this.GridView1.DataBind();
}
```

This sample explicitly defined the Fields that will be exposed by the resultset as MovieTitle and MovieGenre. You can see in Figure 9-1, that because of this change, the column headers in the GridView have changed to match.

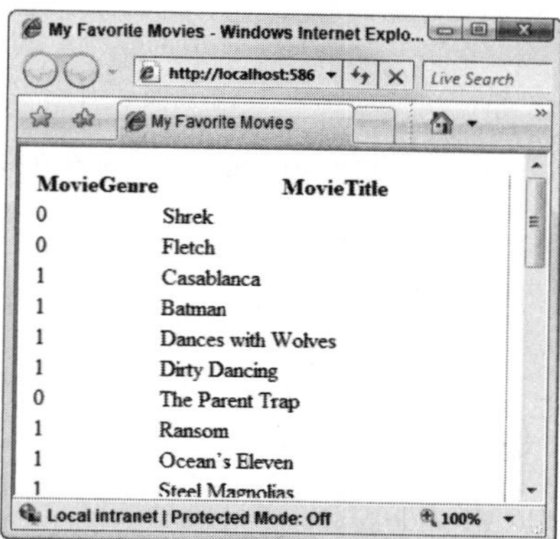

Figure 9-1: Customized GridView column headers as the result of the LINQ projection

Finally the code binds the GridView control to the enumerable list of Movie object returned by the LINQ query.

As shown in Figure 9-2, running the code from Listing 9-6 results in the same vanilla Web page as the one generated by Listing 9-2.

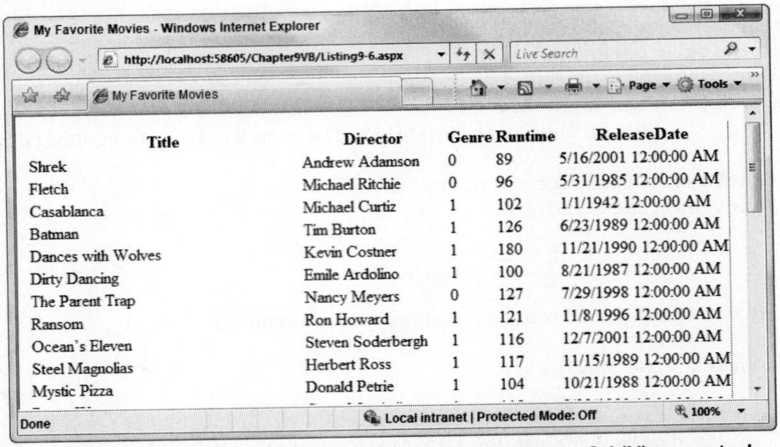

Figure 9-2: The results of a basic LINQ query bound to a GridView control

LINQ also includes the ability to order the results using the order by statement. As with SQL you can choose to order the results in either ascending or descending order, as shown in Listing 9-9.

Listing 9-9: Controlling data ordering using LINQ

VB

```
Protected Sub Page_Load(ByVal sender As Object, ByVal e As System.EventArgs)
    Dim movies = GetMovies()

    Dim query = From m In movies _
                Order By m.Title Descending _
                Select New With {.MovieTitle = m.Title, .MovieGenre = m.Genre}

    Me.GridView1.DataSource = query
    Me.GridView1.DataBind()
End Sub
```

C#

```
protected void Page_Load(object sender, EventArgs e)
{
    var movies = GetMovies();

    var query = from m in movies
                orderby m.Title descending
                select new { MovieTitle = m.Title, MovieGenre = m. Genre };

    this.GridView1.DataSource = query;
    this.GridView1.DataBind();
}
```

Another great feature of the new LINQ syntax is the dramatic improvement in readability and understandability that it makes in your code. LINQ enables you to simply express the intention of your query, indicating to the compiler what you want your code to do, but leaving it up to the compiler to best determine how it should be done.

While these new keywords are what enable you to construct LINQ queries using a simple and clear SQL-like syntax, rest assured there is no magic occurring. These keywords actually map to extension methods on the Movies collection. You could actually write the same LINQ query directly using these extension methods and it would look like this:

VB

```
Dim query = movies.Select( Function(m as Movie) m )
```

C#

```
var query = movies.Select(m => m);
```

This is what the compiler translates the keyword syntax into during its compilation process. You may be wondering how the `Select` *method got added to our generic* `List<Movies>` *collection because if you look at the object structure of* `List<T>`*, there is no* `Select` *method. LINQ adds the* `Select` *method, and many other methods it uses to the base Enumerable class, using Extension Methods. Therefore, any class that implements IEnumerable will be extended by LINQ with these methods. You can see all of the methods added by LINQ by right-clicking on the* `Select` *method in Visual Studio and choosing the View Definition option from the context menu. Doing this causes Visual Studio to display the class metadata for LINQ's* `Enumerable` *class. If you scroll through this class, you will see not only* `Select`*, but other methods such as* `Where`, `Count`, `Min`, `Max`, *and many other methods that LINQ automatically adds to any object that implements the IEnumerable interface.*

Delayed Execution

An interesting feature of LINQ is its delayed execution behavior. This means that even though you may execute the query statements at a specific point in your code, LINQ is smart enough to delay the actual execution of the query until it is accessed. For example, in the previous samples, although the LINQ query was written before the binding of the GridView controls, LINQ will not actually execute the query we have defined until the GridView control begins to enumerate through the query results.

Query Filters

LINQ also supports adding query filters using a familiar SQL-like `where` syntax. You can modify the LINQ query from Listing 9-3 to add filtering capabilities by adding a `where` clause to the query, as shown in Listing 9-10.

Listing 9-10: Adding a filter to a LINQ query

VB

```
Protected Sub Page_Load(ByVal sender As Object, ByVal e As System.EventArgs)
    Dim movies = GetMovies()

    Dim query = From m In movies _
                Where m.Genre = 0 _
                Select m

    Me.GridView1.DataSource = query
    Me.GridView1.DataBind()
```

Continued

```
End Sub
```

C#

```
protected void Page_Load(object sender, EventArgs e)
{
    var movies = GetMovies();

    var query = from m in movies
                where m.Genre==0
                select m;

    this.GridView1.DataSource = query;
    this.GridView1.DataBind();
}
```

By adding this simple `where` clause to the LINQ query, the results returned by the query are filtered to show movies from the 0 genre only, as shown in Figure 9-3.

My Favorite Movies - Windows Internet Explorer

http://localhost:58605/Chapter9VB/Listing9-10.aspx

Title	Director	Genre	Runtime	ReleaseDate
Shrek	Andrew Adamson	0	89	5/16/2001 12:00:00 AM
Fletch	Michael Ritchie	0	96	5/31/1985 12:00:00 AM
The Parent Trap	Nancy Meyers	0	127	7/29/1998 12:00:00 AM
Old School	Todd Phillips	0	91	2/21/2003 12:00:00 AM
Anchorman: The Legend of Ron Burgundy	Adam McKay	0	94	7/9/2004 12:00:00 AM
Bruce Almighty	Tom Shadyac	0	101	5/23/2003 12:00:00 AM
Ace Ventura: Pet Detective	Tom Shadyac	0	86	2/4/1994 12:00:00 AM
Goonies	Richard Donner	0	114	6/7/1985 12:00:00 AM
Weird Science	John Hughes	0	94	8/2/1985 12:00:00 AM
Dazed and Confused	Richard Linklater	0	103	9/24/1993 12:00:00 AM
Monty Python and the Holy Grail	Terry Gilliam	0	91	5/10/1975 12:00:00 AM

Local intranet | Protected Mode: Off

Figure 9-3: A filtered list of Movies

Also, notice that, because LINQ is a first-class member of .NET, Visual Studio is able to provide an excellent coding experience as you are constructing your LINQ queries. In this sample, as you enter the `where` clause, Visual Studio gives you IntelliSense for the possible parameters of `m` (the Movie object), as shown in Figure 9-4.

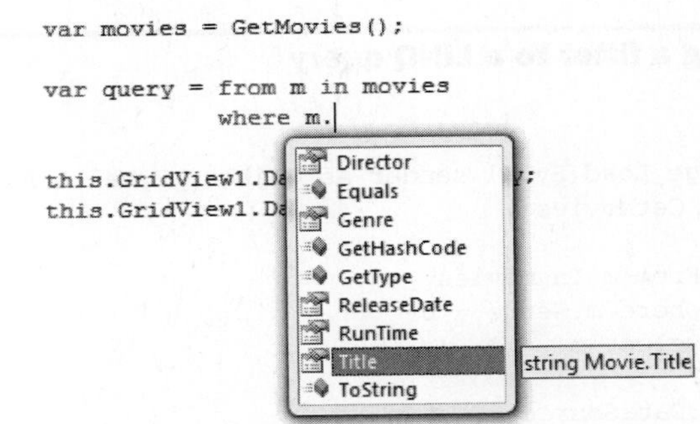

Figure 9-4: Because LINQ is a first class language concept, Visual Studio can give you Intellisense

The `where` clause in LINQ behaves similarly to the SQL `where` clause, enabling you to include sub-queries and multiple where clauses, as shown in Listing 9-11.

Listing 9-11: Adding a Where clause to a LINQ query

VB

```
Protected Sub Page_Load(ByVal sender As Object, ByVal e As System.EventArgs)
    Dim movies = GetMovies()

    Dim query = From m In movies _
                Where m.Genre = 0 And m.Runtime > 92 _
                Select m

    Me.GridView1.DataSource = query
    Me.GridView1.DataBind()
End Sub
```

C#

```
protected void Page_Load(object sender, EventArgs e)
{
    var movies = GetMovies();

    var query = from m in movies
                where m.Genre == 0 && m.RunTime > 92
                select m;

    this.GridView1.DataSource = query;
    this.GridView1.DataBind();
}
```

In this sample, the `where` clause includes two parameters, one restricting the movie genre, the other restricting the movie's runtime.

Data Grouping

LINQ also greatly simplifies grouping data, again using a SQL-like `group` syntax. To show how easy LINQ makes this, you can modify the original Listing 9-4 to use a LINQ query. The modified code is shown in Listing 9-12.

Listing 9-12: Grouping data using a LINQ query

VB

```
Protected Sub Page_Load(ByVal sender As Object, ByVal e As System.EventArgs)
    Dim movies = GetMovies()

    Dim query = From m In movies _
                Group By m.Genre Into g = Group, Count()

    Me.GridView1.DataSource = query
    Me.GridView1.DataBind()
End Sub
```

Continued

C#

```
protected void Page_Load(object sender, EventArgs e)
{
    var movies = GetMovies();

    var query = from m in movies
                group m by m.Genre into g
                select new { Genre = g.Key, Count = g.Count() };

    this.GridView1.DataSource = query;
    this.GridView1.DataBind();
}
```

This LINQ query uses the `group` keyword to group the movie data by genre. Additionally, because a group action does not naturally result in any output, the query creates a custom query projection using the techniques discussed earlier. The results of this query are shown in Figure 9-5.

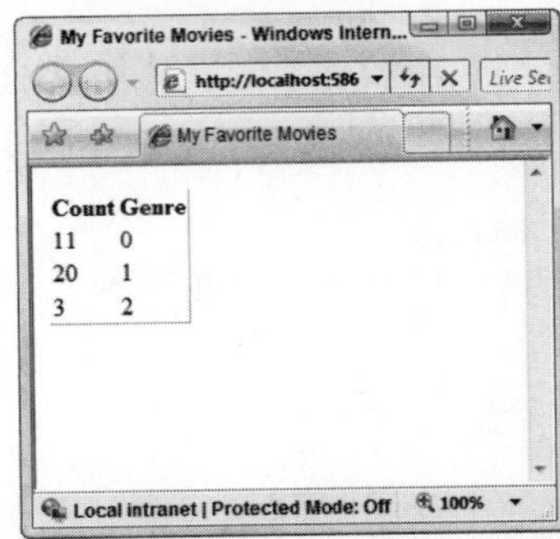

Figure 9-5: Grouped data results

Using LINQ to do this allows you to significantly reduce the lines of code required. If we compare the amount of code required to perform the grouping action in Listing 9-4, with the previous listing using LINQ, you can see that the number of lines of code has dropped from 18 to 3, and the readability and clarity of the code has improved.

Other LINQ Operators

Besides basic selection, filtering and grouping, LINQ also includes many operators you can execute on enumerable objects. Most of these operators are available for you to use and are similar to operators you find in SQL, such as Count, Min, Max, Average, and Sum, as shown in Listing 9-13.

Listing 9-13: Using LINQ query operators

VB

```
Protected Sub Page_Load(ByVal sender As Object, ByVal e As System.EventArgs)
    Dim movies = GetMovies()

    Me.TotalMovies.Text = movies.Count.ToString()
    Me.LongestRuntime.Text = movies.Max(Function(m) m.Runtime).ToString()
    Me.ShortestRuntime.Text = movies.Min(Function(m) m.Runtime).ToString()
    Me.AverageRuntime.Text = movies.Average(Function(m) m.Runtime).ToString()
```

```
End Sub
```

C#

```
protected void Page_Load(object sender, EventArgs e)
{
    var movies = GetMovies();

    this.TotalMovies.Text = movies.Count.ToString();
    this.LongestRuntime.Text = movies.Max(m => m.RunTime).ToString();
    this.ShortestRuntime.Text = movies.Min(m => m.RunTime).ToString();
    this.AverageRuntime.Text = movies.Average(m => m.RunTime).ToString();
}
```

This listing demonstrates the use of the Count, Max, Min, and Average operators with the movies collection. Notice that for all but the Count operator, you need to provide the method with the specific field you want to execute the operation on. This is done using a Lambda expression.

LINQ Joins

LINQ also supports the unioning of data from different collections using a familiar SQL-like join syntax. For example, in our sample data thus far, we have only been able to display the Genre as a numeric ID. It would be preferable to actually display the name of each Genre instead. To do this, you simply create a Genre class, which defines the properties of the genre, as shown in Listing 9-14

Listing 9-14: A simple Genre class

VB

```
Public Class Genre
    Private _id As Integer
    Private _name As String

    Public Property ID() As Integer
        Get
            Return _id
        End Get
        Set(ByVal value As Integer)
            _id = value
        End Set
    End Property

    Public Property Name() As String
        Get
            Return _name
        End Get
        Set(ByVal value As String)
            _name = value
        End Set
    End Property
End Class
```

C#

```
public class Genre
```

Continued

```
{
    public int ID { get; set; }
    public string Name { get; set; }
}
```

Next you can add a `GetGenres` method to your Web page that returns a list of Genre objects, as shown in Listing 9-15.

Listing 9-15: Populating a collection of Genres

VB

```
Public Function GetGenres() As List(Of Genre)
    Dim genres As Genre() = { _
        New Genre With {.ID = 0, .Name = "Comedy"}, _
        New Genre With {.ID = 1, .Name = "Drama"}, _
        New Genre With {.ID = 2, .Name = "Action"} _
    }

    Return New List(Of Genre)(genres)
End Function
```

C#

```
public List<Genre> GetGenres()
{
    return new List<Genre> {
                new Genre { ID=0, Name="Comedy" } ,
                new Genre { ID=1, Name="Drama" } ,
                new Genre { ID=2, Name="Action" }
           };
}
```

Finally, you can modify the Page Load event, including the LINQ query, to retrieve the Genres list and, using LINQ, join that to the Movies list. This is shown in Listing 9-16.

Listing 9-16: Joining Genre data with Movie data using a LINQ query

VB

```
Protected Sub Page_Load(ByVal sender As Object, ByVal e As System.EventArgs)
    Dim movies = GetMovies()
    Dim genres = GetGenres()

    Dim query = From m In movies Join g In genres _
                On m.Genre Equals g.ID _
                Select New With {.Title = m.Title, .Genre = g.Name}

    GridView1.DataSource = query
    GridView1.DataBind()
End Sub
```

C#

```
protected void Page_Load(object sender, EventArgs e)
{
```

```
        var movies = GetMovies();
        var genres = GetGenres();

        var query = from m in movies
                    join g in genres on m.Genre equals g.ID
                    select new { m.Title, Genre = g.Name } ;

        this.GridView1.DataSource = query;
        this.GridView1.DataBind();
    }
```

As you can see in this sample, the join syntax is relatively simple. You tell LINQ to include the genres object, and then tell LINQ which fields it should associate.

Paging Using LINQ

LINQ also makes it much easier to include paging logic in your Web application by exposing the `Skip` and `Take` methods. The `Skip` method enables you to skip a defined number of records in the resultset. The `Take` method enables you to specify the number of records to return from the resultset. By calling `Skip`, and then `Take`, you can return a specific number of records from a specific location of the resultset. This is shown in Listing 9-17.

Listing 9-17: Simple Paging using LINQ methods

VB

```
Protected Sub Page_Load(ByVal sender As Object, ByVal e As System.EventArgs)
    Dim movies = GetMovies()
    Dim genres = GetGenres()

    Dim query = (From m In movies _
                 Join g In genres On m.Genre Equals g.ID _
                 Select New With {m.Title, .Genre = g.Name}).Skip(10).Take(10)

    Me.GridView1.DataSource = query
    Me.GridView1.DataBind()
    End Sub
```

C#

```
protected void Page_Load(object sender, EventArgs e)
{
    var movies = GetMovies();
    var genres = GetGenres();

    var query = (from m in movies
                 join g in genres on m.Genre equals g.ID
                 select new { m.Title, g.Name }).Skip(10).Take(10);

    this.GridView1.DataSource = query;
    this.GridView1.DataBind();
}
```

When running this code, you will see that the results start with the tenth record in the list, and only ten records are displayed.

LINQ to XML

The second flavor of LINQ is called LINQ to XML (or XLINQ). As the name implies, LINQ to XML enables you to use the same basic LINQ syntax to query XML documents. As with the basic LINQ features, the LINQ to XML features of .NET are included as an extension to the basic .NET framework, and do not change any existing functionality. Also, as with the core LINQ features, the LINQ to XML features are contained in their own separate assembly, the System.Xml.Linq assembly.

In this section, to show how you can use LINQ to query XML, we use the same basic Movie data as in the previous section, but converted to XML. Listing 9-18 shows a portion of the Movie data converted to a simple XML document. The XML file containing the complete set of converted data can be found in the downloadable code for this chapter.

Listing 9-18: Sample Movies XML data file

```
<?xml version="1.0" encoding="utf-8" ?>
<Movies>
  <Movie>
    <Title>Shrek</Title>
    <Director>Andrew Adamson</Director>
    <Genre>0</Genre>
    <ReleaseDate>5/16/2001</ReleaseDate>
    <RunTime>89</RunTime>
  </Movie>
  <Movie>
    <Title>Fletch</Title>
    <Director>Michael Ritchie</Director>
    <Genre>0</Genre>
    <ReleaseDate>5/31/1985</ReleaseDate>
    <RunTime>96</RunTime>
  </Movie>
  <Movie>
    <Title>Casablanca</Title>
    <Director>Michael Curtiz</Director>
    <Genre>1</Genre>
    <ReleaseDate>1/1/1942</ReleaseDate>
    <RunTime>102</RunTime>
  </Movie>
</Movies>
```

To get started seeing how you can use LINQ to XML to query XML documents, let's walk through some of the same basic queries we started with in the previous section. Listing 9-19 demonstrates a simple selection query using LINQ to XML.

Listing 9-19: Querying the XML Data file using LINQ

VB

```
<%@ Page Language="VB" %>

<script runat="server">
    Protected Sub Page_Load(ByVal sender As Object, ByVal e As System.EventArgs)
        Dim query = From m In _
                    XElement.Load(MapPath("Movies.xml")).Elements("Movie") _
```

```
                        Select m

            Me.GridView1.DataSource = query
            Me.GridView1.DataBind()
        End Sub
    </script>

    <html xmlns="http://www.w3.org/1999/xhtml">
    <head runat="server">
        <title>My Favorite Movies</title>
    </head>
    <body>
        <form id="form1" runat="server">
        <div>
            <asp:GridView ID="GridView1" runat="server">
            </asp:GridView>
        </div>
        </form>
    </body>
    </html>
```

C#

```
<script runat="server">
    protected void Page_Load(object sender, EventArgs e)
    {
        var query = from m in
                        XElement.Load(MapPath("Movies.xml")).Elements("Movie")
                    select m;

        this.GridView1.DataSource = query;
        this.GridView1.DataBind();
    }
</script>
```

Notice that in this query, you tell LINQ directly where to load the XML data from, and from which elements in that document it should retrieve the data, which in this case are all of the Movie elements. Other than that minor change, the LINQ query is identical to queries we have seen previously.

When you execute this code, you get a page that looks like Figure 9-6.

Notice that the fields included in the resultset of the query don't really show the node data as you might have expected, with each child node as a separate Field in the GridView. This is because the query used in the Listing returns a collection of generic XElement objects, not Movie objects as you might have expected. This is because by itself, LINQ has no way of identifying what object type each node should be mapped to. Thankfully, you can add a bit of mapping logic to the query to tell it to map each node to a Movie object, and how the nodes' sub-elements should map to the properties of the Movie object. This is shown in Listing 9-20.

Listing 9-20: Mapping XML elements using LINQ

VB

```
Protected Sub Page_Load(ByVal sender As Object, ByVal e As System.EventArgs)
    Dim query = From m In XElement.Load(MapPath("Movies.xml")).Elements("Movie") _
```

Continued

```
                    Select New Movie With { _
                                .Title = CStr(m.Element("Title")), _
                                .Director = CStr(m.Element("Director")), _
                                .Genre = CInt(m.Element("Genre")), _
                                .ReleaseDate = CDate(m.Element("ReleaseDate")), _
                                .Runtime = CInt(m.Element("Runtime")) _
                            }

    Me.GridView1.DataSource = query
    Me.GridView1.DataBind()
End Sub
```

C#

```
protected void Page_Load(object sender, EventArgs e)
{
    var query = from m in XElement.Load(MapPath("Movies.xml")).Elements("Movie")
                select new Movie {
                            Title = (string)m.Element("Title"),
                            Director = (string)m.Element("Director"),
                            Genre = (int)m.Element("Genre"),
                            ReleaseDate = (DateTime)m.Element("ReleaseDate"),
                            RunTime = (int)m.Element("RunTime")
                        };

    this.GridView1.DataSource = query;
    this.GridView1.DataBind();
}
```

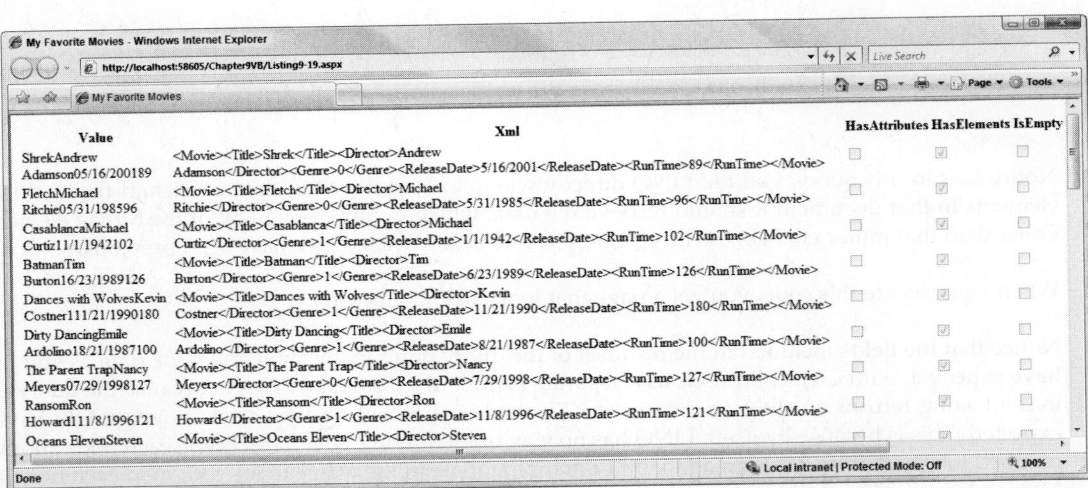

Figure 9-6: LINQ to XML raw query results

As you can see, we have modified the query to include mapping logic so that LINQ knows what our actual intentions are — to create a resultset that contains the values of the Movie elements' inner nodes. Running this code now results in a GridView that contains what we want, as shown in Figure 9-7.

Note that the XElements `Load` method attempts to load the entire XML document; therefore, it is not a good idea to try to load very large XML files using this method.

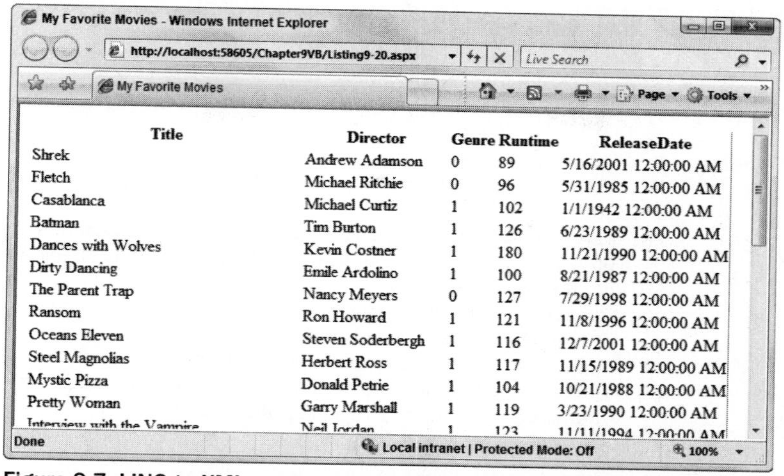
My Favorite Movies - Windows Internet Explorer
http://localhost:58605/Chapter9VB/Listing9-20.aspx
Live Search
My Favorite Movies
Page
Tools
Title
Director
Genre
Runtime
ReleaseDate
Shrek
Andrew Adamson
0
89
5/16/2001 12:00:00 AM
Fletch
Michael Ritchie
0
96
5/31/1985 12:00:00 AM
Casablanca
Michael Curtiz
1
102
1/1/1942 12:00:00 AM
Batman
Tim Burton
1
126
6/23/1989 12:00:00 AM
Dances with Wolves
Kevin Costner
1
180
11/21/1990 12:00:00 AM
Dirty Dancing
Emile Ardolino
1
100
8/21/1987 12:00:00 AM
The Parent Trap
Nancy Meyers
0
127
7/29/1998 12:00:00 AM
Ransom
Ron Howard
1
121
11/8/1996 12:00:00 AM
Oceans Eleven
Steven Soderbergh
1
116
12/7/2001 12:00:00 AM
Steel Magnolias
Herbert Ross
1
117
11/15/1989 12:00:00 AM
Mystic Pizza
Donald Petrie
1
104
10/21/1988 12:00:00 AM
Pretty Woman
Garry Marshall
1
119
3/23/1990 12:00:00 AM
Done
Local intranet | Protected Mode: Off
100%

Figure 9-7: LINQ to XML query with the data properly mapped to a Movie object

Joining XML Data

LINQ to XML supports all of the same query filtering and grouping operations as LINQ to Objects. It also supports joining data and can actually union together data from two different XML documents — a task that previously would have been quite difficult. Let's look at the same basic join scenario as was presented in the LINQ to objects section. Again, our basic XML data includes only an ID value for the Genre. It would, however, be better to show the actual Genre name with our resultset.

In the case of the XML data, rather than being kept in a separate List, the Genre data is actually stored in a completed separate XML file, showing in Listing 9-21.

Listing 9-21: Genres XML data

```
<?xml version="1.0" encoding="utf-8" ?>
<Genres>
    <Genre>
        <ID>0</ID>
        <Name>Comedy</Name>
    </Genre>
    <Genre>
        <ID>1</ID>
        <Name>Drama</Name>
    </Genre>
    <Genre>
        <ID>2</ID>
        <Name>Action</Name>
    </Genre>
</Genres>
```

To join the data together, you can use a very similar join query to that used in Listing 9-16. This is shown in Listing 9-22.

Listing 9-22: Joining XML data using LINQ

VB

```
Protected Sub Page_Load(ByVal sender As Object, ByVal e As System.EventArgs)

    Dim query = From m In _
                XElement.Load(MapPath("Listing9-18.xml")).Elements("Movie") _
                Join g In _
                XElement.Load(MapPath("Listing9-21.xml")).Elements("Genre") _
                    On CInt(m.Element("Genre")) Equals CInt(g.Element("ID")) _
                Select New With { _
                    .Title = CStr(m.Element("Title")), _
                    .Director = CStr(m.Element("Director")), _
                    .Genre = CStr(g.Element("Name")), _
                    .ReleaseDate = CDate(m.Element("ReleaseDate")), _
                    .Runtime = CInt(m.Element("RunTime")) _
                }

    Me.GridView1.DataSource = query
    Me.GridView1.DataBind()
End Sub
```

C#

```
protected void Page_Load(object sender, EventArgs e)
{
    var query = from m in XElement.Load(MapPath("Movies.xml")).Elements("Movie")
                join g in XElement.Load(MapPath("Genres.xml")).Elements("Genre")
                    on (int)m.Element("Genre") equals (int)g.Element("ID")
                select new {
                           Title = (string)m.Element("Title"),
                           Director = (string)m.Element("Director"),
                           Genre = (string)g.Element("Name"),
                           ReleaseDate = (DateTime)m.Element("ReleaseDate"),
                           RunTime = (int)m.Element("RunTime")
                       };

    this.GridView1.DataSource = query;
    this.GridView1.DataBind();
}
```

In this sample, you can see we are using the `XElement.Load` method as part of the LINQ join statement to tell LINQ where to load the Genre data from. Once the data is joined, you can access the elements of the Genre data as you can the elements of the movie data.

LINQ to SQL

LINQ to SQL is the last form of LINQ in this release of .NET. LINQ to SQL, as the name implies, enables you to quickly and easily query SQL-based data sources, such as SQL Server 2005. As with the prior flavors of LINQ, LINQ to SQL is an extension of .NET. Its features are located in the System.Data.Linq assembly.

In addition to the normal Intellisense and strong type checking that every flavor of LINQ gives you, LINQ to SQL also includes a basic Object Relation (O/R) mapper directly in Visual Studio. The O/R mapper enables you to quickly map SQL-based data sources to CLR objects that you can then use LINQ to query. It is the easiest way to get started using LINQ to SQL.

The O/R mapper is used by adding the new Linq to SQL Classes file to your Web site project. The Linq to SQL File document type allows you to easily and visually create data contexts that you can then access and query with LINQ queries. Figure 9-8 shows the Linq to SQL Classes file type in the Add New Item dialog.

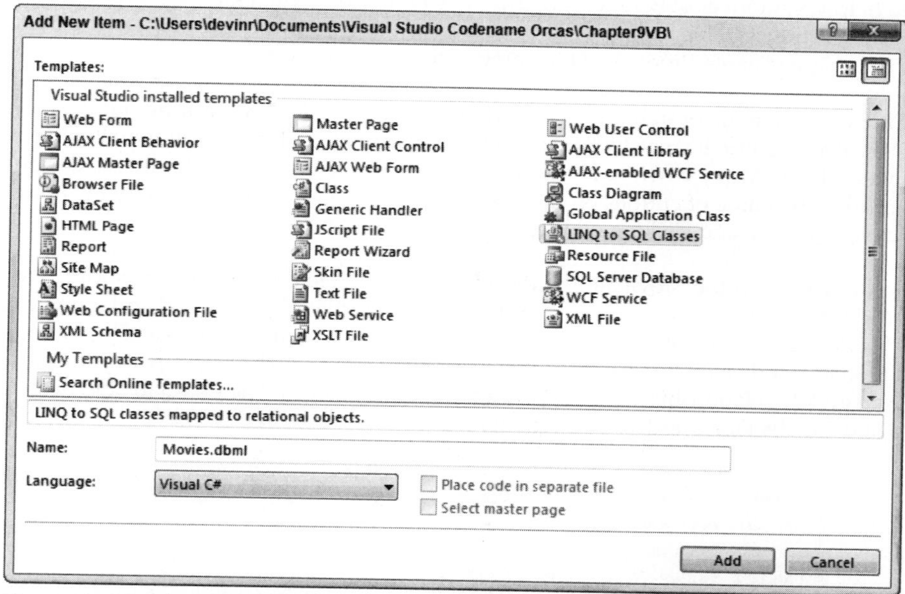

Figure 9-8: The Add New Item dialog includes the new Linq to SQL File type

After clicking the Add New Items dialog's OK button to add the file to your project, Visual Studio notifies you that it wants to add the LINQ to SQL File to your Web site's App_Code directory. By locating the file there, the data context created by the LINQ to SQL Classes file will be accessible from anywhere in your Web site.

Once the file has been added, Visual Studio automatically opens it in the LINQ to SQL design surface. This is a simple Object Relation mapper design tool, enabling you to add, create, remove, and relate data objects. As you modify objects to the design surface, LINQ to SQL is generating object classes that mirror the structure of each of those objects. Later when you are ready to begin writing LINQ queries against the data objects, these classes will allow Visual Studio to provide you with design-time Intellisense support, strong typing and compile-time type checking. Because the O/R mapper is primarily designed to be used with LINQ to SQL, it also makes it easy to create CLR object representations of SQL objects, such as Tables, Views, and Stored Procedures.

To demonstrate using LINQ to SQL, we will use the same sample Movie data used in previous sections of this chapter. For this section, the data is stored in a SQL Server Express database.

A copy of this database is included in the downloadable code from the Wrox Web site (`www.wrox.com`).

After the design surface is open and ready, open the Visual Studio Server Explorer tool and locate the Movies database and expand the database's Tables folder. Drag the Movies table from the Server Explorer onto the design surface. Notice that as soon as you drop the database table onto the design surface, it is automatically interrogated to identify its structure. A corresponding entity class is created by the designer and shown on the design surface.

When you drop table objects onto the LINQ to SQL design surface, Visual Studio examines the entities name and will if necessary, attempt to automatically pluralize the class names it generated. It does this in order to help you more closely following the .NET Framework class naming standards. For example, if you drop the Products table from the Northwind database onto the design surface, it would automatically choose the singular name Product as the name of the generated class.

Unfortunately, while the designer generally does a pretty good job at figuring out the correct pluralization for the class names, it's not 100% accurate. Case in point, simply look at how it incorrectly pluralizes the Movies table to Movy when you drop it into the design surface. Thankfully the designer also allows you to change the name of entities on the design surface. You can do this simply by selecting the entity on the design surface and clicking on the entities name in designer.

Once you have added the Movie entity, drag the Genres table onto the design surface. Again, Visual Studio creates a class representation of this table (and notice it gives it the singular name Genre). Additionally, it detects an existing foreign key relationship between the Movie and Genre. Because it detects this relationship, a dashed line is added between the two tables. The lines arrow indicates the direction of the foreign key relationship that exists between the two tables. The LINQ to SQL design surface with Movies and Genres tables added is shown in Figure 9-9.

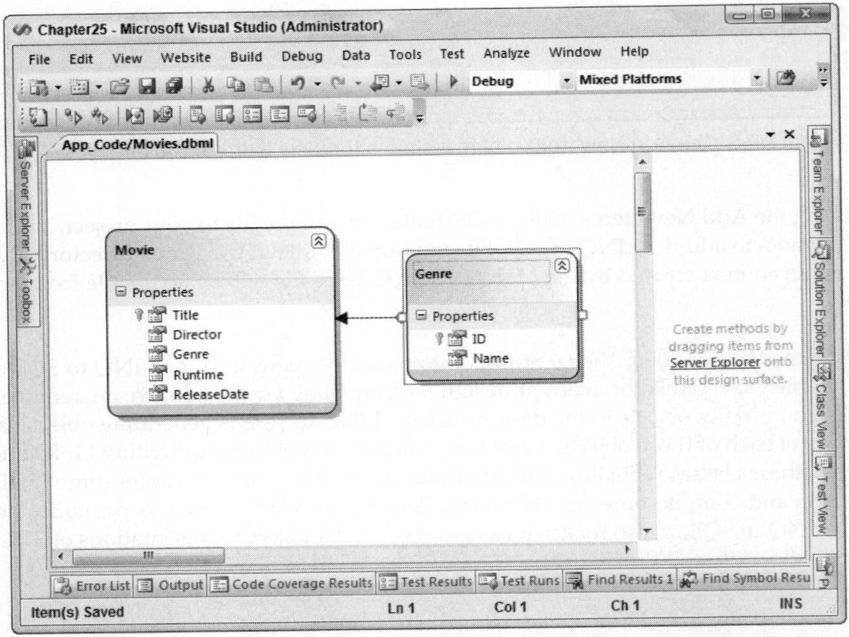

Figure 9-9: The Movies and Genres tables after being added to the LINQ to SQL design surface

Now that you have set up your LINQ to SQL File, accessing its data context and querying its data is simple. To start, you need to create an instance of the data context in the Web page where you will be accessing the data, as shown in Listing 9-23.

Listing 9-23: Creating a new Data Context

VB

```
<%@ Page Language="VB" %>

<script runat="server">
    Protected Sub Page_Load(ByVal sender As Object, ByVal e As System.EventArgs)
        Dim dc As New MoviesDataContext()
    End Sub
</script>

<html xmlns="http://www.w3.org/1999/xhtml">
<head runat="server">
    <title> My Favorite Movies </title>
</head>
<body>
    <form id="form1" runat="server">
    <div>
        <asp:GridView ID="GridView1" runat="server">
        </asp:GridView>

    </div>
    </form>
</body>
</html>
```

C#

```
<script runat="server">
    protected void Page_Load(object sender, EventArgs e)
    {
        MoviesDataContext dc = new MoviesDataContext();

    }
</script>
```

In this case you created an instance of the MoviesDataContext, which is the name of the data context class generated by the LINQ to SQL File you added earlier.

Because the data context class is automatically generated by the LINQ to SQL file, its name will change each time you create a new LINQ to SQL file. The name of this class is determined by appending the name of your LINQ to SQL Class file with the DataContext suffix, so had you named your LINQ to SQL File Northwind.dbml, the data context class would have been NorthwindDataContext.

After you have added the data context to your page, you can begin writing LINQ queries against it. As mentioned earlier, because LINQ to SQL generated object classes mirror the structure of our database tables, you will get Intellisense support as you write your LINQ queries. Listing 9-24 shows the same basic Movie listing query that has been shown in prior sections.

Listing 9-24: Querying Movie data from LINQ to SQL

VB

```
Protected Sub Page_Load(ByVal sender As Object, ByVal e As System.EventArgs)
    Dim dc As New MoviesDataContext()

    Dim query = From m In dc.Movies _
                Select m

    Me.GridView1.DataSource = query
    Me.GridView1.DataBind()
End Sub
```

C#

```
protected void Page_Load(object sender, EventArgs e)
{
    MoviesDataContext dc = new MoviesDataContext();

    var query = from m in dc.Movies
                select m;

    this.GridView1.DataSource = query;
    this.GridView1.DataBind();
}
```

As is shown in Figure 9-10, running the code generates a raw list of the Movies in our database.

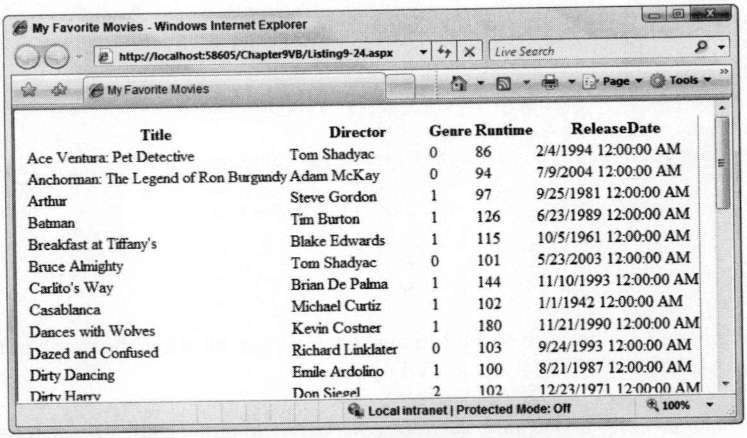

Figure 9-10: Data retrieved from a basic LINQ to SQL query

Note that we did not have to write any of the database access code that would typically have been required to create this page. LINQ has taken care of that for us, even generating the SQL query based on our LINQ syntax. You can see the SQL that LINQ generated for the query by writing the query to the Visual Studio output window, as shown in Listing 9-25.

Listing 9-25: Writing the LINQ to SQL query to the output window

VB

```
Protected Sub Page_Load(ByVal sender As Object, ByVal e As System.EventArgs)
```

```
        Dim dc As New MoviesDataContext()

        Dim query = From m In dc.Movies _
                    Select m

        System.Diagnostics.Debug.WriteLine(query)

        Me.GridView1.DataSource = query
        Me.GridView1.DataBind()
    End Sub
```

C#

```
protected void Page_Load(object sender, EventArgs e)
{
    MoviesDataContext dc = new MoviesDataContext();

    var query = from m in dc.Movies
                select m;

    System.Diagnostics.Debug.WriteLine(query);

    this.GridView1.DataSource = query;
    this.GridView1.DataBind();
}
```

Now, when you debug the Web site using Visual Studio, you can see the SQL query, as shown in Figure 9-11.

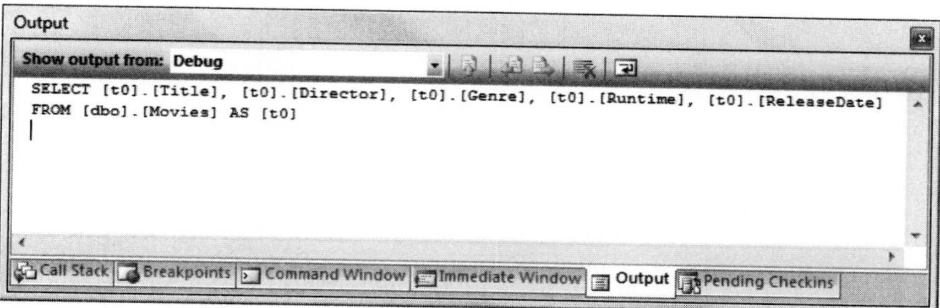

Figure 9-11: The SQL query generated by LINQ to SQL

As you can see, the SQL generated is standard SQL syntax, and LINQ is quite good at optimizing the queries it generates, even for more complex queries such as the grouping query shown in Listing 9-26.

Listing 9-26: Grouping LINQ to SQL data

VB

```
Protected Sub Page_Load(ByVal sender As Object, ByVal e As System.EventArgs)
    Dim dc As New MoviesDataContext()

    Dim query = From m In dc.Movies _
                Group By m.Genre Into g = Group, Count()
```

Continued

```
        System.Diagnostics.Debug.WriteLine(query)

        Me.GridView1.DataSource = query
        Me.GridView1.DataBind()

    End Sub
```

C#

```
protected void Page_Load(object sender, EventArgs e)
{
    MoviesDataContext dc = new MoviesDataContext();

    var query = from m in dc.Movies
                group m by m.Genre into g
                select new { Genre  = g.Key, Count = g.Count() };

    System.Diagnostics.Debug.WriteLine(query);

    this.GridView1.DataSource = query;
    this.GridView1.DataBind();
}
```

The generated SQL for this query is shown in Figure 9-12.

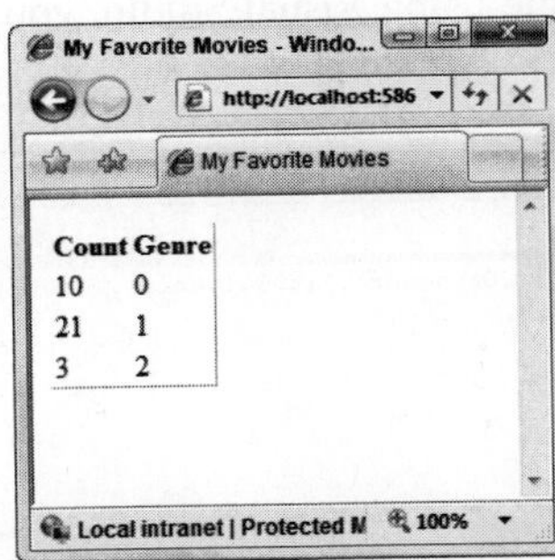

Figure 9-12: Grouping SQL data using LINQ to SQL

Note that SQL to LINQ generates SQL that is optimized for SQL Server 2005.

LINQ also includes a logging option you can enable by setting the Log property of the data context.

While LINQ to SQL does an excellent job generating the SQL query syntax, there may be times where it is more appropriate to use other SQL query methods, such as Stored Procedures, or Views. LINQ supports using the predefined queries as well.

To use a SQL View with LINQ to SQL, you simply drag the View onto the LINQ to SQL design surface just as you would a standard SQL table. Views appear on the design surface, just as the tables we added earlier. Once the View is on the design surface, you can execute queries against it, just as you did the SQL tables. This is shown in Listing 9-27.

Listing 9-27: Querying LINQ to SQL data using a View

VB

```
Protected Sub Page_Load(ByVal sender As Object, ByVal e As System.EventArgs)
    Dim dc As New MoviesDataContext()

    Dim query = From m In dc.AllMovies _
                Select m

    System.Diagnostics.Debug.WriteLine(query)

    Me.GridView1.DataSource = query
    Me.GridView1.DataBind()
End Sub
```

C#

```
protected void Page_Load(object sender, EventArgs e)
{
    MoviesDataContext dc = new MoviesDataContext();

    var query = from m in dc.AllMovies
                select m;

    System.Diagnostics.Debug.WriteLine(query);

    this.GridView1.DataSource = query;
    this.GridView1.DataBind();
}
```

Unlike Tables or Views, which LINQ to SQL exposes as properties, Stored Procedures can require parameters. Therefore, LINQ to SQL exposes them from the data context object as method calls, allowing you to provide method parameter values, which are translated by LINQ into store procedure parameters. Listing 2-28 shows a simple stored procedure you can use to retrieve a specific Genre from the database.

Listing 9-28: Simple SQL Stored procedure

```
CREATE PROCEDURE dbo.GetGenre
    (
    @id int
    )

AS
    SELECT * FROM Genre WHERE ID = @id
```

You can add a Stored Procedure to your LINQ to SQL designer just as you did the Tables and Views, by dragging them from the Server Explorer onto the LINQ to SQL Classes design surface. If you expect your stored procedure to return a collection of data from a table in your database, you should drop the stored procedure onto the LINQ class that represents the types returned by the query. In the case of the stored procedure shown in Listing 9-28, it will return all of the Genre records that match the provided ID, therefore you should drop the GetGenres stored procedure onto the Genres table in the Visual Studio designer. This tells the designer to generate a method that returns a generic collection of Genre objects. Once you drop the stored procedure onto the design surface, unlike the Tables and Views, the Stored Procedure will be displayed in a list on the right-hand side of the design surface. The GetGenre stored procedure is shown after being added in Figure 9-13.

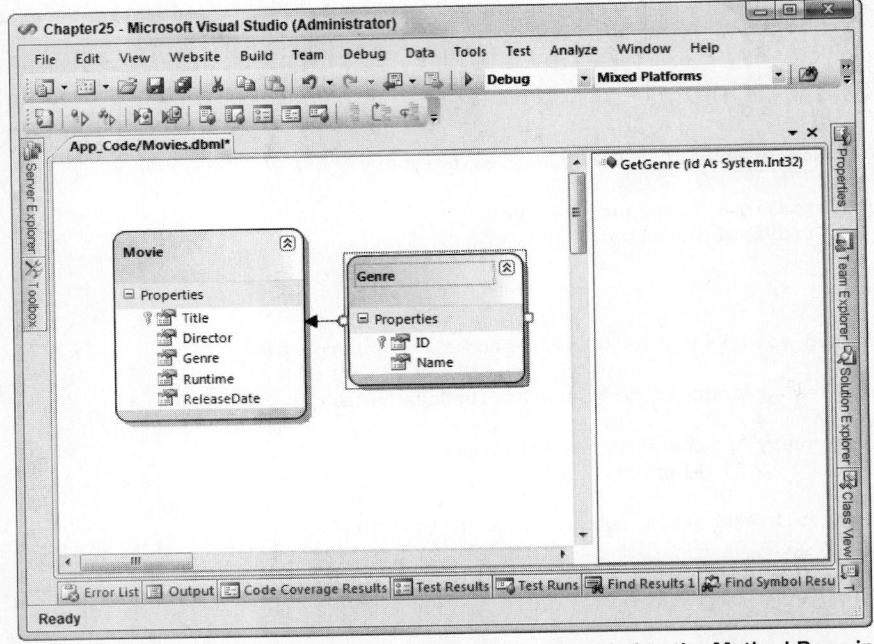

Figure 9-13: The GetGenre stored procedure has been added to the Method Pane in the LINQ to SQL design surface

After you have added the Stored Procedures, you can access them through the data context, just as the Table and Views we accessed. As was stated earlier, however, LINQ to SQL exposes them as method calls. Therefore, they may require you to provide method parameters, as shown in Listing 9-29.

Listing 9-29: Selecting data from a Stored Procedure

VB

```
Protected Sub Page_Load(ByVal sender As Object, ByVal e As System.EventArgs)
    Dim dc As New MoviesDataContext()

    Me.GridView1.DataSource = dc.GetGenre(1)
    Me.GridView1.DataBind()
End Sub
```

C#

```
protected void Page_Load(object sender, EventArgs e)
{
    MoviesDataContext dc = new MoviesDataContext();
```

```
        this.GridView1.DataSource = dc.GetGenre(1);
        this.GridView1.DataBind();
    }
```

Insert, Update, and Delete Queries through LINQ

Not only can LINQ to SQL be used to create powerful queries that select data from a data source, but it can also manage insert, updates, and delete operations. By default, LINQ to SQL does this in much the same manner as selecting data. LINQ to SQL uses the object class representations of the SQL structures and dynamically generates SQL Insert, Update, and Delete commands. As with selection, you can also use Stored Procedures to perform the insert, update, or deletes.

Insert Data Using LINQ

Inserting data using LINQ to SQL is as easy as creating a new instance of the object you want to insert, and adding that to the object collection. The LINQ classes provide two methods called InsertOnSubmit and InsertAllOnSubmit, which make it simple to create and add any object to a LINQ collection. The InsertOnSubmit accepts a single entity as its method parameter, allowing you to insert a single entity, while the InsertAllOnSubmit method accepts a collection as its method parameter, allowing you to insert an entire collection of data in a single method call.

Once you have added your objects, LINQ to SQL does require the extra step of calling the Data Context objects SubmitChanges method. Calling this method tells LINQ to initiate the Insert action. Listing 9-30 shows an example of creating a new Movies object, and then Adding it to the Movies collection and calling SubmitChanges to persist the change back to the SQL database.

Listing 9-30: Inserting data using LINQ to SQL

VB

```
Protected Sub Page_Load(ByVal sender As Object, ByVal e As System.EventArgs)
    Dim dc As New MoviesDataContext()

    Dim m As New Movie With {.Title = "The Princess Bride", _
        .Director = "Rob Reiner", .Genre = 0, _
        .ReleaseDate = DateTime.Parse("9/25/1987"), .Runtime = 98}

    dc.Movies.InsertOnSubmit(m)
    dc.SubmitChanges()

End Sub
```

C#

```
protected void Page_Load(object sender, EventArgs e)
{
    MoviesDataContext dc = new MoviesDataContext();

    Movie m = new Movie { Title="The Princess Bride",
        Director="Rob Reiner", Genre=0,
```

Continued

```
            ReleaseDate=DateTime.Parse("9/25/1987"), Runtime=98 };

        dc.Movies.InsertOnSubmit(m);
        dc.SubmitChanges();
    }
```

Using Stored Procedures to Insert Data

Of course, you may already have a complex stored procedure written to handle the insertion of data into your database table. LINQ makes it simple to use an existing Stored Procedure to insert data into a table. To do this, on the LINQ to SQL design surface, select the entity you want to insert data into, which in this case is the Movies entity. After selecting the entity, open its properties window and locate the Default Methods section, as shown in Figure 9-14.

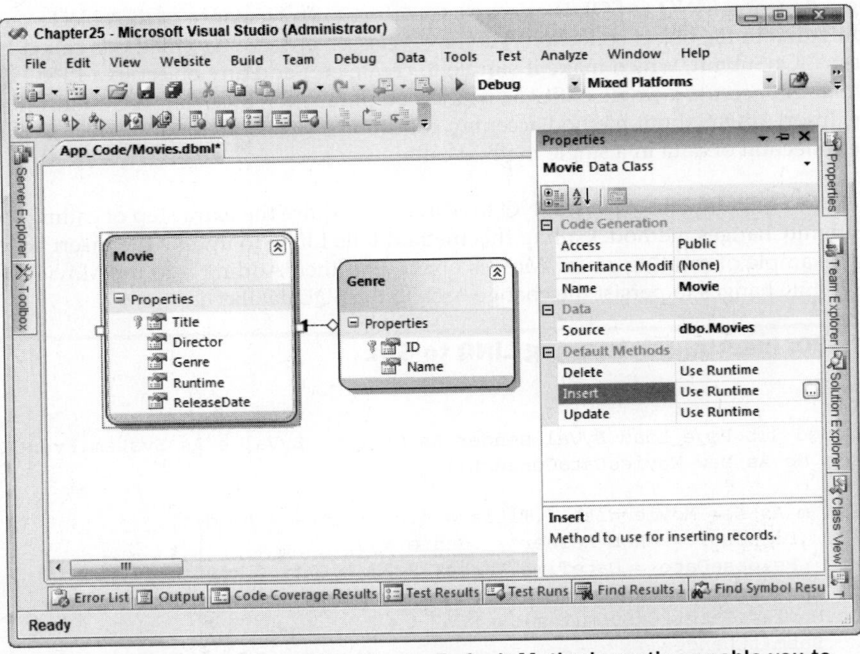

Figure 9-14: The properties of the Movies Default Methods section enable you to configure the Delete, Insert, and Update behavior of LINQ to SQL for this table

The Default Methods section contains three properties, Delete, Insert, and Update, which define the behavior LINQ should use when executing these actions on the Movies table. By default, each property is set to the value `UseRuntime`, which tells LINQ to dynamically generate SQL statements at runtime. Because you want to insert data into the table using a Stored Procedure, open the Insert properties Configure Behavior dialog.

In the dialog, change the Behavior radio button selection from Use Runtime to Customize. Next, select the appropriate stored procedure from the drop-down list below the radio buttons. When you select the stored procedure, LINQ automatically tries to match the table columns to the stored procedure input parameters. However, you can change these manually, if needed.

The final Configure Behavior dialog is shown in Figure 9-15.

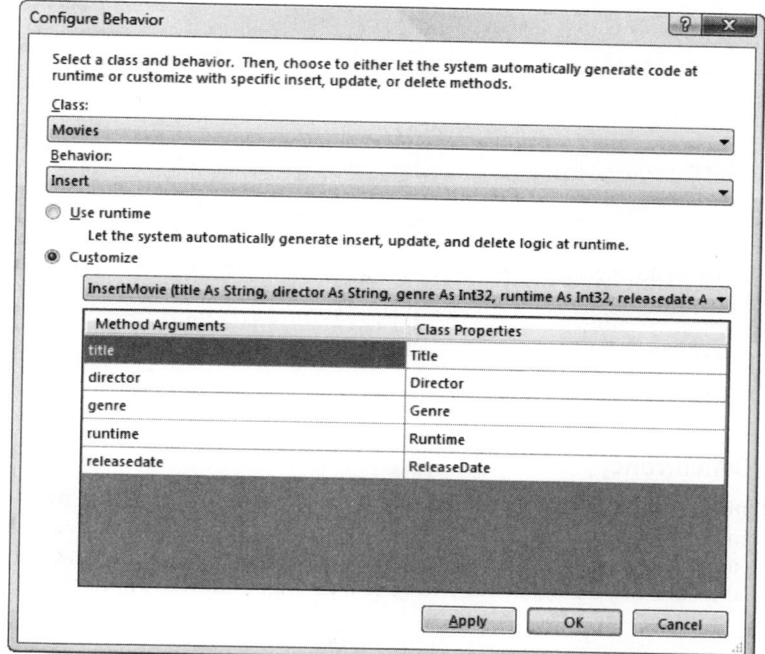

Figure 9-15: Configure Behavior dialog configured for the InsertMovie Stored Procedure

Now, when you run the code from Listing 9-30, LINQ will use the stored procedure you configured instead of dynamically generating a SQL Insert statement.

Update Data Using LINQ

Updating data with LINQ is very similar to inserting data. The first set is to get the specific object you want to update. You can do this by using the Single method of the collection you want to change. The scalar Single method returns a single object from the collection based on its input parameter. If more than one record matches the parameters, the Single method simply returns the first match.

Once you have the record you want to update, you simply change the object's property values, and then call the data context's SubmitChanges method. Listing 9-31 shows the code required to update a specific Movie.

Listing 9-31: Updating data using LINQ to SQL

VB

```
Protected Sub Page_Load(ByVal sender As Object, ByVal e As System.EventArgs)
    Dim dc As New MoviesDataContext()

    Dim movie = dc.Movies.Single(Function(m) m.Title = "Fletch")
    movie.Genre = 1

    dc.SubmitChanges()
End Sub
```

C#

```
protected void Page_Load(object sender, EventArgs e)
{
    MoviesDataContext dc = new MoviesDataContext();

    var movie = dc.Movies.Single(m => m.Title == "Fletch");
    movie.Genre = 1;

    dc.SubmitChanges();
}
```

Handling Data Concurrency

LINQ to SQL also includes and uses by default optimistic concurrency. That means that if two users retrieve the same record from the database and both try to update it, the first user to submit their update to the server wins. If the second user attempts to update the record after the first, LINQ to SQL will detect that the original record has changed and will raise a ChangeConflictException.

Deleting Data Using LINQ

Finally, LINQ to SQL also enables you to delete data from your SQL data source. Each data class object generated by the LINQ to SQL designer also includes two methods that enable you to delete objects from the collection, the `DeleteOnSubmit` and `DeleteAllOnSubmit` methods. As the names imply, the `DeleteOnSubmit` method removes a single object from the collection, whereas the `DeleteAllOnSubmit` method removes all records from the collection.

Listing 9-32 shows how you can use LINQ and the `DeleteOnSubmit` and `DeleteAllOnSubmit` methods to delete data from your data source.

Listing 9-32: Deleting data using LINQ to SQL

VB

```
Protected Sub Page_Load(ByVal sender As Object, ByVal e As System.EventArgs)
    Dim dc As New MoviesDataContext()

    'Select and remove all Action movies
    Dim query = From m In dc.Movies _
                Where (m.Genre = 2) _
                Select m
```

```
        dc.Movies.DeleteAllOnSubmit(query)

        'Select a single movie and remove it
        Dim movie = dc.Movies.Single(Function(m) m.Title = "Fletch")
        dc.Movies.DeleteOnSubmit(movie)

        dc.SubmitChanges()
    End Sub
```

C#

```
protected void Page_Load(object sender, EventArgs e)
{
    MoviesDataContext dc = new MoviesDataContext();

    //Select and remove all Action movies
    var query = from m in dc.Movies
                where m.Genre == 2
                select m;

    dc.Movies.DeleteAllOnSubmit(query);

    //Select a single movie and remove it
    var movie = dc.Movies.Single(m => m.Title == "Fletch");
    dc.Movies.DeleteOnSubmit(movie);

    dc.SubmitChanges();
}
```

As with the other SQL commands, you must remember to call the Data Contexts `SubmitChanges` method in order to commit the changes back to the SQL data source.

Extending LINQ

This chapter focuses primarily on the LINQ capabilities included in the .NET framework, but LINQ is highly extensible and can be used to create query frameworks over just about any data source. While showing you how to implement you own LINQ provider is beyond the scope of this chapter, there are lots of implementations of LINQ that query a wide variety of data stores such as LDAP, Sharepoint, and even `Amazon.com`.

Roger Jennings from Oakleaf Systems maintains a list of third-party LINQ providers on his blog which can be found at `http://oakleafblog.blogspot.com/2007/03/third-party-linq-providers.html`.

Summary

This chapter has introduced you to the new Language Integrated Query, or LINQ, features of .NET 3.5, which greatly simplifies the querying of data in .NET. LINQ makes query a first class concept, embedded directly in .NET.

In this review of LINQ, we first looked at the current methods for performing object queries, including basic data filtering, grouping, and sorting. We looked at the shortcomings of current object query techniques, including the requirement for developers to not only define what the query should do, but also exactly how it should do it. Additionally, we looked at how even simple operations can result in highly complex code that can be difficult to read and maintain.

Next, we began looking at the three basic types of LINQ — LINQ to Objects, LINQ to XML, and LINQ to SQL. Each flavor of LINQ uses the same basic query syntax to dramatically simplify the querying of Objects, XML or SQL. We looked at how you can use the basic SQL-like query syntax for selection, filtering, and grouping. This query syntax is clean and easily readable, and also includes many of the same operator features as SQL.

We also looked at the basic O/R mapper that is included with LINQ to SQL. The O/R mapper makes it easy to create CLR objects that represent SQL structures such as Tables, Views, and Stored Procedures. Once the CLR objects are created, LINQ can be used to query the objects.

Finally we looked at how using LINQ to SQL, you can easily change the data in your database, using generated SQL statements, or using custom Stored Procedures.

10

Working with XML and LINQ to XML

This is not a book about XML, the eXtensible Markup Language; but XML has become such a part of an ASP.NET programmer's life that the topic deserves its own chapter. Although most of the XML functionality in the .NET Framework appears to be in the `System.Xml` namespace, you can find XML's influence throughout the entire Framework, including `System.Data` and `System.Web`.

XML is oft maligned and misunderstood. To some, XML is simply a text-based markup language; to others it is an object serialization format or a document-encoding standard. In fact, XML has become the de facto standard manner in which data passes around the Internet. XML, however, is not really a technology as much as it is a set of standards or guiding principles. It provides a structure within which data can be stored; but the XML specification doesn't dictate how XML processors, parsers, formatters, and data access methods should be written or implemented. `System.Xml`, `System.Xml.Linq`, and other namespaces contain the .NET Framework 3.5's view on how programmers should manipulate XML. Some of its techniques, such as XSLT and XML Schema, are standards-based. Others, like `XmlReader` and `XmlWriter`, started in the world of the .NET Framework and now Java has similar classes. The .NET Framework 3.5 — along with new compilers for C# 3.0 and VB 9 — brings LINQ and LINQ to XML as a Language-Integrated Query over XML to the table.

This is an ASP.NET book, aimed at the professional Web developer, so it can't be a book all about LINQ. However, a single chapter can't do LINQ justice. Rather than making this a chapter that focuses exclusively on just `System.Xml` or `System.Xml.Linq`, this chapter will present the new LINQ model and syntax as a juxtaposition to the way you're used to manipulating XML. The examples will include both the traditional and the new LINQ way of doing things. We recognize that you won't go and rewrite all your `System.Xml` code to use LINQ just because it's cool, but seeing the new syntax alongside what you are used to is an excellent way to learn the syntax, and it also assists you in making decisions on which technology to use going forward.

In this chapter some listings will include a 'q' in the numbering scheme. These listings demonstrate how you can use LINQ to XML to accomplish the same task shown in the previous related listing. For example, Listing 10-5q shows the way you'd accomplish the task from Listing 10-5 using LINQ to XML.

You'll learn more about LINQ and its flexibility in the all new chapter dedicated to the technology. For the purposes of this chapter, know that `System.Xml.Linq` introduces an all new series of objects such as XDocument and XElement that in some ways complement the existing APIs, but in many ways, eclipse them. You'll also see how these new classes have provided "bridges" back and forth between `System.Xml` and `System.Xml.Linq` that will enable you to use many new techniques for clearer, simpler code, while still utilizing the very useful, powerful (and well-tested) features of the `System.Xml` classes you're used to.

Ultimately, however, remember that while the .NET Framework has its own unique style of API around the uses of XML, the XML consumed and produced by these techniques is standards-based and can be used by other languages that consume XML. This chapter covers all the major techniques for manipulating XML provided by the .NET Framework. `XmlReader` and `XmlWriter` offer incredible speed but may require a bit more thought. The XmlDocument or DOM is the most commonly used method for manipulating XML, but you'll pay dearly in performance penalties without careful use. ADO .NET DataSets have always provided XML support, and their deep support continues with .NET 3.5. XML Stylesheet Tree Transformations (XSLT) gained debugging capabilities in Visual Studio 2005, and is improved with new features in Visual Studio 2008, such as XSLT Data Breakpoints and better support in the editor for loading large documents. Additionally, XSLT stylesheets can be compiled into assemblies even more easily with the new command-line stylesheet compiler. ASP.NET continues to make development easier with some simple yet powerful server controls to manipulate XML.

Its flexibility and room for innovation make XML very powerful and a joy to work with.

Note that when the acronym XML appears by itself, the whole acronym is capitalized, but when it appears in a function name or namespace, only the X is capitalized, as in `System.Xml` or `XmlTextReader`. Microsoft's API Design Guidelines dictate that if an abbreviation of three or more characters appears in a variable name, class name, or namespace, the first character is capitalized.

The Basics of XML

Listing 10-1, a `Books.xml` document that represents a bookstore's inventory database, is one of the sample documents used in this chapter. This example document has been used in various MSDN examples for many years.

Listing 10-1: The Books.xml XML document

```
<?xml version='1.0'?>
<!-- This file is a part of a book store inventory database -->
<bookstore xmlns="http://example.books.com">
```

```
    <book genre="autobiography" publicationdate="1981" ISBN="1-861003-11-0">
        <title>The Autobiography of Benjamin Franklin</title>
        <author>
            <first-name>Benjamin</first-name>
            <last-name>Franklin</last-name>
        </author>
        <price>8.99</price>
    </book>
    <book genre="novel" publicationdate="1967" ISBN="0-201-63361-2">
        <title>The Confidence Man</title>
        <author>
            <first-name>Herman</first-name>
            <last-name>Melville</last-name>
        </author>
        <price>11.99</price>
    </book>
    <book genre="philosophy" publicationdate="1991" ISBN="1-861001-57-6">
        <title>The Gorgias</title>
        <author>
            <first-name>Sidas</first-name>
            <last-name>Plato</last-name>
        </author>
        <price>9.99</price>
    </book>
</bookstore>
```

The first line of Listing 10-1, starting with `<?xml version='1.0'?>`, is an XML declaration. This line should always appear before the first element in the XML document and indicates the version of XML with which this document is compliant.

The second line is an XML comment and uses the same syntax as an HTML comment. This isn't a coincidence; remember that XML and HTML are both descendants of SGML, the Standard Generalized Markup Language. Comments are always optional in XML documents

The third line, `<bookstore>`, is the opening tag of the root element or document entity of the XML document. An XML document can have only one root element. The last line in the document is the closing tag `</bookstore>` of the root element. No elements of the document can appear after the final closing tag `</bookstore>`. The `<bookstore>` element contains an `xmlns` attribute such as `xmlns="http://example.books.com"`. Namespaces in XML are similar to namespaces in the .NET Framework because they provide *qualification of elements and attributes*. It's very likely that someone else in the world has created a bookstore XML document before, and it's also likely he or she chose an element such as `<book>` or `<bookstore/>`. A namespace is defined to make your `<book>` element different from any others and to deal with the chance that other `<book>` elements might appear with yours in the same document — it's possible with XML.

This namespace is often a URL (Uniform/Universal Resource Locator), but it actually can be a URI (Uniform/Universal Resource Identifier). A namespace can be a GUID or a nonsense string such as `www-computerzen-com:schema` as long as it is unique. Recently, the convention has been to use a URL because URLs are ostensibly unique, thus making the document's associated schema unique. You will learn more about schemas and namespaces in the next section.

The fourth line is a little different because the `<book>` element contains some additional attributes such as `genre`, `publicationdate`, and `ISBN`. The order of the elements matters in an XML document, but the order of the attributes does not. These attributes are said to be *on* or *contained within* the book element. Consider the following line of code:

```
<book genre="autobiography" publicationdate="1981" ISBN="1-861003-11-0">
```

Notice that every element following this line has a matching end tag, similar to the example that follows:

```
<example>This is a test</example>
```

If no matching end tag is used, the XML is not well formed; technically it isn't even XML! These next two example XML fragments are not well formed because the elements don't match up:

```
<example>This is a test
```

```
<example>This is a test</anothertag>
```

If the `<example>` element is empty, it might appear like this:

```
<example></example>
```

Alternatively, it could appear as a shortcut like this:

```
<example/>
```

The syntax is different, but the semantics are the same. The difference between the syntax and the semantics of an XML document is crucial for understanding what XML is trying to accomplish. XML documents are text files by their nature, but the information — the information set — is representable using text that isn't exact. The set of information is the same, but the actual bytes are not.

> **Note that attributes appear only within start tags or empty elements such as `<book genre="scifi"></book>` or `<book genre = "scifi" />`. Visit the World Wide Web Consortium's (W3C) XML site at `www.w3.org/XML/` for more detailed information on XML.**

The XML InfoSet

The XML InfoSet is a W3C concept that describes what is and isn't significant in an XML document. The InfoSet isn't a class, a function, a namespace, or a language — the InfoSet is a concept.

Listing 10-2 describes two XML documents that are syntactically different but semantically the same.

Listing 10-2: XML syntax versus semantics

XML document

```
<?xml version='1.0'?>
<bookstore>
    <book genre="autobiography" publicationdate="1981" ISBN="1-861003-11-0">
        <title>The Autobiography of Benjamin Franklin</title>
        <author>
```

```
            <first-name>Benjamin</first-name>
            <last-name>Franklin</last-name>
        </author>
        <price></price>
    </book>
</bookstore>
```

XML document that differs in syntax, but not in semantics

```
<?xml version='1.0'?><bookstore><book genre="autobiography"
publicationdate="1981" ISBN="1-861003-11-0"><title>The Autobiography of Benjamin
Franklin</title><author><first-name>Benjamin</first-name>
<last-name>Franklin</last-name></author><price/></book></bookstore>
```

Certainly, the first document in Listing 10-2 is easier for a human to read, but the second document is just as easy for a computer to read. The second document has insignificant white space removed.

Notice also that the empty `<price/>` element is different in the two documents. The first uses the verbose form, whereas the second element uses the shortcut form to express an empty element. However, *both are empty elements.*

You can manipulate XML as elements and attributes. You can visualize XML as a tree of nodes. You rarely, if ever, have to worry about angle brackets or parse text yourself. A text-based differences (diff) tool would report these two documents are different because their character representations are different. An XML-based differences tool would report (correctly) that they are the same document. Each document contains the same InfoSet.

> **You can run a free XML Diff Tool online at** `http://www.deltaxml.com/free/compare/`.

XSD–XML Schema Definition

XML documents must be well formed at the very least. However, just because a document is well formed doesn't ensure that its elements are in the right order, have the right name, or are the correct data types. After creating a well-formed XML document, you should ensure that your document is also *valid*. A *valid* XML document is well formed and also has an associated XML Schema Definition (XSD) that describes what elements, simple types, and complex types are allowed in the document.

The schema for the `Books.xml` file is a glossary or vocabulary for the bookstore described in an XML Schema definition. In programming terms, an XML Schema is a type definition, whereas an XML document is an instance of that type. Listing 10-3 describes one possible XML Schema called `Books.xsd` that validates against the `Books.xml` file.

Listing 10-3: The Books.xsd XML Schema

```
<?xml version="1.0" encoding="utf-8" ?>
<xsd:schema xmlns:xsd="http://www.w3.org/2001/XMLSchema"
xmlns:tns="http://example.books.com"
xmlns="http://example.books.com"
targetNamespace="http://example.books.com"
```

Continued

```
elementFormDefault="qualified">

    <xsd:element name="bookstore" type="bookstoreType"/>

    <xsd:complexType name="bookstoreType">
        <xsd:sequence maxOccurs="unbounded">
            <xsd:element name="book" type="bookType"/>
        </xsd:sequence>
    </xsd:complexType>

    <xsd:complexType name="bookType">
        <xsd:sequence>
            <xsd:element name="title" type="xsd:string"/>
            <xsd:element name="author" type="authorName"/>
            <xsd:element name="price" type="xsd:decimal"/>
        </xsd:sequence>
        <xsd:attribute name="genre" type="xsd:string"/>
        <xsd:attribute name="publicationdate" type="xsd:string"/>
        <xsd:attribute name="ISBN" type="xsd:string"/>
    </xsd:complexType>

    <xsd:complexType name="authorName">
        <xsd:sequence>
            <xsd:element name="first-name" type="xsd:string"/>
            <xsd:element name="last-name" type="xsd:string"/>
        </xsd:sequence>
    </xsd:complexType>
</xsd:schema>
```

The XML Schema in Listing 10-3 starts by including a series of namespace prefixes used in the schema document as attributes on the root element. The prefix `xsd:` is declared on the root element (`xmlns:xsd="http://www.w3.org/2001/XMLSchema"`) and then used on all other elements of that schema. The default namespace assumed for any elements without prefixes is described by the `xmlns` attribute like this:

```
xmlns="http://example.books.com"
```

A namespace-qualified element has a prefix such as `<xsd:element>`. The target namespace for all elements in this schema is declared with the `targetNamespace` attribute.

XML Schema can be daunting at first; but if you read each line to yourself as a *declaration*, it makes more sense. For example, the line

```
<xsd:element name="bookstore" type="bookstoreType"/>
```

declares that an element named `bookstore` has the type `bookstoreType`. Because the `targetNamespace` for the schema is `http://example.books.com`, that is the namespace of each declared type in the `Books.xsd` schema. If you refer to Listing 10-1, you see that the namespace of the `Books.xml` document
is also `http://example.books.com`.

For more detailed information on XML Schema, visit the W3C's XML Schema site at `www.w3.org/XML/Schema`.

Editing XML and XML Schema in Visual Studio 2008

If you start up Visual Studio 2008 and open the `Books.xml` file into the editor, you notice immediately that the Visual Studio editor provides syntax highlighting and formats the XML document as a nicely indented tree. If you start writing a new XML element anywhere, you don't have access to IntelliSense. Even though the `http://example.books.com` namespace is the default namespace, Visual Studio 2008 has no way to find the `Books.xsd` file; it could be located anywhere. Remember that the namespace is *not* a URL. It's a URI — an identifier. Even if it were a URL it wouldn't be appropriate for the editor, or any program you write, to go out on the Web looking for a schema. You have to be explicit when associating XML Schema with instance documents.

Classes and methods are used to validate XML documents when you are working programmatically, but the Visual Studio editor needs a hint to find the `Book.xsd` schema. Assuming the `Books.xsd` file is in the same directory as `Books.xml`, you have three ways to inform the editor:

- ❑ Open the `Books.xsd` schema in Visual Studio in another window while the `Books.xml` file is also open.
- ❑ Include a `schemaLocation` attribute in the `Books.xml` file.
- ❑ If you open at least one XML file with the `schemaLocation` attribute set, Visual Studio uses that schema for any other open XML files that don't include the attribute.
- ❑ Add the `Books.xsd` schema to the list of schemas that Visual Studio knows about internally by adding it to the `Schemas` property in the document properties window of the `Books.xml` file. When schemas are added in this way, Visual Studio checks the document's namespace and determines if it already knows of a schema that matches.

The `schemaLocation` attribute is in a different namespace, so include the `xmlns` namespace attribute and your chosen prefix for the schema's location, as shown in Listing 10-4.

Listing 10-4: Updating the Books.xml file with a schemaLocation attribute

```
<?xml version='1.0'?>
<!-- This file is a part of a book store inventory database -->
<bookstore xmlns="http://example.books.com"
xmlns:xsi="http://www.w3.org/2001/XMLSchema-instance"
xsi:schemaLocation="http://example.books.com Books.xsd">
    <book genre="autobiography" publicationdate="1981" ISBN="1-861003-11-0">
        <title>The Autobiography of Benjamin Franklin</title>
        ...Rest of the XML document omitted for brevity...
```

The format for the `schemaLocation` attribute consists of pairs of strings separated by spaces where the first string in each pair is a namespace URI and the second string is the location of the schema. The location can be relative, as shown in Listing 10-4, or it can be an `http://` URL or `file://` location.

When the `Books.xsd` schema can be located for the `Books.xml` document, Visual Studio 2008's XML Editor becomes considerably more useful. Not only does the editor underline incorrect elements with blue squiggles, it also includes tooltips and IntelliSense for the entire document, as shown in Figure 10-1.

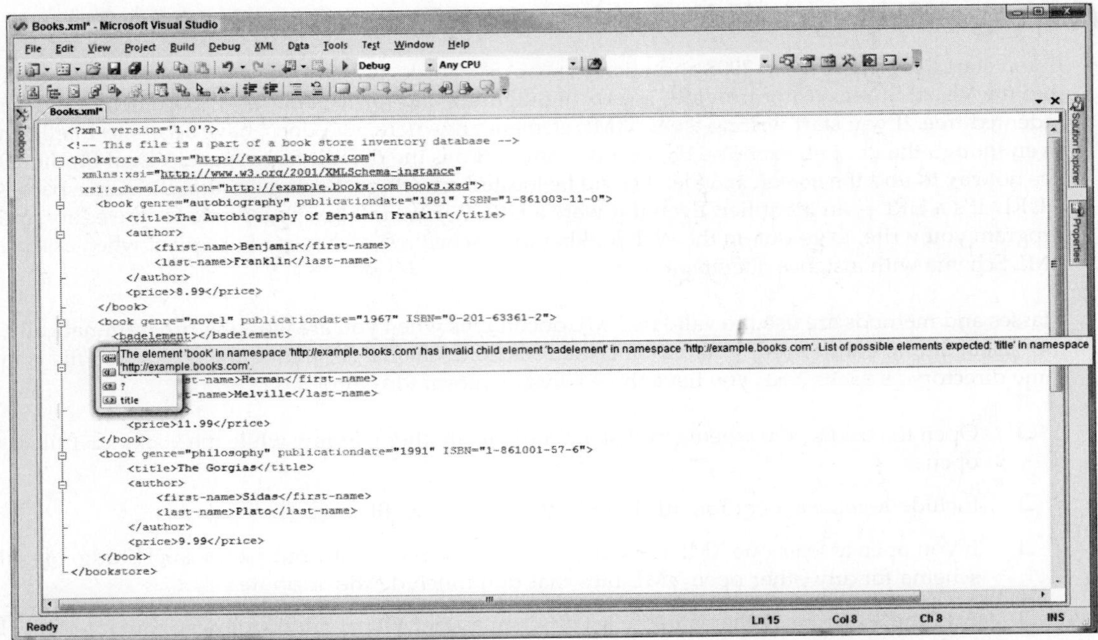

Figure 10-1

When the XML Schema file from Listing 10-3 is loaded into the Visual Studio Editor, the default view in Visual Studio 2008 for standard XSDs is now the XML Editor, rather than the Dataset Designer as in Visual Studio 2005. However, if you right-click on `Books.xsd` in the Solution Explorer and select Open With, you'll get a brief warning that the DataSet Designer might have modified your schema by removing non-dataset XML. Make sure your schema is backed up and select OK, and you'll get a redesigned Dataset Designer that presents the elements and complex types in a format that is familiar if you've edited database schemas before (see Figure 10-2). This Designer view is intended to manipulate DataSets expressed as schema, but it can be a useful visualizer for many XSDs. However, as soon as you use this visualizer to edit your XSD, your document will be turned into a Microsoft DataSet. Therefore the Dataset Designer in Visual Studio 2008 is no longer suitable as a general purpose visual XML Schema Editor.

A greatly enhanced XSD Designer will be released as an add-on soon after the release of Visual Studio. This new XML Schema Editor will include a Schema Explorer toolbox window that will present a comprehensive tree-view of complex schemas in a much more scalable and appropriate way than can a more traditional ER-Diagram. For more details, see Figure 10-3 or go to `http://blogs.msdn.com/xmlteam/archive/2007/08/27/announcing-ctp1-of-the-xml-schema-designer.aspx`.

After you have created an XML Schema that correctly describes an XML document, you're ready to start programmatically manipulating XML. The `System.Xml` and `System.Xml.Linq` namespaces provide a number of ways to create, access, and query XML. XML Schemas provide valuable typing information for all XML consumers who are type aware.

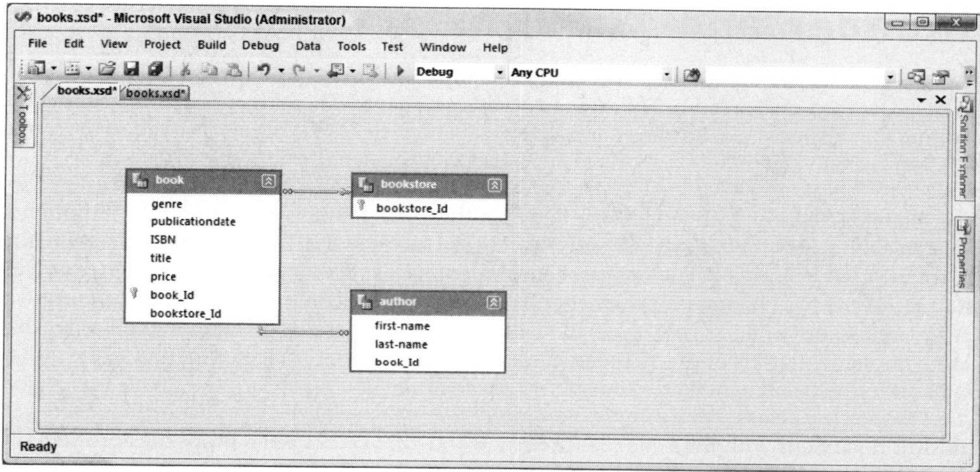

Figure 10-2

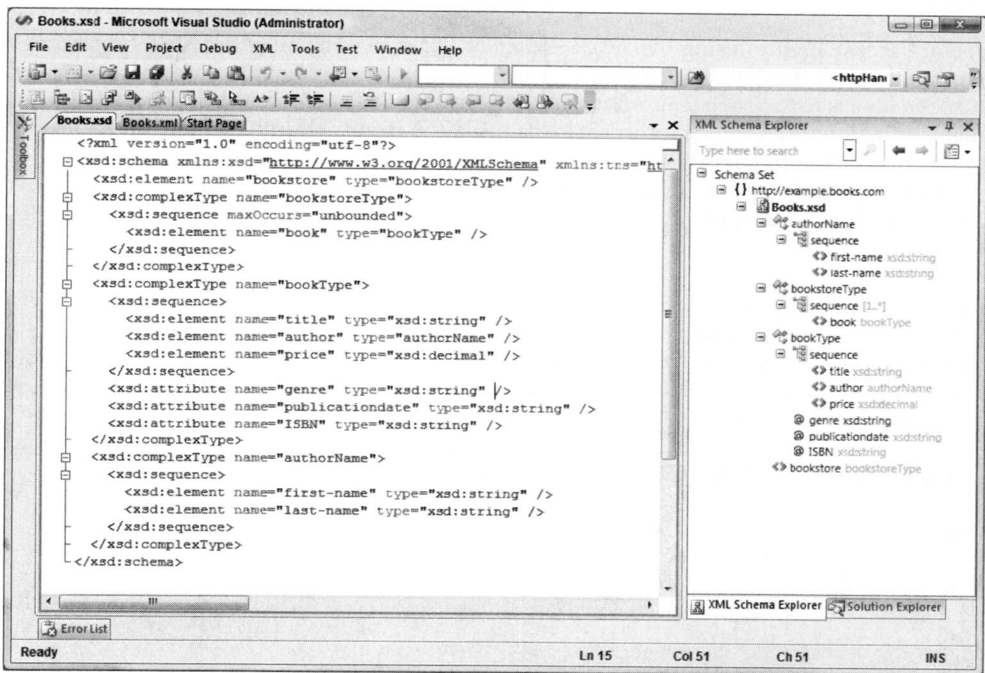

Figure 10-3

XmlReader and XmlWriter

XmlReader offers a *pull-style* API over an XML document that is unique to the .NET Framework. It provides fast, forward-only, read-only access to XML documents. These documents may contain elements in multiple namespaces. XmlReader is actually an abstract class that other classes derive from to provide specific concrete instances like XmlTextReader and XmlNodeReader.

Things changed slightly with XmlReader between the .NET Framework 1.1 and 2.0 although nothing significant changed in the XmlReader and XmlWriter classes in .NET 3.5 as most of the new functionality was around LINQ. Since .NET 1.1, several convenient new methods have been added, and the way you create XmlReader has changed for the better. XmlReader has become a factory. The primary way for you to create an instance of an XmlReader is by using the Static/Shared Create method. Rather than creating concrete implementations of the XmlReader class, you create an instance of the XmlReaderSettings class and pass it to the Create method. You specify the features you want for your XmlReader object with the XmlReaderSettings class. For example, you might want a specialized XmlReader that checks the validity of an XML document with the IgnoreWhiteSpace and IgnoreComments properties pre-set. The Create method of the XmlReader class provides you with an instance of an XmlReader without requiring you to decide which implementation to use. You can also add features to existing XmlReaders by chaining instances of the XmlReader class with each other because the Create method of XmlReader takes another XmlReader as a parameter.

If you are accustomed to using the XmlDocument or DOM to write an entire XML fragment or document into memory, you will find using XmlReader to be a very different process. A good analogy is that XmlReader is to XmlDocument what the ADO ForwardOnly recordset is to the ADO Static recordset. Remember that the ADO Static recordset loads the entire results set into memory and holds it there. Certainly, you wouldn't use a Static recordset if you want to retrieve only a few values. The same basic rules apply to the XmlReader class. If you're going to run through the document only once, you don't want to hold it in memory; you want the access to be as fast as possible. XmlReader is the right decision in this case.

Listing 10-5 creates an XmlReader class instance and iterates forward through it, counting the number of books in the Books.xml document from Listing 10-1. The XmlReaderSettings object specifies the features that are required, rather than the actual kind of XmlReader to create. In this example, IgnoreWhitespace and IgnoreComments are set to True. The XmlReaderSettings object is created with these property settings and then passed to the Create method of XmlReader.

Listing 10-5: Processing XML with an XmlReader

VB

```
Imports System.IO
Imports System.Xml

Partial Class _Default
    Inherits System.Web.UI.Page

    Protected Sub Page_Load(ByVal sender As Object, ByVal e As System.EventArgs) _
            Handles Me.Load
        Dim bookcount As Integer = 0
```

```
        Dim settings As New XmlReaderSettings()

        settings.IgnoreWhitespace = True
        settings.IgnoreComments = True

        Dim booksFile As String = Server.MapPath("books.xml")
        Using reader As XmlReader = XmlReader.Create(booksFile, settings)
            While (reader.Read())
                If (reader.NodeType = XmlNodeType.Element _
                        And "book" = reader.LocalName) Then
                    bookcount += 1
                End If
            End While
        End Using
        Response.Write(String.Format("Found {0} books!", bookcount))
    End Sub
End Class
```

C#

```
using System;
using System.IO;
using System.Xml;

public partial class _Default : System.Web.UI.Page
{
    protected void Page_Load(object sender, EventArgs e)
    {
        int bookcount = 0;
        XmlReaderSettings settings = new XmlReaderSettings();

        settings.IgnoreWhitespace = true;
        settings.IgnoreComments = true;

        string booksFile = Server.MapPath("books.xml");
        using (XmlReader reader = XmlReader.Create(booksFile, settings))
        {
            while (reader.Read())
            {
                if (reader.NodeType == XmlNodeType.Element &&
                        "book" == reader.LocalName)
                {
                    bookcount++;
                }
            }
        }
        Response.Write(String.Format("Found {0} books!", bookcount));
    }
}
```

Notice the use of the `XmlReader.Create` method in Listing 10-5. You may be used to creating concrete implementations of an `XmlReader`, but if you try this technique, you should find it much more flexible because you can reuse the `XmlReaderSettings` objects in the creation of other instances of `XmlReader`. `XmlReader` implements `IDisposable`, so the `Using` keyword is correct in both VB and C#.

In Listing 10-5 the `Books.xml` file is in the same directory as this ASPX page, so a call to `Server.MapPath` gets the complete path to the XML file. The filename with full path is then passed into `XmlReader.Create`, along with the `XmlReaderSettings` instance from a few lines earlier.

The `Read` method continues to return `true` if the node was read successfully. It will return `false` when no more nodes are left to read. From the point of view of an `XmlReader`, everything is a node including white space, comments, attributes, elements, and end elements. If Listing 10-5 had simply spun through the `while` loop incrementing the `bookcount` variable each time `reader.LocalName` equaled `book`, the final value for `bookcount` would have been six. You would have counted both the beginning `book` tag and the ending `book` tag. Consequently, you have to be more explicit, and ensure that the `if` statement is modified to check not only the `LocalName` but also the `NodeType`.

> **The `Reader.LocalName` property contains the non–namespace qualified name of that node. The `Reader.Name` property is different and contains the fully qualified name of that node including namespace. The `Reader.LocalName` property is used in the example in Listing 10-5 for simplicity and ease. You'll hear more about namespaces a little later in the chapter.**

Using XDocument Rather Than XmlReader

The `System.Xml.Linq` namespace introduces a new `XDocument` class that presents a much friendlier face than `XmlDocument` while still allowing for interoperability with `XmlReaders` and `XmlWriters`. Listing10-5q accomplishes the same thing as Listing 10-5 but uses `XDocument` instead. The `XDocument` is loaded just like an `XmlDocument` but the syntax for retrieving the elements we want is significantly different.

The syntax for this query is very clean, but slightly reversed from what you may be used to if you've used T-SQL. Rather than `select...from`, we're using the standard LINQ `from...select` syntax. We ask the `booksXML XDocument` for all its `book` descendants, and they are selected into the `book` range variable. The value of all the book `title` elements is then selected into the `books` variable.

VB takes the opportunity in Visual Studio 2008 to distinguish itself considerably from C# by including a number of bits of ''syntactic sugar,'' which makes the experience of working with Visual Basic and XML more integrated. Notice the use of the `Imports` keyword to declare an XML namespace, as well as the use of ''...<>'' to indicate the method call to `Descendants` and ''.<>'' to call `Elements`. This extraordinary level of XML integration with the compiler really makes working with XML in VB a joy — and this is a C# lover speaking.

Listing 10-5q: Processing XML with a XDocument

VB

```
Imports System.IO
Imports System.Xml
Imports System.Linq
Imports System.Xml.Linq
```

```
Imports <xmlns:b="http://example.books.com">

Partial Class _Default
    Inherits System.Web.UI.Page

    Protected Sub Page_Load(ByVal sender As Object, ByVal e As System.EventArgs) _
            Handles Me.Load

        Dim booksXML = XDocument.Load(Server.MapPath("books.xml"))
        Dim books = From book In booksXML...<b:book> Select book.<b:title>.Value

        Response.Write(String.Format("Found {0} books!", books.Count()))
    End Sub
End Class
```

C#

```
using System;
using System.IO;
using System.Linq;
using System.Xml.Linq;

public partial class _Default : System.Web.UI.Page
{
    protected void Page_Load(object sender, EventArgs e)
    {
        XDocument booksXML = XDocument.Load(Server.MapPath("books.xml"));
        var books = from book in
                        booksXML.Descendants("{http://example.books.com}book")
                        select book.Element("{http://example.books.com}title").Value;
        Response.Write(String.Format("Found {0} books!", books.Count()));
    }
}
```

In both the C# and VB examples, we take advantage of the implicit typing by not indicating the return type in the call to `XDocument.Decendants`. In VB we use `Dim books` and in C# we use `var books`. In this example, because we are using the `from...select` syntax to select our books from the `booksXml` object, the type of the variable `books` is `System.Linq.Enumerable.SelectIterator`, which is ultimately `IEnumerable`. The `count` method is added by LINQ as an extension method, allowing us to retrieve the number of books.

Notice also that the `Books.xml` document has a namespace of `http://examples.books.com`, so elements with this namespace are included in the query using the LINQ for XML format of `namespaceelement`. In later examples we'll use the `XNamespace` object to make the C# syntax slightly cleaner.

Using Schema with XmlTextReader

The code in Listing 10-5 reads any XML document regardless of its schema, and if the document contains an element named `book`, the code counts it. If this code is meant to count books of a particular schema type only, specifically the books from the `Books.xml` file, it should be validated against the `Books.xsd` schema.

Now modify the creation of the `XmlReader` class from Listing 10-5 to validate the `XmlDocument` against the XML Schema used earlier in the chapter. Note that the `XmlValidatingReader` class is now considered obsolete because all reader creation is done using the `Create` method of the `XmlReader` class.

Listing 10-6 shows a concrete example of how easy it is to add schema validation to code using `XmlReaderSettings` and the `XmlReader Create` method.

Listing 10-6: Validating XML with an XmlReader against an XML Schema

VB

```
Imports System.Xml.Schema

Protected Sub Page_Load(ByVal sender As Object, ByVal e As System.EventArgs) _
        Handles Me.Load
    Dim bookcount As Integer = 0
    Dim settings As New XmlReaderSettings()
    Dim booksSchemaFile As String = Server.MapPath("books.xsd")

    settings.Schemas.Add(Nothing, XmlReader.Create(booksSchemaFile))
    settings.ValidationType = ValidationType.Schema
    settings.ValidationFlags = _
        XmlSchemaValidationFlags.ReportValidationWarnings

    AddHandler settings.ValidationEventHandler, _
    AddressOf settings_ValidationEventHandler

    settings.IgnoreWhitespace = True
    settings.IgnoreComments = True

    Dim booksFile As String = Server.MapPath("books.xml")
    Using reader As XmlReader = XmlReader.Create(booksFile, settings)
        While (reader.Read())
            If (reader.NodeType = XmlNodeType.Element _
                    And "book" = reader.LocalName) Then
                bookcount += 1
            End If
        End While
    End Using
    Response.Write(String.Format("Found {0} books!", bookcount))
End Sub

Sub settings_ValidationEventHandler(ByVal sender As Object, _
        ByVal e As System.Xml.Schema.ValidationEventArgs)
    Response.Write(e.Message)
End Sub
```

C#

```
using System.Xml.Schema;

protected void Page_Load(object sender, EventArgs e)
{
    int bookcount = 0;
    XmlReaderSettings settings = new XmlReaderSettings();

    string booksSchemaFile = Server.MapPath("books.xsd");

    settings.Schemas.Add(null, XmlReader.Create(booksSchemaFile));
```

```
        settings.ValidationType = ValidationType.Schema;
        settings.ValidationFlags =

        XmlSchemaValidationFlags.ReportValidationWarnings;
        settings.ValidationEventHandler +=
                new ValidationEventHandler(settings_ValidationEventHandler);

        settings.IgnoreWhitespace = true;
        settings.IgnoreComments = true;

        string booksFile = Server.MapPath( "books.xml");
        using (XmlReader reader = XmlReader.Create(booksFile, settings))
        {
            while (reader.Read())
            {
                if (reader.NodeType == XmlNodeType.Element &&
                        "book" == reader.LocalName)
                {
                    bookcount++;
                }
            }
        }
        Response.Write(String.Format("Found {0} books!", bookcount));
    }

    void settings_ValidationEventHandler(object sender,
            System.Xml.Schema.ValidationEventArgs e)
    {
        Response.Write(e.Message);
    }
```

When validating XML, the validator uses the `schemaLocation` hint found in the XML instance document. If an XML instance document does not contain enough information to find an XML Schema, the instance document expects an `XmlSchemaSet` object on the `XmlReaderSettings` object. In the interest of being explicit, Listing 10-6 shows this technique. The `XmlReaderSettings` object has a `Schemas` collection available as a property and many overloads for the `Add` method. This listing passes `null` into the `Add` method as the first parameter, indicating that the `targetNamespace` is specified in the schema. Optionally, XML documents can also contain their schemas inline.

The validator needs a way to let you know when validation problems occur. The `XmlReaderSettings` object has a validation event handler that notifies you as validation events occur. Listing 10-6 also includes a handler for the validation event that writes the message to the browser.

Validating Against a Schema Using an XDocument

Much of `System.Xml.Linq` is "bridged" to `System.Xml` by using extension methods. For example, the `XDocument` class has an extension `Validate` method that takes a standard `System.Xml.Schema.XmlSchemaSet` as a parameter, allowing us to validate an `XDocument` against an XML Schema.

In Listing 10-6q, the `XmlSchemaSet` is loaded in the standard way, and then passed into the `XDocument`'s validate method.

Listing 10-6q: Validating XML with a LINQ XDocument against an XML Schema

VB

```
Imports System
Imports System.Xml
Imports System.Linq
Imports System.Xml.Linq
Imports System.Xml.Schema

Imports <xmlns:b="http://example.books.com">

Partial Class _Default
    Inherits System.Web.UI.Page

    Protected Sub Page_Load(ByVal sender As Object, ByVal e As System.EventArgs) _
            Handles Me.Load
        Dim schemas = New XmlSchemaSet()
        schemas.Add(Nothing, XmlReader.Create(Server.MapPath("books.xsd")))
        Dim booksXML = XDocument.Load(Server.MapPath("books.xml"))
        booksXML.Validate(schemas, AddressOf ValidationEventHandler, True)

        Dim books = From book In booksXML...<b:book> _
                    Select book.<b:title>.Value

        Response.Write(String.Format("Found {0} books!", books.Count()))
    End Sub

    Sub ValidationEventHandler(ByVal sender As Object, _
            ByVal e As System.Xml.Schema.ValidationEventArgs)
        Response.Write(e.Message)
    End Sub
End Class
```

C#

```
using System;
using System.Xml;
using System.Xml.Linq;
using System.Linq;
using System.Xml.Schema;

public partial class _Default : System.Web.UI.Page
{
    protected void Page_Load(object sender, EventArgs e)
    {
        string booksSchemaFile = Server.MapPath("books.xsd");
        string booksFile = Server.MapPath("books.xml");

        XmlSchemaSet schemas = new XmlSchemaSet();
        schemas.Add(null, XmlReader.Create(booksSchemaFile));
        XDocument booksXML = XDocument.Load(booksFile);
        booksXML.Validate(schemas, (senderParam, eParam) =>
                                   {
                                     Response.Write(eParam.Message);
                                   }, true);
```

```
            XNamespace ns = "http://example.books.com";
            var books = from book in booksXML.Descendants(ns + "book")
                        select book.Element(ns + "title").Value;
            Response.Write(String.Format("Found {0} books!", books.Count()));
        }
    }
```

Notice the unique syntax for an anonymous event handler in the C# example in Listing 10-6q. Rather than creating a separate method and passing it into the call to `Validate`, C# 3.0 programmers can pass the method body anonymously in as a parameter to the `Validate` method. The `(param1, param2) => { method }` syntax can be a bit jarring initially, but it makes for much tidier code.

Including NameTable Optimization

`XmlReader` internally uses a `NameTable` that lists all the known elements and attributes with namespaces that are used in that document. This process is called *atomization*-literally meaning that the XML document is broken up into its atomic parts. There's no need to store the string `book` more than once in the internal structure if you can make `book` an object reference that is held in a table with the names of other elements.

Although this is an internal implementation detail, it is a supported and valid way that you can measurably speed up your use of XML classes, such as `XmlReader` and `XmlDocument`. You add name elements to the `NameTable` that you know will be in the document. Listings 10-5 and 10-6 use string comparisons to compare a string literal with `reader.LocalName`. These comparisons can also be optimized by turning them into object reference comparisons that are many, many times faster. Additionally, an XML `NameTable` can be shared across multiple instances of `System.Xml` classes and even between `XmlReaders` and `XmlDocuments`. This topic is covered shortly.

Because you are counting `book` elements, create a `NameTable` including this element (`book`), and instead of comparing string against string, compare object reference against object reference, as shown in Listing 10-7.

Listing 10-7: Optimizing XmlReader with a NameTable

VB

```
Protected Sub Page_Load(ByVal sender As Object, ByVal e As System.EventArgs) _
        Handles Me.Load
    Dim bookcount As Integer = 0
    Dim settings As New XmlReaderSettings()
    Dim nt As New NameTable()
    Dim book As Object = nt.Add("book")

    settings.NameTable = nt
    Dim booksSchemaFile As String = _
        Path.Combine(Request.PhysicalApplicationPath, "books.xsd")
    settings.Schemas.Add(Nothing, XmlReader.Create(booksSchemaFile))
    settings.ValidationType = ValidationType.Schema
    settings.ValidationFlags = _
    XmlSchemaValidationFlags.ReportValidationWarnings

    AddHandler settings.ValidationEventHandler, _
```

Continued

```
        AddressOf settings_ValidationEventHandler

    settings.IgnoreWhitespace = True
    settings.IgnoreComments = True

    Dim booksFile As String = _
    Path.Combine(Request.PhysicalApplicationPath, "books.xml")
    Using reader As XmlReader = XmlReader.Create(booksFile, settings)
        While (reader.Read())
            If (reader.NodeType = XmlNodeType.Element _
                And book.Equals(reader.LocalName)) Then
                'A subtle, but significant change!
                bookcount += 1
            End If
        End While
    End Using
    Response.Write(String.Format("Found {0} books!", bookcount))
End Sub
```

C#

```
protected void Page_Load(object sender, EventArgs e)
{
    int bookcount = 0;
    XmlReaderSettings settings = new XmlReaderSettings();
    NameTable nt = new NameTable();
    object book = nt.Add("book");

    settings.NameTable = nt;
    string booksSchemaFile = Path.Combine(Request.PhysicalApplicationPath,
        "books.xsd");

    settings.Schemas.Add(null, XmlReader.Create(booksSchemaFile));
    settings.ValidationType = ValidationType.Schema;
    settings.ValidationFlags =
        XmlSchemaValidationFlags.ReportValidationWarnings;

    settings.ValidationEventHandler +=
        new ValidationEventHandler(settings_ValidationEventHandler);

    settings.IgnoreWhitespace = true;
    settings.IgnoreComments = true;

    string booksFile = Path.Combine(Request.PhysicalApplicationPath, "books.xml");
    using (XmlReader reader = XmlReader.Create(booksFile, settings))
    {
        while (reader.Read())
        {
            if (reader.NodeType == XmlNodeType.Element &&
                book.Equals(reader.LocalName)) //A subtle, but significant change!
            {
                bookcount++;
            }
        }
    }
    Response.Write(String.Format("Found {0} books!", bookcount));
}
```

The `NameTable` is added to the `XmlSettings` object and the `Add` method of the `NameTable` returns an object reference to the just-added atom that is stored, in this case, in an object reference named `book`. The `book` reference is then used later to make a comparison to the `reader.LocalName` property. We specifically chose to use the `Equals` method that is present on all objects within that .NET Framework in order to emphasize that this is specifically an object identity check for equality. These two objects are either the same identical atoms or they are not. The `book` object that is returned from the `Add` method on the `NameTable` is the identical object that the reader uses when parsing the `book` element from the `Books.xml` XML document.

In the example of Listing 10-7, in which you count a very small number of books, you probably won't have a measurable performance gain. However, for larger XML documents that approach sizes of 1 MB, you may see performance gains of as much as 10 to 15 percent — especially for the involved calculations and manipulations of `XmlReader`. Additionally, because the `NameTable` is cached within the `XmlReader-Settings` object, that `NameTable` is reused when the `XmlReaderSettings` object is reused for other `System.Xml` objects. This creates additional potential performance gains.

Retrieving .NET CLR Types from XML

It is considerably simpler to retrieve CLR types from an `XmlReader` than it was previously in the 1.*x* Framework. If you've used SQL Server data reader objects before, retrieving data types from `XmlReader` should feel very familiar. Previously the Framework used a helper class called `XmlConvert`. When combined with the `ReadElementString` method on `XmlReader`, this helper class retrieved a strong, simple type, as shown in the following code:

```
//Retrieving a double from an XmlReader in the .NET Framework 1.1
Double price = XmlConvert.ToDouble(reader.ReadElementString());
//Has been replaced by and improved in the .NET Framework 2.0
Double price = reader.ReadElementContentAsDouble();
```

You can see the removal of the unnecessary double method call results in much cleaner and easier-to-read code. Listing 10-8 adds not only the counting of books but also prints the total price of all books using `ReadElementContentAs` when your `XmlReader` is currently on an element, or `ReadContentAs` if on text content. If schema information is available to the reader, `ReadElementContentAsObject` returns the value directly as, in this case, a decimal. If the reader does not have any schema information, it attempts to convert the string to a decimal. A whole series of `ReadElementContentAs` and `ReadContentAs` methods, including `ReadElementContentAsBoolean` and `ReadElementContentAsInt`, are available. Note that the code specific to `XmlSchema` has been removed from Listing 10-8 in the interest of brevity.

Listing 10-8: Using XmlReader.ReadElementContentAs

VB

```
Dim bookcount As Integer = 0
Dim booktotal As Decimal = 0
Dim settings As New XmlReaderSettings()
Dim nt As New NameTable()
Dim book As Object = nt.Add("book")
Dim price As Object = nt.Add("price")

settings.NameTable = nt

Dim booksFile As String = _
```

Continued

```
Path.Combine(Request.PhysicalApplicationPath, "books.xml")
Using reader As XmlReader = XmlReader.Create(booksFile, settings)
    While (reader.Read())
        If (reader.NodeType = XmlNodeType.Element _
            And book.Equals(reader.LocalName)) Then
            bookcount += 1
        End If
        If (reader.NodeType = XmlNodeType.Element _
            And price.Equals(reader.LocalName)) Then
            booktotal += reader.ReadElementContentAsDecimal()
        End If
    End While
End Using

Response.Write(String.Format("Found {0} books that total {1:C}!", _
    bookcount, booktotal))
```

C#

```
int bookcount = 0;
decimal booktotal = 0;
XmlReaderSettings settings = new XmlReaderSettings();
string booksSchemaFile = Path.Combine(Request.PhysicalApplicationPath, "books.xsd");
NameTable nt = new NameTable();
object book = nt.Add("book");
object price = nt.Add("price");

settings.NameTable = nt;

string booksFile = Path.Combine(Request.PhysicalApplicationPath, "books.xml");

using (XmlReader reader = XmlReader.Create(booksFile, settings))
{
    while (reader.Read())
    {
        if (reader.NodeType == XmlNodeType.Element &&
          book.Equals(reader.LocalName))//A subtle, but significant change!
        {
            bookcount++;
        }
        if (reader.NodeType == XmlNodeType.Element &&
        price.Equals(reader.LocalName))
        {
            booktotal +=
                reader.ReadElementContentAsDecimal ();
        }
    }
}

Response.Write(String.Format("Found {0} books that total {1:C}!",
    bookcount, booktotal));
```

The `booktotal` variable from Listing 10-8 is strongly typed as a decimal so that, in the `String.Format` call, it can be formatted as currency using the formatting string `{1:C}`. This results in output from the browser similar to the following:

```
Found 3 books that total $30.97!
```

ReadSubtree and XmlSerialization

Not only does `XmlReader` help you retrieve simple types from XML, it can also help you retrieve more complicated types using XML serialization and `ReadSubtree`.

XML serialization allows you to add attributes to an existing class that give hints to the XML serialization on how to represent an object as XML. XML serialization serializes only the public properties of an object, not the private ones.

When you create an `XmlSerializer`, a `Type` object is passed into the constructor, and the `XmlSerializer` uses reflection to examine whether the object can create a temporary assembly that knows how to read and write this particular object as XML. The `XmlSerializer` uses a concrete implementation of `XmlReader` internally to serialize these objects.

Instead of retrieving the author's first name and last name using `XmlReader.ReadAsString`, Listing 10-10 below uses `ReadSubtree` and a new strongly typed `Author` class that has been marked up with XML serialization attributes, as shown in Listing 10-9. `ReadSubtree` "breaks off" a new `XmlReader` at the current location, and that `XmlReader` is passed to an `XmlSerializer` and a complex type is created. The `Author` class includes `XmlElement` attributes that indicate, for example, that although there is a property called `FirstName`, it should be serialized and deserialized as "first-name."

Listing 10-9: An Author class with XML serialization attributes matching Books.xsd

VB

```
Imports System.Xml.Serialization
<XmlRoot(ElementName:="author", _
Namespace:="http://example.books.com")> Public Class Author
    <XmlElement(ElementName:="first-name")> Public FirstName As String
    <XmlElement(ElementName:="last-name")> Public LastName As String
End Class
```

C#

```
using System.Xml.Serialization;
[XmlRoot(ElementName = "author", Namespace = "http://example.books.com")]
public class Author
{
    [XmlElement(ElementName = "first-name")]
    public string FirstName;

    [XmlElement(ElementName = "last-name")]
    public string LastName;
}
```

Next, this `Author` class is used along with `XmlReader.ReadSubtree` and `XmlSerializer` to output the names of each book's author. Listing 10-10 shows just the additional statements added to the `While` loop.

Listing 10-10: Reading author instances from an XmlReader using XmlSerialization

VB

```
'Create factory early
Dim factory As New XmlSerializerFactory
```

Continued

```
Using reader As XmlReader = XmlReader.Create(booksFile, settings)
    While (reader.Read())
        If (reader.NodeType = XmlNodeType.Element _
            And author.Equals(reader.LocalName)) Then

            'Then use the factory to create and cache serializers
            Dim xs As XmlSerializer = factory.CreateSerializer(GetType(Author))
            Dim a As Author = CType(xs.Deserialize(reader.ReadSubtree), Author)
            Response.Write(String.Format("Author: {1}, {0}<BR/>", _
                a.FirstName, a.LastName))
        End If
    End While
End Using
```

C#

```
//Create factory early
XmlSerializerFactory factory = new XmlSerializerFactory();

using (XmlReader reader = XmlReader.Create(booksFile, settings))
{
    while (reader.Read())
    {
        if (reader.NodeType == XmlNodeType.Element &&
            author.Equals(reader.LocalName))
        {
            //Then use the factory to create and cache serializers
            XmlSerializer xs = factory.CreateSerializer(typeof(Author));
            Author a = (Author)xs.Deserialize(reader.ReadSubtree());
            Response.Write(String.Format("Author: {1}, {0}<BR/>",
                a.FirstName, a.LastName));
        }
    }
}
```

The only other addition to the code, as you can guess, is the `author` object atom (used only in the `Equals` statement) that is added to the `NameTable` just as the book and price were, via `Dim author As Object = nt.Add("author")`.

When you create an `XmlSerializer` instance for a specific type, the Framework uses reflection to create a temporary type-specific assembly to handle serialization and deserialization. The .NET Framework 2.0 includes a new `XmlSerializerFactory` that automatically handles caching of these temporary assemblies. This small factory provides an important layer of abstraction that allows you to structure your code in a way that is convenient without worrying about creating `XmlSerializer` instances ahead of time.

Creating CLR Objects from XML with LINQ to XML

While there isn't a direct bridge between the `XmlSerializer` and `System.Xml.Linq`, there is a very clean way of creating CLR objects within the LINQ to XML syntax. This syntax can also be a little more flexible and more forgiving than the traditional `XmlSerializer`, as shown in Listing 10-10q.

At the time of this writing there is talk of a future bridge technology that will bring strongly typed objects and XML together. It's currently called LINQ to XSD and you can find more information on the XMLTeam's blog at `http://blogs.msdn.com/xmlteam/`.

Listing 10-10q: Reading author instances via LINQ to XML

VB

```
Dim booksXML = XDocument.Load(Server.MapPath("books.xml"))

Dim authors = From book In booksXML...<books:book> Select New Author _
    With {.FirstName = book.<books:author>.<books:first-name>.Value, _
          .LastName = book.<books:author>.<books:last-name>.Value}

    For Each a As Author In authors
    Response.Write(String.Format("Author: {1}, {0}<BR/>", a.FirstName, a.LastName))
Next
```

C#

```
XDocument booksXML = XDocument.Load(Server.MapPath("books.xml"));
XNamespace ns = "http://example.books.com";

var authors = from book in booksXML.Descendants(ns + "author")
              select new Author
              {
                  FirstName = book.Element(ns + "first-name").Value,
                  LastName = book.Element(ns + "last-name").Value
              };
foreach (Author a in authors)
{
    Response.Write(String.Format("Author: {1}, {0}<BR/>", a.FirstName, a.LastName));
}
```

Again, note the unique syntax in the VB example, where "..." is used rather than "descendants." On the C# side, notice how cleanly a new Author object is created with the `select new` syntax, and within the curly braces that new `Author` object has its property values copied over from the XML elements. The VB example assumes the same namespace `Imports` statement as seen in the previous example in Listing 10-6q.

Creating XML with XmlWriter

`XmlWriter` works exactly like `XmlReader` except in reverse. It's very tempting to use string concatenation to quickly create XML documents or fragments of XML, but you should resist the urge! Remember that the whole point of XML is the representation of the InfoSet, not the angle brackets. If you concatenate string literals together with `StringBuilder` to create XML, you are dropping below the level of the InfoSet to the implementation details of the format. Tell yourself that XML documents are not strings!

> **Most people find it helpful (as a visualization tool) to indent the method calls to the `XmlWriter` with the same structure as the resulting XML document. However, VB in Visual Studio is much more aggressive than C# in keeping the code indented a specific way. It does not allow this kind of artificial indentation unless Smart Indenting is changed to either Block or None by using Tools ⇨ Options ⇨ Text Editor ⇨ Basic ⇨ Tabs.**

`XmlWriter` also has a settings class called, obviously, `XmlWriterSettings`. This class has options for indentation, new lines, encoding, and XML conformance level. Listing 10-11 uses `XmlWriter` to create a `bookstore` XML document and output it directly to the ASP.NET `Response.OutputStream`. All the HTML tags in the ASPX page must be removed in order for the XML document to be output correctly. Another way to output XML easily is with an ASHX `HttpHandler`.

The unusual indenting in Listing 10-11 is significant and very common when using `XmlWriter`. It helps the programmer visualize the hierarchical structure of an XML document.

Listing 10-11: Writing out a bookstore with XmlWriter

Default.aspx — C#

```
<%@ Page Language="C#" codefile="Default.aspx.cs" Inherits="Default_aspx" %>
```

Default.aspx — VB

```
<%@ Page Language="VB" codefile="Default.aspx.vb" Inherits="Default_aspx" %>
```

VB

```
Protected Sub Page_Load(ByVal sender As Object, ByVal e As System.EventArgs) _
Handles Me.Load

Dim price As Double = 49.99
Dim publicationdate As New DateTime(2005, 1, 1)
Dim isbn As String = "1-057-610-0"
Dim a As New Author()
a.FirstName = "Scott"
a.LastName = "Hanselman"

Dim settings As New XmlWriterSettings()
settings.Indent = True
settings.NewLineOnAttributes = True

Response.ContentType = "text/xml"

Dim factory As New XmlSerializerFactory()

Using writer As XmlWriter = XmlWriter.Create(Response.OutputStream, settings)

    'Note the artificial, but useful, indenting
    writer.WriteStartDocument()
        writer.WriteStartElement("bookstore")
            writer.WriteStartElement("book")
                writer.WriteStartAttribute("publicationdate")
                    writer.WriteValue(publicationdate)
                writer.WriteEndAttribute()
                writer.WriteStartAttribute("ISBN")
                    writer.WriteValue(isbn)
                writer.WriteEndAttribute()
                writer.WriteElementString("title", "ASP.NET 2.0")
                writer.WriteStartElement("price")
                    writer.WriteValue(price)
                writer.WriteEndElement() 'price
                Dim xs As XmlSerializer = _
                    factory.CreateSerializer(GetType(Author))
                xs.Serialize(writer, a)
            writer.WriteEndElement() 'book
```

```
            writer.WriteEndElement() 'bookstore
        writer.WriteEndDocument()
    End Using

    End Sub
```

C#

```
protected void Page_Load(object sender, EventArgs e)
{
Double price = 49.99;
DateTime publicationdate = new DateTime(2005, 1, 1);
String isbn = "1-057-610-0";
Author a = new Author();
a.FirstName = "Scott";
a.LastName = "Hanselman";

XmlWriterSettings settings = new XmlWriterSettings();
settings.Indent = true;
settings.NewLineOnAttributes = true;

Response.ContentType = "text/xml";

XmlSerializerFactory factory = new XmlSerializerFactory();

using (XmlWriter writer =
        XmlWriter.Create(Response.OutputStream, settings))
{
    //Note the artificial, but useful, indenting
    writer.WriteStartDocument();
        writer.WriteStartElement("bookstore");
            writer.WriteStartElement("book");
                writer.WriteStartAttribute("publicationdate");
                    writer.WriteValue(publicationdate);
                writer.WriteEndAttribute();
                writer.WriteStartAttribute("ISBN");
                    writer.WriteValue(isbn);
                writer.WriteEndAttribute();
                writer.WriteElementString("title", "ASP.NET 2.0");
                writer.WriteStartElement("price");
                    writer.WriteValue(price);
                writer.WriteEndElement(); //price
                XmlSerializer xs = factory.CreateSerializer(typeof(Author));
                xs.Serialize(writer, a);
            writer.WriteEndElement(); //book
        writer.WriteEndElement(); //bookstore
    writer.WriteEndDocument();
}

}
```

The `Response.ContentType` in Listing 10-11 is set to `"text/xml"` to indicate to Internet Explorer that the result is XML. An `XmlSerializer` is created in the middle of the process and serialized directly to `XmlWriter`. The `XmlWriterSettings.Indent` property includes indentation that makes the resulting XML document more palatable for human consumption. Setting both this property and `NewLineOnAttributes` to `false` results in a smaller, more compact document.

Creating XML with LINQ for XML

Listing 10-11q accomplishes the same thing as Listing 10-11 but with LINQ for XML. It won't be as lightening fast as `XmlWriter`, but it will still be extremely fast and it is very easy to read.

Notice the dramatic difference between the VB and C# examples. The VB example uses a new VB9 compiler feature called Xml Literals. The XML structure is typed directly in the code without any quotes. It's not a string. The compiler will turn the XML literal into a tree of XElements similar to the syntax used in the C# example. The underlying LINQ to XML technology is the same — only the syntax differs. One syntax thing to note in the VB example is the exclusion of double-quotes around the attributes for `publicationdate` and `ISBN`. The quotes are considered part of the serialization format of the attribute value and they will be added automatically for you when the final XML is created.

Listing 10-11q: Writing out a bookstore with XElement trees

VB

```
Imports System.Xml
Imports System.Xml.Linq

Partial Class _Default
    Inherits System.Web.UI.Page

    Protected Sub Page_Load(ByVal sender As Object, ByVal e As System.EventArgs)
      Handles Me.Load
        Dim price As Double = 49.99
        Dim publicationdate As New DateTime(2005, 1, 1)
        Dim isbn As String = "1-057-610-0"
        Dim a As New Author()
        a.FirstName = "Scott"
        a.LastName = "Hanselman"

        Response.ContentType = "text/xml"

        Dim books = <bookstore xmlns="http://examples.books.com">
                        <book publicationdate=<%= publicationdate %> ISBN=<%= isbn %>>
                               <title>ASP.NET 2.0</title>
                               <price><%= price %></price>
                               <author>
                                   <first-name><%= a.FirstName %></first-name>
                                   <last-name><%= a.LastName %></last-name>
                               </author>
                        </book>
                    </bookstore>

        Response.Write(books)
    End Sub
End Class
```

C#

```
using System;
using System.Xml.Linq;

public partial class _Default : System.Web.UI.Page
```

```
{
    protected void Page_Load(object sender, EventArgs e)
    {
        Double price = 49.99;
        DateTime publicationdate = new DateTime(2005, 1, 1);
        String isbn = "1-057-610-0";
        Author a = new Author();
        a.FirstName = "Scott";
        a.LastName = "Hanselman";

        Response.ContentType = "text/xml";
        XNamespace ns = "http://example.books.com";
        XDocument books = new XDocument(
            new XElement(ns + "bookstore",
                new XElement(ns + "book",
                    new XAttribute("publicationdate", publicationdate),
                    new XAttribute("ISBN", isbn),
                    new XElement(ns + "title", "ASP.NET 2.0 Book"),
                    new XElement(ns + "price", price),
                    new XElement(ns + "author",
                        new XElement(ns + "first-name", a.FirstName),
                        new XElement(ns + "last-name", a.LastName)
                        )
                    )
                )
            );
        Response.Write(books);
    }
}
```

Even though the C# example appears on multiple lines, it could be all on one line as it is one single expression. The constructors for `XElement` and `XDocument` take an array of parameters that is arbitrarily long, allowing us to create an XML Document structure more declaratively. If you compare this listing to Listing 10-11, you'll notice that the indentation in the `XmlWriter` example makes the sample more readable, but doesn't affect document structure. However, with `XDocument/XElement` declarations, the document structure is expressed by how the objects are nested as they are passed into each other's constructors.

> **There was a "Paste XML as XLinq" feature that didn't make it into the released product but was shipped as a Sample. This add-in adds a menu item to your Visual Studio 2008 Edit Menu that will take XML from the clipboard and paste it into the editor as an XElement expression. You'll find it from within Visual Studio via the Help ➪ Samples ➪ Visual C# Samples folder. The sample is called `PasteXmlAsLinq` and can be compiled and copied to any Visual Studio AddIns folder.**

Bridging XmlSerializer and LINQ to XML

There isn't a direct bridge between `XmlSerialization` and the new LINQ classes; both `XDocument` and `XElement` include a `CreateWriter` method that returns an `XmlWriter`. When that returned `XmlWriter` has its `Close` method called, all the generated XML is turned into XElements and added to the parent `XDocument` or `XElement`. This allows us to mix XElements and XmlSerialization techniques within a single expression. While this could be considered an unusual use case, XmlSerialization happens often, and it's useful to point out how well the new 3.5 classes can get along with the 2.0 classes.

This C# example is the same as Listing 10-11 except it creates an Extension Class to extend `XmlSerializer` with a new `SerializeAsXElement` method that returns an `XElement` containing the result of the serialization. First, the extension:

```
static class XmlSerializerExtension
{
    public static XElement SerializeAsXElement(this XmlSerializer xs, object o)
    {
        XDocument d = new XDocument();
        using (XmlWriter w = d.CreateWriter())
        {
            xs.Serialize(w, o);
        }
        XElement e = d.Root;
        e.Remove();
        return e;
    }
}
```

Notice that the class and method are `static`, and the `this` keyword refers to the class being extended, in this case `XmlSerializer`. An `XDocument` is created and an `XmlWriter` is returned. The `XmlSerializer` then serializes the object to this `XmlWriter`. Then there is a little nuance as the root element is removed from the document. This avoids cloning of the returned element during any subsequent uses within a functional construction.

Now our new extension method on the `XmlSerializer` can be called within the middle of the XElement functional construction, as shown here:

```
XmlSerializer xs = new XmlSerializer(typeof(Author));
XDocument books = new XDocument(
    new XElement(ns + "bookstore",
        new XElement(ns + "book",
            new XAttribute("publicationdate", publicationdate),
            new XAttribute("ISBN", isbn),
            new XElement(ns + "title", "ASP.NET 2.0 Book"),
            new XElement(ns + "price", price),
            xs.SerializeAsXElement(a)
            )
        )
    );
```

The resulting XML is identical to the output of Listing 10-11. Now you've got three different ways to create XML: first with a Writer, second with LINQ to XML, and third as a hybrid of XmlSerialization and LINQ. There are other combinations that you can come up with that maximize existing code reuse and ease of development.

Improvements for XmlReader and XmlWriter in 2.0

A few helper methods and changes make using `XmlReader` and `XmlWriter` even simpler in the .NET Framework 2.0:

- `ReadSubtree`: This method reads the current node of an `XmlReader` and returns a new `XmlReader` that traverses the current node and all its descendants. It allows you to chop off a portion of the XML InfoSet and process it separately.

- ReadToDescendant and ReadToNextSibling: These two methods provide convenient ways to advance the XmlReader to specific elements that appear later in the document.
- Dispose: XmlReader and XmlWriter both implement IDisposable, which means that they support the Using keyword. Using, in turn, calls Dispose, which calls the Close method. These methods are now less problematic because you no longer have to remember to call Close to release any resources. This simple but powerful technique has been used in the listings in this chapter.

XmlDocument and XPathDocument

In the .NET Framework 1.1, the XmlDocument was one of the most common ways to manipulate XML. It is similar to using a static ADO recordset because it parses and loads the entire XmlDocument into memory. Often the XmlDocument is the first class a programmer learns to use and, consequently, as a solution it becomes the hammer in his toolkit. Unfortunately, not every kind of XML problem is a nail. XmlDocuments have been known to use many times their file size in memory. Often an XmlDocument is referred to as the DOM or Document Object Model. The XmlDocument is compliant with the W3C DOM implementation and should be familiar to anyone who has used a DOM implementation.

Problems with the DOM

There are a number of potential problems with the XmlDocument class in the .NET Framework. The data model of the XmlDocument is very different from other XML query languages such as XSLT and XPath. The XmlDocument is editable and provides a familiar API for those who used MSXML in Visual Basic 6. Often, however, people use the XmlDocument to search for data within a larger document, but the XmlDocument isn't designed for searching large amounts of information. The XPathDocument is read-only and optimized for XPath queries or XPath-heavy technologies such as XSLT. In .NET Framework 2.0, the XPathDocument is much, much faster than the XmlDocument for loading and querying XML.

The XPathDocument is very focused around the InfoSet because it has a much-optimized internal structure. Be aware, however, that it does throw away insignificant white spaces and CDATA sections, so it is not appropriate if you want the XPathDocument to maintain the identical number of bytes that you originally created. However, if you're focused more on the set of information that is contained within your document, you can be assured that the XPathDocument contains everything that your source document contains.

A rule of thumb for querying data is that you should use the XPathDocument instead of the XmlDocument — except in situations where you must maintain compatibility with previous versions of the .NET Framework. The new XPathDocument supports all the type information from any associated XML Schema and supports the schema validation via the Validate method. The XPathDocument lets you load XML documents to URLs, files, or streams. The XPathDocument is also the preferred class to use for the XSLT transformations covered later in this chapter.

XPath, the XPathDocument, and XmlDocument

The XPathDocument is so named because it is the most efficient way to use XPath expressions over an in-memory data structure. The XPathDocument implements the IXPathNavigable interface, allowing you to iterate over the underlying XML by providing an XPathNavigator. The XPathNavigator class differs from the XmlReader because rather than forward-only, it provides random access over your XML, similar to a read-only ADO Keyset recordset versus a forward-only recordset.

You typically want to use an XPathDocument to move around freely, forward and backward, within a document. XPathDocument is read-only, while XmlDocument allows read-write access.

The XmlDocument in version 2.0 adds in-memory validation. Using the XmlReader, the only way to validate the XML is from a stream or file. The XmlDocument now allows in-memory validation without the file or stream access using Validate(). XmlDocument also adds capability to subscribe to events like NodeChanged, NodeInserting, and the like.

XPath is a query language best learned by example. You must know it to make good use of the XPath-Document. Here are some valid XPath queries that you can use with the Books.xml file. XPath is a rich language in its own right, with many dozens of functions. As such, fully exploring XPath is beyond the scope of this book, but the following table should give you a taste of what's possible.

Xpath Function	Result
//book[@genre = "novel"]/title	Recursively from the root node, gets the titles of all books whose genre attribute is equal to novel
/bookstore/book[author/last-name = "Melville"]	Gets all books that are children of bookstore whose author's last name is Melville
/bookstore/book/author[last-name = "Melville"]	Gets all authors that are children of book whose last name is Melville
//book[title = "The Gorgias" or title = "The Confidence Man"]	Recursively from the root node, gets all books whose title is either The Gorgias or The Confidence Man
//title[contains(., "The")]	Gets all titles that contain the string The
//book[not(price[.>10.00])]	Gets all books whose prices are not greater than 10.00

Listing 10-12 queries an XPathDocument for books whose prices are less than $10.00 and outputs the price. In order to illustrate using built-in XPath functions, this example uses a greater-than instead of using a less-than. It then inverts the result using the built-in not() method. XPath includes a number of functions for string concatenation, arithmetic, and many other uses. The XPathDocument returns an XPathNavigator as a result of calling CreateNavigator. The XPathNavigator is queried using an XPath passed to the Select method and returns an XPathNodeIterator. That XPathNodeIterator is foreach enabled via IEnumerable. As Listing 10-16 uses a read-only XPathDocument, it will not update the data in memory.

Listing 10-12: Querying XML with XPathDocument and XPathNodeIterator

VB

```
'Load document
Dim booksFile As String = Server.MapPath("books.xml")
Dim document As New XPathDocument(booksFile)
Dim nav As XPathNavigator = document.CreateNavigator()

'Add a namespace prefix that can be used in the XPath expression
Dim namespaceMgr As New XmlNamespaceManager(nav.NameTable)
```

```
namespaceMgr.AddNamespace("b", "http://example.books.com")

'All books whose price is not greater than 10.00
For Each node As XPathNavigator In nav.Select( _
        "//b:book[not(b:price[. > 10.00])]/b:price", namespaceMgr)
    Dim price As Decimal = _
        CType(node.ValueAs(GetType(Decimal)), Decimal)
    Response.Write(String.Format("Price is {0}<BR/>", _
        price))
Next
```

C#

```
//Load document
string booksFile = Server.MapPath("books.xml");

XPathDocument document = new XPathDocument(booksFile);
XPathNavigator nav = document.CreateNavigator();

//Add a namespace prefix that can be used in the XPath expression
XmlNamespaceManager namespaceMgr = new XmlNamespaceManager(nav.NameTable);
namespaceMgr.AddNamespace("b", "http://example.books.com");

//All books whose price is not greater than 10.00
foreach(XPathNavigator node in
    nav.Select("//b:book[not(b:price[. > 10.00])]/b:price",
    namespaceMgr))
{
    Decimal price = (decimal)node.ValueAs(typeof(decimal));
    Response.Write(String.Format("Price is {0}<BR/>",
        price));
}
```

If you then want to modify the underlying XML nodes, in the form of an `XPathNavigator`, you would use an XmlDocument instead of an XPathDocument. Your XPath expression evaluation may slow you down, but you will gain the capability to edit. Beware of this tradeoff in performance. Most often, you will want to use the read-only XPathDocument whenever possible. Listing 10-13 illustrates this change with the new or changed portions appearing in gray. Additionally, now that the document is editable, the price is increased 20 percent.

Listing 10-13: Querying and editing XML with XmlDocument and XPathNodeIterator

VB

```
'Load document
Dim booksFile As String = Server.MapPath("books.xml")

Dim document As New XmlDocument()
document.Load(booksFile)
Dim nav As XPathNavigator = document.CreateNavigator()

'Add a namespace prefix that can be used in the XPath expression
Dim namespaceMgr As New XmlNamespaceManager(nav.NameTable)
namespaceMgr.AddNamespace("b", "http://example.books.com")
'All books whose price is not greater than 10.00
For Each node As XPathNavigator In nav.Select( _
```

Continued

```
            "//b:book[not(b:price[. > 10.00])]/b:price", namespaceMgr)
        Dim price As Decimal = CType(node.ValueAs(GetType(Decimal)), Decimal)
        node.SetTypedValue(price * CDec(1.2))
        Response.Write(String.Format("Price raised from {0} to {1}<BR/>", _
            price, _
            CType(node.ValueAs(GetType(Decimal)), Decimal)))
    Next
```

C#

```
//Load document
string booksFile = Server.MapPath("books.xml");

XmlDocument document = new XmlDocument();
document.Load(booksFile);
XPathNavigator nav = document.CreateNavigator();

//Add a namespace prefix that can be used in the XPath expression
XmlNamespaceManager namespaceMgr = new XmlNamespaceManager(nav.NameTable);
namespaceMgr.AddNamespace("b", "http://example.books.com");

//All books whose price is not greater than 10.00
foreach(XPathNavigator node in
    nav.Select("//b:book[not(b:price[. > 10.00])]/b:price",
    namespaceMgr))
{
    Decimal price = (decimal)node.ValueAs(typeof(decimal));
    node.SetTypedValue(price * 1.2M);
    Response.Write(String.Format("Price inflated raised from {0} to {1}<BR/>",
        price,
        node.ValueAs(typeof(decimal))));
}
```

Listing 10-13 changes the `XPathDocument` to an `XmlDocument`, and adds a call to `XPathNavigator.SetTypedValue` to update the price of the document in memory. The resulting document could then be persisted to storage as needed. If `SetTypedValue` was instead called on the `XPathNavigator` that was returned by `XPathDocument`, a `NotSupportedException` would be thrown as the `XPathDocument` is read-only.

The `Books.xml` document loaded from disk uses `http://example.books.com` as its default namespace. Because the `Books.xsd` XML Schema is associated with the `Books.xml` document, and it assigns the default namespace to be `http://example.books.com`, the XPath must know how to resolve that namespace. Otherwise, you cannot determine if an XPath expression with the word `book` in it refers to a book from this namespace or another book entirely. An `XmlNamespaceManager` is created, and `b` is arbitrarily used as the namespace prefix for the XPath expression.

Namespace resolution can be very confusing because it is easy to assume that your XML file is all alone in the world and that specifying a node named `book` is specific enough to enable the system to find it. However, remember that your XML documents should be thought of as living among all the XML in the world — this makes providing a qualified namespace all the more important. The `XmlNamespaceManager` in Listing 10-12 is passed into the call to `SelectNodes` in order to associate the prefix with the appropriate namespace. Remember, the namespace is unique, not the prefix; the prefix is simply a convenience acting as an alias to the longer namespace. If you find that you're having trouble getting an XPath expression to work and no nodes are being returned, find out if your source XML has a namespace specified and that it matches up with a namespace in your XPath.

Using XPath with XDocuments in LINQ for XML

You can use XPath against an `XDocument` object by adding a reference to the `System.Xml.XPath` namespace via a using or Imports statement. Adding this reference adds new extension methods to the `XDocument` like `CreateNavigator` get to an `XPathNavigator` and the very useful XPathSelectElements. XPathSelectElements is similar to the `SelectNodes` and `SelectSingleNode` methods of the `System.Xml.XmlDocument`. These extension methods are part of the "bridge classes" that provide smooth integration between `System.Xml` and `System.Xml.Linq`.

Listing 10-12q: Querying XDocuments with XPath Expressions

VB

```
Dim booksFile As String = Server.MapPath("books.xml")
Dim document As XDocument = XDocument.Load(booksFile)

'Add a namespace prefix that can be used in the XPath expression
Dim namespaceMgr As New XmlNamespaceManager(New NameTable())
namespaceMgr.AddNamespace("b", "http://example.books.com")

'All books whose price is not greater than 10.00
Dim nodes = document.XPathSelectElements(
    "//b:book[not(b:price[. > 10.00])]/b:price", namespaceMgr)

For Each node In nodes
    Response.Write(node.Value + "<BR/>")
Next
```

C#

```
//Load document
string booksFile = Server.MapPath("books.xml");
XDocument document = XDocument.Load(booksFile);

//Add a namespace prefix that can be used in the XPath expression.
// Note the need for a NameTable. It could be new or come from elsewhere.
XmlNamespaceManager namespaceMgr = new XmlNamespaceManager(new NameTable());
namespaceMgr.AddNamespace("b", "http://example.books.com");

var nodes = document.XPathSelectElements(
    "//b:book[not(b:price[. > 10.00])]/b:price",namespaceMgr);

//All books whose price is not greater than 10.00
foreach (var node in nodes)
{
    Response.Write(node.Value + "<BR/>");
}
```

Notice that the added method in Listing 10-12q, `XPathSelectElements`, still requires an `IXmlNamespaceResolver`, so we create a new `NameTable` and map the namespaces and prefixes explicitly via `XmlNamespaceManager`. When using XElements and simple queries, you're better off using LINQ to XML and the new XElement-specific methods such as `Elements()` and `Descendants()` rather than XPath.

DataSets

The System.Data namespace and System.Xml namespace have started mingling their functionality for some time. DataSets are a good example of how relational data and XML data meet in a hybrid class library. During the COM and XML heyday, the ADO 2.5 recordset sported the capability to persist as XML. The dramatic inclusion of XML functionality in a class library focused entirely on manipulation of relational data was a boon for developer productivity. XML could be pulled out of SQL Server and manipulated.

Persisting DataSets to XML

Classes within System.Data use XmlWriter and XmlReader in a number of places. Now that you're more familiar with System.Xml concepts, be sure to take note of the method overloads provided by the classes within System.Data. For example, the DataSet.WriteXml method has four overloads, one of which takes in XmlWriter. Most of the methods with System.Data are very pluggable with the classes from System.Xml. Listing 10-14 shows another way to retrieve the XML from relational data by loading a DataSet from a SQL command and writing it directly to the browser with the Response object's OutputStream property using DataSet.WriteXml.

Listing 10-14: Extracting XML from a SQL Server with System.Data.DataSet

VB

```
Dim connStr As String = "database=Northwind;Data Source=localhost; " _
        & "User id=sa;pwd=wrox"

Using conn As New SqlConnection(connStr)
    Dim command As New SqlCommand("select * from customers", conn)
    conn.Open()
    Dim ds As New DataSet()
    ds.DataSetName = "Customers"
    ds.Load(command.ExecuteReader(), LoadOption.OverwriteChanges, "Customer")
    Response.ContentType = "text/xml"
    ds.WriteXml(Response.OutputStream)
End Using
```

C#

```
string connStr = "database=Northwind;Data Source=localhost;User id=sa;pwd=wrox";

using (SqlConnection conn = new SqlConnection(connStr))
{
    SqlCommand command = new SqlCommand("select * from customers", conn);
    conn.Open();
    DataSet ds = new DataSet();
    ds.DataSetName = "Customers";
    ds.Load(command.ExecuteReader(), LoadOption.OverwriteChanges, "Customer");
    Response.ContentType = "text/xml";
    ds.WriteXml(Response.OutputStream);
}
```

DataSets have a fairly fixed format, as illustrated in this example. The root node of the document is Customers, which corresponds to the DataSetName property. DataSets contain one or more named DataTable objects, and the names of these DataTables define the wrapper element — in this case,

Customer. The name of the DataTable is passed into the load method of the DataSet. The correlation between the DataSet's name, DataTable's name, and the resulting XML is not obvious when using DataSets. The resulting XML is shown in the browser in Figure 10-4.

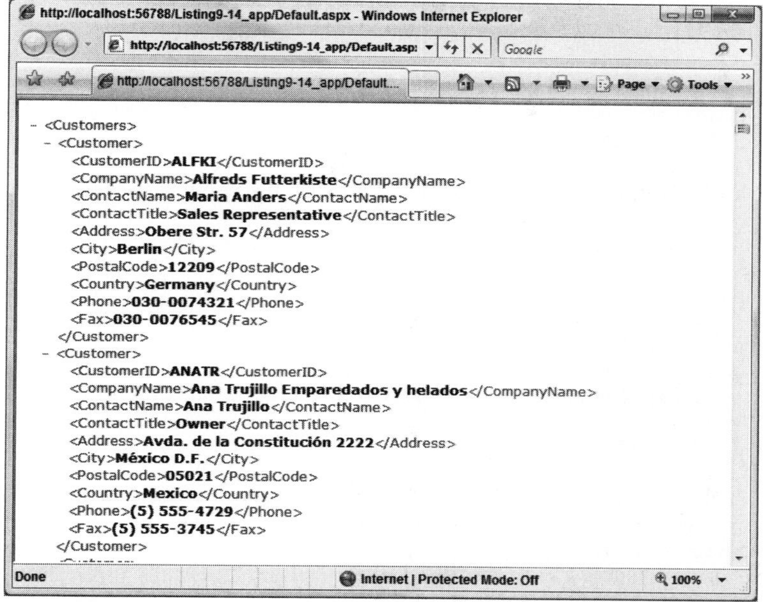

Figure 10-4

DataSets present a data model that is very different from the XML way of thinking about data. Much of the XML-style of thinking revolves around the InfoSet or the DOM, whereas DataSets are row- and column-based. The XmlDataDocument is an attempt to present these two ways of thinking into one relatively unified model.

XmlDataDocument

Although DataSets have their own relatively inflexible format for using XML, the XmlDocument class does not. In order to bridge this gap, an unusual hybrid object, the XmlDataDocument, is introduced. This object maintains the full fidelity of all the XML structure and allows you to access XML via the XmlDocument API without losing the flexibility of a relational API. An XmlDataDocument contains a DataSet of its own and can be called DataSet-aware. Its internal DataSet offers a relational view of the XML data. Any data contained within the XML data document that does not map into the relational view is not lost, but becomes available to the DataSet's APIs.

The XmlDataDocument is a constructor that takes a DataSet as a parameter. Any changes made to the XmlDataDocument are reflected in the DataSet and vice versa.

Now take the DataSet loaded in Listing 10-14 and manipulate the data with the XmlDataDocument and DOM APIs you're familiar with. Next, jump back into the world of System.Data and see that the DataSets underlying DataRows have been updated with the new data, as shown in Listing 10-15.

Listing 10-15: Changing DataSets using the DOM APIs from XmlDataDocument

VB

```
Dim connStr As String = "database=Northwind;Data Source=localhost; " _
      & "User id=sa;pwd=wrox"

Using conn As New SqlConnection(connStr)
    Dim command As New SqlCommand("select * from customers", conn)
    conn.Open()
    Dim ds As New DataSet()
    ds.DataSetName = "Customers"
    ds.Load(command.ExecuteReader(), LoadOption.OverwriteChanges, "Customer")
    'Response.ContentType = "text/xml"
    'ds.WriteXml(Response.OutputStream)

    'Added in Listing 10-15
    Dim doc As New XmlDataDocument(ds)
    doc.DataSet.EnforceConstraints = False
    Dim node As XmlNode = _
    doc.SelectSingleNode("//Customer[CustomerID = 'ANATR']/ContactTitle")
    node.InnerText = "Boss"
    doc.DataSet.EnforceConstraints = True

    Dim dr As DataRow = doc.GetRowFromElement(CType(node.ParentNode, XmlElement))
    Response.Write(dr("ContactName").ToString() & " is the ")
    Response.Write(dr("ContactTitle").ToString())
End Using
```

C#

```
string connStr = "database=Northwind;Data Source=localhost; "
      + "User id=sa;pwd=wrox";
using (SqlConnection conn = new SqlConnection(connStr))
{
    SqlCommand command = new SqlCommand("select * from customers", conn);
    conn.Open();
    DataSet ds = new DataSet();
    ds.DataSetName = "Customers";
    ds.Load(command.ExecuteReader(), LoadOption.OverwriteChanges,"Customer");
    //Response.ContentType = "text/xml";
    //ds.WriteXml(Response.OutputStream);

    //Added in Listing 10-15
    XmlDataDocument doc = new XmlDataDocument(ds);
    doc.DataSet.EnforceConstraints = false;
    XmlNode node = doc.SelectSingleNode(@"//Customer[CustomerID
        = 'ANATR']/ContactTitle");
    node.InnerText = "Boss";
    doc.DataSet.EnforceConstraints = true;

    DataRow dr = doc.GetRowFromElement((XmlElement)node.ParentNode);
    Response.Write(dr["ContactName"].ToString() + " is the ");
    Response.Write(dr["ContactTitle"].ToString());
}
```

Listing 10-15 extends Listing 10-14 by first commenting out changing the HTTP `ContentType` and the call to `DataSet.WriteXml`. After the DataSet is loaded from the database, it is passed to the `XmlDataDocument` constructor. At this point, the `XmlDataDocument` and the DataSet refer to the same set of information. The `EnforceConstraints` property of the DataSet is set to `false` to allow changes to the DataSet. When `EnforceConstraints` is later set to `true`, if any constraint rules were broken, an exception is thrown. An `XPath` expression is passed to the DOM method `SelectSingleNode`, selecting the `ContactTitle` node of a particular customer, and its text is changed to `Boss`. Then by calling `GetRowFromElement` on the `XmlDataDocument`, the context jumps from the world of the `XmlDocument` back to the world of the DataSet. Column names are passed into the `indexing` property of the returned `DataRow`, and the output is shown in this line:

```
Ana Trujillo is the Boss
```

The data is loaded from the SQL server and then manipulated and edited with `XmlDocument`-style methods; a string is then built using a `DataRow` from the underlying DataSet.

XML is clearly more than just angle brackets. XML data can come from files, from databases, from information sets like the DataSet object, and certainly from the Web. Today, however, a considerable amount of data is stored in XML format, so a specific data source control has been added to ASP.NET 2.0 just for retrieving and working with XML data.

The XmlDataSource Control

The `XmlDataSource` control enables you to connect to your XML data and to use this data with any of the ASP.NET data-bound controls. Just like the `SqlDataSource` and the `AccessDataSource` controls, the `XmlDataSource` control also enables you not only to retrieve data, but also to insert, delete, and update data items.

One unfortunate caveat of the `XmlDataSource` is that its `XPath` attribute does not support documents that use namespace qualification. Examples in this chapter use the `Books.xml` file with a default namespace of `http://examples.books.com`. It is very common for XML files to use multiple namespaces, including a default namespace. As you learned when you created an `XPathDocument` and queried it with XPath, the namespace in which an element exists is very important. The regrettable reality is, there is no way to use a namespace qualified XPath expression or to make the XmlDataSource Control aware of a list of prefix/namespace pairs via the `XmlNamespaceManager` class. However, the `XPath` function used in the `ItemTemplate` of the templated `DataList` control *can* take a `XmlNamespaceManager` as its second parameter and query XML returned from the `XmlDataSource` — as long as the control does not include an `XPath` attribute with namespace qualification or you can just omit it all together. That said, in order for these examples to work, you must remove the namespaces from your source XML and use XPath queries that include no namespace qualification, as shown in Listing 10-16.

You can use a `DataList` control or any DataBinding-aware control and connect to an `<asp:XmlDataSource>` control. The technique for binding a control directly to the `Books.xml` file is illustrated in Listing 10-16.

Listing 10-16: Using a DataList control to display XML content

```
<%@ Page Language="VB" AutoEventWireup="false"
CodeFile="Default.aspx.vb" Inherits="Default_aspx" %>
<html xmlns="http://www.w3.org/1999/xhtml" >
    <head id="Head1" runat="server">
        <title>XmlDataSource</title>
    </head>
    <body>
    <form id="form1" runat="server">
        <asp:datalist id="DataList1" DataSourceID="XmlDataSource1" runat="server">
            <ItemTemplate>
                <p><b><%# XPath("author/first-name") %>
                    <%# XPath("author/last-name")%></b>
                    wrote <%# XPath("title") %></p>
            </ItemTemplate>
        </asp:datalist>
        <asp:xmldatasource id="XmlDataSource1" runat="server"
            datafile="~/Books.xml"
            xpath="//bookstore/book"/>
    </form>
    </body>
</html>
```

This is a simple example, but it shows you the ease of using the XmlDataSource control. You should focus on two attributes in this example. The first is the DataFile attribute. This attribute points to the location of the XML file. Because the file resides in the root directory of the application, it is simply ~/Books.xml. The next attribute included in the XmlDataSource control is the XPath attribute. The XmlDataSource control uses the XPath attribute for the filtering of XML data. In this case, the XmlDataSource control is taking everything within the <book> set of elements. The value //bookstore/book means that the XmlDataSource control navigates to the <bookstore> element and then to the <book> element within the specified XML file and returns a list of all books.

The DataList control then must specify its DataSourceID as the XmlDataSource control. In the <ItemTemplate> section of the DataList control, you can retrieve specific values from the XML file by using XPath commands within the template. The XPath commands filter the data from the XML file. The first value retrieved is an element attribute (author/first-name) that is contained in the <book> element. If you are retrieving an attribute of an element, you preface the name of the attribute with an *at* (@) symbol. The next two XPath commands get the last name and the title of the book. Remember to separate nodes with a forward slash (/). When run in the browser, this code produces the results illustrated in the following list:

```
Benjamin Franklin wrote The Autobiography of Benjamin Franklin
Herman Melville wrote The Confidence Man
Sidas Plato wrote The Gorgias
```

Note that if you wrote the actual code, this entire exercise would be done entirely in the ASPX page itself!

Besides working from static XML files such as the Books.xml file shown earlier, the XmlDataSource control has the capability to work from dynamic, URL-accessible XML files. One popular XML format that is pervasive on the Internet today is the *weblog*. These *blogs*, or personal diaries, can be viewed either in the browser, through an RSS-aggregator, or as pure XML.

In Figure 10-5, you can see the XML from my blog's RSS feed. I've saved the XML to a local file and removed a stylesheet so I can see what the XML looks like when viewed directly in the browser. (You can find a lot of blogs to play with for this example at `weblogs.asp.net`.)

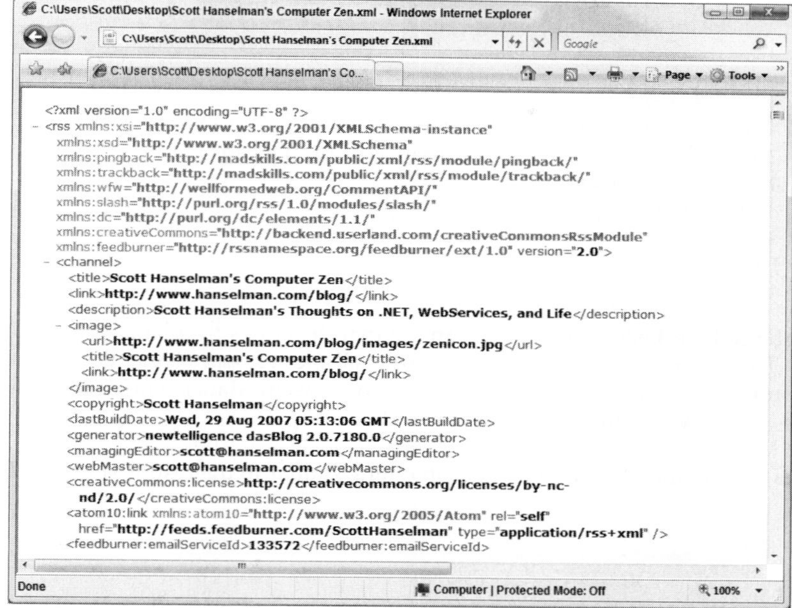

Figure 10-5

Now that you know the location of the XML from the blog, you can use this XML with the `XmlDataSource` control and display some of the results in a `DataList` control. The code for this example is shown in Listing 10-17.

Listing 10-17: Displaying an XML RSS blog feed

```
<%@ Page Language="VB"%>
<html xmlns="http://www.w3.org/1999/xhtml" >
    <head runat="server">
        <title>XmlDataSource</title>
    </head>
    <body>
    <form id="form1" runat="server">
        <asp:DataList ID="DataList1" Runat="server" DataSourceID="XmlDataSource1">
            <HeaderTemplate>
                <table border="1" cellpadding="3">
            </HeaderTemplate>
            <ItemTemplate>
                <tr><td><b><%# XPath("title") %></b><br />
                <i><%# XPath("pubDate") %></i><br />
                <%# XPath("description") %></td></tr>
            </ItemTemplate>
```

Continued

```
            <AlternatingItemTemplate>
                <tr bgcolor="LightGrey"><td><b><%# XPath("title") %></b><br />
                <i><%# XPath("pubDate") %></i><br />
                <%# XPath("description") %></td></tr>
            </AlternatingItemTemplate>
            <FooterTemplate>
                </table>
            </FooterTemplate>
        </asp:DataList>
        <asp:XmlDataSource ID="XmlDataSource1" Runat="server"
        DataFile="http://www.hanselman.com/blog/feed"
        XPath="rss/channel/item">
        </asp:XmlDataSource>
    </form>
    </body>
</html>
```

Looking at the code in Listing 10-17, you can see that the `DataFile` points to a URL where the XML is retrieved. The `XPath` property filters and returns all the `<item>` elements from the RSS feed. The `DataList` control creates an HTML table and pulls out specific data elements from the RSS feed, such as the `<title>`, `<pubDate>`, and `<description>` elements.

Running this page in the browser, you get something similar to the results shown in Figure 10-6.

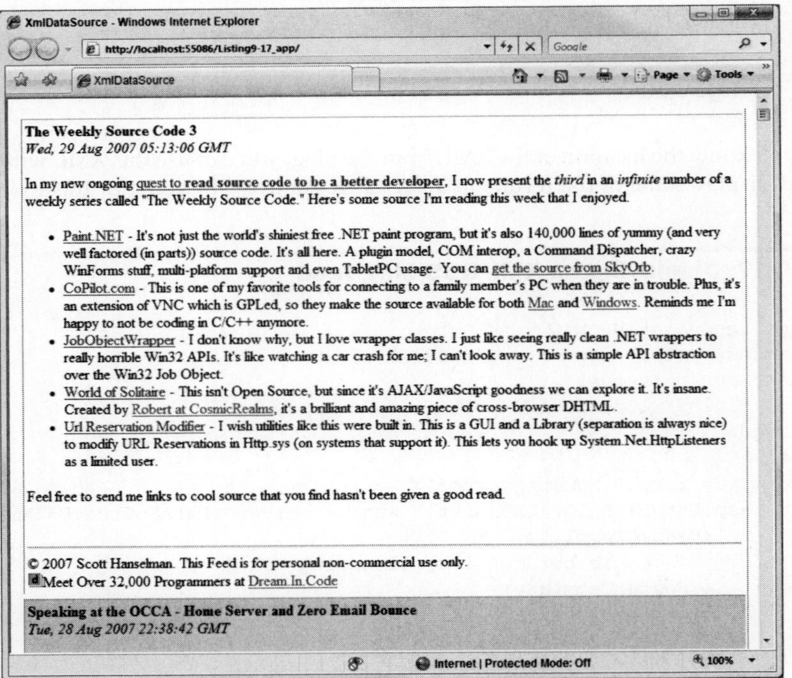

Figure 10-6

This approach also works with XML Web services, even ones for which you can pass in parameters using HTTP-GET. You just set up the `DataFile` property value in the following manner:

```
DataFile="http://www.someserver.com/GetWeather.asmx/ZipWeather?zipcode=63301"
```

There is no end to the number of places you can find and use XML: files, databases, Web sites, and services. Sometimes you will want to manipulate the XML via queries or programmatically, and sometimes you will want to take the XML "tree" and transform it into a tree of a different form.

XSLT

XSLT is a tree transformation language also written in XML syntax. It's a strange hybrid of a declarative and a programmatic language, and some programmers would argue that it's not a language at all. Others, who use a number of XSLT scripting extensions, would argue that it is a very powerful language. Regardless of the controversy, XSLT transformations are very useful for changing the structure of XML files quickly and easily, often using a very declarative syntax.

The best way to familiarize yourself with XSLT is to look at an example. Remember that the `Books.xml` file used in this chapter is a list of books and their authors. The XSLT in Listing 10-18 takes that document and transforms it into a document that is a list of authors.

Listing 10-18: Books.xslt

XSLT

```
<?xml version="1.0" encoding="utf-8" ?>
<xsl:stylesheet xmlns:xsl="http://www.w3.org/1999/XSL/Transform" version="1.0">
    <xsl:template match="/">
        <xsl:element name="Authors">
            <xsl:apply-templates select="//book"/>
        </xsl:element>
    </xsl:template>
    <xsl:template match="book">
        <xsl:element name="Author">
            <xsl:value-of select="author/first-name"/>
            <xsl:text> </xsl:text>
            <xsl:value-of select="author/last-name"/>
        </xsl:element>
    </xsl:template>
</xsl:stylesheet>
```

Remember that XSLT is XML vocabulary in its own right, so it makes sense that it has its own namespace and namespace prefix. XSLT is typically structured with a series of templates that match elements in the source document. The XSLT document doesn't describe what the result looks like as much as it declares what steps must occur for the transformation to succeed. Remembering that your goal is an XML file with a list of authors, you match on the root node of `Books.xml` and output a root element for the resulting document named `<Authors>`. Then `<xsl:apply-templates select = "//book"/>` indicates to the processor that it should continue looking for templates that, in this case, match the XPath expression `//book`. Below the first template is a second template that handles all book matches. It outputs a new element named `<Author>`.

XSLT is very focused on context, so it is often helpful to imagine a cursor that is on a particular element of the source document. Immediately after outputting the `<Author>` element, the processor is in the middle of the template match on the `book` element. All XPath expressions in this example are relative to the `book` element. So the `<xsl:value-of select = "author/first-name">` directive searches for the author's first name relative to the `book` element. The `<xsl:text> </xsl:text>` directive is interesting to note because it is explicit and a reminder that a difference exists between significant white space and insignificant white space. It is important, for example, that a space is put between the author's first and last names, so it must be called out explicitly.

The resulting document is shown in Figure 10-7.

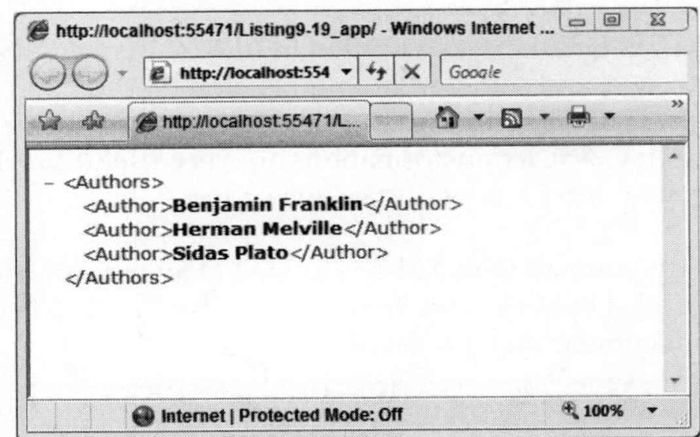

Figure 10-7

This example only scratches the surface of XSLT's power. Although a full exploration of XSLT is beyond the scope of this book, other books by Wrox Press cover the topic more fully. Remember that the .NET Framework implements the 1.0 implementation of XSLT. As of this writing, XSLT 2.0 and XPath 2.0 are W3C Recommendations, and Microsoft is working on CTPs (Community Technology Previews) of XSLT 2 functionality. More details are available on the Microsoft XmlTeam blog at `http://blogs.msdn.com/xmlteam/archive/2007/01/29/xslt-2-0.aspx`.

Figure 10-7 shows the resulting XML as the `Books.xslt` transformation is applied to `Books.xml`. You can apply XSLT transformations in a number of ways, both declarative and programmatic. These are described in the following sections.

XslCompiledTransform

The `XslTransform` class was used in the .NET Framework 1.*x* for XSLT transformation. In the .NET Framework 2.0, the `XslCompiledTransform` class is the new XSLT processor. It is such an improvement that `XslTransform` is deprecated and marked with the `Obsolete` attribute. The compiler will now advise you to use `XslCompiledTransform`. The system generates MSIL code on the call to `Compile()` and the XSLT executes many times faster than previous techniques. This compilation technique also includes full debugging support from within Visual Studio, which is covered a little later in this chapter.

The XPathDocument is absolutely optimized for XSLT transformations and should be used instead of the XmlDocument if you would like a 15 to 30 percent performance gain in your transformations. Remember that XSLT contains XPath, and when you use XPath, use an XPathDocument. According to the team's numbers, XSLT is 400 percent faster in .NET Framework 2.0.

XslCompiledTransform has only two methods: Load and Transform. The compilation happens without any effort on your part. Listing 10-19 loads the Books.xml file into an XPathDocument and transforms it using Books.xslt and an XslCompiledTransform. Even though there are only two methods, there are *14* overrides for Transform and 6 for Load. That may seem a little daunting at first, but there is a simple explanation.

The Load method can handle loading a stylesheet from a string, an XmlReader, or any class that implements IXPathNavigable. An XsltSettings object can be passed in optionally with any of the previous three overloads, giving you six to choose from. XsltSettings includes options to enable the document() XSLT–specific function via the XsltSettings.EnableDocumentFunction property or enable embedded script blocks within XSLT via XsltSettings.EnableScript. These advanced options are disabled by default for security reasons. Alternatively, you can retrieve a pre-populated XslSettings object via the static property XsltSettings.TrustedXslt, which has enabled both these settings.

If you think it is odd that the class that does the work is called the XslCompiledTransform and not the XsltCompiledTransform, but XsltSettings includes the *t*, remember that the *t* in XSLT means *transformation.*

Note in Listing 10-19 that the Response.Output property eliminates an unnecessary string allocation. In the example, Response.Output is a TextWriter wrapped in an XmlTextWriter and passed directly to the Execute method.

Listing 10-19: Executing an XsltCompiledTransform

VB

```
Response.ContentType = "text/xml"

Dim xsltFile As String = Server.MapPath("books.xslt")
Dim xmlFile As String = Server.MapPath("books.xml")

Dim xslt As New XslCompiledTransform()
xslt.Load(xsltFile)

Dim doc As New XPathDocument(xmlFile)
xslt.Transform(doc, New XmlTextWriter(Response.Output))
```

C#

```
Response.ContentType = "text/xml";
```

Continued

```
string xsltFile = Server.MapPath("books.xslt");
string xmlFile = Server.MapPath("books.xml");

XslCompiledTransform xslt = new XslCompiledTransform();
xslt.Load(xsltFile);

XPathDocument doc = new XPathDocument(xmlFile);
xslt.Transform(doc, new XmlTextWriter(Response.Output));
```

Named arguments may be passed into an `XslTransform` or `XslCompiledTransform` if the stylesheet takes parameters. The following code snippet illustrates the use of `XslArgumentList`:

```
XslTransform transformer = new XslTransform();
transformer.Load("foo.xslt");

XslArgumentList args = new XslArgumentList();
args.Add("ID", "SOMEVALUE");

transformer.Transform("foo.xml", args, Response.OutputStream);
```

The XML resulting from an XSLT transformation can be manipulated with any of the `system.XML` APIs that have been discussed in this chapter. One common use of XSLT is to flatten hierarchical and, sometimes, relational XML documents into a format that is more conducive to output as HTML. The results of these transformations to HTML can be placed inline within an existing ASPX document.

The new XSLTC.exe Command-Line Compiler

Compiled stylesheets are very useful but there is a slight performance hit as the stylesheets are compiled at runtime, so the .NET Framework 3.5 has introduced `XSLTC.exe`, a command-line XSLT compiler.

Usage is simple — you simply pass in as many source XSLT files as you like and specify the assembly output file. From a Visual Studio 2008 command prompt, use the following:

```
Xsltc /c:Wrox.Book.CompiledStylesheet books.xslt /out:Books.dll
```

Now, add a reference to the newly created `Books.dll` in your project from Listing 10-19, and change one line:

```
XslCompiledTransform xslt = new XslCompiledTransform();
xslt.Load(typeof(Wrox.Book.MyCompiledStyleSheet));
```

Rather than loading the XSLT from a file, it's now loaded pre-compiled directly from the generated assembly. Using the XSLT Compiler makes deployment much easier as you can put many XSLTs in a single assembly, but most important, you eliminate code-generation time.

If your XSLT uses msxsl:script elements, that code will be compiled into separate assemblies, one per language used. You can merge these resulting assemblies with ILMerge, located at `http://research.microsoft.com/~mbarnett/ILMerge.aspx`, as a post-build step.XML Web Server Control.

XSLT transformations can also be a very quick way to get information out to the browser as HTML. Consider this technique as yet another tool in your toolbox. HTML is a tree, and HTML is a cousin of XML, so an XML tree can be transformed into an HTML tree. A benefit of using XSLT transformations to create large amounts of static text, like HTML tables, is that the XSLT file can be kept external to the application. You can make quick changes to its formatting without a recompile. A problem when using XSLT transformations is that they can become large and very unruly when someone attempts to use them to generate the entire user interface experience. The practice was in vogue in the mid-nineties to use XSLT transformations to generate entire Web sites, but the usefulness of this technique breaks down when complex user interactions are introduced. That said, XSLT has a place, not only for transforming data from one format to another, but also for creating reasonable chunks of your user interface — as long as you don't go overboard.

In the next example, the output of the XSLT is HTML rather than XML. Note the use of the `<xsl:output method = "html">` directive. When this directive is omitted, the default output of an XSLT transformation is XML. This template begins with a match on the root node. It is creating an HTML fragment rather than an entire HTML document. Its first output is the `<h3>` tag with some static text. Next comes a table tag and the header row, and then the `<xsl:apply-template>` element selects all books within the source XML document. For every `book` element in the source document, the second template is invoked with the responsibility of outputting one table row per book. Calls to `<xsl:value-of>` select each of the book's subnodes and output them within the `<td>` tags (see Listing 10-20).

Listing 10-20: BookstoHTML.xslt used with the XML Web Server Control

XSLT

```
<?xml version="1.0" encoding="utf-8" ?>
<xsl:stylesheet xmlns:xsl="http://www.w3.org/1999/XSL/Transform"
        xmlns:b="http://example.books.com" version="1.0">
    <xsl:output method="html"/>
    <xsl:template match="/">
        <h3>List of Authors</h3>
        <table border="1">
            <tr>
                <th>First</th><th>Last</th>
            </tr>
            <xsl:apply-templates select="//b:book"/>
        </table>
    </xsl:template>
    <xsl:template match="b:book">
        <tr>
            <td><xsl:value-of select="b:author/b:first-name"/></td>
            <td><xsl:value-of select="b:author/b:last-name"/></td>
        </tr>
    </xsl:template>
</xsl:stylesheet>
```

ASPX

```
<%@ Page Language="VB" %>
<html xmlns="http://www.w3.org/1999/xhtml" >
    <head runat="server"><title>HTML/XSLT Transformation</title></head>
    <body>
        <form id="form1" runat="server">
            <div>
                <asp:Xml ID="Xml1" Runat="server"
                    DocumentSource="~/Books.xml"
                    TransformSource="~/bookstoHTML.xslt"/>
```

Continued

```
            </div>
        </form>
    </body>
</html>
```

Notice the use of namespace prefixes in Listing 10-20. The source namespace is declared with the prefix b as in `xmlns:b="http://example.books.com"` and the b prefix is subsequently used in XPath expressions like `//b:book`. The XSLT in Listing 10-20 can use the `XSLTCommand` to perform this transformation on the server-side because the entire operation is declarative and requires just two inputs — the XML document and the XSLT document. The XML Web server control makes the transformation easy to perform from the ASPX page and does not require any language-specific features. The `DocumentSource` property of the control holds the path to the `Books.xml` file, whereas the `TransformSource` property holds the path to the `BookstoHTML.xslt` file:

```
<h3>List of Authors</h3>
<table border="1">
    <tr>
        <th>First</th>
        <th>Last</th>
    </tr>
    <tr>
        <td>Benjamin</td>
        <td>Franklin</td>
    </tr>
    <tr>
        <td>Herman</td>
        <td>Melville</td>
    </tr>
    <tr>
        <td>Sidas</td>
        <td>Plato</td>
    </tr>
</table>
```

The results of this transformation are output inline to this HTML document and appear between the two `<div>` tags. You see the results of this HTML fragment in the previous code and in the browser's output shown in Figure 10-8.

Figure 10-8

XSLT Debugging

One of the exciting new additions to ASP.NET 2.0 and Visual Studio was XSLT debugging. Visual Studio 2005 enabled breakpoints on XSLT documents and Visual Studio 2008 adds XSLT Debugger Data Breakpoints — the ability to break on nodes within the source XML document. However, be aware that XSLT debugging is available only in the Professional and Team System versions of Visual Studio and only when using the `XslCompiledTransform` class.

By passing the Boolean value `true` into the constructor of `XslCompiledTransform`, you can step into and debug your XSLT transformations within the Microsoft Development Environment.

```
Dim xslt As New XslCompiledTransform(True)
```

In Listing 10-19, change the call to the constructor of `XslCompiledTransform` to include the value `true` and set a breakpoint on the `Transform` method. When you reach that breakpoint, press F11 to step into the transformation. Figure 10-9 shows a debugging session of the `Books.xslt/Books.xml` transformation in process.

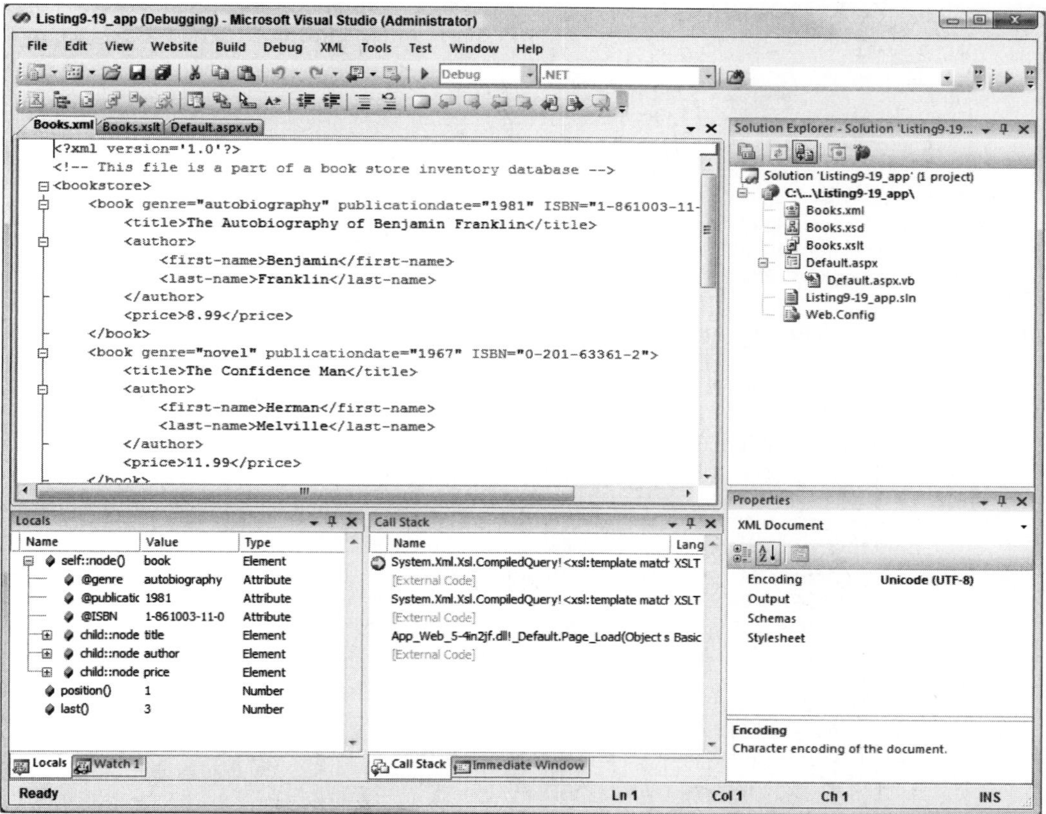

Figure 10-9

In the past, debugging XSLT was largely an opaque process that required a third-party application to troubleshoot. The addition of debugging XSLT to Visual Studio means that your XML experience is just that much more integrated and seamless.

Databases and XML

You have seen that XML can come from any source whether it be a Web service, a file on disk, an XML fragment returned from a Web server, or a database. SQL server and ADO have rich support for XML, starting with the `ExecuteXmlReader` method of the `System.Data.SqlCommand` class. Additional support for XML on SQL Server 2000 is included with SQLXML 3.0 and its XML extensions, and SQL Server 2005 has native XML data type support built right in.

FOR XML AUTO

You can modify a SQL query to return XML with the `FOR XML AUTO` clause. If you take a simple query such as `select * from customers`, you just change the statement like so:

```
select * from customers FOR XML AUTO
```

`XML AUTO` returns XML fragments rather than a full XML document with a document element. Each row in the database becomes one element; each column in the database becomes one attribute on the element. Notice that each element in the following result set is named `Customers` because the `select` clause is `from customers`:

```
<Customers CustomerID="ALFKI" CompanyName="Alfreds Futterkiste"
ContactName="Maria Anders" ContactTitle="Sales Representative"
Address="Obere Str. 57" City="Berlin" PostalCode="12209"
Country="Germany" Phone="030-0074321" Fax="030-0076545" />
<Customers CustomerID="ANATR" CompanyName="Ana Trujillo Emparedados y
helados" ContactName="Ana Trujillo" ContactTitle="Owner" Address="Avda.
de la Constitucion 2222" City="Mexico D.F." PostalCode="05021"
Country="Mexico" Phone="(5) 555-4729" Fax="(5) 555-3745" />
```

If you add `ELEMENTS` to the query like so

```
select * from customers FOR XML AUTO, ELEMENTS
```

you get an XML fragment like this:

```
<Customers>
    <CustomerID>ALFKI</CustomerID>
    <CompanyName>Alfreds Futterkiste</CompanyName>
    <ContactName>Maria Anders</ContactName>
    <ContactTitle>Sales Representative</ContactTitle>
    <Address>Obere Str. 57</Address>
    <City>Berlin</City>
    <PostalCode>12209</PostalCode>
    <Country>Germany</Country>
    <Phone>030-0074321</Phone>
    <Fax>030-0076545</Fax>
</Customers>
<Customers>
    <CustomerID>ANATR</CustomerID>
    <CompanyName>Ana Trujillo Emparedados y helados</CompanyName>
    <ContactName>Ana Trujillo</ContactName>
```

```
        <ContactTitle>Owner</ContactTitle>
        <Address>Avda. de la Constitucion 2222</Address>
        <City>Mexico D.F.</City>
        <PostalCode>05021</PostalCode>
        <Country>Mexico</Country>
        <Phone>(5) 555-4729</Phone>
        <Fax>(5) 555-3745</Fax>
    </Customers>
```

The previous example is just a fragment with no document element. To perform an XSLT transformation, you need a document element (sometimes incorrectly referred to as the "root node"), and you probably want to change the `<Customers>` elements to `<Customer>`. By using an alias like `as Customer` in the `select` statement, you can affect the name of each row's element. The query `select * from Customers as Customer for XML AUTO, ELEMENTS` changes the name of the element to `<Customer>`.

Now, put together all the things you've learned from this chapter and create an `XmlDocument`, edit and manipulate it, retrieve data from SQL Server as an `XmlReader`, and style that information with XSLT into an HTML table all in just a few lines of code.

First, add a document element to the document retrieved by the SQL query `select * from Customers as Customer for XML AUTO, ELEMENTS`, as shown in Listing 10-21.

Listing 10-21: Retrieving XML from SQL Server 2000 using FOR XML AUTO

VB

```
Dim connStr As String = "database=Northwind;Data Source=localhost;" & _
    " User id=sa;pwd=wrox"
Dim x As New XmlDocument()
Dim xpathnav As XPathNavigator = x.CreateNavigator()
Using conn As New SqlConnection(connStr)
    conn.Open()
    Dim command As New SqlCommand("select * from Customers as Customer " & _
        "for XML AUTO, ELEMENTS", conn)
    Using xw As XmlWriter = xpathnav.PrependChild()
        xw.WriteStartElement("Customers")
        Using xr As XmlReader = command.ExecuteXmlReader()
            xw.WriteNode(xr, True)
        End Using
        xw.WriteEndElement()
    End Using
End Using
Response.ContentType = "text/xml"
x.Save(Response.Output)
```

C#

```
string connStr = "database=Northwind;Data Source=localhost;User id=sa;pwd=wrox";
XmlDocument x = new XmlDocument();
XPathNavigator xpathnav = x.CreateNavigator();
using (SqlConnection conn = new SqlConnection(connStr))
{
    conn.Open();
    SqlCommand command = new SqlCommand(
```

Continued

```
            "select * from Customers as Customer for XML AUTO, ELEMENTS", conn);
        using (XmlWriter xw = xpathnav.PrependChild())
        {
            xw.WriteStartElement("Customers");
            using (XmlReader xr = command.ExecuteXmlReader())
            {
                xw.WriteNode(xr, true);
            }
            xw.WriteEndElement();
        }
    }
    Response.ContentType = "text/xml";
    x.Save(Response.Output);
```

This code creates an `XmlDocument` called `Customers`. Then it executes the SQL command and retrieves the XML data into an `XmlReader`. An `XPathNavigator` is created from the `XmlDocument`, and a child node is prepended to the document. A single call to the `WriteNode` method of the `XmlWriter` retrieved from the `XPathDocument` moves the entire XML fragment into the well-formed `XmlDocument`. Because the SQL statement contained `from Customers as Customer` as a table alias, each XML element is named `<Customer>`. Then, for this example, the resulting XML document is output directly to the `Response` object. You see the resulting XML in the browser shown in Figure 10-10.

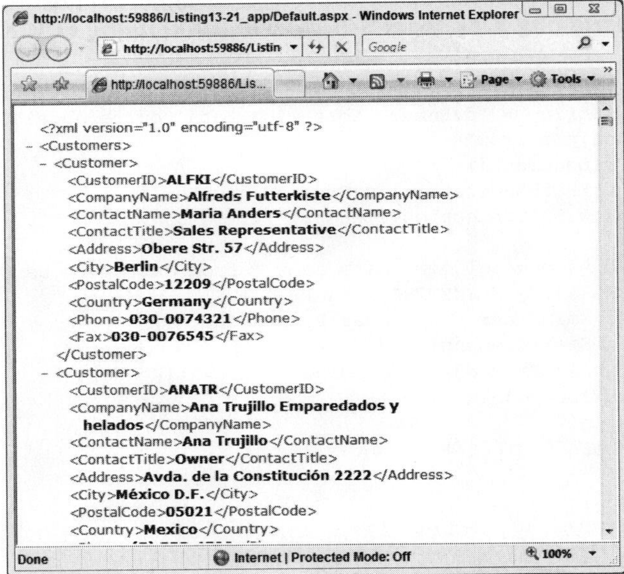

Figure 10-10

Of course, it's nice to see the resulting XML, but it's far more useful to style that information with XSLT. The XML Web Server control mentioned earlier is perfect for this task. However, in Listing 10-22, rather than setting both the `TransformSource` and `DocumentSource` properties as in Listing 10-25, you set only the `TransformSource` property at design time, and the `XmlDocument` is the one created in the code-behind of Listing 10-21.

Listing 10-22: The ASPX Page and XSLT to style the XML from SQL Server

ASPX

```
<%@ Page Language="C#" CodeFile="Default.aspx.cs" Inherits="Default_aspx" %>
<asp:xml id="Xml1" runat="server" transformsource="~/customersToHtml.xslt"/>
```

XSLT

```
<?xml version="1.0" encoding="utf-8" ?>
<xsl:stylesheet xmlns:xsl="http://www.w3.org/1999/XSL/Transform" version="1.0">
    <xsl:output method="html"/>
    <xsl:template match="/">
        <h3>List of Customers</h3>
        <table border="1">
            <tr>
                <th>Company Name</th><th>Contact Name</th><th>Contact Title</th>
            </tr>
            <xsl:apply-templates select="//Customer"/>
        </table>
    </xsl:template>
    <xsl:template match="Customer">
        <tr>
            <td><xsl:value-of select="CompanyName"/></td>
            <td><xsl:value-of select="ContactName"/></td>
            <td><xsl:value-of select="ContactTitle"/></td>
        </tr>
    </xsl:template>
</xsl:stylesheet>
```

VB

```
'Response.ContentType = "text/xml"
'x.Save(Response.Output)
Xml1.XPathNavigator = xpathnav
```

C#

```
//Response.ContentType = "text/xml";
//x.Save(Response.Output);
Xml1.XPathNavigator = xpathnav;
```

In the code-behind file, the lines that set `ContentType` and write the XML to the `Response` object are commented out, and instead the `XPathNavigator` from the `XmlDocument` that is manipulated in Listing 10-21 is set as a property of the XML Web Server control. The control then performs the XSLT `Stylesheet` transformation, and the results are output to the browser, as shown in Figure 10-11.

You have an infinite amount of flexibility within the `System.Xml`, `System.Xml.Linq`, and `System.Data` namespaces. Microsoft has put together a fantastic series of APIs that interoperate beautifully. When you're creating your own APIs that expose or consume XML, compare them to the APIs that Microsoft has provided — if you expose your data over an `XmlReader` or `IXPathNavigable` interface, you are sure to make your users much happier. Passing XML around with these more flexible APIs (rather than as simple and opaque strings) provides a much more comfortable and intuitive expression of the XML information set.

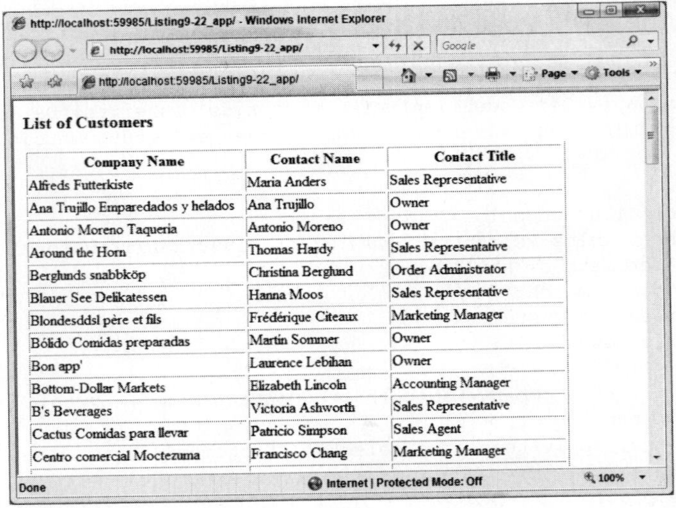

http://localhost:59985/Listing9-22_app/ - Windows Internet Explorer
http://localhost:59985/Listing9-22_app/
Google
http://localhost:59985/Listing9-22_app/
Page
Tools
List of Customers
Company Name
Contact Name
Contact Title
Alfreds Futterkiste
Maria Anders
Sales Representative
Ana Trujillo Emparedados y helados
Ana Trujillo
Owner
Antonio Moreno Taqueria
Antonio Moreno
Owner
Around the Horn
Thomas Hardy
Sales Representative
Berglunds snabbköp
Christina Berglund
Order Administrator
Blauer See Delikatessen
Hanna Moos
Sales Representative
Blondesddsl père et fils
Frédérique Citeaux
Marketing Manager
Bólido Comidas preparadas
Martín Sommer
Owner
Bon app'
Laurence Lebihan
Owner
Bottom-Dollar Markets
Elizabeth Lincoln
Accounting Manager
B's Beverages
Victoria Ashworth
Sales Representative
Cactus Comidas para llevar
Patricio Simpson
Sales Agent
Centro comercial Moctezuma
Francisco Chang
Marketing Manager
Done
Internet | Protected Mode: Off
100%

Figure 10-11

> **Remember that the `XmlReader` that is returned from `SqlCommand.ExecuteXmlReader()` is holding its SQL connection open, so you must call `Close()` when you're done using the `XmlReader`. The easiest way to ensure that this is done is the `using` statement. An `XmlReader` implements `IDisposable` and calls `Close()` for you as the variable leaves the scope of the `using` statement.**

SQL Server 2005 and the XML Data Type

You've seen that retrieving data from SQL Server 2000 is straightforward, if a little limited. SQL Server 2005, originally codenamed Yukon, includes a number of very powerful XML-based features. Dare Obasanjo, a former XML Program Manager at Microsoft has said, "The rise of the ROX [Relational-Object-XML] database has begun." SQL Server 2005 is definitely leading the way.

One of the things that is particularly tricky about mapping XML and the XML information set to the relational structure that SQL Server shares with most databases is that most XML data has a hierarchical structure. Relational databases structure hierarchical data with foreign key relationships. Relational data often has no order, but the order of the elements within `XmlDocument` is very important. SQL Server 2005 introduces a new data type called, appropriately, `XML`. Previously, data was stored in an `nvarchar` or other string-based data type. SQL Server 2005 can now have a table with a column of type `XML`, and each XML data type can have associated XML Schema.

The `FOR XML` syntax is improved to include the `TYPE` directive, so a query that includes `FOR XML TYPE` returns the results as a single XML-typed value. This XML data is returned with a new class called `System.Data.SqlXml`. It exposes its data as an `XmlReader` retrieved by calling `SqlXml.CreateReader`, so you'll find it to be very easy to use because it works like all the other examples you've seen in this chapter.

> **In a DataSet returned from SQL Server 2005, XML data defaults to being a string unless `DataAdapter.ReturnProviderSpecificTypes = true` is set or a schema is loaded ahead of time to specify the column type.**

The `XML` data type stores data as a new internal binary format that is more efficient to query. The programmer doesn't have to worry about the details of how the XML is stored if it continues to be available on the XQuery or in `XmlReader`. You can mix column types in a way that was not possible in SQL Server 2000. You're used to returning data as either a DataSet or an `XmlReader`. With SQL Server 2005, you can return a DataSet where some columns contain XML and some contain traditional SQL Server data types.

Generating Custom XML from SQL 2005

You've seen a number of ways to programmatically generate custom XML from a database. Before reading this book, you've probably used `FOR XML AUTO` to generate fairly basic XML and then modified the XML in post processing to meet your needs. This was formerly a very common pattern. `FOR XML AUTO` was fantastically easy; and `FOR XML EXPLICIT`, a more explicit way to generate XML, was very nearly impossible to use.

SQL Server 2005 adds the new `PATH` method to `FOR XML`, which makes arbitrary XML creation available to mere mortals. SQL 2005's XML support features very intuitive syntax and very clean namespace handling.

Here is an example of a query that returns custom XML. The `WITH XMLNAMESPACES` commands at the start of the query set the stage by defining a default namespace and using column-style name aliasing to associate namespaces with namespace prefixes. In this example, `addr:` is the prefix for `urn:hanselman.com/northwind/address`.

```
use Northwind;
WITH XMLNAMESPACES (
 DEFAULT 'urn:hanselman.com/northwind'
 , 'urn:hanselman.com/northwind/address' as "addr"
)
SELECT CustomerID as "@ID",
           CompanyName,
           Address as "addr:Address/addr:Street",
           City as "addr:Address/addr:City",
           Region as "addr:Address/addr:Region",
           PostalCode as "addr:Address/addr:Zip",
           Country as "addr:Address/addr:Country",
           ContactName as "Contact/Name",
           ContactTitle as "Contact/Title",
           Phone as "Contact/Phone",
           Fax as "Contact/Fax"
FROM Customers
FOR XML PATH('Customer'), ROOT('Customers'), ELEMENTS XSINIL
```

The aliases using the `AS` keyword declaratively describe the elements and their nesting relationships, whereas the `PATH` keyword defines an element for the Customers table. The `ROOT` keyword defines the root node of the document.

The ELEMENTS keyword, along with XSINIL, describes how you handle null. Without these keywords, no XML element is created for a row's column that contains null; this absence of data in the database causes the omission of data in the resulting XML document. When the ELMENTS XSINIL combination is present, an element outputs using an explicit xsi:nil syntax such as <addr:Region xsi:nil="true" />.

When you run the example, SQL 2005 outputs an XML document like the one that follows. Note the namespaces and prefixes are just as you defined them.

```
<Customers xmlns:xsi="http://www.w3.org/2001/XMLSchema-instance"
xmlns:addr="urn:hanselman.com/northwind/address"
xmlns="urn:hanselman.com/northwind">
  <Customer ID="ALFKI">
    <CompanyName>Alfreds Futterkiste</CompanyName>
    <addr:Address>
      <addr:Street>Obere Str. 57</addr:Street>
      <addr:City>Berlin</addr:City>
      <addr:Region xsi:nil="true" />
      <addr:Zip>12209</addr:Zip>
      <addr:Country>Germany</addr:Country>
    </addr:Address>
    <Contact>
      <Name>Maria Anders</Name>
      <Title>Sales Representative</Title>
      <Phone>030-0074321</Phone>
      <Fax>030-0076545</Fax>
    </Contact>
  </Customer>
...the rest of the document removed for brevity...
```

The resulting XML can now be manipulated using an XmlReader or any of the techniques discussed in this chapter.

Adding a Column of Untyped XML

SQL Server can produce XML from a query, and it can now also store XML in a single column. Because XML is a first-class data type within SQL Server 2005, adding a new column to the Customers table of the Northwind Database is straightforward. You can use any SQL Server management tool you like. I use the SQL Server Management Studio Express, a free download that can be used with any SQL SKU (including the free SQL Express 2005). Bring up your Query Analyzer or Management Studio Express and with the Northwind database selected, execute the following query:

```
use Northwind;
BEGIN TRANSACTION
GO
ALTER TABLE dbo.Customers ADD
 Notes xml NULL
GO
COMMIT
```

Note the xml type keyword after Notes in the preceding example. If an XML Schema were already added to the database, you could add this new column and associate it with a named Schema Collection all at once using this syntax.

```
use Northwind;
BEGIN TRANSACTION
GO
ALTER TABLE dbo.Customers ADD
 Notes xml(DOCUMENT dbo.NorthwindCollection)
 GO
COMMIT
```

Here, the word `DOCUMENT` indicates that the column will contain a complete XML document. Use `CONTENT` to store fragments of XML that don't contain a root note. You haven't added a schema yet, so that's the next step. So far, you've added a `Notes` column to the Customers table that can be populated with prose. For example, a customer service representative could use it to describe interactions she's had with the customer, entering text into a theoretical management system.

Adding an XML Schema

Although the user could store untyped XML data in the Notes field, you should really include some constraints on what's allowed. XML data can be stored typed or untyped, as a fragment with no root note or as a document. Because you want store Customer interaction data entered and viewed from a Web site, ostensibly containing prose, XHTML is a good choice.

XML data is validated by XML Schemas, as discussed earlier in the chapter. However, SQL Server 2005 is a database, not a file system. It needs to store the schemas you want to reference in a location it can get to. You add a schema or schemas to SQL Server 2005 using queries formed like this:

```
CREATE XML SCHEMA COLLECTION YourCollection AS 'your complete xml schema here'
```

You'll be using the XHTML 1.0 Strict schema located on the W3C Web site shown here: `http://w3.org/TR/xhtml1-schema/#xhtml1-strict`. Copy the entire schema to a file, or download the schema directly from `http://w3.org/2002/08/xhtml/xhtml1-strict.xsd`.

When executing your query, you include the entire XSD inline in your schema. However, you should watch for few things. First, escape any single quotes so that `'` becomes `''` — that is, two single quotes, *not* one double — using a search and replace. Second, because SQL 2005 uses the MSXML6 XML parser to parse its XML, take into consideration a limitation in that parser. MSXML6 already has the `xml:` namespace prefix and associated namespace hard-coded internally, so you should remove the line from your schema that contains that namespace. This little oddity is documented, but buried within MSDN at `http://msdn2.microsoft.com/ms177489(en-US,SQL.90).aspx` and applies only to a few predefined schemas like this one that uses the `xml:` prefix and/or the `http://www.w3.org/XML/1998/namespace` namespace. In the fragment that follows, I've bolded the line you need to remove.

```
Use Northwind;
CREATE XML SCHEMA COLLECTION NorthwindCollection AS
'<?xml version="1.0" encoding="UTF-8"?>
<xs:schema version="1.0" xml:lang="en"
    xmlns:xs="http://www.w3.org/2001/XMLSchema"
    targetNamespace="http://www.w3.org/1999/xhtml"
    xmlns="http://www.w3.org/1999/xhtml"
    xmlns:xml="http://www.w3.org/XML/1998/namespace"
    elementFormDefault="qualified">
...the rest of the schema has been omitted for brevity...
</xs:schema>';
```

Instead, you want to execute a query like this, noting the single quote and semicolon at the very end.

```
Use Northwind;
CREATE XML SCHEMA COLLECTION NorthwindCollection AS
'<?xml version="1.0" encoding="UTF-8"?>
<xs:schema version="1.0" xml:lang="en"
    xmlns:xs="http://www.w3.org/2001/XMLSchema"
    targetNamespace="http://www.w3.org/1999/xhtml"
    xmlns="http://www.w3.org/1999/xhtml"
    elementFormDefault="qualified">
...the rest of the schema has been omitted for brevity...
</xs:schema>';
```

You may get a few schema validation warnings when you execute this query because of the complexity of the XHTML schema, but you can ignore them. Figure 10-12 shows the new NorthwindCollection schemas added to the Northwind database.

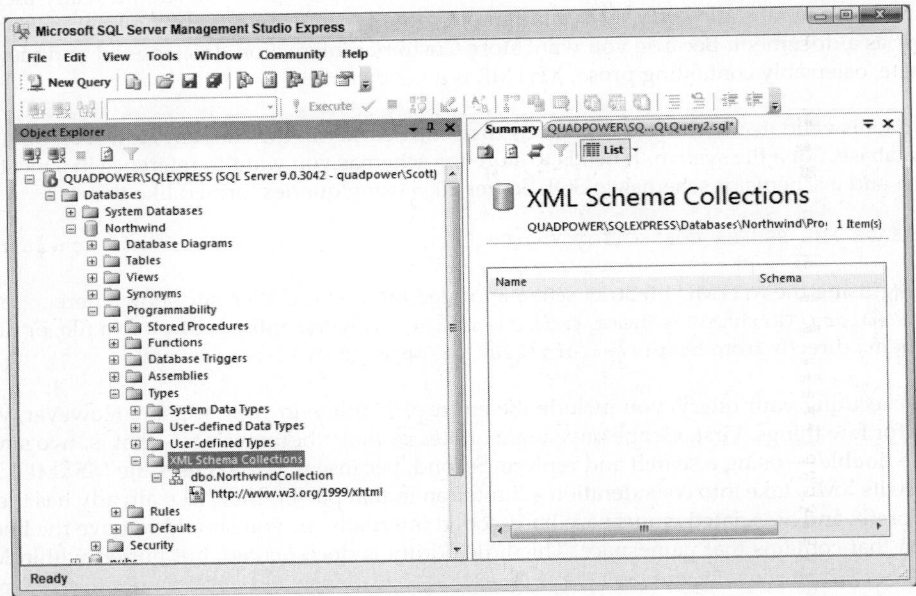

Figure 10-12

Although Figure 10-12 shows the NorthwindCollection within the Object Explorer, you can also confirm that your schema has been added correctly using SQL, as shown in the example that follows:

```
Use Northwind;
SELECT XSN.name
FROM    sys.xml_schema_collections XSC
    JOIN sys.xml_schema_namespaces XSN ON
        (XSC.xml_collection_id = XSN.xml_collection_id)
```

The output of the query is something like the following. You can see that the XHTML namespace appears at the end along with the schemas that already existed in the system.

```
http://www.w3.org/2001/XMLSchema
http://schemas.microsoft.com/sqlserver/2004/sqltypes
http://www.w3.org/XML/1998/namespace
http://www.w3.org/1999/xhtml
```

Next you should associate the new column with the new schema collection. Using the Management Studio, you create one composite script that automates this process. In this case, however, you can continue to take it step by step so you see what's happening underneath.

Associating a XML Typed Column with a Schema

You can use the Microsoft SQLServer Management Studio Express to associate the NorthwindCollection with the new Notes column. Open the Customers table of the Northwind Database and, within its Column collection, right-click and select Modify. Select the Notes column, as shown in Figure 10-13. Within the Notes column's property page, open the XML Type Specification property and select the Northwind-Collection from the Schema Collection dropdown. Also, set the `Is XML Document` property to `Yes`.

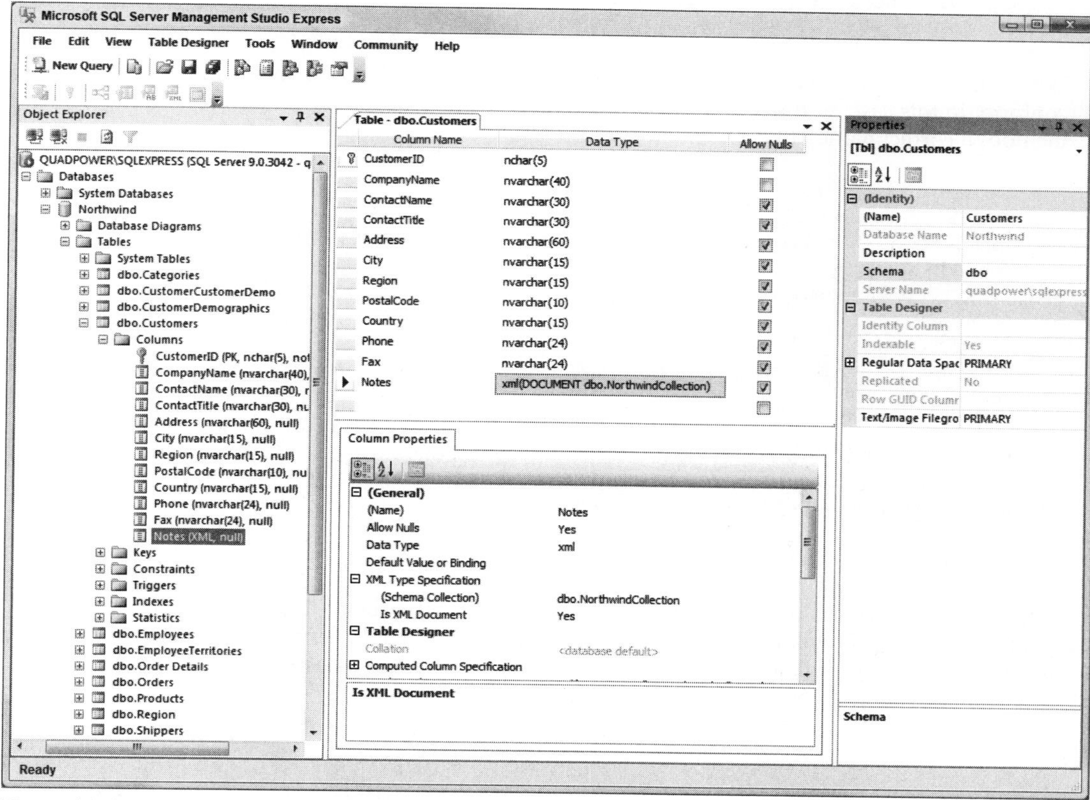

Figure 10-13

At this point, you can save your table and a change script is generated and executed. If you want to see and save the change script after making a modification but before saving the changes, right-click in the grid and select Generate Change Script. Click the Save toolbar button or Ctrl+S to commit your changes to the Customers table.

Now that you've added a new Notes column and associated it with an XHTML schema, you're ready to add some data to an existing row.

Inserting XML Data into an XML Column

You start by adding some data to a row within the Northwind database's Customer table. Add some notes to the famous first row, the customer named Alfreds Futterkiste, specifically CustomerID ALFKI. You add or update data to a column with the XML type just as you add to any data type. For example, you can try an UPDATE query.

```
Use Northwind;
UPDATE Customers SET Notes = N'<HTML></HTML>' WHERE CustomerID = 'ALFKI';
```

Upon executing this query, you get this result:

```
Msg 6913, Level 16, State 1, Line 1
XML Validation: Declaration not found for element 'HTML'. Location: /*:HTML[1]
```

What's this? Oh, yes, you associated a schema with the XML column so the included document must conform, in this case, to the XHTML specification. Now, try again with a valid XHTML document that includes a correct namespace.

```
Use Northwind;
UPDATE Customers SET Notes = N'
<html xmlns="http://www.w3.org/1999/xhtml" xml:lang="en">
 <head>
  <title>Notes about Alfreds</title>
 </head>
 <body>
  <p>He is a nice enough fellow.</p>
 </body>
</html>'
WHERE CustomerID = 'ALFKI';
```

Execute this corrected query and you see a success message.

```
(1 row(s) affected)
```

After you've typed a column as XML and associated an XML Schema, SQL Server 2005 will allow only XML documents that validate. The data can be retrieved from SQL Server using standard System.Data techniques. It can be pulled out of a `DataReader` or a `DataSet` and manipulated with `XmlReaders` or as an `XmlDocument`.

Summary

XML and the XML InfoSet are both pervasive in the .NET Framework and in ASP.NET. All ASP.NET configuration files include associated XML Schema, and the Visual Studio Editor is even smarter about XML documents that use XSDs.

`XmlReader` and `XmlWriter` provide unique and incredibly fast ways to consume and create XML; they now also include even better support for mapping XML Schema types to CLR types, as well as other improvements. The `XmlDocument` and `XPathDocument` return in .NET 2.0 with API additions and numerous performance improvements, while the `XmlDataDocument` straddles the world of `System.Data` and `System.Xml`. ASP.NET and .NET 3.5 include support for XSLT via not only the new `XslCompiledTransform` but also command-line compilation, and tops it all with XSLT debugging support for compiled stylesheets. LINQ to XML introduces the new `System.Xml.Linq` namespace and supporting classes for a tightly integrated IntelliSense-supported coding experience. VB9 takes XML support to the next level with XML literals and XML namespace imports. The bridge classes and extension methods make the transition between `System.Xml` and `System.Xml.Linq` clean and intuitive.

All these ways to manipulate XML via the Base Class Library are married with XML support in SQL Server 2000 and 2005. SQL Server 2005 also includes the XML data type for storing XML in a first class column type validated by XML Schemas stored in the database.

Summary

XML and the XML infoset are both pervasive in the .NET Framework and in ASP.NET. All ASP.NET configuration files include associated XML Schemas, and the Visual Studio Editor is even smarter about XML documents that use XSDs.

XmlReader and XmlWriter provide unique and incredibly fast ways to consume and create XML; they now also include even better support for mapping XML Schema types to CLR types, as well as other improvements. The XmlDocument and XPathDocument return in .NET 2.0 with API additions and numerous performance improvements, while the XmlDataSource control brings the world of declarative data binding and XML together. ASP.NET and .NET 3.5 include support for XSLT via not only the new XslCompiledTransform but also command-line compilation, and tops it all with XSLT debugging support for compiled style sheets. LINQ to XML introduces the new System.Xml.Linq namespace and supporting classes for a tightly integrated IntelliSense-supported coding experience. VB9 takes XML support to the next level with XML literals and XML namespace imports. The bridge classes and extension methods make the transition between System.Xml and System.Xml.Linq clean and intuitive.

All these ways to manipulate XML via the Base Class Library are married with XML support in SQL Server 2000 and 2005. SQL Server 2005 also includes the XML data type for storing XML in a first-class column type validated by XML Schemas stored in the database.

11

IIS7

Internet Information Services 7.0 (IIS7) is the latest version of Microsoft's Web Server. IIS7 has gone through significant architectural changes since the last version. The most notable change for ASP.NET developers is the deep integration of IIS7 and the ASP.NET Framework. This provides both ASP.NET developers and IIS7 administrators with an integrated programming environment that allows them to implement features and functionalities that were not possible before. This chapter will provide you with an overview of the IIS7 and ASP.NET integrated architecture and its constituent components, show you how to install, setup, and configure IIS7, as well as show you how to migrate your existing applications to IIS7.

Modular Architecture of IIS7

The main goal of the Microsoft IIS team for IIS 6.0 was to improve its security, performance, and reliability. For that reason, modularity and extensibility didn't make it to the list of top priorities. That said, IIS 6.0 introduced a very important notion: selective disabling of features such as ISAPI extensions and standard CGI (Common Gateway Interface) components. One of the main problems with the earlier versions of IIS was that every feature had to be installed and enabled. There were no ways to disable specific features not needed by your application scenario.

IIS 6.0 enables only static file serving by default on a clean install of the Web server. In other words, dynamic features such as ISAPI extensions and CGI components are disabled by default unless the administrator explicitly enables them. Such customization of the Web server allows you to decrease the attack surface of your Web server, giving attackers fewer opportunities for attacks.

Disabling unwanted features was the first step toward making the IIS customizable. However, this step didn't go far enough because IIS 6.0 still installs everything, which introduces the following problems:

- Disabled features consume server resources such as memory, and therefore increase the Web server footprint.
- Administrators still need to install service packs that address bugs in the disabled features, even though they're never used.
- Administrators still need to install software updates for the disabled features.

In other words, administrators have to maintain the service features that are never used. All these problems stem from the fact that the architecture of IIS 6.0 is relatively monolithic. The main installation problem with a monolithic architecture is that it's based on an all-or-nothing paradigm where you have no choice but to install the whole system.

IIS 7.0 is modular to the core. Its architecture consists of over 40 feature modules from which you can choose. This allows you to install only feature modules you need to build a highly customized and very thin Web server. This provides the following important benefits:

- Decreases the footprint of your Web server.
- Administrators need to install only those service packs that address bugs in the installed feature modules.
- Administrators need to install software updates for only the installed feature modules.

In other words, administrators have to maintain and service only installed feature modules.

Next, will be an overview of the IIS7 feature modules or components that matter to the `ASP.NET` developer. These feature components are grouped into what is known as *functional areas*, where each functional area maps to a specific IIS package update. In other words, each package update contains one or more feature modules or components. Later you'll use these package updates to custom build your Web server.

> **You can find even more detailed technical information specific to IIS7 at** `http://www.iis.net` **or in Wrox's *Professional IIS7 and ASP.NET Integrated Programming* by Dr. Shahram Khosravi (2007) from which portions of this chapter are adapted.**

The top level IIS update is known as IIS-WebServerRole, and as the name suggests, the IIS-WebServerRole enables Windows Server 2008 and Windows Vista to adapt a Web server role, which enables them to exchange information over the Internet, an intranet, or an extranet. IIS-WebServerRole consists of these sub-roles:

- IIS-WebServer
- IIS-WebServerManagementTools
- IIS-FTPPulishingService

Roles depend on other roles and build a dependency hierarchy.

IIS-WebServer

The system will let you know when you're installing a new role whether that role will require new feature modules. For example, IIS-WebServer requires these modules:

- IIS-CommonHTTPFeatures
- IIS-ApplicationDevelopment

- IIS-HealthAndDiagnostics
- IIS-Security
- IIS-Performance

Let's take a brief look at the feature modules required by the main IIS-WebServer feature.

IIS-CommonHttpFeatures

The IIS-CommonHttpFeatures update contains the feature modules or components described in the following table:

Feature Module	Description
IIS-StaticContent	Use this module to enable your Web server to service requests for static content. Web site resources with file extensions such as `.html`, `.htm`, `.jpg`, and the like that can be serviced without server-side processing are known as static content.
IIS-DefaultDocument	This module allows you to specify a Web resource that will be used as the default resource when the request URL does not contain the name of the requested resource.
IIS-DirectoryBrowsing	Use this module to enable your Web server to display the contents of a specified directory to end users when they directly access the directory and no default document exists in the directory.
IIS-HttpErrors	Use this module to enable your Web server to support sending custom error messages to end users.
IIS-HttpRedirect	Use this module to enable your Web server to support request redirects.

IIS-ApplicationDevelopment

The IIS-ApplicationDevelopment update contains the feature modules that support different application types as described in the following table:

Feature Module	Description
IIS-ASPNET	Use this module to enable your Web server to host ASP.NET applications.
IIS-NetFxExtensibility	Use this module to enable your Web server to host managed modules.
IIS-ASP	Use this module to enable your Web server to host ASP applications.
IIS-CGI	Use this module to enable your Web server to support CGI executables.
IIS-ISAPIExtensions	Use this module to enable your Web server to use ISAPI extension modules to process requests.
IIS-ISAPIFilter	Use this module to enable your Web server to use ISAPI filter to customize the server behavior.
IIS-ServerSideIncludes	Use this module to enable your Web server to support `.stm`, `.shtm`, and `.shtml` include files.

IIS-HealthAndDiagnostics

The IIS-HealthAndDiagnostics package update contains the feature modules described in the following table:

Feature Module	Description
IIS-HttpLogging	Use this module to enable your Web server to log Web site activities.
IIS-LoggingLibraries	Use this module to install logging tools and scripts on your Web server.
IIS-RequestMonitor	Use this module to enable your Web server to monitor the health of the Web server and its sites and applications.
IIS-HttpTracing	Use this module to enable your Web server to support tracing for ASP.NET applications and failed requests.
IIS-CustomLogging	Use this module to enable your Web server to support custom logging for the Web server and its sites and applications.
IIS-ODBCLogging	Use this module to enable your Web server to support logging to an ODBC-compliant database.

IIS-Security

The IIS-Security package update contains the feature modules described in the following table:

Security Feature Module	Description
IIS-BasicAuthentication	Use this module to enable your Web server to support the HTTP 1.1 Basic Authentication scheme. This module authenticates user credentials against Windows accounts.
IIS-WindowsAuthentication	Use this module to enable your Web server to authenticate requests using NTLM or Kerberos.
IIS-DigestAuthentication	Use this module to enable your Web server to support the Digest Authentication scheme. The main difference between Digest and Basic is that Digest sends password hashes over the network as opposed to the passwords themselves.
IIS-ClientCertificateMapping-Authentication	Use this module to enable your Web server to authenticate client certificates with Active Directory accounts.
IIS-IISCertificateMapping-Authentication	Use this module to enable your Web server to map client certificates 1-to-1 or many-to-1 to a Windows security identity.
IIS-URLAuthorization	Use this module to enable your Web server to perform URL authorization.
IIS-RequestFiltering	Use this module to enable your Web server to deny access based on specified configured rules.
IIS-IPSecurity	Use this module to enable your Web server to deny access based on domain name or IP address.

IIS-Performance

The following table describes the performance feature modules:

Performance Feature Module	Description
IIS-HttpCompressionStatic	Use this module to enable your Web server to compress static content before sending it to the client to improve the performance.
IIS-HttpCompressionDynamic	Use this module to enable your Web server to compress dynamic content before sending it to the client to improve the performance.

IIS-WebServerManagementTools

The following table describes the feature modules contained in the IIS-WebServerManagementTools update:

Feature Module	Description
IIS-ManagementConsole	This module installs the Web Server Management Console, which allows administration of local and remote IIS web servers.
IIS-Management-ScriptingTools	Use this module to enable your Web server to support local Web server management via IIS configuration scripts.
IIS-ManagementService	Use this module to enable your Web server to be managed remotely via Web Server Management Console.

The following table presents the feature modules in the IIS-IIS6ManagementCompatibility update:

Feature Module	Description
IIS-Metabase	Use this module to enable your Web server to support metabase calls to the new IIS7 configuration store.
IIS-WMICompatibility	Use this module to install the IIS 6.0 WMI scripting interfaces to enable your Web server to support these interfaces.
IIS-LegacyScripts	Use this module to install the IIS 6.0 configuration scripts, to enable your Web server to support these scripts.
IIS-LegacySnapIn	Use this module to install the IIS 6.0 Management Console to enable administration of remote IIS 6.0 servers from this computer.

IIS-FTPPublishingService

The feature modules contained in the IIS-FTPPublishingService package update are discussed in the following table:

At the time of this writing, Microsoft announced that they'd be releasing a significantly enhanced IIS7 FTP server for Windows Server 2008 and Vista as a separate download. You can get more information on this at `http://go.microsoft.com/fwlink/?LinkId=75371`.

Feature Module	Description
IIS-FTPServer	Use this module to install the FTP service.
IIS-FTPManagement	Use this module to install the FTP Management Console.

Extensible Architecture of IIS7

IIS 6.0 allows you to extend the functionality of the Web server by implementing and plugging in your own custom ISAPI filter and extension modules. Unfortunately, ISAPI suffers from fundamental problems such as:

- Since ISAPI is not a convenient or friendly API, and writing an ISAPI filter or extension module is not an easy task to accomplish, it can take a lot of time and tends to be error-prone
- ISAPI is not a managed API, which means that ASP.NET developers cannot benefit from the rich features of the .NET Framework when they're writing ISAPI filter and extension modules

IIS 7.0 has replaced ISAPI with a new set of convenient object-oriented APIs that make writing new feature modules much easier. These APIs come in two different flavors: managed and native. The native API is a convenient C++ API that you can use to develop and plug native modules into the core Web server. The managed API, on the other hand, allows you to take full advantage of the .NET Framework and its rich environment. This allows both ASP.NET developers and IIS7 administrators to use convenient ASP.NET APIs to extend the core Web server.

IIS7 and ASP.NET Integrated Pipeline

Let's take a moment and talk about how IIS 6.0 and ASP.NET interact with each other. Both IIS 6.0 and ASP.NET have request processing pipelines. Each request processing pipeline is a pipeline of components that are invoked one after another to perform their specific request processing tasks. For example, both IIS 6.0 and ASP.NET pipelines contain an authentication component, which is called to authenticate the request, as shown in Figure 11-1.

A typical incoming HTTP request first goes through the IIS 6.0 pipeline. At some point along this pipeline, IIS 6.0 uses its metabase to map the request to a particular handler. The requests for ASP.NET resources such as ASP.NET pages are mapped to the `aspnet_isapi.dll` handler. This handler then loads the CLR and the target ASP.NET application, if they haven't already been loaded. This is where the ASP.NET request processing pipeline kicks in. To phrase it another way, the request "jumps" over into the ASP.NET world and continues through the ASP.NET pipeline.

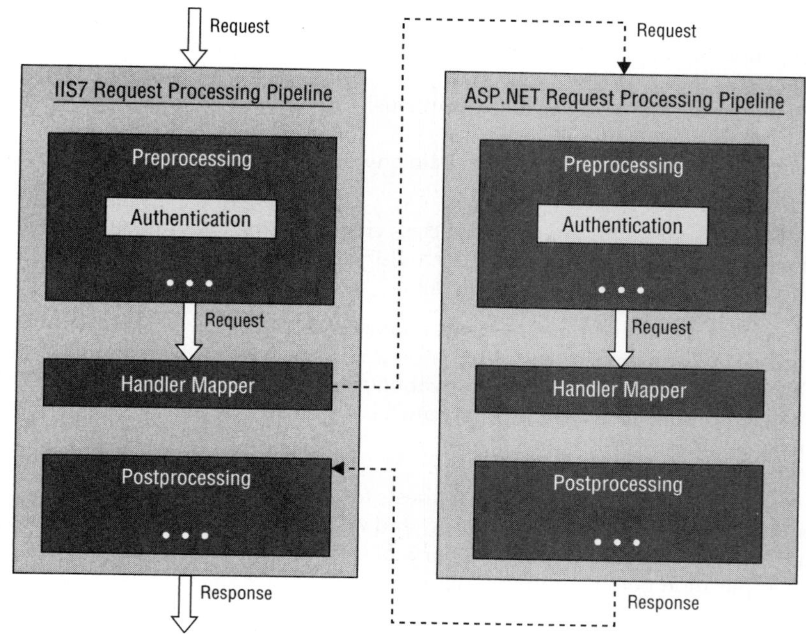

Figure 11-1

At the beginning of the request, ASP.NET allows the components in its request processing pipeline to register one or more event handlers for one or more ASP.NET application-level events. ASP.NET then fires these events one after another and calls these event handlers to allow each component to perform its specific request processing task. At some point along the pipeline, ASP.NET uses the configuration file to map the request to a particular handler. The main responsibility of the handler is to process the request and generate the appropriate markup text, which will then be sent back to the requesting browser.

Having *two separate pipelines*, that is, IIS 6.0 and ASP.NET pipelines, working on the same request introduces the following problems:

- There's a fair amount of duplication. For example, both pipelines contain an authentication component, which means that the same request gets authenticated twice.
- Because the ASP.NET pipeline begins after the IIS pipeline maps the request to the `aspnet_isapi` extension module, the ASP.NET pipeline has no impact on the IIS pipeline steps prior to handler mapping.
- Because the rest of the IIS pipeline steps don't occur until the ASP.NET pipeline finishes, the ASP.NET pipeline has no impact on these IIS pipeline steps either.
- Because the ASP.NET pipeline comes into play when the IIS pipeline maps the request to the `aspnet_isapi` extension module, and because this mapping is done only for requests to ASP.NET content, the ASP.NET pipeline components cannot be applied to requests to non-ASP.NET content such as `.jpg`, `.js`, `.asp`, CGI, and the like. For example, you cannot easily use the ASP.NET authentication and authorization modules to protect the non-ASP.NET contents of your application without a significant performance penalty under IIS6.

IIS7 has changed all that by removing the `aspnet_isapi` extension module and combining the ASP.NET 3.5 and IIS pipelines into a **single integrated request processing pipeline**.

This new integrated design resolves all the previously mentioned problems as follows:

- The integrated pipeline does not contain any duplicate components. For example, the request is authenticated once.
- The ASP.NET modules are now first-class citizens in the integrated pipeline. They can come before, replace, or come after any native IIS7 modules. This allows ASP.NET to intervene at any stage of the request processing pipeline.
- Because the integrated pipeline treats managed modules like native modules, you can apply your ASP.NET managed modules to non-ASP.NET content. For example, you can use the ASP.NET authentication and authorization modules to protect the non-ASP.NET contents of your application, such as `asp` pages much easier than IIS6 and without the performance penalities.

Note however that when IIS7 is processing requests for ASP.NET content there are two different potential request processing pipelines: IIS7 "Integrated" and ASP.NET "Classic." The Classic pipeline basically puts IIS7 into "IIS 6.0" pipeline mode for a particular Application Pool. We'll see more on that when we configure an application pool later in this chapter.

Building a Customized Web Server

To understand IIS7, let's start by setting it up on a fresh system. You can use Windows Vista or Windows Server 2008 for this exercise.

Remember that IIS7 setup is completely modular, allowing you to custom build your Web server from a list of over 40 available feature modules. This ensures that your Web server contains only the feature modules you need, thereby decreasing the attack surface and footprint of your server. In this section, you'll walk through the steps that you need to take to build your very own custom Web server on Windows Vista (including Windows Vista Home Premium, Windows Vista Professional, and Windows Vista Ultimate editions) and Windows Server 2008 operating systems.

In general, there are five different IIS7 setup options:

- Windows Features dialog (Windows Vista only)
- Server Manager tool (Windows Server 2008 only)
- `pkgmgr.exe` command line tool (both Windows Vista and Windows Server 2008)
- Unattended (both Windows Vista and Windows Server 2008)
- Upgrade (both Windows Vista and Windows Server 2008)

Before drilling down into the details of these five setup options, you need to understand the dependencies between the installable updates.

Update Dependencies

When you're installing an update, you must also install the updates that it depends on. In general, there are two types of dependencies: interdependencies and parent-dependencies. The following table presents the update interdependencies:

Update	Depends On
IIS-WebServer	WAS-ProcessModel
IIS-ASP	IIS-ISAPIExtensions IIS-RequestFiltering
IIS-ASPNET	IIS-DefaultDocument IIS-NetFxExtensibility WAS-NetFxEnvironment IIS-ISAPIExtensions IIS-ISAPIFilter IIS-RequestFiltering
IIS-NetFxExtensibility	WAS-NetFxEnvironment IIS-RequestFiltering
IIS-ManagementService	IIS-WebServer IIS-ManagementConsole WAS-NetFxEnvironment WAS-ConfigurationAPI
IIS-ManagementConsole	WAS-ConfigurationAPI
IIS-ManagementScriptingTools	WAS-ConfigurationAPI
IIS-LegacyScripts	IIS-Metabase IIS-WMICompatibility

Every update also depends on its parent update. For example, to install IIS-WebServer, you must also install its parent update, IIS-WebServerRole.

Installing IIS7 on Windows Vista

Under Windows Vista, you install IIS7 from the Programs and Features application and click Turn Windows Features on or off. This dialog does an excellent job illustrating the hierarchy of modules available within IIS7, as shown in Figure 11-2.

Installing IIS7 on Windows Server 2008

You install IIS7 on Window Server 2008 by adding the IIS Server Role from the Server Manager as shown in Figure 11-3. In a clean install of the Windows Server 2008, the server is originally in no roles. The role

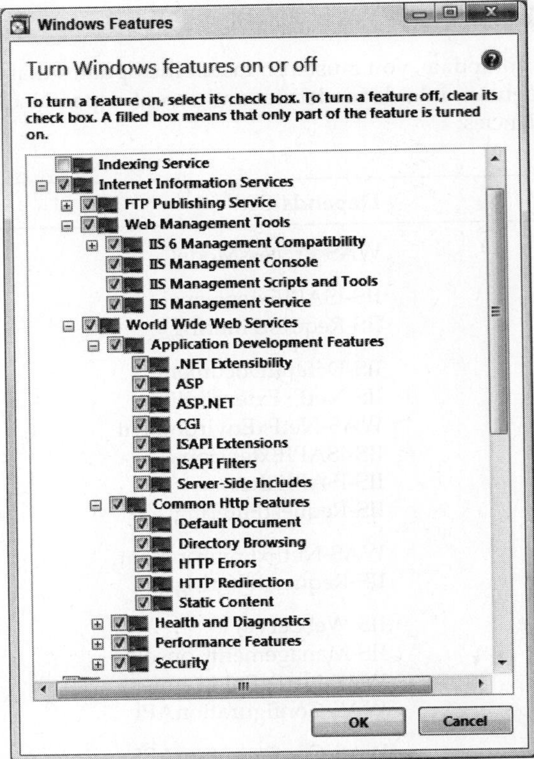

Figure 11-2

that you're interested in is the Web Server role. Recall that this is the role that allows the server to share information on the Internet, an intranet, or an extranet. The first order of business is to launch the Add Roles Wizard from the Server Manager to add this role to your server.

Notice that the same familiar check box list feature hierarchy exists in both Windows Vista and Windows Server 2008.

As you make selections the system will prompt you for dependent features as they are needed. For example, if you select ASP.NET you are prompted to add .Net Extensibility. For a Windows Server 2008 pure development machine, we recommend that you add Application Development, Health and Diagnostics and Security.

Command-Line Setup Options

Windows Vista and Windows Server 2008 come with a new command line tool named `pkgmgr.exe` that you can use to custom install IIS7. The following table describes the available options on this command-line tool:

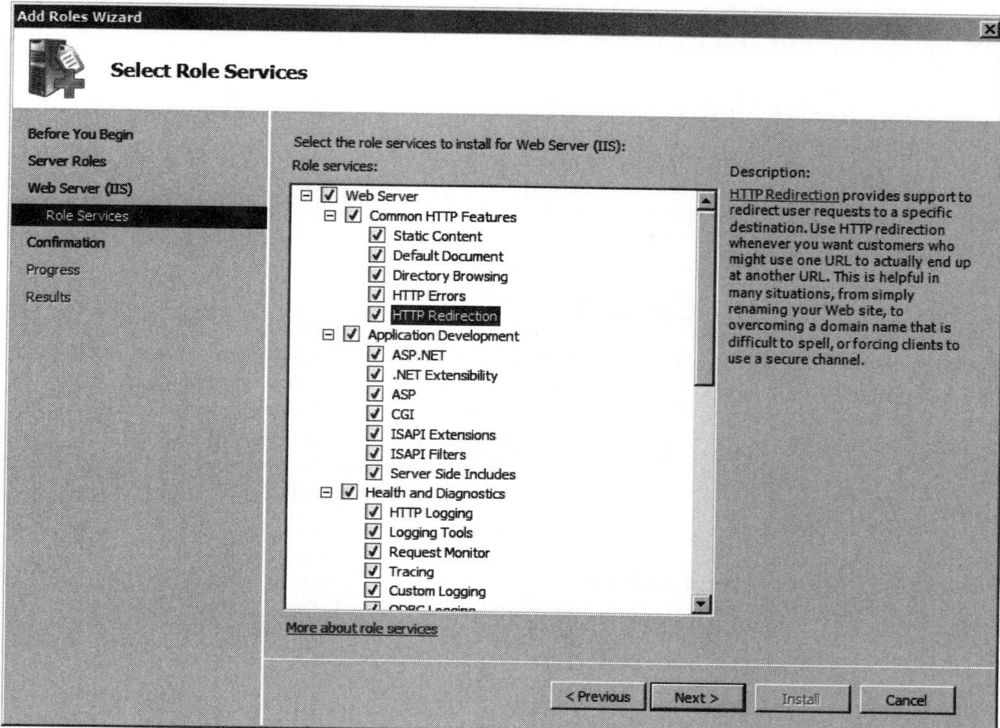

Figure 11-3

Option	Description
`/iu:update1; update2...`	Run the tool with this option to install the specified updates. Notice that the update list contains a semi-colon separated list of the update names discussed in the previous sections.
`/uu:update1; update2...`	Run the tool with this option to uninstall the specified updates. Notice that the update list contains a semi-colon separated list of update names discussed in the previous sections.
`/n:unattend.xml`	Run the tool with this option to install or uninstall the updates specified in the specified `unattend.xml` file. You'll learn about this file in the following section.

When you use the `pkgmgr.exe` command-line tool to install specified updates, you must also explicitly specify and install the updates that your specified updates depend on. For example, if you decide to install the IIS-CommonHttpFeatures update, you must also install its parent update, that is, IIS-WebServer. To install the IIS-WebServer update you must also install its parent update, IIS-WebServerRole, and the update that it depends on, WAS-ProcessModel (see the Update Dependencies table). To install the WAS-ProcessModel update you must also install its parent update, WAS-WindowsActivationService update:

```
start /w pkgmgr.exe /iu:IIS-WebServerRole;WAS-WindowsActivationService;
WAS-ProcessModel;
IIS-WebServer;IIS-CommonHttpFeatures
```

Notice that if you don't specify the `start /w` option, the command-line tool will return immediately and process everything in the background, which means that you won't be able to see when the setup is completed.

Unattended Setup Option

As mentioned earlier, the `pkgmgr.exe` command line tool comes with the `/n:unattend.xml` option. `unattend.xml` is the XML file that contains the updates to be installed or uninstalled. This XML file provides you with two benefits. First, you don't have to directly enter the names of the updates on the command line. Second, you can store this file somewhere for reuse in other Web server machines. This XML file must have the same schema as the XML file shown in Listing 11-1. This listing installs the IIS-CommandHttpFeatures update and the updates that it depends on as discussed in the previous section.

Listing 11-1: The unattend.xml file

```
<?xml version="1.0" ?>
<unattend xmlns="urn:schemas-microsoft-com:unattend"
xmlns:wcm="http://schemas.microsoft.com/WMIConfig/2002/State">
  <servicing>
    <!-- Install a selectable update in a package that is in the
     Windows Foundation namespace -->
    <package action="configure">
      <assemblyIdentity name="Microsoft-Windows-Foundation-Package"
       version="6.0.5308.6" language="neutral" processorArchitecture="x86"
       publicKeyToken="31bf3856ad364e35" versionScope="nonSxS" />

      <selection name="IIS-WebServerRole" state="true"/>
      <selection name="WAS-WindowsActivationService" state="true"/>
      <selection name="WAS-ProcessModel" state="true"/>
      <selection name="IIS-WebServer" state="true"/>
      <selection name="IIS-CommonHttpFeatures" state="true"/>
    </package>
  </servicing>
</unattend>
```

Notice that the `< servicing >` element contains one or more `<package>` elements that contain `<selection>` child elements, and each child element specifies a particular update. The `<selection>` child element features two attributes named `name` and `state`. The `name` attribute contains the update name to be installed or uninstalled. Set the `state` attribute to `true` to install or `false` to uninstall the specified update.

Upgrade

If you're upgrading from the Windows XP to Windows Vista, or from Windows Server 2003 to Windows Server 2008, and if your old operating system has IIS installed, Windows Vista or Windows Server 2008 setup automatically scans through the capabilities of the installed IIS and ensures that the new install of IIS7 supports those features and capabilities. Unfortunately, due to the monolithic architecture of IIS 5.1 and IIS 6.0, this installation ends up installing almost all of the feature modules of IIS7. I highly recommend that after the upgrade you use one of the previously discussed installation options to uninstall the updates that you do not need to decrease the attack surface and footprint of your Web server.

Internet Information Services (IIS) Manager

In this section I'll walk you through different features of the IIS Manager. There are two ways to launch the IIS Manager: GUI-based and command line. If you feel more comfortable with a GUI-based approach, follow these steps to launch the IIS7 Manager:

1. Launch the Control Panel.
2. Click System and Maintenance.
3. Click Administrative Tools.
4. Click the Internet Information Services (IIS) Manager.

If you feel more comfortable with command line tools, use the following command line to launch the IIS Manager:

```
%windir%\system32\inetsrv\inetmgr.exe
```

You can also just type **IIS** into the new Start menu. Make sure to run the IIS7 Manager and not the legacy IIS6 Manager. Note you'll need administration privileges to launch the IIS Manager. If you don't login with the built-in Administrator account, when you try to launch the IIS Manager, Windows launches a dialog. The content of this dialog depends on whether your account has administration privileges. If it does, the dialog simply asks you to confirm the requested action. If it doesn't, the dialog asks for the administrative credentials.

As Figure 11-4 shows, the IIS Manager consists of three panes. The first pane, which is known as the Connections pane, contains a node that represents the Web server. This node has two child nodes:

- Application Pools
- Sites. The label of this node is "Sites" on Windows Server 2008 and "Web Sites" on Windows Vista.

The second pane, which is known as workplace pane, consists of these two tabs:

- **Features View:** If you select a node in the Connections pane, the Features View tab will allow you to edit the features associated with the selected node.
- **Content View:** If you select a node in the Connections pane, the Content View tab will display all the child nodes of the selected node.

The third pane, which is known as Actions pane, contains a bunch of links where each link performs a particular task on the node selected in the first or second pane.

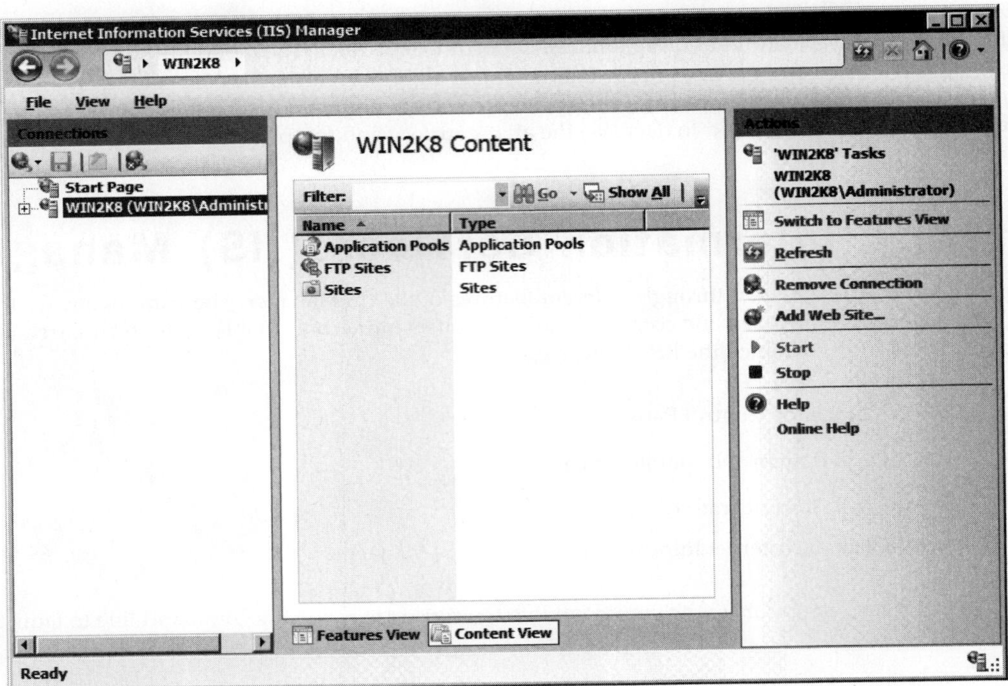

Figure 11-4

Application Pools

Now click the Application Pools node in the Connections pane to display the available application pools as shown in Figure 11-5.

Notice that the Actions pane contains an Add Application Pool link. Click this link to launch the dialog shown in Figure 11-6. This dialog allows you to add a new application pool and to specify its name. It also allows you to specify the .NET version that will be loaded into the application pool. Remember, all ASP.NET applications in the same application pool must use the same .NET version because. NET runtimes of differing versions cannot be loaded into the same worker process.

The Managed pipeline mode drop-down list on this dialog contains two options, Integrated and Classic, as shown in Figure 11-6. This specifies whether the IIS should run in Integrated or Classic mode for this application pool. All applications in the same application pool use the same IIS mode.

After making your selection click OK to commit the changes. Now open the `applicationHost.config` file in `%windir%\system32\inetsrv\config`. You'll need to be an administrator in order to see this file, and you might find it easiest to look for it from an Administrative Command Prompt. You should see the highlighted section shown in Listing 11-2.

Listing 11-2: The applicationHost.config file

```
<system.applicationHost>
  <applicationPools>
```

```
    . . .
    <add name="MyApplicationPool" />
    . . .
  </applicationPools>
</system.applicationHost>
```

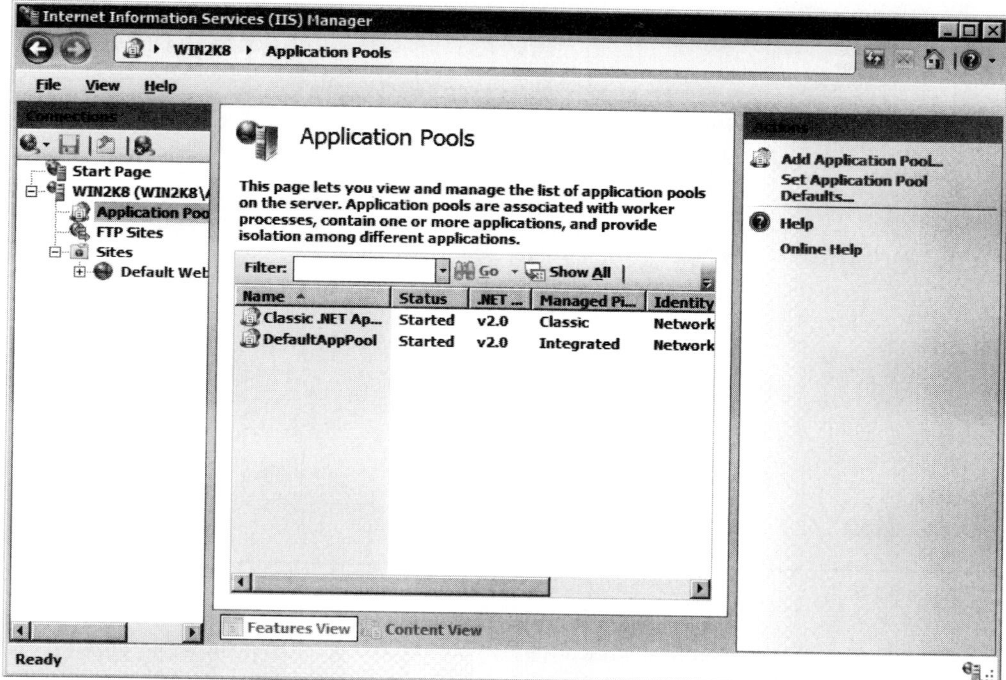

Figure 11-5

Figure 11-6

Click the newly created MyApplicationPool node in the middle pane. You should see new links on the Actions pane, which allow you to edit the properties of the application pool as shown in Figure 11-7.

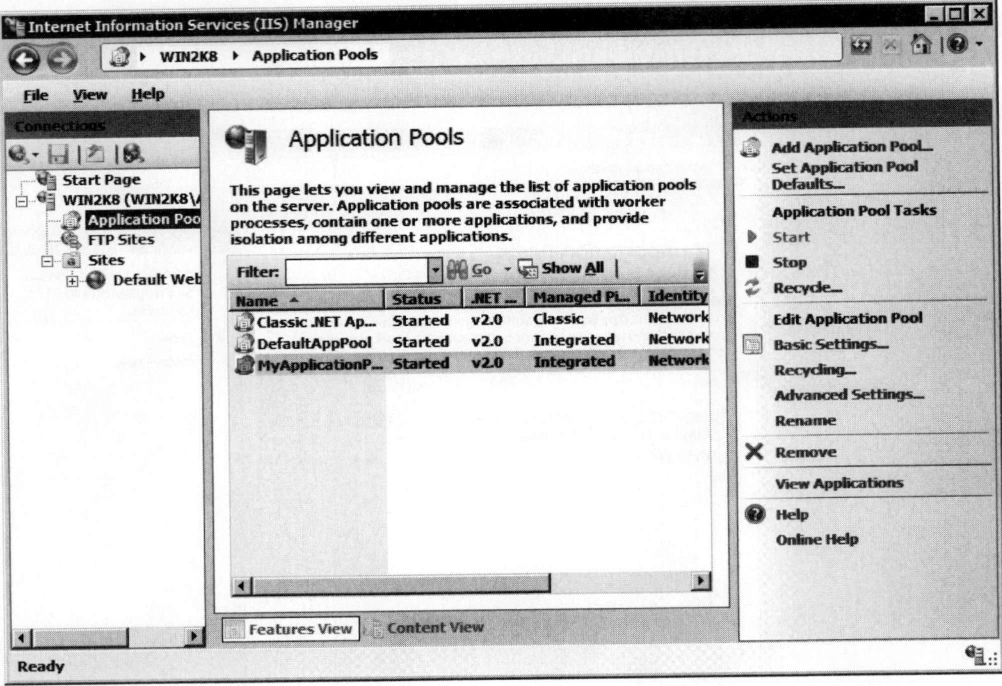

Figure 11-7

Click the Advanced Settings link to launch the Advanced Settings dialog shown in Figure 11-8. Notice that all settings of the newly created application pool have default values. However, as Listing 11-2 shows, none of these values show up in the `applicationHost.config` file. Where are these values stored? As you'll see later, the new IIS7 configuration system maintains the schema of the `applicationHost.config` file in two files named `ASPNET_schema.xml` and `IIS_schema.xml`. These schema files also specify and store the default values for configuration sections, including the `<applicationPools>` section. Storing the default configuration settings in one location as opposed to adding them to every single `<add>` element that represents an application pool keeps the configuration files small and more readable.

> **If you're running a 64-bit OS, make note of the Enable 32-bit Applications option in Advanced Settings. By default, ASP.NET applications will run as 64-bit on 64-bit OSes unless you switch them to 32-bit explicitly. Ninety-nine percent of managed applications will run fine as 64-bit, but if your application is calling into unmanaged code like COM objects or DLLs via `P/Invoke`, you might need to explicitly set aside an application pool for your 32-bit application.**

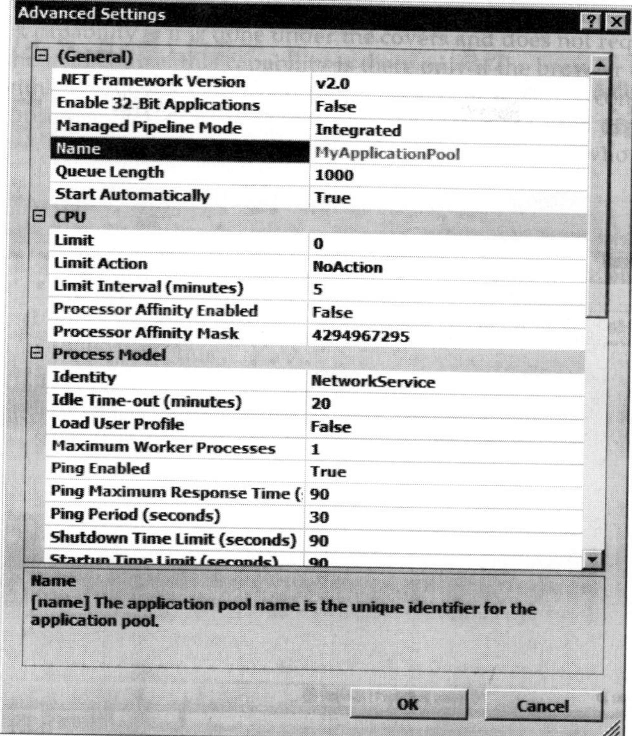

Figure 11-8

Now go to the General section of the Advanced Settings dialog, change the value of the Start Automatically to false (its default of true is shown in Figure 11-8), and click OK. Now if you open the `applicationHost.config` file, you should see the highlighted portion shown in the following code snippet:

```
<system.applicationHost>
  <applicationPools>
    . . .
    <add name="MyApplicationPool" autoStart="false" />
    . . .
  </applicationPools>
</system.applicationHost>
```

In other words, the `applicationHost.config` file records only the values that are different from the default.

Notice that the properties shown in Figure 11-8 map to the XML elements and attributes of the `< applicationPools >` section. When you click the OK button, the callback for this button performs the necessary XML manipulations under the hood to store the changes in the `applicationHost.config` XML file.

Web Sites

Now click the Sites node in the Connections pane of the IIS Manager. In the Actions pane, you should see a link titled Add Web Site, as shown in Figure 11-9. Click the link to launch the dialog shown in Figure 11-10.

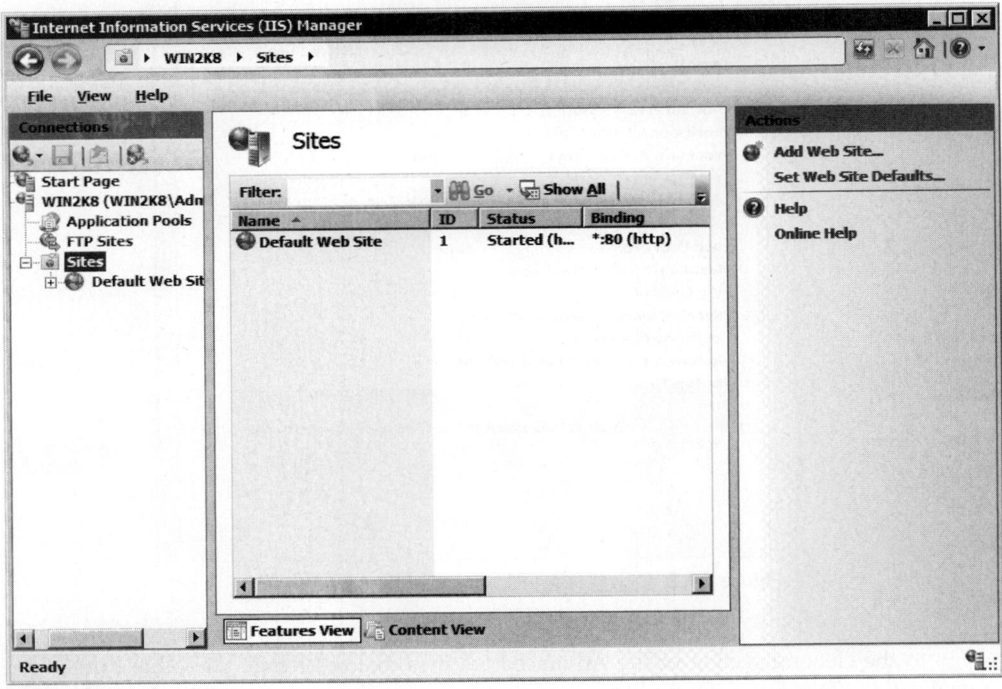

Figure 11-9

This dialog allows you to add a new Web site. Recall that a Web site is a collection of Web applications. Notice that the properties shown in this dialog map to the XML elements and attributes of the `< site >` element. Next, take these steps:

1. Enter a name in the Web site name text field for the new Web site, for example, MySite.
2. Use the Select button to choose the desired application pool.
3. Choose a physical path.
4. Specify a binding including a binding type, an IP address, and a port number.
5. Click the OK button to commit the changes.

Now open the `applicationHost.config` file again. You should see the highlighted portion shown in Listing 11-3.

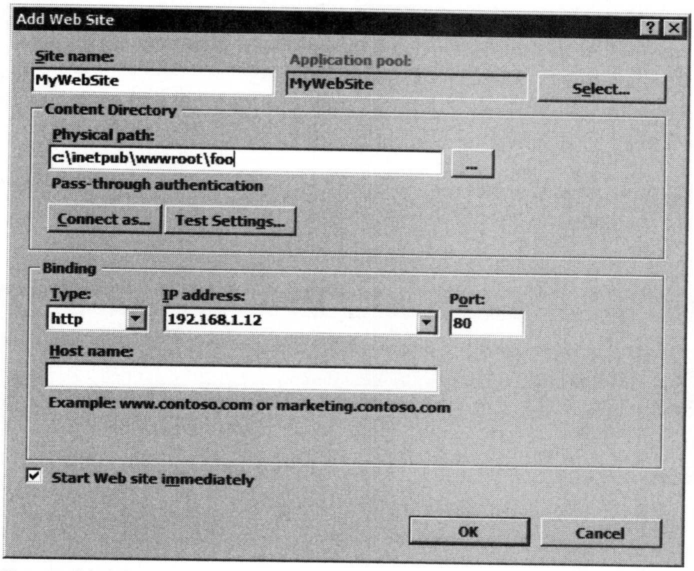

Figure 11-10

Listing 11-3: The applicationHost.config file

```
<configuration>
  <system.applicationHost>
    <sites>
      <site name="MySite" id="1727416169">
        <application path="/">
          <virtualDirectory path="/" physicalPath="C:\inetpub\wwwroot\foo" />
        </application>
        <bindings>
          <binding protocol="http" bindingInformation="192.168.1.12:80:" />
        </bindings>
      </site>
    </sites>
  </system.applicationHost>
</configuration>
```

As Listing 11-3 shows, the dialog shown in Figure 11-10 sets the XML elements and attributes of the `<site>` element that represents the new site. Notice that the dialog automatically created an application with a virtual directory. Every site must have at least one application with the virtual path "/" known as the root application that has at least one virtual directory with the virtual path "/" known as the root virtual directory. This dialog automatically takes care of that requirement behind the scenes.

Hierarchical Configuration

The new IIS7 and ASP.NET 3.5 integrated configuration system consists of a hierarchy of configuration files where lower-level configuration files inherit the configuration settings from higher level configuration files. The lower-level configuration files can override only those inherited configuration settings that are not locked in the higher level configuration files.

In this section, you'll learn how the IIS Manager takes the hierarchical nature of the IIS7 and ASP.NET 3.5 integrated configuration system into account. Let's begin with the ASP.NET 3.5 configuration settings.

Launch the IIS Manager again, select the node that represents the local Web server in the Connections pane and switch to the Features View tab in the workspace pane. The result should look like Figure 11-11.

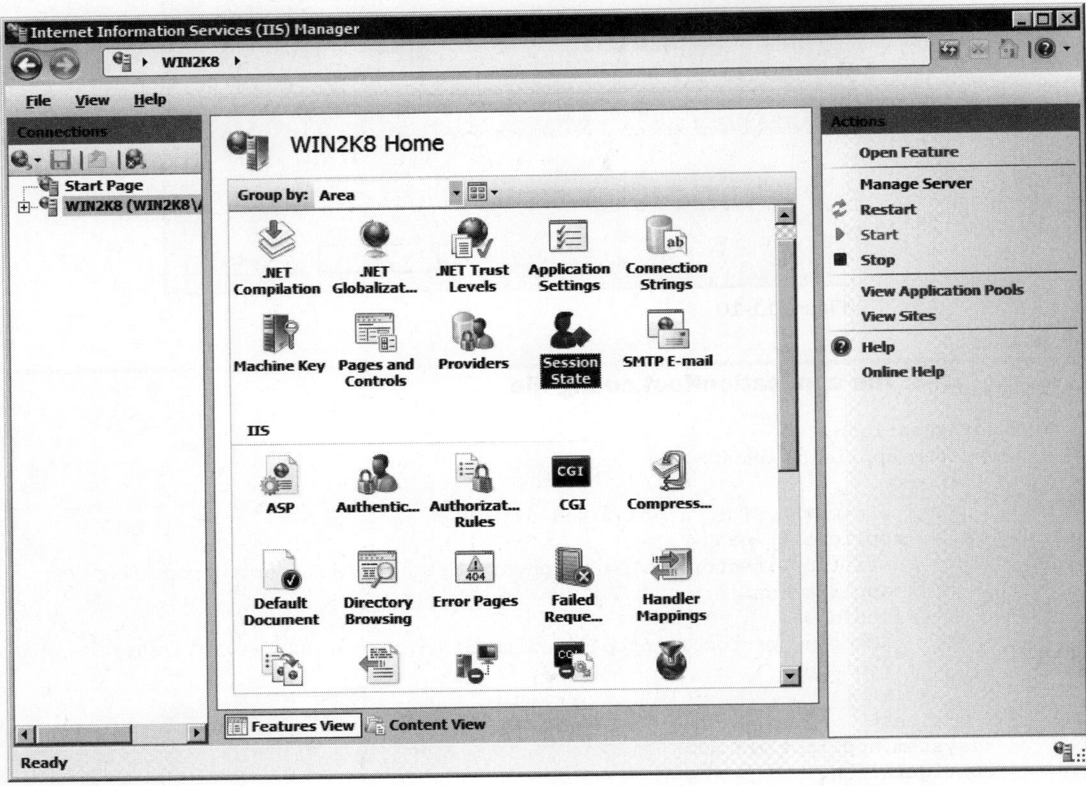

Figure 11-11

Now double-click the Session State icon in the workspace pane. You should see what is shown in Figure 11-12.

Note that the workspace now displays the GUI that allows you to change the session state configuration settings. Go to the Session State Mode Settings section, change the mode to Not enabled, and click the Apply link in the Tasks pane to commit the changes. Now open the root `web.config` file located in the following directory on your machine:

```
%SystemRoot%\Microsoft.NET\Framework\versionNumber\CONFIG\
```

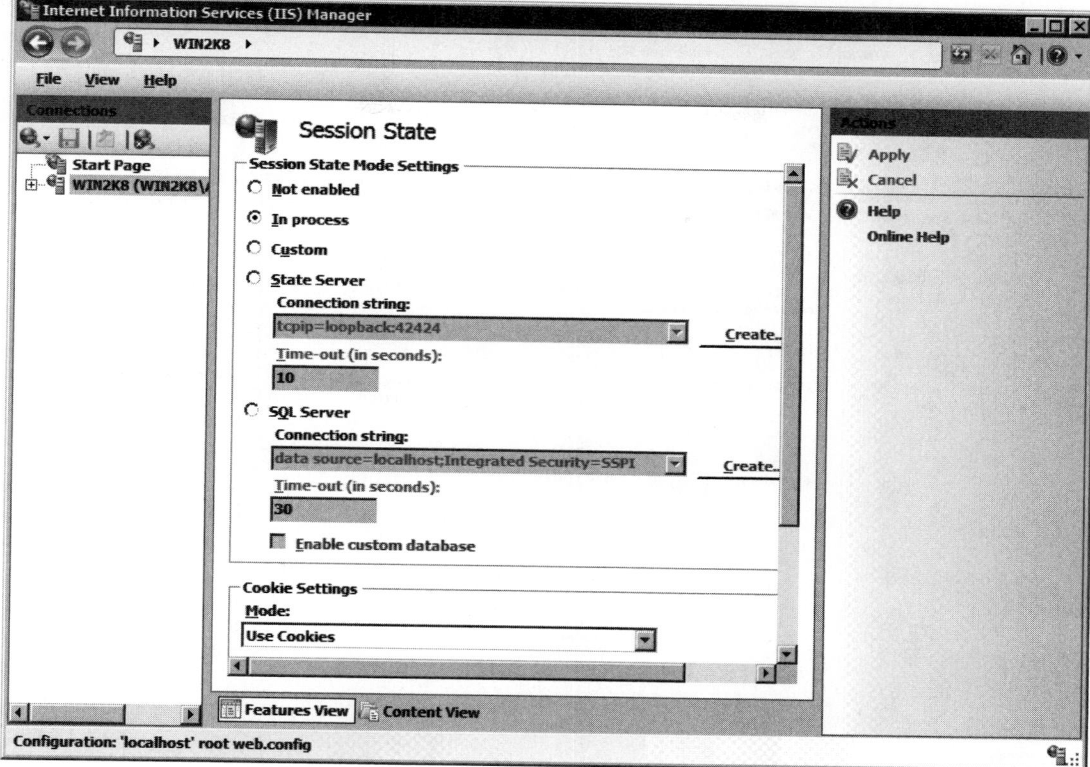

Figure 11-12

You should see the highlighted portion shown in the following listing:

```
<configuration>
  <system.web>
    <sessionState mode="off" />
  </system.web>
</configuration>
```

As this example shows, you can use IIS Manager to specify the ASP.NET configuration settings as you do for the IIS settings. The tool is smart enough to know that the machine-level ASP.NET configuration settings should be saved into the machine level `web.config` file (known as the root `web.config` file) instead of `applicationHost.config`.

The previous example changed the session state configuration settings at the machine level. Now let's change the session state configuration settings at the site level. Go back to the Connections pane, open the node that represents the local Web server, open the Sites node, and select the Default Web Site node. You should see the result shown in Figure 11-13. *Be sure you select the Web Site node and not the node for the entire Web Server.*

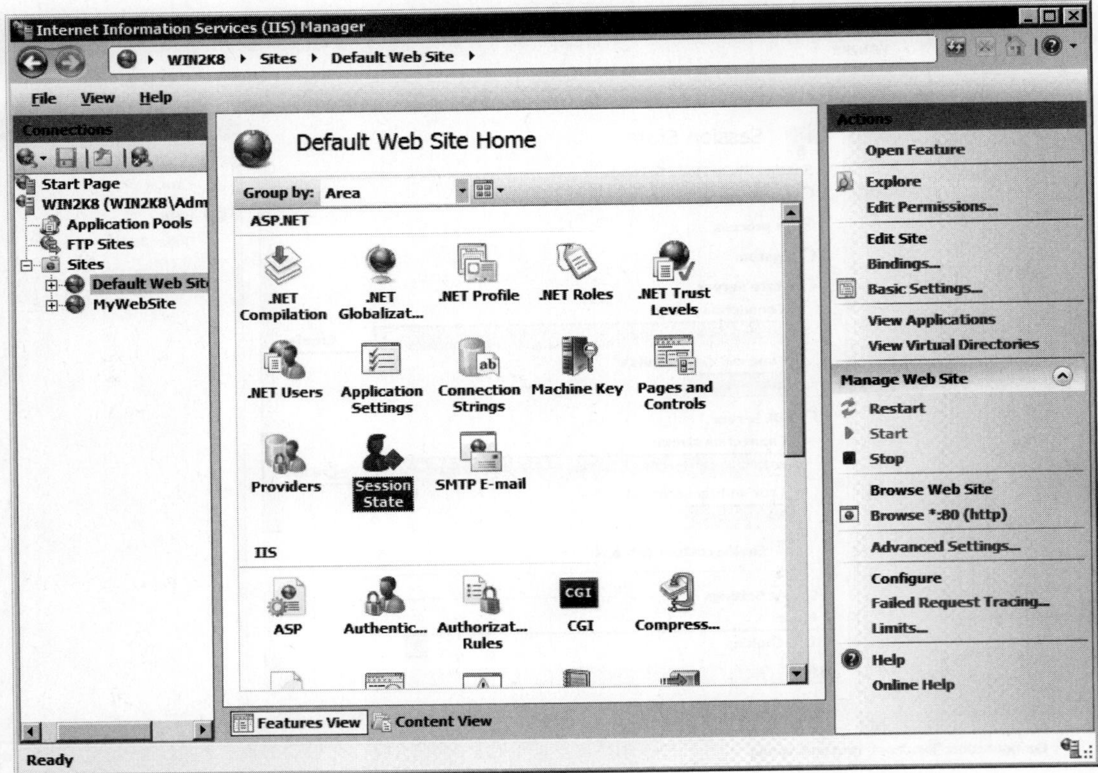

Figure 11-13

Now double-click the Session State icon. Change the Session State Mode settings to Not enabled and click the Apply link on the tasks panel to commit the changes. Now open the `web.config` file in the following directory on your machine:

```
%SystemDrive%\inetpub\wwwroot
```

You should see the highlighted portion of the following code listing:

```
<configuration>
  <system.web>
    <sessionState mode="off" />
  </system.web>
</configuration>
```

As this example shows, the IIS Manager stores the site-level ASP.NET configuration settings to the site-level configuration file. If you repeat the same steps for application level ASP.NET configuration settings, you'll see that the IIS Manager stores these configuration settings into the ASP.NET application level configuration file.

So far you've seen that IIS Manager handles the hierarchical nature of the ASP.NET 3.5 configuration settings. Next, you'll see that the IIS Manager also takes the hierarchical nature of the IIS7 configuration settings into account.

Launch the IIS Manager, click the node that represents the local Web server in the Connections pane, switch to the Features View tab in the workspace, and select the Area option from the Group by combo box to group the items in the workspace by area. You should see the result shown in Figure 11-14.

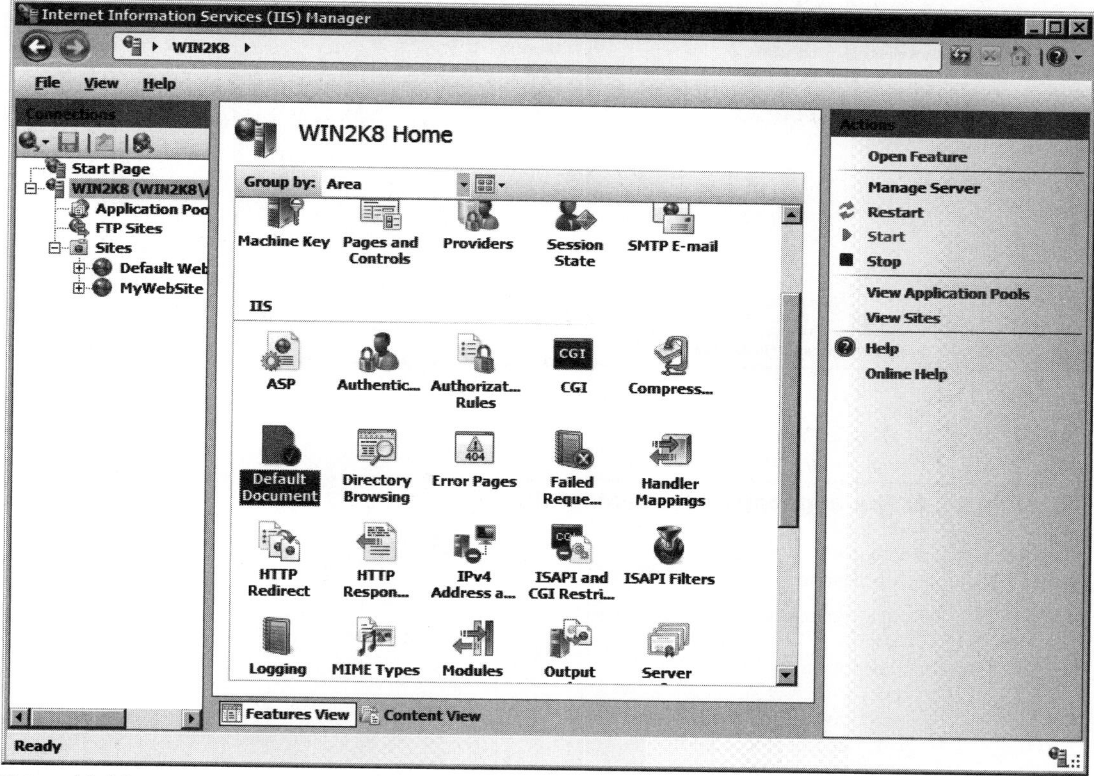

Figure 11-14

Now double-click Default Document. The result should look like Figure 11-15.

Notice that the workspace now contains a text box that displays the list of default documents. Add a new default document named **Welcome.htm** to the list and click the Apply button in the task panel to commit the changes.

If you open the `applicationHost.config` file, you should see the highlighted portion shown in Listing 11-4. Notice that the `< files >` element now contains a new <add> element whose value attribute is set to `Welcome.html`.

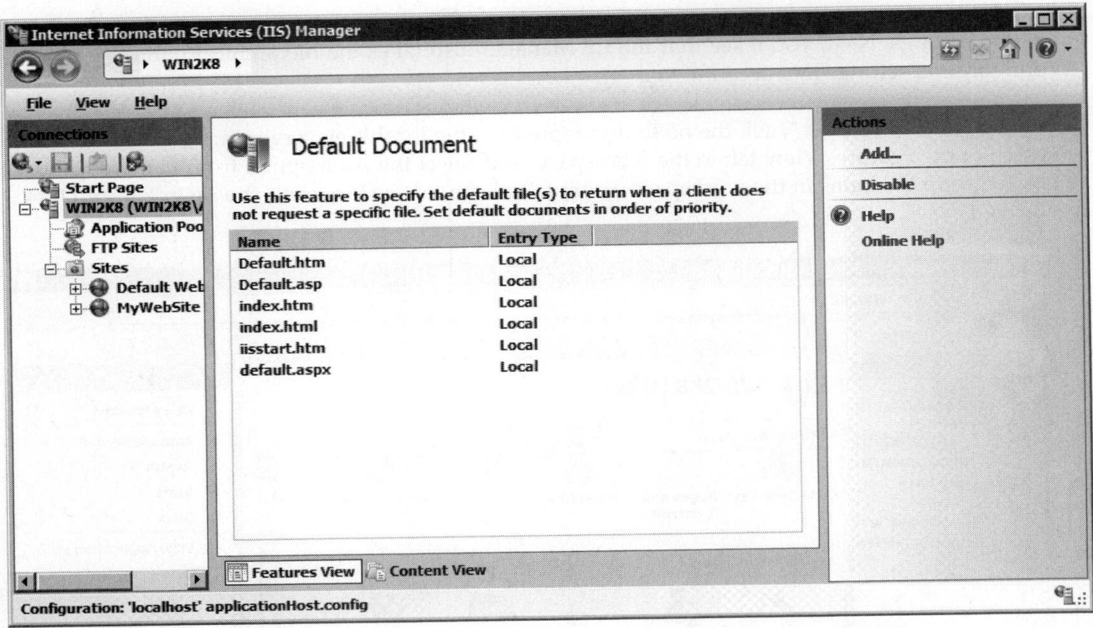

Figure 11-15

Listing 11-4: The applicationHost.config file

```
<configuration>
  <system.webServer>
     <defaultDocument enabled="true">
       <files>
         <clear />
         <add value="Welcome.htm" />
         <add value="Default.asp" />
         <add value="index.htm" />
         <add value="index.html" />
         <add value="iisstart.htm" />
         <add value="default.aspx" />
       </files>
     </defaultDocument>
  </system.webServer>
</configuration>
```

Now select the Default Web Site node from the Connections pane of the IIS Manager and double-click the Default Document icon to go to the page that displays the list of default documents. Note that the list contains the `Welcome.html` default document that you added before. This makes sense because the Default Web Site inherits all the default documents settings from the machine-level `applicationHost.config` file. Now go ahead and remove the `Welcome.html` file from the list, add a new default document named **Start.html**, and click the Apply button to commit the changes. If you open the `web.config` file located in the Default Web Site's root directory, you should see the result shown in Listing 11-5.

Listing 11-5: The root web.config file

```
<configuration>
  <system.webServer>
    <defaultDocument>
      <files>
        <clear />
        <add value="Start.htm" />
        <add value="Default.asp" />
        <add value="index.htm" />
        <add value="index.html" />
        <add value="iisstart.htm" />
        <add value="default.aspx" />
      </files>
    </defaultDocument>
  </system.webServer>
</configuration>
```

Delegation

As Listing 11-5 shows, a site- or application-level `web.config` file now can contain both ASP.NET and IIS configuration sections. This is one of the great new features of IIS7, which provides the following two benefits among many others:

- It allows you to configure IIS7 to meet your application-specific requirements.
- Since these IIS7 custom configuration settings are all stored in the `web.config` file of your application, which is located in the same directory with the rest of your application, you can xcopy this configuration file together with the rest of your application to the test machine, and from there to the production machine. This will allow your testers and clients to start testing and using your applications right away, without going through the tedious task of reconfiguring their Web servers to match the configuration you had on your Web server when you were developing the application.

You may be wondering whether it is a good idea to allow site and application administrators or developers to mess with the Web server settings from a security perspective. IIS7 and ASP.NET 3.5 integrated configuration system has taken this security issue into account. Because of the hierarchical nature of the configuration files, changes made to a configuration file at a certain level of hierarchy apply only to that level and the levels below it. For example, if you make some configuration changes in the `web.config` located in the root directory of a site, it will affect only the applications and virtual directories in that site. Or if you make changes in the `web.config` located in the root directory of an application, it will affect only the virtual directories in that application.

In addition most IIS configuration sections are locked by default at installation, which means that by default only the machine administrator can change these locked IIS configuration sections. However, the machine administrator can remove the lock from selected IIS configuration sections to allow selected sites, applications, or virtual directories to change these configuration sections. This is known as delegation. Let's take a look at an example.

Recall from the previous example (see Listing 11-5) that the Default Web Site administrator was allowed to reconfigure the IIS7 default documents for all the applications and virtual directories of the Default

Web Site. This was possible because by default there is no lock on the IIS7 default documents feature. To see this, take the following steps:

1. Launch the IIS Manager.
2. Click the node that represents the local Web server in the Connections pane.
3. Switch to the Features View tab in the workspace.
4. Select the Area option from the Group by combo box of the workspace.

The result should look like Figure 11-16.

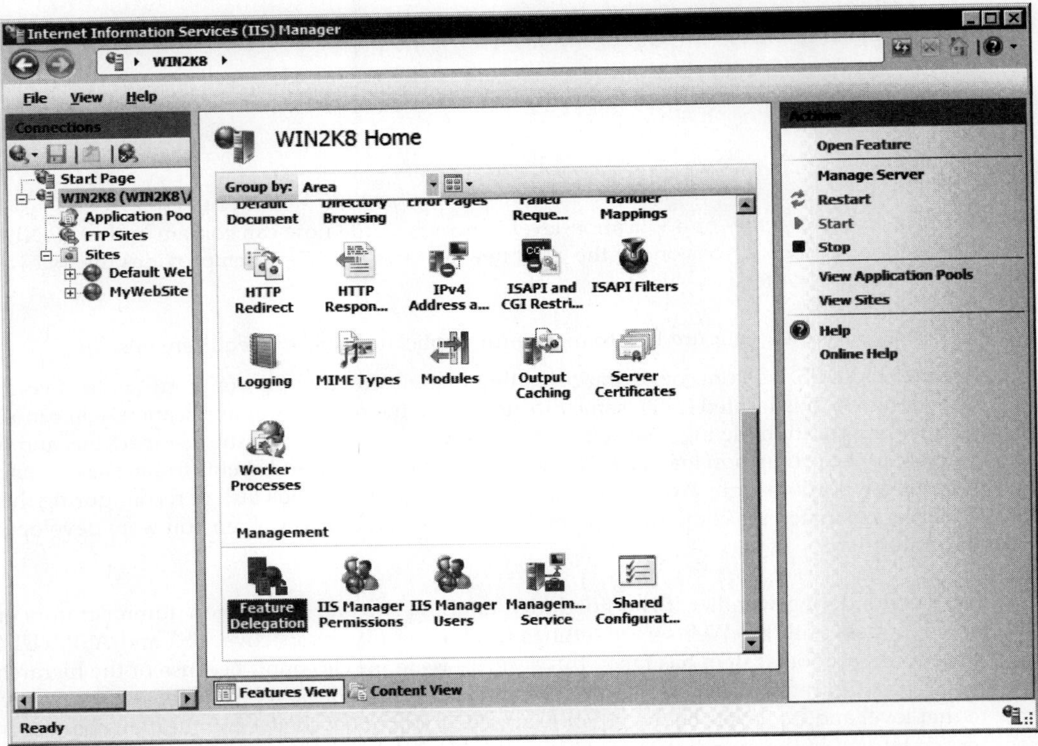

Figure 11-16

Now double-click the Feature Delegation icon in the Management section of the workspace to go to the Feature Delegation page shownin Figure 11-17. As the name implies, the Feature Delegation page allows the machine administrator to delegate the administration of the selected IIS features to site and applications administrators. Select the Delegation option from the Group by combo box and go to the Read/Write section of this page as shown in Figure 11-17. As the title of this section implies, this section contains IIS7 features that can be read and written from the lower-level configuration files. Note that this section contains the Default Document feature.

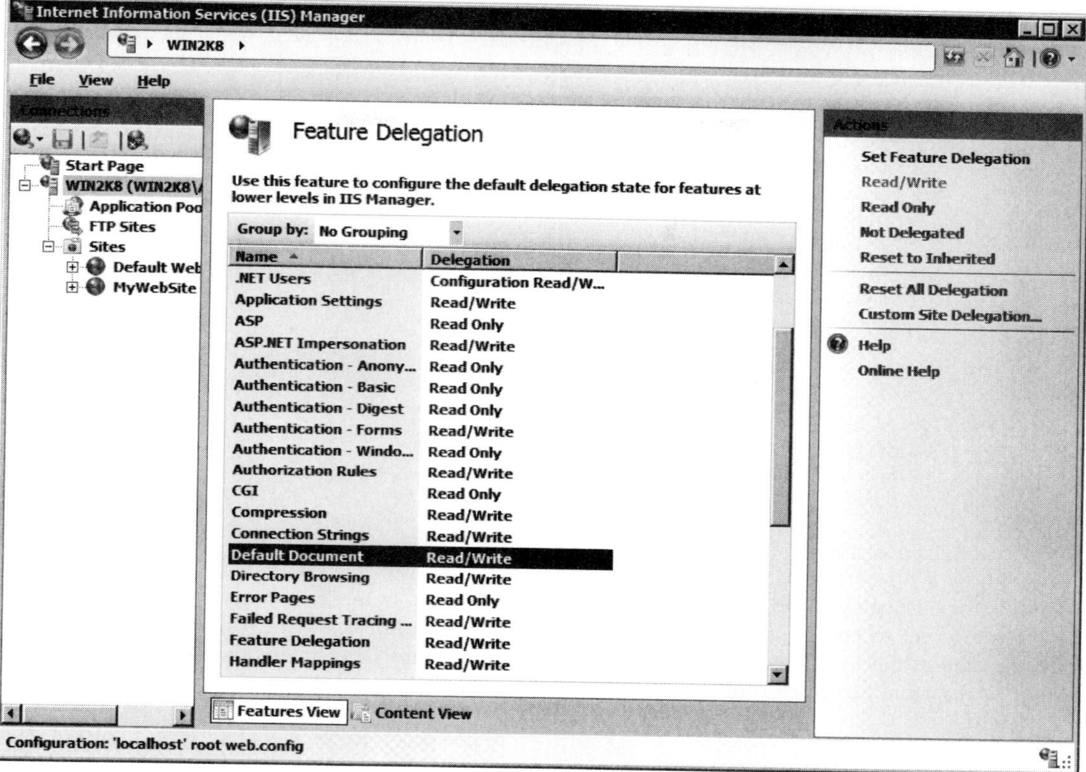

Figure 11-17

Select the Default Document from the Feature Delegation page as shown in Figure 11-17. Notice that the task pane contains a section titled Set Feature Delegation. This section contains six links named:

- Read/Write
- Read Only
- Not Delegated (on Windows Server 2008) or Remove Delegation (on Windows Vista)
- Reset to Inherited
- Reset All Delegation
- Custom Web Site Delegation (This link only exists on Windows Server 2008.)

Note that the Read/Write link in the Actions Pane is grayed out (as is the content-menu item), which means that the lower-level configuration files have the permission to change the IIS7 Default Document feature. Click the Read Only link and open the `applicationHost.config` file. You should see the highlighted portion shown in Listing 11-6. Some parts have been omitted for brevity.

Listing 11-6: The applicationHost.config file

```
<configuration>
  . . .
  <location path="" overrideMode="Deny">
    <system.webServer>
      <defaultDocument enabled="true">
        <files>
          <clear />
          <add value="Welcome.htm" />
          <add value="Default.asp" />
          <add value="index.htm" />
          <add value="index.html" />
          <add value="iisstart.htm" />
          <add value="default.aspx" />
        </files>
      </defaultDocument>
    </system.webServer>
  </location>
  . . .
</configuration>
```

As Listing 11-6 shows, the IIS Manager has added a new < location > tag whose `overrideMode` attribute is set to `Deny` to signal that the machine administrator does not want any lower-level configuration file to change the IIS7 default document feature. This means that every site, application, and virtual directory running on the machine inherits these authorization rules and has to live by them.

Moving an Application from IIS6 to IIS7

If you add a standard ASP.NET application into an IIS application pool that is configured for the Integrated Pipeline, rather than the Classic Pipeline and it contains entries in its `web.config` for < system.web > / < httpModules > , you'll get an informative error message like the one in Figure 11-18.

At this point you have two choices, as clearly outlined in the error message. You can either change the application's `web.config` to move the modules into the IIS7 integrated pipeline, or you can run the application in Classic mode.

The error message actually includes the command line you need to migrate your `web.config`:

```
%systemroot%\system32\inetsrv\APPCMD.EXE migrate config "Default Web Site/DasBlog2"
```

When you run that statement from an administrator command line, you'll see the following output:

```
%systemroot%\system32\inetsrv\APPCMD.EXE migrate config "Default Web Site/DasBlog2"
Successfully migrated section "system.web/httpModules".
Successfully migrated section "system.web/httpHandlers".
```

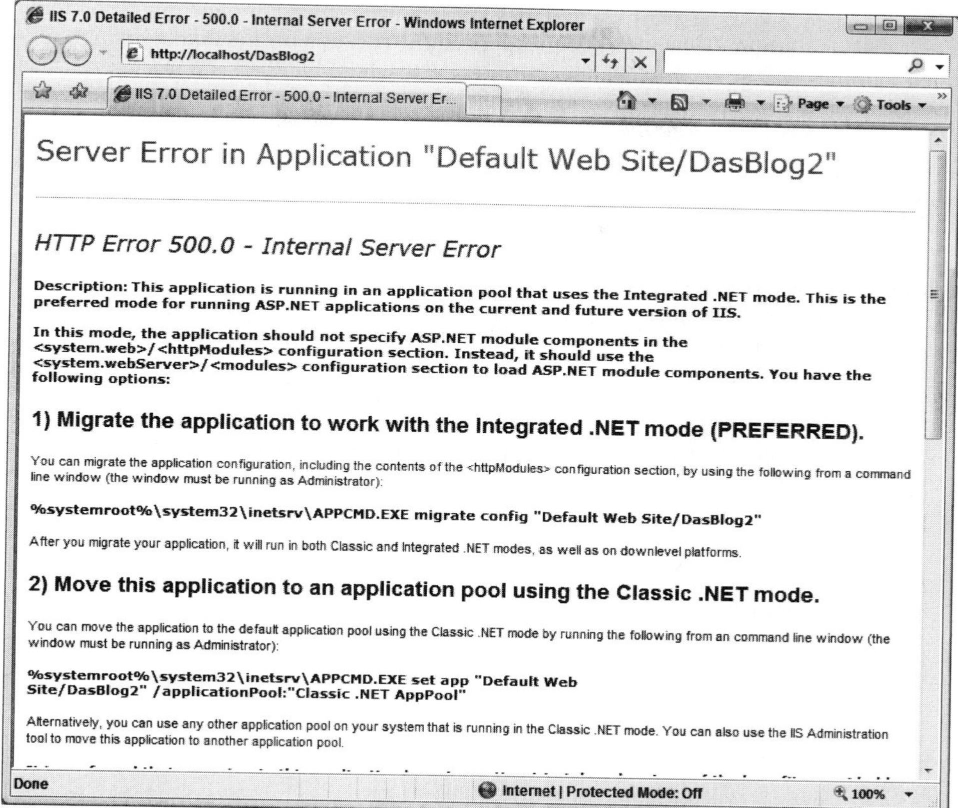

Figure 11-18

Be sure to make a copy of your `web.config` for backup purposes, but also for education as you can compare the two with your favorite diff tool. Notice the creation of a new `system.webServer` section in the following snippet:

```
<system.webServer>
    <modules>
        <add name="UrlMapperModule"
          type="newtelligence.DasBlog.Web.Core.UrlMapperModule,
          newtelligence.DasBlog.Web.Core" preCondition="managedHandler" />
...removed for brevity...
    </modules>
    <handlers>
        <add name="*.blogtemplate_*" path="*.blogtemplate" verb="*"
          type="System.Web.HttpForbiddenHandler"
          preCondition="integratedMode,runtimeVersionv2.0" />
...removed for brevity...
    </handlers>
</system.webServer>
```

Notice also the `preCondition` attribute that was automatically created by the migration tool for both the handlers and the modules. When it is set to `managedHandler`, this means that by default all registered managed modules will be applied only to those requests whose handlers are managed handlers, that is, requests for ASP.NET content.

Summary

IIS7 is easier to install than IIS6 was. When you choose only those modules required for your application, you create a more secure Web Server. IIS7 is easier to configure than IIS6. There's a much richer graphical interface, and command-line interface, and a transparent and hierarchical XML-based configuration system that feels familiar to professional ASP.NET developers. Applications are trivial to migrate and run faster under IIS7.

The skills you've developed writing HttpHandlers and HttpModules can be immediately leveraged within IIS7. You should check out IIS7 on Vista or Windows Server 2008 and pick up *Professional IIS 7 and ASP.NET Integrated Programming* from Wrox for an in-depth look at the IIS 7 programming model.

12

Introduction to the Provider Model

The ASP.NET provider model is an important framework to understand as you build your applications. The ASP.NET provider model was a major change introduced in ASP.NET 2.0, so you probably already know that ASP.NET is a way to build applications for the Internet. *For the Internet* means that an application's display code travels over HTTP, which is a stateless protocol. ASP.NET works with a disconnected architecture. The simple nature of this model means that requests come in and then responses are sent back. On top of that, ASP.NET does not differentiate one request from another. The server containing an ASP.NET application is simply reacting to any request thrown at it.

This means that a developer building a Web application has to put some thought into how users can remain in context between their requests to the server as they work through the application. Keeping a user in context means recording state, the state of the user, to some type of data store. This can be done in multiple ways, and no one way is the *perfect* way. Rather, you have to choose one of the available methods.

You can read about maintaining state in an ASP.NET application in Chapter 22.

State can be stored via multiple methods, some of which include:

- Application State
- Session State
- The Cache Object

You use all these methods on the server, but you can also employ your own custom methods — such as simply storing state in a database using your own custom schema. It is also possible to write state back to the clients, either directly on their computers or by placing state in the HTML output in the response. Some of these methods include:

- Cookies
- Querystrings
- Hidden Fields
- ViewState

Understanding the Provider

These methods work rather well; but most of them are rudimentary and have short life spans. ASP.NET 3.5 includes a handful of systems (such as the new membership and role management systems) that handle state for users between multiple requests/response transactions. In fact, these systems require state management capabilities that go well beyond the limited time frames that are possible in the previously mentioned state management methods. Therefore, many of these systems must record state in more advanced modes — something that is easy to do in ASP.NET 3.5. Recording state to data stores in more advanced modes is accomplished through the use of *providers*.

> **A *provider* is an object that allows for programmatic access to data stores, processes, and more.**

When working with ASP.NET 1.*x*, you might have encountered a rudimentary provider model that was present in the system. This provider model was an object that sat between the `Session` object and the actual place in which the sessions were stored. By default, sessions in ASP.NET are stored `InProc`, meaning in the same process where ASP.NET is running. In ASP.NET 1.*x* (and in ASP.NET 3.5 for that matter), you can simply change the provider used for the `Session` object; this will, in turn, change where the session is stored. The available providers for storing session information include:

- `InProc`
- `StateServer`
- `SQLServer`

Besides `InProc`, you can use `StateServer` that enables you to store sessions in a process that is entirely separate from the one in which ASP.NET runs. This protects your sessions if the ASP.NET process shuts down. You can also store your sessions to disk (in a database for instance) using the `SQLServer` option. This method enables you to store your sessions directly in Microsoft's SQL Server. How do you go about changing the provider that is used for sessions? You can do this in a couple of ways.

One option to change the provider used for sessions is through the Internet Information Services (IIS) Manager, as shown in Figure 12-1.

The other option is to go directly to a system-wide configuration file (such as the `machine.config` file) or to an application configuration file (such as the `web.config`). In the file, change the name of the session state provider that is to be used within the `<sessionState>` section of the configuration document.

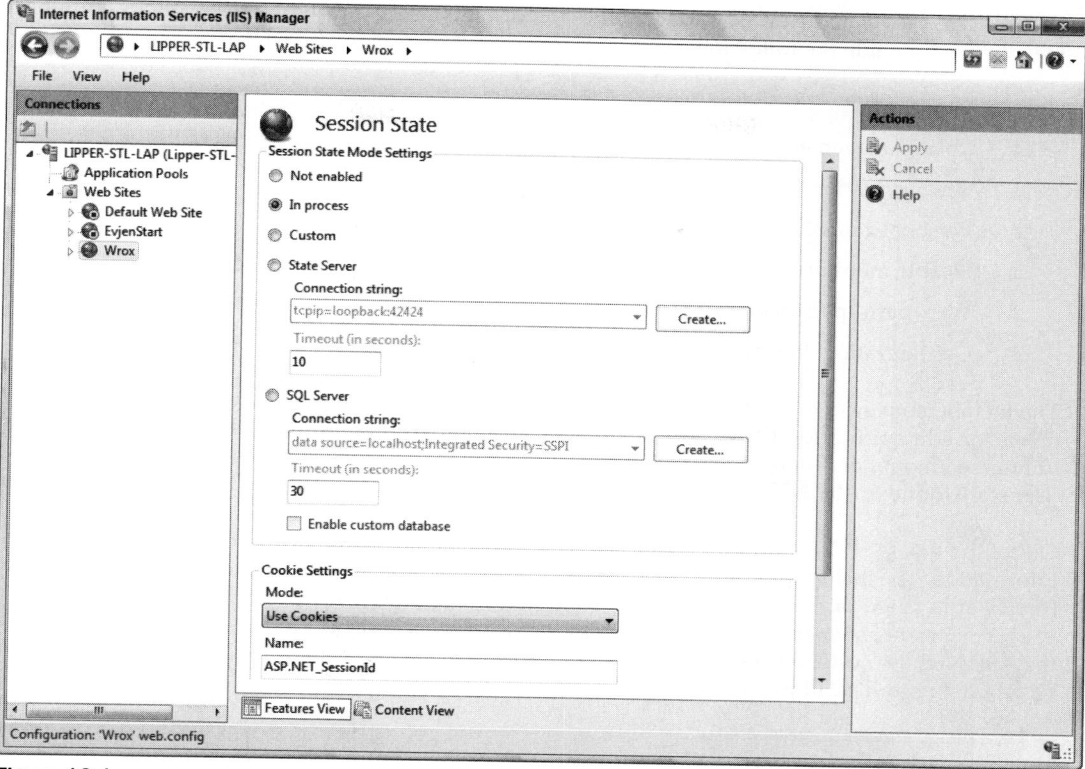

Figure 12-1

Since ASP.NET 2.0, you have been able to take this provider model one step further than you ever could before. You will discover this next.

The Provider Model in ASP.NET 3.5

Back when ASP.NET 2.0 was being developed, plenty of requests came into the ASP.NET team. Users wanted to be able to store sessions by means other than the three methods — `InProc`, `StateServer`, and `SQLServer`. For instance, one such request was for a provider that could store sessions in an Oracle database. This might seem as if it's a logical thing to add to ASP.NET in the days of ASP.NET 1.1. But if the team added a provider for Oracle, they would soon get requests to add even more providers for other databases and data storage methods. For this reason, instead of building providers for each and every possible scenario, the developers designed a provider model that enabled them to add any providers they wished. Thus, the new provider model found in ASP.NET was born.

ASP.NET 3.5 includes a lot of systems that required state storage of some kind. Also, instead of recording state in a fragile mode (the way sessions are stored by default), many of these systems require that their state be stored in more concrete data stores such as databases or XML files. This also allows a longer-lived state for the users visiting an application — something else that is required by these systems.

The systems based upon the provider model found in ASP.NET 3.5 that require advanced state management include the following:

- Membership
- Role management
- Site navigation
- Personalization
- Health monitoring Web events
- Web parts personalization
- Configuration file protection

The membership system is a means to allow ASP.NET to work from a user store of some kind to create, delete, or edit application users. Because it is rather apparent that developers want to work with an unlimited amount of different data stores for their user store, they need a means to change the underlying user store for their ASP.NET applications easily. The provider model found in ASP.NET 3.5 is the answer.

Out of the box, ASP.NET 3.5 provides a couple of membership providers that enable you to store user information. The included providers are the SQL Server and the Active Directory membership providers (found at `System.Web.Security.SqlMembershipProvider` and `System.Web.Security.ActiveDirectoryMembershipProvider`, respectively). In fact, for each of the systems (as well as for some of the ASP.NET 1.*x* systems), a series of providers is available to alter the way the state of that system is recorded. Figure 12-2 illustrates these new providers.

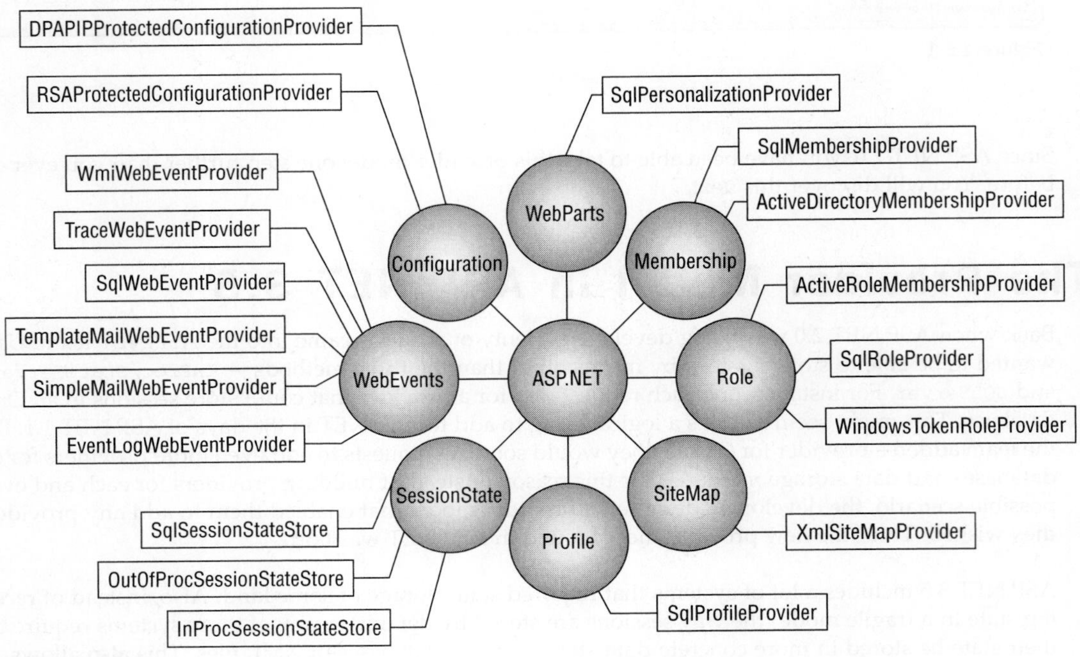

Figure 12-2

As you can see from the diagram, ASP.NET provides a large number of providers out of the box. Some systems have only a single provider (such as the profile system that includes only a provider to connect to SQL Server), whereas other systems include multiple providers (such as the WebEvents provider that includes six separate providers). Next, this chapter reviews how to set up SQL Server to work with a number of the providers presented in this chapter. You can use SQL Server 7.0, 2000, 2005, or 2008 for the backend data store for many of the providers presented (although not all of them). After this explanation, you review each of the available providers built into ASP.NET 3.5.

Setting Up Your Provider to Work with Microsoft SQL Server 7.0, 2000, 2005, or 2008

Quite a number of providers work with SQL Server. For instance, the membership, role management, personalization, and other systems work with SQL Server right out of the box. However, all these systems work with the new Microsoft SQL Server Express Edition file (`.mdf`) by default instead of with one of the full-blown versions of SQL Server such as SQL Server 7.0, SQL Server 2000, SQL Server 2005, or SQL Server 2008.

To work with either of these databases, you must set up the database using the `aspnet_regsql.exe` tool. Working with `aspnet_regsql.exe` creates the necessary tables, roles, stored procedures, and other items needed by the providers. To get at this tool, open up the Visual Studio 2008 Command Prompt by selecting Start ➪All Programs ➪Microsoft Visual Studio 2008 ➪Visual Studio Tools ➪Visual Studio 2008 Command Prompt. This gives you access to the ASP.NET SQL Server Setup Wizard. The ASP.NET SQL Server Setup Wizard is an easy-to-use tool that facilitates setup of the SQL Server to work with many of the systems that are built into ASP.NET 3.5, such as the membership, role management, and personalization systems. The Setup Wizard provides two ways for you to set up the database: using a command-line tool or using a GUI tool. First, look at the command-line version of the tool.

The ASP.NET SQL Server Setup Wizard Command-Line Tool

The command-line version of the Setup Wizard gives the developer optimal control over how the database is created. Working from the command-line using this tool is not difficult, so don't be intimidated by it.

You can get at the actual tool, `aspnet_regsql.exe`, from the Visual Studio Command Prompt if you have Visual Studio 2008. At the command prompt, type `aspnet_regsql.exe -?` to get a list of all the command-line options at your disposal for working this tool.

The following table describes some of the available options for setting up your SQL Server instance to work with the personalization framework.

Command Option	Description
`-?`	Displays a list of available option commands.
`-W`	Uses the Wizard mode. This uses the default installation if no other parameters are used.
`-S <server>`	Specifies the SQL Server instance to work with.
`-U <login>`	Specifies the username to log in to SQL Server. If you use this, you also use the `-P` command.

Command Option	Description
-P <password>	Specifies the password to use for logging in to SQL Server. If you use this, you also use the -U command.
-E	Provides instructions to use the current Windows credentials for authentication.
-C	Specifies the connection string for connecting to SQL Server. If you use this, you can avoid using the -U and -P commands because they are specified in the connection string itself.
-A all	Adds support for all the available SQL Server operations provided by ASP.NET 3.5 including membership, role management, profiles, site counters, and page/control personalization.
-A p	Adds support for working with profiles.
_R all	Removes support for all the available SQL Server operations that have been previously installed. These include membership, role management, profiles, site counters, and page/control personalization.
-R p	Removes support for the profile capability from SQL Server.
-d <database>	Specifies the database name to use with the application services. If you don't specify a name of a database, aspnetdb is used.
/sqlexportonly <filename>	Instead of modifying an instance of a SQL Server database, use this command in conjunction with the other commands to generate a SQL script that adds or removes the features specified. This command creates the scripts in a file that has the name specified in the command.

To modify SQL Server to work with the personalization provider using this command-line tool, you enter a command such as the following:

```
aspnet_regsql.exe -A all -E
```

After you enter the preceding command, the command-line tool creates the features required by all the available ASP.NET 3.5 systems. The results are shown in the tool itself, as you see in Figure 12-3.

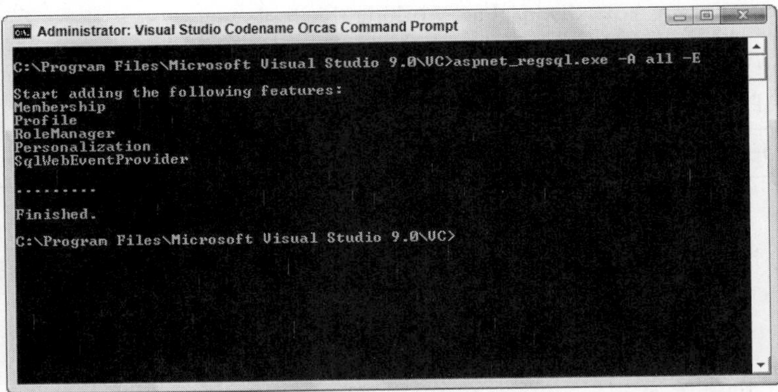

Figure 12-3

When this action is completed, you can see that a new database, `aspnetdb`, has been created in the Microsoft SQL Server Management Studio, which is part of Microsoft SQL Server 2005 (the database used for this example). You now have the appropriate tables for working with all the ASP.NET 3.5 systems that are able to work with SQL Server (see Figure 12-4).

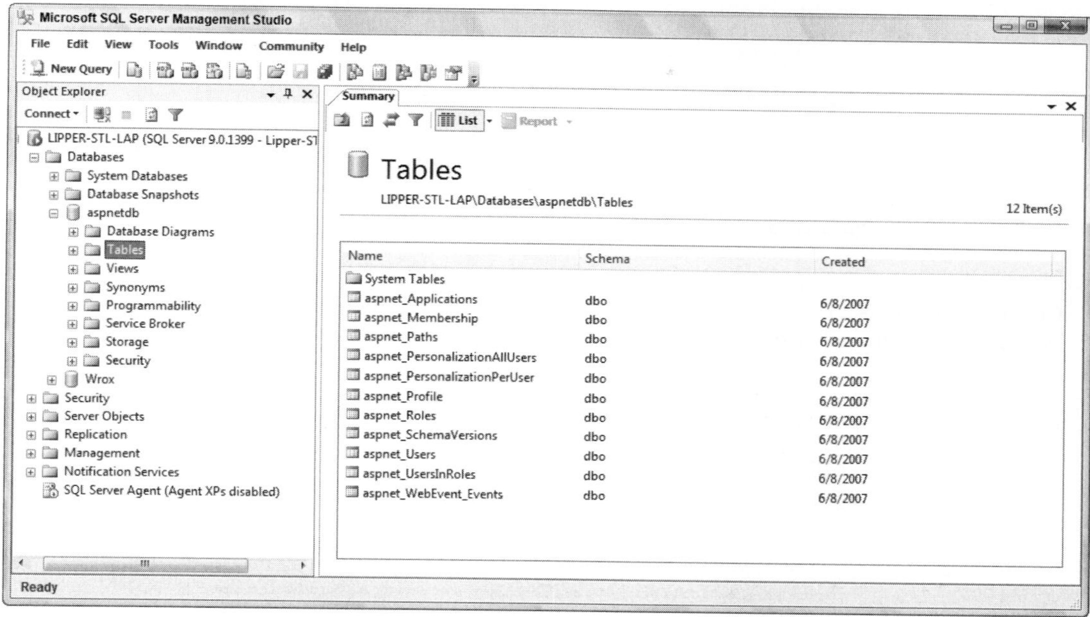

Figure 12-4

One advantage of using the command-line tool rather than the GUI-based version of the ASP.NET SQL Server Setup Wizard is that you can install in the database just the features that you are interested in working with instead of installing everything (as the GUI-based version does). For instance, if you are going to have only the membership system interact with SQL Server 2005 — not any of the other systems (such as role management and personalization) — then you can configure the setup so that only the tables, roles, stored procedures, and other items required by the membership system are established in the database. To set up the database for the membership system only, you use the following command on the command line.

```
aspnet_regsql.exe -A m -E
```

The ASP.NET SQL Server Setup Wizard GUI Tool

Instead of working with the tool through the command line, you can also work with a GUI version of the same wizard. To get at the GUI version, type the following at the Visual Studio command prompt:

```
aspnet_regsql.exe
```

At this point, the ASP.NET SQL Server Setup Wizard welcome screen appears, as shown in Figure 12-5.

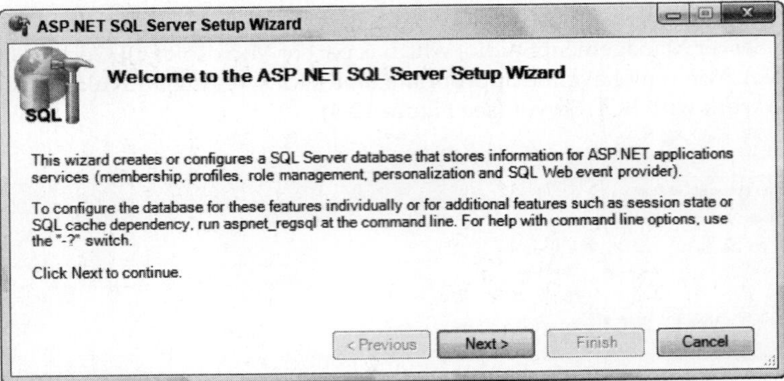

Figure 12-5

Clicking Next gives you a new screen that offers two options: one to install management features into SQL Server and the other to remove them (see Figure 12-6).

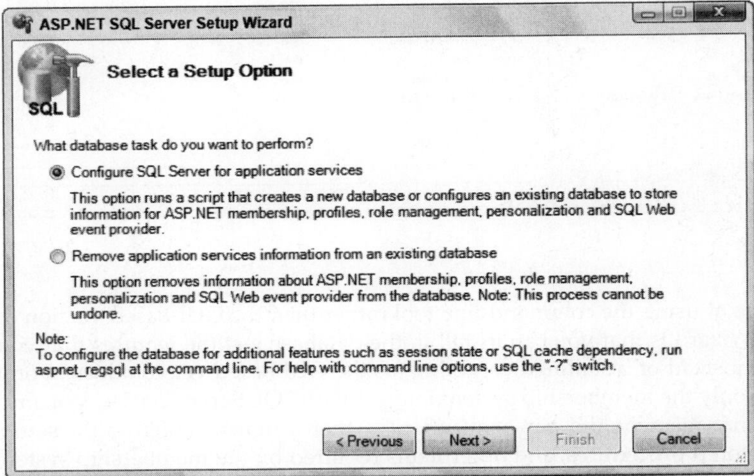

Figure 12-6

From here, choose the Configure SQL Server for application services and click the Next button. The third screen (see Figure 12-7) asks for the login credentials to SQL Server and the name of the database to perform the operations. The Database option is `<default>` — meaning that the wizard creates a database called `aspnetdb`. If you want to choose a different folder, such as the application's database, choose the appropriate option.

After you have made your server and database selections, click Next. The screen shown in Figure 12-8 asks you to confirm your settings. If everything looks correct, click Next — otherwise, click Back and correct your settings.

When this is complete, you are notified that everything was set up correctly.

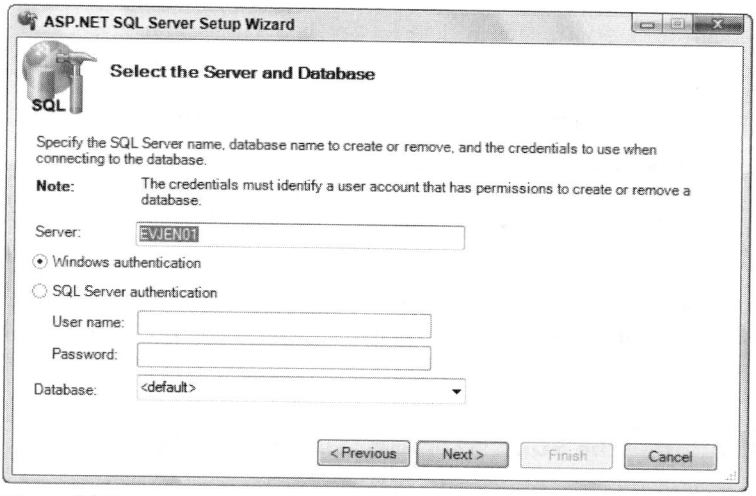

ASP.NET SQL Server Setup Wizard

Select the Server and Database

Specify the SQL Server name, database name to create or remove, and the credentials to use when connecting to the database.

Note: The credentials must identify a user account that has permissions to create or remove a database.

Server: EVJEN01

Windows authentication

SQL Server authentication

User name:

Password:

Database: <default>

< Previous | Next > | Finish | Cancel

Figure 12-7

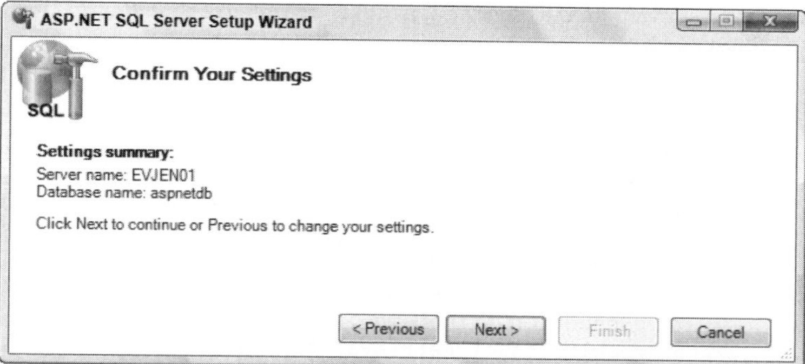

Figure 12-8

Connecting Your Default Provider to a New SQL Server Instance

After you set up the full-blown Microsoft SQL Server to work with the various systems provided by ASP.NET 3.5, you create a connection string to the database in your `machine.config` or `web.config` file. This is illustrated in Listing 12-1.

Listing 12-1: Changing the connection string in the machine.config.comments or your web.config file to work with SQL Server 2005

```
<configuration>

     <connectionStrings>
        <add name="LocalSqlServer"
```

Continued

```
        connectionString="Data Source=127.0.0.1;Integrated Security=SSPI" />
    </connectionStrings>

</configuration>
```

You may want to change the values provided if you are working with a remote instance of SQL Server rather than an instance that resides on the same server as the application. Changing this value in the `machine.config` file changes how each and every ASP.NET application uses this provider. Applying this setting in the `web.config` file causes only the local application to work with this instance.

After the connection string is set up, look further in the `<providers>` section of the section you are going to work with. For instance, if you are using the membership provider, you want to work with the `<membership>` element in the configuration file. The settings to change the SQL Server are shown in Listing 12-2.

Listing 12-2: Altering the SQL Server used via configuration

```
<configuration>

  <connectionStrings>
     <add name="LocalSql2005Server"
      connectionString="Data Source=127.0.0.1;Integrated Security=SSPI" />
  </connectionStrings>

  <system.web>

        <membership defaultProvider="AspNetSql2005MembershipProvider">
            <providers>
                <add name="AspNetSql2005MembershipProvider"
                    type="System.Web.Security.SqlMembershipProvider,
                       System.Web, Version=2.0.0.0, Culture=neutral,
                       PublicKeyToken=b03f5f7f11d50a3a"
                    connectionStringName="LocalSql2005Server"
                    enablePasswordRetrieval="false"
                    enablePasswordReset="true"
                    requiresQuestionAndAnswer="true"
                    applicationName="/"
                    requiresUniqueEmail="false"
                    passwordFormat="Hashed"
                    maxInvalidPasswordAttempts="5"
                    minRequiredPasswordLength="7"
                    minRequiredNonalphanumericCharacters="1"
                    passwordAttemptWindow="10"
                    passwordStrengthRegularExpression="" />
            </providers>
        </membership>

  </system.web>

</configuration>
```

With these changes in place, the SQL Server 2005 instance is now one of the providers available for use with your applications. The name of this provider instance is `AspNetSql2005MembershipProvider`.

You can see that this instance also uses the connection string of `LocalSql2005Server`, which was defined in Listing 12-1.

Pay attention to some important attribute declarations from Listing 12-2. The first is that the provider used by the membership system is defined via the `defaultProvider` attribute found in the main `<membership>` node. Using this attribute, you can specify whether the provider is one of the built-in providers or whether it is a custom provider that you have built yourself or received from a third party. With the code from Listing 12-2 in place, the membership provider now works with Microsoft SQL Server 2005 (as shown in this example) instead of the Microsoft SQL Server Express Edition files.

Next, you look at the providers that come built into the ASP.NET 3.5 install — starting with the membership system providers

Membership Providers

The membership system enables you to easily manage users in your ASP.NET applications. As with most of the systems provided in ASP.NET, it features a series of server controls that interact with a defined provider to either retrieve or record information to and from the data store defined by the provider. Because a provider exists between the server controls and the data stores where the data is retrieved and recorded, it is fairly trivial to have the controls work from an entirely different backend. You just change the underlying provider of the overall system (in this case, the membership system). This can be accomplished by a simple configuration change in the ASP.NET application. It really makes no difference to the server controls.

As previously stated, ASP.NET 3.5 provides two membership providers out of the box.

- `System.Web.Security.SqlMembershipProvider`: Provides you with the capability to use the membership system to connect to Microsoft's SQL Server 2000/2005 as well as with Microsoft SQL Server Express Edition.
- `System.Web.Security.ActiveDirectoryMembershipProvider`: Provides you with the capability to use the membership system to connect to Microsoft's Active Directory.

Both of these membership provider classes inherit from the `MembershipProvider` base class, as illustrated in Figure 12-9.

Next, you review each of these providers.

System.Web.Security.SqlMembershipProvider

The default provider is the `SqlMembershipProvider` instance. You find this default declaration for every ASP.NET application that resides on the application server in the `machine.config` file. This file is found in `C:\WINDOWS\Microsoft.NET\Framework\v2.0.50727\CONFIG`. Listing 12-3 shows the definition of this provider, which is located in the `machine.config` file.

Listing 12-3: A SqlMembershipProvider instance declaration

```
<configuration>
   <system.web>
       <membership>
```

Continued

```
            <providers>
               <add name="AspNetSqlMembershipProvider"
                type="System.Web.Security.SqlMembershipProvider,
                   System.Web, Version=2.0.0.0, Culture=neutral,
                   PublicKeyToken=b03f5f7f11d50a3a"
                connectionStringName="LocalSqlServer"
                enablePasswordRetrieval="false" enablePasswordReset="true"
                requiresQuestionAndAnswer="true" applicationName="/"
                requiresUniqueEmail="false" passwordFormat="Hashed"
                maxInvalidPasswordAttempts="5" minRequiredPasswordLength="7"
                minRequiredNonalphanumericCharacters="1" passwordAttemptWindow="10"
                passwordStrengthRegularExpression=""/>
            </providers>
        </membership>
    </system.web>
</configuration>
```

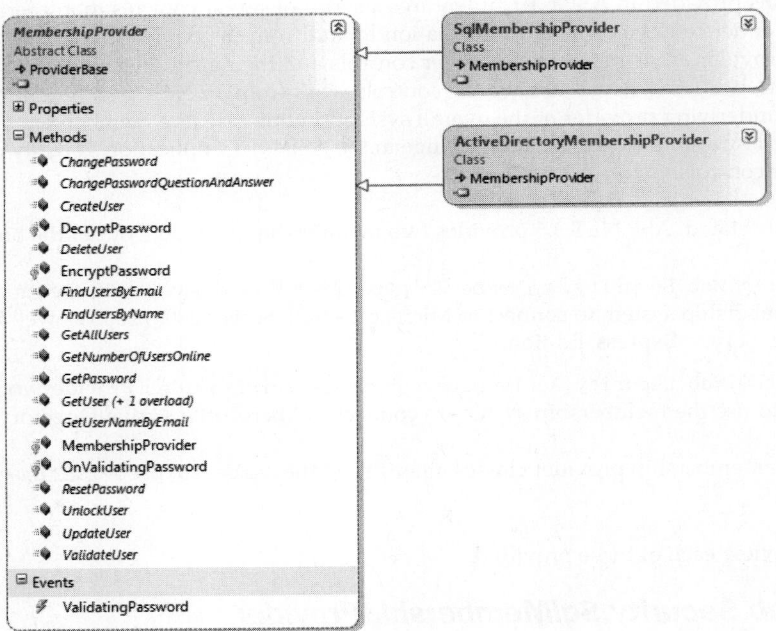

Figure 12-9

From this listing, you can see that a single instance of the `SqlMembershipProvider` object is defined in the `machine.config` file. This single instance is named `AspNetSqlMembershipProvider`. This is also where you find the default behavior settings for your membership system. By default, this provider is also configured to work with a SQL Server Express Edition instance rather than a full-blown version of SQL Server such as SQL Server 2000, 2005, or 2008. You can see this by looking at the defined `connectionStringName` property in the provider declaration from Listing 12-3. In this case, it is set to `LocalSqlServer`. `LocalSqlServer` is also defined in the `machine.config` file as shown in Listing 12-4.

Listing 12-4: The LocalSqlServer defined instance

```
<configuration>
  <connectionStrings>
    <clear />
    <add name="LocalSqlServer"
     connectionString="Data Source=.\SQLEXPRESS;Integrated Security=SSPI;
        AttachDBFilename=|DataDirectory|aspnetdb.mdf;User Instance=true"
     providerName="System.Data.SqlClient" />
  </connectionStrings>
</configuration>
```

You can see this connection string information is set for a local SQL Server Express Edition file (an `.mdf` file). Of course, you are not required to work with only these file types for the `SqlMembershipProvider` capabilities. Instead, you can also set it up to work with either Microsoft's SQL Server 7.0, 2000, 2005, or 2008 (as was previously shown).

System.Web.Security.ActiveDirectoryMembershipProvider

It is also possible for the membership system provided from ASP.NET 3.5 to connect this system to a Microsoft Active Directory instance or even Active Directory Application Mode (ADAM), which is a stand-alone directory product. Because the default membership provider is defined in the `machine.config` files at the `SqlMembershipProvider`, you must override these settings in your application's `web.config` file.

Before creating a defined instance of the `ActiveDirectoryMembershipProvider` in your `web.config` file, you have to define the connection string to the Active Directory store. This is illustrated in Listing 12-5.

Listing 12-5: Defining the connection string to the Active Directory store

```
<configuration>
   <connectionStrings>
      <add name="ADConnectionString"
       connectionString=
       "LDAP://domain.myAdServer.com/CN=Users,DC=domain,DC=testing,DC=com" />
   </connectionStrings>
</configuration>
```

With the connection in place, you can create an instance of the `ActiveDirecotryMembershipProvider` in your `web.config` file that associates itself to this connection string. This is illustrated in Listing 12-6.

Listing 12-6: Defining the ActiveDirectoryMembershipProvider instance

```
<configuration>

   <connectionStrings>
      <add name="ADConnectionString"
       connectionString=
       "LDAP://domain.myAdServer.com/CN=Users,DC=domain,DC=testing,DC=com" />
   </connectionStrings>
```

Continued

```
<system.web>
  <membership
   defaultProvider="AspNetActiveDirectoryMembershipProvider">
   <providers>
     <add name="AspNetActiveDirectoryMembershipProvider"
       type="System.Web.Security.ActiveDirectoryMembershipProvider,
         System.Web, Version=2.0.0.0, Culture=neutral,
         PublicKeyToken=b03f5f7f11d50a3a"
       connectionStringName="ADConnectionString"
       connectionUserName="UserWithAppropriateRights"
       connectionPassword="PasswordForUser"
       connectionProtection="Secure"
       enablePasswordReset="true"
       enableSearchMethods="true"
       requiresQuestionAndAnswer="true"
       applicationName="/"
       description="Default AD connection"
       requiresUniqueEmail="false"
       clientSearchTimeout="30"
       serverSearchTimeout="30"
       attributeMapPasswordQuestion="department"
       attributeMapPasswordAnswer="division"
       attributeMapFailedPasswordAnswerCount="singleIntAttribute"
       attributeMapFailedPasswordAnswerTime="singleLargeIntAttribute"
       attributeMapFailedPassswordAnswerLockoutTime="singleLargeIntAttribute"
       maxInvalidPasswordAttemps = "5"
       passwordAttemptWindow = "10"
       passwordAnswerAttemptLockoutDuration = "30"
       minRequiredPasswordLength="7"
       minRequiredNonalphanumericCharacters="1"
       passwordStrengthRegularExpression="
         @\"(?=.{6,})(?=(.*\d){1,})(?=(.*\W){1,})" />
     />
   </providers>
  </membership>
</system.web>

</configuration>
```

Although not all these attributes are required, this list provides you with the available attributes of the `ActiveDirectoryMembershipProvider`. In fact, you can easily declare the instance in its simplest form, as shown here:

```
<membership defaultProvider="AspNetActiveDirectoryMembershipProvider">
  <providers>
    <add name="AspNetActiveDirectoryMembershipProvider"
      type="System.Web.Security.ActiveDirectoryMembershipProvider,
        System.Web, Version=2.0.0.0, Culture=neutral,
        PublicKeyToken=b03f5f7f11d50a3a"
      connectionStringName="ADConnectionString" />
  </providers>
</membership>
```

Again, with either the `SqlMembershipProvider` or the `ActiveDirectoryMembershipProvider` in place, the membership system server controls (such as the Login server control) as well as the membership API, once configured, will record and retrieve their information via the provider you have established. That is the power of the provider model that the ASP.NET team has established. You continue to see this power as you learn about the rest of the providers detailed in this chapter.

Role Providers

After a user is logged into the system (possibly using the ASP.NET membership system), the ASP.NET role management system enables you to work with the role of that user to authorize him for a particular access to the overall application. The role management system in ASP.NET 3.5, as with the other systems, has a set of providers to store and retrieve role information in an easy manner. This, of course, doesn't mean that you are bound to one of the three available providers in the role management system. Instead, you can extend one of the established providers or even create your own custom provider.

By default, ASP.NET 3.5 offers three providers for the role management system. These providers are defined in the following list:

- `System.Web.Security.SqlRoleProvider`: Provides you with the capability to use the ASP.NET role management system to connect to Microsoft's SQL Server 2000/2005/2008 as well as to Microsoft SQL Server Express Edition.
- `System.Web.Security.WindowsTokenRoleProvider`: Provides you with the capability to connect the ASP.NET role management system to the built-in Windows security group system.
- `System.Web.Security.AuthorizationStoreRoleProvider`: Provides you with the capability to connect the ASP.NET role management system to either an XML file, Active Directory, or in an Active Directory Application Mode (ADAM) store.

These three classes for role management inherit from the `RoleProvider` base class. This is illustrated in Figure 12-10.

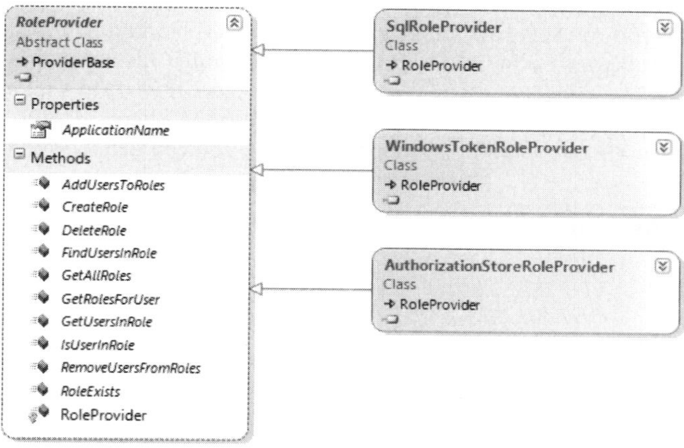

Figure 12-10

System.Web.Security.SqlRoleProvider

The role management system in ASP.NET uses SQL Server Express Edition files by default (just as the membership system does). The connection to the SQL Server Express file uses `SqlRoleProvider`, but you can just as easily configure your SQL Server 7.0, 2000, 2005, or 2008 server to work with the role management system through `SqlRoleProvider`. The procedure for setting up your full-blown SQL Server is described in the beginning of this chapter.

Looking at the `SqlRoleProvider` instance in the `machine.config.comments` file, you will notice the syntax as defined in Listing 12-7. The `machine.config.comments` file provides documentation on the `machine.config` as well as showing you the details of the default settings that are baked into the ASP .NET Framework.

Listing 12-7: A SqlRoleProvider instance declaration

```
<configuration>
  <system.web>
     <roleManager enabled="false" cacheRolesInCookie="false"
      cookieName=".ASPXROLES" cookieTimeout="30" cookiePath="/"
      cookieRequireSSL="false" cookieSlidingExpiration="true"
      cookieProtection="All" defaultProvider="AspNetSqlRoleProvider"
      createPersistentCookie="false" maxCachedResults="25">
        <providers>
           <add name="AspNetSqlRoleProvider"
            connectionStringName="LocalSqlServer" applicationName="/"
            type="System.Web.Security.SqlRoleProvider,
            System.Web, Version=2.0.0.0, Culture=neutral,
            PublicKeyToken=b03f5f7f11d50a3a" />
        </providers>
     </roleManager>
   </system.web>
</configuration>
```

As stated, this is part of the default `<roleManager>` declaration that is baked into the overall ASP.NET Framework (note again that you can change any of these defaults by making a new declaration in your `web.config` file). As you can see, role management is disabled by default through the `enabled` attribute found in the `<roleManager>` node (it is set to `false` by default). Also, pay attention to the `defaultProvider` attribute in the `<roleManager>` element. In this case, it is set to `AspNetSqlRoleProvider`. This provider is defined in the same code example. To connect to the Microsoft SQL Server 2005 instance that was defined earlier (in the membership system examples), you can use the syntax shown in Listing 12-8.

Listing 12-8: Connecting the role management system to SQL Server 2005

```
<configuration>

  <connectionStrings>
     <add name="LocalSql2005Server"
      connectionString="Data Source=127.0.0.1;Integrated Security=SSPI" />
  </connectionStrings>

  <system.web>
        <roleManager enabled="true" cacheRolesInCookie="true"
```

```
            cookieName=".ASPXROLES" cookieTimeout="30" cookiePath="/"
            cookieRequireSSL="false" cookieSlidingExpiration="true"
            cookieProtection="All" defaultProvider="AspNetSqlRoleProvider"
            createPersistentCookie="false" maxCachedResults="25">
               <providers>
                   <clear />
                   <add connectionStringName="LocalSql2005Server" applicationName="/"
                    name="AspNetSqlRoleProvider"
                    type="System.Web.Security.SqlRoleProvider, System.Web,
                      Version=2.0.0.0, Culture=neutral,
                      PublicKeyToken=b03f5f7f11d50a3a" />
               </providers>
          </roleManager>
     </system.web>

</configuration>
```

With this in place, you can now connect to SQL Server 2005. Next is a review of the second provider available to the role management system.

System.Web.Security.WindowsTokenRoleProvider

The Windows operating system has a role system built into it. This Windows security group system is an ideal system to use when you are working with intranet-based applications where you might have all users already in defined roles. This, of course, works best if you have anonymous authentication turned off for your ASP.NET application, and you have configured your application to use Windows Authentication.

Windows Authentication for ASP.NET applications is discussed in Chapter 21.

Some limitations exist when using `WindowsTokenRoleProvider`. This is a read-only provider because ASP.NET is not allowed to modify the settings applied in the Windows security group system. This means that not all the methods provided via the `RoleProvider` abstract class are usable when working with this provider. From the `WindowsTokenRoleProvider` class, the only methods you have at your disposal are `IsUserInRole` and `GetUsersInRole`.

To configure your `WindowsTokenRoleProvider` instance, you use the syntax defined in Listing 12-9.

Listing 12-9: A WindowsTokenRoleProvider instance

```
<configuration>
   <system.web>

      <authentication mode="Windows" />

      <roleManager defaultProvider="WindowsProvider"
       enabled="true"
       cacheRolesInCookie="false">
         <providers>
            <add
             name="WindowsProvider"
```

Continued

```
            type="System.Web.Security.WindowsTokenRoleProvider" />
        </providers>
      </roleManager>

    </system.web>
  </configuration>
```

Remember that you have to declare the default provider using the `defaultProvider` attribute in the `<roleManager>` element to change the assigned provider from the `SqlRoleProvider` association.

System.Web.Security.AuthorizationStoreRoleProvider

The final role provider you have available to you from a default install of ASP.NET is `AuthorizationStoreRoleProvider`. This role provider class allows you to store roles inside of an Authorization Manager policy store. These types of stores are also referred to as AzMan stores. As with `WindowsTokenRoleProvider`, `AuthorizationStoreRoleProvider` is a bit limited because it is unable to support any AzMan business rules.

To use `AuthorizationStoreRoleProvider`, you must first make a connection in your `web.config` file to the XML data store used by AzMan. This is illustrated in Listing 12-10.

Listing 12-10: Making a connection to the AzMan policy store

```
<configuration>
  <connectionStrings>
    <add name="LocalPolicyStore"
         connectionString="msxml://~\App_Data\datafilename.xml" />
  </connectionStrings>
</configuration>
```

Note that when working with these XML-based policy files, it is best to store them in the App_Data folder. Files stored in the App_Data folder cannot be pulled up in the browser.

After the connection string is in place, the next step is to configure your `AuthorizationStoreRoleProvider` instance. This takes the syntax defined in Listing 12-11.

Listing 12-11: Defining the AuthorizationStoreRoleProvider instance

```
<configuration>

  <connectionStrings>
    <add name="MyLocalPolicyStore"
         connectionString="msxml://~\App_Data\datafilename.xml" />
  </connectionStrings>

  <system.web>

    <authentication mode="Windows" />
    <identity impersonate="true" />

    <roleManager defaultProvider="AuthorizationStoreRoleProvider"
      enabled="true"
      cacheRolesInCookie="true"
```

```
        cookieName=".ASPROLES"
        cookieTimeout="30"
        cookiePath="/"
        cookieRequireSSL="false"
        cookieSlidingExpiration="true"
        cookieProtection="All" >
        <providers>
          <clear />
            <add
              name="AuthorizationStoreRoleProvider"
              type="System.Web.Security.AuthorizationStoreRoleProvider"
              connectionStringName="MyLocalPolicyStore"
              applicationName="SampleApplication"
              cacheRefreshInterval="60"
              scopeName="" />
        </providers>
      </roleManager>

    </system.web>

  </configuration>
```

Next, this chapter reviews the single personalization provider available in ASP.NET 3.5.

The Personalization Provider

As with the membership system found in ASP.NET, the personalization system (also referred to as the profile system) is another system that is based on the provider model. This system makes associations between the end user viewing the application and any data points stored centrally that are specific to that user. As stated, these personalization properties are stored and maintained on a per-user basis. ASP.NET provides a single provider for data storage. This provider is detailed here:

- `System.Web.Profile.SqlProfileProvider`: Provides you with the capability to use the ASP .NET personalization system to connect to Microsoft's SQL Server 2000/2005/2008 as well as to the new Microsoft SQL Server Express Edition.

This single class for the personalization system inherits from the `ProfileProvider` base class. This is illustrated in Figure 12-11.

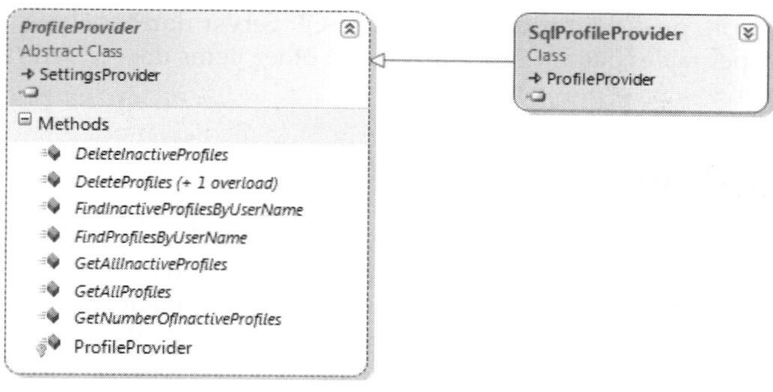

Figure 12-11

As with the other providers covered so far, `SqlProfileProvider` connects to a Microsoft SQL Server Express Edition file by default. Although this is the default, you can change the connection to work with SQL Server 7.0, 2000, 2005, or 2008. For instance, if you are connecting to a SQL Server 2005 database, you define your connection in the `web.config` and then associate your `SqlProfileProvider` declaration to this connection string. This scenario is presented in Listing 12-12.

Listing 12-12: Connecting the SqlProfileProvider to SQL Server 2005

```
<configuration>

    <connectionStrings>
       <add name="LocalSql2005Server"
        connectionString="Data Source=127.0.0.1;Integrated Security=SSPI" />
    </connectionStrings>

    <system.web>

    <profile>
       <providers>
          <clear />
          <add name="AspNetSql2005ProfileProvider"
           connectionStringName="LocalSql2005Server" applicationName="/"
           type="System.Web.Profile.SqlProfileProvider, System.Web,
             Version=2.0.0.0, Culture=neutral,
             PublicKeyToken=b03f5f7f11d50a3a" />
       </providers>

        <properties>
           <add name="FirstName" />
           <add name="LastName" />
           <add name="LastVisited" />
           <add name="Age" />
           <add name="Member" />
        </properties>
    </profile>

   </system.web>

</configuration>
```

Remember that to store profile information in your SQL Server database, you have to configure this database so the proper tables, stored procedures, and other items are created. This task was discussed earlier in the chapter.

The SiteMap Provider

Similar to the personalization provider just discussed, ASP.NET 3.5 provides a single provider to work with sitemaps. Sitemaps are what ASP.NET uses to provide you with a centralized way of maintaining site navigation. By default, the definition of a Web application's navigation is located in a structured XML file. The sitemap provider lets you interact with this XML file, the `.sitemap` file, which you create for your application. The provider available for sitemaps is `System.Web.XmlSiteMapProvider`, which provides you with the capability to use the ASP.NET navigation system to connect to an XML-based file.

This single class for the sitemap system inherits from the `StaticSiteMapProvider` base class, which is a partial implementation of the `SiteMapProvider` base class. This is illustrated in Figure 12-12.

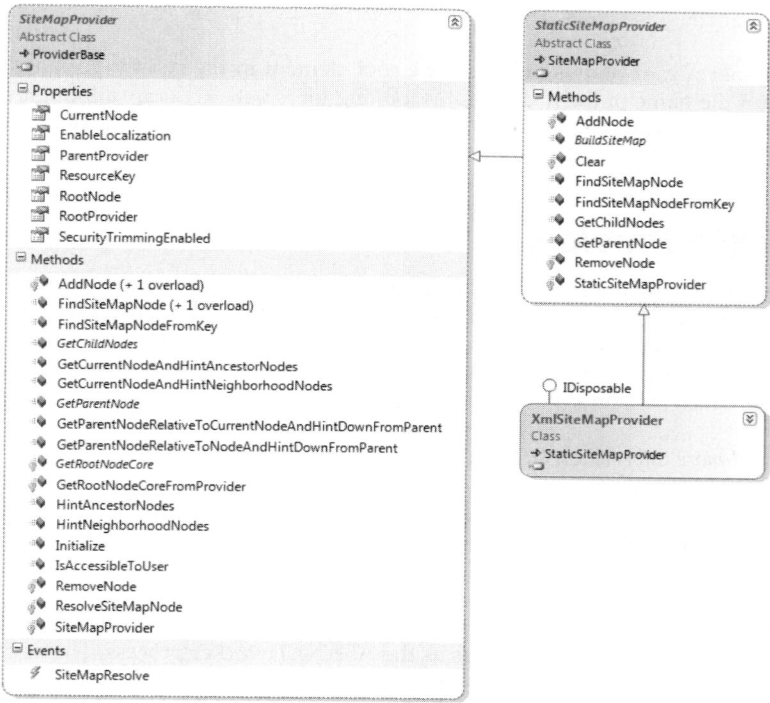

Figure 12-12

This is the first provider introduced so far that does not connect to a SQL Server database by default. Instead, this provider is designed to work with a static XML file. This XML file uses a particular schema and is covered in considerable detail in Chapter 14.

The code required to configure `XmlSiteMapProvider` is presented in Listing 12-13.

Listing 12-13: Defining an XmlSiteMapProvider instance in the web.config

```
<configuration>
   <system.web>

      <siteMap defaultProvider="MyXmlSiteMapProvider" enabled="true">
         <providers>
            <add name="MyXmlSiteMapProvider"
             description="SiteMap provider that reads in .sitemap files."
             type="System.Web.XmlSiteMapProvider, System.Web, Version=2.0.0.0,
               Culture=neutral, PublicKeyToken=b03f5f7f11d50a3a"
             siteMapFile="AnotherWeb.sitemap" />
```

Continued

```
        </providers>
    </siteMap>

  </system.web>
</configuration>
```

The `XmlSiteMapProvider` allows only a single root element in the strictly designed `web.sitemap` file. The default file name of the XML file it is looking for is `web.sitemap`, although you can change this default setting (as you can see in Listing 12-13) by using the `siteMapFile` attribute within the provider declaration in the `web.config` file.

SessionState Providers

As mentioned in the beginning of the chapter, an original concept of a provider model existed when the idea of managing session state in different ways was first introduced with ASP.NET 1.*x*. The available modes of storing session state for your users include `InProc`, `StateServer`, `SQLServer`, or even `Custom`. Each mode has definite pros and cons associated with it, and you should examine each option thoroughly when deciding which session state mode to use.

You can find more information on these session state modes in Chapter 22.

This provider model is a bit different from the others discussed so far in this chapter. The `SessionState-Module` class is a handler provided to load one of the available session state modes. Each of these modes is defined here:

- `System.Web.SessionState.InProcSessionStateStore`: Provides you with the capability to store sessions in the same process as the ASP.NET worker process. This is by far the best-performing method of session state management.
- `System.Web.SessionState.OutOfProcSessionStateStore`: Provides you with the capability to store sessions in a process separate from the ASP.NET worker process. This mode is a little more secure, but a little worse in performance than the InProc mode.
- `System.Web.SessionState.SqlSessionStateStore`: Provides you with the capability to store sessions in SQL Server. This is by far the most secure method of storing sessions, but it is the worst performing mode of the three available methods.

These three modes for session state management are illustrated in Figure 12-13.

Next, this chapter reviews each of the three modes that you can use out of the box in your ASP.NET 3.5 applications.

System.Web.SessionState.InProcSessionStateStore

The `InProcSessionStateStore` mode is the default mode for ASP.NET 1.*x* as well as for ASP.NET 2.0 and 3.5. In this mode, the sessions generated are held in the same process as that being used by the ASP.NET worker process (`aspnet_wp.exe` or `w3wp.exe`). This mode is the best performing, but some problems exist with this mode as well. Because the sessions are stored in the same process, whenever the worker process is recycled, all the sessions are destroyed. Worker processes can be recycled for many reasons (such as a change to the `web.config` file, the `Global.asax` file, or a setting in IIS that requires the process to be recycled after a set time period).

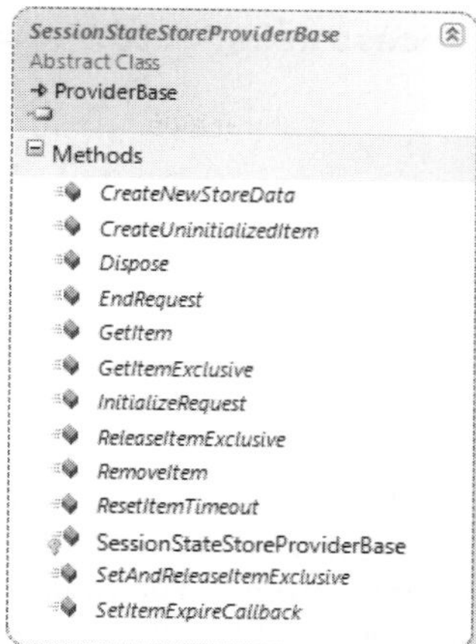

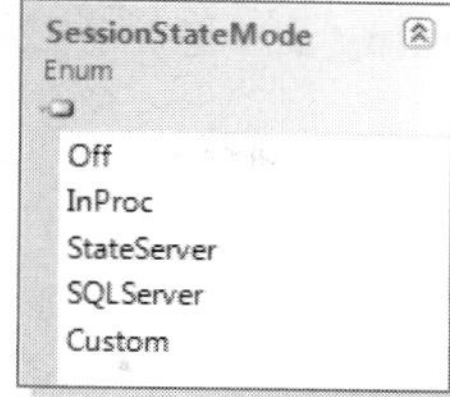

Figure 12-13

An example of the configuration in the `web.config` file for working in the InProc mode is presented in Listing 12-14.

Listing 12-14: Defining the InProc mode for session state management in the web.config

```
<configuration>
   <system.web>

      <sessionState mode="InProc">
      </sessionState>

   </system.web>
</configuration>
```

As you can see, this mode is rather simple. The next method reviewed is the out-of-process mode — also referred to as the StateServer mode.

System.Web.SessionState.OutOfProcSessionStateStore

In addition to the InProc mode, the StateServer mode is an out-of-process method of storing session state. This method does not perform as well as one that stores the sessions in the same process as the ASP.NET worker process. This makes sense because the method must jump process boundaries to work with the sessions you are employing. Although the performance is poorer than in the InProc mode, the `OutOfProcSessionStateStore` method is more reliable than running the sessions using `InProcSessionStateStore`. If your application's worker process recycles, the sessions that this application is working with are still maintained. This is a vital capability for those applications that are critically dependent upon sessions.

An example of using `OutOfProcSessionStateStore` is detailed in Listing 12-15.

Listing 12-15: Running sessions out of process using OutOfProcSessionStateStore

```
<configuration>
   <system.web>

      <sessionState mode="StateServer"
       stateConnectionString="tcpip=127.0.0.1:42424">
      </sessionState>

   </system.web>
</configuration>
```

When using the StateServer mode, you also must define where the sessions are stored using the `stateConnectionString` attribute. In this case, the local server is used, meaning that the sessions are stored on the same machine, but in an entirely separate process. You could have just as easily stored the sessions on a different server by providing the appropriate IP address as a value for this attribute. In addition to the IP address, note that port 42424 is used. This port is required when using the StateServer mode for sessions. Changing the port for the StateServer is detailed in Chapter 22.

System.Web.SessionState.SqlSessionStateStore

The final provider for session state management available to you in ASP.NET is the `SqlSessionStateStore`. This method is definitely the most resilient of the three available modes. With that said, however, it is also the worst performing of the three modes. It is important that you set up your database appropriately if you use this method of session state storage. Again, Chapter 22 shows you how to set up your database.

To configure your application to work with `SqlSessionStateStore`, you must configure the `web.config` as detailed in Listing 12-16.

Listing 12-16: Defining SqlSessionStateStore in the web.config file

```
<configuration>
   <system.web>

      <sessionState mode="SQLServer"
       allowCustomSqlDatabase="true"
       sqlConnectionString="Data Source=127.0.0.1;
         database=MyCustomASPStateDatabase;Integrated Security=SSPI">
      </sessionState>

   </system.web>
</configuration>
```

Next, you review the providers available for the Web events architecture.

Web Event Providers

Among all the available systems provided in ASP.NET 3.5, more providers are available for the health monitoring system than for any other system. The new health monitoring system enables ASP.NET application administrators to evaluate the health of a running ASP.NET application and to capture events (errors and other possible triggers) that can then be stored via one of the available providers. These events are referred to as *Web events*. A large list of events can be monitored via the health monitoring system, and this means that you can start recording items such as authentication failures/successes, all errors generated, ASP.NET worker process information, request data, response data, and more. Recording items means using one of the providers available to record to a data store of some kind.

Health monitoring in ASP.NET 3.5 is covered in Chapter 33.

By default, ASP.NET 3.5 offers seven possible providers for the health monitoring system. This is more than for any of the other ASP.NET systems. These providers are defined in the following list:

- `System.Web.Management.EventLogWebEventProvider`: Provides you with the capability to use the ASP.NET health monitoring system to record security operation errors and all other errors into the Windows event log.
- `System.Web.Management.SimpleMailWebEventProvider`: Provides you with the capability to use the ASP.NET health monitoring system to send error information in an e-mail.
- `System.Web.Management.TemplatedMailWebEventProvider`: Similar to the `SimpleMailWebEventProvider`, the `TemplatedMailWebEventProvider` class provides you with the capability to send error information in a templated e-mail. Templates are defined using a standard `.aspx` page.
- `System.Web.Management.SqlWebEventProvider`: Provides you with the capability to use the ASP.NET health monitoring system to store error information in SQL Server. As with the other SQL providers for the other systems in ASP.NET, the `SqlWebEventProvider` stores error information in SQL Server Express Edition by default.
- `System.Web.Management.TraceWebEventProvider`: Provides you with the capability to use the ASP.NET health monitoring system to send error information to the ASP.NET page tracing system.
- `System.Web.Management.IisTraceWebEventProvider`: Provides you with the capability to use the ASP.NET health monitoring system to send error information to the IIS tracing system.
- `System.Web.Management.WmiWebEventProvider`: Provides you with the capability to connect the new ASP.NET health monitoring system, the Windows Management Instrumentation (WMI) event provider.

These seven providers for the ASP.NET health monitoring system inherit from either the `WebEventProvider` base class, or the `BufferedWebEventProvider` (which, in turn, inherits from `WebEventProvider`). This is illustrated in Figure 12-14.

What is the difference between the `WebEventProvider` class and the `BufferedWebEventProvider`? The big difference is that the `WebEventProvider` writes events as they happen, whereas the `BufferedWebEventProvider` holds Web events until a collection of them is made. The collection is then written to the database or sent in an e-mail in a batch. If you use the `SqlWebEventProvider` class, you actually want this batch processing to occur rather than having the provider make a connection to the database and write to it for each Web event that occurs.

Next, this chapter looks at each of the seven available providers for the health monitoring system.

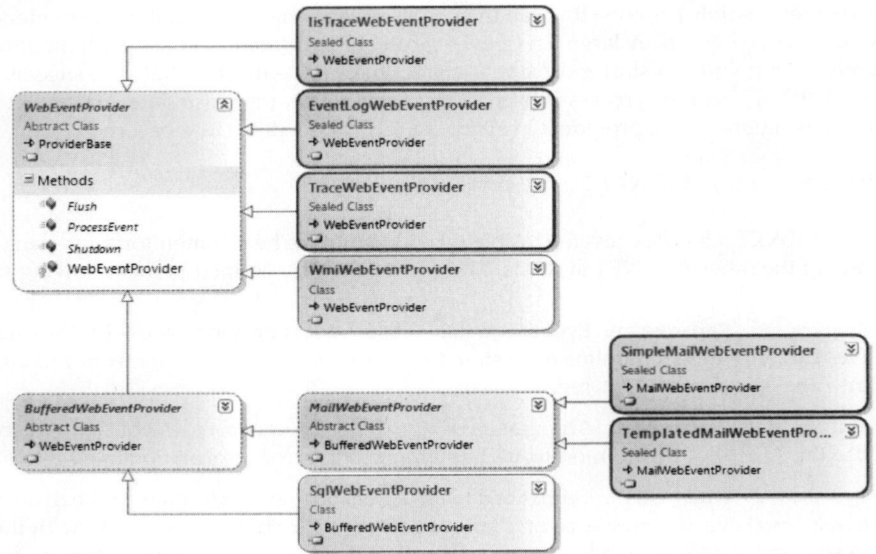

Figure 12-14

System.Web.Management.EventLogWebEventProvider

Traditionally, administrators and developers are used to reviewing system and application errors in the built-in Windows event log. The items in the event log can be viewed via the Event Viewer. This GUI-based tool for viewing events can be found by selecting Administration Tools in the Control Panel and then selecting Event Viewer.

By default, the health monitoring system uses the Windows event log to record the items that are already specified in the server's configuration files or items you have specified in the `web.config` file of your application. If you look in the `web.config.comments` file in the CONFIG folder of the Microsoft .NET Framework installed on your server, you see that the `EventLogWebEventProvider` is detailed in this location. The code is presented in Listing 12-17.

Listing 12-17: The EventLogWebEventProvider declared in the web.config.comments file

```
<configuration>
   <system.web>

      <healthMonitoring heartbeatInterval="0" enabled="true">
         <bufferModes>
            <!-- Removed for clarity -->
         </bufferModes>
         <providers>
            <clear />
            <add name="EventLogProvider"
             type="System.Web.Management.EventLogWebEventProvider,
               System.Web,Version=2.0.0.0,Culture=neutral,
```

```
                PublicKeyToken=b03f5f7f11d50a3a" />
            <!-- Removed for clarity -->
        </providers>
        <profiles>
            <!-- Removed for clarity -->
        </profiles>
        <rules>
            <add name="All Errors Default" eventName="All Errors"
             provider="EventLogProvider" profile="Default" minInstances="1"
             maxLimit="Infinite" minInterval="00:01:00" custom="" />
            <add name="Failure Audits Default" eventName="Failure Audits"
             provider="EventLogProvider" profile="Default" minInstances="1"
             maxLimit="Infinite" minInterval="00:01:00" custom="" />
        </rules>
        <eventMappings>
            <!-- Removed for clarity -->
        </eventMappings>
    </healthMonitoring>

  </system.web>
</configuration>
```

As you can see from Listing 12-17, a lot of possible settings can be applied in the health monitoring system. Depending on the rules and event mappings you have defined, these items are logged into the event log of the server that is hosting the application. Looking closely at the `<rules>` section of the listing, you can see that specific error types are assigned to be monitored. In this section, two types of errors are trapped in the health monitoring system — `All Errors Default` and `Failure Audits Default`.

When one of the errors defined in the `<rules>` section is triggered and captured by the health monitoring system, it is recorded. Where it is recorded depends upon the specified provider. The provider attribute used in the `<add>` element of the `<rules>` section determines this. In both cases in the example in Listing 12-17, you can see that the `EventLogProvider` is the assigned provider. This means that the Windows error log is used for recording the errors of both types.

As you work through the rest of the providers, note that the health monitoring system behaves differently when working with providers than the other systems that have been introduced in this chapter. Using the new health monitoring system in ASP.NET 3.5, you are able to assign more than one provider at a time. This means that you are able to specify in the `web.config` *file that errors are logged not only into the Windows event log, but also into any other data store using any other provider you designate. Even for the same Web event type, you can assign the Web event to be recorded to the Windows event log and SQL Server at the same time (for example).*

System.Web.Management.SimpleMailWebEventProvider

Sometimes when errors occur in your applications, you as an administrator or a concerned developer want e-mail notification of the problem. In addition to recording events to disk using something such as the `EventLogWebEventProvider`, you can also have the error notification e-mailed to you using the `SimpleMailWebEventProvider`. As it states in the provider name, the e-mail is a simply constructed one. Listing 12-18 shows you how you would go about adding e-mail notification in addition to writing the errors to the Windows event log.

Listing 12-18: The SimpleMailWebEventProvider definition

```
<configuration>
   <system.web>

      <healthMonitoring heartbeatInterval="0" enabled="true">
         <bufferModes>
            <add name="Website Error Notification"
             maxBufferSize="100"
             maxFlushSize="20"
             urgentFlushThreshold="1"
             regularFlushInterval="Infinite"
             urgentFlushInterval="00:01:00"
             maxBufferThreads="1" />
         </bufferModes>
         <providers>
            <clear />
            <add name="EventLogProvider"
             type="System.Web.Management.EventLogWebEventProvider,
               System.Web,Version=2.0.0.0,Culture=neutral,
               PublicKeyToken=b03f5f7f11d50a3a" />
            <add name="SimpleMailProvider"
             type="System.Web.Management.SimpleMailWebEventProvider,
              System.Web, Version=2.0.0.0, Culture=neutral,
              PublicKeyToken=b03f5f7f11d50a3a"
             from="website@company.com"
             to="admin@company.com"
             cc="adminLevel2@company.com
             bcc="director@company.com"
             bodyHeader="Warning!"
             bodyFooter="Please investigate ASAP."
             subjectPrefix="Action required."
             buffer="true"
             bufferMode="Website Error Notification"
             maxEventLength="4096"
             maxMessagesPerNotification="1" />
         </providers>
         <profiles>
            <!-- Removed for clarity -->
         </profiles>
         <rules>
            <add name="All Errors Default" eventName="All Errors"
             provider="EventLogProvider" profile="Default" minInstances="1"
             maxLimit="Infinite" minInterval="00:01:00" custom="" />
            <add name="Failure Audits Default" eventName="Failure Audits"
             provider="EventLogProvider" profile="Default" minInstances="1"
             maxLimit="Infinite" minInterval="00:01:00" custom="" />
            <add name="All Errors Simple Mail" eventName="All Errors"
             provider="SimpleMailProvider" profile="Default" />
            <add name="Failure Audits Default" eventName="Failure Audits"
             provider="SimpleMailProvider" profile="Default" />
         </rules>
         <eventMappings>
```

```
            <!-- Removed for clarity -->
         </eventMappings>
      </healthMonitoring>

   </system.web>
</configuration>
```

In this example, the errors that occur are captured and not only written to the event log, but are also e-mailed to the end users specified in the provider definition. One very interesting point of the `SimpleMailWebEventProvider` is that this class inherits from the `BufferedWebEventProvider` instead of from the `WebEventProvider` as the `EventLogWebEventProvider` does. Inheriting from the `BufferedWebEventProvider` means that you can have the health monitoring system build a collection of error notifications before sending them on. The `<bufferModes>` section defines how the buffering works.

System.Web.Management.TemplatedMailWebEventProvider

The aforementioned `SimpleMailWebEventProvider` does exactly what its name states — it sends out a simple, text-based e-mail. To send out a more artistically crafted e-mail that contains even more information, you can use the `TemplatedMailWebEventProvider`. Just like the `SimpleMailWebEventProvider`, you simply define the provider appropriately in the `<healthMonitoring>` section. The model for this is presented in Listing 12-19.

Listing 12-19: The TemplatedMailWebEventProvider definition

```
<providers>
   <clear />
   <add name="EventLogProvider"
    type="System.Web.Management.EventLogWebEventProvider,
      System.Web,Version=2.0.0.0,Culture=neutral,
      PublicKeyToken=b03f5f7f11d50a3a" />
   <add name="TemplatedMailProvider"
    type="System.Web.Management.TemplatedMailWebEventProvider,
      System.Web, Version=2.0.0.0, Culture=neutral,
      PublicKeyToken=b03f5f7f11d50a3a"
    template="../mailtemplates/errornotification.aspx"
    from="website@company.com"
    to="admin@company.com"
    cc="adminLevel2@company.com
    bcc="director@company.com"
    bodyHeader="Warning!"
    bodyFooter="Please investigate ASAP."
    subjectPrefix="Action required."
    buffer="true"
    bufferMode="Website Error Notification"
    maxEventLength="4096"
    maxMessagesPerNotification="1" />
</providers>
```

The big difference between this provider declaration and the `SimpleMailWebEventProvider` is shown in bold in Listing 12-19. The `TemplatedMailWebEventProvider` has a `template` attribute that specifies the location of the template to use for the e-mail that is created and sent from the health monitoring system.

Again, details on using the templated e-mail notification in the health monitoring system appear in Chapter 33.

System.Web.Management.SqlWebEventProvider

In many instances, you may want to write to disk when you are trapping and recording the Web events that occur in your application. The `EventLogWebEventProvider` is an excellent provider because it writes these Web events to the Windows event log on your behalf. However, in some instances, you may want to write these Web events to disk elsewhere. In this case, a good alternative is writing these Web events to SQL Server instead (or even in addition to the writing to an event log).

Writing to SQL Server gives you some benefits over writing to the Windows event log. When your application is running in a Web farm, you might want all the errors that occur across the farm to be written to a single location. In this case, it makes sense to write all Web events that are trapped via the health monitoring system to a SQL Server instance to which all the servers in the Web farm can connect.

By default, the `SqlWebEventProvider` (like the other SQL Server-based providers covered so far in this chapter) uses SQL Server Express Edition as its underlying database. To connect to the full-blown version of SQL Server instead, you need a defined connection as shown in Listing 12-20.

Listing 12-20: The LocalSql2005Server defined instance

```
<configuration>

    <connectionStrings>
       <add name="LocalSql2005Server"
        connectionString="Data Source=127.0.0.1;Integrated Security=SSPI" />
    </connectionStrings>

</configuration>
```

With this connection in place, the next step is to use this connection in your `SqlWebEventProvider` declaration in the `web.config` file. This is illustrated in Listing 12-21.

Listing 12-21: Writing Web events to SQL Server 2005 using the SqlWebEventProvider

```
<configuration>
   <system.web>

      <healthMonitoring>

         <!-- Other nodes removed for clarity -->

         <providers>
            <clear />
            <add name="SqlWebEventProvider"
             type="System.Web.Management.SqlWebEventProvider,System.Web"
             connectionStringName="LocalSql2005Server"
             maxEventDetailsLength="1073741823"
             buffer="true"
             bufferMode="SQL Analysis" />
         </providers>
```

```
    </healthMonitoring>

  </system.web>
</configuration>
```

Events are now recorded in SQL Server 2005 on your behalf. The nice thing about the `SqlWebEventProvider` is that, as with the `SimpleMailWebEventProvider` and the `TemplatedMailWebEventProvider`, the `SqlWebEventProvider` inherits from the `BufferedWebEventProvider`. This means that the Web events can be written in batches as opposed to one by one. This is done by using the `buffer` and `bufferMode` attributes in the provider declaration. It works in conjunction with the settings applied in the `<bufferModes>` section of the `<healthMonitoring>` declarations.

System.Web.Management.TraceWebEventProvider

One method of debugging an ASP.NET application is to use the tracing capability built into the system. Tracing enables you to view details on the request, application state, cookies, the control tree, the form collection, and more. Outputting Web events to the trace output is done via the `TraceWebEventProvider` object. Setting the `TraceWebEventProvider` instance in a configuration file is illustrated in Listing 12-22.

Listing 12-22: Writing Web events to the trace output using TraceWebEventProvider

```
<configuration>
  <system.web>

    <healthMonitoring>

      <!-- Other nodes removed for clarity -->

      <providers>
        <clear />
        <add name="TraceWebEventProvider"
         type="System.Web.Management.TraceWebEventProvider,System.Web"
         maxEventLength="4096"
         maxMessagesPerNotification="1" />
      </providers>

    </healthMonitoring>

  </system.web>
</configuration>
```

Remember, even with the provider in place, you must assign the provider to the particular errors you are wishing to trap. This is accomplished through the `<rules>` section of the health monitoring system. The `IIsTraceWebEventProvider` is the same except that the tracing information is sent to IIS rather than the ASP.NET tracing system.

System.Web.Management.WmiWebEventProvider

The last provider built into the health monitoring system is the `WmiWebEventProvider`. This provider enables you to map any Web events that come from the health monitoring system to Windows Management Instrumentation (WMI) events. When passed to the WMI subsystem, you can represent the events as objects. This mapping to WMI events is accomplished through the `aspnet.mof` file found at `C:\WINDOWS\Microsoft.NET\Framework\v2.0.50727`.

By default, the `WmiWebEventProvider` is already set up for you, and you simply need to map the Web events you are interested in to the already-declared `WmiWebEventProvider` in the `<rules>` section of the health monitoring declaration. This declaration is documented in `web.config.comments` file in the CONFIG folder of the Microsoft .NET Framework install on your server. This is illustrated in Listing 12-23 (the `WmiWebEventProvider` is presented in bold).

Listing 12-23: The WmiWebEventProvider definition in the web.config.comments file

```
<configuration>
   <system.web>

      <healthMonitoring>

         <!-- Other nodes removed for clarity -->

         <providers>
            <clear />
            <add name="EventLogProvider"
             type="System.Web.Management.EventLogWebEventProvider,
               System.Web,Version=2.0.0.0,Culture=neutral,
               PublicKeyToken=b03f5f7f11d50a3a" />
            <add connectionStringName="LocalSqlServer"
             maxEventDetailsLength="1073741823" buffer="false"
             bufferMode="Notification" name="SqlWebEventProvider"
             type="System.Web.Management.SqlWebEventProvider,
               System.Web,Version=2.0.0.0,Culture=neutral,
               PublicKeyToken=b03f5f7f11d50a3a" />
            <add name="WmiWebEventProvider"
             type="System.Web.Management.WmiWebEventProvider,
               System.Web,Version=2.0.0.0,Culture=neutral,
               PublicKeyToken=b03f5f7f11d50a3a" />
         </providers>

      </healthMonitoring>

   </system.web>
</configuration>
```

Remember, the wonderful thing about how the health monitoring system uses the provider model is that it permits more than a single provider for the Web events that the system traps.

Configuration Providers

A wonderful feature of ASP.NET 3.5 is that it enables you to actually encrypt sections of your configuration files. You are able to encrypt defined ASP.NET sections of the `web.config` file as well as custom sections that you have placed in the file yourself. This is an ideal way of keeping sensitive configuration information away from the eyes of everyone who peruses the file repository of your application.

By default, ASP.NET 3.5 provides two possible configuration providers out of the box. These providers are defined in the following list:

- `System.Configuration.DpapiProtectedConfigurationProvider`: Provides you with the capability to encrypt and decrypt configuration sections using the data protection API (DPAPI) that is built into the Windows operating system.

- System.Configuration.RsaProtectedConfigurationProvider: Provides you with the capability to encrypt and decrypt configuration sections using an RSA public-key encryption algorithm.

These two providers used for encryption and decryption of the configuration sections inherit from the ProtectedConfigurationProvider base class. This is illustrated in Figure 12-15.

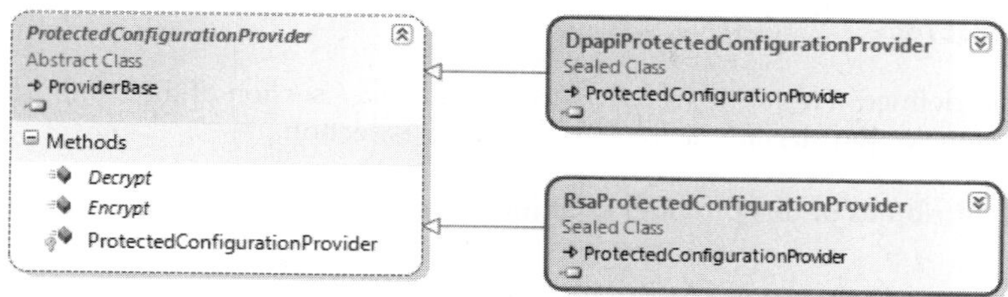

Figure 12-15

You can find information on how to use these providers to encrypt and decrypt configuration sections in Chapter 32.

Next, you review each of these providers.

System.Configuration.DpapiProtectedConfigurationProvider

The DpapiProtectedConfigurationProvider class allows you to encrypt and decrypt configuration sections using the Windows Data Protection API (DPAPI). This provider enables you to perform these encryption and decryption tasks on a per-machine basis. This is not a good provider to use on a Web farm. If you are using protected configuration on your configuration files in a Web farm, you might want to turn your attention to the RsaProtectedConfigurationProvider.

If you look in the machine.config on your server, you see a definition in place for both the DpapiProtectedConfigurationProvider and the RsaProtectedConfigurationProvider. The RsaProtectedConfigurationProvider is set as the default configuration provider. To establish the DpapiProtectedConfigurationProvider as the default provider, you might use the web.config file of your application, or you might change the defaultProvider attribute in the machine.config file for the <configProtectedData> node. Changing it in the web.config is illustrated in Listing 12-24.

Listing 12-24: Using the DpapiProtectedConfigurationProvider in the web.config

```
<configuration>

  <configProtectedData defaultProvider="DataProtectionConfigurationProvider">
    <providers>
      <clear />
      <add name="DataProtectionConfigurationProvider"
       type="System.Configuration.DpapiProtectedConfigurationProvider,
         System.Configuration, Version=2.0.0.0,
         Culture=neutral, PublicKeyToken=b03f5f7f11d50a3a"
```

Continued

```
      description="Uses CryptProtectData and CryptUnProtectData Windows
        APIs to encrypt and decrypt"
      useMachineProtection="true"
      keyEntropy="RandomStringValue" />
    </providers>
  </configProtectedData>

</configuration>
```

The provider is defined within the `<configProtectedData>` section of the configuration file. Note that this configuration section sits *outside* the `< system.web >` section.

The two main attributes of this provider definition are the `useMachineProtection` and the `keyEntropy` attributes.

The `useMachineProtection` attribute by default is set to `true`, meaning that all applications in the server share the same means of encrypting and decrypting configuration sections. This also means that applications residing on the same machine can perform encryption and decryption against each other. Setting the `useMachineProtection` attribute to `false` means that the encryption and decryption are done on an application basis only. This setting also means that you must change the account that the application runs against so it is different from the other applications on the server.

The `keyEntropy` attribute provides a lightweight approach to prevent applications from decrypting each other's configuration sections. The `keyEntropy` attribute can take any random string value to take part in the encryption and decryption processes.

System.Configuration.RsaProtectedConfigurationProvider

The default provider for encrypting and decrypting configuration sections is the `RsaProtectedConfigurationProvider`. You can see this setting in the `machine.config` file on your application server. Code from the `machine.config` file is presented in Listing 12-25.

Listing 12-25: The RsaProtectedConfigurationProvider declaration in the machine.config

```
<configuration>

  <configProtectedData defaultProvider="RsaProtectedConfigurationProvider">
    <providers>
      <add name="RsaProtectedConfigurationProvider"
       type="System.Configuration.RsaProtectedConfigurationProvider,
         System.Configuration, Version=2.0.0.0, Culture=neutral,
         PublicKeyToken=b03f5f7f11d50a3a"
       description="Uses RsaCryptoServiceProvider to encrypt and decrypt"
       keyContainerName="NetFrameworkConfigurationKey" cspProviderName=""
       useMachineContainer="true" useOAEP="false" />
      <add name="DataProtectionConfigurationProvider"
       type="System.Configuration.DpapiProtectedConfigurationProvider,
         System.Configuration, Version=2.0.0.0, Culture=neutral,
         PublicKeyToken=b03f5f7f11d50a3a"
```

```
        description="Uses CryptProtectData and CryptUnProtectData
          Windows APIs to encrypt and decrypt"
        useMachineProtection="true" keyEntropy="" />
    </providers>
  </configProtectedData>

</configuration>
```

The RsaProtectedConfigurationProvider uses Triple-DES encryption to encrypt the specified sections of the configuration file. This provider only has a couple of attributes available to it. These attributes are detailed a bit further on in the chapter.

The keyContainerName attribute is the defined key container that is used for the encryption/decryption process. By default, this provider uses the default key container built into the .NET Framework, but you can easily switch an application to another key container via this attribute.

The cspProviderName attribute is only used if you have specified a custom cryptographic service provider (CSP) to use with the Windows cryptographic API (CAPI). If so, you specify the name of the CSP as the value of the cspProviderName attribute.

The useMachineContainer attribute enables you to specify that you want either a machine-wide or user-specific key container. This attribute is quite similar to the useMachineProtection attribute found in the DpapiProtectedConfigurationProvider.

The useOAEP attribute specifies whether to turn on the Optional Asymmetric Encryption and Padding (OAEP) capability when performing the encryption/decryption process. This is set to false by default only because Windows 2000 does not support this capability. If your application is being hosted on Windows Server 2008, Windows Server 2003, or Windows XP, you can change the value of the useOAEP attribute to true.

The WebParts Provider

Another feature of ASP.NET 3.5 is the capability to build your applications utilizing the new portal framework. The new portal framework provides an outstanding way to build a modular Web site that can be customized with dynamically reapplied settings on a per-user basis. Web Parts are objects in the Portal Framework that the end user can open, close, minimize, maximize, or move from one part of the page to another.

Web parts and the new portal framework are covered in Chapter 17.

The state of these modular components, the Web Parts, must be stored somewhere so they can be re-issued on the next visit for the assigned end user. The single provider available for remembering the state of the Web Parts is System.Web.UI.WebControls.WebParts.SqlPersonalizationProvider, which provides you with the capability to connect the ASP.NET 3.5 portal framework to Microsoft's SQL Server 2000/2005/2008 as well as to the new Microsoft SQL Server Express Edition.

This single class for the portal framework inherits from the PersonalizationProvider base class. This is illustrated in Figure 12-16.

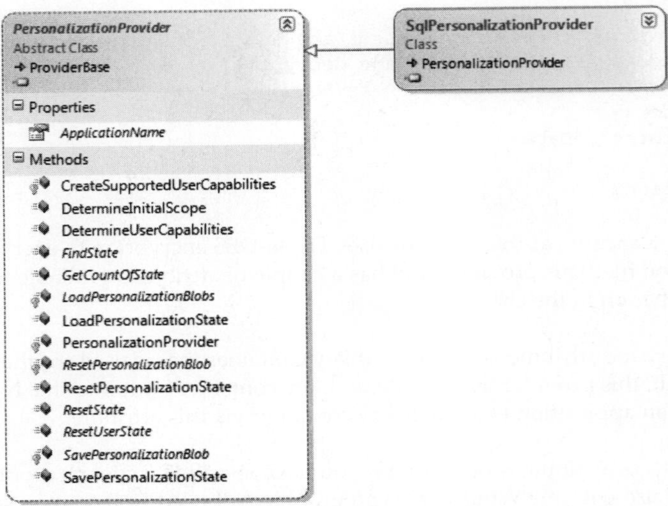

Figure 12-16

You will find the defined `SqlPersonalizationProvider` in the `web.config` file found in the .NET Framework's configuration folder (`C:\WINDOWS\Microsoft.NET\Framework\v2.0.50727\CONFIG`). This definition is presented in Listing 12-26.

Listing 12-26: The SqlPersonalizationProvider definition in the web.config file

```
<configuration>

   <system.web>

        <webParts>
            <personalization>
                <providers>
                    <add connectionStringName="LocalSqlServer"
                     name="AspNetSqlPersonalizationProvider"
                     type="System.Web.UI.WebControls.WebParts.
                       SqlPersonalizationProvider, System.Web,
                       Version=2.0.0.0, Culture=neutral,
                       PublicKeyToken=b03f5f7f11d50a3a" />
                </providers>

                <authorization>
                    <deny users="*" verbs="enterSharedScope" />
                    <allow users="*" verbs="modifyState" />
                </authorization>
            </personalization>

            <transformers>
                <add name="RowToFieldTransformer"
                type="System.Web.UI.WebControls.WebParts.RowToFieldTransformer" />
```

```
                <add name="RowToParametersTransformer"
                type="System.Web.UI.WebControls.WebParts.
                  RowToParametersTransformer" />
            </transformers>
        </webParts>

    </system.web>

</configuration>
```

As you can see the provider declaration is shown in bold in Listing 12-26. As with the other SQL Server–based providers presented in this chapter, this provider works with SQL Server Express Edition by default. To change this to work with SQL Server 2000, 2005, or 2008, you must make a connection to your database within the `<connectionStrings>` section and make an association to this new connection string in the `SqlPersonalizationProvider` declaration using the `connectionStringName` attribute.

Configuring Providers

As you have seen in this chapter, you can easily associate these systems in ASP.NET 3.5 to a large base of available providers. From there, you can also configure the behavior of the associated providers through the attributes exposed from the providers. This can easily be done through either the system-wide configuration files (such as the `machine.config` file) or through more application-specific configuration files (such as the `web.config` file).

You can also just as easily configure providers through the GUI-based configuration systems such as the ASP.NET Web Site Administration Tool or through the new ASP.NET MMC snap-in. Both of these items are covered in detail in Chapter 32. An example of using the ASP.NET MMC snap-in Windows XP to visually configure a provider is presented in Figure 12-17.

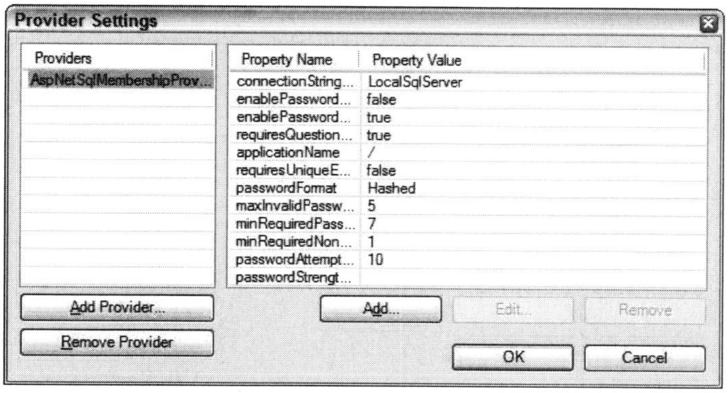

Figure 12-17

From this figure, you can see that you can add and remove providers in the membership system of your application. You can also change the values assigned to individual attributes directly in the GUI.

Summary

This chapter covered the basics of the provider model and what providers are available to you as you start working with the various ASP.NET systems at your disposal. It is important to understand the built-in providers available for each of these systems and how you can fine-tune the behaviors of each provider.

This provider model allows for an additional level of abstraction and permits you to decide for yourself on the underlying data stores to be used for the various systems. For instance, you have the power to decide whether to store the membership and role management information in SQL Server or in Oracle without making any changes to business or presentation logic!

The next chapter shows how to take the provider model to the next level.

13

Extending the Provider Model

The last chapter introduced the provider model found in ASP.NET 3.5 and explained how it is used with the membership and role management systems.

As discussed in the previous chapter, these systems in ASP.NET 3.5 require that some type of user state be maintained for long periods of time. Their time-interval and security requirements for state storage are greater than those for earlier systems that simply used the `Session` object. Out of the box, ASP.NET 3.5 gives you a series of providers to use as the underlying connectors for any data storage needs that arise from state management for these systems.

The providers that come with the default install of the .NET Framework 3.5 include the most common means of state management data storage needed to work with any of the systems. But like most things in .NET, you can customize and extend the providers that are supplied.

This chapter looks at some of the ways to extend the provider model found in ASP.NET 3.5. This chapter also reviews a couple of sample extensions to the provider model. First, however, you look at some of the simpler ways to modify and extend the providers already present in the default install of .NET 3.5.

Providers Are One Tier in a Larger Architecture

Remember from the previous chapter that providers allow you to define the data-access tier for many of the systems in ASP.NET 3.5. They also enable you to define your core business logic implementation on how the data is manipulated or handled. They enable you to use the various controls and APIs that compose these systems in a uniform manner regardless of the underlying data storage method of the provider. The provider model also allows you to easily swap one provider for another without affecting the underlying controls and API that are interacting with the provider. This model is presented in Figure 13-1.

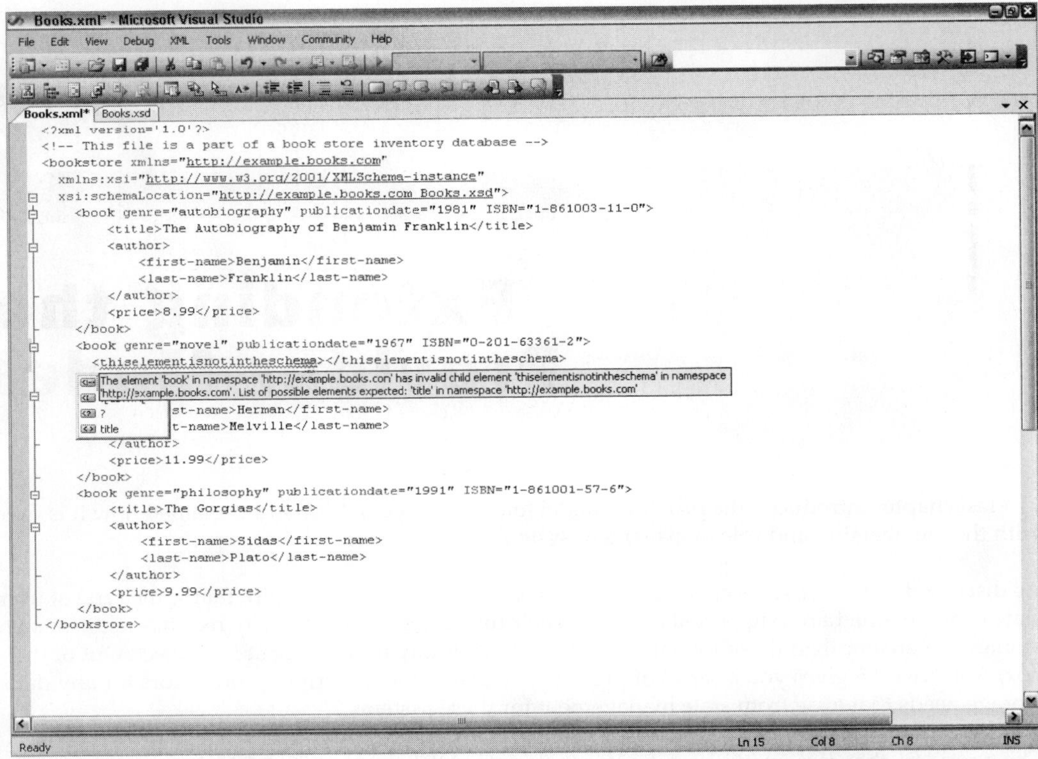

Figure 13-1

From this diagram, you can see that both the controls utilized in the membership system, as well as the Membership API, use the defined provider. Changing the underlying provider does not change the controls or the API, but you can definitely modify how these items behave (as you will see shortly). You can also simply change the location where the state management required by these items is stored. Changing the underlying provider, in this case, does not produce any change whatsoever in the controls or the API; instead, their state management data points are simply rerouted to another data store type.

Modifying Through Attribute-Based Programming

Probably the easiest way to modify the behaviors of the providers built into the .NET Framework 3.5 is through attribute-based programming. In ASP.NET 3.5, you can apply quite advanced behavior modification through attribute usage. You can apply both the server controls and the settings in the various application configuration files. Using the definitions of the providers found in either the `machine.config` files or within the root `web.config` file, you can really change provider behavior. This chapter gives you an example of how to modify the `SqlMembershipProvider`.

Simpler Password Structures Through the SqlMembershipProvider

When you create users with the `SqlMembershipProvider` instance, whether you are using SQL Server Express or Microsoft's SQL Server 2000/2005/2008, notice that the password required to create a user is a semi-strong password. This is evident when you create a user through the ASP.NET Web Site Administration Tool, as illustrated in Figure 13-2.

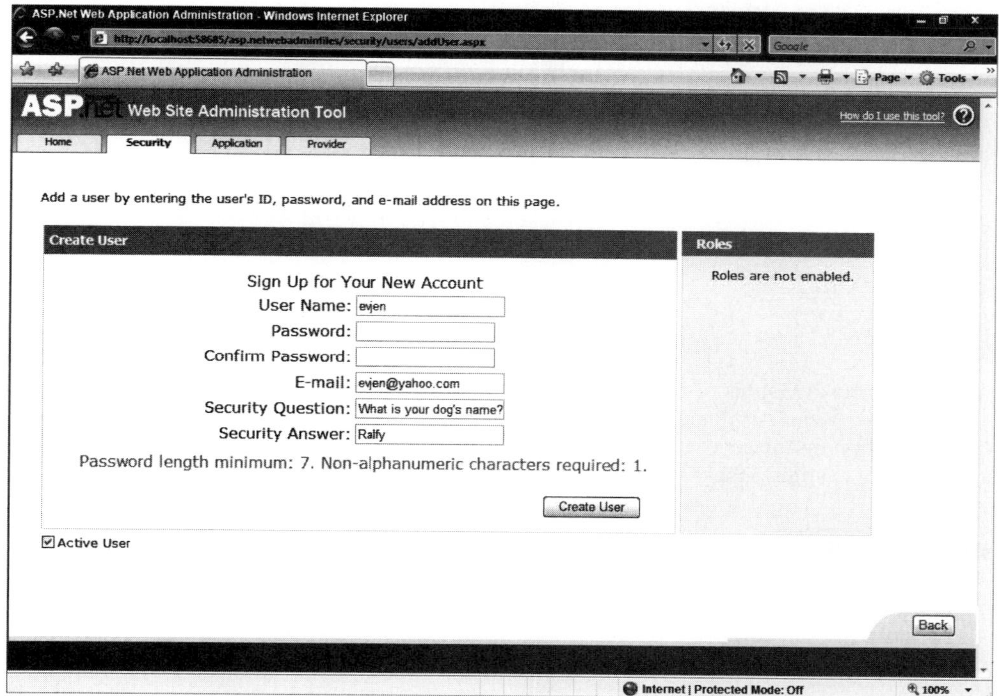

Figure 13-2

On this screen, I attempted to enter a password and was notified that the password did not meet the application's requirements. Instead, I was warned that the minimum password length is seven characters and that at least one non-alphanumeric character is required. This means that a password such as *Bubbles!* is what is required. This kind of behavior is specified by the membership provider and not by the controls or the API used in the membership system. You find the definition of the requirements in the `machine.config.comments` file located at `C:\WINDOWS\Microsoft.NEt\Framework\v20.50727\CONFIG`. This definition is presented in Listing 13-1.

Listing 13-1: The SqlMembershipProvider instance declaration

```
<configuration>
   <system.web>
       <membership defaultProvider="AspNetSqlMembershipProvider"
```

Continued

```
            userIsOnlineTimeWindow="15" hashAlgorithmType="" >
              <providers>
                  <clear />
                  <add connectionStringName="LocalSqlServer"
                    enablePasswordRetrieval="false"
                    enablePasswordReset="true"
                    requiresQuestionAndAnswer="true"
                    applicationName="/"
                    requiresUniqueEmail="false"
                    passwordFormat="Hashed"
                    maxInvalidPasswordAttempts="5"
                    minRequiredPasswordLength="7"
                    minRequiredNonalphanumericCharacters="1"
                    passwordAttemptWindow="10"
                    passwordStrengthRegularExpression=""
                    name="AspNetSqlMembershipProvider"
                    type="System.Web.Security.SqlMembershipProvider,
                       System.Web, Version=2.0.0.0, Culture=neutral,
                       PublicKeyToken=b03f5f7f11d50a3a" />
              </providers>
          </membership>
      </system.web>
  </configuration>
```

Looking over the attributes of this provider, notice the `minRequiredPasswordLength` and the `minRequiredNonalphanumericCharacters` attributes define this behavior. To change this behavior across every application on the server, you simply change these values in this file. The author would, however, suggest simply changing these values in your application's `web.config` file, as shown in Listing 13-2.

Listing 13-2: Changing attribute values in the web.config

```
<configuration>

  <system.web>

      <authentication mode="Forms" />

      <membership>
        <providers>
          <clear />
          <add name="AspNetSqlMembershipProvider"
           type="System.Web.Security.SqlMembershipProvider,
             System.Web, Version=2.0.0.0, Culture=neutral,
             PublicKeyToken=b03f5f7f11d50a3a"
           connectionStringName="LocalSqlServer"
           enablePasswordRetrieval="false"
           enablePasswordReset="true"
           requiresQuestionAndAnswer="true"
           requiresUniqueEmail="false"
           passwordFormat="Hashed"
           maxInvalidPasswordAttempts="5"</b>
           minRequiredPasswordLength="4"
           minRequiredNonalphanumericCharacters="0"
```

```
            passwordAttemptWindow="10" />
        </providers>
      </membership>

  </system.web>

</configuration>
```

In this example, the password requirements are changed through the `minRequiredPasswordLength` and `minRequiredNonalphanumericCharacters` attributes. In this case, the minimum length allowed for a password is four characters, and none of those characters is required to be non-alphanumeric (for example, a special character such as `!`, `$`, or `#`).

Redefining a provider in the application's `web.config` is a fairly simple process. In the example in Listing 13-2, you can see that the `<membership>` element is quite similar to the same element presented in the `machine.config` file.

You have a couple of options when defining your own instance of the `SqlMembershipProvider`. One approach, as presented in Listing 13-2, is to redefine the named instance of the `SqlMembershipProvider` that is defined in the `machine.config` file (`AspNetSqlMembershipProvider`, the value from the name attribute in the provider declaration). If you take this approach, you must *clear* the previous defined instance of `AspNetSqlMembershipProvider`. You must redefine the `AspNetSqlMembershipProvider` using the `< clear / >` node within the `<providers>` section. Failure to do so causes an error to be thrown stating that this provider name is already defined.

After you have cleared the previous instance of `AspNetSqlMembershipProvider`, you redefine this provider using the `<add>` element. In the case of Listing 13-2, you can see that the password requirements are redefined with the use of new values for the `minRequiredPasswordLength` and the `minRequiredNonalphanumericCharacters` attributes (shown in bold).

The other approach to defining your own instance of the `SqlMembershipProvider` is to give the provider defined in the `<add>` element a unique value for the `name` attribute. If you take this approach, you must specify this new named instance as the default provider of the membership system using the `defaultProvider` attribute. This approach is presented in Listing 13-3.

Listing 13-3: Defining your own named instance of the SqlMembershipProvider

```
<membership defaultProvider="MyVeryOwnAspNetSqlMembershipProvider">
   <providers>
      <add name="MyVeryOwnAspNetSqlMembershipProvider"
       type="System.Web.Security.SqlMembershipProvider,
         System.Web, Version=2.0.0.0, Culture=neutral,
         PublicKeyToken=b03f5f7f11d50a3a"
       connectionStringName="LocalSqlServer"
       enablePasswordRetrieval="false"
       enablePasswordReset="true"
       requiresQuestionAndAnswer="true"
       requiresUniqueEmail="false"
       passwordFormat="Hashed"
       maxInvalidPasswordAttempts="5"
       minRequiredPasswordLength="4"
       minRequiredNonalphanumericCharacters="0"
       passwordAttemptWindow="10" />
   </providers>
</membership>
```

In this case, the SqlMembershipProvider instance in the machine.config file (defined under the AspNetSqlMembershipProvider name) is not even redefined. Instead, a completely new named instance (MyVeryOwnAspNetSqlMembershipProvider) is defined here in the web.config.

Stronger Password Structures Through the SqlMembershipProvider

Next, this chapter shows you how to actually make the password structures a little more complicated. You can, of course, accomplish this task in a couple of ways. One approach is to use the same minRequiredPasswordLength and minRequiredNonalphanumericCharacters attributes (as shown earlier) to make the password meet a required length (longer passwords usually mean more secure passwords) and to make the password contain a certain number of non-alphanumeric characters (this also makes for a more secure password).

Another option is to use the passwordStrengthRegularExpression attribute. If the minRequiredPasswordLength and the minRequiredNonalphanumericCharacters attributes cannot give you the password structure you are searching for, then using the passwordStrengthRegularExpression attribute is your next best alternative.

For an example of using this attribute, suppose you require that the user's password is his or her U.S. Social Security number. You can then define your provider as shown in Listing 13-4.

Listing 13-4: A provider instance in the web.config to change the password structure

```
<configuration>

   <system.web>

      <authentication mode="Forms" />

      <membership>
        <providers>
          <clear />
          <add name="AspNetSqlMembershipProvider"
           type="System.Web.Security.SqlMembershipProvider,
             System.Web, Version=2.0.0.0, Culture=neutral,
             PublicKeyToken=b03f5f7f11d50a3a"
           connectionStringName="LocalSqlServer"
           enablePasswordRetrieval="false"
           enablePasswordReset="true"
           requiresQuestionAndAnswer="true"
           requiresUniqueEmail="false"
           passwordFormat="Hashed"
           maxInvalidPasswordAttempts="5"
           passwordAttemptWindow="10"
           passwordStrengthRegularExpression="\d{3}-\d{2}-\d{4}" />
        </providers>
      </membership>

   </system.web>

</configuration>
```

Instead of using the `minRequiredPasswordLength` and the `minRequiredNonalphanumericCharacters` attributes, the `passwordStrengthRegularExpression` attribute is used and given a value of `\d{3}-\d{2}-\d{4}`. This regular expression means that the password should have three digits followed by a dash or hyphen, followed by two digits and another dash or hyphen, finally followed by four digits.

The lesson here is that you have many ways to modify the behaviors of the providers already available in the .NET Framework 3.5 install. You can adapt a number of providers built into the framework to suit your needs by using attribute-based programming. The `SqlMembershipProvider` example demonstrated this, and you can just as easily make similar types of modifications to any of the other providers.

Examining ProviderBase

All the providers derive in some fashion from the class, `ProviderBase`, found in the `System.Configuration.Provider` namespace. `ProviderBase` is an abstract class used to define a base template for inheriting providers. Looking at `ProviderBase`, note that there isn't much to this abstract class, as illustrated in Figure 13-3.

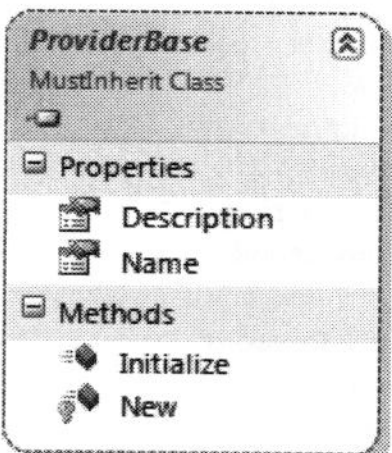

Figure 13-3

As stated, there is not much to this class. It is really just a root class for a provider that exists to allow providers to initialize themselves.

The `Name` property is used to provide a friendly name, such as AspNetSqlRoleProvider. The `Description` property is used to enable a textual description of the provider, which can then be used later by any administration tools. The main item in the `ProviderBase` class is the `Initialize()` method. The constructor for `Initialize()` is presented here:

```
public virtual void Initialize(string name,
   System.Collections.Specialized.NameValueCollection config);
```

Note the two parameters to the `Initialize()` method. The first is the `name` parameter, which is simply the value assigned to the `name` attribute in the provider declaration in the configuration file. The `config` parameter is of type `NameValueCollection`, which is a collection of name/value pairs. These name/value pairs are the items that are also defined in the provider declaration in the configuration file as all the various attributes and their associated values.

When looking over the providers that are included in the default install of ASP.NET 3.5, note that each of the providers has defined a class you can derive from that implements the `ProviderBase` abstract class. For instance, looking at the model in place for the membership system, you can see a base `MembershipProvider` instance that is inherited in the final `SqlMembershipProvider` declaration. The `MembershipProvider`, however, implements `ProviderBase` itself. This model is presented in Figure 13-4.

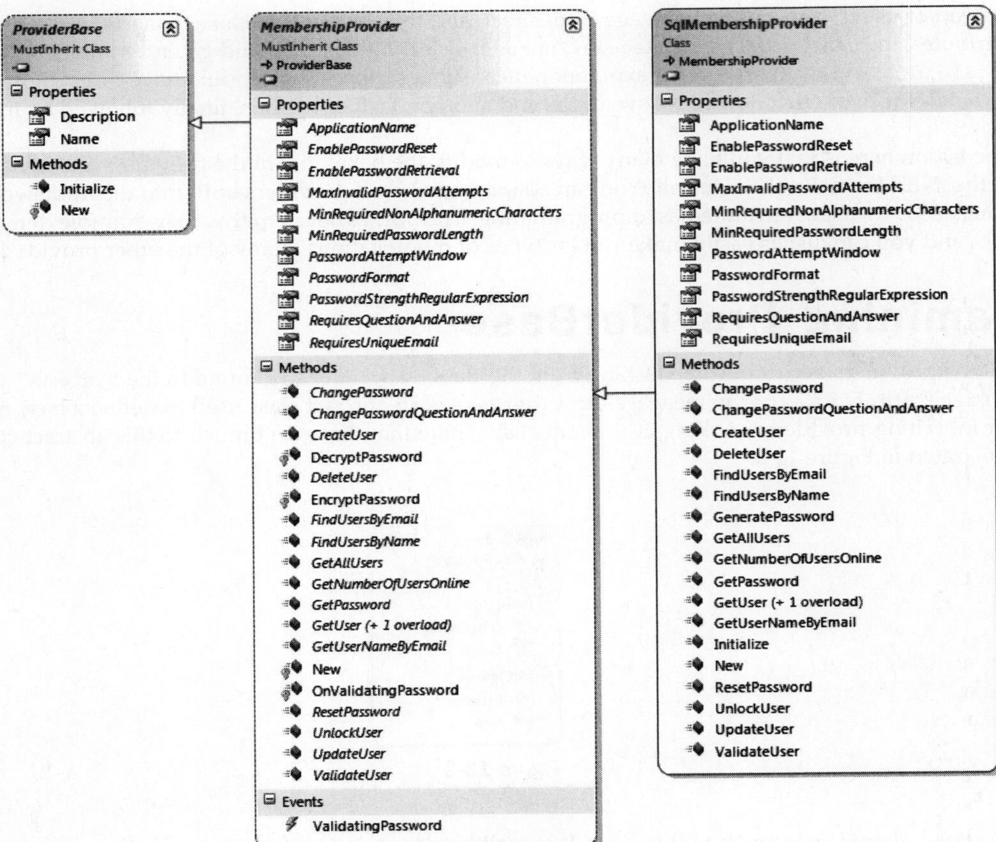

Figure 13-4

Notice that each of the various systems has a specific base provider implementation for you to work with. There really cannot be a single provider that addresses the needs of all the available systems. Looking at Figure 13-4, you can see that the `MembershipProvider` instance exposes some very specific functionality required by the ASP.NET membership system. The methods exposed are definitely not needed by the role management system or the Web parts capability.

With these various base implementations in place, when you are creating your own customizations for working with the ASP.NET membership system, you have a couple of options available to you. First, you can simply create your own provider directly implementing the `ProviderBase` class and working from the ground up. I do not recommend this approach, however, because abstract classes are already in place for you to use with the various systems. So, as I mentioned, you can just implement the `MembershipProvider` instance (a better approach) and work from the model it provides. Finally, if you are working with SQL Server in some capacity and simply want to change the underlying behaviors of this provider, you can inherit from `SqlMembershipProvider` and modify the behavior of the class from this inheritance. Next, this chapter covers the various means of extending the provider model through examples.

Building Your Own Providers

You now examine the process of building your own provider to use within your ASP.NET 3.5 application. Actually, providers are not that difficult to put together (as you will see shortly) and can even be created directly in any of your ASP.NET 3.5 projects. The example demonstrates building a membership provider that works from an XML file. For a smaller Web site, this might be a common scenario. For larger Web sites and Web-based applications, you probably want to use a database of some kind, rather than an XML file, for managing users.

You have a couple of options when building you own membership provider. You can derive from a couple of classes, the `SqlMembershipProvider` class, or the `MembershipProvider` class, to build the functionality you need. You derive from the `SqlMembershipProvider` class only if you want to extend or change the behavior of the membership system as it interacts with SQL. Because the goal here is to build a read-only XML membership provider, deriving from this class is inappropriate. In this case, it is best to base everything on the `MembershipProvider` class.

Creating the CustomProviders Application

For this example, create a new Web site project called CustomProviders in the language of your choice. For this example, you want to build the new membership provider directly in the Web application itself. Another option is to build the provider in a Class Library project and then to reference the generated DLL in your Web project. Either way is fine in the end.

Because you are going to build this directly in the Web site project itself, you create the App_Code folder in your application. This is the location you want to place the class file that you create. The class file is the actual provider in this case.

After the App_Code folder is in place, create a new class in this folder and call the class either `XmlMembershipProvider.vb` or `XmlMembershipProvider.cs`, depending on the language you are using. With this class now in place, have your new `XmlMembershipProvider` class derive from `MembershipProvider`. To accomplish this and to know which methods and properties to override, you can use Visual Studio 2008 to build a skeleton of the class you want to create. You can step through this process starting with the code demonstrated in Listing 13-5.

Listing 13-5: The start of your XmlMembershipProvider class

VB

```
Imports Microsoft.VisualBasic
Imports System.Xml
Imports System.Configuration.Provider
Imports System.Web.Hosting
Imports System.Collections
Imports System.Collections.Generic

Public Class XmlMembershipProvider
    Inherits MembershipProvider

End Class
```

Continued

C#

```
using System;
using System.Web.Hosting;
using System.Web.Security;
using System.Xml;
using System.Collections.Generic;

/// <summary>
/// Summary description for XmlMembershipProvider
/// </summary>
public class XmlMembershipProvider: MembershipProvider
{
 public XmlMembershipProvider()
 {
        //
        // TODO: Add constructor logic here
        //
 }
}
```

You make only a few changes to the basic class, `XmlMembershipProvider`. First, you can see that some extra namespaces are imported into the file. This is done so you can later take advantage of .NET's XML capabilities, generics, and more. Also, notice that this new class, the `XmlMembershipProvider` class, inherits from `MembershipProvider`.

Constructing the Class Skeleton Required

In order to get Visual Studio 2008 to build your class with the appropriate methods and properties, take the following steps (depending on the language you are using). If you are using Visual Basic, all you have to do is press the Enter key. In C#, you first place the cursor on the `MembershipProvider` instance in the document window and then select Edit ➪ IntelliSense ➪ Implement Abstract Class from the Visual Studio menu. After you perform one of these operations, you see the full skeleton of the class in the document window of Visual Studio. Listing 13-6 shows the code that is generated if you are creating a Visual Basic `XmlMembershipProvider` class.

Listing 13-6: Code generated for the XmlMembershipProvider class by Visual Studio

VB (only)

```
Imports Microsoft.VisualBasic
Imports System.Xml
Imports System.Configuration.Provider
Imports System.Web.Hosting
Imports System.Collections
Imports System.Collections.Generic

Public Class XmlMembershipProvider
    Inherits MembershipProvider

    Public Overrides Property ApplicationName() As String
        Get

        End Get
        Set(ByVal value As String)
```

```
        End Set
    End Property

    Public Overrides Function ChangePassword(ByVal username As String, _
      ByVal oldPassword As String, ByVal newPassword As String) As Boolean

    End Function

    Public Overrides Function ChangePasswordQuestionAndAnswer(ByVal username _
      As String, ByVal password As String, ByVal newPasswordQuestion As String, _
      ByVal newPasswordAnswer As String) As Boolean

    End Function

    Public Overrides Function CreateUser(ByVal username As String, _
      ByVal password As String, ByVal email As String, _
      ByVal passwordQuestion As String, ByVal passwordAnswer As String, _
      ByVal isApproved As Boolean, ByVal providerUserKey As Object, _
      ByRef status As System.Web.Security.MembershipCreateStatus) As _
      System.Web.Security.MembershipUser

    End Function

    Public Overrides Function DeleteUser(ByVal username As String, _
      ByVal deleteAllRelatedData As Boolean) As Boolean

    End Function

    Public Overrides ReadOnly Property EnablePasswordReset() As Boolean
        Get

        End Get
    End Property

    Public Overrides ReadOnly Property EnablePasswordRetrieval() As Boolean
        Get

        End Get
    End Property

    Public Overrides Function FindUsersByEmail(ByVal emailToMatch As String, _
      ByVal pageIndex As Integer, ByVal pageSize As Integer, _
      ByRef totalRecords As Integer) As _
      System.Web.Security.MembershipUserCollection

    End Function

    Public Overrides Function FindUsersByName(ByVal usernameToMatch As String, _
      ByVal pageIndex As Integer, ByVal pageSize As Integer, _
      ByRef totalRecords As Integer) As _
      System.Web.Security.MembershipUserCollection

    End Function
```

Continued

```
Public Overrides Function GetAllUsers(ByVal pageIndex As Integer, _
  ByVal pageSize As Integer, ByRef totalRecords As Integer) As _
  System.Web.Security.MembershipUserCollection

End Function

Public Overrides Function GetNumberOfUsersOnline() As Integer

End Function

Public Overrides Function GetPassword(ByVal username As String, _
  ByVal answer As String) As String

End Function

Public Overloads Overrides Function GetUser(ByVal providerUserKey As Object, _
  ByVal userIsOnline As Boolean) As System.Web.Security.MembershipUser

End Function

Public Overloads Overrides Function GetUser(ByVal username As String, _
  ByVal userIsOnline As Boolean) As System.Web.Security.MembershipUser

End Function

Public Overrides Function GetUserNameByEmail(ByVal email As String) As String

End Function

Public Overrides ReadOnly Property MaxInvalidPasswordAttempts() As Integer
    Get

    End Get
End Property

Public Overrides ReadOnly Property MinRequiredNonAlphanumericCharacters() _
  As Integer
    Get

    End Get
End Property

Public Overrides ReadOnly Property MinRequiredPasswordLength() As Integer
    Get

    End Get
End Property

Public Overrides ReadOnly Property PasswordAttemptWindow() As Integer
    Get

    End Get
End Property

Public Overrides ReadOnly Property PasswordFormat() As _
```

```
        System.Web.Security.MembershipPasswordFormat
            Get

            End Get
        End Property

        Public Overrides ReadOnly Property PasswordStrengthRegularExpression() As _
          String
            Get

            End Get
        End Property

        Public Overrides ReadOnly Property RequiresQuestionAndAnswer() As Boolean
            Get

            End Get
        End Property

        Public Overrides ReadOnly Property RequiresUniqueEmail() As Boolean
            Get

            End Get
        End Property

        Public Overrides Function ResetPassword(ByVal username As String, _
          ByVal answer As String) As String

        End Function

        Public Overrides Function UnlockUser(ByVal userName As String) As Boolean

        End Function

        Public Overrides Sub UpdateUser(ByVal user As _
          System.Web.Security.MembershipUser)

        End Sub

        Public Overrides Function ValidateUser(ByVal username As String, _
          ByVal password As String) As Boolean

        End Function
    End Class
```

Wow, that's a lot of code! Although the skeleton is in place, the next step is to build some of the items that will be utilized by the provider that Visual Studio laid out for you — starting with the XML file that holds all the users allowed to access the application.

Creating the XML User Data Store

Because this is an XML membership provider, the intent is to read the user information from an XML file rather than from a database such as SQL Server. For this reason, you must define the XML file structure that the provider can make use of. The structure that we are using for this example is illustrated in Listing 13-7.

Listing 13-7: The XML file used to store usernames and passwords

```
<?xml version="1.0" encoding="utf-8" ?>
<Users>
  <User>
    <Username>BillEvjen</Username>
    <Password>Bubbles</Password>
    <Email>evjen@yahoo.com</Email>
    <DateCreated>11/10/2008</DateCreated>
  </User>
  <User>
    <Username>ScottHanselman</Username>
    <Password>YabbaDabbaDo</Password>
    <Email>123@msn.com</Email>
    <DateCreated>10/20/2008</DateCreated>
  </User>
  <User>
    <Username>DevinRader</Username>
    <Password>BamBam</Password>
    <Email>456@msn.com</Email>
    <DateCreated>9/23/2008</DateCreated>
  </User>
</Users>
```

This XML file holds only three user instances, all of which include the username, password, e-mail address, and the date on which the user is created. Because this is a data file, you should place this file in the `App_Data` folder of your ASP.NET application. You can name the file anything you want; but in this case, we have named the file `UserDatabase.xml`.

Later, this chapter reviews how to grab these values from the XML file when validating users.

Defining the Provider Instance in the web.config File

As you have seen in the last chapter on providers, you define a provider and its behavior in a configuration file (such as the `machine.config` or the `web.config` file). Because this provider is being built for a single application instance, this example defines the provider in the `web.config` file of the application.

The default provider is the `SqlMembershipProvider`, and this is defined in the `machine.config` file on the server. For this example, you must override this setting and establish a new default provider. The XML membership provider declaration in the `web.config` should appear as shown in Listing 13-8.

Listing 13-8: Defining the XmlMembershipProvider in the web.config file

```
<configuration>
   <system.web>

      <authentication mode="Forms"/>

      <membership defaultProvider="XmlFileProvider">
         <providers>
            <add name="XmlFileProvider" type="XmlMembershipProvider"
```

```
            xmlUserDatabaseFile="~/App_Data/UserDatabase.xml"/>
        </providers>
    </membership>

  </system.web>
</configuration>
```

In this listing, you can see that the default provider is defined as the `XmlFileProvider`. Because this provider name will not be found in any of the parent configuration files, you must define `XmlFileProvider` in the `web.config` file.

Using the `defaultProvider` attribute, you can define the name of the provider you want to use for the membership system. In this case, it is `XmlFileProvider`. Then you define the `XmlFileProvider` instance using the `<add>` element within the `<providers>` section. The `<add>` element gives a name for the provider — `XmlFileProvider`. It also points to the class (or type) of the provider. In this case, it is the skeleton class you just created — `XmlMembershipProvider`. These are the two most important attributes.

Beyond this, you can create any attribute in your provider declaration that you wish. Whatever type of provider you create, however, you must address the attributes in your provider and act upon the values that are provided with the attributes. In the case of the simple `XmlMembershipProvider`, only a single custom attribute exists — `xmlUserDatabaseFile`. This attribute points to the location of the user database XML file. For this provider, it is an optional attribute. If you do not provide a value for `xmlUserDatabaseFile`, you have a default value. In Listing 13-8, however, you can see that a value is indeed provided for the XML file to use. Note that the `xmlUserDatabaseFile` is simply the filename and nothing more.

One attribute is not shown in the example, but is an allowable attribute because it is addressed in the `XmlMemberhipProvider` class. This attribute, the `applicationName` attribute, points to the application that the `XmlMembershipProvider` instance should address. The default value, which you can also place in this provider declaration within the configuration file, is illustrated here:

```
applicationName="/"
```

Not Implementing Methods and Properties of the MembershipProvider Class

Now turn your attention to the `XmlMembershipProvider` class. The next step is to implement any methods or properties needed by the provider. You are not required to make any *real* use of the methods contained in this skeleton; instead, you can simply build-out only the methods you are interested in working with. For instance, if you do not allow for programmatic access to change passwords (and, in turn, the controls that use this programmatic access), you either want not to initiate an action or to throw an exception if someone tries to implement this method. This is illustrated in Listing 13-9.

Listing 13-9: Not implementing one of the available methods by throwing an exception

VB

```
Public Overrides Function ChangePassword(ByVal username As String, _
  ByVal oldPassword As String, ByVal newPassword As String) As Boolean
```

Continued

```
        Throw New NotSupportedException()
End Function
```

C#

```
public override bool ChangePassword(string username,
  string oldPassword, string newPassword)
{
   throw new NotSupportedException();
}
```

In this case, a `NotSupportedException` is thrown if the `ChangePassword()` method is invoked. If you do not want to throw an actual exception, you can simply return a `false` value and not take any other action, as shown in Listing 13-10 (although this might annoy a developer who is trying to implement this and does not understand the underlying logic of the method).

Listing 13-10: Not implementing one of the available methods by returning a false value

VB

```
Public Overrides Function ChangePassword(ByVal username As String, _
  ByVal oldPassword As String, ByVal newPassword As String) As Boolean
        Return False
End Function
```

C#

```
public override bool ChangePassword(string username,
  string oldPassword, string newPassword)
{
   return false;
}
```

This chapter does not address every possible action you can take with `XmlMembershipProvider` and, therefore, you may want to work through the available methods and properties of the derived `MembershipProvider` instance and make the necessary changes to any items that you won't be using.

Implementing Methods and Properties of the MembershipProvider Class

Now it is time to implement some of the methods and properties available from the `MembershipProvider` class in order to get the `XmlMembershipProvider` class to work. The first items are some private variables that can be utilized by multiple methods throughout the class. These variable declarations are presented in Listing 13-11.

Listing 13-11: Declaring some private variables in the XmlMembershipProvider class

VB

```
Public Class XmlMembershipProvider
    Inherits MembershipProvider

    Private _AppName As String
```

```
    Private _MyUsers As Dictionary(Of String, MembershipUser)
    Private _FileName As String

    ' Code removed for clarity

End Class
```

C#

```
public class XmlMembershipProvider : MembershipProvider
{
    private string _AppName;
    private Dictionary<string, MembershipUser> _MyUsers;
    private string _FileName;

   ' Code removed for clarity

}
```

The variables being declared are items needed by multiple methods in the class. The `_AppName` variable defines the application using the XML membership provider. In all cases, it is the local application. You also want to place all the members found in the XML file into a collection of some type. This example uses a dictionary generic type named `_MyUsers`. Finally, this example points to the file to use with the `_FileName` variable.

The ApplicationName Property

After the private variables are in place, the next step is to define the `ApplicationName` property. You now make use of the first private variable — `AppName`. The property definition of `ApplicationName` is presented in Listing 13-12.

Listing 13-12: Defining the ApplicationName property

VB

```
Public Overrides Property ApplicationName() As String
   Get
      Return _AppName
   End Get
   Set(ByVal value As String)
      _AppName = value
   End Set
End Property
```

C#

```
public override string ApplicationName
{
   get
   {
      return _AppName;
   }
   set
   {
      _AppName = value;
   }
}
```

Now that the `ApplicationName` property is defined and in place, you next retrieve the values defined in the `web.config` file's provider declaration (`XmlFileProvider`).

Extending the Initialize() Method

You now extend the `Initialize()` method so that it reads in the custom attribute and its associated values as defined in the provider declaration in the `web.config` file. Look through the class skeleton of your `XmlMembershipProvider` class, and note that no `Initialize()` method is included in the list of available items.

The `Initialize()` method is invoked when the provider is first initialized. It is not a requirement to override this method and, therefore, you won't see it in the declaration of the class skeleton. To put the `Initialize()` method in place within the `XmlMembershipProvider` class, simply type `Public Overrides` (for Visual Basic) or `public override` (for C#) in the class. You are then presented with the `Initialize()` method via IntelliSense, as shown in Figure 13-5.

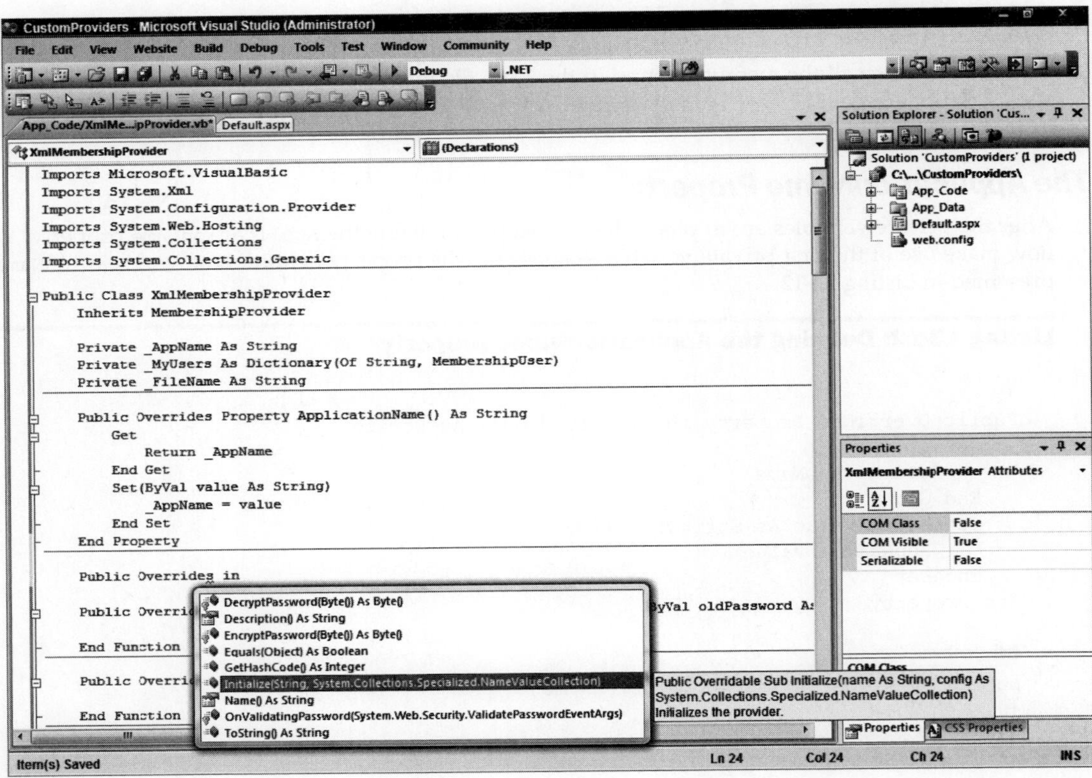

Figure 13-5

Placing the `Initialize()` method in your class in this manner is quite easy. Select the `Initialize()` method from the list in IntelliSense and press the Enter key. This gives you a base construction of the method in your code. This is shown in Listing 13-13.

Listing 13-13: The beginnings of the Initialize method

VB

```
Public Overrides Sub Initialize(ByVal name As String, _
   ByVal config As System.Collections.Specialized.NameValueCollection)
        MyBase.Initialize(name, config)
End Sub
```

C#

```
public override void Initialize(string name,
  System.Collections.Specialized.NameValueCollection config)
{
   base.Initialize(name, config);
}
```

The `Initialize()` method takes two parameters. The first parameter is the name of the parameter. The second is the name/value collection from the provider declaration in the `web.config` file. This includes all the attributes and their values, such as the `xmlUserDatabaseFile` attribute and the value of the name of the XML file that holds the user information. Using `config`, you can gain access to these defined values.

For the `XmlFileProvider` instance, you address the `applicationName` attribute and the `xmlUserDatabaseFile` attribute. You do this as shown in Listing 13-14.

Listing 13-14: Extending the Initialize() method

VB

```
Public Overrides Sub Initialize(ByVal name As String, _
  ByVal config As System.Collections.Specialized.NameValueCollection)
        MyBase.Initialize(name, config)

        _AppName = config("applicationName")

        If (String.IsNullOrEmpty(_AppName)) Then
            _AppName = "/"
        End If

        _FileName = config("xmlUserDatabaseFile")

        If (String.IsNullOrEmpty(_FileName)) Then
            _FileName = "~/App_Data/Users.xml"
        End If
End Sub
```

C#

```
public override void Initialize(string name,
  System.Collections.Specialized.NameValueCollection config)
{
   base.Initialize(name, config);

   _AppName = config["applicationName"];
```

Continued

```
    if (String.IsNullOrEmpty(_AppName))
    {
       _AppName = "/";
    }

    _FileName = config["xmlUserDatabaseFile"];

    if (String.IsNullOrEmpty(_FileName))
    {
       _FileName = "~/App_Data/Users.xml";
    }
}
```

Besides performing the initialization using `MyBase.Initialize()`, you retrieve both the `applicationName` and `xmlUserDatabaseFile` attribute's values using `config`. In all cases, you should first check whether the value is either null or empty. You use the `String.IsNullOrEmpty()` method to assign default values if the attribute is missing for the provider declaration in the `web.config` file. In the case of the `XmlFileProvider` instance, this is, in fact, the case. The `applicationName` attribute in the `XmlFileProvider` declaration is actually not declared and, for this reason, the default value of `/` is actually assigned as the value.

In the case of the `xmlUserDatabaseFile` attribute, a value is provided. If no value is provided in the `web.config` file, the provider looks for an XML file named `Users.xml` found in the App_Data folder.

Validating Users

One of the more important features of the membership provider is that it validates users (it authenticates them). The validation of users is accomplished through the ASP.NET Login server control. This control, in turn, makes use of the `Membership.ValidateUser()` method that ends up using the `ValidateUser()` method in the `XmlMembershipProvider` class.

Now that the `Initialize()` method and private variables are in place, you can start giving the provider some functionality. The implementation of the `ValidateUser()` method is presented in Listing 13-15.

Listing 13-15: Implementing the ValidateUser() method

VB

```
Public Overrides Function ValidateUser(ByVal username As String, _
  ByVal password As String) As Boolean

    If (String.IsNullOrEmpty(username) Or String.IsNullOrEmpty(password)) Then
       Return False
    End If

    Try
       ReadUserFile()

       Dim mu As MembershipUser

       If (_MyUsers.TryGetValue(username.ToLower(), mu)) Then
          If (mu.Comment = password) Then
```

```
                Return True
            End If
        End If

        Return False
    Catch ex As Exception
        Throw New Exception(ex.Message.ToString())
    End Try
End Function
```

C#

```
public override bool ValidateUser(string username, string password)
{
    if (String.IsNullOrEmpty(username) || String.IsNullOrEmpty(password))
    {
        return false;
    }

    try
    {
        ReadUserFile();

        MembershipUser mu;

        if (_MyUsers.TryGetValue(username.ToLower(), out mu))
        {
            if (mu.Comment == password)
            {
                return true;
            }
        }

        return false;
    }
    catch (Exception ex)
    {
        throw new Exception(ex.Message.ToString());
    }
}
```

Looking over the `ValidateUser()` method, you can see that it takes two parameters, the username and the password of the user (both of type `String`). The value returned from `ValidateUser()` is a `Boolean` — just a `True` or `False` value to inform of the success for failure of the validation process.

One of the first operations performed in the `ValidateUser()` method is a check to determine whether either the username or the password is missing from the invocation. If one of these items is missing in the request, a `False` value is returned.

From there, a `Try Catch` is done to check if the user and the user's password are included in the XML file. The process of getting the user information out of the XML file and into the `MyUsers` variable is done by the `ReadUserFile()` method. This method is described shortly, but the important concept is that the `_MyUsers` variable is an instance of the `Dictionary` generic class. The key is a lowercase string value of the username, whereas the value is of type `MembershipUser`, a type provided via the membership system.

After the _MyUsers object is populated with all users in the XML file, a MembershipUser instance is created. This object is the output of a TryGetValue operation. The MembershipUser does not contain the password of the user and, for this reason, the ReadUserFile() method makes the user's password the value of the Comment property of the MembershipUser class. If the username is found in the dictionary collection, then the password of that particular MembershipUser instance is compared to the value in the Comment property. The return value from the ValidateUser() method is True if they are found to be the same.

As you can see, this method really is dependent upon the results that come from the ReadUserFile() method, which is covered next.

Building the ReadUserFile() Method

The ReadUserFile() method reads the contents of the XML file that contains all the users for the application. This method is a custom method, and its work is done outside of the ValidateUser() method. This means it can be reused in other methods you might want to implement (such as the GetAllUsers() method). The only job of the ReadUserFile() method is to read the contents of the XML file and place all the users in the _MyUsers variable, as illustrated in Listing 13-16.

Listing 13-16: The ReadUserFile() method to get all the users of the application

VB

```
Private Sub ReadUserFile()
    If (_MyUsers Is Nothing) Then
        SyncLock (Me)
            _MyUsers = New Dictionary(Of String, MembershipUser)()
            Dim xd As XmlDocument = New XmlDocument()
            xd.Load(HostingEnvironment.MapPath(_FileName))
            Dim xnl As XmlNodeList = xd.GetElementsByTagName("User")

            For Each node As XmlNode In xnl
                Dim mu As MembershipUser = New MembershipUser(Name, _
                    node("Username").InnerText, _
                    Nothing, _
                    node("Email").InnerText, _
                    String.Empty, _
                    node("Password").InnerText, _
                    True, _
                    False, _
                    DateTime.Parse(node("DateCreated").InnerText), _
                    DateTime.Now, _
                    DateTime.Now, _
                    DateTime.Now, _
                    DateTime.Now)

                _MyUsers.Add(mu.UserName.ToLower(), mu)
            Next
        End SyncLock
    End If
End Sub
```

C#

```
private void ReadUserFile()
{
      if (_MyUsers == null)
      {
        lock (this)
        {
         _MyUsers = new Dictionary<string, MembershipUser>();
         XmlDocument xd = new XmlDocument();
         xd.Load(HostingEnvironment.MapPath(_FileName));
         XmlNodeList xnl = xd.GetElementsByTagName("User");

         foreach (XmlNode node in xnl)
         {
            MembershipUser mu = new MembershipUser(Name,
               node["Username"].InnerText,
               null,
               node["Email"].InnerText,
               String.Empty,
               node["Password"].InnerText,
               true,
               false,
               DateTime.Parse(node["DateCreated"].InnerText),
               DateTime.Now,
               DateTime.Now,
               DateTime.Now,
               DateTime.Now);

               _MyUsers.Add(mu.UserName.ToLower(), mu);
         }
      }
   }
}
```

The first action of the `ReadUserFile()` method is to place a lock on the action that is going to occur in the thread being run. This is a unique feature in ASP.NET. When you are writing your own providers, be sure you use thread-safe code. For most items that you write in ASP.NET, such as an HttpModule or an HttpHandler (covered in Chapter 27), you don't need to make them thread-safe. These items may have multiple requests running on multiple threads, and each thread making a request to either the HttpModule or the HttpHandler sees a unique instance of these items.

Unlike an HttpHandler, only one instance of a provider is created and utilized by your ASP.NET application. If there are multiple requests being made to your application, all these threads are trying to gain access to the single provider instance contained in the application. Because more than one request might be coming into the provider instance at the same time, you should create the provider in a thread-safe manner. This can be accomplished by using a lock operation when performing tasks such as a file I/O operation. This is the reason for the use of the `SyncLock` (for Visual Basic) and the `lock` (for C#) statements in the `ReadUserFile()` method.

The advantage to all of this, however, is that a single instance of the provider is running in your application. After the `_MyUsers` object is populated with the contents of the XML file, you have no need to repopulate the object. The provider instance doesn't just disappear after a response is issued to the requestor. Instead, the provider instance is contained in memory and utilized for multiple requests. This is the reason for checking whether `_MyUsers` contains any values before reading the XML file.

If you find that `_MyUsers` is null, use the `XmlDocument` object to get at every `<User>` element in the document. For each `<User>` element in the document, the values are assigned to a `MembershipUser` instance. The `MembershipUser` object takes the following arguments:

```
MembershipUser(
    providerName As String, _
    name As String, _
    providerUserKey As Object, _
    email As String, _
    passwordQuestion As String, _
    comment As String, _
    isApproved As Boolean, _
    isLockedOut As Boolean, _
    creationDate As DateTime, _
    lastLoginDate As DateTime, _
    lastActivityDate As DateTime, _
    lastPasswordChangedDate As DateTime, _
    lastLockoutDate As DateTime)
```

Although you do not provide a value for each and every item in this construction, the values that are really needed are pulled from the XML file using the `XmlNode` object. Then after the `MembershipUser` object is populated with everything you want, the next job is to add this to the `_MyUsers` object using the following:

```
_MyUsers.Add(mu.UserName.ToLower(), mu)
```

With the `ReadUserFile()` method in place, as stated, you can now use this in more than the `ValidateUser()` method. Remember that once the `_MyUsers` collection is populated, you don't need to repopulate the collection again. Instead, it remains in place for the other methods to make use of. Next, this chapter looks at using what has been demonstrated so far in your ASP.NET application.

Using the XmlMembershipProvider for User Login

If you have made it this far in the example, you do not need to do much more to make use of the `XmlMembershipProvider` class. At this point, you should have the XML data file in place that is a representation of all the users of your application (this XML file was presented in Listing 13-7) as well as the `XmlFileProvider` declaration in the `web.config` file of your application (the changes to the `web.config` file are presented in Listing 13-8). Of course, another necessary item is either the `XmlMembershipProvider.vb` or `.cs` class in the `App_Code` folder of your application. However, if you built the provider as a class library, you want to just make sure the DLL created is referenced correctly in your ASP.NET application (which means the DLL is in the Bin folder). After you have these items in place, it is pretty simple to start using the provider.

For a quick example of this, simply create a `Default.aspx` page that has only the text: `You are authenticated!`

Next, you create a `Login.aspx` page, and you place a single Login server control on the page. You won't need to make any other changes to the `Login.aspx` page besides these. Users can now log in to the application.

For information on the membership system, which includes detailed explanations of the various server controls it offers, visit Chapter 16.

When you have those two files in place within your mini-ASP.NET application, the next step is to make some minor changes to the `web.config` to allow for Forms authentication and to deny all anonymous users to view any of the pages. This bit of code is presented in Listing 13-17.

Listing 13-17: Denying anonymous users to view the application in the web.config file

```
<configuration>
   <system.web>

      <authentication mode="Forms"/>
      <authorization>
         <deny users="?"/>
      </authorization>

      <!-- Other settings removed for clarity -->

   </system.web>
</configuration>
```

Now, run the `Default.aspx` page, and you are immediately directed to the `Login.aspx` page (you should have this file created in your application and it should contain only a single Login server control) where you apply one of the username and password combinations that are present in the XML file. It is as simple as that!

The nice thing with the provider-based model found in ASP.NET 3.5 is that the controls that are working with the providers don't know the difference when these large changes to the underlying provider are made. In this example, you have removed the default `SqlMembershipProvider` and replaced it with a read-only XML provider, and the Login server control is really none the wiser. When the end user clicks the Log In button within the Login server control, the control is still simply making use of the `Membership.ValidateUser()` method, which is working with the `XmlMembershipProvider` that was just created. As you should see by now, this is a powerful model.

Extending Pre-Existing Providers

In addition to building your own providers from one of the base abstract classes such as `Membership-Provider`, another option is to simply extend one of the pre-existing providers that come with ASP.NET.

For instance, you might be interested in using the membership and role management systems with SQL Server but want to change how the default providers (`SqlMembershipProvider` or `SqlRoleProvider`) work under the covers. If you are going to work with an underlying data store that is already utilized by one of the providers available out of the box, then it actually makes a lot more sense to change the behavior of the available provider rather than build a brand-new provider from the ground up.

The other advantage of working from a pre-existing provider is that there is no need to override everything the provider exposes. Instead, if you are interested in changing only a particular behavior of a built-in provider, you might only need to override a couple of the exposed methods and nothing more, making this approach rather simple and quick to achieve in your application.

Next, this chapter looks at extending one of the built-in providers to change the underlying functionality of the provider.

Limiting Role Capabilities with a New LimitedSqlRoleProvider Provider

Suppose you want to utilize the new role management system in your ASP.NET application and have every intention of using a SQL Server backend for the system. Suppose you also want to limit what roles developers can create in their applications, and you want to remove their capability to add users to a particular role in the system.

Instead of building a role provider from scratch from the `RoleProvider` abstract class, it makes more sense to derive your provider from `SqlRoleProvider` and to simply change the behavior of a few methods that deal with the creation of roles and adding users to roles.

For this example, create the provider in your application within the `App_Code` folder as before. In reality, however, you probably want to create a Class Library project if you want to use this provider across your company so that your development teams can use a DLL rather than a modifiable class file.

Within the `App_Code` folder, create a class file called `LimitedSqlRoleProvider.vb` or `.cs`. You want this class to inherit from `SqlRoleProvider`, and this gives you the structure shown in Listing 13-18.

Listing 13-18: The beginnings of the LimitedSqlRoleProvider class

VB

```
Imports Microsoft.VisualBasic
Imports System.Configuration.Provider

Public Class LimitedSqlRoleProvider
    Inherits SqlRoleProvider

End Class
```

C#

```
using System;
using System.Web;
using System.Web.Security;
using System.Configuration;
using System.Configuration.Provider;

public class LimitedSqlRoleProvider : SqlRoleProvider
{

}
```

This is similar to creating the `XmlMembershipProvider` class. When you did that, however, you were able to use Visual Studio to build the entire class skeleton of all the methods and properties you had to override to get the new class up and running. In this case, if you try to do the same thing in Visual Studio, you get an error (if using C#) or, perhaps, no result at all (if using Visual Basic) because you are not working with an abstract class. You do not need to override an enormous number of methods and properties. Instead, because you are deriving from a class that already inherits from one of these abstract classes, you can get by with overriding only the methods and properties that you need to work with and nothing more.

To get at this list of methods and properties within Visual Studio, you simply type **Public Overrides** (when using Visual Basic) or **public override** (when using C#). IntelliSense then provides you with a large drop-down list of available methods and properties to work with, as illustrated in Figure 13-6.

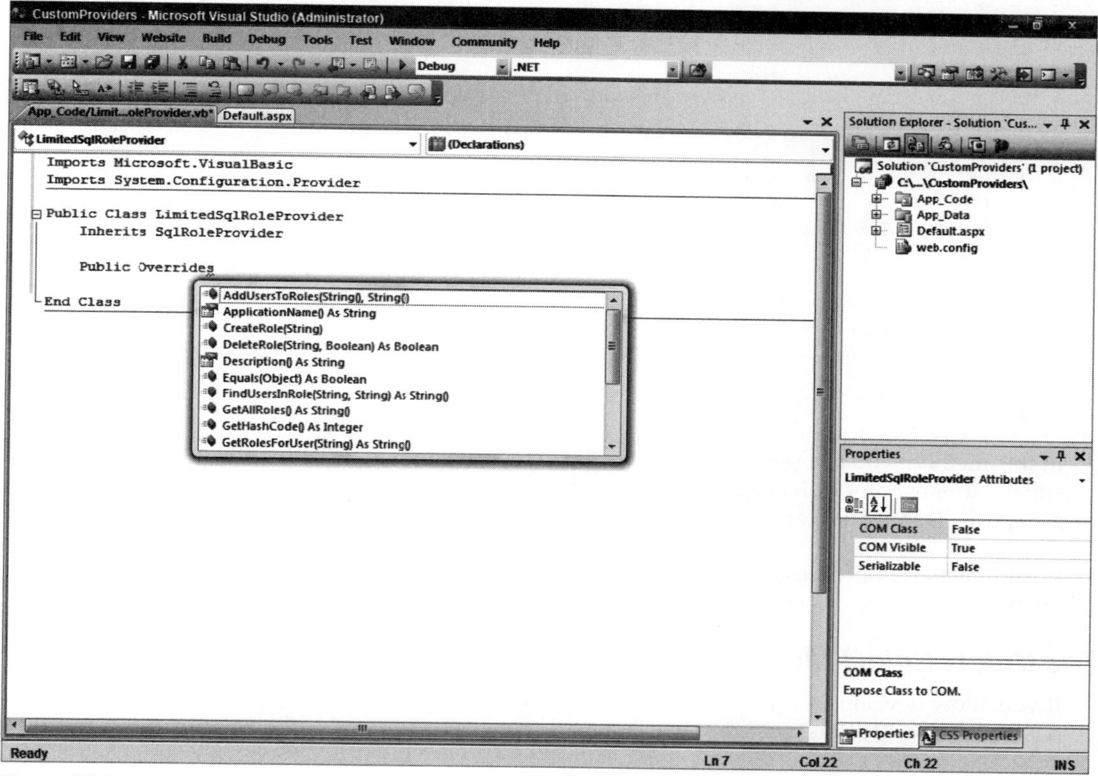

Figure 13-6

For this example, you only override the `CreateRole()`, `AddUsersToRoles()`, and `DeleteRole()` methods. These are described next.

The CreateRole() Method

The `CreateRole()` method in the `SqlRoleProvider` class allows developers to add any role to the system. The only parameter required for this method is a string value that is the name of the role. For this example, instead of letting developers create any role they wish, this provider limits the role creation to only the *Administrator* and *Manager* roles. To accomplish this in the `CreateRole()` method, you code the method as presented in Listing 13-19.

Listing 13-19: Allowing only the Administrator or Manager role in the CreateUser() method

VB

```
Public Overrides Sub CreateRole(ByVal roleName As String)
   If (roleName = "Administrator" Or roleName = "Manager") Then
     MyBase.CreateRole(roleName)
   Else
     Throw New _
      ProviderException("Role creation limited to only Administrator and Manager")
   End If
End Sub
```

C#

```
public override void CreateRole(string roleName)
{
   if (roleName == "Administrator" || roleName == "Manager")
   {
      base.CreateRole(roleName);
   }
   else
   {
     throw new
      ProviderException("Role creation limited to only Administrator and Manager");
   }
}
```

In this method, you can see that a check is first done to determine whether the role being created is either Administrator or Manager. If the role being created is not one of these defined roles, a `ProviderException` is thrown informing the developer of which roles they are allowed to create.

If Administrator or Manager is one of the roles, then the base class (`SqlRoleProvider`) `CreateRole()` method is invoked.

The DeleteRole() Method

If you allow developers using this provider to create only specific roles, you might not want them to delete any role after it is created. If this is the case, you want to override the `DeleteRole()` method of the `SqlRoleProvider` class, as illustrated in Listing 13-20.

Listing 13-20: Disallowing the DeleteRole() method

VB

```
Public Overrides Function DeleteRole(ByVal roleName As String, _
  ByVal throwOnPopulatedRole As Boolean) As Boolean
        Return False
End Function
```

C#

```
public override bool DeleteRole(string roleName, bool throwOnPopulatedRole)
{
   return false;
}
```

Looking at the DeleteRole() method, you can see that deleting any role is completely disallowed. Instead of raising the base class's DeleteRole() and returning the following:

```
Return MyBase.DeleteRole(roleName, throwOnPopulatedRole)
```

a False value is returned and no action is taken. Another approach is to throw a NotSupported-Exception, as shown here:

```
Throw New NotSupportedException()
```

The AddUsersToRoles() Method

As you look over the methods that can be overridden, notice that only one single method allows you to add any number of users to any number of roles. Multiple methods in the Roles class actually map to this method. If you look at the Roles class, notice the AddUserToRole(), AddUserToRoles(), AddUsers-ToRole(), and AddUsersToRoles() methods at your disposal. All these actually map to the AddUsers-ToRoles() method that is available in the RoleProvider base class.

Suppose you want, for example, to enable developers to add users only to the Manager role but not to add any users to the Administrator role. You could accomplish something like this by constructing a method, as shown in Listing 13-21.

Listing 13-21: Disallowing users to be added to a particular role

VB

```
Public Overrides Sub AddUsersToRoles(ByVal usernames() As String, _
  ByVal roleNames() As String)

   For Each roleItem As String In roleNames
      If roleItem = "Administrator" Then
         Throw New _
            ProviderException("You are not authorized to add any users" & _
               " to the Administrator role")
      End If
   Next

   MyBase.AddUsersToRoles(usernames, roleNames)
End Sub
```

C#

```
public override void AddUsersToRoles(string[] usernames, string[] roleNames)
{
   foreach (string roleItem in roleNames)
   {
      if (roleItem == "Administrator")
      {
         throw new ProviderException("You are not authorized to add any users" +
           " to the Administrator role");
      }
   }

   base.AddUsersToRoles(usernames, roleNames);
}
```

This overridden method iterates through all the provided roles, and if one of the roles contained in the string array is the role Administrator, then a `ProviderException` instance is thrown informing the developer that he or she is not allowed to add any users to this particular role. Although it is not shown here, you can also take the same approach with the `RemoveUsersFromRoles()` method exposed from the `RoleProvider` base class.

Using the New LimitedSqlRoleProvider Provider

After you have the provider in place and ready to use, you have to make some modifications to the `web.config` file in order to use this provider in your ASP.NET application. You learn how you add what you need to the `web.config` file for this provider in Listing 13-22.

Listing 13-22: Making the appropriate changes to the web.config file for the provider

```
<configuration>
   <system.web>

     <roleManager defaultProvider="LimitedProvider" enabled="true">
        <providers>
           <add connectionStringName="LocalSqlServer" applicationName="/"
            name="LimitedProvider"
            type="LimitedSqlRoleProvider" />
        </providers>
     </roleManager>

   </system.web>
</configuration>
```

Remember that you have to define the provider to use in your application by providing a value for the `defaultProvider` attribute and defining that provider further in the `<provider>` section. You also have to enable the provider by setting the `enabled` attribute to `true`. By default, the role management system is disabled.

Using the `<add>` element, you can add a provider instance that makes use of the `LimitedSqlRole-Provider` class. Because this provider derives from the `SqlRoleProvider` class, you must use some of the same attributes that this provider requires, such as the `connectionStringName` attribute that points to the connection string to use to connect to the specified SQL instance.

After you have the new `LimitedSqlRoleProvider` instance in place and defined in the `web.config` file, you can use the `Roles` class in your application just as you normally would, but notice the behavior of this class is rather different from the normal `SqlRoleProvider`.

To see it in action, construct a simple ASP.NET page that includes a TextBox, Button, and Label server control. The page should appear as shown in Listing 13-23.

Listing 13-23: Using Roles.CreateRole()

VB

```
<%@ Page Language="VB" %>

<script runat="server">
   Protected Sub Button1_Click(ByVal sender As Object, _
     ByVal e As System.EventArgs)
```

```
        Try
            Roles.CreateRole(TextBox1.Text)
            Label1.Text = "Role successfully created."
        Catch ex As Exception
            Label1.Text = ex.Message.ToString()
        End Try
    End Sub
</script>

<html xmlns="http://www.w3.org/1999/xhtml" >
<head runat="server">
    <title>Main Page</title>
</head>
<body>
    <form id="form1" runat="server">
    <div>
        Role Name:<br />
        <asp:TextBox ID="TextBox1" runat="server"></asp:TextBox><br />
        <br />
        <asp:Button ID="Button1" runat="server" Text="Create Role"
         OnClick="Button1_Click" /><br />
        <br />
        <asp:Label ID="Label1" runat="server"></asp:Label></div>
    </form>
</body>
</html>
```

C#

```
<%@ Page Language="C#" %>

<script runat="server">
    protected void Button1_Click(object sender, EventArgs e)
    {
        try
        {
            Roles.CreateRole(TextBox1.Text);
            Label1.Text = "Role successfully created.";
        }
        catch (Exception ex)
        {
            Label1.Text = ex.Message.ToString();
        }
    }
</script>
```

This simple ASP.NET page enables you to type in a string value in the text box and to attempt to create a new role using this value. Note that anything other than the role Administrator and Manager results in an error. So, when the `Roles.CreateRole()` is called, an error is produced if the rules defined by the provider are not followed. In fact, running this page and typing in a role other than the Administrator or Manager role gives you the results presented in Figure 13-7.

To show this provider in action, create another ASP.NET page that allows you to add users to a particular role. As stated, this can be done with a number of available methods, but in this case, this example uses the `Roles.AddUserToRole()` method. This is illustrated in Listing 13-24.

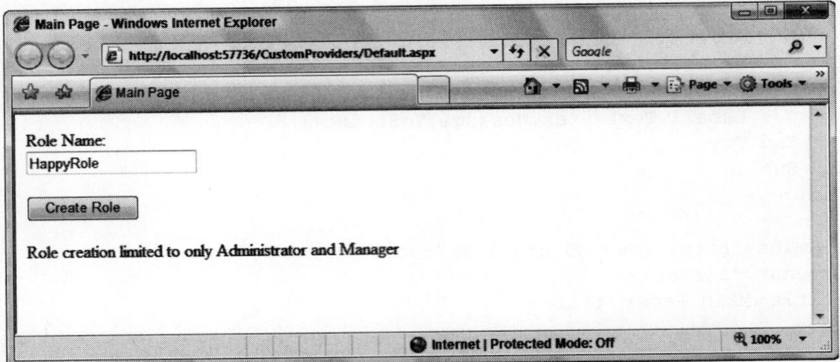

Figure 13-7

Listing 13-24: Attempting to add users to a role through the new role provider

VB

```
<%@ Page Language="VB" %>

<script runat="server">
    Protected Sub Button1_Click(ByVal sender As Object, _
      ByVal e As System.EventArgs)

        Try
            Roles.AddUserToRole(TextBox1.Text, TextBox2.Text)
            Label1.Text = "User successfully added to role"
        Catch ex As Exception
            Label1.Text = ex.Message.ToString()
        End Try
    End Sub
</script>

<html xmlns="http://www.w3.org/1999/xhtml" >
<head runat="server">
    <title>Main Page</title>
</head>
<body>
    <form id="form1" runat="server">
    <div>
        Add the following user:<br />
        <asp:TextBox ID="TextBox1" runat="server"></asp:TextBox><br />
        <br />
        To role:<br />
        <asp:TextBox ID="TextBox2" runat="server"></asp:TextBox><br />
        <br />
        <asp:Button ID="Button1" runat="server" Text="Add User to Role"
         OnClick="Button1_Click" /><br />
```

```
        <br />
        <asp:Label ID="Label1" runat="server"></asp:Label></div>
    </form>
</body>
</html>
```

C#

```
<%@ Page Language="C#" %>

<script runat="server">
    protected void Button1_Click(object sender, EventArgs e)
    {
        try
        {
            Roles.AddUserToRole(TextBox1.Text, TextBox2.Text);
            Label1.Text = "User successfully added to role";
        }
        catch (Exception ex)
        {
            Label1.Text = ex.Message.ToString();
        }
    }
</script>
```

In this example, two text boxes are provided. The first asks for the username and the second asks for the role to add the user to. The code for the button click event uses the `Roles.AddUserToRole()` method. Because you built the provider, you know that an error is thrown if there is an attempt to add a user to the Administrator role. This attempt is illustrated in Figure 13-8.

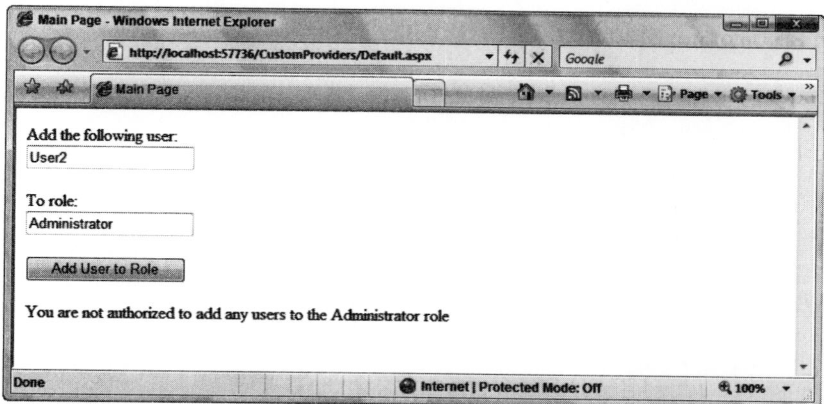

Figure 13-8

In this case, there was an attempt to add User2 to the Administrator role. This, of course, throws an error and returns the error message that is defined in the provider.

Summary

From this chapter and the last chapter, you got a good taste of the provider model and what it means to the ASP.NET 3.5 applications you build today. Although a lot of providers are available to you out of the box to use for interacting with one of the many systems provided in ASP.NET, you are not limited to just these providers. You definitely can either build your own providers or even extend the functionality of the providers already present in the system.

This chapter looked at both of these scenarios. First, you built your own provider to use the membership system with an XML data store for the user data, and then you worked through an example of extending the `SqlRoleProvider` class (something already present in ASP.NET) to change the underlying behavior of this provider.

14

Site Navigation

The Web applications that you develop generally have more than a single page to them. Usually you create a number of Web pages that are interconnected in some fashion. If you also build the navigation around your collection of pages, you make it easy for the end user to successfully work through your application in a straightforward manner.

Currently, you must choose among a number of different ways to expose the paths through your application to the end user. The difficult task of site navigation is compounded when you continue to add pages to the overall application.

The present method for building navigation within Web applications is to sprinkle pages with hyperlinks. Hyperlinks are generally added to Web pages by using include files or user controls. They can also be directly hard-coded onto a page so that they appear in the header or the sidebar of the page being viewed. The difficulties in working with navigation become worse when you move pages around or change page names. Sometimes developers are forced to go to each and every page in the application just to change some aspect of the navigation.

ASP.NET 3.5 tackles this problem by providing a navigation system that makes it quite trivial to manage how end users work through the applications you create. This capability in ASP.NET is complex; but the great thing is that it can be as simple as you need it to be, or you can actually get in deep and control every aspect of how it works.

The site navigation system includes the capability to define your entire site in an XML file that is called a *site map*. After you define a site map, you can work with it programmatically using the `SiteMap` class. Another aspect of the site map capability available in ASP.NET is a data provider that is specifically developed to work with site map files and to bind them to a series of navigation-based server controls. This chapter looks at all these components in the ASP.NET 3.5 navigation system. The following section introduces site maps.

XML-Based Site Maps

Although a site map is not a required element (as you see later), one of the common first steps you take in working with the ASP.NET 3.5 navigation system is building a site map for your application. A site map is an XML description of your site's structure.

You use this site map to define the navigational structure of all the pages in your application and how they relate to one another. If you do this according to the ASP.NET site map standard, you can then interact with this navigation information using either the `SiteMap` class or the SiteMapDataSource control. By using the SiteMapDataSource control, you can then bind the information in the site map file to a variety of data-binding controls, including the navigation server controls provided by ASP.NET.

To create a site map file for your application, add a site map or an XML file to your application. When asked, you name the XML file `Web.sitemap`; this file is already in place if you select the Site Map option. The file is named `Web` and has the file extension of `.sitemap`. Take a look at an example of a `.sitemap` file illustrated here in Listing 14-1.

Listing 14-1: An example of a Web.sitemap file

```
<?xml version="1.0" encoding="utf-8" ?>

<siteMap xmlns="http://schemas.microsoft.com/AspNet/SiteMap-File-1.0" >
   <siteMapNode title="Home" description="Home Page" url="Default.aspx">
      <siteMapNode title="News" description="The Latest News" url="News.aspx">
         <siteMapNode title="U.S." description="U.S. News"
          url="News.aspx?cat=us" />
         <siteMapNode title="World" description="World News"
          url="News.aspx?cat=world" />
         <siteMapNode title="Technology" description="Technology News"
          url="News.aspx?cat=tech" />
         <siteMapNode title="Sports" description="Sports News"
          url="News.aspx?cat=sport" />
      </siteMapNode>
      <siteMapNode title="Finance" description="The Latest Financial Information"
        url="Finance.aspx">
         <siteMapNode title="Quotes" description="Get the Latest Quotes"
          url="Quotes.aspx" />
         <siteMapNode title="Markets" description="The Latest Market Information"
          url="Markets.aspx">
            <siteMapNode title="U.S. Market Report"
             description="Looking at the U.S. Market" url="MarketsUS.aspx" />
            <siteMapNode title="NYSE"
             description="The New York Stock Exchange" url="NYSE.aspx" />
         </siteMapNode>
         <siteMapNode title="Funds" description="Mutual Funds"
          url="Funds.aspx" />
      </siteMapNode>
      <siteMapNode title="Weather" description="The Latest Weather"
       url="Weather.aspx" />
   </siteMapNode>
</siteMap>
```

So what does this file give you? Well, it gives you a logical structure that ASP.NET can now use in the rest of the navigation system it provides. Next, this chapter examines how this file is constructed.

The root node of this XML file is a `<siteMap>` element. Only one `<siteMap>` element can exist in the file. Within the `<siteMap>` element, there is a single root `<siteMapNode>` element. This is generally the start page of the application. In the case of the file in Listing 14-1, the root `<siteMapNode>` points to the `Default.aspx` page, the start page:

```
<siteMapNode title="Home" description="Home Page" url="Default.aspx">
```

The following table describes the most common attributes in the `<siteMapNode>` element.

Attribute	Description
`title`	The `title` attribute provides a textual description of the link. The `String` value used here is the text used for the link.
`description`	The `description` attribute not only reminds you what the link is for, but it is also used for the `ToolTip` attribute on the link. The `ToolTip` attribute is the yellow box that shows up next to the link when the end user hovers the cursor over the link for a couple of seconds.
`url`	The `url` attribute describes where the file is located in the solution. If the file is in the root directory, simply use the file name, such as `"Default.aspx"`. If the file is located in a subfolder, be sure to include the folders in the String value used in this attribute. For example, "`MySubFolder/Markets.aspx`".

After you have the first `<siteMapNode>` in place, you can then nest as many additional `<siteMapNode>` elements as you need within the root `<siteMapNode>` element. You can also create additional link-levels by creating child `<siteMapNode>` elements for any parent `<siteMapNode>` in the structure.

The example in Listing 14-1 gives the application the following navigational structure:

```
Home
   News
      U.S.
      World
      Technology
      Sports
   Finance
      Quotes
      Markets
         U.S. Market Report
         NYSE
      Funds
   Weather
```

You can see that this structure goes down three levels in some places. One of the easiest places to use this file is with the SiteMapPath server control that comes with ASP.NET. The SiteMapPath server control in ASP.NET is built to work specifically with the `.sitemap` files.

SiteMapPath Server Control

It is quite easy to use the `.sitemap` file you just created with the SiteMapPath server control provided with ASP.NET. You can find this control in the Navigation section of the Visual Studio 2008 IDE.

The SiteMapPath control creates navigation functionality that you once might have either created yourself or have seen elsewhere in Web pages on the Internet. The SiteMapPath control creates what some refer to as *breadcrumb navigation*. This is a linear path defining where the end user is in the navigation structure. The `Reuters.com` Web site, shown in Figure 14-1, uses this type of navigation. A black box shows the breadcrumb navigation used on the page.

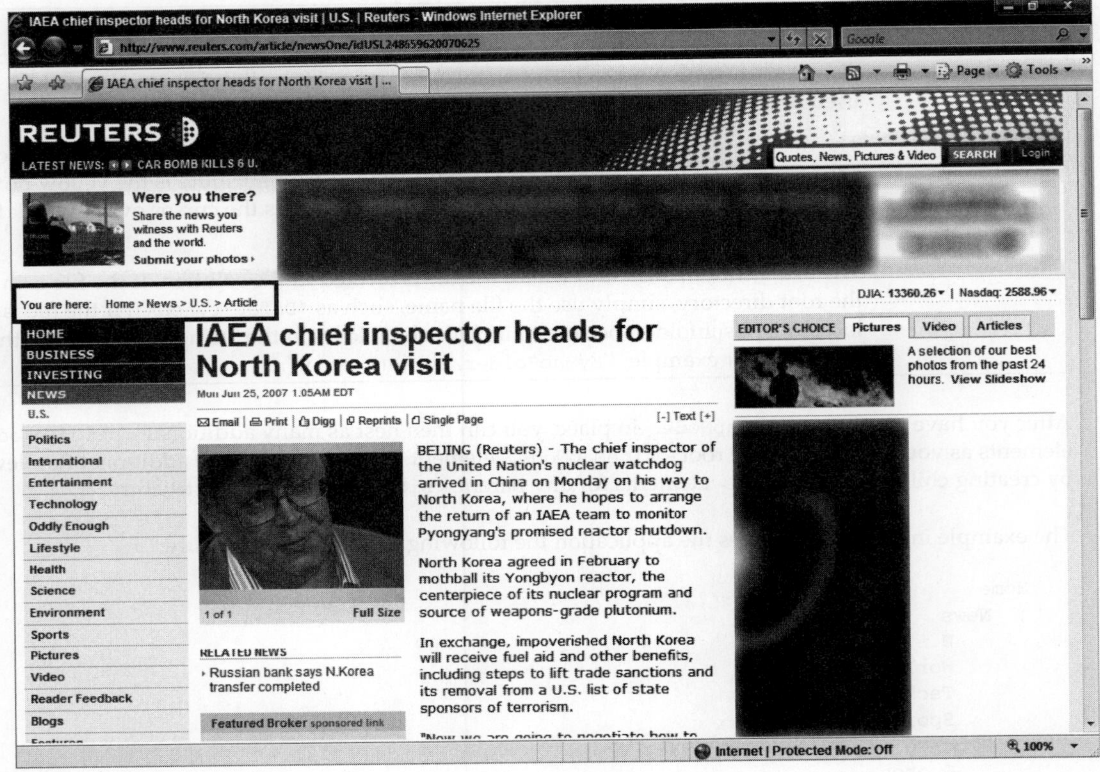

Figure 14-1

The purpose of this type of navigation is to show end users where they are in relation to the rest of the site. Traditionally, coding this kind of navigation has been tricky, to say the least; but now with the introduction of the SiteMapPath server control, you should find coding for this type of navigation a breeze.

You should first create an application that has the `Web.sitemap` file created in Listing 14-1. From there, create a WebForm called `MarketsUS.aspx`. This file is defined in the `Web.sitemap` file as being on the lowest tier of files in the application.

The SiteMapPath control is so easy to work with that it doesn't even require a data source control to hook it up to the `Web.sitemap` file where it infers all its information. All you do is drag-and-drop a SiteMapPath control onto your `MarketsUS.aspx` page. In the end, you should have a page similar to the one shown in Listing 14-2.

Listing 14-2: Using the Web.sitemap file with a SiteMapPath server control

```
<%@ Page Language="VB" %>

<html xmlns="http://www.w3.org/1999/xhtml">
<head runat="server">
    <title>Using the SiteMapPath Server Control</title>
</head>
<body>
    <form id="form1" runat="server">
        <asp:SiteMapPath ID="Sitemappath1" runat="server">
        </asp:SiteMapPath>
    </form>
</body>
</html>
```

Not much to it, is there? It really is that easy. Run this page and you see the results shown in Figure 14-2.

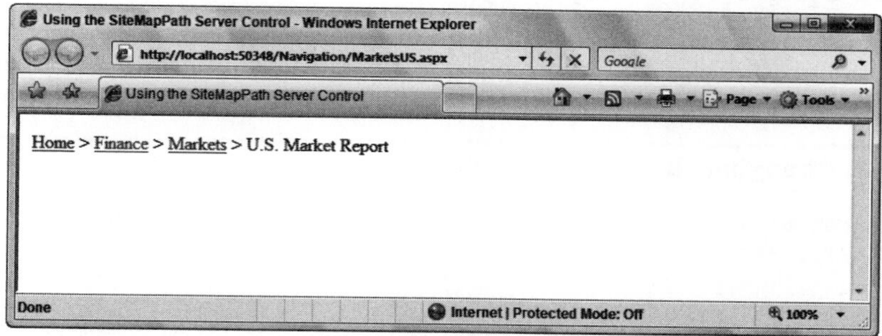

Figure 14-2

This screenshot shows that you are on the U.S. Market Report page at `MarketsUS.aspx`. As an end user, you can see that this page is part of the Markets section of the site; Markets, in turn, is part of the Finance section of the site. With breadcrumb navigation, end users who understand the structure of the site and their place in it can quickly select the links to navigate to any location in the site.

If you hover your mouse over the Finance link, you see a tooltip appear after a couple of seconds, as shown in Figure 14-3.

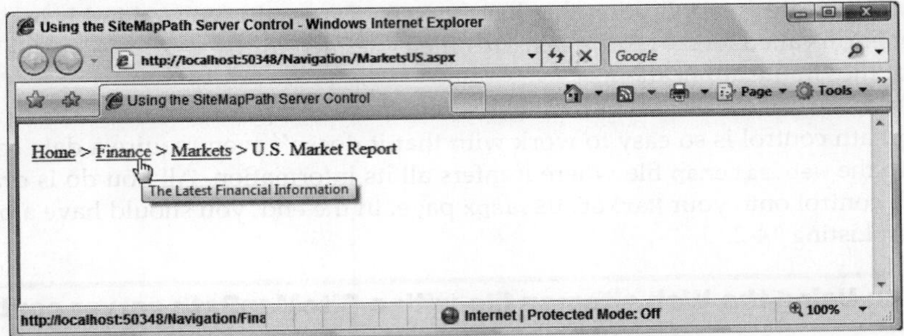

Figure 14-3

This tooltip, which reads `The Latest Financial Information`, comes from the description attribute of the `<siteMapNode>` element in the `Web.sitemap` file.

```
<siteMapNode title="Finance" description="The Latest Financial Information"
 url="Finance.aspx">
```

The SiteMapPath control works automatically requiring very little work on your part. You just add the basic control to your page, and the control automatically creates the breadcrumb navigation you have just seen. However, you can use the properties discussed in the following sections to modify the appearance and behavior of the control.

The PathSeparator Property

One important style property for the SiteMapPath control is the `PathSeparator` property. By default, the SiteMapPath control uses a greater than sign (>) to separate the link elements. You can change this by reassigning a new value to the `PathSeparator` property. Listing 14-3 illustrates the use of this property.

Listing 14-3: Changing the PathSeparator value

```
<asp:SiteMapPath ID="Sitemappath1" runat="server" PathSeparator=" | ">
</asp:SiteMapPath>
```

Or

```
<asp:SiteMapPath ID="Sitemappath1" runat="server">
   <PathSeparatorTemplate> | </PathSeparatorTemplate>
</asp:SiteMapPath>
```

The SiteMapPath control in this example uses the pipe character (|), which is found above the Enter key. When it is rendered, you get the results shown in Figure 14-4.

As you can see, you can use either the `PathSeparator` attribute or the `<PathSeparatorTemplate>` element within the SiteMapPath control.

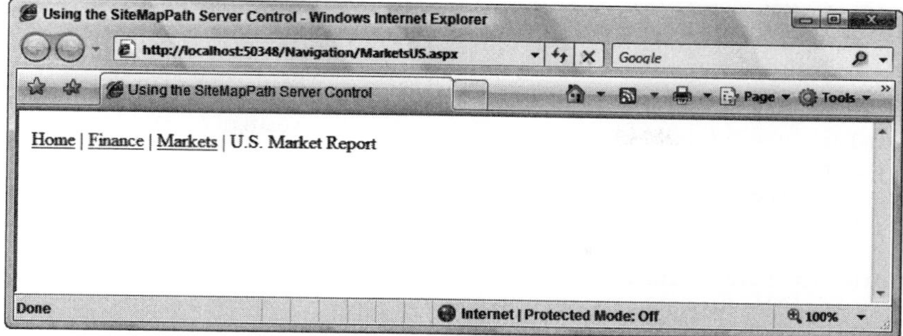

Figure 14-4

With the use of the `PathSeparator` attribute or the `<PathSeparatorTemplate>` element, it is quite easy to specify what you want to use to separate the links in the breadcrumb navigation, but you might also want to give this pipe some visual style as well. You can add a `<PathSeparatorStyle>` node to your SiteMapPath control. An example of this is shown in Listing 14-4.

Listing 14-4: Adding style to the PathSeparator property

```
<asp:SiteMapPath ID="Sitemappath1" runat="server" PathSeparator=" | ">
   <PathSeparatorStyle Font-Bold="true" Font-Names="Verdana" ForeColor="#663333"
    BackColor="#cccc66"></PathSeparatorStyle>
</asp:SiteMapPath>
```

Okay, it may not be pretty, but by using the `<PathSeparatorStyle>` element with the `SiteMapPath` control, we are able to change the visual appearance of the separator elements. The results are shown in Figure 14-5.

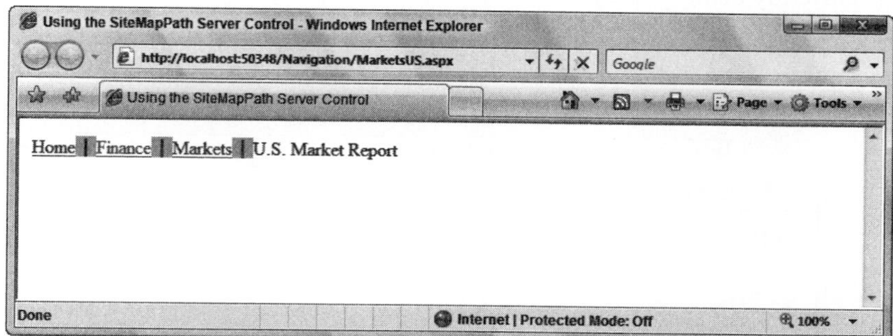

Figure 14-5

Using these constructs, you can also add an image as the separator, as illustrated in Listing 14-5.

Listing 14-5: Using an image as the separator

```
<%@ Page Language="VB" %>

<html xmlns="http://www.w3.org/1999/xhtml">
<head runat="server">
    <title>Using the SiteMapPath Server Control</title>
</head>
<body>
    <form id="form1" runat="server">
        <asp:SiteMapPath ID="SiteMapPath1" runat="server">
            <PathSeparatorTemplate>
                <asp:Image ID="Image1" runat="server" ImageUrl="divider.gif" />
            </PathSeparatorTemplate>
        </asp:SiteMapPath>
    </form>
</body>
</html>
```

To utilize an image as the separator between the links, you use the `<PathSeparatorTemplate>` element and place an Image control within it. In fact, you can place any type of control between the navigation links that the SiteMapPath control produces.

The PathDirection Property

Another interesting property to use with the SiteMapPath control is `PathDirection`. This property changes the direction of the links generated in the output. Only two settings are possible for this property: `RootToCurrent` and `CurrentToRoot`.

The Root link is the first link in the display. This is usually the Home page. The Current link is the link for the page currently being displayed. By default, this property is set to `RootToCurrent`. Changing the example to `CurrentToRoot` produces the results shown in Figure 14-6.

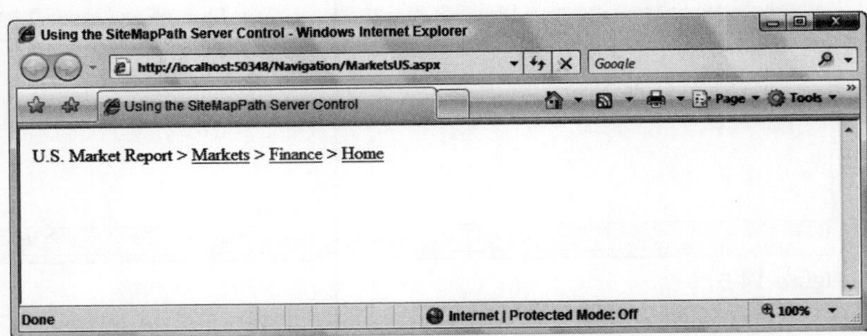

Figure 14-6

The ParentLevelsDisplayed Property

In some cases, your navigation may go quite deep. You can see on the site map, shown in Listing 14-1, that you go three pages deep, which isn't a big deal. Some of you, however, might be dealing with sites that go quite a number of pages deeper. In these cases, it might be a bit silly to use the SiteMapPath control. Doing so would display a huge list of pages.

In a case like this, you can turn to the `ParentLevelsDisplayed` property that is part of the SiteMapPath control. When set, this property displays pages only as deep as specified. Therefore, if you are using the SiteMapPath control with the `Web.sitemap`, as shown in Listing 14-1, and you give the `ParentLevels-Displayed` property a value of `3`, you don't notice any change to your page. It already displays the path three pages deep. If you change this value to `2`, however, the SiteMapPath control is constructed as follows:

```
<asp:SiteMapPath ID="Sitemappath1" runat="server" ParentLevelsDisplayed="2">
</asp:SiteMapPath>
```

Notice the result of this change in Figure 14-7. The SiteMapPath control shows links only two pages deep and doesn't show the Home page link.

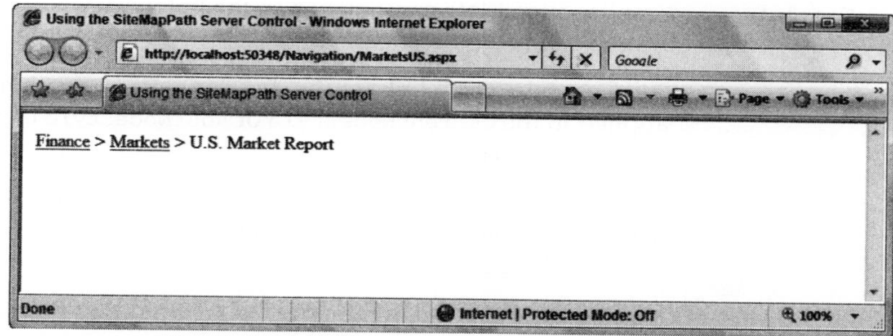

Figure 14-7

By default, no limit is set on the number of links shown, so the SiteMapPath control just generates the specified number of links based on what is labeled in the site map file.

The ShowToolTips Property

By default, the SiteMapPath control generates tooltips for each link if a description property is used within the `Web.sitemap` file. Remember, a tooltip is the text that appears onscreen when an end user hovers the mouse over one of the links in the SiteMapPath control. This capability was shown earlier in this chapter.

There may be times when you do not want your SiteMapPath control to show any tooltips for the links that it generates. For these situations, you can actually turn off this capability in a couple of ways. The first way is to omit any description attributes in the `.sitemap` file. If you remove these attributes from the file, the SiteMapPath has nothing to display for the tooltips on the page.

The other way to turn off the display of tooltips is to set the `ShowToolTips` property to `False`, as shown here:

```
<asp:SiteMapPath ID="Sitemappath1" runat="server" ShowToolTips="false">
</asp:SiteMapPath>
```

This turns off the tooltips capability but still enables you to use the description property in the `.sitemap` file. You may still want to use the description attribute because it allows you to keep track of what the links in your file are used for. This is quite advantageous when you are dealing with hundreds or even thousands of links in your application.

The SiteMapPath Control's Child Elements

You already saw the use of the `<PathSeparatorStyle>` and the `<PathSeparatorTemplate>` child elements for the SiteMapPath control, but additional child elements exist. The following table covers each of the available child elements.

Child Element	Description
`CurrentNodeStyle`	Applies styles to the link in the SiteMapPath navigation for the currently displayed page.
`CurrentNodeTemplate`	Applies a template construction to the link in the SiteMapPath navigation for the currently displayed page.
`NodeStyle`	Applies styles to all links in the SiteMapPath navigation. The settings applied in the `CurrentNodeStyle` or `RootNodeStyle` elements supersede any settings placed here.
`NodeTemplate`	Applies a template construction to all links in the SiteMapPath navigation. The settings applied in the `CurrentNodeTemplate` or `RootNodeTemplate` elements supersede any settings placed here.
`PathSeparatorStyle`	Applies styles to the link dividers in the SiteMapPath navigation.
`PathSeparatorTemplate`	Applies a template construction to the link dividers in the SiteMapPath navigation.
`RootNodeStyle`	Applies styles to the first link (the root link) in the SiteMapPath navigation.
`RootNodeTemplate`	Applies a template construction to the first link in the SiteMapPath navigation.

TreeView Server Control

The TreeView server control is a rich server control for rendering a hierarchy of data, so it is quite ideal for displaying what is contained in your `.sitemap` file. Figure 14-8 shows you how it displays the contents of the site map (again from Listing 14-1) that you have been working with thus far in this chapter. This figure first shows a completely collapsed TreeView control at the top of the screen; the second TreeView control has been completely expanded.

This control can dynamically load the nodes to be displayed as they are selected by the expandable and collapsible framework of the control. If the control can render the TreeView output along with some client-side script, the control can make a call back to the server if someone expands one of the nodes in the control to get the subnodes of the selected item. This is ideal if your site navigation system is large. In this case, loading nodes of the TreeView control dynamically greatly helps performance. One of the great features of this postback capability is it is done under the covers and does not require the ASP.NET page to be completely refreshed. Of course, this capability is there only if the browser accepts the client-side code that goes along with the TreeView control. If the browser does not, the control knows this and renders only what is appropriate (pulling all the information that is required of the entire TreeView control). It only performs these JavaScript-based postbacks for those clients who can work with this client-side script.

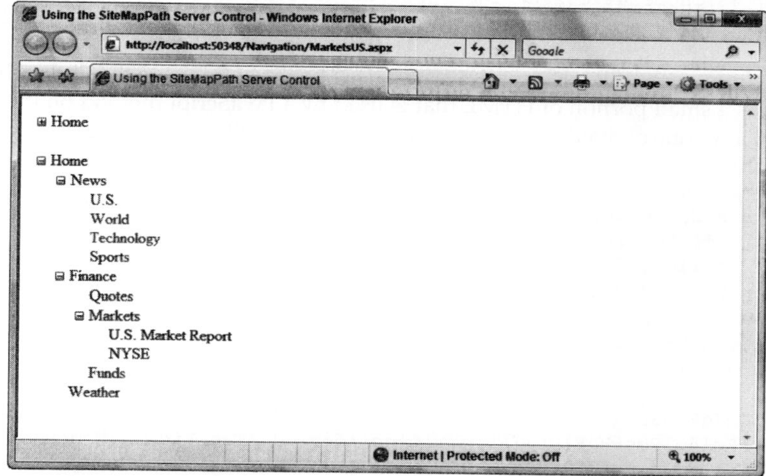

Figure 14-8

You can definitely see this in action if you run the TreeView control on a page that is being monitored by an HTTP sniffer of some kind to monitor the traffic moving across the wire.

I recommend Fiddler by Eric Lawrence of Microsoft that is freely downloadable on the Internet at `fiddlertool.com`.

If your browser allows client-side script and you expand one of the expandable nodes of the TreeView control, your HTTP request will be similar to the following:

```
POST /Navigation/Default.aspx HTTP/1.1
Accept: */*
Accept-Language: en-us
Referrer: http://localhost:1882/Navigation/Default.aspx
Content-Type: application/x-www-form-urlencoded
Accept-Encoding: gzip, deflate
User-Agent: Mozilla/4.0 (compatible; MSIE 7.0; Windows NT 6.0; SLCC1;
.NET CLR 2.0.50727; Media Center PC 5.0; .NET CLR 3.0.04506;
.NET CLR 3.5.20404; .NET CLR 1.1.4322)
Host: localhost:1882
Content-Length: 904
Proxy-Connection: Keep-Alive
Pragma: no-cache
```

```
__EVENTTARGET=&__EVENTARGUMENT=&TreeView1_ExpandState=c&TreeView1_SelectedNode=Tree
View1t0&TreeView1_PopulateLog=&__VIEWSTATE=%2FwEPDwUKLTY0ODk0OTE2Mg9kFgICBA9kFgICAw
88KwAJAgAPFggeDU5ldmVyRXhwYW5kZWRkHgtfIURhdGFCb3VuZGceDFNlbGVjdGVkTm9kZQULVHJlZVZpZ
XcxdDAeCUxhc3RJbmRleAIBZAgUKwACBQMwOjAUKwACFhAeBFRleHQFBEhvbWUeBVZhbHVlBQRIb21lHgtO
YXZpZ2F0ZVVybAUYL05hdmlnYXRpb24vRGVmYXVsdC5hc3B4HgdUb29sVGlwBQlIb21lIFBhZ2UeCERhdGF
QYXRoBRgvbmF2aWdhdGlvbi9kZWZhdWx0LmFzcHgeCURhdGFCb3VuZGceCFNlbGVjdGVkZx4QUG9wdWxhdG
VPbkRlbWFuZGdkZBgBBR5fX0NvbnRyb2xzUmVxdWlyZVBvc3RCYWNrS2V5X18WAwURTG9naW4xJFJlbWVtY
mVyTWUFF0xvZ2luMSRMb2dpbkltYWdlQnV0dG9uBQlUcmVlVmlldzFtwszVpUMxFTDtpERnNjgEIkWWbg%3
D%3D&Login1$UserName=&Login1$Password=&__CALLBACKID=TreeView1&__CALLBACKPARAM=0%7C1
%7Ctft%7C4%7CHome24%7C%2Fnavigation%2Fdefault.aspxHome&__EVENTVALIDATION=%2FwEWBgKg
8Yn8DwKUvNa1DwL666vYDAKC0q%2BkBgKnz4ybCAKn5fLxBaSy6WQwPagNZsHisWRoJfuiopOe
```


The response from your ASP.NET application will *not* be the entire page that holds the TreeView control, but instead it is a small portion of HTML that is used by a JavaScript method on the page and is loaded into the TreeView control dynamically. A sample response is illustrated here:

```
HTTP/1.1 200 OK
Server: ASP.NET Development Server/8.0.0.0
Date: Sat, 11 Feb 2008 17:55:02 GMT
X-AspNet-Version: 2.0.50727
Cache-Control: private, no-store
Content-Type: text/html; charset=utf-8
Content-Length: 1756
Connection: Close

112|/wEWCgKg8Yn8DwKUvNa1DwL666vYDAKC0q+kBgKnz4ybCAKn5fLxBQKAgtPaBALEmcbhCgK8nZDfCAL
M/ZK8AR/nFcl4nlPgp6HcFlU6YiFBfoNM14|nn|<div id="TreeView1n6Nodes"
style="display:none;">
 <table cellpadding="0" cellspacing="0" style="border-width:0;">
        <tr>
                <td><div style="width:20px;height:1px"></div></td><td><div
                 style="width:20px;height:1px"><img
                 src="/Navigation/WebResource.axd?d=GOWKLfnbFU9fYyy
                 PCMT8DIfngU4PXeMiAHxJNuXB-tU1&amp;t=632662834831594592" alt="" />
                </div></td><td><div style="width:20px;height:1px"><img
                 src="/Navigation/WebResource.axd?d=GOWKLfnbFU9fYyyPCMT8DIfngU
                 4PXeMiAHxJNuXB-tU1&amp;t=632662834831594592" alt="" />
                </div></td><td><img
                 src="/Navigation/WebResource.axd?d=GOWKLfnbFU9fYyy
                 PCMT8DCXmyNCWX5x-n_pSXFIW2qE1&amp;t=632662834831594592"
                 alt="" /></td><td style="white-space:nowrap;">
                <a href="/Navigation/MarketsUSasdf.aspx"
                 title="Looking at the U.S. Market" id="TreeView1t12"
                 style="text-decoration:none;">U.S. Market Report</a></td>
        </tr>
 </table><table cellpadding="0" cellspacing="0" style="border-width:0;">
        <tr>
                <td><div style="width:20px;height:1px"></div></td><td><div
                 style="width:20px;height:1px"><img
                 src="/Navigation/WebResource.axd?d=GOWKLfnbFU9fYyyPCMT8DI
                 fngU4PXeMiAHxJNuXB-tU1&amp;t=632662834831594592" alt="" />
                </div></td><td><div style="width:20px;height:1px"><img
                 src="/Navigation/WebResource.axd?d=GOWKLfnbFU9fYyyPCMT8DI
                 fngU4PXeMiAHxJNuXB-tU1&amp;t=632662834831594592" alt="" />
```

```
                    </div></td><td><img
                     src="/Navigation/WebResource.axd?d=GOWKLfnbFU9fY
                     yyPCMT8DGyYai5iS-79vjeYzdeJoiIl&amp;t=632662834831594592"
                     alt="" />
                    </td><td style="white-space:nowrap;">
                    <a href="/Navigation/NYSE.aspx" title="The New York Stock Exchange"
                     id="TreeView1t13" style="text-decoration:none;">NYSE</a></td>
         </tr>
   </table>
  </div>
```

This postback capability is rather powerful, but if you want to disable it (even for browsers that can handle it), you just set the `PopulateNodesFromClient` attribute to `false` in the TreeView control (the default value is `true`).

The TreeView control is quite customizable; but first, take a look at how to create a default version of the control using the `.sitemap` file from Listing 14-1. For this example, continue to use the `MarketsUS.aspx` page you created earlier.

The first step is to create a SiteMapDataSource control on the page. When working with the TreeView control that displays the contents of your `.sitemap` file, you must apply one of these data source controls. The TreeView control doesn't just bind to your site map file automatically as the SiteMapPath control does.

After a basic SiteMapDataSource control is in place, position a TreeView control on the page and set the `DataSourceId` property to `SiteMapDataSource1`. When you have finished, your code should look like Listing 14-6.

Listing 14-6: A basic TreeView control

```
<%@ Page Language="VB" %>

<html xmlns="http://www.w3.org/1999/xhtml">
<head runat="server">
    <title>Using the TreeView Server Control</title>
</head>
<body>
    <form id="form1" runat="server">
        <asp:SiteMapPath ID="SiteMapPath1" runat="server">
        </asp:SiteMapPath>
        <br /><p>
        <asp:TreeView ID="TreeView1" runat="server"
         DataSourceID="SiteMapDataSource1">
        </asp:TreeView>
        <asp:SiteMapDataSource ID="SiteMapDataSource1" runat="server" /></p>
    </form>
</body>
</html>
```

After the page is run and the TreeView control is expanded, the results are displayed as shown in Figure 14-9.

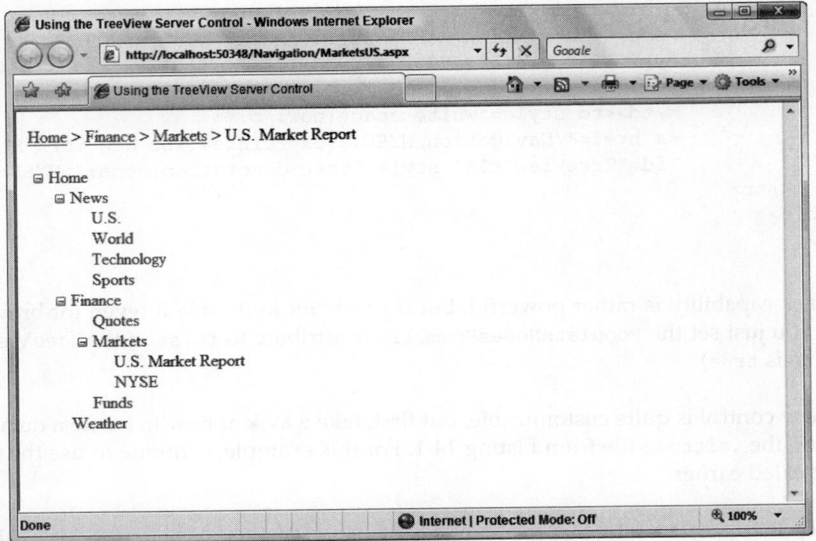

Figure 14-9

This is a very basic TreeView control. The great thing about this control is that it allows for a high degree of customization and even gives you the capability to use some predefined styles that come prepackaged with ASP.NET 3.5.

Identifying the TreeView Control's Built-In Styles

As stated, the TreeView control does come with a number of pre-built styles right out of the box. The best way to utilize these predefined styles is to do so from the Design view of your page. By clicking on the arrow located in the upper right section of the server control in the Design view in Visual Studio 2008, you will find the Auto Format option. Click this option and a number of styles become available to you. Selecting one of these styles changes the code of your TreeView control to adapt to that chosen style. For instance, if you choose `MSDN` from the list of options, the simple one-line TreeView control you created is converted to what is shown in Listing 14-7.

Listing 14-7: A TreeView control with the MSDN style applied to it

```
<asp:TreeView ID="TreeView1" runat="server" DataSourceID="SiteMapDataSource1"
 ImageSet="Msdn" NodeIndent="10">
   <ParentNodeStyle Font-Bold="False" />
   <HoverNodeStyle BackColor="#CCCCCC" BorderColor="#888888" BorderStyle="Solid"
    Font-Underline="True" />
   <SelectedNodeStyle BackColor="White" BorderColor="#888888" BorderStyle="Solid"
    BorderWidth="1px" Font-Underline="False" HorizontalPadding="3px"
    VerticalPadding="1px" />
   <NodeStyle Font-Names="Verdana" Font-Size="8pt" ForeColor="Black"
    HorizontalPadding="5px" NodeSpacing="1px" VerticalPadding="2px" />
</asp:TreeView>
```

As you can see, if you use these built-in styles, it is not too difficult to completely change the look and feel of the TreeView control. When this bit of code is run, you get the results shown in Figure 14-10.

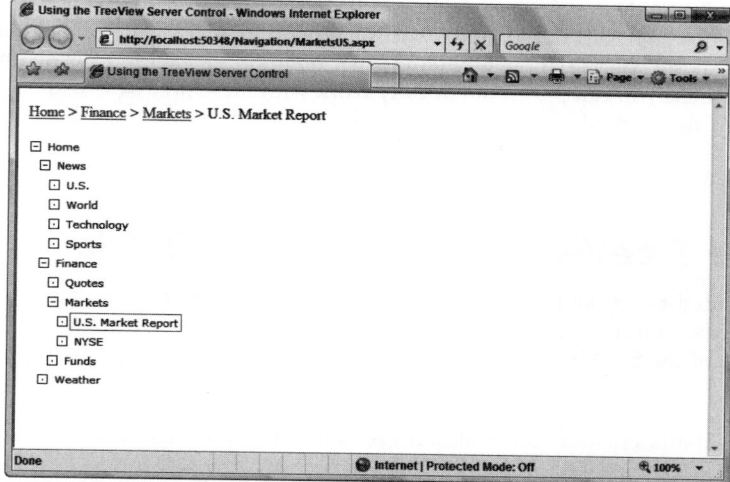

Figure 14-10

Examining the Parts of the TreeView Control

To master working with the TreeView control, you must understand the terminology used for each part of the hierarchical tree that is created by the control.

First, every element or entry in the TreeView control is called a *node*. The uppermost node in the hierarchy of nodes is the *root node*. It is possible for a TreeView control to have multiple root nodes. Any node, including the root node, is also considered a *parent node* if it has any nodes that are directly under it in the hierarchy of nodes. The nodes directly under this parent node are referred to as *child nodes*. Each parent node can have one or more child nodes. Finally, if a node contains no child nodes, it is referred to as a *leaf node*.

The following is based on the site map shown earlier and details the use of this terminology:

```
Home - Root node, parent node
   News - Parent node, child node
      U.S. - Child node, leaf node
      World - Child node, leaf node
      Technology - Child node, leaf node
      Sports - Child node, leaf node
   Finance - Parent node, child node
      Quotes - Child node, leaf node
      Markets - Parent node, child node
         U.S. Market Report - Child node, leaf node
         NYSE - Child node, leaf node
      Funds - Child node, leaf node
   Weather - Child node, leaf node
```

From this listing, you can see what each node is and how it is referred in the hierarchy of nodes. For instance, the `U.S. Market Report` node is a leaf node — meaning that it doesn't have any child nodes associated with it. However, it is also a child node to the `Markets` node, which is a parent node to the `U.S. Market Report` node. If you are working with the `Markets` node directly, it is also a child node to the `Finance` node, which is its parent node. The main point to take away from all this is that each node in the site map hierarchy has a relationship to the other nodes in the hierarchy. You must understand these relationships because you can programmatically work with these nodes (as will be demonstrated later in this chapter), and the methods used for working with them include terms such as `RootNode`, `CurrentNode` and `ParentNode`.

Binding the TreeView Control to an XML File

You are not limited to working with just a `.sitemap` file in order to populate the nodes of your TreeView controls. You have many ways to get this done. One cool way is to use the XmlDataSource control (instead of the SiteMapDataSource control) to populate your TreeView controls from your XML files.

For an example of this, create a hierarchical list of items in an XML file called `Hardware.xml`. An example of this is shown in Listing 14-8.

Listing 14-8: Hardware.xml

```
<?xml version="1.0" encoding="utf-8"?>
<Hardware>
    <Item Category="Motherboards">
        <Option Choice="Asus" />
        <Option Choice="Abit" />
    </Item>
    <Item Category="Memory">
        <Option Choice="128mb" />
        <Option Choice="256mb" />
        <Option Choice="512mb" />
    </Item>
    <Item Category="HardDrives">
        <Option Choice="40GB" />
        <Option Choice="80GB" />
        <Option Choice="100GB" />
    </Item>
    <Item Category="Drives">
        <Option Choice="CD" />
        <Option Choice="DVD" />
        <Option Choice="DVD Burner" />
    </Item>
</Hardware>
```

As you can see, this list is not meant to be used for site navigation purposes, but instead for allowing the end user to make a selection from a hierarchical list of options. This XML file is divided into four categories of available options: `Motherboards`, `Memory`, `HardDrives`, and `Drives`. To bind your TreeView control to this XML file, use an XmlDataSource control that specifies the location of the XML file you are going to use. Then within the TreeView control itself, use the `<asp:TreeNodeBinding>` element to specify which elements to bind in the XML file to populate the nodes of the TreeView control. This is illustrated in Listing 14-9.

Listing 14-9: Binding a TreeView control to the Hardware.xml file

```
<%@ Page Language="VB" %>

<html xmlns="http://www.w3.org/1999/xhtml">
<head runat="server">
    <title>Latest Hardware</title>
</head>
<body>
    <form id="form1" runat="server">
        <asp:TreeView ID="TreeView1" runat="server" DataSourceID="XmlDataSource1">
            <DataBindings>
                <asp:TreeNodeBinding DataMember="Hardware"
                 Text="Computer Hardware" />
                <asp:TreeNodeBinding DataMember="Item" TextField="Category" />
                <asp:TreeNodeBinding DataMember="Option" TextField="Choice" />
            </DataBindings>
        </asp:TreeView>
        <asp:XmlDataSource ID="XmlDataSource1" runat="server"
         DataFile="Hardware.xml">
        </asp:XmlDataSource>
    </form>
</body>
</html>
```

The first item to look at is the `<asp:XmlDataSource>` control. It is just as simple as the previous `<asp:SiteMapDataSource>` control, but it points at the `Hardware.xml` file using the `DataFile` property.

The next step is to create a TreeView control that binds to this particular XML file. You can bind a default TreeView control directly to the XmlDataSource control such as this:

```
<asp:TreeView ID="TreeView1" runat="server" DataSourceId="XmlDataSource1" />
```

Doing this, you get the *incorrect* result shown in Figure 14-11.

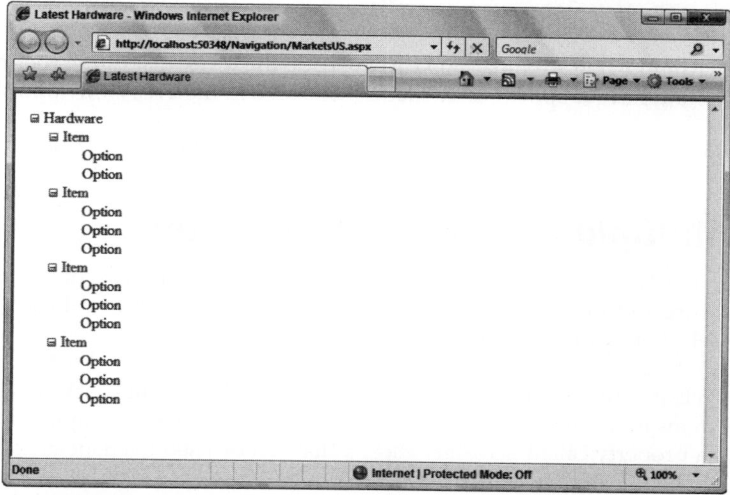

Figure 14-11

As you can see, the TreeView control binds just fine to the `Hardware.xml` file, but looking at the nodes within the TreeView control, you can see that it is simply displaying the names of the actual XML elements from the file itself. Because this isn't what you want, you specify how to bind to the XML file with the use of the `<DataBindings>` element within the TreeView control.

The `<DataBindings>` element encapsulates one or more `TreeNodeBinding` objects. Two of the more important available properties of a `TreeNodeBinding` object are the `DataMember` and `TextField` properties. The `DataMember` property points to the name of the XML element that the TreeView control should look for. The `TextField` property specifies the XML attribute that the TreeView should look for in that particular XML element. If you do this correctly, using the `<DataBindings>` construct, you get the result shown in Figure 14-12.

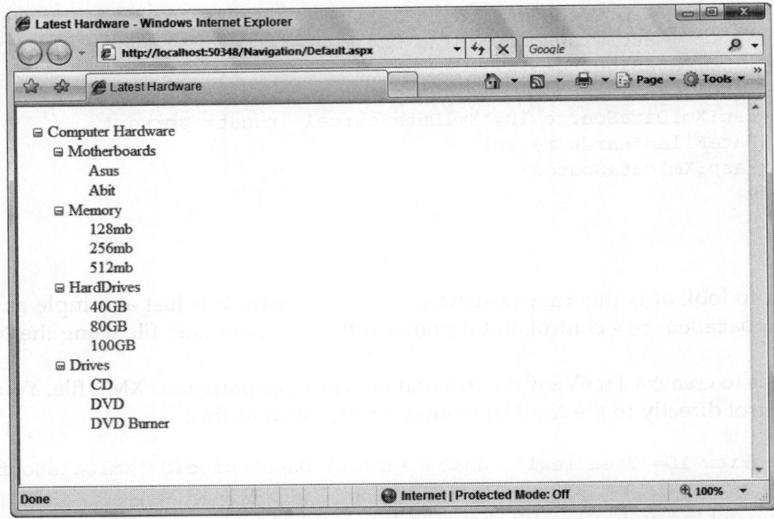

Figure 14-12

You can also see from Listing 14-9 that you can override the text value of the root node from the XML file, `<Hardware>`, and have it appear as `Computer Hardware` in the TreeView control, as follows:

```
<asp:TreeNodeBinding DataMember="Hardware" Text="Computer Hardware" />
```

Selecting Multiple Options in a TreeView

As stated earlier, the TreeView control is not meant to be used exclusively for navigation purposes. You can use it for all sorts of things. In many cases, you can present a hierarchical list from which you want the end user to select one or more items.

One great built-in feature of the TreeView control is the capability to put check boxes next to nodes within the hierarchical items in the list. These boxes enable end users to make multiple selections. The TreeView control contains a property called `ShowCheckBoxes` that can be used to create check boxes next to many different types of nodes within a list of items.

The available values for the `ShowCheckBoxes` property are discussed in the following table.

Value	Description
`All`	Applies check boxes to each and every node within the TreeView control.
`Leaf`	Applies check boxes to only the nodes that have no additional child elements.
`None`	Applies no check boxes to any node within the TreeView control.
`Parent`	Applies check boxes to only the nodes considered parent nodes within the TreeView control. A parent node has at least one child node associated with it.
`Root`	Applies a check box to any root node contained within the TreeView control.

When working with the `ShowCheckBoxes` property, you can set it declaratively in the control itself, as follows:

```
<asp:TreeView ID="Treeview1" runat="server" Font-Underline="false"
 DataSourceID="XmlDataSource1" ShowCheckBoxes="Leaf">
   ...
</asp:TreeViewTreeView>
```

Or you can set it programmatically by using the following code:

VB

```
TreeView1.ShowCheckBoxes = TreeNodeTypes.Leaf
```

C#

```
TreeView1.ShowCheckBoxes = TreeNodeTypes.Leaf;
```

For an example of using check boxes with the TreeView control, let's continue to expand on the computer hardware example from Listing 14-9. Create a hierarchical list that enables people to select multiple items from the list in order to receive additional information about them. Listing 14-10 shows an example of this.

Listing 14-10: Applying check boxes next to the leaf nodes within the hierarchical list of nodes

VB

```
<%@ Page Language="VB" %>

<script runat="server">
   Protected Sub Button1_Click(ByVal sender As Object, ByVal e As System.EventArgs)
        If TreeView1.CheckedNodes.Count > 0 Then
            Label1.Text = "We are sending you information on:<p>"

            For Each node As TreeNode In TreeView1.CheckedNodes
                Label1.Text += node.Text & " " & node.Parent.Text & "<br>"
            Next
        Else
```

Continued

```
                Label1.Text = "You didn't select anything. Sorry!"
            End If
        End Sub
    </script>

    <html xmlns="http://www.w3.org/1999/xhtml">
    <head runat="server">
        <title>Latest Hardware</title>
    </head>
    <body>
        <form runat="server">
        Please select the items you are interested in:
            <p>
            <asp:TreeView ID="TreeView1" runat="server" Font-Underline="False"
             DataSourceID="XmlDataSource1" ShowCheckBoxes="Leaf">
                <DataBindings>
                    <asp:TreeNodeBinding DataMember="Hardware"
                     Text="Computer Hardware" />
                    <asp:TreeNodeBinding DataMember="Item" TextField="Category" />
                    <asp:TreeNodeBinding DataMember="Option" TextField="Choice" />
                </DataBindings>
            </asp:TreeView>
            <p>
            <asp:Button ID="Button1" runat="server" Text="Submit Choices"
             OnClick="Button1_Click" />
            </p>
            <asp:XmlDataSource ID="XmlDataSource1" runat="server"
             DataFile="Hardware.xml">
            </asp:XmlDataSource>
           </p>
           <asp:Label ID="Label1" runat="Server" />
        </form>
    </body>
    </html>
```

C#

```
    <%@ Page Language="C#" %>

    <script runat="server">
        protected void Button1_Click(object sender, System.EventArgs e)
        {
            if (TreeView1.CheckedNodes.Count > 0)
            {
                Label1.Text = "We are sending you information on:<p>";
                foreach (TreeNode node in TreeView1.CheckedNodes)
                {
                    Label1.Text += node.Text + " " + node.Parent.Text + "<br>";
                }
            }
            else
            {
```

```
            Label1.Text = "You didn't select anything. Sorry!";
        }
    }
</script>
```

In this example, you first set the `ShowTextBoxes` property to `Leaf`, meaning that you are interested in having check boxes appear only next to items in the TreeView control that do not contain any child nodes. The items with check boxes next to them should be the last items that can be expanded in the hierarchical list.

After this property is set, you then work with the items that are selected by the end user in the `Button1_Click` event. The first thing you should check is whether any selection at all was made:

```
If TreeView1.CheckedNodes.Count > 0 Then
   ...
End If
```

In this case, the number of checked nodes on the postback needs to be greater than zero, meaning that at least one was selected. If so, you can execute the code within the `If` statement. The `If` statement then proceeds to populate the Label control that is on the page. To populate the Label control with data from the selected nodes, you use a `For Each` statement, as shown here:

```
For Each node As TreeNode In TreeView1.CheckedNodes
   ...
Next
```

This works with an instance of a `TreeNode` object and checks each `TreeNode` object within the `TreeView1` collection of checked nodes.

For each node that is checked, you grab the nodes `Text` value and the `Text` value of this node's parent node to further populate the Label control, as follows:

```
Label1.Text += node.Text & " " & node.Parent.Text & "<br>"
```

In the end, you get a page that produces the results shown in Figure 14-13.

Specifying Custom Icons in the TreeView Control

The TreeView control allows for a high degree of customization. You saw earlier in the chapter that you were easily able to customize the look-and-feel of the TreeView control by specifying one of the built-in styles. Applying one of these styles dramatically changes the appearance of the control. One of the most noticeable changes concerns the icons used for the nodes within the TreeView control. Although it is not as easy as just selecting one of the styles built into the TreeView control, you can apply your own icons to be used for the nodes within the hierarchical list of nodes.

The TreeView control contains the properties discussed in the following table. These properties enable you to specify your own images to use for the nodes of the control.

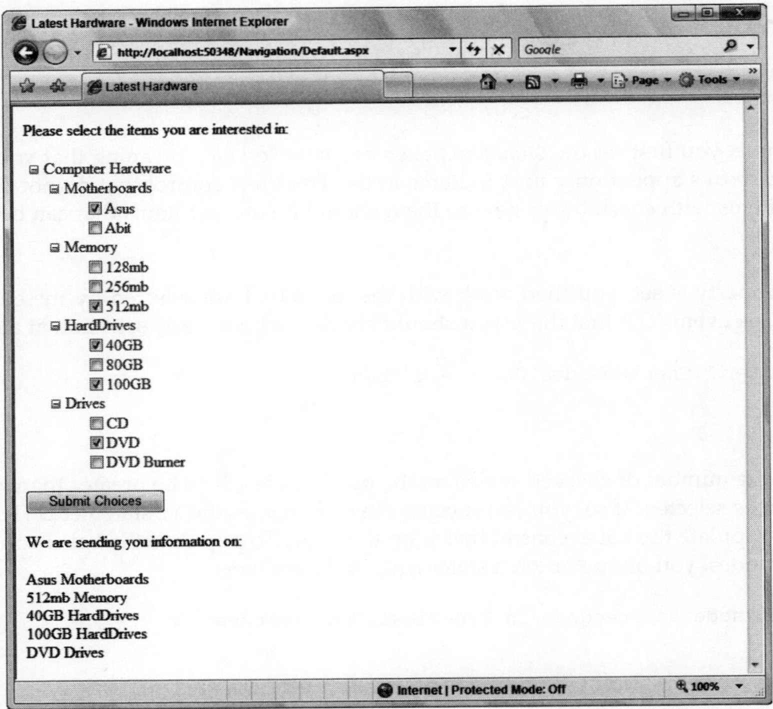

Figure 14-13

Property	Description
`CollapseImageUrl`	Applies a custom image next to nodes that have been expanded to show any of their child nodes and have the capability of being collapsed.
`ExpandImageUrl`	Applies a custom image next to nodes that have the capability of being expanded to display their child nodes.
`LeafNodeStyle-ImageUrl`	Applies a custom image next to a node that has no child nodes and is last in the hierarchical chain of nodes.
`NoExpandImageUrl`	Applies a custom image to nodes that, for programmatic reasons, cannot be expanded or to nodes that are leaf nodes. This is primarily used for spacing purposes to align leaf nodes with their parent nodes.
`ParentNodeStyle-ImageUrl`	Applies a custom image only to the parent nodes within the TreeView control.
`RootNodeStyle-ImageUrl`	Applies a custom image next to only the root nodes within the TreeView control.

Listing 14-11 shows an example of these properties in use.

Listing 14-11: Applying custom images to the TreeView control

```
<asp:TreeView ID="TreeView1" runat="server" Font-Underline="False"
 DataSourceId="XmlDataSource1"
 CollapseImageUrl="Images/CollapseImage.gif"
 ExpandImageUrl="Images/ExpandImage.gif"
 LeafNodeStyle-ImageUrl="Images/LeafImage.gif">
   <DataBindings>
      <asp:TreeNodeBinding DataMember="Hardware" Text="Computer Hardware" />
      <asp:TreeNodeBinding DataMember="Item" TextField="Category" />
      <asp:TreeNodeBinding DataMember="Option" TextField="Choice" />
   </DataBindings>
</asp:TreeView>
```

Specifying these three images to precede the nodes in your control overrides the default values of using a plus (+) sign and a minus (–) sign for the expandable and collapsible nodes. It also overrides simply using an image for any leaf nodes when by default nothing is used. Using the code from Listing 14-11, you get something similar to the results illustrated in Figure 14-14 (depending on the images you use, of course).

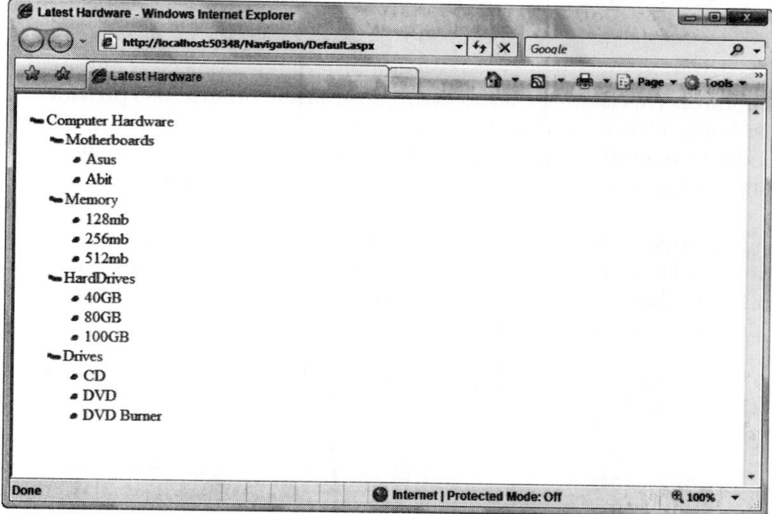

Figure 14-14

Specifying Lines Used to Connect Nodes

Because the TreeView control shows a hierarchical list of items to the end user, you sometimes want to show the relationship between these hierarchical items more explicitly than it is shown by default with the TreeView control. One possibility is to show line connections between parent and child nodes within the display. Simply set the `ShowLines` property of the TreeView control to `True` (by default, this property is set to `False`):

```
<asp:TreeView ID="TreeView1" runat="server" Font-Underline="False"
 DataSourceId="XmlDataSource1" ShowCheckBoxes="Leaf" ShowLines="True">
   ...
</asp:TreeViewTreeView>
```

This code gives the result shown in Figure 14-15.

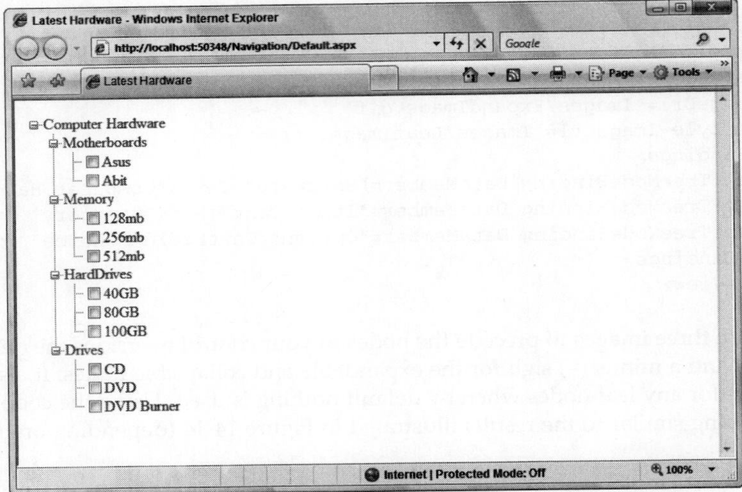

Figure 14-15

If the `ShowLines` property is set to `True`, you can also define your own lines and images within the TreeView control. This is quite easy to do because Visual Studio 2008 provides you with an ASP.NET TreeView Line Image Generator tool. This tool enables you to visually design how you want the lines and corresponding expanding and collapsing images to appear. After you have it set up as you want, the tool then creates all the necessary files for any of your TreeView controls to use.

To get at the tool, move to the Design view of your file and click the smart tag for the TreeView control that is on your page. Here you find the option Customize Line Images. You will not see this option unless the Show Lines check box is checked. Click this and you are presented with the ASP.NET TreeView Line Generator dialog (shown in Figure 14-16).

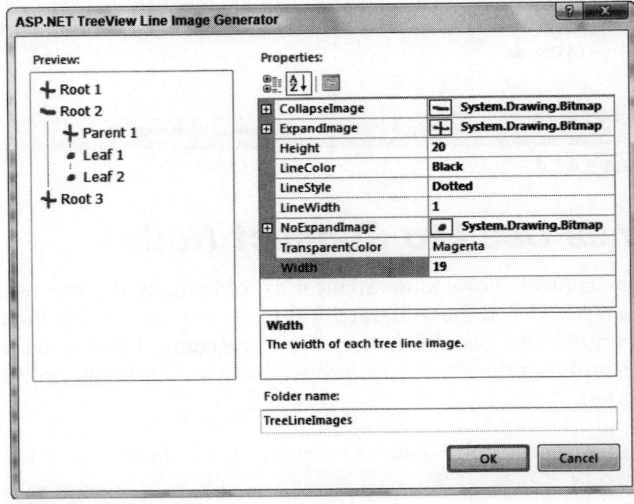

Figure 14-16

From within this dialog, you can select the images used for the nodes that require an Expand, Collapse, or NoCollapse icon. You can also specify the color and style of the lines that connect the nodes. As you create your styles, a sample TreeView control output is displayed for you directly in the dialog box based on how your styles are to be applied. The final step is to choose the output of the files that this dialog will create. When you have completed this step, click OK. This generates a long list of new files to the folder that you specified in the dialog. By default, the ASP.NET TreeView Line Image Generator wants you to name the output folder `TreeLineImages`, but feel free to name it as you wish. If the folder does not exist in the project, you are prompted to allow Visual Studio to create the folder for you. After this is in place, the TreeView control can use your new images and styles if you set the `LineImagesFolder` property as follows:

```
<asp:TreeView ID="TreeView1" runat="server" ShowLines="True"
 DataSourceId="SiteMapDataSource1" LineImagesFolder="TreeViewLineImages">
```

The important properties are shown in bold. The `ShowLines` property must be set to `True`. After it is set, it uses the default settings displayed earlier, unless you have specified a location where it can retrieve custom images and styles using the `LineImagesFolder` property. As you can see, this simply points to the new folder, `TreeViewLineImages`, which contains all the new images and styles you created. Look in the folder — it is interesting to see what is output by the tool.

Working with the TreeView Control Programmatically

So far, with the TreeView control, you have learned how to work with the control declaratively. The great thing about ASP.NET is that you are not simply required to work with its components declaratively, but you can also manipulate these controls programmatically.

The TreeView control has an associated `TreeView` class that enables you to completely manage the TreeView control and how it functions from within your code. The next section looks at how to use some of the more common ways to control the `TreeView` programmatically.

Expanding and Collapsing Nodes Programmatically

One thing you can do with your TreeView control is to expand or collapse the nodes within the hierarchy programmatically. You can accomplish this by using either the `ExpandAll` or `CollapseAll` methods from the `TreeView` class. Listing 14-12 shows you one of the earlier TreeView controls that you used in Listing 14-6, but with a couple of buttons above it that you can now use to initiate the expanding and collapsing of the nodes.

Listing 14-12: Expanding and collapsing the nodes of the TreeView control programmatically

VB

```
<%@ Page Language="VB" %>

<script runat="server">
   Protected Sub Button1_Click(ByVal sender As Object, ByVal e As System.EventArgs)
        TreeView1.ExpandAll()
   End Sub

   Protected Sub Button2_Click(ByVal sender As Object, ByVal e As System.EventArgs)
```

Continued

```
        TreeView1.CollapseAll()
    End Sub
</script>

<html xmlns="http://www.w3.org/1999/xhtml">
<head runat="server">
    <title>TreeView Control</title>
</head>
<body>
    <form id="Form1" runat="server">
        <p>
            <asp:Button ID="Button1" runat="server" Text="Expand Nodes"
             OnClick="Button1_Click" />
            <asp:Button ID="Button2" runat="server" Text="Collapse Nodes"
             OnClick="Button2_Click" />
            <br />
            <br />
        <asp:TreeView ID="TreeView1" runat="server"
         DataSourceId="SiteMapDataSource1">
        </asp:TreeView>
        <asp:SiteMapDataSource ID="SiteMapDataSource1" runat="server" /></p>
    </form>
</body>
</html>
```

C#

```
<%@ Page Language="C#" %>

<script runat="server">
    protected void Button1_Click(object sender, System.EventArgs e)
    {
        TreeView1.ExpandAll();
    }

    protected void Button2_Click(object sender, System.EventArgs e)
    {
        TreeView1.CollapseAll();
    }
</script>
```

Running this page gives you two buttons above your TreeView control. Clicking the first button invokes the `ExpandAll()` method and completely expands the entire list of nodes. Clicking the second button invokes the `CollapseAll()` method and completely collapses the list of nodes (see Figure 14-17).

The example shown in Listing 14-12 is nice, but it expands and collapses the nodes only on end-user actions (when the end user clicks the button). It would be even nicer if you could initiate this action programmatically.

You might want to simply place the `TreeView1.ExpandAll()` command within the `Page_Load` event, but if you try this, you'll see that it doesn't work. Instead, you use the `OnDataBound` attribute within the TreeView control:

```
<asp:TreeView ID="TreeView1" runat="server"
```

```
    DataSourceId="SiteMapDataSource1" OnDataBound="TreeView1_DataBound">
</asp:TreeView>
```

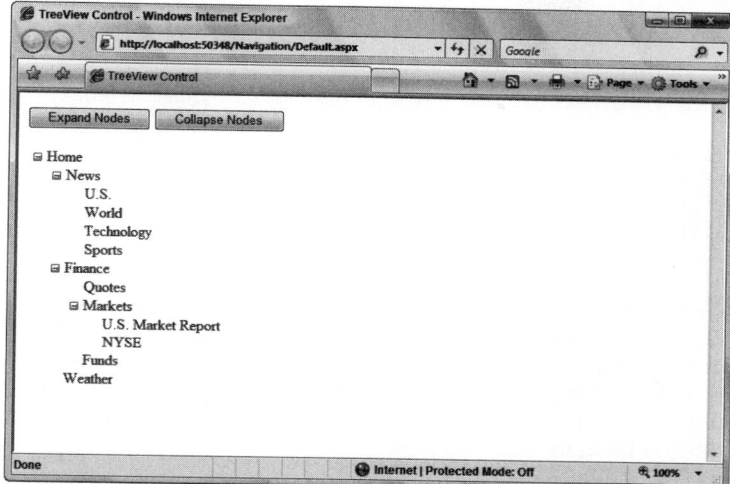

Figure 14-17

The value of this attribute points to a method in your code, as shown here:

VB

```
Protected Sub TreeView1_DataBound(ByVal sender As Object, _
  ByVal e As System.EventArgs)
   TreeView1.ExpandAll()
End Sub
```

C#

```
protected void TreeView1_DataBound(object sender, System.EventArgs e)
{
   TreeView1.ExpandAll();
}
```

Now when you run the page, notice that the TreeView control is completely expanded when the page is first loaded in the browser.

You can also expand specific nodes within the tree instead of just expanding the entire list. For this example, use the `TreeView1_DataBound` method you just created. Using the site map from Listing 14-1, change the `TreeView1_DataBound` method so that it appears as shown in Listing 14-13.

Listing 14-13: Expanding specific nodes programmatically

VB

```
Protected Sub TreeView1_DataBound(ByVal sender As Object, _
```

Continued

```
  ByVal e As System.EventArgs)
   TreeView1.CollapseAll()
   TreeView1.FindNode("Home").Expand()
   TreeView1.FindNode("Home/Finance").Expand()
   TreeView1.FindNode("Home/Finance/Markets").Expand()
End Sub
```

C#

```
protected void TreeView1_DataBound(object sender, System.EventArgs e)
{
   TreeView1.CollapseAll();
   TreeView1.FindNode("Home").Expand();
   TreeView1.FindNode("Home/Finance").Expand();
   TreeView1.FindNode("Home/Finance/Markets").Expand();
}
```

In this case, you use the `FindNode()` method and expand the node that is found. The `FindNode()` method takes a `String` value, which is the node and the path of the node that you want to reference. For instance, `TreeView1.FindNode("Home/Finance").Expand()` expands the `Finance` node. To find the node, it is important to specify the entire path from the root node to the node you want to work with (in this case, the `Finance` node). You separate the nodes within the site map path structure with a forward-slash between each of the nodes in the site map path.

Note that you had to expand each of the nodes individually until you got to the `Finance` node. If you simply used `TreeView1.FindNode("Home/Finance/Markets").Expand()` in the `TreeView1_DataBound()` method, the `Finance` node would indeed be expanded, but the parent nodes above it (the `Finance` and `Home` nodes) would not have been expanded and you wouldn't see the expanded `Markets` node when invoking the page. (Try it; it's interesting.)

Instead of using the `Expand` method, you can just as easily set the `Expanded` property to `True`, as shown in Listing 14-14.

Listing 14-14: Expanding nodes programmatically using the Expanded property

VB

```
Protected Sub TreeView1_DataBound(ByVal sender As Object, _
  ByVal e As System.EventArgs)
   TreeView1.CollapseAll()
   TreeView1.FindNode("Home").Expanded = True
   TreeView1.FindNode("Home/Finance").Expanded = True
   TreeView1.FindNode("Home/Finance/Markets").Expanded = True
End Sub
```

C#

```
protected void TreeView1_DataBound(object sender, System.EventArgs e)
{
   TreeView1.CollapseAll();
   TreeView1.FindNode("Home").Expanded = true;
```

```
        TreeView1.FindNode("Home/Finance").Expanded = true;
        TreeView1.FindNode("Home/Finance/Markets").Expanded = true;
    }
```

Although you focus on the `Expand` method and the `Expanded` property here, you can just as easily programmatically collapse nodes using the `Collapse()` method. No `Collapsed` property really exists. Instead, you simply set the `Expanded` property to `False`.

Adding Nodes

Another interesting thing you can do with the TreeView control is to add nodes to the overall hierarchy programmatically. The TreeView control is made up of a collection of `TreeNode` objects. Therefore, as you see in previous examples, the `Finance` node is actually a `TreeNode` object that you can work with programmatically. It includes the capability to add other `TreeNode` objects.

A `TreeNode` object typically stores a `Text` and `Value` property. The `Text` property is what is displayed in the TreeView control for the end user. The `Value` property is an additional data item that you can use to associate with this particular `TreeNode` object. Another property that you can use (if your TreeView control is a list of navigational links) is the `NavigateUrl` property. Listing 14-15 demonstrates how to add nodes programmatically to the same site map from Listing 14-1 that you have been using.

Listing 14-15: Adding nodes programmatically to the TreeView control

VB

```
<%@ Page Language="VB" %>

<script runat="server">
   Protected Sub Button1_Click(ByVal sender As Object, ByVal e As System.EventArgs)
        TreeView1.ExpandAll()
   End Sub

   Protected Sub Button2_Click(ByVal sender As Object, ByVal e As System.EventArgs)
        TreeView1.CollapseAll()
   End Sub

   Protected Sub Button3_Click(ByVal sender As Object, ByVal e As System.EventArgs)
        Dim myNode As New TreeNode
        myNode.Text = TextBox1.Text
        myNode.NavigateUrl = TextBox2.Text
        TreeView1.FindNode("Home/Finance/Markets").ChildNodes.Add(myNode)
   End Sub
</script>

<html xmlns="http://www.w3.org/1999/xhtml">
<head runat="server">
    <title>TreeView Control</title>
</head>
<body>
```

Continued

```
        <form id="Form1" runat="server">
            <p>
                <asp:Button ID="Button1" runat="server" Text="Expand Nodes"
                 OnClick="Button1_Click" />
                <asp:Button ID="Button2" runat="server" Text="Collapse Nodes"
                 OnClick="Button2_Click" /></p>
            <p>
                <strong>Text of new node:</strong>
                <asp:TextBox ID="TextBox1" runat="server">
                </asp:TextBox>
            </p>
            <p>
                <strong>Destination URL of new node:</strong>
                <asp:TextBox ID="TextBox2" runat="server">
                </asp:TextBox>
                <br />
                <br />
                <asp:Button ID="Button3" runat="server" Text="Add New Node"
                 OnClick="Button3_Click" />
            </p>
            <p>
            <asp:TreeView ID="TreeView1" runat="server"
             DataSourceId="SiteMapDataSource1">
            </asp:TreeView></p>
            <p>
            <asp:SiteMapDataSource ID="SiteMapDataSource1" runat="server" /></p>
        </form>
    </body>
    </html>
```

C#

```
protected void Button3_Click(object sender, System.EventArgs e)
{
   TreeNode myNode = new TreeNode();
   myNode.Text = TextBox1.Text;
   myNode.NavigateUrl = TextBox2.Text;
   TreeView1.FindNode("Home/Finance/Markets").ChildNodes.Add(myNode);
}
```

This page contains two text boxes and a new Button control. The first text box is used to populate the `Text` property of the new node that is created. The second text box is used to populate the `NavigateUrl` property of the new node.

If you run the page, you can expand the entire hierarchy by clicking the `Expand Nodes` button. Then you can add additional child nodes to the `Markets` node. To add a new node programmatically, use the `FindNode` method as you did before to find the `Markets` node. When you find it, you can add additional child nodes by using the `ChildNodes.Add()` method and pass in a `TreeNode` object instance. Submitting `NASDAQ` in the first text box and `Nasdaq.aspx` in the second text box changes your TreeView control as illustrated in Figure 14-18.

After it is added, the node stays added even after the hierarchy tree is collapsed and reopened. You can also add as many child nodes as you want to the `Markets` node. Note that, although you are changing nodes programmatically, this in no way alters the contents of the data source (the XML file, or the `.sitemap` file). These sources remain unchanged throughout the entire process.

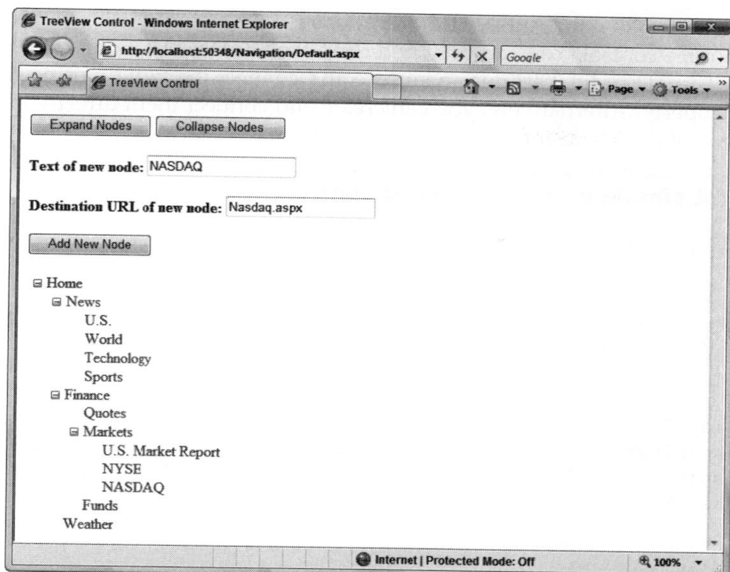

Figure 14-18

Menu Server Control

One of the cooler navigation controls found in ASP.NET 3.5 is the Menu server control. This control is ideal for allowing the end user to navigate a larger hierarchy of options while utilizing very little browser real estate in the process. Figure 14-19 shows you what the menu control looks like when it is either completely collapsed or completely extended down one of the branches of the hierarchy.

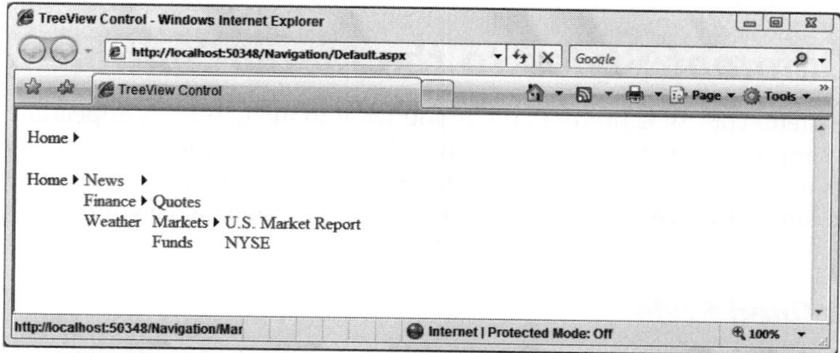

Figure 14-19

From here, you can see that the first Menu control displayed simply shows the Home link with a small arrow to the right of the display. The arrow means that more options are available that relate to this upmost link in the hierarchy. The second Menu control displayed shows what the default control looks like when the end user works down one of the branches provided by the site map.

The Menu control is an ideal control to use when you have lots of options — whether these options are selections the end user can make or navigation points provided by the application in which they are working. The Menu control can provide a multitude of options and consumes little space in the process.

Using the Menu control in your ASP.NET applications is rather simple. The Menu control works with a SiteMapDataSource control. You can drag and drop the SiteMapDataSource control and the Menu control onto the Visual Studio 2008 design surface and connect the two by using the Menu control's `DataSourceId` property. Alternatively, you can create and connect them directly in code. Listing 14-16 shows an example of the Menu control in its simplest form.

Listing 14-16: A simple use of the Menu control

```
<%@ Page Language="VB" %>

<html xmlns="http://www.w3.org/1999/xhtml" >
<head runat="server">
    <title>Menu Server Control</title>
</head>
<body>
    <form id="form1" runat="server">
        <asp:SiteMapDataSource ID="SiteMapDataSource1" runat="server" />
        <asp:Menu ID="Menu1" runat="server" DataSourceID="SiteMapDataSource1">
        </asp:Menu>
    </form>
</body>
</html>
```

From this example, you can see that I'm using a SiteMapDataSource control that automatically works with the application's `Web.sitemap` file. The only other item included is the Menu control, which uses the typical `ID` and `runat` attributes and the `DataSourceID` attribute to connect it with what is retrieved from the SiteMapDataSource control.

Although the default Menu control is pretty simple, you can highly customize how this control looks and works by redefining the properties of the control. The following sections look at some examples of how you can modify the appearance and change the behavior of this control.

Applying Different Styles to the Menu Control

By default, the Menu control is pretty plain. If you want to maintain this appearance, you can use what is provided or simply change the font sizes and styles to make it fit in with your site. You actually have quite a number of ways in which you can modify this control so that it appears unique and fits in with the rest of your site. Either you can customize this control's appearance yourself, or you can use one of the predefined styles that come with the control.

Using a Predefined Style

Visual Studio 2008 includes some predefined styles that you can use with the Menu control to quickly apply a look-and-feel to the displayed menu of items. Some of the provided styles include `Classic` and `Professional` and more. To apply one of these predefined styles, you work with the Menu control from the Design view of your page. Within the Design view, highlight the Menu control and expand the control's smart tag. From here, you see a list of options for working with this control. To change the look-and-feel of the control, click the Auto Format link and select one of the styles.

Performing this operation changes the code of your control by applying a set of style properties. For example, if you select the `Classic` option, you get the results shown in Listing 14-17.

Listing 14-17: Code changes when a style is applied to the Menu control

```
<asp:Menu ID="Menu1" runat="server" DataSourceID="SiteMapDataSource1"
 BackColor="#B5C7DE" ForeColor="#284E98"
 Font-Names="Verdana" Font-Size="0.8em" StaticSubMenuIndent="10px"
 DynamicHorizontalOffset="2">
   <StaticSelectedStyle BackColor="#507CD1"></StaticSelectedStyle>
   <StaticMenuItemStyle HorizontalPadding="5"
    VerticalPadding="2"></StaticMenuItemStyle>
   <DynamicMenuStyle BackColor="#B5C7DE"></DynamicMenuStyle>
   <DynamicSelectedStyle BackColor="#507CD1"></DynamicSelectedStyle>
   <DynamicMenuItemStyle HorizontalPadding="5"
    VerticalPadding="2"></DynamicMenuItemStyle>
   <DynamicHoverStyle ForeColor="White" Font-Bold="True"
    BackColor="#284E98"></DynamicHoverStyle>
   <StaticHoverStyle ForeColor="White" Font-Bold="True"
    BackColor="#284E98"></StaticHoverStyle>
</asp:Menu>
```

You can see a lot of added styles that change the menu items that appear in the control. Figure 14-20 shows how this style selection appears in the browser.

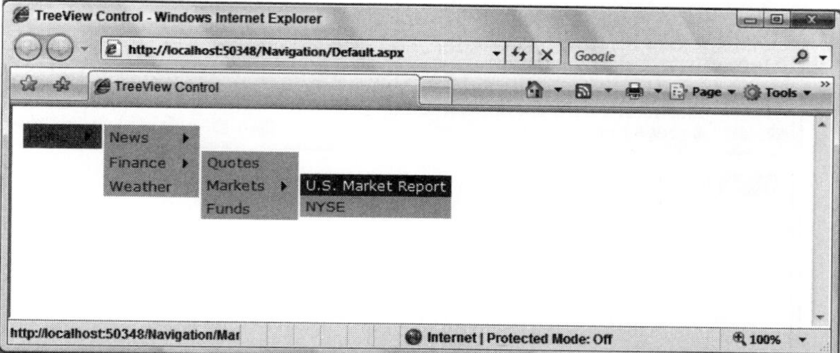

Figure 14-20

Changing the Style for Static Items

The Menu control considers items in the hierarchy to be either *static* or *dynamic*. Static items from this example would be the `Home` link that appears when the page is generated. Dynamic links are the items that appear dynamically when the user hovers the mouse over the `Home` link in the menu. It is possible to change the styles for both these types of nodes in the menu.

To apply a specific style to the static links that appear, you must add a static style element to the Menu control. The Menu control includes the following static style elements:

- `<StaticHoverStyle>`
- `<StaticItemTemplate>`

- <StaticMenuItemStyle>
- <StaticMenuStyle>
- <StaticSelectedStyle>

The important options from this list include the <StaticHoverStyle> and the <StaticMenuItemStyle> elements. The <StaticHoverStyle> is what you use to define the style of the static item in the menu when the end user hovers the mouse over the option. The <StaticMenuItemStyle> is what you use for the style of the static item when the end user is not hovering the mouse over the option.

Listing 14-18 illustrates adding a style that is applied when the end user hovers the mouse over static items.

Listing 14-18: Adding a hover style to static items in the menu control

```
<asp:Menu ID="Menu1" runat="server" DataSourceID="SiteMapDataSource1">
    <StaticHoverStyle BackColor="DarkGray" BorderColor="Black" BorderStyle="Solid"
     BorderWidth="1"></StaticHoverStyle>
</asp:Menu>
```

This little example adds a background color and border to the static items in the menu when the end user hovers the mouse over the item. The result is shown in Figure 14-21.

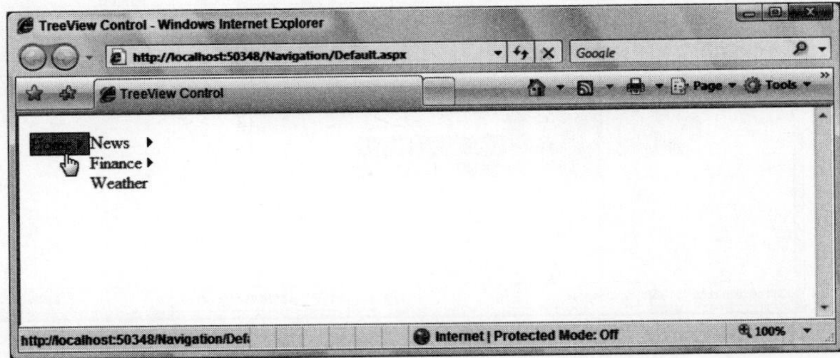

Figure 14-21

Adding Styles to Dynamic Items

Adding styles to the dynamic items of the menu control is just as easy as adding them to static items. The Menu control has a number of different elements for modifying the appearance of dynamic items, including the following:

- <DynamicHoverStyle>
- <DynamicItemTemplate>
- <DynamicMenuItemStyle>
- <DynamicMenuStyle>
- <DynamicSelectedStyle>

These elements change menu items the same way as the static versions of these elements, but they change only the items that dynamically pop-out from the static items. Listing 14-19 shows an example of applying the hover style to dynamic items.

Listing 14-19: Adding a hover style to dynamic items in the menu control

```
<asp:Menu ID="Menu1" runat="server" DataSourceID="Sitemapdatasource1">
   <StaticHoverStyle BackColor="DarkGray" BorderColor="Black" BorderStyle="Solid"
    BorderWidth="1"></StaticHoverStyle>
   <DynamicHoverStyle BackColor="DarkGray" BorderColor="Black" BorderStyle="Solid"
    BorderWidth="1"></DynamicHoverStyle>
</asp:Menu>
```

This code produces the results shown in Figure 14-22.

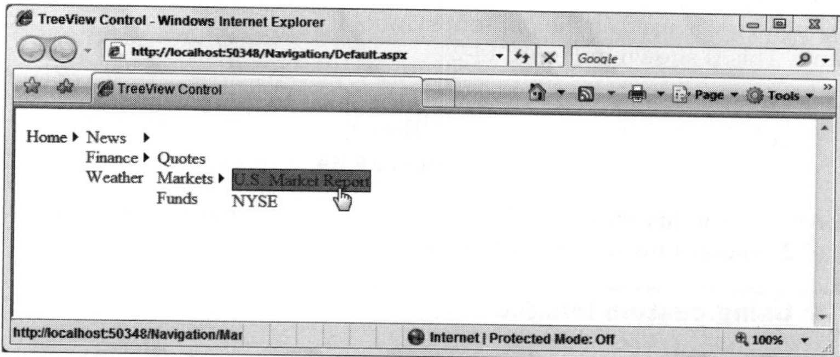

Figure 14-22

Changing the Layout of the Menu Items

By default, the dynamic menu items are displayed from left to right. This means that, as the items in the menu expand, they are continually displayed in a vertical fashion. You can actually control this behavior, but another option is available to you.

The other option is to have the first level of menu items appear directly below the first static item (horizontally). You change this behavior by using the `Orientation` attribute of the Menu control, as shown in Listing 14-20.

Listing 14-20: Forcing the menu items to use a horizontal orientation

```
<asp:Menu ID="Menu1" runat="server" DataSourceID="SiteMapDataSource1"
 Orientation="Horizontal">
</asp:Menu>
```

This code produces the results shown in Figure 14-23.

The `Orientation` attribute can take a value of `Horizontal` or `Vertical` only. The default value is `Vertical`.

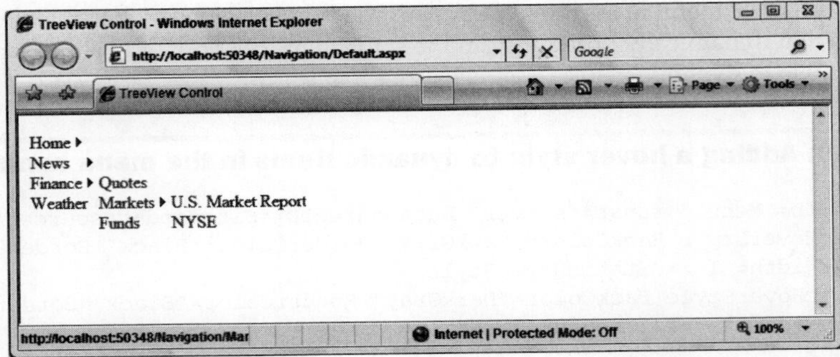

Figure 14-23

Changing the Pop-Out Symbol

As the default, an arrow is used as the pop-out symbol for the menu items generated, whether they are static or dynamic. This is shown in Figure 14-24.

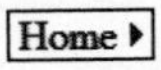

Figure 14-24

You are not forced to use this arrow symbol; in fact, you can change it to an image with relatively little work. Listing 14-21 shows how to accomplish this task.

Listing 14-21: Using custom images

```
<asp:Menu ID="Menu1" runat="server" DataSourceID="SiteMapDataSource1"
 Orientation="Horizontal" DynamicPopOutImageUrl="myArrow.gif"
 StaticPopOutImageUrl="myArrow.gif">
</asp:Menu>
```

To change the pop-out symbol to an image of your choice, you use the `DynamicPopOutImageUrl` or `StaticPopOutImageUrl` properties. The `String` value these attributes take is simply the path of the image you want to use. Depending on the image used, it produces something similar to what you see in Figure 14-25.

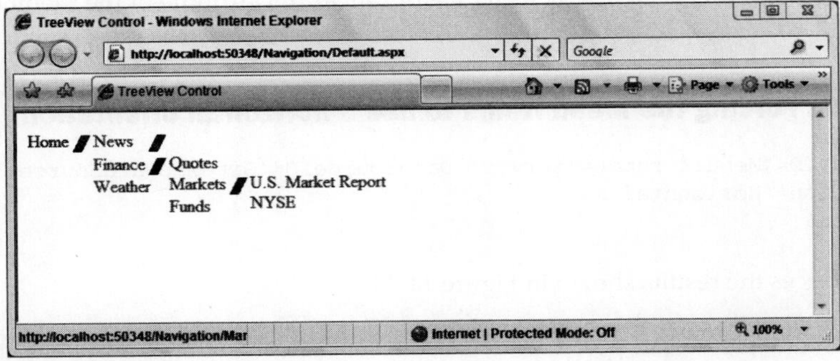

Figure 14-25

Separating Menu Items with Images

Another nice styling option of the Menu control is the capability to add a divider image to the menu items. You use the `StaticBottomSeparatorImageUrl`, `StaticTopSeparatorImageUrl`, `DynamicBottom-SeparatorImageUrl`, and `DynamicTopSeparatorImageUrl` properties depending on where you want to place the separator image.

For example, if you wanted to place a divider image under only the dynamic menu items, you use the `DynamicBottomSeparatorImageUrl` property, as shown in Listing 14-22.

Listing 14-22: Applying divider images to dynamic items

```
<asp:Menu ID="Menu1" runat="server" DataSourceID="SiteMapDataSource1"
 DynamicBottomSeparatorImageUrl="myDivider.gif">
</asp:Menu>
```

All the properties of the Menu control that define the image to use for the dividers take a `String` value that points to the location of the image. The result of Listing 14-22 is shown in Figure 14-26.

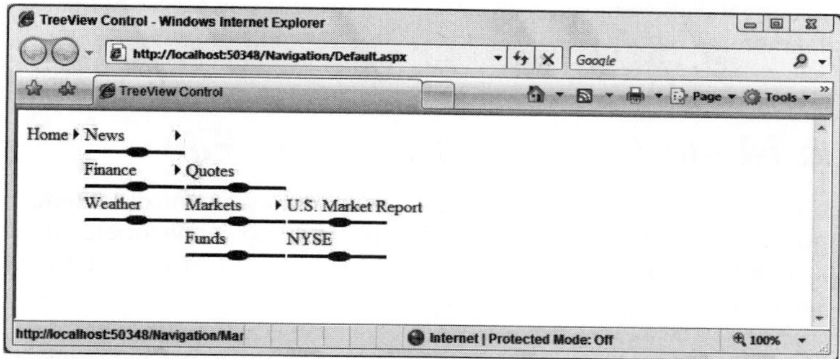

Figure 14-26

Menu Events

The Menu control exposes events such as the following:

- `DataBinding`
- `DataBound`
- `Disposed`
- `Init`
- `Load`
- `MenuItemClick`
- `MenuItemDataBound`
- `PreRender`
- `Unload`

One nice event to be aware of is the `MenuItemClick` event. This event, shown in Listing 14-23, enables you to take some action when the end user clicks one of the available menu items.

Listing 14-23: Using the MenuItemClick event

VB

```
Protected Sub Menu1_MenuItemClick(ByVal sender As Object, _
   ByVal e As System.Web.UI.WebControls.MenuEventArgs)

    ' Code for event here

End Sub
```

C#

```
protected void Menu1_MenuItemClick(object sender, MenuEventArgs e)
{

   // Code for event here

}
```

This delegate uses the `MenuEventArgs` data class and provides you access to the text and value of the item selected from the menu.

Binding the Menu Control to an XML File

Just as with the TreeView control, it is possible to bind the Menu control to items that come from other data source controls provided with ASP.NET 3.5. Although most developers are likely to use the Menu control to enable end users to navigate to URL destinations, you can also use the Menu control to enable users to make selections.

As an example, take the previous XML file, `Hardware.xml`, which was used with the TreeView control from Listing 14-8 earlier in the chapter. For this example, the Menu control works with an XmlDataSource control. When the end user makes a selection from the menu, you populate a Listbox on the page with the items selected. The code for this is shown in Listing 14-24.

Listing 14-24: Using the Menu control with an XML file

VB

```
<%@ Page Language="VB" %>

<script runat="server">
    Protected Sub Menu1_MenuItemClick(ByVal sender As Object, _
       ByVal e As System.Web.UI.WebControls.MenuEventArgs)

        Listbox1.Items.Add(e.Item.Parent.Value & " : " & e.Item.Value)
    End Sub
</script>

<html xmlns="http://www.w3.org/1999/xhtml">
<head runat="server">
    <title>Menu Server Control</title>
</head>
<body>
```

```
        <form id="form1" runat="server">
            <asp:Menu ID="Menu1" runat="server" DataSourceID="XmlDataSource1"
             OnMenuItemClick="Menu1_MenuItemClick">
                <DataBindings>
                    <asp:MenuItemBinding DataMember="Item"
                     TextField="Category"></asp:MenuItemBinding>
                    <asp:MenuItemBinding DataMember="Option"
                     TextField="Choice"></asp:MenuItemBinding>
                </DataBindings>
            </asp:Menu>
            <p>
            <asp:ListBox ID="Listbox1" runat="server">
            </asp:ListBox></p>
            <asp:xmldatasource ID="XmlDataSource1" runat="server"
             datafile="Hardware.xml" />
        </form>
</body>
</html>
```

C#

```
<%@ Page Language="C#" %>

<script runat="server">
   protected void Menu1_MenuItemClick(object sender, MenuEventArgs e)
   {
      Listbox1.Items.Add(e.Item.Parent.Value + " : " + e.Item.Value);
   }
</script>
```

From this example, you can see that instead of using the `<asp:TreeNodeBinding>` elements, as we did with the TreeView control, the Menu control uses the `<asp:MenuItemBinding>` elements to make connections to items listed in the XML file, `Hardware.xml`. In addition, the root element of the Menu control, the `<asp:Menu>` element, now includes the `OnMenuItemClick` attribute, which points to the event delegate `Menu1_MenuItemClick`.

The `Menu1_MenuItemClick` delegate includes the data class `MenuEventArgs`, which enables you to get at both the values of the child and parent elements selected. For this example, both are used and then populated into the Listbox control, as illustrated in Figure 14-27.

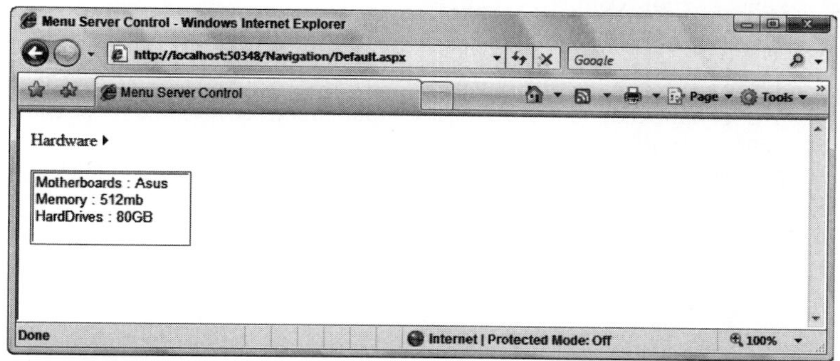

Figure 14-27

SiteMap Data Provider

A series of data providers in the form of DataSource controls are available in ASP.NET 3.5. One of these DataSource controls now at your disposal, which you looked at earlier in the chapter, is the SiteMapDataSource control. This DataSource control was developed to work with site maps and the controls that can bind to them.

Some controls do not need a SiteMapDataSource control in order to bind to the application's site map (which is typically stored in the `Web.sitemap` file). Earlier in the chapter, you saw this in action when using the SiteMapPath control. This control was able to work with the `Web.sitemap` file directly — without the need for this data provider.

Certain navigation controls, however, such as the TreeView control and the DropDownList control, require an intermediary SiteMapDataSource control to retrieve the site navigation information.

The SiteMapDataSource control is simple to use as demonstrated throughout this chapter. The SiteMap-DataSource control in its simplest form is illustrated here:

```
<asp:SiteMapDataSource ID="SiteMapDataSource1" runat="server" />
```

In this form, the SiteMapDataSource control simply grabs the info as a tree hierarchy (as consistently demonstrated so far). Be aware that a number of properties do change how the data is displayed in any control that binds to the data output.

ShowStartingNode

The `ShowStartingNode` property determines whether the root node of the `.sitemap` file is retrieved with the retrieved collection of node objects. This property takes a `Boolean` value and is set to `True` by default. If you are working with the `Web.sitemap` file shown in Listing 14-1, you construct your SiteMapDataSource control as shown in Listing 14-25 to remove the root node from the collection.

Listing 14-25: Removing the root node from the retrieved node collection

```
<%@ Page Language="VB" %>

<html xmlns="http://www.w3.org/1999/xhtml">
<head runat="server">
    <title>Menu Server Control</title>
</head>
<body>
    <form id="form1" runat="server">
        <asp:SiteMapDataSource ID="SiteMapDataSource1" runat="server"
         ShowStartingNode="False" />
        <asp:Menu ID="Menu1" runat="server" DataSourceID="SiteMapDataSource1">
        </asp:Menu>
    </form>
</body>
</html>
```

This code produces a menu like the one shown in Figure 14-28.

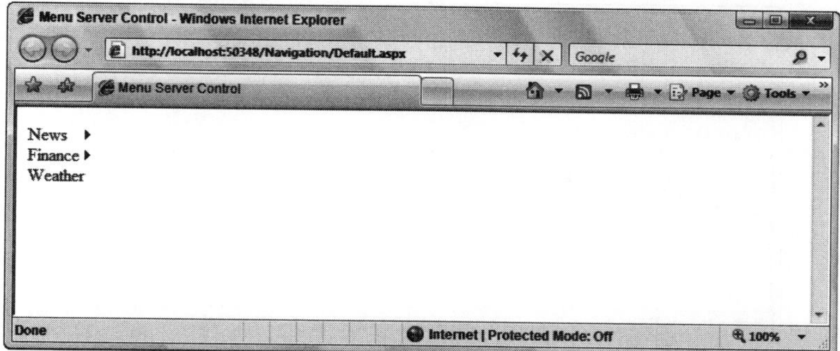

Figure 14-28

From this screenshot, you can see that indeed the root node has been removed, and the menu shown starts by using all the child nodes of the root node.

StartFromCurrentNode

The `StartFromCurrentNode` property causes the SiteMapDataProvider to retrieve only a node collection that starts from the current node of the page being viewed. By default, this is set to `False`, meaning that the SiteMapDataProvider always retrieves all the available nodes (from the root node to the current node).

For an example of this, use the `.sitemap` file from Listing 14-1 and create a page called `Markets.aspx`. This page in the hierarchy of the node collection is a child node of the Finance node, as well as having two child nodes itself: U.S. Market Report and NYSE. An example of setting the `StartFromCurrentNode` property to `True` is shown in Listing 14-26.

Listing 14-26: The Markets.aspx page using the StartFromCurrentNode property

```
<%@ Page Language="VB" %>

<html xmlns="http://www.w3.org/1999/xhtml">
<head runat="server">
    <title>Menu Server Control</title>
</head>
<body>
    <form id="form1" runat="server">
        <asp:SiteMapDataSource ID="SiteMapDataSource1" runat="server"
         StartFromCurrentNode="True" />
        <asp:Menu ID="Menu1" runat="server" DataSourceID="SiteMapDataSource1">
        </asp:Menu>
    </form>
</body>
</html>
```

This simple property addition produces the result shown in Figure 14-29.

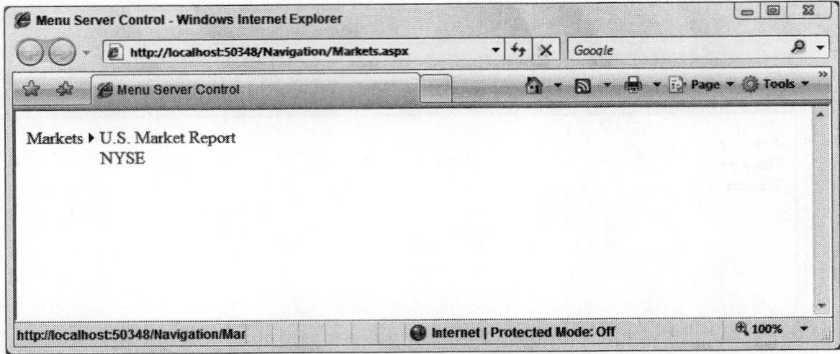

Figure 14-29

StartingNodeOffset

The `StartingNodeOffset` property takes an `Integer` value that determines the starting point of the hierarchy collection. Be default, this property is set to `0`, meaning that the node collection retrieved by the SiteMapDataSource control starts at the root node. Any other value provides the offset from the root node and, in turn, makes this the new starting point. From the example provided in Listing 14-1, you know that the collection starts with the Home page found at `Default.aspx`, a page that you have seen in numerous examples in this chapter.

If you set this property's value to `1`, the starting point of the collection is one space off the default starting point (the Home page starting at `Default.aspx`). For example, if the page using the SiteMapDataSource control is the `MarketsUS.aspx` page, the node collection starts with the Finance page (`Finance.aspx`).

```
Home  Offset 0
   News  Offset 1
      U.S.   Offset 2
      World   Offset 2
      Technology   Offset 2
      Sports   Offset 2
   Finance   Offset 1
      Quotes   Offset 2
      Markets   Offset 2
         U.S. Market Report   Offset 3
         NYSE   Offset 3
      Funds   Offset 2
   Weather   Offset 1
```

From this hierarchy, you can see how much each node is offset from the root node. Therefore, if you set the `StartingNodeOffset` property to `1` and you are browsing on the U.S. Market Report page, you can see that the node collection starts with the Finance page (`Finance.aspx`) and the other child nodes of the root node (News and Weather) are not represented in the node collection as the `Finance.aspx` page is on the direct hierarchical path of the requested page.

StartingNodeUrl

The `StartingNodeUrl` property enables you to specify the page found in the `.sitemap` file from which the node collection should start. By default, the value of this property is empty; but when set to something such as `Finance.aspx`, the collection starts with the Finance page as the root node of the node collection. Listing 14-27 shows an example of using the `StartingNodeUrl` property.

Listing 14-27: Using the StartingNodeUrl property

```
<%@ Page Language="VB" %>

<html xmlns="http://www.w3.org/1999/xhtml">
<head runat="server">
    <title>Menu Server Control</title>
</head>
<body>
    <form id="form1" runat="server">
        <asp:SiteMapDataSource ID="SiteMapDataSource1" runat="server"
         StartingNodeUrl="Finance.aspx" />
        <asp:Menu ID="Menu1" runat="server" DataSourceID="SiteMapDataSource1">
        </asp:Menu>
    </form>
</body>
</html>
```

When the `StartingNodeUrl` property value is encountered, the value is compared against the `url` attributes in the `Web.sitemap` file. When a match is found, the matched page is the one used as the root node in the node collection retrieved by the SiteMapDataSource control.

SiteMap API

The `SiteMap` class is an in-memory representation of the site's navigation structure. This is a great class for programmatically working around the hierarchical structure of your site. The `SiteMap` class comes with a couple of objects that make working with the navigation structure easy. These objects (or public properties) are described in the following table.

Properties	Description
`CurrentNode`	Retrieves a `SiteMapNode` object for the current page
`RootNode`	Retrieves a `SiteMapNode` object that starts from the root node and the rest of the site's navigation structure
`Provider`	Retrieves the default `SiteMapProvider` for the current site map
`Providers`	Retrieves a collection of available, named `SiteMapProvider` objects

Listing 14-28 shows an example of working with some `SiteMap` objects by demonstrating how to use the `CurrentNode` object from the `Markets.aspx` page.

Listing 14-28: Working with the CurrentNode object

VB

```
<%@ Page Language="VB" %>

<script runat="server" language="vb">
    Protected Sub Page_Load(ByVal sender As Object, ByVal e As System.EventArgs)
        Label1.Text = SiteMap.CurrentNode.Description & "<br>" & _
            SiteMap.CurrentNode.HasChildNodes & "<br>" & _
            SiteMap.CurrentNode.NextSibling.ToString() & "<br>" & _
            SiteMap.CurrentNode.ParentNode.ToString() & "<br>" & _
            SiteMap.CurrentNode.PreviousSibling.ToString() & "<br>" & _
            SiteMap.CurrentNode.RootNode.ToString() & "<br>" & _
            SiteMap.CurrentNode.Title & "<br>" & _
            SiteMap.CurrentNode.Url
    End Sub
</script>

<html xmlns="http://www.w3.org/1999/xhtml">
<head runat="server">
    <title>SiteMapDataSource</title>
</head>
<body>
    <form id="form1" runat="server">
        <asp:Label ID="Label1" runat="server"></asp:Label>
    </form>
</body>
</html>
```

C#

```
<%@ Page Language="C#" %>

<script runat="server">
    protected void Page_Load(object sender, System.EventArgs e)
    {
        Label1.Text = SiteMap.CurrentNode.Description + "<br>" +
            SiteMap.CurrentNode.HasChildNodes + "<br>" +
            SiteMap.CurrentNode.NextSibling.ToString() + "<br>" +
            SiteMap.CurrentNode.ParentNode.ToString() + "<br>" +
            SiteMap.CurrentNode.PreviousSibling.ToString() + "<br>" +
            SiteMap.CurrentNode.RootNode.ToString() + "<br>" +
            SiteMap.CurrentNode.Title + "<br>" +
            SiteMap.CurrentNode.Url;
    }
</script>
```

As you can see from this little bit of code, by using the `SiteMap` class and the `CurrentNode` object you can work with a plethora of information regarding the current page. Running this page, you get the following results printed to the screen:

```
The Latest Market Information
True
Funds
Finance
Quotes
```

```
Home
Markets
/SiteNavigation/Markets.aspx
```

Using the `CurrentNode` property, you can actually create your own style of the SiteMapPath control, as illustrated in Listing 14-29.

Listing 14-29: Creating a custom navigation display using the CurrentNode property

VB

```
<%@ Page Language="VB" %>

<script runat="server" language="vb">
    Protected Sub Page_Load(ByVal sender As Object, ByVal e As System.EventArgs)
        Hyperlink1.Text = SiteMap.CurrentNode.ParentNode.ToString()
        Hyperlink1.NavigateUrl = SiteMap.CurrentNode.ParentNode.Url

        Hyperlink2.Text = SiteMap.CurrentNode.PreviousSibling.ToString()
        Hyperlink2.NavigateUrl = SiteMap.CurrentNode.PreviousSibling.Url

        Hyperlink3.Text = SiteMap.CurrentNode.NextSibling.ToString()
        Hyperlink3.NavigateUrl = SiteMap.CurrentNode.NextSibling.Url
    End Sub
</script>

<html xmlns="http://www.w3.org/1999/xhtml" >
<head runat="server">
    <title>SiteMapDataSource</title>
</head>
<body>
    <form id="form1" runat="server">
        Move Up:
        <asp:Hyperlink ID="Hyperlink1" runat="server"></asp:Hyperlink><br />
        <-- <asp:Hyperlink ID="Hyperlink2" runat="server"></asp:Hyperlink> |
        <asp:Hyperlink ID="Hyperlink3" runat="server"></asp:Hyperlink> -->
    </form>
</body>
</html>
```

C#

```
<%@ Page Language="C#" %>

<script runat="server">
    protected void Page_Load(object sender, System.EventArgs e)
    {
        Hyperlink1.Text = SiteMap.CurrentNode.ParentNode.ToString();
        Hyperlink1.NavigateUrl = SiteMap.CurrentNode.ParentNode.Url;

        Hyperlink2.Text = SiteMap.CurrentNode.PreviousSibling.ToString();
        Hyperlink2.NavigateUrl = SiteMap.CurrentNode.PreviousSibling.Url;

        Hyperlink3.Text = SiteMap.CurrentNode.NextSibling.ToString();
        Hyperlink3.NavigateUrl = SiteMap.CurrentNode.NextSibling.Url;
    }
</script>
```

When run, this page gives you your own custom navigation structure, as shown in Figure 14-30.

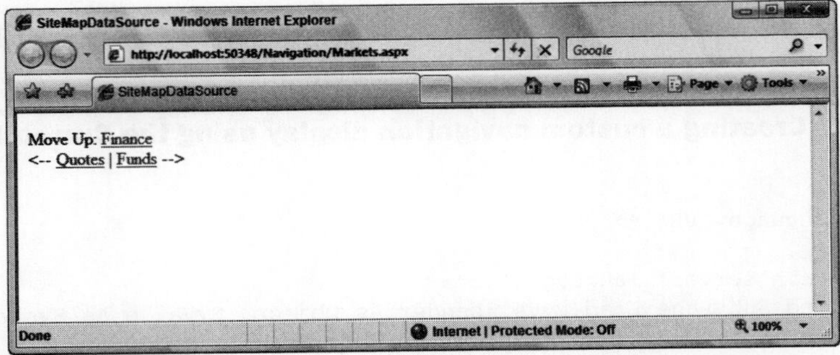

Figure 14-30

URL Mapping

The URLs used by Web pages can sometimes get rather complex as your application grows and grows. Sometimes, you could be presenting Web pages that change their content based on querystrings that are provided via the URL, such as:

```
http://www.asp.net/forums/view.aspx?forumid=12&categoryid=6
```

In other cases, your Web page might be so deep within a hierarchy of folders that the URL has become rather cumbersome for an end user to type or remember when they want to pull up the page later in their browser. There are also moments when you want a collection of pages to look like they are the same page or a single destination.

In cases such as these, you can take advantage of an ASP.NET feature called *URL mapping*. URL mapping enables you to map complex URLs to simpler ones. You accomplish this through settings you apply in the `web.config` file using the `<urlMappings>` element (see Listing 14-30).

Listing 14-30: Mapping URLs using the <urlMappings> element

```
<configuration>

   <system.web>

      <urlMappings>
         <add url="~/Content.aspx" mappedUrl="~/SystemNews.aspx?categoryid=5" />
      </urlMappings>

   </system.web>

</configuration>
```

In this example, we provide a fake URL — `Content.aspx` — that is mapped to a more complicated URL: `SystemNews.aspx?categoryid=5`. With this construction in place, when the end user types URL `Content.aspx`, the application knows to invoke the more complicated URL `SystemNews.aspx?categoryid=5` page. This takes place without the URL even being changed in the browser. Even after the page has completely loaded, the browser will still show the `Content.aspx` page as the destination — thereby tricking the end user in a sense.

It is important to note that in this situation, the end user is routed to `SystemNews.aspx?categoryid=5` no matter what — *even if a* `Content.aspx` *page exists*! Therefore, it is important to map to pages that are not actually contained within your application.

Sitemap Localization

The improved resource files (`.resx`) are a great way to localize ASP.NET applications. This localization of Web applications using ASP.NET is covered in Chapter 31 of this book. However, this introduction focused on applying localization features to the pages of your applications; we didn't demonstrate how to take this localization capability further by applying it to items such as the `Web.sitemap` file.

Structuring the Web.sitemap File for Localization

Just as it is possible to apply localization instructions to the pages of your ASP.NET Web applications, you can also use the same framework to accomplish your localization tasks in the `Web.sitemap` file. To show you this in action, Listing 14-31 constructs a `Web.sitemap` file somewhat similar to the one presented in Listing 14-1, but much simpler.

Listing 14-31: Creating a basic .sitemap file for localization

```
<?xml version="1.0" encoding="utf-8" ?>

<siteMap xmlns="http://schemas.microsoft.com/AspNet/SiteMap-File-1.0"
 enableLocalization="true">
 <siteMapNode url="Default.aspx" resourceKey="Home">
        <siteMapNode url="News.aspx" resourceKey="News">
               <siteMapNode url="News.aspx?cat=us" resourceKey="NewsUS" />
               <siteMapNode url="News.aspx?cat=world" resourceKey="NewsWorld" />
               <siteMapNode url="News.aspx?cat=tech" resourceKey="NewsTech" />
               <siteMapNode url="News.aspx?cat=sport" resourceKey="NewsSport" />
        </siteMapNode>
 </siteMapNode>
</siteMap>
```

Looking at Listing 14-31, you can see that we have a rather simple `Web.sitemap` file. To enable the localization capability from the `Web.sitemap` file, you have to turn this capability on by using the `enable-Localization` attribute in the `<siteMap>` element and setting it to `true`. Once enabled, you can then define each of the navigation nodes as you would normally, using the `<siteMapNode>` element. In this case, however, because you are going to define the contents of these navigation pieces (most notably the `title` and `description` attributes) in various `.resx` files, there is no need to repeatedly define these items in this file. That means you need to define only the `url` attribute for this example. It is important to note, however, that you could also define this attribute through your `.resx` files, thereby forwarding end users to different pages depending on their defined culture settings.

The next attribute to note is the `resourceKey` attribute used in the `<siteMapNode>` elements. This is the key that is used and defined in the various `.resx` files you will implement. Take the following `<siteMapNode>` element as an example:

```
<siteMapNode url="News.aspx" resourceKey="News">
   ...
</siteMapNode>
```

In this case, the value of the `resourceKey` (and the key that will be used in the `.resx` file) is `News`. This means that you are then able to define the values of the `title` and `description` attributes in the `.resx` file using the following syntax:

```
News.Title
News.Description
```

Now that the `Web.sitemap` is in place, the next step is to make some minor modifications to the `Web.config` file, as shown next.

Making Modifications to the Web.config File

Now that the `Web.sitemap` file is in place and ready, the next step is to provide some minor additions to the `Web.config` file. In order for your Web application to make an automatic detection of the culture of the users visiting the various pages you are providing, you need to set the `Culture` and `UICulture` settings in the `@Page` directive, or set these attributes for automatic detection in the `<globalization>` element of the `Web.config` file.

When you are working with navigation and the `Web.sitemap` file, as we are, it is actually best to make this change in the `Web.config` file so that it automatically takes effect on each and every page in your application. This makes it much simpler because you won't have to make these additions yourself to each and every page.

To make these changes, open your `Web.config` file and add a `<globalization>` element, as shown in Listing 14-32.

Listing 14-32: Adding culture detection to the Web.config file

```
<configuration>
   <system.web>

      <globalization culture="auto" uiCulture="auto" />

   </system.web>
</configuration>
```

For the auto-detection capabilities to occur, you simply need to set the `culture` and `uiCulture` attributes to `auto`. You could have also defined the values as `auto:en-US`, which means that the automatic culture detection capabilities should occur, but if the culture defined is not found in the various resource files, then use `en-US` (American English) as the default culture. However, because we are going to define a default `Web.sitemap` set of values, there really is no need for you to bring forward this construction.

Next, you need to create the assembly resources files that define the values used by the `Web.sitemap` file.

Creating Assembly Resource (.resx) Files

To create a set of assembly resource files that you will use with the `Web.sitemap` file, create a folder in your project called `App_GlobalResources`. If you are using Visual Studio 2008 or Visual Web Developer, you can add this folder by right-clicking on the project and selecting Add Folder ➪ App_GlobalResources.

After the folder is in place, the next step is to add two assembly resource files to this folder. Name the first file `Web.sitemap.resx` and the second one `Web.sitemap.fi.resx`. Your goal with these two files is to have a default set of values for the `Web.sitemap` file that will be defined in the `Web.sitemap.resx` file, and a version of these values that has been translated to the Finnish language and is contained in the `Web.sitemap.fi.resx` file.

The `fi` value used in the name will be the file used by individuals who have their preferred language set to `fi-FI`. Other variations of these constructions are shown in the following table.

.resx File	Culture Served
`Web.sitemap.resx`	The default values used when the end user's culture cannot be identified through another `.resx` file
`Web.sitemap.en.resx`	The resource file used for all `en` (English) users
`Web.sitemap.en-gb.resx`	The resource file used for the English speakers of Great Britain
`Web.sitemap.fr-ca.resx`	The resource file used for the French speakers of Canada
`Web.sitemap.ru.resx`	The resource file used for Russian speakers

Now that the `Web.sitemap.resx` and `Web.sitemap.fi.resx` files are in place, the next step is to fill these files with values. To accomplish this task, you use the keys defined earlier directly in the `Web.sitemap` file. Figure 14-31 shows the result of this exercise.

Although the IDE states that these are not valid identifiers, the application still works with this model. After you have the files in place, you can test how this localization endeavor works, as shown in the following section.

Testing the Results

Create a page in your application and place a TreeView server control on the page. In addition to the TreeView control, you also have to include a SiteMapDataSource control to work with the `Web.sitemap` file you created. Be sure to tie the two controls together by giving the TreeView control the attribute `DataSourceID="SiteMapDataSource1"`, as demonstrated earlier in this chapter.

If you have your language preference in Microsoft's Internet Explorer set to `en-us` (American English), you will see the results shown in Figure 14-32.

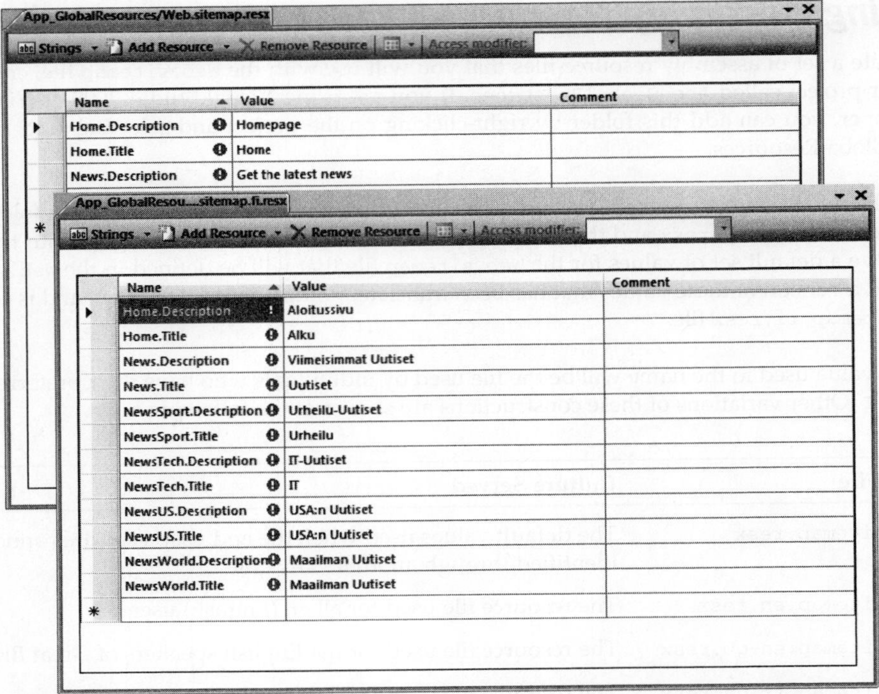

Figure 14-31

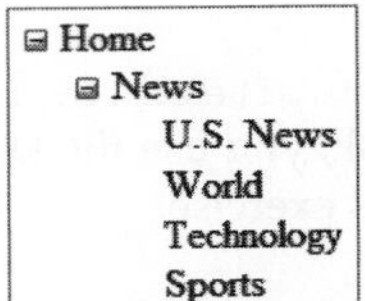

Figure 14-32

When you pull up the page in the browser, the culture of the request is checked. Because the only finely grained preference defined in the example is for users using the culture of `fi` (Finnish), the default `Web.sitemap.resx` is used instead. Because of this, the `Web.sitemap.resx` file is used to populate the values of the TreeView control, as shown in Figure 14-32. If the requestor has a culture setting of `fi`, however, he gets an entirely different set of results.

To test this out, change the preferred language used in IE by selecting Tools ➪ Internet Options in IE. On the first tab (General), click the Languages button at the bottom of the dialog. You are presented with the Language Preferences dialog. Click the Add button and add the Finnish language setting to the list of options. The final step is to use the Move Up button to move the Finnish choice to the top of the list. In the end, you should see something similar to what is shown in Figure 14-33.

With this setting in place, running the page with the TreeView control gives you the result shown in Figure 14-34.

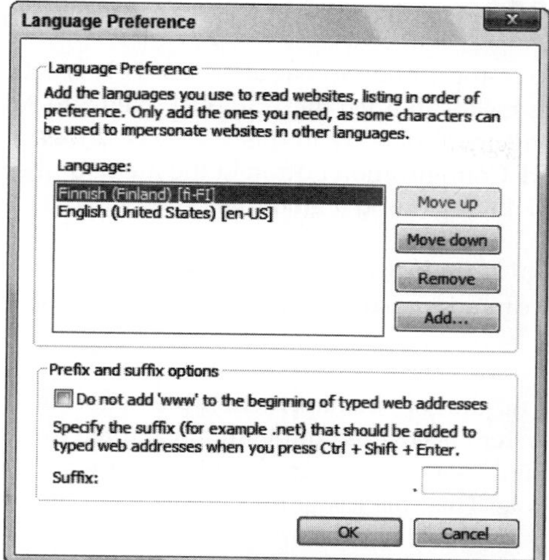

Figure 14-33

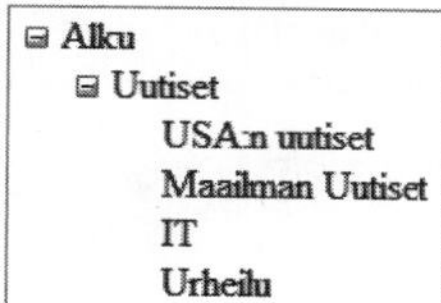

Figure 14-34

Now, when the page is requested, the culture is set to `fi` and correlates to the `Web.sitemap.fi.resx` file instead of to the default `Web.sitemap.resx` file.

Security Trimming

If you have been following the examples so far in this chapter, you might notice that one of the attributes available to a `<siteMapNode>` tag hasn't yet been discussed. The `roles` attribute is a powerful one that allows you to provide an authorization model to the items contained in the navigation system. This really means that you have the capability to display *only* the navigational items that a user is entitled to see and nothing more. The term commonly used for this behavior is *security trimming*. This section looks at how to apply security trimming to the application you are building in ASP.NET 3.5.

This capability is a good example of two ASP.NET 3.5 systems interacting with one another in the site navigation system. Security trimming works only when you have enabled the ASP.NET 3.5 role management system. This system is covered in more detail in Chapter 16. Be sure to check out this chapter because this section does not go into much detail about this system.

As an example of security trimming in your ASP.NET applications, this section shows you how to limit access to the navigation of your application's administration system only to users who are contained within a specific application role.

Setting Up Role Management for Administrators

The first step is to set up your application to handle roles. This is actually a pretty simple process. One easy way to accomplish this task is to open the ASP.NET Web Site Administration Tool for your application and enable role management directly in this Web-based tool. You can get to this administration tool by clicking the ASP.NET Configuration button in the menu of the Solution Explorer in Visual Studio. This button has the logo of a hammer and a globe.

After the ASP.NET Web Site Administration Tool is launched, select the Security tab; this brings you to a screen where you can administer the membership and role management systems for your application.

First, you enable and build up the role management system, and then you also enable the membership system. The membership system is covered in detail in Chapter 16. After you turn on the membership system, you build some actual users in your application. You want a user to log in to your application and be assigned a specific role. This role assignment changes the site navigation system display.

The Security tab in the ASP.NET Web Site Administration Tool is presented in Figure 14-35.

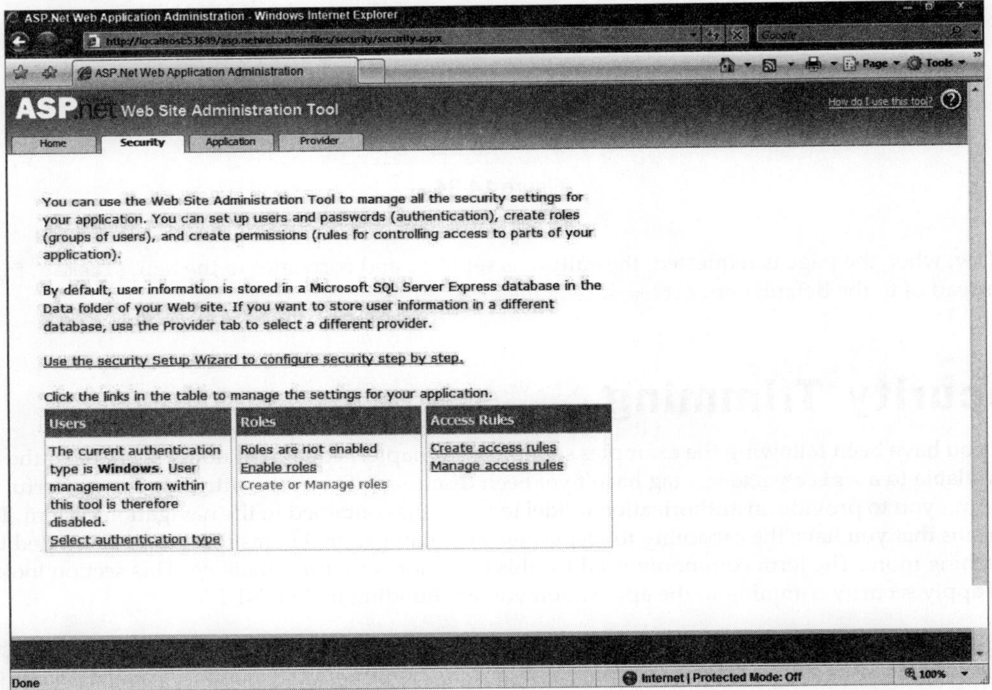

Figure 14-35

On this page, you can easily enable the role management system by selecting the Enable roles link. After you have done this, you are informed that there are no roles in the system. To create the role that you need for the site navigation system, select the Create or Manage roles link. You are then presented with a page where you can create the administrator role. For this example, I named the role Admin.

After adding the Admin role, click the Back button and then select the authentication type that is utilized for the application. You want to make sure that you have selected the From the internet option. This enables you then to create a user in the system. By default, these users are stored in the Microsoft SQL Server Express Edition file that ASP.NET creates in your application. After you have selected the authentication type, you can then create the new user and place the user in the Admin role by making sure the role is selected (using a check box) on the screen where you are creating the user.

After you are satisfied that a user has been created and placed in the Admin role, you can check if the settings are appropriately set in the `web.config` file. This is presented in Listing 14-33.

Listing 14-33: The role management system enabled in the web.config file

```
<configuration>
   <system.web>

      <authentication mode="Forms" />
      <roleManager enabled="true" />

   </system.web>
</configuration>
```

Setting Up the Administrators' Section

The next step is to set up a page for administrators only. For this example, I named the page `AdminOnly.aspx`, and it contains only a simple string value welcoming administrators to the page. This page is locked down only for users who are contained in the Admin role. This is done by making the appropriate settings in the `web.config` file. This lockdown is shown in Listing 14-34.

Listing 14-34: Locking down the AdminOnly.aspx page in the web.config

```
<configuration>
  <location path="AdminOnly.aspx">
    <system.web>
      <authorization>
        <allow roles="Admin" />
        <deny users="*" />
      </authorization>
    </system.web>
  </location>
</configuration>
```

Now, because the `AdminOnly.aspx` page is accessible only to the users who are in the Admin role, the next step is to allow users to log in to the application. The application demo accomplishes this task by creating a `Default.aspx` page that contains a Login server control as well as a TreeView control bound to a SiteMapDataSource control. This simple ASP.NET page is presented in Listing 14-35.

Listing 14-35: The Default.aspx page

```
<%@ Page Language="VB" %>

<html xmlns="http://www.w3.org/1999/xhtml">
<head runat="server">
    <title>Main Page</title>
</head>
<body>
    <form id="form1" runat="server">
    <div>
        <asp:Login ID="Login1" runat="server">
        </asp:Login>
        <br />
        <asp:TreeView ID="TreeView1" runat="server"
         DataSourceID="SiteMapDataSource1" ShowLines="True">
        </asp:TreeView>
        <br />
        <asp:SiteMapDataSource ID="SiteMapDataSource1" runat="server" />
    </div>
    </form>
</body>
</html>
```

With the Default.aspx page in place, another change is made to the Web.sitemap file that was originally presented in Listing 14-1. For this example, you add a <siteMapNode> element that works with the new AdminOnly.aspx page. This node is presented here:

```
<siteMapNode title="Administration" description="The Administrators page"
 url="AdminOnly.aspx" roles="Admin" />
```

After all items are in place in your application, the next step is to enable security trimming for the site navigation system.

Enabling Security Trimming

By default, security trimming is disabled. Even if you start applying values to the roles attribute for any <siteMapNode> element in your web.config file, it does not work. To enable security trimming, you must fine-tune the provider declaration for the site navigation system.

To make the necessary changes to the XmlSiteMapProvider, you need to make these changes high up in the configuration chain, such as to the machine.config file or the default web.config file, or you can make the change lower down, such as in your application's web.config file. This example makes the change in the web.config file.

To alter the XmlSiteMapProvider in the web.config file, you first clear out the already declared instance. After it is cleared, you then redeclare a new instance of the XmlSiteMapProvider, but this time you enable security trimming, as illustrated in Listing 14-36.

Listing 14-36: Enabling security trimming in the provider

```
<configuration>
   <system.web>

      <siteMap>
        <providers>
          <clear />
          <add siteMapFile="web.sitemap" name="AspNetXmlSiteMapProvider"
              type="System.Web.XmlSiteMapProvider, System.Web, Version=2.0.0.0,
                 Culture=neutral, PublicKeyToken=b03f5f7f11d50a3a"
              securityTrimmingEnabled="true" />
        </providers>
      </siteMap>

   </system.web>
</configuration>
```

From this example, you can see that a new XmlSiteMapProvider is defined and the `securityTimming-Enabled` attribute is then set to `true` (shown in bold). With security trimming enabled, the roles attribute in the `<siteMapNode>` element is utilized in the site navigation system.

To test it out for yourself, run the `Default.aspx` page. You are first presented with a page that does not include the link to the administration portion of the page, as illustrated in Figure 14-36.

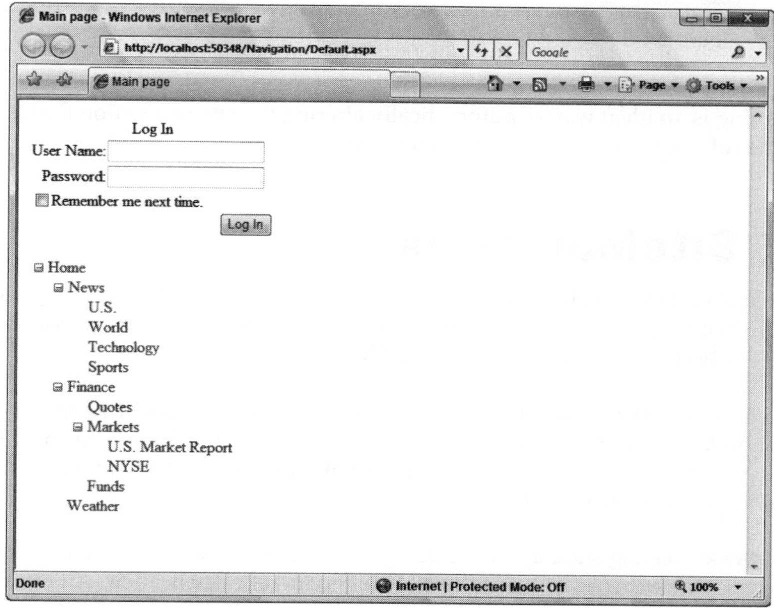

Figure 14-36

From this figure, you can see that the Administration link is not present in the TreeView control. Now, however, log in to the application as a user contained in the Admin role. You then see that, indeed, the site navigation has changed to reflect the role of the user, as presented in Figure 14-37.

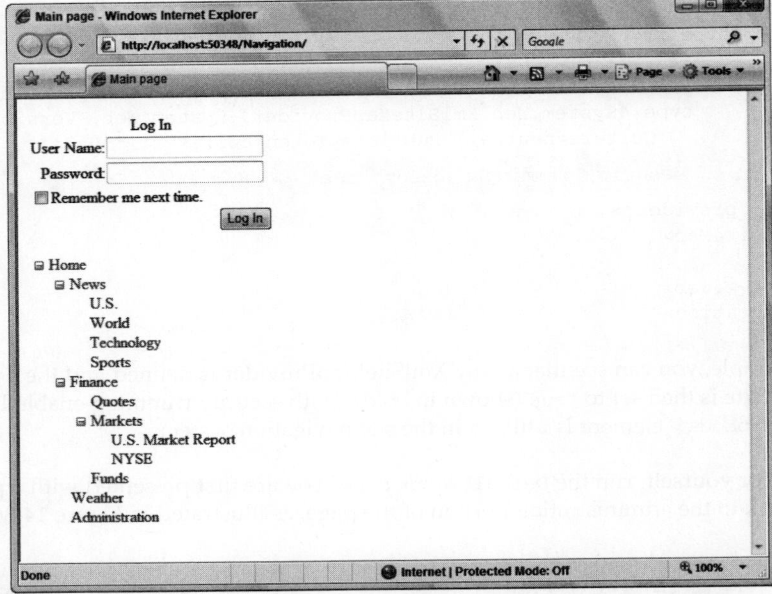

Figure 14-37

Security trimming is an ideal way of automatically altering the site navigation that is presented to users based upon the roles they have in the role management system.

Nesting SiteMap Files

You are not required to place all your site navigation within a single `Web.sitemap` file. In fact, you can spread it out into multiple `.sitemap` files if you wish and then bring them all together into a single `.sitemap` file — also known as *nesting* `.sitemap` files.

For instance, suppose you are using the sitemap file from Listing 14-1 and you have a pretty large amount of site navigation to add under the area of *Entertainment*. You could put all this new information in the current `Web.sitemap` file, or you could keep all the Entertainment links in another sitemap file and just reference that in the main sitemap file.

In the simplest case, nesting sitemap files is easily achievable. To see it in action, create a new `.sitemap` file (called `Entertainment.sitemap`) and place this file in your application. An example `Entertainment.sitemap` file is presented in Listing 14-37.

Listing 14-37: The Entertainment.sitemap

```
<?xml version="1.0" encoding="utf-8" ?>
<siteMap xmlns="http://schemas.microsoft.com/AspNet/SiteMap-File-1.0" >
    <siteMapNode url="Entertainment.aspx" title="Entertainment"
     description="The Entertainment Page">
        <siteMapNode url="Movies.aspx" title="Movies"
         description="The Latest in Movies" />
        <siteMapNode url="Fashion.aspx" title="Fashion"
         description="The Latest in Fashion" />
    </siteMapNode>
</siteMap>
```

You can place the `Entertainment.sitemap` in the root directory where you also have the main `Web.sitemap` file. Now, working from the sitemap file from the earlier Listing 14-1, you make the following addition to the bottom of the list as presented in Listing 14-38.

Listing 14-38: Additions to the Web.sitemap file

```
<siteMapNode siteMapFile="Entertainment.sitemap" />
```

Instead of using the standard `url`, `title`, and `description` attributes, you just point to the other sitemap file to be included in this main sitemap file using the `siteMapFile` attribute. Running this page gives you results similar to those presented in Figure 14-38.

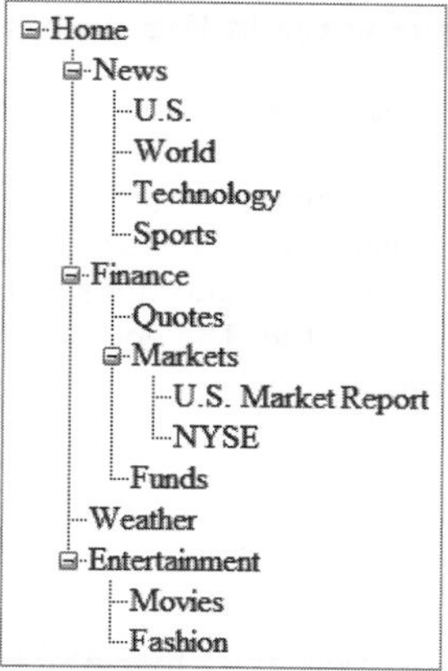

Figure 14-38

Another approach to nesting sitemap files is to build a second provider in the sitemap provider model definitions and to then use the `provider` attribute within the `<siteMapNode>` element to reference this declaration. To accomplish this task, you first add a new sitemap provider reference in the `web.config` file. This is illustrated in Listing 14-39.

Listing 14-39: Using another provider in the same Web.sitemap file

```
<configuration>
   <system.web>

      <siteMap>
        <providers>
          <add siteMapFile="Entertainment.sitemap" name="AspNetXmlSiteMapProvider2"
               type="System.Web.XmlSiteMapProvider, System.Web, Version=2.0.0.0,
                  Culture=neutral, PublicKeyToken=b03f5f7f11d50a3a" />
        </providers>
      </siteMap>

   </system.web>
</configuration>
```

From this bit of code, you can see that a second provider is defined. Defining a second sitemap provider does not mean that you have to use the `<clear />` element in the `<provider>` section, but instead, you simply define a new provider that has a new name. In this case, the name of the provider is `AspNetXml-SiteMapProvider2`. Also, within this provider definition, the `siteMapFile` attribute is used to point to the name of the sitemap file that should be utilized.

With this in place, you can then reference this declaration by using the `provider` attribute within the `<siteMapNode>` element of the `Web.sitemap` file. To add the `Entertainment.sitemap` file in this manner, your `<siteMapNode>` element should take the form presented in Listing 14-40.

Listing 14-40: Using a second provider in the Web.sitemap file

```
<siteMapNode provider="AspNetXmlSiteMapProvider2" />
```

This gives you the same results as those shown in Figure 14-38. Besides providing another way of nesting sitemap files, you gain a lot of power using the `provider` attribute. If you build a new sitemap provider that pulls sitemap navigation information from another source (rather than from an XML file), you can mix those results in the main `Web.sitemap` file. The end result could have items that come from two or more completely different data sources.

Summary

This chapter introduced the navigation mechanics that ASP.NET 3.5 provides. At the core of the navigation capabilities is the power to detail the navigation structure in an XML file, which can then be utilized by various navigation controls — such as the new TreeView and SiteMapPath controls.

The powerful functionality that the navigation capabilities provide saves you a tremendous amount of coding time.

In addition to showing you the core infrastructure for navigation in ASP.NET 3.5, this chapter also described both the TreeView and SiteMapPath controls and how to use them throughout your applications. The great thing about these controls is that, right out of the box, they can richly display your navigation hierarchy and enable the end user to work through the site easily. In addition, these controls are easily changeable so that you can go beyond the standard appearance and functionality that they provide.

Along with the TreeView server control, this chapter also looked at the Menu server control. You will find a lot of similarities between these two controls as they both provide a means to look at hierarchical data.

Finally, this chapter looked at how to achieve URL mapping, as well as how to localize your `Web.sitemap` files and filter the results of the site navigation contents based upon a user's role in the role management system.

15

Personalization

Many Web applications must be customized with information that is specific to the end user who is presently viewing the page. In the past, the developer usually provided storage of personalization properties for end users viewing the page by means of cookies, the `Session` object, or the `Application` object. Cookies enabled storage of persistent items so that when the end user returned to a Web page, any settings related to him were retrieved in order to be utilized again by the application. Cookies are not the best way to approach persistent user data storage, however, mainly because they are not accepted by all computers and also because a crafty end user can easily alter them.

As you will see in Chapter 16, ASP.NET membership and role management capabilities are ways that ASP.NET can conveniently store information about the user. How can you, as the developer, use the same mechanics to store custom information?

ASP.NET 3.5 provides you with an outstanding feature — *personalization*. The ASP.NET personalization engine provided with this latest release can make an automatic association between the end user viewing the page and any data points stored for that user. The personalization properties that are maintained on a per-user basis are stored on the server and not on the client. These items are conveniently placed in a data store of your choice (such as Microsoft's SQL Server) and, therefore, the end user can then access these personalization properties on later site visits.

This feature is an ideal way to start creating highly customizable and user-specific sites without building any of the plumbing beforehand. In this case, the plumbing has been built for you! The personalization feature is yet another way that the ASP.NET team is making developers more productive and their jobs easier.

The Personalization Model

The personalization model provided with ASP.NET 3.5 is simple and, as with most items that come with ASP.NET, it is an extensible model as well. Figure 15-1 shows a simple diagram that outlines the personalization model.

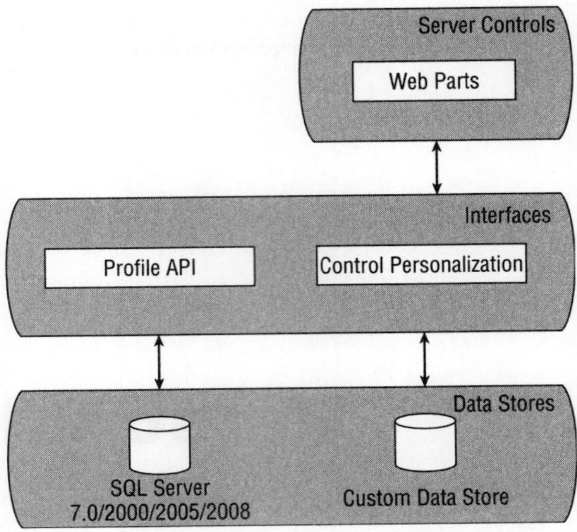

Figure 15-1

From this diagram, you can see the three layers in this model. First, look at the middle layer of the personalization model — the Personalization Services layer. This layer contains the Profile API. This new Profile API layer enables you to program your end user's data points into one of the lower-layer data stores. Also included in this layer are the server control personalization capabilities, which are important for the Portal Framework and the use of Web Parts. The Portal Framework and Web Parts are discussed in Chapter 17.

Although certain controls built into ASP.NET can utilize the personalization capabilities for storing information about the page settings, you can also use this new engine to store your own data points. As with Web Parts, these points can be used within your ASP.NET pages.

Below the Personalization Services layer, you find the default personalization data provider for working with Microsoft's SQL Server 2008, 2005, or 2000, as well as the new Microsoft SQL Server Express Edition files. You are not limited to just this one data store when applying the personalization features of ASP.NET 3.5; you can also extend the model and create a custom data provider for the personalization engine.

You can read about how to create your own providers in Chapter 13.

Now that you have looked briefly at the personalization model, you can begin using it by creating some stored personalization properties that can be used later within your applications.

Creating Personalization Properties

The nice thing about creating custom personalization properties is that you can do it so easily. After these properties are created, you gain the capability to have strongly typed access to them. It is also possible to create personalization properties that are used only by authenticated users, and also some that anonymous users can utilize. These data points are powerful — mainly because you can start using them immediately in your application without building any underlying infrastructures to support them. The first step is to create some simple personalization properties. Later, you learn how to use these personalization properties within your application.

Adding a Simple Personalization Property

The first step is to decide what data items from the user you are going to store. For this example, create a few items about the user that you can use within your application; assume that you want to store the following information about the user:

- First name
- Last name
- Last visited
- Age
- Membership Status

ASP.NET has a heavy dependency on storing configurations inside XML files, and the ASP.NET 3.5 personalization engine is no different. All these customization points concerning the end user are defined and stored within the web.config file of the application. This is illustrated in Listing 15-1.

Listing 15-1: Creating personalization properties in the web.config file

```
<configuration>
  <system.web>

     <profile>

        <properties>

           <add name="FirstName" />
           <add name="LastName" />
           <add name="LastVisited" />
           <add name="Age" />
           <add name="Member" />

        </properties>

     </profile>

     <authentication mode="Windows" />

  </system.web>
</configuration>
```

Within the web.config file and nested within the <system.web> section of the file, you create a <profile> section in order to work with the ASP.NET 3.5 personalization engine. Within this <profile> section of the web.config file, you create a <properties> section. In this section, you can define all the properties you want the personalization engine to store.

From this code example, you can see that it is rather easy to define simple properties using the <add> element. This element simply takes the name attribute, which takes the name of the property you want to persist.

You start out with the assumption that accessing the page you will build with these properties is already authenticated using Windows authentication (you can read more on authentication and authorization in the next chapter). Later in this chapter, you look at how to apply personalization properties to anonymous users as well. The capability to apply personalization properties to anonymous users is disabled by default (for good reasons).

After you have defined these personalization properties, it is just as easy to use them as it is to define them. The next section looks at how to use these definitions in an application.

Using Personalization Properties

Now that you have defined the personalization properties in the web.config file, it is possible to use these items in code. For example, you can create a simple form that asks for some of this information from the end user. On the Button_Click event, the data is stored in the personalization engine. Listing 15-2 shows an example of this.

Listing 15-2: Using the defined personalization properties

VB

```
<%@ Page Language="VB" %>

<script runat="server">
  Protected Sub Button1_Click(ByVal sender As Object, ByVal e As System.EventArgs)
    If Page.User.Identity.IsAuthenticated Then
       Profile.FirstName = TextBox1.Text
       Profile.LastName = TextBox2.Text
       Profile.Age = TextBox3.Text
       Profile.Member = Radiobuttonlist1.SelectedItem.Text
       Profile.LastVisited = DateTime.Now().ToString()

       Label1.Text = "Stored information includes:<p>" & _
          "First name: " & Profile.FirstName & _
          "<br>Last name: " & Profile.LastName & _
          "<br>Age: " & Profile.Age & _
          "<br>Member: " & Profile.Member & _
          "<br>Last visited: " & Profile.LastVisited
    Else
       Label1.Text = "You must be authenticated!"
    End If
  End Sub
</script>

<html xmlns="http://www.w3.org/1999/xhtml">
<head runat="server">
    <title>Storing Personalization</title>
</head>
<body>
```

```
    <form id="form1" runat="server">
        <p>First Name:
        <asp:TextBox ID="TextBox1" Runat="server"></asp:TextBox></p>
        <p>Last Name:
        <asp:TextBox ID="TextBox2" Runat="server"></asp:TextBox></p>
        <p>Age:
        <asp:TextBox ID="TextBox3" Runat="server" Width="50px"
         MaxLength="3"></asp:TextBox></p>
        <p>Are you a member?
        <asp:RadioButtonList ID="Radiobuttonlist1" Runat="server">
            <asp:ListItem Value="1">Yes</asp:ListItem>
            <asp:ListItem Value="0" Selected="True">No</asp:ListItem>
        </asp:RadioButtonList></p>
        <p><asp:Button ID="Button1" Runat="server" Text="Submit"
            OnClick="Button1_Click" />
        </p>
        <hr /><p>
        <asp:Label ID="Label1" Runat="server"></asp:Label></p>
    </form>
</body>
</html>
```

C#

```
<%@ Page Language="C#" %>

<script runat="server">
    protected void Button1_Click(object sender, EventArgs e)
    {
      if (Page.User.Identity.IsAuthenticated)
      {
        Profile.FirstName = TextBox1.Text;
        Profile.LastName = TextBox2.Text;
        Profile.Age = TextBox3.Text;
        Profile.Member = Radiobuttonlist1.SelectedItem.Text;
        Profile.LastVisited = DateTime.Now.ToString();

        Label1.Text = "Stored information includes:<p>" +
            "First name: " + Profile.FirstName +
            "<br>Last name: " + Profile.LastName +
            "<br>Age: " + Profile.Age +
            "<br>Member: " + Profile.Member +
            "<br>Last visited: " + Profile.LastVisited;
      }
      else
      {
        Label1.Text = "You must be authenticated!";
      }
    }
</script>
```

This is similar to the way you worked with the `Session` object in the past, but note that the personalization properties you are storing and retrieving are not key based. Therefore, when working with them you do not need to remember key names.

All items stored by the personalization system are type cast to a particular .NET data type. By default, these items are stored as type `String`, and you have early-bound access to the items stored. To store an item, you simply populate the personalization property directly using the `Profile` object:

```
Profile.FirstName = TextBox1.Text
```

To retrieve the same information, you simply grab the appropriate property of the `Profile` class as shown here:

```
Label1.Text = Profile.FirstName
```

The great thing about using the `Profile` class and all the personalization properties defined in the code view is that this method provides IntelliSense as you build your pages. When you are working with the `Profile` class in this view, all the items you define are listed as available options through the IntelliSense feature, as illustrated in Figure 15-2.

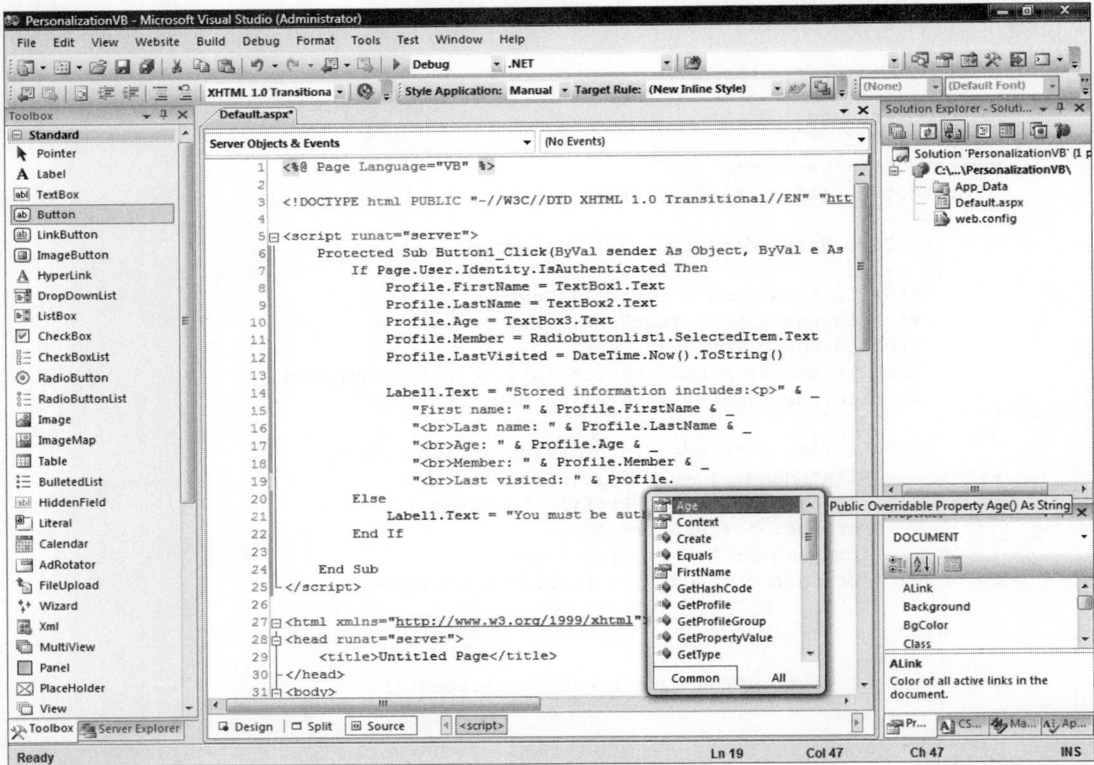

Figure 15-2

All these properties are accessible in IntelliSense because the `Profile` class is hidden and dynamically compiled behind the scenes whenever you save the personalization changes made to the `web.config` file.

After these items are saved in the `web.config` file, these properties are available to you throughout your application in a strongly typed manner.

When run, the page from Listing 15-2 produces the results shown in Figure 15-3.

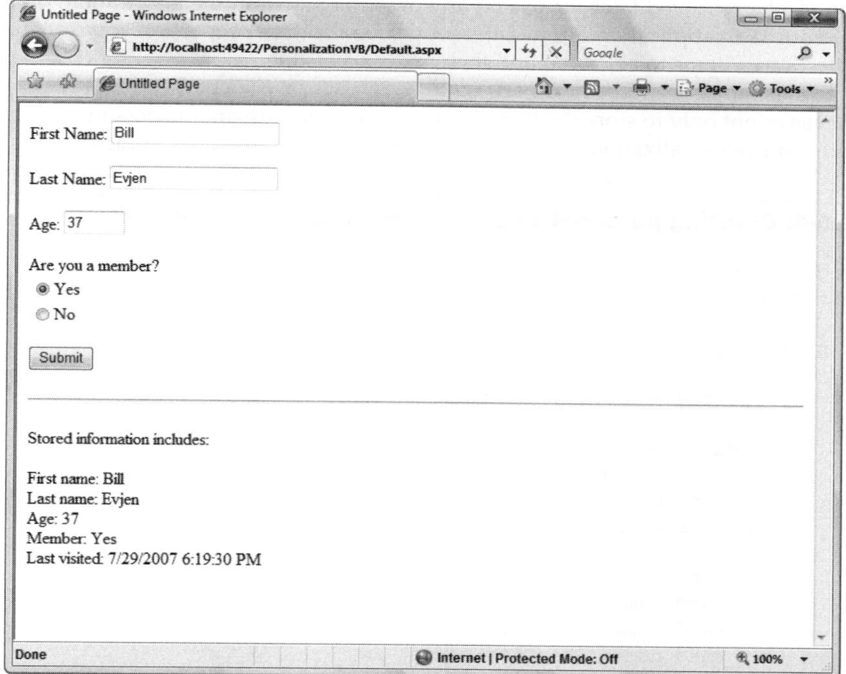

Figure 15-3

In addition to using early-bound access techniques, you can also use late-bound access for the items that you store in the personalization engine. This technique is illustrated in Listing 15-3.

Listing 15-3: Using late-bound access

VB

```
Dim myFirstName As String

myFirstName = Profile.GetPropertyValue("FirstName").ToString()
```

C#

```
string myFirstName;

myFirstName = Profile.GetPropertyValue("FirstName").ToString();
```

Whether it is early-bound access or late-bound access, you can easily store and retrieve personalization properties for a particular user using this capability afforded by ASP.NET 3.5. All this is done in the personalization engine's simplest form — now take a look at how you can customize for specific needs in your applications.

Adding a Group of Personalization Properties

If you want to store a large number of personalization properties about a particular user, remember that you are not just storing personalization properties for a particular page, but for the *entire* application. This means that items you have stored about a particular end user somewhere in the beginning of the application can be retrieved later for use on any other page within the application. Because different sections of your Web applications store different personalization properties, you sometimes end up with a large collection of items to be stored and then made accessible.

To make it easier not only to store the items, but also to retrieve them, the personalization engine enables you to store your personalization properties in groups. This is illustrated in Listing 15-4.

Listing 15-4: Creating personalization groups in the web.config file

```
<configuration>
  <system.web>

     <profile>

        <properties>

           <add name="FirstName" />
           <add name="LastName" />
           <add name="LastVisited" />
           <add name="Age" />

           <group name="MemberDetails">
              <add name="Member" />
              <add name="DateJoined" />
              <add name="PaidDuesStatus" />
              <add name="Location" />
           </group>

           <group name="FamilyDetails">
              <add name="MarriedStatus" />
              <add name="DateMarried" />
              <add name="NumberChildren" />
              <add name="Location" />
           </group>

         </properties>

     </profile>

     <authentication mode="Windows" />

   </system.web>
 </configuration>
```

From the code in Listing 15-4, which is placed within the `web.config` file, you can see that two groups are listed. The first group is the `MemberDetails` group, which has four specific items defined; the second group — `FamilyDetails` — has three other related items defined. Personalization groups are defined using the `<group>` element within the `<properties>` definition. The name of the group is specified using the `name` attribute, just as you specify the `<add>` element. You can have as many groups defined as you deem necessary or as have been recommended as good practice to employ.

Using Grouped Personalization Properties

From Listing 15-4, you can also see that some items are not defined in any particular group. It is possible to mix properties defined from within a group with those that are not. The items not defined in a group in Listing 15-4 can still be accessed in the manner illustrated previously:

```
Label1.Text = Profile.FirstName
```

Now, concerning working with personalization groups, you can access your defined items in a logical manner using nested namespaces:

```
Label1.Text = Profile.MemberDetails.DateJoined

Label2.Text = Profile.FamilyDetails.MarriedStatus
```

From this example, you can see that two separate items from each of the defined personalization groups were accessed in a logical manner. When you study the defined properties in the `web.config` file of your application, you can see that each of the groups in the example has a property with the same name — `Location`. This is possible because they are defined using personalization groups. With this structure, it is now possible to get at each of the `Location` properties by specifying the appropriate group:

```
Label1.Text = Profile.MemberDetails.Location

Label2.Text = Profile.FamilyDetails.Location
```

Defining Types for Personalization Properties

By default, when you store personalization properties, these properties are created as type `System.String`. It is quite easy, however, to change the type to another type altogether through configuration settings within the `web.config` file. To define the name of the personalization property along with its appropriate type, you use the `type` attribute of the `<add>` element contained within the `<properties>` section, as shown in Listing 15-5.

Listing 15-5: Defining types for personalization properties

```
<properties>

   <add name="FirstName" type="System.String" />
   <add name="LastName" type="System.String" />
   <add name="LastVisited" type="System.DateTime" />
   <add name="Age" type="System.Int32" />
   <add name="Member" type="System.Boolean" />

</properties>
```

The first two properties, `FirstName` and `LastName`, are cast as type `System.String`. This is not actually required. Even if you omitted this step, they would still be cast as type `String` because that is the default type of any property defined in the personalization system (if no other type is defined). The next personalization property is the `LastVisited` property, which is defined as type `System.DateTime` and used to store the date and time of the end user's last visit to the page. Beyond that, you can see the rest of the personalization properties are defined using a specific .NET data type.

This is the preferred approach because it gives you type-checking capabilities as you code your application and use the personalization properties you have defined.

Using Custom Types

As you can see from the earlier examples that show you how to define types for the personalization properties, it is quite simple to define properties and type cast them to particular data types that are available in the .NET Framework. Items such as `System.Integer`, `System.String`, `System.DateTime`, `System.Byte`, and `System.Boolean` are easily defined within the `web.config` file. But how do you go about defining complex types?

Personalization properties that utilize custom types are just as easy to define as personalization properties that use simple types. Custom types give you the capability to store complex items such as shopping cart information or other status information from one use of the application to the next. Listing 15-6 first shows a class, `ShoppingCart`, which you use later in one of the personalization property definitions.

Listing 15-6: Creating a class to use as a personalization type

VB

```
<Serializable()> _
Public Class ShoppingCart
    Private PID As String
    Private CompanyProductName As String
    Private Number As Integer
    Private Price As Decimal
    Private DateAdded As DateTime

    Public Property ProductID() As String
        Get
            Return PID
        End Get
        Set(ByVal value As String)
            PID = value
        End Set
    End Property

    Public Property ProductName() As String
        Get
            Return CompanyProductName
        End Get
        Set(ByVal value As String)
            CompanyProductName = value
        End Set
    End Property

    Public Property NumberSelected() As Integer
        Get
            Return Number
        End Get
```

```
        Set(ByVal value As Integer)
            Number = value
        End Set
    End Property

    Public Property ItemPrice() As Decimal
        Get
            Return Price
        End Get
        Set(ByVal value As Decimal)
            Price = value
        End Set
    End Property

    Public Property DateItemAdded() As DateTime
        Get
            Return DateAdded
        End Get
        Set(ByVal value As DateTime)
            DateAdded = value
        End Set
    End Property
End Class
```

C#

```
using System;

[Serializable]
public class ShoppingCart
{
    private string PID;
    private string CompanyProductName;
    private int Number;
    private decimal Price;
    private DateTime DateAdded;

    public ShoppingCart() {}

    public string ProductID
    {
        get {return PID;}
        set {PID = value;}
    }

    public string ProductName
    {
        get { return CompanyProductName; }
        set { CompanyProductName = value; }
    }

    public int NumberSelected
    {
        get { return Number; }
```

Continued

```
            set { Number = value; }
        }

        public decimal ItemPrice
        {
            get { return Price; }
            set { Price = value; }
        }

        public DateTime DateItemAdded
        {
            get { return DateAdded; }
            set { DateAdded = value; }
        }
    }
```

This simple shopping cart construction can now store the end user's shopping cart basket as the user moves around on an e-commerce site. The basket can even be persisted when the end user returns to the site at another time. Be sure to note that the class requires a `Serializable` attribute preceding the class declaration to ensure proper transformation to XML or binary.

Look at how you would specify from within the `web.config` file that a personalization property is this complex type, such as a `ShoppingCart` type. This is illustrated in Listing 15-7.

Listing 15-7: Using complex types for personalization properties

```
<properties>

    <add name="FirstName" type="System.String" />
    <add name="LastName" type="System.String" />
    <add name="LastVisited" type="System.DateTime" />
    <add name="Age" type="System.Int32" />
    <add name="Member" type="System.Boolean" />
    <add name="Cart" type="ShoppingCart" serializeAs="Binary" />

</properties>
```

Just as the basic data types are stored in the personalization data stores, this construction allows you to easily store custom types and to have them serialized into the end data store in the format you choose. In this case, the `ShoppingCart` object is serialized as a binary object into the data store. The `SerializeAs` attribute can take the values defined in the following list:

- **Binary:** Serializes and stores the object as binary data within the chosen data store.
- **ProviderSpecific:** Stores the object based upon the direction of the provider. This simply means that instead of the personalization engine determining the serialization of the object, the serialization is simply left up to the personalization provider specified.
- **String:** The default setting. Stores the personalization properties as a string inside the chosen data store.
- **XML:** Takes the object and serializes it into an XML format before storing it in the chosen data store.

Providing Default Values

In addition to defining the data types of the personalization properties, you can also define their default values directly in the web.config file. By default, the personalization properties you create do not have a value, but you can easily change this using the defaultValue attribute of the <add> element. Defining default values is illustrated in Listing 15-8.

Listing 15-8: Defining default values for personalization properties

```
<properties>

   <add name="FirstName" type="System.String" />
   <add name="LastName" type="System.String" />
   <add name="LastVisited" type="System.DateTime" />
   <add name="Age" type="System.Integer" />
   <add name="Member" type="System.Boolean" defaultValue="false" />

</properties>
```

From this example, you can see that only one of the personalization properties is provided with a default value. The last personalization property, Member in this example, is given a default value of false. This means that when you add a new end user to the personalization property database, Member is defined instead of remaining a blank value within the system.

Making Personalization Properties Read-Only

It is also possible to make personalization properties read-only. To do this, you simply add the readOnly attribute to the <add> element:

```
<add name="StartDate" type="System.DateTime" readOnly="true" />
```

To make the personalization property a read-only property, you give the readOnly attribute a value of true. By default, this property is set to false.

Anonymous Personalization

A great feature in ASP.NET enables anonymous end users to utilize the personalization features it provides. This is important if a site requires registration of some kind. In these cases, end users do not always register for access to the greater application until they have first taken advantage of some of the basic services. For instance, many e-commerce sites allow anonymous end users to shop a site and use the site's shopping cart before the shoppers register with the site.

Enabling Anonymous Identification of the End User

By default, anonymous personalization is turned off because it consumes database resources on popular sites. Therefore, one of the first steps in allowing anonymous personalization is to turn on this feature using the appropriate setting in the web.config file. You also need to make some changes regarding how the properties are actually defined in the web.config file and to determine if you are going to allow anonymous personalization for your application.

As shown in Listing 15-9, you can turn on anonymous identification to enable the personalization engine to identify the unknown end users using the `<anonymousIdentification>` element.

Listing 15-9: Allowing anonymous identification

```
<configuration>
  <system.web>

       <anonymousIdentification enabled="true" />

  </system.web>
</configuration>
```

To enable anonymous identification of the end users who might visit your applications, you add an `<anonymousIdentification>` element to the `web.config` file within the `<system.web>` nodes. Then within the `<anonymousIdentification>` element, you use the `enabled` attribute and set its value to `true`. Remember that by default, this value is set to `false`.

When anonymous identification is turned on, ASP.NET uses a unique identifier for each anonymous user who comes to the application. This identifier is sent with each and every request, although after the end user becomes authenticated by ASP.NET, the identifier is removed from the process.

For an anonymous user, information is stored by default as a cookie on the end user's machine. Additional information (the personalization properties that you enable for anonymous users) is stored in the specified data store on the server.

To see this in action, turn off the Windows Authentication for your example application and, instead, use Forms Authentication. This change is demonstrated in Listing 15-10.

Listing 15-10: Turning off Windows Authentication and using Forms Authentication

```
<configuration>
  <system.web>

       <anonymousIdentification enabled="true" />

       <authentication mode="Forms" />

  </system.web>
</configuration>
```

With this in place, if you run the page from the earlier example in Listing 15-2, you see the header presented in Listing 15-11.

Listing 15-11: Setting an anonymous cookie in the HTTP header

```
HTTP/1.1 200 OK
Server: ASP.NET Development Server/8.0.0.0
Date: Sat, 11 Feb 2008 19:23:37 GMT
X-AspNet-Version: 2.0.50727
Set-Cookie:
.ASPXANONYMOUS=UH5CftJlxgEkAAAAZTJkN2I3YjUtZDhkOS0ONDE2LWFlYjEtOTVjMjVmMzMxZWRmHoBU
```

```
As9A055rziDrMQ1Hu_fC_hM1; expires=Sat, 22-Apr-2008 06:03:36 GMT; path=/; HttpOnly
Cache-Control: private
Content-Type: text/html; charset=utf-8
Content-Length: 1419
Connection: Close
```

From this HTTP header, you can see that a cookie — `.ASPXANONYMOUS` — is set to a hashed value for later retrieval by the ASP.NET personalization system.

Changing the Name of the Cookie for Anonymous Identification

Cookies are used by default under the cookie name `.ASPXANONYMOUS`. You can change the name of this cookie from the `<anonymousIdentification>` element in the `web.config` file by using the `cookieName` attribute, as shown in Listing 15-12.

Listing 15-12: Changing the name of the cookie

```
<configuration>
  <system.web>

       <anonymousIdentification
           enabled="true"
           cookieName=".ASPXEvjenWebApplication" />

  </system.web>
</configuration>
```

Changing the Length of Time the Cookie Is Stored

Also, by default, the cookie stored on the end user's machine is stored for 100,000 minutes (which is almost 70 days). If you want to change this value, you do it within this `<anonymousIdentification>` element using the `cookieTimeout` attribute, as shown in Listing 15-13.

Listing 15-13: Changing the length of time the cookie is stored

```
<configuration>
  <system.web>

       <anonymousIdentification
           enabled="true"
           cookieTimeout="1440" />

  </system.web>
</configuration>
```

In this case, the `cookieTimeout` value was changed to `1440` — meaning 1,440 minutes (or one day). This would be ideal for something like a shopping cart where you do not want to persist the identification of the end user too long.

Changing How the Identifiers Are Stored

Although anonymous identifiers are stored through the use of cookies, you can also easily change this. Cookies are, by far, the preferred way to achieve identification, but you can also do it without the use of cookies. Other options include using the URI or device profiles. Listing 15-14 shows an example of using the URI to place the identifiers.

Listing 15-14: Specifying how cookies are stored

```
<configuration>
  <system.web>

       <anonymousIdentification
           enabled="true"
           cookieless="UseUri" />

  </system.web>
</configuration>
```

Besides `UseUri`, other options include `UseCookies`, `AutoDetect`, and `UseDeviceProfile`. The following list reviews each of the options:

- `UseCookies`: This is the default setting. If you set no value, ASP.NET assumes this is the value. `UseCookies` means that a cookie is placed on the end user's machine for identification.
- `UseUri`: This value means that a cookie *will not* be stored on the end user's machine, but instead the unique identifier will be munged within the URL of the page. This is the same approach used for cookieless sessions in ASP.NET 1.0/1.1. Although this is great if developers want to avoid sticking a cookie on an end user's machine, it does create strange looking URLs and can be an issue when an end user bookmarks pages for later retrieval.
- `AutoDetect`: Using this value means that you are letting the ASP.NET engine decide whether to use cookies or use the URL approach for the anonymous identification. This is done on a per-user basis and performs a little worse than the other two options. ASP.NET must check the end user before deciding which approach to use. My suggestion is to use `AutoDetect` instead of `UseUri` if you absolutely must allow for end users who have cookies turned off (which is rare these days).
- `UseDeviceProfile`: Configures the identifier for the device or browser that is making the request.

Looking at the Anonymous Identifiers Stored

In order to make the anonymous identifiers unique, a globally unique GUID is used. You can also now grab hold of this unique identifier for your own use. In order to retrieve the GUID, the `Request` object has been enhanced with an `AnonymousID` property. The `AnonymousID` property returns a value of type `String`, which can be used in your code as shown here:

```
Label1.Text = Request.AnonymousID
```

Working with Anonymous Identification

In working with the creation of anonymous users, be aware of an important event which you can use form your `Global.asax` file that can be used for managing the process:

- `AnonymousIdentification_Creating`

By using the `AnonymousIdentification_Creating` event, you can work with the identification of the end user as it occurs. For instance, if you do not want to use GUIDs for uniquely identifying the end user, you can change the identifying value from this event instead.

To do so, create the event using the event delegate of type `AnonymousIdentificationEventArgs`, as illustrated in Listing 15-15.

Listing 15-15: Changing the unique identifier of the anonymous user

VB

```
Public Sub AnonymousIdentification_Creating(ByVal sender As Object, _
   ByVal e As AnonymousIDentificationEventArgs)

        e.AnonymousID = "Bubbles " & DateTime.Now()

End Sub
```

C#

```
public void AnonymousIdentification_Creating(object sender,
   AnonymousIDentificationEventArgs e)
{
       e.AnonymousID = "Bubbles " + DateTime.Now;
}
```

The `AnonymousIdentificationEventArgs` event delegate exposes an `AnonymousID` property that assigns the value used to uniquely identify the anonymous user. Now, instead of a GUID to uniquely identify the anonymous user as

```
d13fafec-244a-4d21-9137-b213236ebedb
```

the `AnonymousID` property is changed within the `AnonymousIdentification_Creating` event to

```
Bubbles 2/10/2008 2:07:33 PM
```

Anonymous Options for Personalization Properties

If you have tried to get the anonymous capability working, you might have gotten the error shown in Figure 15-4.

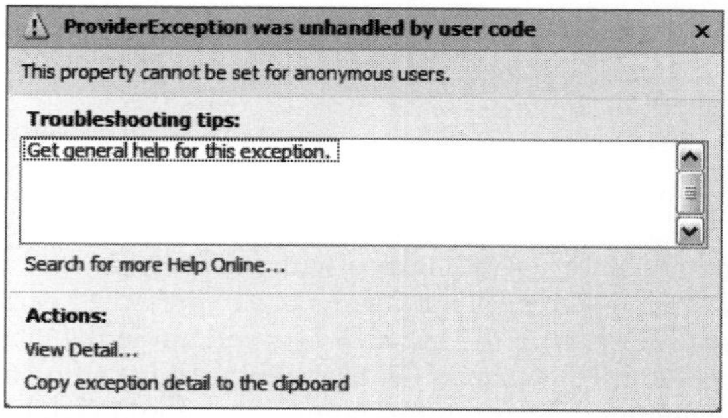

Figure 15-4

To get your application to work with anonymous users, you have to specify which personalization properties you wish to enable for the anonymous users visiting your pages. This is also done through the `web.config` file by adding the `allowAnonymous` attribute to the `<add>` element of the properties you have defined within the `<properties>` section (see Listing 15-16).

Listing 15-16: Turning on anonymous capabilities personalization properties

```
<properties>

    <add name="FirstName" type="System.String" />
    <add name="LastName" type="System.String" />
    <add name="LastVisited" type="System.DateTime" allowAnonymous="true" />
    <add name="Age" type="System.Integer" />
    <add name="Member" type="System.Boolean" />

</properties>
```

In this example, the `LastVisited` property is set to allow anonymous users by setting the `allowAnonymous` attribute to `true`. Because this is the only property that works with anonymous users, the rest of the defined properties do not store information for these types of users.

Warnings about Anonymous User Profile Storage

Taking into account everything said so far about anonymous users, you should be very careful about how you approach this option. Storing profile information about anonymous users can dramatically populate the data store you are using. For instance, in my examples, I am using Microsoft's SQL Server Express Edition, and I stored profile information for one authenticated user and then for a single anonymous user. This puts information for both these users in the aspnet_Profile and the aspnet_Users table.

The two users listed in the aspnet_Users table are shown in Figure 15-5.

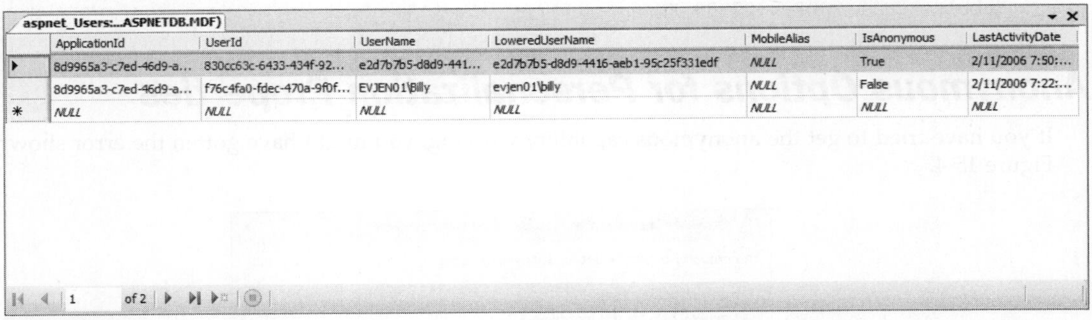

aspnet_Users:...ASPNETDB.MDF)

	ApplicationId	UserId	UserName	LoweredUserName	MobileAlias	IsAnonymous	LastActivityDate
▶	8d9965a3-c7ed-46d9-a...	830cc63c-6433-434f-92...	e2d7b7b5-d8d9-441...	e2d7b7b5-d8d9-4416-aeb1-95c25f331edf	NULL	True	2/11/2006 7:50:...
	8d9965a3-c7ed-46d9-a...	f76c4fa0-fdec-470a-9f0f...	EVJEN01\Billy	evjen01\billy	NULL	False	2/11/2006 7:22:...
*	NULL	NULL	NULL	NULL	NULL	NULL	NULL

1 of 2

Figure 15-5

In this figure, the anonymous user is highlighted with the gray bar, and you can see that this user has a pretty cryptic name, which is the `Request.AnonymousID` presented earlier. The other big difference between the two users is shown with the `IsAnonymous` column in the table. The anonymous user has a setting of `true` for this column while the authenticated user has a setting of `false`. Because your database can fill up quickly with anonymous user information, you should weigh which information you really need to store on these types of users.

Programmatic Access to Personalization

When an ASP.NET page is invoked, ASP.NET creates a class (`ProfileCommon`) by inheriting from the `ProfileBase` class, which it uses to strongly type the profile properties that were defined in the `web.config` file. This created class, meant to deal with the user's profile store, gets and sets profile properties through the use of the `GetPropertyValue` and `SetPropertyValue` methods from the `ProfileBase` class.

As you would expect, ASP.NET provides you with the hooks necessary to get at specific `Profile` events using the `ProfileModule` class. The `ProfileModule` class is what ASP.NET itself uses to create and store profile information in the page's `Profile` object.

The `ProfileModule` class exposes three events that you can use to handle your user's profile situations. These events, `MigrateAnonymous`, `Personalize`, and `ProfileAutoSaving`, are focused around the area of authentication. Because this section just showed you how to work with anonymous users in your applications, this section now looks at how to migrate these users from anonymous users to authenticated users — because you are most likely going to want to move their profile properties as well as change their status.

Migrating Anonymous Users

When working with anonymous users, you must be able to migrate anonymous users to registered users. For example, after an end user fills a shopping cart, he can register on the site to purchase the items. At that moment, the end user switches from being an anonymous user to a registered user.

For this reason, ASP.NET provides a `Profile_MigrateAnonymous` event handler enabling you to migrate anonymous users to registered users. The `Profile_MigrateAnonymous` event requires a data class of type `ProfileMigrateEventArgs`. It is placed either in the page that deals with the migration or within the `Global.asax` file (if it can be used from anywhere within the application). The use of this event is illustrated in Listing 15-17.

Listing 15-17: Migrating anonymous users for particular personalization properties

VB

```
Public Sub Profile_MigrateAnonymous(ByVal sender As Object, _
   ByVal e As ProfileMigrateEventArgs)

      Dim anonymousProfile As ProfileCommon = Profile.GetProfile(e.AnonymousID)
      Profile.LastVisited = anonymousProfile.LastVisited

End Sub
```

C#

```
public void Profile_MigrateAnonymous(object sender,
   ProfileMigrateEventArgs e)
{
      ProfileCommon anonymousProfile = Profile.GetProfile(e.AnonymousID);
      Profile.LastVisited = anonymousProfile.LastVisited
}
```

From this example, you create an instance of the `ProfileCommon` object and populate it with the profile from the visiting anonymous user. Then from there, you can use the instance to get at all the profile properties of that anonymous user. That means that you can then populate a profile through a movement from the anonymous user's profile information to the authenticated user's profile system.

Listing 15-17 shows how to migrate a single personalization property from an anonymous user to the new registered user. In addition to migrating single properties, you can also migrate properties that come from personalization groups. This is shown in Listing 15-18.

Listing 15-18: Migrating anonymous users for items in personalization groups

VB

```
Public Sub Profile_MigrateAnonymous(ByVal sender As Object, _
   ByVal e As ProfileMigrateEventArgs)

      Dim au As ProfileCommon = Profile.GetProfile(e.AnonymousID)

       If au.MemberDetails.DateJoined <> "" Then
          Profile.MemberDetails.DateJoined = DateTime.Now().ToString()
           Profile.FamilyDetails.MarriedStatus = au.FamilyDetails.MarriedStatus
       End If

      AnonymousIdentificationModule.ClearAnonymousIdentifier()
End Sub
```

C#

```
public void Profile_MigrateAnonymous(object sender,
   ProfileMigrateEventArgs e)
{
        ProfileCommon au = Profile.GetProfile(e.AnonymousID);

        if (au.MemberDetails.DateJoined != String.Empty) {
           Profile.MemberDetails.DateJoined = DateTime.Now.ToString();
           Profile.FamilyDetails.MarriedStatus = au.FamilyDetails.MarriedStatus;
        }

        AnonymousIdentificationModule.ClearAnonymousIdentifier();
}
```

Using this event in the `Global.asax` file enables you to logically migrate anonymous users as they register themselves with your applications. The migration process also allows you to pick and choose which items you migrate and to change the values as you wish.

Personalizing Profiles

Besides working with anonymous users from the `Global.asax` file, you can also programmatically personalize the profiles retrieved from the personalization store. This is done through the use of the `Profile_Personalize` event. An example use of this event is shown in Listing 15-19.

Listing 15-19: Personalizing a retrieved profile

VB

```
Public Sub Profile_Personalize(sender As Object, args As ProfileEventArgs)
  Dim checkedProfile As ProfileCommon

  If User Is Nothing Then Return

  checkedProfile = CType(ProfileBase.Create(User.Identity.Name), ProfileCommon)

  If (Date.Now.IsDaylightSavingTime()) Then
    checkedProfile = checkedProfile.GetProfile("TimeDifferenceUser")
  Else
    checkedProfile = checkedProfile.GetProfile("TimeUser")
  End If

  If Not checkedProfile Is Nothing Then
    args.Profile = checkedProfile
  End If
End Sub
```

C#

```
public void Profile_Personalize(object sender, ProfileEventArgs args)
{
  ProfileCommon checkedProfile;

  if (User == null) { return; }

  checkedProfile = (ProfileCommon)ProfileBase.Create(User.Identity.Name);

  if (DateTime.Now.IsDaylightSavingTime()) {
    checkedProfile = checkedProfile.GetProfile("TimeDifferenceUser");
  }
  else {
    checkedProfile = checkedProfile.GetProfile("TimeUser");
  }

  if (checkedProfile != null) {
    args.Profile = checkedProfile;
  }
}
```

In this case, based on a specific parameter (whether it is Daylight Savings Time or something else), you are able to assign a specific profile to the user. You do this by using the `ProfileModule.Personalize` event, which you would usually stick inside the `Global.asax` page.

Determining Whether to Continue with Automatic Saves

When you are working with the profile capabilities provided by ASP.NET, the page automatically saves the profile values to the specified data store at the end of the page's execution. This capability, which is turned on (set to `true`) by default, can be set to `false` through the use of the `automaticSaveEnabled` attribute in the `<profile>` node in the `web.config` file. This is illustrated in Listing 15-20.

Listing 15-20: Working with the automaticSaveEnabled attribute

```
<profile automaticSaveEnabled="false">

   <properties>

      <add name="FirstName" />
      <add name="LastName" />
      <add name="LastVisited" />
      <add name="Age" />
      <add name="Member" />

   </properties>

</profile>
```

If you have set the `automaticSaveEnabled` attribute value to `false`, you will have to invoke the `ProfileBase.Save()` method yourself. In most cases though, you are going to leave this setting on `true`. Once a page request has been made and finalized, the `ProfileModule.ProfileAutoSaving` event is raised. This is an event that you can also work with, as shown in Listing 15-21.

Listing 15-21: Using the ProfileAutoSaving event to turn off the auto-saving feature

VB

```
Public Sub Profile_ProfileAutoSaving(sender As Object, _
 args As ProfileAutoSaveEventArgs)

  If Profile.PaidDueStatus.HasChanged Then
    args.ContinueWithProfileAutoSave = True
  Else
    args.ContinueWithProfileAutoSave = False
  End If
End Sub
```

C#

```
public void Profile_ProfileAutoSaving(object sender, ProfileAutoSaveEventArgs args)
{
  if (Profile.PaidDueStatus.HasChanged)
    args.ContinueWithProfileAutoSave = true;
  else
    args.ContinueWithProfileAutoSave = false;
}
```

In this case, when the `Profile_ProfileAutoSaving` event is triggered, it is then possible to work within this event and change some behaviors. Listing 15-21 looks to see if the `Profile.PaidDueStatus` property has changed. If it has changed, the auto-saving feature of the profile system is continued; if the `Profile.PaidDueStatus` has not changed, the auto-saving feature is turned off.

Personalization Providers

As shown in Figure 15-1 earlier in the chapter, the middle tier of the personalization model, the personalization API layer, communicates with a series of default data providers. By default, the personalization model uses Microsoft SQL Server Express Edition files for storing the personalization properties you define. You are not limited to just this type of data store, however. You can also use the Microsoft SQL Server data provider to allow you to work with Microsoft SQL Server 7.0, 2000, 2005, and SQL Server 2008. Besides the Microsoft SQL Server data provider, the architecture also allows you to create your own data providers if one of these data stores does not fit your requirements.

Working with SQL Server Express Edition

The Microsoft SQL Server data provider does allow you to work with the new SQL Server Express Edition files. The SQL Server data provider is the default provider used by the personalization system provided by ASP.NET. When used with Visual Studio 2008, the IDE places the `ASPNETDB.MDF` file within your application's `App_Data` folder.

As you look through the `machine.config` file, notice the sections that deal with how the personalization engine works with this database. In the first reference to the `LocalSqlServer` file, you find a connection string to this file (shown in Listing 15-22) within the `<connectionStrings>` section of the file.

Listing 15-22: Adding a connection string to the SQL Server Express file

```
<configuration>

    <connectionStrings>
        <clear />
        <add name="LocalSqlServer"
         connectionString="data source=.\SQLEXPRESS;Integrated Security=SSPI;
         AttachDBFilename=|DataDirectory|aspnetdb.mdf;User Instance=true"
         providerName="System.Data.SqlClient" />
    </connectionStrings>

</configuration>
```

In this example, you see that a connection string with the name `LocalSqlServer` has been defined. The location of the file, specified by the `connectionString` attribute, points to the relative path of the file. This means that in every application you build that utilizes the personalization capabilities, the default SQL Server provider should be located in the application's `App_Data` folder and have the name of `ASPNETDB.MDF`.

The SQL Server Express file's connection string is specified through the `LocalSqlServer` declaration within this `<connectionStrings>` section. You can see the personalization engine's reference to this in the `<profile>` section within the `machine.config` file. The `<profile>` section includes a subsection listing all the providers available to the personalization engine. This is shown in Listing 15-23.

Listing 15-23: Adding a new SQL Server data provider

```
<configuration>
  <system.web>
```

Continued

```
        <profile>
            <providers>
                <add name="AspNetSqlProfileProvider"
                 connectionStringName="LocalSqlServer" applicationName="/"
                 type="System.Web.Profile.SqlProfileProvider, System.Web,
                   Version=2.0.0.0, Culture=neutral,
                   PublicKeyToken=b03f5f7f11d50a3a" />
            </providers>
        </profile>

    </system.web>
  </configuration>
```

From this, you can see that a provider is added by using the `<add>` element. Within this element, the `connectionStringName` attribute points to what was declared in the `<connectionString>` attribute from Listing 15-22.

You can specify an entirely different Microsoft SQL Server Express Edition file other than the one specified in the `machine.config` file. First, create a connection string that points to a new SQL Server Express file that is a templated version of the `ASPNETDB.mdb` file. At this point, you can use `<connectionString>` to point to this new file. If you change these values in the `machine.config` file, all the ASP.NET applications that reside on the server will then use this specified file. If you make the changes only to the `web.config` file, however, only the application using this particular `web.config` file uses this new data store. Other applications on the server remain unchanged.

Working with Microsoft's SQL Server 7.0/2000/2005/2008

You will likely find it quite easy to work with the personalization framework using the SQL Server Express files. But when you work with larger applications that require the factors of performance and reliability, you should use the SQL Server personalization provider along with SQL Server 7.0, 2000, 2005, or 2008. If this data store is available, you should always try to use this option instead of the default SQL Server Express Edition files.

If you worked with the SQL Server personalization provider using SQL Server Express files as explained earlier, you probably found it easy to use. The personalization provider works right out of the box — without any set up or configuration on your part. Using the SQL Server personalization provider with a full-blown version of SQL Server, however, is a bit of a different story. Although it is not difficult to work with, you must set up and configure your SQL Server before using it.

ASP.NET 3.5 provides a couple of ways to set up and configure SQL Server for the personalization framework. One way is through the ASP.NET SQL Server Setup Wizard, and the other method is by running some of the SQL Server scripts provided with the .NET Framework 2.0.

Using the ASP.NET SQL Server Setup Wizard is covered in detail in Chapter 12.

To use this wizard to set up your SQL Server for the ASP.NET 3.5 personalization features, you must first open up the aspnet_regsql.exe tool by invoking it from the Visual Studio 2008 Command Prompt. You open this command prompt by selecting Start ➪ All Programs ➪ Visual Studio 2008 ➪ Visual Studio Tools ➪ Visual Studio 2008 Command Prompt. At the prompt, type in `aspnet_regsql.exe` to open the

GUI of the ASP.NET SQL Server Setup Wizard. If you step through the wizard, you can set up your SQL Server instance for many of the ASP.NET systems, such as the personalization system.

Using SQL Scripts to Install Personalization Features

Another option is to use the same SQL scripts that these tools and wizards use. If you look at `C:\WINDOWS\Microsoft.NET\Framework\v2.0.50727\`, from this location, you can see the install and remove scripts — `InstallPersonalization.sql` and `UninstallPersonalization.sql`. Running these scripts provides your database with the tables needed to run the personalization framework. Be forewarned that you must run the `InstallCommon.sql` script before running the personalization script (or any of the new other ASP.NET system scripts).

Configuring the Provider for SQL Server 2005

After you have set up your SQL Server database for the personalization system, the next step is to redefine the personalization provider so that it works with this instance (instead of with the default Microsoft SQL Server Express Edition files).

You accomplish this in the `web.config` file of your application. Here, you want to configure the provider and then define this provider instance as the provider to use. Listing 15-24 shows these additions plus the enlarged `<profile>` section of the `web.config` file.

Listing 15-24: Connecting the SqlProfileProvider to SQL Server 2005

```
<configuration>

     <connectionStrings>
        <add name="LocalSql2005Server"
         connectionString="data source=127.0.0.1;Integrated Security=SSPI" />
     </connectionStrings>

     <profile defaultProvider="AspNetSql2005ProfileProvider">
        <providers>
           <clear />
           <add name="AspNetSql2005ProfileProvider"
            connectionStringName="LocalSql2005Server" applicationName="/"
            type="System.Web.Profile.SqlProfileProvider, System.Web,
              Version=2.0.0.0, Culture=neutral,
              PublicKeyToken=b03f5f7f11d50a3a" />
        </providers>

        <properties>
           <add name="FirstName" />
           <add name="LastName" />
           <add name="LastVisited" />
           <add name="Age" />
           <add name="Member" />
        </properties>
     </profile>

</configuration>
```

The big change you make to this profile definition is to use the `defaultProvider` attribute with a value that is the name of the provider you want to use — in this case the newly created SQL Server provider, `AspNetSql2005ProfileProvider`. You can also make this change to the `machine.config` file by changing the `<profile>` element, as shown in Listing 15-25.

Listing 15-25: Using SQL Server as the provider in the machine.config file

```
<configuration>
  <system.web>

   ...

     <profile enabled="true" defaultProvider="AspNetSql2005ProfileProvider">

       ...

     </profile>

   ...

  </system.web>
</configuration>
```

This change forces each and every application that resides on this server to use this new SQL Server provider instead of the default SQL Server provider (unless this command is overridden in the application's `web.config` file).

Using Multiple Providers

You are not limited to using a single data store or provider. Instead, you can use any number of providers. You can even specify the personalization provider for each property defined. This means that you can use the default provider for most properties, as well as allowing a few of them to use an entirely different provider (see Listing 15-26).

Listing 15-26: Using different providers

```
<configuration>
  <system.web>

     <profile
      defaultProvider="AspNetSqlProvider">

           <properties>

                <add name="FirstName" />
                <add name="LastName" />
                <add name="LastVisited" />
                <add name="Age" />
                <add name="Member" provider="AspNetSql2005ProfileProvider" />

           </properties>
```

```
        </profile>

    </system.web>
</configuration>
```

From this example, you can see that a default provider is specified — `AspNetSqlProvider`. Unless specified otherwise, this provider is used. The only property that changes this setting is the property `Member`. The `Member` property uses an entirely different personalization provider. In this case, it employs the Access provider (`AspNetSql2005ProfileProvider`) through the use of the `provider` attribute of the `<add>` element. With this attribute, you can define a specific provider for each and every property that is defined.

Managing Application Profiles

When you put into production an ASP.NET application that uses profile information, you quickly realize that you need a way to manage all the profile information collected over the lifecycle of the application. As you look at the ASP.NET MMC snap-in or the ASP.NET Web Site Administration Tool, note that neither of these tools gives you a way to delete a specific user's profile information or even to cleanse a database of profile information for users who haven't been active in awhile.

ASP.NET 3.5 gives you the means to manage the profile information that your application stores. This is done through the use of the `ProfileManager` class available in .NET.

Through the use of the `ProfileManager` class, you can build-in the administration capabilities to completely manage the profile information that is stored by your application. In addition to being able to access property values, such as the name of the provider being used by the personalization system or the name of the application in question, you also have a large number of methods available in the `ProfileManager` class to retrieve all sorts of other information concerning your user's profile. Through the `ProfileManager` class, you also have the capability to perform actions on this stored profile information including cleansing the database of old profile information.

Properties of the ProfileManager Class

The properties of the `ProfileManager` class are detailed in the following table.

Properties	Description
`ApplicationName`	Gets or sets the name of the application to work with.
`AutomaticSaveEnabled`	Gets or sets a Boolean value indicating whether the profile information is stored at the end of the page execution.
`Enabled`	Gets or sets a Boolean value indicating whether the application is able to use the personalization system.
`Provider`	Gets the name of the provider being used for the personalization system.
`Providers`	Gets a collection of all the providers available for the ASP.NET application.

You can see that these properties include a bit of information about the personalization system and the providers available to it that you can integrate into any management system you build. Next, this chapter looks at the methods available for the `ProfileManager` class.

Methods of the ProfileManager Class

A good number of methods are available to the `ProfileManager` class that help you manage the profiles of the users of your application. These methods are briefly described in the following table.

Properties	Description
`DeleteInactiveProfiles`	Provides you with the capability to delete any profiles that haven't seen any activity for a specified time period.
`DeleteProfile`	Provides you with the capability to delete a specific profile.
`DeleteProfiles`	Provides you with the capability to delete a collection of profiles.
`FindInactive Profiles ByUserName`	Provides you with all the inactive profiles under a specific username according to a specified date.
`FindProfilesBy UserName`	Provides you with all the profiles from a specific username.
`GetAllInactiveProfiles`	Provides you with all the profiles that have been inactive since a specified date.
`GetAllProfiles`	Provides you with a collection of all the profiles.
`GetNumberOf InactiveProfiles`	Provides you with the number of inactive profiles from a specified date.
`GetNumberOfProfiles`	Provides you with the number of total profiles in the system.

As you can see from this list of methods, you can do plenty to manage to the profile information that is stored in your database.

Next, this chapter looks at building a profile manager administration page for your ASP.NET application. This example builds it as an ASP.NET page, but you can just as easily build it as a console application.

Building the ProfileManager.aspx Page

To create a simple profile manager for your application, create a single ASP.NET page in your application called `ProfileManager.aspx`. You use this page to manage the profiles that are stored in the database for this particular application.

This page includes a number of controls, but the most important is a DropDownList control that holds all the usernames of entities that have profile information in the database. You might see the same username a couple of times depending on what you are doing with your application. Remember that a single user can have multiple profiles in the database.

Using the DropDownList control, you can select a user and see information about his profile stored in your data store. From this page, you can also delete his profile information. You can actually perform very many operations with the `ProfileManager` class, but this is a good example of some basic ones.

The code for the `ProfileManager.aspx` page is presented in Listing 15-27.

Listing 15-27: The ProfileManager.aspx page

VB

```
<%@ Page Language="VB" %>

<script runat="server">
    Protected Sub Page_Load(ByVal sender As Object, ByVal e As System.EventArgs)
        If (DropDownList1.Items.Count = 0) Then
            WriteDropdownList()
            WriteUserOutput()
        End If
    End Sub

    Protected Sub DeleteButton_Click(ByVal sender As Object, _
      ByVal e As System.EventArgs)
        ProfileManager.DeleteProfile(DropDownList1.Text.ToString())
        DropDownList1.Items.Clear()
        WriteDropdownList()
        WriteUserOutput()
    End Sub

    Protected Sub SelectButton_Click(ByVal sender As Object, _
      ByVal e As System.EventArgs)
        WriteUserOutput()
    End Sub

    Protected Sub WriteUserOutput()
        Dim outputInt As Integer
        Dim pic As ProfileInfoCollection = New ProfileInfoCollection()
        pic = ProfileManager.
          FindProfilesByUserName(ProfileAuthenticationOption.All, _
          DropDownList1.Text.ToString(), 0, 1, outputInt)

        DetailsView1.DataSource = pic
        DetailsView1.DataBind()
    End Sub

    Protected Sub WriteDropdownList()
        Dim outputInt As Integer
        Dim pic As ProfileInfoCollection = New ProfileInfoCollection()
        pic = ProfileManager.Provider.
           GetAllProfiles(ProfileAuthenticationOption.All, 0, 10000, outputInt)

        For Each proInfo As ProfileInfo In pic
            Dim li As ListItem = New ListItem()
```

Continued

```
            li.Text = proInfo.UserName.ToString()

            DropDownList1.Items.Add(li)
        Next

        Label1.Text = outputInt.ToString()
    End Sub
</script>

<html xmlns="http://www.w3.org/1999/xhtml" >
<head id="Head1" runat="server">
    <title>ProfileAdmin Page</title>
</head>
<body>
    <form id="form1" runat="server">
    <div>
        <b>Profile Manager<br />
        </b>
        <br />
        Total number of users in system:
        <asp:Label ID="Label1" runat="server"></asp:Label><br />
         <br />
        <asp:DropDownList ID="DropDownList1" runat="server">
        </asp:DropDownList> 
        <asp:Button ID="SelectButton" runat="server"
         OnClick="SelectButton_Click"
            Text="Get User Profile Information" /><br />
        <br />
        <asp:DetailsView ID="DetailsView1" runat="server" CellPadding="4"
         ForeColor="#333333" GridLines="None"
            Height="50px">
            <FooterStyle BackColor="#1C5E55" Font-Bold="True" ForeColor="White" />
            <EditRowStyle BackColor="#7C6F57" />
            <PagerStyle BackColor="#666666" ForeColor="White"
             HorizontalAlign="Center" />
            <HeaderStyle BackColor="#1C5E55" Font-Bold="True" ForeColor="White" />
            <AlternatingRowStyle BackColor="White" />
            <CommandRowStyle BackColor="#C5BBAF" Font-Bold="True" />
            <RowStyle BackColor="#E3EAEB" />
            <FieldHeaderStyle BackColor="#D0D0D0" Font-Bold="True" />
        </asp:DetailsView>
        <br />
        <asp:Button ID="DeleteButton" runat="server"
         Text="Delete Selected User's Profile Information"
         OnClick="DeleteButton_Click" />
    </div>
    </form>
</body>
</html>
```

C#

```
<%@ Page Language="C#" %>
```

```
<script runat="server">

    protected void Page_Load(object sender, EventArgs e)
    {
        if (DropDownList1.Items.Count == 0)
        {
            WriteDropdownList();
            WriteUserOutput();
        }
    }

    protected void DeleteButton_Click(object sender, EventArgs e)
    {
        ProfileManager.DeleteProfile(DropDownList1.Text.ToString());
        DropDownList1.Items.Clear();
        WriteDropdownList();
        WriteUserOutput();
    }

    protected void SelectButton_Click(object sender, EventArgs e)
    {
        WriteUserOutput();
    }

    protected void WriteUserOutput()
    {
        int outputInt;
        ProfileInfoCollection pic = new ProfileInfoCollection();
        pic = ProfileManager.FindProfilesByUserName
           (ProfileAuthenticationOption.All,
            DropDownList1.Text.ToString(), 0, 1, out outputInt);

        DetailsView1.DataSource = pic;
        DetailsView1.DataBind();
    }

    protected void WriteDropdownList()
    {
        int outputInt;
        ProfileInfoCollection pic = ProfileManager.Provider.GetAllProfiles
           (ProfileAuthenticationOption.All, 0, 10000, out outputInt);

        foreach (ProfileInfo proInfo in pic)
        {
            ListItem li = new ListItem();
            li.Text = proInfo.UserName.ToString();

            DropDownList1.Items.Add(li);
        }

        Label1.Text = outputInt.ToString();
    }
</script>
```

Examining the Code of ProfileManager.aspx Page

As you look over the code of the `ProfileManager.aspx` page, note that the `ProfileManager` class is used to perform a couple of different operations.

First, the `ProfileManager` class's `GetAllProfiles()` method is used to populate the DropDownList control that is on the page. The constructor of this method is presented here:

```
GetAllProfiles(
    authenticationOption,
    pageIndex,
    pageSize,
    totalRecords)
```

The `GetAllProfiles()` method takes a number of parameters, the first of which allows you to define whether you are using this method for *all* profiles in the system, or just the anonymous or authenticated user's profiles contained in the system. In the case of this example, all the profiles are retrieved with this method. This is accomplished using the `ProfileAuthenticationOption` enumeration. Then, the other parameters of the `GetAllProfiles()` method require you to specify a page index and the number of records to retrieve from the database. There is not a *get all* option (because of the potential size of the data that might be retrieved); so instead, in this example, I specify the first page of data (using `0`) and that this page contains the first 10,000 records (which is basically a *get all* for my application). The last parameter of the `GetAllProfiles()` method enables you to retrieve the count of the records if you want to use that anywhere within your application or if you want to use that number to iterate through the records. The `ProfileManager.aspx` page uses this number to display within the `Label1` server control.

In return from the `GetAllProfiles()` method, you get a `ProfileInfoCollection` object, which is a collection of `ProfileInfo` objects. Iterating through all the `ProfileInfo` objects in the `ProfileInfoCollection`, you are able to pull out the some of the main properties for a particular user's profile information. In this example, just the `UserName` property of the `ProfileInfo` object is used to populate the DropDownList control on the page.

When the end user selects one of the users from the dropdown list, the `FindProfilesByUserName()` method is used to display the profile of the selected user. Again, a `ProfileInfoCollection` object is returned from this method as well.

To delete the profile of the user selected in the DropDownList control, simply use the `DeleteProfile()` method and pass in the name of the selected user as illustrated here:

```
ProfileManager.DeleteProfile(DropDownList1.Text.ToString())
DropDownList1.Items.Clear()
WriteDropdownList()
WriteUserOutput()
```

After the profile is deleted from the system, that name will not appear in the drop-down list anymore (because the DropDownList control has been redrawn). If you look in the database, particularly at the aspnet_Profile table, you see that the profile of the selected user is, in fact, deleted. However, also notice that the user (even if the user is anonymous) is still stored in the aspnet_Users table.

If you want to delete not only the profile information of the user but also delete the user from the aspnet_Users table, you should invoke the `DeleteUser()` method from the `Membership` class as presented here.

```
ProfileManager.DeleteProfile(DropDownList1.Text.ToString())
Membership.DeleteUser(DropDownList1.Text.ToString())
DropDownList1.Items.Clear()
WriteDropdownList()
WriteUserOutput()
```

This use of the `DeleteUser()` method also deletes the selected user from the aspnet_Users table. You could have also achieved the same thing by using the other constructor of the `DeleteUser()` method as presented here:

```
Membership.DeleteUser(DropDownList1.Text.ToString(), True)
DropDownList1.Items.Clear()
WriteDropdownList()
WriteUserOutput()
```

The second parameter used in this operation of the `DeleteUser()` method deletes all data related to that user across *all* the tables held in the `ASPNETDB.mdf` database.

Running the ProfileManager.aspx Page

When you compile and run this page, you see results similar to those shown in Figure 15-6.

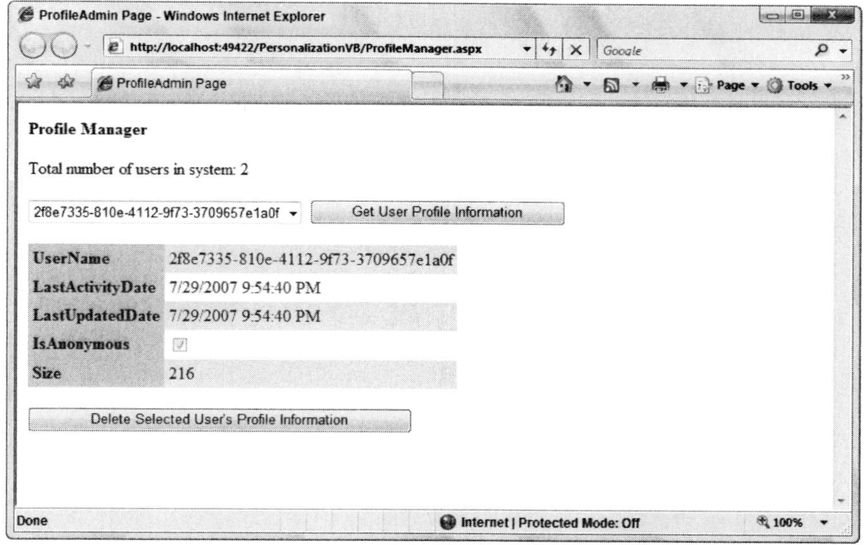

Figure 15-6

From this screen, you can see that this page is dealing with an anonymous user (based upon the GUID for the username). You can also see that the `IsAnonymous` column is indeed checked. From this page, you can then delete this user's profile information by selecting the appropriate button on the page.

Summary

The personalization capabilities provided by ASP.NET 3.5 make it incredibly easy to make your Web applications unique for all end users, whether they are authenticated or anonymous. This system enables you to store everything from basic data types provided by the .NET Framework to custom types that you create. This system is more versatile and extensible than using the `Session` or `Application` objects. The data is stored via a couple of built-in personalization providers that ship with ASP.NET. These providers include ones that connect with either Microsoft's SQL Server Express Edition files or Microsoft SQL Server 2008, 2005, 2000, or 7.0.

You can also use the `ProfileManager` class to manage your system's profile information. This includes the capability to monitor and delete profiles as you deem necessary.

16

Membership and Role Management

The authentication and authorization of users are important functions in many Web sites and browser-based applications. Traditionally, when working with Microsoft's Windows Forms applications (thick-client), you depended on Windows Integrated Authentication; when working with browser-based applications (thin-client), you used forms authentication.

Forms authentication enabled you to take requests that were not yet authenticated and redirect them to an HTML form using HTTP client-side redirection. The user provided his login information and submitted the form. After the application authenticated the request, the user received an HTTP cookie, which was then used on any subsequent requests. This kind of authentication was fine in many ways, but it required developers to build every element and even manage the back-end mechanics of the overall system. This was a daunting task for many developers and, in most cases, it was rather time-consuming.

ASP.NET 3.5 includes an authentication and authorization management service that takes care of the login, authentication, authorization, and management of users who require access to your Web pages or applications. This outstanding *membership and role management service* is an easy-to-implement framework that works out of the box using Microsoft SQL Server as the back-end data store. This framework also includes an API that allows for programmatic access to the capabilities of both the membership and role management services. In addition, a number of membership and role management–focused server controls make it easy to create Web applications that incorporate everything these services have to offer.

Before you look at the membership and role management features of ASP.NET 3.5, here's a quick review of authentication and authorization. This is vital to understand before proceeding.

Authentication

Authentication is a process that determines the identity of a user. After a user has been authenticated, a developer can determine if the identified user has *authorization* to proceed. It is impossible to give an entity authorization if no authentication process has been applied. Authentication is provided in ASP.NET 3.5 using the membership service.

Authorization

Authorization is the process of determining whether an authenticated user is allowed access to any part of an application, access to specific points of an application, or access only to specific datasets that the application provides. When you authenticate and authorize users or groups, you can customize a site based on user types or preferences. Authorization is provided in ASP.NET 3.5 using a role management service.

ASP.NET 3.5 Authentication

ASP.NET 3.5 provides the membership management service to deal with authenticating users to access a page or an entire site. The ASP.NET management service not only provides an API suite for managing users, but it also gives you some server controls, which in turn work with this API. These server controls work with the end user through the process of authentication. You look at the functionality of these controls shortly.

Setting Up Your Web Site for Membership

Before you can use the security controls that are provided with ASP.NET 3.5, you first have to set up your application to work with the membership service. How you do this depends on how you approach the security framework provided.

By default, ASP.NET 3.5 uses the built-in `SqlMembershipProvider` instance for storing details about the registered users of your application. For the initial demonstrations, the examples in this chapter work with forms-based authentication. You can assume for these examples that the application is on the public Internet and, therefore, is open to the public for registration and viewing. If it were an intranet-based application (meaning that all the users are on a private network), you could use Windows Integrated Authentication for authenticating users.

ASP.NET 3.5, as you know, offers a data provider model that handles the detailed management required to interact with multiple types of underlying data stores. Figure 16-1 shows a diagram of the ASP.NET 3.5 membership service.

From the diagram, you can see that, like the rest of the ASP.NET provider models, the membership providers can access a wide variety of underlying data stores. In this diagram, you can see the built-in Microsoft SQL Server data store. You can also build your own membership providers to get at any other custom data stores that work with user credentials. Above the membership providers in the diagram, you can see a collection of security-focused server controls that utilize the access granted by the underlying membership providers to work with the users in the authentication process.

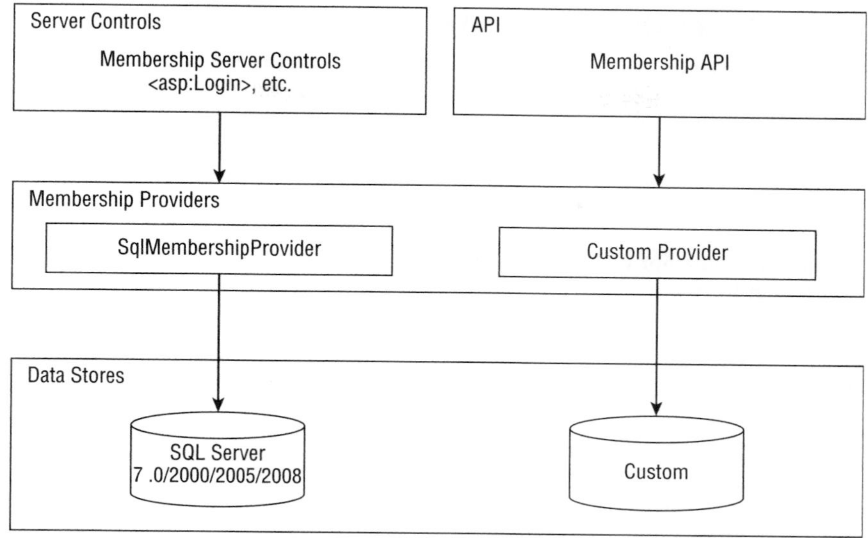

Figure 16-1

Adding an <authentication> Element to the web.config File

In order to have the forms authentication element in your Web application work with the membership service, the first step is to turn on forms authentication within the `web.config` file. To accomplish this, create a `web.config` file (if you do not already have one in your application). Next, add the section shown in Listing 16-1 to this file.

Listing 16-1: Adding forms authentication to the web.config file

```
<?xml version="1.0" encoding="utf-8"?>
<configuration>
    <system.web>
        <authentication mode="Forms" />
    </system.web>
</configuration>
```

The simple addition of the `<authentication>` element to the `web.config` file turns on everything that you need to start using the membership service provided by ASP.NET 3.5. To turn on the forms authentication using this element, you simply give the value `Forms` to the `mode` attribute. This is a forms authentication example, but other possible values of the `mode` attribute include `Windows`, `Passport`, or `None`.

IIS authentication schemes include basic, digest, and Integrated Windows Authentication. Passport authentication points to a centralized service provided by Microsoft that offers a single login and core profile service for any member sites. It costs money to use Passport, which has also recently been depreciated by Microsoft.

Because the `mode` attribute in our example is set to `Forms`, you can move on to the next step of adding users to the data store. You can also change the behavior of the forms authentication system at this point by making some modifications to the `web.config` file. These possibilities are reviewed next.

Adding a <forms> Element to the web.config File

Using forms authentication, you can provide users with access to a site or materials based upon credentials they input into a Web-based form. When an end user attempts to access a Web site, he is entering the site using anonymous authentication, which is the default authentication mode. If he is found to be anonymous, he can be redirected (by ASP.NET) to a specified login page. After the end user inputs the appropriate login information and passes the authentication process, he is provided with an HTTP cookie, which can be used in any subsequent requests.

You can modify the behavior of the forms-based authentication by defining that behavior within a `<forms>` section in the `web.config` file. You can see the possibilities of the forms authentication setting in Listing 16-2, which shows possible changes to the `<forms>` section in the `web.config` file.

Listing 16-2: Modifying the forms authentication behavior

```
<?xml version="1.0" encoding="utf-8"?>
<configuration>
    <system.web>
        <authentication mode="Forms">
            <forms name=".ASPXAUTH"
                   loginUrl="Login.aspx"
                   protection="All"
                   timeout="30"
                   path="/"
                   requireSSL="false"
                   slidingExpiration="true"
                   cookieless="UseDeviceProfile" />
        </authentication>
    </system.web>
</configuration>
```

You can set these as you wish, and you have plenty of options for values other than the ones that are displayed. Also, as stated earlier, these values are not required. You can use the membership service right away with only the configuration setting that is shown in Listing 16-1.

You can find some interesting settings in Listing 16-2, however. You can really change the behavior of the forms authentication system by adding this `<forms>` element to the `web.config` file. If you do this, however, make sure that you have the `<forms>` element nested within the `<authentication>` elements. The following list describes the possible attributes of the `<forms>` element:

- `name`: Defines the name used for the cookie sent to end users after they have been authenticated. By default, this cookie is named `.ASPXAUTH`.
- `loginUrl`: Specifies the page location to which the HTTP request is redirected for logging in the user if no valid authentication cookie (`.ASPXAUTH` or otherwise) is found. By default, it is set to `Login.aspx`.
- `protection`: Specifies the amount of protection that you want to apply to the cookie that is stored on the end user's machine after he has been authenticated. The possible settings include `All`, `None`, `Encryption`, and `Validation`. You should always attempt to use `All`.
- `timeout`: Defines the amount of time (in minutes) after which the cookie expires. The default value is 30 minutes.

- `path`: Specifies the path for cookies issued by the application.
- `requireSSL`: Defines whether you require that credentials be sent over an encrypted wire (SSL) instead of clear text.
- `slidingExpiration`: Specifies whether the timeout of the cookie is on a sliding scale. The default value is `true`. This means that the end user's cookie does not expire until 30 minutes (or the time specified in the `timeout` attribute) after the last request to the application has been made. If the value of the `slidingExpiration` attribute is set to `false`, the cookie expires 30 minutes from the first request.
- `cookieless`: Specifies how the cookies are handled by ASP.NET. The possible values include `UseDeviceProfile`, `UseCookies`, `AutoDetect`, and `UseUri`. The default value is `UseDeviceProfile`. This value detects whether to use cookies based on the user agent of the device. `UseCookies` requires that all requests have the credentials stored in a cookie. `AutoDetect` auto-determines whether the details are stored in a cookie on the client or within the URI (this is done by sending a test cookie first). Finally, `UseUri` forces ASP.NET to store the details within the URI on all instances.

Now that forms authentication is turned on, the next step is adding users to the Microsoft SQL Server Express Edition data store, `ASPNETDB.mdf`.

Adding Users

To add users to the membership service, you can register users into the Microsoft SQL Server Express Edition data store. The first question you might ask is, ''Where is this data store?''

> *Of course, there are a number of editions of Microsoft's SQL Server that you can use to work through the examples in this book. With that said, this chapter uses the default database the membership system uses in creating users.*

The Microsoft SQL Server provider for the membership system can use a SQL Server Express Edition file that is structured specifically for the membership service (and other ASP.NET systems, such as the role management system). ASP.NET is set to automatically create this particular file for you if the appropriate file does not exist already. To create the `ASPNETDB.mdf` file, you work with the ASP.NET server controls that utilize an aspect of the membership service. When the application requires the `ASPNETDB.mdf` file, ASP.NET creates this file on your behalf in the `App_Data` folder.

After the data store is in place, it is time to start adding users to the data store.

Using the CreateUserWizard Server Control

The CreateUserWizard server control is one that can be used in conjunction with the membership service. You can find this and the other controls mentioned in this chapter under the Login section in the Visual Studio 2008 Toolbox. The CreateUserWizard control enables you to plug registered users into your data store for later retrieval. If a page in your application allows end users to register for your site, you want, at a minimum, to retrieve a login and password from the user and place these values in the data store. This enables the end user to access these items later to log in to the application using the membership system.

To make your life as simple as possible, the CreateUserWizard control takes complete control of registration on your behalf. Listing 16-3 shows a simple use of the control.

Listing 16-3: Allowing end users to register with the site

```
<%@ Page Language="VB" %>

<html xmlns="http://www.w3.org/1999/xhtml">
<head runat="server">
    <title>Creating Users</title>
</head>
<body>
    <form id="form1" runat="server">
        <asp:CreateUserWizard ID="CreateUserWizard1" Runat="server"
         BorderWidth="1px" BorderColor="#FFDFAD" BorderStyle="Solid"
         BackColor="#FFFBD6" Font-Names="Verdana">
            <TitleTextStyle Font-Bold="True" BackColor="#990000"
             ForeColor="White"></TitleTextStyle>
        </asp:CreateUserWizard>
    </form>
</body>
</html>
```

This page simply uses the CreateUserWizard control and nothing more. This one control enables you to register end users for your Web application. This particular CreateUserWizard control has a little style applied to it, but this control can be as simple as:

```
<asp:CreateUserWizard ID="CreateUserWizard1" Runat="server">
</asp:CreateUserWizard>
```

When this code is run, an end user is presented with the form shown in Figure 16-2.

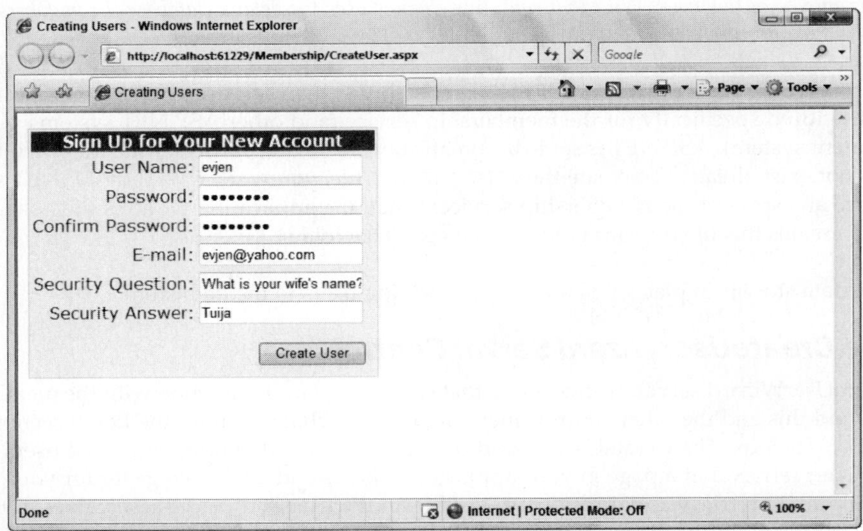

Figure 16-2

This screenshot shows the form as it would appear when filled out by the end user and includes information such as the username, password, e-mail address, as well as a security question-and-answer section. Clicking the Create User button places this defined user information into the data store.

The username and password provided via this control enable the end user to log in to the application later through the Login server control. A Confirm Password text box is also included in the form of the CreateUser server control to ensure that the password provided is spelled correctly. An e-mail address text box is included (in case end users forget their login credentials and want the credentials e-mailed to them at some later point in time). Then finally, the security question and answer are used to verify the identity of the end user before any credentials or user information is changed or later provided via the browser.

After the Create User button on this form is clicked, the end user is presented with a confirmation of the information being stored (see Figure 16-3).

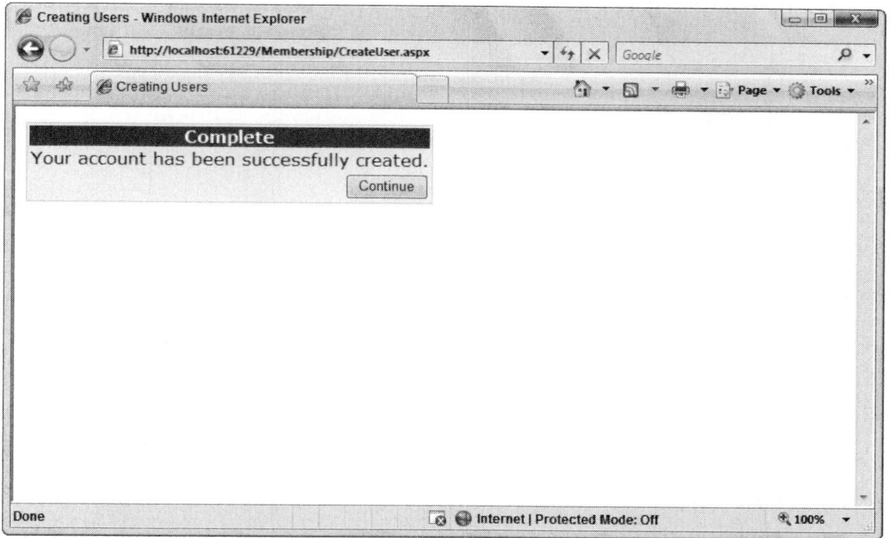

Figure 16-3

Seeing Where Users Are Stored

Now that the CreateUserWizard control has been used to add a user to the membership service, look at where this information is stored. If you used Visual Studio to create the Microsoft SQL Server Express Edition file in which you want to store the user information, the file is created when the previous example is run and you complete the form process as shown in the preceding figures. When the example is run and completed, you can click the Refresh button in the Solution Explorer to find the `ASPNETDB.mdf` file, which is located in the `App_Data` folder of your project. Many different tables are included in this file, but you are interested in the `aspnet_Membership` table only.

When you open the `aspnet_Membership` table (by right-clicking the table in the Server Explorer and selecting Show Table Data), the users you entered are in the system. This is illustrated in Figure 16-4.

The user password in this table is not stored as clear text; instead, it is hashed, which is a one-way form of encryption that cannot be reversed easily. When a user logs in to an application that is using the ASP.NET 3.5 membership service, his or her password is immediately hashed and then compared to the hashed password stored in the database. If the two hashed strings do not compare, the passwords are not considered a match. Storing clear text passwords is considered a security risk, so you should never do so without weighing the risk involved.

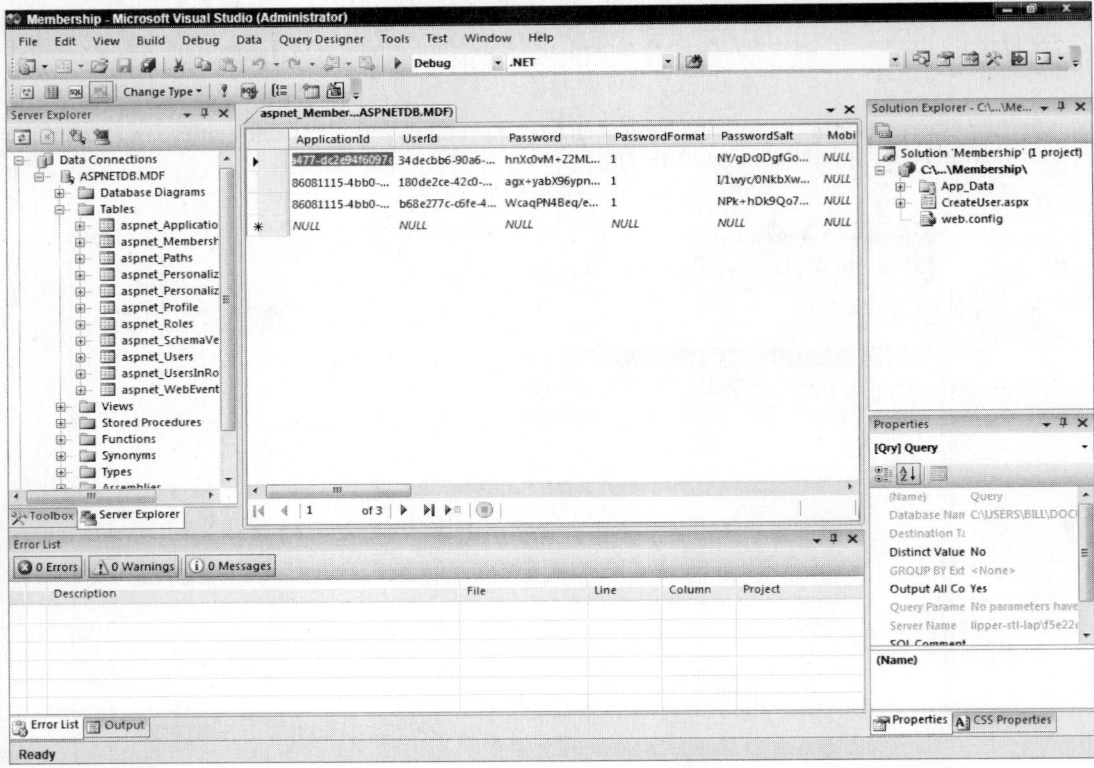

Figure 16-4

A note regarding the passwords used in ASP.NET 3.5: If you are having difficulty entering users because of a password error, it might be because ASP.NET requires strong passwords by default. All passwords input into the system must be at least seven characters, and contain at least one non-alphanumeric character (such as `[ ]`, `!`, `@`, `#`, or `$`). Whew! An example password of this combination is:

```
Bevjen7777$
```

Although this type of password is a heck of a lot more secure, a password like this is sometimes difficult to remember. You can actually change the behavior of the membership provider so that it doesn't require such difficult passwords by reworking the membership provider in the `web.config` file, as illustrated in Listing 16-4.

Listing 16-4: Modifying the membership provider in web.config

```
<configuration>
   <system.web>
```

```
        <membership>
           <providers>
              <clear />
              <add name="AspNetSqlMembershipProvider"
               type="System.Web.Security.SqlMembershipProvider, System.Web,
                 Version=2.0.0.0, Culture=neutral, PublicKeyToken=b03f5f7f11d50a3a"
               connectionStringName="LocalSqlServer"
               requiresQuestionAndAnswer="false"
               requiresUniqueEmail="true"
               passwordFormat="Hashed"
               minRequiredNonalphanumericCharacters="0"
               minRequiredPasswordLength="3" />
           </providers>
        </membership>

    </system.web>
</configuration>
```

In this example, you have reworked the membership provider for SQL Server so that it does not actually require any non-alphanumeric characters and allows passwords as small as three characters in length. You do this by using the `minRequiredNonalphanumericCharacters` and `minRequiredPasswordLength` attributes. With these in place, you can now create users with these password rules as set forth in these configuration settings. Modifying the membership provider is covered in more detail later in this chapter.

Working with the CreateUserWizard Control

When you work with the CreateUserWizard control, be aware of the `ContinueButtonClick()` and the `CreatedUser()` events. The `ContinueButtonClick()` event is triggered when the Continue button on the second page is clicked after the user has been successfully created (see Listing 16-5).

Listing 16-5: The ContinueButtonClick event

VB

```
Protected Sub CreateUserWizard1_ContinueButtonClick(ByVal sender As Object, _
   ByVal e As System.EventArgs)

      Response.Redirect("Default.aspx")
End Sub
```

C#

```
protected void CreateUserWizard1_ContinueButtonClick(object sender, EventArgs e)
{
   Response.Redirect("Default.aspx");
}
```

In this example, after the user has been added to the membership service through the form provided by the CreateUserWizard control, she can click the Continue button to be redirected to another page in the application. This is done with a simple `Response.Redirect` statement. Remember when you use this event, that you must add an `OnContinueButtonClick = "CreateUserWizard1_ContinueButtonClick"` to the `<asp:CreateUserWizard>` control.

The `CreatingUser()` event is triggered when a user is successfully created in the data store. The use of this event is shown in Listing 16-6.

Listing 16-6: The CreateUser event

VB

```
Protected Sub CreateUserWizard1_CreatingUser(ByVal sender As Object, _
   ByVal e As System.EventArgs)

      ' Code here
End Sub
```

C#

```
protected void CreateUserWizard1_CreatingUser(object sender, EventArgs e)
{
   // Code here
}
```

Use this event if you want to take any additional actions when a user is registered to the service.

Incorporating Personalization Properties in the Registration Process

As you saw in the previous chapter on personalization, it is fairly simple to use the personalization management system that comes with ASP.NET 3.5 and store user-specific details. The registration process provided by the CreateUserWizard control is an ideal spot to retrieve this information from the user to store directly in the personalization system. The retrieval is not too difficult to incorporate into your code.

The first step, as you learned in the previous chapter on personalization, is to have some personalization points defined in the application's `web.config` file. This is shown in Listing 16-7.

Listing 16-7: Creating personalization properties in the web.config file

```
<configuration>
  <system.web>

     <profile>

        <properties>

           <add name="FirstName" />
           <add name="LastName" />
           <add name="LastVisited" />
           <add name="Age" />
           <add name="Member" />

        </properties>

     </profile>

  </system.web>
</configuration>
```

Now that these properties are defined in the `web.config` file, you can use them when you create users in the ASP.NET membership system. Again, using the CreateUserWizard control, you can create a process that requires the user to enter his preferred username and password in the first step, and then the second step asks for these custom-defined personalization points. Listing 16-8 shows a CreateUserWizard control that incorporates this idea.

Listing 16-8: Using personalization properties with the CreateUserWizard control

VB

```
<%@ Page Language="VB" %>

<script runat="server">
    Protected Sub CreateUserWizard1_CreatedUser(ByVal sender As Object, _
       ByVal e As System.EventArgs)

        Dim pc As ProfileCommon = New ProfileCommon()
        pc.Initialize(CreateUserWizard1.UserName.ToString(), True)

        pc.FirstName = Firstname.Text
        pc.LastName = Lastname.Text
        pc.Age = Age.Text

        pc.Save()
    End Sub
</script>

<html xmlns="http://www.w3.org/1999/xhtml">
<head id="Head1" runat="server">
    <title>Creating Users with Personalization</title>
</head>
<body>
    <form id="form1" runat="server">
        <asp:CreateUserWizard ID="CreateUserWizard1" Runat="server"
         BorderWidth="1px" BorderColor="#FFDFAD" BorderStyle="Solid"
         BackColor="#FFFBD6" Font-Names="Verdana"
         LoginCreatedUser="true" OnCreatedUser="CreateUserWizard1_CreatedUser" >
            <WizardSteps>
                <asp:WizardStep ID="WizardStep1" Runat="server"
                 Title="Additional Information" StepType="Start">
                    <table width="100%"><tr><td>
                    Firstname: </td><td>
                    <asp:TextBox ID="Firstname" Runat="server"></asp:TextBox>
                    </td></tr><tr><td>
                    Lastname: </td><td>
                    <asp:TextBox ID="Lastname" Runat="server"></asp:TextBox>
                    </td></tr><tr><td>
                    Age: </td><td>
                    <asp:TextBox ID="Age" Runat="server"></asp:TextBox>
                    </td></tr></table>
                </asp:WizardStep>
                <asp:CreateUserWizardStep Runat="server"
                 Title="Sign Up for Your New Account">
                </asp:CreateUserWizardStep>
                <asp:CompleteWizardStep Runat="server" Title="Complete">
                </asp:CompleteWizardStep>
            </WizardSteps>
            <StepStyle BorderColor="#FFDFAD" Font-Names="Verdana"
             BackColor="#FFFBD6" BorderStyle="Solid"
             BorderWidth="1px"></StepStyle>
            <TitleTextStyle Font-Bold="True" BackColor="#990000"
```

Continued

```
            ForeColor="White"></TitleTextStyle>
        </asp:CreateUserWizard>
    </form>
</body>
</html>
```

C#

```
<%@ Page Language="C#" %>

<script runat="server">
    protected void CreateUserWizard1_CreatedUser(object sender, EventArgs e)
    {
        ProfileCommon pc = new ProfileCommon();
        pc.Initialize(CreateUserWizard1.UserName.ToString(), true);

        pc.FirstName = Firstname.Text;
        pc.LastName = Lastname.Text;
        pc.Age = Age.Text;

        pc.Save();
    }
</script>
```

With this change to the standard registration process as is defined by a default instance of the CreateUser-Wizard control, your registration system now includes the request for properties stored and retrieved using the `ProfileCommon` object. Then, using the `ProfileCommon.Initialize()` method, you initialize the property values for the current user. Next, you set the property values using the strongly typed access to the profile properties available via the `ProfileCommon` object. After all the values have been set, you use the `Save()` method to finalize the process.

You can define a custom step within the CreateUserWizard control by using the `<WizardSteps>`element. Within this element, you can construct a series of registration steps in whatever fashion you choose. From the `<WizardSteps>`section, shown in Listing 16-8, you can see that three steps are defined. The first is the custom step in which the end user's personalization properties are requested with the `<asp:WizardStep>` control. Within the `<asp:WizardStep>`control, a table is laid out and a custom form is created.

Two additional steps are defined within Listing 16-7: a step to create the user (using the `<asp:CreateUserWizardStep>` control) and a step to confirm the creation of a new user (using the `<asp:CompleteWizardStep>` control). The order in which these steps appear is the order in which they are presented to the end user.

After the steps are created the way you want, you can then store the custom properties using the CreateUserWizard control's `CreatedUser()` event:

```
Protected Sub CreateUserWizard1_CreatedUser(ByVal sender As Object, _
   ByVal e As System.EventArgs)

    Dim pc As ProfileCommon = New ProfileCommon()
    pc.Initialize(CreateUserWizard1.UserName.ToString(), True)

    pc.FirstName = Firstname.Text
    pc.LastName = Lastname.Text
```

```
        pc.Age = Age.Text

        pc.Save()
    End Sub
```

You are not limited to having a separate step in which you ask for personal bits of information; you can incorporate these items directly into the <asp:CreateUserWizardStep> step itself. An easy way to do this is to switch to the Design view of your page and pull up the smart tag for the CreateUserWizard control. Then click the Customize Create User Step link (shown in Figure 16-5).

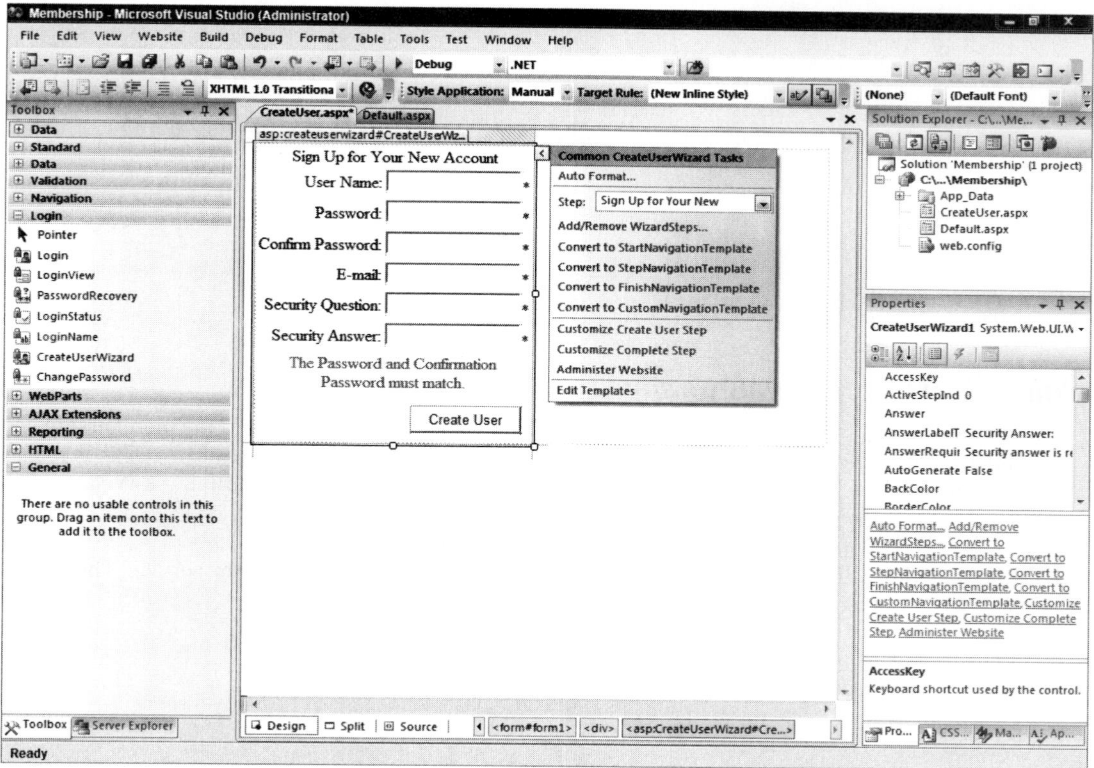

Figure 16-5

Clicking on the Customize Create User Step details the contents of this particular step within a new <ContentTemplate> section that is now contained within the <asp:CreateUserWizardStep> control. Within the <ContentTemplate> element, you can now see the complete default form used for creating a new user. At this point, you are free to change the form by adding your own sections that request the end user's personal information. From this detailed form, you can also remove items. For instance, if you are not interested in asking for the security question and answer, you can remove these two items from the form (remember that you must disable the question-and-answer requirement in the membership provider definition). By changing this default form, you can completely customize the registration process for your end users (see Figure 16-6).

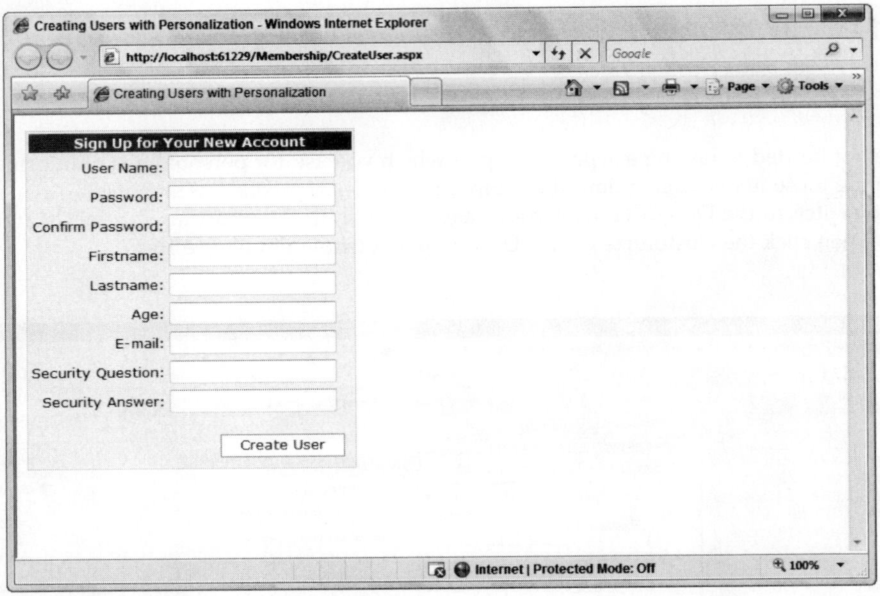

Figure 16-6

Adding Users Programmatically

You are not limited to using only server controls to register or add new users to the membership service. ASP.NET 3.5 provides a Membership API for performing this task programmatically. This is ideal to create your own mechanics for adding users to the service — or if you are modifying a Web application that was created using ASP.NET 1.0/1.1.

The Membership API includes the `CreateUser()` method for adding users to the service. The `CreateUser()` method includes four possible signatures:

```
Membership.CreateUser(username As String, password As String)

Membership.CreateUser(username As String, password As String,
   email As String)

Membership.CreateUser(username As String, password As String,
   email As String, passwordQuestion As String,
   passwordAnswer As String, isApproved As Boolean,
   ByRef status As System.Web.Security.MembershipCreateStatus)

Membership.CreateUser(username As String, password As String,
   email As String, passwordQuestion As String,
   passwordAnswer As String, isApproved As Boolean, providerUserKey As Object
   ByRef status As System.Web.Security.MembershipCreateStatus)
```

You can use this method to create users. The nice thing about this method is that you are not required to create an instance of the `Membership` class; you use it directly. A simple use of the `CreateUser()` method is illustrated in Listing 16-9.

Listing 16-9: Creating users programmatically

VB

```
<%@ Page Language="VB" %>

<script runat="server">
Protected Sub Button1_Click(ByVal sender As Object, ByVal e As System.EventArgs)
   Try
      Membership.CreateUser(TextBox1.Text, TextBox2.Text)
      Label1.Text = "Successfully created user " & TextBox1.Text
   Catch ex As MembershipCreateUserException
      Label1.Text = "Error: " & ex.ToString()
   End Try
End Sub
</script>

<html xmlns="http://www.w3.org/1999/xhtml">
<head runat="server">
    <title>Creating a User</title>
</head>
<body>
    <form id="form1" runat="server">
        <h1>Create User</h1>
        <p>Username<br />
            <asp:TextBox ID="TextBox1" Runat="server"></asp:TextBox>
        </p>
        <p>Password<br />
            <asp:TextBox ID="TextBox2" Runat="server"
             TextMode="Password"></asp:TextBox>
        </p>
        <p>
            <asp:Button ID="Button1" Runat="server" Text="Create User"
             OnClick="Button1_Click" />
        </p>
        <p>
            <asp:Label ID="Label1" Runat="server"></asp:Label>
        </p>
    </form>
</body>
</html>
```

C#

```
<%@ Page Language="C#" %>

<script runat="server">
    protected void Button1_Click(object sender, EventArgs e)
    {
        try
        {
            Membership.CreateUser(TextBox1.Text.ToString(),
               TextBox2.Text.ToString());
            Label1.Text = "Successfully created user " + TextBox1.Text;
        }
```

Continued

```
            catch (MembershipCreateUserException ex)
            {
                Label1.Text = "Error: " + ex.ToString();
            }
        }
    </script>
```

So, use either the CreateUserWizard control or the `CreateUser()` method found in the Membership API to create users for your Web applications with relative ease. This functionality was possible in the past with ASP.NET 1.0/1.1, but it was a labor-intensive task. With ASP.NET 2.0 or 3.5, you can create users either with a single control or with a single line of code.

From this bit of code, you can see that if a problem occurs when creating the user with the `CreateUser()` method, a `MembershipCreateUserException` is thrown. In this example, the exception is written to the screen within a Label server control. An example of an exception written to the screen is presented here:

```
Error: System.Web.Security.MembershipCreateUserException: The password-answer
supplied is invalid. at System.Web.Security.Membership.CreateUser(String username,
String password, String email) at System.Web.Security.Membership.CreateUser(String
username, String password) at ASP.default_aspx.Button1_Click(Object sender,
EventArgs e) in c:\Documents and Settings\BillEvjen\My Documents\Visual Studio
2008\WebSites\Membership\Default.aspx:line 10
```

You might not want such details sent to the end user. You might prefer to return a simpler message to the end user with something like the following construct:

```
Label1.Text = "Error: " & ex.Message.ToString();
```

This gives you results as simple as the following:

```
Error: The password-answer supplied is invalid.
```

You can also capture the specific error using the `MembershipCreateUserException` and returning something that might be a little more appropriate. An example of this is presented in Listing 16-10.

Listing 16-10: Capturing the specific MembershipCreateUserException value

VB

```
<%@ Page Language="VB" %>

<script runat="server">

    Protected Sub Button1_Click(ByVal sender As Object, _
      ByVal e As System.EventArgs)
        Try
            Membership.CreateUser(TextBox1.Text, TextBox2.Text)
            Label1.Text = "Successfully created user " & TextBox1.Text
        Catch ex As MembershipCreateUserException
            Select Case ex.StatusCode
                Case MembershipCreateStatus.DuplicateEmail
                    Label1.Text = "You have supplied a duplicate email address."
                Case MembershipCreateStatus.DuplicateUserName
                    Label1.Text = "You have supplied a duplicate username."
```

```
                Case MembershipCreateStatus.InvalidEmail
                    Label1.Text = "You have not supplied a proper email address."
                Case Else
                    Label1.Text = "ERROR: " & ex.Message.ToString()
            End Select
        End Try
    End Sub
</script>

<html xmlns="http://www.w3.org/1999/xhtml">
<head id="Head1" runat="server">
    <title>Creating a User</title>
</head>
<body>
    <form id="form1" runat="server">
        <h1>Create User</h1>
        <p>Username<br />
            <asp:TextBox ID="TextBox1" Runat="server"></asp:TextBox>
        </p>
        <p>Password<br />
            <asp:TextBox ID="TextBox2" Runat="server"
             TextMode="Password"></asp:TextBox>
        </p>
        <p>
            <asp:Button ID="Button1" Runat="server" Text="Create User"
             OnClick="Button1_Click" />
        </p>
        <p>
            <asp:Label ID="Label1" Runat="server"></asp:Label>
        </p>
    </form>
</body>
</html>
```

C#

```
<%@ Page Language="C#" %>

<script runat="server">
    protected void Button1_Click(object sender, EventArgs e)
    {
        try
        {
            Membership.CreateUser(TextBox1.Text, TextBox2.Text);
            Label1.Text = "Successfully created user " + TextBox1.Text;
        }
        catch (MembershipCreateUserException ex)
        {
            switch(ex.StatusCode)
            {
                case MembershipCreateStatus.DuplicateEmail:
                    Label1.Text = "You have supplied a duplicate email address.";
                    break;
                case MembershipCreateStatus.DuplicateUserName:
                    Label1.Text = "You have supplied a duplicate username.";
```

Continued

```
                    break;
                case MembershipCreateStatus.InvalidEmail:
                    Label1.Text = "You have not supplied a proper email address.";
                    break;
                default:
                    Label1.Text = "ERROR: " + ex.Message.ToString();
                    break;
            }
        }
    }
</script>
```

In this case, you are able to look for the specific error that occurred in the `CreateUser` process. Here, this code is looking for only three specific items, but the list of available error codes includes the following:

- `MembershipCreateStatus.DuplicateEmail`
- `MembershipCreateStatus.DuplicateProviderUserKey`
- `MembershipCreateStatus.DuplicateUserName`
- `MembershipCreateStatus.InvalidAnswer`
- `MembershipCreateStatus.InvalidEmail`
- `MembershipCreateStatus.InvalidPassword`
- `MembershipCreateStatus.InvalidProviderUserKey`
- `MembershipCreateStatus.InvalidQuestion`
- `MembershipCreateStatus.InvalidUserName`
- `MembershipCreateStatus.ProviderError`
- `MembershipCreateStatus.Success`
- `MembershipCreateStatus.UserRejected`

In addition to giving better error reports to your users by defining what is going on, you can use these events to take any actions that might be required.

Changing How Users Register with Your Application

You determine how users register with your applications and what is required of them by the membership provider you choose. You will find a default membership provider and its applied settings are established within the `machine.config` file. If you dig down in the `machine.config` file on your server, you find the code shown in Listing 16-11.

Listing 16-11: Membership provider settings in the machine.config file

```
<membership>
   <providers>
      <add name="AspNetSqlMembershipProvider"
       type="System.Web.Security.SqlMembershipProvider, System.Web,
          Version=2.0.0.0, Culture=neutral, PublicKeyToken=b03f5f7f11d50a3a"
       connectionStringName="LocalSqlServer"
```

```
            enablePasswordRetrieval="false"
            enablePasswordReset="true"
            requiresQuestionAndAnswer="true"
            applicationName="/"
            requiresUniqueEmail="false"
            passwordFormat="Hashed"
            maxInvalidPasswordAttempts="5"
            minRequiredPasswordLength="7"
            minRequiredNonalphanumericCharacters="1"
            passwordAttemptWindow="10"
            passwordStrengthRegularExpression="" />
        </providers>
    </membership>
```

This section of the `machine.config` file shows the default membership provider that comes with ASP.NET 3.5 — named `AspNetSqlProvider`. If you are adding membership providers for server-wide use, add them to this `<membership>` section of the `machine.config` file; if you intend to use them for only a specific application instance, you can add them to your application's `web.config` file.

The important attributes of the SqlMembershipProvider definition include the `enablePasswordRetrieval`, `enablePasswordReset`, `requiresQuestionAndAnswer`, `requiresUniqueEmail`, and `PasswordFormat` attributes. The following table defines these attributes.

Attribute	Description
`enablePasswordRetrieval`	Defines whether the provider supports password retrievals. This attribute takes a `Boolean` value. The default value is `False`. When it is set to `False`, passwords cannot be retrieved although they can be changed with a new random password.
`enablePasswordReset`	Defines whether the provider supports password resets. This attribute takes a `Boolean` value. The default value is `True`.
`requiresQuestionAndAnswer`	Specifies whether the provider should require a question-and-answer combination when a user is created. This attribute takes a `Boolean` value, and the default value is `False`.
`requiresUniqueEmail`	Defines whether the provider should require a unique e-mail to be specified when the user is created. This attribute takes a `Boolean` value, and the default value is `False`. When set to `True`, only unique e-mail addresses can be entered into the data store.
`passwordFormat`	Defines the format in which the password is stored in the data store. The possible values include `Hashed`, `Clear`, and `Encrypted`. The default value is `Hashed`. Hashed passwords use SHA1, whereas encrypted passwords use Triple-DES encryption.

In addition to having these items defined in the `machine.config` file, you can also redefine them again (thus overriding the settings in the `machine.config`) in the `web.config` file.

Asking for Credentials

After you have users that can access your Web application using the membership service provided by ASP.NET, you can then give these users the means to log in to the site. This requires little work on your part. Before you learn about the controls that enable users to access your applications, you should make a few more modifications to the `web.config` file.

Turning Off Access with the <authorization> Element

After you make the changes to the `web.config` file by adding the `<authorization>` and `<forms>` elements (Listings 16-1 and 16-2), your Web application is accessible to each and every user that browses to any page your application contains. To prevent open access, you have to deny unauthenticated users access to the pages of your site.

Denying unauthenticated users access to your site is illustrated in Listing 16-12.

Listing 16-12: Denying unauthenticated users

```
<?xml version="1.0" encoding="utf-8"?>
<configuration>
    <system.web>
        <authentication mode="Forms" />
        <authorization>
           <deny users="?" />
        </authorization>
    </system.web>
</configuration>
```

Using the `<authorization>` and `<deny>` elements, you can deny specific users access to your Web application — or (as in this case) simply deny every unauthenticated user (this is what the question mark signifies).

Now that everyone but authenticated users has been denied access to the site, you want to make it easy for viewers of your application to become authenticated users. To do so, use the Login server control.

Using the Login Server Control

The Login server control enables you to turn unauthenticated users into authenticated users by allowing them to provide login credentials that can be verified in a data store of some kind. In the examples so far, you have used Microsoft SQL Server Express Edition as the data store, but you can just as easily use the full-blown version of Microsoft's SQL Server (such as Microsoft's SQL Server 7.0, 2000, 2005, or 2008).

The first step in using the Login control is to create a new Web page titled `Login.aspx`. This is the default page to which unauthenticated users are redirected to obtain their credentials. Remember that you can change this behavior by changing the value of the `<forms>` element's `loginUrl` attribute in the `web.config` file.

The `Login.aspx` page simply needs an `<asp:Login>` control to give the end user everything he needs to become authenticated, as illustrated in Listing 16-13.

Listing 16-13: Providing a login for the end user using the Login control

```
<%@ Page Language="VB" %>

<html xmlns="http://www.w3.org/1999/xhtml">
<head runat="server">
    <title>Login Page</title>
</head>
<body>
    <form id="form1" runat="server">
        <asp:Login ID="Login1" Runat="server">
        </asp:Login>
    </form>
</body>
</html>
```

In the situation established here, if the unauthenticated user hits a different page in the application, he is redirected to the `Login.aspx` page. You can see how ASP.NET tracks the location in the URL from the address bar in the browser:

```
http://localhost:18436/Membership/Login.aspx?ReturnUrl=%2fMembership%2fDefault.aspx
```

The login page, using the Login control, is shown in Figure 16-7.

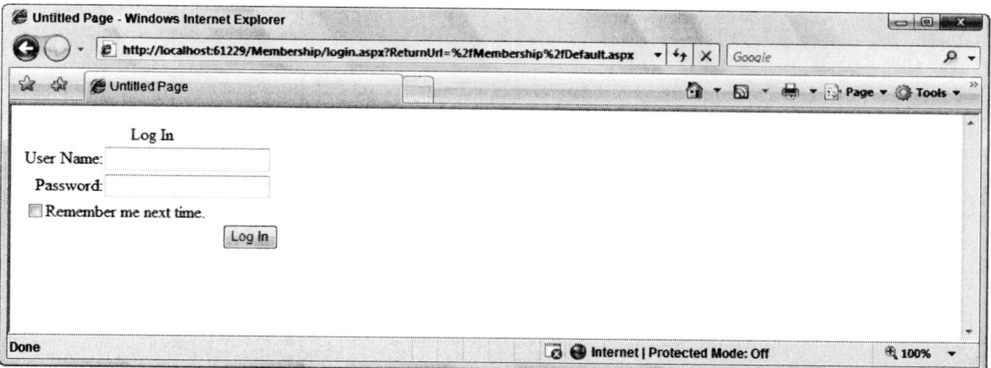

Figure 16-7

From this figure, you can see that the Login control asks the user for a username and password. A check box allows a cookie to be stored on the client machine. This cookie enables the end user to bypass future logins. You can remove the check box and related text created to remember the user by setting the Login control's `DisplayRememberMe` property to `False`.

In addition to the `DisplayRememberMe` property, you can work with this aspect of the Login control by using the `RememberMeText` and the `RememberMeSet` properties. The `RememberMeText` property is pretty self-explanatory because its value simply defines the text set next to the check box. The `RememberMeSet` property, however, is fairly interesting. The `RememberMeSet` property takes a `Boolean` value (by default, it is set to `False`) that specifies whether to set a persistent cookie on the client's machine after a user has logged in using the Login control. If set to `True` when the `DisplayRememberMe` property is also set to `True`, the check box is simply checked by default when the Login control is generated in the browser. If the `DisplayRememberMe` property is set to `False` (meaning the end user does not see the check box or cannot select the option of persisting the login cookie) and the `RememberMeSet` is set to `True`, a cookie is set on the user's machine automatically without the user's knowledge or choice in the matter. You should think carefully about taking this approach because end users sometimes use public computers, and this method would mean you are setting authorization cookies on public machines.

This cookie remains on the client's machine until the user logs out of the application (if this option is provided). With the persisted cookie, and assuming the end user has not logged out of the application, the user never needs to log in again when he returns to the application because his credentials are provided by the contents found in the cookie. After the end user has logged in to the application, he is returned to the page he originally intended to access.

You can also modify the look-and-feel of the Login control just as you can for the other controls. One way to do this is by clicking the Auto Format link in the control's smart tag. There you find a list of options for modifying the look-and-feel of the control (see Figure 16-8).

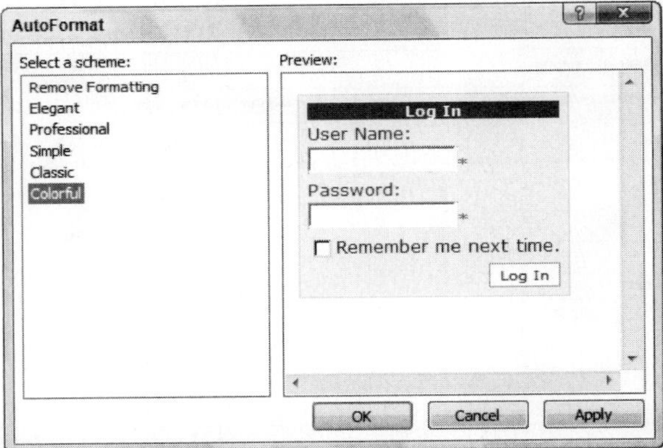

Figure 16-8

Select the Colorful option, for example, and the code is modified. Listing 16-14 shows the code generated for this selection.

Listing 16-14: A formatted Login control

```
<asp:Login ID="Login1" Runat="server" BackColor="#FFFBD6"
 BorderColor="#FFDFAD" BorderPadding="4" BorderStyle="Solid"
 BorderWidth="1px" Font-Names="Verdana" Font-Size="0.8em"
 ForeColor="#333333" TextLayout="TextOnTop">
    <TextBoxStyle Font-Size="0.8em" />
    <LoginButtonStyle BackColor="White" BorderColor="#CC9966"
```

```
        BorderStyle="Solid" BorderWidth="1px" Font-Names="Verdana"
        Font-Size="0.8em" ForeColor="#990000" />
       <InstructionTextStyle Font-Italic="True" ForeColor="Black" />
       <TitleTextStyle BackColor="#990000" Font-Bold="True" Font-Size="0.9em"
        ForeColor="White" />
</asp:Login>
```

From this listing, you can see that there are a number of subelements that are used to modify particular items displayed by the control. The available styling elements for the Login control include the following:

- `<CheckboxStyle>`
- `<FailureTextStyle>`
- `<HyperLinkStyle>`
- `<InstructionTextStyle>`
- `<LabelStyle>`
- `<LoginButtonStyle>`
- `<TextBoxStyle>`
- `<TitleTextStyle>`
- `<ValidatorTextStyle>`

The Login control has numerous properties that allow you to alter how the control appears and behaves. An interesting change you can make is to add some links at the bottom of the control to provide access to additional resources. With these links, you can give users the capability to get help or register for the application so that they can be provided with any login credentials.

You can provide links to do the following:

- Redirect users to a help page using the `HelpPageText`, `HelpPageUrl`, and `HelpPageIconUrl` properties.
- Redirect users to a registration page using the `CreateUserText`, `CreateUserUrl`, and `CreateUserIconUrl` properties.
- Redirect users to a page that allows them to recover their forgotten passwords using the `PasswordRecoveryText`, `PasswordRecoveryUrl`, and `PasswordRecoveryIconUrl` properties.

When used, the Login control looks like what is shown in Figure 16-9.

Logging In Users Programmatically

Besides using the pre-built mechanics of the Login control, you can also perform this task programmatically using the Membership class. To validate credentials that you receive, you use the `ValidateUser()` method of this class. The `ValidateUser()` method takes a single signature:

```
Membership.ValidateUser(username As String, password As String)
```

This method is illustrated in Listing 16-15.

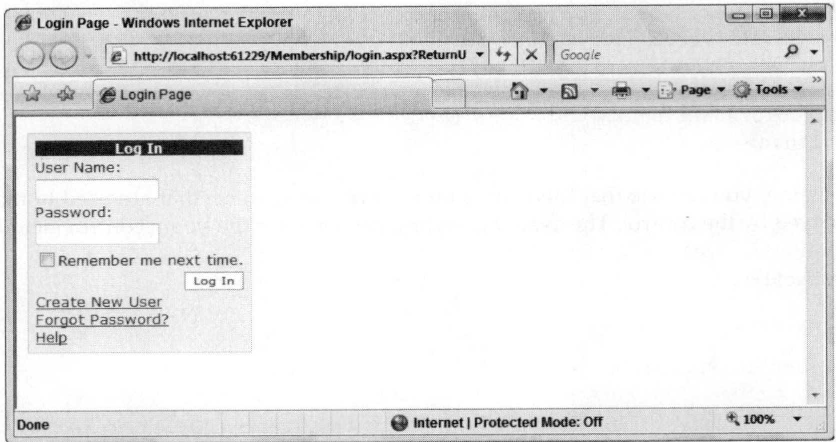

Figure 16-9

Listing 16-15: Validating a user's credentials programmatically

VB

```
If Membership.ValidateUser(TextBox1.Text, TextBox2.Text) Then
   FormsAuthentication.RedirectFromLoginPage(TextBox1.Text, False)
Else
   Label1.Text = "You are not registered with the site."
End If
```

C#

```
if (Membership.ValidateUser(TextBox1.Text, TextBox2.Text) {
   FormsAuthentication.RedirectFromLoginPage(TextBox1.Text.ToString(), false);
}
else {
   Label1.Text = "You are not registered with the site.";
}
```

The `ValidateUser()` method returns a `Boolean` value of `True` if the user credentials pass the test and `False` if they do not. From the code snippet in Listing 16-15, you can see that end users whose credentials are verified as correct are redirected from the login page using the `RedirectFromLoginPage()` method. This method takes the username and a `Boolean` value that specifies whether the credentials are persisted through a cookie setting.

Locking Out Users Who Provide Bad Passwords

When providing a user login form in any application you build, always guard against repeated bogus password attempts. If you have a malicious end user who knows a username, he may try to access the application by repeatedly trying different passwords. You want to guard against this kind of activity. You don't want to allow this person to try hundreds of possible passwords with this username.

ASP.NET has built-in protection against this type of activity. If you look in the aspnet_Membership table, you see two columns focused on protecting against this. These columns are `FailedPasswordAttemptCount` and `FailedPasswordAttemptWindowStart`.

By default, a username can be used with an incorrect password in a login attempt only five times within a 10-minute window. On the fifth failed attempt, the account is locked down. This is done in ASP.NET by setting the `IsLockedOut` column to `True`.

You can actually control the number of password attempts that are allowed and the length of the attempt window for your application. These two items are defined in the SqlMembershipProvider declaration in the `machine.config` file. You can change the values either in the server-wide configuration files or in your application's `web.config` file. Changing these values in your `web.config` file is presented in Listing 16-16.

Listing 16-16: Changing the values for password attempts in the provider declaration

```
<configuration>
   <system.web>

      <membership defaultProvider="AspNetSqlMembershipProvider">
        <providers>
          <clear />
          <add connectionStringName="LocalSqlServer"
           applicationName="/"
           maxInvalidPasswordAttempts="3"
           passwordAttemptWindow="15"
           name="AspNetSqlMembershipProvider"
           type="System.Web.Security.SqlMembershipProvider, System.Web,
             Version=2.0.0.0, Culture=neutral, PublicKeyToken=b03f5f7f11d50a3a" />
        </providers>
      </membership>

   </system.web>
</configuration>
```

To determine the number of password attempts that are allowed, use `maxInvalidPasswordAttempts`. This example changes the value to `3`, meaning that users are allowed to enter an incorrect password three times before being locked out (within the time window defined). The default value of the `maxInvalidPasswordAttempts` attribute is `5`. You can set the time allowed for bad password attempts to `15` minutes using the `passwordAttemptWindow` attribute. The default value of this attribute is `10`, so an extra five minutes is added.

Now that these items are in place, the next step is to test it. Listing 16-17 provides you with an example of the test. It assumes you have an application established with a user already in place.

Listing 16-17: A sample page to test password attempts

VB

```
<%@ Page Language="VB" %>

<script runat="server">
```

Continued

```
    Protected Sub Button1_Click(ByVal sender As Object, _
      ByVal e As System.EventArgs)

        If CheckBox1.Checked = True Then
            Dim user As MembershipUser = Membership.GetUser(TextBox1.Text)
            user.UnlockUser()
        End If

        If Membership.ValidateUser(TextBox1.Text, TextBox2.Text) Then
            Label1.Text = "You are logged on!"
        Else
            Dim user As MembershipUser = Membership.GetUser(TextBox1.Text)
            Label1.Text = "Locked out value: " & user.IsLockedOut.ToString()
        End If
    End Sub
</script>

<html xmlns="http://www.w3.org/1999/xhtml">
<head runat="server">
    <title>Login Page</title>
</head>
<body>
    <form id="form1" runat="server">
    <div>
        <h1>Login User</h1>
        <p>
            <asp:CheckBox ID="CheckBox1" runat="server" Text="Unlock User" />
        </p>
        <p>
            Username<br />
            <asp:TextBox ID="TextBox1" Runat="server"></asp:TextBox>
        </p>
        <p>Password<br />
            <asp:TextBox ID="TextBox2" Runat="server"
             TextMode="Password"></asp:TextBox>
        </p>
        <p>
            <asp:Button ID="Button1" Runat="server" Text="Login"
             OnClick="Button1_Click" />
        </p>
        <p>
            <asp:Label ID="Label1" Runat="server"></asp:Label>
        </p>
    </div>
    </form>
</body>
</html>
```

C#

```
<%@ Page Language="C#" %>

<script runat="server">
    protected void Button1_Click(object sender, EventArgs e)
```

```
        {
            if (CheckBox1.Checked == true)
            {
                MembershipUser user = Membership.GetUser(TextBox1.Text);
                user.UnlockUser();
            }

            if (Membership.ValidateUser(TextBox1.Text, TextBox2.Text))
            {
                Label1.Text = "You are logged on!";
            }
            else
            {
                MembershipUser user = Membership.GetUser(TextBox1.Text);
                Label1.Text = "Locked out value: " + user.IsLockedOut.ToString();
            }
        }
    </script>
```

This page contains two text boxes: one for the username and another for the password. Above these, however, is a check box that can be used to unlock a user after you have locked down the account because of bad password attempts.

If you run this page and enter three consecutive bad passwords for your user, you get the results presented in Figure 16-10.

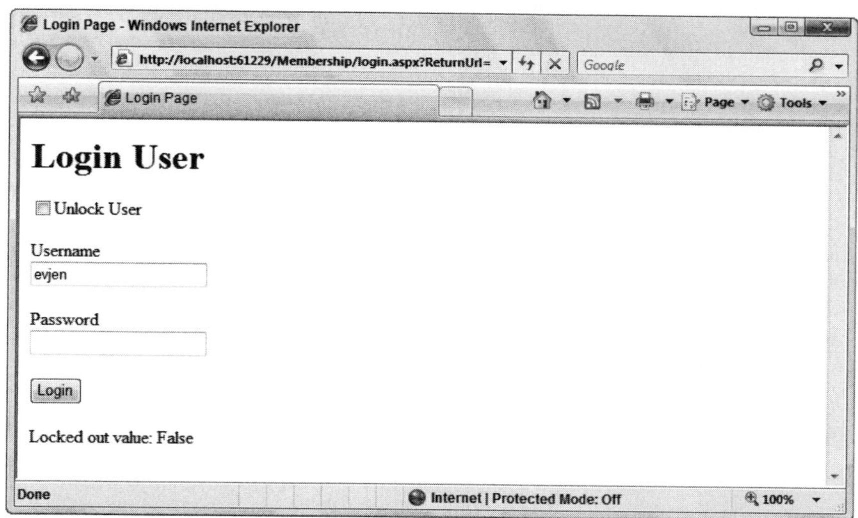

Figure 16-10

The `IsLockedOut` property is read through an instantiation of the `MembershipUser` object. This object allows you programmatic access to the user data points contained in the aspnet_Membership table. In this case, the `IsLockedOut` property is retrieved and displayed to the screen. The `MembershipUser` object also exposes a lot of available methods — one of which is the `UnlockUser()` method. This method is invoked if the check box is checked in the button-click event.

Working with Authenticated Users

After users are authenticated, ASP.NET 3.5 provides a number of different server controls and methods that you can use to work with the user details. Included in this collection of tools are the LoginStatus and the LoginName controls.

The LoginStatus Server Control

The LoginStatus server control enables users to click a link to log in or log out of a site. For a good example of this control, remove the <deny> element from the `web.config` file so that the pages of your site are accessible to unauthenticated users. Then code your `Default.aspx` page so that it is similar to the code shown in Listing 16-18.

Listing 16-18: Login and logout features of the LoginStatus control

```
<%@ Page Language="VB" %>

<html xmlns="http://www.w3.org/1999/xhtml">
<head runat="server">
    <title>Login or Logout</title>
</head>
<body>
    <form id="form1" runat="server">
        <asp:LoginStatus ID="LoginStatus1" Runat="server" />
    </form>
</body>
</html>
```

Running this gives you a simple page that contains only a hyperlink titled `Login`, as shown in Figure 16-11.

Clicking the `Login` hyperlink forwards you to the `Login.aspx` page where you provide your credentials. After the credentials are provided, you are redirected to the `Default.aspx` page — although now the page includes a hyperlink titled `Logout` (see Figure 16-12). The LinkStatus control displays one link when the user is unauthenticated and another link when the user is authenticated. Clicking the `Logout` hyperlink logs out the user and redraws the `Default.aspx` page — but with the `Login` hyperlink in place.

The LoginName Server Control

The LoginName server control enables you to display the username of the authenticated user. This is a common practice today. For an example of this, change the `Default.aspx` page so that it now includes the authenticated user's login name when that user is logged in, as illustrated in Listing 16-19.

Listing 16-19: Displaying the username of the authenticated user

```
<%@ Page Language="VB" %>

<html xmlns="http://www.w3.org/1999/xhtml">
```

```
<head runat="server">
    <title>Login or Logout</title>
</head>
<body>
    <form id="form1" runat="server">
        <asp:LoginStatus ID="LoginStatus1" Runat="server" />
        <p><asp:LoginName ID="LoginName1" Runat="server"
            Font-Bold="True" Font-Size="XX-Large" /></p>
    </form>
</body>
</html>
```

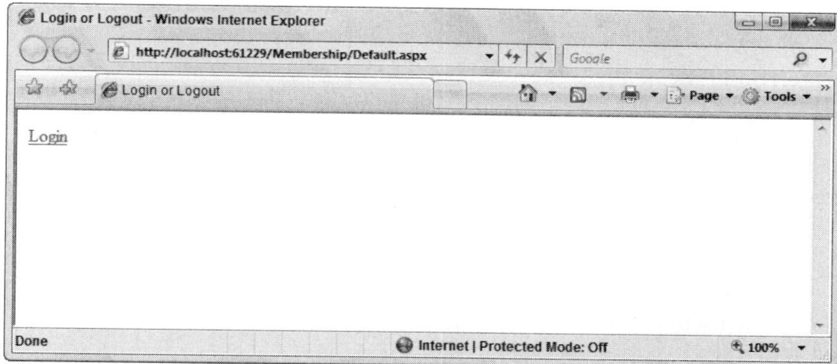

Figure 16-11

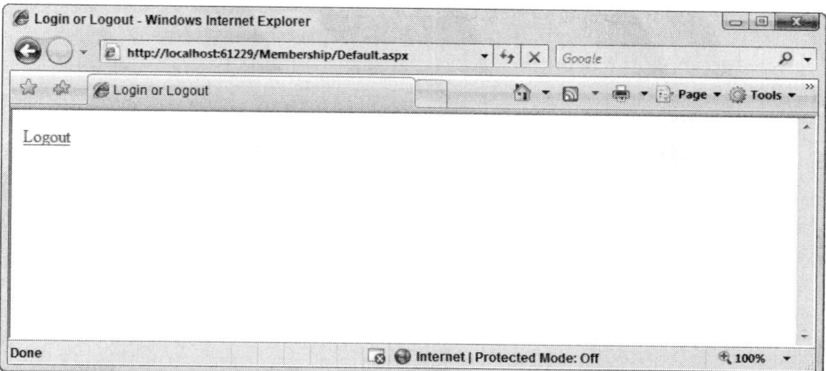

Figure 16-12

When the user logs in to the application and is returned to the `Default.aspx` page, he sees his username displayed, as well as the hyperlink generated by the LoginStatus control (see Figure 16-13).

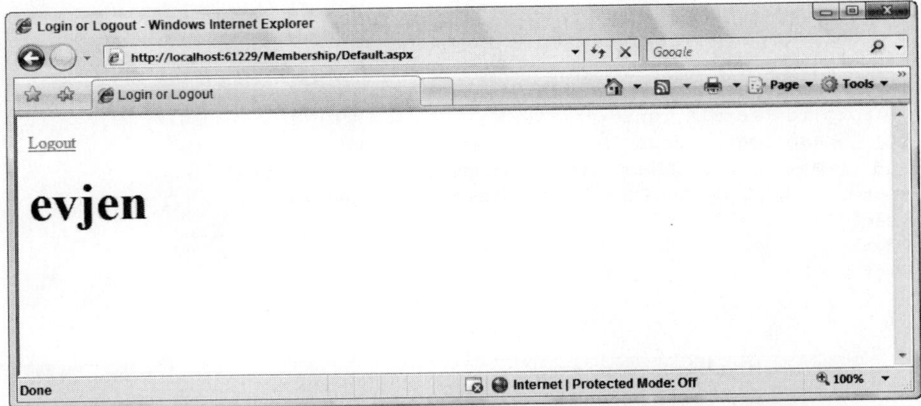

Figure 16-13

In addition to just showing the username of the logged in user, you can also add text by using the LoginName control's `FormatString` property. For instance, to provide a welcome message along with the username, you construct the LoginName control as follows:

```
<asp:LoginName ID="LoginName1" Runat="Server"
 FormatString="Welcome to our Website {0}!" />
```

You can also simply use the following construction in one of the page events. (This is shown in VB; if you are using C#, add a semicolon at the end of the line.)

```
LoginName1.FormatString = "Welcome to the site {0}!"
```

When the page is generated, ASP.NET replaces the `{0}` part of the string with the username of the logged-in user. This provides you with a result similar to the following:

```
Welcome to the site evjen!
```

If you do not want to show the username when using the LoginName control, simply omit the `{0}` aspect of the string. The control then places the `FormatString` property's value on the page.

Showing the Number of Users Online

One cool feature of the membership service is that you can display how many users are online at a given moment. This is an especially popular option for a portal or a forum that wishes to impress visitors to the site with its popularity.

To show the number of users online, you use the `GetNumberOfUsersOnline` method provided by the `Membership` class. You can add to the `Default.aspx` page shown in Figure 16-10 with the code illustrated in Listing 16-20.

Listing 16-20: Displaying the number of users online

VB

```
<%@ Page Language="VB" %>

<script runat="server">
```

```
    Protected Sub Page_Load(ByVal sender As Object, ByVal e As System.EventArgs)
        Label1.Text = Membership.GetNumberOfUsersOnline().ToString()
    End Sub
</script>

<html xmlns="http://www.w3.org/1999/xhtml">
<head runat="server">
    <title>Login or Logout</title>
</head>
<body>
    <form id="form1" runat="server">
        <asp:LoginStatus ID="LoginStatus1" Runat="server" />
        <p><asp:LoginName ID="LoginName1" Runat="server"
            Font-Bold="True" Font-Size="XX-Large" /></p>
        <p>There are <asp:Label ID="Label1" Runat="server" Text="0" />
          users online.</p>
    </form>
</body>
</html>
```

C#

```
<%@ Page Language="C#" %>

<script runat="server">
   protected void Page_Load(object sender, EventArgs e)
   {
      Label1.Text = Membership.GetNumberOfUsersOnline().ToString();
   }
</script>
```

When the page is generated, it displays the number of users who have logged on in the last 15 minutes. An example of what is generated is shown in Figure 16-14.

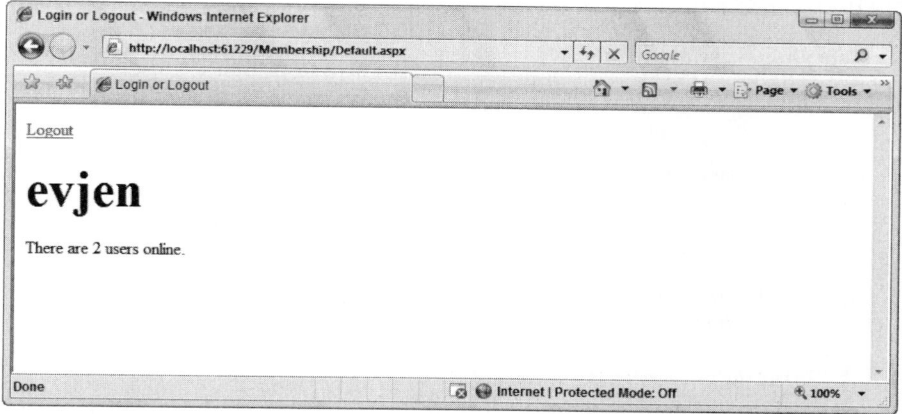

Figure 16-14

You can see that two users have logged on in the last 15 minutes. This 15-minute period is determined in the `machine.config` file from within the `<membership>` element:

```
<membership userIsOnlineTimeWindow="15" >
</membership>
```

By default, the `userIsOnlineTimeWindow` is set to `15`. The number is specified here in minutes. To increase the time window, you simply increase this number. In addition to specifying this number from within the `machine.config` file, you can also set this number in the `web.config` file.

Dealing with Passwords

Many of us seem to spend our lives online and have username/password combinations for many different Web sites on the Internet. For this reason, end users forget passwords or want to change them every so often. ASP.NET provides a couple of server controls that work with the membership service so that end users can either change their passwords or retrieve forgotten passwords.

The ChangePassword Server Control

The ChangePassword server control enables end users to change their passwords directly in the browser. Listing 16-21 shows a use of the ChangePassword control.

Listing 16-21: Allowing users to change passwords

```
<%@ Page Language="VB" %>

<html xmlns="http://www.w3.org/1999/xhtml">
<head runat="server">
    <title>Change Your Password</title>
</head>
<body>
    <form id="form1" runat="server">
        <asp:LoginStatus ID="LoginStatus1" Runat="server" />
        <p><asp:ChangePassword ID="ChangePassword1" Runat="server">
           </asp:ChangePassword><p>
    </form>
</body>
</html>
```

This is a rather simple use of the `<asp:ChangePassword>` control. Running this page produces the results shown in Figure 16-15.

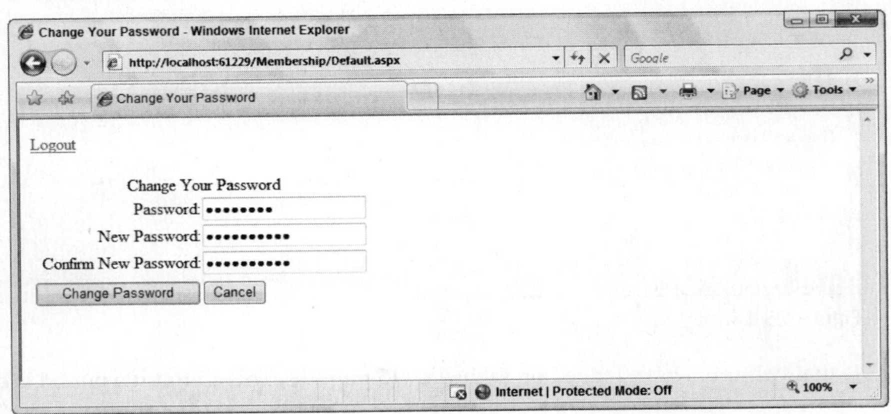

Figure 16-15

The ChangePassword control produces a form that asks for the previous password. It also requires the end user to type the new password twice. Clicking the Change Password button launches an attempt to change the password if the user is logged in. If the end user is not logged in to the application yet, he or she is redirected to the login page. Only a logged-in user can change a password. After the password is changed, the end user is notified (see Figure 16-16).

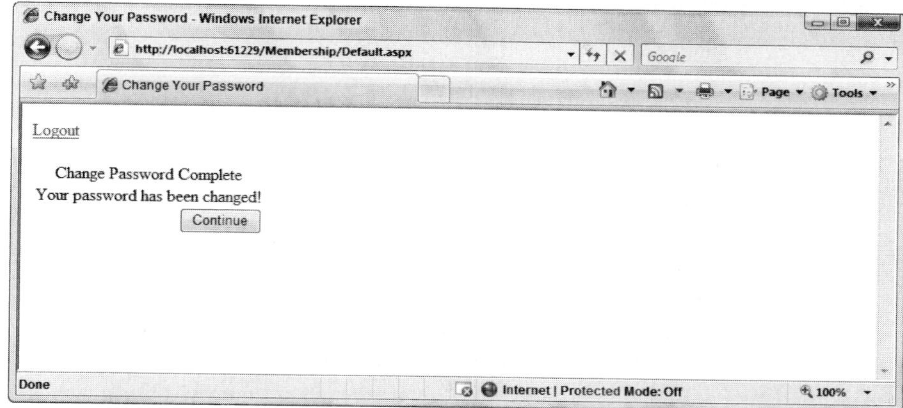

Figure 16-16

Remember that end users are allowed to change their passwords because the `enablePasswordReset` attribute of the membership provider is set to `true`. To deny this capability, set the `enablePasswordReset` attribute to `false`.

You can also specify rules on how the passwords must be constructed when an end user attempts to change her password. For instance, you might want to require that the password contain more than a certain number of characters or that it use numbers and/or special characters in addition to alpha-characters. Using the `NewPasswordRegularExpression` attribute, you can specify the construction required for the new password, as shown here:

```
NewPasswordRegularExpression='@\"(?=.{6,})(?=(.*\d){1,})(?=(.*\W){1,})'
```

Any new passwords created by the end user are checked against this regular expression. If there isn't a match, you can use the `NewPasswordRegularExpressionErrorMessage` attribute (one of the lengthier names for an attribute in ASP.NET) to cause an error message to appear within the control output.

The PasswordRecovery Server Control

People simply forget their passwords. For this reason, you should provide the means to retrieve passwords from your data store. The PasswordRecovery server control provides an easy way to accomplish this task.

Password recovery usually means sending the end user's password to him in an e-mail. Therefore, you need to set up an SMTP server (it might be the same as the application server). You configure for this server in the `web.config` file, as illustrated in Listing 16-22.

Listing 16-22: Configuring passwords to be sent via e-mail in the web.config file

```
<configuration>
   <system.web>
      <!-- Removed for clarity -->
   </system.web>

   <system.net>

      <mailSettings>
         <smtp from="someuser@email.com">
            <network host="localhost" port="25"
             defaultCredentials="true" />
         </smtp>
      </mailSettings>

   </system.net>
</configuration>
```

After you have the `<mailSettings>` element set up correctly, you can start to use the PasswordRecovery control. A simple use of the PasswordRecovery control is shown in Listing 16-23.

Listing 16-23: Using the PasswordRecovery control

```
<%@ Page Language="VB" %>

<html xmlns="http://www.w3.org/1999/xhtml">
<head runat="server">
    <title>Getting Your Password</title>
</head>
<body>
    <form id="form1" runat="server">
        <asp:PasswordRecovery ID="PasswordRecovery1" Runat="server">
            <MailDefinition From="someuser@email.com">
            </MailDefinition>
        </asp:PasswordRecovery>
    </form>
</body>
</html>
```

The `<asp:PasswordRecovery>` element needs a `<MailDefinition>` sub-element. The `<MailDefinition>` element contains details about the e-mail to be sent to the end user. The minimum requirement is that the `From` attribute is used, which provides the e-mail address for the From part of the e-mail. The `String` value of this attribute should be an e-mail address. Other attributes for the `<MailDefinition>` element include the following:

- `BodyFileName`
- `CC`
- `From`
- `IsBodyHtml`

- Priority
- Subject

When you run this page, the PasswordRecovery control asks for the user's username, as shown in Figure 16-17.

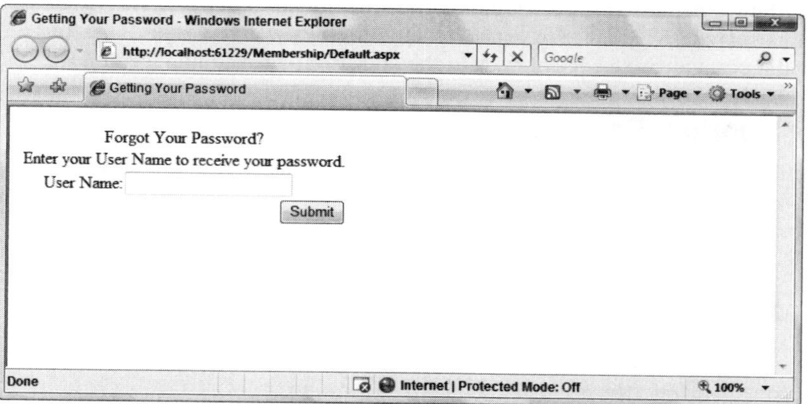

Figure 16-17

When it has the username, the membership service retrieves the question and answer that was earlier entered by the end user and generates the view shown in Figure 16-18.

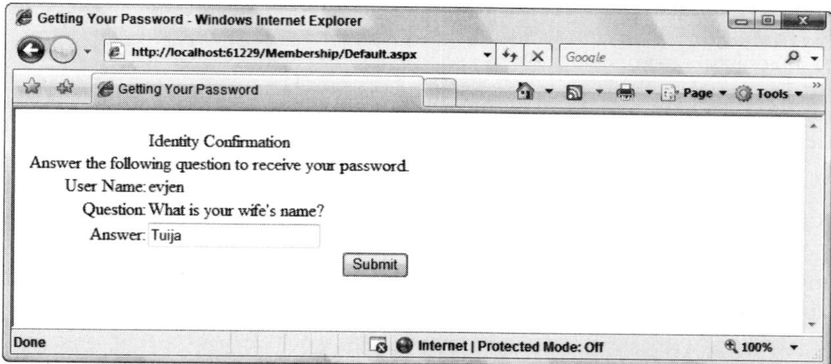

Figure 16-18

If the question is answered correctly (notice that the answer is case sensitive), an e-mail containing the password is generated and mailed to the end user. If the question is answered incorrectly, an error message is displayed. Of course, a question will not be used if you have the Question/Answer feature of the membership system disabled.

It is important to change some of your membership service settings in order for this entire process to work. At present, it will not work because of the way in which a user's password is hashed. The membership service data store is not storing the actual password — just a hashed version of it. Of course, it is useless for an end user to receive a hashed password.

In order for you to be able to send back an actual password to the user, you must change how the passwords are stored in the membership service data store. This is done (as stated earlier in the chapter) by changing the `PasswordFormat` attribute of your membership data provider. The other possible values (besides `Hashed`) are `Clear` and `Encrypted`. Changing the value to either `Clear` or `Encrypted` makes it possible for the passwords to be sent back to the end user in a readable format.

Generating Random Passwords

Certain applications must generate a random password when creating a user. In the days of ASP.NET 1.0/1.1, this was something you had to code yourself. ASP.NET 2.0 and 3.5, on the other hand, include a helper method that enables you to retrieve random passwords. Listing 16-24 shows an example of creating a helper method to pull a random password.

Listing 16-24: Generating a random password

VB

```
Protected Function GeneratePassword() As String
   Dim returnPassword As String
   returnPassword = Membership.GeneratePassword(10, 3)

   Return returnPassword
End Function
```

C#

```
protected string GeneratePassword()
{
   string returnPassword;
   returnPassword = Membership.GeneratePassword(10, 3);

   return returnPassword;
}
```

To generate a password randomly in ASP.NET 2.0 or 3.5, you can use the `GeneratePassword()` helper method. This method allows you to generate a random password of a specified length, and you can specify how many non-alphanumeric characters the password should contain (at minimum). This example utilizes this method five times to produce the results shown here (of course, your results will be different):

- `D](KQg6s2[`
- `$X.M9]*x2-`
- `Q+1Iy2#zD%`
- `%kWZL@zy&f`
- `o]&IhL#iU1`

With your helper method in place, you can create users with random passwords, as shown in Listing 16-25.

Listing 16-25: Creating users with a random password

VB

```
Membership.CreateUser(TextBox1.Text, GeneratePassword().ToString())
```

C#

```
Membership.CreateUser(TextBox1.Text, GeneratePassword().ToString());
```

ASP.NET 3.5 Authorization

Now that you can deal with the registration and authentication of users who want to access your Web applications, the next step is authorization. What are they allowed to see and what roles do they take? These are important questions for any Web application. First, learn how to show only certain items to authenticated users while you show different items to unauthenticated users.

Using the LoginView Server Control

The LoginView server control allows you to control who views what information on a particular part of a page. Using the LoginView control, you can dictate which parts of the pages are for authenticated users and which parts of the pages are for unauthenticated users. Listing 16-26 shows an example of this control.

Listing 16-26: Controlling information viewed via the LoginView control

```
<%@ Page Language="VB" %>

<html xmlns="http://www.w3.org/1999/xhtml">
<head runat="server">
    <title>Changing the View</title>
</head>
<body>
    <form id="form1" runat="server">
        <asp:LoginStatus ID="LoginStatus1" Runat="server" />
        <p>
        <asp:LoginView ID="LoginView1" Runat="server">
            <LoggedInTemplate>
                Here is some REALLY important information that you should know
                about all those people that are not authenticated!
            </LoggedInTemplate>
            <AnonymousTemplate>
                Here is some basic information for you.
            </AnonymousTemplate>
        </asp:LoginView><p>
    </form>
</body>
</html>
```

The `<asp:LoginView>` control is a templated control that takes two possible subelements — the `<LoggedInTemplate>` and `<AnonymousTemplate>` elements. In this case, the information defined in the `<AnonymousTemplate>` section (see Figure 16-19) is for unauthenticated users.

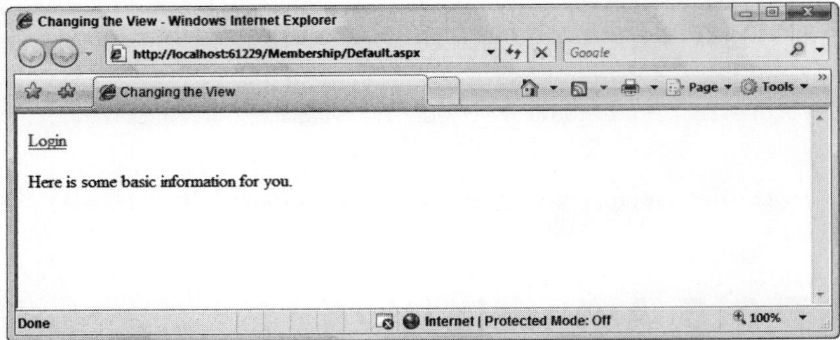

Figure 16-19

It is quite different from what authenticated users see defined in the <LoggedInTemplate> section (see Figure 16-20).

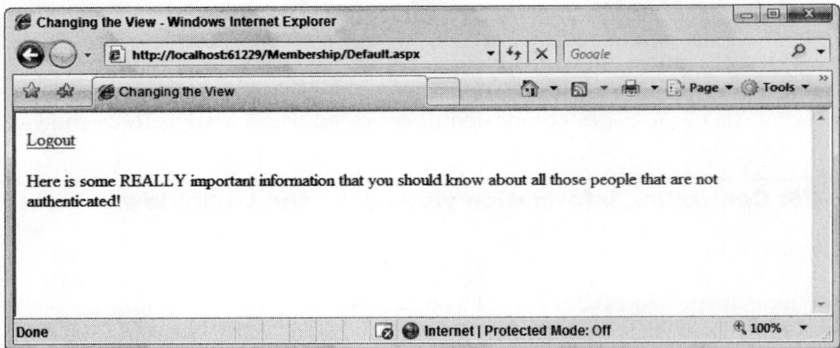

Figure 16-20

Only simple ASCII text is placed inside both of these templates, but you can actually place anything else within the template including additional server controls. This means that you can show entire sections of pages, including forms, from within the templated sections.

Besides using just the <LoggedInTemplate> and the <AnonymousTemplate> of the LoginView control, you can also enable sections of a page or specific content for entities that are part of a particular role — such as someone who is part of the `Admin` group. You can accomplish this by using the <RoleGroups> section of the LoginView control, as shown in Listing 16-27.

Listing 16-27: Providing a view for a particular group

```
<%@ Page Language="VB" %>

<html xmlns="http://www.w3.org/1999/xhtml">
<head runat="server">
    <title>Changing the View</title>
```

```
</head>
<body>
    <form id="form1" runat="server">
        <asp:LoginStatus ID="LoginStatus1" Runat="server" />
        <p>
        <asp:LoginView ID="LoginView1" Runat="server">
            <LoggedInTemplate>
                Here is some REALLY important information that you should know
                about all those people that are not authenticated!
            </LoggedInTemplate>
            <AnonymousTemplate>
                Here is some basic information for you.
            </AnonymousTemplate>
            <RoleGroups>
                <asp:RoleGroup Roles="Admins">
                    <ContentTemplate>
                       You are an Admin!
                    </ContentTemplate>
                </asp:RoleGroup>
                <asp:RoleGroup Roles="CoolPeople">
                    <ContentTemplate>
                       You are cool!
                    </ContentTemplate>
                </asp:RoleGroup>
            </RoleGroups>
        </asp:LoginView><p>
    </form>
</body>
</html>
```

To show content for a particular group of users, you add a `<RoleGroups>` element to the LoginView control. The `<RoleGroups>` section can take one or more RoleGroup controls (you will not find this control in Visual Studio's Toolbox). To provide content to display using the RoleGroup control, you provide a `<ContentTemplate>` element, which enables you to define the content to be displayed for an entity that belongs to the specified role. What is placed in the `<ContentTemplate>` section completely depends on you. You can place raw text (as shown in the example) or even other ASP.NET controls.

Be cautious of the order in which you place the defined roles in the `<RoleGroups>` section. When users log in to a site, they are first checked to see if they match one of the defined roles. The first (uppermost) role matched is the view used for the LoginView control — even if they match more than one role. You can also place more than one role in the `Roles` attribute of the `<asp:RoleGroups>` control, like this:

```
<asp:RoleGroup Roles="CoolPeople, HappyPeople">
   <ContentTemplate>
      You are cool or happy (or both)!
   </ContentTemplate>
</asp:RoleGroup>
```

Setting Up Your Web Site for Role Management

In addition to the membership service just reviewed, ASP.NET provides you with the other side of the end-user management service — the ASP.NET role management service. The membership service covers all the details of authentication for your applications, whereas the role management service covers authorization. Just as the membership service can use any of the data providers listed earlier, the role management service can also use a provider that is focused on SQL Server (SqlRoleProvider) or any custom providers. In fact, this service is comparable to the membership service in many ways. Figure 16-21 shows you a simple diagram that details some particulars of the role management service.

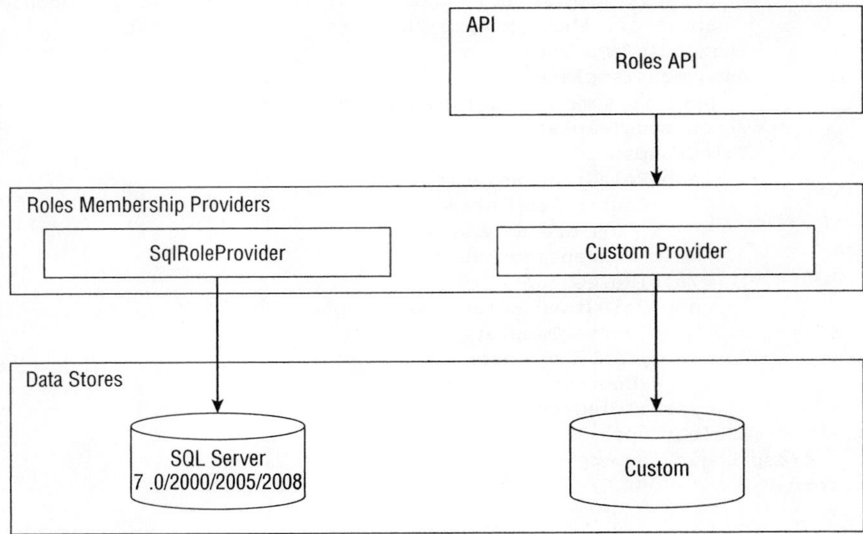

Figure 16-21

Making Changes to the <roleManager> Section

The first step in working with the role management service is to change any of the role management provider's behaviors either in the `machine.config` or from the `web.config` files. If you look in the `machine.config.comments` file, you will see an entire section that deals with the role management service (see Listing 16-28).

Listing 16-28: Role management provider settings in the machine.config.comments file

```
<roleManager
 enabled="false"
 cacheRolesInCookie="false"
 cookieName=".ASPXROLES"
 cookieTimeout="30"
 cookiePath="/"
 cookieRequireSSL="false"
 cookieSlidingExpiration="true"
 cookieProtection="All"
 defaultProvider="AspNetSqlRoleProvider"
```

```
    createPersistentCookie="false"
    maxCachedResults="25">
      <providers>
         <clear />
         <add connectionStringName="LocalSqlServer" applicationName="/"
          name="AspNetSqlRoleProvider" type="System.Web.Security.SqlRoleProvider,
          System.Web, Version=2.0.0.0, Culture=neutral,
          PublicKeyToken=b03f5f7f11d50a3a" />
         <add applicationName="/" name="AspNetWindowsTokenRoleProvider"
          type="System.Web.Security.WindowsTokenRoleProvider, System.Web,
          Version=2.0.0.0, Culture=neutral, PublicKeyToken=b03f5f7f11d50a3a" />
      </providers>
  </roleManager>
```

The role management service defines its settings from within the `machine.config.comments` file, as shown in the previous code listing. You can make changes to these settings either directly in the `machine.config` file or by overriding any of the higher level settings you might have by making changes in the `web.config` file (thereby making changes only to the application at hand).

The main settings are defined in the `<roleManager>` element. Some of the attributes of the `<roleManager>` element are defined in the following table.

Attribute	Description
`enabled`	Defines whether the role management service is enabled for the application. This attribute takes a `Boolean` value and is set to `False` by default. This means that the role management service is disabled by default. This is done to avoid breaking changes that would occur for users migrating from ASP.NET 1.0/1.1 to ASP.NET 2.0 or 3.5. Therefore, you must first change this value to `True` in either the `machine.config` or the `web.config` file.
`cacheRolesInCookie`	Defines whether the roles of the user can be stored within a cookie on the client machine. This attribute takes a `Boolean` value and is set to `True` by default. This is an ideal situation because retrieving the roles from the cookie prevents ASP.NET from looking up the roles of the user via the role management provider. Set it to `False` if you want the roles to be retrieved via the provider for all instances.
`cookieName`	Defines the name used for the cookie sent to the end user for role management information storage. By default, this cookie is named `.ASPXROLES`, and you probably will not change this.
`cookieTimeout`	Defines the amount of time (in minutes) after which the cookie expires. The default value is `30` minutes.
`cookieRequireSSL`	Defines whether you require that the role management information be sent over an encrypted wire (SSL) instead of being sent as clear text. The default value is `False`.

Attribute	Description
cookieSliding-Expiration	Specifies whether the timeout of the cookie is on a sliding scale. The default value is True. This means that the end user's cookie does not expire until 30 minutes (or the time specified in the cookieTimeout attribute) after the last request to the application has been made. If the value of the cookieSlidingExpiration attribute is set to False, the cookie expires 30 minutes from the first request.
createPersistent-Cookie	Specifies whether a cookie expires or if it remains alive indefinitely. The default setting is False because a persistent cookie is not always advisable for security reasons.
cookieProtection	Specifies the amount of protection you want to apply to the cookie stored on the end user's machine for management information. The possible settings include All, None, Encryption, and Validation. You should always attempt to use All.
defaultProvider	Defines the provider used for the role management service. By default, it is set to AspNetSqlRoleProvider.

Making Changes to the web.config File

The next step is to configure your web.config file so that it can work with the role management service. Certain pages or subsections of your application may be accessible only to people with specific roles. To manage this access, you define the access rights in the web.config file. The necessary changes are shown in Listing 16-29.

Listing 16-29: Changing the web.config file

```
<?xml version="1.0" encoding="utf-8"?>
<configuration>

    <system.web>
        <roleManager enabled="true"/>
        <authentication mode="Forms" />
        <authorization>
           <deny users="?" />
        </authorization>
    </system.web>

    <location path="AdminPage.aspx">
        <system.web>
           <authorization>
              <allow roles="AdminPageRights" />
              <deny users="*" />
           </authorization>
        </system.web>
    </location>

</configuration>
```

This `web.config` file is doing a couple of things. First, the function of the first `< system.web >` section is no different from that of the membership service shown earlier in the chapter. The `<deny>` element is denying all unauthenticated users across the board.

The second section of this `web.config` file is rather interesting. The `<location>` element is used to define the access rights of a particular page in the application (`AdminPage.aspx`). In this case, only users contained in the `AdminPageRights` role are allowed to view the page, but all other users — regardless of whether they are authenticated — are not allowed to view the page. When using the asterisk (`*`) as a value of the `users` attribute of the `<deny>` element, you are saying that all users (regardless of whether they are authenticated) are not allowed to access the resource being defined. This overriding denial of access, however, is broken open a bit via the use of the `<allow>` element, which allows users contained within a specific role.

Adding and Retrieving Application Roles

Now that the `machine.config` or the `web.config` file is in place, you can add roles to the role management service. The role management service, just like the membership service, uses data stores to store information about the users. These examples focus primarily on using Microsoft SQL Server Express Edition as the provider because it is the default provider.

One big difference between the role management service and the membership service is that no server controls are used for the role management service. You manage the application's roles and the user's role details through a Roles API or through the Web Site Administration Tool provided with ASP.NET 3.5. Listing 16-30 shows how to use some of the new methods to add roles to the service.

Listing 16-30: Adding roles to the application

VB

```
<%@ Page Language="VB" %>

<script runat="server">
   Protected Sub Page_Load(ByVal sender As Object, ByVal e As System.EventArgs)
       If Not Page.IsPostBack Then
          ListBoxDataBind()
       End If
   End Sub

   Protected Sub Button1_Click(ByVal sender As Object, ByVal e As System.EventArgs)
       Roles.CreateRole(TextBox1.Text)
       ListBoxDataBind()
   End Sub

   Protected Sub ListBoxDataBind()
       ListBox1.DataSource = Roles.GetAllRoles()
       ListBox1.DataBind()
   End Sub
</script>

<html xmlns="http://www.w3.org/1999/xhtml">
<head runat="server">
```

Continued

```
    <title>Role Manager</title>
</head>
<body>
    <form id="form1" runat="server">
        <h1>Role Manager</h1>
        Add Role:<br />
        <asp:TextBox ID="TextBox1" Runat="server"></asp:TextBox>
        <p><asp:Button ID="Button1" Runat="server" Text="Add Role to Application"
            OnClick="Button1_Click" /></p>
        Roles Defined:<br />
        <asp:ListBox ID="ListBox1" Runat="server">
        </asp:ListBox>
    </form>
</body>
</html>
```

C#

```
<%@ Page Language="C#" %>

<script runat="server">
    protected void Page_Load(object sender, EventArgs e)
    {
        if (!Page.IsPostBack)
        {
            ListBoxDataBind();
        }
    }

    protected void Button1_Click(object sender, EventArgs e)
    {
        Roles.CreateRole(TextBox1.Text.ToString());
        ListBoxDataBind();
    }

    protected void ListBoxDataBind()
    {
        ListBox1.DataSource = Roles.GetAllRoles();
        ListBox1.DataBind();
    }
</script>
```

This example enables you to enter roles into the text box and then to submit them to the role management service. The roles contained in the role management service are then displayed in the list box, as illustrated in Figure 16-22.

To enter the roles into the management service, you simply use the `CreateRole()` method of the `Roles` class. As with the `Membership` class, you do not instantiate the `Roles` class. To add roles to the role management service, use the `CreateRole()` method that takes only a single parameter — the name of the role as a `String` value:

```
Roles.CreateRole(rolename As String)
```

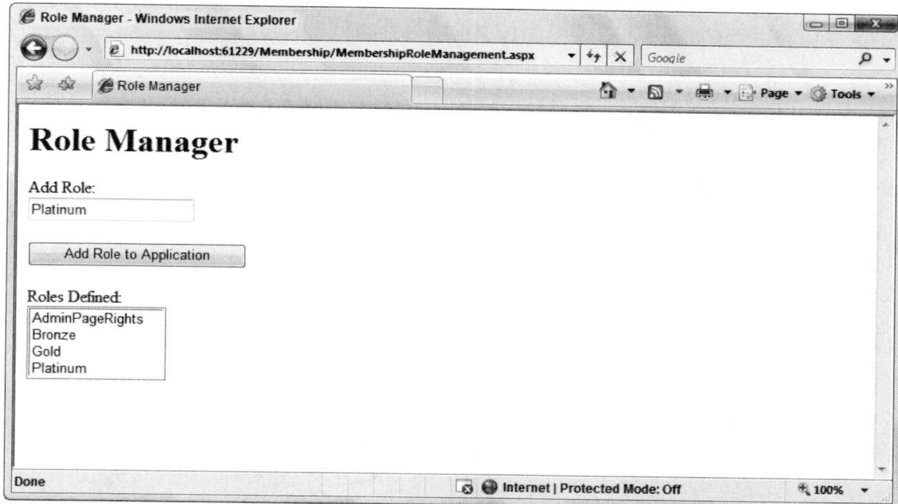

Figure 16-22

With this method, you can create as many roles as you want, but each role must be unique — otherwise an exception is thrown.

To retrieve the roles that are in the application's role management service (such as the list of roles displayed in the list box from the earlier example), you use the `GetAllRoles()` method of the `Roles` class. This method returns a `String` collection of all the available roles in the service:

```
Roles.GetAllRoles()
```

Deleting Roles

It would be just great to sit and add roles to the service all day long. Every now and then, however, you might want to delete roles from the service as well. Deleting roles is just as easy as adding roles to the role management service. To delete a role, you use one of the `DeleteRole()` method signatures. The first option of the `DeleteRole()` method takes a single parameter — the name of the role as a `String` value. The second option takes the name of the role plus a `Boolean` value that determines whether to throw an exception when one or more members are contained within that particular role (so that you don't accidentally delete a role with users in it when you don't mean to):

```
Roles.DeleteRole(rolename As String)

Roles.DeleteRole(rolename As String, throwOnPopulatedRole As Boolean)
```

Listing 16-31 is a partial code example that builds on Listing 16-30. For this example, add an additional button, which initiates a second button-click event that deletes the role from the service.

Listing 16-31: Deleting roles from the application

VB

```
Protected Sub DeleteButton_Click(ByVal sender As Object, _
   ByVal e As System.EventArgs)

   For Each li As ListItem In ListBox1.Items
      If li.Selected = True Then
         Roles.DeleteRole(li.ToString())
      End If
   Next

   ListBoxDataBind()
End Sub
```

C#

```
protected void DeleteButton_Click(object sender, EventArgs e)
{
   foreach (ListItem li in ListBox1.Items) {
      if (li.Selected == true) {
         Roles.DeleteRole(li.ToString());
      }
   }

   ListBoxDataBind();
}
```

This example deletes the selected items from the ListBox control. If more than one selection is made (meaning that you have placed the attribute `SelectionMode = "Multiple"` in the ListBox control), each of the roles is deleted from the service, in turn, in the `For Each` loop. Although `Roles.DeleteRole(li.ToString())` is used to delete the role, `Roles.DeleteRole(li.ToString(), True)` could also be used to make sure that no roles are deleted if that role contains any members.

Adding Users to Roles

Now that the roles are in place and it is possible to delete these roles if required, the next step is adding users to the roles created. A role does not do much good if no users are associated with it. To add a single user to a single role, you use the following construct:

```
Roles.AddUserToRole(username As String, rolename As String)
```

To add a single user to multiple roles at the same time, you use this construct:

```
Roles.AddUserToRoles(username As String, rolenames() As String)
```

To add multiple users to a single role, you use the following construct:

```
Roles.AddUsersToRole(usernames() As String, rolename As String)
```

Then, finally, to add multiple users to multiple roles, you use the following construct:

```
Roles.AddUsersToRoles(usernames() As String, rolenames() As String)
```

The parameters that can take collections, whether they are `usernames()` or `rolenames()`, are presented to the method as `String` arrays.

Getting All the Users of a Particular Role

Looking up information is easy in the role management service, whether you are determining which users are contained within a particular role or whether you want to know the roles that a particular user belongs to.

Methods are available for either of these scenarios. First, look at how to determine all the users contained in a particular role, as illustrated in Listing 16-32.

Listing 16-32: Looking up users in a particular role

VB

```
<%@ Page Language="VB" %>

<script runat="server">
   Protected Sub Page_Load(ByVal sender As Object, ByVal e As System.EventArgs)
       If Not Page.IsPostBack Then
          DropDownDataBind()
       End If
   End Sub

   Protected Sub Button1_Click(ByVal sender As Object, ByVal e As System.EventArgs)
       GridView1.DataSource = Roles.GetUsersInRole(DropDownList1.SelectedValue)
       GridView1.DataBind()
       DropDownDataBind()
   End Sub

   Protected Sub DropDownDataBind()
      DropDownList1.DataSource = Roles.GetAllRoles()
      DropDownList1.DataBind()
   End Sub

</script>

<html xmlns="http://www.w3.org/1999/xhtml">
<head runat="server">
    <title>Role Manager</title>
</head>
<body>
    <form id="form1" runat="server">
        Roles:
        <asp:DropDownList ID="DropDownList1" Runat="server">
        </asp:DropDownList>
        <asp:Button ID="Button1" Runat="server" Text="Get Users In Role"
         OnClick="Button1_Click" />
        <br />
        <br />
        <asp:GridView ID="GridView1" Runat="server">
        </asp:GridView>
```

Continued

```
    </form>
</body>
</html>
```

C#

```
<%@ Page Language="C#" %>

<script runat="server">
    protected void Page_Load(object sender, EventArgs e)
    {
        if (!Page.IsPostBack)
        {
            DropDownDataBind();
        }
    }

    protected void Button1_Click(object sender, EventArgs e)
    {
        GridView1.DataSource = Roles.GetUsersInRole(DropDownList1.SelectedValue);
        GridView1.DataBind();
        DropDownDataBind();
    }

    protected void DropDownDataBind()
    {
        DropDownList1.DataSource = Roles.GetAllRoles();
        DropDownList1.DataBind();
    }
</script>
```

This page creates a drop-down list that contains all the roles for the application. Clicking the button displays all the users for the selected role. Users of a particular role are determined using the `GetUsersInRole()` method. This method takes a single parameter — a `String` value representing the name of the role:

```
Roles.GetUsersInRole(rolename As String)
```

When run, the page looks similar to the page shown in Figure 16-23.

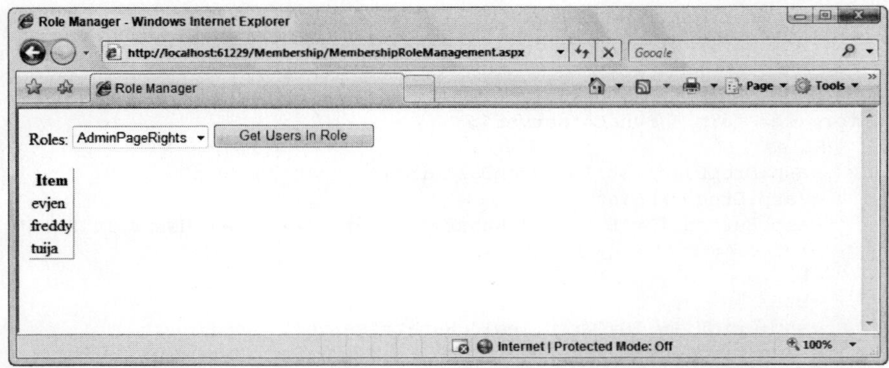

Figure 16-23

Getting All the Roles of a Particular User

To determine all the roles for a particular user, create a page with a single text box and a button. In the text box, you type the name of the user; and a button click initiates the retrieval and populates a GridView control. The button click event (where all the action is) is illustrated in Listing 16-33.

Listing 16-33: Getting all the roles of a specific user

VB

```
Protected Sub Button1_Click(ByVal sender As Object, ByVal e As System.EventArgs)
   GridView1.DataSource = Roles.GetRolesForUser(TextBox1.Text)
   GridView1.DataBind()
End Sub
```

C#

```
protected void Button1_Click(object sender, EventArgs e)
{
   GridView1.DataSource = Roles.GetRolesForUser(TextBox1.Text.ToString());
   GridView1.DataBind();
}
```

The preceding code produces something similar to what is shown in Figure 16-24.

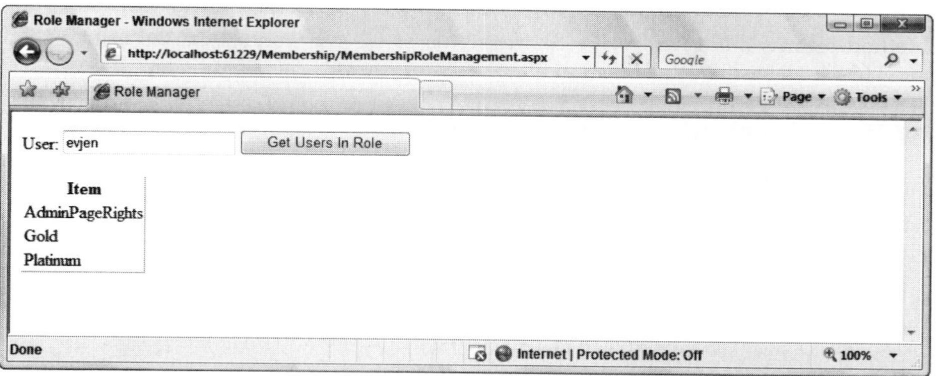

Figure 16-24

To get the roles of a particular user, you simply use the `GetRolesForUser()` method. This method has two possible signatures. The first is shown in the preceding example — a `String` value that represents the name of the user. The other option is an invocation of the method without any parameters listed. This returns the roles of the user who has logged in to the membership service.

Removing Users from Roles

In addition to adding users to roles, you can also easily remove users from roles. To delete or remove a single user from a single role, you use the following construct:

```
Roles.RemoveUserFromRole(username As String, rolename As String)
```

To remove a single user from multiple roles at the same time, you use this construct:

```
Roles.RemoveUserFromRoles(username As String, rolenames() As String)
```

To remove multiple users from a single role, you use the following construct:

```
Roles.RemoveUsersFromRole(usernames() As String, rolename As String)
```

Then, finally, to remove multiple users from multiple roles, you use the following construct:

```
Roles.RemoveUsersFromRoles(usernames() As String, rolenames() As String)
```

The parameters shown as collections, whether they are `usernames()` or `rolenames()`, are presented to the method as `String` arrays.

Checking Users in Roles

One final action you can take is checking whether a particular user is in a role. You can go about this in a couple of ways. The first is using the `IsUserInRole()` method.

The `IsUserInRole()` method takes two parameters — the username and the name of the role:

```
Roles.IsUserInRole(username As String, rolename As String)
```

This method returns a `Boolean` value on the status of the user, and it can be used as shown in Listing 16-34.

Listing 16-34: Checking a user's role status

VB

```
If (Roles.IsUserInRole(TextBox1.Text, "AdminPageRights")) Then
   ' perform action here
End If
```

C#

```
if (Roles.IsUserInRole(TextBox1.Text.ToString(), "AdminPageRights"))
{
   // perform action here
}
```

The other option, in addition to the `IsUserInRole()` method, is to use `FindUsersInRole()`. This method enables you make a name search against all the users in a particular role. The `FindUsersInRole()` method takes two parameters — the name of the role and the username, both as `String` values:

```
Roles.FindUsersInRole(rolename As String, username As String)
```

Listing 16-35 shows an example of this method.

Listing 16-35: Checking for a specific user in a particular role

VB

```
<%@ Page Language="VB" %>

<script runat="server">
   Protected Sub Button1_Click(ByVal sender As Object, ByVal e As System.EventArgs)
       GridView1.DataSource = _
          Roles.FindUsersInRole("AdminPageRights", TextBox1.Text)
       GridView1.DataBind()
   End Sub
</script>

<html xmlns="http://www.w3.org/1999/xhtml" >
<head runat="server">
    <title>Role Manager</title>
</head>
<body>
    <form id="form1" runat="server">
        <asp:TextBox ID="TextBox1" Runat="server"></asp:TextBox>
        <asp:Button ID="Button1" Runat="server" Text="Button"
         OnClick="Button1_Click" />
        <p><asp:GridView ID="GridView1" Runat="server">
        </asp:GridView></p>
    </form>
</body>
</html>
```

C#

```
<%@ Page Language="C#" %>

<script runat="server">
   protected void Button1_Click(object sender, EventArgs e)
   {
        GridView1.DataSource =
           Roles.FindUsersInRole("AdminPageRights", TextBox1.Text.ToString());
        GridView1.DataBind();
   }
</script>
```

Understanding How Roles Are Cached

By default, after you retrieve a user's roles from the data store underlying the role management service, you can store these roles as a cookie on the client machine. This is done so you do not have to access the data store each and every time the application needs a user's role status. There is always a bit of risk in working with cookies because the end user can manipulate the cookie and thereby gain access to information or parts of an application that normally would be forbidden to that particular user.

Although roles are cached in a cookie, the default is that they are cached for only 30 minutes at a time. You can deal with this role cookie in several ways — some of which might help to protect your application better.

One protection for your application is to delete this role cookie, using the `DeleteCookie()` method of the Roles API, when the end user logs on to the site. This is illustrated in Listing 16-36.

Listing 16-36: Deleting the end user's role cookie upon authentication

VB

```
If Membership.ValidateUser(TextBox1.Text, TextBox2.Text) Then
   Roles.DeleteCookie()
   FormsAuthentication.RedirectFromLoginPage(TextBox1.Text, False)
Else
   Label1.Text = "You are not registered with the site."
End If
```

C#

```
if (Membership.ValidateUser(TextBox1.Text.ToString(), TextBox2.Text.ToString()) {
   Roles.DeleteCookie();
   FormsAuthentication.RedirectFromLoginPage(TextBox1.Text.ToString(), false);
}
else {
   Label1.Text = "You are not registered with the site.";
}
```

Using `Roles.DeleteCookie()` does exactly what you would think — it deletes from the client machine any cookie that is used to define the user's roles. If the end user is re-logging into the site, no problem should arise with re-authenticating his exact roles within the application. There is no need to rely on the contents of the cookie. This step provides a little more protection for your site.

Using the Web Site Administration Tool

Many of the actions shown in this chapter can also be performed through the Web Site Administration Tool shown in Figure 16-25. You can get at the ASP.NET Web Site Administration Tool by selecting Website ➪ ASP.NET Configuration from the Visual Studio 2008 menu.

Although you can easily use this tool to perform all the actions for you, often you perform these actions through your own applications as well. It is important to know all the possibilities when programming an ASP.NET application.

The Web Site Administration Tool is detailed in Chapter 34.

Public Methods of the Membership API

The public methods of the Membership API are detailed in the following table. You would use this API when working with the authentication process of your application.

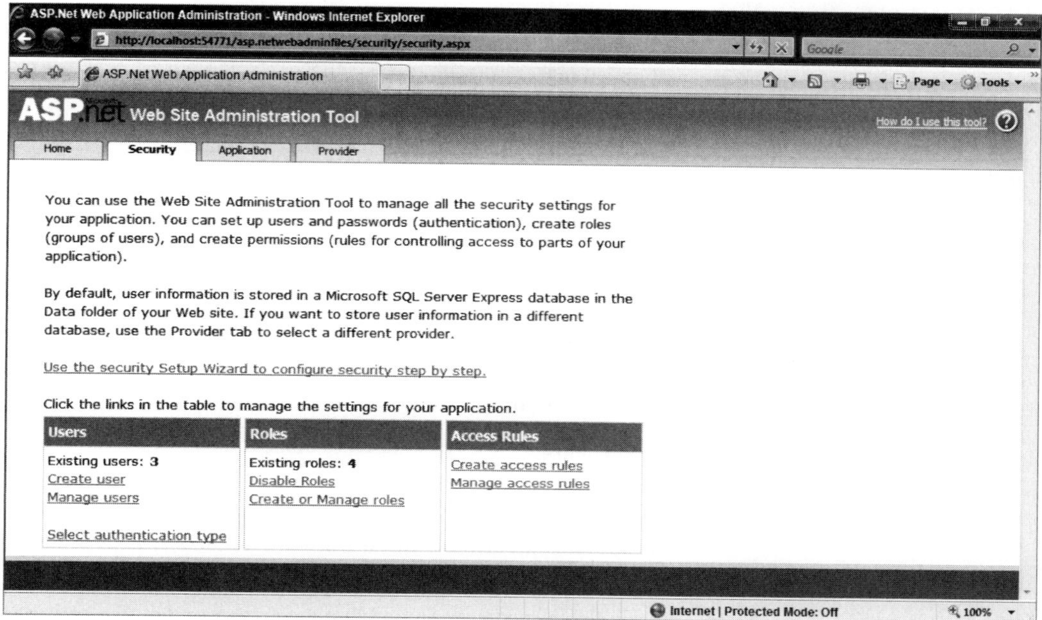

Figure 16-25

Membership Methods	Description
`CreateUser`	Adds a new user to the appointed data store.
`DeleteUser`	Deletes a specified user from the data store.
`FindUsersByEmail`	Returns a collection of users who have an e-mail address to match the one provided.
`FindUsersByName`	Returns a collection of users who have a username to match the one provided.
`GeneratePassword`	Generates a random password of a length that you specify.
`GetAllUsers`	Returns a collection of all the users contained in the data store.
`GetNumberOfUsersOnline`	Returns an Integer that specifies the number of users who have logged in to the application. The time window during which users are counted is specified in the `machine.config` or the `web.config` files.
`GetUser`	Returns information about a particular user from the data store.
`GetUserNameByEmail`	Retrieves a username of a specific record from the data store based on an e-mail address search.
`UpdateUser`	Updates a particular user's information in the data store.
`ValidateUser`	Returns a Boolean value indicating whether a specified set of credentials is valid.

Public Methods of the Roles API

The public methods of the Roles API are detailed in the following table. You would use this API when working with the authorization process of your application.

Roles Methods	Description
`AddUsersToRole`	Adds a collection of users to a specific role.
`AddUsersToRoles`	Adds a collection of users to a collection of roles.
`AddUserToRole`	Adds a specific user to a specific role.
`AddUserToRoles`	Adds a specific user to a collection of roles.
`CreateRole`	Adds a new role to the appointed data store.
`DeleteCookie`	Deletes the cookie on the client used to store the roles to which the user belongs.
`DeleteRole`	Deletes a specific role in the data store. Using the proper parameters for this method, you can also control if roles are deleted or kept intact whether or not that particular role contains users.
`FindUsersInRole`	Returns a collection of users who have a username to match the one provided.
`GetAllRoles`	Returns a collection of all the roles stored in the data store.
`GetRolesForUser`	Returns a collection of roles for a specific user.
`IsUserInRole`	Returns a Boolean value that specifies whether a user is contained in a particular role.
`RemoveUserFromRole`	Removes a specific user from a specific role.
`RemoveUserFromRoles`	Removes a specific user from a collection of roles.
`RemoveUsersFromRole`	Removes a collection of users from a specific role.
`RemoveUsersFromRoles`	Removes a collection of users from a collection of roles.
`RoleExists`	Returns a Boolean value indicating whether a role exists in the data store.

Summary

This chapter covered two outstanding features available to ASP.NET 3.5. The membership and role management services that are now a part of ASP.NET make managing users and their roles almost trivial.

This chapter reviewed both the Membership and Roles APIs and the controls that also utilize these APIs. These controls and APIs follow the same data provider models as the rest of ASP.NET. The examples were presented using Microsoft SQL Server Express Edition for the back-end storage, but you can easily configure these systems to work with another type of data store.

17

Portal Frameworks and Web Parts

Internet and intranet applications have changed considerably since their introduction in the 1990s. Today's applications do not simply display the same canned information to every viewer; they do much more. Because of the wealth of information being exposed to end users, Internet and intranet applications must integrate large amounts of customization and personalization into their offerings.

Web sites that provide a plethora of offerings give end users the option to choose which parts of the site they want to view and which parts they want to hide. Ideally, end users can personalize the pages, deciding for themselves the order in which the content appears on the page. They should be able to move items around on the page as if it were a design surface.

In this situation, after pages are customized and established, end users need the capability to export their final page settings for storage. You certainly would not want an end user who has highly customized a page or a series of pages in your portal to be forced to reapply the settings each time he visits the site. Instead, you want to retain these setting points by moving them to a data store for later exposure.

Adding this kind of functionality is *expensive* — expensive in the sense that it can take a considerable amount of work on the part of the developer. Until ASP.NET 2.0, the developer had to build a personalization framework to be used by each page requiring the functionality. This type of work is error prone and difficult to achieve, which is why in most cases it was not done.

But wait. . .

Introducing Web Parts

To make it easier to retain the page customization settings that your end users apply to your page, Microsoft includes Web Parts as part of ASP.NET. Web Parts, part of the larger Portal Framework, provide an outstanding way to build a modular Web site that can be customized with dynamically reapplied settings on a per-user basis. Web Parts are objects in the Portal Framework which the end user can open, close, minimize, maximize, or move from one part of the page to another.

The Portal Framework enables you to build pages that contain multiple Web Parts — which are part of the ASP.NET server control framework and are used like any other ASP.NET server controls. This means that you can also extend Web Parts if necessary.

The components of the Portal Framework provide the means to build a truly dynamic Web site, whether that site is a traditional Internet site, an intranet site, a browser-based application, or any other typical portal.

When you first look at Web Parts in ASP.NET 3.5, it may remind you of Microsoft's SharePoint offering. Be forewarned, however, that these two technologies are not the same. Web Parts and the resulting Portal Framework, besides being offered in ASP.NET, are also used by the Windows SharePoint Services (WSS). Microsoft, as it often does, is simply creating singular technologies that can be used by other Microsoft offerings. In this process, Microsoft is trying to reach the Holy Grail of computing — *code reuse!*

The modular and customizable sites that you can build with the Portal Framework enable you to place the Web page in view into several possible modes for the end user. The following list describes each of these available modes and what each means to the end user viewing the page:

- **Normal Mode:** Puts the page in a normal state, which means that the end user cannot edit or move sections of the page. This is the mode used for standard page viewing.
- **Edit Mode:** Enables end users to select particular sections on the page for editing. The selected section allows all types of editing capabilities from changing the part's title, the part's color, or even setting custom properties — such as allowing the end user to specify his zip code to pull up a customized weather report.
- **Design Mode:** Enables end users to rearrange the order of the page's modular components. The end user can bring items higher or lower within a zone, delete items from a zone, or move items from one page zone to another.
- **Catalog Mode:** Displays a list of available sections (Web Parts) that can be placed in the page. Catalog mode also allows the end user to select in which zone on the page the items should appear.

Figure 17-1 shows a screenshot of a sample portal utilizing the Portal Framework with the Edit mode enabled.

The Portal Framework is a comprehensive and well-thought-out framework that enables you to incorporate everything you would normally include in your ASP.NET applications. You can apply security using either Windows Authentication or Forms Authentication just as you can with a standard ASP.NET page. This framework also enables you to leverage the other aspects of ASP.NET 3.5, such as applying role management, personalization, and membership features to any portal that you build.

To help you understand how to build your own application on top of the Portal Framework, this chapter begins with the creation of a simple page that makes use of this new framework's utilities.

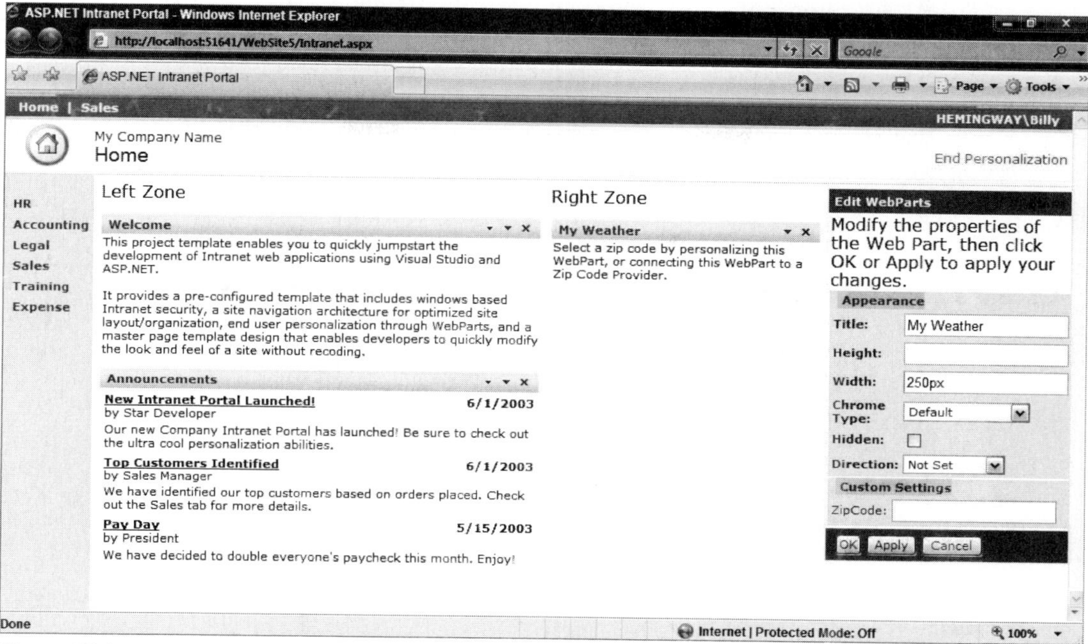

Figure 17-1

Building Dynamic and Modular Web Sites

As you begin using the Portal Framework to build Web sites, note that the framework defines everything in *zones*. There are zones for laying out as well as for editing content. The zones that a page might incorporate are managed by a Portal Framework manager. The Portal framework manager performs the management on your behalf, meaning that you do not have to manage them yourself in any fashion. This makes working with the Portal Framework a breeze.

This framework contains a lot of moving parts and these multiple pieces that are heavily dependent upon each other. For this reason, this section starts at the beginning by examining the Portal Framework manager control: WebPartManager.

Introducing the WebPartManager Control

The WebPartManager control is an ASP.NET server control that completely manages the state of the zones and the content placed in these zones on a per-user basis. This control, which has no visual aspect, can add and delete items contained within each zone of the page. The WebPartManager control can also manage the communications sometimes required between different elements contained in the zones. For example, you can pass a specific name/value pair from one item to another item within the same zone, or between items contained in entirely separate zones. The WebPartManager control provides the capabilities to make this communication happen.

The WebPartManager control must be in place on every page in your application that works with the Portal Framework. A single WebPartManager control does not manage an entire application; instead, it manages on a per-page basis.

You can also place a WebPartManager server control on the master page (if you are using one) to avoid having to place one on each and every content page.

Listing 17-1 shows a WebPartManager control added to an ASP.NET page.

Listing 17-1: Adding a WebPartManager control to an ASP.NET page

```
<%@ Page Language="VB" %>

<html xmlns="http://www.w3.org/1999/xhtml">
<head runat="server">
    <title>Web Parts Example</title>
</head>
<body>
    <form id="form1" runat="server">
        <asp:WebPartManager ID="Webpartmanager1" runat="server">
        </asp:WebPartManager>
    </form>
</body>
</html>
```

If you want to work from the design surface of Visual Studio 2008, you can drag and drop the Web-PartManager control from the Toolbox to the design surface — but remember, it does not have a visual aspect and appears only as a gray box. You can find the WebPartManager control (and the other server controls that are part of the Portal Framework) in the WebParts section of the Toolbox, as shown in Figure 17-2.

Working with Zone Layouts

After you place the WebPartManager control on the page, the next step is to create zones from which you can utilize the Portal Framework. You should give this step some thought because it contributes directly to the usability of the page you are creating. Web pages are constructed in a linear fashion — either horizontally or vertically. Web pages are managed in square boxes — usually using tables that organize the columns and rows in which items appear on the page.

Web zones define specific rows or columns as individual content areas managed by the WebPart-Manager. For an example of a Web page that uses these zones, create a table similar to the one shown in Figure 17-3.

The black sections in Figure 17-3 will represent Web zones. The code used to produce the table with some basic controls in each of the zones is shown in Listing 17-2.

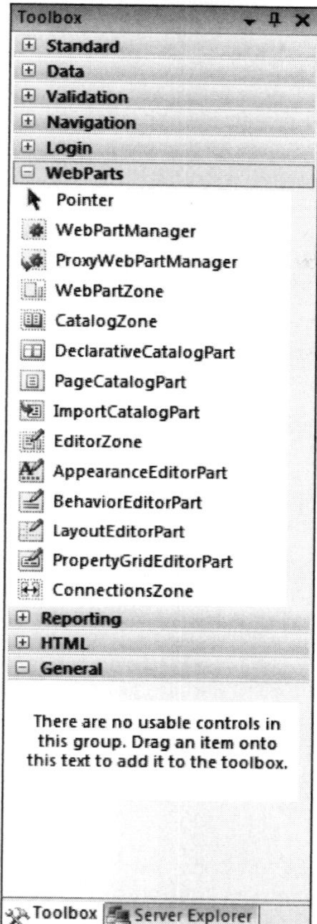

Figure 17-2

Listing 17-2: Creating multiple Web zones

```
<%@ Page Language="VB"%>
<%@ Register Src="DailyLinks.ascx" TagName="DailyLinks" TagPrefix="uc1" %>

<html xmlns="http://www.w3.org/1999/xhtml">
<head runat="server">
    <title>Web Parts Example</title>
</head>
<body>
    <form id="form1" runat="server">
        <asp:WebPartManager ID="Webpartmanager1" runat="server">
        </asp:WebPartManager>
        <table cellpadding="5" border="1">
```

Continued

```
            <tr>
                <td colspan="3">
                    <h1>Bill Evjen's Web Page</h1>
                    <asp:WebPartZone ID="WebPartZone1" runat="server"
                     LayoutOrientation="Horizontal">
                        <ZoneTemplate>
                            <asp:Label ID="Label1" runat="server" Text="Label"
                             Title="Welcome to my web page!">
                             Welcome to the page!
                            </asp:Label>
                        </ZoneTemplate>
                    </asp:WebPartZone>
                </td>
            </tr>
            <tr valign="top">
                <td>
                    <asp:WebPartZone ID="WebPartZone2" runat="server">
                        <ZoneTemplate>
                            <asp:Image ID="Image1" runat="server"
                             ImageUrl="~/Images/Tuija.jpg" Width="150px"
                             Title="Tuija at the Museum">
                            </asp:Image>
                            <uc1:DailyLinks ID="DailyLinks1" runat="server"
                             Title="Daily Links">
                            </uc1:DailyLinks>
                        </ZoneTemplate>
                    </asp:WebPartZone>
                </td>
                <td>
                    <asp:WebPartZone ID="WebPartZone3" runat="server">
                        <ZoneTemplate>
                            <asp:Calendar ID="Calendar1" runat="server"
                             Title="Calendar">
                            </asp:Calendar>
                        </ZoneTemplate>
                    </asp:WebPartZone>
                </td>
                <td><!-- Blank for now -->
                </td>
            </tr>
        </table>
    </form>
</body>
</html>
```

This page now has sections like the ones shown in Figure 17-3: a header section that runs horizontally and three vertical sections underneath the header. Running this page provides the result shown in Figure 17-4.

First, this page includes the `<asp:WebPartManager>` control that manages the items contained in the three zones on this page. Within the table, the `<asp:WebPartZone>` server control specifies three Web zones. You can declare each Web zone in one of two ways. You can use the `<asp:WebPartZone>` element directly in the code, or you can create the zones within the table by dragging and dropping WebPartZone controls onto the design surface at appropriate places within the table. In Figure 17-4, the table border width is intentionally turned on and set to 1 in order to show the location of the Web zones in greater detail. Figure 17-5 shows what the sample from Listing 17-2 looks like in the Design view of Visual Studio 2008.

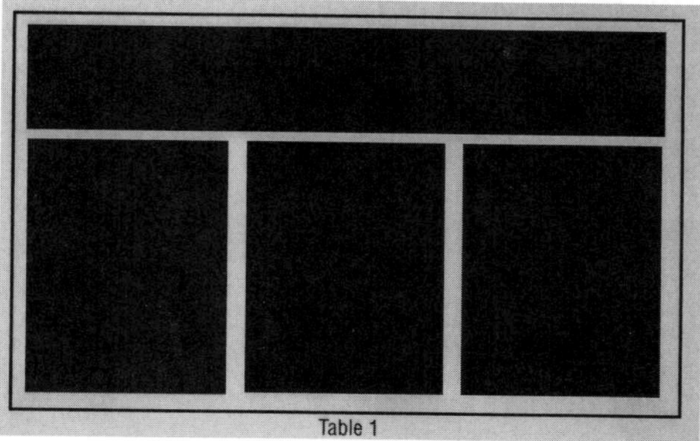

Figure 17-3

Figure 17-4

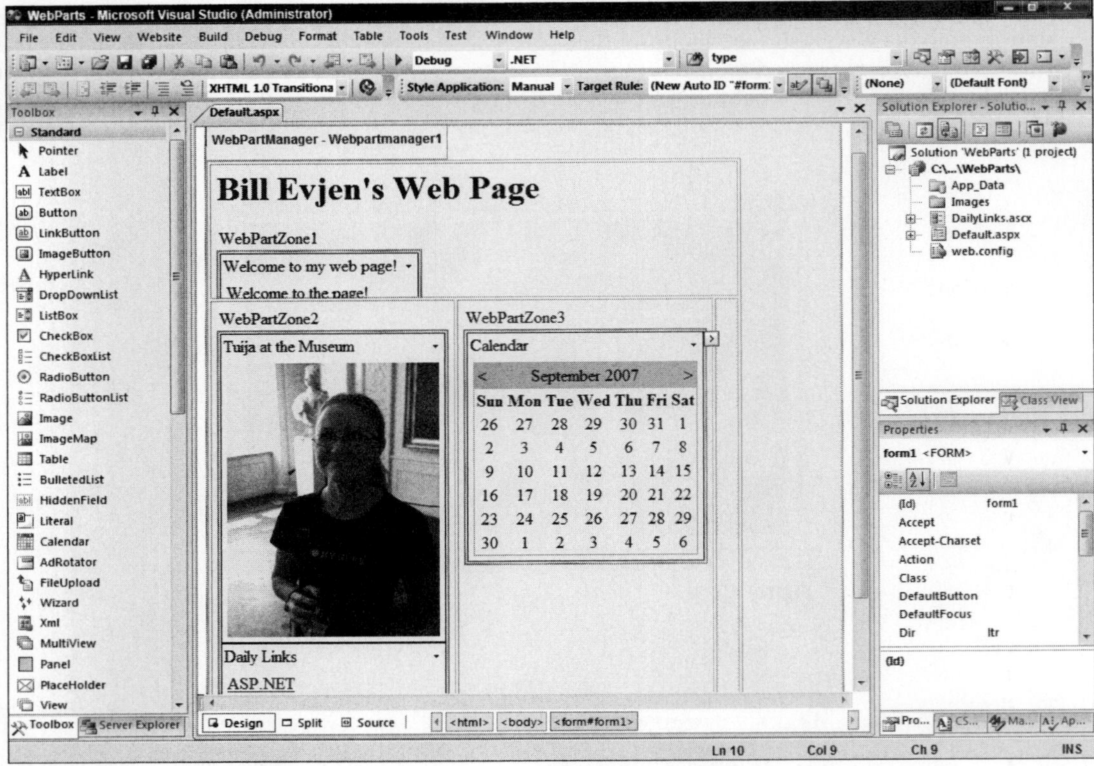

Figure 17-5

When using Visual Studio 2008, note that by default this IDE creates a Microsoft SQL Server Express Edition file called `ASPNETDB.MDF` and stores it in the `App_Data` folder of your Web Project. This database file is where the Portal Framework stores all the customization points.

Note that if you want this portal framework to run from SQL Server 7.0, 2000, 2005, or 2008, you should follow the set-up instructions that are defined in Chapter 12.

Now that you have seen the use of WebPartZone controls, which are managed by the WebPartManager control, the next section takes a closer look at the WebPartZone server control itself.

Understanding the WebPartZone Control

The WebPartZone control defines an area of items, or Web Parts, that can be moved, minimized, maximized, deleted, or added based on programmatic code or user preferences. When you drag and drop WebPartZone controls onto the design surface using Visual Studio 2008, the WebPartZone control is drawn at the top of the zone, along with a visual representation of any of the items contained within the zone.

You can place almost anything in one of the Web zones. For example, you can include the following:

- HTML elements (when putting a `runat = "server"` on the element)
- HTML server controls
- Web server controls
- User controls
- Custom controls

WebPartZone controls are declared like this:

```
<asp:WebPartZone ID="WebPartZone1" Runat="server"></asp:WebPartZone>
```

The LayoutOrientation Attribute

The Web Parts declared within a WebPartZone control can be displayed either horizontally or vertically. By default, all the items are displayed vertically, but to display the items horizontally, you simply add the `LayoutOrientation` attribute to the `<asp:WebPartZone>` element:

```
<asp:WebPartZone ID="WebPartZone1" Runat="server"
 LayoutOrientation="Horizontal"></asp:WebPartZone>
```

The first row in the table from Listing 17-2 uses horizontal orientation, whereas the other two zones use the default vertical orientation.

The ZoneTemplate Element

In order to include items within the templated WebPartZone control, you must include a `<ZoneTemplate>` element.

The `ZoneTemplate` element encapsulates all the items contained within a particular zone. The order in which they are listed in the `ZoneTemplate` section is the order in which they appear in the browser until changed by the end user or by programmatic code. The sample `<ZoneTemplate>` section used earlier is illustrated here:

```
<asp:WebPartZone ID="WebPartZone2" Runat="server">
   <ZoneTemplate>
      <asp:Image ID="Image1" Runat="server"
       ImageUrl="~/Images/Tuija.jpg" Width="150" Title="Tuija at the Museum">
      </asp:Image>
      <uc1:DailyLinks ID="DailyLinks1" runat="server" Title="Daily Links">
      </uc1:DailyLinks>
   </ZoneTemplate>
</asp:WebPartZone>
```

This zone contains two items — an Image server control and a user control consisting of a collection of links that come from an XML file.

Default Web Part Control Elements

By default, when you generate a page using the code from Listing 17-2, you discover that you can exert only minimal control over the Web Parts themselves. In the default view, which is not the most artistic in this case, you are able only to minimize or close a Web Part. You can see these options when you click on the down arrow that is presented next to the name of the Web Part.

Figure 17-6 shows what the Web Part that contains the Calendar control looks like after you minimize it. Notice also that if you opt to close one of the Web Parts, the item completely disappears. There seems to be no way to make it come back — even if you shut down the page and restart it. This is by design — so don't worry. I will show you how to get it back!

Figure 17-6

A few of the items included in the zones have new titles. By default, the title that appears at the top of the Web Part is the name of the control. For instance, you can see that the Calendar control is simply titled Calendar. If you add a Button control or any other control to the zone, at first it is simply titled Untitled. To give better and more meaningful names to the Web Parts that appear in a zone, you simply add a `Title` attribute to the control — just as was done with the Image control and the User control, which both appear on the page. In the preceding code example, the Image control is renamed to `Tuija at the Museum`, and the user control is given the `Title` value `Daily Links`.

Besides this little bit of default functionality, you can do considerably more with the Web Parts contained within this page, but you have to make some other additions. These are reviewed next.

Allowing the User to Change the Mode of the Page

Working with the `WebPartManager` class either directly or through the use of the WebPartManager server control, you can have the mode of the page changed. Changing the mode of the page being viewed allows the user to add, move, or change the pages they are working with. The nice thing about the Web Part capabilities of ASP.NET is that these changes are then recorded to the `ASPNETDB.MDF` database file and are, therefore, re-created the next time the user visits the page.

Using the `WebPartManager` object, you can enable the user to do the following, as defined in this list:

- **Add new Web Parts to the page:** Includes Web Parts not displayed on the page by default and Web Parts that the end user has previously deleted. This aspect of the control works with the catalog capabilities of the Portal Framework, which is discussed shortly.
- **Enter the Design mode for the page:** Enables the end user to drag and drop elements around the page. The end user can use this capability to change the order in which items appear in a zone or to move items from one zone to another.
- **Modify the Web Parts settings:** Enables the end user to customize aspects of the Web Parts, such as their appearance and behavior. It also allows the end user to modify any custom settings that developers apply to the Web Part.
- **Connect Web Parts on the page:** Enables the end user to make a connection between one or more Web Parts on the page. For example, when an end user working in a financial services application enters a stock symbol into an example Web Part, he can use a connection to another Web Part to see a stock chart change or news appear based on that particular stock symbol. All of this is based on the variable defined in the first Web Part.

Building on Listing 17-2, Listing 17-3 adds a DropDownList control to the table's header. This drop-down list provides a list of available modes the user can employ to change how the page is displayed. Again, the mode of the page determines the actions the user can initiate directly on the page (this is demonstrated later in this chapter).

Listing 17-3: Adding a list of modes to the page

VB

```
<%@ Page Language="VB"%>
<%@ Register Src="DailyLinks.ascx" TagName="DailyLinks" TagPrefix="uc1" %>

<script runat="server">
    Protected Sub DropDownList1_SelectedIndexChanged(ByVal sender As Object, _
       ByVal e As System.EventArgs)

      Dim wpDisplayMode As WebParts.WebPartDisplayMode = _
      Webpartmanager1.SupportedDisplayModes(DropDownList1.SelectedValue.ToString())
      Webpartmanager1.DisplayMode = wpDisplayMode
    End Sub

    Protected Sub Page_Init(ByVal sender As Object, ByVal e As System.EventArgs)
      For Each wpMode As WebPartDisplayMode In _
         Webpartmanager1.SupportedDisplayModes
```

Continued

```
            Dim modeName As String = wpMode.Name
            Dim dd_ListItem As ListItem = New ListItem(modeName, modeName)
            DropDownList1.Items.Add(dd_ListItem)
        Next
    End Sub
</script>

<html xmlns="http://www.w3.org/1999/xhtml">
<head id="Head1" runat="server">
    <title>Web Parts Example</title>
</head>
<body>
    <form id="form1" runat="server">
        <asp:WebPartManager ID="Webpartmanager1" Runat="server">
        </asp:WebPartManager>
        <table cellpadding="5" border="1">
            <tr>
                <td colspan="2">
                    <h1>Bill Evjen's Web Page</h1>
                    <asp:WebPartZone ID="WebPartZone1" Runat="server"
                     LayoutOrientation="Horizontal">
                        <ZoneTemplate>
                            <asp:Label ID="Label1" Runat="server" Text="Label"
                             Title="Welcome to my web page!">
                             Welcome to the page!
                            </asp:Label>
                        </ZoneTemplate>
                    </asp:WebPartZone>
                </td>
                <td valign="top">
                    Select mode:
                    <asp:DropDownList ID="DropDownList1" runat="server"
                     AutoPostBack="True"
                     OnSelectedIndexChanged="DropDownList1_SelectedIndexChanged">
                    </asp:DropDownList>
                </td>
            </tr>
            <tr valign="top">
                <td>
                    <asp:WebPartZone ID="WebPartZone2" Runat="server">
                        <ZoneTemplate>
                            <asp:Image ID="Image1" Runat="server"
                             ImageUrl="~/Images/Tuija.jpg" Width="150px"
                             Title="Tuija at the Museum">
                            </asp:Image>
                            <uc1:DailyLinks ID="DailyLinks1" runat="server"
                             Title="Daily Links">
                            </uc1:DailyLinks>
                        </ZoneTemplate>
                    </asp:WebPartZone>
                </td>
                <td>
                    <asp:WebPartZone ID="WebPartZone3" Runat="server">
                        <ZoneTemplate>
```

```
                                <asp:Calendar ID="Calendar1" Runat="server"
                                 Title="Calendar">
                                </asp:Calendar>
                            </ZoneTemplate>
                        </asp:WebPartZone>
                    </td>
                    <td><!-- Blank for now -->
                    </td>
                </tr>
            </table>
        </form>
    </body>
    </html>
```

C#

```
<%@ Page Language="C#"%>
<%@ Register Src="DailyLinks.ascx" TagName="DailyLinks" TagPrefix="uc1" %>

<script runat="server">
    protected void DropDownList1_SelectedIndexChanged(object sender, EventArgs e)
    {
      WebParts.WebPartDisplayMode wpDisplayMode =
     Webpartmanager1.SupportedDisplayModes[DropDownList1.SelectedValue.ToString()];
      Webpartmanager1.DisplayMode = wpDisplayMode;
    }

    protected void Page_Init(object sender, EventArgs e)
    {
      foreach (WebPartDisplayMode wpMode in
         Webpartmanager1.SupportedDisplayModes)
      {
            string modeName = wpMode.Name;
            ListItem dd_ListItem = new ListItem(modeName, modeName);
            DropDownList1.Items.Add(dd_ListItem);
      }
    }
</script>
```

This adds a drop-down list to the top of the table, as shown in Figure 17-7. This drop-down list will allow the end user to switch between the Browse and Design modes.

When the end user clicks the link, a drop-down window of options appears, as shown in Figure 17-8.

Using the `Page_Init` event, the drop-down list is populated with a list of the available page modes that are accessible at this particular time. In this case, it is Browse and Design. The Browse mode is the default mode used when the page is first created. The Design mode causes the ASP.NET page to show the WebPartZone sections. In this mode, the user can drag and drop controls from one section to another with relative ease. Again, the positioning of the elements contained in the page is remembered from one application visit to the next.

It is important to note that the Design mode is only able to work in Internet Explorer browsers.

Figure 17-7

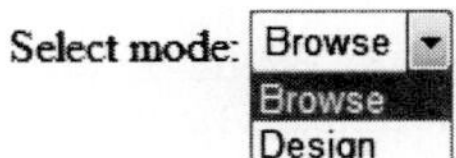

Figure 17-8

The DropDownList control is populated by iterating through a list of available `WebPartDisplayMode` objects contained in the `SupportedDisplayModes` property (which is of type `WebPartDisplayModeCollection`). These modes are available through the `WebPartManager1` control, which was placed on the page and is in charge of managing the modes and change of modes of the page. These `WebPartDisplayMode` objects are then used to populate the DropDownList control.

When the end user selects one of the available modes displayed in the DropDownList control, using the `AutoPostBack` feature of the control, the page is then changed to the selected mode. This is done using the first creating an instance of a `WebPartDisplayMode` object and populating it with the value of the mode selected from the drop-down list. Then, using this `WebPartDisplayMode` object, the `DisplayMode` property of the `WebPartManager` object is assigned with this retrieved value.

The next section covers an important addition to the Portal Framework — the capability to add Web Parts dynamically to a page.

Adding Web Parts to a Page

The next step is to rework the example so that the end user has a built-in way to add Web Parts to the page through the use of the Portal Framework. The ASP.NET Portal Framework enables an end user to add Web Parts, but you must also provide the end user with a list of items he can add. To do this, simply add a Catalog Zone to the last table cell in the bottom of the table, as illustrated in the partial code example in Listing 17-4.

Listing 17-4: Adding a Catalog Zone

```
<tr valign="top">
   <td>
      <asp:WebPartZone ID="WebPartZone2" runat="server">
         <ZoneTemplate>
            <asp:Image ID="Image1" runat="server"
             ImageUrl="~/Images/Tuija.jpg" Width="150px"
             Title="Tuija at the Museum">
            </asp:Image>
            <uc1:DailyLinks ID="DailyLinks1" runat="server"
             Title="Daily Links">
            </uc1:DailyLinks>
         </ZoneTemplate>
      </asp:WebPartZone>
   </td>
   <td>
      <asp:WebPartZone ID="WebPartZone3" runat="server">
         <ZoneTemplate>
            <asp:Calendar ID="Calendar1" runat="server"
             Title="Calendar">
            </asp:Calendar>
         </ZoneTemplate>
      </asp:WebPartZone>
   </td>
   <td>
      <asp:CatalogZone ID="Catalogzone1" runat="server">
         <ZoneTemplate>
            <asp:PageCatalogPart ID="Pagecatalogpart1" runat="server"/>
         </ZoneTemplate>
      </asp:CatalogZone>
   </td>
</tr>
```

Once a Catalog Zone section is present on the page, the page is enabled for the Catalog mode. You need to create a Catalog Zone section by using the `<asp:CatalogZone>` control. This is similar to creating a Web Part Zone, but the Catalog Zone is specifically designed to allow for categorization of the items that can be placed on the page. Notice that Catalog mode does not appear as an option in the drop-down list of available modes until a CatalogZone control is placed on the page. If no CatalogZone control is present on the page, this option is not displayed.

After the Catalog Zone is in place, the next step is to create a `<ZoneTemplate>` section within the Catalog Zone because this is also a templated control. Inside the `<ZoneTemplate>` element is a single control — the PageCatalogPart control. If you run the page after adding the PageCatalogPart control and change the mode to Catalog, you will see the results shown in Figure 17-9.

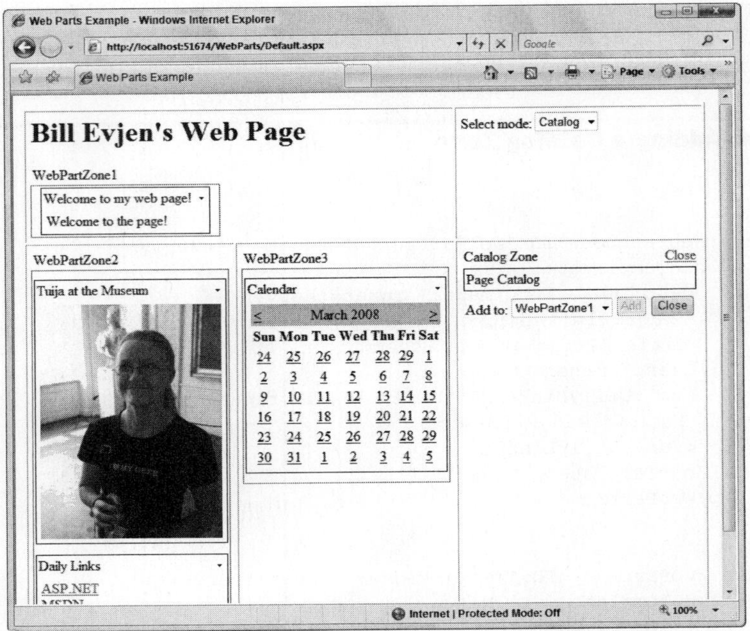

Figure 17-9

To get some items to appear in the list (since none do at present), delete one or more items (any items contained on the page when viewing the page in the browser) from the page's default view and enter the Catalog mode by selecting Catalog from the drop-down list of modes.

At this point, you can see the deleted Web Parts in the Catalog Zone. The PageCatalogPart control contains a title and check box list of items that can be selected. The PageCatalogPart control also includes a drop-down list of all the available Web Part Zones on the page. From here, you can place the selected Web Parts into one of the Web Part Zones available from this list. After you select the Web Parts and the appropriate zone in which you want to place the item, you click the Add button and the items appear in the specified locations.

Moving Web Parts

Not only can the end user change the order in which Web Parts appear in a zone, he can also move Web Parts from one zone to another. By adding the capability to enter the Design mode through the drop-down list that you created earlier, you have already provided the end user with this capability. He simply enters the Design mode, and this allows for this type of movement.

The Design option in the drop-down list changes the page so that the user can see the zones defined on the page, as illustrated in Figure 17-10.

From this figure, you can see the three zones (`WebPartZone1`, `WebPartZone2`, and `WebPartZone3`). At this point, the end user can select one of the Web Parts contained in one of these zones and either change its order in the zone or move it to an entirely different zone on the page. To grab one of the Web

Parts, the user simply clicks and holds the left mouse button on the title of the Web Part. When done correctly, the crosshair, which appears when the end user hovers over the Web Part's title, turns into an arrow. This means that the user has grabbed hold of the Web Part and can drag it to another part of the page. While the user drags the Web Part around the page, a visual representation of the item appears (see Figure 17-11). In this state, the Web Part is a bit transparent and its location in the state of the page is defined with a blue line (the darker line shown at the top of `WebPartZone3`). Releasing the left mouse button drops the Web Part at the blue line's location.

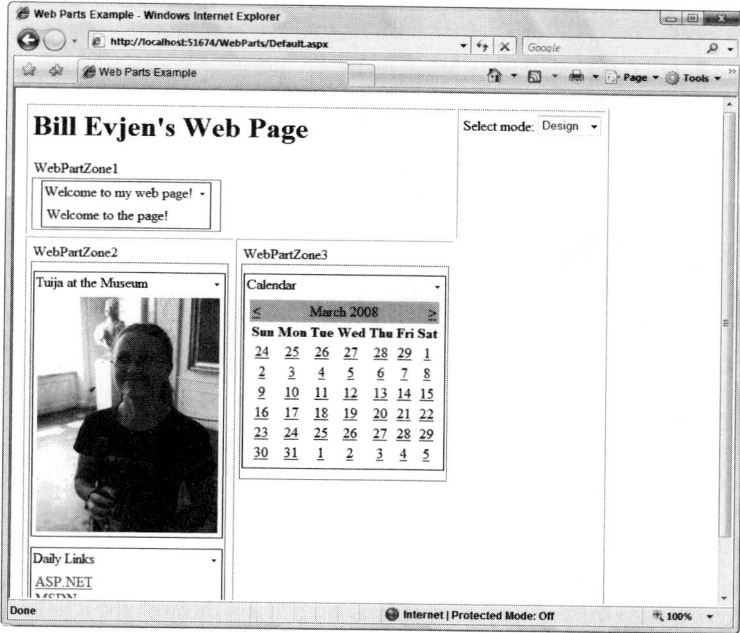

Figure 17-10

After the end user places all the items where he wants them, the locations of the items on the page are saved for later use.

When he reopens the browser, everything is then drawn in the last state in which he left the page. This is done on a per-user basis, so any other users browsing to the same page see either their own modified results or the default view if it is a first visit to the page.

The user can then leave the Design view by opening the list of options from the drop-down list of modes and selecting Browse.

Another way to move Web Parts is to enter the Catalog mode of the page (which is now one of the options in the drop-down list due to the addition of the Catalog Zone section). The Catalog mode enables you to add deleted items to the page, but it also allows you to modify the location of the items on the page by providing the same drag-and-drop capability as the Design mode.

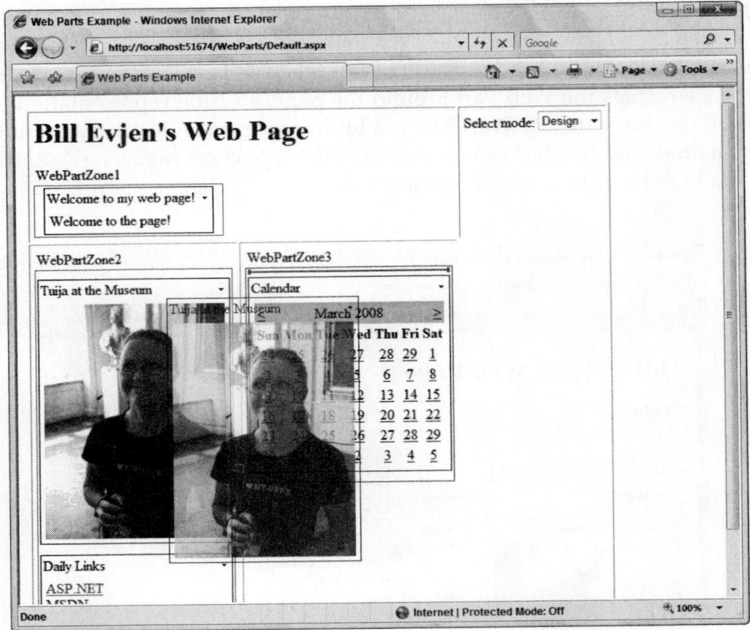

Figure 17-11

Modifying the Web Part Settings

Another option in the list of modes that can be added to the drop-down list is to allow your end users to edit the actual Web Parts themselves to a degree. This is done through the available Edit mode, and this enables the end user to modify settings determining appearance, behavior, and layout for a particular Web Part on the page.

To make this functionality work, you must add an Editor Zone to the page just as you add the Catalog Zone. This is illustrated in Listing 17-5. You place this bit of new code within the same table directly below the Catalog Zone declaration.

Listing 17-5: Adding an Editor Zone to the page

```
<td>
    <asp:CatalogZone ID="Catalogzone1" runat="server">
        <ZoneTemplate>
            <asp:PageCatalogPart ID="Pagecatalogpart1" runat="server"/>
        </ZoneTemplate>
    </asp:CatalogZone>
    <asp:EditorZone ID="Editorzone1" runat="server">
        <ZoneTemplate>
            <asp:AppearanceEditorPart ID="Appearanceeditorpart1" runat="server" />
            <asp:BehaviorEditorPart ID="Behavioreditorpart1" runat="server" />
            <asp:LayoutEditorPart ID="Layouteditorpart1" runat="server" />
            <asp:PropertyGridEditorPart ID="PropertyGridEditorPart1" runat="server" />
```

```
        </ZoneTemplate>
    </asp:EditorZone>
</td>
```

Just like the `<asp:CatalogZone>`, the `<asp:EditorZone>` control is a templated control that requires a `<ZoneTemplate>` section. Within this section, you can place controls that allow for the modification of the appearance, behavior, and layout of the selected Web Part. These controls include `<asp:AppearanceEditorPart>`, `<asp:BehaviorEditorPart>`, `<asp:LayoutEditorPart>`, and `<asp:PropertyGridEditorPart>`.

When you run this new section of code and select Edit from the drop-down list of modes, the arrow that is next to the Web Part title from each of the Web Parts on the page will show an Edit option, as illustrated in Figure 17-12.

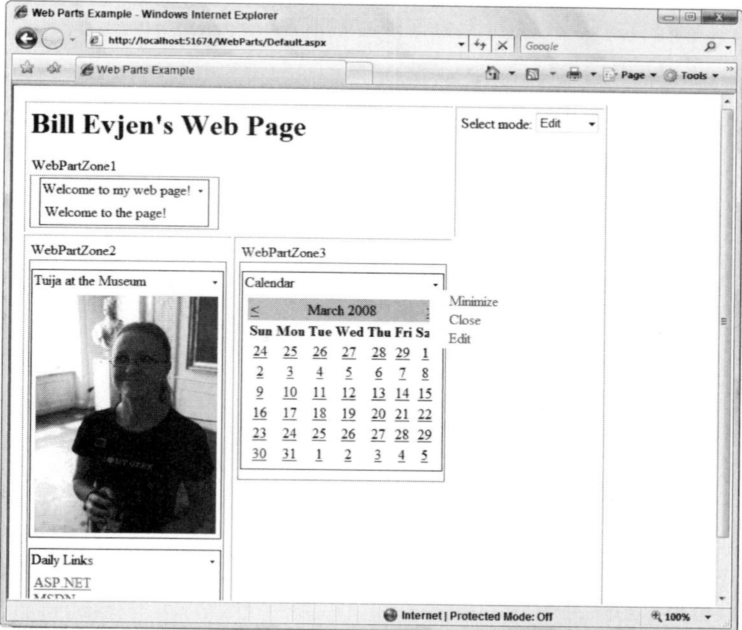

Figure 17-12

After you select the Edit option from this list of three options, the right column of the table shows the various editing sections for this particular Web Part.

The Appearance section enables the end user to change the Web Part's details, including the title, how the title appears, and other appearance-related items such as the item's height and width. The Appearance section is shown in Figure 17-13.

The Behavior section (shown in Figure 17-14) enables the end user to select whether the Web Part can be closed, minimized, or exported. This section allows you to change behavior items for either yourself only (a single user) or for everyone in the system (a shared view of the Web Part). Using the shared view, the

Behavior section is generally used to allow site editors (or admins) to change the dynamics of how end users can modify Web Parts. General viewers of the page most likely will not see this section.

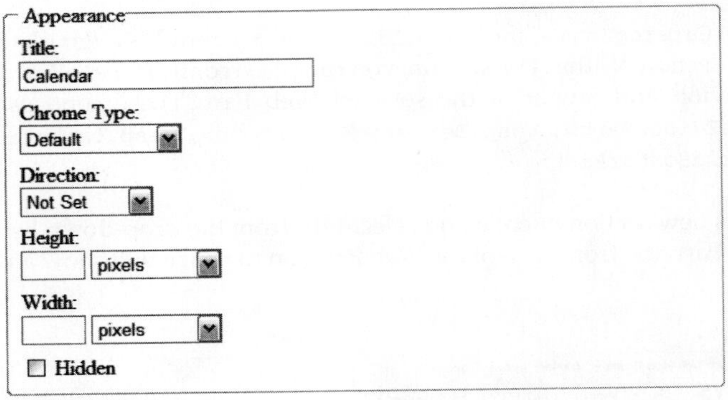

Appearance

Title: Calendar

Chrome Type: Default

Direction: Not Set

Height: pixels

Width: pixels

☐ Hidden

Figure 17-13

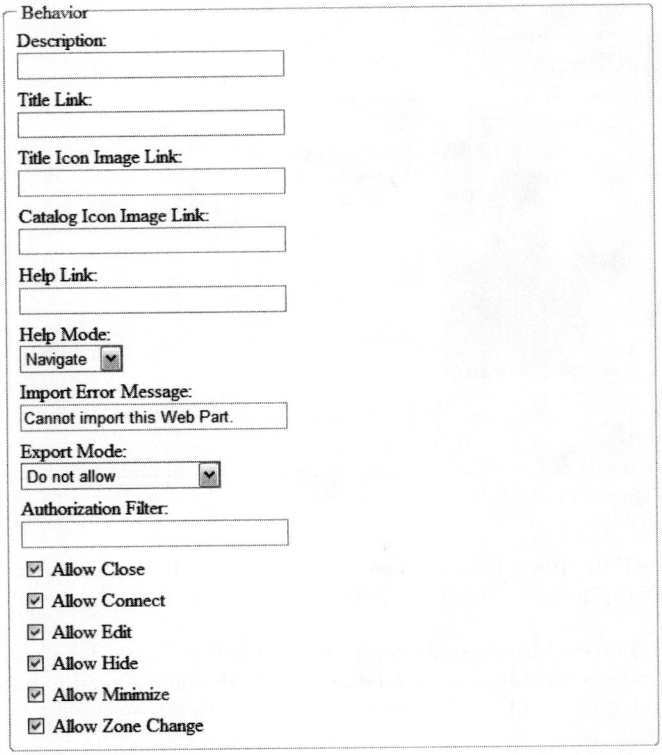

Behavior

Description:

Title Link:

Title Icon Image Link:

Catalog Icon Image Link:

Help Link:

Help Mode: Navigate

Import Error Message: Cannot import this Web Part.

Export Mode: Do not allow

Authorization Filter:

☑ Allow Close

☑ Allow Connect

☑ Allow Edit

☑ Allow Hide

☑ Allow Minimize

☑ Allow Zone Change

Figure 17-14

To get the Behavior section to appear, you first need to make the changes to the `Web.config` files presented in Listing 17-6.

Listing 17-6: Getting the Behavior section to appear through settings in the Web.config

```
<configuration>
   <system.web>
      <webParts>
         <personalization>
            <authorization>
               <allow users="*" verbs="enterSharedScope" />
            </authorization>
         </personalization>
      </webParts>
   </system.web>
</configuration>
```

After the `Web.config` file is in place, the next step is to add a bit of code to your `Page_Load` event, as shown in Listing 17-7.

Listing 17-7: Adding some code to allow the Behavior section to appear

VB

```
If Webpartmanager1.Personalization.Scope = PersonalizationScope.User _
   AndAlso Webpartmanager1.Personalization.CanEnterSharedScope Then

      Webpartmanager1.Personalization.ToggleScope()
End If
```

C#

```
if (Webpartmanager1.Personalization.Scope == PersonalizationScope.User
   && Webpartmanager1.Personalization.CanEnterSharedScope)
{
     Webpartmanager1.Personalization.ToggleScope();
}
```

The Layout section (shown in Figure 17-15) enables the end user to change the order in which Web Parts appear in a zone or move Web Parts from one zone to another. This is quite similar to the drag-and-drop capabilities illustrated previously, but this section allows for the same capabilities through the manipulation of simple form elements.

Figure 17-15

The PropertyGridEditorPart, although not demonstrated yet, allows end users to modify properties that are defined in your own custom server controls. At the end of this chapter, we will look at building a custom Web Part and using the PropertyGridEditorPart to allow end users to modify one of the publicly exposed properties contained in the control.

After you are satisfied with the appearance and layout of the Web Parts and have made the necessary changes to the control's properties in one of the editor parts, simply click OK or Apply.

Connecting Web Parts

One option you do have is to make a connection between two Web Parts using the `<asp:ConnectionsZone>` control. This control enables you to make property connections between two Web Parts on the same page. For example, within the Weather Web Part built into one of ASP.NET's pre-built applications, you can have a separate Web Part that is simply a text box and a button that allows the end user to input a zip code. This, in turn, modifies the contents in the original Weather Web Part.

Modifying Zones

One aspect of the Portal Framework that merits special attention is the capability to modify zones on the page. These zones allow for a high degree of modification — not only in the look-and-feel of the items placed in the zone, but also in terms of the behaviors of zones and the items contained in the zones as well. Following are some examples of what you can do to modify zones.

Turning Off the Capability for Modifications in a Zone

As you have seen, giving end users the capability to move Web Parts around the page is quite easy, whether within a zone or among entirely different zones. When working with the Portal Framework and multiple zones on a page, you do not always want to allow the end user to freely change the items that appear in every zone. You want the items placed in some zones to be left alone. Listing 17-8 shows an example of this.

Listing 17-8: Turning off the zone modification capability

```
<asp:WebPartZone ID="WebPartZone1" runat="server"
 LayoutOrientation="Horizontal" AllowLayoutChange="false">
   <ZoneTemplate>
      <asp:Label ID="Label1" runat="server" Text="Label"
       Title="Welcome to my web page!">
       Welcome to the page!
      </asp:Label>
   </ZoneTemplate>
</asp:WebPartZone>
```

In this example, the first Web Part Zone, `WebPartZone1`, uses the `AllowLayoutChange` attribute with a value of `False`, which turns off the end user's capability to modify this particular Web Part Zone. When you run this page and go to the design mode, notice that you cannot drag and drop any of the Web Parts from the other zones into `WebPartZone1`. Neither can you grab hold of the Label Web Part contained in `WebPartZone1`. No capability exists to minimize and close the Web Parts contained in this zone. It allows absolutely no modifications to the zone's layout.

You may notice another interesting change when you are working in the page catalog mode with the `AllowLayoutChange` attribute set to `False`. After you select items to add to the page through the page catalog, `WebPartZone1` does not appear in the drop-down list of places where you can publish the Web Parts (see Figure 17-16). From this figure, you can see that only `WebPartZone2` and `WebPartZone3` appear and allow modifications.

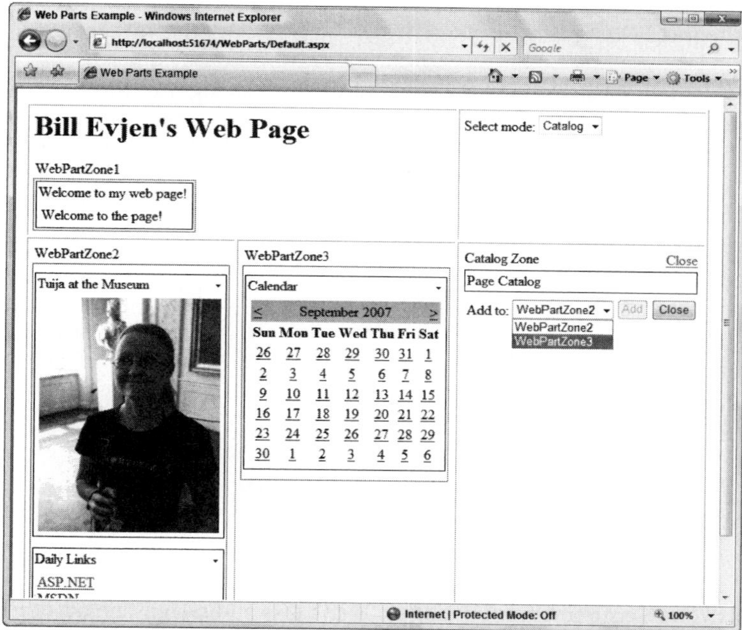

Figure 17-16

Adding Controls through Other Means

Earlier in this chapter, you examined how to use the `<asp:PageCatalogPart>` control to restore controls to a page after they had been deleted. Although the `<asp:PageCatalogPart>` is ideal for this, you might also want to allow the end user to add Web Parts that are not on the page by default. You may want to enable the end user to add more than one of any particular Web Part to a page. For these situations, you work with the `<asp:DeclarativeCatalogPart>` control.

Listing 17-9 shows an example of using this type of catalog system in place of the `<asp:Page-CatalogPart>` control.

Listing 17-9: Using the DeclarativeCatalogPart control

```
<asp:CatalogZone ID="Catalogzone1" Runat="server">
   <ZoneTemplate>
      <asp:DeclarativeCatalogPart ID="Declarativecatalogpart1" Runat="server">
         <WebPartsTemplate>
            <uc1:CompanyContactInfo ID="CompanyContact" Runat="Server"
```

Continued

```
                  Title="Company Contact Info" />
                <uc1:PhotoAlbum ID="PhotoAlbum" Runat="Server" Title="Photo Album" />
                <uc1:Customers ID="Customers" Runat="Server" Title="Customers" />
                <uc1:Locations ID="Locations" Runat="Server" Title="Locations" />
            </WebPartsTemplate>
        </asp:DeclarativeCatalogPart>
    </ZoneTemplate>
</asp:CatalogZone>
```

Instead of using the <asp:PageCatalogPart> control, this catalog uses the <asp:Declarative-CatalogPart> control. This templated control needs a <WebPartsTemplate> section where you can place all the controls you want available as options for the end user. The controls appear in the check box list in the same order in which you declare them in the <WebPartsTemplate> section. Figure 17-17 shows how the catalog looks in the Design view in Visual Studio 2008.

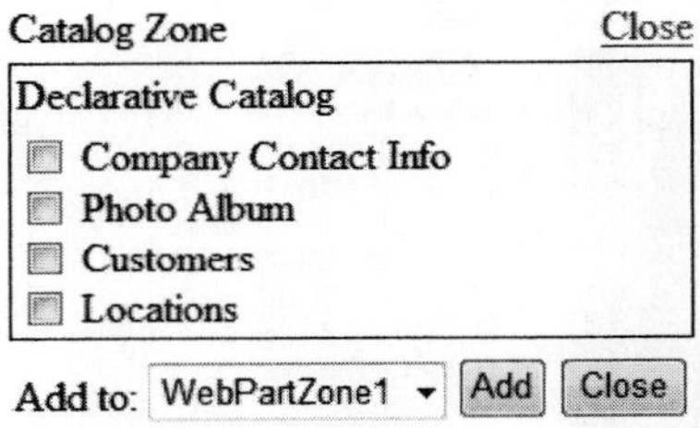

Catalog Zone Close

Declarative Catalog

- [ ] Company Contact Info
- [ ] Photo Album
- [ ] Customers
- [ ] Locations

Add to: WebPartZone1 [Add] [Close]

Figure 17-17

This catalog lets you select items from the list of Web Parts and assign the location of the zone in which they will be placed. After they are placed, notice that the option to add these Web Parts has not disappeared as it did with the earlier PageCatalogPart control. In fact, you can add as many of these items to the page as you deem necessary — even if it is to the same zone within the Portal Framework.

Using the DeclarativeCatalogPart control is not always a completely ideal solution. When the end user closes one of the Web Parts that initially appears on the page, he may not see that control listed in the DeclarativeCatalogPart control's list of elements. You must explicitly specify it should appear when you write the code for the DeclarativeCatalogPart control. In fact, the end user cannot re-add these deleted items. Using both the PageCatalogPart control and the DeclarativeCatalogPart control simultaneously is sometimes the best solution. The great thing about this framework is that it allows you to do that. The Portal Framework melds both controls into a cohesive control that not only enables you to add controls that are not on the page by default, but it also lets you add previously deleted default controls. Listing 17-10 shows an example of this.

Listing 17-10: Combining both catalog types

```
<asp:CatalogZone ID="Catalogzone1" Runat="server">
    <ZoneTemplate>
        <asp:PageCatalogPart ID="Pagecatalogpart1" Runat="server" />
        <asp:DeclarativeCatalogPart ID="Declarativecatalogpart1" Runat="server">
            <WebPartsTemplate>
                <uc1:CompanyContactInfo ID="CompanyContact" Runat="Server"
```

```
            Title="Company Contact Info" />
            <uc1:PhotoAlbum ID="PhotoAlbum" Runat="Server" Title="Photo Album" />
            <uc1:Customers ID="Customers" Runat="Server" Title="Customers" />
            <uc1:Locations ID="Locations" Runat="Server" Title="Locations" />
         </WebPartsTemplate>
      </asp:DeclarativeCatalogPart>
   </ZoneTemplate>
</asp:CatalogZone>
```

In this example, both the PageCatalogPart control and the DeclarativeCatalogPart control are contained within the `<ZoneTemplate>` section. When this page is run, you see the results shown in Figure 17-18.

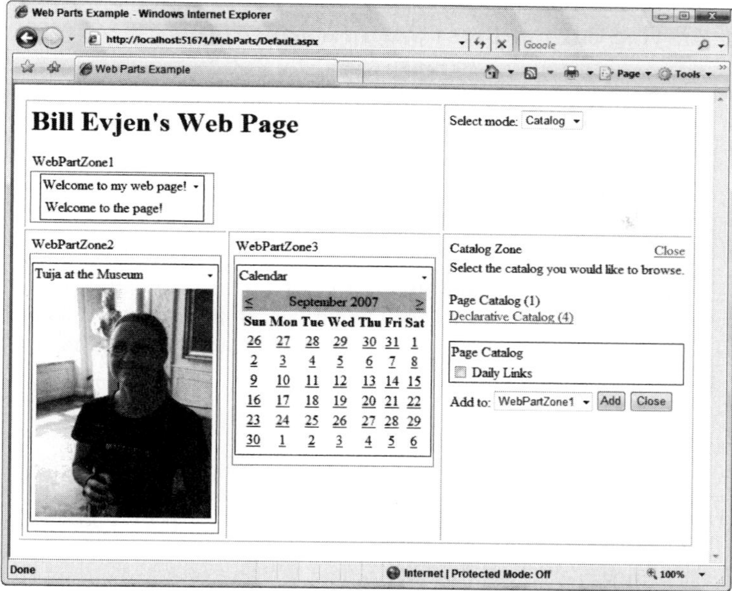

Figure 17-18

You can see that each catalog is defined within the Catalog Zone. Figure 17-18 shows the PageCatalog-Part control's collection of Web Parts (defined as Page Catalog). Also, note that a link to the Declarative Catalog is provided for that particular list of items. Note that the order in which the catalogs appear in the `<ZoneTemplate>` section is the order in which the links appear in the Catalog Zone.

Web Part Verbs

Web Part verbs declare the actions of the items (such as Minimize and Close) that appear in the title. These verbs are basically links that initiate an action for a particular Web Part. The available list of Web Part verbs includes the following:

- `<CloseVerb>`
- `<ConnectVerb>>`
- `<DeleteVerb>`
- `<EditVerb>`

- <ExportVerb>
- <HelpVerb>
- <MinimizeVerb>
- <RestoreVerb>

The `<asp:WebPartZone>` control allows you to control these verbs by nesting the appropriate verb elements within the `<asp:WebPartZone>` element itself. After these are in place, you can manipulate how these items appear in all the Web Parts that appear in the chosen Web Part Zone.

For example, look at graying out the default Close link included with a Web Part. This is illustrated in Listing 17-11.

Listing 17-11: Graying out the Close link in a Web Part

```
<asp:WebPartZone ID="WebPartZone3" Runat="server">
      <CloseVerb Enabled="False" />
      <ZoneTemplate>
         <asp:Calendar ID="Calendar1" Runat="server">
         </asp:Calendar>
      </ZoneTemplate>
</asp:WebPartZone>
```

In this example, you can see that you simply need to set the `Enabled` attribute of the `<CloseVerb>` element to `False` in order to gray out the Close link in any of the generated Web Parts included in this Web Part Zone. If you construct the Web Part Zone in this manner, you achieve the results shown in Figure 17-19.

Figure 17-19

If you do not want to gray out the Close link (or any other verb link contained within the Web Part), you must instead use the `Visible` attribute of the appropriate verb (see Listing 17-12).

Listing 17-12: Removing the Close link in a Web Part

```
<asp:WebPartZone ID="WebPartZone3" Runat="server">
      <CloseVerb Visible="False" />
      <ZoneTemplate>
         <asp:Calendar ID="Calendar1" Runat="server">
         </asp:Calendar>
      </ZoneTemplate>
</asp:WebPartZone>
```

Using the `Visible` attribute produces the screen shown in Figure 17-20.

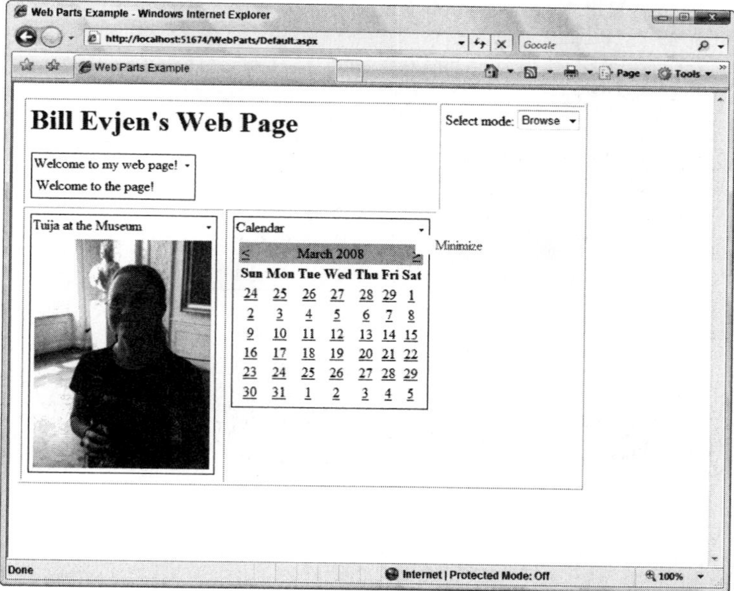

Figure 17-20

Verb elements provide another exciting feature: They give you the capability to use images that would appear next to the text of an item. Using images with the text makes the Web Parts appear more like the overall Windows environment. For instance, you can change the contents of `WebPartZone3` again so that it now uses images with the text for the Close and Minimize links. This is illustrated in Listing 17-13.

Listing 17-13: Using images for the Web Part verbs

```
<asp:WebPartZone ID="WebPartZone3" Runat="server">
      <CloseVerb ImageUrl="Images/CloseVerb.gif" />
```

Continued

```
        <MinimizeVerb ImageUrl="Images/MinimizeVerb.gif" />
        <ZoneTemplate>
            <asp:Calendar ID="Calendar1" Runat="server">
            </asp:Calendar>
        </ZoneTemplate>
    </asp:WebPartZone>
```

To point to an image for the verb, use the `ImageUrl` attribute. This produces something similar to Figure 17-21, depending on the images you use.

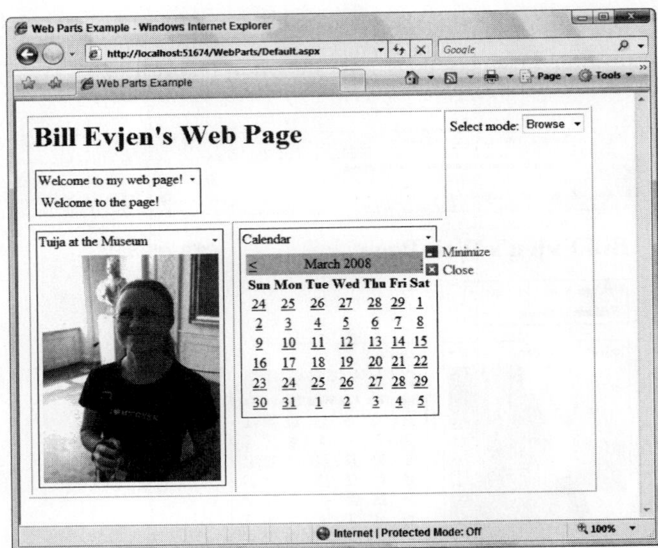

Figure 17-21

This chapter, thus far, has concentrated on creating completely customizable portal applications in a declarative manner using the capabilities provided by the ASP.NET Portal Framework. As with most aspects of ASP.NET, however, not only can you work with appearance and functionality in a declarative fashion, but you can also create the same constructs through server-side code.

Working with Classes in the Portal Framework

The Portal Framework provides three main classes for dealing with the underlying framework presented in this chapter: `WebPartManager`, `WebPartZone`, and `WebPart`.

The `WebPartManager` class allows you to perform multiple operations in your server-side code. The following table shows a partial listing of some of the properties that this class provides.

WebPartManager Class Properties	Description
`Connections`	Provides a collection of all the connections between Web Parts contained on the page.
`DisplayMode`	Allows you to change the page's display mode. Possible choices include `CatalogDisplayMode`, `ConnectDisplayMode`, `DesignDisplayMode`, `EditDisplayMode`, and `BrowseDisplayMode`.
`SelectedWebPart`	Allows you to perform multiple operations on the selected Web Part.
`WebParts`	Provides a collection of all the Web Parts contained on the page.
`Zones`	Provides a collection of all the Web Part Zones contained on the page.

Beyond the properties of the `WebPartManager` class, you also have an extensive list of available methods at your disposal. The following table outlines some of the available methods of the `WebPartManager` class.

WebPartManager Class Methods	Description
`AddWebPart`	Allows you to dynamically add new Web Parts to a particular zone on the page.
`ConnectWebParts`	Allows you to connect two Web Parts together via a common property or value.
`DeleteWebPart`	Allows you to dynamically delete new Web Parts from a particular zone on the page.
`DisconnectWebParts`	Allows you to delete a connection between two Web Parts.
`MoveWebPart`	Allows you to move a Web Part from one zone to another, or allows you to change the index order in which Web Parts appear in a particular zone.

Whereas the `WebPartManager` class allows you to manipulate the location, addition, and deletion of Web Parts that appear in the page as a whole, the `WebPartZone` class allows you to modify a single Web Part Zone on the page. The following table provides a list of some properties available to the `WebPartZone` class.

WebPartZone Class Properties	Description
`AllowLayoutChange`	Takes a `Boolean` value and either enables or disables the Web Part Zone's capability to accept or allow any changes in the Web Parts it contains.
`BackColor, BackImageUrl, BorderColor, BorderStyle, BorderWidth`	Enable you to modify the Web Part Zone's general appearance.

WebPartZone Class Properties	Description
CloseVerb	References the Close verb for a particular Web Part Zone from which you can then manipulate the verb's Description, Enabled, ImageUrl, Text, and Visible properties.
ConnectVerb	References a Web Part Zone's Connect verb from which you can then manipulate the verb's Description, Enabled, ImageUrl, Text, and Visible properties.
DragHighlightColor	Takes a System.Color value that sets the color of the Web Part Zone's border if focused when the moving of Web Parts is in operation. This also changes the color of the line that appears in the Web Part Zone specifying where to drop the Web Part.
EditVerb	References a Web Part Zone's Edit verb from which you can then manipulate the verb's Description, Enabled, ImageUrl, Text, and Visible properties.
EmptyZoneText	Sets the text that is shown in the zone if a Web Part is not set in the zone.
HeaderText	Sets header text.
Height	Sets the height of the Web Part Zone.
HelpVerb	References a Web Part Zone's Help verb from which you can then manipulate the verb's Description, Enabled, ImageUrl, Text, and Visible properties.
MenuLabelStyle, MenuLabelText	Enable you to modify the drop-down menu that appears when end users edit a Web Part. These properties let you apply an image, alter the text, or change the style of the menu.
MinimizeVerb	References a Web Part Zone's Minimize verb from which you can then manipulate the verb's Description, Enabled, ImageUrl, Text, and Visible properties.
LayoutOrientation	Enables you to change the Web Part Zone's orientation from horizontal to vertical or vice versa.
RestoreVerb	References a Web Part Zone's Restore verb, from which you can then manipulate the verb's Description, Enabled, ImageUrl, Text, and Visible properties.
VerbButtonType	Enables you to change the button style. Choices include ButtonType.Button, ButtonType.Image, or ButtonType.Link.
WebParts	Provides a collection of all the Web Parts contained within the zone.
Width	Sets the width of the Web Part Zone.

You have a plethora of options to manipulate the look-and-feel of the Web Part Zone and the items contained therein.

The final class is the `WebPart` class. This class enables you to manipulate specific Web Parts located on the page. The following table details some of the properties available in the `WebPart` class.

WebPart Class Properties	Description
`AllowClose`	Takes a `Boolean` value that specifies whether the Web Part can be closed and removed from the page.
`AllowEdit`	Takes a `Boolean` value that specifies whether the end user can edit the Web Part.
`AllowHide`	Takes a `Boolean` value that specifies whether the end user can hide the Web Part within the Web Part Zone. If the control is hidden, it is still in the zone, but invisible.
`AllowMinimize`	Takes a `Boolean` value that specifies whether the end user can collapse the Web Part.
`AllowZoneChange`	Takes a `Boolean` value that specifies whether the end user can move the Web Part from one zone to another.
`BackColor`, `BackImageUrl`, `BorderColor`, `BorderStyle`, `BorderWidth`	Enable you to modify the Web Part's general appearance.
`ChromeState`	Specifies whether the Web Part chrome is in a normal state or is minimized.
`ChromeType`	Specifies the chrome type that the Web Part uses. Available options include `BorderOnly`, `Default`, `None`, `TitleAndBorder`, and `TitleOnly`.
`Direction`	Specifies the direction of the text or items placed within the Web Part. Available options include `LeftToRight`, `NotSet`, and `RightToLeft`. This property is ideal for dealing with Web Parts that contain Asian text that is read from right to left.
`HelpMode`	Specifies how the help items display when the end user clicks the Help verb. Available options include `Modal`, `Modeless`, and `Navigate`. `Modal` displays the help items within a modal window if the end user's browser supports modal windows. If not, a pop-up window displays. `Modeless` means that a pop-up window displays for every user. `Navigate` redirects the user to the appropriate help page (specified by the `HelpUrl` property) when he clicks on the Help verb.
`HelpUrl`	Used when the `HelpMode` is set to `Navigate`. Takes a `String` value that specifies the location of the page the end user is redirected to when he clicks on the Help verb.
`ScrollBars`	Applies scroll bars to the Web Part. Available values include `Auto`, `Both`, `Horizontal`, `None`, and `Vertical`.

WebPart Class Properties	Description
`Title`	Specifies the text for the Web Part's title. Text appears in the title bar section.
`TitleIconImageUrl`	Enables you to apply an icon to appear next to the title by specifying to the icon image's location as a `String` value of the property.
`TitleUrl`	Specifies the location to direct the end user when the Web Part's title Web Part is clicked. When set, the title is converted to a link; when not set, the title appears as regular text.
`Zone`	Allows you to refer to the zone in which the Web Part is located.

Creating Custom Web Parts

When adding items to a page that utilizes the Portal Framework, you add the pre-existing ASP.NET Web server controls, user controls, or custom controls. In addition to these items, you can also build and incorporate custom Web Parts. Using the `WebParts` class, you can create your own custom Web Parts. Although similar to ASP.NET custom server control development, the creation of custom Web Parts adds some additional capabilities. Creating a class that inherits from the `WebPart` class instead of the `Control` class enables your control to use the new personalization features and to work with the larger Portal Framework, thereby allowing for the control to be closed, maximized, minimized, and more.

To create a custom Web Part control, the first step is to create a project in Visual Studio 2008. From Visual Studio, choose File⇨New Project. This pops open the New Project dialog. From this dialog, select ASP.NET Server Control. Name the project `MyStateListBox` and click OK to create the project. You are presented with a class that contains the basic framework for a typical ASP.NET server control. Ignore this framework; you are going to change it so that your class creates a custom Web Parts control instead of an ASP.NET custom server control. Listing 17-14 details the creation of a custom Web Part control.

Listing 17-14: Creating a custom Web Part control

VB

```
Imports System
Imports System.Web
Imports System.Web.UI.WebControls
Imports System.Web.UI.WebControls.WebParts

Namespace Wrox

    Public Class StateListBox
        Inherits WebPart

        Private _LabelStartText As String = " Enter State Name: "
        Dim StateInput As New TextBox
        Dim StateContents As New ListBox
```

```
        Public Sub New()
            Me.AllowClose = False
        End Sub

        <Personalizable(), WebBrowsable()> _
        Public Property LabelStartText() As String
            Get
                Return _LabelStartText
            End Get
            Set(ByVal value As String)
                _LabelStartText = value
            End Set
        End Property

        Protected Overrides Sub CreateChildControls()
            Controls.Clear()

            Dim InstructionText As New Label
            InstructionText.BackColor = Drawing.Color.LightGray
            InstructionText.Font.Name = "Verdana"
            InstructionText.Font.Size = 10
            InstructionText.Font.Bold = True
            InstructionText.Text = LabelStartText
            Me.Controls.Add(InstructionText)

            Dim LineBreak As New Literal
            LineBreak.Text = "<br />"
            Me.Controls.Add(LineBreak)

            Me.Controls.Add(StateInput)

            Dim InputButton As New Button
            InputButton.Text = "Input State"
            AddHandler InputButton.Click, AddressOf Me.Button1_Click
            Me.Controls.Add(InputButton)

            Dim Spacer As New Literal
            Spacer.Text = "<p>"
            Me.Controls.Add(Spacer)

            Me.Controls.Add(StateContents)

            ChildControlsCreated = True
        End Sub

        Public Sub Button1_Click(ByVal sender As Object, ByVal e As EventArgs)
            StateContents.Items.Add(StateInput.Text)
            StateInput.Text = String.Empty
            StateInput.Focus()
        End Sub

    End Class

End Namespace
```

Continued

C#

```
using System;
using System.Web.UI.WebControls;
using System.Web.UI.WebControls.WebParts;

namespace Wrox
{
    public class StateListBox : WebPart
    {
        private String _LabelStartText = " Enter State Name: ";
        readonly TextBox StateInput = new TextBox();
        readonly ListBox StateContents = new ListBox();

        public StateListBox()
        {
            AllowClose = false;
        }

        [Personalizable, WebBrowsable]
        public String LabelStartText
        {
            get { return _LabelStartText; }
            set { _LabelStartText = value; }
        }

        protected override void CreateChildControls()
        {
            Controls.Clear();

            Label InstructionText = new Label();
            InstructionText.BackColor = System.Drawing.Color.LightGray;
            InstructionText.Font.Name = "Verdana";
            InstructionText.Font.Size = 10;
            InstructionText.Font.Bold = true;
            InstructionText.Text = LabelStartText;
            Controls.Add(InstructionText);

            Literal LineBreak = new Literal();
            LineBreak.Text = "<br />";
            Controls.Add(LineBreak);

            Controls.Add(StateInput);

            Button InputButton = new Button();
            InputButton.Text = "Input State";
            InputButton.Click += this.Button1_Click;
            Controls.Add(InputButton);

            Literal Spacer = new Literal();
            Spacer.Text = "<p>";
            Controls.Add(Spacer);

            Controls.Add(StateContents);
```

```
                ChildControlsCreated = true;
            }

            private void Button1_Click(object sender, EventArgs e)
            {
                StateContents.Items.Add(StateInput.Text);
                StateInput.Text = String.Empty;
                StateInput.Focus();
            }
        }
    }
```

To review, you first import the `System.Web.UI.WebControls.WebParts` namespace. The important step in the creation of this custom control is to make sure that it inherits from the `WebPart` class instead of the customary `Control` class. As stated earlier, this gives the control access to the advanced functionality of the Portal Framework that a typical custom control would not have.

VB

```
Public Class StateListBox
   Inherits WebPart

End Class
```

C#

```
public class StateListBox : WebPart
{

}
```

After the class structure is in place, a few properties are defined, and the constructor is defined as well. The constructor directly uses some of the capabilities that the `WebPart` class provides. These capabilities would not be available if this custom control has the `Control` class as its base class and is making use of the `WebPart.AllowClose` property.

VB

```
Public Sub New()
   Me.AllowClose = False
End Sub
```

C#

```
public StateListBox()
{
   AllowClose = false;
}
```

This constructor creates a control that explicitly sets the control's `AllowClose` property to `False` — meaning that the Web Part will not have a Close link associated with it when generated in the page. Because of the use of the `WebPart` class instead of the `Control` class, you will find, in addition to the `AllowClose` property, other `WebPart` class properties such as `AllowEdit`, `AllowHide`, `AllowMinimize`, `AllowZoneChange`, and more.

In the example shown in Listing 17-14, you see a custom-defined property: `LabelStartText`. This property allows the developer to change the instruction text displayed at the top of the control. The big difference with this custom property is that it is preceded by the `Personalizable` and the `WebBrowsable` attributes.

The `Personalizable` attribute enables the property for personalization, whereas the `WebBrowsable` attribute specifies whether the property should be displayed in the Properties window in Visual Studio. The `Personalizable` attribute can be defined further using a `PersonalizationScope` enumeration. The only two possible enumerations — `Shared` and `User` — can be defined in the following ways:

VB

```
<Personalizable(PersonalizationScope.Shared), WebBrowsable()> _
Public Property LabelStartText() As String
   Get
      Return _LabelStartText
   End Get
   Set(ByVal value As String)
      _LabelStartText = value
   End Set
End Property
```

C#

```
[Personalizable(PersonalizationScope.Shared), WebBrowsable]
public String LabelStartText
{
   get { return _LabelStartText; }
   set { _LabelStartText = value; }
}
```

A `PersonalizationScope` of `User` means that any modifications are done on a per-user basis. This is the default setting and means that if a user makes modifications to the property, the changes are seen only by that particular user and not by the other users who browse the page. If the `PersonalizationScope` is set to `Shared`, changes made by one user can be viewed by others requesting the page.

After you have any properties in place, the next step is to define what gets rendered to the page by overriding the `CreateChildControls` method. From the example in Listing 17-14, the `CreateChildControls` method renders Label, Literal, TextBox, Button, and ListBox controls. In addition to defining the properties of some of these controls, a single event is associated with the Button control (`Button1_Click`) that is also defined in this class.

Now that the custom Web Part control is in place, build the project so that a DLL is created. The next step is to open up the ASP.NET Web project where you want to utilize this new control and, from the Visual Studio Toolbox, add the new control. You can quickly accomplish this task by right-clicking in the Toolbox on the tab where you want the new control to be placed. After right-clicking the appropriate tab, select Choose Items. Click the Browse button and point to the new `MyStateListBox.dll` that you just created. After this is done, the StateListBox control is highlighted and checked in the Choose Toolbox Items dialog, as illustrated in Figure 17-22.

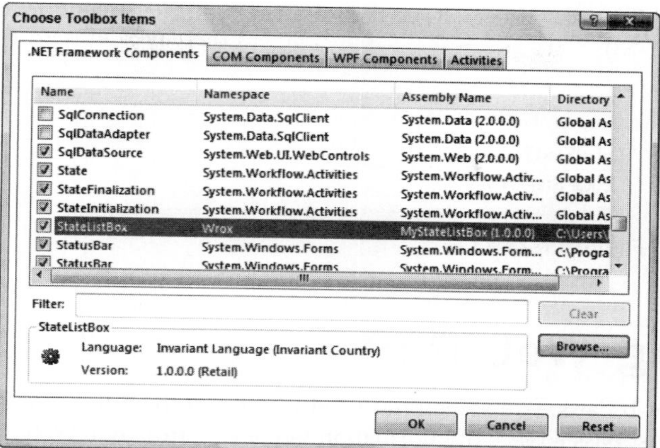

Figure 17-22

Clicking OK adds the control to your Toolbox. Now you are ready to use this new control as a Web Part control. To do this, simply drag and drop the control into one of your Web Part Zone areas. This does a couple of things. First, it registers the control on the page using the Register directive:

```
<%@ Register TagPrefix="cc1" Namespace="MyStateListBox.Wrox"
    Assembly="MyStateListBox" %>
```

Once registered, the control can be used on the page. If dragged and dropped onto the page's design surface, you get a control in the following construct:

```
<cc1:StateListBox Runat="server" ID="StateListBox1"
 LabelStartText=" Enter State Name: " AllowClose="False" />
```

The two important things to notice with this construct is that the custom property, `LabelStartText`, is present and has the default value in place, and the `AllowClose` attribute is included. The `AllowClose` attribute is present only because earlier you made the control's inherited class `WebPart`and not `Control`. Because `WebPart` was made the inherited class, you have access to these Web Part–specific properties. When the StateListBox control is drawn on the page, you can see that, indeed, it is part of the larger Portal Framework and allows for things such as minimization and editing. End users can use this custom Web Part control as if it were any other type of Web Part control. As you can see, you have a lot of power when you create your own Web Part controls.

And because `LabelStartText` uses the `WebBrowsable` attribute, you can use the PropertyGridEditorPart control to allow end users to edit this directly in the browser. With this in place, as was demonstrated earlier in Listing 17-5, an end user will see the following editing capabilities after switching to the Edit mode (see Figure 17-23).

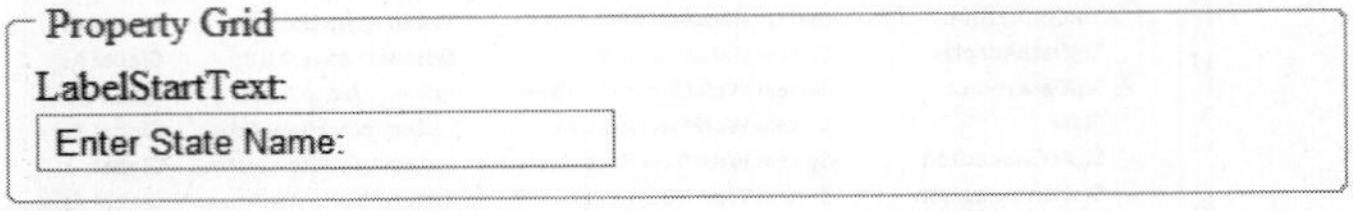

Property Grid
LabelStartText:
Enter State Name:

Figure 17-23

Connecting Web Parts

In working with Web Parts, you sometimes need to connect them in some fashion. *Connecting* them means that you must pass a piece of information (an object) from one Web Part to another Web Part on the page.

For instance, you might want to transfer the text value (such as a zip code or a name) that someone enters in a text box to other Web Parts in the page. Another example is a DropDownList control that specifies all the available currencies in the system. If the end user selects from the drop-down list, this drives changes in all the other Web Parts on that page that deal with this currency value selection. When you need to build constructions in this manner, you can use the Web Part connection capabilities defined here, or you might be able to work with other ASP.NET systems available (such as the personalization capabilities provided through the profile system).

When connecting Web Parts, you should be aware of the specific rules on how these Web Parts interact with one another. First off, if you want to make a connection from one Web Part to another, one of the Web Parts must be the *provider*. This provider Web Part is the component that supplies the piece of information required by any other Web Parts. The Web Parts that require this information are the *consumer* Web Parts. A Web Part provider can supply information to one or more consumer Web Parts; however, a consumer Web Part can only connect with a single provider Web Part. You cannot have a consumer Web Part that connects to more than one provider Web Part.

An example of this scenario is illustrated in Figure 17-24.

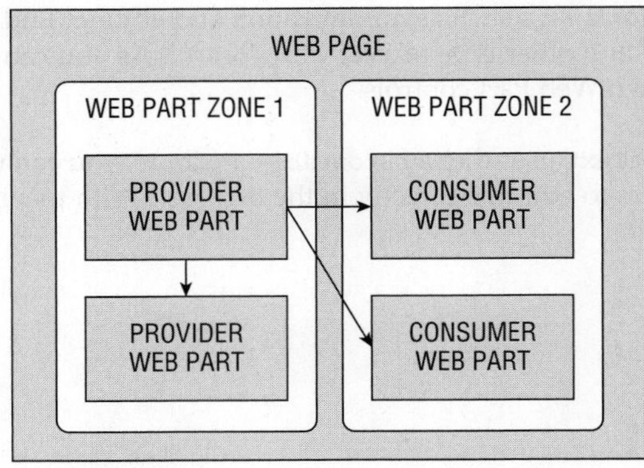

Figure 17-24

From this diagram, you can see that it is possible to use a single provider Web Part with multiple consumer Web Parts regardless of the Web Part Zone area in which the consumer Web Part resides.

When working with provider and consumer Web Parts, be aware that no matter how simple or complicated the Web Part is, you must wrap the Web Part by making it a custom Web Part. You do this to expose the correct item or property from the provider Web Part or to utilize the passed value in the correct manner for the consumer Web Part. This chapter reviews a simple example of connecting Web Parts. Although many steps are required to accomplish this task, you definitely get a lot of value from it as well.

Building the Provider Web Part

In order to build a provider Web Part that can be utilized by any consumer Web Part residing on the page, you first create an interface exposing the item you want to pass from one Web Part to another.

For this example, suppose you want to provide a text box as a Web Part that allows the end user to input a value. This value is then utilized by a calendar control contained within a Web Part in an entirely different Web Part Zone on the page using the Calendar control's `Caption` property.

This interface is demonstrated in Listing 17-15.

Listing 17-15: Building an interface to expose the property used to pass to a Web Part

VB

```
Namespace Wrox.ConnectionManagement
    Public Interface IStringForCalendar
        Property CalendarString() As String
    End Interface
End Namespace
```

C#

```
namespace Wrox.ConnectionManagement
{
    public interface IStringForCalendar
    {
        string CalendarString { get; set;}
    }
}
```

From this bit of code, you can see that the interface, `IStringForCalendar`, is quite simple. It exposes only a single String property — `CalendarString`. This interface is then utilized by the custom provider Web Part shown next.

The custom provider Web Part is built like any other custom Web Part in the manner demonstrated earlier in this chapter. The only difference is that you also provide some extra details so ASP.NET knows what item you are exposing from the Web Part and how this value is retrieved. This custom provider Web Part is illustrated in Listing 17-16.

Listing 17-16: Building a custom provider Web Part

VB

```
Imports Microsoft.VisualBasic
Imports System.Web.UI.WebControls
Imports System.Web.UI.WebControls.WebParts

Namespace Wrox.ConnectionManagement
    Public Class TextBoxChanger
        Inherits WebPart
        Implements IStringForCalendar

        Private myTextBox As TextBox
        Private _calendarString As String = String.Empty

        <Personalizable()> _
        Public Property CalendarString() As String Implements _
          Wrox.ConnectionManagement.IStringForCalendar.CalendarString

            Get
                Return _calendarString
            End Get
            Set(ByVal value As String)
                _calendarString = value
            End Set

        End Property

        <ConnectionProvider("Provider for String From TextBox", _
            "TextBoxStringProvider")> _
        Public Function TextBoxStringProvider() As IStringForCalendar
            Return Me
        End Function

        Protected Overrides Sub CreateChildControls()
            Controls.Clear()
            myTextBox = New TextBox()
            Me.Controls.Add(myTextBox)
            Dim myButton As Button = New Button()
            myButton.Text = "Change Calendar Caption"
            AddHandler myButton.Click, AddressOf Me.myButton_Click
            Me.Controls.Add(myButton)
        End Sub

        Private Sub myButton_Click(ByVal sender As Object, ByVal e As EventArgs)
            If myTextBox.Text <> String.Empty Then
                CalendarString = myTextBox.Text
                myTextBox.Text = String.Empty
            End If
        End Sub
    End Class
End Namespace
```

C#

```
using System;
using System.Web.UI.WebControls;
using System.Web.UI.WebControls.WebParts;

namespace Wrox.ConnectionManagement
{
    public class TextBoxChanger : WebPart, IStringForCalendar
    {
        private TextBox myTextBox;
        private string _calendarString = String.Empty;

        [Personalizable]
        public string CalendarString
        {
            get { return _calendarString; }
            set { _calendarString = value; }
        }

        [ConnectionProvider("Provider for String From TextBox",
            "TextBoxStringProvider")]
        public IStringForCalendar TextBoxStringProvider()
        {
            return this;
        }

        protected override void CreateChildControls()
        {
            Controls.Clear();
            myTextBox = new TextBox();
            Controls.Add(myTextBox);
            Button myButton = new Button();
            myButton.Text = "Change Calendar Caption";
            myButton.Click += this.myButton_Click;

            Controls.Add(myButton);
        }

        private void myButton_Click(object sender, EventArgs e)
        {
            if (myTextBox.Text != String.Empty)
            {
                CalendarString = myTextBox.Text;
                myTextBox.Text = String.Empty;
            }
        }
    }
}
```

Not only does this Web Part inherit the `WebPart` class, this provider Web Part implements the interface, `IStringForCalendar`, which was created earlier in Listing 17-15. From `IStringForCalendar`, the single `String` property is utilized and given the `Personalizable()` attribute. The important bit from the code presented in Listing 17-16 is the `TextBoxStringProvider()` method. This method returns a type of `IStringForCalendar` and is defined even further using the `ConnectionProvider` attribute. This attribute enables you to give a friendly name to the provider as well a programmatic name that can be used within the consumer custom Web Part that will be built shortly.

Using the `CreateChildControls()` method, you layout the design of the Web Part. In this case, a text box and button are the only controls that make up this Web Part. In addition to simply laying out the controls on the design surface, you use this method to assign any specific control events — such as a button-click event by assigning handlers to the controls that require them.

Finally, from within the button-click event of this Web Part (`myButton_Click`), the exposed property of `IStringForCalendar` is assigned a value. Everything is now in place for a consumer Web Part. The construction of this second Web Part is demonstrated next.

Building the Consumer Web Part

After you have a provider Web Part in place on your page, you can utilize the object it supplies for any number of consumer Web Parts on the same page. In this example, however, you are interested in using the `String` value coming from the TextBox control in the provider Web Part. The consumer Web Part takes this `String` and assigns it as the value of the Calendar control's `Caption` property. The construction of the consumer Web Part is illustrated in Listing 17-17.

Listing 17-17: The consumer Web Part

VB

```
Imports Microsoft.VisualBasic
Imports System.Web.UI.WebControls
Imports System.Web.UI.WebControls.WebParts

Namespace Wrox.ConnectionManagement
    Public Class ModifyableCalendar
        Inherits WebPart

        Private _myProvider As IStringForCalendar
        Private _stringTitle As String
        Private myCalendar As Calendar = New Calendar()

        <ConnectionConsumer("Calendar Title Consumer", "CalendarTitleConsumer")> _
        Public Sub RetrieveTitle(ByVal Provider As IStringForCalendar)
            _myProvider = Provider
        End Sub

        Protected Overrides Sub OnPreRender(ByVal e As EventArgs)
            EnsureChildControls()

            If Not (Me._myProvider Is Nothing) Then
                _stringTitle = _myProvider.CalendarString.Trim()
                myCalendar.Caption = _stringTitle
            End If
        End Sub

        Protected Overrides Sub CreateChildControls()
```

```
            Controls.Clear()
            Me.Controls.Add(myCalendar)
        End Sub
    End Class
End Namespace
```

C#

```
using System;
using System.Web.UI.WebControls;
using System.Web.UI.WebControls.WebParts;

namespace Wrox.ConnectionManagement
{
    public class ModifyableCalendar : WebPart
    {
        private IStringForCalendar _myProvider;
        string _stringTitle;
        Calendar myCalendar;

        [ConnectionConsumer("Calendar Title Consumer", "CalendarTitleConsumer")]
        public void RetrieveTitle(IStringForCalendar Provider)
        {
            _myProvider = Provider;
        }

        protected override void OnPreRender(EventArgs e)
        {
            EnsureChildControls();

            if (_myProvider != null)
            {
                _stringTitle = _myProvider.CalendarString.Trim();
                myCalendar.Caption = _stringTitle;
            }
        }

        protected override void CreateChildControls()
        {
            Controls.Clear();
            myCalendar = new Calendar();
            Controls.Add(myCalendar);
        }
    }
}
```

This new custom Web Part, `ModifyableCalendar`, is simply a class that inherits from `WebPart` and nothing more. It requires a reference to the interface `IStringForCalendar`. Because `IStringForCalendar` is part of the same namespace, you can provide a simple reference to this interface.

Your consumer Web Part requires a method that is the connection point for a provider Web Part on the same page. In this case, the `RetrieveTitle()` method is constructed using the `ConnectionConsumer` attribute before the method declaration. Like the `ConnectionProvider` attribute that was utilized in the provider Web Part, the `ConnectionConsumer` Web Part enables you to give your Web Part a friendly name and a reference name to use programmatically.

Then, the value retrieved from the provider Web Part is grabbed from within the `PreRender()` method of the Web Part and assigned to the Calendar control before the actual Calendar control is placed on the page from within the `CreateChildControls()` method.

Now that both a provider and a consumer Web Part are available to you, the next step is to get them both on an ASP.NET page and build the mechanics to tie the two Web Parts together. This is demonstrated next.

Connecting Web Parts on an ASP.NET Page

When in the process of connecting Web Parts, remember that you need a provider Web Part and a consumer Web Part. These items are detailed in Listings 17-16 and 17-17, respectively. When working with the process of connecting Web Parts, it is not simply a matter of placing both of these items on the page to get the connections to take place. In addition to this step, you have to wire the Web Parts together.

This wiring of Web Part connections is done through the WebPartManager control that is discussed at the beginning part of this chapter. The ASP.NET page used for this example is detailed in Listing 17-18.

Listing 17-18: The ASP.NET page that connects two Web Part controls

```
<%@ Page Language="VB" %>
<%@ Register Namespace="Wrox.ConnectionManagement"
    TagPrefix="connectionControls" %>

<html xmlns="http://www.w3.org/1999/xhtml">
<head runat="server">
    <title>Connecting Web Parts</title>
</head>
<body>
    <form id="form1" runat="server">
    <div>
        <asp:WebPartManager ID="WebPartManager1" runat="server">
            <StaticConnections>
                <asp:WebPartConnection ID="WebPartConnection1"
                 ConsumerID="ModifyableCalendar1"
                 ConsumerConnectionPointID="CalendarTitleConsumer"
                 ProviderID="TextBoxChanger1"
                 ProviderConnectionPointID="TextBoxStringProvider">
                </asp:WebPartConnection>
            </StaticConnections>
        </asp:WebPartManager>
        <table cellpadding="3">
            <tr valign="top">
                <td style="width: 100px">
                    <asp:WebPartZone ID="WebPartZone1" runat="server">
                        <ZoneTemplate>
                            <connectionControls:TextBoxChanger
                             ID="TextBoxChanger1"
                             runat="server" Title="Provider Web Part" />
                        </ZoneTemplate>
                    </asp:WebPartZone>
                </td>
                <td style="width: 100px">
```

```
                    <asp:WebPartZone ID="WebPartZone2" runat="server">
                        <ZoneTemplate>
                            <connectionControls:ModifyableCalendar
                             ID="ModifyableCalendar1" runat="server"
                             Title="Consumer Web Part" />
                        </ZoneTemplate>
                    </asp:WebPartZone>
                </td>
            </tr>
        </table>
    </div>
    </form>
</body>
</html>
```

This ASP.NET page that utilizes Web Parts contains a single two-cell table. Each cell in the table contains a single WebPartZone control — `WebPartZone1` and `WebPartZone2`.

Before connecting the Web Parts, the new custom Web Part controls are registered in the ASP.NET page using the `@Register` page directive. This directive simply points to the namespace `Wrox.Connection-Management`. This is the namespace used by the interface and the two custom Web Part controls.

Each of the custom Web Parts is placed within its own WebPartZone control. The two Web Part controls are tied together using the WebPartManager control.

```
<asp:WebPartManager ID="WebPartManager1" runat="server">
   <StaticConnections>
      <asp:WebPartConnection ID="WebPartConnection1"
       ConsumerID="ModifyableCalendar1"
       ConsumerConnectionPointID="CalendarTitleConsumer"
       ProviderID="TextBoxChanger1"
       ProviderConnectionPointID="TextBoxStringProvider">
      </asp:WebPartConnection>
   </StaticConnections>
</asp:WebPartManager>
```

The WebPartManager server control nests the defined connection inside of the `<StaticConnections>` section of the declaration. The definition is actually accomplished using the WebPartConnection server control. This control takes four important attributes required in order to make the necessary connections. The first set of two attributes deals with definitions of the consumer settings. Of these, the `ConsumerID` attribute references the name of the control on the ASP.NET page (through its ID attribute) and the `ConsumerConnectionPointID` references the ID of the object working as the connection point for the consumer. Looking back, you find this is the `RetrieveTitle()` method shown in the following code snippet:

```
<ConnectionConsumer("Calendar Title Consumer", "CalendarTitleConsumer")> _
 Public Sub RetrieveTitle(ByVal Provider As IStringForCalendar)
    _myProvider = Provider
 End Sub
```

The second set of attributes required by the WebPartConnection deals with the provider Web Part. The first attribute of this set is the `ProviderID` attribute that makes reference to the name of the control on the

ASP.NET page, which is considered the provider. The second attribute, `ProviderConnectionPointID` is quite similar to the `ConsumerConnectionPointID` attribute, but the `ProviderConnectionPointID` attribute references the ID of the object working as the provider in the connection process.

```
<ConnectionProvider("Provider for String From TextBox", "TextBoxStringProvider")> _
Public Function TextBoxStringProvider() As IStringForCalendar
    Return Me
End Function
```

Running this page gives you the results illustrated in Figure 17-25.

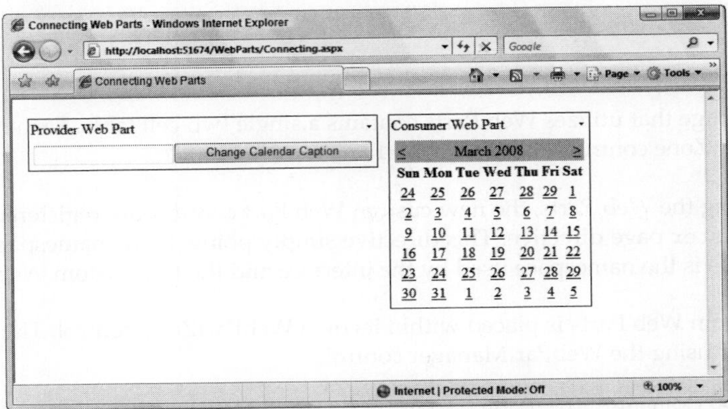

Figure 17-25

If you type any text string in the text box in the provider Web Part on the page and click the button within this control, the Calendar control uses this `String` value as its value for the `Caption` property. This is demonstrated in Figure 17-26.

Consumer Web Part

This is the new caption!

<			March 2008			>
Sun	Mon	Tue	Wed	Thu	Fri	Sat
24	25	26	27	28	29	1
2	3	4	5	6	7	8
9	10	11	12	13	14	15
16	17	18	19	20	21	22
23	24	25	26	27	28	29
30	31	1	2	3	4	5

Figure 17-26

As you can see from this example, you take a lot of steps to take to make this happen, but the steps aren't too difficult. In this example, a simple `String` object was passed from one Web Part to another. You could, however, use the exact same process to pass more complex objects (even custom objects) or larger items such a `DataSet` object.

Understanding the Difficulties in Dealing with Master Pages When Connecting Web Parts

You should note one final consideration about dealing with connecting Web Parts on your ASP.NET pages. You might have already realized that this process gets rather difficult when you are working with ASP.NET pages that make use of the master page capability provided by ASP.NET.

You are allowed only a single WebPartManager control on an ASP.NET page. Many times, when you are working with master pages, it makes a lot of sense to put this control in the master page itself rather than in the content pages that make use of the master page. If you are taking this approach, it does not make much sense to start using WebPartConnection controls within the master page. You can easily have controls with the same ID on multiple content pages. If you do so, the references made within the WebPartConnection control might not be meant for these other controls. For this reason, you need to make use of the ProxyWebPartManager control.

Suppose you have a master page with a WebPartManger control. In this case, the WebPartManager control can be rather simple, as shown here:

```
<asp:WebPartManager ID="WebPartManager1" runat="server">
</asp:WebPartManager>
```

With this WebPartManager control on your `.master` page, you ensure this single instance manages the Web Parts contained in each and every content page making use of this particular master page.

Next, if a content page making use of this master page is attempting to connect some Web Parts, you must place a ProxyWebPartManger control on the content page itself. This instance of the ProxyWeb-PartManager is where you define the connections for the Web Parts on this particular content page. This is illustrated in the following code snippet:

```
<asp:ProxyWebPartManager ID="ProxyWebPartManager1" runat="server">
   <StaticConnections>
      <asp:WebPartConnection ID="WebPartConnection1"
       ConsumerID="ModifyableCalendar1"
       ConsumerConnectionPointID="CalendarTitleConsumer"
       ProviderID="TextBoxChanger1"
       ProviderConnectionPointID="TextBoxStringProvider">
      </asp:WebPartConnection>
   </StaticConnections>
</asp:ProxyWebPartManager>
```

Summary

This chapter introduced you to the WebPartManager, WebPartZone, and the WebPart controls. Not only do these controls allow for easy customization of the look-and-feel of either the Web Parts or the zones in which they are located, but also the framework provided can be used to completely modify the behavior of these items.

This chapter also showed you how to create your own custom Web Part controls. Creating your own controls was always one of the benefits provided by ASP.NET, and this benefit has been taken one step further with the capability to now create Web Part controls. Web Part controls enable you to take advantage of some of the more complex features that you do not get with custom ASP.NET server controls.

You may find the Portal Framework to be one of the more exciting features of ASP.NET 3.5; you may like the idea of creating completely modular and customizable Web pages. End users like this feature, and it is quite easy for developers to implement. Just remember that you do not have to implement every feature explained in this chapter; with the framework provided, however, you can choose the functionality that you want.

18

HTML and CSS Design with ASP.NET

When HTML was first introduced by Tim Berners-Lee, it was intended to be a simple way for researchers using the Internet to format and cross-link their research documents. At the time, the Web was still primarily text-based; therefore, the formatting requirements for these documents were fairly basic. HTML needed only a small handful of basic layout concepts such as a title, paragraph, headers, and lists. As the Web was opened up to the general public, graphical browsers were introduced, and as requirements for formatting Web pages continued to expand, newer versions of HTML were introduced. These newer versions expanded the original capabilities of HTML to accommodate the new, rich graphical browser environment, allowing table layouts, richer font styling, images, and frames.

While all of these improvements to HTML were helpful, HTML still proved to be inadequate for allowing developers to create complex, highly stylized Web pages. Therefore, in 1994 a new technology called Cascading Style Sheets was introduced. CSS served as a complementary technology to HTML, giving developers of Web pages the power they needed to finely control the style of their Web pages.

As the Web has matured, CSS has gained popularity as developers realized that it has significant advantages over standard HTML styling capabilities. Unlike HTML, which was originally conceived as primarily a layout mechanism, CSS was conceived from the beginning to provide rich styling capabilities to Web pages. The cascading nature of CSS makes it easy to apply styles with a broad stroke to an entire application, and only where necessary override those styles. CSS makes it easy to externally define Web site style information, allowing for a clear separation of Web page style and structure. CSS also allows developers to greatly reduce the file size of a Web page, which translates into faster page load times and reduced bandwidth consumption.

While the point of this chapter is not to convince you that CSS is the best solution for styling your Web site, it will help you understand how you can leverage these technologies in your ASP.NET-based Web applications. It will start with a brief overview of CSS and how it works with HTML, and then move into creating Web sites in Visual Studio using HTML and CSS. Finally, you look at how you can use ASP.NET and CSS together.

Caveats

While this chapter includes a lot of great information about HTML and CSS, and how you can use them in conjunction with ASP.NET and Visual Studio 2008, there are several caveats you should be aware of.

First, because there is no way that a single chapter can begin to cover the entire breadth of HTML and CSS, if you are looking for an in-depth discussion of these topics, you can check out the Wrox title *Beginning CSS: Cascading Style Sheets for Web Design, 2nd Edition*, by Richard York (Wiley Publishing, Inc., 2007).

Second, because CSS is simply a specification, it is up to each browser vendor to actually interpret and implement that specification. As is so often the case in Web development, each browser has its own quirks in how it implements (or sometimes does not implement) different CSS features. While the samples in this chapter were tested on Internet Explorer 7, you should make sure to thoroughly test your Web sites in multiple browsers on multiple platforms in order to ensure that your CSS is rendering appropriately in each browser you are targeting.

Finally, the DOCTYPE you use in your Web pages can influence how the browser applies the CSS styles included in your Web page. You should understand how different DOCTYPES influence the browser's rendering process in your Web page.

HTML and CSS Overview

From the beginning of the Web, continuing to today, HTML serves as the primary mechanism for defining the content blocks of your Web page, and is the easiest way to define the layout of your Web page. HTML includes a variety of layout tags you can use, including Table, List, and Grouping elements. You can combine these elements to create highly complex layouts in your Web page. Figure 18-1 illustrates a single Web page that defines a basic layout using a variety of HTML elements.

While this layout is interesting, it lacks all but the most basic styling. To solve this problem, many developers would be tempted to start adding HTML-based formatting tags. For example, if I wanted to change the font and color of the text in the first paragraph, I might change its HTML to something like this:

```
<font face="Arial" Color="Maroon">
```

In fact, in the early days of Web design tools, this is what most of them generated when the user added styling to their Web pages, and for a while, using Font tags looks like a great solution to the problem of styling your Web pages.

Web developers and designers quickly learned, however, that using the Font tag quickly leads to a mess of spaghetti HTML, with font tags being splattered throughout the HTML. Imagine that if, in the previous example, you not only wanted to set the control and color, but some of the work also needed to be bold, others needed to be a different color or font face, some a different font size, some underlined, and some displayed as superscript. Imagine how many font tags you would need then and how it would increase the weight of the Web page and decrease its maintainability. Using Font tags (and other style-related tags) meant that there was no longer a clear and clean separation between the structure and content of the Web page, but instead both were mashed together into a single complex document.

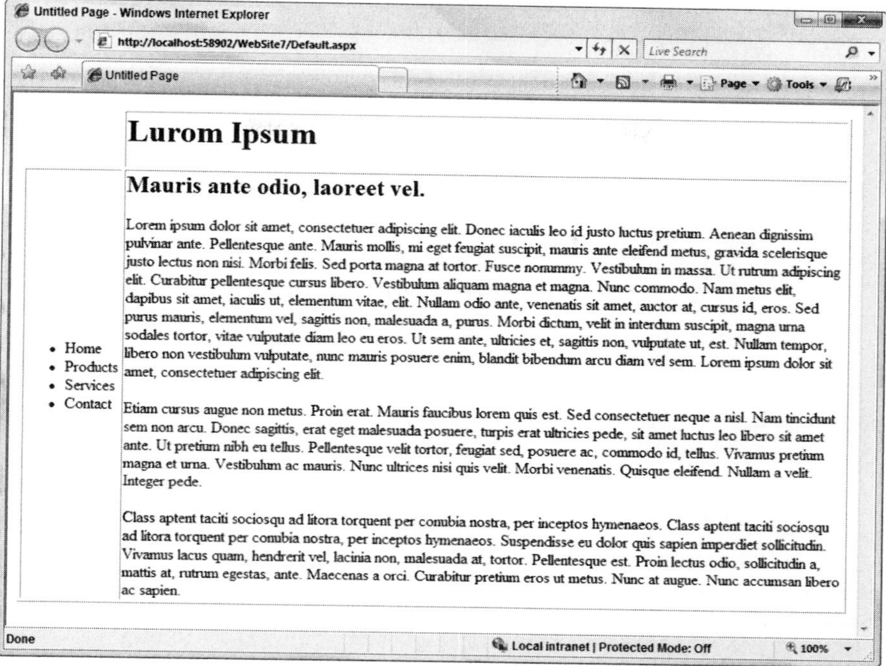

Figure 18-1

Introducing CSS

The introduction of CSS to the Web development and design world brought it back to a clean and elegant solution for styling Web pages. CSS meant a style could be defined in a single location for the entire Web site, and simply referenced on the elements requiring the style. Using CSS brought back the logic separation between Web page content and the styles used to display it.

Creating Style Sheets

Like HTML, CSS is an interpreted language. When a Web page request is processed by a Web server, the server's response can include style sheets, which are simply collections of CSS instructions. The style sheets can be included in the server's response in three different ways: through external style sheet files, internal style sheets embedded directly in the Web page, or inline styles sheets.

External Style Sheets

External Style Sheets are collections of CSS styles stored outside of the Web pages that will use them — generally files using the .css extension. Visual Studio makes it simple to add external style sheet files to your application by including a Style Sheet file template in the Add New Item dialog box, as shown in Figure 18-2.

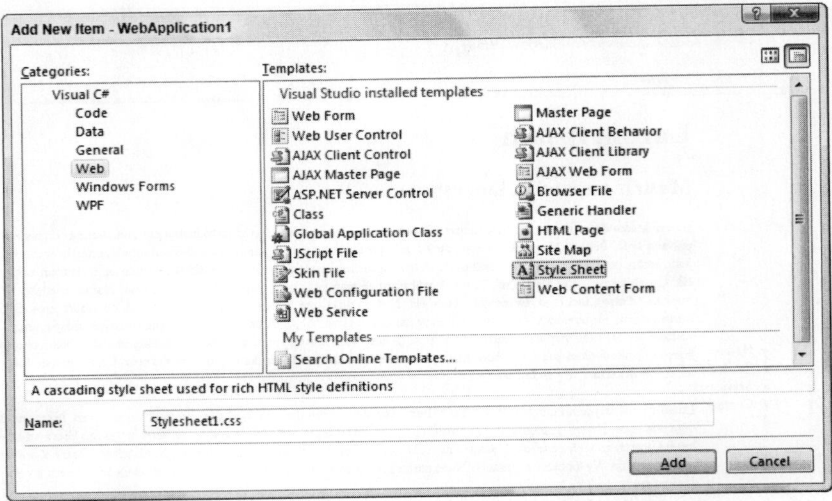

Figure 18-2

Once the Style Sheet is created by Visual Studio, it's easy to insert new styles. Visual Studio even gives you CSS IntelliSense when working with styles in the document, as shown in Figure 18-3.

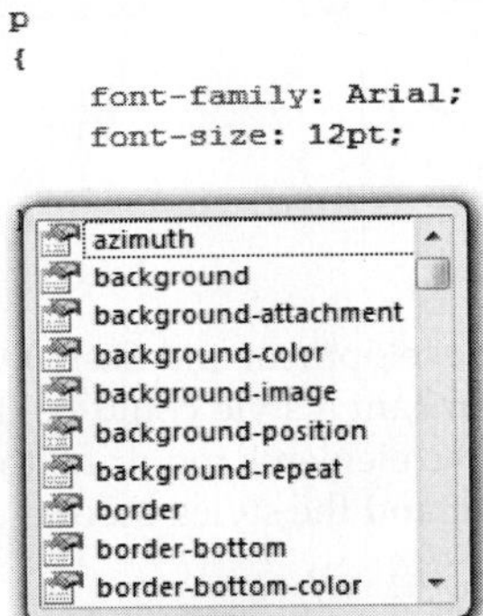

Figure 18-3

External style sheets are linked into Web pages using the HTML `<link>` tag. A single Web page can contain multiple style sheet references, as shown in Listing 18-1.

Listing 18-1: Using external style sheets in a Web page

```
<!DOCTYPE html PUBLIC "-//W3C//DTD XHTML 1.0 Transitional//EN"
"http://www.w3.org/TR/xhtml1/DTD/xhtml1-transitional.dtd">

<html xmlns="http://www.w3.org/1999/xhtml">
<head runat="server">
    <title>CSS Inheritance Sample</title>
    <link href="SampleStyles.css" rel="stylesheet" type="text/css" />
</head>
```

```
<body>
    <form id="form1" runat="server">
       <div>Lorum Ipsum</div>
    </form>
</body>
</html>
```

You can add multiple `link` tags to a single Web page in order to link several different style sheets into the page. You can also use the CSS `import` statement directly in your style sheet to actually link multiple style sheets together.

```
@import url("layout.css");
```

Using the `import` statement has the advantage that you can alter the style sheets linked together without having to modify every Web page in your site. Instead, you can simply link each page to a master external style sheet, which in turn will use the `import` statement to link in other external style sheets. Note that older browsers may not understand this syntax and will simply ignore the command.

Using external style sheets in your Web site offers several advantages. First, because external style sheets are kept outside of the Web pages in your site, it is easier to add a link tag to all of your Web pages rather than trying to manage the styles directly in each page. This also makes maintenance easier because, should you decide to update the style of your Web site in the future, you have a single location in which styles are kept. Finally, using external style sheets can also help the performance of your Web site by allowing the browser to take advantage of its caching capabilities. Like other files downloaded by the browser, the style sheets will be cached on the client once they have been downloaded.

Internal Style Sheets

Internal style sheets are collections of CSS styles that are stored internally in a single Web page. The styles are located inside of the HTML `<style>` tag, which is generally located in the `<head>` section of the Web page. An example of internal style sheets is shown in Listing 18-2.

Listing 18-2: Using internal style sheets in a Web page

```
<!DOCTYPE html PUBLIC "-//W3C//DTD XHTML 1.0 Transitional//EN"
"http://www.w3.org/TR/xhtml1/DTD/xhtml1-transitional.dtd">

<html xmlns="http://www.w3.org/1999/xhtml">
<head runat="server">
    <title>CSS Inheritance Sample</title>
    <style type="text/css">
        div
        {
              font-family:Arial;
        }
    </style>
</head>
<body>
    <form id="form1" runat="server">
       <div>Lorum Ipsum</div>
    </form>
</body>
</html>
```

It is important when you create internal style sheets that when you create style blocks, you make sure to include the `type` attribute with the style tag so the browser knows how to properly interpret the block. Additionally, as with external style sheets, Visual Studio also gives you IntelliSense support to make it easy for you to add properties.

Inline Styles

Inline styles are CSS styles that are applied directly to an individual HTML element using the element's `Style` attribute which is available on most HTML elements. An example of inline styles is shown in Listing 18-3.

Listing 18-3: Using inline styles in a Web page

```
<!DOCTYPE html PUBLIC "-//W3C//DTD XHTML 1.0 Transitional//EN"
"http://www.w3.org/TR/xhtml1/DTD/xhtml1-transitional.dtd">

<html xmlns="http://www.w3.org/1999/xhtml">
<head runat="server">
    <title>CSS Inheritance Sample</title>
</head>
<body>
    <form id="form1" runat="server">
       <div style="font-family:Arial;">Lorum Ipsum</div>
    </form>
</body>
</html>
```

CSS Rules

Regardless of how they are stored, once CSS styles are sent from the server to the client, the browser is responsible for parsing the styles and applying them to the appropriate HTML elements in the Web page. If a style is stored in either an external or internal style sheet, the styles will be defined as a CSS rule. Rules are what the browser uses to determine what styling to apply, and to what HTML elements it should.

Inline styles do not need to be defined as a rule because they are automatically applied to the element they are included with. Therefore, the browser does not need to select the elements to apply it to.

A rule is made up of two parts, the Selector and the Properties. Figure 18-4 shows an example of a CSS rule.

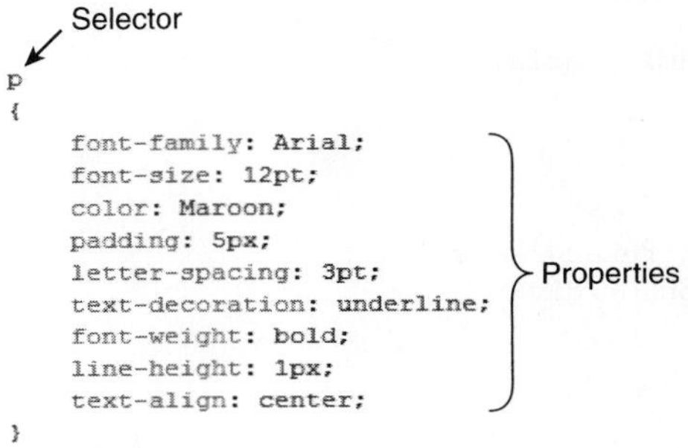

Selector

```
p
{
    font-family: Arial;
    font-size: 12pt;
    color: Maroon;
    padding: 5px;
    letter-spacing: 3pt;
    text-decoration: underline;
    font-weight: bold;
    line-height: 1px;
    text-align: center;
}
```

Properties

Figure 18-4

Selectors

The Selector is the portion of the rule that dictates exactly how the Web browser should select the elements to apply the style to. CSS includes a variety of types of selectors, each of which defines a different element selection technique

Universal Selectors

The Universal Selector indicates that the style should apply to any element in the Web page. The sample that follows shows a Universal Selector, which would change the font of any element that supports the font-family property to Arial.

```
*
{
    font-family:Arial;
}
```

Type Selectors

The Type Selector allows you to create a style that applies to a specific type of HTML element. The style will then be applied to all elements of that type in the Web page. The following sample shows a Type Selector configured for the HTM paragraph tag, which will change the font family of all `<p>` tags in the Web page to Arial.

```
p
{
    font-family:Arial;
}
```

Descendant Selectors

Descendant Selectors allow you to create styles that target HTML elements that are descendants of a specific type of element. The following sample demonstrates a style that will be applied to any `<span>` tag that is a descendant of a `<div>`.

```
div span
{
    font-family:Arial;
}
```

Child Selectors

The Child Selector is similar to the Descendant Selector except unlike the Descendant Selector, which searches the entire descendant hierarchy of an element, the Child Selector restricts its element search to only those elements who are direct children of the parent element. The following code shows a modification of the Descendant Selector, making it a Child Selector.

```
div > span
{
    font-family:Arial;
}
```

Attribute Selectors

An Attribute Selector allows you to define a style that is applied to elements based on the existence of element attributes rather than the actual element name. For example, the following sample creates a style that is applied to any element in the Web page that has the `href` attribute set.

```
*[href]
{
    font-family:Arial;
}
```

Note that Attribute Selectors are not supported by Internet Explorer 6 or earlier, or by the Visual Studio 2008 design surface.

Adjacent Selectors

Adjacent selectors allow you to select HTML elements that are immediately adjacent to another element type. For example, in an unordered list, you may want to highlight the first list item and then have all the following items use a different style. You can use an Adjacent Selector to do this, which is shown in the following sample:

```
li
{
    font-size:xx-large;
}

li+li
{
    font-size:medium;
}
```

In this sample, a default Type Selector has been created for the list item element (`<li>`), which will change the font size of the text in the element to extra, extra large. However, a second Adjacent Selector has been created, which will override the Type Selector for all list items after the first, changing the font size back to normal.

Class Selectors

Class Selectors are a special type of CSS selector that allows you to apply a style to any element with a specific Class name. The Class name is defined in HTML using the Class attribute, which is present on almost every element. Class Selectors are distinguished from other Selector types by prefixing them with a single period (.).

```
.title
{
    font-size:larger;
    font-weight:bold;
}
```

This CSS rule would then be applied to any element whose class attribute value matched the rule name, an example of which is shown here:

```
<div class="title">Lorum Ipsum</div>
```

When creating Class Selectors, note that the class name may not begin with a numeric character. Also, CSS class names can contain only alphanumeric characters. Spaces, symbols, and even underscores are not allowed. Finally, you should make sure that you match the casing of your class name when using it in the HTML. While CSS itself is not case sensitive, some HTML DocTypes dictate that the `class` and `id` attributes be treated as case sensitive.

ID Selectors

ID Selectors are another special type of CSS Selector that allows you to create styles that target elements with specific ID values. ID Selectors are distinguished from other Selector types by prefixing them with a hash mark (#).

```
#title
{
    font-size:larger;
    font-weight:bold;
}
```

This CSS rule would be applied to any element whose `id` attribute value matched the Rule name, an example of which is shown here:

```
<div id="title">Lorum Ipsum</div>
```

Pseudo Classes

CSS also includes a series of pseudo class selectors that give you additional options in creating Style rules. Pseudo classes can be added to other selectors to allow you to create more complex rules.

First-Child Pseudo Class

The first-child pseudo class allows you to indicate that the rule should select the first child element M of an element N. The following is an example of using the first-child pseudo class:

```
#title p:first-child
{
    font-size:xx-small;
}
```

The Rule defined above states that the style should be applied to the first paragraph tag found within any element with an `id` attribute value of `title`. In the following HTML, that means that the text `First Child` would have the style applied to it:

```
<div id="title">Lorum <p>First Child</p><p>Second Child</p> Ipsum</div>
```

Note that the Visual Studio 2008 design surface does not support the first-child pseudo class; therefore, even though the style may be rendered properly in the browser, you may not get an accurate preview on the design surface.

Link Pseudo Classes

CSS includes a number of pseudo classes specifically related to anchor tags. These special pseudo classes allow you to define styles for the different states of an anchor tag.

```
a:link
{
    color:Maroon;
}
a:visited
{
    color:Silver;
}
```

In this sample, two rules have been created, the first of which applies a style to the unvisited links in a page, while the second applies a different style to the visited links.

Dynamic Pseudo Classes

The dynamic pseudo classes are special CSS classes that are applied by the browser based on actions performed by the end user such as hovering over an element, activating an element, or giving an element focus.

```
a:hover
{
    color:Maroon;
}
a:active
{
    color:Silver;
}
a:focus
{
    color:Olive;
}
```

While the sample demonstrates the use of the dynamic pseudo classes with the anchor tag, they can be used with any HTML element. Note, however, that support for the dynamic pseudo classes in different browsers varies.

Language Pseudo Class

The language pseudo class allows you to define specific Rules based on the end user's language settings.

```
:lang(de)
{
    quotes: '«' '»' '\2039' '\203A'
}
```

In this sample, the `lang` pseudo class is used to set the quotes for a Web page that is German. The `lang` pseudo class is not supported by IE 7.

Pseudo Elements

CSS also includes several pseudo elements, which allow you to make selections of items in the Web page that are not true elements.

The pseudo elements available are: first-line, first-letter, before, and after. The following samples demonstrate the use of these.

```
p:first-line
{
    font-style:italic;
}
p:first-letter
{
    font-size:xx-large;
}
```

The pseudo first-line and first-letter elements allow you to apply special styling to the first line and first letter of a content block.

```
p:before
{
    content: url(images/quote.gif);
}
p:after
{
    content: '<<end>>';
}
```

The pseudo `before` and `after` elements allow you to insert content before or after the targeted element, in this case a paragraph element. The content you insert can be a URL, string, Quote character, counter, or the value of an attribute of the element.

Selector Grouping

When creating CSS rules, CSS allows you group several selectors together into a single rule. The following sample demonstrates a single rule that combines three type selectors:

```
h1, h2, h3
{
    color:Maroon;
}
```

This rule then results in the fore-color of the text content of any h1, h2, or h3 tag being maroon.

Selector Combinations

CSS also allows you to combine multiple Selector types. For example, you can create Class selectors that target specific HTML elements in addition to matching the `Class` attribute value.

Listing 18-4: Combining multiple Selector types in a single CSS rule

```
<!DOCTYPE html PUBLIC "-//W3C//DTD XHTML 1.0 Transitional//EN"
"http://www.w3.org/TR/xhtml1/DTD/xhtml1-transitional.dtd">

<html xmlns="http://www.w3.org/1999/xhtml">
<head id="Head1" runat="server">

    <style type="text/css">
        .title
        {
            font-family:Courier New;
        }

        div.title
        {
            font-family:Arial;
        }
    </style>
</head>
<body>
    <form id="form1" runat="server">
        <p class="title">Lorum Ipsum</p>
        <div class="title">Lorum Ipsum</div>
    </form>
</body>
</html>
```

Merged Styles

CSS also merges styles when several style rules are defined that apply to a given HTML element. For example, in the sample code that follows, a Class Selector and a Type Selector are defined. Both of these selectors apply to the paragraph element in the HTML. When the browser interprets the styles, it will merge both onto the element.

Listing 18-5: Merging styles from multiple rules onto a single element

```
<html xmlns="http://www.w3.org/1999/xhtml">
<head id="Head1" runat="server">

    <style type="text/css">
        .title
        {
            font-family:Courier New;
        }

        p
        {
            color:Green;
        }
    </style>
</head>
<body>
```

```
        <form id="form1" runat="server">
            <p class="title">Lorum Ipsum</p>
        </form>
    </body>
    </html>
```

As you can see in Figure 18-5, both the font and the color of the single paragraph element have been styled, even though there were two separate style rules that defined the style.

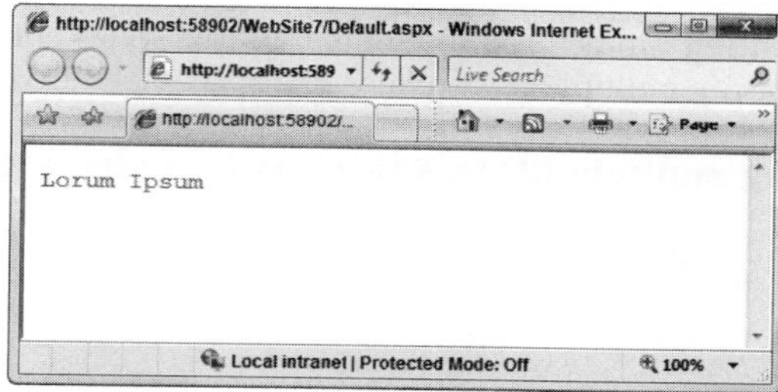

Figure 18-5

You can also merge multiple styles by defining multiple rules using different Selector types. If a single HTML element matches all of the rules, the styles from each rule will be merged together. Listing 18-6 shows an example where a single element matches multiple rules.

Listing 18-6: Multiple Selector matches on a single element

```
<!DOCTYPE html PUBLIC "-//W3C//DTD XHTML 1.0 Transitional//EN"
"http://www.w3.org/TR/xhtml1/DTD/xhtml1-transitional.dtd">

<html xmlns="http://www.w3.org/1999/xhtml">
<head runat="server">
    <title>CSS Inheritance Sample</title>
    <style type="text/css">
        p
        {
            font-family:Arial;
            color:Blue;
        }

        p#book
        {
            font-size:xx-large;
        }

        p.title
        {
            font-family: Courier New;
        }
    </style>
</head>
```

Continued

```
<body>
    <form id="form1" runat="server">
        <p id="book" class="title" style="letter-spacing:5pt;">Lorum Ipsum</p>
    </form>
</body>
</html>
```

In this case, because the paragraph tag defines the `id`, `class`, and `style` attributes, each of the Style rules match; therefore, each of their styles get merged onto the element.

Finally the class attribute itself can be used to merge multiple styles onto the same element. The class attribute allows you to specify multiple class names in a space-delimited string.

Listing 18-7: Assigning multiple Class Selectors to a single element

```
<!DOCTYPE html PUBLIC "-//W3C//DTD XHTML 1.0 Transitional//EN"
"http://www.w3.org/TR/xhtml1/DTD/xhtml1-transitional.dtd">

<html xmlns="http://www.w3.org/1999/xhtml">
<head runat="server">
    <title>CSS Inheritance Sample</title>
    <style type="text/css">
        p.title
        {
            font-family: Courier New;
            letter-spacing:5pt;
        }

        p.summer
        {
            color:Blue;
        }

        p.newproduct
        {
            font-weight:bold;
            color:Red;
        }
    </style>
</head>
<body>
    <form id="form1" runat="server">
        <p class="title newproduct summer">Lorum Ipsum</p>
    </form>
</body>
</html>
```

In this case, the three classes — `title`, `summer`, and `newproduct` — have all been defined in the class attribute. This means that these three styles will be merged onto the paragraph element.

Note that, in this case, the order in which the CSS classes are defined in the internal stylesheet also influences how the styles are merged onto the paragraph tag. Even though the summer class is last in the list of classes defined in the Class attribute, the `newproduct` rule overrides the summer Rules color property because the `newproduct` Rule is defined after the summer rule in the internal style sheet.

CSS Inheritance

CSS includes the concept of style inheritance. This works because the browser views the different locations that a style can be defined in (external, internal, or inline) as a hierarchical structure. Figure 18-6 shows this inheritance by demonstrating how the `font-family` property of a paragraph type selector rule, defined in three different locations, could be overridden by other style rules.

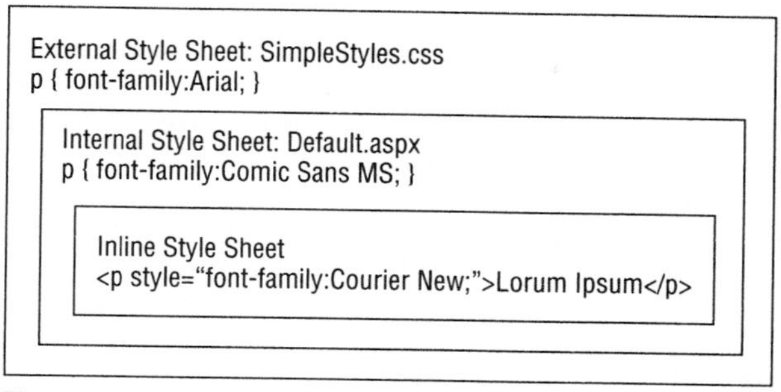

External Style Sheet: SimpleStyles.css
p { font-family:Arial; }

Internal Style Sheet: Default.aspx
p { font-family:Comic Sans MS; }

Inline Style Sheet
<p style="font-family:Courier New;">Lorum Ipsum</p>

Figure 18-6

As you can see from the figure, the rule of thumb is that the closer the style definition is to the element it applies to, the more precedence it will take. In this case, the paragraph text would ultimately be displayed using the Courier New font family because that is defined in the inline style.

Inheritance not only applies to styles kept in separate file locations, but also applies to styles within the same location, which means that sometimes you also need to think about the order in which you define your styles. For example, Listing 18-8 shows a style sheet that contains two Type Selectors, both targeting the paragraph element, both setting the `font-family` style property. Obviously both of these cannot be applied to the same element, so CSS simply chooses the Selector that is closest to the paragraph tags.

Listing 18-8: Using style overriding within the same Internal style sheet

```
<!DOCTYPE html PUBLIC "-//W3C//DTD XHTML 1.0 Transitional//EN"
"http://www.w3.org/TR/xhtml1/DTD/xhtml1-transitional.dtd">

<html xmlns="http://www.w3.org/1999/xhtml">
<head runat="server">

    <style type="text/css">
        p
        {
            font-family:Arial;
        }

        p
        {
            font-family: Courier New;
        }
    </style>
</head>
<body>
```

Continued

```
        <form id="form1" runat="server">
            <p>Lorum Ipsum</p>
        </form>
    </body>
    </html>
```

Running this sample, you will see that the font applied is the Courier New font.

Note that you should be careful when combining styles from external style sheets and internal style sheets. Remember that the browser will ultimately choose the style that is defined closest to the specific elements. This means that as the browser begins to parse the Web page, internal styles defined before external styles are considered further away from the HTML elements. Thus, the browser will use the styles located in the external style sheet. If you plan on storing style rules in both internal and external style sheets, you should remember to include the external style sheets <link> tags before the internal style sheets <style> block in your Web page.

Element Layout and Positioning

CSS is useful not only for styling elements in a page, but also for positioning elements as well. CSS actually gives you a much more flexible system for positioning elements than HTML itself. CSS bases the positioning of elements in a Web page on something called the *box model*. Once an element's box behavior has been determined, it can be positioned using several different techniques.

The CSS Box Model

A core element of positioning in CSS is the box model. The box model defines how every element in HTML is treated by the browser as a rectangular box. The box comprises different parts, including margins, padding, borders, and content. Figure 18-7 shows how all of these elements are combined to form the box.

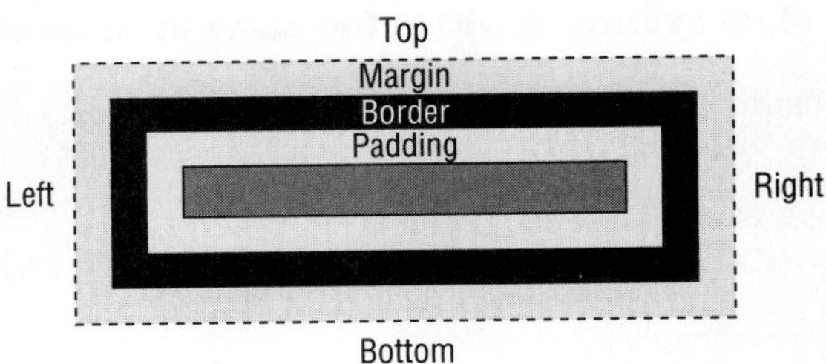

Figure 18-7

All of the separate elements that make up the box can influence its position within the Web page, and unless otherwise specified, each is given a default value of zero. The height and width of the element is equal to the height and width of the outer edge of the margin, which, as you can see in the previous image, is not necessarily the height and width of the content.

HTML provides you with two different types of boxes: the block box and the inline box. Block boxes are typically represented by tags such as `<p>`, `<div>`, or `<table>`. For block boxes, the containing block is used to determine the position of its child blocks. Additionally, block boxes can contain only inline or block boxes, but not both.

Listing 18-9 shows an example of a page containing a single parent block and two child block elements.

Listing 18-9: Creating block box elements

```
<div>
    Lorem ipsum dolor sit amet, consectetuer adipiscing elit.
    <div>
        Donec et velit a risus convallis porttitor.
        Vestibulum nisi metus, imperdiet sed, mollis condimentum, nonummy eu, magna.\
    </div>
    <div>Duis lobortis felis in est. Nulla eu velit ut nisi consequat vulputate.</div>
    Vestibulum vel metus. Integer ut quam. Ut dignissim, sapien sit amet malesuada
aliquam,
    quam quam vulputate nibh, ut pulvinar velit lorem at eros. Sed semper lacinia
diam. In
    faucibus nonummy arcu. Duis venenatis interdum quam. Aliquam ut dolor id leo
    scelerisque convallis. Suspendisse non velit. Quisque nec metus. Lorem ipsum
dolor sit
    amet, consectetuer adipiscing elit. Praesent pellentesque interdum magna.
</div>
```

The second box type is the inline box. Inline boxes are typically represented by tags such as `B`, `I`, and `SPAN` well as and actual text and content. Listing 18-10 shows how the previous listing can be modified to include inline boxes.

Listing 18-10: Creating inline box elements

```
<div>
    Lorem <b>ipsum</b> dolor sit amet, consectetuer adipiscing elit.
    <div>
        Donec et velit a risus <b>convallis</b> porttitor.
        Vestibulum nisi metus, imperdiet sed, mollis condimentum, nonummy eu, magna.
    </div>
    <div>Duis lobortis felis in est.
        <span>Nulla eu velit ut nisi consequat vulputate.</span>
    </div>
    <i>Vestibulum vel metus.</i> Integer ut quam. Ut dignissim, sapien sit amet
malesuada
    aliquam, quam quam vulputate nibh, ut pulvinar velit lorem at eros. Sed semper
lacinia
    diam. In faucibus nonummy arcu. Duis venenatis interdum quam. Aliquam ut dolor
id leo
    scelerisque convallis. Suspendisse non velit. Quisque nec metus. Lorem ipsum
dolor sit
    amet, consectetuer adipiscing elit. Praesent pellentesque interdum magna.
</div>
```

Rendering this page results in each block beginning a new line. Figure 18-8 shows the markup rendered in the browser.

The Visual Studio design surface can help you get a clear picture of the layout of a `div` as well. When you select an individual div element, the design surface highlights the selected element, as shown in Figure 18-9.

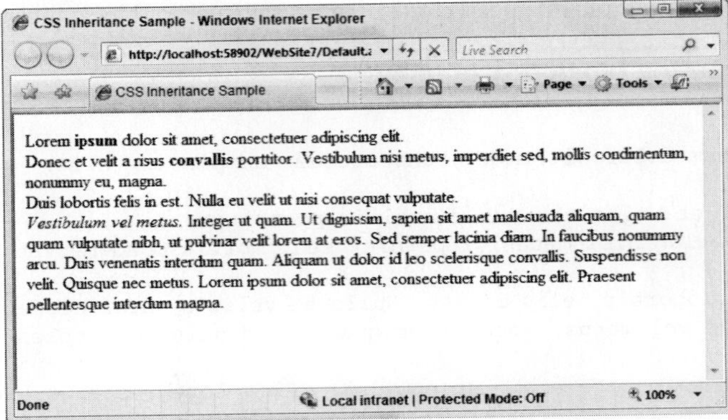

Figure 18-8

div em **ipsum** dolor sit amet, consectetuer adipiscing elit.
Donec et velit a risus **convallis** porttitor. Vestibulum nisi metus, imperdiet sed, mollis condimentum, nonummy eu, magna.
Duis lobortis felis in est. Nulla eu velit ut nisi consequat vulputate.
Vestibulum vel metus. Integer ut quam. Ut dignissim, sapien sit amet malesuada aliquam, quam quam vulputate nibh, ut pulvinar velit lorem at eros. Sed semper lacinia diam. In faucibus nonummy arcu. Duis venenatis interdum quam. Aliquam ut dolor id leo scelerisque convallis. Suspendisse non velit. Quisque nec metus. Lorem ipsum dolor sit amet, consectetuer adipiscing elit. Praesent pellentesque interdum magna.

Figure 18-9

At the beginning of this section, I stated that a block will always container either inline or block boxes, but it's interesting to note that in this case, because the first line of text contains an inline box, and the next contains a block box, it looks like the parent div is violating that rule. However, what is actually happening is that the browser automatically adds an anonymous block box around the first line of text when the page is rendered. Figure 18-10 highlights the block boxes as the browser sees them.

```
<div>
  Lorem <b>ipsum</b> dolor sit amet, consectetuer adipiscing elit.
  <div>Donec et velit a risus <b>convallis</b> porttitor.
  Vestibulum nisi metus, imperdiet sed, mollis condimentum,
  nonummy eu, magna.</div>
  <div>Duis lobortis felis in est. <span>Nulla eu velit ut nisi
  consequat vulputate.</span></div>
  <i>Vestibulum vel metus.</i> Integer ut quam. Ut dignissim,
  sapien sit amet malesuada aliquam, quam quam vulputate nibh,
  ut pulvinar velit lorem at eros. Sed semper lacinia diam. In
  faucibus nonummy arcu. Duis venenatis interdum quam. Aliquam ut
    dolor id leo scelerisque convallis. Suspendisse non velit.
    Quisque nec metus. Lorem ipsum dolor sit amet, consectetuer
    adipiscing elit. Praesent pellentesque interdum magna.
</div>
```

Figure 18-10

You can explicitly set which box behavior an element will exhibit by using the `position` attribute. For example, setting the `position` property on the second div, as shown here, results in the layout of the content changing.

```
<div style="display:inline;">Donec et velit a risus <b>convallis</b> porttitor.
Vestibulum nisi metus, imperdiet sed, mollis condimentum, nonummy eu, magna.</div>
```

Figure 18-11 shows how adding this property changes the rendering of the markup on the Visual Studio design surface. You can see that now, rather than the element being displayed on a new line, its content is simply continued from the previous block.

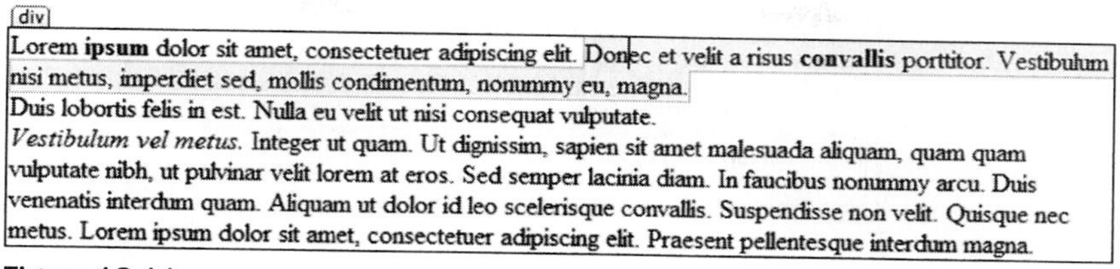

div
Lorem ipsum dolor sit amet, consectetuer adipiscing elit. Donec et velit a risus convallis porttitor. Vestibulum nisi metus, imperdiet sed, mollis condimentum, nonummy eu, magna.
Duis lobortis felis in est. Nulla eu velit ut nisi consequat vulputate.
Vestibulum vel metus. Integer ut quam. Ut dignissim, sapien sit amet malesuada aliquam, quam quam vulputate nibh, ut pulvinar velit lorem at eros. Sed semper lacinia diam. In faucibus nonummy arcu. Duis venenatis interdum quam. Aliquam ut dolor id leo scelerisque convallis. Suspendisse non velit. Quisque nec metus. Lorem ipsum dolor sit amet, consectetuer adipiscing elit. Praesent pellentesque interdum magna.

Figure 18-11

You can also set the display property to `none` to completely remove the element from the Web page layout. If you have elements whose `display` property is set to `none`, or an element whose `visibility` property is set to `hidden`, Visual Studio gives you the option of showing or hiding these elements on its design surface.

As shown in Figure 18-12, there are two options on the View menu that allow you to toggle the design surface visibility of elements with these properties set.

View
Website
Build
Debug
Data
Format
Table
Tools
Test
Developer
Ruler and Grid
Visual Aids
Formatting Marks
Designer
Shift+F7
Markup
Component Designer
Open
Open With...
Synchronize Document Outline
Details
Debug
Mixed Platforms
Show
Block Selection
Visible Borders
Empty Containers
Margins and Padding
CSS Display:none Elements
CSS Visibility:hidden Elements
ASP.NET Non-visual Controls
Template Region Labels

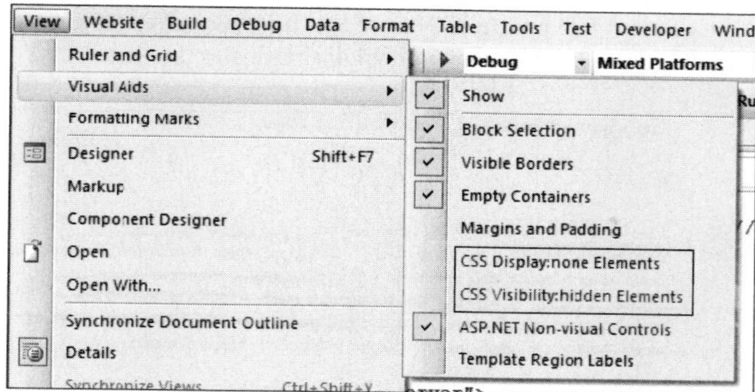

Figure 18-12

Positioning CSS Elements

CSS provides you with three primary positioning mechanisms: Normal, Absolute, and Relative. Each type offers a different behavior you can use to lay out the elements in your page. To specify the type of layout behavior you want an element to use, you can set the CSS `position` property. Each element can have its own position property set, allowing you to use multiple positioning schemes within the same Web page.

Normal Positioning

Using Normal positioning, block items flow vertically, and inline items flow horizontally, left to right. This is the default behavior, and is used when no other value is provided for the position property. Figure 18-13 demonstrates the layout of four separate blocks using Normal positioning.

As you can see, each block item flows vertically as expected.

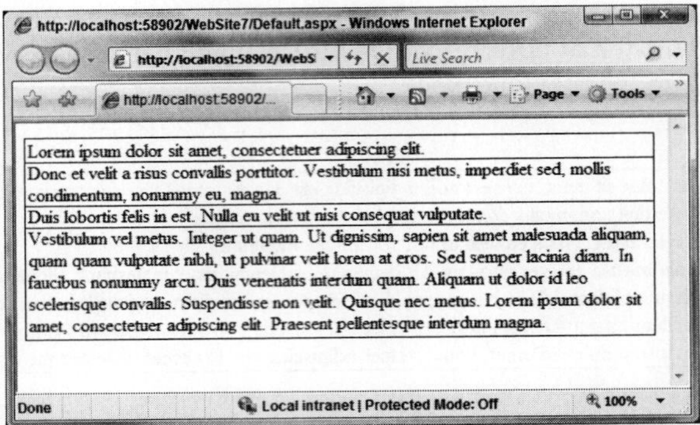

Figure 18-13

Relative Positioning

Using Relative positioning, elements are initially positioned using Normal layout. The surrounding boxes are positioned and then the box is moved based on its offset properties: `top`, `bottom`, `left`, and `right`. Figure 18-14 shows the same content as in the prior section, but now the third block box has been styled to use Relative positioning. Visual Studio is helping you out by providing positioning lines for the block, showing you that its top offset is being calculated based on the normal top position of the block, and the left offset from the normal left position. Visual Studio even lets you visually position the block by grabbing the element's tag label and dragging it over the design surface.

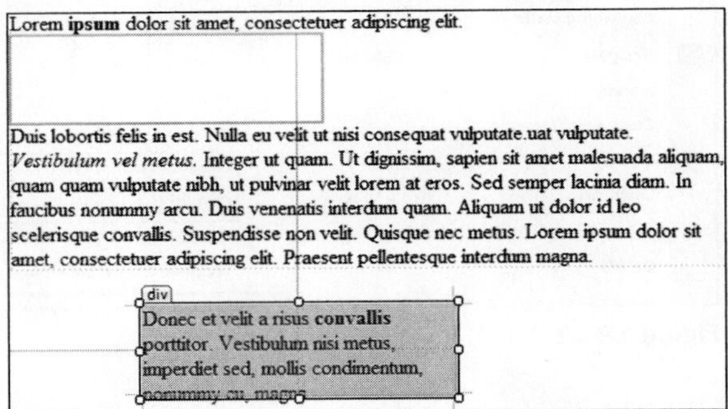

Figure 18-14

As you position the element on the design surface, the element's top and left values are being updated. You will end up with an element looking something like this:

```
<div style="position: relative;top: 214px;left: 62px;width: 239px;height: 81px">
    Donec et velit a risus <b>convallis</b> porttitor. Vestibulum nisi metus,
    imperdiet sed, mollis condimentum, nonummy eu, magna.
</div>
```

If you are using relative positioning and have both left and right offsets defined, the right will generally be ignored.

Absolute Positioning

Absolute positioning works much like relative positioning, except instead of an element calculating its offset position based on its position in the normal positioning scheme, the offsets are calculated based on the position of its closest absolutely positioned ancestor. If no element exists, then the ancestor is the browser window itself.

Figure 18-15 shows how blocks using absolute positioning are displayed on the Visual Studio design surface. As you can see, unlike the display of the relative positioned element shown in the previous section, this time the positioning lines extend all the way to the edge of the design surface. This is because the block is using the browser window to calculate its offset.

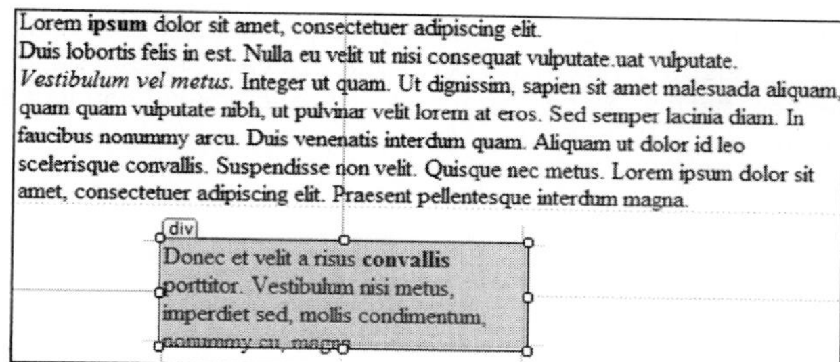

Figure 18-15

As with relative blocks, you can use the element's tag label to position the element on the page, and Visual Studio will automatically update the offset values. The block in Figure 18-15 would output an element that looks something like this:

```
<div style="position: absolute;top: 180px;left:94px;width:239px;height:81px;">
    Donec et velit a risus <b>convallis</b> porttitor. Vestibulum nisi metus,
    imperdiet sed, mollis condimentum, nonummy eu, magna.
</div>
```

Floating Elements

Another option for controlling the position of elements using CSS is the `float` property. The float property allows you to float an element to the left or right side of a block. The floating block is positioned vertically as it would normally be in normal position, but horizontally shifted as far left or right as possible. Listing 18-11 demonstrates floating the same block used in previous samples in this section.

Listing 18-11: Floating a block element to the right

```
<!DOCTYPE html PUBLIC "-//W3C//DTD XHTML 1.0 Transitional//EN"
"http://www.w3.org/TR/xhtml1/DTD/xhtml1-transitional.dtd">

<html xmlns="http://www.w3.org/1999/xhtml">
<head id="Head1" runat="server">
</head>
```

Continued

```
<body>
    <form id="form1" runat="server">
    <div id="asdas" class="werwer">
        Lorem ipsum dolor sit amet, consectetuer adipiscing elit.
    </div>
    <div style="float:right;width: 236px;">
        Donec et velit a risus <b>convallis</b> porttitor. Vestibulum nisi metus,
        imperdiet sed, mollis condimentum, nonummy eu, magna.
    </div>
    <div>Duis lobortis felis in est. Nulla eu velit ut nisi consequat vulputate.</div>
    <div>
        Vestibulum vel metus. Integer ut quam. Ut dignissim, sapien sit amet malesuada
        aliquam, quam quam vulputate nibh, ut pulvinar velit lorem at eros. Sed semper
        lacinia diam. In faucibus nonummy arcu. Duis venenatis interdum quam.
        Aliquam ut dolor id leo scelerisque convallis. Suspendisse non velit.
        Quisque nec metus. Lorem ipsum dolor sit amet, consectetuer adipiscing
        elit. Praesent pellentesque interdum magna.
    </div>

    </form>
</body>
</html>
```

The block has been modified to include the `float` property in its style. When this is done, Visual Studio correctly positions the element to the far right side of the page. This is shown in Figure 18-16.

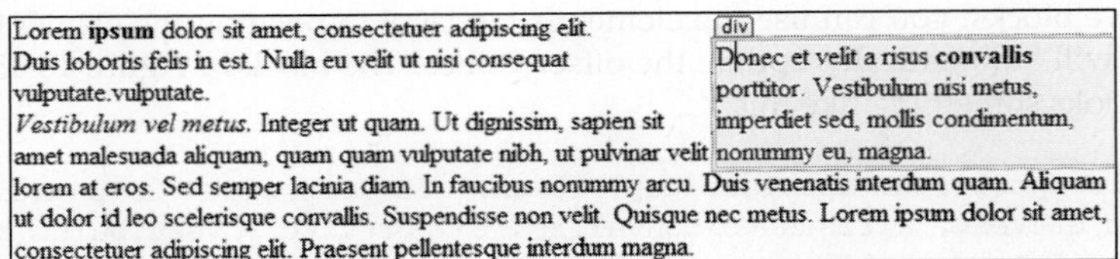

Figure 18-16

The !important Attribute

As you saw earlier in this chapter, the browser will choose to apply the closest style to the element, which can mean that properties of other applied styles may be overridden. As with many other rules in CSS, this too is not absolute. CSS provides a mechanism to circumvent this called the `!important` attribute. Properties that have this attribute applied can prevent other CSS rules from overriding its value. Listing 18-8 showed how the `font-family` property can be overridden. You can see how the `!important` attribute works by modifying this sample to use the attribute. This is shown in Listing 18-12.

Listing 18-12: Using the !important attribute to control style overriding

```
<html xmlns="http://www.w3.org/1999/xhtml">
<head id="Head1" runat="server">

    <style type="text/css">
        p
        {
            font-family:Arial !important;
```

```
        }

        p
        {
            font-family: Courier New;
        }
    </style>
</head>
<body>
    <form id="form1" runat="server">
       <p>Lorum Ipsum</p>
    </form>
</body>
</html>
```

In this case, rather than the paragraph being shown in Courier New, it will use the Arial font because it has been marked with the `!important` attribute.

Working with HTML and CSS in Visual Studio

Working with HTML and CSS to create compelling Web site designs can be quite daunting. Thankfully, Visual Studio provides you with a variety of tools that help simplify page layout and CSS management.

As you are probably already familiar with, Visual Studio includes a great WYSIWYG design surface. In prior versions of Visual Studio, this design surface used Internet Explorer to generate the design view, but with the release of Visual Studio 2008, Microsoft has completely rewritten the design surface to be completely independent of Internet Explorer.

In Visual Studio, when the Design View has focus, two additional menus become available: the Format menu and the Table menu. This is shown in Figure 18-17.

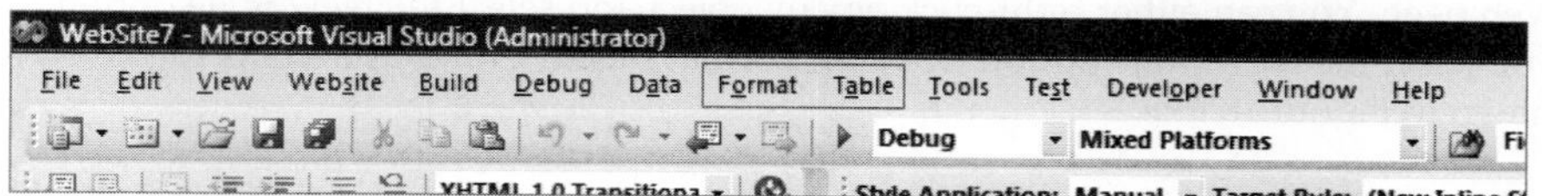

Figure 18-17

The Table menu, as you might guess, includes a set of tools that allow you to Insert, Delete, Select, and Modify the HTML Tables in your Web page. Selecting the Insert Table option from the Table menu opens the Insert Table dialog box shown in Figure 18-18, which allows you to easily specify properties of your table. You can define the number of table rows and columns, the cell padding and spacing, and border attributes, and when you click OK, Visual Studio automatically generates the appropriate table HTML in your Web page.

When you select an existing table in your Web page, the Table menu lets you insert and delete table rows, columns, and cells. The Modify menu option also allows you to split an existing cell into two separate cells, merge two cells into a single cell, and configure row and column sizing.

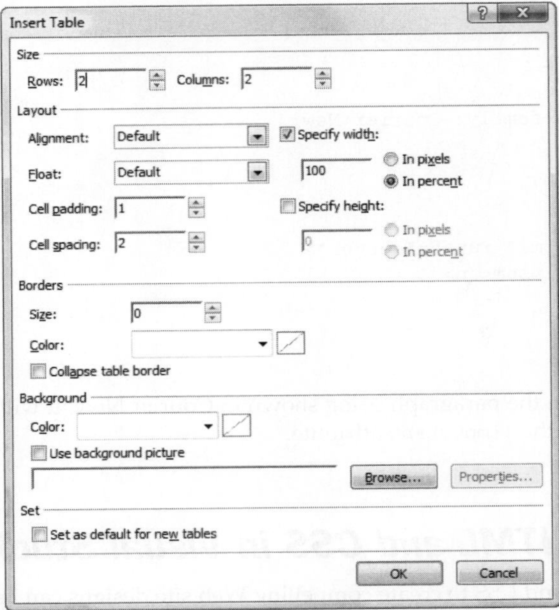

Figure 18-18

The Format menu includes basic element formatting options such as accessing the elements CSS class; setting fore and background colors, font, and position; and converting content to different types of lists.

Working with CSS in Visual Studio

Visual Studio 2008 offers a variety of new tools specifically designed to make working with CSS a much better experience. When working with the Visual Studio design surface, it's easy to create new styles for your Web page. You can either right-click on any object and select the New Style option from the content menu, or select the New Style option from the Format menu. Either option opens the New Style dialog box, shown in Figure 18-19.

This dialog box makes creating a new style a snap. To start, select the type of Selector you want to create from the Selector drop-down list. The list includes all of the available element types, or if you want to create a Class or ID selector, simply type the Style name into the Selector combo box.

Next, you need to select where you want to create the style from the Define In combo box. You can select Current Page to create an internal style sheet, New Style Sheet to create a new external style sheet file, or Existing Style Sheet to insert the style into an existing style sheet file. If you select either New Style Sheet or Existing Style Sheet, you will need to provide a value for the URL combo box.

Once you have entered the Selector you want to use and chosen a location to define the style, you can begin to set the styles properties. Simply select the property category from the Category list box and set the property values. The Preview area gives you a real-time preview of your new style. Additionally, the Description area shows you the actual property syntax created by Visual Studio. Click OK to close the dialog box.

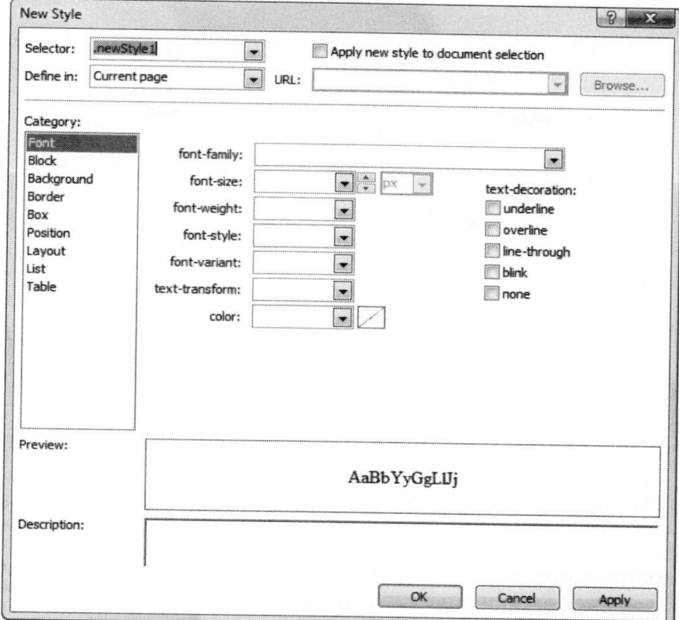

Figure 18-19

After you begin to create styles for your application, you need to be able to manage and apply those styles to elements in your application. Visual Studio 2008 introduces three new tool windows you can use to manage style sheets, apply styles to elements, and easily inspect the style properties applied to an element.

Manage Styles Tool Window

The first tool to explore is the Manage Styles tool window, which can be opened by selecting Manage Styles from the CSS Styles submenu of the view menu. This tool window, shown in Figure 18-20, gives you the birds-eye view of all of the styles available to the current Web page open in Visual Studio.

If you examine the contents of this tool, you see that the top portion includes two important links: New Style, which opens the New Style dialog box and allows you to create a new CSS styles as described earlier in this section, and the Attach Style Sheet link, which allows you to import new style sheets into a Web page. Using this option to attach style sheets to the Web page causes Visual Studio to insert `<link>` tags into your Web page for you.

Remember that you need to be careful about the order of your link tags and style blocks in order to make sure that your styles are applied correctly.

The next portion of the tool window displays all of the styles available to the page. Styles are color coded according to their selector type using colored bullets: blue for Type Selectors, green for Class Selectors, and red for ID Selectors. Styles used within the page are shown with a gray circle surrounding the colored bullet. Should your Web page contain multiple linked style sheets, or inline styles sheets, these styles would be grouped together making it easy to determine where a style is defined.

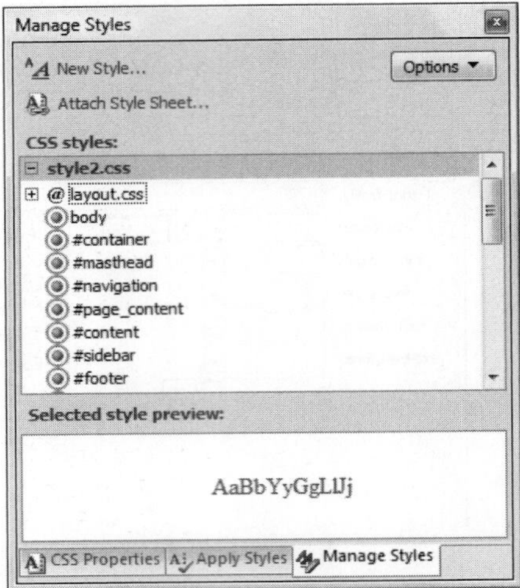

Figure 18-20

Also, as you can see in Figure 18-20, the tool window also allows you to view style sheets attached to the Web page via the CSS Imports statement. By expanding the `layout.css` node in the figure, you can see a listing of all of the styles included in that style sheet.

Finally, the bottom of the tool window includes a preview area, allowing you to see a real-time preview of each style.

Apply Styles Tool Window

The second tool to help you use CSS in Visual Studio 2008 is the Apply Styles tool window. As with the Manage Style tool window, the Apply Styles tool window gives you a much easier way of viewing the CSS Styles available in your application and applying them to elements in a Web page. From the tool window, you can attach CSS files to the Web page, making external CSS Styles available; select page styles to apply or remove from an element; and modify styles. As with the other CSS tool windows, the Apply Styles tool window displays the available styles based on the CSS inheritance order, with external styles being shown first, then the page styles section, and finally the inline styles shown last. The Apply Styles also is contextually sensitive to the currently selected element and will show only those styles in your application that can be applied to the element type. Styles are also grouped according to the CSS Selector style, with a different visual indicator for each Selector type.

The tool window shown in Figure 18-21 shows the styles available for an anchor tag `<a>`. The tool first shows all styles in the attached `styles2.css` file, then the styles in the current page, and finally, if applied, the element's inline styles. You can click on styles in any of these sections to apply them to the element.

The Apply Styles tool also includes the intelligence to properly apply multiple class selectors (hold the Ctrl key down while you click class selectors in the list), but prevent you from selecting multiple ID selectors because that would result in invalid CSS. The tool will also not let you deselect type selectors or inline styles.

Figure 18-21

CSS Properties Tool Window

The final new tool is the CSS Properties tool window shown in Figure 18-22. This handy tool window shows you all of the CSS properties that have been applied to the currently selected element. The tool window is composed of two separate parts: the Applied Rules list and the CSS properties grid.

The Applied Rules list shows all of the CSS rules that are applied to the selected element. The list is automatically sorted to show you the inheritance chain of the applied rules with the outermost rules at the top, moving down to the innermost rules. That means that rules contained in external CSS files are automatically sorted to the top of the list, and inline styles are sorted to the bottom. You can click on each rule in the list and alter the properties that are shown in the CSS Properties grid displayed below.

The CSS Properties grid works in a similar fashion to the standard .NET properties grid, showing you all of the CSS properties available for the element, and properties that have values set being shown in bold. Additionally, you can set property values for a CSS rule directly from the CSS property grid. Also in the CSS Properties tool window is a Summary button that allows you to change the display of the CSS Properties grid to show only properties that have values set. This can be very useful because HTML elements can have a large number of CSS properties.

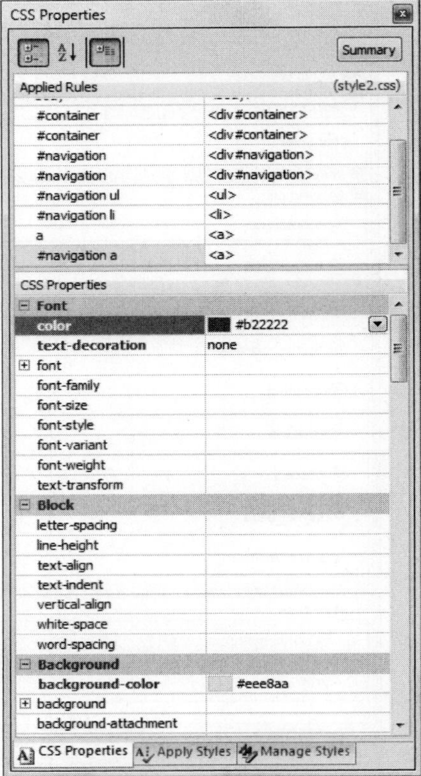

Figure 18-22

Because CSS also includes the concept of property inheritance, which is generally not available in a standard .NET object, the CSS Rules list and CSS Properties grid have been designed to help you fully understand where a specific property value applied to an element is being defined. As you click on each rule in the CSS Rules list, the CSS Properties grid is updated to reflect that rule's properties. What you will notice, however, is that certain properties have a red strikethrough. (See Figure 18-23.)

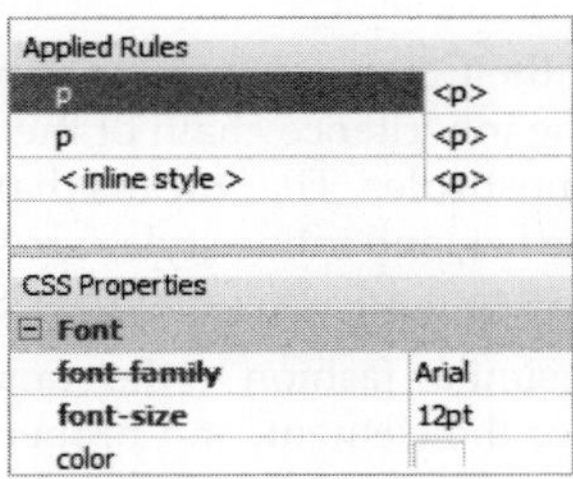

Figure 18-23

The strikethrough of the property indicates that the value of that property is being overridden by a rule closer to the element.

Managing Relative CSS Links in Masterpages

When working with CSS links in a masterpage, it can become difficult to manage the link to the CSS because the `Link` tag will not resolve a relative URL properly. A workaround for this is to define the tag as normal, but give it an ID. Then at runtime, in the Page Load event, simply set the `Href` of the link tag to the proper relative URL.

Styling ASP.NET Controls

Because ASP.NET controls simply render HTML markup, it is fairly easy to use CSS to style them. In fact, by default the controls actually already use inline CSS styles. You can see this in action by looking at the standard ASP.NET Button control. The standard method for styling ASP.NET controls like the Button is to provide values for the style related properties exposed by the control, which is shown here:

```
<asp:Button ID="Button1" runat="server" BackColor="#3333FF"
    BorderColor="Silver" BorderStyle="Double" BorderWidth="3px"
    Font-Bold="True" Font-Size="Large" ForeColor="White" Text="Button" />
```

When ASP.NET processes the Web page containing this control, it converts a button into a standard HTML Input tag, and it also converts the style properties you have set into CSS styles and applies them to the Input tag. The HTML and CSS rendered by the button is shown here:

```
<input type="submit" name="Button1" value="Button" id="Button1"
    style="color:White;background-color:#3333FF;border-color:Silver;
border-width:3px;
            border-style:Double;font-size:Large;font-weight:bold;" />
```

Setting style properties directly on the ASP.NET controls is a fast and simple way to style the ASP.NET controls in your application. Additionally, because these are standard properties on the controls, you can also set them at runtime using code.

```
protected void Page_Load(object sender, EventArgs e)
{
    this.Button1.BackColor = System.Drawing.ColorTranslator.FromHtml("#3333FF");
    this.Button1.BorderColor = System.Drawing.Color.Silver;
    this.Button1.BorderStyle= BorderStyle.Double;
    this.Button1.BorderWidth = Unit.Pixel(3);
    this.Button1.Font.Bold=true;
    this.Button1.Font.Size=FontUnit.Large;
    this.Button1.ForeColor=System.Drawing.Color.White;
}
```

While using properties to set style info is easy and convenient, it does have some drawbacks, especially when you use the same technique with larger repeating controls. First, using inline styles makes it difficult to control the styling of your Web site at a higher, more abstract level. If you want every button in your Web site to have a specific style, generally you would have to manually set that style on every Button control in your entire site. Themes can help solve this but are not always useful, especially when you are mixing ASP.NET controls with standard HTML controls.

Second, for controls that generate a large amount of repetitive HTML, such as the GridView, having inline styles on every element of each iteration of the HTML adds a lot of extra weight to your Web page.

Thankfully, every ASP.NET server control exposes a `CssClass` property. This property allows you to provide one or more Class Selector Rules to the control. While this technique is helpful, and usually better than letting the control render inline styles, it still requires you to be familiar with the HTML that the control will render at runtime. Listing 18-13 shows how you can use the `CssClass` attribute to style the ASP.NET Button control.

Listing 18-13: Styling a standard ASP.NET Button control using CSS

```
<!DOCTYPE html PUBLIC "-//W3C//DTD XHTML 1.0 Transitional//EN"
"http://www.w3.org/TR/xhtml1/DTD/xhtml1-transitional.dtd">

<html xmlns="http://www.w3.org/1999/xhtml">
<head id="Head1" runat="server">

    <link href="SpringStyles.css" rel="stylesheet" type="text/css" />
    <style>
        .search
        {
            color:White;
            font-weight:bolder;
            background-color:Green;
        }
    </style>
</head>
<body>
    <form id="form1" runat="server">
        <asp:Button ID="Button1" CssClass="search" runat="server" Text="Button" />
    </form>
</body>
</html>
```

In this case, the Button will have the search class applied to it.

ASP.NET 2.0 CSS–Friendly Control Adapters

If you are looking for more control over the rendering of the ASP.NET controls, especially so you can leverage more CSS-friendly development techniques, then you may want to look at the ASP.NET 2.0 CSS Friendly Control Adapters toolkit. This free download from Microsoft, available at `www.asp.net/cssadapters/`, leverages the ASP.NET Control Adapter model to allow you to have more control over how the in-box control renders.

The toolkit includes CSS-friendly adapters for five of the standard ASP.NET controls: Menu, TreeView, DetailsView, FormView, and DataList. The CSS controls adapters for these controls modify the HTML they render so that it can be more easily styled with CSS. In fact, when these controls render using the CSS Friendly Control Adapters toolkit, they actually ignore most of the style-related properties that exist on the default control API.

To use CSS with these controls, you simply create a style sheet using the same techniques that have been described earlier in the chapter. Next you create CSS rules that map to the different parts of the control. The documentation included with the adapters gives you a great detailed view of the new control structure and how that maps to the CSS classes you can create.

Summary

CSS is a great way to add style to your Web site. It's a powerful and convenient mechanism that allows you to create complex styles and layouts for your Web site. A full discussion of CSS would require much more time and space than we have here, so this chapter focused on showing you some of the basic concepts of CSS, the tools Visual Studio provides you to work more easily with CSS, and how you can use CSS with ASP.NET server controls. If you are interested in learning more about the details of CSS, we recommended that you pick up the Wrox title *Beginning CSS: Cascading Style Sheets for Web Design, 2nd Edition* by Richard York (Wiley Publishing, Inc., 2007).

This chapter provided an overview of CSS, introducing you to external, internal, and inline style sheets. You learned about the various Selector types the CSS offers and about basic layout and positioning of CSS elements, including how the box model works to influence element positions in your Web page.

Next you reviewed the tools available in Visual Studio that make working with CSS easy. New tools in Visual Studio 2008, including the Style Manager and CSS properties tool windows, make working with CSS easier than ever.

Finally, you looked at how you can use CSS with the ASP.NET server controls, and how you can use the ASP.NET 2.0 CSS Friendly Control Adapters to have more control over the style of the standard ASP.NET server controls.

19

ASP.NET AJAX

AJAX is definitely the hot buzzword in the Web application world at the moment. AJAX is an acronym for *Asynchronous JavaScript and XML* and, in Web application development, it signifies the capability to build applications that make use of the `XMLHttpRequest` object.

The creation and the inclusion of the `XMLHttpRequest` object in JavaScript and the fact that most upper-level browsers support it led to the creation of the AJAX model. AJAX applications, although they have been around for a few years, gained popularity after Google released a number of notable, AJAX-enabled applications such as Google Maps and Google Suggest. These applications demonstrated the value of AJAX.

Shortly thereafter, Microsoft released a beta for a new toolkit that enabled developers to incorporate AJAX features in their Web applications. This toolkit, code-named *Atlas* and later renamed ASP.NET AJAX, makes it extremely simple to start using AJAX features in your applications today.

The ASP.NET AJAX toolkit was *not* part of the default .NET Framework 2.0 install. If you are using the .NET Framework 2.0, it is an extra component that you must download from the Internet. If you are using ASP.NET 3.5, you don't have to worry about installing the ASP.NET AJAX toolkit as everything you need is already in place for you.

Understanding the Need for AJAX

Today, if you are going to build an application, you have the option of creating a thick-client or a thin-client application. A *thick-client* application is typically a compiled executable that end users can run in the confines of their own environment — usually without any dependencies elsewhere (such as an upstream server). Generally, the technology to build this type of application is the Windows Forms technology, or MFC in the C++ world. A *thin-client* application is typically one that has its processing and rendering controlled at a single point (the upstream server) and the results of the view are sent down as HTML to a browser to be viewed by a client. To work, this type of technology generally requires that the end user be connected to the Internet or an intranet of some kind.

Each type of application has its pros and cons. The thick-client style of application is touted as more fluid and more responsive to an end user's actions. In a Web-based application, the complaint has been for many years that every action by an end user takes numerous seconds and results in a jerky page refresh. In turn, the problem with a thick-client style of application has always been that the application sits on the end user's machine and any patches or updates to the application require you to somehow upgrade each and every machine upon which the application sits. In contrast, the thin-client application, or the Web application architecture, includes only one instance of the application. The application in this case is installed on a Web server and any updates that need to occur happen only to this instance. End users who are calling the application through their browsers always get the latest and greatest version of the application. That change model has a lot of power to it.

With this said, it is important to understand that Microsoft is making huge inroads into solving this thick- or thin-client problem and you now have options that completely change this model. For instance, the Windows Presentation Foundation technology recently offered by Microsoft and the new Silverlight technology blur the lines between the two traditional application styles.

Even with the existing Windows Forms and ASP.NET technologies to build the respective thick- or thin-client applications, each of these technologies are advancing to a point where they are even blurring the lines further. ASP.NET AJAX in particular is further removing any of the negatives that would have stopped you from building an application on the Web.

ASP.NET AJAX makes your Web applications seem more fluid than ever before. AJAX-enabled applications are responsive and give the end user immediate feedback and direction through the workflows that you provide. The power of this alone makes the study of this new technology and its incorporation into your projects of the utmost importance.

Before AJAX

So, what is AJAX doing to your Web application? First off, let's take a look at what a Web page does when it *does not* use AJAX. Figure 19-1 shows a typical request and response activity for a Web application.

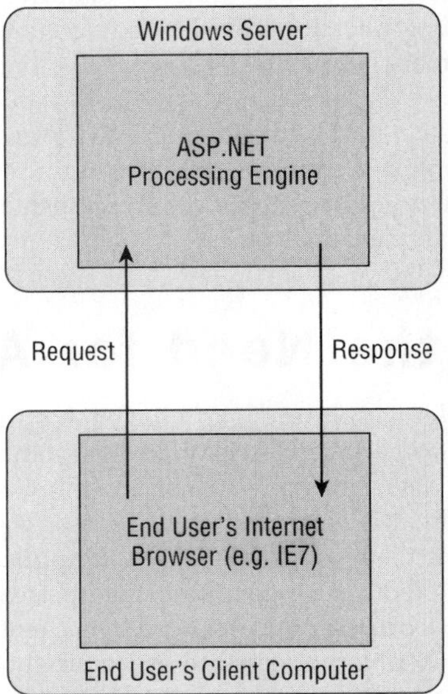

Figure 19-1

In this case, an end user makes a request from his browser to the application that is stored on your Web server. The server processes the request and ASP.NET renders a page, which is then sent to the requestor as a response. The response, once received by the end user, is displayed within the end user's browser.

From here, many events that take place within the application instance as it sits within the end user's browser causes the complete request and response process to reoccur. For instance, the end user might click a radio button, a check box, a button, a calendar, or anything else and this causes the entire Web page to be refreshed or a new page to be provided.

AJAX Changes the Story

On the other hand, an AJAX-enabled Web page includes a JavaScript library on the client that takes care of issuing the calls to the Web server. It does this when it is possible to send a request and get a response for just part of the page and using script; the client library updates that part of the page without updating the entire page. An entire page is a lot of code to send down to the browser to process each and every time. By just processing part of the page, the end user experiences what some people term "fluidity" in the page, which makes the page seem more responsive. The amount of code required to update just a portion of a page is less and produces the responsiveness the end user expects. Figure 19-2 shows a diagram of how this works.

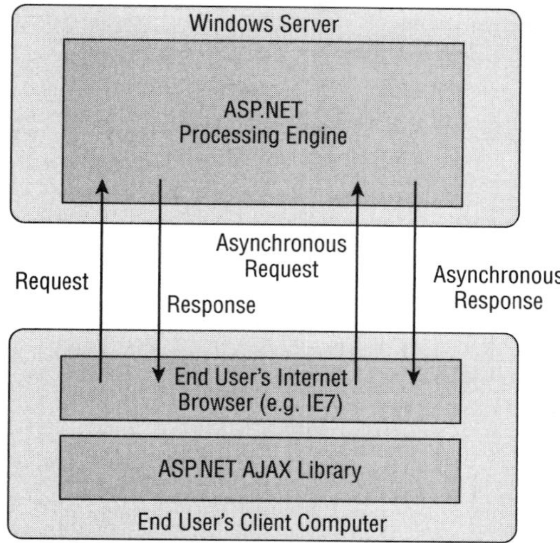

Figure 19-2

Figure 19-2, demonstrates that the first thing that happens is the entire page is delivered in the initial request and response. From there, any partial updates required by the page are done using the client script library. This library can make asynchronous page requests and update just the portion of the page that needs updating. One major advantage to this is that a minimal amount of data is transferred for the updates to occur. Updating a partial page is better than recalling the entire page for what is just a small change to the page.

AJAX is dependent upon a few technologies in order for it to work. The first is the `XMLHttpRequest` object. This object allows the browser to communicate to a back-end server and has been available in the

Microsoft world since Internet Explorer 5 through the MSXML ActiveX component. Of course, the other major component is JavaScript. This technology provides the client-side initiation to communication with the back-end services and takes care of packaging a message to send to any server-side services. Another aspect of AJAX is support for DHTML and the Document Object Model (DOM). These are the pieces that will change the page when the asynchronous response is received from the server. Finally, the last piece is the data that is being transferred from the client to the server. This is done in XML or more important, JSON.

Support for the `XMLHttpRequest` object gives JavaScript functions within the client script library the capability to call server-side events. As stated, typically HTTP requests are issued by a browser. It is also the browser that takes care of processing the response that comes from the server and then usually regenerates the entire Web page in the browser after a response is issued. This process is detailed in Figure 19-3.

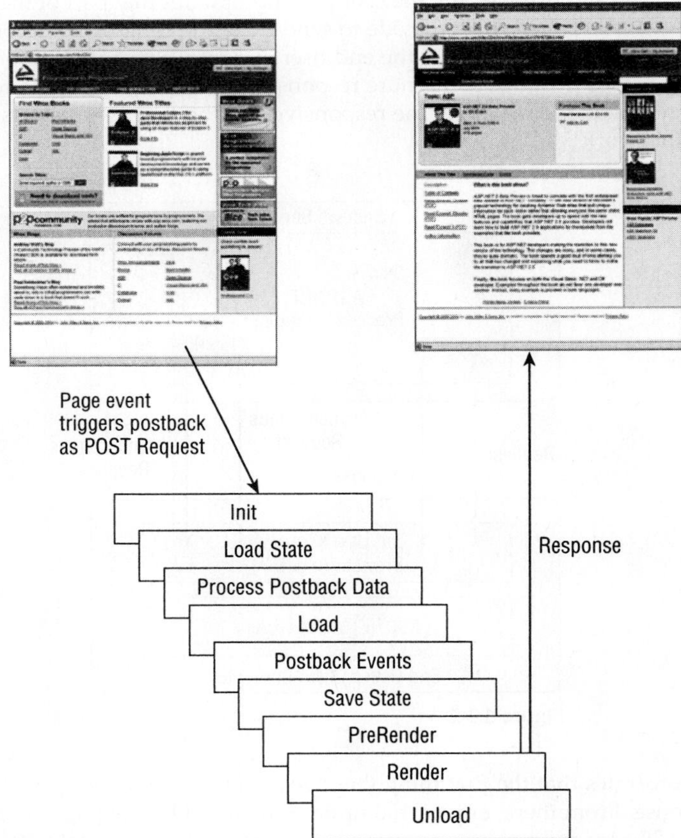

Figure 19-3

If you use the `XMLHttpRequest` object from your JavaScript library, you do not actually issue full page requests from the browser. Instead, you use a client-side script engine (which is basically a JavaScript function) to initiate the request and also to receive the response. Because you are also not issuing a request and response to deal with the entire Web page, you can skip a lot of the page processing because it is not needed. This is the essence of an AJAX Web request. It is illustrated in Figure 19-4.

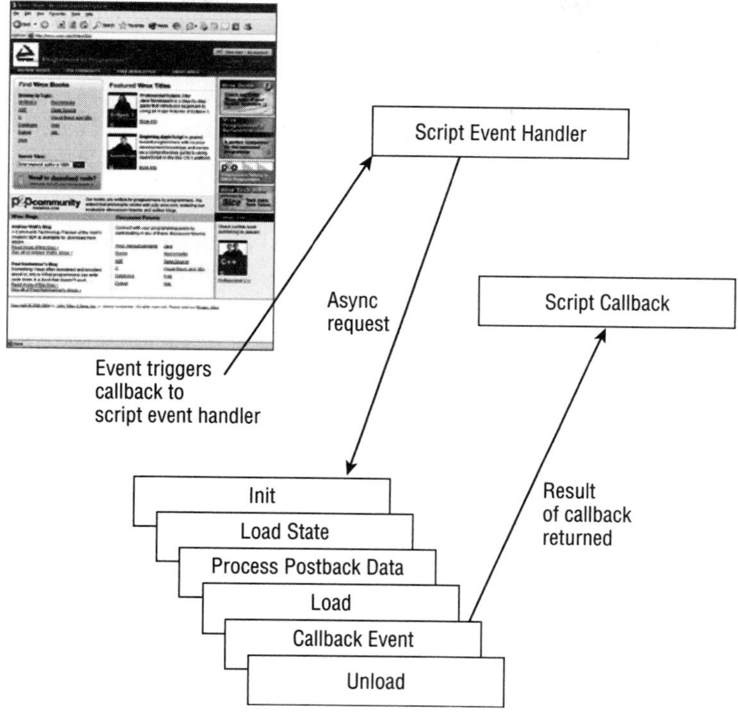

Figure 19-4

As stated, this opens the door to a tremendous number of possibilities. Microsoft has provided the necessary script engines to automate much of the communication that must take place in order for AJAX-style functionality to occur.

ASP.NET AJAX and Visual Studio 2008

Prior to Visual Studio 2008, the ASP.NET AJAX product used to be a separate installation that you were required to install on your machine and the Web server that you were working with. This release gained in popularity quite rapidly and is now a part of the Visual Studio 2008 offering. Not only is it a part of the Visual Studio 2008 IDE, but the ASP.NET AJAX product is also baked into the .NET Framework 3.5. This means that to use ASP.NET AJAX, you don't need to install anything if you are working with ASP.NET 3.5.

If you are using an ASP.NET version that is prior to the ASP.NET 3.5 release, then you need to visit `www.asp.net/AJAX` *to get the components required to work with AJAX.*

ASP.NET AJAX is now just part of the ASP.NET framework. When you create a new Web application, you do not have to create a separate type of ASP.NET application. Instead, all ASP.NET applications that you create are now AJAX-enabled.

If you have already worked with ASP.NET AJAX prior to this 3.5 release, you will find that there is really nothing new to learn. The entire technology is seamlessly integrated into the overall development experience.

Overall, Microsoft has fully integrated the entire ASP.NET AJAX experience so you can easily use Visual Studio and its visual designers to work with your AJAX-enabled pages and even have the full debugging story that you would want to have with your applications. Using Visual Studio 2008, you are now able to debug the JavaScript that you are using in the pages.

In addition, it is important to note that Microsoft focused a lot of attention on cross-platform compatibility with ASP.NET AJAX. You will find that the AJAX-enabled applications that you build upon the .NET Framework 3.5 can work within all the major up-level browsers out there (e.g., Firefox and Opera).

Client-Side Technologies

There really are two parts of the ASP.NET AJAX story. The first is a client-side framework and a set of services that are completely on the client-side. The other part of the story is a server-side framework. Remember that the client-side of ASP.NET AJAX is all about the client communicating asynchronous requests to the server-side of the offering.

For this reason, Microsoft offers a Client Script Library, which is a JavaScript library that takes care of the required communications. The Client Script Library is presented in Figure 19-5.

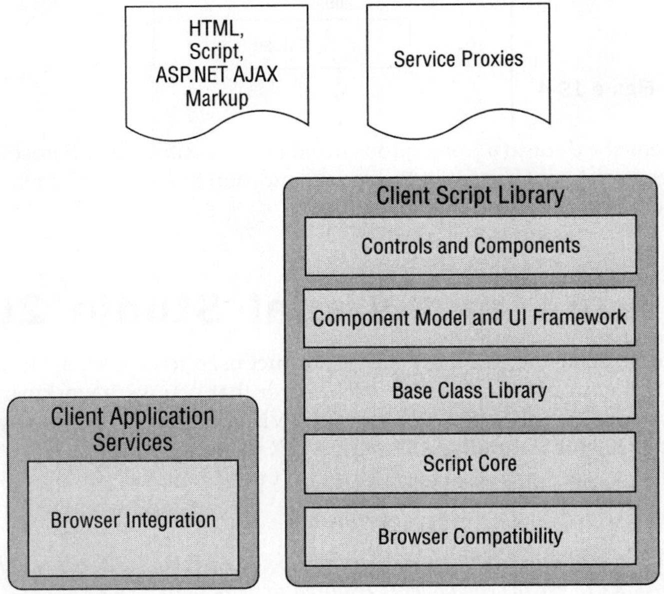

Figure 19-5

The Client Script Library provides a JavaScript, object-oriented interface that is reasonably consistent with aspects of the .NET Framework. Because browser compatibility components are built in, any work that you build in this layer or (in most cases) work that you let ASP.NET AJAX perform for you here will function with a multitude of different browsers. Also, several components support a rich UI infrastructure that produces many things that would take some serious time to build yourself.

The interesting thing about the client-side technologies that are provided by ASP.NET AJAX is that they are completely independent of ASP.NET. In fact, any developer can freely download the Microsoft AJAX Library (again from `asp.net/AJAX`) and use it with other Web technologies such as PHP (`php.net`) and Java Server Pages (JSP). With that said, really the entire Web story is a lot more complete with the server-side technologies that are provided with ASP.NET AJAX.

Server-Side Technologies

As an ASP.NET developer, you will most likely be spending most of your time on the server-side aspect of ASP.NET AJAX. Remember that ASP.NET AJAX is all about the client-side technologies talking back to the server-side technologies. You can actually perform quite a bit on the server-side of ASP.NET AJAX.

The server-side framework knows how to deal with client requests (e.g., putting responses in the correct format). The server-side framework also takes care of the marshalling of objects back and forth between JavaScript objects and the .NET objects that you are using in your server-side code. Figure 19-6 illustrates the server-side framework provided by ASP.NET AJAX.

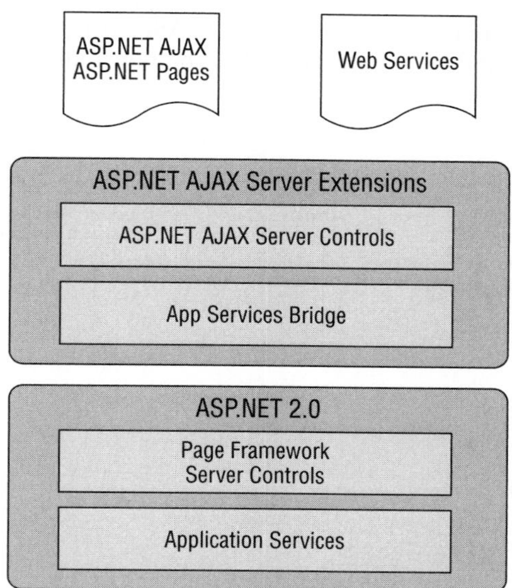

Figure 19-6

When you have the .NET Framework 3.5, you will have the ASP.NET AJAX Server Extensions on top of the core ASP.NET 2.0 Framework, the Windows Communication Foundation, as well as ASP.NET-based Web services (`.asmx`).

Developing with ASP.NET AJAX

There are a couple of types of Web developers out there. There are the Web developers who are used to working with ASP.NET and who have experience working with server-side controls and manipulating these controls on the server-side. Then there are developers who concentrate on the client-side and work with DHTML and JavaScript to manipulate and control the page and its behaviors.

With that said, it is important to realize that ASP.NET AJAX was designed for both types of developers. If you want to work more on the server-side of ASP.NET AJAX, you can use the new ScriptManager control and the new UpdatePanel control to AJAX-enable your current ASP.NET applications with little work on your part. All this work can be done using the same programming models that you are quite familiar with in ASP.NET.

Both the ScriptManager and the UpdatePanel controls are discussed later in this chapter.

In turn, you can also use the Client Script Library directly and gain greater control over what is happening on the client's machine. Next, this chapter looks at building a simple Web application that makes use of AJAX.

ASP.NET AJAX Applications

The next step is to build a basic sample utilizing this new framework. First create a new ASP.NET Web Site application using the New Web Site dialog. Name the project `AJAXWebSite`. You will notice (as shown here in Figure 19-7) that there is not a separate type of ASP.NET project for building an ASP.NET AJAX application because every ASP.NET application that you now build is AJAX-enabled.

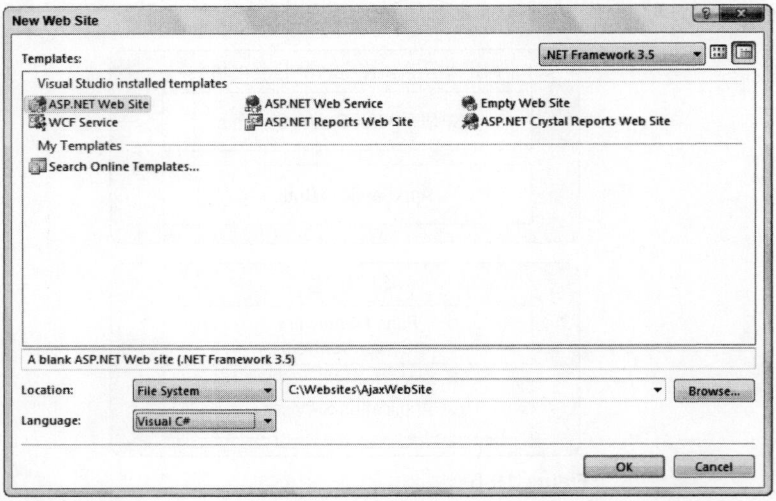

Figure 19-7

After you create the application, you will be presented with what is now a standard Web Site project. However, you may notice some additional settings in the `web.config` file that are new to the ASP.NET

3.5. At the top of the web.config file, there are new configuration sections that are registered that deal with AJAX. This section of web.config is presented in Listing 19-1.

Listing 19-1: The <configSections> element for an ASP.NET 3.5 application

```
<?xml version="1.0"?>

<configuration>
  <configSections>
     <sectionGroup name="system.web.extensions"
       type="System.Web.Configuration.SystemWebExtensionsSectionGroup,
        System.Web.Extensions, Version=3.5.0.0, Culture=neutral,
        PublicKeyToken=31BF3856AD364E35">
        <sectionGroup name="scripting"
          type="System.Web.Configuration.ScriptingSectionGroup,
            System.Web.Extensions, Version=3.5.0.0, Culture=neutral,
            PublicKeyToken=31BF3856AD364E35">
          <section name="scriptResourceHandler"
           type="System.Web.Configuration.ScriptingScriptResourceHandlerSection,
              System.Web.Extensions, Version=3.5.0.0, Culture=neutral,
              PublicKeyToken=31BF3856AD364E35"
            requirePermission="false"
           allowDefinition="MachineToApplication"/>
            <sectionGroup name="webServices"
             type="System.Web.Configuration.ScriptingWebServicesSectionGroup,
               System.Web.Extensions, Version=3.5.0.0, Culture=neutral,
               PublicKeyToken=31BF3856AD364E35">
               <section name="jsonSerialization"
                type="System.Web.Configuration.ScriptingJsonSerializationSection,
                   System.Web.Extensions, Version=3.5.0.0, Culture=neutral,
                   PublicKeyToken=31BF3856AD364E35" requirePermission="false"
                allowDefinition="Everywhere" />
               <section name="profileService"
                type="System.Web.Configuration.ScriptingProfileServiceSection,
                   System.Web.Extensions, Version=3.5.0.0, Culture=neutral,
                   PublicKeyToken=31BF3856AD364E35" requirePermission="false"
                allowDefinition="MachineToApplication" />
              <section name="authenticationService"
               type="System.Web.Configuration.ScriptingAuthenticationServiceSection,
                 System.Web.Extensions, Version=3.5.0.0, Culture=neutral,
                 PublicKeyToken=31BF3856AD364E35" requirePermission="false"
              allowDefinition="MachineToApplication" />
              <section name="roleService"
               type="System.Web.Configuration.ScriptingRoleServiceSection,
                  System.Web.Extensions, Version=3.5.0.0, Culture=neutral,
                  PublicKeyToken=31BF3856AD364E35" requirePermission="false"
               allowDefinition="MachineToApplication" />
            </sectionGroup>
          </sectionGroup>
     </sectionGroup>
  </configSections>

<!-- Configuraiton removed for clarity -->

</configuration>
```

With the `web.config` file in place (as provided by the ASP.NET Web Site project type), the next step is to build a simple ASP.NET page that does not yet make use of AJAX.

Building a Simple ASP.NET Page Without AJAX

The first step is to build a simple page that does not yet make use of the AJAX capabilities offered by ASP.NET 3.5. Your page needs only a Label control and Button server control. The code for the page is presented in Listing 19-2.

Listing 19-2: A simple ASP.NET 3.5 page that does not use AJAX

VB

```
<%@ Page Language="VB" %>

<script runat="server">
    Protected Sub Button1_Click(ByVal sender As Object, _
       ByVal e As System.EventArgs)

        Label1.Text = DateTime.Now.ToString()
    End Sub</script>

<html xmlns="http://www.w3.org/1999/xhtml">
<head runat="server">
    <title>My Normal ASP.NET Page</title>
</head>
<body>
    <form id="form1" runat="server">
    <div>
        <asp:Label ID="Label1" runat="server"></asp:Label>
        <br />
        <br />
        <asp:Button ID="Button1" runat="server" Text="Click to get machine time"
           onclick="Button1_Click" />
    </div>
    </form>
</body>
</html>
```

C#

```
<%@ Page Language="C#" %>

<script runat="server">
    protected void Button1_Click(object sender, EventArgs e)
    {
        Label1.Text = DateTime.Now.ToString();
    }
</script>
```

When you pull this page up in the browser, it contains only a single button. When the button is clicked, the Label control that is on the page is populated with the time from the server machine. Before the button is clicked, the page's code is similar to the code presented in Listing 19-3.

Listing 19-3: The page output for a page that is not using AJAX

```
<!DOCTYPE html PUBLIC "-//W3C//DTD XHTML 1.0 Transitional//EN"
 "http://www.w3.org/TR/xhtml1/DTD/xhtml1-transitional.dtd">

<html xmlns="http://www.w3.org/1999/xhtml">
<head><title>
 My Normal ASP.NET Page
</title></head>
<body>
    <form name="form1" method="post" action="Default.aspx" id="form1">
<div>
<input type="hidden" name="__VIEWSTATE" id="__VIEWSTATE"
 value="/wEPDwULLTE4OTg4OTc0MjVkZIgwrMMmvqXJHfogxzgZ92wTUORS" />
</div>
    <div>
        <span id="Label1"></span>
        <br />
        <br />
        <input type="submit" name="Button1" value="Click to get machine time"
         id="Button1" />
    </div>
<div>

 <input type="hidden" name="__EVENTVALIDATION" id="__EVENTVALIDATION"
  value="/wEWAgLFpoapCAKM54rGBkhUDe2q/7eVsROfd9QCMK6CwiI7" />
</div></form>
</body>
</html>
```

There is not much in this code. There is a little ViewState and a typical form that will be posted back to the `Default.aspx` page. When the end user clicks the button on the page, a full post back to the server occurs and the entire page is reprocessed and returned to the client's browser. Really, the only change made to the page is that the `<span id="Lable1"></span>` element is populated with a value, but in this case, the entire page is returned.

Building a Simple ASP.NET Page with AJAX

The next step is to build upon the page from Listing 19-2 and add AJAX capabilities to it. For this example, you will be adding some additional controls. Two of the controls to add are typical ASP.NET server controls — another Label and Button server control. In addition to these controls, you are going to have to add some ASP.NET AJAX controls.

In the Visual Studio 2008 toolbox, you will find a new section titled AJAX Extensions. This new section is shown in Figure 19-8.

From AJAX Extensions, add a ScriptManager server control to the top of the page and include the second Label and Button control inside the UpdatePanel control. The UpdatePanel control is a template server control and allows you to include any number of items within it (just as other templated ASP.NET server controls). When you have your page set up, it should look something like Figure 19-9.

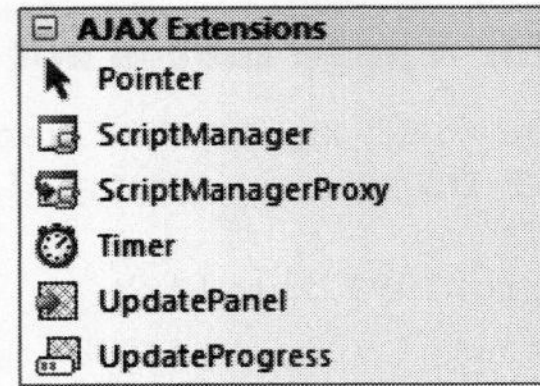

Figure 19-8

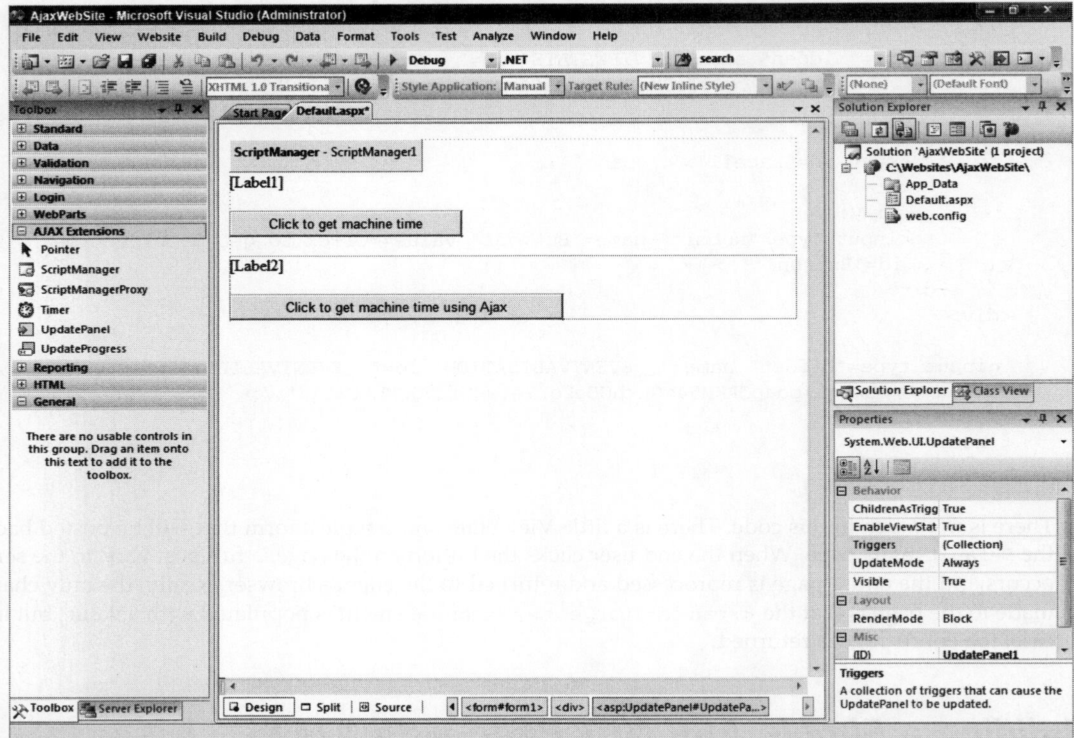

Figure 19-9

The code for this page is shown in Listing 19-4.

Listing 19-4: A simple ASP.NET AJAX page

VB

```
<%@ Page Language="VB" %>

<script runat="server">
    Protected Sub Button1_Click(ByVal sender As Object, _
      ByVal e As System.EventArgs)
        Label1.Text = DateTime.Now.ToString()
```

```
    End Sub

    Protected Sub Button2_Click(ByVal sender As Object, _
       ByVal e As System.EventArgs)
        Label2.Text = DateTime.Now.ToString()
    End Sub
</script>

<html xmlns="http://www.w3.org/1999/xhtml">
<head runat="server">
    <title>My ASP.NET AJAX Page</title>
</head>
<body>
    <form id="form1" runat="server">
    <div>
        <asp:ScriptManager ID="ScriptManager1" runat="server">
        </asp:ScriptManager>
        <asp:Label ID="Label1" runat="server"></asp:Label>
        <br />
        <br />
        <asp:Button ID="Button1" runat="server" Text="Click to get machine time"
            onclick="Button1_Click" />
        <br />
        <br />
        <asp:UpdatePanel ID="UpdatePanel1" runat="server">
            <ContentTemplate>
                <asp:Label ID="Label2" runat="server" Text=""></asp:Label>
                <br />
                <br />
                <asp:Button ID="Button2" runat="server"
                 Text="Click to get machine time using AJAX"
                 onclick="Button2_Click" />
            </ContentTemplate>
        </asp:UpdatePanel>
    </div>
    </form>
</body>
</html>
```

C#

```
<%@ Page Language="C#" %>

<script runat="server">
    protected void Button1_Click(object sender, EventArgs e)
    {
        Label1.Text = DateTime.Now.ToString();
    }

    protected void Button2_Click(object sender, EventArgs e)
    {
        Label2.Text = DateTime.Now.ToString();
    }
</script>
```

When this page is pulled up in the browser, it has two buttons. The first button causes a complete page postback and updates the current time in the Label1 server control. Clicking on the second button causes an AJAX asynchronous postback. Clicking this second button updates the current server time in the Label2 server control. When you click the AJAX button, the time in Label1 will not change at all, as it is outside of the UpdatePanel. A screenshot of the final result is presented in Figure 19-10.

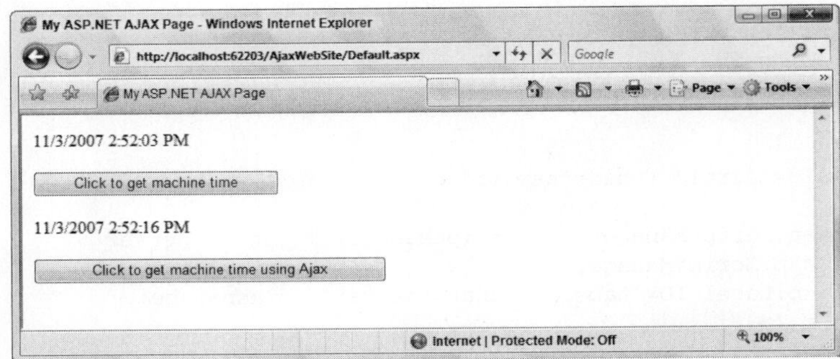

Figure 19-10

When you first pull up the page from Listing 19-4, the code of the page is quite different from the page that was built without using AJAX. Listing 19-5 shows the page results that you will see.

Listing 19-5: The page output for a page that is using AJAX

```
<html xmlns="http://www.w3.org/1999/xhtml">
<head><title>
My ASP.NET AJAX Page
</title></head>
<body>
    <form name="form1" method="post" action="Default.aspx" id="form1">
<div>
<input type="hidden" name="__EVENTTARGET" id="__EVENTTARGET" value="" />
<input type="hidden" name="__EVENTARGUMENT" id="__EVENTARGUMENT" value="" />
<input type="hidden" name="__VIEWSTATE" id="__VIEWSTATE"
 value="/wEPDwULLTE4NzE5NTc5MzRkZDRIzHpPZg4GaO9Hox9A/RnOflkm" />
</div>

<script type="text/javascript">
//<![CDATA[
var theForm = document.forms['form1'];
if (!theForm) {
    theForm = document.form1;
}
function __doPostBack(eventTarget, eventArgument) {
    if (!theForm.onsubmit || (theForm.onsubmit() != false)) {
        theForm.__EVENTTARGET.value = eventTarget;
        theForm.__EVENTARGUMENT.value = eventArgument;
        theForm.submit();
    }
}
```

```
//]]>
</script>

<script src="/AJAXWebSite/WebResource.axd?d=o84znEj-
 n4cYi0Wg0pFXCg2&amp;t=633285028458684000" type="text/javascript"></script>

<script src="/AJAXWebSite/ScriptResource.axd?
 d=FETsh5584DXpx8XqIhEM50YSKyR2GkoMoAqraYEDU5_
 gi1SUmL2Gt7rQTRBAw561SojJRQe0OjVI8SiYDjmpYmFP0
 CO8wBFGhtKKJwm2MeE1&amp;t=633285035850304000" type="text/javascript"></script>
<script type="text/javascript">
//<![CDATA[
if (typeof(Sys) === 'undefined') throw new Error('ASP.NET AJAX client-side
  framework failed to load.');
//]]>
</script>

<script src="/AJAXWebSite/ScriptResource.axd?
 d=FETsh5584DXpx8XqIhEM50YSKyR2GkoMoAqraYEDU5_
 gi1SUmL2Gt7rQTRBAw5617AYfmRViCoO21Z3XwZ33TGiC
 t92e_UOqfrP30mdEYnJYs09ulU1xBLj8TjXOLR1k0&amp;t=633285035850304000"
 type="text/javascript"></script>
    <div>
        <script type="text/javascript">
//<![CDATA[
Sys.WebForms.PageRequestManager._initialize('ScriptManager1',
document.getElementById('form1'));
Sys.WebForms.PageRequestManager.getInstance()._updateControls(['tUpdatePanel1'],
[], [], 90);
//]]>
</script>
        <span id="Label1"></span>
        <br />
        <br />
        <input type="submit" name="Button1" value="Click to get machine time"
         id="Button1" />
        <br />
        <br />
        <div id="UpdatePanel1">

                <span id="Label2"></span>
                <br />
                <br />
                <input type="submit" name="Button2" value="Click to get machine
                 time using AJAX" id="Button2" />
</div>
    </div>
<div>

 <input type="hidden" name="__EVENTVALIDATION" id="__EVENTVALIDATION"
value="/wEWAwLktbDGDgKM54rGBgK7q7GGCMYnNq57VIqmVD2sRDQqfnOsgWQK" />
</div>

<script type="text/javascript">
```

Continued

```
//<![CDATA[
Sys.Application.initialize();
//]]>
</script>
</form>
</body>
</html>
```

From there, if you click Button1 and perform the full-page postback, you get this entire bit of code back in a response — even though you are interested in updating only a small portion of the page! However, if you click Button2 — the AJAX button — you send the request shown in Listing 19-6.

Listing 19-6: The asynchronous request from the ASP.NET AJAX page

```
POST /AJAXWebSite/Default.aspx HTTP/1.1
Accept: */*
Accept-Language: en-US
Referer: http://localhost.:62203/AJAXWebSite/Default.aspx
x-microsoftAJAX: Delta=true
Content-Type: application/x-www-form-urlencoded; charset=utf-8
Cache-Control: no-cache
UA-CPU: x86
Accept-Encoding: gzip, deflate
User-Agent: Mozilla/4.0 (compatible; MSIE 7.0; Windows NT 6.0; SLCC1;
.NET CLR 2.0.50727; Media Center PC 5.0; .NET CLR 1.1.4322; .NET CLR
3.5.21004; .NET CLR 3.0.04506)
Host: localhost.:62203
Content-Length: 334
Proxy-Connection: Keep-Alive
Pragma: no-cache

ScriptManager1=UpdatePanel1%7CButton2&__EVENTTARGET=&__EVENTARGUMENT=&__VIEWSTATE=%
2FwEPDwULLTE4NzE5NTc5MzQPZBYCAgQPZBYCAgMPDxYCHgRUZXh0BRQxMS8zLzIwMDcgMjoxNzo1NSBQTW
RkZHZxUyYQG0M25t8U7vLbHRJuKlcS&__EVENTVALIDATION=%2FwEWAwKCxdk9AoznisYGArursYYI1844
hk7V466AsW31G5yIZ73%2Bc6o%3D&Button2=Click%20to%20get%20machine%20time%20using%20Aj
ax
```

The response for this request is shown in Listing 19-7:

Listing 19-7: The asynchronous response from the ASP.NET AJAX page

```
HTTP/1.1 200 OK
Server: ASP.NET Development Server/9.0.0.0
Date: Sat, 03 Nov 2007 19:17:58 GMT
X-AspNet-Version: 2.0.50727
Cache-Control: private
Content-Type: text/plain; charset=utf-8
Content-Length: 796
Connection: Close

239|updatePanel|UpdatePanel1|
                <span id="Label2">11/3/2007 2:17:58 PM</span>
                <br />
                <br />
                <input type="submit" name="Button2" value="Click to get machine
```

```
                    time using AJAX" id="Button2" />
|172|hiddenField|__VIEWSTATE|/wEPDwULLTE4NzE5NTc5MzQPZBYCAgQPZBYEAgMPDxYCHgRUZXh0BR
QxMS8zLzIwMDcgMjoxNzo1NSBQTWRkAgcPZBYCZg9kFgICAQ8PFgIfAAUUMTEvMy8yMDA3IDI6MTc6NTggU
E1kZGQ4ipZIg91+XSI/dqxFueSUwcrXGw==|56|hiddenField|__EVENTVALIDATION|/wEWAwKCz4mbCA
K7q7GGCAKM54rGBj8b4/mkKNKhV59qX9SdCzqU3AiM|0|asyncPostBackControlIDs|||0|postBackCo
ntrolIDs|||13|updatePanelIDs||tUpdatePanel1|0|childUpdatePanelIDs|||12|panelsToRefr
eshIDs||UpdatePanel1|2|asyncPostBackTimeout||90|12|formAction||Default.aspx|22|page
Title||My ASP.NET AJAX Page|
```

From Listing 19-7 here, you can see that the response is much smaller than an entire Web page! In fact, the main part of the response is only the code that is contained within the UpdatePanel server control and nothing more. The items at the bottom deal with the ViewState of the page (as it has now changed) and some other small page changes.

ASP.NET AJAX's Server-Side Controls

When you look at the AJAX Extensions section in the Visual Studio 2008 toolbox, you will notice that there are not many controls there at your disposal. The controls there are focused on allowing you to AJAX-enable your ASP.NET applications. They are enabling controls. If you are looking for more specific server controls that take advantage of the new AJAX model, then look at the ASP.NET AJAX Control Toolkit — a separate download that is covered in the next chapter.

The new ASP.NET AJAX server controls that come with ASP.NET 3.5 are discussed in the following table.

ASP.NET AJAX Server Control	Description
ScriptManager	A component control that manages the marshalling of messages to the AJAX-enabled server for the parts of the page requiring partial updates. Every ASP.NET page will require a ScriptManager control in order to work. It is important to note that you can have only a single ScriptManager control on a page.
ScriptManagerProxy	A component control that acts as a ScriptManager control for a content page. The ScriptManagerProxy control, which sits on the content page (or sub-page), works in conjunction with a required ScriptManager control that resides on the master page.
Timer	The Timer control will execute client-side events at specific intervals and allows specific parts of your page to update or refresh at these moments.
UpdatePanel	A container control that allows you to define specific areas of the page that are enabled to work with the ScriptManager. These areas can then, in turn, make the partial page postbacks and update themselves outside the normal ASP.NET page postback process.
UpdateProgress	A control that allows you to display a visual element to the end user to show that a partial-page postback is occurring to the part of the page making the update. This is an ideal control to use when you have long-running AJAX updates.

The next few sections of this chapter look at these new controls and how to use them within your ASP.NET pages.

The ScriptManager Control

Probably the most important control in your ASP.NET AJAX arsenal is the ScriptManager server control, which works with the page to allow for partial page rendering. You use a single ScriptManager control on each page that you want to use the AJAX capabilities provided by ASP.NET 3.5. When placed in conjunction with the UpdatePanel server control, AJAX-enabling your ASP.NET applications can be as simple as adding two server controls to the page and then you are ready to go!

The ScriptManager control takes care of managing the JavaScript libraries that are utilized on your page as well as marshalling the messages back and forth between the server and the client for the partial page rendering process. The marshalling of the messages can be done using either SOAP or JSON through the ScriptManager control.

If you place only a single ScriptManager control on your ASP.NET page, it takes care of loading the JavaScript libraries needed by ASP.NET AJAX. The page for this is presented in Listing 19-8.

Listing 19-8: An ASP.NET page that includes only the ScriptManager control

```
<%@ Page Language="VB" %>

<html xmlns="http://www.w3.org/1999/xhtml">
<head runat="server">
    <title>The ScriptManager Control</title>
</head>
<body>
    <form id="form1" runat="server">
    <div>
        <asp:ScriptManager ID="ScriptManager1" runat="server">
        </asp:ScriptManager>
    </div>
    </form>
</body>
</html>
```

From Listing 19-8, you can see that this control is like all other ASP.NET controls and needs only an `ID` and a `runat` attribute to do its work. The page output from this bit of ASP.NET code is presented in Listing 19-9.

Listing 19-9: The page output from the ScriptManager control

```
<html xmlns="http://www.w3.org/1999/xhtml">
<head><title>
 The ScriptManager Control
</title></head>
<body>
    <form name="form1" method="post" action="Default2.aspx" id="form1">
<div>
<input type="hidden" name="__EVENTTARGET" id="__EVENTTARGET" value="" />
<input type="hidden" name="__EVENTARGUMENT" id="__EVENTARGUMENT" value="" />
<input type="hidden" name="__VIEWSTATE" id="__VIEWSTATE"
 value="/wEPDwULLTEzNjQ0OTQ1MDdkZO9dCw2QaeC4D8AwACTbOkD1OX4h" />
</div>
```

```
<script type="text/javascript">
//<![CDATA[
var theForm = document.forms['form1'];
if (!theForm) {
    theForm = document.form1;
}
function __doPostBack(eventTarget, eventArgument) {
    if (!theForm.onsubmit || (theForm.onsubmit() != false)) {
        theForm.__EVENTTARGET.value = eventTarget;
        theForm.__EVENTARGUMENT.value = eventArgument;
        theForm.submit();
    }
}
//]]>
</script>

<script src="/AJAXWebSite/WebResource.axd?d=o84znEj-
 n4cYi0Wg0pFXCg2&amp;t=633285028458684000" type="text/javascript"></script>

<script src="/AJAXWebSite/ScriptResource.axd?d=
 FETsh5584DXpx8XqIhEM50YSKyR2GkoMoAqraYEDU5_gi1SUmL2Gt7rQTRBAw561SojJR
 Qe0OjVI8SiYDjmpYmFP0CO8wBFGhtKKJwm2MeE1&amp;t=633285035850304000"
 type="text/javascript"></script>
<script type="text/javascript">
//<![CDATA[
if (typeof(Sys) === 'undefined') throw new Error('ASP.NET AJAX client-side
 framework failed to load.');
//]]>
</script>

<script
src="/AJAXWebSite/ScriptResource.axd?d=FETsh5584DXpx8XqIhEM50YSKyR2GkoM
oAqraYEDU5
_gi1SUmL2Gt7rQTRBAw5617AYfmRViCoO21Z3XwZ33TGiCt92e_UOqfrP30mdEYnJYs09ulU1xBLj
8TjXOLR1k0&amp;t=633285035850304000" type="text/javascript"></script>
    <div>
        <script type="text/javascript">
//<![CDATA[
Sys.WebForms.PageRequestManager._initialize('ScriptManager1',
 document.getElementById('form1'));
Sys.WebForms.PageRequestManager.getInstance()._updateControls([], [], [], 90);
//]]>
</script>
    </div>

<script type="text/javascript">
//<![CDATA[
Sys.Application.initialize();
//]]>
</script>

</form>
</body>
</html>
```

The page output shows that a number of JavaScript libraries are loaded with the page. You will also notice that the scripts' sources are dynamically registered and available through the HTTP handler provided through the `ScriptResource.axd` handler.

If you are interested in seeing the contents of the JavaScript libraries, you can use the `src` *attribute's URL in the address bar of your browser and you will be prompted to download the JavaScript file that is referenced. You will be prompted to save the* `ScriptResource.axd` *file, but you can rename it to make use of a* `.txt` *or* `.js` *extension if you wish.*

An interesting point about the ScriptManager is that it deals with the scripts that are sent to the client by taking the extra step to compress them.

The ScriptManagerProxy Control

The ScriptManagerProxy control was actually introduced earlier in this book in Chapter 5, as this control deals specifically with master pages. As with the ScriptManager control in the previous section, you need a single ScriptManager control on each page that is going to be working with ASP.NET AJAX. However, with that said, the big question is what do you do when you are utilizing master pages? Do you need to put the ScriptManager control on the master page, and how does this work with the content pages that use the master page?

When you create a new master page from the Add New Item dialog, in addition to an option for a Master Page, there is also an option to add an AJAX Master Page. This option creates the page shown in Listing 19-10.

Listing 19-10: The AJAX Master Page

```
<%@ Master Language="VB" %>

<script runat="server">

</script>

<html xmlns="http://www.w3.org/1999/xhtml">
<head runat="server">
    <title>Untitled Page</title>
    <asp:ContentPlaceHolder id="head" runat="server">
    </asp:ContentPlaceHolder>
</head>
<body>
    <form id="form1" runat="server">
    <div>
        <asp:ScriptManager ID="ScriptManager1" runat="server" />
        <asp:ContentPlaceHolder id="ContentPlaceHolder1" runat="server">

        </asp:ContentPlaceHolder>
    </div>
    </form>
</body>
</html>
```

This code shows that there is indeed a ScriptManager control on the page and that this page will be added to each and every content page that uses this master page. You do not have to do anything special to a content page to use the ASP.NET AJAX capabilities provided by the master page. Instead, you can create a content page that is no different from any other content page that you might be used to creating.

However, if you are going to want to modify the ScriptManager control that is on the master page in any way, then you have to add a ScriptManagerProxy control to the content page, as shown in Listing 19-11.

Listing 19-11: Adding to the ScriptManager control from the content page

```
<%@ Page Language="VB" MasterPageFile="~/AJAXMaster.master" %>

<asp:Content ID="Content1" ContentPlaceHolderID="head" Runat="Server">
</asp:Content>
<asp:Content ID="Content2" ContentPlaceHolderID="ContentPlaceHolder1"
 Runat="Server">
 <asp:ScriptManagerProxy ID="ScriptManagerProxy1" runat="server">
     <Scripts>
         <asp:ScriptReference Path="myOtherScript.js" />
     </Scripts>
 </asp:ScriptManagerProxy>
</asp:Content>
```

In this case, the content page adds to the ScriptManager control that is on the master page by interjecting a script reference from the content page. If you use a ScriptManagerProxy control on a content page and there does not happen to be a ScriptManager control on the master page, you will get an error.

The Timer Control

One common task when working with asynchronous postbacks from your ASP.NET pages is that you might want these asynchronous postbacks to occur at specific intervals in time. To accomplish this, you use the Timer control available to you from the AJAX Extensions part of the toolbox. A simple example to demonstrate how this control works involves putting some timestamps on your page and setting postbacks to occur at specific timed intervals. This example is illustrated in Listing 19-12.

Listing 19-12: Using the Timer control

VB

```
<%@ Page Language="VB" %>

<script runat="server">
    Protected Sub Page_Load(ByVal sender As Object, ByVal e As System.EventArgs)
       If Not Page.IsPostBack
          Label1.Text = DateTime.Now.ToString()
       End If
    End Sub

    Protected Sub Timer1_Tick(ByVal sender As Object, ByVal e As System.EventArgs)
       Label1.Text = DateTime.Now.ToString()
    End Sub
</script>
<html xmlns="http://www.w3.org/1999/xhtml">
<head runat="server">
    <title>Timer Example</title>
</head>
<body>
```

Continued

```
    <form id="form1" runat="server">
    <div>
        <asp:ScriptManager ID="ScriptManager1" runat="server" />
        <asp:UpdatePanel ID="UpdatePanel1" runat="server">
            <ContentTemplate>
                <asp:Label ID="Label1" runat="server" Text="Label"></asp:Label>
                <asp:Timer ID="Timer1" runat="server" OnTick="Timer1_Tick"
                 Interval="10000">
                </asp:Timer>
            </ContentTemplate>
        </asp:UpdatePanel>
    </div>
    </form>
</body>
</html>
```

C#

```
<%@ Page Language="C#" %>

<script runat="server">
    protected void Page_Load(object sender, EventArgs e)
    {
        if (!Page.IsPostBack) {
           Label1.Text = DateTime.Now.ToString();
        }
    }

    protected void Timer1_Tick(object sender, EventArgs e)
    {
        Label1.Text = DateTime.Now.ToString();
    }
</script>
```

In this case, there are only three controls on the page. The first is the ScriptManager control followed by a Label and the Timer control. When this page loads for the first time, the Label control is populated with the `DateTime` value through the invocation of the `Page_Load` event handler. After this initial load of the `DateTime` value to the Label control, the Timer control takes care of changing this value.

The `OnTick` attribute from the Ticker control enables you to accomplish this task. It points to the function that is triggered when the time span specified in the `Interval` attribute is reached.

The `Interval` attribute is set to `10000`, which is 10,000 milliseconds (remember that there are 1,000 milliseconds to every second). This means, that every 10 seconds an asynchronous postback is performed and the `Timer1_Tick()` function is called.

When you run this page, you will see the time change on the page every 10 seconds.

The UpdatePanel Control

The UpdatePanel server control is an AJAX-specific control that is new in ASP.NET 3.5. The UpdatePanel control is the control that you are likely to use the most when dealing with AJAX. This control preserves the postback model and allows you to perform a partial page render.

The UpdatePanel control is a container control, which means that it does not actually have UI-specific items associated with it. It is a way to trigger a partial page postback and update only the portion of the page that the UpdatePanel specifies.

The <ContentTemplate> Element

There are a couple of ways to deal with the controls on the page that initiate the asynchronous page postbacks. The first is by far the simplest and is shown in Listing 19-13.

Listing 19-13: Putting the triggers inside of the UpdatePanel control

VB

```
<%@ Page Language="VB" %>

<script runat="server">
    Protected Sub Button1_Click(ByVal sender As Object,
       ByVal e As System.EventArgs)

       Label1.Text = "This button was clicked on " & DateTime.Now.ToString()
    End Sub
</script>

<html xmlns="http://www.w3.org/1999/xhtml">
<head runat="server">
    <title>UpdatePanel Control</title>
</head>
<body>
    <form id="form1" runat="server">
    <div>
        <asp:ScriptManager ID="ScriptManager1" runat="server">
        </asp:ScriptManager>
        <asp:UpdatePanel ID="UpdatePanel1" runat="server">
            <ContentTemplate>
                <asp:Label ID="Label1" runat="server"></asp:Label>
                <br />
                <br />
                <asp:Button ID="Button1" runat="server"
                 Text="Click to initiate async request"
                 OnClick="Button1_Click" />
            </ContentTemplate>
        </asp:UpdatePanel>
    </div>
    </form>
</body>
</html>
```

C#

```
<%@ Page Language="C#" %>

<script runat="server">
    protected void Button1_Click(object sender, EventArgs e)
    {
        Label1.Text = "This button was clicked on " + DateTime.Now.ToString();
    }
</script>
```

In this case, the Label and Button server controls are contained within the UpdatePanel server control. The `<asp:UpdatePanel>` element has two possible sub-elements: `<ContentTemplate>` and the `<Triggers>` elements. Any content that needs to be changed with the asynchronous page postbacks should be contained within the `<ContentTemplate>` section of the UpdatePanel control.

By default, any type of control trigger (something that would normally trigger a page postback) that is contained within the `<ContentTemplate>` section instead causes the asynchronous page postback. That means, in the case of Listing 19-13, the button on the page will trigger an asynchronous page postback instead of a full-page postback. Each click on the button changes the time displayed in the Label control.

The <Triggers> Element

Listing 19-13 demonstrates one of the big issues with this model: When the asynchronous postback occurs, you are not only sending the date/time value for the Label control, but you are also sending back the entire code for the button that is on the page.

```
265|updatePanel|UpdatePanel1|
     <span id="Label1">This button was clicked on 11/18/2007 11:45:21 AM</span>
     <br />
     <br />
     <input type="submit" name="Button1" value="Click to initiate async request"
      id="Button1" />
|164|hiddenField|__VIEWSTATE|/wEPDwUKLTU2NzQ4MzIwMw9kFgICBA9kFgICAw9kFgJmD2QWAgIBDw
8WAh4EVGV4dAUxVGhpcyBidXR0b24gd2FzIGNsaWNrZWQgb24gMTEvMTgvMjAwNyAxMTo0NToyMSBBTWRkZ
KJIG4WwhyQvUwPCX4PxI5FEUFtC|48|hiddenField|__EVENTVALIDATION|/wEWAgL43YXdBwKM54rGBl
I52OYVl/McOV61BYd/3wSj+RkD|0|asyncPostBackControlIDs|||0|postBackControlIDs|||13|
updatePanelIDs||tUpdatePanel1|0|childUpdatePanelIDs|||12|panelsToRefreshIDs||
UpdatePanel1|2|asyncPostBackTimeout||90|22|formAction||SimpleUpdatePanel.aspx|11|
pageTitle||UpdatePanel|
```

This bit of code that is sent back to the client via the asynchronous postback shows that the entire section contained within the UpdatePanel control is reissued. You can slim down your pages by including only the portions of the page that are actually updating. If you take the button outside of the `<ContentTemplate>` section of the UpdatePanel control, then you have to include a `<Triggers>` section within the control.

The reason for this is that while the content that you want to change with the asynchronous postback is all contained within the `<ContentTemplate>` section, you have to tie up a page event to cause the postback to occur. This is how the `<Triggers>` section of the UpdatePanel control is used. You use this section of the control to specify the various triggers that initiate an asynchronous page postback. Using the `<Triggers>` element within the UpdatePanel control, you can rewrite Listing 19-13 as shown in Listing 19-14.

Listing 19-14: Using a trigger to cause the asynchronous page postback

VB

```
<%@ Page Language="VB" %>

<script runat="server">
    Protected Sub Button1_Click(ByVal sender As Object,
```

```
        ByVal e As System.EventArgs)

        Label1.Text = "This button was clicked on " & DateTime.Now.ToString()
    End Sub
</script>

<html xmlns="http://www.w3.org/1999/xhtml">
<head runat="server">
    <title>UpdatePanel</title>
</head>
<body>
    <form id="form1" runat="server">
    <div>
        <asp:ScriptManager ID="ScriptManager1" runat="server">
        </asp:ScriptManager>
        <asp:UpdatePanel ID="UpdatePanel1" runat="server">
            <ContentTemplate>
                <asp:Label ID="Label1" runat="server"></asp:Label>
            </ContentTemplate>
            <Triggers>
                <asp:AsyncPostBackTrigger ControlID="Button1" EventName="Click" />
            </Triggers>
        </asp:UpdatePanel>
        <br />
        <br />
        <asp:Button ID="Button1" runat="server"
         Text="Click to initiate async request"
         OnClick="Button1_Click" />
    </div>
    </form>
</body>
</html>
```

C#

```
<%@ Page Language="C#" %>

<script runat="server">

    protected void Button1_Click(object sender, EventArgs e)
    {
        Label1.Text = "This button was clicked on " + DateTime.Now.ToString();
    }
</script>
```

In this case, the Button control and the HTML elements are outside of the `<ContentTemplate>` section of the UpdatePanel control and therefore will not be sent back to the client for each asynchronous page postback. The only item contained in the `<ContentTemplate>` section is the only item on the page that needs to change with the postbacks — the Label control. Tying this all together is the `<Triggers>` section.

The `<Triggers>` section can contain two possible controls: AsyncPostBackTrigger and PostBackTrigger. In this case, the AsyncPostBackTrigger is used. The PostBackTrigger control will cause a full page postback, whereas the AsyncPostBackTrigger control will cause only an asynchronous page postback (obviously as described by the names of the controls).

As you can see from the example in Listing 19-14, which uses the AsyncPostBackTrigger element, only two attributes are used to tie the Button control to the trigger for the asynchronous postback: the `ControlID` and the `EventName` attributes. The control you want to act as the initiator of the asynchronous page postback is put here (the control's name as specified by the control's `ID` attribute). The `EventName` attribute's value is the name of the event for the control that is specified in the `ControlID` that you want to be called in the asynchronous request from the client. In this case, the Button control's `Click()` event is called and this is the event that changes the value of the control that resides within the `<ContentTemplate>` section of the UpdatePanel control.

Running this page and clicking on the button gives you a smaller asynchronous response back to the client.

```
108|updatePanel|UpdatePanel1|
   <span id="Label1">This button was clicked on 11/18/2007 11:58:56 AM</span>
|164|hiddenField|__VIEWSTATE|/wEPDwUKMjA2NjQ2MDYzNw9kFgICBA9kFgICAw9kFgJmD2QWAgIBDw
8WAh4EVGV4dAUxVGhpcyBidXR0b24gd2FzIGNsaWNrZWQgb24gMTEvMTgvMjAwNyAxMTo1ODo1NiBBTWRkZ
PJA9uj9wwRaasgTrZo85rVvLnoi|48|hiddenField|__EVENTVALIDATION|/wEWAgKK3YDTDAKM54rGBq
rbjV4/u4ks3aKsn7Xz8xNFE8G/|7|asyncPostBackControlIDs||Button1|0|postBackControlIDs|
||13|updatePanelIDs||tUpdatePanel1|0|childUpdatePanelIDs|||12|panelsToRefreshIDs||
UpdatePanel1|2|asyncPostBackTimeout||90|22|formAction||SimpleUpdatePanel.aspx|11|
pageTitle||UpdatePanel|
```

Although not considerably smaller than the previous example, it is smaller and the size similarity is really due to the size of the page used in this example (pages that are more voluminous would show more dramatic improvements). Pages with heavy content associated with them can show some dramatic size reductions depending on how you structure your pages with the UpdatePanel control.

Building Triggers Using Visual Studio 2008

If you like to work on the design surface of Visual Studio when building your ASP.NET pages, you will find that there is good support for building your ASP.NET AJAX pages, including the creation of triggers in the UpdatePanel control. To see this in action, place a single UpdatePanel server control on your page and view the control in the Properties dialog within Visual Studio. The Triggers item in the list has a button next to it that allows you to modify the items associated with it. This is illustrated in Figure 19-11.

Clicking on the button in the Properties dialog launches the UpdatePanelTrigger Collection Editor, as shown in Figure 19-12. This editor allows you to add any number of triggers and to associate them to a control and a control event very easily.

Clicking the OK button here adds the trigger to the `<Triggers>` section of your UpdatePanel control.

The UpdateProgress Control

The final server control in the AJAX Extensions section of Visual Studio 2008 is the UpdateProgress control. Some asynchronous postbacks take some time to execute because of the size of the response or because of the computing time required to get a result together to send back to the client. The UpdateProgress control allows you to provide a visual signifier to the clients to show that indeed work is being done and they will get results soon (and that the browser simply didn't just lock up).

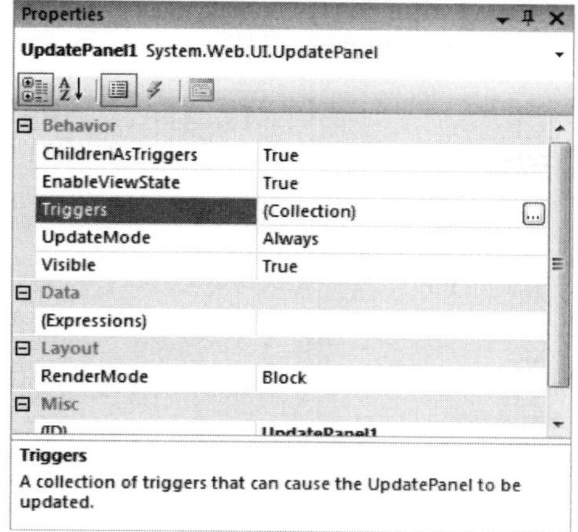

Figure 19-11

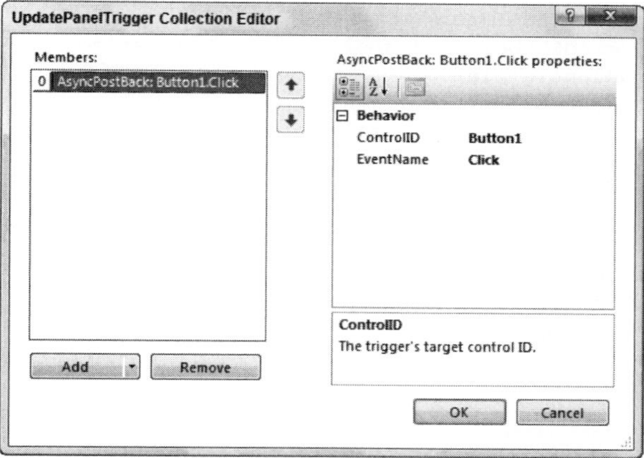

Figure 19-12

Listing 19-15 shows a textual implementation of the UpdateProgress control.

Listing 19-15: Using the UpdateProgess control to show a text message to the client

VB

```
<%@ Page Language="VB" %>

<script runat="server">
    Protected Sub Button1_Click(ByVal sender As Object,
       ByVal e As System.EventArgs)
```

Continued

```
        System.Threading.Thread.Sleep(10000)
        Label1.Text = "This button was clicked on " & DateTime.Now.ToString()
    End Sub
</script>

<html xmlns="http://www.w3.org/1999/xhtml">
<head runat="server">
    <title>UpdatePanel</title>
</head>
<body>
    <form id="form1" runat="server">
    <div>
        <asp:ScriptManager ID="ScriptManager1" runat="server">
        </asp:ScriptManager>
        <asp:UpdateProgress ID="UpdateProgress1" runat="server">
            <ProgressTemplate>
                An update is occurring...
            </ProgressTemplate>
        </asp:UpdateProgress>
        <asp:UpdatePanel ID="UpdatePanel1" runat="server" UpdateMode="Conditional">
            <ContentTemplate>
                <asp:Label ID="Label1" runat="server"></asp:Label>
            </ContentTemplate>
            <Triggers>
                <asp:AsyncPostBackTrigger ControlID="Button1" EventName="Click" />
            </Triggers>
        </asp:UpdatePanel>
        <br />
        <br />
        <asp:Button ID="Button1" runat="server"
         Text="Click to initiate async request"
         OnClick="Button1_Click" />
    </div>
    </form>
</body>
</html>
```

C#

```
<%@ Page Language="C#" %>
<script runat="server">

    protected void Button1_Click(object sender, EventArgs e)
    {
        System.Threading.Thread.Sleep(10000);
        Label1.Text = "This button was clicked on " + DateTime.Now.ToString();
    }
</script>
```

To add some delay to the response (in order to simulate a long running computer process) the Thread. Sleep() method is called. From here, you add an UpdateProgess control to the part of the page where you want the update message to be presented. In this case, the UpdateProgress control was added above the UpdatePanel server control. This control does not go inside the UpdatePanel control; instead, it sits outside of the control. However, like the UpdatePanel control, the UpdateProgress control is a template control.

The UpdateProgress control has only a single sub-element: the `<ProgressTemplate>` element. Whatever you place in this section of the control will appear when the UpdateProgress control is triggered. In this case, the only item present in this section of the control is some text. When you run this page, you will get the update shown in Figure 19-13.

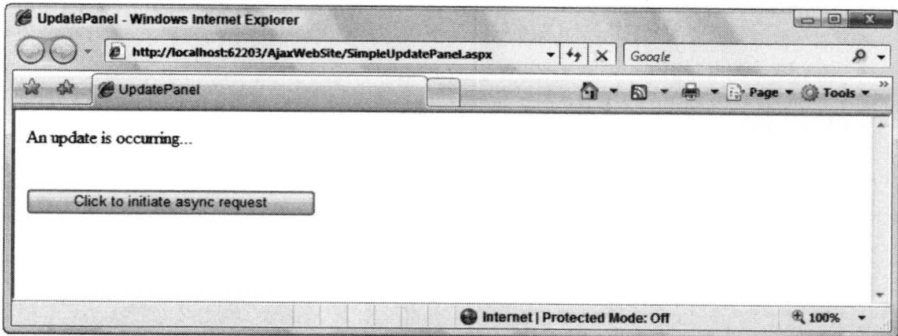

Figure 19-13

The text will appear immediately in this case and will not disappear until the asynchronous postback has finished. The code you put in the `<ProgressTemplate>` section is actually contained in the page, but its display is turned off through CSS.

```
<div id="UpdateProgress1" style="display:none;">
   An update is occurring...
</div>
```

Controlling When the Message Appears

Right now, the UpdateProgress appears as soon as the button is clicked. However, some of your processes might not take that long and you might not always want a progress notification going out to the client. The UpdateProgress control includes a `DisplayAfter` attribute, which allows you to control when the progress update message appears. The use of the `DisplayAfter` attribute is shown in Listing 19-16.

Listing 19-16: Using the DisplayAfter attribute

```
<asp:UpdateProgress ID="UpdateProgress1" runat="server" DisplayAfter="5000">
   <ProgressTemplate>
      An update is occurring...
   </ProgressTemplate>
</asp:UpdateProgress>
```

The value of the `DisplayAfter` property is a number that represents the number of milliseconds that the UpdateProgress control will wait until it displays what is contained within the `<ProgressTemplate>` section. The code in Listing 19-16 specifies that the text found in the `<ProgressTemplate>` section will not be displayed for 5,000 milliseconds (5 seconds).

Adding an Image to the <ProcessTemplate>

The previous examples which make use of the UpdateProgress control use this control with text, but you can put anything you want within this template control. For instance, you can put a spinning wheel image that will show the end user that the request is being processed. The use of the image is shown in Listing 19-17.

Listing 19-17: Using an image in the <ProcessTemplate> section

```
<asp:UpdateProgress ID="UpdateProgress1" runat="server" DisplayAfter="5000">
   <ProgressTemplate>
      <asp:Image ID="Image1" runat="server" ImageUrl="~/spinningwheel.gif" />
   </ProgressTemplate>
</asp:UpdateProgress>
```

Just as the in the text approach, the code for the image is already placed on the client's page instance and is just turned off via CSS.

```
<div id="UpdateProgress1" style="display:none;">
   <img id="Image1" src="spinningwheel.gif" style="border-width:0px;" />
</div>
```

Using Multiple UpdatePanel Controls

So far, this chapter has showed you how to work with a single UpdatePanel control, but it is important to realize that you can have multiple UpdatePanel controls on a single page. This, in the end, will give you the ability to control the output to specific regions of the page when you want.

An example of using more than a single UpdatePanel control is presented in Listing 19-18.

Listing 19-18: Using more than one UpdatePanel control

VB

```
<%@ Page Language="VB" %>

<script runat="server">
    Protected Sub Button1_Click(ByVal sender As Object,
       ByVal e As System.EventArgs)

       Label1.Text = "Label1 was populated on " & DateTime.Now.ToString()
       Label2.Text = "Label2 was populated on " & DateTime.Now.ToString()
    End Sub
</script>

<html xmlns="http://www.w3.org/1999/xhtml">
<head runat="server">
    <title>Multiple UpdatePanel Controls</title>
</head>
<body>
    <form id="form1" runat="server">
    <div>
        <asp:ScriptManager ID="ScriptManager1" runat="server">
        </asp:ScriptManager>
        <asp:UpdatePanel ID="UpdatePanel1" runat="server">
            <ContentTemplate>
                <asp:Label ID="Label1" runat="server"></asp:Label>
            </ContentTemplate>
            <Triggers>
                <asp:AsyncPostBackTrigger ControlID="Button1" EventName="Click" />
            </Triggers>
        </asp:UpdatePanel>
```

```
        <asp:UpdatePanel ID="UpdatePanel2" runat="server">
            <ContentTemplate>
                <asp:Label ID="Label2" runat="server"></asp:Label>
            </ContentTemplate>
        </asp:UpdatePanel>
        <br />
        <br />
        <asp:Button ID="Button1" runat="server"
         Text="Click to initiate async request"
         OnClick="Button1_Click" />
    </div>
    </form>
</body>
</html>
```

C#

```
<%@ Page Language="C#" %>

<script runat="server">
    protected void Button1_Click(object sender, EventArgs e)
    {
        Label1.Text = "Label1 was populated on " + DateTime.Now;
        Label2.Text = "Label2 was populated on " + DateTime.Now;
    }
</script>
```

This is an interesting page. There are two UpdatePanel controls on the page: `UpdatePanel1` and `UpdatePanel2`. Each of these controls contains a single Label control that at one point can take a date/time value from a server response.

The `UpdatePanel1` control has an associated trigger: the Button control on the page. When this button is clicked, the `Button1_Click()` event triggers and does its job. If you run this page, both of the UpdatePanel controls are updated according to the `Button1_Click()` event. This is illustrated in Figure 19-14.

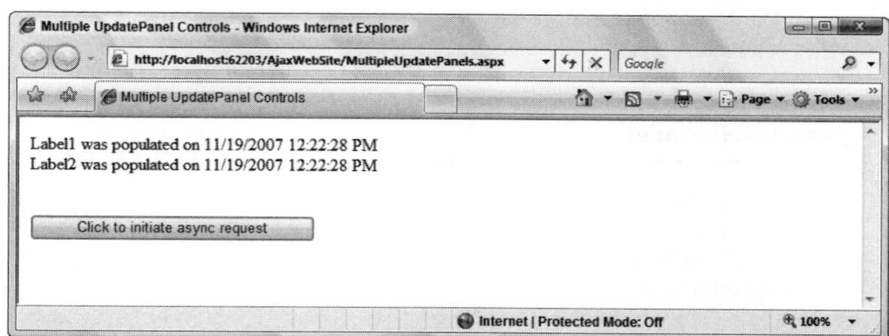

Figure 19-14

Both UpdatePanel sections were updated with the `button-click` event because, by default, all UpdatePanel controls on a single page update with *each* asynchronous postback that occurs. This means that the postback that occurred with the `Button1` button control also causes a postback to occur with the `UpdatePanel2` control.

You can actually control this behavior through the UpdatePanel's `UpdateMode` property. The `UpdateMode` property can take two possible enumerations — `Always` and `Conditional`. If you do not set this property, it uses the value of `Always`, meaning that each UpdatePanel control always updates with each asynchronous request.

The other option is to set the property to `Conditional`. This means that the UpdatePanel updates only if one of the trigger conditions is met. For an example of this, change the UpdatePanel controls on the page so that they are now using an `UpdateMode` of `Conditional`, as shown in Listing 19-19.

Listing 19-19: Using more than one UpdatePanel control

VB

```
<%@ Page Language="VB" %>

<script runat="server">
    Protected Sub Button1_Click(ByVal sender As Object,
       ByVal e As System.EventArgs)

       Label1.Text = "Label1 was populated on " & DateTime.Now.ToString()
       Label2.Text = "Label2 was populated on " & DateTime.Now.ToString()
    End Sub
</script>

<html xmlns="http://www.w3.org/1999/xhtml">
<head runat="server">
    <title>Multiple UpdatePanel Controls</title>
</head>
<body>
    <form id="form1" runat="server">
    <div>
        <asp:ScriptManager ID="ScriptManager1" runat="server">
        </asp:ScriptManager>
        <asp:UpdatePanel ID="UpdatePanel1" runat="server" UpdateMode="Conditional">
            <ContentTemplate>
                <asp:Label ID="Label1" runat="server"></asp:Label>
            </ContentTemplate>
            <Triggers>
                <asp:AsyncPostBackTrigger ControlID="Button1" EventName="Click" />
            </Triggers>
        </asp:UpdatePanel>
        <asp:UpdatePanel ID="UpdatePanel2" runat="server" UpdateMode="Conditional">
            <ContentTemplate>
                <asp:Label ID="Label2" runat="server"></asp:Label>
            </ContentTemplate>
        </asp:UpdatePanel>
        <br />
        <br />
        <asp:Button ID="Button1" runat="server"
         Text="Click to initiate async request"
         OnClick="Button1_Click" />
    </div>
    </form>
```

```
</body>
</html>
```

C#

```
<%@ Page Language="C#" %>

<script runat="server">
    protected void Button1_Click(object sender, EventArgs e)
    {
        Label1.Text = "Label1 was populated on " + DateTime.Now;
        Label2.Text = "Label2 was populated on " + DateTime.Now;
    }
</script>
```

Now that both of the UpdatePanel controls are set to have an `UpdateMode` of `Conditional`, when running this page, you will see the results presented in Figure 19-15.

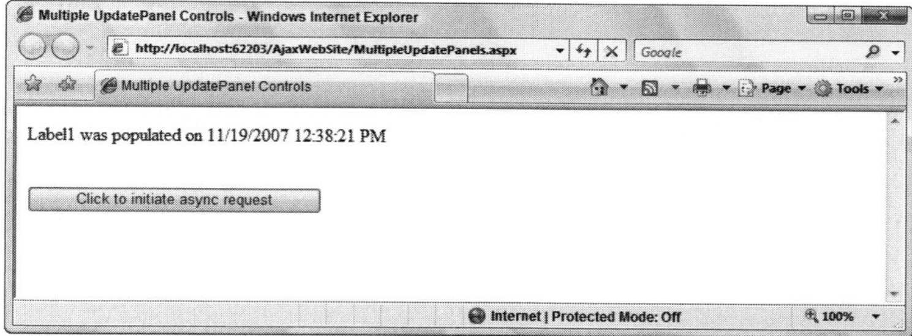

Figure 19-15

In this case, only the right Label control, `Label1`, was updated with the asynchronous request even though the `Button1_Click()` event tries to change the values of both `Label1` and `Label2`. The reason for this is that the UpdatePanel2 control had no trigger that was met.

Summary

ASP.NET AJAX, although it is in its infancy, is an outstanding technology and will fundamentally change the way Web application development is approached. No longer do you need to completely tear down a page and rebuild it for each and every request. Instead, you are able to rebuild the pages slowly in sections as the end user requests them. The line between the thin-client world and the thick-client world just got a lot more opaque.

This chapter took a look at the core foundation of ASP.NET AJAX that is available with the default install of Visual Studio 2008. Beyond that, there is much more. A big addition is the ASP.NET AJAX Control Toolkit, the focus of the next chapter.

20

ASP.NET AJAX Control Toolkit

ASP.NET AJAX applications were introduced in the previous chapter. With the install of the .NET Framework 3.5 and through using Visual Studio 2008, you will find a few controls available that allow you to build ASP.NET applications with AJAX capabilities. This is the framework to take your applications to the next level because there is so much that can be accomplished with it, including adding specific AJAX capabilities to your user and custom server controls. Every AJAX enhancement added to your application will make your application seem more fluid and responsive to the end user.

You might be wondering where the big new AJAX-enabled server controls are for this edition of Visual Studio 2008 if this is indeed a new world for building controls. The reason you do not see a new section of AJAX server controls is that Microsoft has treated them as an open-source project instead of just blending them into Visual Studio 2008.

Developers at Microsoft and in the community have been working on a series of AJAX-capable server controls that you can use in your ASP.NET applications. These controls are collectively called the ASP.NET AJAX Control Toolkit. You will find a link to the control toolkit for download at `www.asp.net/AJAX`. When you choose to download the control toolkit from this page, you will be directed to the ASP.NET AJAX Control Toolkit's page on CodePlex at `www.codeplex.com/Release/ProjectReleases.aspx?ProjectName=AtlasControlToolkit`. This page is shown in Figure 20-1.

Downloading and Installing

Since the ASP.NET AJAX Control Toolkit is not part of the default install of Visual Studio 2008, you have to set up the controls yourself. Again, the control toolkit's site on CodePlex offers a couple of options to you.

First off, you are able to download a control toolkit that is specifically targeted at Visual Studio 2008 or Visual Studio 2005. This chapter focuses on using the control toolkit with Visual Studio 2008.

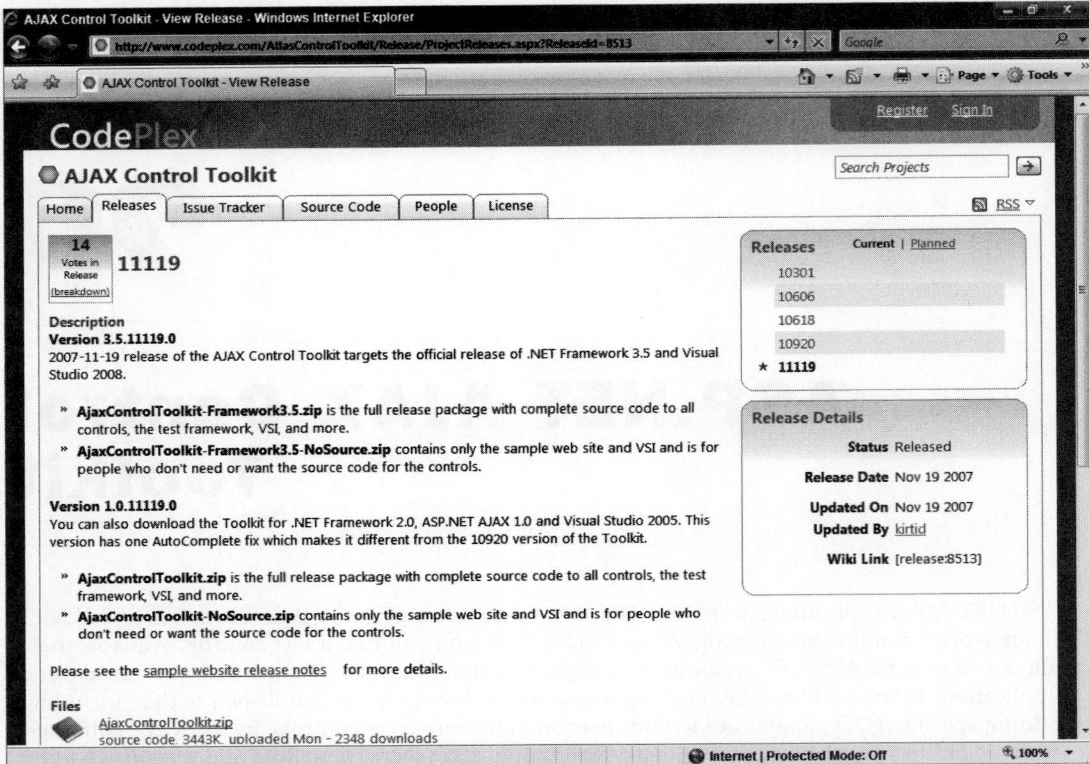

Figure 20-1

The CodePlex page for this project offers two ways to get what you are after. The ASP.NET AJAX Control Toolkit can be downloaded as source code or as a compiled DLL.

The source control option allows you to take the code for the controls and ASP.NET AJAX extenders and change the behavior of the controls or extenders yourself. The DLL option is a single Visual Studio installer file and a sample application.

There are a couple of parts to the install. One part provides a series of new controls that were built with AJAX capabilities in mind. Another part is a series of control extenders (extensions upon pre-existing controls). You will also find some new template additions for your Visual Studio 2008 instance.

To get set up, download the `.zip` file from the CodePlex site and unzip it where you want on your machine. The following sections show you how to work with the various parts provided from the Control Toolkit.

New Visual Studio Templates

Included in the download is a `.vsi` file (Visual Studio Installer) called `AJAXControlExtender.vsi`. This installer will install four new Visual Studio projects for your future use. The installer options are shown in Figure 20-2.

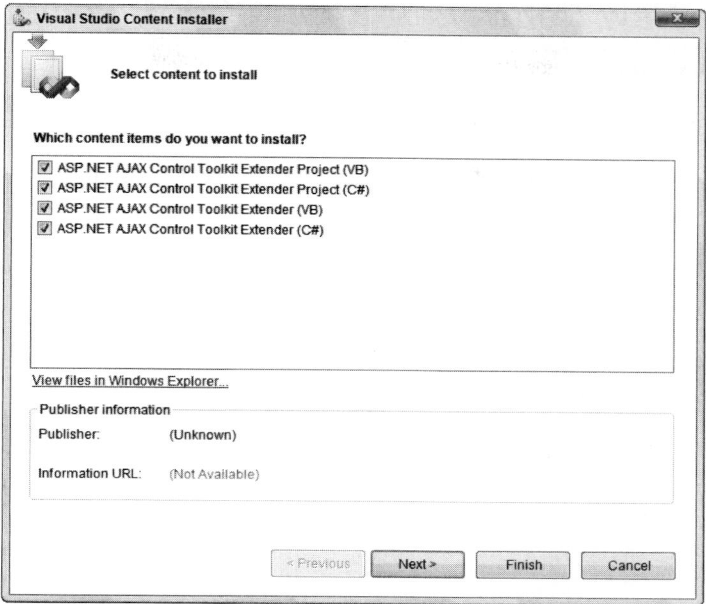

Figure 20-2

After installing these options, you have access to the new project types this provides as illustrated in Figure 20-3.

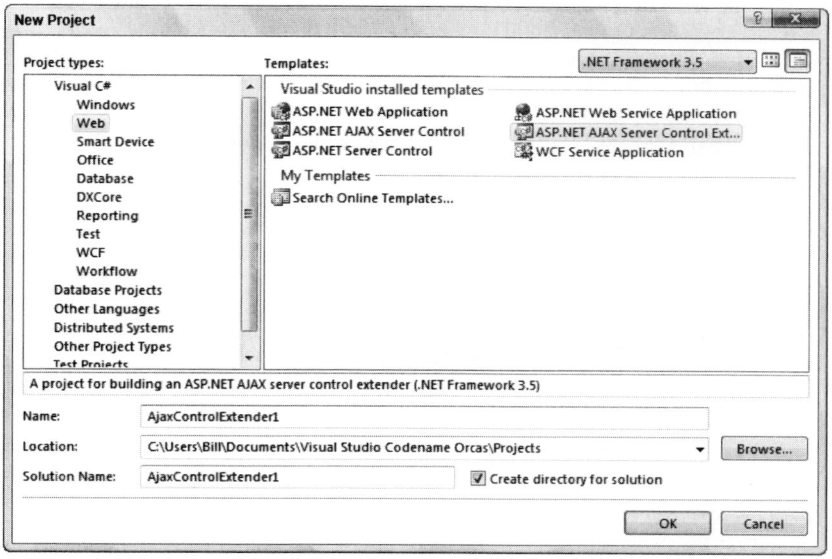

Figure 20-3

Adding the New Controls to the VS2008 Toolbox

In addition to new project types, you can also add the new controls to your Visual Studio 2008 Toolbox. To accomplish this task, right-click in the Toolbox and select Add Tab from the provided menu. Name the tab as you wish, though, for this example the tab was named AJAX Controls.

With the new tab in your Toolbox, right-click the tab and select Choose Items from the provided menu. This action is illustrated in Figure 20-4.

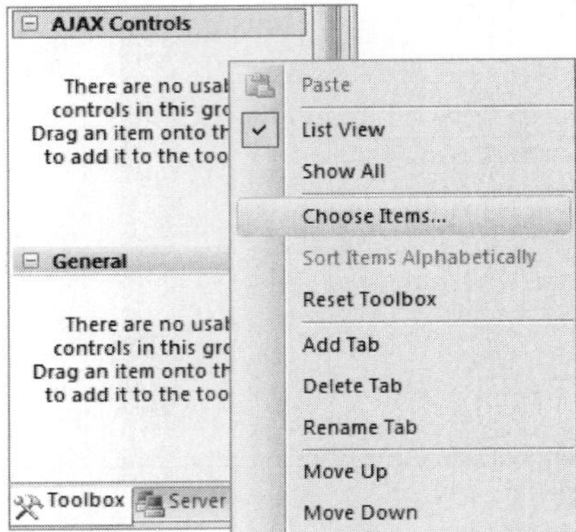

Figure 20-4

Select Choose Items from the menu to open the Choose Toolbox Items dialog. From here, you want to select `AjaxControlToolkit.dll` from the sample application's Bin folder. Remember that the SampleWebSite is a component that was downloaded and unzipped as part of the Control Toolkit. When you find the DLL and click Open. The Choose Toolbox Items dialog changes to include the controls that are contained within this DLL. The controls are highlighted in the dialog and are already selected for you (as shown in Figure 20-5).

From here, click OK and the ASP.NET AJAX Control Toolkit's new controls will be added to your Visual Studio Toolbox. The end result is presented in Figure 20-6.

You will find that there are more than 35 new controls and extenders added to the Toolbox for you to utilize in your ASP.NET applications.

The ASP.NET AJAX Controls

The number of controls and extenders available from the Control Toolkit is large. As stated, there are more than 35 controls and extenders at your disposal. This section will look at these new items and how you can use them in your ASP.NET applications.

When you add an ASP.NET AJAX server control to your page, one thing you will notice is that a number of DLLs focused on localization into a number of languages have been added to the Bin folder of your solution. All the resource files have been organized into language folders within the folder. An example of what you will find is presented in Figure 20-7.

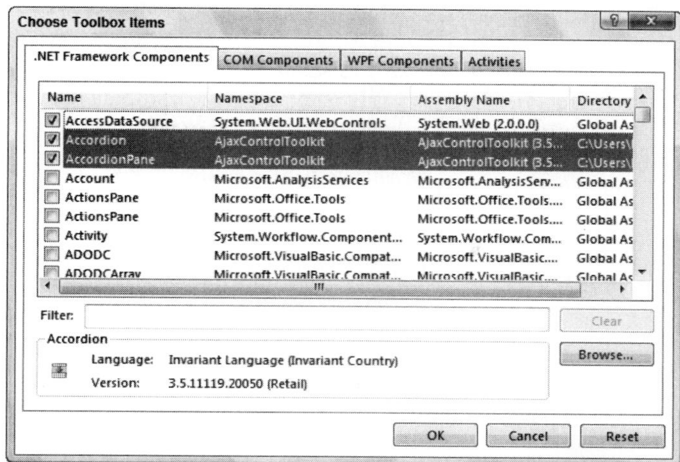

Figure 20-5

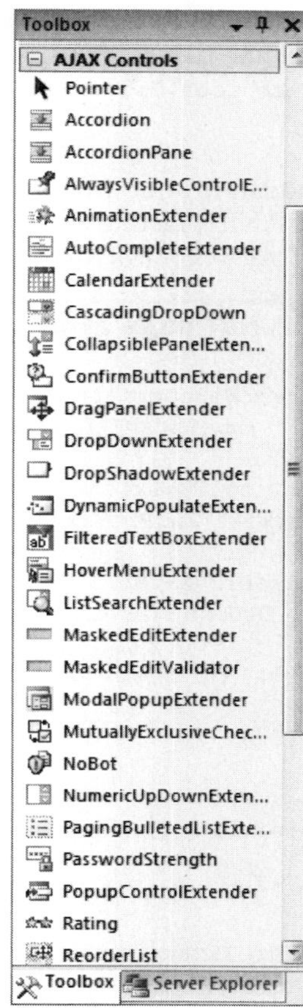

Figure 20-6

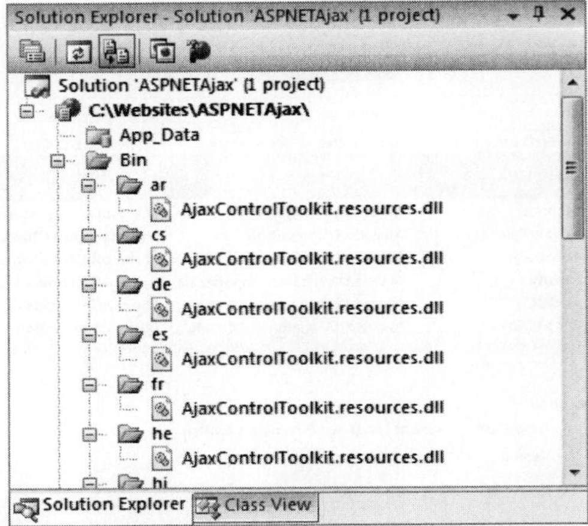

Figure 20-7

Looking at one of the DLLs with Lutz Roeder's .NET Reflector tool (`www.aisto.com/roeder/dotnet/`), you will notice that they are focused on the client-side localization required by many applications. As an example, the `AjaxControlToolkit.resources.dll` for the Russian language within Reflector is shown in Figure 20-8.

In addition to the localization DLLs added to your project, the ASP.NET AJAX control is added just as any other custom server control in ASP.NET. Listing 20-1 shows what your ASP.NET page looks like after the addition of a single ASP.NET AJAX control to it.

Listing 20-1: Changes to the ASP.NET page after adding an ASP.NET AJAX control

```
<%@ Page Language="C#" AutoEventWireup="true"
    CodeFile="Default.aspx.cs" Inherits="_Default" %>

<%@ Register Assembly="AjaxControlToolkit"
    Namespace="AjaxControlToolkit" TagPrefix="cc1" %>

<!DOCTYPE html PUBLIC "-//W3C//DTD XHTML 1.0 Transitional//EN"
 "http://www.w3.org/TR/xhtml1/DTD/xhtml1-transitional.dtd">

<html xmlns="http://www.w3.org/1999/xhtml">
<head runat="server">
    <title>Untitled Page</title>
</head>
<body>
    <form id="form1" runat="server">
    <div>
        <asp:ScriptManager ID="ScriptManager1" runat="server" />

         <cc1:AlwaysVisibleControlExtender
          ID="AlwaysVisibleControlExtender1" runat="server"
          TargetControlID="TextBox1">
         </cc1:AlwaysVisibleControlExtender>
```

```
            <asp:TextBox ID="TextBox1" runat="server"></asp:TextBox>
        </div>
        </form>
    </body>
    </html>
```

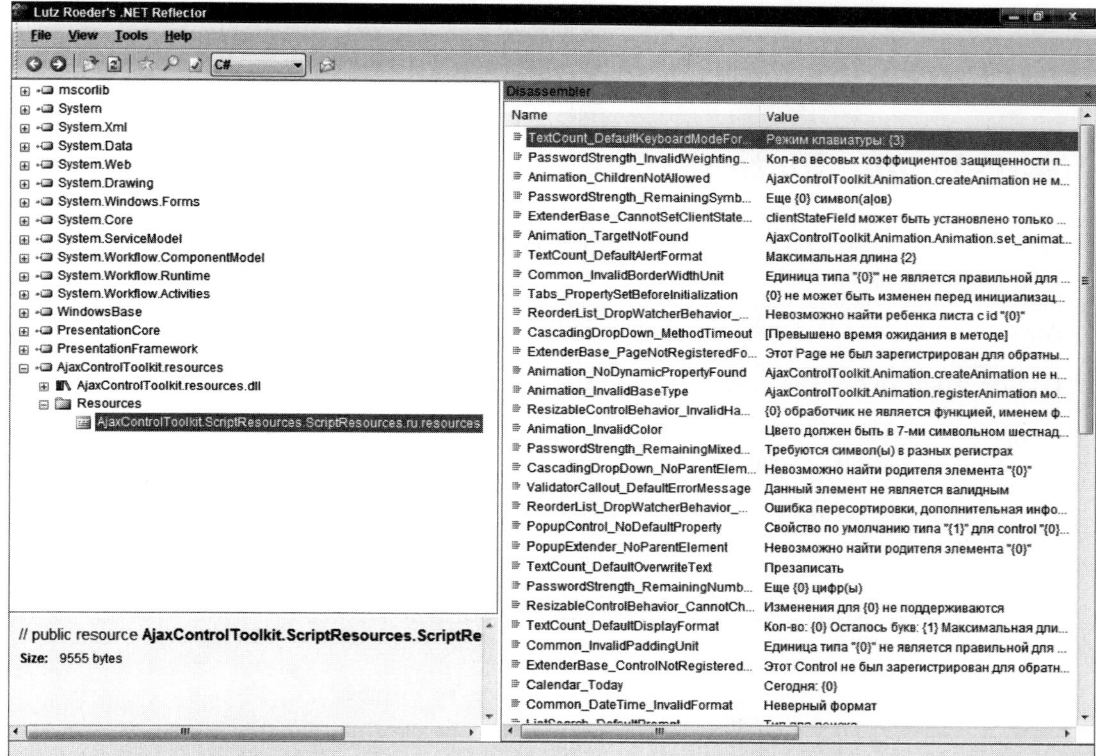

Figure 20-8

In this example, you can see that the ASP.NET AJAX control is registered on the page using the `@Register` directive. This directive points to the `AJAXControlToolkit` assembly and gives all controls that use this assembly reference a tag prefix of `cc1`, which is why you see the AlwaysVisibleControl-Extender control prefixed with a `<cc1:[control name]>`.

ASP.NET AJAX Control Toolkit Extenders

The first set of items you look at includes the new extenders that are part of the ASP.NET AJAX Control Toolkit. Extenders are basically controls that reach out and extend other controls. For an example of this, you can think of the ASP.NET Validation Controls (covered in Chapter 4 of this book) as extender controls themselves. For instance, you can add a `RequiredFieldValidator` server control to a page and associate it to a TextBox control. This extends the TextBox control and changes its behavior.

Normally it would just accept text. Now, if nothing is entered into the control, then the control will trigger an event back to the RequiredFieldValidator control whose client-side behavior is controlled by JavaScript.

The ASP.NET AJAX Control Toolkit's extenders pretty much accomplish the same thing. The controls extend the behavior of the ASP.NET server controls with additional JavaScript on the client as well as some server-side communications.

The ASP.NET AJAX extender controls are built using the ASP.NET AJAX extensions framework. The next few pages focus on using these new extenders within your ASP.NET applications.

AlwaysVisibleControlExtender

The AlwaysVisibleControlExtender allows you to specify controls that will always be present on a long page that requires scrolling. With this control, you can specify a location of the page where the control will always be present, no matter how the end user scrolls the page. Your options are to assign the vertical or horizontal alignment of the control that will always be visible. An example of using the AlwaysVisibleControlExtender is presented in Listing 20-2.

Listing 20-2: Using the AlwaysVisibleControlExtender

VB

```
<%@ Page Language="VB" %>

<%@ Register Assembly="AjaxControlToolkit" Namespace="AjaxControlToolkit"
   TagPrefix="cc1" %>

<!DOCTYPE html PUBLIC "-//W3C//DTD XHTML 1.0 Transitional//EN"
 "http://www.w3.org/TR/xhtml1/DTD/xhtml1-transitional.dtd">

<script runat="server">
    Protected Sub Button1_Click(ByVal sender As Object, _
       ByVal e As System.EventArgs)

        Response.Write("The page has been submitted!")
    End Sub
</script>

<html xmlns="http://www.w3.org/1999/xhtml">
<head runat="server">
    <title>AlwaysVisibleControlExtender</title>
</head>
<body>
    <form id="form1" runat="server">
    <div>
        <asp:ScriptManager ID="ScriptManager1" runat="server" />
        <cc1:AlwaysVisibleControlExtender ID="AlwaysVisibleControlExtender1"
            runat="server" TargetControlID="Panel1" HorizontalOffset="10"
            HorizontalSide="Right" VerticalOffset="10">
        </cc1:AlwaysVisibleControlExtender>
        Form Element :
        <asp:TextBox ID="TextBox1" runat="server"></asp:TextBox>
```

```
        <br />
        Form Element :
        <asp:TextBox ID="TextBox2" runat="server"></asp:TextBox>
        <br />

        <!-- Excessive code removed for clarity -->

        Form Element :
        <asp:TextBox ID="TextBox29" runat="server"></asp:TextBox>
        <br />
        Form Element :
        <asp:TextBox ID="TextBox30" runat="server"></asp:TextBox>
        <br />
        <br />
        <asp:Panel ID="Panel1" runat="server">
            <asp:Button ID="Button1" runat="server" Text="Submit"
             OnClick="Button1_Click" />
            <asp:Button ID="Button2" runat="server" Text="Clear" />
        </asp:Panel>
    </div>
    </form>
</body>
</html>
```

C#

```
<%@ Page Language="C#" %>

<%@ Register Assembly="AjaxControlToolkit" Namespace="AjaxControlToolkit"
    TagPrefix="cc1" %>

<script runat="server">
    protected void Button1_Click(object sender, EventArgs e)
    {
        Response.Write("The page has been submitted!");
    }
</script>
```

This code presents a very long form that requires end users to scroll the page in their browser. The AlwaysVisibleControlExtender control is present and its presence requires that you also have a ScriptManager control on the page (this is the same requirement for all ASP.NET AJAX controls).

The AlwaysVisibleControlExtender1 control extends the `Panel1` control through the use of the `TargetControlID` attribute. In this case, the value of the `TargetControlID` attribute points to the Panel1 control. The Panel1 control contains the form's Submit button. The result of the code from Listing 20-2 is shown in Figure 20-9.

The location of the Submit and Clear buttons on the page is controlled via a combination of a several control attributes. First off, the location on the page is determined by the `HorizontalSide` (possible values include `Center`, `Left`, and `Right`) and `VerticalSide` properties (possible values include `Bottom`, `Middle`, and `Top`). Then a padding is placed around the control using the `HorizontalOffset` and `VerticalOffset` properties, both of which are set to `10` pixels in this example.

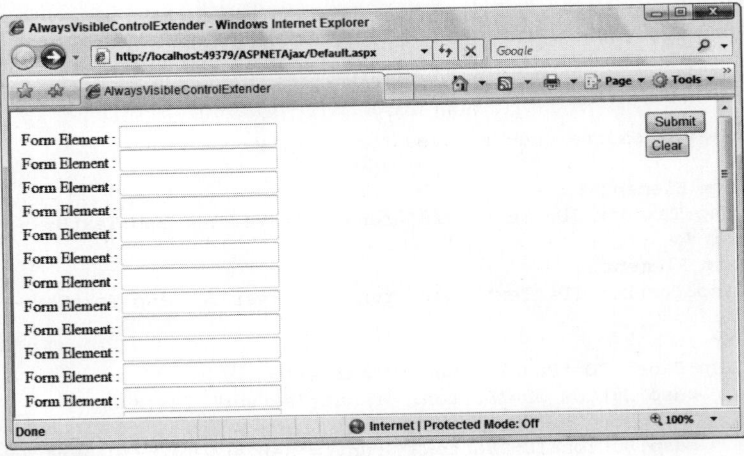

Figure 20-9

AnimationExtender

The AnimationExtender server control provides a tremendous amount of capabilities. It allows you to program fluid animations to the controls that you put on the page. There is a lot that you can do with this control (much more than can be shown in this chapter).

This control allows you to program elements that can move around the page based upon specific end user triggers (such as a button click). There are specific events available for you to program your animations against. These events are as follows:

- OnClick
- OnHoverOver
- OnHoverOut
- OnLoad
- OnMouseOver
- OnMouseOut

Creating animations is not as straightforward as many would like because there is little Visual Studio support (such as wizards or even IntelliSense). For an example of creating your first animation, Listing 20-3 shows how you can fade an element in and out of the page based upon an end user action.

Listing 20-3: Using the AnimationExtender to fade a background color

```
<%@ Page Language="C#" %>

<%@ Register Assembly="AjaxControlToolkit" Namespace="AjaxControlToolkit"
    TagPrefix="cc1" %>
```

```
<html xmlns="http://www.w3.org/1999/xhtml">
<head runat="server">
    <title>AnimationExtender</title>
</head>
<body>
    <form id="form1" runat="server">
    <div>
        <asp:ScriptManager ID="ScriptManager1" runat="server" />
        <cc1:AnimationExtender ID="AnimationExtender1" runat="server"
            TargetControlID="Panel1">
            <Animations>
                <OnClick>
                    <Sequence>
                        <Color PropertyKey="background" StartValue="#999966"
                         EndValue="#FFFFFF" Duration="5.0" />
                    </Sequence>
                </OnClick>
            </Animations>
        </cc1:AnimationExtender>
        <asp:Panel ID="Panel1" runat="server" BorderColor="Black"
            BorderWidth="3px" Font-Bold="True" Width="600px">
            Lorem ipsum dolor sit amet, consectetuer adipiscing elit.
            Donec accumsan lorem. Ut consectetuer tempus metus. Aenean tincidunt
            venenatis tellus. Suspendisse molestie cursus ipsum. Curabitur ut
            lectus. Nulla ac dolor nec elit convallis vulputate. Nullam pharetra
            pulvinar nunc. Duis orci. Phasellus a tortor at nunc mattis congue.
            Vestibulum porta tellus eu orci. Suspendisse quis massa. Maecenas
            varius, erat non ullamcorper nonummy, mauris erat eleifend odio, ut
            gravida nisl neque a ipsum. Vivamus facilisis. Cras viverra. Curabitur
            ut augue eget dolor semper posuere. Aenean at magna eu eros tempor
            pharetra. Aenean mauris.
        </asp:Panel>
    </div>
    </form>
</body>
</html>
```

In this case, when you pull up the page from Listing 20-3, you will see that it uses a single AnimationExtender control that is working off the `Panel1` control. This connection is made using the `TargetControlID` property.

As stated, Intellisense is not enabled when you are typing the code that is contained within the AnimationExtender control, so you are going to have to look in the documentation for the animations that you want to create. In the case of the previous example, the `<OnClick>` element is utilized to define a sequence of events that need to occur when the control is clicked. For this example, there is only one animation defined within the `<Sequence>` element — a color change to the background of the element. Here, the `<Color>` element states that the background CSS property will need to start at the color `#999966` and change completely to color `#FFFFFF` within 5 seconds (defined using the `Duration` property).

When you pull up this page and click on the Panel element, you will see the color change in a five-second duration from the described start color to the end color.

AutoCompleteExtender

The `AutoCompleteExtender` control provides you the ability to help the end user find what they might be looking for when they have to type in search terms within a text box. Like the product Google Suggest (shown in Figure 20-10), once you start typing characters in the text box, you will get results from a datastore that matches what you have typed so far.

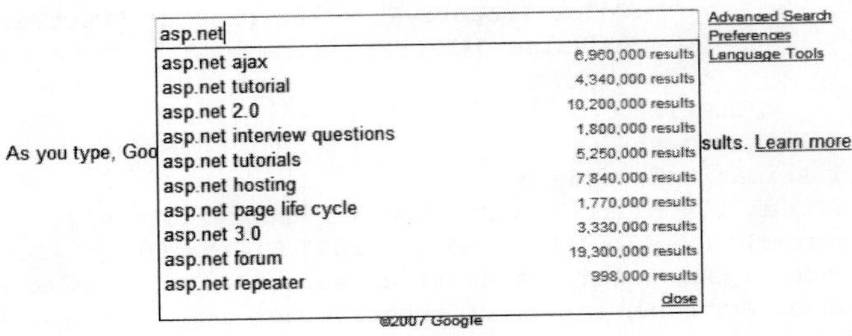

Figure 20-10

To establish something similar for yourself, create a new page that contains only a ScriptManager control, an AutoCompleteExtender control, and a TextBox control. The ASP.NET portion of the page should appear as presented in Listing 20-4.

Listing 20-4: The ASP.NET page

```
<%@ Page Language="C#" AutoEventWireup="true" CodeFile="AutoComplete.aspx.cs"
    Inherits="AutoComplete" %>

<%@ Register Assembly="AjaxControlToolkit" Namespace="AjaxControlToolkit"
    TagPrefix="cc1" %>

<html xmlns="http://www.w3.org/1999/xhtml">
<head runat="server">
    <title>AutoComplete</title>
</head>
<body>
    <form id="form1" runat="server">
    <div>
        <asp:ScriptManager ID="ScriptManager1" runat="server">
        </asp:ScriptManager>
        <cc1:AutoCompleteExtender ID="AutoCompleteExtender1" runat="server"
            TargetControlID="TextBox1" ServiceMethod="GetCompletionList"
            UseContextKey="True">
        </cc1:AutoCompleteExtender>
        <asp:TextBox ID="TextBox1" runat="server"></asp:TextBox>
    </div>
    </form>
</body>
</html>
```

Again, like the other ASP.NET AJAX controls, you extend the TextBox control using the `TargetControlID` property. When you first add these controls to the page, you will not have the `ServiceMethod` property defined in the AutoCompleteExtender control. Using Visual Studio 2008, you can make the framework for a service method and tie the extender control to this method all from the design surface. After expanding the TextBox control's smart tag, select the Add AutoComplete page method option from the provided menu, shown in Figure 20-11.

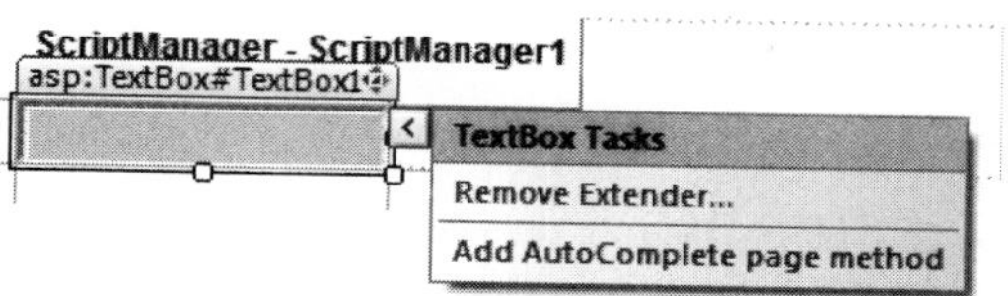

Figure 20-11

This action creates a service method in the code-behind for your page. Listing 20-4 shows the steps necessary to complete this method to call the company names from the Northwind database.

Instructions on downloading and using the Northwind database can be found in Chapter 8.

Listing 20-4: The code-behind that sets up the service method for auto-complete

VB

```
Imports System.Data
Imports System.Data.SqlClient

Partial Class AutoComplete
    Inherits System.Web.UI.Page

    <System.Web.Services.WebMethodAttribute(), _
     System.Web.Script.Services.ScriptMethodAttribute()> _
    Public Shared Function GetCompletionList(ByVal prefixText As String, _
      ByVal count As Integer) As String()
        Dim conn As SqlConnection
        Dim cmd As SqlCommand
        Dim cmdString As String =
            "Select CompanyName from Customers WHERE CompanyName LIKE '" & _
            prefixText & "%'"
        conn = New SqlConnection("Data Source=.\SQLEXPRESS;
            AttachDbFilename=|DataDirectory|\NORTHWND.MDF;
            Integrated Security=True;User Instance=True")
        ' Put this string on one line in your code
        cmd = New SqlCommand(cmdString, conn)
        conn.Open()

        Dim myReader As SqlDataReader
        Dim returnData As List(Of String) = New List(Of String)
        myReader = cmd.ExecuteReader(CommandBehavior.CloseConnection)

        While myReader.Read()
```

Continued

```
            returnData.Add(myReader("CompanyName").ToString())
        End While

        Return returnData.ToArray()
    End Function
End Class
```

C#

```
using System.Collections.Generic;
using System.Data;
using System.Data.SqlClient;

public partial class AutoComplete : System.Web.UI.Page
{
    [System.Web.Services.WebMethodAttribute(),
     System.Web.Script.Services.ScriptMethodAttribute()]
    public static string[] GetCompletionList(string prefixText, int count,
       string contextKey)
    {
        SqlConnection conn;
        SqlCommand cmd;
        string cmdString =
           "Select CompanyName from Customers WHERE CompanyName LIKE '" +
           prefixText + "%'";
        conn = new
            SqlConnection(@"Data Source=.\SQLEXPRESS;
            AttachDbFilename=|DataDirectory|\NORTHWND.MDF;
            Integrated Security=True;User Instance=True");
        // Put this string on one line in your code
        cmd = new SqlCommand(cmdString, conn);
        conn.Open();

        SqlDataReader myReader;
        List<string> returnData = new List<string>();

        myReader = cmd.ExecuteReader(CommandBehavior.CloseConnection);

        while (myReader.Read())
        {
            returnData.Add(myReader["CompanyName"].ToString());
        }

        return returnData.ToArray();
    }
}
```

When you run this page and type the characters **alf** into the text box, the `GetCompletionList()` method is called, passing in these characters. These characters are retrievable through the `prefixText` parameter (you can also use the `count` parameter, which is defaulted at `10`). The Northwind database is called using the `prefixText` value and this is what is returned back to the TextBox1 control. In the end, you get a drop-down list of the items that match the first three characters that were entered into the text box. This is illustrated in Figure 20-12.

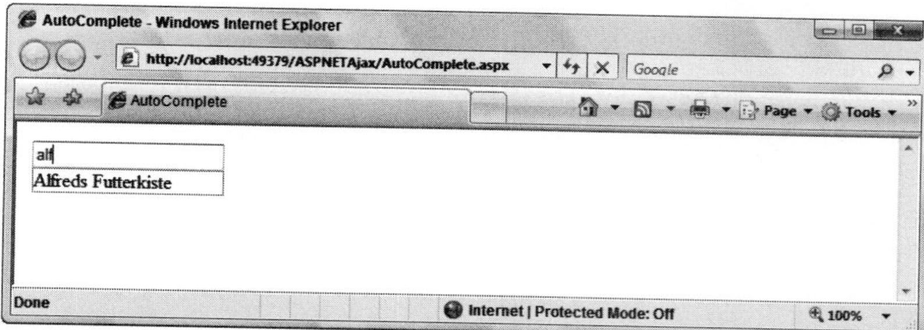

Figure 20-12

It is good to know that the results, once called the first time, are cached. This caching is controlled via the `EnableCaching` property (it is defaulted to `true`). You can also change the style of the drop-down auto-complete list, configure how many elements appear, and many more points of this feature. One more important point is that you are not required to call a method that is exposed out on the same page as the control as the example in this book demonstrates, but you can also call another server-side method on another page, or a Web method.

CalendarExtender

If there is one problem with a form that slows form submission up, it is selecting dates and trying to figure out which format of the date the form requires. The CalendarExtender control is a solution that makes it simple for your end users to select a date within a form.

The quickest way for end users to select a date in a form is to have a calendar that they can navigate to find the date they require. The calendar date can then be translated to a textual date format in the text box. The CalendarExtender control gives you all the client-side code required for this kind of action. Listing 20-5 shows you an example of providing a calendar control off your textbox controls.

Listing 20-5: Using a calendar control from a TextBox control

```
<%@ Page Language="VB" %>

<%@ Register Assembly="AjaxControlToolkit" Namespace="AjaxControlToolkit"
    TagPrefix="cc1" %>

<html xmlns="http://www.w3.org/1999/xhtml">
<head runat="server">
    <title>CalendarExtender</title>
</head>
<body>
    <form id="form1" runat="server">
    <div>
```

Continued

```
            <asp:ScriptManager ID="ScriptManager1" runat="server">
            </asp:ScriptManager>
            <cc1:CalendarExtender ID="CalendarExtender1" runat="server"
             TargetControlID="TextBox1">
            </cc1:CalendarExtender>
            <asp:TextBox ID="TextBox1" runat="server"></asp:TextBox>
        </div>
        </form>
    </body>
    </html>
```

When you run this page, the result will be a single text box on the page and the text box will appear no different from any other text box. However, when the end user clicks inside of the text box, a calendar appears directly below it as shown in Figure 20-13.

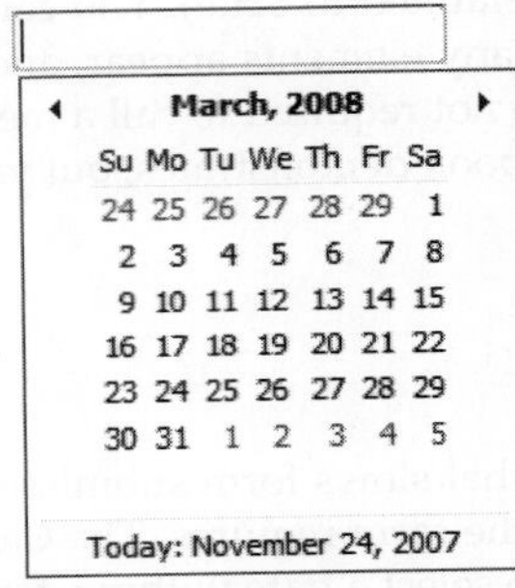

Figure 20-13

Then, when the end user selects a date from the calendar, the date is placed as text within the text box as illustrated in Figure 20-14.

3/8/2008

Figure 20-14

Some of the properties exposed from this control are `FirstDayOfWeek` and `PopupPosition` (which has the options `BottomLeft`, `BottomRight`, `TopLeft`, and `TopRight`). You can also change how the calendar is initiated on the client. Some sites offer a calendar button next to the text box and only popup the calendar option when the end user clicks the button. If this is something that you would like to do on your pages, then you should use the `PopupButtonID` property, which you must point to the ID of the image or button that you are using.

CollapsiblePanelExtender

The CollapsiblePanelExtender server control allows you to collapse one control into another. When working with two Panel server controls, you can provide a nice way to control any real estate issues that you might be experiencing on your ASP.NET page.

An example of using the CollapsiblePanelExtender control with two Panel controls is illustrated here in Listing 20-6.

Listing 20-6: Using CollapsiblePanelExtender with two Panel controls

```
<%@ Page Language="C#" %>

<%@ Register Assembly="AjaxControlToolkit" Namespace="AjaxControlToolkit"
    TagPrefix="cc1" %>

<!DOCTYPE html PUBLIC "-//W3C//DTD XHTML 1.0 Transitional//EN"
 "http://www.w3.org/TR/xhtml1/DTD/xhtml1-transitional.dtd">

<html xmlns="http://www.w3.org/1999/xhtml">
<head runat="server">
    <title>CollapsiblePanelExtender</title>
</head>
<body>
    <form id="form1" runat="server">
    <div>
        <asp:ScriptManager ID="ScriptManager1" runat="server">
        </asp:ScriptManager>
        <cc1:CollapsiblePanelExtender ID="CollapsiblePanelExtender1" runat="server"
         TargetControlID="Panel2" Collapsed="True" ExpandControlID="Panel1"
         CollapseControlID="Panel2">
        </cc1:CollapsiblePanelExtender>
        <asp:Panel ID="Panel1" runat="server" BackColor="#000066"
         ForeColor="White">
            <asp:Label ID="Label2" runat="server"
             Text="This is my title"></asp:Label>
            <asp:Label ID="Label1" runat="server"
             Text="[Click to expand or collapse]"></asp:Label>
        </asp:Panel>
        <asp:Panel ID="Panel2" runat="server">
            Lorem ipsum dolor sit amet, consectetuer adipiscing elit.
            Donec accumsan lorem. Ut consectetuer tempus metus. Aenean tincidunt
            venenatis tellus. Suspendisse molestie cursus ipsum. Curabitur ut
            lectus. Nulla ac dolor nec elit convallis vulputate. Nullam pharetra
            pulvinar nunc. Duis orci. Phasellus a tortor at nunc mattis congue.
            Vestibulum porta tellus eu orci. Suspendisse quis massa. Maecenas
            varius, erat non ullamcorper nonummy, mauris erat eleifend odio, ut
            gravida nisl neque a ipsum. Vivamus facilisis. Cras viverra. Curabitur
            ut augue eget dolor semper posuere. Aenean at magna eu eros tempor
            pharetra. Aenean mauris.
        </asp:Panel>
    </div>
    </form>
</body>
</html>
```

In this case, when the page is pulled up for the first time you will only see the contents of `Panel1` — the title panel. By default, you would usually see both controls, but since the `Collapsed` property is set to `True` in the control, you will only see Panel1. Clicking the Panel control will then expose the contents of Panel2. In fact, the contents will slide out from the Panel1 control. Tying these two controls together to do this action is accomplished through the use of the CollapsiblePanelExtender control. This control's `TargetControlID` is assigned to the second Panel control — Panel2, as this is the control that needs to expand onto the page. The `ExpandControlID` property is the control that initiates the expansion.

Once expanded, it is when the end user clicks on the Panel2 that the contents will disappear by sliding back into Panel1. This is accomplished through the use of the `CollapseControlID` property being assigned to `Panel2`.

The CollapsiblePanelExtender control has a number of properties that allow you to fine-tune how the expanding and collapsing occur. For instance, you could have also set the Label1 control to be the initiator of this process and even change the text of the Label control depending on the whether the Panel2 is collapsed or expanded. This use is illustrated in Listing 20-7.

Listing 20-7: Using a Label control to expand or collapse the Panel control

```
<cc1:CollapsiblePanelExtender ID="CollapsiblePanelExtender1" runat="server"
 TargetControlID="Panel2" Collapsed="True" ExpandControlID="Label1"
 CollapseControlID="Label1"
 CollapsedText="[Click to expand]"
 ExpandedText="[Click to collapse]"
 TextLabelID="Label1">
</cc1:CollapsiblePanelExtender>
```

In this case, when the end user clicks on the Label1 control, not only will Panel2 expand and collapse, but the text within the Label1 control will change accordingly.

ConfirmButtonExtender and ModalPopupExtender

Usually before allowing your end users to make deletions of data via a browser application, you want to confirm with the end user upon such actions. ConfirmButtonExtender allows you to question the end user's action and reconfirm that they want the action to occur. Listing 20-8 shows how to use this control.

Listing 20-8: Using the ConfirmButtonExtender control to reconfirm a user action

```
<%@ Page Language="C#" %>

<%@ Register Assembly="AjaxControlToolkit" Namespace="AjaxControlToolkit"
    TagPrefix="cc1" %>

<html xmlns="http://www.w3.org/1999/xhtml">
<head runat="server">
    <title>ConfirmButtonExtender</title>
</head>
<body>
    <form id="form1" runat="server">
    <div>
        <asp:ScriptManager ID="ScriptManager1" runat="server">
        </asp:ScriptManager>
        <cc1:ConfirmButtonExtender ID="ConfirmButtonExtender1" runat="server"
         TargetControlID="Button1"
         ConfirmText="Are you sure you wanted to click this button?">
        </cc1:ConfirmButtonExtender>
```

```
            <asp:Button ID="Button1" runat="server" Text="Button" />
        </div>
        </form>
    </body>
    </html>
```

In this case, the ConfirmButtonExtender extends the Button1 server control and adds a confirmation dialog using the text defined with the `ConfirmText` property. This page is shown in Figure 20-15.

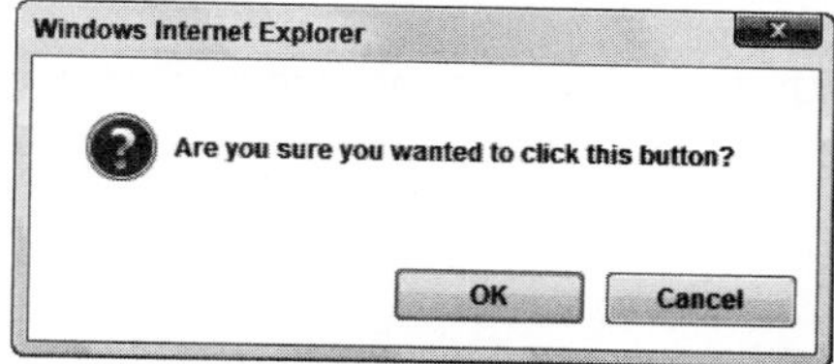

Figure 20-15

If the end user clicks OK in this instance, then the page will function normally as if the dialog never occurred. However, if Cancel is clicked, by default the dialog will disappear and the form will not be submitted (it will be as if the button was not clicked at all). In this case, you can also capture the Cancel button being clicked and perform a client-side operation by using the `OnClientClick` event and giving it a value of a client-side JavaScript function.

Instead of using the browsers modal dialogs, you can even go as far as creating your own to use as the confirmation form. To accomplish this task, you will need to use the new ModalPopupExtender server control. The `ModalPopupExtender` control points to another control to use for the confirmation. Listing 20-9 shows how to make use of this control.

Listing 20-9: Using the ModalPopupExtender control to create your own confirmation form

```
<%@ Page Language="C#" %>

<%@ Register Assembly="AjaxControlToolkit" Namespace="AjaxControlToolkit"
 TagPrefix="cc1" %>

<html xmlns="http://www.w3.org/1999/xhtml">
<head runat="server">
    <title>ConfirmButtonExtender</title>
</head>
<body>
    <form id="form1" runat="server">
    <div>
        <asp:ScriptManager ID="ScriptManager1" runat="server">
        </asp:ScriptManager>
        <cc1:ConfirmButtonExtender ID="ConfirmButtonExtender1" runat="server"
         TargetControlID="Button1"
         DisplayModalPopupID="ModalPopupExtender1">
        </cc1:ConfirmButtonExtender>
```

Continued

```
            <cc1:ModalPopupExtender ID="ModalPopupExtender1" runat="server"
                CancelControlID="ButtonNo" OkControlID="ButtonYes"
                PopupControlID="Panel1"
                TargetControlID="Button1">
            </cc1:ModalPopupExtender>
            <asp:Button ID="Button1" runat="server" Text="Button" />
            <asp:Panel ID="Panel1" runat="server"
             style="display:none; background-color:White; width:200;
             border-width:2px; border-color:Black; border-style:solid; padding:20px;">
             Are you sure you wanted to click this button?<br />
             <asp:Button ID="ButtonYes" runat="server" Text="Yes" />
             <asp:Button ID="ButtonNo" runat="server" Text="No" />
            </asp:Panel>
        </div>
        </form>
    </body>
    </html>
```

In this example, the ConfirmButtonExtender still points to the Button1 control on the page, meaning that when the button is clicked, then the ConfirmButtonExtender will take action. Instead of using the `ConfirmText` property, the `DisplayModalPopupID` property is used. In this case, it points to the ModalPopupExtender1 control — another extender control.

The ModalPopupExtender control, in turn, references the Panel1 control on the page through the use of the `PopupControlID` property. The contents of this Panel control is used for the confirmation on the button click. For this to work, the ModalPopupExtender control has to have a value for the `OkControlID` and the `CancelControlID` properties. In this case, these two properties point to the two Button controls that are contained within the Panel control. When you run this page, you will get the results shown in Figure 20-16.

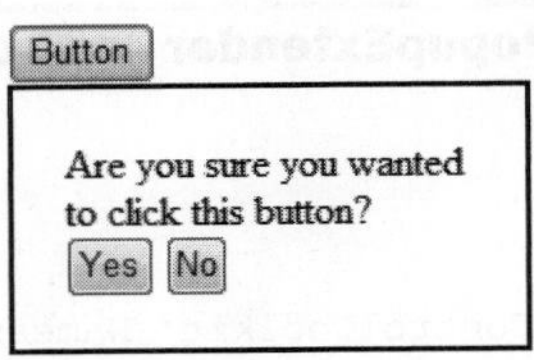

Figure 20-16

DragPanelExtender

The DragPanelExtender enables you define areas where end users can move elements around the page as they wish. The end user actually has the ability to drag and drop the element anywhere on the browser page.

To enable this feature, you have to do a few things. The first suggestion is to create a `<div>` area on the page that is large enough for to drag the item around in. From here, you need to specify what will be used as the drag handle and another control that will follow the drag handle around. In the example in Listing 20-10, the Label control is used as the drag handle, and the Panel2 control is the content that is dragged around the screen.

Listing 20-10: Dragging a Panel control around the page

```
<%@ Page Language="C#" %>

<%@ Register Assembly="AjaxControlToolkit" Namespace="AjaxControlToolkit"
    TagPrefix="cc1" %>

<html xmlns="http://www.w3.org/1999/xhtml">
<head runat="server">
    <title>DragPanel control</title>
</head>
<body>
    <form id="form1" runat="server">
    <div>
        <asp:ScriptManager ID="ScriptManager1" runat="server">
        </asp:ScriptManager>
        <div style="height: 600px;">
            <cc1:DragPanelExtender ID="DragPanelExtender1" runat="server"
             DragHandleID="Label1" TargetControlID="Panel1">
            </cc1:DragPanelExtender>
            <asp:Panel ID="Panel1" runat="server" Width="450px">
                <asp:Label ID="Label1" runat="server"
                 Text="Drag this Label control to move the control"
                 BackColor="DarkBlue" ForeColor="White"></asp:Label>
                <asp:Panel ID="Panel2" runat="server" Width="450px">
            Lorem ipsum dolor sit amet, consectetuer adipiscing elit.
            Donec accumsan lorem. Ut consectetuer tempus metus. Aenean tincidunt
            venenatis tellus. Suspendisse molestie cursus ipsum. Curabitur ut
            lectus. Nulla ac dolor nec elit convallis vulputate. Nullam pharetra
            pulvinar nunc. Duis orci. Phasellus a tortor at nunc mattis congue.
            Vestibulum porta tellus eu orci. Suspendisse quis massa. Maecenas
            varius, erat non ullamcorper nonummy, mauris erat eleifend odio, ut
            gravida nisl neque a ipsum. Vivamus facilisis. Cras viverra. Curabitur
            ut augue eget dolor semper posuere. Aenean at magna eu eros tempor
            pharetra. Aenean mauris.
                </asp:Panel>
            </asp:Panel>
        </div>
    </div>
    </form>
</body>
</html>
```

This example creates a <div> element that has a height of 600 pixels. Within this defined area, the example uses a DragPanelExtender control and targets the Panel1 control through the use of the TargetControlID property being assigned to this control.

Within the Panel1 control are two other server controls — a Label and another Panel control. The Label control is assigned to be the drag handle using the DragHandleID property of the DragPanelExtender control. With this little bit of code in place, you are now able to drag the Panel1 control around on your browser window. Figure 20-17 shows the Label control being used as a handle to drag around the Panel control.

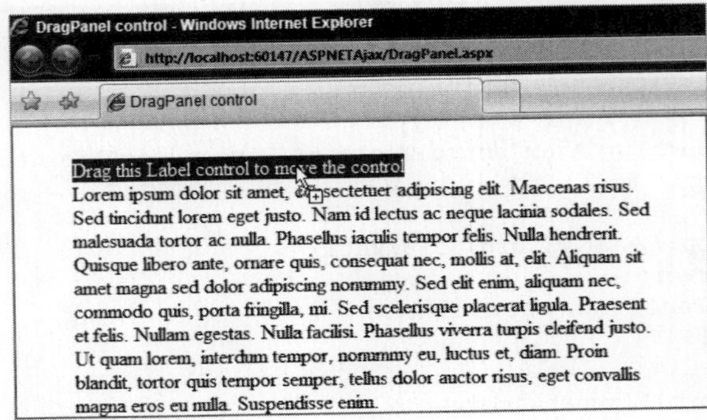

Figure 20-17

DropDownExtender

The DropDownExtender control allows you to take any control and provide a drop-down list of options below it for selection. It provides a different framework than a typical drop-down list control as it allows for an extreme level of customization. Listing 20-11 shows how you can even use an image as the initiator of drop-down list of options.

Listing 20-11: Using an Image control as an initiator of a drop-down list

VB

```
<%@ Page Language="VB" %>

<%@ Register Assembly="AjaxControlToolkit" Namespace="AjaxControlToolkit"
    TagPrefix="cc1" %>

<script runat="server">
    Protected Sub Page_Load(ByVal sender As Object, ByVal e As System.EventArgs)
        Image1.ImageUrl = "Images/Creek.jpg"
    End Sub

    Protected Sub Option_Click(ByVal sender As Object, ByVal e As System.EventArgs)
        Image1.ImageUrl = "Images/" & DirectCast(sender, LinkButton).Text & ".jpg"
    End Sub
</script>

<html xmlns="http://www.w3.org/1999/xhtml">
<head runat="server">
    <title>DropDownExtender Control</title>
</head>
<body>
    <form id="form1" runat="server">
    <div>
        <asp:ScriptManager ID="ScriptManager1" runat="server">
```

```
        </asp:ScriptManager>
        <asp:UpdatePanel ID="UpdatePanel1" runat="server">
            <ContentTemplate>
                <cc1:DropDownExtender ID="DropDownExtender1" runat="server"
                 DropDownControlID="Panel1" TargetControlID="Image1">
                </cc1:DropDownExtender>
                <asp:Image ID="Image1" runat="server">
                </asp:Image>
            <asp:Panel ID="Panel1" runat="server" Height="50px" Width="125px">
                <asp:LinkButton ID="Option1" runat="server"
                 OnClick="Option_Click">Creek</asp:LinkButton>
                <asp:LinkButton ID="Option2" runat="server"
                 OnClick="Option_Click">Dock</asp:LinkButton>
                <asp:LinkButton ID="Option3" runat="server"
                 OnClick="Option_Click">Garden</asp:LinkButton>
            </asp:Panel>
            </ContentTemplate>
        </asp:UpdatePanel>
    </div>
    </form>
</body>
</html>
```

C#

```
<%@ Page Language="C#" %>

<%@ Register Assembly="AjaxControlToolkit" Namespace="AjaxControlToolkit"
    TagPrefix="cc1" %>

<script runat="server">
    protected void Page_Load(object sender, EventArgs e)
    {
        Image1.ImageUrl = "Images/Creek.jpg";
    }

    protected void Option_Click(object sender, EventArgs e)
    {
        Image1.ImageUrl = "Images/" + ((LinkButton)sender).Text + ".jpg";
    }
</script>
```

In this case, a DropDownExtender control is tied to an Image control that on the `Page_Load()` event displays a specific image. The DropDownExtender control has two specific properties that need to be filled. The first is the `TargetControlID` property that defines the control that becomes the initiator of the drop-down list. The second property is the `DropDownControlID` property, which defines the element on the page that will be used for the drop-down items that appear below the control. In this case, it is a Panel control with three LinkButton controls.

Each of the LinkButton controls designates a specific image that should appear on the page. Selecting one of the options changes the image to the choice through the `Option_Click()` method. Running this page gives you the results illustrated in Figure 20-18.

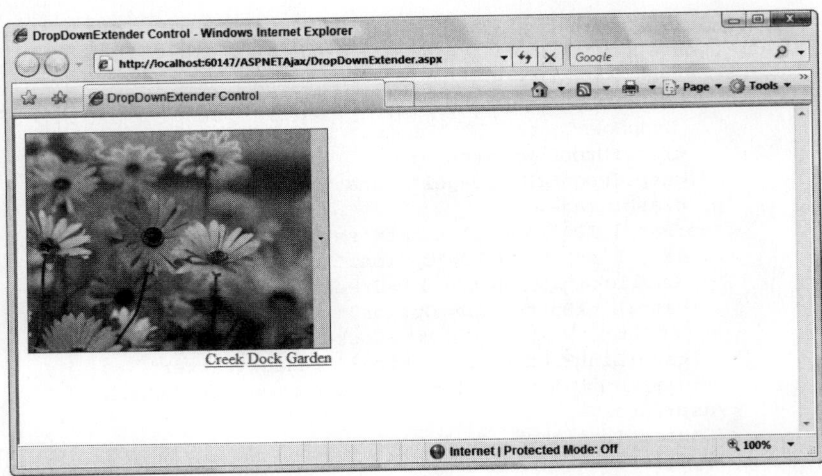

Figure 20-18

DropShadowExtender

The DropShadowExtender control allows you to put a drop shadow on any control you choose as the target. The first thought is an image (as shown here in Listing 20-12), but you can use it for any control that you wish.

Listing 20-12: Using DropShadowExtender with an Image control

```
<%@ Page Language="C#" %>

<%@ Register Assembly="AjaxControlToolkit" Namespace="AjaxControlToolkit"
    TagPrefix="cc1" %>

<html xmlns="http://www.w3.org/1999/xhtml">
<head runat="server">
    <title>DropShadowExtender Control</title>
</head>
<body>
    <form id="form1" runat="server">
    <div>
        <asp:ScriptManager ID="ScriptManager1" runat="server">
        </asp:ScriptManager>
        <cc1:DropShadowExtender ID="DropShadowExtender1" runat="server"
         TargetControlID="Image1">
        </cc1:DropShadowExtender>
        <asp:Image ID="Image1" runat="server" ImageUrl="Images/Garden.jpg" />
    </div>
    </form>
</body>
</html>
```

In this example, it is as simple as using the DropShadowExtender control with a `TargetControlID` of `Image1`. With this in place, the image will appear in the browser as shown in Figure 20-19.

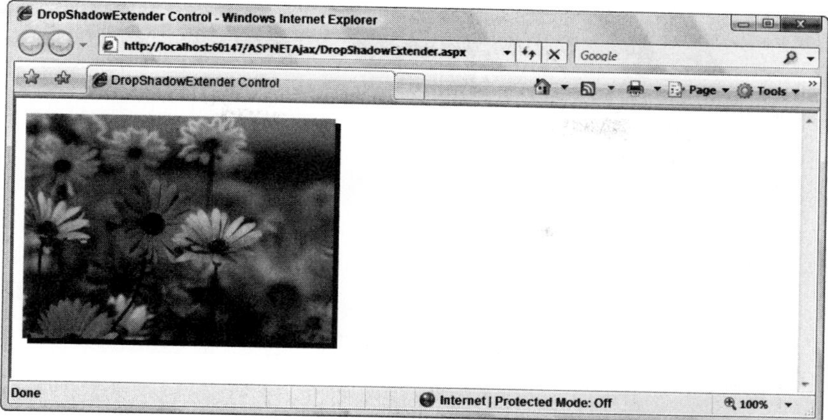

Figure 20-19

As stated, in addition to images, you can use DropShadowExtender for almost anything. Listing 20-13 shows how to use it with a Panel control.

Listing 20-13: Using the DropShadowExtender with a Panel control

```
<%@ Page Language="C#" %>

<%@ Register Assembly="AjaxControlToolkit" Namespace="AjaxControlToolkit"
    TagPrefix="cc1" %>

<html xmlns="http://www.w3.org/1999/xhtml">
<head runat="server">
    <title>DropShadowExtender Control</title>
</head>
<body>
    <form id="form1" runat="server">
    <div>
        <asp:ScriptManager ID="ScriptManager1" runat="server">
        </asp:ScriptManager>
        <cc1:DropShadowExtender ID="DropShadowExtender1" runat="server"
         TargetControlID="Panel1" Rounded="True">
        </cc1:DropShadowExtender>
        <asp:Panel ID="Panel1" runat="server" BackColor="Orange" Width="300"
         HorizontalAlign="Center">
            <asp:Login ID="Login1" runat="server">
            </asp:Login>
        </asp:Panel>
    </div>
    </form>
</body>
</html>
```

In this case, a Panel control with a Login control is extended with the DropShadowExtender control. The result is quite similar to that of the Image control's result. However, one addition to the DropShadow-Extender control here is that the `Rounded` property is set to `True` (by default, it is set to `False`). This produces the look shown in Figure 20-20.

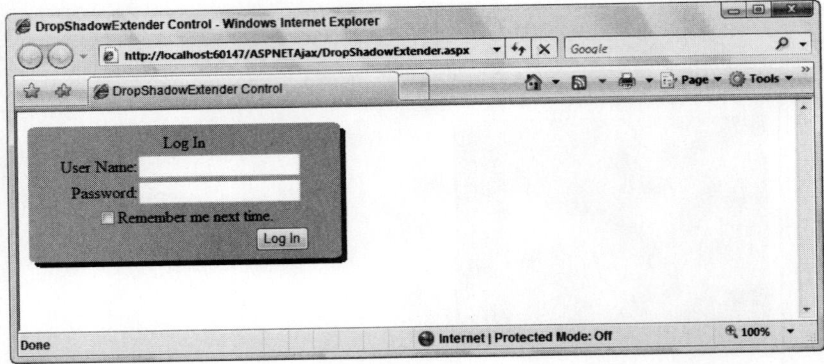

Figure 20-20

As you can see from Figure 20-20, not only are the edges of the drop shadow rounded, but also the entire Panel control has rounded edges. Other style properties that you can work with include the `Opacity` property, which controls the opacity of the drop shadow only, and the `Radius` property, which controls the radius used in rounding the edges and obviously works only if the `Rounded` property is set to `True`. By default, the `Opacity` setting is set at `1`, which means 100% visible. To set it at, say, 50% opacity, you have to set the `Opacity` value to `.5`.

DynamicPopulateExtender

The DynamicPopulateExtender control allows you to send dynamic HTML output to a Panel control. For this to work, you need one control or event that triggers a call back to the server to get the HTML that in turn gets pushed into the `Panel` control, thereby making a dynamic change on the client.

As with the AutoCompleteExtender control, you need a server-side event that returns something back to the client asynchronously. Listing 20-14 shows the code required to use this control on the `.aspx` page.

Listing 20-14: Using the DynamicPopulateExtender control to populate a Panel control

.ASPX

```
<%@ Page Language="VB" AutoEventWireup="true"
    CodeFile="DynamicPopulateExtender.aspx.vb"
    Inherits="DynamicPopulateExtender" %>

<%@ Register Assembly="AjaxControlToolkit, Version=3.5.11119.20050,
    Culture=neutral, PublicKeyToken=28f01b0e84b6d53e"
    Namespace="AjaxControlToolkit" TagPrefix="cc1" %>

<html xmlns="http://www.w3.org/1999/xhtml">
<head runat="server">
    <title>DynamicPopulateExtender Control</title>
    <script type="text/javascript">
      function updateGrid(value) {
        var behavior = $find('DynamicPopulateExtender1');
        if (behavior) {
            behavior.populate(value);
        }
      }
```

```
    </script>
</head>
<body>
    <form id="form1" runat="server">
    <div>
        <asp:ScriptManager ID="ScriptManager1" runat="server" />
        <cc1:DynamicPopulateExtender ID="DynamicPopulateExtender1" runat="server"
            TargetControlID="Panel1" ServiceMethod="GetDynamicContent">
        </cc1:DynamicPopulateExtender>
        <div onclick="updateGrid(this.value);" value='0'>
        <asp:LinkButton ID="LinkButton1" runat="server"
         OnClientClick="return false;">Customers</asp:LinkButton></div>
        <div onclick="updateGrid(this.value);" value='1'>
        <asp:LinkButton ID="LinkButton2" runat="server"
         OnClientClick="return false;">Employees</asp:LinkButton></div>
        <div onclick="updateGrid(this.value);" value='2'>
        <asp:LinkButton ID="LinkButton3" runat="server"
         OnClientClick="return false;">Products</asp:LinkButton></div>
        <asp:Panel ID="Panel1" runat="server">
        </asp:Panel>
    </div>
    </form>
</body>
</html>
```

This `.aspx` page is doing a lot. First off, there is a client-side JavaScript function called `updateGrid()`. This function calls the DynamicPopulateExtender control that is on the page. You will also find three LinkButton server controls, each of which is encased within a `<div>` element that calls the `updateGrid()` function and provides a value that is passed into the function. Since you want the `<div>` element's `onclick` event to be triggered with a click and not the `LinkButton` control's click event, each LinkButton contains an `OnClientClick` attribute that simply does nothing. This is accomplished using `return false;`.

The DynamicPopulateExtender control on the page targets the Panel1 control as the container that will take the HTML that comes from the server on an asynchronous request. The DynamicPopulateExtender control knows where to go get the HTML using the `ServiceMethod` attribute. The value of this attribute calls the `GetDynamicContent()` method, which is in the page's code-behind file.

Once you have the `.aspx` page in place, the next step is to create the code-behind page. This page will contain the server-side method that is called by the DynamicPopulateExtender control. This is presented in Listing 20-15.

Listing 20-15: The code-behind page of the DynamicPopulateExtender.aspx page

VB

```
Imports System.Data
Imports System.Data.SqlClient
Imports System.IO

Partial Class DynamicPopulateExtender
    Inherits System.Web.UI.Page

    <System.Web.Services.WebMethodAttribute()> _
```

Continued

```
    <System.Web.Script.Services.ScriptMethodAttribute()> _
    Public Shared Function GetDynamicContent(ByVal contextKey As System.String) _
      As System.String
        Dim conn As SqlConnection
        Dim cmd As SqlCommand
        Dim cmdString As String = "Select * from Customers"

        Select Case contextKey
            Case "1"
                cmdString = "Select * from Employees"
            Case "2"
                cmdString = "Select * from Products"
        End Select

        conn = New SqlConnection("Data Source=.\SQLEXPRESS;
            AttachDbFilename=|DataDirectory|\NORTHWND.MDF;
            Integrated Security=True;User Instance=True")
            ' Put this string on one line in your code
        cmd = New SqlCommand(cmdString, conn)
        conn.Open()

        Dim myReader As SqlDataReader
        myReader = cmd.ExecuteReader(CommandBehavior.CloseConnection)

        Dim dt As New DataTable
        dt.Load(myReader)
        myReader.Close()

        Dim myGrid As New GridView
        myGrid.ID = "GridView1"
        myGrid.DataSource = dt
        myGrid.DataBind()

        Dim sw As New StringWriter
        Dim htw As HtmlTextWriter = New HtmlTextWriter(sw)

        myGrid.RenderControl(htw)
        htw.Close()

        Return sw.ToString()
    End Function
End Class
```

C#

```
using System.Data;
using System.Data.SqlClient;
using System.IO;
using System.Web.UI;
using System.Web.UI.WebControls;

public partial class DynamicPopulateExtender : System.Web.UI.Page
{
    [System.Web.Services.WebMethodAttribute(),
     System.Web.Script.Services.ScriptMethodAttribute()]
```

```
        public static string GetDynamicContent(string contextKey)
        {
            SqlConnection conn;
            SqlCommand cmd;
            string cmdString = "Select * from Customers";

            switch (contextKey)
            {
                case ("1"):
                    cmdString = "Select * from Employees";
                    break;
                case ("2"):
                    cmdString = "Select * from Products";
                    break;
            }

            conn = new
                SqlConnection(@"Data Source=.\SQLEXPRESS;
                   AttachDbFilename=|DataDirectory|\NORTHWND.MDF;
                   Integrated Security=True;User Instance=True");
                   // Put this string on one line in your code
            cmd = new SqlCommand(cmdString, conn);
            conn.Open();

            SqlDataReader myReader;
            myReader = cmd.ExecuteReader(CommandBehavior.CloseConnection);

            DataTable dt = new DataTable();
            dt.Load(myReader);
            myReader.Close();

            GridView myGrid = new GridView();
            myGrid.ID = "GridView1";
            myGrid.DataSource = dt;
            myGrid.DataBind();

            StringWriter sw = new StringWriter();
            HtmlTextWriter htw = new HtmlTextWriter(sw);

            myGrid.RenderControl(htw);
            htw.Close();

            return sw.ToString();
        }
    }
```

This code is the code-behind page for the `DynamicPopulateExtender.aspx` page and contains a single method that is callable asynchronously. The `GetDynamicContent()` method takes a single parameter, `contextKey`, a string value that can be used to determine what link the end user clicked.

Based upon the selection, a specific command string is used to populate a `DataTable` object. From here, the `DataTable` object is used as the data source for a programmatic GridView control that is rendered and returned as a string to the client. The client will take the large string and use the text to populate the Panel1 control that is on the page. The result of clicking one of the links is shown in Figure 20-21.

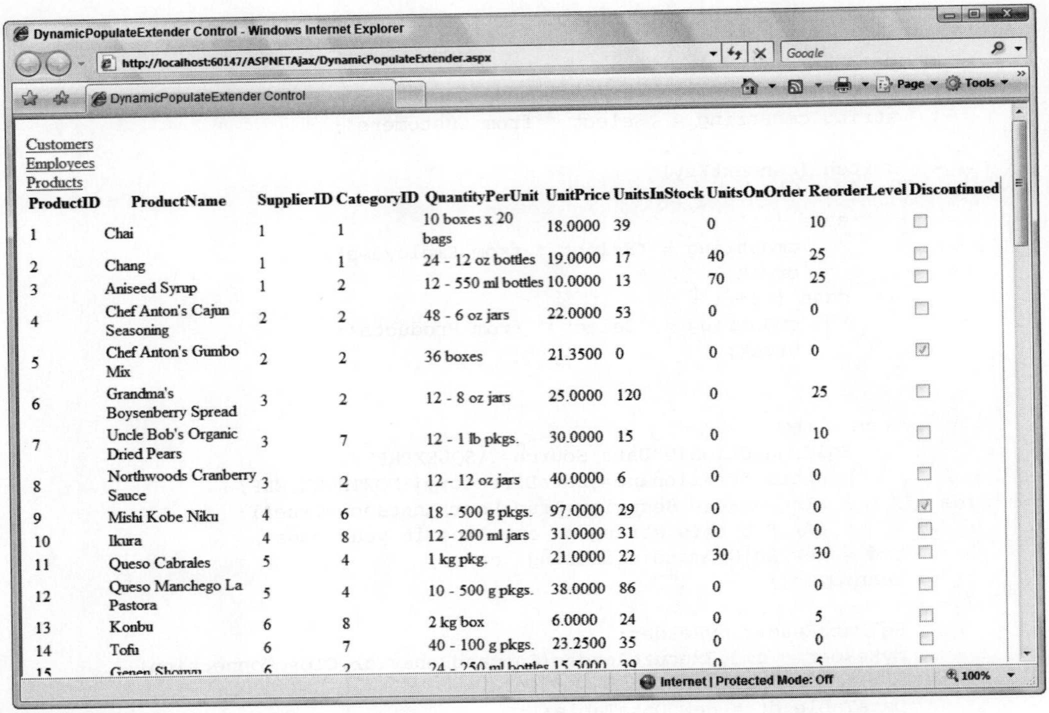

Figure 20-21

FilteredTextBoxExtender

The FilteredTextBoxExtender control works off a `TextBox` control to specify the types of characters the end user can input into the control. For instance, if you want the end user to be able to enter only numbers into the text box, then you can associate a FilteredTextBoxExtender to the `TextBox` control and specify such behavior. An example of this is presented in Listing 20-16.

Listing 20-16: Filtering a text box to use only numbers

```
<%@ Page Language="C#" %>

<%@ Register Assembly="AjaxControlToolkit" Namespace="AjaxControlToolkit"
   TagPrefix="cc1" %>

<html xmlns="http://www.w3.org/1999/xhtml">
<head runat="server">
    <title>FilteredTextBoxExtender Control</title>
</head>
<body>
    <form id="form1" runat="server">
    <div>
        <asp:ScriptManager ID="ScriptManager1" runat="server">
        </asp:ScriptManager>
```

```
            <cc1:FilteredTextBoxExtender ID="FilteredTextBoxExtender1" runat="server"
             TargetControlID="TextBox1" FilterType="Numbers">
            </cc1:FilteredTextBoxExtender>
            <asp:TextBox ID="TextBox1" runat="server"></asp:TextBox>
        </div>
        </form>
    </body>
    </html>
```

In this case, a FilteredTextBoxExtender control is attached to the TextBox1 control through the use of the `TargetControlID` property. The FilteredTextBoxExtender control has a property called `FilterType` that has the possible values of `Custom`, `LowercaseLetters`, `Numbers`, and `UppercaseLetters`.

This example uses a `FilterType` value of `Numbers`, meaning that only numbers can be entered into the text box. If the end user tries to enter any other type of information, then nothing happens — it will seem to the end user as if the key doesn't even function.

Another property the FilteredTextBoxExtender control exposes is the `FilterMode` and the `InvalidChars` properties. An example of using these two properties is presented here:

```
<cc1:FilteredTextBoxExtender ID="FilteredTextBoxExtender1" runat="server"
 TargetControlID="TextBox1" InvalidChars="*" FilterMode="InvalidChars">
</cc1:FilteredTextBoxExtender>
```

The default value of the `FilterMode` property is `ValidChars`. When set to `ValidChars`, the control works from the `FilterType` property and only allows what this property defines. When set to `InvalidChars`, you then use the `InvalidChars` property and put the characters here (multiple characters all go together with no space or item between them).

HoverMenuExtender

The HoverMenuExtender control allows you to make a hidden control appear on the screen when the end user hovers on another control. This means that you can build either elaborate ToolTips or provide extra functionality when an end user hovers somewhere in your application.

One example is to change a ListView control so that when the end user hovers over a product name, the Edit button for that row of data appears on the screen. The code for the `<ItemTemplate>` in the ListView control is partially shown in Listing 20-17.

Listing 20-17: Adding a hover button to the ListView control's ItemTemplate

```
<ItemTemplate>
   <tr style="background-color:#DCDCDC;color: #000000;">
      <td>
         <cc1:HoverMenuExtender ID="HoverMenuExtender1" runat="server"
          TargetControlID="ProductNameLabel" PopupControlID="Panel1"
          PopDelay="25" OffsetX="-50">
         </cc1:HoverMenuExtender>
         <asp:Panel ID="Panel1" runat="server" Height="50px" Width="125px">
            <asp:Button ID="EditButton" runat="server"
```

Continued

```
                CommandName="Edit" Text="Edit" />
            </asp:Panel>
        </td>
        <td>
            <asp:Label ID="ProductIDLabel" runat="server"
             Text='<%# Eval("ProductID") %>' />
        </td>
        <td>
            <asp:Label ID="ProductNameLabel" runat="server"
             Text='<%# Eval("ProductName") %>' />
        </td>

        <!-- Code removed for clarity -->

    </tr>
</ItemTemplate>
```

Here, a HoverMenuExtender control is attached to the Label control with the `ID` of `ProductNameLabel`, which appears in each row of the ListView control. This is done using the `TargetControlID` property, while the `PopupControlID` property is used to assign the control that appears dynamically when a user hovers the mouse over the targeted control.

The HoverMenuExtender control exposes several properties that control the style and behaviors of the popup. First off, the `PopDelay` property is used in this example and provides a means to delay the popup from occurring (in milliseconds). The `OffsetX` and `OffsetY` properties specify the location of the popup based upon the targeted control. In this case, the offset is set to `-50` (pixels). The results of the operation are shown in Figure 20-22.

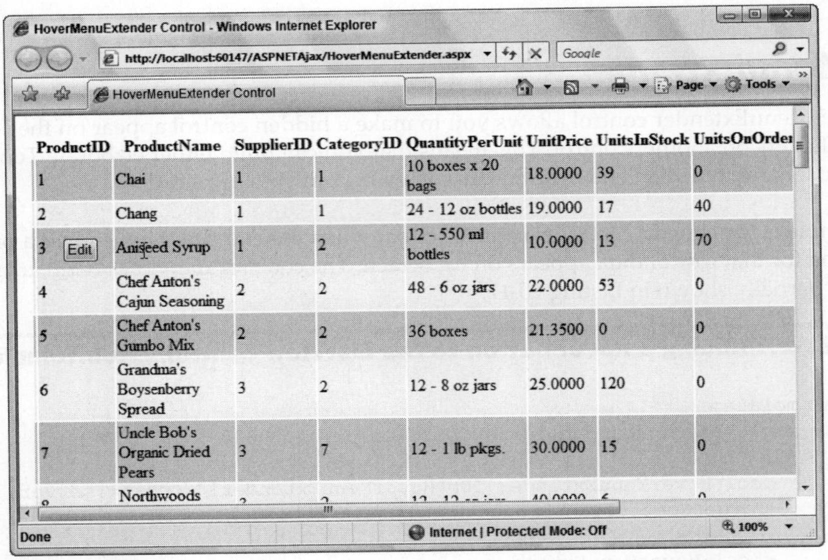

Figure 20-22

ListSearchExtender

The ListSearchExtender control extends either a ListBox or a DropDownList control, though not always with the best results in browsers such as Opera and Safari. This extender allows you to provide search capabilities through large collections that are located in either of these controls. This alleviates the need for the end users to search through the collection to find the item they are looking for.

When utilized, the extender adds a search text that shows the characters the end user types for their search area above the control. Listing 20-18 shows the use of this extender.

Listing 20-18: Extending a ListBox control with the ListSearchExtender control

```
<%@ Page Language="C#" %>

<%@ Register Assembly="AjaxControlToolkit" Namespace="AjaxControlToolkit"
    TagPrefix="cc1" %>

<html xmlns="http://www.w3.org/1999/xhtml">
<head runat="server">
    <title>ListSearchExtender Control</title>
</head>
<body>
    <form id="form1" runat="server">
    <div>
        <asp:ScriptManager ID="ScriptManager1" runat="server">
        </asp:ScriptManager>
        <cc1:ListSearchExtender ID="ListSearchExtender1" runat="server"
         TargetControlID="ListBox1">
        </cc1:ListSearchExtender>
        <asp:ListBox ID="ListBox1" runat="server" Width="150">
            <asp:ListItem>Aardvark</asp:ListItem>
            <asp:ListItem>Bee</asp:ListItem>
            <asp:ListItem>Camel</asp:ListItem>
            <asp:ListItem>Dog</asp:ListItem>
            <asp:ListItem>Elephant</asp:ListItem>
        </asp:ListBox>
    </div>
    </form>
</body>
</html>
```

In this case, the only property used in the ListSearchExtender control is the `TargetControlID` property to associate which control it extends. Running this page produces the results shown in Figure 20-23.

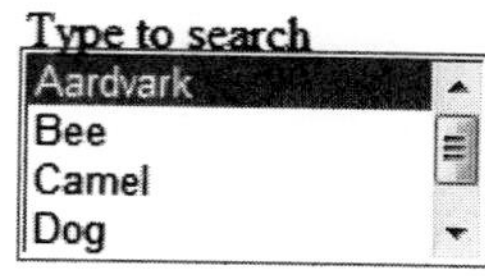

Figure 20-23

Then, as an end user, when you start typing, you will see what you are typing in the text above the control (as shown in Figure 20-24).

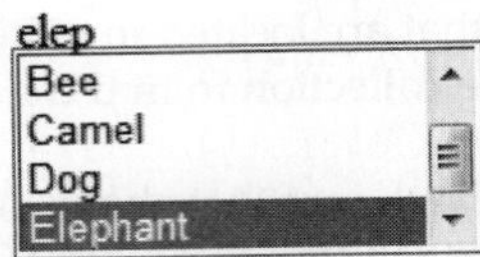

Figure 20-24

You can customize the text that appears at the top of the control with the `PromptCssClass`, `PromptPosition`, and `PromptText` properties. By default, the `PromptPosition` is set to `Top` (the other possible value is `Bottom`) and the `PromptText` value is `Type to search`.

MaskedEditExtender and MaskedEditValidator

The MaskedEditExtender control is similar to the FilteredTextBoxExtender control in that it restricts the end user from entering specific text within a TextBox control. This control takes the process one step further in that it provides the end user a template within the text box for them to follow. If the end users do not follow the template, they will be unable to proceed and might get a validation warning from the control using the MaskedEditValidator control.

Listing 20-19 provides an example of using both of these controls.

Listing 20-19: Using both the MaskedEditExtender and the MaskedEditValidator controls

```
<%@ Page Language="C#" %>

<%@ Register Assembly="AjaxControlToolkit, Version=3.5.11119.20050,
    Culture=neutral, PublicKeyToken=28f01b0e84b6d53e"
    Namespace="AjaxControlToolkit" TagPrefix="cc1" %>

<html xmlns="http://www.w3.org/1999/xhtml">
<head runat="server">
    <title>MaskedEditExtender Control</title>
</head>
<body>
    <form id="form1" runat="server">
    <div>
        <asp:ScriptManager ID="ScriptManager1" runat="server">
        </asp:ScriptManager>
        <cc1:MaskedEditExtender ID="MaskedEditExtender1" runat="server"
         TargetControlID="TextBox1" MaskType="Number" Mask="999">
        </cc1:MaskedEditExtender>
        <asp:TextBox ID="TextBox1" runat="server"></asp:TextBox>
        <cc1:MaskedEditValidator ID="MaskedEditValidator1" runat="server"
```

```
        ControlExtender="MaskedEditExtender1" ControlToValidate="TextBox1"
        IsValidEmpty="False" EmptyValueMessage="A three digit number is required!"
        Display="Dynamic"></cc1:MaskedEditValidator>
    </div>
    </form>
</body>
</html>
```

In this case, the MaskedEditExtender control uses the `TargetControlID` to associate itself with the TextBox1 control. The `MaskType` property supplies the type of mask or filter to place on the text box. The possible values include:

- `None` — means that no validation will be performed.
- `Date` — means date validation will occur.
- `DateTime` — means date and time validation will occur.
- `Number` — means a number validation will occur.
- `Time` — means a time validation will occur

Listing 20-19 uses `Number` and then specifies the mask or template the numbers need to take. This is done through the use of the `Mask` property. In this case, the `Mask` property is set to `999`. This means that all numbers can be only three digits in length.

Using `999` as a value to the `Mask` property means that when end user enters a value in the text box, he will be presented with three underscores inside the text box. This is the template for entering items. This is shown in Figure 20-25.

Figure 20-25

If the `Mask` property is changed to `99,999.99` as follows:

```
<cc1:MaskedEditExtender ID="MaskedEditExtender1" runat="server"
 TargetControlID="TextBox1" MaskType="Number" Mask="99,999.99">
</cc1:MaskedEditExtender>
```

. . . the textbox template appears as illustrated in Figure 20-26.

Figure 20-26

From Figure 20.26, you can see that the comma and the period are present in the template. As the end users type, they do not need to retype these values. The cursor will simply move to the next section of numbers required.

As you can see from the Mask property value, numbers are represented by the number 9. When working with other MaskType values, you also need to be aware of the other mask characters. These are provided here in the following list:

- 9 — Only a numeric character
- L — Only a letter
- $ — Only a letter or a space
- C — Only a custom character (case sensitive)
- A — Only a letter or a custom character
- N — Only a numeric or custom character
- ? — Any character

In addition to the character specifications, the delimiters used in the template are detailed in the following list:

- / is a date separator
- : is a time separator
- . is a decimal separator
- , is a thousand separator
- \ is the escape character
- { is the initial delimiter for repetition of masks
- } is the final delimiter for repetition of masks

Using some of these items, you can easily change MaskedEditExtender to deal with a DateTime value:

```
<cc1:MaskedEditExtender ID="MaskedEditExtender1" runat="server"
 TargetControlID="TextBox1" MaskType="DateTime" Mask="99/99/9999 99:99:99">
</cc1:MaskedEditExtender>
```

The template created in the text box for this is shown in Figure 20-27.

Figure 20-27

The MaskedEditExtender control has a ton of properties that are exposed to control and manipulate the behavior and style of the text box. The MaskedEditExtender control can work in conjunction with the MaskedEditValidator control, which provides validation against the text box controls.

In the earlier example, the validation was accomplished through an instance of the MaskedEditValidator control.

```
<cc1:MaskedEditValidator ID="MaskedEditValidator1" runat="server"
 ControlExtender="MaskedEditExtender1" ControlToValidate="TextBox1"
```

```
IsValidEmpty="False" EmptyValueMessage="A three digit number is required!"
Display="Dynamic"></cc1:MaskedEditValidator>
```

This control uses the ControlExtender property to associate itself with the MaskedEditExtender control and uses the `ControlToValidate` property to watch a specific control on the form. By default, the `IsValidEmpty` property is set to `True`, but changing it to `False` means that the end user will be required to enter some value in the text box in order to pass validation and not get the error message that is presented in the `EmptyValueMessage` property.

Triggering the MaskedEditValidator control gives you something like the message shown in Figure 20-28. It is important to remember that you can style the control in many ways to produce the validation message appearance that you are looking for.

A three digit number is required!

Figure 20-28

MutuallyExclusiveCheckBoxExtender

Often you want to offer a list of check boxes that behave as if they are radio buttons. That is, when you have a collection of check boxes, you will only want the end user to make a single selection from the provided list of items. However, unlike a radio button, you also want to enable the end user to deselect an item or to make no selection whatsoever.

Using the MutuallyExclusiveCheckBoxExtender control, you can perform such an action. Listing 20-20 shows you how to accomplish this task.

Listing 20-20: Using the MutuallyExclusiveCheckBoxExtender control with check boxes

```
<%@ Page Language="C#" %>

<%@ Register Assembly="AjaxControlToolkit" Namespace="AjaxControlToolkit"
    TagPrefix="cc1" %>

<html xmlns="http://www.w3.org/1999/xhtml">
<head runat="server">
    <title>MutuallyExclusiveCheckBoxExtender Control</title>
</head>
<body>
    <form id="form1" runat="server">
    <div>
        <asp:ScriptManager ID="ScriptManager1" runat="server">
        </asp:ScriptManager>
        <cc1:MutuallyExclusiveCheckBoxExtender
         ID="MutuallyExclusiveCheckBoxExtender1" runat="server"
         TargetControlID="CheckBox1" Key="MyCheckboxes" />
        <asp:CheckBox ID="CheckBox1" runat="server" Text="Blue" /><br />
        <cc1:MutuallyExclusiveCheckBoxExtender
         ID="MutuallyExclusiveCheckBoxExtender2" runat="server"
         TargetControlID="CheckBox2" Key="MyCheckboxes" />
```

Continued

```
            <asp:CheckBox ID="CheckBox2" runat="server" Text="Brown" /><br />
            <cc1:MutuallyExclusiveCheckBoxExtender
             ID="MutuallyExclusiveCheckBoxExtender3" runat="server"
             TargetControlID="CheckBox3" Key="MyCheckboxes" />
            <asp:CheckBox ID="CheckBox3" runat="server" Text="Green" /><br />
            <cc1:MutuallyExclusiveCheckBoxExtender
             ID="MutuallyExclusiveCheckBoxExtender4" runat="server"
             TargetControlID="CheckBox4" Key="MyCheckboxes" />
            <asp:CheckBox ID="CheckBox4" runat="server" Text="Orange" /><br />
        </div>
        </form>
    </body>
    </html>
```

It is impossible to associate a MutuallyExclusiveCheckBoxExtender control with a CheckBoxList control, therefore, each of the check boxes needs to be laid out with CheckBox controls as the previous code demonstrates. You need to have one MutuallyExclusiveCheckBoxExtender control for each CheckBox control on the page.

You form a group of CheckBox controls by using the `Key` property. All the check boxes that you want in one group need to have the same `Key` value. In the example is Listing 20-20, all the check boxes share a `Key` value of `MyCheckboxes`.

Running this page, results in a list of four check boxes. When you select one of the check boxes, a check mark appears. Then, when you select another check box, the first checkbox you selected gets deselected. The best part is that you can even deselect what you have selected in the group, thereby selecting nothing in the check box group.

NumericUpDownExtender

The NumericUpDownExtender control allows you to put some up/down indicators next to a TextBox control that enable the end user to more easily control a selection.

A simple example of this is illustrated here in Listing 20-21.

Listing 20-21: Using the NumericUpDownExtender control

```
<%@ Page Language="C#" %>

<%@ Register Assembly="AjaxControlToolkit" Namespace="AjaxControlToolkit"
    TagPrefix="cc1" %>

<html xmlns="http://www.w3.org/1999/xhtml">
<head runat="server">
    <title>NumericUpDownExtender Control</title>
</head>
<body>
    <form id="form1" runat="server">
    <div>
        <asp:ScriptManager ID="ScriptManager1" runat="server">
        </asp:ScriptManager>
        <cc1:NumericUpDownExtender ID="NumericUpDownExtender1" runat="server"
         TargetControlID="TextBox1" Width="150" Maximum="10" Minimum="1">
```

```
        </cc1:NumericUpDownExtender>
        <asp:TextBox ID="TextBox1" runat="server"></asp:TextBox>
    </div>
    </form>
</body>
</html>
```

The NumericUpDownExtender control here extends the TextBox control on the page. When using the NumericUpDownExtender control, you have to specify the width of the control with the `Width` property. Otherwise, you will see only the up and down arrow keys and not the text box area. In this case, the `Width` property is set to `150` (pixels). The `Maximum` and `Minimum` properties provide the range used by the up and down indicators.

With a `Maximum` value setting of `10` and a `Minimum` value of `1`, the only range in the control will be 1 through 10. Running this page produces the results shown in Figure 20-29.

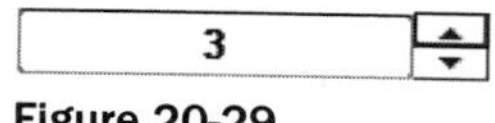

Figure 20-29

In addition to numbers as is shown with Listing 20-21, you can also use text as is illustrated here in Listing 20-22.

Listing 20-22: Using characters instead of numbers with NumericUpDownExtender

```
<cc1:NumericUpDownExtender ID="NumericUpDownExtender1" runat="server"
 TargetControlID="TextBox1" Width="150"
 RefValues="Blue;Brown;Green;Orange;Black;White">
</cc1:NumericUpDownExtender>
```

In this case, the words are defined within the `RefValues` property (all separated with a semicolon). This gives you the results presented in Figure 20-30.

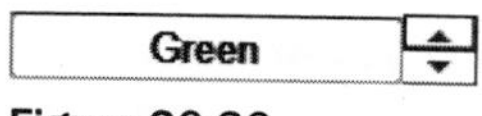

Figure 20-30

PagingBulletedListExtender

The PagingBulletedListExtender control allows you to take long bulleted lists and easily apply alphabetic paging to the list. For an example of this, Listing 20-23 will work off of the Customers table within the Northwind database.

Listing 20-23: Paging a bulleted list from the Northwind database

```
<%@ Page Language="C#" %>

<%@ Register Assembly="AjaxControlToolkit" Namespace="AjaxControlToolkit"
    TagPrefix="cc1" %>

<html xmlns="http://www.w3.org/1999/xhtml">
```

Continued

```
<head runat="server">
    <title>PagingBulletedListExtender Control</title>
</head>
<body>
    <form id="form1" runat="server">
    <div>
        <asp:ScriptManager ID="ScriptManager1" runat="server">
        </asp:ScriptManager>
        <cc1:PagingBulletedListExtender ID="PagingBulletedListExtender1"
         runat="server" TargetControlID="BulletedList1">
        </cc1:PagingBulletedListExtender>
        <asp:SqlDataSource ID="SqlDataSource1" runat="server"
            ConnectionString="Data Source=.\SQLEXPRESS;
               AttachDbFilename=|DataDirectory|\NORTHWND.MDF;
               Integrated Security=True;User Instance=True"
            ProviderName="System.Data.SqlClient"
            SelectCommand="SELECT [CompanyName] FROM [Customers]">
        </asp:SqlDataSource>
        <asp:BulletedList ID="BulletedList1" runat="server"
            DataSourceID="SqlDataSource1" DataTextField="CompanyName"
            DataValueField="CompanyName">
        </asp:BulletedList>
    </div>
    </form>
</body>
</html>
```

This code pulls all the `CompanyName` values from the Customers table of the Northwind database and binds those values to the BulletList control on the page. Running this page gives you the results illustrated in Figure 20-31.

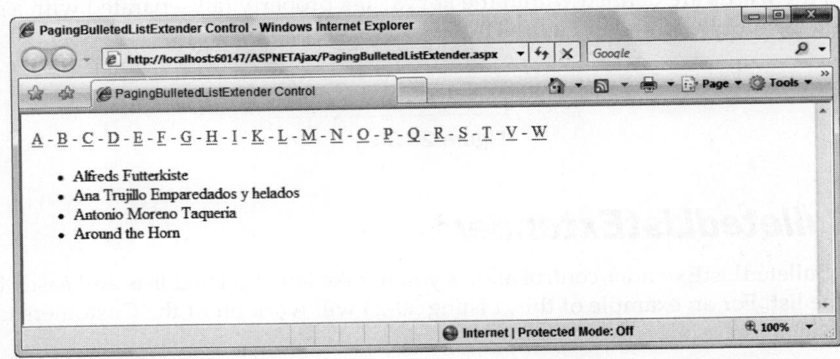

Figure 20-31

From this figure, you can see that the paging is organized alphabetically on the client side. Only the letters for which there are values appear in the linked list of letters. Clicking any of the letters gives you the items from the bulleted list that start with that character.

PopupControlExtender

The PopupControlExtender control allows you to create a popup for any control on your page. For instance, you can completely mimic the CalendarExtender control that was presented earlier by creating a popup containing a Calendar control off a TextBox control. Listing 20-24 mimics this behavior.

Listing 20-24: Creating a CalendarExtender control with PopupControlExtender

VB

```
<%@ Page Language="VB" %>

<%@ Register Assembly="AjaxControlToolkit" Namespace="AjaxControlToolkit"
    TagPrefix="cc1" %>

<script runat="server">
    Protected Sub Calendar1_SelectionChanged(ByVal sender As Object, _
      ByVal e As System.EventArgs)
        PopupControlExtender1.Commit(Calendar1.SelectedDate.ToShortDateString())
    End Sub
</script>

<html xmlns="http://www.w3.org/1999/xhtml">
<head runat="server">
    <title>PopupControlExtender Control</title>
</head>
<body>
    <form id="form1" runat="server">
    <div>
        <asp:ScriptManager ID="ScriptManager1" runat="server">
        </asp:ScriptManager>
        <cc1:PopupControlExtender ID="PopupControlExtender1" runat="server"
         TargetControlID="TextBox1" PopupControlID="UpdatePanel1" OffsetY="25">
        </cc1:PopupControlExtender>
        <asp:TextBox ID="TextBox1" runat="server"></asp:TextBox>
        <asp:UpdatePanel ID="UpdatePanel1" runat="server">
            <ContentTemplate>
                <asp:Calendar ID="Calendar1" runat="server" BackColor="White"
                 BorderColor="White" BorderWidth="1px" Font-Names="Verdana"
                 Font-Size="9pt" ForeColor="Black" Height="190px"
                 NextPrevFormat="FullMonth" Width="350px"
                 OnSelectionChanged="Calendar1_SelectionChanged">
                    <SelectedDayStyle BackColor="#333399" ForeColor="White" />
                    <TodayDayStyle BackColor="#CCCCCC" />
                    <OtherMonthDayStyle ForeColor="#999999" />
                    <NextPrevStyle Font-Bold="True" Font-Size="8pt"
                     ForeColor="#333333" VerticalAlign="Bottom" />
                    <DayHeaderStyle Font-Bold="True" Font-Size="8pt" />
                    <TitleStyle BackColor="White" BorderColor="Black"
                     BorderWidth="4px" Font-Bold="True" Font-Size="12pt"
                     ForeColor="#333399" />
```

Continued

```
                </asp:Calendar>
            </ContentTemplate>
        </asp:UpdatePanel>
    </div>
    </form>
</body>
</html>
```

C#

```
<%@ Page Language="C#" %>

<%@ Register Assembly="AjaxControlToolkit" Namespace="AjaxControlToolkit"
    TagPrefix="cc1" %>

<script runat="server">
    protected void Calendar1_SelectionChanged(object sender, EventArgs e)
    {
        PopupControlExtender1.Commit(Calendar1.SelectedDate.ToShortDateString());
    }
</script>
```

When running this page, you get a single text box on the page. Click within the text box and a pop-up calendar appears so you can select a date that will be populated back into the text box (as illustrated in Figure 20-32).

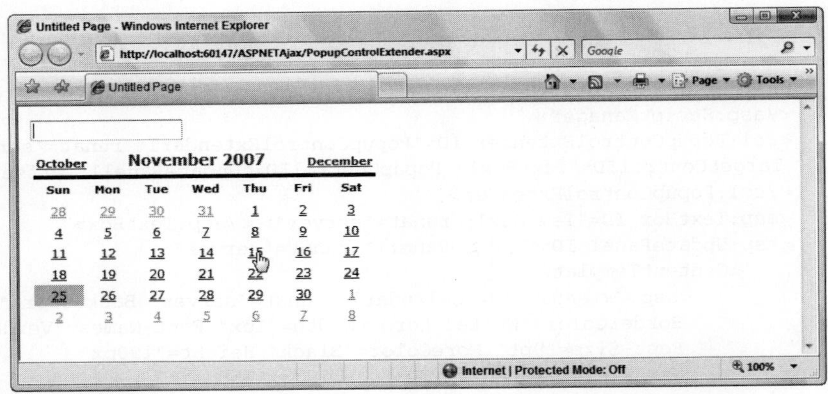

Figure 20-32

You will want to place your pop-up control within an ASP.NET AJAX UpdatePanel control and to pass the value from the pop-up control back to the target control (the TextBox1 control), so you use the `Commit()` method:

```
PopupControlExtender1.Commit(Calendar1.SelectedDate.ToShortDateString())
```

ResizableControlExtender

The ResizableControlExtender control allows you to take a Panel control and give end users the ability to grab a handle and change the size of the element (smaller or bigger). Anything you put inside the `Panel` control will then change in size depending on how the end user extends the item. For this to work, you have to create a handle for the end user to use. Listing 20-25 shows you how to use ResizableControlExtender with an image.

Listing 20-25: Using the ResizableControlExtender control with an image

```
<%@ Page Language="C#" %>

<%@ Register Assembly="AjaxControlToolkit" Namespace="AjaxControlToolkit"
    TagPrefix="cc1" %>

<html xmlns="http://www.w3.org/1999/xhtml">
<head runat="server">
    <title>ResizableControlExtender Control</title>
    <style type="text/css">
        .handle
        {
         width:10px;
         height:10px;
         background-color:Black;
        }
        .resizable
        {
            border-style:solid;
            border-width:2px;
            border-color:Black;
        }
    </style>
</head>
<body>
    <form id="form1" runat="server">
    <div>
        <asp:ScriptManager ID="ScriptManager1" runat="server">
        </asp:ScriptManager>
        <cc1:ResizableControlExtender ID="ResizableControlExtender1" runat="server"
         TargetControlID="Panel1" HandleCssClass="handle"
         ResizableCssClass="resizable">
        </cc1:ResizableControlExtender>
        <asp:Panel ID="Panel1" runat="server" Width="300" Height="225">
            <asp:Image ID="Image1" runat="server" ImageUrl="Images/Garden.jpg"
             style="width:100%; height:100%"/>
        </asp:Panel>
    </div>
    </form>
</body>
</html>
```

In this example, the ResizableControlExtender control depends upon CSS to create the handle for the end user to grab to resize the `Panel` control. The `TargetControlID` property points to the control to be resized.

There are two CSS references in the ResizableControlExtender control. One deals with the control as it sits on the screen with no end user interaction. This is really to show the end user that there is an ability to resize the element. This is done through the `HandleCssClass` property. The value of this property points to the CSS class `handle` contained within the same file. The second CSS reference deals with the control as it is clicked and held (when the end user does not let up with the mouse click performed). This one is done with the `ResizableCssClass` property. The value of this property points to the CSS class `resizable`.

When compiled and run, the code should generate the same page presented in Figure 20-33.

Figure 20-33

You can see in the top screenshot how the image looks when there is no end user interaction. In this case, there is a black square (as defined by the CSS) in the lower-right corner of the image. The screenshot on the bottom shows what happens when the end user grabs the handle and starts changing the shape of the image.

RoundedCornersExtender

The RoundedCornersExtender control allows you to put rounded corners on the elements on your page. As with the ResizableControlExtender control, you put the element you are interested in working with inside of a Panel control. Listing 20-26 shows this done with a Login server control.

Listing 20-26: Rounding the corners of the Panel control containing a Login server control

```
<%@ Page Language="C#" %>

<%@ Register Assembly="AjaxControlToolkit" Namespace="AjaxControlToolkit"
    TagPrefix="cc1" %>

<html xmlns="http://www.w3.org/1999/xhtml">
<head runat="server">
    <title>RoundedCornersExtender Control</title>
</head>
<body>
    <form id="form1" runat="server">
    <div>
        <asp:ScriptManager ID="ScriptManager1" runat="server">
        </asp:ScriptManager>
        <cc1:RoundedCornersExtender ID="RoundedCornersExtender1" runat="server"
         TargetControlID="Panel1">
        </cc1:RoundedCornersExtender>
        <asp:Panel ID="Panel1" runat="server" Width="250px"
         HorizontalAlign="Center" BackColor="Orange">
            <asp:Login ID="Login1" runat="server">
            </asp:Login>
        </asp:Panel>
    </div>
    </form>
</body>
</html>
```

Here, the RoundedCornersExtender control simply points to the Panel control with the `TargetControlID` property. This Panel control has a background color of orange to show that the corners are indeed rounded. The result of this bit of code is illustrated in Figure 20-34.

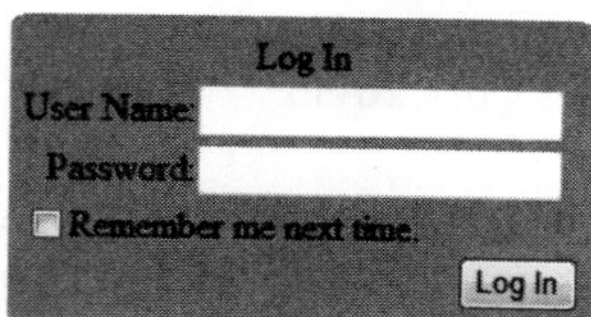

Figure 20-34

You can control the degree of the rounded corners using the `Radius` property of the RoundedCorners-Extender control. By default, this property is set to a value of `5`. You can even go as far as choosing the corners that you want to round using the `Corners` property. The possible values of the `Corners` property include `All`, `Bottom`, `BottomLeft`, `BottomRight`, `Left`, `None`, `Right`, `Top`, `TopLeft`, and `TopRight`.

SliderExtender

The SliderExtender control actually extends a TextBox control to make it look like nothing it normally does. This ASP.NET AJAX control gives you the ability to create a true slider control that allows the end user to select a range of numbers using a mouse instead of typing in the number. Listing 20-27 shows a simple example of using the slider.

Listing 20-27: Using the SliderExtender control

```
<%@ Page Language="C#" %>

<%@ Register Assembly="AjaxControlToolkit" Namespace="AjaxControlToolkit"
    TagPrefix="cc1" %>

<html xmlns="http://www.w3.org/1999/xhtml">
<head runat="server">
    <title>SliderExtender Control</title>
</head>
<body>
    <form id="form1" runat="server">
    <div>
        <asp:ScriptManager ID="ScriptManager1" runat="server">
        </asp:ScriptManager>
        <cc1:SliderExtender ID="SliderExtender1" runat="server"
         TargetControlID="TextBox1">
        </cc1:SliderExtender>
        <asp:TextBox ID="TextBox1" runat="server"></asp:TextBox>
    </div>
    </form>
</body>
</html>
```

This little bit of code to tie a SliderExtender control to a typical TextBox control is simple and produces the result presented in Figure 20-35.

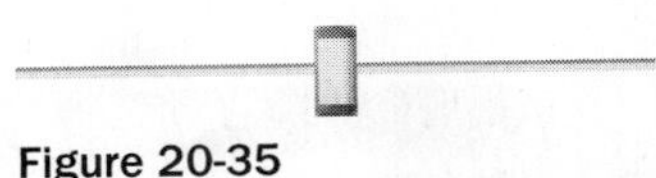

Figure 20-35

This is fine, but it is hard for the end users to tell what number they are selecting. Therefore, you might find it better to give a signifier to the end user. Adding a Label control to the page (called `Label1`) and changing the SliderExtender control to include a `BoundControlID` property gives you this result. The code for this change is presented here:

```
<cc1:SliderExtender ID="SliderExtender1" runat="server" TargetControlID="TextBox1"
 BoundControlID="Label1">
</cc1:SliderExtender>
```

This small change produces see the result (with the appropriate Label control on the page) shown in Figure 20-36.

Figure 20-36

Now when the end users slide the handle on the slider, they see the number that they are working with quite easily. Some of the following properties are available to the SliderExtender control.

- `Decimal` — Allows you to specify the number of decimals the result should take. The more decimals you have, the more unlikely the end user will be able to pick an exact number.
- `HandleCssClass` — The CSS class that you are using the design the handle.
- `HandleImageUrl` — The image file you are using to represent the handle.
- `Length` — The length of the slider in pixels. The default value is `150`.
- `Maximum` — The maximum number represented in the slider. The default value is `100`.
- `Minimum` — The minimum number represented in the slider. The default value is `0`.
- `Orientation` — The orientation of the slider. The possible values include `Horizontal` and `Vertical`. The default value is `Horizontal`.
- `RailCssClass` — The CSS class that you are using to design the rail of the slider.
- `ToolTipText` — The ToolTip when the end user hovers over the slider. Using `0` within the text provides the means show the end user the position the slider is currently in.

SlideShowExtender

The SlideShowExtender control allows you to put an image slideshow in the browser. The slideshow controls allow the end user to move to the next or previous images as well as simply play the images as a slideshow with a defined wait between each image. Listing 20-28 shows an example of creating a slideshow.

Listing 20-28: Creating a slideshow with three images

.ASPX

```
<%@ Page Language="VB" AutoEventWireup="true" CodeFile="SlideShowExtender.aspx.vb"
    Inherits="SlideShowExtender" %>

<%@ Register Assembly="AjaxControlToolkit" Namespace="AjaxControlToolkit"
    TagPrefix="cc1" %>

<html xmlns="http://www.w3.org/1999/xhtml">
<head runat="server">
    <title>SlideShowExtender Control</title>
</head>
<body>
    <form id="form1" runat="server">
```

Continued

```
    <div>
        <asp:ScriptManager ID="ScriptManager1" runat="server">
        </asp:ScriptManager>
        <asp:Panel ID="Panel1" runat="server" Width="300px"
         HorizontalAlign="Center">
            <cc1:SlideShowExtender ID="SlideShowExtender1" runat="server"
                ImageTitleLabelID="LabelTitle" TargetControlID="Image1"
                UseContextKey="True" NextButtonID="ButtonNext"
                PlayButtonID="ButtonPlay"
                PreviousButtonID="ButtonPrevious"
                SlideShowServiceMethod="GetSlides"
                ImageDescriptionLabelID="LabelDescription">
            </cc1:SlideShowExtender>
            <asp:Label ID="LabelTitle" runat="server" Text="Label"
             Font-Bold="True"></asp:Label><br /><br />
            <asp:Image ID="Image1" runat="server"
             ImageUrl="Images/Garden.jpg" /><br />
            <asp:Label ID="LabelDescription" runat="server"
             Text="Label"></asp:Label><br /><br />
            <asp:Button ID="ButtonPrevious" runat="server" Text="Previous" />
            <asp:Button ID="ButtonNext" runat="server" Text="Next" />
            <asp:Button ID="ButtonPlay" runat="server" />
        </asp:Panel>
    </div>
    </form>
</body>
</html>
```

The SlideShowExtender control has a lot of available properties available. You can specify the location where you are defining the image title and description using the `ImageTitleLabelID` and the `ImageDescriptionLabelID` properties. In addition to that, this page contains three Button controls. One to act as the Previous button, another for the Next button, and the final one as the Play button. However, it is important to note that when the Play button is clicked (to start the slideshow), it turns into the Stop button.

The `SlideShowServiceMethod` property is important because it points to the server-side method that returns the images that are part of the slide show. In this case, it is referring to a method called GetSlides, which is represented here in Listing 20-29.

Listing 20-29: The GetSlides method implementation

VB

```
Partial Class SlideShowExtender
    Inherits System.Web.UI.Page

    <System.Web.Services.WebMethodAttribute()> _
    <System.Web.Script.Services.ScriptMethodAttribute()> _
    Public Shared Function GetSlides(ByVal contextKey As System.String) _
      As AjaxControlToolkit.Slide()

             Return New AjaxControlToolkit.Slide() { _
                New AjaxControlToolkit.Slide("Images/Creek.jpg",
```

```
                    "The Creek", "This is a picture of a creek."),
                New AjaxControlToolkit.Slide("Images/Dock.jpg",
                    "The Dock", "This is a picture of a Dock."),
                New AjaxControlToolkit.Slide("Images/Garden.jpg",
                    "The Garden", "This is a picture of a Garden.") }
    End Function
End Class
```

C#

```
public partial class SlideShowExtender : System.Web.UI.Page
{
    [System.Web.Services.WebMethodAttribute(),
     System.Web.Script.Services.ScriptMethodAttribute()]
    public static AjaxControlToolkit.Slide[] GetSlides(string contextKey)
    {
        return new AjaxControlToolkit.Slide[] {
            new AjaxControlToolkit.Slide("Images/Creek.jpg",
              "The Creek", "This is a picture of a creek."),
            new AjaxControlToolkit.Slide("Images/Dock.jpg",
              "The Dock", "This is a picture of a Dock."),
            new AjaxControlToolkit.Slide("Images/Garden.jpg",
              "The Garden", "This is a picture of a Garden.") };
    }
}
```

With the code-behind in place, the SlideShowExtender has a server-side method to call for the photos. This method, called `GetSlides()`, returns an array of `Slide` objects which require the location of the object (the path), the title, and the description. When running this page, you get something similar to the following results shown in Figure 20-37.

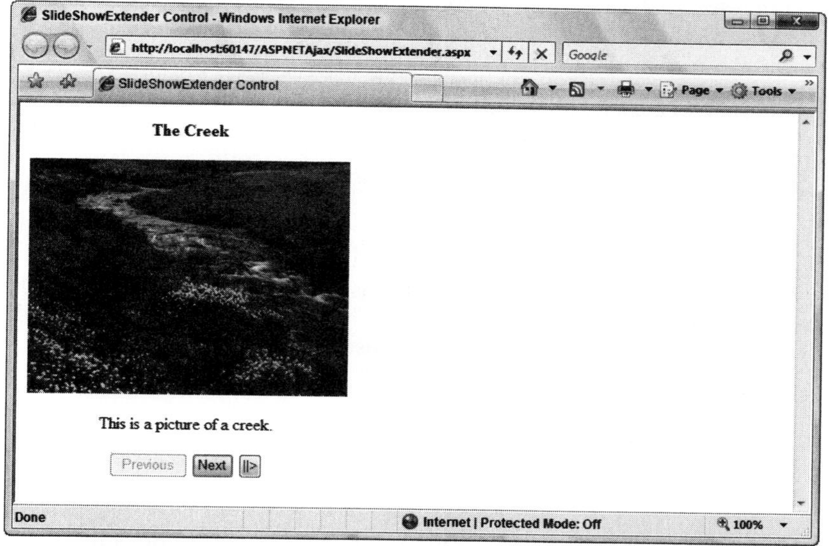

Figure 20-37

Pressing the Play button on the page will rotates the images until they are done. They will not repeat in a loop unless you have the SlideShowExtender control's `Loop` property set to `True`. (It is set to `False` by default.)

The other important property to pay attention to is the `PlayInterval` property. The value of this property is an integer that represents the number of milliseconds that the browser will take to change to the next photo in the series of images. By default, this is set to `3000` milliseconds.

TextBoxWatermarkExtender

The TextBoxWatermarkExtender control allows you to put instructions within controls for the end users, which gives them a better understanding of what to use the control for. This can be text or even images (when using CSS). Listing 20-30 shows an example of using this control with a TextBox server control.

Listing 20-30: Using the TextBoxWatermarkExtender control with a TextBox control

```
<%@ Page Language="C#" %>

<%@ Register Assembly="AjaxControlToolkit" Namespace="AjaxControlToolkit"
    TagPrefix="cc1" %>

<html xmlns="http://www.w3.org/1999/xhtml">
<head runat="server">
    <title>TextBoxWatermarkExtender Control</title>
</head>
<body>
    <form id="form1" runat="server">
    <div>
        <asp:ScriptManager ID="ScriptManager1" runat="server">
        </asp:ScriptManager>
        <cc1:TextBoxWatermarkExtender ID="TextBoxWatermarkExtender1" runat="server"
         WatermarkText="Enter in something here!" TargetControlID="TextBox1">
        </cc1:TextBoxWatermarkExtender>
        <asp:TextBox ID="TextBox1" runat="server"></asp:TextBox>
    </div>
    </form>
</body>
</html>
```

In this case, the TextBoxWatermarkExtender control is associated with a simple TextBox control and uses the `WatermarkText` property to provide the text that will appear inside the actual TextBox control. Figure 20-38 shows the results of the code from this listing.

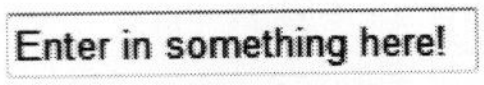

Enter in something here!

Figure 20-38

The text in the image from Figure 20-38 is straight text with no style inside of the TextBox control. When the end user clicks inside of the TextBox control, the text will disappear and the cursor will be properly placed at the beginning of the text box.

To apply some style to the content that you use as a watermark, you can use the `WatermarkCssClass` property. You can change the code to include a bit of style as shown in Listing 20-31.

Listing 20-31: Applying style to the watermark

```
<%@ Page Language="C#" %>

<%@ Register Assembly="AjaxControlToolkit" Namespace="AjaxControlToolkit"
    TagPrefix="cc1" %>

<html xmlns="http://www.w3.org/1999/xhtml">
<head runat="server">
    <title>TextBoxWatermarkExtender Control</title>
    <style type="text/css">
        .watermark
        {
         width:150px;
         font:Verdana;
         font-style:italic;
         color:GrayText;
        }

    </style>
</head>
<body>
    <form id="form1" runat="server">
    <div>
        <asp:ScriptManager ID="ScriptManager1" runat="server">
        </asp:ScriptManager>
        <cc1:TextBoxWatermarkExtender ID="TextBoxWatermarkExtender1" runat="server"
         WatermarkText="Enter in something here!" TargetControlID="TextBox1"
         WatermarkCssClass="watermark">
        </cc1:TextBoxWatermarkExtender>
        <asp:TextBox ID="TextBox1" runat="server"></asp:TextBox>
    </div>
    </form>
</body>
</html>
```

This time, the WatermarkCssClass property is used and points to the inline CSS class, `watermark`, which is on the page. Running this page, you will see the style applied as shown in Figure 20-39.

Enter in something here!

Figure 20-39

ToggleButtonExtender

The ToggleButtonExtender control works with CheckBox controls and allows you to use an image of your own instead of the standard check box images that the CheckBox controls typically use. Using the ToggleButtonExtender control, you are able to specify images for checked, unchecked, and disabled statuses. Listing 20-32 shows an example of using this control.

Listing 20-32: Using the ToggleButtonExtender control

```
<%@ Page Language="C#" %>

<%@ Register Assembly="AjaxControlToolkit" Namespace="AjaxControlToolkit"
    TagPrefix="cc1" %>

<html xmlns="http://www.w3.org/1999/xhtml">
<head runat="server">
    <title>ToggleButtonExtender Control</title>
</head>
<body>
    <form id="form1" runat="server">
    <div>
        <asp:ScriptManager ID="ScriptManager1" runat="server">
        </asp:ScriptManager>
        <cc1:MutuallyExclusiveCheckBoxExtender
         ID="MutuallyExclusiveCheckBoxExtender1" runat="server" Key="MyCheckBoxes"
         TargetControlID="CheckBox1">
        </cc1:MutuallyExclusiveCheckBoxExtender>
        <cc1:MutuallyExclusiveCheckBoxExtender
         ID="MutuallyExclusiveCheckBoxExtender2" runat="server" Key="MyCheckBoxes"
         TargetControlID="CheckBox2">
        </cc1:MutuallyExclusiveCheckBoxExtender>
        <cc1:ToggleButtonExtender ID="ToggleButtonExtender1" runat="server"
         TargetControlID="CheckBox1" UncheckedImageUrl="Images/Unchecked.gif"
         CheckedImageUrl="Images/Checked.gif" CheckedImageAlternateText="Checked"
         UncheckedImageAlternateText="Not Checked" ImageWidth="25"
         ImageHeight="25">
        </cc1:ToggleButtonExtender>
        <asp:CheckBox ID="CheckBox1" runat="server" Text=" Option One" />
        <cc1:ToggleButtonExtender ID="ToggleButtonExtender2" runat="server"
         TargetControlID="CheckBox2" UncheckedImageUrl="Images/Unchecked.gif"
         CheckedImageUrl="Images/Checked.gif" CheckedImageAlternateText="Checked"
         UncheckedImageAlternateText="Not Checked" ImageWidth="25"
         ImageHeight="25">
        </cc1:ToggleButtonExtender>
        <asp:CheckBox ID="CheckBox2" runat="server" Text=" Option Two" />
    </div>
    </form>
</body>
</html>
```

This page has two CheckBox controls. Each check box has an associated ToggleButtonExtender control along with a MutuallyExclusiveCheckBoxExtender control to tie the two check boxes together. The ToggleButtonExtender control uses the `CheckedImageUrl` and the `UncheckedImageUrl` properties to specify the appropriate images to use. Then, if images are disabled by the end user's browser instance, the text that is provided in the `CheckedImageAlternateText` and `UncheckedImageAlternateText` properties is used instead. You will also have to specify values for the `ImageWidth` and `ImageHeight` properties for the page to run.

Running this page, you get results similar to those presented in Figure 20-40.

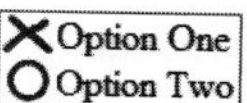

Figure 20-40

UpdatePanelAnimationExtender

The UpdatePanelAnimationExtender control allows you to apply an animation to a Panel control for two specific events. The first is the `OnUpdating` event and the second is the `OnUpdated` event. You can then use the animation framework provided by ASP.NET AJAX to change the page's style based on these two events. Listing 20-33 shows an example of using the `OnUpdated` event when the end user clicks a specific date within a `Calendar` control contained within the UpdatePanel control on the page.

Listing 20-33: Using animations on the OnUpdated event

VB

```
<%@ Page Language="VB" %>

<%@ Register Assembly="AjaxControlToolkit" Namespace="AjaxControlToolkit"
    TagPrefix="cc1" %>

<script runat="server">
    Protected  Sub Calendar1_SelectionChanged(ByVal sender As Object, _
      ByVal e As EventArgs)
        Label1.Text = "The date selected is " &
           Calendar1.SelectedDate.ToLongDateString()
    End Sub
</script>

<html xmlns="http://www.w3.org/1999/xhtml">
<head runat="server">
    <title>UpdatePanelAnimationExtender Control</title>
</head>
<body>
    <form id="form1" runat="server">
    <div>
        <asp:ScriptManager ID="ScriptManager1" runat="server">
        </asp:ScriptManager>
        <cc1:UpdatePanelAnimationExtender ID="UpdatePanelAnimationExtender1"
         runat="server" TargetControlID="UpdatePanel1">
            <Animations>
                <OnUpdated>
                    <Sequence>
                        <Color PropertyKey="background" StartValue="#999966"
                         EndValue="#FFFFFF" Duration="5.0" />
                    </Sequence>
                </OnUpdated>
            </Animations>
        </cc1:UpdatePanelAnimationExtender>
        <asp:UpdatePanel ID="UpdatePanel1" runat="server">
            <ContentTemplate>
                <asp:Label ID="Label1" runat="server"></asp:Label><br />
```

Continued

```
                <asp:Calendar ID="Calendar1" runat="server"
                    onselectionchanged="Calendar1_SelectionChanged"></asp:Calendar>
            </ContentTemplate>
        </asp:UpdatePanel>
    </div>
    </form>
</body>
</html>
```

C#

```
<%@ Page Language="C#" %>

<%@ Register Assembly="AjaxControlToolkit" Namespace="AjaxControlToolkit"
    TagPrefix="cc1" %>

<script runat="server">
    protected void Calendar1_SelectionChanged(object sender, EventArgs e)
    {
        Label1.Text = "The date selected is " +
           Calendar1.SelectedDate.ToLongDateString();
    }
</script>
```

With this bit of code, when you click a date within the Calendar control, the entire background of the UpdatePanel holding the calendar changes color from one to another for a five-second duration as specified in the animation you built. The animations you define can get pretty complex, and building deluxe animations are beyond the scope of this chapter.

ValidatorCalloutExtender

The last extender control covered is the ValidatorCalloutExtender control. This control allows you to add a more noticeable validation message to end users working with a form. You associate this control not with the control that is being validated, but instead with the validation control itself. An example of associating the ValidatorCalloutExtender control with a RegularExpressionValidator control is presented in Listing 20-34.

Listing 20-34: Creating validation callouts with the ValidatorCalloutExtender

```
<%@ Page Language="C#" %>

<%@ Register Assembly="AjaxControlToolkit" Namespace="AjaxControlToolkit"
    TagPrefix="cc1" %>

<html xmlns="http://www.w3.org/1999/xhtml">
<head runat="server">
    <title>ValidatorCalloutExtender Control</title>
</head>
<body>
    <form id="form1" runat="server">
    <div>
        <asp:ScriptManager ID="ScriptManager1" runat="server">
```

```
            </asp:ScriptManager>
            <cc1:ValidatorCalloutExtender ID="ValidatorCalloutExtender1" runat="server"
                TargetControlID="RegularExpressionValidator1">
            </cc1:ValidatorCalloutExtender>
            Email Address: 
            <asp:TextBox ID="TextBox1" runat="server"></asp:TextBox>
            <asp:RegularExpressionValidator ID="RegularExpressionValidator1"
             runat="server"
             ErrorMessage="You must enter an email address" Display="None"
             ControlToValidate="TextBox1"
             ValidationExpression="\w+([-+.']\w+)*@\w+([-.]\w+)*\.\w+([-.]\w+)*">
            </asp:RegularExpressionValidator><br />
            <asp:Button ID="Button1" runat="server" Text="Submit" />
        </div>
        </form>
    </body>
    </html>
```

This page has a single text box for the form, a Submit button and a RegularExpressionValidator control. The RegularExpressionValidator control is built as you normally would, except you make use of the `Display` property and set it to `None`. You do not want the normal ASP.NET validation control to also display its message, as it will collide with the one displayed with the ValidatorCalloutExtender control. Although the `Display` property is set to `None`, you still use the `ErrorMessage` property to provide the error message. Running this page produces the results presented in Figure 20-41.

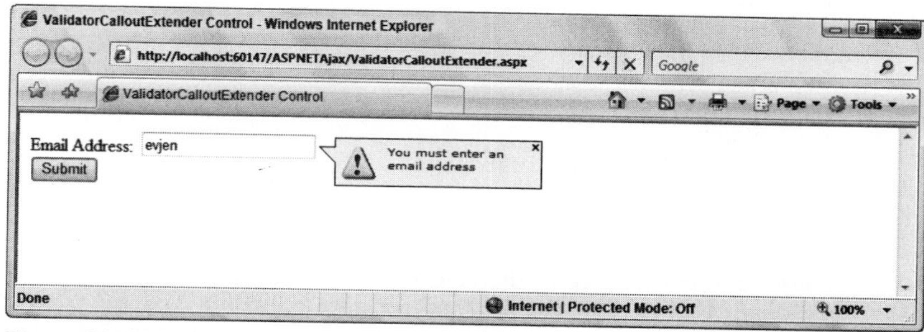

Figure 20-41

ASP.NET AJAX Control Toolkit Server Controls

The next set of ASP.NET AJAX controls actually do not always extend other ASP.NET controls, but instead, are controls themselves. The following sections detail these controls.

Accordion Control

The `Accordion` control gives you the ability to provide a series of collapsible panes to the end user. This control is ideal when you have a lot of content to present in a limited space. The `Accordion` control is a template control and contains panes represented as AccordionPane controls. Listing 20-35 shows an Accordion control that contains two AccordionPane controls.

Listing 20-35: An Accordion control with two AccordionPane controls

```
<%@ Page Language="C#" %>

<%@ Register Assembly="AjaxControlToolkit" Namespace="AjaxControlToolkit"
   TagPrefix="cc1" %>

<html xmlns="http://www.w3.org/1999/xhtml">
<head runat="server">
    <title>Accordion Control</title>
    <style type="text/css">
        .titlebar
        {
         background-color:Blue;
         color:White;
         font-size:large;
         font-family:Verdana;
         border:solid 3px Black;
        }
    </style>
</head>
<body>
    <form id="form1" runat="server">
    <div>
        <asp:ScriptManager ID="ScriptManager1" runat="server">
        </asp:ScriptManager>
        <cc1:Accordion ID="Accordion1" runat="server" HeaderCssClass="titlebar"
         HeaderSelectedCssClass="titlebar">
            <Panes>
            <cc1:AccordionPane runat="server">
                <Header>
                    This is the first pane
                </Header>
                <Content>
            Lorem ipsum dolor sit amet, consectetuer adipiscing elit.
            Donec accumsan lorem. Ut consectetuer tempus metus. Aenean tincidunt
            venenatis tellus. Suspendisse molestie cursus ipsum. Curabitur ut
            lectus. Nulla ac dolor nec elit convallis vulputate. Nullam pharetra
            pulvinar nunc. Duis orci. Phasellus a tortor at nunc mattis congue.
            Vestibulum porta tellus eu orci. Suspendisse quis massa. Maecenas
            varius, erat non ullamcorper nonummy, mauris erat eleifend odio, ut
            gravida nisl neque a ipsum. Vivamus facilisis. Cras viverra. Curabitur
            ut augue eget dolor semper posuere. Aenean at magna eu eros tempor
            pharetra. Aenean mauris.
                </Content>
            </cc1:AccordionPane>
            <cc1:AccordionPane runat="server">
                <Header>
                    This is the second pane
                </Header>
                <Content>
            Lorem ipsum dolor sit amet, consectetuer adipiscing elit.
            Donec accumsan lorem. Ut consectetuer tempus metus. Aenean tincidunt
```

```
            venenatis tellus. Suspendisse molestie cursus ipsum. Curabitur ut
            lectus. Nulla ac dolor nec elit convallis vulputate. Nullam pharetra
            pulvinar nunc. Duis orci. Phasellus a tortor at nunc mattis congue.
            Vestibulum porta tellus eu orci. Suspendisse quis massa. Maecenas
            varius, erat non ullamcorper nonummy, mauris erat eleifend odio, ut
            gravida nisl neque a ipsum. Vivamus facilisis. Cras viverra. Curabitur
            ut augue eget dolor semper posuere. Aenean at magna eu eros tempor
            pharetra. Aenean mauris.
                </Content>
            </cc1:AccordionPane>
            </Panes>
        </cc1:Accordion>
    </div>
    </form>
</body>
</html>
```

There is a single CSS class defined in the document and this class, `titlebar`, is used as the value of the `HeaderCssClass` and the `HeaderSelectedCssClass` properties. The Accordion control here contains two AccordionPane controls. The subelements of the AccordionPane control are the `<Header>` and the `<Content>` elements. The items placed in the `<Header>` section will be in the clickable pane title, while the items contained within the `<Content>` section will slide out and be presented when the associated header is selected.

Running this page produces the results illustrated here in Figure 20-42.

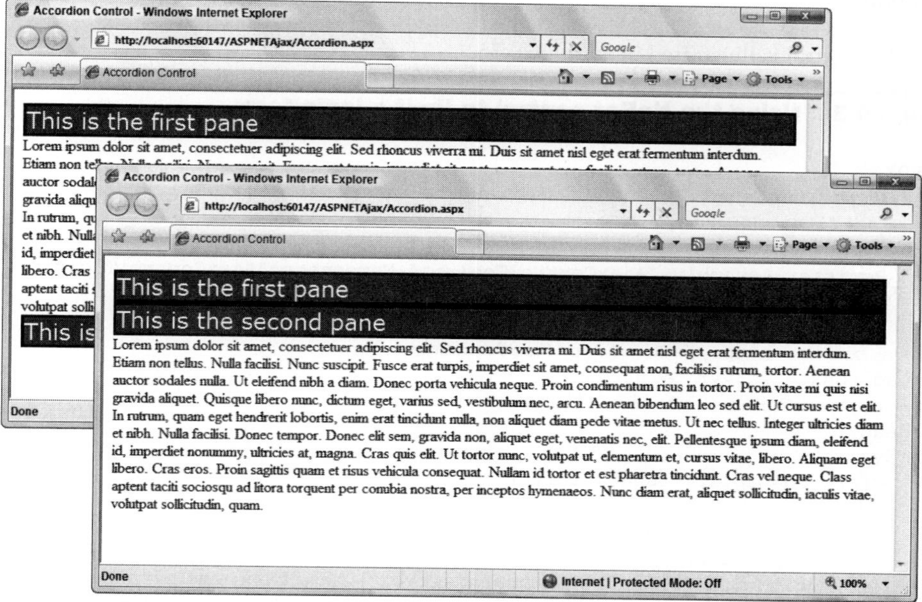

Figure 20-42

This figure shows a screenshot of each of the panes selected. Some of the more important properties are described in the following list:

- AutoSize — Defines how the control deals with its size expansion and shrinkage. The possible values include None, Fill, and Limit. The default is None and when used, items below the control may move to make room for the control expansion. A value of Fill works with the Height property and the control will fill to the required Height. This means that some of the panes may have to grow to accommodate the space while other panes might have to shrink and include a scrollbar to handle the limited space from the height restriction. A value of Limit also works with the Height property and will never grow larger than this value. It is possible that the pane might be smaller than the specified height.
- TransitionDuration — The number of milliseconds it takes to transition to another pane.
- FramesPerSecond — The number of frames per second to use to transition to another pane.
- RequireOpenedPane — Specifies that at least one pane is required to be open at all times. The default setting of this property is True. A value of False means that all panes can be collapsed.

Finally, the properties of DataSource, DataSourceID, and DataMember allow you to bind to this control from your code.

NoBot Control

The NoBot control works to determine how entities interact with your forms and to help you make sure that actual humans are working with your forms and some automated code isn't working through your application.

The NoBot control is illustrated in Listing 20-36.

Listing 20-36: Using the NoBot control to limit a login form

.ASPX

```
<%@ Page Language="VB" AutoEventWireup="true" CodeFile="NoBot.aspx.vb"
    Inherits="NoBot" %>

<%@ Register Assembly="AjaxControlToolkit" Namespace="AjaxControlToolkit"
    TagPrefix="cc1" %>

<html xmlns="http://www.w3.org/1999/xhtml">
<head runat="server">
    <title>NoBot Control</title>
</head>
<body>
    <form id="form1" runat="server">
    <div>
        <asp:ScriptManager ID="ScriptManager1" runat="server">
        </asp:ScriptManager>
        <cc1:NoBot ID="NoBot1" runat="server" CutoffMaximumInstances="3"
            CutoffWindowSeconds="15" ResponseMinimumDelaySeconds="10"
            OnGenerateChallengeAndResponse="NoBot1_GenerateChallengeAndResponse" />
        <asp:Login ID="Login1" runat="server">
        </asp:Login>
```

```
        <asp:Label ID="Label1" runat="server"></asp:Label>
    </div>
    </form>
</body>
</html>
```

The NoBot control has three important properties to be aware of when controlling how your forms are submitted. These properties include the `CutoffMaximumInstances`, `CutoffWindowSeconds`, and the `ResponseMinimumDelaySeconds` properties.

The `CutoffMaximumInstances` is the number of times the end user is allowed to try to submit the form within the number of seconds specified by the `CutoffWindowSeconds` property. The `ResponseMinimum-DelaySeconds` property defines the minimum number of seconds the end user has to submit the form. If you know the form you are working with will take some time, then setting this property to a value (even if it is `5` seconds) will help stop submissions that are not made by humans.

The `OnGenerateChallengeAndResponse` property allows you to define the server-side method that works with the challenge and allows you to provide a response based on the challenge. This property is used in Listing 20-36 and posts back to the user the status of the form submission.

The code-behind for this page is represented in Listing 20-37.

Listing 20-37: The code-behind page for the NoBot control's OnGenerateChallengeAndResponse

VB

```
Imports System
Imports AjaxControlToolkit

Public partial Class NoBot
 Inherits System.Web.UI.Page
    Protected Sub NoBot1_GenerateChallengeAndResponse(ByVal sender As Object, _
      ByVal void As AjaxControlToolkit.NoBotEventArgs) _
      Handles NoBot1.GenerateChallengeAndResponse

        Dim state As NoBotState
        NoBot1.IsValid(state)

        Label1.Text = state.ToString()
    End Sub
End Class
```

C#

```
using System;
using AjaxControlToolkit;

public partial class NoBot : System.Web.UI.Page
{
    protected void NoBot1_GenerateChallengeAndResponse(object sender,
        AjaxControlToolkit.NoBotEventArgs e)
    {
```

Continued

```
            NoBotState state;
            NoBot1.IsValid(out state);

            Label1.Text = state.ToString();
        }
    }
```

Running this page and trying to submit the form before the ten-second minimum time results in an invalid submission. In addition, trying to submit the form more than three times within 15 seconds results in an invalid submission.

PasswordStrength Control

The PasswordStrength control allows you to check the contents of a password in a TextBox control and validate its strength. It will also then give a message to the end user about whether the strength is reasonable. A simple example of the PasswordStrength control is presented in Listing 20-38.

Listing 20-38: Using the PasswordStrength control with a TextBox control

```
<%@ Page Language="C#" %>

<%@ Register Assembly="AjaxControlToolkit" Namespace="AjaxControlToolkit"
    TagPrefix="cc1" %>

<html xmlns="http://www.w3.org/1999/xhtml">
<head runat="server">
    <title>Password Strength Control</title>
</head>
<body>
    <form id="form1" runat="server">
    <div>
        <asp:ScriptManager ID="ScriptManager1" runat="server">
        </asp:ScriptManager>
        <cc1:PasswordStrength ID="PasswordStrength1" runat="server"
         TargetControlID="TextBox1">
        </cc1:PasswordStrength>
        <asp:TextBox ID="TextBox1" runat="server"></asp:TextBox>
    </div>
    </form>
</body>
</html>
```

This simple page produces a single text box and when end users start typing in the text box, they will be notified on the strength of the submission as they type. This is illustrated in Figure 20-43.

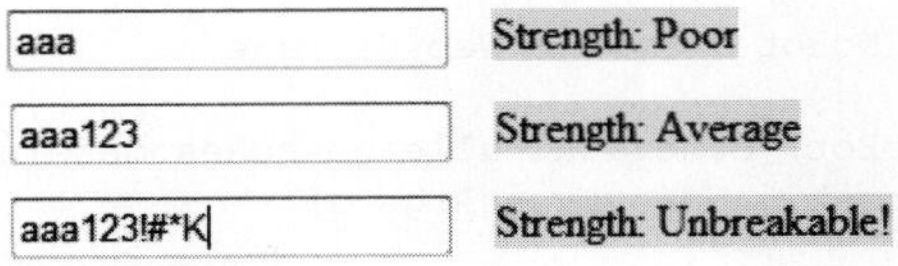

aaa | Strength: Poor
aaa123 | Strength: Average
aaa123!#*K | Strength: Unbreakable!

Figure 20-43

Some of the important properties to work with here include MinimumLowerCaseCharacters, Minimum-NumericCharacters, MinimumSymbolCharacters, MinimumUpperCaseCharacters, and PreferredPass-wordLength.

Rating Control

The Rating control gives your end users the ability to view and set ratings (such as star ratings). You have control over the number of ratings, the look of the filled ratings, the look of the empty ratings, and more. Listing 20-39 shows you a page that shows a five-star rating system that gives end users the ability to set the rating themselves.

Listing 20-39: A rating control that the end user can manipulate

```
<%@ Page Language="C#" %>

<%@ Register Assembly="AjaxControlToolkit" Namespace="AjaxControlToolkit"
    TagPrefix="cc1" %>

<html xmlns="http://www.w3.org/1999/xhtml">
<head runat="server">
    <title>Rating Control</title>
    <style type="text/css">
        .ratingStar {
            font-size: 0pt;
            width: 13px;
            height: 12px;
            margin: 0px;
            padding: 0px;
            cursor: pointer;
            display: block;
            background-repeat: no-repeat;
        }

        .filledRatingStar {
            background-image: url(Images/FilledStar.png);
        }

        .emptyRatingStar {
            background-image: url(Images/EmptyStar.png);
        }

        .savedRatingStar {
            background-image: url(Images/SavedStar.png);
        }
    </style>
</head>
<body>
    <form id="form1" runat="server">
    <div>
        <asp:ScriptManager ID="ScriptManager1" runat="server">
        </asp:ScriptManager>
```

Continued

```
            <cc1:Rating ID="Rating1" runat="server" StarCssClass="ratingStar"
             WaitingStarCssClass="savedRatingStar"
             FilledStarCssClass="filledRatingStar" EmptyStarCssClass="emptyRatingStar">
            </cc1:Rating>
        </div>
        </form>
    </body>
    </html>
```

Here, the Rating control uses a number of CSS classes to define its look and feel in various states. In addition to the CSS class properties (`StarCssClass`, `WaitingStarCssClass`, `FilledStarCssClass`, and `EmptyCssClass`), you can also specify rating alignments, the number of rating items (the default is `5`), the width, the current rating, and more. The code presented in Listing 20-39 produces the results shown in Figure 20-44.

Figure 20-44

TabContainer Control

Tabs are another great way to control a page that has a lot of content to present. The `TabContainer` control can contain one or more TabPanel controls that provide you with a set of tabs that show content one tab at a time.

You are able to control the width and the height of the panels and to specify whether there are scrollbars as well. Each `TabPanel` control has `<HeaderTemplate>` and `<ContentTemplate>` subelements that you can define. Listing 20-40 shows an example of a TabContainer control with three TabPanel controls.

Listing 20-40: Showing three tabs in a TabContainer control

```
<%@ Page Language="C#" %>

<%@ Register Assembly="AjaxControlToolkit" Namespace="AjaxControlToolkit"
    TagPrefix="cc1" %>

<html xmlns="http://www.w3.org/1999/xhtml">
<head runat="server">
    <title>TabContainer Control</title>
</head>
<body>
    <form id="form1" runat="server">
    <div>
        <asp:ScriptManager ID="ScriptManager1" runat="server">
        </asp:ScriptManager>
        <cc1:TabContainer ID="TabContainer1" runat="server" Height="300px">
            <cc1:TabPanel runat="server">
                <HeaderTemplate>Tab 1</HeaderTemplate>
```

```
                <ContentTemplate>Here is some tab one content.</ContentTemplate>
            </cc1:TabPanel>
            <cc1:TabPanel runat="server">
                <HeaderTemplate>Tab 2</HeaderTemplate>
                <ContentTemplate>Here is some tab two content.</ContentTemplate>
            </cc1:TabPanel>
            <cc1:TabPanel runat="server">
                <HeaderTemplate>Tab 3</HeaderTemplate>
                <ContentTemplate>Here is some tab three content.</ContentTemplate>
            </cc1:TabPanel>
        </cc1:TabContainer>
    </div>
    </form>
</body>
</html>
```

The result of this simple page is presented in Figure 20-45.

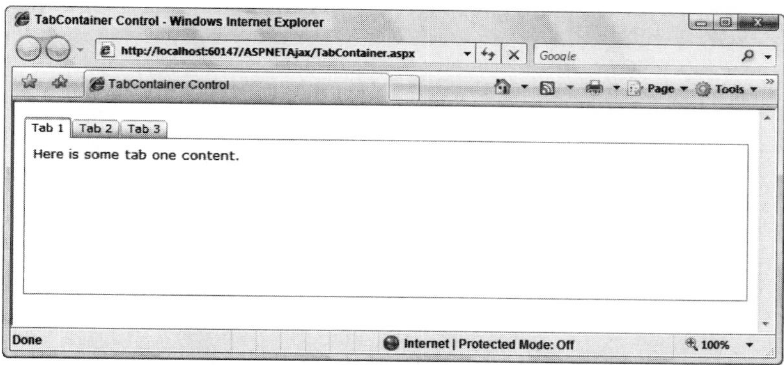

Figure 20-45

Summary

As you can see, there are a ton of new controls at your disposal. The best thing about this is that this is a community effort along with Microsoft and the list of available ASP.NET AJAX controls is only going to grow over time.

This chapter looked at a lot of the new ASP.NET AJAX controls and how to use them in your ASP.NET applications. Remember to visit the CodePlex page for these controls often and take advantage of the newest offerings out there.

21

Security

Not every page that you build with ASP.NET is meant to be open and accessible to everyone on the Internet. Sometimes, you want to build pages or sections of an application that are accessible to only a select group of your choosing. For this reason, you need the security measures explained in this chapter. They can help protect the data behind your applications and the applications themselves from fraudulent use.

Security is a very wide-reaching term. During every step of the application-building process, you must, without a doubt, be aware of how mischievous end users might attempt to bypass your lockout measures. You must take steps to ensure that no one can take over the application or gain access to its resources. Whether it involves working with basic server controls or accessing databases, you should be thinking through the level of security you want to employ to protect yourself.

How security is applied to your applications is truly a measured process. For instance, a single ASP.NET page on the Internet, open to public access, has different security requirements than does an ASP.NET application that is available to only selected individuals because it deals with confidential information such as credit card numbers or medical information.

The first step is to apply the appropriate level of security for the task at hand. Because you can take so many different actions to protect your applications and the resources, you have to decide for yourself which of these measures to employ. This chapter looks at some of the possibilities for protecting your applications.

Notice that security is discussed throughout this book. In addition, a couple chapters focus on specific security frameworks provided by ASP.NET 3.5 that are not discussed in this chapter. Chapters 15 and 16 discuss ASP.NET's membership and role management frameworks, as well as the personalization features in this version. These topics are aspects of security that can make it even easier for you to build safe applications. Although these new security frameworks are provided with this latest release of ASP.NET, you can still build your own measures as you did in the previous versions of ASP.NET. This chapter discusses how to do so.

An important aspect of security is how you handle the authentication and authorization for accessing resources in your applications. Before you begin working through some of the authentication/authorization possibilities in ASP.NET, you should know exactly what we mean by those two terms.

Authentication and Authorization

As discussed in Chapter 16, *authentication* is the process that determines the identity of a user. After a user has been authenticated, a developer can determine if the identified user has authorization to proceed. It is impossible to give an entity authorization if no authentication process has been applied.

Authorization is the process of determining whether an authenticated user is permitted access to any part of an application, access to specific points of an application, or access only to specified datasets that the application provides. Authenticating and authorizing users and groups enable you to customize a site based on user types or preferences.

Applying Authentication Measures

ASP.NET provides many different types of authentication measures to use within your applications, including basic authentication, digest authentication, forms authentication, Passport, and Integrated Windows authentication. You also can develop your own authentication methods. You should never authorize access to resources you mean to be secure if you have not applied an authentication process to the requests for the resources.

The different authentication modes are established through settings that can be applied to the application's `web.config` file or in conjunction with the application server's Internet Information Services (IIS) instance.

ASP.NET is configured through a series of `.config` files on the application server. These are XML-based files that enable you to easily change how ASP.NET behaves. This is an ideal way to work with the configuration settings you require. ASP.NET configuration files are applied in a hierarchal manner. The .NET Framework provides a server-level configuration file called the `machine.config` file, which can be found at `C:\Windows\Microsoft.NET\Framework\v2.0.50727\CONFIG`. The folder contains the `machine.config` file. This file provides ASP.NET application settings at a server-level, meaning that the settings are applied to each and every ASP.NET application that resides on the particular server.

A `web.config` file is another XML-based configuration file that resides in the root of the Web application. The settings applied in the `web.config` file override the same settings applied in the higher-level `machine.config` file.

You can even nest the `web.config` files so that the main application `web.config` file is located in the root directory of your application, but additional `web.config` files reside in some of the application's subdirectories (see Figure 21-1). The `web.config` files contained in any of the subdirectories supersede the root directory's `web.config` file. Therefore, any settings applied through a subdirectory's `web.config` file change whatever was set in the application's main `web.config` file.

In many of the examples in this chapter, you use the `web.config` file to apply the authentication and authorization mechanics you want in your applications. You also can work with IIS to apply settings directly to your applications.

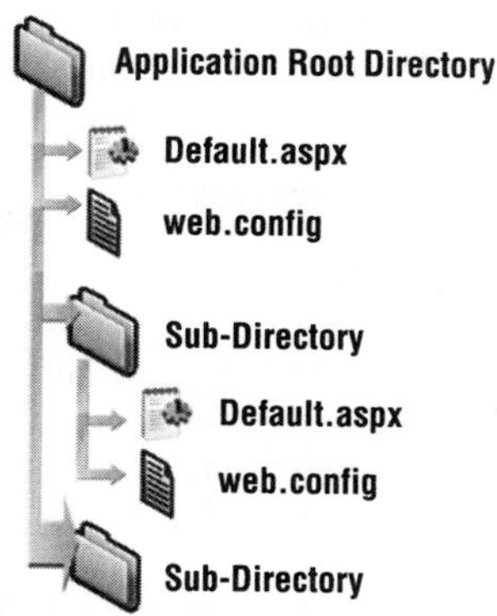

Figure 21-1

IIS is the Web server that handles all the incoming HTTP requests that come into the server. You must modify IIS to perform as you want. IIS hands a request to the ASP.NET engine only if the page has a specific file extension (for example, `.aspx`). In this chapter, you will work with IIS 7.0, as well.

The <authentication> Node

You use the `<authentication>` node in the application's `web.config` file to set the type of authentication your ASP.NET application requires:

```
<system.web>
   <authentication mode="Windows|Forms|Passport|None">

   </authentication>
</system.web>
```

The `<authentication>` node uses the `mode` attribute to set the form of authentication that is to be used. Options include `Windows`, `Forms`, `Passport`, and `None`. Each option is explained in the following table.

Provider	Description
`Windows`	Windows authentication is used together with IIS authentication. Authentication is performed by IIS in the following ways: basic, digest, or Integrated Windows Authentication. When IIS authentication is complete, ASP.NET uses the authenticated identity to authorize access. This is the default setting.
`Forms`	Requests that are not authenticated are redirected to an HTML form using HTTP client-side redirection. The user provides his login information and submits the form. If the application authenticates the request, the system issues a form that contains the credentials or a key for reacquiring the identity.
`Passport`	A centralized authentication service provided by Microsoft that offers single login and core profile services for member sites. This mode of authentication was de-emphasized by Microsoft at the end of 2004.
`None`	No authentication mode is in place with this setting.

As you can see, a couple of methods are at your disposal for building an authentication/authorization model for your ASP.NET applications. We start by examining the Windows mode of authentication.

Windows-Based Authentication

Windows-based authentication is handled between the Windows server where the ASP.NET application resides and the client machine. In a Windows-based authentication model, the requests go directly to IIS to provide the authentication process. This type of authentication is quite useful in an intranet environment where you can let the server deal completely with the authentication process — especially in environments where users are already logged onto a network. In this scenario, you simply grab and utilize the credentials that are already in place for the authorization process.

IIS first takes the user's credentials from the domain login. If this process fails, IIS displays a pop-up dialog box so the user can enter or re-enter his login information. To set up your ASP.NET application to work with Windows-based authentication, begin by creating some users and groups.

Creating Users

You use aspects of Windows-based authentication to allow specific users who have provided a domain login to access your application or parts of your application. Because it can use this type of authentication, ASP.NET makes it quite easy to work with applications that are deployed in an intranet environment. If a user has logged onto a local computer as a domain user, he will not need to be authenticated again when accessing a network computer in that domain.

The following steps show you how to create a user. It is important to note that you must have sufficient rights to be authorized to create users on a server. If you are authorized, the steps to create users are as follows:

1. Within your Windows XP or Windows Server 2003 server, choose Start ➪ Control Panel ➪ Administrative Tools ➪ Computer Management. If you are using Windows Vista, choose Start ➪ Control Panel ➪ System and Maintenance ➪ Administrative Tools ➪ Computer Management. Either one opens the Computer Management utility. It manages and controls resources on the local Web server. You can accomplish many things using this utility, but the focus here is on the creation of users.
2. Expand the System Tools node.
3. Expand the Local Users and Groups node.
4. Select the Users folder. You see something similar to the results shown in Figure 21-2.
5. Right-click the Users folder and select New User. The New User dialog appears, as shown in Figure 21-3.
6. Give the user a name, password, and description stating that this is a test user. In this example, the user is called **Bubbles**.
7. Clear the check box that requires the user to change his password at the next login.
8. Click the Create button. Your test user is created and presented in the Users folder of the Computer Management utility, as shown in Figure 21-4.

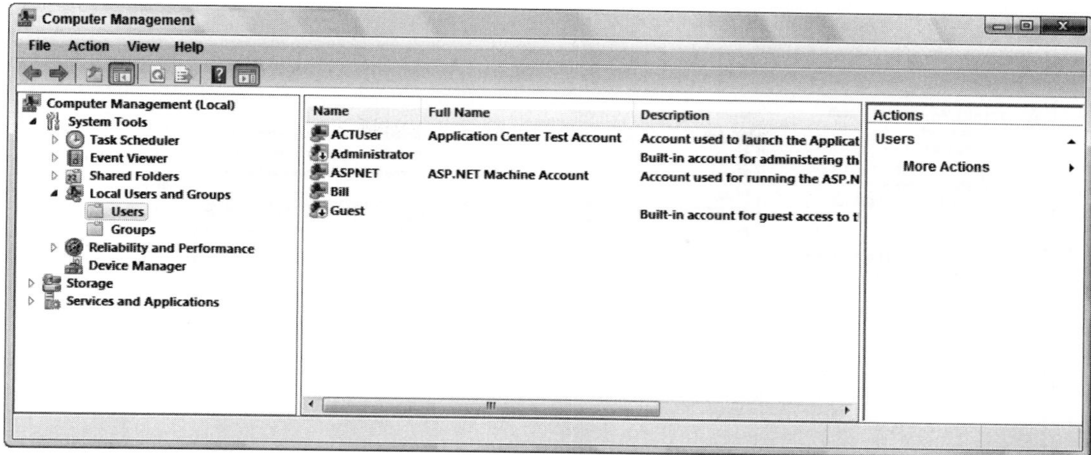

Figure 21-2

Figure 21-3

Now create a page to work with this user.

Authenticating and Authorizing a User

Now create an application that enables the user to enter it. You work with the application's `web.config` file to control which users are allowed to access the site and which users are not allowed.

Add the section presented in Listing 21-1 to your `web.config` file.

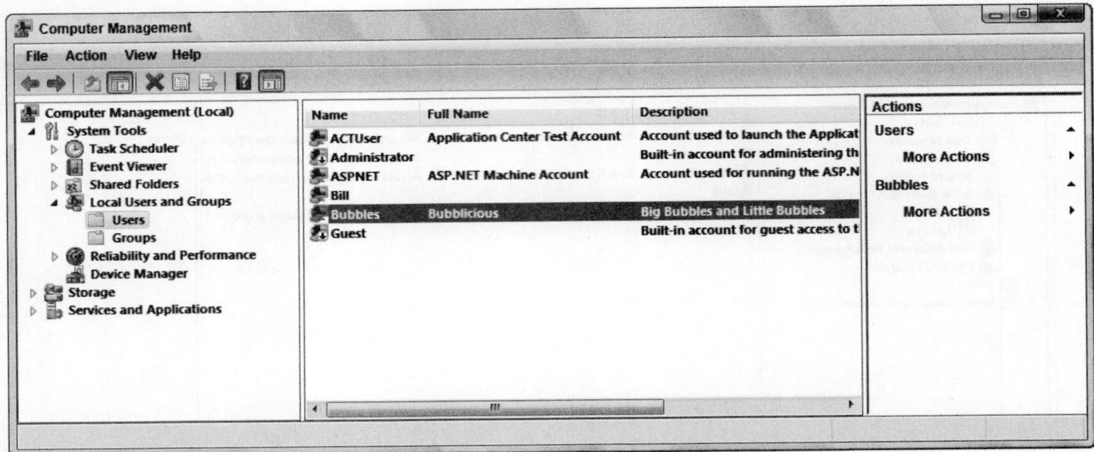

Figure 21-4

Listing 21-1: Denying all users through the web.config file

```
<system.web>
   <authentication mode="Windows" />
   <authorization>
      <deny users="*" />
   </authorization>
</system.web>
```

In this example, the `web.config` file is configuring the application to employ Windows-based authentication using the `<authentication>` element's mode attribute. In addition, the `<authorization>` element is used to define specifics about the users or groups who are permitted access to the application. In this case, the `<deny>` element specifies that all users (even if they are authenticated) are denied access to the application. Not permitting specific users with the `<allow>` element does not make much sense, but for this example, leave it as it is. The results are illustrated in Figure 21-5.

Any end user — authenticated or not — who tries to access the site sees a large ''Access is denied'' statement in his browser window, which is just what you want for those not allowed to access your application!

In most instances, however, you want to allow at least some users to access your application. Use the `<allow>` element in the `web.config` file to allow a specific user. Here is the syntax:

```
<allow users="Domain\Username" />
```

Listing 21-2 shows how the user is permitted access.

Listing 21-2: Allowing a single user through the web.config file

```
<system.web>
   <authentication mode="Windows" />
   <authorization>
```

```
        <allow users="REUTERS-EVJEN\Bubbles"/>
        <deny users="*"/>
      </authorization>
   </system.web>
```

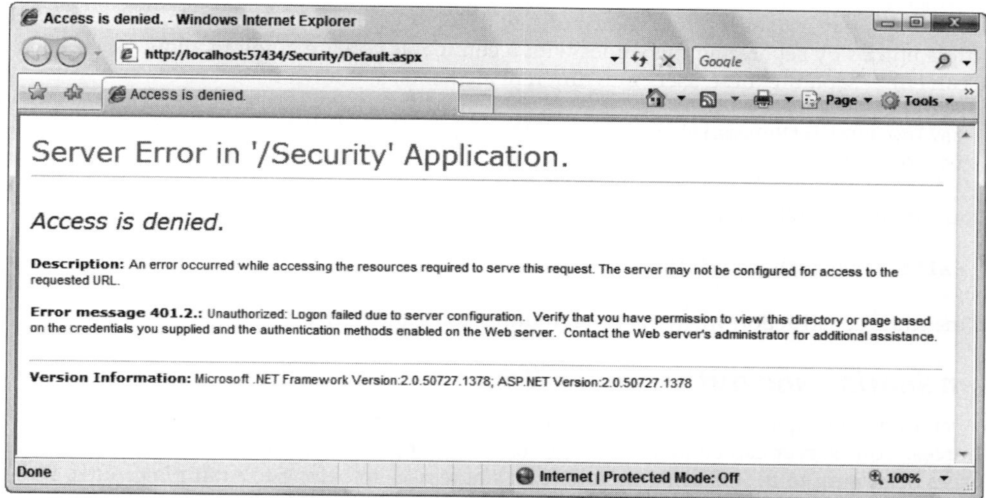

Figure 21-5

Even though all users (even authenticated ones) are denied access through the use of the `<deny>` element, the definitions defined in the `<allow>` element take precedence. In this example, a single user — `Bubbles` — is allowed.

Now, if you are logged on to the client machine as the user Bubbles and run the page in the browser, you get access to the application.

Looking Closely at the <allow> and <deny> Nodes

The `<allow>` and `<deny>` nodes enable you to work not only with specific users, but also with groups. The elements support the attributes defined in the following table.

Attribute	Description
`Users`	Enables you to specify users by their domain and/or name.
`Roles`	Enables you to specify access groups that are allowed or denied access.
`Verbs`	Enables you to specify the HTTP transmission method that is allowed or denied access.

When using any of these attributes, you can specify all users with the use of the asterisk (*):

```
<allow roles="*" />
```

In this example, all roles are allowed access to the application. Another symbol you can use with these attributes is the question mark (?), which represents all anonymous users. For example, if you want to block all anonymous users from your application, use the following construction:

```
<deny users="?" />
```

When using users, roles, or verbs attributes with the <allow> or <deny> elements, you can specify multiple entries by separating the values with a comma. If you are going to allow more than one user, you can either separate these users into different elements, as shown here:

```
<allow users="MyDomain\User1" />
<allow users="MyDomain\User2" />
```

or you can use the following:

```
<allow users="MyDomain\User1, MyDomain\User2" />
```

Use the same construction when defining multiple roles and verbs.

Authenticating and Authorizing a Group

You can define groups of individuals allowed or denied access to your application or the application's resources. Your server can contain a number of different groups, each of which can have any number of users belonging to it. It is also possible for a single user to belong to multiple groups. Pull up the Computer Management utility to access the list of the groups defined on the server you are working with. Simply click the Groups folder in the Computer Management utility, and the list of groups is displayed, as illustrated in Figure 21-6.

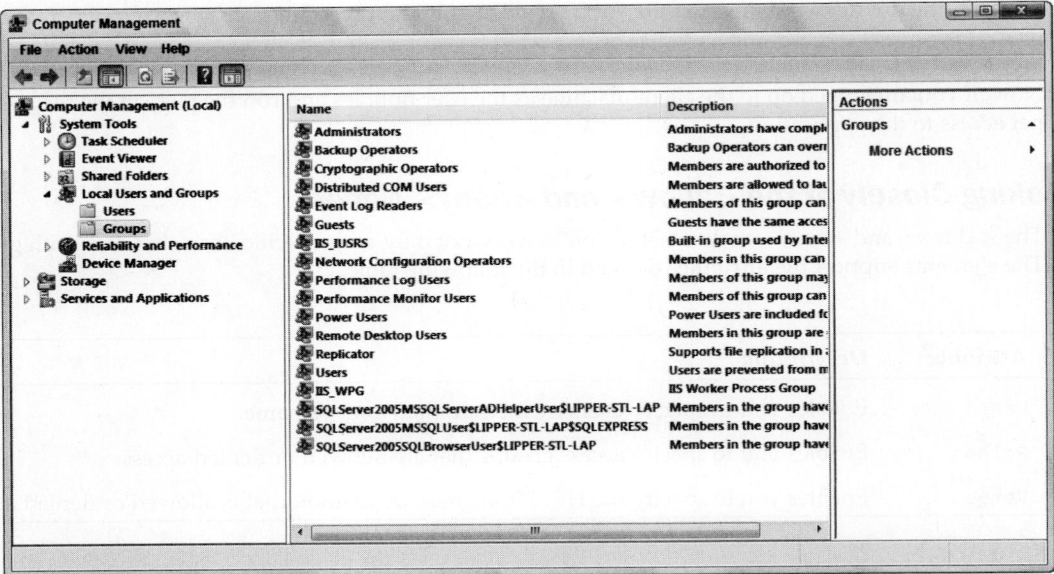

Figure 21-6

Right-click in the Groups folder to select New Group. The New Group dialog displays (see Figure 21-7).

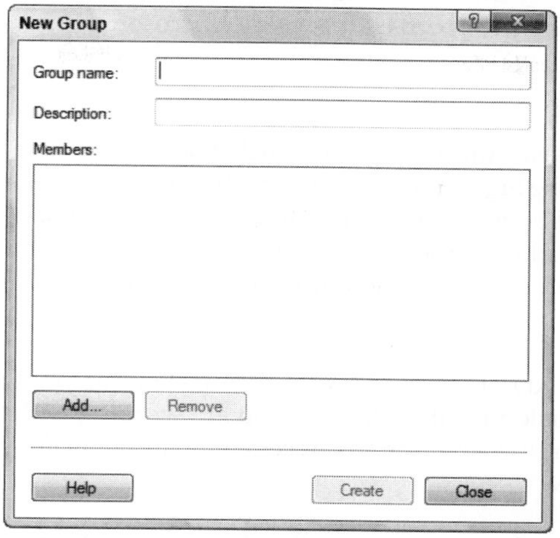

Figure 21-7

To create a group, give it a name and description; then click the Add button and select the users whom you want to be a part of the group. After a group is created, you can allow it access to your application like this:

```
<allow roles="MyGroup" />
```

You can use the `roles` attribute in either the `<allow>` or `<deny>` element to work with a group that you have created or with a specific group that already exists.

Authenticating and Authorizing an HTTP Transmission Method

In addition to authenticating and authorizing specific users or groups of users, you can also authorize or deny requests that come via a specific HTTP transmission protocol. This is done using the `verb` attribute in the `<allow>` and `<deny>` elements.

```
<deny verbs="GET, DEBUG" />
```

In this example, requests that come in using the HTTP GET or HTTP DEBUG protocols are denied access to the site. Possible values for the `verbs` attribute include `POST`, `GET`, `HEAD`, and `DEBUG`.

Integrated Windows Authentication

So far, you have been using the default Integrated Windows authentication mode for the authentication/ authorization process. This is fine if you are working with an intranet application and each of the clients is using Windows, the only system that the authentication method supports. This system of authentication also requires the client to be using Microsoft's Internet Explorer, which might not always be possible.

Integrated Windows authentication was previously known as NTLM or Windows NT Challenge/Response authentication. This authentication model has the client prove its identity by sending a hash of its credentials to the server that is hosting the ASP.NET application. Along with Microsoft's Active Directory, a client can also use Kerberos if it is using Microsoft's Internet Explorer 5 or higher.

Basic Authentication

Another option is to use Basic authentication, which also requires a username and password from the client for authentication. The big plus about Basic authentication is that it is part of the HTTP specification and therefore is supported by most browsers. The negative aspect of Basic authentication is that it passes the username and password to the server as clear text, meaning that the username and password are quite visible to prying eyes. For this reason, it is important to use Basic authentication along with SSL (*Secure Sockets Layer*).

If you are using IIS 5 or 6, to implement Basic authentication for your application, you must pull up IIS and open the Properties dialog for the Web site you are working with. Select the Directory Security tab and click the Edit button in the Anonymous Access and Authentication Control box. The Authentication Methods dialog box opens.

Uncheck the Integrated Windows Authentication check box at the bottom and check the Basic Authentication check box above it (see Figure 21-8). When you do, you are warned that this method transmits usernames and passwords as clear text.

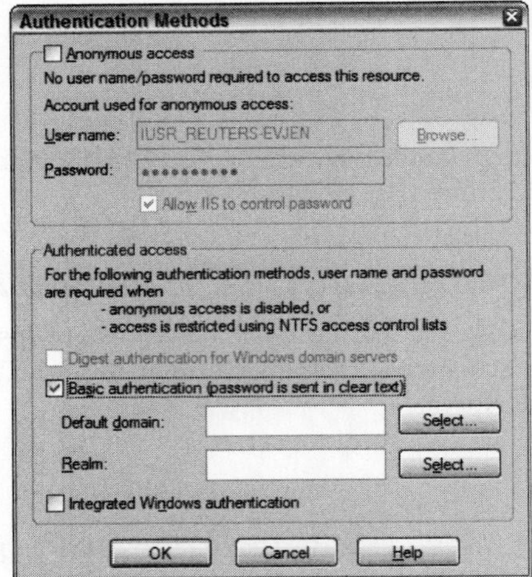

Figure 21-8

End by clicking OK in the dialog. Now your application uses Basic authentication instead of Integrated Windows authentication.

If you are using Windows Vista, it is not easy to find the option to enable Basic authentication. Instead, you first have to enable IIS 7 to use Basic authentication by selecting Start ➪ Control Panel ➪ Programs ➪ Programs and Features ➪ Turn Windows features on or off. From the provided dialog box, navigate to the Internet Information Services section and expand until you arrive at World Wide Web Services ➪ Security. From here, check the Basic Authentication option and press OK to install. This option is presented in Figure 21-9.

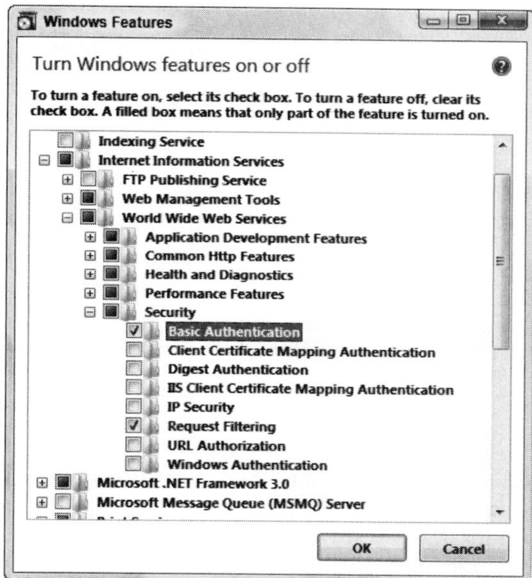

Figure 21-9

Once this option is installed, you can then return to the Internet Information Services (IIS) Manager and select the Authentication option in the IIS section for the virtual directory you are focusing on. From there, highlight the Basic Authentication option and select Enable from the Actions pane. This is illustrated in Figure 21-10.

Digest Authentication

Digest authentication is the final mode you explore in this chapter. The model alleviates the Basic authentication problem of passing the client's credentials as clear text. Instead, Digest authentication uses an algorithm to encrypt the client's credentials before they are sent to the application server.

To use Digest authentication, you are required to have a Windows domain controller. One of the main issues that arises with Digest authentication is that it is not supported on all platforms and requires browsers that conform to the HTTP 1.1 specification. Digest authentication, however, not only works well with firewalls, but it is also compatible with proxy servers.

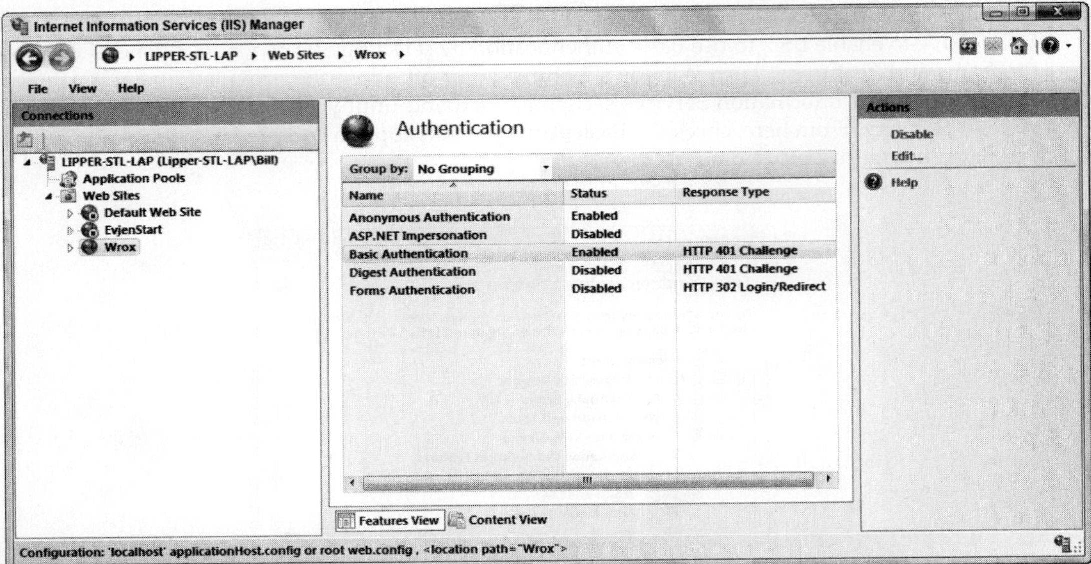

Figure 21-10

You can select Digest authentication as the choice for your application in the same Authentication Methods dialog — simply select the Digest Authentication check box from the properties dialog if you are using IIS 5 or 6. If you are using IIS 7, you need to install Digest Authentication just as you installed Basic Authentication. Once installed, you will find this option and will be able to enable it from the Authentication section within the IIS Manager.

Forms-Based Authentication

Forms-based authentication is a popular mode of authenticating users to access an entire application or specific resources within an application. Using it enables you to put the login form directly in the application so that the end user simply enters his username and password into an HTML form contained within the browser itself. One negative aspect of forms-based authentication is that the usernames and passwords are sent as clear text unless you are using SSL.

It is easy and relatively straightforward to implement forms-based authentication in your Web application. To begin with, you make some modifications to your application's `web.config` file, as illustrated in Listing 21-3.

Listing 21-3: Modifying the web.config file for forms-based authentication

```
<system.web>
   <authentication mode="Forms">
      <forms name="Wrox" loginUrl="Login.aspx" path="/" />
   </authentication>

   <authorization>
```

```
      <deny users="?" />
    </authorization>
  </system.web>
```

You must apply this structure to the web.config file. First, using the <authorization> element described earlier, you are denying access to the application to all anonymous users. Only authenticated users are allowed to access any page contained within the application.

If the requestor is not authenticated, what is defined in the <authentication> element is put into action. The value of the mode attribute is set to Forms to employ forms-based authentication for your Web application. The next attribute specified is loginUrl, which points to the page that contains the application's login form. In this example, Login.aspx is specified as a value. If the end user trying to access the application is not authenticated, his request is redirected to Login.aspx so that the user can be authenticated and authorized to proceed. After valid credentials have been provided, the user is returned to the location in the application where he originally made the request. The final attribute used here is path. It simply specifies the location in which to save the cookie used to persist the authorized user's access token. In most cases, you want to leave the value as /. The following table describes each of the possible attributes for the <forms> element.

Attribute	Description
name	This name is assigned to the cookie saved in order to remember the user from request to request. The default value is .ASPXAUTH.
loginUrl	Specifies the URL to which the request is redirected for login if no valid authentication cookie is found. The default value is Login.aspx.
protection	Specifies the amount of protection you want to apply to the authentication cookie. The four available settings are: ❑ All: The application uses both data validation and encryption to protect the cookie. This is the default setting. ❑ None: Applies no encryption to the cookie. ❑ Encryption: The cookie is encrypted but data validation is not performed on it. Cookies used in this manner might be subject to plain text attacks. ❑ Validation: The opposite of the Encryption setting. Data validation is performed, but the cookie is not encrypted.
path	Specifies the path for cookies issued by the application. In most cases you want to use /, which is the default setting.
timeout	Specifies the amount of time, in minutes, after which the cookie expires. The default value is 30.
cookieless	Specifies whether the forms-based authentication process should use cookies when working with the authentication/authorization process.
defaultUrl	Specifies the default URL.

Attribute	Description
domain	Specifies the domain name to be sent with forms authentication cookies.
slidingExpiration	Specifies whether to apply a sliding expiration to the cookie. If set to True, the expiration of the cookie is reset with each request made to the server. The default value is False.
enableCross AppsRedirect	Specifies whether to allow for cross-application redirection.
requireSSL	Specifies whether a Secure Sockets Layer (SSL) connection is required when transmitting authentication information.

After the web.config file is in place, the next step is to create a typical page for your application that people can access. Listing 21-4 presents a simple page.

Listing 21-4: A simple page — Default.aspx

```
<%@ Page Language="VB" %>

<html xmlns="http://www.w3.org/1999/xhtml">
<head runat="server">
    <title>The Application</title>
</head>
<body>
    <form id="form1" runat="server">
    <div>
       Hello World
    </div>
    </form>
</body>
</html>
```

As you can see, this page simply writes Hello World to the browser. The real power of forms authentication is shown in the Login.aspx page presented in Listing 21-5.

Listing 21-5: The Login.aspx page

VB

```
<%@ Page Language="VB" %>

<script runat="server">
    Protected Sub Button1_Click(ByVal sender As Object, _
      ByVal e As System.EventArgs)

        If (TextBox1.Text = "BillEvjen" And TextBox2.Text = "Bubbles") Then
            FormsAuthentication.RedirectFromLoginPage(TextBox1.Text, True)
        Else
            Response.Write("Invalid credentials")
```

```
        End If
    End Sub
</script>

<html xmlns="http://www.w3.org/1999/xhtml">
<head runat="server">
    <title>Login Page</title>
</head>
<body>
    <form id="form1" runat="server">
    <div>
        Username<br />
        <asp:TextBox ID="TextBox1" runat="server"></asp:TextBox><br />
        <br />
        Password<br />
        <asp:TextBox ID="TextBox2" runat="server"
         TextMode="Password"></asp:TextBox><br />
        <br />
        <asp:Button ID="Button1" OnClick="Button1_Click" runat="server"
         Text="Submit" />
    </div>
    </form>
</body>
</html>
```

C#

```
<%@ Page Language="C#"%>

<script runat="server">
   protected void Button1_Click(object sender, EventArgs e)
    {
        if (TextBox1.Text == "BillEvjen" && TextBox2.Text == "Bubbles") {
            FormsAuthentication.RedirectFromLoginPage(TextBox1.Text, true);
        }
        else {
            Response.Write("Invalid credentials");
        }
    }
</script>
```

`Login.aspx` has two simple TextBox controls and a Button control that asks the user to submit his username and password. The `Button1_Click` event uses the `RedirectFromLoginPage` method of the `FormsAuthentication` class. This method does exactly what its name implies — it redirects the request from `Login.aspx` to the original requested resource.

`RedirectFromLoginPage` takes two arguments. The first is the name of the user, used for cookie authentication purposes. This argument does not actually map to an account name and is used by ASP.NET's URL authorization capabilities. The second argument specifies whether a durable cookie should be issued. If set to `True`, the end user does not need to log in again to the application from one browser session to the next.

Using the three pages you have constructed, each request for the `Default.aspx` page from Listing 21-4 causes ASP.NET to check that the proper authentication token is in place. If the proper token is not found, the request is directed to the specified login page (in this example, `Login.aspx`). Looking at the URL in the browser, you can see that ASP.NET is using a querystring value to remember where to return the user after he has been authorized to proceed:

```
http://localhost:35089/Security/Login.aspx?ReturnUrl=%2fSecurity%2fDefault.aspx
```

Here, the querystring `ReturnUrl` is used with a value of the folder and page that was the initial request.

Look more closely at the `Login.aspx` page from Listing 21-5, and note that the values placed in the two text boxes are checked to make sure they abide by a specific username and password. If they do, the `RedirectFromLoginPage` method is invoked; otherwise, the `Response.Write()` statement is used. In most cases, you do not want to hardcode a username and password in your code. Many other options exist for checking whether usernames and passwords come from authorized users. Some of the other options follow.

Authenticating Against Values Contained in the web.config File

The previous example is not the best approach for dealing with usernames and passwords offered for authentication. It is never a good idea to hardcode these things directly into your applications. Take a quick look at storing these values in the `web.config` file itself.

The `<forms>` element in `web.config` that you worked with in Listing 21-3 can also take a sub-element. The sub-element, `<credentials>`, allows you to specify username and password combinations directly in the `web.config` file. You can choose from a couple of ways to add these values. The simplest method is shown in Listing 21-6.

Listing 21-6: Modifying the web.config file to add username/password values

```
<system.web>
   <authentication mode="Forms">
      <forms name="Wrox" loginUrl="Login.aspx" path="/">
         <credentials passwordFormat="Clear">
            <user name="BillEvjen" password="Bubbles" />
         </credentials>
      </forms>
   </authentication>

   <authorization>
      <deny users="?" />
   </authorization>
</system.web>
```

The `<credentials>` element has been included to add users and their passwords to the configuration file. `<credentials>` takes a single attribute — `passwordFormat`. The possible values of `passwordFormat` are `Clear`, `MD5`, and `SHA1`. The following list describes each of these options:

- `Clear`: Passwords are stored in clear text. The user password is compared directly to this value without further transformation.
- `MD5`: Passwords are stored using a Message Digest 5 (MD5) hash digest. When credentials are validated, the user password is hashed using the MD5 algorithm and compared for equality with

this value. The clear-text password is never stored or compared. This algorithm produces better performance than SHA1.

- SHA1: Passwords are stored using the SHA1 hash digest. When credentials are validated, the user password is hashed using the SHA1 algorithm and compared for equality with this value. The clear-text password is never stored or compared. Use this algorithm for best security.

In the example from Listing 21-6, you use a setting of Clear. This is not the most secure method, but it is used for demonstration purposes. A sub-element of <credentials> is <user>; that is where you define the username and password for the authorized user with the attributes name and password.

The next step is to change the Button1_Click event on the Login.aspx page shown earlier. This is illustrated in Listing 21-7.

Listing 21-7: Changing the Login.aspx page to work with the web.config file

VB

```
<%@ Page Language="VB" %>

<script runat="server">
    Protected Sub Button1_Click(ByVal sender As Object, _
      ByVal e As System.EventArgs)

        If FormsAuthentication.Authenticate(TextBox1.Text, TextBox2.Text) Then
            FormsAuthentication.RedirectFromLoginPage(TextBox1.Text, True)
        Else
            Response.Write("Invalid credentials")
        End If
    End Sub
</script>
```

C#

```
<%@ Page Language="C#"%>

<script runat="server">
    protected void Button1_Click(object sender, EventArgs e)
    {
        if (FormsAuthentication.Authenticate(TextBox1.Text, TextBox2.Text)) {
            FormsAuthentication.RedirectFromLoginPage(TextBox1.Text, true);
        }
        else {
            Response.Write("Invalid credentials");
        }
    }
</script>
```

In this example, you simply use the Authenticate() method to get your ASP.NET page to look at the credentials stored in the web.config file for verification. The Authenticate() method takes two parameters — the username and the password that you are passing in to be checked. If the credential lookup is successful, the RedirectFromLoginPage method is invoked.

It is best not to store your users' passwords in the web.config file as clear text as the preceding example did. Instead, use one of the available hashing capabilities so you can keep the end user's password out of sight of prying eyes. To do this, simply store the hashed password in the configuration file as shown in Listing 21-8.

Listing 21-8: Using encrypted passwords

```
<forms name="Wrox" loginUrl="Login.aspx" path="/">
   <credentials passwordFormat="SHA1">
      <user name="BillEvjen" password="58356FB4CAC0B801F011B397F9DFF45ADB863892" />
   </credentials>
</forms>
```

Using this kind of construct makes it impossible for even the developer to discover a password because the clear text password is never used. The `Authenticate()` method in the `Login.aspx` page hashes the password using SHA1 (because it is the method specified in the `web.config`'s `<credentials>` node) and compares the two hashes for a match. If a match is found, the user is authorized to proceed.

When using SHA1 or MD5, the only changes you make are in the `web.config` file and nowhere else. You do not have to make any changes to the login page or to any other page in the application. To store hashed passwords, however, you use the `FormsAuthenticationHashPasswordForStoringInConfigFile` method (probably the longest method name in the .NET Framework). You accomplish this in the following manner:

```
FormsAuthentication.HashPasswordForStoringInConfigFile(TextBox2.Text, "SHA1")
```

Authenticating Against Values in a Database

Another common way to retrieve username/password combinations is by getting them directly from a datastore of some kind. This enables you, for example, to check the credentials input by a user against values stored in Microsoft's SQL Server. The code for this is presented in Listing 21-9.

Listing 21-9: Checking credentials in SQL Server (Login.aspx)

VB

```
<%@ Page Language="VB" %>
<%@ Import Namespace="System.Data" %>
<%@ Import Namespace="System.Data.SqlClient" %>

<script runat="server">
    Protected Sub Button1_Click(ByVal sender As Object, _
      ByVal e As System.EventArgs)

        Dim conn As SqlConnection
        Dim cmd As SqlCommand
        Dim cmdString As String = "SELECT [Password] FROM [AccessTable] WHERE" & _
           " (([Username] = @Username) AND ([Password] = @Password))"

        conn = New SqlConnection("Data Source=localhost;Initial " & _
           "Catalog=Northwind;Persist Security Info=True;User ID=sa")
        cmd = New SqlCommand(cmdString, conn)

        cmd.Parameters.Add("@Username", SqlDbType.VarChar, 50)
        cmd.Parameters("@Username").Value = TextBox1.Text
```

```
        cmd.Parameters.Add("@Password", SqlDbType.VarChar, 50)
        cmd.Parameters("@Password").Value = TextBox2.Text

        conn.Open()

        Dim myReader As SqlDataReader

        myReader = cmd.ExecuteReader(CommandBehavior.CloseConnection)

        If myReader.Read() Then
           FormsAuthentication.RedirectFromLoginPage(TextBox1.Text, False)
        Else
           Response.Write("Invalid credentials")
        End If

        myReader.Close()
    End Sub
</script>
```

C#

```
<%@ Page Language="C#"%>
<%@ Import Namespace="System.Data" %>
<%@ Import Namespace="System.Data.SqlClient" %>

<script runat="server">
    protected void Button1_Click(object sender, EventArgs e)
    {
       SqlConnection conn;
       SqlCommand cmd;
       string cmdString = "SELECT [Password] FROM [AccessTable] WHERE" +
          " (([Username] = @Username) AND ([Password] = @Password))";

       conn = new SqlConnection("Data Source=localhost;Initial " +
          "Catalog=Northwind;Persist Security Info=True;User ID=sa");
       cmd = new SqlCommand(cmdString, conn);

       cmd.Parameters.Add("@Username", SqlDbType.VarChar, 50);
       cmd.Parameters["@Username"].Value = TextBox1.Text;
       cmd.Parameters.Add("@Password", SqlDbType.VarChar, 50);
       cmd.Parameters["@Password"].Value = TextBox2.Text;

       conn.Open();

       SqlDataReader myReader;

       myReader = cmd.ExecuteReader(CommandBehavior.CloseConnection);

       if (myReader.Read()) {
          FormsAuthentication.RedirectFromLoginPage(TextBox1.Text, false);
       }
       else {
          Response.Write("Invalid credentials");
       }
```

Continued

```
        myReader.Close();
    }
</script>
```

Leave everything else from the previous examples the same, except for the `Login.aspx` page. You can now authenticate usernames and passwords against data stored in SQL Server. In the `Button1_Click` event, a connection is made to SQL Server. (For security reasons, you should store your connection string in the `web.config` file.) Two parameters are passed in — the inputs from `TextBox1` and `TextBox2`. If a result is returned, the `RedirectFromLoginPage()` method is invoked.

Using the Login Control with Forms Authentication

You have seen how to use ASP.NET forms authentication with standard ASP.NET server controls, such as simple TextBox and Button controls. You can also use the ASP.NET server controls — such as the Login server control — with your custom-developed forms-authentication framework instead of using other controls. This really shows the power of ASP.NET — you can combine so many pieces to construct the solution you want.

Listing 21-10 shows a modified `Login.aspx` page using the new Login server control.

Listing 21-10: Using the Login server control on the Login.aspx page

VB

```
<%@ Page Language="VB" %>

<script runat="server">
    Protected Sub Login1_Authenticate(ByVal sender As Object, _
      ByVal e As System.Web.UI.WebControls.AuthenticateEventArgs)

        If (Login1.UserName = "BillEvjen" And Login1.Password = "Bubbles") Then
            FormsAuthentication.RedirectFromLoginPage(Login1.UserName, _
               Login1.RememberMeSet)
        Else
            Response.Write("Invalid credentials")
        End If
    End Sub
</script>

<html xmlns="http://www.w3.org/1999/xhtml" >
<head runat="server">
    <title>Login Page</title>
</head>
<body>
    <form id="form1" runat="server">
    <div>
        <asp:Login ID="Login1" runat="server" OnAuthenticate="Login1_Authenticate">
        </asp:Login>
    </div>
    </form>
</body>
</html>
```

C#

```
<%@ Page Language="C#" %>
```

```
<script runat="server">
    protected void Login1_Authenticate(object sender, AuthenticateEventArgs e)
    {
        if (Login1.UserName == "BillEvjen" && Login1.Password == "Bubbles") {
            FormsAuthentication.RedirectFromLoginPage(Login1.UserName,
               Login1.RememberMeSet);
        }
        else {
            Response.Write("Invalid credentials");
        }
    }
</script>
```

Because no Button server control is on the page, you use the Login control's `OnAuthenticate` attribute to point to the authentication server-side event — `Login1_Authenticate`. The event takes care of the authorization lookup (although the values are hardcoded in this example). The username text box of the Login control can be accessed via the `Login1.UserName` declaration, and the password can be accessed using `Login1.Password`. The `Login1.RememberMeSet` property is used to specify whether to persist the authentication cookie for the user so that he is remembered on his next visit.

This example is a bit simpler than creating your own login form using TextBox and Button controls. You can give the Login control a predefined look-and-feel that is provided for you. You can also get at the subcontrol properties of the Login control a bit more easily. In the end, it really is up to you as to what methods you employ in your ASP.NET applications.

Looking Closely at the FormsAuthentication Class

As you can tell from the various examples in the forms authentication part of this chapter, a lot of what goes on depends on the `FormsAuthentication` class itself. For this reason, you should learn what that class is all about.

`FormsAuthentication` provides a number of methods and properties that enable you to read and control the authentication cookie as well as other information (such as the return URL of the request). The following table details some of the methods and properties available in the `FormsAuthentictation` class.

Method/Property	Description
`Authenticate`	This method is used to authenticate credentials that are stored in a configuration file (such as the `web.config` file).
`Decrypt`	Returns an instance of a valid, encrypted authentication ticket retrieved from an HTTP cookie as an instance of a `FormsAuthenticationTicket` class.
`Encrypt`	Creates a string which contains a valid encrypted authentication ticket that can be used in an HTTP cookie.
`FormsCookieName`	Returns the name of the cookie for the current application.
`FormsCookiePath`	Returns the cookie path (the location of the cookie) for the current application.
`GetAuthCookie`	Provides an authentication cookie for a specified user.

Method/Property	Description
`GetRedirectUrl`	Returns the URL to which the user is redirected after being authorized by the login page.
`HashPasswordFor Storing InConfigFile`	Creates a hash of a provided string password. This method takes two parameters — one is the password and the other is the type of hash to perform on the string. Possible hash values include `SHA1` and `MD5`.
`Initialize`	Performs an initialization of the `FormsAuthentication` class by reading the configuration settings in the `web.config` file, as well as getting the cookies and encryption keys used in the given instance of the application.
`RedirectFromLogin Page`	Performs a redirection of the HTTP request back to the original requested page. This should be performed only after the user has been authorized to proceed.
`RenewTicketIfOld`	Conditionally updates the sliding expiration on a `FormsAuthenticationTicket` instance.
`RequireSSL`	Specifies whether the cookie should be transported via SSL only (HTTPS).
`SetAuthCookie`	Creates an authentication ticket and attaches it to a cookie that is contained in the outgoing response.
`SignOut`	Removes the authentication ticket.
`SlidingExpiration`	Provides a Boolean value indicating whether sliding expiration is enabled.

Passport Authentication

Another method for the authentication of your end users is using Microsoft's Passport identity system. Users with a passport account can have a single sign-on solution, meaning that he needs only those credentials to log in to your site and into other Passport-enabled sites and applications on the Internet.

When your application is enabled for Passport authentication, the request is actually redirected to the Microsoft Passport site where the user can enter his credentials. If the authentication is successful, the user is then authorized to proceed, and the request is redirected back to your application.

Very few Internet sites and applications use Microsoft's Passport technologies. In fact, Microsoft has completely de-emphasized Passport in 2005, and most companies interested in global authentication/authorization standards are turning toward the Project Liberty endeavors for a solution (`www.projectliberty.org`).

Authenticating Specific Files and Folders

You may not want to require credentials for each and every page or resource in your application. For instance, you might have a public Internet site with pages anyone can access without credentials, although you might have an administration section as part of your application that may require authentication/authorization measures.

URL authorization enables you to use the `web.config` file to apply the settings you need. Using URL authorization, you can apply any of the authentication measures to only specific files or folders. Listing 21-11 shows an example of locking down a single file.

Listing 21-11: Applying authorization requirements to a single file

```
<configuration>
   <system.web>
      <authentication mode="None" />

      <!-- The rest of your web.config file settings go here -->

   </system.web>

   <location path="AdminPage.aspx">
      <system.web>
         <authentication mode="Windows" />

         <authorization>
            <allow users="ReutersServer\EvjenB" />
            <deny users="*" />
         </authorization>
      </system.web>
   </location>
</configuration>
```

This `web.config` construction keeps the Web application open to the general public while, at the same time, it locks down a single file contained within the application — the `AdminPage.aspx` page. This is accomplished through the `<location>` element. `<location>` takes a single attribute (`path`) to specify the resource defined within the `<system.web>` section of the `web.config` file.

In the example, the `<authentication>` and `<authorization>` elements are used to provide the authentication and authorization details for the `AdminPage.aspx` page. For this page, Windows authentication is applied, and the only user allowed access is `EvjenB` in the `ReutersServer` domain. You can have as many `<location>` sections in your `web.config` file as you want.

Programmatic Authorization

So far, you have seen a lot of authentication examples that simply provide a general authorization to a specific page or folder within the application. Yet, you may want to provide more granular authorization measures for certain items on a page. For instance, you might provide a link to a specific document only for users who have an explicit Windows role. Other users may see something else. You also might want additional commentary or information for specified users, while other users see a condensed version of the information. Whatever your reason, this role-based authorization practice is possible in ASP.NET by working with certain objects.

You can use the `Page` object's `User` property, which provides an instance of the `IPrincipal` object. The `User` property provides a single method and a single property:

- `Identity`: This property provides an instance of the `System.Security.Principal.IIdentity` object for you to get at specific properties of the authenticated user.

- `IsInRole`: This method takes a single parameter, a string representation of the system role. It returns a Boolean value that indicates whether the user is in the role specified.

Working with User.Identity

The `User.Identity` property enables you to work with some specific contextual information about the authorized user. Using the property within your ASP.NET applications enables you to make resource-access decisions based on the information the object provides.

With `User.Identity`, you can gain access to the user's name, his authentication type, and whether he is authenticated. The following table details the properties provided through `User.Identity`.

Attribute	Description
`Authentication Type`	Provides the authentication type of the current user. Example values include `Basic`, `NTLM`, `Forms`, and `Passport`.
`IsAuthenticated`	Returns a Boolean value specifying whether the user has been authenticated.
`Name`	Provides the username of the user as well as the domain of the user (only if he logged on with a Windows account).

For some examples of working with the `User` object, take a look at checking the user's login name. To do this, you use code similar to that shown in Listing 21-12.

Listing 21-12: Getting the username of the logged-in user

VB

```
Dim UserName As String
UserName = User.Identity.Name
```

C#

```
string userName;
userName = User.Identity.Name;
```

Another task you can accomplish with the `User.Identity` object is checking whether the user has been authenticated through your application's authentication methods, as illustrated in Listing 21-13.

Listing 21-13: Checking whether the user is authenticated

VB

```
Dim AuthUser As Boolean
AuthUser = User.Identity.IsAuthenticated
```

C#

```
bool authUser;
authUser = User.Identity.IsAuthenticated;
```

This example provides you with a Boolean value indicating whether the user has been authenticated. You can also use the `IsAuthenticated` method in an `If/Then` statement, as shown in Listing 21-14.

Listing 21-14: Using an If/Then statement that checks authentication

VB

```
If (User.Identity.IsAuthenticated) Then
   ' Do some actions here for authenticated users
Else
   ' Do other actions here for unauthenticated users
End If
```

C#

```
if (User.Identity.IsAuthenticated) {
   // Do some actions here for authenticated users
}
else {
   // Do other actions here for unauthenticated users
}
```

You can also use the `User` object to check the authentication type of the user. This is done with the `AuthenticationType` property illustrated in Listing 21-15.

Listing 21-15: Using the AuthenticationType property

VB

```
Dim AuthType As String
AuthType = User.Identity.AuthenticationType
```

C#

```
string authType;
authType = User.Identity.AuthenticationType;
```

Again, the result is `Basic`, `NTLM`, `Forms`, or `Passport`.

Working with User.IsInRole()

If you are using Windows-based authentication, you can check to make sure that an authenticated user is in a specific Windows role. For example, you might want to show specific information only for users in the `Subscribers` group in the Computer Management Utility. To accomplish that, you can use the `User` object's `IsInRole` method, as shown in Listing 21-16.

Listing 21-16: Checking whether the user is part of a specific role

VB

```
If (User.IsInRole("ReutersServer\Subscribers")) Then
   ' Private information for subscribers
Else
   ' Public information
End If
```

C#

```
if (User.IsInRole("ReutersServer\\Subscribers")) {
   // Private information for subscribers
```

Continued

```
}
else {
   // Public information
}
```

The `IsInRole` method's parameter provides a string value that represents the domain and the group (Windows role). In this case, you specify that any user in the `Subscribers` Windows role from the `ReutersServer` domain is permitted to see some information not available to users who don't belong to that specific role.

Another possibility is to specify some of the built-in groups available to you. Ever since Windows 2000, Windows has included a series of built-in accounts such as Administrator, Guest, PrintOperator, and User. You can access these built-in accounts in a couple of ways. One is to specify the built-in account with the domain directly:

```
User.IsInRole("ReutersServer\Administrator")
```

The other possibility is to use the `BUILTIN` keyword:

```
User.IsInRole("BUILTIN\Administrator")
```

Pulling More Information with WindowsIdentity

So far, in working with the user's identity information, you have used the standard `Identity` object that is part of ASP.NET by default. If you are working with Windows-based authentication, you also have the option of using the `WindowsIdentity` object and other objects. To gain access to these richer objects, create a reference to the `System.Security.Principal` object in your application.

Used in combination with the `Identity` object from the preceding examples, these additional objects make certain tasks even easier. For instance, if you are working with roles, `System.Security.Principal` provides access to the `WindowsBuiltInRole` enumeration.

Listing 21-17 is an example of using the `WindowsBuiltInRole` enumeration.

Listing 21-17: Using the WindowsBuiltInRole enumeration

VB

```
Dim AdminUser As Boolean
AdminUser = User.IsInRole(WindowsBuiltInRole.Administrator.ToString())
```

C#

```
bool adminUser;
adminUser = User.IsInRole(WindowsBuiltInRole.Administrator.ToString());
```

Instead of specifying a string value of the domain and the role, you can use the `WindowsBuiltInRole` enumeration to easily access specific roles on the application server. When working with this and other enumerations, you also have IntelliSense (see Figure 21-11) to help you make your selections easily.

The roles in the `WindowsBuiltInRole` enumeration include the following:

- ❑ AccountOperator
- ❑ Administrator

- BackupOperator
- Guest
- PowerUser
- PrintOperator
- Replicator
- SystemOperator
- User

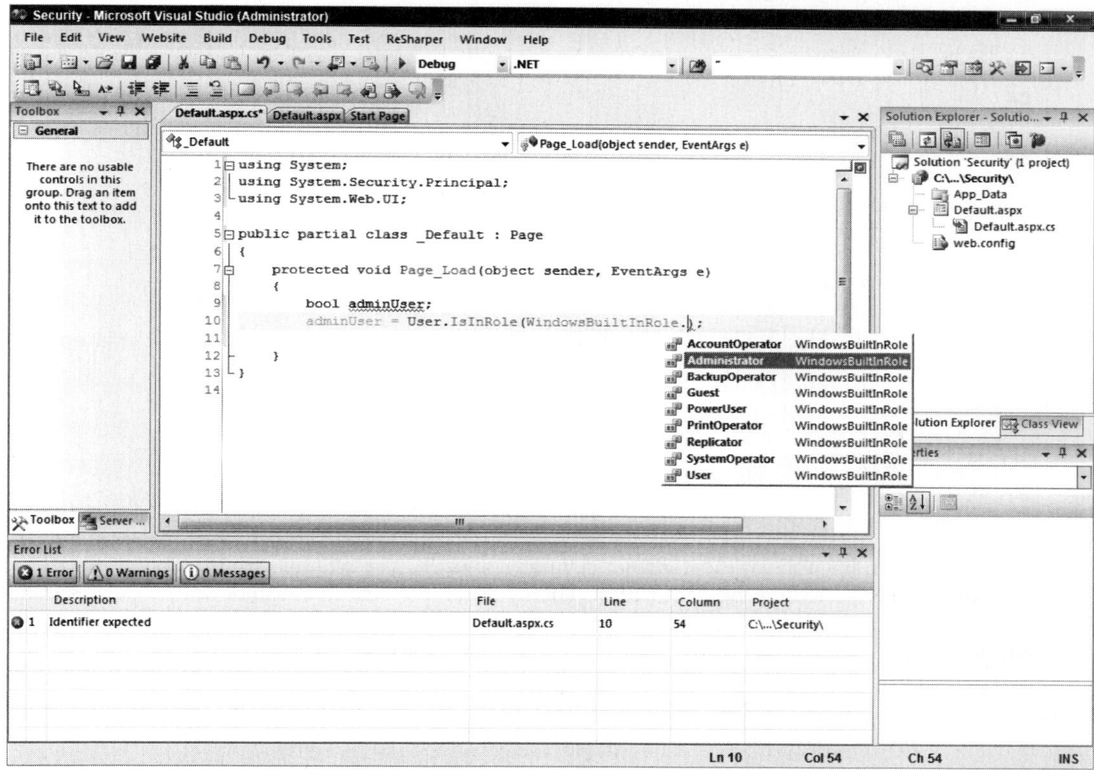

Figure 21-11

Using `System.Security.Principal`, you have access to the `WindowsIdentity` object, which is much richer than working with the default `Identity` object. Listing 21-18 lists some of the additional information you can get through the `WindowsIdentity` object.

Listing 21-18: Using the WindowsIdentity object

VB

```
<%@ Page Language="VB" %>
<%@ Import Namespace="System.Security.Principal" %>
```

Continued

```
<script runat="server">
    Protected Sub Page_Load(ByVal sender As Object, _
      ByVal e As System.EventArgs)

        Dim AuthUser As WindowsIdentity = WindowsIdentity.GetCurrent()
        Response.Write(AuthUser.AuthenticationType.ToString() & "<br>" & _
           AuthUser.ImpersonationLevel.ToString() & "<br>" & _
           AuthUser.IsAnonymous.ToString() & "<br>" & _
           AuthUser.IsAuthenticated.ToString() & "<br>" & _
           AuthUser.IsGuest.ToString() & "<br>" & _
           AuthUser.IsSystem.ToString() & "<br>" & _
           AuthUser.Name.ToString())
    End Sub
</script>
```

C#

```
<%@ Page Language="C#" %>
<%@ Import Namespace="System.Security.Principal" %>

<script runat="server">
    protected void Page_Load(object sender, EventArgs e)
    {
        WindowsIdentity AuthUser = WindowsIdentity.GetCurrent();
        Response.Write(AuthUser.AuthenticationType.ToString() + "<br>" +
           AuthUser.ImpersonationLevel.ToString() + "<br>" +
           AuthUser.IsAnonymous.ToString() + "<br>" +
           AuthUser.IsAuthenticated.ToString() + "<br>" +
           AuthUser.IsGuest.ToString() + "<br>" +
           AuthUser.IsSystem.ToString() + "<br>" +
           AuthUser.Name.ToString());
    }
</script>
```

In this example, an instance of the `WindowsIdentity` object is created and populated with the current identity of the user accessing the application. Then you have access to a number of properties that are written to the browser using a `Response.Write()` statement. The displayed listing shows information about the current user's credentials, such as if the user is authenticated, anonymous, or running under a guest account or a system account. It also gives you the user's authentication type and login name. A result is shown in Figure 21-12.

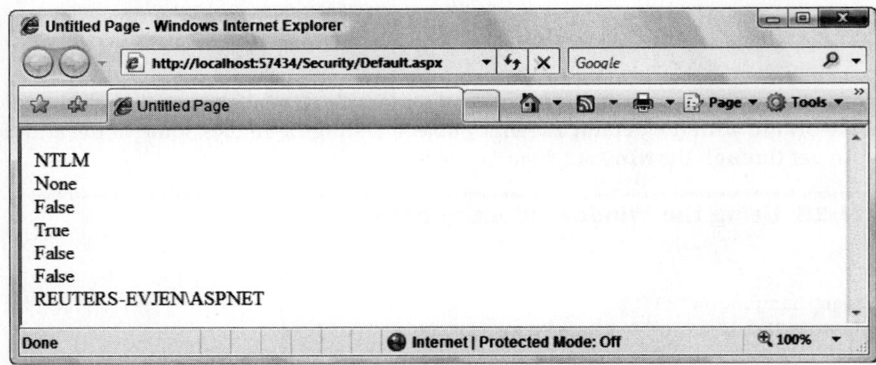

Figure 21-12

Identity and Impersonation

By default, ASP.NET runs under an account that has limited privileges. For instance, you may find that although the account can gain access to a network, it cannot be authenticated to any other computer on the network. The account setting is provided in the `machine.config` file:

```
<processModel
 enable="true"
 userName="machine"
 password="AutoGenerate" />
```

These settings force ASP.NET to run under the system account (ASPNET or Network Service). This is really specified through the `userName` attribute that contains a value of `machine`. The other possible value you can have for this attribute is `system`. Here's what each entails:

- `machine`: The most secure setting. You should have good reasons to change this value. It's the ideal choice mainly because it forces the ASP.NET account to run under the fewest number of privileges possible.
- `system`: Forces ASP.NET to run under the local SYSTEM account, which has considerably more privileges to access networking and files.

It is also possible to specify an account of your choosing using the `<processModel>` element in either the `machine.config` or `web.config` files:

```
<processModel
 enable="true"
 userName="MySpecifiedUser"
 password="MyPassword" />
```

In this example, ASP.NET is run under a specified administrator or user account instead of the default ASPNET or Network Service account. It inherits all the privileges this account offers. You should consider encrypting this section of the file. Encrypting sections of a configuration file are covered in Chapter 32.

You can also change how ASP.NET behaves in whatever account it is specified to run under through the `<identity>` element in the `web.config` file. The `<identity>` element in the `web.config` file allows you to turn on *impersonation*. Impersonation provides ASP.NET with the capability to run as a process using the privileges of another user for a specific session. In more detail, impersonation allows ASP.NET to run under the account of the entity making the request to the application. To turn on this impersonation capability, you use the `impersonate` attribute in the `<identity>` element as shown here:

```
<configuration>
   <system.web>

      <identity impersonate="true" />

   </system.web>
</configuration>
```

By default, the `impersonate` attribute is set to `false`. Setting this property to `true` ensures that ASP.NET runs under the account of the person making the request to the application. If the requestor is an anonymous user, ASP.NET runs under the IUSR_MachineName account. To see this in action, run the example shown in Listing 21-18, but this time with impersonation turned on (`true`). Instead of getting a username of `REUTERS-EVJEN\ASPNET` as the user, you get the name of the user who is requesting the page — `REUTERS-EVJEN\Administrator` in this example — as shown in Figure 21-13.

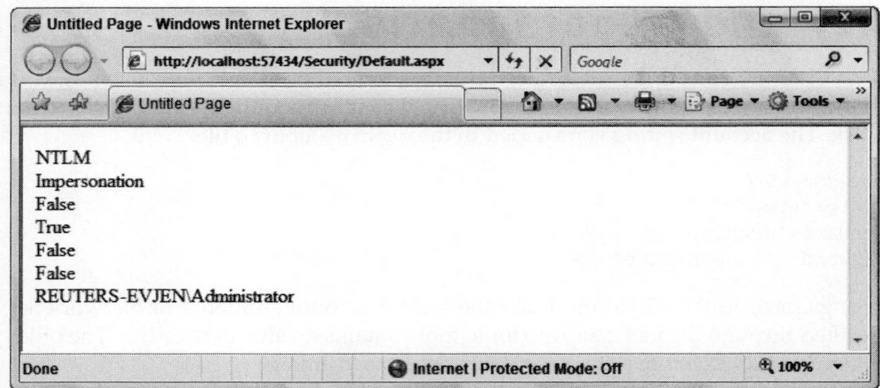

Figure 21-13

You also have the option of running ASP.NET under a specified account that you declare using the `<identity>` element in the `web.config` file:

```
<identity impersonate="true" userName="MySpecifiedUser" password="MyPassword" />
```

As shown, you can run the ASP.NET process under an account that you specify through the `userName` and `password` attributes. These values are stored as clear text in the `web.config` file.

Look at the root `web.config` file, and you can see that ASP.NET runs under full trust, meaning that it has some pretty high-level capabilities to run and access resources. Here is the setting:

```
<system.web>

    <location allowOverride="true">
        <system.web>
            <securityPolicy>
                <trustLevel name="Full" policyFile="internal"/>
                <trustLevel name="High" policyFile="web_hightrust.config"/>
                <trustLevel name="Medium" policyFile="web_mediumtrust.config"/>
                <trustLevel name="Low" policyFile="web_lowtrust.config"/>
                <trustLevel name="Minimal" policyFile="web_minimaltrust.config"/>
            </securityPolicy>
            <trust level="Full" originUrl=""/>
        </system.web>
    </location>

</system.web>
```

Five possible settings exist for the level of trust that you give ASP.NET — `Full`, `High`, `Medium`, `Low`, and `Minimal`. The level of trust applied is specified through the `<trust>` element's `level` attribute. By default, it is set to `Full`. Each one points to a specific configuration file for the policy in which the level can find its trust level settings. The `Full` setting does not include a policy file because it simply skips all the code access security checks.

Securing Through IIS

ASP.NET works in conjunction with IIS; not only can you apply security settings directly in ASP.NET (through code or configuration files), but you can also apply additional security measures in IIS itself. IIS enables you to apply access methods you want by working with users and groups (which were discussed earlier in the chapter), working with restricting IP addresses, file extensions, and more. Security through IIS is deserving of a chapter in itself, but the major topics are explored here.

IP Address and Domain Name Restrictions

You can work with the restriction of IP addresses and domain names in Windows Server 2003, Windows 2000 Server, or Windows NT. Through IIS 6.0, you can apply specific restrictions based on a single computer's IP address, a group of computers, or even a specific domain name.

To access this capability, pull up the Internet Information Services (IIS) Manager and right-click on either the Web site you are interested in working with or on the Default Web Site node to simply apply the settings to every Web application on the server. From the menu, choose Properties and select the Directory Security tab.

Click the Edit button in the IP Address and domain name restrictions box and a dialog appears. The resulting dialog enables you to grant or restrict access based on an IP address or domain name. These dialogs are shown in Figure 21-14.

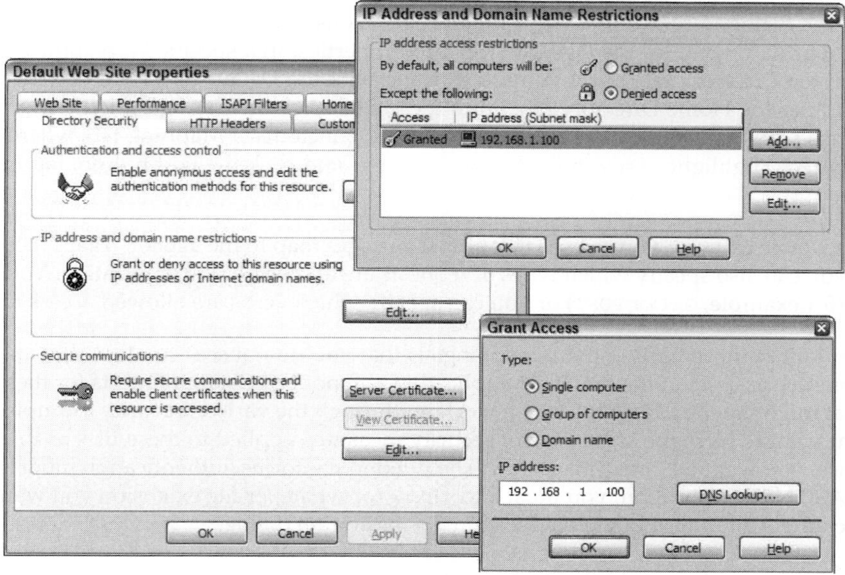

Figure 21-14

Think twice about restricting based on a domain name. It can hinder performance when the reverse DNS lookup is performed on each request to check the domain.

You not only can restrict specific IP addresses and domain names, but you can also restrict everyone and just allow specified entities based on the same items. Although Figure 21-14 shows restricting a specific IP address, you can restrict or grant access to an entire subnet as well. Figure 21-15 shows how to grant access just to the servers on the 192.168.1.0 subnet (defined by a Linksys router).

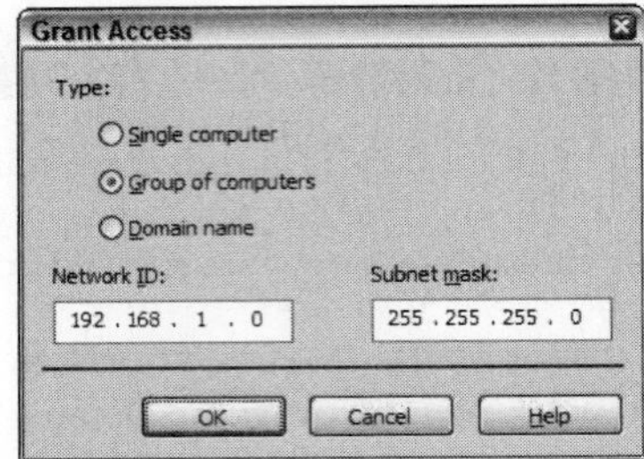

Figure 21-15

Working with File Extensions

You can work with many types of files in ASP.NET. These files are defined by their extensions. For example, you know that `.aspx` is a typical ASP.NET page, and `.asmx` is an ASP.NET Web service file extension. These files are actually mapped by IIS to the ASP.NET DLL, `aspnet_isapi.dll`.

To access the dialog in IIS 6.0 that maps the file extensions, pull up the Properties dialog of your Web application in IIS or pull up the Default Web Site Properties. In a specific Web application, you must work from the Directory tab; but if you are working with the Default Web Site Properties dialog, you can instead use the Home Directory tab. From these tabs, click the Configuration button in the Application Settings box. The Application Configuration dialog includes a Mapping tab, where the mappings are configured. Highlight `.aspx` in the list of mappings and click the Edit button. Figure 21-16 shows the result.

In the Executable text box, you can see that all `.aspx` pages map to the `aspnet_isapi.dll` from ASP.NET, and that you can also specify which types of requests are allowed in the application. You can allow either all verbs (for example, `GET` or `POST`) or you can specify which verbs are allowed access to the application.

One important point regarding these mappings is that you do not see `.html`, `.htm`, `.jpg`, or other file extensions such as `.txt` in the list. Your application will not be passing requests for these files to ASP .NET. That might not be a big deal, but in working through the various security examples in this chapter, you might want to have the same type of security measures applied to these files as to `.aspx` pages. If, for instance, you want all `.html` pages to be included in the forms authentication model that you require for your ASP.NET application, you must add `.html` (or whatever file extension you want) to the list. To do so, click the Add button in the Application Configuration dialog.

In the next dialog, you can add the ASP.NET DLL to the Executable text box, and the appropriate file extension and verbs to the list before adding the mapping to your application's mapping table. This example is illustrated in Figure 21-17.

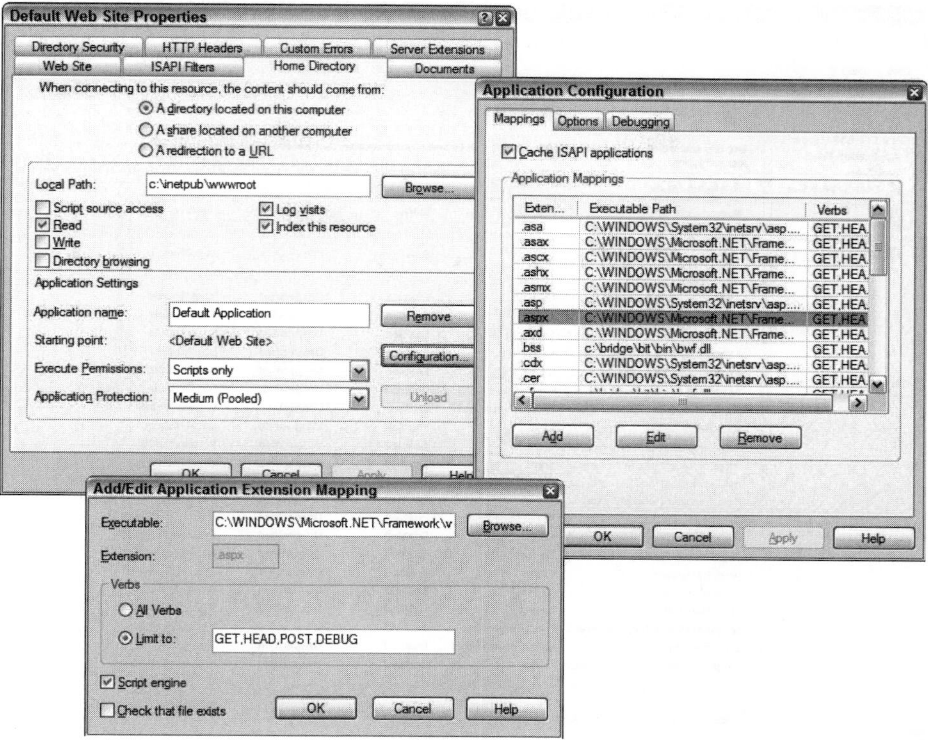

Figure 21-16

Figure 21-17

When dealing with the security of your site, you have to remember all the files that might not be included in the default mapping list and add the ones you think should fall under the same security structure.

If you are working with Windows Vista, you can get to the same functionality through the IIS Manager. In this tool, select Handler Mappings in the IIS section. You will find a large list of mappings that have already been provided. This is illustrated in Figure 21-18.

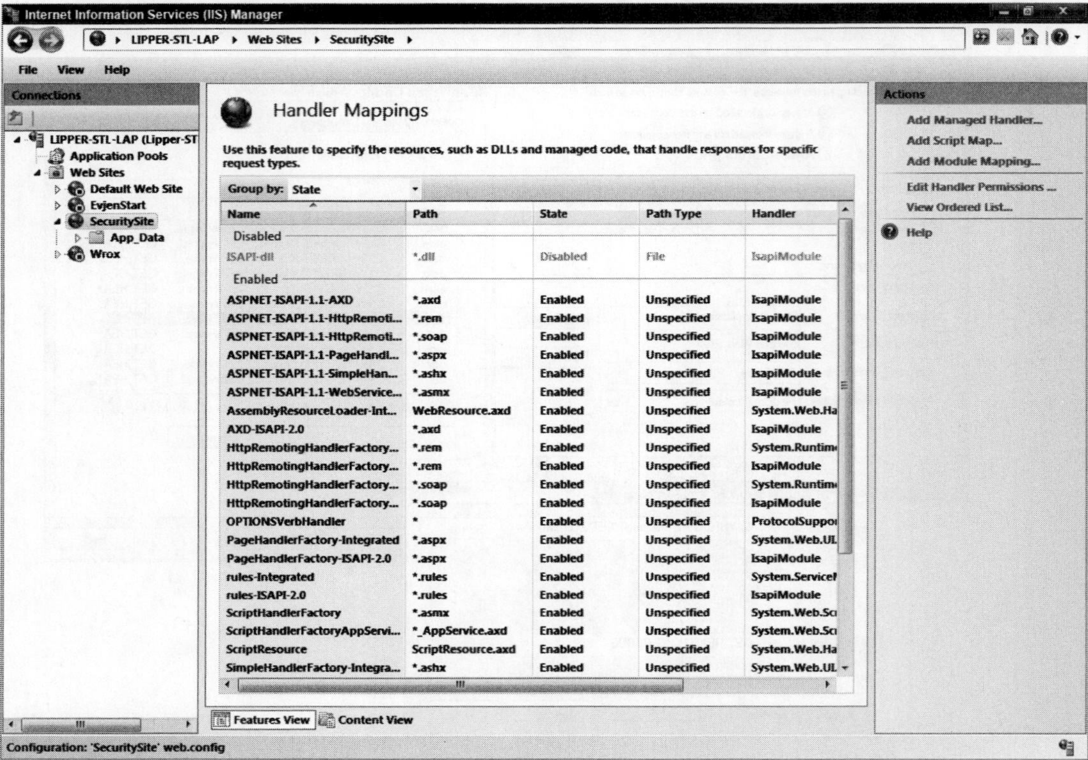

Figure 21-18

By highlighting the `*.aspx` option and pressing the Edit button, you see that this extension is mapped to `%windir%\Microsoft.NET\Framework\v2.0.50727\aspnet_isapi.dll`, as shown in Figure 21-19.

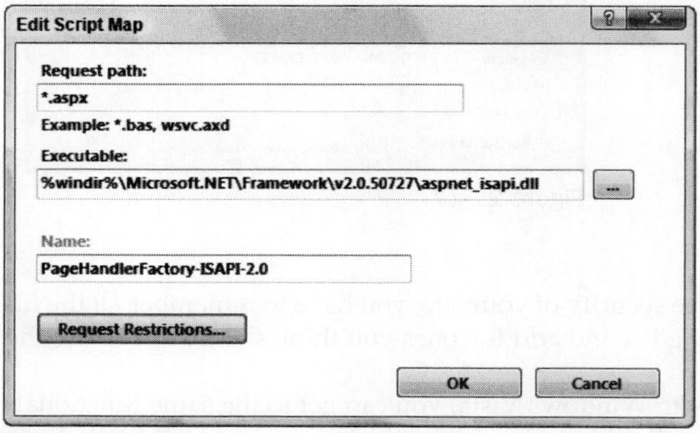

Edit Script Map

Request path:

*.aspx

Example: *.bas, wsvc.axd

Executable:

%windir%\Microsoft.NET\Framework\v2.0.50727\aspnet_isapi.dll

Name:

PageHandlerFactory-ISAPI-2.0

Request Restrictions...

OK Cancel

Figure 21-19

Pressing the Request Restrictions button provides a dialog that enables you to select the verbs allowed (as shown in Figure 21-20).

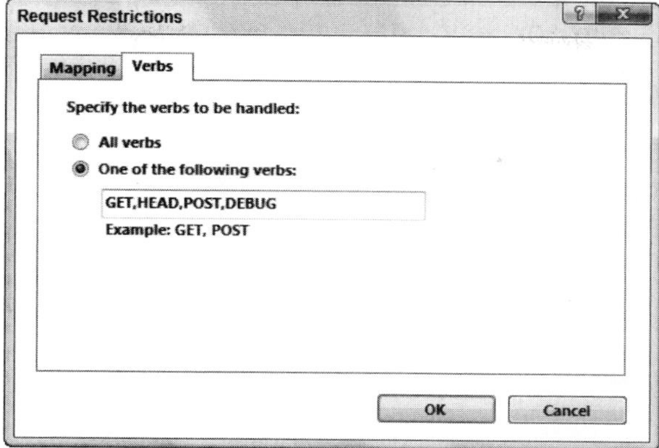

Figure 21-20

Using the ASP.NET MMC Snap-In

The ASP.NET MMC console (covered in more detail in Chapter 34) enables you to edit the `web.config` and `machine.config` files using an easy-to-use GUI instead of having to dig through the text of those files yourself to make the necessary changes. This option is only available in either Windows Server 2003 or Windows XP. Most of the items examined in this book can also be modified and changed using this dialog. The plug-in is available on the ASP.NET tab (see Figure 21-21) of your Web application running under IIS.

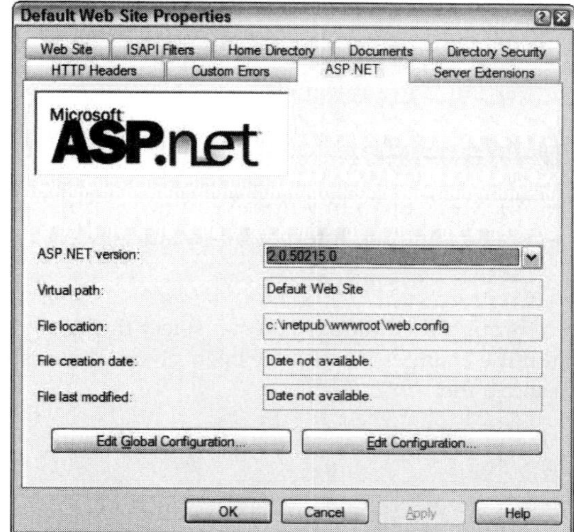

Figure 21-21

When you make the changes directly in the dialog, you are also making the hardcoded changes to the actual configuration files.

Click the Edit Configuration button on the ASP.NET tab, and the ASP.NET Configuration Settings dialog opens. There you can modify how your forms authentication model works in the GUI without going to the application's `web.config` file directly. Figure 21-22 shows an example of working with forms authentication in the GUI.

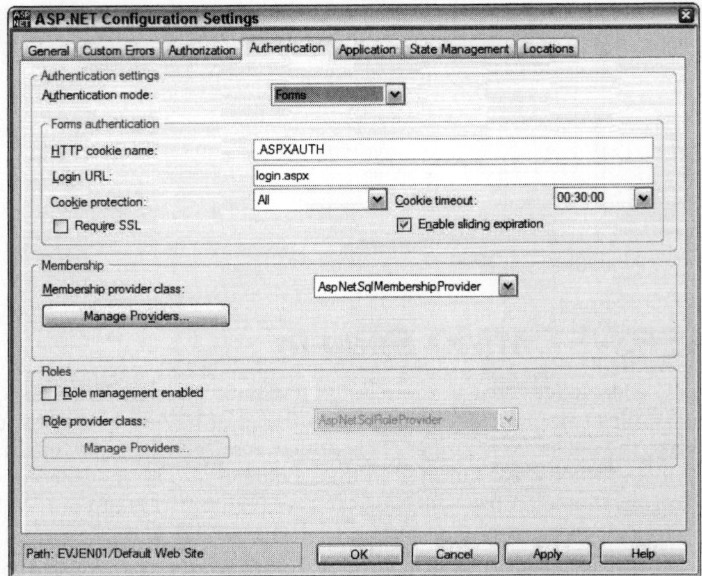

Figure 21-22

Using the IIS 7.0 Manager

You will not find the ASP.NET MMC Snap In within Windows Vista. Instead, you will be able to make all the same site modifications through the Internet Information Services (IIS) Manager (as shown in Figure 21-23).

After making any changes through this dialog, you can select the Apply Changes link in the Actions pane and it will notify you if the changes made have been saved. When successful, the changes made are applied to the site's `web.config` file.

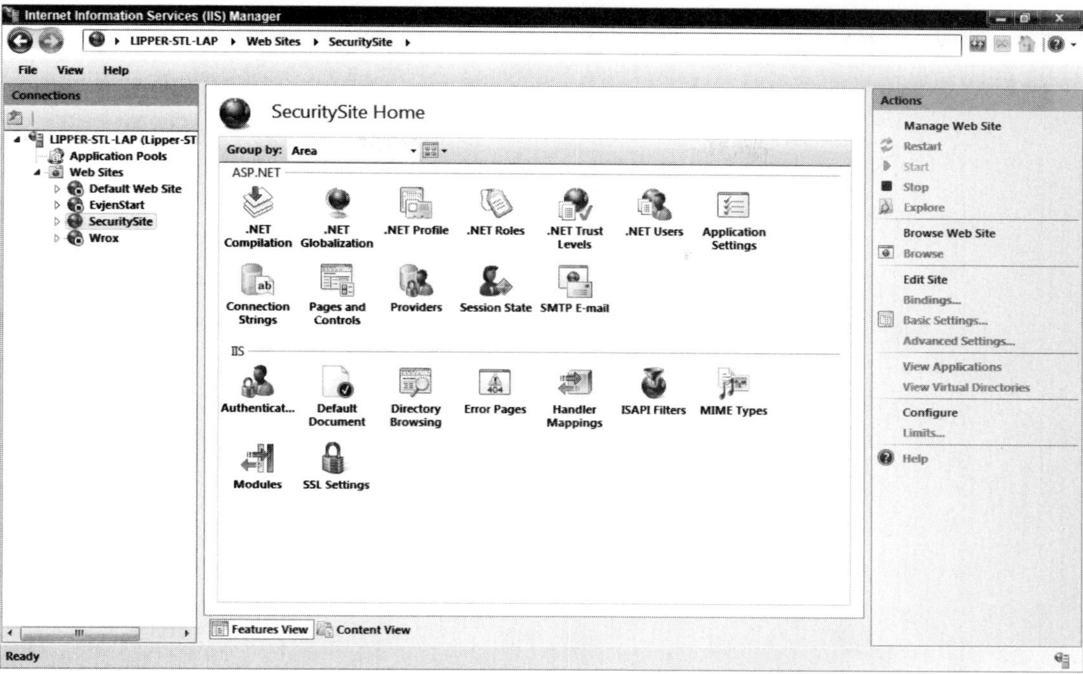

Figure 21-23

Summary

This chapter covered some of the foundation items of ASP.NET security and showed you how to apply both authentication and authorization to your Web applications. It reviewed some of the various authentication and authorization models at your disposal, such as Basic, Digest, and Windows Integrated Authentication. Other topics included forms-based authentication and how to construct your own forms-based authentication models outside of the ones provided via ASP.NET 3.5 by using the membership and role management capabilities it provides. The chapter also discussed how to use authentication properties within your applications and how to authorize users and groups based on those properties.

22

State Management

Why is state management such a difficult problem that it requires an entire chapter in a book on programming? In the old days (about 15 years ago), using standard client-server architecture meant using a fat client and a fat server. Perhaps your Visual Basic 6 application could talk to a database. The state was held either on the client-side or in the server-side database. Typically, you could count on a client having a little bit of memory and a hard drive of its own to manage state. The most important aspect of traditional client/server design, however, was that the client was *always* connected to the server. It's easy to forget, but HTTP is a stateless protocol. For the most part, a connection is built up and torn down each time a call is made to a remote server. Yes, HTTP 1.1 includes a keep-alive technique that provides optimizations at the TCP level. Even with these optimizations, the server has no way to determine that subsequent connections came from the same client.

Although the Web has the richness of DHTML and Ajax, JavaScript, and HTML 4.0 on the client side, the average high-powered Intel Core Duo with a few gigabytes of RAM is still being used only to render HTML. It's quite ironic that such powerful computers on the client side are still so vastly underutilized when it comes to storing state. Additionally, although many individuals have broadband, it is not universally used. Developers must still respect and pay attention to the dial-up users of the world. When was the last time that your project manager told you that bandwidth was not an issue for your Web application?

The ASP.NET concept of a Session that is maintained over the statelessness of HTTP is not a new one, and it existed before ASP.NET and even before classic ASP. It is, however, a very effective and elegant way to maintain state. There are, however, a number of different choices available to you, of which the ASP.NET session is just one. There have been a few subtle changes between ASP.NET 1.*x* and 2.0/3.5 that will be covered in this chapter. The `Session` object remains as before, but the option to plug in your own session state provider is now available.

What Are Your Choices?

Given a relatively weak client, a stateless protocol such as HTTP, and ASP.NET on the server side, how do you manage state on the Web? Figure 22-1 is a generalized diagram that identifies the primary means available for managing state. The problem is huge, and the solution range is even larger. This chapter assumes that you are not using Java applets or ActiveX controls to manage state. Although these options are certainly valid (although complex) solutions to the state problem, they are beyond the scope of this book.

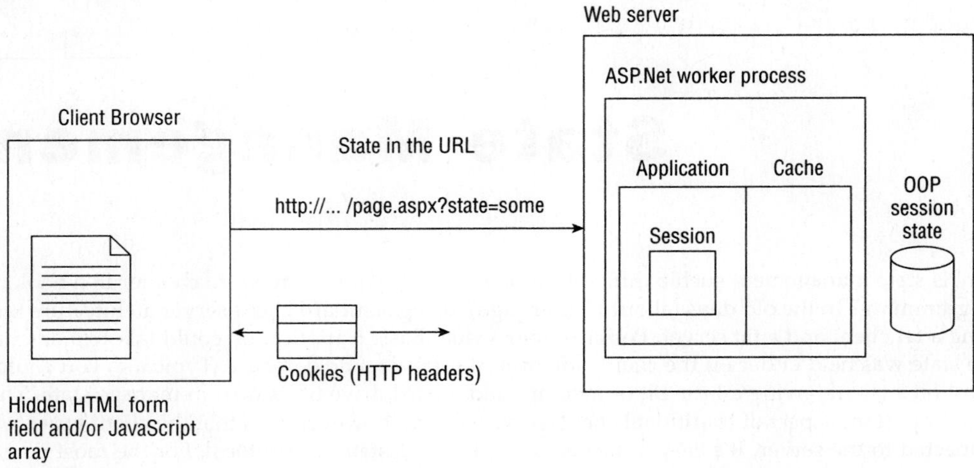

Figure 22-1

If you remember one thing about state management, remember this: There is no right answer. Some answers are more right than others, certainly; but there are many, many ways to manage state. Think about your last project. How many days were spent trying to decide where you should manage state? The trick is to truly understand the pros and cons of each method.

To make an educated decision about a method, you should understand the lifecycle of a request and the opportunities for state management at each point in the process:

1. A Web browser makes an `HTTP GET` request for a page on your server, `http://myserver/myapp/mypage.aspx`. This client Web browser has *never* visited your site before.
2. IIS and your ASP.NET application respond by returning HTML rendered by `mypage.aspx`. Additionally `mypage.aspx` returns a cookie with a unique ID to track this Web browser. Remember that a cookie is actually a slightly abstract concept. The cookie is set by returning a Set-Cookie HTTP Header to the client. The client then promises to return the values of the cookie in every subsequent HTTP call in the HTTP header. The *state* in this example is actually an agreement between the client and server to bounce the cookie back-and-forth on every request in response.
3. The HTML that is returned may contain hidden text boxes such as `<input type="hidden" value="somestate"/>`. These text boxes are similar to cookies because they are passed back to the server if the form on this page is submitted. Cookies are set per domain; hidden form fields are set per page.

4. Upon the next request, the previously set cookies are returned to the server. If this request was the submission of the form as an HTTP POST, all fields in the Form are returned — hidden or otherwise.

5. The unique identifier that was set earlier as a cookie can now be used as a key into any kind of server-side state mechanism. That state might be as simple as an in-memory hashtable, or as complicated as a SQL database.

One of the repeating themes you might notice is the agreement between the client and the server to pass information back and forth. That information can be in the URL, in HTTP headers, or even in the submitted Form as an input field.

On the server side, you have a few options. You'll want to weigh the options based on the amount of memory you have available, the amount of data you want to store, and how often you'll require access to the data.

The following tables express each of the server-side and client-side options and list a few pros and cons for each.

Server-Side Option	Pros	Cons
Application State	Fast. Shared among all users.	State is stored once per server in multiple server configurations.
Cache Object (Application Scope)	Like the Application State but includes expiration via Dependencies (see Chapter 23 on caching).	State is stored once per server in multiple server configurations.
Session State	Three choices: in process, out of process, DB-backed. Can be configured as cookieless.	Can be abused. You pay a serialization cost when objects leave the process. In process requires Web Server affinity. Cookieless configuration makes it easier to hijack.
Database	State can be accessed by any server in a Web farm.	Pay a serialization and persistence cost when objects leave the process. Requires a SQL Server license.

On the client side, every available option costs you in bandwidth. Each option involves passing data back and forth from client to server. Every byte of data you store will be paid for twice: once when it is passed to the server and once when it is passed back.

Client-Side Option	Pros	Cons
Cookie	Simple	Can be rejected by browser. Not appropriate for large amounts of data. Inappropriate for sensitive data. Size cost is paid on *every* HTTP Request and Response.
Hidden Field	Simple for page-scoped data	Not appropriate for large amounts of data. Inappropriate for sensitive data.

Client-Side Option	Pros	Cons
ViewState	Simple for page-scoped data	Encoding of serialized object as binary Base64-encoded data adds approximately 30 percent overhead. Small serialization cost. Has a negative reputation, particularly with DataGrids.
ControlState	Simple for page-scoped control-specific data	Like ViewState, but used for controls that require ViewState even if the developer has turned it off.
QueryString (URL)	Incredibly simple and often convenient if you want your URLs to be modified directly by the end user	Comparatively complex. Can't hold a lot of information. Inappropriate for sensitive data. Easily modified by the end user.

These tables provided you with some of the server-side and client-side options. The improvements to caching in ASP.NET 2.0/3.5 are covered in Chapter 23.

Understanding the Session Object in ASP.NET

In classic ASP, the `Session` object was held in-process (as was everything) to the IIS process. The user received a cookie with a unique key in the form of a GUID. The Session key was an index into a dictionary where object references could be stored.

In all versions of ASP.NET the `Session` object offers an in-process option, but also includes an out-of-process and database-backed option. Additionally, the developer has the option to enable *cookieless* session state where the Session key appears in the URL rather than being sent as a cookie.

Sessions and the Event Model

The `HttpApplication` object raises a series of events during the life of the HTTP protocol request:

- `BeginRequest`: This event fires at the beginning of every request.
- `AuthenticateRequest`: This event is used by the security module and indicates that a request is about to be authenticated. This is where the security module, or you, determines who the user is.
- `AuthorizeRequest`: This event is used by the security module and indicates that a request is about to be authorized. This is where the security module, or you, determines what the user is allowed to do.
- `ResolveRequestCache`: This event is used by the caching module to determine whether this now-authorized request can bypass any additional processing.
- `AcquireRequestState`: This event indicates that all session state associated with this HTTP request is about to be acquired.

> **Session state is available to you, the developer, *after* the `AcquireRequestState` event fires. The session state key that is unique to each user is retrieved either from a cookie or from the URL.**

- `PreRequestHandlerExecute`: This is the last event you get before the `HttpHandler` class for this request is called.

> **Your application code, usually in the form of a Page, executes at this point in the process.**

- `PostRequestHandlerExecute`: This is the event that fires just after the `HttpHandler` is called.
- `ReleaseRequestState`: Indicates that the session state should be stored. Session state is persisted at this point, using whatever Session-state module is configured in `web.config`.
- `UpdateRequestCache`: All work is complete, and the resulting output is ready to be added to the cache.
- `EndRequest`: This is the last event called during a request.

You can see from the preceding list that `AcquireRequestState` and `ReleaseRequestState` are two significant events in the life of the `Session` object.

By the time your application code executes, the `Session` object has been populated using the Session key that was present in the cookie, or as you see later, from the URL. If you want to handle some processing at the time the Session begins, rather than handling it in `AcquireRequestState`, you can define an event handler for the `Start` event of a SessionState HttpModule.

```
Sub Session_OnStart()
    'this fires after session state has been acquired by the SessionStateModule.
End Sub
```

> **The `Session` object includes both `Start` and `End` events that you can hook event handlers to for your own needs. However, the `Session_OnEnd` event is supported only in the In-Process Session State mode. This event will not be raised if you use out-of-process State Server or SQL Server modes. The `Session` ends, but your handlers will never hear about it.**

Pre- and post-events occur at almost every point within the life of an HTTP request. Session state can be manipulated at any point after `AcquireRequestState`, including in the `Global.asax` within the `Session_OnStart` event.

The `HttpSessionState` object can be used within any event in a subclass of the `Page` object. Because the pages you create in ASP.NET derive from `System.Web.UI.Page`, you can access Session State as a collection because `System.Web.SessionState.HttpSessionState` implements `ICollection`.

The Page has a public property aptly named Session that automatically retrieves the Session from the current HttpContext. Even though it seems as if the Session object lives inside the page, it actually lives in the HttpContext, and the page's public Session property actually retrieves the reference to the session state. This convenience not only makes it more comfortable for the classic ASP programmer, but saves you a little typing as well.

The Session object can be referred to within a page in this way:

```
Session["SomeSessionState"] = "Here is some data";
```

or

```
HttpContext.Current.Session["SomeSessionState"] = "Here is some data";
```

The fact that the Session object actually lives in the current HTTP context is more than just a piece of trivia. This knowledge enables you to access the Session object in contexts other than the page (such as in your own HttpHandler).

Configuring Session State Management

All the code within a page refers to the Session object using the dictionary-style syntax seen previously, but the HttpSessionState object uses a Provider Pattern to extract possible choices for session state storage. You can choose between the included providers by changing the sessionState element in web.config. ASP.NET ships with the following three storage providers:

- **In-Process Session State Store:** Stores sessions in the ASP.NET in-memory cache.
- **Out-Of-Process Session State Store:** Stores sessions in the ASP.NET State Server service aspnet_state.exe.
- **Sql Session State Store:** Stores sessions in Microsoft SQL Server database and is configured with aspnet_regsql.exe.

The format of the web.config file's sessionState element is shown in the following code:

```
<configuration>
   <system.web>
      <sessionState mode="Off|InProc|StateServer|SQLServer|Custom" ../>
   </system.web>
...
```

Begin configuring session state by setting the mode="InProc" attribute of the sessionState element in the web.config of a new Web site. This is the most common configuration for session state within ASP.NET 2.0 and is also the fastest, as you see next.

In-Process Session State

When the configuration is set to InProc, session data is stored in the HttpRuntime's internal cache in an implementation of ISessionStateItemCollection that implements ICollection. The session state key is a 120-bit value string that indexes this global dictionary of object references. When session state is in process, objects are stored as live references. This is an incredibly fast mechanism because no serialization occurs, nor do objects leave the process space. Certainly, your objects are not garbage-collected if they exist in the `In-Process Session` object because a reference is still being held.

Additionally, because the objects are stored (held) in memory, they use up memory until that session times out. If a user visits your site and hits one page, he might cause you to store a 40 MB `XmlDocument` in in-process session. If that user never comes back, you are left sitting on that large chunk of memory for the next 20 minutes or so (a configurable value) until the Session ends, even if the user never returns.

InProc Gotchas

Although the InProc Session model is the fastest, the default, and the most common, it does have a significant limitation. If the worker process or application domain recycles, all session state data is lost. Also, the ASP.NET application may restart for a number of reasons, such as the following:

- You've changed the `web.config` or `Global.asax` file or "touched" it by changing its modified date.
- You've modified files in the `\bin` or `\App_Code` directory.
- The `processModel` element has been set in the `web.config` or `machine.config` file indicating when the application should restart. Conditions that could generate a restart might be a memory limit or request-queue limit.
- Antivirus software modifies any of the previously mentioned files. This is particularly common with antivirus software that *innoculates* files.

This said, In-Process Session State works great for smaller applications that require only a single Web server, or in situations where IP load balancing is returning each user to the server where his original Session was created.

If a user already has a Session key, but is returned to a different machine than the one on which his session was created, a new Session is created on that new machine using the session ID supplied by the user. Of course, that new Session is empty and unexpected results may occur. However if `regenerate-ExpiredSessionId` is set to `True` in the `web.config` file, a new Session ID is created and assigned to the user.

Web Gardening

Web gardening is a technique for multiprocessor systems wherein multiple instances of the ASP.NET worker process are started up and assigned with processor affinity. On a larger Web server with as many as four CPUs, you could have anywhere from one to four worker processes hosting ASP.NET. *Processor affinity* means literally that an ASP.NET worker process has an affinity for a particular CPU. It's "pinned" to that CPU. This technique is usually enabled only in very large Web farms.

Don't forget that In-Process Session State is just that — in-process. Even if your Web application consists of only a single Web server and all IP traffic is routed to that single server, you have no guarantee that each subsequent request will be served on the same processor. A Web garden must follow many of the same rules that a Web farm follows.

> **If you're using Web gardening on a multiprocessor system, you must not use In-Process Session State or you lose Sessions. In-Process Session State is appropriate only where there is a 1:1 ratio of applications to application domains.**

Storing Data in the Session Object

In the following simple example, in a `Button_Click` event the content of the text box is added to the `Session` object with a specific key. The user then clicks to go to another page within the same application, and the data from the `Session` object is retrieved and presented in the browser.

Note the use of the `<asp:HyperLink>` control. Certainly, that markup could have been hard-coded as HTML, but this small distinction will serve us well later. Additionally, the URL is relative to this site, not absolute. Watch for it to help you later in this chapter.

Listing 22-1 illustrates how simple it is to use the `Session` object. It behaves like any other `IDictionary` collection and allows you to store keys of type `String` associated with any kind of object. The `Retrieve.aspx` file referenced will be added in Listing 22-2.

Listing 22-1: Setting values in session state

ASP.NET

```
<%@ Page Language="C#" CodeFile="Default.aspx.cs" Inherits="_Default" %>
```

ASP.NET — VB.NET

```
<%@ Page Language="VB" AutoEventWireup="false" CodeFile="Default.aspx.vb"
    Inherits="_Default" %>
```

ASP.NET

```
<!DOCTYPE html PUBLIC "-//W3C//DTD XHTML 1.1//EN" "http://www.w3.org/TR/xhtml11/DTD/
xhtml11.dtd">
<html xmlns="http://www.w3.org/1999/xhtml" >
<head runat="server">
    <title>Session State</title>
</head>
<body>
    <form id="form1" runat="server">
    <div>
        <asp:TextBox ID="TextBox1" Runat="server"></asp:TextBox>
        <asp:Button ID="Button1" Runat="server" Text="Store in Session"
        OnClick="Button1_Click" />
        <br />
        <asp:HyperLink ID="HyperLink1" Runat="server"
         NavigateUrl="Retrieve.aspx">Next Page</asp:HyperLink>
    </div>
    </form>
</body>
</html>
```

VB

```
Partial Class _Default
   Inherits System.Web.UI.Page

    Protected Sub Button1_Click(ByVal sender As Object, _
            ByVal e As System.EventArgs)
        Session("mykey") = TextBox1.Text
    End Sub

End Class
```

C#

```
public partial class _Default : System.Web.UI.Page
{
    protected void Button1_Click(object sender, EventArgs e)
    {
        Session["mykey"] = TextBox1.Text;
    }
}
```

The page from Listing 22-1 renders in the browser as shown in Figure 22-2. The `Session` object is accessed as any dictionary indexed by a string key.

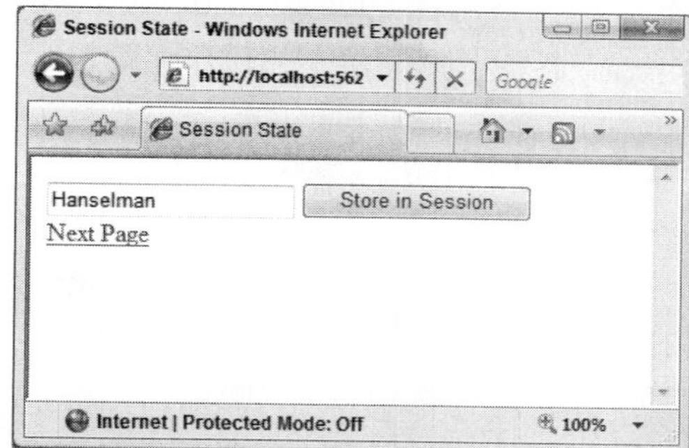

Figure 22-2

More details about the page and the `Session` object can be displayed to the developer if page tracing is enabled. You add this element to your application's `web.config` file inside the `<system.web>` element, as follows:

```
<trace enabled="true" pageOutput="true"/>
```

Now tracing is enabled, and the tracing output is sent directly to the page. More details on tracing and debugging are given in Chapter 24. For now, make this change and refresh your browser.

In Figure 22-3, the screenshot is split to show both the top and roughly the middle of the large amount of trace information that is returned when trace is enabled. Session State is very much baked into the fabric of ASP.NET. You can see in the Request Details section of the trace that not only was this page the result of an HTTP POST but the Session ID was as well — elevated to the status of first-class citizen. However, the ASP.NET Session ID lives as a cookie by default, as you can see in the `Cookies` collection at the bottom of the figure.

The default name for that cookie is `ASP.NET_SessionId`, but its name can be configured via the `cookieName` attribute of the `<sessionState>` element in `web.config`. Some large enterprises allow only certain named cookies past their proxies, so you might need to change this value when working on an extranet or a network with a gateway server; but this would be a very rare occurrence. The `cookieName` is changed to use the name "Foo" in the following example:

```
<sessionState cookieName="Foo" mode="InProc"></sessionState>
```

The trace output shown in Figure 22-3 includes a section listing the contents of the `Session State` collection. In the figure, you can see that the name `mykey` and the value `Hanselman` are currently stored. Additionally, you see the CLR data type of the stored value; in this case, it's `System.String`.

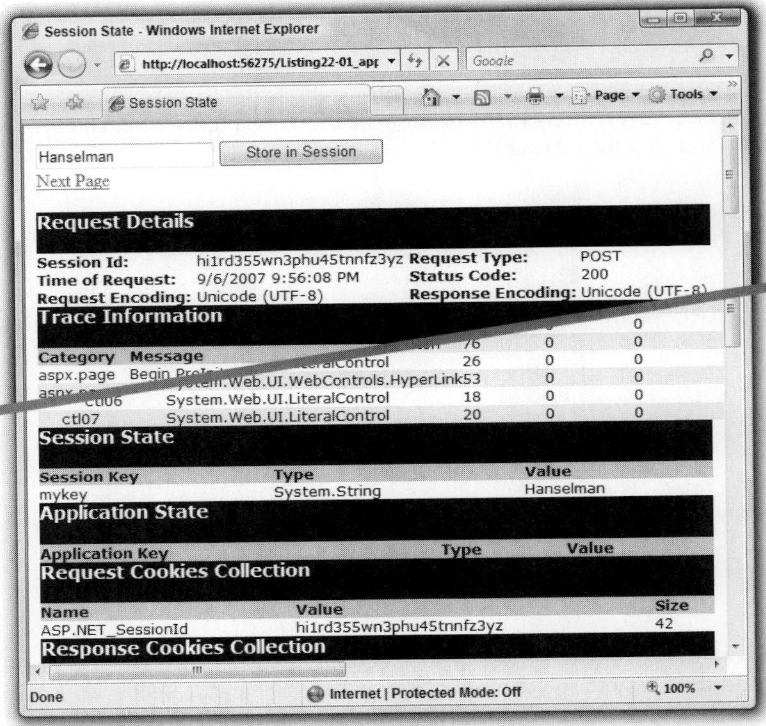

Figure 22-3

> **The Value column of the trace output comes from a call to the contained object's `ToString()` method. If you store your own objects in the Session, you can override `ToString()` to provide a text-friendly representation of your object that might make the trace results more useful.**

Now add the next page, `retrieve.aspx`, which pulls this value out of the session. Leave the `retrieve.aspx` page as the IDE creates it and add a `Page_Load` event handler, as shown in Listing 22-2.

Listing 22-2: Retrieving values from the session

VB

```
Partial Class Retrieve
    Inherits System.Web.UI.Page

    Protected Sub Page_Load(ByVal sender As Object, ByVal e As System.EventArgs) _
```

```
        Handles Me.Load

        Dim myValue As String = CType(Session("mykey"), String)
        Response.Write(myValue)
    End Sub
End Class
```

C#

```
public partial class Retrieve : System.Web.UI.Page
{
    protected void Page_Load(object sender, EventArgs e)
    {
        string myValue = (string)Session["mykey"];
        Response.Write(myValue);
    }
}
```

Because the session contains object references, the resulting object is converted to a string by way of a cast in C# or the `CType` or `CStr` function in VB.

Making Sessions Transparent

It is unfortunate that a cast is usually required to retrieve data from the `Session` object. Combined with the string key used as an index, it makes for a fairly weak contract between the page and the `Session` object. You can create a session helper that is specific to your application to hide these details, or you can add properties to a base `Page` class that presents these objects to your pages in a friendlier way. Because the generic `Session` object is available as a property on `System.Web.UI.Page`, add a new class derived from `Page` that exposes a new property named `MyKey`.

Start by right-clicking your project and selecting Add New Item from the context menu to create a new class. Name it `SmartSessionPage` and click OK. The IDE may tell you that it would like to put this new class in the `/App_Code` folder to make it available to the whole application. Click Yes.

Your new base page is very simple. Via derivation, it does everything that `System.Web.UI.Page` does, plus it has a new property, as shown in Listing 22-3.

Listing 22-3: A more session-aware base page

VB

```
Imports Microsoft.VisualBasic
Imports System
Imports System.Web

Public Class SmartSessionPage
    Inherits System.Web.UI.Page

    Private Const MYSESSIONKEY As String = "mykey"
    Public Property MyKey() As String
        Get
            Return CType(Session(MYSESSIONKEY), String)
        End Get
```

Continued

```
        Set(ByVal value As String)
            Session(MYSESSIONKEY) = value
        End Set
    End Property
End Class
```

C#

```
using System;
using System.Web;

public class SmartSessionPage : System.Web.UI.Page
{
    private const string MYKEY = "mykey";
    public string MyKey
    {
        get
        {
            return (string)Session[MYKEY];
        }
        set
        {
            Session[MYKEY] = value;
        }
    }
}
```

Now, return to your code from Listing 22-1 and derive your pages from this new base class. To do this, change the base class in the code-beside files to inherit from `SmartSessionPage`. Listing 22-4 shows how the class in the code-behind file derives from the `SmartSessionPage`, which in turn derives from `System.Web.UI.Page`. Listing 22-4 outlines the changes to make to Listing 22-1.

Listing 22-4: Deriving from the new base page

VB — ASPX

```
<%@ Page Language="VB" AutoEventWireup="false" CodeFile="Default.aspx.vb"
    Inherits="_Default" %>
```

VB — Default.aspx.vb Code

```
Partial Class _Default
    Inherits SmartSessionPage

   Protected Sub Button1_Click(ByVal sender As Object, ByVal e As System.EventArgs)
        ' Session("mykey") = TextBox1.Text
        MyKey = TextBox1.Text
   End Sub
End Class
```

C# — ASPX

```
<%@ Page Language="C#" CodeFile="Default.aspx.cs" Inherits="_Default" %>
```

C# — Default.aspx.cs Code

```
public partial class _Default : SmartSessionPage
```

```
{
    protected void Button1_Click(object sender, EventArgs e)
    {
        //Session["mykey"] = TextBox1.Text;
        MyKey = TextBox1.Text;
    }
}
```

In this code, you change the access to the `Session` object so it uses the new public property. After the changes in Listing 22-3, all derived pages have a public property called `MyKey`. This property can be used without any concern about casting or Session key indexes. Additional specific properties can be added as other objects are included in the Session.

Here's an interesting language note: In Listing 22-3 the name of the private string value collides with the public property in VB because they differ only in case. In C#, a private variable named `MYKEY` and a public property named `MyKey` are both acceptable. Be aware of things like this when creating APIs that will be used with multiple languages. Aim for CLS compliance.

Advanced Techniques for Optimizing Session Performance

By default, all pages have write access to the `Session`. Because it's possible that more than one page from the same browser client might be requested at the same time (using frames, more than one browser window on the same machine, and so on), a page holds a reader/writer lock on the same `Session` for the duration of the page request. If a page has a writer lock on the same `Session`, all other pages requested in the same `Session` must wait until the first request finishes. To be clear, the `Session` is locked only for that SessionID. These locks don't affect other users with different `Sessions`.

In order to get the best performance out of your pages that use `Session`, ASP.NET allows you declare exactly what your page requires of the `Session` object via the `EnableSessionState @Page` attribute. The options are `True`, `False`, or `ReadOnly`:

- `EnableSessionState="True"`: The page requires read and write access to the `Session`. The `Session` with that SessionID will be locked during each request.
- `EnableSessionState="False"`: The page does not require access to the `Session`. If the code uses the `Session` object anyway, an `HttpException` is thrown stopping page execution.
- `EnableSessionState="ReadOnly"`: The page requires read-only access to the Session. A reader lock is held on the `Session` for each request, but concurrent reads from other pages can occur. The order that locks are requested is essential. As soon as a writer lock is requested, even before a thread is granted access, all subsequent reader lock requests are blocked, regardless of whether a reader lock is currently held or not. While ASP.NET can obviously handle multiple requests, only one request at a time gets write access to a Session.

By modifying the `@Page` direction in `default.aspx` and `retrieve.aspx` to reflect each page's actual need, you affect performance when the site is under load. Add the `EnableSessionState` attribute to the pages, as shown in the following code:

VB — Default.aspx

```
<%@ Page Language="VB" EnableSessionState="True" AutoEventWireup="false"
```

```
    CodeFile="Default.aspx.vb" Inherits="_Default" %>
```

VB — Retrieve.aspx

```
<%@ Page Language="VB" EnableSessionState="ReadOnly" AutoEventWireup="false"
    CodeFile="Retrieve.aspx.vb" Inherits="Retrieve" %>
```

C# — Default.asp

```
<%@ Page Language="C#" EnableSessionState="True"
    CodeFile="Default.aspx.cs" Inherits="_Default"%>
```

C# — Retrieve.aspx

```
<%@ Page Language="C#" EnableSessionState="ReadOnly"
    CodeFile="Retrieve.aspx.cs" Inherits="Retrieve" %>
```

Under the covers, ASP.NET is using marker interfaces from the `System.Web.SessionState` namespace to keep track of each page's needs. When the partial class for `default.aspx` is generated, it implements the `IRequiresSessionState` interface, whereas `Retrieve.aspx` implements `IReadOnlySessionState`. All `HttpRequests` are handled by objects that implement `IHttpHandler`. Pages are handled by a `PageHandlerFactory`. You can find more on HttpHandlers in Chapter 25. Internally, the `SessionStateModule` is executing code similar to the pseudocode that follows:

```
If TypeOf HttpContext.Current.Handler Is IReadOnlySessionState Then
    Return SessionStateStore.GetItem(itemKey)
Else 'If TypeOf HttpContext.Current.Handler Is IRequiresSessionState
    Return SessionStateStore.GetItemExclusive(itemKey)
End If
```

As the programmer, you know things about the intent of your pages at compile time that ASP.NET can't figure out at runtime. By including the `EnableSessionState` attribute in your pages, you allow ASP.NET to operate more efficiently. Remember, ASP.NET always makes the most conservative decision unless you give it more information to act upon.

> ***Performance Tip*: If you're coding a page that doesn't require anything of the Session, by all means, set `EnableSessionState="False"`. This causes ASP.NET to schedule that page ahead of pages that require Session and helps with the overall scalability of your app. Additionally, if your application doesn't use Session at all, set `Mode="Off"` in your `web.config` file to reduce overhead for the entire application.**

Out-of-Process Session State

Out-of-process session state is held in a process called `aspnet_state.exe` that runs as a Windows Service. You can start the ASP.NET state service by using the Services MMC snap-in or by running the following `net` command from an administrative command line:

```
net start aspnet_state
```

By default, the State Service listens on TCP port 42424, but this port can be changed at the registry key for the service, as shown in the following code. The State Service is not started by default.

```
HKEY_LOCAL_MACHINE\SYSTEM\CurrentControlSet\Services\
aspnet_state\Parameters\Port
```

Change the `web.config`'s settings from `InProc` to `StateServer`, as shown in the following code. Additionally, you must include the `stateConnectionString` attribute with the IP address and port on which the Session State Service is running. In a Web farm (a group of more than one Web server), you could run the State Service on any single server or on a separate machine entirely. In this example, the State Server is running on the local machine, so the IP address is the localhost IP 127.0.0.1. If you run the State Server on another machine, make sure the appropriate port is open — in this case, TCP port 42424.

```
<configuration>
   <system.web>
      <sessionState mode="StateServer"
          stateConnectionString="tcpip=127.0.0.1:42424"/>
   </system.web>
</configuration>
```

The State Service used is always the most recent one installed with ASP.NET. That means that if you are running ASP.NET 2.0/3.5 and 1.1 on the same machine, all the states stored in `Session` objects for any and all versions of ASP.NET are kept together in a single instance of the ASP.NET State Service.

Because your application's code runs in the ASP.NET Worker Process (`aspnet_wp.exe`, or `w3wp.exe`) and the State Service runs in the separate `aspnet_state.exe` process, objects stored in the Session can't be stored as references. Your objects must physically leave the worker process via binary serialization.

For a world-class, highly available, and scalable Web site, consider using a Session model other than InProc. Even if you can guarantee via your load-balancing appliance that your Sessions will be *sticky*, you still have application-recycling issues to contend with. The out-of-process state service's data is persisted across application pool recycles but not computer reboots. However, if your state is stored on a different machine entirely, it will survive Web Server recycles and reboots.

Only classes that have been marked with the `[Serializable]` attribute may be serialized. In the context of the `Session` object, think of the `[Serializable]` attribute as a permission slip for instances of your class to leave the worker process.

Update the `SmartSessionPage` file in your `\App_Code` directory to include a new class called `Person`, as shown in Listing 22-5. Be sure to mark it as `Serializable` or you will see the error shown in Figure 22-4.

As long as you've marked your objects as `[Serializable]`, they'll be allowed out of the ASP.NET process. Notice that the objects in Listing 22-5 are marked `[Serializable]`.

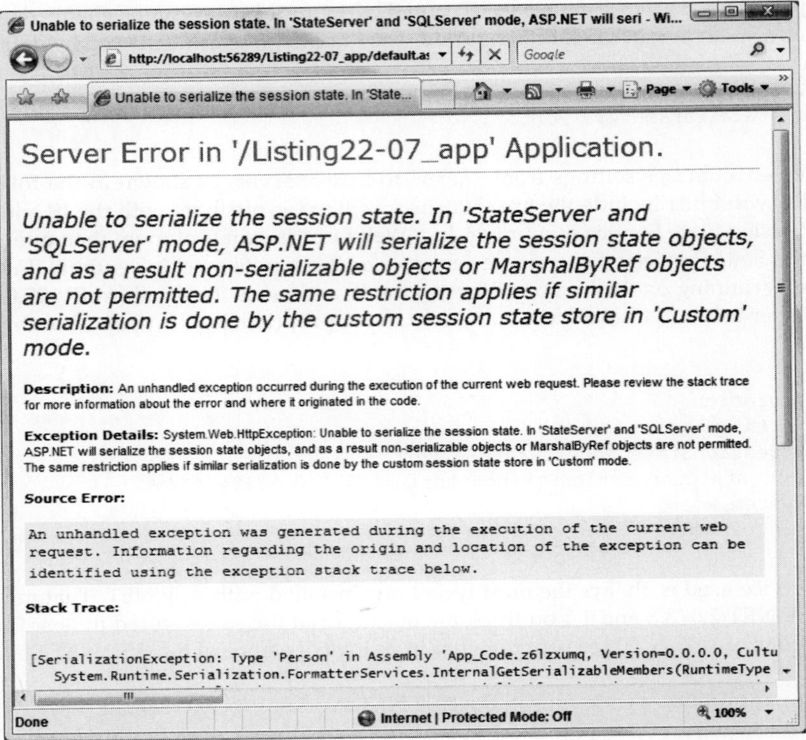

Figure 22-4

Listing 22-5: A serializable object that can be used in the out-of-process Session

VB

```
<Serializable()> _
Public Class Person
    Public firstName As String
    Public lastName As String

    Public Overrides Function ToString() As String
        Return String.Format("Person Object: {0} {1}", firstName, lastName)
    End Function
End Class
```

C#

```
[Serializable]
public class Person
{
   public string firstName;
   public string lastName;
```

```
    public override string ToString()
    {
        return String.Format("Person Object: {0} {1}", firstName, lastName);
    }
}
```

Because you put an instance of the `Person` class from Listing 22-5 into the `Session` object that is currently configured as `StateServer`, you should add a strongly typed property to the base `Page` class from Listing 22-3. In Listing 22-6 you see the strongly typed property added. Note the cast on the property `Get`, and the strongly typed return value indicating that this property deals only with objects of type `Person`.

Listing 22-6: Adding a strongly typed property to SmartSessionPage

VB

```
Public Class SmartSessionPage
    Inherits System.Web.UI.Page

    Private Const MYSESSIONPERSONKEY As String = "myperson"

    Public Property MyPerson() As Person
        Get
            Return CType(Session(MYSESSIONPERSONKEY), Person)
        End Get
        Set(ByVal value As Person)
            Session(MYSESSIONPERSONKEY) = value
        End Set
    End Property

End Class
```

C#

```
public class SmartSessionPage : System.Web.UI.Page
{
    private const string MYPERSON = "myperson";

    public Person MyPerson
    {
        get
        {
            return (Person)Session[MYPERSON];
        }
        set
        {
        Session[MYPERSON] = value;
        }
    }
}
```

Now, add code to create a new `Person`, populate its fields from the text box, and put the instance into the now-out-of-process Session State Service. Then, retrieve the `Person` and write its values out to the browser using the overloaded `ToString()` method from Listing 22-5.

Certain classes in the Framework Class Library are not marked as serializable. If you use objects of this type within your own objects, these objects are *not* serializable at all. For example, if you include a DataRow field in a class and add your object to the State Service, you receive a message telling you it ". . . is not marked as serializable" because the DataRow includes objects that are not serializable.

In Listing 22-7, the value of the `TextBox` is split into a string array and the first two strings are put into a `Person` instance. For example, if you entered `"Scott Hanselman"` as a value, `"Scott"` is put into `Person.firstName` and `"Hanselman"` is put into `Person.lastName`. The values you enter should appear when they are retrieved later in `Retrieve.aspx` and written out to the browser with the overloaded `ToString` method.

Listing 22-7: Setting and retrieving objects from the Session using State Service and a base page

VB — Default.aspx.vb

```
Partial Class _Default
    Inherits SmartSessionPage

   Protected Sub Button1_Click(ByVal sender As Object, ByVal e As System.EventArgs)
        Dim names As String()
        names = TextBox1.Text.Split(" "c) ' " "c creates a char
        Dim p As New Person()
        p.firstName = names(0)
        p.lastName = names(1)
        Session("myperson") = p
   End Sub
End Class
```

VB — Retrieve.aspx.vb

```
Partial Class Retrieve
        Inherits SmartSessionPage
    Protected Sub Page_Load(ByVal sender As Object, ByVal e As System.EventArgs) _
            Handles Me.Load
        Dim p As Person = MyPerson
        Response.Write(p) ' ToString will be called!
    End Sub
End Class
```

C# — Default.aspx.cs

```
public partial class _Default : SmartSessionPage
{
    protected void Button1_Click(object sender, EventArgs e)
    {
        string[] names = TextBox1.Text.Split(' ');
        Person p = new Person();
```

```
            p.firstName = names[0];
            p.lastName = names[1];

            Session["myperson"] = p;
        }
    }
```

C# — Retrieve.aspx.cs

```
public partial class Retrieve : SmartSessionPage
{
    protected void Page_Load(object sender, EventArgs e)
    {
        Person p = MyPerson;
        Response.Write(p); //ToString will be called!
    }
}
```

Now, launch the browser, enter your name (or `"Scott Hanselman"` if you like), click the button to store it in the `Session`, and then visit `Retrieve.aspx` via the hyperlink. You see the result of the `ToString()` method via `Response.Write`, as shown in Figure 22-5.

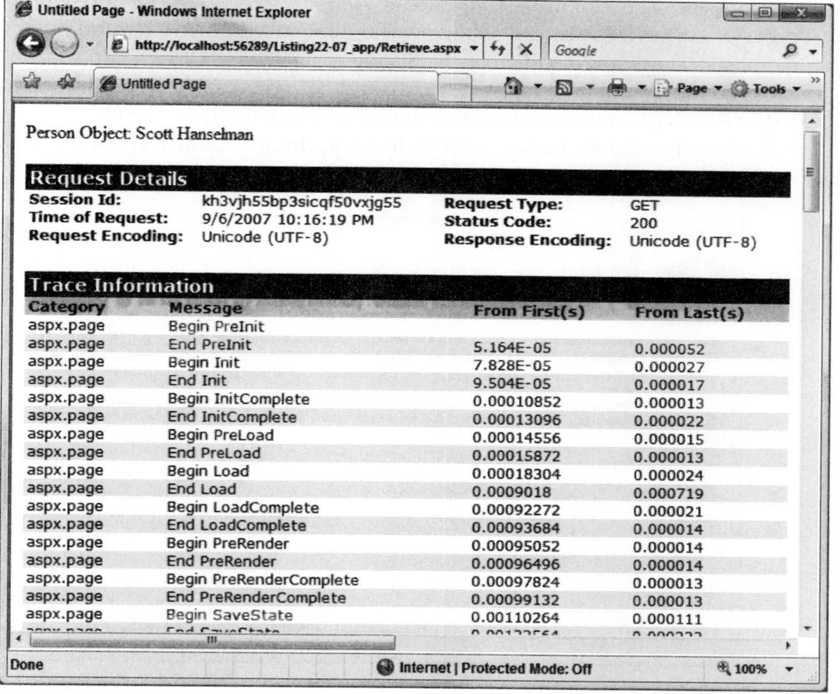

Figure 22-5

The completed code and techniques shown in Listing 22-7 illustrate a number of best practices for session management:

- Mark your objects as `Serializable` if you might ever use non-In-Proc session state.
- Even better, do all your development with a local session state server. This forces you to discover non-serializable objects early, gives you a sense of the performance and memory usages of `aspnet_state.exe`, and allows you to choose from any of the session options at deployment time.
- Use a base `Page` class or helper object with strongly typed properties to simplify your code. It enables you to hide the casts made to session keys otherwise referenced throughout your code.

These best practices apply to all state storage methods, including SQL session state.

SQL-Backed Session State

ASP.NET sessions can also be stored in a SQL Server database. InProc offers speed, StateServer offers a resilience/speed balance, and storing sessions in SQL Server offers resilience that can serve sessions to a large Web farm that persists across IIS restarts, if necessary.

SQL-backed session state is configured with `aspnet_regsql.exe`. This tool adds and removes support for a number of ASP.NET features such as cache dependency (see Chapter 23) and personalization/membership (see Chapters 17 and 18) as well as session support. When you run `aspnet_regsql.exe` from the command line without any options, surprisingly, it pops up a GUI as shown in Figure 22-6. This utility is located in the .NET Framework's installed directory, usually `c:\windows\microsoft.net\framework\2.0`. Note that the Framework 3.5 includes additional libraries, but this wizard is still in the 2.0 directory.

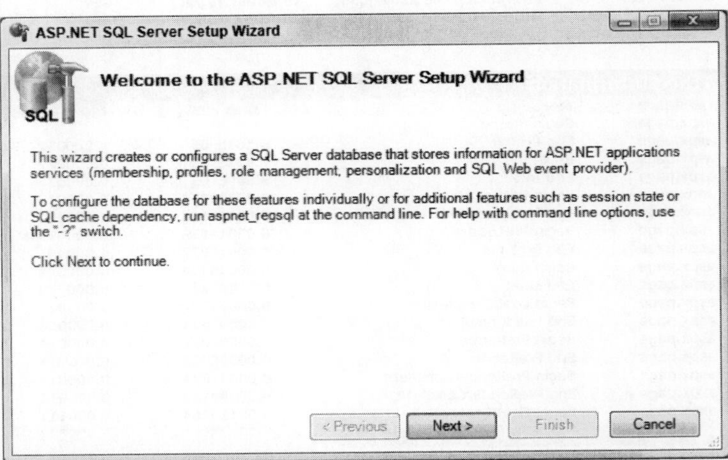

Figure 22-6

The text of the dialog shown in Figure 22-6 contains instructions to run `aspnet_regsql` from the command line with a `"-?"` switch. You have a huge number of options, so you'll want to pipe it through in a form like `aspnet_regsql -? | more`. You see the session-state–specific options shown here:

```
                          -- SESSION STATE OPTIONS --

-ssadd                    Add support for SQLServer mode session state.

-ssremove                 Remove support for SQLServer mode session state.

-sstype t|p|c             Type of session state support:

                          t: temporary. Session state data is stored in the
                          "tempdb" database. Stored procedures for managing
                          session are installed in the "ASPState" database.
                          Data is not persisted if you restart SQL. (Default)

                          p: persisted. Both session state data and the stored
                          procedures are stored in the "ASPState" database.

                          c: custom. Both session state data and the stored
                          procedures are stored in a custom database. The
                          database name must be specified.

-d <database>             The name of the custom database to use if -sstype is
                          "c".
```

Three options exist for session state support: `t`, `p`, and `c`. The most significant difference is that the `-sstype t` option does not persist session state data across SQL Server restarts, whereas the `-sstype p` option does. Alternatively, you can specify a custom database with the `-c` option and give the database name with `-d database`.

The following command-line example configures your system for SQL session support with the SQL Server on localhost with an sa password of *wrox* and a persistent store in the ASPState database. (Certainly, you know not to deploy your system using sa and a weak password, but this simplifies the example. Ideally you'd use Windows Integration Authentication and give the Worker Process Identity access to the ASPState database.) If you're using SQL Express, replace "localhost" with ".\SQLEXPRESS". If you aren't using Windows Authentication, you may need to explicitly enable the sa account from the Management Studio, run this tool, and then disable the sa account for security reasons.

```
C:\ >aspnet_regsql -S localhost -U sa -P wrox -ssadd -sstype p
Start adding session state.
...........
Finished.
```

Next, open up Enterprise Manager and look at the newly created database. Two tables are created — ASPStateTempApplications and ASPStateTempSessions — as well as a series of stored procedures to support moving the session back and forth from SQL to memory.

If your SQL Server has its security locked down tight, you might get an Error 15501 after executing `aspnet_regsql.exe` that says "An error occurred during the execution of the SQL file 'InstallSqlState.sql'." The SQL error number is 15501 and the SqlException message is:

```
This module has been marked OFF. Turn on 'Agent XPs' in order to be able to access the
module. If the job does not exist, an error from msdb.dbo.sp_delete_job is expected.
```

This is a rather obscure message, but aspnet_regsql.exe is trying to tell you that the extended stored procedures it needs to enable session state are not enabled for security reasons. You'll need to allow them explicitly. To do so, execute the following commands within the SQL Server 2005 Query Analyzer or the SQL Server 2005 Express Manager:

```
USE master
EXECUTE sp_configure 'show advanced options', 1
RECONFIGURE WITH OVERRIDE
GO
EXECUTE sp_configure 'Agent XPs', 1
RECONFIGURE WITH OVERRIDE
GO
EXECUTE sp_configure 'show advanced options', 0
RECONFIGURE WITH OVERRIDE
GO
```

Now, change the web.config <sessionState> element to use SQL Server, as well as the new connection string:

```
<sessionState mode="SQLServer" sqlConnectionString="data source=127.0.0.1;user
id=sa;password=Wrox"/>
```

The session code shown in Listing 22-7 continues to work as before. However, if you open up the ASPStateTempSessions table, you see the serialized objects. Notice in Figure 22-7 that the Session ID from the trace appears as a primary key in a row in the ASPStateTempSessions table.

Figure 22-7 shows the SessionId as seen in the Request Details of ASP.NET tracing. That SessionId appears in the SessionId column of the ASPStateTempSessions table in the ASPState database just created. Notice also the ASPStateTempApplications table that keeps track of each IIS application that may be using the same database to manage sessions.

If you want to use your own database to store session state, you specify the database name with the -d <database> switch of aspnet_regsql.exe and include the allowCustomSqlDatabase="true" attribute and the name of the database in the connection string:

```
<sessionState allowCustomSqlDatabase="true" mode="SQLServer"
sqlConnectionString="data source=127.0.0.1; database=MyCustomASPStateDatabase;"/>
```

The user ID and password can be included in the connection string; or Windows Integrated Security can be used if the ASP.NET Worker Process's identity is configured with access in SQL Server.

Extending Session State with Other Providers

ASP.NET Session State is built on a new, extensible, provider-based storage model. You can implement custom providers that store session data in other storage mechanisms simply by deriving from SessionStateStoreProviderBase. This extensibility feature also allows you to generate session IDs via your own algorithms by implementing ISessionIDManager.

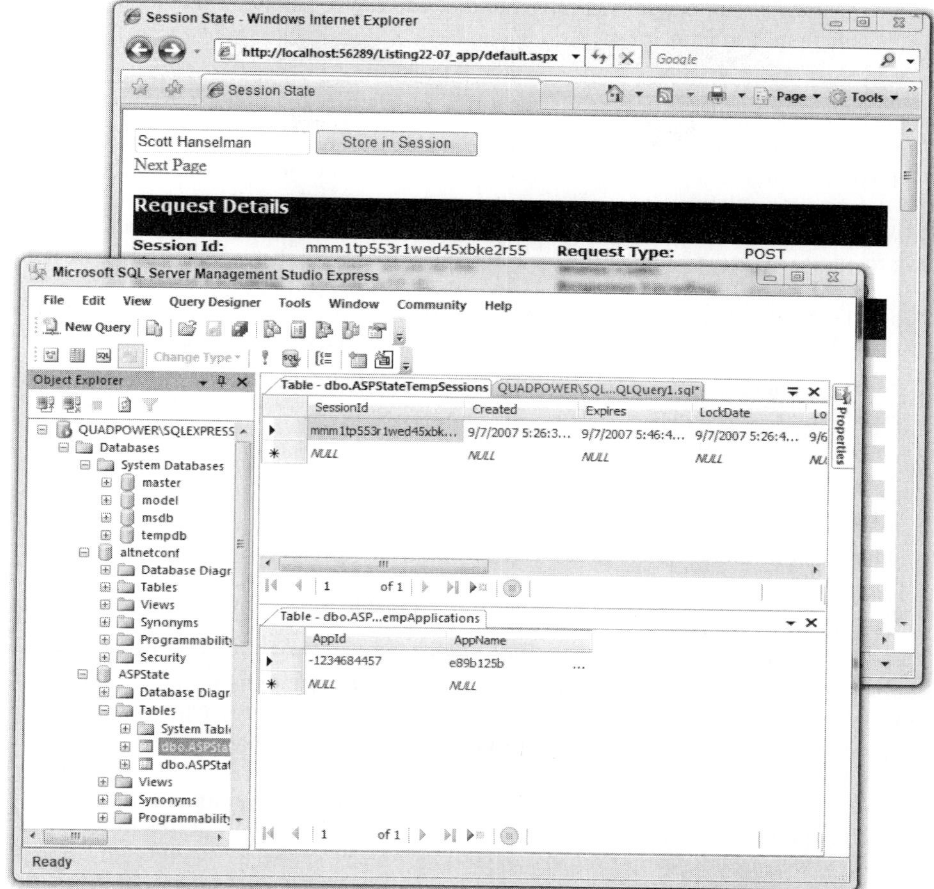

Figure 22-7

You start by creating a class that inherits from `SessionStateStoreProviderBase`. The session module will call methods on any session provider as long as it derives from `SessionStateStoreProviderBase`. Register your custom provider in your application's `web.config`, as in the following example:

```
<sessionState mode ="Custom" customProvider ="WroxProvider">
    <providers >
        <add name ="WroxProvider" type ="Wrox.WroxStore, WroxSessionSupplier"/>
    </providers>
</sessionState>
```

ASP.NET initializes the `SessionStateModule`, and these methods are called on any custom implementation:

- `Initialize`: This method is inherited ultimately from `System.Configuration.Provider.ProviderBase` and is called immediately after the constructor. With this method, you set your provider name and call up to the base implementation of `Initialize`.

- `SetItemExpireCallback`: With this method, you can register any methods to be called when a session item expires.
- `InitializeRequest`: This method is called by the `SessionStateModule` for each request. This is an early opportunity to get ready for any requests for data that are coming.
- `CreateNewStoreData`: With this method, you create a new instance of `SessionStateStoreData`, the data structure that holds session items, the session timeout values, and any static items.

When a session item is requested, ASP.NET calls your implementation to retrieve it. Implement the following methods to retrieve items:

- `GetItemExclusive`: This method enables you to get `SessionStateStoreData` from your chosen store. You may have created an Oracle provider, stored data in XML, or stored data elsewhere.
- `GetItem`: This is your opportunity to retrieve it as you did in `GetItemExclusive` except without exclusive locking. You may or may not care, depending on what backing store you've chosen.

When it's time to store an item, the following method is called:

- `SetAndReleaseItemExculsive`: Here you should save the `SessionStateStoreData` object to your custom store.

A number of third-party session state providers are available — both open source and for sale.

> **ScaleOut Software released the first third-party ASP.NET State Provider in the form of their StateServer product. It fills a niche between the ASP.NET included singleton StateServer and the SQL Server Database State Provider. ScaleOut Software's StateServer is an out-of-process service that runs on each machine in the Web farm and ensures that session state is stored in a transparent and distributed manner among machines in the farm. You can learn more about StateServer and their ASP.NET 2.0 Session Provider at** `www.scaleoutsoftware.com/`.
>
> **Another commercial product is StrangeLoop Network's AppScaler. It includes an ASP.NET Session Provider that plugs into their network acceleration appliance. Their product also optimizes ViewState among other things and won a "Best of TechEd 2007" award. Details are at** `www.strangeloopnetworks.com/`.

The derivation-based provider module for things such as session state will no doubt continue to create a rich ecosystem of enthusiasts who will help push the functionality to new places Microsoft did not expect.

Cookieless Session State

In the previous example, the ASP.NET Session State ID was stored in a cookie. Some devices don't support cookies, or a user may have turned off cookie support in his browser. Cookies are convenient because the values are passed back and forth with every request and response. That means every `HttpRequest` contains cookie values, and every `HttpResponse` contains cookie values. What is the only other thing that is passed back and forth with every `Request` and `Response`? The URL.

If you include the `cookieless="UseUri"` attribute in the `web.config`, ASP.NET does not send the ASP.NET Session ID back as a cookie. Instead, it modifies every URL to include the Session ID just before the requested page:

```
<sessionState mode="SQLServer" cookieless="UseUri" sqlConnectionString="data
source=127.0.0.1;user id=sa;password=Wrox"></sessionState>
```

Notice that the Session ID appears in the URL as if it were a directory of its own situated between the actual Web site virtual directory and the page. With this change, server-side user controls such as the `HyperLink` control, used in Listing 22-1, have their properties automatically modified. The link in Listing 22-1 could have been hard-coded as HTML directly in the Designer, but then ASP.NET could not modify the target URL shown in Figure 22-8.

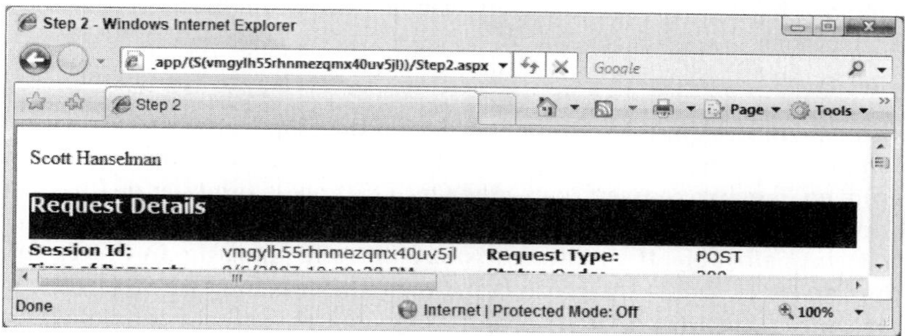

Figure 22-8

The Session ID is a string that contains only the ASCII characters allowed in a URL. That makes sense when you realize that moving from a cookie-based Session-State system to a cookieless system requires putting that Session State value in the URL.

Notice in Figure 22-8 that the request URL contains a Session ID within parentheses. One disadvantage to cookieless Sessions is how easily they can be tampered with. Certainly, cookies can be tampered with using HTTP sniffers, but URLS can be edited by anyone. The only way Session State is maintained is if *every* URL includes the Session ID in this way.

Additionally, all URLS *must* be relative. Remember that the Session ID appears as if it were a directory. The Session is lost if an absolute URL such as `/myapp/retrieve.aspx` is invoked. If you are generating URLs on the server side, use `HttpResponse.ApplyAppPathModifier()`. It changes a URL when the Session ID is embedded, as shown here:

```
Response.Write(Response.ApplyAppPathModifier("foo/bar.aspx"));
```

The previous line generates a URL similar to the following:

```
/myapp/ (S(avkbnbml4n1n5mi5dmfqnu45))/foo/bar.aspx
```

Notice that not only was session information added to the URL, but it was also converted from a relative URL to an absolute URL, including the application's virtual directory. This method can be useful when you need to use `Response.Redirect` or build a URL manually to redirect from an HTTP page to an HTTPS page while still maintaining cookieless session state.

Choosing the Correct Way to Maintain State

Now that you're familiar with the variety of options available for maintaining state in ASP.NET 2.0, here's some real-world advice from production systems. The In-Process (InProc) Session provider is the fastest method, of course, because everything held in memory is a live object reference. This provider is held in the `HttpApplication's` cache and, as such, it is susceptible to application recycles. If you use Windows 2000 Server or Windows XP, the `aspnet_wp.exe` process manages the ASP.NET HTTP pipeline. If you're running Windows 2003 Server or Vista, `w3wp.exe` is the default process that hosts the runtime.

You must find a balance between the robustness of the out-of-process state service and the speed of the in-process provider. In our experience, the out-of-process state service is usually about 15 percent slower than the in-process provider because of the serialization overhead and marshaling. SQL Session State is about 25 percent slower than InProc. Of course your mileage will likely vary. Don't let these numbers concern you too much. Be sure to do scalability testing on your applications before you panic and make inappropriate decisions.

> **It's worth saying again: We recommend that all developers use Out-Of-Process Session State during development, even if this is not the way your application will be deployed. Forcing yourself to use the Out-Of-Process provider enables you to catch any potential problems with custom objects that do not carry the `Serializable` attribute. If you design your entire site using the In-Process provider and then discover, late in the project, that requirements force you to switch to the SQL or Out-Of-Process providers, you have no guarantee that your site will work as you wrote it. Developing with the Out-Of-Process provider gives you the best of both worlds and does not affect your final deployment method. Think of it as an insurance policy that costs you nothing upfront.**

The Application Object

The `Application` object is the equivalent of a bag of global variables for your ASP.NET application. Global variables have been considered harmful for many years in other programming environments, and ASP.NET is no different. You should give some thought to what you want to put in the `Application` object and why. Often, the more flexible `Cache` object that helps you control an object's lifetime is the more useful. Caching is discussed in depth in Chapter 23.

The `Application` object is not global to the machine; it's global to the `HttpApplication`. If you are running in the context of a Web farm, each ASP.NET application on each Web server has its own `Application` object. Because ASP.NET applications are multithreaded and are receiving requests that are being handled by your code on multiple threads, access to the `Application` object should be managed using the `Application.Lock` and `Application.Unlock` methods. If your code doesn't call Unlock directly (which it should, shame on you) the lock is removed implicitly at the end of the `HttpRequest` that called Lock originally.

This small example shows you how to lock the `Application` object just before inserting an object. Other threads that might be attempting to write to the `Application` will wait until it is unlocked. This example assumes there is an integer already stored in `Application` under the key `GlobalCount`.

VB

```
Application.Lock()
Application("GlobalCount") = CType(Application("GlobalCount"), Integer) + 1
Application.UnLock()
```

C#

```
Application.Lock();
Application["GlobalCount"] = (int)Application["GlobalCount"] + 1;
Application.UnLock();
```

Object references can be stored in the `Application`, as in the `Session`, but they must be cast back to their known types when retrieved (as shown in the preceding sample code).

QueryStrings

The URL, or QueryString, is the ideal place for navigation-specific — not user-specific — data. The QueryString is the most hackable element on a Web site, and that fact can work for you or against you. For example, if your navigation scheme uses your own page IDs at the end of a query string (such as `/localhost/mypage.aspx?id = 54`) be prepared for a user to play with that URL in his browser, and try every value for `id` under the sun. Don't blindly cast `id` to an int, and if you do, have a plan if it fails. A good idea is to return `Response.StatusCode=404` when someone changes a URL to an unreasonable value. Another fine idea that Amazon.com implemented was the *Smart 404*. Perhaps you've seen these: They say "Sorry you didn't find what you're looking for. Did you mean _____?"

Remember, your URLs are the first thing your users may see, even before they see your HTML. *Hackable* URLs — hackable even by my mom — make your site more accessible. Which of these URLs is friendlier and more hackable (for the *right* reason)?

```
http://reviews.cnet.com/Philips_42PF9996/4505-6482_7-31081946.html?tag=cnetfd.sd
```

or

```
http://www.hanselman.com/blog/CategoryView.aspx?category=Movies
```

Cookies

Do you remember the great cookie scare of 1997? Most users weren't quite sure just what a cookie was, but they were all convinced that cookies were evil and were storing their personal information. Back then, it was likely personal information was stored in the cookie! Never, ever store sensitive information, such as a user ID or password, in a cookie. Cookies should be used to store only non-sensitive information, or information that can be retrieved from an authoritative source. Cookies shouldn't be trusted, and their contents should be able to be validated. For example, if a Forms Authentication cookie has been tampered with, the user is logged out and an exception is thrown. If an invalid Session ID cookie is passed in for an expired Session, a new cookie can be assigned.

When you store information in cookies, remember that it's quite different from storing data in the `Session` object:

- Cookies are passed back and forth on *every* request. That means you are paying for the size of your cookie during *every* HTTP GET and HTTP POST.
- If you have ten 1-pixel spacer GIFs on your page used for table layouts, the user's browser is sending the same cookie *eleven* times: once for the page itself, and once for each spacer GIF, even if the GIF is already cached.
- Cookies can be stolen, sniffed, and faked. If your code counts on a cookie's value, have a plan in your code for the inevitability that cookie will get corrupted or be tampered with.
- What is the expected behavior of your application if a cookie doesn't show? What if it's 4096 bytes? Be prepared. You should design your application around the "principle of least surprise." Your application should attempt to heal itself if cookies are found missing or if they are larger than expected.
- Think twice before Base64 encoding anything large and placing it in a cookie. If your design depends on this kind of technique, rethink using either the Session or another backing-store.

PostBacks and Cross-Page PostBacks

In classic ASP, in order to detect logical events such as a button being clicked, developers had to inspect the `Form` collection of the `Request` object. Yes, a button was clicked in the user's browser, but no object model was built on top of stateless HTTP and HTML. ASP.NET 1.*x* introduced the concept of the postback, wherein a server-side event was raised to alert the developer of a client-side action. If a button is clicked on the browser, the Form collection is POSTed back to the server, but now ASP.NET allowed the developer to write code in events such as `Button1_Click` and `TextBox1_Changed`.

However, this technique of posting *back* to the same page is counter-intuitive, especially when you are designing user interfaces that aim to create wizards to give the user the sense of forward motion.

This chapter is about all aspects of state management. Postbacks and cross-page postbacks, however, are covered extensively in Chapter 3 so this chapter touches on them only in the context of state management. Postbacks were introduced in ASP.NET 1.*x* to provide an eventing subsystem for Web development. It was inconvenient to have only single-page postbacks in 1.*x*, however, and that caused many developers to store small objects in the `Session` on a postback and then redirect to the next page to pick up the stored data. With cross-page postbacks, data can be posted "forward" to a different page, often obviating the need for storing small bits of data that could be otherwise passed directly.

ASP.NET 2.0 and above includes the notion of a `PostBackUrl` to all the Button controls including LinkButton and ImageButton. The `PostBackUrl` property is both part of the markup when a control is presented as part of the ASPX page, as seen in the following, and is a property on the server-side component that's available in the code-behind:

```
<asp:Button PostBackUrl="url" ..>
```

When a button control with the `PostBackUrl` property set is clicked, the page does not post back to itself; instead, the page is posted to the URL assigned to the button control's `PostBackUrl` property. When a cross-page request occurs, the `PreviousPage` property of the current `Page` class holds a reference to the page that caused the postback. To get a control reference from the `PreviousPage`, use the `Controls` property or use the `FindControl` method.

Create a fresh site with a `Default.aspx` (as shown in Listing 22-8). Put a `TextBox` and a `Button` on it, and set the `Button PostBackUrl` property to `Step2.aspx`. Then create a `Step2.aspx` page with a single `Label` and add a `Page_Load` handler by double-clicking the HTML Designer.

Listing 22-8: Cross-page postbacks

Default.aspx

```
<!DOCTYPE html PUBLIC "-//W3C//DTD XHTML 1.1//EN" "http://www.w3.org/TR/
xhtml11/DTD/xhtml11.dtd">
<html xmlns="http://www.w3.org/1999/xhtml" >
<head runat="server">
    <title>Cross-page PostBacks</title>
</head>
<body>
    <form id="form1" runat="server">
    <div>
        <asp:TextBox ID="TextBox1" Runat="server"></asp:TextBox>
        <asp:Button ID="Button1" Runat="server" Text="Button"
            PostBackUrl="~/Step2.aspx" />
    </div>
    </form>
</body>
</html>
```

Step2.aspx

```
<!DOCTYPE html PUBLIC "-//W3C//DTD XHTML 1.0 Transitional//EN"
"http://www.w3.org/TR/xhtml1/DTD/xhtml1-transitional.dtd">
<html xmlns="http://www.w3.org/1999/xhtml" >
<head runat="server">
    <title>Step 2</title>
</head>
<body>
    <form id="form1" runat="server">
    <div>
        <asp:Label ID="Label1" runat="server" Text="Label"></asp:Label>
    </div>
    </form>
</body>
 </html>
```

VB — Step2.aspx.vb

```
Partial Class Step2
    Inherits System.Web.UI.Page

    Protected Sub Page_Load(ByVal sender As Object, ByVal e As System.EventArgs) _
            Handles Me.Load

        If PreviousPage IsNot Nothing AndAlso PreviousPage.IsCrossPagePostBack Then
            Dim text As TextBox = _
                    CType(PreviousPage.FindControl("TextBox1"), TextBox)
            If text IsNot Nothing Then
                Label1.Text = text.Text
```

Continued

```
            End If
        End If

    End Sub

End Class
```

CS — Step2.aspx.cs

```
using System;
using System.Web.UI.WebControls;

public partial class Step2 : System.Web.UI.Page
{
    protected void Page_Load(object sender, EventArgs e)
    {
        if (PreviousPage != null && PreviousPage.IsCrossPagePostBack)
        {
            TextBox text = PreviousPage.FindControl("TextBox1") as TextBox;
            if (text != null)
            {
                Label1.Text = text.Text;
            }
        }
    }

}
```

In Listing 22-8, `Default.aspx` posts *forward* to `Step2.aspx`, which can then access the `Page.PreviousPage` property and retrieve a populated instance of the `Page` that caused the postback. A call to `FindControl` and a cast retrieves the `TextBox` from the previous page and copies its value into the Label of `Step2.aspx`.

Hidden Fields, ViewState, and ControlState

Hidden input fields such as `<input type=""hidden" name="foo">` are sent back as name/value pairs in a Form POST exactly like any other control, except they are not rendered. Think of them as hidden text boxes. Figure 22-9 shows a HiddenField control on the Visual Studio Designer with its available properties. Hidden fields are available in all versions of ASP.NET.

ViewState, on the other hand, exposes itself as a collection of key/value pairs like the `Session` object, but renders itself as a hidden field with the name `"__VIEWSTATE"` like this:

```
<input type="hidden" name="__VIEWSTATE" value="/AAASSDAS...Y/lOI=" />
```

Any objects put into the ViewState must be marked `Serializable`. ViewState serializes the objects with a special binary formatter called the LosFormatter. LOS stands for limited object serialization. It serializes any kind of object, but it is optimized to contain strings, arrays, and hashtables.

To see this at work, create a new page and drag a `TextBox`, `Button`, and `HiddenField` onto it. Double-click in the Designer to create a `Page_Load` and include the code from Listing 22-9. This example adds a string to `HiddenField.Value`, but adds an instance of a `Person` to the `ViewState` collection. This listing illustrates that while ViewState is persisted in a single HTML `TextBox` on the client, it can contain both simple types such as strings, and complex types such as `Person`. This technique has been around since ASP.NET 1.*x* and continues to be a powerful and simple way to persist small pieces of data without utilizing server resources.

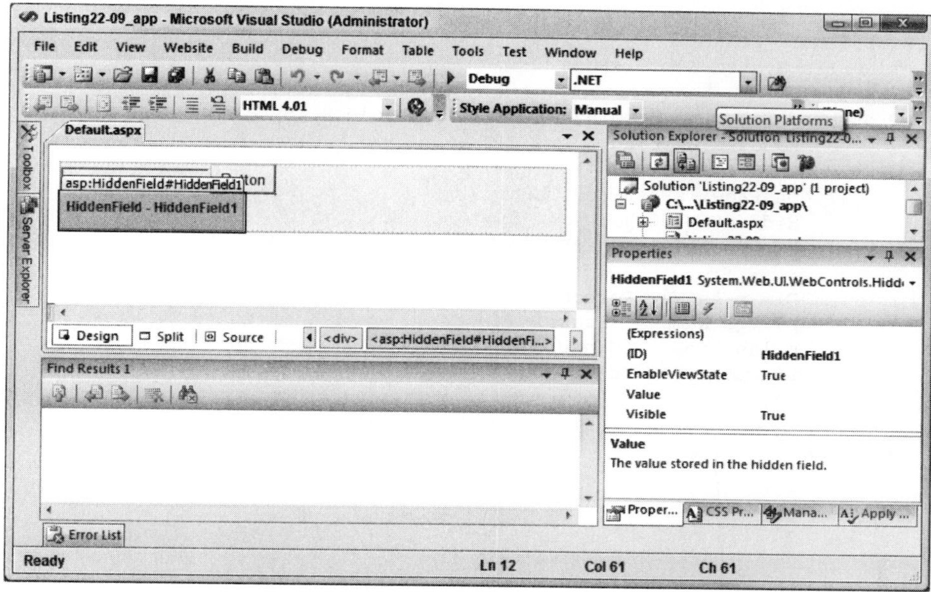

Figure 22-9

Listing 22-9: Hidden fields and ViewState

ASPX

```
<!DOCTYPE html PUBLIC "-//W3C//DTD XHTML 1.1//EN"
 "http://www.w3.org/TR/xhtml11/DTD/xhtml11.dtd">
<html xmlns="http://www.w3.org/1999/xhtml" >
<head runat="server">
    <title>Hidden Fields and ViewState</title>
</head>
<body>
    <form id="form1" runat="server">
    <div>
        <asp:TextBox ID="TextBox1" Runat="server"></asp:TextBox>
        <asp:Button ID="Button1" Runat="server" Text="Button"  />
        <asp:HiddenField ID="HiddenField1" Runat="server" />
    </div>
    </form>
</body>
</html>
```

Continued

VB

```
<Serializable> _
Public Class Person
    Public firstName As String
    Public lastName As String
End Class

Partial Class _Default
    Inherits System.Web.UI.Page

    Protected Sub Page_Load(ByVal sender As Object, ByVal e As System.EventArgs) _
            Handles Me.Load

        If Not Page.IsPostBack Then
            HiddenField1.Value = "foo"
            ViewState("AnotherHiddenValue") = "bar"

            Dim p As New Person
            p.firstName = "Scott"
            p.lastName = "Hanselman"
            ViewState("HiddenPerson") = p
        End If

    End Sub

End Class
```

C#

```
using System;
using System.Web.UI.WebControls;
using System.Web.UI.HtmlControls;

[Serializable]
public class Person
{
    public string firstName;
    public string lastName;
}

public partial class _Default : System.Web.UI.Page
{

    protected void Page_Load(object sender, EventArgs e)
    {
        if (!Page.IsPostBack)
        {
            HiddenField1.Value = "foo";
            ViewState["AnotherHiddenValue"] = "bar";

            Person p = new Person();
            p.firstName = "Scott";
            p.lastName = "Hanselman";
```

```
                ViewState["HiddenPerson"] = p;
            }
        }
    }
```

In Listing 22-9, a string is added to a `HiddenField` and to the `ViewState` collection. Then a `Person` instance is added to the `ViewState` collection with another key. A fragment of the rendered HTML is shown in the following code:

```
<form method="post" action="Default.aspx" id="form1">
<div>
<input type="hidden" name="__VIEWSTATE"
value="/wEPDwULLTIxMjQ3OTEzODcPFgQeEkFub3RoZXJIaWRkZW5WYWx1ZQUDYmFyHgxIaWRkZW5QZXJz
b24ypwEAAQAAAP////8BAAAAAAAAAAAwCAAAAP3ZkcTVqYzdxLCBWZXJzaW9uPTAuMC4wLjAsIEN1bHR1cmU
9bmV1dHJhbCwgUHVibGljS2V5VG9rZW49bnVsbAUBAAAAE0RlZmF1bHRfYXNweCtQZXJzb24CAAAACWZpcn
N0TmFtZQhsYXN0TmFtZQEBAgAAAAYDAAAABVNjb3R0BgQAAAAJSGFuc2VsbWFuC2RkI/CLauUviFo58BF8v
pSNsjY/lOI=" />
</div>
    <div>
        <input name="TextBox1" type="text" id="TextBox1" />
        <input type="submit" name="Button1" value="Button" id="Button1" />
        <input type="hidden" name="HiddenField1" id="HiddenField1" value="foo" />
    </div>
</form>
```

Notice that the `ViewState` value uses only valid ASCII characters to represent all its contents. Don't let the sheer mass of it fool you. It is big and it appears to be opaque. However, it's just a hidden text box and is automatically POSTed back to the server. The entire `ViewState` collection is available to you in the `Page_Load`. The value of the `HiddenField` is stored as plain text.

Neither ViewState nor Hidden Fields are acceptable for any kind of sensitive data.

> **People often complain about the size of ViewState and turn if off completely without realizing its benefits. ASP.NET 2.0 cut the size of serialized ViewState nearly in half. You can find a number of tips on using ViewState on my blog by Googling for "Hanselman ViewState". Fritz Onion's free ViewStateDecoder tool from `www.pluralsight.com` is a great way to gain insight into what's stored in your pages' ViewState. Note also Nikhil Kotari's detailed blog post on ViewState improvements at `www.nikhilk.net/ViewStateImprovements.aspx`.**

By default, the ViewState field is sent to the client with a *salted hash* to prevent tampering. Salting means that the ViewState's data has a unique value appended to it before it's encoded. As Keith Brown says "Salt is just one ingredient to a good stew." The technique used is called HMAC, or hashed message authentication code. As shown in the following code, you can use the `<machineKey>` element of the `web.config file` to specify the `validationKey`, as well as the algorithm used to protect ViewState. This section of the file and the `decryptionKey` attribute also affect how Forms Authentication cookies are encrypted (see Chapter 21 for more on forms authentication).

```
<machineKey validationKey="AutoGenerate,IsolateApps"
 decryptionKey="AutoGenerate,IsolateApps" validation="SHA1" />
```

If you are running your application in a Web farm, `<validationKey>` and `<decryptionKey>` have to be manually set to the same value. Otherwise, ViewState generated from one machine could be POSTed back to a machine in the farm with a different key! The keys should be 128 characters long (the maximum) and generated totally by random means. If you add `IsolateApps` to these values, ASP.NET generates a unique encrypted key for each application using each application's application ID.

I like to use security guru Keith Brown's GenerateMachineKey tool, which you can find at `www.pluralsight.com/tools.aspx`*, to generate these keys randomly.*

The `validation` attribute can be set to SHA1 or MD5 to provide tamper-proofing, but you can include added protection by encrypting ViewState as well. In ASP.NET 1.1 you can encrypt ViewState only by using the value 3DES in the `validation` attribute, and ASP.NET 1.1 will use the key in the `decryptionKey` attribute for encryption. However, ASP.NET 2.0 adds a new decryption attribute that is used exclusively for specifying the encryption and decryption mechanisms for forms authentication tickets, and the `validation` attribute is used exclusively for ViewState, which can now be encrypted using 3DES or AES and the key stored in the `validationKey` attribute.

ASP.NET 2.0 also adds the `ViewStateEncryptionMode` attribute to the `<pages>` configuration element with two possible values, `Auto` or `Always`. Setting the attribute to `Always` will force encryption of ViewState, whereas setting it to `Auto` will encrypt ViewState only if a control requested encryption using the new `Page.RegisterRequiresViewStateEncryption` method.

Added protection can be applied to ViewState by setting `Page.ViewStateUserKey` in the `Page_Init` to a unique value such as the user's ID. This must be set in `Page_Init` because the key should be provided to ASP.NET before ViewState is loaded or generated. For example:

```
protected void Page_Init (Object sender, EventArgs e)
{
    if (User.Identity.IsAuthenticated)
      ViewStateUserKey = User.Identity.Name;
}
```

When optimizing their pages, ASP.NET programmers often disable ViewState for many controls when that extra bit of state isn't absolutely necessary. However, in ASP.NET 1.*x*, disabling ViewState was a good way to break many third-party controls, as well as the included DataGrid's sorting functionality. ASP.NET now includes a second, parallel ViewState-like collection called `ControlState`. This dictionary can be used for round-tripping crucial information of limited size that should not be disabled even when ViewState is. You should only store data in the `ControlState` collection that is absolutely critical to the functioning of the control.

Recognize that ViewState, and also ControlState, although not secure, is a good place to store small bits of a data and state that don't quite belong in a cookie or the `Session` object. If the data that must be stored is relatively small and local to that specific instance of your page, ViewState is a much better solution than littering the `Session` object with lots of transient data.

Using HttpContext.Current.Items for Very Short-Term Storage

The `Items` collection of `HttpContext` is one of ASP.NET's best-kept secrets. It is an `IDictionary` key/value collection of objects that's shared across the life of a single `HttpRequest`. That's a *single* `HttpRequest`. Why would you want to store state for such a short period of time? Consider these reasons:

- **When you share content between IHttpModules and IHttpHandlers:** If you write a custom IHttpModule, you can store context about the user for use later in a page.
- **When you communicate between two instances of the same UserControl on the same page:** Imagine you are writing a UserControl that serves banner ads. Two instances of the same control could select their ads from `HttpContext.Items` to prevent showing duplicates on the same page.
- **When you store the results of expensive calls that might otherwise happen twice or more on a page:** If you have multiple UserControls that each show a piece of data from a large, more expensive database retrieval, those UserControls can retrieve the necessary data from `HttpContext.Items`. The database is hit only once.
- **When individual units within a single HttpRequest need to act on the same or similar data:** If the lifetime of your data is just one request, consider using `HttpContext.Items`, as a short term cache.

The `Items` collection holds objects, just like many of the collections that have been used in this chapter. You need to cast those objects back to their specific type when they are retrieved.

Within a Web-aware Database Access Layer, per-request caching can be quickly implemented with the simple coding pattern shown here. Note that this sample code is a design pattern and there is no `MyData` class; it's for illustration.

VB

```
Public Shared Function GetExpensiveData(ID As Integer) As MyData
  Dim key as string = "data" & ID.ToString()
  Dim d as MyData = _
      CType(HttpContext.Current.Items(key), MyData)
  If d Is Nothing Then
    d = New Data()
    'Go to the Database, do whatever...
    HttpContext.Current.Items(key) = d
  End If
  Return d
End Function
```

C#

```
public static MyData GetExpensiveData(int ID)
{
  string key = "data" + ID.ToString();
  MyData d = (MyData) HttpContext.Current.Items[key];
  if (d == null)
```

```
    {
      d = new Data();
      //Go to the Database, do whatever...
      HttpContext.Current.Items[key] = d;
    }
    return d;
  }
```

This code checks the `Items` collection of the current `HttpContext` to see if the data is already there. If not, the data is retrieved from the appropriate backing store and then stored in the `Items` collection. Subsequent calls to this function within the same `HttpRequest` receive the already-cached object.

As with all optimizations and caching, premature optimization is the root of all evil. Measure your need for caching, and measure your improvements. Don't cache just because it *feels right*; cache because it makes sense.

Summary

This chapter explored the many ways to manage State within your ASP.NET application. The `Session` object and its providers offer many choices. Each has its own pros and cons for managing state in the form of object references and serialized objects in a way that can be made largely transparent to the application. Server-side Session state data can have its unique identifying key stored in a cookie or the key can be carried along in the URL. Cookies can also be used independently to store small amounts of data and persist it between visits, albeit in much smaller amounts and with simpler types. Hidden fields, ViewState, ControlState, postbacks, and new cross-page postbacks offer new possibilities for managing small bits of state within a multi-page user experience. `HttpContext.Current.Items` offers a perfect place to hold transient state, living the life of only a single `HttpRequest`. QueryStrings are an old standby for holding non-private state that is appropriate for navigation.

ASP.NET has improved on ASP.NET 1.*x*'s state management options with a flexible Session State Provider module, the addition of Control State for user controls, and cross-page postbacks for a more mature programming model.

23

Caching

Performance is a key requirement for any application or piece of code that you develop. The browser helps with client-side caching of text and images, whereas the server-side caching you choose to implement is vital for creating the best possible performance. *Caching* is the process of storing frequently used data on the server to fulfill subsequent requests. You will discover that grabbing objects from memory is much faster than re-creating the Web pages or items contained in them from scratch each time they are requested. Caching increases your application's performance, scalability, and availability. The more you fine-tune your application's caching approach, the better it performs.

This chapter focuses on caching, including the SQL invalidation caching capabilities that ASP.NET provides. This chapter takes a close look at this unique aspect of caching. When you are using SQL cache invalidation, if the result set from SQL Server changes, the output cache can be triggered to change automatically. This ensures that the end user always sees the latest result set, and the data presented is never stale. After introducing SQL cache invalidation, this chapter also covers other performance enhancements. It discusses the new Post-Cache Substitution feature, which caches entire pages while dynamically replacing specified bits of content. Lastly, this chapter covers a new capability that enables a developer to create custom dependencies.

Caching

There are several ways to deal with caching in ASP.NET. First, you can cache an entire HTTP response (the entire Web page) using a mechanism called output caching. Two other methods are partial page caching and data caching. The following sections describe these methods.

Output Caching

Output caching is a way to keep the dynamically generated page content in the server's memory or disk for later retrieval. This type of cache saves post-rendered content so it won't have to be regenerated again the next time it's requested. After a page is cached, it can be served up again when any subsequent requests are made to the server. You apply output caching by inserting an `OutputCache` page directive at the top of an `.aspx` page, as follows:

```
<%@ OutputCache Duration="60" VaryByParam="None" %>
```

The `Duration` attribute defines the number of seconds a page is stored in the cache. The `VaryByParam` attribute determines which versions of the page output are actually cached. You can generate different responses based on whether an HTTP-POST or HTTP-GET response is required. Other than the attributes for the `OutputCache` directive, ASP.NET includes the `VaryByHeader`, `VaryByCustom`, `VaryByControl`, and `Location` attributes. Additionally, the `Shared` attribute can affect UserControls, as you'll see later.

Caching in ASP.NET is implemented as an `HttpModule` that listens to all `HttpRequests` that come through the ASP.NET worker process. The `OutputCacheModule` listens to the application's `ResolveRequestCache` and `UpdateRequestCache` events, handles cache hits and misses, and returns the cached HTML, bypassing the Page Handler if need be.

VaryByParam

The `VaryByParam` attribute can specify which `QueryString` parameters cause a new version of the page to be cached:

```
<%@ OutputCache Duration="90" VaryByParam="pageId;subPageId" %>
```

For example, if you have a page called `navigation.aspx` that includes navigation information in the `QueryString`, such as `pageId` and `subPageId`, the `OutputCache` directive shown here caches the page for every different value of `pageId` and `subPageId`. In this example, the number of pages is best expressed with an equation:

```
cacheItems = (num of pageIds) * (num of subPageIds)
```

where `cacheItems` is the number of rendered HTML pages that would be stored in the cache. Pages are cached only after they're requested and pass through the `OutputCacheModule`. The maximum amount of cache memory in this case is used only after every possible combination is visited at least once. Although these are just *potential* maximums, creating an equation that represents your system's potential maximum is an important exercise.

If you want to cache a new version of the page based on any differences in the `QueryString` parameters, use `VaryByParam = "*"`, as in the following code.

```
<%@ OutputCache Duration="90" VaryByParam="*" %>
```

It's important to "do the math" when using the VaryBy attributes. For example, you could add `VaryByHeader` and cache a different version of the page based on the browser's reported `User-Agent` HTTP Header.

```
<%@ OutputCache Duration="90" VaryByParam="*" VaryByHeader="User-Agent"%>
```

The `User-Agent` identifies the user's browser type. ASP.NET can automatically generate different renderings of a given page that are customized to specific browsers, so it makes sense in many cases to save these various renderings in the cache. A Firefox user might have slightly different HTML than an IE user, so we don't want to send all users the exact same post-rendered HTML. Literally dozens, if not hundreds, of `User-Agent` strings exist in the wild because they identify more than just the browser type;

this `OutputCache` directive could multiply into thousands of different versions of this page being cached, depending on server load. In this case, you should measure the cost of the caching against the cost of re-creating the page dynamically.

> **Always cache what will give you the biggest performance gain, and prove that assumption with testing. Don't "cache by coincidence" using attributes like `VaryByParam = "*"`. A common rule of thumb is to cache the least possible amount of data at first and add more caching later if you determine a need for it. Remember that the server memory is a limited resource so you may want configure the use of disk caching in some cases. Be sure to balance your limited resources with security as a primary concern; don't put sensitive data on the disk.**

VaryByControl

`VaryByControl` can be a very easy way to get some serious performance gains from complicated User-Controls that render a lot of HTML that doesn't change often. For example, imagine a UserControl that renders a ComboBox showing the names of all the countries in the world. Perhaps those names are retrieved from a database and rendered in the combo box as follows:

```
<%@ OutputCache Duration="2592000" VaryByControl="comboBoxOfCountries" %>
```

Certainly the names of the world's countries don't change that often, so the `Duration` might be set to a month (in seconds). The rendered output of the UserControl is cached, allowing a page using that control to reap performance benefits of caching the control while the page itself remains dynamic.

VaryByCustom

Although the `VaryBy` attributes offer a great deal of power, sometimes you need more flexibility. If you want to take the `OutputCache` directive from the previous navigation example and cache by a value stored in a cookie, you can add `VaryByCustom`. The value of `VaryByCustom` is passed into the `GetVaryByCustomString` method that can be added to the `Global.asax.cs`. This method is called every time the page is requested, and it is the function's responsibility to return a value.

A different version of the page is cached for each unique value returned. For example, say your users have a cookie called `Language` that has three potential values: en, es, and fr. You want to allow users to specify their preferred language, regardless of their language reported by their browser. `Language` also has a fourth potential value — it may not exist! Therefore, the `OutputCache` directive in the following example caches many versions of the page, as described in this equation:

```
cacheItems = (num of pageIds) * (num of subPageIds) * (4 possible Language values)
```

To summarize, suppose there were 10 potential values for `pageId`, five potential `subPageId` values for each `pageId`, and 4 possible values for `Language`. That adds up to 200 different potential cached versions of this single navigation page. This math isn't meant to scare you away from caching, but you should realize that with great (caching) power comes great responsibility.

The following `OutputCache` directive includes `pageId` and `subPageId` as values for `VaryByParam`, and `VaryByCustom` passes in the value of `"prefs"` to the `GetVaryByCustomString` callback function in Listing 23-1:

```
<%@ OutputCache Duration="90" VaryByParam="pageId;subPageId" VaryByCustom="prefs"%>
```

Caching in ASP.NET involves a tradeoff between CPU and memory: how hard is it to make this page, versus whether you can afford to hold 200 versions of it. If it's only 5 KB of HTML, a potential megabyte of memory could pay off handsomely versus thousands and thousands of database accesses. Since most pages will hit the database at least once during a page cycle, every page request served from the cache saves you a trip to the database. Efficient use of caching can translate into cost savings if fewer database servers and licenses are needed.

The code in Listing 23-1 returns the value stored in the `Language` cookie. The `arg` parameter to the `GetVaryByCustomString` method contains the string `"prefs"`, as specified in `VaryByCustom`.

Listing 23-1: GetVaryByCustomString callback method in the HttpApplication

VB

```
Overrides Function GetVaryByCustomString(ByVal context As HttpContext, _
    ByVal arg As String) As String
    If arg.ToLower() = "prefs" Then
        Dim cookie As HttpCookie = context.Request.Cookies("Language")
        If cookie IsNot Nothing Then
            Return cookie.Value
        End If
    End If
    Return MyBase.GetVaryByCustomString(context, arg)
End Function
```

C#

```
public override string GetVaryByCustomString(HttpContext context, string arg)
{
    if(arg.ToLower() == "prefs")
    {
      HttpCookie cookie = context.Request.Cookies["Language"];
      if(cookie != null)
      {
          return cookie.Value;
      }
    }
    return base.GetVaryByCustomString(context, arg);
}
```

The `GetVaryByCustomString` method in Listing 23-1 is used by the `HttpApplication` in `Global.asax.cs` and will be called for every page that uses the `VaryByCustom` `OutputCache` directive. If your application has many pages that use `VaryByCustom`, you can create a switch statement and a series of helper functions to retrieve whatever information you want from the user's HttpContext and to generate unique values for cache keys.

Partial Page (UserControl) Caching

Similar to output caching, *partial page caching* enables you to cache only specific blocks of a Web page. You can, for example, cache only the center of the page the user sees. Partial page caching is achieved with the caching of user controls so you can build your ASP.NET pages to utilize numerous user controls and then apply output caching to the selected user controls. This, in essence, caches only the parts of the page that you want, leaving other parts of the page outside the reach of caching. This is a nice feature and, if done correctly, it can lead to pages that perform better. This requires a modular design to be planned up front so you can partition the components of the page into logical units composed of user controls.

Typically, UserControls are designed to be placed on multiple pages to maximize reuse of common functionality. However, when these UserControls (ASCX files) are cached with the `@OutputCache` directive's default attributes, they are cached on a per-page basis. That means that even if a UserControl outputs the identical HTML when placed on `pageA.aspx` as it does when placed on `pageB.aspx`, its output is cached twice. By enabling the `Shared = "true"` attribute, the UserControl's output can be shared among multiple pages and on sites that make heavy use of shared UserControls:

```
<%@ OutputCache Duration="300" VaryByParam="*" Shared="true" %>
```

The resulting memory savings can be surprisingly large since you only cache one copy of the post-rendered user control instead of caching a copy for each page. As with all optimizations, you need to test both for correctness of output as well as memory usage.

> **If you have an ASCX UserControl using the `OutputCache` directive, remember that the UserControl *exists only for the first request*. If a UserControl has its HTML retrieved from the `OutputCache`, the control doesn't really exist on the ASPX page. Instead, a PartialCachingControl is created that acts as a proxy or *ghost* of that control.**

Any code in the ASPX page that requires a UserControl to be constantly available will fail if that control is reconstituted from the `OutputCache`. So be sure to always check for this type of caching before using any control. The following code fragment illustrates the kind of logic required when accessing a potentially cached UserControl:

VB

```
Protected Sub Page_Load()
    If Not PossiblyCachedUserControl is Nothing Then
       " Place code manipulating PossiblyCachedUserControl here.
    End If
End Sub
```

C#

```
protected void Page_Load()
{
    if (PossiblyCachedUserControl != null)
    {
       // Place code manipulating PossiblyCachedUserControl here.
    }
}
```

Post-Cache Substitution

Output caching has typically been an all-or-nothing proposition. The output of the entire page is cached for later use. However, often you want the benefits of output caching, but you also want to keep a small bit of dynamic content on the page. It would be a shame to cache a page but be unable to output a dynamic ''Welcome, Scott!''

ASP.NET 2.0 added post-cache substitution as an opportunity to affect the about-to-be-rendered page. A control is added to the page that acts as a placeholder. It calls a method that you specify after the cached content has been returned. The method returns any string output you like, but you should be careful not to abuse the feature. If your post-cache substitution code calls an expensive stored procedure, you could easily lose any performance benefits you might have expected.

Post-cache substitution is an easy feature to use. It gives you two ways to control the substitution:

- Call the new `Response.WriteSubstitution` method, passing it a reference to the desired substitution method callback.
- Add a `<asp:Substitution>` control to the page at the desired location, and set its `methodName` attribute to the name of the callback method.

To try this feature, create a new Web site with a `Default.aspx`. Drag a label control and a substitution control to the design surface. The code in Listing 23-2 updates the label to display the current time, but the page is cached immediately and future requests return that cached value. Set the `methodName` property in the substitution control to `GetUpdatedTime`, meaning the name of the static method that is called after the page is retrieved from the cache.

The callback function must be static because the page that is rendered doesn't really exist at this point (an instance of it doesn't). Because you don't have a page instance to work with, this method is limited in its scope. However, the current `HttpContext` is passed into the method, so you have access to the `Session`, `Request`, and `Response`. The string returned from this method is injected into the `Response` in place of the substitution control.

Listing 23-2: Using the substitution control

ASPX

```
<%@ Page Language="C#" CodeFile="Default.aspx.cs" Inherits="_Default" %>
<%@ OutputCache Duration="30" VaryByParam="None" %>

<html xmlns="http://www.w3.org/1999/xhtml" >
<head >
    <title>Substitution Control</title>
</head>
<body>
    <form id="form1" runat="server">
    <div>
        <asp:Label ID="Label1" Runat="server" Text="Label"></asp:Label>
        <br />
        <asp:Substitution ID="Substitution1" Runat="server"
            methodName="GetUpdatedTime" />
        <br />
    </div>
    </form>
</body>
</html>
```

VB

```
Partial Class _Default
    Inherits System.Web.UI.Page
```

```
        Public Shared Function GetUpdatedTime(ByVal context As HttpContext) As String
            Return DateTime.Now.ToLongTimeString() + " by " + _
                    context.User.Identity.Name
        End Function

        Protected Sub Page_Load(ByVal sender As Object, ByVal e As System.EventArgs) _
                Handles Me.Load
            Label1.Text = DateTime.Now.ToLongTimeString()
        End Sub
    End Class
```

C#

```
public partial class _Default : System.Web.UI.Page
{
    public static string GetUpdatedTime(HttpContext context)
    {
        return DateTime.Now.ToLongTimeString() + " by " +
                context.User.Identity.Name;
    }
    protected void Page_Load(object sender, EventArgs e)
    {
        Label1.Text = DateTime.Now.ToLongTimeString();
    }
}
```

The ASPX page in Listing 23-2 has a label and a Post-Cache Substitution Control. The control acts as a placeholder in the spot where you want fresh content injected after the page is returned from the cache. The very first time the page is visited only the label is updated because no cached content is returned. The second time the page is visited, however, the entire page is retrieved from the cache — the page handler isn't called and, consequently, none of the page-level events fire. However, the `GetUpdatedTime` method is called after the cache module completes its work. Figure 23-1 shows the result if the first line is cached and the second line is created dynamically.

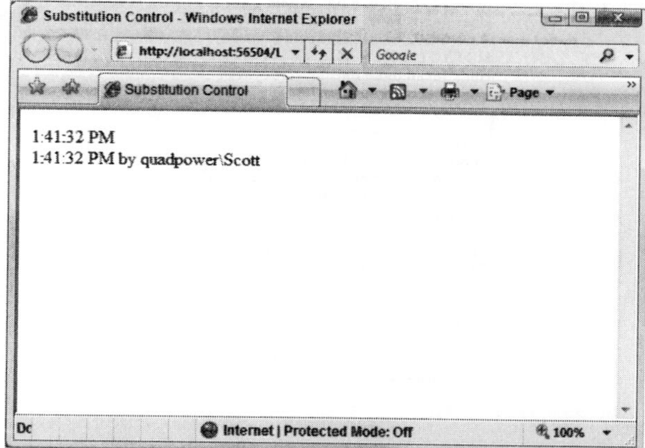

Figure 23-1

HttpCachePolicy and Client-Side Caching

Caching is more than just holding data in memory on the server-side. A good caching strategy should also include the browser and its client-side caches, controlled by the Cache-Control HTTP Header. HTTP Headers are hints and directives to the browser on how to handle a request.

Some people recommend using HTML `<META>` tags to control caching behavior. Be aware that neither the browsers nor routers along the way are obligated to pay attention to these directives. You might have more success using HTTP Headers to control caching.

Because HTTP Headers travel outside the body of the HTTP message, you have several options for viewing them. You can enable tracing (see Chapter 21) and view the Headers from the tracing output. In Figure 23-2 I'm using the free TcpTrace redirector from `PocketSoap.com`.

> **For background information on HTTP headers and controlling caching, see the document RFC 2616: Hypertext Transfer Protocol - HTTP/1.1, available on the World Wide Web Consortium's site at `www.w3c.org`. You might also check out Fiddler at `www.fiddlertool.com/fiddler` and FireBug for Firefox at `www.getfirebug.com`. Commercial tools such as HttpWatch from `www.httpwatch.com` add more features.**

Create a `Default.aspx` that writes the current time in its `Load` event. Now, view the default HTTP Headers used by ASP.NET, as in Figure 23-2 with page-level tracing turned on. Note that one header, `Cache-Control: private`, indicates to routers and other intermediates that this response is intended only for you (private).

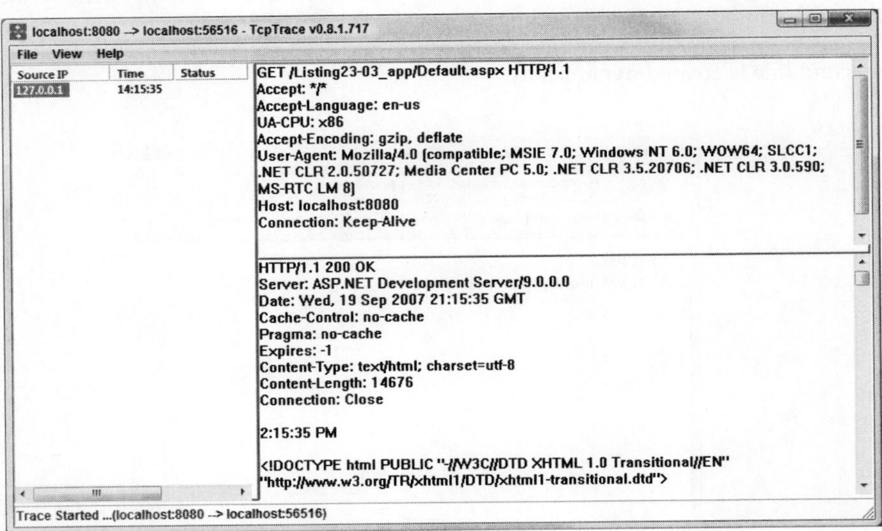

Figure 23-2

The `HttpCachePolicy` class gives you an object model for managing client-side state that insulates you from adding HTTP headers yourself. Add the lines from Listing 23-3 to your `Page_Load` to influence the Response's headers and the caching behavior of the browser. This listing tells the browser not to cache this Response in memory nor store it on disk. It also directs the Response to expire immediately.

Listing 23-3: Using HTTP Headers to force the browser not to cache on the client-side

VB

```
Protected Sub Page_Load(ByVal sender As Object, _
  ByVal e As System.EventArgs) Handles Me.Load

    Response.Cache.SetCacheability(HttpCacheability.NoCache)
    Response.Cache.SetNoStore()
    Response.Cache.SetExpires(DateTime.MinValue)

    Response.Write(DateTime.Now.ToLongTimeString())
End Sub
```

C#

```
protected void Page_Load(object sender, EventArgs e)
{
    Response.Cache.SetCacheability(HttpCacheability.NoCache);
    Response.Cache.SetNoStore();
    Response.Cache.SetExpires(DateTime.MinValue);

    Response.Write(DateTime.Now.ToLongTimeString());
}
```

Compare the results of running Listing 23-3 in the *before* Figure 23-2 and then in the *after* Figure 23-3. Two new HTTP headers have been injected directing the client's browser and the `Cache-Control` Header has changed to `no-cache, no-store`. The Output Caching HttpModule will respect these HTTP headers, so sending `no-cache, no store` to the browser also advises the HttpModule to record the response as a cache miss.

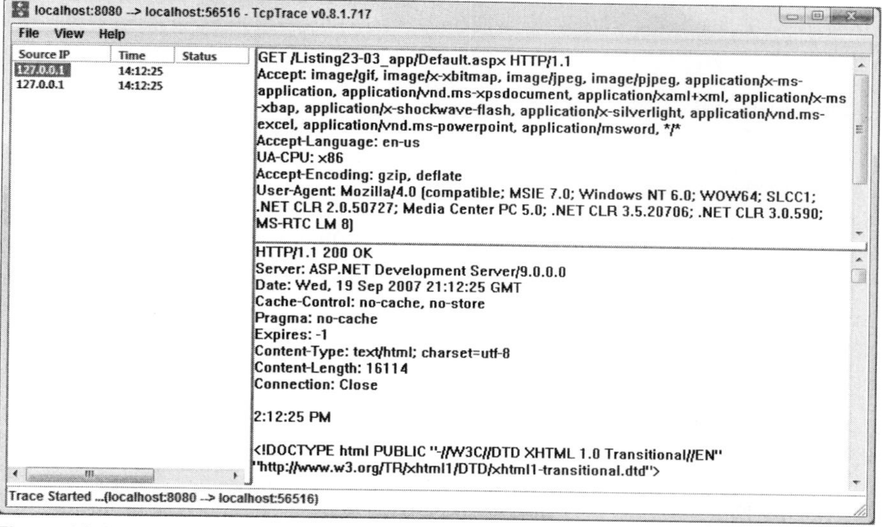

Figure 23-3

If your ASP.NET application contains a considerable number of relatively static or non–time-sensitive pages, consider what your client-side caching strategy is. It's better to take advantage of the disk space and the memory of your users' powerful client machines rather than burdening your server's limited resources.

Caching Programmatically

Output Caching is a very declarative business. UserControls and Pages can be marked up with `OutputCache` directives and dramatically change the behavior of your site. Declarative caching controls the life cycle of HTML markup, but ASP.NET also includes deep imperative programmatic support for caching objects.

Data Caching Using the Cache Object

Another method of caching is to use the `Cache` object to start caching specific data items for later use on a particular page or group of pages. The `Cache` object enables you to store everything from simple name/value pairs to more complex objects such as datasets and entire `.aspx` pages.

> **Although this is quite similar to Session state, the `Cache` object is shared by all users of the particular web server's app domain that is hosting this application. So if you put a particular item in the `Cache`, all users will be able to see that object. This may not work as expected in a server farm scenario since you can't be assured of which server the user will hit next, and even if there's only one server involved there may be more than one app domain running this application. Also, the server is free to invalidate any cached item at any time if it needs to reclaim some of the memory.**

You use the `Cache` object in the following fashion:

VB

```
Cache("WhatINeedToStore") = myDataSet
```

C#

```
Cache["WhatINeedToStore"] = myDataSet;
```

After an item is in the cache, you can retrieve it later as shown here:

VB

```
Dim ds As New DataSet
ds = CType(Cache("WhatINeedToStore"), DataSet)
```

C#

```
DataSet ds = new DataSet();
ds = (DataSet)Cache["WhatINeedToStore"];
```

Using the `Cache` object is an outstanding way to cache your pages and is, in fact, what the `OutputCache` directive uses under the covers. This small fragment shows the simplest use of the `Cache` object. Simply put an object reference in it. However, the real power of the `Cache` object comes with its capability to invalidate itself. That's where cache dependencies come in.

> **You must always follow the pattern of testing to see if an item is in the Cache, and if not, you need to do whatever processing is necessary to re-create the object. Once re-created, you can insert it back into the Cache to become available for the next request.**

Controlling the ASP.NET Cache

Ordinarily the default parameters set by ASP.NET for the caching subsystem are appropriate for general use. They are configurable, however, within the machine.config or web.config. These options let you make changes like preventing cached items from expiring when the system is under memory pressure, or turning off item expiration completely. You can set the maximize size of the application's private bytes before the cache begins to flush items.

```
<system.web>
  <cache disableMemoryCollection="false"
  disableExpiration="false" privateBytesLimit="0"
  percentagePhysicalMemoryUsedLimit="90"
  privateBytesPollTime="00:02:00" />
...snip...
```

I encourage you to leave the default values as they are unless you've done formal profiling of your application and understand how it utilizes the Cache. More detail on this section can be found on MSDN here: `http://msdn2.microsoft.com/en-us/library/ms228248.aspx`.

Cache Dependencies

Using the `Cache` object, you can store and also invalidate items in the cache based on several different dependencies. In ASP.NET 1.0/1.1, the only possible dependencies were the following:

- File-based dependencies
- Key-based dependencies
- Time-based dependencies

When inserting items into the cache using the `Cache` object, you set the dependencies with the `Insert` method, as shown in the following example:

```
Cache.Insert("DSN", connectionString, _
   New CacheDependency(Server.MapPath("myconfig.xml")))
```

By using a *dependency* when the item being referenced changes, you remove the cache for that item from memory.

Cache Dependencies were improved in ASP.NET 2.0 with the addition of the `AggregateCacheDependency` class, the newly extendable `CacheDependency` class, and the capability to create your own custom `CacheDependency` classes. These three things are discussed in the following sections.

The AggregateCacheDependency Class

The `AggregateCacheDependency` class is like the `CacheDependency` class but it enables you to create an association connecting an item in the cache with many disparate dependencies of *different types*. For example, if you have a cached data item that is built from XML from a file and you also have information from a SQL database table, you can create an `AggregateCacheDependency` with inserted `CacheDependency` objects for each subdependency. To do this, you call `Cache.Insert` and add the `AggregateCacheDependency` instance. For example:

```
Dim agg as new AggregateCacheDependency()
agg.Insert(New CacheDependency(Server.MapPath("myconfig.xml")))
agg.Insert(New SqlCacheDependency("Northwind", "Customers"))
Cache.Insert("DSN", connectionString, agg)
```

Note that `AggregateCacheDependency` is meant to be used with *different* kinds of `CacheDependency` classes. If you simply want to associate one cached item with multiple files, use an overload of `CacheDependency`, as in this example:

VB

```
Cache.Insert("DSN", yourObject, _
    New System.Web.Caching.CacheDependency( _
        New String() _
       { _
         Server.MapPath("foo.xml"), _
         Server.MapPath("bar.xml") _
       } _
    ) _
)
```

C#

```
Cache.Insert("DSN", yourObject,
    new System.Web.Caching.CacheDependency(
        new string[]
        {
            Server.MapPath("foo.xml"),
            Server.MapPath("bar.xml")
        }
    )
);
```

The `AggregateCacheDependency` class is made possible by the new support for extending the previously sealed `CacheDependency` class. You can use this innovation to create your own custom `CacheDependency`.

The Unsealed CacheDependency Class

A big change in caching in ASP.NET 2.0 was that the `CacheDependency` class has been refactored and unsealed (or made overrideable). This allows us to create classes that inherit from the `CacheDependency` class and create more elaborate dependencies that are not limited to the `Time`, `Key`, or `File` dependencies.

When you create your own cache dependencies, you have the option to add procedures for such things as Web services data, only-at-midnight dependencies, or textual string changes within a file. The dependencies you create are limited only by your imagination. The unsealing of the `CacheDependency` class puts you in the driver's seat to let you decide when items in the `Cache` need to be invalidated.

Along with the unsealing of the `CacheDependency` class, the ASP.NET team has also built a SQL Server cache dependency — `SqlCacheDependency`. A SQL cache dependency was the caching feature most requested by ASP.NET 1.0/1.1 developers. When a cache becomes invalid because a table changes within the underlying SQL Server, you now know it immediately.

Because `CacheDependency` is now unsealed, you can derive your own custom Cache Dependencies; that's what you do in the next section.

Creating Custom Cache Dependencies

ASP.NET has time-based, file-based, and SQL-based `CacheDependency` support. You might ask yourself why you would write your own `CacheDependency`. Here are a few ideas:

- Invalidate the cache from the results of an Active Directory lookup query
- Invalidate the cache upon arrival of an MSMQ or MQSeries message
- Create an Oracle-specific `CacheDependency`
- Invalidate the cache using data reported from an XML Web service
- Update the cache with new data from a Stock Price service

The new version of the `CacheDependency` class, while introducing no breaking changes to existing ASP.NET 1.1 code, exposes three new members and a constructor overload that developers can use:

- `GetUniqueID`: When overridden, enables you to return a unique identifier for a custom cache dependency to the caller.
- `DependencyDispose`: Used for disposing of resources used by the custom cache dependency class. When you create a custom cache dependency, you are required to implement this method.
- `NotifyDependencyChanged`: Called to cause expiration of the cache item dependent on the custom cache dependency instance.
- New Public Constructor.

Listing 23-4 creates a new `RssCacheDependency` that invalidates a cache key if an RSS (Rich Site Summary) XML Document has changed.

Listing 23-4: Creating an RssCacheDependency class

VB

```
Imports System
Imports System.Web
Imports System.Threading
```

Continued

```
Imports System.Web.Caching
Imports System.Xml

Public Class RssCacheDependency
    Inherits CacheDependency

    Dim backgroundThread As Timer
    Dim howOften As Integer = 900
    Dim RSS As XmlDocument
    Dim RSSUrl As String

    Public Sub New(ByVal URL As String, ByVal polling As Integer)
        howOften = polling
        RSSUrl = URL
        RSS = RetrieveRSS(RSSUrl)

        If backgroundThread Is Nothing Then
            backgroundThread = New Timer( _
                New TimerCallback(AddressOf CheckDependencyCallback), _
                Me, (howOften * 1000), (howOften * 1000))
        End If
    End Sub

    Function RetrieveRSS(ByVal URL As String) As XmlDocument
        Dim retVal As New XmlDocument
        retVal.Load(URL)
        Return retVal
    End Function

    Public Sub CheckDependencyCallback(ByVal Sender As Object)
        Dim CacheDepends As RssCacheDependency = _
            CType(Sender, RssCacheDependency)
        Dim NewRSS As XmlDocument = RetrieveRSS(RSSUrl)
        If Not NewRSS.OuterXml = RSS.OuterXml Then
            CacheDepends.NotifyDependencyChanged(CacheDepends, EventArgs.Empty)
        End If
        End Sub

    Protected Overrides Sub DependencyDispose()
        backgroundThread = Nothing
        MyBase.DependencyDispose()
    End Sub

    Public ReadOnly Property Document() As XmlDocument
        Get
            Return RSS
        End Get
    End Property
End Class
```

C#

```
using System;
using System.Web;
using System.Threading;
using System.Web.Caching;
using System.Xml;
```

```
public class RssCacheDependency : CacheDependency
{
    Timer backgroundThread;
    int howOften = 900;
    XmlDocument RSS;
    string RSSUrl;

    public RssCacheDependency(string URL, int polling)
    {
        howOften = polling;
        RSSUrl = URL;
        RSS = RetrieveRSS(RSSUrl);

        if (backgroundThread == null)
        {
            backgroundThread = new Timer(
                   new TimerCallback(CheckDependencyCallback),
                   this, (howOften * 1000), (howOften * 1000));
        }
    }

    public XmlDocument RetrieveRSS(string URL)
    {
        XmlDocument retVal = new XmlDocument();
        retVal.Load(URL);
        return retVal;
    }

    public void CheckDependencyCallback(object sender)
    {
        RssCacheDependency CacheDepends = sender as RssCacheDependency;
        XmlDocument NewRSS = RetrieveRSS(RSSUrl);
        if (NewRSS.OuterXml != RSS.OuterXml)
        {
            CacheDepends.NotifyDependencyChanged(CacheDepends, EventArgs.Empty);
        }
    }

    override protected void DependencyDispose()
    {
        backgroundThread = null;
        base.DependencyDispose();
    }

    public XmlDocument Document
    {
        get
        {
            return RSS;
        }
    }
}
```

Create a new Web site and put the `RssCacheDependency` class in a `/Code` folder. Create a `default.aspx` and drag two text boxes, a label, and a button onto the HTML Design view. Execute the Web site and enter an RSS URL for a blog (like mine at `www.hanselman.com/blog/SyndicationService.asmx/`

GetRss), and click the button. The program checks the Cache object using the URL itself as a key. If the XmlDocument containing RSS doesn't exist in the cache, a new RssCacheDependency is created with a 10-minute (600-second) timeout. The XmlDocument is then cached, and all future requests within the next 10 minutes to this page retrieve the RSS XmlDocument from the cache.

Next, your new RssCacheDependency class from Listing 23-4 is illustrated in the following fragment. The RssCacheDependency is created and passed into the call to Cache.Insert. The Cache object handles the lifetime and calling of the methods of the RssCacheDependency instance:

VB

```
<%@ Page Language="VB" ValidateRequest="false" %>

<html>
<head runat="server">
    <title>Custom Cache Dependency Example</title>
</head>
<body>
    <form runat="server"> RSS URL:
        <asp:TextBox ID="TextBox1" Runat="server"/>
        <asp:Button ID="Button1" onclick="Button1_Click" Runat="server"
         Text="Get RSS" />
         Cached:<asp:Label ID="Label2" Runat="server"></asp:Label><br />
         RSS:<br />
         <asp:TextBox ID="TextBox2" Runat="server" TextMode="MultiLine"
          Width="800px" Height="300px"></asp:TextBox>
    </form>
</body>
</html>

<script runat="server">
    Sub Button1_Click(ByVal sender As Object, ByVal e As System.EventArgs)
        Dim RSSUrl As String = TextBox1.Text
        Label2.Text = "Loaded From Cache"
        If Cache(TextBox1.Text) Is Nothing Then
            Label2.Text = "Loaded Fresh"
            Dim itDepends As New RssCacheDependency(RSSUrl, 600)
            Cache.Insert(RSSUrl, itDepends.Document, itDepends)
        End If
        TextBox2.Text = CType(Cache(TextBox1.Text), _
            System.Xml.XmlDocument).OuterXml
    End Sub
</script>
```

C#

```
<%@ Page Language="C#" ValidateRequest="false" %>
<script runat="server">
    void Button1_Click(object sender, System.EventArgs e)
    {
        string RSSUrl = TextBox1.Text;
        Label2.Text = "Loaded From Cache";
        if (Cache[TextBox1.Text] == null)
        {
            Label2.Text = "Loaded Fresh";
            RssCacheDependency itDepends = new RssCacheDependency(RSSUrl, 600);
```

```
            Cache.Insert(RSSUrl, itDepends.Document, itDepends);
        }
        TextBox2.Text = ((System.Xml.XmlDocument)Cache[TextBox1.Text]).OuterXml;
    }
</script>
```

The `RssCacheDependency` class creates a `Timer` background thread to poll for changes in the RSS feed. If it detects changes, the `RssCacheDependency` notifies the caching subsystem with the `NotifyDependencyChanged` event. The cached value with that key clears, and the next page view forces a reload of the requested RSS from the specified feed.

Using the SQL Server Cache Dependency

To utilize the SQL Server Cache Dependency feature in ASP.NET, you must perform a one-time setup of your SQL Server database. To set up your SQL Server, use the `aspnet_regsql.exe` tool found at `C:\Windows\MicroSoft.NET\Framework\v2.0.50727/`. This tool makes the necessary modifications to SQL Server so that you can start working with the new SQL cache invalidation features.

Follow these steps when using the new SQL Server Cache Dependency features:

1. Enable your database for SQL Cache Dependency support.
2. Enable a table or tables for SQL Cache Dependency support.
3. Include SQL connection string details in the ASP.NET application's `web.config`.
4. Utilize the SQL Cache Dependency features in one of the following ways:
    - Programmatically create a `SqlCacheDependency` object in code.
    - Add a `SqlDependency` attribute to an `OutputCache` directive.
    - Add a `SqlCacheDependency` instance to the Response object via `Response.AddCacheDependency`.

This section explains all the steps required and the operations available to you.

To start, you need to get at the `aspnet_regsql.exe` tool. Open up the Visual Studio Command Prompt by choosing Start ➪ All Programs ➪ Microsoft Visual Studio 2008 ➪ Visual Studio Tools ➪ Visual Studio Command Prompt from the Windows Start menu. After the prompt launches, type this command:

```
aspnet_regsql.exe -?
```

This code outputs the help command list for this command-line tool, as shown in the following:

```
                        -- SQL CACHE DEPENDENCY OPTIONS --

-d <database>               Database name for use with SQL cache dependency. The
                            database can optionally be specified using the
                            connection string with the -c option instead.
                            (Required)

-ed                         Enable a database for SQL cache dependency.
```

`-dd`	`Disable a database for SQL cache dependency.`
`-et`	`Enable a table for SQL cache dependency. Requires -t option.`
`-dt`	`Disable a table for SQL cache dependency. Requires -t option.`
`-t <table>`	`Name of the table to enable or disable for SQL cache dependency. Requires -et or -dt option.`
`-lt`	`List all tables enabled for SQL cache dependency.`

The following sections show you how to use some of these commands.

Enabling Databases for SQL Server Cache Invalidation

To use SQL Server cache invalidation with SQL Server 7 or 2000, begin with two steps. The first step enables the appropriate database. In the second step, you enable the tables that you want to work with. You must perform both steps for this process to work. If you want to enable your databases for SQL cache invalidation and you are working on the computer where the SQL Server instance is located, you can use the following construct. If your SQL instance is on another computer, change `localhost` in this example to the name of the remote machine.

```
aspnet_regsql.exe -S localhost -U sa -P password -d Northwind -ed
```

This produces something similar to the following output:

```
Enabling the database for SQL cache dependency.
..
Finished.
```

From this command prompt, you can see that we simply enabled the Northwind database (the sample database that comes with SQL Server) for SQL cache invalidation. The name of the SQL machine was passed in with `-S`, the username with `-U`, the database with `-d`, and most importantly, the command to enable SQL cache invalidation was `-ed`.

Now that you have enabled the database for SQL cache invalidation, you can enable one or more tables contained within the Northwind database.

Enabling Tables for SQL Server Cache Invalidation

You enable more tables by using the following command:

```
aspnet_regsql.exe -S localhost -U sa -P password -d Northwind -t Customers -et

aspnet_regsql.exe -S localhost -U sa -P password -d Northwind -t Products -et
```

You can see that this command is not much different from the one for enabling the database, except for the extra `-t Customers` entry and the use of `-et` to enable the table rather than `-ed` to enable a database. `Customers` is the name of the table that is enabled in this case.

Go ahead and enable both the Customers and Product tables. You run the command once per table. After a table is successfully enabled, you receive the following response:

```
Enabling the table for SQL cache dependency.
.
Finished.
```

After the table is enabled, you can begin using the SQL cache invalidation features. However, before you do, the following section shows you what happens to SQL Server when you enable these features.

Looking at SQL Server 2000

Now that the Northwind database and the Customers and Products tables have all been enabled for SQL cache invalidation, look at what has happened in SQL Server. If you open up the SQL Server Enterprise Manager, you see a new table contained within the Northwind database — `AspNet_SqlCacheTablesForChangeNotification` (whew, that's a long one!). Your screen should look like Figure 23-4. Note that SQL Server 2000 isn't supported on Vista, so this is a screenshot of a *remote* SQL 2000 machine viewed from the SQL Management Studio running on Vista.

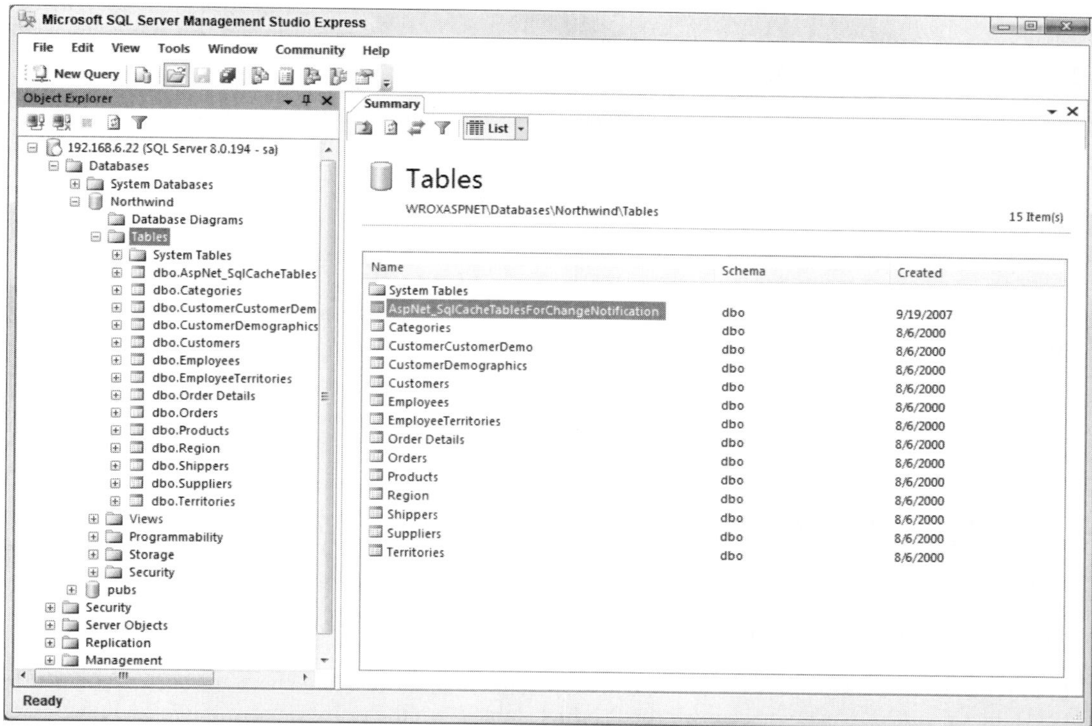

Figure 23-4

At the top of the list of tables in the right-hand pane, you see the `AspNet_SqlCacheTablesForChangeNotification` table. This is the table that ASP.NET uses to learn which tables are being monitored for change notification and also to make note of any changes to the tables being monitored. The table is actually quite simple when you look at the details, as illustrated in Figure 23-5.

Table - dbo.Asp...ngeNotification | Summary

	tableName	notificationCreated	changeId
▶	Customers	9/19/2007 1:38:17 PM	0
	Products	9/19/2007 1:38:43 PM	0
*	NULL	NULL	NULL

Figure 23-5

In this figure, you can see three columns in this new table. The first is the `tableName` column. This column simply shows a `String` reference to the names of the tables contained in the same database. Any table named here is enabled for SQL cache invalidation.

The second column, `notificationCreated`, shows the date and time when the table was enabled for SQL cache invalidation. The final column, `changeId`, is used to communicate to ASP.NET any changes to the included tables. ASP.NET monitors this column for changes and, depending on the value, either uses what is stored in memory or makes a new database query.

Looking at the Tables That Are Enabled

Using the `aspnet_regsql.exe` tool, you can see (by using a simple command) which tables are enabled in a particular database. If you are working through the preceding examples, you see that so far you have enabled the Customers and Products tables of the Northwind database. To get a list of the tables that are enabled, use something similar to the following command:

```
aspnet_regsql.exe -S localhost -U sa -P password -d Northwind -lt
```

The `-lt` command produces a simple list of tables enabled for SQL cache invalidation. Inputting this command produces the following results:

```
Listing all tables enabled for SQL cache dependency:
Customers
Products
```

Disabling a Table for SQL Server Cache Invalidation

Now that you know how to enable your SQL Server database for SQL Server cache invalidation, take a look at how you remove the capability for a specific table to be monitored for this process. To remove a table from the SQL Server cache invalidation process, use the `-dt` command.

In the preceding example, using the `-lt` command showed that you have both the Customers and Products tables enabled. Next, you remove the Products table from the process using the following command:

```
aspnet_regsql.exe -S localhost -U sa -P password -d Northwind -t Products -dt
```

You can see that all you do is specify the name of the table using the `-t` command followed by a `-dt` command (disable table). The command line for disabling table caching will again list the tables that are enabled for SQL Server cache invalidation; this time, the Products table is not listed — instead, Customers, the only enabled table, is listed.

Disabling a Database for SQL Server Cache Invalidation

Not only can you pick and choose the tables that you want to remove from the process, but you can also disable the entire database for SQL Server cache invalidation. In order to disable an entire database, you use the `-dd` command (disable database).

Note that disabling an entire database for SQL Server cache invalidation also means that every single table contained within this database is also disabled.

This example shows the Northwind database being disabled on my computer:

```
C:\>aspnet_regsql -S localhost -U sa -P wrox -d Northwind -dd
Disabling the database for SQL cache dependency.
..
Finished.
```

To ensure that the table is no longer enabled for SQL Server cache invalidation, we attempted to list the tables that were enabled for cache invalidation using the `-lt` command. We received the following error:

```
C:\ >aspnet_regsql -S localhost -U sa -P wrox -d Northwind -lt
An error has happened. Details of the exception:
The database is not enabled for SQL cache notification. To enable a database for
SQL cache notification, please use SQLCacheDependencyAdmin.EnableNotifications
method, or the command line tool aspnet_regsql.exe.
```

If you now open the Northwind database in the SQL Server Enterprise Manager, you can see that the `AspNet_SqlCacheTablesForChangeNotification` table has been removed for the database.

SQL Server 2005 Cache Invalidation

As you've seen, standard SQL Server 2000 cache invalidation uses a table-level mechanism using a polling model every few seconds to monitor what tables have changed. SQL Server 2000's technique not only requires preparation of the database, its polling is rather expensive and its caching is quite coarse.

SQL Server 2005 supports a different, more granular series of notification that doesn't require polling. Direct notification of changes is a built-in feature of SQL Server 2005 and is presented via the ADO.NET `SqlCommand`. For example:

```
Protected Sub Page_Load(ByVal sender as Object, ByVal e as System.EventArgs)

    Response.Write("Page created: " + DateTime.Now.ToLongTimeString())
    Dim connStr As String =
ConfigurationManager.ConnectionStrings("AppConnectionString1").ConnectionString
    SqlDependency.Start(connStr)
    Dim connection As New SqlConnection(connStr)
    Dim command as New SqlCommand("Select * FROM Customers", connection)
```

```
    Dim depends as New SqlCacheDependency(command)

    Connection.Open
    GridView1.DataSource = command.ExecuteReader()
    GridView1.DataBind()

    Connection.Close

     "Now, do what you want with the sqlDependency object like:
    Response.AddCacheDependency(depends)

End Sub
```

SQL Server 2005 supports both programmatic and declarative techniques when caching. Use the string `"CommandNotification"` in the `OutputCache` directive to enable notification-based caching for a page as in this example. You can specify SQL caching options either programmatically or declaratively, but not both. Note that you must first call `System.Data.SqlClient.SqlDependency.Start`, passing in the connection string, to start the SQL notification engine.

```
<%@ OutputCache Duration="3600" VaryByParam="none"
    SqlDependency="CommandNotification"%>
```

Or, if you're using a SqlDataSource control from within your ASP.NET page:

```
<asp:SqlDataSource EnableCaching="true" SqlCacheDependency="CommandNotification"
    CacheDuration="2600" />
```

As data changes within SQL Server 2005, SQL and ADO.NET automatically invalidate data cached on the Web server.

Configuring Your ASP.NET Application

After you enable a database for SQL Server cache invalidation and also enable a couple of tables within this database, the next step is to configure your application for SQL Server cache invalidation.

To configure your application to work with SQL Server cache invalidation, the first step is to make some changes to the `web.config` file. In the `web.config` file, specify that you want to work with the Northwind database, and you want ASP.NET connected to it.

Listing 23-5 shows an example of how you should change your `web.config` file to work with SQL Server cache invalidation. The `pollTime` attribute isn't needed if you're using SQL Server 2005 notification because it uses database events instead of the polling needed for earlier versions.

Listing 23-5: Configuring the web.config file

```
<configuration xmlns="http://schemas.microsoft.com/.NetConfiguration/v2.0">

   <connectionStrings>
      <add name="AppConnectionString1" connectionString="Data Source=localhost;
        User ID=sa;Password=wrox;Database=Northwind;Persist Security Info=False"
```

```
        providerName="System.Data.SqlClient" />
    </connectionStrings>

    <system.web>

      <caching>
        <sqlCacheDependency enabled="true">
          <databases>
            <add name="Northwind" connectionStringName="AppConnectionString1"
             pollTime="500" />
          </databases>
        </sqlCacheDependency>
      </caching>

    </system.web>
</configuration>
```

From this listing, you can see that the first thing established is the connection string to the Northwind database using the <connectionStrings> element in the web.config file. Note the name of the connection string because it is utilized later in the configuration settings for SQL Server cache invalidation.

The SQL Server cache invalidation is configured using the new <caching> element. This element must be nested within the <system.web> elements. Because you are working with a SQL Server cache dependency, you must use a <sqlCacheDependency> child node. You enable the entire process by using the enabled = "true" attribute. After this attribute is enabled, you work with the <databases> section. You use the <add> element, nested within the <databases> nodes, to reference the Northwind database. The following table explains all the attributes of the <add> element.

Attribute	Description
Name	The name attribute provides an identifier to the SQL Server database.
connectionStringName	The connectionStringName attribute specifies the name of the connection. Because the connection string in the preceding example is called AppConnectionString1, you use this value for the connectionStringName attribute as well.
pollTime	The pollTime attribute specifies the time interval from one SQL Server poll to the next. The default is .5 seconds or 500 milliseconds (as shown in the example). This is not needed for SQL Server 2005 notification.

Now that the web.config file is set up correctly, you can start using SQL Server cache invalidation on your pages. ASP.NET makes a separate SQL Server request on a completely different thread to the AspNet_SqlCacheTablesForChangeNotification table to see if the changeId number has been incremented. If the number is changed, ASP.NET knows that an underlying change has been made to the SQL Server table and that a new result set should be retrieved. When it checks to see if it should make a SQL Server call, the request to the small AspNet_SqlCacheTablesForChangeNotification table has a single result. With SQL Server cache invalidation enabled, this is done so quickly that you really notice the difference.

Testing SQL Server Cache Invalidation

Now that the web.config file is set up and ready to go, the next step is to actually apply these new capabilities to a page. Listing 23-6 is an example of a page using the SQL Server cache invalidation process.

Listing 23-6: An ASP.NET page utilizing SQL Server cache invalidation

VB

```
<%@ Page Language="VB" %>
<%@ OutputCache Duration="3600" VaryByParam="none"
    SqlDependency="Northwind:Customers"%>

<script runat="server">
    Protected Sub Page_Load(ByVal sender As Object, ByVal e As System.EventArgs)
        Label1.Text = "Page created at " & DateTime.Now.ToShortTimeString ()
    End Sub
</script>

<html xmlns="http://www.w3.org/1999/xhtml" >
<head runat="server">
    <title>Sql Cache Invalidation</title>
</head>
<body>
    <form id="form1" runat="server">
        <asp:Label ID="Label1" Runat="server"></asp:Label><br />
        <br />
        <asp:GridView ID="GridView1" Runat="server" DataSourceID="SqlDataSource1">
        </asp:GridView>
        <asp:SqlDataSource ID="SqlDataSource1" Runat="server"
         SelectCommand="Select * From Customers"
         ConnectionString="<%$ ConnectionStrings:AppConnectionString1 %>"
        ProviderName="<%$ ConnectionStrings:AppConnectionString1.providername %>">
        </asp:SqlDataSource>
    </form>
</body>
</html>
```

C#

```
<%@ Page Language="C#" %>
<%@ OutputCache Duration="3600" VaryByParam="none"
    SqlDependency="Northwind:Customers"%>

<script runat="server">
    protected void Page_Load(object sender, System.EventArgs e)
    {
        Label1.Text = "Page created at " + DateTime.Now.ToShortTimeString();
    }
</script>
```

The first and most important part of this page is the OuputCache page directive that is specified at the top of the file. Typically, the OutputCache directive specifies how long the page output is held in the cache using the `Duration` attribute. Next is the `VaryByParam` attribute. The new addition is the `SqlDependency` attribute. This enables a particular page to use SQL Server cache invalidation. The following line shows the format of the value for the `SqlDependency` attribute:

```
SqlDependency="database:table"
```

The value of `Northwind:Customers` specifies that you want the SQL Server cache invalidation enabled for the Customers table within the Northwind database. The `Duration` attribute of the `OutputCache` directive shows you that, typically, the output of this page is stored in the cache for a long time — but this cache is invalidated immediately if the Customers table has any underlying changes made to the data that it contains.

A change to any of the cells in the Customers table of the Northwind database invalidates the cache, and a new cache is generated from the result, which now contains a new SQL Server database request. Figure 23-6 shows an example of the page generated the first time it is run.

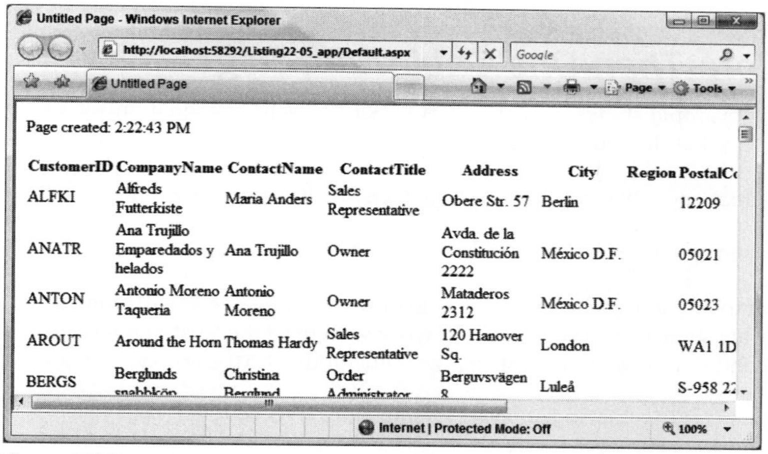

Figure 23-6

From this figure, you can see the contents of the customer with the `CustomerID` of `ALFKI`. For this entry, go to SQL Server and change the value of the `ContactName` from `Maria Anders` to `Mary Anders`. If we weren't using SQL Server cache invalidation, this change would have done nothing to the output cache. The original page output in the cache would still be present and the end user would still see the `Maria Anders` entry for the duration specified in the page's `OutputCache` directive. But because we're using SQL Server cache invalidation, after the underlying information in the table is changed, the output cache is invalidated, a new result set is retrieved, and the new result set is cached. When a change has been made, you see the results as shown in Figure 23-7.

Notice also that the text "Page created at" includes an updated time indicating when this page was rendered. Need to stop working so late, eh?

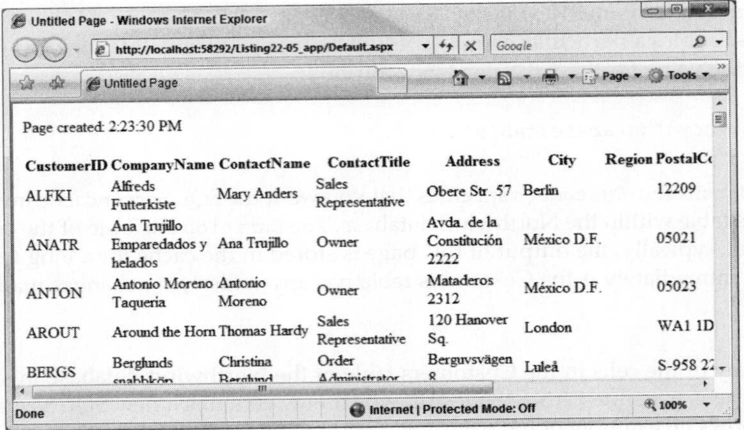

Figure 23-7

Adding More Than One Table to a Page

The preceding example shows how to use SQL Server cache invalidation for a single table on the ASP.NET page. What do you do if your page is working with two or more tables?

To add more than one table, you use the `OutputCache` directive shown here:

```
SqlDependency="database:table;database:table"
```

From this example, you can see that the value of the `SqlDependency` attribute separates the databases and tables with a semicolon. If you want to work with both the Customers table and the Products table of the Northwind database, you construct the value of the `SqlDependency` attribute as follows:

```
SqlDependency="Northwind:Customers;Northwind:Products"
```

Attaching SQL Server Cache Dependencies to the Request Object

In addition to changing settings in the `OutputCache` directive to activate SQL Server cache invalidation, you can also set the SQL Server cache invalidation programmatically. To do so, use the `SqlCacheDependency` class, which is illustrated in Listing 23-7.

Listing 23-7: Working with SQL Server cache invalidation programmatically

VB

```
Dim myDependency As SqlCacheDependency = _
    New SqlCacheDependency("Northwind", "Customers")
Response.AddCacheDependency(myDependency)
Response.Cache.SetValidUntilExpires(true)
Response.Cache.SetExpires(DateTime.Now.AddMinutes(60))
```

```
Response.Cache.SetCacheability(HttpCacheability.Public)
```

C#

```
SqlCacheDependency myDependency = new SqlCacheDependency("Northwind", "Customers");
Response.AddCacheDependency(myDependency);
Response.Cache.SetValidUntilExpires(true);
Response.Cache.SetExpires(DateTime.Now.AddMinutes(60));
Response.Cache.SetCacheability(HttpCacheability.Public);
```

You first create an instance of the `SqlCacheDependency` object, assigning it the value of the database and the table at the same time. The `SqlCacheDependency` class takes the following parameters:

```
SqlCacheDependency(databaseEntryName As String, tablename As String)
```

You use this parameter construction if you are working with SQL Server 7.0 or with SQL Server 2000. If you are working with SQL Server 2005, you use the following construction:

```
SqlCacheDependency(sqlCmd As System.Data.SqlClient.SqlCommand)
```

After the `SqlCacheDependency` class is in place, you add the dependency to the `Cache` object and set some of the properties of the `Cache` object as well. You can do this either programmatically or through the `OutputCache` directive.

Attaching SQL Server Cache Dependencies to the Cache Object

In addition to attaching SQL Server cache dependencies to the `Request` object, you can attach them to the `Cache` object for data that can be cached much longer. The `Cache` object is contained within the `System.Web.Caching` namespace, and it enables you to work programmatically with the caching of any type of objects. Listing 23-8 shows a page that utilizes the `Cache` object with the `SqlDependency` object.

Listing 23-8: Using the Cache object with the SqlDependency object

VB

```
<%@ Page Language="VB" %>
<%@ Import Namespace="System.Data"%>
<%@ Import Namespace="System.Data.SqlClient"%>

<script runat="server">
    Protected Sub Page_Load(ByVal sender As Object, ByVal e As System.EventArgs)
        Dim myCustomers As DataSet
        myCustomers = CType(Cache("firmCustomers"), DataSet)

        If myCustomers Is Nothing Then
           Dim conn As SqlConnection = _
            New SqlConnection( _
 ConfigurationManager.ConnectionStrings("AppConnectionString1").ConnectionString)
           Dim da As SqlDataAdapter = _
```

Continued

```
            New SqlDataAdapter("Select * From Customers", conn)

           myCustomers = New DataSet
           da.Fill(myCustomers)

           Dim myDependency As SqlCacheDependency = _
              New SqlCacheDependency("Northwind", "Customers")
           Cache.Insert("firmCustomers", myCustomers, myDependency)

           Label1.Text = "Produced from database."
        Else
           Label1.Text = "Produced from Cache object."
        End If

        GridView1.DataSource = myCustomers
        GridView1.DataBind()
    End Sub
</script>

<html xmlns="http://www.w3.org/1999/xhtml" >
<head runat="server">
    <title>Sql Cache Invalidation</title>
</head>
<body>
    <form id="form1" runat="server">
        <asp:Label ID="Label1" Runat="server"></asp:Label><br />
        <br />
        <asp:GridView ID="GridView1" Runat="server"></asp:GridView>
    </form>
</body>
</html>
```

C#

```
<%@ Page Language="C#" %>
<%@ Import Namespace="System.Data" %>
<%@ Import Namespace="System.Data.SqlClient" %>

<script runat="server">
    protected void Page_Load(object sender, System.EventArgs e)
    {
       DataSet myCustomers;
       myCustomers = (DataSet)Cache["firmCustomers"];

       if (myCustomers == null)
       {
          SqlConnection conn = new
           SqlConnection(
  ConfigurationManager.ConnectionStrings["AppConnectionString1"].ConnectionString);
          SqlDataAdapter da = new
             SqlDataAdapter("Select * from Customers", conn);

          myCustomers = new DataSet();
```

```
            da.Fill(myCustomers);

            SqlCacheDependency myDependency = new
               SqlCacheDependency("Northwind", "Customers");
            Cache.Insert("firmCustomers", myCustomers, myDependency);

            Label1.Text = "Produced from database.";
         }
         else
         {
            Label1.Text = "Produced from Cache object.";
         }

         GridView1.DataSource = myCustomers;
         GridView1.DataBind();
   }
   </script>
```

In this example, the `SqlCacheDependency` class associated itself to the Customers table in the Northwind database as before. This time, however, you use the `Cache` object to insert the retrieved dataset along with a reference to the `SqlCacheDependency` object. The `Insert` method of the `Cache` class is constructed as follows:

```
Cache.Insert(key As String, value As Object,
   dependencies As System.Web.Caching.CacheDependency)
```

You can also insert more information about the dependency using the following construct:

```
Cache.Insert(key As String, value As Object,
   dependencies As System.Web.Caching.CacheDependency
   absoluteExpiration As Date, slidingExpiration As System.TimeSpan)
```

And finally:

```
Cache.Insert(key As String, value As Object,
   dependencies As System.Web.Caching.CacheDependency
   absoluteExpiration As Date, slidingExpiration As System.TimeSpan)
   priority As System.Web.Caching.CacheItemPriority,
   onRemoveCallback As System.Web.Caching.CacheItemRemovedCallback)
```

The SQL Server cache dependency created comes into action and does the same polling as it would have done otherwise. If any of the data in the Customers table has changed, the `SqlCacheDependency` class invalidates what is stored in the cache. When the next request is made, the `Cache("firmCustomers")` is found to be empty and a new request is made to SQL Server. The `Cache` object again repopulates the cache with the new results generated.

When the ASP.NET page from Listing 23-8 is called for the first time, the results generated are shown in Figure 23-8.

Because this is the first time that the page is generated, nothing is in the cache. The `Cache` object is, therefore, placed in the result set along with the association to the SQL Server cache dependency. Figure 23-9 shows the result for the second request. Notice that the HTML table is identical because it was generated from the identical `DataSet`, but the first line of the page has changed to indicate that this output was produced from cache.

On the second request, the dataset is already contained within the cache; therefore, it is retrievable. You aren't required to hit SQL Server to get the full results again. If any of the information has changed within SQL Server itself, however, the `Cache` object returns nothing; a new result set is retrieved.

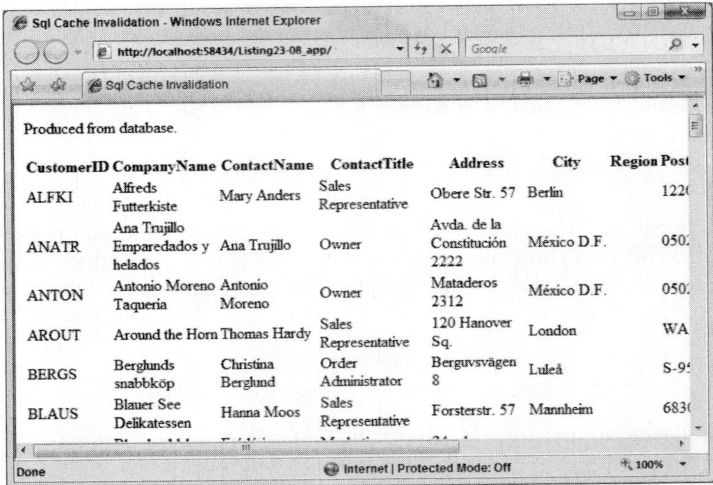

Figure 23-8

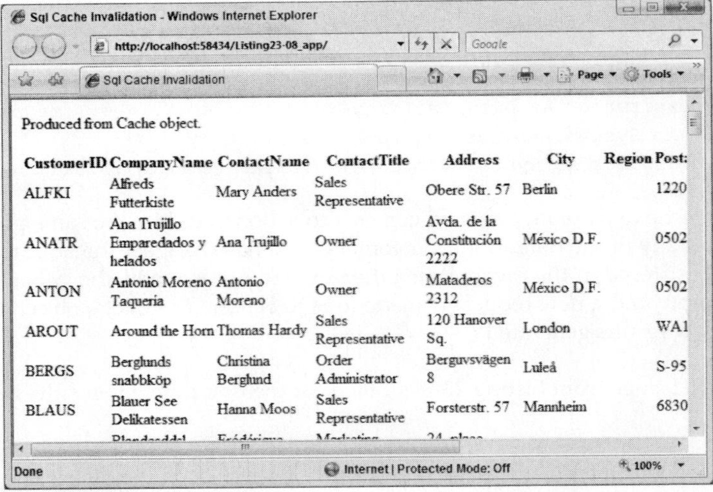

Figure 23-9

Summary

SQL Server cache invalidation is an outstanding feature of ASP.NET that enables you to invalidate items stored in the cache when underlying changes occur to the data in the tables being monitored. Post-Cache Substitution fills in an important gap in ASP.NET's technology, enabling you to have both the best highly dynamic content and a high-performance Web site with caching.

When you are monitoring changes to the database, you can configure these procedures easily in the `web.config` file, or you can work programmatically with cache invalidation directly in your code. These changes are possible because the `CacheDependency` object has been unsealed. You can now inherit from this object and create your own cache dependencies. The SQL Server cache invalidation process is the first example of this capability.

24

Debugging and Error Handling

Your code always runs exactly as you wrote it, and you will *never* get it right the first time. So, expect to spend about 30 percent of your time debugging and, to be a successful debugger, learn to use the available tools effectively. Visual Studio has upped the ante, giving you a host of new features that greatly improve your debugging experience. So many of these new features, however, can be overwhelming at first. This chapter breaks down all the techniques available to you, one at a time, while presenting a holistic view of Visual Studio, the Common Language Runtime (CLR), and the Base Class Library (BCL).

> *Everyone knows that debugging is twice as hard as writing a program in the first place. So if you're as clever as you can be when you write it, how will you ever debug it?*
>
> — ***Brian Kernighan***

Additionally, because debugging is more than stepping through code, this chapter discusses efficient error and exception handling, tracing and logging, and cross-language (C#, Visual Basic, client-side JavaScript, XSLT, and SQL Stored Procedure) debugging.

Design-Time Support

Visual Studio has always done a good job of warning you of potential errors at design time. *Syntax notifications* or *squiggles* underline code that won't compile or that might cause an error before you have compiled the project. A *new error notification* pops up when an exception occurs during a debugging session and recommends a course of action that prevents the exception. At every step, Visual Studio tries to be smarter, anticipating your needs and catching common mistakes.

Rico Mariani, the Chief Architect of Visual Studio, has used the term "The Pit of Success" to describe the experience Microsoft wants you to have with Visual Studio. When Microsoft designed these new features, they wanted the customer to simply fall into winning practices. The company tried to achieve this by making it more difficult for you to write buggy code or make common mistakes. Microsoft's developers put a great deal of thought into building APIs that point you in the right direction.

Syntax Notifications

Both the Visual Basic and C# editors show squiggles and tooltips for many syntax errors well before compilation, as illustrated in Figure 24-1.

```
for(int i; i < 5; i++;)
{                              Invalid expression term ')'
    Response.Wite();
}
```

Figure 24-1

Syntax notifications aren't just for CLR programming languages; Visual Studio has also greatly improved the XML Editor since its original release with enhancements like the following:

- Full XML 1.0 syntax checking
- Support for XSD and DTD validation and IntelliSense
- Support for XSLT 1.0 syntax checking

Figure 24-2 shows a detailed tooltip indicating that the element `<junk>` doesn't have any business being in the `web.config` file. The editor knows this because of a combination of the XSD validation support in the XML Editor and the addition of schemas for configuration files such as `web.config`. This is a welcome change for anyone who, when manually editing a `web.config` file, has wondered if he guessed the right elements. See Chapter 10 for more details on these XML-related features.

```
<?xml version='1.0'?>
<!-- This file is a part of a book store inventory database -->
<bookstore xmlns="http://example.books.com"
  xmlns:xsi="http://www.w3.org/2001/XMLSchema-instance"
  xsi:schemaLocation="http://example.books.com Books.xsd">
  <junk></junk>
  <The element 'bookstore' in namespace 'http://example.books.com' has invalid child element 'junk' in namespace 'http://example.books.com'.
   List of possible elements expected: 'book' in namespace 'http://example.books.com'.
      <author>
          <first-name>Benjamin</first-name>
          <last-name>Franklin</last-name>
      </author>
      <price>8.99</price>
  </book>
```

Figure 24-2

The ASPX/HTML Editor benefits from these improvements as well; for example, Figure 24-3 shows a warning that the `<hanselman/>` element is not available in the active schema. Code that appears in `<script runat="Server"/>` blocks in ASP.NET pages is also parsed and marked with squiggles. This makes including code in your pages considerably easier. Notice also that the ASP.NET page in Figure 24-3 has an XHTML DOCTYPE declaration on the first line, and the HTML element has a default XHTML namespace. This HTML page is treated as XML because XHTML has been targeted.

XHTML is the HTML vocabulary of markup expressed with all the syntax rules of XML. For example, in HTML you could create a `<br>` tag and never close it. In XHTML you use the closing tag `<br />`. XHTML documents look exactly like HTML documents because they *are*, in fact, expressing the same semantics. Because XHTML documents are XML, they require a namespace on their root element and should have a `DOCTYPE` as well.

```
<!DOCTYPE html PUBLIC "-//W3C//DTD XHTML 1.0 Transitional//EN"
<html xmlns="http://www.w3.org/1999/xhtml" >
<head runat="server">
    <title>Untitled Page</title>
</head>
<body>
    <hanselman></hanselman>
    <Validation (XHTML 1.0 Transitional): Element 'hanselman' is not supported.
    <div>

    </div>
    </form>
</body>
</html>
```

Figure 24-3

To add a `hanselman` element, you must put it in its own namespace and add a namespace declaration in the root HTML element.

The Visual Basic Editor takes assistance to the next level with a *smart tag* like the pulldown/button that appears when you hover your mouse over a squiggle. A very nicely rendered modeless window appears with your code in a box along with some suggested changes to make your code compile. Figure 24-4 shows a recommendation to insert a missing `End If`; making the correction is simple — just click `Insert the missing 'End If'`.

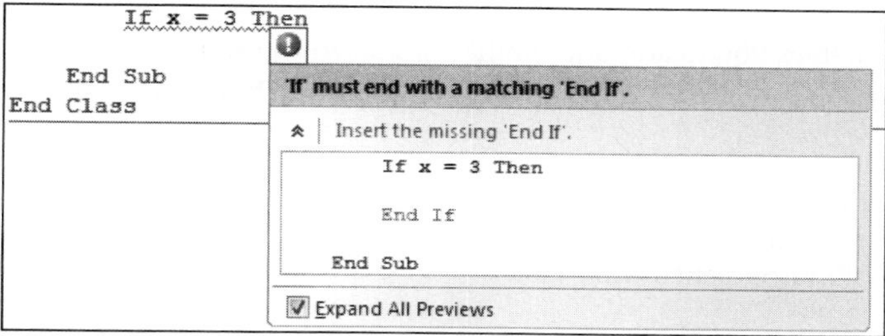

Figure 24-4

All these design-time features exist to help you ensure better code while it's being written, before it's been compiled and run. Two related features help you run arbitrary code within the development environment as well as organize the tasks still to be performed.

Immediate and Command Window

The Immediate Window lets you run arbitrary bits of code in Design mode without compiling your application. You can evaluate code at design time or while you're debugging. It can be a great way to test a line of code or a static method quickly. The Immediate mode of this window is used primarily for debugging.

Access the Immediate Window from Debug ➪ Windows ➪ Immediate. To evaluate a variable or run a method, simply click in the Immediate Window and type a question mark (?) followed by the expression, variable, or method you want to evaluate.

The immediate window can also be switched into the Command Window by prefacing commands with a greater-than sign (>). When you enter a greater-than sign in the Immediate/Command Window, an IntelliSense drop-down appears exposing the complete Visual Studio object model as well as any macros that you may have recorded. Command mode of this window is used for executing Visual Studio Commands without using the menus. You can also execute commands that may not have a menu item.

If you type `>alias` into the Command window, you receive a complete list of all current aliases and their definitions. Some useful command aliases include the following:

- `>Log filename /overwrite /on|off`: The `Log` command starts logging all output from the command window to a file. If no filename is included for logging, go to `cmdline.log`. This is one of the more useful and least-used features of the debugger, and reason enough to learn a few things about the immediate/Command Window.
- `>Shell args /command /output /dir:folder`: The `Shell` command allows you to launch executable programs from within the Visual Studio Command window such as utilities, command shells, batch files, and so on.

Task List

The Task list in Visual Studio is more useful than you might think. People who haven't given it much attention are missing out on a great feature. The Task list supports two views: User Tasks and Comments.

User Tasks view enables you to add and modify tasks, which can include anything from "Remember to Test" to "Buy Milk." These tasks are stored in the .suo (solution user options) that is a parallel partner to the .sln files.

The Comments view shows text from the comments in your code where those lines are prefixed with a specific token. Visual Studio comes configured to look for the `TODO:` token, but you can add your own in Tools ➪ Options ➪ Environment ➪ Task List.

In Figure 24-5, the comment token `HACK` has been added in the Options dialog box. A comment appears in the source with `HACK:` preceding it, so that comment line automatically appears in the Task List in the docked window at the bottom of Visual Studio. The three circles in Figure 24-5 illustrate the connection between the word `HACK` added to the Options dialog box and its subsequent appearance in the source code and Task List. You and your team can add as many of these tokens as you'd like.

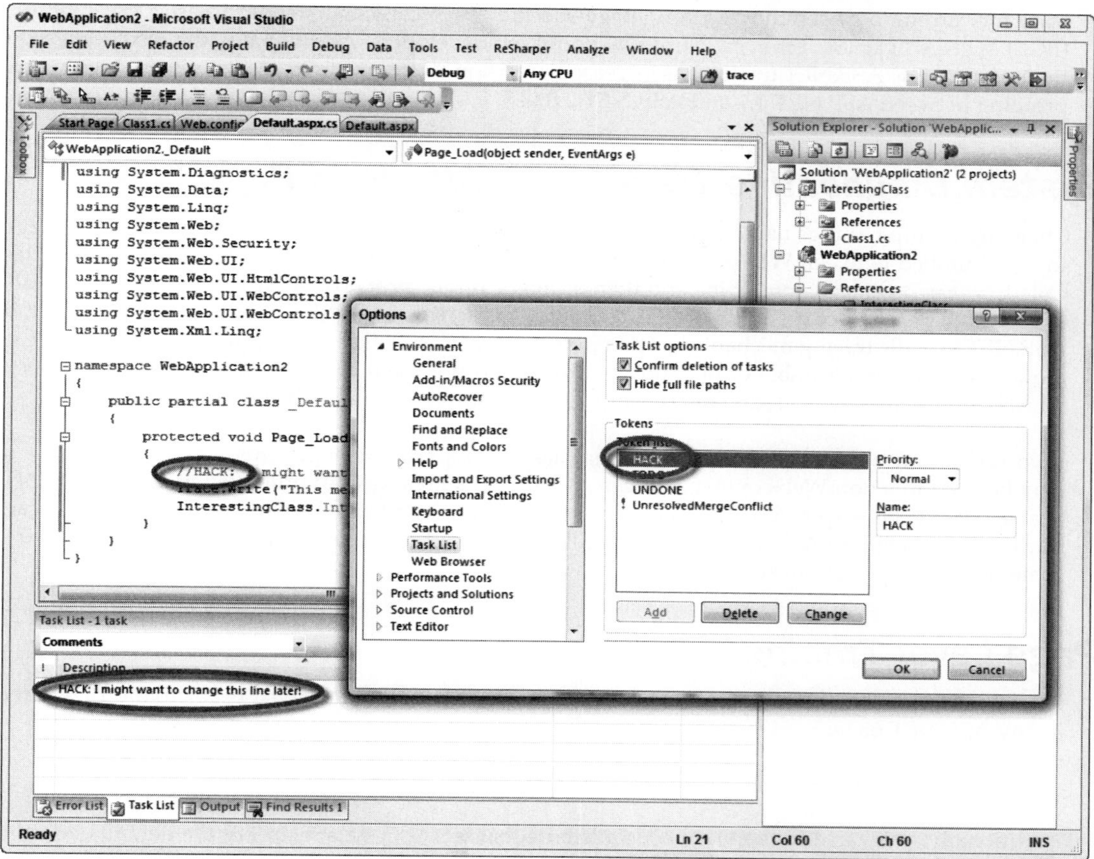

Figure 24-5

Tracing

Tracing is a way to monitor the execution of your ASP.NET application. You can record exception details and program flow in a way that doesn't affect the program's output. In classic ASP, tracing and debugging facilities were nearly nonexistent, forcing developers to use "got here" debugging in the form of many `Response.Write` statements that litter the resulting HTML with informal trace statements announcing to the programmer that the program "got here" and "got there" with each new line executed. This kind of intrusive tracing was very inconvenient to clean up and many programmers ended up creating their own informal trace libraries to get around these classic ASP limitations.

In ASP.NET, there is rich support for tracing. The destination for trace output can be configured with TraceListeners like the `EventLogTraceListener`. Configuration of TraceListeners is covered later in this section. ASP.NET also includes a number of small improvements to tracing over ASP.NET 1.*x*, including trace forwarding between the ASP.NET page-specific `Trace` class and standard Base Class Library's (BCL) `System.Diagnostics.Trace` used by non–Web developers. Additionally, the resolution of the timing output by ASP.NET tracing has increased precision — from 6 digits to 18 digits for highly accurate profiling between ASP.NET 1.1 and ASP.NET 2.0/3.5.

System.Diagnostics.Trace and ASP.NET's Page.Trace

There are multiple things named *Trace* in the whole of the .NET Framework, so it may appear that tracing isn't unified between Web and non-Web applications. Don't be confused because there is a class called `System.Diagnostics.Trace` and there is also a public property on `System.Web.UI.Page` called `Trace`. The `Trace` property on the `Page` class gives you access to the `System.Web.TraceContext` and the ASP.NET-specific tracing mechanism. The `TraceContext` class collects all the details and timing of a Web request. It contains a number of methods, but the one you'll use the most is `Write`. It also includes `Warn`, which simply calls `Write()`, and also ensures that the output generated by `Warn` is colored red.

If you're writing an ASP.NET application that has no supporting components or other assemblies that may be used in a non-Web context, you can usually get a great deal of utility using only the ASP.NET `TraceContext`. However, ASP.NET support tracing is different from the rest of the base class library's tracing. You'll explore ASP.NET's tracing facilities first, and then learn how to bridge the gap and see some new features that make debugging even easier.

Page-Level Tracing

ASP.NET tracing can be enabled on a page-by-page basis by adding `Trace="true"` to the Page directive in any ASP.NET page:

```
<%@ Page Language="C#" Inherits="System.Web.UI.Page" Trace="true" %>
```

Additionally, you can add the `TraceMode` attribute that sets `SortByCategory` or the default, `SortByTime`. You might include a number of categories, one per subsystem, and use `SortByCategory` to group them, or you might use `SortByTime` to see the methods that take up the most CPU time for your application. You can enable tracing programmatically as well, using the `Trace.IsEnabled` property. The capability to enable tracing programmatically means you can enable tracing via a querystring, cookie, or IP address; it's up to you.

Application Tracing

Alternatively, you can enable tracing for the entire application by adding tracing settings in `web.config`. In the following example, `pageOutput="false"` and `requestLimit="20"` are used, so trace information is stored for 20 requests, but not displayed on the page:

```
<configuration>
    <system.web>
        <trace enabled="true" pageOutput="false" requestLimit="20"
            traceMode="SortByTime" localOnly="true" />
    </system.web>
</configuration>
```

The page-level settings take precedence over settings in `web.config`, so if `enabled="false"` is set in `web.config` but `trace="true"` is set on the page, tracing occurs.

Viewing Trace Data

Tracing can be viewed for multiple page requests at the application level by requesting a special page (of sorts) called `trace.axd`. Note that `trace.axd` doesn't actually exist; it is actually provided by `System.Web.Handlers.TraceHandler`, a special `IHttpHandler` to which `trace.axd` is bound. When ASP.NET detects an HTTP Request for `trace.axd`, that request is handled by the `TraceHandler` rather than by a page.

Create a Web site and a page, and in the `Page_Load` event, call `Trace.Write()`. Enable tracing in the `web.config` as shown in Listing 24-1.

Listing 24-1: Tracing using Page.Trace

Web.config

```
<configuration>
   <system.web>
       <trace enabled="true" pageOutput="true" />
   </system.web>
</configuration>
```

VB

```
Protected Sub Page_Load(ByVal sender As Object, ByVal e As System.EventArgs)
   Handles Me.Load 'All on one line!
       Trace.Write("This message is from the START OF the Page_Load method!")
End Sub
```

C#

```
protected void Page_Load(object sender, EventArgs e)
{
   Trace.Write("This message is from the START of the Page_Load method!");
}
```

Hit the page in the browser a few times and notice that, although this page doesn't create any HTML to speak of, a great deal of trace information is presented in the browser, as shown in Figure 24-6, because the setting is `pageOutput="true"`.

The message from `Trace.Write` appears after Begin Load and before End Load — it's right in the middle of the `Page_Load` method where you put it. The page was automatically JIT-compiled as you ran it, and that initial performance hit is over. Now that it's been compiled into native code, a subsequent run of this same page, performed by clicking Refresh in the browser, took only 0.000167 seconds on my laptop because the page had already compiled. It's very easy and very useful to collect this kind of very valuable performance timing data between Trace statements.

> **Incidentally, this simple page is more than 100 times faster than when the first edition of this book was written in 2004. Both computers and the JITter continue to improve!**

Eleven different sections of tracing information provide a great deal of detail and specific insight into the ASP.NET page-rendering process, as described in the following table.

Section	Description
Request Details	Includes the ASP.NET Session ID, the character encoding of the request and response, and the HTTP conversation's returned status code. Be aware of the request and response encoding, especially if you're using any non-Latin character sets. If you're returning languages other than English, you'll want your encoding to be UTF-8. Fortunately that is the default.
Trace Information	Includes all the `Trace.Write` methods called during the lifetime of the HTTP request and a great deal of information about timing. This is probably the most useful section for debugging. The timing information located here is valuable when profiling and searching for methods in your application that take too long to execute.
Control Tree	Presents an HTML representation of the ASP.NET Control Tree. Shows each control's unique ID, runtime type, the number of bytes it took to be rendered, and the bytes it requires in ViewState and ControlState. Don't undervalue the usefulness of these two sections, particularly of the three columns showing the weight of each control. The weight of the control indicates the number of bytes occupied in ViewState and/or ControlState by that particular Control. Be aware of the number of bytes that each of your controls uses, especially if you write your own custom controls, as you want your controls to return as few bytes as possible to keep overall page weight down.
Session State	Lists all the keys for a particular user's session, their types, and their values. Shows only the current user's Session State.
Application State	Lists all the keys in the current application's Application object and their types and values.
Request Cookies	Lists all the cookies passed in during the page's request.
Response Cookies	Lists all the cookies that were passed back during the page's response.
Headers Collection	Shows all the headers that might be passed in during the request from the browser, including Accept-Encoding, indicating whether the browser supports compressed HTTP responses; Accept-Languages, a list of ISO language codes that indicate the order of the user's language preferences; and User-Agent, the identifying string for the user's browser. The string also contains information about the user's operating system and the version or versions of the .NET Framework he is running (on IE).
Form Collection	Displays a complete dump of the Form collection and all its keys and values.
Querystring Collection	Displays a dump of the Querystring collection and all its contained keys and values.
Server Variables	A complete dump of name-value pairs of everything that the Web server knows about the application and the requesting browser.

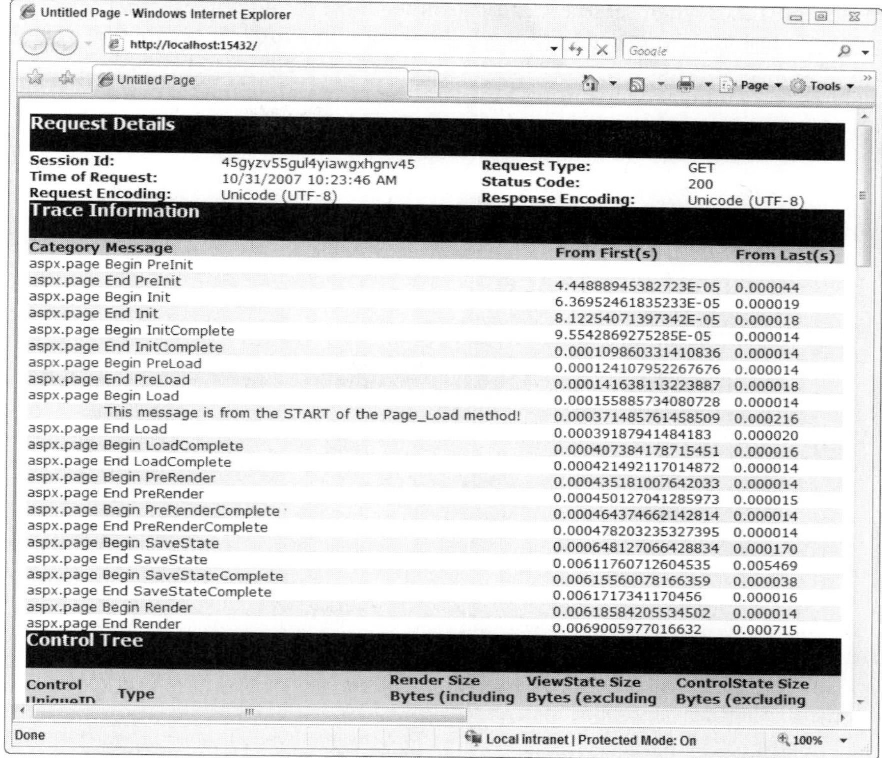

Figure 24-6

Page output of tracing shows only the data collected for the current page request. However, when visiting `http://localhost/yoursite/trace.axd` you'll see detailed data collected for all requests to the site thus far. If you're using the built-in ASP.NET Development Server, remove the current page from the URL and replace it with `trace.axd`. Don't change the automatically selected port or path.

Again, `trace.axd` is an internal handler, not a real page. When it's requested from a local browser, as shown in Figure 24-7, it displays all tracing information for all requests up to a preset limit.

Figure 24-7 shows that nine requests have been made to this application and the right side of the header indicates "Remaining: 1". That means that there is one more request remaining before tracing stops for this application. After that final request, tracing data is not saved until an application recycle or until you click "Clear current trace" from the `trace.axd` page. The request limit can be raised in `web.config` at the expense of memory:

```
<trace requestLimit="100" pageOutput="true" enabled="true"/>
```

The maximum request limit value is 10000. If you try to use any greater value, ASP.NET uses 10000 anyway and gives you no error. However, a new property called `mostRecent` was added to the trace section in ASP.NET 2.0. When set to `true`, it shows the most recent requests that are stored in the trace log up to the request limit — instead of showing tracing in the order it occurs (the default) — without using up a lot of memory. Setting `mostRecent` to true causes memory to be used only for the trace information it stores and automatically throws away tracing information over the `requestLimit`.

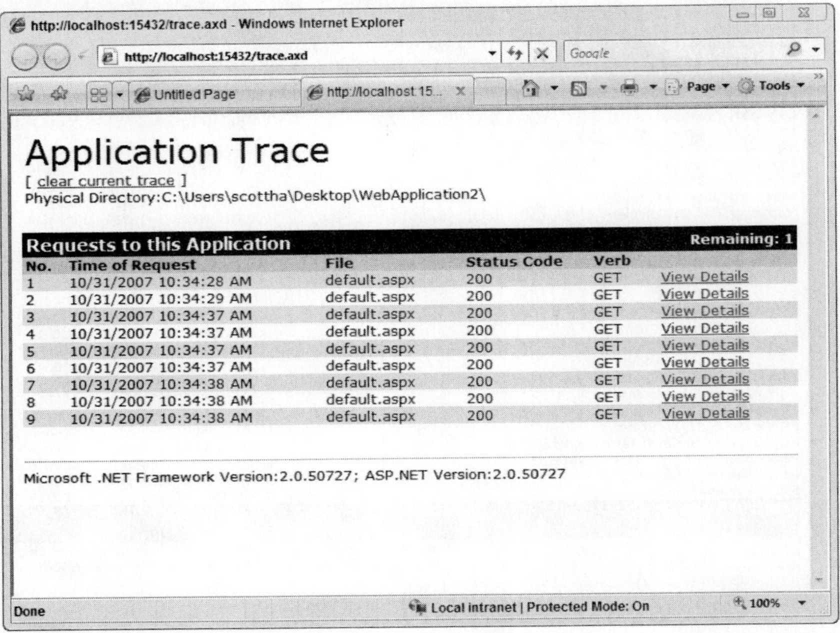

Figure 24-7

Clicking View Details from `Trace.axd` on any of these requests takes you to a request-specific page with the same details shown in Figure 24-6.

Tracing from Components

The tracing facilities of ASP.NET are very powerful and can stand alone. However, previously we mentioned `System.Diagnostics.Trace`, the tracing framework in the Base Class Library that is not Web-specific and that receives consistent and complete tracing information when an ASP.NET application calls a non–Web-aware component. This can be confusing. Which should you use?

`System.Diagnostics.Trace` is the core .NET Framework tracing library. Along with `System.Diagnostics.Debug`, this class provides flexible, non-invasive tracing and debug output for any application. But, as mentioned earlier, there is rich tracing built into the `System.Web` namespace. As a Web developer, you'll find yourself using ASP.NET's tracing facilities. You may need to have ASP.NET-specific tracing forwarded to the base framework's `System.Diagnostics.Trace`, or more likely, you'll want to have your non–Web-aware components output their trace calls to ASP.NET so you can take advantage of `trace.axd` and other ASP.NET specific features.

Additionally, some confusion surrounds Trace.Write and Debug.Write functions. Look at the source code for Debug.Write, and you see something like this:

```
[Conditional("DEBUG")]
public static void Write(string message)
{
     TraceInternal.Write(message);
}
```

Notice that Debug.Write calls a function named TraceInternal.Write, which has a conditional attribute indicating that Debug.Write is compiled only if the debug preprocessor directive was set. In other words, you can put as many calls to Debug.Write as you want in your application without affecting your performance when you compile in Release mode. This enables you to be as verbose as you want to be during the debugging phase of development.

TraceInternal cycles through all attached trace listeners, meaning all classes that derive from the TraceListener base class and are configured in that application's configuration file. The default TraceListener lives in the aptly named DefaultTraceListener class and calls the Win32 API OutputDebugString. OutputDebugString sends your string into the abyss and, if a debugger is listening, it is displayed. If no debugger is listening, OutputDebugString does nothing. Everyone knows the debugger listens for output from OutputDebugString so this can be a very effective way to listen in on debug versions of your application.

For quick and dirty no-touch debugging, try using DbgView from SysInternals at www.sysinternals.com/ntw2k/freeware/debugview.shtml**. DbgView requires no installation, works great with all your calls to Debug.Writer, and has lots of cool features such as highlighting and logging to a file.**

Now, if you look at the source code for Trace.Write (that's TRACE not DEBUG), you see something like this:

```
[Conditional("TRACE")]
public static void Write(string message)
{
     TraceInternal.Write(message);
}
```

The only difference between Debug.Write and Trace.Write given these two source snippets is the conditional attribute indicating the preprocessor directive TRACE. You can conditionally compile your assemblies to include tracing statements, debug statements, both, or neither. Most people keep TRACE defined even for release builds and use the configuration file to turn tracing on and off. More than likely, the benefits you gain from making tracing available to your users far outweigh any performance issues that might arise.

Because Trace.Write calls the DefaultTraceListener just like Debug.Write, you can use any debugger to tap into tracing information. So, what's the difference?

When designing your application, think about your deployment model. Are you going to ship debug builds or release builds? Do you want a way for end users or systems engineers to debug your application using log files or the event viewer? Are there things you want only the developer to see?

Typically, you want to use tracing and `Trace.Write` for any formal information that could be useful in debugging your application in a production environment. `Trace.Write` gives you everything that `Debug.Write` does, except it uses the `TRACE` preprocessor directive and is not affected by debug or release builds.

This means you have four possibilities for builds: Debug On, Trace On, Both On, or Neither On. You choose what's right for you. Typically, use Both On for debug builds and Trace On for production builds. You can specify these conditional attributes in the property pages or the command line of the compiler, as well as with the C# `#define` keyword or `#CONST` keyword for Visual Basic.

Trace Forwarding

You often find existing ASP.NET applications that have been highly instrumented and make extensive use of the ASP.NET `TraceContext` class. ASP.NET version 2.0 introduces a new attribute to the `web.config` `<trace>` element that allows you to route messages emitted by ASP.NET tracing to `System.Diagnostics.Trace`: `writeToDiagnosticsTrace`.

```
<trace writeToDiagnosticsTrace="true" pageOutput="true" enabled="true"/>
```

When you set `writeToDiagnosticsTrace` to `true`, all calls to `System.Web.UI.Page.Trace.Write` (the ASP.NET TraceContext) also go to `System.Diagnostics.Trace.Write`, enabling you to use all the standard TraceListeners and tracing options that are covered later in this chapter. The simple `writeToDiagnoticsTrace` setting connects the ASP.NET tracing functionality with the rest of the base class library. I use this feature when I'm deep in debugging my pages, and it's easily turned off using this configuration switch. I believe that more information is better than less, but you may find the exact page event information too verbose. Try it and form your own opinion.

TraceListeners

Output from `System.Diagnostics.Trace` methods is routable by a TraceListener to a text file, to ASP.NET, to an external monitoring system, even to a database. This powerful facility is a woefully underused tool in many ASP.NET developers' tool belts. In ASP.NET 1.1, some component developers who knew their components were being used within ASP.NET would introduce a direct reference to `System.Web` and call `HttpContext.Current.Trace`. They did this so that their tracing information would appear in the developer-friendly ASP.NET format. All components called within the context of an `HttpRequest` automatically receive access to that request's current context, enabling the components to talk directly to the request and retrieve cookies or collect information about the user.

However, assuming an `HttpContext` will always be available is dangerous for a number of reasons. First, you are making a big assumption when you declare that your component can be used only within the context of an HttpRequest. Notice that this is said within the context of *a request*, not within the context of *an application*. If you access `HttpContext.Current` even from within the `Application_Start`, you will be surprised to find that `HttpContext.Current` is null. Second, marrying your component's functionality to `HttpContext` makes it tricky if not impossible to use your application in any non-Web context, and unit testing becomes particularly difficult.

If you have a component that is being used by a Web page, but it also needs to be unit tested outside of Web context or must be called from any other context, don't call `HttpContext.Current.Trace`. Instead, use the standard `System.Diagnostics.Trace` and redirect output to the ASP.NET tracing facilities using the new WebPageTraceListener described in the next section. Using the standard trace mechanism means your component can be used in any context, Web or otherwise. You'll still be able to view the component's trace output with a TraceListener.

The framework comes with a number of very useful TraceListeners; you can add them programmatically or via a `.config` file. For example, you can programmatically add a TraceListener log to a file, as shown in Listing 24-2. These snippets required the `System.Diagnostics` and `System.IO` namespaces.

Listing 24-2: Configuring TraceListeners

VB

```
Dim myTextListener As New TextWriterTraceListener(File.Create("c:\myListener.log"))
Trace.Listeners.Add(myTextListener)
```

C#

```
TextWriterTraceListener myTextListener = new
  TextWriterTraceListener(File.Create(@"c:\myListener.log"));
Trace.Listeners.Add(myTextListener);
```

You can do the same thing declaratively in `web.config` via an `add` element that passes in the type of TraceListener to use, along with any initializing data it might need. TraceListeners already configured in `machine.config` or a parent `web.config` can also be removed using the `remove` tag, along with their name:

```
<configuration>
 <system.diagnostics>
     <trace autoflush="false" indentsize="4">
         <listeners>
            <add name="myListener"
                type="System.Diagnostics.TextWriterTraceListener"
                initializeData="c:\myListener.log" />
            <remove name="Default" />
         </listeners>
     </trace>
 </system.diagnostics>
</configuration>
```

TraceListeners, such as `TextWriterTraceListener`, that access a resource (such as a file, event log, or database) require that the ASP.NET worker process be run as a user who has sufficient access. In order to write to `c:\foo\example.log`, for example, the ASP.NET worker process requires explicit write access in the Access Control List (ACL) of that file.

Notice the preceding example also optionally removes the default TraceListener. If you write your own TraceListener, you must provide a fully qualified assembly name in the `type` attribute.

The New ASP.NET WebPageTraceListener

The new ASP.NET `WebPageTraceListener` derives from `System.Diagnostics.TraceListener` and automatically forwards tracing information from any component calls to `System.Diagnostics.Trace.Write`.

This enables you to write your components using the most generic trace provider and to see its tracing output in the context of your ASP.NET application.

The `WebPageTraceListener` is added to the `web.config` as shown in the following example. Note that we use the fully qualified assembly name for System.Web:

```
<configuration>
 <system.diagnostics>
     <trace autoflush="false" indentsize="4">
         <listeners>
             <add name="webListener"
                type="System.Web.WebPageTraceListener, System.Web, Version=2.0.0.0,
                      Culture=neutral, PublicKeyToken=b03f5f7f11d50a3a"/>
         </listeners>
     </trace>
 </system.diagnostics>
 <system.web>
        <trace enabled="true" pageOutput="false" localOnly="true" />
 </system.web>
</configuration>
```

Figure 24-8 shows output from a call to `System.Diagnostics.Trace.Write` from a referenced library. It appears within ASP.NET's page tracing. The line generated from the referenced library is circled in this figure.

EventLogTraceListener

Tracing information can also be sent to the event log using the EventLogTraceListener. This can be a little tricky because ASP.NET requires explicit write access to the event log:

```
<configuration>
 <system.diagnostics>
     <trace autoflush="false" indentsize="4">
         <listeners>
            <add name="EventLogTraceListener"
                type="System.Diagnostics.EventLogTraceListener"
                initializeData="Wrox"/>
         </listeners>
     </trace>
 </system.diagnostics>
</configuration>
```

Notice that `"Wrox"` is passed in as a string to the `initializeData` attribute as the TraceListener is added. The string `"Wrox"` appears as the application or *source* for this event. This works fine when debugging your application; most likely, the debugging user has the appropriate access. However, when your application is deployed, it will probably run under a less privileged account, so you must give explicit write access to a registry key such as `HKLM\System\CurrentControlSet\Services\EventLog\Application\Wrox`, where `"Wrox"` is the same string passed in to `initializeData`. Remember that registry keys have ACLs (Access Control Lists) just as files do. Use `RegEdit.exe` to change the permissions on a registry key by right-clicking the key and selecting Properties, and setting the ACL just like you would for a file.

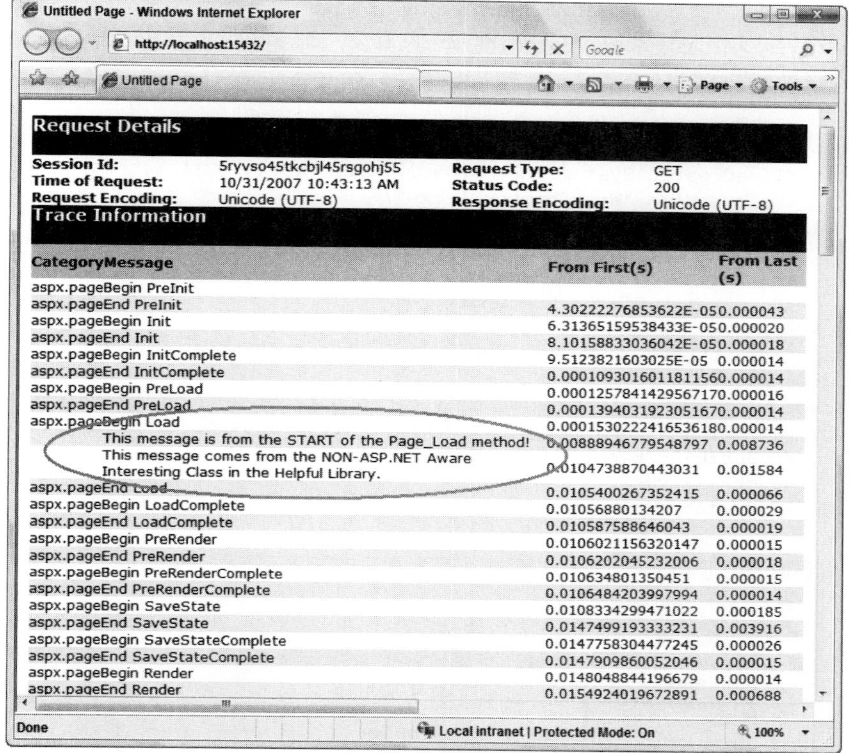

Figure 24-8

Be careful when using the EventLogTraceListener because your event log can fill up fairly quickly if you have a particularly chatty application. Figure 24-9 shows the same tracing output used in Figure 24-8, this time in the event log. The Event Viewer has changed in Windows Vista and you'll need to create a simple Custom View that shows only "Wrox" events.

Other Useful Listeners

The .NET 2.0 Framework added two TraceListeners in addition to the WebPageTraceListener:

- **XmlWriterTraceListener:** Derives from `TextWriterTraceListener` and writes out a strongly typed XML file.
- **DelimitedListTraceListener:** Also derives from `TextWriterTraceListener`; writes out comma-separated values (CSV) files.

One of the interesting things to note about the XML created by the XmlWriterTraceListener — it's not well-formed XML! Specifically, it doesn't have a root node; it's just a collection of peer nodes, as shown in the following code. This may seem like it goes against many of the ideas you've been told about XML, but think of each event as a document. Each stands alone and can be consumed alone. They just happen to be next to each other in one file. Certainly, the absence of an ultimate closing tag cleverly dodges the issue of wellformedness and allows easy appending to a file.

```
<E2ETraceEvent xmlns=\"http://schemas.microsoft.com/2004/06/E2ETraceEvent\">
    <System xmlns=\"http://schemas.microsoft.com/2004/06/windows/eventlog/system\">
        <EventID>0</EventID>
        <Type>3</Type>
        <SubType Name="Information">0</SubType>
        <Level>8</Level>
        <TimeCreated SystemTime="2005-11-05T12:43:44.4234234Z">
        <Source Name="WroxChapter21.exe"/>
        <Correlation ActivityID="{00000000-0000-0000-0000-000000000000>
        <Execution ProcessName="WroxChapter21.exe" ProcessID="4234" ThreadID="1"/>
        <Channel/>
        <Computer>SCOTTPC</Computer>
    </System>
    <ApplicationData>Your Text Here</ApplicationData>
</E2ETraceEvent>
<E2ETraceEvent xmlns=\"http://schemas.microsoft.com/2004/06/E2ETraceEvent\">
    <System xmlns=\"http://schemas.microsoft.com/2004/06/windows/eventlog/system\">
        <EventID>0</EventID>
        <Type>3</Type>
...the XML continues...
```


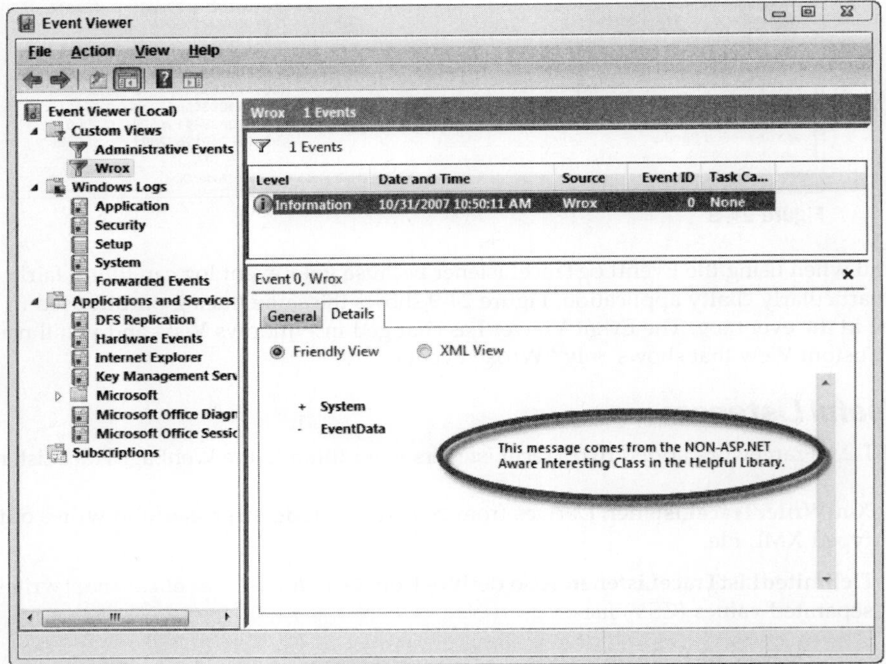

Figure 24-9

The "E2E" in `E2ETraceEvent` stands for end-to-end. Notice that it includes information such as your computer name and a "correlation id." Microsoft will include TraceViewer tools with coming products, such as the product codenamed *Indigo* and the managed WinFX API that will consume this XML Schema and help you diagnose problems with operations that span multiple machines in a Web farm. If your ASP.NET application makes calls to an Indigo service, you may want your app to supply its tracing information in this format to make aggregated analysis easier.

The .NET 3.5 Framework added one additional TraceListener, the IisTraceListener. This new TraceListener has been added to the System.Web Assembly in the .NET 3.5 but that assembly is still versioned as 2.0. Consequently, this class is available only on systems that have the .NET Framework 3.5 installed. Remember that the .NET Framework 3.5 includes fixes for the 2.0 Framework as well as some new functionality, like the `IisTraceListener`.

Much like the `WebPageTraceListener` bridges Diagnostics Tracing with ASP.NET tracing, the `IisTraceListener` bridges the tracing mechanism of ASP.NET with IIS 7.0. This listener lets us raise events to the IIS 7.0 infrastructure. See Chapter 11 on IIS7 for more details on this new class and its use.

Diagnostic Switches

It's often not convenient to recompile your application just because you want to change tracing characteristics. Sometimes you may want to change your configuration file to add and remove TraceListeners. At other times, you may want to change a configuration parameter or "flip a switch" to adjust the amount of detail the tracing produces. That's where `Switch` comes in. `Switch` is an abstract base class that supports a series of diagnostic switches that you can control by using the application's configuration file.

BooleanSwitch

To use a `BooleanSwitch`, create an instance and pass in the switch name that appears in the application's `config` file (see Listing 24-3).

Listing 24-3: Using diagnostic switches

```
<configuration>
 <system.diagnostics>
  <switches>
    <add name="ImportantSwitch" value="1" /> <!-- This is for the BooleanSwitch -->
    <add name="LevelSwitch" value="3" />     <!-- This is for the TraceSwitch -->
    <add name="SourceSwitch" value="4" />    <!-- This is for the SourceSwitch -->
  </switches>
 </system.diagnostics>
</configuration>
```

Switches can be used in an `if` statement for any purpose, but they are most useful in the context of tracing along with `System.Diagnostics.Trace.WriteIf`:

VB

```
Dim aSwitch As New BooleanSwitch("ImportantSwitch", "Show errors")
System.Diagnostics.Trace.WriteIf(aSwitch.Enabled, "The Switch is enabled!")
```

C#

```
BooleanSwitch aSwitch = new BooleanSwitch("ImportantSwitch", "Show errors");
System.Diagnostics.Trace.WriteIf(aSwitch.Enabled, "The Switch is enabled!");
```

If `ImportantSwitch` is set to `1`, or a non-zero value, in the `config` file, the call to `WriteIf` sends a string to trace output.

TraceSwitch

TraceSwitch offers five levels of tracing from 0 to 4, implying an increasing order: Off, Error, Warning, Info, and Verbose. You construct a `TraceSwitch` exactly as you create a `BooleanSwitch`:

VB

```
Dim tSwitch As New TraceSwitch("LevelSwitch", "Trace Levels")
System.Diagnostics.Trace.WriteIf(tSwitch.TraceInfo, "The Switch is 3 or more!")
```

C#

```
TraceSwitch tSwitch = new TraceSwitch("LevelSwitch", "Trace Levels");
System.Diagnostics.Trace.WriteIf(tSwitch.TraceInfo, "The Switch is 3 or more!");
```

A number of properties on the `TraceSwitch` class return `true` if the switch is at the same level or at a higher level than the property's value. For example, the `TraceInfo` property will return `true` if the switch's value is set to 3 or more.

SourceSwitch

New with .NET 2.0 is `SourceSwitch`, which is similar to `TraceSwitch` but provides a greater level of granularity. You call `SourceSwitch.ShouldTrace` with an EventType as the parameter:

VB

```
Dim sSwitch As New SourceSwitch("SourceSwitch", "Even More Levels")
System.Diagnostics.Trace.WriteIf(sSwitch.ShouldTrace(TraceEventType.Warning), _
                                 "The Switch is 3 or more!")
```

C#

```
SourceSwitch sSwitch = new SourceSwitch("SourceSwitch", " Even More Levels");
System.Diagnostics.Trace.WriteIf(sSwitch.ShouldTrace(TraceEventType.Warning),
                                 "The Switch is 4 or more!");
```

Web Events

It doesn't exactly qualify as debugging, but a series of new application-monitoring and health-monitoring tools within the system has been added in ASP.NET's `System.Web.Management` namespace in ASP.NET 2.0. These tools can be as valuable as tracing information in helping you monitor, maintain, and diagnose the health of your application. The system has a whole new event model and event engine that can update your application with runtime details. There are a number of built-in events, including application lifetime events such as start and stop and a heartbeat event. You can take these base classes and events and build on them to create events of your own. For example, you might want to create an event that tells you when a user downloads a particularly large file or when a new user is created in your personalization database. You can have your application send an e-mail to you once a day with statistics.

For instance, you can create your own event by deriving from `System.Web.Management.WebBaseEvent`, as shown in Listing 24-4.

Listing 24-4: Web events

VB

```
Imports System
Imports System.Web.Management

Namespace Wrox
    Public Class WroxEvent
       Inherits WebBaseEvent

        Public Const WroxEventCode As Integer = WebEventCodes.WebExtendedBase + 1
        Public Sub New(ByVal message As String, ByVal eventSource As Object)
            MyBase.New(message, eventSource, WroxEventCode)
        End Sub
    End Class
End Namespace
```

C#

```
namespace Wrox
{
    using System;
    using System.Web.Management;

    public class WroxEvent: WebBaseEvent
    {
        public const int WroxEventCode = WebEventCodes.WebExtendedBase + 1;
        public WroxEvent(string message, object eventSource) :
             base(message, eventSource, WroxEventCode){}
     }
}
```

Later, in a sample `Page_Load`, you raise this event to the management subsystem:

VB

```
Protected Sub Page_Load(sender As Object, e As EventArgs)
    ' Raise a custom event
    Dim anEvent As Wrox.WroxEvent = New Wrox.WroxEvent("Someone visited here", Me)
    anEvent.Raise()
  End Sub
```

C#

```
protected void Page_Load(Object sender, EventArgs e)
{
    // Raise a custom event
    Wrox.WroxEvent anEvent = new Wrox.WroxEvent("Someone visited here!", this);
    anEvent.Raise();
}
```

The event is caught by the management subsystem and can be dispatched to different providers based on a number of rules. This is a much more formal kind of tracing than a call to `Trace.WriteLine`, so you create a strongly typed event class for events specific to your application:

Web.config

```
<?xml version="1.0"?>
<configuration>
    <system.web>
        <healthMonitoring enabled="true">
            <providers>
                <add name="WroxDatabaseLoggingProvider"
                    type="System.Web.Management.SqlWebEventProvider"
                    connectionStringName="QuickStartSqlServer"
                    maxEventDetailsLength="1073741823"
                    buffer="false"/>
            </providers>
            <rules>
                <add
                    name="Application Lifetime Events Rule"
                    eventName="All Events"
                    provider="WroxDatabaseLoggingProvider"
                    profile="Critical" />
            </rules>
        </healthMonitoring>
    </system.web>
</configuration>
```

Debugging

Visual Studio includes two configurations by default: *debug* and *release*. The debug configuration automatically defines the debug and trace constants, enabling your application to provide context to a troubleshooter. The option to generate debugging information is turned on by default, causing a program database (or debug) file (PDB) to be generated for each assembly and your solution. They appear in the same `\bin` folder as your assemblies. Remember, however, that the actual compilation to native code does not occur in Visual Studio, but rather at runtime using just-in-time compilation (JIT). The JIT will automatically optimize your code for speed. Optimized code, however, is considerably harder to debug because the operations that are generated may not correspond directly to lines in your source code. For debug purposes, this option is set to `false`.

What's Required

The PDBs are created when either the C# compiler (`CSC.EXE`) or Visual Basic compiler (`VBC.EXE`) is invoked with the `/debug:full` command lines switch. As an option, if you use `/debug:pdbonly`, you will generate PDBs but still direct the compiler to produce release-mode code.

Debug versus Release

The debug and release configurations that come with Visual Studio are generally sufficient for your needs. However, these configurations control only the compilation options of the code behind files. Remember that, depending on how you've chosen to design your ASP.NET application, the ASP.NET `.aspx` files may be compiled the first time they're hit, or the entire application may compile the first time a page is hit. You can control these compilation settings via the compilation elements within the

`<system.web>` section of your application's `web.config`. Set `<compilation debug="true">` to produce binaries as you do when using the `/debug:full` switches. PDBs are also produced.

The average developer is most concerned with the existence of PDB files. When these files exist in your ASP.NET applications `\bin` folder, the runtime provides you with line numbers. Of course, line numbers greatly assist in debugging. You can't step through source code during an interactive debugging session without these files.

> **An interesting CLR Internals trick: Call `System.Diagnostics.Debugger.Launch` within your assembly, even if the assembly was compiled via `/debug:pdbonly`, and the debugger pops up. The JIT compiler compiles code on the first call to a method, and the code that it generates is debuggable because JIT knows that a debugger is attached.**

Debugging and the JIT Dialog

When an unhandled error occurs in an ASP.NET application, the default error handler for the ASP.NET worker process catches it and tries to output some HTML that expresses what happened. However, when you are debugging components outside of ASP.NET, perhaps within the context of unit testing, the debug dialog box appears when the .NET application throws an unhandled exception.

If something has gone horribly wrong with an ASP.NET application, it's conceivable that you may find a Web server with the dialog box popped up waiting for your input. This can be especially inconvenient if the machine has no keyboard or monitor hooked up. The day may come when you want to turn off the debug dialog box that appears, and you have two options to do this:

- You can disable JIT Debugging from the registry. The proper registry key is `HKLM\Software\Microsoft\.NETFramework\DbgJITDebugLaunchSetting`. There are three possible values for the option:
  - `0`: Prompts the user by means of a message box. The choices presented include Continue, which results in a stack dump and process termination, and Attach a Debugger, which means the runtime spawns the debugger listed in the DbgManagedDebugger registry key. If no key exists, the debugger releases control and the process is terminated.
  - `1`: Does not display a dialog box. This results in a stack dump and then process termination.
  - `2`: Launches the debugger listed in the DbgManagedDebugger registry key.

For this option, the registry entry must to be set to `0` for the dialog box to show up.

- To disable the JIT debug dialog box and still present an error dialog box, within Visual Studio.NET, choose Tools ➪ Options ➪ Debugging ➪ Just-In-Time and deselect Common Language Runtime. Instead of the Select a Debugger dialog box, an OK/Cancel dialog box will appear during an unhandled exception.

IIS versus ASP.NET Development Server

ASP.NET greatly simplifies your Web developing experience by enabling you to develop applications without IIS (Internet Information Server — the Web server) on your developer machine. Rather than the traditional style of creating a virtual directory and mapping it to a physical directory, a directory can be opened as a Web site simply by telling Visual Studio that it is a Web site. When you open a Web site from the File menu, the first option on the list of places to open from is the file system. Visual Studio considers any folder that you open to be the root of a Web site. Other options, of course, are opening Web sites from your local IIS instance, FTP, or source control.

Using the IIS option works much as it does in previous versions of Visual Studio with a few convenient changes such as the capability to create a Web site or map a virtual directory directly from the Open Web Site dialog. However, more interesting stuff happens after you open a Web site from the file system.

By default, Web sites that exist only on the file system have a "just-in-time" Web server instantiated called the ASP.NET Development Server. The small Web server hosts the exact same ASP.NET page rendering at runtime that is hosted within IIS on a deployed production site. The page rendering behavior should be identical under the small server as it is under IIS. You should be aware of a few important differences and specific caveats to ensure a smooth transition from development to production.

Create a new Web site by selecting File ⇨ New Web Site and immediately pressing F5 to begin a debugging session. You are greeted with a Debugging Not Enabled dialog box. The first option automatically adds a new `web.config` file with debugging enabled. (Earlier versions of Visual Studio required a tedious manual process.) Click OK and balloon help appears in the system tray announcing that the ASP.NET Development Server has started up. It also shows what random high-number port the Web server has selected on the local host. When you close your browser and stop your debugging session, the tiny Web server shuts down.

The ASP.NET Development Server is an application, not a service. It is not a replacement for IIS, nor does it try to be. It's really just a broker that sits between the developer and the ASP.NET page renderer, and it contains very few, if any, of the security benefits that IIS includes. It is loosely based on a .NET 1.*x* project, code-named Cassini, which is downloadable from `http://asp.net/Projects/Cassini/Download/Default.aspx`. This project was a sample meant to illustrate how to use the `System.Web.Hosting` namespace. The Cassini project was the grandparent, and now the ASP.NET Development Server is a first-class member of the Visual Studio product family. Including this tiny Web server with the Development Environment also allows Visual Studio to be used on Windows XP Home systems that are unable to run IIS.

The small Web server runs under the same user context that runs Visual Studio. If your application requires a specific security context, such as an anonymous user or specific domain user, consider using IIS as your development Web server. Additionally, because the Web server starts up on a port other than port 80, be sure to use best practices while developing your site's navigation scheme. Often, developers assume their site's URL will not include a port number (it will default to port 80), that their site may appear within a specific subdomain (`bar.foo.com`), or that their site will appear within a subdirectory (`www.foo.com/bar`). Consider making your navigation relative to the virtual root of your application so your application is resilient enough to be run in many contexts.

Starting a Debugging Session

There are a number of ways to enter an interactive debugging session with ASP.NET. Visual Studio can fire up the ASP.NET Worker Process, load your newly compiled Web site and attach the debugging to the Worker Process automatically. Or, you can attach a debugger to a site that is already running. Visual Studio also includes a new simpler remote debugging tool for cross-machine debugging.

F5 Debugging

When you start debugging an ASP.NET application, Visual Studio takes into consideration all the Start options within your project properties. Just as ASP.NET 1.*x* Visual Studio can be set to launch the browser on a specific page, the new version allows you to start debugging using the currently selected page. The specific page has been selected so that the Visual Studio debugger can automatically attach the correct process, which might be the Visual Studio Web Server, the ASP.NET Worker Process, or a remote debug monitor.

Attaching to a Process

It's often convenient to jump into an interactive debugging session of a Web site that is already running, and at known state, rather than starting an application from scratch each time you debug. To begin debugging a site that is already running, from Visual Studio's Debug menu, select Attach to Process. The dialog has been improved from previous versions of Visual Studio and now includes a Refresh button and simplifies most common debugging use cases by showing only those processes that belong to the user and that are in the currently running session.

Also included is a transport drop-down with the default transport selected. The default allows you to select processes on your computer or on a remote computer that's running the Remote Debugging Monitor. Other options are there for smart client or unmanaged debugging.

> *The only difference between starting a Debug session via F5 and attaching to a process manually is that when you debug via F5, Visual Studio automatically starts up a browser or external application for you. Remember that if you use Attach to Process, it is assumed that you have already done the work of starting up the process. The ASP.NET Worker Processes under IIS will start up when the site has been hit with an* `HttpRequest` *at least once. The debugger can now attach to the running Worker Process.*

Sometimes you want to debug an ASP.NET application that is already running on your computer. If that application was not started by Visual Studio and you want to attach to it, select Attach to Process from the Debug menu and choose either `ASPNET_WP.exe` (if you're running Windows XP) or `W3WP.exe` (if you are running Windows 2003 server). Be careful that you are not trying to debug an application that is actively servicing other users or you may ruin their experience.

Simpler Remote Debugging

Remote debugging got simpler with Visual Studio 2005. However, in the interest of security, you must have the appropriate credentials to perform remote debugging. You'll find a `Remote Debugger` folder in `C:\Program Files\Microsoft Visual Studio 8\Common7\IDE`. In Figure 24-10, Explorer is shown open and the `Remote Debugger` folder is selected and has been configured as a shared directory for access over the local network.

To begin, remote debugging must be set up on the machine that contains the application you want to debug. Rather than performing a complicated installation, you can now use the Remote Debug Monitor, and an application that can simply be run off a file share. The easiest scenario has you sharing these components directly from your Visual Studio machine and then running `msvsmon.exe` off the share, as shown in Figure 24-11.

Simply running the Remote Debug Monitor executable off the file share can make remote ASP.NET debugging of an already-deployed applications much simpler, although you still need to manually attach to the ASP.NET worker process because automatic attaching is not supported. Do note that there are now two versions of the debugger, one for x86 processes and one for x64 processes, so make sure you're using the right debugger for your process.

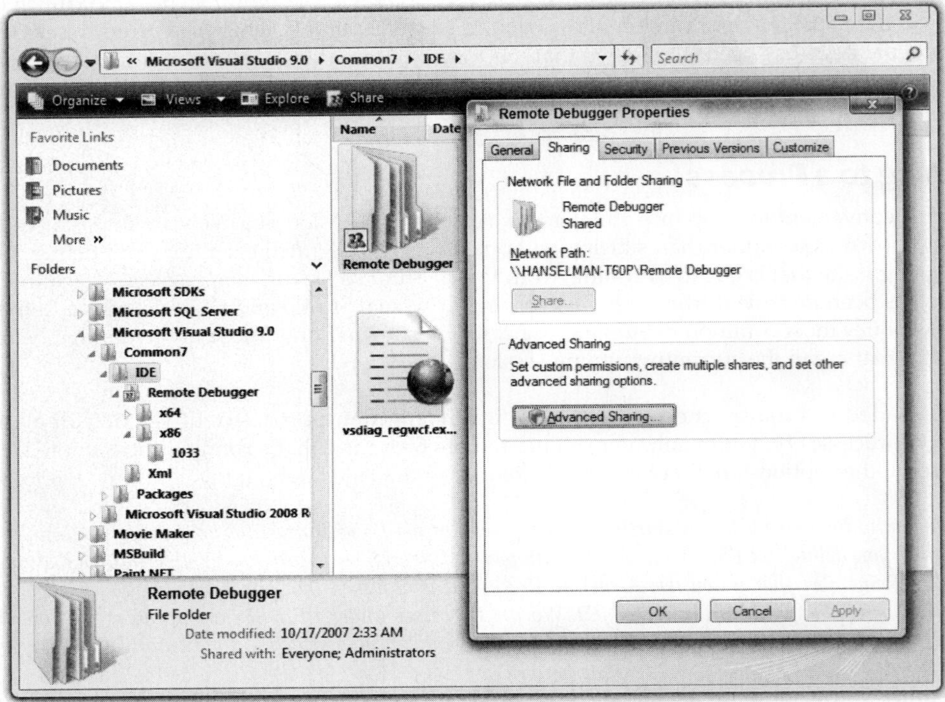

Figure 24-10

You are allowed to debug a process that's running under your account and password without any special permissions. If you need to debug a process running under another account name, such as an ASP.NET worker process running as a user who is not you, you must be an administrator on the machine running the process.

The most important thing to remember when debugging remotely is this: You need to get the user account that is running as Visual Studio to map somehow to a legitimate user account on the machine running the Remote Debug Monitor (`msvsmon.exe`) machine and vice versa. The easiest way to do this is to create a local user account on both computers with the same username and password. To run `msvsmon` as a user other than Visual Studio, you must create two user accounts on each computer.

If one of the machines is located on a domain, be aware that domain account can be mapped to a local account. You create a local user account on both computers. However, if you pick the same username and password as your domain account, Visual Studio can be run as a domain account. Figure 24-12 shows the machine name is SCOTTPC and the username is Wrox. A Wrox user was created on both machines with the same password on each.

For Windows XP machines on a workgroup, the security option entitled Network Security: Shared and Security Model for Local Accounts affects your use of the Remote Debug Monitor. If this option is set to Guest Only — Local Users Authenticate As Guest, then remote debugging fails and shows you a dialog box. Configure this via the Local Security Policy MMC-based administrative tool. The warning doesn't affect Windows 2000 or Windows Server 2003, Windows XP, or Vista-based computers that are joined to a domain.

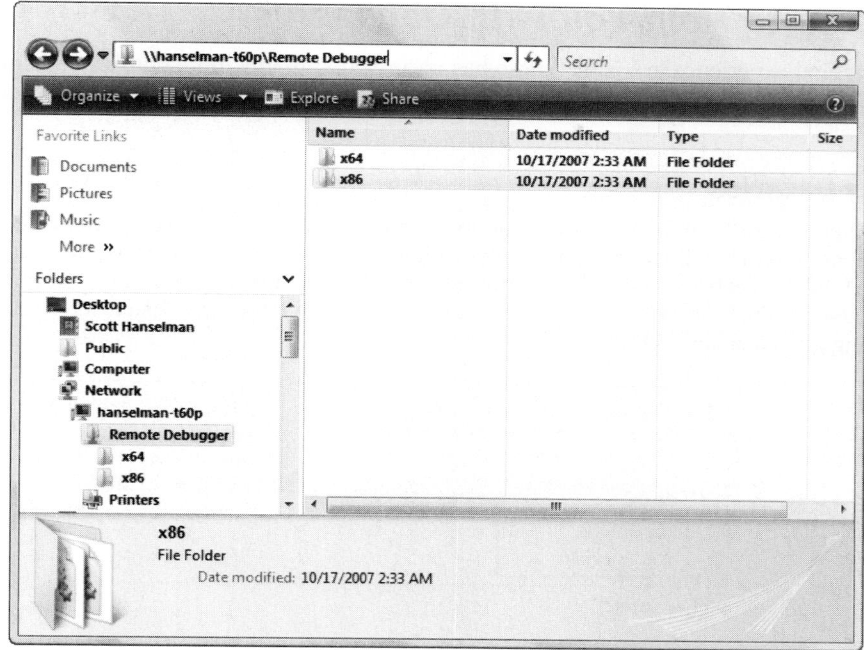

Figure 24-11

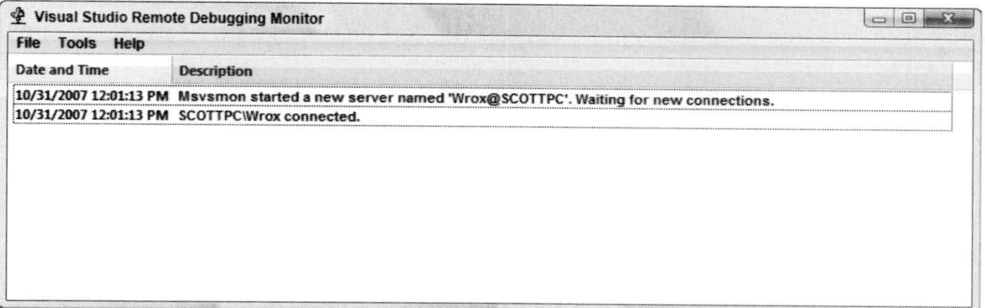

Figure 24-12

Debugging Running Windows XP Service Pack 2

Make sure that TCP Port 80 is set to allow ASP.NET and IIS to communicate with the remote machine. Try to keep the scope limited, using options such as Local Subnet Only, and avoid exposing your Web server to the Internet during development. Also include TCP Port 135, which allows DCOM to communicate with remote machines as well as with UDP Ports 4500 and 500 for IPSec-based security. Last, confirm that the Remote Debug Monitor (`msvsmon.exe`) is in the list of exceptions to the firewall. Again, avoid exposing your debugging session to the outside world. Remote debugging is usually a last resort if the bug isn't reproducible for whatever reason on the developer workstation.

New Tools to Help You with Debugging

The debugging experience in Visual Studio has improved arguably more than any other aspect of the environment. A number of new tools, some obvious, some more subtle, assist you in every step of the debug session.

Debugger Datatips

Previous versions of Visual Studio gave you tooltips when the user hovered the mouse over variables of simple types. Visual Studio 2005 offers *datatips*, allowing. complex types to be explored using a modeless tree-style view that acts like a tooltip and provides much more information. After you traverse the tree to the node that you're interested in, that simple type can be viewed using a visualizer by clicking the small magnifying glass icon, as seen in Figure 24-13.

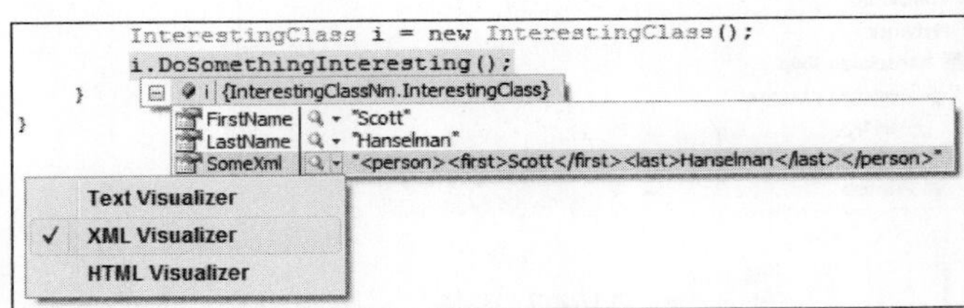

Figure 24-13

Data Visualizers

As you see in Figure 24-13, a simple type can be viewed using any number of data visualizers. For example, if a simple variable such as a string contains a fragment of XML, you might want to visualize that data in a style that's more appropriate for the data's native format, as shown in Figure 24-14.

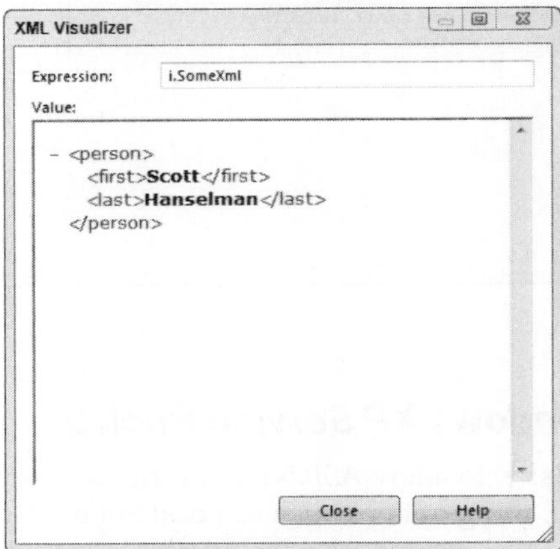

Figure 24-14

The visualizers are straightforward to write and, although Visual Studio ships with default visualizers for text, HTML, XML, and DataSets, expect to see a flood of new visualizers appearing on the Internet with support for images, collection classes, and more. The result is a rich, unparalleled debugging experience.

Error Notifications

During an interactive debugging session, Visual Studio now strives to assist you with informative Error Notifications. These notifications not only report on events such as unhandled exceptions, but also offer context-sensitive troubleshooting tips and next steps for dealing with the situation. Figure 24-15 shows an unhandled `NullReferenceException` along with the good advice that we might try using the "new" keyword to create an object instance before using it. Oops!

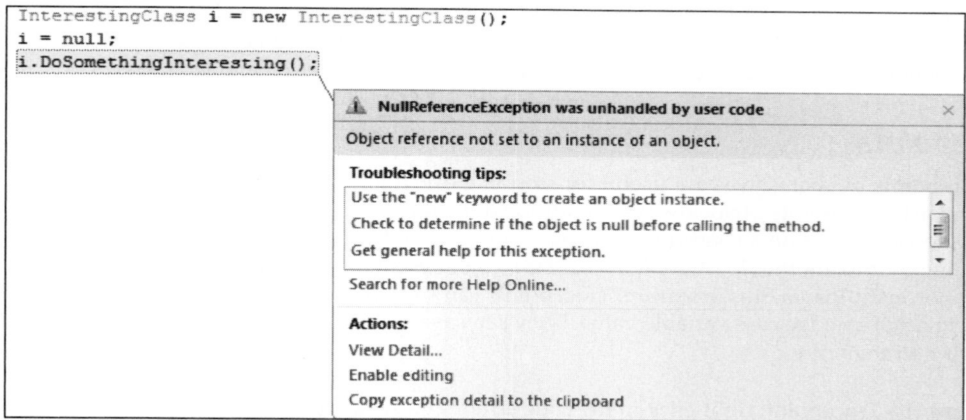

Figure 24-15

Edit and Continue (Lack of) Support, or Edit and Refresh

Visual Basic 6 was all about developing things quickly, and its most powerful feature was the Edit and Continue feature, which gave you capability to change code during a debugging session without restarting the session. In break mode, you could modify code fix bugs and move on. The 2.0 version of the CLR has restored this feature for both C# and Visual Basic. Although this has a large number of developers cheering, unfortunately this feature is not available to ASP.NET developers.

In ASP.NET, your assembly is compiled not by Visual Studio, but by the ASP.NET runtime using the same technique it does during a normal Web page request by a browser. To cooperate with the debugger and support Edit and Continue within ASP.NET, a number of fantastically complex modifications to ASP.NET runtime would have been required by the development team. Rather than including support for this feature, ASP.NET developers can use *page recycling*.

This means that code changes are made during a debugging session, and then the whole page is refreshed via F5, automatically recompiled, and re-executed. Basically, ASP.NET 2.0 includes much improved support for Edit and Refresh, but not for Edit and Continue.

Just My Code Debugging

A new concept in the .NET 2.0 CLR is called *Just My Code* debugging. Any method in code can be explicitly marked with the new attribute `[DebuggerNonUserCode]`. Using this explicit technique and a number of other heuristic methods internal to the CLR, the debugger silently skips over code that isn't important to the code at hand. You can find the new preference Enable Just My Code in Tools ➪ Options ➪ Debugging.

The `[DebuggerHidden]` attribute is still available in .NET 2.0 and hides methods from the debugger, regardless of the user's Just My Code preference. The 1.1 attribute `[DebuggerStepThrough]` tells the debugger to step through, rather than into, any method to which it's applied; the `[DebuggerNonUserCode]` attribute is a much more pervasive and complete implementation that works at runtime on delegates, virtual functions, and any arbitrarily complex code.

Be aware that these attributes and this new user option exist to help you debug code effectively and not be fooled by any confusing call stacks. While these can be very useful, be sure not to use them on your components until you're sure you won't accidentally hide the very error you're trying to debug. Typically these attributes are used for components such as proxies or thin shim layers.

Tracepoints

Breakpoints by themselves are useful for stopping execution either conditionally or unconditionally. Standard breakpoints break always. Conditional breakpoints cause you to enter an interactive debugging session based on a condition. Tracing is useful to output the value of a variable or assertion to the debugger or to another location. If you combine all these features, what do you get? Tracepoints, a new and powerful Visual Studio feature. Tracepoints can save you from hitting breakpoints dozens of times just to catch an edge case variable value. They can save you from covering your code with breakpoints to catch a strange case.

To insert a Tracepoint, right-click in the code editor and select Breakpoint ➪ Insert Tracepoint. You'll get the dialog shown in Figure 24-16. The icon that indicates a breakpoint is a red circle, and the icon for a Tracepoint is a red diamond. Arbitrary strings can be created from the dialog using pseudo-variables in the form of keywords such as `$CALLSTACK` or `$FUNCTION`, as well as the values of variables in scope placed in curly braces. In Figure 24-16, the value of `i.FirstName` (placed in curly braces) is shown in the complete string with the Debug output of Visual Studio.

Client-side Javascript Debugging

Excellent client-side Javascript Debugging is new in Visual Studio 2008. If you run an ASP.NET application in a debugging session in Internet Explorer you'll need to enable script debugging. If not, you'll receive a dialog similar to the one in Figure 24-17.

After you've turned on Script Debugging, try a simple ASPX page with some Javascript that changes the text in a textbox to UPPERCASE when the button is pressed.

Listing 24-5: Simple Javascript debugging test

ASPX

```
<!DOCTYPE html PUBLIC "-//W3C//DTD XHTML 1.0 Transitional//EN" "http://www.w3.org/TR/
xhtml1/DTD/xhtml1-transitional.dtd">
<html xmlns="http://www.w3.org/1999/xhtml" >
```

```
<head runat="server">
    <script type="text/javascript">
        function MakeItUpper()
        {
            newText = document.getElementById("TextBox1").value.toUpperCase();
            document.getElementById("TextBox1").value = newText;
         }
    </script>
</head>
<body>
    <form id="form1" runat="server">
        <div>
            <input type="button" id="Button1" value="Upper"
                onclick="javascript:MakeItUpper()" />
            <input type="text" id="TextBox1" runat="server"/>
        </div>
    </form>
</body>
</html>
```

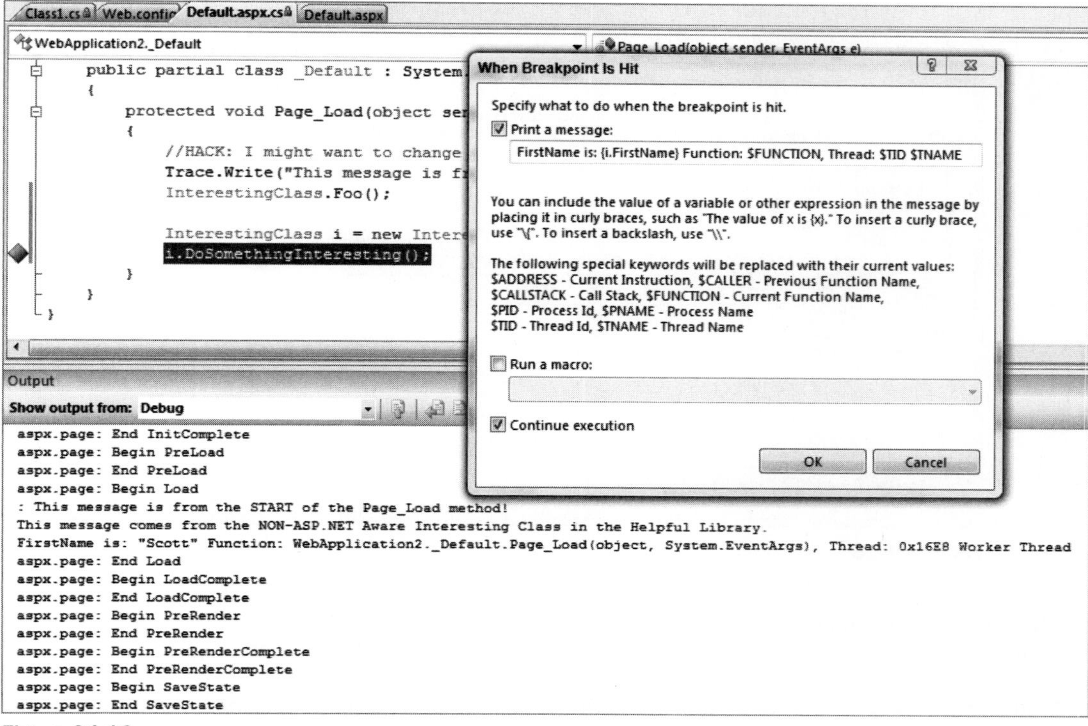

Figure 24-16

Put a breakpoint on one of the lines of *client-side* Javascript. Note that this is code that runs in the browser, not on the Web server. Start a debugging session with the page from Listing 24-5. Visual Studio will break at that point, as shown in Figure 24-18.

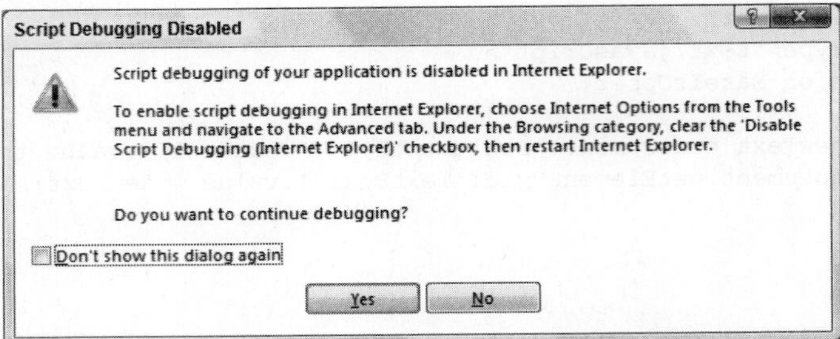

Figure 24-17

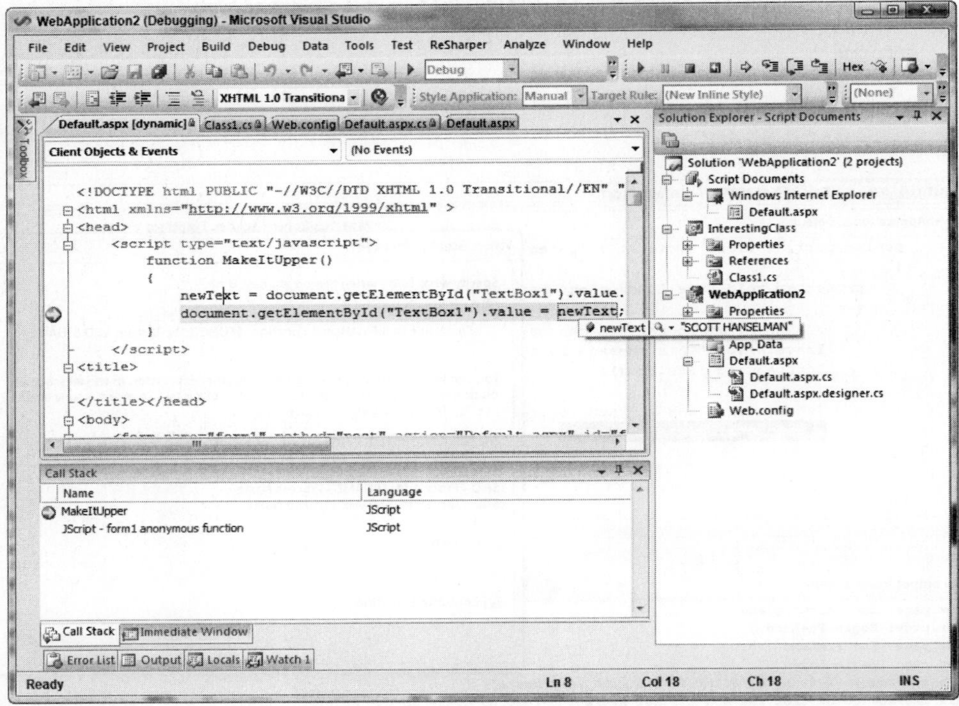

Figure 24-18

The Javascript debugger in Visual Studio 2008 supports variable tooltips, visualizers, call stacks, locals, watches, and all the features you're used to when debugging .NET-based languages.

Notice in the figure that `Default.aspx` has the word [dynamic] listed on the tab, indicating that this isn't the same `default.aspx` that was edited earlier; you can see that `default.aspx` listed on the final tab.

Rather, this is the dynamically generated `default.aspx` that was delivered to the browser, including ViewState and other generated elements. Dynamically generated documents and scripts appear during the debug session in the Solution Explorer.

This rich debugging support on the client side makes creating today's Javascript-heavy AJAX applications much easier.

SQL Stored Proc Debugging

Database projects are file-based projects that let you manage and execute database queries. You can add your existing SQL scripts to the project or create new ones and edit them within Visual Studio. Database projects and SQL debugging are not available in the Express or Standard versions of Visual Studio. They are available only in the Professional or Team Edition Visual Studio SKUs/versions.

When debugging database applications, you can't use Step Into (F11) to step between code in the application tier into the code in SQL Server 2005 (be it T-SQL or CLR SQL). However, you can set a breakpoint in the stored procedure code and use Continue (F5) to execute code to that set break point.

When debugging SQL on SQL Server 2005, be aware of any software or hardware firewalls you may be running. Windows XP SP2's software firewall will warn you what you're trying to do. Be sure to select "unblock" in any warning dialogs to ensure that SQL Server 2005 and Visual Studio can communicate.

If you are using a SQL account to connect to the SQL Server, make sure the Windows User Account you run Visual Studio under is also an administrator on the SQL Server machine. You can add accounts to SQL Server's `sysadmin` privilege using the SQL command `sp_addsrvrolemember 'Domain\Name', 'sysadmin'`. Of course, never do this in production; and better yet, do your debugging on a machine with everything installed locally.

If you're using the NT Authentication model on the SQL Server 2005, make sure that account has permissions to run the `sp_enable_sql_debug` stored procedure. You can give account access to this stored procedure by using the SQL commands `CREATE USER UserName FOR LOGIN 'Domain\Name'` followed by `GRANT EXECUTE ON sp_enable_sql_debug TO UserName`. This creates a SQL user that is associated directly with a specific Windows User and then explicitly grants permissions to debug TSQL to that user. On SQL Server 2000, the user must have access to the extended stored procedure `sp_sdidebug`.

For slightly older installations such as Windows 2000 and Windows NT 4, or if you are using SQL 2000, be sure to visit MSDN for the latest details and tools in this space. The MSDN URL for debugging SQL Server is `http://msdn2.microsoft.com/library/zefbf0t6`.

Exception and Error Handling

When an exception occurs in your ASP.NET application code, you can handle it in a number of ways, but the best approach is a multi-pronged one:

- Catch what you expect:
  - Use a `Try/Catch` around error-prone code. This can always catch specific exceptions that you can deal with, such as `System.IO.FileNotFoundException`

    - Rather than catching exceptions around specific chunks of code at the page level, consider using the page-level error handler to catch specific exceptions that might happen anywhere on the page.
- But prepare for unhandled exceptions:
    - Set the `Page.Error` property if a specific page should show a specific error page for any unhandled exception. This can also be done using the `<%@ Page >` directive or the code behind the property.
    - Have default error pages for 400 and 500 errors set in your `web.config`.
    - Have a boilerplate `Application_OnError` handler that takes into consideration both specific exceptions that you can do something about, as well as all unhandled exceptions that you may want logged to either the event log, a text file, or other instrumentation mechanism.

The phrase *unhandled exception* may be alarming, but remember that you don't do anyone any good catching an exception that you can't recover from. Unhandled exceptions are okay if they are just that — exceptional. For these situations, rely on global exception handlers for logging and friendly error pages that you can present to the user.

> **Why try to catch an exception by adding code everywhere if you can catch and log exceptions all in one place? A common mistake is creating a try/catch block around some arbitrary code and catching the least specific exception type — `System.Exception`. A rule of thumb is, don't catch any exception that you can't do anything about. Just because an exception *can* be thrown by a particular method doesn't mean you have to catch it. It's *exceptional*, remember? Also, there are exception handlers at both the page and the application level. Catch exceptions in these two centralized locations rather than all over.**

Handling Exceptions on a Page

To handle exceptions at a page level, override the `OnError` method that `System.Web.UI.Page` inherits from the `TemplateControl` class (see Listing 24-6). Calling `Server.GetLastError` gives you access to the exception that just occurred. Be aware that a chain of exceptions may have occurred, and you can use the `ExceptionGetBaseException` method to return the root exception.

Listing 24-6: Page-level error handling

VB

```
Protected Overrides Sub OnError(ByVal e As System.EventArgs)
    Dim AnError As System.Exception = Server.GetLastError()
    If (TypeOf AnError.GetBaseException() Is SomeSpecificException) Then
        Response.Write("Something bad happened!")
        Response.StatusCode = 200
        Server.ClearError()
        Response.End()
    End If
End Sub
```

C#

```
protected override void OnError(EventArgs e)
{
    System.Exception anError = Server.GetLastError();
    if (anError.GetBaseException() is SomeSpecificException)
    {
        Response.Write("Something bad happened!");
        Response.StatusCode = 200;
        Server.ClearError();
        Response.End();
    }
}
```

Handling Application Exceptions

The technique of catching exceptions in a centralized location can be applied to error handling at the application level in `Global.asax`, as shown in Listing 24-7. If an exception is not caught on the page, the `web.config` is checked for an alternate error page; if there isn't one, the exception bubbles up to the application and your user sees a complete call stack.

Listing 24-7: Application-level error handling

VB

```
Protected Sub Application_Error(sender as Object, ByVal e As System.EventArgs)
    Dim bigError As System.Exception = Server.GetLastError()
    'Example checking for HttpRequestValidationException
    If (TypeOf bigError.GetBaseException() Is HttpRequestValidationException) Then
        System.Diagnostics.Trace.WriteLine(bigError.ToString)
        Server.ClearError()
    End If
End Sub
```

C#

```
protected void Application_Error(Object sender, EventArgs e)
{
   System.Exception bigError = Server.GetLastError();
   //Example checking for HttpRequestValidationException
   if(bigError.GetBaseException() is HttpRequestValidationException )
   {
     System.Diagnostics.Trace.WriteLine(bigError.ToString());
    Server.ClearError();
   }
}
```

Unhandled application errors turn into HTTP Status Code 500 and display errors in the browser. These errors, including the complete callstack and other technical details, may be useful during development, but are hardly useful at production time. Most often, you want to create an error handler (as shown previously) to log your error and to give the user a friendlier page to view.

If you ever find yourself trying to catch exceptions of type `System.Exception`, take a look at the code to see whether you can avoid it. There's almost never a reason to catch such a non-specific exception, and you're more likely to swallow exceptions that can provide valuable debugging. Check the API documentation for the framework method you are calling — a section specifically lists what exceptions an API call might throw. Never rely on an exception occurring to get a standard code path to work.

Http Status Codes

Every `HttpRequest` results in an `HttpResponse`, and every `HttpResponse` includes a status code. The following table describes 11 particularly interesting HTTP status codes.

Status Code	Explanation
200 OK	Everything went well.
301 Moved Permanently	Reminds the caller to use a new, permanent URL rather than the one he used to get here.
302 Found	Returned during a Response.Redirect. This is the way to say "No, no, look over here right now."
304 Not Modified	Returned as the result of a conditional `GET` when a requested document hasn't been modified. It is the basis of all browser-based caching. An HTTP message-body must not be returned when using a 304.
307 Temporary Redirect	Redirects calls to ASMX Web services to alternate URLs. Rarely used with ASP.NET.
400 Bad Request	Request was malformed.
401 Unauthorized	Request requires authentication from the user.
403 Forbidden	Authentication has failed, indicating that the server understood the requests but cannot fulfill it.
404 Not Found	The server has not found an appropriate file or handler to handle this request. The implication is that this may be a temporary state. This happens in ASP.NET not only because a file cannot be found, but also because it may be inappropriately mapped to an IHttpHandler that was not available to service the request.
410 Gone	The equivalent of a permanent 404 indicating to the client that it should delete any references to this link if possible. 404s usually indicate that the server does not know whether the condition is permanent.

Status Code	Explanation
500 Internal Server Error	The official text for this error is ''The server encountered an unexpected condition which prevented it from fulfilling the request,'' but this error can occur when any unhandled exception bubbles all the way up to the user from ASP.NET.

Any status code greater than or equal to 400 is considered an error and, unless you configure otherwise, the user will likely see an unfriendly message in his browser. If you have not already handled these errors inside of the ASP.NET runtime by checking their exception types, or if the error occurred outside of ASP.NET and you want to show the user a friendly message, you can assign pages to any status code within `web.config`, as the following example shows:

```
<customErrors mode ="On" >
    <error statusCode ="500" redirect ="FriendlyMassiveError.aspx" />
</customErrors>
```

After making a change to the customer errors section of your `web.config`, make sure a page is available to be shown to the user. A classic mistake in error redirection is redirecting the user to a page that will cause an error, thereby getting him stuck in a loop. Use a great deal of care if you have complicated headers or footers in your application that might cause an error if they appear on an error page. Avoid hitting the database or performing any other backend operation that requires either user authorization or that the user's session be in any specific state. In other words, make sure that the error page is a reliable standalone.

Any status code greater than or equal to 400 increments the ASP.NET Requests Failed performance counter. 401 increments Requests Failed and Requests Not Authorized. 404 and 414 increment both Requests Failed and Requests Not Found. Requests that result in a 500 status code increment Requests Failed and Requests Timed Out. If you're going to return status codes, you must realize their effects and their implications.

Summary

This chapter examined the debugging tools available to you for creating robust ASP.NET applications. A successful debugging experience includes not only interactive debugging with new features such as datatips, data visualizers, and error notifications, but also powerful options around configurable tracing and logging of information.

Remote debugging is easier than ever with ASP.NET, and the capability to write and debug ASP.NET pages without installing IIS removes yet another layer of complexity from the development process.

Visual Studio and its extensible debugging mechanisms continue to be expanded by intrepid bloggers and enthusiasts, making debugging even less tedious than it has been in the past.

25

File I/O and Streams

Although most of this book concentrates specifically on learning and using the features of ASP.NET 3.5, .NET provides an enormous amount of additional functionality in other areas of the Base Class Library (BCL). This chapter examines a few of the common base classes that you can use to enhance your ASP.NET applications. First, you look at using the frameworks `System.IO` namespace to manage files on the local file system. Next, you explore how to use the various Stream classes within the framework to read from and write different data formats to memory and the local file system. Finally, you learn how to use the .NET Framework to communicate with other computers across the Internet using common protocols such as HTTP and FTP.

A Word about I/O Security

Although this chapter is not specifically about ASP.NET security, you need to understand the impact of local system security on what the ASP.NET Worker Process is allowed to do inside of the IO namespace. Remember that generally, when your code is executed by IIS, it executes under the context of the ASP.NET Worker Process user account (ASPNET) and, therefore, your application may be restricted by that account's security rights. For example, by default, the ASP.NET Worker Process does not have rights to write to the local disk. The two main areas that you should look at to get a very basic understanding of the impact of security on an application are impersonation and user account ACLs. ASP.NET security is discussed thoroughly in Chapter 18.

Additionally, this chapter demonstrates how to use classes in the BCL to delete files and directories and to modify the permissions of directories and files. Recognize that it is entirely possible to permanently delete important data from your hard drive or change the permissions of a resource, which would result in you losing the ability to access the resource. *Be very careful* when using these classes against the file system.

Working with Drives, Directories, and Files

Many times in your ASP.NET applications, you need to interact with the local file system, reading directory structures, reading and writing to files, or performing many other tasks. The `System.IO` namespace within the .NET Framework makes working with file system directories and files very easy. While working with the classes in the `System.IO` namespace, keep in mind that because your ASP.NET applications are executing on the server, the file system you are accessing is the one your Web application is running on. You, of course, cannot use an ASP.NET application to access the end user's file system.

The DriveInfo Class

You can start working with the `System.IO` namespace at the top of the directory tree by using a great new addition to the .NET 3.5 class libraries, the `DriveInfo` class. This class supplements the `GetLogicalDrives()` method of the `Directory` class included in prior versions of the .NET Framework. It provides you with extended information on any drive registered with the server's local file system. You can get information such as the name, type, size, and status of each drive. Listing 25-1 shows you how to create a `DriveInfo` object and display local drive information on a Web page.

Listing 25-1: Displaying local drive information

VB

```
<script runat="server">
    Protected Sub Page_Load(ByVal sender As Object, ByVal e As System.EventArgs)
        Dim drive As New System.IO.DriveInfo("C:\")
        lblDriveName.Text = drive.Name
        lblDriveType.Text = drive.DriveType.ToString()
        lblAvailableFreeSpace.Text = drive.AvailableFreeSpace.ToString()
        lblDriveFormat.Text = drive.DriveFormat
        lblTotalFreeSpace.Text = drive.TotalFreeSpace.ToString()
        lblTotalSize.Text = drive.TotalSize.ToString()
        lblVolumeLabel.Text = drive.VolumeLabel
    End Sub
</script>

<html xmlns="http://www.w3.org/1999/xhtml" >
<head runat="server">
    <title>Displaying Drive Information</title>
</head>
<body>
    <form id="form1" runat="server">
    <div>
        <table>
            <tr><td>Drive Name:</td><td>
                <asp:Label ID="lblDriveName" runat="server" Text="Label" />
            </td></tr>
            <tr><td>Drive Type:</td><td>
                <asp:Label ID="lblDriveType" runat="server" Text="Label"/>
            </td></tr>
            <tr><td>Available Free Space:</td><td>
               <asp:Label ID="lblAvailableFreeSpace" runat="server" Text="Label" />
            </td></tr>
```

```
            <tr><td>Drive Format:</td><td>
                <asp:Label ID="lblDriveFormat" runat="server" Text="Label" />
            </td></tr>
            <tr><td>Total Free Space:</td><td>
                <asp:Label ID="lblTotalFreeSpace" runat="server" Text="Label" />
            </td></tr>
            <tr><td>Total Size:</td><td>
                <asp:Label ID="lblTotalSize" runat="server" Text="Label" />
            </td></tr>
            <tr><td>Volume Label</td><td>
                <asp:Label ID="lblVolumeLabel" runat="server" Text="Label" />
            </td></tr>
        </table>
    </div>
    </form>
</body>
</html>
```

C#

```
<script runat="server">
    protected void Page_Load(object sender, EventArgs e)
    {
        System.IO.DriveInfo drive = new System.IO.DriveInfo(@"C:\");
        lblDriveName.Text = drive.Name;
        lblDriveType.Text = drive.DriveType.ToString();
        lblAvailableFreeSpace.Text = drive.AvailableFreeSpace.ToString();
        lblDriveFormat.Text = drive.DriveFormat;
        lblTotalFreeSpace.Text = drive.TotalFreeSpace.ToString();
        lblTotalSize.Text = drive.TotalSize.ToString();
        lblVolumeLabel.Text = drive.VolumeLabel;
    }
</script>
```

One of the more interesting properties in the sample is the `DriveType` enumeration. This read-only enumeration tells you what the drive type is, for example CD-ROM, Fixed, Ram, or Removable. Figure 25-1 shows you what the page looks like when you view it in a browser.

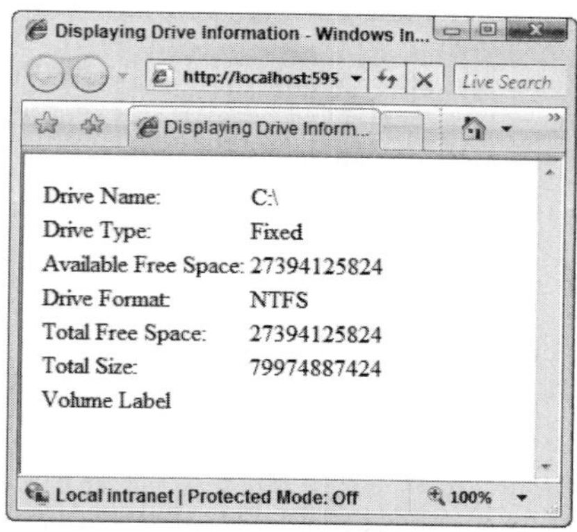

Figure 25-1

You can also enumerate through all the drives on the local file system by using the `DriveInfo`'s static `GetDrives()` method. Listing 25-2 shows an example of enumerating through the local file system drives and adding each drive as a root node to a TreeView control.

Listing 25-2: Enumerating through local file system drives

VB

```
<script runat="server">
    Protected Sub Page_Load(ByVal sender As Object, ByVal e As System.EventArgs)
        If (Not Page.IsPostBack) Then

        For Each drive As System.IO.DriveInfo In System.IO.DriveInfo.GetDrives()

            Dim node As TreeNode = New TreeNode()
            node.Value = drive.Name

            ' Make sure the drive is ready before we access it
            If (drive.IsReady) Then
                node.Text = drive.Name & _
                            " - (free space: " & drive.AvailableFreeSpace & ")"
            Else
                node.Text = drive.Name & " - (not ready)"
            End If

            Me.TreeView1.Nodes.Add(node)
        Next

        End If
    End Sub
</script>

<html xmlns="http://www.w3.org/1999/xhtml" >
<head runat="server">
    <title>Enumerate Local System Drives</title>
</head>
<body>
    <form id="form1" runat="server">
    <div>
        <table>
            <tr>
                <td style="width: 100px" valign="top">
                    <asp:TreeView ID="TreeView1" runat="server"></asp:TreeView>
                </td>
            </tr>
        </table>
    </div>
    </form>
</body>
</html>
```

C#

```
<script runat="server">
    protected void Page_Load(object sender, EventArgs e)
```

```
        Catch ex As System.IO.IOException
            parent.Text += " (Unknown Error: " + ex.Message + ")"
        End Try
    End Sub
</script>
```

C#

```
<script runat="server">
    protected void Page_Load(object sender, EventArgs e)
    {
        if (!Page.IsPostBack)
        {

        foreach (System.IO.DriveInfo drive in System.IO.DriveInfo.GetDrives())
        {
            TreeNode node = new TreeNode();
            node.Value = drive.Name;

            if (drive.IsReady)
            {
                node.Text = drive.Name +
                            " - (free space: " + drive.AvailableFreeSpace + ")";

                LoadDirectories(node, drive.Name);
            }
            else
                node.Text = drive.Name + " - (not ready)";

            this.TreeView1.Nodes.Add(node);
        }

        }

        this.TreeView1.CollapseAll();
    }

    private void LoadDirectories(TreeNode parent, string path)
    {
        System.IO.DirectoryInfo directory = new System.IO.DirectoryInfo(path);

        try
        {
            foreach (System.IO.DirectoryInfo d in directory.GetDirectories())
            {
                TreeNode node = new TreeNode(d.Name, d.FullName);

                parent.ChildNodes.Add(node);

                //Recurs the current directory
                LoadDirectories(node, d.FullName);
            }
        }
        catch (System.UnauthorizedAccessException e)
        {
            parent.Text += " (Access Denied)";
```

```
        }
        catch (System.IO.IOException e)
        {
            parent.Text += " (Unknown Error: " + e.Message + ")";
        }
    }
</script>
```

Figure 25-3 shows what the page should look like in the browser. You should now be able to browse the directory tree, much as you do in Windows Explorer, by opening and closing the TreeView nodes.

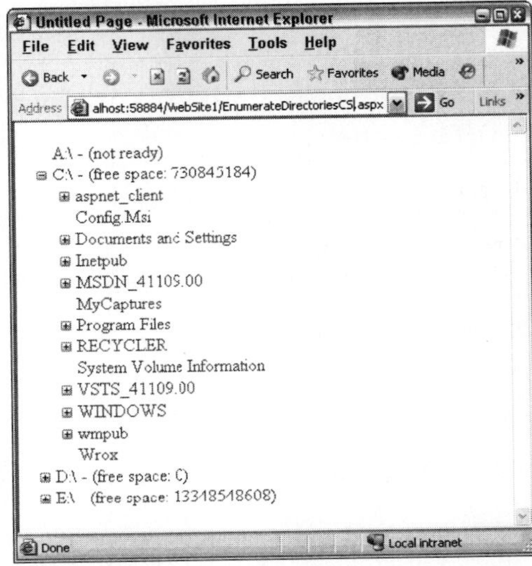

Figure 25-3

Notice that the example continuously creates new instances of the `DirectoryInfo` class each time the method executes in order to continue to enumerate the directory tree. You could also extend this example by displaying some additional properties as part of the `Node` text, such as the `CreationTime` or `Attributes`.

To perform only a specific action, you don't have to create an instance of the `DirectoryInfo` class. You can simply use the static methods exposed by the `Directory` class. These methods allow you to create, read properties from, and delete a directory. Rather than creating an object instance that represents a specific path and exposes methods that act on that path, the static methods exposed by the `Directory` class generally require you to pass the path as a method parameter. Listing 25-4 shows how you can use the static methods exposed by the `Directory` class to create, read properties from, and delete a directory.

> **Remember to be very careful when deleting a folder from your hard drive. It is possible to permanently delete important data from your system or change the permissions of a resource, which would result in your losing the ability to access the resource.**

Listing 25-4: Working with the static methods of the Directory class

VB

```
<%@ Import Namespace="System.IO" %>

<script runat="server">

    Protected Sub Page_Load(ByVal sender As Object, ByVal e As System.EventArgs)

        Directory.CreateDirectory("C:\Wrox")

        If Directory.Exists("C:\Wrox") Then

            Me.Label1.Text = _
                    Directory.GetCreationTime("C:\Wrox").ToString()
            Me.Label2.Text = _
                    Directory.GetLastAccessTime("C:\Wrox").ToString()
            Me.Label3.Text = _
                   Directory.GetLastWriteTime("C:\Wrox").ToString()

            Directory.Delete("C:\Wrox")
        End If
    End Sub
</script>

<html xmlns="http://www.w3.org/1999/xhtml" >
<head runat="server">
    <title>Using Static Methods</title>
</head>
<body>
    <form id="form1" runat="server">
    <div>
        Creation Time:
             <asp:Label ID="Label1" runat="server" Text="Label"></asp:Label><br />
        Last Access Time:
             <asp:Label ID="Label2" runat="server" Text="Label"></asp:Label><br />
        Last Write Time:
              <asp:Label ID="Label3" runat="server" Text="Label"></asp:Label>
    </div>
    </form>
</body>
</html>
```

C#

```
<%@ Import Namespace="System.IO" %>

<script runat="server">

    protected void Page_Load(object sender, EventArgs e)
    {
        Directory.CreateDirectory(@"C:\Wrox");

        if (Directory.Exists(@"C:\Wrox") )
```

Continued

```
            {
                this.Label1.Text =
                        Directory.GetCreationTime(@"C:\Wrox").ToString();
                this.Label2.Text =
                        Directory.GetLastAccessTime(@"C:\Wrox").ToString();
                this.Label3.Text =
                        Directory.GetLastWriteTime(@"C:\Wrox").ToString();

                Directory.Delete(@"C:\Wrox");
            }
        }
    </script>
```

When you load this page in the browser, you will see that the `Creation Time`, `Last Access Time`, and `Last Write Time` are displayed. Additionally, if you open Windows Explorer, you will see that the Wrox directory has been deleted.

Using Relative Paths and Setting and Getting the Current Directory

When an ASP.NET page is executed, the thread used to execute the code that generates the page, by default, has a current working directory. It uses this directory as its base directory if you have specified relative paths in your application. Therefore, if you pass a relative filename into any `System.IO` class, the file is assumed to be located in the current working directory.

For example, the default working directory for the ASP.NET Development Server is a directory under your Visual Studio install root. If you installed Visual Studio in `C:\Program Files`, your ASP.NET Development Server working directory would be `c:\Program Files\Microsoft Visual Studio 9.0\Common7\IDE`.

You can find the location of your working directory by using the `Directory` class's `GetCurrentDirectory()` method. In addition, you can change the current working directory using the `Directory` class's `SetCurrentDirectory()` method.

Listing 25-5 shows you how to set and then display your working directory.

Listing 25-5: Setting and displaying the application's working directory

VB

```
<%@ Import Namespace="System.IO" %>

<script runat="server">

    Protected Sub Page_Load(ByVal sender As Object, ByVal e As System.EventArgs)
        Me.Label1.Text = Directory.GetCurrentDirectory()
        Directory.SetCurrentDirectory("C:\Wrox")
        Me.Label2.Text = Directory.GetCurrentDirectory()
    End Sub
</script>

<html xmlns="http://www.w3.org/1999/xhtml" >
<head runat="server">
    <title>Set and Display the Working Directory</title>
```

```
</head>
<body>
    <form id="form1" runat="server">
    <div>
        Old Working Directory:
            <asp:Label ID="Label1" runat="server" Text="Label"></asp:Label><br />
        New Working Directory:
            <asp:Label ID="Label2" runat="server" Text="Label"></asp:Label>
    </div>
    </form>
</body>
</html>
```

C#

```
<script runat="server">

    protected void Page_Load(object sender, EventArgs e)
    {
        this.Label1.Text = Directory.GetCurrentDirectory();
        Directory.SetCurrentDirectory(@"C:\Wrox");
        this.Label2.Text = Directory.GetCurrentDirectory();
    }
</script>
```

Note that the directory parameter you specify in the `SetCurrentDirectory()` method must already exist; otherwise, ASP.NET throws an exception. Knowing this, it would probably be a good idea to use the `Exists()` method of the `Directory` class to make sure the directory you are specifying does, in fact, already exist before you try to change the working directory.

When you execute this code, you should see that it displays the original working directory, and then displays the new working directory after you change it. Figure 25-4 shows what the page looks like when executed.

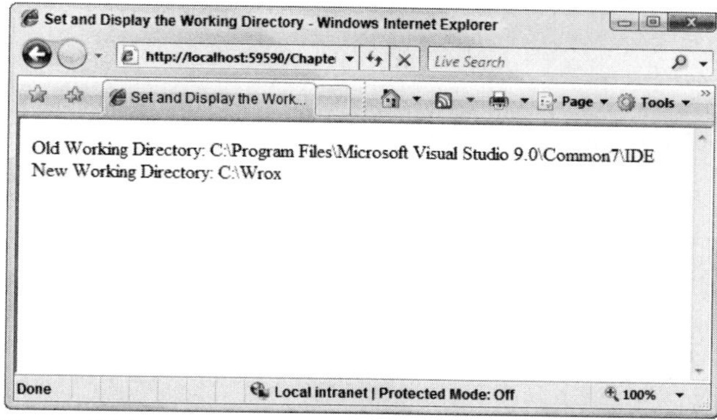

Figure 25-4

File and FileInfo

Now that you can effectively display and browse a directory tree, you can expand the example even further by displaying the files located in the directory that is currently selected in your TreeView control.

The simplest way to display the files is to bind a `FileInfo` array to a `GridView`. This example uses the `GetFiles()` method of the `DirectoryInfo` class because it returns an array of `FileInfo` objects. You want to use this method because the `FileInfo` object enables you to display some properties of each file. (If you want to display only the filenames, you could use the `Directory` class's `GetFiles()` method, which returns a simple string array of filenames.)

Listing 25-6 shows how to use the TreeView control's `SelectedNodeChanged` event to bind your `GridView` with the file information.

Listing 25-6: Binding a GridView to directory files

VB

```
<script runat="server">

    Protected Sub Page_Load(ByVal sender As Object, ByVal e As System.EventArgs)

        If (Not Page.IsPostBack) Then

        For Each drive As System.IO.DriveInfo In System.IO.DriveInfo.GetDrives()

            Dim node As TreeNode = New TreeNode()
            node.Value = drive.Name

            If (drive.IsReady) Then
                node.Text = drive.Name & _
                            " - (free space: " & drive.AvailableFreeSpace & ")"

                LoadDirectories(node, drive.Name)
            Else
                node.Text = drive.Name & " - (not ready)"
            End If

            Me.TreeView1.Nodes.Add(node)
        Next

        End If

        Me.TreeView1.CollapseAll()

    End Sub

    Private Sub LoadDirectories(ByVal parent As TreeNode, ByVal path As String)

        Dim directory As System.IO.DirectoryInfo = _
                New System.IO.DirectoryInfo(path)

        Try
            For Each d As System.IO.DirectoryInfo In directory.GetDirectories()

                Dim node As TreeNode = New TreeNode(d.Name, d.FullName)

                parent.ChildNodes.Add(node)

                'Recurse the current directory
```

```
                LoadDirectories(node, d.FullName)
            Next
        Catch ex As System.UnauthorizedAccessException
            parent.Text += " (Access Denied)"
        Catch ex As Exception
            parent.Text += " (Unknown Error: " + ex.Message + ")"
        End Try
    End Sub

    Protected Sub TreeView1_SelectedNodeChanged _
        (ByVal sender As Object, ByVal e As System.EventArgs)

        Dim directory As System.IO.DirectoryInfo = _
                    New System.IO.DirectoryInfo(Me.TreeView1.SelectedNode.Value)

        Me.GridView1.DataSource = directory.GetFiles()
        Me.GridView1.DataBind()
    End Sub
</script>

<html xmlns="http://www.w3.org/1999/xhtml" >
<head runat="server">
    <title>Binding a Gridview </title>
</head>
<body>
    <form id="form1" runat="server">
    <div>
        <table>
            <tr>
                <td style="width: 100px" valign="top">
                   <asp:TreeView ID="TreeView1" runat="server"
                         OnSelectedNodeChanged="TreeView1_SelectedNodeChanged">
                   </asp:TreeView>
                </td>
                <td valign=top>
                    <asp:GridView ID="GridView1" runat="server"
                          AutoGenerateColumns=False GridLines=None CellPadding=3>
                        <Columns>
                            <asp:BoundField DataField="Name" HeaderText="Name"
                                 HeaderStyle-HorizontalAlign=Left
                                 HeaderStyle-Font-Bold=true />
                            <asp:BoundField DataField="Length" HeaderText="Size"
                                 ItemStyle-HorizontalAlign=Right
                                 HeaderStyle-HorizontalAlign=Right
                                 HeaderStyle-Font-Bold=true />
                            <asp:BoundField DataField="LastWriteTime"
                                 HeaderText="Date Modified"
                                 HeaderStyle-HorizontalAlign=Left
                                 HeaderStyle-Font-Bold=true />
                        </Columns>
                    </asp:GridView>
                </td>
            </tr>
        </table>
```

Continued

```
    </div>
    </form>
</body>
</html>
```

C#

```
<script runat="server">
    protected void Page_Load(object sender, EventArgs e)
    {

        if (!Page.IsPostBack)
        {

        foreach (System.IO.DriveInfo drive in System.IO.DriveInfo.GetDrives())
        {
            TreeNode node = new TreeNode();
            node.Value = drive.Name;

            // Make sure the drive is ready before we access it
            if (drive.IsReady)
            {
                node.Text = drive.Name +
                            " - (free space: " + drive.AvailableFreeSpace + ")";

                LoadDirectories(node, drive.Name);
            }
            else
                node.Text = drive.Name + " - (not ready)";

            this.TreeView1.Nodes.Add(node);
        }

        }

        this.TreeView1.CollapseAll();
    }

    private void LoadDirectories(TreeNode parent, string path)
    {
        System.IO.DirectoryInfo directory = new System.IO.DirectoryInfo(path);

        try
        {
            foreach (System.IO.DirectoryInfo d in directory.GetDirectories())
            {
                TreeNode node = new TreeNode(d.Name, d.FullName);

                parent.ChildNodes.Add(node);

                //Recurse the current directory
                LoadDirectories(node, d.FullName);
            }
        }
        catch (System.UnauthorizedAccessException e)
        {
```

```
                parent.Text += " (Access Denied)";
            }
            catch (Exception e)
            {
                parent.Text += " (Unknown Error: " + e.Message + ")";
            }
        }

        protected void TreeView1_SelectedNodeChanged(object sender, EventArgs e)
        {
            System.IO.DirectoryInfo directory =
                      new System.IO.DirectoryInfo(this.TreeView1.SelectedNode.Value);

            this.GridView1.DataSource = directory.GetFiles();
            this.GridView1.DataBind();
        }
    </script>
```

Figure 25-5 shows what your Web page looks like after you have selected a directory and your grid has been bound to the `FileInfo` array.

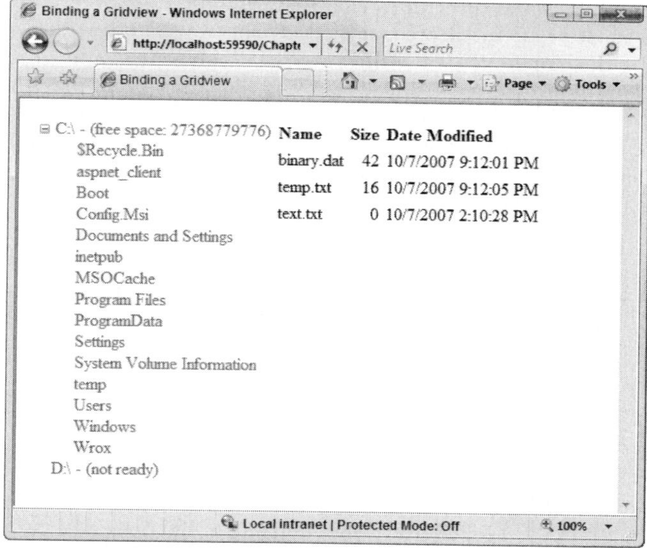

Figure 25-5

Keep in mind that, as in the Load Directory example, you can also enumerate though the `FileInfo` array to display the information. Listing 25-7 shows you how to enumerate through the `FileInfo` array and display the properties to the page.

Listing 25-7: Manually enumerating directory files

VB

```
Dim dir as New System.IO.DirectoryInfo("C:\")
```

Continued

```
For Each file as System.IO.FileInfo In dir.GetFiles("*.*")
     Response.Write(file.Name & "<BR>")
     Response.Write(file.LastWriteTime.ToString() & "<BR>")
     Response.Write(file.Attributes.ToString() & "<BR>")
Next
```

C#

```
System.IO.DirectoryInfo dir = new System.IO.DirectoryInfo(@"C:\");
foreach (System.IO.FileInfo file in dir.GetFiles("*.*"))
{
     Response.Write(file.Name + "<BR>");
     Response.Write(file.LastWriteTime.ToString() + "<BR>");
     Response.Write(file.Attributes.ToString() + "<BR>");
}
```

Listing 25-7 also shows that you can provide a file filter to the `GetFiles()` method. This allows you to limit the results from the method to specific file extensions or to files matching a specific filename part.

Working with Paths

Although working with files and directories has been pretty easy, even going all the way back to good old ASP, one of the most problematic areas has always been working with paths. Many lines of code have been written by developers to deal with concatenating partial paths together, making sure files have extensions, evaluating those extensions, stripping filenames off of paths, and even more.

Thankfully, the .NET Framework provides you with a class just for dealing with paths. The `System.IO.Path` class exposes a handful of static methods that make dealing with paths a snap. The following table lists the static methods exposed by the `Path` class.

Method	Description
`ChangeExtension`	Changes the extension of the provided path string to the provided new extension.
`Combine`	Returns a single combined path from two partial path strings.
`GetDirectoryName`	Returns the directory or directories of the provided path.
`GetExtension`	Returns the extension of the provided path.
`GetFileName`	Returns the filename of the provided path.
`GetFileNameWithoutExtension`	Returns the filename without its extension of the provided path.
`GetFullPath`	Given a non-rooted path, returns a rooted pathname based on the current working directory. For example, if the path passed in is `"temp"` and the current working directory is `c:\MyWebsite`, the method returns `C:\MyWebsite\temp`.
`GetInvalidFileNameChars`	Returns an array of characters that are not allowed in filenames for the current system.

Method	Description
`GetInvalidPathChars`	Returns an array of characters that are not allowed in pathnames for the current system.
`GetPathRoot`	Returns the root path.
`GetTempFileName`	Returns a temporary filename, located in the temporary directory returned by `GetTempPath`.
`GetTempPath`	Returns the temporary directory name.
`HasExtension`	Returns a Boolean value indicating whether a path has an extension.
`IsPathRooted`	Returns a Boolean indicating if a path is rooted.

As an example of using the `Path` class, the application shown in Figure 25-6 lets you enter a path and then displays the component parts of the path such as the root path (logical drive), the directory, filename, and extension.

The `GetInvalidPathChars` *and* `GetInvalidFileNameChars` *methods return an array of characters that are not allowed in path and filenames, respectively. Although the specific invalid characters are dependent on the platform the application is running on, the arrays returned by these methods will most likely contain elements such as non-printable characters, special Unicode characters, or characters from non-Latin–based character sets. The characters that your browser is capable of rendering will depend on your specific platform setup. Characters that your browser is incapable of rendering properly will display as the generic square box shown in Figure 25-6.*

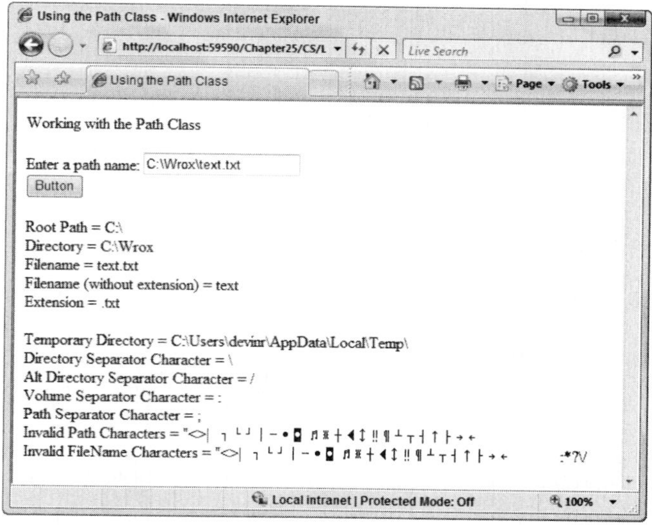

Figure 25-6

The code in Listing 25-8 shows how the various methods and constant properties of the `Path` class have been used to create the application shown in Figure 25-6.

Listing 25-8: Using the Path class

VB

```
<%@ Import Namespace="System.IO" %>

<script runat="server">

    Protected Sub Page_Load(ByVal sender As Object, ByVal e As System.EventArgs)
        If Page.IsPostBack Then
            Me.lblRootPath.Text = Path.GetPathRoot(Me.txtPathName.Text)
            Me.lblDirectoryName.Text = Path.GetDirectoryName(Me.txtPathName.Text)
            Me.lblFileName.Text = Path.GetFileName(Me.txtPathName.Text)
            Me.lblFileNameWithoutExtension.Text = _
                     Path.GetFileNameWithoutExtension(Me.txtPathName.Text)
            Me.lblExtension.Text = Path.GetExtension(Me.txtPathName.Text)

            Me.lblTemporaryPath.Text = Path.GetTempPath()
            Me.lblDirectorySeparatorChar.Text = _
                     Path.DirectorySeparatorChar.ToString()
            Me.lblAltDirectorySeparatorChar.Text = _
                     Path.AltDirectorySeparatorChar.ToString()
            Me.lblVolumeSeparatorChar.Text = Path.VolumeSeparatorChar.ToString()
            Me.lblPathSeparator.Text = Path.PathSeparator.ToString()

            Me.lblInvalidChars.Text = _
                 HttpUtility.HtmlEncode(New String(Path.GetInvalidPathChars()))
            Me.lblInvalidFileNameChars.Text = _
                 HttpUtility.HtmlEncode(New String(Path.GetInvalidFileNameChars()))

        End If
    End Sub
</script>

<html xmlns="http://www.w3.org/1999/xhtml" >
<head runat="server">
    <title>Using the Path Class</title>
</head>
<body>
    <form id="form1" runat="server">
    <div>
        Working with the Path Class<br />
        <br />
        Enter a path name:
        <asp:TextBox ID="txtPathName" runat="server"></asp:TextBox><br />
        <asp:Button ID="Button1" runat="server" Text="Button" /><br />
        <br />
        Root Path =
        <asp:Label ID="lblRootPath" runat="server" Text="Label" />
        <br />
        Directory =
        <asp:Label ID="lblDirectoryName" runat="server" Text="Label" />
```

```
        <br />
        Filename =
        <asp:Label ID="lblFileName" runat="server" Text="Label" />
        <br />
        Filename (without extension) =
        <asp:Label ID="lblFileNameWithoutExtension" runat="server" Text="Label" />
        <br />
        Extension =
        <asp:Label ID="lblExtension" runat="server" Text="Label" />
        <br />
        <br />
        Temporary Directory =
        <asp:Label ID="lblTemporaryPath" runat="server" Text="Label" />
        <br />
        Directory Separator Character =
        <asp:Label ID="lblDirectorySeparatorChar" runat="server" Text="Label" />
        <br />
        Alt Directory Separator Character =
        <asp:Label ID="lblAltDirectorySeparatorChar" runat="server" Text="Label" />
        <br />
        Volume Separator Character =
        <asp:Label ID="lblVolumeSeparatorChar" runat="server" Text="Label" />
        <br />
        Path Separator Character =
        <asp:Label ID="lblPathSeparator" runat="server" Text="Label" />
        <br />
        Invalid Path Characters =
        <asp:Label ID="lblInvalidChars" runat="server" Text="Label" />
        <br />
        Invalid FileName Characters =
        <asp:Label ID="lblInvalidFileNameChars" runat="server" Text="Label" />

    </div>
    </form>
</body>
</html>
```

C#

```
<%@ Import Namespace="System.IO" %>

<script runat="server">

    protected void Page_Load(object sender, EventArgs e)
    {
        if (Page.IsPostBack)
        {
            this.lblRootPath.Text =
                            Path.GetPathRoot(this.txtPathName.Text);
            this.lblDirectoryName.Text =
                            Path.GetDirectoryName(this.txtPathName.Text);
            this.lblFileName.Text =
                            Path.GetFileName(this.txtPathName.Text);
            this.lblFileNameWithoutExtension.Text =
```

Continued

```
                    Path.GetFileNameWithoutExtension(this.txtPathName.Text);
            this.lblExtension.Text =
                    Path.GetExtension(this.txtPathName.Text);

            this.lblTemporaryPath.Text = Path.GetTempPath();
            this.lblDirectorySeparatorChar.Text =
                    Path.DirectorySeparatorChar.ToString();
            this.lblAltDirectorySeparatorChar.Text =
                    Path.AltDirectorySeparatorChar.ToString();
            this.lblVolumeSeparatorChar.Text = Path.VolumeSeparatorChar.ToString();
            this.lblPathSeparator.Text = Path.PathSeparator.ToString();

            this.lblInvalidChars.Text =
              HttpUtility.HtmlEncode( new String(Path.GetInvalidPathChars() ) );
            this.lblInvalidFileNameChars.Text =
              HttpUtility.HtmlEncode( new String(Path.GetInvalidFileNameChars()));
        }
    }
</script>
```

File and Directory Properties, Attributes, and Access Control Lists

Finally, this section explains how you can access and modify file and directory properties, attributes, and Access Control Lists.

Samples in this section use a simple text file called `TextFile.txt` *to demonstrate the concepts. You can either create this file or substitute your own file in the sample code. The samples assume the file has been added to the Web site and use the* `Server.MapPath` *method to determine the full filepath.*

Properties and Attributes

Files and directories share certain properties that you can use to determine the age of a file or directory, when it was last modified, and what attributes have been applied. These properties can be viewed by opening the file's Properties dialog. You can open this dialog from Windows Explorer by either right-clicking on the file and selecting Properties from the context menu, or selecting Properties from the File menu. Figure 25-7 shows the file's Properties window for the text document.

Both the `DirectoryInfo` and the `FileInfo` classes let you access these properties and modify them. Listing 25-9 shows you an example of displaying the file properties.

Listing 25-9: Displaying and modifying the file properties

VB

```
Dim file As New System.IO.FileInfo(Server.MapPath("TextFile.txt"))
Response.Write("Location: " & file.FullName & "<BR>")
Response.Write("Size: " & file.Length & "<BR>")
Response.Write("Created: " & file.CreationTime & "<BR>")
```

```
Response.Write("Modified: " & file.LastWriteTime & "<BR>")
Response.Write("Accessed: " & file.LastAccessTime & "<BR>")
Response.Write("Attributes: " & file.Attributes)
```

C#

```
System.IO.FileInfo file = new System.IO.FileInfo(Server.MapPath("TextFile.txt"));
Response.Write("Location: " + file.FullName + "<BR>");
Response.Write("Size: " + file.Length + "<BR>");
Response.Write("Created: " + file.CreationTime + "<BR>");
Response.Write("Modified: " + file.LastWriteTime + "<BR>");
Response.Write("Accessed: " + file.LastAccessTime + "<BR>");
Response.Write("Attributes: " + file.Attributes);
```

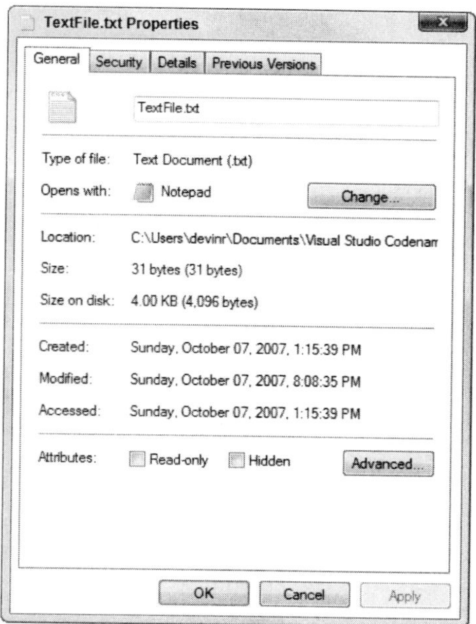

Figure 25-7

Access Control Lists

Although getting the properties and attributes is useful, what many developers need is the capability to actually change the Access Control Lists, or ACLs — pronounced *Ackels* — on directories and files. ACLs are the way resources such as directories and files are secured in the NTFS file system, which is the file system used by Windows XP, NT 4.0, 2000, and 2003. You can view a file's ACLs by selecting the Security tab from the file's Properties dialog. Figure 25-8 shows the ACLs set for the `TextFile.txt` file you created.

Using the new `System.AccessControl` namespace in the .NET Framework, you can query the file system for the ACL information and display it in a Web page, as shown in Listing 25-10.

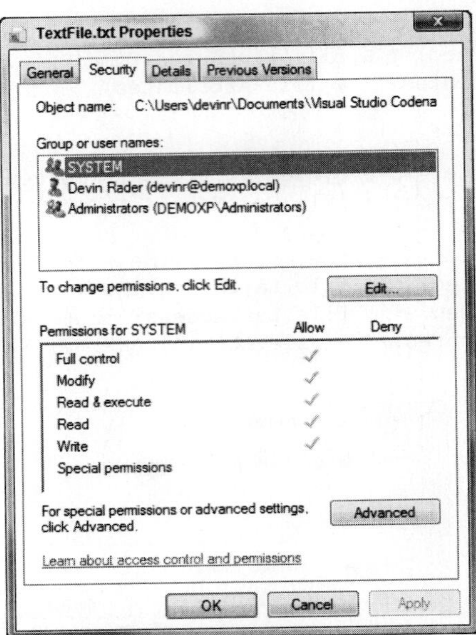

Figure 25-8

Listing 25-10: Access Control List information

VB

```
<script runat="server">

    Protected Sub Page_Load(ByVal sender As Object, ByVal e As System.EventArgs)
        ' retrieve the AccessControl information for this file
        Dim sec As System.Security.AccessControl.FileSecurity
        sec = System.IO.File.GetAccessControl(Server.MapPath("TextFile.txt"))

        Me.Label1.Text = _
                 sec.GetOwner(GetType(System.Security.Principal.NTAccount)).Value

        ' retrieve the collection of access rules
        Dim auth As System.Security.AccessControl.AuthorizationRuleCollection = _
                                    sec.GetAccessRules(true, true, _
                                    GetType(System.Security.Principal.NTAccount))

        Dim tc As TableCell
        ' loop through the rule collection and add a table row for each rule
        For Each r As System.Security.AccessControl.FileSystemAccessRule In auth

            Dim tr As New TableRow()

            tc = New TableCell()
            tc.Text = r.AccessControlType.ToString() ' deny or allow
            tr.Cells.Add(tc)

            tc = New TableCell()
            tc.Text = r.IdentityReference.Value ' who
```

```
            tr.Cells.Add(tc)

            tc = New TableCell()
            tc.Text = r.InheritanceFlags.ToString()
            tr.Cells.Add(tc)

            tc = New TableCell()
            tc.Text = r.IsInherited.ToString()
            tr.Cells.Add(tc)

            tc = New TableCell()
            tc.Text = r.PropagationFlags.ToString()
            tr.Cells.Add(tc)

            tc = New TableCell()
            tc.Text = r.FileSystemRights.ToString()
            tr.Cells.Add(tc)

            Table1.Rows.Add(tr)
        Next
    End Sub
</script>

<html xmlns="http://www.w3.org/1999/xhtml" >
<head runat="server">
    <title>Displaying ACL Information</title>
</head>
<body>
    <form id="form1" runat="server">
    <div>
        <p><b>File Owner:</b>
              <asp:Label ID="Label1" runat="server" Text="Label" /></p>
        <p>
        Access Rules:<br />
        <asp:Table ID="Table1" runat="server" CellPadding="2" GridLines="Both">
            <asp:TableRow>
                <asp:TableHeaderCell>Control Type</asp:TableHeaderCell>
                <asp:TableHeaderCell>Identity</asp:TableHeaderCell>
                <asp:TableHeaderCell>Inheritance Flags</asp:TableHeaderCell>
                <asp:TableHeaderCell>Is Inherited</asp:TableHeaderCell>
                <asp:TableHeaderCell>Propagation Flags</asp:TableHeaderCell>
                <asp:TableHeaderCell>File System Rights</asp:TableHeaderCell>
            </asp:TableRow>
        </asp:Table>
        </p>
    </div>
    </form>
</body>
</html>
```

C#

```
<script runat="server">

    protected void Page_Load(object sender, EventArgs e)
    {
```

```
        // retrieve the AccessControl information for this file
        System.Security.AccessControl.FileSecurity sec =
                System.IO.File.GetAccessControl(Server.MapPath("TextFile.txt"));

        this.Label1.Text =
                sec.GetOwner( typeof(System.Security.Principal.NTAccount) ).Value;

        // retrieve the collection of access rules
        System.Security.AccessControl.AuthorizationRuleCollection auth =
                                    sec.GetAccessRules(true, true,
                                    typeof (System.Security.Principal.NTAccount));

        TableCell tc;
        // loop through the rule collection and add a table row for each rule
        foreach (System.Security.AccessControl.FileSystemAccessRule r in auth)
        {
            TableRow tr = new TableRow();

            tc = new TableCell();
            tc.Text = r.AccessControlType.ToString(); // deny or allow
            tr.Cells.Add(tc);

            tc = new TableCell();
            tc.Text = r.IdentityReference.Value; // who
            tr.Cells.Add(tc);

            tc = new TableCell();
            tc.Text = r.InheritanceFlags.ToString();
            tr.Cells.Add(tc);

            tc = new TableCell();
            tc.Text = r.IsInherited.ToString();
            tr.Cells.Add(tc);

            tc = new TableCell();
            tc.Text = r.PropagationFlags.ToString();
            tr.Cells.Add(tc);

            tc = new TableCell();
            tc.Text = r.FileSystemRights.ToString();
            tr.Cells.Add(tc);

            Table1.Rows.Add(tr);
        }
    }
</script>
```

Figure 25-9 shows what the page looks like when it is executed. Note that the Identity column might be different depending on whom you are logged in as when you run the page and what security mode the application is running under (Integrated Windows Authentication, Basic, or Anonymous).

Now let's look at actually modifying the ACL lists. In this example, you give a user explicit Full Control rights over the `TextFile.txt` file. You can use either an existing user or create a new test User account in Windows to run this sample. Listing 25-11 shows how to add an access rule to the `TextFile.txt` file.

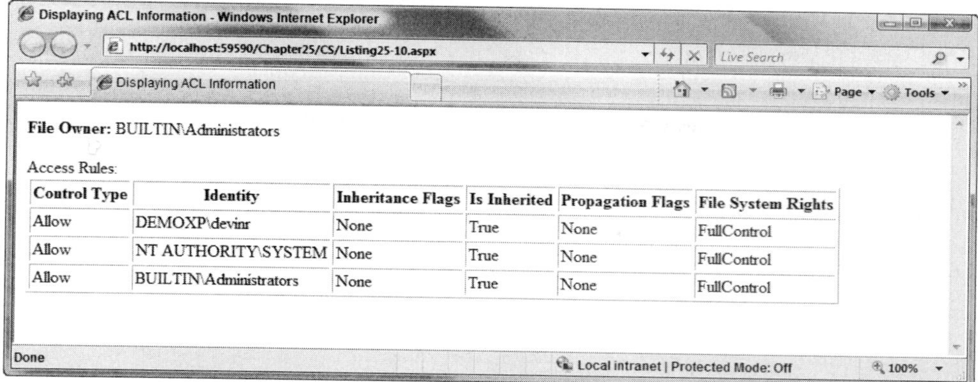

Figure 25-9

Listing 25-11: Adding a rule to the Access Control List

VB

```
Dim sec As System.Security.AccessControl.FileSecurity = _
        System.IO.File.GetAccessControl(Server.MapPath("TextFile.txt"))

sec.AddAccessRule( _
        New System.Security.AccessControl.FileSystemAccessRule( _
                "DEMOXP\TestUser", _
                System.Security.AccessControl.FileSystemRights.FullControl, _
                System.Security.AccessControl.AccessControlType.Allow _
                ) _
        )

System.IO.File.SetAccessControl(Server.MapPath("TextFile.txt"),sec)
```

C#

```
System.Security.AccessControl.FileSecurity sec =
        System.IO.File.GetAccessControl(Server.MapPath("TextFile.txt"));

sec.AddAccessRule(
        new System.Security.AccessControl.FileSystemAccessRule(
                @"DEMOXP\TestUser",
                System.Security.AccessControl.FileSystemRights.FullControl,
                System.Security.AccessControl.AccessControlType.Allow
                )
        );

System.IO.File.SetAccessControl(Server.MapPath("TextFile.txt"),sec);
```

There are several things to notice in this code sample. First, notice that you are passing three parameters to the `FileSystemAccessRule` constructor. The first parameter is the user you want to give rights to; change this value to a user on your specific system. Also notice that you must specify the full DOMAIN\USERNAME for the user. Next, notice that, in the code, you are using the `FileSystemRights` enumeration to specify exactly which rights you want to give to this user. You can specify multiple rights by using a bitwise `Or` operator, as shown in the following:

```
new System.Security.AccessControl.FileSystemAccessRule(
    "DEMOXP\TestUser",
    System.Security.AccessControl.FileSystemRights.Read &
        System.Security.AccessControl.FileSystemRights.Write,
    System.Security.AccessControl.AccessControlType.Allow
)
```

After running Listing 25-11, take a look at the Security tab in the file's Properties dialog and you should see that the user has been added to the Access Control List and allowed Full Control. Figure 25-10 shows what the dialog should look like.

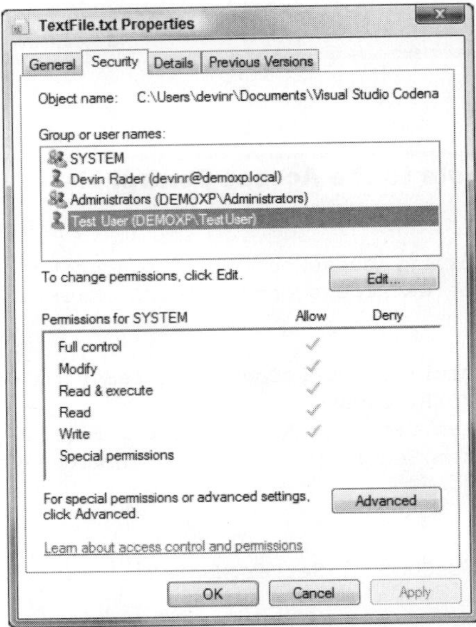

Figure 25-10

Now remove the ACL you just added by running essentially the same code, but using the `RemoveAccessRule` method rather than the `AddAccessRule` method. Listing 25-12 shows this code.

Listing 25-12: Removing the rule from the Access Control List

VB

```
Dim sec As System.Security.AccessControl.FileSecurity = _
        System.IO.File.GetAccessControl(Server.MapPath("TextFile.txt"))

sec.RemoveAccessRule( _
        new System.Security.AccessControl.FileSystemAccessRule( _
                "DEMOXP\TestUser", _
                System.Security.AccessControl.FileSystemRights.FullControl, _
                System.Security.AccessControl.AccessControlType.Allow _
                ) _
        )
```

```
System.IO.File.SetAccessControl(Server.MapPath("TextFile.txt"),sec)
```

C#

```
System.Security.AccessControl.FileSecurity sec =
        System.IO.File.GetAccessControl(Server.MapPath("TextFile.txt"));
sec.RemoveAccessRule(
        new System.Security.AccessControl.FileSystemAccessRule(
                @"DEMOXP\TestUser",
                System.Security.AccessControl.FileSystemRights.FullControl,
                System.Security.AccessControl.AccessControlType.Allow)
        );

System.IO.File.SetAccessControl(Server.MapPath("TextFile.txt"),sec);
```

If you open the file Properties dialog again, you see that the user has been removed from the Access Control List.

Reading and Writing Files

Now that you have learned how to manage the files on the local system, this section shows you how to use the .NET Framework to perform input/output (I/O) operations, such as reading and writing, on those files. The .NET Framework makes performing I/O very easy because it uses a common model of reading or writing I/O data; so regardless of the source, virtually the same code can be used. The model is based on two basic concepts, Stream classes and Reader/Writer classes. Figure 25-11 shows the basic I/O model .NET uses and how Streams, Readers, and Writers work together to make it possible to transfer data to and from any number of sources in any number of formats. Note that the diagram shows only some of the Streams and Reader/Writer pairs in the .NET Framework.

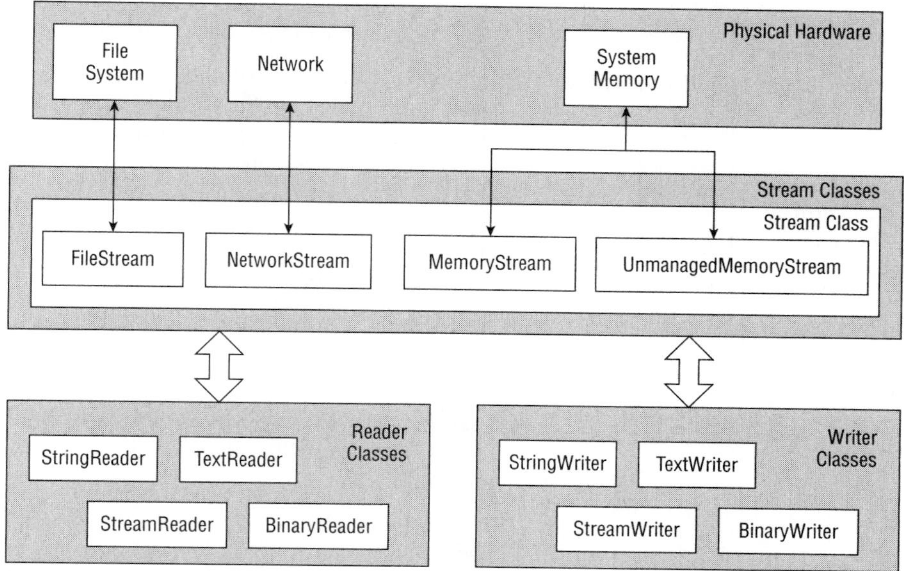

Figure 25-11

In this section, you dive deeper into learning how Streams, Readers, and Writers work and how .NET makes it easy to use them to transfer data.

Streams

Regardless of the type of I/O operation you are performing in .NET, if you want to read or write data you eventually use a stream of some type. Streams are the basic mechanism .NET uses to transfer data to and from its underlying source, be it a file, communication pipe, or TCP/IP socket. The `Stream` class provides the basic functionality to read and write I/O data, but because the `Stream` class is marked as abstract, you most likely need to use one of the several classes derived from `Stream`. Each `Stream` derivation is specialized to make it easy to transfer data from a specific source. The following table lists some of the classes derived from the `Stream` class.

Class	Description
`System.IO.FileStream`	Reads and writes files on a file system, as well as other file-related operating system handles (including pipes, standard input, standard output, and so on).
`System.IO.MemoryStream`	Creates streams that have memory as a backing store instead of a disk or a network connection. This can be useful in eliminating the need to write temporary files to disk or to store binary blob information in a database.
`System.IO.UnmanagedMemoryStream`	Supports access to unmanaged memory using the existing stream-based model and does not require that the contents in the unmanaged memory be copied to the heap.
`System.IO.BufferedStream`	Extends the `Stream` class by adding a buffering layer to read and write operations on another stream. The stream performs reads and writes in blocks (4096 bytes by default), which can result in improved efficiency.
`System.Net.Sockets.NetworkStream`	Implements the standard .NET Framework stream to send and receive data through network sockets. It supports both synchronous and asynchronous access to the network data stream.
`System.Security .Cryptography.CryptoStream`	Enables you to read and write data through cryptographic transformations.
`System.IO.Compression.GZipStream`	Enables you to compress data using the GZip data format.
`System.IO .Compression.DeflateStream`	Enables you to compress data using the `Deflate` algorithm. For more information, see the RFC 1951: DEFLATE 1.3 Specification.
`System.Net.Security.NegotiateStream`	Uses the Negotiate security protocol to authenticate the client, and optionally the server, in client-server communication.
`System.Net.Security.SslStream`	Necessary for client-server communication that uses the Secure Socket Layer (SSL) security protocol to authenticate the server and optionally the client.

As an example, you can use the `FileStream` to read a local system file from disk. To prepare for this sample, open the `TextFile.txt` you created for the samples in the previous section, enter some text, and save the file. Listing 25-13 shows the code to read this simple text file.

Listing 25-13: Using a FileStream to read a system file

VB

```
Dim fs As New FileStream (Server.MapPath("TextFile.txt"), FileMode.Open)
Dim data(fs.Length) As Byte
fs.Read(data, 0, fs.Length)
fs.Close()
```

C#

```
FileStream fs = new FileStream(Server.MapPath("TextFile.txt"), FileMode.Open);
byte[] data = new byte[fs.Length];
fs.Read(data, 0, (int)fs.Length);
fs.Close();
```

There are several items of note in this code. First, notice that you are creating a byte array the length of the stream, using the `Length` property to properly size the array, and then passing it to the `Read` method. The `Read` method fills the byte array with the stream data, in this case reading the entire stream into the byte array. If you want to read only a chunk of the stream or to start at a specific point in the stream, just change the parameters you pass to the `Read` method.

Streams use byte arrays as the basic means of transporting data to and from the underlying data source. You use a byte array to read data in this sample and, later in the chapter, you learn how to create a byte array that contains data you can write to a stream.

Second, note that you are explicitly closing the `FileStream` using the `Close` method. Streams must always be explicitly closed in order to release the resources they are using, which in this case is the file. Failing to explicitly close the stream can cause memory leaks, and it may also deny other users and applications access to the resource.

A good way to ensure that your streams will always be closed once you are done using them is to wrap them in a `Using` *statement.* `Using` *automatically calls the stream objects* `Dispose()` *method once the* `Using` *statement is closed. For the stream object, calling the* `Dispose` *method also automatically calls the streams* `Close()` *method. Utilizing the* `Using` *statement with stream objects is a good way to ensure that even if you do forget to explicitly add a call to close the stream, the object will be closed and the underlying resources released before the object is disposed.*

Finally, notice that in the `FileStream` constructor, you are passing two parameters, the first being the path to the file you want to read and the other indicating the type of access you want to use when opening the file. The `FileMode` enumeration lets you specify how the stream should be opened, for reading, writing, or both reading and writing.

Thinking about *how* you will use the opened file can become very important. Here are some issues you might want to consider when working with files using `FileStream`:

- ❑ Will you be reading, writing, or both?
- ❑ Are you creating a new file, or appending or truncating an existing file?

- Should other programs be allowed to access the file while you are using it?
- How are you going to read or write the data in the file? Are you looking for a specific location in the file, or simply reading the entire file from beginning to end?

Thankfully, the `FileStream` constructor includes a number of overloads that let you explicitly specify how you will use the file. The IO namespace also includes four enumerations that can help you control how the `FileStream` accesses your file:

- **FileMode:** The `FileMode` enumeration lets you control whether the file is appended, truncated, created, or opened.
- **FileAccess:** The `FileAccess` enumeration controls whether the file is opened for reading, writing, or both.
- **FileOptions:** The `FileOptions` enumeration controls several other miscellaneous options, such as random or sequential access, file encryption, or asynchronous file writing.
- **FileShare:** The `FileShare` enumeration controls the access that other users and programs have to the file while your application is using it.

Listing 25-14 shows how you can use all these enumerations in the `FileStream` constructor to write data to the text file you created earlier. Notice that you are supplying the `FileStream` constructor with much more information on how you want to open the file. In this sample, you append another text string to the file you just read. To do this, set the `FileMode` to Append and the `FileAccess` to Write.

Listing 25-14: Using I/O enumerations to control file behavior when writing a file

VB

```
Dim fs As New System.IO.FileStream(Server.MapPath("TextFile.txt"), _
    System.IO.FileMode.Append, System.IO.FileAccess.Write, _
    System.IO.FileShare.Read, 8, System.IO.FileOptions.None)
Dim data() As Byte = _
            System.Text.Encoding.ASCII.GetBytes("This is an additional string")
fs.Write(data, 0, data.Length)
fs.Flush()
fs.Close()
```

C#

```
System.IO.FileStream fs =
    new System.IO.FileStream(Server.MapPath("TextFile.txt"),
        System.IO.FileMode.Append, System.IO.FileAccess.Write,
        System.IO.FileShare.Read, 8, System.IO.FileOptions.None);
byte[] data = System.Text.Encoding.ASCII.GetBytes("This is an additional string");
fs.Write(data, 0, data.Length);
fs.Flush();
fs.Close();
```

You can write your text to the file by encoding a string to a byte array, which contains the information you want to write. Then, using the `Write` method, write your byte array to the `FileStreams` buffer and use the `Flush` method to instruct the `FileStream` to clear its buffer, causing any buffered data to be committed to the underlying data store. Finally, close the `FileStream`, releasing any resources it is using. If you open the `TextFile.txt` file in Notepad, you should see your string has been appended to the existing text in the file.

Note that using the `Flush` method in this scenario is optional because the `Close` method also calls `Flush` internally to commit the data to the data store. However, because the `Flush` method does not release the `FileStream` resources as `Close` does, it can be very useful if you are going to perform multiple write operations and do not want to release and then reacquire the resources for each write operation.

As you can see, so far reading and writing to files is really quite easy. The good thing is that, as mentioned earlier, because .NET uses the same basic `Stream` model for a variety of data stores, you can use these same techniques for reading and writing to any of the `Stream` derived classes. Listing 25-15 shows how you can use the same basic code to write to a `MemoryStream`, and Listing 25-16 demonstrates reading a Telnet server response using the `NetworkStream`.

Listing 25-15: Writing to a MemoryStream

VB

```
Dim data() As Byte = System.Text.Encoding.ASCII.GetBytes("This is a string")
Dim ms As New System.IO.MemoryStream()
ms.Write(data, 0, data.Length)
ms.Close()
```

C#

```
byte[] data = System.Text.Encoding.ASCII.GetBytes("This is a string");
System.IO.MemoryStream ms = new System.IO.MemoryStream();
ms.Write(data, 0, data.Length);
ms.Close();
```

Listing 25-16: Reading from a NetworkStream

VB

```
Dim client As New System.Net.Sockets.TcpClient()

' Note: You can find a large list of Telnet accessible
' BBS systems at http://www.dmine.com/telnet/brieflist.htm

' The WCS Online BBS (http://bbs.wcssoft.com)
Dim addr As System.Net.IPAddress = System.Net.IPAddress.Parse("65.182.234.52")
Dim endpoint As New System.Net.IPEndPoint(addr, 23)

client.Connect(endpoint)
Dim ns As System.Net.Sockets.NetworkStream = client.GetStream()

If (ns.DataAvailable) Then
     Dim data(client.ReceiveBufferSize) As Byte
     ns.Read(data, 0, client.ReceiveBufferSize)
     Dim response As String = System.Text.Encoding.ASCII.GetString(data)
End If
ns.Close()
```

C#

```
System.Net.Sockets.TcpClient client = new System.Net.Sockets.TcpClient();

// Note: You can find a large list of Telnet accessible
// BBS systems at http://www.dmine.com/telnet/brieflist.htm
```

Continued

```
// The WCS Online BBS (http://bbs.wcssoft.com)
System.Net.IPAddress addr = System.Net.IPAddress.Parse("65.182.234.52");
System.Net.IPEndPoint endpoint = new System.Net.IPEndPoint(addr,23);

client.Connect(endpoint);
System.Net.Sockets.NetworkStream ns = client.GetStream();

if (ns.DataAvailable)
{
    byte[] bytes = new byte[client.ReceiveBufferSize];
    ns.Read(bytes, 0, client.ReceiveBufferSize);
    string data = System.Text.Encoding.ASCII.GetString(bytes);
}
ns.Close();
```

Notice that the concept in both examples is virtually identical. You create a `Stream` object, read the bytes into a byte array for processing, and then close the stream. The code varies only in the implementation of specific Streams.

Readers and Writers

Other main parts of I/O in the .NET Framework are `Reader` and `Writer` classes. These classes help insulate you from having to deal with reading and writing individual bytes to and from Streams, enabling you to concentrate on the data you are working with. The .NET Framework provides a wide variety of reader and writer classes, each designed for reading or writing according to a specific set of rules. The first table following shows a partial list of the readers available in the .NET Framework. The second table lists the corresponding writer classes.

Class	Description
`System.IO.TextReader`	Abstract class that enables the reading of a sequential series of characters.
`System.IO.StreamReader`	Reads characters from a byte stream. Derived from `TextReader`.
`System.IO.StringReader`	Reads textual information as a stream of in-memory characters. Derived from `TextReader`.
`System.IO.BinaryReader`	Reads primitive data types as binary values from a stream.
`System.Xml.XmlTextReader`	Provides fast, non-cached, forward-only access to XML.

Class	Description
`System.IO.TextWriter`	Abstract class that enables the writing of a sequential series of characters.
`System.IO.StreamWriter`	Writes characters to a stream. Derived from `TextWriter`.

Class	Description
System.IO.StringWriter	Writes textual information as a stream of in-memory characters. Derived from TextWriter.
System.IO.BinaryWriter	Writes primitive data types in binary to a stream.
System.Xml.XmlTextWriter	Provides a fast, non-cached, forward-only way of generating XML streams or files.

Now look at using several different types of readers and writers, starting with a simple example. Listing 25-17 shows you how to use a StreamReader to read a FileStream.

Listing 25-17: Reading and writing a text file with a StreamReader

VB

```
Dim streamwriter As New System.IO.StreamWriter( _
    System.IO.File.Open("C:\Wrox\temp.txt", System.IO.FileMode.Open) )
streamwriter.Write("This is a string")
streamwriter.Close()

Dim reader As New System.IO.StreamReader( _
    System.IO.File.Open("C:\Wrox\temp.txt", System.IO.FileMode.Open) )
Dim tmp As String = reader.ReadToEnd()
reader.Close()
```

C#

```
System.IO.StreamWriter streamwriter =
             new System.IO.StreamWriter(
             System.IO.File.Open(@"C:\Wrox\temp.txt", System.IO.FileMode.Open) );
streamwriter.Write("This is a string");
streamwriter.Close();

System.IO.StreamReader reader =
             new System.IO.StreamReader(
             System.IO.File.Open(@"C:\Wrox\temp.txt",System.IO.FileMode.Open) );
string tmp = reader.ReadToEnd();
reader.Close();
```

Notice that when you create a StreamReader, you must pass an existing stream instance as a constructor parameter. The reader uses this stream as its underlying data source. In this sample, you use the File class's static Open method to open a writable FileStream for your StreamWriter.

Also notice that you no longer have to deal with byte arrays. The StreamReader takes care of converting the data to a type that's more user-friendly than a byte array. In this case, you are using the ReadToEnd method to read the entire stream and convert it to a string. The StreamReader provides a number of different methods for reading data that you can use depending on exactly how you want to read the data, from reading a single character using the Read method, to reading the entire file using the ReadToEnd method.

Figure 25-12 shows the results of your writing when you open the file in Notepad.

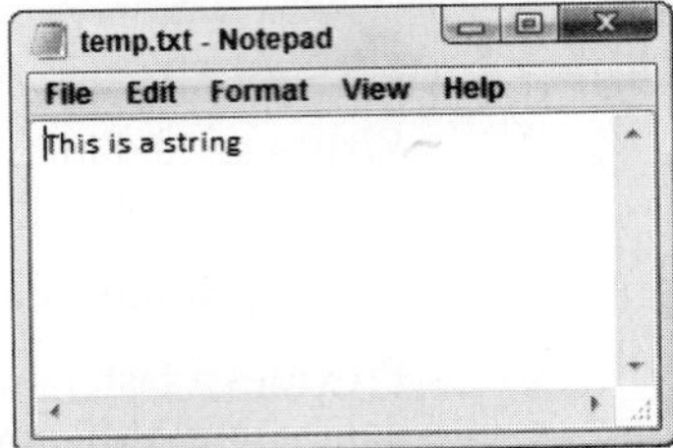

Figure 25-12

Now use the `BinaryReader` and `BinaryWriter` classes to read and write some primitive types to a file. The `BinaryWriter` writes primitive objects in their native format, so in order to read them using the `BinaryReader`, you must select the appropriate `Read` method. Listing 25-18 shows you how to do that; in this case, you are writing a value from a number of different primitive types to the text file, then reading the same value.

Listing 25-18: Reading and writing binary data

VB

```
Dim binarywriter As New System.IO.BinaryWriter( _
    System.IO.File.Create("C:\Wrox\binary.dat"))

binarywriter.Write("a string")
binarywriter.Write(&H12346789ABCDEF)
binarywriter.Write(&H12345678)
binarywriter.Write("c"c)
binarywriter.Write(1.5F)
binarywriter.Write(100.2D)
binarywriter.Close()

Dim binaryreader As New System.IO.BinaryReader( _
    System.IO.File.Open("C:\Wrox\binary.dat", System.IO.FileMode.Open))

Dim a As String = binaryreader.ReadString()
Dim l As Long = binaryreader.ReadInt64()
Dim i As Integer = binaryreader.ReadInt32()
Dim c As Char = binaryreader.ReadChar()
Dim f As Double = binaryreader.ReadSingle()
Dim d As Decimal = binaryreader.ReadDecimal()
binaryreader.Close()
```

C#

```
System.IO.BinaryWriter binarywriter =
            new System.IO.BinaryWriter(
                System.IO.File.Create(@"C:\Wrox\binary.dat") );
binarywriter.Write("a string");
binarywriter.Write(0x12346789abcdef);
binarywriter.Write(0x12345678);
binarywriter.Write('c');
binarywriter.Write(1.5f);
binarywriter.Write(100.2m);
binarywriter.Close();
```

```
System.IO.BinaryReader binaryreader =
            new System.IO.BinaryReader(
                System.IO.File.Open(@"C:\Wrox\binary.dat",
                    System.IO.FileMode.Open));

string a = binaryreader.ReadString();
long l = binaryreader.ReadInt64();
int i = binaryreader.ReadInt32();
char c = binaryreader.ReadChar();
float f = binaryreader.ReadSingle();
decimal d = binaryreader.ReadDecimal();
binaryreader.Close();
```

If you open this file in Notepad, you should see that the `BinaryWriter` has written the nonreadable binary data to the file. Figure 25-13 shows what the content of the file looks like. The `BinaryReader` provides a number of different methods for reading various kinds of primitive types from the stream. In this sample, you use a different `Read` method for each primitive type that you write to the file.

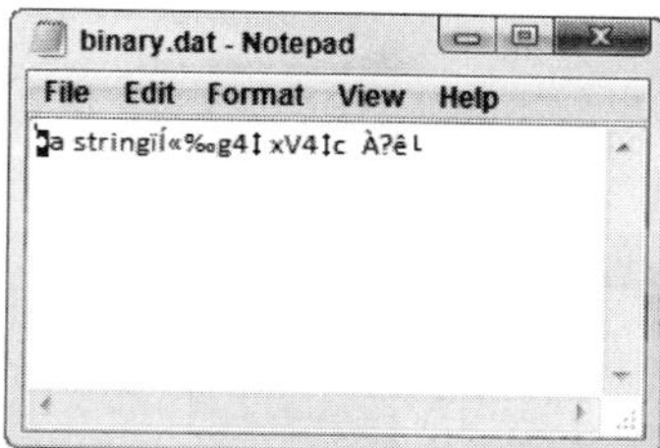

Figure 25-13

Finally, notice that the basic usage of both the `StreamReader`/`StreamWriter` and `BinaryReader`/`BinaryWriter` classes is virtually identical. You can apply the same basic ideas to use any of the reader or writer classes.

Encodings

The `StreamReader` by default attempts to determine the encoding format of the file. If one of the supported encodings such as UTF-8 or UNICODE is detected, it is used. If the encoding is not recognized, the default encoding of UTF-8 is used. Depending on the constructor you call, you can change the default encoding used and optionally turn off encoding detection. The following example shows how you can control the encoding that the `StreamReader` uses.

```
StreamReader reader =
            new StreamReader(@"C:\Wrox\text.txt",System.Text.Encoding.Unicode);
```

The default encoding for the `StreamWriter` is also UTF-8, and you can override it in the same manner as the `StreamReader` class.

I/O Shortcuts

Although knowing how to create and use streams is always very useful and worth studying, the .NET Framework provides you with numerous shortcuts for common tasks like reading and writing to files.

For instance, if you want to read the entire file, you can simply use one of the static Read All methods of the `File` class. Using these methods, you cause .NET to handle the process of creating the `Stream` and `StreamReader` for you, and simply return the resulting string of data. This is just one example of the shortcuts that the .NET Framework provides. Listing 25-19 shows some of the others, with explanatory comments. Keep in mind that Listing 25-19 is showing individual code snippets; do not try to run the listing as a single block of code.

Listing 25-19: Using the static method of the File and Directory classes

VB

```
' Opens a file and returns a FileStream
Dim fs As System.IO FileStream = _
    System.IO.File.Open("C:\Wrox\temp.txt", System.IO.FileMode.Open)


' Opens a file and returns a StreamReader for reading the data
Dim sr As System.IO.StreamReader = System.IO.File.OpenText("C:\Wrox\temp.txt")


' Opens a filestream for reading
Dim fs As System.IO.FileStream = System.IO.File.OpenRead("C:\Wrox\temp.txt")


' Opens a filestream for writing
Dim fs As System.IO.FileStream = System.IO.File.OpenWrite("C:\Wrox\temp.txt")


' Reads the entire file and returns a string of data
Dim data As String = System.IO.File.ReadAllText("C:\Wrox\temp.txt")


' Writes the string of data to the file
System.IO.File.WriteAllText("C:\Wrox\temp.txt", data)
```

C#

```
// Opens a file and returns a FileStream
System.IO.FileStream fs =
    System.IO.File.Open(@"C:\Wrox\temp.txt", System.IO.FileMode.Open);


// Opens a file and returns a StreamReader for reading the data
System.IO.StreamReader sr = System.IO.File.OpenText(@"C:\Wrox\temp.txt");


// Opens a filestream for reading
System.IO.FileStream fs = System.IO.File.OpenRead(@"C:\Wrox\temp.txt");


// Opens a filestream for writing
System.IO.FileStream fs = System.IO.File.OpenWrite(@"C:\Wrox\temp.txt");


// Reads the entire file and returns a string of data
```

```
string data = System.IO.File.ReadAllText(@"C:\Wrox\temp.txt");

// Writes the string of data to the file
System.IO.File.WriteAllText(@"C:\Wrox\temp.txt", data);
```

Compressing Streams

Introduced in the .NET 2.0 Framework, the System.IO.Compression namespace includes classes for compressing and decompressing data using either the `GZipStream` or the `DeflateStream` classes.

GZip Compression

Because both new classes are derived from the `Stream` class, using them should be relatively similar to using the other `Stream` operations you have examined so far in this chapter. Listing 25-20 shows an example of compressing your text file using the `GZipStream` class.

Listing 25-20: Compressing a file using GZipStream

VB

```
' Read the file we are going to compress into a FileStream
Dim filename As String = Server.MapPath("TextFile.txt")

Dim infile As System.IO.FileStream = System.IO.File.OpenRead(filename)
Dim buffer(infile.Length) As Byte
infile.Read(buffer, 0, buffer.Length)
infile.Close()

' Create the output file
Dim outfile As System.IO.FileStream = _
    System.IO.File.Create(System.IO.Path.ChangeExtension(filename, "zip"))

' Compress the input stream and write it to the output FileStream
Dim gzipStream As New System.IO.Compression.GZipStream(
    outfile, System.IO.Compression.CompressionMode.Compress)
gzipStream.Write(buffer, 0, buffer.Length)
gzipStream.Close()
```

C#

```
// Read the file we are going to compress into a FileStream
string filename = Server.MapPath("TextFile.txt");

System.IO.FileStream infile = System.IO.File.OpenRead(filename);
byte[] buffer = new byte[infile.Length];
infile.Read(buffer, 0, buffer.Length);
infile.Close();

// Create the output file
System.IO.FileStream outfile =
    System.IO.File.Create(System.IO.Path.ChangeExtension(filename, "zip"));

// Compress the input stream and write it to the output FileStream
```

Continued

```
System.IO.Compression.GZipStream gzipStream =
    new System.IO.Compression.GZipStream(outfile,
        System.IO.Compression.CompressionMode.Compress);
gzipStream.Write(buffer, 0, buffer.Length);
gzipStream.Close();
```

Notice that the `GZipStream` constructor requires two parameters, the stream to write the compressed data to, and the `CompressionMode` enumeration, which tells the class if you want to compress or decompress data. After the code runs, be sure there is a file called `text.zip` in your Web site directory.

Deflate Compression

The `Compression` namespace also allows to you decompress a file using the `GZip` or `Deflate` methods. Listing 25-21 shows an example of decompressing a file using the `Deflate` method.

Listing 25-21: Decompressing a file using DeflateStream

VB

```
Dim filename As String = Server.MapPath("TextFile.zip")

Dim infile As System.IO.FileStream = System.IO.File.OpenRead(filename)
Dim deflateStream As New System.IO.Compression.DeflateStream( _
    infile, System.IO.Compression.CompressionMode.Decompress)
Dim buffer(infile.Length + 100) As Byte

Dim offset As Integer = 0
Dim totalCount As Integer = 0
While True
    Dim bytesRead As Integer = deflateStream.Read(buffer, offset, 100)
    If bytesRead = 0 Then
        Exit While
    End If
    offset += bytesRead
    totalCount += bytesRead
End While

Dim outfile As System.IO.FileStream = _
    System.IO.File.Create(System.IO.Path.ChangeExtension(filename, "txt"))
outfile.Write(buffer, 0, buffer.Length)
outfile.Close()
```

C#

```
string filename = Server.MapPath("TextFile.zip");

System.IO.FileStream infile = System.IO.File.OpenRead(filename);
System.IO.Compression.DeflateStream deflateStream =
    new System.IO.Compression.DeflateStream(infile,
        System.IO.Compression.CompressionMode.Decompress);
byte[] buffer = new byte[infile.Length + 100];

int offset = 0;
int totalCount = 0;
while (true)
```

```
{
    int bytesRead = deflateStream.Read(buffer, offset, 100);
    if (bytesRead == 0)
    { break; }

    offset += bytesRead;
    totalCount += bytesRead;
}

System.IO.FileStream outfile =
    System.IO.File.Create(System.IO.Path.ChangeExtension(filename, "txt"));
outfile.Write(buffer, 0, buffer.Length);
outfile.Close();
```

Compressing HTTP Output

Besides compressing files, one other very good use of the compression features of the .NET Framework in an ASP.NET application is to implement your own `HttpModule` class that compresses the HTTP output of your application. This is easier than it might sound, and it will save you precious bandwidth by compressing the data that is sent from your Web server to the browsers that support the HTTP 1.1 Protocol standard (which most do). The browser can then decompress the data before rendering it.

IIS 6 does offer built-in HTTP compression capabilities, and there are several third-party HTTP compression modules available, such as the Blowery Http Compression Module (`www.blowery.org`).

Start by creating a Windows Class library project. Add a new class to your project called `CompressionModule`. This class is your compression `HttpModule`. Listing 25-22 shows the code for creating the class.

Listing 25-22: Compressing HTTP output with an HttpModule

VB

```
Imports System
Imports System.Collections.Generic
Imports System.Text
Imports System.Web
Imports System.IO
Imports System.IO.Compression

Namespace Wrox.Demo.Compression

Public Class CompressionModule
    Implements IHttpModule

    Public Sub Dispose() Implements System.Web.IHttpModule.Dispose
        Throw New Exception("The method or operation is not implemented.")
    End Sub

    Public Sub Init(ByVal context As System.Web.HttpApplication) _
       Implements System.Web.IHttpModule.Init
        AddHandler context.BeginRequest, AddressOf context_BeginRequest
    End Sub

    Public Sub context_BeginRequest(ByVal sender As Object, ByVal e As EventArgs)
        Dim app As HttpApplication = CType(sender, HttpApplication)
```

```
        'Get the Accept-Encoding HTTP header from the request.
        'The requesting browser sends this header which we will use
        ' to determine if it supports compression, and if so, what type
        ' of compression algorithm it supports
        Dim encodings As String = app.Request.Headers.Get("Accept-Encoding")

        If (encodings = Nothing) Then
            Return
        End If

        Dim s As Stream = app.Response.Filter

        encodings = encodings.ToLower()

        If (encodings.Contains("gzip")) Then
            app.Response.Filter = New GZipStream(s, CompressionMode.Compress)
            app.Response.AppendHeader("Content-Encoding", "gzip")
            app.Context.Trace.Warn("GZIP Compression on")
        Else
            app.Response.Filter = _
                          New DeflateStream(s, CompressionMode.Compress)
            app.Response.AppendHeader("Content-Encoding", "deflate")
            app.Context.Trace.Warn("Deflate Compression on")
        End If
    End Sub
End Class

End Namespace
```

C#

```
using System;
using System.Collections.Generic;
using System.Text;
using System.Web;
using System.IO;
using System.IO.Compression;

namespace Wrox.Demo.Compression
{
    public class CompressionModule : IHttpModule
    {

        #region IHttpModule Members

        void IHttpModule.Dispose()
        {
            throw new Exception("The method or operation is not implemented.");
        }

        void IHttpModule.Init(HttpApplication context)
        {
            context.BeginRequest += new EventHandler(context_BeginRequest);
        }

        void context_BeginRequest(object sender, EventArgs e)
```

```
            {
                HttpApplication app = (HttpApplication)sender;

                //Get the Accept-Encoding HTTP header from the request.
                //The requesting browser sends this header which we will use
                // to determine if it supports compression, and if so, what type
                // of compression algorithm it supports
                string encodings = app.Request.Headers.Get("Accept-Encoding");

                if (encodings == null)
                    return;

                Stream s = app.Response.Filter;

                encodings = encodings.ToLower();

                if (encodings.Contains("gzip"))
                {
                    app.Response.Filter = new GZipStream(s, CompressionMode.Compress);
                    app.Response.AppendHeader("Content-Encoding", "gzip");
                    app.Context.Trace.Warn("GZIP Compression on");
                }
                else
                {
                    app.Response.Filter =
                                   new DeflateStream(s, CompressionMode.Compress);
                    app.Response.AppendHeader("Content-Encoding", "deflate");
                    app.Context.Trace.Warn("Deflate Compression on");
                }
            }

            #endregion
        }
    }
```

After you create and build the module, add the assembly to your Web site's `Bin` directory. After that's done, you let your Web application know that it should use the `HttpModule` when it runs. Do this by adding the module to the `web.config` file. Listing 25-23 shows the nodes to add to the `web.config` `system.web` configuration section.

Listing 25-23: Adding an HttpCompression module to the web.config

```
<httpModules>
      <add name="HttpCompressionModule"
       type="Wrox.Demo.Compression.CompressionModule, HttpCompressionModule"/>
</httpModules>

<trace enabled="true" />
```

Notice that one other change you are making is to enable page tracing. You use this to demonstrate that the page is actually being compressed. When you run the page, you should see the trace output shown in Figure 25-14. Notice a new entry under the trace information showing that the GZip compression has been enabled on this page.

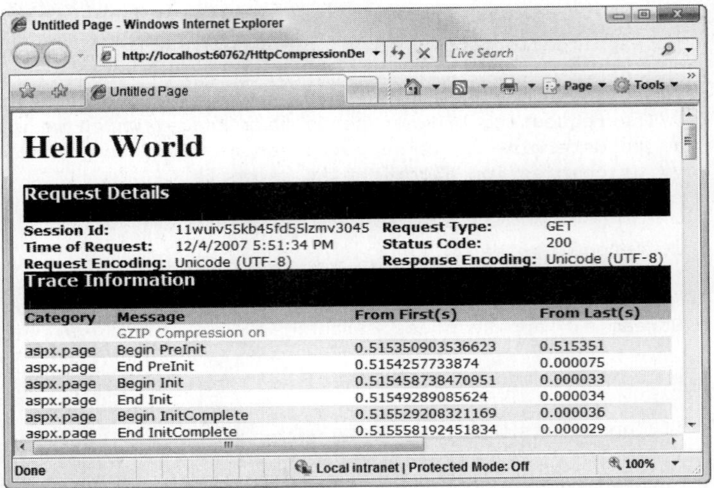

Figure 25-14

Working with Serial Ports

Also introduced in the .NET 2.0 Framework was the `System.IO.Ports` namespace. This namespace contains classes that enable you to work with and communicate through serial ports.

.NET provides a `SerialPort` component that you can add to the Component Designer of your Web page. Adding this component enables your application to communicate via the serial port. Listing 25-24 shows how to write some text to the serial port.

Listing 25-24: Writing text to the serial port

VB

```
<script runat="server">
    Dim SerialPort1 As New System.IO.Ports.SerialPort()

    Protected Sub Page_Load(ByVal sender As Object, ByVal e As System.EventArgs)

        Me.SerialPort1.PortName = "COM1"

        If (Not Me.SerialPort1.IsOpen()) Then
            Me.SerialPort1.Open()
        End If

        Me.SerialPort1.Write("Hello World")
        Me.SerialPort1.Close()

    End Sub
</script>
```

C#

```
<script runat="server">
```

```
    System.IO.Ports.SerialPort SerialPort1 = new System.IO.Ports.SerialPort();

    protected void Page_Load(object sender, EventArgs e)
    {
        this.SerialPort1.PortName = "COM1";

        if (!this.SerialPort1.IsOpen)
        {
            this.SerialPort1.Open();
        }

        this.SerialPort1.Write("Hello World");
        this.SerialPort1.Close();
    }

</script>
```

This code simply attempts to open the serial port COM1 and write a bit of text. The `SerialPort` component gives you control over most aspects of the serial port, including baud rate, parity, and stop bits.

Network Communications

Finally, this chapter takes you beyond your own systems and talks about how you can use the .NET Framework to communicate with other systems. The .NET Framework contains a rich set of classes in the `System.Net` namespace that allow you to communicate over a network using a variety of protocols and communications layers. You can perform all types of actions, from DNS resolution to programmatic HTTP Posts to sending e-mail through SMTP.

WebRequest and WebResponse

The first series of classes to discuss are the `WebRequest` and `WebResponse` classes. You can use these two classes to develop applications that can make a request to a Uniform Resource Identifier (URI) and receive a response from that resource. The .NET Framework provides three derivatives of the `WebRequest` and `WebResponse` classes, each designed to communicate to a specific type of end point via HTTP, FTP, and file:// protocols.

HttpWebRequest and HttpWebResponse

The first pair of classes are the `HttpWebRequest` and `HttpWebResponse` classes. As you can probably guess based on their names, these two classes are designed to communicate using the HTTP protocol. Perhaps the most famous use of the `HttpWebRequest` and `HttpWebResponse` classes is to write applications that can make requests to other Web pages via HTTP and parse the resulting text to extract data. This is known as *screen scraping*.

For an example of using the `HttpWebRequest` and `HttpWebResponse` classes to screen scrape, you can use the following code to build a Web page that will serve as a simple Web browser. You also learn how another Web page can be displayed inside of yours using an `HttpWebRequest`. In this example, you scrape the wrox.com home page and display it in a panel on your Web page. Listing 25-25 shows the code.

Listing 25-25: Using an HttpWebRequest to retrieve a Web page

VB

```
<%@ Page Language="VB" %>
<%@ Import Namespace=System.IO %>
<%@ Import Namespace=System.Net %>

<script runat="server">
    Protected Sub Page_Load(ByVal sender As Object, ByVal e As System.EventArgs)
        Dim uri As New Uri("http://www.wrox.com/")
        If (uri.Scheme = uri.UriSchemeHttp) Then
            Dim request As HttpWebRequest = HttpWebRequest.Create(uri)
            request.Method = WebRequestMethods.Http.Get
            Dim response As HttpWebResponse = request.GetResponse()
            Dim reader As New StreamReader(response.GetResponseStream())
            Dim tmp As String = reader.ReadToEnd()
            response.Close()

            Me.Panel1.GroupingText = tmp
        End If
    End Sub
</script>

<html xmlns="http://www.w3.org/1999/xhtml" >
<head runat="server">
    <title>Untitled Page</title>
</head>
<body>
    <form id="form1" runat="server">
    <div>
        <p>This is the wrox.com website:</p>
        <asp:Panel ID="Panel1" runat="server"
          Height="355px" Width="480px" ScrollBars=Auto>
        </asp:Panel>
    </div>
    </form>
</body>
</html>
```

C#

```
<script runat="server">
    protected void Page_Load(object sender, EventArgs e)
    {
        Uri uri = new Uri("http://www.wrox.com/");
        if (uri.Scheme == Uri.UriSchemeHttp)
        {
            HttpWebRequest request = (HttpWebRequest)HttpWebRequest.Create( uri );
            request.Method = WebRequestMethods.Http.Get;
            HttpWebResponse response = (HttpWebResponse)request.GetResponse();
            StreamReader reader = new StreamReader(response.GetResponseStream());
            string tmp = reader.ReadToEnd();
            response.Close();
```

```
            this.Panel1.GroupingText = tmp;
        }
    }
</script>
```

Figure 25-15 shows what the Web page look likes when you execute the code in Listing 25-25. The `HttpWebRequest` to the Wrox.com home page returns a string containing the scraped HTML. The sample assigns the value of this string to the `GroupingText` property of the Panel control. When the final page is rendered, the browser renders the HTML that was scraped as literal content on the page.

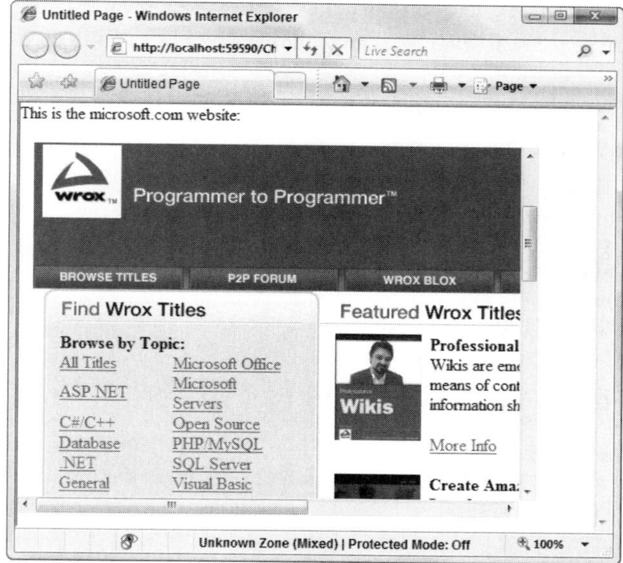

Figure 25-15

One other use of the `HttpWebRequest` and `HttpWebResponse` classes is to programmatically post data to another Web page, as shown in Listing 25-26.

Listing 25-26: Using an HttpWebRequest to post data to a remote Web page

VB

```
<%@ Page Language="VB" %>
<%@ Import Namespace=System.IO %>
<%@ Import Namespace=System.Net %>

<script runat="server">

    Protected Sub Page_Load(ByVal sender As Object, ByVal e As System.EventArgs)
        Dim uri As New Uri("http://www.amazon.com/" & _
                        "exec/obidos/search-handle-form/102-5194535-6807312")
```

Continued

```
        Dim data As String = "field-keywords=Professional ASP.NET 3.5"
        If (uri.Scheme = uri.UriSchemeHttp) Then

            Dim request As HttpWebRequest = HttpWebRequest.Create(uri)
            request.Method = WebRequestMethods.Http.Post
            request.ContentLength = data.Length
            request.ContentType = "application/x-www-form-urlencoded"

            Dim writer As New StreamWriter(request.GetRequestStream())
            writer.Write(data)
            writer.Close()

            Dim response As HttpWebResponse = request.GetResponse()
            Dim reader As New StreamReader(response.GetResponseStream())
            Dim tmp As String = reader.ReadToEnd()
            response.Close()

            Me.Panel1.GroupingText = tmp
        End If
    End Sub
</script>

<html xmlns="http://www.w3.org/1999/xhtml" >
<head runat="server">
    <title>Untitled Page</title>
</head>
<body>
    <form id="form1" runat="server">
    <div>
        <asp:Panel ID="Panel1" runat="server"
            Height="355px" Width="480px" ScrollBars=Auto>
        </asp:Panel>
    </div>
    </form>
</body>
</html>
```

C#

```
<script runat="server">

    protected void Page_Load(object sender, EventArgs e)
    {
        Uri uri = new Uri("http://www.amazon.com/" +
                        "exec/obidos/search-handle-form/102-5194535-6807312");
        string data = "field-keywords=Professional ASP.NET 3.5";
        if (uri.Scheme == Uri.UriSchemeHttp)
        {
            HttpWebRequest request = (HttpWebRequest)HttpWebRequest.Create(uri);
            request.Method = WebRequestMethods.Http.Post;
            request.ContentLength = data.Length;
            request.ContentType = "application/x-www-form-urlencoded";

            StreamWriter writer = new StreamWriter( request.GetRequestStream() );
```

```
            writer.Write(data);
            writer.Close();

            HttpWebResponse response = (HttpWebResponse)request.GetResponse();
            StreamReader reader = new StreamReader(response.GetResponseStream());
            string tmp = reader.ReadToEnd();
            response.Close();

            this.Panel1.GroupingText = tmp;
        }
    }
</script>
```

You can see that the preceding code posts a search query to Amazon.com and receives the HTML as the response. As in the example shown earlier in Listing 25-25, you can simply use a Panel to display the resulting text as HTML. The results of the query are shown in Figure 25-16.

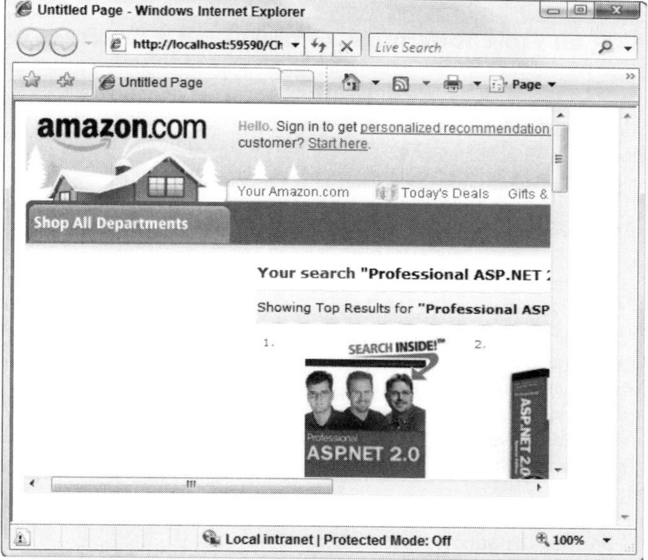

Figure 25-16

FtpWebRequest and FtpWebResponse

The next pair of classes are the `FtpWebRequest` and `FtpWebResponse` classes. These two classes were new additions to the .NET 2.0 Framework, and they make it easy to execute File Transfer Protocol (FTP) commands from your Web page. Using these classes, it is now possible to implement an entire FTP client right from your Web application. Listing 25-27 shows an example of downloading a text file from the public Microsoft.com FTP site. (See Figure 25-17.)

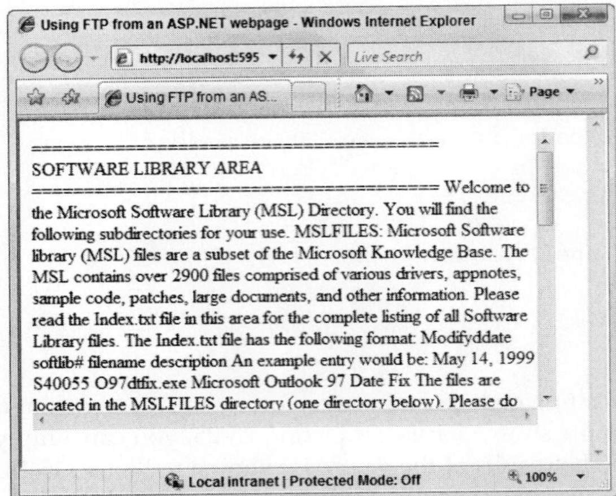

Figure 25-17

Listing 25-27: Using an FtpWebRequest to download a file from an FTP site

VB

```
<%@ Page Language="VB" %>
<%@ Import Namespace=System.IO %>
<%@ Import Namespace=System.Net %>

<script runat="server">

    Protected Sub Page_Load(ByVal sender As Object, ByVal e As System.EventArgs)
        Dim uri As New Uri("ftp://ftp.microsoft.com/SoftLib/ReadMe.txt")
        If (uri.Scheme = uri.UriSchemeFtp) Then
            Dim request As FtpWebRequest = FtpWebRequest.Create(uri)
            request.Method = WebRequestMethods.Ftp.DownloadFile
            Dim response As FtpWebResponse = request.GetResponse()
            Dim reader As New StreamReader(response.GetResponseStream())
            Dim tmp As String = reader.ReadToEnd()
            response.Close()

            Me.Panel1.GroupingText = tmp
        End If
    End Sub
</script>

<html xmlns="http://www.w3.org/1999/xhtml" >
<head runat="server">
    <title>Using FTP from an ASP.NET webpage</title>
</head>
<body>
    <form id="form1" runat="server">
    <div>
        <div runat="server" id="ftpContent"
            style="overflow:scroll; height: 260px; width: 450px;">
        </div>
    </div>
```

```
    </form>
</body>
</html>
```

C#

```
<script runat="server">

    protected void Page_Load(object sender, EventArgs e)
    {
        Uri uri = new Uri("ftp://ftp.microsoft.com/SoftLib/ReadMe.txt ");
        if (uri.Scheme == Uri.UriSchemeFtp)
        {
            FtpWebRequest request = (FtpWebRequest)FtpWebRequest.Create(uri);
            request.Method = WebRequestMethods.Ftp.DownloadFile;
            FtpWebResponse response = (FtpWebResponse)request.GetResponse();
            StreamReader reader = new StreamReader(response.GetResponseStream());
            string tmp = reader.ReadToEnd();
            response.Close();

            this.Panel1.GroupingText = tmp;
        }
    }
</script>
```

FileWebRequest and FileWebResponse

Next, look at the `FileWebRequest` and `FileWebResponse` classes. These classes provide a file system implementation of the WebRequest and WebResponse classes and are designed to make it easy to transfer files using the file:// protocol, as shown in Listing 25-28.

Listing 25-28: Using the FileWebRequest to write to a remote file

VB

```
Dim uri As New Uri("file://DEMOXP/Documents/lorum.txt")
If (uri.Scheme = uri.UriSchemeFile) Then
    Dim request As System.Net.FileWebRequest = _
        System.Net.FileWebRequest.Create(uri)
    Dim response As System.Net.FileWebResponse = request.GetResponse()
    Dim reader As New System.IO.StreamReader(response.GetResponseStream())
    Dim tmp As String = reader.ReadToEnd()
    response.Close()
End If
```

C#

```
Uri uri = new Uri("file://DEMOXP/Documents/lorum.txt ");
if (uri.Scheme == Uri.UriSchemeFile)
{
    System.Net.FileWebRequest request =
        (System.Net.FileWebRequest)System.Net.FileWebRequest.Create(uri);
    System.Net.FileWebResponse response =
        (System.Net.FileWebResponse)request.GetResponse();
    System.IO.StreamReader reader =
        new System.IO.StreamReader(response.GetResponseStream());
```

```
        string tmp = reader.ReadToEnd();
        response.Close();
    }
```

In this listing, we are requesting the `lorum.txt` file that exists in the `Documents` folder on the DEMOXP machine on our local network.

Sending Mail

Finally, consider a feature common to many Web applications — the capability to send e-mail from a Web page. The capability to send mail was part of the 1.0 Framework and located in the `System.Web.Mail` namespace. In the 2.0 Framework, this functionality was enhanced and moved to the `System.Net.Mail` namespace. Listing 25-29 shows an example of sending an e-mail.

Listing 25-29: Sending mail from a Web page

VB

```
Dim message As _
    New System.Net.Mail.MailMessage("webmaster@ineta.org", "webmaster@ineta.org")
message.Subject = "Sending Mail with ASP.NET 3.5"
message.Body = _
    "This is a sample email which demonstrates sending email using ASP.NET 3.5"

Dim smtp As New System.Net.Mail.SmtpClient("localhost")
smtp.Send(message)
```

C#

```
System.Net.Mail.MailMessage message =
    new System.Net.Mail.MailMessage("webmaster@ineta.org","webmaster@ineta.org");
message.Subject = "Sending Mail with ASP.NET 3.5";
message.Body =
    "This is a sample email which demonstrates sending email using ASP.NET 3.5";
System.Net.Mail.SmtpClient smtp = new System.Net.Mail.SmtpClient("localhost");
smtp.Send(message);
```

In this sample, you first create a `MailMessage` object, which is the class that contains the actual message you want to send. The `MailMessage` class requires the To and From address be provided to its constructor, and you can either provide the parameters as strings, or you can use the `MailAddressCollection` class to provide multiple recipients' e-mail addresses.

After you create the `Message`, you use the `SmtpClient` class to actually send the message to your local SMTP server. The `SmtpClient` class allows you to specify the SMTP Server from which you want to relay your e-mail.

Summary

In this chapter, you looked at some of the other classes in the .NET Framework. You looked at managing the local file system by using classes in the `System.IO` namespace such as `DirectoryInfo` and the `FileInfo`, and you learned how to enumerate the local file system and manipulate both directory and file properties and directory and file Access Control Lists. Additionally, the chapter discussed the rich functionality .NET provides for working with paths.

The chapter also covered how the .NET Framework enables you to read and write data to a multitude of data locations, including the local file system, network file system, and even system memory through a common `Stream` architecture. The Framework provides you with specialized classes to deal with each kind of data location. Additionally, the Framework makes working with streams even easier by providing `Reader` and `Writer` classes. These classes hide much of the complexity of reading from and writing to underlying streams. Here, too, the Framework provides you with a number of different `Reader` and `Writer` classes that give you the power to control exactly how your data is read or written, be it character, binary, string, or XML.

You were also introduced to a new feature of the .NET 2.0 Framework that allows you to communicate with serial ports.

Finally, you learned about the variety of network communication options the .NET Framework provides. From making and sending Web requests over HTTP, FTP, and File, to sending mail, the .NET Framework offers you a full plate of network communication services.

26

User and Server Controls

In an object-oriented environment like .NET, the encapsulation of code into small, single-purpose, reusable objects is one of the keys to developing a robust system. For instance, if your application deals with customers, you might want to consider creating a customer's object that encapsulates all the functionality a customer might need. The advantage is that you create a single point with which other objects can interact, and you have only a single point of code to create, debug, deploy, and maintain. In this scenario, the customer object is typically known as a business object because it encapsulates all the business logic needed for a customer.

Several other types of reusable objects are available in .NET. In this chapter, we concentrate on discussing and demonstrating how you can create reusable visual components for an ASP.NET application. The two types of reusable components in ASP.NET are user controls and server controls.

A *user control* encapsulates existing ASP.NET controls into a single container control, which you can easily reuse throughout your Web project.

A *server control* encapsulates the visual design, behavior, and logic for an element that the user interacts with on the Web page.

Visual Studio ships with a large number of server controls that you are probably already familiar with, such as the Label, Button, and TextBox controls. This chapter talks about how you can create custom server controls and extend existing server controls.

Because the topics of user controls and server controls are so large, and because discussing the intricacies of each could easily fill an entire book by itself, this chapter can't possibly investigate every option available to you. Instead, it attempts to give you a brief overview of building and using user controls and server controls and demonstrates some common scenarios for each type of control. By the end of this chapter, you should have learned enough that you can get started building basic controls of each type and be able to continue to learn on your own.

User Controls

User controls represent the simplest form of ASP.NET control encapsulation. Because they are the simplest, they are also the easiest to create and use. Essentially a *user control* is the grouping of existing server controls into a single-container control. This enables you to create powerful objects that you can easily use throughout an entire Web project.

Creating User Controls

Creating user controls is very simple in Visual Studio 2008. To create a new user control, you first add a new User Control file to your Web site. From the Website menu, select the Add New Item option. After the Add New File dialog appears, select the Web User Control File template from the list and click OK. Notice that after the file is added to the project, the file has an `.ascx` extension. This extension signals to ASP.NET that this file is a user control. If you attempt to load the user control directly into your browser, ASP.NET returns an error telling you that this type of file cannot be served to the client.

If you look at the HTML source (shown in Listing 26-1) for the user control, you see several interesting differences from a standard ASP.NET Web page.

Listing 26-1: A Web user control file template

```
<%@ Control Language="VB" ClassName="WebUserControl1" %>

<script runat="server">

</script>
```

First, notice that the source uses the `@Control` directive rather than the `@Page` directive, which a standard Web page would use. Second, notice that unlike a standard ASP.NET Web page, no other HTML tags besides the `<script>` tags exist in the control. The Web page containing the user control provides the basic HTML, such as the `<body>` and `<form>` tags. In fact, if you try to add a server-side form tag to the user control, ASP.NET returns an error when the page is served to the client. The error message tells you that only one server-side form tag is allowed in your Web page.

To add controls to the form, simply drag them from the Toolbox onto your user control. Listing 26-2 shows the user control after a Label and a Button have been added.

Listing 26-2: Adding controls to the Web user control

```
<%@ Control Language="VB" ClassName="WebUserControl2" %>

<script runat="server">

</script>

<asp:Label ID="Label1" runat="server" Text="Label"></asp:Label>
<asp:Button ID="Button1" runat="server" Text="Button" />
```

After you add the controls to the user control, you put the user control onto a standard ASP.NET Web page. To do this, drag the file from the Solution Explorer onto your Web page.

If you are familiar with using user controls in prior versions of Visual Studio, you probably remember the gray control representation that appeared in the page designer when you dropped a user control onto a Web page. In Visual Studio 2005, this experience was improved and user controls are now fully rendered on the host Web page during design time. This allows you to see an accurate representation of what the entire page will look like after it is rendered to the client.

Figure 26-1 shows the user control after it has been dropped onto a host Web page.

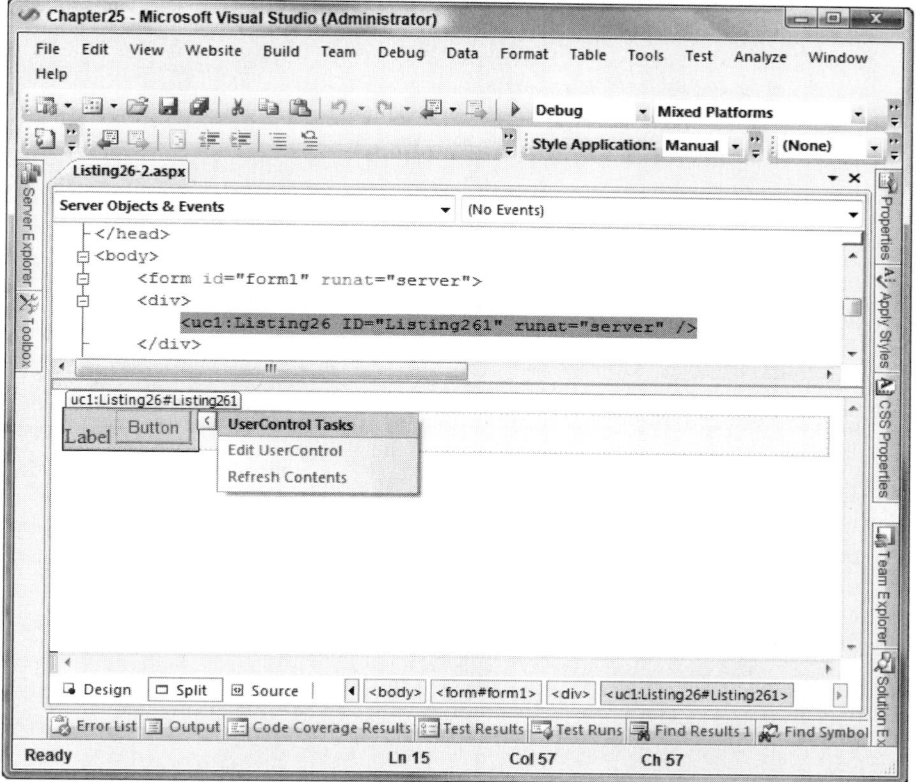

Figure 26-1

After you have placed the user control onto a Web page, open the page in a browser to see the fully rendered Web page.

User controls fully participate in the page-rendering lifecycle, and controls contained within a user control behave identically to controls placed onto a standard ASP.NET Web page. This means that the user control has its own page execute events (such as Init, Load, and Prerender) that execute as the page is processed. It also means that child control events, such as a button-click event, will behave identically. Listing 26-3 shows how to use the User Controls `Page_Load` event to populate the label and to handle the button-click event.

Listing 26-3: Creating control events in a user control

VB

```
<%@ Control Language="VB" ClassName="WebUserControl1" %>

<script runat="server">

    Protected Sub Page_Load(ByVal sender As Object, ByVal e As System.EventArgs)
        Me.Label1.Text = "The quick brown fox jumped over the lazy dog"
    End Sub

    Protected Sub Button1_Click(ByVal sender As Object, _
       ByVal e As System.EventArgs)
        Me.Label1.Text = "The quick brown fox clicked the button on the page"
    End Sub
</script>

<asp:Label ID="Label1" runat="server" Text="Label"></asp:Label>
<asp:Button ID="Button1" runat="server" Text="Button" OnClick="Button1_Click" />
```

C#

```
<%@ Control Language="C#" ClassName="WebUserControl1" %>

<script runat="server">

    protected void Page_Load(object sender, EventArgs e)
    {
        this.Label1.Text = "The quick brown fox jumped over the lazy dog";
    }

    protected void Button1_Click(object sender, EventArgs e)
    {
        this.Label1.Text = "The quick brown fox clicked the button on the page";
    }
</script>

<asp:Label ID="Label1" runat="server" Text="Label"></asp:Label>
<asp:Button ID="Button1" runat="server" Text="Button" OnClick="Button1_Click" />
```

Now when you render the Web page, you see that the text of the label changes as the user control loads, and again when you click the bottom of the page. In fact, if you put a breakpoint on either of these two events, you can see that ASP.NET does indeed break, even inside the user control code when the page is executed.

Interacting with User Controls

So far, you have learned how you can create user controls and add them to a Web page. You have also learned how user controls can execute their own code. Most user controls, however, are not islands on their parent page. Many scenarios require that the host Web page be able to interact with user controls that have been placed on it. For instance, you may decide that the text you want to load in the label must be given to the user control by the host page. To do this, you simply add a public property to the user control, and then assign text using the property. Listing 26-4 shows the modified user control.

Listing 26-4: Exposing user control properties

VB

```
<%@ Control Language="VB" ClassName="WebUserControl" %>

<script runat="server">

    Private _text As String

    Public Property Text() As String
        Get
            Return _text
        End Get
        Set(ByVal value As String)
            _text = value
        End Set
    End Property

    Protected Sub Page_Load(ByVal sender As Object, ByVal e As System.EventArgs)
        Me.Label1.Text = Me.Text
    End Sub

    Protected Sub Button1_Click(ByVal sender As Object, _
      ByVal e As System.EventArgs)
        Me.Label1.Text = "The quick brown fox clicked the button on the page"
    End Sub

</script>

<asp:Label ID="Label1" runat="server" Text="Label"></asp:Label>
<asp:Button ID="Button1" runat="server" Text="Button" OnClick="Button1_Click" />
```

C#

```
<%@ Control Language="C#" ClassName="WebUserControl" %>

<script runat="server">

    private string _text;

    public string Text
    {
        get {
            return _text;
        }
        set {
            _text = value;
        }
    }

    protected void Page_Load(object sender, EventArgs e)
    {
        this.Label1.Text = this.Text;
    }
```

Continued

```
    protected void Button1_Click(object sender, EventArgs e)
    {
        this.Label1.Text = "The quick brown fox clicked the button on the page";
    }

</script>

<asp:Label ID="Label1" runat="server" Text="Label"></asp:Label>
<asp:Button ID="Button1" runat="server" Text="Button" OnClick="Button1_Click" />
```

After you modify the user control, you simply populate the property from the host Web page. Listing 26-5 shows how to set the `Text` property in code, but public properties exposed by user controls will also be exposed by the Property Browser.

Listing 26-5: Populating user control properties from the host Web page

VB

```
Protected Sub Page_Load(ByVal sender As Object, ByVal e As System.EventArgs)
    Me.WebUserControl1.Text = "The quick brown fox jumped over the lazy dog"
End Sub
```

C#

```
protected void Page_Load(object sender, EventArgs e)
{
    this.WebUserControl1.Text = "The quick brown fox jumped over the lazy dog";
}
```

User controls are simple ways of creating powerful, reusable components in ASP.NET. They are easy to create using the built-in templates. Because they participate fully in the page lifecycle, you can create controls that can interact with their host page and even other controls on the host page.

Loading User Controls Dynamically

User controls can also be created and added to the Web form dynamically at runtime. The ASP.NET `Page` object includes the `LoadControl` method, which allows you to load user controls at runtime by providing the method with a virtual path to the user control you want to load. The method returns a generic `Control` object that you can then add to the page's `Controls` collection. Listing 26-6 demonstrates how you can use the `LoadControl` method to dynamically add a user control to a Web page.

Listing 26-6: Dynamically adding a user control

VB

```
<%@ Page Language="VB" %>

<script runat="server">
    Protected Sub Page_Load(ByVal sender As Object, ByVal e As System.EventArgs)
        Dim myForm As Control = Page.FindControl("form1")
        Dim c1 As Control = LoadControl("~/WebUserControl.ascx")
        myForm.Controls.Add(c1)
    End Sub
</script>
```

```
<html xmlns="http://www.w3.org/1999/xhtml" >
<head runat="server">
    <title>Untitled Page</title>
</head>
<body>
    <form id="form1" runat="server">
    <div>
    </div>
    </form>
</body>
</html>
```

C#

```
<script runat="server">
    void Page_Load(object sender, EventArgs e)
    {
        Control myForm = Page.FindControl("Form1");
        Control c1 = LoadControl("~/WebUserControl.ascx");
        myForm.Controls.Add(c1);
    }
</script>
```

The first step in adding a user control to the page is to locate the page's Form control using the `FindControl` method. Should the user control contain ASP.NET controls that render form elements such as a button or text box, this user control must be added to the Form element's `Controls` collection.

It is possible to add user controls containing certain ASP.NET elements such as a Label, HyperLink, or Image directly to the `Page` *object's* `Controls` *collection; however, it is generally safer to be consistent and add them to the Form. Adding a control that must be contained within the Form, such as a Button control, to the* `Pages Controls` *collection results in a runtime parser error.*

After the form has been found, the sample uses the Page's `LoadControl()` method to load an instance of the user control. The method accepts a virtual path to the user control you want to load and returns the loaded user control as a generic `Control` object.

Finally, the control is added to the `Form` object's `Controls` collection. You can also add the user control to other container controls that may be present on the Web page, such as a Panel or Placeholder control.

Remember that you need to re-add your control to the ASP.NET page each time the page performs a postback.

After you have the user control loaded, you can also work with its object model, just as you can with any other control. To access properties and methods that the user control exposes, you cast the control from the generic Control type to its actual type. To do that, you also need to add the `@Reference` directive to the page. This tells ASP.NET to compile the user control and link it to the ASP.NET page so that the page knows where to find the user control type. Listing 26-7 demonstrates how you can access a custom property of your user control by casting the control after loading it. The sample loads a modified user control that hosts an ASP.NET TextBox control and exposes a public property that allows you to access the TextBox control's `Text` property.

Listing 26-7: Casting a user control to its native type

VB

```
<%@ Page Language="VB" %>
<%@ Reference Control="~/WebUserControl.ascx" %>

<script runat="server">
    Protected Sub Page_Load(ByVal sender As Object, ByVal e As System.EventArgs)
        Dim myForm As Control = Page.FindControl("form1")
        Dim c1 As WebUserControl = _
            CType(LoadControl("~/WebUserControl.ascx"), WebUserControl)
        myForm.Controls.Add(c1)

        c1.ID = "myWebUserControl1"
        c1.Text = "My users controls text"
    End Sub
</script>
```

C#

```
<%@ Page Language="C#" %>
<%@ Reference Control="~/WebUserControl.ascx" %>

<script runat="server">
    void Page_Load(object sender, EventArgs e)
    {
        Control myForm = Page.FindControl("Form1");
        WebUserControl c1 =
            (WebUserControl)LoadControl("WebUserControl.ascx");
        myForm.Controls.Add(c1);

        c1.ID = "myWebUserControl1";
        c1.Text = "My users controls text";
    }
</script>
```

Notice that the sample adds the control to the Form's `Controls` collection and then sets the `Text` property. This ordering is actually quite important. After a page postback occurs the control's ViewState is not calculated until the control is added to the `Controls` collection. If you set the `Text` value (or any other property of the user control) before the control's ViewState, the value is not persisted in the ViewState. One twist to dynamically adding user controls occurs when you are also using Output Caching to cache the user controls. In this case, after the control has been cached, the `LoadControl` method does not return a new instance of the control. Instead, it returns the cached copy of the control. This presents problems when you try to cast the control to its native type because, after the control is cached, the `LoadControl` method returns it as a `PartialCachingControl` object rather than as its native type. Therefore, the cast in the previous sample results in an exception being thrown.

To solve this problem, you simply test the object type before attempting the cast. This is shown in Listing 26-8.

Listing 26-8: Detecting cached user controls

VB

```
<script runat="server">
    Protected Sub Page_Load(ByVal sender As Object, ByVal e As System.EventArgs)
        Dim myForm As Control = Page.FindControl("form1")
```

```
        Dim c1 As Control = LoadControl("~/WebUserControl.ascx")
        myForm.Controls.Add(c1)

        If (c1.GetType() Is GetType(WebUserControl)) Then
            'This control is not participating in OutputCache
            CType(c1, WebUserControl).ID = "myWebUserControl1"
            CType(c1, WebUserControl).Text = "My users controls text"

        ElseIf (c1.GetType() Is GetType(PartialCachingControl) And _
            ((CType(c1, PartialCachingControl)).CachedControl IsNot Nothing)) Then

            'The control is participating in output cache, but has expired
            Dim myWebUserControl as WebUserControl = _
                CType((CType(c1, PartialCachingControl).CachedControl), _
                WebUserControl)

            myWebUserControl.ID = "myWebUserControl1"
            myWebUserControl.Text = "My users controls text"
        End If

    End Sub
</script>
```

C#

```
<script runat="server">
    void Page_Load(object sender, EventArgs e)
    {
        Control myForm = Page.FindControl("Form1");
        Control c1 = LoadControl("WebUserControl.ascx");
        myForm.Controls.Add(c1);

        if (c1 is WebUserControl)
        {
            //This control is not participating in OutputCache
            ((WebUserControl)c1).ID = "myWebUserControl1";
            ((WebUserControl)c1).Text = "My users controls text";
        }
        else if ((c1 is PartialCachingControl) &&
            ((PartialCachingControl)c1).CachedControl != null)
        {
            //The control is participating in output cache, but has expired
             WebUserControl myWebUserControl =
                ((WebUserControl)((PartialCachingControl)c1).CachedControl);
            myWebUserControl.ID = "myWebUserControl1";
            myWebUserControl.Text = "My users controls text";
        }
    }
</script>
```

The sample demonstrates how you can test to see what type the `LoadControl` returns and set properties based on the type. For more information on caching, check out Chapter 23.

Finally, in all the previous samples that demonstrate dynamically adding user controls, the user controls have been added during the `Page_Load` event. But there may be times when you want to add the control based on other events, such as a button's `Click` event or the `SelectedIndexChanged` event of a DropDownList control. Using these events to add user controls dynamically presents challenges. Specifically, because the events may not be raised each time a page postback occurs, you need to create a way to track when a user control has been added so that it can be re-added to the Web page as additional postbacks occur.

A simple way to do this is to use the ASP.NET session to track when the user control is added to the Web page. Listing 26-9 demonstrates this.

Listing 26-9: Tracking added user controls across postbacks

VB

```
<%@ Page Language="VB" %>

<script runat="server">
   Protected Sub Button1_Click(ByVal sender As Object, ByVal e As System.EventArgs)
        'Make sure the control has not already been added to the page
        If ((Session("WebUserControlAdded") Is Nothing) Or _
            (Not CBool(Session("WebUserControlAdded")))) Then

            Dim myForm As Control = Page.FindControl("Form1")
            Dim c1 As Control = LoadControl("WebUserControl.ascx")
            myForm.Controls.Add(c1)

            Session("WebUserControlAdded") = True
        End If
    End Sub

    Protected Sub Page_Load(ByVal sender As Object, ByVal e As System.EventArgs)
        'Check to see if the control should be added to the page
        If ((Session("WebUserControlAdded") IsNot Nothing) And _
            (CBool(Session("WebUserControlAdded")))) Then

            Dim myForm As Control = Page.FindControl("Form1")
            Dim c1 As Control = LoadControl("WebUserControl.ascx")
            myForm.Controls.Add(c1)
        End If
    End Sub
</script>

<html xmlns="http://www.w3.org/1999/xhtml" >
<head id="Head1" runat="server">
    <title>Untitled Page</title>
</head>
<body>
    <form id="form1" runat="server">
    <div>
        <asp:Button ID="Button1" runat="server" Text="Button"
            OnClick="Button1_Click" />
        <asp:Button ID="Button2" runat="server" Text="Button" />
    </div>
    </form>
</body>
</html>
```

C#

```
<%@ Page Language="C#" %>

<script runat="server">
    protected void Button1_Click(object sender, EventArgs e)
    {
        //Make sure the control has not already been added to the page
        if ((Session["WebUserControlAdded"] == null) ||
            (!(bool)Session["WebUserControlAdded"]))
        {
            Control myForm = Page.FindControl("Form1");
            Control c1 = LoadControl("WebUserControl.ascx");
            myForm.Controls.Add(c1);

            Session["WebUserControlAdded"] = true;
        }
    }

    protected void Page_Load(object sender, EventArgs e)
    {
        //Check to see if the control should be added to the page
        if ((Session["WebUserControlAdded"] != null) &&
            ((bool)Session["WebUserControlAdded"]))
        {
            Control myForm = Page.FindControl("Form1");
            Control c1 = LoadControl("WebUserControl.ascx");
            myForm.Controls.Add(c1);
        }
    }
</script>
```

This sample used a simple `Session` variable to track whether the user control has been added to the page. When the Button1 `Click` event fires, the session variable is set to `True`, indicating that the user control has been added. Then, each time the page performs a postback, the `Page_Load` event checks to see if the session variable is set to `True`, and if so, it re-adds the control to the page.

Server Controls

The power to create server controls in ASP.NET is one of the greatest tools you can have as an ASP.NET developer. Creating your own custom server controls and extending existing controls are actually both quite easy. In ASP.NET 3.5, all controls are derived from two basic classes: `System.Web.UI.WebControls.WebControl` or `System.Web.UI.ScriptControl`. Classes derived from the `WebControl` class have the basic functionality required to participate in the Page framework. These classes include most of the common functionality needed to create controls that render a visual HTML representation and provide support for many of the basic styling elements such as Font, Height, and Width. Because the `WebControl` class derives from the `Control` class, the controls derived from it have the basic functionality to be a designable control, meaning they can be added to the Visual Studio Toolbox, dragged onto the page designer, and have their properties and events displayed in the Property Browser.

Controls derived from the `ScriptControl` class build on the functionality that the `WebControl` class provides by including additional features designed to make working with client-side script libraries easier. The class tests to ensure that a ScriptManager control is present in the hosting page during the control's PreRender stage, and also ensures that derived controls call the the proper ScriptManager methods during the Render event.

WebControl Project Setup

This section demonstrates just how easy it is to create custom server controls by creating a very simple server control that derives from the `WebControl` class. In order to create a new server control, you create a new ASP.NET Server Control project. You can use this project to demonstrate concepts throughout the rest of this chapter. In Visual Studio, choose File ➪ New Project to open the New Project dialog box. From the Project Types tree, open either the Visual Basic or Visual C# nodes and select the Web node. Figure 26-2 shows the New Project dialog with a Visual C# ASP.NET Server Control project template selected.

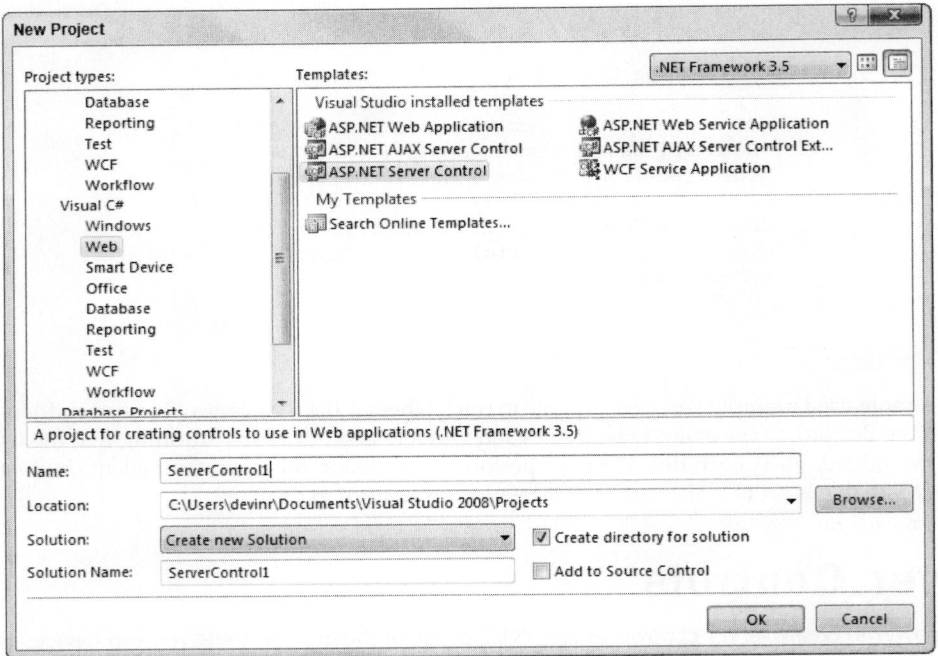

Figure 26-2

When you click OK in the New Project dialog box, Visual Studio creates a new ASP.NET Server Control project for you. Notice that the project includes a template class that contains a very simple server control. Listing 26-10 shows the code for this template class.

Listing 26-10: The Visual Studio ASP.NET Server Control class template

VB

```
Imports System
Imports System.Collections.Generic
Imports System.ComponentModelImports System.Text
Imports System.Web
Imports System.Web.UI
Imports System.Web.UI.WebControls

<DefaultProperty("Text"), _
 ToolboxData("<{0}:ServerControl1 runat=server></{0}:ServerControl1>")> _
Public Class ServerControl1
    Inherits WebControl

    <Bindable(True), Category("Appearance"), DefaultValue(""), Localizable(True)> _
    Property Text() As String
        Get
            Dim s As String = CStr(ViewState("Text"))
            If s Is Nothing Then
                Return "[" + Me.ID + "]"
            Else
                Return s
            End If
        End Get

        Set(ByVal Value As String)
            ViewState("Text") = Value
        End Set
    End Property

    Protected Overrides Sub RenderContents(ByVal output As HtmlTextWriter)
        output.Write(Text)
    End Sub

End Class
```

C#

```
using System;
using System.Collections.Generic;
using System.ComponentModel;
using System.Linq;
using System.Text;
using System.Web.UI;
using System.Web.UI.WebControls;

namespace ServerControl1
```

Continued

```
{
    [DefaultProperty("Text")]
    [ToolboxData("<{0}:ServerControl1 runat=server></{0}:ServerControl1>")]
    public class ServerControl1 : WebControl
    {
        [Bindable(true)]
        [Category("Appearance")]
        [DefaultValue("")]
        [Localizable(true)]
        public string Text
        {
            get
            {
                String s = (String)ViewState["Text"];
                return ((s == null) ? "[" + this.ID + "]" : s);
            }
            set
            {
                ViewState["Text"] = value;
            }
        }

        protected override void RenderContents(HtmlTextWriter output)
        {
            output.Write(Text);
        }
    }
}
```

This template class creates a basic server control that exposes one property called `Text` and renders the value of that property to the screen. Notice that you override the `RenderContents` method of the control and write the value of the `Text` property to the pages output stream. We talk more about rendering output later in the chapter.

> *Note that creating a server control project is not the only way to create an ASP.NET server control. Visual Studio 2008 also provides a basic ASP.NET Server Control file template that you can add to either an existing ASP.NET Server Control project, or to any other standard class library project. This template, however, differs slightly from the template used to create the default server control included in the ASP.NET Server control project. It uses a different filename scheme and includes slightly different code in the default Text properties getter.*

Now, take this class and use it in a sample Web application by adding a new Web Project to the existing solution. The default Web page, created by Visual Studio, serves as a test page for the server control samples in this chapter.

Visual Studio 2008 will automatically add any controls contained in projects in the open Solution to the Toolbox for you. To see this, simply build the Solution and then open the default Web page of the Web Project you just added. The Toolbox should contain a new section called WebControlLibrary1 .Components, and the new server control should be listed in this section (see Figure 26-3).

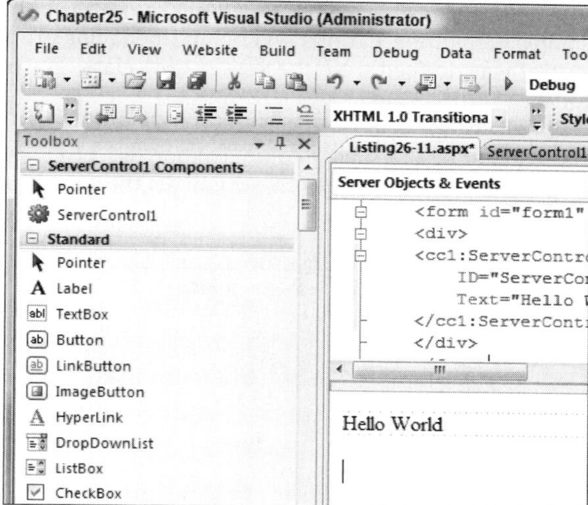

Figure 26-3

Now, all you have to do is drag the control onto the Web Form, and the control's assembly is automatically added to the Web project for you. When you drag the control from the Toolbox onto the designer surface, the control adds itself to the Web page. Listing 26-11 shows you what the Web page source code looks like after you have added the control.

Listing 26-11: Adding a Web Control Library to a Web page

```
<%@ Register Assembly="MyServerControl"
    Namespace="ServerControl1" TagPrefix="cc1" %>

<!DOCTYPE html PUBLIC "-//W3C//DTD XHTML 1.1//EN"
"http://www.w3.org/TR/xhtml11/DTD/xhtml11.dtd">

<html xmlns="http://www.w3.org/1999/xhtml" >
<head runat="server">
    <title>Adding a Custom Web Control</title>
</head>
<body>
    <form id="form1" runat="server">
    <div>
        <cc1:ServerControl1 ID="ServerControl1" runat="server" />
    </div>
    </form>
</body>
</html>
```

After you drag the control onto the Web form, take a look at its properties in the Properties Window. Figure 26-4 shows the properties of your custom control.

Notice that in addition to the `Text` property you defined in the control, the control has all the basic properties of a visual control, including various styling and behavior properties. The properties are exposed because the control was derived from the `WebControl` class. The control also inherits the base events exposed by `WebControl`.

Make sure the control is working by entering a value for the `Text` property and viewing the page in a browser. Figure 26-5 shows what the page looks like if you set the `Text` property to `"Hello World!"`.

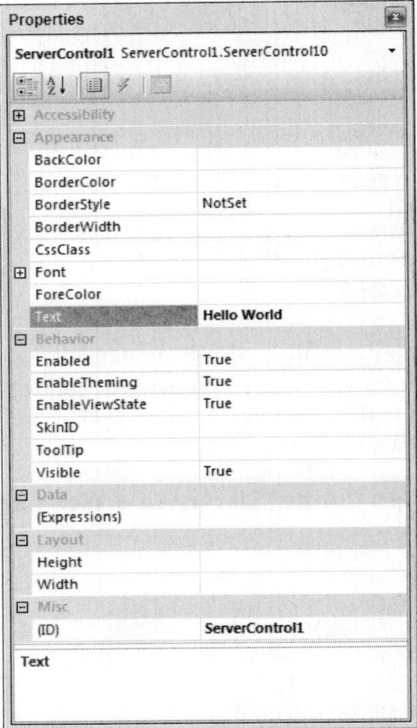

Figure 26-4

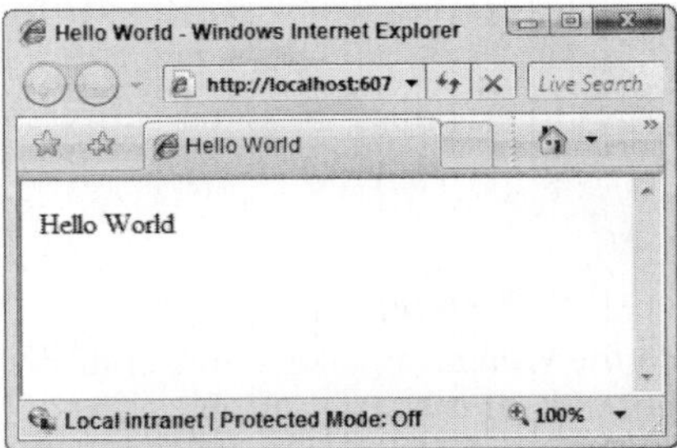

Figure 26-5

As expected, the control has rendered the value of the Text property to the Web page. If you view the HTML source of this sample, you will see that not only has ASP.NET added the value of the Text property to the HTML markup, but it has surrounded the text with a <SPAN> block. If you look at the code for the WebControl class's render method, you can see why.

```
protected internal override void Render(HtmlTextWriter writer)
{
    this.RenderBeginTag(writer);
    this.RenderContents(writer);
    this.RenderEndTag(writer);
}
```

You can see that, by default, the Render method, which calls the RenderContents method, also includes the RenderBeginTag and RenderEndTag methods, causing the Span tags to be added. If you have provided an ID value for your control, then the Span tag will also, by default, render an ID attribute. Having the Span tags can sometimes be problematic, so if you want to prevent this in ASP.NET, you simply override the RenderMethod and call the RenderContents method directly.

VB

```
Protected Overrides Sub Render(ByVal writer As System.Web.UI.HtmlTextWriter)
    Me.RenderContents(writer)
End Sub
```

C#

```
protected override void Render(HtmlTextWriter writer)
{
    this.RenderContents(writer);
}
```

This prevents ASP.NET from automatically adding the Span tags.

The samples in this section demonstrate just how easy it is to create a simple server control. Of course, this control does not have much functionality and lacks many of the features of a server control. The following section shows how you can use attributes to enhance this server control to make it more useful and user-friendly.

Control Attributes

A key enhancement to the design-time experience for users utilizing server controls is achieved by adding attributes to the class level and to the control's classes and properties. Attributes define much of how the control behaves at design time in Visual Studio. For instance, when you look at the default control template from the previous section (Listing 26-6), notice that attributes have been applied to both the Class and to the Text property. In this section, you study these attributes and how they affect the behavior of the control.

Class Attributes

Class attributes generally control how the server control behaves in the Visual Studio Toolbox and when placed on the design surface. The class attributes can be divided into three basic categories: attributes that help the Visual Studio designer know how to render the control at design time, attributes that help you tell ASP.NET how to render nested controls, and attributes that tell Visual Studio how to display the control in the Toolbox. The following table describes some of these attributes.

Attribute	Description
`Designer`	Indicates the designer class this control should use to render a design-time view of the control on the Visual Studio design surface
`TypeConverter`	Specifies what type to use as a converter for the object
`DefaultEvent`	Indicates the default event created when the user double-clicks the control on the Visual Studio design surface
`DefaultProperty`	Indicates the default property for the control
`ControlBuilder`	Specifies a `ControlBuilder` class for building a custom control in the ASP.NET control parser
`ParseChildren`	Indicates whether XML elements nested within the server controls tags will be treated as properties or as child controls
`TagPrefix`	Indicates the text the control is prefixed with in the Web page HTML

Property/Event Attributes

Property attributes are used to control a number of different aspects of server controls. You can use attributes to control how your properties and events behave in the Visual Studio Property Browser. You can also use attributes to control how properties and events are serialized at design time. The following table describes some of the property and event attributes you can use.

Obviously, the class and property/event attribute tables present a lot of information upfront. You already saw a demonstration of some of these attributes in Listing 26-1; now, as you go through the rest of the chapter, you will spend time working with most of the attributes listed in the tables.

Control Rendering

Now that that you have seen the large number of options you have for working with a server control at design-time, look at what you need to know to manage how your server control renders its HTML at runtime.

Attribute	Description
`Bindable`	Indicates that the property can be bound to a data source
`Browsable`	Indicates whether the property should be displayed at design time in the Property Browser
`Category`	Indicates the category this property should be displayed under in the Property Browser
`Description`	Displays a text string at the bottom of the Property Browser that describes the purpose of the property
`EditorBrowsable`	Indicates whether the property should be editable when shown in the Property Browser
`DefaultValue`	Indicates the default value of the property shown in the Property Browser
`DesignerSerializationVisibility`	Specifies the visibility a property has to the design-time serializer
`NotifyParentProperty`	Indicates that the parent property is notified when the value of the property is modified
`PersistChildren`	Indicates whether, at design-time, the child controls of a server control should be persisted as nested inner controls
`PersistanceMode`	Specifies how a property or an event is persisted to the ASP.NET page
`TemplateContainer`	Specifies the type of INamingContainer that will contain the template once it is created
`Editor`	Indicates the UI Type Editor class this control should use to edit its value
`Localizable`	Indicates that the property contains text that can be localized
`Themable`	Indicates whether this property can have a theme applied to it

The Page Event Lifecycle

Before we talk about rendering HTML, you must understand the lifecycle of a Web page. As the control developer, you are responsible for overriding methods that execute during the lifecycle and implementing your own custom rendering logic.

Remember that when a Web browser makes a request to the server, it is using HTTP, a stateless protocol. ASP.NET provides a page-execution framework that helps create the illusion of state in a Web application. This framework is basically a series of methods and events that execute every time an ASP.NET page is processed. You may have seen diagrams showing this lifecycle for ASP.NET 1.0. Since ASP.NET 2.0, a variety of additional events have been available to give you more power over the behavior of the control. Figure 26-6 shows the events and methods called during the control's lifecycle.

Many events and members are executed during the control's lifecycle, but you should concentrate on the more important among them.

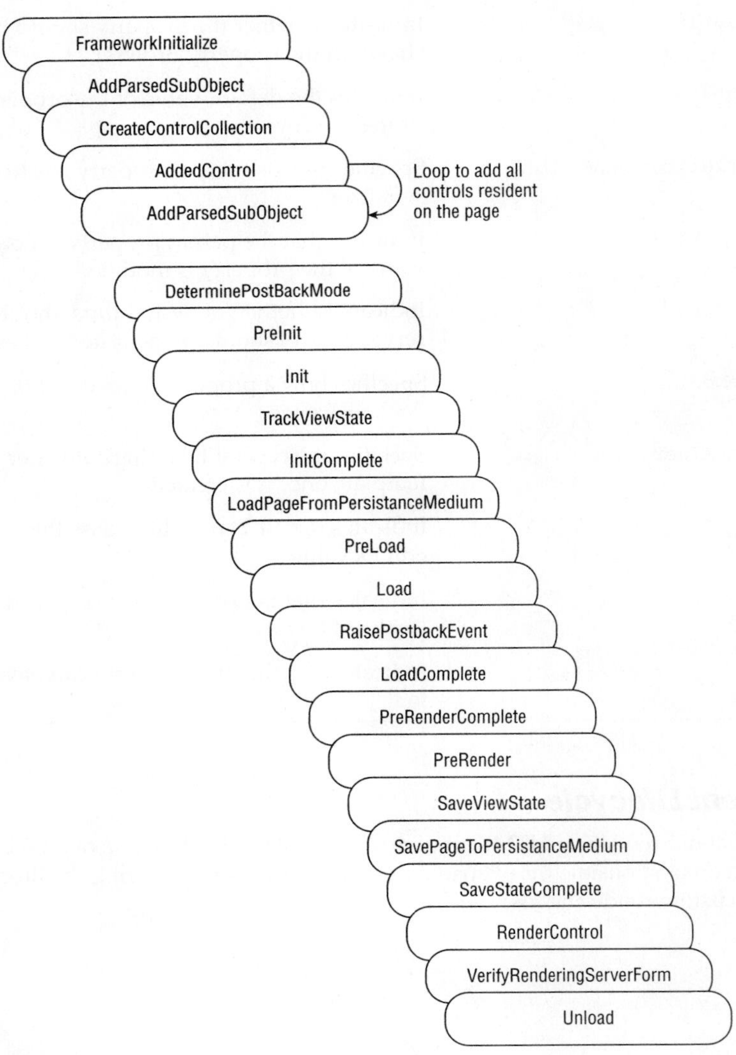

Figure 26-6

Rendering Services

The main job of a server control is to render some type of markup language to the HTTP output stream, which is returned to and displayed by the client. If your client is a standard browser, the control should emit HTML; if the client is something like a mobile device, the control may need to emit a different type of markup, such as WAP, or WML. As I stated earlier, it is your responsibility as the control developer to tell the server control what markup to render. The overridden `RenderContents` method, called during the control's lifecycle, is the primary location where you tell the control what you want to emit to the client. In Listing 26-12, notice that the `RenderContents` method is used to tell the control to print the value of the `Text` property.

Listing 26-12: Overriding the Render method

VB

```
Protected Overrides Sub RenderContents(ByVal output As HtmlTextWriter)
    output.Write(Text)
End Sub
```

C#

```
protected override void RenderContents(HtmlTextWriter output)
{
    output.Write(Text);
}
```

Also notice that the `RenderContents` method has one method parameter called `output`. This parameter is an `HtmlTextWriter` class, which is what the control uses to render HTML to the client. This special writer class is specifically designed to emit HTML 4.0–compliant HTML to the browser. The `HtmlTextwriter` class has a number of methods you can use to emit your HTML, including `RenderBeginTag` and `WriteBeginTag`. Listing 26-13 shows how you can modify the control's `Render` method to emit an HTML `<input>` tag.

Listing 26-13: Using the HtmlTextWriter to render an HTML tag

VB

```
Protected Overrides Sub RenderContents(ByVal output As HtmlTextWriter)
    output.RenderBeginTag(HtmlTextWriterTag.Input)
    output.RenderEndTag()
End Sub
```

C#

```
protected override void RenderContents(HtmlTextWriter output)
{
    output.RenderBeginTag(HtmlTextWriterTag.Input);
    output.RenderEndTag();
}
```

First, notice that the `RenderBeginTag` method is used to emit the HTML. The advantage of using this method to emit HTML is that it requires you to select a tag from the `HtmlTextWriterTag` enumeration. Using the `RenderBeginTag` method and the `HtmlTextWriterTag` enumeration enables you to have your control automatically support downlevel browsers that cannot understand HTML 4.0 syntax. If a downlevel browser is detected by ASP.NET, the control automatically emits HTML 3.2 syntax instead of HTML 4.0.

Second, notice that the `RenderEndTag` method is also used. As the name suggests, this method renders the closing tag. Notice, however, that you do not have to specify in this method which tag you want to close. The `RenderEndTag` automatically closes the last begin tag rendered by the `RenderBeginTag` method, which in this case is the `<input>` tag. If you want to emit multiple HTML tags, make sure you order your `Begin` and `End` render methods properly. In Listing 26-14, for example, you add a `<div>` tag to the control. The `<div>` tag surrounds the `<input>` tag when rendered to the page.

Listing 26-14: Using the HtmlTextWriter to render multiple HTML tags

VB

```
Protected Overrides Sub RenderContents(ByVal output As HtmlTextWriter)
    output.RenderBeginTag(HtmlTextWriterTag.Div)
    output.RenderBeginTag(HtmlTextWriterTag.Input)
    output.RenderEndTag()
    output.RenderEndTag()
End Sub
```

C#

```
protected override void RenderContents(HtmlTextWriter output)
{
    output.RenderBeginTag(HtmlTextWriterTag.Div);
    output.RenderBeginTag(HtmlTextWriterTag.Input);
    output.RenderEndTag();
    output.RenderEndTag();
}
```

Now that you have a basic understanding of how to emit simple HTML, look at the output of your control. You can do this by viewing the test HTML page containing the control in a browser and choosing View ➪ Source. Figure 26-7 shows the source for the page.

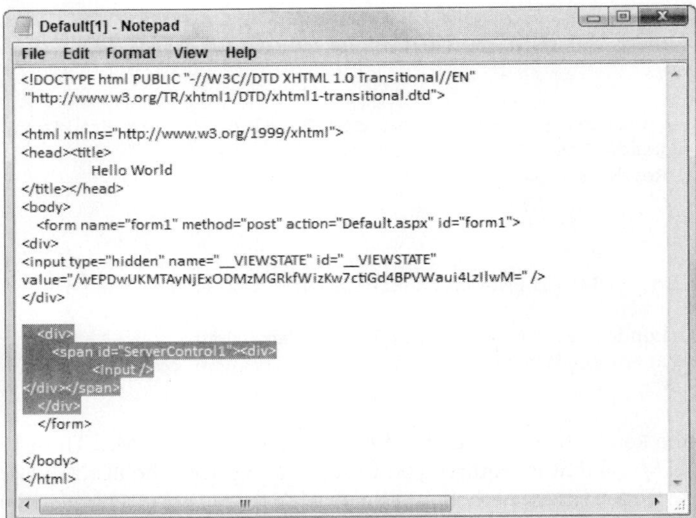

Figure 26-7

You can see that the control emitted some pretty simple HTML markup. Also notice (in the highlighted area) that the control was smart enough to realize that the input control did not contain any child controls and, therefore, the control did not need to render a full closing tag. Instead, it automatically rendered the shorthand / > , rather than </input>.

Adding Tag Attributes

Emitting HTML tags is a good start to building the control, but perhaps this is a bit simplistic. Normally, when rendering HTML you would emit some tag attributes (such as ID or Name) to the client in addition to the tag. Listing 26-15 shows how you can easily add tag attributes.

Listing 26-15: Rendering HTML tag attributes

VB

```
Protected Overrides Sub RenderContents(ByVal output As HtmlTextWriter)
    output.RenderBeginTag(HtmlTextWriterTag.Div)

    output.AddAttribute(HtmlTextWriterAttribute.Type, "text")
    output.AddAttribute(HtmlTextWriterAttribute.Id, Me.ClientID & "_i")
    output.AddAttribute(HtmlTextWriterAttribute.Name, Me.ClientID & "_i")
    output.AddAttribute(HtmlTextWriterAttribute.Value, Me.Text)
    output.RenderBeginTag(HtmlTextWriterTag.Input)
    output.RenderEndTag()

    output.RenderEndTag()
End Sub
```

C#

```
protected override void RenderContents(HtmlTextWriter output)
{
    output.RenderBeginTag(HtmlTextWriterTag.Div);

    output.AddAttribute(HtmlTextWriterAttribute.Type, "text");
    output.AddAttribute(HtmlTextWriterAttribute.Id, this.ClientID + "_i");
    output.AddAttribute(HtmlTextWriterAttribute.Name, this.ClientID + "_i");
    output.AddAttribute(HtmlTextWriterAttribute.Value, this.Text);
    output.RenderBeginTag(HtmlTextWriterTag.Input);
    output.RenderEndTag();

    output.RenderEndTag();
}
```

You can see that by using the AddAttribute method, you have added three attributes to the <input> tag. Also notice that, once again, you are using an enumeration, HtmlTextWriterAttribute, to select the attribute you want to add to the tag. This serves the same purpose as using the HtmlTextWriterTag enumeration, allowing the control to degrade its output to downlevel browsers.

As with the Render methods, the order in which you place the AddAttributes methods is important. You place the AddAttributes methods directly before the RenderBeginTag method in the code. The AddAttributes method associates the attributes with the next HTML tag that is rendered by the RenderBeginTag method — in this case the <input> tag.

Now browse to the test page and check out the HTML source with the added tag attributes. Figure 26-8 shows the HTML source rendered by the control.

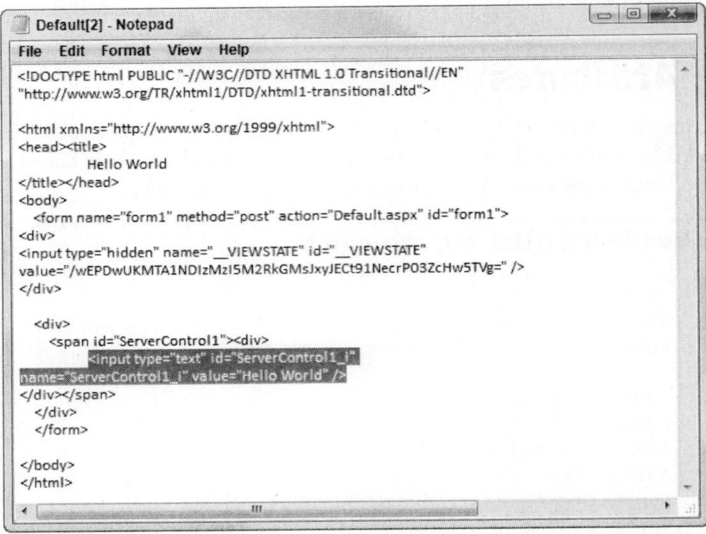


```
<!DOCTYPE html PUBLIC "-//W3C//DTD XHTML 1.0 Transitional//EN"
"http://www.w3.org/TR/xhtml1/DTD/xhtml1-transitional.dtd">

<html xmlns="http://www.w3.org/1999/xhtml">
<head><title>
        Hello World
</title></head>
<body>
  <form name="form1" method="post" action="Default.aspx" id="form1">
<div>
<input type="hidden" name="__VIEWSTATE" id="__VIEWSTATE"
value="/wEPDwUKMTA1NDIzMzI5M2RkGMsJxyJECt91NecrP03ZcHw5TVg=" />
</div>

  <div>
    <span id="ServerControl1"><div>
        <input type="text" id="ServerControl1_i"
name="ServerControl1_i" value="Hello World" />
</div></span>
  </div>
  </form>

</body>
</html>
```

Figure 26-8

You can see that the tag attributes you added in the server control are now included as part of the HTML tag rendered by the control.

A Word about Control IDs

Notice that in Listing 26-11 it's important to use the control's `ClientID` property as the value of both the `Id`and `Name` attributes. Controls that derive from the `WebControl` class automatically expose three different types of ID properties: `ID`, `UniqueID`, and `ClientID`. Each of these properties exposes a slightly altered version of the control's ID for use in a specific scenario.

The `ID` property is the most obvious. Developers use it to get and set the control's ID. It must be unique to the page at design time.

The `UniqueID` property is a read-only property generated at runtime that returns an ID that has been prepended with the containing control's ID. This is essential so that ASP.NET can uniquely identify each control in the page's control tree, even if the control is used multiple times by a container control such as a Repeater or GridView. For example, if you add this custom control to a repeater, the `UniqueID` for each custom control rendered by the Repeater is modified to include the Repeater's ID when the page executed:

```
MyRepeater:Ctrl0:MyCustomControl
```

> The `ClientID` property is essentially identical to the `UniqueID` property with one important exception. The `ClientID` property always uses an underscore (_) to separate the ID values, rather than using the value of the `IdSeparator` property. This is because the ECMAScript standard disallows the use of colons in ID attribute values, which is the default value of the `IdSeparator` property. Using the underscore ensures that a control can be used by client-side JavaScript.
>
> Additionally, in order to ensure that controls can generate a unique ID, they should implement the INamingContainer interface. This is a marker interface only, meaning that it does not require any additional methods to be implemented; it does, however, ensure that the ASP.NET runtime guarantees the control always has a unique name within the page's tree hierarchy, regardless of its container.

Styling HTML

So far, you have seen how easy it is to build a simple HTML control and emit the proper HTML, including attributes. In this section, we discuss how you can have your control render style information. As mentioned at the very beginning of this section, you are creating controls that inherit from the `WebControl` class. Because of this, these controls already have the basic infrastructure for emitting most of the standard CSS-style attributes. In the Property Browser for this control, you should see a number of style properties already listed, such as background color, border width, and font. You can also launch the style builder to create complex CSS styles. These basic properties are provided by the `WebControl` class, but it is up to you to tell your control to render the values set at design time. To do this, you simply execute the `AddAttributesToRender` method. Listing 26-16 shows you how to do this.

Listing 26-16: Rendering style properties

VB

```
Protected Overrides Sub RenderContents(ByVal output As HtmlTextWriter)
   output.RenderBeginTag(HtmlTextWriterTag.Div)

    output.AddAttribute(HtmlTextWriterAttribute.Type, "text")
    output.AddAttribute(HtmlTextWriterAttribute.Id, Me.ClientID & "_i")
    output.AddAttribute(HtmlTextWriterAttribute.Name, Me.ClientID & "_i")
    output.AddAttribute(HtmlTextWriterAttribute.Value, Me.Text)
    Me.AddAttributesToRender(output)

    output.RenderBeginTag(HtmlTextWriterTag.Input)
    output.RenderEndTag()

    output.RenderEndTag()
End Sub
```

C#

```
protected override void RenderContents(HtmlTextWriter output)
{
    output.RenderBeginTag(HtmlTextWriterTag.Div);
```

Continued

```
        output.AddAttribute(HtmlTextWriterAttribute.Type, "text");
        output.AddAttribute(HtmlTextWriterAttribute.Id, this.ClientID + "_i");
        output.AddAttribute(HtmlTextWriterAttribute.Name, this.ClientID + "_i");
        output.AddAttribute(HtmlTextWriterAttribute.Value, this.Text);
        this.AddAttributesToRender(output);

        output.RenderBeginTag(HtmlTextWriterTag.Input);
        output.RenderEndTag();

        output.RenderEndTag();
    }
```

Executing this method tells the control to render any style information that has been set.

Note that executing this method not only causes the style-related properties to be rendered, but also several other attributes, including `ID`, `tabindex`, and `tooltip`. If you are manually rendering these attributes earlier in your control, then you may end up with duplicate attributes being rendered. Additionally, be careful about where you use the `AddAttributesToRender` method. In Listing 26-26, it is executed immediately before the `Input` tag is rendered, which means that the attributes will be rendered both on the `Input` element and on the `Span` element surrounding the Input element.

Try placing the method call before the beginning DIV tag is rendered, or after the DIV's end tag is rendered. You will see that in the case of the former, the attributes are now applied to the DIV and its surrounding span and in the case of the latter, only the SPAN has the attribute applied.

Using the Property Browser, you can set the background color of the control to `Red` and the font to `Bold`. When you set these properties, they are automatically added to the control tag in the ASP.NET page. After you have added the styles, the control tag looks like this:

```
<cc1:ServerControl1 BackColor="Red" Font-Bold=true
 ID="ServerControl11" runat="server" />
```

The style changes have been persisted to the control as attributes. When you execute this page in the browser, the style information should be rendered to the HTML, making the background of the text box red and its font bold. Figure 26-9 shows the page in the browser.

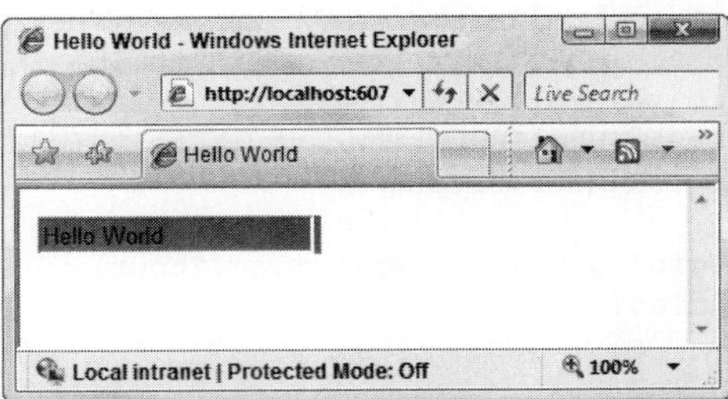

Figure 26-9

Once again, look at the source for this page. The style information has been rendered to the HTML as a style tag. Figure 26-10 shows the HTML emitted by the control.

If you want more control over the rendering of styles in your control you can use the HtmlTextWriters `AddStyleAttribute` method. Similar to the `AddAttribute` method, the `AddStyleAttribute` method enables you to specify CSS attributes to add to a control using the `HtmlTextWriterStyle` enumeration. However, unlike the `AddAttribute` method, attributes added using `AddStyleAttribute` are defined inside of a style attribute on the control. Listing 26-17 demonstrates the use of the `AddStyleAttribute` method.

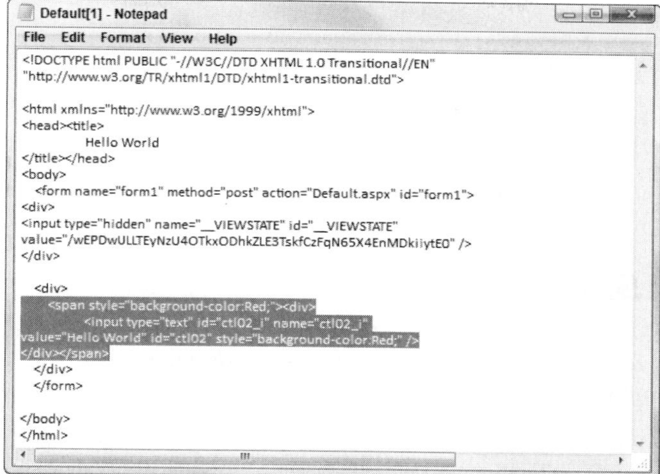


```
<!DOCTYPE html PUBLIC "-//W3C//DTD XHTML 1.0 Transitional//EN"
"http://www.w3.org/TR/xhtml1/DTD/xhtml1-transitional.dtd">

<html xmlns="http://www.w3.org/1999/xhtml">
<head><title>
        Hello World
</title></head>
<body>
  <form name="form1" method="post" action="Default.aspx" id="form1">
<div>
<input type="hidden" name="__VIEWSTATE" id="__VIEWSTATE"
value="/wEPDwULLTEyNzU4OTkxODhkZLE3TskfCzFqN65X4EnMDkiiytE0" />
</div>

  <div>
    <span style="background-color:Red;"><div>
        <input type="text" id="ctl02_i" name="ctl02_i"
value="Hello World" id="ctl02" style="background-color:Red;" />
</div></span>
  </div>
  </form>

</body>
</html>
```

Figure 26-10

Listing 26-17: Adding control styes using AddStyleAttribute

VB

```
Protected Overrides Sub RenderContents(ByVal output As HtmlTextWriter)
    output.RenderBeginTag(HtmlTextWriterTag.Div)

    output.AddAttribute(HtmlTextWriterAttribute.Type, "text")
    output.AddAttribute(HtmlTextWriterAttribute.Id, Me.ClientID & "_i")
    output.AddAttribute(HtmlTextWriterAttribute.Name, Me.ClientID & "_i")
    output.AddAttribute(HtmlTextWriterAttribute.Value, Me.Text)

    output.AddStyleAttribute(HtmlTextWriterStyle.BackgroundColor, "Red")

    output.RenderBeginTag(HtmlTextWriterTag.Input)
    output.RenderEndTag()

    output.RenderEndTag()
End Sub
```

C#

```
protected override void RenderContents(HtmlTextWriter output)
{
    output.RenderBeginTag(HtmlTextWriterTag.Div);

    output.AddAttribute(HtmlTextWriterAttribute.Type, "text");
```

Continued

```
        output.AddAttribute(HtmlTextWriterAttribute.Id, this.ClientID + "_i");
        output.AddAttribute(HtmlTextWriterAttribute.Name, this.ClientID + "_i");
        output.AddAttribute(HtmlTextWriterAttribute.Value, this.Text);

        output.AddStyleAttribute(HtmlTextWriterStyle.BackgroundColor, "Red");

        output.RenderBeginTag(HtmlTextWriterTag.Input);
        output.RenderEndTag();

        output.RenderEndTag();
    }
```

Running this sample will result in the same red background color being applied to the control.

Themes and Skins

A great feature added in ASP.NET 2.0, and introduced to you in Chapter 6, is themes and skins. This feature allows you to create visual styles for your Web applications. In this section, you learn what you need to know about themes and skins when creating a server control.

As you saw in Chapter 6, skins are essentially a way to set default values for the UI elements of controls in your Web application. You simply define the control and its properties in a `.skin` file and the values are applied to the control at runtime. Listing 26-18 shows a sample skin.

Listing 26-18: Sample ASP.NET skin

```
<%@ Register Assembly="WebControlLibrary1" Namespace="WebControlLibrary1"
    TagPrefix="cc1" %>

<cc1:webcustomcontrol1 BackColor="Green" runat="server" />
```

By default, ASP.NET allows all control properties to be defined in the skin file, but obviously this is not always appropriate. Most exposed properties are non-UI related; therefore, you do not apply a theme to them. By setting the `Themeable` attribute to `False` on each of these properties, you prevent the application of a theme. Listing 26-19 shows how to do this in your control by disabling themes on the `Text` property.

Listing 26-19: Disabling theme support on a control property

VB

```
<Bindable(True), Category("Appearance"), DefaultValue(""), _
Localizable(True), Themeable(False)> _
Property Text() As String
    Get
        Dim s As String = CStr(ViewState("Text"))
        If s Is Nothing Then
            Return "[" + Me.ID + "]"
        Else
            Return s
        End If
    End Get
```

```
        Set(ByVal Value As String)
            ViewState("Text") = Value
        End Set
    End Property
```

C#

```
[Bindable(true)]
[Category("Appearance")]
[DefaultValue("")]
[Localizable(true)]
[Themeable(false)]
public string Text
    {
        get
        {
            String s = (String)ViewState["Text"];
            return ((s == null) ? "["+ this.ID + "]": s);
        }
        set
        {
            ViewState["Text"] = value;
        }
    }
```

Now, if a developer attempts to define this property in his skin file, he receives a compiler error when the page is executed.

Adding Client-Side Features

Although the capability to render and style HTML is quite powerful by itself, other resources can be sent to the client, such as client-side scripts, images, and resource strings. ASP.NET 3.5 provides you with some powerful new tools for using client-side scripts in your server controls and retrieving other resources to the client along with the HTML your control emits. Additionally, ASP.NET now includes an entire model that allows you to make asynchronous callbacks from your Web page to the server.

Emitting Client-Side Script

Having your control emit client-side script such as VBScript or JavaScript enables you to add powerful client-side functionality to your control. Client-side scripting languages take advantage of the client's browser to create more flexible and easy-to-use controls. Although ASP.NET 1.0 provided some simple methods to emit client-side script to the browser, ASP.NET has since enhanced these capabilities and now provides a wide variety of methods for emitting client-side script that you can use to control where and how your script is rendered.

If you have already used ASP.NET 1.0 to render client-side script to the client, you are probably familiar with a few methods such as the `Page.RegisterClientScriptBlock` and the `Page.RegisterStartup Script` methods. Since ASP.NET 2.0, these classes have been deprecated. Instead, ASP.NET now uses the `ClientScriptManager` class, which you can access using `Page.ClientScript`. This class exposes various static client-script rendering methods that you can use to render client-side script.

Listing 26-20 demonstrates how you can use the `RegisterStartupScriptMethod` method to render JavaScript to the client. This listing adds the code into the `OnPreRender` method, rather than into the

Render method used in previous samples. This method allows every control to inform the page about the client-side script it needs to render. After the Render method is called, the page is able to render all the client-side script it collected during the OnPreRender method. If you call the client-side script registration methods in the Render method, the page has already completed a portion of its rendering before your client-side script can render itself.

Listing 26-20: Rendering a client-side script to the browser

VB

```
Protected Overrides Sub OnPreRender(ByVal e As System.EventArgs)
    Page.ClientScript.RegisterStartupScript(GetType(Page), _
       "ControlFocus", "document.getElementById('" & Me.ClientID & _
           "_i" & "').focus();", _
       True)
End Sub
```

C#

```
protected override void OnPreRender(EventArgs e)
{
    Page.ClientScript.RegisterStartupScript( typeof(Page),
        "ControlFocus","document.getElementById('" + this.ClientID +
            "_i" + "').focus();",
        true);
}
```

In this listing, the code emits client-side script to automatically move the control focus to the TextBox control when the Web page loads. When you use the RegisterStartupScript method, notice that it now includes an overload that lets you specify if the method should render surrounding script tags. This can be handy if you are rendering more than one script to the page.

Also notice that the method requires a key parameter. This parameter is used to uniquely identify the script block; if you are registering more than one script block in the Web page, make sure that each block is supplied a unique key. You can use the IsStartupScriptRegistered method and the key to determine if a particular script block has been previously registered on the client using the RegisterStatupScript method.

When you execute the page in the browser, notice that the focus is automatically placed into a text box. If you look at the source code for the Web page, you should see that the JavaScript was written to the bottom of the page, as shown in Figure 26-11.

If you want the script to be rendered to the top of the page, you use the RegisterClientScriptBlock method that emits the script block immediately after the opening <form> element.

Keep in mind that the browser parses the Web page from top to bottom, so if you emit client-side script at the top of the page that is not contained in a function, any references in that code to HTML elements further down the page will fail. The browser has not parsed that portion of the page yet.

Being able to render script that automatically executes when the page loads is nice, but it is more likely that you will want the code to execute based on an event fired from an HTML element on your page, such as the Click, Focus, or Blur events. In order to do this, you add an attribute to the HTML element you want the event to fire from. Listing 26-21 shows you how you can modify your control's Render and PreRender methods to add this attribute.

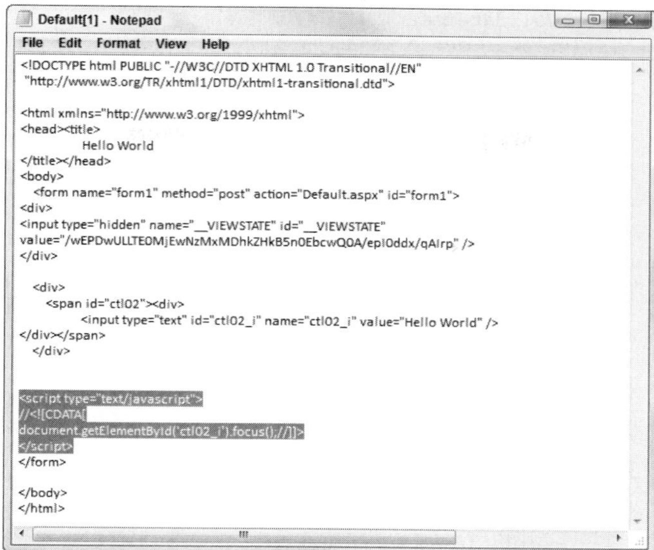

Figure 26-11

Listing 26-21: Using client-side script and event attributes to validate data

VB

```
Protected Overrides Sub RenderContents(ByVal output As HtmlTextWriter)
    output.RenderBeginTag(HtmlTextWriterTag.Div)

    output.AddAttribute(HtmlTextWriterAttribute.Type, "text")
    output.AddAttribute(HtmlTextWriterAttribute.Id, Me.ClientID & "_i")
    output.AddAttribute(HtmlTextWriterAttribute.Name, Me.ClientID & "_i")
    output.AddAttribute(HtmlTextWriterAttribute.Value, Me.Text)

    output.AddAttribute("OnBlur", "ValidateText(this)")

    output.RenderBeginTag(HtmlTextWriterTag.Input)
    output.RenderEndTag()

    output.RenderEndTag()

End Sub

Protected Overrides Sub OnPreRender(ByVal e As System.EventArgs)
    Page.ClientScript.RegisterStartupScript(GetType(Page), _
        "ControlFocus", "document.getElementById('" & Me.ClientID & _
            "_i" & "').focus();", _
       True)

    Page.ClientScript.RegisterClientScriptBlock( _
        GetType(Page), _
        "ValidateControl", _
```

Continued

```
            "function ValidateText() {" & _
                "if (ctl.value==") {" & _
                    "alert('Please enter a value.');ctl.focus();} " & _
            "}", _
            True)
    End Sub
```

C#

```
protected override void RenderContents(HtmlTextWriter output)
{
    output.RenderBeginTag(HtmlTextWriterTag.Div);
    output.AddAttribute(HtmlTextWriterAttribute.Type, "text");
    output.AddAttribute(HtmlTextWriterAttribute.Id, this.ClientID + "_i");
    output.AddAttribute(HtmlTextWriterAttribute.Name, this.ClientID + "_i");
    output.AddAttribute(HtmlTextWriterAttribute.Value, this.Text);

    output.AddAttribute("OnBlur", "ValidateText(this)");

    output.RenderBeginTag(HtmlTextWriterTag.Input);
    output.RenderEndTag();
    output.RenderEndTag();
}

protected override void OnPreRender(EventArgs e)
{
    Page.ClientScript.RegisterStartupScript(
        typeof(Page),
        "ControlFocus","document.getElementById("' + this.ClientID +
            "_i" + "').focus();",
        true);

    Page.ClientScript.RegisterClientScriptBlock(
        typeof(Page),
        "ValidateControl",
        "function ValidateText(ctl) {" +
            "if (ctl.value==") {" +
                "alert('Please enter a value.');ctl.focus();} " +
        "}",
        true);
}
```

As you can see, the TextBox control is modified to check for an empty string. We have also included an attribute that adds the JavaScript `OnBlur` event to the text box. The `OnBlur` event fires when the control loses focus. When this happens, the client-side `ValidateText` method is executed, which we rendered to the client using `RegisterClientScriptBlock`.

The rendered HTML is shown in Figure 26-12.

Embedding JavaScript in the page is powerful, but if you are writing large amounts of client-side code, you might want to consider storing the JavaScript in an external file. You can include this file in your HTML by using the `RegisterClientScriptInclude` method. This method renders a script tag using the URL you provide to it as the value of its `src` element.

```
<script src="[url]" type="text/javascript"></script>
```

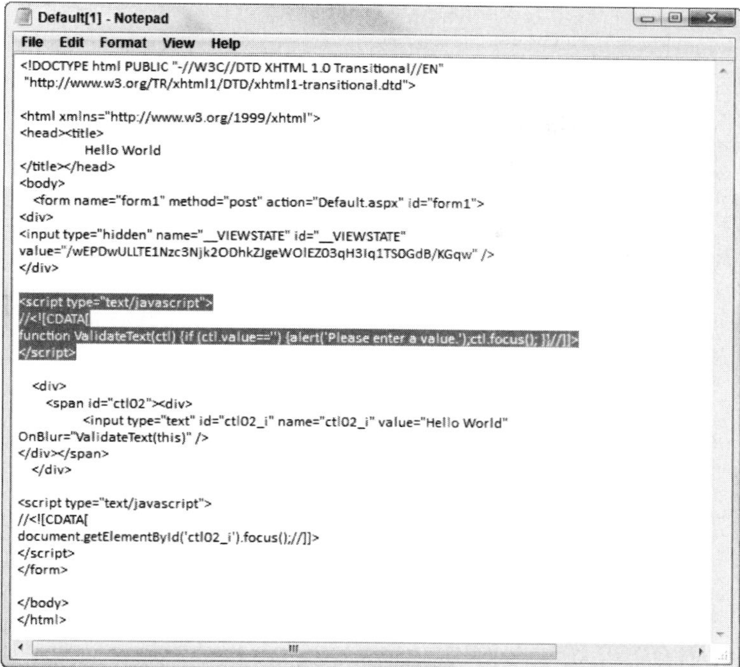

Figure 26-12

Listing 26-22 shows how you can modify the validation added to the TextBox control in Listing 26-20; but this time, the JavaScript validation function is stored in an external file.

Listing 26-22: Adding client-side script include files to a Web page

VB

```
Protected Overrides Sub OnPreRender(ByVal e As System.EventArgs)
    Page.ClientScript.RegisterClientScriptInclude( _
       "UtilityFunctions", "JScript.js")

    Page.ClientScript.RegisterStartupScript(GetType(Page), _
        "ControlFocus", "document.getElementById('" & Me.ClientID & _
            "_i" & "').focus();", _
       True)
End Sub
```

C#

```
protected override void OnPreRender(EventArgs e)
{
    Page.ClientScript.RegisterClientScriptInclude(
        "UtilityFunctions", "JScript.js");

    Page.ClientScript.RegisterStartupScript(
        typeof(Page),
```

Continued

```
            "ControlFocus","document.getElementById("' + this.ClientID +
                "_i" + "').focus();",
            true);
    }
```

You have modified the `OnPreRender` event to register a client-side script file include, which contains the `ValidateText` function. You need to add a JScript file to the project and create the `ValidateText` function, as shown in Listing 26-23.

Listing 26-23: The validation JavaScript contained in the Jscript file

```
// JScript File

function ValidateText(ctl)
{
   if (ctl.value=='') {
        alert('Please enter a value.');
        ctl.focus();
    }
}
```

The `ClientScriptManager` also provides methods for registering hidden HTML fields and adding script functions to the `OnSubmit` event.

Accessing Embedded Resources

A great way to distribute application resources like JavaScript files, images, or resource files is to embed them directly into the compiled assembly. While this was possible in ASP.NET 1.0, it was very difficult to access these resources as part of the page request process. ASP.NET 2.0 solved this problem by including the `RegisterClientScriptResource` method as part of the ClientScriptManager.

This method makes it possible for your Web pages to retrieve stored resources — like JavaScript files — from the compiled assembly at runtime. It works by using an HttpHandler to retrieve the requested resource from the assembly and return it to the client. The `RegisterClientScriptResource` method emits a `<script>` block whose `src` value points to this HttpHandler:

```
<script
     language="javascript"
     src="WebResource.axd?a=s&r=WebUIValidation.js&t=631944362841472848"
     type="text/javascript">
</script>
```

As you can see, the `WebResource.axd` handler is used to return the resource — in this case, the JavaScript file. You can use this method to retrieve any resource stored in the assembly, such as images or localized content strings from resource files.

Asynchronous Callbacks

Finally, ASP.NET also includes a convenient mechanism for enabling basic AJAX behavior, or client-side callbacks, in a server control. Client-side callbacks enable you to take advantage of the XmlHttp components found in most modern browsers to communicate with the server without actually performing a complete postback. Figure 26-13 shows how client-side callbacks work in the ASP.NET Framework.

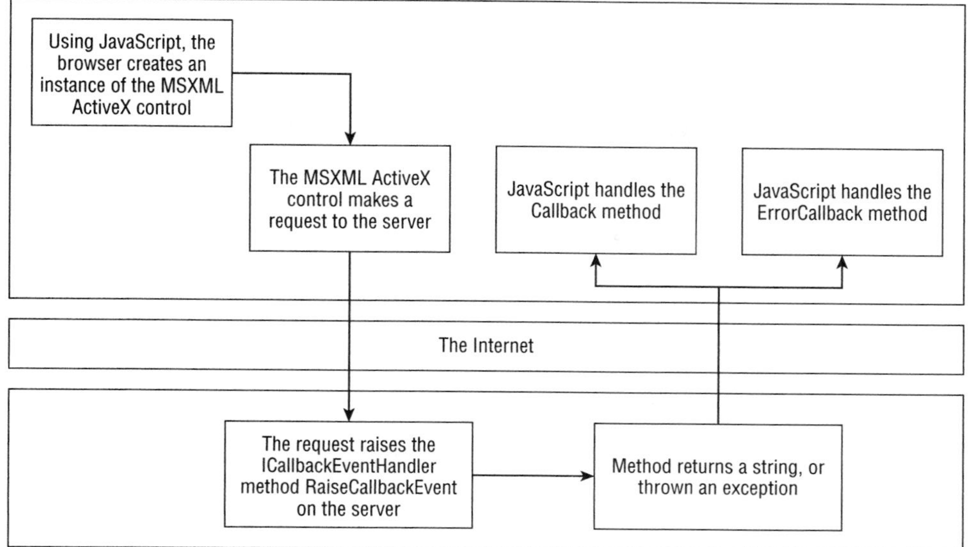

Figure 26-13

In order to enable callbacks in your server control, you implement the `System.Web.UI.ICallBackEventHander` interface. This interface requires you to implement two methods, the `RaiseCallbackEvent` method and the `GetCallbackResult method`. These are the server-side events that fire when the client executes the callback. After you implement the interface, you want to tie your client-side events back to the server. You do this by using the `Page.ClientScript.GetCallbackEventReference` method. This method allows you to specify the two client-side functions: one to serve as the callback handler and one to serve as an error handler. Listing 26-24 demonstrates how you can modify the TextBox control's `Render` methods and add the `RaiseCallBackEvent` method to use callbacks to perform validation.

Listing 26-24: Adding an asynchronous callback to validate data

VB

```
Protected Overrides Sub RenderContents(ByVal output As HtmlTextWriter)
    output.RenderBeginTag(HtmlTextWriterTag.Div)

    output.AddAttribute(HtmlTextWriterAttribute.Type, "text")
    output.AddAttribute(HtmlTextWriterAttribute.Id, Me.ClientID & "_i")
    output.AddAttribute(HtmlTextWriterAttribute.Name, Me.ClientID & "_i")
    output.AddAttribute(HtmlTextWriterAttribute.Value, Me.Text)

    output.AddAttribute("OnBlur", "ClientCallback();")
    Me.AddAttributesToRender(output)

    output.RenderBeginTag(HtmlTextWriterTag.Input)
    output.RenderEndTag()

    output.RenderEndTag()

End Sub
```

Continued

```
Protected Overrides Sub OnPreRender(ByVal e As System.EventArgs)
    Page.ClientScript.RegisterStartupScript(GetType(Page), _
        "ControlFocus", "document.getElementById('" & _
            Me.ClientID & "_i" & "').focus();", _
       True)

    Page.ClientScript.RegisterStartupScript( _
        GetType(Page), "ClientCallback", _
        "function ClientCallback() {" & _
            "args=document.getElementById('" & Me.ClientID & "_i" & "').value;" & _
            Page.ClientScript.GetCallbackEventReference(Me, "args", _
                "CallbackHandler", Nothing, "ErrorHandler", True) + "}", _
        True)
End Sub

Public Sub RaiseCallbackEvent(ByVal eventArgument As String) _
    Implements System.Web.UI.ICallbackEventHandler.RaiseCallbackEvent

    Dim result As Int32
    If (Not Int32.TryParse(eventArgument, result)) Then
        Throw New Exception("The method or operation is not implemented.")
    End If
End Sub

Public Function GetCallbackResult() As String _
    Implements System.Web.UI.ICallBackEventHandler.GetCallbackResult

    Return "Valid Data"
End Function
```

C#

```
protected override void RenderContents(HtmlTextWriter output)
{
    output.RenderBeginTag(HtmlTextWriterTag.Div);

    output.AddAttribute(HtmlTextWriterAttribute.Type, "text");
    output.AddAttribute(HtmlTextWriterAttribute.Id, this.ClientID + "_i");
    output.AddAttribute(HtmlTextWriterAttribute.Name, this.ClientID + "_i");
    output.AddAttribute(HtmlTextWriterAttribute.Value, this.Text);

    output.AddAttribute("OnBlur", "ClientCallback();");
    this.AddAttributesToRender(output);

    output.RenderBeginTag(HtmlTextWriterTag.Input);
    output.RenderEndTag();

    output.RenderEndTag();
}
protected override void OnPreRender(EventArgs e)
{
    Page.ClientScript.RegisterStartupScript(
        typeof(Page),
        "ControlFocus","document.getElementById('" +
            this.ClientID + "_i" + "').focus();",
```

```
            true);

        Page.ClientScript.RegisterStartupScript(
            typeof(Page), "ClientCallback",
            "function ClientCallback() {" +
                "args=document.getElementById('" + this.ClientID + "_i" + "').value;" +
                Page.ClientScript.GetCallbackEventReference(this, "args",
                    "CallbackHandler", null,"ErrorHandler",true) + "{",
            true);
    }

    #region ICallbackEventHandler Members

    public void RaiseCallbackEvent(string eventArgument)
    {
        int result;
        if (!Int32.TryParse(eventArgument,out result) )
            throw new Exception("The method or operation is not implemented.");
    }

    public string GetCallbackResult()
    {
        return "Valid Data";
    }

    #endregion
```

As you can see, the `OnBlur` attribute has again been modified, this time by simply calling the `ClientCallback` method. This method is created and rendered during the `PreRender` event. The main purpose of this event is to populate the client-side `args` variable and call the client-side callback method.

You are using the `GetCallbackEventReference` method to generate the client-side script that actually initiates the callback. The parameters passed to the method indicate which control is initiating the callback, the names of the client-side callback method, and the name of the callback method parameters. The following table provides more details on the `GetCallbackEventReference` arguments.

Parameter	Description
`Control`	Server control that initiates the callback.
`Argument`	Client-side variable used to pass arguments to the server-side event handler.
`ClientCallback`	Client-side function serving as the `Callback`method. This method fires when the server-side processing has completed successfully.
`Context`	Client-side variable that gets passed directly to the receiving client-side function. The context does not get passed to the server.
`ClientErrorCallback`	Client-side function serving as the `Callback` error-handler method. This method fires when the server-side processing encounters an error.

In the code, two client-side methods are called: `CallbackHandler` and `ErrorHandler`, respectively. The two method parameters are `args` and `ctx`.

In addition to the server control code changes, the two client-side callback methods have been added to the JavaScript file. Listing 26-25 shows these new functions.

Listing 26-25: The client-side callback JavaScript functions

```
// JScript File
var args;
var ctx;

function ValidateText(ctl)
{
    if (ctl.value=='') {
        alert('Please enter a value.');
        ctl.focus();
     }
}

function CallbackHandler(args,ctx)
{
    alert("The data is valid");
}

function ErrorHandler(args,ctx)
{
    alert("Please enter a number");
}
```

Now, when you view your Web page in the browser, as soon as the text box loses focus, you perform a client-side callback to validate the data. The callback raises the `RaiseCallbackEvent` method on the server, which validates the value of the text box that was passed to it in the `eventArguments`. If the value is valid, you return a string and the client-side `CallbackHandler` function fires. If the value is invalid, you throw an exception, which causes the client-side `ErrorHandler` function to execute.

Detecting and Reacting to Browser Capabilities

So far in the chapter we have described many powerful features, such as styling and emitting client-side scripts, that you can utilize when writing your own custom control. But if you are taking advantage of these features, you must also consider how you can handle certain browsers, often called downlevel browsers, that might not understand these advanced features or might not have them enabled. Being able to detect and react to downlevel browsers is an important consideration when creating your control. ASP.NET includes some powerful tools you can use to detect the type and version of the browser making the page request, as well as what capabilities the browser supports.

.browser files

ASP.NET 2.0 introduced a new and highly flexible method for configuring, storing, and discovering browser capabilities. All browser identification and capability information is now stored in `.browser` files. ASP.NET stores these files in the `C:\Windows\Microsoft.NET\Framework\v2.0.[xxxx]\CONFIG\Browsers` directory. If you open this folder, you see that ASP.NET provides you with a variety of `.browser` files that describe the capabilities of most of today's common desktop browsers, as well as information on browsers in devices such as PDAs and cellular phones. Open one of the browser files, and you see that the file contains all the identification and capability information for the browser. Listing 26-26 shows you the contents of the WebTV capabilities file.

Listing 26-26: A sample browser capabilities file

```
<browsers>
    <!-- sample UA "Mozilla/3.0 WebTV/1.2(Compatible;MSIE 2.0)" -->
    <browser id="WebTV" parentID="IE2">
        <identification>
            <userAgent
           match="WebTV/(?'version'(?'major'\d+)(?'minor'\.\d+)(?'letters'\w*))" />
        </identification>

        <capture>
        </capture>

        <capabilities>
            <capability name="backgroundsounds"    value="true" />
            <capability name="browser"             value="WebTV" />
            <capability name="cookies"             value="true" />
            <capability name="isMobileDevice"      value="true" />
            <capability name="letters"             value="\${letters}" />
            <capability name="majorversion"        value="\${major}" />
            <capability name="minorversion"        value="\${minor}" />
            <capability name="tables"              value="true" />
            <capability name="type"                value="WebTV\${major}" />
            <capability name="version"             value="\${version}" />
        </capabilities>

        <controlAdapters markupTextWriterType="System.Web.UI.Html32TextWriter">
    </controlAdapters>
    </browser>

    <browser id="WebTV2" parentID="WebTV">
        <identification>
            <capability name="minorversion" match="2" />
        </identification>

        <capture>
        </capture>

        <capabilities>
            <capability name="css1"                value="true" />
            <capability name="ecmascriptversion"   value="1.0" />
            <capability name="javascript"          value="true" />
        </capabilities>
    </browser>

    <gateway id="WebTVbeta" parentID="WebTV">
        <identification>
            <capability name="letters" match="^b" />
```

Continued

```
        </identification>

        <capture>
        </capture>

        <capabilities>
            <capability name="beta"    value="true" />
        </capabilities>
    </gateway>
</browsers>
```

The advantage of this new method for storing browser capability information is that as new browsers are created or new versions are released, developers simply create or update a `.browser` file to describe the capabilities of that browser.

Accessing Browser Capability Information

Now that you have seen how ASP.NET stores browser capability information, we want to discuss how you can access this information at runtime and program your control to change what it renders based on the browser. To access capability information about the requesting browser, you can use the `Page.Request.Browser` property. This property gives you access to the `System.Web.HttpBrowserCapabilities` class, which provides information about the capabilities of the browser making the current request. The class provides you with a myriad of attributes and properties that describe what the browser can support and render and what it requires. Lists use this information to add capabilities to the TextBox control. Listing 26-27 shows how you can detect browser capabilities to make sure a browser supports JavaScript.

Listing 26-27: Detecting browser capabilities in server-side code

VB

```
Protected Overrides Sub OnPreRender(ByVal e As System.EventArgs)
    If (Page.Request.Browser.EcmaScriptVersion.Major > 0) Then
        Page.ClientScript.RegisterStartupScript( _
            GetType(Page), "ClientCallback", _
            "function ClientCallback() {" & _
                "args=document.getElementById('" & _
                    Me.ClientID & "_i" & "').value;" & _
                Page.ClientScript.GetCallbackEventReference(Me, "args", _
                    "CallbackHandler", Nothing, "ErrorHandler", True) + "}", _
            True)

        Page.ClientScript.RegisterStartupScript(GetType(Page), _
            "ControlFocus", "document.getElementById('" & _
            Me.ClientID & "').focus();", _
            True)
    End If
End Sub
```

C#

```
protected override void OnPreRender(EventArgs e)
{
```

```
        if (Page.Request.Browser.EcmaScriptVersion.Major > 0)
        {
            Page.ClientScript.RegisterClientScriptInclude(
                "UtilityFunctions", "JScript.js");

            Page.ClientScript.RegisterStartupScript(
                typeof(Page),
                "ControlFocus","document.getElementById('" +
                    this.ClientID + "_i" + "').focus();",
                true);

            Page.ClientScript.RegisterStartupScript(
                typeof(Page), "ClientCallback",
                "function ClientCallback() {" +
                    "args=document.getElementById('" +
                        this.ClientID + "_i" + "').value;" +
                    Page.ClientScript.GetCallbackEventReference(this, "args",
                        "CallbackHandler", null,"ErrorHandler",true) + "}",
                true);
        }
    }
```

This is a very simple sample, but it gives you an idea of what is possible using the `HttpBrowserCapabilities` class.

Using ViewState

When developing Web applications, remember that they are built on the stateless HTTP protocol. ASP.NET gives you a number of ways to give users the illusion that they are using a stateful application, including Session State and cookies. Additionally, ASP.NET 1.0 introduced a new way of creating the state illusion called ViewState. ViewState enables you to maintain the state of the objects and controls that are part of the Web page through the page's lifecycle by storing the state of the controls in a hidden form field that is rendered as part of the HTML. The state contained in the form field can then be used by the application to reconstitute the page's state when a postback occurs. Figure 26-14 shows how ASP.NET stores ViewState information in a hidden form field.

Notice that the page contains a hidden form field named `_ViewState`. The value of this form field is the ViewState for your Web page. By default, ViewState is enabled in all in-box server controls shipped with ASP.NET. If you write customer server controls, however, you are responsible for ensuring that a control is participating in the use of ViewState by the page.

The ASP.NET ViewState is basically a StateBag that enables you to save and retrieve objects as key/value pairs. As you see in Figure 26-14, these objects are then serialized by ASP.NET and persisted as an encrypted string, which is pushed to the client as a hidden HTML form field. When the page posts back to the server, ASP.NET can use this hidden form field to reconstitute the StateBag, which you can then access as the page is processed on the server.

Because the ViewState can sometimes grow to be very large and can therefore affect the overall page size, you might consider an alternate method of storing the ViewState information. You can create your own persistence mechanism by deriving a class from the `System.Web.UI.PageStatePersister` *class and overriding its* `Load` *and* `Save` *methods.*

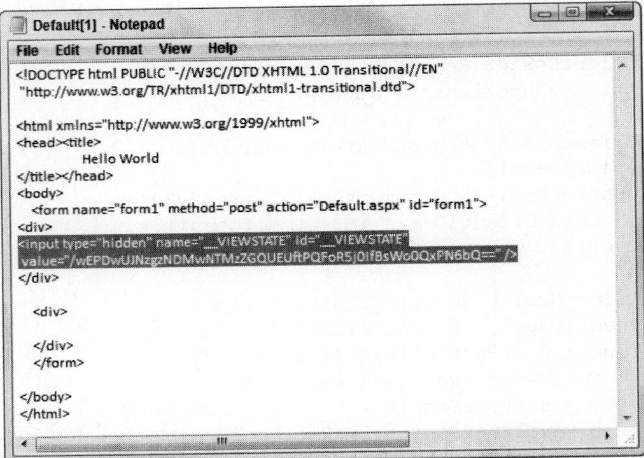

Figure 26-14

As shown in Listing 26-28, by default, the Text property included with the ASP.NET Server Control template is set up to store its value in ViewState.

Listing 26-28: The Text property's use of ViewState

VB

```
Property Text() As String
    Get
        Dim s As String = CStr(ViewState("Text"))
        If s Is Nothing Then
            Return "[" + Me.ID + "]"
        Else
            Return s
        End If
    End Get

    Set(ByVal Value As String)
        ViewState("Text") = Value
    End Set
End Property
```

C#

```
public string Text
{
    get
    {
        String s = (String)ViewState["Text"];
        return ((s == null) ? "[" + this.ID + "]": s);
    }
    set
    {
        ViewState["Text"] = value;
    }
}
```

When creating new properties in an ASP.NET server control, you should remember to use this same technique in order to ensure that the values set by the end user in your control will be persisted across page postbacks.

Note that the loading of ViewState happens after the `OnInit` event has been raised by the page. If your control makes changes to itself or another server control before the event has been raised, the changes are not saved to the ViewState.

Types and ViewState

As mentioned in the preceding section, the ViewState is basically a generic collection of objects, but not all objects can be added to the ViewState. Only types that can be safely persisted can be used in the ViewState, so objects such as database connections or file handles should not be added to the ViewState.

Additionally, certain data types are optimized for use in the ViewState. When adding data to the ViewState, try to package the data into these types:

- Primitive Types (Int32, Boolean, and so on)
- Arrays of Primitive Types
- ArrayList, HashTable
- Pair, Triplet
- Color, DataTime
- String, IndexedString
- HybridDictionary of these types
- Objects that have a TypeConverter available. Be aware, however, that there is a reduction in performance if you use these types.
- Objects that are serializable (marked with the `Serializable` attribute)

ASP.NET 2.0 introduced new ViewState features that improve performance. For example, the .NET 1.1 ViewState used the LosFormatter to serialize objects, but starting with.NET 2.0, ViewState no longer uses this serializer. Instead, it uses the ObjectStateFormatter, which results in dramatic improvements in the speed with which objects are serialized and deserialized. It also decreases the overall byte size of the resulting serialization. Additionally, beginning with ASP.NET 2.0, ViewState was modified to be written out as bytes rather than strings, thereby saving the cost of converting to a string.

Control State

At times, your control must store critical, usually private information across postbacks. In ASP.NET 1.0, you might have considered using ViewState, but a developer using your control could disable ViewState. ASP.NET solved this problem by introducing a new kind of ViewState called ControlState. ControlState is essentially a private ViewState for your control only, and it is not affected when ViewState is turned off.

Two new methods, `SaveViewState` and `LoadViewState`, provide access to ControlState; however, the implementation of these methods is left up to you. Listing 26-29 shows how you can use the `LoadControlState` and `SaveViewState` methods.

Listing 26-29: Using ControlState in a server control

VB

```
Imports System
Imports System.Collections.Generic
Imports System.ComponentModel
Imports System.Text
Imports System.Web
Imports System.Web.UI
Imports System.Web.UI.WebControls

<DefaultProperty("Text")> _
<ToolboxData("<{0}:ServerControl1 runat=server></{0}:ServerControl1>")> _
Public Class ServerControl1
    Inherits WebControl

    Dim s As String
    Protected Overrides Sub OnInit(ByVal e As System.EventArgs)
        Page.RegisterRequiresControlState(Me)
        MyBase.OnInit(e)
    End Sub

    Protected Overrides Sub LoadControlState(ByVal savedState As Object)
        s = CStr(savedState)
    End Sub

    Protected Overrides Function SaveControlState() As Object
        Return CType("FOO", Object)
    End Function

    Protected Overrides Sub Render(ByVal output As System.Web.UI.HtmlTextWriter)
        output.Write("Control State: " & s)
    End Sub

End Class
```

C#

```
using System;
using System.Collections.Generic;
using System.ComponentModel;
using System.Linq;
using System.Text;
using System.Web;
using System.Web.UI;
using System.Web.UI.WebControls;

namespace ServerControl1
{
    [DefaultProperty("Text")]
    [ToolboxData("<{0}:ServerControl1 runat=server></{0}:ServerControl1>")]
    public class ServerControl1 : WebControl
```

```
        {
            string s;
            protected override void OnInit(EventArgs e)
           {
               Page.RegisterRequiresControlState(this);
               base.OnInit(e);
           }

            protected override void LoadControlState(object savedState)
            {
                s = (string)savedState;
            }

            protected override object SaveControlState()
            {
                return (object)"FOO";
            }

            protected override void Render(HtmlTextWriter output)
            {
                output.Write("Control State: " + s);
            }
        }
    }
```

Controls intending to use ControlState must call the `Page.RegisterRequiresControlState` method before attempting to save control state data. Additionally, the `RegisterRequiresControlState` method must be called for each page load because the value is not retained through page postbacks.

Raising PostBack Events

As you have seen in this chapter, ASP.NET provides a very powerful set of tools you can use to develop server controls and emit them to a client browser. But this is still one-way communication because the server only pushes data to the client. It would be useful if the server control could send data back to the server. The process of sending data back to the server is generally known as a *page postback*. You experience a page postback any time you click a form button or link that causes the page to make a new request to the Web server.

ASP.NET provides a rich framework for handling postbacks from ASP.NET Web pages. Additionally, ASP.NET attempts to give you a development model that mimics the standard Windows Forms event model. It enables you to use controls that, even though they are rendered in the client browser, can raise events in server-side code. It also provides an easy mechanism for plugging the server control into that framework, allowing you to create controls that can cause a page postback. Figure 26-15 shows the ASP.NET postback framework.

In order to initiate a postback, ASP.NET uses client-side scripting. You can add the proper script to your control by using the `GetPostBackEventReference` method and emitting the results to the client during the controls render method. Listing 26-30 shows how you can add that to a new server control that emits an HTML button.

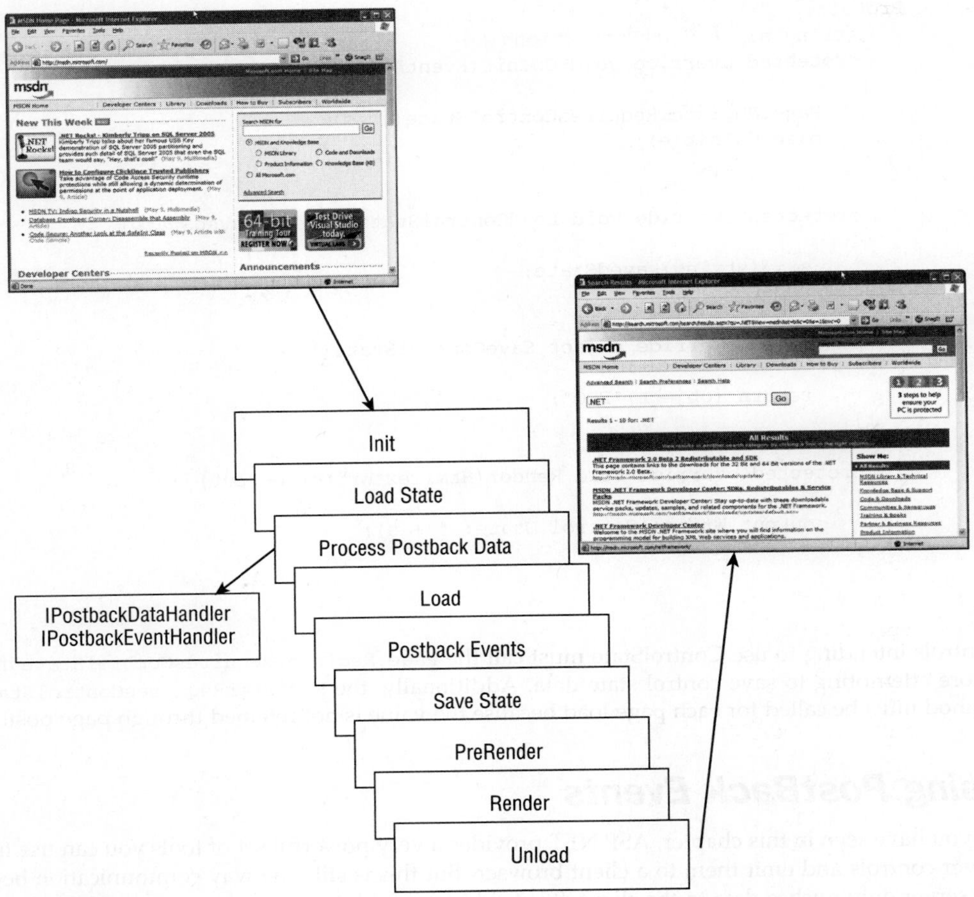

Figure 26-15

Listing 26-30: Adding PostBack capabilities to a server control

VB

```
Imports System
Imports System.Collections.Generic
Imports System.ComponentModel
Imports System.Text
Imports System.Web
Imports System.Web.UI
Imports System.Web.UI.WebControls

<DefaultProperty("Text")> _
<ToolboxData("<{0}:ServerControl1 runat=server></{0}:ServerControl1>")> _
Public Class ServerControl1
    Inherits WebControl
```

```
    Protected Overrides Sub RenderContents(ByVal output As HtmlTextWriter)
        Dim p As New PostBackOptions(Me)

        output.AddAttribute(HtmlTextWriterAttribute.Onclick, _
            Page.ClientScript.GetPostBackEventReference(p))

        output.AddAttribute(HtmlTextWriterAttribute.Value, "My Button")
        output.AddAttribute(HtmlTextWriterAttribute.Id, Me.ClientID & "_i")
        output.AddAttribute(HtmlTextWriterAttribute.Name, Me.ClientID & "_i")
        output.RenderBeginTag(HtmlTextWriterTag.Button)
        output.RenderEndTag()
    End Sub
End Class
```

C#

```
Using System;
Using System.Collections.Generic;
using System.ComponentModel;
using System.Linq;
using System.Text;
using System.Web;
using System.Web.UI;
using System.Web.UI.WebControls;

namespace ServerControl1
{
    [DefaultProperty("Text")]
    [ToolboxData("<{0}:ServerControl1 runat=server></{0}:ServerControl1>")]
    public class ServerControl1 : WebControl
    {
        protected override void RenderContents(HtmlTextWriter output)
        {
            PostBackOptions p = new PostBackOptions(this);

            output.AddAttribute(HtmlTextWriterAttribute.Onclick,
                Page.ClientScript.GetPostBackEventReference(p));
            output.AddAttribute(HtmlTextWriterAttribute.Value, "My Button");
            output.AddAttribute(HtmlTextWriterAttribute.Id, this.ClientID + "_i");
            output.AddAttribute(HtmlTextWriterAttribute.Name,
                this.ClientID + "_i");
            output.RenderBeginTag(HtmlTextWriterTag.Button);
            output.RenderEndTag();
        }
    }
}
```

As you can see, this code adds the postback event reference to the client-side OnClick event, but you are not limited to that. You can add the postback JavaScript to any client-side event. You could even add the code to a client-side function if you want to include some logic code.

Now that you can create a postback, you may want to add events to your control that execute during the page postback. To raise server-side events from a client-side object, you implement the System.Web.IPostBackEventHandler interface. Listing 26-31 shows how to do this for a button control. You also create a server-side Click event you can handle when the page posts back.

Listing 26-31: Handling postback events in a server control

VB

```
Imports System
Imports System.Collections.Generic
Imports System.ComponentModel
Imports System.Text
Imports System.Web
Imports System.Web.UI
Imports System.Web.UI.WebControls

<DefaultProperty("Text")> _
<ToolboxData("<{0}:ServerControl1 runat=server></{0}:ServerControl1>")>  _
Public Class ServerControl1
    Inherits System.Web.UI.WebControls.WebControl
    Implements IPostBackEventHandler

    '. . . Code removed for clarity . . .

    Public Event Click()
    Public Sub OnClick(ByVal args As EventArgs)
        RaiseEvent Click()
    End Sub

    Public Sub RaisePostBackEvent(ByVal eventArgument As String) _
      Implements System.Web.UI.IPostBackEventHandler.RaisePostBackEvent
        OnClick(EventArgs.Empty)
    End Sub
End Class
```

C#

```
using System;
using System.Collections.Generic;
using System.ComponentModel;
using System.Linq;
using System.Text;
using System.Web;
using System.Web.UI;
using System.Web.UI.WebControls;

namespace ServerControl1
{
    [DefaultProperty("Text")]
    [ToolboxData("<{0}:ServerControl1 runat=server></{0}:ServerControl1>")]
    public class ServerControl1 : WebControl, IPostBackEventHandler
    {

        //. . . Code removed for clarity . . .

        #region IPostBackEventHandler Members
        public event EventHandler Click;

        public virtual void OnClick(EventArgs e)
```

```
        {
            if (Click != null)
            {
                Click(this,e);
            }
        }

        public void RaisePostBackEvent(string eventArgument)
        {
            OnClick(EventArgs.Empty);
        }

        #endregion
    }
}
```

Now, when the user clicks the button and the page posts back, the server-side Click event fires, allowing you to add server-side handling code to the event.

Handling PostBack Data

Now that you have learned how to store data in ViewState and add postback capabilities to a control, look at how you can enable the control to interact with data the user enters into one of its form fields. When a page is posted back to the server by ASP.NET, all the form data is also posted to the server. If the control can interact with data that is passed with a page, you can store the information in ViewState and complete the illusion of a stateful application.

To interact with postback data, your control must be able to access the data. To do this, it implements the System.Web.IPostBackDataHandler interface. This interface allows your control to examine the form data that is passed back to the server during the postback.

The IPostBackDataHandler interface requires that you implement two methods: `LoadPostData` and `RaisePostBackDataChangedEvent`. The `LoadPostData` method is called for all server controls on the page that have postback data. If a control does not have any postback data, the method is not called; however, you can explicitly ask for the method to be called by using the `RegisterRequiresPostBack` method.

Listing 26-32 shows how you implement the IPostBackDataHandler interface method in a text box.

Listing 26-32: Accessing Postback data in a server control

VB

```
Imports System
Imports System.Collections.Generic
Imports System.ComponentModel
Imports System.Text
Imports System.Web
Imports System.Web.UI
Imports System.Web.UI.WebControls

<DefaultProperty("Text")> _
<ToolboxData("<{0}:ServerControl1 runat=server></{0}:ServerControl1>")> _
```

```
Public Class ServerControl1
    Inherits SystemWebControl
    Implements IPostBackEventHandler, IPostBackDataHandler

    '. . . Code removed for clarity . . .

    Public Function LoadPostData(ByVal postDataKey As String, _
        ByVal postCollection As _
            System.Collections.Specialized.NameValueCollection) _
        As Boolean Implements System.Web.UI.IPostBackDataHandler.LoadPostData

        Me.Text = postCollection(postDataKey)
        Return False
    End Function

    Public Sub RaisePostDataChangedEvent() _
        Implements System.Web.UI.IPostBackDataHandler.RaisePostDataChangedEvent

    End Sub

End Class
```

C#

```
using System;
using System.Collections.Generic;
using System.ComponentModel;
using System.Linq;
using System.Text;
using System.Web;
using System.Web.UI;
using System.Web.UI.WebControls;

namespace ServerControl1
{
    [DefaultProperty("Text")]
    [ToolboxData("<{0}:ServerControl1 runat=server></{0}:ServerControl1>")]
    public class ServerControl1 : WebControl,
        IPostBackEventHandler, IPostBackDataHandler
    {

        //. . . Code removed for clarity . . .

        public bool LoadPostData(string postDataKey,
            System.Collections.Specialized.NameValueCollection postCollection)
        {
            this.Text = postCollection[postDataKey];
            return false;
        }

        public void RaisePostDataChangedEvent()
        {
        }
    }
}
```

As you can see, the `LoadPostData` method passes any form data submitted to the method as a name value collection that the control can access. The `postDataKey` parameter allows the control to access the postback data item specific to it. You use these parameters to save text to the `Text` property of the TextBox control. If you remember the earlier ViewState example, the `Text` property saves the new value to ViewState; when the page renders, the TextBox value automatically repopulates.

In addition to the input parameters, the `LoadPostData` method also returns a Boolean value. This value indicates whether the `RaisePostBackDataChangedEvent` method is also called after the `LoadPostData` method completes execution. In the sample, it returns `false` because no events exist, but if you create a `TextChanged` event to indicate the Textbox text has changed, you raise that event in the `RaisePostDataChangedEvent` method.

Composite Controls

So far, in looking at Server controls, you have concentrated on emitting a single HTML control; but this can be fairly limiting. Creating extremely powerful controls often requires that you nest several HTML elements together. ASP.NET allows you to easily create controls that serve as a container for other controls. These types of controls are called *composite controls*.

To demonstrate how easy creating a composite control can be, try to change an existing control into a composite control. Listing 26-33 shows how you can do this.

Listing 26-33: Creating a composite control

VB

```
Imports System
Imports System.Collections.Generic
Imports System.ComponentModel
Imports System.Text
Imports System.Web
Imports System.Web.UI
Imports System.Web.UI.WebControls

<DefaultProperty("Text")> _
<ToolboxData("<{0}:ServerControl1 runat=server></{0}:ServerControl1>")> _
Public Class ServerControl1
    Inherits System.Web.UI.WebControls.CompositeControl

    Protected textbox As TextBox

    Protected Overrides Sub CreateChildControls()
        Me.Controls.Add(textbox)
    End Sub

End Class
```

C#

```
using System;
using System.Collections.Generic;
```

Continued

```
using System.ComponentModel;
using System.Linq;
using System.Text;
using System.Web;
using System.Web.UI;
using System.Web.UI.WebControls;

namespace ServerControl1
{
    [DefaultProperty("Text")]
    [ToolboxData("<{0}:ServerControl1 runat=server></{0}:ServerControl1>")]
    public class ServerControl1 : CompositeControl
    {
        protected TextBox textbox = new TextBox();

        protected override void CreateChildControls()
        {
            this.Controls.Add(textbox);
        }
    }
}
```

A number of things in this listing are important. First, notice that the control class is now inheriting from `CompositeControl`, rather than `WebControl`. Deriving from `CompositeControl` gives you a few extra features specific to this type of control.

Second, notice that no `Render` method appears in this code. Instead, you simply create an instance of another type of server control and add that to the `Controls` collection in the `CreateChildControls` method. When you run this sample, you see that it renders a text box just like the last control did. In fact, the HTML that it renders is almost identical.

Exposing Child Control Properties

When you drop a composite control (such as the text box from the last sample) onto the design surface, notice that even though you are using a powerful ASP.NET TextBox control within the control, none of that control's properties are exposed to you in the Properties Explorer. In order to expose child control properties through the parent container, you must create corresponding properties in the parent control. For example, if you want to expose the ASP.NET text box `Text` property through the parent control, you create a `Text` property. Listing 26-34 shows how to do this.

Listing 26-34: Exposing control properties in a composite control

VB

```
Imports System
Imports System.Collections.Generic
Imports System.ComponentModel
Imports System.Text
Imports System.Web
Imports System.Web.UI
Imports System.Web.UI.WebControls

<DefaultProperty("Text")> _
```

```
<ToolboxData("<{0}:ServerControl1 runat=server></{0}:ServerControl1>")> _
Public Class ServerControl1
    Inherits System.Web.UI.WebControls.CompositeControl

    Protected textbox As TextBox

    Public Property Text() As String
        Get
            EnsureChildControls()
            Return textbox.Text
        End Get
        Set(ByVal value As String)
            EnsureChildControls()
            textbox.Text = value
        End Set
    End Property

    Protected Overrides Sub CreateChildControls()
        Me.Controls.Add(textbox)
        Me.ChildControlsCreated=True
    End Sub

End Class
```

C#

```
using System;
using System.Collections.Generic;
using System.ComponentModel;
using System.Linq;
using System.Text;
using System.Web;
using System.Web.UI;
using System.Web.UI.WebControls;

namespace ServerControl1
{
    [DefaultProperty("Text")]
    [ToolboxData("<{0}:ServerControl1 runat=server></{0}:ServerControl1>")]
    public class ServerControl1 : CompositeControl
    {

        protected TextBox textbox = new TextBox();

        public string Text
        {
            get
            {
                EnsureChildControls();
                return textbox.Text;
            }
            set
            {
                EnsureChildControls();
```

Continued

```
                textbox.Text = value;
            }
        }

        protected override void CreateChildControls()
        {
            this.Controls.Add(textbox);
            this.ChildControlsCreated=true;
        }
    }
}
```

Notice that you use this property simply to populate the underlying control's properties. Also notice that before you access the underlying control's properties, you always call the `EnsureChildControls` method. This method ensures that children of the container control have actually been initialized before you attempt to access them.

Templated Controls

In addition to composite controls, you can also create templated controls. *Templated controls* allow the user to specify a portion of the HTML that is used to render the control, and to nest other controls inside of a container control. You might be familiar with the Repeater or DataList control. These are both templated controls that let you specify how you want the bound data to be displayed when the page renders.

To demonstrate a templated control, the following code gives you a simple example of displaying a message from a user on a Web page. Because the control is a templated control, the developer has complete control over how the message is displayed.

To get started, create the Message server control that will be used as the template inside of a container control. Listing 26-35 shows the class which simply extends the existing Panel control by adding two additional properties, Name and Text, and a new constructor.

Listing 26-35: Creating the templated control's inner control class

VB

```
Public Class Message
    Inherits System.Web.UI.WebControls.Panel
    Implements System.Web.UI.INamingContainer

    Private _name As String
    Private _text As String

    Public Sub New(ByVal name As String, ByVal text As String)
        _text = text
        _name = name
    End Sub

    Public ReadOnly Property Name() As String
        Get
            Return _name
        End Get
    End Property
```

```
        Public ReadOnly Property Text() As String
            Get
                Return _text

            End Get
        End Property
    End Class
```

C#

```
using System;
using System.Text;
using System.Web;
using System.Web.UI;
using System.Web.UI.WebControls;

namespace ServerControl1
{
    public class Message : Panel, INamingContainer
    {
        private string _name;
        private string _text;

        public Message(string name, string text)
        {
            _text = text;
            _name = name;
        }

        public string Name
        {
            get { return _name;}
        }

        public string Text
        {
            get { return _text;}
        }
    }
}
```

As you will see in a moment, you can access the public properties exposed by the `Message` class in order to insert dynamic content into the template. You will also see how you can display the values of the `Name` and `Text` properties as part of the rendered template control.

Next, as shown in Listing 26-36, create a new server control which will be the container for the `Message` control. This server control is responsible for rendering any template controls nested in it.

Listing 26-36: Creating the template control container class

VB

```
Imports System
Imports System.Collections.Generic
```

Continued

```
Imports System.ComponentModel
Imports System.Text
Imports System.Web
Imports System.Web.UI
Imports System.Web.UI.WebControls

<DefaultProperty("Text")> _
<ToolboxData("<{0}:TemplatedControl runat=server></{0}:TemplatedControl>")> _
Public Class TemplatedControl
    Inherits System.Web.UI.WebControls.WebControl

    Private _name As String
    Private _text As String

    Private _message As Message
    Private _messageTemplate As ITemplate

    <Browsable(False)> Public ReadOnly Property Message() As Message
        Get
            Return _message
        End Get
    End Property

    <PersistenceMode(PersistenceMode.InnerProperty), _
        TemplateContainer(GetType(Message))> _
    Public Property MessageTemplate() As ITemplate
        Get
            Return _messageTemplate
        End Get
        Set(ByVal value As ITemplate)
            _messageTemplate = value
        End Set
    End Property

    <Bindable(True), DefaultValue("")> Public Property Name() As String
        Get
            Return _name
        End Get
        Set(ByVal value As String)
            _name = value
        End Set
    End Property

    <Bindable(True), DefaultValue("")> Public Property Text() As String
        Get
            Return _text
        End Get
        Set(ByVal value As String)
            _text = value
        End Set
    End Property

    Public Overrides Sub DataBind()
        CreateChildControls()
```

```
            ChildControlsCreated = True

            MyBase.DataBind()
        End Sub

        Protected Overrides Sub CreateChildControls()

            Me.Controls.Clear()

            _message = New Message(Name, Text)

            If Me.MessageTemplate Is Nothing Then
                Me.MessageTemplate = New DefaultMessageTemplate()
            End If

            Me.MessageTemplate.InstantiateIn(_message)
            Controls.Add(_message)
        End Sub

        Protected Overrides Sub RenderContents( _
            ByVal writer As System.Web.UI.HtmlTextWriter)

            EnsureChildControls()
            ChildControlsCreated = True

            MyBase.RenderContents(writer)
        End Sub
    End Class
```

C#

```
using System;
using System.Collections.Generic;
using System.ComponentModel;
using System.Linq;
using System.Text;
using System.Web;
using System.Web.UI;
using System.Web.UI.WebControls;

namespace ServerControl1
{
    [DefaultProperty("Text")]
    [ToolboxData("<{0}:TemplatedControl runat=server></{0}: TemplatedControl >")]
    public class TemplatedControl : WebControl
    {
        private string _name;
        private string _text;

        private Message _message;
        private ITemplate _messageTemplate;

        [Browsable(false)]
        public Message Message
        {
```

Continued

```
        get
        {
            return _message;
        }
    }

    [PersistenceMode(PersistenceMode.InnerProperty)]
    [TemplateContainer(typeof(Message))]
    public virtual ITemplate MessageTemplate
    {
        get { return _messageTemplate;}
        set { _messageTemplate = value;}
    }

    [Bindable(true)]
    [DefaultValue("")]
    public string Name
    {
        get { return _name;}
        set { _name = value;}
    }

    [Bindable(true)]
    [DefaultValue("")]
    public string Text
    {
        get { return _text;}
        set { _text = value;}
    }

    public override void DataBind()
    {
        CreateChildControls();
        ChildControlsCreated = true;

        base.DataBind();
    }

    protected override void CreateChildControls()
    {
        this.Controls.Clear();

        _message = new Message(Name,Text);

        if (this.MessageTemplate == null)
        {
            this.MessageTemplate = new DefaultMessageTemplate();
        }
        this.MessageTemplate.InstantiateIn(_message);
        Controls.Add(_message);
    }

    protected override void RenderContents(HtmlTextWriter writer)
    {
```

```
                EnsureChildControls();
                ChildControlsCreated = true;

                base.RenderContents(writer);
            }
        }
    }
```

To start to dissect this sample, first notice the `MessageTemplate` property. This property allows Visual Studio to understand that the control can contain a template, and allows it to display the IntelliSense for that template. The property has been marked with the `PersistanceMode` attribute indicating that the template control should be persisted as an inner property within the control's tag in the ASPX page. Additionally, the property is marked with the `TemplateContainer` attribute, which helps ASP.NET figure out what type of template control this property represents. In this case, it's the Message template control you created earlier.

The container control exposes two public properties, Name and Text. These properties are used to populate the `Name` and `Text` properties of the Message control since that class does not allow developers to set the properties directly.

Finally, the `CreateChildControls` method, called by the `DataBind` method, does most of the heavy lifting in this control. It creates a new `Message` object, passing the values of `Name` and `Text` as constructor values. Once the `CreateChildControls` method completes, the base DataBind operation continues to execute. This is important because that is where the evaluation of the Name and Text properties occurs, which allows you to insert these properties values into the template control.

After the control and template are created, you can drop them onto a test Web page. Listing 26-37 shows how the control can be used to customize the display of the data.

Listing 26-37: Adding a templated control to a Web page

VB

```
<%@ Page Language="VB" %>

<%@ Register Assembly="WebControlLibrary1" Namespace="WebControlLibrary1"
    TagPrefix="cc1" %>

<script runat="server">
    Protected Sub Page_Load(ByVal sender As Object, ByVal e As System.EventArgs)
        Me.TemplatedControl1.DataBind()
    End Sub
</script>

<html xmlns="http://www.w3.org/1999/xhtml" >
<head runat="server">
    <title>Templated Web Controls</title>
</head>
<body>
    <form id="form1" runat="server">
    <div>
        <cc1:TemplatedControl Name="John Doe" Text="Hello World!"
```

Continued

```
            ID="TemplatedControl1" runat="server">
            <MessageTemplate>The user '<%# Container.Name %>'
                has a message for you: <br />"<%#Container.Text%>"
            </MessageTemplate>
        </cc1:TemplatedControl>

    </div>
    </form>
</body>
</html>
```

C#

```
<script runat="server">
    protected void Page_Load(object sender, EventArgs e)
    {
        this.TemplatedControl1.DataBind();
    }
</script>
```

As you can see in the listing, the `<cc1:TemplatedControl>` control contains a `MessageTemplate` within it, which has been customized to display the `Name` and `Text` values. Figure 26-16 shows this page after it has been rendered in the browser.

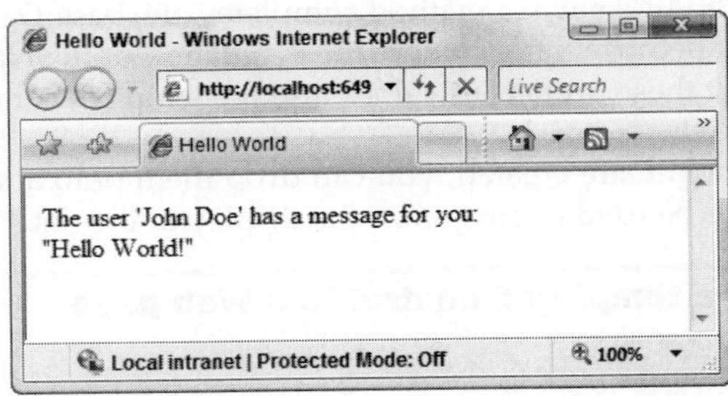

Figure 26-16

One item to consider when creating templated controls is what happens if the developer does not include a template control inside of the container control. In the previous example, if you removed the MessageTemplate control from the TemplateContainer, a NullReferenceException would occur when you tried to run your Web page because the container control's MessageTemplate property would return a null value. In order to prevent this, you can include a default template class as part of the container control. An example of a default template is shown in Listing 26-38.

Listing 26-38: Creating the templated control's default template class

VB

```
Friend Class DefaultMessageTemplate
    Implements ITemplate

    Public Sub InstantiateIn(ByVal container As System.Web.UI.Control) _
            Implements System.Web.UI.ITemplate.InstantiateIn
```

```
        Dim l As New Literal()
        l.Text="No MessageTemplate was included."
        container.Controls.Add(l)
    End Sub
End Class
```

C#

```
internal sealed class DefaultMessageTemplate : ITemplate
{
    public void InstantiateIn(Control container)
    {
        Literal l = new Literal();
        l.Text="No MessageTemplate was included.";
        container.Controls.Add(l);
    }
}
```

Notice that the DefaultMessageTemplate implements the ITemplate interface. This interface requires that the `InstantiateIn` method be implemented, which we use to provide the default template content.

To include the default template, simply add the class to the `TemplatedControl` class. You will also need to modify the `CreateChildControls` method to detect the null MessageTemplate and instead create an instance of and use the default template.

VB

```
If template = Nothing Then
    template = New DefaultMessageTemplate()
End If
```

C#

```
if (template == null)
{
    template = new DefaultMessageTemplate();
}
```

Creating Control Design-Time Experiences

So far in this chapter, you concentrated primarily on what gets rendered to the client's browser, but the browser is not the only consumer of server controls. Visual Studio and the developer using a server control are also consumers, and you need to consider their experiences when using your control.

Note that beginning with Visual Studio 2008, the Web Page Design Surface used to provide Web page designers with a WYSIWYG design experience has been completely rewritten. The design surface, which in prior versions was derived from the core Internet Explorer rendering engine has been replaced by a completely independent and new rendering engine. This is good news for Web page developers because they are no longer subject to the quirks of IE rendering. If you have existing controls you should be sure to test them thoroughly on the new design-surface to ensure compatibility. From a control design perspective, all of the previous functionality has been retained. Therefore, any controls you have written to take advantage of design-time tools such as SmartTags or Designer regions should function normally on the new design surface.

ASP.NET offers numerous improvements in the design-time experience you give to developers using your control. Some of these improvements require no additional coding, such as the WYSIWYG rendering of user controls and basic server controls; but for more complex scenarios, ASP.NET includes a number of tools that give the developer an outstanding design-time experience.

When you write server controls, a priority should be to give the developer a design-time experience that closely replicates the runtime experience. This means altering the appearance of the control on the design surface in response to changes in control properties and the introduction of other server controls onto the design surface. Three main components are involved in creating the design-time behaviors of a server control:

- `Type Converters`
- `Designers`
- `UI Type Editors`

Because a chapter can be written for each one of these topics, in this section I attempt to give you only an overview of each, how they tie into a control's design-time behavior, and some simple examples of their use.

Type Converters

`TypeConverter` is a class that allows you to perform conversions between one type and another. Visual Studio uses type converters at design time to convert object property values to String types so that they can be displayed on the Property Browser, and it returns them to their original types when the developer changes the property.

ASP.NET includes a wide variety of type converters you can use when creating your control's design-time behavior. These range from converters that allow you to convert most number types, to converters that let you convert Fonts, Colors, DataTimes, and Guids. The easiest way to see what type converters are available to you in the .NET Framework is to search for types in the framework that derive from the `TypeConverter` class using the MSDN Library help.

After you have found a type converter that you want to use on a control property, mark the property with a `TypeConverter` attribute, as shown in Listing 26-39.

Listing 26-39: Applying the TypeConverter attribute to a property

VB

```
<Bindable(True)> _
<Category("Appearance")> _
<DefaultValue("")> _
<TypeConverter(GetType(GuidConverter))> _
Property BookId() As System.Guid
    Get
        Return _bookid
    End Get

    Set(ByVal Value As System.Guid)
```

```
            _bookid = Value
        End Set
End Property
```

C#

```
[Bindable(true)]
[Category("Appearance")]
[DefaultValue("")]
[TypeConverter(typeof(GuidConverter))]
public Guid BookId
{
    get
    {
        return _bookid;
    }

    set
    {
        _bookid = value;
    }
}
```

In this example, a property is exposed that accepts and returns an object of type Guid. The Property Browser cannot natively display a Guid object, so you convert the value to a string so that it can be displayed properly in the property browser. Marking the property with the `TypeConverter` attribute and, in this case, specifying the GuidConverter as the type converter you want to use, allows complex objects like a Guid to display properly in the Property Browser.

Custom Type Converters

It is also possible to create your own custom type converters if none of the in-box converters fit into your scenario. Type converters derive from the `System.ComponentModel.TypeConverter` class. Listing 26-40 shows a custom type converter that converts a custom object called `Name` to and from a string.

Listing 26-40: Creating a custom type converter

VB

```
Imports System
Imports System.ComponentModel
Imports System.Globalization

Public Class Name

    Private _first As String
    Private _last As String

    Public Sub New(ByVal first As String, ByVal last As String)
        _first = first
        _last = last
    End Sub
```

Continued

```
    Public Property First() As String
        Get
            Return _first
        End Get
        Set(ByVal value As String)
            _first = value
        End Set
    End Property

    Public Property Last() As String
        Get
            Return _last
        End Get
        Set(ByVal value As String)
            _last = value
        End Set
    End Property
End Class

Public Class NameConverter
    Inherits TypeConverter

    Public Overrides Function CanConvertFrom(ByVal context As _
      ITypeDescriptorContext, ByVal sourceType As Type) As Boolean

        If (sourceType Is GetType(String)) Then
            Return True
        End If

        Return MyBase.CanConvertFrom(context, sourceType)
    End Function

    Public Overrides Function ConvertFrom( _
            ByVal context As ITypeDescriptorContext, _
            ByVal culture As CultureInfo, ByVal value As Object) As Object
        If (value Is GetType(String)) Then
            Dim v As String() = (CStr(value).Split(New [Char]() {" "c}))
            Return New Name(v(0), v(1))
        End If
        Return MyBase.ConvertFrom(context, culture, value)
    End Function

    Public Overrides Function ConvertTo( _
            ByVal context As ITypeDescriptorContext, _
            ByVal culture As CultureInfo, ByVal value As Object, _
            ByVal destinationType As Type) As Object
        If (destinationType Is GetType(String)) Then
            Return (CType(value, Name).First + " " + (CType(value, Name).Last))
        End If
        Return MyBase.ConvertTo(context, culture, value, destinationType)
    End Function
End Class
```

C#

```
using System;
using System.ComponentModel;
using System.Globalization;

public class Name
{
    private string _first;
    private string _last;

    public Name(string first, string last)
    {
        _first=first;
        _last=last;
    }

    public string First
    {
        get{ return _first;}
        set { _first = value;}
    }
    public string Last
    {
        get { return _last;}
        set { _last = value;}
    }
}

public class NameConverter : TypeConverter
{

   public override bool CanConvertFrom(ITypeDescriptorContext context,
      Type sourceType) {

      if (sourceType == typeof(string)) {
         return true;
      }
      return base.CanConvertFrom(context, sourceType);
   }

   public override object ConvertFrom(ITypeDescriptorContext context,
      CultureInfo culture, object value) {
      if (value is string) {
         string[] v = ((string)value).Split(new char[] {' '});
         return new Name(v[0],v[1]);
      }
      return base.ConvertFrom(context, culture, value);
   }

   public override object ConvertTo(ITypeDescriptorContext context,
      CultureInfo culture, object value, Type destinationType) {
```

Continued

```
        if (destinationType == typeof(string)) {
            return ((Name)value).First + " " + ((Name)value).Last;
        }
        return base.ConvertTo(context, culture, value, destinationType);
    }
}
```

The NameConverter class overrides three methods, CanConvertFrom, ConvertFrom, and ConvertTo. The CanConvertFrom method allows you to control what types the converter can convert from. The ConvertFrom method converts the string representation back into a Name object, and ConvertTo converts the Name object into a string representation.

After you have built your type converter, you can use it to mark properties in your control with the TypeConverter attribute, as you saw in Listing 26-35.

Control Designers

Controls that live on the Visual Studio design surface depend on *control designers* to create the design-time experience for the end user. Control designers, for both WinForms and ASP.NET, are classes that derive from the System.ComponentModel.Design.ComponentDesigner class. .NET provides an abstracted base class specifically for creating ASP.NET control designers called the System.Web.UI.Design .ControlDesigner. In order to access these classes you will need to add a reference to the System .Design.dll assembly to your project.

.NET includes a number of in-box control designer classes that you can use when creating a custom control; but as you develop server controls, you see that .NET automatically applies a default designer. The designer it applies is based on the type of control you are creating. For instance, when you created your first TextBox control, Visual Studio used the ControlDesigner class to achieve the WYSIWYG design-time rendering of the text box. If you develop a server control derived from the ControlContainer class, .NET automatically use the ControlContainerDesigner class as the designer.

You can also explicitly specify the designer you want to use to render your control at design time using the Designer attribute on your control's class, as shown in Listing 26-41.

Listing 26-41: Adding a Designer attribute to a control class

VB

```
<DefaultProperty("Text")> _
<ToolboxData("<{0}:WebCustomControl1 runat=server></{0}:WebCustomControl1>")> _
<Designer(GetType(System.Web.UI.Design.ControlDesigner))> _
Public Class WebCustomControl1
    Inherits System.Web.UI.WebControls.WebControl
```

C#

```
[DefaultProperty("Text")]
[ToolboxData("<{0}:WebCustomControl1 runat=server></{0}:WebCustomControl1>")]
[Designer(typeof(System.Web.UI.Design.ControlDesigner))]
public class WebCustomControl1 : WebControl
```

Notice that the Designer attribute has been added to the WebCustomControl1 class. You have specified that the control should use the ControlDesigner class as its designer. Other in-box designers you could have specified are:

- CompositeControlDesigner
- TemplatedControlDesigner
- DataSourceDesigner

Each designer provides a specific design-time behavior for the control, and you can select one that is appropriate for the type of control you are creating.

Design-Time Regions

As you saw earlier, ASP.NET allows you to create server controls that consist of other server controls and text. In ASP.NET 1.0, a server control developer could use the `ReadWriteControlDesigner` class to enable the user of the server control to enter text or drop other server controls into a custom server control at design time. An example of this is the ASP.NET Panel control, which enables developers to add content to the panel at design time.

Since ASP.NET 2.0, however, creating a control with this functionality has changed. The `ReadWriteControlDesigner` class was marked as obsolete, and a new and improved way was included to allow the developer to create server controls that have design-time editable portions. The new technique, called *designer regions*, is an improvement over the `ReadWriteControlDesigner` in several ways. First, unlike the `ReadWriteControlDesigner` class, which allowed only a single editable area, designer regions enable you to create multiple, independent regions defined within a single control. Second, designer classes can now respond to events raised by a design region. This might be the designer drawing a control on the design surface or the user clicking an area of the control or entering or exiting a template edit mode.

To show how you can use designer regions, create a container control to which you can apply a custom control designer (as shown in Listing 26-42).

Listing 26-42: Creating a composite control with designer regions

VB

```
<Designer(GetType(MultiRegionControlDesigner))> _
<ToolboxData("<{0}:MultiRegionControl runat=server width=100%>" & _
    "</{0}:MultiRegionControl>")> _
Public Class MultiRegionControl
    Inherits CompositeControl

    ' Define the templates that represent 2 views on the control
    Private _view1 As ITemplate
    Private _view2 As ITemplate

    ' These properties are inner properties
    <PersistenceMode(PersistenceMode.InnerProperty), DefaultValue("")> _
    Public Overridable Property View1() As ITemplate
        Get
            Return _view1
        End Get
        Set(ByVal value As ITemplate)
            _view1 = value
```

Continued

```
        End Set
    End Property

    <PersistenceMode(PersistenceMode.InnerProperty), DefaultValue("")> _
    Public Overridable Property View2() As ITemplate
        Get
            Return _view2
        End Get
        Set(ByVal value As ITemplate)
            _view2 = value
        End Set
    End Property

    ' The current view on the control; 0= view1, 1=view2, 2=all views
    Private _currentView As Int32 = 0
    Public Property CurrentView() As Int32
        Get
            Return _currentView
        End Get
        Set(ByVal value As Int32)
            _currentView = value
        End Set
    End Property

    Protected Overrides Sub CreateChildControls()
        MyBase.CreateChildControls()

        Controls.Clear()

        Dim template As ITemplate = View1
        If (_currentView = 1) Then
            template = View2
        End If

        Dim p As New Panel()
        Controls.Add(p)

        If (Not template Is Nothing) Then
            template.InstantiateIn(p)
        End If

    End Sub

End Class
```

C#

```
[Designer(typeof(MultiRegionControlDesigner))]
[ToolboxData("<{0}:MultiRegionControl runat=\"server\" width=\"100%\">" +
    "</{0}:MultiRegionControl>")]
public class MultiRegionControl : CompositeControl {

    // Define the templates that represent 2 views on the control
    private ITemplate _view1;
    private ITemplate _view2;
```

```
        // These properties are inner properties
        [PersistenceMode(PersistenceMode.InnerProperty), DefaultValue(null)]
        public virtual ITemplate View1 {
            get { return _view1;}
            set { _view1 = value;}
        }

        [PersistenceMode(PersistenceMode.InnerProperty), DefaultValue(null)]
        public virtual ITemplate View2 {
            get { return _view2;}
            set { _view2 = value;}
        }

        // The current view on the control; 0= view1, 1=view2, 2=all views
        private int _currentView = 0;
        public int CurrentView {
            get { return _currentView;}
            set { _currentView = value;}
        }

        protected override void CreateChildControls()
        {
            Controls.Clear();

            ITemplate template = View1;
            if (_currentView == 1)
                template = View2;

            Panel p = new Panel();
            Controls.Add(p);

            if (template != null)
                template.InstantiateIn(p);
        }
    }
```

The container control creates two `ITemplate` objects, which serve as the controls to display. The `ITemplate` objects are the control containers for this server control, allowing you to drop other server controls or text into this control. The control also uses the `Designer` attribute to indicate to Visual Studio that it should use the `MultiRegionControlDesigner` class when displaying this control on the designer surface.

Now you create the control designer that defines the regions for the control. Listing 26-43 shows the designer class.

Listing 26-43: A custom designer class used to define designer regions

VB

```
Public Class MultiRegionControlDesigner
    Inherits System.Web.UI.Design.WebControls.CompositeControlDesigner

    Protected _currentView As Int32 = 0
    Private myControl As MultiRegionControl
```

```
Public Overrides Sub Initialize(ByVal component As IComponent)
    MyBase.Initialize(component)
    myControl = CType(component, MultiRegionControl)
End Sub

Public Overrides ReadOnly Property AllowResize() As Boolean
    Get
        Return True
    End Get
End Property

Protected Overrides Sub OnClick(ByVal e As DesignerRegionMouseEventArgs)

    If (e.Region Is Nothing) Then
        Return
    End If

    If ((e.Region.Name = "Header0") And (Not _currentView = 0)) Then
        _currentView = 0
        UpdateDesignTimeHtml()
    End If

    If ((e.Region.Name = "Header1") And (Not _currentView = 1)) Then

        _currentView = 1
        UpdateDesignTimeHtml()
    End If
End Sub

Public Overrides Function GetDesignTimeHtml( _
        ByVal regions As DesignerRegionCollection) As String
    BuildRegions(regions)
    Return BuildDesignTimeHtml()
End Function

Protected Overridable Sub BuildRegions( _
        ByVal regions As DesignerRegionCollection)

    regions.Add(New DesignerRegion(Me, "Header0"))
    regions.Add(New DesignerRegion(Me, "Header1"))

    ' If the current view is for all, we need another editable region
    Dim edr0 As New EditableDesignerRegion(Me, "Content" & _currentView, False)
    edr0.Description = "Add stuff in here if you dare:"
    regions.Add(edr0)

    ' Set the highlight, depending upon the selected region
    If ((_currentView = 0) Or (_currentView = 1)) Then
        regions(_currentView).Highlight = True
    End If
End Sub

Protected Overridable Function BuildDesignTimeHtml() As String
```

```
        Dim sb As New StringBuilder()
        sb.Append(BuildBeginDesignTimeHtml())
        sb.Append(BuildContentDesignTimeHtml())
        sb.Append(BuildEndDesignTimeHtml())

        Return sb.ToString()
    End Function

    Protected Overridable Function BuildBeginDesignTimeHtml() As String
        ' Create the table layout
        Dim sb As New StringBuilder()
        sb.Append("<table ")

        ' Styles that we'll use to render for the design-surface
        sb.Append("height='" & myControl.Height.ToString() & "' width='" & _
            myControl.Width.ToString() & "'>")

        ' Generate the title or caption bar
        sb.Append("<tr height='25px' align='center' " & _
            "style='font-family:tahoma;font-size:10pt;font-weight:bold;'>" & _
            "<td style='width:50%' " & _
            DesignerRegion.DesignerRegionAttributeName & "='0'>")
        sb.Append("Page-View 1</td>")
        sb.Append("<td style='width:50%' " & _
            DesignerRegion.DesignerRegionAttributeName & "='1'>")
        sb.Append("Page-View 2</td></tr>")

        Return sb.ToString()
    End Function

    Protected Overridable Function BuildEndDesignTimeHtml() As String
        Return ("</table>")
    End Function

    Protected Overridable Function BuildContentDesignTimeHtml() As String

        Dim sb As New StringBuilder()
        sb.Append("<td colspan='2' style='")
        sb.Append("background-color:" & _
            myControl.BackColor.Name.ToString() & ";' ")

        sb.Append(DesignerRegion.DesignerRegionAttributeName & "='2'>")

        Return sb.ToString()
    End Function

    Public Overrides Function GetEditableDesignerRegionContent( _
            ByVal region As EditableDesignerRegion) As String

        Dim host As IDesignerHost = _
            CType(Component.Site.GetService(GetType(IDesignerHost)), IDesignerHost)

        If (Not host Is Nothing) Then
            Dim template As ITemplate = myControl.View1
```

Continued

```
            If (region.Name = "Content1") Then
                template = myControl.View2
            End If

            If (Not template Is Nothing) Then
                Return ControlPersister.PersistTemplate(template, host)
            End If

        End If

        Return String.Empty
    End Function

    Public Overrides Sub SetEditableDesignerRegionContent( _
        ByVal region As EditableDesignerRegion, ByVal content As String)

        Dim regionIndex As Int32 = Int32.Parse(region.Name.Substring(7))

        If (content Is Nothing) Then

            If (regionIndex = 0) Then
                myControl.View1 = Nothing
            ElseIf (regionIndex = 1) Then
                myControl.View2 = Nothing
                Return
            End If

            Dim host As IDesignerHost = _
                CType(Component.Site.GetService(GetType(IDesignerHost)),
                    IDesignerHost)

            If (Not host Is Nothing) Then
                Dim template = ControlParser.ParseTemplate(host, content)

                If (Not template Is Nothing) Then
                    If (regionIndex = 0) Then
                        myControl.View1 = template
                    ElseIf (regionIndex = 1) Then
                        myControl.View2 = template
                    End If
                End If
            End If
        End If
    End Sub
End Class
```

C#

```
public class MultiRegionControlDesigner :
    System.Web.UI.Design.WebControls.CompositeControlDesigner {

    protected int _currentView = 0;

    private MultiRegionControl myControl;
    public override void Initialize(IComponent component)
```

```
    {
        base.Initialize(component);
        myControl = (MultiRegionControl)component;
    }

    public override bool AllowResize { get { return true;}}

    protected override void OnClick(DesignerRegionMouseEventArgs e)
    {
        if (e.Region == null)
            return;

        if (e.Region.Name == "Header0" && _currentView != 0) {
            _currentView = 0;
            UpdateDesignTimeHtml();
        }

        if (e.Region.Name == "Header1" && _currentView != 1) {
            _currentView = 1;
            UpdateDesignTimeHtml();
        }
    }

    public override String GetDesignTimeHtml(DesignerRegionCollection regions)
    {
        BuildRegions(regions);
        return BuildDesignTimeHtml();
    }

    protected virtual void BuildRegions(DesignerRegionCollection regions)
    {
        regions.Add(new DesignerRegion(this, "Header0"));
        regions.Add(new DesignerRegion(this, "Header1"));

        // If the current view is for all, we need another editable region
        EditableDesignerRegion edr0 = new
            EditableDesignerRegion(this, "Content" + _currentView, false);
        edr0.Description = "Add stuff in here if you dare:";
        regions.Add(edr0);

        // Set the highlight, depending upon the selected region
        if (_currentView ==0 || _currentView==1)
            regions[_currentView].Highlight = true;
    }

    protected virtual string BuildDesignTimeHtml()
    {
        StringBuilder sb = new StringBuilder();
        sb.Append(BuildBeginDesignTimeHtml());
        sb.Append(BuildContentDesignTimeHtml());
        sb.Append(BuildEndDesignTimeHtml());

        return sb.ToString();
    }
```

```
protected virtual String BuildBeginDesignTimeHtml()
{
    // Create the table layout
    StringBuilder sb = new StringBuilder();
    sb.Append("<table ");

    // Styles that we'll use to render for the design-surface
    sb.Append("height='" + myControl.Height.ToString() + "' width='" +
        myControl.Width.ToString() +  "'>");

    // Generate the title or caption bar
    sb.Append("<tr height='25px' align='center' " +
        "style='font-family:tahoma;font-size:10pt;font-weight:bold;'>" +
        "<td style='width:50%' " + DesignerRegion.DesignerRegionAttributeName +
        "='0'>");
    sb.Append("Page-View 1</td>");
    sb.Append("<td style='width:50%' " +
        DesignerRegion.DesignerRegionAttributeName + "='1'>");
    sb.Append("Page-View 2</td></tr>");

    return sb.ToString();
}

protected virtual String BuildEndDesignTimeHtml()
{
    return ("</table>");
}

protected virtual String BuildContentDesignTimeHtml()
{
    StringBuilder sb = new StringBuilder();
    sb.Append("<td colspan='2' style='");
    sb.Append("background-color:" + myControl.BackColor.Name.ToString() +
        ";' ");

    sb.Append(DesignerRegion.DesignerRegionAttributeName + "='2'>");

    return sb.ToString();
}

public override string GetEditableDesignerRegionContent
    (EditableDesignerRegion region)
{
    IDesignerHost host =
        (IDesignerHost)Component.Site.GetService(typeof(IDesignerHost));

    if (host != null) {
        ITemplate template = myControl.View1;

        if (region.Name == "Content1")
            template = myControl.View2;
```

```
                if (template != null)
                    return ControlPersister.PersistTemplate(template, host);
            }

            return String.Empty;
        }

        public override void SetEditableDesignerRegionContent
             (EditableDesignerRegion region, string content)
        {
            int regionIndex = Int32.Parse(region.Name.Substring(7));

            if (content == null)
            {
                if (regionIndex == 0)
                    myControl.View1 = null;
                else if (regionIndex == 1)
                    myControl.View2 = null;
                return;
            }

            IDesignerHost host =
                (IDesignerHost)Component.Site.GetService(typeof(IDesignerHost));

            if (host != null)
            {
                ITemplate template = ControlParser.ParseTemplate(host, content);

                if (template != null)
                {
                    if (regionIndex == 0)
                        myControl.View1 = template;
                    else if (regionIndex == 1)
                        myControl.View2 = template;
                }
            }
        }
    }
```

The designer overrides the `GetDesignTimeHtml` method, calling the `BuildRegions` and `BuildDesignTimeHtml` methods to alter the HTML that the control renders to the Visual Studio design surface.

The BuildRegions method creates three design regions in the control, two header regions and an editable content region. The regions are added to the `DesignerRegionCollection`. The `BuildDesignTimeHtml` method calls three methods to generate the actual HTML that will be generated by the control at design time.

The designer class also contains two overridden methods for getting and setting the editable designer region content: `GetEditableDesignerRegionContent` and `SetEditableDesignerRegionContent`. These methods get or set the appropriate content HTML, based on the designer region template that is currently active.

Finally, the class contains an `OnClick` method that it uses to respond to click events fired by the control at design time. This control uses the OnClick event to switch the current region being displayed by the control at design time.

When you add the control to a Web form, you see that you can toggle between the two editable regions, and each region maintains its own content. Figure 26-17 shows what the control looks like on the Visual Studio design surface.

As you can see in Figure 26-17, the control contains three separate design regions. When you click design regions 1 or 2, the `OnClick` method in the designer fires and redraws the control on the design surface, changing the template area located in design region 3.

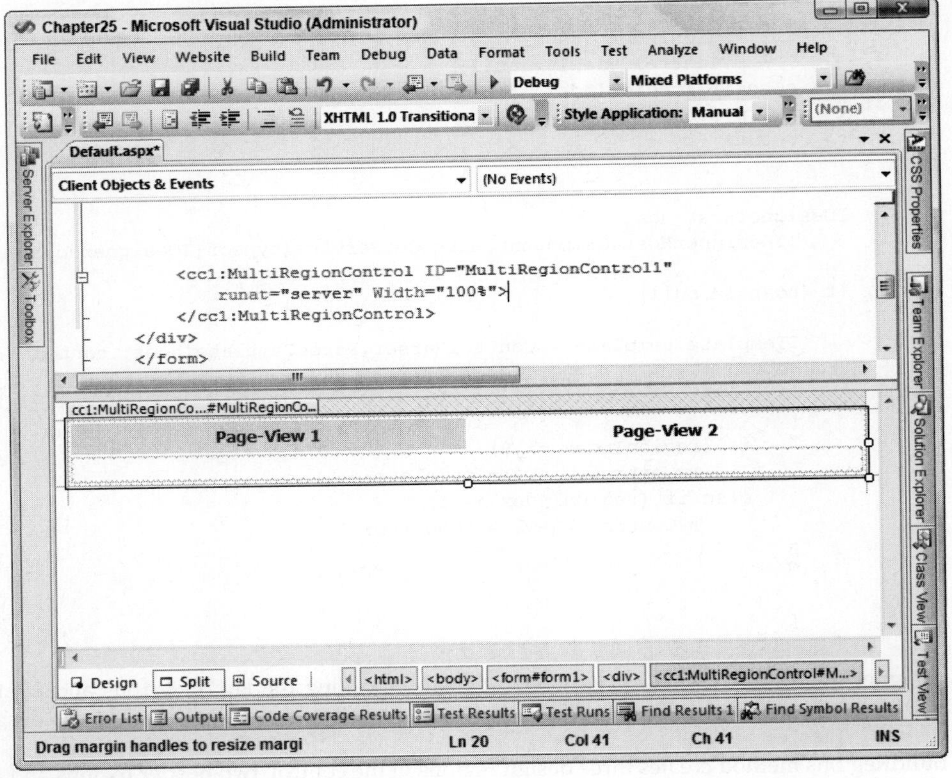

Figure 26-17

Designer Actions

Another great feature of ASP.NET design-time support is control smart tags. Smart tags give developers using a control quick access to common control properties. Smart tags are actually a new and improved implementation of the Designer Verbs functionality that was available in ASP.NET 1.0.

To add menu items to a server control's smart tag, you create a new class that inherits from the `DesignerActionList` class. The `DesignerActionList` contains the list of designer action items that are displayed by a server control. Classes that derive from the DesignerActionList class can override the GetSortedActionItems method, creating their own DesignerActionItemsCollection object to which designer action items can be added.

You can add several different types of DesignerActionItems types to the collection:

- DesignerActionTextItem
- DesignerActionHeaderItem
- DesignerActionMethodItem
- DesignerActionPropertyItem

Listing 26-44 shows a control designer class that contains a private class deriving from DesignerActionList.

Listing 26-44: Adding designer actions to a control designer

VB

```
Imports System.Web.UI.Design
Imports System.ComponentModel.Design

Public Class TestControlDesigner
    Inherits ControlDesigner

    Public Overrides ReadOnly Property ActionLists() _
            As DesignerActionListCollection
        Get
            Dim lists As New DesignerActionListCollection()
            lists.AddRange(MyBase.ActionLists)
            lists.Add(New TestControlList(Me))
            Return lists
        End Get
    End Property

    Private NotInheritable Class TestControlList
        Inherits DesignerActionList

        Public Sub New(ByVal c As TestControlDesigner)
            MyBase.New(c.Component)
        End Sub

        Public Overrides Function GetSortedActionItems() _
                As DesignerActionItemCollection

            Dim c As New DesignerActionItemCollection()
            c.Add(New DesignerActionTextItem("FOO", "FOO"))
            Return c
```

Continued

```
        End Function
    End Class

End Class
```

C#

```
using System;
using System.Collections.Generic;
using System.ComponentModel;
using System.ComponentModel.Design;
using System.Linq;
using System.Text;
using System.Web;
using System.Web.UI;
using System.Web.WebControls;
using System.Web.UI.Design;

public class TestControlDesigner : ControlDesigner
{
    public override DesignerActionListCollection ActionLists
    {
        get
        {
            DesignerActionListCollection actionLists =
                new DesignerActionListCollection();
            actionLists.AddRange(base.ActionLists);
            actionLists.Add(new TestControlList(this));
            return actionLists;
        }
    }

    private sealed class TestControlList : DesignerActionList
    {
        public TestControlList(TestControlDesigner c) : base(c.Component)
        {
        }

        public override DesignerActionItemCollection GetSortedActionItems()
        {
            DesignerActionItemCollection c = new DesignerActionItemCollection();
            c.Add(new DesignerActionTextItem("FOO", "FOO"));
            return c;
        }
    }
}
```

The control designer class overrides the `ActionsLists` property. The property creates an instance of the `TextControlList` class, which derives from `DesignerActionList` and overrides the `GetSortedActionItems`method. The method creates a new `DesignerActionListCollection`, and a `DesignerActionTextItem` is added to the collection (see Figure 26-18). The `DesignerActionTextItem` class allows you to add text menu items to the smart tag.

As shown in Figure 26-18, when you add the control to a Web page, the control now has a smart tag with the `DesignerActionTextItem` class as content.

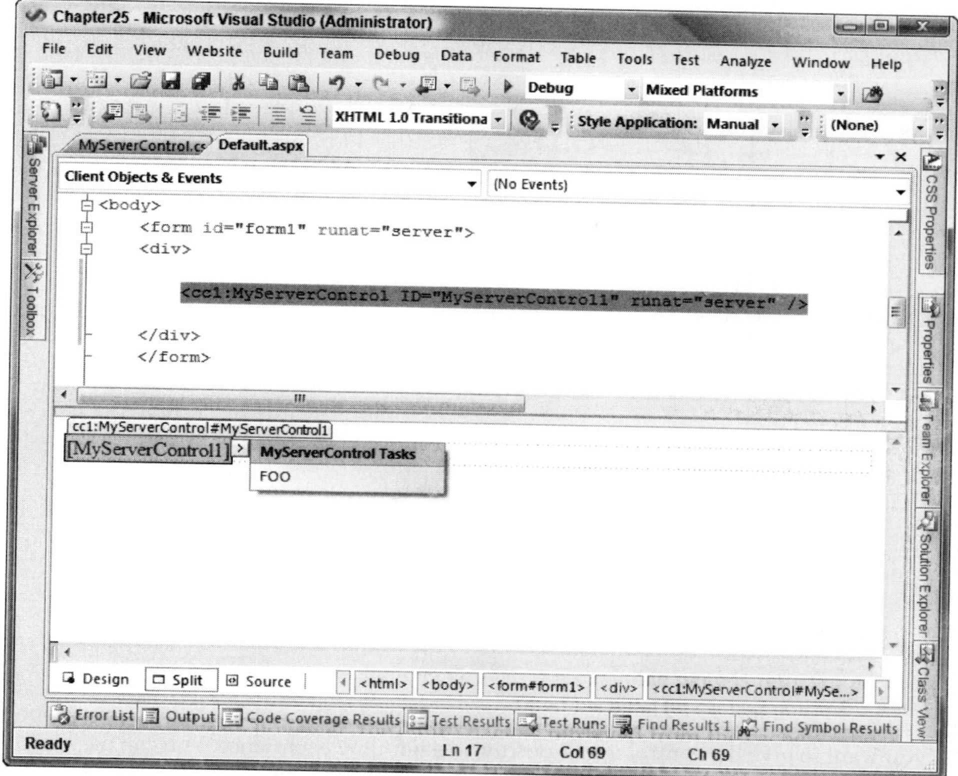

Figure 26-18

UI Type Editors

A UI type editor is a way to provide users of your controls with a custom interface for editing properties directly from the Property Browser. One type of UI type editor you might already be familiar with is the Color Picker you see when you want to change the `ForeColor` attribute that exists on most ASP.NET controls. ASP.NET provides a wide variety of in-box UI type editors that make it easy to edit more complex property types. The easiest way to find what UI type editors are available in the .NET Framework is to search for types derived from the `UITypeEditor` class in the MSDN Library help.

After you find the type editor you want to use on your control property, you simply apply the UI Type Editor to the property using the `Editor` attribute. Listing 26-45 shows how to do this.

Listing 26-45: Adding a UI type editor to a control property

VB

```
<Bindable(True), Category("Appearance"), DefaultValue(""), _
Editor( _
        GetType(System.Web.UI.Design.UrlEditor), _
        GetType(System.Drawing.Design.UITypeEditor))> _
```

Continued

```
Public Property Url() As String
    Get
        Return _url
    End Get
    Set(ByVal value As String)
        _url = value
    End Set
End Property
```

C#

```
[Bindable(true)]
[Category("Appearance")]
[DefaultValue("")]
[Editor(typeof(System.Web.UI.Design.UrlEditor),
    typeof(System.Drawing.Design.UITypeEditor))]
public string Url
{
    get
    {
        return url;
    }
    set
    {
        url = value;
    }
}
```

In this sample, you have created a `Url` property for a control. Because you know this property will be a URL, you want to give the control user a positive design-time experience. You can use the UrlEditor type editor to make it easier for users to select a URL. Figure 26-19 shows the Url Editor that appears when the user edits the control property.

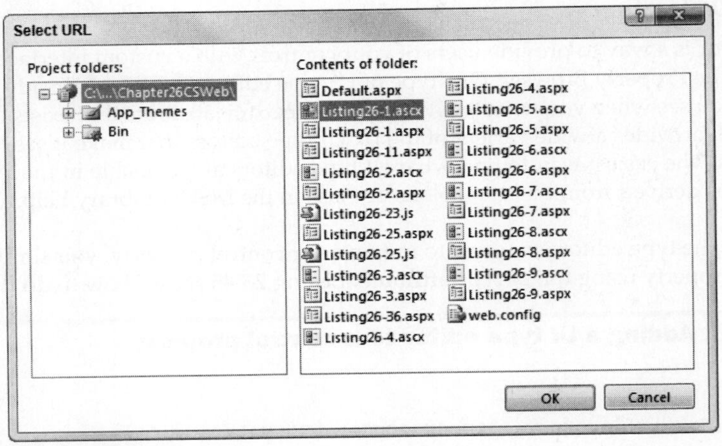

Figure 26-19

Summary

In this chapter, you learned a number of ways you can create reusable, encapsulated chunks of code. You first looked at user controls, the simplest form of control creation. You learned how to create user controls and how you can make them interact with their host Web pages. Creating user controls is quite easy, but they lack the portability of other control-creation options.

Then, you saw how you can create your own custom server controls. You looked at many of the tools you can create by writing custom server controls. These range from tools for emitting HTML and creating CSS styles and JavaScript to those applying themes. The chapter also discussed the type of server controls you can create, ranging from server controls that simply inherit from the `WebControl` class to templated controls that give users of the control the power to define the display of the server control.

Finally, you looked at ways you can give the users of your server control a great design-time experience by providing them with TypeConvertors, design surface interactions, and custom property editors in your server control.

27

Modules and Handlers

Sometimes, just creating dynamic Web pages with the latest languages and databases does not give you, the developer, enough control over an application. At times, you need to be able to dig deeper and create applications that can interact with the Web server itself. You want to be able to interact with the low-level processes, such as how the Web server processes incoming and outgoing HTTP requests.

Before ASP.NET, to get this level of control using IIS, you were forced to create ISAPI extensions or filters. This proved to be quite a daunting and painful task for many developers because creating ISAPI extensions and filters required knowledge of C/C++ and knowledge of how to create native Win32 DLLs. Thankfully, in the .NET world, creating these types of low-level applications is really no more difficult than most other tasks you would normally perform. This chapter looks at two methods of manipulating how ASP.NET processes HTTP requests, the HttpModule, and the HttpHandler. Each method provides a unique level of access to the underlying processing of ASP.NET and can be a powerful tool for creating Web applications.

Processing HTTP Requests

Before starting to write Handlers or Modules, it's helpful to know how IIS and ASP.NET normally process incoming HTTP requests and what options you have for plugging custom logic into those requests. IIS is the basic endpoint for incoming HTTP requests. At a very high level, its job is to listen for and validate incoming HTTP requests. Then it routes them to the appropriate module for processing and returns any results to the original requestor. ASP.NET is one of the modules that IIS may pass requests to for processing. However, exactly how that processing happens and how you can integrate your own logic into the pipeline differs based on the version of IIS you are using.

IIS 5/6 and ASP.NET

If you are using IIS 5 or IIS 6, the HTTP request processing pipeline is fairly black box to a managed code developer. IIS basically treats ASP.NET as one of the modules that it can pass requests to for processing rather than as an integrated part of the IIS request processing pipeline. Figure 27-1 shows the basic request processing pipeline of IIS 5/6 and ASP.NET.

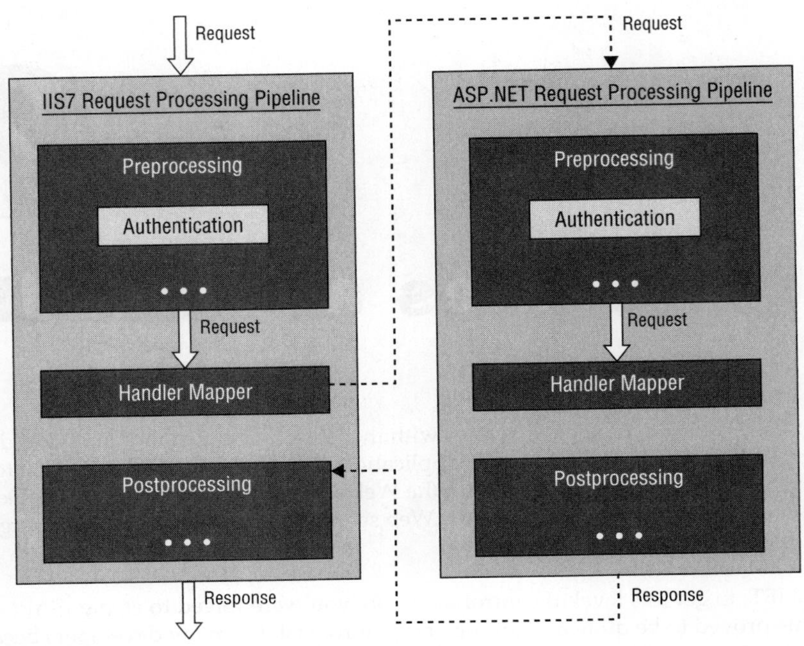

Figure 27-1

As you can see, the IIS and ASP.NET request pipelines are very similar and several tasks, such as authentication, are even duplicated between the two pipelines. Furthermore, while you can write Handlers and Modules using managed code, they are still processed in the isolated context of the ASP.NET process. If you wanted to integrate deeper into the IIS pipeline you are forced to create modules using native code.

IIS 7 and ASP.NET

Starting with IIS 7, the request processing pipeline in IIS has been completely re-architected using an open and highly extensible module based system. Now, instead of IIS seeing ASP.NET as a separate entity, ASP.NET has been deeply integrated into the IIS request processing pipeline. As shown in Figure 27-2, the request processing pipeline has been streamlined to eliminate duplicate processes and to allow you to integrate managed modules in the pipeline.

Because ASP.NET modules are first-class citizens, you can place them at any point in the pipeline, or even completely replace existing modules with your own custom functionality. Features that previously required you to write custom ISAPI modules in unmanaged code can now simply be replaced by managed code modules containing your logic. If you are interested in learning more about the integration of ASP.NET and IIS 7, check out the Wrox title *Professional IIS 7 and ASP.NET Integrated Programming* by Shahram Khosravi (Wiley Publishing, Inc., 2007).

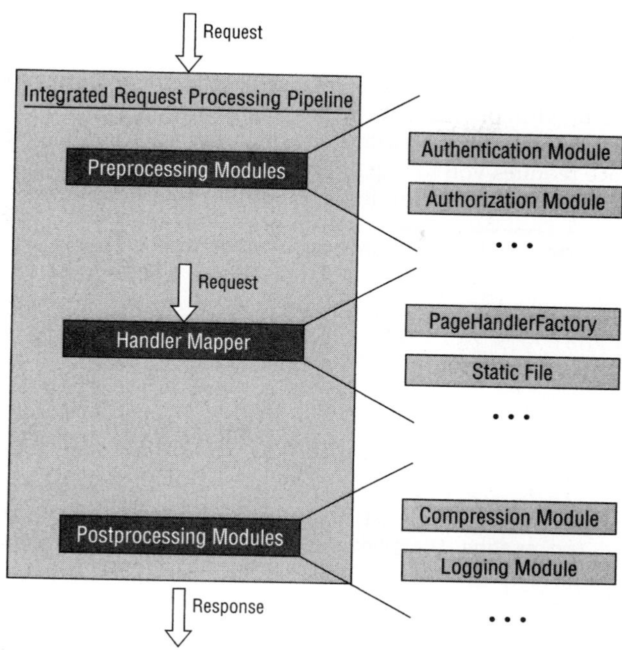

Figure 27-2

ASP.NET Request Processing

Regardless of the IIS version, the basic HTTP request pipeline model has two core mechanisms for handling requests: HttpModules and HttpHandlers. ASP.NET uses those two mechanisms to process incoming ASP.NET requests, generate a response, and return that response to the client. In fact, you are probably already familiar with HttpModules and HttpHandlers — although you might not know it. If you have ever used the Inbox caching or the authentication features of ASP.NET, you have used several different HttpModules. Additionally, if you have ever served up an ASP.NET application, even something as simple as a *Hello World* Web page and viewed it in a browser, you have used an HttpHandler. ASP.NET uses handlers to process and render ASPX pages and other file extensions. Modules and handlers allow you to plug into the request-processing pipeline at different points and interact with the actual requests being processed by IIS.

As you can see in both Figures 27-1 and 27-2, ASP.NET passes each incoming request through a layer of preprocessing HttpModules in the pipeline. ASP.NET allows multiple modules to exist in the pipeline for each request. After the incoming request has passed through each module, it is passed to the HttpHandler, which serves the request. Notice that although a single request may pass through many different modules, it can be processed by one handler only. The handler is generally responsible for creating a response to the incoming HTTP request. After the handler has completed execution and generated a response, the response is passed back through a series of post-processing modules, before it is returned to the client.

You should now have a basic understanding of the IIS and ASP.NET request pipeline — and how you can use HttpModules and HttpHandlers to interact with the pipeline. The following sections take an in-depth look at each of these.

HttpModules

HttpModules are simple classes that can plug themselves into the request-processing pipeline. They do this by hooking into a handful of events thrown by the application as it processes the HTTP request. To create an HttpModule, you simply create a class that derives from the `System.Web.IHttpModule` interface. This interface requires you to implement two methods: `Init` and `Dispose`. Listing 27-1 shows the class stub created after you implement the `IHttpModule` interface.

Listing 27-1: Implementing the IHttpModule Interface

VB

```
Imports Microsoft.VisualBasic
Imports System.Web

Namespace Demo

    Public Class SimpleModule
        Implements IHttpModule

        Public Overridable Sub Init(ByVal context As HttpApplication) _
                Implements IHttpModule.Init

        End Sub

        Public Overridable Sub Dispose() Implements IHttpModule.Dispose

        End Sub
    End Class

End Namespace
```

C#

```
using System;
using System.Collections.Generic;
using System.Text;
using System.Web;
namespace Demo
{
    class SimpleModule : IHttpModule
    {
        #region IHttpModule Members

        public void Dispose()
        {
            throw new Exception("The method or operation is not implemented.");
        }

        public void Init(HttpApplication context)
        {
            throw new Exception("The method or operation is not implemented.");
        }

        #endregion
    }
}
```

The Init method is the primary method you use to implement functionality. Notice that it has a single method parameter, an HttpApplication object named context. This parameter gives you access to the current HttpApplication context, and it is what you use to wire up the different events that fire during the request processing. The following table shows the events that you can register in the Init method.

Event Name	Description
AcquireRequestState	Raised when ASP.NET runtime is ready to acquire the Session State of the current HTTP request.
AuthenticateRequest	Raised when ASP.NET runtime is ready to authenticate the identity of the user.
AuthorizeRequest	Raised when ASP.NET runtime is ready to authorize the user for the resources user is trying to access.
BeginRequest	Raised when ASP.NET runtime receives a new HTTP request.
Disposed	Raised when ASP.NET completes the processing of HTTP request.
EndRequest	Raised just before sending the response content to the client.
Error	Raised when an unhandled exception occurs during the processing of HTTP request.
PostRequestHandlerExecute	Raised just after HTTP handler finishes execution.
PreRequestHandlerExecute	Raised just before ASP.NET begins executing a handler for the HTTP request. After this event, ASP.NET forwards the request to the appropriate HTTP handler.
PreSendRequestContent	Raised just before ASP.NET sends the response contents to the client. This event allows you to change the contents before it gets delivered to the client. You can use this event to add the contents, which are common in all pages, to the page output. For example, a common menu, header, or footer.
PreSendRequestHeaders	Raised just before ASP.NET sends the HTTP response headers to the client. This event allows you to change the headers before they get delivered to the client. You can use this event to add cookies and custom data into headers.

Modifying HTTP Output

Take a look at some examples of using HttpModules. The first example shows a useful way of modifying the HTTP output stream before it is sent to the client. This can be a simple and useful tool if you want to add text to each page served from your Web site, but you do not want to modify each page. For the first example, create a Web project in Visual Studio and add a class to the App_Code directory. The code for this first module is shown in Listing 27-2.

Listing 27-2: Altering the output of an ASP.NET Web page

VB

```
Imports Microsoft.VisualBasic
Imports System.Web

Namespace Demo

    Public Class AppendMessage
        Implements IHttpModule

        Dim WithEvents _application As HttpApplication = Nothing

        Public Overridable Sub Init(ByVal context As HttpApplication) _
            Implements IHttpModule.Init
            _application = context
        End Sub

        Public Overridable Sub Dispose() Implements IHttpModule.Dispose

        End Sub

        Public Sub context_PreSendRequestContent(ByVal sender As Object, _
            ByVal e As EventArgs) Handles _application.PreSendRequestContent

            'alter the outgoing content by adding a HTML comment.
            Dim message As String = "<!-- This page has been post processed at " & _
                                    System.DateTime.Now.ToString() & _
                                    " by a custom HttpModule.-->"

            _application.Context.Response.Output.Write(message)

        End Sub
    End Class

End Namespace
```

C#

```
using System;
using System.Collections.Generic;
using System.Text;
using System.Web;

namespace Demo
{
    public class AppendMessage : IHttpModule
    {
        private HttpContext _current = null;

        #region IHttpModule Members

        public void Dispose()
        {
            throw new Exception("The method or operation is not implemented.");
        }
```

```
            public void Init(System.Web.HttpApplication context)
            {
                _current = context.Context;

                context.PreSendRequestContent +=
                    new EventHandler(context_PreSendRequestContent);
            }

            void context_PreSendRequestContent(object sender, EventArgs e)
            {
                //alter the outgoing content by adding a HTML comment.
                string message = "<!-- This page has been post processed at " +
                                 System.DateTime.Now.ToString() +
                                 " by a custom HttpModule.-->";

                _current.Response.Output.Write(message);
            }

            #endregion
        }
    }
```

You can see that the class stub from Listing 27-2 is expanded here. In the `Init` method, you register the `PreSendRequestContent` event. This event fires right before the content is sent to the client, and you have one last opportunity to modify it.

In the `PreSendRequestContent` handler method, you simply create a string containing an HTML comment that contains the current time. You take this string and write it to the current HTTP requests output stream. The HTTP request is then sent back to the client.

In order to use this module, you must let ASP.NET know that you want to include the module in the request-processing pipeline. You do this is by modifying the `web.config` to contain a reference to the module. Listing 27-3 shows how you can add an httpModules section to your `web.config`.

Listing 27-3: Adding the httpModule configuration to web.config

```
<configuration>
    <system.web>
      <httpModules>
        <add name="AppendMessage" type="Demo.AppendMessage, App_code" />
      </httpModules>
    </system.web>
</configuration>
```

The generic format of the httpModules section is

```
<httpModules>
  <add name="modulename" type="namespace.classname, assemblyname" />
</httpModules>
```

If you are deploying your application to an IIS 7 server, you must also add the module configuration to the <system.webServer> configuration section.

```
<modules>
    <add name="AppendMessage" type="Demo.AppendMessage, App_code"/>
</modules>
```

If you have created your HttpModule in the `App_Code` directory of an ASP.NET web site, you might wonder how you know what the `assemblyname` value should be, considering ASP.NET now dynamically compiles this code at runtime. The solution is to use the text `App_Code` as the assembly name. This tells ASP.NET that your module is located in the dynamically created assembly.

You can also create HttpModules as a separate class library in which case you simply use the assembly name of the library.

After you have added this section to your `web.config` file, simply view one of the Web pages from your project in the browser. When you view the page in the browser, you should not notice any difference. But if you view the source of the page, notice the comment you added at the bottom of the HTML. Figure 27-3 shows what you should see when you view the page source.

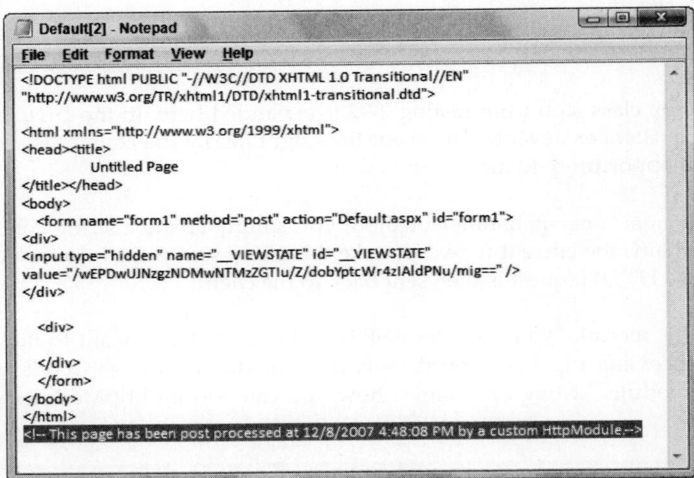

Figure 27-3

URL Rewriting

Another interesting use of an HttpModule is to perform URL rewriting. *URL rewriting* is a technique that allows you to intercept the HTTP request and change the path that was requested to an alternative one. This can be very useful for creating pseudo Web addresses that simplify a URL for the user. For example, the MSDN Library is well known for its extremely long and cryptic URL paths, such as

```
http://msdn.microsoft.com/library/default.asp?url=/library/en-us/cpref/html/
frlrfSystemWebIHttpModuleClassTopic.asp
```

The problem with this URL is that it is not easy to remember; and even if you do somehow remember it, it is very difficult to type into the browser's Address field. URL rewriting allows you to create friendly URLs that you can parse and redirect to the appropriate resource. The MSDN Library now uses URL rewriting to create friendly URLs. Instead of the cryptic URL you saw previously, you can now use the following URL to access the same resource:

```
http://msdn2.microsoft.com/library/system.web.ihttpmodule.aspx
```

This URL is much shorter, easier to remember, and easier to type into a browser's Address field. You can create your own URL rewriter module to learn how this is done.

To demonstrate this, you create three new Web pages in your project. The first Web page is used to construct a URL using two text boxes. The second serves as the page that accepts the unfriendly querystring, like the MSDN URL shown previously. The third page is used to trick IIS into helping you serve the request. Shortly, we talk about this trick and how to get around it.

Listing 27-4 shows the first Web page you add to the project; it's called `friendlylink.aspx`.

Listing 27-4: The friendlylink.aspx Web page

```
<html xmlns="http://www.w3.org/1999/xhtml" >
<head runat="server">
    <title>Untitled Page</title>
</head>
<body>
    <form id="form1" runat="server">
    <div>
    <a href="John/Smith/trickiis.aspx">Click this friendly link</a>
    </div>
    </form>
</body>
</html>
```

As you can see, you simply created a hyperlink that links to a friendly, easily remembered URL.

Now, create the second page called `unfriendly.aspx`. This is the page that the handle actually executes when a user clicks the hyperlink in the `friendlylink.aspx` page. Listing 27-5 shows how to create `unfriendly.aspx`.

Listing 27-5: The unfriendly.aspx Web page

VB

```
<%@ Page Language="VB" %>

<script runat="server">
    Protected Sub Page_Load(ByVal sender As Object, _
            ByVal e As System.EventArgs) Handles Me.Load
        Label1.Text = Request("firstname").ToString() & _
            " " & Request("lastname").ToString()
    End Sub
</script>
<html xmlns="http://www.w3.org/1999/xhtml" >
<head runat="server">
    <title>Unfriendly Web Page</title>
</head>
```

Continued

```
<body>
    <form id="form1" runat="server">
        <div>
        Welcome to the unfriendly URL page <asp:Label ID="Label1"
            runat="server" Text="Label"></asp:Label>
        </div>
    </form>
</body>
</html>
```

C#

```
<script runat="server">
    protected void Page_Load(object sender, EventArgs e)
    {
        Label1.Text = Request["firstname"].ToString() +
            " " + Request["lastname"].ToString();
    }
</script>
```

Next, you create the directory and file that the hyperlink in `friendlyurl.aspx` points to. The `trickiis.aspx` page can simply be an empty Web page because you are not really going to execute it.

Finally, you create a new module that parses the request path and rewrites the URL to the page you want to execute. To do this, create another class in the `App_Code` directory called `SimpleRewriter`. Listing 27-6 shows the code for this.

Listing 27-6: A sample URL rewriting HttpModule

VB

```
Imports Microsoft.VisualBasic
Imports System.Web

Namespace Demo
    Public Class SimpleRewriter
        Implements System.Web.IHttpModule

        Dim WithEvents _application As HttpApplication = Nothing

        Public Overridable Sub Init(ByVal context As HttpApplication) _
                Implements IHttpModule.Init
            _application = context
        End Sub

        Public Overridable Sub Dispose() Implements IHttpModule.Dispose

        End Sub

        Public Sub context_BeginRequest(ByVal sender As Object, _
            ByVal e As EventArgs) Handles _application.BeginRequest

            Dim requesturl As String = _
                _application.Context.Request.Path.Substring(0, _
                _application.Context.Request.Path.LastIndexOf("/"c))
```

```
            'Here is where we parse the original request url to determine
            ' the querystring parameters for the unfriendly url
            Dim parameters() As String = _
                requesturl.Split(New [Char]() {"/"c}, _
                    StringSplitOptions.RemoveEmptyEntries)

            If (parameters.Length > 1) Then
                Dim firstname As String = parameters(1)
                Dim lastname As String = parameters(2)

                'Rewrite the request path
                _application.Context.RewritePath("~/unfriendly.aspx?firstname=" & _
                    firstname & "&lastname=" & lastname)
            End If
        End Sub
    End Class

End Namespace
```

C#

```
using System.Web;

namespace Demo
{
    public class SimpleRewriter: System.Web.IHttpModule
    {

        HttpApplication _application = null;

        public void Init(HttpApplication context)
        {
            context.BeginRequest+=new System.EventHandler(context_BeginRequest);
            _application = context;
        }

        public void Dispose()
        {
        }

        private void context_BeginRequest(object sender, System.EventArgs e)
        {
            string requesturl =
                _application.Context.Request.Path.Substring(0,
                    _application.Context.Request.Path.LastIndexOf("//")
                );

            //Here is where we parse the original request url to determine
            //the querystring parameters for the unfriendly url
            string[] parameters = requesturl.Split(new char[] {'/'});

            if (parameters.Length > 1)
            {
                string firstname = parameters[1];
                string lastname = parameters[2];
```

Continued

```
                    //Rewrite the request path
                    _application.Context.RewritePath("~/unfriendly.aspx?firstname=" +
                        firstname + "&lastname=" + lastname);
                }
            }
        }
    }
```

As you can see from the listing, in this sample you use the BeginRequest event in the HttpModule to parse the incoming HTTP request path and create a new URL that you execute. Normally, when you click the hyperlink on `friendlyurl.aspx`, an HTTP request is sent to the server for execution and then IIS returns the page asked for in the hyperlink. In this case, you make a request for this page:

```
http://localhost:1234/WebProject1/John/Smith/trickiis.aspx
```

But, because you put the HttpModule in the request-processing pipeline, you can modify the HTTP request and change its behavior. The code in the `BeginRequest` method of the module parses the request path to create a querystring that the `unfriendly.aspx` page can understand and execute. So when you execute the code in the listing, you convert the original path into the following:

```
http://localhost:1234/WebProject1/unfriendly.aspx?var1=John&var2=Smith
```

This URL is, as the page name states, not very friendly; and the user is less likely to remember and be able to type this URL. Finally, the module uses the `RewritePath` method to tell ASP.NET that you want to rewrite the path to execute for this request.

After you have completed creating the code for this sample, try loading `friendlylink.aspx` into a browser. When you click the hyperlink on the page, you should notice two things. First, notice that the URL in the browser's address bar shows that you have been served the page you requested, `trickiis.aspx`, but the contents of the page show that you are actually served `unfriendly.aspx`. Figure 27-4 shows what the browser looks like.

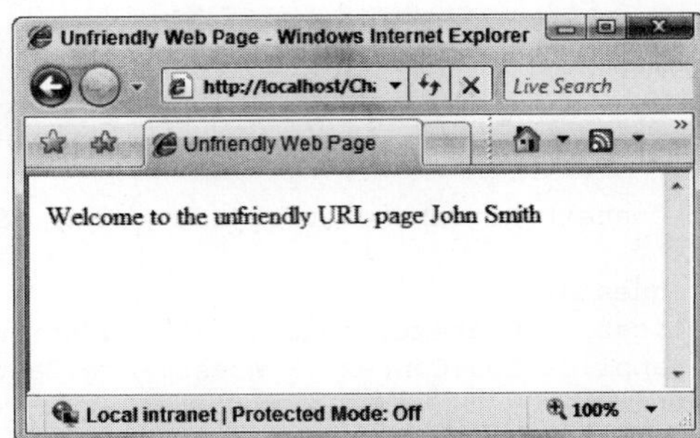

Figure 27-4

IIS WildCards

There is, however, a drawback to this type of URL rewriting. When IIS receives a request to serve a resource, it first checks to see if the resource exists. If the resource does exist, the request is passed to the appropriate handler; in this case, the handler is ASP.NET, which processes the request. IIS then returns the results to the client. However, if the requested resource does not exist, IIS returns a `404 File Not`

Found error to the client. It never hands the request to ASP.NET. In order for a module to execute, you must create an endpoint that actually exists on the Web server.

In the case of the previous example, you had to actually create the `/WebProject1/John/Smith/trickiis.aspx` path so that IIS would know which handler to give the request to. Had you not created the path, IIS would have simply returned a 404 error. Unfortunately, having to create the physical paths can be a problem if you find you are creating a large number of directories or resources just to enable URL rewriting. Thankfully, however, a solution to this problem exists in IIS: wildcards. *Wildcards* allow you to tell IIS that it should use a particular handler to process all incoming requests, regardless of the requested paths or file extensions. In the previous example, adding a wildcard would keep you from having to actually create the dummy end point for the module.

Adding Wildcards in IIS 5

To add a wildcard mapping in IIS 5, start by opening the IIS Management Console. After the console is open, right-click on the Web site or virtual directory you want to modify and select the Properties option from the context menu. When the Properties dialog box opens, select the Configuration button from the Home Directory Tab. The Configuration dialog is where you can create new or modify existing application extension mappings. If you take a moment to look at the existing mappings, you see that most of the familiar file extensions (such as `.aspx`, `.asp`, and `.html`) are configured.

To add the wildcard that you need to create a new mapping, click the Add button. The Add Application Extension Mapping dialog box is shown in Figure 27-5. You create a mapping that directs IIS to use the ASP.NET ISAPI DLL to process every incoming request. To do this, simply put the full path to the ISAPI DLL (usually something such as `C:\WINDOWS\Microsoft.NET\Framework\v1.1.4322\aspnet_isapi.dll`) in the Executable field. For the extension, simply use .*, which indicates any file extension.

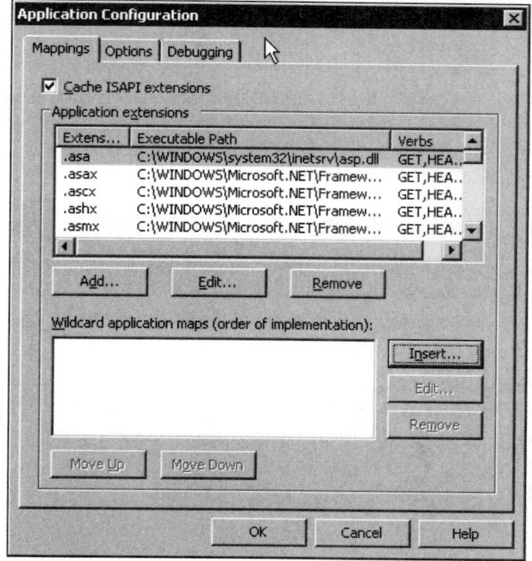

Figure 27-5

Additionally, you uncheck the Check That File Exists check box to tell IIS not to check whether the requested file exists before processing (because you know that it doesn't).

Now you don't have to add the stub file to your Web site. IIS will pass any request that it receives to ASP.NET for processing, regardless of whether the file exists.

Adding Wildcards in IIS 6

Adding Wildcards in IIS 6 is similar to adding wildcards in IIS 5. Open the IIS Management Console, and then open the Properties dialog box for the Web site or virtual directory you want to modify. Next, click the Configuration button on the Home Directory tab.

The Application Extension Configuration dialog in IIS is slightly different. Wildcard application maps now have their own separate listing, as shown in Figure 27-6.

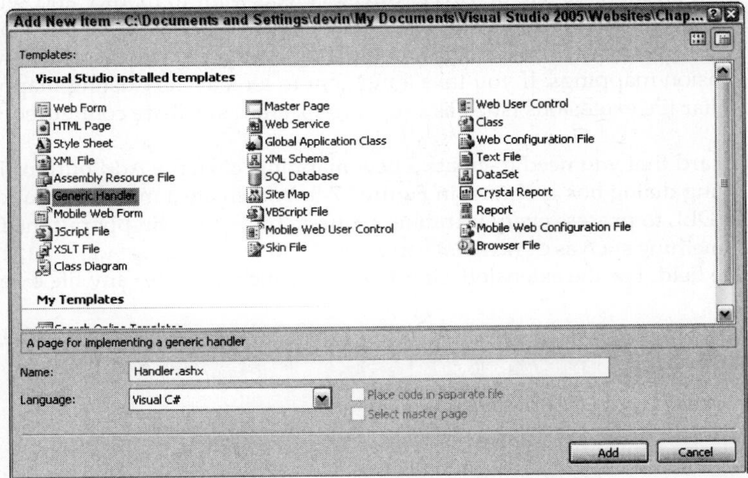

Figure 27-6

To add a wildcard mapping, click the Insert button, add the path to the ASP.NET ISAPI DLL, and make sure the Verify That File Exists check box is unchecked.

HttpHandlers

HttpHandlers differ from HttpModules, not only because of their positions in the request-processing pipeline (refer to Figure 27-3), but also because they must be mapped to a specific file extension. Handlers are the last stop for incoming HTTP requests and are ultimately the point in the request-processing pipeline that is responsible for serving up the requested content, be it an ASPX page, HTML, plain text, or an image. Additionally, HttpHandlers can offer significant performance gains.

In this section, we demonstrate two different ways to create a simple HttpHandler that you can use to serve up dynamic images. First, you look at creating an HttpHandler using an ASHX file extension. Then you learn how you get even more control by mapping your HttpHandler to a custom file extension using IIS.

Generic Handlers

In early versions of Visual Studio, HttpHandlers were somewhat hard to understand and create because little documentation was included to help developers understand handlers. In addition, Visual Studio did not provide any friendly methods for creating them.

Since Visual Studio 2005, however, this has changed with Visual Studio now providing a standard template for HttpHandlers to help you get started. To add an HttpHandler to your project, you simply select the Generic Handler file type from the Add New Item dialog. Figure 27-7 shows this dialog box with the file type selected.

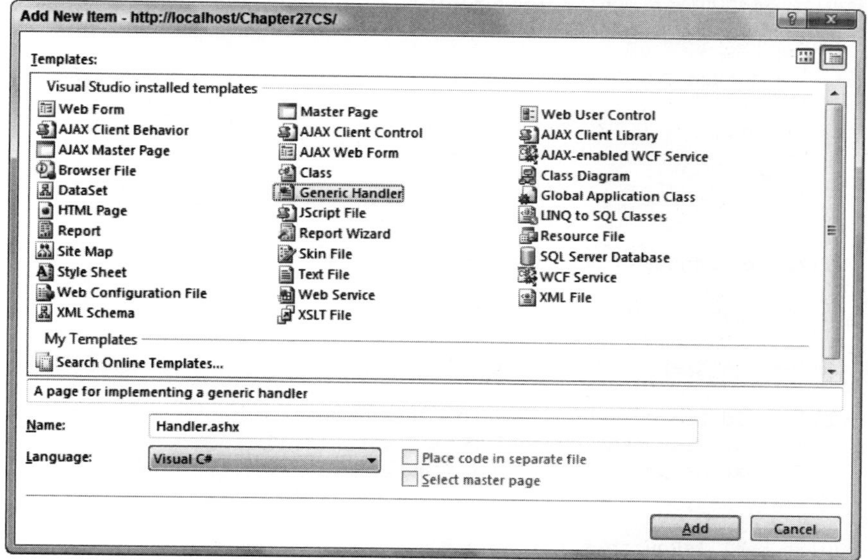

Figure 27-7

You can see that when you add the Generic Handler file to your project, it adds a file with an `.ashx` extension. The `.ashx` file extension is the default HttpHandler file extension set up by ASP.NET. Remember that HttpHandlers must be mapped to a unique file extension, so by default ASP.NET uses the `.ashx` extension. This is convenient because, otherwise, you would be responsible for adding the file extension yourself. This is obviously not always possible, nor is it practical. Using the Custom Handler file type helps you avoid any extra configuration.

Notice the class stub that the file type automatically creates for you. Listing 27-7 shows the class.

Listing 27-7: The HttpHandler page template

VB

```
<%@ WebHandler Language="VB" Class="Handler" %>

Imports System.Web

Public Class Handler
   Implements IHttpHandler

    Public Sub ProcessRequest(ByVal context As HttpContext) _
            Implements IHttpHandler.ProcessRequest
        context.Response.ContentType = "text/plain"
        context.Response.Write("Hello World")
    End Sub

    Public ReadOnly Property IsReusable() As Boolean _
            Implements IHttpHandler.IsReusable
        Get
            Return False
        End Get
    End Property

End Class
```

C#

```
<%@ WebHandler Language="C#" Class="Handler" %>

using System.Web;

public class Handler : IHttpHandler {

    public void ProcessRequest (HttpContext context) {
        context.Response.ContentType = "text/plain";
        context.Response.Write("Hello World");
    }

    public bool IsReusable {
        get {
            return false;
        }
    }
}
```

Notice that the stub implements the IHttpHandler interface, which requires the `ProcessRequest` method and `IsReusable` property. The `ProcessRequest` method is the method we use to actually process the incoming HTTP request. By default, the class stub changes the content type to plain and then writes the "Hello World" string to the output stream. The IsReusable property simply lets ASP.NET know if incoming HTTP requests can reuse the sample instance of this HttpHandler.

By default, this handler is ready to run right away. Try executing the handler in your browser and see what happens. The interesting thing to note about this handler is that because it changes the content to text/plain, browsers handle the responses from this handler in potentially very different ways depending on a number of factors:

- Browser type and version
- Applications loaded on the system that may map to the MIME type
- Operating system and service pack level

Based on these factors, you might see the text returned in the browser, you might see Notepad open and display the text, or you might receive the Open/Save/Cancel prompt from IE. Make sure you understand the potential consequences of changing the ContentType header.

You can continue the example by modifying it to return an actual file. In this case, you use the handler to return an image. To do this, you simply modify the code in the ProcessRequest method, as shown in Listing 27-8.

Listing 27-8: Outputting an image from an HttpHandler

VB

```
<%@ WebHandler Language="VB" Class="Handler" %>

Imports System.Web

Public Class Handler : Implements IHttpHandler

    Public Sub ProcessRequest(ByVal context As HttpContext) _
            Implements IHttpHandler.ProcessRequest
        'Logic to retrieve the image file
        context.Response.ContentType = "image/jpeg"
        context.Response.WriteFile("Garden.jpg")
    End Sub

    Public ReadOnly Property IsReusable() As Boolean _
            Implements IHttpHandler.IsReusable
        Get
            Return False
        End Get
    End Property

End Class
```

C#

```
<%@ WebHandler Language="C#" Class="Handler" %>
```

Continued

```
using System.Web;

public class Handler : IHttpHandler {

    public void ProcessRequest (HttpContext context) {
        //Logic to retrieve the image file
        context.Response.ContentType = "image/jpeg";
        context.Response.WriteFile("Garden.jpg");
    }

    public bool IsReusable {
        get {
            return false;
        }
    }
}
```

As you can see, you simply change the ContentType to image/jpeg to indicate that you are returning a JPEG image; then you use the `WriteFile()` method to write an image file to the output stream. Load the handler into a browser, and you see that the handler displays the image. Figure 27-8 shows the resulting Web page.

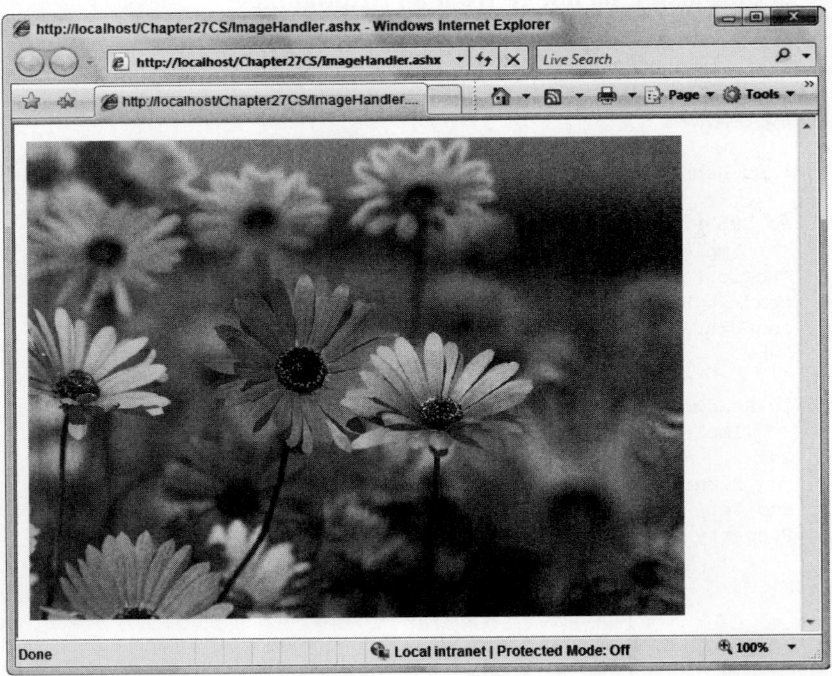

Figure 27-8

Now, you create a simple Web page to display the image handler. Listing 27-9 shows code for the Web page.

Listing 27-9: A sample Web page using the HttpHandler for the image source

```
<!DOCTYPE html PUBLIC "-//W3C//DTD XHTML 1.1//EN" "http://www.w3.org/TR/xhtml11/DTD/
xhtml11.dtd">

<html xmlns="http://www.w3.org/1999/xhtml" >
<head runat="server">
    <title>HttpHandler Serving an Image</title>
</head>
<body>
    <form id="form1" runat="server">
    <div>
        <img src="Handler.ashx" />
    </div>
    </form>
</body>
</html>
```

Although this sample is simple, you can enhance it by passing querystring parameters to your handler and using them to perform additional logic in the handler. For instance, you can pass an ID in to dynamically retrieve an image from a SQL database and return it to the client, like this:

```
<img src="Handler.ashx?imageid=123" />
```

Mapping a File Extension in IIS

Although using the `.ashx` file extension is convenient, you might want to create an HTTP handler for a custom file extension or even for a commonly used extension. Use the code from the image handler to demonstrate this.

Create a new class in the `App_Code` directory of your Web project. You can simply copy the code from the existing image handler control into this class, as shown in Listing 27-10. Notice that you removed the `WebHandler` directive because this is only a class and not a generic handler control. Other than that, the code is the same.

Listing 27-10: The class-based image HttpHandler

VB

```
Imports System.Web

Public Class MappedHandler : Implements IHttpHandler

    Public Sub ProcessRequest(ByVal context As HttpContext) _
            Implements IHttpHandler.ProcessRequest
        context.Response.ContentType = "image/jpeg"
        context.Response.WriteFile("Garden.jpg")
    End Sub

    Public ReadOnly Property IsReusable() As Boolean _
            Implements IHttpHandler.IsReusable
```

Continued

```
        Get
            Return False
        End Get
    End Property

End Class
```

C#

```
using System.Web;

public class MappedHandler : IHttpHandler {

    public void ProcessRequest (HttpContext context) {
        //Logic to retrieve the image file
        context.Response.ContentType = "image/jpeg";
        context.Response.WriteFile("Garden.jpg");
    }

    public bool IsReusable {
        get {
            return false;
        }
    }

}
```

After your class is added, configure the application to show which file extension this handler serves. You do this by adding an httpHandlers section to `web.config`. Listing 27-11 shows the section to add for the image handler.

Listing 27-11: Adding the HttpHandler configuration information to web.config

```
<httpHandlers>
    <add verb="*" path="ImageHandler.img" type="MappedHandler, App_Code" />
</httpHandlers>
```

In the configuration section, you direct the application to use the `MappedHandler` class to process incoming requests for `ImageHandler.img`. You can also specify wildcards for the path. Specifying `*.img` for the path indicates that you want the application to use the `MappedHandler` class to process any request with the `.img` file extension. Specifying `*` indicates that you want all requests to the application to be processed using the handler.

As with HttpModules, if you are running your Web application using IIS 7, then you will also need to add the HttpHandler configuration section to the `<system.webServer>` configuration section of your applications config file. When adding the handler configuration in this section, you also need to include the name attribute.

```
<add name="ImageHandler" verb="*" path="ImageHandler.img"
    type="MappedHandler, App_Code" />
```

Load the `ImageHandler.img` file into a browser and, again, you should see that it serves up the image. Figure 27-9 shows the results. Notice the path in the browser's address bar leads directly to the `ImageHandler.img` file.

Figure 27-9

Summary

In this chapter, you learned a number of ways you can create modules which allow you to interact with the ASP.NET request processing pipeline. First you worked with HttpModules, which give you the power to plug yourself directly into the ASP.NET page-processing pipeline. The events provided to an HttpModule give you great power and flexibility to customize your applications.

Finally, you looked at HttpHandlers. Handlers allow you to skip the ASP.NET page-processing pipeline completely and have 100 percent control over how the framework serves up requested data. You learned how to create your own image handler and then map the handler to any file or file extension you want. Using these features of ASP.NET can help you create features in your application which exercise great control over the standard page processing which ASP.NET uses.

28

Using Business Objects

One of the best practices in programming is to separate your application into workable and separate components — also known as *business objects*. This makes your applications far easier to manage and enables you to achieve the goal of code reuse because you can share these components among different parts of the same application or between entirely separate applications.

Using business components enables you to build your ASP.NET applications using a true three-tier model where the business tier is in the middle between the presentation and data tiers. In addition, using business objects enables you to use multiple languages within your ASP.NET applications. Business objects can be developed in one programming language while the code used for the presentation logic is developed in another.

If you are moving any legacy applications or aspects of these applications to an ASP.NET environment, you might find that you need to utilize various COM components. This chapter shows you how to use both .NET and COM components in your ASP.NET pages and code.

This chapter also explains how you can mingle old ActiveX (COM) DLLs with new .NET components. So when all is said and done, you should feel somewhat relieved. You will see that you have not wasted all the effort you put into building componentized applications using the ''latest'' ActiveX technologies.

Using Business Objects in ASP.NET 3.5

Chapter 1 of this book provides an introduction to using .NET business objects within your ASP.NET 3.5 applications. ASP.NET now includes a folder, `\App_Code`, which you can place within your ASP.NET applications to hold all your .NET business objects. The nice thing about the `App_Code` folder is that you can simply place your uncompiled .NET objects (such as `Calculator.vb` or `Calculator.cs`) into this folder and ASP.NET takes care of compiling the objects into usable .NET business objects.

Chapter 1 also shows how you can place within the `App_Code` folder multiple custom folders that enable you to use business objects written in different programming languages. Using this method enables ASP.NET to compile each business object into the appropriate DLLs to be used by your ASP.NET applications.

Creating Precompiled .NET Business Objects

Even though the `App_Code` folder is there for your use, you might choose instead to precompile your business objects into DLLs to be used by your ASP.NET applications. This is the method that was utilized prior to ASP.NET 2.0 and is still a method that is available today. You also might not have a choice if you are receiving your .NET business objects only as DLLs.

First look at how to create a simple .NET business object using Visual Studio 2008. The first step is not to create an ASP.NET project but to choose File ➪ New ➪ Project from the Visual Studio menu. This launches the New Project dialog. From this dialog, select Class Library as the project type and name the project `Calculator` (see Figure 28-1).

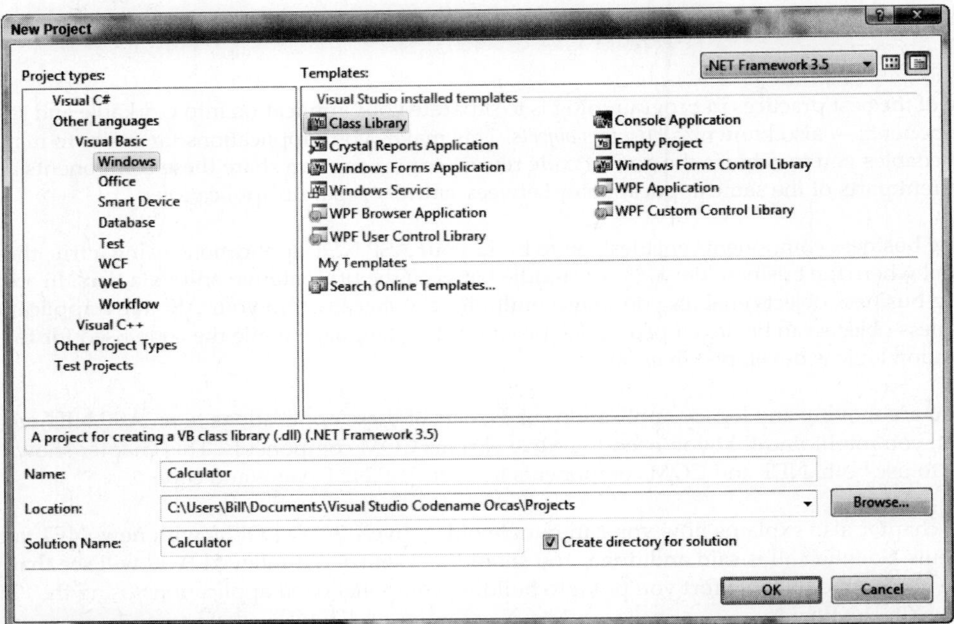

Figure 28-1

Using the `Class1.vb` or `Class1.cs` file that is created in the project for you, modify the class to be a simple calculator with `Add`, `Subtract`, `Multiply`, and `Divide` functions. This is illustrated using Visual Basic in Figure 28-2.

One point to pay attention to when you build your .NET components is the assembly's metadata that is stored along with the assembly. Looking at the project's properties, click the Application tab (the first tab available). Note that you can get to the project's properties by right-clicking on the project title in the Solution Explorer. On this tab's page, you will find a button labeled Assembly Information. Clicking this button gives you a dialog where you can put in the entire business object's metadata, including the assembly's versioning information (see Figure 28-3).

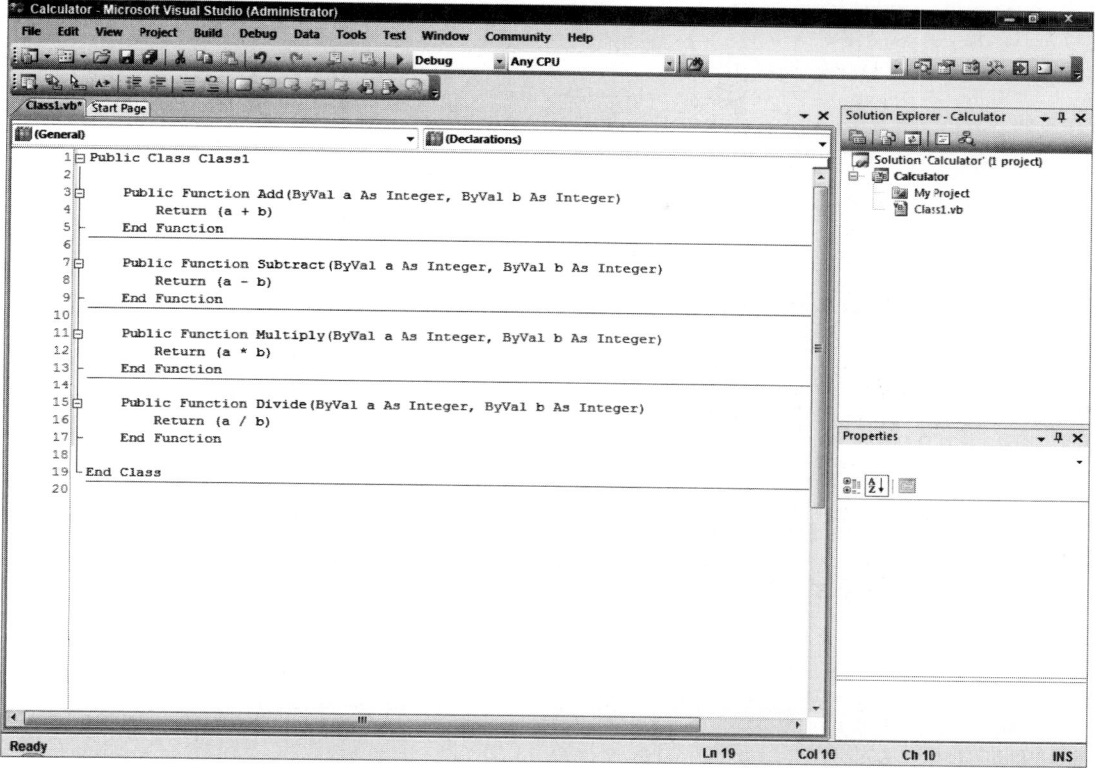

Figure 28-2

You are now ready to compile the business object into a usable object. To accomplish this task, choose Build ➪ Build Calculator from the Visual Studio menu. This process compiles everything contained in this solution down to a `Calculator.dll` file. You will find this DLL in your project's `bin\debug` folder. By default, that will be `C:\Users\[user]\Documents\Visual Studio 2008\Projects\Calculator\Calculator\bin\Debug\Calculator.dll`, only if you are using Windows Vista.

Besides using Visual Studio 2008 to build and compile your business objects into DLLs, you can also accomplish this yourself manually. In Notepad, you simply create the same class file as was shown in Figure 28-2 and save the file as `Calculator.vb` or `Calculator.cs` depending on the language you are using. After saving the file, you need to compile the class into an assembly (a DLL).

The .NET Framework provides you with a compiler for each of the targeted languages. This book focuses on the Visual Basic 2008 and C# 2008 compilers that come with the Framework.

To compile this class, open the Visual Studio 2008 Command Prompt found at All Programs ➪ Microsoft Visual Studio 2008 ➪ Visual Studio Tools ➪ Visual Studio 2008 Command Prompt. From the provided DOS prompt, navigate to the directory that is holding your `Calculator` class (an example navigation command is `cd c:\My Files`). From the DOS prompt, type the following command if you are using the Visual Basic compiler:

```
vbc /t: library Calculator.vb
```

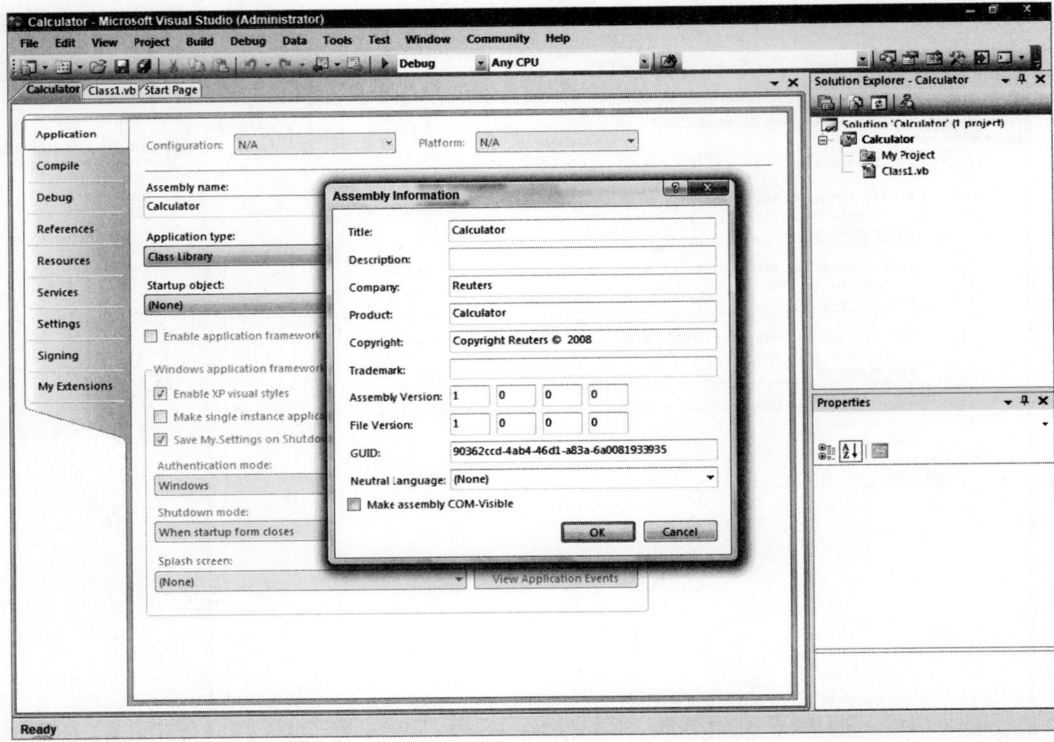

Figure 28-3

If your class is in C#, you use the following command:

```
csc /t:library Calculator.cs
```

As stated, each language uses its own compiler. Visual Basic uses the `vbc.exe` compiler found at `C:\Windows\Microsoft.NET\Framework\v3.5\`. You will find the C# compiler, `csc.exe`, contained in the same folder. In the preceding examples, `/t:library` states that you are interested in compiling the `Calculator.vb` (or `.cs`) class file into a DLL and not an executable (`.exe`), which is the default. Following the `t:/library` command is the name of the file to be compiled.

There are many different commands you can give the compiler — even more than Visual Studio 2008 offers. For example, if you want to make references to specific DLLs in your assembly, you will have to add commands such as `/r:system.data.dll`*. To get a full list of all the compiler options, check out the MSDN documentation.*

After you have run the commands through the compiler, the DLL is created and ready to go.

Using Precompiled Business Objects in Your ASP.NET Applications

To use any DLLs in your ASP.NET 3.5 project, you need to create a `Bin` folder in the root directory of your application by right-clicking on the project within the Solution Explorer and selecting Add ASP.NET

Folder ➪ Bin. In Visual Studio 2008, the `Bin` directory's icon appears as a gray folder with a gear next to it. Add your new DLL to this folder by right-clicking on the folder and selecting the Add Reference option from the menu provided. This launches the Add Reference dialog. From this dialog, select the Browse tab and browse until you find the `Calculator.dll`. When you find it, highlight the DLL and press OK to add it to the `Bin` folder of your project. This dialog is illustrated in Figure 28-4.

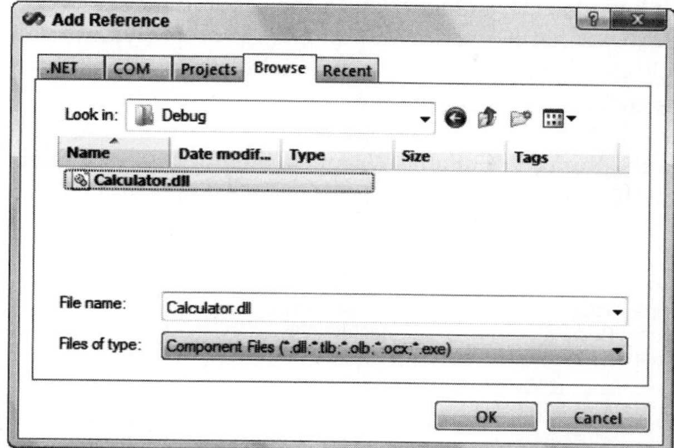

Figure 28-4

`Calculator.dll` is added to your project and is now accessible by the entire project. This means that you now have access to all the functions exposed through this interface. Figure 28-5 shows an example of how IntelliSense makes exploring this .NET component easier than ever.

Default.aspx.vb* | Default.aspx* | Start Page

Button1 | Click

```
Partial Class _Default
    Inherits System.Web.UI.Page

    Protected Sub Button1_Click(ByVal sender As Object, ByVal e As Sys
        Dim myCalc As New Calculator.Class1()
        Label1.Text = myCalc.Add(
    End Sub          Add (a As Integer, b As Integer) As Object
End Class
```

Figure 28-5

As you can see, it is rather simple to create .NET components and use them in your ASP.NET applications. Next, let's look at using COM components.

COM Interop: Using COM Within .NET

Microsoft knows that every one of its legions of developers out there would be quite disappointed if they couldn't use the thousands of COM controls that it has built, maintained, and improved over the years. Microsoft knows that nobody would get up and walk away from these controls to a purely .NET world.

To this end, Microsoft has provided us with COM Interoperability. COM Interop (for short) is a technology that enables .NET to wrap the functionality of a COM object with the interface of a .NET component so that your .NET code can communicate with the COM object without having to use COM techniques and interfaces in your code.

Figure 28-6 illustrates the Runtime Callable Wrapper, the middle component that directs traffic between the .NET code and the COM component.

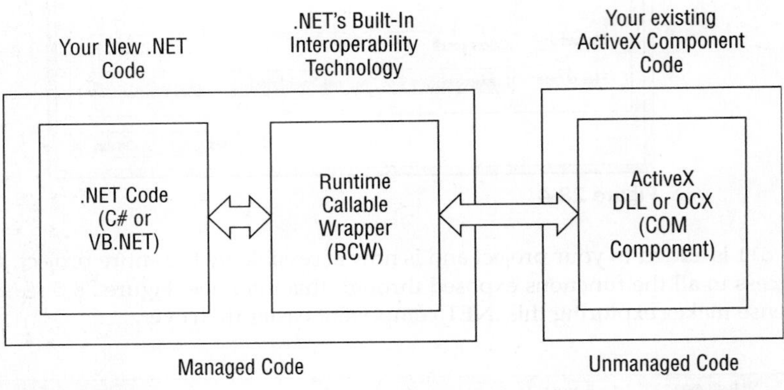

Figure 28-6

The Runtime Callable Wrapper

The Runtime Callable Wrapper, or RCW, is the magic piece of code that enables interaction to occur between .NET and COM. One RCW is created for each COM component in your project. To create an RCW for a COM component, you can use Visual Studio 2008.

To add an ActiveX DLL to the References section of your project, choose Website ➪ Add Reference or choose the Add Reference menu item that appears when you right-click the root node of your project in the Solution Explorer.

The Add Reference dialog box appears with five tabs: .NET, COM, Projects, Browse, and Recent, as shown in Figure 28-7. For this example, select the COM tab and locate the component that you want to add to your .NET project. After you have located the component, highlight the item and click OK to add a reference to the component to your project. The newly added component will then be found inside a newly created `Bin` folder in your project.

Your Interop library is automatically created for you from the ActiveX DLL that you told Visual Studio 2008 to use. This Interop library is the RCW component customized for your ActiveX control, as shown previously in Figure 28-6. The name of the Interop file is simply `Interop.OriginalName.DLL`.

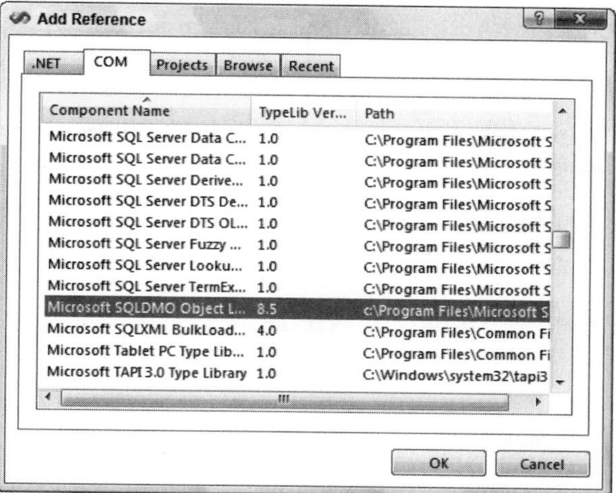

Figure 28-7

It is also possible to create the RCW files manually instead of doing it through Visual Studio 2008. In the .NET Framework, you will find a method to create RCW Interop files for controls manually through a command-line tool called the Type Library Importer. You invoke the Type Library Importer by using the `tlbimp.exe` executable.

For example, to create the Interop library for the SQLDMO object used earlier, start up a Visual Studio 2008 Command Prompt from the Microsoft Visual Studio 2008 ➪ Visual Studio Tools group within your Start Menu. From the comment prompt, type

```
tlbimp sqldmo.dll /out:sqldmoex.dll
```

In this example, the `/out:` parameter specifies the name of the RCW Interop library to be created. If you omit this parameter, you get the same name that Visual Studio would generate for you.

The Type Library Importer is useful when you are not using Visual Studio 2008 as your development environment, if you want to have more control over the assemblies that get created for you, or if you are automating the process of connecting to COM components.

The Type Library Importer is a wrapper application around the `TypeLibConvertor` class of the `System.Runtime.InteropServices` namespace.

Using COM Objects in ASP.NET Code

To continue working through some additional examples, you next take a look at a simple example of using a COM object written in Visual Basic 6 within an ASP.NET page.

In the first step, you create an ActiveX DLL that you can use for the upcoming examples. Add the Visual Basic 6 code shown in Listing 28-1 to a class called `NameFunctionsClass` and compile it as an ActiveX DLL called `NameComponent.dll`.

Listing 28-1: VB6 code for ActiveX DLL, NameComponent.DLL

```
Option Explicit

Private m_sFirstName As String
Private m_sLastName As String

Public Property Let FirstName(Value As String)
  m_sFirstName = Value
End Property

Public Property Get FirstName() As String
  FirstName = m_sFirstName
End Property

Public Property Let LastName(Value As String)
  m_sLastName = Value
End Property

Public Property Get LastName() As String
  LastName = m_sLastName
End Property

Public Property Let FullName(Value As String)
  m_sFirstName = Split(Value, " ")(0)
  If (InStr(Value, " ") > 0) Then
    m_sLastName = Split(Value, " ")(1)
  Else
    m_sLastName = ""
  End If
End Property

Public Property Get FullName() As String
  FullName = m_sFirstName + " " + m_sLastName
End Property

Public Property Get FullNameLength() As Long
  FullNameLength = Len(Me.FullName)
End Property
```

Now that you have created an ActiveX DLL to use in your ASP.NET pages, the next step is to create a new ASP.NET project using Visual Studio 2008. Replace the HTML code in the `Default.aspx` file with the HTML code illustrated in Listing 28-2. This adds a number of text boxes and labels to the HTML page, as well as the Visual Basic or C# code for the functionality.

Listing 28-2: Using NameComponent.dll

VB

```
<%@ Page Language="VB" %>

<script runat="server">
  Protected Sub AnalyzeName_Click(ByVal sender As Object, _
      ByVal e As System.EventArgs)
```

```
      Dim Name As New NameComponent.NameFunctionsClass()

      If (FirstName.Text.Length > 0) Then
        Name.FirstName = FirstName.Text
      End If

      If (LastName.Text.Length > 0) Then
        Name.LastName = LastName.Text
      End If

      If (FullName.Text.Length > 0) Then
        Name.FullName = FullName.Text
      End If

      FirstName.Text = Name.FirstName
      LastName.Text = Name.LastName
      FullName.Text = Name.FullName
      FullNameLength.Text = Name.FullNameLength.ToString

    End Sub
</script>

<html xmlns="http://www.w3.org/1999/xhtml" >
  <head runat="server">
     <title>Using COM Components</title>
  </head>
  <body>
    <form id="form1" runat="server">
      <p>
        <asp:Label ID="Label1" runat="server">First Name:</asp:Label>
         
        <asp:TextBox ID="FirstName" runat="server"></asp:TextBox>
      </p>
      <p>
        <asp:Label ID="Label2" runat="server">Last Name:</asp:Label>
         
        <asp:TextBox ID="LastName" runat="server"></asp:TextBox>
      </p>
      <p>
        <asp:Label ID="Label3" runat="server">Full Name:</asp:Label>
         
        <asp:TextBox ID="FullName" runat="server"></asp:TextBox>
      </p>
      <p>
        <asp:Label ID="Label4" runat="server">Full Name Length:</asp:Label>
         
        <asp:Label ID="FullNameLength" runat="server"
         Font-Bold="True">0</asp:Label>
      </p>
      <p>
        <asp:Button ID="AnalyzeName" runat="server"
         OnClick="AnalyzeName_Click" Text="Analyze Name"></asp:Button>
      </p>
```

Continued

```
    </form>
  </body>
</html>
```

C#

```
<%@ Page Language="C#" %>

<script runat="server">
  protected void AnalyzeName_Click(object sender, System.EventArgs e)
  {
    NameComponent.NameFunctionsClass Name =
        new NameComponent.NameFunctionsClass();

    if (FirstName.Text.Length > 0)
    {
      string firstName = FirstName.Text.ToString();
      Name.set_FirstName(ref firstName);
    }

    if (LastName.Text.Length > 0)
    {
      string lastName = LastName.Text.ToString();
      Name.set_LastName(ref lastName);
    }

    if (FullName.Text.Length > 0)
    {
      string fullName = FullName.Text.ToString();
      Name.set_FullName(ref fullName);
    }

    FirstName.Text = Name.get_FirstName();
    LastName.Text = Name.get_LastName();
    FullName.Text = Name.get_FullName();
    FullNameLength.Text = Name.FullNameLength.ToString();
  }
</script>
```

Now you need to add the reference to the ActiveX DLL that you created in the previous step. To do so, follow these steps:

1. Right-click your project in the Solution Explorer dialog.
2. Select the Add Reference menu item.
3. In the Add Reference dialog box, select the fourth tab, Browse.
4. Locate the `NameComponent.dll` object by browsing to its location.
5. Click OK to add `NameComponent.dll` to the list of selected components and close the dialog box.

If you are not using Visual Studio 2008 or code-behind pages, you can still add a reference to your COM control by creating the RCW manually using the Type Library Converter and then placing an `Imports` *statement (VB) or* `using` *statement (C#) in the page.*

After you have selected your component using the Add Reference dialog, an RCW file is created for the component and added to your application.

That's all there is to it! Simply run the application to see the COM interoperability layer in action.

Figure 28-8 shows the ASP.NET page that you created. When the Analyze Name button is clicked, the fields in the First Name, Last Name, and Full Name text boxes are sent to the RCW to be passed to the `NameComponent.DLL` ActiveX component. Data is retrieved in the same manner to repopulate the text boxes and to indicate the length of the full name.

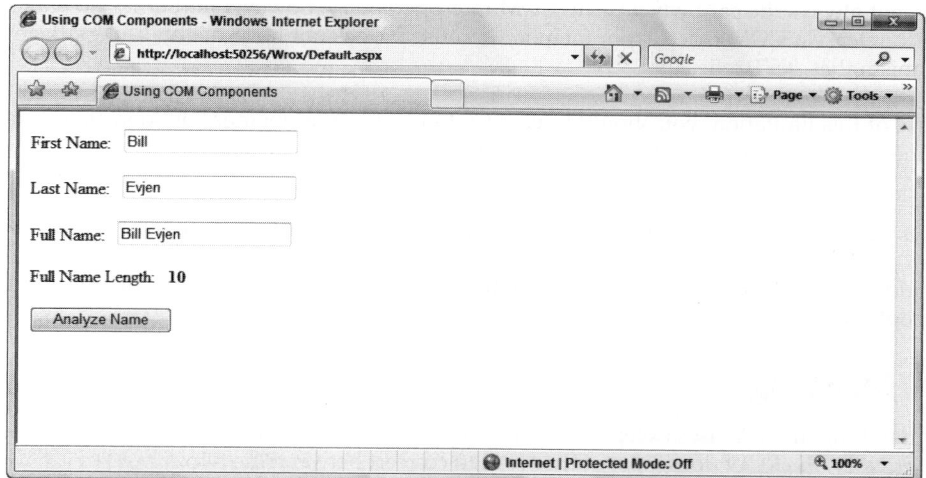

Figure 28-8

Accessing Tricky COM Members in C#

Sometimes, some members of COM objects do not expose themselves properly to C#. In the preceding examples, the `String` properties did not expose themselves, but the `Long` property (`FullNameLength`) did.

You know when there is a problem because, although you can see the property, you cannot compile the application. For instance, instead of the code shown in Listing 28-2 for C#, use the following piece of code to set the `FirstName` property of the `NameComponent.dll` ActiveX component:

```
if (FirstName.Text.Length > 0)
  Name.FirstName = FirstName.Text.ToString();
```

When you try to compile this code, you get the following error:

```
c:\inetpub\wwwroot\wrox\Default.aspx.cs(67): Property, indexer, or event
'FirstName' is not supported by the language; try directly calling accessor methods
'NameComponent.NameFunctionsClass.get_FirstName()' or
'NameComponent.NameFunctionsClass.set_FirstName(ref string)'
```

The `FirstName` property seems to be fine. It shows up in IntelliSense, but you can't use it. Instead, you must use `set_FirstName` (and `get_FirstName` to read). These methods do not show up in IntelliSense, but rest assured, they exist.

Furthermore, these methods expect a `ref string` parameter rather than a `String`. In the example from Listing 28-2, two steps are used to do this properly. First, `String` is assigned to a local variable, and then the variable is passed to the method using `ref`.

Releasing COM Objects Manually

One of the great things about .NET is that it has its own garbage collection — it can clean up after itself. This is not always the case when using COM interoperability, however. .NET has no way of knowing when to release a COM object from memory because it does not have the built-in garbage collection mechanism that .NET relies on.

Because of this limitation, you should release COM objects from memory as soon as possible using the `ReleaseComObject` class of the `System.Runtime.InteropServices.Marshal` class:

C#

```
System.Runtime.InteropServices.Marshal.ReleaseComObject(Object);
```

It should be noted that if you attempt to use this object again before it goes out of scope, you would raise an exception.

Error Handling

Error handling in .NET uses exceptions instead of the HRESULT values used by Visual Basic 6 applications. Luckily, the RCW does most of the work to convert between the two.

Take, for instance, the code shown in Listing 28-3. In this example, a user-defined error is raised if the numerator or the denominator is greater than 1000. Also notice that we are not capturing a divide-by-zero error. Notice what happens when the ActiveX component raises the error on its own.

Begin this example by compiling the code listed in Listing 28-3 into a class named `DivideClass` within an ActiveX component called `DivideComponent.dll`.

Listing 28-3: Raising errors in VB6

```
Public Function DivideNumber(Numerator As Double, _
                             Denominator As Double) As Double

  If ((Numerator > 1000) Or (Denominator > 1000)) Then
      Err.Raise vbObjectError + 1, _
                "DivideComponent:Divide.DivideNumber", _
                "Numerator and denominator both have to " + _
                "be less than or equal to 1000."

  End If

  DivideNumber = Numerator / Denominator

End Function
```

Next, create a new ASP.NET project; add a reference to the `DivideComponent.dll` (invoking Visual Studio 2008 to create its own copy of the RCW). Remember, you can also do this manually by using the `tlbimp` executable.

Now add the code shown in Listing 28-4 to an ASP.NET page.

Listing 28-4: Error handling in .NET

VB

```
<%@ Page Language="VB" %>

<script runat="server">
  Protected Sub Calculate_Click(ByVal sender As Object, _
     ByVal e As System.EventArgs)

     Dim Divide As New DivideComponent.DivideClass()

     Try
        Answer.Text = Divide.DivideNumber(Numerator.Text, Denominator.Text)
     Catch ex As Exception
        Answer.Text = ex.Message.ToString()
     End Try

     System.Runtime.InteropServices.Marshal.ReleaseComObject(Divide)

  End Sub
</script>

<html xmlns="http://www.w3.org/1999/xhtml">
  <head runat="server">
     <title>Using COM Components</title>
  </head>
  <body>
    <form id="form1" runat="server">
      <p>
        <asp:Label ID="Label1" runat="server">Numerator:</asp:Label>
         
        <asp:TextBox ID="Numerator" runat="server"></asp:TextBox>
      </p>
      <p>
        <asp:Label ID="Label2" runat="server">Denominator:</asp:Label>
         
        <asp:TextBox ID="Denominator" runat="server"></asp:TextBox>
      </p>
      <p>
        <asp:Label ID="Label3" runat="server">
         Numerator divided by Denominator:</asp:Label>
         
        <asp:Label ID="Answer" runat="server" Font-Bold="True">0</asp:Label>
      </p>
      <p>
        <asp:Button ID="Calculate"
         runat="server"
```

Continued

```
            OnClick="Calculate_Click"
            Text="Calculate">
          </asp:Button>
        </p>
      </form>
    </body>
</html>
```

C#

```
<%@ Page Language="C#" %>

<script runat="server">
  protected void Calculate_Click(object sender, System.EventArgs e)
  {

    DivideComponent.DivideClass myDivide = new DivideComponent.DivideClass();

    try
    {
      double numerator = double.Parse(Numerator.Text);
      double denominator = double.Parse(Denominator.Text);
      Answer.Text = myDivide.DivideNumber(ref numerator,
         ref denominator).ToString();
    }

    catch (Exception ex)
    {
      Answer.Text = ex.Message.ToString();
    }

    System.Runtime.InteropServices.Marshal.ReleaseComObject(myDivide);

  }
</script>
```

The code in Listing 28-4 passes the user-entered values for the `Numerator` and `Denominator` to the `DivideComponent.dll` ActiveX component for it to divide. Running the application with invalid data gives the result shown in Figure 28-9.

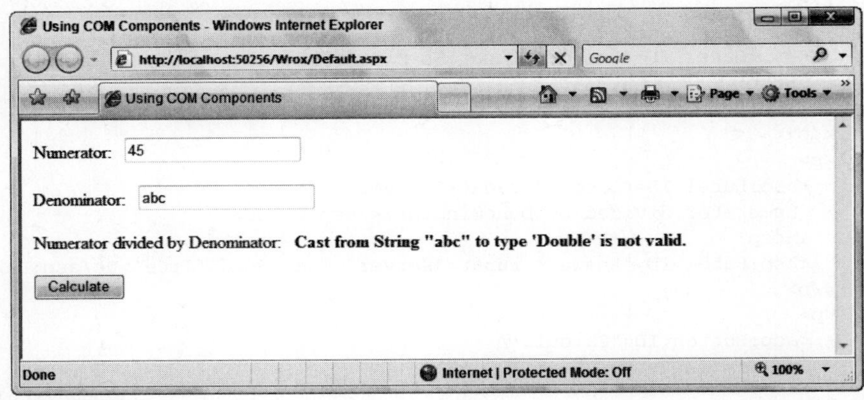

Figure 28-9

Depending on the language that you are using to run the ASP.NET application, you will see different values for different sets of data. For valid inputs, you will always see the correct result, of course, and for any input that is over 1000, you see the Visual Basic 6 appointed error description of `Numerator and denominator both have to be less than or equal to 1000`.

However, for invalid Strings, Visual Basic 2008 reports `Cast from string "abc" to type 'Double' is not valid.` whereas C# reports `Input string was not in a correct format`. For a divide by zero, they both report `Divide by Zero` because the error is coming directly from the Visual Basic 6 runtime.

Deploying COM Components with .NET Applications

Deploying COM components with your .NET applications is very easy; especially when compared to just deploying ActiveX controls. Two scenarios are possible when deploying .NET applications with COM components:

- Using private assemblies
- Using shared assemblies

Private Assemblies

Installing all or parts of the ActiveX component local to the .NET application is considered installing private assemblies. In this scenario, each installation of your .NET application on the same machine has, at least, its own copy of the Interop library for the ActiveX component you are referencing, as shown in Figure 28-10.

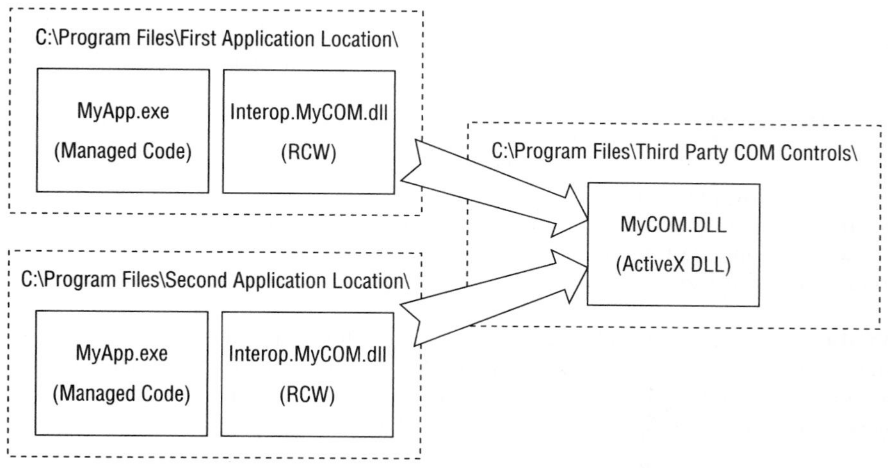

Figure 28-10

It is up to you whether you decide to install the ActiveX component as local to the application or in a shared directory for all calling applications.

It was once considered proper practice to separate ActiveX components into their own directory so that if these components were referenced again by other applications, you did not have to register or install the file for a second time. Using this method meant that when you upgraded a component, you automatically upgraded all the utilizing applications. However, this practice didn't work out so well. In fact, it became a very big contributor to DLL hell and the main reason why Microsoft began promoting the practice of installing private .NET component assemblies.

After you have your components physically in place, the only remaining task is to register the ActiveX component using regsvr32, just as you would when deploying an ActiveX-enabled application.

Public Assemblies

The opposite of a private assembly is a public assembly. Public assemblies share the RCW Interop DLL for other applications. In order to create a public assembly, you must put the RCW file into the *Global Assembly Cache* (GAC), as shown in Figure 28-11.

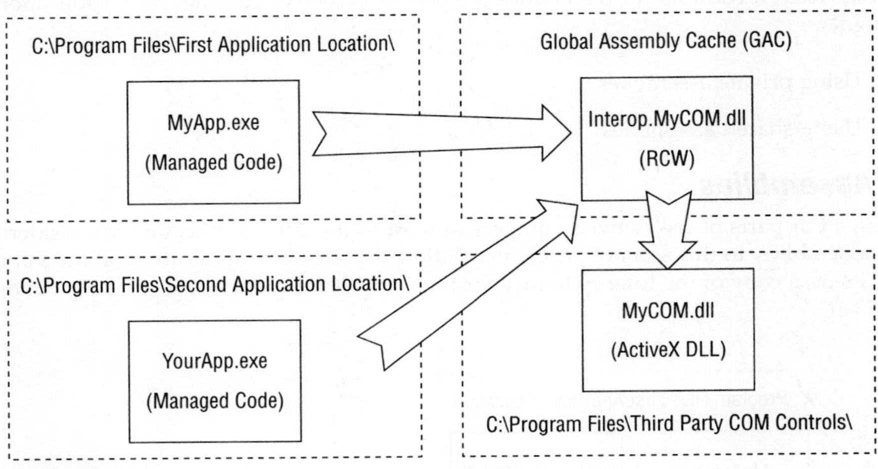

Figure 28-11

You can find the GAC at `C:\Windows\assembly`. Installing items in the GAC can be as simple as dragging-and-dropping the item into this folder through Windows Explorer. Although the GAC is open to everyone, it is not recommended that you blindly install your components into this section unless you have a very good reason to do so.

You can also add items to the GAC from the command line using the Global Assembly Cache Tool (Gacutil.exe). It enables you to view and manipulate the contents of the global assembly cache and download cache. While the Explorer view of the GAC provides similar functionality, you can use Gacutil.exe from build scripts, makefile files, and batch files.

It is hard to find a very good reason to install your ActiveX Interop Assemblies into the GAC. If we had to pick a time to do this, it would be if and when we had a highly shared ActiveX component that many .NET applications would be utilizing on the same machine. In a corporate environment, this might occur when you are upgrading existing business logic from ActiveX to .NET enablement on a server that many applications use. In a commercial setting, we avoid using the GAC.

Using .NET from Unmanaged Code

.NET provides the opposite of COM interoperability by enabling you to use your newly created .NET components within unmanaged code. This section discusses using .NET components with Visual Basic 6 executables. The techniques shown in this section are identical when you are using ActiveX OCXs or DLLs instead of executables.

The COM-Callable Wrapper (CCW) is the piece of the .NET Framework that enables unmanaged code to communicate with your .NET component. The CCW, unlike the RCW, is not a separate DLL that you distribute with your application. Instead, the CCW is part of the .NET Framework that gets instantiated once for each .NET component that you are using.

Figure 28-12 shows how the CCW marshals the communication between the unmanaged code and the .NET component in much the same way that the RCW marshals the code between managed code and COM code.

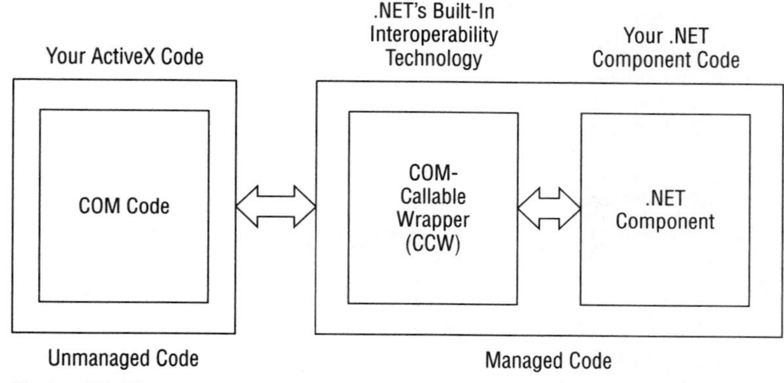

Figure 28-12

The COM-Callable Wrapper

The COM-Callable Wrapper or CCW, as previously stated, is not a separate DLL like the RCW. Instead, the CCW uses a specially created type library based on the .NET component. This type library is called an Interop Type Library. The Interop Type Library is statically linked with the unmanaged code so that this code can communicate with the CCW about the .NET component included in your application.

In order for a .NET component to generate an Interop Type Library, you tell Visual Studio 2008 to generate it when the component is built. Both Visual Basic and C# projects have a setting in the Compile properties section of the Class Library project's Property Pages dialog.

Right-click the project in the Solution Explorer and choose Properties to see the project's properties. Figure 28-13 shows the project's properties for a Visual Basic 2008 Class Library application. This is shown directly in the Visual Studio document window.

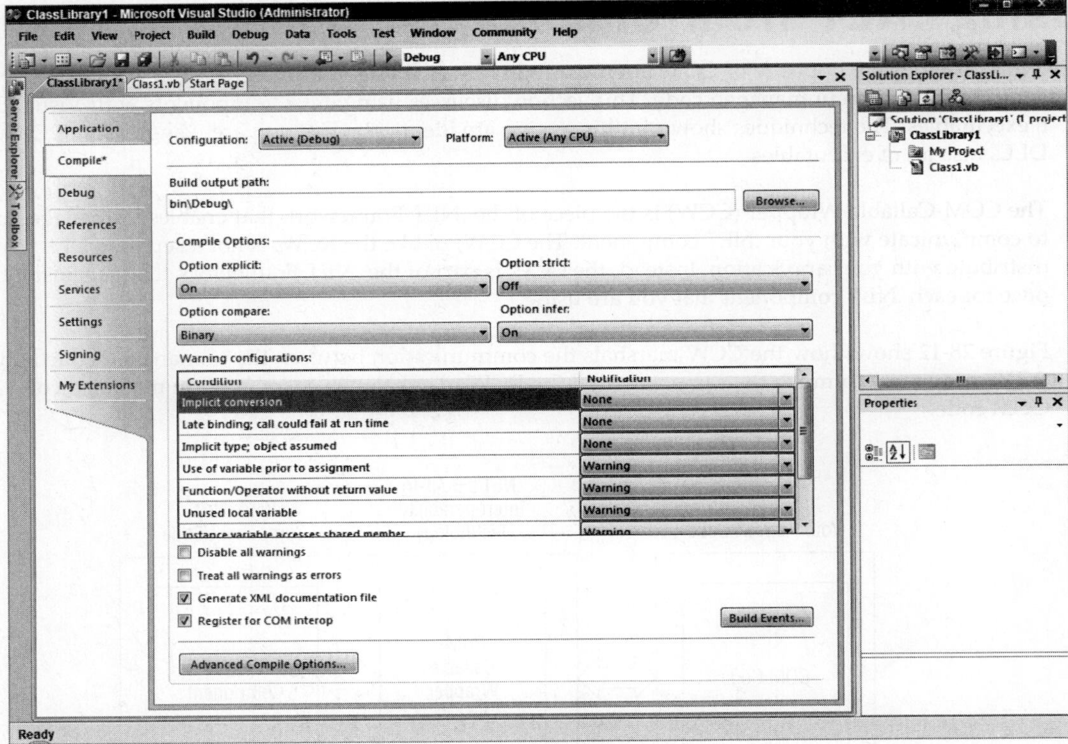

Figure 28-13

C# has a slightly different dialog, as shown in Figure 28-14. In both dialogs, the property is called Register for COM Interop. In Visual Basic, you can find this property on the Compile page; in C#, you can find it on the Build tab of the properties pages.

After you set this option by checking the check box, when you build the project a separate type library file (`.tlb`) is generated for the DLL that you are building. This `.tlb` file is your key to including .NET components in COM applications.

Normally in Visual Basic, when you add a reference to a DLL, you navigate from the References section of the Visual Basic project to find the ActiveX DLL that you want to add. If you use .NET components, they cannot be properly referenced in this manner because they are not ActiveX. Instead, you reference the Interop Type Library, which makes the functionality of the corresponding .NET component available to your application.

The .NET Framework also gives you a method to create Interop Type Library files manually for .NET components. You do this through a command-line tool called the Type Library Exporter (as compared to the Type Library Importer used for COM Interoperability). The Type Library Exporter is invoked using the `tlbexp.exe` executable.

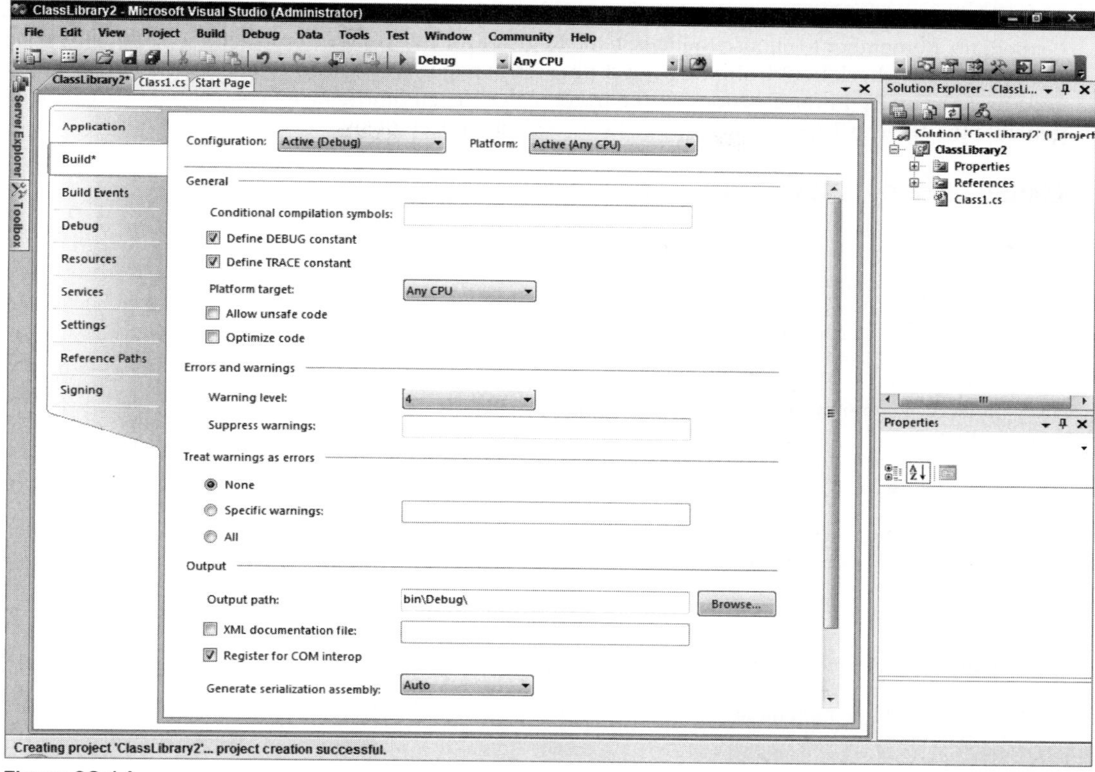

Figure 28-14

For example, to create the Interop Type Library for the `NameComponent.dll` in the next example, you use the following command:

```
tlbexp NameComponent.dll /out:NameComponentEx.tlb
```

The `/out:` parameter specifies the name of the Interop Type Library that is to be created. If you omit this parameter, you get a file with the same name as the ActiveX component, but with a `.tlb` extension.

The Type Library Exporter is useful when you are not using Visual Studio 2008 as your development environment, if you want to have more control over the assemblies that get created for you, or if you are automating the process of connecting to .NET components.

Using .NET Components Within COM Objects

The next example illustrates how .NET components can be utilized within COM code. To begin, create and compile the .NET code found in Listing 28-5 in either Visual Basic or C#.

After you have typed your code into your Class Library project, build the component and call it `NameComponent`. Remember to choose to include the Register for the COM Interop setting of True (by checking the appropriate check box) from the project properties pages, as shown in Figure 28-13 for Visual Basic code and Figure 28-14 for C# code. If you aren't using Visual Studio 2008, you can use `tblexp.exe` to generate the Interop Type Library manually as described previously.

Listing 28-5: The .NET component

VB

```
Public Class NameFunctions

  Private m_FirstName As String
  Private m_LastName As String

  Public Property FirstName() As String
    Get
      Return m_FirstName
    End Get

    Set(ByVal Value As String)
      m_FirstName = Value
    End Set
  End Property

  Public Property LastName() As String
    Get
      Return m_LastName
    End Get

    Set(ByVal Value As String)
      m_LastName = Value
    End Set
  End Property

  Public Property FullName() As String
    Get
      Return m_FirstName + " " + m_LastName
    End Get

    Set(ByVal Value As String)
      m_FirstName = Split(Value, " ")(0)
      m_LastName = Split(Value, " ")(1)
    End Set
  End Property

  Public ReadOnly Property FullNameLength() As Long
    Get
      FullNameLength = Len(Me.FullName)
    End Get
  End Property

End Class
```

C#

```
using System;
using System.Runtime.InteropServices;

namespace NameComponent
{
  [ComVisible(true)]
  public class NameFunctions
  {

    private string m_FirstName;
    private string m_LastName;

    public string FirstName
    {
      get
      {
        return m_FirstName;
      }
      set
      {
        m_FirstName=value;
      }
    }

    public string LastName
    {
      get
      {
        return m_LastName;
      }
      set
      {
        m_LastName=value;
      }
    }

    public string FullName
    {
      get
      {
        return m_FirstName + " " + m_LastName;
      }
      set
      {
        m_FirstName=value.Split(' ')[0];
        m_LastName=value.Split(' ')[1];
      }
    }

    public long FullNameLength
```

Continued

```
        {
          get
          {
            return this.FullName.Length;
          }
        }

      }
    }
```

After you have created the .NET component, you can then create the consuming Visual Basic 6 code shown in Listing 28-6.

Listing 28-6: VB6 code using the .NET component

```
Option Explicit

Public Sub Main()

  Dim o As NameComponent.NameFunctions

  Set o = New NameComponent.NameFunctions

  o.FirstName = "Bill"
  o.LastName = "Evjen"

  MsgBox "Full Name is: " + o.FullName

  MsgBox "Length of Full Name is: " + CStr(o.FullNameLength)

  o.FullName = "Scott Hanselman"

  MsgBox "First Name is: " + o.FirstName

  MsgBox "Last Name is: " + o.LastName

  o.LastName = "Evjen"

  MsgBox "Full Name is: " + o.FullName

  Set o = Nothing

End Sub
```

Remember to add a reference to the .NET component. You choose Project ➪ References and select the .NET component that was created either by Visual Studio or by manually using `tlbexp.exe`.

When you run the code in Listing 28-6, you see that Visual Basic 6 does not miss a beat when communicating with the .NET component.

It is also possible to register the assemblies yourself. Earlier you learned how to manually create Interop Type Libraries with the Type Library Exporter. This tool does not register the assemblies created but instead generates only the type library.

To register the assemblies yourself, you use the Assembly Registration Tool (`regasm.exe`). This tool is similar the `regsvr32.exe` for .NET components.

To use `regasm.exe`, use a command syntax similar to the following example:

```
regasm NameComponent.dll /tlb:NameComponentEx.tlb /regfile:NameComponent.reg
```

The `/tlb:` option specifies the name of the type library, and the `/regfile:` option specifies the name of a registry file to be created that can be used later in an installation and deployment application.

Early versus Late Binding

The preceding example illustrates the use of early binding, the technique most Visual Basic 6 developers are used to. However, in some cases, it is desirable to use late binding. Performing late binding with .NET components is similar to performing late binding with ActiveX components, as shown in Listing 28-7.

Listing 28-7: Late binding with VB6

```
Option Explicit

Public Sub Main()

  Dim o As Object

  Set o = CreateObject("NameComponent.NameFunctions")

  o.FirstName = "Bill"
  o.LastName = "Evjen"

  MsgBox "Full Name is: " + o.FullName

  MsgBox "Length of Full Name is: " + CStr(o.FullNameLength)

  o.FullName = "Scott Hanselman"

  MsgBox "First Name is: " + o.FirstName

  MsgBox "Last Name is: " + o.LastName

  o.LastName = "Evjen"

  MsgBox "Full Name is: " + o.FullName

  Set o = Nothing

End Sub
```

Error Handling

Handling errors that are raised from .NET components in Visual Basic 6 is easily accomplished via the Interop functionality. Listing 28-8 shows code for both Visual Basic and C# to throw exceptions for a custom error. When the `Numerator` or the `Denominator` parameters are greater than 1000 in the `Divide` function, a custom exception is thrown up to the calling code, which is Visual Basic 6 in this example.

Notice how the divide-by-zero error possibility is not handled in this example. This is done intentionally to demonstrate how interoperability handles unhandled errors.

Listing 28-8: Raising errors

VB

```
Public Class CustomException
  Inherits Exception

  Sub New(ByVal Message As String)
    MyBase.New(Message)
  End Sub
End Class

Public Class DivideFunction

  Public Function Divide(ByVal Numerator As Double, _
                         ByVal Denominator As Double) As Double

    If ((Numerator > 1000) Or (Denominator > 1000)) Then
      Throw New CustomException("Numerator and denominator both " & _
                          "have to be less than or equal to 1000.")
    End If

    Divide = Numerator / Denominator

  End Function

End Class
```

C#

```
using System;

namespace DivideComponent
{
    public class CustomException:Exception
    {
      public CustomException(string message):base(message)
      {
      }
    }

  public class DivideFunction
  {
    public double Divide(double Numerator, double Denominator)
    {
      if ((Numerator > 1000) || (Denominator > 1000))
        throw new CustomException("Numerator and denominator " +
                    "both have to be less than or equal to 1000.");
```

```
            return Numerator / Denominator;
        }
    }
}
```

Now that you have the code for the .NET component, compile it with the Register for COM Interop flag set to True in the project's Property Pages dialog and call the component `DivideComponent`.

The consuming Visual Basic 6 code is shown in Listing 28-9. Remember to add a reference to the Interop Type Library of the `DivideComponent` generated by Visual Studio.

Listing 28-9: VB6 experiencing .NET errors

```
Option Explicit

Public Sub Main()

  Dim o As DivideComponent.DivideFunction

  Set o = New DivideComponent.DivideFunction

  MsgBox "1 divided by 3: " + CStr(o.divide(1, 3))

  MsgBox "1 divided by 0: " + CStr(o.divide(1, 0))

  MsgBox "2000 divided by 3000: " + CStr(o.divide(2000, 3000))

  Set o = Nothing

End Sub
```

The Visual Basic 6 code example in Listing 28-9 does not handle the errors thrown by the .NET component, but it can easily do so using `On Error`, Visual Basic 6's method for trapping raised errors.

Instead of trapping the errors, make sure that the Error Trapping setting in the Options dialog of Visual Basic 6 is set to Break in Class Module.

When the application is run, the first example of 1 divided by 3 works fine; you see the output properly. The second example, which you would expect to end in a divide-by-zero error, does not. Instead, an invalid property value is returned to Visual Basic 6. The final example, which does not pass the custom error handling in the .NET component, raises a Visual Basic error, as you would expect.

Deploying .NET Components with COM Applications

Deploying .NET components with COM applications is similar to deploying COM components. There are two scenarios in this deployment scheme:

- Using private assemblies
- Using shared assemblies

The following sections discuss these two scenarios.

Private Assemblies

Private assemblies mean the deployment of the .NET component is installed in each individual directory where the application is installed, within the same machine. The only needed component is the .NET DLL and the calling application. The Interop Type Library that you created earlier with Visual Studio 2008 or `tlbexp.exe` is statically linked with the component or application that references the .NET component.

The only additional task you must complete is to properly register the .NET assembly using `regasm.exe`. This is an extra step that is not needed in 100 percent .NET applications; it is required only for the interoperability for the unmanaged code to reference the managed code. Figure 28-15 illustrates using private assemblies.

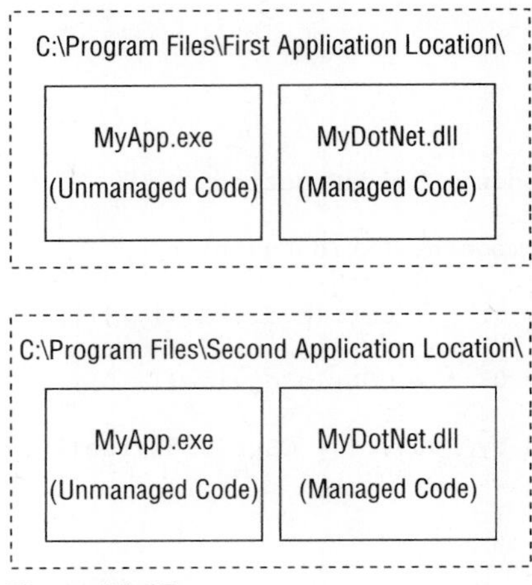

Figure 28-15

Public Assemblies

The use of a public assembly is illustrated in Figure 28-16. This scenario involves installing the .NET component into the Global Assembly Cache (GAC).

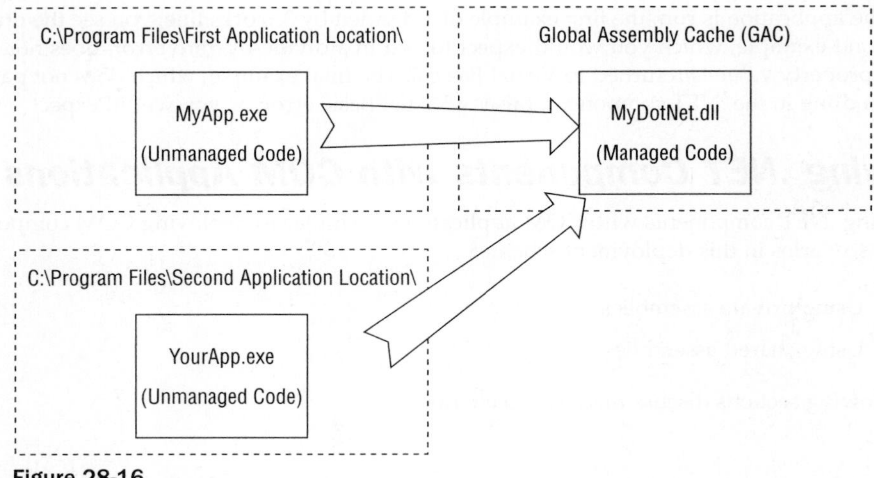

Figure 28-16

As with private assemblies, the .NET component and the consuming unmanaged code are the only requirements for deployment — besides the need to register the interop assembly using `regasm.exe`.

Summary

When .NET was introduced, there was some initial concern about existing ActiveX controls and their place in Microsoft's vision for the future of component development. Immediately, Microsoft stepped up to the bat and offered the robust and solid .NET Interop functionality to provide a means to communicate not only from .NET managed code to COM unmanaged code, but also from COM unmanaged code to .NET managed code. The latter was an unexpected, but welcome, feature for many Visual Basic 6 developers and future .NET component builders.

This layer of interoperability has given Microsoft the position to push .NET component development as a solution for not only newly created applications, but also applications that are currently in development and ones that have already been rolled out and are now in the maintenance phase.

Interoperability has given .NET developers a means to gradually update applications without rewriting them entirely, and it has given them a way to start new .NET projects without having to wait for all the supporting components to be developed in .NET.

29

Building and Consuming Services

When the .NET Framework 1.0 was first introduced, much of the hype around its release was focused on XML Web services. In fact, Microsoft advertised that the main purpose of the newly released .NET Framework 1.0 was to enable developers to build and consume XML Web services with ease. Unfortunately, the new Web services model was slow to be accepted by the development community because it was so radically different from those that came before. Decision makers in the development community regarded this new Web services model with a cautious eye.

Since then, Microsoft has stopped trumpeting that .NET is all about Web services and instead has really expanded the power of .NET and its relation to applications built within the enterprise. Still, the members of the IT community continued to look long and hard at the Web services model (Microsoft is no longer alone in hyping this new technology), examining how it could help them with their current issues and problems.

This chapter looks at building XML Web services and how you can consume XML Web service interfaces and integrate them into your ASP.NET applications. It begins with the foundations of XML Web services in the .NET world by examining some of the underlying technologies such as SOAP, WSDL, and more.

Communication Between Disparate Systems

It is a diverse world. In a major enterprise, very rarely do you find that the entire organization and its data repositories reside on a single vendor's platform. In most instances, organizations are made up of a patchwork of systems — some based on Unix, some on Microsoft, and some on other systems. There probably will not be a day when everything resides on a single platform where all the data moves seamlessly from one server to another. For that reason, these various systems must be able to talk to one another. If disparate systems can communicate easily, moving unique datasets around the enterprise becomes a simple process — alleviating the need for replication systems and data stores.

When XML (eXtensible Markup Language) was introduced, it became clear that the markup language would be the structure to bring the necessary integration into the enterprise. XML's power comes from the fact that it can be used regardless of the platform, language, or data store of the system using it to expose DataSets.

XML has its roots in the Standard Generalized Markup Language (SGML), which was created in 1986. Because SGML was so complex, something a bit simpler was needed — thus the birth of XML.

XML is considered ideal for data representation purposes because it enables developers to structure XML documents as they see fit. For this reason, it is also a bit chaotic. Sending self-structured XML documents between dissimilar systems does not make a lot of sense — you would have to custom build the exposure and consumption models for each communication pair.

Vendors and the industry as a whole soon realized that XML needed a specific structure that put some rules in place to clarify communication. The rules defining XML structure make the communication between the disparate systems just that much easier. Tool vendors can now automate the communication process, as well as provide for the automation of the possible creation of all the components of applications using the communication protocol.

The industry settled on using SOAP (Simple Object Access Protocol) to make the standard XML structure work. Previous attempts to solve the communication problem that arose included component technologies such as Distributed Component Object Model (DCOM), Remote Method Invocation (RMI), Common Object Request Broker Architecture (CORBA), and Internet Inter-ORB Protocol (IIOP). These first efforts failed because each of these technologies was either driven by a single vendor or (worse yet) very vendor-specific. It was, therefore, impossible to implement them across the entire industry.

SOAP enables you to expose and consume complex data structures, which can include items such as DataSets, or just tables of data that have all their relations in place. SOAP is relatively simple and easy to understand. Like ASP.NET, XML Web services are also primarily engineered to work over HTTP. The DataSets you send or consume can flow over the same Internet wires (HTTP), thereby bypassing many firewalls (as they move through port 80).

So what is actually going across the wire? ASP.NET Web services generally use SOAP over HTTP using the HTTP Post protocol. An example SOAP request (from the client to the Web service residing on a Web server) takes the structure shown in Listing 29-1.

Listing 29-1: A SOAP request

```
POST /MyWebService/Service.asmx HTTP/1.1
Host: www.wrox.com
Content-Type: text/xml; charset=utf-8
Content-Length: 19
SOAPAction: "http://tempuri.org/HelloWorld"

<?xml version="1.0" encoding="utf-8"?>
<soap:Envelope xmlns:xsi="http://www.w3.org/2001/XMLSchema-instance"
 xmlns:xsd="http://www.w3.org/2001/XMLSchema"
 xmlns:soap="http://schemas.xmlsoap.org/soap/envelope/">
```

```
    <soap:Body>
      <HelloWorld xmlns="http://tempuri.org/" />
    </soap:Body>
  </soap:Envelope>
```

The request is sent to the Web service to invoke the `HelloWorld` WebMethod (WebMethods are discussed later in this chapter). The SOAP response from the Web service is shown in Listing 29-2.

Listing 29-2: A SOAP response

```
HTTP/1.1 200 OK
Content-Type: text/xml; charset=utf-8
Content-Length: 14

<?xml version="1.0" encoding="utf-8"?>
<soap:Envelope xmlns:xsi="http://www.w3.org/2001/XMLSchema-instance"
 xmlns:xsd="http://www.w3.org/2001/XMLSchema"
 xmlns:soap="http://schemas.xmlsoap.org/soap/envelope/">
  <soap:Body>
    <HelloWorldResponse xmlns="http://tempuri.org/">
      <HelloWorldResult>Hello World</HelloWorldResult>
    </HelloWorldResponse>
  </soap:Body>
</soap:Envelope>
```

In the examples from Listings 29-1 and 29-2, you can see that what is contained in this message is an XML file. In addition to the normal XML declaration of the `<xml>` node, you see a structure of XML that is the SOAP message. A SOAP message uses a root node of `<soap:Envelope>` that contains the `<soap:Body>` or the body of the SOAP message. Other elements that can be contained in the SOAP message include a SOAP header, `<soap:Header>`, and a SOAP fault — `<soap:Fault>`.

For more information about the structure of a SOAP message, be sure to check out the SOAP specifications. You can find them at the W3C Web site, `www.w3.org/tr/soap`.

Building a Simple XML Web Service

Building an XML Web service means that you are interested in exposing some information or logic to another entity either within your organization, to a partner, or to your customers. In a more granular sense, building a Web service means that you, as a developer, simply make one or more methods from a class you create that is enabled for SOAP communication.

You can use Visual Studio 2008 to build an XML Web service. The first step is to actually create a new Web site by selecting File ➪ New ➪ Web Site from the IDE menu. The New Web Site dialog opens. Select ASP.NET Web Service, as shown in Figure 29-1.

Visual Studio creates a few files you can use to get started. In the Solution Explorer of Visual Studio (see Figure 29-2) is a single XML Web service named `Service.asmx`; its code-behind file, `Service.vb` or `Service.cs`, is located in the `App_Code` folder.

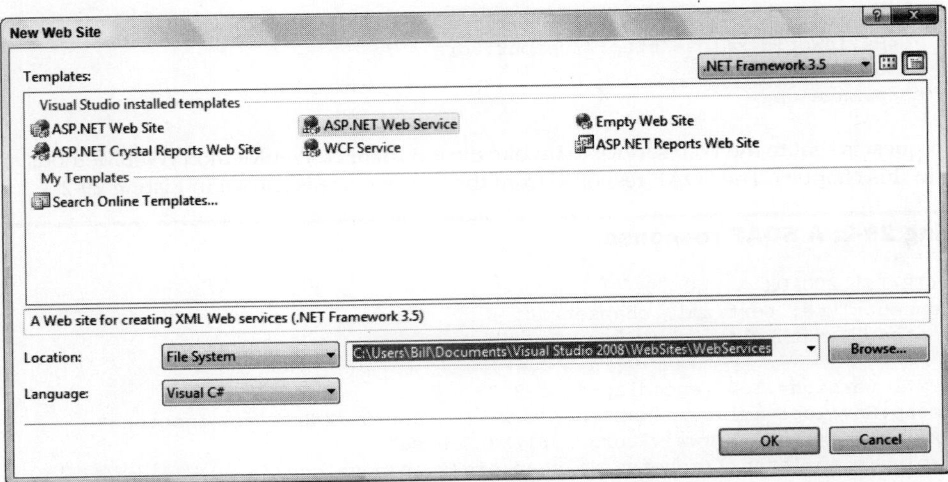

Figure 29-1

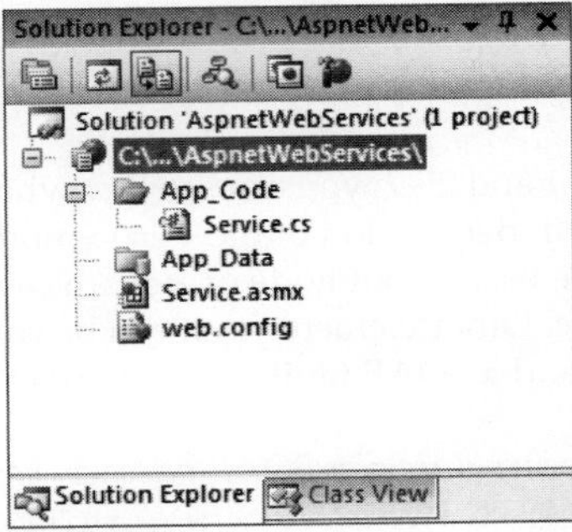

Figure 29-2

Check out the `Service.asmx` file. All ASP.NET Web service files use the `.asmx` file extension instead of the `.aspx` extension used by typical ASP.NET pages.

The WebService Page Directive

Open the `Service.asmx` file in Visual Studio, and you see that the file contains only the `WebService` page directive, as illustrated in Listing 29-3.

Listing 29-3: Contents of the Service.asmx file

```
<%@ WebService Language="VB" CodeBehind="~/App_Code/Service.vb"
    Class="Service" %>
```

You use the `@WebService` directive instead of the `@Page` directive.

The simple `WebService` directive has only four possible attributes. The following list explains these attributes:

- `Class`: Required. It specifies the class used to define the methods and data types visible to the XML Web service clients.
- `CodeBehind`: Required only when you are working with an XML Web service file using the code-behind model. It enables you to work with Web services in two separate and more manageable pieces instead of a single file. The `CodeBehind` attribute takes a string value that represents the physical location of the second piece of the Web service — the class file containing all the Web service logic. In ASP.NET, it is best to place the code-behind files in the `App_Code` folder, starting with the default Web service created by Visual Studio when you initially opened the Web service project.
- `Debug`: Optional. It takes a setting of either `True` or `False`. If the `Debug` attribute is set to `True`, the XML Web service is compiled with debug symbols in place; setting the value to `False` ensures that the Web service is compiled without the debug symbols in place.
- `Language`: Required. It specifies the language that is used for the Web service.

Looking at the Base Web Service Class File

Now look at the `WebService.vb` or `WebService.cs` file — the code-behind file for the XML Web. By default, a structure of code is already in place in the `WebService.vb` or `WebService.cs` file, as shown in Listing 29-4.

Listing 29-4: Default code structure provided by Visual Studio for your Web service

VB

```
Imports System.Web
Imports System.Web.Services
Imports System.Web.Services.Protocols

' To allow this Web Service to be called from script, using ASP.NET AJAX, uncomment
' the following line.
' <System.Web.Script.Services.ScriptService()> _
<WebService(Namespace:="http://tempuri.org/")> _
<WebServiceBinding(ConformsTo:=WsiProfiles.BasicProfile1_1)> _
<Global.Microsoft.VisualBasic.CompilerServices.DesignerGenerated()> _
Public Class Service
     Inherits System.Web.Services.WebService

    <WebMethod()> _
    Public Function HelloWorld() As String
        Return "Hello World"
    End Function

End Class
```

Continued

C#

```
using System;
using System.Linq;
using System.Web;
using System.Web.Services;
using System.Web.Services.Protocols;
using System.Xml.Linq;

[WebService(Namespace = "http://tempuri.org/")]
[WebServiceBinding(ConformsTo = WsiProfiles.BasicProfile1_1)]
// To allow this Web Service to be called from script, using ASP.NET AJAX,
// uncomment the following line.
// [System.Web.Script.Services.ScriptService]
public class Service : System.Web.Services.WebService
{
    public Service () {

        //Uncomment the following line if using designed components
        //InitializeComponent();
    }

    [WebMethod]
    public string HelloWorld() {
        return "Hello World";
    }

}
```

Some minor changes to the structure have been made since the .NET 3.5 release. You will notice that the `System.Linq` and `System.Xml.Linq` namespaces are now included in the C# solution. In addition, the other change in this version is the inclusion of the commented `System.Web.Script.Services.ScriptService` object to work with ASP.NET AJAX scripts. To make use of this attribute, you simply uncomment the item.

Since the .NET 1.0/1.1 days, there also have been some big changes. First, the `System.Web.Services.Protocols` namespace is included by default. Therefore, in working with SOAP headers and other capabilities provided via this namespace, you do not need to worry about including it.

The other addition is the new `<WebServiceBinding>` attribute. It builds the XML Web service responses that conform to the WS-I Basic Profile 1.0 release (found at `www.ws-i.org/Profiles/BasicProfile-1.0-2004-04-16.html`).

Besides these minor changes, very little has changed in this basic *Hello World* structure.

Exposing Custom Datasets as SOAP

To build your own Web service example, delete the `Service.asmx` file and create a new file called `Customers.asmx`. This Web service will expose the Customers table from SQL Server. Then jump into the code shown in Listing 29-5.

Listing 29-5: An XML Web service that exposes the Customers table from Northwind

VB

```
Imports System.Web
Imports System.Web.Services
Imports System.Web.Services.Protocols
Imports System.Data
Imports System.Data.SqlClient

<WebService(Namespace := "http://www.wrox.com/customers")> _
<WebServiceBinding(ConformsTo:=WsiProfiles.BasicProfile1_1)> _
Public Class Customers
     Inherits System.Web.Services.WebService

    <WebMethod()> _
    Public Function GetCustomers() As DataSet
        Dim conn As SqlConnection
        Dim myDataAdapter As SqlDataAdapter
        Dim myDataSet As DataSet
        Dim cmdString As String = "Select * From Customers"

        conn = New SqlConnection("Server=localhost;uid=sa;pwd=;database=Northwind")
        myDataAdapter = New SqlDataAdapter(cmdString, conn)

        myDataSet = New DataSet()
        myDataAdapter.Fill(myDataSet, "Customers")

        Return myDataSet
    End Function

End Class
```

C#

```
using System;
using System.Web;
using System.Web.Services;
using System.Web.Services.Protocols;
using System.Data;
using System.Data.SqlClient;

[WebService(Namespace = "http://www.wrox.com/customers")]
[WebServiceBinding(ConformsTo = WsiProfiles.BasicProfile1_1)]
public class Customers : System.Web.Services.WebService
{

    [WebMethod]
    public DataSet GetCustomers() {
       SqlConnection conn;
       SqlDataAdapter myDataAdapter;
```

Continued

```
            DataSet myDataSet;
            string cmdString = "Select * From Customers";


            conn = new SqlConnection("Server=localhost;uid=sa;pwd=;database=Northwind");
            myDataAdapter = new SqlDataAdapter(cmdString, conn);

            myDataSet = new DataSet();
            myDataAdapter.Fill(myDataSet, "Customers");

            return myDataSet;
        }

    }
```

The WebService Attribute

All Web services are encapsulated within a class. The class is defined as a Web service by the `WebService` attribute placed before the class declaration. Here is an example:

```
<WebService(Namespace := "http://www.wrox.com/customers")> _
```

The `WebService` attribute can take a few properties. By default, the `WebService` attribute is used in your Web service along with the `Namespace` property, which has an initial value of `http://tempuri.org/`. This is meant to be a temporary namespace and should be replaced with a more meaningful and original name, such as the URL where you are hosting the XML Web service. In the example, the `Namespace` value was changed to `www.wrox.com/customers`. Remember that it does not have to be an actual URL; it can be any string value you want. The idea is that it should be unique. It is common practice to use a URL because a URL is always unique.

Notice that the two languages define their properties within the `WebService` attribute differently. Visual Basic 2008 uses a colon and an equal sign to set the property:

```
Namespace:="http://www.wrox.com/customers"
```

C# uses just an equal sign to assign the properties within the `WebService` attribute values:

```
Namespace="http://www.wrox.com/customers"
```

Other possible `WebService` properties include `Name` and `Description`. `Name` enables you to change how the name of the Web service is presented to the developer via the ASP.NET test page (the test page is discussed a little later in the chapter). `Description` allows you to provide a textual description of the Web service. The description is also presented on the ASP.NET Web service test page. If your `WebService` attribute contains more than a single property, separate the properties using a comma. Here's an example:

```
<WebService(Namespace:="http://www.wrox.com/customers", Name:="GetCustomers")> _
```

The WebMethod Attribute

In Listing 29-5, the class called `Customers` has only a single `WebMethod`. A `WebService` class can contain any number of `WebMethods`, or a mixture of standard methods along with methods that are enabled to be WebMethods via the use of the attribute preceding the method declaration. The only methods that are accessible across the HTTP wire are the ones to which you have applied the WebMethod attribute.

As with the WebService attribute, WebMethod can also contain some properties, which are described in the following list:

- BufferResponse: When BufferResponse is set to True, the response from the XML Web service is held in memory and sent as a complete package. If it is set to False, the default setting, the response is sent to the client as it is constructed on the server.
- CacheDuration: Specifies the number of seconds that the response should be held in the system's cache. The default setting is 0, which means that caching is disabled. Putting an XML Web service's response in the cache increases the Web service's performance.
- Description: Applies a text description to the WebMethod that appears on the .aspx test page of the XML Web service.
- EnableSession: Setting EnableSession to True enables session state for a particular WebMethod. The default setting is False.
- MessageName: Applies a unique name to the WebMethod. This is a required step if you are working with overloaded WebMethods (discussed later in the chapter).
- TransactionOption: Specifies the transactional support for the WebMethod. The default setting is Disabled. If the WebMethod is the root object that initiated the transaction, the Web service can participate in a transaction with another WebMethod that requires a transaction. Other possible values include NotSupported, Supported, Required, and RequiresNew.

The XML Web Service Interface

The Customers Web service from Listing 29-5 has only a single WebMethod that returns a DataSet containing the complete Customers table from the SQL Server Northwind database.

Running Customers.asmx in the browser pulls up the ASP.NET Web service test page. This visual interface to your Web service is really meant either for testing purposes or as a reference page for developers interested in consuming the Web services you expose. The page generated for the Customers Web service is shown in Figure 29-3.

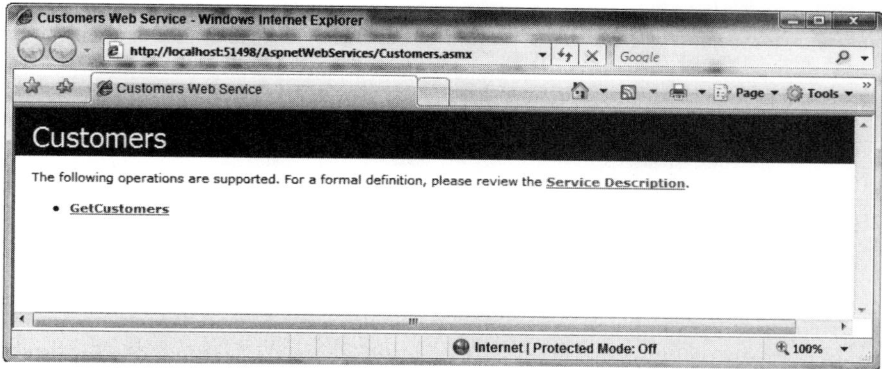

Figure 29-3

The interface shows the name of the Web service in the blue bar (the dark bar in this black and white image) at the top of the page. By default, the name of the class is used unless you changed the value through the `Description` property of the `WebService` attribute, as defined earlier. A bulleted list of links to the entire Web service's `WebMethods` is displayed. In this example, there is only one `WebMethod`: `GetCustomers`.

A link to the Web service's Web Services Description Language (WSDL) document is also available (the link is titled Service Description in the figure). The WSDL file is the actual interface with the Customers Web service. The XML document (shown in Figure 29-4) is not really meant for human consumption; it is designed to work with tools such as Visual Studio, informing the tool what the Web service requires to be consumed. Each Web service requires a request that must have parameters of a specific type. When the request is made, the Web service response comes back with a specific set of data defined using specific data types. Everything you need for the request and a listing of exactly what you are getting back in a response (if you are the consumer) is described in the WSDL document.

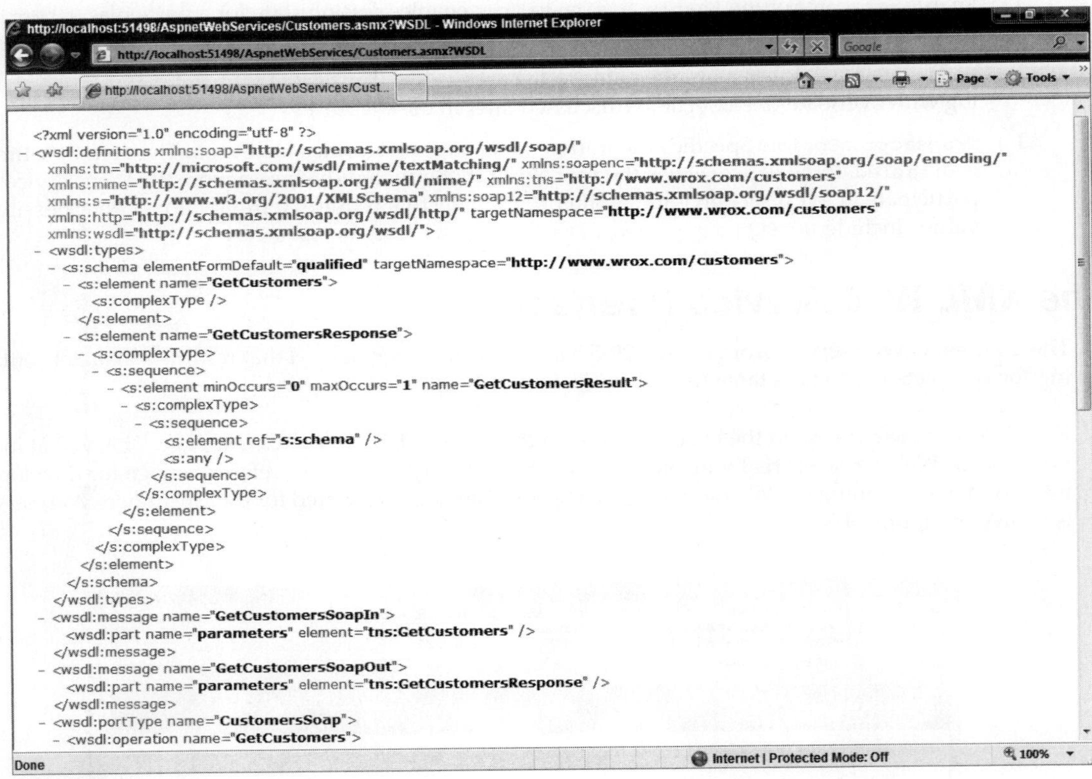

Figure 29-4

Clicking the `GetCustomers` link gives you a new page, shown in Figure 29-5, that not only describes the `WebMethod` in more detail, but it also allows you to test the `WebMethod` directly in the browser.

At the top of the page is the name of the XML Web service (`Customers`); below that is the name of this particular `WebMethod` (`GetCustomers`). The page shows you the structure of the SOAP messages that are required to consume the `WebMethod`, as well as the structure the SOAP message takes for the response. Below the SOAP examples is an example of consuming the XML Web service using HTTP Post (with name/value pairs). It is possible to use this method of consumption instead of using SOAP. (This is discussed later in the "Transport Protocols for Web Services" section of this chapter.)

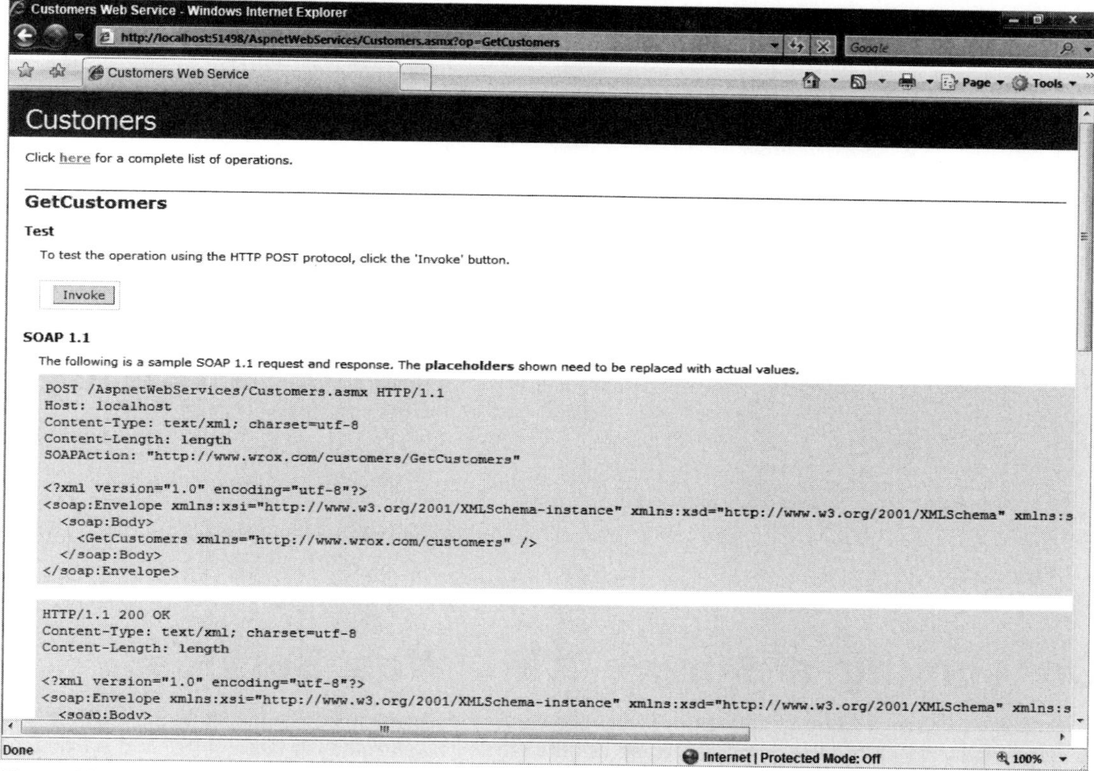

Figure 29-5

You can test the `WebMethod` directly from the page. In the Test section, you find a form. If the `WebMethod` you are calling requires an input of some parameters to get a response, you see some text boxes included so you can provide the parameters before clicking the Invoke button. If the `WebMethod` you are calling does not require any parameters, you see only the Invoke button and nothing more.

Clicking Invoke is actually sending a SOAP request to the Web service, causing a new browser instance with the result to appear, as illustrated in Figure 29-6.

Now that everything is in place to expose the XML Web service, you can consume it in an ASP.NET application.

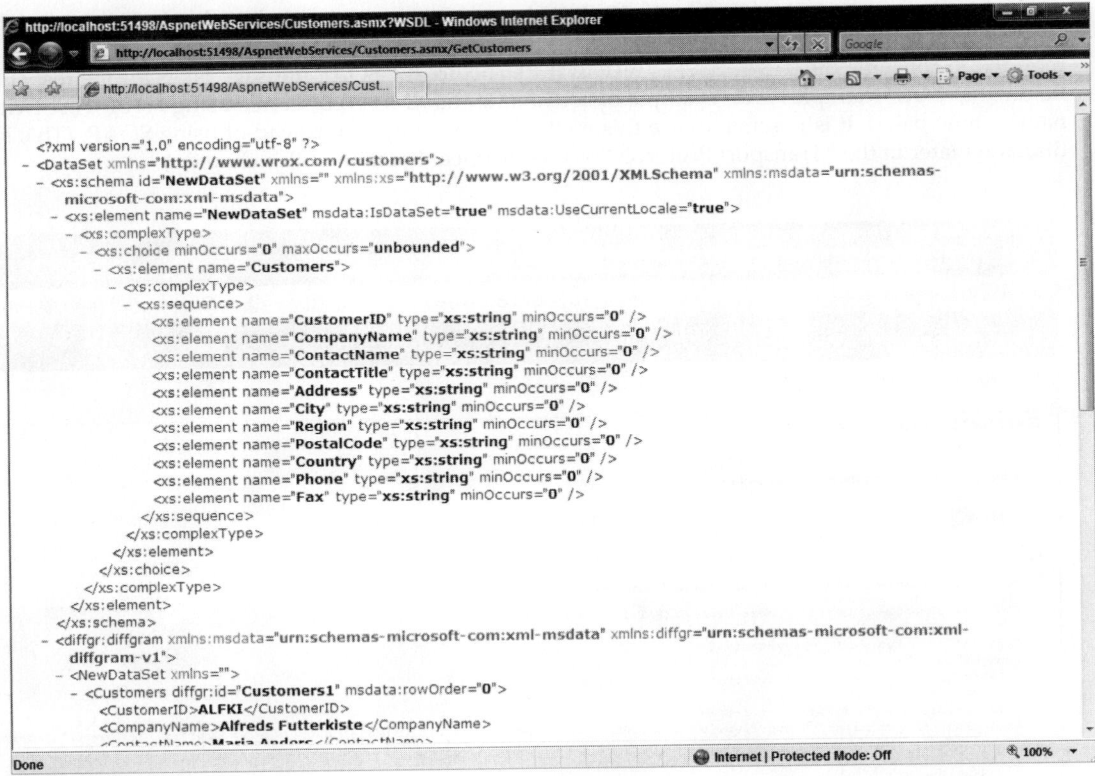

Figure 29-6

Consuming a Simple XML Web Service

So far, you have seen only half of the XML Web service story. Exposing data and logic as SOAP to disparate systems across the enterprise or across the world is a simple task using .NET and particularly ASP.NET. The other half of the story is the actual consumption of an XML Web service into an ASP.NET application.

You are not limited to consuming XML Web services only into ASP.NET applications; but because this is an ASP.NET book, it focuses on that aspect of the consumption process. Consuming XML Web services into other types of applications is not that difficult and, in fact, is rather similar to how you would consume them using `ASP.NET`. Remember that the Web services you come across can be consumed in Windows Forms, mobile applications, databases, and more. You can even consume XML Web services with other Web services so you can have a single Web service made up of what is basically an aggregate of other Web services.

Adding a Web Reference

To consume the Customers Web service that you created earlier in this chapter, create a new ASP.NET Web site called `CustomerConsumer`. The first step in consuming an XML Web service in an ASP.NET application is to make a reference to the remote object — the Web service. This is done by right-clicking on the root node of your project from within the Solution Explorer of Visual Studio and selecting Add Web Reference. This pulls up the Add Web Reference dialog box, shown in Figure 29-7.

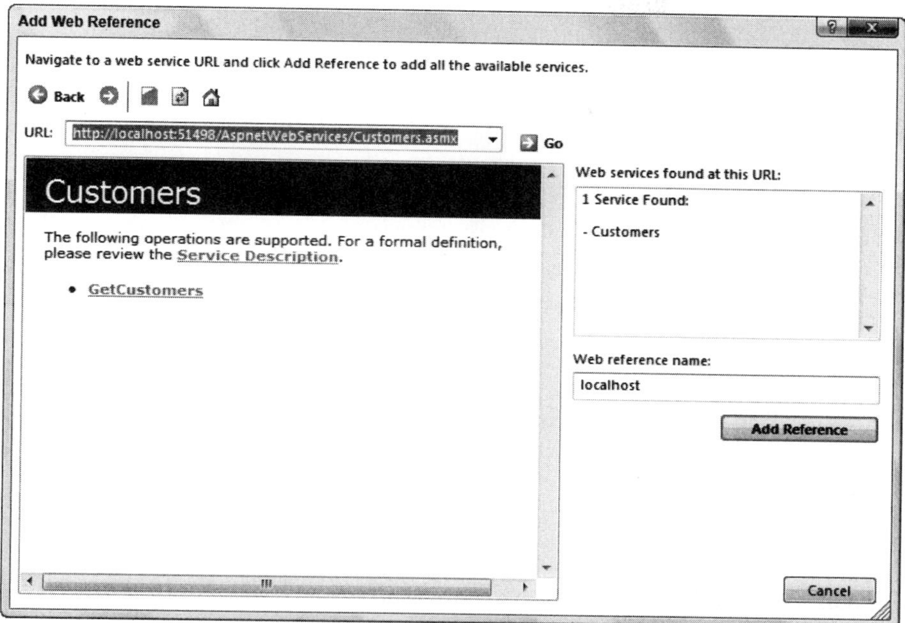

Figure 29-7

The Add Web Reference dialog box enables you to point to a particular `.asmx` file to make a reference to it. Understand that the Add Web Reference dialog box is really looking for WSDL files. Microsoft's XML Web services automatically generate WSDL files based on the `.asmx` files themselves. To pull up the WSDL file in the browser, simply type in the URL of your Web service's `.asmx` file and add a `?WSDL` at the end of the string. For example, you might have the following construction (this is not an actual web service, but simply an example):

```
http://www.wrox.com/MyWebService/Customers.asmx?WSDL
```

Because the Add Web Reference dialog box automatically finds where the WSDL file is for any Microsoft-based XML Web service, you should simply type in the URL of the actual WSDL file for any non–Microsoft-based XML Web service.

If you are using Microsoft's Visual Studio and its built-in Web server instead of IIS, you will be required to also interject the port number the Web server is using into the URL. In this case, your URL would be structured similar to `http://localhost:5444/MyWebService/Customers.asmx?WSDL`.

In the Add Web Reference dialog box, change the reference from the default name to something a little more meaningful. If you are working on a single machine, the Web reference might have the name of `localhost`; if you are actually working with a remote Web service, the name is the inverse of the URL, such as com.wrox.www. In either case, it is best to rename it so that the name makes a little more sense and is easy to use within your application. In the example here, the Web reference is renamed WroxCustomers.

Clicking the Add Reference button causes Visual Studio to make an actual reference to the Web service from the web.config file of your application (shown in Figure 29-8). You may find some additional files under the App_WebReferences folder — such as a copy of the Web service's WSDL file.

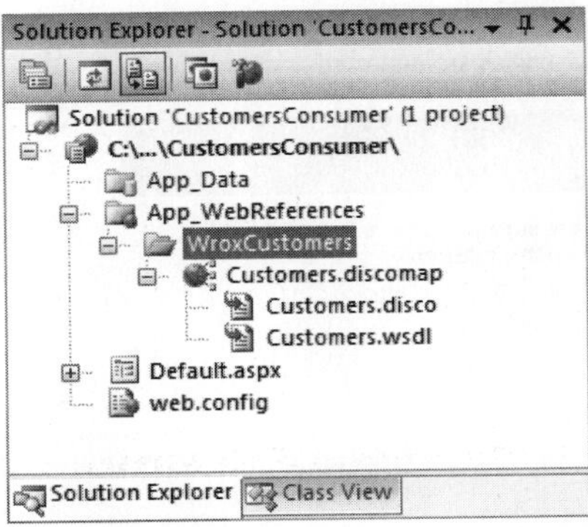

Figure 29-8

Your consuming application's web.config file contains the reference to the Web service in its <appSettings> section. The addition is shown in Listing 29-6.

Listing 29-6: Changes to the web.config file after making a reference to the Web service

```
<configuration xmlns="http://schemas.microsoft.com/.NetConfiguration/v2.0">
   <appSettings>
      <add key="WroxCustomers.Customers"
       value="http://www.wrox.com/MyWebService/Customers.asmx"/>
   </appSettings>
</configuration>
```

You can see that the WroxCustomers reference has been made along with the name of the Web service, providing a key value of WroxCustomers.Customers. The value attribute takes a value of the location of the Customers Web service, which is found within the Customers.asmx page.

Invoking the Web Service from the Client Application

Now that a reference has been made to the XML Web service, you can use it in your ASP.NET application. Create a new Web Form in your project. With this page, you can consume the Customers table from the remote Northwind database directly into your application. The data is placed in a GridView control.

On the design part of the page, place a Button and a GridView control so that your page looks something like the one shown in Figure 29-9.

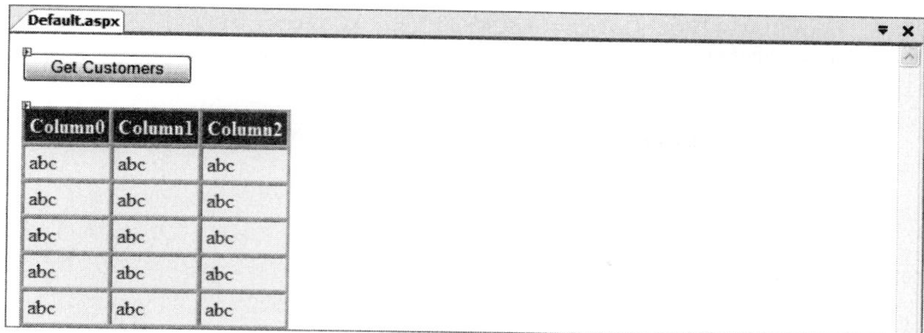

Figure 29-9

The idea is that, when the end user clicks the button contained on the form, the application sends a SOAP request to the Customers Web service and gets back a SOAP response containing the Customers table, which is then bound to the GridView control on the page. Listing 29-7 shows the code for this simple application.

Listing 29-7: Consuming the Customers Web service in an ASP.NET page

VB

```
<%@ Page Language="VB" %>

<script runat="server">
   Protected Sub Button1_Click(ByVal sender As Object, ByVal e As System.EventArgs)
        Dim ws As New WroxCustomers.Customers()
        GridView1.DataSource = ws.GetCustomers()
        GridView1.DataBind()
   End Sub
</script>

<html xmlns="http://www.w3.org/1999/xhtml" >
<head runat="server">
    <title>Web Service Consumer Example</title>
</head>
<body>
    <form id="form1" runat="server">
    <div>
        <asp:Button ID="Button1" Runat="server" Text="Get Customers"
         OnClick="Button1_Click" />
        <br />
        <br />
        <asp:GridView ID="GridView1" Runat="server" BorderWidth="1px"
         BackColor="#DEBA84" CellPadding="3" CellSpacing="2" BorderStyle="None"
         BorderColor="#DEBA84">
            <FooterStyle ForeColor="#8C4510" BackColor="#F7DFB5"></FooterStyle>
            <PagerStyle ForeColor="#8C4510" HorizontalAlign="Center"></PagerStyle>
            <HeaderStyle ForeColor="White" Font-Bold="True"
             BackColor="#A55129"></HeaderStyle>
            <SelectedRowStyle ForeColor="White" Font-Bold="True"
             BackColor="#738A9C"></SelectedRowStyle>
```

Continued

```
            <RowStyle ForeColor="#8C4510" BackColor="#FFF7E7"></RowStyle>
        </asp:GridView>
    </div>
    </form>
</body>
</html>
```

C#

```
<%@ Page Language="C#" %>

<script runat="server">
    protected void Button1_Click(Object sender, EventArgs e) {
       WroxCustomers.Customers ws = new WroxCustomers.Customers();
        GridView1.DataSource = ws.GetCustomers();
        GridView1.DataBind();
    }
</script>
```

The end user is presented with a simple button. Clicking it causes the ASP.NET application to send a SOAP request to the remote XML Web service. The returned DataSet is bound to the GridView control, and the page is redrawn, as shown in Figure 29-10.

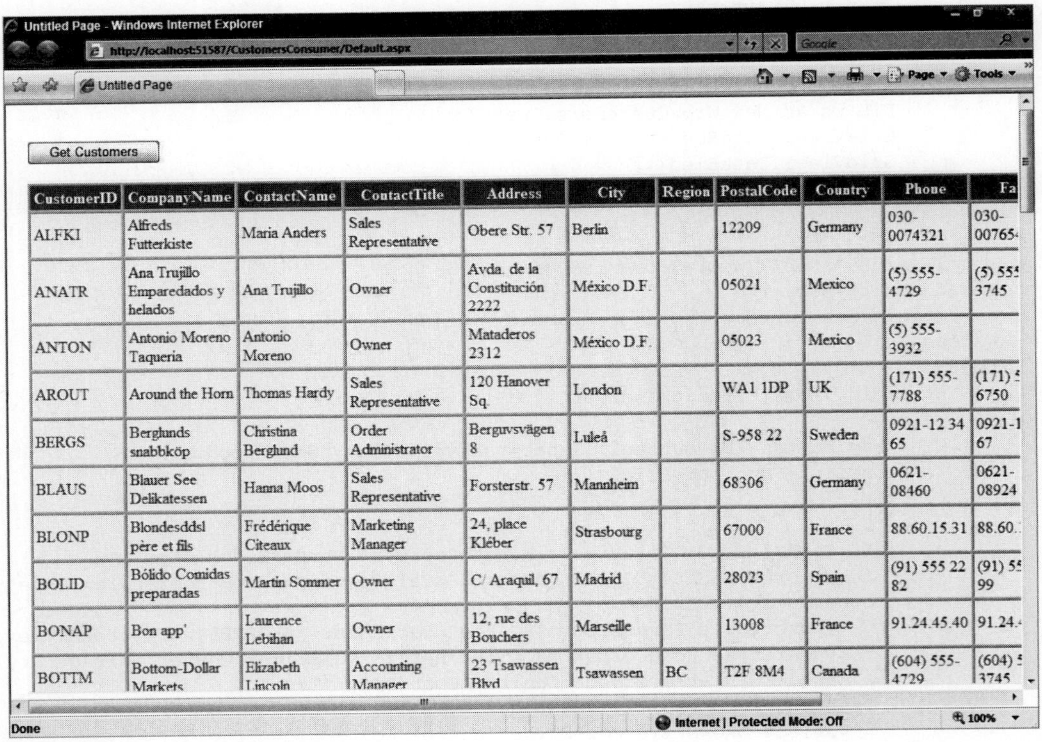

Untitled Page - Windows Internet Explorer

http://localhost:51587/CustomersConsumer/Default.aspx

Get Customers

CustomerID	CompanyName	ContactName	ContactTitle	Address	City	Region	PostalCode	Country	Phone	Fa
ALFKI	Alfreds Futterkiste	Maria Anders	Sales Representative	Obere Str. 57	Berlin		12209	Germany	030-0074321	030-00765
ANATR	Ana Trujillo Emparedados y helados	Ana Trujillo	Owner	Avda. de la Constitución 2222	México D.F.		05021	Mexico	(5) 555-4729	(5) 555 3745
ANTON	Antonio Moreno Taquería	Antonio Moreno	Owner	Mataderos 2312	México D.F.		05023	Mexico	(5) 555-3932	
AROUT	Around the Horn	Thomas Hardy	Sales Representative	120 Hanover Sq.	London		WA1 1DP	UK	(171) 555-7788	(171) 5 6750
BERGS	Berglunds snabbköp	Christina Berglund	Order Administrator	Berguvsvägen 8	Luleå		S-958 22	Sweden	0921-12 34 65	0921-1 67
BLAUS	Blauer See Delikatessen	Hanna Moos	Sales Representative	Forsterstr. 57	Mannheim		68306	Germany	0621-08460	0621-08924
BLONP	Blondesddsl père et fils	Frédérique Citeaux	Marketing Manager	24, place Kléber	Strasbourg		67000	France	88.60.15.31	88.60.
BOLID	Bólido Comidas preparadas	Martín Sommer	Owner	C/ Araquil, 67	Madrid		28023	Spain	(91) 555 22 82	(91) 55 99
BONAP	Bon app'	Laurence Lebihan	Owner	12, rue des Bouchers	Marseille		13008	France	91.24.45.40	91.24.
BOTTM	Bottom-Dollar Markets	Elizabeth Lincoln	Accounting Manager	23 Tsawassen Blvd	Tsawassen	BC	T2F 8M4	Canada	(604) 555-4729	(604) 5 3745

Done | Internet \| Protected Mode: Off | 100%

Figure 29-10

The Customers Web service is invoked by the instantiation of the `WroxCustomers.Customers` proxy object:

```
Dim ws As New WroxCustomers.Customers()
```

Then you can use the `ws` object like any other object within your project. In the code example from Listing 29-7, the results of the `ws.GetCustomers()` method call is assigned to the `DataSource` property of the GridView control:

```
GridView1.DataSource = ws.GetCustomers()
```

As you develop or consume more Web services within your applications, you will see more of their power and utility.

Transport Protocols for Web Services

XML Web services use standard wire formats such as HTTP for transmitting SOAP messages back and forth, and this is one of the reasons for the tremendous popularity of Web services. Using HTTP makes using Web services one of the more accessible and consumable messaging protocols when working between disparate systems.

The transport capabilities of Web services are a fresh new addition to the evolutionary idea of a messaging format to use between platforms. DCOM, an older messaging technology that was developed to address the same issues, uses a binary protocol that consists of a method-request layer riding on top of a proprietary communication protocol. One of the problems with using DCOM and similar methods for calling remote objects is that the server's firewall usually gets in the way because DCOM flows through some odd port numbers.

Web services, on the other hand, commonly use a port that is typically open on almost every server — port 80. The port is used for HTTP or Internet traffic. Moving messages from one system to another through port 80 over HTTP is sensible and makes consumption of Web services easy.

An interesting note about XML Web services is that, although many people still think of Web services as SOAP going over HTTP, you can actually consume the Web service in a couple of different ways. Three wire formats are available to Web services: HTTP-GET, HTTP-POST, and SOAP.

Listing 29-8 shows how to work with these different wire formats by consuming a simple Addition Web service.

Listing 29-8: The Addition Web service

VB

```
Imports System.Web
Imports System.Web.Services
Imports System.Web.Services.Protocols

<WebService(Namespace := "http://www.wrox.com/addition/")> _
```

Continued

```
<WebServiceBinding(ConformsTo:=WsiProfiles.BasicProfile1_1)> _
Public Class WroxMath
     Inherits System.Web.Services.WebService

    <WebMethod()> _
    Public Function Addition(ByVal a As Integer, ByVal b As Integer) As Integer
        Return (a + b)
    End Function

End Class
```

C#

```
using System;
using System.Web;
using System.Web.Services;
using System.Web.Services.Protocols;

[WebService(Namespace = "http://www.wrox.com/addition/")]
[WebServiceBinding(ConformsTo = WsiProfiles.BasicProfile1_1)]
public class WroxMath : System.Web.Services.WebService
{

    [WebMethod]
    public int Addition(int a, int b) {
        return a + b;
    }

}
```

The Addition Web service takes two parameters: `a` and `b`. The Web service then adds these numbers and returns the result in a SOAP message. You might typically consume this Web service by sending a request SOAP message to the service. Now look at some of the other means of consumption.

HTTP-GET

The use of HTTP-GET has been rather popular for quite awhile. It enables you to send your entire request, along with any required parameters, all contained within the URL submission. Here is an example of a URL request that is passing a parameter to the server that will respond:

```
http://www.reuters.com?newscategory=world
```

In this example, a request from the `Reuters.com` Web site is made, but in addition to a typical Web request, it is also passing along a parameter. Any parameters that are sent along using HTTP-GET can only be in a name/value pair construction — also known as querystrings. This means that you can have only a single value assigned to a single parameter. You cannot provide hierarchal structures through querystrings. As you can tell from the previous URL construction, the name/value pair is attached to the URL by ending the URL string with a question mark, followed by the variable name.

Using querystrings, you can also pass more than a single name/value pair with the URL request as the following example shows:

```
http://www.reuters.com?newscategory=world&language=en
```

In this example, the URL construction includes two name/value pairs. The name/value pairs are separated with an ampersand (&).

Now turn your attention to working with the Addition Web service using HTTP-GET. To accomplish this task, you must enable HTTP-GET from within the Web service application because it is disabled by default.

HTTP-GET requests have been disabled by default since ASP.NET 1.1. ASP.NET 1.0 did allow for HTTP-GET and even ran the Web service test interface page using it.

You should possibly consider using HTTP-GET for non-secure data that you want the end user to get a hold of as simply as possible. To enable HTTP-GET, make changes to your `web.config` file as shown in Listing 29-9.

Listing 29-9: Enabling HTTP-GET in your Web service applications

```
<configuration xmlns="http://schemas.microsoft.com/.NetConfiguration/v2.0">
   <system.web>
      <webServices>
         <protocols>
            <add name="HttpGet"/>
         </protocols>
      </webServices>
   </system.web>
</configuration>
```

Creating a `<protocols>` section in your `web.config` file enables you to add or remove protocol communications. For example, you can add missing protocols (such as HTTP-GET) by using the syntax shown previously, or you can remove protocols as the following example shows:

```
<configuration xmlns="http://schemas.microsoft.com/.NetConfiguration/v2.0">
   <system.web>
      <webServices>
         <protocols>
            <remove name="HttpGet"/>
            <remove name="HttpPost"/>
            <remove name="HttpSoap"/>
            <remove name="Documentation"/>
         </protocols>
      </webServices>
   </system.web>
</configuration>
```

You do not want to remove everything shown in this code because that would leave your Web service with basically no capability to communicate; but you can see the construction required for any of the protocols that you do want to remove. HTTP-POST and SOAP are covered shortly, but the node removing `Documentation` is interesting in that it can eliminate the ability to invoke the Web services interface test page if you do not want to make that page available.

After you have enabled your Web service to receive HTTP-GET requests, you build a page that uses that protocol to communicate with the Addition Web service. The Web page is shown in Listing 29-10.

Listing 29-10: Invoking the Addition Web service using HTTP-GET

```
<html>
<head>
   <title>HTTP-GET Example</title>
</head>
<body>
    <a href="http://www.wrox.com/WroxMath.asmx/Addition?a=5&b=2">
     http://www.wrox.com/WroxMath.asmx/Addition?a=5&b=2</a>
</body>
</html>
```

This is a simple page with the single hyperlink pointing at the Addition Web service. When the page is run, you get the result shown in Figure 29-11.

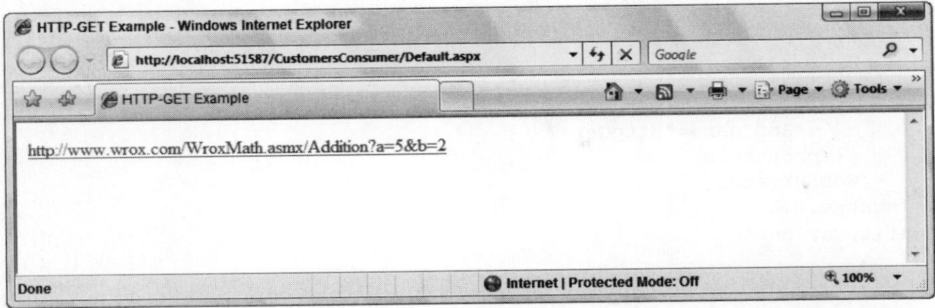

Figure 29-11

To call a Web service using HTTP-GET, you call the actual file (`WroxMath.asmx`), followed by the method name (in this case, `/Addition`), and followed by a querystring list of required parameters. In the example, values for `a` and `b` are passed in the URL. The diagram in Figure 29-12 details the construction of the URL.

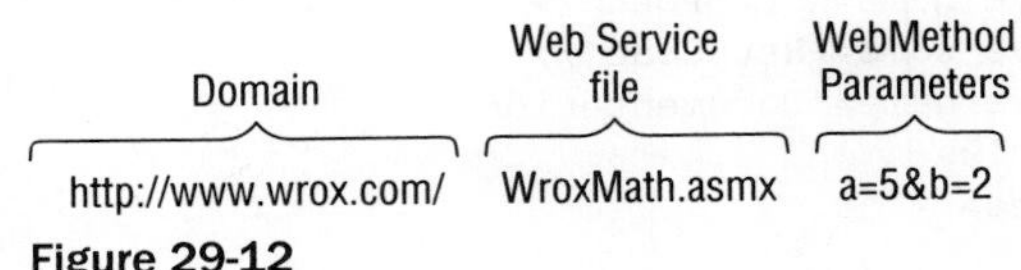

Figure 29-12

Pull up the `WroxMath.aspx` page and click the link to produce the following text result in the browser:

```
<?xml version="1.0" encoding="utf-8" ?>
<int xmlns="http://www.wrox.com/addition/">7</int>
```

One little caveat when constructing your URL string is that the `WebMethod` name in the URL construction is case-sensitive. If you type `addition` instead of `Addition`, you get an error. Also, be sure to consider when it makes sense to use HTTP-GET; it can be a security risk. It is quite easy to alter values in the querystring to either input false values or values that might cause harm to a server. That's why HTTP-GET capabilities were removed from the default settings of the Web services model.

HTTP-POST

The HTTP-POST protocol is similar to HTTP-GET in that you are sending name/value pairs to the server for processing. The big difference is that HTTP-POST places these name/value pairs within a request header so that they are not visible; HTTP-GET sends these same items within a viewable, open URL string.

Setting up a standard HTML page to communicate with the Addition Web service using HTTP-POST is relatively simple, as illustrated in Listing 29-11.

Listing 29-11: Using HTTP-POST to send a request to an XML Web service

```
<html>
<head>
   <title>HTTP-POST Example</title>
</head>
<body>
   <form method="post" action="http://www.wrox.com/WroxMath.asmx/Addition">
      <p><input type="text" name="a"></p>
      <p><input type="text" name="b"></p>
      <p><input type="submit" value="Call Web Service"></p>
   </form>
</body>
</html>
```

This example puts two text boxes and a button on the form. In order to provide the form elements to be posted in the request, the construction of the text boxes and the `<form>` element are important when working with an XML Web service using HTTP-POST. The `<form>` element here contains two attributes. The first is `method`, which specifies that the form is using HTTP-POST for the request. The `action` attribute provides a link to the `WebMethod` that will be called. As with HTTP-GET, the construction of the URL takes the format of the `.asmx` page followed by the name of the `WebMethod` (`Addition`).

The two text boxes are typical text boxes. This process uses the `name` attribute, giving it a value of the parameter name required by the Web service. In the example, the two required parameters are `a` and `b`.

Posting this page (by clicking the Submit button), produces the same results as the HTTP-GET request:

```
<?xml version="1.0" encoding="utf-8" ?>
<int xmlns="http://tempuri.org/">7</int>
```

Again, this code demonstration is purely an example and you won't find the actual endpoint out there on the Internet.

SOAP

The final method of communicating with an XML Web service is by using SOAP, which was discussed earlier in the chapter. The SOAP message is actually sent in an HTTP request, but does not use the name/value pair construction.

Representing data as SOAP messages brings a lot more value than the simple construction of name/value pairs. SOAP enables you to represent data in a hierarchical manner — something you cannot do when using name/value pairs. For instance, how would you send the Customers table from the Northwind database if you were limited to using name/value pairs? It would be impossible to represent the data properly. SOAP permits this type of data representation. In addition, as you get into more advanced Web service scenarios, you can expand the SOAP messages and allow for authentication/authorization capabilities, SOAP routing, partial encryption capabilities, and more. The expandability of SOAP is a powerful feature.

Web Services Enhancements (WSE) is a powerful toolset from Microsoft that enables you to build advanced Web services for specialized situations, as described previously. You can find more information on the WSE at `http://msdn.microsoft.com/webservices/`.

Overloading WebMethods

In the object-oriented world of .NET, it is quite possible to use method overloading in the code you develop. A true object-oriented language has support for *polymorphism* of which method overloading is a part. Method overloading enables you to have multiple methods that use the same name but have different signatures. With method overloading, one method can be called, but the call is routed to the appropriate method based on the full signature of the request. An example of standard method overloading is illustrated in Listing 29-12.

Listing 29-12: Method overloading in .NET

VB

```
Public Function HelloWorld() As String
   Return "Hello"
End Function

Public Function HelloWorld(ByVal FirstName As String) As String
   Return "Hello " & FirstName
End Function
```

C#

```
public string HelloWorld() {
   return "Hello";
}

public string HelloWorld(string FirstName) {
   return "Hello " + FirstName;
}
```

In this example, both methods have the same name, `HelloWorld`. So, which one is called when you invoke `HelloWorld`? Well, it depends on the signature you pass to the method. For instance, you might provide the following:

```
Label1.Text = HelloWorld()
```

This yields a result of just `Hello`. However, you might invoke the `HelloWorld()` method using the following signature:

```
Label1.Text = HelloWorld("Bill Evjen")
```

Then you get back a result of `Hello Bill Evjen`. As you can see, method overloading is a great feature that can be effectively utilized by your ASP.NET applications — but how do you go about overloading `WebMethods`?

If you have already tried to overload any of your WebMethods, you probably got the following error when you pulled up the Web service in the browser:

```
Both System.String HelloWorld(System.String) and System.String HelloWorld() use the
message name 'HelloWorld'. Use the MessageName property of the WebMethod custom
attribute to specify unique message names for the methods.
```

As this error states, the extra step you have to take to overload `WebMethods` is to use the `MessageName` property. Listing 29-13 shows how.

Listing 29-13: WebMethod overloading in .NET

VB

```
<WebMethod(MessageName:="HelloWorld")> _
Public Function HelloWorld() As String
   Return "Hello"
End Function

<WebMethod(MessageName:="HelloWorldWithFirstName")> _
Public Function HelloWorld(ByVal FirstName As String) As String
   Return "Hello " & FirstName
End Function
```

C#

```
[WebMethod(MessageName="HelloWorld")]
public string HelloWorld() {
   return "Hello";
}

[WebMethod(MessageName="HelloWorldWithFirstName")]
public string HelloWorld(string FirstName) {
   return "Hello " + FirstName;
}
```

In addition to adding the `MessageName` property of the `WebMethod` attribute, you have to disable your Web service's adherence to the WS-I Basic Profile 1.0 specification — which it wouldn't be doing if you perform WebMethod overloading with your Web services. You can disable the conformance to the WS-I Basic Profile specification in a couple of ways. The first way is to add the `<WebServiceBinding>` attribute to your code, as illustrated in Listing 29-14.

Listing 29-14: Changing your Web service so it does not conform to the WS-I Basic Profile spec

VB

```
<WebServiceBinding(ConformsTo := WsiProfiles.None)> _
Public Class MyOverloadingExample
   ' Code here
End Class
```

Continued

C#

```
[WebServiceBinding(ConformsTo = WsiProfiles.None)]
public class WroxMath : System.Web.Services.WebService
{
   // Code here
}
```

The other option is to turn off the WS-I Basic Profile 1.0 capability in the `web.config` file, as shown in Listing 29-15.

Listing 29-15: Turning off conformance using the web.config file

```
<configuration>
  <system.web>
    <webServices>
      <conformanceWarnings>
        <remove name="BasicProfile1_1" />
      </conformanceWarnings>
    </webServices>
  </system.web>
</configuration>
```

After you have enabled your Web service to overload `WebMethods`, you can see both `WebMethods` defined by their `MessageName` value properties when you pull up the Web service's interface test page in the browser (see Figure 29-13).

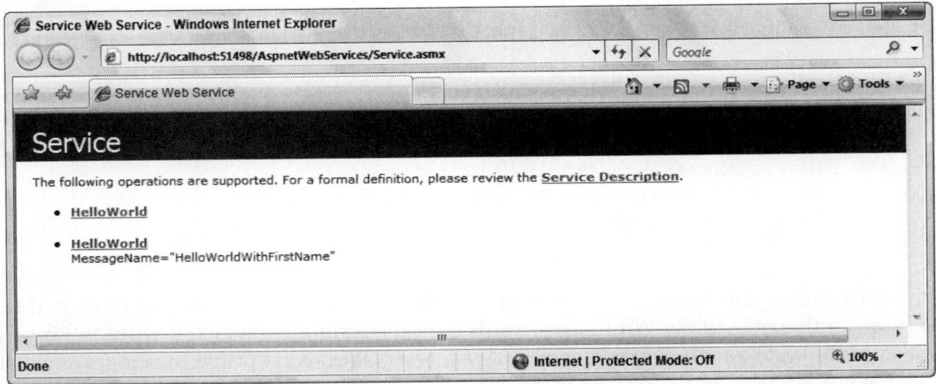

Figure 29-13

Although you can see the names of the `WebMethods` as the same, the `MessageName` property shows that they are distinct methods. When the developer consuming the Web service makes a Web reference to your Web service, he will see only a single method name available (in this example, `HelloWorld`). This is shown in the IntelliSense of Visual Studio 2008 in the application consuming these methods (see Figure 29-14).

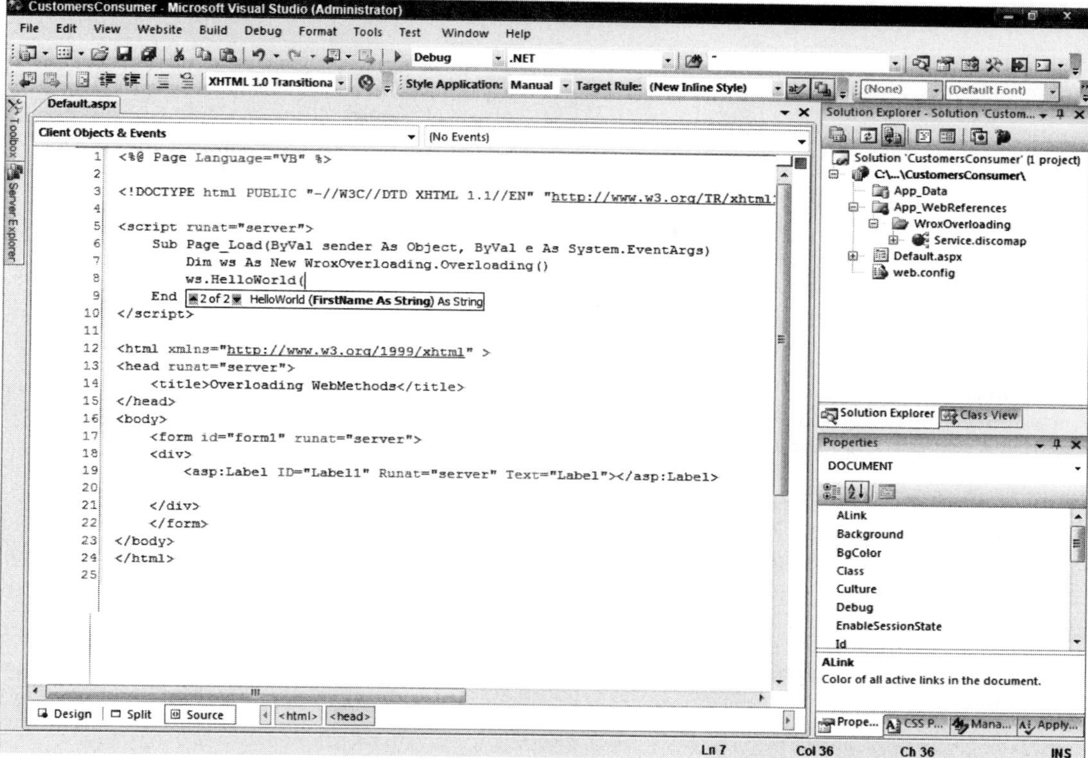

Figure 29-14

In the yellow box that pops up to guide developers on the signature structure, you can see two options available — one is an empty signature, and the other requires a single string.

Caching Web Service Responses

Caching is an important feature in almost every application that you build with .NET. Most of the caching capabilities available to you in ASP.NET are discussed in Chapters 19 and 20, but a certain feature of Web services in .NET enables you to cache the SOAP response sent to any of the service's consumers.

First, by way of review, remember that caching is the capability to maintain an in-memory store where data, objects, and various items are stored for reuse. This feature increases the responsiveness of the applications you build and manage. Sometimes, returning cached results can greatly affect performance.

XML Web services use an attribute to control caching of SOAP responses — the `CacheDuration` property. Listing 29-16 shows its use.

Listing 29-16: Utilizing the CacheDuration property

VB

```
<WebMethod(CacheDuration:=60)> _
Public Function GetServerTime() As String
   Return DateTime.Now.ToLongTimeString()
End Function
```

C#

```
[WebMethod(CacheDuration=60)]
public string GetServerTime() {
   return DateTime.Now.ToLongTimeString();
}
```

As you can see, `CacheDuration` is used within the `WebMethod` attribute much like the `Description` and `Name` properties. `CacheDuration` takes an `Integer` value that is equal to the number of seconds during which the SOAP response is cached.

When the first request comes in, the SOAP response is cached by the server, and the consumer gets the same timestamp in the SOAP response for the next minute. After that minute is up, the stored cache is discarded, and a new response is generated and stored in the cache again for servicing all other requests for the next minute.

Among the many benefits of caching your SOAP responses, you will find that the performance of your application is greatly improved when you have a response that is basically re-created again and again without any change.

SOAP Headers

One of the more common forms of extending the capabilities of SOAP messages is to add metadata of the request to the SOAP message itself. The metadata is usually added to a section of the SOAP envelope called the *SOAP header*. Figure 29-15 shows the structure of a SOAP message.

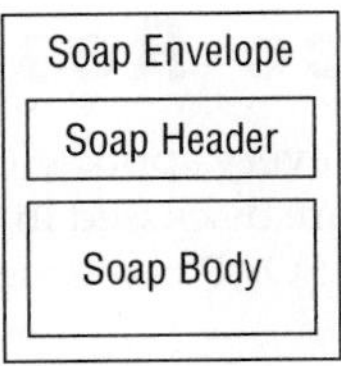

Figure 29-15

The entire SOAP message is referred to as a *SOAP envelope*. Contained within the SOAP message is the *SOAP body* — a piece of the SOAP message that you have been working with in every example thus far. It is a required element of the SOAP message.

The one optional component of the SOAP message is the SOAP header. It is the part of the SOAP message in which you can place any metadata about the overall SOAP request instead of incorporating it in the signature of any of your `WebMethods`. It is important to keep metadata separate from the actual request.

What kind of information? It could include many things. One of the more common items placed in the SOAP header is any authentication/authorization functionality required to consume your Web service or to get at specific pieces of logic or data. Placing usernames and passwords inside the SOAP headers of your messages is a good example of what you might include.

Building a Web Service with SOAP Headers

You can build upon the sample `HelloWorld` Web service that is presented in the default `.asmx` page when it is first pulled up in Visual Studio (from Listing 29-4). Name the new `.asmx` file `HelloSoapHeader.asmx`. The initial step is to add a class that is an object representing what is to be placed in the SOAP header by the client, as shown in Listing 29-17.

Listing 29-17: A class representing the SOAP header

VB

```
Public Class HelloHeader
   Inherits System.Web.Services.Protocols.SoapHeader

   Public Username As String
   Public Password As String
End Class
```

C#

```
public class HelloHeader : System.Web.Services.Protocols.SoapHeader
{
   public string Username;
   public string Password;
}
```

The class, representing a SOAP header object, has to inherit from the `SoapHeader` class from `System.Web.Services.Protocols.SoapHeader`. The `SoapHeader` class serializes the payload of the `<soap:header>` element into XML for you. In the example in Listing 29-17, you can see that this SOAP header requires two elements — simply a username and a password, both of type `String`. The names you create in this class are those used for the subelements of the SOAP header construction, so it is important to name them descriptively.

Listing 29-18 shows the Web service class that instantiates an instance of the `HelloHeader` class.

Listing 29-18: A Web service class that utilizes a SOAP header

VB

```
<WebService(Namespace:="http://www.wrox.com/helloworld")> _
<WebServiceBinding(ConformsTo:=WsiProfiles.BasicProfile1_1, _
  EmitConformanceClaims:=True)> _
Public Class HelloSoapHeader
    Inherits System.Web.Services.WebService

    Public myHeader As HelloHeader

    <WebMethod(), SoapHeader("myHeader")> _
```

Continued

```
    Public Function HelloWorld() As String
        If (myHeader Is Nothing) Then
            Return "Hello World"
        Else
            Return "Hello " & myHeader.Username & ". " & _
                "<br>Your password is: " & myHeader.Password
        End If
    End Function

End Class
```

C#

```
[WebService(Namespace = "http://www.wrox.com/helloworld")]
[WebServiceBinding(ConformsTo = WsiProfiles.BasicProfile1_1)]
public class HelloSoapHeader : System.Web.Services.WebService
{

    public HelloHeader myHeader;

    [WebMethod]
    [SoapHeader("myHeader")]
    public string HelloWorld() {
        if (myHeader == null) {
            return "Hello World";
        }
        else {
            return "Hello " + myHeader.Username + ". " +
                "<br>Your password is: " + myHeader.Password;
        }
    }

}
```

The Web service, `HelloSoapHeader`, has a single `WebMethod` — `HelloWorld`. Within the Web service class, but outside of the `WebMethod` itself, you create an instance of the `SoapHeader` class. This is done with the following line of code:

```
Public myHeader As HelloHeader
```

Now that you have an instance of the `HelloHeader` class that you created earlier called `myHeader`, you can use that instantiation in your `WebMethod`. Because Web services can contain any number of `WebMethods`, it is not a requirement that all `WebMethods` use an instantiated SOAP header. You specify whether a `WebMethod` will use a particular instantiation of a SOAP header class by placing the `SoapHeader` attribute before the WebMethod declaration.

```
<WebMethod(), SoapHeader("myHeader")> _
Public Function HelloWorld() As String
    ' Code here
End Function
```

In this example, the `SoapHeader` attribute takes a `string` value of the name of the instantiated `SoapHeader` class — in this case, `myHeader`.

From here, the `WebMethod` actually makes use of the `myHeader` object. If the `myHeader` object is not found (meaning that the client did not send in a SOAP header with his constructed SOAP message), a simple "`Hello World`" is returned. However, if values are provided in the SOAP header of the SOAP request, those values are used within the returned `string` value.

Consuming a Web Service Using SOAP Headers

It really is not difficult to build an ASP.NET application that makes a SOAP request to a Web service using SOAP headers. Just as with the Web services that do not include SOAP headers, you make a Web Reference to the remote Web service directly in Visual Studio.

For the ASP.NET page, create a simple page with a single Label control. The output of the Web service is placed in the Label control. The code for the ASP.NET page is shown in Listing 29-19.

Listing 29-19: An ASP.NET page working with an XML Web service using SOAP headers

VB

```
<%@ Page Language="VB" %>

<script runat="server">
    Protected Sub Page_Load(ByVal sender As Object, ByVal e As System.EventArgs)
        Dim ws As New localhost.HelloSoapHeader()
        Dim wsHeader As New localhost.HelloHeader()

        wsHeader.Username = "Bill Evjen"
        wsHeader.Password = "Bubbles"
        ws.HelloHeaderValue = wsHeader

        Label1.Text = ws.HelloWorld()
    End Sub
</script>

<html xmlns="http://www.w3.org/1999/xhtml" >
<head runat="server">
    <title>Working with SOAP headers</title>
</head>
<body>
    <form id="form1" runat="server">
    <div>
        <asp:Label ID="Label1" Runat="server"></asp:Label>
    </div>
    </form>
</body>
</html>
```

C#

```
<%@ Page Language="C#" %>

<script runat="server">
    protected void Page_Load(object sender, System.EventArgs e) {
        localhost.HelloSoapHeader ws = new localhost.HelloSoapHeader();
        localhost.HelloHeader wsHeader = new localhost.HelloHeader();
```

Continued

```
            wsHeader.Username = "Bill Evjen";
            wsHeader.Password = "Bubbles";
            ws.HelloHeaderValue = wsHeader;

            Label1.Text = ws.HelloWorld();
        }
    </script>
```

Two objects are instantiated. The first is the actual Web service, `HelloSoapHeader`. The second, which is instantiated as `wsHeader`, is the `SoapHeader` object. After both of these objects are instantiated and before making the SOAP request in the application, you construct the SOAP header. This is as easy as assigning values to the `Username` and `Password` properties of the `wsHeader` object. After these properties are assigned, you associate the `wsHeader` object to the `ws` object through the use of the `HelloHeaderValue` property. After you have made the association between the constructed SOAP header object and the actual `WebMethod` object (`ws`), you can make a SOAP request just as you would normally do:

```
Label1.Text = ws.HelloWorld()
```

Running the page produces the result in the browser shown in Figure 29-16.

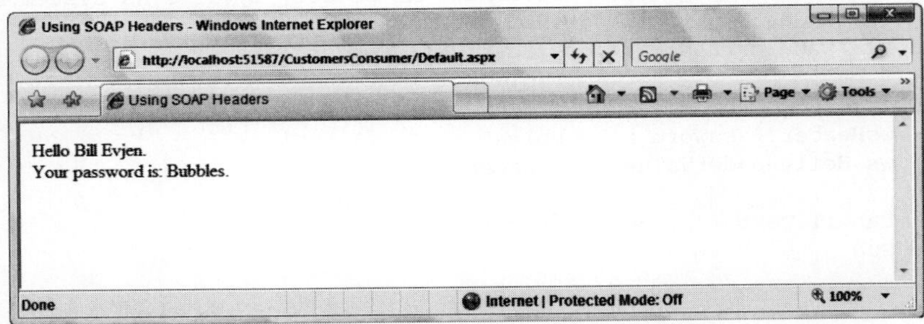

Figure 29-16

What is more interesting, however, is that the SOAP request reveals that the SOAP header was indeed constructed into the overall SOAP message, as shown in Listing 29-20.

Listing 29-20: The SOAP request

```
<?xml version="1.0" encoding="utf-8" ?>
<soap:Envelope xmlns:soap="http://schemas.xmlsoap.org/soap/envelope/"
 xmlns:xsi="http://www.w3.org/2001/XMLSchema-instance"
 xmlns:xsd="http://www.w3.org/2001/XMLSchema">
   <soap:Header>
      <HelloHeader xmlns="http://www.wrox.com/helloworld/">
         <Username>Bill Evjen</Username>
         <Password>Bubbles</Password>
      </HelloHeader>
   </soap:Header>
   <soap:Body>
      <HelloWorld xmlns="http://www.wrox.com/helloworld/" />
   </soap:Body>
</soap:Envelope>
```

This returns the SOAP response shown in Listing 29-21.

Listing 29-21: The SOAP response

```
<?xml version="1.0" encoding="utf-8" ?>
<soap:Envelope xmlns:soap="http://schemas.xmlsoap.org/soap/envelope/"
 xmlns:xsi="http://www.w3.org/2001/XMLSchema-instance"
 xmlns:xsd="http://www.w3.org/2001/XMLSchema">
   <soap:Body>
      <HelloWorldResponse xmlns="http://www.wrox.com/helloworld/">
         <HelloWorldResult>Hello Bill Evjen. Your password is:
          Bubbles</HelloWorldResult>
      </HelloWorldResponse>
   </soap:Body>
</soap:Envelope>
```

Requesting Web Services Using SOAP 1.2

Most Web services out there use SOAP version 1.1 for the construction of their messages. With that said, SOAP 1.2 became a W3C recommendation in June 2003 (see `www.w3.org/TR/soap12-part1/`). The nice thing about XML Web services in the .NET Framework platform is that they are capable of communicating in both the 1.1 and 1.2 versions of SOAP.

In an ASP.NET application that is consuming a Web service, you can control whether the SOAP request is constructed as a SOAP 1.1 message or a 1.2 message. Listing 29-22 changes the previous example so that the request uses SOAP 1.2 instead of the default setting of SOAP 1.1.

Listing 29-22: An ASP.NET application making a SOAP request using SOAP 1.2

VB

```
<%@ Page Language="VB" %>

<script runat="server">
    Protected Sub Page_Load(ByVal sender As Object, ByVal e As System.EventArgs)
        Dim ws As New localhost.HelloSoapHeader()
        Dim wsHeader As New localhost.HelloHeader()

        wsHeader.Username = "Bill Evjen"
        wsHeader.Password = "Bubbles"
        ws.HelloHeaderValue = wsHeader

        ws.SoapVersion = System.Web.Services.Protocols.SoapProtocolVersion.Soap12

        Label1.Text = ws.HelloWorld()
    End Sub
</script>
```

C#

```
<%@ Page Language="C#" %>

<script runat="server">
```

Continued

```
    protected void Page_Load(object sender, System.EventArgs e) {
        localhost.HelloSoapHeader ws = new localhost.HelloSoapHeader();
        localhost.HelloHeader wsHeader = new localhost.HelloHeader();

        wsHeader.Username = "Bill Evjen";
        wsHeader.Password = "Bubbles";
        ws.HelloHeaderValue = wsHeader;

        ws.SoapVersion = System.Web.Services.Protocols.SoapProtocolVersion.Soap12;

        Label1.Text = ws.HelloWorld();
    }
</script>
```

In this example, you first provide an instantiation of the Web service object and use the new `SoapVersion` property. The property takes a value of `System.Web.Services.Protocols.SoapProtocolVersion.Soap12` to work with SOAP 1.2 specifically.

With this bit of code in place, the SOAP request takes the structure shown in Listing 29-23.

Listing 29-23: The SOAP request using SOAP 1.2

```
<?xml version="1.0" encoding="utf-8"?>
<soap:Envelope xmlns:soap="http://www.w3.org/2003/05/soap-envelope"
 xmlns:xsi="http://www.w3.org/2001/XMLSchema-instance"
 xmlns:xsd="http://www.w3.org/2001/XMLSchema">
    <soap:Header>
        <HelloHeader xmlns="http://www.wrox.com/helloworld/">
            <Username>Bill Evjen</Username>
            <Password>Bubbles</Password>
        </HelloHeader>
    </soap:Header>
    <soap:Body>
        <HelloWorld xmlns="http://www.wrox.com/helloworld/" />
    </soap:Body>
</soap:Envelope>
```

One difference between the two examples is the `xmlns:soap` namespace that is used. The difference actually resides in the HTTP header. When you compare the SOAP 1.1 and 1.2 messages, you see a difference in the `Content-Type` attribute. In addition, the SOAP 1.2 HTTP header does not use the `soapaction` attribute because this is now combined with the `Content-Type` attribute.

You can turn off either SOAP 1.1 or 1.2 capabilities with the Web services that you build by making the proper settings in the `web.config` file, as shown in Listing 29-24.

Listing 29-24: Turning off SOAP 1.1 or 1.2 capabilities

```
<configuration xmlns="http://schemas.microsoft.com/.NetConfiguration/v2.0">
    <system.web>
        <webServices>
            <protocols>
                <remove name="HttpSoap"/> <!-- Removes SOAP 1.1 abilities -->
                <remove name="HttpSoap1.2"/> <!-- Removes SOAP 1.2 abilities -->
```

```
        </protocols>
      </webServices>
    </system.web>
</configuration>
```

Consuming Web Services Asynchronously

All the Web services that you have been working with in this chapter have been done *synchronously*. This means that after a request is sent from the code of an ASP.NET application, the application comes to a complete standstill until a SOAP response is received.

The process of invoking a `WebMethod` and getting back a result can take some time for certain requests. At times, you are not in control of the Web service from which you are requesting data and, therefore, you are not in control of the performance or response times of these services. For these reasons, you should consider consuming Web services *asynchronously*.

An ASP.NET application that makes an asynchronous request can work on other programming tasks while the initial SOAP request is awaiting a response. When the ASP.NET application is done working on the additional items, it can return to get the result from the Web service.

The great news is that to build an XML Web service that allows asynchronous communication, you don't have to perform any additional actions. All `.asmx` Web services have the built-in capability for asynchronous communication with consumers. The Web service in Listing 29-25 is an example.

Listing 29-25: A slow Web service

VB

```
Imports System.Web
Imports System.Web.Services
Imports System.Web.Services.Protocols

<WebServiceBinding(ConformsTo:=WsiProfiles.BasicProfile1_1,
  EmitConformanceClaims:=True)> _
Public Class Async
    Inherits System.Web.Services.WebService

    <WebMethod()> _
    Public Function HelloWorld() As String
        System.Threading.Thread.Sleep(1000)
        Return "Hello World"
    End Function

End Class
```

C#

```
using System;
using System.Web;
using System.Web.Services;
using System.Web.Services.Protocols;
```

Continued

```
[WebService(Namespace = "http://www.wrox.com/AsyncHelloWorld")]
[WebServiceBinding(ConformsTo = WsiProfiles.BasicProfile1_1)]
public class Async : System.Web.Services.WebService
{

    [WebMethod]
    public string HelloWorld() {
        System.Threading.Thread.Sleep(1000);
        return "Hello World";
    }

}
```

This Web service returns a simple `Hello World` as a string, but before it does, the Web service makes a 1000-millisecond pause. This is done by putting the Web service thread to sleep using the `Sleep` method.

Next, take a look at how an ASP.NET application can consume this slow Web service asynchronously, as illustrated in Listing 29-26.

Listing 29-26: An ASP.NET application consuming a Web service asynchronously

VB

```
<%@ Page Language="VB" %>

<script runat="server">
    Protected Sub Page_Load(ByVal sender As Object, ByVal e As System.EventArgs)
        Dim ws As New localhost.Async()
        Dim myIar As IAsyncResult

        myIar = ws.BeginHelloWorld(Nothing, Nothing)

        Dim x As Integer = 0

        Do Until myIar.IsCompleted = True
            x += 1
        Loop

        Label1.Text = "Result from Web service: " & ws.EndHelloWorld(myIar) & _
           "<br>Local count while waiting: " & x.ToString()
    End Sub
</script>

<html xmlns="http://www.w3.org/1999/xhtml" >
<head runat="server">
    <title>Async consumption</title>
</head>
<body>
    <form id="form1" runat="server">
    <div>
        <asp:Label ID="Label1" Runat="server"></asp:Label>
    </div>
    </form>
</body>
</html>
```

C#

```
<%@ Page Language="C#" %>

<script runat="server">
    protected void Page_Load(object sender, System.EventArgs e) {
        localhost.Async ws = new localhost.Async();
        IAsyncResult myIar;

        myIar = ws.BeginHelloWorld(null, null);

        int x = 0;

        while (myIar.IsCompleted == false) {
            x += 1;
        }

        Label1.Text = "Result from Web service: " + ws.EndHelloWorld(myIar) +
           "<br>Local count while waiting: " + x.ToString();
    }
</script>
```

When you make the Web reference to the remote Web service in the consuming ASP.NET application, you not only see the `HelloWorld` `WebMethod` available to you in IntelliSense, but you also see a `BeginHelloWorld` and an `EndHelloWorld`. To work with the Web service asynchronously, you must utilize the `BeginHelloWorld` and `EndHelloWorld` methods.

Use the `BeginHelloWorld` method to send a SOAP request to the Web service, but instead of the ASP.NET application waiting idly for a response, it moves on to accomplish other tasks. In this case, it is not doing anything that important — just counting the amount of time it is taking in a loop.

After the SOAP request is sent from the ASP.NET application, you can use the `IAsyncResult` object to check whether a SOAP response is waiting. This is done by using `myIar.IsCompleted`. If the asynchronous invocation is not complete, the ASP.NET application increases the value of `x` by one before making the same check again. The ASP.NET application continues to do this until the XML Web service is ready to return a response. The response is retrieved using the `EndHelloWorld` method call.

Results of running this application are similar to what is shown in Figure 29-17.

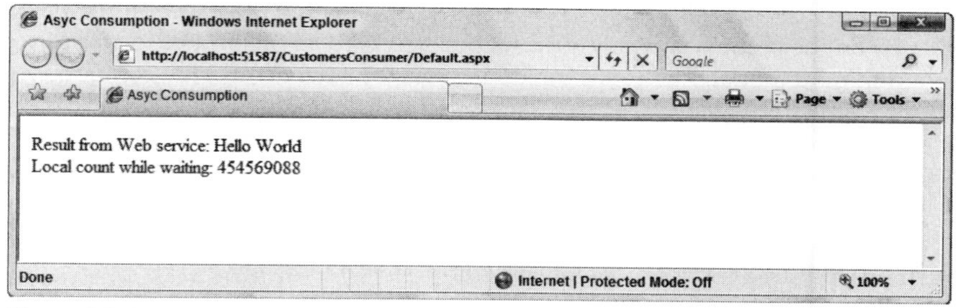

Figure 29-17

Windows Communication Foundation

Since the introduction of the .NET Framework 3.0, Microsoft has made available a new way to build Web services beyond the ASP.NET-based Web services presented in this chapter.

Until the .NET Framework 3.0 came out, it was not a simple task to build components that were required to communicate a message from one point to another because Microsoft offered more than one technology that you could use for such an action.

For instance, you could have used ASP.NET Web services (as just seen), Web Service Enhancements 3.0 (WSE), MSMQ, Enterprise Services, .NET Remoting, and even the `System.Messaging` namespace. Each technology has its own pros and cons. ASP.NET Web Services (also known as *ASMX Web Services*) provided the capability to easily build interoperable Web services. The WSE enabled you to easily build services that took advantage of some of the WS-* message protocols. MSMQ enabled the queuing of messages, making it easy to work with solutions that were only intermittently connected. Enterprise Services, provided as a successor to COM+, offered an easy means to build distributed applications. .NET Remoting was a fast way to move messages from one .NET application to another. Moreover, these are Microsoft options only. This does not include all the options available in other environments, such as the Java world.

With so many options available to a Microsoft developer, it can be tough to decide which path to take with the applications you are trying to build. With this in mind, Microsoft has created the Windows Communication Foundation (WCF).

WCF is a new framework for building service-oriented applications. Microsoft wanted to provide its developers with a framework to quickly get a proper service-oriented architecture up and running. Using the WCF, you will be able to take advantage of all the items that make distribution technologies powerful. WCF is the answer and the successor to all these other message distribution technologies.

The Larger Move to SOA

Upon examining WCF, you will find that it is part of a larger movement that organizations are making toward the much talked about *service-oriented architecture*, or *SOA*. An SOA is a message-based service architecture that is vendor agnostic. As a result, you have the capability to distribute messages across a system, and the messages are interoperable with other systems that would otherwise be considered incompatible with the provider system.

Looking back, you can see the gradual progression to the service-oriented architecture model. In the 1980s, the revolution arrived with the concept of everything being an object. When object-oriented programming came on the scene, it was enthusiastically accepted as the proper means to represent entities within a programming model. The 1990s took that one step further, and the component-oriented model was born. This enabled objects to be encapsulated in a tightly coupled manner. It was only recently that the industry turned to a service-oriented architecture because developers and architects needed to take components and have them distributed to other points in an organization, to their partners, or to their customers. This distribution system needed to have the means to transfer messages between machines that were generally incompatible with one another. In addition, the messages had to include the ability to express the metadata about how a system should handle a message.

If you ask 10 people what an SOA is, you'll probably get 11 different answers, but there are some common principles that are considered to be foundations of a service-oriented architecture:

- **Boundaries are explicit:** Any datastore, logic, or entity uses an interface to expose its data or capabilities. The interface provides the means to hide the behaviors within the service, and the interface front-end enables you to change this behavior as required without affecting downstream consumers.
- **Services are autonomous:** All the services are updated or versioned independently of one another. Thus, you do not upgrade a system in its entirety; instead, each component of these systems is an individual entity within itself and can move forward without waiting for other components to progress forward. Note that with this type of model, once you publish an interface, that interface must remain unchanged. Interface changes require new interfaces (versioned, of course).
- **Services are based upon contracts, schemas, and policies:** All services developed require a contract regarding what is required to consume items from the interface (usually done through a WSDL document). Along with a contract, schemas are required to define the items passed in as parameters or delivered through the service (using XSD schemas). Finally, policies define any capabilities or requirements of the service.
- **Service compatibility that is based upon policy:** The final principle enables services to define policies (decided at runtime) that are required to consume the service. These policies are usually expressed through WS-Policy.

If your own organization is considering establishing an SOA, the WCF is a framework that works on these principles and makes it relatively simple to implement. The next section looks at what the WCF offers. Then you can dive into building your first WCF service.

WCF Overview

As stated, the Windows Communication Foundation is a means to build distributed applications in a Microsoft environment. Although the distributed application is built upon that environment, this does not mean that consumers are required to be Microsoft clients or to take any Microsoft component or technology to accomplish the task of consumption. On the other hand, building WCF services means you are also building services that abide by the principles set forth in the aforementioned SOA discussion and that these services are vendor agnostic — thus, they are able to be consumed by almost anyone.

You can build WCF services using Visual Studio 2008. Note that because this is a .NET Framework 3.0 component, you are actually limited to the operating systems in which you can run a WCF service. Whereas the other Microsoft distribution technologies mentioned in this chapter do not have too many limitations on running on Microsoft operating systems, an application built with WCF can only run on Windows XP SP2, Windows Vista, or Windows Server 2008.

Building a WCF Service

Building a WCF service is not hard to accomplish. If you are working from a .NET Framework 2.0 environment, you need to install the .NET Framework 3.0. If you have installed the . NET Framework 3.5, then you will find that both the .NET Framework 2.0 and 3.0 have been installed also.

From there, it is easy to build WCF services directly in Visual Studio 2008 because it is already geared to work with this application type. If you are working with Visual Studio 2005, you need to install the Visual Studio 2005 extensions for .NET Framework 3.0 (WCF and WPF). Download these Visual Studio extensions, if you are using Visual Studio 2005. Installing the extensions into Visual Studio 2005 adds a WCF project to your IDE. If you are using Visual Studio 2008, the view of the project from the New Web Site dialog box is presented in Figure 29-18.

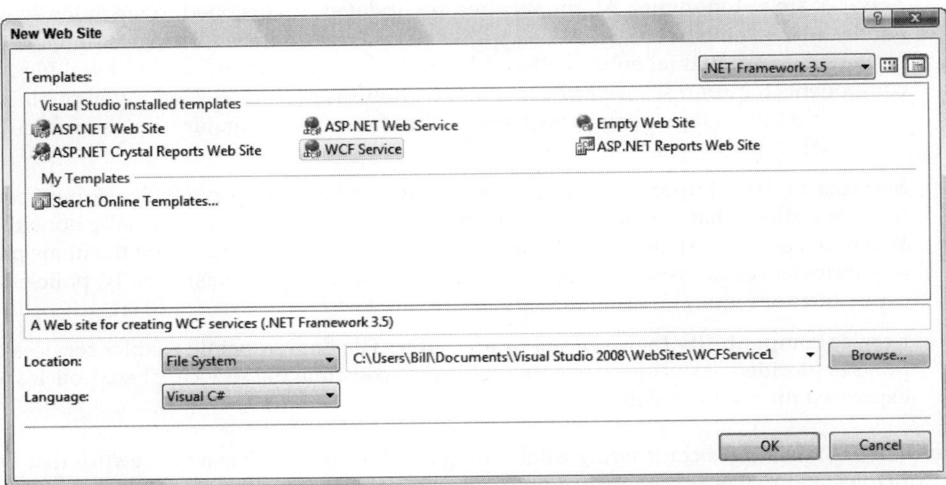

Figure 29-18

When you build a WCF project in this manner, the idea is that you build a traditional class library that is compiled down to a DLL that can then be added to another project. The separation of code and project is a powerful division on larger projects. That said, you can, however, just as easily build a WCF service directly in your .NET project, whether that is a console application or a Windows Forms application. The approach taken for the examples in this chapter show you how to build a WCF service that is hosted in a console application. Keep in mind that for the services you actually build and deploy, it is usually better to build them directly as a WCF Service Library project and use the created DLL in your projects or in IIS itself.

Before we jump into building a WCF service, first consider what makes up a service built upon the WCF framework.

What Makes a WCF Service

When looking at a WCF service, it is important to understand that it is made up of three parts: the service, one or more endpoints, and an environment in which to host the service.

A service is a class that is written in one of the .NET-compliant languages. The class can contain one or more methods that are exposed through the WCF service. A service can have one or more endpoints. An endpoint is used to communicate through the service to the client.

Endpoints themselves are also made up of three parts. These parts are usually defined by Microsoft as the ABC of WCF. Each letter of WCF means something in particular in the WCF model, including the following:

- "A" is for address
- "B" is for binding
- "C" is for contract

Basically, you can think of this as follows: "A" is the *where*, "B" is the *how*, and "C" is the *what*. Finally, a hosting environment is where the service is contained. This constitutes an application domain and process. All three of these elements (the service, the endpoints, and the hosting environment) are put together to create a WCF service offering, as depicted in Figure 29-19.

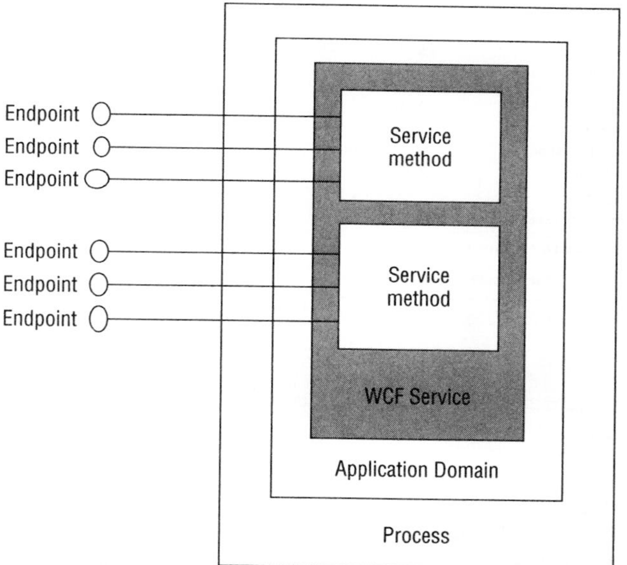

Figure 29-19

The next step is to create a basic service using the WCF framework.

Creating Your First WCF Service

To build your service, prior to hosting it, you must perform two main steps. First, you need to create a service contract. Second, you must create a data contract. The service contract is really a class with the methods that you want to expose from the WCF service. The data contract is a class that specifies the structure you want to expose from the interface.

Once you have a service class in place, you can host it almost anywhere. When running this from Visual Studio 2008, you will be able to use the same built-in hosting mechanisms that are used by any standard ASP.NET application. To build your first WCF application, select File ➪ New ➪ Web Site from the Visual Studio 2008 menu and call the project `WCFService1`.

The example this chapter will run through here demonstrates how to build the WCF service by building the interface, followed by the service itself.

Creating the service framework

The first step is to create the services framework in the project. To do this, right-click on the project and select Add New Item from the provided menu. From this dialog box, select WCF Service, and name the service Calculator.svc, as illustrated in Figure 29-20.

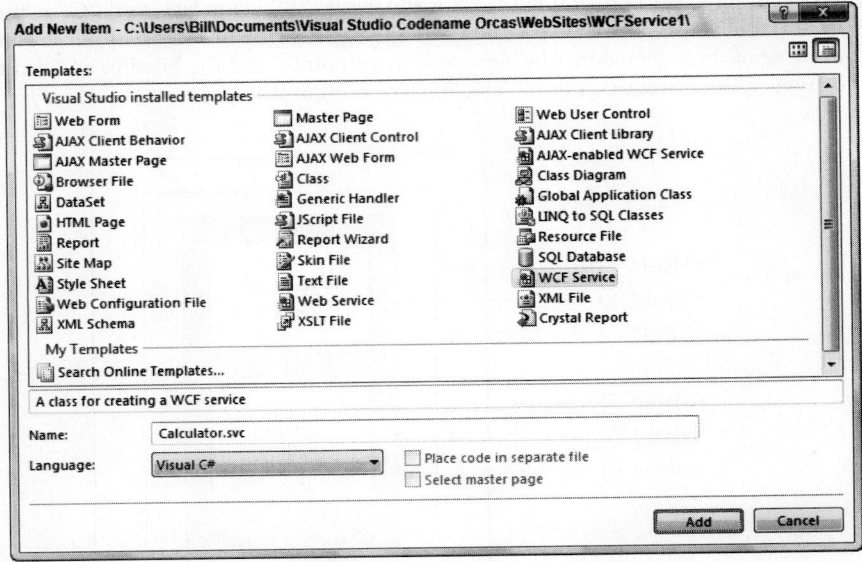

Figure 29-20

This step creates a `Calculator.svc` file, a `Calculator.cs` file, and an `ICalculator.cs` file. The `Calculator.svc` file is a simple file that includes only the page directive, whereas the `Calculator.cs` does all the heavy lifting. The `Calculator.cs` file is an implementation of the `ICalculator.cs` interface.

Working with the Interface

To create your service you need a service contract. The service contract is the interface of the service. This consists of all the methods exposed, as well as the input and output parameters that are required to invoke the methods. To accomplish this task, turn to the `ICalculator.vb` or `ICalculator.cs` (depending on the language you are using). The interface you need to create is presented in Listing 29-27.

Listing 29-27: Creating the interface

VB

```
Imports System
Imports System.ServiceModel

<ServiceContract()> _
```

```
Public Interface ICalculator
    <OperationContract()> _
    Function Add(ByVal a As Integer, ByVal b As Integer) As Integer

    <OperationContract()> _
    Function Subtract(ByVal a As Integer, ByVal b As Integer) As Integer

    <OperationContract()> _
    Function Multiply(ByVal a As Integer, ByVal b As Integer) As Integer

    <OperationContract()> _
    Function Divide(ByVal a As Integer, ByVal b As Integer) As Integer
End Interface
```

C#

```
using System.ServiceModel;

[ServiceContract]
public interface ICalculator
{
    [OperationContract]
    int Add(int a, int b);

    [OperationContract]
    int Subtract(int a, int b);

    [OperationContract]
    int Multiply(int a, int b);

    [OperationContract]
    int Divide(int a, int b);
}
```

This is pretty much the normal interface definition you would expect, but with a couple of new attributes included. To gain access to these required attributes, you need to make a reference to the `System.ServiceModel` namespace. This will give you access to the `<ServiceContract()>` and `<OperationContract()>` attributes.

The `<ServiceContract()>` attribute is used to define the class or interface as the service class, and it needs to precede the opening declaration of the class or interface. In this case, the example in the preceding code is based upon an interface:

```
<ServiceContract()> _
Public Interface ICalculator

   ' Code removed for clarity

End Interface
```

Within the interface, four methods are defined. Each method is going to be exposed through the WCF service as part of the service contract. For this reason, each method is required to have the `<OperationContract()>` attribute applied.

```
<OperationContract()> _
Function Add(ByVal a As Integer, ByVal b As Integer) As Integer
```

Utilizing the Interface

The next step is to create a class that implements the interface. Not only is the new class implementing the defined interface, but it is also implementing the service contract. For this example, add this class to the same `Calculator.vb` or `.cs` file. The following code, illustrated in Listing 29-28, shows the implementation of this interface.

Listing 29-28: Implementing the interface

VB

```
Public Class Calculator
    Implements ICalculator

    Public Function Add(ByVal a As Integer, ByVal b As Integer) As Integer _
       Implements ICalculator.Add

        Return (a + b)
    End Function

    Public Function Subtract(ByVal a As Integer, ByVal b As Integer) As Integer _
       Implements ICalculator.Subtract

        Return (a - b)
    End Function

    Public Function Multiply(ByVal a As Integer, ByVal b As Integer) As Integer _
       Implements ICalculator.Multiply

        Return (a * b)
    End Function

    Public Function Divide(ByVal a As Integer, ByVal b As Integer) As Integer _
       Implements ICalculator.Divide

        Return (a / b)
    End Function
End Class
```

C#

```
public class Calculator : ICalculator
{
    public int Add(int a, int b)
    {
        return (a + b);
    }

    public int Subtract(int a, int b)
    {
        return (a - b);
    }
```

```
        public int Multiply(int a, int b)
        {
            return (a * b);
        }

        public int Divide(int a, int b)
        {
            return (a / b);
        }
    }
```

From these new additions, you can see that you don't have to do anything different to the `Calculator` class. It is a simple class that implements the `ICalculator` interface and provides implementations of the `Add()`, `Subtract()`, `Multiply()`, and `Divide()` methods.

With the interface and the class available, you now have your WCF service built and ready to go. The next step is to get the service hosted. Note that this is a simple service — it exposes only simple types, rather than a complex type. This enables you to build only a service contract and not have to deal with the construction of a data contract. The construction of data contracts is presented later in this chapter.

Hosting the WCF Service in a Console Application

The next step is to take the service just developed and host it in some type of application process. You have many available hosting options, including the following:

- Console applications
- Windows Forms applications
- Windows Presentation Foundation applications
- Managed Windows Services
- Internet Information Services (IIS) 5.1
- Internet Information Services (IIS) 6.0
- Internet Information Services (IIS) 7.0 and the Windows Activation Service (WAS)

As stated earlier, this example hosts the service in the developer Web server provided by Visual Studio 2008. There are a couple of ways to activate hosting — either through the direct coding of the hosting behaviors or through declarative programming (usually done via the configuration file).

Compiling and running this application produces the results illustrated in Figure 29-21.

You will notice that this is quite similar to how it appears when you build an ASP.NET Web service.

Reviewing the WSDL Document

The page presented in Figure 29-21 was the information page about the service. In the image, notice that there is also a link to the WSDL file of the service. As with ASP.NET Web services, you find that a WCF service can also auto-generate the WSDL file. Clicking on the WSDL link shows the WSDL in the browser, as illustrated in Figure 29-22.

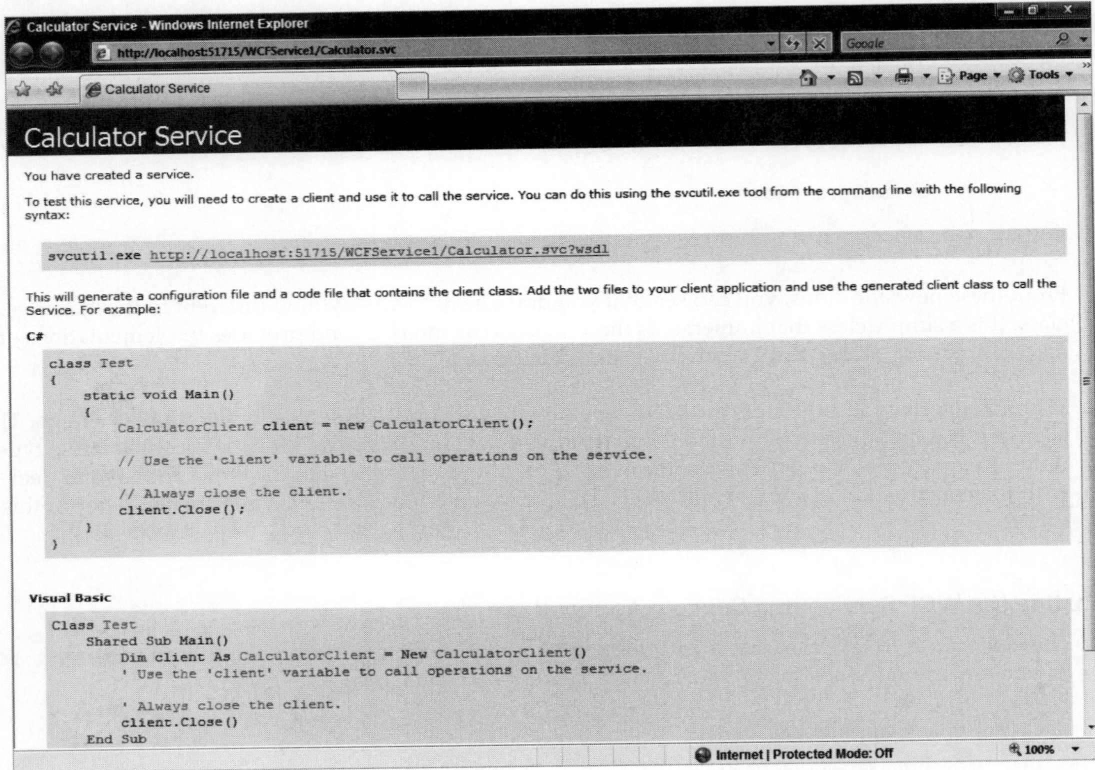

Figure 29-21

With this WSDL file, you can consume the service it defines through an HTTP binding. Note the following element at the bottom of the document, as shown in Listing 29-29.

Listing 29-29: The part of the WSDL file showing the service's endpoint

```
<wsdl:service name="Calculator">
   <wsdl:port name="WSHttpBinding_ICalculator"
    binding="tns:WSHttpBinding_ICalculator">
      <soap12:address
       location="http://localhost:51715/WCFService1/Calculator.svc" />
      <wsa10:EndpointReference>
         <wsa10:Address>http://localhost:51715/WCFService1/Calculator.svc
         </wsa10:Address>
         <Identity
         xmlns="http://schemas.xmlsoap.org/ws/2006/02/addressingidentity">
         <Upn>Lipper-STL-LAP\Bill</Upn>
         </Identity>
      </wsa10:EndpointReference>
   </wsdl:port>
</wsdl:service>
```

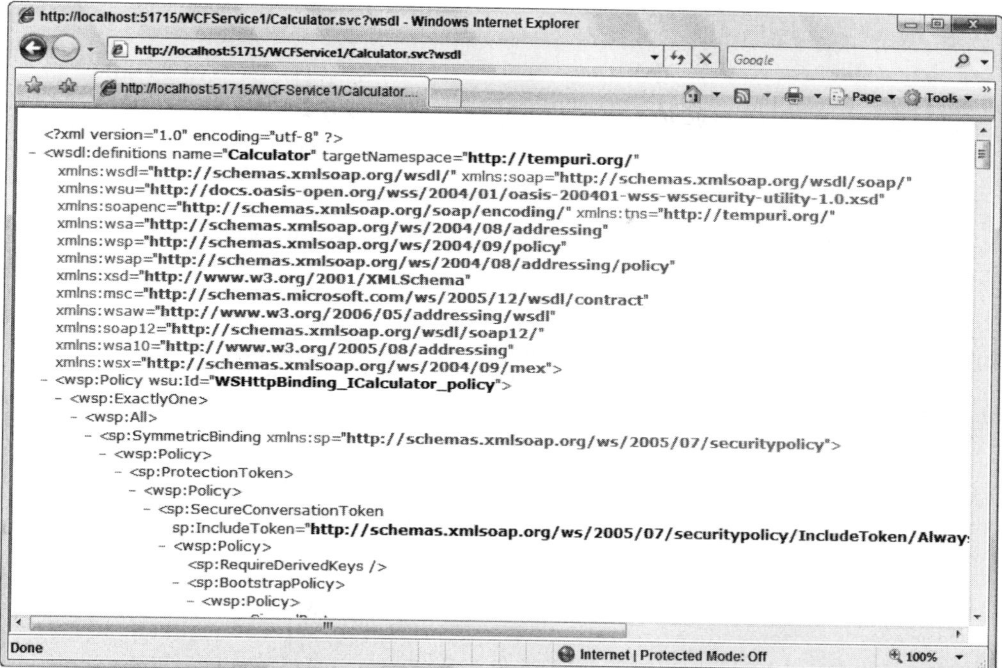

Figure 29-22

This element in the XML document indicates that in order to consume the service, the end user needs to use SOAP 1.2 over HTTP. This is presented through the use of the `<soap12:address>` element in the document. The `<wsa10:EndpointReference>` is a WS-Addressing endpoint definition.

Using this simple WSDL document, you can now build a consumer that makes use of this interface.

Building the WCF Consumer

Now that an HTTP service is out there, which you built using the WCF framework, the next step is to build a consumer application in ASP.NET that uses the simple `Calculator` service. The consumer sends its request via HTTP using SOAP. This section describes how to consume this service. The first step is to open Visual Studio 2008 and create a new ASP.NET application. Although we are using an ASP.NET application, you can make this consumer call through any other application type within .NET as well.

Call the new ASP.NET application `WCFConsumer`. This application consumes the `Calculator` service, so it should be laid out with two text boxes and a button to initiate the service call. For this example, we will only use the `Add()` method of the service.

Adding a Service Reference

Once you have laid out your ASP.NET page, make a reference to the new WCF service. You do this in a manner quite similar to how it is done with XML Web service references. Right-click on the solution name from the Solution Explorer in Visual Studio and select Add Service Reference from the dialog box. This capability to add a service reference is new to Visual Studio 2008 — previously, you had only the Add Reference and Add Web Reference options.

Once you have selected Add Service Reference, you are presented with the dialog box shown in Figure 29-23.

The Add Service Reference dialog box asks you for two things: the Service URI or Address (basically a pointer to the WSDL file) and the name you want to give to the reference. The name you provide the reference is the name that will be used for the instantiated object that enables you to interact with the service.

Referring to Figure 29-23, you can see that the name provided to the Service Address setting is what is used for the running service from earlier in this chapter. Press OK in the Add Service Reference dialog box. This adds to your project a Service References folder containing some proxy files, as shown in Figure 29-24.

Indeed, the Service References folder is added and two files are contained within this folder: `CalculatorService.map` and `CalculatorService.vb`. The other important addition to note is the `System.ServiceModel` reference, made for you in the References folder. This reference was not there before you made reference to the service through the Add Service Reference dialog.

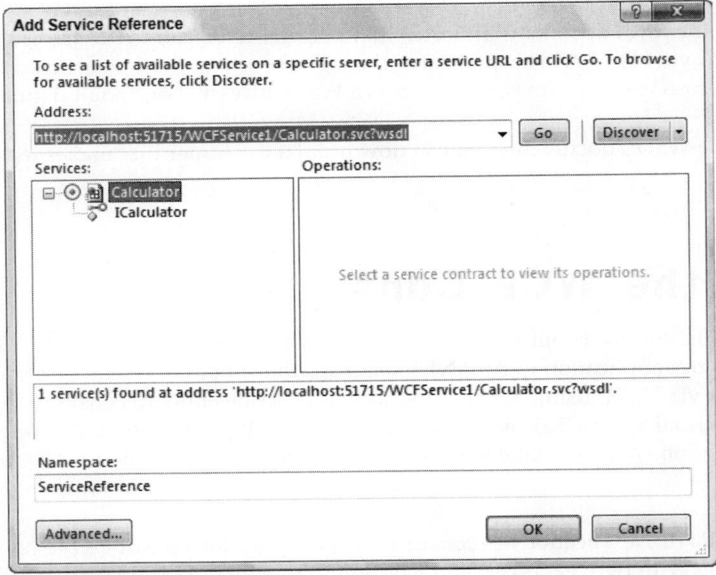

Figure 29-23

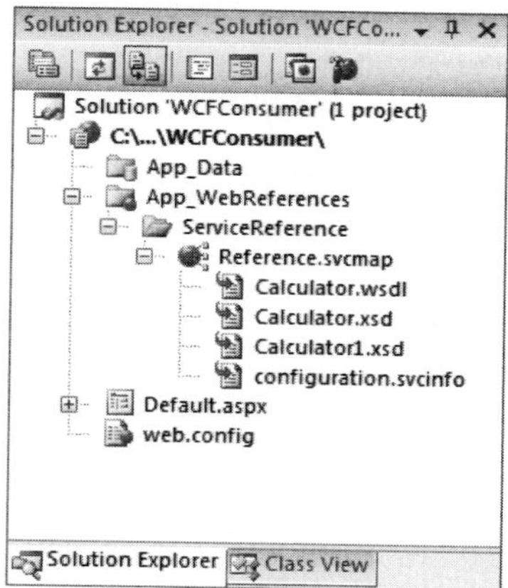

Figure 29-24

Configuration File Changes

Looking at the `web.config` file, you can see that Visual Studio has placed information about the service inside the document, as illustrated in Listing 29-30.

Listing 29-30: Additions made to the web.config file by Visual Studio

```
<system.serviceModel>
   <bindings>
      <wsHttpBinding>
         <binding name="WSHttpBinding_ICalculator" closeTimeout="00:01:00"
          openTimeout="00:01:00" receiveTimeout="00:10:00" sendTimeout="00:01:00"
          bypassProxyOnLocal="false" transactionFlow="false"
          hostNameComparisonMode="StrongWildcard" maxBufferPoolSize="524288"
          maxReceivedMessageSize="65536" messageEncoding="Text"
          textEncoding="utf-8" useDefaultWebProxy="true" allowCookies="false">
            <readerQuotas maxDepth="32" maxStringContentLength="8192"
             maxArrayLength="16384" maxBytesPerRead="4096"
             maxNameTableCharCount="16384"/>
            <reliableSession ordered="true" inactivityTimeout="00:10:00"
             enabled="false"/>
            <security mode="Message">
               <transport clientCredentialType="Windows" proxyCredentialType="None"
                realm=""/>
               <message clientCredentialType="Windows"
                negotiateServiceCredential="true" algorithmSuite="Default"
                establishSecurityContext="true"/>
            </security>
         </binding>
      </wsHttpBinding>
   </bindings>
   <client>
```

Continued

```
        <endpoint address="http://localhost:51715/WCFService1/Calculator.svc"
         binding="wsHttpBinding" bindingConfiguration="WSHttpBinding_ICalculator"
         contract="ServiceReference.ICalculator" name="WSHttpBinding_ICalculator">
           <identity>
              <userPrincipalName value="Lipper-STL-LAP\Bill"/>
           </identity>
        </endpoint>
     </client>
  </system.serviceModel></ServiceReference>
```

The important part of this configuration document is the `<client>` element. This element contains a child element called `<endpoint>` that defines the *where* and *how* of the service consumption process.

The `<endpoint>` element provides the address of the service — `http://localhost:51715/WCFService1/Calculator.svc` — and it specifies which binding of the available WCF bindings should be used. In this case, the `wsHttpBinding` is the required binding. Even though you are using an established binding from the WCF framework, from the client side you can customize how this binding behaves. The settings that define the behavior of the binding are specified using the `bindingConfiguration` attribute of the `<endpoint>` element. In this case, the value provided to the `bindingConfiguration` attribute is `WSHttpBinding_ICalculator`, which is a reference to the `<binding>` element contained within the `<wsHttpBinding>` element:

As demonstrated, the Visual Studio 2008 enhancements for WCF do make the consumption of these services fairly trivial. The next step is to code the consumption of the service interface to the GUI that was created as one of the first steps.

Writing the Consumption Code

The code to consume the interface is quite minimal. The end user places a number in each of the two text boxes provided and clicks the button to call the service to perform the designated operation on the provided numbers. Listing 29-31 is the code from the button click event.

Listing 29-31: The button click event to call the service

VB

```
Protected Sub Button1_Click(ByVal sender As Object, ByVal e As System.EventArgs)
  Handles Button1.Click

  Dim ws As New ServiceReference.CalculatorClient()
  Dim result As Integer

   result = ws.Add(TextBox1.Text, TextBox2.Text)
   Response.Write(result.ToString())

   ws.Close()
End Sub
```

C#

```
protected void Button1_Click(object sender, EventArgs e)
{
   ServiceReference.CalculatorClient ws = new ServiceReference.CalculatorClient();
```

```
        int result = ws.Add(int.Parse(TextBox1.Text), int.Parse(TextBox2.Text));
        Response.Write(result);

        ws.Close();
    }
```

This is quite similar to what is done when working with Web references from the XML Web services world. First is an instantiation of the proxy class, as shown with the creation of the `svc` object:

```
Dim ws As New ServiceReference.CalculatorClient()
```

Working with the `ws` object now, the IntelliSense options provide you with the appropriate `Add()`, `Subtract()`, `Multiply()`, and `Divide()` methods.

As before, the requests and responses are sent over HTTP as SOAP 1.2. This concludes the short tutorial demonstrating how to build your own WCF service using the HTTP protocol and consume this service directly into an ASP.NET application.

Working with Data Contracts

Thus far, when building the WCF services, the defined data contract has relied upon simple types or primitive datatypes. In the case of the earlier WCF service, a .NET type of `Integer` was exposed, which in turn was mapped to an XSD type of `int`. While you may not be able to see the input and output types defined in the WSDL document provided via the WCF-generated one, they are there. These types are actually exposed through an imported `.xsd` document (`Calculator.xsd` and `Calculator1.xsd`). This bit of the WSDL document is presented in Listing 29-32.

Listing 29-32: Imported types in the WSDL document

```
<wsdl:types>
   <xsd:schema targetNamespace="http://tempuri.org/Imports">
      <xsd:import
       schemaLocation="http://localhost:51715/WCFService1/Calculator.svc?xsd=xsd0"
       namespace="http://tempuri.org/" />
      <xsd:import
       schemaLocation="http://localhost:51715/WCFService1/Calculator.svc?xsd=xsd1"
       namespace="http://schemas.microsoft.com/2003/10/Serialization/" />
   </xsd:schema>
</wsdl:types>
```

Typing in the XSD location of `http://localhost:51715/WCFService1/Calculator.svc?xsd=xsd0` gives you the input and output parameters of the service. For instance, looking at the definition of the `Add()` method, you will see the following bit of code, as shown in Listing 29-33.

Listing 29-33: Defining the required types in the XSD

```
<xs:element name="Add">
  <xs:complexType>
    <xs:sequence>
      <xs:element minOccurs="0" name="a" type="xs:int" />
```

Continued

```
        <xs:element minOccurs="0" name="b" type="xs:int" />
      </xs:sequence>
    </xs:complexType>
  </xs:element>
  <xs:element name="AddResponse">
    <xs:complexType>
      <xs:sequence>
        <xs:element minOccurs="0" name="AddResult" type="xs:int" />
      </xs:sequence>
    </xs:complexType>
  </xs:element>
```

This bit of XML code indicates that there are two required input parameters (a and b) that are of type int; in return, the consumer gets an element called <AddResult>, which contains a value of type int.

As a builder of this WCF service, you did not have to build the data contract because this service used simple types. When using complex types, you have to create a data contract in addition to your service contract.

Building a Service with a Data Contract

For an example of working with data contracts, create a new WCF service (another WCF service project) called WCF_WithDataContract. In this case, you still need an interface that defines your service contract, and then another class that implements that interface. In addition to these items, you also need another class that defines the data contract.

As with the service contract, which makes use of the <ServiceContract()> and the <Operation-Contract()> attributes, the data contract uses the <DataContract()> and <DataMember()> attributes. To gain access to these attributes, you have to make a reference to the System.Runtime.Serialization namespace in your project and import this namespace into the file.

The custom type in this case is a Customer type, as presented in Listing 29-34.

Listing 29-34: Building the Customer type

VB

```
Imports System
Imports System.ServiceModel
Imports System.Runtime.Serialization

<DataContract()> _
Public Class Customer
    <DataMember()> _
    Public FirstName As String

    <DataMember()> _
    Public LastName As String
End Class

<ServiceContract()> _
Public Interface IHelloCustomer
```

```
    <OperationContract()> _
    Function HelloFirstName(ByVal cust As Customer) As String

    <OperationContract()> _
    Function HelloFullName(ByVal cust As Customer) As String
End Interface
```

C#

```
using System.Runtime.Serialization;
using System.ServiceModel;

[DataContract]
public class Customer
{
    [DataMember]
    public string Firstname;

    [DataMember]
    public string Lastname;
}

[ServiceContract] IHelloCustomer
public interface IWithContract
{
    [OperationContract]
    string HelloFirstName(Customer cust);

    [OperationContract]
    string HelloFullName(Customer cust);
}
```

Here, you can see that the `System.Runtime.Serialization` namespace is also imported, and the first class in the file is the data contract of the service. This class, the `Customer` class, has two members: `FirstName` and `LastName`. Both of these properties are of type `String`. You specify a class as a data contract through the use of the `<DataContract()>` attribute:

```
<DataContract()> _
Public Class Customer

    ' Code removed for clarity

End Class
```

Now, any of the properties contained in the class are also part of the data contract through the use of the `<DataMember()>` attribute:

```
<DataContract()> _
Public Class Customer
    <DataMember()> _
    Public FirstName As String

    <DataMember()> _
    Public LastName As String
End Class
```

Finally, the `Customer` object is used in the interface, as well as the class that implements the `IHelloCustomer` interface, as shown in Listing 29-35.

Listing 29-35: Implementing the interface

VB

```
Public Class HelloCustomer
    Implements IHelloCustomer

    Public Function HelloFirstName(ByVal cust As Customer) As String _
      Implements IHelloCustomer.HelloFirstName
        Return "Hello " & cust.FirstName
    End Function

    Public Function HelloFullName(ByVal cust As Customer) As String _
      Implements IHelloCustomer.HelloFullName
        Return "Hello " & cust.FirstName & " " & cust.LastName
    End Function
End Class
```

C#

```
public class HelloCustomer: IHelloCustomer
{
    public string HelloFirstName(Customer cust)
    {
        return "Hello " + cust.Firstname;
    }

    public string HelloFullName(Customer cust)
    {
        return "Hello " + cust.Firstname + " " + cust.Lastname;
    }
}
```

Building the Consumer

Now that the service is running and in place, the next step is to build the consumer. To begin, build a new ASP.NET application from Visual Studio 2008 and call the project `HelloWorldConsumer`. Again, right-click on the solution and select Add Service Reference from the options provided in the menu.

From the Add Service Reference dialog box, add the location of the WSDL file for the service and press OK. This adds the changes to the references and the `web.config` file just as before, enabling you to consume the service. The following code, as presented in Listing 29-36, shows what is required to consume the service if you are using a Button control to initiate the call.

Listing 29-36: Consuming a custom type through a WCF service

VB

```
Protected Sub Button1_Click(ByVal sender As Object, ByVal e As System.EventArgs)
  Handles Button1.Click

    Dim ws As New ServiceReference.HelloCustomerClient()
    Dim myCustomer As New ServiceReference.Customer()
```

```
        myCustomer.Firstname = "Bill"
        myCustomer.Lastname = "Evjen"

        Response.Write(ws.HelloFullName(myCustomer))

        ws.Close()
    End Sub
```

C#

```
protected void Button1_Click(object sender, EventArgs e)
{
    ServiceReference.HelloCustomerClient ws = new
        ServiceReference.HelloCustomerClient();
    ServiceReference.Customer myCustomer = new ServiceReference.Customer();

    myCustomer.Firstname = "Bill";
    myCustomer.Lastname = "Evjen";

    Response.Write(ws.HelloFullName(myCustomer));

    ws.Close();
}
```

As a consumer, once you make the reference, you will notice that the service reference provides both a `HelloCustomerClient` object andthe `Customer` object, which was defined through the service's data contract.

Therefore, the preceding code block just instantiates both of these objects and builds the `Customer` object before it is passed into the `HelloFullName()` method provided by the service.

Looking at WSDL and the Schema for HelloCustomerService

When you make a reference to the `HelloCustomer` service, you will find the following XSD imports in the WSDL:

```
<wsdl:types>
   <xsd:schema targetNamespace="http://tempuri.org/Imports">
    <xsd:import
     schemaLocation="http://localhost:51715/WCFService1/HelloCustomer.svc?xsd=xsd0"
     namespace="http://tempuri.org/" />
    <xsd:import
     schemaLocation="http://localhost:51715/WCFService1/HelloCustomer.svc?xsd=xsd1"
     namespace="http://schemas.microsoft.com/2003/10/Serialization/" />
    <xsd:import
     schemaLocation="http://localhost:51715/WCFService1/HelloCustomer.svc?xsd=xsd2"
     namespace="http://schemas.datacontract.org/2004/07/" />
   </xsd:schema>
</wsdl:types>
```

`http://localhost:51715/WCFService1/HelloCustomer.svc?xsd=xsd2` provides the details on your `Customer` object. The code from this file is shown here:

```
<?xml version="1.0" encoding="utf-8" ?>
<xs:schema elementFormDefault="qualified"
```

```
    targetNamespace="http://schemas.datacontract.org/2004/07/"
    xmlns:xs="http://www.w3.org/2001/XMLSchema"
    xmlns:tns="http://schemas.datacontract.org/2004/07/">
      <xs:complexType name="Customer">
         <xs:sequence>
            <xs:element minOccurs="0" name="Firstname" nillable="true"
             type="xs:string" />
            <xs:element minOccurs="0" name="Lastname" nillable="true"
             type="xs:string" />
         </xs:sequence>
      </xs:complexType>
      <xs:element name="Customer" nillable="true" type="tns:Customer" />
   </xs:schema>
```

This is an XSD description of the `Customer` object. Making a reference to the WSDL includes the XSD description of the `Customer` object and gives you the ability to create local instances of this object.

Using this model, you can easily build your services with your own defined types.

Namespaces

Note that the services built in the chapter have no defined namespaces. If you looked at the WSDL files that were produced, you would see that the namespace provided is `http://tempuri.org`. Obviously, you do not want to go live with this default namespace. Instead, you need to define your own namespace.

To accomplish this task, the interface's `<ServiceContract()>` attribute enables you to set the namespace, as shown here:

```
<ServiceContract(Namespace:="http://www.lipperweb.com/ns/")> _
Public Interface IHelloCustomer
    <OperationContract()> _
    Function HelloFirstName(ByVal cust As Customer) As String

    <OperationContract()> _
    Function HelloFullName(ByVal cust As Customer) As String
End Interface
```

Here, the `<ServiceContract()>` attribute uses the `Namespace` property to provide a namespace.

Summary

This chapter was a whirlwind tour of XML Web services in the .NET platform. It is definitely a topic that merits an entire book of its own. The chapter showed you the power of exposing your data and logic as SOAP and also how to consume these SOAP messages directly in the ASP.NET applications you build.

In addition to pointing out the power you have for building and consuming basic Web services, the chapter spent some time helping you understand caching, performance, the use of SOAP headers, and more. A lot of power is built into this model; every day the Web services model is starting to make stronger inroads into various enterprise organizations. It is becoming more likely that to get at some data or logic you need for your application, you will employ the tactics presented here.

This chapter also looked at one of the newest capabilities provided to the .NET Framework world. The .NET Framework 3.5 and WCF are a great combination for building advanced services that take ASP.NET Web services, .NET Remoting, Enterprise Services, and MSMQ to the next level.

While not exhaustive, this chapter broadly outlined the basics of the framework. As you start to dig deeper in the technology, you will find capabilities that are strong and extensible.

30

Localization

Developers usually build Web applications in their native language and then, as the audience for the application expands, they realize the need to globalize the application. Of course, the ideal is to build the Web application to handle an international audience right from the start — but, in many cases, this may not be possible because of the extra work it requires.

It is good to note that with the ASP.NET 3.5 framework, a considerable effort has been made to address the internationalization of Web applications. You quickly realize that changes to the API, the addition of capabilities to the server controls, and even Visual Studio itself equip you to do the extra work required more easily to bring your application to an international audience. This chapter looks at some of the important items to consider when building your Web applications for the world.

Cultures and Regions

The ASP.NET page that is pulled up in an end user's browser runs under a specific culture and region setting. When building an ASP.NET application or page, the defined culture in which it runs is dependent upon both a culture and region setting coming from the server in which the application is run or from a setting applied by the client (the end user). By default, ASP.NET runs under a culture setting defined by the server.

The world is made up of a multitude of cultures, each of which has a language and a set of defined ways in which it views and consumes numbers, uses currencies, sorts alphabetically, and so on. The .NET Framework defines cultures and regions using the *Request for Comments 1766* standard definition (tags for identification of languages) that specifies a language and region using two-letter codes separated by a dash. The following table provides examples of some culture definitions.

Culture Code	Description
en-US	English language; United States
en-GB	English language; United Kingdom (Great Britain)
en-AU	English language; Australia
en-CA	English language; Canada

Looking at the examples in this table, you can see that four distinct cultures are defined. These four cultures have some similarities and some differences. All four cultures speak the same language (English). For this reason, the language code of `en` is used in each culture setting. After the language setting comes the region setting. Even though these cultures speak the same language, it is important to distinguish them further by setting their region (such as `US` for the United States, `GB` for the United Kingdom, `AU` for Australia, and `CA` for Canada). As you are probably well aware, the English language in the United States is slightly different from the English language that is used in the United Kingdom, and so forth. Beyond language, differences exist in how dates and numerical values are represented. This is why a culture's language and region are presented together.

The differences do not break down by the country only. Many times, countries contain more than a single language and each area has its own preference for notation of dates and other items. For example, `en-CA` specifies English speakers in Canada. Because Canada is not only an English-speaking country, it also includes the culture setting of `fr-CA` for French-speaking Canadians.

Understanding Culture Types

The culture definition you have just seen is called a *specific culture* definition. This definition is as detailed as you can possibly get — defining both the language and the region. The other type of culture definition is a *neutral culture* definition. Each specific culture has a specified neutral culture that it is associated with. For instance, the English language cultures shown in the previous table are separate, but they also all belong to one neutral culture EN (English). The diagram presented in Figure 30-1 displays how these culture types relate to one another.

From this diagram, you can see that many specific cultures belong to a neutral culture. Higher in the hierarchy than the neutral culture is an *invariant culture,* which is an agnostic culture setting that should be utilized when passing items (such as dates and numbers) around a network. When performing these kinds of operations, make your back-end data flows devoid of user-specific culture settings. Instead, apply these settings in the business and presentation layers of your applications.

Also, pay attention to the neutral culture when working with your applications. Invariably, you are going to build applications with views that are more dependent on a neutral culture rather than on a specific culture. For instance, if you have a Spanish version of your application, you probably make this version available to all Spanish speakers regardless of their regions. In many applications, it will not matter if the Spanish speaker is from Spain, Mexico, or Argentina. In a case where it does make a difference, use the specific culture settings.

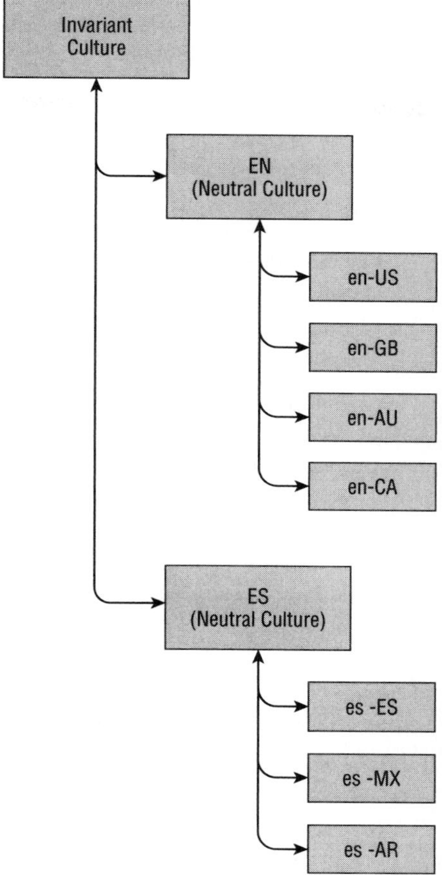

Figure 30-1

The ASP.NET Threads

When the end user requests an ASP.NET page, this Web page is executed on a thread from the thread pool. The thread has a culture associated with it. You can get information about the culture of the thread programmatically and then check for particular details about that culture. This is illustrated in Listing 30-1.

Listing 30-1: Checking the culture of the ASP.NET thread

VB

```
Protected Sub Page_Load(ByVal sender As Object, ByVal e As System.EventArgs)
   Dim ci As CultureInfo = System.Threading.Thread.CurrentThread.CurrentCulture
   Response.Write("<b><u>CURRENT CULTURE'S INFO</u></b>")
   Response.Write("<p><b>Culture's Name:</b> " & ci.Name.ToString() & "<br>")
```

Continued

```
    Response.Write("<b>Culture's Parent Name:</b> " & ci.Parent.Name.ToString() & _
       "<br>")
    Response.Write("<b>Culture's Display Name:</b> " & ci.DisplayName.ToString() & _
       "<br>")
    Response.Write("<b>Culture's English Name:</b> " & ci.EnglishName.ToString() & _
       "<br>")
    Response.Write("<b>Culture's Native Name:</b> " & ci.NativeName.ToString() & _
       "<br>")
    Response.Write("<b>Culture's Three Letter ISO Name:</b> " & _
       ci.Parent.ThreeLetterISOLanguageName.ToString() & "<br>")
    Response.Write("<b>Calendar Type:</b> " & ci.Calendar.ToString() & "</p >")
End Sub
```

C#

```
protected void Page_Load(object sender, EventArgs e)
{
    CultureInfo ci = System.Threading.Thread.CurrentThread.CurrentCulture;
    Response.Write("<b><u>CURRENT CULTURE'S INFO</u></b>");
    Response.Write("<p><b>Culture's Name:</b> " + ci.Name.ToString() + "<br>");
    Response.Write("<b>Culture's Parent Name:</b> " + ci.Parent.Name.ToString() +
       "<br>");
    Response.Write("<b>Culture's Display Name:</b> " + ci.DisplayName.ToString() +
       "<br>");
    Response.Write("<b>Culture's English Name:</b> " + ci.EnglishName.ToString() +
       "<br>");
    Response.Write("<b>Culture's Native Name:</b> " + ci.NativeName.ToString() +
       "<br>");
    Response.Write("<b>Culture's Three Letter ISO Name:</b> " +
       ci.Parent.ThreeLetterISOLanguageName.ToString() + "<br>");
    Response.Write("<b>Calendar Type:</b> " + ci.Calendar.ToString() + "</p >");
}
```

This bit of code in the `Page_Load` event checks the `CurrentCulture` property. You can place the result of this value in a `CultureInfo` object. To get at this object, you import the `System.Globalization` namespace into your Web page. The `CultureInfo` object contains a number of properties that provides you with specific culture information. The following items, which are displayed in a series of simple `Response.Write` statements, are only a small sampling of what is actually available. Running this page produces results similar to what is shown in Figure 30-2.

From this figure, you can see that the en-US culture is the default setting in which the ASP.NET thread executes. In addition to this, you can use the `CultureInfo` object to get at a lot of other descriptive information about the culture.

You can always change a thread's culture on the overloads provided via a new instantiation of the `CultureInfo` object. This is presented in Listing 30-2.

Listing 30-2: Changing the culture of the thread using the CultureInfo object

VB

```
Protected Sub Page_Load(ByVal sender As Object, ByVal e As System.EventArgs)
    System.Threading.Thread.CurrentThread.CurrentCulture = New CultureInfo("th-TH")
```

```
    Dim ci As CultureInfo = System.Threading.Thread.CurrentThread.CurrentCulture
    Response.Write("<b><u>CURRENT CULTURE'S INFO</u></b>")
    Response.Write("<p><b>Culture's Name:</b> " & ci.Name.ToString() & "<br>")
    Response.Write("<b>Culture's Parent Name:</b> " & ci.Parent.Name.ToString() & _
       "<br>")
    Response.Write("<b>Culture's Display Name:</b> " & ci.DisplayName.ToString() & _
       "<br>")
    Response.Write("<b>Culture's English Name:</b> " & ci.EnglishName.ToString() & _
       "<br>")
    Response.Write("<b>Culture's Native Name:</b> " & ci.NativeName.ToString() & _
       "<br>")
    Response.Write("<b>Culture's Three Letter ISO Name:</b> " & _
       ci.Parent.ThreeLetterISOLanguageName.ToString() & "<br>")
    Response.Write("<b>Calendar Type:</b> " & ci.Calendar.ToString() & "</p >")
End Sub
```

C#

```
protected void Page_Load(object sender, EventArgs e)
{
    System.Threading.Thread.CurrentThread.CurrentCulture = new CultureInfo("th-TH");
    CultureInfo ci = System.Threading.Thread.CurrentThread.CurrentCulture;
    Response.Write("<b><u>CURRENT CULTURE'S INFO</u></b>");
    Response.Write("<p><b>Culture's Name:</b> " + ci.Name.ToString() + "<br>");
    Response.Write("<b>Culture's Parent Name:</b> " + ci.Parent.Name.ToString() +
       "<br>");
    Response.Write("<b>Culture's Display Name:</b> " + ci.DisplayName.ToString() +
       "<br>");
    Response.Write("<b>Culture's English Name:</b> " + ci.EnglishName.ToString() +
       "<br>");
    Response.Write("<b>Culture's Native Name:</b> " + ci.NativeName.ToString() +
       "<br>");
    Response.Write("<b>Culture's Three Letter ISO Name:</b> " +
       ci.Parent.ThreeLetterISOLanguageName.ToString() + "<br>");
    Response.Write("<b>Calendar Type:</b> " + ci.Calendar.ToString() + "</p>");
}
```

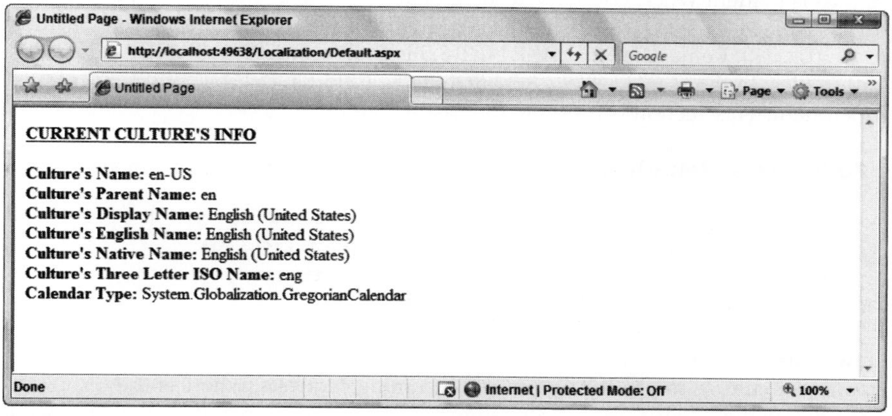

Figure 30-2

In this example, only a single line of code is added to assign a new instance of the `CultureInfo` object to the `CurrentCulture` property of the thread being executed by ASP.NET. The culture setting enables the `CultureInfo` object to define the culture you want to utilize. In this case, the Thai language of Thailand is assigned, and the results produced in the browser are illustrated in Figure 30-3.

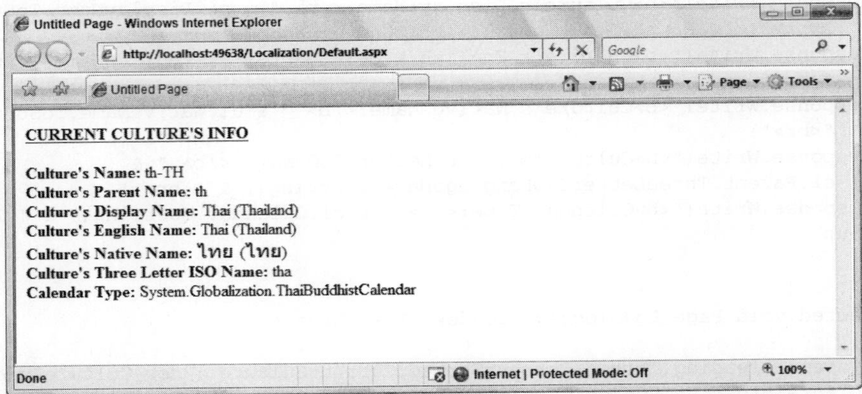

Figure 30-3

From this figure, you can see that the .NET Framework goes so far as to provide the native name of the language used even if it is not a Latin-based letter style. In this case, the results are presented for the Thai language in Thailand, and some of the properties that are associated with this culture (such as an entirely different calendar than is the one used in Western Europe and the United States). Remember that you reference `System.Globalization` to get at the `CultureInfo` object.

Server-Side Culture Declarations

ASP.NET enables you to easily define the culture that is used either by your entire ASP.NET application or by a specific page within your application. You can specify the culture for any of your ASP.NET applications by means of the appropriate configuration files. In the default install of ASP.NET, no culture is specified as is evident when you look at the global `web.config.comments` file (meant for documentation purposes) found in the ASP.NET 2.0 CONFIG folder (`C:\WINDOWS\Microsoft.NET\Framework\v2.0.50727\CONFIG`). Remember that ASP.NET 3.5 is built on top of ASP.NET 2.0 and uses the same configuration files. In the `web.config.comments` file, you find a `<globalization>` section of the configuration document. This section is presented in Listing 30-3.

Listing 30-3: The <globalization> section in the web.config.comments file

```
<globalization requestEncoding="utf-8" responseEncoding="utf-8" fileEncoding=""
  culture="" uiCulture="" enableClientBasedCulture="false"
  responseHeaderEncoding="utf-8" resourceProviderFactoryType=""
  enableBestFitResponseEncoding="false" />
```

Note the two attributes represented in bold — `culture` and `uiCulture`. The `culture` attribute enables you to define the culture to use for processing incoming requests, whereas the `uiCulture` attribute enables you define the default culture needed to process any resource files in the application. (The use of these attributes will be covered later in the chapter.)

As you look at the configuration declaration in Listing 30-3, you can see that nothing is specified for the culture settings. One option you have when specifying a culture on the server is to define this culture in the server version of the `web.config` file found in the CONFIG folder. This causes every ASP.NET 3.5 application on this server to adopt this particular culture setting. The other option is to specify these settings in the `web.config` file of the application as illustrated in Listing 30-4.

Listing 30-4: Defining the <globalization> section in the web.config file

```
<configuration>
   <system.web>

      <globalization culture="ru-RU" uiCulture="ru-RU" />

   </system.web>
</configuration>
```

In this case, the culture established for just this ASP.NET application is the Russian language in the country of Russia. In addition to setting the culture at either the server-wide the application-wide level, another option is to set the culture at the page-level. This is illustrated in Listing 30-5.

Listing 30-5: Defining the culture at the page level @page using the directive

```
<%@ Page Language="VB" UICulture="ru-RU" Culture="ru-RU" %>
```

This example determines that the Russian language and culture settings are used for everything on the page. You can see this in action by using this `@Page` directive and a simple calendar control on the page. Figure 30-4 shows the output.

<			Август 2008 г.			>
Пн	Вт	Ср	Чт	Пт	Сб	Вс
28	29	30	31	1	2	3
4	5	6	7	8	9	10
11	12	13	14	15	16	17
18	19	20	21	22	23	24
25	26	27	28	29	30	31
1	2	3	4	5	6	7

Figure 30-4

Client-Side Culture Declarations

In addition to using server-side setting to define the culture for your ASP.NET pages, you also have the option of defining the culture with what the client has set as his preference in a browser instance.

When end users install Microsoft's Internet Explorer and some of the other browsers, they have the option to select their preferred cultures in a particular order (if they have selected more than a single culture preference). To see this in action in IE, select Tools ➪ Internet Options from the IE menu. On the first tab provided (General), you see a Languages button at the bottom of the dialog. Select this button and you are provided with the Language Preference dialog shown in Figure 30-5.

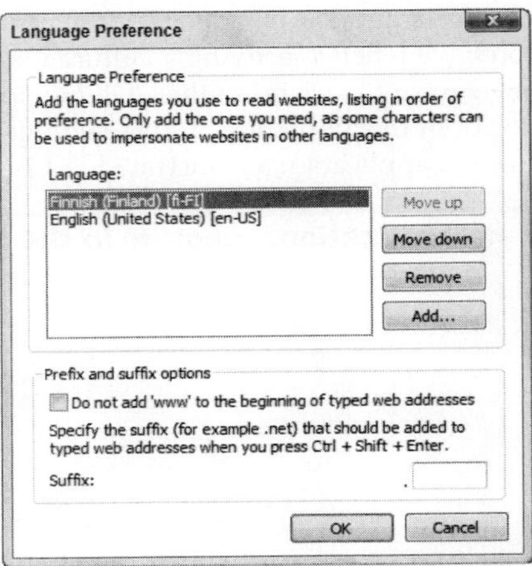

Figure 30-5

In this figure, you can see that two cultures are selected from the list of available cultures. To add any additional cultures to the list, select the Add button from the dialog and select the appropriate culture from the list. After you have selected cultures that are present in the list, you can select the order in which you prefer to use them. In the case of Figure 30-5, the Finnish culture is established as the most preferred culture, whereas the U.S. version of English is selected as the second preference. A user with this setting gets the Finnish language version of the application before anything else; if a Finnish version is not available, a U.S. English version is presented.

After the end user selects, you can use the auto feature provided in ASP.NET 3.5. Instead of specifying a distinct culture in any of the configuration files or from the `@Page` directive, you can also state that ASP.NET should automatically select the culture provided by the end user requesting the page. This is done using the `auto` keyword, as illustrated in Listing 30-6.

Listing 30-6: Changing the culture to the end user's selection

```
<%@ Page Language="VB" UICulture="auto" Culture="auto" %>
```

With this construction in your page, the dates, calendars, and numbers now appear in the preferred culture of the requestor. What happens, however, if you have translated resources in resource files (shown later in the chapter) that depend on a culture specification? What if you only have specific translations and so cannot handle every possible culture that might be returned to your ASP.NET page? In this case, you can specify the auto option with an additional fallback option if ASP.NET cannot find the culture settings of the user (such as culture-specific resource files). This usage is illustrated in Listing 30-7.

Listing 30-7: Providing a fallback culture from the auto option

```
<%@ Page Language="VB" UICulture="auto:en-US" Culture="auto:en-US" %>
```

In this case, the automatic detection is utilized, but if the culture the end user prefers is not present, then en-US is used.

Translating Values and Behaviors

In the process of globalizing your ASP.NET application, you may notice a number of items that are done differently than building an application that is devoid of globalization, including how dates are represented and currencies are shown. This next section touches upon some of these topics.

Understanding Differences in Dates

Different cultures specify dates and time very differently. For instance, take the following date as an example:

```
08/11/2008
```

What is this date exactly? Is it August 11, 2008 or is it November 8, 2008? I repeat: When storing values such as date/time stamps in a database or other some type of back-end system, you should always use the same culture (or invariant culture) for these items so that you avoid any mistakes. It should be the job of the business logic layer or the presentation layer to convert these items for use by the end user.

Setting the culture at the server-level or in the `@Page` directive (as was discussed earlier) enables ASP.NET to make these conversions for you. You can also simply assign a new culture to the thread in which ASP.NET is running. For instance, look at the code listing presented in Listing 30-8.

Listing 30-8: Working with date/time values in different cultures

VB

```
Protected Sub Page_Load(ByVal sender As Object, ByVal e As System.EventArgs)
   Dim dt As DateTime = New DateTime(2008, 8, 11, 11, 12, 10, 10)
   System.Threading.Thread.CurrentThread.CurrentCulture = New CultureInfo("en-US")
   Response.Write("<b><u>en-US</u></b><br>")
   Response.Write(dt.ToString() & "<br>")

   System.Threading.Thread.CurrentThread.CurrentCulture = New CultureInfo("ru-RU")
   Response.Write("<b><u>ru-RU</u></b><br>")
   Response.Write(dt.ToString() & "<br>")

   System.Threading.Thread.CurrentThread.CurrentCulture = New CultureInfo("fi-FI")
   Response.Write("<b><u>fi-FI</u></b><br>")
   Response.Write(dt.ToString() & "<br>")

   System.Threading.Thread.CurrentThread.CurrentCulture = new CultureInfo("th-TH")
   Response.Write("<b><u>th-TH</u></b><br>")
   Response.Write(dt.ToString())
End Sub
```

C#

```
protected void Page_Load(object sender, EventArgs e)
{
   DateTime dt = new DateTime(2008, 8, 11, 11, 12, 10, 10);
   System.Threading.Thread.CurrentThread.CurrentCulture = new CultureInfo("en-US");
   Response.Write("<b><u>en-US</u></b><br>");
   Response.Write(dt.ToString() + "<br>");
```

Continued

```
        System.Threading.Thread.CurrentThread.CurrentCulture = new CultureInfo("ru-RU");
        Response.Write("<b><u>ru-RU</u></b><br>");
        Response.Write(dt.ToString() + "<br>");

        System.Threading.Thread.CurrentThread.CurrentCulture = new CultureInfo("fi-FI");
        Response.Write("<b><u>fi-FI</u></b><br>");
        Response.Write(dt.ToString() + "<br>");

        System.Threading.Thread.CurrentThread.CurrentCulture = new CultureInfo("th-TH");
        Response.Write("<b><u>th-TH</u></b><br>");
        Response.Write(dt.ToString());
    }
```

In this case, four different cultures are utilized, and the date/time construction used by that culture is written to the browser screen using a `Response.Write` command. The result from this code operation is presented in Figure 30-6.

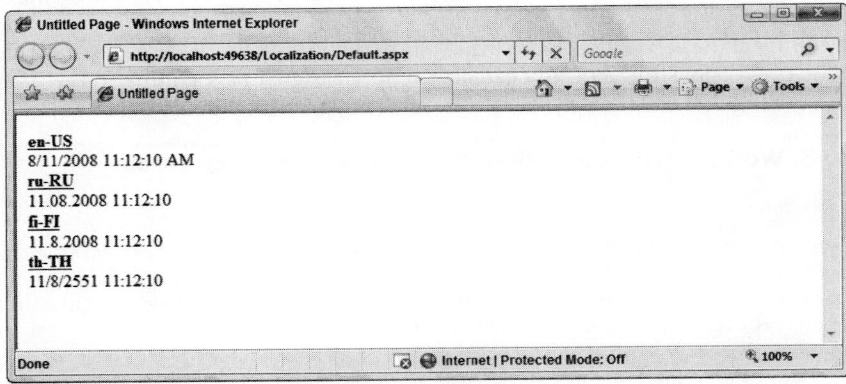

Figure 30-6

As you can see, the formats used to represent a date/time value are dramatically different from one another — and one of the cultures, the Thai culture (th-TH), even uses an entirely different calendar that labels this year as 2551.

Understanding Differences in Numbers and Currencies

In addition to date/time values, numbers are constructed quite differently from one culture to the next. How can a number be represented differently in different cultures? Well, it has less to do with the actual number (although certain cultures use different number symbols), and more to do with how the number separators are used for decimals or for showing amounts such as thousands, millions, and more. For instance, in the English culture of the United States (en-US), you see numbers represented in the following fashion:

```
5,123,456.00
```

From this example, you can see that the en-US culture uses a comma as a separator for thousands and a period for signifying the start of any decimals that might appear after the number is presented. It is quite different when working with other cultures. Listing 30-9 shows you an example of representing numbers in other cultures.

Listing 30-9: Working with numbers in different cultures

VB

```
Protected Sub Page_Load(ByVal sender As Object, ByVal e As System.EventArgs)
   Dim myNumber As Double = 5123456.00
   System.Threading.Thread.CurrentThread.CurrentCulture = New CultureInfo("en-US")
   Response.Write("<b><u>en-US</u></b><br>")
   Response.Write(myNumber.ToString("n") & "<br>")

   System.Threading.Thread.CurrentThread.CurrentCulture = new CultureInfo("vi-VN")
   Response.Write("<b><u>vi-VN</u></b><br>")
   Response.Write(myNumber.ToString("n") & "<br>")

   System.Threading.Thread.CurrentThread.CurrentCulture = new CultureInfo("fi-FI")
   Response.Write("<b><u>fi-FI</u></b><br>")
   Response.Write(myNumber.ToString("n") & "<br>")

   System.Threading.Thread.CurrentThread.CurrentCulture = new CultureInfo("fr-CH")
   Response.Write("<b><u>fr-CH</u></b><br>")
   Response.Write(myNumber.ToString("n"))
End Sub
```

C#

```
protected void Page_Load(object sender, EventArgs e)
{
   double myNumber = 5123456.00;
   System.Threading.Thread.CurrentThread.CurrentCulture = new CultureInfo("en-US");
   Response.Write("<b><u>en-US</u></b><br>");
   Response.Write(myNumber.ToString("n") + "<br>");

   System.Threading.Thread.CurrentThread.CurrentCulture = new CultureInfo("vi-VN");
   Response.Write("<b><u>vi-VN</u></b><br>");
   Response.Write(myNumber.ToString("n") + "<br>");

   System.Threading.Thread.CurrentThread.CurrentCulture = new CultureInfo("fi-FI");
   Response.Write("<b><u>fi-FI</u></b><br>");
   Response.Write(myNumber.ToString("n") + "<br>");

   System.Threading.Thread.CurrentThread.CurrentCulture = new CultureInfo("fr-CH");
   Response.Write("<b><u>fr-CH</u></b><br>");
   Response.Write(myNumber.ToString("n"));
}
```

Running this short example produces the results presented in Figure 30-7.

From this example, you can see that the other cultures represented here show numbers in quite a different format than that of the en-US culture. The second culture listed in the figure, vi-VN (Vietnamese in Vietnam), constructs a number exactly the opposite from the way it is constructed in en-US. The Vietnamese culture uses periods for the thousand separators and a comma for signifying decimals. Finnish, on the other hand, uses spaces for the thousand separators and a comma for the decimal separator, whereas the French-speaking Swiss use a high comma for separating thousands and a period for the decimal separator. As you can see, it is important to "translate" numbers to the proper construction so that users of your application can properly understand the numbers represented.

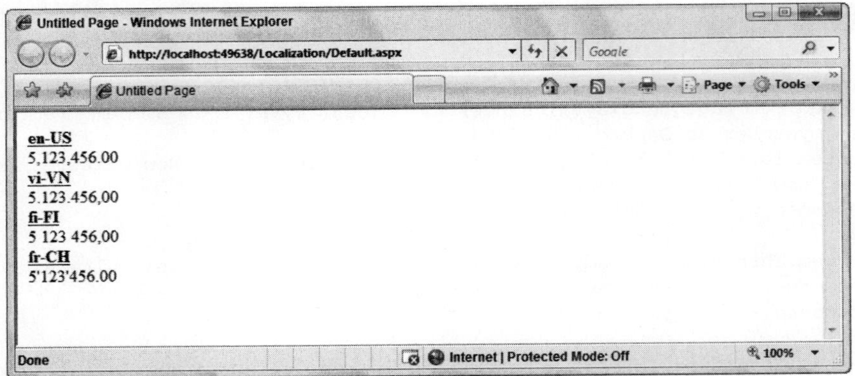

Figure 30-7

You also represent numbers is when working with currencies. It is one thing to *convert* currencies so that end users understand the proper value of an item, but it is another to translate the construction of the currency just as you would a basic number.

Each culture has a distinct currency symbol used to signify that a number represented is an actual currency value. For instance, the en-US culture represents a currency in the following format:

```
$5,123,456.00
```

The en-US culture uses a U.S. Dollar symbol ($), and the location of this symbol is just as important as the symbol itself. For en-US, the $ symbol directly preceeds the currency value (with no space in between the symbol and the first character of the number). Other cultures use different symbols to represent a currency and often place those currency symbols in different locations. Change the previous Listing 30-9 so that it now represents the number as a currency. The necessary changes are presented in Listing 30-10.

Listing 30-10: Working with currencies in different cultures

VB

```
Protected Sub Page_Load(ByVal sender As Object, ByVal e As System.EventArgs)
    Dim myNumber As Double = 5123456.00
    System.Threading.Thread.CurrentThread.CurrentCulture = New CultureInfo("en-US")
    Response.Write("<b><u>en-US</u></b><br>")
    Response.Write(myNumber.ToString("c") & "<br>")

    System.Threading.Thread.CurrentThread.CurrentCulture = new CultureInfo("vi-VN")
    Response.Write("<b><u>vi-VN</u></b><br>")
    Response.Write(myNumber.ToString("c") & "<br>")

    System.Threading.Thread.CurrentThread.CurrentCulture = new CultureInfo("fi-FI")
    Response.Write("<b><u>fi-FI</u></b><br>")
    Response.Write(myNumber.ToString("c") & "<br>")

    System.Threading.Thread.CurrentThread.CurrentCulture = new CultureInfo("fr-CH")
    Response.Write("<b><u>fr-CH</u></b><br>")
    Response.Write(myNumber.ToString("c"))
```

```
End Sub
```

C#

```
protected void Page_Load(object sender, EventArgs e)
{
   double myNumber = 5123456.00;
   System.Threading.Thread.CurrentThread.CurrentCulture = new CultureInfo("en-US");
   Response.Write("<b><u>en-US</u></b><br>");
   Response.Write(myNumber.ToString("c") + "<br>");

   System.Threading.Thread.CurrentThread.CurrentCulture = new CultureInfo("vi-VN");
   Response.Write("<b><u>vi-VN</u></b><br>");
   Response.Write(myNumber.ToString("c") + "<br>");

   System.Threading.Thread.CurrentThread.CurrentCulture = new CultureInfo("fi-FI");
   Response.Write("<b><u>fi-FI</u></b><br>");
   Response.Write(myNumber.ToString("c") + "<br>");

   System.Threading.Thread.CurrentThread.CurrentCulture = new CultureInfo("fr-CH");
   Response.Write("<b><u>fr-CH</u></b><br>");
   Response.Write(myNumber.ToString("c"));
}
```

Run this example to see how these cultures represent currency values, as illustrated in Figure 30-8.

From this figure, you can see that not only are the numbers constructed quite differently from one another, but the currency symbol and the location of the symbol in regard to the number are quite different as well.

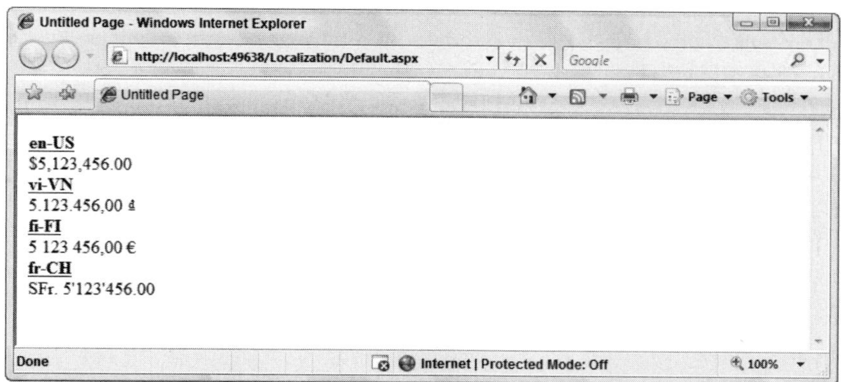

Figure 30-8

When working with currencies, note that when you are using currencies on an ASP.NET page, you have provided an automatic culture setting for the page as a whole (such as setting the culture in the `@Page` directive). You must specify a specific culture for the currency that is the same in all cases *unless* you are actually doing a currency conversion. For instance, if you are specifying a U.S. Dollar currency value on your ASP.NET page, you do not want to specify that the culture of the currency is something else (for example, the Euro). An exception would be if you actually performed a currency conversion and showed the appropriate Euro value along with the culture specification of the currency. Therefore, if you are using an automatic culture setting on your ASP.NET page and you are *not* converting the currency, you perform something similar to what is illustrated in Listing 30-11 for currency values.

Listing 30-11: Reverting to a specific culture when displaying currencies

VB

```
Dim myNumber As Double = 5123456.00
Dim usCurr As CultureInfo = New CultureInfo("en-US")
Response.Write(myNumber.ToString("c", usCurr))
```

C#

```
double myNumber = 5123456.00;
CultureInfo usCurr = new CultureInfo("en-US");
Response.Write(myNumber.ToString("c", usCurr));
```

Understanding Differences in Sorting Strings

You have learned to translate textual values and alter the construction of the numbers, date/time values, currencies, and more when you are globalizing an application. You should also take note when applying culture settings to some of the programmatic behaviors that you establish for values in your applications. One operation that can change based upon the culture setting applied is how .NET sorts strings. You might think that all cultures sort strings in the same way (and generally they do), but sometimes differences exist in how sorting occurs. To give you an example, Listing 30-12 shows you a sorting operation occurring in the en-US culture.

Listing 30-12: Working with sorting in different cultures

VB

```
Protected Sub Page_Load(ByVal sender As Object, ByVal e As System.EventArgs)
   System.Threading.Thread.CurrentThread.CurrentCulture = New CultureInfo("en-US")

   Dim myList As List(Of String) = New List(Of String)

   myList.Add("Washington D.C.")
   myList.Add("Helsinki")
   myList.Add("Moscow")
   myList.Add("Warsaw")
   myList.Add("Vienna")
   myList.Add("Tokyo")

   myList.Sort()

   For Each item As String In myList
      Response.Write(item.ToString() + "<br>")
   Next
End Sub
```

C#

```
protected void Page_Load(object sender, EventArgs e)
{
   System.Threading.Thread.CurrentThread.CurrentCulture = new CultureInfo("en-US");
```

```
        List<string> myList = new List<string>();
        myList.Add("Washington D.C.");
        myList.Add("Helsinki");
        myList.Add("Moscow");
        myList.Add("Warsaw");
        myList.Add("Vienna");
        myList.Add("Tokyo");

        myList.Sort();

        foreach (string item in myList)
        {
           Response.Write(item.ToString() + "<br>");
        }
    }
```

For this example to work, you have to import the `System.Collections` and the `System.Collections.Generic` namespaces because this example makes use of the `List(Of String)` object.

In this example, a generic list of capitals from various countries of the world is created in random order. Then the `Sort()` method of the generic `List(Of String)` object is invoked. This sorting operation sorts the strings based upon how sorting is done for the defined culture in which the ASP.NET thread is running. Listing 30-12 shows the sorting as it is done for the en-US culture. The result of this operation is presented in Figure 30-9.

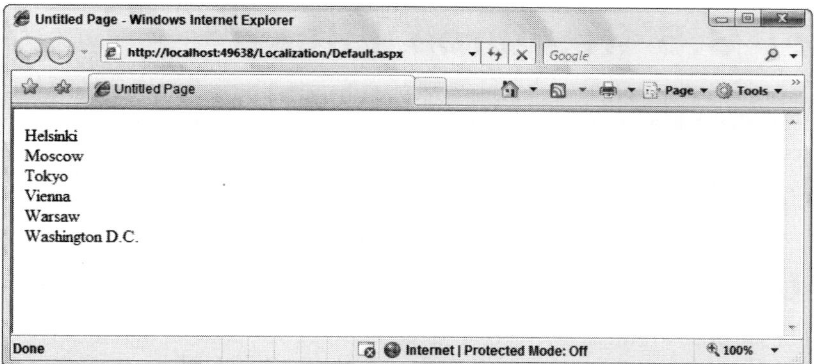

Figure 30-9

This is pretty much what you would expect. Now, however, change the previous example from Listing 30-12 so that the culture is set to Finnish, as shown in Listing 30-13.

Listing 30-13: Changing the culture to Finnish

VB

```
System.Threading.Thread.CurrentThread.CurrentCulture = New CultureInfo("fi-FI")
```

C#

```
System.Threading.Thread.CurrentThread.CurrentCulture = new CultureInfo("fi-FI");
```

If you run the same bit of code under the Finnish culture setting, you get the results presented in Figure 30-10.

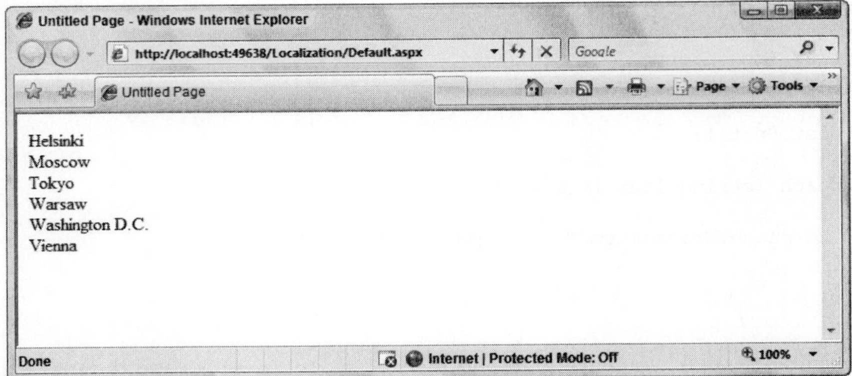

Figure 30-10

If you examine the difference between the Finnish culture sorting done in Figure 30-10 and the U.S. English culture sorting done in Figure 30-9, you see that the city of Vienna is in a different place in the Finnish version. This is because, in the Finnish language, there is no difference between the letter V and the letter W. Because no difference exists, if you are sorting using the Finnish culture setting, then `Vi` comes after `Wa` and thus Vienna comes last in the list of strings in the sorting operation.

ASP.NET 3.5 Resource Files

When you work with ASP.NET 3.5, all resources are handled by a resource file. A resource file is an XML-based file that has a `.resx` extension. You can have Visual Studio 2008 help you construct this file. Resource files provide a set of items that are utilized by a specified culture. In your ASP.NET 3.5 applications, you store resource files as either local resources or global resources. The following sections look at how to use each type of resource.

Making Use of Local Resources

You would be surprised how easily you can build an ASP.NET page so that it can be *localized* into other languages. Really, the only thing you need to do is build the ASP.NET page as you normally would and then use some built-in capabilities from Visual Studio 2008 to convert the page to a format that allows you to plug in other languages easily.

To see this in action, build a simple ASP.NET page as presented in Listing 30-14.

Listing 30-14: Building the basic ASP.NET page to localize

```
<%@ Page Language="VB" %>

<script runat="server">
    Protected Sub Button1_Click(ByVal sender As Object, _
      ByVal e As System.EventArgs)
```

```
            Label2.Text = TextBox1.Text
        End Sub
    </script>

    <html xmlns="http://www.w3.org/1999/xhtml" >
    <head runat="server">
        <title>Sample Page</title>
    </head>
    <body>
        <form id="form1" runat="server">
        <div>
            <asp:Label ID="Label1" runat="server"
             Text="What is your name?"></asp:Label><br />
            <br />
            <asp:TextBox ID="TextBox1" runat="server"></asp:TextBox>
            <asp:Button ID="Button1" runat="server" Text="Submit Name" /><br />
            <br />
            <asp:Label ID="Label2" runat="server"></asp:Label>
        </div>
        </form>
    </body>
    </html>
```

As you can see, there is not much to this page. It is composed of a couple of Label controls, as well as TextBox and Button controls. The end user enters her name into the text box, and then the `Label2` server control is populated with the inputted name and a simple greeting.

The next step is what makes Visual Studio so great. To change the construction of this page so that it can be localized easily from resource files, open the page in Visual Studio and select Tools ➪ Generate Local Resource from the Visual Studio menu. Note that you can select this tool only when you are in the Design view of your page. It will not work in the split view or the code view of the page.

Selecting the Generate Local Resource from the Tool menu option causes Visual Studio to create an App_LocalResouces folder in your project if you already do not have one. A `.resx` file based upon this ASP.NET page is then placed in the folder. For instance, if you are working with the `Default.aspx` page, the resource file is named `Default.aspx.resx`. These changes are shown in Figure 30-11.

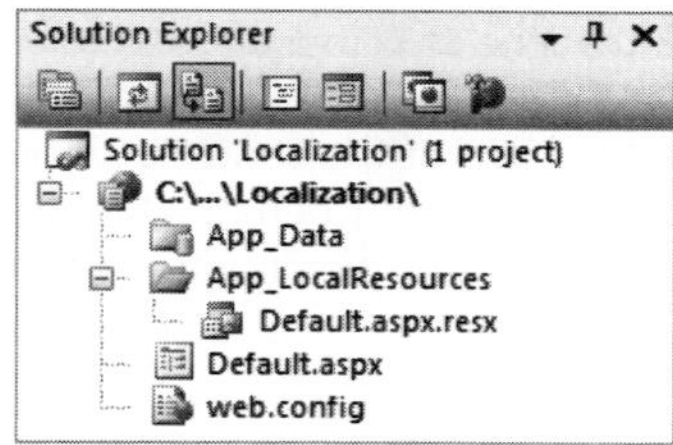

Figure 30-11

If you right-click on the `.resx` file and select View Code, notice that the `.resx` file is nothing more than an XML file with an associated schema at the beginning of the document. The resource file that is generated for you takes every possible property of every translatable control on the page and gives each item a key value that can be referenced in your ASP.NET page. If you look at the code of the page, notice that all the text values that you placed in the page have been left in the page, but they have also been placed inside the resource file. You can see how Visual Studio changed the code of the `Default.aspx` page in Listing 30-15.

Listing 30-15: Looking at how Visual Studio altered the page code

```
<%@ Page Language="VB" Culture="auto" meta:resourcekey="PageResource1"
    UICulture="auto" %>

<script runat="server">
    Protected Sub Button1_Click(ByVal sender As Object, _
      ByVal e As System.EventArgs)
        Label2.Text = TextBox1.Text
    End Sub
</script>

<html xmlns="http://www.w3.org/1999/xhtml" >
<head runat="server">
    <title>Sample Page</title>
</head>
<body>
    <form id="form1" runat="server">
    <div>
        <asp:Label ID="Label1" runat="server" Text="What is your name?"
         meta:resourcekey="Label1Resource1"></asp:Label><br />
        <br />
        <asp:TextBox ID="TextBox1" runat="server"
         meta:resourcekey="TextBox1Resource1"></asp:TextBox> 
        <asp:Button ID="Button1"
         runat="server" Text="Submit Name"
         meta:resourcekey="Button1Resource1" /><br />
        <br />
        <asp:Label ID="Label2" runat="server"
         meta:resourcekey="Label2Resource1"></asp:Label>
    </div>
    </form>
</body>
</html>
```

From this bit of code, you can see that the `Culture` and `UICulture` attributes have been added to the `@Page` directive with a value of `auto`, thus enabling this application to be localized. Also, the attribute `meta:resourcekey` has been added to each of the controls along with an associated value. This is the key from the `.resx` file that was created on your behalf. Double-clicking on the `Default.aspx.resx` file opens the resource file in the Resource Editor, which you will find is built into Visual Studio. This new editor is presented in Figure 30-12.

In the figure, note that a couple of properties from each of the server controls have been defined in the resource file. For instance, the Button server control has its `Text` and `ToolTip` properties exposed in this resource file, and the Visual Studio localization tool has pulled the default `Text` property value from the control based on what you placed there. Looking more closely at the Button server control constructions in this file, you can see that both the `Text` and `ToolTip` properties have a defining `Button1Resource1` value preceding the property name. This key is used in the Button server control you saw earlier.

```
<asp:Button ID="Button1"
 runat="server" Text="Submit Name"
 meta:resourcekey="Button1Resource1" />
```

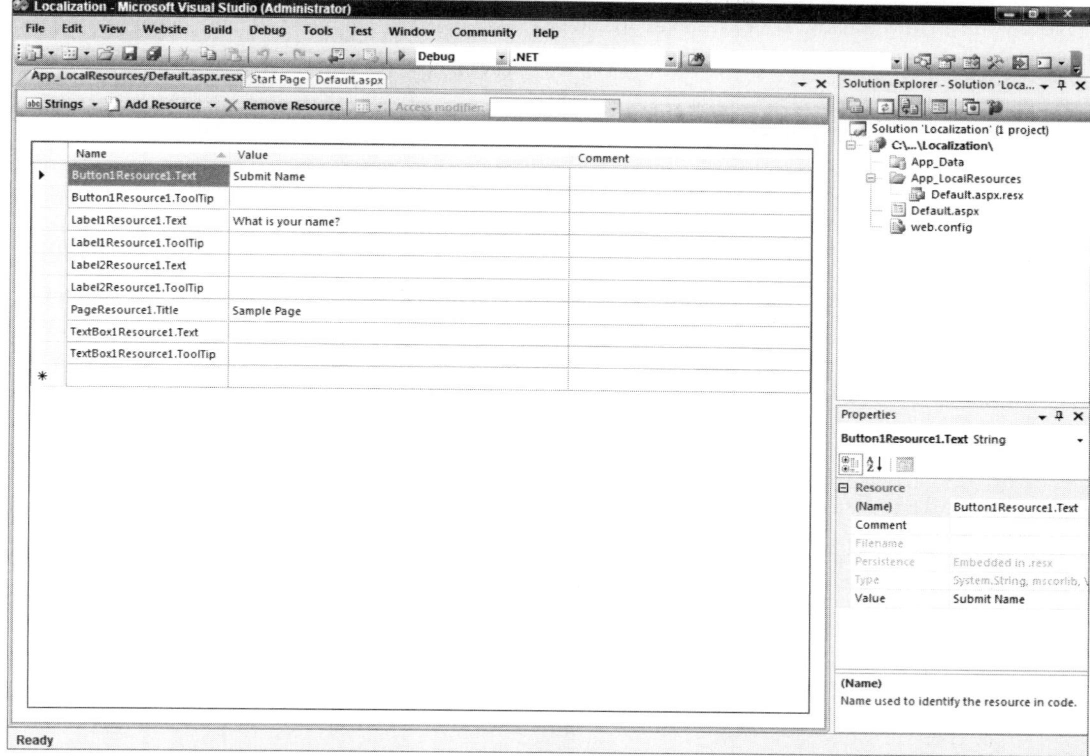

Figure 30-12

You can see that a `meta:resourcekey` attribute has been added and, in this case, it references `Button1Resource1`. All the properties using this key in the resource file (for example, the `Text` and `ToolTip` properties) are applied to this Button server control at runtime.

Adding Another Language Resource File

Now that the `Default.aspx.resx` file is in place, this is a file for an invariant culture. No culture is assigned to this resource file. If no culture can be determined, this resource file is then utilized. To add another resource file for the `Default.aspx` page that handles another language altogether, you copy and paste the `Default.aspx.resx` file into the same App_LocalResources folder and rename the newly copied file. If you use `Default.aspx.fi-FI.resx`, you give the following keys the following values to make a Finnish language resource file.

```
Button1Resource1.Text   Lähetä Nimi
Label1Resource1.Text    Mikä sinun nimi on?
PageResource1.Title     Näytesivu
```

You want to create a custom resource in both resource files using the key `Label2Answer`. The `Default.aspx.resx` file should have the following new key:

```
Label2Answer    Hello
```

Now you can add the key `Label2Answer` to the `Default.aspx.fi-FI.resx` file as shown here:

```
Label2Answer    Hei
```

You now have resources for specific controls and a resource that you can access later programmatically.

Finalizing the Building of the Default.aspx Page

Finalizing the `Default.aspx` page, you want to add a `Button1_Click` event so that when the end user enters a name into the text box and clicks the Submit button, the `Label2` server control provides a greeting to him or her that is pulled from the local resource files. When all is said and done, you should have a `Default.aspx` page that resembles the one in Listing 30-16.

Listing 30-16: The final Default.aspx page

VB

```
<%@ Page Language="VB" Culture="auto" meta:resourcekey="PageResource1"
    UICulture="auto" %>

<script runat="server">
    Protected Sub Button1_Click(ByVal sender As Object, _
      ByVal e As System.EventArgs)

       Label2.Text = GetLocalResourceObject("Label2Answer").ToString() & _
          " " & TextBox1.Text
    End Sub
</script>

<html xmlns="http://www.w3.org/1999/xhtml" >
<head runat="server">
    <title>Sample Page</title>
</head>
<body>
    <form id="form1" runat="server">
    <div>
        <asp:Label ID="Label1" runat="server" Text="What is your name?"
         meta:resourcekey="Label1Resource1"></asp:Label><br />
        <br />
        <asp:TextBox ID="TextBox1" runat="server"
         meta:resourcekey="TextBox1Resource1"></asp:TextBox> 
        <asp:Button ID="Button1"
         runat="server" Text="Submit Name"
         meta:resourcekey="Button1Resource1" OnClick="Button1_Click" /><br />
        <br />
        <asp:Label ID="Label2" runat="server"
         meta:resourcekey="Label2Resource1"></asp:Label>
    </div>
    </form>
```

```
</body>
</html>
```

C#

```
<%@ Page Language="C#" Culture="auto" meta:resourcekey="PageResource1"
    UICulture="auto" %>

<script runat="server">
    protected void Button1_Click(object sender, EventArgs e)
    {
        Label2.Text = GetLocalResourceObject("Label2Answer").ToString() + " " +
           TextBox1.Text;
    }
</script>
```

In addition to pulling local resources using the `meta:resourcekey` attribute in the server controls on the page to get at the exposed attributes, you can also get at any property value contained in the local resource file by using the `GetLocalResourceObject`. When using `GetLocalResourceObject`, you simply use the name of the key as a parameter as shown here:

```
GetLocalResourceObject("Label2Answer")
```

You could just as easily get at any of the control's property values from the resource file programmatically using the same construct:

```
GetLocalResourceObject("Button1Resource1.Text")
```

With the code from Listing 30-16 in place and the resource files completed, you can run the page, entering a name in the text box and then clicking the button to get a response, as illustrated in Figure 30-13.

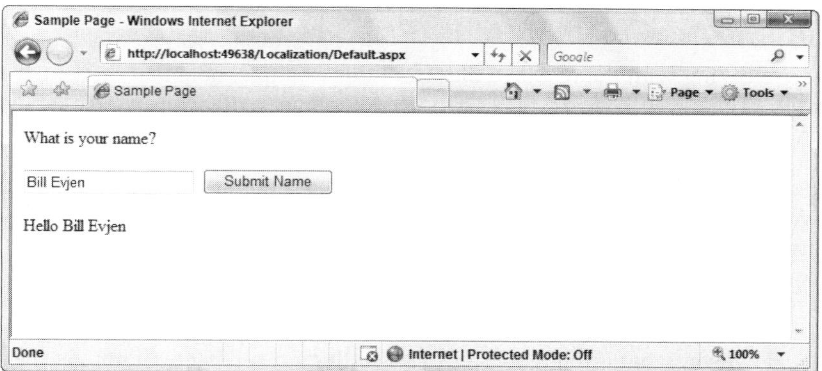

Figure 30-13

What happened behind the scenes that caused this page to be constructed in this manner? First, only two resource files, `Default.aspx.resx` and `Default.aspx.fi-FI.resx`, are available. The `Default.aspx.resx` resource file is the invariant culture resource file, whereas the `Default.aspx.fi-FI.resx` resource file is for a specific culture (fi-FI). Because I requested the `Default.aspx` page and my browser is set to en-US as my preferred culture, ASP.NET found the local resources for the `Default.aspx` page. From there, ASP.NET made a check for an en-US–specific version of the `Default.aspx` page.

Because there is not a specific page for the en-US culture, ASP.NET made a check for an EN (neutral culture) specific page. Not finding a page for the EN neutral culture, ASP.NET was then forced to use the invariant culture resource file of `Default.aspx.resx`, producing the page presented in Figure 30-13.

Now, if you set your IE language preference as fi-FI and rerun the `Default.aspx` page, you see a Finnish version of the page, as illustrated in Figure 30-14.

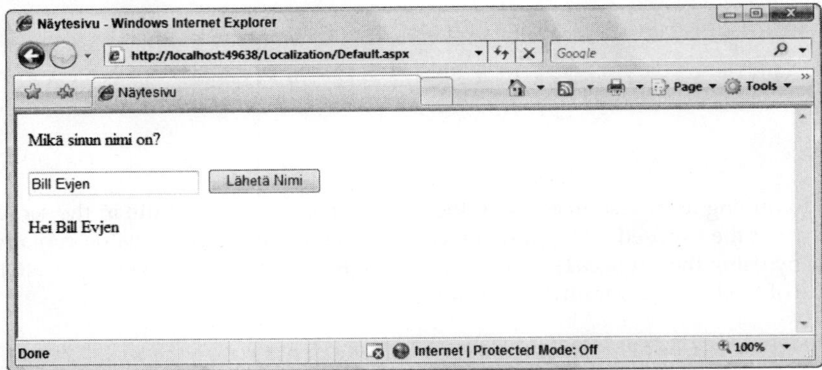

Figure 30-14

In this case, having set my IE language preference to fi-FI, I am presented with this culture's page instead of the invariant culture page that was presented earlier. ASP.NET found this specific culture through use of the `Default.aspx.fi-FI.resx` resource file.

You can see that all the control properties that were translated and placed within the resource file are utilized automatically by ASP.NET including the page title presented in the title bar of IE.

Neutral Cultures Are Generally More Preferred

When you are working with the resource files from this example, note that one of the resources is for a *specific culture*. The `Default.aspx.fi-FI.resx` file is for a specific culture — the Finnish language as spoken in Finland. Another option would be to make this file work not for a specific culture, but instead for a neutral culture. To accomplish this task, you simply name the file `Default.aspx.FI.resx` instead. In this example, it really does not make that much difference because no other countries speak Finnish. It would make sense for languages such as German, Spanish, or French. These languages are spoken in multiple countries. For instance, if you are going to have a Spanish version of the `Default.aspx` page, you could definitely build it for a specific culture, such as `Default.aspx.es-MX.resx`. This construction is for the Spanish language as spoken in Mexico. With this in place, if someone requests the `Default.aspx` page with the language setting of es-MX, that user is provided with the contents of this resource file. However, what if the requestor has a setting of es-ESHe will not get the `Default.aspx.es-MX.resx` resource file, but instead gets the invariant culture resource file of `Default.aspx.resx`. If you are going to make only a single translation into German, Spanish, or another language for your site or any of your pages, you want to construct the resource files to be for neutral cultures rather than for specific cultures.

If you have the resource file `Default.aspx.ES.resx`, then it won't matter if the end user's preferred setting is set to es-MX, es-ES, or even es-AR — the user gets the appropriate ES neutral culture version of the page.

Making Use of Global Resources

Besides using only local resources that specifically deal with a particular page in your ASP.NET application, you also have the option of creating *global* resources that can be used across multiple pages. To create a resource file that can be utilized across the entire application, right-click on the solution in the Solution Explorer of Visual Studio and select Add New Item. From the Add New Item dialog, select Resource file.

Selecting this option provides you with a `Resource.resx` file. Visual Studio places this file in a new folder called App_GlobalResources. Again, this first file is the invariant culture resource file. Add a single string resource giving it the key of `PrivacyStatement` and a value of some kind (a long string).

After you have the invariant culture resource file completed, the next step is to add another resource file, but this time name it `Resource.fi-FI.resx`. Again, for this resource file, give a string key of `PrivacyStatement` and a different value altogether from the one you used in the other resource file.

The idea of a global resource file is that you have access to these resources across your entire application. You can gain access to the values that you place in these files in several ways. One way is to work the value directly into any of your server control declarations. For instance, you can place this privacy statement in a Label server control as presented in Listing 30-17.

Listing 30-17: Using a global resource directly in a server control

```
<asp:Label ID="Label1" runat="server"
 Text='<%$ Resources: Resource, PrivacyStatement %>'></asp:Label>
```

With this construction in place, you can now grab the appropriate value of the `PrivacyStatement` global resource depending upon the language preference of the end user requesting the page. To make this work, you use the keyword Resources followed by a colon. Next, you specify the name of the resource file class. In this case, the name of the resource file is `Resource` because this statement goes to the `Resource.resx` and `Resource.fi-FI.resx` files in order to find what it needs. After specifying the particular resource file to use, the next item in the statement is the key — in this case, `PrivacyStatement`.

Another way of achieving the same result is to use some built-in dialogs within Visual Studio. To accomplish this task, highlight the server control you want in Visual Studio from Design view so that the control appears within the Properties window. For my example, I highlighted a Label server control. From the Properties window, you click the button within the Expressions property. This launches the Expressions dialog and enables you to bind the `PrivacyStatement` value to the `Text` property of the control. This is illustrated in Figure 30-15.

To make this work, highlight the Text property in the Bindable properties list. You then select an expression type from a drop-down list on the right-hand side of the dialog. Your options include AppSettings, ConnectionStrings, and Resources. Select the Resources option and you are then asked for the `ClassKey` and `ResourceKey` property values. The `ClassKey` is the name of the file that should be utilized. In this example, the name of the file is `Resource.resx`. Therefore, use the `Resource` keyword as a value. You are provided with a drop-down list in the `ResourceKey` property section with all the keys available in this file. Because only a single key exists at this point, you find only the `PrivacyStatement` key in this list. Make this selection and click the OK button. The Label server control changes and now appears as it was presented earlier in Listing 30-17.

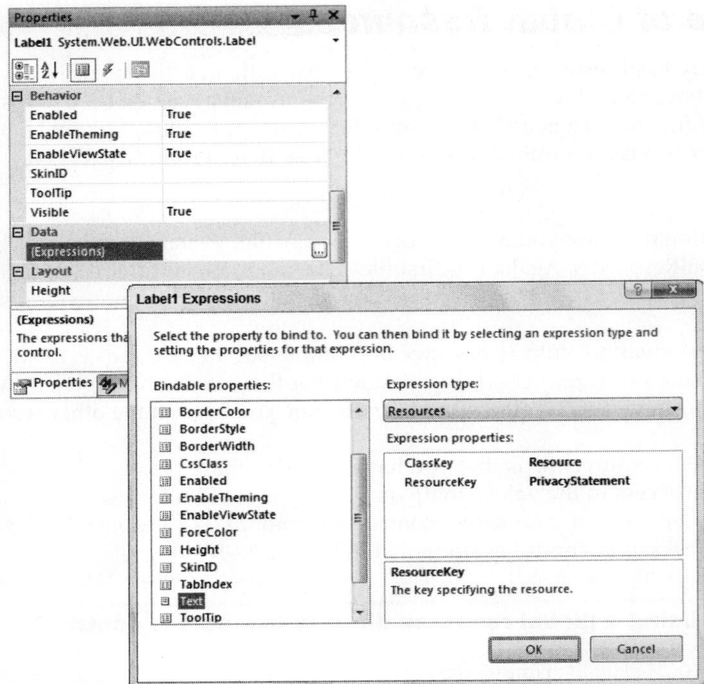

Figure 30-15

One nice feature is that the resources provided via global resources are available in a strongly typed manner. For instance, you can programmatically get at a global resource value by using the construction presented in Listing 30-18.

Listing 30-18: Programmatically getting at global resources

VB

```
Label1.Text = Resources.Resource.PrivacyStatement
```

C#

```
Label1.Text = Resources.Resource.PrivacyStatement;
```

In Figure 30-16, you can see that you have full intelliSense for these resource values.

Looking at the Resource Editor

Visual Studio 2008 provides an editor for working with resource files. You have already seen some of the views available from this editor. Resources are categorized visually by the data type of the resource. So far, this chapter has dealt only with the handling of strings, but other categories exist (as well as images, icons, audio files, miscellaneous files, and other items). These options are illustrated in Figure 30-17.

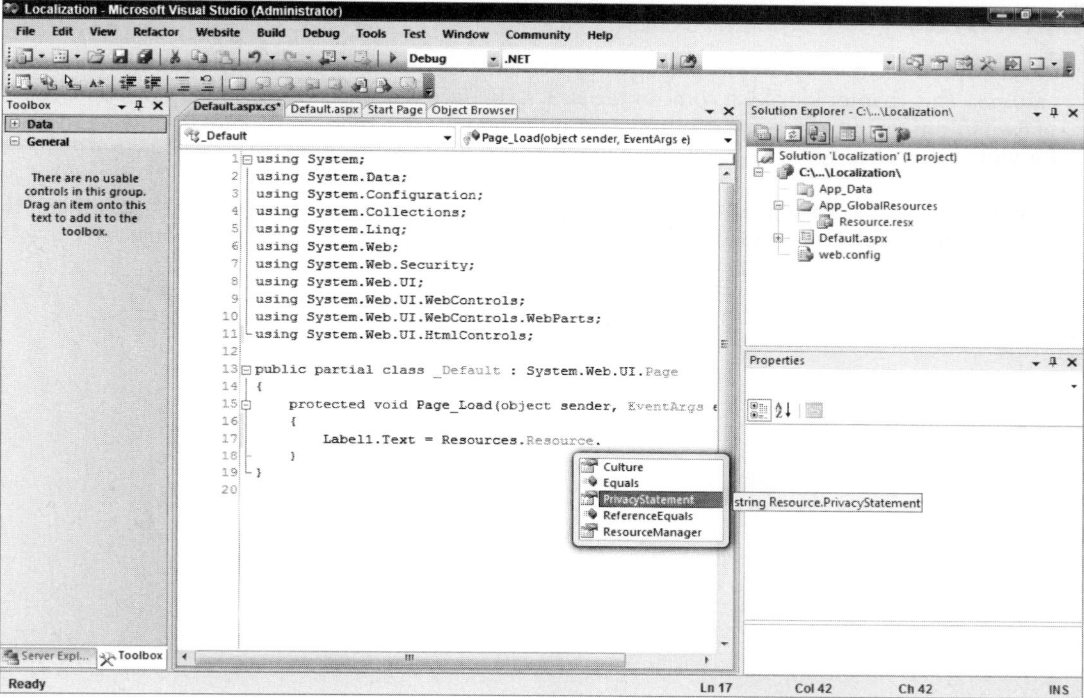

Figure 30-16

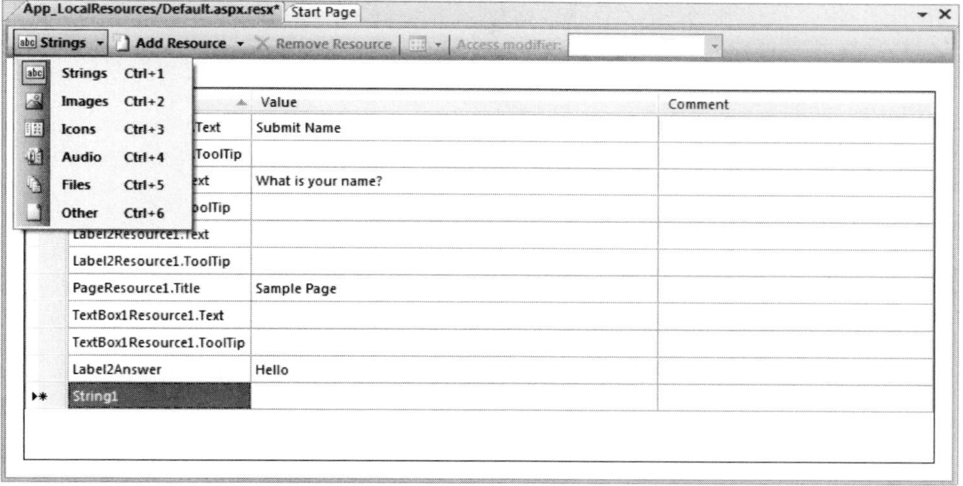

Figure 30-17

Summary

We hope you see the value in localizing your ASP.NET applications so that they can handle multiple cultures. This chapter looked at some of the issues you face when localizing your applications and some of the built-in tools provided via both Visual Studio and the .NET Framework to make this process easier for you.

It really is almost as easy as taking ASP.NET pages that have been already created and running the appropriate Visual Studio tool over the files to rebuild the pages to handle translations.

31

Configuration

Those of you who remember the "Classic" ASP days know that ASP's configuration information was stored in a binary repository called the Internet Information Services (IIS) metabase. To configure a classic ASP application, you had to modify the metabase, either through script or, more commonly, through the IIS Microsoft Management Console (MMC) snap-in.

Unlike classic ASP, all the available versions of ASP.NET do not require extensive use of the IIS metabase. Instead, ASP.NET uses an XML file-based configuration system that is much more flexible, accessible, and easier to use. When building ASP.NET, the ASP.NET team wanted to improve the manageability of the product. Although the release of ASP.NET 1.0 was a huge leap forward in Web application development, it really targeted the developer. What was missing was the focus on the administrator — the person who takes care of Web applications after they are built and deployed. ASP.NET today makes it quite easy for you to configure an ASP.NET application by working either directly with the various configuration files or by using GUI tools that, in turn, interact with configuration files. Before examining the various GUI-based tools in detail in Chapter 34, you first take an in-depth look at how to work directly with the XML configuration files to change the behavior of your ASP.NET applications.

This chapter covers the following:

- Introduction to the ASP.NET configuration file
- An overview of the ASP.NET configuration settings
- How to encrypt portions of your configuration files
- An examination of the ASP.NET 3.5 configuration APIs
- How to store and retrieve sensitive information

The journey into these new configuration enhancements starts with an overview of configuration in ASP.NET.

Configuration Overview

ASP.NET configuration is stored in two primary XML-based files in a hierarchal fashion. XML is used to describe the properties and behaviors of various aspects of ASP.NET applications.

The ASP.NET configuration system supports two kinds of configuration files:

- Server or machine-wide configuration files such as the `machine.config` file
- Application configuration files such as the `web.config` file

Because the configuration files are based upon XML, the elements that describe the configuration are, therefore, case-sensitive. Moreover, the ASP.NET configuration system follows camel-casing naming conventions. If you look at the session state configuration example shown in Listing 31-1, for example, you can see that the XML element that deals with session state is presented as `<sessionState>`.

Listing 31-1: Session state configuration

```
<?xml version="1.0" encoding="UTF-8" ?>
<configuration>
<system.web>
    <sessionState
        mode="InProc"
        stateConnectionString="tcpip=127.0.0.1:42424"
        stateNetworkTimeout="10"
        sqlConnectionString="data source=127.0.0.1; user id=sa; password=P@55worD"
        cookieless="false"
        timeout="20" />
  </system.web>
</configuration>
```

The benefits of having an XML configuration file instead of a binary metabase include the following:

- The configuration information is human-readable and can be modified using a plain text editor such as Notepad, although it is recommended to use Visual Studio 2008 or another XML-aware editor. Unlike a binary metabase, the XML-based configuration file can be easily copied from one server to another, as with any simple file. This feature is extremely helpful when working in a Web farm scenario.
- When some settings are changed in the configuration file, ASP.NET automatically detects the changes and applies them to the running ASP.NET application. ASP.NET accomplishes this by creating a new instance of the ASP.NET application and directing end users to this new application.
- The configuration changes are applied to the ASP.NET application without the need for the administrator to stop and start the Web server. Changes are completely transparent to the end user.
- The ASP.NET configuration system is extensible.
- Application-specific information can be stored and retrieved very easily.
- The sensitive information stored in the ASP.NET configuration system can optionally be encrypted to keep it from prying eyes.

Server Configuration Files

Every ASP.NET server installation includes a series of configuration files, such as the `machine.config` file. This file is installed as a part of the default .NET Framework installation. You can find `machine.config` and the other server-specific configuration files in `C:\Windows\Microsoft.NET\Framework\v2.0.50727\CONFIG`. They represent the default settings used by all ASP.NET Web applications installed on the server.

Some of the server-wide configuration files include the following:

- `machine.config`
- `machine.config.comments`
- `machine.config.default`
- `web.config`
- `web.config.comments`
- `web.config.default`
- `web_hightrust.config`
- `web_hightrust.config.default`
- `web_lowtrust.config`
- `web_lowtrust.config.default`
- `web_mediumtrust.config`
- `web_mediumtrust.config.default`
- `web_minimaltrust.config`
- `web_minimaltrust.config.default`

The system-wide configuration file, `machine.config`, is used to configure common .NET Framework settings for all applications on the machine. As a rule, it is not a good idea to edit or manipulate the `machine.config` file unless you know what you are doing. Changes to this file can affect all applications on your computer (Windows, Web, and so on).

Because the .NET Framework supports side-by-side execution mode, you might find more than one installation of the machine.config file if you have multiple versions of the .NET Framework installed on the server. If you have .NET Framework versions 1.0, 1.1, and 2.0 running on the server, for example, each .NET Framework installation has its own machine.config file. This means that you will find three machine.config file installations on that particular server. It is interesting to note that the .NET Framework 3.5 is really just a bolt-on to the .NET Framework 2.0. (It includes extra DLLs, which are sometimes referred to as extensions.) Thus, the .NET Framework 3.5 uses the same machine.config file as the .NET Framework 2.0.

In addition to the `machine.config` file, the .NET Framework installer also installs two more files called `machine.config.default` and `machine.config.comments`. The `machine.config.default` file acts as a backup for the `machine.config` file. If you want to revert to the factory setting for `machine.config`, simply copy the settings from the `machine.config.default` to the `machine.config` file.

The machine.config.comments file contains a description for each configuration section and explicit settings for the most commonly used values. machine.config.default and machine.config.comment files are not used by the .NET Framework runtime; they're installed in case you want to revert back to default factory settings and default values.

You will also find a root-level web.config file in place within the same CONFIG folder as the machine.config. When making changes to settings on a server-wide basis, you should always attempt to make these changes in the root web.config file rather than in the machine.config file. You will find that files like the machine.config.comments and the machine.config.default files also exist for the web.config (web.config.comments and web.config.default).

By default, your ASP.NET Web applications run under a *full trust* setting. You can see this by looking at the <securityPolicy> and <trust> sections in the root-level web.config file. This section is presented in Listing 31-2.

Listing 31-2: The root web.config showing the trust level

```
<configuration>

    <location allowOverride="true">
        <system.web>
            <securityPolicy>
                <trustLevel name="Full" policyFile="internal" />
                <trustLevel name="High" policyFile="web_hightrust.config" />
                <trustLevel name="Medium" policyFile="web_mediumtrust.config" />
                <trustLevel name="Low"  policyFile="web_lowtrust.config" />
                <trustLevel name="Minimal" policyFile="web_minimaltrust.config" />
            </securityPolicy>
            <trust level="Full" originUrl="" />
        </system.web>
    </location>

</configuration>
```

The other policy files are defined at specific trust levels. These levels determine the code-access security (CAS) allowed for ASP.NET. To change the trust level in which ASP.NET applications can run on the server, you simply change the <trust> element within the document or within your application's instance of the web.config file. For example, you can change to a medium trust level using the code shown in Listing 31-3.

Listing 31-3: Changing the trust level to medium trust

```
<configuration>

    <location allowOverride="false">
        <system.web>
            <securityPolicy>
                <trustLevel name="Full" policyFile="internal" />
                <trustLevel name="High" policyFile="web_hightrust.config" />
                <trustLevel name="Medium" policyFile="web_mediumtrust.config" />
                <trustLevel name="Low" policyFile="web_lowtrust.config" />
                <trustLevel name="Minimal" policyFile="web_minimaltrust.config" />
```

```
            </securityPolicy>
            <trust level="Medium" originUrl="" />
        </system.web>
    </location>

</configuration>
```

In this case, not only does this code mandate use of the `web_mediumtrust.config` file, but also (by setting the `allowOverride` attribute to `false`) it forces this trust level upon every ASP.NET application on the server. Individual application instances are unable to change this setting by overriding it in their local `web.config` files because this setting is in the root-level `web.config` file.

If you look through the various trust level configuration files (such as the `web_mediumtrust.config` file), notice that they define what kinds of actions you can perform through your code operations. For instance, the `web_hightrust.config` file allows for open FileIO access to any point on the server as illustrated in Listing 31-4.

Listing 31-4: The web_hightrust.config file's definition of FileIO CAS

```
<IPermission
   class="FileIOPermission"
   version="1"
   Unrestricted="true"
/>
```

If, however, you look at the medium trust `web.config` file (`web_mediumtrust.config`), you see that this configuration file restricts ASP.NET to *only* those FileIO operations within the application directory. This definition is presented in Listing 31-5.

Listing 31-5: FileIO restrictions in the web_mediumtrust.config file

```
<IPermission
   class="FileIOPermission"
   version="1"
   Read="\$AppDir\$"
   Write="\$AppDir\$"
   Append="\$AppDir\$"
   PathDiscovery="\$AppDir\$"
/>
```

It is always a good idea to see in which trust level you can run your ASP.NET applications and to change the `<trust>` section to enable the appropriate level of CAS.

Application Configuration File

Unlike the `machine.config` file, each and every ASP.NET application has its own copy of configuration settings stored in a file called `web.config`. If the Web application spans multiple subfolders, each subfolder can have its own `web.config` file that inherits or overrides the parent's file settings.

To update servers in your farm with these new settings, you simply copy this `web.config` file to the appropriate application directory. ASP.NET takes care of the rest — no server restarts and no local server access is required — and your application continues to function normally, except that it now uses the new settings applied in the configuration file.

How Configuration Settings Are Applied

When the ASP.NET runtime applies configuration settings for a given Web request, `machine.config` (as well as any of the `web.config` files configuration information) is merged into a single unit, and that information is then applied to the given application. Configuration settings are inherited from any parent `web.config` file or `machine.config`, which is the root configuration file or the ultimate parent. An example of this is presented in Figure 31-1.

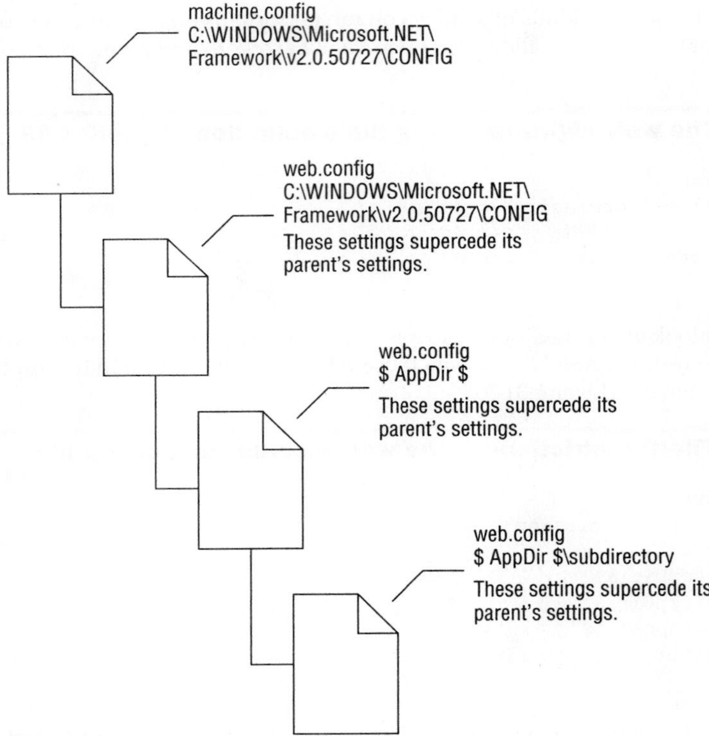

Figure 31-1

The configuration for each Web application is unique; however, settings are inherited from the parent. For example, if the `web.config` file in the root of your Web site defines a session timeout of 10 minutes, then that particular setting overrides the default ASP.NET setting inherited from the `machine.config` or the root `web.config` file. The `web.config` files in the subdirectories or subfolders can override these settings or inherit the settings (such as the 10-minute session timeout).

The configuration settings for virtual directories are independent of the physical directory structure. Unless the manner in which the virtual directories are organized is exclusively specified, configuration problems can result.

Note that these inheritance/override rules can be blocked in most cases by using the `allowOverride = "false"` mechanism shown in Listing 31-3.

Detecting Configuration File Changes

ASP.NET automatically detects when configuration files, such as `machine.config` or `web.config`, are changed. This logic is implemented based on listening for file-change notification events provided by the operating system.

When an ASP.NET application is started, the configuration settings are read and stored in the ASP.NET cache. A file dependency is then placed on the entry within the cache in the `machine.config` and/or `web.config` configuration file. When the configuration file update is detected in the `machine.config`, ASP.NET creates a new application domain to service new requests. The old application domain is destroyed as soon as it completes servicing all its outstanding requests.

Configuration File Format

The main difference between `machine.config` and `web.config` is the filename. Other than that, their schemas are the same. Configuration files are divided into multiple groups. The root-level XML element in a configuration file is named `<configuration>`. This pseudo `web.config` file has a section to control ASP.NET, as shown in Listing 31-6.

Listing 31-6: A pseudo web.config file

```
<?xml version="1.0" encoding="UTF-8"?>
<configuration>
  <configSections>
    <section name="[sectionSettings]" type="[Class]"/>
    <sectionGroup name="[sectionGroup]">
      <section name="[sectionSettings]" type="[Class]"/>
    </sectionGroup>
  </configSections>
</configuration>
```

Values within brackets [ ] have unique values within the real configuration file.

The root element in the XML configuration file is always `<configuration>`. Each of the section handlers and settings are optionally wrapped in a `<sectionGroup>`. A `<sectionGroup>` provides an organizational function within the configuration file. It allows you to organize configuration into unique groups — for instance, the `<system.web>` section group is used to identify areas within the configuration file specific to ASP.NET.

Config Sections

The `<configSections>` section is the mechanism to group the configuration section handlers associated with each configuration section. When you want to create your own section handlers, you must declare them in the `<configSections>` section. The `<httpModules>` section has a configuration handler that is set to `System.Web.Caching.HttpModulesSection`, and the `<sessionState>` section has a configuration handler that is set to `System.Web.SessionState.SessionStateSection` classes, as shown in Listing 31-7.

Listing 31-7: HTTP Module configuration setting from the machine.config file

```
<configSections>
   <sectionGroup>
      <section name="httpModules"
       type="System.Web.Configuration.HttpModulesSection,
          System.Web, Version=2.0.0.0, Culture=neutral,
          PublicKeyToken=b03f5f7f11d50a3a"/>
   </sectionGroup>
</configSections>
```

Common Configuration Settings

The ASP.NET applications depend on a few common configuration settings. These settings are common to both the `web.config` and `machine.config` files. In this section, you look at some of these common configuration settings.

Connecting Strings

In ASP.NET 1.0 and 1.1, all the connection string information was stored in the `<appSettings>` section. However, ever since ASP.NET 2.0, a section called `<connectionStrings>` was included that stores all kinds of connection-string information. Even though storing connection strings in the `<appSettings>` element works fine, it poses the following challenges:

- When connection strings are stored in `appSettings` section, it is impossible for a data-aware control such as `SqlCacheDependency` or `MembershipProvider` to discover the information.
- Securing connection strings using cryptographic algorithms is a challenge.
- Last, but not least, this feature does not apply to ASP.NET only; rather, it applies to all the .NET application types including Windows Forms, Web Services, and so on.

Because the connection-string information is stored independently of the `appSettings` section, it can be retrieved using the strongly typed collection method `ConnectionStrings`. Listing 31-8 gives an example of how to store connecting strings.

Listing 31-8: Storing a connection string

```
<configuration>
  <connectionStrings>
    <add
        name = "ExampleConnection"
        connectionString = "server=401kServer;database=401kDB;
        uid=WebUser;pwd=P@$$worD9" />
  </connectionStrings>
</configuration>
```

Listing 31-9 shows how to retrieve the connection string (`ExampleConnection`) in your code.

Listing 31-9: Retrieving a connection string

VB

```
Public Sub Page_Load (sender As Object, e As EventArgs)
    ...
    Dim dbConnection as New _
      SqlConnection(ConfigurationManager.ConnectionStrings("ExampleConnection")
             .ConnectionString)
    ...
End Sub
```

C#

```
public void Page_Load (Object sender, EventArgs e)
{
    ...
    SqlConnection dbConnection = new
      SqlConnection(ConfigurationManager.ConnectionStrings["ExampleConnection"]
             .ConnectionString);
    ...
}
```

This type of construction has a lot of power. Instead of hard-coding your connection strings into each and every page within your ASP.NET application, you can store one instance of the connection string centrally (in the `web.config` file for instance). Now, if you have to make a change to this connection string, you can make this change in only *one* place rather than in multiple places.

Configuring Session State

Because Web-based applications utilize the stateless HTTP protocol, you must store the application-specific state or user-specific state where it can persist. The `Session` object is the common store where user-specific information is persisted. Session store is implemented as a `Hashtable` and stores data based on key/value pair combinations.

ASP.NET 1.0 and 1.1 had the capability to persist the session store data in `InProc`, `StateServer`, and `SqlServer`. ASP.NET 2.0 and 3.5 adds one more capability called `Custom`. The `Custom` setting gives the developer a lot more control regarding how the session state is persisted in a permanent store. For example, out of the box ASP.NET 3.5 does not support storing session data on non-Microsoft databases such as Oracle, DB2, or Sybase. If you want to store the session data in any of these databases or in a custom store such as an XML file, you can implement that by writing a custom provider class. (See the section ''Custom State Store'' later in this chapter and Chapter 22 to learn more about the new session state features in ASP.NET 3.5.)

You can configure the session information using the `<sessionState>` element as presented in Listing 31-10.

Listing 31-10: Configuring session state

```
<sessionState
 mode="StateServer"
 cookieless="false"
```

Continued

```
    timeout="20"
    stateConnectionString="tcpip=ExampleSessionStore:42424"
    stateNetworkTimeout="60"
    sqlConnectionString=""
  />
```

The following list describes each of the attributes for the <sessionState> element shown in the preceding code:

- `mode`: Specifies whether the session information should be persisted. The mode setting supports five options: `Off`, `InProc`, `StateServer`, `SQLServer`, and `Custom`. The default option is `InProc`.
- `cookieless`: Specifies whether HTTP cookieless Session key management is supported.
- `timeout`: Specifies the `Session` lifecycle time. The `timeout` value is a sliding value; at each request, the timeout period is reset to the current time plus the timeout value. For example, if the `timeout` value is 20 minutes and a request is received at 10:10 AM, the timeout occurs at 10:30 AM.
- `stateConnectionString`: When `mode` is set to `StateServer`, this setting is used to identify the TCP/IP address and port to communicate with the Windows Service providing state management.
- `stateNetworkTimeout`: Specifies the timeout value (in seconds) while attempting to store state in an out-of-process session store such as `StateServer`.
- `sqlConnectionString`: When `mode` is set to `SQLServer`, this setting is used to connect to the SQL Server database to store and retrieve session data.

Web Farm Support

Multiple Web servers working as a group are called a Web farm. If you would like to scale out your ASP.NET application into multiple servers inside a Web farm, ASP.NET supports this kind of deployment out of the box. However, the session data needs to be persisted in an out-of-process session state such as `StateServer` or `SQLServer`.

State Server

Both `StateServer` and `SQLServer` support the out-of-process session state. However, the `StateServer` stores all the session information in a Windows Service, which stores the session data in memory. Using this option, if the server that hosts the session state service goes down in the Web farm, all the ASP.NET clients that are accessing the Web site fail; there is no way to recover the session data.

You can configure the session state service using the Services dialog available by choosing Start ➪ Settings ➪ Control Panel ➪ Administrative Tools ➪ Computer Management if you are using Windows XP, and Start ➪ Control Panel ➪ System and Maintenance ➪ Administrative Tools ➪ Services if you are using Windows Vista (as shown in Figure 31-2).

Alternatively, you can start the session state service by using the command prompt and entering the `net start` command, like this:

```
C:\Windows\Microsoft.NET\Framework\v2.0.50727\> net start aspnet_state

The ASP.NET State Service service is starting.

The ASP.NET State Service service was started successfully.
```

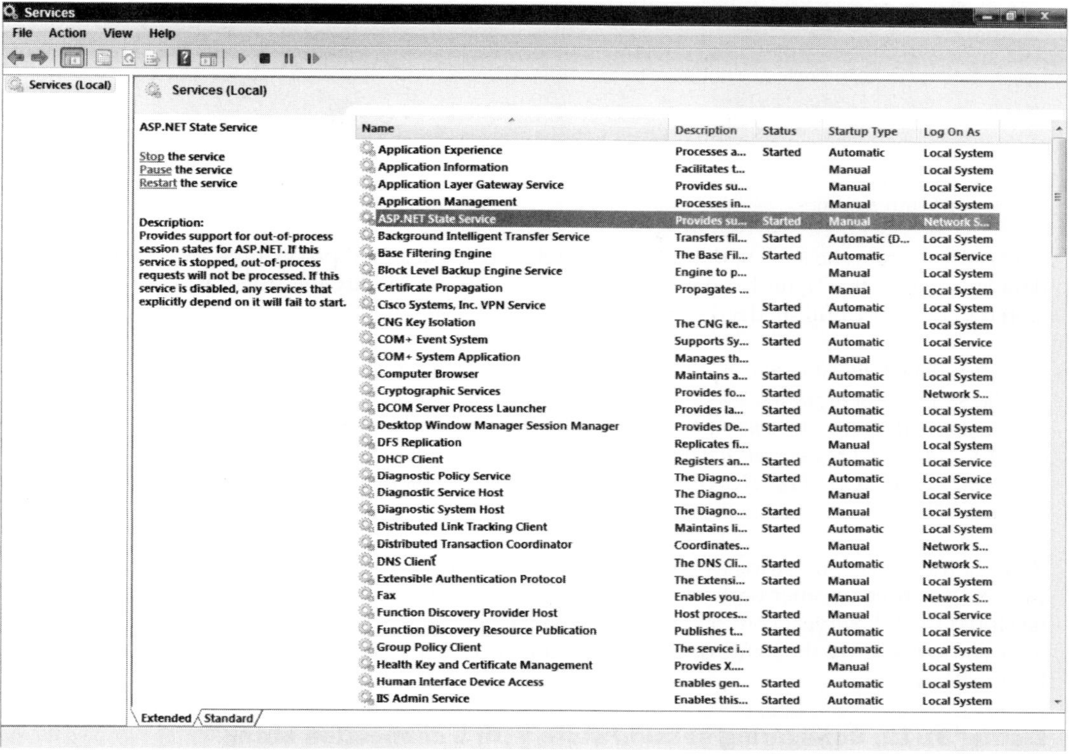

Figure 31-2

All compatible versions of ASP.NET share a single state service instance, which is the service installed with the highest version of ASP.NET. For example, if you have installed ASP.NET 2.0 on a server where ASP.NET 1.0 and 1.1 are already running, the ASP.NET 2.0 installation replaces the ASP.NET 1.1's state server instance. The ASP.NET 2.0 service is guaranteed to work for all previous compatible versions of ASP.NET.

SQL Server

When you choose the `SQLServer` option, session data is stored in a Microsoft SQL Server database. Even if SQL Server goes down, the built-in SQL Server recovery features enable you to recover all the session data. Configuring ASP.NET to support SQL Server for session state is just as simple as configuring the Windows Service. The only difference is that you run a T-SQL script that ships with ASP.NET, `InstallSqlState.sql`. The T-SQL script that uninstalls ASP.NET SQL Server support, called `Uninstall-SqlState.sql`, is also included. The install and uninstall scripts are available in the Framework folder. An example of using the SQL Server option is presented in Listing 31-11.

Listing 31-11: Using the SQLServer option for session state

```
<configuration>
  <system.web>
    <sessionStaet
```

Continued

```
      mode="SQLServer"
      sqlConnectionString="data source=ExampleSessionServer;
      user id=ExampleWebUser;password=P@55worD"
      cookieless="false"
      timeout="20"
    />
  </system.web>
</configuration>
```

ASP.NET accesses the session data stored in SQL Server via stored procedures. By default, all the session data is stored in the Temp DB database. However, you can modify the stored procedures so they are stored in tables in a full-fledged database other than Temp DB.

Even though the SQL Server–based session state provides a scalable use of session state, it could become the single point of failure. This is because SQL Server session state uses the same SQL Server database for all applications in the same ASP.NET process. This problem has been fixed ever since ASP.NET 2.0, and you can configure different databases for each application. Now you can use the `aspnet_regsql.exe` *utility to configure this. However, if you are looking for a solution for older .NET Frameworks, a fix is available at* `http://support.microsoft.com/default.aspx?scid = kb;EN-US;836680.`

Because the connection strings are stored in the strongly typed mode, the connection string information can be referenced in other parts of the configuration file. For example, when configuring session state to be stored in SQL Server, you can specify the connection string in the `connectionStrings` section, and then you can specify the name of the connection string in the `<sessionState>` element, as shown in Listing 31-12.

Listing 31-12: Configuring session state with a connection string

```
<configuration>

  <connectionStrings>
    <add name = "ExampleSqlSessionState"
         connectionString = "data source=ExampleSessionServer;
         user id=ExampleWebUser;password=P@55worD" />
  </connectionStrings>

  <system.web>
    <sessionState
      mode="SQLServer"
      sqlConnectionString="ExampleSqlSessionState"
      cookieless="false"
      timeout="20"
    />
  </system.web>

</configuration>
```

Custom State Store

The session state in ASP.NET 3.5 is based on a pluggable architecture with different providers that inherit the `SessionStateStoreProviderBase` class. If you want to create your own custom provider or use a third-party provider, you must set the mode to `Custom`.

You specify the custom provider assembly that inherits the `SessionStateStoreProviderBase` class, as shown in Listing 31-13.

Listing 31-13: Working with your own session state provider

```
<configuration>
   <system.web>

      <sessionState
          mode="Custom"
          customProvider="CustomStateProvider">
         <providers>
           <add name="CustomStateProvider"
            type="CustomStateProviderAssembly,
              CustomStateProviderNamespace.CustomStateProvider"/>
         </providers>
      </sessionState>

   </system.web>
</configuration>
```

In the previous example, you have configured the session state mode as custom because you have specified the provider name as `CustomStateProvider`. From there, you add the provider element and include the type of the provider with namespace and class name.

You can read more about the provider model and custom providers in Chapters 12 and 13.

Compilation Configuration

ASP.NET supports the dynamic compilation of ASP.NET pages, Web services, HttpHandlers, ASP.NET application files (such as the `Global.asax` file), source files, and so on. These files are automatically compiled on demand when they are first required by an ASP.NET application.

Any changes to a dynamically compiled file causes all affected resources to become automatically invalidated and recompiled. This system enables developers to quickly develop applications with a minimum of process overhead because they can just press Save to immediately cause code changes to take effect within their applications.

The ASP.NET 1.0 and 1.1 features are extended in ASP.NET 2.0 and 3.5 to account for other file types, including class files. The ASP.NET compilation settings can be configured using the `<compilation>` section in `web.config` or `machine.config`. The ASP.NET engine compiles the page when necessary and saves the generated code in code cache. This cached code is used when executing the ASP.NET pages. Listing 31-14 shows the syntax for the `<compilation>` section.

Listing 31-14: The compilation section

```
<!-- compilation Attributes -->
<compilation
  tempDirectory="directory"
  debug="[true|false]"
```

Continued

```
    strict="[true|false]"
    explicit="[true|false]"
    batch="[true|false]"
    batchTimeout="timeout in seconds"
    maxBatchSize="max number of pages per batched compilation"
    maxBatchGeneratedFileSize="max combined size in KB"
    numRecompilesBeforeAppRestart="max number of recompilations "
    defaultLanguage="name of a language as specified in a <compiler/> element below"
      <compilers>
         <compiler language="language"
                   extension="ext"
                   type=".NET Type"
                   warningLevel="number"
                   compilerOptions="options"/>
      </compilers>
      <assemblies>
         <add assembly="assembly"/>
      </assemblies>
      <codeSubDirectories>
        <codeSubDirectory directoryName="sub-directory name"/>
      </codeSubDirectories>
      <buildproviders>
        <buildprovider
          extension="file extension"
          type="type reference"/>
      </buildproviders>
  </compilation>
```

Now take a more detailed look at these `<compilation>` attributes:

- `batch`: Specifies whether the batch compilation is supported. The default value is `true`.
- `maxBatchSize`: Specifies the maximum number of pages/classes that can be compiled into a single batch. The default value is 1000.
- `maxBatchGeneratedFileSize`: Specifies the maximum output size of a batch assembly compilation. The default value is 1000 KB.
- `batchTimeout`: Specifies the amount of time (minutes) granted for batch compilation to occur. If this timeout elapses without compilation being completed, an exception is thrown. The default value is 15 minutes.
- `debug`: Specifies whether to compile production assemblies or debug assemblies. The default is `false`.
- `defaultLanguage`: Specifies the default programming language, such as `VB` or `C#`, to use in dynamic compilation files. Language names are defined using the `<compiler>` child element. The default value is `VB`.
- `explicit`: Specifies whether the Microsoft Visual Basic code compile option is explicit. The default is `true`.
- `numRecompilesBeforeAppRestart`: Specifies the number of dynamic recompiles of resources that can occur before the application restarts.
- `strict`: Specifies the setting of the Visual Basic strict compile option.

- `tempDirectory`: Specifies the directory to use for temporary file storage during compilation. By default, ASP.NET creates the temp file in the `[WinNT\Windows]\Microsoft.NET\Framework\[version]\Temporary ASP.NET` Files folder.
- `compilers`: The `<compilers>` section can contain multiple `<compiler>` subelements, which are used to create a new compiler definition:
  - The `language` attribute specifies the languages (separated by semicolons) used in dynamic compilation files. For example, `C#; VB`.
  - The `extension` attribute specifies the list of filename extensions (separated by semicolons) used for dynamic code. For example, `.cs; .vb`.
  - The `type` attribute specifies .NET type/class that extends the `CodeDomProvider` class used to compile all resources that use either the specified language or the file extension.
  - The `warningLevel` attribute specifies how the .NET compiler should treat compiler warnings as errors. Five levels of compiler warnings exist, numbered 0 through 4. When the compiler transcends the warning level set by this attribute, compilation fails. The meaning of each warning level is determined by the programming language and compiler you're using; consult the reference specification for your compiler to get more information about the warning levels associated with compiler operations and what events trigger compiler warnings.
  - The `compilerOptions` attribute enables you to include compiler's command-line switches while compiling the ASP.NET source.
- `assemblies`: Specifies assemblies that are used during the compilation process.
- `codeSubDirectories`: Specifies an ordered collection of subdirectories containing files compiled at runtime. Adding the `codeSubDirectories` section creates separate assemblies.
- `buildproviders`: Specifies a collection of build providers used to compile custom resource files.

Browser Capabilities

Identifying and using the browser's capabilities is essential for Web applications. The browser capabilities component was designed for the variety of desktop browsers, such as Microsoft's Internet Explorer, Netscape, Opera, and so on. The `<browserCaps>` element enables you to specify the configuration settings for the browser capabilities component. The `<browserCaps>` element can be declared at the machine, site, application, and subdirectory level.

> *The* `HttpBrowserCapabilities` *class contains all the browser properties. The properties can be set and retrieved in this section. The* `<browserCaps>` *element has been deprecated since ASP.NET 2.0 and now you should instead focus on using* `.browser` *files.*

When a request is received from a browser, the browser capabilities component identifies the browser's capabilities from the request headers.

For each browser, compile a collection of settings relevant to applications. These settings may either be statically configured or gathered from request headers. Allow the application to extend or modify the capabilities settings associated with browsers and to access values through a strongly typed object model. The ASP.NET mobile capabilities depend on the browser capabilities component.

In ASP.NET 3.5, all the browser capability information is represented in browser definition files. The browser definitions are stored in `*.browser` file types and specified in XML format. A single file may contain one or more browser definitions. The `*.browser` files are stored in the `Config\Browsers` subdirectory of the Framework installation directory (for example, `[WinNT\Windows]\Microsoft.NET\Framework\v2.0.50727\CONFIG\Browsers`), as shown in Figure 31-3. Application-specific browser definition files are stored in the `/Browsers` subdirectory of the application.

In ASP.NET 1.0 and 1.1, the browser cap information was stored in the `machine.config` *and* `web.config` *files themselves.*

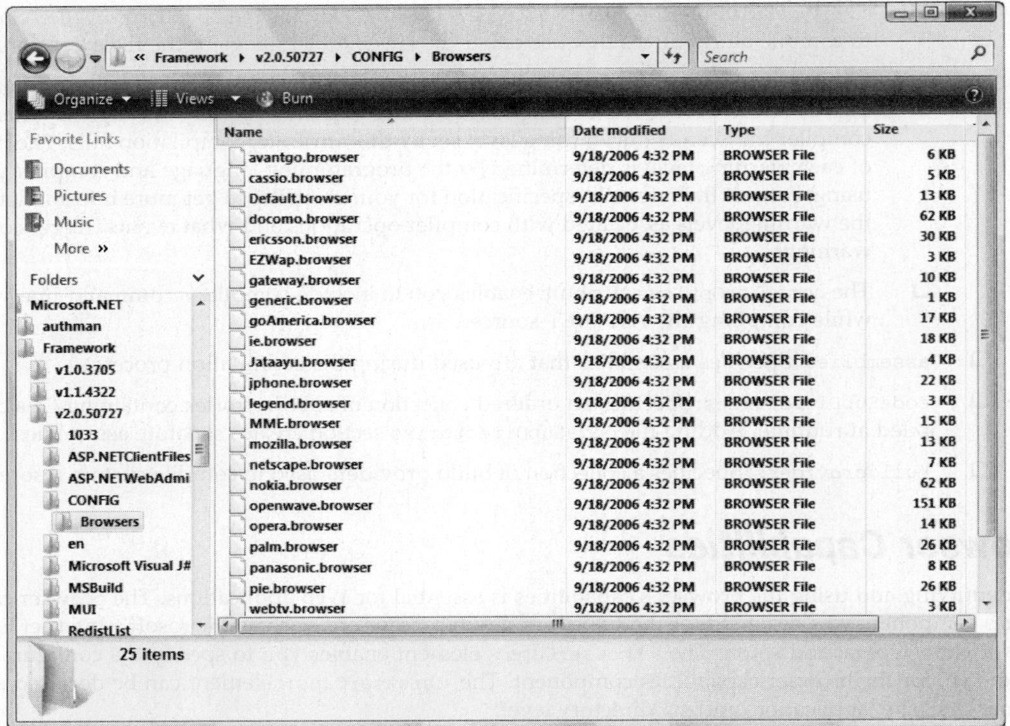

Figure 31-3

The browser definition file format defines each browser as an entity, self-contained in a `<browser>` XML element. Each browser has its own ID that describes a class of browser and its parent class. The root node of a browser definition file is the `<browsers>` element and multiple browser entries identified using the `id` attribute of the `<browser>` element.

Listing 31-15 shows a section of the `ie.browser` file.

Listing 31-15: Content of IE.browser file

```
<browsers>
    <browser id="IE" parentID="Mozilla">
        <identification>
```

```
            <userAgent match="^Mozilla[^(]*\([C|c]ompatible;\s*MSIE
        (?'version'(?'major'\d+)(?'minor'\.\d+)(?'letters'\w*))(?'extra'[^)]*)" />
            <userAgent nonMatch="Opera" />
            <userAgent nonMatch="Go\.Web" />
            <userAgent nonMatch="Windows CE" />
            <userAgent nonMatch="EudoraWeb" />
        </identification>
        <capture>
        </capture>
        <capabilities>

            <capability name="browser"                  value="IE" />
            <capability name="extra"                    value="${extra}" />
            <capability name="isColor"                  value="true" />
            <capability name="letters"                  value="${letters}" />
            <capability name="majorversion"             value="${major}" />
            <capability name="minorversion"             value="${minor}" />
            <capability name="screenBitDepth"           value="8" />
            <capability name="type"                     value="IE${major}" />
            <capability name="version"                  value="${version}" />

        </capabilities>
    </browser>
    ...
```

The `id` attribute of the `<browser>` element uniquely identifies the class of browser. The `parentID` attribute of the `<browser>` element specifies the unique ID of the parent browser class. Both the `id` and the `parentID` are required values.

Before running an ASP.NET application, the framework compiles all the browser definitions into an assembly and installs the compilation in GAC. When the browser definition files at the system level are modified, they do not automatically reflect the change in each and every ASP.NET application. Therefore, it becomes the responsibility of the developer or the installation tool to update this information. You can send the updated browser information to all the ASP.NET applications by running the `aspnet_regbrowsers.exe` *utility provided by the framework. When the* `aspnet_regbrowsers.exe` *utility is called, the browser information is recompiled and the new assembly is stored in the GAC; this assembly is reused by all the ASP.NET applications. Nevertheless, browser definitions at the application level are automatically parsed and compiled on demand when the application is started. If any changes are made to the application's* `/Browsers` *directory, the application is automatically recycled.*

Custom Errors

When the ASP.NET application fails, the ASP.NET page can show the default error page with the source code and line number of the error. However, this approach has a few problems:

- The source code and error message may not make any sense to a less-experienced end user.
- If the same source code and the error messages are displayed to a hacker, subsequent damage could result.

Displaying too much error information could provide important implementation details that you are in most cases going to want to keep from the public. Figure 31-4 shows an example of this.

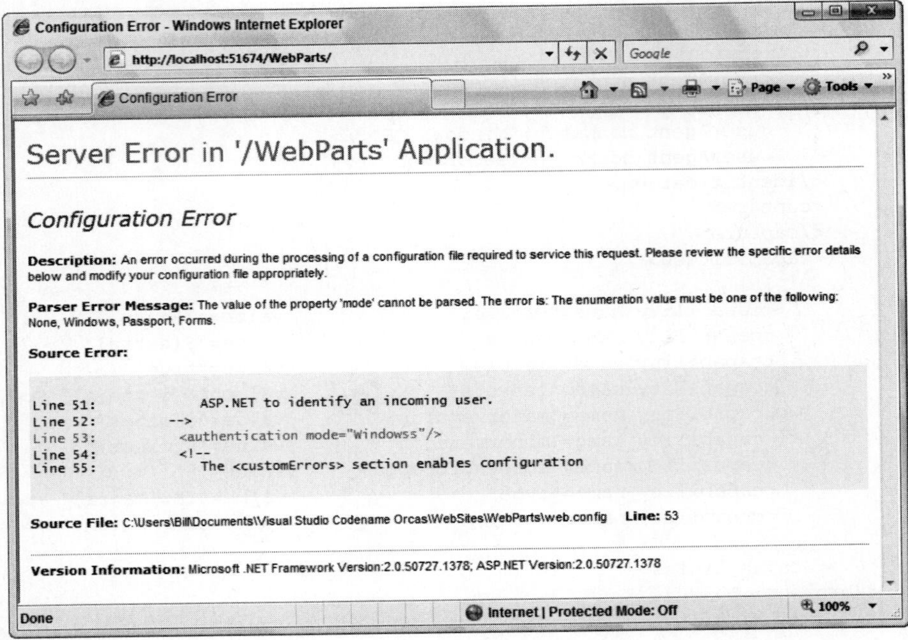

Figure 31-4

However, ASP.NET provides excellent infrastructure to prevent this kind of error information. The <customErrors> section provides a means for defining custom error messages in an ASP.NET application. The syntax is as follows:

```
<customErrors defaultRedirect="[url]" mode="[on/off/remote]">
   <error statusCode="[statuscode]" redirect="[url]" />
</customErrors>
```

- defaultRedirect: Specifies the default URL to which the client browser should be redirected if an error occurs. This is an optional setting.
- mode: Specifies if the status of the custom errors is enabled, disabled, or shown only to remote machines. The possible values are On, Off, RemoteOnly. On indicates that the custom errors are enabled. Off indicates that the custom errors are disabled. RemoteOnly indicates that the custom errors are shown only to remote clients.
- customErrors: The <customErrors> section supports multiple <error> subelements that are used to define custom errors. Each <error> subelement can include a statusCode attribute and a URL.

Authentication

In Chapter 21, you see the authentication process in detail. In this section, you can review configuration-specific information. Authentication is a process that verifies the identity of the user and establishes the identity between the server and a request. Because HTTP is a stateless protocol, the authentication information is persisted somewhere in the client or the server; ASP.NET supports both of these.

You can store the server-side information in `Session` objects. When it comes to client side, you have many options:

- Cookies
- ViewState
- URL
- Hidden fields

ASP.NET 3.5 supports following authentication methods out of the box:

- Windows authentication
- Passport authentication
- Forms Authentication

If you would like to disable authentication, you can use the setting `mode = "None"`:

```
<authentication mode="None" />
```

Windows Authentication

ASP.NET relies on IIS's infrastructure to implement Windows authentication, and Windows authentication enables you to authenticate requests using Windows Challenge/Response semantics. When the Web server receives a request, it initially denies access to the request (which is a challenge). This triggers the browser to pop up a window to collect the credentials; the request responds with a hashed value of the Windows credentials, which the server can then choose to authenticate.

To implement Windows authentication, you configure the appropriate Web site or virtual directory using IIS. You can then use the `<authentication>` element to mark the Web application or virtual directory with Windows authentication. This is illustrated in Listing 31-16.

Listing 31-16: Setting authentication to Windows authentication

```
<configuration>
   <system.web>

      <authentication mode="Windows">

   </system.web>
</configuration>
```

The `<authentication>` element can be declared only at the machine, site, or application level. Any attempt to declare it in a configuration file at the subdirectory or page level results in a parser error message.

Passport Authentication

ASP.NET 3.5 relies on the Passport SDK to implement Passport authentication, which is promoted by Microsoft Corporation. Passport is a subscription-based authentication mechanism that allows end users to remember a single username/password pair across multiple Web applications that implement Passport authentication.

ASP.NET 3.5 authenticates users based on the credentials presented by users. The Passport service sends a token back to authenticate. The token is stored in a site-specific cookie after it has been authenticated with `login.passport.com`. Using the `redirectUrl` attribute of the `<passport>` authentication option, you can control how non-authenticated Passport users are directed, as in the following example:

```
<passport redirectUrl="/Passport/SignIn.aspx" />
```

Forms Authentication

Forms Authentication is the widely used authentication mechanism. Forms Authentication can be configured using the `<authentication>` section along with the `<forms>` subsection. The structure of an `<authentication>` section that deals with forms authentication in the configuration file is presented in Listing 31-17.

Listing 31-17: The <authentication> section working with forms authentication

```
<configuration>
   <system.web>

      <authentication mode="Forms">
         <forms
            name="[name]"
            loginUrl="[url]"
            protection="[All|None|Encryption|Validation]"
            timeout="30"
            path="/"
            requireSSL="[true|false]"
            slidingExpiration="[true|false]"
            cookieless="UseCookies|UseUri|AutoDetect|UseDeviceProfile"
            defaultUrl="[url]"
            domain="string">
            <credentials passwordFormat="[Clear, SHA1, MD5]">
               <user name="[UserName]" password="[password]"/>
            </credentials>
         </forms>
      </authentication>

   </system.web>
</configuration>
```

Each attribute is shown in detail in the following list:

- `name`: Specifies the name of the HTTP authentication ticket. The default value is `.ASPXAUTH`.
- `loginUrl`: Specifies the URL to which the request is redirected if the current request doesn't have a valid authentication ticket.
- `protection`: Specifies the method used to protect cookie data. Valid values are `All`, `None`, `Encryption`, and `Validation`.

  - `Encryption`: Specifies that content of the cookie is encrypted using `TripleDES` or `DES` cryptography algorithms in the configuration file. However, the data validation is not done on the cookie.
  - `Validation`: Specifies that content of the cookie is not encrypted, but validates that the cookie data has not been altered in transit.
  - `All`: Specifies that content of the cookie is protected using both data validation and encryption. The configured data validation algorithm is used based on the `<machineKey>` element, and Triple DES is used for encryption. The default value is `All`, and it indicates the highest protection available.
  - `None`: Specifies no protection mechanism is applied on the cookie. Web applications that do not store any sensitive information and potentially use cookies for personalization can look at this option. When `None` is specified, both encryption and validation are disabled.
- `timeout`: Specifies cookie expiration time in terms of minutes. The `timeout` attribute is a sliding value, which expires `n` minutes from the time the last request was received. The default value is 30 minutes.
- `path`: Specifies the path to use for the issued cookie. The default value is `/` to avoid difficulties with mismatched case in paths because browsers are strictly case-sensitive when returning cookies.
- `requireSSL`: Specifies whether Forms Authentication should happen in a secure HTTPS connection.
- `slidingExpiration`: Specifies whether valid cookies should be updated periodically when used. When false, a ticket is good for only the duration of the period for which it is issued, and a user must re-authenticate even during an active session.
- `cookieless`: Specifies whether cookieless authentication is supported. Supported values are `UseCookies`, `UseUri`, `Auto`, and `UseDeviceProfile`. The default value is `UseDeviceProfile`.
- `defaultUrl`: Specifies the default URL used by the login control to control redirection after authentication.
- `domain`: Specifies the domain name string to be attached in the authentication cookie. This attribute is particularly useful when the same authentication cookie is shared among multiple sites across the domain.

It is strongly recommended that the `loginUrl` *should be an SSL URL (*`https://`*) to keep secure credentials secure from prying eyes.*

Anonymous Identity

Many application types require the capability to work with anonymous users, although this is especially true for e-commerce Web applications. In these cases, your site must support *both* anonymous and authenticated users. When anonymous users are browsing the site and adding items to a shopping cart, the Web application needs a way to uniquely identify these users. For example, if you look at busy e-commerce Web sites such as `Amazon.com` or `BN.com`, they do not have a concept called anonymous users. Rather these sites assign a unique identity to each user.

In ASP.NET 1.0 and 1.1, no out-of-the box feature existed to enable a developer to achieve this identification of users. Most developers used `SessionID` to identify users uniquely. They experienced a few pitfalls inherent in this method. Since the introduction of ASP.NET 2.0, ASP.NET has had anonymous identity support using the `<anonymousIdentification>` section in the configuration file. The following listing here in Listing 31-18 shows the `<anonymousIdentification>` configuration section settings.

Listing 31-18: Working with anonymous identification in the configuration file

```
<configuration>
  <system.web>

    <anonymousIdentification
                 enabled="false"
                 cookieName=".ASPXANONYMOUS
                 cookieTimeout="100000"
                 cookiePath="/"
                 cookieRequireSSL="false"
                 cookieSlidingExpiration = "true"
                 cookieProtection = "Validation"
                 cookieLess="UseCookies|UseUri|AutoDetect|UseDeviceProfile"
                 domain="... ."     />

  </system.web>
</configuration>
```

The `enabled` attribute within the `<anonymousIdentification>` section specifies whether the anonymous access capabilities of ASP.NET are enabled. The other attributes are comparable to those in the authentication section from Listing 31-17. When working with anonymous identification, it is possible that the end user will have cookies disabled in their environments. When cookies are not enabled by the end user, the identity of the user is then stored in the URL string within the end user's browser.

Authorization

The authorization process verifies whether a user has the privilege to access the resource he is trying to request. ASP.NET 3.5 supports both file and URL authorization. The authorization process dictated by an application can be controlled by using the `<authorization>` section within the configuration file. The `<authorization>` section, as presented in Listing 31-19, can contain subsections that either allow or deny permission to a user, a group of users contained within a specific role in the system, or a request that is coming to the server in a particular fashion (such as an HTTP GET request). Optionally, you can also use the `<location>` section to grant special authorization permission to only a particular folder or file within the application.

Listing 31-19: Authorization capabilities from the configuration file

```
<authorization>
   <allow users="" roles="" verbs="" />
   <deny users="" roles="" verbs="" />
</authorization>
```

URL Authorization

The URL Authorization is a service provided by `URLAuthorizationModule` (inherited from `HttpModule`) to control the access to resources such as `.aspx` files. The URL Authorization is very useful if you want to allow or deny certain parts of your ASP.NET application to certain people or roles.

For example, you may want to restrict the administration part of your ASP.NET application only to administrators and deny access to others. You can achieve this very easily with URL Authorization. URL Authorization can be configurable based on the user, the role, or HTTP verbs such as HTTP GET request or HTTP POST request.

You can configure URL Authorization in the `web.config` file with `<allow>` and `<deny>` attributes. For example, the following code (Listing 31-20) shows how you can allow the user `Bubbles` and deny the groups `Sales` and `Marketing` access to the application.

Listing 31-20: An example of allowing and denying entities from the <authorization> section

```
<system.web>
    <authorization>
        <allow users="Bubbles" />
        <deny roles="Sales, Marketing" />
    </authorization>
</system.web>
```

The `<allow>` and `<deny>` elements support `users`, `roles`, and `verbs` values. As you can see from the previous code example, you can add multiple users and groups by separating them with commas.

Two special characters, an asterisk (`*`) and a question mark (`?`), are supported by `URLAuthorizationModule`. The asterisk symbol represents all users (anonymous and registered) and the question mark represents only anonymous users. The following code example in Listing 31-21 denies access to all anonymous users and grants access to anyone contained within the Admin role.

Listing 31-21: Denying anonymous users

```
<system.web>
    <authorization>
        <allow roles="Admin" />
        <deny users="?" />
    </authorization>
</system.web>
```

You can also grant or deny users or groups access to certain HTTP methods. In the example in Listing 31-22, access to the HTTP GET method is denied to the users contained within the Admin role, whereas access to the HTTP POST method is denied to all users.

Listing 31-22: Denying users and roles by verb

```
<system.web>
    <authorization>
        <deny verbs="GET" roles="Admin" />
        <deny verbs="POST" users="*" />
    </authorization>
</system.web>
```

File Authorization

It is possible to construct the authorization section within the configuration file so that what is specified can be applied to a specific file or directory using the <location> element. For example, suppose you have a root directory called Home within your application and nested within that root directory you have a subdirectory called Documents. Suppose you want to allow access to the Documents subdirectory only to those users contained within the Admin role. This scenario is illustrated in Listing 31-23.

Listing 31-23: Granting access to the Documents subdirectory for the Admin role

```
<configuration>
    <location path="Documents">
        <system.web>
            <authorization>
                <allow roles="Admin" />
                <deny users="*" />
            </authorization>
        </system.web>
    </location>
</configuration>
```

The ASP.NET application does not verify the path specified in the path attribute. If the given path is invalid, ASP.NET does not apply the security setting.

You can also set the security for a single file as presented in Listing 31-24.

Listing 31-24: Granting access to a specific file for the Admin role

```
<configuration>
    <location path="Documents/Default.aspx">
        <system.web>
            <authorization>
                <allow roles="Admin" />
                <deny users="*" />
            </authorization>
        </system.web>
    </location>
</configuration>
```

Locking-Down Configuration Settings

ASP.NET's configuration system is quite flexible in terms of applying configuration information to a specific application or folder. Even though the configuration system is flexible, in some cases you may want to limit the configuration options that a particular application on the server can control. For example, you could decide to change the way in which the ASP.NET session information is stored. This lock-down process can be achieved using the <location> attributes allowOverride and allowDefinition, as well as the path attribute.

Listing 31-25 illustrates this approach. A <location> section in this machine.config file identifies the path "Default Web Site/ExampleApplication" and allows any application to override the <trace> setting through the use of the allowOverride attribute.

Listing 31-25: Allowing a <trace> section to be overridden in a lower configuration file

```
<configuration>
    <location path="Default Web Site/ExampleApplication" allowOverride="true">
        <trace enabled="false"/>
    </location>
</configuration>
```

The trace attribute can be overridden because the `allowOverride` attribute is set to `true`. You are able to override the tracing setting in the `ExampleApplication`'s `web.config` file and enable the local `<trace>` element, thereby overriding the settings presented in Listing 31-25.

However, if you had written the attribute as `allowOverride = "false"` in the `<location>` section of the `machine.config` file, the `web.config` file for `ExampleApplication` is unable to override that specific setting.

ASP.NET Page Configuration

When an ASP.NET application has been deployed, the `<pages>` section of the configuration file enables you to control some of the default behaviors for each and every ASP.NET page. These behaviors include options such as whether you should buffer the output before sending it or whether session state should be enabled for the entire application. An example of using the `<pages>` section is presented in Listing 31-26.

Listing 31-26: Configuring the <pages> section

```
<configuration>
  <system.web>

    <pages buffer="true"
           enableSessionState="true"
           enableViewState="true"
           enableViewStateMac="false"
           autoEventWireup="true"
           smartNavigation="false"
           masterPageFile="~/ExampleApplicationMasterPage.master"
           pageBaseType="System.Web.UI.Page"
           userControlBaseType="System.Web.UI.UserControl"
           compilationMode="Auto"
           validateRequest="true" >
        <namespaces>
           <add namespace="Wrox.ExampleApplication"/>
        </namespaces>
        <controls />
        <tagMapping />
    </pages>

  </system.web>
</configuration>
```

The following list gives you the ASP.NET page configuration information elements in detail:

- `buffer`: Specifies whether the requests must be buffered on the server before it is sent it to the client.
- `enableSessionState`: Specifies whether the session state for the current ASP.NET application should be enabled. The possible values are `true`, `false`, or `readonly`. The `readonly` value means that the application can read the session values but cannot modify them.
- `enableViewState`: Specifies whether the ViewState is enabled for all the controls. If the application does not use ViewState, you can set the `value` to `false` in the application's `web.config` file.
- `autoEventWireup`: Specifies whether ASP.NET can automatically wire-up common page events such as Load or Error.
- `smartNavigation`: Smart navigation is a feature that takes advantage of IE as a client's browser to prevent the redrawing that occurs when a page is posted back to itself. Using smart navigation, the request is sent through an `IFRAME` on the client, and IE redraws only the sections of the page that have changed. By default, this option is set to `false`. When it is enabled, it is available only to Internet Explorer browsers — all other browsers get the standard behavior.
- `masterPageFile`: Identifies the master page for the current ASP.NET application. If you wish to apply the master page template to only a specific subset of pages (such as pages contained within a specific folder of your application), you can use the `<location>` element within the `web.config` file:

```
<configuration>
    <location path="ExampleApplicationAdmin">
        <system.web>
            <pages masterPageFile="~/ExampleApplicationAdminMasterPage.master" />
        </system.web>
    </location>
</configuration>
```

- `pageBaseType`: Specifies the base class for all the ASP.NET pages in the current ASP.NET application. By default, this option is set to `System.Web.UI.Page`. However, if you want all ASP.NET pages to inherit from some other base class, you can change the default via this setting.
- `userControlBaseType`: Specifies the base class for all the ASP.NET user controls in the current ASP.NET application. The default is `System.Web.UI.UserControl`. You can override the default option using this element.
- `validateRequest`: Specifies whether ASP.NET should validate all the incoming requests that are potentially dangerous like the cross-site script attack and the script injection attack. This feature provides out-of-the-box protection against cross-site scripting and script injection attacks by automatically checking all parameters in the request, ensuring that their content does not include HTML elements. For more information about this setting, visit `http://www.asp.net/faq/RequestValidation.aspx`.
- `namespaces`: Optionally, you can import a collection of assemblies that can be included in the precompilation process.
- `compilationMode`: Specifies how ASP.NET should compile the current Web application. Supported values are `Never`, `Always`, and `Auto`. When you set `compilationMode = "Never"`, this

means that the pages should never be compiled. A part error occurs if the page has constructs that require compilation. When you set `compilationMode = "Always"`, this means that the pages are always compiled. When you set `compilationMode = "Auto"`, ASP.NET does not compile the pages if that is possible.

Include Files

Unlike ASP.NET 1.0 and 1.1, ASP.NET 2.0 and 3.5 support *include* files in both the `machine.config` and the `web.config` files. When configuration content is to be included in multiple places or inside the location elements, an include file is an excellent way to encapsulate the content.

Any section in a configuration file can include content from a different file using the `configSource` attribute in the `<pages>` section. The value of the attribute indicates a virtual relative filename to the include file. Listing 31-27 is an example of such a directive.

Listing 31-27: Adding additional content to the web.config file

```
<configuration>
    <system.web>
        <pages configSource="SystemWeb.config" />
    </system.web>
</configuration>
```

The configuration include files can contain information that applies to a single section, and a single include file cannot contain more than one configuration section or a portion of a section. If the `config-Source` attribute is present, the section element in the source file should not contain any other attribute or any child element.

Nevertheless, the include file is not a full configuration file. It should contain only the include section, as presented in Listing 31-28.

Listing 31-28: The SystemWeb.config file

```
<pages authentication mode="Forms" />
```

The `configSource` attribute cannot be nested. An include file cannot nest another file inside it using the `configSource` attribute.

When an ASP.NET configuration file is changed, the application is restarted at runtime. When an external include file is used within the configuration file, the configuration reload happens without restarting the application.

Configuring ASP.NET Runtime Settings

The general configuration settings are those that specify how long a given ASP.NET resource, such as a page, is allowed to execute before being considered timed-out. The other settings specify the maximum size of a request (in kilobytes) or whether to use fully qualified URLs in redirects. These settings can be specified using the `<httpRuntime>` section within a configuration file. The `<httpRuntime>` element is applied at the ASP.NET application at the folder level. Listing 31-29 shows the default values used in the `<httpRuntime>` section.

Listing 31-29: The <httpRuntime> section

```
<configuration>
  <system.web>

    <httpRuntime
      useFullyQualifiedRedirectUrl="false"
      enable="true"
      executionTimeout="90"
      maxRequestLength="4096"
      requestLengthDiskThreshold="512"
      appRequestQueueLimit="5000"
      minFreeThreads="8"
      minLocalRequestFreeThreads="4"
      enableKernelOutputCache="true" />

  </system.web>
</configuration>
```

Enabling and Disabling ASP.NET Applications

The `enable` attribute specifies whether the current ASP.NET application is enabled. When set to `false`, the current ASP.NET application is disabled, and all the clients trying to connect to this site receive the HTTP 404 — File Not Found exception. This value should be set only at the machine or application level. If you set this value in any other level (such as subfolder level), it is ignored. This great feature enables the administrators to bring down the application for whatever reason without starting or stopping IIS. The default value is `true`.

Outside of this setting, it is also possible to take applications offline quickly by simply placing an `App_Offline.htm` *file in the root of your application. This* `.htm` *file does not need to actually contain anything (it will not make any difference). Just having the file in the root directory causes the application domain to come down, and all requests to the application get a Page Not Found error.*

Fully Qualified Redirect URLs

The `useFullyQualifiedRedirectUrl` attribute specifies whether the client-side redirects should include the fully qualified URL. When you are programming against the mobile devices, some devices require specifying fully qualified URLs. The default value is `false`.

Request Time-Out

The `executionTimeout` setting specifies the timeout option for an ASP.NET request time-out. The value of this attribute is the amount of time in seconds during which a resource can execute before ASP.NET times the request out. The default setting is 110 seconds. If you have a particular ASP.NET page or Web service that takes longer than 110 seconds to execute, you can extend the time limit in the configuration.

Maximum Request Length

The `maxRequestLength` attribute specifies the maximum file-size upload accepted by ASP.NET runtime. For example, if the ASP.NET application is required to process huge files, it is better to change this setting. The default is 4096. This number represents kilobytes (KB or around 4 MB).

Web applications are prone to attacks these days. The attacks range from a script injection attack to a denial of service (DoS) attack. The DoS is a typical attack that bombards the Web server with requests for large files. This huge number of requests ultimately brings down the Web server. The `maxRequestLength` attribute could save you from a DoS attack by setting a restriction on the size of requests.

Buffer Uploads

In ASP.NET 1.0 or 1.1, when a HTTP post is made (either a normal ASP.NET form post, file upload, or an XMLHTTP client-side post), the entire content is buffered in memory. This works out fine for smaller posts. However, when memory-based recycling is enabled, a large post can cause the ASP.NET worker process to recycle before the upload is completed. To avoid the unnecessary worker process recycling, ASP.NET 3.5 includes a setting called `requestLengthDiskThreshold`. This setting enables an administrator to configure the file upload buffering behavior without affecting the programming model. Administrators can configure a threshold below which requests will be buffered into memory. After a request exceeds the limit, it is transparently buffered on disk and consumed from there by whatever mechanism is used to consume the data. The valid values for this setting are numbers between `1` and `Int32.MaxSize` in KB.

When file buffering is enabled, the files are uploaded to the `codegen` folder. The default path for the `codegen` folder is the following:

```
[WinNT\Windows]\Microsoft.NET\Framework\[version]\Temporary ASP.NET Files\
[ApplicationName]
```

The files are buffered using a random name in a subfolder within the `codegen` folder called `Uploads`. The location of the `codegen` folder can be configured on a per application basis using the `tempDirectory` attribute of the `<compilation>` section.

This is not a change in ASP.NET; rather it is an internal change. When an ASP.NET 1.0 or 1.1 application is migrated to the .NET Framework 2.0 or 3.5, the ASP.NET application automatically takes advantage of this feature.

Thread Management

ASP.NET runtime uses free threads available in its thread pool to fulfill requests. The `minFreeThreads` attribute indicates the number of threads that ASP.NET guarantees is available within the thread pool. The default number of threads is eight. For complex applications that require additional threads to complete processing, this simply ensures that the threads are available and that the application will not be blocked while waiting for a free thread to schedule more work. The `minLocalRequestFreeThreads` attribute controls the number of free threads dedicated for local request processing; the default is four.

Application Queue Length

The `appRequestQueueLimit` attribute specifies the maximum number of requests that ASP.NET queues for the current ASP.NET application. ASP.NET queues requests when it does not have enough free threads to process them. The `minFreeThreads` attribute specifies the number of free threads the ASP.NET application should maintain, and this setting affects the number of items stored in the queue.

When the number of requests queued exceeds the limit set in the `appRequestQueueLimit` *setting, all the incoming requests are rejected and an* `HTTP 503 - Server Too Busy` *error is thrown back to the browser.*

Output Caching

The `enableKernelOutputCache` specifies whether the output caching is enabled at the IIS kernel level (`Http.sys`). At present, this setting applies only to Web servers IIS6 and higher.

Configuring the ASP.NET Worker Process

When a request for an ASP.NET page is received by IIS, it passes the request to an unmanaged DLL called `aspnet_isapi.dll`. The `aspnet_isapi.dll` further passes the request to a separate worker process, `aspnet_wp.exe` if you are working with IIS5, which runs all the ASP.NET applications. With IIS6 and higher, however, all the ASP.NET applications are run by the `w3wp.exe` process. The ASP.NET worker process can be configured using the `<processModel>` section in the `machine.config` file.

All the configuration sections talked about so far are read by managed code. On the other hand, the `<processModel>` *section is read by the* `aspnet_isapi.dll` *unmanaged DLL. Because the configuration information is read by an unmanaged DLL, the changed process model information is applied to all ASP.NET applications only after an IIS restart.*

The code example in Listing 31-30 shows the default format for the `<processModel>` section.

Listing 31-30: The structure of the <processModel> element

```
<processModel
    enable="true|false"
    timeout="hrs:mins:secs|Infinite"
    idleTimeout="hrs:mins:secs|Infinite"
    shutdownTimeout="hrs:mins:secs|Infinite"
    requestLimit="num|Infinite"
    requestQueueLimit="num|Infinite"
    restartQueueLimit="num|Infinite"
    memoryLimit="percent"
    cpuMask="num"
    webGarden="true|false"
    userName="username"
    password="password"
    logLevel="All|None|Errors"
    clientConnectedCheck="hrs:mins:secs|Infinite"
    responseDeadlockInterval="hrs:mins:secs|Infinite"
    responseRestartDeadlockInterval="hrs:mins:secs|Infinite"
    comAuthenticationLevel="Default|None|Connect|Call|
    Pkt|PktIntegrity|PktPrivacy"
    comImpersonationLevel="Default|Anonymous|Identify|
    Impersonate|Delegate"
    maxWorkerThreads="num"
    maxIoThreads="num"
/>
```

The following section looks at each of these attributes in more detail:

- `enable`: Specifies whether the process model is enabled. When set to `false`, the ASP.NET applications run under IIS's process model.

When ASP.NET is running under IIS6 or higher in native mode, the IIS6 or higher process model is used and most of the `<processModel>` *section within the configuration file is simply ignored. The* `autoConfig` *and* `requestQueueLimit` *attributes are still applied in this case.*

- `timeout`: Specifies how long the worker process lives before a new worker process is created to replace the current worker process. This value can be extremely useful if a scenario exists where the application's performance starts to degrade slightly after running for several weeks, as in the case of a memory leak. Rather than your having to manually start and stop the process, ASP.NET can restart automatically. The default value is `Infinite`.
- `idleTimeout`: Specifies how long the worker process should wait before it is shut down. You can shut down the ASP.NET worker process automatically using the `idleTimeout` option. The default value is `Infinite`. You can also set this value to a time using the format, HH:MM:SS:.
- `shutdownTimeout`: Specifies how long the worker process is given to shut itself down gracefully before ASP.NET calls the `Kill` command on the process. `Kill` is a low-level command that forcefully removes the process. The default value is 5 seconds.
- `requestLimit`: Specifies when the ASP.NET worker process should be recycled after a certain number of requests are served. The default value is `Infinite`.
- `requestQueueLimit`: Instructs ASP.NET to recycle the worker process if the limit for queued requests is exceeded. The default setting is 5000.
- `memoryLimit`: Specifies how much physical memory the worker process is allowed to consume before it is considered to be misbehaving or leaking memory. The default value is 60 percent of available physical memory.
- `username` **and** `password`: By default, all ASP.NET applications are executed using the ASPNET identity. If you want an ASP.NET application to run with a different account, you can provide the username and the password pair using these attributes.
- `logLevel`: Specifies how the ASP.NET worker process logs events. The default setting is to log errors only. However, you can also disable logging by specifying `None` or you can log everything using `All`. All the log items are written to the Windows Application Event Log.
- `clientConnectedCheck`: The `clientConnectedCheck` setting enables you to check whether the client is still connected at timed intervals before performing work. The default setting is 5 seconds.
- `responseDeadlockInterval`: Specifies how frequently the deadlock check should occur. A deadlock is considered to exist when requests are queued and no responses have been sent during this interval. After a deadlock, the process is restarted. The default value is 3 minutes.
- `responseRestartDeadlockInterval`: Specifies, when a deadlock is detected by the runtime, how long the runtime should wait before restarting the process. The default value is 9 minutes.
- `comAuthenticationLevel`: Controls the level of authentication for DCOM security. The default is set to `Connect`. Other values are `Default`, `None`, `Call`, `Pkt`, `PktIntegrity`, and `PktPrivacy`.
- `comImpersonationLevel`: Controls the authentication level for COM security. The default is set to `Impersonate`. Other values are `Default`, `Anonymous`, `Identify`, and `Delegate`.
- `webGarden`: Specifies whether Web Garden mode is enabled. The default setting is `false`. A Web Garden lets you host multiple ASP.NET worker processes on a single server, thus providing

the application with better hardware scalability. Web Garden mode is supported only on multi-processor servers.

- cpuMask: Specifies which processors should be affinities to ASP.NET worker processes when webGarden = "true". The cpuMask is a hexadecimal value. The default value is all processors, shown as 0xFFFFFFFF.
- maxWorkerThreads: Specifies the maximum number of threads that exist within the ASP.NET worker process thread pool. The default is 20.
- maxIoThreads: Specifies the maximum number of I/O threads that exist within the ASP.NET worker process. The default is 20.

Running Multiple Web Sites with Multiple Versions of Framework

In the same context, multiple Web sites within the given Web server can host multiple Web sites, and each of these sites can be bound to a particular version of a .NET Framework. This is typically done using the aspnet_regiis.exe utility. The aspnet_regiis.exe utility is shipped with each version of the framework.

This utility has multiple switches. Using the -s switch allows you to install the current version of the .NET Framework runtime on a given Web site. Listing 31-31 shows how to install .NET Framework version 1.1 on the ExampleApplication Web site.

Listing 31-31: Installing .NET Framework version 1.1 on the ExampleApplication Web site

```
C:\WINDOWS\Microsoft.NET\Framework\v1.1.4322>
   aspnet_regiis -s W3SVC/1ROOT/ExampleApplication
```

Storing Application-Specific Settings

Every Web application must store some application-specific information for its runtime use. The <appSettings> section of the web.config file provides a way to define custom application settings for an ASP.NET application. The section can have multiple <add> subelements. Its syntax is as follows:

```
<appSettings>
   <add key="[key]" value="[value]"/>
</appSettings>
```

The <add> subelement supports two attributes:

- key: Specifies the key value in an appSettings hash table
- value: Specifies the value in an appSettings hash table

Listing 31-32 shows how to store an application-specific connection string. The key value is set to ApplicationInstanceID, and the value is set to the ASP.NET application instance and the name of the server on which the application is running.

Listing 31-32: Application instance information

```
<appSettings>
    <add key="ApplicationInstanceID" value="Instance1onServerOprta"/>
</appSettings>
```

Programming Configuration Files

In ASP.NET 1.0 and 1.1 versions of the Framework provided APIs that enabled you only to read information from the configuration file. You had no way to write information into the configuration file because no out-of-the-box support was available. However, some advanced developers wrote their own APIs to write the information back to the configuration files. Because the web.config file is an XML file, developers were able to open configuration file using the XmlDocument object, modify the settings, and write it back to the disk. Even though this approach worked fine, the way to access the configuration settings were not strongly typed. Therefore, validating the values was always a challenge.

However, ASP.NET 3.5 includes APIs (ASP.NET Management Objects) to manipulate the configuration information settings in machine.config and web.config files. ASP.NET Management Objects provide a strongly typed programming model that addresses targeted administrative aspects of a .NET Web Application Server. They also govern the creation and maintenance of the ASP.NET Web configuration. Using the ASP.NET Management Objects, you can manipulate the configuration information stored in the configuration files in the local or remote computer. These can be used to script any common administrative tasks or the writing of installation scripts.

All of the ASP.NET Management Objects are stored in the System.Configuration and System.Web.Configuration namespaces. You can access the configuration using the WebConfigurationManager class. The System.Configuration.Configuration class represents a merged view of the configuration settings from the machine.config and hierarchical web.config files. The System.Configuration and System.Web.Configuration namespaces have multiple classes that enable you to access pretty much all the settings available in the configuration file. The main difference between System.Configuration and System.Web.Configuration namespaces is that the System.Configuration namespace contains all the classes that apply to all the .NET applications. On the other hand, the System.Web.Configuration namespace contains the classes that are applicable only to ASP.NET Web applications. The following table shows the important classes in System.Configuration and their uses.

Class Name	Purpose
Configuration	Enables you to manipulate the configuration stored in the local computer or a remote one.
ConfigurationElementCollection	Enables you to enumerate the child elements stored inside the configuration file.
AppSettingsSection	Enables you to manipulate the <appSettings> section of the configuration file.
ConnectionStringsSettings	Enables you to manipulate the <connectionStrings> section of the configuration file.

Class Name	Purpose
ProtectedConfigurationSection	Enables you to manipulate the <protectedConfiguration> section of the configuration file.
ProtectedDataSection	Enables you to manipulate the <protectedData> section of the configuration file.

The next table shows classes from the System.Web.Configuration and their uses.

Class Name	Purpose
AuthenticationSection	Enables you to manipulate the <authentication> section of the configuration file.
AuthorizationSection	Enables you to manipulate the <authorization> section of the configuration file.
CompilationSection	Enables you to manipulate the <compilation> section of the configuration file.
CustomErrorsSection	Enables you to manipulate the <customErrors> section of the configuration file.
FormsAuthenticationConfiguration	Enables you to manipulate the <forms> section of the configuration file.
GlobalizationSection	Enables you to manipulate the <globalization> section of the configuration file.
HttpHandlersSection	Enables you to manipulate the <httpHandlers> section of the configuration file.
HttpModulesSection	Enables you to manipulate the <httpModules> section of the configuration file.
HttpRuntimeSection	Enables you to manipulate the <httpRuntime> section of the configuration file.
MachineKeySection	Enables you to manipulate the <machineKey> section of the configuration file.
MembershipSection	Enables you to manipulate the <membership> section of the configuration file.
PagesSection	Enables you to manipulate the <pages> section of the configuration file.
ProcessModelSection	Enables you to manipulate the <processModel> section of the configuration file.
WebPartsSection	Enables you to manipulate the <webParts> section of the configuration file.

All the configuration classes are implemented based on simple object-oriented based architecture that has an entity class that holds all the data and a collection class that has methods to add, remove, enumerate, and so on. Start your configuration file programming with a simple connection string enumeration, as shown in the following section.

Enumerating Connection Strings

In a Web application, you can store multiple connection strings. Some of them are used by the system and the others may be application-specific. You can write a very simple ASP.NET application that enumerates all the connection strings stored in the `web.config` file, as shown in Listing 31-33.

Listing 31-33: The web.config file

```
<?xml version="1.0" ?>
<configuration>

    <appSettings>
        <add key="symbolServer" value="192.168.1.1" />
    </appSettings>
    <connectionStrings>
        <add name="ExampleApplication"
        connectionString="server=ExampleApplicationServer;
        database=ExampleApplicationDB;uid=WebUser;pwd=P@$$worD9"
        providerName="System.Data.SqlClient"
        />
    </connectionStrings>
    <system.web>
        <compilation debug="false" />
        <authentication mode="None" />
    </system.web>

</configuration>
```

As shown in Listing 31-33, one application setting points to the symbol server, and one connection string is stored in the `web.config` file. Use the `ConnectionStrings` collection of the `System.Web.Configuration.WebConfigurationManager` class to read the connection strings, as seen in Listing 31-34.

Listing 31-34: Enum.aspx

VB

```
Protected Sub Page_Load(ByVal sender As Object, ByVal e As System.EventArgs)
    GridView1.DataSource = _
        System.Web.Configuration.WebConfigurationManager.ConnectionStrings
    GridView1.DataBind()
End Sub
```

C#

```
protected void Page_Load(object sender, EventArgs e)
{
    GridView1.DataSource =
       System.Web.Configuration.WebConfigurationManager.ConnectionStrings;
    GridView1.DataBind();
}
```

As shown in Listing 31-34, you've bound the `ConnectionStrings` property collection of the `WebConfigurationManager` class into the GridView control. The `WebConfigurationManager` class returns an instance of the `Configuration` class and the `ConnectionStrings` property is a static (shared in Visual Basic) property. Therefore, you are just binding the property collection into the GridView control. Figure 31-5 shows the list of connection strings stored in the ASP.NET application.

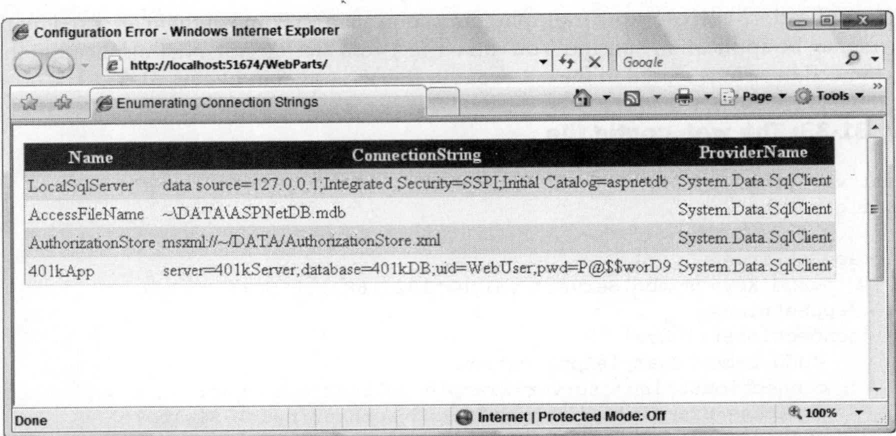

Figure 31-5

Adding a connection string at runtime is also a very easy task. If you do it as shown in Listing 31-35, you get an instance of the configuration object. Then you create a new `connectionStringSettings` class. You add the new class to the collection and call the update method. Listing 31-35 shows examples of this in both VB and C#.

Listing 31-35: Adding a connection string

VB

```
Protected Sub Button1_Click(ByVal sender As Object, ByVal e As System.EventArgs)
    ' Get the file path for the current web request
    Dim webPath As String = Request.ApplicationPath

    Try
        ' Get configuration object of the current web request
        Dim config As Configuration = _
          System.Web.Configuration.WebConfigurationManager.OpenWebConfiguration
(webPath)

        ' Create new connection setting from text boxes
        Dim newConnSetting As New _
        ConnectionStringSettings(txtName.Text, txtValue.Text, txtProvider.Text)

        ' Add the connection string to the collection
        config.ConnectionStrings.ConnectionStrings.Add(newConnSetting)

        ' Save the changes
        config.Save()
```

```
    Catch cEx As ConfigurationErrorsException
        lblStatus.Text = "Status: " + cEx.ToString()
    Catch ex As System.UnauthorizedAccessException
        ' The ASP.NET process account must have read/write access to the directory
        lblStatus.Text = "Status: " + "The ASP.NET process account must have
        read/write access to the directory"
    Catch eEx As Exception
        lblStatus.Text = "Status: " + eEx.ToString()
    End Try

    ShowConnectionStrings()
End Sub
```

C#

```
protected void Button1_Click(object sender, EventArgs e)
{
    // Get the file path for the current web request
    string webPath = Request.ApplicationPath;

    // Get configuration object of the current web request
    Configuration config =
    System.Web.Configuration.WebConfigurationManager.OpenWebConfiguration(webPath);

    // Create new connection setting from text boxes
    ConnectionStringSettings newConnSetting = new
    ConnectionStringSettings(txtName.Text, txtValue.Text, txtProvider.Text);

    try
    {
        // Add the connection string to the collection
        config.ConnectionStrings.ConnectionStrings.Add(newConnSetting);

        // Save the changes
        config.Save();
    }
    catch (ConfigurationErrorsException cEx)
    {
        lblStatus.Text = "Status: " + cEx.ToString();
    }
    catch (System.UnauthorizedAccessException uEx)
    {
        // The ASP.NET process account must have read/write access to the directory
        lblStatus.Text = "Status: " + "The ASP.NET process account must have" +
           "read/write access to the directory";
    }
    catch (Exception eEx)
    {
        lblStatus.Text = "Status: " + eEx.ToString();
    }

    // Reload the connection strings in the list box
    ShowConnectionStrings();
}
```

Manipulating a machine.config File

The `OpenMachineConfiguration` method of the `System.Configuration.ConfigurationManager` class provides a way to manipulate the `machine.config` file. The `OpenMachineConfiguration` method is a static method.

Listing 31-36 shows a simple example that enumerates all the section groups stored in the `machine.config` file. As shown in this listing, you're getting an instance of the configuration object using the `OpenMachineConfiguration` method. Then you are binding the `SectionGroups` collection with the GridView control.

Listing 31-36: Configuration groups from machine.config

VB

```
Protected Sub Button2_Click(ByVal sender As Object, ByVal e As System.EventArgs)
    ' List all the SectionGroups in machine.config file
    Dim configSetting As Configuration = _
      System.Configuration.ConfigurationManager.OpenMachineConfiguration()
    GridView1.DataSource = configSetting.SectionGroups
    GridView1.DataBind()
End Sub
```

C#

```
protected void Button2_Click(object sender, EventArgs e)
{
    // List all the SectionGroups in machine.config file
    Configuration configSetting =
      System.Configuration.ConfigurationManager.OpenMachineConfiguration();
    GridView1.DataSource = configSetting.SectionGroups;
    GridView1.DataBind();
}
```

In the same way, you can list all the configuration sections using the `Sections` collections, as shown in Listing 31-37.

Listing 31-37: Configuration sections from machine.config

VB

```
Protected Sub Button2_Click(ByVal sender As Object, ByVal e As System.EventArgs)
    ' List all the SectionGroups in machine.config file
    Dim configSetting As Configuration = _
      System.Configuration.ConfigurationManager.OpenMachineConfiguration()
    GridView1.DataSource = configSetting.Sections
    GridView1.DataBind()
End Sub
```

C#

```
protected void Button2_Click(object sender, EventArgs e)
{
    // List all the SectionGroups in machine.config file
    Configuration configSetting =
      System.Configuration.ConfigurationManager.OpenMachineConfiguration();
```

```
        GridView1.DataSource = configSetting.Sections;
        GridView1.DataBind();
    }
```

Manipulating web.config from Remote Servers

The ASP.NET Management Objects also provide a way to read configuration information from remote servers.

For example, if you would like to manipulate the Expense Web application's configuration file located on the imaginary `Optra.Microsoft.com` site, you can do so as shown in Listing 31-38.

Listing 31-38: Manipulating a remote server's web.config

VB

```
' Connect to the web application Expense on Optra.Microsoft.com server
Dim configSetting As Configuration = _
   System.Web.Configuration.WebConfigurationManager.OpenWebConfiguration _
      ("/Expense", "1", "Optra.Microsoft.com")

Dim section As System.Configuration.ConfigurationSection = _
   configSetting.GetSection("appSettings")

Dim element As KeyValueConfigurationElement = _
   CType(configSetting.AppSettings.Settings("keySection"), _
     KeyValueConfigurationElement)

If Not element Is Nothing Then
   Dim value As String = "New Value"
   element.Value = value

   Try
      config.Save()
   Catch ex As Exception
      Response.Write(ex.Message)
   End Try
End If
```

C#

```
// Connect to the web application Expense on Optra.Microsoft.com server
Configuration configSetting =
   System.Web.Configuration.WebConfigurationManager.OpenWebConfiguration
   ("/Expense", "1", "Optra.Microsoft.com");

ConfigurationSection section = configSetting.GetSection("appSettings");

KeyValueConfigurationElement element =
   configSetting.AppSettings.Settings["keySection"];

if (element != null)
{
   string value = "New Value";
   element.Value = value;
```

Continued

```
    try
    {
       configSetting.Save();
    }
       catch (Exception ex)
    {
       Response.Write(ex.Message);
    }
}
```

The code in Listing 31-38 demonstrates how to give the machine address in the constructor method to connect to the remote server. Then you change a particular `appSettings` section to a new value and save the changes.

Protecting Configuration Settings

When ASP.NET 1.0 was introduced, all the configuration information was stored in human-readable, clear-text format. However, ASP.NET 1.1 introduced a way to store the configuration information inside the registry using the Data Protection API (or DPAPI).

For example, Listing 31-39 shows how you can store a process model section's username and password information inside the registry.

Listing 31-39: Storing the username and password in the registry and then referencing these settings in the machine.config

```
<processModel
    userName="registry:HKLM\SOFTWARE\ExampleApp\Identity\ASPNET_SETREG,userName"
    password="registry:HKLM\SOFTWARE\ExampleApp\Identity\ASPNET_SETREG,password"
/>
```

ASP.NET 1.0 also acquired this functionality as a fix. Visit the following URL for more information: `http://support.microsoft.com/default.aspx?scid=kb;en-us;329290`.

ASP.NET 3.5 includes a system for protecting sensitive data stored in the configuration system. It uses industry-standard XML encryption to encrypt specified sections of configuration that contain any sensitive data.

Developers often feel apprehensive about sticking sensitive items such as connection strings, passwords, and more in the `web.config` file. For this reason, ASP.NET makes it possible to store these items in a format that is not readable by any human or machine process without intimate knowledge of the encryption techniques and keys used in the encryption process.

One of the most encrypted items in the web.config is the `<connectionStrings>` section. Listing 31-40 shows an example of a `web.config` file with an exposed connection string.

Listing 31-40: A standard connection string exposed in the web.config file

```
<?xml version="1.0"?>

<configuration>
```

```
    <appSettings/>

    <connectionStrings>
      <add name="Northwind"
   connectionString="Server=localhost;Integrated Security=True;Database=Northwind"
        providerName="System.Data.SqlClient" />
    </connectionStrings>

  <system.web>

        <compilation debug="false" />

        <authentication mode="Forms">
           <forms name="Wrox" loginUrl="Login.aspx" path="/">
              <credentials passwordFormat="Clear">
                 <user name="BillEvjen" password="Bubbles" />
              </credentials>
           </forms>
        </authentication>

    </system.web>
</configuration>
```

In this case, you might want to encrypt this connection string to the database. To accomplish this, the install of ASP.NET provides a tool called *aspnet_regiis.exe*. You find this tool at `C:\WINDOWS\Microsoft.NET\Framework\v2.0.50727`. To use this tool to encrypt the <connectionStrings> section, open a command prompt and navigate to the specified folder using `cd C:\WINDOWS\Microsoft.NET\Framework\v2.0.50727`. Another option is to just open the Visual Studio 2008 Command Prompt. After you are in one of these environments, you use the syntax presented in Listing 31-41 to encrypt the `<connectionStrings>` section.

Listing 31-41: Encrypting the <connectionString> section

```
aspnet_regiis -pe "connectionString" -app "/EncryptionExample"
```

Running this bit of script produces the results presented in Figure 31-6.

Looking over the script used in the encryption process, you can see that the `-pe` command specifies the section in the `web.config` file to encrypt, whereas the `-app` command specifies which application to actually work with. If you look back at the `web.config` file and examine the encryption that occurred, you see something similar to the code in Listing 31-42.

Listing 31-42: The encrypted <connectionStrings> section of the web.config

```
<?xml version="1.0"?>

<configuration>

    <appSettings/>

    <connectionStrings
```

Continued

```
        configProtectionProvider="RsaProtectedConfigurationProvider">
          <EncryptedData Type="http://www.w3.org/2001/04/xmlenc#Element"
             xmlns="http://www.w3.org/2001/04/xmlenc#">
             <EncryptionMethod
              Algorithm="http://www.w3.org/2001/04/xmlenc#tripledes-cbc" />
             <KeyInfo xmlns="http://www.w3.org/2000/09/xmldsig#">
                <EncryptedKey xmlns="http://www.w3.org/2001/04/xmlenc#">
                   <EncryptionMethod
                    Algorithm="http://www.w3.org/2001/04/xmlenc#rsa-1_5" />
                   <KeyInfo xmlns="http://www.w3.org/2000/09/xmldsig#">
                      <KeyName>Rsa Key</KeyName>
                   </KeyInfo>
                   <CipherData>
                      <CipherValue>
                       0s99STuGx+CdDXmWaOVc0prBFA65
                       Yub0VxDS7nOSQ79AAYcxKG7Alq1o
                       M2BqZGSmElc7c4w93qgZn0CNN
                       VHGhDLE1OjHPV942HaYhcddK5
                       5XY5j7L3WSEJFj68E2Ng9+EjU
                       o+oAGJVhCAuG8owQBaQ2Bri3+
                       tfUB/Q8LpOW4kP8=
                      </CipherValue>
                   </CipherData>
                </EncryptedKey>
             </KeyInfo>
             <CipherData>
                <CipherValue>
                O3/PtxajkdVD/5TLGddc1/
                C8cg8RFYl8MiRXh71h4ls=
                </CipherValue>
             </CipherData>
          </EncryptedData>
        </connectionStrings>

      <system.web>

          <compilation debug="false" />

          <authentication mode="Forms">
             <forms name="Wrox" loginUrl="Login.aspx" path="/">
                <credentials passwordFormat="Clear">
                   <user name="BillEvjen" password="Bubbles" />
                </credentials>
             </forms>
          </authentication>

        </system.web>
    </configuration>
```

Now when you work with a connection string in your ASP.NET application, ASP.NET itself automatically decrypts this section in order to utilize the values stored. Looking at the `web.config` file, you can see a subsection within the `<system.web>` section that exposes a username and password as clear text. This is also something that you might want to encrypt in order to keep it away from prying eyes. Because it is a subsection, you use the script presented in Listing 31-43.

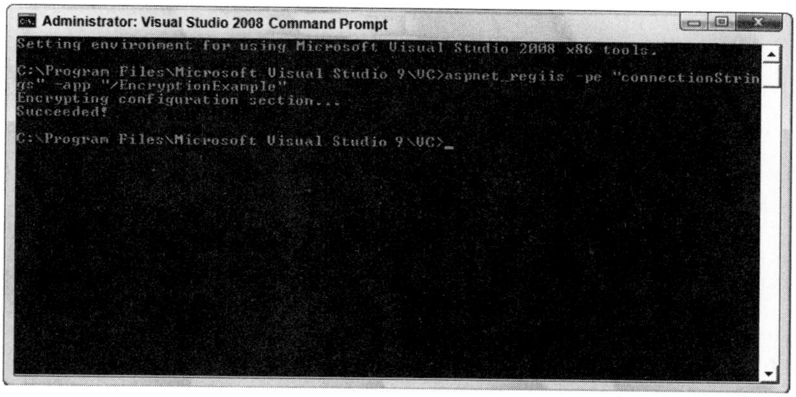

```
Administrator: Visual Studio 2008 Command Prompt
Setting environment for using Microsoft Visual Studio 2008 x86 tools.

C:\Program Files\Microsoft Visual Studio 9\VC>aspnet_regiis -pe "connectionStrin
gs" -app "/EncryptionExample"
Encrypting configuration section...
Succeeded!

C:\Program Files\Microsoft Visual Studio 9\VC>_
```

Figure 31-6

Listing 31-43: Encrypting the <authentication> section

```
aspnet_regiis -pe "system.web/authentication" -app "/EncryptionExample"
```

This code gives you the partial results presented in Listing 31-44.

Listing 31-44: The encrypted <authentication> section of the web.config

```
<authentication configProtectionProvider="RsaProtectedConfigurationProvider">
   <EncryptedData Type="http://www.w3.org/2001/04/xmlenc#Element"
    xmlns="http://www.w3.org/2001/04/xmlenc#">
      <EncryptionMethod
       Algorithm="http://www.w3.org/2001/04/xmlenc#tripledes-cbc" />
         <KeyInfo xmlns="http://www.w3.org/2000/09/xmldsig#">
            <EncryptedKey xmlns="http://www.w3.org/2001/04/xmlenc#">
               <EncryptionMethod
                Algorithm="http://www.w3.org/2001/04/xmlenc#rsa-1_5" />
               <KeyInfo xmlns="http://www.w3.org/2000/09/xmldsig#">
                  <KeyName>Rsa Key</KeyName>
               </KeyInfo>
               <CipherData>
                  <CipherValue>
                   GzTlMc89r3ees9EoMedFQrLo3FI5p3JJ9DMONWe
                   ASIww89UADkihLpmzCUPa3YtiCfKXpodr3Xt3RI
                   4zpveulZs5gIZUoX8aCl48U89dajudJn7eoJqai
                   m6wuXTGI5XrUWTgYdELCcFCloW1c+eGMRBZpNi9
                   cir4xkkh2SsHBDE=
                  </CipherValue>
               </CipherData>
            </EncryptedKey>
         </KeyInfo>
         <CipherData>
            <CipherValue>
             3MpRm+Xs+x5YsndH201Zau8/t+3RuaGv5+nTFoRXaV
             tweKdgrAVeB+PXnTjydq/u4LBXKMKmHzaBtxrqEHRD
```

Continued

```
            mNZgigLWVtfIRQ6P8cgBwtdIFhFmjm3B4tg/rA8dpJ
            ivDav2kDPp+SZ6yZ9LJzhBIe9TdJvwBQ9gJTGNVRft
            QOvdvH8c4KwYfiwZa9WCqys9WOZmw6g1a5jdW3hM//
            jiMizY1MwCECVh+T+y+f/vpP0xCkoKT9GGgHRMMrQd
            PqHUd5s7rUYp1ijQgrh1oPIXr6mx/XtzdXV8bQiEsg
            CLhsqphoVVwxkvmUKEmDQdOzdrB4sqmKgoHR3wCPyB
            npH58g==
           </CipherValue>
         </CipherData>
      </EncryptedData>
   </authentication>
```

After you have sections of your `web.config` file encrypted, you need a process to decrypt these sections to their original unencrypted values. To accomplish this task, you use the aspnet_regiis tool illustrated in Listing 31-45.

Listing 31-45: Decrypting the <connectionStrings> section in the web.config file

```
aspnet_regiis -pd "connectionString" -app "/EncryptionExample"
```

Running this script returns the encrypted values to original values.

Editing Configuration Files

So far in this chapter, you have learned about configuration files and what each configuration entry means. Even though the configuration entries are in an easy, human-readable XML format, editing these entries can be cumbersome. To help with editing, Microsoft ships three tools:

- Visual Studio 2008 IDE
- Web Site Administration Tool
- ASP.NET Snap-In for IIS 6.0 or Windows Vista's Internet Information Services (IIS) Manager

One of the nice capabilities of the Visual Studio 2008 IDE is that it supports IntelliSense-based editing for configuration files, as shown in Figure 31-7.

The Visual Studio 2008 IDE also supports XML element syntax checking, as shown in Figure 31-8.

XML element syntax checking and IntelliSense for XML elements are accomplished using the XSD-based XML validation feature available for all the XML files inside Visual Studio 2008. The configuration XSD file is located at `<drive>:\Program Files\Microsoft Visual Studio 9.0\Xml\Schemas\DotNetConfig.xsd`.

The Visual Studio 2008 IDE also adds two new useful features via the XML toolbar options that can help you with formatting the configuration settings:

- **Reformat Selection:** This option reformats the current XML notes content.
- **Format the whole document:** This option formats the entire XML document.

The Web Site Administration Tool and the ASP.NET Snap-In for IIS 6.0 or Window Vista's IIS Manager allow you to edit the configuration entries without knowing the XML element names and their corresponding values. Chapter 24 covers these tools in more detail.

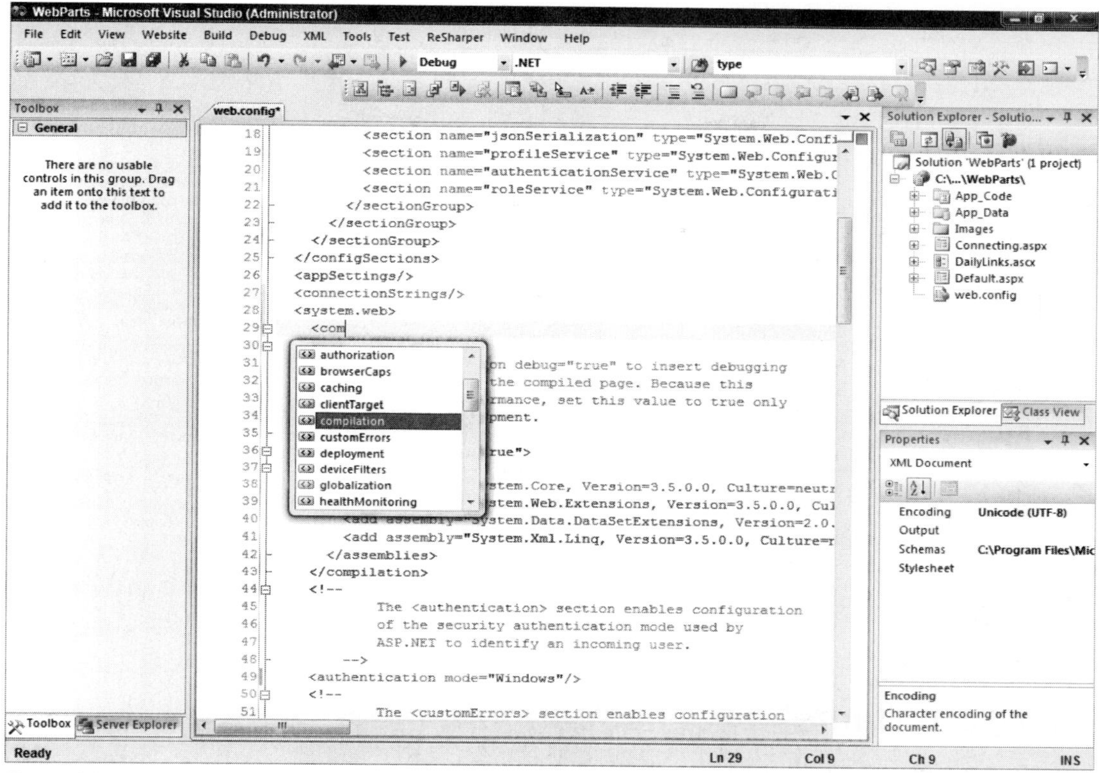

Figure 31-7

Creating Custom Sections

In addition to using the `web.config` file as discussed, you can also extend it and add your own custom sections to the file that you can make use of just as the other sections.

One way of creating custom sections is to use some built-in handlers that enable you to read key-value pairs from the `.config` file. All three of the following handlers are from the `System.Configuration` namespace:

- `NameValueFileSectionHandler`: This handler works with the current `<appSettings>` section of the `web.config` file. You are able to use this handler to create new sections of the configuration file that behave in the same manner as the `<appSettings>` section.
- `DictionarySectionHandler`: This handler works with a dictionary collection of key-value pairs.
- `SingleTagSectionHandler`: This handler works from a single element in the configuration file and allows you to read key-value pairs that are contained as attributes and values.

Next, this chapter looks at each of these handlers and some programmatic ways to customize the configuration file.

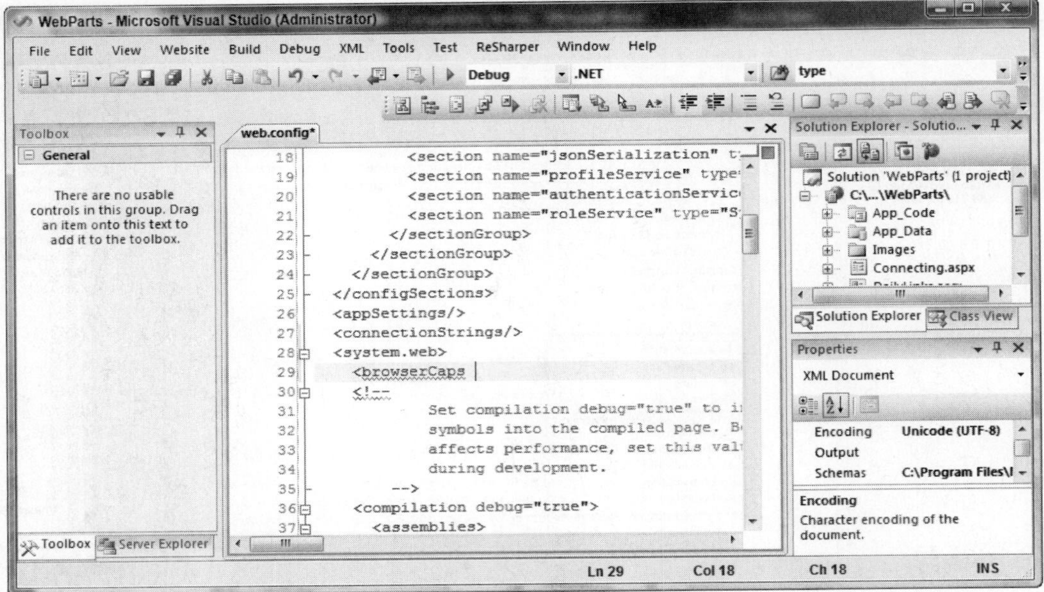

Figure 31-8

Using the NameValueFileSectionHandler Object

If you are looking to create a custom section that behaves like the `<appSettings>` section of the `web.config` file, then using this handler is the way to go. Above the `<system.web>` section of the `web.config` file, make a reference to the `NameValueFileSectionHandler` object, along with the other default references you will find in an ASP.NET 3.5 application. This additional reference is shown in Listing 31-46.

Listing 31-46: Creating your own custom section of key-value pairs in the web.config

```
<configSections>
  <section name="MyCompanyAppSettings"
   type="System.Configuration.NameValueFileSectionHandler, System,
     Version=2.0.0.0, Culture=neutral, PublicKeyToken=b77a5c561934e089"
   restartOnExternalChanges="false" />
  <sectionGroup name="system.web.extensions"
   type="System.Web.Configuration.SystemWebExtensionsSectionGroup,
     System.Web.Extensions, Version=3.5.0.0, Culture=neutral,
     PublicKeyToken=31BF3856AD364E35">
    <sectionGroup name="scripting"
     type="System.Web.Configuration.ScriptingSectionGroup, System.Web.Extensions,
       Version=3.5.0.0, Culture=neutral, PublicKeyToken=31BF3856AD364E35">
      <section name="scriptResourceHandler"
       type="System.Web.Configuration.ScriptingScriptResourceHandlerSection,
         System.Web.Extensions, Version=3.5.0.0, Culture=neutral,
         PublicKeyToken=31BF3856AD364E35"
```

```
          requirePermission="false" allowDefinition="MachineToApplication"/>
         <sectionGroup name="webServices"
          type="System.Web.Configuration.ScriptingWebServicesSectionGroup,
             System.Web.Extensions, Version=3.5.0.0, Culture=neutral,
             PublicKeyToken=31BF3856AD364E35">
           <section name="jsonSerialization"
            type="System.Web.Configuration.ScriptingJsonSerializationSection,
               System.Web.Extensions, Version=3.5.0.0, Culture=neutral,
               PublicKeyToken=31BF3856AD364E35"
            requirePermission="false" allowDefinition="Everywhere"/>
           <section name="profileService"
            type="System.Web.Configuration.ScriptingProfileServiceSection,
               System.Web.Extensions, Version=3.5.0.0, Culture=neutral,
               PublicKeyToken=31BF3856AD364E35"
            requirePermission="false" allowDefinition="MachineToApplication"/>
           <section name="authenticationService"
            type="System.Web.Configuration.ScriptingAuthenticationServiceSection,
               System.Web.Extensions, Version=3.5.0.0, Culture=neutral,
               PublicKeyToken=31BF3856AD364E35"
            requirePermission="false" allowDefinition="MachineToApplication"/>
           <section name="roleService"
            type="System.Web.Configuration.ScriptingRoleServiceSection,
               System.Web.Extensions, Version=3.5.0.0, Culture=neutral,
               PublicKeyToken=31BF3856AD364E35"
            requirePermission="false" allowDefinition="MachineToApplication"/>
         </sectionGroup>
      </sectionGroup>
   </sectionGroup>
</configSections>
```

Once you have made this reference to the `System.Configuration.NameValueFileSectionHandler` object and have given it a name (in this case, `MyCompanyAppSettings`), then you can create a section in your `web.config` that makes use of this reference. This is illustrated in Listing 31-47.

Listing 31-47: Creating your own custom key-value pair section in the web.config

```
<configuration>

   <MyCompanyAppSettings>
      <add key="Key1" value="This is value 1" />
      <add key="Key2" value="This is value 2" />
   </MyCompanyAppSettings>

   <system.web>

      <!-- Removed for clarity -->

   </system.web>

</configuration>
```

After you have this in place within your `web.config` file, you can then programmatically get access to this section, as illustrated in Listing 31-48.

Listing 31-48: Getting access to your custom section in the web.config file

VB

```
Dim nvc As NameValueCollection = New NameValueCollection()
nvc = System.Configuration.ConfigurationManager.GetSection("MyCompanyAppSettings")

Response.Write(nvc("Key1") + "<br />")
Response.Write(nvc("Key2"))
```

C#

```
NameValueCollection nvc = new NameValueCollection();
nvc = ConfigurationManager.GetSection("MyCompanyAppSettings") as
   NameValueCollection;

Response.Write(nvc["Key1"] + "<br />");
Response.Write(nvc["Key2"]);
```

For this to work, you are going to have to import the `System.Collections.Specialized` namespace into the file, as this is where you will find the `NameValueCollection` object.

Using the DictionarySectionHandler Object

The `DictionarySectionHandler` works nearly the same as the `NameValueFileSectionHandler`. The difference, however, is that the `DictionarySectionHandler` returns a `HashTable` object instead of returning an `Object`.

This handler is presented in Listing 31-49.

Listing 31-49: Making a reference to the DictionarySectionHandler object

```
<configSections>
   <section name="MyCompanyAppSettings"
    type="System.Configuration.DictionarySectionHandler, System,
       Version=2.0.0.0, Culture=neutral, PublicKeyToken=b77a5c561934e089"
    restartOnExternalChanges="false" />

   <!-- Removed for clarity -->

</configSections>
```

Once in place, you can then make the same `MyCompanyAppSettings` section in the `web.config` file, as shown in Listing 31-50.

Listing 31-50: Creating your own custom key-value pair section in the web.config

```
<configuration>

   <MyCompanyAppSettings>
      <add key="Key1" value="This is value 1" />
      <add key="Key2" value="This is value 2" />
```

```
    </MyCompanyAppSettings>

    <system.web>

       <!-- Removed for clarity -->

    </system.web>

</configuration>
```

Now that the `web.config` file is ready, you can call the items from code using the `Configuration` API, as illustrated in Listing 31-51.

Listing 31-51: Getting access to your custom section in the web.config file

VB

```
Dim ht As Hashtable = New Hashtable()
ht = System.Configuration.ConfigurationManager.GetSection("MyCompanyAppSettings")

Response.Write(ht("Key1") + "<br />")
Response.Write(ht("Key2"))
```

C#

```
Hashtable ht = new Hashtable();
ht = ConfigurationManager.GetSection("MyCompanyAppSettings") as
   Hashtable;

Response.Write(ht["Key1"] + "<br />");
Response.Write(ht["Key2"]);
```

Using the SingleTagSectionHandler Object

The `SingleTagSectionHandler` works almost the same as the previous `NameValueFileSectionHandler` and `DictionarySectionHandler`. However, this object looks to work with a single element that contains the key-value pairs as attributes.

This handler is presented in Listing 31-52.

Listing 31-52: Making a reference to the DictionarySectionHandler object

```
<configSections>
   <section name="MyCompanyAppSettings"
    type="System.Configuration.SingleTagSectionHandler, System,
       Version=2.0.0.0, Culture=neutral, PublicKeyToken=b77a5c561934e089"
    restartOnExternalChanges="false" />

   <!-- Removed for clarity -->

</configSections>
```

Once in place, you can make a different `MyCompanyAppSettings` section in the `web.config` file, as presented in Listing 31-53.

Listing 31-53: Creating your own custom key-value pair section in the web.config

```
<configuration>

 <MyCompanyAppSettings Key1="This is value 1" Key2="This is value 2" />

   <system.web>

      <!-- Removed for clarity -->

   </system.web>

</configuration>
```

Now that the `web.config` file is complete, you can call the items from code using the `Configuration` API, as illustrated in Listing 31-54.

Listing 31-54: Getting access to your custom section in the web.config file

VB

```
Dim ht As Hashtable = New Hashtable()
ht = System.Configuration.ConfigurationManager.GetSection("MyCompanyAppSettings")

Response.Write(ht("Key1") + "<br />")
Response.Write(ht("Key2"))
```

C#

```
Hashtable ht = new Hashtable();
ht = ConfigurationManager.GetSection("MyCompanyAppSettings") as
   Hashtable;

Response.Write(ht["Key1"] + "<br />");
Response.Write(ht["Key2"]);
```

Using Your Own Custom Configuration Handler

You can also create your own custom configuration handler. To do this, you first need to create a class that represents your section in the `web.config` file. In your App_Code folder, create a class called `MyCompanySettings`. This class is presented in Listing 31-55.

Listing 31-55: The MyCompanySettings class

VB

```
Public Class MyCompanySettings
    Inherits ConfigurationSection

    <ConfigurationProperty("Key1", DefaultValue:="This is the value of Key 1", _
       IsRequired:=False)> _
    Public ReadOnly Property Key1() As String
        Get
            Return MyBase.Item("Key1").ToString()
```

```
        End Get
    End Property

    <ConfigurationProperty("Key2", IsRequired:=True)> _
    Public ReadOnly Property Key2() As String
        Get
            Return MyBase.Item("Key2").ToString()
        End Get
    End Property

End Class
```

C#

```
using System.Configuration;

public class MyCompanySettings : ConfigurationSection
{
    [ConfigurationProperty("Key1", DefaultValue = "This is the value of Key 1",
     IsRequired = false)]
    public string Key1
    {
        get
        {
            return this["Key1"] as string;
        }
    }

    [ConfigurationProperty("Key2", IsRequired = true)]
    public string Key2
    {
        get
        {
            return this["Key2"] as string;
        }
    }
}
```

You can see that this class inherits from the `ConfigurationSection` and the two properties that are created using the `ConfigurationProperty` attribute. You can use a couple of attributes here, such as the `DefaultValue`, `IsRequired`, `IsKey`, and `IsDefaultCollection`.

Once you have this class in place, you can configure your application to use this handler, as illustrated in Listing 31-56.

Listing 31-56: Making a reference to the MyCompanySettings object

```
<configSections>

   <section name="MyCompanySettings" type="MyCompanySettings" />

   <!-- Removed for clarity -->

</configSections>
```

You can now use this section in your `web.config` file, as illustrated in Listing 31-57.

Listing 31-57: Creating your own custom key-value pair section in the web.config

```
<configuration>

   <MyCompanySettings Key2="Here is a value for Key2" />

   <system.web>

      <!-- Removed for clarity -->

   </system.web>

</configuration>
```

From there, you can programmatically access this from code, as illustrated in Listing 31-58.

Listing 31-58: Getting access to your custom section in the web.config file

VB

```
Dim cs As MyCompanySettings = New MyCompanySettings()
cs = ConfigurationManager.GetSection("MyCompanySettings")

Response.Write(cs.Key1 + "<br />")
Response.Write(cs.Key2)
```

C#

```
MyCompanySettings cs = ConfigurationManager.GetSection("MyCompanySettings") as
   MyCompanySettings;

Response.Write(cs.Key1 + "<br />");
Response.Write(cs.Key2);
```

Summary

In this chapter, you have seen the ASP.NET configuration system and learned how it does not rely on the IIS metabase. Instead, ASP.NET uses an XML configuration system that is human-readable.

You also looked at the two different ASP.NET XML configuration files:

- machine.config
- web.config

The machine.config file applies default settings to all Web applications on the server. However, if the server has multiple versions of the framework installed, the machine.config file applies to a particular framework version. On the other hand, a particular Web application can customize or override its own configuration information using web.config files. Using a web.config file, you can also configure the applications on an application-by-application or folder-by-folder basis.

Next, you looked at some typical configuration settings that can be applied to an ASP.NET application, such as configuring connecting strings, session state, browser capabilities, and so on. Then you looked at an overview of new ASP.NET Admin Objects and learned how to program configuration files. Finally, you learned how to protect the configuration section using cryptographic algorithms.

32

Instrumentation

Many ASP.NET developers do more than just build an application and walk away. They definitely think about how the application will behave after it is deployed. *Instrumentation* is the task that developers undertake to measure and monitor their ASP.NET applications. Depending on the situation, some instrumentation operations occur at design time, whereas others are ongoing processes that begin at runtime.

ASP.NET 3.5 gives you greater capability to apply instrumentation techniques to your applications. You will find that the ASP.NET framework includes a large series of performance counters, the capability to work with the Windows Event Tracing system, possibilities for application tracing (covered in Chapter 24), and the most exciting part of this discussion — a health monitoring system that allows you to log a number of different events over an application's lifetime.

You can monitor a deployed application in several ways. First, you learn how to work with the Windows event log.

Working with the Event Log

When working with Visual Studio 2008, you can use the event log in the Server Explorer of the IDE in a couple of different ways. You can get to the event log section in the Server Explorer by expanding the view of the server you want to work with (by clicking the plus sign next to the server) until you see the Event Logs section. You also have the option to right-click the Event Logs node and select Launch Event Viewer from the list of available options. This selection displays the same Event Viewer you are familiar with. From the Event Viewer or from the Server Explorer you can work directly with events recorded to your system.

The other option available from the Server Explorer is to expand the Event Logs node of the tree view in the Server Explorer so that you can see the additional nodes such as Application, Security, and System. If you are on Windows Vista, you will see a series of additional event categories. Expanding any of these sub-nodes allows you to see all the events that have been registered in the event log. These events are arranged by type, which makes browsing for specific events rather easy, as illustrated in Figure 32-1.

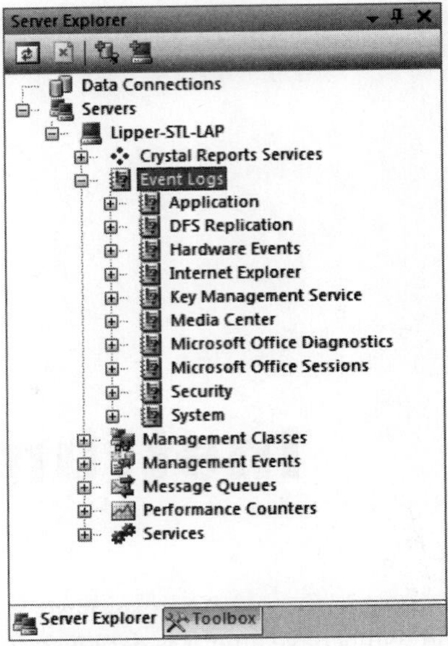

Figure 32-1

Reading from the Event Log

It is possible to read and to write events to and from the event log from your .NET application. If you are interested in reading events from the event log, you can do so rather simply by using the `EventLog` object that is provided by .NET in the `System.Diagnostics` namespace.

To see an example of using this object, you can create an ASP.NET page that displays all the entries contained within a specified event log. To create it, you need a DropDownList control, a Button control, and a GridView control. In Visual Studio .NET 2002 and 2003, a Components tab was located within the Toolbox, and you could simply drag and drop the Event Log component onto your design surface in order to start working with it. In Visual Studio 2005, you won't find this tab within the Toolbox, but it still isn't too hard to find the objects you need. Listing 32-1 shows the simple ASP.NET page that enables you to easily display the contents of the event log.

Listing 32-1: Displaying the contents of the event logs within the browser

VB

```
<%@ Page Language="VB" %>
<%@ Import Namespace="System.Diagnostics" %>

<script runat="server">
    Protected Sub Button1_Click(ByVal sender As Object, _
      ByVal e As System.EventArgs)

        Dim el As EventLog = New EventLog()
        el.Source = DropDownList1.SelectedItem.Text

        GridView1.DataSource = el.Entries
        GridView1.DataBind()
    End Sub
```

```
</script>

<html xmlns="http://www.w3.org/1999/xhtml" >
<head runat="server">
    <title>Working with Event Logs</title>
</head>
<body>
    <form id="form1" runat="server">
    <div>
        <asp:DropDownList ID="DropDownList1" runat="server">
            <asp:ListItem>Application</asp:ListItem>
            <asp:ListItem>Security</asp:ListItem>
            <asp:ListItem>System</asp:ListItem>
        </asp:DropDownList>
        <asp:Button ID="Button1" runat="server" OnClick="Button1_Click"
         Text="Submit" /><br />
        <br />
        <asp:GridView ID="GridView1" runat="server"
         BackColor="LightGoldenrodYellow" BorderColor="Tan"
            BorderWidth="1px" CellPadding="2" ForeColor="Black" GridLines="None">
            <FooterStyle BackColor="Tan" />
            <SelectedRowStyle BackColor="DarkSlateBlue" ForeColor="GhostWhite" />
            <PagerStyle BackColor="PaleGoldenrod" ForeColor="DarkSlateBlue"
             HorizontalAlign="Center" />
            <HeaderStyle BackColor="Tan" Font-Bold="True" />
            <AlternatingRowStyle BackColor="PaleGoldenrod" />
            <RowStyle VerticalAlign="Top" />
        </asp:GridView>
    </div>
    </form>
</body>
</html>
```

C#

```
<%@ Page Language="C#" %>
<%@ Import Namespace="System.Diagnostics" %>

<script runat="server">
    protected void Button1_Click(object sender, EventArgs e)
    {
        EventLog el = new EventLog();
        el.Source = DropDownList1.SelectedItem.Text;

        GridView1.DataSource = el.Entries;
        GridView1.DataBind();
    }
</script>
```

Note that you are going to have to run this with credentials that have administrative rights for this code sample to work.

For this code to work, you import the `System.Diagnostics` namespace if you are not interested in fully qualifying your declarations. After you do so, you can create an instance of the `EventLog` object to give you access to the `Source` property. In assigning a value to this property, you use the `SelectedItem.Text` property from the DropDownList control on the page. Next, you can provide all the `EventLog` entries as the data source value to the GridView control. Finally, you bind this data source to the GridView. In the end, you get something similar to the results illustrated in Figure 32-2.

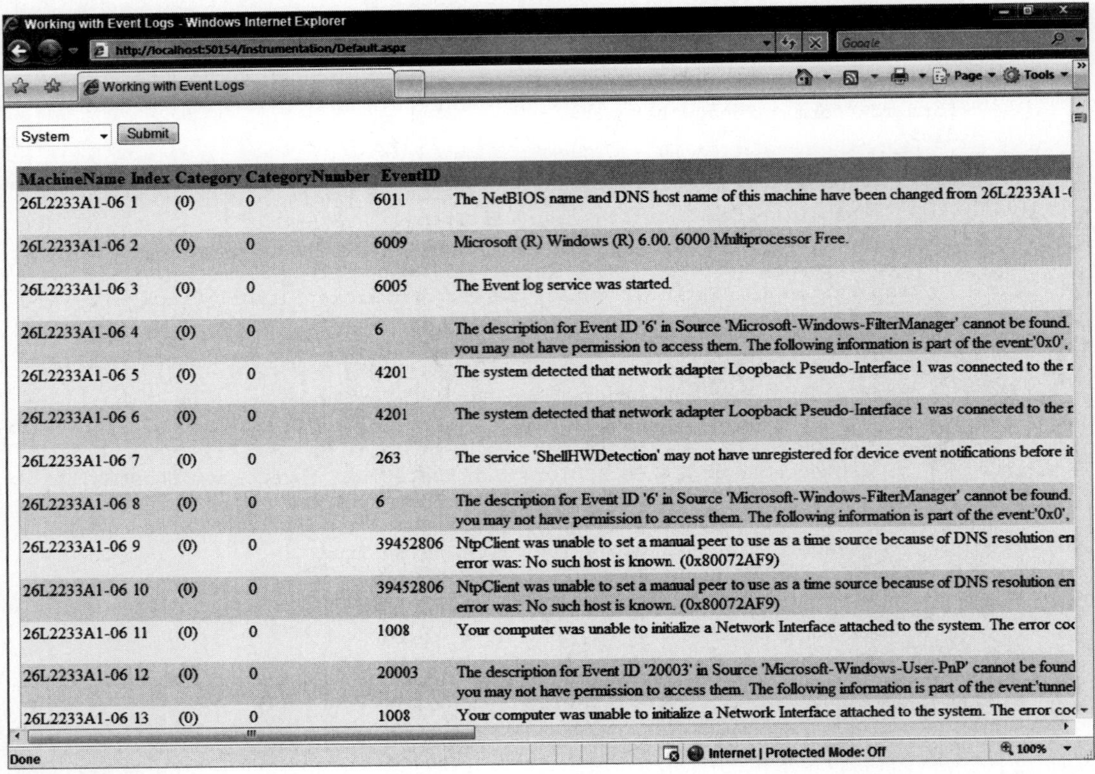

Figure 32-2

As you can see, it is simple to pull all the events from the event log and write them to the browser screen. The next section looks at writing values back to the event log.

Writing to the Event Logs

Not only can you read from the event logs, but you can write to them as well. This can be quite handy if you want to record specific events in an event log. The following table provides a short description of the main event logs available to you. Windows Vista has other event categories, but these are the main event categories that you will use.

Event Log	Description
Application	Enables you to record application-specific events, including whether a certain event was fired, a page was loaded, or a customer made a specific purchase
Security	Enables you to track security-related issues such as security changes and breaches
System	Enables you to track system-specific items such as issues that arise with components or drivers

From your code, you can write to any of the event logs defined in the preceding table as well as to any custom event logs that you might create. To accomplish this task, create an example ASP.NET page that contains a multiline TextBox control and a Button control. On the `Button1_Click` event, you register the text you want placed in the text box directly into the Application event log. Your ASP.NET page should be similar to what is presented in Listing 32-2.

Listing 32-2: Writing to the Application event log

VB

```
<%@ Page Language="VB" %>
<%@ Import Namespace="System.Diagnostics" %>

<script runat="server">
    Protected Sub Page_Load(ByVal sender As Object, _
      ByVal e As System.EventArgs)

        If Not EventLog.SourceExists("My Application") Then
            EventLog.CreateEventSource("My Application", "Application")
        End If
    End Sub

    Protected Sub Button1_Click(ByVal sender As Object, _
      ByVal e As System.EventArgs)

        Dim el As EventLog = New EventLog()
        el.Source = "My Application"
        el.WriteEntry(TextBox1.Text)

        Label1.Text = "ENTERED: " & TextBox1.Text
    End Sub
</script>

<html xmlns="http://www.w3.org/1999/xhtml" >
<head runat="server">
    <title>Working with Event Logs</title>
</head>
<body>
    <form id="form1" runat="server">
    <div>
        <asp:TextBox ID="TextBox1" runat="server" Height="75px"
         TextMode="MultiLine" Width="250px"></asp:TextBox><br />
        <br />
        <asp:Button ID="Button1" runat="server" OnClick="Button1_Click"
         Text="Submit to custom event log" /><br />
        <br />
        <asp:Label ID="Label1" runat="server"></asp:Label> </div>
    </form>
</body>
</html>
```

C#

```
<%@ Page Language="C#" %>
<%@ Import Namespace="System.Diagnostics" %>
```

Continued

```
<script runat="server">
    protected void Page_Load(object sender, EventArgs e)
    {
        if (!EventLog.SourceExists("My Application"))
        {
            EventLog.CreateEventSource("My Application", "Application");
        }
    }

    protected void Button1_Click(object sender, EventArgs e)
    {
        EventLog el = new EventLog();
        el.Source = "My Application";
        el.WriteEntry(TextBox1.Text);

        Label1.Text = "ENTERED: " + TextBox1.Text;
    }
</script>
```

Again, for this to work, you must import the `System.Diagnostics` namespace. In the `Page_Load` event of the page, ASP.NET is checking whether the event source exists for `My Application`. If no such source exists in the Application event log, it is created using the `CreateEventSource()` method.

```
el.CreateEventSource("My Application", "Application")
```

The first parameter of the method takes the name of the source that you are creating. The second parameter of this method call takes the name of the event log that you are targeting. After this source has been created, you can start working with the `EventLog` object to place an entry into the system. First, the `EventLog` object is assigned a source. In this case, it is the newly created `My Application`. Using the `WriteEntry()` method, you can write to the specified event log. You can also assign the source and the message within the `WriteEntry()` method in the following manner:

```
el.WriteEntry("My Application", TextBox1.Text);
```

The ASP.NET page produces something similar to what is illustrated in Figure 32-3.

After this is done, you can look in the Event Viewer and see your entry listed in the Application event log. Figure 32-4 illustrates what happens when you double-click the entry.

Later in this chapter, you see some of the automatic ways in which ASP.NET can record events for you in the event log and in some other data stores (such as Microsoft's SQL Server). Next, it is time to turn your attention to working with performance counters.

Using Performance Counters

Utilizing performance counters is important if you want to monitor your applications as they run. What exactly is monitored is up to you. A plethora of available performance counters are at your disposal in Windows and you will find that there are more than 60 counters specific to ASP.NET.

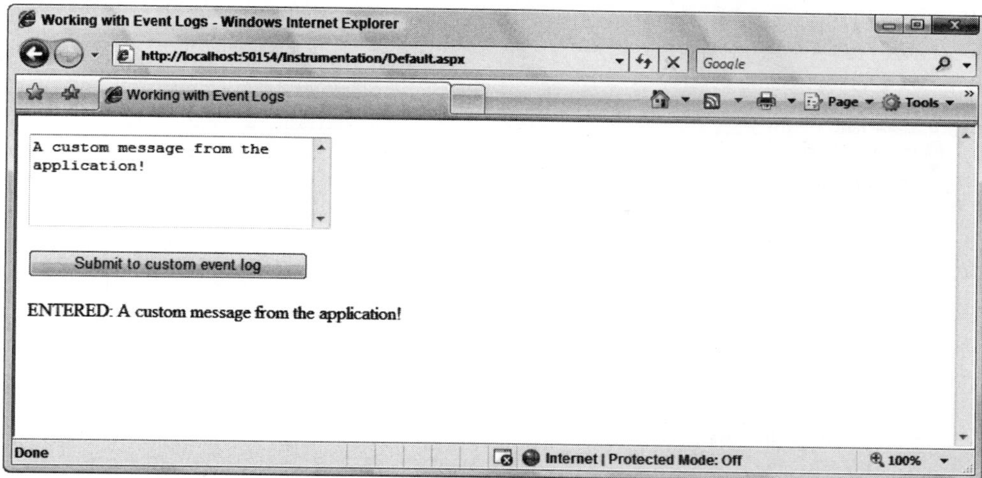

Figure 32-3

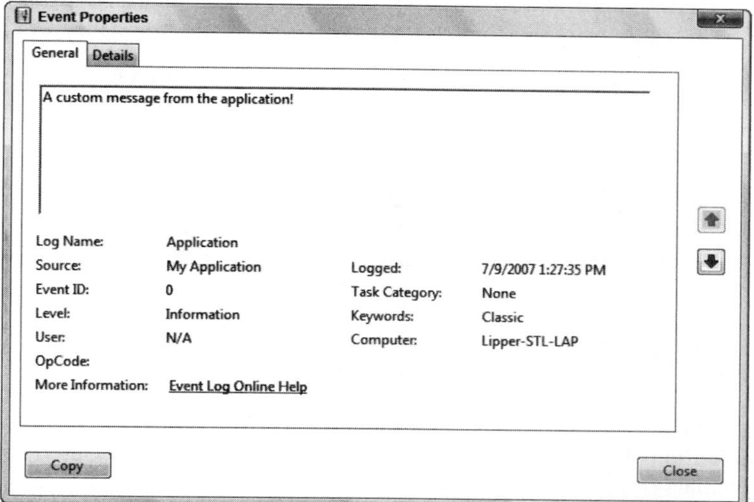

Figure 32-4

Viewing Performance Counters Through an Administration Tool

You can see these performance counters by opening the Performance dialog found in the Control Panel and then Administration Tools if you are using Windows XP. If you are using Windows Vista, select Control Panel ➪ System and Maintenance ➪ Performance Information and Tools ➪ Advanced Tools ➪ Open Reliability and Performance Monitor. Figure 32-5 shows the dialog opened in Windows Vista.

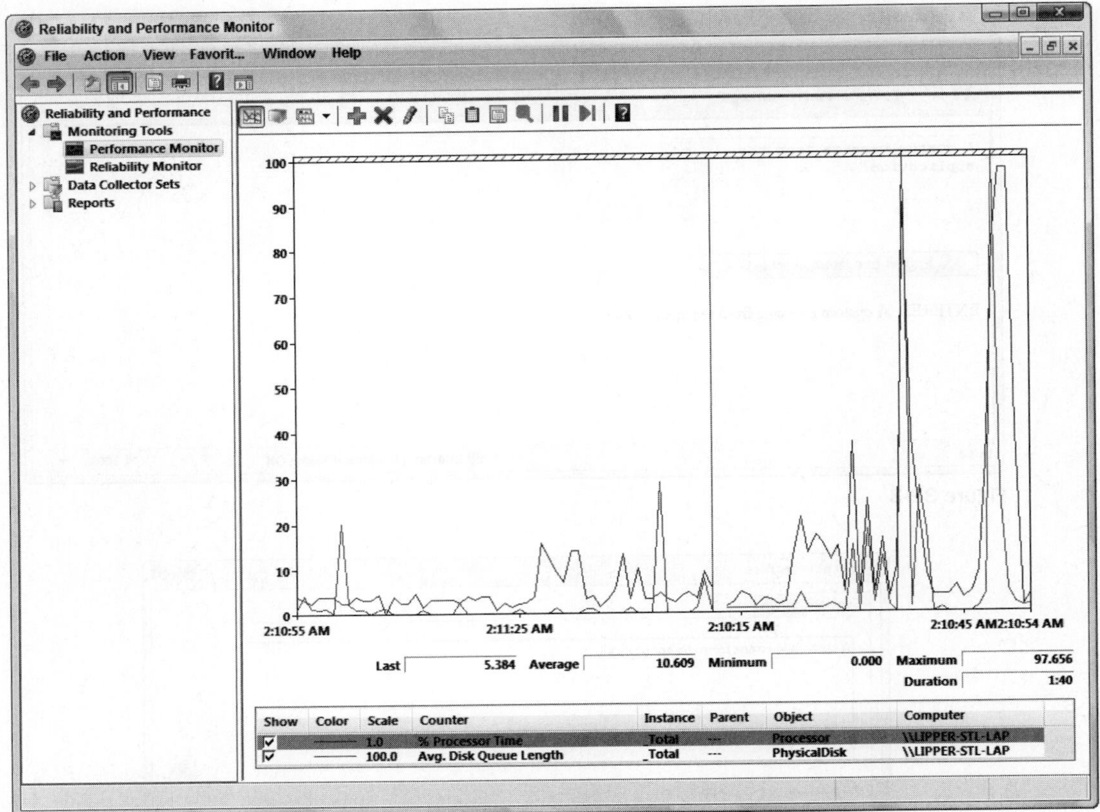

Figure 32-5

Clicking the plus sign in the menu enables you to add more performance counters to the list. You will find a number of ASP.NET–specific counters in the list illustrated in Figure 32-6.

The following list details some of the ASP.NET–specific performance counters that are at your disposal along with a definition of the counter (also available by checking the Show Description check box in Vista from within the dialog).

- **Application Restarts:** Number of times the application has been restarted during the Web server's lifetime.
- **Applications Running:** Number of currently running Web applications.
- **Audit Failure Events Raised:** Number of audit failures in the application since it was started.
- **Audit Success Events Raised:** Number of audit successes in the application since it was started.
- **Error Events Raised:** Number of error events raised since the application was started.
- **Infrastructure Error Events Raised:** Number of HTTP error events raised since the application was started.

- **Request Error Events Raised:** Number of runtime error events raised since the application was started.
- **Request Execution Time:** The number of milliseconds it took to execute the most recent request.
- **Request Wait Time:** The number of milliseconds the most recent request was waiting in the queue.
- **Requests Current:** The current number of requests, including those that are queued, currently executing, or waiting to be written to the client. Under the ASP.NET process model, when this counter exceeds the `requestQueueLimit` defined in the `processModel` configuration section, ASP.NET begins rejecting requests.
- **Requests Disconnected:** The number of requests disconnected because of communication errors or user terminations.
- **Requests Queued:** The number of requests waiting to be processed.
- **Requests Rejected:** The number of requests rejected because the request queue was full.
- **State Server Sessions Abandoned:** The number of sessions that have been explicitly abandoned.
- **State Server Sessions Active:** The current number of sessions currently active.
- **State Server Sessions Timed Out:** The number of sessions timed out.
- **State Server Sessions Total:** The number of sessions total.
- **Worker Process Restarts:** Number of times a worker process has restarted on the machine.
- **Worker Processes Running:** Number of worker processes running on the machine.

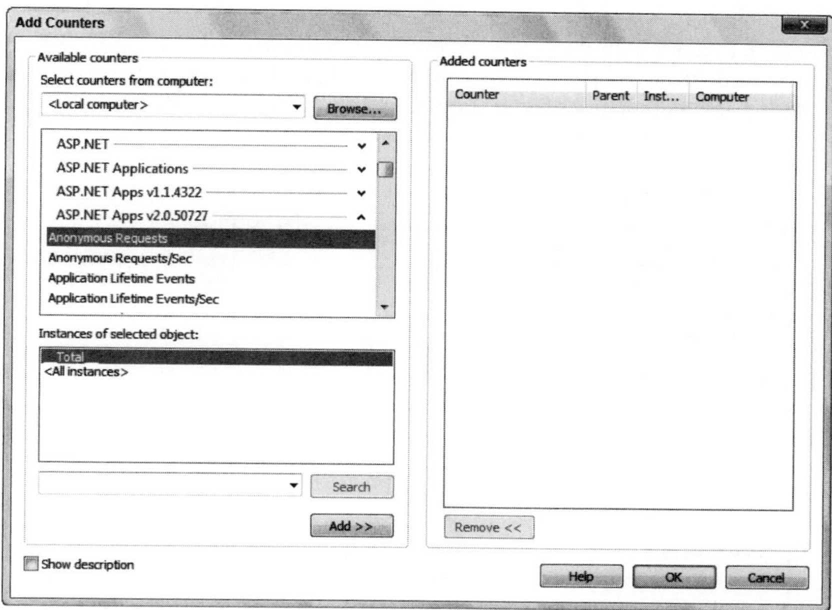

Figure 32-6

These are the performance counters for just the ASP.NET v2.0.50727 category. Here you will find categories for other ASP.NET–specific items such as:

- ASP.NET
- ASP.NET Applications
- ASP.NET Apps v1.0.3705.288
- ASP.NET Apps v2.0.50727
- ASP.NET State Service
- ASP.NET v1.0.3705.288
- ASP.NET v2.0.50727

Performance counters can give you a pretty outstanding view of what is happening in your application. The data retrieved by a specific counter is not a continuous thing because the counter is really taking a snapshot of the specified counter every 400 milliseconds, so be sure to take that into account when analyzing the data produced.

Building a Browser-Based Administrative Tool

In addition to viewing the performance counters available to you through the Performance dialog, you can also get at the performance counter values programmatically. This is possible by working with the `System.Diagnostics` namespace in the .NET Framework. This namespace gives you access to performance-counter-specific objects such as the `PerformanceCounterCategory` and `PerformanceCounter` objects.

To show you how to work with these objects, this next example creates an ASP.NET page that enables you to view any value from a performance counter directly in the browser. To accomplish this task, create a basic ASP.NET page that includes three DropDownList controls, a Button control, and a Label control. This gives you the results presented in Figure 32-7.

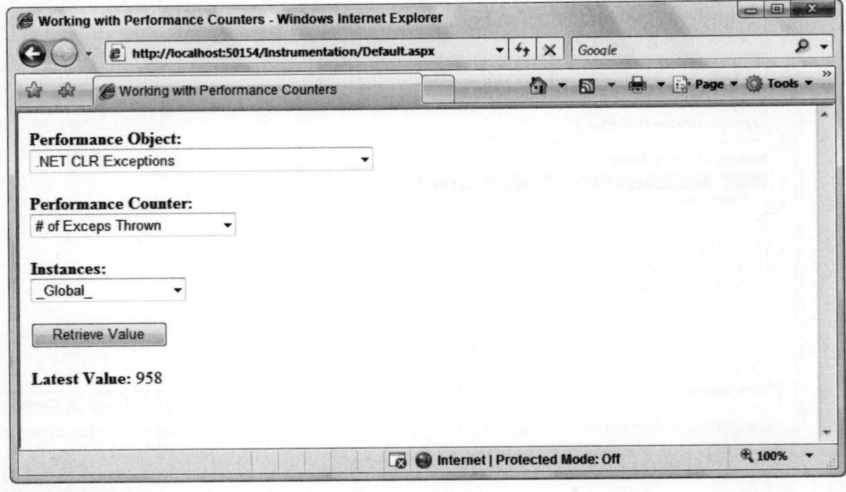

Figure 32-7

Listing 32-3 shows the code required for this figure.

Listing 32-3: Working with performance counters in ASP.NET

VB

```
<%@ Page Language="VB" %>
<%@ Import Namespace="System.Diagnostics" %>
<%@ Import Namespace="System.Collections.Generic" %>

<script runat="server">
    Protected Sub Page_Load(ByVal sender As Object, ByVal e As System.EventArgs)
        If Not Page.IsPostBack Then
            Dim pcc As List(Of String) = New List(Of String)

            For Each item As PerformanceCounterCategory In _
              PerformanceCounterCategory.GetCategories()
                pcc.Add(item.CategoryName)
            Next

            pcc.Sort()
            pcc.Remove(".NET CLR Data")

            DropDownList1.DataSource = pcc
            DropDownList1.DataBind()

            Dim myPcc As PerformanceCounterCategory
            myPcc = New PerformanceCounterCategory(DropDownList1.SelectedItem.Text)

            DisplayCounters(myPcc)
        End If
    End Sub

    Protected Sub DisplayCounters(ByVal pcc As PerformanceCounterCategory)
        DisplayInstances(pcc)

        Dim myPcc As List(Of String) = New List(Of String)

        If DropDownList3.Items.Count > 0 Then
            For Each pc As PerformanceCounter In _
              pcc.GetCounters(DropDownList3.Items(0).Value)
                myPcc.Add(pc.CounterName)
            Next
        Else
            For Each pc As PerformanceCounter In pcc.GetCounters()
                myPcc.Add(pc.CounterName)
            Next
        End If

        myPcc.Sort()

        DropDownList2.DataSource = myPcc
        DropDownList2.DataBind()
    End Sub
```

Continued

```
    Protected Sub DisplayInstances(ByVal pcc As PerformanceCounterCategory)
        Dim listPcc As List(Of String) = New List(Of String)

        For Each item As String In pcc.GetInstanceNames()
            listPcc.Add(item.ToString())
        Next

        listPcc.Sort()

        DropDownList3.DataSource = listPcc
        DropDownList3.DataBind()
    End Sub

    Protected Sub DropDownList1_SelectedIndexChanged(ByVal sender As Object, _
      ByVal e As System.EventArgs)
        Dim pcc As PerformanceCounterCategory
        pcc = New PerformanceCounterCategory(DropDownList1.SelectedItem.Text)

        DropDownList2.Items.Clear()
        DropDownList3.Items.Clear()

        DisplayCounters(pcc)
    End Sub

    Protected Sub Button1_Click(ByVal sender As Object, _
      ByVal e As System.EventArgs)
        Dim pc As PerformanceCounter

        If DropDownList3.Items.Count > 0 Then
            pc = New PerformanceCounter(DropDownList1.SelectedItem.Text, _
              DropDownList2.SelectedItem.Text, DropDownList3.SelectedItem.Text)
        Else
            pc = New PerformanceCounter(DropDownList1.SelectedItem.Text, _
              DropDownList2.SelectedItem.Text)
        End If

        Label1.Text = "<b>Latest Value:</b> " & pc.NextValue().ToString()
    End Sub
</script>

<html xmlns="http://www.w3.org/1999/xhtml">
<head runat="server">
    <title>Working with Performance Counters</title>
</head>
<body>
    <form id="form1" runat="server">
    <div>
        <strong>Performance Object:</strong><br />
        <asp:DropDownList ID="DropDownList1" runat="server" AutoPostBack="True"
         OnSelectedIndexChanged="DropDownList1_SelectedIndexChanged">
        </asp:DropDownList><br />
        <br />
        <strong>Performance Counter:</strong><br />
```

```
        <asp:DropDownList ID="DropDownList2" runat="server">
        </asp:DropDownList><br />
        <br />
        <strong>Instances:</strong><br />
        <asp:DropDownList ID="DropDownList3" runat="server">
        </asp:DropDownList><br />
        <br />
        <asp:Button ID="Button1" runat="server" OnClick="Button1_Click"
         Text="Retrieve Value" /><br />
        <br />
        <asp:Label ID="Label1" runat="server"></asp:Label></div>
    </form>
</body>
</html>
```

C#

```
<%@ Page Language="C#" %>
<%@ Import Namespace="System.Diagnostics" %>
<%@ Import Namespace="System.Collections.Generic" %>

<script runat="server">
    protected void Page_Load(object sender, EventArgs e)
    {
        if (!Page.IsPostBack)
        {
            List<string> pcc = new List<string>();

            foreach (PerformanceCounterCategory item in
               PerformanceCounterCategory.GetCategories())
            {
                pcc.Add(item.CategoryName);
            }

            pcc.Sort();
            pcc.Remove(".NET CLR Data");

            DropDownList1.DataSource = pcc;
            DropDownList1.DataBind();

            PerformanceCounterCategory myPcc;
            myPcc = new
               PerformanceCounterCategory(DropDownList1.SelectedItem.Text);

            DisplayCounters(myPcc);
        }
    }

    void DisplayCounters(PerformanceCounterCategory pcc)
    {
        DisplayInstances(pcc);

        List<string> myPcc = new List<string>();
```

```
    if (DropDownList3.Items.Count > 0)
    {
        foreach (PerformanceCounter pc in
           pcc.GetCounters(DropDownList3.Items[0].Value))
        {
            myPcc.Add(pc.CounterName);
        }
    }
    else
    {
        foreach (PerformanceCounter pc in pcc.GetCounters())
        {
            myPcc.Add(pc.CounterName);
        }
    }

    myPcc.Sort();

    DropDownList2.DataSource = myPcc;
    DropDownList2.DataBind();
}

void DisplayInstances(PerformanceCounterCategory pcc)
{
    List<string> listPcc = new List<string>();

    foreach (string item in pcc.GetInstanceNames())
    {
        listPcc.Add(item.ToString());
    }

    listPcc.Sort();

    DropDownList3.DataSource = listPcc;
    DropDownList3.DataBind();
}

protected void DropDownList1_SelectedIndexChanged(object sender, EventArgs e)
{
    PerformanceCounterCategory pcc;
    pcc = new PerformanceCounterCategory(DropDownList1.SelectedItem.Text);

    DropDownList2.Items.Clear();
    DropDownList3.Items.Clear();

    DisplayCounters(pcc);
}

protected void Button1_Click(object sender, EventArgs e)
{
    PerformanceCounter pc;
    if (DropDownList3.Items.Count > 0)
```

```
            {
                pc = new PerformanceCounter(DropDownList1.SelectedItem.Text,
                  DropDownList2.SelectedItem.Text, DropDownList3.SelectedItem.Text);
            }
            else
            {
                pc = new PerformanceCounter(DropDownList1.SelectedItem.Text,
                  DropDownList2.SelectedItem.Text);
            }

            Label1.Text = "<b>Latest Value:</b> " + pc.NextValue().ToString();
        }
    </script>
```

To make this work, you have to deal with only a couple of performance-counter objects such as the `PerformanceCounterCategory` and the `PerformanceCounter` objects. The first drop-down list is populated with all the categories available. These values are first placed in a `List(Of String)` object that enables you to call a `Sort()` method and also allows you to remove any categories you aren't interested in by using the `Remove()` method before binding to the DropDown list control.

The category selected in the first drop-down list drives what is displayed in the second and third drop-down lists. The second drop-down list displays a list of counters that are available for a particular category. You might tend to think that the third drop-down list of instances is based upon the counter that is selected, but instances are set at the category level.

When the button on the page is clicked, a new instance of the `PerformanceCounter` object is created and, as you can see from the example, it can be instantiated in several ways. The first constructor takes just a category name and a counter name, whereas the second constructor takes these two items plus the instance name utilized. After a `PerformanceCounter` is created, the `NextValue()` method pulls a sample from the specified item, thus producing the results that are illustrated in Figure 32-7.

Application Tracing

ASP.NET does an excellent job of displaying trace information either directly on the requested pages of your ASP.NET application or in a trace log that can be found at `http://[server]/[application]/trace.axd`. Sample screenshots of both of these scenarios appear in Figure 32-8.

You can get a lot of detailed information on working with tracing for instrumentation in Chapter 24.

Understanding Health Monitoring

One of the more exciting instrumentation capabilities provided by ASP.NET is the health monitoring system introduced with ASP.NET 2.0. ASP.NET health monitoring is built around various health monitoring events (which are referred to as *Web events*) occurring in your application. Using the health monitoring system enables you to use the event logging for Web events such as failed logins, application starts and stops, or any unhandled exceptions. The event logging can occur in more than one place; therefore, you can log to the event log or even back to a database. In addition to this disk-based logging, you can also use the system to e-mail health monitoring information.

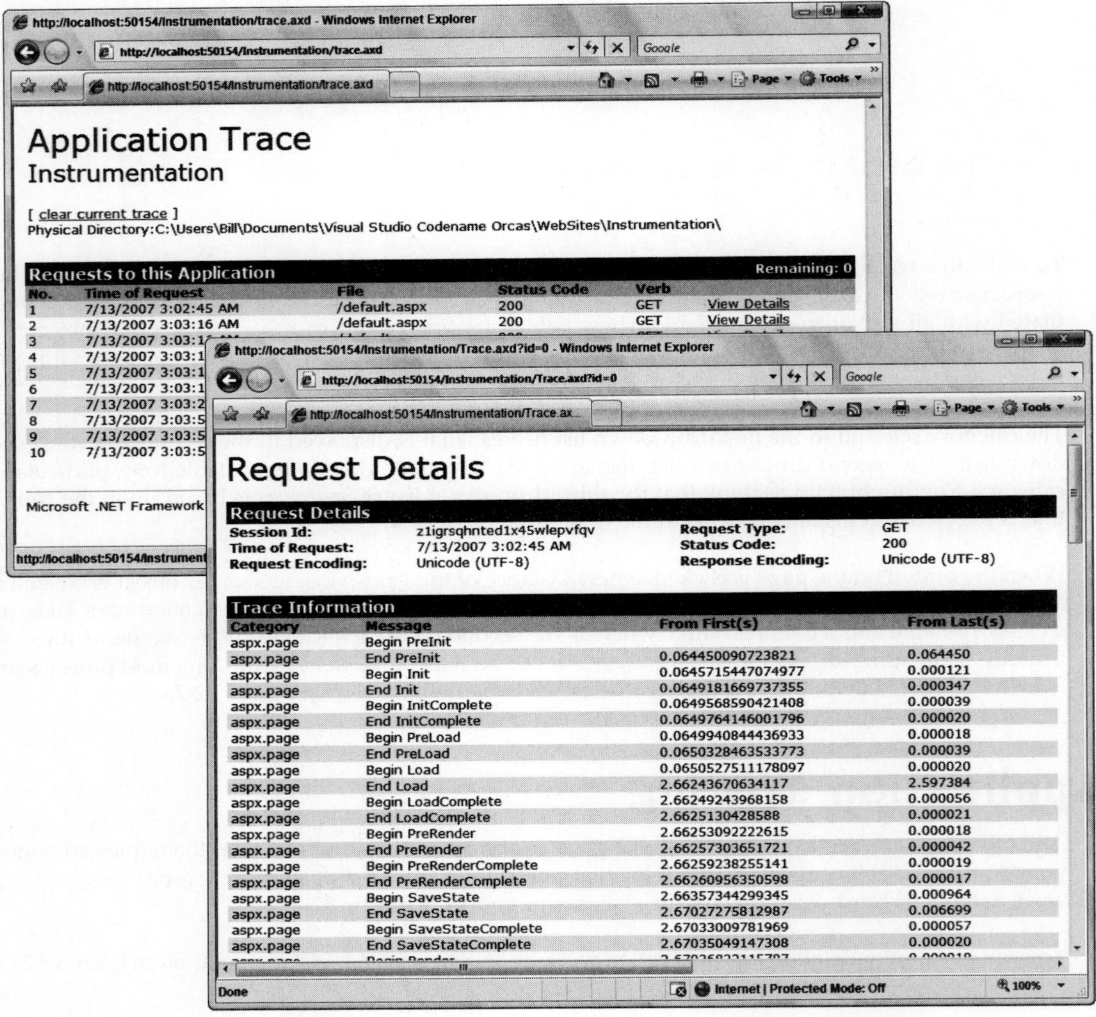

Figure 32-8

By default, the health monitoring system is already enabled. All default errors and failure audits are logged into the event logs on your behalf. For instance, throwing an error produces an entry in the event log, as illustrated in Figure 32-9.

By default, these errors are registered in the event logs, but you can also record these events in a couple of other places. You define where you record these event messages through the various providers available to the health monitoring system. These providers are briefly covered next.

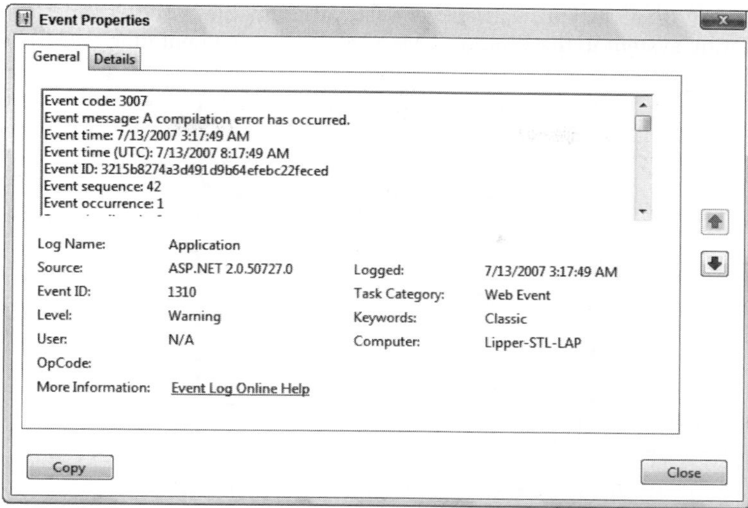

Figure 32-9

The Health Monitoring Provider Model

Quite a bit of information about what a provider model is and how the health monitoring system works with providers is covered in Chapter 12, but a short review of the providers available to the health monitoring system is warranted here as well.

The health monitoring system has the most built-in providers in ASP.NET. A diagram of the available providers is shown in Figure 32-10.

Seven providers are available to the health monitoring system right out of the box:

- `System.Web.Management.EventLogWebEventProvider`: Enables you to use the ASP.NET health monitoring system to record security operation errors and all other errors into the Windows event log.
- `System.Web.Management.SimpleMailWebEventProvider`: Allows you to use the ASP.NET health monitoring system to send error information in an e-mail.
- `System.Web.Management.TemplatedMailWebEventProvider`: Similar to the `SimpleMailWebEventProvider`, the `TemplatedMailWebEventProvider` class lets you send error information in a templated e-mail. Templates are defined using a standard `.aspx` page.
- `System.Web.Management.SqlWebEventProvider`: Enables you to use the ASP.NET health monitoring system to store error information in SQL Server. Like the other SQL providers for the other systems in ASP.NET, the `SqlWebEventProvider` stores error information in SQL Server Express Edition by default.
- `System.Web.Management.TraceWebEventProvider`: Enables you to use the ASP.NET health monitoring system to send error information to the ASP.NET page tracing system.
- `System.Web.Management.IisTraceWebEventProvider`: Provides you with the capability to use the ASP.NET health monitoring system to send error information to the IIS tracing system.

- `System.Web.Management.WmiWebEventProvider`: Enables you to connect the ASP.NET health monitoring system to the Windows Management Instrumentation (WMI) event provider.

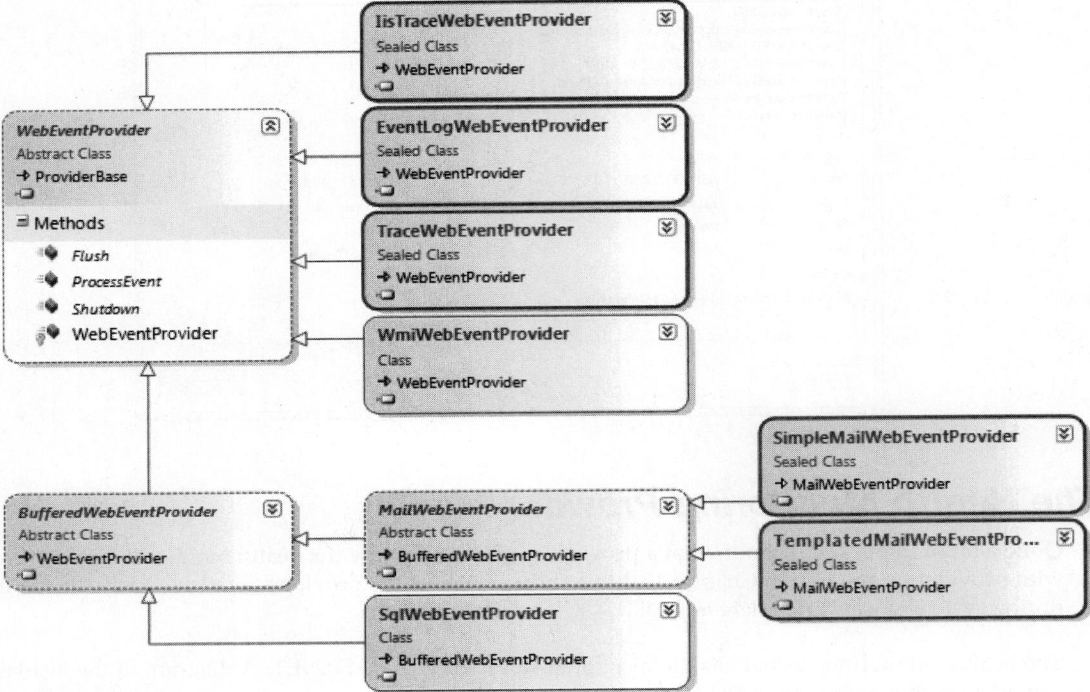

Figure 32-10

Health Monitoring Configuration

By default, the `EventLogWebEventProvider` object is what is utilized for all errors and failure audits. These rules are defined along with the providers and what Web events to trap in the root `web.config` file found at `C:\WINDOWS\Microsoft.NET\Framework\v2.0.50727\CONFIG`. All the information for the health monitoring section is defined within the `<healthMonitoring>` section of this file. Even though these items are defined in the root `web.config` file, you can also override these settings and define them yourself in your application's `web.config` file.

To define the health monitoring capabilities and behaviors in your `web.config` file, place a `<healthMonitoring>` section within the `<system.web>` section of your configuration file:

```
<configuration>
   <system.web>

     <healthMonitoring enabled="true">

     </healthMonitoring>

   </system.web>
</configuration>
```

The <healthMonitoring> section can include a number of subsections, including the following:

- <bufferModes>
- <eventMappings>
- <profiles>
- <providers>
- <rules>

You will look next at some of the core sections and how you can use these sections to define health monitoring tasks in your application's web.config file.

<eventMappings>

The <eventMappings> section of the health monitoring system allows you to define friendly names for specific events that can be captured. You can declare a number of events in this section, but doing so doesn't mean that they are utilized automatically. Remember that when placing events in this section, you are just simply defining them in this configuration file for reuse in other sections. Listing 32-4 shows an example of event mapping.

Listing 32-4: Using the <eventMappings> section

```
<configuration>
   <system.web>

      <healthMonitoring enabled="true">

         <eventMappings>

            <clear />

            <add name="All Events"
             type="System.Web.Management.WebBaseEvent,System.Web,
               Version=2.0.0.0,Culture=neutral,PublicKeyToken=b03f5f7f11d50a3a"
             startEventCode="0" endEventCode="2147483647" />
            <add name="Heartbeats"
             type="System.Web.Management.WebHeartbeatEvent,System.Web,
               Version=2.0.0.0,Culture=neutral,PublicKeyToken=b03f5f7f11d50a3a"
             startEventCode="0" endEventCode="2147483647" />
            <add name="Application Lifetime Events"
             type="System.Web.Management.WebApplicationLifetimeEvent,System.Web,
               Version=2.0.0.0,Culture=neutral,PublicKeyToken=b03f5f7f11d50a3a"
             startEventCode="0" endEventCode="2147483647" />
            <add name="Request Processing Events"
             type="System.Web.Management.WebRequestEvent,System.Web,
               Version=2.0.0.0,Culture=neutral,PublicKeyToken=b03f5f7f11d50a3a"
             startEventCode="0" endEventCode="2147483647" />
            <add name="All Errors"
             type="System.Web.Management.WebBaseErrorEvent,System.Web,
               Version=2.0.0.0,Culture=neutral,PublicKeyToken=b03f5f7f11d50a3a"
             startEventCode="0" endEventCode="2147483647" />
```

Continued

```
            <add name="Infrastructure Errors"
             type="System.Web.Management.WebErrorEvent,System.Web,
               Version=2.0.0.0,Culture=neutral,PublicKeyToken=b03f5f7f11d50a3a"
             startEventCode="0" endEventCode="2147483647" />
            <add name="Request Processing Errors"
             type="System.Web.Management.WebRequestErrorEvent,System.Web,
               Version=2.0.0.0,Culture=neutral,PublicKeyToken=b03f5f7f11d50a3a"
             startEventCode="0" endEventCode="2147483647" />
            <add name="All Audits"
             type="System.Web.Management.WebAuditEvent,System.Web,
               Version=2.0.0.0,Culture=neutral,PublicKeyToken=b03f5f7f11d50a3a"
             startEventCode="0" endEventCode="2147483647" />
            <add name="Failure Audits"
             type="System.Web.Management.WebFailureAuditEvent,System.Web,
               Version=2.0.0.0,Culture=neutral,PublicKeyToken=b03f5f7f11d50a3a"
             startEventCode="0" endEventCode="2147483647" />
            <add name="Success Audits"
             type="System.Web.Management.WebSuccessAuditEvent,System.Web,
               Version=2.0.0.0,Culture=neutral,PublicKeyToken=b03f5f7f11d50a3a"
             startEventCode="0" endEventCode="2147483647" />
         </eventMappings>

      </healthMonitoring>

   </system.web>
</configuration>
```

From this section, you can see that a number of different event types are defined within this `<eventMappings>` section. Not all these definitions are required, just the ones you are interested in working with. Because these definitions are important, look at how the first one is listed:

```
<add name="All Events"
 type="System.Web.Management.WebBaseEvent,System.Web,
   Version=2.0.0.0,Culture=neutral,PublicKeyToken=b03f5f7f11d50a3a"
 startEventCode="0" endEventCode="2147483647" />
```

The `<add>` element takes a number of different attributes. The first, `name`, allows you to give a user-friendly name that can be used later in one of the other sections of the document. In this case, the friendly name provided is `All Events`.

The next attribute is the `type` attribute. This enables you to define the .NET event object with which this event mapping is associated. In this case, it is the base event used by all the other event types as a base class. Although the object definition with the `type` attribute is shown on multiple lines in this book, you should define it on a single line in order for it to work. All the possible Web events it might associate with are found in the `System.Web.Management` namespace.

Each Web Event that is recorded has a code associated with it, and you can use the `startEventCode` attribute to define a starting point for this code definition. In the preceding example, the event code starts at `0` and increments from there until it reaches the number defined in the `endEventCode` attribute. In this case, the ending event code is `2147483647`.

The following table defines each event type you can find in the `System.Web.Management` namespace.

Web Event (System.Web.Management)	Description
`WebBaseEvent`	The `WebBaseEvent` class is the base class for all Web event types. You can, therefore, use this instance within the `<eventMappings>` section in order to create a definition to capture all events.
`WebHeartbeatEvent`	This event defines Web events that are recorded only at specific intervals instead of every time they occur.
`WebApplicationLifetimeEvent`	This event defines Web events that occur on the scale of the application and its lifecycle. These types of events include application starts and stops as well as compilation starts and stops.
`WebRequestEvent`	This event defines Web events that occur during a request cycle and include items such as when a transaction for a request is committed or aborted.
`WebBaseErrorEvent`	The `WebBaseErrorEvent` class is the base class for all Web events that deal with error types. You can, therefore, use this instance within the `<eventMappings>` section to create a definition to capture all error events.
`WebErrorEvent`	This event defines Web events that occur because of configuration errors or any compilation or parsing errors.
`WebRequestErrorEvent`	This event defines Web events that occur because requests are aborted or requests are larger than allowable as defined by the `maxRequestLength` attribute in the configuration file. It also includes any validation errors or any unhandled exceptions.
`WebAuditEvent`	The `WebAuditEvent` class is the base class for all Web events that deal with login attempts. These attempts can either fail or succeed. You can use this instance within the `<eventMappings>` section to write a definition to capture all login attempts.
`WebFailureAuditEvent`	This event defines Web events that occur because of failed login attempts.

Now that all the error definitions are in place within the `<eventMappings>` section, the next step is to further define the structure your health monitoring system will take by detailing the `<providers>` section, which is also found within the `<healthMonitoring>` section.

<providers>

As you saw earlier in Figure 32-10, seven different providers that you can use within the health monitoring system are available to you out of the box. By default, ASP.NET records these events to the event logs using the EventLogWebEventProvider, but you can also modify the provider model so that it uses any of the other providers available. You can also build your own custom providers so you can record these Web events to any data store you want.

You can find more information on building custom providers in Chapter 13.

Providers are declared within the <providers> section, which is nested within the <healthMonitoring> section of the document. Within the root web.config file found at C:\WINDOWS\Microsoft.NET\Framework\v2.0.50727\CONFIG, you find a short list of declared providers. You can also declare other providers in your application's web.config file as presented in Listing 32-5.

Listing 32-5: Using the <providers> section

```
<configuration>
   <system.web>

      <healthMonitoring enabled="true">

         <eventMappings>
            <!-- Code removed for clarity -->
         </eventMappings>

         <providers>

            <clear />

            <add name="EventLogProvider"
             type="System.Web.Management.EventLogWebEventProvider,System.Web,
               Version=2.0.0.0,Culture=neutral,PublicKeyToken=b03f5f7f11d50a3a" />
            <add name="SqlWebEventProvider"
             connectionStringName="LocalSqlServer"
             maxEventDetailsLength="1073741823"
             buffer="false" bufferMode="Notification"
             type="System.Web.Management.SqlWebEventProvider,System.Web,
               Version=2.0.0.0,Culture=neutral,PublicKeyToken=b03f5f7f11d50a3a" />
            <add name="WmiWebEventProvider"
             type="System.Web.Management.WmiWebEventProvider,System.Web,
             Version=2.0.0.0,Culture=neutral,PublicKeyToken=b03f5f7f11d50a3a" />

         </providers>

      </healthMonitoring>

   </system.web>
</configuration>
```

In this example, you see three separate health monitoring providers declared in the web.config file. A provider is defined for storing Web events in the event logs, another for storing in SQL Server, and finally another for the Windows Management Instrumentation (WMI) system.

By declaring these providers within the <providers> section of the web.config file, you don't ensure that these providers are *actually* utilized. Instead, they are simply defined and ready for you to use. You specify which providers to use within the <rules> section of the <healthMonitoring> section, which is defined shortly.

You can add defined providers by using the `<add />` element within the `<providers>` section. Within the `<add />` element, you find a series of available attributes. The first one is the `name` attribute. This allows you to provide a friendly name to the defined provider instance that you will use later when specifying the provider to actually use. The name can be anything you want. The `type` attribute allows you to define the class used for the provider. In some cases, this is all you need (for example, for the event log provider). If you are working with a database-linked provider, however, you must further define things like the `connectionString` attribute along with the `buffer` and `bufferMode` attributes. These are covered in more detail later.

After your providers are defined in the `<healthMonitoring>` section of the document, the next step is to determine which Web events to work with and which provider(s) should be utilized in the monitoring of these events. Both these operations are accomplished from within the `<rules>` section.

<rules>

The `<rules>` section allows you to define the Web events to monitor and the providers to tie them to when one of the monitored Web events is actually triggered. When you are using the health monitoring system, you can actually assign multiple providers to watch for the same Web events. This means that you can store the same Web event in both the event logs *and* in SQL Server. That is pretty powerful. Listing 32-6 provides an example of using the `<rules>` section within your application's `web.config` file.

Listing 32-6: Using the <rules> section

```
<configuration>
   <system.web>

      <healthMonitoring enabled="true">

         <eventMappings>
            <!-- Code removed for clarity -->
         </eventMappings>

         <providers>
            <!-- Code removed for clarity -->
         </providers>

         <rules>

            <clear />

            <add name="All Errors Default" eventName="All Errors"
             provider="EventLogProvider"
             profile="Default" minInstances="1" maxLimit="Infinite"
             minInterval="00:01:00" custom="" />
            <add name="Failure Audits Default" eventName="Failure Audits"
             provider="EventLogProvider" profile="Default" minInstances="1"
             maxLimit="Infinite" minInterval="00:01:00" custom="" />

         </rules>

      </healthMonitoring>

   </system.web>
</configuration>
```

In this example, two types of Web events are being recorded. You specify rules (the Web events to monitor) by using the <add /> element within the <rules> section. The name attribute allows you to provide a friendly name for the rule definition. The eventName is an important attribute because it takes a value of the Web event to monitor. These names are the friendly names that you defined earlier within the <eventMappings> section of the <healthMonitoring> section. The first <add /> element provides a definition of monitoring for All Errors via the eventName attribute. Looking back, you can see that this was, indeed, defined in the <eventMappings> section.

```
<eventMappings>
    <add name="All Errors"
     type="System.Web.Management.WebBaseErrorEvent,System.Web,
        Version=2.0.0.0,Culture=neutral,PublicKeyToken=b03f5f7f11d50a3a"
     startEventCode="0" endEventCode="2147483647" />
</eventMappings>
```

After specifying which Web event to work with through the eventName attribute, the next step is to define which provider to use for this Web event. You do this using the provider attribute. In the case of the first <add /> element, the EventLogProvider is utilized. Again, this is the friendly name that was used for the provider definition in the <providers> section, as shown here:

```
<providers>
    <add name="EventLogProvider"
     type="System.Web.Management.EventLogWebEventProvider,System.Web,
       Version=2.0.0.0,Culture=neutral,PublicKeyToken=b03f5f7f11d50a3a" />
</providers>
```

The three attributes discussed so far are required attributes. The rest are considered optional attributes. The minInstances attribute defines the minimum number of times this Web event must occur before it is logged. The maxLimit attribute defines the maximum number of instances of the defined Web event that can be recorded. If instances are likely to occur because of some continuous loop, you might want to add a value here. The minInterval attribute denotes the minimum time allowed between log entries. This means that if the minInterval is set to 00:01:00 and two Web events being monitored occur within 15 seconds of each other, the first one is recorded but the second instance is discarded because it falls within the 1-minute setting.

Within the <rules> section, you can also see a profile attribute defined in the <add /> elements of the rules defined. The value of this attribute comes from a definition that is supplied from the <profiles> section of the <healthMonitoring> section. This section is discussed next.

<profiles>

The <profiles> section enables you to define some of the behaviors for Web event monitoring. These definitions are utilized by any number of rule definitions within the <rules> section. An example use of the <profiles> section is illustrated in Listing 32-7.

Listing 32-7: Using the <profiles> section

```
<configuration>
   <system.web>

      <healthMonitoring enabled="true">
```

```
            <eventMappings>
               <!-- Code removed for clarity -->
            </eventMappings>

            <providers>
               <!-- Code removed for clarity -->
            </providers>

            <rules>
               <!-- Code removed for clarity -->
            </rules>

            <profiles>

               <clear />

               <add name="Default" minInstances="1" maxLimit="Infinite"
                minInterval="00:01:00" custom="" />
               <add name="Critical" minInstances="1" maxLimit="Infinite"
                minInterval="00:00:00" custom="" />

            </profiles>

         </healthMonitoring>

      </system.web>
   </configuration>
```

As with the other sections, you add a profile definition by using the `<add />` element within the `<profiles>` section. The `name` attribute allows you to provide a friendly name that is then utilized from the definitions placed within the `<rules>` section, as illustrated here:

```
<rules>
   <add name="All Errors Default" eventName="All Errors"
    provider="EventLogProvider"
    profile="Default" minInstances="1" maxLimit="Infinite"
    minInterval="00:01:00" custom="" />
</rules>
```

The definitions in the `<profiles>` section also use the attributes `minInstances`, `maxLimit`, and `minInterval`. These have the same meanings as if they were used directly in the `<rules>` section (see the explanation in the previous section). The idea here, however, is that you can more centrally define these values and use them across multiple rule definitions.

Writing Events via Configuration: Running the Example

Using the sample `<healthMonitoring>` section (illustrated in the previous listings in this chapter), you can now write all errors as well as audits that fail (failed logins) to the event log automatically.

To test this construction in the `<healthMonitoring>` section, create a simple ASP.NET page that allows you to divide two numbers and then show the result of the division on the screen. An example ASP.NET page is presented in Figure 32-11.

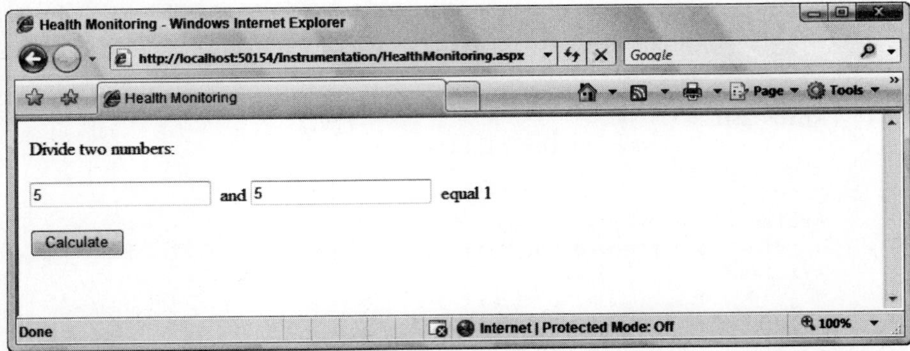

Figure 32-11

As you can see from this page, you can enter a single number in the first text box and another in the second text box and press the calculate button. This allows the two numbers to be divided. The result appears in a Label control on the page. In this example, the code intentionally does not use any exception handling. Therefore, if the end user tried to divide 5 by 0 (zero), an exception is thrown. This event, in turn, causes the exception to be written to the event log. In fact, if you run a similar example and look in the event log, you find that the error has indeed been written as you have specified it should be within the `web.config` file. The report from the event log is presented in Figure 32-12.

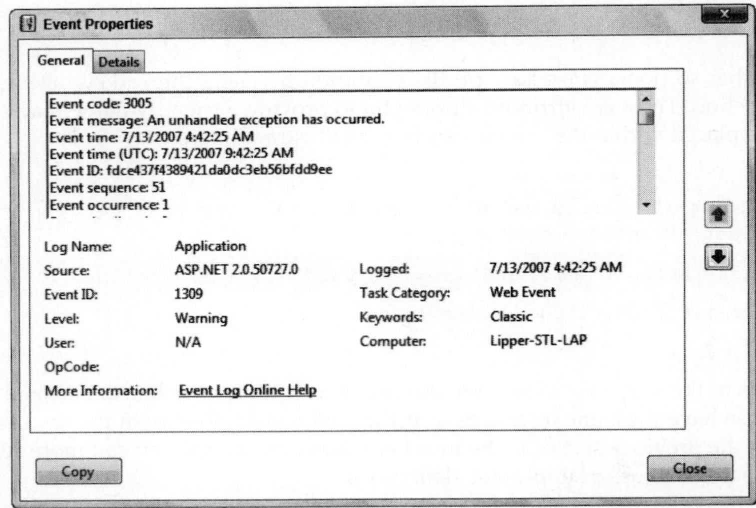

Figure 32-12

Routing Events to SQL Server

Pushing Web events to the event log is something most Web applications do and is also something you should consider if you have overridden these built-in (and default) features. Even more powerful than writing them to the event log, however, is being able to write them to a database.

Writing them to a database allows you to actually create a larger history, makes them more secure, and allows you to more easily retrieve the values and use them in any type of administration application that you might create.

This capability was briefly introduced in Chapter 1 and is not that difficult to work with. If you work from the same <healthMonitoring> section created earlier in this chapter, writing the events to SQL Server is as simple as adding some <add /> elements to the various sections.

As shown in the previous <providers> section, a declaration actually exists for recording events into SQL Server. It is presented here again:

```
<providers>

   <clear />

   <add name="EventLogProvider"
    type="System.Web.Management.EventLogWebEventProvider,System.Web,
      Version=2.0.0.0,Culture=neutral,PublicKeyToken=b03f5f7f11d50a3a" />

   <add name="SqlWebEventProvider"
    connectionStringName="LocalSqlServer"
    maxEventDetailsLength="1073741823"
    buffer="false" bufferMode="Notification"
    type="System.Web.Management.SqlWebEventProvider,System.Web,
      Version=2.0.0.0,Culture=neutral,PublicKeyToken=b03f5f7f11d50a3a" />
   <add name="WmiWebEventProvider"
    type="System.Web.Management.WmiWebEventProvider,System.Web,
      Version=2.0.0.0,Culture=neutral,PublicKeyToken=b03f5f7f11d50a3a" />

</providers>
```

If you look over this bit of code, you see the definition to record events into SQL Server is presented in the bold section within the <providers> section. The section in bold shows a connection to the SQL Server instance that is defined by the `LocalSqlServer` connection string name. You can find this connection string in the `machine.config` file, and you see that it points to an auto-generated SQL Server Express file that ASP.NET can work with.

```
<connectionStrings>
   <add name="LocalSqlServer" connectionString="data source=.\SQLEXPRESS;Integrated
    Security=SSPI;AttachDBFilename=|DataDirectory|aspnetdb.mdf;User Instance=true"
    providerName="System.Data.SqlClient" />
</connectionStrings>
```

To work with Microsoft's SQL Server 2005, you simply create a new connection string within your ASP.NET application's `web.config` *file and reference the friendly name provided to this connection from the* <add /> *element of the* <providers> *section.*

Although this SQL Server instance is declared and defined, it is not utilized by any of the rules that you have established. Looking at the previous sections, you can see that within the <rules> section of the health monitoring section of the `web.config`, only two rules exist: a rule to write all errors to the event log and another rule to write failure audits to the event log. To add a new rule to write errors (all errors again) to SQL Server, you use the construction shown in Listing 32-8.

Listing 32-8: Creating a rule to write events to SQL Server

```
<configuration>
   <system.web>
      <healthMonitoring enabled="true">

         <eventMappings>
            <!-- Code removed for clarity -->
         </eventMappings>

         <providers>
            <!-- Code removed for clarity -->
         </providers>

         <rules>

            <clear />

            <add name="All Errors Default" eventName="All Errors"
             provider="EventLogProvider"
             profile="Default" minInstances="1" maxLimit="Infinite"
             minInterval="00:01:00" custom="" />
            <add name="Failure Audits Default" eventName="Failure Audits"
             provider="EventLogProvider" profile="Default" minInstances="1"
             maxLimit="Infinite" minInterval="00:01:00" custom="" />
            <add name="All Errors SQL Server" eventName="All Errors"
             provider="SqlWebEventProvider"
             profile="Default" minInstances="1" maxLimit="Infinite"
             minInterval="00:01:00" custom="" />

         </rules>

      </healthMonitoring>

   </system.web>
</configuration>
```

To be able to write to SQL Server, you must create a new `<add />` element within the `<rules>` section of the document. The friendly name provided via the `name` attribute must be unique in the list of defined rules or you encounter an error. In this case, the name of the rule is `All Errors SQL Server` and like the `All Errors Default` rule, it points to the event mapping of `All Errors` as shown via the `eventName` attribute. The `provider` attribute then points to the SQL Server definition contained within the `<providers>` section. In this case, it is `SqlWebEventProvider`.

With all this in place, run the ASP.NET page (shown earlier) that allows you to throw an error by dividing by zero. If you run this page a couple of times, you see that ASP.NET has automatically created an `ASPNETDB.MDF` file in your project (if you didn't already have one).

You can then open the SQL Server Express Edition database and expand the Tables node in the Server Explorer of Visual Studio. In this list of available tables, you find a new table called `aspnet_WebEvent_Events`. Right-click this table and select Show Table Data from the menu. This gives you something similar to what is illustrated in Figure 32-13.

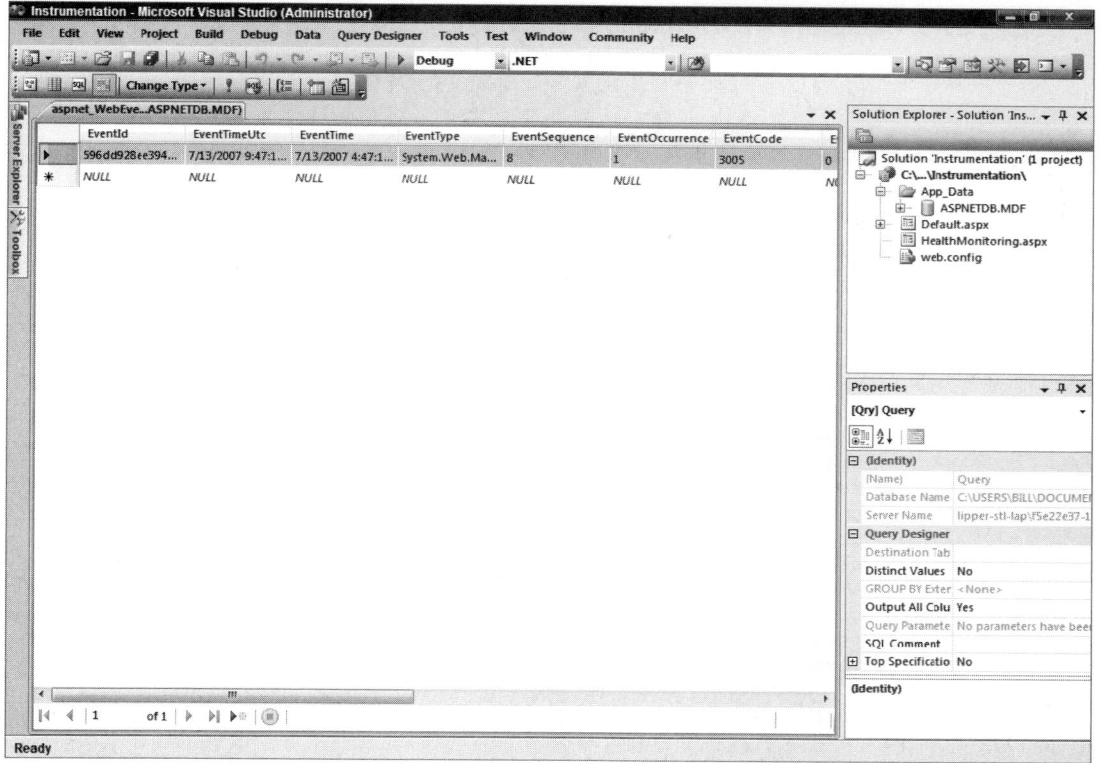

Figure 32-13

As you can see from this figure, the entire event is now stored within SQL Server (it is the first and only event at the moment). One of the nice things about this example is that not only is this event recorded to the database, but it is also written to the event log because you can use more than a single provider for each event. You can just as easily use a provider that comes from `MailWebEventProvider` and send the error out as an e-mail message.

Buffering Web Events

When you start working with Web events that you want to write to a database (such as SQL Server) or sent via an e-mail, you soon realize that doing so can really lock up your database or result in a huge amount of e-mail (especially if your application is sent into some perpetual loop of errors). For this reason, you can see why these providers inherit from `BufferedWebEventProvider`.

`BufferedWebEventProvider` does exactly what it says — it *buffers* (or queues) your collected Web events before performing the specified action upon them. The reason you might want to buffer is to eliminate the possibility of your database being pounded or your e-mail box being flooded.

Definitions of how the buffering should occur are located in the `<bufferModes>` section within the `<healthMonitoring>` section of the `web.config` file. An example of the `<bufferModes>` section is presented in Listing 32-9.

Listing 32-9: Using the <bufferModes> section

```
<configuration>
   <system.web>

      <healthMonitoring enabled="true">

         <bufferModes>

            <clear />

            <add name="Critical Notification" maxBufferSize="100" maxFlushSize="20"
             urgentFlushThreshold="1" regularFlushInterval="Infinite"
             urgentFlushInterval="00:01:00"
             maxBufferThreads="1" />
            <add name="Notification" maxBufferSize="300" maxFlushSize="20"
             urgentFlushThreshold="1" regularFlushInterval="Infinite"
             urgentFlushInterval="00:01:00"
             maxBufferThreads="1" />
            <add name="Analysis" maxBufferSize="1000" maxFlushSize="100"
             urgentFlushThreshold="100" regularFlushInterval="00:05:00"
             urgentFlushInterval="00:01:00" maxBufferThreads="1" />
            <add name="Logging" maxBufferSize="1000" maxFlushSize="200"
             urgentFlushThreshold="800"
             regularFlushInterval="00:30:00" urgentFlushInterval="00:05:00"
             maxBufferThreads="1" />

         </bufferModes>

         <eventMappings>
            <!-- Code removed for clarity -->
         </eventMappings>

         <providers>
            <!-- Code removed for clarity -->
         </providers>

         <rules>
            <!-- Code removed for clarity -->
         </rules>

         <profiles>
            <!-- Code removed for clarity -->
         </profiles>

      </healthMonitoring>

   </system.web>
</configuration>
```

In this code, you can see four buffer modes defined. Each mode has a friendly name defined using the `name` attribute. For each mode, a number of different attribute can be applied. To examine these attributes, take a closer look at the `Logging` buffer mode.

```
<add name="Logging"
 maxBufferSize="1000"
 maxFlushSize="200"
 urgentFlushThreshold="800"
 regularFlushInterval="00:30:00"
 urgentFlushInterval="00:05:00"
 maxBufferThreads="1" />
```

This buffer mode is called *Logging* and, based on the values assigned to its attributes, any provider using this buffer mode sends the messages to the database or via e-mail every 30 minutes. This is also referred to as *flushing* the Web events. The time period of 30 minutes is defined using the `regularFlushInterval` attribute. Therefore, every 30 minutes, ASP.NET sends 200 messages to the database (or via e-mail). It will not send more than 200 messages at a time because of what is specified in the `maxFlushSize` attribute. Well, what happens if more than 200 messages are waiting within that 30-minute time period? ASP.NET still sends only 200 messages every 30 minutes and holds additional messages when the number exceeds 200. The maximum number of messages held in the queue cannot exceed 1,000 messages. This number is set through the `maxBufferSize` attribute. However, after the total in the queue hits 800 messages, ASP.NET starts flushing the messages every 5 minutes instead of every 30 minutes. The change in frequency of messages is determined by the `urgentFlushThreshold` attribute, and the time interval used to send messages when the `urgentFlushThreshold` is hit is determined by the `urgentFlushInterval` attribute.

After you have defined the buffering modes you want to use, the next step is to apply them. To analyze the process, look back on how the `SqlWebEventProvider` is declared.

```
<providers>

   <clear />

   <add name="EventLogProvider"
    type="System.Web.Management.EventLogWebEventProvider,System.Web,
      Version=2.0.0.0,Culture=neutral,PublicKeyToken=b03f5f7f11d50a3a" />

   <add name="SqlWebEventProvider"
    connectionStringName="LocalSqlServer"
    maxEventDetailsLength="1073741823"
    buffer="false" bufferMode="Notification"
    type="System.Web.Management.SqlWebEventProvider,System.Web,
      Version=2.0.0.0,Culture=neutral,PublicKeyToken=b03f5f7f11d50a3a" />

   <add name="WmiWebEventProvider"
    type="System.Web.Management.WmiWebEventProvider,System.Web,
      Version=2.0.0.0,Culture=neutral,PublicKeyToken=b03f5f7f11d50a3a" />

</providers>
```

Again, this event is shown in bold. First, the most important attribute is the `buffer` attribute. By default, buffering of messages is turned off. This is done by setting the `buffer` attribute to `false`. The `bufferMode` attribute allows you to assign one of the defined buffer modes created within the `<bufferModes>` section. In this case, the `Notification` buffer mode is referenced. Changing the buffer attribute to `true` enables the events to be sent only to SQL Server according to the time intervals defined by the `Notification` buffer mode.

E-mailing Web Events

When monitoring a server for Web events, you are not *always* going to be networked into a server or actively monitoring it every second. This doesn't mean that you won't want to know immediately if something is going very wrong with your ASP.NET application. For this reason, you will find the `SimpleMailWebEventProvider` and the `TemplatedMailWebEventProvider` objects quite beneficial.

Using the SimpleMailProvider

The `SimpleMailWebEventProvider` sends Web events as a simple text e-mail, as shown in Figure 32-14.

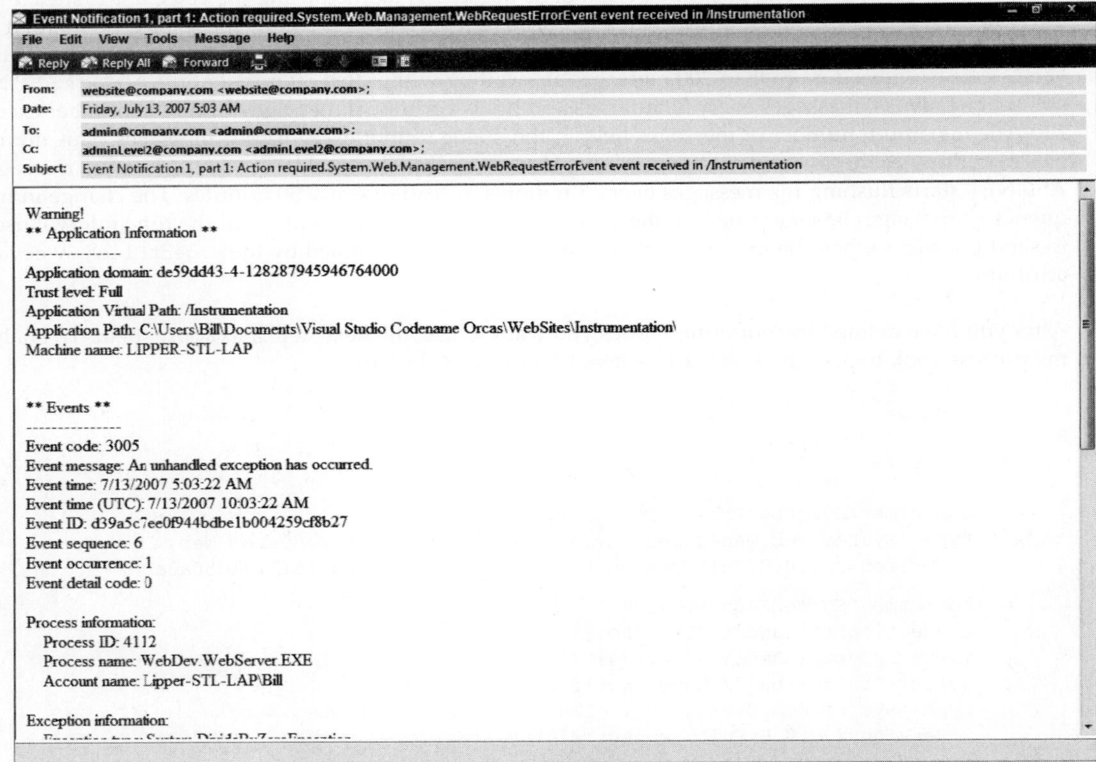

Figure 32-14

To set up this provider, you place an additional `<add />` element within the `<providers>` section, as illustrated in Listing 32-10.

Listing 32-10: Adding a SimpleMailWebEventProvider instance

```
<add name="SimpleMailProvider"
 type="System.Web.Management.SimpleMailWebEventProvider, System.Web,
   Version=2.0.0.0, Culture=neutral, PublicKeyToken=b03f5f7f11d50a3a"
 from="website@company.com"
 to="admin@company.com"
 cc="adminLevel2@company.com"
 bcc="director@company.com"
```

```
    bodyHeader="Warning!"
    bodyFooter="Please investigate ASAP."
    subjectPrefix="Action required."
    buffer="false"
    maxEventLength="4096"
    maxMessagesPerNotification="1" />
```

After the provider is added, you also add a rule that uses this provider in some fashion (as you do with all the other providers). This is done by referencing the `SimpleMailWebEventProvider` name within the provider attribute of the `<add />` element contained in the `<rules>` section.

For this to work, be sure that you set up the SMTP capabilities correctly in your `web.config` file. An example is presented in Listing 32-11.

Listing 32-11: Setting up SMTP in the web.config file

```
<configuration>

  <system.web>
     <!-- Code removed for clarity -->
  </system.web>

  <system.net>
    <mailSettings>
      <smtp deliveryMethod="Network">
        <network
          host="localhost"
          port="25"
          defaultCredentials="true"
        />
      </smtp>
    </mailSettings>
  </system.net>

</configuration>
```

If you do not have a quick way of setting up SMTP and still want to test this, you can also have ASP.NET create e-mail messages and store them to disk by setting up the `<smtp>` section as illustrated in Listing 32-12.

Listing 32-12: Another option for setting up the SMTP section

```
<configuration>

  <system.web>
     <!-- Code removed for clarity -->
  </system.web>

  <system.net>
    <mailSettings>
      <smtp deliveryMethod="SpecifiedPickupDirectory">
        <specifiedPickupDirectory pickupDirectoryLocation ="C:\"/>
      </smtp>
```

Continued

```
    </mailSettings>
  </system.net>

</configuration>
```

In this scenario, the e-mails will be just placed within the `C:\` root directory.

Using the TemplatedMailWebEventProvider

Another option for e-mailing Web events is to use the `TemplatedMailWebEventProvider` object. This works basically the same as the `SimpleMailWebEventProvider`, but the `TemplatedMailWebEventProvider` allows you to create more handsome e-mails (they might get noticed more). As with the other providers, you use the `<add />` element within the `<providers>` section to add this provider. This process is illustrated in Listing 32-13.

Listing 32-13: Adding a TemplatedMailWebEventProvider

```
<add name="TemplatedMailProvider"
 type="System.Web.Management.TemplatedMailWebEventProvider, System.Web,
   Version=2.0.0.0, Culture=neutral, PublicKeyToken=b03f5f7f11d50a3a"
 template="../MailTemplates/ErrorNotification.aspx"
 from="website@company.com"
 to="admin@company.com"
 cc="adminLevel2@company.com"
 bcc="director@company.com"
 subjectPrefix="Action required."
 buffer="false"
 detailedTemplateErrors="true"
 maxMessagesPerNotification="1" />
```

After the provider is added, you also need to add a rule that uses this provider in some fashion (as you do with all the other providers). You add it by referencing the `TemplatedMailWebEventProvider` name within the provider attribute of the `<add />` element contained in the `<rules>` section. Be sure to set up the `<smtp>` section, just as you did with the `SimpleMailWebEventProvider`.

After these items are in place, the next step is to create an `ErrorNotification.aspx` page. This page construction is illustrated in Listing 32-14.

Listing 32-14: Creating the ErrorNotification.aspx page

VB

```
<%@ Page Language="VB" %>
<%@ Import Namespace="System.Web.Management" %>

<script runat="server">
    Protected Sub Page_Load(ByVal sender As Object, ByVal e As System.EventArgs)
        Dim meni As MailEventNotificationInfo = _
          TemplatedMailWebEventProvider.CurrentNotification
        Label1.Text = "Events Discarded By Buffer: " & _
          meni.EventsDiscardedByBuffer.ToString()
        Label2.Text = "Events Discarded Due To Message Limit: " & _
          meni.EventsDiscardedDueToMessageLimit.ToString()
        Label3.Text = "Events In Buffer: " & meni.EventsInBuffer.ToString()
        Label4.Text = "Events In Notification: " & _
```

```
            meni.EventsInNotification.ToString()
          Label5.Text = "Events Remaining: " & meni.EventsRemaining.ToString()
          Label6.Text = "Last Notification UTC: " & _
            meni.LastNotificationUtc.ToString()
          Label7.Text = "Number of Messages In Notification: " & _
            meni.MessagesInNotification.ToString()

          DetailsView1.DataSource = meni.Events
          DetailsView1.DataBind()
      End Sub
</script>

<html xmlns="http://www.w3.org/1999/xhtml">
   <head></head>
   <body>
      <form id="form1" runat="server">
         <asp:label id="Label1" runat="server"></asp:label><br />
         <asp:label id="Label2" runat="server"></asp:label><br />
         <asp:label id="Label3" runat="server"></asp:label><br />
         <asp:label id="Label4" runat="server"></asp:label><br />
         <asp:label id="Label5" runat="server"></asp:label><br />
         <asp:label id="Label6" runat="server"></asp:label><br />
         <asp:label id="Label7" runat="server"></asp:label><br />

         <br />

         <asp:DetailsView ID="DetailsView1" runat="server" Height="50px"
          Width="500px" BackColor="White" BorderColor="#E7E7FF" BorderStyle="None"
          BorderWidth="1px" CellPadding="3" GridLines="Horizontal">
            <FooterStyle BackColor="#B5C7DE" ForeColor="#4A3C8C" />
            <EditRowStyle BackColor="#738A9C" Font-Bold="True"
             ForeColor="#F7F7F7" />
            <RowStyle BackColor="#E7E7FF" ForeColor="#4A3C8C" />
            <PagerStyle BackColor="#E7E7FF" ForeColor="#4A3C8C"
             HorizontalAlign="Right" />
            <HeaderStyle BackColor="#4A3C8C" Font-Bold="True"
             ForeColor="#F7F7F7" />
            <AlternatingRowStyle BackColor="#F7F7F7" />
         </asp:DetailsView>
      </form>
   </body>
</html>
```

C#

```
<%@ Page Language="C#" %>
<%@ Import Namespace="System.Web.Management" %>

<script runat="server">
    protected void Page_Load(object sender, EventArgs e)
    {
        MailEventNotificationInfo meni =
          TemplatedMailWebEventProvider.CurrentNotification;
        Label1.Text = "Events Discarded By Buffer: " +
          meni.EventsDiscardedByBuffer.ToString();
```

Continued

```
            Label2.Text = "Events Discarded Due To Message Limit: " +
              meni.EventsDiscardedDueToMessageLimit.ToString();
            Label3.Text = "Events In Buffer: " + meni.EventsInBuffer.ToString();
            Label4.Text = "Events In Notification: " +
              meni.EventsInNotification.ToString();
            Label5.Text = "Events Remaining: " + meni.EventsRemaining.ToString();
            Label6.Text = "Last Notification UTC: " +
              meni.LastNotificationUtc.ToString();
            Label7.Text = "Number of Messages In Notification: " +
              meni.MessagesInNotification.ToString();

            DetailsView1.DataSource = meni.Events;
            DetailsView1.DataBind();
        }
    </script>
```

To work with the `TemplatedMailWebEventProvider`, you first import the `System.Web.Management` namespace. This is done so you can work with the `MailEventNotificationInfo` and `TemplatedMailWebEventProvider` objects. You first create an instance of the `MailEventNotificationInfo` object and assign it a value of the `TemplatedMailWebEventProvider.CurrentNotification` property. Now, you have access to an entire series of values from the Web event that was monitored.

This e-mail message is displayed in Figure 32-15.

As you can see in this figure, the e-mail message is more readable in this format.

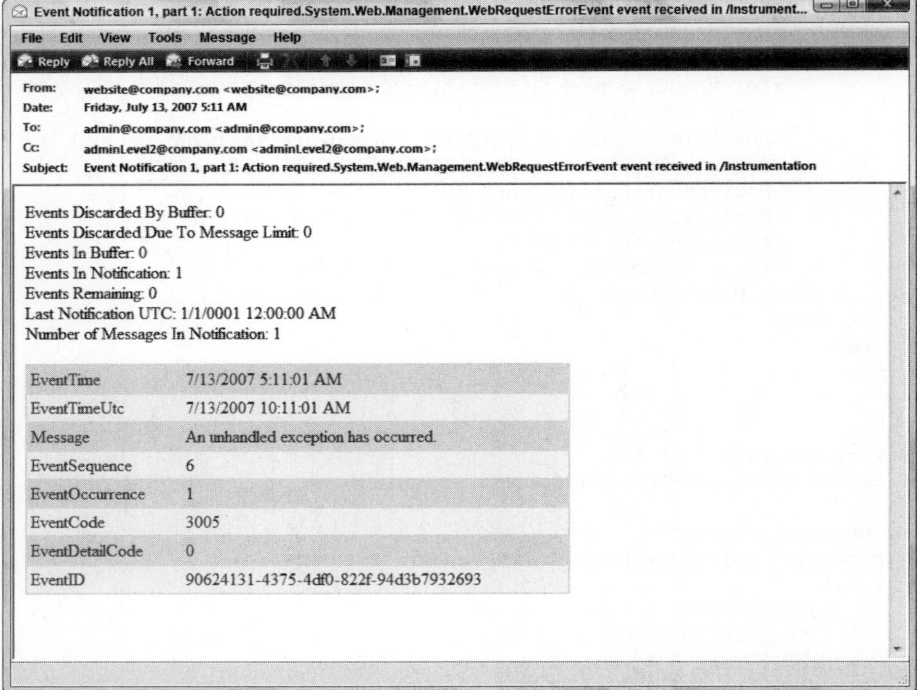

Figure 32-15

Summary

Whereas ASP.NET 1.*x* was really focused on the developer, ASP.NET 2.0 and 3.5 have made tremendous inroads into making life easier for the administrator of the deployed ASP.NET application. In addition to a number of GUI-based management and administration tools (covered in the next chapter), you can now record and send notifications about the health (good or bad) of your ASP.NET applications using the ASP.NET health monitoring capabilities.

33

Administration and Management

You have almost reached the end of this book; you have been introduced to ASP.NET 3.5 with its wonderful features designed to help you become a better and more efficient programmer. However, with all advancement comes complexity, as is the case in the areas of ASP.NET configuration and management. The good news is that the ASP.NET development team realized this and provided tools and APIs that enable developers to configure and manage ASP.NET–based applications with reliability and comfort.

This chapter covers these tools in great detail in an effort to educate you about some of the options available to you. This chapter explores two powerful configuration tools: the ASP.NET Web Site Administration Tool, a Web-based application, and the IIS Manager, which is used to configure your ASP.NET applications.

The ASP.NET Web Site Administration Tool

When ASP.NET was first released, it introduced the concept of an XML-based configuration file for its Web applications. This `web.config` file is located in the same directory as the application itself. It is used to store a number of configuration settings, some of which can override configuration settings defined in `machine.config` file or in the root server's `web.config` file. Versions of ASP.NET before ASP.NET 2.0, however, did not provide an administration tool to make it easy to configure the settings. Because of this, a large number of developers around the world ended up creating their own configuration tools to avoid having to work with the XML file manually.

The ASP.NET Web Site Administration Tool enables you to manage Web site configuration through a simple, easy-to-use Web interface. It eliminates the need for manually editing the `web.config` file. If no `web.config` file exists when you use the administration tool for the first time, it creates one. By default, the ASP.NET Web Site Administration Tool also creates the standard `ASPNETDB.MDF` SQL Server Express Edition file in the `App_Data` folder of your Web site to store application data.

The changes made to most settings in the ASP.NET Web Site Administration Tool take effect immediately. You find them reflected in the `web.config` file.

The default settings are automatically inherited from any configuration files that exist in the root folder of a Web server. The ASP.NET Web Site Administration Tool enables you to create or update your own settings for your Web application. You can also override the settings inherited from uplevel configuration files, if an override for those settings is allowed. If overriding is not permitted, the setting appears dimmed in the administration tool.

The ASP.NET Web Site Administration Tool is automatically installed during installation of the .NET Framework version 3.5. To use the administration tool to administer your own Web site, you must be logged in as a registered user of your site and you must have read and write permissions to `web.config`.

You cannot access the ASP.NET Web Site Administration Tool remotely or even locally through IIS. Instead, you access it with Visual Studio 2008, which, in turn, uses its integrated web server (formally named Cassini) to access the administration tool.

In order to access this tool through Visual Studio 2008, open the website and click the ASP.NET Configuration button found in the menu located at the top of the Solution Explorer pane. Another way to launch this tool is to select ASP.NET Configuration from the Website option in the main Visual Studio menu. Figure 33-1 shows the ASP.NET Web Site Administration Tool's welcome page.

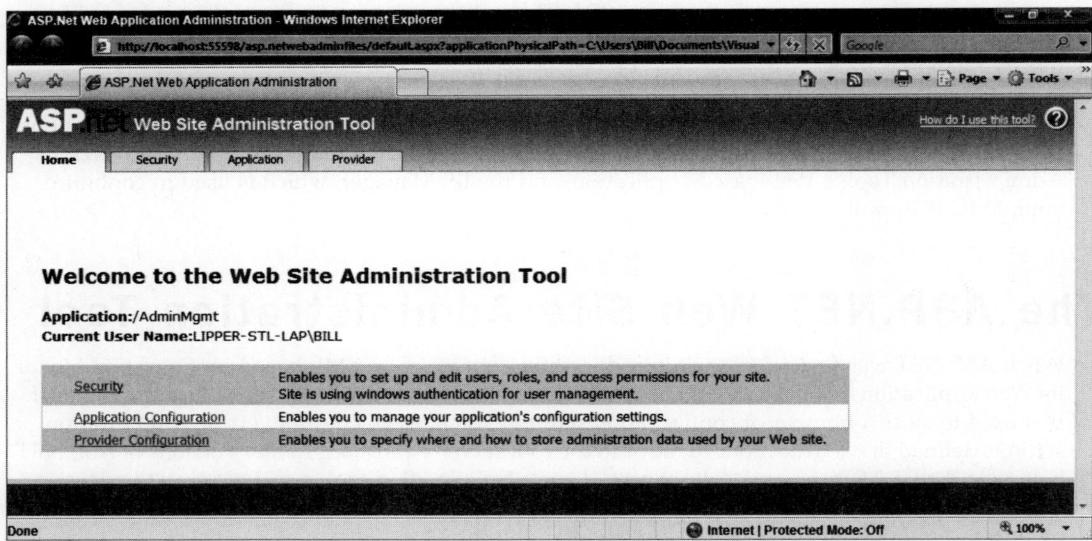

Figure 33-1

The ASP.NET Web Site Administration Tool features a tabbed interface that groups related configuration settings. The tabs and the configuration settings that they manage are described in the following sections.

The Home Tab

The Home tab (shown previously in Figure 33-1) is a summary that supplies some basic information about the application you are monitoring or modifying. It provides the name of the application and the current user context in which you are accessing the application. In addition, you see links to the other administration tool tabs that provide you with summaries of their settings. To make any changes to your Web application, you simply click the appropriate tab or link.

Remember that most changes to configuration settings made using this administration tool take effect immediately, causing the Web application to be restarted and currently active sessions to be lost if you are using an InProc session. The best practice for administrating ASP.NET is to make configuration changes to a development version of your application and later publish these changes to your production application. That's why this tool can't be used outside of Visual Studio.

Some settings (those in which the administration tool interface has a dedicated Save button) do not save automatically. You can lose the information typed in these windows if you do not click the Save button to propagate the changes you made to the `web.config` file. The ASP.NET Web Site Administration Tool also times out after a period of inactivity. Any settings that do not take effect immediately and are not saved will be lost if this occurs.

As extensive as the ASP.NET Web Site Administration Tool is, it manages only some of the configuration settings that are available for your Web application. All other settings require modification of configuration files manually, by using the Microsoft Management Console (MMC) snap-in for ASP.NET if you are using Windows XP, using the Internet Information Services (IIS) Manager if you are using Windows Vista, or by using the `Configuration` API.

The Security Tab

Use the Security tab to manage access permissions to secure sections of your Web application, user accounts, and roles. From this tab, you can select whether your Web application is accessed on an intranet or from the Internet. If you specify the intranet, Windows-based authentication is used; otherwise, forms-based authentication is configured. The latter mechanism relies on you to manage users in a custom data store, such as SQL Server database tables. The Windows-based authentication employs the user's Windows logon for identification.

User information is stored in a SQL Server Express database by default (`ASPNETDB.MDF`). The database is automatically created in the `App_Data` folder of the Web application. It is recommended that you store such sensitive information on a different and more secure database, perhaps located on a separate server. Changing the data store might mean that you also need to change the underlying data provider. To accomplish this, you simply use the Provider tab to select a different data provider. The Provider tab is covered later in this chapter.

You can configure security settings on this tab in two ways: select the Setup Wizard, or simply use the links provided for the Users, Roles, and Access Management sections. Figure 33-2 shows the Security tab.

You can use the wizard to configure initial settings. Later, you learn other ways to create and modify security settings.

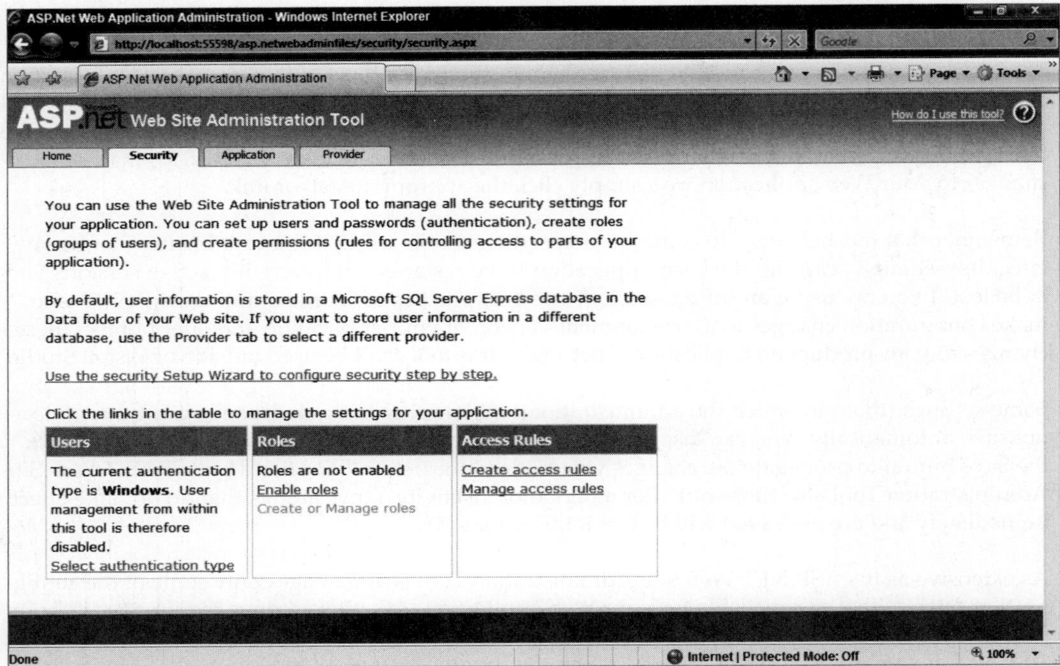

Figure 33-2

The Security Setup Wizard

The Security Setup Wizard provides a seven-step process ranging from selecting the way the user will be authenticated to selecting a data source for storing user information. This is followed by definitions of roles, users, and access rules.

> **Be sure to create all folders that need special permissions *before* you engage the wizard.**

Follow these steps to use the Security Setup Wizard:

1. The wizard welcome screen (shown in Figure 33-3) is informational only. It educates you on the basics of security management in ASP.NET. When you finish reading the screen, click Next.
2. Select your access method (authentication mechanism). You have two options:
    - **From the Internet:** Indicates you want forms-based authentication. You must use your own database of user information. This option works well in scenarios where non-employees need to access the Web application.
    - **From a Local Area Network:** Indicates users of this application are already authenticated on the domain. You do not have to use your own user information database. Instead, you can use the Windows web server domain user information.

    Figure 33-4 shows the screen for Step 2 of the process.

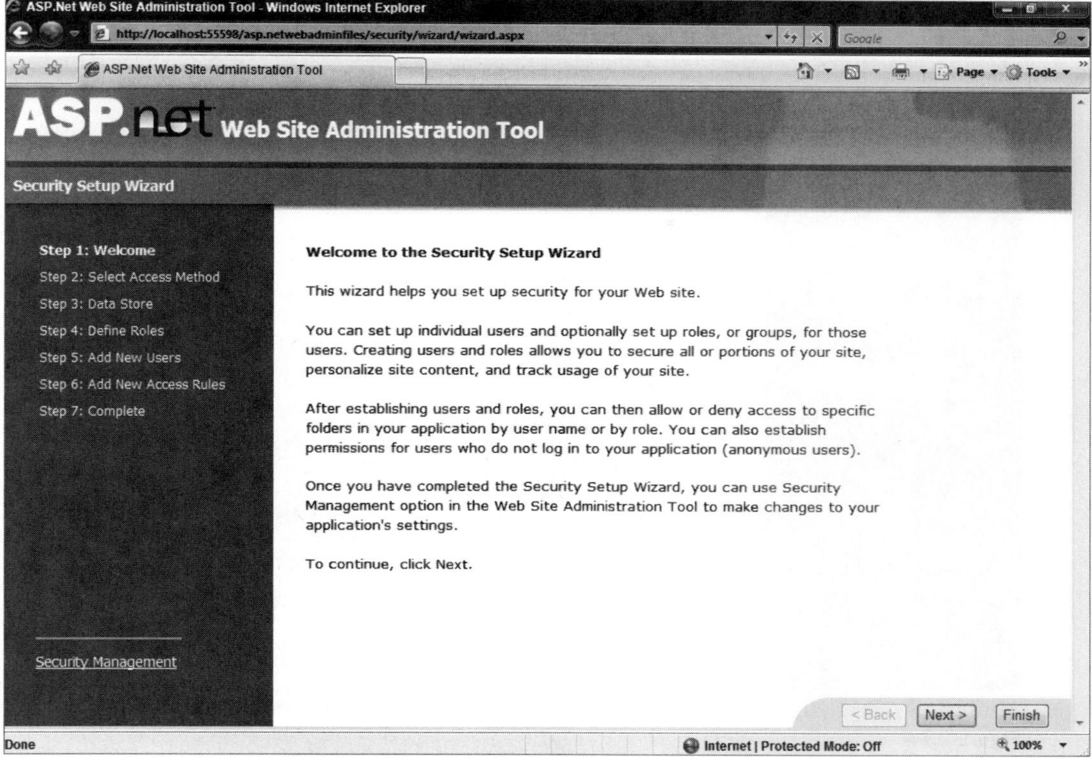

Figure 33-3

Select **From the Internet**, and click the Next button.

3. Select Access Method. As mentioned earlier, the ASP.NET Web Site Administration Tool uses SQL Server Express Edition by default. You can configure additional providers on the Providers tab. In the Step 3 screen shown in Figure 33-5, only an advanced provider is displayed because no other providers have been configured yet. Click Next.

4. Define Roles. If you are happy with all users having the same access permission, you can simply skip this step by deselecting the Enable Roles for This Web Site check box. If this box is not checked, clicking the Next button takes you directly to the User Management screens. Check this box to see how to define roles using this wizard.

   The screen from Step 4 is shown in Figure 33-6. When you are ready, click Next.

   The next screen (see Figure 33-7) in the wizard enables you to create and delete roles. The roles simply define categories of users. Later, you can provide users and access rules based on these roles. Go ahead and create roles for Administrator, Human Resources, Sales, and Viewer. Click Next.

5. Add New Users. Earlier, you selected the From the Internet option, so the wizard assumes that you want to use forms authentication and provides you with the option of creating and managing users. The From a Local Area Network option, remember, uses Windows-based authentication.

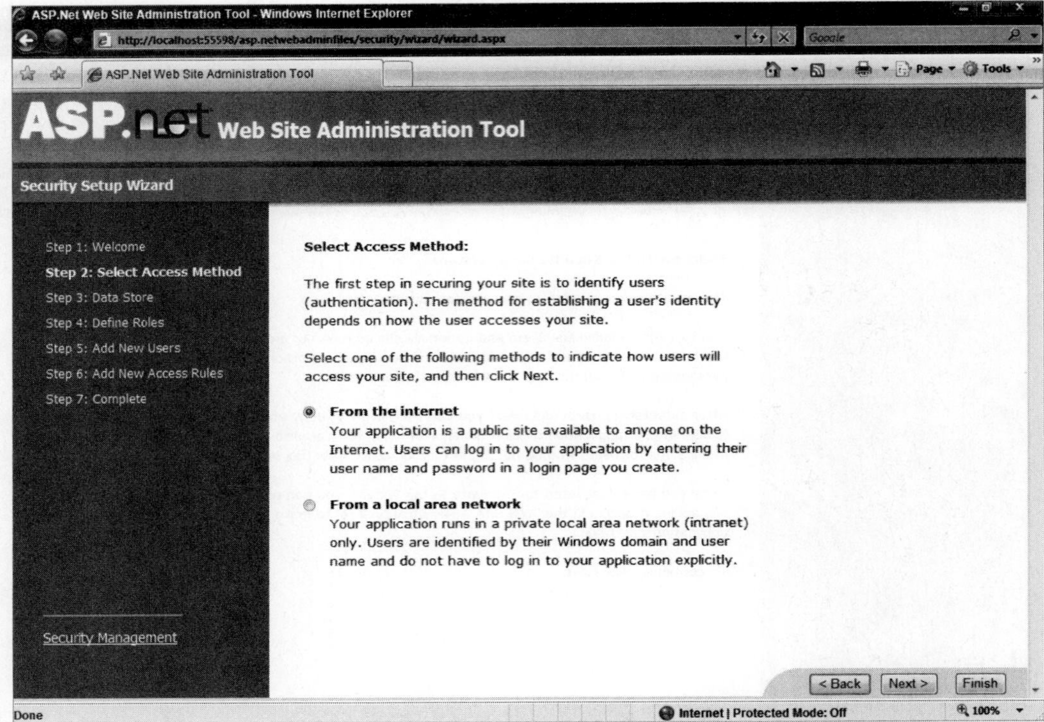

Figure 33-4

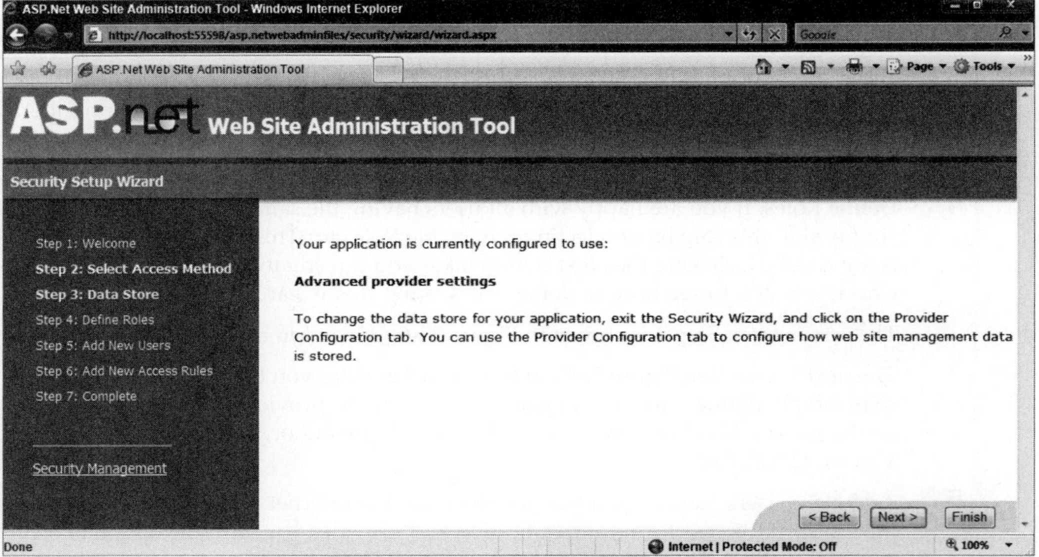

Figure 33-5

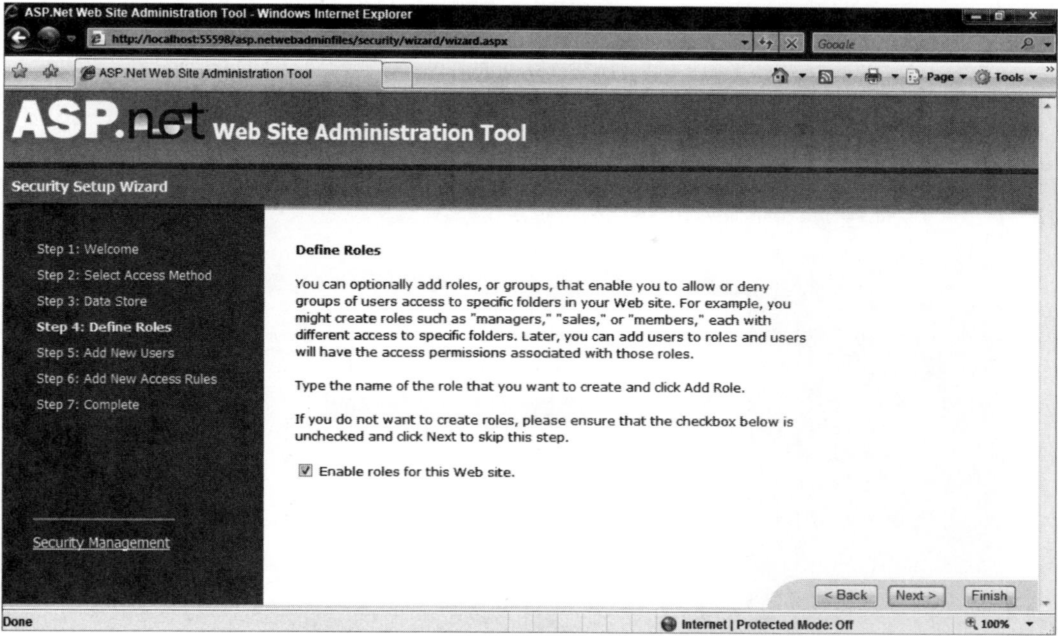

Figure 33-6

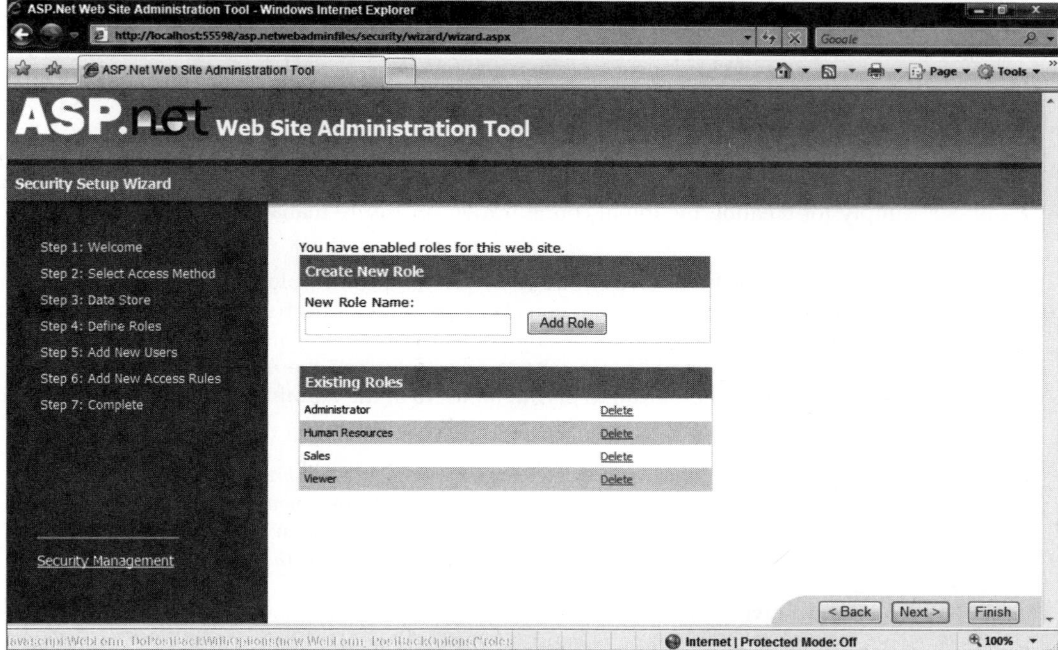

Figure 33-7

The Add New Users screen (see Figure 33-8) enables you to enter the username, password, e-mail address, and a security question and answer.

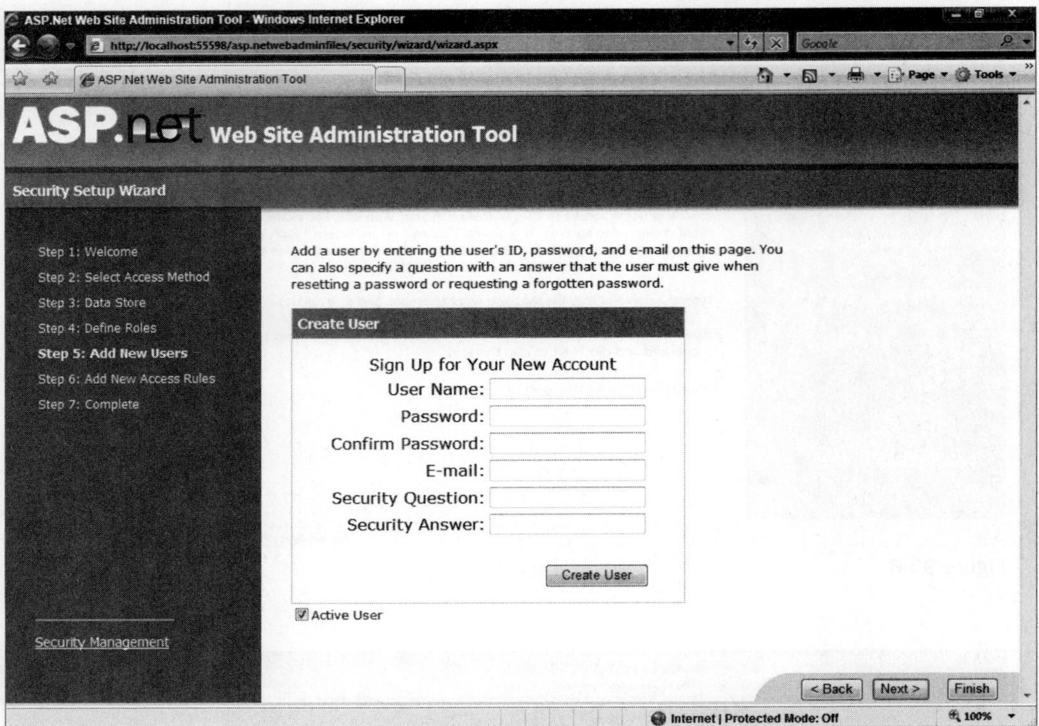

Figure 33-8

You can create as many users as you like; but to delete or update information for users, you must leave the wizard and manage the users separately. As mentioned earlier, the wizard is simply for creating the initial configuration for future management.
Click Next.

6. Add New Access Rules (see Figure 33-9). First, select the folder in the Web application that needs special security settings. Then choose the role or user(s) to whom the rule will apply. Select the permission (Allow or Deny) and click the Add This Rule button. For example, if you had a folder named `Secure` you could select it and the Administrator role, and then click the Allow radio button to permit all users in the Administrator role to access to the `Secure` folder.

> *All folders that need special permissions must be created ahead of time. The information shown in the wizard is cached and is not updated if you decide to create a new folder inside your Web application while you are already on this screen so remember to create your special security folders before starting the wizard.*

The wizard gives you the capability to apply access rules to either roles or specific users. The Search for Users option is handy if you have defined many users for your Web site and want to search for a specific user.

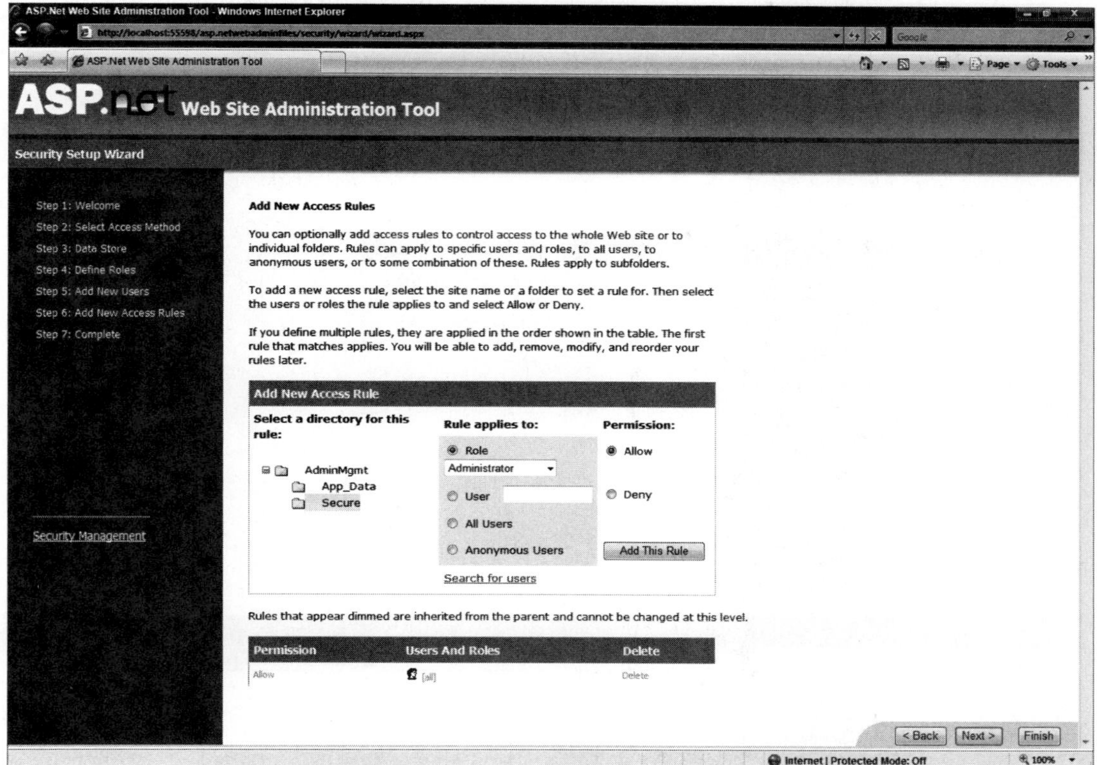

Figure 33-9

All access rules are shown at the bottom on the screen, and you can delete a specific rule and start again. Rules are shown dimmed if they are inherited from the parent configuration and cannot be changed here.

When you are ready, click Next.

7. The last screen in the Security Setup Wizard is an information page. Click the Finish button to exit the wizard.

Creating New Users

The ASP.NET Web Site Administration Tool's Security tab provides ways to manage users without using the wizard and is very helpful for ongoing maintenance of users, roles, and access permissions.

To create a new user, simply click the Create User link on the main page of the Security tab (as you saw earlier in Figure 33-2). The Create User screen, shown in Figure 33-10, is displayed, enabling you to provide username, password, confirmation of password, e-mail, and the security question and answer. You can assign a new user to any number of roles in the Roles list; these are roles currently defined for your Web application. Use this tool to create users named Admin, HRUser and SalesUser and assign them the corresponding roles.

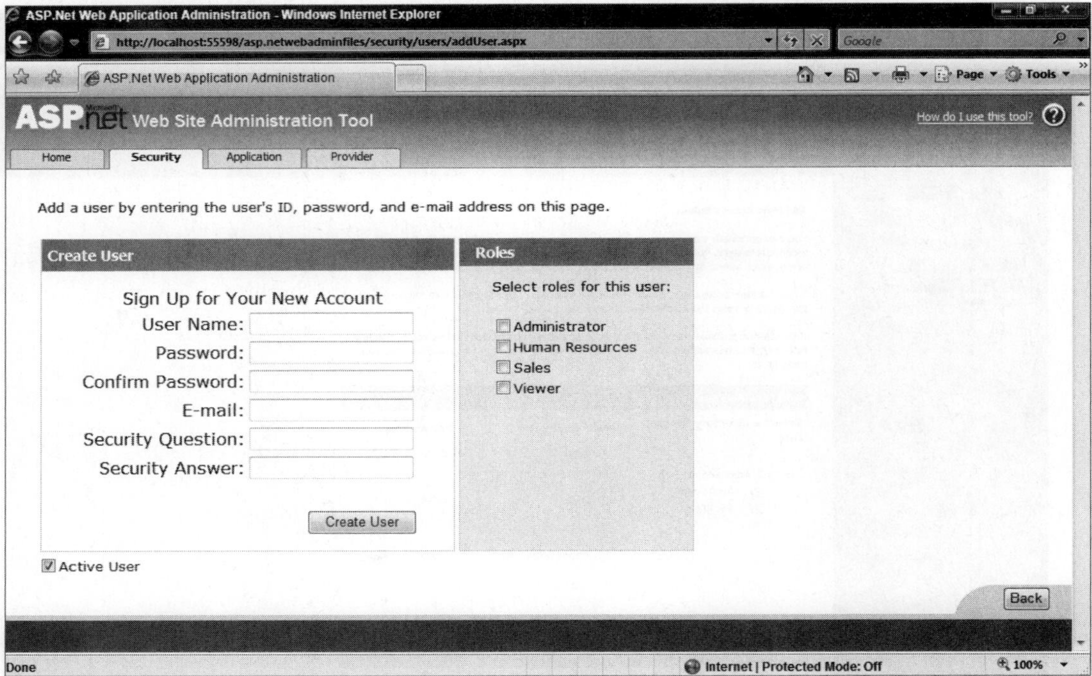

Figure 33-10

Managing Users

You can manage existing users by clicking the Manage Users link on the Security tab. A new screen displays a list of all existing users (see Figure 33-11). A search option is available, which makes it easier to find a specific user if the list is long.

Find the user you want to manage, then you can update his information, delete the user, reassign roles, or set the user to active or inactive.

Managing Roles

Two links are provided in the Security tab for managing roles: Disable Roles and Create or Manage Roles. Clicking Disable Roles does just that — disables role management in the Web application; it also dims the other link.

Click the Create or Manage Roles link to start managing roles and user assignments to specific roles. A screen displays all roles you have defined so far. You have options to add new roles, delete existing roles, or manage specific roles.

Click the Manage link next to a specific role, and a screen shows all the users currently assigned to that role (see Figure 33-12). You can find other users by searching for their names, and you can then assign them to or remove them from a selected role.

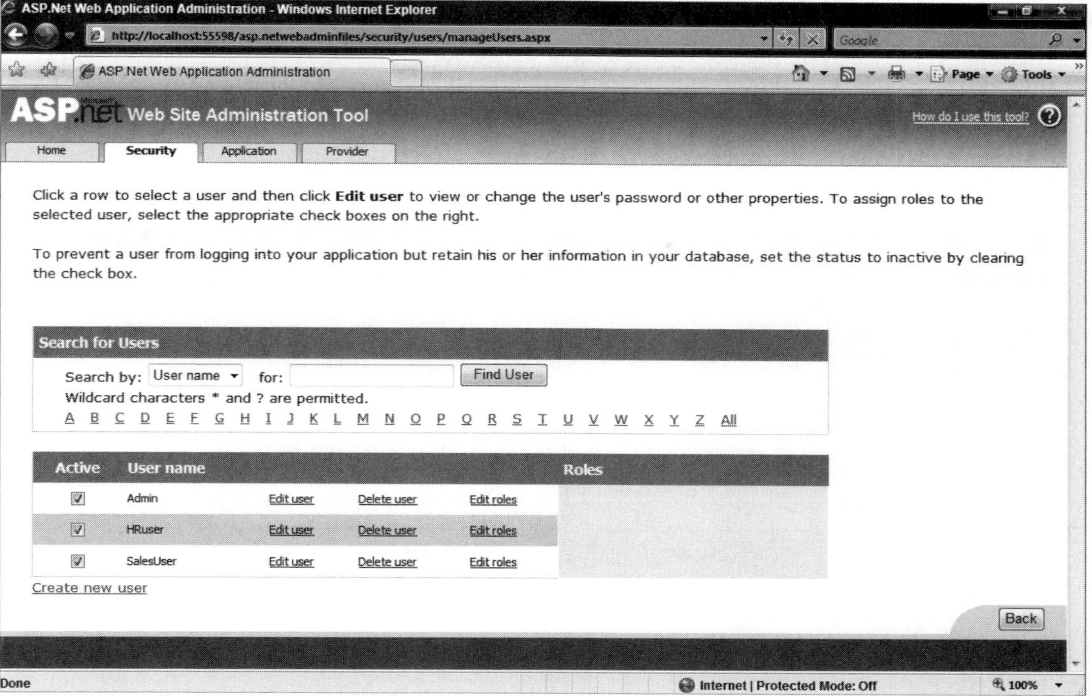

Figure 33-11

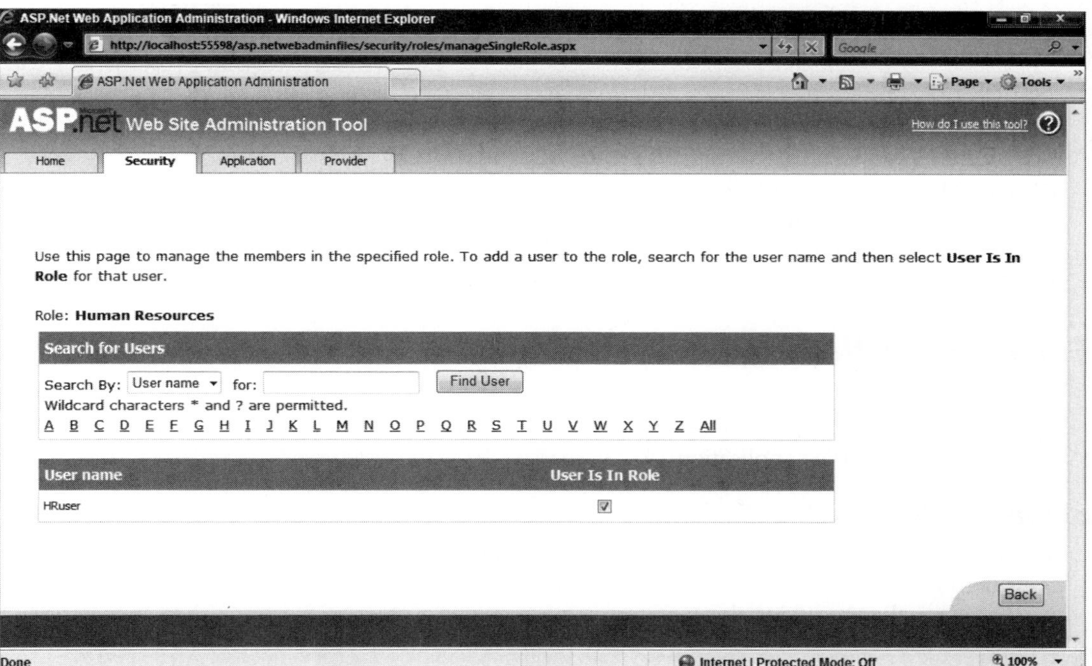

Figure 33-12

Managing Access Rules

The Security tab provides options for creating and managing access rules. Access rules are applied either to an entire Web application or to specific folders inside it. Clicking the Create Access Rules link takes you to a screen where you can view a list of the folders inside your Web application. You can select a specific folder, select a role or a user, and then choose whether you want to enable access to the selected folder. Figure 33-13 shows the Add New Access Rule screen.

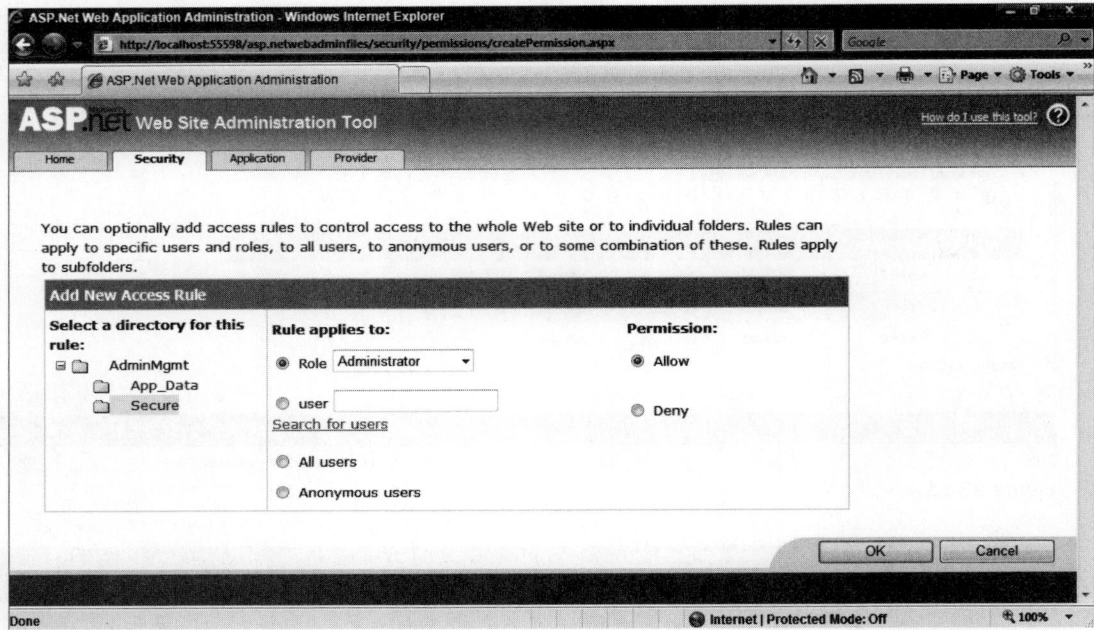

Figure 33-13

Clicking Manage Access Rules on the Security tab takes you to a screen that shows all existing access rules. You can remove any of these rules and add new ones. You can also readjust the list of access rules if you want to apply them in a specific order. The Manage Access Rules screen is shown in Figure 33-14.

The Application Tab

The Application tab provides a number of application-specific configurations, including the configuration of appSettings, SMTP mail server settings, debugging and trace settings, and starting/stopping the entire Web application.

Managing Application Settings

The left side of the screen shows links for creating and managing application settings. The settings are stored in the `<appSettings>` section of the `web.config`. Most ASP.NET programmers are used to manually modifying this tag in previous versions of ASP.NET. Figure 33-15 shows the Application tab.

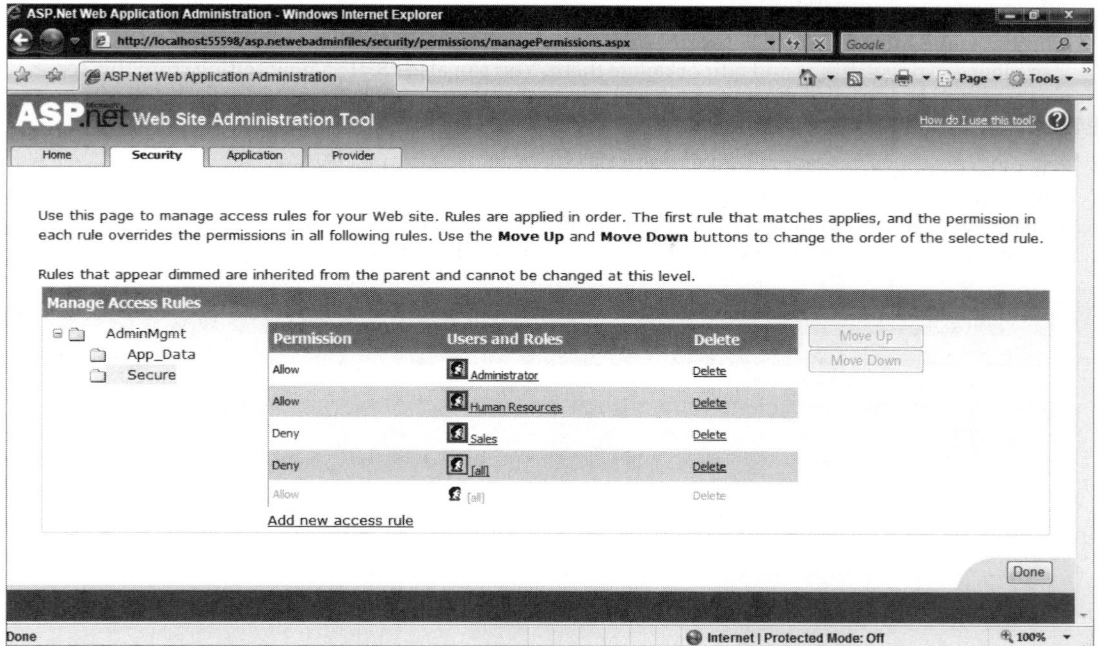

Figure 33-14

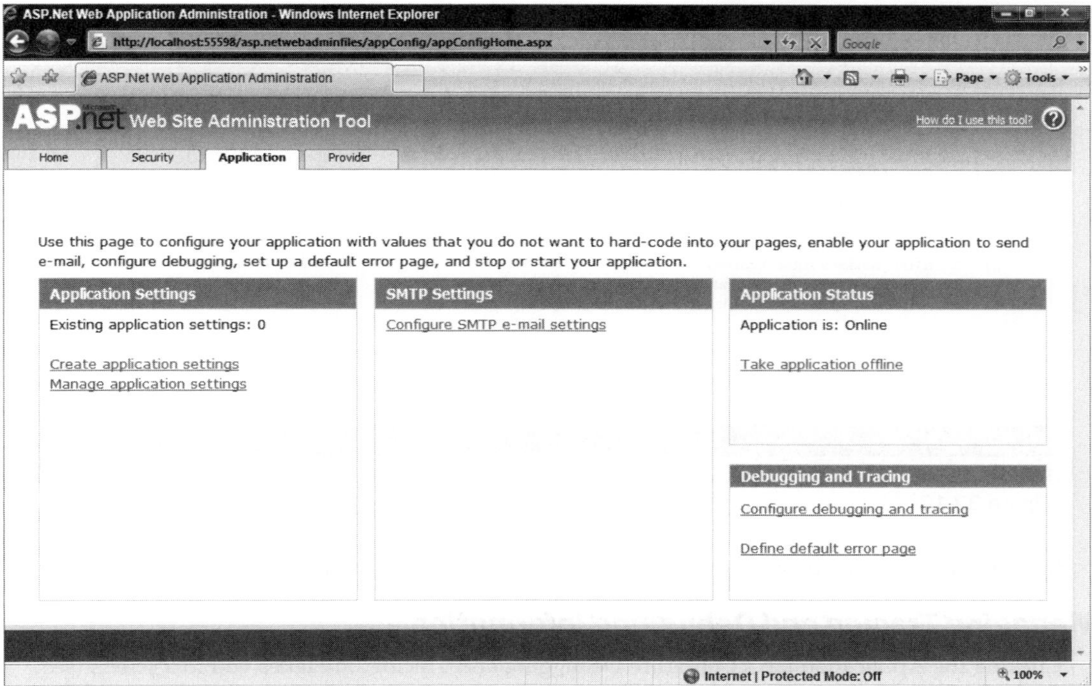

Figure 33-15

Clicking the Create Application Settings link takes you to a screen where you can provide the name and the value information. Clicking Manage Application Settings takes you to a screen where you can view existing settings and edit or delete them. You can also create a new setting from this screen.

Managing SMTP Configuration

Click the Configure SMTP E-Mail Settings link to view a screen like the one shown in Figure 33-16. The configure SMTP mail settings feature is useful if your Web application can send autogenerated e-mails. Instead of denoting SMTP server configuration in the code, you can spell it out in the configuration file by entering values here in the administration tool.

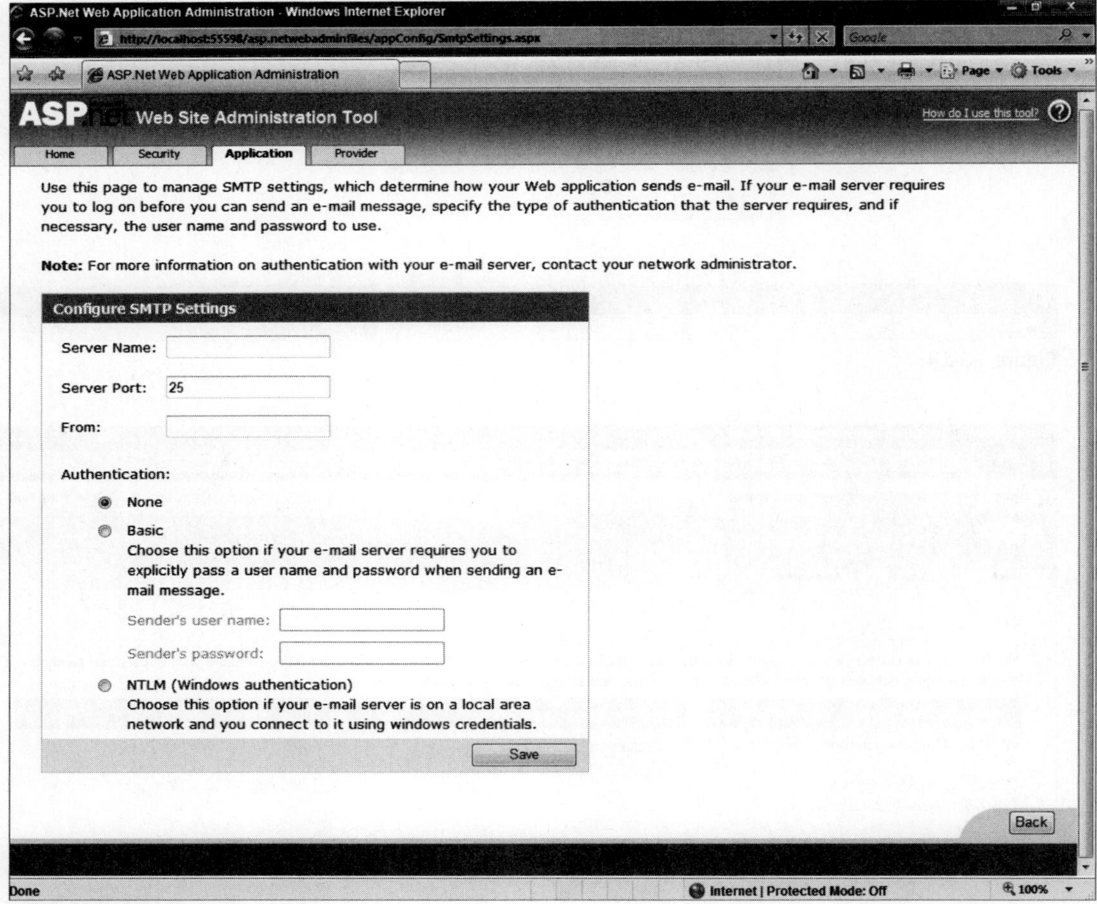

Figure 33-16

Specify the server name, port, sender e-mail address, and authentication type.

Managing Tracing and Debugging Information

Clicking the Application tab's Configure Debugging and Tracing link takes you to a screen (see Figure 33-17) where you can enable or disable tracing and debugging. Select whether you want to display trace information on each page. You can also specify whether to track just local requests or all requests, as well as trace sorting and caching configuration.

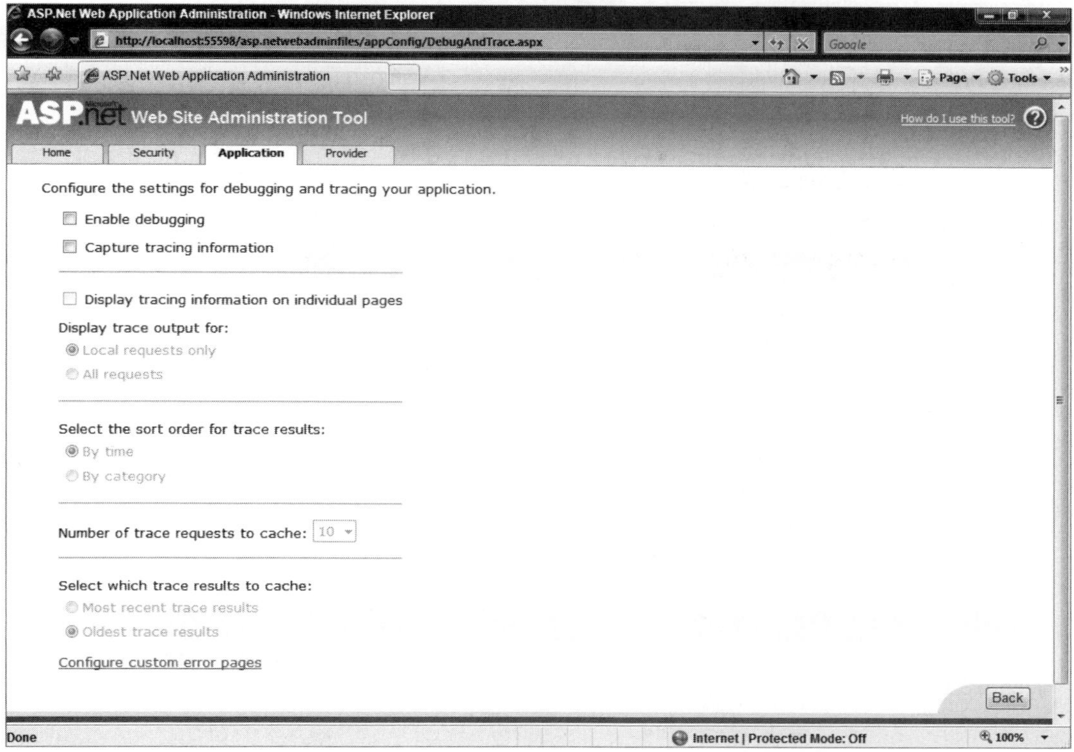

Figure 33-17

To configure default error pages, you simply click Define Default Error Page on the screen you saw in Figure 33-15. This takes you to a screen where you can select a URL that is used for redirection in case of an error condition (see Figure 33-18).

Taking an Application Offline

You can take your entire Web application offline simply by clicking the Take Application Offline link (again, refer to Figure 33-15). The link stops the app domain for your Web application. It is useful if you want to perform a scheduled maintenance for an application.

The Provider Tab

The final tab in the ASP.NET Web Site Administration Tool is Provider, shown in Figure 33-19. You use it to set up additional providers and to determine the providers your application will use.

The Provider page is simple, but it contains an important piece of information: the default data provider with which your application is geared to work. In Figure 33-19, the application is set up to work with the `AspNetSqlProvider` provider, the default data provider.

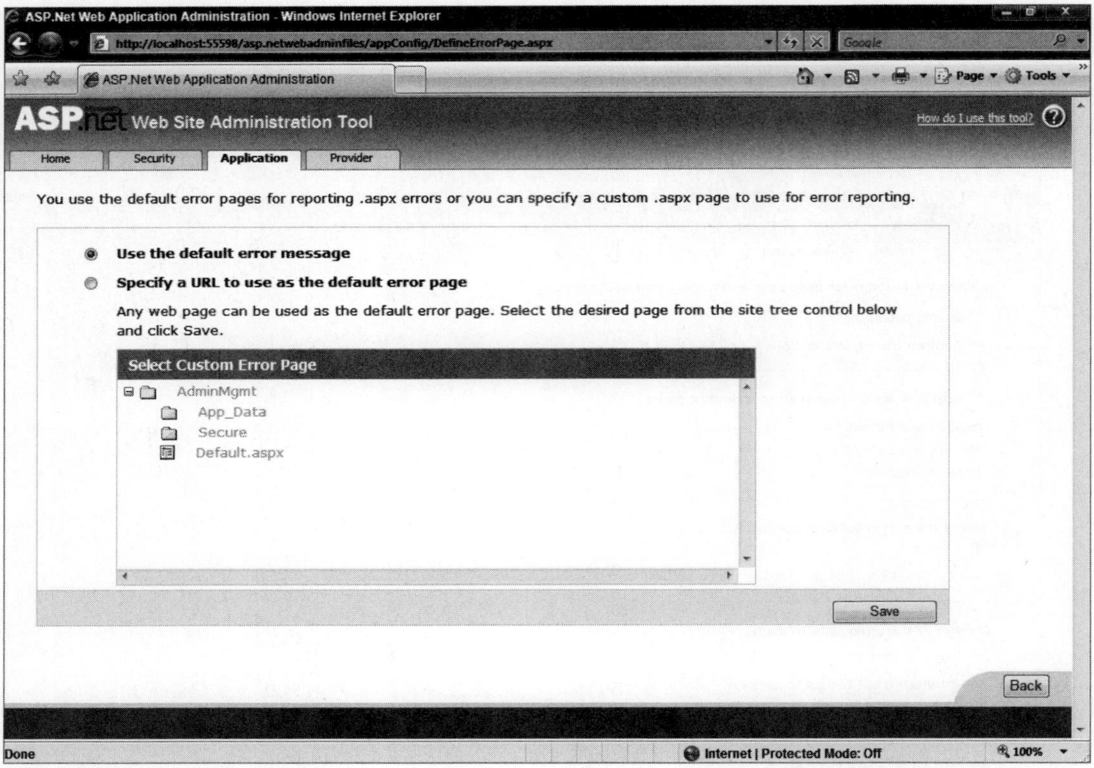

ASP.Net Web Application Administration - Windows Internet Explorer
http://localhost:55598/asp.netwebadminfiles/appConfig/DefineErrorPage.aspx
ASP.Net Web Application Administration
ASP.net Web Site Administration Tool
How do I use this tool?
Home
Security
Application
Provider
You use the default error pages for reporting .aspx errors or you can specify a custom .aspx page to use for error reporting.
Use the default error message
Specify a URL to use as the default error page
Any web page can be used as the default error page. Select the desired page from the site tree control below and click Save.
Select Custom Error Page
AdminMgmt
App_Data
Secure
Default.aspx
Save
Back
Done
Internet | Protected Mode: Off
100%

Figure 33-18

ASP.Net Web Application Administration - Windows Internet Explorer
http://localhost:55598/asp.netwebadminfiles/providers/chooseProviderManagement.aspx
ASP.Net Web Application Administration
ASP.net Web Site Administration Tool
How do I use this tool?
Home
Security
Application
Provider
Use this page to configure how Web site management data such as membership is stored. You can use a single provider for all the management data for your site or you can specify a different provider for each feature.
Your application is currently configured to use the provider: AspNetSqlProvider
Select a single provider for all site management data
Select a different provider for each feature (advanced)
Done
Internet | Protected Mode: Off
100%

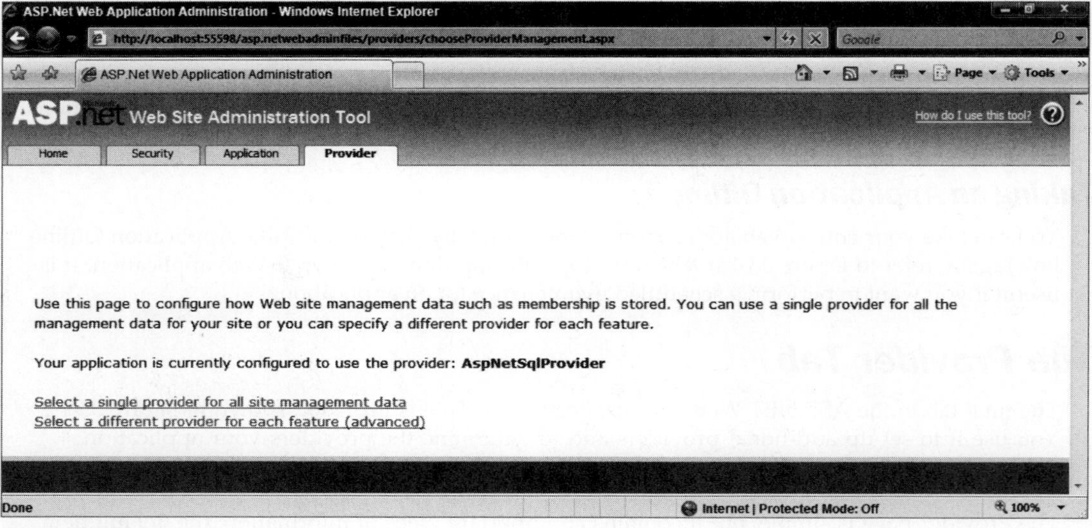

Figure 33-19

The two links on this tab let you set up either a single data provider or a specific data provider for each of the features in ASP.NET that requires a data provider. If you click the latter, you are presented with the screen shown in Figure 33-20. It enables you to pick the available providers separately for Membership and Role management.

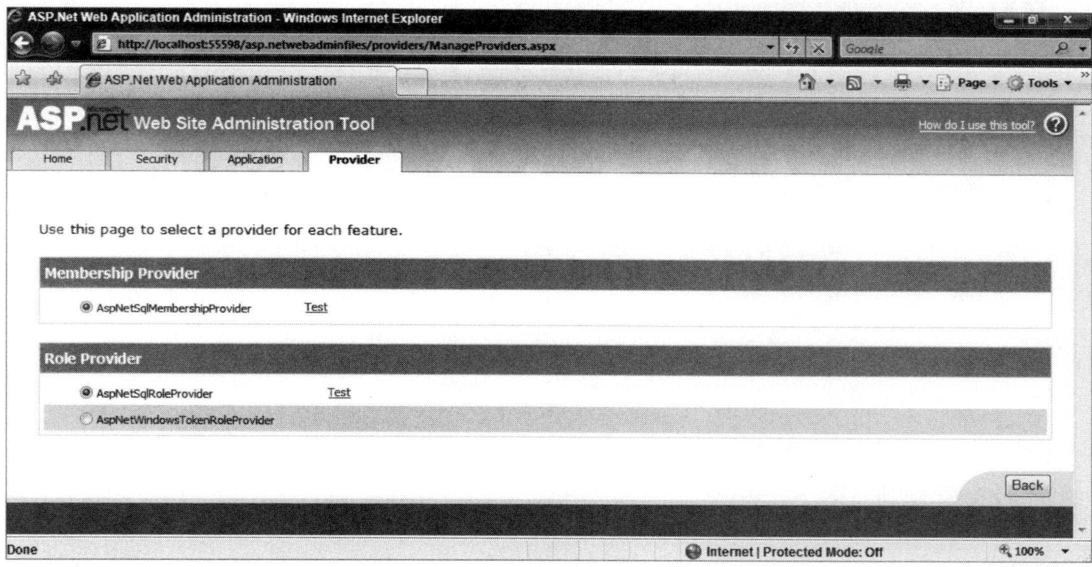

Figure 33-20

As you can see from the screenshots and brief explanations provided here, you could now handle a large portion of the necessary configurations through a GUI. You no longer have to figure out which setting must be placed in the `web.config` file. This functionality becomes even more important as the `web.config` file grows. In ASP.NET 1.0/1.1, the `web.config` file was a reasonable size, but with all the features provided by ASP.NET 2.0 or 3.5, the `web.config` file has the potential to become very large. These GUI-based tools are an outstanding way to configure some of the most commonly needed settings. However, there are many settings that can not be modified with the Web Server Administration Tool, such as the AJAX settings, so you will still need to edit web.config in many cases.

Configuring ASP.NET in IIS on Vista

If you are using IIS as the basis of your ASP.NET applications, you will find that it is quite easy to configure the ASP.NET application directly through the Internet Information Services (IIS) Manager if you are using Windows Vista. To access the ASP.NET configurations, open IIS and expand the `Web Sites` folder, which contains all the sites configured to work with IIS. Remember that not all your Web sites are configured to work in this manner because it is also possible to create ASP.NET applications that make use of the new ASP.NET built-in Web server.

Once you have expanded the IIS Web Sites folder, right-click one of the applications in this folder and you will notice that the options you have available to you for configuration will appear in the IIS Manager (see Figure 33-21).

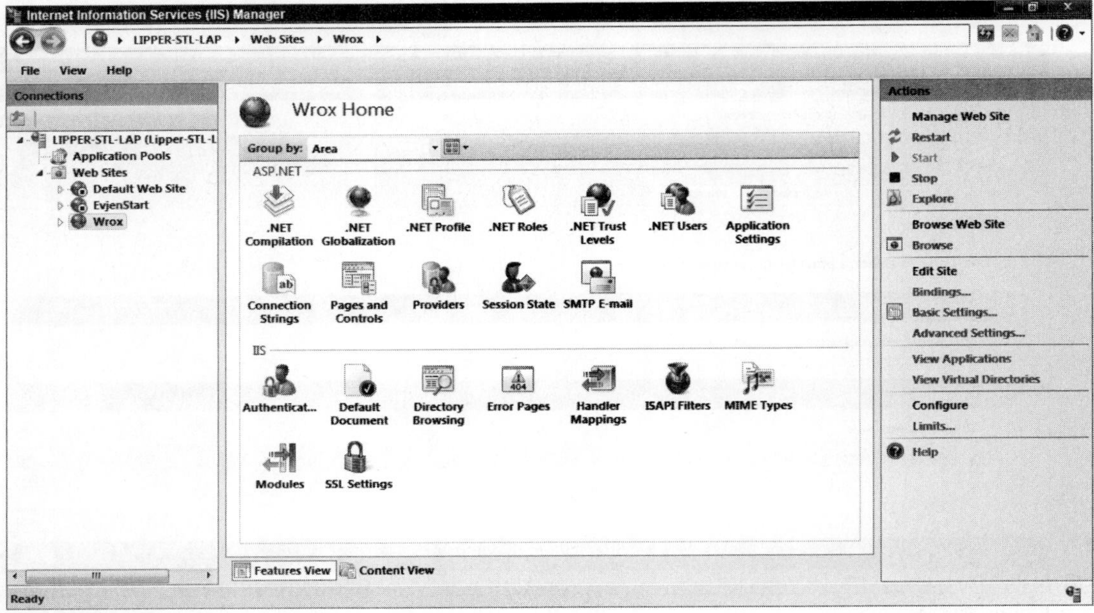

Figure 33-21

The options available to you enable you to completely configure ASP.NET or even configure IIS itself. The focus of this chapter is on the ASP.NET section of the options. In addition to the options you can select from one of the available icons, you can also configure some basic settings of the application by clicking the Basic Settings link in the Actions pane on the right-hand side of the IIS Manager. When clicking the Basic Settings link, you will get a dialog box, as shown in Figure 33-22.

Changes you are making in the IIS Manager are actually being applied to the `web.config` *file of your application; making changes to the Default Web site (the root node) lets you edit the* `machine.config` *file.*

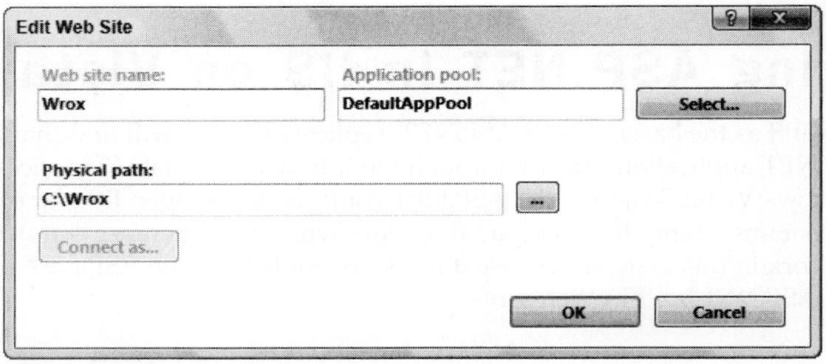

Figure 33-22

The dialog enables you to change the following items:

- **Web site name:** The name of the Web site. In the case of Figure 33-22, naming the Web site "Wrox" means that the URL will be `http://[IP address or domain name]/Wrox`.
- **Application pool:** The application pool you are going to use for the application. You will notice that you have three options by default — DefaultAppPool (which uses the .NET Framework 2.0 and an integrated pipeline mode), Classic .NET AppPool (which uses the .NET Framework 2.0 and a classic pipeline mode), and ASP.NET 1.1 (which uses the .NET Framework 1.1 as it states and a classic pipeline mode).
- **Physical path:** The folder location where the ASP.NET application can be found. In this case, it is `C:\Wrox`.

The sections that follow review some of the options available to you through the icons in the IIS Manager.

.NET Compilation

Use the Application tab to make changes that are more specific to the pages in the context of your application. From this dialog, shown in Figure 33-23, you can change how your pages are compiled and run. You can also make changes to global settings in your application.

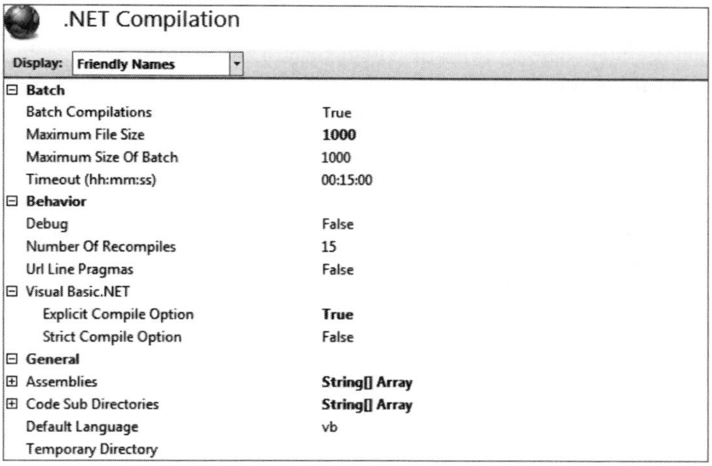

.NET Compilation

Display: Friendly Names

Setting	Value
⊟ **Batch**	
Batch Compilations	True
Maximum File Size	**1000**
Maximum Size Of Batch	1000
Timeout (hh:mm:ss)	00:15:00
⊟ **Behavior**	
Debug	False
Number Of Recompiles	15
Url Line Pragmas	False
⊟ Visual Basic.NET	
Explicit Compile Option	**True**
Strict Compile Option	False
⊟ **General**	
⊞ Assemblies	**String[] Array**
⊞ Code Sub Directories	**String[] Array**
Default Language	vb
Temporary Directory	

Figure 33-23

This section deals with compilation of the ASP.NET application as well as how some of the pages of the application will behave. The Batch section deals with the batch compilation of the application — first, whether or not it is even supported, and then details on batch sizes and the time it takes to incur the compilation.

The Behavior section deals with whether or not the compilation produces a release or debug build; you will also find some Visual Basic–specific compilation instructions on whether Option Explicit or Option Script are enabled across the entire application.

The General section focuses on the assemblies that are referenced as well as your code subdirectories if you are going to break up your App_Code folder into separate compiled instances (required for when you want to incorporate Visual Basic and C# code in the same application). You can also specify the default language that is used in the compilation process — such as `VB` or `C#`.

.NET Globalization

The .NET Globalization option enables you to customize how your ASP.NET application deals with culture and the encoding of the requests and responses. Figure 33-24 shows the options available in this section.

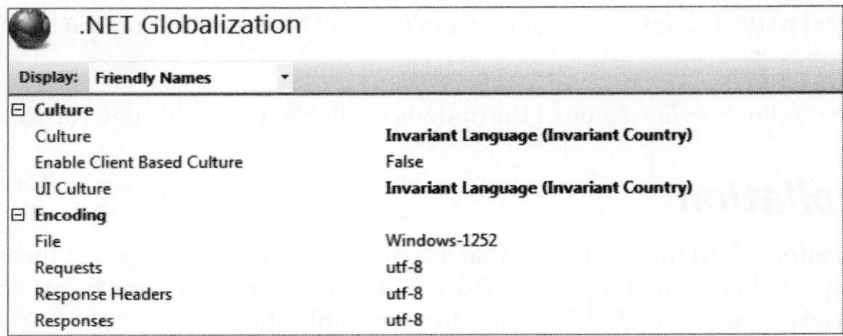

Figure 33-24

In addition to picking a specific Culture or UI Culture setting, you can also select Auto Detect, which will pick up the culture of the client if it is available. By default, you can also see that the encoding of the requests and the responses are set to `utf-8`, which will work fine for most Latin-based languages.

.NET Profile

The .NET Profile options enable you to customize how your ASP.NET application deals with the ASP.NET personalization system. This system was discussed earlier in Chapter 15 of this book. Figure 33-25 shows the dialog that is provided when you add a new profile to the personalization system.

Add .NET Profile Property
Name:
Firstname
Data Type:
System.String
Default value:
Serialization option:
String
Read only
Available for anonymous users
OK
Cancel

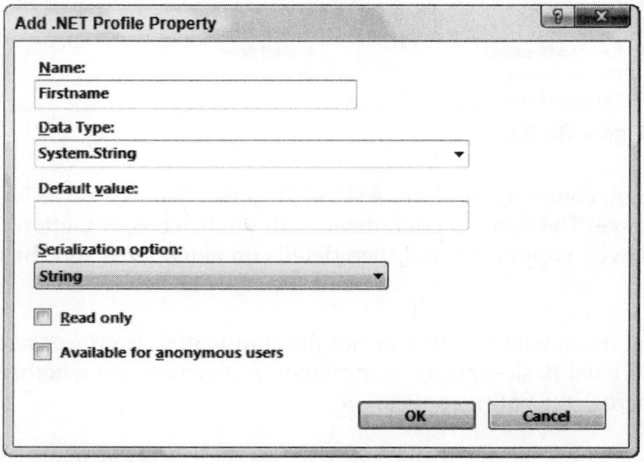

Figure 33-25

In this case, as presented in Figure 33-25, you can specify the name of the personalization property, the data type used, its default value, how it is serialized, and whether or not it is read-only or available for anonymous users. To better understand these settings, it is important to review Chapter 15.

In addition to building properties to use in the personalization system, you can also specify the provider that is used by the system as a whole. By default, it will be using the AspNetSqlProfileProvider, as illustrated in Figure 33-26.

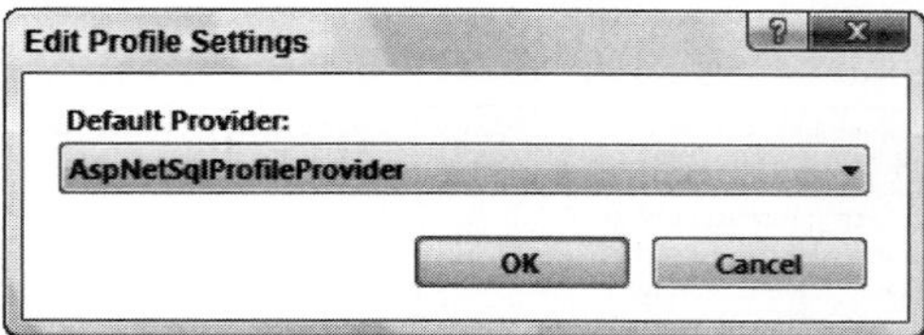

Figure 33-26

.NET Roles

You can enable role-based management by adding roles to your application from the .NET Roles section. Figure 33-27 shows an example of adding a role called Admin to the application.

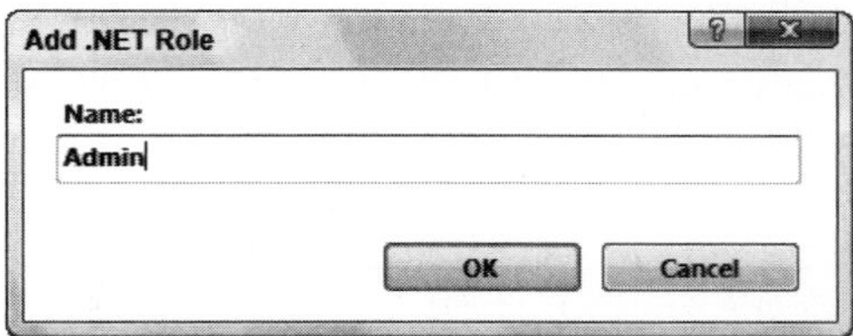

Figure 33-27

Pressing OK will add the role to the system and the role will then be shown in a list of roles from the main screen of the section, as illustrated in Figure 33-28.

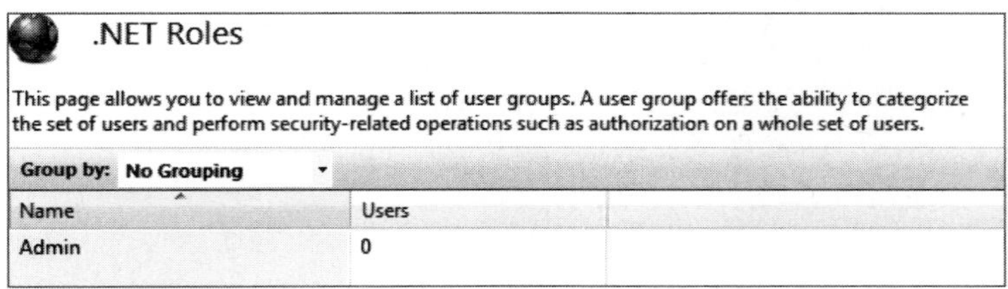

Figure 33-28

By default, there will be no users added to the role. You will be able to add users to roles through the .NET Users section, discussed shortly.

.NET Trust Levels

The .NET Trust Levels section allows you to specify the level of security to apply to your application through the selection of a specific pre-generated configuration file. This is illustrated in the list of options presented in Figure 33-29.

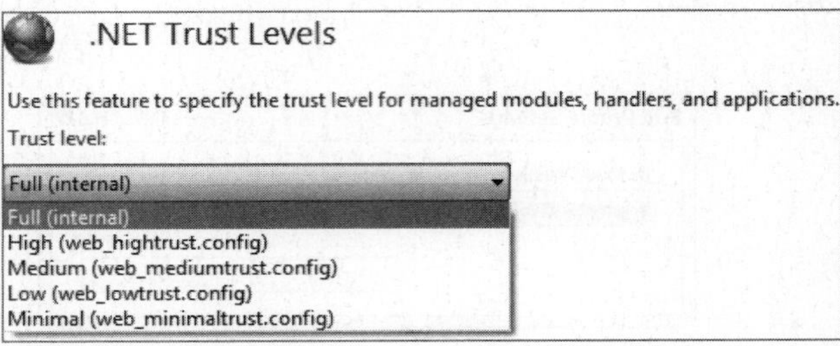

Figure 33-29

By default, your application makes use of the `web.config` file, but specifying a different trust level will cause the application to use a different `.config` file. All of these `.config` files are found at `C:\Windows\Microsoft.NET\Framework\v2.0.50727\CONFIG`.

.NET Users

Probably one of the easiest ways to work with the ASP.NET membership system (covered in Chapter 16 of this book) is to create your users in the .NET Users section of IIS. Adding a user is easy through the dialogs provided, as illustrated in Figure 33-30.

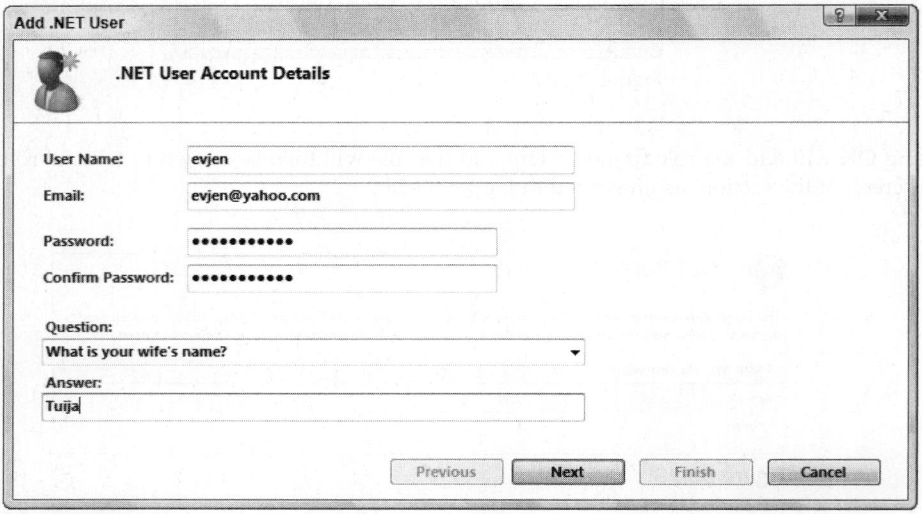

Figure 33-30

In Figure 33-30, you can provide the username, password, and security question and answer in a simple wizard. Figure 33-31 shows the second screen of the wizard.

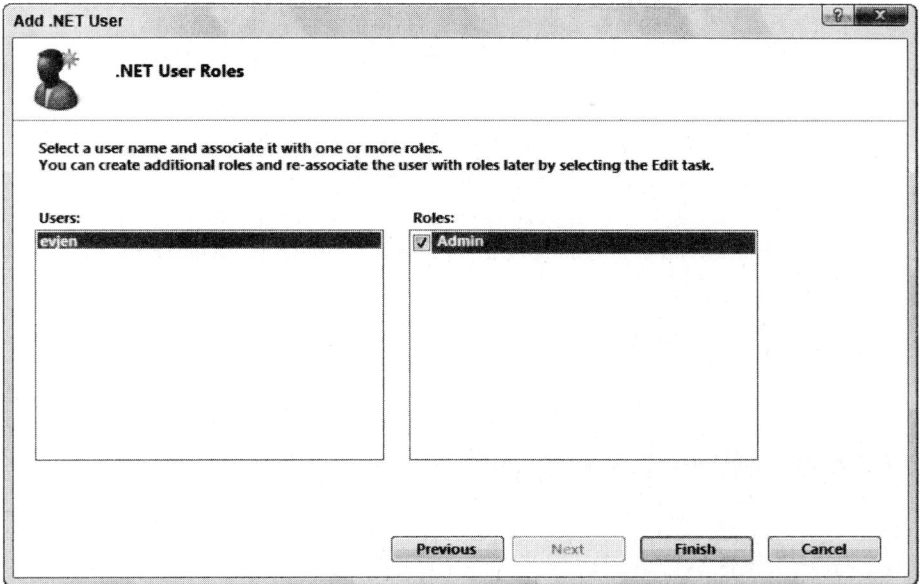

Figure 33-31

In this second screen of the wizard, you can assign users to specific roles that are present in the role management system. Because the Admin role was created earlier in this chapter, I am able to assign the user to this particular role as it exists in the system.

Once a user is created, you can then see the entire list of users for this particular application from the main .NET Users screen, as illustrated in Figure 33-32.

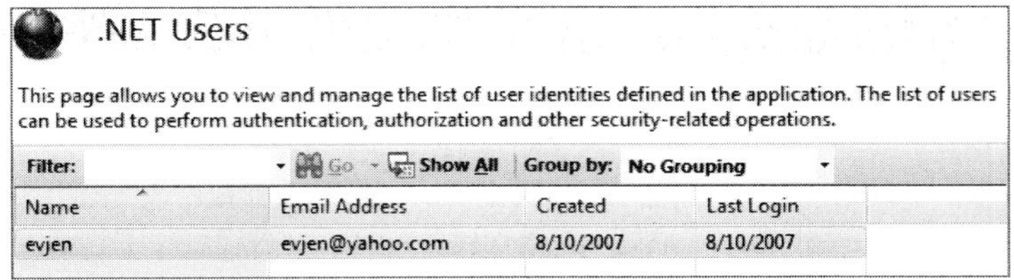

Figure 33-32

Application Settings

Another section is the Application Settings section. Click its Add or Edit button, and the Edit/Add Application Settings dialog opens (see Figure 33-33).

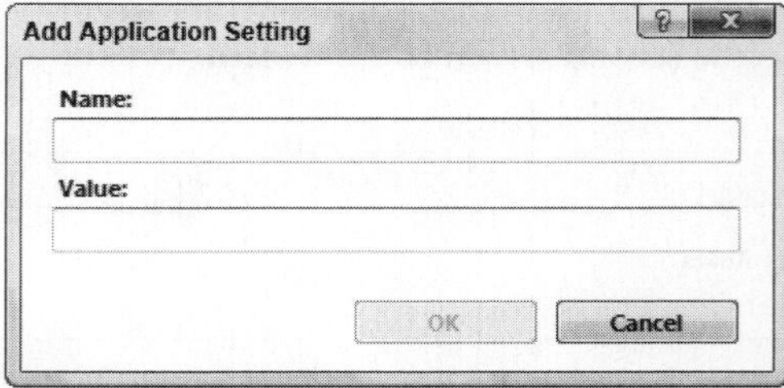

Figure 33-33

After you enter a key and value pair, click OK; the settings appear in the list in the main dialog. Then you can edit or delete the settings from the application.

Connection Strings

The next section is the Connection Strings section. To add a connection string to your application, just click its Add button. You also can edit or remove existing connection strings. Figure 33-34 shows the Edit Connection String dialog for the default connection string — LocalSqlServer.

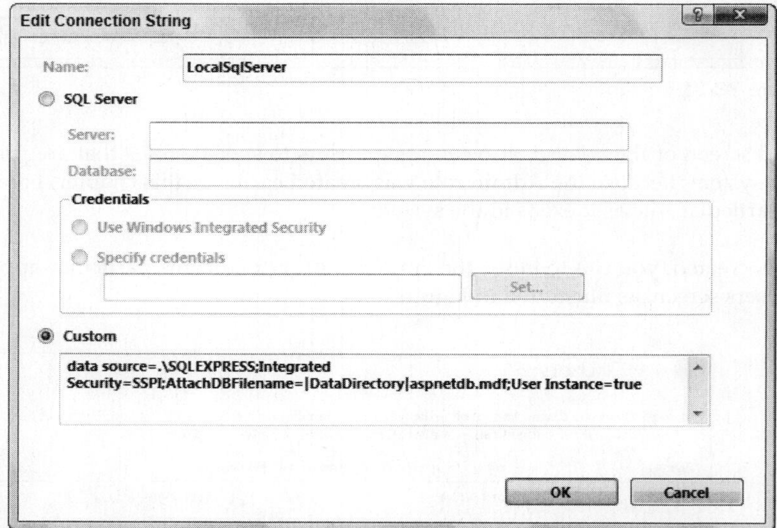

Figure 33-34

It is also rather simple to add a brand new connection, as illustrated in Figure 33-35.

Pages and Controls

The Pages and Controls section deals with a group of settings that control the overall ASP.NET pages (`.aspx`) and user controls in the application (`.ascx`). Figure 33-36 shows the available settings for this section.

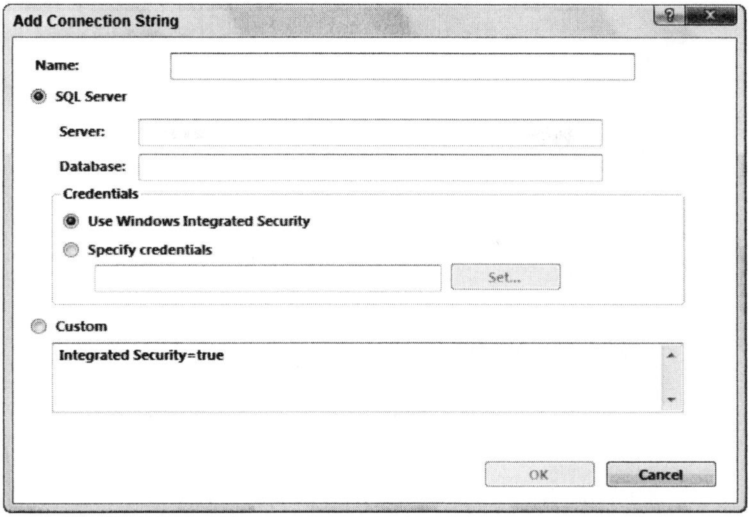

Figure 33-35

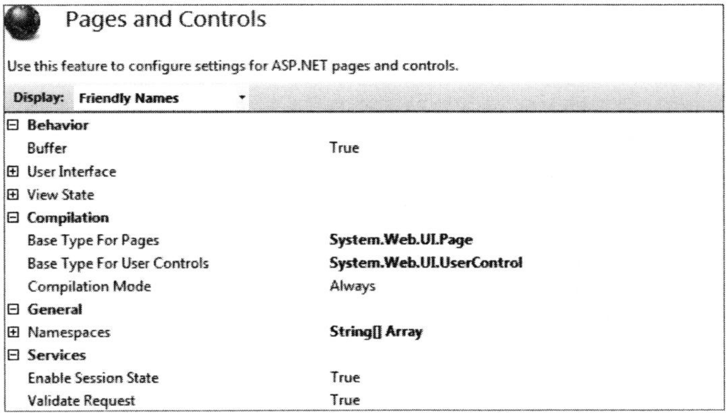

Figure 33-36

Providers

The Providers section deals with all the providers that are defined within the application. From the example in Figure 33-37, you can see that there are only two providers defined for the .NET Roles engine — a SQL Server role provider and a Windows Token role provider.

You can look at all the other engines found in ASP.NET by selecting the option in the drop-down list at the top of the dialog.

Session State

ASP.NET applications, being stateless in nature, are highly dependent on how state is stored. The Session State section (see Figure 33-38) enables you to change a number of different settings that determine how state management is administered.

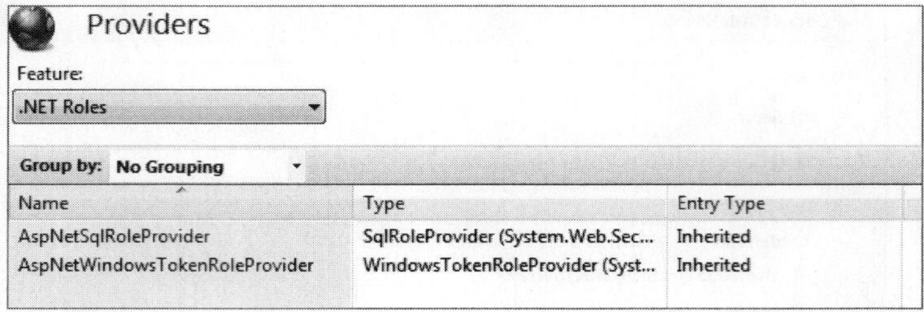

Figure 33-37

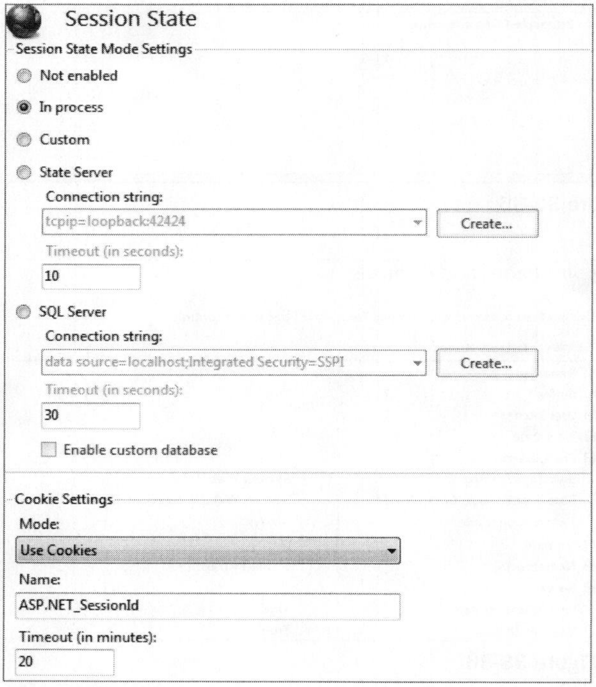

Figure 33-38

You can apply state management to your applications in a number of ways, and this dialog allows for a number of different settings — some of which are enabled or disabled based on what is selected. The following list describes the items available in the Session State Settings section:

- **Session state mode:** Determines how the sessions are stored by the ASP.NET application. The default option (shown in Figure 33-38) is InProc. Other options include Off, StateServer, and SQLServer. Running sessions in-process (InProc) means that the sessions are stored in the same process as the ASP.NET worker process. Therefore, if IIS is shut down and then brought up again, all the sessions are destroyed and unavailable to end users. StateServer means that sessions are stored out-of-process by a Windows service called ASPState. SQLServer is by far the most secure way to deal with your sessions — it stores them directly in SQL Server. StateServer is also the least performance-efficient method.

- **Cookieless mode:** Changes how the identifiers for the end user are stored. The default setting uses cookies (UseCookies). Other possible settings include UseUri, AutoDetect, and UseDeviceProfile.
- **Session timeout:** Sessions are stored for only a short period of time before they expire. For years, the default has been 20 minutes. Modifying the value here changes how long the sessions created by your application are valid.

SMTP E-mail

If you need to work with an application that delivers e-mail, then you must specify the settings to do this. Sending e-mail and the settings required are defined in the SMTP E-mail section (see Figure 33-39).

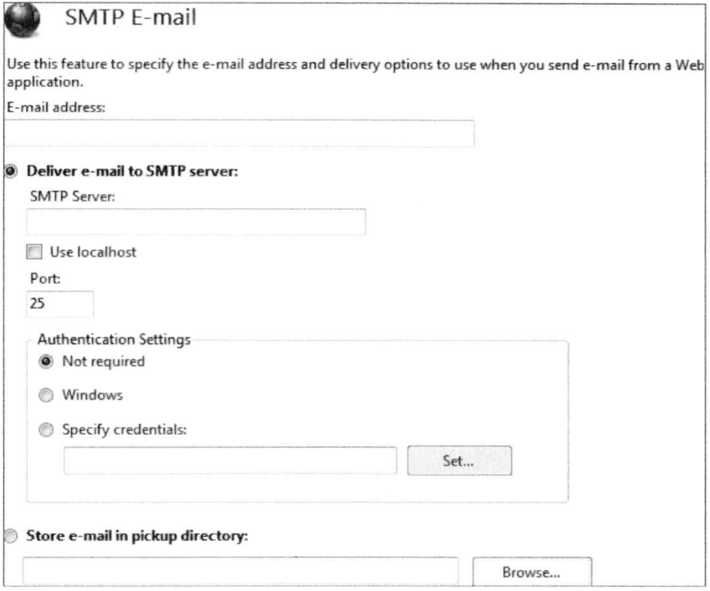

Figure 33-39

Summary

This chapter showed you some of the new management tools that come with the latest release of ASP.NET. These tools make the ever-increasing size of the `web.config` file more manageable because they take care of setting the appropriate values in the application's configuration file.

The new IIS Manager console in Windows Vista is a welcome addition for managing applications that are configured to work with IIS. The ASP.NET Web Site Administration Tool provides even more value to administrators and developers by enabling them to easily manage settings.

34

Packaging and Deploying ASP.NET Applications

Packaging and deploying ASP.NET applications are topics that usually receive little attention. This chapter is going to take a more in-depth look at how you can package and deploy your ASP.NET applications after they are built. After you have developed your ASP.NET application on a development computer, you will need to deploy the finished product to a quality assurance or staging server, and eventually on a production server.

An important reason to consider the proper packaging and deploying of your ASP.NET applications is that many applications are built as saleable products, starter kits, or solutions. In this case you may have to allow complete strangers to download and install these products in their own — environments that you have absolutely no control over. If this is the case, it is ideal to give the consumer a single installer file that ensures proper installation of the application in any environment.

But regardless of whether you will distribute your web application outside your company you still need a way to deploy it to another server where it can be tested before production deployment. You should never assume that it will be perfect just because it worked on your computer. Most of the time we just develop using the internal web server in Visual Studio, so we will need a full test using IIS before we assume all is well. Even if you do test with IIS on your computer there are still deployment related factors that need to be ironed out and fully tested before the application goes to production.

Before you start, you should understand the basics of packaging and deploying ASP.NET applications. In the process of packaging your ASP.NET applications, you are putting your applications into a package and utilizing a process of deployment that is initiated through a deployment procedure, such as using a Windows installer.

Deployment Pieces

So what are you actually deploying? ASP.NET contains a lot of pieces that are all possible parts of the overall application and need to be deployed with the application in order for it to run properly. The following list details some of the items that are potentially part of your ASP.NET application and need deployment consideration when you are moving your application:

- `.aspx` pages
- The code-behind pages for the `.aspx` pages (`.aspx.vb` or `.aspx.cs` files)
- User controls (`.ascx`)
- Web service files (`.asmx` and `.wsdl` files)
- `.htm` or `.html` files
- Image files such as `.jpg` or `.gif`
- ASP.NET system folders such as `App_Code` and `App_Themes`
- JavaScript files (`.js`)
- Cascading Style Sheets (`.css`)
- Configuration files such as the `web.config` file
- .NET components and compiled assemblies
- Data files such as `.mdb` files

Steps to Take before Deploying

Before deploying your ASP.NET Web applications, you should take some basic steps to ensure that your application is *ready* for deployment. These steps are often forgotten and are mentioned here to remind you of how you can ensure that your deployed application performs at its best.

The first step you should take is to *turn off* debugging in the `web.config` file. You do this by setting the `debug` attribute in the `<compilation>` element to `false`, as shown in Listing 34-1.

Listing 34-1: Setting debug to false before application deployment

```
<configuration xmlns="http://schemas.microsoft.com/.NetConfiguration/v2.0">
   <system.web>

      <compilation debug="false" />

   </system.web>
</configuration>
```

By default, most developers set the `debug` attribute to `true` when developing their applications. Doing this inserts debug symbols into the compiled ASP.NET pages. These symbols degrade the performance of any application. After the application is built and ready to be deployed, it is unnecessary to keep these debug symbols in place.

For those who have been coding ASP.NET for some time now, it is important to note that the Debug option in the drop-down list in the Visual Studio menu does not accomplish much in changing the configuration file or anything similar (shown here in Figure 34-1). In the ASP.NET 1.0 and 1.1 days, Visual Studio .NET (as it was called at that time) actually controlled the compilation of the ASP.NET project to a DLL. Now, and ever since ASP.NET 2.0, it is actually ASP.NET itself that controls the compilation process at runtime. Therefore, while the drop-down with the Debug designation is present, it really has no meaning in the context of building an ASP.NET project. You completely control the compilation designation through what is set in the `web.config` file, as shown in Listing 34-1.

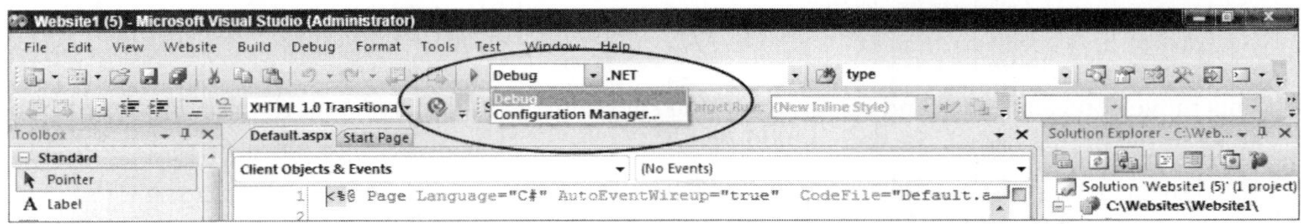

Figure 34-1

Methods of Deploying Web Applications

Remember that deployment is the last step in a process. The first is setting up the program — packaging the program into a component that is best suited for the deployment that follows. You can actually deploy a Web application in a number of ways. You can use the XCopy capability that simply wows audiences when demonstrated (because of its simplicity). A second method is to use Visual Studio 2008's capability to copy a Web site from one location to another using the Copy Web Site feature, as well as an alternative method that uses Visual Studio to deploy a precompiled Web application. The final method uses Visual Studio to build an installer program that can be launched on another machine. After reviewing each of the available methods, you can decide which is best for what you are trying to achieve. Start by looking at the simplest of the three methods: XCopy.

Using XCopy

Because of the nature of the .NET Framework, it is considerably easier to deploy .NET applications now than it was to deploy applications constructed using Microsoft's predecessor technology — COM. Applications in .NET compile down to assemblies, and these assemblies contain code that is executed by the Common Language Runtime (CLR). One great thing about assemblies is that they are self-describing. All the details about the assembly are stored within the assembly itself. In the Windows DNA world, COM stored all its self-describing data within the server's registry, so installing (as well as uninstalling) COM components meant shutting down IIS. Because a .NET assembly stores this information within itself, XCOPY deployment is possible and no registry settings are needed. Installing an assembly is as simple as copying it to another server and you do not need to stop or start IIS while this is going on.

We mention XCOPY here because it is the command-line way of basically doing a copy-and-paste of the files you want to move. XCOPY, however, provides a bit more functionality than just a copy-and-paste, as you will see shortly. XCOPY enables you to move files, directories, and even entire drives from one point to another.

The default syntax of the XCOPY command is as follows:

```
xcopy [source] [destination] [/w] [/p] [/c] [/v] [/q] [/f] [/l] [/g]
   [/d[:mm-dd-yyyy]] [/u] [/i] [/s [/e]] [/t] [/k] [/r] [/h] [{/a|/m}] [/n] [/o]
   [/x] [/exclude:file1[+[file2]][+file3]] [{/y|/-y}] [/z]
```

To see an example of using the XCOPY feature, suppose you are working from your developer machine (`C:\`) and want to copy your ASP.NET application to a production server (`Z:\`). In its simplest form, the following command would do the job:

```
xcopy c:\Websites\Website1 y:\Websites\ /f /e /k /h
```

This move copies the files and folders from the source drive to the destination drive. Figure 34-2 shows an example of this use on the command line.

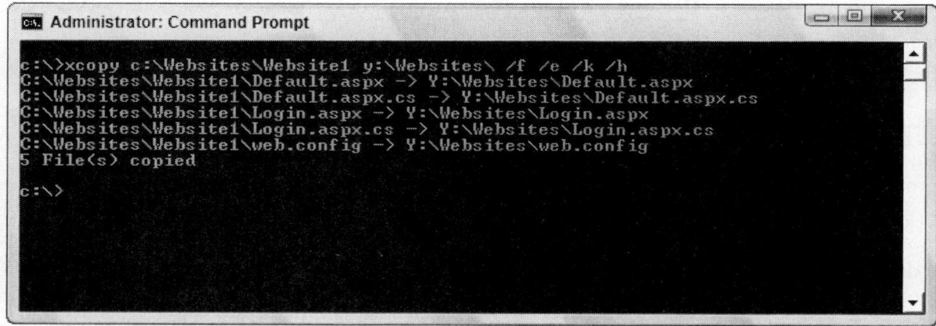

Figure 34-2

When you copy files using XCOPY, be aware that this method does not allow for the automatic creation of any virtual directories in IIS. When copying a new web application, you also need to create a virtual directory in the destination server and associate this virtual directory with the application you are copying. It is a simple process, but you must take these extra steps to finalize the site copy actions.

You can provide a number of parameters to this XCOPY command to get it to behave as you want it to. The following table details these parameters.

Parameter	Description
`/w`	Displays the message: `Press any key to begin copying file(s)`. It waits for your response to start the copying process.
`/p`	Asks for a confirmation on each file being copied. This is done in a file-by-file manner.
`/c`	Ignores errors that might occur in the copying process.
`/v`	Performs a verification on the files being copied to make sure they are identical to the source files.

Parameter	Description
`/q`	Suppresses any display of the XCOPY messages.
`/f`	Displays the file names for the source and destination files while the copying process is occurring.
`/l`	Displays a list of the files to be copied to the destination drive.
`/g`	Builds decrypted files for the destination drive.
`/d`	When used as simply `/d`, the only files copied are those newer than the existing files located in the destination location. Another alternative is to use `/d[:mm-dd-yyyy]`, which copies files that have been modified either on or after the specified date.
`/u`	Copies only source files that already exist in the destination location.
`/i`	If what is being copied is a directory or a file that contains wildcards and the same item does not exist in the destination location, a new directory is created. The XCOPY process also copies all the associated files into this directory.
`/s`	Copies all directories and their subdirectories only if they contain files. All empty directories or subdirectories are not copied in the process.
`/e`	Copies all subdirectories regardless of whether these directories contain files.
`/t`	Copies the subdirectories only and not the files they might contain.
`/k`	By default, the XCOPY process removes any read-only settings that might be contained in the source files. Using `/k` ensures that these read-only settings remain in place during the copying process.
`/r`	Copies only the read-only files to the destination location.
`/h`	Specifies that the hidden and system files, which are usually excluded by default, are included.
`/a`	Copies only files that have their archive file attributes set, and leaves the archive file attributes in place at the XCOPY destination.
`/m`	Copies only files that have their archive file attributes set, and turns off the archive file attributes.
`/n`	Copies using the NTFS short file and short directory names.
`/o`	Copies the discretionary access control list (DACL) in addition to the files.
`/x`	Copies the audit settings and the system access control list (SACL) in addition to the files.
`/exclude`	Allows you to exclude specific files. The construction used for this is `exclude:File1.aspx + File2.aspx + File3.aspx`.
`/y`	Suppresses any prompts from the XCOPY process that ask whether to overwrite the destination file.

Parameter	Description
`/-y`	Adds prompts in order to confirm an overwrite of any existing files in the destination location.
`/z`	Copies files and directories over a network in restartable mode.
`/?`	Displays help for the XCOPY command.

Using XCOPY is an easy way to move your applications from one server to another with little work on your part. If you have no problem setting up your own virtual directories, this mode of deployment should work just fine for you.

When the Web application is copied (and if placed in a proper virtual directory), it is ready to be called from a browser.

Using the VS Copy Web Site Option

The next option for copying a Web site is to use a GUI provided by Visual Studio 2008. This Copy Web Site GUI enables you to copy Web sites from your development server to either the same server or a remote server (as you can when you use the XCOPY command).

You can pull up this Copy Web Site dialog in Visual Studio in two ways. The first way is to click in the Copy Web Site icon in the Visual Studio Solution Explorer. This icon is shown in Figure 34-3.

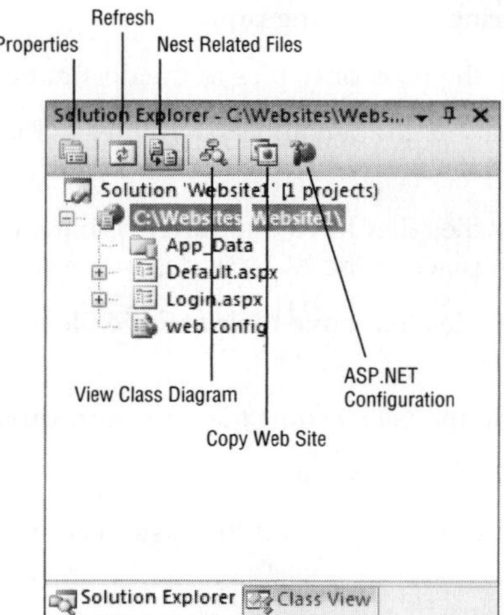

Figure 34-3

The other way to open the Copy Web Site GUI is to choose Website ➪ Copy Web Site from the Visual Studio menu. Using either method pulls up the Copy Web Site GUI in the Document window, as illustrated in Figure 34-4.

From this GUI, you can click the Connect To a Remote Server button (next to the Connections text box). This action brings up the Open Web Site dialog shown in Figure 34-5.

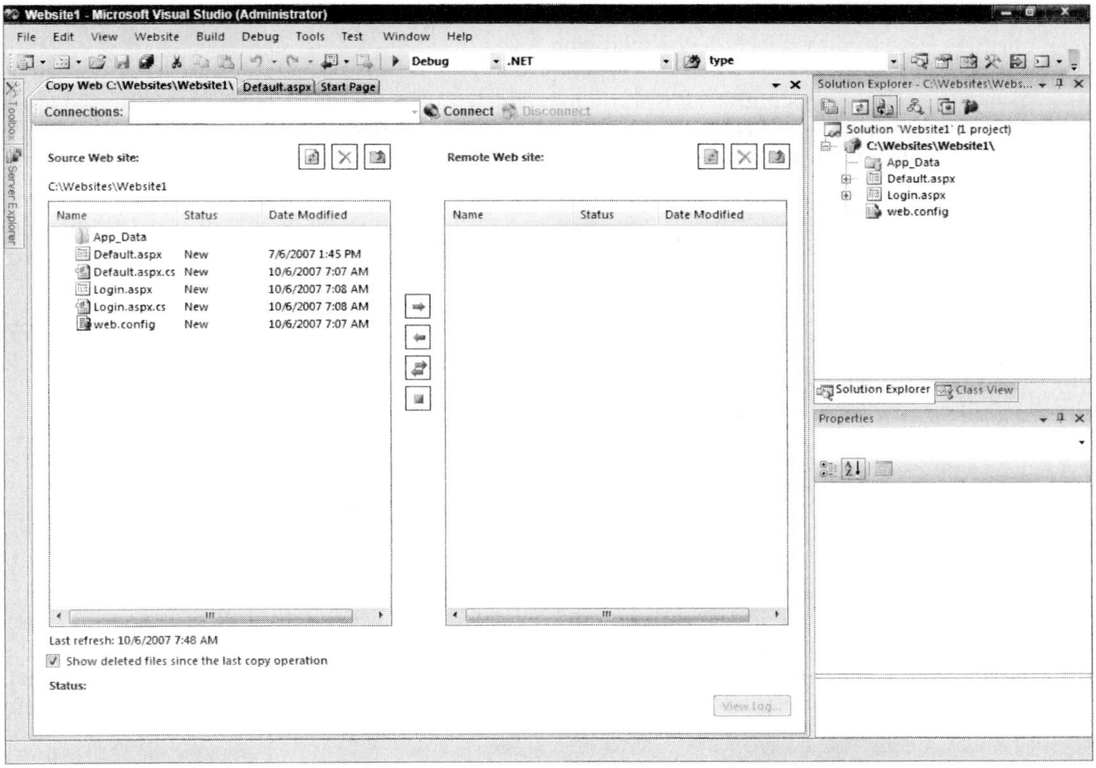

Figure 34-4

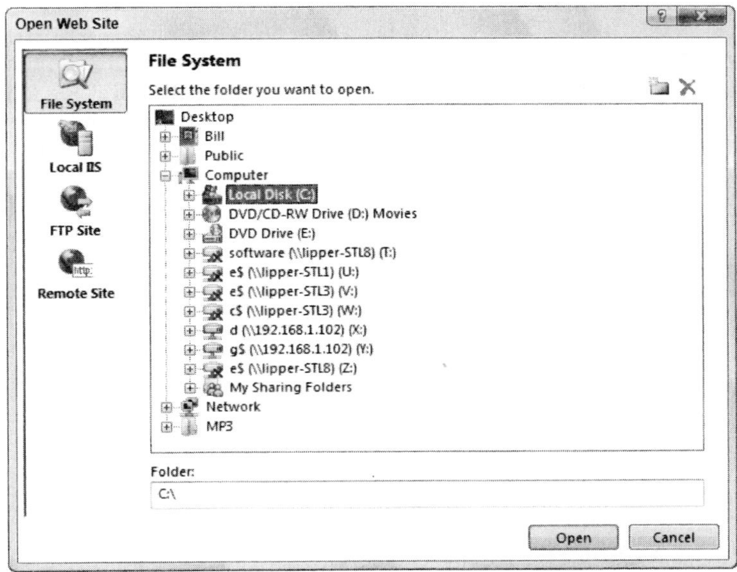

Figure 34-5

As you can see from this dialog, you have a couple of options to connect to and copy your Web application. These options include the following:

- **File System:** This option allows you to navigate through a file explorer view of the computer. If you are going to install on a remote server from this view, you must have already mapped a drive to the installation location.
- **Local IIS:** This option enables you to use your local IIS in the installation of your Web application. From this part of the dialog, you can create new applications as well as new virtual directories directly. You can also delete applications and virtual directories from the same dialog. The Local IIS option does not permit you to work with IIS installations on any remote servers.
- **FTP Site:** This option enables you to connect to a remote server using FTP capabilities. From this dialog, you can specify the server that you want to contact using a URL or IP address, the port you are going to use, and the directory on the server that you will work with. From this dialog, you can also specify the username and password that may be required to access the server via FTP. Note that if you access this server with this dialog via FTP and provide a username and password, the items are transmitted in plain text.
- **Remote Site:** This option enables you to connect to a remote site using FrontPage Server Extensions. From this option in the dialog, you can also choose to connect to the remote server using Secure Sockets Layer (SSL).

After being connected to a server, you can copy the contents of your Web application to it by selecting all or some of the files from the Source Web Site text area. After you select these files in the dialog, some of the movement arrows become enabled. Clicking the right-pointing arrow copies the selected files to the destination server. In Figure 34-6 you can see that, indeed, the files have been copied to the remote destination.

If you pull up the same copy dialog later, after working on the files, you see an arrow next to the files that have been changed in the interim and are, therefore, newer than those on the destination server (see Figure 34-7).

These arrows enable you to select only the files that must be copied again and nothing more. All the copying actions are recorded in a log file. You can view the contents of this log file from the Copy Web Site dialog by clicking the View Log button at the bottom of the dialog. This pulls up the `CopyWebSite.log` text file. From the copy that you made previously, you can see the transaction that was done. An example log entry is shown here:

```
Copy from 'C:\Websites\Website1' to 'Y:\Websites' started at 10/6/2007 7:52:31 AM.
            Create folder App_Data in the remote Web site.


            Copy file Default.aspx from source to remote Web site.
            Copy file Default.aspx.cs from source to remote Web site.
            Copy file Login.aspx from source to remote Web site.
            Copy file Login.aspx.cs from source to remote Web site.
            Copy file web.config from source to remote Web site.

Copy from 'C:\Websites\Website1' to 'Y:\Websites' is finished. Completed at 10/6/2007
7:52:33 AM.
```

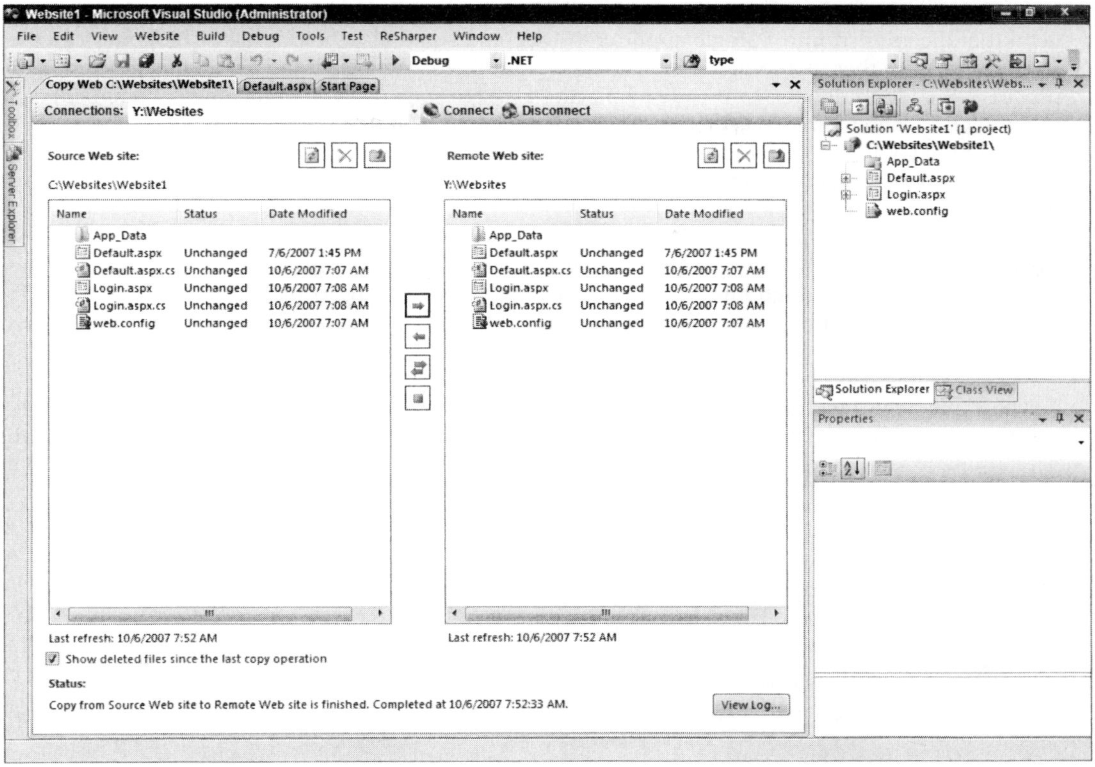

Figure 34-6

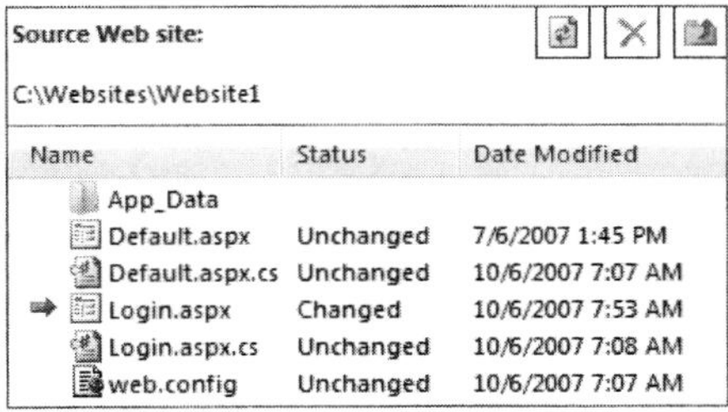

Figure 34-7

Deploying a Precompiled Web Application

In addition to using Visual Studio to copy a Web application from one location to another, it is also possible to use this IDE to deploy a precompiled application. The process of precompiling a Web application is explained in Chapter 1. ASP.NET 3.5 includes a precompilation process that allows for a process referred to as *precompilation for deployment*.

What happens in the precompilation for deployment process is that each page in the Web application is built and compiled into a single application DLL and some placeholder files. These files can then be deployed together to another server and run from there. The nice thing about this precompilation process is that it obfuscates your code by placing all page code (as well as the page's code-behind code) into the DLL, thereby making it more difficult for your code to be stolen or changed if you select this option in the compilation process. This is an ideal situation when you are deploying applications your customers are paying for, or applications that you absolutely do not want changed in any manner after deployment.

Chapter 1 showed you how to use the command-line tool `aspnet_compiler.exe` to accomplish the task of precompilation. Although this is a great method for precompiling your Web applications and deploying them to remote servers, you can also use Visual Studio 2008 to accomplish the precompilation and deployment process.

To accomplish this task, open up the project you want to deploy and get the application ready for deployment by turning off the debugging capabilities as described earlier in the chapter. Then pull up the precompilation and deployment dialog by choosing Build ➪ Publish Web Site in the Visual Studio menu. This opens the Publish Web Site dialog shown in Figure 34-8.

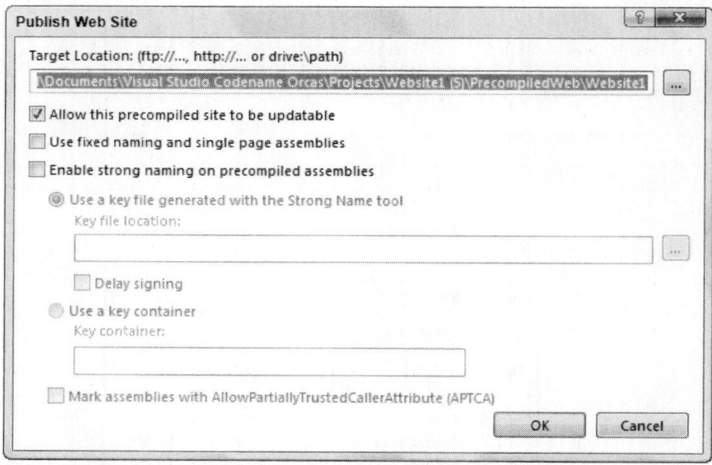

Figure 34-8

Using the Browse (. . .) button in this dialog, you can choose any remote location to which you want to deploy the application. As in earlier examples, your options are a file system location, a place in the local IIS, a location accessed using FTP, or a location accessed via FrontPage Server Extensions.

Other options in this dialog include the Allow this precompiled site to be updateable check box. When checked, the site will be compiled and copied without any changes to the `.aspx` pages. This means that after the precompilation process, you can still make minor changes to the underlying pages and the application will work and function as normal. If this check box is unchecked, all the code from the pages is stripped out and placed inside a single DLL. In this state, the application is not updateable because it is impossible to update any of the placeholder files from this compilation process.

Another option in this dialog is to assign a strong name to the DLL that is created in this process. You can select the appropriate check box and assign a key to use in the signing process. The created DLL from the precompilation will then be a strong-assembly — signed with the key of your choice.

When you are ready to deploy, click OK in the dialog and then the open application is built and published. *Published* means that the application is deployed to the specified location. Looking at this location, you can see that a `bin` directory has now been added that contains the precompiled DLL, which is your Web application. This is illustrated in Figure 34-9.

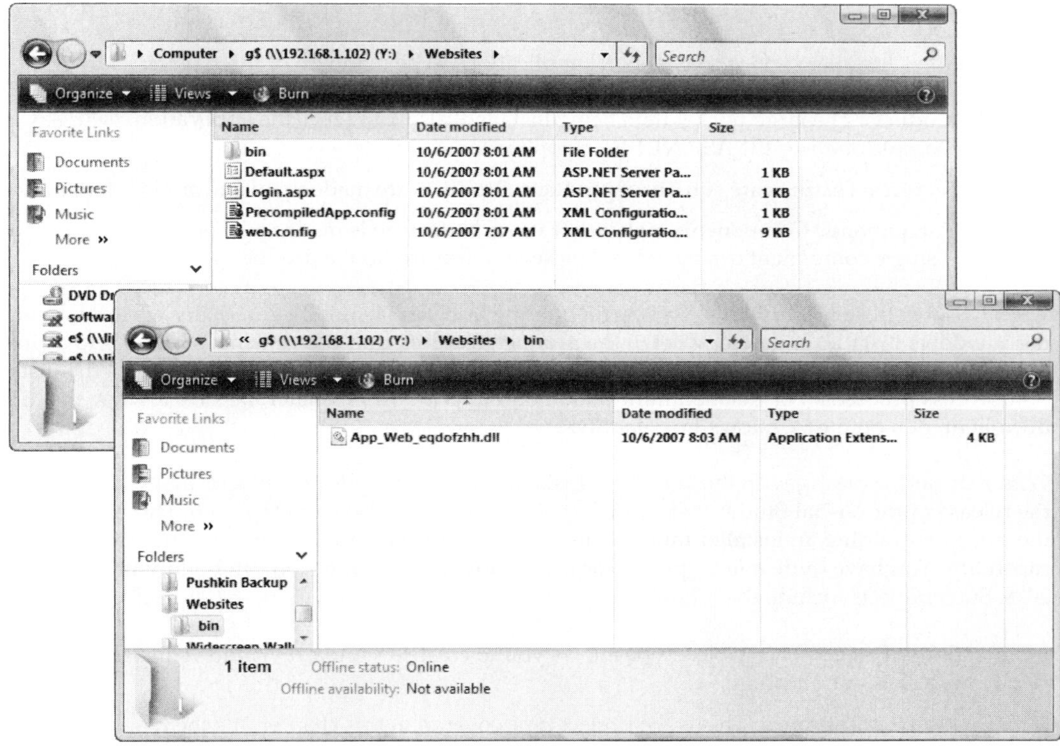

Figure 34-9

In this state, the code contained in any of the ASP.NET-specific pages is stripped out and placed inside the DLL. The files that you see are actually just placeholders that the DLL needs for reference.

Building an Installer Program

The final option you should look at is how to use Visual Studio to build an installation program. After the program is constructed, a consumer can run the installation program on a server where it performs a series of steps to install the Web application.

Packaging your Web application into an installer program works in many situations. For instance, if you sell your Web application, one of the simpler ways for the end user to receive the application is as an executable that can be run on the computer and installed — all without much effort on his part.

The Windows Installer

The Windows Installer service was introduced with Windows 2000, although it is also available in Windows XP, Windows Server 2003, and Windows Server 2008. This service was introduced to make the installation process for your Windows-based applications as easy as possible.

You use the Windows Installer technology not only for ASP.NET applications but also for any type of Windows-based application. The Windows Installer service works by creating a set of rules that determine how the application is to be installed. These rules are packaged into a Windows Installer Package File that uses the `.msi` file extension.

The Windows Installer service considers all applications to be made up of three parts:

- **Products:** The large-bucket item being installed, also known as the application itself. An example of this is the ASP.NET Web application.
- **Features:** Features are subsets of products. Products are made up of one or more features.
- **Components:** Components make up features. A feature is made up of one or more components. A single component can be utilized by several features in the product.

The Windows Installer service is a powerful offering and can be modified in many ways. Not only does the Windows Installer technology detail the product, features, and components of what is to be installed, but it can also take other programmatic actions or show a sequence of user interfaces as the installation process proceeds. For detailed information on the Windows Installer, be sure to view the MSDN documentation on the Windows Installer SDK.

With that said, working with the Windows Installer SDK is complicated at best; that was the reason for the release of the Visual Studio Installer (VSI) as an add-on with Visual Studio 6. This addition made the steps for building an installer much easier to follow. Visual Studio 2008 continues to expand on this capability. You have quite a few options for the deployment projects you can build with Visual Studio 2008. Such projects include the following:

- **Setup Project:** This project type allows you to create a standard Windows Installer setup for a Windows application.
- **Web Setup Project:** This is the project type covered in this chapter. It's the type of setup project you use to create an installer for an ASP.NET Web application.
- **Merge Module Project:** This project type creates a merge module similar to a cabinet file. A merge module, such as a cabinet file, allows you to package a group of files for distribution but not for installation. The idea is that you use a merge module file with other setup programs. This project type produces a file type with an extension of `.msm`.
- **Setup Wizard:** This selection actually gives you a wizard to assist you through one of the other defined project types.
- **Cab Project:** This project type creates a cabinet file (`.cab`) that packages a group of files for distribution. It is similar to a merge module file, but the cabinet file is different in that it allows for installation of the files contained in the package.
- **Smart Device Cab Project:** This new project type allows for the creation of a cabinet file that is installed on a smart device instead of on a typical operating system.

Although you have a number of different setup and deployment project types at your disposal, the Web Setup Project is the only one covered in this chapter because it is the project you use to build an installer for an ASP.NET Web application.

Actions of the Windows Installer

You might already be thinking that using the Windows Installer architecture for your installation program seems a lot more complicated than using the methods shown previously in this chapter. Yes, it is a bit more complicated — mainly because of the number of steps required to get the desired result; but in the end, you are getting a lot more control over how your applications are installed.

Using an installer program gives you programmatic logic over how your applications are installed. You also gain other advantages, such as:

- The capability to check if the .NET Framework is installed, as well as which version of the Framework is installed
- The capability to read or write values to the registry
- The capability to collect information from the end user during the installation process
- The capability to run scripts
- The capability to include such features such as dialogs and splash screens during the installation process

Creating a Basic Installation Program

You can apply a tremendous amount of customization to the installation programs you build. Let's start, however, by looking at how to create a basic installation program for your ASP.NET Web application. To create an installer for your application, first open up the project for which you want to create a deployment project in Visual Studio. The next step is to add an installer program to the solution. To do this, you add the setup program as a new project contained within the same solution. Choose File ➪ New ➪ Project from the Visual Studio menu. This launches the New Project dialog.

From the New Project dialog, first expand Other Project Types from the left-hand pane in the dialog and then select Setup and Deployment. This provides you with a list of all the available setup and deployment projects in Visual Studio. For our purposes, select Web Setup Project (shown in Figure 34-10).

Clicking OK in this dialog adds the Web Setup Project type to your solution. It uses the default name of `WebSetup1`. Visual Studio also opens up the File System Editor in the document window, which is shown in Figure 34-11.

The File System Editor shows a single folder: the Web Application Folder. This is a representation of what is going to be installed on the target machine. The first step is to add the files from the WebSite1 project to this folder. You do this by choosing Project ➪ Add ➪ Project Output from the Visual Studio menu. This pulls up the Add Project Output Group dialog. This dialog (shown in Figure 34-12) enables you to select the items you want to include in the installer program.

From this dialog, you can see that the project, Wrox, is already selected. Highlight the Content Files option and click OK. This adds all the files from the Wrox project to the WebSetup1 installer program. This addition is then represented in the File System Editor as well.

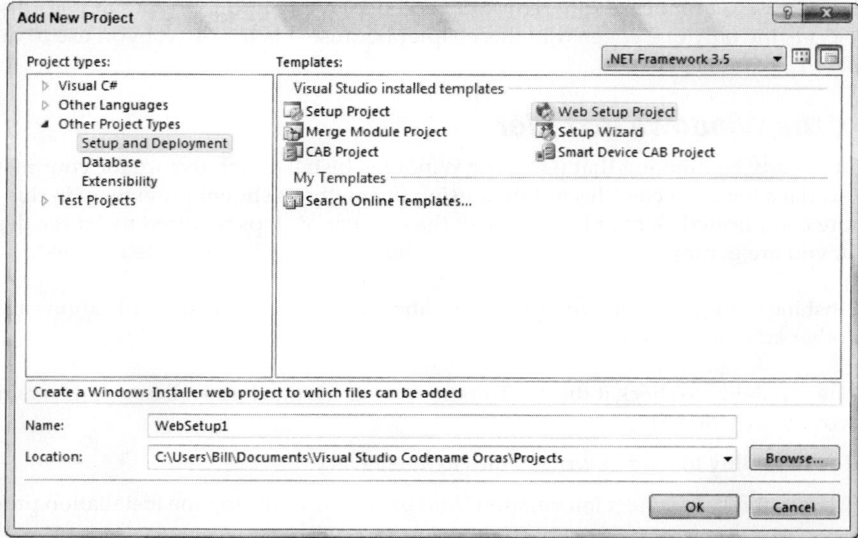

Figure 34-10

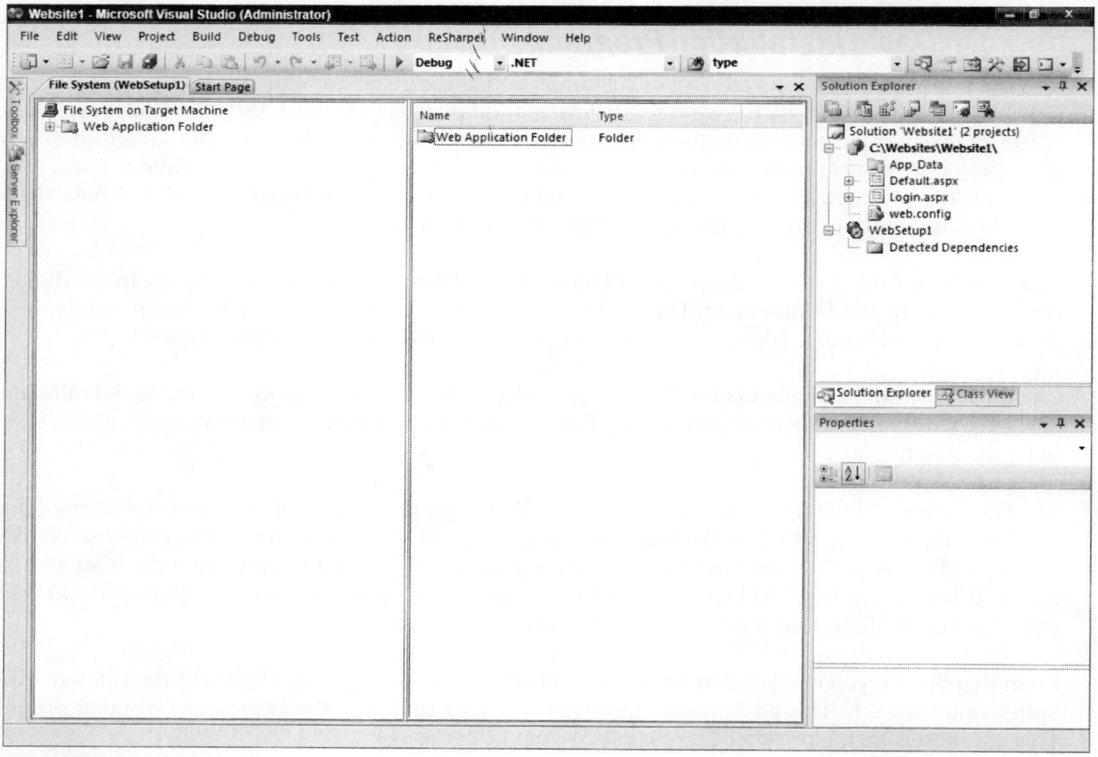

Figure 34-11

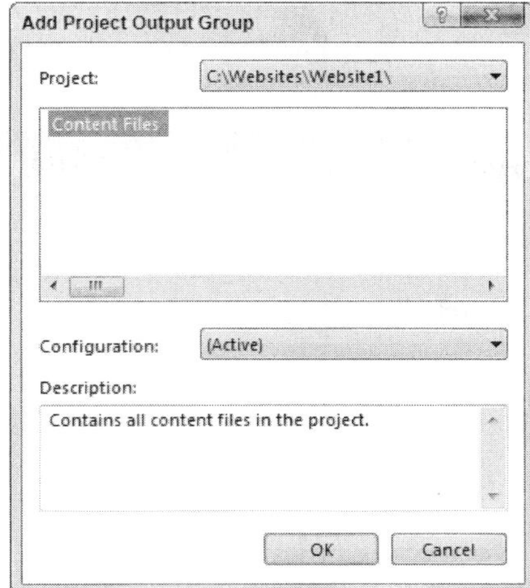

Figure 34-12

After the files are added to the installer program, the next step is to click the Launch Conditions Editor button in the Solution Explorer (see Figure 34-13) to open the editor. The Launch Conditions Editor is also displayed in Visual Studio's document window. From this editor, you can see that a couple of conditions are already defined for you. Obviously, for Web applications, it is important that IIS be installed. Logically, one of the defined conditions is that the program must perform a search to see if IIS is installed before installing the application. You should also stipulate that the installation server must have version 3.5 of the .NET Framework installed.

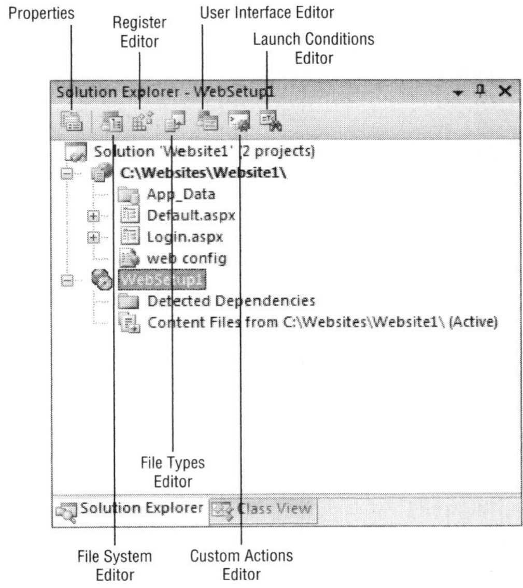

Figure 34-13

To establish this condition, right-click the Requirements On Target Machine node. Then select Add .NET Framework Launch Condition (as shown in Figure 34-14).

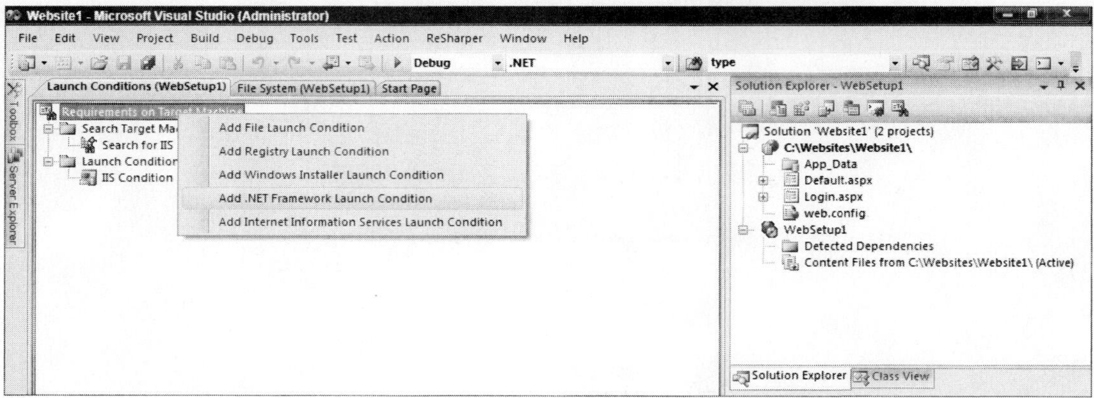

Figure 34-14

This adds the .NET Framework requirement to the list of launch conditions required for a successful installation of the Web application.

As a final step, highlight the WebSetup1 program in the Visual Studio Solution Explorer so you can modify some of the properties that appear in the Properties window. For now, you just change some of the self-explanatory properties, but you will review these again later in this chapter. For this example, however, just change the following properties:

- `Author`: Wrox
- `Description`: This is a test project.
- `Manufacturer`: Wrox
- `ManufacturerUrl`: `http://www.wrox.com`
- `SupportPhone`: 1-800-555-5555
- `SupportUrl`: `http://www.wrox.com/support/`

Now the installation program is down to its simplest workable instance. Make sure Release is selected as the active solution configuration in the Visual Studio toolbar; then build the installer program by choosing Build ➪ Build WebSetup1 from the menu.

Looking in `C:\Documents and Settings\<username>\My Documents\Visual Studio 2008\Projects\Wrox\WebSetup1\Release`, you find the following files:

- `Setup.exe`: This is the installation program. It is meant for machines that do not have the Windows Installer service installed.
- `WebSetup1.msi`: This is the installation program for those that have the Windows Installer service installed on their machine.

That's it! You now have your ASP.NET Web application wrapped up in an installation program that can be distributed in any manner you want. It can then be run and installed automatically for the end user. Take a quick look in the following section at what happens when the consumer actually fires it up.

Installing the Application

Installing the application is a simple process (as it should be). Double-click the `WebSetup1.msi` file to launch the installation program. This pulls up the Welcome screen shown in Figure 34-15.

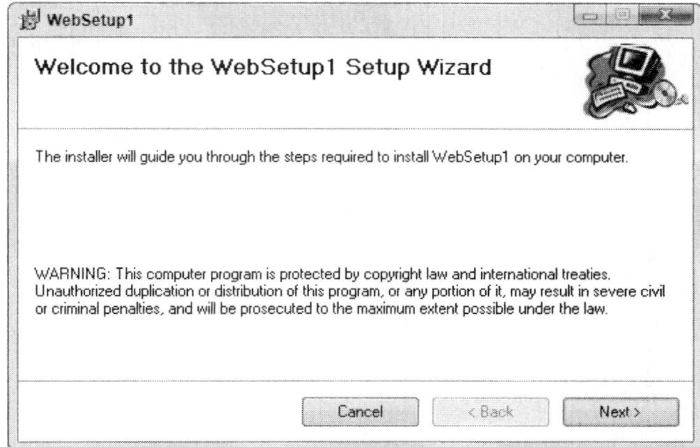

Figure 34-15

From this dialog, you can see that the name of the program being installed is `WebSetup1`. Clicking Next gives you the screen shown in Figure 34-16.

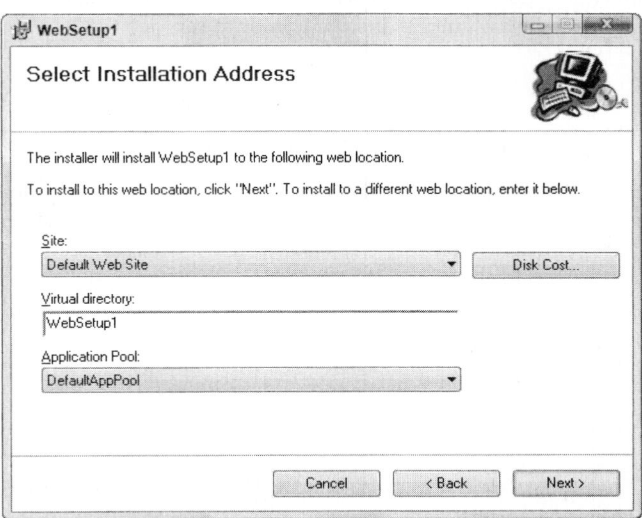

Figure 34-16

This screen tells you what you are installing (the Default Web Site) as well as the name of the virtual directory created for the deployed Web application. The consumer can feel free to change the name of the virtual directory in the provided text box. A button in this dialog allows for an estimation of the disk cost (space required) for the installed application. In .NET 3.5, the installer also allows the end user to choose the application pool he or she is interested in using for the application. The next series of screens install the `WebSetup1` application (shown in Figure 34-17).

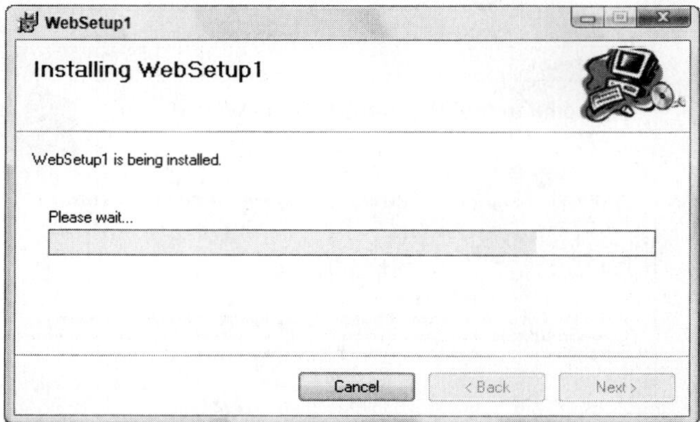

Figure 34-17

After the application is installed, you can find the `WebSetup1` folder and application files located in the `C:\Inetpub\wwwroot` folder (within IIS). The application can now be run on the server from this location.

Uninstalling the Application

To uninstall the application, the consumer has a couple of options. First, he can relaunch the `.msi` file and use the option to either repair the current installation or to remove the installation altogether (as shown in Figure 34-18).

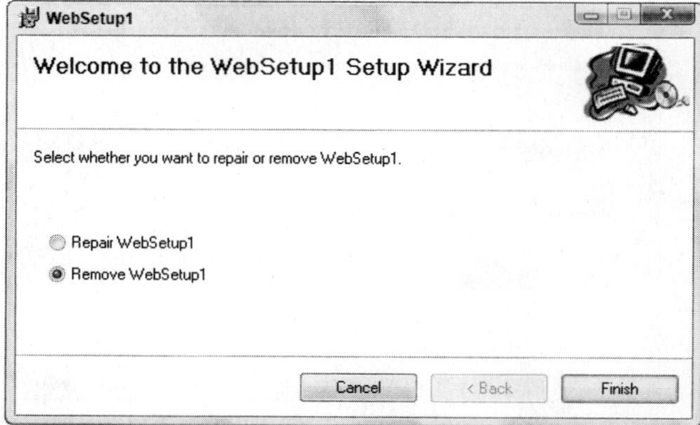

Figure 34-18

The other option is to pull up the Add/Remove Programs dialog from the server's Control Panel. On the Control Panel, you see `WebSetup1` listed (as shown in Figure 34-19).

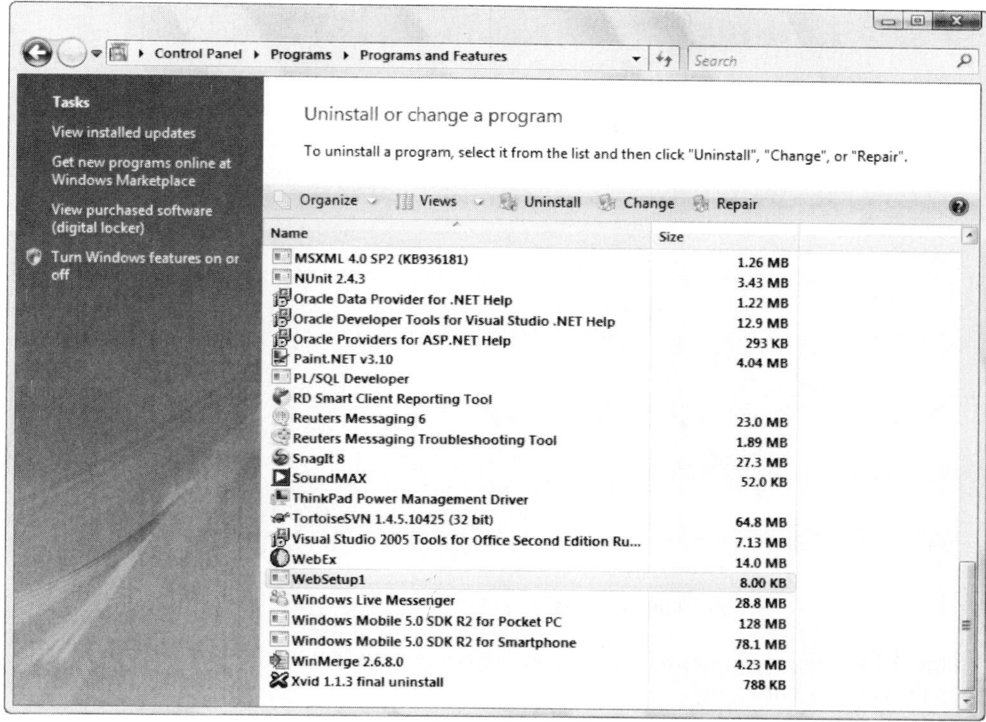

Figure 34-19

This dialog holds information about the size of the installed application and, if you are using Windows XP, it will also show you how often the application is used. Also, if you are using Windows XP, clicking the support link pulls up the Support Info dialog, which shows the project's properties that you entered a little earlier (see Figure 34-20).

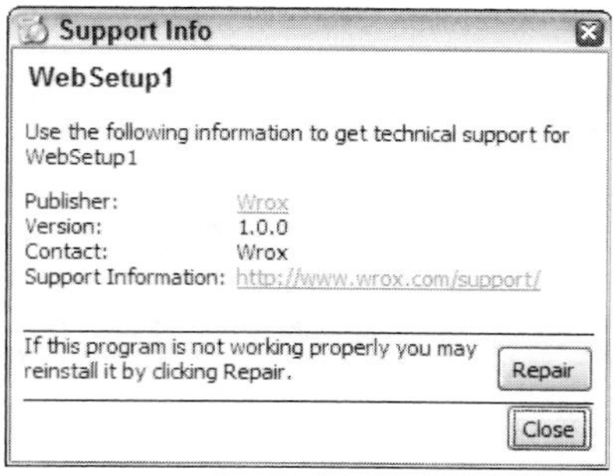

Support Info
WebSetup1
Use the following information to get technical support for WebSetup1
Publisher: Wrox
Version: 1.0.0
Contact: Wrox
Support Information: http://www.wrox.com/support/
If this program is not working properly you may reinstall it by clicking Repair.
Repair
Close

Figure 34-20

However, if you are using Windows Vista, you can get at the same information by right-clicking on the column headers and selecting the More option from the provided menu. This gives you a list of options (shown here in Figure 34-21), providing the same information as what you can see in Windows XP.

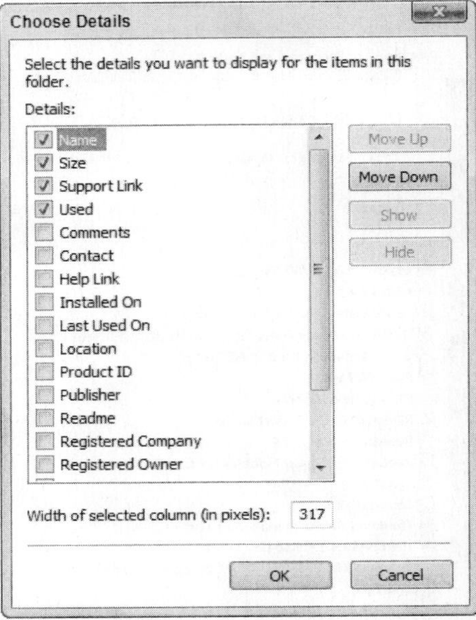

Figure 34-21

From the Add/Remove Programs dialog, you can remove the installation by clicking the Remove button of the selected program.

Looking More Closely at Installer Options

The Windows Installer service easily installs a simple ASP.NET Web application. The installer takes care of packaging the files into a nice `.msi` file from which it can then be distributed. Next, the `.msi` file takes care of creating a virtual directory and installing the application files. The installer also makes it just as easy to uninstall the application from the server. All these great services are provided with very little work on the user's part.

Even though this approach addresses almost everything needed for an ASP.NET installer program, the setup and deployment project for Web applications provided by Visual Studio really provides much more in the way of options and customizations. This next section looks at the various ways you can work with modifying the installer program.

Working with the Deployment Project Properties

You can work with the project properties of the installer from Visual Studio in several ways. The first way is by right-clicking the installer project from the Solution Explorer of Visual Studio and selecting Properties from the menu. This pulls up the WebSetup1 Properties Pages dialog shown in Figure 34-22.

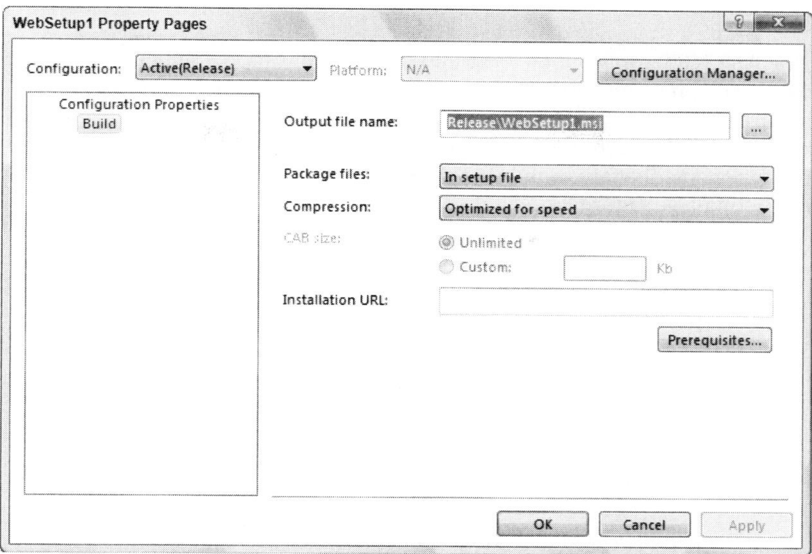

Figure 34-22

This dialog has some important settings for your installer application. Notice that, like other typical projects, this setup and deployment project allows for different active build configuration settings. For instance, you can have the active build configuration set to either Release or Debug. You can also click on the Configuration Manager button to get access to configuration settings for all the projects involved. In addition, this dialog enables you to add or remove build configurations from the project.

The Output File Name

The Output File Name setting lets you set the name of the `.msi` file that is generated. By default, it is the name of the project, but you can change this value to anything you want. This section also allows you to modify the location where the built `.msi` is placed on the system after the build process occurs.

Package Files

The Package files section of this properties page enables you to specify how the application files are packaged in the `.msi` file. The available options include the following:

- **As loose, uncompressed files:** This option builds the project so that a resulting `.msi` file is created without the required application files. Instead, these application files are kept separate from the `.msi` file but copied to the same location as the `.msi` file. With this type of structure, you must distribute both the `.msi` file and the associated application files.
- **In setup file:** This option (which is the default option) packages the application files inside the `.msi` file. This makes distribution an easy task because only a single file is distributed.
- **In cabinet file(s):** This option packages all the application files into a number of cabinet files. The size of the cabinet files can be controlled through this same dialog (discussed shortly). This is an ideal type of installation process to use if you have to spread the installation application over a number of DVDs, CDs, or floppy disks.

Installation URL

Invariably, the ASP.NET applications you build have some component dependencies. In most cases, your application depends on some version of the .NET Framework. The installation of these dependencies, or components, can be made part of the overall installation process. This process is also referred to as *bootstrapping*. Clicking the Prerequisites button next to the Installation URL text box gives you a short list of available components that are built into Visual Studio in order to bootstrap to the installation program you are constructing (see Figure 34-23).

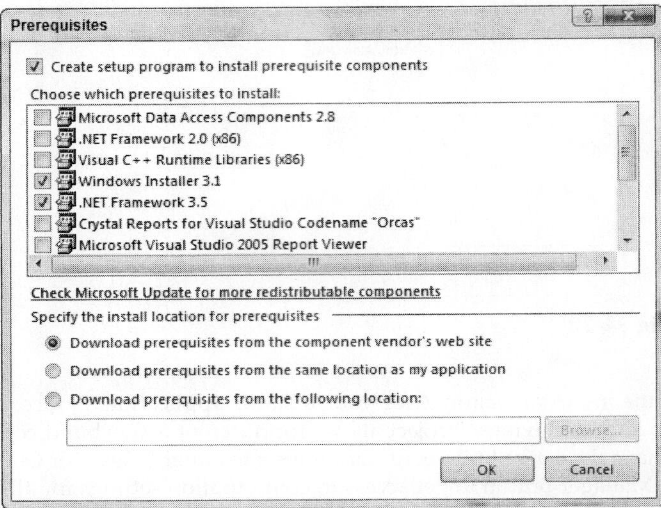

Figure 34-23

As you can see from when you first enter this settings dialog, the .NET Framework 3.5 and the Windows Installer 3.1 options are enabled by default, and you check the other components (thereby enabling them) only if your Web application has some kind of dependency on them.

From this dialog, you can also set how the dependent components are downloaded to the server where the installation is occurring. The options include downloading from Microsoft, from the server where the application originated, or from a defined location (URL) specified in the provided text box.

Compression

The Windows Installer service can work with the compression of the application files included in the build process so that they are optimized for either speed or size. You also have the option to turn off all compression optimizations. The default setting is Optimized for Speed.

CAB Size

The CAB Size section of the properties page is enabled only if you select In Cabinet File(s) from the Package Files drop-down list, as explained earlier. If this is selected, it is enabled with the `Unlimited` radio button selected. As you can see from this section, the two settings are `Unlimited` and `Custom`:

- `Unlimited`: This selection means that only a single cabinet file is created. The size of this file is dependent on the size of the collection of application files in the Web application and the type of compression selected.

- `Custom`: This selection allows you to break up the installation across multiple cabinet files. If the `Custom` radio button is selected, you can enter the maximum size of the cabinet files allowed in the provided text box. The measure of the number you place in the text box is in kilobytes (KB).

Additional Properties

You learned one place where you can apply settings to the installer program; however, at another place in Visual Studio you can find even more properties pertaining to the entire installer program. By selecting the `WebSetup1` installer program in the Solution Explorer, you can work with the installer properties directly from the Properties window of Visual Studio. The following table lists the properties that appear in the Properties window.

Property	Description
`AddRemoveProgramsIcon`	Defines the location of the icon used in the Add/Remove Programs dialog found through the system's Control Panel.
`Author`	The author of the installer. This could be the name of a company or individual.
`Description`	Allows for a textual description of the installer program.
`DetectNewerInstalledVersion`	Instructs the installer to make a check on the installation server if a newer version of the application is present. If one is present, the installation is aborted. The default setting is `True` (meaning that the check will be made).
`Keywords`	Defines the keywords used when a search is made for an installer.
`Localization`	Defines the locale for any string resources and the runtime user interface. An example setting is `English (United States)`.
`Manufacturer`	Defines the name of the company that built or provided the installer program.
`ManufacturerUrl`	Defines the URL of the company that built or provided the installer program.
`PostBuildEvent`	Specifies a command line executed after the build ends.
`PreBuildEvent`	Specifies a command line executed before the build begins.
`ProductCode`	Defines a string value that is the unique identifier for the application. An example value is `{885D2E86-6247-4624-9DB1-50790E3856B4}`.
`ProductName`	Defines the name of the program being installed.
`RemovePreviousVersions`	Specifies as a `Boolean` value whether any previous versions of the application should be uninstalled prior to installing the fresh version. The default setting is `False`.
`RestartWWWService`	Specifies as a `Boolean` value whether or not IIS should be stopped and restarted for the installation process. The default value is `False`.

Property	Description
RunPostBuildEvent	Defines when to run the post-build event. The default setting is On successful build. The other possible value is Always.
SearchPath	Defines the path to use to search for any files, assemblies, merge modules on the development machine.
Subject	Allows you to provide additional descriptions for the application.
SupportPhone	Specifies the support telephone number for the installed program.
SupportUrl	Specifies the URL by which the end user can get support for the installed application.
TargetPlatform	Defines the target platform of the installer. Possible values include x86, x64, and Itanium.
Title	Defines the title of the installer program.
UpgradeCode	Defines a shared identifier that can be used from build to build. An example value is {A71833C7-3B76-4083-9D34-F074A4FFF544}.
Version	Specifies the version number of the installer, cabinet file, or merge module. An example value is 1.0.1.

The following sections look at the various editors provided to help you build and customize the construction of the installer. You can get at these editors by clicking the appropriate icon in the Solution Explorer in Visual Studio or by choosing View ➪ Editor in the Visual Studio menu. These editors are explained next.

The File System Editor

The first editor that comes up when you create your installer program is the File System Editor. The File System Editor enables you to add folders and files that are to be installed on the destination server. In addition to installing folders and files, it also facilitates the creation of shortcuts. This editor is shown in Figure 34-24.

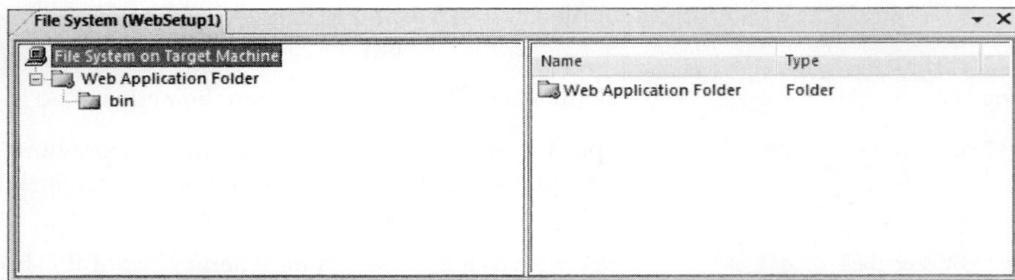

Figure 34-24

The File System Editor has two sections. The left section is the list of folders to be installed during the installation process. By default, only the Web Application Folder is shown. Highlighting this folder, or one of the other folders, gives you a list of properties for that folder in the Properties window of Visual Studio. The following table details some of the properties you might find in the Properties window.

Property	Description
`AllowDirectoryBrowsing`	Allows browsing of the selected directory in IIS. The default value is `False`.
`AllowReadAccess`	Specifies whether the selected folder should have Read access. The default value is `True`.
`AllowScriptSourceAccess`	Specifies the script source access of the selected folder. The default value is `False`.
`AllowWriteAccess`	Specifies whether the selected folder should have Write access. The default value is `False`.
`ApplicationProtection`	Defines the IIS Application Protection property for the selected folder. Possible values include `vsdapLow`, `vsdapMedium`, and `vsdapHigh`. The default value is `vsdapMedium`.
`AppMappings`	Enables you to define the IIS application mappings for the selected folder.
`DefaultDocument`	Defines the default document of the selected folder. The default value is `Default.aspx`.
`ExecutePermissions`	Defines the IIS Execute Permissions property. Possible values include `vsdepNone`, `vsdepScriptsOnly`, `vsdepScriptsAnd-Executables`. The default value is `vsdepScriptsOnly`.
`Index`	Specifies the IIS Index of this resource property for the selected folder. The default value is `True`.
`IsApplication`	Specifies whether an IIS application root is created for the installed application. The default value is `True`.
`LogVisits`	Specifies the IIS Log Visits property for the selected folder. The default value is `True`.
`VirtualDirectory`	Defines the name of the virtual directory created. The default value is the name of the project.

Adding Items to the Output

You can add files, folders, and assemblies to the installer output quite easily. To add some of these items to the output list, right-click the folder and select Add from the menu. You have four choices: Web Folder, Project Output, File, and Assembly.

If you want to add a custom folder to the output (for example, an Images folder), you can select Web Folder and provide the name of the folder. This enables you to create the folder structure you want.

If you want to add system folders, you highlight the File System on Target Machine node and then choose Action ➪ Add Special Folder. This provides you with a large list of folders that are available for you to add to the installer program. You can also get at this list of folders by simply right-clicking a blank portion of the left pane of the File System Editor (see Figure 34-25).

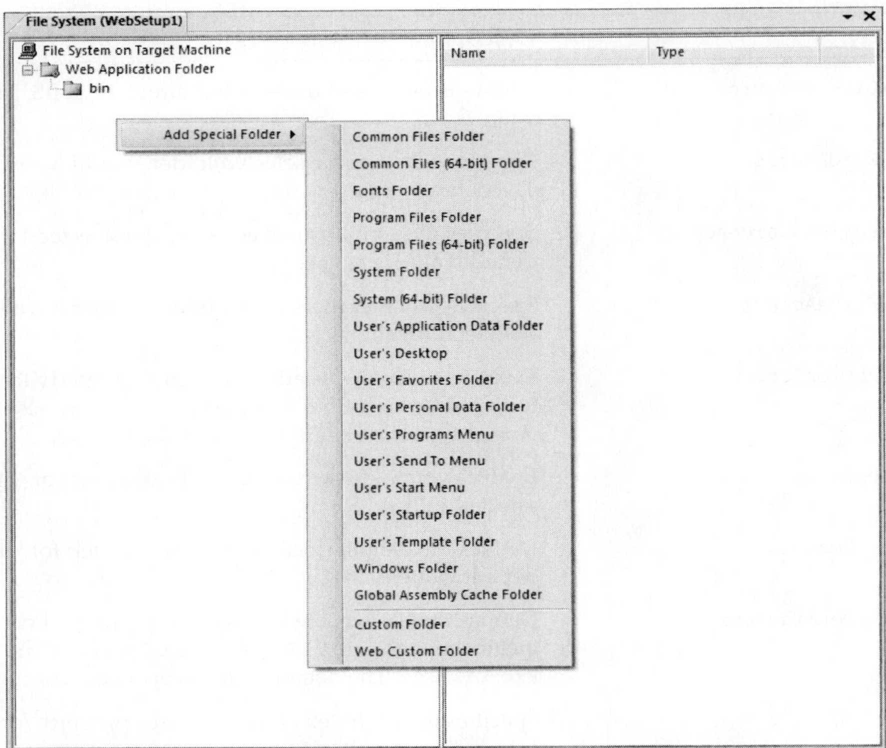

Figure 34-25

The following table defines the possible folders you can add to the installer structure you are building.

Folders and Menus	Description
Common Files Folder	Meant for non–system files not shared by multiple applications.
Common Files (64-bit) Folder	Meant for non–system files on a 64-bit machine not shared by multiple applications.
Fonts Folder	Meant for only fonts you want installed on the client's machine.
Program Files Folder	A Windows Forms application would be a heavy user of this folder because most applications are installed here.
Program Files (64-bit) Folder	A Programs Files folder meant for 64-bit machines.

Folders and Menus	Description
System Folder	Meant for storing files considered shared system files.
System (64-bit) Folder	Meant for storing files on 64-bit machines considered shared system files.
User's Application Data Folder	A hidden folder meant for storing data that is application- and user-specific.
User's Desktop	Meant for storing files on a user's desktop (also stores these files in the My Desktop folder).
User's Favorites Folder	Meant for storing files in a user's Favorites folder (browser-specific).
User's Personal Data Folder	Meant for storing personal data specific to a single user. This is also referred to as the My Documents folder.
User's Programs Menu	Meant for storing shortcuts, which then appear in the user's program menu.
User's Send To Menu	Meant for storing files that are presented when a user attempts to send a file or folder to a specific application (by right-clicking the folder or file and selecting Send To).
User's Start Menu	Meant for storing files in the user's Start menu.
User's Startup Folder	Meant for storing files that are initiated whenever a user logs into his machine.
User's Template Folder	Meant for storing templates (applications like Microsoft's Office).
Windows Folder	Meant for storing files in the Windows root folder. These are usually system files.
Global Assembly Cache Folder	Meant for storing assemblies that can then be utilized by all the applications on the server (shared assemblies).
Custom Folder	Another way of creating a unique folder.
Web Custom Folder	Another way of creating a unique folder that also contains a bin folder.

Creating a Desktop Shortcut to the Web Application

For an example of using one of these custom folders, look at placing a shortcut to the Web application on the user's desktop. The first step is to right-click on a blank portion of the left-hand pane in the File System Editor and choose Add Special Folder ⇨ User's Desktop. This adds that folder to the list of folders presented in the left-hand pane.

Because you want to create a desktop shortcut to the Web Application Folder and not to the desktop itself, the next step is to right-click the Web Application folder and select Create Shortcut to Web Application Folder. The created shortcut appears in the right-hand pane. Right-click the shortcut and rename it to something a little more meaningful, such as Wrox Application. Because you do not want to keep the shortcut in this folder, drag the shortcut from the Web Application Folder and drop it onto the User's Desktop folder.

With this structure in place, this installer program not only installs the application (as was done previously), but it also installs the application's shortcut on the user's desktop.

The Registry Editor

The next editor is the Registry Editor. This editor enables you to work with the client's registry in an easy and straightforward manner. Using this editor, you can perform operations such as creating new registry keys, providing values for already existing registry keys, and importing registry files. The Registry Editor is presented in Figure 34-26.

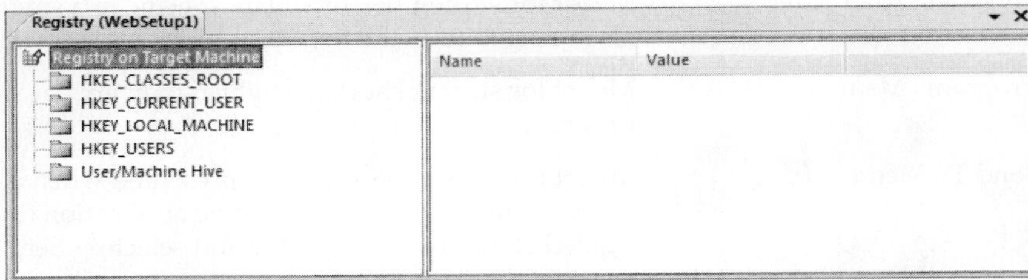

Figure 34-26

From this figure, you can see that the left-hand pane provides the standard registry folders, such as HKEY_CLASSES_ROOT and HKEY_LOCAL_MACHINE, as well as others. Right-clicking one of these folders, you can add a new key from the menu selection. This creates a new folder in the left-hand pane where it is enabled for renaming. By right-clicking this folder, you can add items such as those illustrated in Figure 34-27.

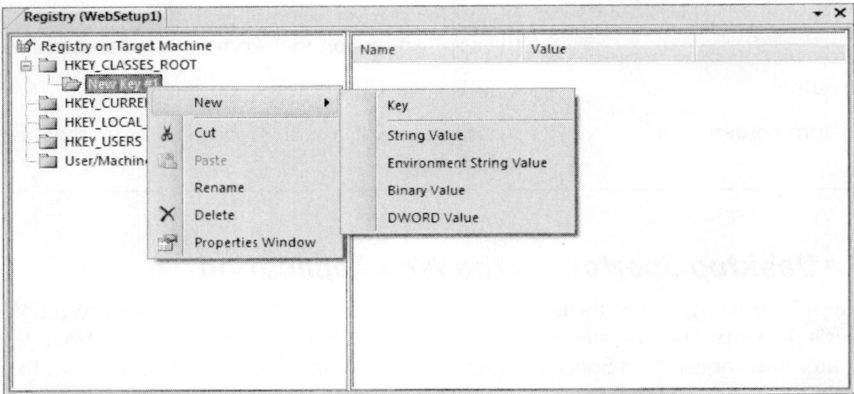

Figure 34-27

As you can see in the figure, you can add items such as the following:

- Key
- String Value
- Environment String Value
- Binary Value
- DWORD Value

Selecting String Value allows you to apply your settings for this in the right-hand pane, as illustrated in Figure 34-28.

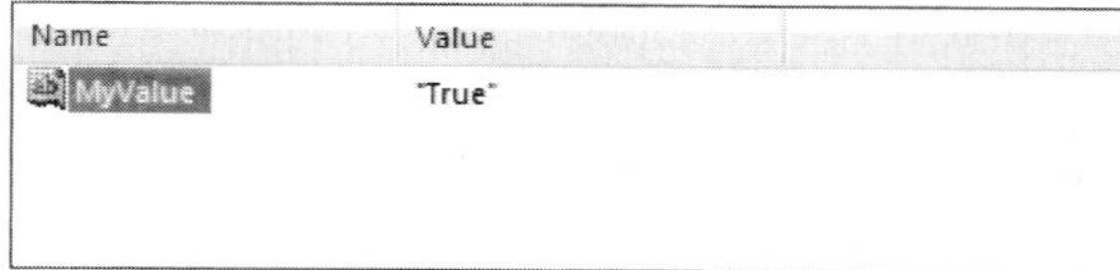

Figure 34-28

The other values work in a similar manner.

The File Types Editor

All files on a Windows operating system use file extensions to uniquely identify themselves. A file such as `Default.aspx`, for example, uses the file extension `.aspx`. This file extension is then associated with ASP.NET. Another example is `.xls`. This file extension is associated with Microsoft Excel. When someone attempts to open an `.xls` file, the file is passed to the Excel program because of mappings that have been made on the computer to associate these two entities.

Using the File Types Editor in Visual Studio, you can also make these mappings for the applications you are trying to install. Right-clicking the File Types On Target Machine allows you to add a new file type. From here, you can give your file type a descriptive name and provide a file extension (shown in Figure 34-29).

Figure 34-29

Highlighting the defined file type provides some properties that you can set in the Visual Studio Properties window, as shown in the following table.

Property	Description
`Name`	Specifies a name used in the File System Editor to identify a file type and its associated settings.
`Command`	Specifies the executable file (`.exe`) that is launched when the specified file extension is encountered.
`Description`	Defines a textual description for the file type.
`Extensions`	Defines the file extension associated with the executable through the `Command` property. An example is `wrox`. You should specify the extension without the period in front of it. If you are going to specify multiple extensions, you can provide a list separated by semicolons.
`Icon`	Defines the icon used for this file extension.
`MIME`	Specifies the MIME type associated with this file type. An example is `application/msword`.

The User Interface Editor

The User Interface Editor defines the dialogs used in the installation process. You can change the installation process greatly with the dialogs you decide to use or not use. By default, these dialogs (shown in Figure 34-30) are presented in your installer.

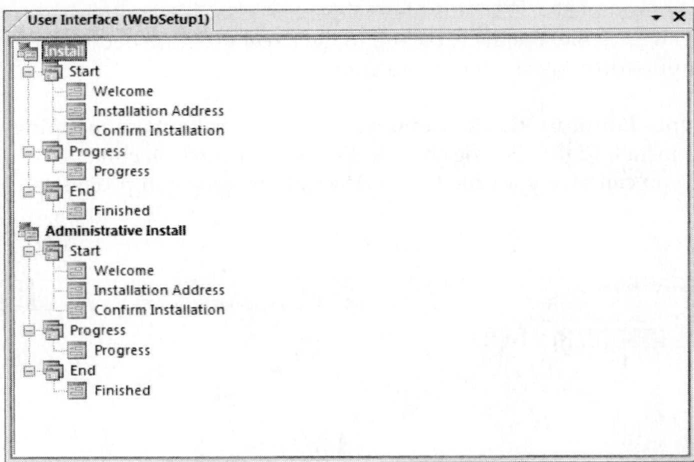

Figure 34-30

From this figure, you can see how the dialogs are divided into two main sections. The first section, labeled Install, is the dialog sequence used for a typical install. However, because some applications might require it, a second installation process is defined through the Administrative Install. The

Administrative Install process is initiated only if the user is logged onto the machine under the Administrator account. If this is not the case, the Install section is used instead.

By default, the Install and Administrative Install sections are exactly the same. Both the Install and Administrative Install sections are further divided into three subsections: Start, Progress, and End. These sections are defined in the following list:

- **Start:** A sequence of dialogs that appears before the installation occurs. By default, the Start section includes a welcome screen, a definition stating where the application is to be installed, and a dialog asking for an installation confirmation.
- **Progress:** The second stage, the Progress stage, is the stage in which the actual installation occurs. Throughout this stage no interaction occurs between the installer program and the end user. This is the stage where the end user can watch the installation progress through a progress bar.
- **End:** The End stage specifies to the end user whether the installation was successful. Many installer programs use this stage to present the customer with release notes and `ReadMe.txt` files, as well as the capability to launch the installed program directly from the installer program itself.

Adding Dialogs to the Installation Process

Of course, you are not limited to just the dialogs that appear in the User Interface Editor by default. You have a number of other dialogs that can be added to the installation process. For instance, right-click the Start node and select Add Dialog (or highlight the Start node and choose Action ⇨ Add Dialog). This pulls up the Add Dialog dialog, as shown in Figure 34-31.

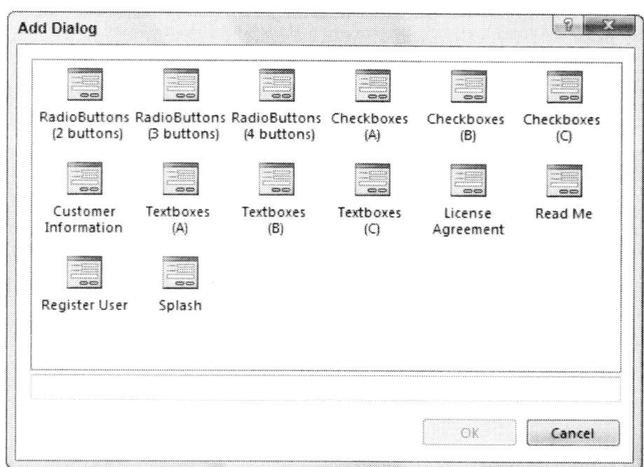

Figure 34-31

As you can see from this image, you can add quite a number of different steps to the installation process, such as license agreements and splash screens. After adding a dialog to the process, you can highlight the dialog to get its properties to appear in the Properties window so that you can assign the items needed. For example, you can assign the image to use for the splash screen or the `.rtf` file to use for the license agreement.

When you add an additional dialog to the installation process (for instance, to the Install section), be sure to also install the same dialog on the Administrative Install (if required). If no difference exists between the two user types in the install process, be sure to add the dialogs in unison in order to keep them the same.

Changing the Order in Which the Dialogs Appear in the Process

In working with the dialogs in the Start, Process, and End sections of the User Interface Editor, you can always determine the order in which these dialogs appear. Even if you are working with the default dialogs, you can easily change their order by right-clicking the dialog and selecting Move Up or Move Down, as shown in Figure 34-32.

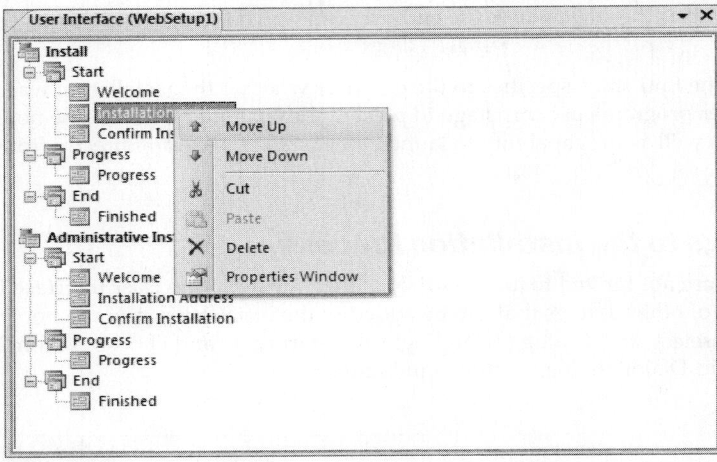

Figure 34-32

The Custom Actions Editor

The Custom Actions Editor is a powerful editor that enables you to take the installer one step further and perform custom actions during various events of the installation cycle (but always *after* the installation process is completed) such as Install, Commit, Rollback, and Uninstall. The Custom Actions Editor is presented in Figure 34-33.

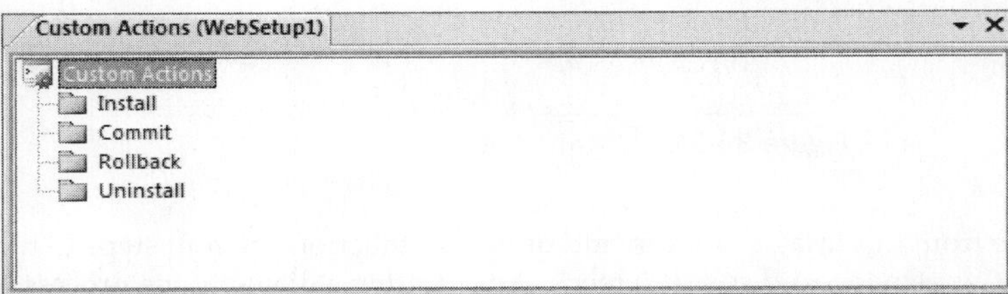

Figure 34-33

The idea is that you can place a reference to a `.dll`, `.exe`, or `.vbs` file from one of the folders presented here in the Custom Actions Editor to perform a custom action. For example, you can insert a custom action to install a database into Microsoft's SQL Server in the Commit folder (after the install has actually been committed).

The four available folders are explained in the following list:

- **Install:** This is the point at which the installation of the files for the Web application are finished being installed. Although the files are installed, this point is right before the installation has been committed.
- **Commit:** This is the point at which the actions of the installation have been actually committed (taken) and are considered successful.
- **Rollback:** This is the point at which the installation has failed and the computer must return to the same state that it was in before the installation occurred.
- **Uninstall:** This is the point at which a successfully installed application is uninstalled for a machine.

Using these capabilities, you can take the installation process to the level of complexity you need for a successfully installed application.

The Launch Conditions Editor

Certain conditions are required in order for your Web application to run on another server automatically. Unless your application is made up of HTML files only, you must make sure that the .NET Framework is installed on the targeted machine in order to consider the install a success. The Launch Conditions Editor is an editor that you can use to make sure that everything that needs to be in place on the installation computer for the installation to occur is there. The Launch Conditions Editor is presented in Figure 34-34.

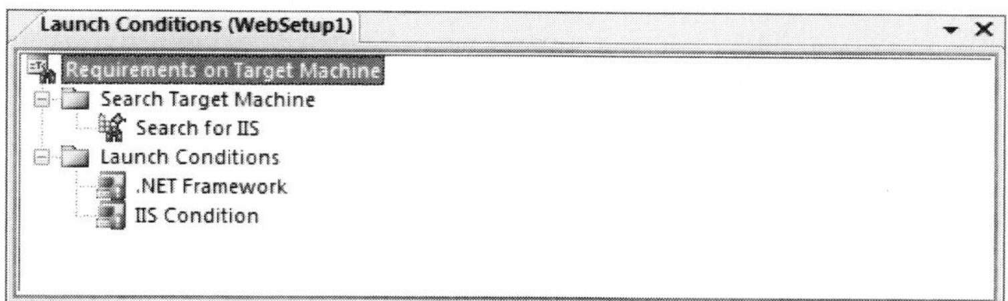

Figure 34-34

From this image, you can see some of the conditions required in this instance. The first folder defines the items that must be in place on the computer where the installation is to occur. A search is done on the computer to see whether IIS is installed. It can also check if any files or registry keys are present on the computer before the installation occurs.

The second folder is an important one because certain conditions must be in place before the installation. This folder shows two conditions. One is that the .NET Framework must be installed, and the second is that IIS must be installed. You can add these types of launch conditions by right-clicking the Requirements On Target Machine node in the dialog. You are then presented with a short list of conditions.

After a condition is in place, you can highlight the condition to see the property details of this condition in the Properties window. For instance, highlighting the IIS Condition gives you some basic properties in the Properties window. One of these is the `Condition` property. By default, for an IIS Condition, the value of the `Condition` property is the following:

```
IISVERSION >= "#4"
```

This means that the requirement for this installation is that IIS must be equal to or greater than version 4. If it is not, the installation fails. If the IIS version is 4, 5, or 6, the installation can proceed. You can feel free to change this value to whatever you deem necessary. You can change the value to `IISVERSION >= "#5"`, for example, to ensure it is either IIS 5.0, 6.0, or 7.0 at a minimum.

Another example of fine-tuning these launch conditions is the .NET Framework condition that enables you to set the minimum version of the .NET Framework you want to allow. You do this by setting the `Version` property of the condition.

Summary

As you can see, you have many possibilities for installing your ASP.NET applications! From the simplest mode of just copying the files to a remote server — sort of a save-and-run mode — to building a complex installer program that can run side events, provide dialogs, and even install extra items such as databases and more.

Just remember that when working on the installation procedures for your Web applications, you should be thinking about making the entire process logical and easy for your customers to understand. You do not want to make people's lives too difficult when they are required to programmatically install items on another machine.

Migrating Older ASP.NET Projects

In some cases, you build your ASP.NET 3.5 applications from scratch — starting everything new. In many instances, however, this is not an option. You need to take an ASP.NET application that was previously built on the 1.0, 1.1, or 2.0 versions of the .NET Framework and migrate the application so that it can run on the .NET Framework 3.5.

This appendix focuses on migrating ASP.NET 1.*x* or 2.0 applications to the 3.5 framework.

Migrating Is Not Difficult

Be aware that Microsoft has done a lot of work to ensure that the migration process from ASP.NET 1.*x* is as painless as possible. In most cases, your applications run with no changes needed.

When moving a 1.*x* or 2.0 application to 3.5, you don't have to put the ASP.NET application on a new server or make any changes to your present server beyond installing the .NET Framework 3.5.

After you install the .NET Framework 3.5, you see the framework versions on your server at C:\WINDOWS\Microsoft.NET\Framework, as illustrated in Figure A-1.

In this case, you can see that all five official versions of the .NET Framework installed, including v1.0.3705, v1.1.4322, v2.0.50727, v3.0, and v3.5.

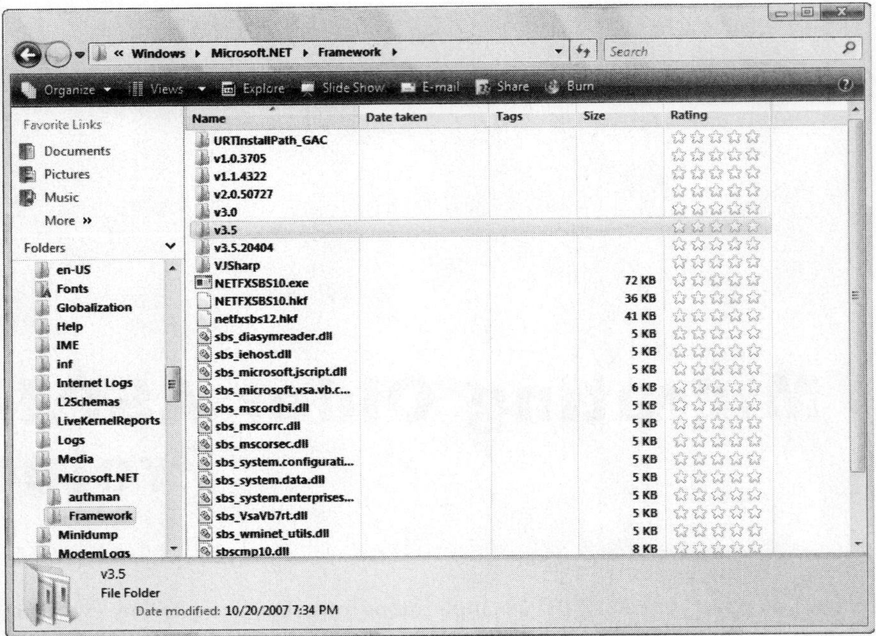

Figure A-1

Running Multiple Versions of the Framework Side by Side

From this figure, you can see that it is possible to run multiple versions of the .NET Framework side by side. ASP.NET 1.0, ASP.NET 1.1, ASP.NET 2.0, and ASP.NET 3.5 applications can all run from the same server. Different versions of ASP.NET applications that are running on the same server run in their own worker processes and are isolated from one another.

Upgrading Your ASP.NET Applications

When you install the .NET Framework 3.5, it does not remap all your ASP.NET applications so that they now run off of the new framework instance. Instead, you selectively remap applications to run off of the ASP.NET 3.5 framework.

To accomplish this task if you are migrating ASP.NET 1.*x* applications to ASP.NET 2.0, you use the ASP.NET MMC Snap-In that is a part of the .NET Framework 2.0 install. You get to this GUI-based administration application by right-clicking and selecting Properties from the provided menu using Windows XP when you are working with your application domain in Microsoft's Internet Information Services (IIS). After selecting the MMC console (the Properties option), select the ASP.NET tab and you are provided with something similar to what is shown in Figure A-2.

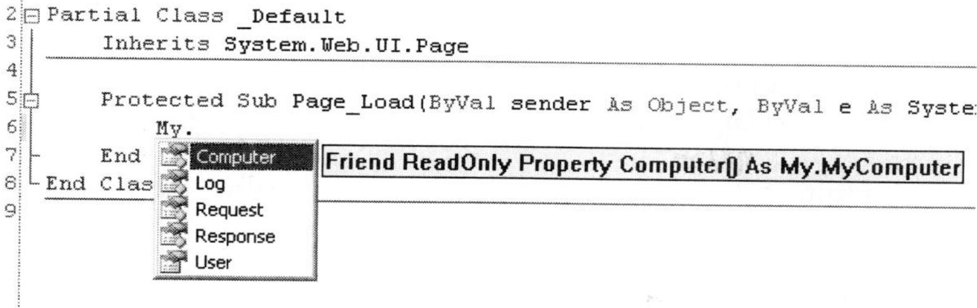

Figure A-2

You can see from this figure that an option exists for selecting the application's ASP.NET version (the top-most option). This allows you to select the version of the .NET Framework in which this ASP.NET application should run. In this case, the Wrox application on my machine was retargeted to the 2.0 release of ASP.NET when I selected 2.0.50727 in the drop-down list.

You should always test your older ASP.NET application by first running on the newer version of ASP.NET in a developer or staging environment. Do not change the version to a newer version on a production system without first testing for any failures.

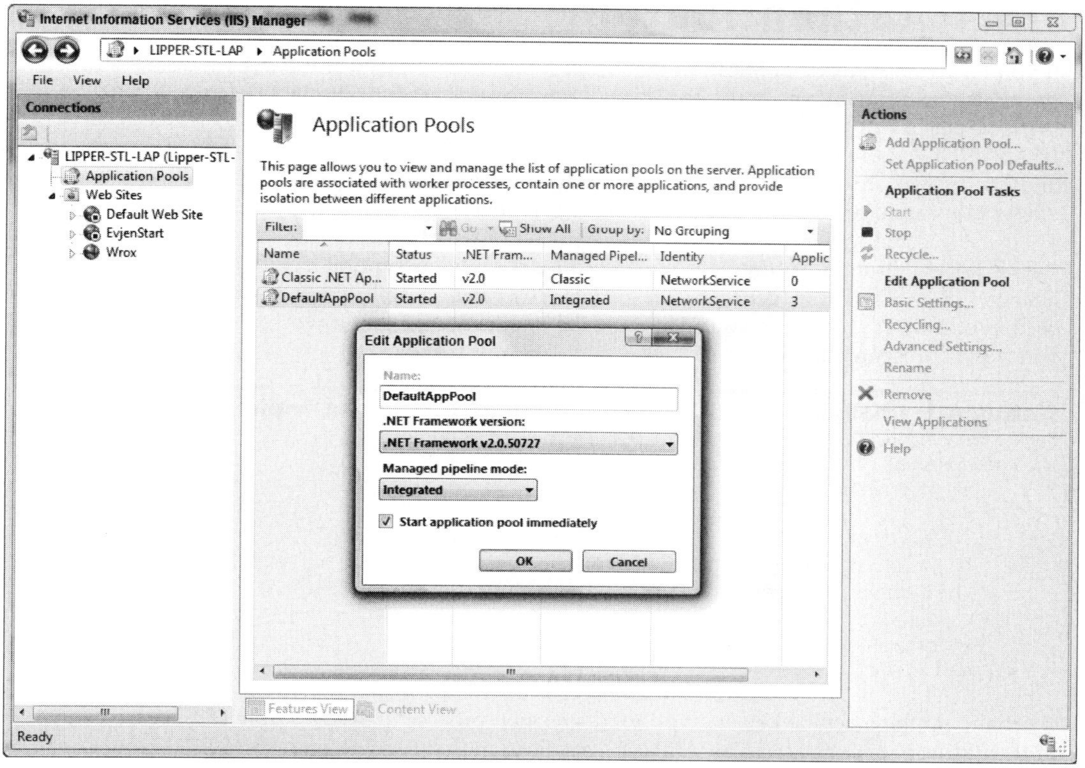

Figure A-3

If you are not ready to upgrade your entire application to a newer version of ASP.NET, one option is to create additional virtual directories in the root virtual directory of your application and target the portions of the application to the versions of the .NET Framework that you want them to run on. This enables you to take a stepped approach in your upgrade process.

If you are upgrading from ASP.NET 2.0 to ASP.NET 3.5, there really is very little that you have to do. It is true that the System.Web DLL in both versions of the framework is the same. The major differences between these two versions of the framework for ASP.NET are the use of a different language compiler and the inclusion of the `System.Core` and the `System.Web.Extensions` DLLs.

The differences are even more self-evident when working with the new IIS Manager on Windows Vista. From this management tool, you can see that the DefaultAppPool is running off the same version 2.0.50727 of the .NET Framework, as shown in Figure A-3.

Upgrading your application to ASP.NET 3.5 using Visual Studio 2008 will cause the IDE to make all the necessary changes to the application's configuration file. This is illustrated later in this appendix.

When Mixing Versions — Forms Authentication

If you have an ASP.NET application that utilizes multiple versions of the .NET Framework then, as was previously mentioned, you must be aware of how forms authentication works in ASP.NET 2.0 and 3.5.

In ASP.NET 1.*x*, the forms authentication process uses Triple DES encryption (3DES) for the encryption and decryption process of the authentication cookies. ASP.NET 2.0 and 3.5, on the other hand, use an encryption technique — AES (*Advanced Encryption Standard*).

AES is faster and more secure. However, because the two encryption techniques are different, you must change how ASP.NET 3.5 generates these keys. You can accomplish this by changing the `<machineKey>` section of the `web.config` in your ASP.NET 3.5 application so that it works with Triple DES encryption instead (as presented in Listing A-1).

Listing A-1: Changing your ASP.NET 3.5 application to use Triple DES encryption

```
<configuration>
   <system.web>

      <machineKey validation="3DES" decryption="3DES"
       validationKey="1234567890123456789012345678901234567890"
       decryptionKey="1234567890123456789012345678901234567890" />

   </system.web>
</configuration>
```

By changing the machine key encryption/decryption process to utilize Triple DES, you enable the forms authentication to work across an ASP.NET application that is using both the .NET Framework 1.*x* and 3.5. Also, this example shows the `validationKey` and `decryptionKey` attributes using a specific set of keys. These keys should be the same as those you utilize in your ASP.NET 1.*x* application.

It is important to understand that you are not required to make these changes when you are upgrading an ASP.NET 2.0 application to ASP.NET 3.5 because both are enabled to use AES encryption and are not using Triple DES encryption. If you are mixing an ASP.NET 1.*x* application along with ASP.NET 2.0 and 3.5, then you are going to have to move everything to use Triple DES encryption, as shown in Listing A-1.

Upgrading — ASP.NET Reserved Folders

As described in Chapter 1 of this book, ASP.NET 3.5 includes a number of application folders that are specific to the ASP.NET framework. In addition to the `\Bin` folder that was a reserved folder in ASP.NET 1.*x*, the following folders are all reserved in ASP.NET 2.0 and 3.5:

- `\Bin` : This folder stores the application DLL and any other DLLs used by the application. This folder was present in both ASP.NET 1.0 and 1.1. It is also present in both ASP.NET 2.0 and 3.5.
- `\App_Code` : This folder is meant to store your classes, `.wsdl` files, and typed datasets. Any items stored in this folder are automatically available to all the pages within your solution.
- `\App_Data` : This folder holds the data stores utilized by the application. It is a good, central spot to store all the data stores used by your application. The `\App_Data` folder can contain Microsoft SQL Express files (`.mdf files`), Microsoft Access files (`.mdb files`), XML files, and more.
- `\App_Themes` : Themes are a new way of providing a common look-and-feel to your site across every page. You implement a theme by using a `.skin file`, CSS files, and images used by the server controls of your site. All these elements can make a theme, which is then stored in the `\App_Themes` folder of your solution.
- `\App_GlobalResources` : This folder enables you to store resource files that can serve as data dictionaries for your applications if these applications require changes in their content (based on things such as changes in culture). You can add Assembly Resource Files (`.resx`) to the `\App_GlobalResources` folder, and they are dynamically compiled and made part of the solution for use by all the .aspx pages in the application.
- `\App_LocalResources` : Quite similar to the `\App_GlobalResources` folder, the `\App_LocalResources` folder is a pretty simple method to incorporate resources that can be used for a specific page in your application.
- `\App_WebReferences` : You can use the `\App_WebReferences` folder and have automatic access to the remote Web services referenced from your application.
- `\App_Browsers` : This folder holds `.browser` files, which are XML files used to identify the browsers making requests to the application and to elucidate the capabilities these browsers have.

The addition of the `App_` prefix to the folder names ensures that you already do not have a folder with a similar name in your ASP.NET 1.*x* applications. If, by chance, you do have a folder with one of the names you plan to use, you should change the name of your previous folder to something else because these ASP.NET 3.5 application folder names are unchangeable.

ASP.NET 3.5 Pages Come as XHTML

ASP.NET 3.5, by default, constructs its pages to be XHTML-compliant. You can see the setting for XHTML 1.0 Transitional in the Visual Studio 2008 IDE. This is illustrated in Figure A-4.

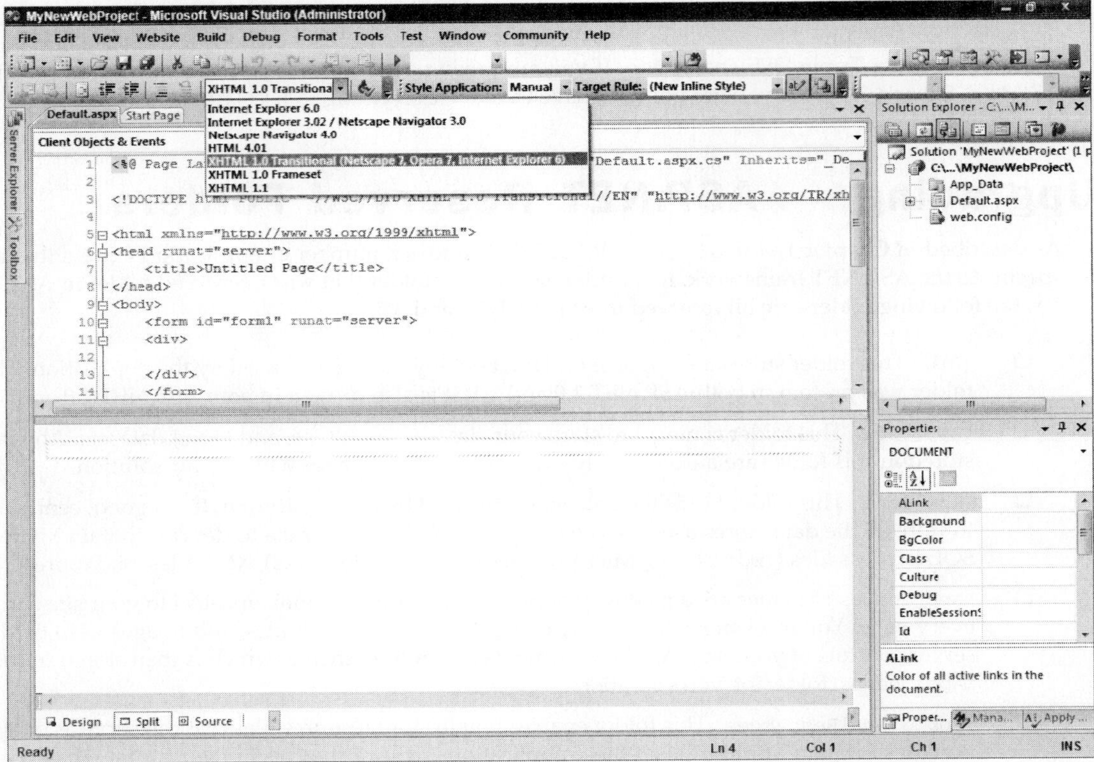

Figure A-4

In this case, you can see that you have a list of options for determining how the ASP.NET application outputs the code for the pages. By default, it is set to `XHTML 1.0 Transitional (Netscape 7, Opera 7, Internet Explorer 6)`. You can also make a change to the `web.config` file so that the output is not XHTML-specific (as illustrated in Listing A-2).

Listing A-2: Reversing the XHTML capabilities of your ASP.NET 3.5 application

```
<configuration>
   <system.web>

      <xhtmlConformance mode="Legacy" />

   </system.web>
</configuration>
```

Setting the `mode` attribute to `Legacy` ensures that XHTML is not used, but instead, ASP.NET 3.5 defaults to what was used in ASP.NET 1.*x*.

It is important to note that using the `Legacy` setting as a value for the `mode` attribute will sometimes cause you problems for your application if you are utilizing AJAX. One of the symptoms that you might experience is that instead of doing a partial page update (as AJAX does), you will get a full-page postback instead. This is due to the fact that the page is not XHTML compliant. The solution is to set the mode property to `Traditional` or `Strict` and to make your pages XHTML compliant.

If you take this approach, you also have to make some additional changes to any new ASP.NET 3.5 pages that you create in Visual Studio 2008. Creating a new ASP.NET 3.5 page in Visual Studio 2008 produces the results illustrated in Listing A-3.

Listing A-3: A typical ASP.NET 3.5 page

```
<%@ Page Language="VB" %>

<!DOCTYPE html PUBLIC "-//W3C//DTD XHTML 1.0 Transitional//EN"
 "http://www.w3.org/TR/xhtml1/DTD/xhtml1-transitional.dtd">

<script runat="server">

</script>

<html xmlns="http://www.w3.org/1999/xhtml">
<head runat="server">
    <title>Untitled Page</title>
</head>
<body>
    <form id="form1" runat="server">
    <div>

    </div>
    </form>
</body>
</html>
```

From this, you can see that a `<!DOCTYPE ...>` element is included at the top of the page. This element signifies to some browsers (such as Microsoft's Internet Explorer) that the page is XHTML-compliant. If this is not the case, then you want to remove this element altogether from your ASP.NET 3.5 page. In addition to the `<!DOCTYPE>` element, you also want to change the `<html>` element on the page from:

```
<html xmlns="http://www.w3.org/1999/xhtml">
```

to the following:

```
<html>
```

The original also signifies that the page is XHTML-compliant (even if it is not) and must be removed if your pages are not XHTML-compliant.

No Hard-Coded .js Files in ASP.NET 3.5

ASP.NET 1.*x* provides some required JavaScript files as hard-coded `.js` files. For instance, in ASP.NET a JavaScript requirement was necessary for the validation server controls and the smart navigation capabilities to work. If you are utilizing either of these features in your ASP.NET 1.*x* applications, ASP.NET could pick up the installed `.js` files and use them directly.

These `.js` files are found at `C:\WINDOWS\Microsoft.NET\Framework\v1.0.3705\ASP.NETClientFiles`. Looking at this folder, you see three `.js` files — two of which deal with the smart navigation feature (`SmartNav.js and SmartNavIE5.js`) and one that deals with the validation server controls (`WebUIValidation.js`). Because they are hard-coded `.js` files, it is possible to open them and change or alter the code in these files to better suit your needs. In some cases, developers have done just that.

If you have altered these JavaScript files in any manner, you must change some code when migrating your ASP.NET application to ASP.NET 2.0 or 3.5. ASP.NET 3.5 dynamically includes `.js` files from the System.Web.dll instead of hard-coding them on the server. In ASP.NET 3.5, the files are included via a new handler — WebResource.axd.

Converting ASP.NET 1.*x* Applications in Visual Studio 2008

As previously mentioned, if you have a pre-existing ASP.NET 1.*x* application, you can run the application on the ASP.NET 2.0 runtime by simply making the appropriate changes in IIS to the application pool. Using the IIS manager or the MMC Snap-In, you can select the appropriate framework on which to run your application from the provided drop-down list.

ASP.NET 3.5 applications work with the Visual Studio 2008 IDE. If you still intend to work with ASP.NET 1.0 or 1.1 applications, you should keep Visual Studio .NET 2002 or 2003, respectively, installed on your machine. Installing Visual Studio 2008 gives you a complete, new copy of Visual Studio and does not upgrade the previous Visual Studio .NET 2002 or 2003 IDEs. All copies of Visual Studio can run side by side.

If you want to run ASP.NET 1.*x* applications on the .NET Framework, but you also want to convert the entire ASP.NET project for the application to ASP.NET 3.5, you can use Visual Studio 2008 to help you with the conversion process. After the project is converted in this manner, you can take advantage of the features that ASP.NET 3.5 offers.

To convert your ASP.NET 1.*x* application to an ASP.NET 3.5 application, you simply open up the solution in Visual Studio 2008. This starts the conversion process. It is important to note that Visual Studio 2008 converts the application to an ASP.NET 2.0 application first and then asks if you want to take the extra step to convert the application to an ASP.NET 3.5 application.

When you open the solution in Visual Studio 2008, it warns you that your solution will be upgraded if you continue. It does this by popping up the Visual Studio Conversion Wizard, as presented in Figure A-5.

Notice that the upgrade wizard has been dramatically improved from Visual Studio .NET 2003 to this newer one provided by Visual Studio 2008. To start the conversion process of your ASP.NET 1.*x* applications, click the Next button in the wizard. This example uses the open source Issue Tracker Starter Kit — an ASP.NET 1.1 starter kit found on the ASP.NET Web site at `www.asp.net`.

The first step in the process is deciding whether you want the Visual Studio 2008 Conversion Wizard to create a backup of the ASP.NET 1.1 application before it attempts to convert it to an ASP.NET 2.0 application (remember that it first converts to an ASP.NET 2.0 application before asking you to convert it to an ASP.NET 3.5 application). Definitely, if this is your only copy of the application, you want to make a backup copy even though this conversion wizard does a good job in the conversion process. The conversion wizard also enables you to specify the location where you want to store the backup copy. This step is presented in Figure A-6.

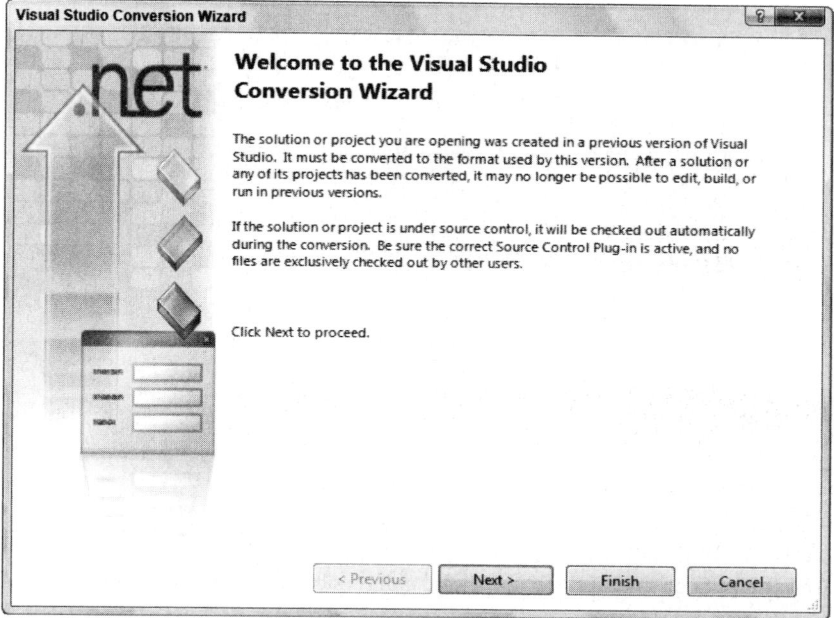

Figure A-5

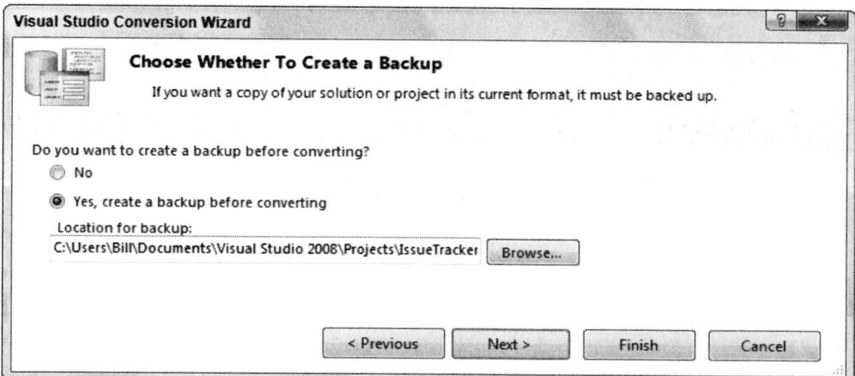

Figure A-6

The final step is a warning on how to handle the project if it is controlled by a source control system. If it is, you want to ensure that the project or any of its components are checked out by someone. You also want to ensure that the check-in capabilities are enabled. This warning is shown in Figure A-7.

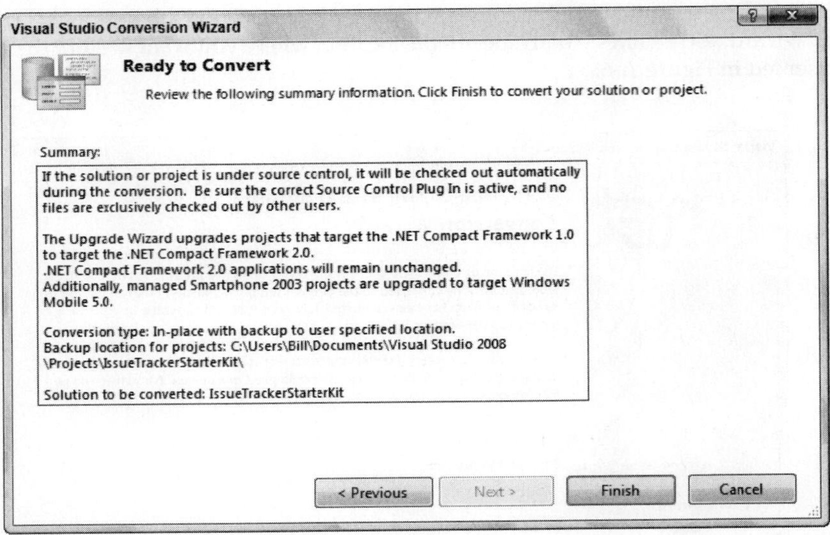

Figure A-7

When you are ready to convert the project, click the Finish button. The actual conversion process could take some time, so allow a few minutes for it. When the process is complete, you are offered a completion notification that also enables you to see the conversion log that was generated from the conversion process (Figure A-8).

After the project is converted, you are presented with the conversion log, as shown in Figure A-9.

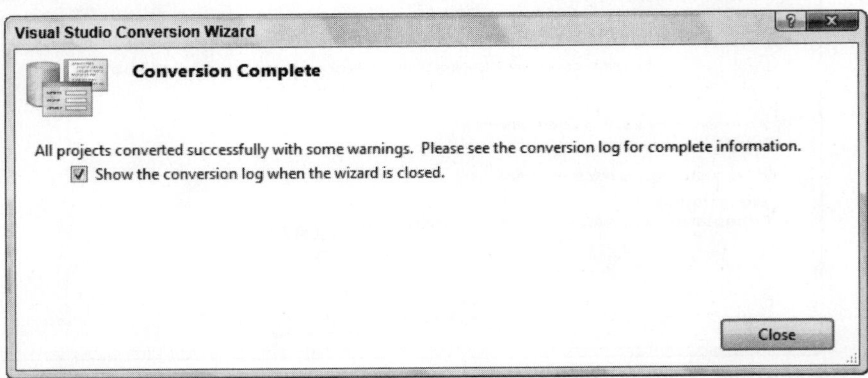

Figure A-8

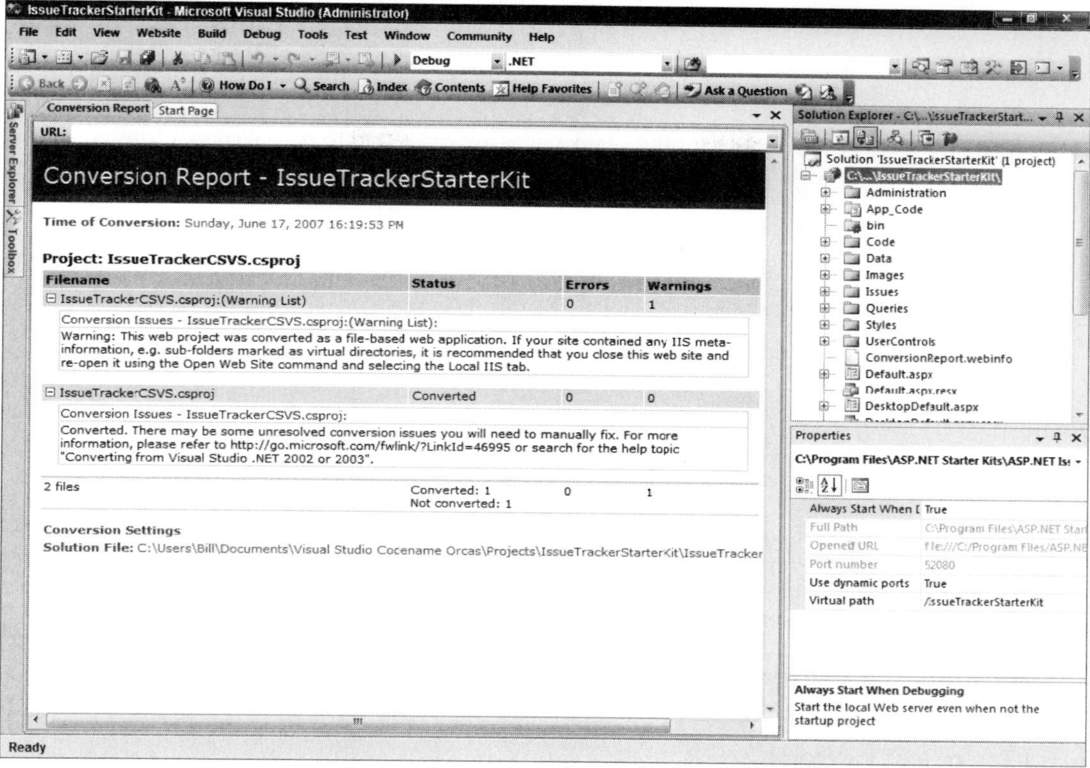

Figure A-9

As you look over the project in the Solution Explorer, notice that some major changes have been made to the project. Some of these changes include the following:

- All class files are removed from their folders and placed in the new `App_Code` folder. The folder from which the class files were removed is left in place, even if the folder is empty after all the class files are removed.
- All the Visual Studio .NET 2002/2003 Web project files are deleted because Visual Studio 2008 does not use these any longer.
- The application's DLL is deleted from the `Bin` folder.
- All the `.aspx` pages have had their `@Page` directives changed. An example from the `Default.aspx` page shows that the previousc `@Page` directive was constructed as:

```
<%@ Page Language="c#" CodeBehind="Default.aspx.cs" AutoEventWireup="false"
  Inherits="ASPNET.StarterKit.IssueTracker._Default" %>
```

- After the conversion process, the @Page directive now appears as:

```
<%@ Page Language="c#" Inherits="ASPNET.StarterKit.IssueTracker._Default"
   CodeFile="Default.aspx.cs" %>
```

- The code-behind classes for the `.aspx` pages are converted to partial classes (presented here in C#). This is what the code behind for the `Default.aspx` page looked like before the conversion:

```
public class _Default : System.Web.UI.Page
{
  // Code removed for clarity
}
```

- After the conversion process, the page class appears as shown here:

```
public partial class _Default : System.Web.UI.Page
{
  // Code removed for clarity
}
```

For a full list of changes, look for a `ConversionReport.webinfo` file in the root of your solution. The partial text from this example conversion is presented in Listing A-4. This conversion report can get quite large, but pay attention to everything that was done to your project. In the following listing, some of the four pages of this conversion report are shown.

Listing A-4: The ConversionReport.webinfo file

```
This report shows the steps taken to convert your Web application from ASP.NET 1.1
to ASP.NET 2.0.
There may be some unresolved conversion issues you will need to manually fix.
For more information, please refer to http://go.microsoft.com/fwlink/?LinkId=46995
or search for the help topic "Converting from Visual Studio .NET 2002 or 2003".
Conversion Started on project file IssueTrackerCSVS.csproj at April 17 2008,
16:48:39.

=========================ERRORS===================

=========================WARNINGS=================
Warning: This web project was converted as a file-based web application. If your
site contained any IIS meta-information, e.g. sub-folders marked as virtual
directories, it is recommended that you close this web site and re-open it using
the Open Web Site command and selecting the Local IIS tab.

=========================COMMENTS=================
Web.Config: Added 'xhtmlConformance' attribute.
Web.Config: added a reference for assembly System.DirectoryServices.
Removed attribute AutoEventWireup from file Default.aspx.
Removed attribute CodeBehind from file Default.aspx.
Removed attribute AutoEventWireup from file DesktopDefault.aspx.
Removed attribute CodeBehind from file DesktopDefault.aspx.
Warning: Access level of 'Page_Load' changed to 'protected' in file
DesktopDefault.aspx.cs (Line 55).
Warning: Access level of 'Login' changed to 'protected' in file
```

```
DesktopDefault.aspx.cs (Line 62).
Warning: Access level of 'btnRegister_Click' changed to 'protected' in file
DesktopDefault.aspx.cs (Line 74).
Removed attribute Codebehind from file Global.asax.
Removed attribute AutoEventWireup from file LogOff.aspx.
Removed attribute CodeBehind from file LogOff.aspx.
Warning: Access level of 'Page_Load' changed to 'protected' in file LogOff.aspx.cs
(Line 49).
Removed attribute AutoEventWireup from file NoProjects.aspx.
Removed attribute CodeBehind from file NoProjects.aspx.
Removed attribute AutoEventWireup from file Register.aspx.
Removed attribute CodeBehind from file Register.aspx.
Warning: Access level of 'SaveUser' changed to 'protected' in file Register.aspx.cs
(Line 55).
Removed attribute AutoEventWireup from file administration\projects\addproject.aspx.
Removed attribute CodeBehind from file administration\projects\addproject.aspx.
Warning: Access level of 'Page_Load' changed to 'protected' in file
Removed file Bin\ASPNET.StarterKit.IssueTracker.dll.
Removed file IssueTrackerCSVS.csproj.
Removed file IssueTrackerCSVS.csproj.webinfo.
Project IssueTrackerCSVS.csproj has been converted successfully at April 17 2008,
16:50:12.
```

After the project is converted, you can build and run the application from Visual Studio 2008. The application is now built and run on the ASP.NET 2.0 runtime.

Remember: Do not upgrade production solutions without testing your programs first in a staging environment to ensure that your application is not affected by the changes between versions 1.0/1.1 and 2.0 or 3.5 of the .NET Framework.

Migrating from ASP.NET 2.0 to 3.5

Visual Studio 2008 is the first version of the IDE that enables you to build applications at more than one framework. For instance, Visual Studio .NET 2002 would only let you build 1.0 applications. If you wanted to build .NET Framework 1.1 applications, then you were required to install and use Visual Studio .NET 2003. At the same time, Visual Studio .NET 2003 would not enable you to build .NET Framework 1.0 applications, meaning that if you were dealing with applications that made use of either framework, then you were required to have both IDEs on your computer.

When you create a new project in Visual Studio 2008, you have the option of targeting the project at any of the following frameworks:

- .NET Framework 2.0
- .NET Framework 3.0
- .NET Framework 3.5

Although you can open your .NET 2.0 applications and work with them directly in Visual Studio 2008, when you first open an ASP.NET 2.0 application in the IDE, you will be prompted to update the application to ASP.NET 3.5. The dialog box that you are presented with is shown in Figure A-10.

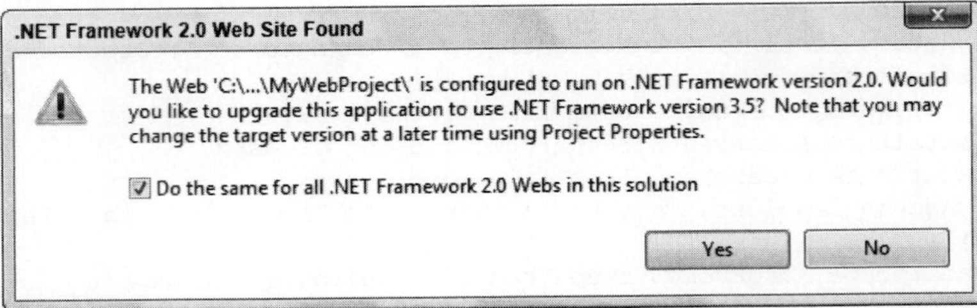

Figure A-10

Selecting Yes from this dialog box upgrades your ASP.NET 2.0 application to ASP.NET 3.5. You can also right-click on the project in the Solution Explorer and select Property Pages from the provided menu. This gives you a dialog box that enables you to change the target framework of the application. In this case, you can see the default options on a Microsoft Vista computer (as shown in Figure A-11).

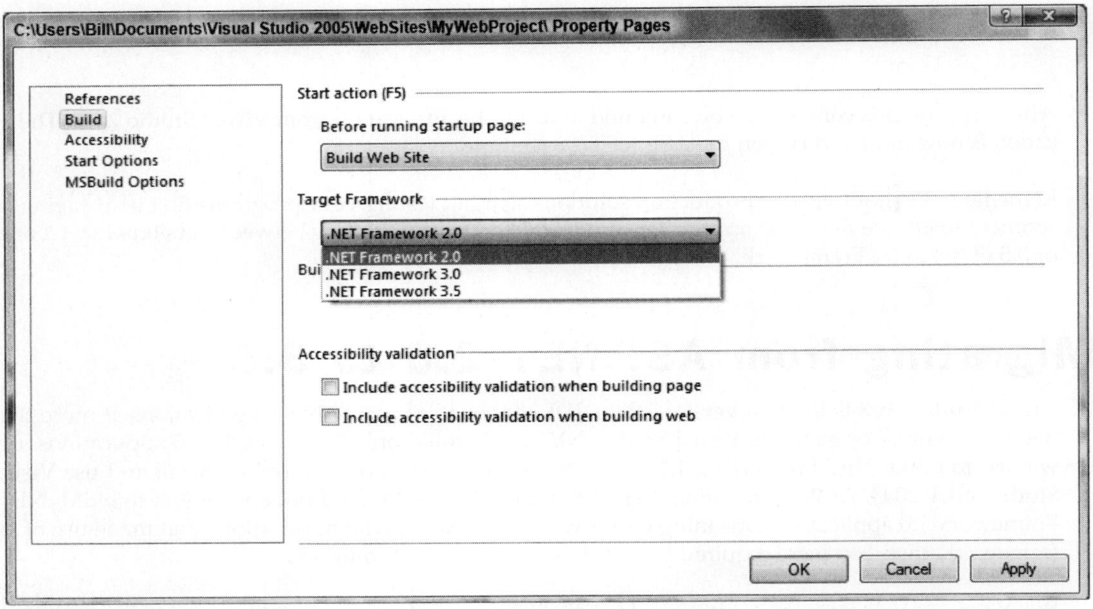

C:\Users\Bill\Documents\Visual Studio 2005\WebSites\MyWebProject\ Property Pages

References
Build
Accessibility
Start Options
MSBuild Options

Start action (F5)
Before running startup page:
Build Web Site
Target Framework
.NET Framework 2.0
.NET Framework 2.0
.NET Framework 3.0
.NET Framework 3.5
Accessibility validation
Include accessibility validation when building page
Include accessibility validation when building web
OK
Cancel
Apply

Figure A-11

Although you can change the target framework as is illustrated in Figure A-11, you will find that it is better to use Visual Studio 2008, as is shown in Figure A-10, to upgrade your ASP.NET applications. Although ASP.NET 2.0 and ASP.NET 3.5 use the same .NET Framework 2.0 runtime, there are some extra bolted-on additions available to ASP.NET 3.5 applications. The hooks into these extra capabilities are established through changes made by Visual Studio 2008 to the `web.config` file in the upgrade process. Some of the changes are detailed in the next few listings.

The first major change to the `web.config` file is presented here in Listing A-5.

Listing A-5: Adding the .NET 3.5 language compilers

```
<system.codedom>
   <compilers>
      <compiler language="c#;cs;csharp" extension=".cs"
       type="Microsoft.CSharp.CSharpCodeProvider,System, Version=2.0.0.0,
       Culture=neutral, PublicKeyToken=b77a5c561934e089" compilerOptions="/w:1">
         <providerOption name="CompilerVersion" value="v3.5"/>
      </compiler>
      <compiler language="vb;vbs;visualbasic;vbscript" extension=".vb"
       type="Microsoft.VisualBasic.VBCodeProvider, System, Version=2.0.0.0,
       Culture=neutral, PublicKeyToken=b77a5c561934e089"
       compilerOptions="/optioninfer+">
         <providerOption name="CompilerVersion" value="v3.5"/>
      </compiler>
   </compilers>
</system.codedom>
```

From this bit of the `web.config`, you can see that there are two new compilers provided in this configuration code. Both the C# 3.5 and Visual Basic 3.5 compilers are targeted with ASP.NET 3.5.

The next important change is in the `<compilation>` section of the `web.config`, as shown here in Listing A-6.

Listing A-6: Adding new DLLs to ASP.NET with the 3.5 release

```
<compilation debug="true">
   <assemblies>
      <add assembly="System.Core, Version=2.0.0.0, Culture=neutral,
       PublicKeyToken=B77A5C561934E089"/>
      <add assembly="System.Web.Extensions, Version=2.0.0.0, Culture=neutral,
       PublicKeyToken=31BF3856AD364E35"/>
   </assemblies>
</compilation>
```

In ASP.NET 3.5, the `System.Core` and `System.Web.Extensions` DLLs are added and made available to this new version of the framework.

In addition to these two major additions to the `web.config`, you will find large sections of other changes that mainly deal with the new AJAX capabilities that ASP.NET 3.5 provides. If you are not using ASP.NET AJAX in your applications, you can then delete these sections from the configuration file.

B

ASP.NET Ultimate Tools

I've always believed that I'm only as good as my tools. I've spent years combing the Internet for excellent tools to help me be a more effective developer. There are thousands of tools out there to be sure, many overlapping in functionality with others. Some tools do one thing incredibly well and others aim to be a Swiss Army knife with dozens of small conveniences packed into their tiny toolbars. Here is a short, exclusive list of some of the ASP.NET tools that I keep turning back to. These are tools that I find myself using consistently while developing ASP.NET-based Web sites. I recommend that you give them a try if they sound useful. Many are free; some are not. In my opinion, each is worth at least a trial on your part, and many are worth your hard-earned money as they'll save you precious time.

These tools can be easily searched for in your favorite search engine and found in the first page. For those that are harder to find, I've included URLs. I also encourage you to check out my annually updated Ultimate Tools List at `www.hanselman.com/tools` and you might also enjoy my weekly podcast at `www.hanselminutes.com` as we often discover and share new tools for the developer enthusiast.

Enjoy!

–Scott Hanselman

Debugging Made Easier

"There has never been an unexpectedly short debugging period in the history of computers."
— Steven Levy

Firebug

There are so many great things about this application one could write a book about it. Firebug is actually a Firefox plug-in, so you'll need to download and install Firefox to use it.

The screenshot below shows Firebug analyzing all the network traffic required to download my page. This shows a very detailed graph of when each asset is downloaded and how long it took from first byte to last byte as seen in Figure B-1.

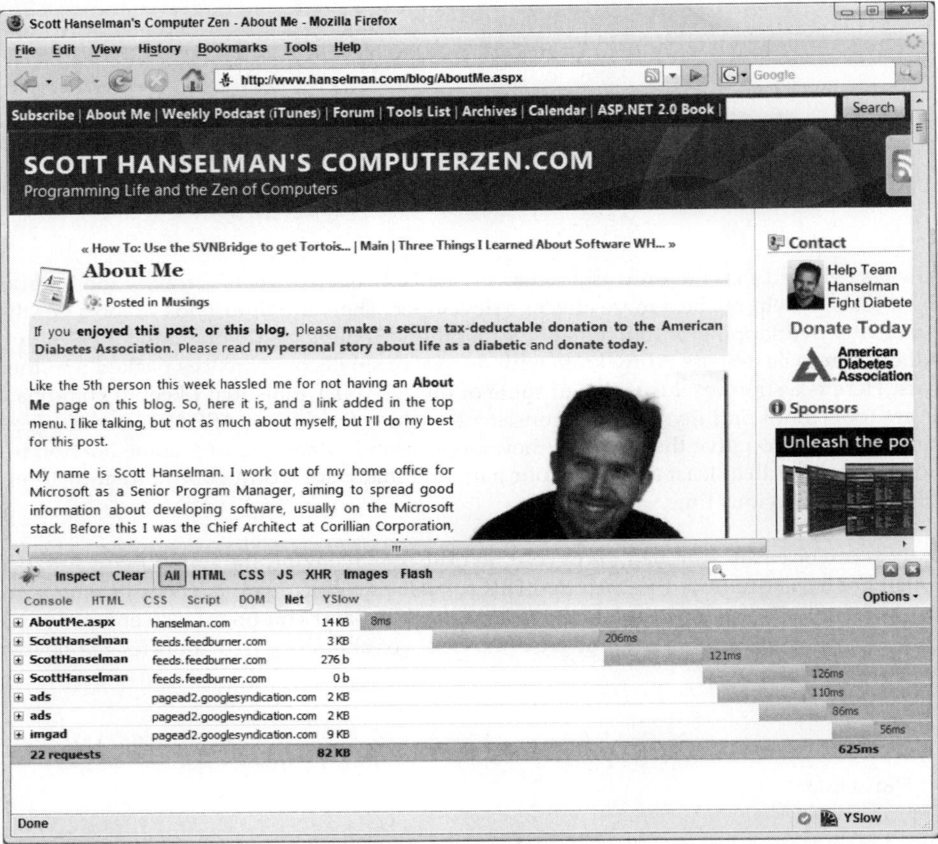

Figure B-1

It has a wealth of interesting features that allow you to inspect HTML and deeply analyze your CSS, including visualization of some more complicated CSS techniques such as offsets, margins, borders, and padding. Firebug also includes a powerful JavaScript debugger that will enable you to debug JavaScript within Firefox. Even more interesting is its JavaScript profiler and a very detailed error handler that helps you chase down even the most obscure bugs.

Finally, Firebug includes an interactive console feature like the Visual Studio Immediate window that lets you execute JavaScript on-the-fly, as well as console debugging that enables classic "got here" debugging. Firebug is indispensable for the Web developer and it's highly recommended.

> **There is also Firebug Lite in the form of a JavaScript file. You can add it to the pages in which you want a console debugger to work in Internet Explorer, Opera, or Safari. This file will enable you to do "got here" debugging using the Firebug JavaScript `console.log` method.**

YSlow

YSlow is an add-on to an add-on. Brought to you by Yahoo!, YSlow extends Firebug and analyzes your Web pages using Yahoo!'s 13 rules for fast Web sites. In Figure B-2, you can see Yahoo!'s YSlow analyzing my blog.

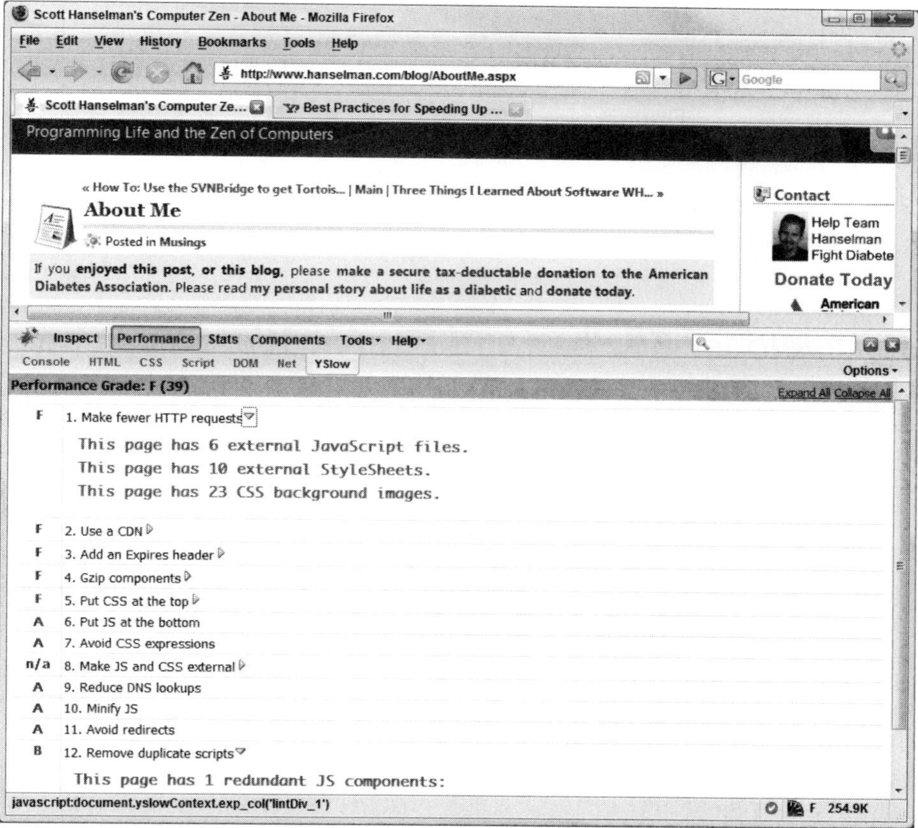

Figure B-2

In some instances, I do well, but in others I receive a failing grade. For example, rule number one says to make fewer HTTP requests. My site has too many external assets. Each one of these requires an HTTP request, so I suspect I could speed up my site considerably with some refactoring.

Not every rule will apply to you exactly, but Yahoo! knows what they're doing and it's worth your time to use this tool and consider your grades in each category. At the very least, you'll gain insight into how your application behaves. For example, Figure B-3 shows how many HTTP requests and bytes are transmitted with an empty cache versus a primed one.

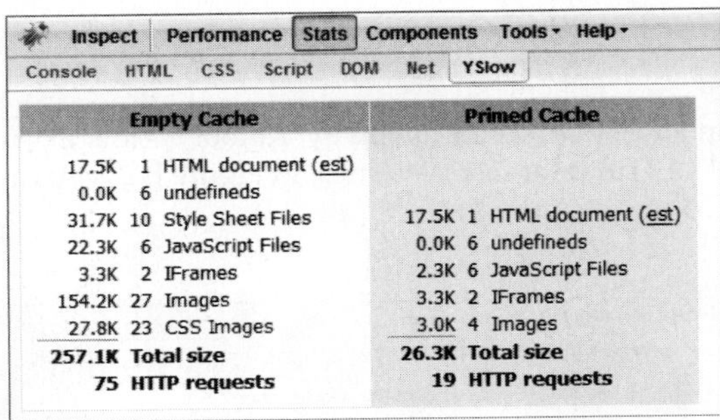

Figure B-3

YSlow is free and is an excellent resource to help you get a clear understanding about how hard the client's browser must work in order to view your Web site.

IE WebDeveloper Toolbar and Firefox WebDeveloper

Both of these toolbars are free and absolutely essential for Web development. The IE Web Developer Toolbar is from Microsoft and extends Internet Explorer with a docked "Explorer Bar" offering features such as DOM inspection and element outlining. You can edit the CSS and see what styles are applied to specific elements as seen in Figure B-4.

Firefox has a similar but even more powerful Web Developer Toolbar created by Chris Pederick. It takes a slightly different direction for its user interface by including a number of menus, each literally chock full of menu options. You can disable cookies, CSS, images, inspect elements, form inputs, and outline tables, as shown in Figure B-5.

ASP.NET developers today need their sites to look great in both browsers. These two toolbars put a host of usefulness at your fingertips. Highly recommended.

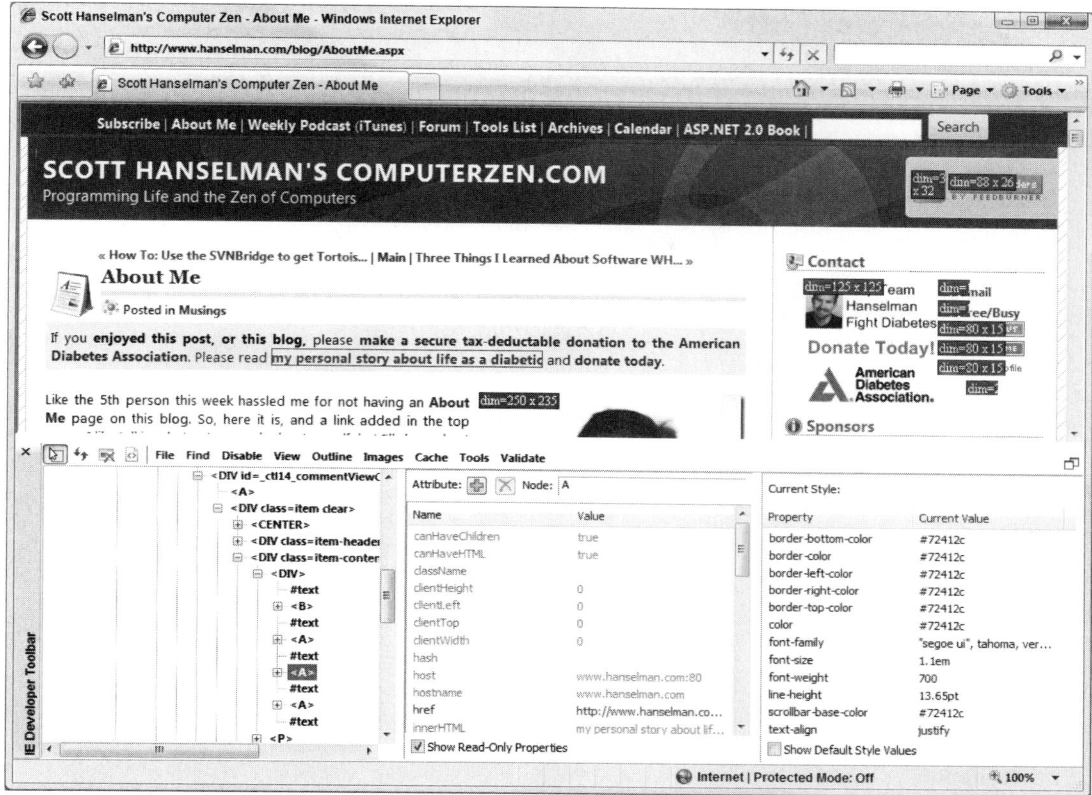

Figure B-4

Aptana Studio — JavaScript IDE

Aptana offers a pay-for Professional Edition and a Free Community Edition. It's a Web development environment based on the Eclipse codebase. It's not optimized for ASP.NET, but it includes some amazing JavaScript-specific support that makes it worth looking at for AJAX or JavaScript heavy sites.

One of Aptana's most compelling features is its understanding of browser compatibility of JavaScript properties and functions. Aptana's IntelliSense includes icons for the various browsers and dims them out appropriately for unsupported features, for not only JavaScript, but also HTML and CSS, as well.

The Professional Edition also includes a JSON (JavaScript Object Notation) editor with syntax highlighting for JSON datasets. This is a great feature if you're passing a large and deep dataset back and forth via AJAX.

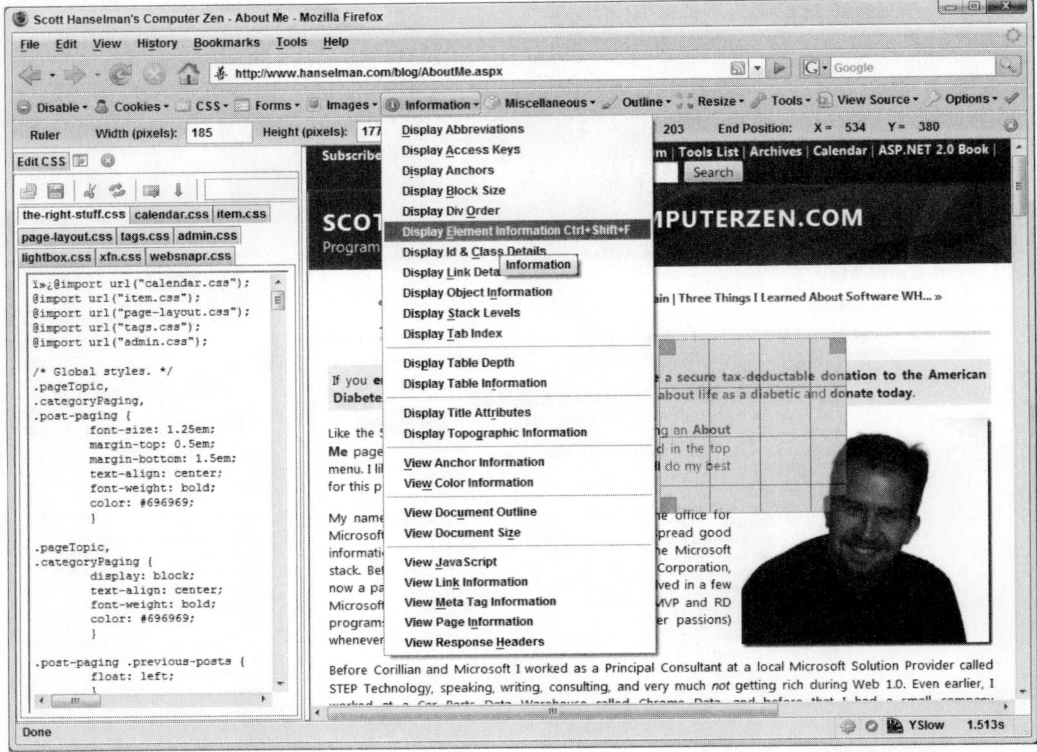

Figure B-5

Aptana also includes all the major open source AJAX libraries such as Prototype and Scriptaculous, as shown in Figure B-6. Adding support for them simply requires checking a check box. It also integrates with Firebug. The Pro edition integrates with Internet Explorer.

Profilers: dotTrace or ANTS

If you're not measuring your code with a good profiler you really don't realize what you're missing out on. Only a profiler can give you extensive metrics and a clear understanding of what your code is doing.

Visual Studio Team System 2008 includes a Profiler in the top-level Analyze menu. If you're not running VSTS, there are excellent third-party profilers such as JetBrains' dotTrace and Red Gate Software's ANTS that are worth your 10-day trial.

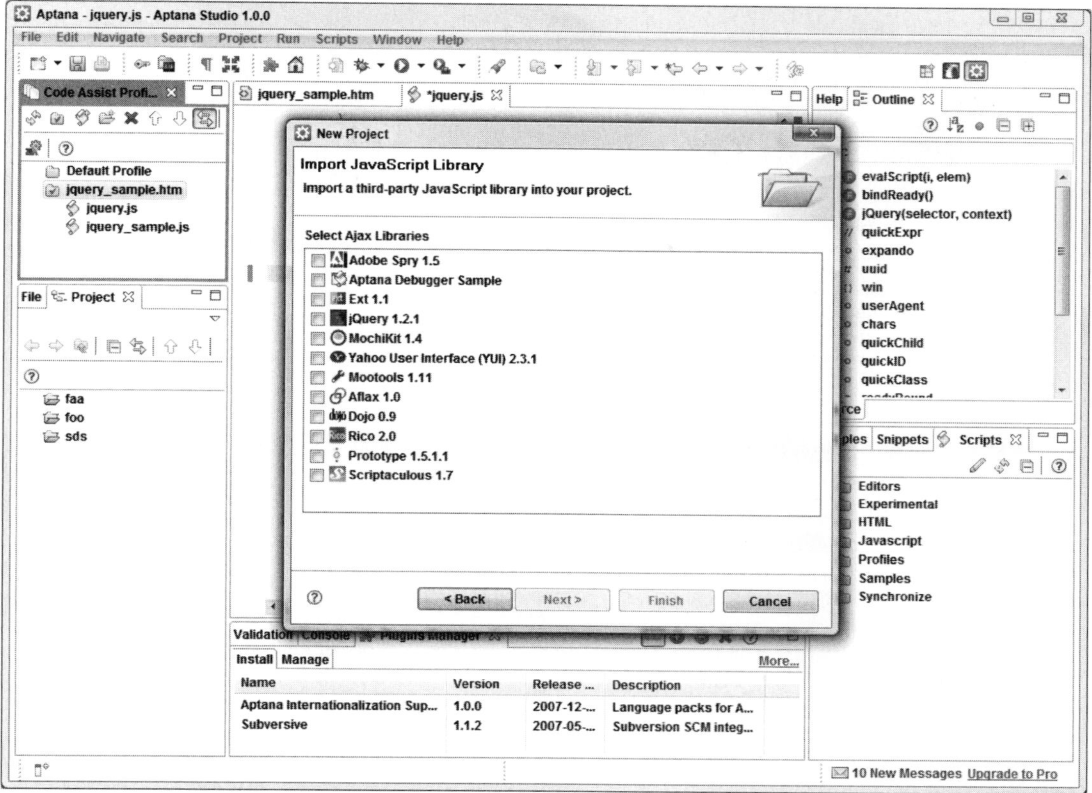

Figure B-6

.NET Profilers instruments a runtime session of your code and measure how many times each line is hit and how much time is spent executing that line, as shown in Figure B-7. They create a hierarchical series of reports that allow you to analyze time spent not only within a method, but within child methods executed through the stack. Reports can be saved and multiple versions can be analyzed as you improve your applications, revision after revision.

If you haven't already done so, consider adding profiling of your ASP.NET application to your software development lifecycle. You'd be surprised to learn how few developers formally analyze and profile their applications. Set aside some time to profile an application that you've never looked at before and you'll be surprised how much faster it can be made using analysis from a tool such as ANTS or dotTrace.

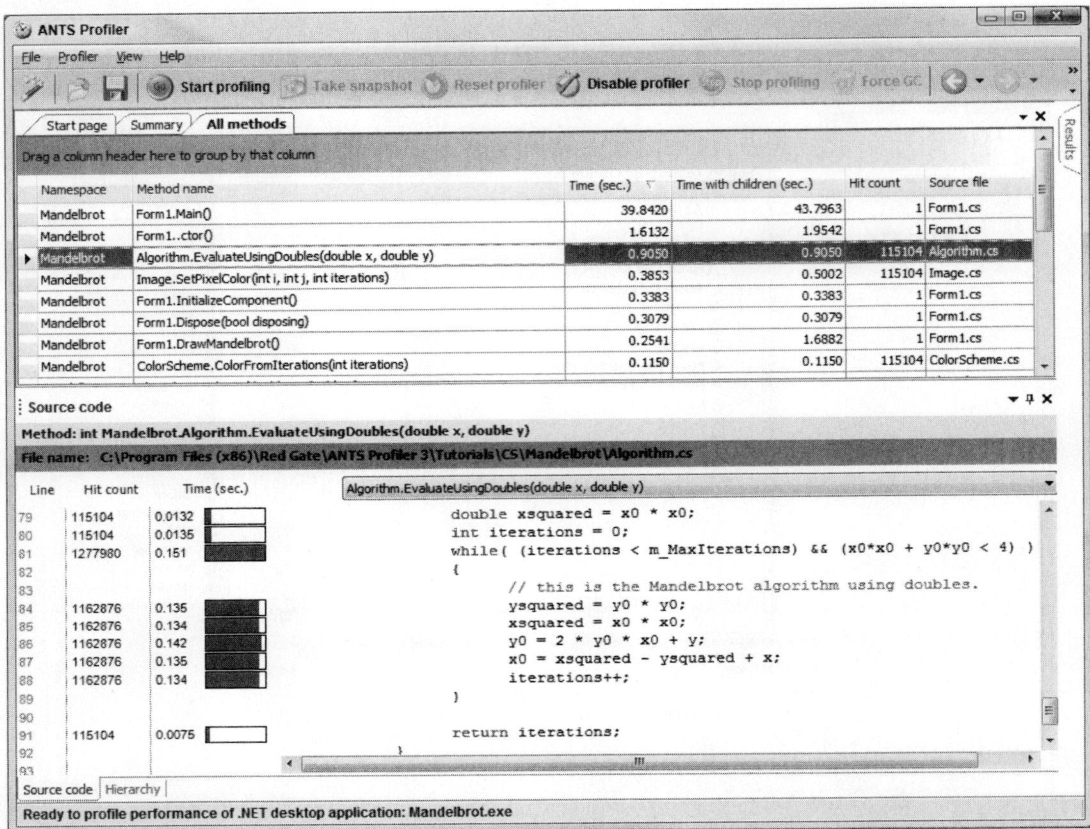

Figure B-7

References

"He who lends a book is an idiot. He who returns the book is more of an idiot." — Anonymous, Arabic Proverb

PositionIsEverything.net, QuirksMode.org, and HTMLDog.com

When you're creating Web sites that need to look nice on all browsers, you're bound to bump into bugs, "features," and general differences in the popular browsers. Web pages are composed of a large combination of standards (HTML, CSS, JS). These standards are not only open to interpretation, but their implementations can differ in subtle ways, especially when they interact.

Reference Web sites, such as PositionIsEverything and QuirksMode, collect hundreds of these hacks and workarounds. Then they catalog them for your benefit. Many of these features aren't designed, but rather discovered or stumbled upon.

HTMLDog is a fantastic Web designer's resource for HTML and CSS. It's full of tutorials, articles, and a large reference section specific to XHTML. QuirksMode includes many resources for learning JavaScript and CSS and includes many test and demo pages demonstrating the quirks. PositionIsEverything is hosted by John and Holly Bergevin and showcases some of the most obscure bugs and browser oddities with demo examples for everything.

Visibone

Visibone is known for its amazing reference cards and charts that showcase Color, Fonts, HTML, JavaScript, and CSS. Visibone reference cards and booklets are available online and are very reasonably priced. The best value is the Browser Book available at `www.visibone.com/products/browserbook.html`. I recommend the laminated version. Be sure to put your name on it because your co-workers will make it disappear.

www.asp.net

I work for Microsoft on the team that runs `www.asp.net`. The site is a huge resource for learning about ASP.NET and the various technologies around it. Figure B-8 shows part of the Community page for the site, where you'll link to my Weblog, among others, and links to other community resources. The `www.asp.net/learn/` section includes dozens and dozens of videos about general ASP.NET and how to use it.

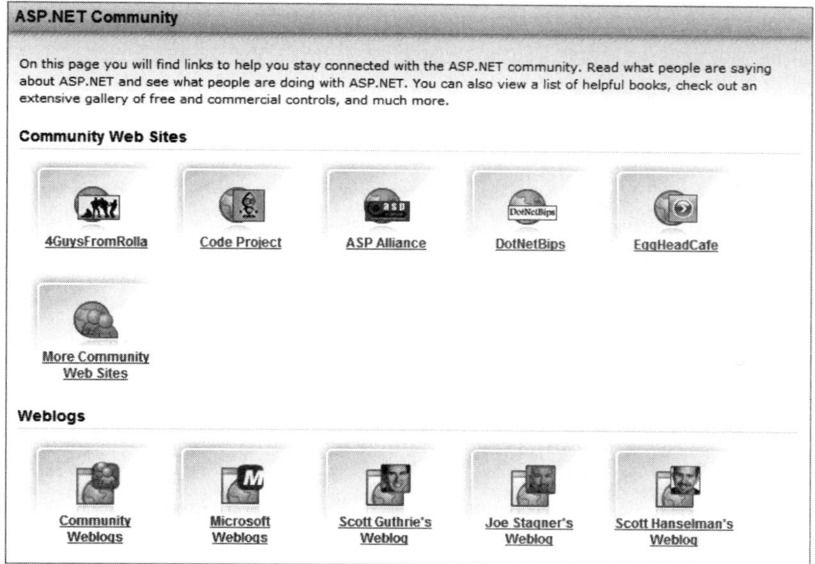

Figure B-8

Tidying Up Your Code

"After every war someone has to tidy up." — Wislawa Szymborska

Refactor! for ASP.NET from Devexpress

Refactoring support in Visual Studio 2008 continues to get better. The third-party utilities continue to push the envelope adding value to the IDE. Refactor! for ASP.NET adds refactoring to the ASP.NET source view.

For example, in Figure B-9 while hovering over the Refactor! context menu and selecting the "Extract UserControl" refactoring, a preview of the changes that *would* be made appear within the source view. A new UserControl would be created in a new file `WebUserControl0.ascx`. The currently selected label control would turn into a `WebUserControl0` control. You can then choose a new name for the UserControl immediately after the refactoring.

The most amazing thing about Refactor! for ASP.NET is that it's a free download from `www.devexpress.com/Products/NET/IDETools/RefactorASP/`. It includes 28 refactorings that make it easier to simplify your code and your ASP.NET markup.

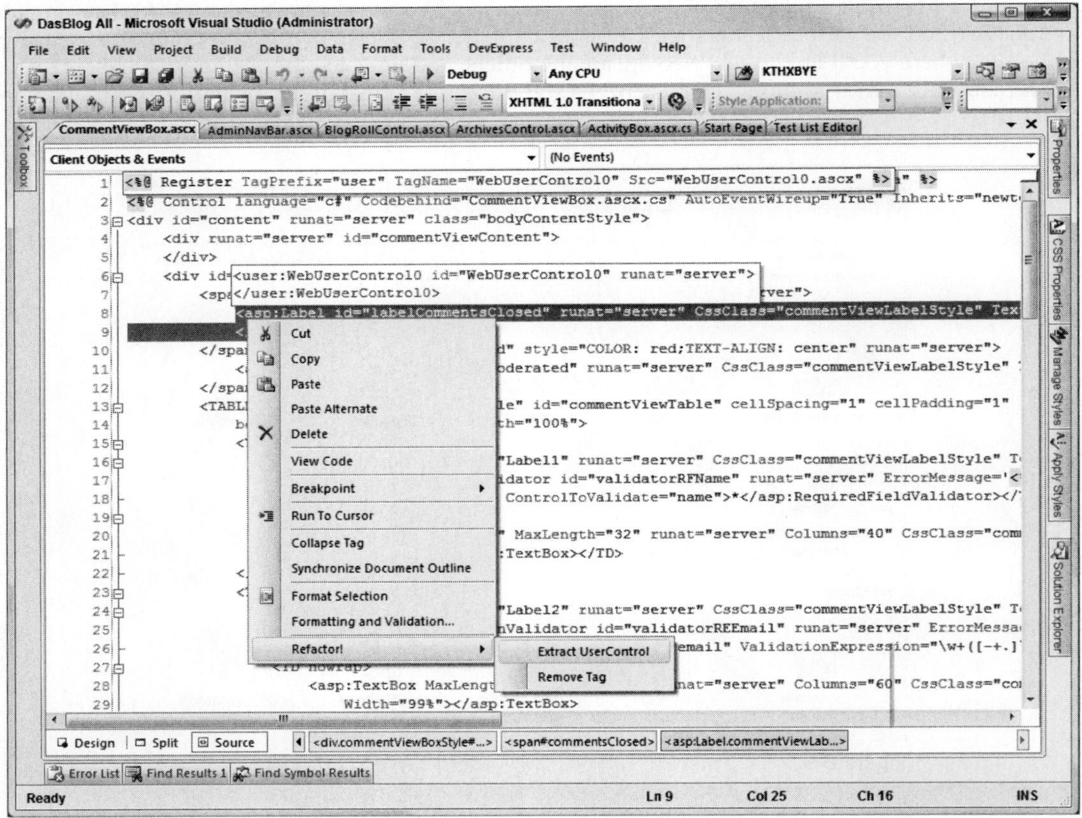

Figure B-9

Code Style Enforcer

Code Style Enforcer from Joel Fjordén does just that. It's a DXCore Plugin that enforces code style rules that you configure. DXCore is the free engine from DevExpress that Refactor! uses to extend Visual Studio.

Every team has a coding standard that they'd like programmers to follow, but it's not only hard to keep track of all the rules, it's tedious. Are methods supposed to be CamelCased or pascalCased? Are we putting "m_" in front of member fields?

Code Style Enforcer is a lot like Microsoft Word's spelling and grammar checker except for code. As shown in Figure B-10, identifiers that do not meet the code style guidelines are underlined in red. You can right-click on each error and Code Style Enforcer will use DxCore to refactor and fix each violation.

Style guidelines are configurable and the default uses Juval Lowy's excellent C# Code Style Guidelines available from `www.idesign.net`. The latest version will also generate code rule violation reports for a solution using XML and XSLT providing customizable different templates. Code Style Enforcer is an excellent tool to add to your team's toolbox.

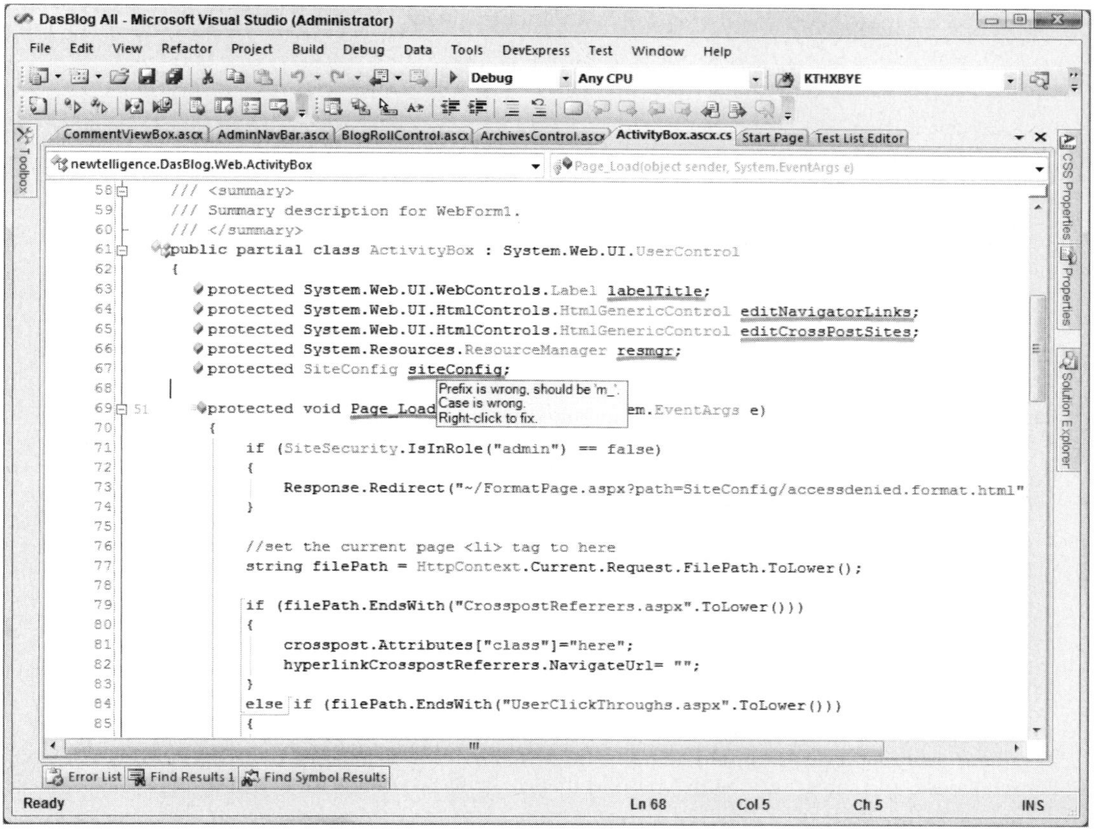

Figure B-10

Packer for .NET — JavaScript Minimizer

When creating an ASP.NET Web site, you often find yourself creating custom JavaScript files. During development, you want these files to be commented and easy to read. During production, however, every byte counts and it's nice to reduce the size of your JavaScript files with a JavaScript "minimizer."

Packer for .NET is a C# application that offers compression of JavaScript or simple "minification" by stripping comments and white space.

You'd be surprised how well these techniques work. For example, Steve Kallestad reported that a copy of the JavaScript library Prototype 1.50 was 70K before JavaScript-specific compression. It became 30K after the process, and then reached only 14K when gzip HTTP compression was applied. From 70K to 14K is a pretty significant savings.

JavaScript-specific compression does things such as renaming variables to single letters, being aware of global variable renaming vs. local variable renaming, as well as stripping unnecessary white space and comments.

Packer includes utilities for compression at both the command line and within MSBuild projects. The MSBuild targets can be added to your build process. Consequently, your integration server is continuous so you receive these benefits automatically and unobtrusively.

As an example, a JavaScript library might start out looking like this:

```
var Prototype = {
  Version: '1.5.0',
  BrowserFeatures: {
    XPath: !!document.evaluate
  },

  ScriptFragment: '(?:<script.*?>)((\n|\r|.)*?)(?:<\/script>)',
  emptyFunction: function() {},
  K: function(x) { return x }
}
```

Packed, the JavaScript might end up looking like this (as an example). . .but it will still work!

```
(c(){f 7.2q(/<\\/?[^>]+>/5a,"")}),2C:(c(){f 7.2q(P 5d(1m.5s,"9n"),"")}),9j:(c(){k
9m=P 5d(1m.5s,"9n");k 9k=P
5d(1m.5s,"ce");f(7.E(9m)||[]).1F((c(91){f(91.E(9k)||["",""])[1]}))}),3P:(c(){f
7.9j().1F((c(4s){f 6A(4s)}))}),cd:(c(){k 1h=N.4f("1h");k 2V=N.cc(7);1h.63(2V);f
1h.2P}),cb:(c(){k 1h=N.4f("1h");1h.2P=7.9i();f
1h.2O[0]?(1h.2O.o>1?$A(1h.2O).2A("",(c(3Y,1G){f
3Y+1G.4j})):1h.2O[0].4j):""}),6J:(c(9h){k E=7.4d().E(/([^?#]*)(#.*)?$/);h(!E){f{}}f
E[1].3m(9h||"&").2A({},(c(2E,Q){h((Q=Q.3m("="))[0]){k v=9g(Q[0]);k
1=Q[1]?9g(Q[1]):1b;h(2E[v]!==1b){h(2E[v].3k!=1M){2E[v]=[2E[v>}h(1){2E[v].M(1)}}1k
{2E[v]=1}}f 2E}))}),2F:(c(){f 7.3m("")})
```

There are many JavaScript minimizing libraries available; this is just one of them. However, it's options, completeness, and integration with MSBuild that make Packer for .NET worth trying out.

Visual Studio Add-ins

"If I had eight hours to chop down a tree, I'd spend six sharpening my axe." — Abraham Lincoln

ASPX Edit Helper Add-In for Visual Studio

Sometimes an add-in does something so small and so simple that you might dismiss it at first glance. But when you find yourself doing the same action over and over again, you'll be thankful for the ingenuity of developers who create time savers like this little gem.

The ASPX Edit Helper does two things, and it does them well. Not everyone likes to use the visual designer in Visual Studio 2008. Some users prefer to type ASPX markup directly in the source view. This add-in automatically fills in `"runat="server"` and `id="randomid"` when you type a server control. It also includes short codes for automatic insertion of snippets.

For example, if you type `/lbl` and press Enter, you'll get:

```
<asp:Label runat="server" id="lbl5394" Text="" />
```

A nice touch is that the cursor will be automatically positioned within the id attribute in the random ID selected so you can immediately begin typing a new ID for the control. This thoughtful design will allow you to create complicated forms with minimal typing very quickly. Figure B-11 shows the moment just before I press Enter after typing the `/txt` short code.

Installation is easy. Just unzip into your Visual Studio Add-ins folder. As an aside, the authors also include source code, which is useful if you're interested in writing your own Add-in.

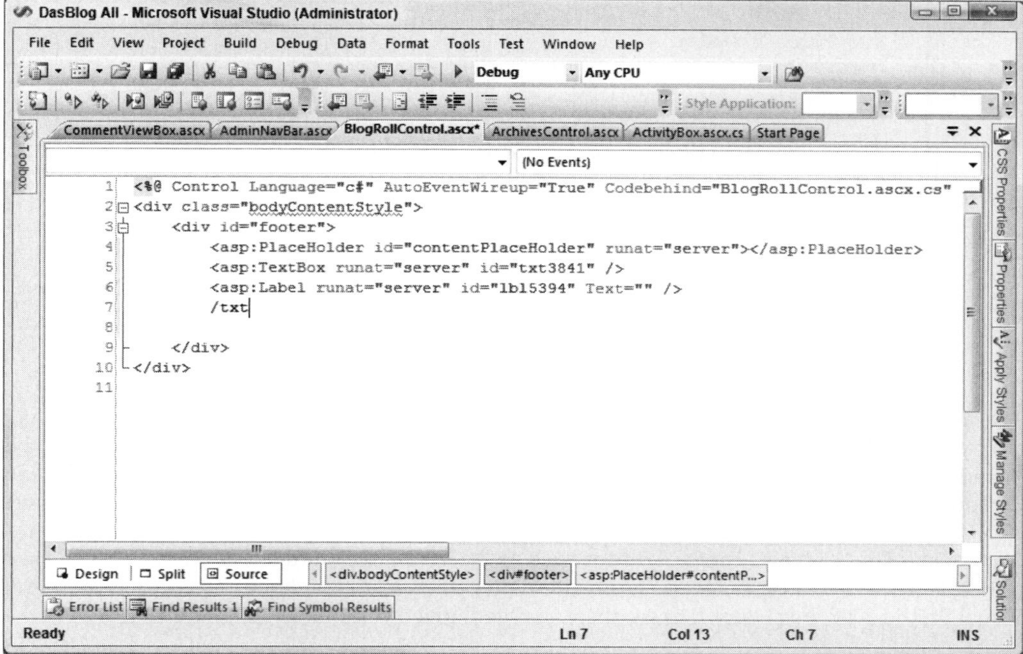

Figure B-11

Power Toys Pack Installer

What's better than a useful Visual Studio Add-in? Why, an automatic installer that downloads a list of useful add-ins and lets you select them and install at once, that's what! The Power Toys Pack Installer, shown in Figure B-12, is an open source CodePlex project that downloads a feed full of at least three dozen projects, samples, starter kits, and extensions that can be selected and installed *en masse*.

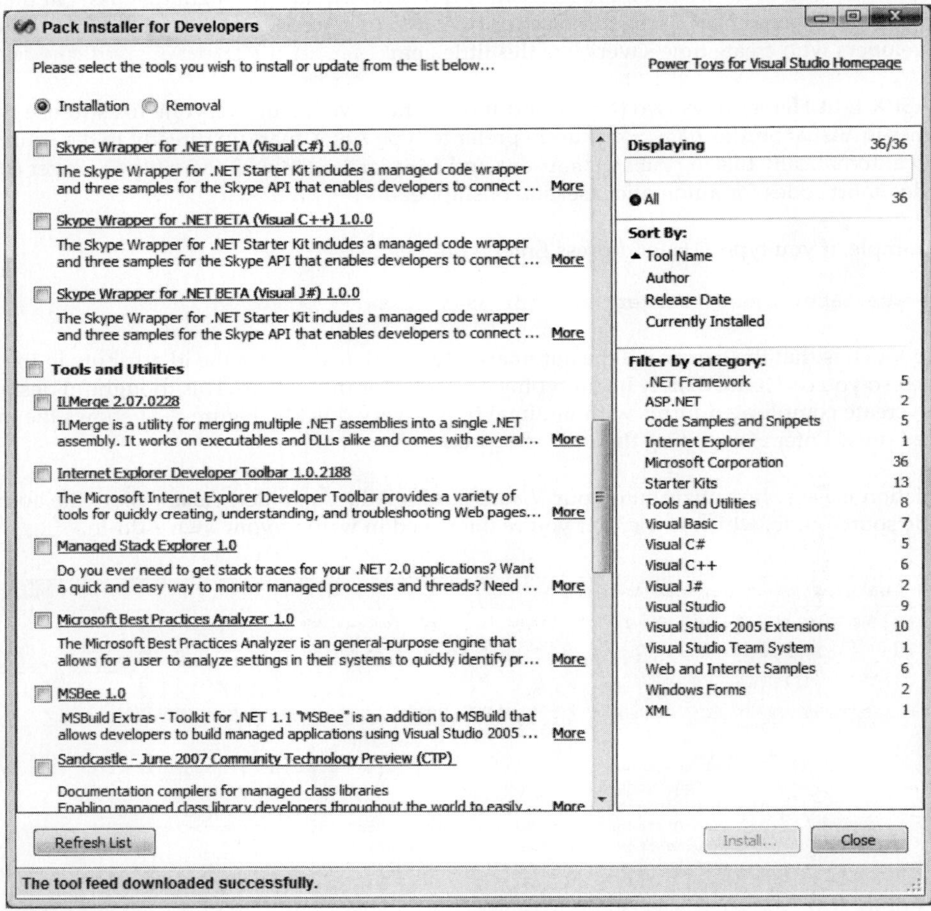

Figure B-12

The selection is cherry-picked from projects and downloads all over Microsoft. Some highlights include Microsoft .NET Interfaces for Skype and starter kits for creating your own shareware. Developer tools include ILMerge, a utility for merging multiple .NET assemblies into a single assembly, the Internet Explorer Developer Toolbar mentioned earlier in this chapter, a Managed Stack Explorer for investigating application hangs, and XML Notepad 2007, an experimental interface for browsing and editing XML documents. There are also choice Add-Ins such as the VS Source Outliner, giving you a tree view of your project's member and types for use as an alternative navigational method. A few tools aren't ready for Visual Studio 2008, but I expect to see them updated, given community pressure.

Extending ASP.NET

"Oh man! :-) I have shoot into my foot myself ;-) Sorry!" — matz."

ASP.NET AJAX Control Toolkit

The AJAX Control Toolkit is a collaboration between Microsoft and the larger ASP.NET community. Its goal was to provide the largest collection of Web client components available. It includes excellent examples if you want to learn how to write ASP.NET Ajax yourself, and then it gives you the opportunity to give back and have your code shared within the community.

There are literally dozens of controls that build on and extend the ASP.NET Ajax framework. Some of the controls are simple and provide those nice "little touches" such as drop shadows, rounded corners, watermarks, and animations. Others provide highly functional controls such as calendars, popups, and sliders.

Complete source is available for all the controls so that they can be extended and improved by you. These controls are more than just samples; they are complete and ready to be used in your applications.

There's a complete demo site available at `http://ajax.asp.net/ajaxtoolkit/` showcasing examples of each control so you can try each one to see if it meets your needs, as illustrated in Figure B-13, for example.

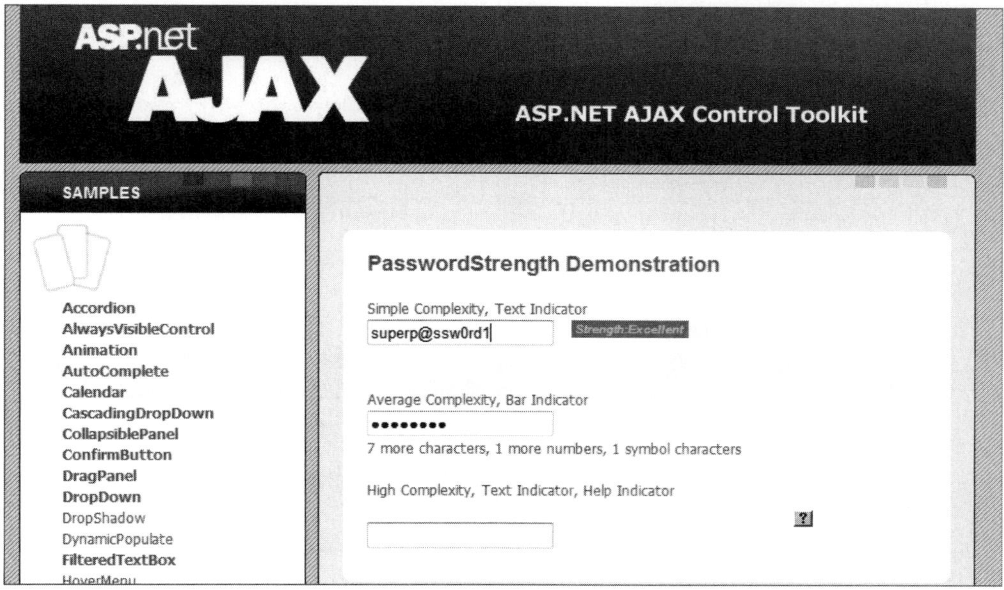

Figure B-13

Note that there are two versions, one for Visual Studio 2005 and one for Visual Studio 2008. Features that are specific to the 2008 version include "reference tags" for toolkit JavaScript files providing more complete JavaScript IntelliSense support within Visual Studio.

Atif Aziz's ELMAH — Error Logging Modules and Handlers

Troubleshooting errors and unhandled exceptions in your applications can be a full-time job. Rather than writing your own custom global exception handlers every time, consider looking at the ELMAH (Error Logging Modules And Handlers) from Atif Aziz. It's a very flexible application-wide error logging facility with pluggable extension points to the interfaces at nearly every location. You can even configure it in your application without re-compilation or even redeployment. Simply modify your `web.config` to include the error logging modules and handlers, and then you'll receive a single Web page to remotely review the entire log of unhandled exceptions.

ELMAH captures so much information about exceptions that it can reconstitute the original "yellow screen of death" that ASP.NET would have generated given an exception, even if customErrors was turned off. It's almost like TiVo for your exceptions! Figure B-14 shows ELMAH, providing a developer's view, including all the details you might need to debug this error.

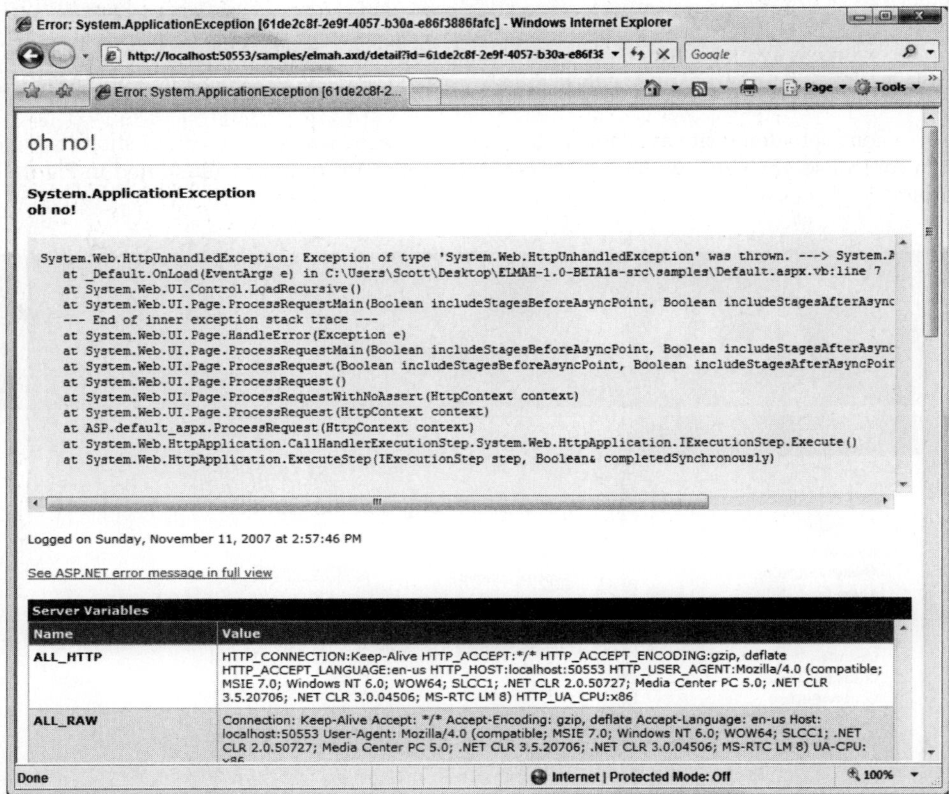

Figure B-14

Another clever feature is an RSS feed that shows the last 15 years from your log. This flexible tool is open source and the recent beta includes support for medium trust environments. You can plug in SQL Server or use an XML file to manage your error logs. I highly recommend you take the time to learn about ELMAH.

Helicon's ISAPI_Rewrite

Users of the Apache Web server sing the praises of the power of `mod_rewrite`, their URL rewriting mechanism. IIS users have this available to them in the form of the ISAPI_Rewrite module from Helicon. It's incredibly fast because it's written in pure C. It integrates nicely with ASP.NET because URLs are rewritten before ASP.NET realizes anything has happened.

Because it uses regular expressions, it can initially be very frustrating due to its terse syntax. However, if you are patient, it can be an incredibly powerful tool for your tool belt.

I recently discovered that there were a dozen ways to visit my blog that all lead to the same location. This was a confusing Google because it appeared that my blog had multiple addresses. I wanted not only to canonicalize my URL but also send back a 301 HTTP redirect to search indexes, thereby raising my standing within the search by appearing to have only one official URL.

For example, all of these links were valid ways to reach my blog:

- `www.hanselman.com/blog/`
- `www.hanselman.com/blog/default.aspx`
- `www.hanselman.com/blog`
- `http://hanselman.com/blog/`
- `http://hanselman.com/blog/default.aspx`
- `http://hanselman.com/blog`
- `www.hanselman.com/blog/Default.aspx`
- `www.computerzen.com/blog/`
- `www.computerzen.com`
- `http://computerzen.com/blog/`
- `http://computerzen.com/`

Notice that there's a difference between a trailing slash and no trailing slash in the eyes of a search engine. Using ISAPI Rewrite, I created this rather terse but very effective configuration file:

```
[ISAPI_Rewrite]
RewriteRule /blog/default\.aspx http\://www.hanselman.com/blog/ [I,RP]
RewriteCond Host: ^hanselman\.com
RewriteRule (.*) http\://www.hanselman.com$1 [I,RP]
RewriteCond Host: ^computerzen\.com
RewriteRule (.*) http\://www.hanselman.com$1 [I,RP]
RewriteCond Host: ^www.computerzen\.com
RewriteRule (.*) http\://www.hanselman.com/blog/ [I,RP]
```

The I and RP at the end of the line indicate that this match is case insensitive and the redirect should be permanent rather than temporary. The rules that include a $1 at the end of line cause the expression to include any path after the domain name. This allows the rule to apply site-wide and provides these benefits to every single page on my site. It's powerful and that's worth your time.

General Purpose Developer Tools

"If you get the dirty end of the stick, sharpen it and turn it into a useful tool." — Colin Powell

Telerik's Online Code Converter

Creating samples that should appear in both C# and Visual Basic can be very tedious without the assistance of something like Telerik's CodeChanger.com.

While it's not an officially supported tool, this little application will definitely get you 80 percent of the way when converting between Visual Basic and C#.

It also understands a surprising number of rather obscure syntaxes, as shown in Figure B-15, where I tried to convert an immediate `if` from C#'s `?:` syntax to VB's `IIf` syntax. It's not only useful for the writer, and blog author, but also anyone who's trying to switch projects between the two languages.

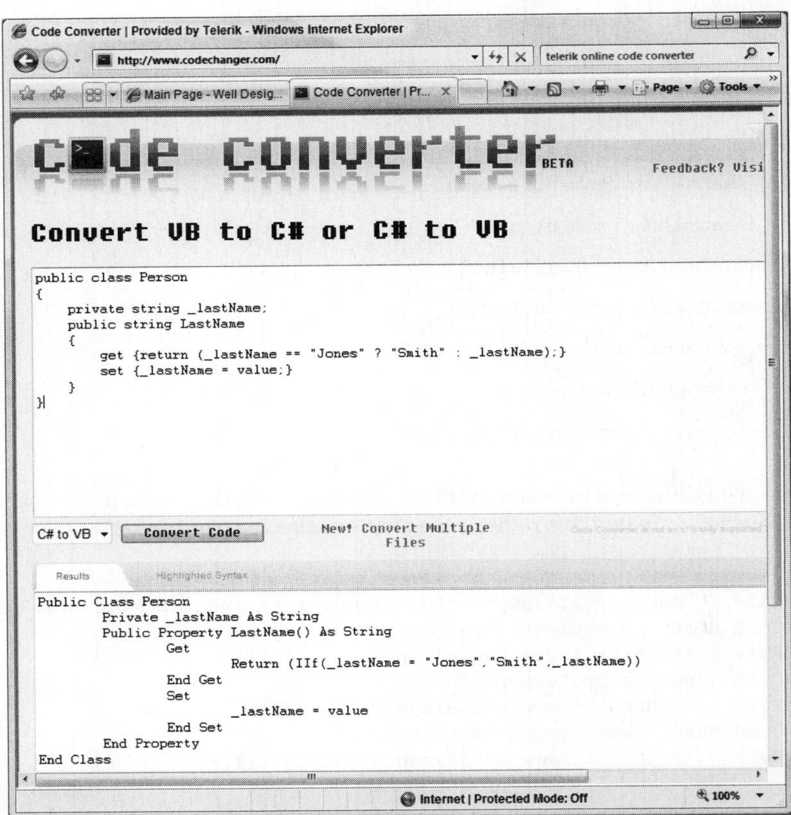

Figure B-15

WinMerge and Differencing Tools

Everyone has their favorite merge tool. Whether yours is WinMerge (Figure B-16), or Beyond Compare, or the old standby WinDiff, just make sure that you have one in your list of tools that you're very familiar with. When managing large numbers of changes across large numbers of individuals on software development teams, a good merge tool can help you untangle even the most complicated conflicting checkins.

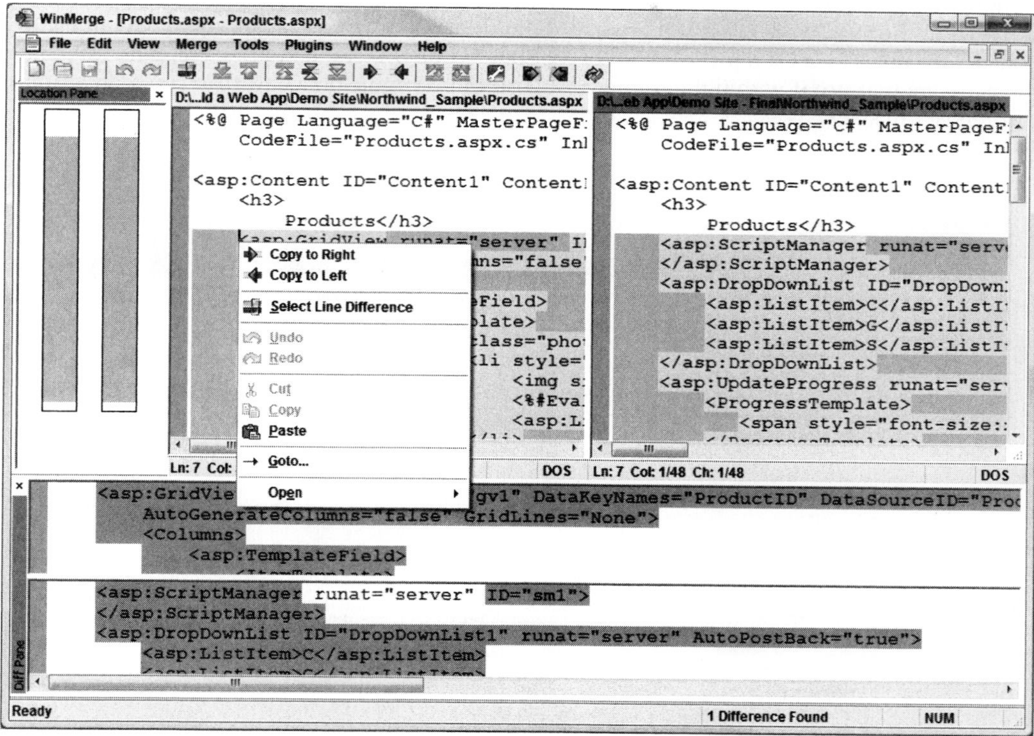

Figure B-16

A number of different plug-ins are available for WinMerge that extend its functionality to include comparison of Word and Excel documents and XML files.

Other highly recommended merge tools include Beyond Compare from Scooter Software and DiffMerge from SourceGear. Each of these three tools integrates with Windows Explorer, so the comparing files are as easy as a right-click.

Reflector

If you're not using Reflector, your .NET developer experience is lesser for it. Reflector is an object browser, decompiler, help system, powerful plug-in host, and incredible learning tool. This tiny utility from Microsoft developer Lutz Roeder is consistently listed as the number one most indispensable tool available to the .NET developer after Visual Studio.

Reflector is amazing because it not only gives you a representation of the programmer's intent by transforming IL back into C# or VB, but it includes analysis tools that help you visualize dependencies between methods in the .NET Base Class Library and within your code or any third-party code. In Figure B-17, you can see not only a C# representation of the code inside System. RolePrincipal, but more importantly the methods that use it within the framework. You can continue on as deep as you want within the theoretical call stack.

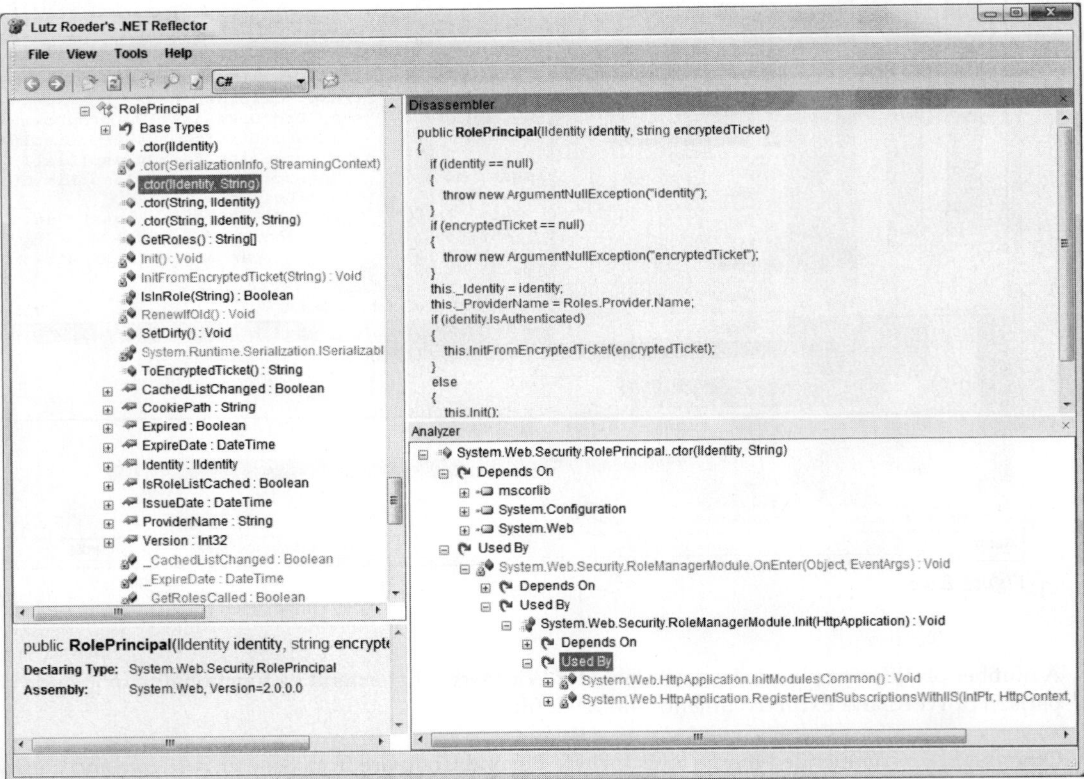

Figure B-17

While Reflector's decompilation abilities may become less useful with the release of the Base Class Library source code under the Microsoft Reference License, its abilities as an object browser and its vibrant plug-in community will keep this tool on the top shelf for years to come.

CR_Documentor

CR_Documentor (Figure B-18) is another free plug-in that uses the DxCore extension technology from DevExpress. This tool is a collaboration between developer Travis Illig and Reflector author Lutz Roeder.

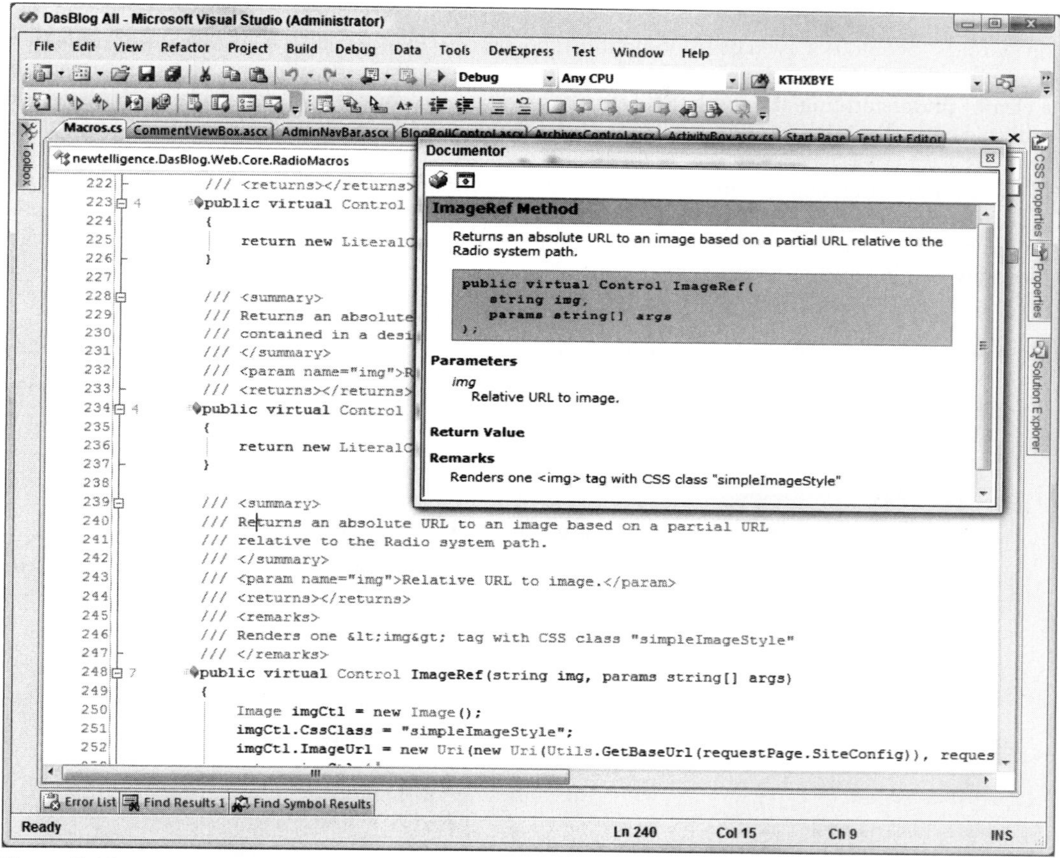

Figure B-18

This add-on allows you to see a preview of your XML document comments in real time as you edit them within your source code in Visual Studio.

CR_Documentor lets you choose your level of compliance including support for the now-defunct-but-still-useful NDoc project, as well as Microsoft specific tags for use with the Microsoft ''Sandcastle'' Documentation building suite of tools.

CR_Documentor also includes context menu support with snippets and helpful templates making it much easier to visualize complicated documentation. XML documentation source code provides all the tools and tags needed to make MSDN-quality help. CR_Documentor provides that last missing piece in the form of excellent and accurate visualization. It's indispensable if you intend on building compiled help files from your source code.

Process Explorer

Last, but unquestionably not least, is Process Explorer from Mark Russinovich. To call it "Task Manager on steroids" would not even begin to do it justice. Process Explorer puts Windows itself under a microscope by allowing you to peer inside your active processes, their threads, and the environment to get a clearer understanding about what is actually going on. Advanced and detailed use of this tool, along with the entire SysInternals Suite of Tools, should be required for all developers.

In Figure B-19, I'm looking at the Properties dialog box of an application running under the Visual Studio 2008 Web Server while a debugging session is in process. I can see the process tree, the DLLs loaded into the Web server's process, their versions, and their paths, making this an excellent tool for debugging assembly loading and versioning issues.

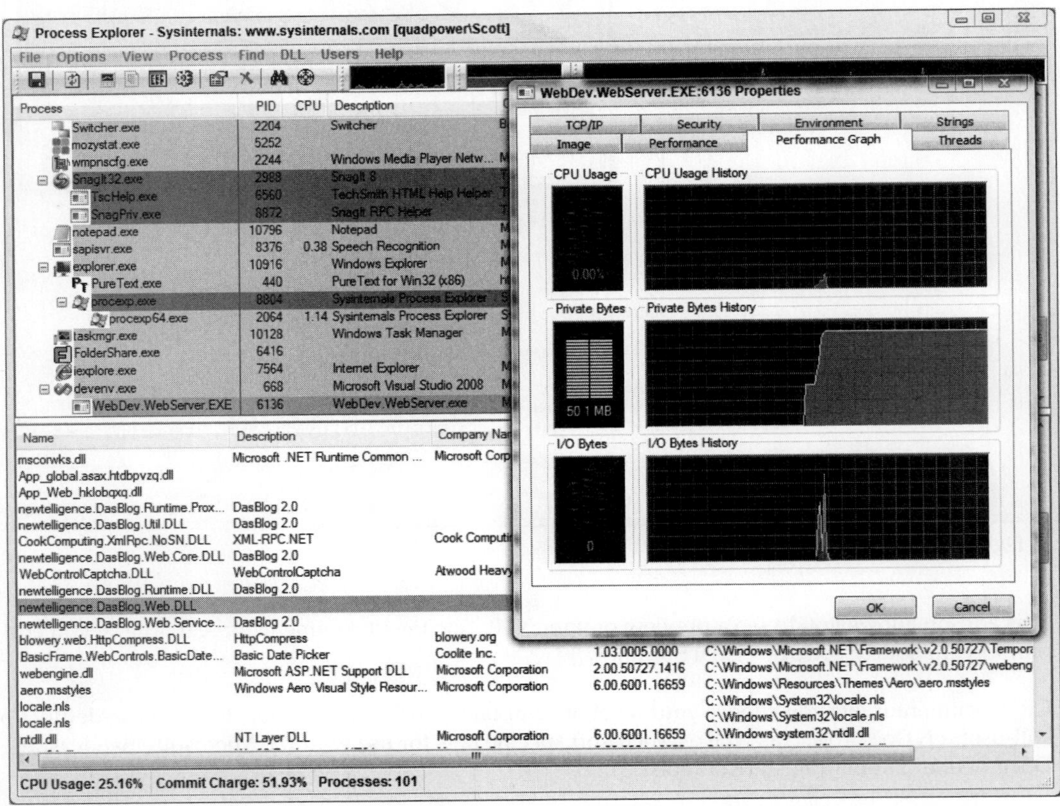

Figure B-19

Summary

Having the right tools can mean the difference between a week of time spent with your head against the wall versus five minutes of quick analysis in debugging. The right tool can mean the difference between a tedious and keyboard-heavy code slogging or a refactoring session that is actually pleasant. I encourage you to try each of the tools listed here, as well as to explore the ecosystem of available tools to find those that make your development experience not just more productive but more enjoyable.

C

Silverlight

Silverlight is a lightweight browser plug-in from Microsoft that runs not only on all major browsers on Windows, but also on the Mac. Silverlight 1.0 was released in September of 2007. Many books have been written already on the subject. And now, Silverlight 2.0 is fast on the heels of version 1.0. Microsoft also announced "Moonlight," a partnership with Novell and the Open Source Mono Project to bring Silverlight-like technology to Linux — you already know this, don't you?

It is outside the scope of this book to give more than an introduction to Silverlight. Rather than just offering the standard "Hello World" example, however, we thought we'd try something more pragmatic. As this is a book on Professional ASP.NET, why not explore the scenario that a typical ASP.NET programmer (not a designer or an artist) would find herself in? Along the way you'll learn about Silverlight and its capabilities, and perhaps it will inspire you to include Silverlight in your applications. You should read books such as *Silverlight 1.0* (Wiley Publishing, Inc., 2007) to familiarize yourself with this deceptively deep new technology.

Thank you to Eilon Lipton for his help with this application!

Extending ASP.NET Apps with Silverlight

Let's begin with a theoretical application for patients signing into a chiropractic clinic. They need to sign in and indicate to the doctor what part of their body hurts as seen in Figure C-1. This is a very typical application using Web Controls to present a form and collect the feedback via a Form POST.

The page uses conventional ASP.NET techniques including validation controls. One interesting thing to note is that this page's Submit button sends its data back to another page using a Cross Page PostBack. The page that receives the Form POST is seen in Figure C-2.

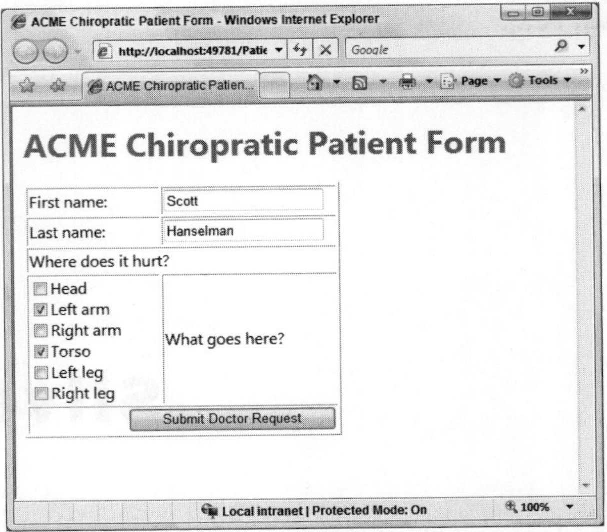

Figure C-1

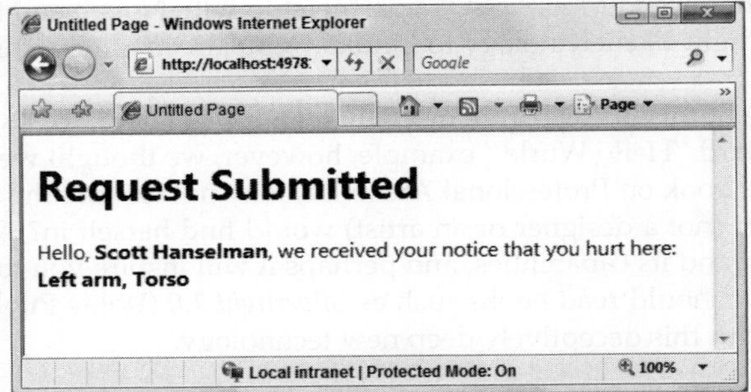

Figure C-2

Step 1: A Basic ASP.NET Application

Figure C-1 shows our generic Patient Form for our Chiropractic Clinic.

The code for the patient form as seen in Listing C-1 has an empty code-behind class. We've removed some minor markup for the sake of brevity.

You see applications like this every day that are created by composing basic HTML input elements into more and more complicated forms. What can be done with a simple application like this to make it not only a more compelling user experience, but ultimately more *usable?*

Listing C-1: Patient Form

ASPX

```
<%@ Page Language="C#" AutoEventWireup="true" CodeBehind=
"PatientForm.aspx.cs" Inherits="SLPersonProject.PatientForm" %>
<html xmlns="http://www.w3.org/1999/xhtml">
<head runat="server">
    <title>ACME Chiropratic Patient Form</title>
</head>
<body>
    <form id="form1" runat="server">
    <h1>ACME Chiropratic Patient Form</h1>
    <div>
        <table border="1">
            <tr>
                <td>First name:</td>
                <td>
                    <asp:TextBox ID="FirstName" runat="server"></asp:TextBox>
                    <asp:RequiredFieldValidator ID="RequiredFieldValidator1"
                        runat="server" ControlToValidate="FirstName"
                        ErrorMessage="*"></asp:RequiredFieldValidator>
                </td>
            </tr>
            <tr>
                <td>Last name:</td>
                <td>
                    <asp:TextBox ID="LastName" runat="server"></asp:TextBox>
                    <asp:RequiredFieldValidator ID="RequiredFieldValidator2"
                        runat="server" ControlToValidate="LastName"
                        ErrorMessage="*"></asp:RequiredFieldValidator>
                </td>
            </tr>
            <tr><td colspan="2">Where does it hurt? </td></tr>
            <tr>
                <td style="width: 125px">
      <asp:CheckBox ID="headCheckBox" runat="server" Text="Head" /><br />
      <asp:CheckBox ID="leftarmCheckBox" runat="server" Text="Left arm" /><br />
      <asp:CheckBox ID="rightarmCheckBox" runat="server" Text="Right arm" />
<br />
      <asp:CheckBox ID="torsoCheckBox" runat="server" Text="Torso" /><br />
      <asp:CheckBox ID="leftlegCheckBox" runat="server" Text="Left leg" /><br />
      <asp:CheckBox ID="rightlegCheckBox" runat="server" Text="Right leg" />
                </td>
                <td>What goes here?</td>
            </tr>
            <tr>
                <td colspan="2" align="right">
                   <asp:Button ID="SubmitButton" runat="server"
                    Text="Submit Doctor Request" PostBackUrl="~/Complete.aspx" />
```

Continued

```
                    </td>
                </tr>
            </table>
        </div>
        </form>
    </body>
    </html>
```

Finding Vector-Based Content

A professional ASP.NET programmer will often find themselves adding an "active element" to an existing application to make the end-user experience richer. Let's add a picture of a human body that users can click on to indicate their areas of pain, but you'll add the constraint that the picture should interact with the existing checkboxes so that server-side code won't need to change.

You may not be an artist, so you can start by looking for some vector-based clip art that you can leverage in the application. Bitmaps are exactly that — maps of bits. When you scale a 100 by 100 image to 400 by 400, each pixel is resampled or resized to be 4x larger, but additional information isn't created. Small pixels simply become larger pixels. Vectors, on the other hand, are represented using mathematical equations and can scale to any size without degradation in quality.

Silverlight uses XAML (eXtensible Application Markup Language) to represent vector graphics. For example, this snippet of XAML draws a gray circle:

```
<Ellipse Width="340" Height="340"  Canvas.Left="50" Canvas.Top="50"
Fill="#FF000000" Opacity="0.3"/>
```

Let's head over to `iStockPhoto.com` and search for "Adult Vector Diagram" and download this vector image of a cartoon version of Leonardo da Vinci's *Vitruvian Man* (see Figure C-3). Because it's a vector and not a bitmap it's in EPS (Encapsulated Postscript) format rather than the more familiar PNG, JPG, GIF, or BMP formats that you use every day.

Next, let's download a trial edition of Adobe Illustrator and open the downloaded EPS as shown in Figure C-4.

If you'd like a free alternative to our Cartoon Virtruvian Man, there is a Public Domain alternative at `http://www.hanselman.com/book/asp.net/assets/SilverlightMan.zip`**. If you'd rather not use Adobe Illustrator, try the Open Source InkScape at** `http://www.inkscape.org/`.

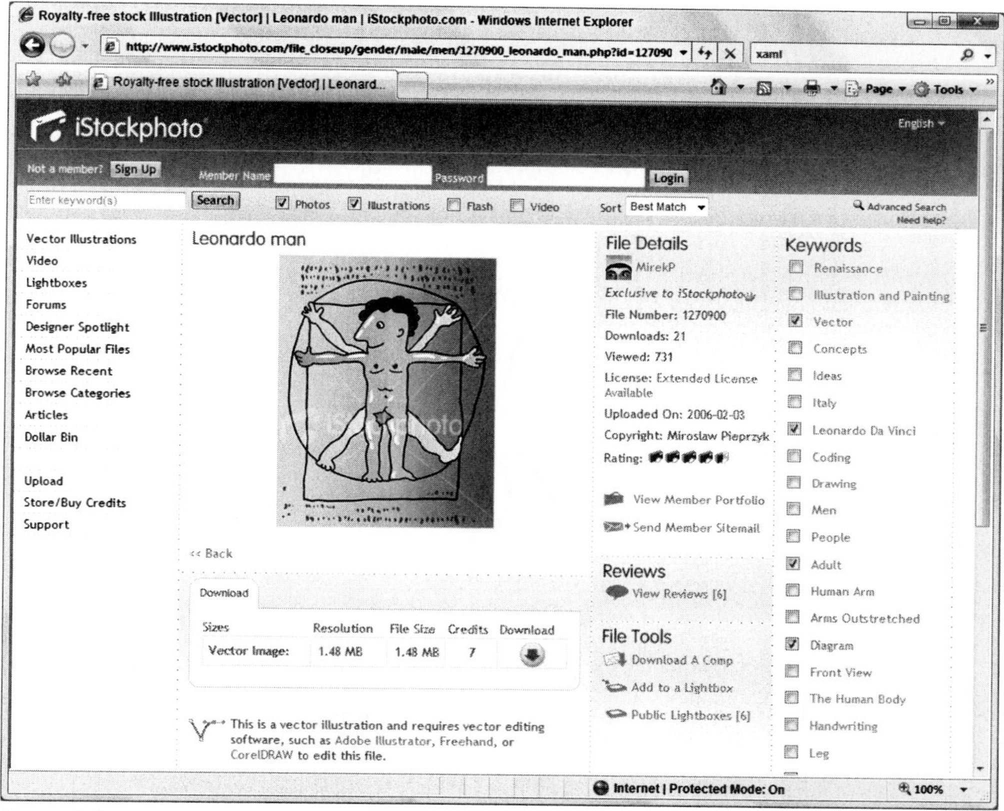

Figure C-3

"Leonardo man" copyright 2006 Miroslaw Pieprzyk, licensed by `iStockphoto.com`.

Zooming in to 300 percent, as shown in Figure C-5, underscores the fact that vectors can be scaled to any resolution.

Converting Vector Content to XAML

We downloaded Mike Swanson's excellent Illustrator to XAML Export plug-in from his site at `www.mikeswanson.com/xamlexport/`. It has some limitations, and they are listed on his site, but it is an excellent tool for bringing vector content into Silverlight.

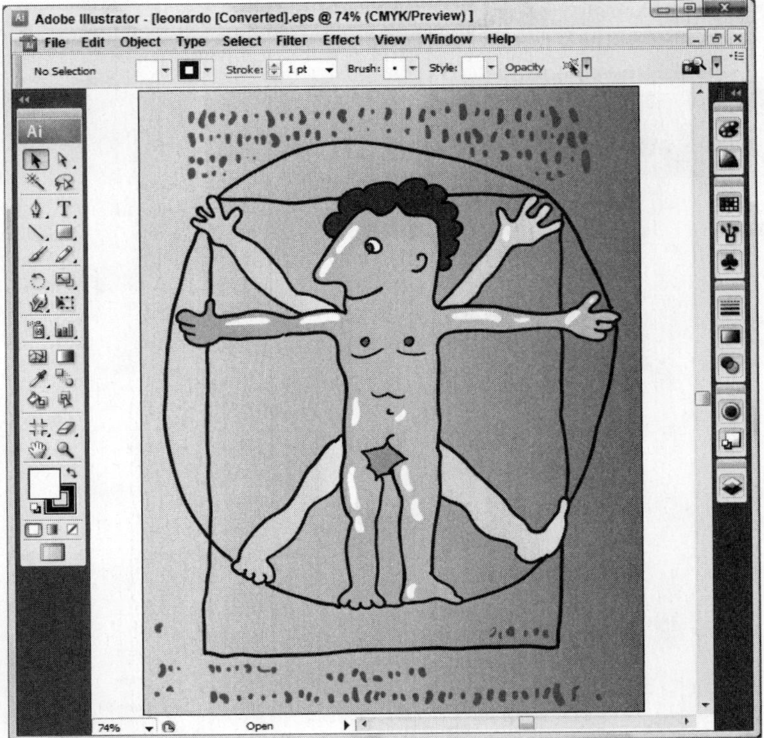

Figure C-4

Installation of Mike's plug-in is simple, just drop the .AIP file into `C:\Program Files\Adobe\Adobe Illustrator CS3\Plug-ins\Illustrator Formats` and you'll see new options appear in the File ➪ Export dialog box within Illustrator, as shown in Figure C-6.

There are two options, one for WPF XAML usable in a .NET 3.0 Windows Application and one using the old code-name for Silverlight, Windows Presentation Foundation/Everywhere or WPF/E. You'll select the last one as you're using Silverlight. The only difference in the documents is the root node of the XML.

The resulting XAML document is about 256 KB and starts out like this:

```
<!-- Generated by Adobe Illustrator CS -> XAML Export Plug-In Version 0.16      -->
<!-- For questions, contact Mike Swanson: http://www.mikeswanson.com/XAMLExport -->

<Canvas Width="612.000000" Height="792.000000"
  xmlns="http://schemas.microsoft.com/client/2007"
  xmlns:x="http://schemas.microsoft.com/winfx/2006/xaml">
  <Canvas>
  <!-- Layer 1/<Path> -->
  <Path Data="F1 M 612.000000,792.000000 L 0.000000,792.000000 L
0.000000,0.000000 L 612.000000,0.000000 L 612.000000,792.000000 Z">
...the other 255k removed...
```

Figure C-5

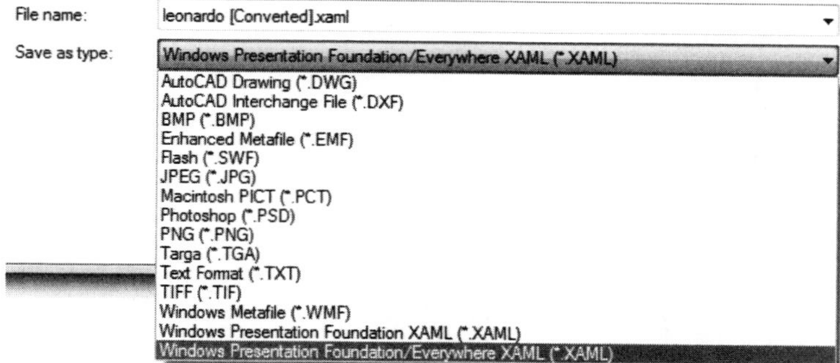

Figure C-6

How do you know if the export succeeded and our little man looks correct? There are a few ways.

Tools for Viewing and Editing XAML

There are a number of ways for you to view or edit our newly created XAML file. You can use Internet Explorer, Visual Studio 2008's XAML Editor, or Microsoft Expression Blend.

Internet Explorer with a Minimal Silverlight Page

First, you create a minimal static HTML page to view your XAML, as shown in Figure C-7.

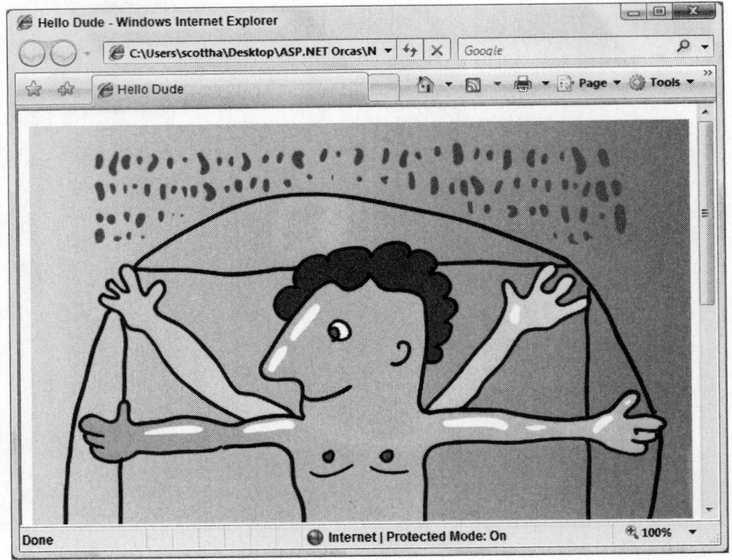

Figure C-7

The code is fairly simple. First, the `default.html` file shown in Listing C-2a includes a `div` to hold the Silverlight control.

Listing C-2a: Helloworld.html

HTML

```
<!DOCTYPE HTML PUBLIC "-//W3C//DTD HTML 4.01 Transitional//EN"
"http://www.w3c.org/TR/1999/REC-html401-19991224/loose.dtd">
<html xmlns="http://www.w3.org/1999/xhtml">
<head>
  <title>Hello Dude</title>
  <script type="text/javascript" src="Silverlight.js"></script>
  <script type="text/javascript" src="HelloWorld.js"></script>
  <script type="text/javascript" src="Dude.xaml.js"></script>
  <style type="text/css">
        .silverlightHost {
               height: 792px;
               width: 612px;
        }
```

```
    </style>
  </head>
  <body>
            <div id="SilverlightControlHost" class="silverlightHost">
             <script type="text/javascript">
                   createSilverlight();
            </script>
    </div>
  </body>
  </html>
```

The div with the ID SilverlightControlHost calls a method called createSilverlight that lives in HelloWorld.js, shown in Listing C-2b. We've separated the JavaScript files for the sake of tidiness, but you're welcome to lay the files out however you like.

Listing C-2b: Helloworld.js

JavaScript

```
function createSilverlight()
{
  var scene = new HelloWorld.Page();
  Silverlight.createObjectEx({
          source: "Dude.xaml",
          parentElement: document.getElementById("SilverlightControlHost"),
          id: "SilverlightControl",
          properties: {
                 width: "100%",
                 height: "100%",
                 version: "1.0"
          },
          events: {
                 onLoad: Silverlight.createDelegate(scene, scene.handleLoad)
          }
  });
}


if (!window.Silverlight)
  window.Silverlight = {};

Silverlight.createDelegate = function(instance, method) {
  return function() {
          return method.apply(instance, arguments);
  }
}
```

Notice the three lines called out in Listing C-2b. The ID of the div from our HTML file is referenced in the call to getElementById above. Our XAML file is referenced in the source: property.

You can hook up JavaScript events to Silverlight, as shown in Listing C-2c. A good naming convention is to put these events in a file named `yourxamlfile.xaml.js`, so I've named mine `Dude.xaml.js`.

Listing C-2c: Dude.xaml.js

JavaScript

```
if (!window.HelloWorld)
 window.HelloWorld = {};

HelloWorld.Page = function() {}

HelloWorld.Page.prototype = {
 handleLoad: function(control, userContext, rootElement)
 {
        this.control = control;
        // Sample event hookup:
        rootElement.addEventListener("MouseLeftButtonDown",
           Silverlight.createDelegate(this, this.handleMouseDown));
 },
// Sample event handler
 handleMouseDown: function(sender, eventArgs) {
        // The following line of code shows how to find an
        // element by name and call a method on it.
        // this.control.content.findName("something").Begin();
 }
}
```

Visual Studio 2008's Built-in XAML Editor

Visual Studio 2008 includes an XAML editor for editing WPF XAML rather than Silverlight. However, it'll let you move things around and confirm our layout if you change the `http://schemas.microsoft.com/winfx/2007` namespace to `http://schemas.microsoft.com/winfx/2006/xaml/presentation` in our XAML file. This isn't recommended, but it's an interesting exercise in exploring the subtle differences between WPF and Silverlight's implementation of XAML. Figure C-8 shows our XAML file edited in Visual Studio in a split-screen.

Microsoft Expression Blend

At the time of this writing, Expression Blend 2 was in Beta and not yet released. Blend is a designer focused editor for XAML files, animations, and Silverlight projects. Blend shares the same project file format as Visual Studio, so you can open CSPROJ files and SLN files and move seamlessly between Blend and VS.

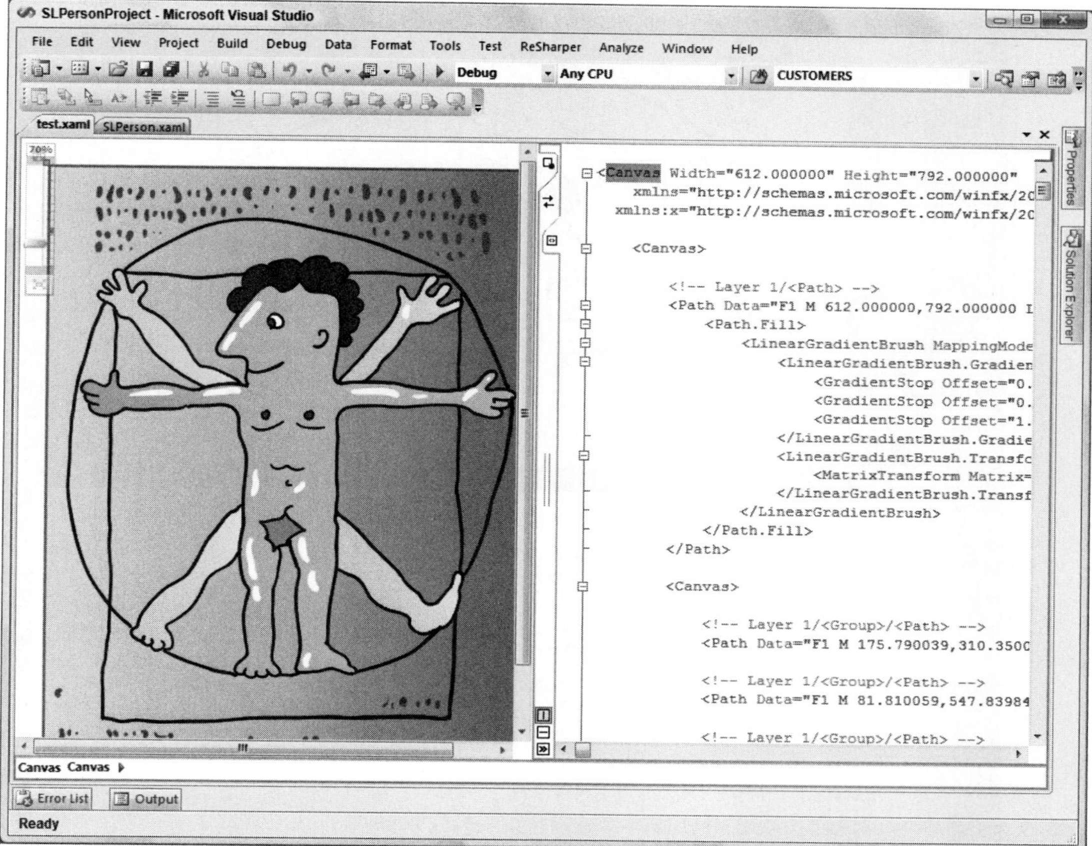

Figure C-8

Figure C-9 shows our XAML file being edited in Expression Blend. Blend gives you complete control over XAML files, and you'll use it to extend the image for your application. For the application, you'll add red dots over each of the body parts represented in the original applications by checkboxes. You'll name them so they are accessible from JavaScript and hook up events to both the checkboxes and within Silverlight so they both stay in sync.

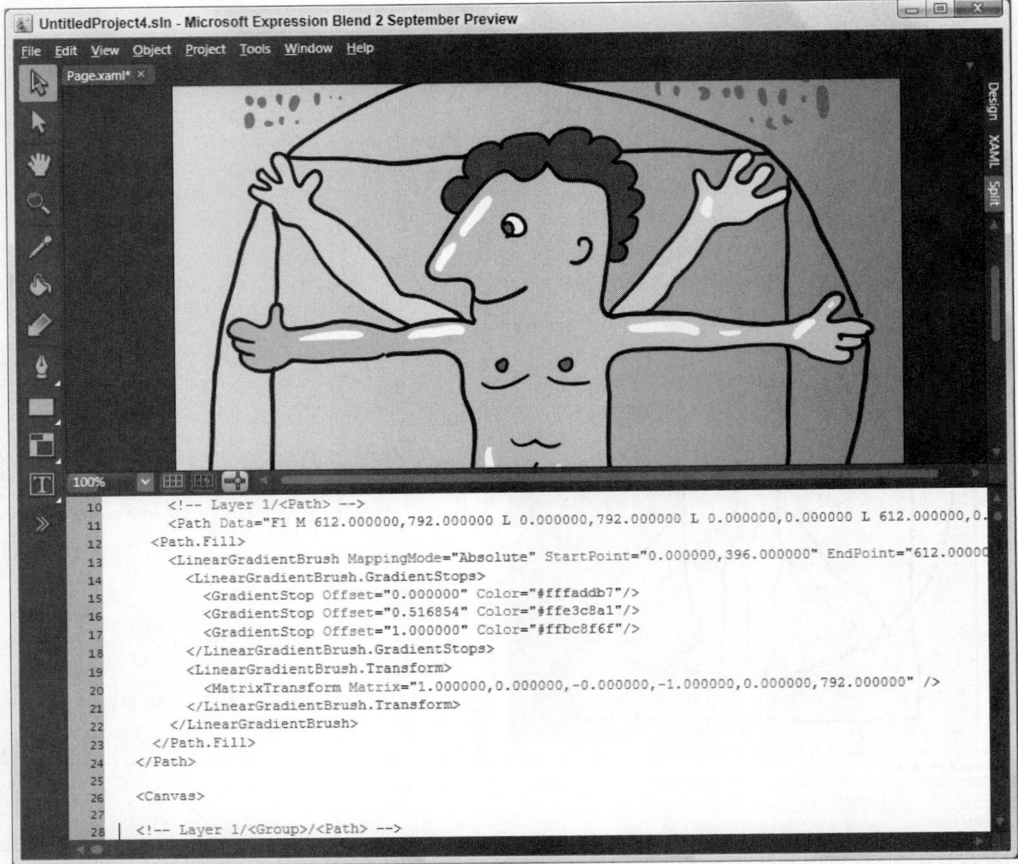

Figure C-9

Adding Active Elements with Blend

Open up your exported XAML file in Blend and perform the following tasks:

1. Using the basic drawing tools in the toolbox, draw a circle over the left and right arms, left and right legs, the head, and the torso. Feel free to color them any way you like. I've used a gradient.
2. Name each of the newly drawn circles leftLeg, rightArm, and so on, by selecting them and typing in a name in the Properties pane.

You'll notice while Blend is all black and has a different UI than you're used to, the metaphors of object selection, properties panes, and naming are familiar from your experience using Visual Studio. Blend is almost like "Visual Studio for Designers."

Alternatively, if you don't like using the visual editor in Blend as seen in Figure C-10, you can just copy and paste the XAML directly.

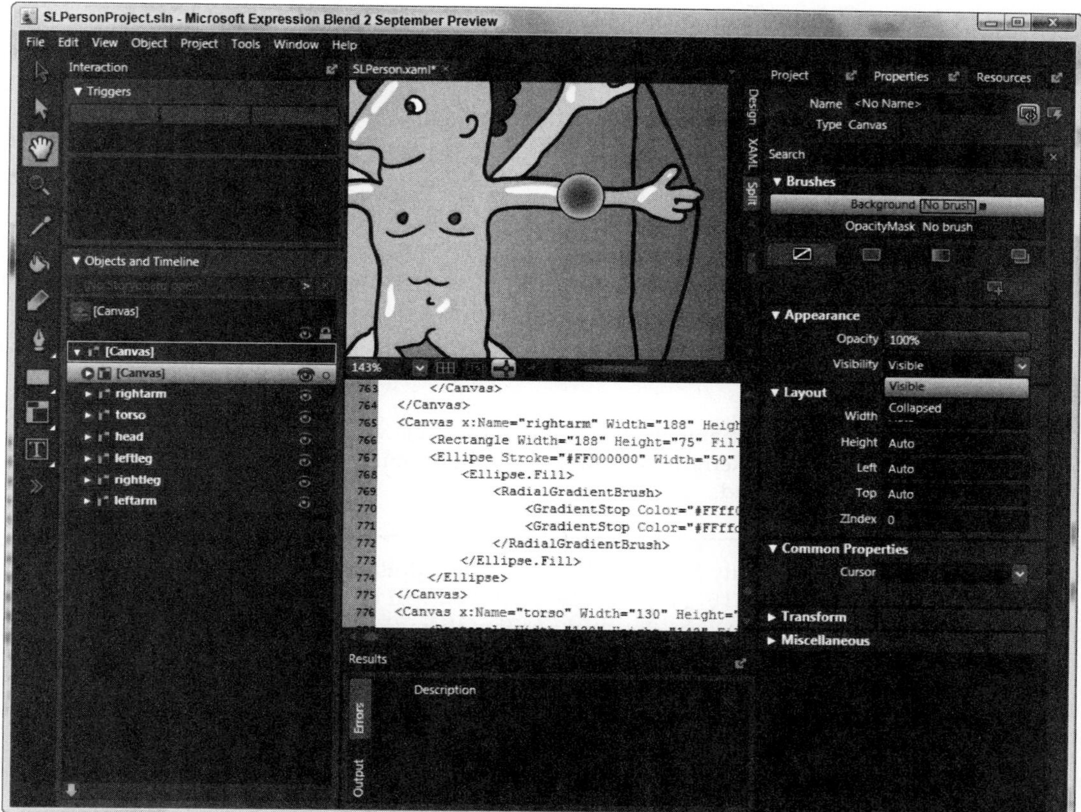

Figure C-10

Editing in Notepad

You can edit in your favorite XML editor or even Notepad. Each "pain dot" is a snippet of XAML that resembles Listing C-3:

Listing C-3: An XAML Ellipse

```
<Canvas x:Name="leftarm" Width="193" Height="60" Canvas.Left="377.762"
Canvas.Top="261.857">
    <Rectangle Width="193" Height="60" Fill="Transparent"></Rectangle>
    <Ellipse Stroke="#FF000000" Width="50" Height="50"
        Visibility="Collapsed"
```

Continued

```
         Canvas.Left="57" Canvas.Top="8">
        <Ellipse.Fill>
            <RadialGradientBrush>
                <GradientStop Color="#FFff0000" Offset="0"/>
                <GradientStop Color="#FFffddaa" Offset="1"/>
            </RadialGradientBrush>
        </Ellipse.Fill>
    </Ellipse>
</Canvas>
```

Listing C-3 is an example of an ellipse with a filled gradient between red and a shade of light-gray. The only differences between the six pain dots are these:

- `x:Name` attribute: In order for a Silverlight element to be "addressable" from JavaScript, it should have a name.
- `Canvas.Left="x" Canvas.Top="y"` attributes: These indicate the position of the elements within the larger canvas.

You can certainly edit XAML manually in Notepad and preview your changes in Internet Explorer via the very repetitive "Edit, Refresh in Browser, Edit, Refresh in Browser," technique if you like, but we recommend using Blend.

> **Notice also the Visibility attribute. You want these dots to be initially invisible, so they are marked as `Visibility="Collapsed"`. You will toggle the dot's visibility in JavaScript code. Draw all the dots and position them first before you make their `Visibility="Collapsed"`. Just before you hit the dots, you'll have a person that resembles Figure C-11.**

Integrating with Your Existing ASP.NET Site

All right, now that you have our imported and edited "Chiro Dude," let's add him to the site. You have a few choices. You can copy over the Silverlight.js and the other assets and simply add them to your Visual Studio Project as content. The JavaScript files can be added as standard script references on your ASPX pages and the Silverlight `div` added manually.

However, Microsoft often has "Futures Releases" or "Previews" that showcase coming technologies that make things easier. The ASP.NET 3.5 Extensions Preview at the time of this writing is available at `http://www.asp.net/downloads/3.5-extensions/`. It includes a preview of some new controls that will arrive around the first half of 2008 as a downloadable add-on to the .NET Framework 3.5. These controls will simply be added into the Visual Studio Toolbox and make things easier. You should be able to get these controls within a few months of the publication of this very book!

Remember earlier when we created three JavaScript files and needed to check ID attributes to instantiate a new Silverlight Control? The `asp:Silverlight`and improved `asp:ScriptManager`controls will likely make that process easier.

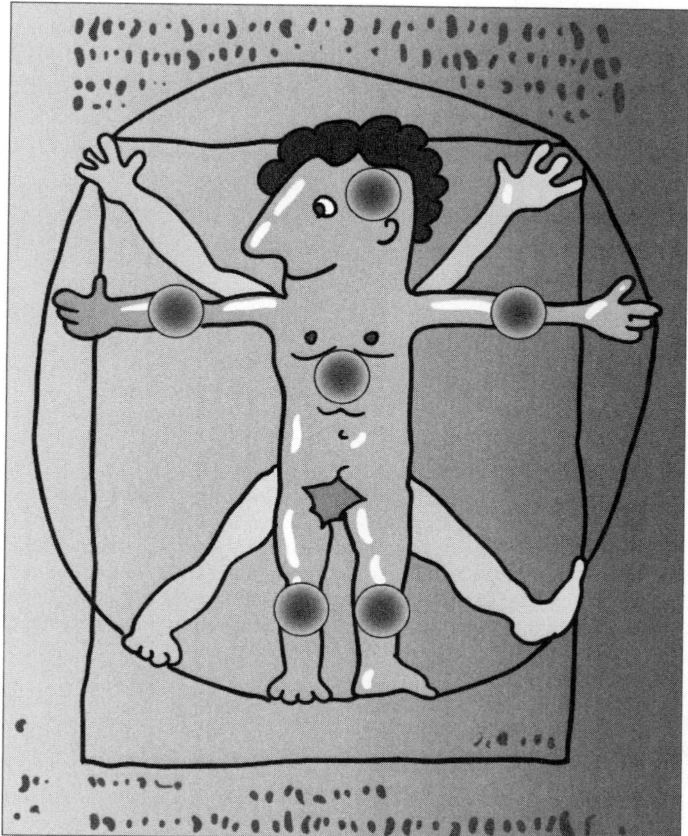

Figure C-11

An update of Listing C-1 using these controls looks like Listing C-4, with some repetition removed for brevity. Pay special attention to the `ScriptReferences` in the `ScriptManager`. One uses `Name=` and one `Path=`. That is not a typo. The Silverlight JavaScript is referred to by name and is served from an Assembly Resource. It's compiled into a DLL and served from there by `ScriptResource.axd`, an HttpHandler for doing just that. The `Dude.xaml.js` will be served up directly from disk like any other JavaScript file, except you didn't have to write the `script` tag because it's handled for you.

Listing C-4: Markup using ASP.NET 3.5 Extensions

ASPX

```
<html xmlns="http://www.w3.org/1999/xhtml">
<head runat="server">
    <title>Untitled Page</title>
</head>
```

Continued

```
<body>
    <form id="form1" runat="server">
     <asp:ScriptManager ID="ScriptManager1" runat="server">
         <Scripts>
             <asp:ScriptReference Name="SilverlightControl.js" />
             <asp:ScriptReference Path="Dude.xaml.js" />
         </Scripts>
     </asp:ScriptManager>
     <h1>Patient Form</h1>
     <div>
         <table border="1">
 ...OMMITED...
             <tr>
                 <td colspan="2">Where does it hurt? </td>
             </tr>
             <tr>
                 <td style="width: 125px">
     <asp:CheckBox ID="headCheckBox" runat="server" Text="Head" /><br />
     <asp:CheckBox ID="leftarmCheckBox" runat="server" Text="Left arm" /><br />
     <asp:CheckBox ID="rightarmCheckBox" runat="server" Text="Right arm" /><br />
     <asp:CheckBox ID="torsoCheckBox" runat="server" Text="Torso" /><br />
     <asp:CheckBox ID="leftlegCheckBox" runat="server" Text="Left leg" /><br />
     <asp:CheckBox ID="rightlegCheckBox" runat="server" Text="Right leg" />
                 </td>
                 <td>
                     <asp:Silverlight runat="server" ID="Xaml1" Height="475"
                            Width="367" Source="Dude.xaml"
                         ClientType="Custom.SLPerson"></asp:Silverlight>
                 </td>
             </tr>
             <tr>
                 <td colspan="2" align="right">
                       <asp:Button ID="SubmitButton" runat="server" Text="Submit
  Doctor Request" PostBackUrl="~/Complete.aspx" />
                 </td>
             </tr>
         </table>
     </div>
    </form>
 </body>
 </html>
```

In order to get Listing C-4 to work, you'll need the ASP.NET 3.5 Extensions from `http://www.asp.net/downloads/3.5-extensions/`**. The release date of this new package was not available at the time of this writing, but watch** `www.asp.net` **for all the latest details.**

At this point, you've added the control but there's no interactivity. He's on the page, but he doesn't do anything. You need to expose the named dots that you created earlier. You will use JavaScript to find them within the XAML document and assign them to JavaScript variables. Silverlight is very good at being transparent. Once you've gotten hold of a Silverlight object within JavaScript, you can treat it just like any other JavaScript object. Notice that the ID in this case of the Silverlight object is "Xaml1."

Receiving Silverlight Events in JavaScript

You start your JavaScript by creating a "class" called `personElements` with each of the dots. They are initially set to null because you find them in the `initializeComponent` method that acts as your constructor. Notice how `slhost` is passed into `initializeComponent`. Then you access its `content` node and use `findName` to grab each of the named body part dots, storing them away in variables as seen in Listing C-5.

Listing C-5: Dude.xaml.js

JavaScript

```
/// <reference name="MicrosoftAjax.js"/>
/// <reference name="SilverlightControl.js"/>

personElements = function() {
    this.leftarm = null;
    this.rightarm = null;
    this.head = null;
    this.leftleg = null;
    this.rightleg = null;
    this.torso = null;
}
personElements.prototype = {
    initializeComponent: function(slhost) {
        var host = slhost.content;

        this.leftarm = host.findName("leftarm");
        this.rightarm = host.findName("rightarm");
        this.head = host.findName("head");
        this.leftleg = host.findName("leftleg");
        this.rightleg = host.findName("rightleg");
        this.torso = host.findName("torso");

    }
}

Type.registerNamespace("Custom");

Custom.SLPerson = function(element) {
    Custom.SLPerson.initializeBase(this, [element]);
```

Continued

```
        this._designer = new personElements();
    }

    Custom.SLPerson.prototype = {
        initialize : function() {
            Custom.SLPerson.callBaseMethod(this, 'initialize');

            // Call on the component initialized to get the
            // specific component's XAML element fields.
            this._designer.initializeComponent(this.get_element());

            // Hookup event handlers as required in this custom type.

            var onClick = Function.createDelegate(this, this._onPersonClick);

        this.addEventListener(this._designer.leftarm, "mouseLeftButtonUp", onClick);
        this.addEventListener(this._designer.rightarm, "mouseLeftButtonUp", onClick);
        this.addEventListener(this._designer.head, "mouseLeftButtonUp", onClick);
        this.addEventListener(this._designer.leftleg, "mouseLeftButtonUp", onClick);
        this.addEventListener(this._designer.rightleg, "mouseLeftButtonUp", onClick);
        this.addEventListener(this._designer.torso, "mouseLeftButtonUp", onClick);
        },

        _onPersonClick : function(sender, e) {
            var region = sender.Name;
            this.toggleVisibility(region);

            var elem = $get(region + "CheckBox");
            elem.checked = !elem.checked;
        },

        toggleVisibility : function(region) {
            var elem = this._designer[region];
            var wasVisible = (elem.children.getItem(1).Visibility == "Visible");
            elem.children.getItem(1).Visibility = wasVisible ? "Collapsed" : "Visible";
        }
    }
    Custom.SLPerson.registerClass('Custom.SLPerson', Sys.UI.Silverlight.Control);
```

After finding those parts, you hook up to the `mouseLeftButtonUp` event and attach it to `_onPersonClick`. That method will get called each time you click a dot.

Within `_onPersonClick` you call a new method `toggleVisibility` that will not only change the visibility of the dot, but also use an ASP.NET Ajax JavaScript method `$get()` to grab onto a similarly named HTML checkbox and toggle its `checked` property.

At this point, clicking on the Chiro Dude in certain spots toggles the dots and checkboxes simultaneously. However, you also need to hook event handlers up to the checkboxes themselves so that they toggle the dots within the Chiro Dude.

Accessing Silverlight Elements from JavaScript Events

You can use the `$find()` method to access our Silverlight control. What's this? There's `$find()` and `$get()`? What's the difference between these two methods?

Well, `$find()` is a shortcut for `Sys.Application.findComponent`, whereas `$get()` is an alias for the `getElementById` method. The `$get()` method will work on any browser, even those without support for `getElementById`. Generally, `$find()` is useful for getting a reference to a Silverlight control from within JavaScript, whereas `$get()` is typically used for getting references to standard HTML controls, DIVS, and SPANS.

Now, let's add these attributes to our check boxes:

```
<asp:CheckBox ID="headCheckBox" runat="server" Text="Head"
OnClick="$find('Xaml1').toggleVisibility('head')" />
<br />
<asp:CheckBox ID="leftarmCheckBox" runat="server" Text="Left arm"
OnClick="$find('Xaml1').toggleVisibility('leftarm')" />
<br />
<asp:CheckBox ID="rightarmCheckBox" runat="server" Text="Right arm"
OnClick="$find('Xaml1').toggleVisibility('rightarm')" />
<br />
<asp:CheckBox ID="torsoCheckBox" runat="server" Text="Torso"
 OnClick="$find('Xaml1').toggleVisibility('torso')" />
<br />
<asp:CheckBox ID="leftlegCheckBox" runat="server" Text="Left leg"
OnClick="$find('Xaml1').toggleVisibility('leftleg')" />
<br />
<asp:CheckBox ID="rightlegCheckBox" runat="server" Text="Right leg"
OnClick="$find('Xaml1').toggleVisibility('rightleg')" />
```

Here you've added a `$find()` call to grab your Silverlight controls. Then you call the `toggleVisbility` method that you added in Listing C-5. You've completed the cycle and now users can click the check boxes or the Chiro Dude in order to make their selection. And, because the resulting Form POST still uses the values of the check boxes, you haven't had to change any server-side code.

The completed application is shown in Figure C-12. Notice that the check boxes and Chiro Dude's pain dots are in sync.

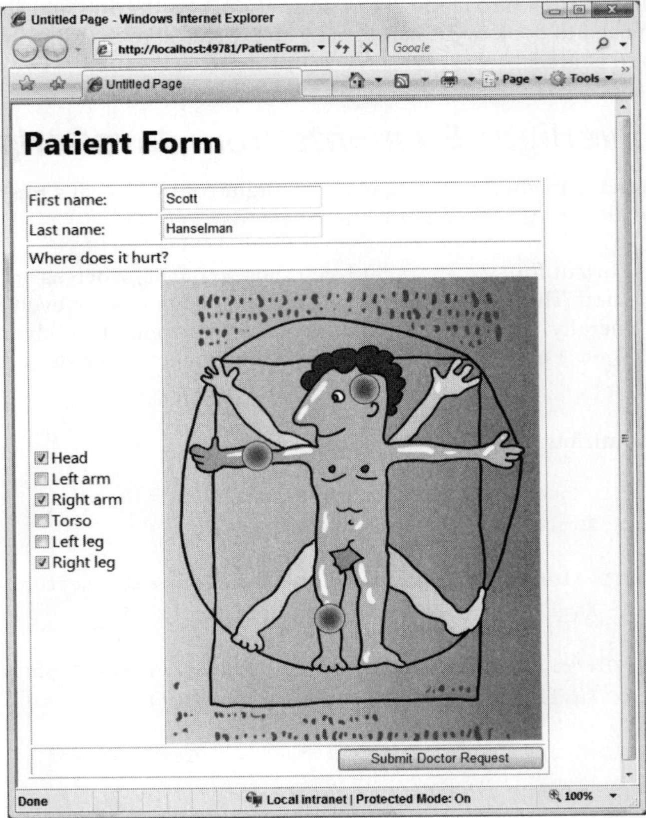

Figure C-12

Summary

Silverlight 1.0 has a very clean, very natural programming model that feels familiar to developers who have programmed against the JavaScript DOM or worked with AJAX code of any kind. The bridge between Silverlight and JavaScript is seamless, allowing ASP.NET developers to mix and match Silverlight and HTML as they like.

Programming with Silverlight will get even easier in the near future when a minor release adds Silverlight Server Controls and an improved ScriptManager to ASP.NET 3.5.

ASP.NET Online Resources

Author Blogs

Bill Evjen: www.geekswithblogs.net/evjen

Scott Hanselman: www.hanselman.com/blog/

Devin Rader: www.geekswithblogs.net/devin

ASP.NET Influential Blogs

Kent Sharkey: www.acmebinary.com/blog

Rob Howard: weblogs.asp.net/rhoward/

Scott Guthrie: weblogs.asp.net/scottgu

Steve Smith: blogs.aspadvice.com/ssmith/

G. Andrew Duthie: blogs.msdn.com/gduthie/

Scott Mitchell: scottonwriting.net/sowBlog/

Scott Watermasysk: scottwater.com/blog/

Nikhil Kothari: www.nikhilk.net/

Dave Sussman: www.daveandal.net/daveroom/diary.asp

Mike Pope: www.mikepope.com/blog/

Web Sites

123ASPX Directory: www.123aspx.com

4 Guys from Rolla: www.4guysfromrolla.com

Angry Coder: www.angrycoder.com

ASP 101: www.asp101.com

ASP Alliance: www.aspalliance.com

ASP Alliance Lists: www.aspadvice.com

The ASP.NET Developer Portal: msdn2.microsoft.com/asp.net

ASP.NET Homepage: www.asp.net

ASP.NET Resources: www.aspnetresources.com

ASP.NET World: www.aspnetworld.com

DotNetJunkies: www.dotnetjunkies.com

GotDotNet: www.gotdotnet.com

International .NET Association: www.ineta.org

Microsoft's ASP.NET AJAX Site: www.asp.net/ajax/

Microsoft's Classic ASP Site: msdn2.microsoft.com/en-us/library/aa286483.aspx

Microsoft Developer Centers: msdn2.microsoft.com/developercenters

Microsoft Forums: forums.microsoft.com

Microsoft Newsgroups: msdn.microsoft.com/newsgroups/

Microsoft's Open Source Project Community: www.codeplex.com

.NET 247: www.dotnet247.com

RegExLib: www.regexlib.com

The ServerSide .NET: www.theserverside.net

XML for ASP.NET: www.xmlforasp.net

Index

SYMBOLS & NUMBERS

$ (dollar sign), currency translation, 1358
*** (asterisk), URL Authorization, 1395**
"... <>", calling descendants, 488–489
"<>", calling elements, 488–489
?, URL Authorization, 1395
400 errors, exception handling, 1102

A

<a> **element, 263**
Absolute positioning, CSS elements, 855
accelerator keys, 105
Access Control Lists. *See* ACLs (Access Control Lists)
access rules, 1466–1471, 1474
AccessDataSource control, 294
AccessKey **attribute, hot-keys, 106**
Accordion control, AJAX, 955–958
AccordionPane controls, 955–957
ACLs (Access Control Lists)
adding rules to, 1130–1131
overview of, 1127–1133
querying information about, 1127–1128
removing rules from, 1132
AcquireRequestState, Session **object, 1006**
acronyms, design guidelines, 478
Actions pane, IIS Manager, 549
Activate **event, Wizard server control, 177**
Active Directory Application Mode (ADAM), 579–581
Active Server Pages (ASP), 61
ActiveDirectoryMembershipProvider, **579–581**
ActiveX component, installing private assembiles, 1277–1278
ActiveX DLL
adding to References section of project, 1269–1270
using COM objects in ASP.NET, 1269–1270, 1272–1273
ADAM (Active Directory Application Mode), 579–581
adapters, CSS Friendly Control Adapters toolkit, 864
Add Application Extensions Mapping dialog, IIS 5, 1253
Add Connection dialog box, 402–403
Add Field dialog, GridView, 315–317
Add Reference dialog, 1267, 1269, 1272
Add Service Reference dialog, 1336, 1342
Add Web Reference dialog, 1303
<add> **element**
adding profiles with, 1449
adding providers with, 1447
adding rules with, 1448
adding SQL Server data provider, 722
application-specific settings, 1404
<eventMappings> configuration, 1444
SQL Server cache invalidation, 1061
working with personalization properties, 702, 707, 711
AddAccessRule( ) **method, ACLs, 1131–1132**
AddAttribute( ) **method, server controls, 1181**
AddAttributesToRender( ) **method, server controls, 1183–1186**
AddRemoveProgramsIcon **property, installer properties, 1513**
AddStyleAttribute**, server controls, 1185**

`AddUsersToRole( )` method, `Roles` class, 633–634, 636–637, 778–779
Adjacent Selectors, CSS, 842
administration
- security trimming, 691–692
- setting up `AdminOnly.aspx` page, 692
- using Web Site Administration Tool. *See* Web Site Administration Tool

Administration Tool
- building browser-based, 1434–1439
- viewing performance counters through, 1431–1434

ADO.NET
- asynchronous command execution. *See* asynchronous command execution
- asynchronous connections, 435
- common tasks, 362–366
- `DataAdapter` object, 373–376
- DataList server control, 387–393
- `DataReader` object, 371–373
- `DataSet` and `DataTable`, 379–384
- deleting data, 366
- inserting data, 364–365
- ListView server control, 393–402
- namespaces and classes, 367–368
- Oracle as database with ASP.NET 3.5, 384–387
- parameters, 376–379
- selecting data, 362–364
- updating data, 365–366
- using `Command` object, 370–371
- using `Connection` object, 368–370

ADO.NET, using Visual Studio, 402–413
- creating connection to data source, 402–404
- using `CustomerOrders` DataSet, 409–413
- working with DataSet Designer, 404–409

AdRotator server control, 145–146, 351
Advanced Settings dialog, IIS Manager, 552–553
`after` element, CSS, 845
`AggregateCacheDependency` class, 1050
AJAX (Asynchronous JavaScript and XML)
- applications, 874–876
- Aptana open source libraries for, 1545–1546
- building ASP.NET page with, 877–883
- building ASP.NET page without, 876–877
- development of, 868–871
- need for, 867–868
- overview of, 867
- Visual Studio 2008 and, 871–874

AJAX (Asynchronous JavaScript and XML), server-side controls, 883–899
- overview of, 883–884
- ScriptManager control, 883–886
- ScriptManagerProxy control, 886–887
- Timer control, 887–888
- UpdatePanel control, 888–892
- UpdateProgress control, 892–896
- using multiple UpdatePanel controls, 896–899

AJAX Control Toolkit
- adding controls to VS2008 Toolbox, 904
- ASP.NET controls, 904–906
- downloading and installing, 901–902
- new Visual Studio templates, 902–903
- overview of, 1555

AJAX Control Toolkit control extenders, 907–955
- AlwaysVisibleControlExtender control, 908–910
- AnimationExtender server control, 910–911
- AutoCompleteExtender control, 912–915
- CalendarExtender control, 915–916
- CollapsiblePanelExtender server control, 916–918
- ConfirmButtonExtender control, 918–920
- DragPanelExtender control, 920–922
- DropDownExtender control, 922–924
- DropShadowExtender control, 924–926
- DynamicPopulateExtender control, 926–930
- FilteredTextBoxExtender control, 930–931
- HoverMenuExtender control, 931–932
- ListSearchExtender control, 933–934
- MaskedEditExtender and MaskedEditValidator controls, 934–937
- ModalPopUpExtender control, 919–920
- MutuallyExclusiveCheckBoxExtender control, 937–938

NumericUpDownExtender control, 938–939
overview of, 907–908
PagingBulletedListExtender control, 939–940
PopUpControlExtender control, 941–942
ResizableControlExtender control, 942–944
RoundedCornersExtender control, 944–945
SliderExtender control, 946–947
SlideShowExtender control, 947–950
TextBoxWatermarkExtender control, 950–951
ToggleButtonExtender control, 951–952
UpdatePanelAnimationExtender control, 953–954
ValidatorCalloutExtender control, 954–955
AJAX Control Toolkit server controls, 955–963
Accordion control, 955–958
Extensions, 877–883
NoBot control, 958–960
PasswordStrength control, 960–961
Rating control, 961–962
TabContainer control, 962–963
`AJAXControlExtender.vsi` **file, 902**
`AJAXToolkit.resources.dll`**, 906**
aliases, listing of current, 1074
`All` **attribute, Forms Authentication, 1393**
`<allow>` **node**
authenticating/authorizing groups, 973
authenticating/authorizing HTTP transmission, 973
authenticating/authorizing users, 971–972
URL Authorization, 1395
`allowAnonymous` **attribute, personalization, 716**
`AllowClose` **property,** `WebPart` **class, 821, 823**
`allowDefinition` **attribute, locking-down configuration, 1396–1397**
`AllowDirectoryBrowsing` **property, File System Editor, 1515**
`AllowLayoutChange` **attribute, Web Parts, 809**
`allowOverride` **attribute, locking-down configuration, 1396–1397**
`AllowReadAccess` **property, File System Editor, 1515**
`AllowReturn` **attribute, Wizard server control, 172**
`AllowScriptSourceAccess` **property, File System Editor, 1515**
`AllowWriteAccess` **property, File System Editor, 1515**
AlternatingItemTemplate, DataList server control, 390–392
AlwaysVisibleControlExtender control, 908–910
animations, extender controls, 910–911, 953–954
anonymous authentication, 583
anonymous identity, 1393–1394
anonymous personalization. *See* personalization, anonymous
anonymous users, URL Authorization, 1395
`AnonymousID` **property, anonymous identifier storage, 714**
`AnonymousIdentification_Creating` **event, 715**
`<anonymousIdentification>` **section, configuration, 1394**
<AnonymousTemplate>, LoginView control, 769–770
ANTS profiler, Red Gate Software, 1546–1547
Apache Web Server, and `mod_rewrite`**, 1557**
`-app` **command, 1413**
`\App_Browsers` **folder, 38–39**
`\App_Code` **folder, 32–37, 1263**
`\App_Data folder`**, 37**
`\App_GlobalResources` **folder, 38**
`\App_LocalResources` **folder, 38**
`\App_prefix`**, reserved folders, 1529**
`\App_Themes` **folder, 37–38, 258–259**
`\App_WebReferences` **folder, 38**
Appearance section, Web Parts, 805
Application Configuration dialog, IIS, 996–999
application configuration files, 1377–1378
`@Application` **directive,** `Global.asax` **file, 51–52**
application event logs, writing to, 1428–1430
Application Extension Configuration dialog, IIS 6, 1254

application frameworks
adding `Global.asax` file, 50–53
application location options, 1–5
build providers, 43–50
compilation, 39–43
folders, 32–39
working with classes through VS2008, 53–59
`Application` **object, 1028–1029**
application packaging and deploying
with Copy Web Site, 1496–1501
Custom Actions Editor, 1522–1523
deployment pieces, 1492
File System Editor, 1514–1518
File Types Editor, 1519–1520
installation programs, 1501–1507
Launch Conditions Editor, 1523–1524
overview of, 1491
precompiled Web applications, 1499–1501
Registry Editor, 1518–1519
steps to take before, 1492–1493
summary review, 1524
User Interface Editor, 1520–1522
Windows Installer options, 1510–1514
XCOPY, 1493–1496
application pools, IIS Manager, 550–553, 1481
Application Restarts performance counter, 1432
Application Settings, IIS Manager, 1485–1486
Application tab, Web Site Administration Tool, 1474–1475
`Application_onError` **handler, 1102**
`applicationHost.config` **file, IIS Manager**
adding Web site, 554–555
delegation, 564
hierarchical configuration, 559–561
overview of, 550–553
`ApplicationName` **property,** `MembershipProvider` **class, 621–622**
`ApplicationProtection` **property, File System Editor, 1515**
applications
configuring for SQL Server cache invalidation, 1060–1061
error and exception handling, 1103–1104
storing settings specific to, 1404–1405
tracing, 1076–1080, 1439
Applications Running performance counter, 1432
Applied Rules list, CSS Properties Tool window, 861–862
Apply Styles tool window, Visual Studio, 860–861
`AppMappings` **property, File System Editor, 1515**
`appRequestQueueLimit` **attribute, runtime, 1401**
AppScaler, 1026
`<appSettings>`, `web.config` **file, 1380–1381, 1404, 1474–1475**
Aptana Studio, JavaScript IDE, 1545–1546
architecture, IIS 7
extensible, 542
modular, 537–538
`.ascx` **file extension, user controls, 1160**
`.ashx` **file extension, HttpHandlers, 1255**
`.asmx` **file extension, Web service files, 1294, 1303**
ASMX Web Services, 1326
ASP (Active Server Pages), 61
ASP.NET
AJAX. *See* AJAX (Asynchronous JavaScript and XML)
application packaging and deploying. *See* application packaging and deploying
configuration settings, 1397–1399
Extensions Preview, 1578–1581
forms-based authentication, 1528
IIS 7 integrated pipeline with, 542–544
localization threads, 1349–1352
Machine account, 160
Management Objects, 1405–1412
migrating from 1x to 2.0, 1526–1528
migrating from 2.0 to 3.5, 1528
runtime configuration settings, 1399–1402

Snap-In for IIS 6.0 or Windows Vista's IIS Manager, 1416–1417
TreeView Line Generator dialog, 663
Web Site Administration Tool. *See* Web Site Administration Tool
Web Site Configuration Tool, 603
worker process configuration settings, 1402–1404

ASP.NET Development Server, 1091–1092

ASP.NET MMC snap-in
configuring providers in, 603
migrating from 1x to 2.0, 1526–1528
security through IIS, 999–1000

ASP.NET SQL Server Setup Wizard
command-line tool, 571–573
configuring personalization framework, 722
configuring SQL-backed session state, 1022–1024
defined, 571
as GUI tool, 573–575

`aspnet_compiler.exe` **tool, 41**
`aspnet_isapi` **extension module, IIS 7, 544**
`aspnet_regiis.exe` **tool, 1404, 1413**
`aspnet_regsql.exe` **tool, 571–574, 1022–1024, 1055–1060**
`AspNet_SqlCacheTablesForChangeNotification` **table, 1061**
`aspnet_state.exe` **tool, 1016**
`aspnet_wp.exe`**, 1017, 1028**
`ASPNETDB.mdf` **file, 721–722, 737**
`AspNetSql2005ProfileProvider`**, 724**
`AspNetSqlProfileProvider`**, 751**

ASPX Edit Helper for Visual Studio, 1553

`.aspx` **extension**
caching with master pages, 248–249
content page basics, 221
content page coding, 226–229
converting ASP.NET 1.x in Visual Studio 2008, 1536

assemblies
adding to installer output, 1515–1516
LINQ, 446
private, 1277–1278, 1288
public, 1278, 1288–1289

`assemblies` **attribute, compilation, 1387**
`@Assembly` **directive, 12, 21, 51–52**

Assembly Registration Tool (`regasm.exe`**), 1285, 1288**

assembly resource (.resx) files, 687

`AsyncCallback` **class, 416**

asynchronous command execution, 414–435
with `AsyncCallback` class, 416
callback approach to, 432–434, 1192–1196
canceling, 434
consuming Web services, 1323–1325
`IAsyncResult` interface and, 415–416
methods of `SqlCommand` class, 414–415
overview of, 414
poll approach to, 417–420
using multiple wait handles, 423–432
wait approach to, 420–423
`WaitHandle` class, 416–417

Asynchronous JavaScript and XML. *See* AJAX (Asynchronous JavaScript and XML)

asynchronous postbacks
UpdatePanel control, 890–892
using Timer control for, 887–888

`Asynchronous` **property,** `SqlConnection` **class, 435**

AsyncPostBackTrigger, 892

atomization, 493

Attach to Process, Debug menu, 1093

Attribute Selectors, CSS, 842

attributes
`<add/>`, 1447
`@Assembly` directive, 21
`<browser>`, 1388–1389
buffering Web events, 1455
code-behind pages, 11
`<compilation>`, 1386–1387
`@Control` directive, 17–18
`<eventMappings>`, 1445
`<form>`, 736–737
Forms Authentication, 1392–1393
`@Implements` directive, 20
locking-down configuration, 1396–1397
`@Master` directive, 16
`@MasterType` directive, 21

attributes *(continued)*
modifying file and directory, 1126–1127
modifying provider behaviors, 606–611
@OutputCache directive, 22
@Page directive, 13–15
@PreviousPageType directive, 21
<processModel> element, 1402–1404
@Reference directive, 22
@Register directive, 20
rendering HTML tag, 1181–1183
<rolemanager>, 772–773
<rules>, 1447–1448
runtime settings configuration, 1399–1402
server control, 1175–1176
<sessionState>, 1382
<siteMapNode>, 641
SqlMembershipProvider, 751
storing application-specific settings, 1404–1405
@WebService directive, 1295
XML document, 479–480
Audit Failure Events Raised performance counter, 1432
Audit Success Events Raised performance counter, 1432
Australia, culture codes, 1348
Authenticate( ) **method, forms authentication, 982**
authentication, 734–769
applying measures, 966–967
authorization vs., 966
configuring, 1390–1393
configuring WindowsTokenRoleProvider, 583–584
credentials, 752–760
defined, 734
forms-based. *See* Forms-based authentication
IIS 6 interaction with ASP.NET, 542–544
MembershipProvider class, 624–626
Passport. *See* Passport authentication
passwords and, 764–768
setting <authentication> node, 967–968
showing number of users online, 762–764
of specific files and folders, 986–987
users, adding, 737–751
users, authenticating, 969–971
users, working with authenticated, 760–762
using ASP.NET MMC snap-in, 999–1000
using Security Setup Wizard, 1466–1471
Web site setup for, 734–737
Windows-based. *See* Windows-based authentication
WindowsIdentity object and, 990–992
author blogs, online resources, 1585
Author **property, installer properties, 1513**
authorization, 769–785
applying to single file, 987
authentication vs., 966
configuration settings, 1394–1396
defined, 734
with LoginView server control, 769–771
roles, adding and retrieving application, 775–777
roles, adding users to, 778–779
roles, caching of, 783–785
roles, checking for specific user in, 782–783
roles, deleting, 777–778
roles, getting all users of particular, 779–780
roles, getting for specific user, 781
roles, removing users from, 781–782
roles, setting up Web site for managing, 771–775
of specific files and folders, 987
Windows-based, 969–973
authorization, programmatic, 987–992
overview of, 987–988
with User.Identity property, 988–989
using User.IsInRole( ) method, 989–990
with WindowsIdentity, 990–992
<authorization> **element, 752**
AuthorizationStoreRoleProvider**, 584–585**
Auto Format, TreeView server control, 652–653
AutoCompleteExtender control, 912–915
AutoDetect **value, storing identifiers, 714**
autoEventWireup **element, page configuration, 1398**

AutoGenerateDeleteButton **property, 327, 335–336**
AutoGenerateEditButton **attribute, 322**
automaticSaveEnabled **attribute,** <profile> **node, 720**
AutoPostBack **property**
DropDownList control, 118
RadioButton server control, 130
TextBox server control, 108–110

B

Base Class Library (BCL), 1107
Basic authentication, 974–975
batch **attribute, compilation configuration, 1386**
Batch section, .NET compilation, 1481–1482
batchTimeout **attribute, compilation configuration, 1386**
BCL (Base Class Library), 1107
before element, CSS, 845
BeginExecuteReader**, asynchronous commands, 417–420**
***Beginning JavaScript, Third Edition* (Wiley Publishing, Inc.), 86**
Beyond Compare, 1559
Bin **folder, 1267**
binary metabase, 1374
BinaryReader **class, 1140**
BinaryWriter **class, 1140**
Bind **method, data binding, 353**
binding
early vs. late, 1285
Menu server control to XML file, 676–678
TreeView control to XML file, 654–656
Blend, Microsoft, 1574–1576
block boxes, 851
blogs (weblogs), and XmlDataSource **control, 515–517**
blogs (weblogs), online resources, 1585–1586
Blowery Http Compression Module, 1145
<body> **tag, 263**
BooleanSwitch**, 1087–1088**
bootstrapping, 1512
borders, CheckBoxList control, 128
Bound List controls
AdRotator control, 351
DetailsView server control, 330–335
DropDownList control, 350
FormView, 345–350
GridView control. *See* GridView control
ListBox control, 350
ListView control. *See* ListView server control
Menu control, 351
overview of, 304
RadioButtonList control, 350
TreeView control, 350–351
box model, CSS, 850–853
breadcrumb navigation, SiteMapPath control, 642
.browser **files, 1196–1198, 1388–1389**
browsers
Administrative Tool and, 1434–1439
\App_Browsers folder, 38–39
ASP.NET server controls and, 62
client-side caching and, 1046–1048
configuration settings, 1387–1389
container-specific master pages and, 246–248
displaying event log contents, 1426–1428
downlevel, 1196–1199
implementing CSS, 836
internal stylesheets and, 73
limitations of classic ASP, 61–62
state management and, 1004
supporting Basic authentication, 974
buffer **element, 1398**
buffer uploads, 1401
BufferedWebEventProvider**, 591, 595, 597, 1453–1455**
buffering, Web events, 1453–1455
Build Calculator, 1265
build providers, 43–50
compilation configuration, 1387
constructing own, 45–50
overview of, 43
using built-in, 44–45

built-in Web server, 2
BulletedList server control, 150–155
business objects, .NET
COM Interoperability with. *See* COM Interop
defined, 1263
using from unmanaged code. *See*.NET from unmanaged code
using in ASP.NET 3.5, 1263–1267
Button server control
`CausesValidation` property, 111
`CommandName` property, 111–112
ImageButton server control, 115–116
LinkButton server control, 114–115
overview of, 111–114
working with client-side JavaScript, 112–114
`Button_Command` **event, 112**
buttons
events, 66–67
Wizard navigation, 174
`Byte` **arrays, 165–166, 1135**

C

Cab Project, 1502
CAB Size, 1512–1513
cabinet files, 1512–1513
`Cache` **object**
`Application` object vs., 1028–1029
attaching SQL Server cache dependencies to, 1065–1068
cache dependencies, 1049–1055
data caching using, 1048–1049
Cache-Control HTTP Header, 1046–1048
`CacheDependency`**, 1049–1055**
`AggregateCacheDependency` class, 1050
creating custom, 1051–1055
defined, 1049
setting dependencies with `Insert` method, 1049
`SqlCacheDependency` class, 1055, 1060–1061, 1065–1068
`UnsealedCacheDependency` class, 1050–1051
`CacheDuration` **property, SOAP responses, 1315–1316**
caching
data source control, 300–301
defined, 1039
detecting cached user controls, 1166–1168
`HttpCachePolicy` class and client-side, 1046–1048
with master pages, 248–249
output, 1039–1040
overview of, 1039
partial page, 1042–1043
post-cache substitution, 1043–1045
programmatically, 1048–1055
roles, 783–785
testing SQL Server invalidation, 1062–1068
using AnimationExtender control, 915
using SQL Server Cache Dependency, 1055–1060
Web service responses, 1315–1316
Calendar server control, 137–144
date format, 138–139
date ranges, 139–141
date selection, 137–138
day, week or month selections, 139
overview of, 136
style and behavior, 141–144
CalendarExtender control, 915–916
Canada, culture codes, 1348
`Cancel` **method, asynchronous processing, 434**
CAPI (cryptographic API), 601
`Caption` **attribute, Table server control, 135–136**
Cascading Style Sheets. *See* CSS (Cascading Style Sheets)
Cassini Web server, 1092
casting, user control to its native type, 1166
Catalog Mode, Portal Framework Web pages, 788, 801–802, 803
`CausesValidation` **property, Button server control, 111**
CCW (Com-Callable Wrapper), 1279–1281
`.cd` **file extension (class designer), 53–59**

Cell property, DayRenderEventArgs class, 144
ChangeConflictException, 474
ChangePassword server control, 764–765
check boxes, in TreeView, 656–659
CheckBox server control
CheckBoxList server control vs., 127
overview of, 124–126
RadioButton server control vs., 129
with ToggleButtonExtender control, 951–952
using MutuallyExclusiveCheckBoxExtender control with, 937–938
CheckBoxList server control, 127–129
visually removing items from collections, 119–121
Checked property, CheckBox server control, 126
child elements, SiteMapPath server control, 648
child nodes, TreeView control, 653
Child Selectors, CSS, 841
Choose Location dialog, 2–5
Choose Toolbox Items dialog, Visual Studio 2008 Toolbox, 904
class designer (.cd file extension), 53–59
Class Selectors, CSS, 842–843
classes
\App_Code folder for, 32–37
basic ADO.NET, 367–368
configuration file programming, 1405–1406
CSS pseudo, 843–844
derived from Stream class, 1134
in LINQ to SQL, 463
Portal Framework, 814–818
working with, 53–59
classic ASP
ASP.NET today vs., 61–62
event model, 65–66
include files in, 219–221
Session object in, 1006
Client Script Library, AJAX, 872–873
ClientID property, server controls, 1182
ClientScriptManager class, 1187–1192
client-side, adding features to server controls, 1187–1196
accessing embedded resources, 1192
asynchronous callbacks, 1192–1196
emitting client-side script, 1187–1192
client-side AJAX, 872–873
client-side authentication settings, 1391
client-side caching, 1046–1048
client-side callback, 87–101
complex example of, 95–101
overview of, 86
simple approach for, 87–92
typical postback vs., 86–87
using single parameter, 92–95
client-side culture declarations, 1353–1354
client-side Javascript debugging, 1098–1101
client-side state management, 1005–1006
client-side validation
CustomValidator control with, 202–208
server-side validation vs., 186–187
turning off, 211–212
Close( ) method
Stream class, 1135
XmlReader, 528
XmlReader and XmlWriter, 505
CLR objects, creating from XML, 498–499
cmd.ExecuteNonQuery( ) command, ADO.NET, 365
code
content pages, 225–229
in-line pages, 7–9
master pages, 223–225
online converter tool for, 1558
server controls, 64–65
tools for tidying up, 1550–1552
Code Converter, online, 1558
Code Style Enforcer, 1551
code-access security (CAS), 1376–1377
code-behind pages
for AutoCompleteExtender, 913–915
creating new page using, 9–11
for CustomerOrders page, 411
for DynamicPopulateExtender control, 927–929

code-behind pages *(continued)*
for NoBot control, 959–960
overview of, 9–11
for XML Web, 1295
CodeExpression **class, 356**
CodeFile **attribute,** Page **directive, 11**
codegen **folder, buffer uploads, 1401**
codeSubDirectories **attribute, compilation configuration, 1386**
CollapseAll( ) **method,** TreeView **class, 663–667**
Collapsed **property, CollapsiblePanelExtender control, 917**
CollapsiblePanelExtender server control, 916–918
collections, visually removing items from, 119–121
Color Picker, 1237
columns
DataList control, creating multiple, 392–393
Grid View control, sorting, 310–312
GridView control, customizing, 314–317
GridView control, editing row data, 320–323
GridView control, using TemplateField, 317–320
inserting XML data into, 534
COM Interop, 1268–1278
assessing tricky members in C#, 1273–1274
deploying components with .NET apps, 1277–1278
error handling, 1274–1277
overview of, 1268
releasing COM objects manually, 1274
Runtime Callable Wrapper, 1268–1269
using COM objects in ASP.NET code, 1269–1274
Com-Callable Wrapper (CCW), 1279–1281
Command and Parameter Editor dialog, 282
Command **object**
defined, 367–368
using DataReader object, 371–373
using in ADO.NET, 370–371
Command window, 1074
CommandField**, 322**
CommandName **property, Button server control, 111–112**
comments
internal stylesheets using HTML, 73
in XML documents, 479
Comments view, Task List, 1074
CompareValidator server control, 188, 194–197
compilation
configuration, 1385–1387
configuration settings, 1385–1387
.NET Compilation in IIS Manager, 1481–1482
overview of, 39–43
precompilation for deployment, 1499–1501
precompilation of .NET business objects, 1264–1266
compilationMode, <pages> **configuration, 1398**
components, tracing from, 1080–1082
composite controls, 1209–1212, 1225–1227
compression, deployment project, 1512
compression, streams
HTTP output, 1145–1147
using Deflate( ) method, 1144–1145
using GZipStream, 1143–1144
Computer Management utility, group authentication, 972–973
concurrency, LINQ to SQL, 474
<configSections> **element, 875, 1379–1380**
configSource **attribute, include files configuration, 1398**
configuration
altering SQL Server versions, 576–577
anonymous identity, 1393–1394
application file, 1377–1378
applying in hierarchal manner, 966
applying settings, 1378–1379
ASP.NET pages, 1397–1399
ASP.NET runtime settings, 1399–1402
ASP.NET worker process, 1402–1404
authentication, 1390–1393
authorization, 1394–1396
browser capabilities, 1387–1389
compilation, 1385–1387

connecting strings, 1380–1381
custom errors, 1389–1390
custom sections, 1417–1424
detecting changes, 1379
editing files, 1416–1417
file format, 1379–1380
health monitoring, 1442–1449
with IIS Manager. *See* IIS (Internet Information Service) Manager
include files, 1399
locking-down settings, 1396–1397
overview of, 1373–1374
programming files, 1405–1412
protecting settings, 1412–1416
of providers, 603
server configuration files, 1375–1377
session state, 1381–1385
storing application-specific settings, 1404–1405
summary review, 1424
with Web Site Administration Tool. *See* Web Site Administration Tool
writing events via, 1449–1450

configuration files, session state and, 1374

configuration providers, 598–601

Configure Behavior dialog, 473

Configure Data Source Wizard, 277–281, 286–288

Configure Data Wizard, 294–295

Configure ListView dialog, 338

ConfirmButtonExtender control, 918–920

`ConflictDetection` **property, SqlDataSource control, 282–285**

`Connection` **object**
defined, 367
executing SQL queries with, 370
using `DataReader` object, 371–373
using in ADO.NET, 368–370

connection strings
configuration settings, 1380–1381
connecting `SqlProfileProvider` to SQL Server 2005, 586
creating `ActiveDirectoryMembershipProvider`, 579
enumerating, 1408–1409
IIS Manager, 1486
protecting configuration settings, 1412–1416
session state configuration, 1384
storing connection information, 301–304
using `Connection` object in ADO.NET, 368–370
using `ConnectionStringBuilder` for, 304

connections
asynchronous, 435
to data source, 402–404
to Oracle Database, 384–387
SqlDataSource control, 277–281
between WebParts. *See* Web Parts, connecting

Connections pane, IIS Manager, 549–555
Application Pools node, 550–553
overview of, 549
Sites node, 554–555

`ConnectionString` **property, SqlDataSource control, 279, 281, 288–289, 722**

`ConnectionStringBuilder` **class, 304**

`connectionStringName` **attribute,** `<add>` **element, 1061**

constants, validating against, 196–197

consumer Web Parts, 824–825, 828–830

consuming XML Web services. ***See*** **XML Web services, consuming**

`Container.DataItem` **syntax, 353**

containers, ListView, 342–343

container-specific master pages, 246–248

content areas, 221–223, 240–241

content pages
basics, 221–223
caching with master pages, 248–249
coding, 225–229
mixing languages/master pages with, 229–231
programmatically assigning master pages to, 241–243
working with page title on, 232

ContentPlaceholder **server control, 240–241, 244–246**

<ContentTemplate>**, LoginView control, 771**

<ContentTemplate>**, UpdatePanel server control, 889–890**

ContinueButtonClick( ) **event, CreateUserWizard control, 741–742**

Control **class, 68**

control designers, 1224–1237
- designer actions, 1234–1236
- designer regions, 1225–1234
- overview of, 1224

@Control **directive**
- defined, 12
- overview of, 17–18
- for user controls, 1160

control IDs, 1182

ControlContainer **class, 1224**

controls
- data source. *See* data source controls
- IIS Manager, 1486–1487
- master page, 233–239
- server. *See* server controls
- styling ASP.NET, 863–864

Controls **collection, 1164–1166**

ControlState
- client-side state management, 1006
- state management and, 1036
- using in server controls, 1201–1203

ControlToValidate **property**
- CompareValidator control, 194–197
- CustomValidator control, 205
- Regular Expression validator control, 202
- RequiredFieldValidator control, 190, 193

conversion, currency, 1358–1360

ConversionReport.webinfo **file, 1536–1537**

cookieless **attribute, Forms Authentication, 1393**

cookieless session state, 1026–1027, 1382, 1489

cookieName **attribute, 712–713, 1011**

cookies
- achieving identification without, 713–714
- changing length of time stored, 713
- changing name for anonymous identification, 713
- client-side state management, 1004–1005
- with Login control, 754
- persistent user data storage and, 699
- roles cached in, 783–785
- setting anonymous, 712–713
- storing only non-sensitive information in, 1029–1030

cookieTimeout **attribute, anonymous personlization, 712–713**

Copy Web Site GUI, deployment option, 1496–1501
- precompiled Web applications, 1499–1501

copy-and-paste deployment, XCOPY, 1493–1496

Corners **property, RoundedCornersExtender control, 945**

counters, performance, 1430–1439

CR_Documentor, 1561–1562

Create( ) **method,** XmlReader**, 486–488**

Create or Manage Roles link, ASP.NET Web Site Administration Tool, 690–691

CreateChildControls( ) **method, Web Parts, 822, 828, 830**

CreateEventSource()**, writing to event log, 1430**

CreateNewStoreData( ) **method,** SessionStateModule**, 1026**

CreateRole( ) **method,** Roles **class, 631–632, 634–635, 776**

createSilverlight( ) **method, 1573**

CreateUser( ) **event, CreateUserWizard control, 741–742, 745–746**

CreateUser( ) **method, Membership API, 746**

CreateUserWizard server control
- adding user to membership service, 737–739
- overview of, 737–739
- seeing where users are stored, 739–741
- using personalization properties, 742–746
- working with, 741–742

credentials
- authenticating against values in database, 982–984

authenticating against values in web.config file, 980–982
Basic authentication, 974–975
Digest authentication, 975–976
locking out users with bad passwords, 756–760
logging in users programmatically, 755–756
remote debugging, 1093–1094
turning off access with <authorization> element, 752
using Login server control, 752–755, 984–985

cross-page postbacks
Button server control, 114
overview of, 25–32
state management and, 1030–1032

cryptographic API (CAPI), 601

cryptographic service provider (CSP), 601

CsaProviderName **attribute,** RsaProtectedConfigurationProvider**, 601**

CSP (cryptographic service provider), 601

CSS (Cascading Style Sheets)
changing styles using, 70–73
creating files for themes, 261–264
designing. *See* HTML and CSS design
incorporating images into themes using, 264–267
references in ResizableControlExtender control, 943–944
styling HTML for server controls, 1183–1186

CSS properties grid, CSS Properties Tool window, 861–862

CSS Properties tool window, Visual Studio, 861–862

CssClass **property, ASP.NET server controls, 864**

culture **attribute,** Web.config **file, 686**

culture **attribute,** web.config.comments **file, 1352–1353**

culture declarations
client-side, 1353–1354
server-side, 1352–1353

culture types
localization, 1348–1349
.NET globalization, 1482

CultureInfo **object, ASP.NET threads, 1349–1352**

currency, localization, 1356–1360

CurrentNode **property,** SiteMap **class, 681–684**

Custom Actions Editor, 1522–1523

custom sections, configuration, 1417–1424

custom server controls, 270–274

<customErrors> **section, configuration settings, 1389–1390**

Customize Line Images, TreeView control, 662

CustomProviders, 613–614

CustomValidator server control, 188, 202–208

CutoffMaximumInstances **property, NoBot control, 959**

CutoffWindowSeconds **property, NoBot control, 959**

D

data binding
expressions and expression builders, 354–359
inline data-binding syntax, 352
ListView, 343–344
using data source controls. *See* data source controls

data caching, 1048–1049

data concurrency, 284–285, 293

data context, LINQ to SQL, 465

data contract, WCF service, 1329, 1339–1342

data item rendering, ListView, 340–341

data management, with ADO.NET. ***See*** **ADO.NET**

Data Protection API (or DPAPI), 1412–1416

Data Provider **classes, ADO.NET, 367**

data providers. ***See*** **providers**

data source controls
AccessDataSource control, 294
configuring caching, 300–301
LinqDataSource control, 289–294
ObjectDataSource control, 295–300
overview of, 275–277
SiteMapDataSource control, 300
`SqlDataSource` control. *See* `SqlDataSource` control
storing connection information, 301–304
using Bound List controls with. *See* Bound List controls
XmlDataSource control, 294–295
data source, creating connection to, 402–404
data stores, 37, 154
data visualizers, debugging using, 1096–1097
`DataAdapter` **object, 367–368, 373–376**
databases, 524–534
authenticating against values in, 982–984
debugging, 1101
enabling for SQL Server cache invalidation, 1056
routing events to SQL server, 1450–1453
SQL Server cache invalidation, 1059
XML and, 524–528
XML data type and SQL Server 2005, 528–534
`DataBind()` **method, list controls, 304**
data-binding, GridView control, 319
`DataFile` **property, AccessDataSource control, 294**
DataGrid control, 310, 312–314
`DataKeyNames` **property, GridView control, 322–323**
DataList server control, 387–393
available templates, 387
ItemTemplate, 388–390
multiple columns, 392–393
other layout templates, 390–392
styling with CSS-Friendly Control Adapters, 864
DataPager control, 344–345
`DataReader` **object**
in ADO.NET, 371–373
`DataSet` vs., 382–384
defined, 367–368
loading `DataTable` from, 380–382
reading data from SQL database, 362
Dataset Designer view, 484
DataSets
building, 409–413
defined, 379
overview of, 510
persisting to XML, 510–511
typed, 384
when to use, 382–384
`XmlDataDocument`, 511–513
`DataSourceMode` **property, SqlDataSource control, 281**
`DataTable` **objects, 379–384, 510–511**
datatips, debugger, 1096
dates
Calendar control. *See* Calendar server control
CalendarExtender control, 915–916
localization, 1355–1356
`Day` **property,** `DayRenderEventArgs` **class, 144**
`DayRender` **event, Calendar control, 142–144**
DbgView, debugging using, 1081
DCOM, 1307
`debug` **attribute, compilation configuration, 1386**
debug configuration, Visual Studio, 1090–1091
debugging, 1090–1101
in Application tab, 1476–1477
client-side Javascript, 1098–1101
datatips, 1096
debug vs. release, 1090–1091
design-time support for, 1071–1074
IIS vs. ASP.NET Development Server, 1091–1092
JIT dialog and, 1091
new tools for, 1096–1098
overview of, 1090
remote, 1093–1094
SQL stored proc and, 1101

starting session of, 1092–1096
tools, 1541–1547
tracing and. *See* tracing
turning off before deploying, 1492–1493
XSLT, 523
Debug.Write **function, 1081–1082**
declarations, culture, 1352–1354
declarations, XML documents, 479
DeclarativeCatalogPart control, 809
decryption, ViewState, 1035–1036
Default.asp**, 1010, 1015–1016**
Default.aspx **page**
adding language to, 1365–1366
finalizing localization, 1366–1368
local resource files, 1366–1367
setting up administrators' section, 692–693
user login, 628–629
DefaultDocument **property, File System Editor, 1515**
defaultLanguage **attribute, compilation configuration, 1386**
defaultProvider **attribute**
connecting to new SQL Server instance, 575–577
defining provider instance, 618–619
installing personalization, 724
SqlMembershipProvider, 577
SqlRoleProvider, 584
defaultRedirect**, custom errors configuration settings, 1390**
defaultUrl **attribute, Forms authentication, 1393**
defaultValue **attribute, personalization, 711**
Deflate( ) **method, streams, 1144–1145**
delayed execution, LINQ, 451
delegation, IIS Manager, 561–564
DeleteAllOnSubmit **method, LINQ to SQL, 474–475**
DeleteCommand**, DetailsView control, 336**
DeleteCookie( ) **method, Roles API, 784–785**
DeleteOnSubmit **method, LINQ to SQL, 474–475**
DeleteProfile( ) **method,** ProfileManager**, 730**
DeleteRole( ) **method,** Roles **class, 632–633, 777–778**
DeleteUser( ) **method,** ProfileManager**, 731**
deleting, users from roles, 781–782
deleting data
from SQL Server, 366
using DetailsView server control, 335–336
using GridView control, 327–330
using LINQ to SQL, 474–475
using SqlDataSource control, 328
DelimitedListTraceListener, 1085
denial of service (DoS) attacks, 161, 1401
<deny> **node**
authenticating/authorizing groups, 973
authenticating/authorizing HTTP transmission, 973
authenticating/authorizing users, 971–972
denying unauthenticated users, 752
URL authorization, 1395
dependencies, 1049–1055
AggregateCacheDependency class, 1050
creating custom, 1051–1055
IIS 7 update, 545
setting dependencies with Insert method, 1049
testing SQL Server cache invalidation, 1064–1068
UnsealedCacheDependency class, 1050–1051
using SQL Server Cache Dependency, 1055–1060
deployment. *See* application packaging and deploying
Descendant Selectors, CSS, 841
Description **property, installer properties, 1513**
Description **property,** ProviderBase **class, 611**
DescriptionUrl **attribute, Image server control, 133**
Design Mode, Portal Framework Web pages, 788, 797, 802–804

Design view
applying styles to Menu control in, 670–671
dragging and dropping controls in, 63–64
HTML and CSS in, 857–858
HTML server controls in, 74
server control events in, 66–67
viewing nested master pages in, 245–246
Designer **attribute, 1224–1225, 1227**
designer regions
creating composite control with, 1225–1227
customizing designer class to define, 1227–1234
overview of, 1225
DesignerActionList class, 1234–1236
design-time
syntax notifications, 1072–1073
Task List views, 1074–1075
tracing. *See* tracing
using Immediate and Command window at, 1074
design-time, server control behaviors at, 1219–1239
custom type converters, 1221–1223
designers, 1224–1237
overview of, 1219
type converters, 1220–1224
UI type editors, 1237–1238
desktop shortcuts, 1517–1518
DetailsView server control, 330–335
CSS-Friendly Control Adapters for styling, 864
customizing display of, 331
with GridView control, 331–335
inserting, updating and deleting data, 335–336
overview of, 330–331
SelectParameters vs. FilterParameters, 334
DetectNewerInstalledVersion **property, installer properties, 1513**
developers
ASP.NET AJAX and, 874
tools for, 1558–1562
diagnostic switches, 1087–1088
dialog boxes, reporting validation errors, 210–211
dialogs, adding to installation process, 1521–1522
DictionarySectionHandler**, 1417, 1421**
DiffMerge, 1559
Digest authentication, 975–976
Direction **attribute, Panel server control, 149**
directives
Global.asax file, 51–52
page. *See* page directives
directories
browsing with Directory/DirectoryInfo, 1111–1116
displaying files using File/FileInfo, 1117–1122
enumerating file system directories, 1112–1114
getting/setting current, 1116–1117
I/O shortcuts, 1141–1143
modifying Access Control Lists, 1127–1133
modifying properties and attributes, 1126–1127
working with DriveInfo class, 1108–1111
Directory **class, 1111–1116**
DirectoryInfo **class**
browsing directory structure with, 1111–1116
displaying files in directory, 1117–1122
modifying file and directory properties with, 1126–1127
Disconnected **classes, ADO.NET, 367**
Display **property, CSS box model, 853**
Display **property, ValidatorCalloutExtender control, 955**
DisplayAfter **attribute, UpdateProgress control, 895**
DisplayMode **property, BulletedList control, 152–153**
DisplayMode **property, ValidationSummary control, 210**
DisplayRememberMe **property, Login control, 753–754**
Dispose **method, IHttpModule interface, 1244–1245**

Dispose **statement, 1135**
<div> element, DragPanelExtender control, 920–921
DLLs
in ASP.NET applications, 1267
localization, using AJAX controls, 906
precompiling business objects into, 1264–1266
DOCTYPES, 836
dollar symbol ($), currency translation, 1358
domain **attribute, Forms authentication, 1393**
domain name restrictions, 995–996
DoS (denial of service) attacks, 161, 1401
dotTrace profiler, Jetbrain, 1546–1547
DPAPI (Data Protection API), 1412–1416
DpapiProtectedConfigurationProvider, **598**
drag and drop, server controls, 63–64
DragPanelExtender control, 920–922
DriveInfo **class, 1108–1111**
drives, 1108–1111
DriveType **enumeration, 1109**
drop-down lists, validating, 193–194
DropDownExtender control, 922–924
DropDownList control
adding list of modes to Web page, 797–800
building ProfileManager.aspx page with, 726–729
as databound control, 350
reading from event log, 1426–1428
DropDownList server control
ListBox server control vs., 121–124
overview of, 117–119
using ListSearchExtender control, 933–934
visually removing items from collections, 119–121
DropShadowExtender control, 924–926
Duration **attribute, output caching, 1040**
dynamic compilation configuration, 1385–1387
dynamic links, menu styles
adding styles to dynamic items, 672–673
overview of, 671
dynamic pseudo classes, CSS, 844
DynamicBottomSeparatorImageUrl **property, Menu control, 675**
DynamicPopOutImageUrl **property, Menu control, 674**
DynamicPopulateExtender control, 926–930
DynamicTopSeparatorImageUrl **property, Menu control, 675**

E

early-bound access, personalization, 705
Edit and Continue, debugging, 1097
Edit and Refresh, debugging, 1097
Edit Columns, GridView control, 315
Edit Mode, Portal Framework Web pages, 788, 804–808
Edit Templates, GridView, 308–309
editing configuration files, 1416–1417
EditItemTemplate, ListView, 342–343, 398–399
editor, resource, 1370–1371
Editor **attribute, UI type editors, 1237–1238**
Editor Zone, adding to page, 804–807
editors
Custom Actions Editor, 1522–1523
File System Editor, 1514–1518
File Types Editor, 1519–1520
Launch Conditions Editor, 1523–1524
Registry Editor, 1518–1519
User Interface Editor, 1520–1522
EditTemplate, GridView control, 320
ELMAH (Error Logging Modules and Handlers), 1556
e-mail
notification, 593–596
password recovery using, 765–768
sending from Web page, 1156
SMTP e-mail in IIS Manager, 1489
Web events, 1456–1460
embedded resources, accessing, 1192
empty elements, XML, 481
EmptyDataTemplate **property, GridView, 308–310**
EmptyDataText **property, GridView, 308–310**

EmptyItem **template, ListView, 342–343, 399**
Enable 32-bit Applications, IIS Manager, 552
enable **attribute, runtime settings configuration, 1400**
EnableCaching **property, AnimationExtender control, 915**
EnableDelete **property, LinqDataSource control, 290**
EnableInsert **property, LinqDataSource control, 290**
enableLocalization **attribute,** <siteMap> **element, 685**
EnableSessionState **attribute,** <pages> **configuration, 1398**
EnableSessionState **attribute,** Session **performance, 1015–1016**
EnableSortingAndPagingCallbacks **property, GridView, 314**
EnableTheming **attribute, 256**
EnableUpdate **property, LinqDataSource control, 290**
enableViewState **element,** <pages> **configuration, 1398**
encryption
  configuration settings, 1412–1416
  Digest authentication with, 975–976
  Forms authentication and, 1393
  Forms-based authentication with, 982
  ViewState, 1035–1036
End **events,** Session **object, 1007**
EndExecuteReader**, asynchronous commands, 417–420**
endpoints, WCF service, 1328
English-speaking culture codes, 1348
EnsureChildControls() **method, composite controls, 1212**
Enterprise Services, 1326
Error Events Raised performance counter, 1432
error handling
  adding users programmatically, 748–750
  configuration settings, 1389–1390
  <customErrors> syntax for, 1389–1390
  design-time support for, 1071–1074
  health monitoring and. *See* health monitoring
  in .NET, 1274–1277
  in .NET from unmanaged code, 1285–1287
  overview of, 1101–1104
  SQL-backed session state, 1023–1024
  tracing and. *See* tracing
  using data source control events for database, 285–286
Error Logging Modules and Handlers (ELMAH), 1556
error notifications
  debugging using, 1097
  design-time support for, 1071–1072
  e-mail Web events, 1458–1460
  using images and sounds for, 212–213
Error **property,** Page **class, 1102**
ErrorMessage **property, ValidationSummary control, 209**
Eval **method, data binding syntax, 353**
EvaluateExpression **property, expression builders, 357–358**
event logs
  health monitoring. *See* health monitoring
  instrumentation overview, 1425
  reading, 1426–1428
  writing, 1428–1430
EventLogTraceListener, 1084–1085
EventLogWebEventProvider
  defined, 591
  health monitoring configuration, 1442
  overview of, 592–593
<eventMappings>**, health monitoring configuration, 1443–1445**
eventName **attribute,** <rules> **configuration, 1448**
events
  AnimationExtender control, 910–911
  anonymous identification, 715
  buffering Web, 1453–1455
  CreateUserWizard control, 741–742
  e-mailing Web, 1456–1460
  global application, 51
  GridView control, 306–307, 314
  Init method registering, 1244–1245

LinqDataSource control, 293–294
master page, 248
Menu server control, 675–676
ObjectDataSource control, 300
page, 23–24
postback, 1203–1207
`ProfileModule` class, 717
server control, 65–68
server controls, 1176
sessions and, 1006–1008
Silverlight, 1583–1584
SQL server, 1450–1453
SqlDataSource control, 285
UpdatePanelAnimationExtender control, 953–954
user control, 1162, 1167–1168
validation, 188
Web, 1088–1090
Wizard server control, 174–176
writing via configuration, 1449–1450
XmlDataSource control, 294–295

exception handling, 1101–1104
application-level, 1103–1104
HTTP Status Codes, 1104–1105
methods for, 1101–1102
page-level, 1102–1103

`ExceptionHandled` **property, database errors, 285–286**

Execute methods, `Command` **object, 370–371**

`ExecuteNonQuery( )` **command, SQL Server, 366**

`ExecutePermissions` **property, File System Editor, 1515**

`executionTimeout` **property, 162, 1400**

`ExpandAll( )` **method,** `TreeView` **class, 663–667**

`ExpandControlID` **property, CollapsiblePanelExtender control, 917**

`explicit` **attribute, compilation configuration, 1386**

Expression Blend, Microsoft, 1574–1576

expression builders, 354–359

expressions, 354–359

extending ASP.NET, tools for, 1555–1557

extensible architecture, IIS 7, 542

eXtensible Markup Language. ***See*** **XML (eXtensible Markup Language)**

Extensions Preview, ASP.NET 3.5, 1578–1581

external style sheets, CSS
combining with internal style sheets, 850
creating, 72
overview of, 837–839

F

F5, starting debug session, 1093

Fiddler tool, 649, 1046

field names, LINQ queries, 449–450

file buffering, runtime configuration, 1401

file extensions
`.ascx` (user controls), 1160
`.ashx` (HttpHandlers), 1255
`.asmx` (Web service files), 1294, 1303
`.aspx` pages, 221–223, 226–229, 248–249, 1536
`.cd` (class designer), 53–59
`.js` (JavaScript), 1531–1532
mapping in IIS, 1259–1260
mapping with File Types Editor, 1519–1520
`.master` (master pages), 221–223
`.mdf`. *See* SQL Server Express Edition (`.mdf` file)
`.msi` (Windows Installer), 1502
`.resx` (resource files), 1362
using AJAX, 1280–1281
`.vsi (AJAXControlExtender)`, 902
working with, 996–999
`.wsdl` (Web Services Description Language), 32–37

file I/O and streams, 1108–1133
`Directory` and `DirectoryInfo` classes, 1111–1116
`DriveInfo` class, 1108–1111
`File` and `FileInfo` objects, 1117–1122
modifying Access Control Lists, 1127–1133
modifying properties and attributes, 1126–1127

file I/O and streams *(continued)*
network communications. *See* network communications
security and, 1107
using relative paths and setting/getting current directory, 1116–1117
working with paths, 1122–1126
working with serial ports, 1148–1149
file I/O and streams, reading and writing files, 1133–1148
compressing streams, 1143–1148
encodings, 1141
I/O shortcuts, 1141–1143
overview of, 1133–1134
`Reader` and `Writer` classes, 1138–1141
streams, 1134–1138
File System Editor, 1503, 1514–1518
File System setting, Copy Web Site, 1498
File Transfer Protocol. *See* FTP (File Transfer Protocol)
File Types Editor, 1519–1520
`FileInfo` **class, 1117–1122, 1126–1127**
FileIO access, server configuration, 1377
files
adding to installer output, 1515–1516
authenticating specific, 986–987
authorization of, 1396
configuration of. *See* configuration
`File/FileInfo` displaying directory, 1117–1122
I/O shortcuts, 1141–1143
modifying ACLs in, 1127–1133
modifying properties and attributes, 1126–1127
`FileStream`
reading system file with, 1135–1136
Streamreader and, 1139–1140
FileUpload server control, 156–166
file size limitations, 161–162
overview of, 156–157
permissions, 160
uploading file contents into `Byte` array, 165–166
uploading file contents into `Stream` object, 164–165
uploading files using, 157–159
uploading multiple files from same page, 162–164
`FileWebRequest` **class, 1155–1156**
`FileWebResponse` **class, 1155–1156**
FilteredTextBoxExtender control, 930–931
filtering
adding to LINQ query, 451–453
traditional query methods, 444
using `SelectParameter` controls, 281–282
`FilterMode` **property, FilteredTextBoxExtender control, 931**
`FilterParameters`**, DetailsView control, 334**
`FilterType` **property, FilteredTextBoxExtender control, 931**
`$find( )` **method, Silverlight control, 1583**
`FindControl( )` **method**
cross-page posting, 27
dynamically adding user control to Web page, 1165
getting at server controls on master page, 234
`FindNode( )` **method,** `TreeView` **control, 666, 669**
`FindProfilesByUserName( )` **method,** `ProfileManager` **class, 730**
`FindUsersInRole ( )` **method,** `Roles` **class, 782–783**
`FinishButtonClick` **event, Wizard server control, 175–176**
FireBug, 1046
Firebug, 1542–1543
Firebug Lite, 1543
firewalls, debugging SQL, 1101
first letter pseudo element, CSS, 845
first-child pseudo classes, CSS, 843
first-line pseudo element, CSS, 845
500 errors, exception handling, 1102
`float` **property, CSS elements, 855–856**
flushing Web events, 1455
`Focus( )` **method, TextBox server control, 108**

folders
adding to installer output, 1515–1516
authenticating specific, 986–987
creating proper structure for themes, 258–259
folders, application, 32–39
\App_Browsers, 38–39
\App_Code, 32–37
\App_Data, 37
\App_GlobalResources, 38
\App_LocalResources, 38
\App_Themes, 37–38
\App_WebReferences, 38
Font tags, HTML, 836
FOR XML AUTO, **524–528**
FOR XML PATH, **529**
FOR XML TYPE, **528**
ForceCopyBuildProvider, **44–45**
foreach **loop, queries, 444**
form elements, Wizard server control, 176–180
Format menu, Visual Studio Design view, 858
Format whole document option, XML toolbar, 1416
FormatString property, LoginName control, 762
formatting, configuration files, 1379–1380
<forms> **element, 977**
FormsAuthentication **class, 979, 985–986**
FormsAuthenticationHashPasswordForStoringInConfigFile( ) **method, 982**
Forms-based authentication, 976–986
adding users to membership service, 737–751
configuration settings, 1392–1393
configuring, 1392–1393
defined, 967
FormsAuthentication class, 979, 985–986
mixing versions of .NET Framework, 1528–1529
overview of, 976–978
Security Setup Wizard, 1466–1467
setting up Web site for membership, 734–737
using Login control with, 984–985
against values in database, 982–984
against values in web.config file, 980–982
FormView server control, 345–350, 864
400 errors, exception handling, 1102
Framework Class Library, 1020
Friendly Control Adapters, CSS, 864
from **statement, LINQ syntax, 448**
FrontPage Extensions, 5
FTP (File Transfer Protocol)
changing application location with, 3–5
Copy Web Site GUI option, 1498
using FtpWebRequest/FtpWebResponse, 1153–1156
FtpWebRequest **class, 1153–1156**
FtpWebResponse **class, 1153–1156**
full trust settings, server configuration files, 1376–1377
fully qualified redirect URLs, runtime settings configuration, 1400
functional areas, IIS 7, 538

G

GAC (Global Assembly Cache), 1278, 1288
Gacutil.exe, 1278
garbage collection, .NET, 1274
General section, .NET compilation, 1482
GenerateMachineKey tool, 1036
GeneratePassword( ) **method, creating users, 768–769**
generic handlers, 1255–1259
GetAllProfiles( ) **method,** ProfileManager **class, 730**
GetAllRoles( ) **method,** Roles **class, 777**
GetCallBackEventReference **arguments, 1195**
GetCallBackResult( ) **method, asynchronous callbacks, 1192–1196**
GetCallbackResults **method,** ICallbackEventHandler**, 94**
GetCodeExpression **method, expressions, 356**

GetCompletionList( ) **method, AnimationExtender control, 914**
GetCurrentDirectory( ) **method,** Directory **class, 1116–1117**
GetDirectories( ) **method,** DirectoryInfo **class, 1112–1114**
GetDynamicContent( ) **method, DynamicPopulateExtender control, 927**
GetFiles( ) **method,** DirectoryInfo **class, 1117–1122**
GetInvalidFileNameChars **method,** Path **class, 1123**
GetInvalidPathChars **method,** Path **class, 1123**
GetItem( ) **method,** SessionStateModule, **1026**
GetItemExclusive( ) **method,** SessionStateModule, **1026**
GetNumberOfUsersOnline( ) **method,** Membership **class, 762–764**
GetSlides( ) **method, SlideShowExtender control, 948–950**
GetUpdatedTime **method, Post-Cache Substitution Control, 1045**
GetUsersForRole ( ) **method,** Roles **class, 781**
GetUsersInRole ( ) **method,** Roles **class, 583, 780**
GetXmlDocument **method, XmlDataSource control, 295**
Global Application Class, 50–53
Global Assembly Cache (GAC), 1278, 1288
global resources, localization, 1369–1370
Global.asax **file, 50–53**
globalization
- .NET Globalization in IIS Manager, 1482
- server-side culture declarations, 1352–1353
- through localization. *See* localization

GridView control
- adding paging to, 312–314
- adding sorting to, 310–312
- binding to directory files, 1118–1121
- creating LINQ query bound to, 447–450
- customizing columns in, 314–317
- deleting data, 327–330
- DetailsView server control vs., 330
- displaying data with, 304–308
- errors when updating data, 323–325
- other formatting features, 329–330
- overview of, 304
- reading from event log, 1426–1428
- row data, 320–323
- TemplateField EditItem template, 325–327
- in traditional query methods, 439–443
- using EmptyDataText and EmptyDataTemplate properties, 308–310
- using TemplateField column, 317–320
- using with DetailsView server control, 331–335

Group Container, ListView, 342–343
grouping data
- with group keyword in LINQ, 453–454
- LINQ to Objects, 453–454
- LINQ to SQL, 467–469
- LinqDataSource control, 292
- traditional query methods, 444–446

GroupName **property, RadioButton control, 130**
groups
- authenticating/authorizing, 972–973
- CSS selector, 845–846
- personalization, 706–707, 718
- rendering in ListView, 341–342
- validation, 213–217

GUI tool, SQL Server Setup Wizard, 573–575
GUIDs (unique identifiers), 233–234, 714
GZipStream, **1143–1144**

H

HandleCssClass **property, ResizableControlExtender control, 943**
handlers
- custom configuration, 1422–1424
- custom section creation, 1417–1424
- HttpHandlers. *See* HttpHandlers
- processing HTTP requests, 1241–1244

hashed message authentication code (HMAC), 1035
header, Wizard server control, 173
`HeaderText` **attribute, Wizard server control, 173**
health monitoring
buffering Web events, 1453–1455
configuration, 1442–1449
e-mailing Web events, 1456–1460
overview of, 1439–1441
provider model, 1441–1442
routing events to SQL server, 1450–1453
using Web event providers for, 591
writing events via configuration, 1449–1450
HiddenField server control, 155–156, 1032–1035
hierarchical configuration, IIS Manager, 555–561
hierarchical structure, of XML data, 528
HMAC (hashed message authentication code), 1035
Home tab, Web Site Administration Tool, 1465
`HorizontalAlign` **attribute, Panel server control, 149**
hosting, WCF service in console application, 1333
hot-keys, 105–106
hotspots, ImageMap control, 182
hover style, Menu control, 671–672
HoverMenuExtender control, 931–932
HRESULT values, 1274
HTML
compiling, 43
rendering server controls at runtime, 1176–1181
in state management, 1004
styling server controls, 1183–1186
syle-chaning elements, 70
user controls vs. standard Web page, 1160
HTML and CSS design
caveats, 836
external style sheets, 837–839
Friendly Control Adapters, 864
HTML vs. CSS, 835
inline styles, 840
internal style sheets, 839–840
introducing CSS, 837
limitations of styling HTML, 836
style inheritance, 849–850
HTML and CSS design, CSS rules, 840–848
merged styles, 846–848
overview of, 840
pseudo classes, 843–844
pseudo elements, 845
Selector combinations, 845–846
Selector grouping, 845
Selectors, 841–843
styling ASP.NET controls using, 863–864
HTML and CSS design, element layout and positioning, 850–856
controlling style overriding with `!important` attribute, 856–857
CSS box model, 850–853
overview of, 850
positioning CSS elements, 853–856
HTML and CSS design, in Visual Studio, 857–864
Apply Styles tool window, 860–861
CSS Properties tool window, 861–862
Manage Styles tool window, 859–860
managing relative CSS links in masterpages, 863
overview of, 857–858
styling ASP.NET controls, 863–864
working with CSS, 858–862
HTML elements
applying styles directly to, 70–71
turning into server controls, 73–76
HTML server controls, 73–80
HTML classes for working with, 78–79
`HtmlContainerControl` base class, 77–78
`HtmlControl` base class, 76–77
`HtmlGenericControl` class, 79–80
turning HTML elements into, 73–76
Web server controls vs., 62–63, 103–104
`HtmlContainerControl` **class, 77–78**
`HtmlControl` **base class, 76–77**
HTMLDog Web site, 1548–1549

HtmlGenericControl **class, 79–80**
HtmlTextWriter **class, 1178–1181, 1184–1185**
HTTP GET **requests, state management, 1004**
HTTP Headers, 1004
HTTP Headers, controlling caching with, 1046–1048
HTTP output, 1145–1147, 1245–1248
HTTP requests, processing
ASP.NET request processing, 1244–1245
IIS 5/6 and ASP.NET, 1241–1242
overview of, 1241
using HttpHandlers. *See* HttpHandlers
using HttpModules. *See* HttpModules
HTTP Status Codes, 1104–1105
HTTP transmission, authenticating/authorizing, 973
HttpApplication **object, 1006–1007**
HttpCachePolicy **class, 1046–1048**
HttpContext**, 1008**
HttpContext.Current.Items**, 1037–1038**
HttpFileCollection **class, 163**
HTTP-GET, 1308–1310
HttpHandlers
generic handlers, 1255–1259
HTTP pipeline model handling requests with, 1244–1245
mapping file extensions in IIS, 1259–1260
HttpModules, 1244–1260
compressing HTTP output, 1145–1147
configuration settings, 1380
creating, 1244–1245
HttpHandlers vs., 1254–1255
IIS wildcards, 1252–1254
implementing IHttpModule interface, 1244–1245
modifying HTTP output with, 1245–1248
performing URL rewriting with, 1248–1252
HTTP-POST, 1311
<httpRuntime> **section, 1400**
HttpSessionState **object, 1008**
HttpWebRequest **class, 1149–1153**
HttpWebResponse **class, 1149–1153**
HyperLink server control, 116
HyperLinkField control, 317
hyperlinks
appearance of, 263–264
attaching styles sheets in Manage Style Tool window, 859–860
managing CSS in masterpages, 863

I

IAsyncResult **interface, 415–416, 1325**
ICallbackEventHandler**, 86, 93–94**
icons, TreeView control, 659–661
id **attribute,** <browser> **element, 1389**
ID **attribute, server controls, 104, 1182**
ID Selectors, CSS, 843
identification, anonymous user, 1393–1394
<identity> **element, 993–994**
IDisposable**, 505, 528**
IE Web Developer Toolbar, Microsoft, 1544–1545
ie.browser **files, configuration settings, 1388–1389**
IEnumerable interface, 451
If Then **statement, CheckBox control, 126**
IgnoreFileBuildProvider**, 44–45**
IHttpHandler interface, 1257–1258
IHttpModule interface, 1244–1245
IIS (Internet Information Server)
ASP.NET Development Server vs., 1091–1092
authentication schemes, 735
changing where application is saved, 3
mapping file extensions, 1259–1260
state management, 1004
Windows authentication. *See* Windows-based authentication
working with file extensions, 996–999
IIS (Internet Information Service) Manager, 1479–1489
Application Pools node, 550–553
Application Settings, 1485–1486
changing provider for sessions using, 568–569
configuring on Vista, 1479–1482

Connection Strings, 1486
delegation, 561–564
hierarchical configuration, 555–561
.NET Compilation, 1481–1482
.NET Globalization, 1482
.NET Profile, 1482–1483
.NET Roles, 1483
.NET Trust Levels, 1484
.NET Users, 1484–1485
overview of, 549–550
Pages and Controls, 1486–1487
Providers, 1487
Session State, 1487–1489
Sites node, 554–555
SMTP e-mail, 1489
summary review, 1489
using IIS 7.0 Manager, 1000–1001

IIS 5 (Internet Information Server 5.0)
adding wildcards in, 1253–1254
processing HTTP requests, 1241–1242

IIS 6 (Internet Information Server 6.0)
adding wildcards in, 1254
interaction with ASP.NET, 542–544
main features of, 537–538
moving to IIS 7, 564–566
processing HTTP requests, 1241–1242
security, 995–1000

IIS 7 (Internet Information Server 7.0)
ASP.NET integrated pipeline with, 542–544
building customized Web server, 544–549
extensible architecture of, 542
IIS Manager. *See* IIS (Internet Information Service) Manager
IIS-WebServer, 538–541
modular architecture of, 537–538
moving application from IIS6 to, 564–566
overview of, 537
processing HTTP requests, 1242

IIS-ApplicationDevelopment update, 539
IIS-CommonHttpFeatures update, 539
IIS-HealthAndDiagnostics update, 540
IIS-IIS6ManagementCompatibility update, 541
IIS-Performance update, 541
IIS-Security update, 540
IisTraceListener, 1087
`IisWebEventProvider`**, 591, 597**
IIS-WebServer, 538–541
IIS-ApplicationDevelopment update, 539
IIS-CommonHttpFeatures update, 539
IIS-HealthAndDiagnostics update, 540
IIS-Performance update, 541
IIS-Security update, 540
IIS-WebServerManagementTools update, 541
ISS-FTPPublishingService, 542
overview of, 538–539
update dependencies, 545

IIS-WebServerManagementTools update, 541
IIS-WebServerRole, 538
ILMerge, 520
Image server control, 132–134
ImageButton server control, 115–116
ImageMap server control, 180–182
images
BulletedList control, 151–152
DropDownExtender control, 922–924
error notification, 212–213
Hyperlink control, 116
menu item, 674–675
ResizableControlExtender control, 943–944
SlideShowExtender, 947–948
themes, 264–267
TreeView control icons, 659–661
UpdateProgress control, 895–896
Web Part verbs, 813–814

`Images` **folder, themes, 264–267**
`ImageUrl` **property**
Image server control, 132
ImageButton server control, 115
Web Part verbs, 814

Immediate window, 1074
impersonation, 993–994
`@Implements` **directive, 12, 20**
`@Import` **directive, 12, 18–20, 51–52**
`import` **statement, CSS, 839**
`!important` **attribute, 856–857**
`Imports` **keyword, XML namespace, 488–489**
`include` **files, 219–221, 1399**
indentation, VB in Visual Studio, 499

Index **property, File System Editor, 1515**
influential blogs, online resources, 1585–1586
Infrastructure Error Events Raised performance counter, 1432
inheritance
  applying configuration files, 1378–1379
  CSS Properties Tool window and, 861–862
  CSS style, 849–850
Inherits **attribute,** Page **directive, 11**
Init **method, IHttpModule interface, 1244–1245**
Initialize( ) **method**
  ProviderBase class, 611
  SessionStateModule, 1025
  XmlMembershipProvider class, 622–624
InitializeRequest( ) **method,** SessionStateModule**, 1026**
InitialValue **property, RequiredFieldValidator control, 192–193**
inline boxes, 851–853
inline styles, 70, 840, 864
InnerHtml **property,** HtmlContainerControl **class, 78**
InnerText **property,** HtmlContainerControl **class, 78**
in-place precompilation, 40
InProc **provider, 568**
In-Process Session State
  limitation of, 1009
  maintaining state, 1028
  overview of, 1008–1009
  Session_OnEnd event in, 1008–1009
  storing data in Session object, 1010–1013
  Web gardening and, 1009
InProcSessionStateStore
  configuring sessionState management, 1008
  defined, 588
  overview of, 1008–1015
  working with, 588–589
Insert **method, cache dependencies, 1049**
InsertCommand**, DetailsView control, 335–336**
inserting data
  into SQL Server, 364–365
  using DetailsView server control, 335–336
  using LINQ to SQL, 471–473
  using stored procedures, 472–473
InsertItemTemplate, ListView control, 344, 399–400
InsertTemplate, GridView control, 320
installation
  AJAX Control Toolkit, 901–902
  building programs, 1501–1507
  using Windows Installer service. *See* Windows Installer service
installation program
  creating, 1503–1507
  installing application with, 1507–1508
  uninstalling application with, 1508–1510
Installation URL property, deployment projects, 1512
instrumentation
  application tracing, 1439
  browser-based Administrative Tool building, 1434–1439
  buffering Web events, 1453–1455
  e-mailing Web events, 1456–1460
  event log, 1425–1426
  event log reading, 1426–1428
  event log writing, 1428–1430
  health monitoring configuration, 1442–1449
  health monitoring provider model, 1441–1442
  performance counter viewing through Administration Tool, 1431–1434
  routing events to SQL server, 1450–1453
  summary review, 1461
  writing events via configuration, 1449–1450
Integrated Windows authentication, 973–974
IntelliSense
  for CSS, 838, 840
  for inline coding, 9
  for LINQ to SQL, 462–463
  for personalization properties, 704–705
  for server controls, 64–65

interfaces
creating for provider Web Part, 825–828
WCF service contract, 1330–1332
XML Web service, 1299–1302
internal style sheets, CSS
combining with external style sheets, 850
creating, 72–73
overview of, 839–840
internationalization, through localization. *See* localization
Internet Explorer
client-side culture declarations, 1353–1354
Design mode only in, 799
viewing or editing XAML using, 1572–1574
Internet Information Server. *See* IIS (Internet Information Server)
Internet Information Service Manager. *See* IIS (Internet Information Service) Manager
Interop Type Library, 1279–1281
`InvalidChars` **property, FilteredTextBoxExtender control, 931**
invariant cultures, 1348–1349, 1367
IP addresses, restrictions, 995–996
IPostBackDataHandler interface, 1207–1209
IPostbackEventHandler, 86
ISAPI Rewrite module, Helicon, 1557
`IsApplication` **property, File System Editor, 1515**
`IsAuthenticated` **property,** `User.Identity`**, 988–989**
`IsCrossPagePostBack` **property, cross-page posting, 30**
`IsEnabled` **property, page-level tracing, 1076**
`IsLockedOut` **property,** `MembershipUser` **object, 757, 759**
`IsPostBack` **property,** `Page` **class, 25**
`IsReusable` **property, IHttpHandler interface, 1256**
ISS-FTPPublishingService, 542
`IsUserInRole ( )` **method,** `Roles` **class, 583, 782**
Item Container, ListView, 342–343
ItemTemplate
DataList control, 388–390
GridView control, 318
ListView control, 398
`IXPathNavigable`, `XslCompiledTransform` **class, 519**

J

JavaScript. *See also* AJAX (Asynchronous JavaScript and XML)
accessing Silverlight elements from events in, 1583–1584
AJAX client-side technologies, 872–873
AJAX dependency on, 869–871
Aptana Studio tools for, 1545–1546
buttons for client-side, 112–114
client-side callback functions, 1196
client-side debugging, 1098–1101
compressor for, 1552
hard-coded .js files and ASP.NET 3.5, 1531–1532
hooking up events to Silverlight, 1574
libraries, 884
manipulating server controls, 80–86
receiving Silverlight events in, 1581–1583
resource for, 86
in Web applications, 250–251
JavaScript Object Notation (JSON) editor, 1545
JIT (just-in-time) compiler, 1090–1091
joins
LINQ to Objects, 455–457
LINQ to XML, 461–462
`.js` **(JavaScript) file extension, 1531–1532**
Just My Code debugging, 1098
just-in-time (JIT) compiler, 1090–1091

K

`keyContainerName` **attribute,** `RsaProtectedConfigurationProvider`**, 601**
`keyEntropy` **attribute,** `DpapiProtectedConfigurationProvider`**, 600**
keywords, LINQ query syntax, 448

L

Label server control
FileUpload control using, 159
Literal control vs., 106
overview of, 104–106
using with DragPanelExtender control, 921
Label2Answer **key, resource files, 1366**
LabelStartText **property,** WebPart **class, 822, 823**
language pseudo classes, CSS, 844
languages
cultures and regions, 1347–1349
resource files, 1365–1366
setting preferences, 1353–1354
late-bound access, personalization, 705
Launch Conditions Editor, 1505, 1523–1524
layout
DataList control template, 387–393
menu item, 673–674
Web Part settings, 808
Web zone, 790–794
WebPartZone control, 795
layout, CSS elements, 850–856
controlling style overriding, 856–857
CSS box model, 850–853
overview of, 850
positioning, 853–856
LayoutTemplate, ListView control, 338–340, 396–398
Legacy **setting, XHTML, 1530**
limited object serialization formatter (LosFormatter), 1032
LimitedSqlRoleProvider **provider, 630–631, 634–637**
line numbers, and debugging, 1091
LineImagesFolder **property, TreeView control, 663**
link pseudo classes, CSS, 844
link **tags, HTML, 838–839**
LinkButton server control, 114–115, 927
links. ***See*** **hyperlinks**
LINQ (Language Integrated Query)
extending, 475
LINQ to Objects. *See* LINQ to Objects
LINQ to SQL. *See* LINQ to SQL
LINQ to XML. *See* LINQ to XML (XLINQ)
summary review, 475–476
traditional query methods, 437–446
LINQ to Objects, 437–446
adding query filters, 451–453
defined, 437
delayed execution behavior, 451
grouping data, 453–454
joins, 455–457
operators used by, 454–455
paging, 457
replacing traditional queries, 446–451
traditional query methods, 437–446
LINQ to SQL, 462–471
adding new data context, 465
deleting data, 474–475
inserting data, 471–473
overview of, 462–465
setting up file, 463
updating data, 473–474
writing LINQ queries, 466–467
LINQ to XML (XLINQ)
bridging XmlSerializer and, 503–504
creating CLR objects from XML, 498–499
creating XML, 502–504
joining XML data, 461–462
overview of, 477–478
using XDocument vs. XmlReader, 488–489
using XPath with XDocuments, 509
validating against schema with XDocument, 491–493
working with, 458–461
LINQ to XSD, 498
LinqDataSource Configuration Wizard, 289–291
LinqDataSource control, 289–294
data concurrency, 293
events, 293–294
overview of, 289–291
query operations, 291–292

ListBox server control, 121–124
adding items to collection, 124
allowing users to select multiple items, 121–122
as databound control, 350
example, 122–123
overview of, 121
using ListSearchExtender control, 933–934
ListSearchExtender control, 933–934
ListView server control, 336–345
data binding and commands, 343–344
data item rendering, 340–341
getting started with, 338–340
group rendering, 341–342
overview of, 336–337
paging and DataPager control, 344–345
results of, 400–402
ListView server control, templates, 393–402
creating EditItemTemplate, 398–399
creating EmptyItemTemplate, 399
creating InsertItemTemplate, 399–400
creating ItemTemplate, 398
creating LayoutTemplate, 396–398
data item rendering using templates, 340–341
defining templates, 340
group rendering using templates, 341–342
list of available templates, 393–394
overview of, 340
using, 394–396
using EmptyItem template, 342–343
Literal server control, 106–107
`Load`**, page event, 23–24**
`Load` **method,** `XslCompiledTransform` **class, 519–522**
`LoadControl( )` **method, to Web page, 1164–1169**
`LoadPostData( )` **method, IPostBackDataHandler interface, 1207–1209**
Local IIS setting, Copy Web Site GUI, 1498
local resource files, 1362–1365
localization
ASP.NET threads, 1349–1352
client-side culture declarations, 1353–1354
culture types, 1348–1349
date translation, 1355–1356
`Default.aspx` page finalization, 1366–1368
DLLs, AJAX controls, 906
global resources, 1369–1370
language resource files, 1365–1366
local resource files, 1362–1365
neutral cultures, 1368
number and currency translation, 1356–1360
overview of, 1347
resource editor, 1370–1371
server-side culture declarations, 1352–1353
site map, 685–689
sorting strings translation, 1360–1362
`Localization` **property, installer properties, 1513**
`LocalName` **property,** `Reader`**, 488**
`LocalSqlServer`**,** `SqlMembershipProvider`**, 579**
location options, application
authorization configuration, 1394
built-in Web server, 2
file authorization, 1396
using FrontPage Extensions for remote sites, 5
using FTP, 3–5
using IIS, 3
`Lock( )` **method,** `Application`**, 1028**
lock statement, `ReadUserFile( )` **method, 627**
lock-down configuration settings, 1396–1397
`Log` **command, 1074**
`<LoggedInTemplate>`**, LoginView control, 769–770**
Logging buffer mode, 1455
login, 752–760
denying unauthenticated users, 752
locking out users with bad passwords, 756–760
logging in users programmatically, 755–756

login *(continued)*
using Login server control, 752–755
using XmlMembershipProvider, 628–629
Login server control, 752, 984–985
LoginName server control, 760–762
LoginStatus server control, 760
loginURL **attribute, Forms authentication, 1392**
LoginView server control, 769–771
LogVisits **property, File System Editor, 1515**
LosFormatter (limited object serialization formatter), 1032

M

m **variable, LINQ syntax, 448**
machine.config **file**
adding SQL data provider, 721–722
changing SQL Server 2005 connection string, 575–576
configuration files. *See* configuration
configuring providers, 603
controlling ASP.NET cache, 1049
creating SqlMembershipProvider, 577–579
creating SqlRoleProvider, 582–583
defined, 966
membership provider settings, 750–751
using RsaProtectedConfigurationProvider, 600–601
using SQL Server as provider, 724
<machinekey>, web.config **file, 1035**
<MailDefinition> **element, PasswordRecovery control, 766**
MaMaskedEditValidator control, 934–937
Manage Styles tool window, Visual Studio, 859–860
management
with IIS Manager. *See* IIS (Internet Information Service) Manager
with Web Site Administration Tool. *See* Web Site Administration Tool
Management Objects, ASP.NET, 1405–1412
Manufacturer **property, installer properties, 1513**
ManufacturerUrl **property, installer properties, 1513**
mapping
file extension in IIS, 1259–1260
file extensions, 996–999
with File Types Editor, 1519–1520
IIS wildcard, 1253–1254
LINQ to XML, 459–461
URLs, 684–685
MARS (Multiple Active Result Sets)
asynchronous command execution using, 414
defined, 435
using multiple wait handles, 423–432
MaskedEditExtender control, 934–937
@Master **directive, 12, 15–17**
.master **file extension, 221–223**
master pages
ASP.NET AJAX and, 249–251
basics, 221–223
caching, 248–249
coding, 223–225
coding content pages, 225–229
connecting to Web Parts, 833
container-specific, 246–248
development of, 219–221
event ordering, 248
managing CSS links, 863
mixing page types and languages, 229–231
nesting, 243–246
placing WebPartManager control on, 790
programmatically assigning, 241–243
specifying default content in, 240–241
specifying which one to use, 231–232
working with controls and properties from, 233–239
working with page title, 232
working with ScriptManagerProxy control, 886–887
MasterPageFile **attribute, content page, 227–228, 246–248, 1398**

@MasterType **directive, 12, 21**
maxBatchGeneratedFileSize **attribute, compilation configuration, 1386**
maxBatchSize **attribute, compilation configuration, 1386**
MaximumValue **property, RangeValidator control, 198**
maxInvalidPasswordAttempts **attribute, 757**
maxRequestLength **property**
  changing file-size limitation setting, 162
  runtime settings configuration, 1400–1401
.mdf **files. *See* SQL Server Express Edition (.mdf file)**
medium trust setting, 1376–1377
Membership API, 746, 784
membership management service
  adding users, 737–751
  asking for credentials, 752–760
  authorization vs. authentication, 734
  dealing with passwords, 764–768
  overview of, 733
  public methods of Membership API, 784
  role management service vs., 772
  setting up Web site for, 734–737
  showing number of users online, 762–764
  using Web Site Administration Tool, 784–786
  working with authenticated users, 760–762
membership providers, 577–581
  changing password requirements, 738
  in machine.config file, 750–751
  .NET Users, 1484–1485
  overview of, 570–571
  setting up Web site for, 734–737
  System.Web.Security.ActiveDirectoryMembershipProvider, 579–581
  System.Web.Security.SqlMembershipProvider, 577–579
  using multiple skin options, 577
membership system, role management, 690–691
MembershipCreateUserException**, 748–750**
MembershipProvider **class**
  building own providers, 613
  constructing class skeleton, 614–617
  creating CustomProviders application, 613–614
  creating XML user data store, 617–618
  defining provider instance in web.config file, 618–619
  implementing methods/properties of, 620–628
  not implementing methods/properties of, 619–620
MembershipUser **object, user login, 759**
memory
  caching and, 1042
  releasing COM objects and, 1274
MemoryStream**, writing to, 1137**
Menu server control, 669–678
  binding to XML file, 676–678
  as databound control, 351
  events, 675–676
  menu items, layout, 673–674
  menu items, separating with images, 675
  overview of, 669–670
  pop-out symbol, 674
  styles, adding to dynamic items, 672–673
  styles, for static items, 671–672
  styles, predefined, 670–671
  styles, with CSS-Friendly Control Adapters, 864
MenuItemClick **event, 675–676**
Merge Module Project, 1502
merge tools, 1559
merged styles, CSS, 846–848
methods
  DirectoryInfo class, 1112
  extending session state with other providers, 1025–1026
  FormsAuthentication class, 985–986
  Membership API public, 784
  overloading Web, 1312–1315
  Path class, 1122
  ProfileManager class, 726
  Roles API public, 786
  WebPartManager class, 815
Microsoft programs. *See* by individual names

migrating older ASP.NET projects
ASP.NET 3.5 pages as XHTML, 1529–1531
converting ASP.NET 1.x in VS 2008, 1532–1537
Forms authentication for mixing versions, 1528–1529
migrating from 2.0 to 3.5, 1537–1540
no hard-coded .js files in 3.5, 1531–1532
overview of, 1525
reserved folders, 1529
running multiple versions side-by-side, 1526
upgrading applications, 1526–1528
MinimumValue **property, RangeValidator control, 198**
minRequiredNonalphanumericCharacters **attribute, passwords, 608–610, 741**
minRequiredPasswordLength **attribute, passwords, 610, 741**
mod_rewrite, **Apache Web Server, 1557**
ModalPopUpExtender control, 919–920
mode **attribute**
<authentication> node, 967–968
custom errors configuration settings, 1390
Literal server control, 106–107
<sessionState> configuration, 1382
modes, Web page
changing. *See* WebPartManager control
modifying Web Part settings, 804–808
possible, 788
session state settings, 1487–1489
modules
architecture of IIS 7, 537–538
HttpModules. *See* HttpModules
money, currency translation, 1358–1360
monitoring, health. *See* health monitoring
mostRecent **property, trace data, 1080**
.msi **file extension, Windows Installer service, 1502**
MSMQ, 1326
multiline text boxes, 107–108
Multiple Active Result Sets. *See* MARS (Multiple Active Result Sets)
MultiView server control, 166–170
MutuallyExclusiveCheckBoxExtender control, 937–938
MYKEY private variable, 1015
MyKey property, 1013–1015
myRead.Read( ) **method,** DataReader **class, 364**

N

name **attribute**
<add> element, 1061
Forms authentication, 1392
<profiles> configuration, 1449
<rules> configuration, 1448
Name **property,** ProviderBase **class, 611**
Name **property,** Reader**, 488**
namespaces
ADO.NET, 367–368
LINQ, 447
<pages> configuration, 1398
namespaces, XML
building Web services, 1344
declaring, 488–489
defined, 479
overcoming XmlDataSource control limitations, 513
resolution, 508–509
NameTable **optimization, XML, 493–495**
NameValueFileSectionHandler**, 1417**
naming conventions, LINQ to SQL, 464
NavigateUrl **attribute, ImageMap control, 182**
NavigateUrl **property,** TreeNode **object, 667–669**
navigation, Wizard control, 173–174
nesting
master pages, 243–246
.sitemap files, 694–696
web.config files, 966
.NET
Compilation, 1481–1482
deploying COM components with, 1277–1278
Globalization, 1482
.NET Roles in IIS Manager, 1483

.NET Trust Levels in IIS Manager, 1484
.NET Users in IIS Manager, 1484–1485
Profile, 1482–1483
Remoting, 1326
running multiple Web sites with multiple versions of, 1404
server configuration files, 1375–1377

.NET from unmanaged code, 1279–1289
COM-Callable Wrapper, 1279–1281
deploying .NET components with COM apps, 1287–1289
early vs. late binding, 1285
error handling, 1285–1287
overview of, 1279
using .NET components within COM objects, 1281–1285

`net start` **command, 1382**

.NET Users, IIS, 1484–1485

network communications, 1149–1156
defined, 1149
`FileWebRequest` and `FileWebResponse`, 1155–1156
`FtpWebRequest` and `FtpWebResponse`, 1153–1156
`HttpWebRequest` and `HttpWebResponse`, 1149–1153
sending mail, 1156

`NetworkStream`**, reading to, 1137–1138**

neutral cultures, 1348–1349, 1368

New Group dialog, authentication/authorization, 973

New Project dialog, 1170, 1264

New Style dialog box, Visual Studio, 859

New User dialog, Windows authentication, 968–969

New Web Site dialog, 874, 1293–1294

`NewPasswordRegularExpression` **attribute, ChangePassword control, 765**

`NextView` **method, MultiView and View controls, 168**

NoBot control, AJAX, 958–960

nodes, TreeView control
adding programmatically, 667–669
expanding and collapsing programmatically, 663–667
overview of, 653–654
specifying lines used to connect, 661–663

None, authentication, 967, 1393

Normal Mode, Portal Framework Web pages, 788

Normal positioning, CSS elements, 853–854

Northwind.mdf file, locating, 362

Notepad, editing XAML in, 1577–1578

NT authentication, SQL Server 2005, 1101

NTLM, 974

`Null` **value, GridView control, 314**

numbers, localizing, 1356–1360

NumericUpDownExtender control, 938–939

`numRecompilesBeforeAppRestart` **attribute, compilation, 1386**

O

OAEP (Optional Asymmetric Encryption and Padding), 601

Object Relation (O/R) mapper, LINQ to XML, 462–463

Object Test Bench, 53, 58

ObjectDataSource control, 295–300

ODP (Oracle Data Provider), 286

offline, taking application, 1477

`OnClientClick` **attribute, Button control, 113**

`OnCommand` **event, Button control, 111**

`OnDataBound` **attribute, TreeView control, 664–665**

`OnGenerateChallengeandResponse` **property, NoBot control, 959**

online, displaying number of users, 762–764

online resources
advanced Web services, 1312
AJAX Control Toolkit download, 901–902
ASP.NET 3.5 Extensions Preview, 1578–1581
author blogs, 1585
built-in Web server, 2
Cassini built-in Web server, 1092

online resources *(continued)*
DbgView, 1081
extending LINQ, 475
Fiddler tool, 649
Friendly Control Adapters toolkit, CSS, 864
GenerateMachineKey tool, 1036
HTTP Headers and controlling caching, 1046
IIS 7 and ASP.NET integration, 1242
ILMerge, 520
influential blogs, 1585–1586
JavaScript for controls, 82
LINQ to XSD, 498
MSDN URL for debugging SQL Server, 1101
Northwind database, 362
regular expression strings, 202
third-party session-state providers, 1026
third-party validation server controls, 188
Ultimate Tools List updates, 1541
ViewState, 1035
ViewStateDecoder tool, 1035
W3C on XML, 480
Web sites, 1586
working with HTML, 70
working with JavaScript, 86
www.asp.net, 1549
XML Schema Editor, 484
XSLT, 518
OnServerValidate **attribute, CustomValidator control, 207**
OnUpdating **event, UpdatePanelAnimationExtender control, 953–954**
Opacity **property, DropDownExtender control, 926**
OpenMachineConfiguration **method,** machine.config, **1410**
Operator **property, CompareValidator control, 197**
operators, LINQ query, 454–455
Optimistic Currency, SqlDataSource control, 280
Optional Asymmetric Encryption and Padding (OAEP), 601
O/R (Object Relation) mapper, LINQ to XML, 462–463
Oracle Data Provider (ODP), 286
Oracle database, 286–288, 384–387
order by **statement, LINQ query, 450–451**
OrderBy **clause, LinqDataSource control, 291–292**
Orientation **attribute, Menu control, 673**
Out-of-Process Session State
configuration settings, 1382–1385
configuring sessionState management, 1008
maintaining state using, 1028
working with, 1016–1022
OutOfProcSessionStateStore
defined, 588
working with, 589–590
output, installer adding items to, 1515–1516
output caching
overview of, 1039–1040
runtime settings configuration, 1402
testing SQL Server cache invalidation, 1062–1068
VaryByControl attribute, 1041
VaryByCustom attribute, 1041–1042
VaryByParam attribute, 1040–1041
Output File Name property, deployment projects, 1511
@OutputCache **directive, 12, 22, 249**
OutputCacheModule, 1040
OutputDebugString, **1081**
overloading WebMethods, 1312–1315
override rules, configuration files, 1379

P

package files, deployment projects, 1511
packaging. *See* application packaging and deploying
Packer for .NET, 1552
page, cross posting, 25
Page **class**
adding strongly typed property to, 1019–1020
converting ASP.NET 1.x in VS 2008, 1536

Error property, 1102
making sessions transparent, 1013–1015
Trace property, 1076

page compilation, 39–43

@Page **directive**
adding tracing to, 1076
converting ASP.NET 1.x in Visual Studio 2008, 1536
defined, 12
optimizing Session performance, 1015–1016
overview of, 12–15
server-side culture declarations, 1353

page directives, 11–22
@Assembly directive, 21
@Control directive, 17–18
@Implements directive, 20
@Import directive, 18–20
@Master directive, 15–17
@MasterType directive, 21
@OutputCache directive, 22
@PreviousPageType directive, 21
@Reference directive, 12, 22
@Register directive, 12, 20–21

page events, 23–24

page exception handling, 1102–1103

page postbacks, 24–25
raising, 1203–1207

page recycling, 1097

page structure options, ASP.NET
code-behind model, 9–11
inline coding, 7–9
overview of, 5–7

page tracing, 1076

Page_Init **event, 799**

Page_Load **event**
disabling client-side validation, 211–212
DropDownExtender control, 923
example of, 66
getting at server controls on master page, 235
working with simple callback, 93

Page_LoadComplete **event handler, controls on master page, 235**

pageBaseType **element,** <pages> **configuration, 1398**

PageCatalogPart control, 802, 810

PageClientScript **property, applying JavaScript to controls, 81**

PageIndexingChanged **event, GridView control, 314**

PageIndexingChanging **event, GridView control, 314**

Page.MasterPageFile **property, 241–243**

Page.RegisterClientScriptBlock **method, 82**

Page.RegisterStartupScript **method, 82**

PagerSettings **property, GridView control, 313–314**

PagerStyle **property, GridView control, 313–314**

pages, applying themes to Web. *See* themes

Pages and Controls, IIS Manager, 1486–1487

<pages>**, configuration settings, 1397–1399**

Page.Trace, 1076–1077

paging
DataPager control, 344–345
DetailsView control, 331
GridView control, 312–314
LINQ, 457

PagingBulletedListExtender control, 939–940

Panel server control
adding CollapsiblePanelExtender control, 916–918
adding DragPanelExtender control, 921
adding DropDownExtender control with, 925–926
adding DynamicPopulateExtender control, 926–930
adding ResizableControlExtender control, 942–944
adding RoundedCornersExtender control, 944–945
adding UpdatePanelAnimationExtender control, 953–954
overview of, 147–149

parameters
client-side callback, 92–95
configuring SQL statements, 376–379
XCOPY, 1494–1496

parent node, TreeView control, 653
`parentID` **attribute, browsers, 1389**
`ParentLevelsDisplayed` **property, SiteMapPath control, 646–647**
`ParseExpression` **method, expressions, 356–357**
`Partial` **keyword, code-behind pages, 11**
partial page caching, 1042–1043
Passport authentication
  configuration settings, 1391–1392
  defined, 967
  limitations of, 735
  overview of, 986
PasswordRecovery server control, 765–768
passwords
  adding user to membership service, 737–739
  authenticating against values in database, 982–984
  authenticating against values in `web.config` file, 980–982
  ChangePassword server control, 764–765
  generating random, 768–769
  inputting on form with TextBox control, 107
  limitations of Basic authentication, 974
  locking out users with bad, 756–760
  PasswordRecovery server control, 765–768
  protecting configuration settings, 1412
  seeing and modifying, 738
  using `SqlMembershipProvider`, 607–610
PasswordStrength control, AJAX, 960–961
`passwordStrengthRegularExpression` **attribute, 610–611**
"Paste XML as XLinq" feature, 503
`path` **attribute, 1393, 1396**
`PathDirection` **property, SiteMapPath control, 646**
paths
  changing in IIS Manager, 1481
  `Path` class, 1122–1126
  structuring pages with, 5
  working with, 1122–1126
`PathSeparator` **property, SiteMapPath control, 644–646**
PDB (program database or debug) file, 1090–1091
`-pe` **command, 1413**
performance. ***See also*** **caching**
performance, state management and, 1015–1016
performance counters, 1430–1439
permissions, uploading files, 160
`Personalizable` **attribute, custom Web Parts, 822**
personalization
  model for, 699–700
  past ways of providing end user, 699
  programmatic access to, 717–720
  providers, 721–725
personalization, anonymous, 711–716
  defined, 711
  enabling identification of end user, 711–713
  migration to authenticated users, 717–720
  options for personalization properties, 715–716
  user profile storage warnings, 716
  working with, 714–715
personalization, managing application profiles, 725–731
  overview of, 725
  `ProfileManager` class methods, 726
  `ProfileManager` class properties, 725
  `ProfileManager.aspx` page, building, 726–729
  `ProfileManager.aspx` page, examining code of, 730–731
  `ProfileManager.aspx` page, running, 731–732
personalization properties, 702–711
  anonymous options for, 715–716
  creating, 700–701
  making read-only, 711
  migrating anonymous users for particular, 718
  providing default values, 711
  registering users in membership service with, 742–746
  storing in groups, 706–707

using, 702–705
using custom types, 708–710
personalization provider
.NET Profile, 1482–1483
overview of, 585–586
Personalization Services layer, personalization model, 700
PersonalizationScope**, custom Web Parts, 822**
pkmgr.exe**, 546–547**
Placeholder server control, 150
PlayInterval **property, SlideShowExtender control, 950**
Poll approach, asynchronous commands, 417–420
pollTime **attribute,** <add> **element, 1061**
polymorphism, and method overloading, 1312
pop-out symbol, Menu control, 674
PopUpControlExtender control, 941–942
PopUpControlID **property, ModalPopUpExtender control, 920**
Portal Framework
overview of, 787–788
Web Parts. *See* Web Parts
working with classes in, 814–818
ports
session state service, 1017
Web services using port 80, 1307
working with serial, 1148–1149
position **attribute, CSS box model, 852**
positioning CSS elements
Absolute, 855
Normal, 853–854
overview of, 853
Relative, 854
using float property, 855–856
PositionIsEverything Web site, 1548–1549
postbacks
accessing data in server controls, 1207–1209
client-side vs. typical, 86–87
dealing with, 24–25
handling events in server controls, 1203–1207
state management and, 1030–1032
tracking user controls across, 1168–1169
using Timer control for asynchronous, 887–888
using triggers for asynchronous, 890–892
PostBackTrigger, 892
PostBackUrl **attribute, Button control, 114, 1030**
PostBackValue **attribute, ImageMap control, 182**
PostBuildEvent **property, installer properties, 1513**
Post-Cache Substitution Control, 1043–1045
Power Toys Pack Installer, 1554
PreBuildEvent **property, installer properties, 1513**
precompilation
for business objects, 1264–1267
for deployment, 41, 1499–1501
predefined styles, Menu control, 670–671
pre-existing providers. *See* providers, extending pre-existing
PreInit **event, assigning master pages, 241–243**
PreRender( ) **method, server controls, 1188**
presentation logic, inline coding and, 9
@PreviousPageType **directive, 12, 21**
private assemblies, 1277–1278, 1288
privileges, authorization configuration, 1394–1396
Process Explorer, 1562
<processModel> **element, configuration, 1402–1404**
processor affinity, 1009
ProcessRequest( ) **method, IHttpHandler interface, 1257**
<ProcessTemplate> **element, UpdateProgress control, 895–896**
ProductCode **property, installer properties, 1513**
ProductName **property, installer properties, 1513**
***Professional IIS 7 and ASP.NET Integrated Programming* (Khosravi), 1242**

Profile API layer, personalization model, 700
Profile **class, personalization properties, 704–705**
Profile_MigrateAnonymous **event, 717**
Profile_Personalization **event, 718–719**
<profile> **section,** web.config **file, 704–705**
ProfileCommon object, 744
ProfileManager **class, 725–731**
  methods, 726
  overview of, 725
  ProfileManager.aspx page, building, 726–729
  ProfileManager.aspx page, examining code, 730–731
  ProfileManager.aspx page, running, 731–732
  properties, 725
ProfileModule **class, 717–720**
Profile.ProfileAutoSaving **event, 720**
profiler tools, 1546–1547
profiles
  managing application. *See* ProfileManager class
  .NET Profile in IIS Manager, 1482–1483
  programmatic access to personalization, 717–720
<profiles>**, health monitoring, 1448–1449**
program database or debug (PDB) file, 1090–1091
programming
  authorization. *See* authorization, programmatic
  configuration files, 1405–1412
  mixing languages on content/master pages, 229–231
<ProgressTemplate> **element, UpdateProgress control, 895**
properties
  Accordion control, 958
  CalendarExtender control, 916
  CheckBoxList control, 128–129
  composite controls, 1210–1212
  cross-page posting, 27–32
  CSS Properties Tool window, 861–862
  custom controls, 272–274
  custom server controls, 1173–1174
  custom Web Part control, 821–823
  deployment projects, 1510–1514
  dragging and dropping controls, 63–64
  DropDownExtender control, 926
  file and directory, 1126–1127
  File System Editor, 1514–1518
  File Types Editor, 1520
  FormsAuthentication class, 985–986
  GridView control style, 329–330
  HoverMenuExtender control, 932
  HTML server control styles, 1183–1186
  HtmlContainerControl class, 78
  HtmlControl base class, 77
  ListSearchExtender control, 933–934
  Login control, 755
  MaskedEditExtender control, 935–937
  master page, 235–237
  NoBot control, 959–960
  NumericUpDownExtender control, 939
  PasswordStrength control, 961
  personalization. *See* personalization properties
  ProfileManager class, 725
  RequiredFieldValidator control, 190–191
  server controls, 68–70, 1176–1177
  SliderExtender control, 947
  SlideShowExtender control, 948–950
  SqlCommand class, 370
  styling ASP.NET controls, 863–864
  ToggleButtonExtender control, 952
  user controls, 1162–1164
  WebMethod attribute, 1298–1299
  WebPart class, 817–818
  WebPartManager class, 815–816
  WebPartZone class, 815–817
  WebService attribute, 1298
PropertyGridEditorPart, 808
protection, configuration settings, 1412–1416
protection **attribute, Forms authentication, 1392**

protocols, Web services transport, 1307–1312
provider model
in ASP.NET 3.5, 569–571
configuration providers, 598–601
configuring providers, 603
health monitoring, 1441–1442
membership providers, 577–581
overview of, 567–568
personalization provider, 585–586
role providers, 581–585
SessionState providers, 588–590
setting up for SQL Server versions, 571–577
SiteMap provider, 586–588
understanding providers, 568–569
Web event providers. *See* Web event providers
WebParts provider, 601–603
provider model, extending
building providers. *See* providers, building
modifying with attributes, 606–611
as one tier in larger architecture, 605–606
pre-existing providers. *See* providers, extending pre-existing
`ProviderBase` class, 611–612
Provider pattern, `HttpSessionState` **object, 1008**
`Provider` **property,** `SiteMap` **class, 681**
Provider tab, Web Site Administration Tool, 1477–1479
`ProviderBase` **class, 611–612**
providers
custom, 1384–1385
e-mailing Web events, 1456–1460
extending session state with, 1024–1026
IIS Manager, 1487
personalization, 700, 721–725
`<providers>` configuration, 1445–1447
`<rules>` configuration, 1447–1448
SqlDataSource control connections, 278
understanding, 568–569
Web Part, 825–828, 830–833
providers, building, 613–629
building `ReadUserFile( )` method, 626–628
constructing class skeleton, 614–617
creating CustomProviders application, 613–614
creating XML user data store, 617–618
defining provider instance in `web.config` file, 618–619
`MembershipProvider` class, 620–628
user login, 628–629
validating users, 624–626
providers, extending pre-existing, 629–637
`AddUsersToRole( )` method, 633–634
`CreateRole( )` method, 631–632
`DeleteRole( )` method, 632–633
limiting role capabilities, 630–631
using `LimitedSqlRoleProvider` provider, 634–637
`Providers` **property,** `SiteMap` **class, 681**
`<providers>`
health monitoring, 1445–1447
routing events to SQL server, 1451
ProxyWebPartManager control, 833
pseudo classes, CSS, 843–844
pseudo elements, CSS, 845
pseudo `web.config` **files, 1379–1380**
public assemblies, 1278, 1288–1289
Publish Web Site, 1499–1501

Q

queries, 437–446. *See also* LINQ (Language Integrated Query)
QueryString (URL), 1029
client-side state management, 1006
queues, buffering Web events, 1453–1455
queues, runtime settings configuration, 1401
QuirksMode Web site, 1548–1549

R

RadioButton server control, 129–131
RadioButtonList server control
as databound control, 350
DropDownList control vs., 117
overview of, 131–132

RadioButtonList server control *(continued)*
RadioButton control vs., 131
visually removing items from collections, 119–121
Radius **property, DropDownExtender control, 926**
Radius **property, RoundedCornersExtender control, 945**
RaiseCallBackEvent( ) **method, asynchronous callbacks, 1192–1196**
RaiseCallbackEvent **method,** ICallbackEventHandler**, 94, 100**
RaisePostBackDataChangedEvent( ) **method, IPostBackDataHandler interface, 1207–1209**
random passwords, 768–769
RangeValidator server control, 188, 198–201
Rating control, AJAX, 961–962
RCW (Runtime Callable Wrapper)
adding reference to COM control manually, 1272
Com-Callable Wrapper vs., 1279
defined, 1268
deploying COM with public assemblies, 1278
error handling in .NET, 1274
overview of, 1268–1269
Read( ) **method,** Stream **class, 1135**
ReadContentAs( ) **method,** XmlReader**, 495–496**
ReadElementContentAs( ) **method,** XmlReader**, 495–496**
ReadElementString( ) **method,** XmlReader**, 495**
Reader **class**
encodings, 1141
I/O shortcuts, 1141–1143
overview of, 1138–1141
working with Writers and Streams, 1133–1134
reading, with event log, 1426–1428
read-only, personalization, 711
readOnly **attribute, personalization properties, 711**
ReadSubTree**, 497–498, 504**
ReadToDescendant**,** XmlReader**, 505**
ReadToNextSibling**,** XmlReader**, 505**
ReadUserFile( ) **method, 626–628**
ReadWriteControlDesigner **class, 1225**
RedirectFromLoginPage( ) **method,** FormsAuthentication**, 979, 984**
redirectUrl **attribute, authentication, 1392**
Refactor! for ASP.NET, Devexpress, 1550
@Reference **directive, 12, 22, 1165**
references
adding WCF consumer service reference, 1336–1337
consuming XML Web services by adding, 1302–1304
tools, 1548–1549
Reflector, 1560
Reformat Selection option, XML toolbar, 1416
regasm.exe **(Assembly Registration Tool), 1285, 1288**
RegExLib Web site, 202
regions, localization. *See* localization
@Register **directive**
creating custom Web Part control, 823
defined, 12
overview of, 20–21
registering AJAX control on page, 907
RegisterClientScriptBlock **method, server controls, 82–83**
RegisterClientScriptInclude **method, server controls, 85–86**
RegisterStartupScript **method, server controls, 83–85**
RegisterStartupScriptMethod( ) **method, server controls, 1187–1192**
Registry Editor, 1518–1519
Regular Expression Editor, 202
RegularExpressionValidator server control, 188, 201–202, 954–955
relational database structure, SQL Server, 528
relative positioning, CSS, 854
release configuration, Visual Studio, 1090–1091

ReleaseComObject **class, memory, 1274**
ReleaseRequestState, Session **object, 1007**
RememberMeSet **property, Login control, 753–754**
RememberMeText **property, Login control, 753–754**
Remote Debug Monitor (msvsmon.exe)**, 1093–1094**
remote debugging, 1093–1094
remote servers, web.config **file, 1411–1412**
Remote Site, Copy Web Site GUI, 1498
remote sites, FrontPage Extensions, 5
RemoveAccessRule( ) **method, 1132**
RemovePreviousVersions **property, installer properties, 1513**
RemoveUserFromRole( ) method, Roles **class, 781–782**
Render( ) **method, server controls, 1187–1192**
RenderContents( ) **method, overriding, 1178**
RenderContents( ) **method, server controlz, 1175**
rendering, ListView, 340–342
rendering HTML, server controls
- defined, 1176–1177
- overview of, 1178–1181
- page event lifecycle, 1177–1178

RepeatColumn **property, CheckBoxList control, 128–129**
RepeatColumn **property, RadioButtonList control, 132**
RepeatColumns **property, DataList control, 392**
RepeatDirection **property**
- CheckBoxList control, 128–129
- DataList control, 392–393
- RadioButtonList control, 132

RepeatLayout **property, DataList control, 390**
Request Error Events Raised performance counter, 1433
Request Execution Time performance counter, 1433
request limit, for trace data, 1080
Request **object, 1064–1065**
request time-out, runtime, 1400
Request Wait Time performance counter, 1433
requestLengthDiskThreshold**, runtime, 1401**
Requests Current performance counter, 1433
Requests Disconnected performance counter, 1433
Requests Failed performance counter, HTTP Status Codes, 1105
Requests Queued performance counter, 1433
Requests Rejected performance counter, 1433
RequiredFieldValidator server control, 189–194
- blank entries and, 193
- defined, 188
- overview of, 189–190
- using InitialValue property, 192–193
- validating drop-down lists, 193–194
- viewing results, 191–192

requireSSL **attribute, Forms authentication, 1393**
reserved folders, ASP.NET, 1529
ResizableControlExtender control, 942–944
ResizableCssClass **property, ResizableControlExtender control, 944**
Resource Editor, 1367, 1370–1371
resource files
- global, 1369–1370
- localization, 1362–1365
- .resx extension for, 687, 1362
- storing, 38

resourceKey **attribute,** <siteMapNode> **element, 686**
ResponseMinimumDelaySeconds **property, NoBot control, 959**
Response.Write **command, 1356**
RestartWWWService **property, installer properties, 1513**

`.resx` **extensions (resource files), 687, 1362**
`Retrieve.aspx`**, 1012**
`RetrieveTitle()` **method, consumer Web Parts, 829**
`RewritePath()` **method, URL rewriting, 1252**
role management service
adding and retrieving application roles, 775–777
adding users to roles, 778–779
caching roles, 783–785
checking users in roles, 782–783
deleting roles, 777–778
getting all roles of particular user, 781
getting all users of particular role, 779–780
membership management service vs., 772
overview of, 733
public methods of Roles API, 786
removing users from roles, 781–782
setting up Web site for role management, 771–775
using LoginView server control, 769–771
using Web Site Administration Tool, 784
role providers, 581–585
`LimitedSqlRoleProvider`, 630–631
overview of, 581
`SqlRoleProvider`, 582–583
<RoleGroups>, LoginView control, 770–771
<rolemanager>, setting up Web site, 771–775
roles
adding and retrieving application, 775–777
adding users to, 778–779
caching, 783–785
checking users in, 782–783
defining with Security Setup Wizard, 1467
deleting, 777–778
enabling security trimming, 692–694
getting all users of particular, 779–780
getting for particular user, 781
IIS-WebServerRole, 538
managing, 690–692, 771–775, 1472
.NET Roles in IIS Manager, 1483
.NET Users, 1484–1485
public methods of Roles API, 786
removing users from, 781–782
Wizard server control, 179–180
Roles API
deleting end user's role cookie, 784–785
public methods of, 786
role management service with, 772
root element, XML documents, 479
root node, TreeView control, 653
`RootNode` **property,** `SiteMap` **class, 681**
`Rounded` **property, DropDownExtender control, 926**
RoundedCornersExtender control, 944–945
routing, events to SQL server, 1450–1453
`RowDataBound` **event, GridView control, 307, 325–327**
`RowDeleted` **event, GridView control, 328–329**
rows
GridView control, 320–323
Table server control, 134–135
`RowState` **property, GridView control, 326**
`RowUpdated` **event, DataGrid view, 324**
`RowUpdating` **event, GridView control, 327**
`RsaProtectedConfigurationProvider`**, 599**
RSS feeds
viewing using ELMAH, 1556
XmlDataSource control and, 294–295, 515–517
`RssCacheDependency` **class, custom cache dependencies, 1051–1055**
rules
adding/removing ACL, 1130–1133
CSS. *See* HTML and CSS design, CSS rules
health monitoring, 1447–1448
managing access rules in Security tab, 1474
Windows Installer, 1502
XML, 1292
`<rules>`**, routing events to SQL server, 1451–1452**
Run As Server Control, Visual Studio, 74–75
`runat='server"` **attribute declaration**
creating skin using, 259
HTML server controls requiring, 74–76
Web server controls requiring, 104

`RunPostBuildEvent` **property, installer properties, 1514**

runtime
- applying configuration files, 1378–1379
- configuration settings, 1399–1402
- loading user controls dynamically at, 1164–1169
- server controls rendering HTML at, 1176–1181

Runtime Callable Wrapper. *See* RCW (Runtime Callable Wrapper)

S

salted hash, 1035

`Save` **method,** `XmlDataSource` **control, 295**

ScaleOut Software, 1026

schema, XML
- adding in SQL Server 2005, 531–533
- associating XML typed column with, 533
- editing, 483–485
- using with `XmlTextReader`, 489–491
- using XML Schema Definition (XSD), 481–482
- validating against with `XDocument`, 491–493

`schemaLocation` **attribute, editing XML and XML schema, 483–485**

`ScriptControl` **class, 1169**

ScriptManager server control, AJAX, 249–251, 883–886

ScriptManagerProxy server control, AJAX, 251, 883, 886–887

scripts
- adding features to server controls, 1187–1192
- installing personalization features, 723

scrollbars, Panel server control, 148–149

`SearchPath` **property, installer properties, 1514**

security
- authentication. *See* authentication
- authorization. *See* authorization
- Basic authentication, 974–975
- client-side vs. server-side validation and, 186–187
- Forms-based authentication. *See* Forms-based authentication
- identity and impersonation, 993–994
- I/O, 1107
- membership management. *See* membership management service
- .NET Trust Levels, 1484
- overview of, 965–966
- Passport authentication. *See* Passport authentication
- personalization. *See* personalization
- programmatic authorization. *See* authorization, programmatic
- protecting configuration settings, 1412–1416
- role management. *See* role management service
- through IIS, 995–1000
- Windows-based authentication, 968–976

Security event log, 1428

Security Setup Wizard, 1466–1471
- authentication options, 1466–1468
- role definition, 1467
- users, adding, 1467, 1470

Security tab, Web Site Administration Tool
- creating users, 1471
- enabling role management in, 690–691
- managing access rules, 1474
- managing roles, 1472
- managing users, 1472
- overview of, 1465
- Security Setup Wizard, 1466–1471

security trimming, 689–696
- enabling, 692–694
- overview of, 689
- setting up administrators' section, 691–692
- setting up role management for administrators, 690–691

`securityTrimmingEnabled` **attribute, XmlSiteMapProvider, 693**

Select a Master Page dialog, 225–229

SELECT statement
- LINQ query syntax, 448
- SqlDataSource control connections, 279

selecting data, from SQL database, 362–364

SelectionMode **attribute, Calendar control, 137–138**
SelectionMode **attribute, ListBox control, 121**
Selectors, CSS
combinations, 846
grouping, 845–846
merging styles, 846–848
overview of, 841–843
working with CSS in Visual Studio, 858–859
SelectParameters**, DetailsView server control, 334**
SelectParameters **property, SqlDataSource control, 281–282**
semantics, XML syntax vs., 480–481
SeparatorTemplate, DataList control, 390–392
serial ports, 1148–1149
Serializable **attribute**
Out-of-Process Session State, 1017–1019
ViewState, 1032
serialization, XML, 497–498
server configuration files, 1375–1377
server controls. *See also* validation server controls
AJAX. *See* AJAX (Asynchronous JavaScript and XML), server-side controls
AJAX Control Toolkit. *See* AJAX Control Toolkit server controls
attributes of, 1175–1176
building pages with, 63–65
client-side callback, working with. *See* client-side callback
client-side features, adding to, 1187–1196
composite controls, 1209–1212
control designers, 1224–1237
defined, 1159
detecting and reacting to downlevel browsers, 1196–1199
events, 65–68
HTML, 73–80
HTML, styling, 1183–1186
manipulating with JavaScript, 80–86
overview of, 61–62, 1169–1170
postback data, 1207–1209
postback events, 1203–1207
rendering, 1176–1181
skins, 259–261, 1186–1187
styles applied to, 68–73
tag attributes, 1181–1183
templated, 1212–1219
themes, 256, 1186–1187
types of, 62–63
UI type editors, 1237–1238
using ControlState, 1201–1203
using type converters, 1220–1224
using ViewState, 1199–1201
WebControl project setup, 1170–1175
Server Explorer, event logs. *See* event logs
Server Extensions, ASP.NET AJAX, 873
servers
routing events to SQL, 1450–1453
state management options, 1005
server-side technologies
AJAX, 873
authentication, 1391
culture declarations, 1352–1353
validation, 205–208
service contract, WCF service
creating interface for, 1330–1332
defined, 1329
implementing interface for, 1332–1333
setting namespace, 1344
Service.asmx **file, 1294–1295**
ServiceMethod **attribute, DynamicPopulateExtender control, 927**
service-oriented architecture (SOA), 1326–1327
services
WCF. *See* WCF (Windows Communication Foundation)
XML Web. *See* XML Web services
Session **object, 1006–1028**
in classic ASP, 1006
configuring session state management, 1008
cookieless session state and, 1026–1027
event model and, 1006–1008
extending session state with other providers, 1024–1026

in-process session state and, 1008–1015
maintaining, 1028
making transparent, 1013–1015
optimizing performance, 1015–1016
Out-of-Process session state, 1016–1022
SQL-backed session state, 1022–1024

session state
configuration settings, 1374, 1381–1385
configuring management, 1008
cookieless, 1026–1027
extending with other providers, 1024–1026
in IIS Manager, 556, 1487–1489
In-Process, 1008–1015
Out-of-Process, 1016–1022
provider model in ASP.NET 3.5 for, 569–571
providers, 568–569, 588–590
Session State Settings for, 1487–1489
SQL-backed, 1022–1024
storing, 567–568

`SessionStateModule`, **1025**

`SessionStateStoreProviderBase`, **1024–1025**

Set-Cookie HTTP Header, state, 1004

`SetCurrentDirectory( )` **method,** `Directory` **class, 1116–1117**

SetFocusOnError property, validation groups, 216

`SetItemExpireCallback( )` **method,** `SessionStateModule`**, 1026**

Setup Project, Windows Installer service, 1502

Setup Wizard, Windows Installer service, 1502

SGML (Standard Generalized Markup Language), 479, 1292

`Shared` **classes, ADO.NET, 367**

`Shell` **command, 1074**

shortcuts, desktop, 1517–1518

`ShowCheckBoxes` **property, TreeView control, 656–659**

`ShowLines` **property, TreeView control, 661–663**

`ShowStartingNode` **property, SiteMapDataSource control, 678–679**

`ShowToolTips` **property, SiteMapPath server control, 647–648**

Silverlight, 1565–1584
accessing from JavaScript events, 1583–1584
basic ASP.NET application, 1566–1568
converting vector content to XAML, 1569–1571
extending application with, 1565–1566
finding vector-based content in, 1568–1569
integrating with existing ASP.NET site, 1578–1581
overview of, 1565
receiving events in JavaScript, 1581–1583
viewing and editing XAML, 1571–1581

`SimpleMailWebEventProvider`, **591, 593–595, 1456–1457**

`SingleTagSectionHandler`, **1417, 1421**

site maps
defined, 639
localization of, 685–689
nesting, 694–696
URL mapping, 684–685
using SiteMapDataSource control, 678–681
using SiteMapPath control. *See* SiteMapPath server control
using TreeView control. *See* TreeView server control
XML-based, 640–641

site navigation
nesting `.sitemap` files, 694–696
security trimming and, 689–696
using Menu server control. *See* Menu server control
using SiteMap API, 681–684
using sitemap localization, 685–689
using SiteMapDataSource control, 678–681
using SiteMapPath control, 642–648
using TreeView server control. *See* TreeView server control
using URL mapping, 684–685
using XML-based site maps, 640–641

SiteMap API, 681–684

`SiteMap` **class, 639, 640, 681**

.sitemap file. *See* site maps
SiteMap provider, 586–588
SiteMapDataSource control
applying to Menu control, 669–670
applying to TreeView control, 651
data source controls, 300
interacting with site maps using, 640
overview of, 678
`ShowStartingNode` property, 678–679
`StartFromCurrentNode` property, 679–680
`StartingNodeOffset` property, 680
`StartingNodeUrl` property, 681
testing site map localization results, 687–689
`<siteMapNode>` **element, XML-based site maps, 640–641**
SiteMapPath server control, 642–648
child elements of, 648
creating own style for, 683–684
overview of, 642–644
`ParentLevelsDisplayed` property, 646–647
`PathDirection` property, 646
`PathSeparator` property, 644–646
`ShowToolTips` property, 647–648
Sites node, IIS Manager, 554–555
size limitations, files, 161–162
`SkinID` **attribute, 268–269, 270**
skins
creating for server controls, 259–261
creating multiple options for, 267–269
creating server controls with, 1186–1187
in custom controls, 270–274
incorporating images into themes using, 264–267
`Skip` **method, LINQ, 457**
SliderExtender control, 946–947
SlideShowExtender control, 947–950
`slidingExpiration` **attribute, Forms authentication, 1393**
smart controls, 62
Smart Device Cab Project, Windows Installer, 1502
smart tags
server control, 1234–1235
syntax notification at design-time, 1073
`smartNavigation` **element, 1398**
SMTP
configuring in Application tab, 1476
IIS Manager, 1489
set-up for e-mailing Web events, 1457–1458
SOA (service-oriented architecture), 1326–1327
SOAP (Simple Object Access Protocol)
caching responses, 1315–1316
communicating with XML Web service using, 1311–1312
defining XML structure through, 1292
exposing custom datasets as, 1296–1299
requests, 1292–1293
responses, 1293
XML Web service interface displaying messages, 1301
SOAP headers, 1316–1321
building Web services with, 1317–1319
consuming Web services with, 1319–1321
overview of, 1316–1317
requesting Web services with SOAP 1.2, 1321–1323
SortByCategory, page-level tracing, 1076
SortByTime, page-level tracing, 1076
sorting data
adding to GridView control, 310–312
strings in different cultures, 1360–1362
in traditional query methods, 444–446
sounds, in error notification, 212–213
Source view
coding server controls in, 65
GridView control columns in, 317
HTML server controls in, 74–76
`SourceSwitch`**, 1088**
`Span` **tag, server controls, 1175**
specific culture definitions
currency translation, 1360
defined, 1348
vs. neutral cultures, 1368
SQL Server
debugging, 1101
setting up providers for versions of, 571–577
writing Web events to, 596–597

SQL Server 2000
cache dependency, 1057–1058
cache invalidation, 1065
caching in, 1057–1058
creating users with SqlMembershipProvider, 607
locating Northwind.mdf file in, 362
membership provider for, 577, 578
personalization provider for, 586, 722–723
retrieving XML from, 525–526
role provider for, 581
setting up provider to work with, 571–577
SQL stored proc debugging, 1101
support for XML on, 524
Web Parts provider for, 601
SQL Server 2005
cache invalidation, 1059–1060, 1065
connecting role management system to, 583
creating users with SqlMembershipProvider, 607
debugging, 1101
membership provider for, 577, 578
personalization provider for, 585–586, 722–723
`pollTime` attribute and, 1061
role provider for, 581
routing events to SQL server, 1451
setting up provider to work with, 571–577
SQL stored proc debugging, 1101
SQL to LINQ generating SQL optimized for, 468
Web Parts provider for, 601
writing Web events to, 596–597
SQL Server 2005, and `XML` data type, 528–534
adding column of untyped XML, 530–531
adding XML schema, 531–533
associating XML typed column with schema, 533
generating custom XML, 529–530
inserting XML data into XML column, 534
overview of, 528–529
SQL Server 2008
creating users with SqlMembershipProvider, 607
membership provider for, 578
personalization provider for, 586, 722–723
role provider for, 581
setting up provider to work with, 571–577
Web Parts provider for, 601
SQL Server 7.0
cache invalidation, 1065
personalization provider for, 722–723
setting up provider to work with, 571–577
SQL Server Cache Dependency, 1055–1060
cache invalidation, 1059–1060
disabling databases for cache invalidation, 1058–1059
disabling table for cache invalidation, 1058–1059
enabled tables, 1058
enabling databases for cache invalidation, 1056
enabling table for cache invalidation, 1056–1057
overview of, 1055–1056
and SQL Server 2000, 1057–1058
SQL Server cache invalidation. *See also* SQL Server Cache Dependency
configuring applications for, 1060–1061
testing, 1062–1068
SQL Server Express Edition (`.mdf` file)
adding users to membership service, 737–751
personalization provider, 721–722
personalization provider for, 585–586
providers working with, 571
role providers, 581–585
`SqlMembershipProvider` in, 578
Web site setup for membership, 734–737
SQL Server scripts, installing personalization features, 723
SQL* Plus, 385
`SqlCacheDependency` **class**
attaching SQL cache dependencies to `Request` object, 1065–1068
configuring ASP.NET application, 1060–1061
defined, 1055

SqlCommand **class, 414–415**
properties, 370
SqlConnection **class**
asynchronous connections, 435
overview of, 368–369
using DataReader object, 371–373
sqlConnectionString **attribute, 1382**
SqlDataAdapter **class, 373–376**
SqlDataSource control
adding UpdateCommand to, 321–322
configuring data connection, 277–281
ConflictDetection property, 282–285
DataSourceMode property, 281
events, 285
filtering data using SelectParameters, 281–282
overview of, 277
SqlDependency **object, 1064–1068**
SqlMembershipProvider, 751
SqlMembershipProvider **class**
building providers, 613
overview of, 577–579
simpler password structures, 607–610
stronger password structures, 610–611
Web site set up for membership, 734–737
SqlParameter **class, 376–379**
SqlPersonalizationProvider**, 601–603**
SqlProfileProvider**, 585–586**
SqlProfileProvider**, connecting to SQL Server 2005, 723–724**
SqlRoleProvider **class, 582–583**
AddUsersToRole( ) **method, 633–634**
CreateRole( ) method, 631–632
DeleteRole( ) method, 632–633
role management service with, 771–775
working with LimitedSqlRoleProvider, 630–631
SQLServer
provider, 568
session state configuration, 1383–1384
SqlSessionStateStore
configuring sessionState management, 1008
defined, 588
working with, 590
SqlWebEventProvider
buffering Web events, 1455
defined, 591
overview of, 596–597
squiggles (syntax notifications), 1071–1073
Standard Generalized Markup Language (SGML), 479, 1292
Start **events,** Session **object, 1007**
StartFromCurrentNode **property, SiteMapDataSource control, 679–680**
StartingNodeOffset **property, SiteMapDataSource control, 680**
StartingNodeUrl **property, SiteMapDataSource control, 681**
state management
Application object, 1028–1029
ControlState, 1036
cookies, 1029–1030
deciding on method for, 1004–1006
hidden fields, 1032–1035
overview of, 1003
postbacks and cross-page postbacks, 1030–1032
QueryStrings, 1029
using HttpContext.Current.Items for short-term storage, 1037–1038
ViewState, 1032–1036
state management, Session **object in, 1006–1028**
choosing correct way to maintain, 1028
configuring sessionState management, 1008
cookieless session state, 1026–1027
event model and, 1006–1008
extending session state with other providers, 1024–1026
in-process session state, 1008–1015
making transparent, 1013–1015
optimizing performance, 1015–1016
Out-of-Process Session State, 1016–1022
SQL-backed session state, 1022–1024
State **property,** SqlConnection **class, 435**

State Server Sessions Abandoned performance counter, 1433
State Server Sessions Active performance counter, 1433
State Server Sessions Timed Out performance counter, 1433
State Server Sessions Total performance counter, 1433
State Service, 1017, 1020–1022
stateConnectionString **attribute, <sessionState>, 1382**
stateNetworkTimeout **attribute, <sessionState>, 1382**
StateServer**, 568, 1382–1383**
static links, Menu control styles for, 671–672
StaticBottomSeparatorImageUrl **property, Menu control, 675**
<StaticHoverStyle>, Menu control, 671–672
<StaticMenuItemStyle>, Menu control, 671–672
StaticPopOutImageUrl **property, Menu control, 674**
StaticTopSeparatorImageUrl **property, Menu control, 675**
StepType **attribute, Wizard server control, 172–173**
stored procedures
- inserting data into SQL Server, 472–473
- simple SQL and, 469–471

storing
- application-specific settings, 1404–1405
- connection strings, 1380–1381
- session state, 1381–1385

StrangeLoop Network, AppScaler, 1026
Stream **class**
- classes derived from, 1134
- compressing, 1143–1148
- compressing streams, 1143–1148
- encodings, 1141
- I/O shortcuts, 1141–1143
- overview of, 1134–1138
- Reader and Writer classes, 1138–1141
- reading and writing I/O data with, 1133–1134

Stream **object, 164–165**
StreamReader**, 1139–1140, 1141**
StreamWriter**, 1141**
strict **attribute, compilation configuration, 1386**
strings, sorting, 1360–1362
Style Builder, 71–72
<style> tag, HTML, 839–840
styles
- adding to PathSeparator property, 645
- applying to HTML elements, 70–71
- BulletedList server control, 151
- Calendar server control, 141–144
- DataList control template, 391–392
- displaying in Manage Style Tool window, 859–860
- GridView control, 329–330
- HTML for server controls, 1183–1186
- limitations of HTML for, 836
- Login control, 755
- Menu control, 670–675
- TreeView control, 652–653
- using Apply Styles tool window, 860–861
- using CSS for. *See* CSS (Cascading Style Sheets)
- using themes. *See* themes
- watermark, 950

StyleSheetTheme **attribute,** Page **directive, 258**
Subject **property, installer properties, 1514**
submaster pages, 244–246
subpages. *See* content pages
Subscribers **group,** IsInRole **method, 989–990**
Substitution Control, Post-Cache, 1043–1045
SupportPhone **property, installer properties, 1514**
SupportsEvaluate **property, expression builders, 357–358**
SupportUrl **property, installer properties, 1514**
Switch **class**
- aspnet_regiis.exe utility, 1404
- BooleanSwitch, 1087–1088
- for diagnostic switches, 1087

Switch **class (continued)**
SourceSwitch, 1088
TraceSwitch, 1088
Synclock statement, 627
syntax
notifications (squiggles), 1071–1073
VB in Visual Studio 2008 vs. C#, 488
XML semantics vs., 480–481
System event log, writing to, 1428
System.AccessControl **namespace, 1127–1128**
System.ComponentModel.TypeConverter **class, 1221**
System.Configuration**, 598–601, 1405–1412, 1417–1424**
System.Core.dll **assembly, LINQ, 446**
System.Data.OracleClient**, 384–387**
System.Diagnostics**, 1426–1428, 1434–1439**
System.Diagnostics.Trace**, 1076, 1080**
System.Exception**, 1104**
System.IO **namespace, 1108–1117**
System.IO.Compression **, 1143**
System.IO.Path**, 1122–1126**
System.IO.Ports**, 1148–1149**
System.Net **namespace**
defined, 1149
FileWebRequest and FileWebResponse classes, 1155–1156
FtpWebRequest and FtpWebResponse classes, 1153–1156
HttpWebRequest and HttpWebResponse classes, 1149–1153
sending mail, 1156
System.Net.Mail **namespace, 1156**
SystemWeb.config **, 1399**
System.Web.Configuration**, 1405–1412**
System.Web.HttpBrowserCapabilities**, 1198**
System.Web.Mail**, 1156**
System.Web.Management
event types, 1445
Web event providers, 591
System.Web.Management.EventLogWebEventProvider**, 592–593, 1441**
System.Web.Management.IisTraceWebEventProvider-**, 591, 1441**
System.Web.Management.SimpleMailWebEventProvider**, 591, 593–595, 1441**
System.Web.Management.SqlWebEventProvider**, 591, 596–597, 1441**
System.Web.Management.TemplatedMailWebEventProvider**, 591, 595–596, 1441**
System.Web.Management.TraceWebEventProvider**, 591, 597, 1441**
System.Web.Management.WmiWebEventProvider**, 591, 597–598, 1442**
System.Web.Script.Services.ScriptService**, 1296**
System.Web.Security.ActiveDirectoryMembershipProvider**, 579–581**
System.Web.Security.AuthorizationStoreRoleProvider**, 584–585**
System.Web.Security.SqlMembershipProvider**, 577–579**
System.Web.Security.SqlProfileProvider**, 585–586**
System.Web.Security.SqlRoleProvider**, 582–583**
System.Web.Security.WindowsTokenRoleProvider**, 583–584**
System.Web.Services.Protocols**, 1296**
System.Web.SessionState**, 588–590**
System.Web.UI.ICallBackEventHandler **interface, 1192–1196**
System.Web.UI.ScriptControl**, 1169**
System.Web.UI.WebControls**, 1169**
System.Web.UI.WebControls.WebParts.SqlPersonalizationProvider**, 601–603**

T

TabContainer control, AJAX, 962–963
Table menu, Visual Studio Design view, 857–858
Table server control, 134–136

TableAdapter Configuration wizard, 406
TableAdapter **object, 405–406, 413**
tables
  disabling for SQL Server cache invalidation, 1058–1059
  enabling for cache invalidation, 1056–1057
  enabling for SQL Server cache invalidation, 1058
  SQL Server cache invalidation and, 1064
TabPanel controls, 962–963
tags
  rendering HTML, 1180–1181
  rendering HTML attributes, 1181–1183
  user control, 1160
Take **method, LINQ, 457**
TargetControlID **property**
  AlwaysVisibleControlExtender control, 909
  AnimationExtender control, 911
  CollapsiblePanelExtender control, 917
  DragPanelExtender control, 921
  DropDownExtender control, 923
  DropShadowExtender control, 924
  FilteredTextBoxExtender control, 931
  ListSearchExtender control, 933
  MaskedEditExtender control, 934
  ResizableControlExtender control, 943
  RoundedCornersExtender control, 945
TargetPlatform **property, installer properties, 1514**
Task List views, 1074–1075
Temp DB database, 1384
tempDirectory **attribute, compilation configuration, 1387**
templated controls, 1212–1219
TemplatedMailWebEventProvider, **591, 595–596, 1458–1460**
TemplateField column, GridView control, 317–320
TemplateField EditItem template, GridView control, 325–327
TemplatePagerField, ListView paging, 344–345
templates. *See also* master pages
  AJAX Control Toolkit, 902–903
  ASP.NET Server Control class, 1170–1173
  controls, 308–309
  DataList server control. *See* DataList server control
  GridView control, 308–309
  ListView server control, 393–394
testing
  health monitoring, 1449–1450
  migration from ASP.NET 1x to 2.0, 1527
  site map localization, 687–689
  SQL Server cache invalidation, 1062–1068
text
  aligning around check box, 126
  compiling, 43
  Hyperlink control, 116
  Label control, 104–106
  Literal control, 106–107
  TextBox control, 107–111
  UpdateProgress control, 893–895
Text **property**
  CompareValidator control, 196
  Regular Expression validator control, 202
  RequiredFieldValidator control, 190–191
  TreeNode object, 667–669
  validation control with, 209–210
  ViewState, 1200–1201
TextAlign **property, CheckBox control, 126**
TextBox server control, 107–111
  AutoPostBack, 108–110
  with FilteredTextBoxExtender control, 930–931
  Focus( ) method, 108
  with NumericUpDownExtender control, 939
  overview of, 107–108
  with PasswordStrength control, 960–961
  with SliderExtender control, 946–947
  with TextBoxWatermarkExtender control, 950–951
  using AutoCompleteType, 110–111
TextBoxStringProvider( ) **method, provider Web Parts, 828**

TextBoxWatermarkExtender control, 950–951
`Themeable` **attribute, 271–274**
themes
- assigning skin programmatically, 270
- assigning to entire application, 255
- assigning to page programmatically, 269–270
- assigning to single ASP.NET page, 253–255
- creating proper folder structure, 258–259
- creating server controls with, 1186–1187
- creating skin, 259–261
- custom controls, skins and, 270–274
- defining multiple skin options, 267–269
- folder for storing, 37–38
- master pages using, 257
- removing from server controls, 256
- removing from web pages, 257
- `StyleSheetTheme` attribute, 258
- using CSS files in, 261–264
- using images in, 264–267

thick-client applications, 867–868
thin-client applications, 867–868
third-party vendors
- DbgView, 1081
- extending LINQ, 475
- GenerateMachineKey tool, 1036
- HTTP compression modules, 1145
- HTTP Headers and controlling caching, 1046
- session state providers, 1024–1026
- validation server controls, 188
- ViewStateDecoder tool, 1035

threads, ASP.NET, 1349–1352, 1401
time, culture differences, 1355–1356
timeouts
- Forms authentication, 1393
- runtime settings configuration, 1400–1401
- session state configuration, 1382
- Session State Settings, 1489

Timer server control, AJAX, 883, 887–888
titles
- content page, 232
- custom content page, 232

titles, installer properties, 1514
`.tlb` **file extension (type library file), 1280–1281**
`tlbexp.exe`**, 1280–1284**
ToggleButtonExtender control, 951–952
tools
- configuration file editing, 1416–1417
- debugging, 1541–1547
- extending ASP.NET, 1555–1557
- general purpose developer, 1558–1562
- IIS Manager. *See* IIS (Internet Information Service) Manager
- references, 1548–1549
- resource editor, 1370–1371
- tidying up code, 1550–1552
- Visual Studio add-ins, 1553–1554
- Web Site Administration Tool. *See* Web Site Administration Tool
- Windows Installer service. *See* Windows Installer service

ToolTips
- SiteMapPath server control, 647–648
- for syntax errors at design-time, 1072
- using HoverMenuExtender, 931

`ToShortDateString( )` **method, Calendar control, 138**
trace forwarding, 1082
`Trace` **property,** `Page` **class, 1076**
`<trace>` **setting, locking-down configuration, 1396**
`trace.axd`**, 1077–1080**
`TraceContext` **class, 1076**
`Trace.IsEnabled` **property, page-level tracing, 1076**
TraceListeners
- configuring, 1082–1083
- defined, 1075–1076
- DelimitedListTraceListener, 1085
- EventLogTraceListener, 1084–1085
- IisTraceListener, 1087
- listening in on debugging with, 1081
- new WebPageTraceListener, 1083–1084
- XmlWriterTraceListener, 1085–1086

TraceMode attribute, page-level tracing, 1076
Tracepoints, 1098

`TraceSwitch`, **1088**
`TraceWebEventProvider`, **591, 597**
`Trace.Write` **function, 1077, 1081–1082**
tracing, 1075–1090
- application, 1076, 1439
- ASP.NET's `Page.Trace`, 1076
- from components, 1080–1082
- configuring TraceListeners, 1082–1083
- DelimitedListTraceListener, 1085
- diagnostic switches, 1087–1088
- EventLogTraceListener, 1084–1085
- managing in Application tab, 1476–1477
- new ASP.NET WebPageTraceListener, 1083–1084
- overview of, 1075–1076
- page-level, 1076
- storing data in `Session` object, 1011–1012
- `System.Diagnostics.Trace`, 1076
- trace forwarding, 1082
- viewing trace data, 1077–1080
- Web events, 1088–1090
- XmlWriterTraceListener, 1085–1086

`Transform` **method,** `XslCompiledTransform` **class, 519–522**
translation
- dates, 1355–1356
- number and currency, 1356–1360
- sorting strings, 1360–1362

transport protocols, Web services, 1307–1312
`TreeNode` **objects, TreeView control, 667–669**
TreeView class, TreeView control, 663–669
TreeView Line Generator dialog, 663
TreeView server control, 648–669
- binding to XML file, 654–656
- built-in styles of, 652–653
- as databound control, 350–351
- incorporating images into themes, 264–265
- overview of, 648–652
- parts of, 653–654
- programmatically working with, 663–669
- selecting multiple options, 656–660
- specifying custom icons, 659–661
- specifying lines used to connect nodes, 661–663
- styling with CSS-Friendly Control Adapters, 864
- testing site map localization results, 687–689

`TreeView1_DataBound( )` **method, 665**
`TreeViewLineImages` **property, TreeView control, 663**
triggers, UpdatePanel control, 890–892, 897
Triple DES encryption, 601
trust levels
- .NET Trust Levels in IIS Manager, 1484
- security and, 994
- server configuration files, 1376–1377

`Try/Catch`**, in exception handling, 1101–1102**
two-way data binding, 353
type converters, 1220–1224
type libraries, 1279–1281
Type Library Exporter, 1280–1281, 1284
Type Library Importer, 1269, 1272
`Type` **property, CompareValidator server control, 197**
`Type` **property, RangeValidator server control, 198**
Type Selectors, CSS, 841
typed datasets, 32–37, 384
types
- personalization properties, 707–710
- ViewState and, 1201

U

UI type editors, 1237–1238
`uiculture` **attribute,** `Web.config` **file, 686**
`uiculture` **attribute,** `Web.config.comments` **file, 1352–1353**
`unattend.xml` **file, 548**
unhandled exceptions, 1102
Uniform Resource Locator. ***See*** **URL (Uniform Resource Locator)**
Uniform/Universal Resource Identifier (URI), 479, 714
uninstalling applications, Windows Installer, 1508–1510

unique identifiers (GUIDs), 233–234, 714
UniqueID **property, server controls, 1182**
United Kingdom, culture codes, 1348
United States, culture codes, 1348
Universal Selectors, CSS, 841
Unlock( ) **method,** Application**, 1028**
unmanaged code. *See*. NET from unmanaged code
UnsealedCacheDependency **class, 1050–1051**
UpdateCommand
  DetailsView control, 336
  SqlDataSource control, 321
updateGrid ( ) function, DynamicPopulateExtender control, 927
UpdateMode **property, UpdatePanel, 898**
UpdatePanel server control, AJAX, 888–892
UpdatePanelAnimationExtender control, 953–954
UpdatePanelTrigger Collection Editor, 892
UpdateParameters**, SqlDataSource control, 321–322**
UpdateProgress server control, AJAX, 883, 892–896
updates
  browser configuration, 1389
  in DetailsView control, 335–336
  handling errors in GridView control during, 323–325
  IIS 7 dependencies and, 545
  LINQ to SQL, 473–474
  in SQL Server, 365–366
  using AJAX on Web page, 869
  using pkmgr.exe to install specific, 547
UpgradeCode **property, installer properties, 1514**
upgrades
  to ASP.NET 3.5 using VS 2008, 1528
  to ASP.NET applications, 1526–1528
  to IIS 7, 548–549
  using ASP.NET reserved folders, 1529
  using stepped approach in, 1528
upload buffering, 1401
uploading files. *See* FileUpload server control
URI (Uniform/Universal Resource Identifier), 479, 714
URL (Uniform Resource Locator)
  Installation URL, 1512
  mapping, 684–685
  state management and, 1005
  XML namespaces as, 479
URL Authorization, 1395
URL rewriting, 1248–1252
URLAuthorizationModule**, 1395**
UseCookies **value, storing identifiers, 714**
UseDeviceProfile **value, storing identifiers, 714**
useFullyQualifiedRedirectUrl **attribute, runtime, 1400**
useMachineContainer **attribute,** RsaProtectedConfigurationProvider, **601**
useMachineProtection **attribute,** DpapiProtectedConfigurationProvider, **600**
useOAEP **attribute,** RsaProtectedConfigurationProvider, **601**
user controls
  creating, 1160–1162
  defined, 1159
  interacting with, 1162–1164
  loading dynamically, 1164–1169
  problems with in ASP.NET 1.0, 221
User Interface Editor, 1520–1522
User **property,** Page **object, 987–988**
User Tasks view, Task List, 1074
userControlBaseType **element,** <pages> **configuration, 1398**
UserControls (ASCX), 1043
User.Identity **property, 988–989**
User.IsInRole( ) **method, 989–990**
usernames
  adding users to membership service, 737–739
  authenticating against values in database, 982–984

authenticating against values in web.config file, 980–982
Basic authentication limitation, 974
locking out users with bad passwords, 756–760
with LoginName server control, 760–762
protecting configuration settings, 1412
using Login control with Forms authentication, 984–985

users
adding with Security Setup Wizard, 1467, 1470
allowing to change Web page mode, 797–808
authentication. *See* authentication; membership management service
authorization. *See* authorization; role management service
creating, 1471
creating and placing in Admin role, 690–691
managing, 1472
membership providers validating, 624–626
.NET Users in IIS Manager, 1484–1485
personalization properties for. *See* personalization properties
rating control manipulated by, 961–962
ReadUserFile( ) method, 626–628
using XmlMembershipProvider for login, 628–629
Windows authentication. *See* Windows-based authentication

UseURI **value, storing identifiers with, 714**

Using **statement**
closing streams with, 1135
XmlReader and XmlWriter, 505
XmlReader implementing, 528

V

ValidateNumber **function, CustomValidator control, 207**

validateRequest **element,** <pages> **configuration, 1398**

ValidateUser( ) **method**
Membership class, 755–756
MembershipProvider class, 624–626

validation
CustomValidator control, 202–208
Forms authentication and, 1393
MaskedEditValidator control, 936–937
with membership providers, 624–626
against schema with XDocument, 491–493
ValidatorCalloutExtender control, 954–955
of XML, 481–482, 490–493

Validation and More (VAM) server control, 188

validation server controls
client-side vs. server-side, 186–187
CompareValidator, 194–197
CustomValidator, 202–208
defined, 185
as extender controls, 907–908
overview of, 187–188
RangeValidator, 198–201
RegularExpressionValidator, 201–202
RequiredFieldValidator, 189–194
turning off client-side validation, 211–212
understanding validation, 185–186
using images and sounds for error notifications, 212–213
validation causes, 188–189
ValidationSummary, 208–211
working with validation groups, 213–217

ValidationExpression **property, Regular Expression validator control, 202**

ValidationGroup **property, validation groups, 214**

<validationkey>, web.config **file, 1035**

ValidationSummary server control, 188, 208–211

ValidatorCalloutExtender control, 954–955

Value **property,** TreeNode **object, 667**

ValueChanged **event, HiddenField control, 156**

value-required rule, RequiredFieldValidator control, 189

ValueToCompare **property, CompareValidator control, 197**

VAM (Validation and More) server control, 188

`VaryByControl` **attribute, output caching, 1041**
`VaryByCustom` **attribute, output caching, 1041–1042**
`VaryByParam` **attribute, output caching, 1040–1041, 1063**
vector graphics, 1568–1571
verbs
URL Authorization configuration, 1395
Web Part, 811–814
`Version` **property, installer properties, 1514**
View server control, 166–170
views
querying LING to SQL data using, 468–469
of trace data, 1077–1080
ViewState
client-side state management, 1006
state management, 1032–1036
tips for, 1035
using ControlState in server controls, 1201–1203
using in server controls, 1199–1201
ViewStateDecoder tool, 1035
virtual directories, 1379
`VirtualDirectory` **property, File System Editor, 1515**
`visibility` **property, CSS box model, 853**
Visibone Web site, 1549
Visual Studio
ADO.NET tasks with, 402–413
classes, 53–59
configuration file editing tools, 1416–1417
global resource files, 1369–1370
HTML and CSS in. *See* HTML and CSS design, in Visual Studio
HTML server controls, 73–76
release and debug configurations, 1090–1091
Resource Editor, 1370–1371
Style Builder, 71–72
Visual Studio 2008
add-in tools, 1553–1554
AJAX, working with. *See* AJAX (Asynchronous JavaScript and XML)
AJAX Control Toolkit and. *See* AJAX Control Toolkit
ASP.NET 1.x applications, converting, 1532–1537
ASP.NET 2.0 to 3.5, migrating from, 1537–1540
ASP.NET 3.5, upgrading application to, 1528
ASP.NET projects, creating new, 1270–1273
configuration files, editing, 1416
Copy Web Site deployment option, 1496–1501
CSS, working with, 858–862
CSS Attribute Selectors not supported in, 842
design surface, 855
event log, working with, 1425–1430
first-child pseudo class not supported in, 843
installer program, building, 1501–1507
Interop Type Library, generating in, 1279–1281
JavaScript debugger, 1100–1101
.NET business objects, creating, 1264–1266
precompilation for deployment, 1499–1501
RCW for COM component, creating, 1269
refactoring support in, 1550
resource files, 1362–1368
server controls, creating ASP.NET, 1170
triggers, building, 892
UpdateProgress control, 892–896
WCF service, building, 1327–1328
Web Page Design Surface, 1219
Web Part controls, creating custom, 818–819
Web Site Administration Tool access, 784, 1464
WebPartManager control, 790
WebPartZone controls, dragging and dropping in, 794
XAML, viewing and editing in, 1571–1578
XHTML in, 1529–1531
XML Web service. *See* XML Web Services, building
zone layouts, 794
Visual Studio Conversion Wizard, 1532–1537

Visual Studio Toolbox, 904
visualizers, data, 1096–1097
.vsi **file extension, 902**

W

W3C (World Wide Web Consortium), 480, 482
w3wp.exe**, 1017, 1028**
Wait approach
multiple wait handles, 423–432
overview of, 420–423
WaitAny **method, asynchronous processes, 428–432**
WaitHandle **class, 416–417**
WaitOne **method,** WaitHandle **class, 420–423**
Warn( ) **method,** TraceContext **class, 1076**
WatermarkText **property, TextBoxWatermarkExtender control, 950**
WCF (Windows Communication Foundation), 1326–1335
building service, 1327–1328
creating interface, 1330–1332
creating service framework, 1330
development of, 1326
hosting service in console application, 1333
larger move to SOA, 1326–1327
overview of, 1327
reviewing WSDL document, 1333–1335
service components, 1328–1329
utilizing interface, 1332–1333
WCF (Windows Communication Foundation), building consumer application, 1335–1344
adding service reference, 1336–1337
building consumer, 1342–1343
configuration file changes, 1337–1338
namespaces, 1344
working with data contracts, 1339–1342
writing consumption code, 1338–1339
WSDL and schema for HelloCustomer service, 1343–1344
Web Developer Toolbar, Firefox, 1544–1545
Web event providers
EventLogWebEventProvider, 592–593
IisWebEventProvider, 597
list of, 591
overview of, 591–592
SimpleMailWebEventProvider, 593–595
SqlWebEventProvider, 596–597
TemplatedMailWebEventProvider, 595–596
TraceWebEventProvider, 597
WmiWebEventProvider, 597–598
Web events
defined, 591
health monitoring. *See* health monitoring
tracing using, 1088–1090
Web Farm, session state configuration, 1382–1385
Web gardening, 1009
Web Page Design Surface, Visual Studio 2008, 1219
Web pages
adding templated controls to, 1217–1218
adding user controls to, 1161–1162
dynamically adding user controls to, 1164–1169
limitations of using HTML for styling, 836
sending e-mail from, 1156
using external style sheets in, 838–839
using inline styles in, 840
using internal style sheets in, 839–840
Web Parts
allowing user to change mode of page, 797–808
creating custom, 818–824
modifying zones, 808–814
overview of, 787–788
using WebPartManager control, 789–790
using WebPartZone control, 794–796
verbs, 811–814
working with zone layouts, 790–794
Web Parts, connecting, 824–833
on ASP.NET page, 830–833
building consumer Web Part, 828–830
building provider Web Part, 825–828

Web Parts, connecting *(continued)*
dealing with master pages when, 833
overview of, 824–825
Web server
built-in, 2
customizing with IIS 7, 544–549
Web server controls, 103–184
AdRotator, 145–146
BulletedList, 150–155
Button, 111–114
Calendar, 137–144
CheckBox, 124–126
CheckBoxList, 127–129
DropDownList, 117–119
FileUpload, 156–166
HiddenField, 155–156
HyperLink, 116
Image, 132–134
ImageButton, 115–116
ImageMap, 180–182
Label, 104–106
LinkButton, 114–115
ListBox, 121–124
Literal, 106–107
MultiView, 166–170
overview of, 103–104
Panel, 147–149
Placeholder, 150
RadioButton, 129–131
RadioButtonList, 131–132
Table, 134–136
TextBox, 107–111
using HTML server controls vs., 62–63
View, 166–170
visually removing items from collections, 119–121
Wizard, 170–180
Xml, 146–147
Web services. *See* XML Web services
Web Services Description Language. *See* WSDL (Web Services Description Language) files
Web Services Enhancements (WSE), 1312, 1326
Web Setup Project, Windows Installer, 1502
Web Site Administration Tool
Application tab, 1474–1475
configuration file editing, 1416–1417
Home tab, 1465
overview of, 1463–1464
Provider tab, 1477–1479
role management service with, 775
Security Setup Wizard, 1466–1471
Security tab, creating users, 1471
Security tab, managing access rules, 1474
Security tab, managing roles, 1472
Security tab, managing users, 1472
Security tab, overview of, 1465
using, 784
Web sites
adding in IIS Manager, 554–555
building with Portal Framework. *See* Portal Framework
changing name of in IIS Manager, 1481
membership management set up, 734–737
online resources, 1586
role management set up, 771–775
running with multiple versions of .NET, 1404
Web user control, 1161–1162
`web.config` **file**
`ActiveDirectoryMembershipProvider` in, 579–581
administrator section, 691–692
ASP.NET cache, 1049
attribute values, 608–609
`<authentication>` node setting, 967–968
`AuthorizationStoreRoleProvider`, 584–585
configuration files. *See* configuration
connection strings, 369–370, 575–576
defined, 966
`DpapiProtectedConfigurationProvider`, 599–600
file-size limitation, 162
Forms authentication. *See* Forms-based authentication
health monitoring, 1442
HttpHandler, 1260

HttpModule, 1147–1148, 1247–1248
InProcSessionStateStore, 588–589
localization, 686
master page, 231–232
multiple languages, 36–37
personalization properties, 700–701
provider instances, 618–619
providers, 603
role management, 691
role management service, 772–773
<rules>, 1447–1448
security trimming, 692–694
SMTP setup for emailing Web events, 1457–1458
SQL Server cache invalidation, 1060–1061
SqlPersonalizationProvider, 601–603
SqlSessionStateStore, 590
storing connection information, 301–304
System.LINQ namespace, 447
themes, 255, 257
WCF consumer, 1337–1338
Web event providers. *See* Web event providers
Web site membership, 735–737
Windows authentication. *See* Windows-based authentication
WindowsTokenRoleProvider, 583–584
XmlSiteMapProvider, 586–588
web.config.comments **file, 1352–1353**
WebControl **class, 68, 1169–1175**
WebEventProvider **class, 591**
weblogs (blogs), and XmlDataSource **control, 515–517**
weblogs (blogs), online resources, 1585–1586
WebMethod **attribute**
overloading, 1312–1315
specifying SOAP header for, 1318–1319
XML Web service, 1298–1299
WebPageTraceListener, 1083–1084
WebPart **class**
building consumer Web Part, 828–830
building provider Web Part, 825–828
creating custom Web Part control, 818–824
working with, 817–818
WebPartManager **class, 815**
WebPartManager control
adding Web Parts to page, 800–802
connecting Web Parts, 808
connecting Web Parts using, 830–833
dealing with master pages, 833
modifying Web Part settings, 804–808
moving Web Parts, 802–804
overview of, 789–790, 797
WebParts provider, 601–603
<WebPartsTemplate>**, DeclarativeCatalogPart control, 809–810**
WebPartZone **class, 816–818**
WebPartZone control
connecting Web Parts on page, 831
controlling Web Part verbs, 811–814
default elements, 796
working with, 794–796
WebRequest **class**
defined, 1155–1156
FileWebRequest class, 1155–1156
FtpWebRequest class, 1153–1156
HttpWebRequest class, 1149–1153
WebResource.axd **handler, 1192**
WebResponse **class**
defined, 1155–1156
FileWebResponse class, 1155–1156
FtpWebResponse class, 1153–1156
HttpWebResponse class, 1149–1153
WebService **attribute, 1298**
@WebService **directive, 1295**
<WebServiceBinding> **attribute, 1296**
WebService.cs **file, 1295**
WebService.vb**, 1295**
Web.sitemap **file**
for localization, 685–686
nesting, 694–696
setting up administrators' section, 692
Web.sitemap.fi.resx **file, 687–689**
Web.sitemap.resx **file, 687–689**
where **clause**
LINQ query, 452–453
LinqDataSource control, 291–292
wildcards, IIS,1252–1254

WinDiff, 1559
Windows Communication Foundation. *See* WCF (Windows Communication Foundation)
Windows Installer service
actions of, 1503
Custom Actions Editor, 1522–1523
defined, 1502–1503
File System Editor, 1514–1518
File Types Editor, 1519–1520
Launch Conditions Editor, 1523–1524
options, 1510
Output File Name, 1511
Registry Editor, 1518–1519
User Interface Editor, 1520–1522
working with deployment project properties, 1510–1514
Windows NT Challenge/Response authentication, 974, 1391
Windows Presentation Foundation (WPF), 868
Windows Server 2008
command-line setup options, 546–548
installing IIS 7 on, 545–546
Windows Services, 1382–1383
Windows Vista
command-line setup options, 546–548
configuration file editing tools, 1416–1417
IIS Manager. *See* IIS (Internet Information Service) Manager
installing IIS 7 on, 545
using Basic authentication option in, 975
using IIS 7.0 Manager in, 1000–1001
working with file extensions, 997
Windows XP, remote debugging and, 1094
Windows-based authentication, 968–976
`<allow>` and `<deny>` nodes, 971–972
authenticating/authorizing groups, 972–973
authenticating/authorizing HTTP transmission method, 973
authenticating/authorizing users, 969–971
Basic authentication, 974–975
configuring, 1391
creating users, 968–969
defined, 967
Digest authentication, 975–976
Integrated Windows authentication, 973–974
overview of, 968
Security Setup Wizard, 1467
`WindowsIdentity` object, 990–992
`WindowsBuiltInRole` **enumeration, 990–991**
`WindowsIdentity` **object, 990–992**
`WindowsTokenRoleProvider`**, 583–584**
WinMerge, 1559
Wizard server control, 170–180
adding header to, 173
`AllowReturn` attribute, 172
customizing side navigation, 171–172
events, 174–176
navigation system for, 173–174
overview of, 170–171
showing form elements with, 176–180
`StepType` attribute, 172–173
<WizardSteps> element, 744
`WmiWebEventProvider`**, 591, 597–598**
worker process, configuration settings, 1402–1404
Worker Process Restarts performance counter, 1433
Worker Processes Running performance counter, 1433
workplace pane, IIS Manager, 549
World Wide Web Consortium (W3C), 480, 482
WPF (Windows Presentation Foundation), 868
`Wrap` **attribute, multiline text boxes, 108**
`Write()` **method**
`Stream` class, 1136–1137
`TraceContext` class, 1076
writing to `MemoryStream`, 1137
`WriteEntry()`**, writing to event log, 1430**
`Writer` **class, 1133–1134, 1138–1141**
writing events
with event log, 1428–1430
routing events to SQL server, 1450–1453
via configuration, 1449–1450

`Wrox.master` file, 228–229, 246–248
`WroxOpera.master` file, 246–248
***Wrox's Beginning Web Programming with HTML, XHTML, and CSS* (Wiley Publishing, Inc.), 70**
WSDL (Web Services Description Language) files
- consuming XML Web services, 1303
- schema for `HelloCustomer` service, 1343–1344
- WCF service linking to, 1333–1335
- XML Web services linking to, 1300

`.wsdl` file extension, 32–37
WSE (Web Services Enhancements), 1312, 1326
WS-I Basic Profile spec, 1313–1314
WS-Policy, 1327
www.asp.net, 1549
WYSIWYG design, of Visual Studio, 857

X

XAML
- converting vector content to, 1569–1571
- editing in Notepad, 1577–1578
- Export plug-in, 1569
- using XAML editor, 1574
- viewing or editing with Expression Blend, 1574–1576
- viewing or editing with Internet Explorer, 1572–1574

XCOPY, deploying with, 1493–1496
`XDocument`
- processing XML with, 488–489
- querying with `XPath`, 509
- validating against schema with, 491–493

XHTML, 1072–1073, 1529–1531
XLINQ. *See* LINQ to XML (XLINQ)
XML (eXtensible Markup Language). *See also* AJAX (Asynchronous JavaScript and XML)
- acronym design and, 478
- basics of, 478–480
- binding Menu server control to, 676–678
- binding TreeView control to, 654–656
- configuration files, 1374
- creating CLR objects from, 498–499
- creating with `XmlWriter`, 499–501
- data binding, 353–354
- and databases, `FOR XML AUTO` clause, 524–528
- DataSets, 510–513
- integration with, 1292
- LINQ to. *See* LINQ to XML (XLINQ)
- `NameTable` optimization, 493–495
- overview of, 477–478
- retrieving .NET CLR types from, 495–496
- schema, editing, 483–485
- schema, using with `XmlTextReader`, 489–491
- schema, validating against with `XDocument`, 491–493
- serialization, 497–498
- site maps based on, 640–641
- using AdRotator control, 145–146
- using `XDocument` vs. `XmlReader`, 488–489
- `XML` data type and SQL Server 2005, 528–534
- Xml InfoSet, 480–481
- `XmlDataSource` control, 513–517
- `XmlDocument` and `XPathDocument`, 505–509
- `XmlReader` and `XmlWriter`, 486–488, 504–505
- XSD, 481–482
- XSLT, 517–523

XML Editor, 483–485, 1072–1073
Xml InfoSet, 480–481
XML Literals, 502
XML Schema Definition. *See* XSD (XML Schema Definition)
XML Schema Editor, 484
XML server control, 146–147
XML Web services
- caching responses, 1315–1316
- communication between disparate systems, 1291–1293

XML Web services *(continued)*
overloading Web methods, 1312–1315
overview of, 1291
SOAP headers, 1316–1317
Windows Communication Foundation for. *See* WCF (Windows Communication Foundation)
XML Web services, building, 1293–1302
contents of `Service.asmx` file, 1294–1295
exposing custom datasets as SOAP, 1296–1299
interface, 1299–1302
overview of, 1293–1294
`WebService.vb` or `WebService.cs` file, 1295–1296
XML Web services, consuming
adding Web reference, 1302–1304
asynchronously, 1323–1325
invoking from client application, 1304–1307
overview of, 1302
transport protocols for, 1307–1312
using SOAP headers, 1319–1321
`XmlConvert` **class, 495**
`XmlDataDocument` **class, 511–513**
`XmlDataSource` **server control**
binding TreeView control to XML file using, 654–656
data binding and, 155
overview of, 294–295, 513–517
`XmlDocument`
databases and XML, 524–528
`XDocument` vs., 488–489
`XPathDocument` and, 505–509
XmlHTTP, 92
`XMLHttpRequest` **object, 867, 869–870**
`XmlMembershipProvider` **class**
constructing class skeleton, 614–617
creating CustomProviders application, 613–614
creating XML user data store, 617–618
defining provider instance in web.config file, 618–619
implementing methods/properties of, 620–621
not implementing methods/properties of, 619–620
`XmlNamespaceManager`**, 513**
`XmlReader`
calling `Close( )` when done with, 528
improvements in 2.0, 504–505
optimizing with `NameTable`, 493–495
overview of, 486–488
`ReadSubTree` and XML serialization, 497–498
retrieving .NET CLR types from, 495–496
`XDocument` vs., 488–489
`XmlReaderSettings` **object, 486–488**
`XmlSerializer`**, 497–498, 503–504**
XmlSiteMapProvider, 586–588, 692–694
`XmlTextReader`**, 489–491**
`XmlWriter`**, 486–488, 499–501, 504–505**
`XmlWriterSettings` **class, 499–501**
XmlWriterTraceListener, 1085–1086
`XPath`**, 509, 513**
`XPathBinder` **class, XML data binding, 354**
`XPathDocument`**, 505–509, 519**
`XPathNavigator` **class, 505–508**
`XPathNodeIterator`**, 506–509**
XSD (XML Schema Definition)
LINQ to XSD, 498
overview of, 481–482
working with WCFservice, data contracts, 1339
WSDL and, 1343–1344
XML Editor as default view for, 484
XSD Designer, 484
`XslCompiledTransform` **class, 519–522, 523**
XSLT, 517–523
debugger, 523
overview of, 517–518
speed of, 519

styling XML from SQL Server, 527–528
XslCompiledTransform class, 519–522
XSLTC.exe command-line compiler, 520–522
XSLTC.exe command-line compiler, 520–522
XSLTCommand, 522
XsltSettings object, 519

Y

YSlow, by Yahoo!, 1543–1544

Z

zones, Web
adding Web Parts to page, 801–802
defining, 789
layouts, 790–794
modifying, 808–814
moving Web Parts between, 802–804
using WebPartZone control, 794–796
WebPartManager control managing, 789–790
ZoneTemplate attribute, WebPartZone control, 795

.NET Domain-Driven Design with C#

.NET Domain-Driven Design with C#

Problem – Design – Solution

Tim McCarthy

Wiley Publishing, Inc.

.NET Domain-Driven Design with C#

Published by
Wiley Publishing, Inc.
10475 Crosspoint Boulevard
Indianapolis, IN 46256
www.wiley.com

Published simultaneously in Canada

ISBN: 978–0–470–14756–6

Manufactured in the United States of America

10 9 8 7 6 5 4 3 2 1

For general information on our other products and services or to obtain technical support, please contact our Customer Care Department within the U.S. at (800) 762-2974, outside the U.S. at (317) 572-3993 or fax (317) 572-4002.

Library of Congress Cataloging-in-Publication Data is available from the publisher.

Wiley also publishes its books in a variety of electronic formats. Some content that appears in print may not be available in electronic books.

About the Author

Tim McCarthy is a freelance consultant who architects, designs and builds highly scalable layered web and smart client applications utilizing the latest Microsoft platforms and technologies. Tim is a Microsoft MVP in Solutions Architecture, and his expertise covers a wide range of Microsoft technologies, including, but not limited to, the following: .NET Framework (ASP.NET/Smart Clients/VSTO/Workflow/Web Services, Windows Presentation Foundation), SQL Server, Active Directory, MS Exchange development, UDDI, SharePoint, and Service Oriented Architecture (SOA) applications. Tim has worked as both a project technical lead/member as well as being in a technical consulting role for several Fortune 500 companies. He has held the Microsoft Certified Solution Developer (MCSD) and Microsoft Certified Trainer (MCT) certifications for several years, and was one of the first wave of developers to earn the Microsoft Certified Application Developer (MCAD) for .NET and MCSD for .NET certifications. He also holds the Microsoft Certified Database Administrator certification for SQL Server 2000. Tim is also certified as an IEEE Certified Software Development Professional, and he is one of only 550 people to hold this certification in the world.

Tim has been an author and technical reviewer for several books from Wrox Press. His other books include being a lead author on *Professional VB 2005*, several editions of *Professional VB.NET*, *Professional Commerce Server 2000*, and *Professional ADO 2.5 Programming*. He also has written and presented a DVD titled *SharePoint Portal Services Programming 2003*. Tim has written numerous articles for the Developer .NET Update newsletter, developed packaged presentations for the Microsoft Developer Network (MSDN), and wrote a whitepaper for Microsoft on using COM+ services in .NET. He has also written articles for *SQL Server Magazine* and *Windows & .NET Magazine*.

Tim has spoken at technical conferences around the world and several San Diego area user groups (including both .NET and SQL Server groups, and several Code Camps), and he has been a regular speaker at the Microsoft Developer Days conference in San Diego for the last several years. Tim has also delivered various MSDN webcasts, many of which were repeat requests from Microsoft. He also teaches custom .NET classes to companies in need of expert .NET mentoring and training.

Tim holds a B.B.A. in Marketing from the Illinois Institute of Technology as well as an M.B.A. in Marketing from National University. Before becoming an application developer, Tim was an officer in the United States Marine Corps. Tim's passion for .NET is only surpassed by his passion for Notre Dame Athletics.

Tim can be reached via email at `tmccart1@san.rr.com`.

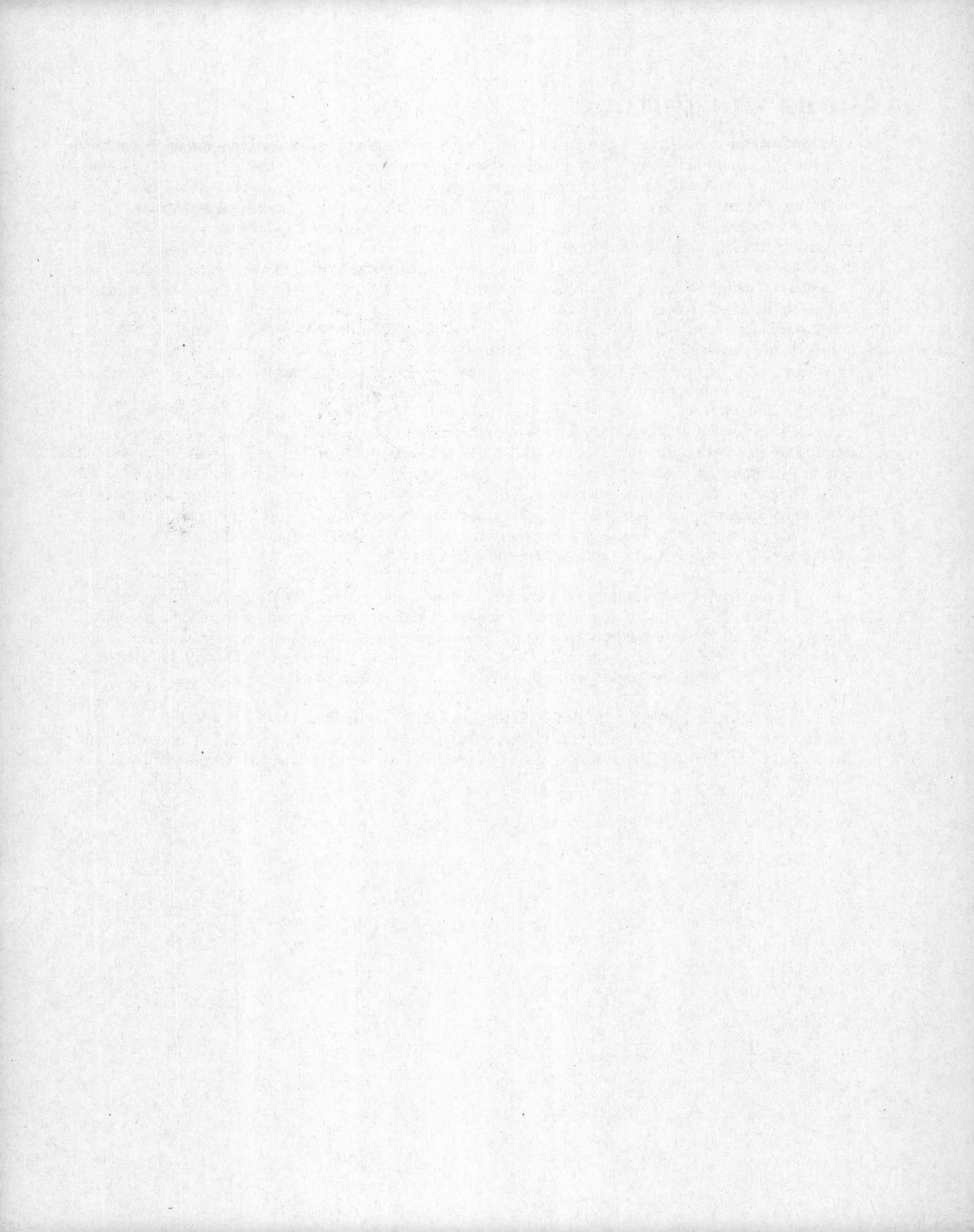

Credits

Acquisitions Editor
Katie Mohr

Development Editor
Christopher J. Rivera

Technical Editor
Doug Holland

Production Editor
Rachel McConlogue

Copy Editor
Foxxe Editorial Services

Editorial Manager
Mary Beth Wakefield

Production Manager
Tim Tate

Vice President and Executive Group Publisher
Richard Swadley

Vice President and Executive Publisher
Joseph B. Wikert

Project Coordinator, Cover
Lynsey Standford

Proofreader
Jen Larsen, Word One

Indexer
Jack Lewis

Cover Image
Leandra Hosier

.NET Domain-Driven Design with C#

Acknowledgments xv
Introduction xvii

Chapter 1: Introducing the Project: The SmartCA Application ... 1
Chapter 2: Designing the Layered Architecture 13
Chapter 3: Managing Projects 55
Chapter 4: Companies and Contacts 109
Chapter 5: Submittal Transmittals 157
Chapter 6: Requests for Information 199
Chapter 7: Proposal Requests 233
Chapter 8: Change Orders 265
Chapter 9: Construction Change Directives 295
Chapter 10: Synchronizing With the Server 327
Chapter 11: The Client Membership System 357

Index 391

Contents

Acknowledgments xv
Introduction xvii

Chapter 1: Introducing the Project: The SmartCA Application **1**

The Problem **1**
The Design **4**
Reliability and Availability 4
Scalability 5
Maintainability 5
Rich Client Application Functionality 5
Offline Capable 5
Web Access 5
Intelligent Installation and Auto-Update Functionality 5
Additional Client Device Support 5
The Solution **6**
Fulfilling the Reliability, Availability, Scalability, Offline Capable, and Additional Client Device Support Requirements 6
Fulfilling the Maintainability Requirement 7
Fulfilling the Rich Client Application Functionality Requirement 9
Fulfilling the Web Access Requirement 11
Fulfilling the Intelligent Installation and Auto-Update Functionality Requirement 11
Summary **11**

Chapter 2: Designing the Layered Architecture **13**

The Problem **13**
The Design **13**
Designing the Visual Studio Solution 13
Designing the Architectural Layers 14
The Solution **18**
Implementing the Visual Studio Solution 19
Implementing the Architectural Layers 19
Summary **53**

Chapter 3: Managing Projects **55**

The Problem **55**
The Design **55**
Designing the Domain Model 56
Defining the Project Aggregate 56
Defining the Aggregate Boundaries 57
Designing the Repositories 58
Writing the Unit Tests 60
The Solution **65**
The Project Class 65
The Repository Implementations 77
The Service Class Implementations 90
The Project Information ViewModel Implementation 92
The Project Information View Implementation 102
Summary **107**

Chapter 4: Companies and Contacts **109**

The Problem **109**
The Design **109**
Designing the Domain Model 110
Defining the Company and Contact Aggregates 110
Defining the Aggregate Boundaries 111
Designing the Repositories 112
Writing the Unit Tests 114
The Solution **119**
The Company Class 119
The Contact Class 121
The ProjectContact Class 123
The Repository Implementations 124
The Service Class Implementations 134
The Company ViewModel 137
The Company View 144
The Project Contact View Model 148
The Project Contact View 154
Summary **156**

Chapter 5: Submittal Transmittals **157**

The Problem **157**
The Design **158**
Designing the Domain Model 158
Defining the Submittal Aggregate 159

Defining the Aggregate Boundaries 159
Designing the Repository 160
Writing the Unit Tests 161
The Solution **164**
The Submittal Repository Implementation 178
The Submittal Service Implementation 187
The Submittal View Model 188
The Submittal View 192
Summary **197**

Chapter 6: Requests for Information **199**

The Problem **199**
The Design **200**
Designing the Domain Model 200
Defining the RFI Aggregate 201
Defining the Aggregate Boundaries 202
Designing the Repository 203
Writing the Unit Tests 204
The Solution **207**
The RFI Repository Implementation 213
The RFI Service Implementation 223
The RFI ViewModel Classes 224
The RFI View 231
Summary **232**

Chapter 7: Proposal Requests **233**

The Problem **233**
The Design **234**
Designing the Domain Model 234
Designing the Proposal Request Aggregate 235
Defining the Aggregate Boundaries 236
Designing the Repository 237
Writing the Unit Tests 239
The Solution **242**
The Proposal Request Class Private Fields and Constructors 242
The ProposalRequest Properties 245
The Validate Method 248
The Proposal Request Repository Implementation 253
The Proposal Request Service Implementation 257
The Proposal Request View Model Class 258
The Proposal Request View 260
Summary **263**

Chapter 8: Change Orders **265**

The Problem **265**
The Design **266**
Designing the Domain Model 266
Designing the Change Order Aggregate 267
Defining the Aggregate Boundaries 268
Designing the Repository 268
Writing the Unit Tests 271
The Solution **271**
The Change Order Repository Implementation 283
The Change Order Service Implementation 288
The Change Order View Model Class 289
The Change Order View 292
Summary **293**

Chapter 9: Construction Change Directives **295**

The Problem **295**
The Design **295**
Designing the Domain Model 296
Designing the Construction Change Directive Aggregate 297
Defining the Aggregate Boundaries 298
Designing the Repository 299
Writing the Unit Tests 300
The Solution **300**
The Construction Change Directive Class Private Fields and Constructors 300
The Construction Change Directive Repository Implementation 307
The Construction Change Directive Service Implementation 313
The Construction Change Directive ViewModel Class 314
The Construction Change Directive View 324
Summary **325**

Chapter 10: Synchronizing With the Server **327**

The Problem **327**
The Design **327**
Redesigning the Unit of Work 328
Designing the Synchronization 330
Writing the Unit Tests 331

The Solution **333**
Unit of Work Refactoring 333
Synchronizing with the Synchronizer Class 349
Summary **356**

Chapter 11: The Client Membership System **357**

The Problem **357**
The Design **357**
Password Security 358
Designing the Client Membership System 358
The Solution **359**
The Client Membership System Domain Model Classes 360
Client Membership System Unit Tests 388
Summary **389**

Index **391**

Acknowledgments

First of all, I would like to thank my family. To my wife Miriam and my daughter Jasmine—thank you for putting up with me the past year or so while I worked on this book. Everything I do is always with you guys in mind! I love you both! Jasmine, I think you may be writing books someday, too! To my Mom and Dad, who taught me the value of hard work, never giving up, and always believing in myself—thank you and I love you!

I also would like to thank my development editor, Christopher Rivera, who did a brilliant job of shielding me from things that I did not need to be bothered with and always kept me on track and kept on encouraging me the whole way. Thank you Christopher! To my technical reviewer, Doug Holland—Doug you did awesome work and were a pleasure to work with. I hope to work with you on another project some day, thank you! To my acquisitions editor, Katie Mohr—Katie, thank you for never giving up on my idea for this book and pushing it through! Also, thank you for your always kind words of encouragement; it always made me feel like I was appreciated.

I also would like to thank some of my friends at InterKnowlogy. To Kevin Kennedy—Kevin, thank you for taking the time to come up with a decent design for the layout of the WPF forms; you did more in 15 minutes with WPF than I would have done in hours! A big thank you to Dale Bastow and Staci Lopez—thank you so much for being so patient with me, and for always taking your time to educate me about the Architecture industry. To Dan Hanan and John Bowen—Guys, thank you for always taking time out for me whenever I had a WPF question, I really appreciated it. P.S. Don't forget to override GetHashcode and Equals. To Tim Huckaby—Tim, thank you for always encouraging me to write about whatever I was passionate about, and also for always being a good friend to me.

—Tim

Introduction

After reading Eric Evans' book *Domain-Driven Design, Tackling Complexity in the Heart of Software,* my way of designing software systems completely changed. Before that, I used to design software object models in a very data-centric way, and I did not really focus on how to combine behavior and data in objects. I was so inspired with this new way of thinking that I started trying to find any code samples I could get my hands on that demonstrated the concepts from Eric's awesome book. I did the usual Googling for answers to my Domain-Driven Design (DDD) questions, and I usually did find something that would help me, but I still thirsted for more knowledge on the subject.

I had to search for DDD answers in .NET because Eric's book is technology-agnostic. The main point of the book was the architectural concepts. There were code samples here and there in Java and Smalltalk, but that was about it. Then along came Jimmy Nilsson's book *Applying Domain-Driven Design and Patterns,* and it was then that I started to see a lot more of the patterns that could be used in conjunction with the DDD concepts. Jimmy tied together some of the concepts from Martin Fowler's excellent book *Patterns of Enterprise Application Architecture* and showed how they could help with good DDD design principles. Jimmy also did a great job providing lots of good .NET code examples in his book, as well as leading the reader down several paths to accomplish things the DDD way. Right after I finished Jimmy's book, I started subscribing to the DDD RSS Group feed on Yahoo! Groups, and this also helped me a great deal. One of the things I discovered while on the DDD group was that people kept asking for a .NET reference application that would showcase the DDD principles. After reading these posts for a while, I decided that I should write this book and give the developer community my take on how to build .NET applications using DDD techniques. I guess I probably felt a little bit guilty because I read so many other people's posts on the group, and I never posted very often. So now, instead of posting, I have written a book! Maybe this will be my catalyst to get more involved with the group.

My main goal in writing this book was to take the ideas and patterns from Eric's, Martin's, and Jimmy's books and use the ideas and concepts from them to build an actual end-to-end .NET application. I really wanted to show some of my ideas of how to build a domain model in .NET using DDD principles, but, I did not want to build just any old .NET application; I also wanted to try out some of the latest technologies from Microsoft in building the application, such as Visual Studio 2008 and the .NET 3.5 Framework.

Who This Book Is For

This book is targeted at experienced .NET developers who are looking to hone their object-oriented design skills and learn about DDD. If you are not at that level, that is okay, but I recommend that you at least have some experience writing .NET code or even Java code. If you have not written any .NET code before, this book may be a little bit hard to follow.

I also recommend that you read the books that I mentioned earlier from Eric Evans, Jimmy Nilsson, and Martin Fowler. You do not have to do this, but I highly recommend it, as it will help you understand better many of the designs and patterns in this book.

Since each chapter in this book builds upon the previous chapter, I recommend that you read the book in chapter order.

What This Book Covers

Chapter 1, "Introducing the Project: The SmartCA Application" —This chapter introduces you to the application that I am building, the SmartCA application. I outline the problems of the legacy application and the requirements for the new application, as well as what technologies and designs I plan to use to satisfy all of the requirements.

Chapter 2, "Designing the Layered Architecture" — This chapter covers the architectural foundations that will be used in the rest of the book. Several patterns are introduced in the chapter, which include the Layered Supertype pattern, the Separated Interface pattern, and the Model-View-ViewModel pattern. I also identify and explain several important DDD concepts. This also is the first chapter where I start to write the application code, with a focus on the infrastructure layer.

Chapter 3, "Managing Projects" — In this chapter, I start implementing the functionality for managing Projects in the application. I also discuss the concept of Contractors and how they relate to Projects as well as introducing the first iteration of code for the Model-View-ViewModel pattern.

Chapter 4, "Companies and Contacts" — In this chapter, I define and model Companies, Contacts, and Project Contacts. I also show how I deal with saving Entities that are not their own Aggregate Root. This was demonstrated by the techniques I used to save Project Contacts within the Project Aggregate. Last, I show a technique I came up with for displaying and editing Value objects in the UI.

Chapter 5, "Submittal Transmittals" — In this chapter, I introduce the concept of a Submittal Transmittal as used in the construction industry, and then I use the concept to model the Submittal Aggregate. I add a new concept to both the domain layer and the infrastructure layer, illustrating how to deal with saving child collections from the Entity Root repository. I also cover building User Controls that use the Xceed Data Grid Control.

Chapter 6, "Requests for Information" — In this chapter, I introduce the construction industry concept of a Request for Information (RFI). I also introduce a new pattern to the domain called the Specification pattern. I also do some major refactoring in this chapter on the Repositories and View Models for dealing with Transmittals.

Chapter 7, "Proposal Requests" — In this chapter, I introduce the concept of a Proposal Request in the construction industry. In this chapter, I start adding more behavior to the domain model and demonstrating richer Domain Model classes. I also cover handling broken business rules inside of my Domain Model classes, and tie in the Specification functionality.

Chapter 8, "Change Orders" — In this chapter, I introduce the concept of a Change Order in the construction industry. I continue to add more behavior to my Domain Model classes in this chapter, and continue to develop richer Domain Model classes. Two important interfaces are introduced in this chapter, the `IEntity` interface and the `IAggregateRoot` interface. This causes quite a bit of good refactoring throughout the domain model. Last, I create some more advanced `Specification` classes.

Chapter 9, "Construction Change Directives" — In this chapter, I introduce the concept of a Construction Change Directive in the construction industry. I do a lot of refactoring in this chapter, mostly focused on the various `ViewModel` classes. In this chapter, I demonstrate the power of combining interfaces with Generics.

Chapter 10, "Synchronizing with the Server" — In this chapter, I design and implement how to synchronize the client's offline data with the server. I show how to store transaction messages on the client, and also show how to synchronize those messages on the client with the messages on the server. I also show how to make sure that all of the synchronization logic is implemented in the domain model.

Chapter 11, "The Client Membership System" — In this chapter, I show you how to allow users to be able to perform membership-related tasks in an offline scenario by creating what I call my Client Membership System. This involves a very rich domain model for representing the Users and their membership data, as well as a new concept of using a Provider instead of a Repository for interacting with the data store. I also show how to take advantage of the Synchronization code from Chapter 10.

How This Book Is Structured

This book is essentially a very large case study. Throughout the chapters, a complete application is built from start to finish. The structure for each chapter is the same; it is generally a self-contained module with a problem, design, and solution that adds some new aspect of functionality to the application that is being built, followed by a summary at the end of the chapter.

Most of the time, the Problem sections are fairly short, whereas the Design and Solution sections make up most of the bulk of the chapters. The Solution section will always contain the code that implements what was designed in the Design section.

What You Need to Use This Book

You will need Visual Studio 2008 (which includes the .NET 3.5 Framework in its installation) in order to run all of the code samples in the book. I highly recommend using Visual Studio 2008 Professional Edition so that you can run all of the unit tests I have written as part of the code base.

In addition, you will need to install the following applications and components:

- **SQL Server Compact 3.5 (SQL CE)** — This is freely downloadable from the Microsoft SQL Server web site (`www.microsoft.com/sql/editions/compact/downloads.mspx`).
- **Version 1.3 of the Xceed DataGrid Control for WPF** — This also freely downloadable from the Xceed web site (`http://xceed.com/Grid_WPF_New.html`).
- **One of the available versions of SQL Server 2008** — This is necessary if you want to be able to use the SQL Server Management Studio to make changes to the SQL CE database. The Express Edition is freely downloadable from `www.microsoft.com/sql/2008/prodinfo/download.mspx`.

Source Code

As you work through the examples in this book, you may choose either to type in all the code manually or to use the source code files that accompany the book. All of the source code used in this book is available for downloading at `www.wrox.com`. Once at the site, simply locate the book's title (either by using the Search box or by using one of the title lists) and click the Download Code link on the book's detail page to obtain all the source code for the book.

Because many books have similar titles, you may find it easiest to search by ISBN; this book's ISBN is 978-0-470-14756-6.

Once you download the code, just decompress it with your favorite compression tool. Alternately, you can go to the main Wrox code download page at `www.wrox.com/dynamic/books/download.aspx` to see the code available for this book and all other Wrox books.

Also, if you are interested in seeing how the code continues to iterate and grow after you finish the book, please visit my CodePlex site for this book's code at `www.codeplex.com/dddpds`. Here you will find new code that was written after the book was published.

Errata

We make every effort to ensure that there are no errors in the text or in the code. Nevertheless, no one is perfect, and mistakes do occur. If you find an error in one of our books, such as a spelling mistake or faulty piece of code, we would be very grateful for your feedback. By sending in errata you may save another reader hours of frustration, and at the same time you will be helping us provide even higher-quality information.

To find the errata page for this book, go to `www.wrox.com` and locate the title using the Search box or one of the title lists. Then, on the book details page, click the Book Errata link. On this page you can view all errata that has been submitted for this book and posted by Wrox editors. A complete book list including links to each book's errata is also available at `www.wrox.com/misc-pages/booklist.shtml`.

If you don't spot "your" error on the Book Errata page, go to `www.wrox.com/contact/techsupport.shtml` and complete the form there to send us the error you have found. We'll check the information and, if appropriate, post a message to the book's errata page and fix the problem in subsequent editions of the book.

p2p.wrox.com

For author and peer discussion, join the P2P forums at `p2p.wrox.com`. The forums are a web-based system for you to post messages relating to Wrox books and related technologies and interact with other readers and technology users. The forums offer a subscription feature to email you topics of interest of your choosing when new posts are made to the forums. Wrox authors, editors, other industry experts, and your fellow readers are present on these forums.

At `http://p2p.wrox.com` you will find a number of different forums that will help you not only as you read this book but also as you develop your own applications. To join the forums, just follow these steps:

1. Go to `p2p.wrox.com` and click the Register link.
2. Read the terms of use and click Agree.
3. Complete the required information to join, as well as any optional information you wish to provide, and click Submit.
4. You will receive an email with information describing how to verify your account and complete the joining process.

You can read messages in the forums without joining P2P, but in order to post your own messages, you must join.

Once you join, you can post new messages and respond to messages that other users post. You can read messages at any time on the web. If you would like to have new messages from a particular forum emailed to you, click the Subscribe to this Forum icon by the forum name in the forum listing.

For more information about how to use the Wrox P2P, be sure to read the P2P FAQs for answers to questions about how the forum software works as well as many common questions specific to P2P and Wrox books. To read the FAQs, click the FAQ link on any P2P page.

1

Introducing the Project: The SmartCA Application

The project for this book is based on a real application for a real company. The names of the company and the application have been changed for privacy reasons. The fictional company name will be Smart Design, and the name of their new application will be called SmartCA. Smart Design is a growing architectural, engineering, and interior design firm. One of its many service offerings is construction administration, which in its case consists mostly of document management, cost control, and project portfolio management.

The Problem

To manage its construction administration (CA) data and processes, Smart Design has been getting by for 10 years on a home-grown Microsoft Access database application, called the Construction Administration Database, which lives on its corporate network. The company has grown accustomed to this application, both the good parts and the bad. When the application was originally written, there were only a few users, the requirements were very simple, they already had licenses for Microsoft Office, and they had a very small budget. All of this made using Microsoft Access a good technology choice. Figure 1.1 shows the main screen of the application.

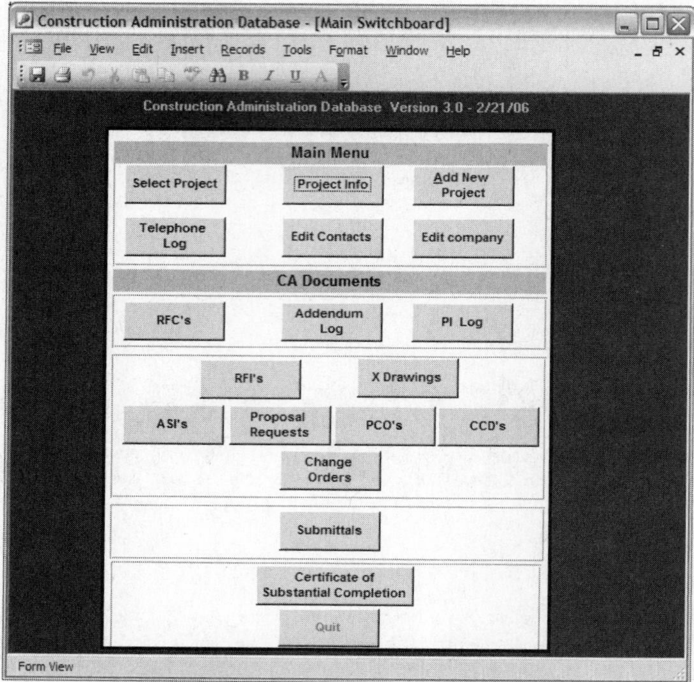

Figure 1.1: Legacy Construction Administration application main screen.

As the years went by, the application became more and more important. It was modified many times, both with code and tweaks to the design of the user interface (UI). This led to UI forms with lots of logic embedded in them as well as some embedded logic in the database queries. The application is now, essentially, a poster child for the Smart Client anti-pattern.

The Smart Client anti-pattern is defined by Eric Evans as "Put all the business logic into the user interface. Chop the application into small functions and implement them as separate user interfaces, embedding the business rules into them. Use a relational database as a shared repository of the data. Use the most automated UI building and visual programming tools available" (Evans, *Domain-Driven Design: Tackling Complexity in the Heart of Software* [Addison-Wesley, 2004], 77).

Figure 1.2 shows the architecture of the current application.

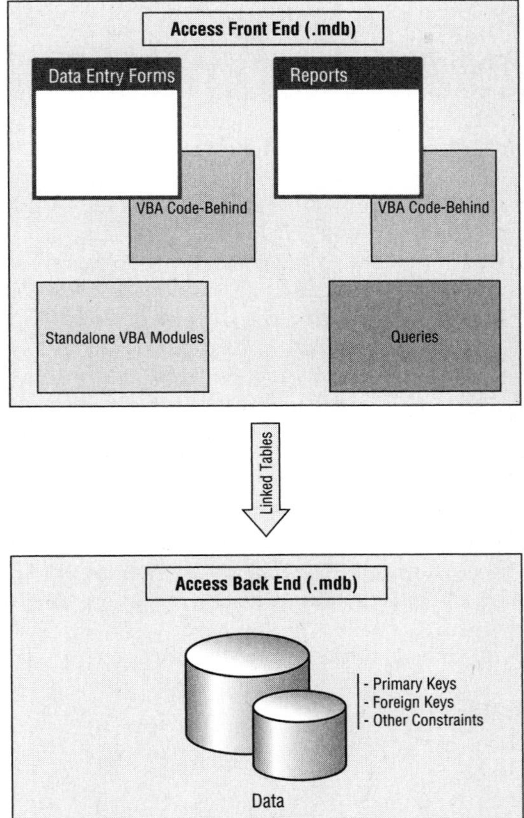

Figure 1.2: Legacy Construction Administration application architecture.

Recently, Smart Design merged with another architectural design company, and as a result the CA application became even more important. It is now being used more often than before by many more users from several remote offices. The increased use has caused scalability and performance problems with the application.

The problem with the Access application is that it has so much logic embedded into its forms, queries, and reports. This makes it very hard to maintain as well as very difficult to add new features to the application.

The Design

As far as a Microsoft Access application goes, the architecture is really not that bad. As shown in Figure 1.2, it is a two-tier application, with all of the UI, business logic, and queries in the first tier (which is a separate `.mdb` file), and all of the database tables in the second tier (also a separate `.mdb` file). Although the current solution for construction administration might have been a good fit 10 years ago, Smart Design has outgrown the application and needs a new solution that will support its new needs. Ten years ago, their needs were fairly simple—they just needed an organized way to capture information and be able to print reports on that information to send out to various people on various projects.

Originally, the main requirement was for a very simple information tracking and reporting tool. The first version of the application was made without any IT involvement, just a stakeholder and one Access programmer. Many changes were made to the program over the years, both by the stakeholder, and by the Access programmer. Several of the changes resulted in denormalized data structures, repetitious code, and various other code smells. Often, changes were made to the application that the Access programmer was not even aware of, and changing things to make them right would have taken a lot of time and effort, so the application just kept on moving along. As the data being tracked started to get larger, an archiving solution was put in place, which resulted in more Microsoft Access data files being created. In the end, almost every attempt to enhance the application has resulted in some type of "one-off" solution that has become very difficult to maintain over the years.

Now that the CA application has been deemed critical to Smart Design's business by their chief operating officer, it has become very apparent that it has greatly outgrown its original design. Smart Design has decided that they do not want to buy an off-the-shelf product; instead they want to rewrite the current application onto a different platform that will meet their growing needs.

Here are their most prevalent needs, in order of importance:

- Reliability and Availability
- Scalability
- Maintainability
- Rich client application functionality
- Offline capable
- Web access
- Intelligent installation and auto-update functionality
- Additional client device support

Reliability and Availability

One of the problems with the current application is that the database sometimes becomes corrupt and must be compacted or repaired regularly, which causes the application to be down for periods of time. The new system's database should be able to be backed up while the system is still in use, and should not be prone to data corruption issues.

Scalability

The system should be able to handle demands from a growing number of users and processes.

Maintainability

Because the code for the application is not correctly partitioned, updating the current application sometimes requires updating the same code and logic in several different places. The new application must be designed it such a way that the domain logic is centralized and is never duplicated.

Rich Client Application Functionality

Users are used to the current Microsoft Access application's rich controls and responsiveness, and they would like to continue to improve upon this type of user experience.

Offline Capable

The new application must be able to work even when the user is not connected to the network. For those users running the application with occasional or intermittent connectivity — such as those used by on-site construction managers, where connectivity cannot be guaranteed at all times — being able to work while disconnected is very important.

Web Access

The firm would like some parts of the application exposed to the web, such as reporting. Also, in the future, some parts of the application may need to be exposed to outside contractors. Another nice-to-have would be the ability to extend the application to support some type of an executive dashboard for showing key performance indicators (KPIs) or similar information to management.

Intelligent Installation and Auto-Update Functionality

Currently, the Smart Design IT department is challenged with making sure that users of the application have the right version on their desktops. IT has also had a tough time getting the application pushed out when new changes have been made to the application. IT would definitely prefer a deployment method similar to that of web applications, and would like SmartCA to be easily installed by clicking on a URL from their intranet. The application must be able to be updated while it is still running, and the updates should guarantee the integrity of the application and its related files.

Additional Client Device Support

The new application should be designed in such a way as to be able to reuse a good part of its core logic modules for different UI devices, such as personal digital assistants (PDAs), smart phones, and the like.

The current application and platform will not easily support these requirements. Therefore, Smart Design has decided to start from scratch and completely reengineer the new application to be able to meet the new requirements. The old Access application has served the company well for more than 10 years. Actually, it can still serve the company well by being the basis for the new design. There are lots of business rules captured in the old application that are not documented anywhere else, so the old application will be used as a guide in fleshing out some of the requirements for the new system.

The Solution

The new application, SmartCA, will be written using Microsoft Visual Studio 2008 (which includes the Microsoft .NET Framework 3.5) technologies for both the client-side and server-side partitions.

Fulfilling the Reliability, Availability, Scalability, Offline Capable, and Additional Client Device Support Requirements

Most of the current problems in the areas of reliability, availability, and scalability lie in the fact that the legacy application was implemented in Microsoft Access and used Access for its data store. The new solution going forward will be using both a database on the server as well as a database on the client.

On the Server

In order to support the Reliability and Availability requirements, the database server will be a SQL Server instance. All of the data from the legacy application will need to be migrated to the new SQL Server database. A SQL migration script or .NET program will be written that will facilitate this data transfer. This will allow the old application to continue working while the new application is still being built, since the script or migration tool will make it easier to refresh data on a regular basis from the production Access database into the development, testing, and staging database environments. Moving to a server-based relational database (SQL Server) will also lend itself well to the Scalability requirement, although the application design has just as much to do with that as the idea of using a database server instead an Access `.mdb` file for a data store.

On the Client

Yes, that's right, you see it correctly, a database on the client. You are probably saying to yourself, "That is worse than the original Access application's two-tier architecture, where at least the database lived on a network share!" Not so fast, my friend. One of the requirements of the application is to be able to support users who are not always connected to the network, such as those construction managers who may be inside of a construction trailer with no available connectivity, a.k.a. the Offline Capable requirement. The database used on the client will be a SQL Server Compact Edition 3.5 (SQL CE) database. Although SQL CE was originally only targeted for mobile platforms, such as PDAs and Tablet PCs, it now runs on all client platforms. According to Microsoft, SQL CE is a "low maintenance, compact embedded database for single-user client applications for all Windows platforms including tablet PCs, pocket PCs, smart phones and desktops. Just as with SQL Server Mobile, SQL Server Compact is a free, easy-to-use, lightweight, and embeddable version of SQL Server 2005 for developing desktop and mobile applications."

Another benefit of having a database on the client is the fact that it can help take some of the load off the database server, thus helping with the Scalability requirement.

At this point, you may be asking yourself, "Why not use SQL Server Express? At least with SQL Server Express I can use stored procedures!" While it is true that SQL Server Express supports stored procedures, while SQL CE does not, the real reason for using SQL CE is that I want to support multiple devices, not just Windows machines. With SQL CE I can reuse the same database on both a PC and a mobile device, and this functionality maps directly to the Additional Client Device Support requirement. I can live without stored procedures on the client.

Instead of using traditional replication to keep the schema and data between the database on the client and the database server in sync, the application will use Microsoft Synchronization Services for ADO .NET. The Synchronization Services application programming interface (API) provides a set of components to synchronize data between data services and a local store. Equally important is the need to synchronize the local copy of the data with a central server when a network connection is available. The Synchronization Services API, which is modeled after ADO.NET data access APIs, is a much more intelligent, service-based way of synchronizing the data. It makes building applications for occasionally connected environments a logical extension of building applications for which you can count on a consistent network connection. Think about how Microsoft Outlook works, and you will get the picture of the online/offline functionality that the Synchronization Services API will enable.

It should be noted that I will not be talking much about databases in this book, since the focus of this book is on Domain-Driven Design. One of the main tenants of Domain-Driven Design is persistence ignorance, and therefore, while the application is being designed, as far as you and I are concerned, the data could be coming from a text file. Therefore, from this point on, I will only talk about the 10,000 foot view when it comes to the database.

Fulfilling the Maintainability Requirement

In order to avoid embedding business logic in the behavior of the UI elements, such as the various forms, controls, and reports, or even embedded inside of database queries, a layered architecture (ibid., 69) will be used. Because the legacy application was implemented with such a Smart UI anti-pattern, the domain-related code became very difficult to decipher and track down. Unit testing was impossible, and sometimes trying to change one business rule meant tracing of UI code, Visual Basic for Applications (VBA) module code, and embedded SQL code. The layered architecture's main principle is that any element of a layer depends only on other elements in the same layer, or on elements of the layers beneath it. Using a layered architecture will make the code for this application much more maintainable, which maps directly to the Maintainability requirement. The layers that will be used in the SmartCA application will be:

- **UI (presentation layer)** — Probably the easiest to understand, this layer is responsible for showing information to the user and interpreting the user's commands. Sometimes, instead of a human, the user could be another system.
- **Application layer** — This layer is meant to be very thin and is used for coordinating the actions of the domain model objects. It is not supposed to contain business rules or domain knowledge, or even maintain state — that is what the domain model is for. The application layer is very useful for coordinating tasks and delegating actions to the domain model. Although it is not to be used to maintain state of a business entity, it can maintain the state that tracks the current task being performed by the user or system. It is very important that the application layer does not interfere or get in the way of the domain model representing the important parts of the business model (`http://weblogs.asp.net`)

- **Domain layer** — This is where the business logic and rules of an application live, and it is the heart of the software. The domain layer controls and uses the state of a particular business concept or situation, but how it is stored is actually delegated to the infrastructure layer. It is absolutely critical in Domain-Driven Design that the domain layer contains the business model, and that the domain logic is not scattered across any other layers.
- **Infrastructure layer** — This is where general technical, plumbing-related code happens, such as persisting objects to a database, sending messages, logging, and other general cross-cutting concerns. It can also serve as a place for an architectural framework for the pattern of interactions between the four layers. In the next chapter, you will see an example of a framework for the SmartCA domain model that is contained in the infrastructure layer.

Generically, Figure 1.3 shows what the SmartCA layered application architecture looks like.

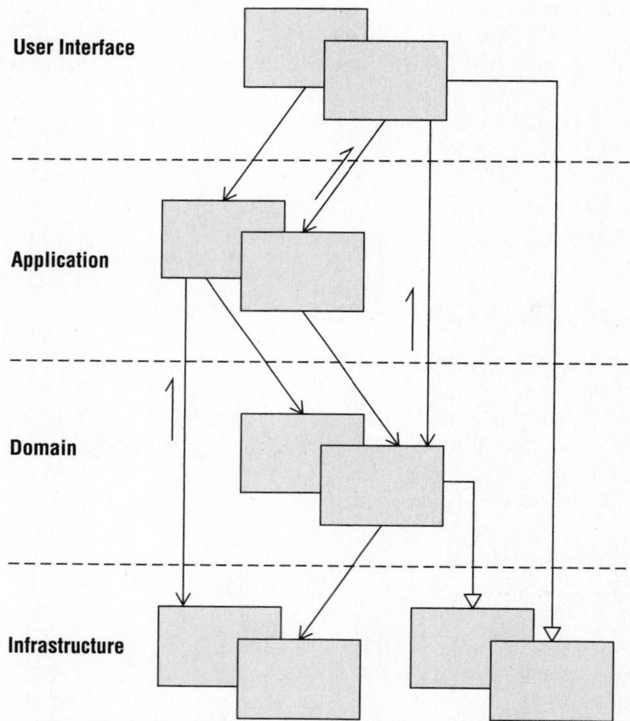

Figure 1.3: The layered architecture (adapted from Evans, 68).

Figure 1.4 shows what the application architecture looks like with all of the technologies and patterns layered on top of the layered architecture model.

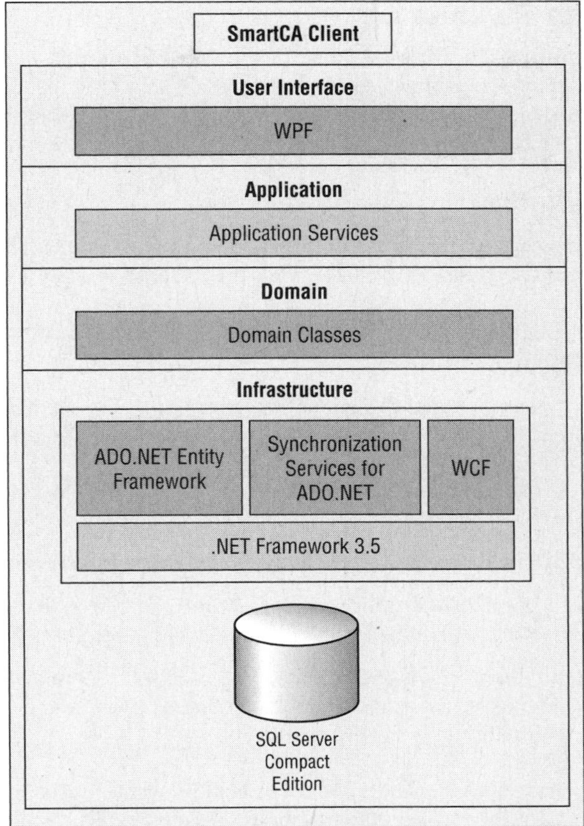

Figure 1.4: The SmartCA application architecture.

Fulfilling the Rich Client Application Functionality Requirement

Since the users of the current application have become used to a Windows application, the new application will also be Windows-based, but it will be much more than just a traditional Windows application. The SmartCA application will be a smart client application implemented using the Windows Presentation Foundation (WPF). You might be asking yourself, OK, what exactly do you mean by smart client?

A smart client is a type of application that combines the best of both Windows applications and web applications.

Windows Application Benefits

The advantages of Windows applications are that they are able to provide a rich user experience, they are not too complex to develop, and they can use local resources. Using local resources allows Windows applications to be responsive, interact with connected devices, and do other things that web applications cannot do (at least not very easily).

Web Application Benefits

The positive aspects of a web application are that it is easy to deploy and manage, since you deploy it to a server not to the client computer, and it has a very broad reach — even PDAs and cell phones can access a web application!

Smart Client Definition

The term "smart client" means different things to different people. For the purposes of this book, I will classify a smart client application (note this is adapted from the MSDN Smart Client FAQ) as follows:

- It uses local resources and provides a rich user experience. This satisfies the rich client application functionality requirement.
- It is a connected application that can exchange data on the Internet or on an enterprise network.
- Even though it is a connected application, it is offline capable so that it can be used even if it is not currently connected. This satisfies the Offline Capable requirement.
- It has an intelligent deployment and update story, maintaining relatively the same ease of deployment and management as web applications, thus satisfying the Intelligent Installation and Auto-Update Functionality requirement.

Intelligent deployment means that the smart client application is deployed to an application server, and from there it is deployed onto the local client system. Intelligent update means that the application on the client system is able to receive updates that are deployed to the server.

Windows Presentation Foundation (WPF)

WPF is intended to be the next-generation graphics API for Windows applications on the desktop. Applications written in WPF are visually of a higher quality than Windows Forms applications. Some of the relevant highlights of WPF for the SmartCA application are:

- **Resolution independence** — Because of WPF's use of vector graphics, unlike most Windows-based applications of today, graphics and text that are viewed in a higher resolution do not get smaller; they actually get better! This means that a user can literally shrink or enlarge elements on the screen independently of the screen's resolution.
- **Declarative programming** — Windows Forms do not have built-in support for declarative UI definitions. The .NET Framework as a whole has allowed developers to use declarative custom attributes classes, methods, and assemblies, as well as XML-based resource and configuration files. WPF takes this declarative-based model to a new level with Extensible Application Markup Language (XAML). Using XAML in WPF is very similar to using HTML to define a UI for a web page, yet it is much better than that analogy. Not only does XAML give a great range of expressiveness for the look and feel of a UI, but it also allows for parts of the behavior of the UI to be declarative.

- **Rich composition and customization** — It is very easy to customize controls in WPF with little or no code. Almost any type of control can be composed with another control. There literally are no boundaries here; for example, you could bind a media clip to a text box if you wanted to, or make it spin around, and so on. It is also very easy to "skin" applications with very different looks, without requiring any code. These advantages help satisfy the Rich Client Application Functionality requirement.
- **Easy deployment** — Using the .NET Framework's ClickOnce technology will provide a way to install and run SmartCA on the client machines simply by clicking on a URL. ClickOnce ensures that installation will not affect other applications because all files required for the application are placed in an isolated area and it also prevents any custom registration.

Fulfilling the Web Access Requirement

Although I have not talked much about the server-side partition of this application, the mere fact that there will be a server-side implementation means that it is possible for the application's data and behavior to be exposed to the web via a web application or even via web services. In fact, I will show later in the book how each SmartCA client application instance will be using web services to synchronize its transactions with the server.

Fulfilling the Intelligent Installation and Auto-Update Functionality Requirement

The SmartCA application will take advantage of the Visual Studio 2008's ClickOnce deployment tools and .NET Framework technology to satisfy the Intelligent Installation requirement. Since the .NET Framework also has built-in support for automatic updates and for rolling back to previous versions, the Auto-Update requirement will also be satisfied.

Since SQL CE is so lightweight (it only eats up about 1.5 MB worth of hard disk space), it will be very easy to deploy, which will also help support the Intelligent Installation requirement.

Summary

In this chapter, I introduced you to the fictitious company Smart Design, and more importantly, the new application that I am building for them, the SmartCA application. I also outlined the problems of the legacy application, the requirements for the new application, as well as what technologies and designs I plan to use to satisfy all of the requirements. In the next chapter, I will delve into the details of the layered architecture model and implementation for the SmartCA application.

2

Designing the Layered Architecture

Since I have decided that the application architecture will use a layered approach, it is time to create the Visual Studio solution to host these layers.

The Problem

In order to implement the layered approach correctly, there are some steps that I will need to follow:

1. The Visual Studio solution must be organized make it very obvious where the layers have been implemented in the code modules.
2. Each individual layer needs to be designed as well, and needs to include the design patterns and technologies for each layer.
3. I need to decide what functionality belongs in each of the layers.
4. An application framework needs to be built that will simplify coding the application.

The Design

In this chapter, there are two main items that need to be designed, and those items are the Visual Studio solution and the actual architectural layers of the SmartCA application.

Designing the Visual Studio Solution

As stated earlier, the first step in implementing the layered architecture is to create a Visual Studio solution that will support the approach.

The initial skeleton for the solution will hold four projects, one for each layer of the application. Figure 2.1 below shows this initial design.

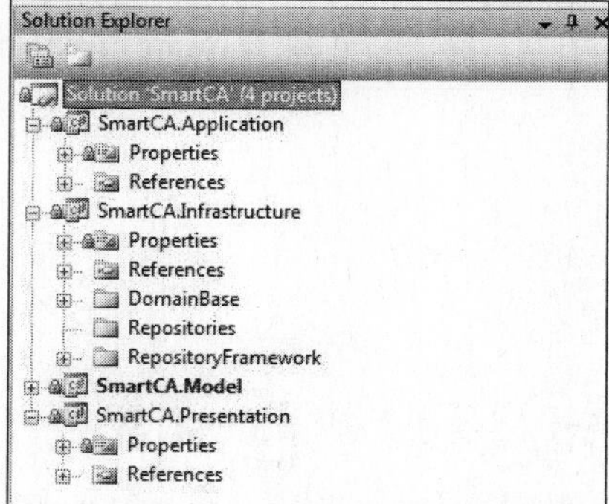

Figure 2.1: Initial code skeleton design.

The first three projects in the solution are basic C# Class Library projects, and the last project, SmartCA. Presentation, is actually a WPF project.

As can be seen from the names of the projects in the solution, the namespace pattern that will be used is always `SmartCA.`*`<Layer Name>`*. There will be cases where an extra project may be required even though it still belongs in one of the four layers. Usually, this happens in the infrastructure layer, where you may be implementing some functionality that needs to be separated from the rest of the Infrastructure project. In that particular case, the naming standard that I will follow is `SmartCA.`*`<Layer Name>`*`.`*`<Some other functionality name>`*. An example is a project with a name and namespace combination of `SmartCA.Infrastructure.Caching`. These types of projects can be added later if and when they are needed.

Designing the Architectural Layers

Now that the namespace naming pattern has been established for the layers, it is time to start the layers. Just to refresh your memory from Chapter 1, the layers I will be building are the application, domain, infrastructure, and presentation (a.k.a. UI) layers.

Designing the Application Layer

I would like to approach the application layer as an application programming interface (API), or almost a façade, to the domain model. The reason I say *almost* a façade is because the application will be doing a little bit more than just making it simple to use the domain model; it will also be coordinating actions between different domain objects as well as maintaining the state of a particular task. The classes in this layer will be composed of mostly static methods, thus making it easy for a class in the presentation layer to do some work. An example is having a `ProjectService` class in the application layer that has very simple methods to load and save a Project, such as `Project.GetProject(1)` and `Project.Save(project)`. This could also be the layer that web service methods would call to get or save their data. Another example is using the application layer to coordinate actions between domain objects and infrastructure objects, such as saving a project and then sending an email to all of the interested parties in management.

Designing the Domain Layer

The domain layer will be designed using the POCO approach (POCO stands for Plain-Old CLR Objects). It is my intent to make the domain model as free from any distractions as possible, including having to implement several persistence-related interfaces or inherit from classes that have nothing to do with the business model. The idea is for the classes in the domain layer to be as persistent-ignorant as possible.

Important Domain-Driven Design Concepts

Before getting too deep into the design of the SmartCA application, there are some common Domain-Driven Design terms and concepts that must be discussed. Although I am not going to go into great detail about them here, they still need to be talked about before moving forward. In order to get a deeper understanding of these concepts I highly recommend reading *Domain-Driven Design: Tackling Complexity in the Heart of Software* (Addison-Wesley, 2004) by Eric Evans; *Applying Domain-Driven Design and Patterns, With Examples in C# and .NET* (Addison-Wesley, 2006) by Jimmy Nilsson; and *Patterns of Enterprise Application Architecture* (Addison-Wesley, 2003) by Martin Fowler. The main point of this book is to adhere to these concepts as much as possible while building the SmartCA application.

Entities

One of the most important fundamental concepts to understand is the definition of Entity in Domain-Driven Design. According to Evans "An object primarily defined by its identity is called an Entity." Entities are very important in the domain model, and need to be designed carefully. Sometimes what people think of as an entity in one system is not an entity in another system; for example, an address. In some systems, an address may not have an identity at all; it may only represent attributes of a person or company. In other systems, such as a cable television company or a utility company, the address could be very important. In those systems, the address is important as an identity because the billing may be tied directly to the address. In that case, the address would definitely be classified as an entity. In other systems, such as an e-commerce web site, the address may only be used for determining where to send an order, and the identity of the address may not really matter much, just the attributes of the address so that the order can be fulfilled. In those types of cases, the address becomes what is called in Domain-Driven Design a Value object.

Value Objects

Unlike Entity objects, Value objects have no identity. There is no need to track the object's identity, and it is very easy to create and discard. Most of the time, Value objects usually contain either just data or just behavior. The ones that contain only data are also known as Data Transfer Objects (DTOs) (Fowler, *Patterns of Enterprise Application Architecture*, 401). A very common scenario is for an Entity to contain other Value objects. There are also times where Value objects can contain other Value objects, even other Entity objects. Most of the time, as in the case of the address example used earlier, they are a group of attributes that make up a conceptual whole but without an identity.

It is recommended that Value objects be immutable, that is, they are created with a constructor, with all properties being read-only. To get a different value for the object, a new one must be created. A perfect example of this is the `System.String` class. Value objects do not always have to be immutable, but the main rule to follow is that if the object is going to be shared, then it needs to be immutable.

In distinguishing between Entity objects and Value objects, if the object does not have an identity that I care about, then I classify it as a Value object.

Services

Sometimes, when designing a domain model, you will have certain types of behavior that do not fit into any one class. Trying to tack on the behavior to a class to which it really does not belong will only cloud the domain model, but .NET, and all other object-oriented languages, requires the behavior to live in some type of object, so it cannot be a separate function on its own (as you might find in JavaScript or other scripting languages). The type of class that becomes the home for this behavior is known in Domain-Driven Design as a Service.

A `Service` class has no internal state and can simply act as an interface implementation that provides operations. This concept is very similar to web services. Services typically coordinate the work of one or more domain objects, and present the coordination as a well-known operation. It is also important to note that some services may live in the application layer, some may live in the domain layer, and others may live in the infrastructure layer.

Application Layer Services

The services that live in the application layer typically coordinate the work of other services in other layers. Consider an order fulfillment service. This service probably takes in an order message in the format of XML data, calls a factory to transform the XML into an object, and then sends the object to the domain layer for processing. After processing has been completed, the service may need to send out a notification to a user, and it may delegate that to an infrastructure layer service.

Domain Layer Services

In keeping with the order fulfillment example, the domain layer service would be responsible for interacting with the right Entity objects, Value objects, and other domain layer objects necessary to process the order in the domain. Ultimately, the service would return some type of result from the operation so that the calling service could take the necessary actions.

Infrastructure Layer Services

In the same order fulfillment scenario, the infrastructure layer service may need to do things like sending the user an order confirmation email letting them know that their order is being processed. These types of activities belong in the infrastructure layer.

Aggregates

In Domain-Driven Design speak, an Aggregate is a term used to define object ownership and the boundaries between objects and their relationships. It is used to define a group of associated objects that are to be treated as one unit in regard to data changes. For example, an `Order` class and its associated line items can be considered to be part of the same Order Aggregate, with the `Order` class being the root of the Aggregate. That brings me to a very important rule, and that is each Aggregate can only have one root object, and that object is an Entity object. The root of an Aggregate can hold references to the roots of other Aggregates, and objects inside of an Aggregate can hold references to one another, but nothing outside of the Aggregate boundary can access the objects inside of the Aggregate without going through that Aggregate's root object.

It is easier to understand this concept with an example. The example I always use is the canonical Order Aggregate. An Order object is the root of its own Aggregate, and it contains objects such as Line Items (which can contain Products) and Customers. To get to a Line Item object, I would have to go through the Order Aggregate root object, the Order object. If I only wanted get some data about a Customer, and not the Order, I might choose to start from the Customer Aggregate. I could move from the Order Aggregate to the Customer Aggregate, since the Order Aggregate contains an instance of a Customer object. On the other hand, I could get to a Customer's Order by going through the Customer Aggregate first, and then traversing the relationship between a Customer and his Orders. In this case, the relationship is bidirectional, and I could choose to start from the Customer Aggregate or from the Order Aggregate, depending on the use case. The key to remember is that both the Customer and the Order are the roots of their own Aggregate, and can also hold references to other Aggregate roots. I could not go directly from a Customer to a Line Item; I would first need to go to the Customer's Order, and then travel from there to the Line Item.

Defining the Aggregates in a domain model is one of the hardest activities to get right in Domain-Driven Design, and this is where you really need the help of an expert in the business domain that you are dealing with to determine the right boundaries and associations. It is also an area that I end up refactoring a lot as I begin to understand more about the business model of an application.

Repositories

According to Eric Evans, a repository "represents all objects of a certain type as a conceptual set (usually emulated)" (Evans, *Domain-Driven Design: Tackling Complexity in the Heart of Software*, 151). He also goes on to say that for every object that is an Aggregate, create a repository for the object and give it the look and feel of an in-memory collection of objects of that particular type. The access to the repository must be through a well-known interface. The main point of repositories is to keep the developer focused on the domain model logic, and hide the plumbing of data access behind well-known repository interfaces. This concept is also known as *persistence ignorance*, meaning that the domain model is ignorant of how its data is saved or retrieved from its underlying data store or stores.

Factories

As the Entities and their associated Aggregates start to grow in the domain layer, it becomes increasingly more difficult to build up objects consistently just using constructors. Lots of times there is intimate knowledge needed to construct an Aggregate and all of its relationships, constraints, rules, and the like. Instead of making the Entity objects themselves responsible for this creation, it is better to have a Factory that knows how to build these types of objects, and thus avoid clouding up the code of an Entity object.

In Domain-Driven Design, there are two types of Factories, those for building the root Entity of an Aggregate (usually from some type of resultset data) and those for building Value objects (usually from some type of configuration data).

Using Repositories in the Domain Layer

If I can get away with it, I will try not to let any of my domain model classes know about any of the repositories. This goes a long way towards persistence ignorance, but it is not always an easy thing to accomplish. I would like to restrict repositories so that only their interfaces will live in the domain layer. If I am successful, a domain model class can talk to a repository interface if it really needs to, yet the implementation of the actual repositories will be in the infrastructure layer. This is better known as the Separated Interface pattern (Fowler, *Patterns of Enterprise Application Architecture*, 476–479), where the interface is defined in a separate assembly from its implementation. My goal can also be aided by having a factory provide the implementation of the interface requested, and therefore the domain model classes may need to have an extra dependency on the Repository Factory if they need to create and use the repository implementation classes.

Using the Layered Supertype Pattern

Since Evans defines an Entity as "an object that is distinguished by identity, rather than its attributes" (Evans, *Domain-Driven Design: Tackling Complexity in the Heart of Software*, 92), we know that all of our entity classes are going to need some type of data type to distinguish their identities. This would be a good opportunity to use Fowler's Layered Supertype pattern, which is defined as "a type that acts as the supertype for all types in its layer" (Fowler, *Patterns of Enterprise Application Architecture*, 475). Having all entities inherit from an entity base class type will help eliminate some duplicate properties and behavior in the domain entity classes. The use of this base class is purely for convenience, and I feel that it will not distract our model at all; in fact, it will be easier to distinguish between which classes are entities and which ones are value objects.

Designing the Infrastructure Layer

The infrastructure layer is where all of the SmartCA application's *plumbing* lives. Any type of framework, data access code, calls to web service calls, and so forth will live in this layer. A perfect example of this is the SmartCA application's Repository Framework implementation, which I will dive into in the Solution section of this chapter, that lives inside of the infrastructure layer. Not only can the infrastructure layer hold infrastructure for the domain layer, but it can also hold infrastructure code and logic for any of the other layers, including those that meet its own needs.

Designing the Presentation Layer

The goal in designing the presentation layer is to keep it as thin as possible, very similarly to the application layer. One of the main pitfalls to avoid is embedding any business logic in the presentation layer. The presentation layer has two main responsibilities:

1. Interpret the user's commands and send the user's requests down to the application layer or domain layer.
2. Show information to the user.

In order to help the presentation layer carry out its responsibilities, I will be using a new pattern developed by John Gossman of the Microsoft WPF team, called the Model-View-ViewModel pattern. The implementation of this pattern will be discussed in the Solution section.

The Solution

Now that I have detailed how the Visual Studio solution and all of the architectural layers should be designed, it is time to start implementing these designs. That means I finally get to do my favorite thing, which is writing code!

Implementing the Visual Studio Solution

In keeping with the layered architecture diagram in Figure 1.2, the dependencies of the layers can only go down from higher levels to lower levels, that is, the presentation layer can depend on the application layer, but the application layer cannot have a dependency on the presentation layer. Figure 2.2 illustrates the dependencies by showing the references between the projects.

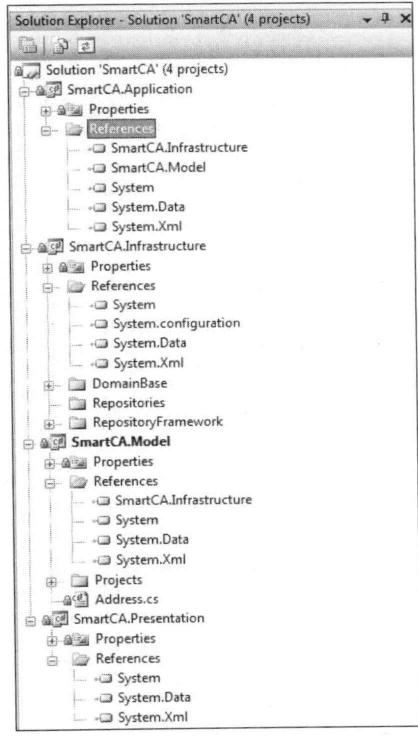

Figure 2.2: Initial code skeleton design with dependencies.

The project that is really the root of dependencies is the `SmartCA.Infrastructure` project, as it is referred to by all of the other assemblies and it does not refer to any of the other assemblies.

Implementing the Architectural Layers

This section may sound a little bit misleading, because if I were to implement all of the architectural layers here, then the application would be finished and the book would be over! What I am going to show you in this section is a lot of Infrastructure code that the other layers of the application will be using. I will first start with the Layered Supertype implementation, followed by the Repository Framework, and lastly I will conclude with the Model-View-ViewModel pattern implementation that will be used in the presentation layer.

Layered Supertype

The layered supertype I will use is an abstract class named `EntityBase`, with the intention that all Entity classes in the domain model will need to inherit from this class to gain their identity. This class will live in the `SmartCA.Infrastructure` project, as it is not really part of the domain logic, but it is providing necessary functionality to the domain model. Here is the code for this class:

```
using System;

namespace SmartCA.Infrastructure.DomainBase
{
    public abstract class EntityBase
    {
        private object key;

        /// <summary>
        /// Default Constructor.
        /// </summary>
        protected EntityBase()
            : this(null)
        {
        }

        /// <summary>
        /// Overloaded constructor.
        /// </summary>
        /// <param name="key">An <see cref="System.Object"/> that
        /// represents the primary identifier value for the
        /// class.</param>
        protected EntityBase(object key)
        {
            this.key = key;
        }

        /// <summary>
        /// An <see cref="System.Object"/> that represents the
        /// primary identifier value for the class.
        /// </summary>
        public object Key
        {
            get
            {
                return this.key;
            }
        }
```

The first part of the class contains a default constructor and an overloaded constructor that allow a key value to be passed in. The key that was passed in is also exposed as a read-only property. Currently, I am leaving the `Key` property's type as a `System.Object`, because I am not really sure yet if the keys to the entities will be Guids, Integers, an so on. Also, some key data types on entity objects may be different from others, and so for right now this gives me the most flexibility.

The next part of the code implements all of the necessary equality tests to determine whether two entity objects are equal to each other. These come in very handy later when comparing entity values in collections, trying to find matches, and so forth.

```
        #region Equality Tests

        /// <summary>
        /// Determines whether the specified entity is equal to the
        /// current instance.
        /// </summary>
        /// <param name="entity">An <see cref="System.Object"/> that
        /// will be compared to the current instance.</param>
        /// <returns>True if the passed in entity is equal to the
        /// current instance.</returns>
        public override bool Equals(object entity)
        {
            if (entity == null || !(entity is EntityBase))
            {
                return false;
            }
            return (this == (EntityBase)entity);
        }

        /// <summary>
        /// Operator overload for determining equality.
        /// </summary>
        /// <param name="base1">The first instance of an
        /// <see cref="EntityBase"/>.</param>
        /// <param name="base2">The second instance of an
        /// <see cref="EntityBase"/>.</param>
        /// <returns>True if equal.</returns>
        public static bool operator ==(EntityBase base1,
            EntityBase base2)
        {
            // check for both null (cast to object or recursive loop)
            if ((object)base1 == null && (object)base2 == null)
            {
                return true;
            }

            // check for either of them == to null
            if ((object)base1 == null || (object)base2 == null)
            {
                return false;
            }

            if (base1.Key != base2.Key)
```

(continued)

(continued)

```
            {
                return false;
            }

            return true;
        }

        /// <summary>
        /// Operator overload for determining inequality.
        /// </summary>
        /// <param name="base1">The first instance of an
        /// <see cref="EntityBase"/>.</param>
        /// <param name="base2">The second instance of an
        /// <see cref="EntityBase"/>.</param>
        /// <returns>True if not equal.</returns>
        public static bool operator !=(EntityBase base1,
            EntityBase base2)
        {
            return (!(base1 == base2));
        }

        /// <summary>
        /// Serves as a hash function for this type.
        /// </summary>
        /// <returns>A hash code for the current Key
        /// property.</returns>
        public override int GetHashCode()
        {
            return this.key.GetHashCode();
        }

        #endregion
    }
}
```

This behavior is necessary for comparing, sorting, and matching entity objects. This is nice because this *plumbing* type of code is encapsulated in the infrastructure layer and keeps the domain layer's entity objects free from these distractions.

Repository Framework

For the SmartCA application, I have decided to implement a hybrid Repository Framework. By hybrid, I mean a cross between a pure Repository Framework, where all repositories have the same interface, and a custom repository implementation for each aggregate root.

The Interfaces

The hybrid framework will contain a generic `IRepository<T>` interface, which will live in the `SmartCA.Infrastructure.RepositoryFramework` namespace in the `SmartCA.Infrastructure` assembly, which has the following signature:

```
using System;
using SmartCA.Infrastructure.DomainBase;

namespace SmartCA.Infrastructure.RepositoryFramework
{
    public interface IRepository<T> where T : EntityBase
    {
        T FindBy(object key);
        void Add(T item);
        T this[object key] { get; set; }
        void Remove(T item);
    }
}
```

Using .NET Generics helps a great deal here, as it allows for the `IRepository<T>` interface to be reused in many places of the application, and because of the `where` clause on `T`, it restricts the data type to being a class that derives from `EntityBase`, the domain model's layered supertype. An interesting note about this interface is that there is actually an indexer (`T this[object key] { get; set; }`). I added this to emphasize the concept that a repository should emulate a collection of objects in memory.

You may have noticed that I did not put a `Find` or `FindBy` method on this interface that takes some type of generic predicate or expression. I did this intentionally. Based on my previous experience, this can get pretty complicated, and so I have decided to put all of the `Find` type of methods in Aggregate-specific types of repositories, an example of which would look like the `IProjectRepository` interface shown below:

```
using System;
using System.Collections.Generic;
using SmartCA.Infrastructure.RepositoryFramework;

namespace SmartCA.Model.Projects
{
    public interface IProjectRepository : IRepository<Project>
    {
        IList<Project> FindBy(object sector, object segment,
            bool completed);
    }
}
```

This way, if you want to program against the general interface (`IRepository<T>`) you can, but you can also program against a more specific interface if you need to add more specialized methods to your repository, such as more granular `Find` methods. It essentially gives you the option to refactor things later without too much pain.

The Repository Factory

Earlier in the Design section of this chapter I talked about the importance of the domain model classes being able to use a particular `Repository` interface without needing a reference to the associated repository implementation in the infrastructure layer. This concept was defined as the Separated Interface pattern, and I mentioned that I would need a Factory to provide the implementation of the `Repository` interface that was requested. That Factory is called the Repository Factory and is exactly what I going to implement in this section.

Configuration Section

In order to eliminate any hard-coding of repository class names in the Repository Factory, I have chosen to use configuration along with the Factory to make it very easy to change what repositories get created at runtime by changing a few configuration settings. Not only does this make use of the previously mentioned Separated Interface pattern, but it also very closely resembles the ASP.NET Provider pattern, in that the provider's Factory creates its objects based upon configuration settings.

Here is what the configuration section for the Repository Factory looks like:

```
<?xml version="1.0" encoding="utf-8" ?>
<configuration>
  <configSections>
    <section name="repositoryMappingsConfiguration"

type="SmartCA.Infrastructure.RepositoryFramework.Configuration.RepositorySettings,
SmartCA.Infrastructure, Version=1.0.0.0, Culture=neutral, PublicKeyToken=null"/>
  </configSections>
  <repositoryMappingsConfiguration>
    <repositoryMappings>
      <repositoryMapping interfaceShortTypeName="IProjectRepository"

repositoryFullTypeName="SmartCA.Infrastructure.Repositories.ProjectRepository,
SmartCA.Infrastructure.Repositories, Version=1.0.0.0, Culture=neutral,
PublicKeyToken=null" />
    </repositoryMappings>
  </repositoryMappingsConfiguration>
</configuration>
```

The configuration section is really just storing the mappings of interface types to their implementations, as can be seen in the `repositoryMapping` element in the configuration file. What this means is that a repository implementation could be changed in the application's configuration file without having to recompile the application.

Configuration Section Handling

In order to support this functionality, I have added a `Configuration` folder under the `RepositoryFramework` folder of the `SmartCA.Infrastructure` project (see Figure 2.3).

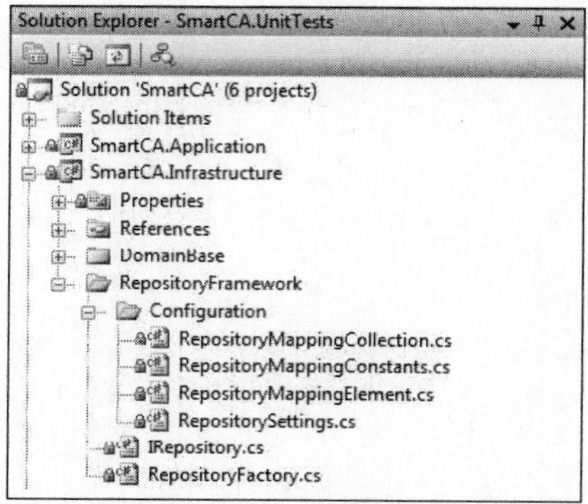

Figure 2.3: RepositoryFramework Configuration folder.

The job of the classes in the Configuration folder is to read and copy the settings from the `repositoryMappingsConfiguration` configuration section into a nice object model that the `RepositoryFactory` can consume in order to do its job. The root class for this configuration-section-handling functionality is the `RepositorySettings` class, which inherits from the .NET Framework `ConfigurationSection` class.

```
using System;
using System.Configuration;

namespace SmartCA.Infrastructure.RepositoryFramework.Configuration
{
    public class RepositorySettings : ConfigurationSection
    {

[ConfigurationProperty(RepositoryMappingConstants.ConfigurationPropertyName,
            IsDefaultCollection = true)]
        public RepositoryMappingCollection RepositoryMappings
        {
            get { return
(RepositoryMappingCollection)base[RepositoryMappingConstants.ConfigurationProperty
Name]; }
        }
    }
}
```

The class is very simple, since the .NET Framework's `ConfigurationSection` class does most of the work. Its main purpose is to return the collection of repositories defined in configuration into a `RepositoryMappingCollection` data type. I have defined the name of the configuration element that represents the collection of repositories in a separate class named `RepositoryMappingConstants`.

```
using System;

namespace SmartCA.Infrastructure.RepositoryFramework.Configuration
{
    internal static class RepositoryMappingConstants
    {
        public const string ConfigurationPropertyName = "repositoryMappings";
        public const string ConfigurationElementName = "repositoryMapping";
        public const string InterfaceShortTypeNameAttributeName =
"interfaceShortTypeName";
        public const string RepositoryFullTypeNameAttributeName =
"repositoryFullTypeName";
        public const string RepositoryMappingsConfigurationSectionName =
"repository
MappingsConfiguration";
    }
}
```

Since I have to refer to these string values more than once in the Repository Framework configuration code, it's a lot easier to define them with a static constants class. Note that the `RepositoryMappingConstants` class is marked `internal`, as the only code needing to know about these constants is in the `SmartCA.Infrastructure` assembly.

The `RepositoryMappingCollection` is a little bit more complicated than the `RepositorySettings` class. Its job is to wrap the `repositoryMappings` element from the configuration section, and expose it as a strongly typed collection.

```
using System;
using System.Configuration;

namespace SmartCA.Infrastructure.RepositoryFramework.Configuration
{
    public sealed class RepositoryMappingCollection :
ConfigurationElementCollection
    {
        protected override ConfigurationElement CreateNewElement()
        {
            return new RepositoryMappingElement();
        }

        protected override object GetElementKey(ConfigurationElement element)
        {
            return ((RepositoryMappingElement)element).InterfaceShortTypeName;
        }

        public override ConfigurationElementCollectionType CollectionType
        {
            get { return ConfigurationElementCollectionType.BasicMap; }
        }

        protected override string ElementName
        {
            get { return RepositoryMappingConstants.ConfigurationElementName; }
        }

        public RepositoryMappingElement this[int index]
        {
            get { return (RepositoryMappingElement)this.BaseGet(index); }
            set
            {
                if (this.BaseGet(index) != null)
                {
                    this.BaseRemoveAt(index);
                }
                this.BaseAdd(index, value);
            }
        }

        public new RepositoryMappingElement this[string interfaceShortTypeName]
        {
            get { return
(RepositoryMappingElement)this.BaseGet(interfaceShortTypeName); }
        }

        public bool ContainsKey(string keyName)
```

```
        {
            bool result = false;
            object[] keys = this.BaseGetAllKeys();
            foreach (object key in keys)
            {
                if ((string)key == keyName)
                {
                    result = true;
                    break;

                }
            }
            return result;
        }
    }
}
```

Like the `RepositorySettings` class, it too inherits from one of the `Sytem.Configuration` classes, this time the `ConfigurationElementCollection` class. There is really nothing very special about this class; it is basically just overriding various methods and properties on its base class. One thing that might look a little bit odd is the indexer property for the class.

```
public new RepositoryMappingElement this[string interfaceShortTypeName]
        {
            get { return
(RepositoryMappingElement)this.BaseGet(interfaceShortTypeName); }
        }
```

It is actually hiding the base class indexer (by using the `new` keyword) in order to make it strongly typed instead of exposing the collection item as a `System.Object`.

The child members that the `RepositoryMappingCollection` contains are `RepositoryMappingElement` instances. The `RepositoryMappingElement` class is what actually holds the mapping between an interface type name and a concrete repository type name.

```
using System;
using System.Configuration;

namespace SmartCA.Infrastructure.RepositoryFramework.Configuration
{
    public sealed class RepositoryMappingElement : ConfigurationElement
    {
[ConfigurationProperty(RepositoryMappingConstants.InterfaceShortTypeName
AttributeName,
            IsKey = true, IsRequired = true)]
        public string InterfaceShortTypeName
        {
            get
            {
                return (string)this[RepositoryMappingConstants.Interface
ShortTypeNameAttributeName];
            }
            set
```

(continued)

(continued)

```
            {
   
this[RepositoryMappingConstants.InterfaceShortTypeNameAttributeName] = value;
            }
        }

[ConfigurationProperty(RepositoryMappingConstants.RepositoryFullTypeName
AttributeName,
            IsRequired = true)]
        public string RepositoryFullTypeName
        {
            get
            {
                return
(string)this[RepositoryMappingConstants.RepositoryFullTypeNameAttributeName];
            }
            set
            {
                
this[RepositoryMappingConstants.RepositoryFullTypeNameAttributeName] = value;
            }
        }
    }
}
```

Like the other repository mapping configuration classes, this class also inherits from one of the `System.Configuration` classes, the `ConfigurationElement` class. With the help of some `System.Configuration` attributes decorating it, the `RepositoryMappingElement` class exposes two properties, `InterfaceShortTypeName` and `RepositoryFullTypeName`.

The RepositoryFactory Class

Now that the configuration is finished, the `RepositoryFactory` can use it to create repositories. The `RepositoryFactory` uses Generic type parameters combined with the mappings from the configuration in order to determine what kind of repository to create. The `RepositoryFactory` is a static class with one static method, `GetRepository`.

```
using System;
using System.Collections.Generic;
using SmartCA.Infrastructure;
using SmartCA.Infrastructure.DomainBase;
using SmartCA.Infrastructure.RepositoryFramework.Configuration;
using System.Configuration;

namespace SmartCA.Infrastructure.RepositoryFramework
{
    public static class RepositoryFactory
    {
        // Dictionary to enforce the singleton pattern
        private static Dictionary<string, object> repositories = new
Dictionary<string, object>();
```

```
        /// <summary>
        /// Gets or creates an instance of the requested interface. Once a
        /// repository is created and initialized, it is cached, and all
        /// future requests for the repository will come from the cache.
        /// </summary>
        /// <typeparam name="TRepository">The interface of the repository
        /// to create.</typeparam>
        /// <typeparam name="TEntity">The type of the EntityBase that the
        /// repository is for.</typeparam>
        /// <returns>An instance of the interface requested.</returns>
        public static TRepository GetRepository<TRepository, TEntity>()
            where TRepository : class, IRepository<TEntity>
            where TEntity : EntityBase
        {
            // Initialize the provider's default value
            TRepository repository = default(TRepository);

            string interfaceShortName = typeof(TRepository).Name;

            // See if the provider was already created and is in the cache
            if (!RepositoryFactory.repositories.ContainsKey(interfaceShortName))
            {
                // Not there, so create it

                // Get the repositoryMappingsConfiguration config section
                RepositorySettings settings =
(RepositorySettings)ConfigurationManager.GetSection(RepositoryMappingConstants
.RepositoryMappingsConfigurationSectionName);

                // Create the repository, and cast it to the interface specified
                repository =
Activator.CreateInstance(Type.GetType(settings.RepositoryMappings[interfaceShortName]
.RepositoryFullTypeName)) as TRepository;

                // Add the new provider instance to the cache
                RepositoryFactory.repositories.Add(interfaceShortName, repository);
            }
            else
            {
                // The provider was in the cache, so retrieve it
                repository =
(TRepository)RepositoryFactory.repositories[interfaceShortName];
            }
            return repository;
        }
    }
}
```

The signature of this method is interesting because it uses two Generic type parameters, `TRepository` and `TEntity`, with the restrictions that `TRepository` is a class and implements the `IRepository<TEntity>` interface, and that `TEntity` derives from the `EntityBase` class. Because the Repository Framework is supporting interfaces other than just `IRepository<T>`, the method cannot just return a type of `IRepository<T>` for the `Repository` instance. It must also support returning any interface that implements `IRepository<T>`, since the repository interface being used can also have additional methods defined in it; that is why `TRepository` has been declared as a Generic type, so that the factory can support the Repository Framework requirements of being able to pass in a valid `Repository` interface type and get an instance of the interface (as long as it has been properly defined in the application's configuration file).

The code for the method first uses reflection to get the short type name of the interface type passed in via the Generic `TRepository` parameter. It then does a lookup in its static dictionary of repositories that have already been created to see if it can pull it out of memory. If it cannot, it then begins the process of using the custom repository configuration objects to find the right repository type to create based on the values in the mappings configuration. When the type is found, the method then uses the reflection capabilities of the Activator object to create an instance of the correct repository based on the mapped type from configuration. Then, after the repository has been created, it is put into the static dictionary of repositories so that it will be available the next time it is requested. Once the repository has been retrieved from memory or created, the instance is returned to the caller.

I decided to use a static dictionary to hold the repositories in order to make them behave like singletons. This is very important for performance reasons, since it can be expensive to build a Repository Factory using reflection every time you need one, especially in Domain-Driven Design architectures, where repositories are used quite frequently. Also, because the repositories are guaranteed to have only one instance per type, I can now do other interesting things, such as enable domain model objects to be cached, refresh the cache when I choose to, and so on. This functionality can have a very positive impact on the performance of the application.

Unit of Work

Since I will be using several repositories to pull data in and out of the database (and possibly other resources), I need a way to keep track of what has been changed. I also need a way to define what sequences of events define a transaction and to be able to commit those sequences of events as a single transaction. One way of doing this is simply to avoid the problem altogether and every time an object changes, just write the change to the data store; however, this pattern usually does not work very well, especially when you need to group actions together into a single transaction.

The answer to this requirement that I am going to use is the Unit of Work pattern, as defined by Martin Fowler (Fowler, *Patterns of Enterprise Application Architecture*, 184). According to Martin, the Unit of Work "maintains a list of objects affected by a business transaction and coordinates the writing out of changes and the resolution of concurrency problems." The Unit of Work needs to know what objects it should keep track of, and Martin goes on to describe two basic ways this can be accomplished:

- **Caller registration** — The user of the object has to remember to register with the Unit of Work.
- **Object registration** — The objects register themselves with the Unit of Work.

Jimmy Nilsson describes a different approach to the Unit of Work, and that is to let the repositories delegate all of their work to a Unit of Work, and then the Unit of Work then makes all necessary database calls (or other types of resource calls) on behalf of the repositories (Nilsson, *Applying Domain-Driven Design and Patterns, With Examples in C# and .NET*, 200). One major benefit of this approach is that the messages sent to the Unit of Work are invisible to the consumer of the repositories, since the repositories are reporting what has been asked of them to the Unit of Work. This also helps promote persistence ignorance in the domain objects, which is what I am striving for.

In his solution, Jimmy implemented object persistence outside of the repository in his Unit of Work implementation. The reasoning for not letting the repositories completely hide the Unit of Work was that he wanted to synchronize changes across several Aggregates (and their respective repositories) in a single logical unit. In order for this to work, the repositories need to have a Unit of Work injected into them at creation time.

I really like Jimmy's idea of hiding the Unit of Work calls in the repositories because it eliminates lots of plumbing calls inside of domain objects or from application-level code. This way, the plumbing stays inside the repository, which itself represents plumbing, and shields the domain object from having to deal with the noise. With that being said, I also would like to have my cake and eat it too. What I mean by that is that I would like to keep the spirit of Jimmy's solution but also still have the repositories be responsible for the data persistence. In order to do that, I have created a few interfaces to help out. The first one being the obvious one, the `IUnitOfWork` interface:

```
using System;
using SmartCA.Infrastructure.DomainBase;
using SmartCA.Infrastructure.RepositoryFramework;

namespace SmartCA.Infrastructure
{
    public interface IUnitOfWork
    {
        void RegisterAdded(EntityBase entity, IUnitOfWorkRepository repository);
        void RegisterChanged(EntityBase entity, IUnitOfWorkRepository repository);
        void RegisterRemoved(EntityBase entity, IUnitOfWorkRepository repository);
        void Commit();
    }
}
```

The `IUnitOfWork` interface identifies for use the entities that have been added, changed, or removed from the repositories. An instance of this interface must be passed to all repositories that are to participate in a Unit of Work. Then, once all work is completed, I simply call `Commit` on the interface to commit all of my changes to the appropriate data stores. You may be asking yourself, how in the world can the Unit of Work implementation commit the changes if the repositories are supposed to do the work? The answer is to have the repositories implement a second interface to which the Unit of Work refers. That interface is the `IUnitOfWorkRepository` interface:

```
using System;
using SmartCA.Infrastructure.DomainBase;

namespace SmartCA.Infrastructure.RepositoryFramework
{
    public interface IUnitOfWorkRepository
    {
        void PersistNewItem(EntityBase item);
        void PersistUpdatedItem(EntityBase item);
        void PersistDeletedItem(EntityBase item);
    }
}
```

Because the repositories will implement the `IUnitOfWorkRepository` interface, the Unit of Work implementation will now be able to call back in to the repositories to make changes to the data store (or stores).

I have created a Unit of Work implementation class called `UnitofWork` (I know, very creative). It essentially keeps a list of the three types of changes, and then cycles through each of them during commit time and talks to the right repository to persist the changes.

```
using System;
using System.Collections.Generic;
using SmartCA.Infrastructure.DomainBase;
using SmartCA.Infrastructure.RepositoryFramework;
using System.Transactions;

namespace SmartCA.Infrastructure
{
    public class UnitOfWork : IUnitOfWork
    {
        private Dictionary<EntityBase, IUnitOfWorkRepository> addedEntities;
        private Dictionary<EntityBase, IUnitOfWorkRepository> changedEntities;
        private Dictionary<EntityBase, IUnitOfWorkRepository> deletedEntities;

        public UnitOfWork()
        {
            this.addedEntities = new Dictionary<EntityBase,
                                     IUnitOfWorkRepository>();
            this.changedEntities = new Dictionary<EntityBase,
                                       IUnitOfWorkRepository>();
            this.deletedEntities = new Dictionary<EntityBase,
                                       IUnitOfWorkRepository>();
        }

        #region IUnitOfWork Members

        public void RegisterAdded(EntityBase entity,
            IUnitOfWorkRepository repository)
        {
            this.addedEntities.Add(entity, repository);
        }

        public void RegisterChanged(EntityBase entity,
            IUnitOfWorkRepository repository)
        {
            this.changedEntities.Add(entity, repository);
        }

        public void RegisterRemoved(EntityBase entity,
            IUnitOfWorkRepository repository)
        {
            this.deletedEntities.Add(entity, repository);
        }

        public void Commit()
        {
            using (TransactionScope scope = new TransactionScope())
            {
                foreach (EntityBase entity in this.deletedEntities.Keys)
                {
                    this.deletedEntities[entity].PersistDeletedItem(entity);
                }

                foreach (EntityBase entity in this.addedEntities.Keys)
                {
```

```
                    this.addedEntities[entity].PersistDeletedItem(entity);
                }

                foreach (EntityBase entity in this.changedEntities.Keys)
                {
                    this.changedEntities[entity].PersistDeletedItem(entity);
                }

                scope.Complete();
            }

            this.deletedEntities.Clear();
            this.addedEntities.Clear();
            this.changedEntities.Clear();
        }

        #endregion
    }
}
```

The methods in the `IUnitOfWork Members` region of the class will get called by the repositories, and the repositories actually pass in their own instances to the `UnitOfWork` class when they call these methods. When these methods are called, the entity and its associated `IUnitOfWorkRepository` instance are added to their respective dictionary object, depending whether the call was an add, change, or remove registration.

Then, in the `Commit` method, the `UnitOfWork` cycles through all of the deletions, additions, and updates, respectively, and calls back on the associated `IUnitOfWorkRepository` instance to persist the changes to the correct data store. The entire operation is wrapped up in a transaction using the .NET Framework's `TransactionScope` class, which knows how to enlist the right type of transaction properly, be it just a local transaction or a distributed transaction. Once everything has been committed, the entity-repository dictionaries are then reset to empty.

The Repository Base Classes

In order to eliminate a lot of duplicate code, I have decided to put in some abstract base classes from which the repositories will inherit common code. This should make it easier to code the concrete repository classes.

The RepositoryBase<T> Class

This is the first repository base class and its main job is to lend a helping hand to its derived repositories in regard to implementing the Unit of Work pattern. It also helps out with the indexer implementation of the `IRepository<T>` interface.

```
using System;
using SmartCA.Infrastructure.DomainBase;

namespace SmartCA.Infrastructure.RepositoryFramework
{
    public abstract class RepositoryBase<T>
        : IRepository<T>, IUnitOfWorkRepository where T : EntityBase
```

(continued)

(continued)

```
    {
        private IUnitOfWork unitOfWork;

        protected RepositoryBase()
            : this(null)
        {
        }

        protected RepositoryBase(IUnitOfWork unitOfWork)
        {
            this.unitOfWork = unitOfWork;
        }

        #region IRepository<T> Members

        public abstract T FindBy(object key);

        public void Add(T item)
        {
            if (this.unitOfWork != null)
            {
                this.unitOfWork.RegisterAdded(item, this);
            }
        }

        public void Remove(T item)
        {
            if (this.unitOfWork != null)
            {
                this.unitOfWork.RegisterRemoved(item, this);
            }
        }

        public T this[object key]
        {
            get
            {
                return this.FindBy(key);
            }
            set
            {
                if (this.FindBy(key) == null)
                {
                    this.Add(value);
                }
                else
                {
                    this.unitOfWork.RegisterChanged(value, this);
                }
            }
        }
```

```
        #endregion

        #region IUnitOfWorkRepository Members

        public void PersistNewItem(EntityBase item)
        {
            this.PersistNewItem((T)item);
        }

        public void PersistUpdatedItem(EntityBase item)
        {
            this.PersistUpdatedItem((T)item);
        }

        public void PersistDeletedItem(EntityBase item)
        {
            this.PersistDeletedItem((T)item);
        }

        #endregion

        protected abstract void PersistNewItem(T item);
        protected abstract void PersistUpdatedItem(T item);
        protected abstract void PersistDeletedItem(T item);
    }
}
```

This class implements both the `IRepository<T>` interface and the `IUnitOfWorkRepository` interface, and it is optionally injected with the `IUnitOfWork` interface in its constructor. Its main job in implementing the `IRepository<T>` interface is mainly to call back into the `IUnitOfWork` interface instance to let it know when something has been added, removed, or changed. The other `IRepository<T>` method without an implementation in this class, `T FindBy(object key)`, is actually declared as an abstract method to be implemented by one of the derived repository classes.

All of the methods on the `IUnitOfWorkRepository` interface are implemented in this class, but really as a pass-through to some more abstract methods that the derived repositories have to implement. I did this to avoid having to cast from `EntityBase` to the types being used inside all of the repository implementations. Instead, the casting is performed in this class and then delegated to the more strongly typed, Generic-enabled abstract methods (`protected abstract void PersistNewItem(T item)`, `protected abstract void PersistUpdatedItem(T item)`, and `protected abstract void PersistDeletedItem(T item)`). This way, the code for the casting is centralized, and the concrete repositories can deal with the strongly typed entities that they know and represent.

The SqlCeRepositoryBase<T> Class

Since the architecture of this application dictates that we write and read all data to and from a local SQL Server CE database, a lot of duplicate SQL data access type of code can be eliminated in the `Repository` classes by building a base class to handle these types of operations. I decided to name this class

SqlCeRepositoryBase, in order to make its purpose obvious. This class makes it very easy for its derived Repository classes to talk to the local SQL CE database.

```
using System;
using System.Collections.Generic;
using SmartCA.Infrastructure.RepositoryFramework;
using SmartCA.Infrastructure.DomainBase;
using Microsoft.Practices.EnterpriseLibrary.Data.SqlCe;
using Microsoft.Practices.EnterpriseLibrary.Data;
using System.Data;
using System.Data.Common;
using SmartCA.Infrastructure.EntityFactoryFramework;

namespace SmartCA.Infrastructure.Repositories
{
    public abstract class SqlCeRepositoryBase<T> : RepositoryBase<T>
        where T : EntityBase
    {
        #region AppendChildData Delegate

        /// <summary>
        /// The delegate signature required for callback methods
        /// </summary>
        /// <param name="entityAggregate"></param>
        /// <param name="childEntityKey"></param>
        public delegate void AppendChildData(T entityAggregate,
            object childEntityKeyValue);

        #endregion

        #region Private Members

        private Database database;
        private IEntityFactory<T> entityFactory;
        private Dictionary<string, AppendChildData> childCallbacks;

        #endregion

        #region Constructors

        protected SqlCeRepositoryBase()
            : this(null)
        {
        }

        protected SqlCeRepositoryBase(IUnitOfWork unitOfWork)
            : base(unitOfWork)
        {
            this.database = DatabaseFactory.CreateDatabase();
            this.entityFactory = EntityFactoryBuilder.BuildFactory<T>();
            this.childCallbacks = new Dictionary<string, AppendChildData>();
            this.BuildChildCallbacks();
        }
```

```
        #endregion

        #region Abstract Methods

        protected abstract void BuildChildCallbacks();
        public abstract override T FindBy(object key);
        protected abstract override void PersistNewItem(T item);
        protected abstract override void PersistUpdatedItem(T item);
        protected abstract override void PersistDeletedItem(T item);

        #endregion

        #region Properties

        protected Database Database
        {
            get { return this.database; }
        }

        protected Dictionary<string, AppendChildData> ChildCallbacks
        {
            get { return this.childCallbacks; }
        }

        #endregion

        #region Protected Methods

        protected IDataReader ExecuteReader(string sql)
        {
            DbCommand command = this.database.GetSqlStringCommand(sql);
            return this.database.ExecuteReader(command);
        }

        protected virtual T BuildEntityFromSql(string sql)
        {
            T entity = default(T);
            using (IDataReader reader = this.ExecuteReader(sql))
            {
                if (reader.Read())
                {
                    entity = this.BuildEntityFromReader(reader);
                }
            }
            return entity;
        }

        protected virtual T BuildEntityFromReader(IDataReader reader)
        {
            T entity = this.entityFactory.BuildEntity(reader);
            if (this.childCallbacks != null && this.childCallbacks.Count > 0)
            {
                object childKeyValue = null;
                DataTable columnData = reader.GetSchemaTable();
                foreach (string childKeyName in this.childCallbacks.Keys)
```

(continued)

(continued)

```
                {
                    if (DataHelper.ReaderContainsColumnName(columnData,
                        childKeyName))
                    {
                        childKeyValue = reader[childKeyName];
                    }
                    else
                    {
                        childKeyValue = null;
                    }
                    this.childCallbacks[childKeyName](entity, childKeyValue);
                }
            }
            return entity;
        }

        protected virtual List<T> BuildEntitiesFromSql(string sql)
        {
            List<T> entities = new List<T>();
            using (IDataReader reader = this.ExecuteReader(sql))
            {
                while (reader.Read())
                {
                    entities.Add(this.BuildEntityFromReader(reader));
                }
            }
            return entities;
        }

        #endregion
    }
}
```

The class inherits from `RepositoryBase<T>` and does not implement any of its abstract methods; it simply overrides them and passes them on as abstract again. The real value it adds is in all of its protected methods to get data in and out of the local SQL CE database. One of the most interesting things about this class is that it is delegating out to a factory for building domain entity objects (`EntityBase`) from `IDataReader` instances.

When looking at the constructors, the first thing to notice is that I am using the Microsoft Enterprise Library 3.0 for data access, hence the use of the library's abstract `Database` class and its `DatabaseFactory` to create the `Database` class instance from configuration.

```
        #region Constructors

        protected SqlCeRepositoryBase()
            : this(null)
        {
        }

        protected SqlCeRepositoryBase(IUnitOfWork unitOfWork)
            : base(unitOfWork)
```

```
{
    this.database = DatabaseFactory.CreateDatabase();
    this.entityFactory = EntityFactoryBuilder.BuildFactory<T>();
    this.childCallbacks = new Dictionary<string,
                                SqlCeRepositoryBase<T>.AppendChildData>();
    this.BuildChildCallbacks();
}

#endregion
```

When doing this I actually get a `SqlCeDatabase` instance, which is the Enterprise Library's nice encapsulation of common actions with a SQL Server CE database. The next item of interest is the instantiation of the `IEntityFactory<T>` interface instance; I will discuss the purpose of that interface in the next section of this chapter. The last thing the constructor does is delegate to its derived class and call its abstract method `BuildChildCallbacks`. This method initializes the private `Dictionary<string, AppendChildData> childCallbacks` member and represents a key-value pair of the name of a field in an `IDataReader` instance and a delegate of type `AppendChildData(T entityAggregate, object childEntityKeyValue)`. This will be talked about later, but it is used for allowing the `SqlCeRepository<T>` base class to call the method encapsulated in the delegate in order to help populate an aggregate object with data from another query in addition to the main query's results. It is very flexible in that it allows the derived class to use the base class's code for retrieving an entity, yet still leaves the door open for the derived class to append data on to the entity created by the base class.

The next section of code defines all of the abstract methods of the class:

```
#region Abstract Methods

protected abstract void BuildChildCallbacks();
public abstract override T FindBy(object key);
protected abstract override void PersistNewItem(T item);
protected abstract override void PersistUpdatedItem(T item);
protected abstract override void PersistDeletedItem(T item);

#endregion
```

The `BuildChildCallbacks` method was just discussed, and it really is optional for the derived classes to put working code into it. What I mean by that is that the derived classes must implement the method signature, but they may decide to leave the body of the method blank if the derived class does not have a need for any methods to be called back when building its entities. The rest of the methods are just passing on the strongly typed Unit of Work methods defined on the `RepositoryBase<T>` class.

The two read-only protected properties on the class, `Database` and `ChildCallbacks`, are simply just encapsulating their respective private members. The next four protected methods are really the heart of the class. The first method, `ExecuteReader`, shown below, simply takes a SQL string and executes against the SQL CE database and returns an `IDataReader` instance.

```
protected IDataReader ExecuteReader(string sql)
{
    DbCommand command = this.database.GetSqlStringCommand(sql);
    return this.database.ExecuteReader(command);
}
```

The next method, `BuildEntityFromSql`, uses the `ExecuteReader` method to help build an entity instance from a SQL statement.

```
protected virtual T BuildEntityFromSql(string sql)
{
    T entity = default(T);
    using (IDataReader reader = this.ExecuteReader(sql))
    {
        if (reader.Read())
        {
            entity = this.BuildEntityFromReader(reader);
        }
    }
    return entity;
}
```

It starts off by first getting an `IDataReader` from the `ExecuteReader` method, and then uses that `IDataReader` and passes it to the main method, `BuildEntityFromReader`, to build the entity. The Generic entity instance that is returned is a derivative of the `EntityBase` type.

The `BuildEntityFromReader` method is a little bit more complicated than the other methods in the class.

```
protected virtual T BuildEntityFromReader(IDataReader reader)
{
    T entity = this.entityFactory.BuildEntity(reader);
    if (this.childCallbacks != null && this.childCallbacks.Count > 0)
    {
        object childKeyValue = null;
        DataTable columnData = reader.GetSchemaTable();
        foreach (string childKeyName in this.childCallbacks.Keys)
        {
            if (DataHelper.ReaderContainsColumnName(columnData,
                childKeyName))
            {
                childKeyValue = reader[childKeyName];
            }
            else
            {
                childKeyValue = null;
            }
            this.childCallbacks[childKeyName](entity, childKeyValue);
        }
    }
    return entity;
}
```

It starts by delegating to the class's `IEntityFactory<T>` instance to build and map an entity from an `IDataReader`. I will discuss this *Entity Factory Framework* in the next section. It then checks the dictionary of child callback delegates (`Dictionary<string, AppendChildData> childCallbacks`) defined in the derived class to see whether any callback delegates have been defined. If there are some entries present in the dictionary, it iterates through the keys of the collection, which are really database foreign key field names from the derived class's main query. While iterating, it uses the `DataHelper` class to check to see whether the field name actually exists in the `IDataReader`'s set of fields (I will discuss the DataHelper class in the next paragraph). If it does exist, it then retrieves the value of the field name from the IDataReader instance. Once that foreign key value has been extracted, it then passes the value back to the callback method, along with the partially populated entity object, and executes the method, thus filling another part of the entity object. This is particularly useful for populating aggregate objects with many child objects attached to them.

The DataHelper class is used by the various Repositories and Factories to get data to and from ADO .NET objects, such as the IDataReader. In the code example above, I was using the DataHelper's ReaderContainsColumnName method to determine whether a particular column name (or field name) existed in the DataReader's set of data. Here is the method:

```
public static bool ReaderContainsColumnName(DataTable schemaTable,
    string columnName)
{
    bool containsColumnName = false;
    foreach (DataRow row in schemaTable.Rows)
    {
        if (row["ColumnName"].ToString() == columnName)
        {
            containsColumnName = true;
            break;
        }
    }
    return containsColumnName;
}
```

The next method, BuildEntitiesFromSql, is very similar to BuildEntityFromSql, except that instead of just returning a single entity instance, it returns a generic list (IList<T>) of them.

```
protected virtual List<T> BuildEntitiesFromSql(string sql)
{
    List<T> entities = new List<T>();
    using (IDataReader reader = this.ExecuteReader(sql))
    {
        while (reader.Read())
        {
            entities.Add(this.BuildEntityFromReader(reader));
        }
    }
    return entities;
}
```

The method starts by initializing the list of entities to be returned, and then similarly to BuildEntityFromSql, it calls the class's ExecuteReader method to get an IDataReader instance from the SQL statement passed in. It then iterates over the IDataReader instance and uses the BuildEntityFromReader method to build the entity and add it to its list.

The Entity Factory Framework

When I was originally building this application, I had hoped to be using the ADO.NET Entity Framework as my object-relational (OR) mapping solution. Since it was pulled from the Visual Studio 2008 release, I have decided to roll my own pseudo-mapping factory type of framework.

The IEntityFactory<T> Interface

The main concept of what I need the framework to do is extremely simple: to map field names contained in an instance of an `IDataReader` to fields of an object instance. Actually, it's really just mapping field names to class property names. To promote the simplicity of what I wanted, I created an interface, `IEntityFactory<T>`, to show my intent.

```
using System;
using SmartCA.Infrastructure.DomainBase;
using System.Data;

namespace SmartCA.Infrastructure.EntityFactoryFramework
{
    public interface IEntityFactory<T> where T : EntityBase
    {
        T BuildEntity(IDataReader reader);
    }
}
```

This interface is extremely simple, its one method, `BuildEntity`, takes an `IDataReader` and returns an object that derives from `EntityBase`. Now, since I have this interface in place, I need to have a way of figuring out how to get the right object instances of this interface. I will use a factory class to do this, named `EntityFactoryBuilder`.

Configuration Section

Just like the `RepositoryFactory`, I have chosen to use configuration along with my EntityFactoryBuilder. This keeps things very flexible.

Here is what the application configuration file with added support for the Entity Factory Framework looks like:

```
<?xml version="1.0" encoding="utf-8" ?>
<configuration>
  <configSections>
    <section name="dataConfiguration" type="Microsoft.Practices.EnterpriseLibrary
.Data.Configuration.DatabaseSettings, Microsoft.Practices.EnterpriseLibrary.Data,
Version=3.0.0.0, Culture=neutral, PublicKeyToken=null"/>
    <section name="repositoryMappingsConfiguration"

type="SmartCA.Infrastructure.RepositoryFramework.Configuration
.RepositorySettings, SmartCA.Infrastructure, Version=1.0.0.0, Culture=neutral,
PublicKeyToken=null"/>
    <section name="entityMappingsConfiguration"

type="SmartCA.Infrastructure.EntityFactoryFramework.Configuration
.EntitySettings,
SmartCA.Infrastructure, Version=1.0.0.0, Culture=neutral, PublicKeyToken=null"/>
  </configSections>
  <dataConfiguration defaultDatabase="SmartCA"/>

  <connectionStrings>
```

```
    <add name="SmartCA" connectionString="Data Source=|DataDirectory|\SmartCA.sdf"
         providerName="System.Data.SqlServerCe.3.5"/>
  </connectionStrings>

  <repositoryMappingsConfiguration>
    <repositoryMappings>
      <repositoryMapping interfaceShortTypeName="IProjectRepository"

repositoryFullTypeName="SmartCA.Infrastructure.Repositories.ProjectRepository,
SmartCA.Infrastructure.Repositories, Version=1.0.0.0, Culture=neutral,
PublicKeyToken=null" />
      <repositoryMapping interfaceShortTypeName="IEmployeeRepository"

repositoryFullTypeName="SmartCA.Infrastructure.Repositories.EmployeeRepository,
SmartCA.Infrastructure.Repositories, Version=1.0.0.0, Culture=neutral,
PublicKeyToken=null" />
      <repositoryMapping interfaceShortTypeName="ICompanyRepository"

repositoryFullTypeName="SmartCA.Infrastructure.Repositories.CompanyRepository,
SmartCA.Infrastructure.Repositories, Version=1.0.0.0, Culture=neutral,
PublicKeyToken=null" />
      <repositoryMapping interfaceShortTypeName="IContactRepository"

repositoryFullTypeName="SmartCA.Infrastructure.Repositories.ContactRepository,
SmartCA.Infrastructure.Repositories, Version=1.0.0.0, Culture=neutral,
PublicKeyToken=null" />
    </repositoryMappings>
  </repositoryMappingsConfiguration>

  <entityMappingsConfiguration>
    <entityMappings>
      <entityMapping entityShortTypeName="Project"

entityFactoryFullTypeName="SmartCA.Infrastructure.Repositories.ProjectFactory,
SmartCA.Infrastructure.Repositories, Version=1.0.0.0, Culture=neutral,
PublicKeyToken=null" />
      <entityMapping entityShortTypeName="Employee"

entityFactoryFullTypeName="SmartCA.Infrastructure.Repositories.EmployeeFactory,
SmartCA.Infrastructure.Repositories, Version=1.0.0.0, Culture=neutral,
PublicKeyToken=null" />
      <entityMapping entityShortTypeName="Company"

entityFactoryFullTypeName="SmartCA.Infrastructure.Repositories.CompanyFactory,
SmartCA.Infrastructure.Repositories, Version=1.0.0.0, Culture=neutral,
PublicKeyToken=null" />
    </entityMappings>
  </entityMappingsConfiguration>

</configuration>
```

Configuration Section Handling

Again, just as with the Repository Framework configuration, I have added a `Configuration` folder under the `EntityFactoryFramework` folder of the `SmartCA.Infrastructure` project (see Figure 2.4).

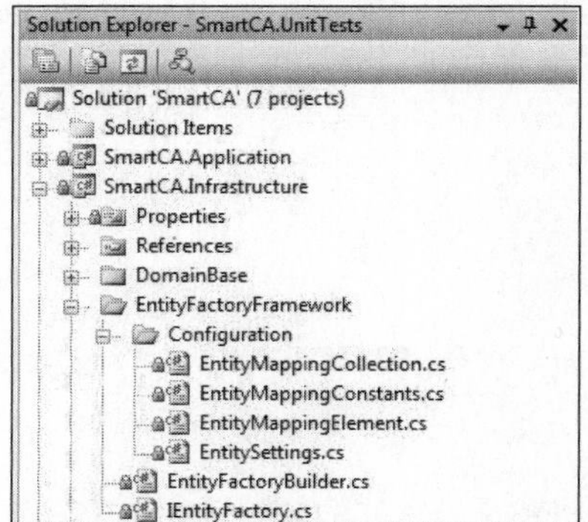

Figure 2.4: EntityFactoryFramework Configuration folder.

I am not going to show the configuration code for the Entity Factory Framework because it is almost exactly the same as the configuration code for the Repository Framework.

The EntityFactoryBuilder Class

Now that the configuration is finished, the `EntityFactoryBuilder` can use it to create repositories. The way the `EntityFactoryBuilder` works is that it uses a Generic type parameter representing the type of the entity that needs to be mapped, combined with the mappings from the configuration in order to determine what kind of `IEntityFactory<T>` to create. The `EntityFactoryBuilder` class is a static class with one static method, `BuildFactory`.

```
using System;
using System.Collections.Generic;
using SmartCA.Infrastructure.DomainBase;
using SmartCA.Infrastructure.EntityFactoryFramework.Configuration;
using System.Configuration;

namespace SmartCA.Infrastructure.EntityFactoryFramework
{
    public static class EntityFactoryBuilder
    {
        // Dictionary used for caching purposes
        private static Dictionary<string, object> factories =
            new Dictionary<string, object>();

        public static IEntityFactory<T> BuildFactory<T>() where T : EntityBase
        {
            IEntityFactory<T> factory = null;

            // Get the key from the Generic parameter passed in
            string key = typeof(T).Name;
```

```
            // See if the factory is in the cache
            if (EntityFactoryBuilder.factories.ContainsKey(key))
            {
                // It was there, so retrieve it from the cache
                factory = EntityFactoryBuilder.factories[key] as IEntityFactory<T>;
            }
            else
            {
                // Create the factory

                // Get the entityMappingsConfiguration config section
EntitySettings settings = (EntitySettings)ConfigurationManager.GetSection
(EntityMappingConstants.EntityMappingsConfigurationSectionName);

                // Get the type to be created using reflection
                Type entityFactoryType =
Type.GetType(settings.EntityMappings[key].EntityFactoryFullTypeName);

                // Create the factory using reflection
                factory = Activator.CreateInstance(entityFactoryType) as
IEntityFactory<T>;

                // Put the newly created factory in the cache
                EntityFactoryBuilder.factories[key] = factory;
            }

            // Return the factory
            return factory;
        }
    }
}
```

The signature of this method is much simpler than the `RepositoryFactory` class's `GetRepository<TRepository, TEntity>` method. It has only one Generic type parameter, `T`, and that is the type of entity for which the factory was created. The `T` parameter has a restriction that it must be derived from the `EntityBase` class.

First, the code for the method uses .NET Reflection to find the short type name of the Generic parameter type being passed in via the `T` parameter. Then, the code looks in its static dictionary of entity factories to see whether it can pull the particular Factory out of memory. If it cannot, it then uses the custom Entity Factory Framework configuration objects to find the right entity factory type to create based on the values in the mappings configuration. When the type is found, the method then uses the reflection capabilities of the Activator object to create an instance of the correct Factory based on the mapped type from configuration. Then, after the Factory has been created, it is put into the static dictionary of repositories so it will be available the next time it has been requested. Once the Factory has been retrieved from memory or created, the instance is then returned to the caller.

The Model-View-ViewModel Pattern

Traditional Presentation Patterns

So far, I have covered the various patterns and principles being followed in the domain layer and the infrastructure layer. Since this book is about Domain-Driven Design, that is a good thing, but I still have an application to build; it cannot just be all domain objects and unit tests. I actually have to make the application present something fairly compelling to the user. If you remember, in Chapter 1 I stated that I was going to be using WPF for the presentation technology. That is all well and good, but there must be some type of strategy for hooking up domain objects to the user interface. Some very common presentation patterns are the Model-View-Controller (MVC) and the Model-View-Presenter (MVP). These patterns are very good, and I highly encourage you to study more about them; however, in my opinion, they have one major drawback when used with WPF: they do not take into account data-binding technology at all. What I mean by that, is that in those patterns, the Controller or the Presenter is responsible for acting upon the View, such as filling TextBoxes with text, loading ListBoxes, filling a grid, and so on. It just so happens that one of WPF's greatest strengths is its rich data-binding capabilities. By implementing either the MVC or the MVP pattern, I would be completely bypassing the data-binding facilities in WPF. There must be some way to make this concept of separating the View from the Model work in WPF without bypassing a whole slew of rich WPF features!

Model-View-ViewModel Definition

That way is the Model-View-ViewModel pattern. I first learned about this pattern by reading John Gossman's blog entries about it. He was a member of the Microsoft Expression Blend team and is currently on the WPF team at Microsoft. In his blog entries, he talks about how his team has created this new pattern, called Model-View-ViewModel, to separate the Model from the View but, at the same time, to take full advantage of WPF's features. According to John "The pattern was to take a pure Model, create an abstract view that contained state, and data bind a View created with a visual designer to that abstract view. That's a nice clean, formal pattern." In this case, the visual designer is the Microsoft Expression Blend tool, and the abstract view is the ViewModel. The key point is that there is a two-way connection between the View and the ViewModel via data binding. When properly set up, this means that every View will consist of almost nothing but pure XAML and very little procedural code, which is exactly what I want.

Because this pattern separates out the View and the Model so nicely, there are a lot of opportunities for graphic artist types to work in Blend all day, hand the XAML off to a developer working on the domain model, and have the developer wire everything up to the domain model. Shortly, I will show how I implemented this pattern for the SmartCA application.

What's a ViewModel?

You must be asking yourself this question by now. When I first read about it and looked at some sample code, it took me a while to grasp the full power of it. The purpose in life for a ViewModel is to adapt the Model to the View. This may mean that you have a method in the domain model that returns an `IList<Project>` type, but you would really like to convert that into a more WPF-friendly class for data binding purposes. Enter the ViewModel. In this case the ViewModel would transform the `IList<Project>` type from the domain model into something like a `CollectionView` class for a WPF UI Element to bind data to. The key is to expose public properties on the ViewModel for the things that the View needs to bind data to. Also, like a Controller, the ViewModel can be used to hold the View's state, as well as any commands that the View needs.

Since WPF natively implements the Command pattern, by which I mean certain UI elements such as Button controls, there is a property called `Command` that is of the WPF-defined `ICommand` type. I can place Commands into my ViewModel and expose them as public properties for my View to bind to. This is extremely powerful, as it allows me to bind executable code to a Button on a form without having to write any code to wire up the Button. WPF's Command pattern along with a public `Command` property on my ViewModel take care of this.

An Example

In order to understand this a little better, I will show you a part of the SmartCA application. The use case is extremely simple; it is to display a form to the user to show a list of projects, and have the user pick a project, and remember what project was selected. The selected project is what the user will be working on in his or her session until the user decides to change to another project. Since the point of this example is the Model-View-ViewModel presentation pattern, I will focus a little bit less on the domain and a little bit more on the presentation items.

To start off with, I first create a `Service` class in my domain model, called `ProjectService`. `ProjectService` has one method we care about right now, and that is `GetProjects`.

```
using System;
using System.Collections.Generic;
using SmartCA.Model.Projects;
using SmartCA.Infrastructure.RepositoryFramework;

namespace SmartCA.Model.Projects
{
    public static class ProjectService
    {
        public static IList<Project> GetAllProjects()
        {
            IProjectRepository repository =
RepositoryFactory.GetRepository<IProjectRepository, Project>();
            return repository.FindAll();
        }
    }
}
```

The code is pretty straightforward; it is simply acting as a façade to the `IProjectRepository` instance and gets a list of all of the repository's Projects. So far so good; I now have a way of getting the data that I need.

The next step is to build a View for displaying the list of Projects to the user in the form of a dropdown list. Figure 2.5 shows what I want the form to look like.

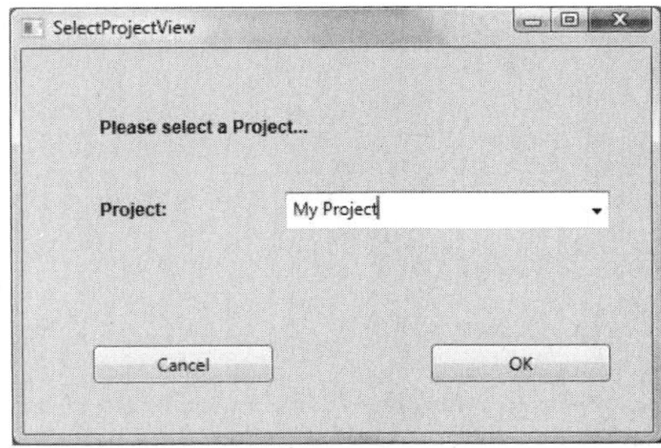

Figure 2.5: The SelectProjectView view

In order to get to this point, I need to build a ViewModel class that I can have the `SelectProjectView` class bind to. I only need to expose a list and two commands, one per button.

```
using System;
using System.Collections.Generic;
using SmartCA.Model.Projects;
using System.Windows.Data;
using SmartCA.Infrastructure.UI;
using SmartCA.Presentation.Views;
using SmartCA.Application;

namespace SmartCA.Presentation.ViewModels
{
    public class SelectProjectViewModel
    {
        private CollectionView projects;
        private DelegateCommand selectCommand;
        private DelegateCommand cancelCommand;
        private IView view;

        public SelectProjectViewModel()
            : this(null)
        {
        }

        public SelectProjectViewModel(IView view)
        {
            this.view = view;
            this.projects = new CollectionView(ProjectService.GetAllProjects());
            this.selectCommand = new DelegateCommand(this.SelectCommandHandler);
            this.cancelCommand = new DelegateCommand(this.CancelCommandHandler);
        }

        public CollectionView Projects
        {
            get { return this.projects; }
        }

        public DelegateCommand SelectCommand
        {
            get { return this.selectCommand; }
        }

        public DelegateCommand CancelCommand
        {
            get { return this.cancelCommand; }
        }

        private void SelectCommandHandler(object sender, EventArgs e)
        {
            Project project = this.projects.CurrentItem as Project;
            UserSession.CurrentProject = project;
            this.view.Close();
        }
```

```
        private void CancelCommandHandler(object sender, EventArgs e)
        {
            this.view.Close();
        }
    }
}
```

The first thing to note about this class is its overloaded constructor. It first gives a reference to the View via the `IView` interface. This interface currently has two methods, `Show` and `Close`, and it just so happens that the WPF Window class happens to implement both of these methods.

```
using System;

namespace SmartCA.Presentation.Views
{
    public interface IView
    {
        void Show();
        void Close();
    }
}
```

This interface allows me to open and close the form from my ViewModel.

The next thing that the `SelectProjectViewModel` constructor does is to transform the `IList<Project>` list of projects into a WPF-friendly `CollectionView` class. This `CollectionView` is then exposed via the `Projects` public property.

```
        public SelectProjectViewModel(IView view)
        {
            this.view = view;
            this.projects = new CollectionView(ProjectService.GetAllProjects());
            this.selectCommand = new DelegateCommand(this.SelectCommandHandler);
            this.cancelCommand = new DelegateCommand(this.CancelCommandHandler);
        }
```

The next two lines are interesting not in that they are setting up the two `ICommand` properties for the two Buttons, but rather that they are using a class called `DelegateCommand` to represent the `ICommand` instances. The `DelegateCommand` class not only implements the `ICommand` interface but also allows a delegate to be called when the `ICommand`'s `Execute` method is called.

```
using System;
using System.Windows.Input;

namespace SmartCA.Infrastructure.UI
{
    public class DelegateCommand : ICommand
    {
        public delegate void SimpleEventHandler(object sender, EventArgs e);

        private SimpleEventHandler handler;
        private bool isEnabled = true;
```

(continued)

(continued)

```
        public DelegateCommand(SimpleEventHandler handler)
        {
            this.handler = handler;
        }

        #region ICommand implementation

        /// <summary>
        /// Executing the command is as simple as calling that method
        /// we were handed on creation.
        /// </summary>
        /// <param name="parameter">Data used by the command. If the
        /// command does not require data to be passed,
        /// this object can be set to null.</param>
        public void Execute(object parameter)
        {
            this.handler(this, EventArgs.Empty);
        }

        /// <summary>
        /// Determines whether the command can execute in its
        /// current state.
        /// </summary>
        /// <param name="parameter">Data used by the command. If the
        /// command does not require data to be passed,
        /// this object can be set to null.</param>
        /// <returns>True if the command can be executed.</returns>
        public bool CanExecute(object parameter)
        {
            return this.IsEnabled;
        }

        /// <summary>
        /// This is the event that WPF's command architecture listens to so
        /// it knows when to update the UI on command enable/disable.
        /// </summary>
        public event EventHandler CanExecuteChanged;

        #endregion

        /// <summary>
        /// Public visibility of the isEnabled flag - note that when it is
        /// set, need to raise the event so that WPF knows to update
        /// any UI that uses this command.
        /// </summary>
        public bool IsEnabled
        {
            get { return this.isEnabled; }
            set
            {
                this.isEnabled = value;
                this.OnCanExecuteChanged();
```

```
            }
        }

        /// <summary>
        /// Simple event propagation that makes sure someone is
        /// listening to the event before raising it.
        /// </summary>
        private void OnCanExecuteChanged()
        {
            if (this.CanExecuteChanged != null)
            {
                this.CanExecuteChanged(this, EventArgs.Empty);
            }
        }
    }
}
```

As advertised, the real power of this class is that, when its `Execute` method is called, it calls the delegate method that was passed in via the constructor. The reason why this is so powerful is that I can define the method handler for the delegate right inside of my ViewModel class, which keeps all of the presentation logic glue right where I want it.

So going back to the `SelectProjectViewModel` class, here are the handler methods for the two `DelegateCommand` properties.

```
private void SelectCommandHandler(object sender, EventArgs e)
{
    Project project = this.projects.CurrentItem as Project;
    UserSession.CurrentProject = project;
    this.view.Close();
}

private void CancelCommandHandler(object sender, EventArgs e)
{
    this.view.Close();
}
```

The handler for the `SelectCommand` property is a true example of why the ViewModel shines. Instead of having to talk to an element on the UI to know which project was selected, it simply asks the `CollectionView` for its `CurrentItem` property to get the selected project. This is made possible by the default two-way binding in the XAML, which I will show shortly. The handler method then sets the `CurrentProject` property of the application layer's `UserSession` class. Then, since its work is done, it tells the View to go away via the `Close` method of the `IView` interface.

The handler for the `CancelCommand` property is much simpler. It simply tells the View to close itself via the `IView` interface.

Now that the ViewModel class for the use case `SelectProjectViewModel` has been detailed, it's time to look at how the View actually uses it and communicates with it. The View class, `SelectProjectView`, has very little code behind in it. The only code that I wrote for it was in the constructor for wiring up the `DataContext` property of the form's `Window` element.

```
using System;
using System.Windows;
using System.Windows.Controls;
using SmartCA.Presentation.ViewModels;

namespace SmartCA.Presentation.Views
{
    public partial class SelectProjectView : Window, IView
    {
        public SelectProjectView()
        {
            this.InitializeComponent();
            this.DataContext = new SelectProjectViewModel(this);
        }
    }
}
```

The first thing to notice is that I added the implementation of the `IView` interface to the class. This was easy since the `System.Windows.Window` class already implemented the `Close` and `Show` methods. Then, in the constructor, after the auto-generated call to `InitializeComponent`, I set the `Window`'s `DataContext` property to the `SelectProjectViewModel` class, passing in the `Window` instance (`this`) as the `IView` instance expected in `SelectProjectViewModel`'s constructor. Finally, the form is wired up for data binding to the ViewModel.

The XAML markup for the View contains the ComboBox declaration, a few Label declarations, as well as a few Button declarations.

```
<Window x:Class="SmartCA.Presentation.Views.SelectProjectView"
    xmlns="http://schemas.microsoft.com/winfx/2006/xaml/presentation"
    xmlns:x="http://schemas.microsoft.com/winfx/2006/xaml"
    xmlns:vm="clr-namespace:SmartCA.Presentation.ViewModels"
    Title="SelectProjectView" Height="300" Width="437"
    Background="{DynamicResource FormBackgroundBrush}">
    <Grid>
    <ComboBox  Height="26" Margin="175.993333333333,98,28.006666666667,0"
         Name="projectsComboBox" VerticalAlignment="Top"
         IsSynchronizedWithCurrentItem="True"
         TextSearch.TextPath="Name"
         ItemsSource="{Binding Path=Projects}" IsTextSearchEnabled="True"
         IsEditable="True">
         <ComboBox.ItemTemplate>
              <DataTemplate>
                   <Grid ShowGridLines="True" >
                        <Grid.ColumnDefinitions>
                             <ColumnDefinition Width="50" />
                             <ColumnDefinition />
                        </Grid.ColumnDefinitions>
                        <TextBlock Grid.Column="0" Text="{Binding
Path=Number}"/>
                       <TextBlock Grid.Column="1" Text="{Binding Path=Name}" />
                   </Grid>
              </DataTemplate>
```

```
      <ComboBox.ItemTemplate>
      </ComboBox>
      <Label Margin="47,42,0,0" Name="selectProjectLabel"
           Style="{StaticResource boldLabelStyle}"
           VerticalAlignment="Top" HorizontalAlignment="Left"
           Width="153">Please select a Project...</Label>
      <Label Margin="47,98.04,0,0" Name="projectLabel"
           Style="{StaticResource boldLabelStyle}">Project:</Label>
      <Button Margin="47,0,0,35" Name="cancelButton"
           Command="{Binding Path=CancelCommand}" Style="{StaticResource baseButton}"
           HorizontalAlignment="Left" VerticalAlignment="Bottom">Cancel</Button>
      <Button Margin="0,0,28.006666666667,35" Name="okButton"
           Command="{Binding Path=SelectCommand}" Style="{StaticResource baseButton}"
           HorizontalAlignment="Right" VerticalAlignment="Bottom">OK</Button>
    </Grid>
  </Window>
```

The first interesting thing to note about the ComboBox declaration is that it is bound to the `Projects CollectionView` property of the `SelectProjectViewModel`, and that its `IsSynchronizedWithCurrentItem` property is set to `True`. What this means is that whenever I change a selection in the ComboBox, I can always get the item selected from the `CollectionView` in the ViewModel to which it is bound, in this case the `Projects` property. The way I get that is by checking the `SelectedItem` property of that `CollectionView`. That is cool because I do not need to be tightly coupled to the UI elements in the ViewModel; data binding takes care of giving me the state that I need.

The next interesting thing about the ComboBox declaration is its use of a `DataTemplate` element to format how the dropdown will be displayed. In this case, the dropdown will show two columns instead of one, and each one of the columns is bound to properties of the child `Property` objects via the `Path` property of the `Binding` declaration. What's nice about using this pattern is that I can make the code for the UI View be more declarative, that is, keep most of it in XAML, and really get a good separation between the View and the Model, while at the same time take advantage of WPF's binding features to reduce the amount of code that I would have had to write to do this manually.

Summary

I covered quite a bit of ground in this chapter. I started out by designing the Visual Studio solution that will be used throughout the rest of the book, and then began the design for the four architectural layers, which were the application, domain, infrastructure, and presentation layers. In designing and implementing the layers, I introduced a few patterns that will be used throughout the book, such as the Layered Supertype pattern, the Separated Interface pattern, and the Model-View-ViewModel pattern. Also, when talking about the domain layer, I covered some very important Domain-Driven Design terms, which will be used throughout the remainder of the book.

I also wrote some code in this chapter! I started writing code for the infrastructure layer with the Layered Supertype implementation, followed by the Repository Framework and the Entity Factory Framework, and ending with the Model-View-ViewModel pattern implementation for the presentation layer. Overall, there is a good foundation on which to build for the rest of the application.

3

Managing Projects

Since I have just built the application architecture, it is time to start implementing the functionality of the application. Actually, the application architecture is not fully developed yet; in fact, I will probably refactor parts of it based on the needs of the application as I go along. In last chapter's example of a View and a ViewModel, I introduced what I will be talking about this chapter, the SmartCA's concept of Projects. I intentionally did not show you the `Project` class because that is the focus of this chapter. I will also be talking about the concept of Contractors and how they relate to Projects.

The Problem

Smart Design is an architectural, engineering, and interior design firm that is known for its expertise in the design and construction of complex facilities, such as hospitals and universities. Because they are involved from beginning to end in the construction projects, they are, by default, the "general contractor," meaning that they are the ones in charge of making sure that the facilities are built properly, according to both customer's and government's specifications. In order to carry out this large responsibility, they must manage several other parties involved in carrying out their architectural and engineering plans. This usually involves a lot of administration, mostly for keeping track of costs, project communications, documentation (such as requests for information, change orders, and proposal requests), and more. This construction administration is designed to ensure that the construction process is in general conformance with the architectural and engineering design documents as well as the applicable codes and standards. It is exactly these types of activities that the SmartCA application is intended to track and manage.

In the SmartCA domain, a Project is the center of all behavior: almost everything in the domain relates to a Project in one way or another. Construction Projects are, after all, what other companies hire Smart Design to do for them. A Project is a part of SmartCA's *core domain*.

The Design

In the SmartCA domain, the purpose of a Project is to bring together and manage all of the people involved in the construction process. In the next few sections I will be designing the domain model, determining the Project Aggregate and its boundaries, and designing the repository for Projects.

Designing the Domain Model

Listed below is a drawing showing the Entities that make up the Project Domain:

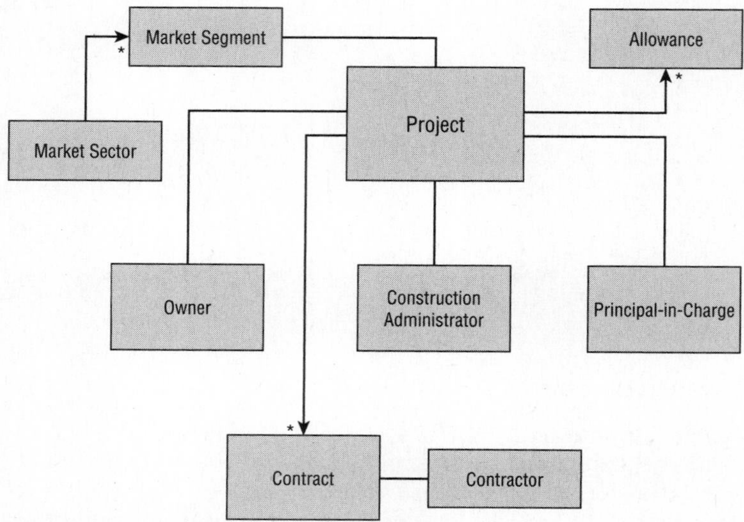

Figure 3.1: The Project Domain and its parts.

As you can see from Figure 3.1, every Project must have an Owner. An Owner is an outside party for whom the Project is being built. Other entities represented in every Project are the Construction Administrator and the Principal-in-Charge. These two roles will always be occupied by Smart Design employees. The Principal-in-Charge is the project director, the person who is ultimately responsible for the success or failure of the Project. The Construction Administrator will be using the SmartCA application the most. This person, and usually their assistant, is the domain expert of a Project.

One of the most important parts of the application is keeping track of the Contracts between Smart Design and the Contractors on the Project. Many of the aspects of the SmartCA application deal in communicating with the Contractors and documenting all of their costs in order to know what the current cost of the Project is and what the estimated cost of the Project will be.

One of the other items that must be tracked about a Project is what Market Segment the construction is for, that is, if it is for a university, a high school, a woman's hospital, and so on. Market Segments belong to Market Sectors, and are a bit more specific than Market Sectors. For example, a high school building would be classified in the education Market Sector, as would a university. A woman's hospital would be classified in the health care Market Sector. This information is later used by Smart Design management to analyze the company's portfolio of projects to identify trends within a particular Market Sector or Segment.

Defining the Project Aggregate

Now that the Project domain model has been designed, I need to design the Project Aggregate with the actual classes that will be used. Figure 3.2 shows a class diagram showing the classes that will be used in the Project Aggregate.

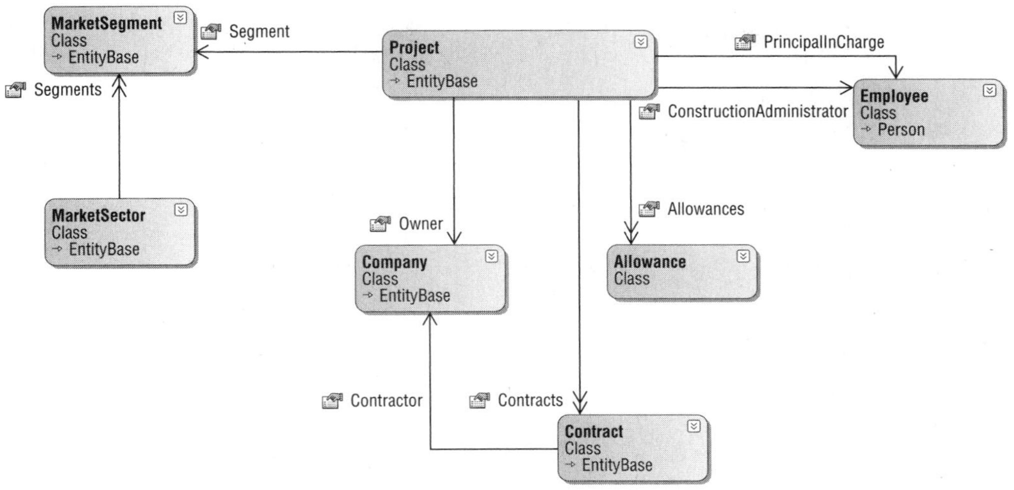

Figure 3.2: Classes constituting the Project Aggregate.

As you can tell from Figure 3.2, the class names are staying true to the model that I created in the previous section. There are some subtle differences though. For example, in the previous diagram, there was an association between the Project entity and the Principal-in-Charge entity. In the class diagram above, the association to Principal-in-Charge is a property on the Project class that is associated with an Employee class. The same pattern follows for the association to Construction Administrator. This is because the `PrincipalInCharge` and `ConstructionAdministrator` properties are both instances of an Employee class. The main idea here is to keep the code as consistent with the model as possible, and to strive to make the code become as easy to read as the model.

Defining the Aggregate Boundaries

Now that I have defined the Project Aggregate, it is time to determine where the boundaries are on this Aggregate. This is very important for when I start to design the Project repository in the next section.

Obviously, all of the classes in this diagram are part of the Project Aggregate, but the Project Aggregate also holds some references to the roots of other Aggregates. Figure 3.3 shows the Aggregate boundaries that I have determined so far in the domain model.

In Figure 3.3, I have identified two additional Aggregate Roots, `Company` and `Employee`. There is definitely a need to get `Company` and `Employee` information outside the context of a `Project`. In the context of a particular `Project`, if I wanted to get some detailed information about the `ConstructionAdministrator`, even though that represents an `Employee` instance, and `Employee` is an Aggregate Root, I would still need to navigate from the `Project` class to the `ConstructionAdministrator` property to get that information. If I just wanted to find some data about an `Employee` not in the context of a `Project`, I would go directly to the `Employee` aggregate itself, via the repository for the `Employee` aggregate. The same concept applies to accessing `Company` information; if you are in the context of a `Project`, for example wanting to find about the `Owner` of a `Project`, then you should go through the `Project` Aggregate's repository, but, if you just need information on a particular `Company` outside the concerns of a `Project`, then go directly to the repository for the `Company` Aggregate.

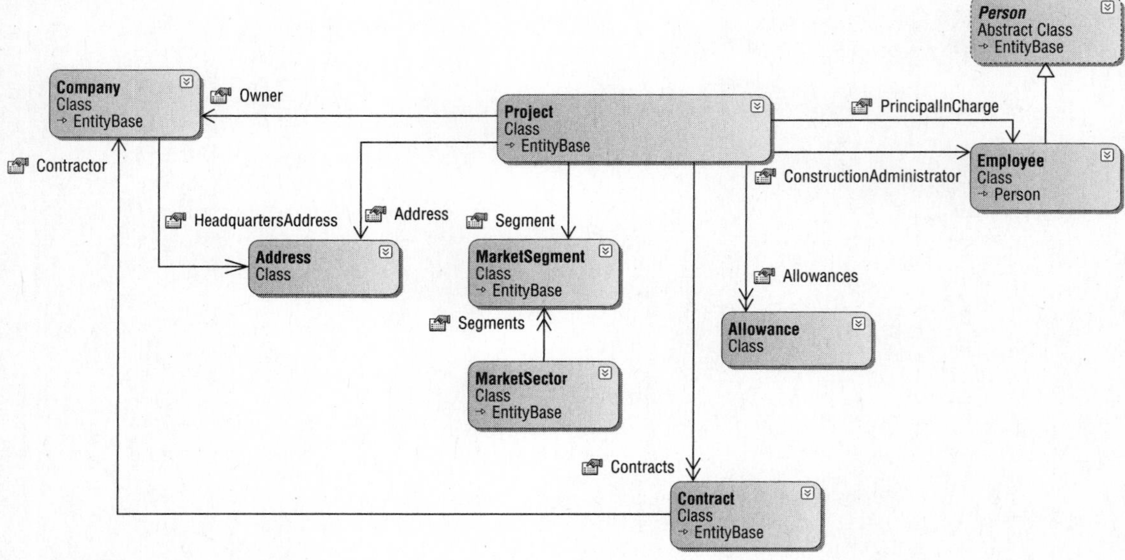

Figure 3.3: The Project Aggregate boundaries.

Designing the Repositories

Since I have just defined the boundaries for the Project Aggregate, identifying the classes that need Repositories is easy. The rule is that each Aggregate Root gets its own repository. Very simply, if a class has been identified as the Entity Root of an Aggregate, then a repository will be made for that class. This means that in the current domain model, we will have three repositories: one for the Project Aggregate, one for the Company Aggregate, and one for the Employee Aggregate (see Figure 3.4).

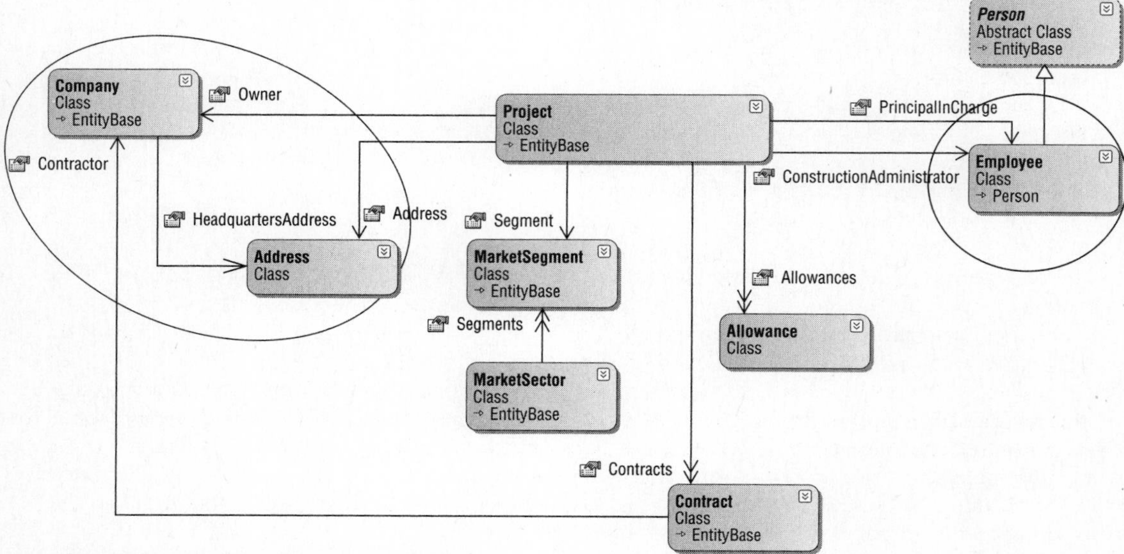

Figure 3.4: The Project Aggregate Repositories.

Because I will be covering Companies in the next chapter, I will not be showing the details of the Company Aggregate nor its respective repository in this chapter.

The IProjectRepository Interface

The `IProjectRepository` interface is the front to instances of Project Repositories. Currently, I have two implementations of this interface, one designed as a mock implementation, and the other one designed as real. As I was developing, I quickly decided that the mock implementations were not really necessary since I was writing to a local SQL CE database anyway, so my tests did not slow down at all. Here is the `IProjectRepository` interface:

```
using System;
using System.Collections.Generic;
using SmartCA.Infrastructure.RepositoryFramework;

namespace SmartCA.Model.Projects
{
    public interface IProjectRepository : IRepository<Project>
    {
        IList<Project> FindBy(IList<MarketSegment> segments, bool completed);
        Project FindBy(string projectNumber);
        IList<MarketSegment> FindAllMarketSegments();
    }
}
```

Notice how the `IProjectRepository` interface implements the `IRepository<T>` interface. This functionality is all handled by the `RepositoryBase<T>` class and the `SqlCeRepositoryBase<T>` class, which I showed in Chapter 2.

The IEmployeeRepository Interface

The `IEmployeeRepository` interface is the interface for instances of Employee Repositories. Here is the `IEmployeeRepository` interface:

```
using System;
using System.Collections.Generic;
using SmartCA.Infrastructure.RepositoryFramework;

namespace SmartCA.Model.Employees
{
    public interface IEmployeeRepository : IRepository<Employee>
    {
        IList<Employee> GetConstructionAdministrators();
        IList<Employee> GetPrincipals();
    }
}
```

Just like the `IProjectRepository` interface, the `IEmployeeRepository` interface also implements the `IRepository<T>` interface.

Writing the Unit Tests

Before implementing the solution for managing Projects, I am going to write some unit tests for what I expect of the Project and Employee repository implementations. I am not going to write any tests, yet, for the Project and Employee classes, just for their respective Repositories. You may be wondering how I can write these tests when the classes do not even exist yet. Since I have written the interfaces for these Repositories, and since I also have a Repository Factory implemented, I can write test code against the interfaces. The tests will fail, and that is what I expect. After the code is written for the repository implementations later on in the Solution section, then the tests should pass. The goal is to write code in the Solution section that will ultimately make the unit tests pass.

Setting Up the Unit Tests Project

For all of my unit tests, I have decided to use Visual Studio Team System (VSTS) to create my unit test projects. There is an excellent project template for doing this, and it is fairly straightforward. I simply add a new project to my Visual Studio solution, and choose "Test Project," as shown in Figure 3.5.

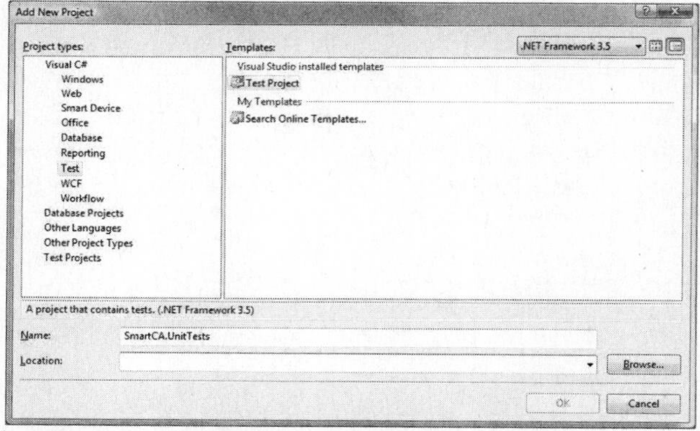

Figure 3.5: Creating the Visual Studio test project.

The next thing to do is to delete the default `UnitTest1.cs` file and create a real unit test file. In order to make things a little better organized, I have created folders in my test project for both Projects and Employees (see Figure 3.6).

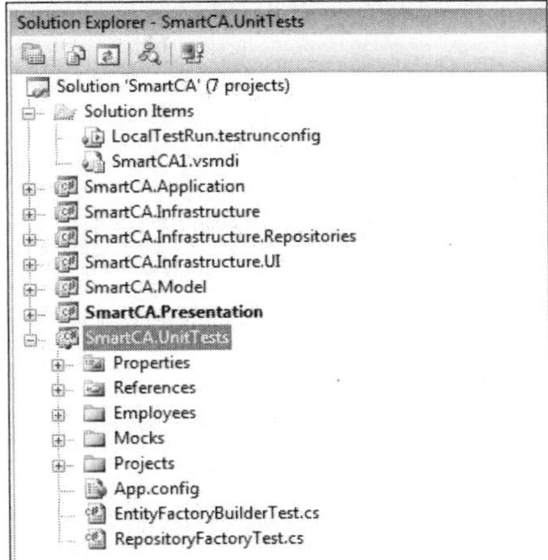

Figure 3.6: The SmartCA.UnitTests Project with folders.

The IProjectRepository Unit Tests

In order to get a jump start on writing the unit tests for the `IProjectRepository` interface, I use the VSTS New Unit Test Wizard to write test stubs automatically for each method in the `IProjectRepository` interface that I choose to test (see Figure 3.7).

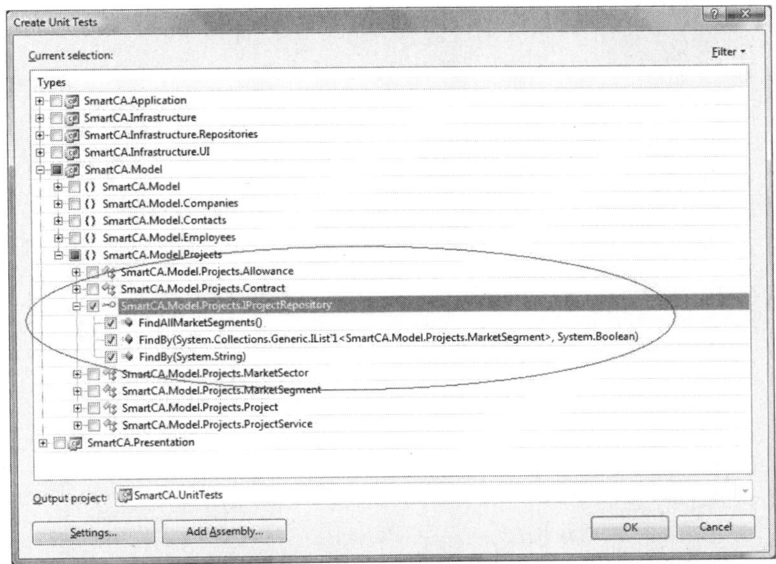

Figure 3.7: Creating Unit Tests for the IProjectRepository interface.

The next step is to modify the file created to use the `RepositoryFactory` class to build instances of the `IProjectRepository` interface. I have created a private class field for the unit test class to hold this reference, and I initialize it in the `MyTestInitialize` method of the unit test class. Here are the declarations for the private class fields:

```
using SmartCA.Infrastructure.Repositories;
using Microsoft.VisualStudio.TestTools.UnitTesting;
using SmartCA.Model.Projects;
using System.Collections.Generic;
using SmartCA.Infrastructure.RepositoryFramework;
using SmartCA.Infrastructure;

namespace SmartCA.UnitTests
{
    /// <summary>
    ///This is a test class for ProjectRepositoryTest and is intended
    ///to contain all ProjectRepositoryTest Unit Tests
    ///</summary>
    [TestClass()]
    public class ProjectRepositoryTest
    {
        private TestContext testContextInstance;
        private UnitOfWork unitOfWork;
        private IProjectRepository repository;
```

As you can see, I am also using a `UnitOfWork` private field (`unitOfWork`), and a `TestContext` private field (`testContextInstance`). The `testContextInstance` field was added automatically by the Visual Studio Wizard.

The next step is to initialize these fields in the `MyTestInitialize` method:

```
        /// <summary>
        /// Use TestInitialize to run code before running each test
        /// </summary>
        [TestInitialize()]
        public void MyTestInitialize()
        {
            this.unitOfWork = new UnitOfWork();
            this.repository = RepositoryFactory.GetRepository<IProjectRepository,
                Project>(this.unitOfWork);
        }
```

The code to create the `IProjectRepository` interface instance should look familiar to you, since I just covered that in the last chapter.

Now that the initialization is taken care of, it is time to fix the unit test methods that the Visual Studio Wizard generated.

The FindBySegmentsAndNotCompletedTest Method

The purpose of this test is to verify that I can query the `IProjectRepository` interface for all Projects that match the given Market Segments but have not been completed.

```
/// <summary>
///A test for FindBy(object sector, object segment, bool completed)
///</summary>
[DeploymentItem("SmartCA.sdf"), TestMethod()]
public void FindBySegmentsAndNotCompletedTest()
{
    // Create a list of Market Segments
    List<MarketSegment> segments = new List<MarketSegment>();
    segments.Add(new MarketSegment(1, null, "test", "test"));

    // Pass the Market Segments into the FindBy method, and
    // specify Projects that have NOT completed yet
    IList<Project> projects = this.repository.FindBy(segments, false);

    // Make sure there is one project that matches the criteria
    Assert.AreEqual(1, projects.Count);
}
```

The first thing to notice about this method is how it is decorated with the two different attributes, the `DeploymentItem` attribute and the `TestMethod` attribute. The `DeploymentItem` attribute lets the VSTS test host know to copy the `SmartCA.sdf` SQL CE project file to the output directory of the unit test project. This is important because otherwise I would not be able to connect to the database in the test. The `TestMethod` attribute lets VSTS know that this is a unit test, and it will be recognized as such by the VSTS unit testing UI.

This test code starts out by creating a dummy `MarketSegment` instance and adds it to a generic List of type `MarketSegment`. I then pass the list of Market Segments into the `IProjectRepository`'s overloaded `FindBy` method to have an `IList` of type `Project` returned. The test occurs on the last line, when I assert that there should be one Project returned from the `IProjectRepository` method. If the assertion is true, then the test will pass. As of this point in the chapter, this test (and all others in this class) should fail because I have not written the `IProjectRepository` implementation, yet.

The FindByProjectNumberTest Method

This method validates the ability to get a Project instance based on the Number of a Project:

```
/// <summary>
///A test for FindBy(string projectNumber)
///</summary>
[DeploymentItem("SmartCA.sdf"), TestMethod()]
public void FindByProjectNumberTest()
{
    // The Project Number
    string projectNumber = "12345.00";

    // Try to get the Project
    Project project = this.repository.FindBy(projectNumber);

    // Verify the Project is there and is the right one
    Assert.AreEqual("My Project", project.Name);
}
```

The method first starts out by initializing a Project Number string value. It then passes that value to the `IProjectRepository` in order to retrieve a Project with that particular Number value. Once the `Project` instance is returned from the repository, the Project's name is validated.

The FindAllMarketSegmentsTest Method

This method tests the last method on the `IProjectRepository` interface, the `FindAllMarketSegments` method:

```
/// <summary>
///A test for FindAllMarketSegments()
///</summary>
[DeploymentItem("SmartCA.sdf"), TestMethod()]
public void FindAllMarketSegmentsTest()
{
    // Get the list of all Market Segments
    IList<MarketSegment> segments =
        this.repository.FindAllMarketSegments();

    // Make sure there is at least one item in the list
    Assert.AreEqual(true, segments.Count > 0);
}
```

The code for this method is pretty straightforward; it simply calls the `IProjectRepository` interface to get the list of all Market Segments and then asserts that at least one has been returned.

The IEmployeeRepository Unit Tests

There are only two tests necessary for the `IEmployeeRepository`, and those are the tests for the `GetConstructionAdministrators` method and the `GetPrincipals` method. I am not going to go over the steps for creating the `EmployeeRepositoryTest` class; the steps are exactly the same as those I just outlined for the `IProjectRepository` unit tests.

The GetPrincipalsTest Method

This method tests the `GetPrincipals` method of the `IEmployeeRepository` interface:

```
/// <summary>
///A test for GetPrincipals
///</summary>
[TestMethod()]
public void GetPrincipalsTest()
{
    // Get the list of all Principals
    IList<Employee> principals = this.repository.GetPrincipals();

    // Make sure there is at least one item in the list
    Assert.AreEqual(true, principals.Count > 0);
}
```

This method is very similar to the `FindAllMarketSegmentsTest` method on the `ProjectRepositoryTest` class shown previously. It just validates that at least one `Employee` instance was returned from the `GetPrincipals` method of the `IEmployeeRepository` interface.

The GetConstructionAdministratorsTest Method

The code for this test is almost identical to the last test, only this time I am testing the `GetConstructionAdministrators` method of the `IEmployeeRepository` interface:

```
        /// <summary>
        ///A test for GetConstructionAdministrators
        ///</summary>
        [DeploymentItem("SmartCA.sdf"), TestMethod()]
        public void GetConstructionAdministratorsTest()
        {
            // Get the list of all Construction Administrators
            IList<Employee> administrators =
                this.repository.GetConstructionAdministrators();

            // Make sure there is at least one item in the list
            Assert.AreEqual(true, administrators.Count > 0);
        }
```

This method validates that at least one `Employee` instance was returned from the `GetConstructionAdministrators` method.

The Solution

Now that the design is in place for the Project domain model, the Project Aggregate has been defined and its boundaries have been determined, and the Repositories have been designed with their associated tests, it is time to start the code implementation. In this section, I will be implementing these designs, as well as implementing the ViewModel and the View for Projects.

The Project Class

Currently, the Project class does not have any behavior. It only contains data at the moment, but this will change as I get further into the domain model. One of the things that should jump out at you about the Project class is that there is no persistence code in it, no code that calls any file operations, database operations, and the like. It is a Plain-Old CLR Object (POCO), and because of this it helps me to focus on the domain logic of a Project rather than worrying about persistence-related things. Those types of concerns will be left to the infrastructure layer.

The Private Fields and Constructors

Here are the private fields and constructors for the `Project` class:

```
using System;
using System.Collections.Generic;
using SmartCA.Infrastructure.DomainBase;
using SmartCA.Model.Companies;
using SmartCA.Model.Employees;

namespace SmartCA.Model.Projects
```

(continued)

(continued)

```
{
    public class Project : EntityBase
    {
        #region Private Fields

        private string number;
        private string name;
        private Address address;
        private Company owner;
        private Employee constructionAdministrator;
        private Employee principalInCharge;
        private DateTime? contractDate;
        private DateTime? estimatedStartDate;
        private DateTime? estimatedCompletionDate;
        private DateTime? adjustedCompletionDate;
        private DateTime? currentCompletionDate;
        private DateTime? actualCompletionDate;
        private decimal contingencyAllowanceAmount;
        private decimal testingAllowanceAmount;
        private decimal utilityAllowanceAmount;
        private decimal originalConstructionCost;
        private int totalChangeOrderDays;
        private decimal adjustedConstructionCost;
        private decimal totalChangeOrdersAmount;
        private int totalSquareFeet;
        private int percentComplete;
        private string remarks;
        private decimal aeChangeOrderAmount;
        private string contractReason;
        private string agencyApplicationNumber;
        private string agencyFileNumber;
        private MarketSegment segment;
        private List<Allowance> allowances;
        private List<Contract> contracts;

        #endregion

        #region Constructors

        public Project(string number, string name)
            : this(null, number, name)
        {
        }

        public Project(object key, string number, string name)
            : base(key)
        {
            this.number = number;
            this.name = name;
            this.address = null;
            this.owner = new Company();
            this.constructionAdministrator = null;
            this.principalInCharge = null;
```

```
        this.contractDate = null;
        this.estimatedStartDate = null;
        this.estimatedCompletionDate = null;
        this.currentCompletionDate = null;
        this.actualCompletionDate = null;
        this.contingencyAllowanceAmount = 0;
        this.testingAllowanceAmount = 0;
        this.utilityAllowanceAmount = 0;
        this.originalConstructionCost = 0;
        this.totalChangeOrderDays = 0;
        this.adjustedConstructionCost = 0;
        this.totalChangeOrdersAmount = 0;
        this.totalSquareFeet = 0;
        this.percentComplete = 0;
        this.remarks = string.Empty;
        this.aeChangeOrderAmount = 0;
        this.contractReason = string.Empty;
        this.agencyApplicationNumber = string.Empty;
        this.agencyFileNumber = string.Empty;
        this.segment = null;
        this.allowances = new List<Allowance>();
        this.contracts = new List<Contract>();
    }

    #endregion
```

Since the `Project` class is an Entity, it inherits from the `EntityBase` type. Again, this is not to give the `Project` class any type of infrastructure functionality from its base class, it is merely to eliminate the duplicate code of having to decorate every `Entity` class with an `Id` property. This was mentioned before in Chapter 2, and it is my implementation of a Layer Supertype.

When analyzing the constructors for the Project class, you will notice that there are two overloads, one that requires a key value and one that does not. I used the two overloads because sometimes I may be loading an existing `Project` from a data store, and other times I may be creating a new `Project` that does not yet exist in the data store. When loading from the data store, I will use the key value to retrieve the `Project`.

The Properties

Currently, the `Project` class has several properties, which may make it a candidate to be split up into further classes later.

The Name and Number Properties

The first two properties, `Name` and `Number`, are actually read-only:

```
    public string Number
    {
        get { return this.number; }
    }

    public string Name
    {
        get { return this.name; }
    }
```

This means that once a number and name have been assigned to a `Project`, they cannot be changed. To change the name or number, you must delete the old `Project` instance and create a new one. The project number and project name are very important parts of a `Project`; many other parts of the application will refer to these properties later. Currently, the only way to set these values of the class is through the constructor.

Since C# 2.0, it is possible to add a private or protected set accessor to properties, but I have decided not to do that because right now I do not need it.

The Address Property

The next property, `Address`, actually represents a Value Object type.

```
public Address Address
{
    get { return this.address; }
    set { this.address = value; }
}
```

Since address information will be used on several other objects, it was put into its own class, so I only had to write the code for address information once. This class is a Value Object type because it has no conceptual identity that the SmartCA domain model cares about; it is simply holding the atomic value of an address.

Please do not confuse the term Value Object with a .NET Value type. .NET Value types are data types such as integers and DateTime structures. Strictly speaking in .NET terms, a Value Object is still a Reference type. In the Address example, the `Address` *class is a Value Object in DDD terms, but in .NET terms it is still a Reference type.*

A nice consequence of making the `Address` class a Value Object is that I do not have to write any code to track its identity. Here is the code for the `Address` class:

```
using System;

namespace SmartCA.Model
{
    /// <summary>
    /// This is an immutable Value class.
    /// </summary>
    public class Address
    {
        private string street;
        private string city;
        private string state;
        private string postalCode;

        public Address(string street, string city, string state, string postalCode)
        {
            this.street = street;
            this.city = city;
            this.state = state;
            this.postalCode = postalCode;
        }

        public string Street
```

```
        {
            get { return this.street; }
        }

        public string City
        {
            get { return this.city; }
        }

        public string State
        {
            get { return this.state; }
        }

        public string PostalCode
        {
            get { return this.postalCode; }
        }
    }
}
```

The interesting thing about this class is that it is immutable. What this means is that once it is created, it can never be changed. This is exactly how the .NET Framework's `System.String` class behaves, also. When I change the value of a `String`, or call a method on the `String` class to modify the `String`, I get an entirely new `String` returned to me. According to Eric Evans, if a class meets the requirements to be a Value Object, it should be conceptually whole (Evans, *Domain-Driven Design, Tackling Complexity in the Heart of Software*, 99). In the case of the class, it is conceptually whole and cannot be changed; it can only be copied or have new instances of it created.

In order to make sure that the address data from the constructor is valid, I have added some validation code to the `Address` class to make sure that only valid `Address` instances will be created:

```
using System;

namespace SmartCA.Model
{
    /// <summary>
    /// This is an immutable Value class.
    /// </summary>
    public class Address
    {
        private string street;
        private string city;
        private string state;
        private string postalCode;

        public Address(string street, string city, string state, string postalCode)
        {
            this.street = street;
            this.city = city;
```

(continued)

(continued)

```
                this.state = state;
                this.postalCode = postalCode;
                this.Validate();
            }

            public string Street
            {
                get { return this.street; }
            }

            public string City
            {
                get { return this.city; }
            }

            public string State
            {
                get { return this.state; }
            }

            public string PostalCode
            {
                get { return this.postalCode; }
            }

            private void Validate()
            {
                if (string.IsNullOrEmpty(this.street) ||
                    string.IsNullOrEmpty(this.city) ||
                    string.IsNullOrEmpty(this.state) ||
                    string.IsNullOrEmpty(this.postalCode))
                {
                    throw new InvalidOperationException("Invalid address.");
                }
            }
        }
    }
```

Later, when I write the ViewModel for editing `Projects`, I will show a strategy for how to change the `Project`'s `Address` property value from the UI.

The Owner Property

The next property, `Owner`, represents a `Company` instance. A `Company` is an Entity that is also the root of its own Aggregate. This is not a problem, as we are only referring to the `Company` instance (`Owner`), and all information requested about the `Company` instance will need to go through its respective repository. I will show how I deal with this later in the chapter when looking at the repositories for the Aggregate Roots.

The code for `Company` is very simple right now, and following the principle of YAGNI (You Ain't Gonna Need It) (Wikipedia -`http://en.wikipedia.org/wiki/You_Ain't_Gonna_Need_It`), it only contains the code we need for the moment.

```
using System;
using SmartCA.Infrastructure.DomainBase;

namespace SmartCA.Model.Companies
{
    public class Company : EntityBase
    {
        private string name;
        private string abbreviation;
        private Address address;

        public Company()
            : this(null)
        {
        }

        public Company(object key)
            : base(key)
        {
        }

        public string Name
        {
            get { return this.name; }
            set { this.name = value; }
        }

        public string Abbreviation
        {
            get { return this.abbreviation; }
            set { this.abbreviation = value; }
        }

        public Address HeadquartersAddress
        {
            get { return this.address; }
            set { this.address = value; }
        }
    }
}
```

The main note of interest in the `Company` class is that it is using the immutable `Address` class also being used by the `Project` class. This is great because we are getting immediate reuse of the `Address` class.

The ConstructionAdministrator and PrincipalInCharge Properties

The `ConstructionAdministrator` and `PrincipalInCharge` properties are both instances of the `Employee` class, which is also the root of its own Aggregate.

```
using System;

namespace SmartCA.Model.Employees
{
    public class Employee : Person
```

(continued)

(continued)

```
    {
        private string jobTitle;

        public Employee(object key)
            : this(key, string.Empty, string.Empty)
        {
        }

        public Employee(object key, string firstName, string lastName)
            : base(key, firstName, lastName)
        {
            this.jobTitle = string.Empty;
        }

        public string JobTitle
        {
            get { return this.jobTitle; }
            set { this.jobTitle = value; }
        }
    }
}
```

The interesting thing to notice about the `Employee` class is that it inherits from the `Person` class. The `Person` class is mainly to share common properties for some of the classes coming up in later chapters that are also people, such as `Contacts`.

```
using System;
using SmartCA.Infrastructure.DomainBase;

namespace SmartCA.Model
{
    public abstract class Person : EntityBase
    {
        private string firstName;
        private string lastName;
        private string initials;

        protected Person()
            : this(null)
        {
        }

        protected Person(object key)
            : this(key, string.Empty, string.Empty)
        {
        }

        protected Person(object key, string firstName, string lastName)
            : base(key)
        {
            this.firstName = firstName;
            this.lastName = lastName;
            this.initials = string.Empty;
        }
```

```
        public string FirstName
        {
            get { return this.firstName; }
            set { this.firstName = value; }
        }

        public string LastName
        {
            get { return this.lastName; }
            set { this.lastName = value; }
        }

        public string Initials
        {
            get { return this.initials; }
            set { this.initials = value; }
        }
    }
}
```

The main thing to note about the `Person` class is that it is abstract, that is, it cannot be created directly. I really just wanted this class to reuse some of the property code, but who knows, later on having it as an abstract class might turn out to be useful in other ways via polymorphism.

The Segment Property

The next property in the `Project` class, `Segment`, represents what market segment the Project is in:

```
using System;
using SmartCA.Infrastructure.DomainBase;

namespace SmartCA.Model.Projects
{
    public class MarketSegment : EntityBase
    {
        private MarketSector parentSector;
        private string name;
        private string code;

        public MarketSegment(MarketSector parentSector, string name, string code)
            : this(null, parentSector, name, code)
        {
        }

        public MarketSegment(object key, MarketSector parentSector, string name,
            string code) : base(key)
        {
            this.parentSector = parentSector;
            this.name = name;
            this.code = code;
        }

        public string Name
```

(continued)

(continued)

```
        {
            get { return this.name; }
            set { this.name = value; }
        }

        public string Code
        {
            get { return this.code; }
            set { this.code = value; }
        }

        public MarketSector ParentSector
        {
            get { return this.parentSector; }
        }
    }
}
```

The `MarketSegment` class holds a reference to the market sector in which it belongs, and this relationship is represented by the `ParentSector` property.

```
using System;
using System.Collections.Generic;
using SmartCA.Infrastructure.DomainBase;

namespace SmartCA.Model.Projects
{
    public class MarketSector : EntityBase
    {
        private string name;
        private List<MarketSegment> segments;

        public MarketSector(string name)
            : this(null, name)
        {
            this.name = name;
        }

        public MarketSector(object key, string name)
            : base(key)
        {
            this.name = name;
            this.segments = new List<MarketSegment>();
        }

        public string Name
        {
            get { return this.name; }
            set { this.name = value; }
        }
```

```
        public IList<MarketSegment> Segments
        {
            get { return this.segments; }
        }
    }
}
```

As you can see in the code for the `MarketSector` class, there is a bidirectional relationship between `MarketSegment` and `MarketSector`. `MarketSector` can contain zero or more `MarketSegment` instances, and `MarketSegment` refers to the appropriate market sector via its `MarketSector` property.

The ContingencyAllowanceAmount, TestingAllowanceAmount, and UtilityAllowanceAmount Properties

You may notice in the `Project` class that there are properties for `ContingencyAllowanceAmount`, `TestingAllowanceAmount`, and `UtilityAllowanceAmount`, and also one called `Allowances`. The first three are of type `System.Decimal` (for money), and the last one, `Allowances`, is an `IList<Allowance>`, which is just a list of name-value pairs of allowance names and allowance amounts. This gives the Construction Administrator the flexibility to have other allowance amounts without having to have them be hard-coded into the `Project` class.

```
using System;

namespace SmartCA.Model.Projects
{
    public class Allowance
    {
        private string title;
        private decimal amount;

        public Allowance(string title, decimal amount)
        {
            this.title = title;
            this.amount = amount;
        }

        public string Title
        {
            get { return this.title; }
        }

        public decimal Amount
        {
            get { return this.amount; }
        }
    }
}
```

Hopefully, from the code above you can ascertain that the `Allowance` class is a `Value` class. Because of its read-only properties and constructor, it has been made immutable. Just as with the other `Value` classes, the only way to change its value is to create another instance of the class.

The Contracts Property

The `Contracts` property represents a list of Contract types. The contract represents an agreement between the main or general contractor, in this case Smart Design, and another contractor:

```
using System;
using SmartCA.Infrastructure.DomainBase;
using SmartCA.Model.Companies;

namespace SmartCA.Model.Projects
{
    public class Contract : EntityBase
    {
        private Company contractor;
        private string scopeOfWork;
        private string bidPackageNumber;
        private DateTime? contractDate;
        private DateTime? noticeToProceedDate;
        private decimal contractAmount;

        public Contract()
            : this(null)
        {
        }

        public Contract(object key)
            : base(key)
        {
            this.contractor = new Company();
            this.scopeOfWork = string.Empty;
            this.bidPackageNumber = string.Empty;
            this.contractAmount = 0;
        }

        public Company Contractor
        {
            get { return this.contractor; }
            set { this.contractor = value; }
        }

        public string ScopeOfWork
        {
            get { return this.scopeOfWork; }
            set { this.scopeOfWork = value; }
        }

        public string BidPackageNumber
```

```
        {
            get { return this.bidPackageNumber; }
            set { this.bidPackageNumber = value; }
        }

        public DateTime? ContractDate
        {
            get { return this.contractDate; }
            set { this.contractDate = value; }
        }

        public DateTime? NoticeToProceedDate
        {
            get { return this.noticeToProceedDate; }
            set { this.noticeToProceedDate = value; }
        }

        public decimal ContractAmount
        {
            get { return this.contractAmount; }
            set { this.contractAmount = value; }
        }
    }
}
```

As you can see, the `Contract` class contains the scope of work to be performed, how much the work will cost, when the contract is in effect, and when the contractor can start the work. The `BidPackageNumber` property allows the Contract to be tied back to the original bid for the work. Most important, the class contains a `Contractor` property, which represents the instance of the `Company` doing the work. More will be covered on the `Company` class in the next chapter.

The Repository Implementations

The next code to start writing is for the repositories. In this section I will be writing the code for the Project and Employee repositories.

The Project Repository

In order to implement the concrete `ProjectRepository` class, I just need to inherit from `SqlCeRepositoryBase<T>`, and also implement the `IProjectRepository` interface that I showed earlier in the Design section:

```
namespace SmartCA.Infrastructure.Repositories
{
    public class ProjectRepository : SqlCeRepositoryBase<Project>,
        IProjectRepository
    {
...
```

Refactoring the FindAll and FindBy Methods

During the process of writing the code for the `ProjectRepository` class and testing the Repository Framework, I noticed a nice refactoring I could do by putting the `FindAll` method inside of the `IRepository` interface:

```
using System;
using SmartCA.Infrastructure.DomainBase;
using System.Collections.Generic;

namespace SmartCA.Infrastructure.RepositoryFramework
{
    public interface IRepository<T> where T : EntityBase
    {
        T FindBy(object key);
        IList<T> FindAll();
        void Add(T item);
        T this[object key] { get; set; }
        void Remove(T item);
    }
}
```

To implement the `FindAll` method, I put in an abstract method in the `RepositoryBase<T>` class and then did an override of the method in the `SqlCeRepositoryBase<T>` class. Here is the signature in `RepositoryBase<T>`:

```
public abstract IList<T> FindAll();
```

Here is the implementation in the `SqlCeRepositoryBase<T>` class:

```
        public override IList<T> FindAll()
        {
            StringBuilder builder = this.GetBaseQueryBuilder();
            builder.Append(";");
            return this.BuildEntitiesFromSql(builder.ToString());
        }
```

The `baseQuery` variable is a private string variable in the `SqlCeRepositoryBase<T>` class that I have added. It gets set by an abstract Template Method, `GetBaseQuery()`, which returns a string:

```
protected abstract string GetBaseQuery();
```

This allows all of the derived `SqlCeRepositoryBase<T>` classes to define their own base queries for their respective Aggregates. The `GetBaseQuery()` method is called from the constructor of `SqlCeRepositoryBase<T>`:

```
        protected SqlCeRepositoryBase(IUnitOfWork unitOfWork)
            : base(unitOfWork)
        {
            this.database = DatabaseFactory.CreateDatabase();
            this.entityFactory = EntityFactoryBuilder.BuildFactory<T>();
```

```
        this.childCallbacks = new Dictionary<string, AppendChildData>();
        this.BuildChildCallbacks();
        this.baseQuery = this.GetBaseQuery();
    }
```

I also noticed another refactoring opportunity, and that was to change the `FindBy` method in `SqlCeRepositoryBase<T>` from abstract to an implemented public method. Here was the old signature for the method in the `SqlCeRepositoryBase<T>` class:

```
public abstract T FindBy(object key);
```

Here is the new implementation of the method in the `SqlCeRepositoryBase<T>` class:

```
    public override T FindBy(object key)
    {
        StringBuilder builder = this.GetBaseQueryBuilder();
        builder.Append(this.BuildBaseWhereClause(key));
        return this.BuildEntityFromSql(builder.ToString());
    }
```

The `BuildBaseWhereClause` method is a private method in the `SqlCeRepositoryBase<T>` class:

```
    protected virtual string BuildBaseWhereClause(object key)
    {
        return string.Format(this.baseWhereClause, key);
    }
```

This method uses the private string variable, `baseWhereClause`, in the `SqlCeRepositoryBase<T>` class to substitute in a key value for the Aggregate's base query. It is set by another abstract Template Method, `GetBaseWhereClause()`, which returns a string, just like `GetBaseQuery()`:

```
protected abstract string GetBaseWhereClause();
```

This also allows all of the derived `SqlCeRepositoryBase<T>` classes to define their own `where` clauses for their respective Aggregate queries. The `GetBaseWhereClause()` method is also called from the constructor of `SqlCeRepositoryBase<T>`:

```
    protected SqlCeRepositoryBase(IUnitOfWork unitOfWork)
        : base(unitOfWork)
    {
        this.database = DatabaseFactory.CreateDatabase();
        this.entityFactory = EntityFactoryBuilder.BuildFactory<T>();
        this.childCallbacks = new Dictionary<string, AppendChildData>();
        this.BuildChildCallbacks();
        this.baseQuery = this.GetBaseQuery();
        this.baseWhereClause = this.GetBaseWhereClause();
    }
```

The end result of this refactoring is that now I do not have to implement the `FindAll` and `FindBy` methods in any of my concrete repositories, it is already done for me by the `SqlCeRepositoryBase<T>` class. This could save quite a bit of coding and testing in the long run.

The Organization of the ProjectRepository Class

Before going any further into the implementation of the ProjectRepository class, I wanted to take a moment to show you how I have it organized. I have divided the class into several collapsible regions (via the `#region` and `#endregion` keywords), as shown in Figure 3.8.

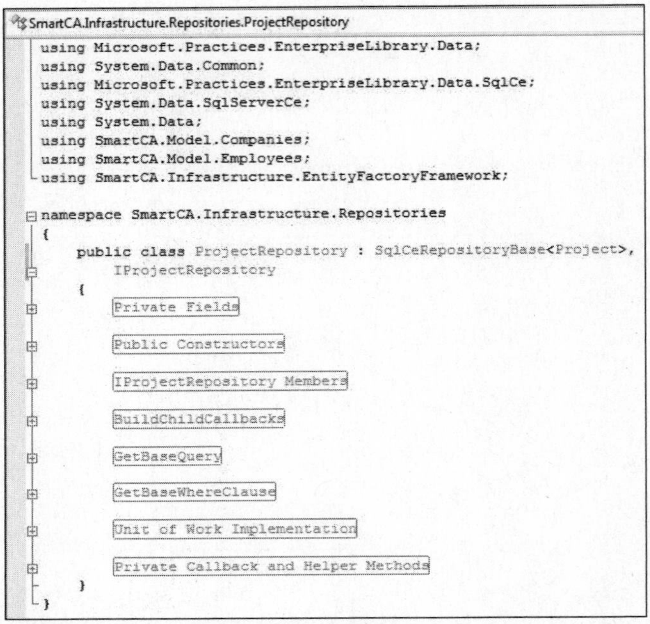

```
SmartCA.Infrastructure.Repositories.ProjectRepository
using Microsoft.Practices.EnterpriseLibrary.Data;
using System.Data.Common;
using Microsoft.Practices.EnterpriseLibrary.Data.SqlCe;
using System.Data.SqlServerCe;
using System.Data;
using SmartCA.Model.Companies;
using SmartCA.Model.Employees;
using SmartCA.Infrastructure.EntityFactoryFramework;

namespace SmartCA.Infrastructure.Repositories
{
    public class ProjectRepository : SqlCeRepositoryBase<Project>,
        IProjectRepository
    {
        Private Fields

        Public Constructors

        IProjectRepository Members

        BuildChildCallbacks

        GetBaseQuery

        GetBaseWhereClause

        Unit of Work Implementation

        Private Callback and Helper Methods
    }
}
```

Figure 3.8: Repository code organization.

This type of code organization helps me quite a bit when I need to refactor code or just get to something quickly in the class.

The Constructors

There are two public constructors for the `ProjectRepository` class, a default constructor, and one that takes an `IUnitOfWork` instance (defined earlier in Chapter 2).

```
#region Public Constructors

        public ProjectRepository()
            : this(null)
        {
        }

        public ProjectRepository(IUnitOfWork unitOfWork)
            : base(unitOfWork)
        {
        }

        #endregion
```

These are very simple, and just pass on their data to the `SqlCeRepositoryBase<T>` constructor.

The IProjectRepository Implementation

Because of the infrastructure I have already built, the actual implementation of methods for almost all of the `Repository` interfaces are fairly simple. The usual pattern they follow is to build a SQL string, and then have the base class execute the SQL and return instances of Entity object(s) to the derived `Repository`. The `IProjectRepository` interface dictates that I need to implement three methods, `FindBy(IList<MarketSegment> segments, bool completed)`, `FindBy(string projectNumber)`, and `FindAllMarketSegments()`. The first one is the most complex of the three:

```
        public IList<Project> FindBy(IList<MarketSegment> segments, bool completed)
        {
            StringBuilder builder = this.GetBaseQueryBuilder();
            if (completed)
            {
                builder.Append(" WHERE p.ActualCompletionDate IS NOT NULL AND
p.PercentComplete > 99");
            }
            else
            {
                builder.Append(" WHERE p.ActualCompletionDate IS NULL AND
p.PercentComplete < 100");
            }
            if (segments ! = null || segments.Count > 0)
            {
                builder.Append(string.Format(" AND p.MarketSegmentID IN ({0})",
                    DataHelper.EntityListToDelimited(segments).ToString()));
            }
            builder.Append(";");
            return this.BuildEntitiesFromSql(builder.ToString());
        }
```

This method first filters the list of `Projects` based on whether the `Project` has been completed. It then builds another filter based on what `MarketSegment` instances were passed in to it. It uses the `DataHelper` class to help transform the `IList<MarketSegment>` object into a comma-delimited SQL `IN` clause via the `EntityListToDelimited` method. Finally, it passes the SQL it has built up to its base class, `SqlCeRepositoryBase<T>` for processing.

The next method, `FindBy(string projectNumber)`, is the simplest, thanks to the base class functionality in `SqlCeRepository<T>`:

```
        public Project FindBy(string projectNumber)
        {
            StringBuilder builder = this.GetBaseQueryBuilder();
            return this.BuildEntityFromSql(builder.Append(string.Format(" WHERE
p.ProjectNumber = N'{0}';",
                projectNumber)).ToString());
        }
```

It does not have any logic in it except to build the SQL `WHERE` clause for the Project Number. It then follows the normal pattern of sending the SQL statement to the base class and getting an Entity back.

The last `IProjectRepository` method to look at is the `FindAllMarketSegments()` method. I was trying to decide whether `MarketSegment` objects belonged in their own repository, but right now they are not used outside of the Project Aggregate, so I have decided to leave them in the `ProjectRepository`.

```
        public IList<MarketSegment> FindAllMarketSegments()
        {
            List<MarketSegment> segments = new List<MarketSegment>();
            string query = "SELECT * FROM MarketSegment mst INNER JOIN MarketSector
msr ON mst.MarketSectorID = msr.MarketSectorID;";
            IEntityFactory<MarketSegment> factory =
EntityFactoryBuilder.BuildFactory<MarketSegment>();
            using (IDataReader reader = this.ExecuteReader(query))
            {
                while (reader.Read())
                {
                    segments.Add(factory.BuildEntity(reader));
                }
            }
            return segments;
        }
```

This method is a little bit different in that it must build its own full SQL statement, use its own `IEntityFactory<T>` instance, `IEntityFactory<MarketSegment>`, and builds the list of `MarketSegment` instances "by hand." The `IEntityFactory<MarketSegment>` instance created by the `EntityFactoryBuilder` is actually a `MarketSegmentFactory` instance. In Chapter 2, I went over the Entity Factory Framework, and now you will see it actually put to use.

```
using System;
using SmartCA.Model.Projects;
using SmartCA.Infrastructure.EntityFactoryFramework;
using System.Data;

namespace SmartCA.Infrastructure.Repositories
{
    internal class MarketSegmentFactory : IEntityFactory<MarketSegment>
    {
        #region Field Names

        internal static class FieldNames
        {
            public const string MarketSegmentId = "MarketSegmentID";
            public const string MarketSectorId = "MarketSectorID";
            public const string Code = "Code";
            public const string MarketSegmentName = "MarketSegmentName";
            public const string MarketSectorName = "MarketSectorName";
        }

        #endregion

        #region IEntityFactory<MarketSegment> Members

        public MarketSegment BuildEntity(IDataReader reader)
```

```
        {
            return new MarketSegment(reader[FieldNames.MarketSegmentId],
                                            new
MarketSector(reader[FieldNames.MarketSectorId],
reader[FieldNames.MarketSectorName].ToString()),
reader[FieldNames.MarketSegmentName].ToString(),
                                            reader[FieldNames.Code].ToString());
        }

        #endregion
    }
}
```

This class uses an internal static class, `FieldNames`, to hold the field names used in the mapping from database table field names to the class property names. The interface method `BuildEntity` uses the `IDataReader` instance passed to it along with the `FieldNames` static class to build an instance of a `MarketSegment` class. That is all there is to it, very nice and simple to maintain. The rest of the objects that get build by the repositories will all follow this same pattern.

The BuildChildCallbacks Method

Now that I have finished going over the `IProjectRepository` implementation, it is time to go back to how the `Project` class actually gets built. If you recall, this functionality was moved up into the base class, `SqlCeRepositoryBase<T>`, but it does make use of the Template Method pattern, and `BuildChildCallbacks` is one of those abstract template methods that the `ProjectRepository` must implement.

```
        #region BuildChildCallbacks

        protected override void BuildChildCallbacks()
        {
            this.ChildCallbacks.Add(ProjectFactory.FieldNames.OwnerCompanyId,
                this.AppendOwner);

            this.ChildCallbacks.Add(
                ProjectFactory.FieldNames.ConstructionAdministratorEmployeeId,
                this.AppendConstructionAdministrator);

            this.ChildCallbacks.Add(ProjectFactory.FieldNames.PrincipalEmployeeId,
                this.AppendPrincipal);

            this.ChildCallbacks.Add("allowances",
                delegate(Project project, object childKeyName)
                {
                    this.AppendProjectAllowances(project);
                });

        }

        #endregion
```

To refresh your memory from Chapter 2, the `ChildCallbacks` property of `SqlCeRepositoryBase<T>` is a dictionary of type `Dictionary<string, AppendChildData>`, with `AppendChildData` being a delegate type with the following signature:

```
#region AppendChildData Delegate

/// <summary>
/// The delegate signature required for callback methods
/// </summary>
/// <param name="entityAggregate"></param>
/// <param name="childEntityKey"></param>
public delegate void AppendChildData(T entityAggregate,
    object childEntityKeyValue);

#endregion
```

This takes in the entity Aggregate type, in this case a `Project` instance, and an entity key value, in this case the value of the primary key of the child entity's corresponding table. In the first example of `AppendOwner`, this would be the field name on the Project table representing the `Owner`.

The code in the `BuildChildCallbacks` method just adds entries to the `ChildCallbacks` dictionary, with the appropriate field names and delegate methods. The last entry is the most interesting, because the `AppendProjectAllowances` method has no parameters, so an anonymous delegate is used to make it fit:

```
this.ChildCallbacks.Add("allowances",
delegate(Project project, object childKeyName)
{
    this.AppendProjectAllowances(project);
});
```

Since it has no parameters, it does not need a field name on the Project table either; it will use the `Id` property of the Project class (I will show this method shortly). I added the `"allowances"` string value in order to give it a valid key value in the `ChildCallbacks` dictionary.

The AppendOwner Callback Method

The first entry made in the `ChildCallbacks` dictionary was for the `AppendOwner` method. This method uses the Company Repository to find the matching `Company` that represents the Owner of the Project:

```
private void AppendOwner(Project project, object ownerCompanyId)
{
    ICompanyRepository repository
        = RepositoryFactory.GetRepository<ICompanyRepository, Company>();
    project.Owner = repository.FindBy(ownerCompanyId);
}
```

As you can see, it follows the same pattern I have been using and is actually using the `IRepository<T>` interface's `FindBy(object key)` method implemented in `SqlCeRepositoryBase<T>`.

The AppendConstructionAdministrator and AppendPrincipal Callback Methods

These methods both need to get and set an `Employee` instance value on their respective properties in the `Project` class:

```
private void AppendConstructionAdministrator(Project project,
    object constructionAdministratorId)
{
    project.ConstructionAdministrator =
        this.GetEmployee(constructionAdministratorId);
}

private void AppendPrincipal(Project project, object principalId)
{
    project.PrincipalInCharge = this.GetEmployee(principalId);
}
```

Following the "Don't Repeat Yourself" (DRY) principle, I created a `GetEmployee(object employeeId)` method that the two methods could share:

```
private Employee GetEmployee(object employeeId)
{
    IEmployeeRepository repository
        = RepositoryFactory.GetRepository<IEmployeeRepository, Employee>();
    return repository.FindBy(employeeId);
}
```

This method is very similar to the `AppendOwner` method in that it also uses the `IRepository<T>` interface's `FindBy(object key)` method implemented in `SqlCeRepositoryBase<T>` in order to build the Employee instance.

The AppendProjectAllowances Callback Method

As mentioned earlier, the `AppendProjectAllowances` method is a little bit different from the previous three callback methods:

```
private void AppendProjectAllowances(Project project)
{
    string sql =
        string.Format("SELECT * FROM ProjectAllowance WHERE ProjectID =
'{0}'", project.Key);
    using (IDataReader reader = this.ExecuteReader(sql))
    {
        while (reader.Read())
        {
            project.Allowances.Add(ProjectFactory.BuildAllowance(reader));
        }
    }
}
```

The Project Allowance data does not belong to another repository; it is part of the `ProjectRepository`. Therefore, since it is not covered by the base query for the `ProjectRepository`, the `Allowance` instances must be built by hand, very similarly to the `FindAllMarketSegments` method seen earlier in this chapter. In fact, this method is almost identical except for the SQL statement and the ProjectFactory method used to build the Entity. In this case the method is using a static method on the ProjectFactory class to build the Entity.

```
        public static Allowance BuildAllowance(IDataReader reader)
        {
            return new Allowance(reader[FieldNames.AllowanceTitle].ToString(),
                       DataHelper.GetDecimal(reader[FieldNames.AllowanceAmount]));
        }
```

As you can see in the code for the method, it is a very simple mapping. I had to make it a static method in the ProjectFactory class because the Allowance class is not an Entity, it is a Value class; therefore, it cannot use the Entity Factory Framework.

The GetBaseQuery Method

The next abstract Template Method that the SqlCeRepositoryBase<T> calls is the GetBaseQuery method. Here is the ProjectRepository class's override of the abstract method:

```
        #region GetBaseQuery

        protected override string GetBaseQuery()
        {
            return "SELECT * FROM Project p INNER JOIN MarketSegment ms ON
p.MarketSegmentID = ms.MarketSegmentID";
        }

        #endregion
```

This simply returns the SQL statement for the Project Aggregate. By abstracting the base query out, the SqlCeRepositryBase<T> class is able to pull in the two "FindBy" methods, thus eliminating repetitive code in all of the derived repositories.

The GetBaseWhereClause Method

The GetBaseWhereClause method is very similar to the GetBaseQuery method just shown, only this time the string returned is just a formatted SQL WHERE clause for the Project Aggregate with a placeholder for the ProjectID field.

```
        #region GetBaseWhereClause

        protected override string GetBaseWhereClause()
        {
            return " WHERE ProjectID = '{0}';";
        }

        #endregion
```

The SqlCeRepositoryBase<T> class handles filling in the ProjectID placeholder at runtime.

The Unit of Work Implementation

In order to implement the Repository Framework's Unit of Work defined in Chapter 2, I only need to override three methods, `PersistNewItem(Project item)`, `PersistUpdatedItem(Project item)`, and `PersistDeletedItem(Project item)`. I am not going to show all of the code for `PersistNewItem`, since it is rather lengthy, but here is an abbreviated version of it:

```
        protected override void PersistNewItem(Project item)
        {
            StringBuilder builder = new StringBuilder(100);
            builder.Append(string.Format("INSERT INTO Project
({0},{1},{2},{3},{4},{5},{6},{7},{8},{9},{10},{11},{12},{13},{14},{15},{16},{17},
{18},{19},{20},{21},{22},{23},{24},{25},{26}) ",
                ProjectFactory.FieldNames.ProjectId,
                ProjectFactory.FieldNames.ProjectNumber,
                ProjectFactory.FieldNames.ProjectName,
```

....

```
                DataHelper.GetSqlValue(item.AgencyFileNumber),
                item.Segment.Key));

 this.Database.ExecuteNonQuery(this.Database.GetSqlStringCommand(builder
.ToString()));
        }
```

The code is building up an insert statement composed of the values from the `Project` instance and then executing the query using the Microsoft Enterprise Library's `Database` object.

`PersistUpdatedItem` is very similar, only it does an update to the table:

```
protected override void PersistUpdatedItem(Project item)
        {
            StringBuilder builder = new StringBuilder(100);
            builder.Append("UPDATE Project SET ");

            builder.Append(string.Format("{0} = {1}",
                ProjectFactory.FieldNames.ConstructionAdministratorEmployeeId,
                item.ConstructionAdministrator.Key));

            builder.Append(string.Format(",{0} = {1}",
                ProjectFactory.FieldNames.PrincipalEmployeeId,
                item.PrincipalInCharge.Key));
            builder.Append(string.Format(",{0} = {1}",
                ProjectFactory.FieldNames.AgencyFileNumber,
                DataHelper.GetSqlValue(item.AgencyFileNumber)));

            builder.Append(string.Format(",{0} = {1}",
                ProjectFactory.FieldNames.MarketSegmentId,
                item.Segment.Key));
```

(continued)

(continued)

```
            builder.Append(" ");
            builder.Append(this.BuildBaseWhereClause(item.Key));

   this.Database.ExecuteNonQuery(this.Database.GetSqlStringCommand(builder
  .ToString()));
        }
```

The last method to implement, `PersistDeletedItem`, follows the same pattern:

```
        protected override void PersistDeletedItem(Project item)
      {
            string query = string.Format("DELETE FROM ProjectAllowance {0}",
                this.BuildBaseWhereClause(item.Key));
            this.Database.ExecuteNonQuery(this.Database.GetSqlStringCommand(query));
            query = string.Format("DELETE FROM Project {0}",
                this.BuildBaseWhereClause(item.Key));
            this.Database.ExecuteNonQuery(this.Database.GetSqlStringCommand(query));
        }
```

It is a little different from the other two persistence methods in that it actually has to execute two SQL statements, one to delete rows from the `ProjectAllowance` table and then one for deleting the single row from the `Project` table. Notice, also, how the last two methods make use of the `SqlCeRepositoryBase<T>` class's `BuildBaseWhereClause` method. The refactoring of code into `SqlCeRepositoryBase<T>` keeps paying off.

The Employee Repository

Similar to the `ProjectRepository` class, in order to implement the concrete `EmployeeRepository` class I just need to inherit from `SqlCeRepositoryBase<T>`, and also to implement the `IEmployeeRepository` interface shown earlier in the Design section of this chapter:

```
namespace SmartCA.Infrastructure.Repositories
{
    public class EmployeeRepository : SqlCeRepositoryBase<Employee>,
        IEmployeeRepository
    {
...
```

The Constructors

The public constructors for the `EmployeeRepository` class are exactly the same as those in the `ProjectRepository` class:

```
        #region Public Constructors

        public EmployeeRepository()
            : this(null)
        {
        }

        public EmployeeRepository(IUnitOfWork unitOfWork)
            : base(unitOfWork)
```

```
        {
        }

        #endregion
```

The IEmployeeRepository Implementation

The `IEmployeeRepository` interface dictates that I need to implement two methods, `GetConstructionAdministrators()` and `GetPrincipals()`. Both of these methods are fairly simple, and both return a type of `IList<Employee>`.

```
        #region IEmployeeRepository Members

        public IList<Employee> GetConstructionAdministrators()
        {
            //Construction Administrator
            StringBuilder builder = this.GetBaseQueryBuilder ();
            return this.BuildEntitiesFromSql(builder.Append
                (" WHERE JobTitle LIKE '%Construction Administrator%';")
.ToString());
        }

        public IList<Employee> GetPrincipals()
        {
            //Principal-in-Charge
            StringBuilder builder = this.GetBaseQueryBuilder();
            return this.BuildEntitiesFromSql(builder.Append
                (" WHERE JobTitle LIKE '%Principal%';").ToString());
        }

        #endregion
```

I am not going to worry about the string matching going on in the SQL `WHERE` clauses of these two methods because that is not my concern right now. This can always be refactored later to get rid of the string references and made to use a more normalized table structure with foreign key relationships.

The GetBaseQuery Method

Here is the `EmployeeRepository` class's override of the `GetBaseQuery` abstract method:

```
        #region GetBaseQuery

        protected override string GetBaseQuery()
        {
            return "SELECT * FROM Employee";
        }

        #endregion
```

This just follows the same Template Method pattern I have shown all along.

The GetBaseWhereClause Method

Again, I am just following the Template Method pattern for implementing the `GetBaseWhereClause` method:

```
        #region GetBaseWhereClause

        protected override string GetBaseWhereClause()
        {
            return " WHERE EmployeeID = {0};";
        }

        #endregion
```

The Service Class Implementations

The only `Service` classes I have implemented up to this point are all Service classes that live in the domain model layer and are acting as facades to their respective `Repository` interfaces. These `Service` classes are intended to be called directly from the `ViewModel` classes; the idea is that they will greatly simplify access to the domain model operations. In this section, I will cover the `ProjectService` and the `EmployeeService` classes.

The ProjectService Class

The `ProjectService` class is responsible for retrieving and saving `Project` instances, as well as retrieving `MarketSegment` instances:

```
using System;
using System.Collections.Generic;
using SmartCA.Model.Projects;
using SmartCA.Infrastructure.RepositoryFramework;
using SmartCA.Infrastructure;

namespace SmartCA.Model.Projects
{
    public static class ProjectService
    {
        private static IProjectRepository repository;
        private static IUnitOfWork unitOfWork;

        static ProjectService()
        {
            ProjectService.unitOfWork = new UnitOfWork();
            ProjectService.repository =
                RepositoryFactory.GetRepository<IProjectRepository,
                Project>(ProjectService.unitOfWork);
        }

        public static IList<Project> GetAllProjects()
        {
            return ProjectService.repository.FindAll();
        }
```

```
        public static IList<MarketSegment> GetMarketSegments()
        {
            return ProjectService.repository.FindAllMarketSegments();
        }

        public static void SaveProject(Project project)
        {
            ProjectService.repository[project.Key] = project;
            ProjectService.unitOfWork.Commit();
        }
    }
}
```

The first thing to notice about this class is that it is a static class with all static methods. Again, the idea is to make it very easy to use. The next interesting part of the class is its static constructor. This is where the instance to the `IProjectRepository` is created via the `RepositoryFactory`. Also note that when the `IProjectRepository` is created it is injected with a `UnitOfWork` instance. This is necessary since I will be saving `Project` instances in this class and want that operation to be wrapped in a transaction.

The rest of the class is just acting as a façade in front of the `IProjectRepository` instance. The next interesting method is the `SaveProject` method. Notice how the collection-like functionality of the `IProjectRepository` instance is utilized by calling the indexer (see Chapter 2 for more information). What's nice about having the indexer is that the `RepositoryBase<T>` class will figure out whether it is a new `Project` or an existing one. Also, after updating the `IProjectRepository` with the newly updated `Project` instance, the `Commit` method is called on the `UnitOfWork` instance to commit the transaction.

The EmployeeService Class

Currently, the only thing that the `EmployeeService` class does is to wrap the `IEmployeeRepository` calls for the `GetConstructionAdministrators` and `GetPrincipals` methods.

```
using System;
using System.Collections.Generic;
using SmartCA.Infrastructure;
using SmartCA.Infrastructure.RepositoryFramework;

namespace SmartCA.Model.Employees
{
    public static class EmployeeService
    {
        private static IEmployeeRepository repository;
        private static IUnitOfWork unitOfWork;

        static EmployeeService()
        {
            EmployeeService.unitOfWork = new UnitOfWork();
            EmployeeService.repository
                = RepositoryFactory.GetRepository<IEmployeeRepository,
                Employee>(EmployeeService.unitOfWork);
        }

        public static IList<Employee> GetConstructionAdministrators()
```

(continued)

(continued)

```
            {
                return EmployeeService.repository.GetConstructionAdministrators();
            }

            public static IList<Employee> GetPrincipals()
            {
                return EmployeeService.repository.GetPrincipals();
            }
        }
    }
```

This code should look very similar to the `ProjectService` class. It literally is acting like a façade for now, but there is plenty of room for it to grow later. Right now, we do not need any additional functionality in it yet.

The Project Information ViewModel Implementation

As I showed in Chapter 2, with the `SelectProjectViewModel` example, the ViewModel class is used for adapting the domain model to the UI, or View.

The ViewModel Class Revisited

Since writing Chapter 2, I went in and did some refactoring on this concept and made an abstract `ViewModel` class for all of the new ViewModel classes to inherit from.

```
using System;
using System.ComponentModel;

namespace SmartCA.Infrastructure.UI
{
    public abstract class ViewModel : INotifyPropertyChanged
    {
        private IView view;
        private DelegateCommand cancelCommand;
        private ObjectState currentObjectState;
        private const string currentObjectStatePropertyName = "CurrentObjectState";

        protected ViewModel()
            : this(null)
        {
        }

        protected ViewModel(IView view)
        {
            this.view = view;
            this.cancelCommand = new DelegateCommand(this.CancelCommandHandler);
            this.currentObjectState = ObjectState.Existing;
        }

        public enum ObjectState
```

```
        {
            New,
            Existing,
            Deleted
        }

        public DelegateCommand CancelCommand
        {
            get { return this.cancelCommand; }
        }

        public ObjectState CurrentObjectState
        {
            get { return this.currentObjectState; }
            set
            {
                if (this.currentObjectState != value)
                {
                    this.currentObjectState = value;
                    this.OnPropertyChanged(
                        ViewModel.currentObjectStatePropertyName);
                }
            }
        }

        protected virtual void OnPropertyChanged(string propertyName)
        {
            if (this.PropertyChanged != null)
            {
                this.PropertyChanged(this,
                    new PropertyChangedEventArgs(propertyName));
            }
        }

        protected virtual void CancelCommandHandler(object sender, EventArgs e)
        {
            this.CloseView();
        }

        protected void CloseView()
        {
            if (this.view != null)
            {
                this.view.Close();
            }
        }

        #region INotifyPropertyChanged Members

        public event PropertyChangedEventHandler PropertyChanged;

        #endregion
    }
}
```

This class implements the `INotifyPropertyChanged` interface, which tells the WPF UI when certain object properties have changed so that the UI will automatically be updated. Again, this is all part of adapting the domain model to the UI. It also contains properties for a `CancelCommand` and an `ObjectState` property, so the View can know whether its domain object is new, deleted, or updated. It can then act appropriately based on those states. I will show an example of this with the `ProjectInformationView` a little bit later.

The constructor for the `ViewModel` class takes care of getting a reference to the passed in `IView` instance, as well as wiring up the `CancelCommand`'s `DelegateCommand` to the `CancelCommandHandler` method. This class is very simple, yet it gives me a lot of necessary functionality that I need in all of my `ViewModel` classes.

The ProjectInformationViewModel Class

Now, I can create my `ProjectInformationViewModel` class and inherit from the new `ViewModel` abstract class:

```
using System;
using SmartCA.Presentation.Views;
using SmartCA.Model.Projects;
using SmartCA.Application;
using System.Windows.Data;
using SmartCA.Infrastructure.UI;
using System.ComponentModel;
using SmartCA.Model.Employees;
using SmartCA.Model.Companies;

namespace SmartCA.Presentation.ViewModels
{
    public class ProjectInformationViewModel : ViewModel
    {
        private static class Constants
        {
            public const string CurrentProjectPropertyName = "CurrentProject";
            public const string ProjectAddressPropertyName = "ProjectAddress";
            public const string OwnerHeadquartersAddressPropertyName =
                "ProjectOwnerHeadquartersAddress";
        }

        private Project currentProject;
        private string newProjectNumber;
        private string newProjectName;
        private MutableAddress projectAddress;
        private MutableAddress projectOwnerHeadquartersAddress;
        private CollectionView owners;
        private CollectionView marketSegments;
        private CollectionView constructionAdministrators;
        private CollectionView principals;
        private DelegateCommand saveCommand;
        private DelegateCommand newCommand;

        public ProjectInformationViewModel()
            : this(null)
```

```
        {
        }

        public ProjectInformationViewModel(IView view)
            : base(view)
        {
            this.currentProject = UserSession.CurrentProject;
            this.newProjectNumber = string.Empty;
            this.newProjectName = string.Empty;

            this.projectAddress = new MutableAddress
              {
                  Street = this.currentProject.Address.Street,
                  City = this.currentProject.Address.City,
                  State = this.currentProject.Address.State,
                  PostalCode = this.currentProject.Address.PostalCode
              };

            this.projectOwnerHeadquartersAddress = new MutableAddress
              {
                  Street = this.currentProject.Owner.HeadquartersAddress.Street,
                  City = this.currentProject.Owner.HeadquartersAddress.City,
                  State = this.currentProject.Owner.HeadquartersAddress.State,
                  PostalCode =
                  this.currentProject.Owner.HeadquartersAddress.PostalCode
              };

            this.CurrentObjectState =
                (this.currentProject != null ?
                ObjectState.Existing : ObjectState.New);

            this.owners = new CollectionView(CompanyService.GetOwners());

            this.marketSegments =
                new CollectionView(ProjectService.GetMarketSegments());

            this.constructionAdministrators =
                new CollectionView(
                    EmployeeService.GetConstructionAdministrators());

            this.principals = new CollectionView(EmployeeService.GetPrincipals());
            this.saveCommand = new DelegateCommand(this.SaveCommandHandler);
            this.newCommand = new DelegateCommand(this.NewCommandHandler);
        }

        public Project CurrentProject
        {
            get { return this.currentProject; }
        }

        public string NewProjectNumber
        {
            get { return this.newProjectNumber; }
            set
```

(continued)

(continued)

```
            {
                if (this.newProjectNumber != value)
                {
                    this.newProjectNumber = value;
                    this.VerifyNewProject();
                }
            }
        }

        public string NewProjectName
        {
            get { return this.newProjectName; }
            set
            {
                if (this.newProjectName != value)
                {
                    this.newProjectName = value;
                    this.VerifyNewProject();
                }
            }
        }

        public MutableAddress ProjectAddress
        {
            get { return this.projectAddress; }
        }

        public MutableAddress ProjectOwnerHeadquartersAddress
        {
            get { return this.projectOwnerHeadquartersAddress; }
        }

        public CollectionView Owners
        {
            get { return this.owners; }
        }

        public CollectionView MarketSegments
        {
            get { return this.marketSegments; }
        }

        public CollectionView ConstructionAdministrators
        {
            get { return this.constructionAdministrators; }
        }

        public CollectionView Principals
```

```
        {
            get { return this.principals; }
        }

        public DelegateCommand SaveCommand
        {
            get { return this.saveCommand; }
        }

        public DelegateCommand NewCommand
        {
            get { return this.newCommand; }
        }

        private void SaveCommandHandler(object sender, EventArgs e)
        {
            this.currentProject.Address = this.projectAddress.ToAddress();

            this.currentProject.Owner.HeadquartersAddress =
                this.projectOwnerHeadquartersAddress.ToAddress();

            ProjectService.SaveProject(this.currentProject);

            this.OnPropertyChanged(
                Constants.CurrentProjectPropertyName);

            this.CurrentObjectState = ObjectState.Existing;
        }

        private void NewCommandHandler(object sender, EventArgs e)
        {
            this.currentProject = null;
            this.projectAddress = new MutableAddress();

            this.OnPropertyChanged(
                Constants.ProjectAddressPropertyName);

            this.newProjectNumber = string.Empty;
            this.newProjectName = string.Empty;
            this.projectOwnerHeadquartersAddress = new MutableAddress();

            this.OnPropertyChanged(
                Constants.OwnerHeadquartersAddressPropertyName);

            this.CurrentObjectState = ObjectState.New;

            this.OnPropertyChanged(
                Constants.CurrentProjectPropertyName);
        }

        private void VerifyNewProject()
```

(continued)

(continued)

```
            {
                if (this.newProjectNumber.Length > 0 &&
                    this.newProjectName.Length > 0)
                {
                    this.currentProject = new Project(this.newProjectNumber,
                                                      this.newProjectName);
                    this.OnPropertyChanged(
                        Constants.CurrentProjectPropertyName);
                }
            }
        }
    }
```

The Constructors

Notice that there is quite a bit going on in the constructor. Just like the `SelectProjectViewModel` class in Chapter 2, the `ProjectInformationViewModel` class is a `Value` class.

```
        public ProjectInformationViewModel()
            : this(null)
        {
        }

        public ProjectInformationViewModel(IView view)
            : base(view)
        {
            this.currentProject = UserSession.CurrentProject;
            this.newProjectNumber = string.Empty;
            this.newProjectName = string.Empty;
            this.projectAddress = new MutableAddress
              {
                  Street = this.currentProject.Address.Street,
                  City = this.currentProject.Address.City,
                  State = this.currentProject.Address.State,
                  PostalCode = this.currentProject.Address.PostalCode
              };
            this.projectOwnerHeadquartersAddress = new MutableAddress
              {
                  Street = this.currentProject.Owner.HeadquartersAddress.Street,
                  City = this.currentProject.Owner.HeadquartersAddress.City,
                  State = this.currentProject.Owner.HeadquartersAddress.State,
                  PostalCode =
                  this.currentProject.Owner.HeadquartersAddress.PostalCode
              };
            this.CurrentObjectState =
                (this.currentProject != null ?
                ObjectState.Existing : ObjectState.New);

            this.owners = new CollectionView(CompanyService.GetOwners());

            this.marketSegments =
                new CollectionView(ProjectService.GetMarketSegments());
```

```
        this.constructionAdministrators =
            new CollectionView(
                EmployeeService.GetConstructionAdministrators());

        this.principals = new CollectionView(EmployeeService.GetPrincipals());
        this.saveCommand = new DelegateCommand(this.SaveCommandHandler);
        this.newCommand = new DelegateCommand(this.NewCommandHandler);
    }
```

In the constructor code above, all of the read-only properties of the class are being initialized. Probably the most important one is the `Project` instance coming from the `UserSession`'s `CurrentProject` property, since editing the `Project` instance is the whole point of the form. Remember from Chapter 2 that the `CurrentProject` property of the `UserSession` class gets set when you select a Project from the `SelectProjectView`.

The MutableAddress Class

The next thing that should stand out to you is that I am creating an instance of a `MutableAddress` class. This class is a mutable companion to the immutable `Address` class, and it allows the UI to have two-way binding to its read-write properties.

```
using System;
using SmartCA.Model;

namespace SmartCA.Presentation.ViewModels
{
    public class MutableAddress
    {
        private string street;
        private string city;
        private string state;
        private string postalCode;

        public string Street
        {
            get { return this.street; }
            set { this.street = value; }
        }

        public string City
        {
            get { return this.city; }
            set { this.city = value; }
        }

        public string State
        {
            get { return this.state; }
            set { this.state = value; }
        }

        public string PostalCode
```

(continued)

(continued)

```
            {
                get { return this.postalCode; }
                set { this.postalCode = value; }
            }

            public Address ToAddress()
            {
                return new Address(this.street, this.city,
                          this.state, this.postalCode);
            }
        }
    }
```

The purpose of this class is to make it easy for the presentation layer to deal with the `Address` Value object, since binding to and setting properties on an immutable class is impossible (believe me, I learned the hard way about that). As you can see, it is also a Value object, but not immutable. The `ToAddress` method actually creates an instance of the `Address` Value object, and this is what we will be using from the `ProjectInformationViewModel`.

Using the C# 3.0 Initializer Features

Going back to the `ProjectInformationViewModel`, notice how the `MutableAddress` class is being initialized; I am taking advantage of the new C# 3.0 object initializer features:

```
this.projectAddress = new MutableAddress
  {
      Street = this.currentProject.Address.Street,
      City = this.currentProject.Address.City,
      State = this.currentProject.Address.State,
      PostalCode = this.currentProject.Address.PostalCode
  };
this.projectOwnerHeadquartersAddress = new MutableAddress
  {
      Street = this.currentProject.Owner.HeadquartersAddress.Street,
      City = this.currentProject.Owner.HeadquartersAddress.City,
      State = this.currentProject.Owner.HeadquartersAddress.State,
      PostalCode =
      this.currentProject.Owner.HeadquartersAddress.PostalCode
  };
```

Transforming the Model Objects into View Objects

The rest of the `ProjectInformationViewModel` is transforming `IList<T>` types from the domain model into WPF-friendly `CollectionView` objects and setting up a few `DelegateCommand` instances.

```
this.CurrentObjectState =
    (this.currentProject != null ?
    ObjectState.Existing : ObjectState.New);

this.owners = new CollectionView(CompanyService.GetOwners());

this.marketSegments =
```

```
            new CollectionView(ProjectService.GetMarketSegments());

        this.constructionAdministrators =
            new CollectionView(
                EmployeeService.GetConstructionAdministrators());

        this.principals = new CollectionView(EmployeeService.GetPrincipals());
        this.saveCommand = new DelegateCommand(this.SaveCommandHandler);
        this.newCommand = new DelegateCommand(this.NewCommandHandler);
```

Notice how I am taking full advantage of the `Service` classes I have created that stand in front of the Company and Employee repositories.

The Properties

All of the properties in the `ProjectInformationViewModel` class are read-only except for two, `ProjectName` and `ProjectNumber`. These properties are actually taking the place of the same properties on the `Project` class, kind of like what I did with the `MutableAddress` class shown earlier.

```
public string NewProjectNumber
{
    get { return this.newProjectNumber; }
    set
    {
        if (this.newProjectNumber != value)
        {
            this.newProjectNumber = value;
            this.VerifyNewProject();
        }
    }
}

public string NewProjectName
{
    get { return this.newProjectName; }
    set
    {
        if (this.newProjectName != value)
        {
            this.newProjectName = value;
            this.VerifyNewProject();
        }
    }
}
```

The setters for these two properties both call the `VerifyNewProject` method, and this method checks to make sure that there is both a valid `ProjectNumber` value set and a valid `ProjectName` value set:

```
        private void VerifyNewProject()
        {
            if (this.newProjectNumber.Length > 0 &&
                this.newProjectName.Length > 0)
            {
                this.currentProject = new Project(this.newProjectNumber,
                                          this.newProjectName);
                this.OnPropertyChanged(
                    ProjectInformationViewModel.currentProjectPropertyName);
            }
        }
```

If the validation passes, it then sets the `CurrentProject` property value of the `ProjectInformationViewModel` class to an instance of a new `Project` class, passing in the two values to the `Project` constructor. Then, in order to signal the UI to refresh, it raises the `PropertyChanged` event. In the next section, you will see how I deal with this functionality in the UI in order to change the display when a new Project is created.

The Project Information View Implementation

The View that is associated with the `ProjectInformationViewModel`, the `ProjectInformationView` class (which consists of XAML plus code-behind), is very similar to the `SelectProjectView` class, in that it has very little code behind in it:

```
using System;
using System.Windows;
using SmartCA.Presentation.ViewModels;
using SmartCA.Infrastructure.UI;

namespace SmartCA.Presentation.Views
{
 public partial class ProjectInformationView : Window, IView
    {
        public ProjectInformationView()
        {
            this.InitializeComponent();
            this.DataContext = new ProjectInformationViewModel(this);
        }
    }
}
```

In fact it is almost identical to the code in the `SelectProjectView` class, except that it initializes the `DataContext` of the View with a `ProjectInformationViewModel` instead of a `SelectProjectViewModel`. The XAML for the form is fairly complex, so first I want to show what the form looks like at run time. Then, you can get a better picture of what I am building, as shown in Figure 3.9.

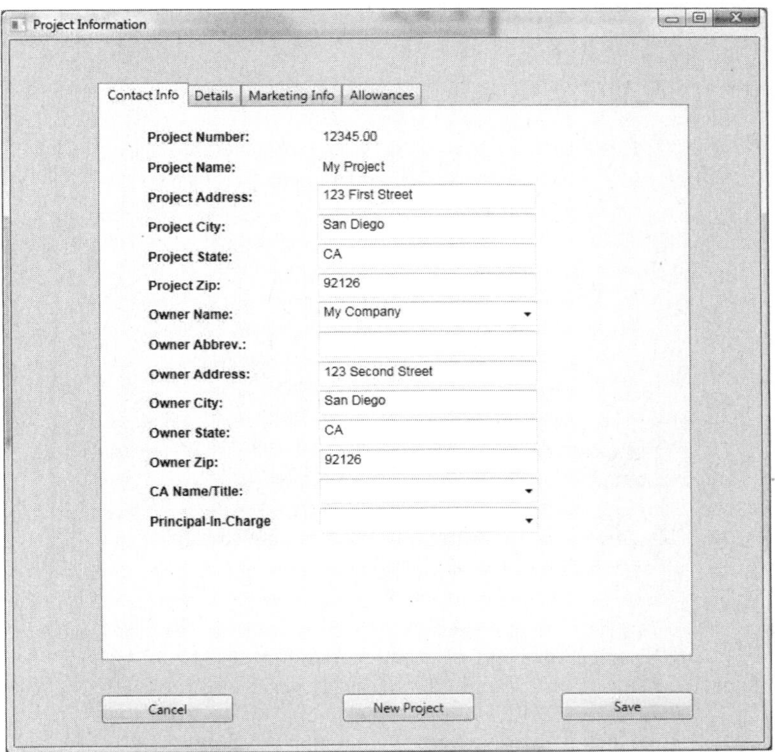

Figure 3.9: The Project Information View

As you can see, it utilizes a tabbed view in order to take better advantage of the screen real estate. Also, notice that the Project Number and Project Name fields are displayed with a label instead of a textbox, thus indicating that they are read-only fields. In this instance of the form, the two fields are bound to the `ProjectNumber` and `ProjectName` properties of the `ProjectInformationViewModel's` `CurrentProject` property (which is an instance of the `Project` domain object), but when I click on the New Project button, you will see that they both change into textboxes in order to support adding a new Project (see Figure 3.10).

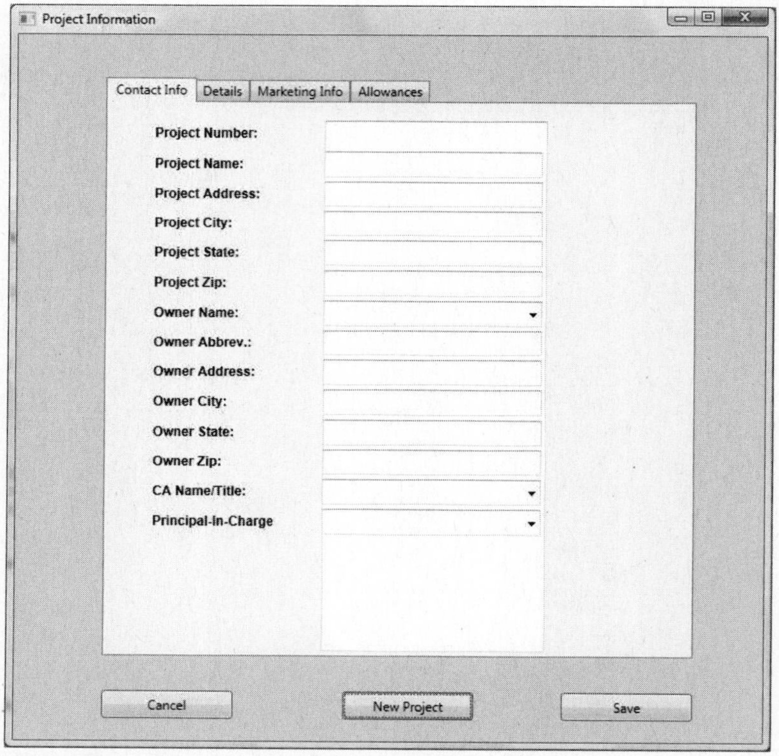

Figure 3.10: The Project Information View for a new Project

This is all made possible through the `ProjectInformationViewModel` and the XAML of the `ProjectInformationView`. Specifically, I am using a data template with a data trigger element embedded inside of it, which is bound to properties in the `ProjectInformationViewModel`.

```
<DataTemplate x:Key="projectNameAndNumber">
<Grid>

     <Label Margin="35,13.04,0,0" Content="Project Number:"
            Style="{StaticResource boldLabelStyle}"/>

     <Label Margin="195,13.04,131,0"
            Content="{Binding Path=CurrentProject.Number}"
            x:Name="projectNumber"
            Style="{StaticResource baseLabelStyle}"/>

     <TextBox Margin="195,13.04,131,0" Visibility="Hidden"
            Text="{Binding Path=NewProjectNumber}"
            x:Name="newProjectNumber"/>
```

```
                <Label Margin="35,41.04,0,0" Content="Project Name:"
                       Style="{StaticResource boldLabelStyle}"/>

                <Label Margin="195,41.04,0,0"
                       Content="{Binding Path=CurrentProject.Name}"
                       x:Name="projectName"
                       Style="{StaticResource baseLabelStyle}"/>

                <TextBox Margin="195,41.04,0,0" Visibility="Hidden"
                       x:Name="newProjectName"
                       Text="{Binding Path=NewProjectName}"
                       Style="{StaticResource baseTextBoxStyle}"/>

            </Grid>
            <DataTemplate.Triggers>
                <DataTrigger Binding="{Binding Path=CurrentObjectState}"
                       Value="New">

                       <Setter Property="Visibility" Value="Visible"
                               TargetName="newProjectNumber" />

                       <Setter Property="Visibility" Value="Visible"
                               TargetName="newProjectName" />

                       <Setter Property="Visibility" Value="Hidden"
                               TargetName="projectNumber" />

                       <Setter Property="Visibility" Value="Hidden"
                               TargetName="projectName" />

                </DataTrigger>
            </DataTemplate.Triggers>
```

The data trigger is actually listening for changes to the `CurrentObjectState` property in the `ProjectInformationViewModel`. Based upon the value of that property it either shows textboxes or labels for the Project Name and Project Number fields. Also cool is how this data template is integrated into the rest of the XAML for the tab control:

```
<Grid x:Name="LayoutRoot">
        <TabControl Margin="80,40,64,80" IsSynchronizedWithCurrentItem="True">
                <TabItem Header="Contact Info">
                        <Grid>
                                <ContentControl Content="{Binding}"
ContentTemplate="{StaticResource projectNameAndNumber}"/>
```

All I have to do is place the name of the data template into the `ContentTemplate` attribute of a `ContentControl` element to make it show up in the right place. Setting the `Content` attribute value to `{Binding}` means that the data binding will honor what binding paths I have already set in the `projectNameAndNumber` data template.

I promised earlier to show how I was going to deal with the Address Value objects in the XAML code, so here it goes. I already showed how I am handling this in the ProjectInformationViewModel, so now it is time to show it in the XAML:

```
<Label Margin="35,69.04,0,0" Content="Project Address:"
    Style="{StaticResource boldLabelStyle}"/>

<TextBox Margin="195,69.15,0,0"
    Text="{Binding Path=ProjectAddress.Street}"
    Style="{StaticResource baseTextBoxStyle}"/>

<Label Margin="35,97.04,0,0" Content="Project City:"
    Style="{StaticResource boldLabelStyle}"/>

<TextBox Margin="195,97.15,0,0"
    Text="{Binding Path=ProjectAddress.City}"
    Style="{StaticResource baseTextBoxStyle}"/>

<Label Margin="35,125.04,0,0" Content="Project State:"
    Style="{StaticResource boldLabelStyle}"/>

<TextBox Margin="195,125.15,0,0"
    Text="{Binding Path=ProjectAddress.State}"
    Style="{StaticResource baseTextBoxStyle}"/>

<Label Margin="35,153.04,0,0" Content="Project Zip:"
    Style="{StaticResource boldLabelStyle}"/>

<TextBox Margin="195,153.15,0,0"
    Text="{Binding Path=ProjectAddress.PostalCode}"
    Style="{StaticResource baseTextBoxStyle}"/>
```

The way this works is that I am not actually binding to the CurrentProject property of the ProjectInformationViewModel; instead I am binding to the properties of the ProjectAddress property of the ProjectInformationViewModel. Remember, the ProjectAddress property is actually an instance of the MutableAddress type, so I can change the properties through data binding. The code inside of the ProjectInformationViewModel translates this into my immutable Address Value object, and the data going into the Address Value object's constructor is validated inside of the constructor in order to make sure that I am entering a valid address.

I love the fact that I can bind to my ViewModel and get the type of functionality that I just showed in these examples without having to write any procedural code in my View!

For the sake of brevity, I am not going to show all of the XAML code for the ProjectInformationView; there is just too much. There is nothing really special going on with the rest of it; it is the same pattern as I showed in Chapter 2 with the SelectProjectView XAML.

Summary

The end result in the UI is not that spectacular, but I certainly covered a lot of ground in getting there. In this chapter, I first defined and modeled all of the objects that make up what a Project is and then started analyzing the classes further in order to define the Aggregate Boundaries. Once the Aggregate Boundaries were defined, the Aggregate Roots were chosen, and then I defined what the various repositories were for the Aggregates. After the repositories were designed and implemented, I then designed and implemented the ViewModel and the View for the use case scenario of editing Projects. I know it may not sound like much, but I actually wrote a lot of code and refactored a lot of code in the process of getting to where I am now. The rest of the way should be well-paved for code reuse in the SmartCA application.

Companies and Contacts

Last chapter I showed how both Companies and Contacts were part of the Project Aggregate. Since the focus was on the Project Aggregate, not much was done with these two Entities. This chapter, I will dive in and take a deeper look at the Company and Contact Aggregates, and I will show how they relate to the Project Aggregate.

The Problem

One of the problems with the legacy application is that it does not handle tracking Companies, Contacts, and their associated Addresses very well. The current system does not allow multiple Addresses per Company or Contact, and as a result the users are often entering the same Companies and Contacts into the system as duplicate records in order to show a different Address for the Company or Contact.

With that being said, it sounds like a database issue of having denormalized data. It is not the point of this book to dwell on the database design; I believe that the focus of the problem needs to be on the domain model. If the domain model is designed properly, it can handle this problem. Remember, one of the tenets of Domain-Driven Design, which I discussed in Chapter 2, is *persistence ignorance*. Therefore, the application's data store could be a text file for all I care, because it is abstracted away by the Repository Framework.

The Design

In the SmartCA domain, the purpose of a Project is to bring together and manage all of the people involved in the construction process. In the next few sections, I will be designing the domain model, determining the Project Aggregate and its boundaries, and designing the repository for Projects.

Designing the Domain Model

Companies and Contacts are extremely important in the SmartCA domain, as they ensure that the right construction documents get to the right people in a timely manner. There is a slight distinction between a Contact and a ProjectContact. A ProjectContact is a Contact that happens to be part of a Project, whereas a Contact may or may not be on a Project.

Companies and Contacts both have multiple Addresses, but Companies also must have one of their Addresses designated as their headquarters address. Figure 4.1 is a diagram showing the relationships between Companies, Contacts, ProjectContacts, and Addresses.

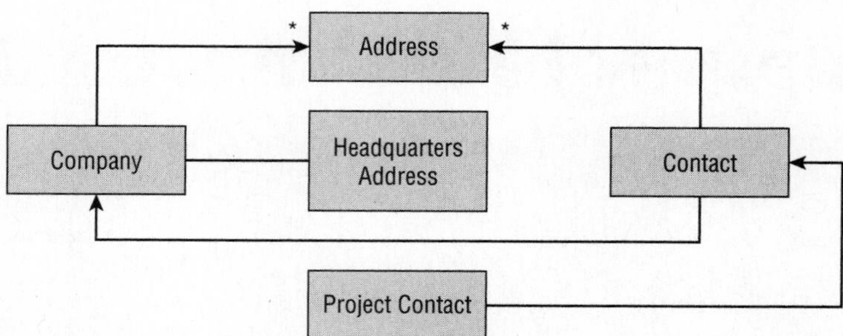

Figure 4.1: Company and Contact Aggregates.

Each contact belongs to a single Company, but people move around, and therefore Contacts often change companies over the course of time. You may notice that in this diagram that a ProjectContact contains a Contact, but does not inherit from a Contact. This is purely my preference to stick with the Gang-of-Four advice by favoring composition over inheritance.

> *The Gang-of-Four, also known as GoF, refers to the four authors who wrote the classic software-engineering book* Design Patterns: Elements of Reusable Object-Oriented Software. *The book's authors are Erich Gamma, Richard Helm, Ralph Johnson, and John Vlissides.*

Defining the Company and Contact Aggregates

Even though the `Contact` class maintains a relationship to the `Company` class, both the `Company` class and the `Contact` class are the roots of their own Aggregates, with both containing instances of the `Address Value` class. ProjectContact is not the root of an aggregate; it is an Entity, but it actually belongs to the Project Aggregate (see Figure 4.2).

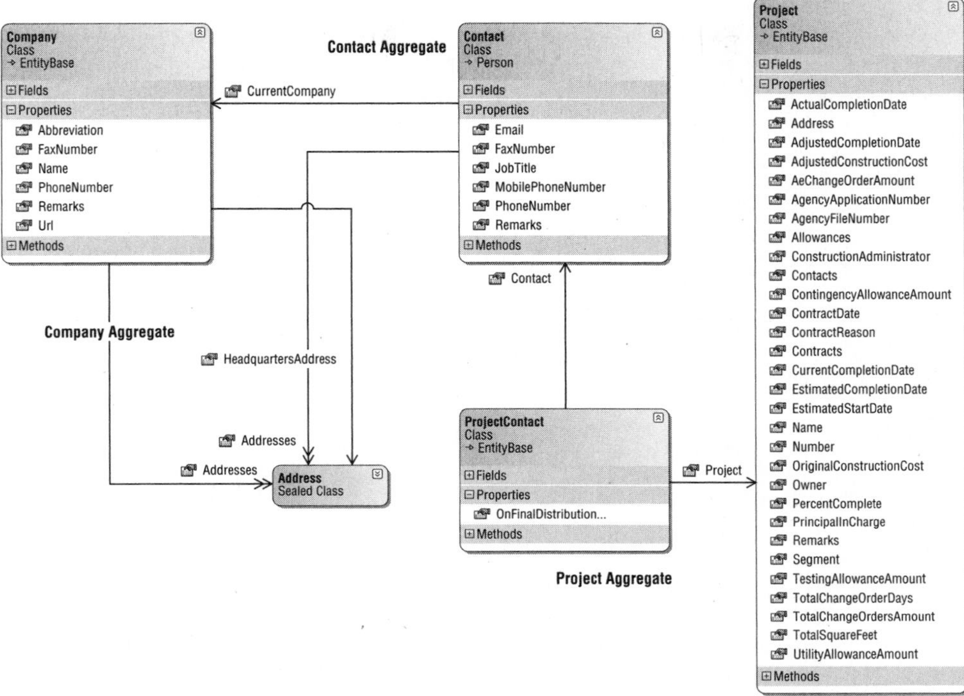

Figure 4.2: Classes composing the Company and Contact Aggregates.

Defining the Aggregate Boundaries

As mentioned before, both the Company and Contact Aggregates share the `Address` class (see Figure 4.3). Since the `Contact` class has a `Company` property, there are two ways to get to a particular company. The first way is to go to the Company Aggregate, and the second way is to go to the Contact Aggregate, navigate to a particular Contact, and then from the Contact navigate to a Company via the `CurrentCompany` property.

The third Aggregate in the figure is one I have already shown, the Project Aggregate. This time around, I have refactored the domain model to include the `ProjectContact` class as part of the Project Aggregate and have defined its relationship with the Contact Aggregate to be one of composition.

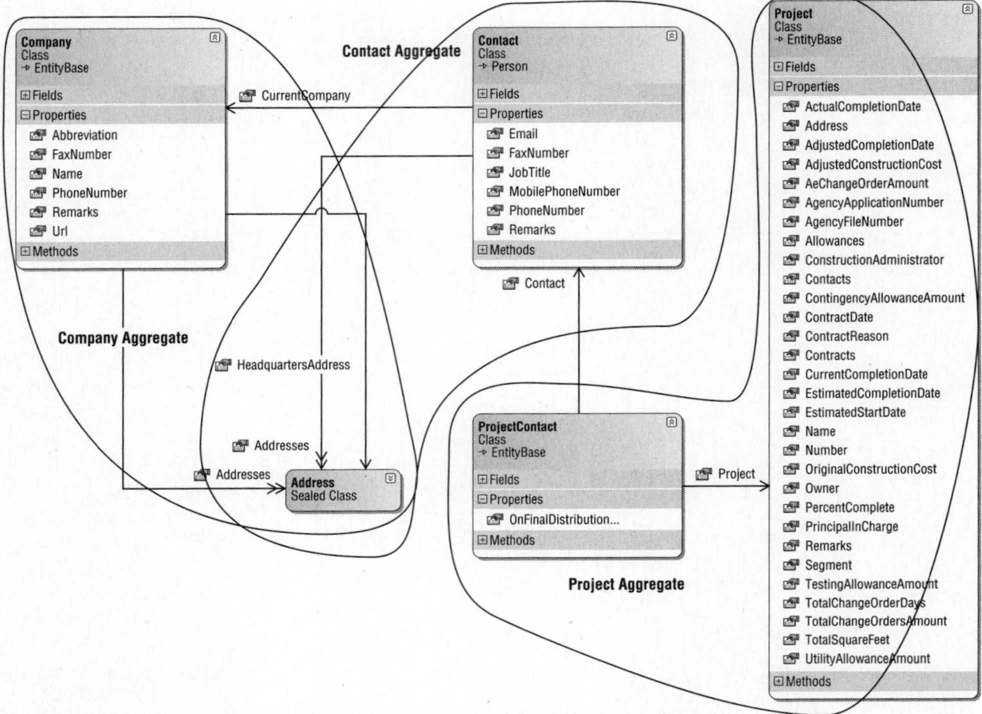

Figure 4.3: The Company and Contact Aggregate boundaries.

Designing the Repositories

Following the one repository per Aggregate rule, there are three repositories to look at in this chapter, the `CompanyRepository`, the `ContactRepository`, and last a revised `ProjectRepository`. Figure 4.4 shows the company and contact repositories.

I did not show the Project Aggregate Repository classes since they are still the same, they will just have some new behavior added to them.

The ICompanyRepository Interface

The `ICompanyRepository` interface is the interface to instances of Company Repositories. Because of the previous refactoring to `IRepository` and `SqlCeRepositoryBase<T>`, the `ICompanyRepository` is currently empty. Here is the `ICompanyRepository` interface:

```
using System;
using SmartCA.Infrastructure.RepositoryFramework;

namespace SmartCA.Model.Companies
{
    public interface ICompanyRepository : IRepository<Company>
    {
    }
}
```

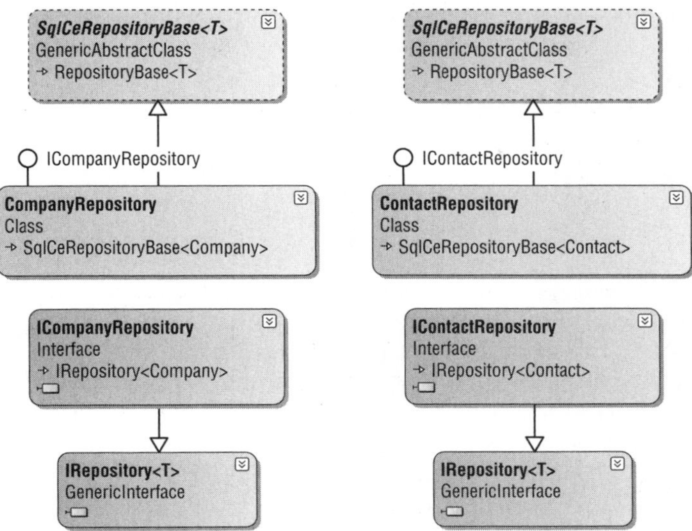

Figure 4.4: The Company and Contact Aggregate Repositories.

The IContactRepository Interface

Just like the `ICompanyRepository` interface, the `IContactRepository` interface is also empty. Here is the `IContactRepository` interface:

```
using System;
using SmartCA.Infrastructure.RepositoryFramework;

namespace SmartCA.Model.Companies
{
    public interface IContactRepository : IRepository<Contact>
    {
    }
}
```

The IProjectRepository Interface Revisited

The `IProjectRepository` interface has a new method added to it in order to support ProjectContacts:

```
using System;
using System.Collections.Generic;
using SmartCA.Infrastructure.RepositoryFramework;

namespace SmartCA.Model.Projects
{
    public interface IProjectRepository : IRepository<Project>
```

(continued)

(continued)

```
        {
            IList<Project> FindBy(IList<MarketSegment> segments, bool completed);
            Project FindBy(string projectNumber);
            IList<MarketSegment> FindAllMarketSegments();
            void SaveContact(ProjectContact contact);

        }
    }
```

The new method added is `SaveContact`, which takes an instance of the `ProjectContact` class as its argument. You may be wondering where a `FindProjectContacts` method is, but the fact that `ProjectContact` is not an Aggregate Root and is part of the Project Aggregate means that I must traverse to `ProjectContact` instances from the Project Entity root. This is because the `ProjectContact` class is just an Entity in the Project Aggregate; it is not its own Aggregate Root.

Writing the Unit Tests

Just as in the last chapter, before implementing the solution for managing Companies and Contacts, I am first going to write some unit tests of what I expect of the Company and Contact Repository implementations. It is important to remember that these tests will compile correctly, but they will also fail when run, and that is what I expect. They will pass once I write the code for the Repository implementations in the Solution section.

The ICompanyRepository Unit Tests

I have already created the `CompanyRepositoryTest` class for the `ICompanyRepository` unit tests. I am not going to go over the steps of creating this class, as I covered that in Chapter 3. I am not going to show how I created the instance of the `ICompanyRepository` interface either, as that is explained in the previous chapter.

Since the `ICompanyRepository` interface has no methods in it, and since it does extend the `IRepository<Company>` interface, I am going to test the methods from the `IRepository<Company>` interface.

The FindByKeyTest Method

The purpose of this test is to verify that I can query the `IProjectRepository` interface for all Projects that match the given Market Segments and have not completed.

```
        /// <summary>
        ///A test for FindBy(object key)
        ///</summary>
        [DeploymentItem("SmartCA.sdf"), TestMethod()]
        public void FindByKeyTest()
        {
            // Set the Key value
            object key = "8b6a05be-6106-45fb-b6cc-b03cfa5ab74b";
```

```
        // Find the Company
        Company company = this.repository.FindBy(key);

        // Verify the Company's name
        Assert.AreEqual("My Company", company.Name);
    }
```

The method first starts out by initializing a unique identifier string value. It then passes that value to the `ICompanyRepository` interface instance in order to retrieve a Company with that particular `Key` value. Once the Company instance is returned from the repository, the Company's name is validated.

The FindAllTest Method

The purpose of the `FindAllTest` method is to validate that the correct number of `Company` instances have been returned by the Company Repository:

```
    /// <summary>
    ///A test for FindAll()
    ///</summary>
    [DeploymentItem("SmartCA.sdf"), TestMethod()]
    public void FindAllTest()
    {
        // Get all of the Companies
        IList<Company> companies = this.repository.FindAll();

        // Make sure there are two
        Assert.AreEqual(2, companies.Count);
    }
```

This method is pretty short; it simply gets all of the `Company` instances and checks the total count. What is not seen here is that when the `ICompanyRepository` interface is implemented, it will test the ability of the repository to map the data correctly from the data store into Company instances. Later in the chapter, when the `ICompanyRepository` interface is implemented, I can run the test again to see what I messed up when the test fails.

The AddTest Method

The purpose of the `AddTest` method is to test adding a new Company to the Company Repository:

```
    /// <summary>
    ///A test for Add(Company item)
    ///</summary>
    [DeploymentItem("SmartCA.sdf"), TestMethod()]
    public void AddTest()
    {
        // Create a new Company and give it a fake name
        Company company = new Company();
        company.Name = "My Test Company";

        // Add the Company to the Repository
        this.repository.Add(company);
```

(continued)

(continued)

```
            // Commit the transaction
            this.unitOfWork.Commit();

            // Reload the Company and verify it's name
            Company savedCompany = this.repository.FindBy(company.Key);
            Assert.AreEqual("My Test Company", savedCompany.Name);

            // Clean up
            this.repository.Remove(savedCompany);
            this.unitOfWork.Commit();
        }
```

This test is a little bit more involved than the previous tests. It starts out by instantiating a new `Company` instance and setting its `Name` property. It then tries to add the Company to the repository, and then commits the transaction by calling the `Commit` method on the `IUnitOfWork` instance.

The `Commit` method is important because that method calls back into the Company Repository to tell it to write the Company's data to the data store.

Once the Company has been saved, it is then reloaded and the Company's `Name` property is checked to verify that the `Add` and `Commit` methods worked properly. The last task that the method needs to perform is to remove the Company. Removing the Company that was just created leaves the data store in the same state as it was in before the method started, which is important for the rest of the tests that may depend on a known state of the data store. Otherwise, some of the other tests may fail because there was data in the data store that was not expected.

The UpdateTest Method

The purpose of the `UpdateTest` method is to find a Company and update it with a different name, and then verify that the change was persisted properly:

```
        /// <summary>
        ///A test for Updating a Company
        ///</summary>
        [DeploymentItem("SmartCA.sdf"), TestMethod()]
        public void UpdateTest()
        {
            // Set the Key value
            object key = "59427e22-0c9e-4821-95d6-9c9f541bf37a";

            // Find the Company
            Company company = this.repository.FindBy(key);

            // Change the Company's Name
            company.Name = "My Updated Company";

            // Update the Repository
            this.repository[company.Key] = company;
```

```
        // Commit the transaction
        this.unitOfWork.Commit();

        // Verify that the change was saved
        Company savedCompany = this.repository.FindBy(company.Key);
        Assert.AreEqual("My Updated Company", savedCompany.Name);
    }
```

The first few lines of the method should look familiar; I am just using the same `Key` value I used before to find a Company. Once I have found the Company, I then change its `Name` property, and then call the indexer method of the `ICompanyRepository`. After the call to the indexer, I use the `IUnitOfWork` interface to commit the transaction. Last, I verify that the change actually made it to the data store by reloading the same Company and checking to see whether its `Name` property value is the same one that I just assigned earlier in the method.

The RemoveTest Method

The purpose of the `RemoveTest` method is to test the process of removing a Company from the data store:

```
    /// <summary>
    ///A test for Remove(Company item)
    ///</summary>
    [DeploymentItem("SmartCA.sdf"), TestMethod()]
    public void RemoveTest()
    {
        // Set the Key value
        object key = "8b6a05be-6106-45fb-b6cc-b03cfa5ab74b";

        // Find the Company
        Company company = this.repository.FindBy(key);

        // Remove the Company from the Repository
        this.repository.Remove(company);

        // Commit the transaction
        this.unitOfWork.Commit();

        // Verify that there is now one less Company in the data store
        IList<Company> companies = this.repository.FindAll();
        Assert.AreEqual(1, companies.Count);
    }
```

Again, the first few lines of the method should look familiar; I am just using the same `Key` value I used before to find a Company. Once I have found the Company, I remove it from the repository. After removing it from the repository, I then use the `IUnitOfWork` interface to commit the transaction. Last, I verify that the change actually made it to the data store by using the repository to find all of the Company instances and making sure that there is now one fewer Company than before.

The IContactRepository Unit Tests

Since the `IContactRepository` is identical to the `ICompanyRepository` in that it does not implement any new methods, I have decided not to show any of the unit test code for it. Its test class will have all of the exact same methods tested as the `ICompanyRepository` test class, only the Entity being passed around will be a Contact instead of a Company.

The IProjectRepository Unit Test

Since the `IProjectRepository` has been refactored with a new method, the `SaveContact` method, I will only unit test that method.

I have created a new method in the `ProjectRepositoryTest` class called `SaveProjectContactTest`. The purpose of the method is to test creating a new `ProjectContact` instance that is then saved to the `IProjectRepository` instance.

```
/// <summary>
///A test for SaveContact(ProjectContact contact)
///</summary>
[DeploymentItem("SmartCA.sdf"), TestMethod()]
public void SaveProjectContactTest()
{
    // The Project Number
    string projectNumber = "12345.00";

    // Try to get the Project
    Project project = this.repository.FindBy(projectNumber);

    // Get the old count of Project Contacts
    int oldCount = project.Contacts.Count;

    // Get a Contact
    IContactRepository contactRepository =
        RepositoryFactory.GetRepository<IContactRepository, Contact>();
    object contactKey = "cae9eb86-5a86-4965-9744-18326fd56a3b";
    Contact contact = contactRepository.FindBy(contactKey);

    // Create a Project Contact
    ProjectContact projectContact = new ProjectContact(project,
        Guid.NewGuid(), contact);

    // Save the Project Contact
    this.repository.SaveContact(projectContact);

    // Commit the transaction
    this.unitOfWork.Commit();

    // Reload the the Project
    Project updatedProject = this.repository.FindBy("12345.00");

    // Verify that there is a new ProjectContact now
    Assert.AreEqual(oldCount, updatedProject.Contacts.Count - 1);
}
```

The first part of the code should remind you of the test code from the last chapter, where I tested finding a Project by a `Project Number` value. The next step is to get the count of `ProjectContact` instances the Project currently contains. Next, I use the `IContactRepository` interface instance to find a Contact, and then I use that contact to create an instance of the `ProjectContact` class. Once I have the new `ProjectContact` instance, I then save it to the `IProjectRepository` instance and commit the transaction on the `IUnitOfWork` instance.

Now that the `ProjectContact` instance is saved, I will reload the same Project from the repository, and make sure that the new count of `ProjectContact` instances is one more than the old count.

The Solution

The design is in place for the Company and Contact domain models, the Company and Contact Aggregates have been defined and their boundaries have been determined, and the repositories have been designed with their associated tests. It is time to start the code implementation. In this section, I will be implementing these designs, as well as implementing the ViewModel and the View for Companies and Contacts.

The Company Class

Like the `Project` class, the `Company` class does not have any behavior yet. I have already shown the `Company` class in Chapter 3, but now I have added some more properties to it:

```
using System;
using SmartCA.Infrastructure.DomainBase;
using System.Collections.Generic;

namespace SmartCA.Model.Companies
{
    public class Company : EntityBase
    {
        private string name;
        private string abbreviation;
        private Address headquartersAddress;
        private List<Address> addresses;
        private string phoneNumber;
        private string faxNumber;
        private string url;
        private string remarks;

        public Company()
            : this(null)
        {
        }

        public Company(object key)
            : base(key)
```

(continued)

(continued)

```
        {
            this.name = string.Empty;
            this.abbreviation = string.Empty;
            this.headquartersAddress = null;
            this.addresses = new List<Address>();
            this.phoneNumber = string.Empty;
            this.faxNumber = string.Empty;
            this.url = string.Empty;
            this.remarks = string.Empty;
        }

        public string Name
        {
            get { return this.name; }
            set { this.name = value; }
        }

        public string Abbreviation
        {
            get { return this.abbreviation; }
            set { this.abbreviation = value; }
        }

        public Address HeadquartersAddress
        {
            get { return this.headquartersAddress; }
            set
            {
                if (this.headquartersAddress != value)
                {
                    this.headquartersAddress = value;
                    if (!this.addresses.Contains(value))
                    {
                        this.addresses.Add(value);
                    }
                }
            }
        }

        public IList<Address> Addresses
        {
            get { return this.addresses; }
        }

        public string PhoneNumber
        {
            get { return this.phoneNumber; }
            set { this.phoneNumber = value; }
        }

        public string FaxNumber
```

```
        {
            get { return this.faxNumber; }
            set { this.faxNumber = value; }
        }

        public string Url
        {
            get { return this.url; }
            set { this.url = value; }
        }

        public string Remarks
        {
            get { return this.remarks; }
            set { this.remarks = value; }
        }
    }
}
```

The interesting thing to note about the `Company` class is its `HeadquartersAddress` property. The address is really just one of its addresses that has been deemed as a headquarters address. In the setter for this property, I included logic to make sure that the value of the `Address` being passed in is actually contained in the internal list of `Addresses`. If it is not present, then the `Address` is added to the collection. The rest of the properties of the `Company` class are all very straightforward.

I am not going to go into the detail of the constructors of the `Company` class; they follow the pattern of having two constructors, a default constructor and a parameterized constructor containing the Key value for the instance. Again, as with the `Project` class before, this is because sometimes I may need to load an existing `Company` from a data store and sometimes I may be creating a new `Company` that does not yet exist in the data store.

The Contact Class

Aside from the names of its properties, the `Contact` class is almost completely the same as the `Company` class:

```
using System;
using System.Collections.Generic;
using System.Text;
using SmartCA.Model.Companies;

namespace SmartCA.Model.Contacts
{
    public class Contact : Person
    {
        private string jobTitle;
        private string email;
        private string phoneNumber;
        private string mobilePhoneNumber;
        private string faxNumber;
        private string remarks;
```

(continued)

(continued)

```
        private Company currentCompany;
        private IList<Address> addresses;

        public Contact()
            : this(null)
        {
        }

        public Contact(object key)
            : this(key, null, null)
        {
        }

        public Contact(object key, string firstName, string lastName)
            : base(key, firstName, lastName)
        {
            this.jobTitle = string.Empty;
            this.email = string.Empty;
            this.phoneNumber = string.Empty;
            this.mobilePhoneNumber = string.Empty;
            this.faxNumber = string.Empty;
            this.remarks = string.Empty;
            this.currentCompany = null;
            this.addresses = new List<Address>();
        }

        public string JobTitle
        {
            get { return this.jobTitle; }
            set { this.jobTitle = value; }
        }

        public string Email
        {
            get { return this.email; }
            set { this.email = value; }
        }

        public string PhoneNumber
        {
            get { return this.phoneNumber; }
            set { this.phoneNumber = value; }
        }

        public string MobilePhoneNumber
        {
            get { return this.mobilePhoneNumber; }
            set { this.mobilePhoneNumber = value; }
        }
```

```
        public string FaxNumber
        {
            get { return this.faxNumber; }
            set { this.faxNumber = value; }
        }

        public string Remarks
        {
            get { return this.remarks; }
            set { this.remarks = value; }
        }

        public Company CurrentCompany
        {
            get { return this.currentCompany; }
            set { this.currentCompany = value; }
        }

        public IList<Address> Addresses
        {
            get { return this.addresses; }
        }
    }
}
```

The main difference between the `Contact` and `Company` classes is that the `Contact` class's `CurrentCompany` property contains a reference to a `Company` instance. The `Company` class, however, does not contain a reference to any `Contact` instances.

The ProjectContact Class

As I mentioned before, the `ProjectContact` class actually contains a `Contact` instance and then adds one other property to it to distinguish it as a `ProjectContact`:

```
using System;
using SmartCA.Model.Contacts;
using SmartCA.Infrastructure.DomainBase;

namespace SmartCA.Model.Projects
{
    public class ProjectContact : EntityBase
    {
        private Project project;
        private bool onFinalDistributionList;
        private Contact contact;

        public ProjectContact(Project project, object key,
            Contact contact) : base(key)
```

(continued)

(continued)

```
        {
            this.project = project;
            this.contact = contact;
            this.onFinalDistributionList = false;
        }

        public Project Project
        {
            get { return this.project; }
        }

        public Contact Contact
        {
            get { return this.contact; }
        }

        public bool OnFinalDistributionList
        {
            get { return this.onFinalDistributionList; }
            set { this.onFinalDistributionList = value; }
        }
    }
}
```

In fact, you cannot create an instance of the `ProjectContact` class without passing an instance of a `Contact` in its constructor, as well as a `Project` instance and a `Key` value. The property that distinguishes the `ProjectContact` class from the `Contact` class is the `OnFinalDistributionList` property. This property is used to designate which Contacts in a Project are to receive copies of documents for things like Submittal Transmittals, Change Orders, and so on once they become final. The `ProjectContact` class also maintains a reference to the Project to which it belongs via the `Project` property, as well as what Contact it contains via its `Contact` property.

The Repository Implementations

In this section, I will be writing the code for the Company and Contact Repositories, as well as refactoring part of the Project Repository.

The Company Repository

To implement the concrete `CompanyRepository` class, just like the other Repository implementations before, I inherit from the `SqlCeRepositoryBase<T>` class, and also implement the `ICompanyRepository` interface:

```
namespace SmartCA.Infrastructure.Repositories
{
    public class CompanyRepository : SqlCeRepositoryBase<Company>,
        ICompanyRepository
    {
...
```

Public Constructors

Just like the `ProjectRepository` class, there are also two public constructors for the `CompanyRepository` class:

```
#region Public Constructors

public CompanyRepository()
    : this(null)
{
}

public CompanyRepository(IUnitOfWork unitOfWork)
    : base(unitOfWork)
{
}

#endregion
```

All Repository implementations will follow this same pattern.

BuildChildCallbacks

Now that I have finished going over the `IProjectRepository` implementation, it is time to go back to how the `Project` class is actually built. If you recall, this functionality was moved up into the base class, `SqlCeRepositoryBase<T>`, but it does make use of the Template Method pattern, and `BuildChildCallbacks` is one of those abstract template methods that the `ProjectRepository` must implement.

```
#region BuildChildCallbacks

protected override void BuildChildCallbacks()
{
    this.ChildCallbacks.Add("addresses",
        delegate(Company company, object childKeyName)
        {
            this.AppendAddresses(company);
        });
}

#endregion
```

The AppendAddresses Callback

The only entry made in the `ChildCallbacks` dictionary was for the `AppendAddresses` method. This method queries the CompanyAddress table to get the list of addresses for the Company:

```
private void AppendAddresses(Company company)
{
    string sql = string.Format
        ("SELECT * FROM CompanyAddress WHERE CompanyID = '{0}'",
        company.Key);
    using (IDataReader reader = this.ExecuteReader(sql))
```

(continued)

(continued)

```
            {
                Address address = null;
                while (reader.Read())
                {
                    address = AddressFactory.BuildAddress(reader);
                    company.Addresses.Add(address);
                    if (CompanyFactory.IsHeadquartersAddress(reader))
                    {
                        company.HeadquartersAddress = address;
                    }
                }
            }
        }
```

This method is using the `AddressFactory` static class to build the `Address` instance from the `IDataReader` instance using static field mappings. It then asks the `CompanyFactory` class whether the data for the Address contained in the `IDataReader` contains a Headquarters Address.

```
        internal static bool IsHeadquartersAddress(IDataReader reader)
        {
            return DataHelper.GetBoolean(reader[FieldNames.IsHeadquarters]);
        }
```

If the data does contain a Headquarters Address, the method then sets the `HeadquartersAddress` property of the `Company` instance.

GetBaseQuery

The next abstract Template Method that the `SqlCeRepositoryBase<T>` calls is the `GetBaseQueryMethod`. Here is the `CompanyRepository` class's override of the abstract method:

```
        #region GetBaseQuery

        protected override string GetBaseQuery()
        {
            return "SELECT * FROM Company";
        }

        #endregion
```

This simply returns the SQL statement for the Company Aggregate. Again, just as I mentioned before, by abstracting this, the `SqlCeRepositryBase<T>` class is able to pull in the two `"FindBy"` methods from the `IRepository<T>` interface, thereby eliminating the code from `CompanyRepository`.

GetBaseWhereClause

This is very similar to the `GetBaseQuery` method just shown, only this time the string returned is just a formatted SQL `WHERE` clause for the Company Aggregate with a placeholder for the `CompanyID` field:

```
#region GetBaseWhereClause

protected override string GetBaseWhereClause()
{
    return " WHERE CompanyID = '{0}';";
}

#endregion
```

The `SqlCeRepositoryBase<T>` class handles filling in the `CompanyID` placeholder at runtime.

Unit of Work Implementation

As I demonstrated in Chapter 3, in order to implement the Repository Framework's Unit of Work, I only need to override three methods, `PersistNewItem(Company item)`, `PersistUpdatedItem(Company item)`, and `PersistDeletedItem(Company item)`. Here is the code for `PersistNewItem`:

```
protected override void PersistNewItem(Company item)
{
    StringBuilder builder = new StringBuilder(100);
    builder.Append(string.Format("INSERT INTO Company
({0},{1},{2},{3},{4},{5},{6}) ",
        CompanyFactory.FieldNames.CompanyId,
        CompanyFactory.FieldNames.CompanyName,
        CompanyFactory.FieldNames.CompanyShortName,
        CompanyFactory.FieldNames.Phone,
        CompanyFactory.FieldNames.Fax,
        CompanyFactory.FieldNames.Url,
        CompanyFactory.FieldNames.Remarks));
    builder.Append(string.Format("VALUES ({0},{1},{2},{3},{4},{5},{6});",
        DataHelper.GetSqlValue(item.Key),
        DataHelper.GetSqlValue(item.Name),
        DataHelper.GetSqlValue(item.Abbreviation),
        DataHelper.GetSqlValue(item.PhoneNumber),
        DataHelper.GetSqlValue(item.FaxNumber),
        DataHelper.GetSqlValue(item.Url),
        DataHelper.GetSqlValue(item.Remarks)));

    this.Database.ExecuteNonQuery(
        this.Database.GetSqlStringCommand(builder.ToString()));

    // Now do the addresses
    this.InsertAddresses(item);
}
```

The code is building up an insert statement composed of the values from the `Company` instance and then executing the query using the Microsoft Enterprise Library's `Database` object. After the insert statement has been executed, the Company's addresses are saved to the database via the `InsertAddresses` method:

```
        private void InsertAddresses(Company company)
        {
            foreach (Address address in company.Addresses)
            {
                this.InsertAddress(address, company.Key,
                    (company.HeadquartersAddress == address));
            }
        }
```

`InsertAddresses` just iterates the `Addresses` property of the `Company` instance and calls `InsertAddress` on each one. `InsertAddress` then saves the address to the database:

```
        private void InsertAddress(Address address, object key,
            bool isHeadquartersAddress)
        {
            StringBuilder builder = new StringBuilder(100);
            builder.Append(string.Format("INSERT INTO CompanyAddress
({0},{1},{2},{3},{4},{5}) ",
                CompanyFactory.FieldNames.CompanyId,
                AddressFactory.FieldNames.Street,
                AddressFactory.FieldNames.City,
                AddressFactory.FieldNames.State,
                AddressFactory.FieldNames.PostalCode,
                CompanyFactory.FieldNames.IsHeadquarters));
            builder.Append(string.Format("VALUES ({0},{1},{2},{3},{4},{5});",
                DataHelper.GetSqlValue(key),
                DataHelper.GetSqlValue(address.Street),
                DataHelper.GetSqlValue(address.City),
                DataHelper.GetSqlValue(address.State),
                DataHelper.GetSqlValue(address.PostalCode),
                DataHelper.GetSqlValue(isHeadquartersAddress)));

            this.Database.ExecuteNonQuery(
                this.Database.GetSqlStringCommand(builder.ToString()));
        }
```

`InsertAddress` is also very similar to the first part of `PersistNewItem`, in that it builds up its insert statement and executes it against the database in the same manner.

`PersistUpdatedItem` first does an update to the Company table:

```
        protected override void PersistUpdatedItem(Company item)
        {
            StringBuilder builder = new StringBuilder(100);
            builder.Append("UPDATE Company SET ");

            builder.Append(string.Format("{0} = {1}",
                CompanyFactory.FieldNames.CompanyName,
```

```
            DataHelper.GetSqlValue(item.Name)));

        builder.Append(string.Format(",{0} = {1}",
            CompanyFactory.FieldNames.CompanyShortName,
            DataHelper.GetSqlValue(item.Abbreviation)));

        builder.Append(string.Format(",{0} = {1}",
            CompanyFactory.FieldNames.Phone,
            DataHelper.GetSqlValue(item.PhoneNumber)));

        builder.Append(string.Format(",{0} = {1}",
            CompanyFactory.FieldNames.Fax,
            DataHelper.GetSqlValue(item.FaxNumber)));

        builder.Append(string.Format(",{0} = {1}",
            CompanyFactory.FieldNames.Url,
            DataHelper.GetSqlValue(item.Url)));

        builder.Append(string.Format(",{0} = {1}",
            CompanyFactory.FieldNames.Remarks,
            DataHelper.GetSqlValue(item.Remarks)));

        builder.Append(" ");
        builder.Append(this.BuildBaseWhereClause(item.Key));

        this.Database.ExecuteNonQuery(
            this.Database.GetSqlStringCommand(builder.ToString()));

        // Now do the addresses

        // First, delete the existing ones
        this.DeleteAddresses(item);

        // Now, add the current ones
        this.InsertAddresses(item);
    }
```

The second part of the method uses `DeleteAddresses` to delete the existing addresses for the Company and then uses the familiar `InsertAddresses` method to add the addresses from the Company's `Addresses` property to the database. `DeleteAddresses` runs a query against the `CompanyAddress` table to remove all entries with a matching `CompanyID` field value:

```
    private void DeleteAddresses(Company company)
    {
        string query = string.Format("DELETE FROM CompanyAddress {0}",
            this.BuildBaseWhereClause(company.Key));
        this.Database.ExecuteNonQuery(
            this.Database.GetSqlStringCommand(query));
    }
```

The last method in `CompanyRepository` to override, `PersistDeletedItem`, follows the same pattern as `DeleteAddresses`:

```
protected override void PersistDeletedItem(Company item)
{
    // Delete the company addresses first
    this.DeleteAddresses(item);

    // Now delete the company
    string query = string.Format("DELETE FROM Company {0}",
        this.BuildBaseWhereClause(item.Key));
    this.Database.ExecuteNonQuery(
        this.Database.GetSqlStringCommand(query));
}
```

This method actually takes advantage of the `DeleteAddresses` method in the first part of its body in order to remove the entries from the `CompanyAddress` table before deleting a row from the `Company` table. The rest of the code in the method should look very familiar as it is building up a standard delete statement for removing a row from the `Company` table and then executing the statement.

The Contact Repository

To implement the concrete `ContactRepository` class, just as before, I inherit from the `SqlCeRepositoryBase<T>` class, and also implement the `IContactRepository` interface:

```
namespace SmartCA.Infrastructure.Repositories
{
    public class ContactRepository : SqlCeRepositoryBase<Contact>,
        IContactRepository
    {
...
```

Public Constructors

The public constructors for the `ContactRepository` class are exactly the same as the `CompanyRepository` class:

```
#region Public Constructors

public ContactRepository()
    : this(null)
{
}

public ContactRepository(IUnitOfWork unitOfWork)
    : base(unitOfWork)
{
}

#endregion
```

GetBaseQuery

Here is the ContactRepository class's override of the GetBaseQuery abstract method:

```
#region GetBaseQuery

protected override string GetBaseQuery()
{
    return "SELECT * FROM Contact";
}

#endregion
```

This just follows the same Template Method pattern I have shown all along.

GetBaseWhereClause

Again, I am just following the Template Method pattern for implementing the GetBaseWhereClause method:

```
#region GetBaseWhereClause

protected override string GetBaseWhereClause()
{
    return " WHERE ContactID = '{0}';";
}

#endregion
```

Unit of Work Implementation

Since the code for the ContactRepository's Unit of Work implementation is almost identical to the CompanyRepository's implementation, I am not going to show it here. It is follows all of the same patterns, so there is nothing new to see with it.

The Refactored Project Repository Implementation

```
public void SaveContact(ProjectContact contact)
{
    // Get the list of contacts
    List<ProjectContact> contacts =
        new List<ProjectContact>(
            this.FindBy(contact.Project.Key).Contacts);

    if (contacts.Where(c => c.Key.Equals(contact.Key)).Count() > 0)
    {
        // The contact exists, so update it
        this.UnitOfWork.RegisterChanged(contact, this);
    }
    else
    {
        // The contact is new, so add it
        this.UnitOfWork.RegisterAdded(contact, this);
    }
}
```

The `SaveContact` method first uses the `FindBy` method to find the correct Project based on a Project Key property passed in from the `ProjectContact` argument. Once the Project is found, I then call the `Contacts` property getter to get the list of `ProjectContact` instances for the Project. When the list has been obtained, a LINQ query is performed on the list to see if it contains any `ProjectContact` instances that match that being passed from the method's argument contact argument. To perform the query, I am using a lambda expression (`c => c.Key.Equals(contact.Key)`) to find the list of ProjectContacts that meet the criteria, and then using the `Count` method extension on the `IEnumerable` interface (which `List<ProjectContact>` implements) to see whether the results are greater than zero. If the results are greater than zero, then I know that the ProjectContact already exists, and I can go ahead and update it. If not, then I know that the ProjectContact is new and needs to be added.

The way that I am handling the actual changes to the data store is by telling the `UnitOfWork` property of the `RepositoryBase<T>` instance to register the items as either changed or added. Then, once the `Commit` method on the `IUnitOfWork` instance is called, the items will be properly persisted and the transaction will be committed.

Calling the `IUnitOfWork` instance directly should look strange, since in every other Repository implementation I just had the `RepositoryBase<T>` class abstract that away for me. This case is different, because I am not dealing with an object that is an Entity Root. I have to tell the `IUnitOfWork` instance about the Entity explicitly in order for it to be part of the transaction. I also had to refactor a little bit more of the `ProjectRepository` in order for the transaction to work. Normally, when `Commit` is called on the `IUnitOfWork` instance, the `IUnitOfWork` instance will cycle through all of the entities in its deleted, added, and changed Entity collections, and call the proper `Persist*` method on each one (e.g., `PersistNewItem`). In this case, it's a little bit of a challenge because I want to save one of the Project's ProjectContact items, but not the whole entire Project. In the current implementation of the `ProjectRepository`, if one of the `Persist*` overrides is called, it will cause an error because it will try to convert a `ProjectContact` instance into a `Project` instance. The way around that was to declare the `RepositoryBase<T>`'s `Persist*` methods as virtual and override them, thereby effectively bypassing the `RepositoryBase<T>`'s translation from `EntityBase` to `Project` by casting the Entity to the proper type using the `T` generic parameter. I then exposed the `IUnitOfWork` instance as a protected property. Here is what I am talking about on `RepositoryBase<T>`:

```
#region IUnitOfWorkRepository Members

    public virtual void PersistNewItem(EntityBase item)
    {
        this.PersistNewItem((T)item);
    }

    public virtual void PersistUpdatedItem(EntityBase item)
    {
        this.PersistUpdatedItem((T)item);
    }

    public virtual void PersistDeletedItem(EntityBase item)
    {
        this.PersistDeletedItem((T)item);
    }

    #endregion
```

```
        protected IUnitOfWork UnitOfWork
        {
            get { return this.unitOfWork; }
        }

        protected abstract void PersistNewItem(T item);
        protected abstract void PersistUpdatedItem(T item);
        protected abstract void PersistDeletedItem(T item);
```

By overriding the `PersistNewItem(EntityBase item)`, `PersistUpdatedItem(EntityBase item)`, and `PersistDeletedItem(EntityBase item)` methods, the abstract `PersistNewItem(T item)`, `PersistUpdatedItem(T item)`, and `PersistDeletedItem(T item)` methods never get called. I have to call them myself within the `ProjectRepository`:

```
        public override void PersistNewItem(EntityBase item)
        {
            Project project = item as Project;
            if (project != null)
            {
                this.PersistNewItem(project);
            }
            else
            {
                ProjectContact contact = item as ProjectContact;
                this.PersistNewItem(contact);
            }
        }
```

In the example above, I have to test to see what is getting passed in to the method from the `IUnitOfWork` instance; it could either be a `Project` instance or a `ProjectContact` instance. If it is a `Project` instance, then I just call the existing `PersistNewItem(Project item)` method. If it is a `ProjectContact` instance, then I need to call the new method, `PersistNewItem(ProjectContact item)`.

```
        protected void PersistNewItem(ProjectContact contact)
        {
            StringBuilder builder = new StringBuilder(100);
            builder.Append(string.Format(
                "INSERT INTO ProjectContact ({0},{1},{2}) ",
            ProjectFactory.FieldNames.ProjectId,
            ContactFactory.FieldNames.ContactId,
            ProjectFactory.FieldNames.OnFinalDistributionList));
            builder.Append(string.Format("VALUES ({0},{1},{2});",
                DataHelper.GetSqlValue(contact.Project.Key),
                DataHelper.GetSqlValue(contact.Contact.Key),
                DataHelper.GetSqlValue(contact.OnFinalDistributionList)));
            this.Database.ExecuteNonQuery(
                this.Database.GetSqlStringCommand(builder.ToString()));
        }
```

The other methods, `PersistUpdatedItem` *and* `PersistDeletedItem` *follow the exact same pattern so I am not going to show them.*

Everything is still cleanly broken out and easy to maintain. The Repository Framework still works and I now have a pattern for saving Entities off of the aggregate root. That wasn't too painful of a refactoring, and it was actually pretty fun.

The Service Class Implementations

In this application, the only `Service` classes I have implemented up to this point are those that live in the domain model layer and act as facades to their respective Repository interfaces.

The CompanyService Class

The `CompanyService` class is responsible for retrieving and saving `Company` instances.

```
using System;
using System.Collections.Generic;
using SmartCA.Infrastructure;
using SmartCA.Infrastructure.RepositoryFramework;

namespace SmartCA.Model.Companies
{
    public static class CompanyService
    {
        private static ICompanyRepository repository;
        private static IUnitOfWork unitOfWork;

        static CompanyService()
        {
            CompanyService.unitOfWork = new UnitOfWork();
            CompanyService.repository =
                RepositoryFactory.GetRepository<ICompanyRepository,
                Company>(CompanyService.unitOfWork);
        }

        public static IList<Company> GetOwners()
        {
            return CompanyService.GetAllCompanies();
        }

        public static IList<Company> GetAllCompanies()
        {
            return CompanyService.repository.FindAll();
        }

        public static void SaveCompany(Company company)
        {
            CompanyService.repository[company.Key] = company;
            CompanyService.unitOfWork.Commit();
        }
    }
}
```

The first thing to notice about this class is that it is a static class with all static methods. Again, the idea is to make it very easy to use. The next interesting part of the class is its static constructor. This is where the instance to the `IProjectRepository` is created via the `RepositoryFactory`. Also note that when the `IProjectRepository` is created it is injected with a `UnitOfWork` instance. This is necessary since I will be saving `Project` instances in this class and want that operation to be wrapped in a transaction.

The rest of the class is just acting as a façade in front of the `IProjectRepository` instance. The next interesting method is the `SaveProject` method. Notice how the collection-like functionality of the `IProjectRepository` instance is utilized by calling the indexer (see Chapter 2 for more information on this). What's nice about having the indexer is that the `RepositoryBase<T>` class will figure out if it is a new `Project` or an existing one. Also, after updating the `IProjectRepository` with the newly updated `Project` instance, the `Commit` method is called on the `UnitOfWork` instance to commit the transaction.

The ContactService Class

Currently, the only thing that the `ContactService` class does is to wrap the `IContactRepository` call for saving a Contact:

```
using System;
using SmartCA.Infrastructure;
using SmartCA.Infrastructure.RepositoryFramework;

namespace SmartCA.Model.Contacts
{
    public static class ContactService
    {
        private static IContactRepository repository;
        private static IUnitOfWork unitOfWork;

        static ContactService()
        {
            ContactService.unitOfWork = new UnitOfWork();
            ContactService.repository =
                RepositoryFactory.GetRepository<IContactRepository,
                Contact>(ContactService.unitOfWork);
        }

        public static void SaveContact(Contact contact)
        {
            ContactService.repository[contact.Key] = contact;
            ContactService.unitOfWork.Commit();
        }
    }
}
```

Right now, this code does not need any additional functionality, so I am going to leave it alone for a while.

The ProjectService Class

In order to save a ProjectContact, since it is part of the Project Aggregate, the `SaveProjectContact` method was added to the `ProjectService` class:

```
using System;
using System.Collections.Generic;
using SmartCA.Model.Projects;
using SmartCA.Infrastructure.RepositoryFramework;
using SmartCA.Infrastructure;
using SmartCA.Model.Contacts;

namespace SmartCA.Model.Projects
{
    public static class ProjectService
    {
        private static IProjectRepository projectRepository;
        private static IContactRepository contactRepository;
        private static IUnitOfWork unitOfWork;

        static ProjectService()
        {
            ProjectService.unitOfWork = new UnitOfWork();
            ProjectService.projectRepository =
                RepositoryFactory.GetRepository<IProjectRepository,
                Project>(ProjectService.unitOfWork);
            ProjectService.contactRepository =
                RepositoryFactory.GetRepository<IContactRepository,
                Contact>(ProjectService.unitOfWork);
        }

        public static IList<Project> GetAllProjects()
        {
            return ProjectService.projectRepository.FindAll();
        }

        public static IList<MarketSegment> GetMarketSegments()
        {
            return ProjectService.projectRepository.FindAllMarketSegments();
        }

        public static void SaveProject(Project project)
        {
            ProjectService.projectRepository[project.Key] = project;
            ProjectService.unitOfWork.Commit();
        }

        public static void SaveProjectContact(ProjectContact contact)
        {
            ProjectService.contactRepository[contact.Contact.Key]
                = contact.Contact;
```

```
                // Add/Update the project contact
                ProjectService.projectRepository.SaveContact(contact);
                ProjectService.unitOfWork.Commit();
            }
        }
    }
```

The method first calls the `IContactRepository` instance's indexer to save the `Contact` instance. I thought about having this call the `ContactService`'s `SaveContact` method, but then I would lose my Unit of Work context, so I decided to keep the code here for now. After talking to the `IContactRepository` instance, the code then calls the `SaveContact` method on the `IProjectRepository`'s instance. Once both of those calls are made, the Unit of Work is committed.

The Company ViewModel

Following the same patterns as before, the `CompanyViewModel` class adapts the Company Aggregate from the domain model to the UI. To start out, just like my previous examples, I inherit from the `ViewModel` abstract class:

```
using System;
using SmartCA.Infrastructure.UI;
using System.Windows.Data;
using SmartCA.Model.Companies;
using System.Collections.Generic;
using SmartCA.Model;
using System.Collections.ObjectModel;
using System.Collections.Specialized;
using System.ComponentModel;
using Xceed.Wpf.DataGrid;

namespace SmartCA.Presentation.ViewModels
{
    public class CompanyViewModel : ViewModel
    {
        #region Constants

        private static class Constants
        {
            public const string CurrentCompanyPropertyName = "CurrentCompany";
            public const string AddressesPropertyName = "Addresses";
            public const string HeadquartersAddressPropertyName =
                "HeadquartersAddress";
        }

        #endregion

        #region Private Fields

        private CollectionView companies;
        private IList<Company> companiesList;
        private Company currentCompany;
```

(continued)

(continued)

```
        private BindingList<MutableAddress> addresses;
        private MutableAddress headquartersAddress;
        private DelegateCommand saveCommand;
        private DelegateCommand newCommand;
        private DelegateCommand deleteAddressCommand;

        #endregion

        #region Constructors

        public CompanyViewModel()
            : this(null)
        {
        }

        public CompanyViewModel(IView view)
            : base(view)
        {
            this.companiesList = CompanyService.GetAllCompanies();
            this.companies = new CollectionView(companiesList);
            this.currentCompany = null;
            this.addresses = new BindingList<MutableAddress>();
            this.headquartersAddress = null;
            this.saveCommand = new DelegateCommand(this.SaveCommandHandler);
            this.saveCommand.IsEnabled = false;
            this.newCommand = new DelegateCommand(this.NewCommandHandler);
            this.deleteAddressCommand =
                new DelegateCommand(this.DeleteAddressCommandHandler);
        }

        #endregion

        #region Public Properties

        public CollectionView Companies
        {
            get { return this.companies; }
        }

        public Company CurrentCompany
        {
            get { return this.currentCompany; }
            set
            {
                if (this.currentCompany != value)
                {
                    this.currentCompany = value;
                    this.OnPropertyChanged(Constants.CurrentCompanyPropertyName);
                    this.saveCommand.IsEnabled = (this.currentCompany != null);
```

```
                this.PopulateAddresses();
                this.HeadquartersAddress =
                    new MutableAddress(
                        this.currentCompany.HeadquartersAddress);
            }
        }
    }

    public BindingList<MutableAddress> Addresses
    {
        get { return this.addresses; }
    }

    public MutableAddress HeadquartersAddress
    {
        get { return this.headquartersAddress; }
        set
        {
            if (this.headquartersAddress != value)
            {
                this.headquartersAddress = value;
                this.OnPropertyChanged(
                    Constants.HeadquartersAddressPropertyName);
            }
        }
    }

    public DelegateCommand NewCommand
    {
        get { return this.newCommand; }
    }

    public DelegateCommand SaveCommand
    {
        get { return this.saveCommand; }
    }

    public DelegateCommand DeleteAddressCommand
    {
        get { return this.deleteAddressCommand; }
    }

    #endregion

    #region Private Methods

    private void SaveCommandHandler(object sender, EventArgs e)
    {
        this.currentCompany.Addresses.Clear();
        foreach (MutableAddress address in this.addresses)
```

(continued)

(continued)

```
            {
                this.currentCompany.Addresses.Add(address.ToAddress());
            }
            this.currentCompany.HeadquartersAddress =
                this.headquartersAddress.ToAddress();
            CompanyService.SaveCompany(this.currentCompany);
        }

        private void NewCommandHandler(object sender, EventArgs e)
        {
            Company company = new Company();
            company.Name = "{Enter Company Name}";
            this.companiesList.Add(company);
            this.companies.Refresh();
            this.companies.MoveCurrentToLast();
        }

        private void DeleteAddressCommandHandler(object sender,
            DelegateCommandEventArgs e)
        {
            MutableAddress address = e.Parameter as MutableAddress;
            if (address != null)
            {
                this.addresses.Remove(address);
            }
        }

        private void PopulateAddresses()
        {
            if (this.currentCompany != null)
            {
                this.addresses.Clear();
                foreach (Address address in this.currentCompany.Addresses)
                {
                    this.addresses.Add(new MutableAddress(address));
                }
                this.OnPropertyChanged(Constants.AddressesPropertyName);
            }
        }

        #endregion
    }
}
```

Constructor

The interesting thing to note in this class, which is a little different from the other `ViewModel` classes, is the initialization of the `BindingList<MutableAddress>` (the addresses variable) type in the constructor that is used to represent the list of addresses for the Company.

```
#region Constructors

public CompanyViewModel()
    : this(null)
{
}

public CompanyViewModel(IView view)
    : base(view)
{
    this.companiesList = CompanyService.GetAllCompanies();
    this.companies = new CollectionView(companiesList);
    this.currentCompany = null;
    this.addresses = new BindingList<MutableAddress>();
    this.headquartersAddress = null;
    this.saveCommand = new DelegateCommand(this.SaveCommandHandler);
    this.saveCommand.IsEnabled = false;
    this.newCommand = new DelegateCommand(this.NewCommandHandler);
    this.deleteAddressCommand =
        new DelegateCommand(this.DeleteAddressCommandHandler);
}

#endregion
```

The `MutableAddress` type should look familiar, as I have already used that in last chapter's `ProjectInformationViewModel` class. The reason I had to use this type of object, and not something like a `CollectionView`, is because I have decided to display the Company's addresses in the form of a data grid, and the data grid I am using (more on that in the next section) requires that the data bound to it implement the `IBindingList` interface. Since the `BindingList` class gives me that implementation for free, I have decided to use it.

You may be wondering why I am maintaining an `IList<Company>` variable (`companiesList`) as well as the `CollectionView` of the list. In the UI form I am going to be displaying a list of Companies to choose from, but I am also supporting adding new Companies, which need to be added the list. Therefore, I need access to the `IList` interface so that I can add new Companies to the list. Just as when I had to deal with addresses in the previous chapter, I am also maintaining a `MutableAddress` instance for the Company's `HeadquartersAddress` property. The rest of the constructor code should look very familiar; I am just doing the standard wire-up code for the `DelegateCommand` instances.

Properties

The `CurrentCompany` property indicates the current `Company` instance that is being edited:

```
public Company CurrentCompany
{
    get { return this.currentCompany; }
    set
    {
        if (this.currentCompany != value)
```

(continued)

(continued)

```
                {
                    this.currentCompany = value;
                    this.OnPropertyChanged(Constants.CurrentCompanyPropertyName);
                    this.saveCommand.IsEnabled = (this.currentCompany != null);
                    this.PopulateAddresses();
                    this.HeadquartersAddress =
                        new MutableAddress(
                            this.currentCompany.HeadquartersAddress);
                }
            }
        }
```

Whenever a new Company is selected in the UI, the `CurrentProperty` setter is called (I will show you how this is done in the XAML in a few paragraphs). Once that has happened, the `PropertyChanged` event for the `CurrentCompany` property is raised, thus letting the UI know to refresh itself. Next, the `SaveCommand`'s `IsEnabled` property is set to the boolean value of the Current Company. Then the `PopulateAddresses` method is called:

```
        private void PopulateAddresses()
        {
            if (this.currentCompany != null)
            {
                this.addresses.Clear();
                foreach (Address address in this.currentCompany.Addresses)
                {
                    this.addresses.Add(new MutableAddress(address));
                }
                this.OnPropertyChanged(Constants.AddressesPropertyName);
            }
        }
```

This is necessary because the Addresses contained in the Company's `Addresses` property are the immutable Address types, and in order to be able to edit the Addresses I have to convert them into `MutableAddress` types. Once this is done, then the `PropertyChanged` event for the `Addresses` property is raised so the UI can refresh itself.

The `CurrentCompany` property setter then finishes by resetting the `HeadquartersAddress` property. This is necessary because the `HeadquartersAddress` property is also a converter between the current Company's immutable `Address` type and a `MutableAddress`:

```
        public MutableAddress HeadquartersAddress
        {
            get { return this.headquartersAddress; }
            set
            {
                if (this.headquartersAddress != value)
```

```
                {
                    this.headquartersAddress = value;
                    this.OnPropertyChanged(
                        Constants.HeadquartersAddressPropertyName);
                }
            }
        }
```

The code for the property setter ensures that when the property changes the `PropertyChanged` event is fired for the UI to consume.

The rest of the properties in the `CompanyView` class are the read-only `DelegateCommand` properties for creating New Companies, saving Companies, and deleting Addresses from a Company.

Command Handler Methods

The handlers for the `DelegateCommand` properties are pretty interesting. The `NewCommandHandler` method has to do a lot of housekeeping:

```
        private void NewCommandHandler(object sender, EventArgs e)
        {
            Company company = new Company();
            company.Name = "{Enter Company Name}";
            this.companiesList.Add(company);
            this.companies.Refresh();
            this.companies.MoveCurrentToLast();
        }
```

It first has to create a new instance of a `Company`, set its `Name` property to some default text, and then add it to the internal list of companies. Once the internal list has been updated, it then calls `Refresh` on the `CollectionView` companies variable in order to have the UI be refreshed. Finally, by calling the `MoveCurrentToLast` method on the `CollectionView`, the new Company will appear last in the list in the UI.

The `DeleteAddressCommandHandler` method is interesting because it gets the `MutableAddress` that must be deleted passed in to it from the `DelegateCommandEventArgs` parameter.

```
        private void DeleteAddressCommandHandler(object sender,
            DelegateCommandEventArgs e)
        {
            MutableAddress address = e.Parameter as MutableAddress;
            if (address != null)
            {
                this.addresses.Remove(address);
            }
        }
```

It then checks to see whether it is null, and if it is not, it removes it from the `BindingList<MutableAddress>` collection (the addresses are variable). Once this happens, the data grid that is bound to it is automatically updated.

The Company View

The View that is associated with the `CompanyViewModel`, the `CompanyView` class (which consists of XAML plus code-behind), is very similar to the `ProjectInformationView` class, in that it has very little code behind it:

```
using System;
using System.Windows;
using SmartCA.Presentation.ViewModels;
using SmartCA.Infrastructure.UI;

namespace SmartCA.Presentation.Views
{
 public partial class CompanyView : Window, IView
    {
        public CompanyView()
        {
            this.InitializeComponent();
             this.DataContext = new CompanyViewModel(this);
        }
    }
}
```

From this point forward, I will not show the code-behind any more for the Views, since they are almost always going to be identical. Before diving into the XAML for the `CompanyView`, take a look at Figure 4.5, which shows what the form looks like at run time.

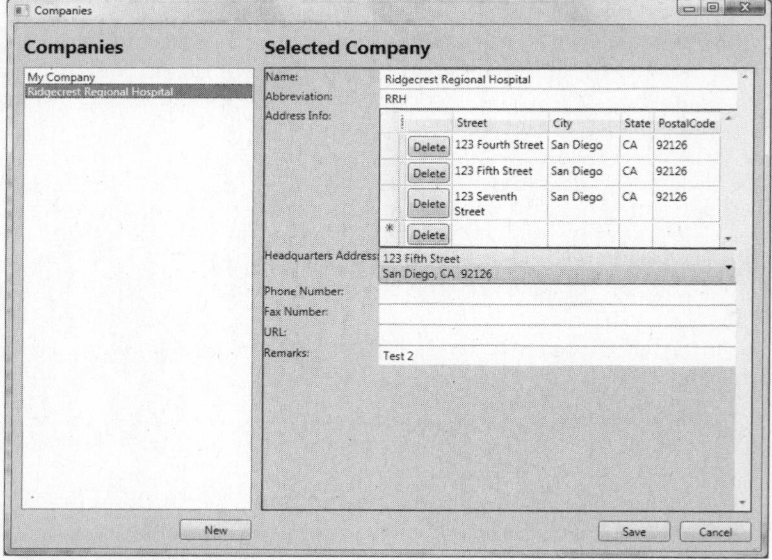

Figure 4.5: The Company View

The form is split into two parts; the one on the left is for selecting a Company to edit, and the one on the right is for actually editing the Company. The New button adds a new Company to the list. The Save and Cancel buttons both deal with the currently selected Company. There are two things that should stand out to you while looking at this form. One, I am using a data grid to display and edit the addresses, and two, the dropdown for the headquarters address looks pretty cool, doesn't it?

For the grid, I am using the Xceed DataGrid for WPF component. Xceed recognized that Microsoft did not include a data grid implementation in WPF, and so they made one themselves. The nice part is that their product is licensed for free, with an unlimited number of licenses per company. Kudos to them, I think that this was a very smart marketing move on their part, since most developers are going to want to use a data grid control at some point when working in WPF.

Using the Xceed Data Grid

Since the XAML code for displaying lists of addresses will be needed for Contacts as well as Companies, I have created the `Addresses` reusable `UserControl` to display editable Address data in a grid. Because I am using the Xceed DataGrid control, it was fairly easy to create the `Addresses UserControl` to display the list of editable addresses. In order to get the look and feel shown in Figure 4.5 the `UserControl` contains the following XAML:

```
<UserControl x:Class="SmartCA.Presentation.Views.Addresses"
    xmlns="http://schemas.microsoft.com/winfx/2006/xaml/presentation"
    xmlns:xcdg="http://schemas.xceed.com/wpf/xaml/datagrid"
    xmlns:x="http://schemas.microsoft.com/winfx/2006/xaml">
    <xcdg:DataGridControl ItemsSource="{Binding}">
        <xcdg:DataGridControl.Columns>
               <xcdg:Column Width="50" FieldName="DeleteButton"
                      DisplayMemberBinding="{Binding .}">
                      <xcdg:Column.CellContentTemplate>
                             <DataTemplate>
                                    <Button Content="Delete"
                                           Command="{Binding
                                           RelativeSource={RelativeSource
                                           FindAncestor, AncestorType={x:Type
Window}},
Path=DataContext.DeleteAddressCommand}">
                                           <Button.CommandParameter>
                                                  <Binding Path="."/>
                                           </Button.CommandParameter>
                                    </Button>
                             </DataTemplate>
                      </xcdg:Column.CellContentTemplate>
               </xcdg:Column>
               <xcdg:Column FieldName="Street" Width="100" TextWrapping="Wrap"/>
               <xcdg:Column FieldName="City" Width="75" TextWrapping="Wrap"/>
               <xcdg:Column FieldName="State"  MaxWidth="35"/>
               <xcdg:Column FieldName="PostalCode" MaxWidth="70"/>
        </xcdg:DataGridControl.Columns>
```

(continued)

(continued)

```
            <xcdg:DataGridControl.View>
                <xcdg:TableView HorizontalGridLineThickness="1"
                    VerticalGridLineThickness="1">
                    <xcdg:TableView.HorizontalGridLineBrush>
                        <SolidColorBrush Color="Orange"/>
                    </xcdg:TableView.HorizontalGridLineBrush>
                    <xcdg:TableView.VerticalGridLineBrush>
                        <SolidColorBrush Color="Orange"/>
                    </xcdg:TableView.VerticalGridLineBrush>
                    <xcdg:TableView.Footers>
                        <DataTemplate>
                            <xcdg:InsertionRow/>
                      </DataTemplate>
                    </xcdg:TableView.Footers>
                    <xcdg:TableView.FixedHeaders>
                        <xcdg:ClearHeadersFooters/>
                        <DataTemplate>
                            <xcdg:ColumnManagerRow/>
                        </DataTemplate>
                    </xcdg:TableView.FixedHeaders>
                </xcdg:TableView>
            </xcdg:DataGridControl.View>
    </xcdg:DataGridControl>
</UserControl>
```

The first thing to notice is that, at the top of the XAML, I am setting the `ItemsSource` property of the `DataGridControl` to a value of `"{Binding}"`. This allows the `DataGridControl` to take advantage of the current Window's `DataContext`. The next interesting thing to note is the Delete button that shows up in every row of the addresses grid. The grid column containing repeating Delete buttons has its `DisplayMemberBinding` set to a value of `"{Binding .}"`, and the Button itself has its `Command` property's binding set to `"{Binding RelativeSource={RelativeSource FindAncestor, AncestorType={x:Type Window}}, Path=DataContext.DeleteAddressCommand}"`. These settings allow each Delete Button to traverse up the binding tree to the `Window`, descend from the `Window` to the `DataContext`, and then bind to the `DeleteAddressCommand` property of the `DataContext`, which in this case is the `CompanyViewModel`. The next thing I need, once I get the Delete Button's `Command` property bound, is to have it pass as a parameter to the item that is being deleted. This is done by the following code inside of the Button element:

```
<Button.CommandParameter>
    <Binding Path="."/>
</Button.CommandParameter>
```

This allows the Button's `Command` property to receive the item being deleted; in this case it is an `Address` instance.

The Headquarters Address Addresses Dropdown

As far as the dropdown for the headquarters address, this is made possible by a little refactoring to both the `Address` and `MutableAddress` classes and some WPF magic.

Here is the `ToString` override in the `Address` class:

```
public override string ToString()
{
    StringBuilder builder = new StringBuilder(300);
    builder.Append(this.street);
    builder.Append("\r\n");
    builder.Append(this.city);
    builder.Append(", ");
    builder.Append(this.state);
    builder.Append(" ");
    builder.Append(this.postalCode);
    return builder.ToString();
}
```

In the `MutableAddress` class, it is even easier:

```
public override string ToString()
{
    return this.ToAddress().ToString();
}
```

In WPF, by not specifying the `DisplayMemberPath` property of the `ComboBox` control, what is rendered for the text of the items in the list is the `ToString()` result of each item in the list. In .NET, the default value specified on the `System.Object` class is the type name of the class, that is, "System.Object" or "System.String", and so on, but, if your class overrides the `ToString` method, then WPF will use that for the value of the list item.

Here is the XAML for the Headquarters Address `ComboBox`:

```
<ComboBox Grid.Row="3" Grid.Column="1"
    SelectedItem="{Binding Path=HeadquartersAddress}"
    ItemsSource="{Binding Path=Addresses}">
</ComboBox>
```

This XAML declares that the `SelectedItem` of the `ComboBox` will set the `HeadquartersAddress` property in the `CompanyViewModel` class (remember that a `CompanyViewModel` instance has been set as the `DataContext` for the whole `Window`). It also declares that the `ItemsSource` property is bound to the `Addresses` property in the `CompanyViewModel`, and that property is a `BindingList <MutableAddress>` type.

The rest of the XAML for the `CompanyView` is fairly vanilla, so I will not show it here for the sake of brevity.

The Project Contact View Model

The ProjectContactViewModel is very similar to the CompanyViewModel, and is actually a little bit simpler. Because both the CompanyViewModel and ProjectContactViewModel need to contain an Addresses property and the necessary behavior around that property, I was able to factor that functionality out from the CompanyViewModel into a new abstract class called AddressesViewModel.

```
using System;
using System.Collections.Generic;
using SmartCA.Infrastructure.UI;
using System.ComponentModel;

namespace SmartCA.Presentation.ViewModels
{
    public abstract class AddressesViewModel : ViewModel
    {
        #region Constants

        private static class Constants
        {
            public const string AddressesPropertyName = "Addresses";
        }

        #endregion

        #region Private Fields

        private BindingList<MutableAddress> addresses;
        private DelegateCommand deleteAddressCommand;

        #endregion

        #region Constructors

        protected AddressesViewModel()
            : this(null)
        {
        }

        protected AddressesViewModel(IView view)
            : base(view)
        {
            this.addresses = new BindingList<MutableAddress>();
            this.deleteAddressCommand =
                new DelegateCommand(this.DeleteAddressCommandHandler);
        }

        #endregion

        #region Public Properties

        public BindingList<MutableAddress> Addresses
```

```
        {
            get { return this.addresses; }
        }

        public DelegateCommand DeleteAddressCommand
        {
            get { return this.deleteAddressCommand; }
        }

        #endregion

        #region Private Methods

        private void DeleteAddressCommandHandler(object sender,
            DelegateCommandEventArgs e)
        {
            MutableAddress address = e.Parameter as MutableAddress;
            if (address != null)
            {
                this.addresses.Remove(address);
            }
        }

        #endregion

        #region Virtual Methods

        protected virtual void PopulateAddresses()
        {
            this.OnPropertyChanged(Constants.AddressesPropertyName);
        }

        #endregion
    }
}
```

This class should look very similar to the parts of the `CompanyViewModel` that dealt with Addresses. In fact, I copied and pasted most of the code from that class into the `AddressesViewModel`. It is an abstract class, so the `CompanyViewModel` class changed to inherit from `AddressesViewModel` instead of `ViewModel`. The only method that I needed to change was `PopulateAddressses`; I had to change it to raise only the `PropertyChanged` event for the `Addresses` property, and then I marked it as virtual so I could override it and call it from `CompanyViewModel` and `ProjectContactViewModel`.

Here is the code for the `ProjectContactViewModel` using the new `AddressesViewModel` class:

```
using System;
using System.Collections.Generic;
using SmartCA.Infrastructure.UI;
using System.Windows.Data;
using SmartCA.Application;
using SmartCA.Model.Companies;
using SmartCA.Model.Projects;
```

(continued)

(continued)

```
using System.ComponentModel;
using SmartCA.Model.Contacts;
using SmartCA.Model;

namespace SmartCA.Presentation.ViewModels
{
    public class ProjectContactViewModel : AddressesViewModel
    {
        #region Constants

        private static class Constants
        {
            public const string CurrentContactPropertyName = "CurrentContact";
        }

        #endregion

        private CollectionView contacts;
        private IList<ProjectContact> contactsList;
        ProjectContact currentContact;
        private CollectionView companies;
        private DelegateCommand saveCommand;
        private DelegateCommand newCommand;

        #region Constructors

        public ProjectContactViewModel()
            : this(null)
        {
        }

        public ProjectContactViewModel(IView view)
            : base(view)
        {
            this.contactsList = UserSession.CurrentProject.Contacts;
            this.contacts = new CollectionView(contactsList);
            this.currentContact = null;
            this.companies = new CollectionView(CompanyService.GetAllCompanies());
            this.saveCommand = new DelegateCommand(this.SaveCommandHandler);
            this.newCommand = new DelegateCommand(this.NewCommandHandler);
        }

        #endregion

        public CollectionView Contacts
        {
            get { return this.contacts; }
        }

        public ProjectContact CurrentContact
```

```
        {
            get { return this.currentContact; }
            set
            {
                if (this.currentContact != value)
                {
                    this.currentContact = value;
                    this.OnPropertyChanged(Constants.CurrentContactPropertyName);
                    this.saveCommand.IsEnabled = (this.currentContact != null);
                    this.PopulateAddresses();
                }
            }
        }

        public CollectionView Companies
        {
            get { return this.companies; }
        }

        public DelegateCommand SaveCommand
        {
            get { return this.saveCommand; }
        }

        public DelegateCommand NewCommand
        {
            get { return this.newCommand; }
        }

        private void SaveCommandHandler(object sender, EventArgs e)
        {
            this.currentContact.Contact.Addresses.Clear();
            foreach (MutableAddress address in this.Addresses)
            {
                this.currentContact.Contact.Addresses.Add(address.ToAddress());
            }
            ProjectService.SaveProjectContact(this.currentContact);
        }

        private void NewCommandHandler(object sender, EventArgs e)
        {
            ProjectContact contact = new ProjectContact(UserSession.CurrentProject,
                                         null, new Contact(null,
                                                "{First Name}", "{Last Name}"));
            this.contactsList.Add(contact);
            this.contacts.Refresh();
            this.contacts.MoveCurrentToLast();
        }

        protected override void PopulateAddresses()
```

(continued)

(continued)

```
            {
                if (this.currentContact != null)
                {
                    this.Addresses.Clear();
                    foreach (Address address in this.currentContact.Contact.Addresses)
                    {
                        this.Addresses.Add(new MutableAddress(address));
                    }
                    base.PopulateAddresses();
                }
            }
        }
    }
```

As you can see, it inherits from the `AddressesViewModel` class, thus eliminating several lines of code from the class.

Constructor

The constructor is almost exactly the same as the `CompanyViewModel` constructor, only this time I am dealing with ProjectContacts instead of Companies. There is a variable and property for Companies, but that is used as a dropdown list in the UI to assign a ProjectContact to a Company.

```
        #region Constructors

        public ProjectContactViewModel()
            : this(null)
        {
        }

        public ProjectContactViewModel(IView view)
            : base(view)
        {
            this.contactsList = UserSession.CurrentProject.Contacts;
            this.contacts = new CollectionView(contactsList);
            this.currentContact = null;
            this.companies = new CollectionView(CompanyService.GetAllCompanies());
            this.saveCommand = new DelegateCommand(this.SaveCommandHandler);
            this.newCommand = new DelegateCommand(this.NewCommandHandler);
        }

        #endregion
```

Just like the `CompanyView` class, I am also maintaining an `IList<T>` variable (contactsList) as well as the `CollectionView` of the list. There is a `CollectionView` containing `Company` instances, and this is used by the UI to select the Company to which a Contact belongs.

Properties

The `CurrentContact` property indicates the current `ProjectContact` instance that is being edited.

```
public ProjectContact CurrentContact
{
    get { return this.currentContact; }
    set
    {
        if (this.currentContact != value)
        {
            this.currentContact = value;
            this.OnPropertyChanged(Constants.CurrentContactPropertyName);
            this.saveCommand.IsEnabled = (this.currentContact != null);
            this.PopulateAddresses();
        }
    }
}
```

Whenever a new ProjectContact is selected in the UI, then this property's setter is called. Once that has happened, then the `PropertyChanged` event for the `CurrentContact` property is raised, thus letting the UI know to refresh itself. The next thing to happen is to set the `SaveCommand`'s `IsEnabled` property to the boolean value of the Current ProjectContact. Then the `PopulateAddresses` method is called:

```
protected override void PopulateAddresses()
{
    if (this.currentContact != null)
    {
        this.Addresses.Clear();
        foreach (Address address in this.currentContact.Contact.Addresses)
        {
            this.Addresses.Add(new MutableAddress(address));
        }
        base.PopulateAddresses();
    }
}
```

This is now changed to account for the `PopulateAddresses` method in the `AddressesViewModel` base class.

The rest of the properties in the `ProjectContactView` class are the `Companies CollectionView` property and the read-only `DelegateCommand` properties for creating New ProjectContacts and saving ProjectContacts.

Command Handler Methods

The handlers for the `DelegateCommand` properties are pretty interesting. The `NewCommandHandler` method has to do a lot of housekeeping:

```
private void NewCommandHandler(object sender, EventArgs e)
{
    ProjectContact contact = new ProjectContact(UserSession.CurrentProject,
                                null, new Contact(null,
                                          "{First Name}", "{Last Name}"));
    this.contactsList.Add(contact);
    this.contacts.Refresh();
    this.contacts.MoveCurrentToLast();
}
```

It first has to create a new instance of a `ProjectContact`, and then add it to the internal list of ProjectContacts. Once the internal list has been updated, it then calls `Refresh` on the `CollectionView` contacts variable in order to have the UI refreshed. Finally, by calling the `MoveCurrentToLast` method on the `CollectionView`, the ProjectContact will appear last in the list in the UI.

The `SaveCommandHandler` first has to swap out the addresses from the `Addresses` property into the `Addresses` property of the `ProjectContact`.

```
private void SaveCommandHandler(object sender, EventArgs e)
{
    this.currentContact.Contact.Addresses.Clear();
    foreach (MutableAddress address in this.Addresses)
    {
        this.currentContact.Contact.Addresses.Add(address.ToAddress());
    }
    ProjectService.SaveProjectContact(this.currentContact);
}
```

It then finishes up by using the `ProjectService` class to save the current `ProjectContact` instance. Again, it is nice how this `Service` class makes it very easy for the UI code to concentrate on display rather than the plumbing of saving a ProjectContact.

The Project Contact View

The View that is associated with the `ProjectContactViewModel`, the `ProjectContactView` class (which consists of XAML plus code-behind), is almost identical to the `CompanyView` class shown previously in this chapter. Figure 4.6 shows what the form looks like at run time.

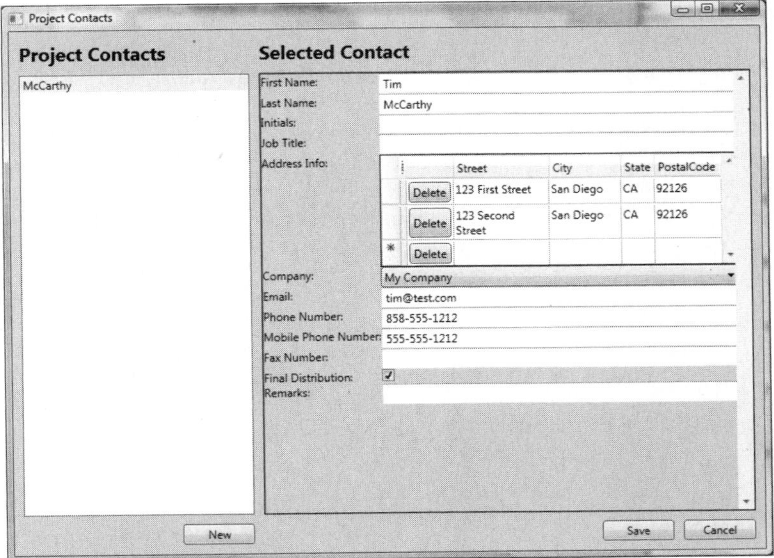

Figure 4.6: The ProjectContact View

The main difference between this form and `CompanyView` form is that now I am dealing with ProjectContacts instead of Companies. Everything else is almost identical, from the selection of items to edit to using the `UserControl` for Addresses to saving and adding new ProjectContacts.

There is one more difference, and that is that this View has a dropdown for choosing what Company a ProjectContact belongs to.

Here is the XAML for the Company `ComboBox`:

```
<ComboBox Grid.Row="5" Grid.Column="1"
    SelectedItem="{Binding Path=CurrentContact.Contact.CurrentCompany}"
    DisplayMemberPath="Name"
    ItemsSource="{Binding Path=Companies}">
</ComboBox>
```

This XAML declares that the `SelectedItem` of the ComboBox will set the `CurrentCompany` property in the `ProjectContactViewModel` class. It also declares that the `ItemsSource` property is bound to the `Companies` property in the `ProjectContactViewModel`, and the property that will be displayed to the user in the `ComboBox` will be the `Name` property on the `Company` instances.

The rest of the XAML for the `ProjectContactView` is so similar to the `CompanyView` that it is not worth showing here.

Summary

In this chapter I defined and modeled Companies, Contacts, and ProjectContacts, and then defined the Aggregate Boundaries for these classes in the domain model. A new concept was added to both the Domain Layer and Infrastructure Layer that allowed saving Entities that are not their own Aggregate Root. This was demonstrated by the techniques I used to save ProjectContacts within the Project Aggregate. Also covered was how to deal with `Address` Value Objects using the Xceed DataGrid control. I showed how to wrap this functionality into a reusable `UserControl` for Addresses. Furthermore, there was also a lot of good refactoring going on with the `ProjectRepository` and the new `ViewModel` classes.

5

Submittal Transmittals

In the last chapter, I took a deep look at Companies and Contacts, mainly because they are building blocks to be used in other parts of the SmartCA domain model. In this chapter, I will show what Submittal Transmittals are and how they also depend on Contacts, Companies, and several other classes in the domain model.

The Problem

In the construction administration world, submittal requirements are part of the project specifications. The book of specifications for construction projects is very large and describes "how the project is to be constructed and what results are to be achieved."

Architects and engineers prepare the specifications. Almost all specifications used in the United States and Canada are based on a format called the "MasterFormat" developed by the Construction Specifications Institute. Some design firms use the 16 division MasterFormat from the 1995 version. Other design firms have adopted the 2004 edition, which has 20 divisions.

As a rule, submittal requirements are set forth in project specifications. Another section lays out specific submittal procedures. At the beginning of a project, the general contractor will prepare a submittal schedule. The schedule, sometimes called a submittal log, indicates the specification sections, due dates, and responsible party for each required submittal. The design firm then approves this schedule.

The specification details the time requirements for the architect's review of each submittal and the type of cover sheets and transmittal memos needed to identify them. Examples of some common submittals for specifications are items such as product data and shop drawings.

The Design

A Submittal Transmittal is made up of many parts, but probably the most important part is the tracking of the status of the specification sections. It is very important for the Smart Design firm to know the status of all of their submittals, such as which have been received and which are still pending.

Designing the Domain Model

Figure 5.1 is a drawing showing the relationships between the classes that combine to make up a Submittal Transmittal.

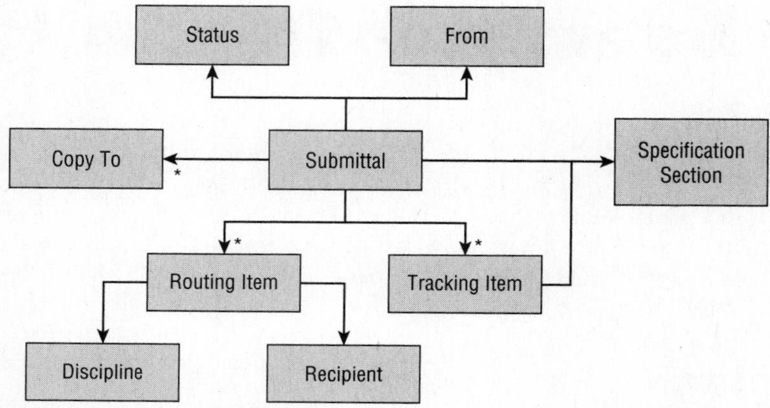

Figure 5.1: Submittal Aggregate.

Obviously, the root of this Aggregate is the `Submittal` class. Probably its most important relationship is the one to the Specification Section. This is the whole purpose of the submittal transmittal, to track the actual materials and labor against the project specifications. The `Status` class is used to convey the overall status of the Submittal. Also, notice that each Tracking Item is related to an individual Specification Section: this is how the domain model determines the status of each specification item in the Submittal.

The next important part of the diagram is the Submittal's relationship to the Routing Item. This is how Smart Design determines to whom each Submittal has been routed for action, and that person's Discipline, such as an architect, engineer, or a construction administrator. Also, notice that there is a Copy To relationship from a Submittal; this represents the list of Recipients who need to be copied on all correspondence having to do with the Submittal.

Defining the Submittal Aggregate

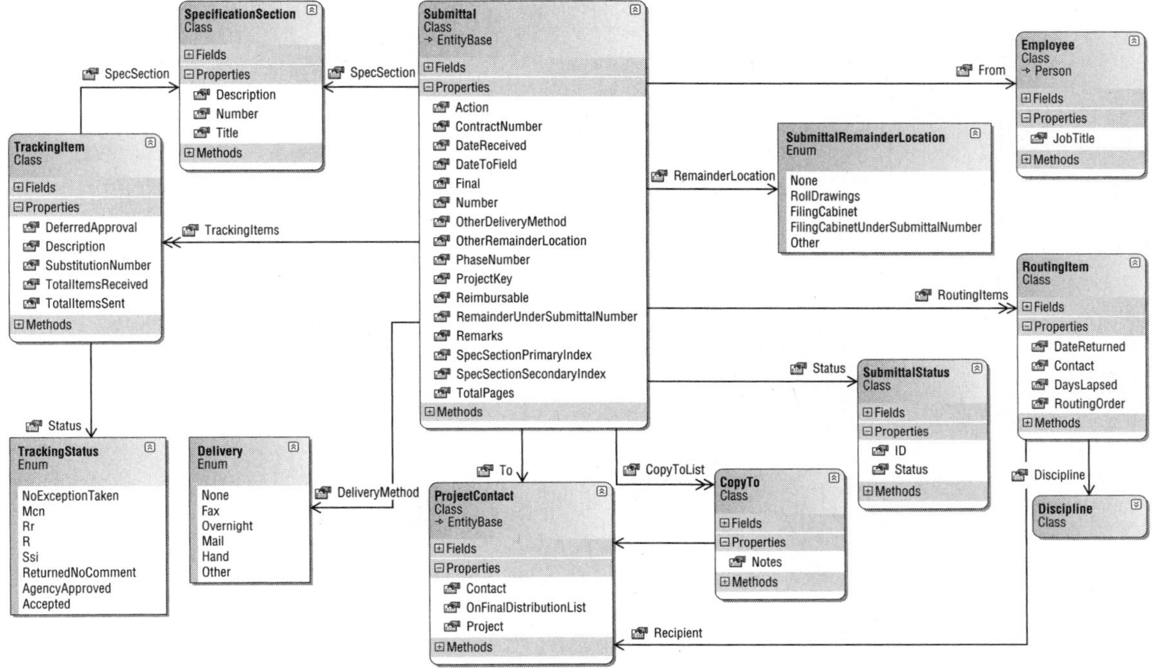

Figure 5.2: Classes composing the Submittal Aggregate.

As you can see from the diagram of the Submittal Aggregate in Figure 5.2, there are a lot of moving parts in this Aggregate. Notice how I am starting to make use of some of the other Entities introduced in previous chapters, such as the `ProjectContact` class, which is used to represent the `To` property of the `Submittal` class, the `Recipient` property of the `RoutingItem` class, and the `Contact` property of the `CopyTo` class. Also, the `Employee` class is used in the Submittal's `From` property to represent the Employee that originated the Submittal.

Defining the Aggregate Boundaries

The Submittal class has its own identity and is definitely the root of its own Aggregate. All of the other classes in the diagram in Figure 5.3, except for `ProjectContact` and `Employee`, belong to the Submittal Aggregate. As shown in earlier chapters, `ProjectContact` belongs to the Project Aggregate, and `Employee` is the root of its own Aggregate.

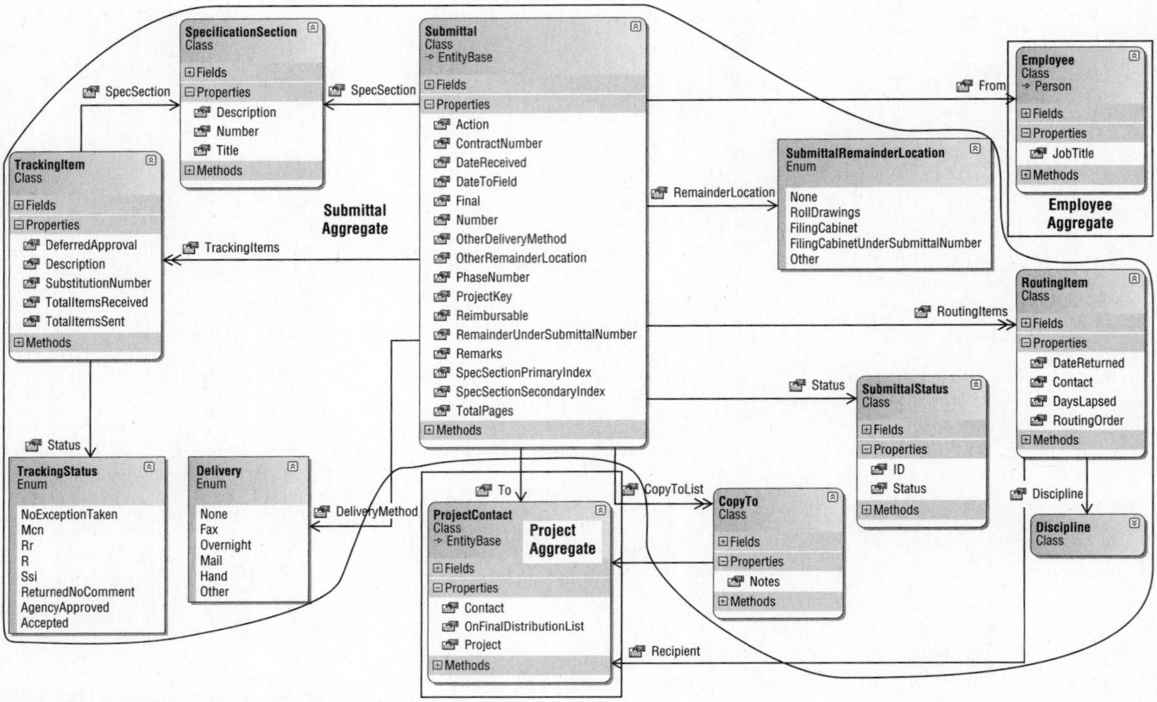

SpecificationSection
Class
Fields
Properties
Description
Number
Title
Methods
Submittal
Class
EntityBase
Fields
Properties
Action
ContractNumber
DateReceived
DateToField
Final
Number
OtherDeliveryMethod
OtherRemainderLocation
PhaseNumber
ProjectKey
Reimbursable
RemainderUnderSubmittalNumber
Remarks
SpecSectionPrimaryIndex
SpecSectionSecondaryIndex
TotalPages
Methods
Employee
Class
Person
Fields
Properties
JobTitle
Methods
Employee Aggregate
SubmittalRemainderLocation
Enum
None
RollDrawings
FilingCabinet
FilingCabinetUnderSubmittalNumber
Other
TrackingItem
Class
Fields
Properties
DeferredApproval
Description
SubstitutionNumber
TotalItemsReceived
TotalItemsSent
Methods
Submittal Aggregate
SpecSection
SpecSection
From
RemainderLocation
TrackingItems
RoutingItems
RoutingItem
Class
Fields
Properties
DateReturned
Contact
DaysLapsed
RoutingOrder
Methods
Status
SubmittalStatus
Class
Fields
Properties
ID
Status
Methods
Status
TrackingStatus
Enum
NoExceptionTaken
Mcn
Rr
R
Ssi
ReturnedNoComment
AgencyApproved
Accepted
Delivery
Enum
None
Fax
Overnight
Mail
Hand
Other
DeliveryMethod
To
ProjectContact
Class
EntityBase
Project Aggregate
Fields
Properties
Contact
OnFinalDistributionList
Project
Methods
CopyToList
CopyTo
Class
Fields
Properties
Notes
Methods
Discipline
Discipline
Class
Recipient

Figure 5.3: Submittal Aggregate boundaries.

Designing the Repository

Since Submittal is its own Aggregate root, it will have its own repository, as shown in Figure 5.4.

SqlCeRepositoryBase<T>
GenericAbstractClass
RepositoryBase<T>
ISubmittalRepository
SubmittalRepository
Class
SqlCeRepositoryBase<Submittal>
ISubmittalRepository
Interface
IRepository<Submittal>
IRepository<T>
GenericInterface

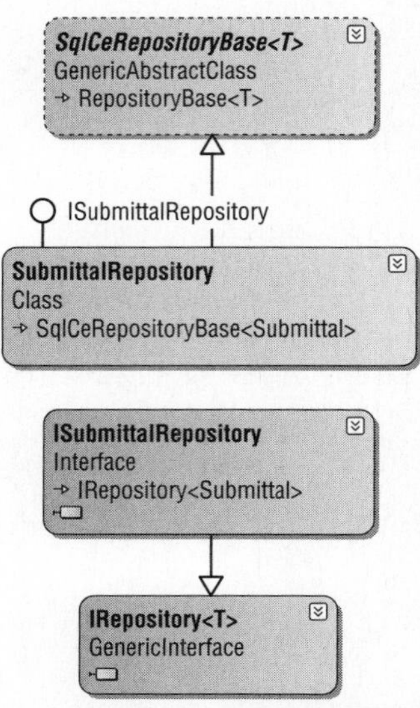

Figure 5.4: Submittal Aggregate repository.

Although the Project Aggregate and the Employee Aggregate are part of the Submittal Aggregate, I will not be covering their respective repositories here because they have already been covered in Chapter 3. I will only be covering the Submittal repository in this chapter.

The `ISubmittalRepository` interface is the interface into instances of Submittal repositories. Here is the `ISubmittalRepository` interface:

```
using System.Collections.Generic;
using SmartCA.Infrastructure.RepositoryFramework;
using SmartCA.Model.Projects;

namespace SmartCA.Model.Submittals
{
    public interface ISubmittalRepository : IRepository<Submittal>
    {
        IList<Submittal> FindBy(Project project);
        IList<SpecificationSection> FindAllSpecificationSections();
        IList<SubmittalStatus> FindAllSubmittalStatuses();
        IList<Discipline> FindAllDisciplines();
    }
}
```

The first method, `FindBy`, will be called fairly often, as most Submittals will only be looked at on a per-project basis. The `FindAllSpecificationSections`, `FindAllSubmittalStatuses`, and `FindAllDisciplines` methods all return lists of their respective Value objects from the data store. These lists will be used later in the UI for lookup purposes.

Writing the Unit Tests

In this section, I will be writing some unit tests of what I expect of the Submittal repository implementation. As noted before, these tests will compile correctly, but they will also fail until I write the code for the Repository implementation later on in the Solution section.

There will be more unit tests in the accompanying code for this chapter, but for brevity's sake I am showing the tests that I think are important here.

The FindSubmittalsByProjectTest Method

The purpose of the `FindSubmittalsByProjectTest` method is to validate that the correct number of `Submittal` instances have been returned by the Submittal repository for a given Project:

```
        /// <summary>
        /// A test for FindBy(Project project)
        /// </summary>
        [DeploymentItem("SmartCA.sdf"), TestMethod()]
        public void FindSubmittalsByProjectTest()
        {
            // Get a Project reference
            Project project =
                ProjectService.GetProject("5704f6b9-6ffa-444c-9583-35cc340fce2a");
```

(continued)

(continued)

```
        // FIns all of the Submittals for the Project
        IList<Submittal> submittals = this.repository.FindBy(project);

        // Verify that at least one Submittal was returned
        Assert.IsTrue(submittals.Count > 0);
    }
```

This method starts out by getting a `Project` instance from the `ProjectService` class. It then calls the `FindBy` method on the repository to get the list of Submittals for the given `Project` instance. The method finishes by checking that the repository returned at least one `Submittal`.

The AddSubmittalTest Method

The purpose of the `AddSubmittalTest` method is to test adding a new Submittal to the Submittal repository:

```
    /// <summary>
    ///A test for Add(Submittal item)
    ///</summary>
    [DeploymentItem("SmartCA.sdf"), TestMethod()]
    public void AddSubmittalTest()
    {
        // Create a new Submittal
        IList<SpecificationSection> specSections =
            this.repository.FindAllSpecificationSections();
        Guid projectKey = new Guid("5704f6b9-6ffa-444c-9583-35cc340fce2a");
        Submittal submittal = new Submittal(specSections[0], projectKey);
        submittal.To = ProjectService.GetProject(projectKey).Contacts[0];
        submittal.From = EmployeeService.GetEmployees()[0];
        IList<SubmittalStatus> statuses =
            this.repository.FindAllSubmittalStatuses();
        submittal.Status = statuses[0];

        // Add the Submittal to the Repository
        this.repository.Add(submittal);

        // Commit the transaction
        this.unitOfWork.Commit();

        // Reload the Submittal and verify it's number
        Submittal savedSubmittal = this.repository.FindBy(submittal.Key);
        Assert.AreEqual("00 11 13.01.00", savedSubmittal.Number);

        // Clean up
        this.repository.Remove(savedSubmittal);
        this.unitOfWork.Commit();
    }
```

This test is a little bit more involved than the previous test. It starts out by getting the list of all `SpecificationSection` instances. It then creates a Project Key value, and then passes the first `SpecificationSection` from the `specSections` list variable as well as the Project Key value into the constructor of the `Submittal` class. The next step is to initialize the `To` and `From` properties of the `Submittal` instance with a `ProjectContact` instance and an `Employee` instance. Once those properties are set, the next property that needs to be set is the `Status` property. The `Status` property is set the value of the first `SubmittalStatus` in the list of all `SubmittalStatus` instances.

The next step is to add the Submittal to the repository, and then to commit the transaction by calling the `Commit` method on the `IUnitOfWork` instance. The `Commit` method is important because that method calls back into the Submittal repository to tell it to write the Submittal's data to the data store.

Once the Submittal has been saved, it is then reloaded, and the Submittal's `Number` property is checked to verify that the `Add` and `Commit` methods worked properly. The last task that the method needs to perform is to remove the Submittal. Removing the Submittal that was just created leaves the data store in the same state it was in before the method started, which is important for the rest of the tests that may depend on a known state of the data store. Otherwise, some of the other tests may fail because there was unexpected Submittal's data in the data store.

The UpdateSubmittalTest Method

The purpose of the `UpdateTest` method is to find a Submittal and update it with a different `DateReceived` property value and then verify that the change was persisted properly:

```
/// <summary>
///A test for Updating a Submittal
///</summary>
[DeploymentItem("SmartCA.sdf"), TestMethod()]
public void UpdateSubmittalTest()
{
    // Get the list of all Submittals
    IList<Submittal> submittals = this.repository.FindAll();

    // Change the first Submittal's DateReceived value
    DateTime dateReceived = DateTime.Now;
    submittals[0].DateReceived = dateReceived;

    // Update the Repository
    this.repository[submittals[0].Key] = submittals[0];

    // Commit the transaction
    this.unitOfWork.Commit();

    // Verify that the change was saved
    IList<Submittal> refreshedSubmittals = this.repository.FindAll();
    Assert.AreEqual(dateReceived.Date,
        refreshedSubmittals[0].DateReceived.Value.Date);
}
```

In this method I start out by getting the entire list of Submittals from the data store. I then proceed to change the `DateReceived` property value on the first Submittal in the list, and then call the indexer method of the `ISubmittalRepository`. After the call to the indexer, I then use the `IUnitOfWork` interface to commit the transaction. Last, I verify that the change actually made it to the data store by reloading the same Submittal and checking to see if its `DateReceived` property value is the same calendar date that I just assigned to the Submittal earlier in the method.

The RemoveSubmittalTest Method

The purpose of the `RemoveTest` method is to test the process of removing a Submittal from the data store:

```
/// <summary>
///A test for Remove(Submittal item)
///</summary>
[DeploymentItem("SmartCA.sdf"), TestMethod()]
public void RemoveSubmittalTest()
{
    // Get the list of all Submittals
    IList<Submittal> submittals = this.repository.FindAll();

    // Remove the Submittal from the Repository
    this.repository.Remove(submittals[0]);

    // Commit the transaction
    this.unitOfWork.Commit();

    // Verify that there is now one less Submittal in the data store
    IList<Submittal> refreshedSubmittals = this.repository.FindAll();
    Assert.AreEqual(0, refreshedSubmittals.Count);

    // Reset the state
    this.AddSubmittalTest();
}
```

The first line of this method should look familiar; I am getting the entire list of Submittals from the data store. I then remove the first Submittal in the list from the repository. After removing the Submittal from the repository, I then use the `IUnitOfWork` interface to commit the transaction. Last, I verify that the change actually made it to the data store by using the repository to find all of the Submittal instances and making sure there is now one less Submittal than before. Last, I call the `AddSubmittalTest` method to add the Submittal I just deleted back into the data store in order to reset the original state of the data store.

The Solution

Now that the design is in place for the Submittal domain model, the Submittal Aggregate has been defined and its boundaries have been determined, and the repository has been designed with its associated tests, it is time to start the code implementation. In this section, I will be implementing these designs, as well as implementing the ViewModel and the View for Submittals.

Implementing the Submittal Class Private Fields and Constructors

There are two constructors for the `Submittal` class, and they both take a `projectKey` parameter of type `System.Object` and a `specSection` parameter of type `SpecificationSection`. Every Submittal must be associated with a Specification Section. That is why it is in both constructors. The `projectKey` parameter links the Submittal with a particular Project.

I decided to use a key value for a Project instead of a full blown `Project` instance, since I can always get to the Project via the `ProjectService` class. The second constructor takes a key argument of type `System.Object`, thus following the pattern I have laid out before for creating instances of existing Entity classes.

```
using System;
using System.Collections.Generic;
using System.Text;
using SmartCA.Infrastructure.DomainBase;
using SmartCA.Model.Employees;
using SmartCA.Model.Projects;

namespace SmartCA.Model.Submittals
{
    public class Submittal : EntityBase
    {
        private object projectKey;
        private SpecificationSection specSection;
        private string specSectionPrimaryIndex;
        private string specSectionSecondaryIndex;
        private ProjectContact to;
        private DateTime transmittalDate;
        private Employee from;
        private int totalPages;
        private Delivery deliveryMethod;
        private string otherDeliveryMethod;
        private string phaseNumber;
        private bool reimbursable;
        private bool final;
        private List<CopyTo> copyToList;
        private DateTime? dateReceived;
        private string contractNumber;
        private List<TrackingItem> trackingItems;
        private List<RoutingItem> routingItems;
        private string remarks;
        private ActionStatus action;
        private SubmittalStatus status;
        private DateTime? dateToField;
        private SubmittalRemainderLocation remainderLocation;
        private string remainderUnderSubmittalNumber;
        private string otherRemainderLocation;

        public Submittal(SpecificationSection specSection, object projectKey)
            : this(null, specSection, projectKey)
        {
        }

        public Submittal(object key, SpecificationSection specSection,
            object projectKey) : base(key)
        {
            this.projectKey = projectKey;
```

(continued)

(continued)

```
            this.specSection = specSection;
            this.specSectionPrimaryIndex = "01";
            this.specSectionSecondaryIndex = "00";
            this.to = null;
            this.transmittalDate = DateTime.Now;
            this.from = null;
            this.totalPages = 1;
            this.deliveryMethod = Delivery.None;
            this.otherDeliveryMethod = string.Empty;
            this.phaseNumber = string.Empty;
            this.reimbursable = false;
            this.final = false;
            this.copyToList = new List<CopyTo>();
            this.dateReceived = null;
            this.contractNumber = string.Empty;
            this.trackingItems = new List<TrackingItem>();
            this.routingItems = new List<RoutingItem>();
            this.remarks = string.Empty;
            this.action = ActionStatus.NoExceptionTaken;
            this.status = null;
            this.dateToField = null;
            this.remainderLocation = SubmittalRemainderLocation.None;
            this.remainderUnderSubmittalNumber = string.Empty;
            this.otherRemainderLocation = string.Empty;
            this.Validate();
        }
```

All of the data for the `Submittal` class are initialized and validated in the second constructor, which gets called by the first constructor. The default value for `specSectionPrimaryIndex` is "01"; this signifies the first submittal associated with a particular Specification Section. The default value for `specSectionSecondaryIndex` is "00"; the default value is retained unless another Submittal is created for the same Specification Section.

The Submittal Properties

The `Submittal` class does not have much behavior yet, aside from the getter for the `Number` property, which concatenates values in the submittal in order to produce a Submittal Number:

```
    public object ProjectKey
        {
            get { return this.projectKey; }
        }

        public SpecificationSection SpecSection
        {
            get { return this.specSection; }
            set { this.specSection = value; }
        }

        public string SpecSectionPrimaryIndex
```

```
        {
            get { return this.specSectionPrimaryIndex; }
            set { this.specSectionPrimaryIndex = value; }
        }

        public string SpecSectionSecondaryIndex
        {
            get { return this.specSectionSecondaryIndex; }
            set { this.specSectionSecondaryIndex = value; }
        }

        public string Number
        {
            get
            {
                return string.Format("{0}.{1}.{2}",
                    this.specSection.Number, this.specSectionPrimaryIndex,
                    this.specSectionSecondaryIndex);
            }
        }

        public ProjectContact To
        {
            get { return this.to; }
            set { this.to = value; }
        }

        public DateTime TransmittalDate
        {
            get { return this.transmittalDate; }
            set { this.transmittalDate = value; }
        }

        public Employee From
        {
            get { return this.from; }
            set { this.from = value; }
        }

        public int TotalPages
        {
            get { return this.totalPages; }
            set { this.totalPages = value; }
        }

        public Delivery DeliveryMethod
        {
            get { return this.deliveryMethod; }
            set { this.deliveryMethod = value; }
        }

        public string OtherDeliveryMethod
```

(continued)

(continued)

```
        {
            get { return this.otherDeliveryMethod; }
            set { this.otherDeliveryMethod = value; }
        }

        public string PhaseNumber
        {
            get { return this.phaseNumber; }
            set { this.phaseNumber = value; }
        }

        public bool Reimbursable
        {
            get { return this.reimbursable; }
            set { this.reimbursable = value; }
        }

        public bool Final
        {
            get { return this.final; }
            set { this.final = value; }
        }

        public IList<CopyTo> CopyToList
        {
            get { return this.copyToList; }
        }

        public DateTime? DateReceived
        {
            get { return this.dateReceived; }
            set { this.dateReceived = value; }
        }

        public string ContractNumber
        {
            get { return this.contractNumber; }
            set { this.contractNumber = value; }
        }

        public IList<TrackingItem> TrackingItems
        {
            get { return this.trackingItems; }
        }

        public IList<RoutingItem> RoutingItems
        {
            get { return this.routingItems; }
        }
```

```
        public string Remarks
        {
            get { return this.remarks; }
            set { this.remarks = value; }
        }

        public ActionStatus Action
        {
            get { return this.action; }
            set { this.action = value; }
        }

        public SubmittalStatus Status
        {
            get { return this.status; }
            set { this.status = value; }
        }

        public DateTime? DateToField
        {
            get { return this.dateToField; }
            set { this.dateToField = value; }
        }

        public SubmittalRemainderLocation RemainderLocation
        {
            get { return this.remainderLocation; }
            set { this.remainderLocation = value; }
        }

        public string RemainderUnderSubmittalNumber
        {
            get { return this.remainderUnderSubmittalNumber; }
            set { this.remainderUnderSubmittalNumber = value; }
        }

        public string OtherRemainderLocation
        {
            get { return this.otherRemainderLocation; }
            set { this.otherRemainderLocation = value; }
        }
```

Actually, this code could be simplified considerably because the properties currently do nothing other than setting or getting the backing field. In C# 3.0 the backing field can be created automatically by the compiler in these situations; however, I do actually want the private fields in this class because later I intend to add more behavior to this class and that behavior will be acting on the private fields.

The SpecSection Property

The `SpecSection` property represents a `SpecificationSection` class instance. The `SpecificationSection` class is a value class composed of a number, a title, and a description:

```
using System;

namespace SmartCA.Model.Projects
{
    public class SpecificationSection
    {
        private string number;
        private string title;
        private string description;

        public SpecificationSection(string number, string title,
            string description)
        {
            this.number = number;
            this.title = title;
            this.description = description;
        }

        public string Number
        {
            get { return this.number; }
        }

        public string Title
        {
            get { return this.title; }
        }

        public string Description
        {
            get { return this.description; }
        }
    }
}
```

Although the concept of a Specification Section is very important to Submittals, it is still a value class because it is only representing values. This may change later, but, for now, it makes things simple to keep this as a `Value` class.

The DeliveryMethod Property

The `DeliveryMethod` property of the Submittal class is represented by the `Delivery` enumeration:

```
using System;

namespace SmartCA.Model.Submittals
{
    [Flags]
    public enum Delivery
```

```
    {
        None = 0,
        Fax = 1,
        Overnight = 2,
        Mail = 4,
        Hand = 8,
        Other = 16
    }
}
```

Take a look at the `Flags` attribute on the enumeration. This means that the values of this enumeration can be combined, and when `ToString()` is called on the enumeration, it will render a comma-separated list of enumeration values, such as "Fax, Mail."

> *This is very handy when displaying the combination of values selected. I could do the same thing without the `Flags` attribute, but then the `ToString()` method would only render the value 5.*

Using the enumeration in this way shows that the same Submittal can be delivered in a combination of ways, such as Fax and Mail, or Hand and Overnight.

The CopyToList Property

The `CopyToList` property represents all of the people that get a copy of the Submittal once it is transmitted. It is actually a `List` of type `CopyTo`. The `CopyTo` class is also a value class, containing read-only properties for a `ProjectContact` and notes about the `ProjectContact` being copied:

```
using SmartCA.Model.Projects;

namespace SmartCA.Model.Submittals
{
    public class CopyTo
    {
        private ProjectContact contact;
        private string notes;

        public CopyTo(ProjectContact contact, string notes)
        {
            this.contact = contact;
            this.notes = notes;
        }

        public ProjectContact Contact
        {
            get { return this.contact; }
        }

        public string Notes
        {
            get { return this.notes; }
        }

        public override bool Equals(object obj)
```

(continued)

(continued)

```
        {
            return obj != null
                && obj.GetType() == typeof(CopyTo)
                && this == (CopyTo)obj;
        }

        public static bool operator ==(CopyTo one, CopyTo other)
        {
            // check for both null (cast to object to avoid recursive loop)
            if ((object)one == null && (object)other == null)
            {
                return true;
            }

            // check for either of them equal to null
            if ((object)one == null || (object)other == null)
            {
                return false;
            }

            if (one.Contact != other.Contact
                || one.Notes != other.Notes)
            {
                return false;
            }

            return true;
        }

        public static bool operator !=(CopyTo one, CopyTo other)
        {
            return !(one == other);
        }

        public override int GetHashCode()
        {
            return this.contact.GetHashCode()
                ^ this.notes.GetHashCode();
        }

        public override string ToString()
        {
            return string.Format("{0} - {1}",
                this.contact.Contact.LastName, this.notes);
        }
    }
}
```

As you will see in later chapters, it makes sense to have this class as a `Value` class, especially since it will be reused later in other parts of the domain model.

The TrackingItems Property

The `TrackingItems` property represents a List of type `TrackingItem`. The `TrackingItem` class is not a Value class, but it must be constructed with a `SpecificationSection` instance.

```
namespace SmartCA.Model.Submittals
{
    public class TrackingItem
    {
        private int totalItemsReceived;
        private int totalItemsSent;
        private int deferredApproval;
        private int substitutionNumber;
        private string description;
        private ActionStatus status;

        public TrackingItem()
        {
            this.totalItemsReceived = 0;
            this.totalItemsSent = 0;
            this.deferredApproval = 0;
            this.description = string.Empty;
            this.status = ActionStatus.NoExceptionTaken;
        }

        public int TotalItemsReceived
        {
            get { return this.totalItemsReceived; }
            set
            {
                if (value != this.totalItemsReceived)
                {
                    this.totalItemsReceived = value;
                    // Default to making the total number
                    // of items sent equal to what was received
                    this.totalItemsSent = value;
                }
            }
        }

        public int TotalItemsSent
        {
            get { return this.totalItemsSent; }
            set { this.totalItemsSent = value; }
        }

        public int DeferredApproval
        {
            get { return this.deferredApproval; }
            set { this.deferredApproval = value; }
        }

        public int SubstitutionNumber
```

(continued)

(continued)

```
        {
            get { return this.substitutionNumber; }
            set { this.substitutionNumber = value; }
        }

        public string Description
        {
            get { return this.description; }
            set { this.description = value; }
        }

        public ActionStatus Status
        {
            get { return this.status; }
            set { this.status = value; }
        }
    }
}
```

The Constructor

The reason the `TrackingItem` class must be passed a `SpecificationSection` instance in its constructor is because that is what the `TrackingItem` class is providing information about, and it must have a value in order to do that.

The TotalItemsSent and TotalItemsReceived Properties

The `TotalItemsSent` property has logic in its setter to update automatically the `TotalItemsReceived` property to the same value as was received. This is a business rule specified by the Smart Design firm, and one that used to reside in the user interface code of the legacy application.

The DeferredApproval Property

There is nothing special, codewise, about this property, except that I need to explain the concept of Deferred Approval. The Deferred Approvals are documents that are prepared by others that are "deferred" agency submittal until the manufacturer is selected. These could be things like fire sprinkler systems, bleachers, and elevator guide rails. Once those plans are approved they become part of the Contract Documents.

They are typically listed on the General Sheet of the Smart Design firm's Drawings under a Deferred Approval section and are listed like:

1. Fire Sprinkler System
2. Bleachers
3. Elevator Guide Rails

The number they assign follows the number listed on the General Sheet. So, in this case, Fire Sprinkler System would have a Deferred Approval value of 1, Bleachers would have a value of 2, and so on.

The Status Property

The `Status` property is using the `ActionStatus` enumeration type. This type is fairly self-evident:

```
using System;

namespace SmartCA.Model.Submittals
{
    public enum ActionStatus
    {
        Accepted,
        AgencyApproved,
        MakeCorrectionsNoted,
        NoExceptionTaken,
        ReceiptAcknowledgedNoActionTaken,
        Rejected,
        ReturnedNoComment,
        ReviseResubmit,
        SubmitSpecificItem,
    }
}
```

The RoutingItems Property

The `RoutingItems` property represents a `List` of type `RoutingItem`. The `RoutingItem` class keeps track of who has seen a particular document, when the document was seen, and how long the document was held before it was returned. The `RoutingItem` class is not a `Value` class, but it must be constructed with the discipline of the person being routed to, who the person is and in what order they are in the routing, and when the item was sent to them.

```
using System;
using SmartCA.Model.Projects;

namespace SmartCA.Model.Submittals
{
    public class RoutingItem
    {
        private object key;
        private Discipline discipline;
        private int routingOrder;
        private ProjectContact recipient;
        private DateTime dateSent;
        private DateTime? dateReturned;
        private int daysLapsed;

        public RoutingItem(object key, Discipline discipline,
            int routingOrder, ProjectContact recipient,
            DateTime dateSent)
        {
            this.key = key;
            this.discipline = discipline;
            this.routingOrder = routingOrder;
            this.recipient = recipient;
```

(continued)

(continued)

```
        this.dateSent = dateSent;
        this.dateReturned = null;
        this.daysLapsed = 0;
    }

    public object Key
    {
        get { return this.key; }
    }

    public Discipline Discipline
    {
        get { return this.discipline; }
    }

    public int RoutingOrder
    {
        get { return this.routingOrder; }
    }

    public ProjectContact Recipient
    {
        get { return this.recipient; }
    }

    public DateTime DateSent
    {
        get { return this.dateSent; }
    }

    public DateTime? DateReturned
    {
        get { return this.dateReturned; }
        set
        {
            if (value != this.dateReturned && value.HasValue)
            {
                this.dateReturned = value;
                this.CalculateDaysLapsed();
            }
        }
    }

    public int DaysLapsed
    {
        get { return this.daysLapsed; }
    }

    private void CalculateDaysLapsed()
    {
        if (this.dateReturned.HasValue &&
            this.dateReturned.Value > this.dateSent)
```

```
                {
                    this.daysLapsed =
                        this.dateReturned.Value.Subtract(this.dateSent).Days;
                }
            }
        }
    }
```

The Constructor

The reason that the `RoutingItem` class must pass a `Discipline` instance, a `RoutingOrder` value, a `ProjectContact` instance, and a `DateTime` value in its constructor is that the `RoutingItem` class needs to know who the item is being routed to (`ProjectContact recipient`), what that person's discipline (`Discipline discipline`) is, and when (`DateTime dateSent`) it was sent to them. Without these values, the `RoutingItem` instance is useless.

The Properties

The `Discipline`, `RoutingOrder`, `Recipient`, and `DateSent` properties are all read-only, as their values can only be set in the constructor. In order to change these values, you must construct a new `RoutingItem` instance. The `DateReturned` value is the only property in the class that is not read-only, and when it is changed, it calls the `CalculateDaysLapsed` method if the value being passed to it is different from the original value. The `CalculateDaysLapsed` method figures out the number of days between when the item was sent and when it was returned, and then updates the value for the read-only `DaysLapsed` property.

The Status Property

The `Status` property indicates the overall status of the Submittal, such as whether it is complete or whether it has even been accepted yet. The `Status` property is represented by a `SubmittalStatus` instance. The `SubmittalStatus` class is a `Value` class, composed of an integer identification value and a status value of type `string`.

```
using System;

namespace SmartCA.Model.Submittals
{
    public class SubmittalStatus
    {
        private int id;
        private string status;

        public SubmittalStatus(int id, string status)
        {
            this.id = id;
            this.status = status;
        }

        public int Id
        {
            get { return this.id; }
        }

        public string Status
```

(continued)

(continued)

```
            {
                get { return this.status; }
            }
        }
    }
```

The values for the `SubmittalStatus` class will come from the database.

The RemainderLocation Property

The `RemainderLocation` property is represented by the `SubmittalRemainderLocation` enumeration:

```
    using System;

    namespace SmartCA.Model.Submittals
    {
        [Flags]
        public enum SubmittalRemainderLocation
        {
            None,
            RollDrawings,
            FilingCabinet,
            FilingCabinetUnderSubmittalNumber,
            Other
        }
    }
```

This property indicates the location of the rest of the items associated with the Submittal. This is for Smart Design's use only and is not to be seen by third parties. This property allows Smart Design to tie together papers associated with the electronic Submittal in a timely fashion. They are not ready to go paperless just yet, and so this process is one way to allow them at least to track the location of their Submittal paper documents.

The Submittal Repository Implementation

After going over the `ISubmittalRepository` interface in the Design section, it is now time to explain how the `Submittal` class actually gets persisted to and from the data store by the Submittal repository. In this section, I will be writing the code for the Submittal repository.

Most of the work for building a Submittal instance from the data store is done in the `SqlCeReposiotryBase<T>` class. If you recall, the Template Method pattern I have been using in the repositories for getting Entity Root instances, the `BuildChildCallbacks` method, must be overridden in the `SubmittalRepository`.

```
            #region BuildChildCallbacks

            protected override void BuildChildCallbacks()
            {
                this.ChildCallbacks.Add(SubmittalFactory.FieldNames.EmployeeId,
                    this.AppendFrom);
```

```
        this.ChildCallbacks.Add(SubmittalFactory.FieldNames.ProjectContactId,
            this.AppendTo);
        this.ChildCallbacks.Add("CopyToList",
            delegate(Submittal submittal, object childKeyName)
            {
                this.AppendCopyToList(submittal);
            });
        this.ChildCallbacks.Add("TrackingItems",
            delegate(Submittal submittal, object childKeyName)
            {
                this.AppendTrackingItems(submittal);
            });
        this.ChildCallbacks.Add("RoutingItems",
            delegate(Submittal submittal, object childKeyName)
            {
                this.AppendRoutingItems(submittal);
            });
    }

    #endregion
```

The AppendFrom Callback

The first entry made in the `ChildCallbacks` dictionary is for the `AppendFrom` method. Thanks to the `EmployeeService` class's `GetEmployee` method, this method's code is very simple:

```
    private void AppendFrom(Submittal submittal, object fromEmployeeId)
    {
        submittal.From = EmployeeService.GetEmployee(fromEmployeeId);
    }
```

You may recall the `GetEmployee` private method in the `ProjectRepository` class from Chapter 3. I have since refactored the code from the `GetEmployee` method into the `EmployeeService` class where it really belongs:

```
    public static Employee GetEmployee(object employeeKey)
    {
        return EmployeeService.repository.FindBy(employeeKey);
    }
```

This method simply delegates to the `IEmployeeRepository` interface instance to find an Employee by the method's `employeeKey` argument.

The AppendTo Callback

This method is very similar to the `AppendFrom` method; instead of retrieving an Employee, however, it retrieves and adds a `ProjectContact` to the Submittal:

```
private void AppendTo(Submittal submittal, object fromProjectContactKey)
    {
        submittal.To = ProjectService.GetProjectContact(submittal.ProjectKey,
            fromProjectContactKey);
    }
```

This uses the ProjectContactService's class newly added GetProjectContact method to find the right ProjectContact based on the key value:

```
public static ProjectContact GetProjectContact(object projectKey,
    object projectContactKey)
{
    // Get the list of contacts for the project
    List<ProjectContact> contacts = new List<ProjectContact>(
            ProjectService.projectRepository.FindBy(projectKey).Contacts);
    // Return the one that matches the key
    return contacts.Where(c => c.Key.Equals(projectContactKey)).Single();
}
```

The GetProjectContact method first uses the ProjectRepository's FindBy method to get the correct Project instance, and it then gets the Contacts property (which is an IList<ProjectContact> type) of the found Project. I then take the IList<ProjectContact> instance and use it to initialize a List<ProjectContact> type. I then turn the IList<ProjectContact> type into a List<ProjectContact> type. The reason why I do this is so that I can use a LINQ query on the List<ProjectContact> instance to easily find the ProjectContact I am trying to traverse to:

```
// Return the one that matches the key
return contacts.Where(c => c.Key.Equals(projectContactKey)).Single();
```

The above code uses a lambda expression (c => c.Key.Equals(projectContactKey)) as an argument for the Where extension method on the List<T> class to return a type of IEnumerable <ProjectContactContact>. The Single extension method of the IEnumerable<T> class is then used to return a single ProjectContact instance. Pretty cool, huh? That LINQ query saved me several lines of code, and I think that it makes the intent of what I am trying to do much more obvious.

The AppendCopyToList Callback

The AppendCopyToList method has to perform a query on the database to get a list of CopyTo instances and then adds the items from the list to the CopyToList property on the Submittal class:

```
private void AppendCopyToList(Submittal submittal)
{
    StringBuilder builder = new StringBuilder(100);
    builder.Append("SELECT * FROM SubmittalCopyList");
    builder.Append(string.Format(" WHERE SubmittalID = '{0}';",
        submittal.Key));
    using (IDataReader reader = this.ExecuteReader(builder.ToString()))
    {
        while (reader.Read())
        {
            submittal.CopyToList.Add(SubmittalFactory.BuildCopyTo(
                submittal.ProjectKey, reader));
        }
    }
}
```

As the code iterates through the `IDataReader` results of the query, I use the SubmittalFactory's `BuildCopyTo` method to build the `CopyTo` instance from the `IDataReader`'s current position. The `BuildCopyTo` method is also fairly interesting, as it uses the `ProjectContactService` class to help it get its job done:

```
internal static CopyTo BuildCopyTo(object projectKey, IDataReader reader)
{
    ProjectContact contact = ProjectService.GetProjectContact(projectKey,
        reader[FieldNames.ProjectContactId]);
    return new CopyTo(contact, reader[FieldNames.Notes].ToString());
}
```

The `GetProjectContact` method being called should look familiar, since I just showed that earlier in the chapter. Notice, also, that the `CopyTo` class is a `Value` class, as evidenced by having to supply all of the data for the class to its constructor.

The AppendTrackingItems Callback

This method is very similar to the `AppendCopyToList` method just shown:

```
private void AppendTrackingItems(Submittal submittal)
{
    StringBuilder builder = new StringBuilder(100);
    builder.Append("SELECT * FROM SubmittalTrackingItem");
    builder.Append(string.Format(" WHERE SubmittalID = '{0}';",
        submittal.Key));
    using (IDataReader reader = this.ExecuteReader(builder.ToString()))
    {
        while (reader.Read())
        {
            submittal.TrackingItems.Add(
                SubmittalFactory.BuildTrackingItem(reader));
        }
    }
}
```

It also uses a `StringBuilder` to build up a SQL statement, and then uses `SqlCeRepositoryBase<T>` to get an `IDataReader` instance. While iterating through the `IDataReader`, it also uses the `SubmittalFactory`, this time calling the `BuildTrackingItem` method.

```
private void AppendTrackingItems(Submittal submittal)
{
    StringBuilder builder = new StringBuilder(100);
    builder.Append("SELECT * FROM SubmittalTrackingItem sti");
    builder.Append(" INNER JOIN SpecificationSection ss");
    builder.Append(" ON sti.SpecificationSectionID =");
    builder.Append( "ss.SpecificationSectionID");
    builder.Append(string.Format(" WHERE SubmittalID = '{0}';",
        submittal.Key));
    using (IDataReader reader = this.ExecuteReader(builder.ToString()))
    {
        while (reader.Read())
```

(continued)

(continued)

```
                {
                    submittal.TrackingItems.Add(
                        SubmittalFactory.BuildTrackingItem(reader));
                }
            }
        }
```

The `BuildTrackingItem` method first builds a `SpecificationSection` object to pass in to the `TrackingItem` class's constructor, and then it populates the rest of the class's properties:

```
        internal static TrackingItem BuildTrackingItem(IDataReader reader)
        {
            TrackingItem item = new TrackingItem(
                                SubmittalFactory.BuildSpecSection(reader));
            item.TotalItemsReceived = DataHelper.GetInteger(
                reader[FieldNames.TotalItemsReceived]);
            item.TotalItemsSent = DataHelper.GetInteger(
                reader[FieldNames.TotalItemsSent]);
            item.DeferredApproval = DataHelper.GetInteger(
                reader[FieldNames.DeferredApproval]);
            item.SubstitutionNumber = DataHelper.GetInteger(
                reader[FieldNames.SubstitutionNumber]);
            item.Description = reader[FieldNames.Description].ToString();
            item.Status = DataHelper.GetEnumValue<ActionStatus>(
                reader[FieldNames.Status].ToString());
            return item;
        }
```

I get some nice code reuse when building the `SpecificationSection` instance via the `BuildSpecSection` method of the factory. The rest of this factory method is just setting properties on the `TrackingItem` from the `IDataReader` instance.

The AppendRoutingItems Callback

This method is also similar to the previous callback methods, following the same pattern of executing a SQL statement and delegating to the factory to build `RoutingItem` instances:

```
        private void AppendRoutingItems(Submittal submittal)
        {
            StringBuilder builder = new StringBuilder(100);
            builder.Append("SELECT * FROM SubmittalRoutingItem sri ");
            builder.Append(" INNER JOIN RoutingItem ri ON");
            builder.Append(" sri.RoutingItemID = ri.RoutingItemID");
            builder.Append(" INNER JOIN Discipline d ON");
            builder.Append(" ri.DisciplineID = d.DisciplineID");
            builder.Append(string.Format(" WHERE sri.SubmittalID = '{0}';",
                submittal.Key));
            using (IDataReader reader = this.ExecuteReader(builder.ToString()))
```

```
            {
                while (reader.Read())
                {
                    submittal.RoutingItems.Add(SubmittalFactory.BuildRoutingItem(
                        submittal.ProjectKey, reader));
                }
            }
        }
```

This code should look very familiar to you by now, except for the SQL statement requiring a few more joins to get all of the necessary data into the `IDataReader` instance. I am not going to show the `BuildRoutingItem` method of the `SubmittalFactory` class, since it is very similar to the `BuildCopyTo` method just shown.

Unit of Work Implementation

Following the same steps that I have shown before to implement the Unit of Work pattern, I only need to override three methods, `PersistNewItem(Submittal item)`, `PersistUpdatedItem(Submittal item)`, and `PersistDeletedItem(Submittal item)`.

The PersistNewItem Method

The first method override for the `SubmittalRepository`'s Unit of Work implementation is the `PersistNewItem` method:

```
protected override void PersistNewItem(Submittal item)
        {
            StringBuilder builder = new StringBuilder(100);
            builder.Append(string.Format("INSERT INTO Submittal
({0},{1},{2},{3},{4},{5},{6},{7},{8},{9},{10},{11},{12},{13},{14},{15},{16},{17},
{18},{19},{20},{21}) ",
                SubmittalFactory.FieldNames.SubmittalId,
                ProjectFactory.FieldNames.ProjectId,
                SubmittalFactory.FieldNames.SpecificationSectionId,
                SubmittalFactory.FieldNames.SpecificationSectionPrimaryIndex,
                SubmittalFactory.FieldNames.SpecificationSectionSecondaryIndex,
                SubmittalFactory.FieldNames.ProjectContactId,
                SubmittalFactory.FieldNames.EmployeeId,
                SubmittalFactory.FieldNames.TotalPages,
                SubmittalFactory.FieldNames.DeliveryMethod,
                SubmittalFactory.FieldNames.OtherDeliveryMethod,
                SubmittalFactory.FieldNames.PhaseNumber,
                SubmittalFactory.FieldNames.Reimbursable,
                SubmittalFactory.FieldNames.Final,
                SubmittalFactory.FieldNames.DateReceived,
                SubmittalFactory.FieldNames.ContractNumber,
                SubmittalFactory.FieldNames.Remarks,
                SubmittalFactory.FieldNames.Action,
                SubmittalFactory.FieldNames.SubmittalStatusId,
                SubmittalFactory.FieldNames.DateToField,
                SubmittalFactory.FieldNames.RemainderLocation,
                SubmittalFactory.FieldNames.RemainderUnderSubmittalNumber,
```

(continued)

(continued)

```
                SubmittalFactory.FieldNames.OtherRemainderLocation));
            builder.Append(string.Format("VALUES ({0},{1},{2},{3},{4},{5},{6},{7},
{8},{9},{10},{11},{12},{13},{14},{15},{16},{17},{18},{19},{20},{21});",
                DataHelper.GetSqlValue(item.Key),
                DataHelper.GetSqlValue(item.ProjectKey),
                DataHelper.GetSqlValue(item.SpecSection.Key),
                DataHelper.GetSqlValue(item.SpecSectionPrimaryIndex),
                DataHelper.GetSqlValue(item.SpecSectionSecondaryIndex),
                DataHelper.GetSqlValue(item.To.Key),
                DataHelper.GetSqlValue(item.From.Key),
                DataHelper.GetSqlValue(item.TotalPages),
                DataHelper.GetSqlValue(item.DeliveryMethod),
                DataHelper.GetSqlValue(item.OtherDeliveryMethod),
                DataHelper.GetSqlValue(item.PhaseNumber),
                DataHelper.GetSqlValue(item.Reimbursable),
                DataHelper.GetSqlValue(item.Final),
                DataHelper.GetSqlValue(item.DateReceived),
                DataHelper.GetSqlValue(item.ContractNumber),
                DataHelper.GetSqlValue(item.Remarks),
                DataHelper.GetSqlValue(item.Action),
                DataHelper.GetSqlValue(item.Status.Id),
                DataHelper.GetSqlValue(item.DateToField),
                DataHelper.GetSqlValue(item.RemainderLocation),
                DataHelper.GetSqlValue(item.RemainderUnderSubmittalNumber),
                DataHelper.GetSqlValue(item.OtherRemainderLocation)));

            this.Database.ExecuteNonQuery(
                this.Database.GetSqlStringCommand(builder.ToString()));

            // Now do the child objects
            this.InsertCopyToList(item);
            this.InsertRoutingItems(item);
            this.InsertTrackingItems(item);
        }
```

The code builds up a large insert statement composed of the values from the `Submittal` instance, and then executes the query using the Microsoft Enterprise Library's `Database` object. After the insert statement has been executed, I also need to insert the `CopyTo`, `RoutingItem`, and `TrackingItem` instances for the Submittal. I do this by calling the `InsertCopyToList`, `InsertRoutingItems`, and `InsertTrackingItems` methods, which all take a Submittal instance as an argument.
The `InsertCopyToList` method saves all of the Submittal's `CopyTo` items in the database:

```
        private void InsertCopyToList(Submittal submittal)
        {
            foreach (CopyTo copyTo in submittal.CopyToList)
            {
                this.InsertCopyTo(copyTo, submittal.Key);
            }
        }
```

The `InsertCopyToList` method just iterates the `CopyToList` property of the `Submittal` instance and calls `InsertCopyTo` on each item in the list. `InsertCopyTo` then saves the `CopyTo` instance to the database:

```
        private void InsertCopyTo(CopyTo copyTo, object key)
        {
            StringBuilder builder = new StringBuilder(100);
            builder.Append(string.Format("INSERT INTO SubmittalCopyList
({0},{1},{2}) ",
                SubmittalFactory.FieldNames.SubmittalId,
                SubmittalFactory.FieldNames.ProjectContactId,
                SubmittalFactory.FieldNames.Notes));
            builder.Append(string.Format("VALUES ({0},{1},{2});",
                DataHelper.GetSqlValue(key),
                DataHelper.GetSqlValue(copyTo.Contact.Key),
                DataHelper.GetSqlValue(copyTo.Notes)));

            this.Database.ExecuteNonQuery(
                this.Database.GetSqlStringCommand(builder.ToString()));
        }
```

The code for `InsertCopyTo` should look very familiar; it follows the same pattern of building a SQL insert string and then executing it against the database.

I am not going to show the code for the `InsertRoutingItems` and `InsertTrackingItems` methods because they and their helper methods are almost identical to the `InsertCopyToList` method and its helper methods.

The PersistUpdatedItem Method

`PersistUpdatedItem` first does an update to the Submittal table:

```
protected override void PersistUpdatedItem(Submittal item)
        {
            StringBuilder builder = new StringBuilder(100);
            builder.Append("UPDATE Submittal SET ");

            builder.Append(string.Format("{0} = {1}",
                SubmittalFactory.FieldNames.SpecificationSectionId,
                DataHelper.GetSqlValue(item.SpecSection.Key)));

            builder.Append(string.Format(",{0} = {1}",
                SubmittalFactory.FieldNames.SpecificationSectionPrimaryIndex,
                DataHelper.GetSqlValue(item.SpecSectionPrimaryIndex)));

          *******************************************************************

            builder.Append(string.Format(",{0} = {1}",
                SubmittalFactory.FieldNames.OtherRemainderLocation,
                DataHelper.GetSqlValue(item.OtherRemainderLocation)));
```

(continued)

(continued)

```
            builder.Append(" ");
            builder.Append(this.BuildBaseWhereClause(item.Key));

            this.Database.ExecuteNonQuery(
                this.Database.GetSqlStringCommand(builder.ToString()));

            // Now do the child objects

            // First, delete the existing ones
            this.DeleteCopyToList(item);
            this.DeleteRoutingItems(item);
            this.DeleteTrackingItems(item);

            // Now, add the current ones
            this.InsertCopyToList(item);
            this.InsertRoutingItems(item);
            this.InsertTrackingItems(item);
        }
```

I have omitted several lines of repetitive code building the SQL update statement in the middle of the code in order save you from the boring code. The omitted lines are represented by the stars (***********).

The second part of the method uses the `DeleteCoyToList`, `DeleteRoutingItems`, and `DeleteTrackingItems` helper methods to delete all of the child objects of the Submittal, and then uses the familiar `InsertCopyToList`, `InsertRoutingItems`, and `InsertTrackingItems` helper methods to add the existing child objects from the Submittal to the database. `DeleteCopyToList` runs a query against the `SubmittalCopyList` table to remove all entries with a matching `SubmittalID` field value.

```
        private void DeleteCopyToList(Submittal submittal)
        {
            string query = string.Format("DELETE FROM SubmittalCopyList {0}",
                this.BuildBaseWhereClause(submittal.Key));
            this.Database.ExecuteNonQuery(
                this.Database.GetSqlStringCommand(query));
        }
```

The `DeleteRoutingItems` and `DeleteTrackingItems` are very similar to the `DeleteCopyToList` method, so I will not show the code for those methods here.

The PersistDeletedItem Method

The last method in `SubmittalRepository` to override, `PersistDeletedItem`, follows the same pattern that I have shown for the `PersistDeletedItem` override in the other Repository classes:

```
        protected override void PersistDeletedItem(Submittal item)
        {
            // Delete the child objects first
            this.DeleteCopyToList(item);
            this.DeleteRoutingItems(item);
```

```
            this.DeleteTrackingItems(item);

            // Now delete the submittal
            string query = string.Format("DELETE FROM Submittal {0}",
                this.BuildBaseWhereClause(item.Key));
            this.Database.ExecuteNonQuery(
                this.Database.GetSqlStringCommand(query));
        }
```

This code deletes all of the child objects from the Submittal first, and then deletes the Submittal record from the database.

The Submittal Service Implementation

The only `Service` classes I have implemented up to this point are the `Service` classes that live in the domain model layer and act as facades for their respective Repository interfaces.

The `SubmittalService` class is responsible for retrieving and saving `Submittal` instances:

```
using System.Collections.Generic;
using SmartCA.Infrastructure;
using SmartCA.Infrastructure.RepositoryFramework;
using SmartCA.Model.Projects;

namespace SmartCA.Model.Submittals
{
    public static class SubmittalService
    {
        private static ISubmittalRepository repository;
        private static IUnitOfWork unitOfWork;

        static SubmittalService()
        {
            SubmittalService.unitOfWork = new UnitOfWork();
            SubmittalService.repository =
                RepositoryFactory.GetRepository<ISubmittalRepository,
                Submittal>(SubmittalService.unitOfWork);
        }

        public static IList<Submittal> GetSubmittals(Project project)
        {
            return SubmittalService.repository.FindBy(project);
        }

        public static IList<SpecificationSection> GetSpecificationSections()
        {
            return SubmittalService.repository.FindAllSpecificationSections();
        }
```

(continued)

(continued)

```
        public static IList<SubmittalStatus> GetSubmittalStatuses()
        {
            return SubmittalService.repository.FindAllSubmittalStatuses();
        }

        public static void SaveSubmittal(Submittal submittal)
        {
            SubmittalService.repository[submittal.Key] = submittal;
            SubmittalService.unitOfWork.Commit();
        }

        public static IList<Discipline> GetDisciplines()
        {
            return SubmittalService.repository.FindAllDisciplines();
        }
    }
}
```

This class, like the other `Service` classes in the application, is just acting as a façade for the `ISubmittalRepository` instance. All of the methods from the `ISubmittalRepository` interface are now exposed as static methods, which, as you will see in the next section covering the `SubmittalViewModel` class, make it very easy to interact with the repository.

The Submittal View Model

Following the same patterns as before, the `SubmittalViewModel` class adapts the Submittal Aggregate from the domain model to the UI. Like all previously shown `ViewModel` classes, I start out by inheriting from the `ViewModel` abstract class:

```
using System;
using System.Collections.Generic;
using SmartCA.Infrastructure.UI;
using SmartCA.Model.Submittals;
using System.Windows.Data;
using SmartCA.Application;
using SmartCA.Model.Employees;
using System.ComponentModel;
using SmartCA.Model.Projects;

namespace SmartCA.Presentation.ViewModels
{
    public class SubmittalViewModel : ViewModel
    {
```

The Constructor

As you have already seen in the `CompanyViewModel` and `ProjectContactViewModel` classes, anywhere that there is a parent-child relationship in the Aggregate, such as Company and Addresses, a `BindingList<T>` must be used to represent the child list in the ViewModel. This is because the Xceed DataGrid needs to bind to the `IBindingList<T>` interface to be able to add records to the grid dynamically. In the `SubmittalViewModel`, that means I need to use a `BindingList<T>` for the `CopyToList`, `RoutingItems`, and `TrackingItems` Submittal properties.

```
#region Constructors

public SubmittalViewModel()
    : this(null)
{
}

public SubmittalViewModel(IView view)
    : base(view)
{
    this.currentSubmittal = null;
    this.submittalsList = new List<Submittal>(
                            SubmittalService.GetSubmittals(
                            UserSession.CurrentProject));
    this.submittals = new CollectionView(this.submittalsList);
    this.specificationSections
        = SubmittalService.GetSpecificationSections();
    this.submittalStatuses = SubmittalService.GetSubmittalStatuses();
    this.toList = UserSession.CurrentProject.Contacts;
    this.mutableCopyToList = new BindingList<MutableCopyTo>();
    this.routingItems = new BindingList<RoutingItem>();
    this.trackingItems = new BindingList<TrackingItem>();
    this.fromList = EmployeeService.GetEmployees();
    this.trackingStatusValues = new CollectionView(
                            Enum.GetNames(typeof(ActionStatus)));
    this.deliveryMethods = new CollectionView(
                            Enum.GetNames(typeof(Delivery)));
    this.disciplines = SubmittalService.GetDisciplines();
    this.saveCommand = new DelegateCommand(this.SaveCommandHandler);
    this.newCommand = new DelegateCommand(this.NewCommandHandler);
    this.deleteCopyToCommand =
        new DelegateCommand(this.DeleteCopyToCommandHandler);
    this.deleteRoutingItemCommand =
        new DelegateCommand(this.DeleteRoutingItemCommandHandler);
    this.deleteTrackingItemCommand =
        new DelegateCommand(this.DeleteTrackingItemCommandHandler);
}

#endregion
```

The `MutableCopyTo` type is very similar to the `MutableAddress` type shown in previous chapters, and it is used to edit the values for the `CopyTo` Value type. Remember, in WPF, I cannot use two-way binding with read-only objects, so the `MutableCopyTo` gives me that flexibility without changing any of my domain objects.

Similarly to what I did to maintain the list of Contacts and Companies in the last chapter, I am again maintaining both a `List<Submittal>` variable (`submittalsList`) and the `CollectionView` variable (`submittals`) of the list. This allows me the benefit of using the `CollectionView` to know when a Submittal has been selected from the `CollectionView` (without having to write any code) and to be able to add new Submittals, which need to be added to the list. Using the `List<Submittal>` type, I am easily able to add new Submittal instances and then subsequently refresh the `CollectionView`. The other pattern I am following in this constructor is to initialize all of my property data, such as the data used to display all of the dropdowns in the UI (i.e., Employees, ProjectContacts, etc.). The rest of the constructor code is the standard wire-up code for the `DelegateCommand` instances.

The Properties

The `CurrentSubmittal` property indicates the current `Submittal` instance that is being edited:

```
public Submittal CurrentSubmittal
{
    get { return this.currentSubmittal; }
    set
    {
        if (this.currentSubmittal != value)
        {
            this.currentSubmittal = value;
            this.OnPropertyChanged(Constants.CurrentSubmittalPropertyName);
            this.saveCommand.IsEnabled = (this.currentSubmittal != null);
            this.PopulateSubmittalChildren();
        }
    }
}
```

Just as with Contacts and Companies, whenever a Submittal is selected from the list box in the UI, the property's setter is called. Once that has happened, the `PropertyChanged` event for the `CurrentSubmittal` property is raised, letting the UI know to refresh itself. The next thing to happen is to set the `SaveCommand`'s `IsEnabled` property to `true` if the current Submittal is null; otherwise, it is set to `false`. Then the `PopulateSubmittalChildren` method is called:

```
private void PopulateSubmittalChildren()
{
    this.PopulateMutableCopyToList();
    this.PopulateRoutingItems();
    this.PopulateTrackingItems();
}
```

This is essentially a controller method, as it calls three more methods to populate the collections representing the children of the Submittal Aggregate.

The `PopulateMutableCopyToList` method is very similar to the `PopulateAddresses` method used in the last chapter:

```
private void PopulateMutableCopyToList()
{
    if (this.currentSubmittal != null)
    {
        this.mutableCopyToList.Clear();
        foreach (CopyTo copyTo in this.currentSubmittal.CopyToList)
        {
            this.mutableCopyToList.Add(new MutableCopyTo(copyTo));
        }
        this.OnPropertyChanged(Constants.MutableCopyToListPropertyName);
    }
}
```

This is necessary because the `CopyTo` instances contained in the Submittal's `CopyToList` property are the immutable `CopyTo` types, and in order to be able to edit the `CopyToList`, I have to convert them into `MutableCopyTo` types. Once this is done, the `PropertyChanged` event for the `MutableCopyToList` property is raised so that the UI can refresh itself.

The `PopulateRoutingItems` and `PopulateTrackingItems` methods are almost identical, so I will just show `PopulateRoutingItems` method:

```
private void PopulateRoutingItems()
{
    if (this.currentSubmittal != null)
    {
        this.routingItems.Clear();
        foreach (RoutingItem item in this.currentSubmittal.RoutingItems)
        {
            this.routingItems.Add(item);
        }
        this.OnPropertyChanged(Constants.RoutingItemsPropertyName);
    }
}
```

You may be asking yourself, "Why can't we just use the `RoutingItems` property of the Submittal class? Why do we have to create a whole new separate property for that and have to maintain the state between the two?" That's a good question, and the answer is because I need the `RoutingItems` property to be in the form of a `BindingList<RoutingItem>` rather than an `IList<RoutingItem>`. The reason I need it to be in that form is because that is the type that my data grid (Xceed Data Grid for WPF) is looking for in order to get the nice functionality of adding rows to the grid at run time without writing any code.

The rest of the properties in the `SubmittalViewModel` class are simple read-only properties representing lookup lists, and the `DelegateCommand` instances for creating New Submittals, saving Submittals, and deleting `RoutingItems`, `TrackingItems`, and `CopyTo` instances from the Submittal Aggregate.

Command Handler Methods

The handlers for the `DelegateCommand` properties are pretty interesting. The `NewCommandHandler` method has to do a lot of housekeeping:

```
private void NewCommandHandler(object sender, EventArgs e)
        {
            Submittal newSubmittal = new Submittal(
                                          this.currentSubmittal.SpecSection,
                                          this.currentSubmittal.ProjectKey);
            newSubmittal.SpecSectionSecondaryIndex = "01";

            this.currentSubmittal = null;
            this.mutableCopyToList.Clear();
            this.routingItems.Clear();
            this.trackingItems.Clear();
```

(continued)

(continued)

```
            this.CurrentObjectState = ObjectState.New;
            this.OnPropertyChanged(
                Constants.CurrentSubmittalPropertyName);

            this.submittalsList.Add(newSubmittal);
            this.submittals.Refresh();
            this.submittals.MoveCurrentToLast();
        }
```

It first has to create a new instance of a `Submittal` and initialize its `SpecSection` constructor argument to be the same as the current Submittal, as well as feed it the same Project key as the current Submittal. This is necessary because a Submittal cannot be created without knowing the Specification Section or to what Project it belongs. The Specification Section value can be changed via a property setter later, but to start I need to put something there. As far as the Project key, that cannot be changed unless a different project is selected altogether. Once the Submittal has been created, it is given a default Specification Section Secondary Index of "01". This is to prevent any duplicate entries, and once again, can be changed via property setters later.

The next steps are to clear the current Submittal data and then to clear out the `MutableCopyToList`, `RoutingItems`, and `TrackingItems` lists. Once that is done, the state of the ViewModel is set to `New`, and the `PropertyChanged` event is raised for the UI to refresh itself.

Next, the newly created Submittal is added to the current list of Submittals, and then the `Refresh` method is called on the `CollectionView` submittals variable in order to have the UI refreshed. Finally, by calling the `MoveCurrentToLast` method on the `CollectionView`, the Submittal will appear last in the list in the UI.

The `DeleteCopyToCommandHandler` method is interesting because it gets the `MutableCopyTo` instance that must be deleted passed to it from the `DelegateCommandEventArgs` parameter:

```
        private void DeleteCopyToCommandHandler(object sender,
            DelegateCommandEventArgs e)
        {
            MutableCopyTo copyTo = e.Parameter as MutableCopyTo;
            if (copyTo != null)
            {
                this.mutableCopyToList.Remove(copyTo);
            }
        }
```

It then checks to see whether the `MutableCopyTo` instance is null, and if it is not, it removes it from the `BindingList<MutableCopyTo>` collection (the `mutableCopyToList` variable). Once this happens, the data grid that is bound to it is automatically updated. The `DeleteCopyToCommandHandler` and `DeleteCopyToCommandHandler` methods are almost identical to the `DeleteCopyToCommandHandler` method, so I will not show them here.

The Submittal View

The View for Submittals is the most complicated view encountered so far, because it has to manage all of the parent-child relationships in the Aggregate. Before diving into the XAML for the `SubmittalView`, take a look at Figure 5.5, which shows what the form looks like at run time:

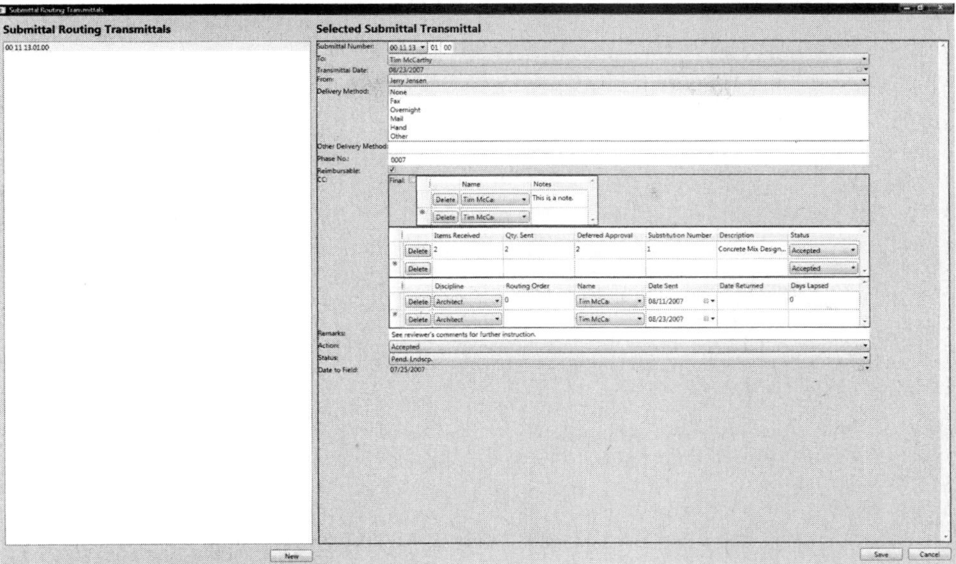

Figure 5.5: The Submittal view.

The form is not the most elegant looking in the world, but it is functional.

Like the form for Companies and Contacts, this form is split into two parts: the one on the left is for selecting a Submittal to edit and the one on the right is for editing the selected Submittal. The New button adds a new Submittal to the list. The Save and Cancel buttons both deal with the currently selected Submittal.

In the form, you will see three grid areas, one for the `CopyToList`, one for `TrackingItems`, and one for `RoutingItems`. These have all been implemented as separate user controls, so that they may be reused in other parts of the UI that require routing, tracking, and copying.

The XAML for this form is pretty large, so I am only going to show the sections that are implemented differently from what has been done so far in the UI.

Using the StackPanel Element

The first interesting part WPF-wise is the very top field, the Submittal Number field:

```
<Label Grid.Row="0" Grid.Column="0" Content="Submittal Number:"
Style="{StaticResource baseLabelStyle}"/>

<StackPanel Orientation="Horizontal" Grid.Row="0" Grid.Column="1">
    <ComboBox SelectedItem="{Binding Path=CurrentSubmittal.SpecSection}"
        IsSynchronizedWithCurrentItem="True"
        DisplayMemberPath="Number"
        ItemsSource="{Binding Path=SpecificationSections}">
    </ComboBox>
```

(continued)

(continued)

```
        <TextBox
            Text="{Binding Path=CurrentSubmittal.SpecSectionPrimaryIndex}"/>
        <TextBox
            Text="{Binding Path=CurrentSubmittal.SpecSectionSecondaryIndex}"/>
    </StackPanel>
```

The first part is just the label for the field. The second part needs to squeeze a combo box and two textboxes right next to each other. In WPF, this is not possible to do in a single cell of a `Grid`, but the way around that limitation is to wrap a `StackPanel` around the three elements, and then the `StackPanel` becomes the only child element in the grid cell. `StackPanel` elements allow you to group more than one element together. This is a good thing to remember when building WPF applications.

Using the Xceed DatePicker Control

In order to allow users to edit date fields, I am using the Xceed DatePicker control, which comes for free with the free WPF Data Grid control. The first occasion I need to use it is for the Transmittal Date field:

```
<Label Grid.Row="2" Grid.Column="0" Content="Transmittal Date:"
    Style="{StaticResource baseLabelStyle}"/>
<xcdg:DatePicker Grid.Row="2" Grid.Column="1"
    SelectedDate="{Binding Path=CurrentSubmittal.TransmittalDate}"
    SyncCalendarWithSelectedDate="True" />
```

The first part of the XAML is just for the label, but the second part contains the `DatePicker` element, which supports binding to `DateTime` properties (in this case, I am binding to the `TransmittalDate` property of the Submittal). Also, it has a nice feature that syncs the calendar with the selected date, which looks like Figure 5.6.

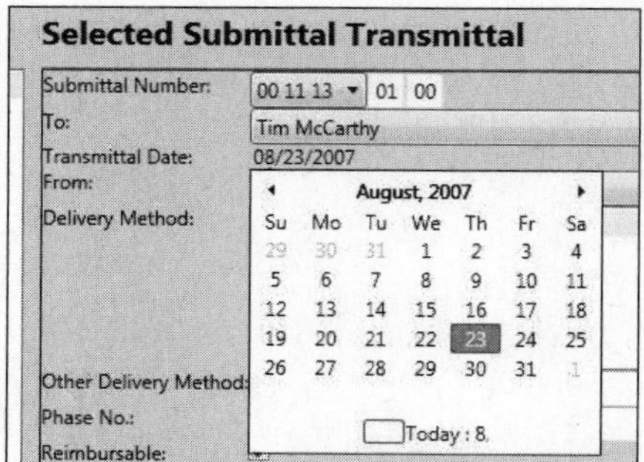

Figure 5.6: The DatePicker control.

This is great, because once again, I do not have to write that UI plumbing code, Xceed has already done a great job for me.

The CopyToList Section

The next interesting part of the XAML for the form is the section that displays the `CopyTo` child items, as shown in Figure 5.7.

Figure 5.7: The CopyToList section.

This requires using a `StackPanel` element again in order to stack the Final checkbox field next to the grid:

```
<Border BorderBrush="Black" Padding="1" BorderThickness="1"
 Grid.Row="8" Grid.Column="1">
    <StackPanel Orientation="Horizontal">
        <Label Content="Final: " Style="{StaticResource baseLabelStyle}"/>
        <CheckBox IsChecked="{Binding Path=CurrentSubmittal.Final}" />
        <presentation:CopyToList DataContext="{Binding Path=MutableCopyToList}"/>
    </StackPanel>
</Border>
```

Also included in the mix for this section is the `Border` element that wraps the `StackPanel`. This is what gives the border line around the controls. Then, inside of the `StackPanel` is the label for the checkbox, the actual checkbox itself, and then the `CopyTo` grid. The `CopyTo` grid is actually a new user control, the `CopyToList` user control. Here is the XAML for the `CopyToList` control:

```
<UserControl x:Class="SmartCA.Presentation.Views.CopyToList"
    xmlns="http://schemas.microsoft.com/winfx/2006/xaml/presentation"
    xmlns:xcdg="http://schemas.xceed.com/wpf/xaml/datagrid"
    xmlns:x="http://schemas.microsoft.com/winfx/2006/xaml">
    <xcdg:DataGridControl ItemsSource="{Binding}">
        <xcdg:DataGridControl.Columns>
                <xcdg:Column Width="50" FieldName="DeleteButton"
                        DisplayMemberBinding="{Binding .}">
                        <xcdg:Column.CellContentTemplate>
                                <DataTemplate>
                                        <Button Content="Delete"
                                            Command="{Binding
                                            RelativeSource=
                                            {RelativeSource FindAncestor,
                                            AncestorType={x:Type Window}},
                                            Path=DataContext.DeleteCopyToCommand}">
                                                <Button.CommandParameter>
                                                        <Binding Path="."/>
                                                </Button.CommandParameter>
                                        </Button>
                                </DataTemplate>
                        </xcdg:Column.CellContentTemplate>
                </xcdg:Column>
```

(continued)

(continued)

```
                <xcdg:Column FieldName="ProjectContact" Title="Name">
                    <xcdg:Column.CellContentTemplate>
                        <DataTemplate>
                            <ComboBox
                                ItemsSource="{Binding
                                RelativeSource=
                                {RelativeSource FindAncestor,
                                AncestorType={x:Type Window}},
                                Path=DataContext.ToList}"
                                SelectedItem="{Binding .}"
                                IsSynchronizedWithCurrentItem="True">
                                <ComboBox.ItemTemplate>
                                    <DataTemplate>
                                        <Grid>

<Grid.ColumnDefinitions>

<ColumnDefinition />

<ColumnDefinition />

<ColumnDefinition />

</Grid.ColumnDefinitions>

            <TextBlock Grid.Column="0" Text="{Binding Path=Contact.FirstName}"/>
            <TextBlock Grid.Column="1" Text=" " />
            <TextBlock Grid.Column="2" Text="{Binding Path=Contact.LastName}"/>
                                            </Grid>
                                        </DataTemplate>
                                    </ComboBox.ItemTemplate>
                                </ComboBox>
                            </DataTemplate>
                        </xcdg:Column.CellContentTemplate>
                </xcdg:Column>
                <xcdg:Column FieldName="Notes"
                    Title="Notes" Width="100" TextWrapping="Wrap"/>
            </xcdg:DataGridControl.Columns>
            <xcdg:DataGridControl.View>
                <xcdg:TableView HorizontalGridLineThickness="1"
                    VerticalGridLineThickness="1">
                    <xcdg:TableView.HorizontalGridLineBrush>
                        <SolidColorBrush Color="Orange"/>
                    </xcdg:TableView.HorizontalGridLineBrush>
                    <xcdg:TableView.VerticalGridLineBrush>
                        <SolidColorBrush Color="Orange"/>
                    </xcdg:TableView.VerticalGridLineBrush>
                    <xcdg:TableView.Footers>
                        <DataTemplate>
                            <xcdg:InsertionRow/>
                        </DataTemplate>
                    </xcdg:TableView.Footers>
```

```
                        <xcdg:TableView.FixedHeaders>
                              <xcdg:ClearHeadersFooters/>
                              <DataTemplate>
                                    <xcdg:ColumnManagerRow/>
                              </DataTemplate>
                        </xcdg:TableView.FixedHeaders>
                  </xcdg:TableView>
            </xcdg:DataGridControl.View>
    </xcdg:DataGridControl>
   </ UserControl>
```

The XAML for this control is very similar to the XAML for the `Addresses` user control shown in the previous chapter. Probably the most important things to pay attention to here are the bindings for the various elements in the control. The Delete button is pretty much the same as the `Addresses` control's delete button, but this is the first time that I have had to use a nested combo box inside of the Xceed DataGrid. I have to say that it handled it very well, with the only caveat that you have to make sure that you specify the binding for the `SelectedItem` property like this: `SelectedItem="{Binding .}"`. Other than having to figure that out, it was pretty easy to put together and use.

The Routing Items and Tracking Items sections both follow the same pattern used for the `CopyToList` section, so I am not going to show the code for those here.

Summary

In this chapter, I introduced the concept of a Submittal Transmittal in the construction industry, and then I used that concept to model the Submittal Aggregate. I then defined the boundaries for the Submittal Aggregate, as well as implemented all of the necessary domain model and `Infrastructure` classes necessary to work with those classes. A new concept was added to the both the domain layer and infrastructure layer, and that was how to deal with saving child collections from the Entity Root repository. The concept was demonstrated by the techniques I used to save `CopyTo`, `RoutingItem`, and `TrackingItem` instances of the Submittal Aggregate. I also covered how to deal with `CopyTo` Value objects using the Xceed DataGrid control, and I showed how to wrap this functionality up into a reusable `UserControl` for the CopyToList, RoutingItems and Tacking Items. On top of those items, I threw in a few little WPF UI tricks. There was also some refactoring again in this chapter, particularly with the service classes being used almost like a façade in front of the repositories from all of the `ViewModel` classes.

6

Requests for Information

In the last chapter, I dove into some of the important domain logic for the SmartCA application by covering Submittal Transmittals. In this chapter, I will continue that trend by introducing another important new concept to the domain, the Request for Information (RFI). As you will see, the RFI is similar to a Submittal Transmittal in that they share a lot of the same classes: this will also prompt some refactoring.

The Problem

Contractors can have many questions throughout a project that may concern documents, construction, materials, and so on. In the old days, these questions were answered with a phone call or an informal conversation with the architect in charge. Nowadays, however, it is necessary to document every request and reply between project contractors and the firm that is running the project, which in this case is Smart Design. This documentation is necessary because significant costs and complications may arise during the question/answer process, and the RFI can be used as a tool to shape the project's direction.

Some of the uses of RFIs do not have cost implications, such as a simple non-change request for more information about something shown in the specifications. They can also be used to let the architect know about an occurrence of something on the job site, or to let the architect know about latent or unknown conditions. The most important rule for an RFI is that it must contain all of the necessary information and not be too brief. If a contractor has a question for the architect, the architect needs to know exactly what the question is so that it may be answered properly.

Each RFI needs to be numbered in the sequence issued, per project. The RFI number is later used as a reference for members of the project when the architect answers the questions or resolves the issues. The RFI is a time-sensitive document, and it must include the date that it was sent, as well as the date that a response is needed. It is important that there are no duplicate RFI numbers per project and that there are no gaps between RFI numbers. RFI numbers can be reused across other projects.

The Design

In the SmartCA domain, an RFI contains several important business concepts that must be closely followed. In the next few sections, I will be designing the domain model, determining the RFI Aggregate and its boundaries, and designing the Repository for RFIs.

Designing the Domain Model

As stated earlier, the most important parts of the RFI are the Date Received, Date Requested By, Date to Field, Question, and Answer properties. Since these are properties, it is a little bit difficult to model their expected behavior in a diagram. This can be remedied by using a Specification (Evans, *Domain-Driven Design, Tackling Complexity in the Heart of Software*, 225) class to specify the rules for these properties, and actually make the specification part of the domain. This helps convey to the business domain experts what the intended logic is instead of burying it inside of the Request for Information class.

Figure 6.1 shows a drawing showing the relationships among the classes that combine to make up a Request for Information.

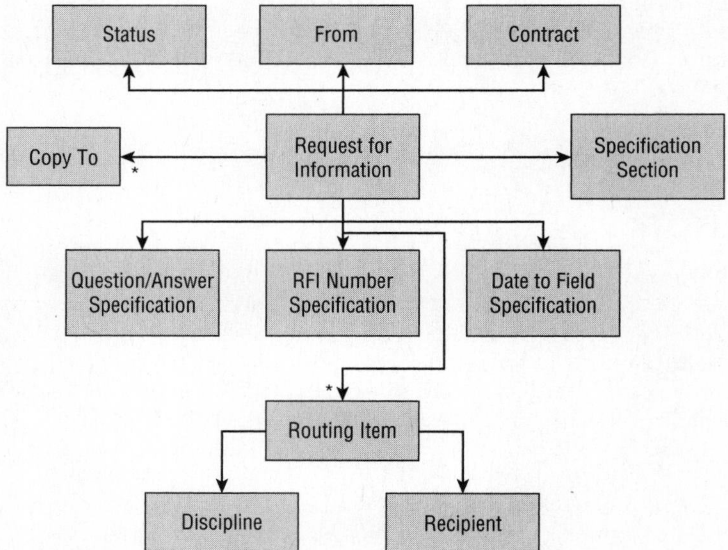

Figure 6.1: RFI Aggregate.

Obviously, the root of this aggregate is the Request for Information class. Note the relationships to the Question/Answer Specification, Date to Field Specification, and RFI Number Specification. These relationships make it very clear to the domain experts that there are rules being modeled for these important concepts.

The relationship to the Status class shows exactly what state the RFI is in, such as completed, pending an architect review, and so on. The relationship to the "From" class represents who the RFI is from, and to go along with who it is from is what Contract is associated with the RFI. The relationship to the

Specification Section is not as important for an RFI as it was for a Submittal Transmittal. It is quite possible that the RFI may not require a reference to a Specification Section, as the RFI could be requesting information about something else that may have nothing to do with a Specification Section, such as an incident.

The next important part of the diagram is the RFI's relationship to the Routing Item. This is how Smart Design knows to whom each RFI has been routed for action, and the Discipline of that person, such as architect, engineer, or construction administrator. Just like the Submittal Transmittal Aggregate, there is a Copy To relationship from an RFI which represents the list of Recipients who need to be copied on all correspondence having to do with the RFI.

Defining the RFI Aggregate

As you can see from the diagram of the RFI Aggregate in Figure 6.2, there are a lot of moving parts.

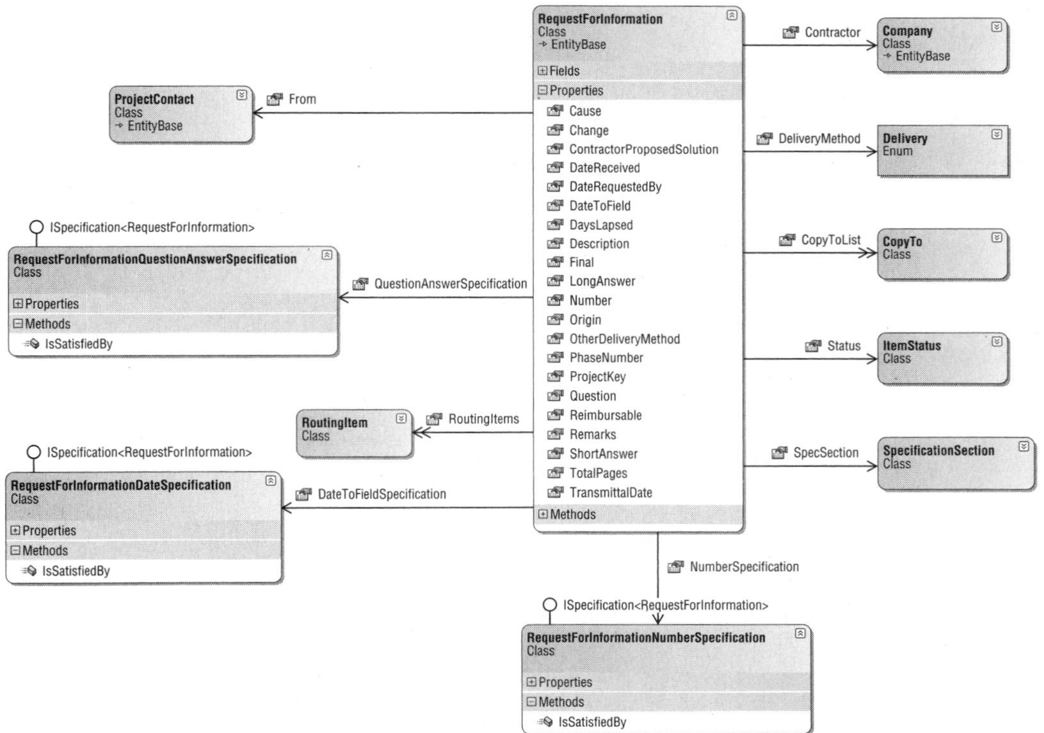

Figure 6.2: Classes constituting the RFI Aggregate.

Notice how I am starting to make use of some of the other Entities introduced in previous chapters, such as the `ProjectContact` class, which is used to represent the To property of the Submittal class, the Recipient property of the RoutingItem class, and the Contact property of the CopyTo class. Also, the `ProjectContact` class is used in the RFI's From property to represent the person originating the RFI.

Defining the Aggregate Boundaries

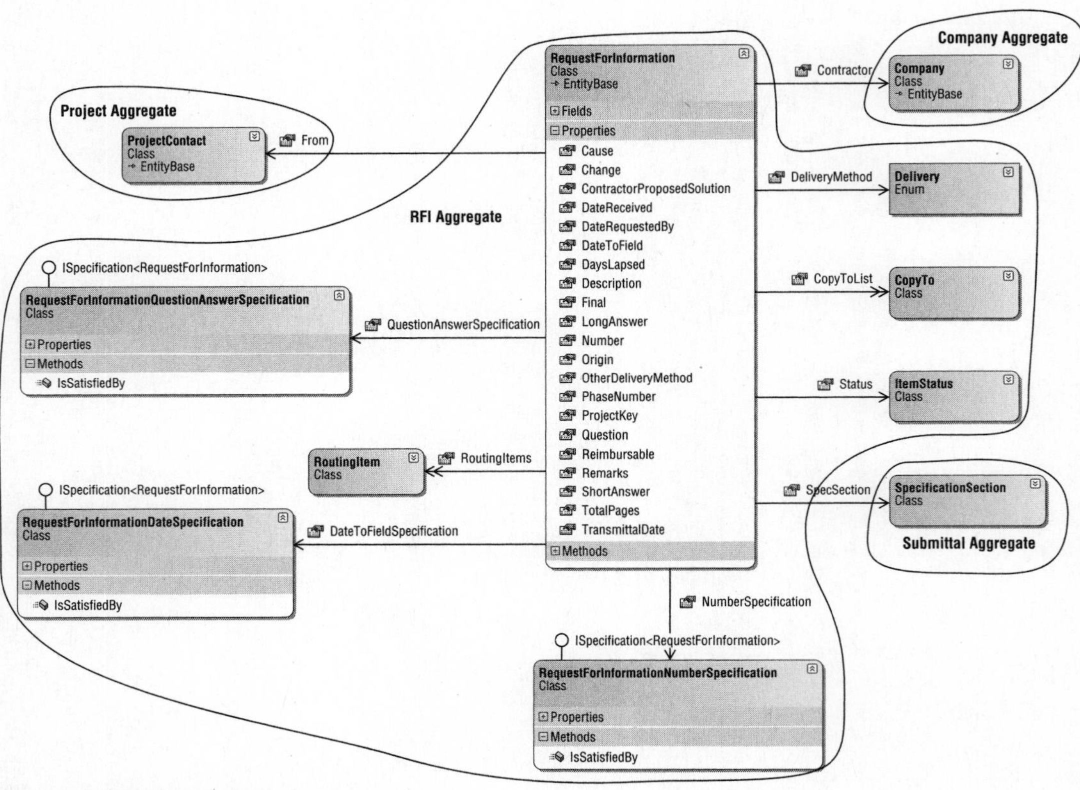

Figure 6.3: RFI Aggregate boundaries.

The RequestForInformation class has its own identity and is definitely the root of its own Aggregate (see Figure 6.3). All of the other classes in the diagram, except for ProjectContact, Company, and SpecificationSection, belong to the RFI Aggregate. As shown in earlier chapters, ProjectContact belongs to the Project Aggregate, Company is the root of its own Aggregate, and the SpecificationSection class is part of the Submittal Aggregate.

Designing the Repository

Since the RequestForInformation class is its own Aggregate root, it will have its own Repository, as shown in Figure 6.4.

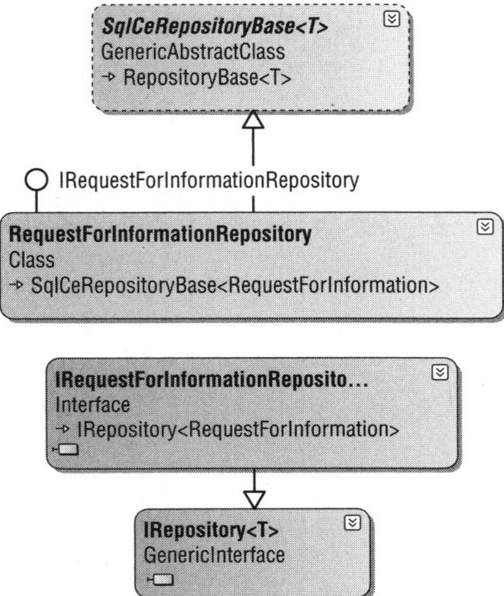

Figure 6.4: RFI Aggregate Repository.

Although the Project Aggregate, Company Aggregate, and Submittal Aggregate are part of the RFI Aggregate, I will not be covering their respective Repositories here because they have already been covered in the previous chapters. I will only be covering the RFI Repository in this chapter.

The `IRequestForInformationRepository` interface provides access to instances of RFI Repositories. Here is the `IRequestForInformationRepository` interface:

```
using System;
using System.Collections.Generic;
using SmartCA.Infrastructure.RepositoryFramework;
using SmartCA.Model.Projects;

namespace SmartCA.Model.RFI
{
    public interface IRequestForInformationRepository
        : IRepository<RequestForInformation>
    {
        IList<RequestForInformation> FindBy(Project project);
    }
}
```

Its only unique method, `FindBy`, should be called fairly often, as almost all of the time RFIs will only be looked at on a per-project basis.

Writing the Unit Tests

In this section, I will be writing some unit tests of what I expect of the Submittal Repository implementation. As noted before, these tests will compile correctly, but they will also fail until I write the code for the Repository implementation later on in the Solution section.

Please note that there will be more unit tests in the accompanying code for this chapter, but for brevity's sake I am showing the tests that I think are important here.

The FindRfisByProjectTest Method

The purpose of the `FindSubmittalsByProjectTest` method is to validate that the correct number of `Submittal` instances have been returned by the Submittal Repository for a given Project.

```
/// <summary>
/// A test for FindBy(Project project)
/// </summary>
[DeploymentItem("SmartCA.sdf"), TestMethod()]
public void FindRfisByProjectTest()
{
    // Get a Project reference
    Project project =
        ProjectService.GetProject("5704f6b9-6ffa-444c-9583-35cc340fce2a");

    // Find all of the RFI's for the Project
    IList<RequestForInformation> rfis = this.repository.FindBy(project);

    // Verify that at least one RFI was returned
    Assert.IsTrue(rfis.Count > 0);
}
```

This method starts out by getting a `Project` instance from the `ProjectService` class. It then calls the `FindBy` method on the repository to get the list of RFI's for the given `Project` instance. The method finishes by checking that the repository returned at least one `RequestForInformation`.

The AddRfiTest Method

The purpose of the `AddRfiTest` method is to test adding a new RFI to the RFI Repository:

```
/// <summary>
///A test for Add(RequestForInformation item)
///</summary>
[DeploymentItem("SmartCA.sdf"), TestMethod()]
public void AddRfiTest()
{
    // Create a new RequestForInformation
    Guid projectKey = new Guid("5704f6b9-6ffa-444c-9583-35cc340fce2a");
    RequestForInformation rfi = new RequestForInformation(projectKey, 2);
    IList<ItemStatus> statuses = SubmittalService.GetItemStatuses();
    rfi.From = ProjectService.GetProject(projectKey).Contacts[0];
    rfi.Status = statuses[0];
    rfi.Contractor = CompanyService.GetAllCompanies()[0];
    IList<SpecificationSection> specSections =
```

```
            SubmittalService.GetSpecificationSections();
        rfi.SpecSection = specSections[0];

        // Add the RFI to the Repository
        this.repository.Add(rfi);

        // Commit the transaction
        this.unitOfWork.Commit();

        // Reload the RFI and verify it's number
        RequestForInformation savedRfi = this.repository.FindBy(rfi.Key);
        Assert.AreEqual(2, savedRfi.Number);

        // Clean up
        this.repository.Remove(savedRfi);
        this.unitOfWork.Commit();
    }
```

This test is a little more complicated than the last test. It starts out by creating a Project Key value, and then passes the Project Key value as well as an RFI number into the constructor of the `RequestForInformation` class. Now that I have an initialized the `RequestForInformation` instance, the next step is to set the `From` property of the `RequestForInformation` instance with a `ProjectContact` instance. The next property that needs to be set is the `Status` property. The `Status` property is set to the value of the first `ItemStatus` in the list of all `ItemStatus` instances. I then set the `Contractor` property with a `Company` instance that is retrieved by the `CompanyService` class. Last, I get the list of all Specification Sections from the `SubmittalService` class and set the RFI's `SpecSection` property to the first value in the list of Specification Sections.

The next step is to add the RFI to the repository, and then to commit the transaction by calling the `Commit` method on the `IUnitOfWork` instance. The `Commit` method is important because that method calls back into the RFI Repository to tell it to write the RFI's data to the data store.

Once the RFI has been saved, it is then reloaded and the RFI's `Number` property is checked to verify that the `Add` and `Commit` methods worked properly. The last task that the method needs to perform is to remove the RFI. Removing the RFI that was just created leaves the data store in the same state as it was in before the method started, which is important for the rest of the tests that may depend on a known state of the data store.

The UpdateRfiTest Method

The purpose of the `UpdateTest` method is to find an RFI and update it with a different `DateReceived` property value, and then verify that the change was persisted properly.

```
        /// <summary>
        ///A test for Updating an RFI
        ///</summary>
        [DeploymentItem("SmartCA.sdf"), TestMethod()]
        public void UpdateRfiTest()
        {
            IList<RequestForInformation> rfis = this.repository.FindAll();

            // Change the RFI's DateReceived value
```

(continued)

(continued)

```
        DateTime dateReceived = DateTime.Now;
        rfis[0].DateReceived = dateReceived;

        // Update the Repository
        this.repository[rfis[0].Key] = rfis[0];

        // Commit the transaction
        this.unitOfWork.Commit();

        // Verify that the change was saved
        IList<RequestForInformation> refreshedRfis = this.repository.FindAll();
        Assert.AreEqual(dateReceived.Date,
            refreshedRfis[0].DateReceived.Value.Date);
    }
```

In this method I start out by getting the entire list of RFIs from the data store. I then proceed to change the `DateReceived` property value on the first RFI in the list, and then call the indexer method of the `IRequestForInformationRepository`. After the call to the indexer, I then use the `IUnitOfWork` interface to commit the transaction. Last, I verify that the change actually made it to the data store by reloading the same RFI and checking to see if its `DateReceived` property value is the same calendar date that I just assigned to the RFI earlier in the method.

The RemoveRfiTest Method

The purpose of the `RemoveRfiTest` method is to test the process of removing an RFI from the data store.

```
    /// <summary>
    ///A test for Remove(RequestForInformation item)
    ///</summary>
    [DeploymentItem("SmartCA.sdf"), TestMethod()]
    public void RemoveRfiTest()
    {
        IList<RequestForInformation> rfis = this.repository.FindAll();

        // Remove the RFI from the Repository
        this.repository.Remove(rfis[0]);

        // Commit the transaction
        this.unitOfWork.Commit();

        // Verify that there is now one less RFI in the data store
        IList<RequestForInformation> refreshedRfis = this.repository.FindAll();
        Assert.AreEqual(0, refreshedRfis.Count);

        // Reset the state
        this.AddRfiTest();
    }
```

The first line of this method should look familiar; I am getting the entire list of RFIs from the data store. I then remove the first RFI in the list from the repository. After removing the RFI from the repository, I then use the `IUnitOfWork` interface to commit the transaction. Next, I verify that the change actually made it to the data store by using the repository to find all of the RFI instances and making sure there is now one less RFI than before. Last, I call the `AddRfiTest` method to add the RFI I just deleted back into the data store in order to reset the original state of the data store.

The Solution

Now that I have finished going over the design the RFI domain model, Aggregate, and repository, it's time to do my favorite thing: write some code! In this section I will be implementing these designs, as well as implementing the ViewModel and the View for RFIs.

The RFI Class Private Fields and Constructors

There are two constructors for the RFI class, and they both take a `projectKey` parameter of type `System.Object` and a number (`integer`) parameter. Every RFI must have a number and belong to a Project, so that is why those arguments are in both constructors.

Again, as in the last chapter, I am using a key value for a Project instead of a full blown Project instance, since I can always get to the Project via the `ProjectService` class. The second constructor takes a key argument of type `System.Object`, thus following the existing pattern for creating instances of existing Entity classes.

```
using System;
using SmartCA.Infrastructure.DomainBase;
using SmartCA.Model.Submittals;
using SmartCA.Model.Employees;
using SmartCA.Model.Projects;
using System.Collections.Generic;
using System.Text;
using SmartCA.Model.Companies;

namespace SmartCA.Model.RFI
{
    public class RequestForInformation : EntityBase
    {
        private object projectKey;
        private int number;
        private DateTime transmittalDate;
        private ProjectContact from;
        private int totalPages;
        private Delivery deliveryMethod;
        private string otherDeliveryMethod;
        private string phaseNumber;
        private bool reimbursable;
        private bool final;
        private List<CopyTo> copyToList;
        private DateTime? dateReceived;
        private DateTime? dateRequestedBy;
        private Company contractor;
```

(continued)

(continued)

```
        private SpecificationSection specSection;
        private List<RoutingItem> routingItems;
        private string question;
        private string description;
        private string contractorProposedSolution;
        private bool change;
        private int cause;
        private int origin;
        private ItemStatus status;
        private DateTime? dateToField;
        private string shortAnswer;
        private string longAnswer;
        private string remarks;
        private RequestForInformationNumberSpecification numberSpecification;
        private RequestForInformationDateSpecification dateToFieldSpecification;
        private RequestForInformationQuestionAnswerSpecification
questionAnswerSpecification;

        public RequestForInformation(object projectKey, int number)
            : this(null, projectKey, number)
        {
        }

        public RequestForInformation(object key, object projectKey,
            int number) : base(key)
        {
            this.projectKey = projectKey;
            this.number = number;
            this.transmittalDate = DateTime.Now;
            this.from = null;
            this.totalPages = 1;
            this.deliveryMethod = Delivery.None;
            this.otherDeliveryMethod = string.Empty;
            this.phaseNumber = string.Empty;
            this.reimbursable = false;
            this.final = false;
            this.copyToList = new List<CopyTo>();
            this.dateReceived = null;
            this.dateRequestedBy = null;
            this.contractor = null;
            this.specSection = null;
            this.routingItems = new List<RoutingItem>();
            this.question = string.Empty;
            this.description = string.Empty;
            this.contractorProposedSolution = string.Empty;
            this.change = false;
            this.cause = 0;
            this.origin = 0;
            this.status = null;
            this.dateToField = null;
            this.shortAnswer = string.Empty;
            this.longAnswer = string.Empty;
```

```
            this.remarks = string.Empty;
            this.numberSpecification = new
RequestForInformationNumberSpecification();
            this.dateToFieldSpecification = new
RequestForInformationDateSpecification();
            this.questionAnswerSpecification = new
RequestForInformationQuestionAnswerSpecification();
            this.Validate();
        }
```

All of the data for the `RequestForInformation` class is initialized and validated in the second constructor, which is called by the first constructor.

The RFI Properties

The properties of the `RequestForInformation` class are very similar to those of the `Submittal` class, so I am only going to show the differences here. Most of the properties in this class are fairly straightforward.

```
        public DateTime? DateRequestedBy
        {
            get { return this.dateRequestedBy; }
            set { this.dateRequestedBy = value; }
        }

        public int DaysLapsed
        {
            get
            {
                int daysLapsed = 0;
                if (this.dateReceived.HasValue &&
                    this.dateToField.HasValue)
                {
                    daysLapsed =
this.dateToField.Value.Subtract(this.dateReceived.Value).Days;
                }
                return daysLapsed;
            }
        }

        public Company Contractor
        {
            get { return this.contractor; }
            set { this.contractor = value; }
        }

        public string Question
        {
            get { return this.question; }
            set { this.question = value; }
        }
```

(continued)

(continued)

```
        public string Description
        {
            get { return this.description; }
            set { this.description = value; }
        }

        public string ContractorProposedSolution
        {
            get { return this.contractorProposedSolution; }
            set { this.contractorProposedSolution = value; }
        }

        public bool Change
        {
            get { return this.change; }
            set { this.change = value; }
        }

        public int Cause
        {
            get { return this.cause; }
            set { this.cause = value; }
        }

        public int Origin
        {
            get { return this.origin; }
            set { this.origin = value; }
        }

        public string ShortAnswer
        {
            get { return this.shortAnswer; }
            set { this.shortAnswer = value; }
        }

        public string LongAnswer
        {
            get { return this.longAnswer; }
            set { this.longAnswer = value; }
        }

        public RequestForInformationNumberSpecification NumberSpecification
        {
            get { return this.numberSpecification; }
        }

        public RequestForInformationDateSpecification DateToFieldSpecification
        {
            get { return this.dateToFieldSpecification; }
        }
```

```
        public RequestForInformationQuestionAnswerSpecification
QuestionAnswerSpecification
        {
            get { return this.questionAnswerSpecification; }
        }
```

The DaysLapsed Property

This read-only property represents the difference in time from when the RFI was received to when it was sent to the field.

The NumberSpecification Property

This property is designed to model the business rules about the proper numbering of RFIs. The `NumberSpecification` property is represented by the `RequestForInformationNumberSpecification` class. Its only job is to validate that the RFI adheres to the numbering rules, which are, if you remember, that all RFIs must be numbered consecutively within a Project, and there cannot be duplicate RFI numbers within a Project.

```
using System;
using SmartCA.Infrastructure.Specifications;
using System.Collections.Generic;
using SmartCA.Model.Projects;
using System.Linq;

namespace SmartCA.Model.RFI
{
    public class RequestForInformationNumberSpecification
        : Specification<RequestForInformation>
    {
        public override bool IsSatisfiedBy(RequestForInformation candidate)
        {
            bool isSatisfiedBy = true;

            // Make sure that the same RFI number has not been used for the
            // current project, and that there are no gaps between RFI numbers

            // First get the project associated with the RFI
            Project project = ProjectService.GetProject(candidate.ProjectKey);

            // Next get the list of RFIs for the project
            IList<RequestForInformation> requests =
RequestForInformationService.GetRequestsForInformation(project);

            // Determine if the RFI number has been used before
            isSatisfiedBy = (requests.Where(rfi =>
rfi.Number.Equals(candidate.Number)).Count() < 1);

            // See if the candidate passed the first test
            if (isSatisfiedBy)
```

(continued)

(continued)

```
            {
                // First test passed, now make sure that there are no gaps
                isSatisfiedBy = (candidate.Number - requests.Max(rfi =>
rfi.Number) == 1);
            }

            return isSatisfiedBy;
        }
    }
}
```

This code starts out by getting the list of RFIs for the current Project, which is the Project that is associated with the RFI. Once it has the list of RFIs, it then uses a LINQ query to determine whether the count of RFIs in the list that matches the candidate RFI's `Number` property is less than one. If the count is less than one, then the test passes.

The next test is to make sure that the candidate RFI will not introduce any numbering gaps within RFIs of the current Project. This is done with another LINQ query to get the highest RFI number (`Max`) in the list; then that number is subtracted from the candidate RFI's `Number` property. If the result equals one, then the test passes.

The DateToFieldSpecification Property

This property is designed to model the business rule about the dates associated with RFIs. The `DateToFieldSpecification` property is represented by the `RequestForInformationDateSpecification` class. Its only job is to validate that the RFI has both a date received value and a date requested by value.

```
using System;
using SmartCA.Infrastructure.Specifications;

namespace SmartCA.Model.RFI
{
    public class RequestForInformationDateSpecification
        : Specification<RequestForInformation>
    {
        public override bool IsSatisfiedBy(RequestForInformation candidate)
        {
            // Each RFI must have a date received and a date
            // that the response is needed
            return (candidate.DateReceived.HasValue &&
                candidate.DateRequestedBy.HasValue);
        }
    }
}
```

This code is much simpler than the first Specification class, as it only needs to perform two simple `Boolean` checks for the two dates.

The QuestionAnswerSpecification Property

This property is designed to model the business rule question and answer associated with RFIs. The `QuestionAnswerSpecification` property is represented by the `RequestForInformationQuestionAnswerSpecification` class. Its only job is to validate that the RFI has a question entered and either a short answer or a long answer entered.

```
using System;
using SmartCA.Infrastructure.Specifications;

namespace SmartCA.Model.RFI
{
    public class RequestForInformationQuestionAnswerSpecification
        : Specification<RequestForInformation>
    {
        public override bool IsSatisfiedBy(RequestForInformation candidate)
        {
            // The RFI must have a question and answer

            // The answer could be the short answer or
            // the long answer
            return (!string.IsNullOrEmpty(candidate.Question) &&
                (!string.IsNullOrEmpty(candidate.ShortAnswer) ||
                !string.IsNullOrEmpty(candidate.LongAnswer)));
        }
    }
}
```

This code is also performing `Boolean` comparisons by ensuring that the `Question` property is valid and that either the `ShortAnswer` or the `LongAnswer` property is valid.

The RFI Repository Implementation

After going over the `IRequestForInformationRepository` interface in the Design section, it is now time to explain how the `RequestForInformation` class is actually persisted to and from the data store by the RFI Repository. In this section, I will be writing the code for the RFI Repository.

The BuildChildCallbacks Method

If you have been following along, you know that the application's Template Method pattern implementation that I have been using in the repositories for getting Entity Root instances, the `BuildChildCallbacks` method, must be overridden in the `RequestForInformationRepository`.

```
        #region BuildChildCallbacks

        protected override void BuildChildCallbacks()
        {
            this.ChildCallbacks.Add(ProjectFactory.FieldNames.ProjectContactId,
                this.AppendFrom);
            this.ChildCallbacks.Add("CopyToList",
                delegate(RequestForInformation rfi, object childKeyName)
```

(continued)

(continued)

```
                {
                    this.AppendCopyToList(rfi);
                });
            this.ChildCallbacks.Add("RoutingItems",
                delegate(RequestForInformation rfi, object childKeyName)
                {
                    this.AppendRoutingItems(rfi);
                });
        }

        #endregion
```

The AppendFrom Callback

The first entry made in the `ChildCallbacks` dictionary is for the `AppendFrom` method. Thanks to the `ProjectService` class's `GetProjectContact` method, this method's code is very simple:

```
private void AppendFrom(RequestForInformation rfi, object fromProjectContactKey)
{
    rfi.From = ProjectService.GetProjectContact(rfi.ProjectKey,
        fromProjectContactKey);
}
```

The AppendCopyToList and AppendRoutingItems Callbacks

You have probably noticed that the `AppendCopyToList` and `AppendRoutingItems` callbacks look identical to those from the Submittal Repository. Well, you are right! This signals me that I need to do some refactoring of classes and methods. In order to prevent code duplication, I have identified the "area" that needs refactoring, and that "area" is any code that deals with the transmittal aspect of a Submittal or an RFI. I will cover this refactoring in the next few paragraphs.

The Transmittal Refactoring

The whole reason for needing to do a refactoring was the RFI Repository was just about ready to have the same code as the Submittal Repository, and that code was for handling the `CopyTo` list and the `RoutingItems` list associated with the RFI. Looking at this a little bit further, it seems as if there is more in common between Submittals and RFIs. They both happen to be a document transmittal, and there is certain data around that transmittal that is common. The first step to refactor this was to put everything they have in common into an interface, and I decided to name this interface the `ITransmittal` interface.

```
using System;
using System.Collections.Generic;
using SmartCA.Model;

namespace SmartCA.Model.Transmittals
{
    public interface ITransmittal
    {
        object ProjectKey { get; }
        DateTime TransmittalDate { get; set; }
        int TotalPages { get; set; }
        Delivery DeliveryMethod { get; set; }
```

```
            string OtherDeliveryMethod { get; set; }
            string PhaseNumber { get; set; }
            bool Reimbursable { get; set; }
            bool Final { get; set; }
            IList<CopyTo> CopyToList { get; }
        }
    }
```

This interface contains all of the common properties associated with a document Transmittal, including the associated Project.

You may have noticed that there are no Routing Items in this interface, and that is because when I did my analysis of the existing application, I noticed that not all transmittals were always routable. To account for transmittals that could be routed, I created another interface, the `IRoutableTransmittal` interface:

```
using System;
using System.Collections.Generic;

namespace SmartCA.Model.Transmittals
{
    public interface IRoutableTransmittal : ITransmittal
    {
        IList<RoutingItem> RoutingItems { get; }
    }
}
```

This interface simply adds to the existing `ITransmittal` interface and adds a property for the Routing Items. The next step in the refactoring was to modify the `Submittal` and `RequestForInformation` classes to implement these interfaces. Luckily, these classes already contain all of these properties, so it was a very simple refactoring to change the class signatures:

```
public class RequestForInformation : EntityBase, IRoutableTransmittal

public class Submittal : EntityBase, IRoutableTransmittal
```

Remember, in the .NET Framework, you can only inherit from one base class, but you can implement as many interfaces as you like.

The next step was to add a new Repository to the inheritance chain so that the Transmittal-related behavior could be shared by both the `SubmittalRepository` and the `RequestForInformationRepository` classes. So I made a new Repository and called it `SqlCeTransmittalRepository<T>`. This Repository is an abstract class that inherits from `SqlCeRepositoryBase<T>`.

Here is the signature for the Repository:

```
public abstract class SqlCeTransmittalRepository<T> : SqlCeRepositoryBase<T>
        where T : EntityBase, ITransmittal
```

The next thing to add to this new class was the pass-through constructors to the SqlCeRepositoryBase<T> class:

```
#region Constructors

 protected SqlCeTransmittalRepository()
     : this(null)
 {
 }

 protected SqlCeTransmittalRepository(IUnitOfWork unitOfWork)
     : base(unitOfWork)
 {
 }

 #endregion
```

Figure 6.5 shows a diagram of what the new RFI Aggregate Repository inheritance chain looks like now.

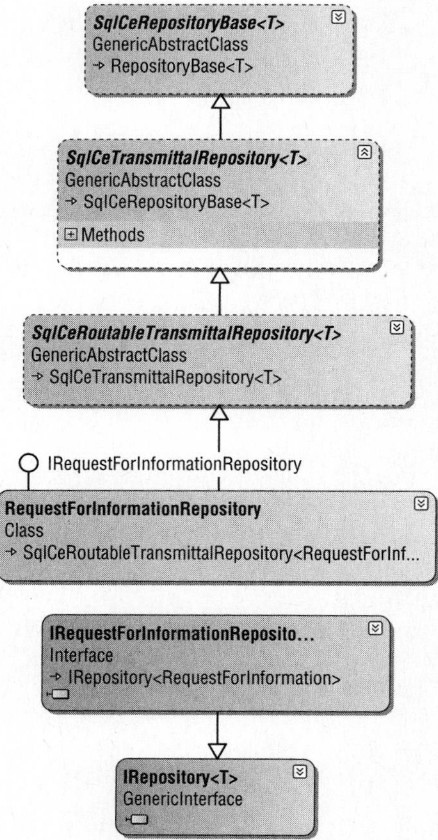

Figure 6.5: Newly refactored RFI Aggregate Repository.

The next function that I needed to perform was splitting out the code that deals with the CopyTo instances.

The AppendCopyToList Method

This method is now refactored to take a type of EntityBase and ITransmittal for its arguments:

```
protected void AppendCopyToList(T transmittal)
{
    StringBuilder builder = new StringBuilder(100);
    builder.Append(string.Format("SELECT * FROM {0}CopyList",
        this.EntityName));
    builder.Append(string.Format(" WHERE {0} = '{1}';",
        this.KeyFieldName,
        transmittal.Key));
    using (IDataReader reader = this.ExecuteReader(builder.ToString()))
    {
        while (reader.Read())
        {
            transmittal.CopyToList.Add(TransmittalFactory.BuildCopyTo(
                transmittal.ProjectKey, reader));
        }
    }
}
```

This code is essentially the same as the code from the old version of the SubmittalRepository, but instead of being hard-coded to a Submittal instance or a RequestForInformation instance, it now only relies upon EntityBase and ITransmittal. The queries have been changed to be more generic as well. An important thing to note about this change is that I needed also to refactor the SqlCeRepositoryBase<T> class a little bit, with the addition of the EntityName and KeyFieldName properties. Also, all classes deriving from SqlCeRepositoryBase<T> now need to implement the following new abstract methods:

```
protected abstract string GetEntityName();
protected abstract string GetKeyFieldName();
```

Here is an example of how the RequestForInformationRepository class is implementing the methods:

```
#region GetEntityName

protected override string GetEntityName()
{
    return "RequestForInformation";
}

#endregion

#region GetKeyFieldName

protected override string GetKeyFieldName()
```

(continued)

(continued)

```
            {
                return RequestForInformationFactory.FieldNames.RequestForInformationId;
            }

            #endregion
```

These follow the same Template Method Pattern that the `SqlCeRepositoryBase<T>` class has been implementing all along, as two more calls have been added to its constructor:

```
            protected SqlCeRepositoryBase(IUnitOfWork unitOfWork)
                : base(unitOfWork)
            {
                this.database = DatabaseFactory.CreateDatabase();
                this.entityFactory = EntityFactoryBuilder.BuildFactory<T>();
                this.childCallbacks = new Dictionary<string, AppendChildData>();
                this.BuildChildCallbacks();
                this.baseQuery = this.GetBaseQuery();
                this.baseWhereClause = this.GetBaseWhereClause();
                this.entityName = this.GetEntityName();
                this.keyFieldName = this.GetKeyFieldName();
            }
```

The DeleteCopyToList Method

This method has been refactored very similarly to the `AppendCopyToList` method.

```
            protected void DeleteCopyToList(T transmittal)
            {
                string query = string.Format("DELETE FROM {0}CopyList {1}",
                    this.EntityName, this.BuildBaseWhereClause(transmittal.Key));
                this.Database.ExecuteNonQuery(
                    this.Database.GetSqlStringCommand(query));
            }
```

The only change in this method is that, just like the `AppendCopyToList` method, it has been made more generic and relies upon the `EntityBase` class as well as the `ITransmittal` interface in order to build its SQL query.

The InsertCopyToList and InsertCopyTo Methods

These methods keep following the same pattern in their refactoring as the others:

```
            protected void InsertCopyToList(T transmittal)
            {
                foreach (CopyTo copyTo in transmittal.CopyToList)
                {
                    this.InsertCopyTo(copyTo, transmittal.Key);
                }
            }
            private void InsertCopyTo(CopyTo copyTo, object key)
```

```
        {
            StringBuilder builder = new StringBuilder(100);
            builder.Append(string.Format("INSERT INTO {0}CopyList ({1},{2},{3}) ",
                this.EntityName,
                this.KeyFieldName,
                TransmittalFactory.FieldNames.ProjectContactId,
                TransmittalFactory.FieldNames.Notes));
            builder.Append(string.Format("VALUES ({0},{1},{2});",
                DataHelper.GetSqlValue(key),
                DataHelper.GetSqlValue(copyTo.Contact.Key),
                DataHelper.GetSqlValue(copyTo.Notes)));

            this.Database.ExecuteNonQuery(
                this.Database.GetSqlStringCommand(builder.ToString()));
        }
```

Like the other methods, these methods are also aided by the new interface and the new properties and abstract methods of the `SqlCeRepositoryBase<T>` class.

The next piece of functionality that needed refactoring was the notion of routable Transmittals. As shown earlier, the `IRoutableTransmital` interface shows that a routable Transmittal is one that has `RoutingItems` associated with it.

```
public interface IRoutableTransmittal : ITransmittal
{
    IList<RoutingItem> RoutingItems { get; }
}
```

So the next logical step was to add a new abstract Repository to house the necessary code for `RoutingItems`. That class is the `SqlCeRoutableTransmittalRepository<T>` class, and its signature is shown here:

```
public abstract class SqlCeRoutableTransmittalRepository<T> :
        SqlCeTransmittalRepository<T>
        where T : EntityBase, IRoutableTransmittal
```

I am not going to show its pass-through constructors, since they are almost identical to the constructors in the `SqlCeTransmittalRepository<T>` class. As you might expect, this class is intended to isolate the code that deals with `RoutingItem` instances. It has three protected methods in it, `AppendRoutingItems`, `DeleteRoutingItems`, and `InsertRoutingItems`, and two private methods, `DeleteRoutingItem` and `InsertRoutingItem`. I am not going to show the code for these methods, as they are nearly identical to the old methods, and they have simply been modified, like all of the other newly refactored methods, to be more generic. Instead of depending upon the `ITransmittal` interface, the new methods in the `SqlCeRoutableTransmittalRepository<T>` class depend upon the `IRoutableTransmittal` interface.

Unit of Work Implementation

Following the same steps that I have shown before to implement the Unit of Work pattern, I need to override the following three methods: `PersistNewItem(RequestForInformation item)`, `PersistUpdatedItem(RequestForInformation item)`, and `PersistDeletedItem(RequestForInformation item)`.

The PersistNewItem Method

The first method override for the `RequestForInformationRepository`'s Unit of Work implementation is the `PersistNewItem` method:

```
        protected override void PersistNewItem(RequestForInformation item)
        {
            StringBuilder builder = new StringBuilder(100);
            builder.Append(string.Format("INSERT INTO RequestForInformation
({0},{1},{2},{3},{4},{5},{6},{7},{8},{9},{10},{11},{12},{13},{14},{15},{16},{17},
{18},{19},{20},{21},{22},{23},{24},{25}) ",
            RequestForInformationFactory.FieldNames.RequestForInformationId,
            ProjectFactory.FieldNames.ProjectId,
            RequestForInformationFactory.FieldNames.RequestForInformationNumber,
            RequestForInformationFactory.FieldNames.TransmittalDate,
            RequestForInformationFactory.FieldNames.ProjectContactId,
            RequestForInformationFactory.FieldNames.TotalPages,
            RequestForInformationFactory.FieldNames.DeliveryMethod,
            RequestForInformationFactory.FieldNames.OtherDeliveryMethod,
            RequestForInformationFactory.FieldNames.PhaseNumber,
            RequestForInformationFactory.FieldNames.Reimbursable,
            RequestForInformationFactory.FieldNames.Final,
            RequestForInformationFactory.FieldNames.DateReceived,
            RequestForInformationFactory.FieldNames.DateRequestedBy,
            CompanyFactory.FieldNames.CompanyId,
            SubmittalFactory.FieldNames.SpecificationSectionId,
            RequestForInformationFactory.FieldNames.Question,
            RequestForInformationFactory.FieldNames.Description,
            RequestForInformationFactory.FieldNames.ContractorProposedSolution,
            RequestForInformationFactory.FieldNames.NoChange,
            RequestForInformationFactory.FieldNames.Cause,
            RequestForInformationFactory.FieldNames.Origin,
            RequestForInformationFactory.FieldNames.ItemStatusId,
            RequestForInformationFactory.FieldNames.DateToField,
            RequestForInformationFactory.FieldNames.ShortAnswer,
            RequestForInformationFactory.FieldNames.LongAnswer,
            RequestForInformationFactory.FieldNames.Remarks
            ));
            builder.Append(string.Format("VALUES
({0},{1},{2},{3},{4},{5},{6},{7},{8},{9},{10},{11},{12},{13},{14},{15},{16},{17},
{18},{19},{20},{21},{22},{23},{24},{25});",
                DataHelper.GetSqlValue(item.Key),
                DataHelper.GetSqlValue(item.ProjectKey),
                DataHelper.GetSqlValue(item.Number),
                DataHelper.GetSqlValue(item.TransmittalDate),
                DataHelper.GetSqlValue(item.From.Key),
                DataHelper.GetSqlValue(item.TotalPages),
                DataHelper.GetSqlValue(item.DeliveryMethod),
                DataHelper.GetSqlValue(item.OtherDeliveryMethod),
                DataHelper.GetSqlValue(item.PhaseNumber),
                DataHelper.GetSqlValue(item.Reimbursable),
                DataHelper.GetSqlValue(item.Final),
                DataHelper.GetSqlValue(item.DateReceived),
                DataHelper.GetSqlValue(item.DateRequestedBy),
```

```
                DataHelper.GetSqlValue(item.Contractor),
                DataHelper.GetSqlValue(item.SpecSection),
                DataHelper.GetSqlValue(item.Question),
                DataHelper.GetSqlValue(item.Description),
                DataHelper.GetSqlValue(item.ContractorProposedSolution),
                DataHelper.GetSqlValue(item.Change),
                DataHelper.GetSqlValue(item.Cause),
                DataHelper.GetSqlValue(item.Origin),
                DataHelper.GetSqlValue(item.Status.Id),
                DataHelper.GetSqlValue(item.DateToField),
                DataHelper.GetSqlValue(item.ShortAnswer),
                DataHelper.GetSqlValue(item.LongAnswer),
                DataHelper.GetSqlValue(item.Remarks)));

            this.Database.ExecuteNonQuery(
                this.Database.GetSqlStringCommand(builder.ToString()));

            // Now do the child objects
            this.InsertCopyToList(item);
            this.InsertRoutingItems(item);
        }
```

The code builds up a large insert statement composed of the values from the `RequestForInformation` instance and then executes the query using the Microsoft Enterprise Library's `Database` object. After the insert statement has been executed, I have to account for inserting the `CopyTo` and `RoutingItem` instances for the RFI. I do this by calling the newly refactored `InsertCopyToList` and `InsertRoutingItems` methods, which all take an `IRoutableTransmittal` instance (which the RFI class implements) as their only argument.

The PersistUpdatedItem Method

`PersistUpdatedItem` first does an update to the `RequestForInformation` table:

```
        protected override void PersistUpdatedItem(RequestForInformation item)
        {
            StringBuilder builder = new StringBuilder(100);
            builder.Append("UPDATE RequestForInformation SET ");

            builder.Append(string.Format("{0} = {1}",
                RequestForInformationFactory.FieldNames
.RequestForInformationNumber,
                DataHelper.GetSqlValue(item.Number)));

            builder.Append(string.Format(",{0} = {1}",
                RequestForInformationFactory.FieldNames.TransmittalDate,
                DataHelper.GetSqlValue(item.TransmittalDate)));
************************************************************************
builder.Append(string.Format(",{0} = {1}",
                RequestForInformationFactory.FieldNames.Remarks,
                DataHelper.GetSqlValue(item.Remarks)));

            builder.Append(" ");
```

(continued)

(continued)

```
            builder.Append(this.BuildBaseWhereClause(item.Key));

            this.Database.ExecuteNonQuery(
                this.Database.GetSqlStringCommand(builder.ToString()));

            // Now do the child objects

            // First, delete the existing ones
            this.DeleteCopyToList(item);
            this.DeleteRoutingItems(item);

            // Now, add the current ones
            this.InsertCopyToList(item);
            this.InsertRoutingItems(item);
        }
```

I have omitted several lines of repetitive code building the SQL update statement in the middle of the code in order save you from the boring code. The removed lines are represented by a single line of asterisks.

The second part of the method then uses the newly refactored `DeleteCopyToList` and `DeleteRoutingItems` helper methods to delete all of the child objects of the RFI, and then uses the also newly refactored `InsertCopyToList` and `InsertRoutingItems` helper methods to add the existing child objects from the RFI to the database.

PersistDeletedItem

As I was writing the last method in `RequestForInformationRepository` to override, `PersistDeletedItem`, I realized that I could refactor that back into the base classes as well. Originally, the code I wrote looked like this:

```
        protected override void PersistDeletedItem(RequestForInformation item)
        {
            // Delete the child objects first
            this.DeleteCopyToList(item);
            this.DeleteRoutingItems(item);

            // Now delete the RFI
            string query = string.Format("DELETE FROM RequestForInformation {0}",
                this.BuildBaseWhereClause(item.Key));
            this.Database.ExecuteNonQuery(
                this.Database.GetSqlStringCommand(query));
        }
```

After analyzing the code, I saw another opportunity to refactor it back into the `SqlCeRepositoryBase<T>` and `SqlCeRoutableTransmittalRepository<T>` classes. I will start with the `SqlCeRepositoryBase<T>` implementation:

```
        protected override void PersistDeletedItem(T item)
        {
            // Delete the Entity
            string query = string.Format("DELETE FROM {0} {1}",
```

```
                this.entityName,
                this.BuildBaseWhereClause(item.Key));
            this.Database.ExecuteNonQuery(
                this.Database.GetSqlStringCommand(query));
        }
```

This was made possible by the Template Method Pattern implemented in the earlier refactoring for the `EntityName` and `EntityKey` properties of the `SqlCeRepositoryBase<T>` class. This method is now generic enough to delete any Entity from the database. So the logical question now is, "what about when the Entity has children that must be deleted first?" The answer comes in overriding the `PersistDeletedItem` method in derived classes. I took this a step further with the concept of deleting Transmittals and added functionality in the `SqlCeRoutableTransmittalRepository<T>` class to do just this:

```
        protected override void PersistDeletedItem(T transmittal)
        {
            // Delete the child objects first
            this.DeleteCopyToList(transmittal);
            this.DeleteRoutingItems(transmittal);

            // Delete the transmittal entity
            base.PersistDeletedItem(transmittal);
        }
```

This is great because now I can delete whatever child objects I want to delete first, and then call the base class, in this case `SqlCeRepositoryBase<T>`, to do the rest. So in the `SubmittalRepository`, the implementation now becomes:

```
        protected override void PersistDeletedItem(Submittal item)
        {
            // Delete the child objects first
            this.DeleteTrackingItems(item);

            // Now delete the submittal and its associated
            // transmittal objects
            base.PersistDeletedItem(item);
        }
```

Because Tracking Items are not part of the `ITransmittal` interface, I needed to delete these first, and then by calling the base class, in this case the `SqlCeRoutableTransmittalRepository<T>` class, I am able to delete the rest of the child objects (the `CopyToList` and the `RoutingItems`) as well as the Entity itself. What is even better is that in the `RequestForInformationRepository` class (and in a few other repositories), the need to override the `PersistDeletedItem` method goes away completely!

The RFI Service Implementation

Still in this application, the only `Service` classes I have implemented up to this point are all `Service` classes that live in the domain model layer and are acting as facades to their respective Repository interfaces.

The RequestForInformationService class is responsible for retrieving and saving RequestForInformation instances.

```
using System;
using SmartCA.Infrastructure;
using SmartCA.Infrastructure.RepositoryFramework;
using SmartCA.Model.Projects;
using System.Collections.Generic;

namespace SmartCA.Model.RFI
{
    public static class RequestForInformationService
    {
        private static IRequestForInformationRepository repository;
        private static IUnitOfWork unitOfWork;

        static RequestForInformationService()
        {
            RequestForInformationService.unitOfWork = new UnitOfWork();
            RequestForInformationService.repository =
                RepositoryFactory.GetRepository<IRequestForInformationRepository,
                RequestForInformation>(RequestForInformationService.unitOfWork);
        }

        public static IList<RequestForInformation>
            GetRequestsForInformation(Project project)
        {
            return RequestForInformationService.repository.FindBy(project);
        }

        public static void SaveRequestForInformation(RequestForInformation rfi)
        {
            RequestForInformationService.repository[rfi.Key] = rfi;
            RequestForInformationService.unitOfWork.Commit();
        }
    }
}
```

This class is mainly just acting as a façade in front of the IRequestForInformationRepository instance. There is nothing really new in this Service class compared to the other ones.

The RFI ViewModel Classes

Following the same patterns for all ViewModel classes as before, the RequestForInformationViewModel class adapts the RFI Aggregate from the domain model to the UI. When I started coding the ViewModel for the RFI I noticed that there was a lot in common between the SubmittalViewModel and the RequestForInformationViewModel, so I did another major refactoring and created a new abstract ViewModel class called, you guessed it, the TransmittalViewModel<T> class.

The TransmittalViewModel<T> Class

This class is very similar to the SqlCeTransmittalRepository<T> and SqlCeRoutableTransmittalRepository<T> classes that I showed earlier. It is the same concept again, which is to refactor common functionality into an abstract base class and have future classes that share the same functionality inherit them from the new base class. In this case, just like with the Repository classes and the SqlCeRepositoryBase<T> class, there is already an abstract base class that my ViewModel classes inherit from, and that is the ViewModel class. The TransmittalViewModel<T> class will be extending this class and it will be abstract as well. Here is the signature for the class:

```
public abstract class TransmittalViewModel<T> : ViewModel
        where T : EntityBase, IRoutableTransmittal
```

This is following the same pattern as the SqlCeTransmittalRepository<T> and SqlCeRoutableTransmittalRepository<T> classes, since it is a generic class and is using constraints to make sure that the generic class is an EntityBase that implements the IRoutableTransmittal interface.

The Constructor

My goal with this class was to lift all of the Transmittal behavior out of the SubmittalViewModel class and put it into this class. Therefore, the constructor code you see below should look very much like the old SubmittalViewModel code, with all references to anything named "submittal" changed to "transmittal."

```
#region Constructors

public TransmittalViewModel()
    : this(null)
{
}

public TransmittalViewModel(IView view)
    : base(view)
{
    this.currentTransmittal = null;
    this.transmittalList = this.GetTransmittals();
    this.transmittals = new CollectionView(this.transmittalList);
    this.specificationSections
        = SubmittalService.GetSpecificationSections();
    this.itemStatuses = SubmittalService.GetItemStatuses();
    this.mutableCopyToList = new BindingList<MutableCopyTo>();
    this.routingItems = new BindingList<RoutingItem>();
    this.deliveryMethods = new CollectionView(
                                Enum.GetNames(typeof(Delivery)));
    this.disciplines = SubmittalService.GetDisciplines();
    this.saveCommand = new DelegateCommand(this.SaveCommandHandler);
    this.newCommand = new DelegateCommand(this.NewCommandHandler);
    this.deleteCopyToCommand =
        new DelegateCommand(this.DeleteCopyToCommandHandler);
    this.deleteRoutingItemCommand =
        new DelegateCommand(this.DeleteRoutingItemCommandHandler);
}

#endregion
```

I was able to reuse almost everything in the old constructor, except for the Tracking Items, which are not part of what I have defined for a Transmittal. I decided for now to leave the calls in to the `SubmittalService`, although that class is also a candidate for refactoring.

Notice how the `GetTransmittals` method is called in order to initialize the list of Transmittals. This is an abstract method of the `TransmittalViewModel<T>` class, and thus I am once again using the Template Method pattern. I will show more on this method later.

The Properties

The `CurrentTransmittal` property is extremely similar to the old `CurrentSubmittal` property of the `SubmitalViewModel` class:

```
        public T CurrentTransmittal
        {
            get { return this.currentTransmittal; }
            set
            {
                if (this.currentTransmittal != value)
                {
                    this.currentTransmittal = value;
                    this.OnPropertyChanged(Constants
    .CurrentTransmittalPropertyName);
                    this.OnPropertyChanged("Status");
                    this.saveCommand.IsEnabled = (this.currentTransmittal != null);
                    this.PopulateTransmittalChildren();
                }
            }
        }
```

The only difference between this code and the `SubmitalViewModel CurrentTransmittal` property code is that this code is more generic. Don't you just love Generics? I bet you can't tell that I do!

The `PopulateSubmittalChildren` method has been changed to the `PopulateSubmittalChildren` method. Here is the old method:

```
        private void PopulateSubmittalChildren()
        {
            this.PopulateMutableCopyToList();
            this.PopulateRoutingItems();
            this.PopulateTrackingItems();
        }
```

And here is the new method:

```
        protected virtual void PopulateTransmittalChildren()
        {
            this.PopulateMutableCopyToList();
            this.PopulateRoutingItems();
        }
```

The only difference in this method is that it no longer tries to populate the Tracking Items data, and that is exactly why I made it virtual, because derived classes may need to override this method in order to populate their own child objects as necessary.

The `PopulateMutableCopyToList` method has been changed from this:

```
private void PopulateMutableCopyToList()
{
    if (this.currentSubmittal != null)
    {
        this.mutableCopyToList.Clear();
        foreach (CopyTo copyTo in this.currentSubmittal.CopyToList)
        {
            this.mutableCopyToList.Add(new MutableCopyTo(copyTo));
        }
        this.OnPropertyChanged(Constants.MutableCopyToListPropertyName);
    }
}
```

To this:

```
private void PopulateMutableCopyToList()
{
    if (this.currentTransmittal != null)
    {
        this.mutableCopyToList.Clear();
        foreach (CopyTo copyTo in this.currentTransmittal.CopyToList)
        {
            this.mutableCopyToList.Add(new MutableCopyTo(copyTo));
        }
        this.OnPropertyChanged(Constants.MutableCopyToListPropertyName);
    }
}
```

I am not going to show the `PopulateRoutingItems` method because it follows the exact same pattern as the `PopulateMutableCopyToList` method.

The Command Handler Methods

Refactoring the Command Handler methods was a little bit trickier than some of the other methods in the `TransmittalViewModel` class. The `SaveCommandHandler` and the `NewCommandHandler` methods both had to be marked as virtual, and that is because I could only pull so much out of them into this, and the rest that is specific to the derived class must be overridden.

For example, the `NewCommandHandler` went from this:

```
private void NewCommandHandler(object sender, EventArgs e)
{
    Submittal newSubmittal = new Submittal(
                                 this.currentSubmittal.SpecSection,
                                 this.currentSubmittal.ProjectKey);
```

(continued)

(continued)

```
            newSubmittal.SpecSectionSecondaryIndex = "01";

            this.currentSubmittal = null;
            this.mutableCopyToList.Clear();
            this.routingItems.Clear();
            this.trackingItems.Clear();
            this.CurrentObjectState = ObjectState.New;
            this.OnPropertyChanged(
                Constants.CurrentSubmittalPropertyName);

            this.submittalsList.Add(newSubmittal);
            this.submittals.Refresh();
            this.submittals.MoveCurrentToLast();
        }
```

To this:

```
        protected virtual void NewCommandHandler(object sender, EventArgs e)
        {
            this.currentTransmittal = null;
            this.mutableCopyToList.Clear();
            this.routingItems.Clear();
            this.CurrentObjectState = ObjectState.New;
            this.OnPropertyChanged(
                Constants.CurrentTransmittalPropertyName);
        }
```

The code that initializes the new Entity (i.e., the `Submittal` class in the first example above) had to be removed and must be overridden in the derived `ViewModel`. I also needed to remove the code that added the Submittal to the list of Submittals because I needed that to happen last in the derived class, after this code executes.

The GetTransmittals Template Pattern Method

As seen in the constructor, the `GetTransmittals` abstract method is called in order to initialize the list of Transmittals for the class. Here is the signature of this method:

```
    protected abstract List<T> GetTransmittals();
```

This is great because by doing this I am delegating the derived class to get the right list of objects, yet I can still code against that list in my base class. Combining the Template Method pattern with Generics is a great thing!

The RequestForInformationViewModel Class

Now the fruits of our ViewModel refactoring labor start to pay off. The code inside of the `RequestForInformationViewModel` and `SubmittalViewModel` classes has been reduced significantly. Here is what the signature of the `RequestForInformationViewModel` class looks like when deriving from the `TransmittalViewModel<T>` class:

```
    public class RequestForInformationViewModel
        : TransmittalViewModel<RequestForInformation>
```

Notice how the generic parameter from the `TransmittalViewModel<T>` class is replaced by the `RequestForInformation` class.

The Constructor

The constructors for the `RequestForInformationViewModel` class now are mostly pass-through. Here is the old `SubmittalViewModel` constructor:

```
#region Constructors

public SubmittalViewModel()
    : this(null)
{
}

public SubmittalViewModel(IView view)
    : base(view)
{
    this.currentSubmittal = null;
    this.submittalsList = new List<Submittal>(
                            SubmittalService.GetSubmittals(
                            UserSession.CurrentProject));
    this.submittals = new CollectionView(this.submittalsList);
    this.specificationSections
        = SubmittalService.GetSpecificationSections();
    this.submittalStatuses = SubmittalService.GetSubmittalStatuses();
    this.toList = UserSession.CurrentProject.Contacts;
    this.mutableCopyToList = new BindingList<MutableCopyTo>();
    this.routingItems = new BindingList<RoutingItem>();
    this.trackingItems = new BindingList<TrackingItem>();
    this.fromList = EmployeeService.GetEmployees();
    this.trackingStatusValues = new CollectionView(
                                    Enum.GetNames(typeof(ActionStatus)));
    this.deliveryMethods = new CollectionView(
                                Enum.GetNames(typeof(Delivery)));
    this.disciplines = SubmittalService.GetDisciplines();
    this.saveCommand = new DelegateCommand(this.SaveCommandHandler);
    this.newCommand = new DelegateCommand(this.NewCommandHandler);
    this.deleteCopyToCommand =
        new DelegateCommand(this.DeleteCopyToCommandHandler);
    this.deleteRoutingItemCommand =
        new DelegateCommand(this.DeleteRoutingItemCommandHandler);
    this.deleteTrackingItemCommand =
        new DelegateCommand(this.DeleteTrackingItemCommandHandler);
}

#endregion
```

Here are the new constructors for the `RequestForInformationViewModel` class:

```
#region Constructors

public RequestForInformationViewModel()
    : this(null)
{
}

public RequestForInformationViewModel(IView view)
    : base(view)
{
    this.toList = UserSession.CurrentProject.Contacts;
    this.fromList = UserSession.CurrentProject.Contacts;
}

#endregion
```

That's quite a reduction in code! The `toList` and `fromList` private fields are not contained in the base class and therefore need to be initialized here.

The Properties

There are not many properties left to implement in the `RequestForInformationViewModel` class. Here is all of the code for the properties:

```
#region Properties

public IList<ProjectContact> ToList
{
    get { return this.toList; }
}

public IList<ProjectContact> FromList
{
    get { return this.fromList; }
}

#endregion
```

The Command Handler Methods

The only command handler methods that I need to override in the `RequestForInformationViewModel` class are the `NewCommandHandler` and `SaveCommandHandler` methods. The `DeleteCommandHandler` method is completely taken care of by the base class.

Because the `NewCommandHandler` method in the base class was marked as virtual, I am still able to use it as well as add my own functionality:

```
        protected override void NewCommandHandler(object sender, EventArgs e)
        {
            base.NewCommandHandler(sender, e);
            RequestForInformation newRfi = new RequestForInformation(
                                         this.CurrentTransmittal.ProjectKey,
                                         this.CurrentTransmittal.Number + 1);
            this.TransmittalList.Add(newRfi);
            this.Transmittals.Refresh();
            this.Transmittals.MoveCurrentToLast();
        }
```

Notice how on the first line of the method I call the same method in the base class. This allows me to reuse the common code yet gives me the flexibility to do my own housekeeping when creating the new `RequestForInformation` instance.

The GetTransmittals Template Pattern Method

As I mentioned before, the `GetTransmittals` method is overridden in the derived classes because only they know where to get their data; the base class does not need to know about that:

```
#region GetTransmittals

        protected override List<RequestForInformation> GetTransmittals()
        {
            return new
List<RequestForInformation>(RequestForInformationService.GetRequestsForInformation(
                                         UserSession.CurrentProject));
        }

        #endregion
```

In this case of the `RequestForInformationViewModel` class's override, I am simply calling out to the `RequestForInformationService` to get the list of `RequestForInformation` instances.

The RFI View

The View for RFIs is almost exactly identical to that for Submittals. Figure 6.6 shows what the form looks like at run time.

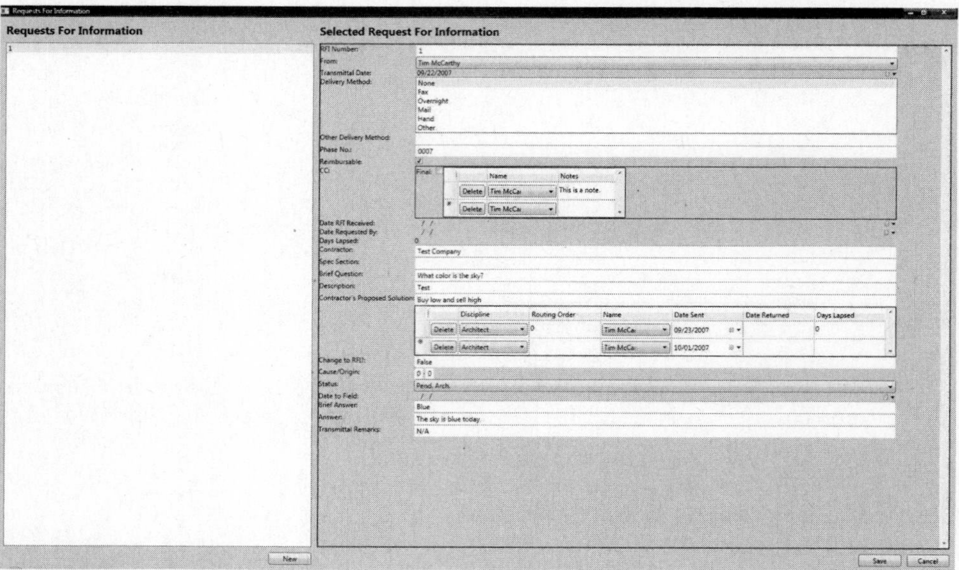

Figure 6.6: The RFI View.

Following the same pattern as before, the form is split into two parts: the one on the left is for selecting an RFI to edit, and the one on the right is for editing the selected RFI. The New button adds a new RFI to the list. The Save and Cancel buttons both deal with the currently selected RFI.

I really do not need to show any of the XAML code for this form because there is really not much in it that is different from the Submittal form.

Summary

In this chapter, I introduced the concept of a Request for Information (RFI) in the construction industry and then used that concept to model the RFI Aggregate. I also introduced a new concept into the domain, called the Specification Pattern. This made some of the business rule modeling very clear by bringing business rules out from underneath class methods and placing them into their own `Specification` classes. I then defined the boundaries for the RFI Aggregate, as well as implementing all of the necessary domain model and `Infrastructure` classes necessary to work with those classes. I also did some major refactoring in this chapter for the repositories and ViewModels dealing with the new concept of Transmittals.

7 Proposal Requests

In the last chapter, I covered the ins and outs of the Request for Information (RFI) document. In this chapter, I will cover another concept that is similar to an RFI but has a different intent. That concept is the Proposal Request.

The Problem

In the construction industry, just like the software industry, projects rarely finish exactly as planned; there are usually changes that have to be made along the way. In software, it could be that the application you are working on has some features that the business no longer needs, or doesn't have new features discovered while the application is still in development. Likewise, in the construction industry, there are many factors in a project that may necessitate a change to the original contract.

A Contractor can discover physical or economic situations, usually unanticipated, that may make it impossible to follow the contract documents. Architects could find it necessary to recommend changes in the contract documents because of errors in the contract documents. Other sources of changes could be weather damage such as wind and rain, natural disasters such as an earthquake, labor and material shortages, and fire and explosion.

When these types of events occur, it means that there needs to be a Change Order issued for the project. In the construction industry, there is an action that must occur before the Change Order is drafted. That action is known officially as the Work Changes Proposal Request. For the purposes of this chapter, I will refer to this as a Proposal Request.

A Proposal Request is a one page form that identifies the change and all the parties involved in the contract. The form is prepared by the architect and is directed to the Contractor. It is essentially a request for a price and time proposal for carrying out the proposed change. A copy of it should be sent to all parties involved and a record kept of all recipients. A Proposal Request is not an authorization to do the work. It is not a Change Order. It is only a special type of request for information that will be needed by the owner and architect to decide whether to make the change, modify it, or to cancel it.

The form includes a time limit for the Contractor's submission of the proposal or for a commitment of the date on which the completed Proposal Request will be submitted. Like the RFI, each Proposal Request should be serially numbered by project.

The Design

In the SmartCA domain, an RFI contains several important business concepts that must be closely followed. In the next few sections, I will be designing the domain model, determining the RFI Aggregate and its boundaries, and designing the Repository for RFIs.

Designing the Domain Model

As stated earlier, the most important parts of the Proposal Request are the Expected Return Date from the Contractor, the Description of the Proposal Request, and the proper ordering of the Proposal Request Number. Just as in the last chapter, I will be using the Specification pattern to specify the rules for these properties, and the specifications that I create will also be part of the domain model.

Below is a drawing showing the relationships between the classes that combine to make up a Proposal Request:

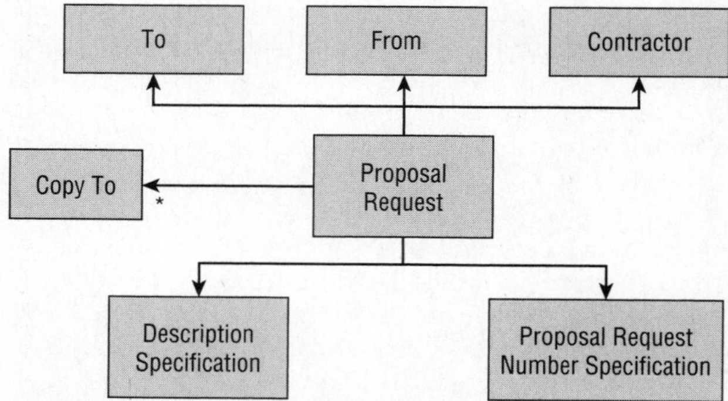

Figure 7.1: Proposal Request Aggregate.

In the diagram, it should be pretty clear that the Proposal Request class is the root of the Aggregate. The relationships to the Description Specification and Proposal Request Number Specification classes help model the important rules of the Proposal Request.

The relationship to the "From" class represents from whom the Proposal Request came, and with which Contractor it is associated. The "To" class represents for what Project Contact the Proposal Request is intended.

Just as with the Submittal Transmittal and RFI Aggregates, there is a Copy To relationship from a Proposal Request, which represents the list of Recipients who need to be copied on all correspondence having to do with the Proposal Request.

Designing the Proposal Request Aggregate

You may have expected this, but as I was analyzing the Proposal Request class from Figure 7.1, I noticed that it had a lot of the same properties as the `RequestForInformation` and `Submittal` classes. Namely, all of the properties that make up the `ITransmittal` interface that I introduced in the last chapter. Instead of having all of these classes implement the `ITransmittal` interface and have all of that duplicate code, I decided to refactor the common code into a new abstract class, the `Transmittal` class.

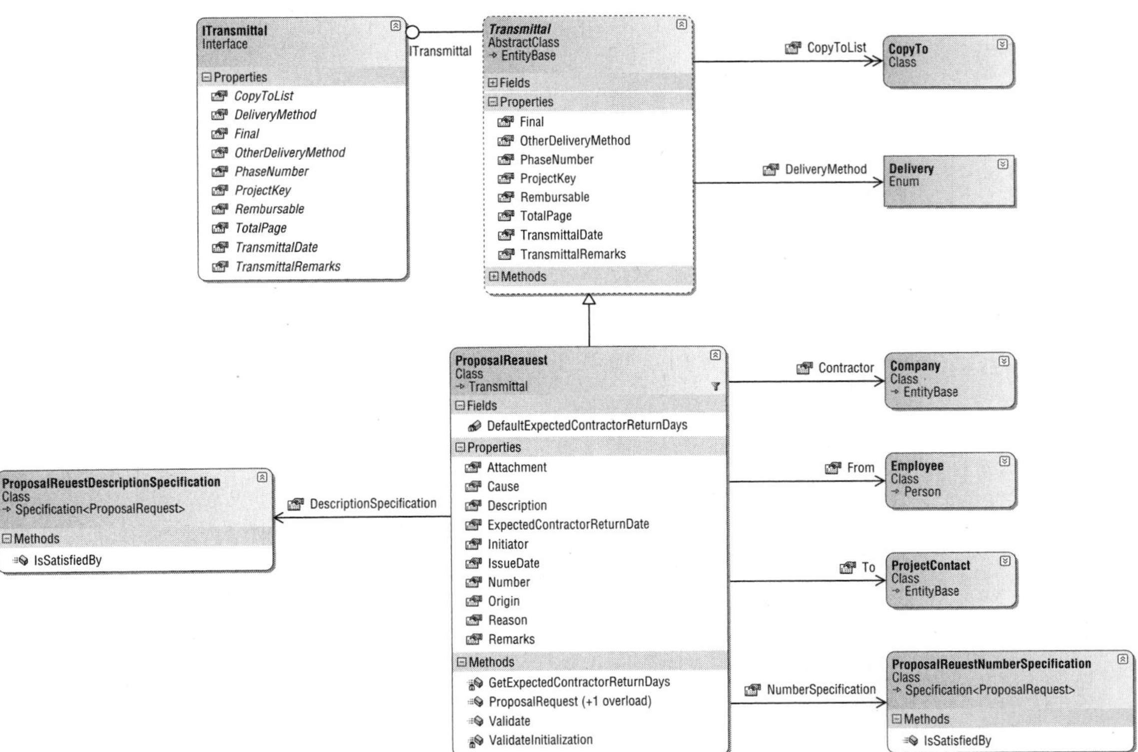

Figure 7.2: Classes constituting the Proposal Request Aggregate.

As shown in Figure 7.2, the `ProposalRequest` class inherits from the `Transmittal` class. Since `ProposalRequest` Transmittals do not have Routing Items, and the `RequestForInformation` and `Submittal` classes do, I made another abstract class for those classes to inherit from, and that class is the `RoutableTransmittal` class. I refactored the `RequestForInformation` and `Submittal` classes to inherit from the `RoutableTransmittal` class. Figure 7.3 details the relationships and hierarchy between the Transmittal and Routable Transmittal interfaces and abstract classes.

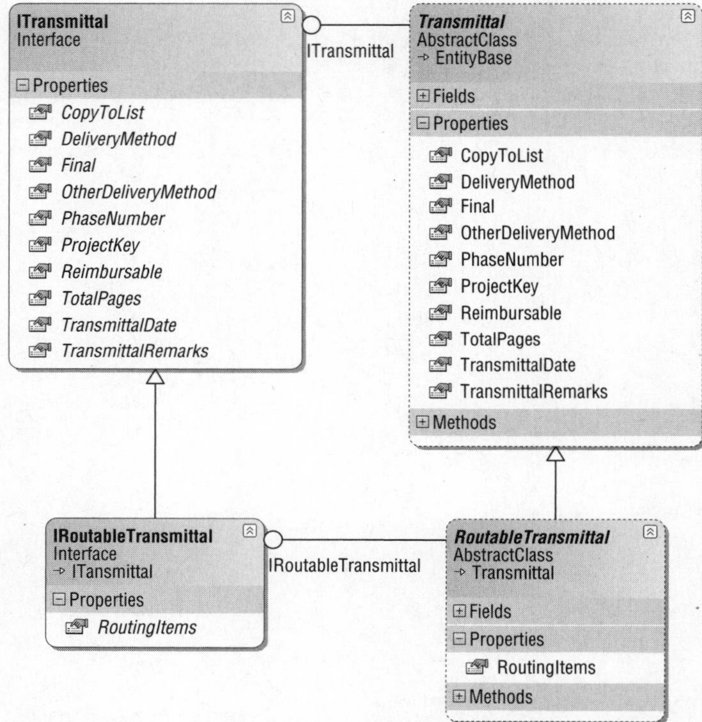

Figure 7.3: Transmittal and RoutableTransmittal classes.

Since the Transmittal and `RoutableTransmittal` classes respectively implement the `ITransmittal` and `IRoutableTransmittal` interfaces, everything will still work as before with their associated repositories.

Defining the Aggregate Boundaries

The `ProposalRequest` class has its own identity and is definitely the root of its own Aggregate. All of the other classes in Figure 7.4, except for `ProjectContact`, `Company`, and `Employee`, belong to the

Proposal Request Aggregate. As shown in earlier chapters, `ProjectContact` belongs to the Project Aggregate, `Company` is the root of its own Aggregate, and the `Employee` class is part of the Employee Aggregate.

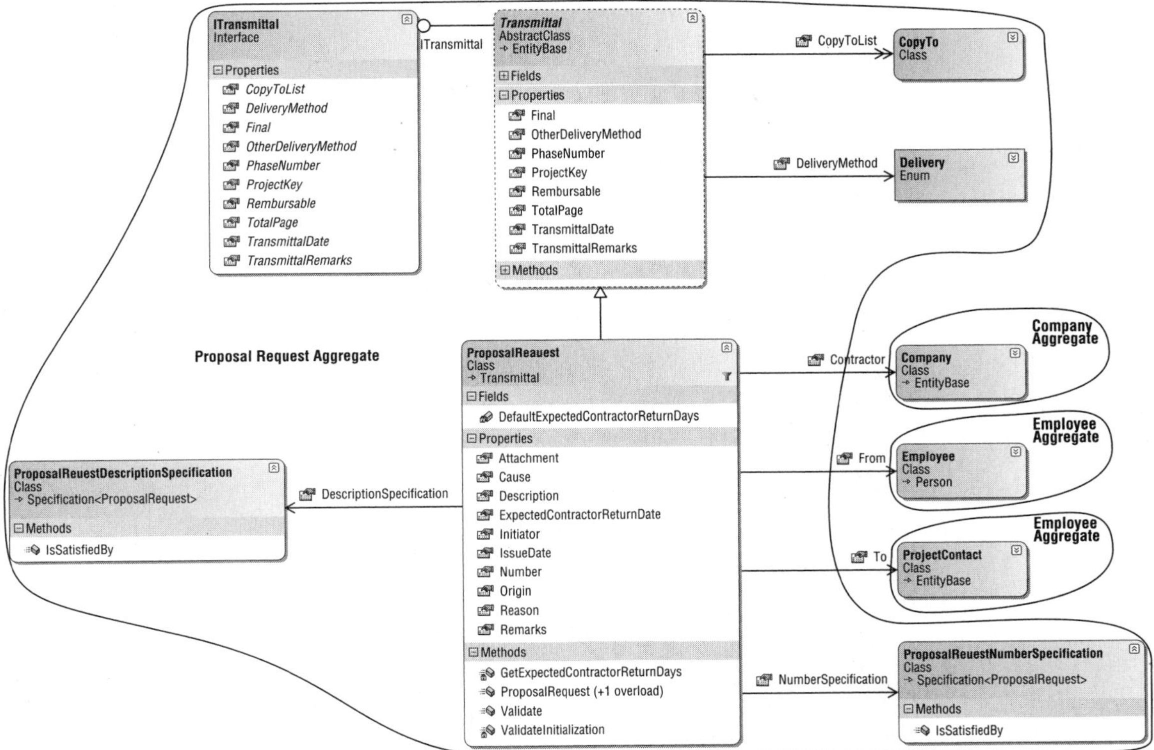

Figure 7.4: Proposal Request Aggregate boundaries.

Designing the Repository

This should be getting familiar by now, but I will say it again: since the `ProposalRequest` class is its own Aggregate root, it will have its own Repository (as shown in Figure 7.5).

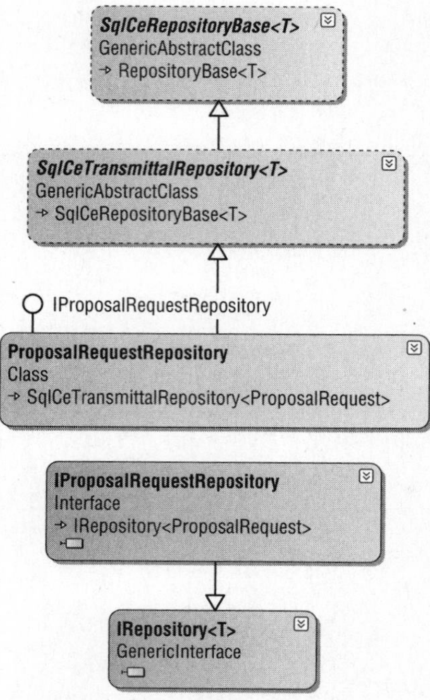

Figure 7.5: Proposal Request Repository.

The `IProposalRequestRepository` interface is the interface for instances of Proposal Request Repositories. Here is the `IProposalRequestRepository` interface:

```
using System;
using System.Collections.Generic;
using SmartCA.Infrastructure.RepositoryFramework;
using SmartCA.Model.Projects;

namespace SmartCA.Model.ProposalRequests
{
    public interface IProposalRequestRepository
        : IRepository<ProposalRequest>
    {
        IList<ProposalRequest> FindBy(Project project);
        int GetExpectedContractorReturnDays();
    }
}
```

Like the Repository interfaces for Submittals and RFIs, this Repository interface also has a `FindBy` method. In addition, it has the `GetExpectedContractorReturnDays` method, which I will go over in detail later in the chapter.

Writing the Unit Tests

In this section, I will be writing some unit tests for what I expect of the Proposal Request Repository implementation. As noted before, these tests will compile correctly, but they will also fail until I write the code for the Repository implementation later on, in the Solution section.

There will be more unit tests in the accompanying code for this chapter, but for brevity's sake I am showing the tests that I think are important here.

The FindProposalRequestsByProjectTest Method

The purpose of the `FindProposalRequestsByProjectTest` method is to validate that the correct number of `ProposalRequest` instances have been returned by the Proposal Request Repository for a given Project.

```
/// <summary>
/// A test for FindBy(Project project)
/// </summary>
[DeploymentItem("SmartCA.sdf"), TestMethod()]
public void FindProposalRequestsByProjectTest()
{
    // Get a Project reference
    Project project =
        ProjectService.GetProject("5704f6b9-6ffa-444c-9583-35cc340fce2a");

    // Finds all of the Proposal Requests for the Project
    IList<ProposalRequest> proposalRequests =
        ProposalRequestRepositoryUnitTest.repository.FindBy(project);

    // Verify that at least one ProposalRequest was returned
    Assert.IsTrue(proposalRequests.Count > 0);
}
```

This method starts out by getting a `Project` instance from the `ProjectService` class. It then calls the `FindBy` method on the Repository to get the list of Proposal Requests for the given `Project` instance. The method finishes by checking that the repository returned at least one `ProposalRequest`.

The AddProposalRequestTest Method

The purpose of the `AddProposalRequestTest` method is to test adding a new Proposal Request to the Proposal Request Repository.

```
/// <summary>
///A test for Add(ProposalRequest item)
///</summary>
[DeploymentItem("SmartCA.sdf"), TestMethod()]
public void AddProposalRequestTest()
{
    IList<ProposalRequest> proposalRequests =
        ProposalRequestRepositoryUnitTest.repository.FindAll();

    // Create a new ProposalRequest
```

(continued)

(continued)

```
            Guid projectKey = new Guid("5704f6b9-6ffa-444c-9583-35cc340fce2a");
            ProposalRequest pr = new ProposalRequest(projectKey, 2);
            pr.From = EmployeeService.GetEmployees()[0];
            pr.Contractor = CompanyService.GetAllCompanies()[0];
            pr.To = ProjectService.GetProject(projectKey).Contacts[0];

            // Add the ProposalRequest to the Repository
            ProposalRequestRepositoryUnitTest.repository.Add(pr);

            // Commit the transaction
            ProposalRequestRepositoryUnitTest.unitOfWork.Commit();

            // Reload the ProposalRequest and verify it's number
            ProposalRequest savedPr =
                ProposalRequestRepositoryUnitTest.repository.FindBy(pr.Key);
            Assert.AreEqual(2, savedPr.Number);
        }
```

This test is a little more complicated than the last test. It starts out by creating a Project Key value, and then passes the Project Key value as well as a Proposal Request number into the constructor of the `ProposalRequest` class. Now that I have an initialized `ProposalRequest` instance, the next step is to set the `From` property of the `ProposalRequest` instance with an `Employee` instance. I then set the `Contractor` property with a `Company` instance that is retrieved by the `CompanyService` class. After those steps, I assign the `To` property value to the first `ProjectContact` instance for the `Project`.

The next step is to add the Proposal Request to the Repository and then to commit the transaction by calling the `Commit` method on the `IUnitOfWork` instance. The `Commit` method is important because that method calls back into the Proposal Request Repository to tell it to write the Proposal Request's data to the data store.

Once the Proposal Request has been saved, it is then reloaded and the Proposal Request's `Number` property is checked to verify that the `Add` and `Commit` methods worked properly.

The UpdateProposalRequestTest Method

The purpose of the `UpdateProposalRequestTest` method is to find a Proposal Request and update it with a different `Description` property value, and then verify that the change was persisted properly.

```
        /// <summary>
        ///A test for Updating a Proposal Request
        ///</summary>
        [DeploymentItem("SmartCA.sdf"), TestMethod()]
        public void UpdateProposalRequestTest()
        {
            IList<ProposalRequest> proposalRequests =
                ProposalRequestRepositoryUnitTest.repository.FindAll();

            // Change the Proposal Request's Description value
            proposalRequests[0].Description = "Test Description";

            // Update the Repository
```

```
        ProposalRequestRepositoryUnitTest.repository[proposalRequests[0].Key]
            = proposalRequests[0];

        // Commit the transaction
        ProposalRequestRepositoryUnitTest.unitOfWork.Commit();

        // Verify that the change was saved
        IList<ProposalRequest> refreshedProposalRequests =
            ProposalRequestRepositoryUnitTest.repository.FindAll();
        Assert.AreEqual("Test Description",
            refreshedProposalRequests[0].Description);
    }
```

In this method, I start by getting the entire list of Proposal Requests from the data store. I then change the `Description` property value on the first Proposal Request in the list, and then call the indexer method of the `IProposalRequestRepository`. After the call to the indexer, I then use the `IUnitOfWork` interface to commit the transaction. Finally, I verify that the change actually made it to the data store by reloading the same Proposal Request and checking to see whether its `Description` property value is the same value as the one I assigned to the Proposal Request earlier in the method.

The RemoveProposalRequestTest Method

The purpose of the `RemoveProposalRequestTest` method is to test the process of removing a Proposal Request from the data store.

```
    /// <summary>
    ///A test for Remove(ProposalRequest item)
    ///</summary>
    [DeploymentItem("SmartCA.sdf"), TestMethod()]
    public void RemoveProposalRequestTest()
    {
        IList<ProposalRequest> proposalRequests =
            ProposalRequestRepositoryUnitTest.repository.FindAll();

        int expectedCount = proposalRequests.Count - 1;

        // Remove the Proposal Request from the Repository
        ProposalRequestRepositoryUnitTest.repository.Remove(
            proposalRequests[0]);

        // Commit the transaction
        ProposalRequestRepositoryUnitTest.unitOfWork.Commit();

        // Verify that there is now one less Proposal Request in the data store
        IList<ProposalRequest> refreshedProposalRequests =
            ProposalRequestRepositoryUnitTest.repository.FindAll();
        Assert.AreEqual(expectedCount, refreshedProposalRequests.Count);
    }
```

The first line of this method should look familiar; I am getting the entire list of Proposal Requests from the data store. I then remove the first Proposal Request in the list from the repository. After removing the Proposal Request from the repository, I use the `IUnitOfWork` interface to commit the transaction. Finally, I verify that the change actually made it to the data store by using the repository to find all of the Proposal Request instances and making sure that there is now one fewer Proposal Request.

The Solution

Now for the fun part! I have just shown some very interesting refactoring taking place in the Proposal Request domain model, and now I get to show you how those designs are going to be implemented, as well as how they affect the Proposal Request Repository implementation. In this section, I will also be implementing the ViewModel and the View for Proposal Requests.

The Proposal Request Class Private Fields and Constructors

The `ProposalRequest` class inherits from the `Transmittal` class, and passes its values from its constructors straight through to the Transmittal base class.

```
using System;
using SmartCA.Infrastructure.DomainBase;
using SmartCA.Model.Transmittals;
using SmartCA.Model.Projects;
using System.Collections.Generic;
using SmartCA.Model.Companies;
using SmartCA.Model.Submittals;
using SmartCA.Model.Employees;
using System.Text;

namespace SmartCA.Model.ProposalRequests
{
    public class ProposalRequest : Transmittal
    {
        private int number;
        private ProjectContact to;
        private Employee from;
        private DateTime? issueDate;
        private DateTime expectedContractorReturnDate;
        private Company contractor;
        private string description;
        private string attachment;
        private string reason;
        private string initiator;
        private int cause;
        private int origin;
        private string remarks;
        private ProposalRequestNumberSpecification numberSpecification;
        private ProposalRequestDescriptionSpecification descriptionSpecification;
        private int expectedContractorReturnDays;

        private const int DefaultExpectedContractorReturnDays = 7;

        public ProposalRequest(object projectKey, int number)
            : this(null, projectKey, number)
        {
        }

        public ProposalRequest(object key, object projectKey,
```

```
        int number) : base(key, projectKey)
    {
        this.number = number;
        this.to = null;
        this.from = null;
        this.issueDate = null;
        this.GetExpectedContractorReturnDays();
        this.expectedContractorReturnDate =
            this.TransmittalDate.AddDays(this.expectedContractorReturnDays);
        this.contractor = null;
        this.description = string.Empty;
        this.attachment = string.Empty;
        this.reason = string.Empty;
        this.initiator = string.Empty;
        this.cause = 0;
        this.origin = 0;
        this.remarks = string.Empty;
        this.numberSpecification =
            new ProposalRequestNumberSpecification();
        this.descriptionSpecification =
            new ProposalRequestDescriptionSpecification();
        this.ValidateInitialization();
    }
```

Just as in the `Submittal` and `RequestForInformation` classes, all of the data for the `ProposalRequest` class is initialized and validated in the second constructor, which is called by the first constructor.

The GetExpectedContractorReturnDays Method

On the fifth line of the second constructor, there is a call to the `GetExpectedContractorReturnDays` method. This private method determines the threshold for how long a Contractor has before he or she must return the Proposal Request to the issuer:

```
    private void GetExpectedContractorReturnDays()
    {
        // First go with the default value
        this.expectedContractorReturnDays =
            ProposalRequest.DefaultExpectedContractorReturnDays;

        // Now try to get the real value from the service
        int expectedContractorReturnDays =
            ProposalRequestService.GetExpectedContractorReturnDays();

        // If the service returned a valid value, then use it instead
        // of the default value
        if (expectedContractorReturnDays > 0)
        {
            this.expectedContractorReturnDays =
                expectedContractorReturnDays;
        }
    }
```

To start with, the method sets the class variable, expectedContractorReturnDays, to whatever default value is defined for it, by accessing the DefaultExpectedContractorReturnDays class constant value.

```
private const int DefaultExpectedContractorReturnDays = 7;
```

In this case, the class default value is seven days. After getting the default value, the next step is to use the ProposalRequestService class's GetExpectedContractorReturnDays method. I'll cover that method later in this chapter. For now, I don't really care where the value comes from, as long as I know that I have a Service method that I can call to get the value.

After getting the value from the ProposalRequestService class, I then check to see whether it has a value greater than zero; if it does, then I reset the expectedContractorReturnDays class variable to use that value. If it does not, then I do nothing, and the class uses the default value.

Initializing the expectedContractorReturnDate Class Variable

Now that I have just shown how the expectedContractorReturnDays class variable is set, it is time to use it to set the value of the expectedContractorReturnDays class variable. That happens in this line of the second constructor:

```
this.expectedContractorReturnDate =
                this.TransmittalDate.AddDays(this.expectedContractorReturnDays);
```

This line of code sets the expectedContractorReturnDays class variable value to the TransmittalDate property value of the base class and adds to it the number from the expectedContractorReturnDays class variable value. Here is the TransmittalDate property from the Transmittal base class:

```
public DateTime TransmittalDate
{
    get { return this.transmittalDate; }
    set { this.transmittalDate = value; }
}
```

Here is the code that initializes the TransmittalDate value in the Transmittal base class:

```
protected Transmittal(object key, object projectKey)
    : base(key)
{
    this.projectKey = projectKey;
    this.transmittalDate = DateTime.Now;
    this.totalPages = 1;
    this.deliveryMethod = Delivery.None;
    this.otherDeliveryMethod = string.Empty;
    this.phaseNumber = string.Empty;
    this.reimbursable = false;
    this.final = false;
    this.copyToList = new List<CopyTo>();
    this.transmittalRemarks = string.Empty;
}
```

As you can see, the highlighted second line of the `Transmittal` constructor initializes the `TransmittalDate` property.

The ValidateInitialization Method

The last action that happens in the `ProposalRequest` class initialization process is validation. A check is made via the `ValidateInitialization` method to ensure either that the class is passed a key value or that the class has a valid Proposal Request number and is associated with a Project.

```
private void ValidateInitialization()
{
    if (this.Key == null &&
        (this.number < 1 || this.ProjectKey == null))
    {
        StringBuilder builder = new StringBuilder(100);
        builder.Append("Invalid Proposal Request. ");
        builder.Append("The Proposal Request must have ");
        builder.Append("a valid Proposal Request number ");
        builder.Append("and be associated with a Project.");
        throw new InvalidOperationException(builder.ToString());
    }
}
```

The ProposalRequest Properties

The properties of the `ProposalRequest` class are very similar to those covered in previous Domain Model classes, so I am only going to show the differences here. Most of the properties in this class are fairly straightforward.

```
public DateTime? IssueDate
{
    get { return this.issueDate; }
    set { this.issueDate = value; }
}

public DateTime ExpectedContractorReturnDate
{
    get { return this.expectedContractorReturnDate; }
}

public string Description
{
    get { return this.description; }
    set { this.description = value; }
}

public string Attachment
{
    get { return this.attachment; }
    set { this.attachment = value; }
}

public string Reason
```

(continued)

(continued)

```
        {
            get { return this.reason; }
            set { this.reason = value; }
        }

        public string Initiator
        {
            get { return this.initiator; }
            set { this.initiator = value; }
        }

        public int Cause
        {
            get { return this.cause; }
            set
            {
                // Cause must be a positive number
                if (value > 0)
                {
                    this.cause = value;
                }
            }
        }

        public int Origin
        {
            get { return this.origin; }
            set
            {
                // Origin must be a positive number
                if (value > 0)
                {
                    this.origin = value;
                }
            }
        }

        public ProposalRequestNumberSpecification NumberSpecification
        {
            get { return this.numberSpecification; }
        }

        public ProposalRequestDescriptionSpecification DescriptionSpecification
        {
            get { return this.descriptionSpecification; }
        }
```

The Cause and Origin Properties

Both of these properties have a check in their setter to make sure that any value entered must be a positive number. Slowly, I am starting to put more behavior into the Domain Model classes. More behavior will come with this class in the next few sections.

The NumberSpecification Property

This property is designed to model the business rules about the proper numbering of Proposal Requests. The `NumberSpecification` property is represented by the `ProposalRequestNumberSpecification` class. Its only job is to validate that the Proposal Request adheres to the numbering rules, which are, if you remember, that all Proposal Requests must be numbered consecutively within a Project, and there cannot be duplicate Proposal Request numbers within a Project.

```
using System;
using SmartCA.Infrastructure.Specifications;
using System.Collections.Generic;
using SmartCA.Model.Projects;
using System.Linq;

namespace SmartCA.Model.ProposalRequests
{
    public class ProposalRequestNumberSpecification
        : Specification<ProposalRequest>
    {
        public override bool IsSatisfiedBy(ProposalRequest candidate)
        {
            bool isSatisfiedBy = true;

            // Make sure that the same Proposal Request number has not
            // been used for the current project, and that there are no
            // gaps between Proposal Request numbers

            // First get the project associated with the Proposal Request
            Project project = ProjectService.GetProject(candidate.ProjectKey);

            // Next get the list of Proposal Requests for the project
            IList<ProposalRequest> requests =
                ProposalRequestService.GetProposalRequests(project);

            // Determine if the Proposal Request number has been used before
            isSatisfiedBy =
                (requests.Where(pr => pr.Number.Equals(candidate.Number)).Count() <
1);

            // See if the candidate passed the first test
            if (isSatisfiedBy)
            {
                // First test passed, now make sure that there are no gaps
                isSatisfiedBy =
                    (candidate.Number - requests.Max(pr => pr.Number) == 1);
            }

            return isSatisfiedBy;
        }
    }
}
```

This code starts out by getting the list of Proposal Requests for the current Project, which is the Project that is associated with the Proposal Request. Once I have the list of Proposal Requests, I then use a LINQ query to determine whether the count of Proposal Requests in the list that match the candidate Proposal Request's Number property is less than one. If the count is less than one, then the test passes.

The next test is to make sure that the candidate Proposal Request will not introduce any numbering gaps within Proposal Requests of the current Project. This is done with another LINQ query to get the highest Proposal Requests number (`Max`) in the list, and then subtract that from the candidate Proposal Request's `Number` property. If the result equals one, then the test passes.

The DescriptionSpecification Property

This property is designed to model the business rule about the dates associated with RFIs. The `DateToFieldSpecification` property is represented by the `RequestForInformationDateSpecification` class. Its only job is to validate that the RFI has both a date received value and a date requested by value.

```
using System;
using SmartCA.Infrastructure.Specifications;

namespace SmartCA.Model.ProposalRequests
{
    public class ProposalRequestDescriptionSpecification
        : Specification<ProposalRequest>
    {
        public override bool IsSatisfiedBy(ProposalRequest candidate)
        {
            // The Proposal Request must have a description
            return (!string.IsNullOrEmpty(candidate.Description));
        }
    }
}
```

This code is much simpler than the first `Specification` class, as it only needs to perform two simple `Boolean` checks for the two dates.

The Validate Method

Since I have been starting to add more behavior to the Domain Model classes, one of the things that I really need to add is some type of validation before trying to save an Entity. In the `ProposalRequest` class I have added a `Validate` method to do just this:

```
        protected override void Validate()
        {
            if (!this.numberSpecification.IsSatisfiedBy(this))
            {
                this.AddBrokenRule(
                    ProposalRequestRuleMessages.MessageKeys.InvalidNumber);
            }
            if (!this.descriptionSpecification.IsSatisfiedBy(this))
            {
```

```
                this.AddBrokenRule(
                    ProposalRequestRuleMessages.MessageKeys.InvalidDescription);
            }
            if (this.to == null)
            {
                this.AddBrokenRule(
                    ProposalRequestRuleMessages.MessageKeys.InvalidProjectContact);
            }
            if (this.from == null)
            {
                this.AddBrokenRule(
                    ProposalRequestRuleMessages.MessageKeys.InvalidEmployee);
            }
            if (this.contractor == null)
            {
                this.AddBrokenRule(
                    ProposalRequestRuleMessages.MessageKeys.InvalidContractor);
            }
            base.Validate();
        }
```

Wait a second, why is it an override, and where is the `Boolean` return value? Ok, I admit it, I did some more refactoring. I made an abstract method in the `EntityBase` class called `Validate`. I also came up with a little mini-framework for dealing with the concept of Broken Rules, which I am borrowing (although simplifying it a bit here) from Rocky Lhotka's CSLA Framework (CSLA). Here is the `BrokenRule` class:

```
using System;

namespace SmartCA.Infrastructure.DomainBase
{
    public class BrokenRule
    {
        private string name;
        private string description;

        public BrokenRule(string name, string description)
        {
            this.name = name;
            this.description = description;
        }

        public string Name
        {
            get { return this.name; }
        }

        public string Description
        {
            get { return this.description; }
        }
    }
}
```

The BrokenRule class is a Value class for holding information about a broken business rule. Next, I needed some way for my Domain Model classes to get at the list of possible BrokenRule instances, so I made another class to capture that functionality:

```
using System;
using System.Collections.Generic;

namespace SmartCA.Infrastructure.DomainBase
{
    public abstract class BrokenRuleMessages
    {
        private Dictionary<string, string> messages;

        protected Dictionary<string, string> Messages
        {
            get { return this.messages; }
        }

        protected BrokenRuleMessages()
        {
            this.messages = new Dictionary<string, string>();
            this.PopulateMessages();
        }

        protected abstract void PopulateMessages();

        public string GetRuleDescription(string messageKey)
        {
            string description = string.Empty;
            if (this.messages.ContainsKey(messageKey))
            {
                description = this.messages[messageKey];
            }
            return description;
        }
    }
}
```

This class is fairly simple; its job is to hold a key-value dictionary of messages, and to provide a way to get messages out of the dictionary via the GetRuleDescription method. It also calls the abstract PopulateMessages method in its constructor, which means that the deriving class is responsible for putting the messages into the dictionary.

The BrokenRuleMessages abstract class is then used inside the EntityBase class, and here are the parts of the EntityBase class that have been refactored to accommodate this new functionality:

```
    public abstract class EntityBase
    {
        private object key;
        private List<BrokenRule> brokenRules;

        /// <summary>
```

```
        /// Default Constructor.
        /// </summary>
        protected EntityBase()
            : this (null)
        {
        }

        /// <summary>
        /// Overloaded constructor.
        /// </summary>
        /// <param name="key">An <see cref="System.Object"/> that
        /// represents the primary identifier value for the
        /// class.</param>
        protected EntityBase(object key)
        {
            this.key = key;
            if (this.key == null)
            {
                this.key = EntityBase.NewKey();
            }
            this.brokenRules = new List<BrokenRule>();
        }

        protected List<BrokenRule> BrokenRules
        {
            get { return this.brokenRules; }
        }

        protected abstract void Validate();

        public ReadOnlyCollection<BrokenRule> GetBrokenRules()
        {
            this.Validate();
            return this.brokenRules.AsReadOnly();
        }
    }
```

So now the `EntityBase` class holds a list of broken business rules and has a public method for consumers of Entity classes to call, which is the `GetBrokenRules` method. Notice how the `Validate` method is declared as abstract; this is because it is the responsibility of the derived Entity class to validate itself. The `GetBrokenRules` method calls the abstract `Validate` method (which is the very method in the `ProposalRequest` class that brought us into this refactoring rant of mine), which will be implemented in the derived class, and then it returns the list of broken business rules as a read-only collection.

So what this design implies is that I can set up a special class in my domain model to hold all of the particular business rules for a particular Entity, and normally that Entity will be an Aggregate Root.

In the case of Proposal Requests, the Aggregate Root is the `ProposalRequest` class, and therefore I have a `ProposalRequestRuleMessages` class:

```
using System;
using System.Collections.Generic;
using SmartCA.Infrastructure.DomainBase;

namespace SmartCA.Model.ProposalRequests
{
    internal class ProposalRequestRuleMessages : BrokenRuleMessages
    {
        internal static class MessageKeys
        {
            public const string InvalidNumber = "Invalid Proposal Request Number";
            public const string InvalidDescription = "Invalid Proposal Request " +
                "Description";
            public const string InvalidProjectContact = "Must Have " +
                "ProjectContact Assigned";
            public const string InvalidEmployee = "Must Have Employee Assigned";
            public const string InvalidContractor = "Must Have Contractor " +
                "Assigned";
        }

        protected override void PopulateMessages()
        {
            // Add the rule messages
            this.Messages.Add(MessageKeys.InvalidNumber,
                "The same Proposal Request number cannot be used for the " +
                "current project, and there cannot be any gaps between " +
                "Proposal Request numbers.");

            this.Messages.Add(MessageKeys.InvalidDescription,
                "The Proposal Request must have a description");

            this.Messages.Add(MessageKeys.InvalidProjectContact,
                "The Proposal Request must have a ProjectContact assigned " +
                "to the To property.");

            this.Messages.Add(MessageKeys.InvalidEmployee,
                "The Proposal Request must have an Employee assigned to the " +
                "From property.");

            this.Messages.Add(MessageKeys.InvalidContractor,
                "The Proposal Request must have a Company assigned to the " +
                "Contractor property.");
        }
    }
}
```

This class helps build all of the messages that I will use to represent the broken business rules of a Proposal Request. This brings us full circle back to the `ProposalRequest` class's `Validate` method:

```
protected override void Validate()
{
    if (!this.numberSpecification.IsSatisfiedBy(this))
    {
        this.AddBrokenRule(
            ProposalRequestRuleMessages.MessageKeys.InvalidNumber);
    }
    if (!this.descriptionSpecification.IsSatisfiedBy(this))
    {
        this.AddBrokenRule(
            ProposalRequestRuleMessages.MessageKeys.InvalidDescription);
    }
    if (this.to == null)
    {
        this.AddBrokenRule(
            ProposalRequestRuleMessages.MessageKeys.InvalidProjectContact);
    }
    if (this.from == null)
    {
        this.AddBrokenRule(
            ProposalRequestRuleMessages.MessageKeys.InvalidEmployee);
    }
    if (this.contractor == null)
    {
        this.AddBrokenRule(
            ProposalRequestRuleMessages.MessageKeys.InvalidContractor);
    }
    base.Validate();
}
```

This method makes use of the mini-validation framework that I have just shown. It first uses the Specification classes and tests to see whether the `ProposalRequest` instance satisfies its criteria. If not, the broken rules are added to the class instance. The rest of the validation is making sure that there are values for the `To`, `From`, and `Contractor` properties. I also added a little helper method to make adding broken rules a little less repetitive:

```
private void AddBrokenRule(string messageKey)
{
    this.BrokenRules.Add(new BrokenRule(messageKey,
        this.brokenRuleMessages.GetRuleDescription(messageKey)));
}
```

This method just allows me not to have to repeat the same verbose code in each of the validations.

The Proposal Request Repository Implementation

After going over the `IProposalRequestRepository` interface in the Design section, it is now time to explain how the `ProposalRequest` class is actually persisted to and from the data store by the Proposal Request Repository. In this section, I will be writing the code for the Proposal Request Repository.

The BuildChildCallbacks Method

As expected from the previous chapters, the `BuildChildCallbacks` method must be overridden as part of the Template Method pattern implementation in the `RequestForInformationRepository`.

```
#region BuildChildCallbacks

protected override void BuildChildCallbacks()
{
    this.ChildCallbacks.Add(
        ProposalRequestFactory.FieldNames.ProjectContactId,
        this.AppendTo);
    this.ChildCallbacks.Add(
        ProposalRequestFactory.FieldNames.EmployeeId,
        this.AppendFrom);
    base.BuildChildCallbacks();
}

#endregion
```

The AppendTo Callback

The first entry made in the `ChildCallbacks` dictionary is for the `AppendFrom` method. Thanks to the `ProjectService` class's `GetProjectContact` method, this method's code is very simple:

```
private void AppendTo(ProposalRequest proposalRequest,
    object toProjectContactKey)
{
    proposalRequest.To = ProjectService.GetProjectContact(
        proposalRequest.ProjectKey, toProjectContactKey);
}
```

The AppendFrom Callback

The first entry made in the `ChildCallbacks` dictionary is for the `AppendFrom` method. Thanks to the `EmployeeService` class's `GetEmployee` method, this method's code is also very simple:

```
private void AppendFrom(ProposalRequest proposalRequest,
    object fromEmployeeKey)
{
    proposalRequest.From =
        EmployeeService.GetEmployee(fromEmployeeKey);
}
```

Unit of Work Implementation

Following the same steps that I have shown before to implement the Unit of Work pattern, I need to override the following three methods: `PersistNewItem(ProposalRequest item)`, `PersistUpdatedItem(ProposalRequest item)`, and `PersistDeletedItem (ProposalRequest item)`.

The PersistNewItem Method

The first method override for the Proposal Request's Unit of Work implementation is the `PersistNewItem` method:

```
        protected override void PersistNewItem(ProposalRequest item)
        {
            StringBuilder builder = new StringBuilder(100);
            builder.Append(string.Format("INSERT INTO RequestForInformation ({0},
{1},{2},{3},{4},{5},{6},{7},{8},{9},{10},{11},{12},{13},{14},{15},{16},{17},{18},
{19},{20},{21},{22}) ",
                ProposalRequestFactory.FieldNames.ProposalRequestId,
                ProjectFactory.FieldNames.ProjectId,
                ProposalRequestFactory.FieldNames.ProposalRequestNumber,
                ProposalRequestFactory.FieldNames.TransmittalDate,
                ProposalRequestFactory.FieldNames.ProjectContactId,
                ProposalRequestFactory.FieldNames.EmployeeId,
                ProposalRequestFactory.FieldNames.TotalPages,
                ProposalRequestFactory.FieldNames.DeliveryMethod,
                ProposalRequestFactory.FieldNames.OtherDeliveryMethod,
                ProposalRequestFactory.FieldNames.PhaseNumber,
                ProposalRequestFactory.FieldNames.Reimbursable,
                ProposalRequestFactory.FieldNames.Final,
                ProposalRequestFactory.FieldNames.IssueDate,
                CompanyFactory.FieldNames.CompanyId,
                ProposalRequestFactory.FieldNames.Description,
                ProposalRequestFactory.FieldNames.Attachment,
                ProposalRequestFactory.FieldNames.Reason,
                ProposalRequestFactory.FieldNames.Initiator,
                ProposalRequestFactory.FieldNames.Cause,
                ProposalRequestFactory.FieldNames.Origin,
                ProposalRequestFactory.FieldNames.Remarks,
                ProposalRequestFactory.FieldNames.TransmittalRemarks
                ));
            builder.Append(string.Format("VALUES ({0},{1},{2},{3},{4},{5},{6},{7},
{8},{9},{10},{11},{12},{13},{14},{15},{16},{17},{18},{19},{20},{21},{22});",
                DataHelper.GetSqlValue(item.Key),
                DataHelper.GetSqlValue(item.ProjectKey),
                DataHelper.GetSqlValue(item.Number),
                DataHelper.GetSqlValue(item.TransmittalDate),
                DataHelper.GetSqlValue(item.To.Key),
                DataHelper.GetSqlValue(item.From.Key),
                DataHelper.GetSqlValue(item.TotalPages),
                DataHelper.GetSqlValue(item.DeliveryMethod),
                DataHelper.GetSqlValue(item.OtherDeliveryMethod),
                DataHelper.GetSqlValue(item.PhaseNumber),
                DataHelper.GetSqlValue(item.Reimbursable),
                DataHelper.GetSqlValue(item.Final),
                DataHelper.GetSqlValue(item.IssueDate),
                DataHelper.GetSqlValue(item.Contractor.Key),
                DataHelper.GetSqlValue(item.Description),
                DataHelper.GetSqlValue(item.Attachment),
                DataHelper.GetSqlValue(item.Reason),
                DataHelper.GetSqlValue(item.Initiator),
                DataHelper.GetSqlValue(item.Cause),
```

(continued)

(continued)

```
                DataHelper.GetSqlValue(item.Origin),
                DataHelper.GetSqlValue(item.Remarks),
                DataHelper.GetSqlValue(item.TransmittalRemarks)));

            this.Database.ExecuteNonQuery(
                this.Database.GetSqlStringCommand(builder.ToString()));

            // Now do the child objects
            this.InsertCopyToList(item);
        }
```

The code builds up a large insert statement composed of the values from the `ProposalRequest` instance and then executes the query using the Microsoft Enterprise Library's `Database` object. After the insert statement has been executed, I have to account for inserting the `CopyTo` instances for the `ProposalRequest`. I do this by calling the base class `InsertCopyToList` method, which takes an `ITransmittal` instance (which the `ProposalRequest`'s base class, `Transmittal`, implements) as its only argument.

The PersistUpdatedItem Method

`PersistUpdatedItem` first does an update to the `ProposalRequest` table:

```
        protected override void PersistUpdatedItem(ProposalRequest item)
        {
            StringBuilder builder = new StringBuilder(100);
            builder.Append("UPDATE ProposalRequest SET ");

            builder.Append(string.Format("{0} = {1}",
                ProposalRequestFactory.FieldNames.ProposalRequestNumber,
                DataHelper.GetSqlValue(item.Number)));

            builder.Append(string.Format(",{0} = {1}",
                ProposalRequestFactory.FieldNames.TransmittalDate,
                DataHelper.GetSqlValue(item.TransmittalDate)));

            **************************************************************

            builder.Append(string.Format(",{0} = {1}",
                ProposalRequestFactory.FieldNames.Remarks,
                DataHelper.GetSqlValue(item.Remarks)));

            builder.Append(string.Format(",{0} = {1}",
                ProposalRequestFactory.FieldNames.TransmittalRemarks,
                DataHelper.GetSqlValue(item.TransmittalRemarks)));

            builder.Append(" ");
            builder.Append(this.BuildBaseWhereClause(item.Key));

            this.Database.ExecuteNonQuery(
                this.Database.GetSqlStringCommand(builder.ToString()));

            // Now do the child objects

            // First, delete the existing ones
```

```
            this.DeleteCopyToList(item);

            // Now, add the current ones
            this.InsertCopyToList(item);
        }
```

I have omitted several lines of repetitive code building the SQL update statement in the middle of the code in order save you from the boring code.

The second part of the method uses the newly refactored `DeleteCopyToList` helper method to delete all of the `CopyTo` child objects of the Proposal Request and then uses the also newly refactored `InsertCopyToList` helper method to add the existing `CopyTo` child objects from the Proposal Request to the database.

The Proposal Request Service Implementation

Like the other Service classes shown in the domain model so far, the `ProposalRequestService` class is responsible for retrieving and wrapping the methods of its associated Repository interface, in this case the `IProposalRequestRepository` instance.

```
using System;
using System.Collections.Generic;
using SmartCA.Infrastructure;
using SmartCA.Infrastructure.RepositoryFramework;
using SmartCA.Model.Projects;

namespace SmartCA.Model.ProposalRequests
{
    public static class ProposalRequestService
    {
        private static IProposalRequestRepository repository;
        private static IUnitOfWork unitOfWork;

        static ProposalRequestService()
        {
            ProposalRequestService.unitOfWork = new UnitOfWork();
            ProposalRequestService.repository =
                RepositoryFactory.GetRepository<IProposalRequestRepository,
                ProposalRequest>(ProposalRequestService.unitOfWork);
        }

        public static IList<ProposalRequest>
            GetProposalRequests(Project project)
        {
            return ProposalRequestService.repository.FindBy(project);
        }

        public static void SaveProposalRequest(ProposalRequest proposalRequest)
        {
            ProposalRequestService.repository[proposalRequest.Key] =
                proposalRequest;
```

(continued)

(continued)

```
                ProposalRequestService.unitOfWork.Commit();
            }

            public static int GetExpectedContractorReturnDays()
            {
                return ProposalRequestService.repository
.GetExpectedContractorReturnDays();
            }
        }
    }
```

The Proposal Request View Model Class

Following the same patterns as before for all `ViewModel` classes, the `ProposalRequestViewModel` class adapts the Proposal Request Aggregate from the domain model to the UI. In the last chapter, I did some major refactoring and created the `TransmittalViewModel<T>` class for adapting Transmittal Entities to the UI, and now I get to use it again.

Just like the code for the RFI and Submittal ViewModels, the code inside of the `ProposalRequestViewModel` class has been reduced significantly. Here is what the signature of the `ProposalRequestViewModel` class looks like when deriving from the `TransmittalViewModel<T>` class:

```
public class ProposalRequestViewModel
    : TransmittalViewModel<ProposalRequest>
```

Notice how the generic parameter from the `TransmittalViewModel<T>` class is replaced with the `ProposalRequest` class.

The Constructor

Because of the recent refactoring, the constructors for the `ProposalRequestViewModel` class now are very small. Here are the constructors for the `ProposalRequestViewModel` class:

```
        #region Constructors

        public ProposalRequestViewModel()
            : this(null)
        {
        }

        public ProposalRequestViewModel(IView view)
            : base(view)
        {
            this.toList = UserSession.CurrentProject.Contacts;
            this.fromList = EmployeeService.GetEmployees();
        }

        #endregion
```

Just like with the `RequestForInformationViewModel` class, the `toList` and `fromList` private fields are not contained in the base class and therefore need to be initialized here.

The Properties

There are not many properties left to implement in the `ProposalRequestViewModel` class. Here is all of the code for the properties:

```
#region Properties

public IList<ProjectContact> ToList
{
    get { return this.toList; }
}

public IList<Employee> FromList
{
    get { return this.fromList; }
}

#endregion
```

The Command Handler Methods

The only command handler methods that I need to override in the `ProposalRequestViewModel` class are the `SaveCommandHandler` and `NewCommandHandler` methods. Again, if you remember from before, the `DeleteCommandHandler` method is completely taken care of by the base class.

The NewCommandHandler Method

Here is the code for the `NewCommandHandler` method:

```
protected override void NewCommandHandler(object sender, EventArgs e)
{
    base.NewCommandHandler(sender, e);
    ProposalRequest newProposalRequest = new ProposalRequest(
                                this.CurrentTransmittal.ProjectKey,
                                this.CurrentTransmittal.Number + 1);
    this.TransmittalList.Add(newProposalRequest);
    this.Transmittals.Refresh();
    this.Transmittals.MoveCurrentToLast();
}
```

On the first line of the method, I call the same method of the base class. This allows me to reuse the common code for managing the new Transmittal state and yet it still gives me the flexibility to do my own housekeeping for creating the new `ProposalRequest` instance.

The SaveCommandHandler Method

This method is much simpler, since it first calls the same method on the base class, and then proceeds to save the `ProposalRequest` instance:

```
protected override void SaveCommandHandler(object sender, EventArgs e)
{
    base.SaveCommandHandler(sender, e);
    ProposalRequestService.SaveProposalRequest(this.CurrentTransmittal);
}
```

Now, one thing that I am not taking advantage of here is the new validation functionality that I just built. Here is what the call will look like now:

```
protected override void SaveCommandHandler(object sender, EventArgs e)
{
    if (this.CurrentTransmittal.GetBrokenRules().Count == 0)
    {
        base.SaveCommandHandler(sender, e);
        ProposalRequestService.SaveProposalRequest(
            this.CurrentTransmittal);
    }
}
```

This really needs to be refactored a little bit more in order to display the list of broken rules to the user in an easily consumable manner. I will leave this as an exercise to do later.

The GetTransmittals Template Pattern Method

Here is the `GetTransmittals` method override:

```
#region GetTransmittals

protected override List<ProposalRequest> GetTransmittals()
{
    return new List<ProposalRequest>(
                ProposalRequestService.GetProposalRequests(
                UserSession.CurrentProject));
}

#endregion
```

In this method, just as in the last chapter, I am simply calling out to the `Service` class (the `ProposalRequestService` class) to get the list of instances (`ProposalRequest` instances).

The Proposal Request View

The View for Proposal Requests is almost exactly identical to the ones for Submittals and RFIs. Figure 7.6 shows what the form looks like at run time:

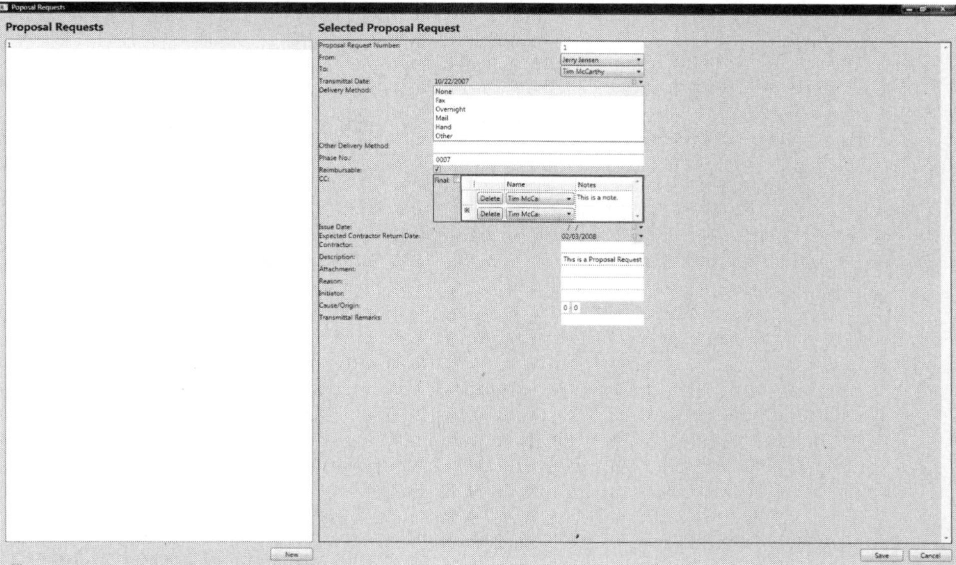

Figure 7.6: Proposal Request View.

Well, I have been doing a lot of refactoring lately regarding the common functionality of Transmittals and Routable Transmittals, and there is no reason that refactoring cannot continue in the UI. So, instead of having to repeat the same XAML over and over for Submittals, RFIs, and now Proposal Requests, I have decided to refactor the XAML that makes up the Transmittal sections of those Entities into some WPF UserControls. These are very similar to the UserControls that I created for Addresses, CopyToList, RoutingItems, and TrackingItems; in fact it is the same concept once again.

The Transmittal User Control

Once again, there is no code for this User Control, only XAML. The XAML for the `Transmittal` User Control is just a `Grid` element with all of the fields that are part of a Transmittal:

```
<UserControl
 x:Class="SmartCA.Presentation.Views.Transmittal"
 xmlns:presentation="clr-namespace:SmartCA.Presentation.Views"
    xmlns="http://schemas.microsoft.com/winfx/2006/xaml/presentation"
    xmlns:xcdg="http://schemas.xceed.com/wpf/xaml/datagrid"
    xmlns:x="http://schemas.microsoft.com/winfx/2006/xaml">

    <Grid>

        <Grid.RowDefinitions>
            <RowDefinition Height="Auto" />
            <RowDefinition Height="Auto" />
            <RowDefinition Height="Auto" />
            <RowDefinition Height="Auto" />
            <RowDefinition Height="Auto" />
            <RowDefinition Height="Auto" />
```

(continued)

(continued)

```
        </Grid.RowDefinitions>

        <Grid.ColumnDefinitions>
               <ColumnDefinition Width="200" />
               <ColumnDefinition Width="Auto" />
        </Grid.ColumnDefinitions>

        <Label Grid.Row="0" Grid.Column="0" Content="Transmittal Date:"
               Style="{StaticResource baseLabelStyle}"/>
        <xcdg:DatePicker Grid.Row="0" Grid.Column="1"
               SelectedDate="{Binding Path=CurrentTransmittal.TransmittalDate}"
               SyncCalendarWithSelectedDate="True" />

        <Label Grid.Row="1" Grid.Column="0" Content="Delivery Method:"
               Style="{StaticResource baseLabelStyle}"/>
        <ListBox Grid.Row="1" Grid.Column="1"
               SelectedItem="{Binding Path=CurrentTransmittal.DeliveryMethod}"
               IsSynchronizedWithCurrentItem="True"
               ItemsSource="{Binding Path=DeliveryMethods}"
               SelectionMode="Multiple"/>

        <Label Grid.Row="2" Grid.Column="0" Content="Other Delivery Method:"
               Style="{StaticResource baseLabelStyle}"/>
        <TextBox Grid.Row="2" Grid.Column="1"
               Text="{Binding Path=CurrentTransmittal.OtherDeliveryMethod}"/>

        <Label Grid.Row="3" Grid.Column="0" Content="Phase No.:"
               Style="{StaticResource baseLabelStyle}"/>
        <TextBox Grid.Row="3" Grid.Column="1"
               Text="{Binding Path=CurrentTransmittal.PhaseNumber}"/>

        <Label Grid.Row="4" Grid.Column="0" Content="Reimbursable:"
               Style="{StaticResource baseLabelStyle}"/>
        <CheckBox Grid.Row="4" Grid.Column="1"
               IsChecked="{Binding Path=CurrentTransmittal.Reimbursable}"/>

        <Label Content="CC:" Grid.Row="5" Grid.Column="0"
                                   Style="{StaticResource baseLabelStyle}"/>
        <Border BorderBrush="Black" Padding="1" BorderThickness="1"
               Grid.Row="5" Grid.Column="1">
               <StackPanel Orientation="Horizontal">
                      <Label Content="Final: "
                                   Style="{StaticResource baseLabelStyle}"/>
                      <CheckBox IsChecked=
                                 "{Binding Path=CurrentTransmittal.Final}" />
                      <presentation:CopyToList
                                DataContext="{Binding Path=MutableCopyToList}"/>
               </StackPanel>
        </Border>

</Grid>

</UserControl>
```

The RoutableTransmittal User Control

Since a Routable Transmittal is just a Transmittal that contains Routing Items, it should follow that I should be able to use the `Transmittal` User Control shown above, plus the `RoutingItems` User Control from a few chapters back to make one composite User Control. In fact, that is exactly what I did for the `RoutableTransmittal` UserControl:

```
<UserControl
 x:Class="SmartCA.Presentation.Views.RoutableTransmittal"
 xmlns:presentation="clr-namespace:SmartCA.Presentation.Views"
    xmlns="http://schemas.microsoft.com/winfx/2006/xaml/presentation"
    xmlns:x="http://schemas.microsoft.com/winfx/2006/xaml">
    <Grid>

         <Grid.RowDefinitions>
                <RowDefinition Height="Auto" />
                <RowDefinition Height="Auto" />
         </Grid.RowDefinitions>

         <Grid.ColumnDefinitions>
                <ColumnDefinition Width="200"/>
                <ColumnDefinition Width="Auto" />
         </Grid.ColumnDefinitions>

         <presentation:Transmittal Grid.Row="0"
                Grid.Column="0" Grid.ColumnSpan="2"
                DataContext="{Binding Path= .}"/>

         <Label Grid.Row="1" Grid.Column="0" Content="Routing:"
                   Style="{StaticResource baseLabelStyle}"/>
         <presentation:RoutingItems Grid.Row="1" Grid.Column="1"
                   DataContext="{Binding Path=RoutingItems}"/>

    </Grid>
</UserControl>
```

Nothing really new here, I am just enjoying the fact that not only can I get good code re-use out of my domain model, but now I can also get it in my UI code as well!

Summary

In this chapter, I introduced the concept of a Proposal Request in the construction industry, and then I used that concept to model the Proposal Request Aggregate. Up until this point, the classes in the domain model had been a little bit anemic, but by adding lots of behavior to them in this chapter, they are starting to become rich Domain Model classes. I also introduced a new concept into the domain this chapter in regard to handling broken business rules inside my Domain Model classes. Then I put in some validation to exercise both the broken rule functionality as well as the Specification functionality, showing how the two can play nicely together. I also continued my constant refactoring in this chapter, only this time I showed how to refactor some of the UI UserControls to handle some of the Transmittal concepts.

Change Orders

In the last chapter, I covered Proposal Requests, which must precede Change Orders in the construction industry. In this chapter, I am going to cover the actual Change Order itself.

The Problem

If it turns out that a Proposal Request that was submitted was acceptable to the owner, or becomes acceptable after adjustment of the scope, negotiation of the price, and/or the adjustment of the Contract time, then a Change Order can be prepared. After execution by the Owner and Contractor, and countersignature by the Architect, it becomes a modification of the construction Contract. It authorizes the Contractor to do the work and obligates the Owner to pay for it.

There are two types of Change Orders:

1. **Change in Contract Price** — Any change, up or down, in the Contract price should be agreed and entered into the Change Order form.
2. **Change in Contract Time** — Any change, up or down, in the Contract time should be agreed on and entered into the Change Order form. If there is no change in time, then the change order should state that there is no change in Contract time. It is a big mistake to leave the time blank, as this will often result in a dispute. The Owner will assume that the blank means no change in time, while the Contractor reasons that the blank means that it will be discussed later.

When there is to be a change in Contract time only, but with no change in Contract price, it is good practice to handle it as a Change Order complete with a Change Order form and signatures of the Owner and Contractor. The form should clearly state the change in Contract time and that the Contract price is unchanged.

Like RFIs and Proposal Requests, each Change Order should be serially numbered by Project.

The Design

In the SmartCA domain, a Change Order is one of the most important concepts for the entire application, and it also contains several important business concepts that must be closely tracked. In the next few sections I will be designing the domain model, determining the Change Order Aggregate and its boundaries, and designing the Repository for Change Orders.

Designing the Domain Model

As stated earlier, the most important parts of the Change Order are the changes in Contract time or price, as well as the proper ordering of the Change Order Number. I will be using the Specification pattern to govern the rules for the Number property, and the Specification that I create will also be part of the domain model. It is very important that the logic inside of the Change Order be correct for calculating the total price or time whenever one of those items is changed.

Figure 8.1 shows a drawing showing the relationships between the classes that combine to make up a Change Order:

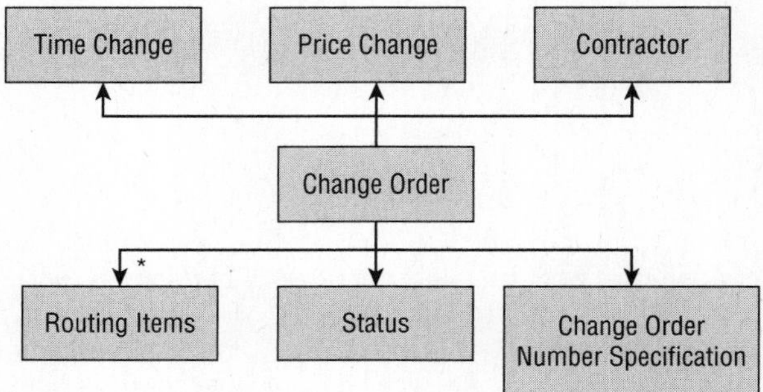

Figure 8.1: Change Order Aggregate.

In the diagram, the Change Order class is clearly the root of the Aggregate. The two most important attributes of the Change Order are the amount of time being changed and the amount of money being added. These are both represented in the diagram by the Time Change and Price Change relationships, respectively. The relationship to the Contractor class shows what Contractor has requested the Change Order.

The next important part of the diagram is the Change Order's relationship to the Routing Items. It is important for Smart Design to know to whom each Change Order has been routed internally for action, and that person's Discipline, such as architect, engineer, or construction administrator. This was already created and used in Chapter 6; I am just reusing the same concept in this Aggregate.

The relationship to the `Status` class shows exactly the state of the Change Order, such as completed or pending an architect review. The relationship to the Change Order Number Specification helps model the numbering rules of the Change Order.

Designing the Change Order Aggregate

The Change Order Aggregate does not have as many classes in it as some of the other Aggregates, but it does contain some important concepts that I will show later in the Solution section (see Figure 8.2).

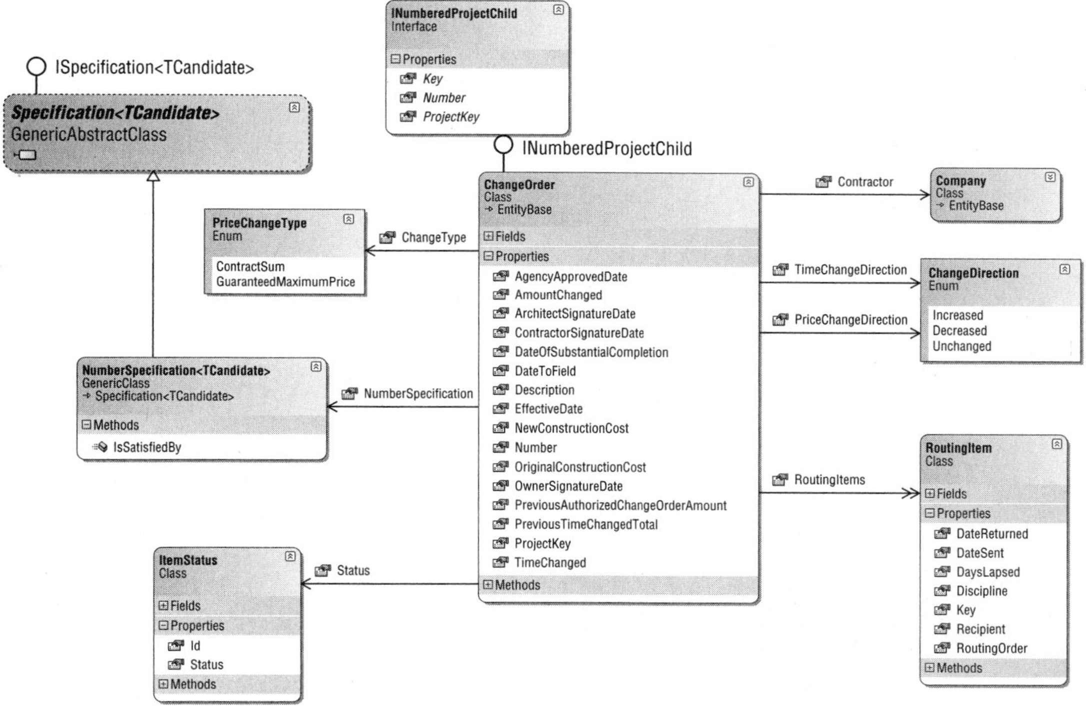

Figure 8.2: Classes Constituting the Change Order Aggregate.

As shown in the diagram, the `ChangeOrder` class inherits from the `EntityBase` class and implements the `INumberedProjectChild` interface. I will talk more about this interface and how it is used in relation to the other parts of the domain model later in the chapter.

Defining the Aggregate Boundaries

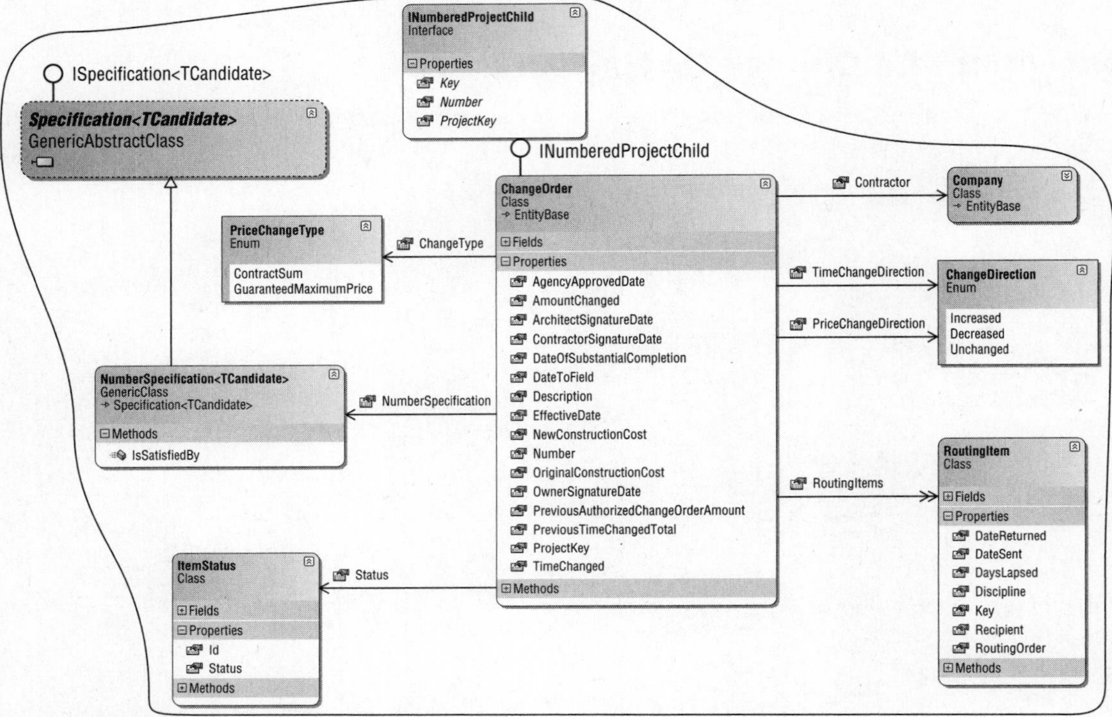

Figure 8.3: Change Order Aggregate boundaries.

The `ChangeOrder` class has its own identity and is definitely the root of its own Aggregate (see Figure 8.3). All of the other classes in the diagram, except for the `Company` class, belong to the Change Order Aggregate. The `Company` class is the root of its own Aggregate.

Designing the Repository

Since the `ChangeOrder` class is its own Aggregate root, it will have its own repository (see Figure 8.4).

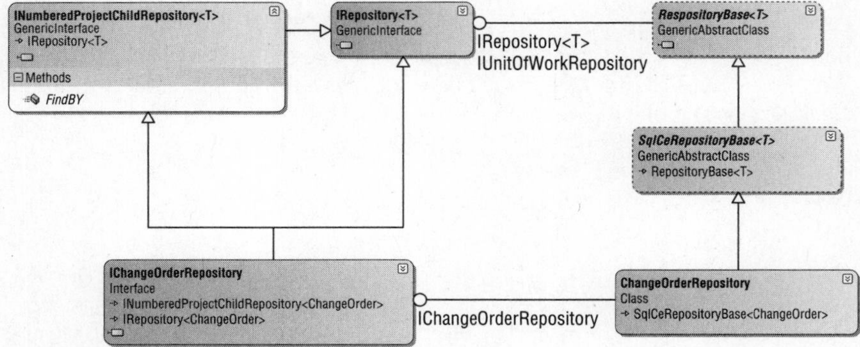

Figure 8.4: The Change Order Repository.

Designing the IChangeOrderRepository Interface

The `IChangeOrderRepository` interface is the interface into instances of Change Order Repositories. Here is the `IChangeOrderRepository` interface:

```
using System;
using System.Collections.Generic;

namespace SmartCA.Model.ChangeOrders
{
    public interface IChangeOrderRepository :
        INumberedProjectChildRepository<ChangeOrder>
    {
        decimal GetPreviousAuthorizedAmountFrom(ChangeOrder co);
        int GetPreviousTimeChangedTotalFrom(ChangeOrder co);
    }
}
```

The `GetPreviousAuthorizedAmountFrom` and the `GetPreviousTimeChangedTotal` methods should look pretty familiar as the `ChangeOrder` class implementation has been calling these methods indirectly via the `ChangeOrderService` class.

The most interesting thing to notice about this interface is that it extends the `INumberedProjectChildRepository<T>` interface, as previously shown in Figure 8.4.

Designing the INumberedProjectChild Interface

You probably saw this coming, since I had the `INumberedProjectChild` interface already. It turned out that all created instances of the `INumberedProjectChild` interface were usually a result of the `FindBy(Project project)` method, so I put this method into its own interface and factored it out of the `IChangeOrderRepository` interface. As a result, I factored this method out of the `IProposalRequestRepository` and `IRequestForInformationRepository` interfaces as well. Here is the `INumberedProjectChildRepository<T>` interface:

```
using System;
using System.Collections.Generic;
using SmartCA.Infrastructure.RepositoryFramework;
using SmartCA.Model.Projects;
using SmartCA.Infrastructure.DomainBase;

namespace SmartCA.Model
{
    public interface INumberedProjectChildRepository<T>
        : IRepository<T> where T : IAggregateRoot, INumberedProjectChild
    {
        IList<T> FindBy(Project project);
    }
}
```

Notice how it is extending the `IRepository<T>` interface; that is expected, but the constraints on the Generic parameter should look different. I am actually able to constrain the Entity (the `T` Generic parameter) that has to implement the `INumberedProjectChild` interface, as well as the `IAggregateRoot` interface, which I will cover next.

I thought about using a custom attribute instead of an empty interface, but I decided I really like the use of interfaces more. They seem to me to be much more explicit, and they allow me to use Generic constraints on them, which I will explain later.

Designing the IAggregateRoot Interface

This should really jump out at you. What is this `IAggregateRoot` interface? Here is what it looks like:

```
using System;

namespace SmartCA.Infrastructure.DomainBase
{
    /// <summary>
    /// This is a marker interface that indicates that an
    /// Entity is an Aggregate Root.
    /// </summary>
    public interface IAggregateRoot : IEntity
    {
    }
}
```

It does not look like much—it is just a marker interface that simply extends the `IEntity` interface—but conceptually, this is huge. By using this interface as a constraint on a repository, I can now enforce the DDD rule that only the Aggregate Root is allowed to have a repository associated with it. This is huge from a DDD standpoint! I refactored the `IRepository<T>` interface to make sure that it uses this constraint as well:

```
using System;
using SmartCA.Infrastructure.DomainBase;
using System.Collections.Generic;

namespace SmartCA.Infrastructure.RepositoryFramework
{
    public interface IRepository<T> where T : IAggregateRoot
    {
        T FindBy(object key);
        IList<T> FindAll();
        void Add(T item);
        T this[object key] { get; set; }
        void Remove(T item);
    }
}
```

I also refactored all of the classes that have been deemed Aggregate Root classes to extend this interface. I did not mention it earlier in the chapter, but some of you may have noticed that the signature of the `ChangeOrder` class also extends this interface:

```
public class ChangeOrder : EntityBase, IAggregateRoot, INumberedProjectChild
```

I also refactored the `RepositoryFactory` class to honor this new concept.

```
public static TRepository GetRepository<TRepository, TEntity>(IUnitOfWork
unitOfWork)
            where TRepository : class, IRepository<TEntity>
            where TEntity : IAggregateRoot
```

This new interface and subsequent refactoring really helps clarify the domain model and enforce the DDD concepts that I have been implementing.

Writing the Unit Tests

I am not going to show the unit tests here in this section because they are essentially the same as most of the unit tests written in previous chapters. The main point is that they are there to guide me along my way as I refactor the code; every time I refactor I try to make sure to run my unit tests in order to make sure that I do not break any pieces in the application.

The Solution

The classes used to make up the Change Order Aggregate should look very familiar to you; I am at the point in the application architecture where I am starting to reuse many of the classes. The thing that is a little bit different from previous chapters is that now there is much more business logic to implement inside of the classes. Change Orders deal with money and time, and these types of documents may literally be dealing with millions of dollars.

The Change Order Class Private Fields and Constructors

The `ChangeOrder` class inherits from the `Transmittal` class and passes its values from its constructors straight through to the `Transmittal` base class.

```
using System;
using SmartCA.Model.Companies;
using SmartCA.Infrastructure.DomainBase;
using System.Collections.Generic;
using SmartCA.Model.Transmittals;
using System.Text;
using SmartCA.Model.Projects;

namespace SmartCA.Model.ChangeOrders
{
    public class ChangeOrder : EntityBase, INumberedProjectChild
    {
        #region Private Fields

        private object projectKey;
        private int number;
        private DateTime effectiveDate;
        private Company contractor;
        private string description;
        private Project currentProject;
        private PriceChangeType? changeType;
```

(continued)

(continued)

```
        private ChangeDirection priceChangeDirection;
        private decimal? previousAuthorizedChangeOrderAmount;
        private decimal amountChanged;
        private ChangeDirection timeChangeDirection;
        private int? previousTimeChangedTotal;
        private int timeChanged;
        private List<RoutingItem> routingItems;
        private ItemStatus status;
        private DateTime? agencyApprovedDate;
        private DateTime? dateToField;
        private DateTime? ownerSignatureDate;
        private DateTime? architectSignatureDate;
        private DateTime? contractorSignatureDate;
        private NumberSpecification<ChangeOrder> numberSpecification;
        private BrokenRuleMessages brokenRuleMessages;

        #endregion

        #region Constructors

        public ChangeOrder(object projectKey, int number)
            : this(null, projectKey, number)
        {
        }

        public ChangeOrder(object key, object projectKey,
            int number) : base(key)
        {
            this.projectKey = projectKey;
            this.number = number;
            this.effectiveDate = DateTime.Now;
            this.contractor = null;
            this.description = string.Empty;
            this.changeType = null;
            this.priceChangeDirection = ChangeDirection.Unchanged;
            this.previousAuthorizedChangeOrderAmount = 0;
            this.previousTimeChangedTotal = 0;
            this.amountChanged = 0;
            this.timeChangeDirection = ChangeDirection.Unchanged;
            this.timeChanged = 0;
            this.routingItems = new List<RoutingItem>();
            this.status = null;
            this.agencyApprovedDate = null;
            this.dateToField = null;
            this.ownerSignatureDate = null;
            this.architectSignatureDate = null;
            this.contractorSignatureDate = null;
            this.numberSpecification =
                new NumberSpecification<ChangeOrder>();
            this.ValidateInitialization();
            this.brokenRuleMessages = new ChangeOrderRuleMessages();
        }

        #endregion
```

Just like the `Submittal` and `RequestForInformation` classes, all of the data for the `ChangeOrder` class is initialized and validated in the second constructor, which is called by the first constructor.

The ValidateInitialization Method

The last action that happens in the `ChangeOrder` class initialization process is validation. A check is made via the `ValidateInitialization` method to ensure that, if the class is not passed in a key value, then the class has a valid Change Order number and is associated with a Project.

```
private void ValidateInitialization()
{
    NumberedProjectChildValidator.ValidateInitialState(this,
        "Change Order");
}
```

The old code for this method would have looked like this:

```
private void ValidateInitialization()
{
    if (this.Key == null &&
        (this.number < 1 || this.ProjectKey == null))
    {
        StringBuilder builder = new StringBuilder(100);
        builder.Append("Invalid Change Order. ");
        builder.Append("The Change Order must have ");
        builder.Append("a valid Change Order number ");
        builder.Append("and be associated with a Project.");
        throw new InvalidOperationException(builder.ToString());
    }
}
```

This method's code has been factored out into a new class, the `NumberedProjectChildValidator` class. This new static class has one method, `ValidateInitialState`, which helps reduce the repetitive initialization validation code that I implemented in some of the other Entity classes:

```
using System;
using System.Text;

namespace SmartCA.Model
{
    public static class NumberedProjectChildValidator
    {
        /// <summary>
        /// This method throws an exception if the initial state is not valid.
        /// </summary>
        /// <param name="child">The Entity instance, which must implement the
        /// INumberedProjectChild interface.</param>
        /// <param name="entityFriendlyName">The friendly name of the Entity,
        /// such as "Change Order".</param>
        public static void ValidateInitialState(INumberedProjectChild child,
            string entityFriendlyName)
        {
            if (child.Key == null &&
```

(continued)

(continued)

```
                    (child.Number < 1 || child.ProjectKey == null))
                {
                    StringBuilder builder = new StringBuilder(100);
                    builder.Append(string.Format("Invalid {0}. ",
                        entityFriendlyName));
                    builder.Append(string.Format("The {0} must have ",
                        entityFriendlyName));
                    builder.Append(string.Format("a valid {0} number ",
                        entityFriendlyName));
                    builder.Append("and be associated with a Project.");
                    throw new InvalidOperationException(builder.ToString());
                }
            }
        }
    }
```

The logic is exactly the same as before, but this method takes as its arguments an instance of the `INumberedProjectChild` interface and the friendly name of the Entity to validate. By factoring this logic out into a separate class, I am now able to reuse it across several of the Entity classes that fall into this category, such as Proposal Requests or RFIs.

The `INumberedProjectChild` interface is a nice way to represent all Entities that belong to a Project and have a `Number` property. Here is what its signature looks like:

```
using System;
using SmartCA.Infrastructure.DomainBase;

namespace SmartCA.Model
{
    public interface INumberedProjectChild : IEntity
    {
        object ProjectKey { get; }
        int Number { get; set; }
    }
}
```

Something that should catch your eye right away is that this interface implements the `IEntity` interface. The `IEntity` interface represents an Entity:

```
using System;

namespace SmartCA.Infrastructure.DomainBase
{
    public interface IEntity
    {
        object Key { get; }
    }
}
```

This is something I probably should have done before, but I was not quite sure about it. After working with this domain model for a while now, this just feels like the right thing to do. I have also refactored the `EntityBase` class to implement the `IEntity` interface as well.

```
public abstract class EntityBase : IEntity
```

I did not have to change any of the other code in the `EntityBase` class, since it already implements the `Key` property required by the `IEntity` interface.

I also changed a lot of other places in the code where an `EntityBase` class was used, in any part of any method argument or class property, to an `IEntity` interface instead. When I was first pondering this change, I thought it might be a risky move, especially since the `EntityBase` class is referred to almost everywhere in the code, but it turned out that really the dependency was only on the `EntityBase` class's `Key` property. When I decided to make the changes, it really was not too big a deal; once I was able to get everything to compile, I re-ran all of the unit tests until each one passed.

Making the change to `IEntity` actually makes the domain model a lot better; for example, when I cover how to synchronize with the server in Chapter 10, I introduce a `Transaction` class that does not need a lot of validation logic in it. So instead of the `Transaction` class inheriting from the `EntityBase` class and having to implement required functionality for `BrokenRule` logic, it can simply implement the `IEntity` interface and avoid all of that code that does not quite fit with what it is trying to represent.

The ChangeOrder Properties

A lot of the properties of the `ChangeOrder` class are very similar to those covered in previous Domain Model classes, so I am only going to cover those that contain behavior here.

The OriginalConstructionCost Property

The first property I will cover, the `OriginalConstructionCost` property, represents the original cost of the Project from the time it started. It is used as a baseline to compare against the sum of the current Change Orders to date.

```
        public decimal OriginalConstructionCost
        {
            get
            {
                this.GetCurrentProject();
                return this.currentProject.OriginalConstructionCost;
            }
        }
```

This is a read-only property, and it uses the private `currentProject` field to get the value from the Project instance. Before doing so, it calls the `GetCurrentProject` private method to make sure that the `currentProject` field has been populated:

```
        private void GetCurrentProject()
        {
            if (this.currentProject == null)
            {
                this.currentProject = ProjectService.GetProject(this.projectKey);
            }
        }
```

This method implements lazy-load functionality on the `currentProject` field; if it is a null value, then it uses the `ProjectService` class to load it up via its `GetProject` method.

The PreviousAuthorizedAmount Property

The `PreviousAuthorizedAmount` property is another read-only property that represents what has been previously authorized from all of the previous Change Orders before the date of the current Change Order.

```
public decimal PreviousAuthorizedAmount
{
    get
    {
        this.GetPreviousAuthorizedAmount();
        return this.previousAuthorizedAmount.HasValue ?
            this.previousAuthorizedAmount.Value : 0;
    }
}
```

Very similar to the `OriginalConstructionCost` property, this property also calls a private method to get the value in a lazy-load type manner. The `previousAuthorizedAmount` field is a Nullable type, so if it has a value, then the value is used; otherwise, the property returns a value of zero. The private method the property calls is the `GetPreviousAuthorizedAmount` method:

```
private void GetPreviousAuthorizedAmount()
{
    if (!this.previousAuthorizedAmount.HasValue)
    {
        this.previousAuthorizedAmount =
            ChangeOrderService.GetPreviousAuthorizedAmountFrom(this);
    }
}
```

This method implements its lazy-load functionality by checking to see whether the `previousAuthorizedAmount` field has a value; if it does not have a value, then it sets its value using the `GetPreviousAuthorizedAmountFrom` method of the `ChangeOrderService`.

The NewConstructionCost Property

This property is read-only and represents what the new construction cost is as of the date of the current Change Order.

```
public decimal NewConstructionCost
{
    get
    {
        this.GetPreviousAuthorizedAmount();
        return this.OriginalConstructionCost +
            this.PreviousAuthorizedAmount +
            this.amountChanged;
    }
}
```

This property starts out by calling the method I just showed, the `GetPreviousAuthorizedAmount` method. It then adds up the value of the `OriginalConstructionCost` property, the `PreviousAuthorizedAmount` property, and the `amountChanged` private field. The `amountChanged` private field is changed by the setter on the `AmountChanged` property. These values added together represent the new construction cost of a Project at the particular point in time of the current Change Order.

The PreviousTimeChangedTotal Property

This is another read-only property that represents the total amount of days that have been added or subtracted from the Project as of the date of the current Change Order.

```
public int PreviousTimeChangedTotal
{
    get
    {
        this.GetPreviousTimeChangedTotal();
        return this.previousTimeChangedTotal.HasValue ?
            this.previousTimeChangedTotal.Value : 0;
    }
}
```

The logic for this property is pretty much the same as for the `PreviousAuthorizedAmount` property. It also calls a private method to get the value in a lazy-load type manner. The `previousTimeChangedTotal` field is a Nullable type, so if it has a value, then the value is used; otherwise, the property returns a value of zero. The private method the property calls is the `GetPreviousTimeChangedTotal` method:

```
private void GetPreviousTimeChangedTotal()
{
    if (!this.previousTimeChangedTotal.HasValue)
    {
        this.previousTimeChangedTotal =
            ChangeOrderService.GetPreviousTimeChangedTotalFrom(this);
    }
}
```

As you would expect, the logic for this method is very similar to the logic for the `GetPreviousAuthorizedAmount` method. This method also implements lazy-load functionality by checking to see whether the `previousTimeChangedTotal` field has a value; if it does not have a value, then it sets its value using the `GetPreviousTimeChangedTotalFrom` method of the `ChangeOrderService`.

The DateOfSubstantialCompletion Property

This read-only property represents the date that the Project will be completed as of the current Change order. This takes into account all of the days added or subtracted from the Project by previous Change Orders.

```
public DateTime? DateOfSubstantialCompletion
{
    get
    {
        DateTime? completionDate = null;
        this.GetCurrentProject();
        if (this.currentProject.EstimatedCompletionDate.HasValue)
        {
            this.GetPreviousTimeChangedTotal();
            completionDate =
                this.currentProject.EstimatedCompletionDate.Value.AddDays(
                this.PreviousTimeChangedTotal + this.timeChanged);
        }
        return completionDate;
    }
}
```

This getter starts by setting up a `Nullable DateTime` variable to use as the return value and sets it to null. The next step is to check whether the `currentProject` instance's `EstimatedCompletionDate` property value has a value, but before doing that, I have to call the `GetCurrentProject` method to make sure that the `currentProject` field is properly initialized. If the Project has an `EstimatedCompletionDate` value, I then call the `GetPreviousTimeChangedTotal` method to get the number of days that have been added to or subtracted from the current Project as of the date of the current Change Order. I then add the value of the `PreviousTimeChangedTotal` property and the `timeChanged` class field value to add the right number of days to the Project's `EstimatedCompletionDate` property and then return that value. The `timeChanged` field value is set via the `TimeChanged` property.

The NumberSpecification Property

This property is designed to model the business rules about the proper numbering of Change Orders. The `NumberSpecification` property is represented by the `ChangeOrderNumberSpecification` class. Its only job is to validate that the Change Order adheres to the numbering rules, which are, if you remember, that all Change Orders must be numbered consecutively within a Project and that there cannot be duplicate Change Order numbers within a Project.

```
public NumberSpecification<ChangeOrder> NumberSpecification
{
    get { return this.numberSpecification; }
}
```

This is very similar to the other Number Specification implementations in the last two chapters, so, seeing that, I felt this needed some more refactoring in order to eliminate the duplicate code. As a result, I created a generic Number Specification class; actually it is a .NET Generic `NumberSpecification<TCandidate>` class.

```
using System;
using System.Collections.Generic;
using System.Linq;
using SmartCA.Infrastructure.Specifications;
using SmartCA.Model.Projects;
using SmartCA.Infrastructure.RepositoryFramework;
using SmartCA.Infrastructure.DomainBase;

namespace SmartCA.Model
{
    public class NumberSpecification<TCandidate>
        : Specification<TCandidate> where TCandidate : IAggregateRoot,
        INumberedProjectChild
    {
        public override bool IsSatisfiedBy(TCandidate candidate)
        {
            bool isSatisfiedBy = true;

            // Make sure that the same entity number has not
            // been used for the current project, and that there are no
            // gaps between entity numbers

            // First get the project associated with the entity
            Project project = ProjectService.GetProject(candidate.ProjectKey);

            // Next get the list of items for the project

            // First get the correct Repository
            INumberedProjectChildRepository<TCandidate> repository =
                RepositoryFactory.GetRepository
                <INumberedProjectChildRepository<TCandidate>, TCandidate>();

            // Now use the Repository to find all of the items by the Project
            IList<TCandidate> items = repository.FindBy(project);

            // Use a LINQ query to determine if the entity number has been
            // used before
            isSatisfiedBy =
                (items.Where(item => item.Number.Equals(candidate.Number)).Count()
                    < 1);

            // See if the candidate passed the first test
            if (isSatisfiedBy)
            {
                // First test passed, now use another LINQ query to make sure that
                // there are no gaps
                isSatisfiedBy =
                    (candidate.Number - items.Max(item => item.Number) == 1);
            }

            return isSatisfiedBy;
        }
    }
}
```

This code is almost the same as the other Number Specification implementations, only it uses .NET Generics to give it reusability. Let me start out by comparing the signature of this class to the non-Generic class that would have been created.

Here is the old way of implementing this:

```
public class ChangeOrderNumberSpecification : Specification<ChangeOrder>
```

Here, again, is the new way:

```
public class NumberSpecification<TCandidate> : Specification<TCandidate> where
    TCandidate : IAggregateRoot, INumberedProjectChild
```

The trick here is using the constraints on the `TCandidate` Generic parameter. By declaring that the `TCandidate` Generic parameter has to implement the `INumberedProjectChild` interface, I now have strongly typed access to its properties (via the `TCandidate` candidate argument) in the `IsSatisfied` method. I then proceed to use the `ProjectKey` property to get the correct `Project` instance via the `ProjectService` class. I get an instance of the `INumberedProjectChildRepository` interface and then use that to get the list of all of the items (in this case, it would be `ChangeOrder` instances) for the given Project. Finally, in the LINQ queries I use the `Number` property of the `INumberedProjectChild` interface instance to make sure that the Number has not been used before and that there are no gaps between the last item (in this case `ChangeOrder`) `Number` and this item (again, `ChangeOrder`) `Number`.

I also went back and refactored the `NumberSpecification` properties on the `ProposalRequest` and `RequestForInformation` classes to use the new `NumberSpecification<TCandidate>` class.

The Validate Method

Taking advantage of the mini-validation framework that was built in the last chapter, here is the `Validate` method override for the `ChangeOrder` class:

```
protected override void Validate()
{
    if (!this.numberSpecification.IsSatisfiedBy(this))
    {
        this.AddBrokenRule(
            ChangeOrderRuleMessages.MessageKeys.InvalidNumber);
    }
    if (this.contractor == null)
    {
        this.AddBrokenRule(
            ChangeOrderRuleMessages.MessageKeys.InvalidContractor);
    }
}
```

If you remember in the last chapter, there was a little bit more to this implementation than just overriding the `Validate` method of the `EntityBase` class. Well, I know this is hard to believe, but I did a little bit more refactoring since then. I moved the `brokenRuleMessages` field into the `EntityBase` class, as well as the `AddBrokenRule` method.

Here are the new changes to the `EntityBase` class:

```
public abstract class EntityBase : IEntity
{
    private object key;
    private List<BrokenRule> brokenRules;
    private BrokenRuleMessages brokenRuleMessages;

    /// <summary>
    /// Overloaded constructor.
    /// </summary>
    /// <param name="key">An <see cref="System.Object"/> that
    /// represents the primary identifier value for the
    /// class.</param>
    protected EntityBase(object key)
    {
        this.key = key;
        if (this.key == null)
        {
            this.key = EntityBase.NewKey();
        }
        this.brokenRules = new List<BrokenRule>();
        this.brokenRuleMessages = this.GetBrokenRuleMessages();
    }

    #region Validation and Broken Rules

    protected abstract void Validate();

    protected abstract BrokenRuleMessages GetBrokenRuleMessages();

    protected List<BrokenRule> BrokenRules
    {
        get { return this.brokenRules; }
    }

    public ReadOnlyCollection<BrokenRule> GetBrokenRules()
    {
        this.Validate();
        return this.brokenRules.AsReadOnly();
    }

    protected void AddBrokenRule(string messageKey)
    {
        this.brokenRules.Add(new BrokenRule(messageKey,
            this.brokenRuleMessages.GetRuleDescription(messageKey)));
    }

    #endregion
```

There is also a new abstract method in the EntityBase class, the GetBrokenRulesMessages method. This allows the EntityBase class to separate the brokenRuleMessages field completely from the derived classes; all they have to do is implement the GetBrokenRuleMessages method and return a BrokenRuleMessages instance. Here is how it is implemented in the ChangeOrder class:

```
        protected override BrokenRuleMessages GetBrokenRuleMessages()
        {
            return new ChangeOrderRuleMessages();
        }
```

This is another implementation of the Template Method pattern, and as you can see it really helps to encapsulate the logic of managing BrokenRule instances. Here is the ChangeOrderRuleMessages class:

```
using System;
using SmartCA.Infrastructure.DomainBase;

namespace SmartCA.Model.ChangeOrders
{
    public class ChangeOrderRuleMessages : BrokenRuleMessages
    {
        internal static class MessageKeys
        {
            public const string InvalidNumber = "Invalid Change Order Number";
            public const string InvalidDescription = "Invalid Change Order " +
                "Description";
            public const string InvalidStatus = "Must Have " +
                "Status Assigned";
            public const string InvalidContractor = "Must Have Contractor " +
                "Assigned";
        }

        protected override void PopulateMessages()
        {
            // Add the rule messages
            this.Messages.Add(MessageKeys.InvalidNumber,
                "The same Change Order number cannot be used for the " +
                "current project, and there cannot be any gaps between " +
                "Change Order numbers.");

            this.Messages.Add(MessageKeys.InvalidDescription,
                "The Change Order must have a description");

            this.Messages.Add(MessageKeys.InvalidContractor,
                "The Change Order must have a Company assigned to the " +
                "Contractor property.");
        }
    }
}
```

The main idea to take away from this class is that it inherits the BrokenRuleMessages class, and because of this I am able to return an instance of it from the ChangeOrder class's GetBrokenRuleMessages method override.

The end result of this refactoring is that now my Entity classes can be validated with even less code in them, and they are even more focused on nothing but the business logic.

The Change Order Repository Implementation

After going over the `IChangeOrderRepository` interface in the Design section, it is now time to explain how the `ChangeOrder` class is actually persisted to and from the data store by the Change Order Repository. In this section, I will be writing the code for the Change Order Repository.

The BuildChildCallbacks Method

It should be like clockwork now: it is time to implement the Template Method pattern that I have been using in the repositories for getting Entity Root instances, and that means that the `BuildChildCallbacks` method has to be overridden in the `ChangeOrderRepository`.

```
#region BuildChildCallbacks

protected override void BuildChildCallbacks()
{
    this.ChildCallbacks.Add(CompanyFactory.FieldNames.CompanyId,
        this.AppendContractor);
    this.ChildCallbacks.Add("RoutingItems",
        delegate(ChangeOrder co, object childKeyName)
        {
            this.AppendRoutingItems(co);
        });
}

#endregion
```

The AppendContractor Callback

The first entry made in the `ChildCallbacks` dictionary is for the `AppendContractor` method. Thanks to the `CompanyService` class's `GetCompany` method, this method's code is very simple:

```
private void AppendContractor(ChangeOrder co, object contractorKey)
{
    co.Contractor = CompanyService.GetCompany(contractorKey);
}
```

The AppendRoutingItems Callback

The last entry made in the `ChildCallbacks` dictionary is for the `AppendRoutingItems` method. Thanks to the `ProjectService` class's `GetProjectContact` method, this method's code is very simple:

```
private void AppendRoutingItems(ChangeOrder co)
{
    StringBuilder builder = new StringBuilder(100);
    builder.Append(string.Format("SELECT * FROM {0}RoutingItem tri ",
        this.EntityName));
    builder.Append(" INNER JOIN RoutingItem ri ON");
    builder.Append(" tri.RoutingItemID = ri.RoutingItemID");
```

(continued)

(continued)

```
            builder.Append(" INNER JOIN Discipline d ON");
            builder.Append(" ri.DisciplineID = d.DisciplineID");
            builder.Append(string.Format(" WHERE tri.{0} = '{1}';",
                this.KeyFieldName, co.Key));
            using (IDataReader reader = this.ExecuteReader(builder.ToString()))
            {
                while (reader.Read())
                {
                    co.RoutingItems.Add(TransmittalFactory.BuildRoutingItem(
                        co.ProjectKey, reader));
                }
            }
        }
```

This code is almost identical to the code for the `AppendRoutingItems` in the `SqlCeRoutableTransmittalRepository` class. In fact, it actually uses the `TransmittalFactory` class to build the instances of the `RoutingItem` class from the `IDataReader` instance.

The FindBy Method

The `FindBy` method is very similar to the other `FindBy` methods in the other Repository implementations. The only part that is really different is the SQL query that is being used.

```
        public IList<ChangeOrder> FindBy(Project project)
        {
            StringBuilder builder = this.GetBaseQueryBuilder();
            builder.Append(string.Format(" WHERE ProjectID = '{0}';",
                project.Key));
            return this.BuildEntitiesFromSql(builder.ToString());
        }
```

This method should also probably be refactored into a separate class, but I will leave that as an exercise to be done later.

The GetPreviousAuthorizedAmountFrom Method

The purpose of this method is to get the total number of Change Orders for the particular Project that occurred before the current Change Order being passed in.

```
        public decimal GetPreviousAuthorizedAmountFrom(ChangeOrder co)
        {
            StringBuilder builder = new StringBuilder(100);
            builder.Append("SELECT SUM(AmountChanged) FROM ChangeOrder ");
            builder.Append(string.Format("WHERE ProjectID = '{0}' ",
                co.ProjectKey.ToString()));
            builder.Append(string.Format("AND ChangeOrderNumber < '{1}';",
                co.Number));
            object previousAuthorizedAmountResult =
                this.Database.ExecuteScalar(
                this.Database.GetSqlStringCommand(builder.ToString()));
            return previousAuthorizedAmountResult != null ?
                Convert.ToDecimal(previousAuthorizedAmountResult) : 0;
        }
```

It builds an SQL statement to get the total amount from the `ChangeOrder` table, and then uses the Microsoft Enterprise Library's `ExecuteScalar` method to retrieve the value from the query. It then checks to see whether the value is null, and if it is null, it returns a value of zero instead.

The GetPreviousTimeChangedTotalFrom Method

This method is very similar in implementation to the previous method. Its purpose is to get the total number of days that have been added or subtracted from the Project before the current Change Order being passed in.

```
public int GetPreviousTimeChangedTotalFrom(ChangeOrder co)
{
    StringBuilder builder = new StringBuilder(100);
    builder.Append("SELECT SUM(TimeChangedDays) FROM ChangeOrder ");
    builder.Append(string.Format("WHERE ProjectID = '{0}' ",
        co.ProjectKey.ToString()));
    builder.Append(string.Format("AND ChangeOrderNumber < '{0}';",
        co.Number));
    object previousTimeChangedTotalResult =
        this.Database.ExecuteScalar(
        this.Database.GetSqlStringCommand(builder.ToString()));
    return previousTimeChangedTotalResult != null ?
        Convert.ToInt32(previousTimeChangedTotalResult) : 0;
}
```

It also builds an SQL query, only this query is to get the total number of days that have been added or subtracted, and it also uses the Microsoft Enterprise Library's `ExecuteScalar` method to get the result of the query. As before, I make a check to see whether the value is null, and if the value is null, then I return a value of zero.

Unit of Work Implementation

Following the same steps that I have shown before to implement the Unit of Work pattern, I only need to override the `PersistNewItem(ChangeOrder item)` and `PersistUpdatedItem(ChangeOrder item)` methods.

The `PersistNewItem` Method

The first method override for the Change Order's Unit of Work implementation is the `PersistNewItem` method:

```
protected override void PersistNewItem(ChangeOrder item)
{
    StringBuilder builder = new StringBuilder(100);
    builder.Append(string.Format("INSERT INTO ChangeOrder
({0},{1},{2},{3},{4},{5},{6},{7},{8},{9},{10},{11},{12},{13},{14},{15},{16}) ",
        ChangeOrderFactory.FieldNames.ChangeOrderId,
        ProjectFactory.FieldNames.ProjectId,
        ChangeOrderFactory.FieldNames.ChangeOrderNumber,
        ChangeOrderFactory.FieldNames.EffectiveDate,
        CompanyFactory.FieldNames.CompanyId,
        ChangeOrderFactory.FieldNames.Description,
        ChangeOrderFactory.FieldNames.PriceChangeType,
```

(continued)

(continued)

```
                    ChangeOrderFactory.FieldNames.PriceChangeTypeDirection,
                    ChangeOrderFactory.FieldNames.AmountChanged,
                    ChangeOrderFactory.FieldNames.TimeChangeDirection,
                    ChangeOrderFactory.FieldNames.TimeChangedDays,
                    ChangeOrderFactory.FieldNames.ItemStatusId,
                    ChangeOrderFactory.FieldNames.AgencyApprovedDate,
                    ChangeOrderFactory.FieldNames.DateToField,
                    ChangeOrderFactory.FieldNames.OwnerSignatureDate,
                    ChangeOrderFactory.FieldNames.ArchitectSignatureDate,
                    ChangeOrderFactory.FieldNames.ContractorSignatureDate
                    ));
                builder.Append(string.Format("VALUES
({0},{1},{2},{3},{4},{5},{6},{7},{8},{9},{10},{11},{12},{13},{14},{15},{16});",
                    DataHelper.GetSqlValue(item.Key),
                    DataHelper.GetSqlValue(item.ProjectKey),
                    DataHelper.GetSqlValue(item.Number),
                    DataHelper.GetSqlValue(item.EffectiveDate),
                    DataHelper.GetSqlValue(item.Contractor.Key),
                    DataHelper.GetSqlValue(item.Description),
                    DataHelper.GetSqlValue(item.ChangeType),
                    DataHelper.GetSqlValue(item.PriceChangeDirection),
                    DataHelper.GetSqlValue(item.AmountChanged),
                    DataHelper.GetSqlValue(item.TimeChangeDirection),
                    DataHelper.GetSqlValue(item.TimeChanged),
                    DataHelper.GetSqlValue(item.Status.Id),
                    DataHelper.GetSqlValue(item.AgencyApprovedDate),
                    DataHelper.GetSqlValue(item.DateToField),
                    DataHelper.GetSqlValue(item.OwnerSignatureDate),
                    DataHelper.GetSqlValue(item.ArchitectSignatureDate),
                    DataHelper.GetSqlValue(item.ContractorSignatureDate)));

                this.Database.ExecuteNonQuery(
                    this.Database.GetSqlStringCommand(builder.ToString()));

                // Now do the child objects
                this.InsertRoutingItems(item);
            }
```

The code builds up a large insert statement composed of the values from the `ChangeOrder` instance and then executes the query using the Microsoft Enterprise Library's `Database` object. After the insert statement has been executed, I then have to account for inserting the `RoutingItem` instances for the `ChangeOrder`. I do this by calling the `InsertRoutingItems` method, which is almost identical to the same method in the `SqlCeRoutableTransmittalRepository` class:

```
        private void InsertRoutingItems(ChangeOrder co)
        {
            foreach (RoutingItem item in co.RoutingItems)
            {
                this.InsertRoutingItem(item, co.Key);
            }
        }
```

And this code does a basic loop through all of the `RoutingItem` instances in the list and calls the `InsertRoutingItem` method for each one. I am not going to show the code for that method as it is identical to the one in the `SqlCeRoutableTransmittalRepository` class. This definitely signals to me that this code needs to be refactored, but for now I will just flag it to be refactored at a later time.

The PersistUpdatedItem Method

`PersistUpdatedItem` first does an update to the `ChangeOrder` table:

```
protected override void PersistUpdatedItem(ChangeOrder item)
        {
            StringBuilder builder = new StringBuilder(100);
            builder.Append("UPDATE ChangeOrder SET ");

            builder.Append(string.Format("{0} = {1}",
                ChangeOrderFactory.FieldNames.ChangeOrderNumber,
                DataHelper.GetSqlValue(item.Number)));

            builder.Append(string.Format(",{0} = {1}",
                ChangeOrderFactory.FieldNames.EffectiveDate,
                DataHelper.GetSqlValue(item.EffectiveDate)));

            builder.Append(string.Format(",{0} = {1}",
                ChangeOrderFactory.FieldNames.OwnerSignatureDate,
                DataHelper.GetSqlValue(item.OwnerSignatureDate)));

            /*************************************************************/

            builder.Append(string.Format(",{0} = {1}",
                ChangeOrderFactory.FieldNames.ArchitectSignatureDate,
                DataHelper.GetSqlValue(item.ArchitectSignatureDate)));

            builder.Append(string.Format(",{0} = {1}",
                ChangeOrderFactory.FieldNames.ContractorSignatureDate,
                DataHelper.GetSqlValue(item.ContractorSignatureDate)));

            builder.Append(" ");
            builder.Append(this.BuildBaseWhereClause(item.Key));

            this.Database.ExecuteNonQuery(
                this.Database.GetSqlStringCommand(builder.ToString()));

            // Now do the child objects

            // First, delete the existing ones
            this.DeleteRoutingItems(item);

            // Now, add the current ones
            this.InsertRoutingItems(item);
        }
```

I have omitted several lines of repetitive code building the SQL update statement in the middle of the code in order to try to save you from the boring code.

The second part of the method then uses the `DeleteRoutingItems` helper method to delete all of the `RoutingItem` child objects of the Change Order and then uses the also newly refactored `InsertRoutingItems` helper method to add the existing `RoutingItem` child objects from the Change Order to the database.

The Change Order Service Implementation

Like the other Service classes shown in the domain model so far, the `ChangeOrderService` class is responsible for retrieving and wrapping the methods of its associated Repository interface, in this case the `IChangeOrderRepository` instance:

```
using System;
using System.Collections.Generic;
using SmartCA.Model.Projects;
using SmartCA.Infrastructure;
using SmartCA.Infrastructure.RepositoryFramework;

namespace SmartCA.Model.ChangeOrders
{
    public static class ChangeOrderService
    {
        private static IChangeOrderRepository repository;
        private static IUnitOfWork unitOfWork;

        static ChangeOrderService()
        {
            ChangeOrderService.unitOfWork = new UnitOfWork();
            ChangeOrderService.repository =
                RepositoryFactory.GetRepository<IChangeOrderRepository,
                ChangeOrder>(ChangeOrderService.unitOfWork);
        }

        public static IList<ChangeOrder>
            GetChangeOrders(Project project)
        {
            return ChangeOrderService.repository.FindBy(project);
        }

        public static void SaveChangeOrder(ChangeOrder co)
        {
            ChangeOrderService.repository[co.Key] = co;
            ChangeOrderService.unitOfWork.Commit();
        }

        public static decimal GetPreviousAuthorizedAmountFrom(ChangeOrder co)
        {
            return
                ChangeOrderService.repository.GetPreviousAuthorizedAmountFrom(co);
        }

        public static int GetPreviousTimeChangedTotalFrom(ChangeOrder co)
        {
            return
```

```
                ChangeOrderService.repository.GetPreviousTimeChangedTotalFrom(co);
            }
        }
    }
```

These are the only methods needed for now, but others could easily be added later, such as a method for removing Change Orders.

The Change Order View Model Class

Following the same patterns for all `ViewModel` classes as before, the `ChangeOrderViewModel` class adapts the Change Order Aggregate from the domain model to the UI. It follows the usual pattern of inheriting from the `ViewModel` class introduced previously:

```
using System;
using System.Collections.Generic;
using SmartCA.Infrastructure.UI;
using SmartCA.Model.ChangeOrders;
using System.Windows.Data;
using SmartCA.Model;
using SmartCA.Model.Transmittals;
using System.ComponentModel;
using SmartCA.Application;
using SmartCA.Model.Submittals;
using SmartCA.Model.Companies;

namespace SmartCA.Presentation.ViewModels
{
    public class ChangeOrderViewModel : ViewModel
```

The Constructor

Again, there are not any new concepts being introduced in the constructor code for this class, I am just following the same patterns as laid out in the previous chapters. Here are the constructors for the `ChangeOrderViewModel` class:

```
        #region Constructors

        public ChangeOrderViewModel()
            : this(null)
        {
        }

        public ChangeOrderViewModel(IView view)
            : base(view)
        {
            this.currentChangeOrder = null;
            this.changeOrderList = new List<ChangeOrder>(
                ChangeOrderService.GetChangeOrders(UserSession.CurrentProject));
            this.changeOrders = new CollectionView(this.changeOrderList);
            this.contractors = CompanyService.GetAllCompanies();
```

(continued)

(continued)

```
            this.priceChangeTypesView = new
                CollectionView(Enum.GetNames(typeof(PriceChangeType)));
            string[] changeDirections = Enum.GetNames(typeof(ChangeDirection));
            this.priceChangeDirections = new CollectionView(changeDirections);
            this.timeChangeDirections = new CollectionView(changeDirections);
            this.itemStatuses = SubmittalService.GetItemStatuses();
            this.routingItems = new BindingList<RoutingItem>();
            this.disciplines = SubmittalService.GetDisciplines();
            this.saveCommand = new DelegateCommand(this.SaveCommandHandler);
            this.newCommand = new DelegateCommand(this.NewCommandHandler);
            this.deleteRoutingItemCommand =
                new DelegateCommand(this.DeleteRoutingItemCommandHandler);
        }

        #endregion
```

I am making good use of the `ChangeOrderService` and the `SubmittalService` classes to retrieve the necessary data for the dropdowns in the UI. Note how I am also exposing the enumeration data types as `CollectionView` instances here. You may wonder why I am using two different `CollectionView` objects to represent the `ChangeDirection` enumeration. I am using them to represent two different properties, `PriceChangeDirection` and `TimeChangeDirection`, and because of the synchronization that WPF uses, if I do not use two separate instances, whenever one is changed, the other will change its value to be the same as the first.

The Properties

All of the properties in the `ChangeOrderViewModel` class are read-only, except for the `CurrentChangeOrder` property:

```
        public ChangeOrder CurrentChangeOrder
        {
            get { return this.currentChangeOrder; }
            set
            {
                if (this.currentChangeOrder != value)
                {
                    this.currentChangeOrder = value;
                    this.OnPropertyChanged(
                        Constants.CurrentChangeOrderPropertyName);
                    this.saveCommand.IsEnabled =
                        (this.currentChangeOrder != null);
                    this.PopulateRoutingItems();
                }
            }
        }
```

The getter for the property is pretty simple, but the property's setter is a little bit more interesting. It is following the same pattern as before, by first checking to see whether the value being set is actually a different `ChangeOrder` instance. If it is, then the `currentChangeOrder` field is set to the setter's value, and the `PropertyChanged` event is raised. Also, the `saveCommand` field's `IsEnabled` property is set to true if the `currentChangeOrder` field's value is not null. Last, the `RoutingItems` property value is initialized based on the `currentChangeOrder` field's `RoutingItems` property value via the `PopulateRoutingItems` private method.

The Command Handler Methods

The only command handler methods that I need to override in the `ChangeOrderViewModel` class are the `SaveCommandHandler` and `NewCommandHandler` methods. Again, I do not have to worry about deletes because the `DeleteCommandHandler` method is completely taken care of by the base class.

The NewCommandHandler method

Here is the code for the `NewCommandHandler` method:

```
protected void NewCommandHandler(object sender, EventArgs e)
{
    object projectKey = this.currentChangeOrder.ProjectKey;
    this.currentChangeOrder = null;
    this.routingItems.Clear();
    this.CurrentObjectState = ObjectState.New;
    this.OnPropertyChanged(
        Constants.CurrentChangeOrderPropertyName);
    ChangeOrder newChangeOrder = new ChangeOrder(
                                projectKey,
                                this.currentChangeOrder.Number + 1);
    this.changeOrderList.Add(newChangeOrder);
    this.changeOrders.Refresh();
    this.changeOrders.MoveCurrentToLast();
}
```

This method starts out by obtaining the `ProjectKey` property value of the old Change Order instance (the `currentChangeOrder` field). It then sets the `currentChangeOrder` field to null, clears the `RoutingItems` property, and sets the state of the `ViewModel` to `New`. Next, it raises the `PropertyChanged` event so the UI can clear its screen. Then, a new `ChangeOrder` instance is created and initialized with the old `ProjectKey` property value saved on the first line of the method, and the current Change Order Number plus one. Finally, the new `ChangeOrder` instance is added to the list of Change Orders (the `changeOrdersList` field), and the wrapping `changeOrders CollectionView` field is then refreshed and directed to move the current Change Order to the last position.

The SaveCommandHandler Method

This method is responsible for validating and saving the currently selected Change Order instance.

```
protected void SaveCommandHandler(object sender, EventArgs e)
{
    if (this.currentChangeOrder != null &&
        this.currentChangeOrder.GetBrokenRules().Count == 0)
    {
        foreach (RoutingItem item in this.routingItems)
        {
            this.currentChangeOrder.RoutingItems.Add(item);
        }
        ChangeOrderService.SaveChangeOrder(this.currentChangeOrder);
    }
    this.CurrentObjectState = ObjectState.Existing;
}
```

It begins by making sure that the current Change Order is not null, and also calls the `GetBrokenRules` method to validate the state of the Change Order. Currently, I do not have anything wired up to handle any of the broken rules, but the hook is there for it. I probably would add another property to the ViewModel for the broken rules so the XAML could easily bind to it.

The next step after passing validation is to add all of the `RoutingItem` instances into the current Change Order, and then finally, to save the Change Order.

The Change Order View

The View for Change Orders is very similar to what has been seen in the past few chapters, where the list of Change Orders is on the left, and the currently selected Change Order is on the right. Following is what the form looks like at run time (see Figure 8.5).

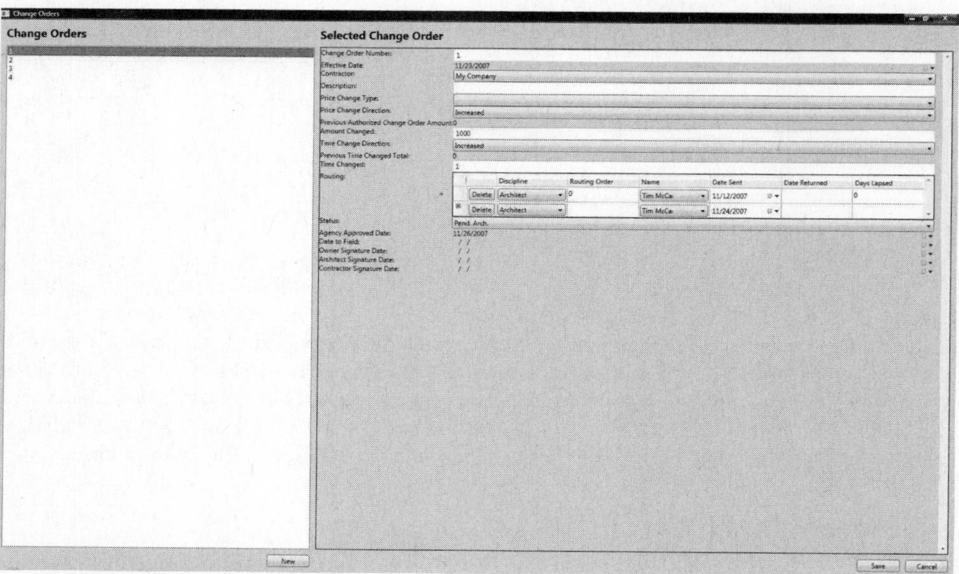

Figure 8.5: Change Order View.

There certainly is a lot more that I could be doing in the UI regarding validation, but that really is not the focus of this chapter or book. I want to keep the focus on the domain model, but at some point this application will definitely need to wire the validation for the domain model into the UI in an elegant way. The Microsoft Patterns and Practices team has actually built a Validation application block that I have not really tapped into in this book, but I imagine that I will later in the life of this code base.

Summary

In this chapter, I introduced the concept of a Change Order in the construction industry, and then I used this concept to model the Change Order Aggregate. I added quite a bit more behavior to my classes in this chapter, and the current Domain Model classes are certainly starting to get much richer than they were before. I also created a nice way of distinguishing the Aggregate Roots in the domain model by way of the `IAggregateRoot` interface. This concept is also heavily reinforced in the various Repository classes through the use of Generic Constraints constraining the repositories to use the `IAggregateRoot` interface for the Entity Roots that they are supporting. While I was refactoring again, I changed a good portion of the code base to rely on the `IEntity` interface instead of the `EntityBase` class. In fact, the `EntityBase` class itself implements the `IEntity` interface. Also involved in the refactoring was the creation of the new Generic `NumberSpecification<TCandidate>` class, which made nice use of the new `INumberedProjectChild` interface.

9

Construction Change Directives

In the last two chapters, I covered Proposal Requests and Change Orders, and in this chapter I will be showing you the last of the Change Order–related concepts, the Construction Change Directive.

The Problem

Sometimes a Change Order will be approved and signed off on by the Architect and the Owner, but not by the Contractor. The Contractor may not agree with the change in work, contract price, contract time, or both. This type of Change Order will be signed by the Owner and Architect but not by the Contractor. When this happens, the Contractor is obligated to go ahead with the work, with the price and time adjustments to be determined later by the Architect, utilizing standard industry guidelines.

The means to capture this type of change is the Construction Change Directive. At any time that the contractor later agrees to its terms or mutual agreement is obtained by adjustment of its terms, it is then turned into a Change Order. In the event that the contractor finds it impossible to accept the Architect's determination of changed cost and time, the Contractor's only other alternative at that point is mediation and arbitration.

Like RFIs, Proposal Requests, and Change Orders, each Construction Change Directive should also be serially numbered by Project.

The Design

In the SmartCA domain, a Change Order is one of the most important concepts for the entire application, and it also contains several important business concepts that must be closely tracked. In the next few sections, I will be designing the domain model, determining the Change Order Aggregate and its boundaries, and designing the Repository for Change Orders.

Designing the Domain Model

As stated earlier, the most important parts of the Construction Change Directive are the changes in contract time or price, as well as the proper ordering of the Construction Change Directive Number. I again will be using the Specification pattern to define the rules for the `Number` property, and the Specification that I create will also be part of the domain model. It is very important that the logic inside of the Construction Change Directive be correct for calculating the total price and time whenever one of those items is changed from the Construction Change Directive.

Figure 9.1 shows a drawing showing the relationships between the classes that combine to make up a Construction Change Directive.

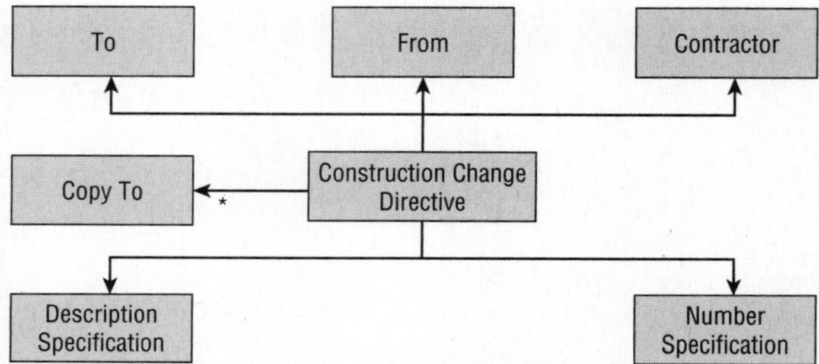

Figure 9.1: Construction Change Directive Aggregate.

In the diagram, the Construction Change Directive class is clearly the root of the Aggregate. The two most important attributes of the Construction Change Directive are the amount of time being changed and the amount of money being added. These are represented in the diagram by the Time Change and Price Change relationships, respectively. The relationship to the `Contractor` class shows the Contractor that has requested the Construction Change Directive.

The next important part of the diagram is the Construction Change Directive's relationship to the Routing Items. It is important for Smart Design to know to whom each Construction Change Directive has been routed internally, and the Discipline of that person, such as architect, engineer, or construction administrator. This was already created and used in Chapter 6; I am just reusing the same concept again in this Aggregate.

The relationship to the `Status` class shows exactly the state of the Construction Change Directive, such as completed or pending an architect review. The relationship to the Construction Change Directive Number Specification helps model the numbering rules of the Construction Change Directive.

Designing the Construction Change Directive Aggregate

The Construction Change Directive Aggregate does not have as many classes in it as some of the other Aggregates, but it definitely uses a lot of interfaces (see Figure 9.2)!

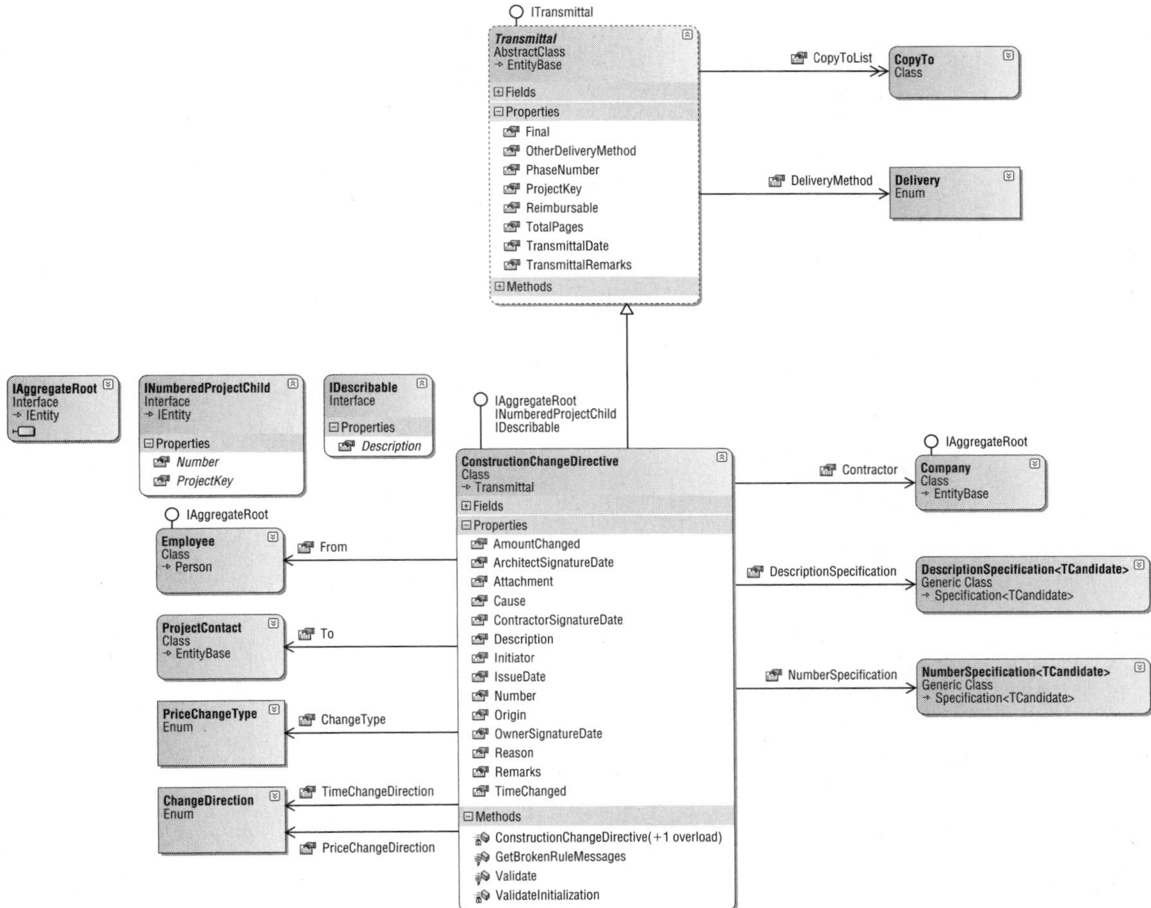

Figure 9.2: Classes Constituting the Construction Change Directive Aggregate.

As shown in the diagram, the `ConstructionChangeDirective` class inherits from the `Transmittal` class and implements the `IAggregateRoot`, `INumberedProjectChild`, and `IDescribable` interfaces. I have already covered what all of these interfaces are for, except for the `IDescribable` interface. This interface goes hand in hand with the `DescriptionSpecification<TCandidate>` class, and I will cover both of these later in the chapter.

Defining the Aggregate Boundaries

The `ConstructionChangeDirective` class has its own identity and is definitely the root of its own Aggregate (see Figure 9.3).

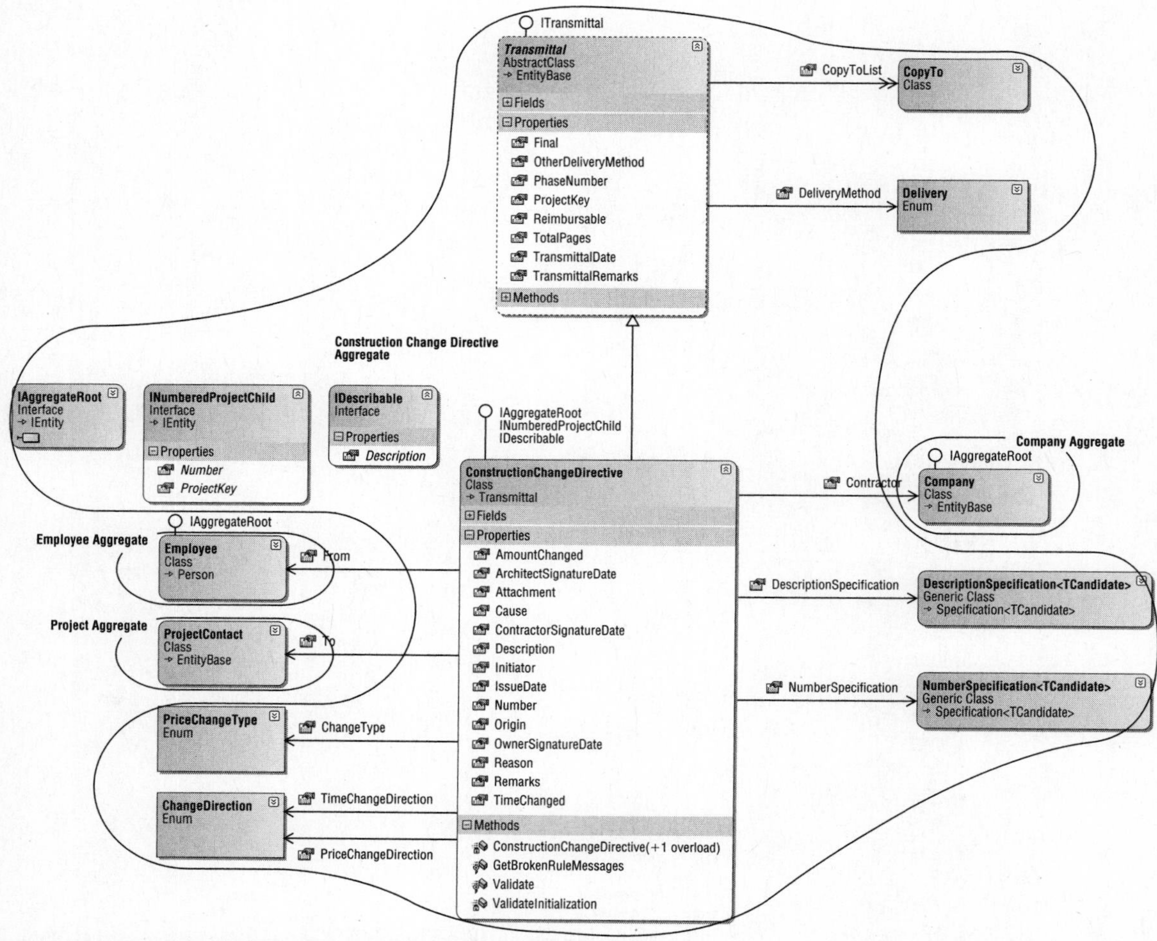

Figure 9.3: Construction Change Directive Aggregate Boundaries.

All of the other classes in the diagram, except for `Company`, `Employee`, and `ProjectContact` classes, belong to the Construction Change Directive Aggregate. The `Company` and `Employee` classes are actually the root of their own Aggregates, and the `ProjectContact` class is part of the Project Aggregate.

Designing the Repository

As you should definitely know by now, since the `ConstructionChangeDirective` class is its own Aggregate root, it will have its own repository.

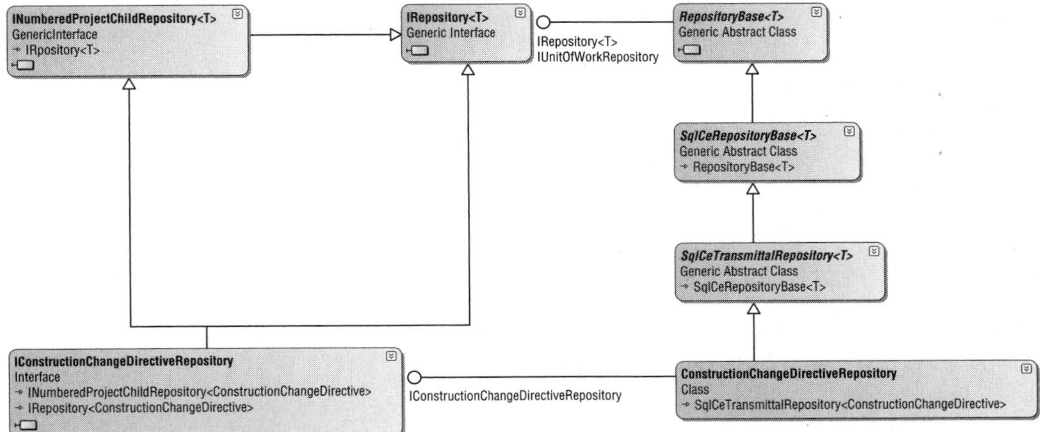

Figure 9.4: Construction Change Directive Repository.

Figure 9.4 should look familiar to you, as it is very similar to the Change Order Repository diagram from the last chapter.

The `IConstructionChangeDirectiveRepository` interface is the interface into instances of Construction Change Directive Repositories. Here is the `IConstructionChangeDirectiveRepository` interface:

```
using System;
using SmartCA.Model.NumberedProjectChildren;

namespace SmartCA.Model.ConstructionChangeDirectives
{
    public interface IConstructionChangeDirectiveRepository
        : INumberedProjectChildRepository<ConstructionChangeDirective>
    {
    }
}
```

As you can see, since the `ConstructionChangeDirective` class implements the `INumberedProjectChild` interface, it follows that the `IConstructionChangeDirectiveRepository` interface extends the `INumberedProjectChildRepository` interface. There are no methods in the `IConstructionChangeDirectiveRepository` interface, as you can see it is just merely extending the `INumberedProjectChildRepository` interface.

Writing the Unit Tests

Again, in this chapter, I am not going to show the unit tests in this section because they are essentially the same as most of the unit tests written in previous chapters. They are important; in fact I rely upon them very much as I refactor the code.

The Solution

The classes used to make up the Construction Change Directive Aggregate should look very familiar to you; I am at the point in the application architecture where I am starting to reuse many of the classes. The thing that is a little bit different from previous chapters is that now there is much more business logic to implement inside of the classes. This is because the Construction Change Directives deal with money, and these types of documents may literally be dealing with millions of dollars.

The Construction Change Directive Class Private Fields and Constructors

The `ConstructionChangeDirective` class inherits from the `Transmittal` class and passes its values from its constructors straight through to the `Transmittal` base class.

```
using System;
using SmartCA.Model.Transmittals;
using SmartCA.Infrastructure.DomainBase;
using SmartCA.Model.Companies;
using SmartCA.Model.Employees;
using SmartCA.Model.Projects;
using SmartCA.Model.ChangeOrders;
using SmartCA.Model.Description;
using SmartCA.Model.NumberedProjectChildren;

namespace SmartCA.Model.ConstructionChangeDirectives
{
    public class ConstructionChangeDirective
        : Transmittal, IAggregateRoot, INumberedProjectChild, IDescribable
    {
        private int number;
        private ProjectContact to;
        private Employee from;
        private DateTime? issueDate;
        private Company contractor;
        private string description;
        private string attachment;
        private string reason;
        private string initiator;
        private int cause;
        private int origin;
        private string remarks;
        private PriceChangeType? changeType;
        private ChangeDirection priceChangeDirection;
```

```
        private decimal amountChanged;
        private ChangeDirection timeChangeDirection;
        private int timeChanged;
        private DateTime? ownerSignatureDate;
        private DateTime? architectSignatureDate;
        private DateTime? contractorSignatureDate;
        private NumberSpecification<ConstructionChangeDirective>
numberSpecification;
        private DescriptionSpecification<ConstructionChangeDirective>
descriptionSpecification;
        private object changeOrderKey;
        private BrokenRuleMessages brokenRuleMessages;

        public ConstructionChangeDirective(object projectKey, int number)
            : this(null, projectKey, number)
        {
        }

        public ConstructionChangeDirective(object key, object projectKey,
            int number) : base(key, projectKey)
        {
            this.number = number;
            this.to = null;
            this.from = null;
            this.issueDate = null;
            this.contractor = null;
            this.description = string.Empty;
            this.attachment = string.Empty;
            this.reason = string.Empty;
            this.initiator = string.Empty;
            this.cause = 0;
            this.origin = 0;
            this.remarks = string.Empty;
            this.changeType = null;
            this.priceChangeDirection = ChangeDirection.Unchanged;
            this.amountChanged = 0;
            this.timeChangeDirection = ChangeDirection.Unchanged;
            this.timeChanged = 0;
            this.ownerSignatureDate = null;
            this.architectSignatureDate = null;
            this.contractorSignatureDate = null;
            this.numberSpecification =
                new NumberSpecification<ConstructionChangeDirective>();
            this.descriptionSpecification =
                new DescriptionSpecification<ConstructionChangeDirective>();
            this.changeOrderKey = null;
            this.ValidateInitialization();
            this.brokenRuleMessages =
                new ConstructionChangeDirectiveRuleMessages();
        }
```

Just like the `Submittal` and `RequestForInformation` classes, all of the data for the `ConstructionChangeDirective` class is initialized and validated in the second constructor, which is called by the first constructor.

The ValidateInitialization Method

The last action that happens in the `ConstructionChangeDirective` class initialization process is validation. A check is made via the `ValidateInitialization` method to ensure that, if the class is not passed in a `key` value, it contains a valid Construction Change Directive `number` and is associated with a `Project`.

```
            private void ValidateInitialization()
            {
                NumberedProjectChildValidator.ValidateInitialState(this,
                    "Construction Change Directive");
            }
```

The ConstructionChangeDirective Properties

A lot of the properties of the `ConstructionChangeDirective` class are very similar to those covered in previous Domain Model classes, so I am only going to cover those that are new here and also those that contain behavior.

The DescriptionSpecification Property

This property is designed to make sure that Construction Change Directives have a description associated with them. The `DescriptionSpecification` property is represented by the `DescriptionSpecification<T>` Generic class.

```
    public DescriptionSpecification<ConstructionChangeDirective>
    DescriptionSpecification
            {
                get { return this.descriptionSpecification; }
            }
```

Just as with the previously refactored `NumberSpecification< TCandidate>` class in last chapter, I have another situation with Description Specification implementations repeating themselves in the last couple of chapters, so I decided to refactor it, as well. As a result, I created the Generic Description Specification class; actually it is a .NET Generic `DescriptionSpecification<TCandidate>` class.

```
using System;
using SmartCA.Infrastructure.Specifications;
using SmartCA.Infrastructure.DomainBase;
using SmartCA.Model.Description;

namespace SmartCA.Model.Description
{
    public class DescriptionSpecification<TCandidate>
        : Specification<TCandidate> where TCandidate : IDescribable
    {
        public override bool IsSatisfiedBy(TCandidate candidate)
        {
            // The candidate must have a description
            return (!string.IsNullOrEmpty(candidate.Description));
        }
    }
}
```

This code is almost the same as the other Description Specification implementations, but again, I am using .NET Generics to make it reusable. I will compare the signature of this class to the non-Generic class that would have been created. Here is the old way of implementing this:

```
public class ConstructionChangeDirectiveDescriptionSpecification :
Specification<ConstructionChangeDirective>
```

Here is the new way:

```
public class DescriptionSpecification<TCandidate> : Specification<TCandidate> where
    TCandidate : IDescribable
```

Again, just like the `NumberSpecification<TCandidate>` class, the trick here is using the constraints on the `TCandidate` Generic parameter. By declaring that the `TCandidate` Generic parameter has to implement the `IDescribable` interface, I now have strongly typed access to its properties (via the `TCandidate candidate` argument) in the `IsSatisfied` method. All I want is access to the `Description` property so that I can validate it, and the `IDescribable` interface gives me exactly that:

```
using System;

namespace SmartCA.Model.Description
{
    public interface IDescribable
    {
        string Description { get; set; }
    }
}
```

The signature for the `ConstructionChangeDirective` class shows that it now implements this interface:

```
public class ConstructionChangeDirective
        : Transmittal, IAggregateRoot, INumberedChild, IDescribable
```

I also went back and refactored the `DescriptionSpecification` properties on the `ProposalRequest` and `RequestForInformation` classes to use the new `DescriptionSpecification<TCandidate>` class.

The HasBeenTransformedToChangeOrder Property

This property signifies whether the `ConstructionChangeDirective` has been converted to a `ChangeOrder` instance. If you remember from the beginning of the chapter, one of the interesting characteristics of a Construction Change Directive is that once the Contractor agrees with the terms of the Construction Change Directive, it can then be turned into a Change Order. This property represents whether or not that transformation has happened.

```
        public bool HasBeenTransformedToChangeOrder
        {
            get { return (this.changeOrderKey != null); }
        }
```

The way I am keeping track of this is by using the `changeOrderKey` field; this field will get populated once the `ConstructionChangeDirective` has been transformed into a `ChangeOrder`, and it will contain the value of the key for the `ChangeOrder`.

The Validate Method

Taking advantage of the mini-validation framework that was built in the last chapter, here is the `Validate` method override for the `ConstructionChangeDirective` class:

```
        protected override void Validate()
        {
            if (!this.numberSpecification.IsSatisfiedBy(this))
            {
                this.AddBrokenRule(
                    NumberedProjectChildrenRuleMessageKeys.InvalidNumber);
            }
            if (!(this.descriptionSpecification.IsSatisfiedBy(this)))
            {
                this.AddBrokenRule(
                    DescriptionRuleMessageKeys.InvalidDescription);
            }
            if (this.contractor == null)
            {
                this.AddBrokenRule(

ConstructionChangeDirectiveRuleMessages.MessageKeys.InvalidContractor);
            }
        }
```

You may notice in the code block above that I am now putting the rule constants classes with their respective class families, that is, the description messages are now centralized in the `DescriptionRuleMessageKeys` class:

```
using System;

namespace SmartCA.Model.Description
{
    internal static class DescriptionRuleMessageKeys
    {
        public const string InvalidDescription =
            "Invalid Description property value";
    }
}
```

Here is the `ConstructionChangeDirectiveRuleMessages` class:

```
using System;
using SmartCA.Infrastructure.DomainBase;
using SmartCA.Model.NumberedProjectChildren;
using SmartCA.Model.Description;

namespace SmartCA.Model.ConstructionChangeDirectives
{
```

```
    public class ConstructionChangeDirectiveRuleMessages
        : BrokenRuleMessages
    {
        internal static class MessageKeys
        {
            public const string InvalidContractor = "Must Have Contractor " +
                "Assigned";
        }

        protected override void PopulateMessages()
        {
            // Add the rule messages
            this.Messages.Add(DescriptionRuleMessageKeys.InvalidDescription,
                "The Construction Change Directive must have a description");

            this.Messages.Add(MessageKeys.InvalidContractor,
                "The Construction Change Directive must have a Company assigned " +
                "to the Contractor property.");
        }
    }
}
```

Just as in the last chapter, this class inherits from the `BrokenRuleMessages` class, and because of this I am able to return an instance of it from the `ConstructionChangeDirective` class's `GetBrokenRuleMessages` method override.

The TransformToChangeOrder Method

As mentioned already, this method essentially promoted the `ConstructionChangeDirective` up to a `ChangeOrder` instance:

```
        public ChangeOrder TransformToChangeOrder()
        {
            ChangeOrder co = null;

            // See if it has already been transformed into a
            // Change Order...it can only be changed once!
            if (!this.HasBeenTransformedToChangeOrder)
            {
                Project project = ProjectService.GetProject(this.ProjectKey);
                co = NumberedProjectChildFactory.CreateNumberedProjectChild
                    <ChangeOrder>(project);
                co.AmountChanged = this.amountChanged;
                co.ArchitectSignatureDate = this.architectSignatureDate;
                co.ChangeType = this.changeType;
                co.Contractor = this.contractor;
                co.ContractorSignatureDate = this.contractorSignatureDate;
                co.Description = this.description;
                co.OwnerSignatureDate = this.ownerSignatureDate;
                co.PriceChangeDirection = this.priceChangeDirection;
                co.TimeChanged = this.timeChanged;
                co.TimeChangeDirection = this.timeChangeDirection;
            }
```

(continued)

(continued)

```
            else
            {
                // It was already changed, so get the Change Order that it was
                // changed into
                co = ChangeOrderService.GetChangeOrder(this.changeOrderKey);
            }

            // Get the key of the Change Order
            this.changeOrderKey = co.Key;

            // Return the instance
            return co;
        }
```

This method starts out by first testing whether the `ConstructionChangeDirective` has already been transformed. If it has not, then a new instance is created, and if it has, then it uses the `changeOrderKey` field to pass into the `ChangeOrderService`'s `GetChangeOrder` method to get the existing `ChangeOrder` instance.

The interesting part about the method is where it has to create a new instance of the `ChangeOrder`. Specifically, it uses a new `Factory` class to get a correctly initialized ChangeOrder instance with the correct `Number` value applied to it. This class is the `NumberedProjectChildFactory` class.

The NumberedProjectChildFactory Class

The sole responsibility of this class is to create instances of classes that implement the `INumberedProjectChild` interface that are properly numbered:

```
using System;
using SmartCA.Infrastructure.DomainBase;
using SmartCA.Infrastructure.RepositoryFramework;
using System.Collections.Generic;
using System.Linq;
using SmartCA.Model.Projects;

namespace SmartCA.Model.NumberedProjectChildren
{
    public static class NumberedProjectChildFactory
    {
        public static T CreateNumberedProjectChild<T>(Project project)
            where T : EntityBase, IAggregateRoot, INumberedProjectChild
        {
            // Initialize the NumberedProjectChild return value
            T newNumberedProjectChild = default(T);

            // Get the correct repository using the Repository Factory
            INumberedProjectChildRepository<T> repository =
                RepositoryFactory.GetRepository
                <INumberedProjectChildRepository<T>, T>();

            // Get all of the items in the Aggregate from the FindBy method
```

```
            IList<T> numberedProjectChildren = repository.FindBy(project);

            // Use LINQ to get the last numbered item in the list
            // and increment it by 1
            int newNumber = numberedProjectChildren.Last().Number + 1;

            // Create the instance, passing in the projectKey value as well
            // as the new number to the constructor of the INumberedProjectChild
            // instance, and then casting it to the correct type (T)
            newNumberedProjectChild = Activator.CreateInstance(typeof(T),
                new object[] { project.Key, newNumber }) as T;

            // Return the newly initialized object
            return newNumberedProjectChild;
        }
    }
}
```

Notice that the `CreateNumberedProjectChild` method is a Generic method and that it is using constraints on the Generic parameter `T` to ensure that the parameter is an `EntityBase` type that implements the `IAggregateRoot` and `INumberedProjectChild` interfaces. It has to implement `IAggregateRoot` in order to have a repository associated with it, and it must implement the `INumberedProjectChild` interface in order to be able to call the `FindBy(Project project)` method on the repository.

The method starts out by declaring and initializing the `newNumberedProjectChild` variable to its default value. It then uses the `RepositoryFactory` to get the correct `INumberedProjectChildRepository` instance. Once the repository is retrieved, then it uses it to get the list of all items in the repository by Project. I next use a LINQ extension method (`Last`) on the `List<T>` class to find the last item in the list, then get the `Number` property of the item and add one to its value to create the new number for the soon-to-be-created `INumberedProjectChild` instance. I then use Reflection to create the `INumberedProjectChild` instance, and pass the new number value as well as the `Key` value of the `Project` instance to the `INumberedProjectChild` instance's constructor in the `CreateInstance` method. Finally, the newly created and initialized `INumberedProjectChild` instance, represented by the `newNumberedProjectChild` variable, is returned.

The Construction Change Directive Repository Implementation

After going over the `IConstructionChangeDirectiveRepository` interface in the Design section, it is now time to show in code how the `ConstructionChangeDirective` class actually gets persisted to and from the data store by the Construction Change Directive Repository. In this section, I will be writing the code for the Construction Change Directive Repository.

The BuildChildCallbacks Method

Now that I have finished going over the `IConstructionChangeDirectiveRepository` interface, it is time to build the `ConstructionChangeDirective` class. Again, most of the work is done in the `SqlCeRepositoryBase<T>` class. If you have been following along, you know that from the application's Template Method pattern implementation that I have been using in the Repositories for getting Entity Root instances, the `BuildChildCallbacks` method must be overridden in the `ConstructionChangeDirectiveRepository`.

```
#region BuildChildCallbacks

protected override void BuildChildCallbacks()
{
    this.ChildCallbacks.Add(
        ProposalRequestFactory.FieldNames.ProjectContactId,
        this.AppendTo);
    this.ChildCallbacks.Add(
        ProposalRequestFactory.FieldNames.EmployeeId,
        this.AppendFrom);
    this.ChildCallbacks.Add(CompanyFactory.FieldNames.CompanyId,
        this.AppendContractor);
    base.BuildChildCallbacks();
}

#endregion
```

There is nothing really new in this method; it is just following the same pattern as laid out in earlier chapters.

The AppendTo Callback

```
private void AppendTo(ConstructionChangeDirective ccd,
    object toProjectContactKey)
{
    ccd.To = ProjectService.GetProjectContact(
        ccd.ProjectKey, toProjectContactKey);
}
```

Again, this method is very similar to the other `AppendTo` methods from some of the other Repositories.

The AppendFrom Callback

```
private void AppendFrom(ConstructionChangeDirective ccd,
    object fromEmployeeKey)
{
    ccd.From =
        EmployeeService.GetEmployee(fromEmployeeKey);
}
```

Same thing here with the `AppendFrom` method—it is nice that all of this stuff is already built for me!

The AppendContractor Callback

The last entry made in the `ChildCallbacks` dictionary is for the `AppendContractor` method. Thanks to the `CompanyService` class's `GetCompany` method, this method's code is also very simple:

```
private void AppendContractor(ConstructionChangeDirective ccd,
    object contractorKey)
{
    ccd.Contractor = CompanyService.GetCompany(contractorKey);
}
```

The FindBy Method

I talked about refactoring this method in the last chapter. The same code is repeated for it in different repositories, so here is the newly refactored method.

```
        public IList<ConstructionChangeDirective> FindBy(Project project)
        {
            return
                NumberedProjectChildRepositoryHelper.FindBy
                <ConstructionChangeDirective>(this, project);
        }
```

As you can see, all of the functionality of the method has been factored out into the `NumberedProjectChildRepositoryHelper` class. This class is a static class with one Generic method, `FindBy`:

```
using System;
using System.Collections.Generic;
using SmartCA.Model.Projects;
using System.Text;
using SmartCA.Infrastructure.DomainBase;
using SmartCA.Model.NumberedProjectChildren;

namespace SmartCA.Infrastructure.Repositories.NumberedProjectChildren
{
    public static class NumberedProjectChildRepositoryHelper
    {
        public static IList<T> FindBy<T>(SqlCeRepositoryBase<T> repository,
            Project project) where T : IAggregateRoot, INumberedProjectChild
        {
            StringBuilder builder = new StringBuilder(100);
            builder.Append(repository.BaseQuery);
            builder.Append(string.Format(" WHERE ProjectID = '{0}';",
                project.Key));
            return repository.BuildEntitiesFromSql(builder);
        }
    }
}
```

This code looks pretty similar to the `CreateNumberedProjectChild` method of the `NumberedProjectChildFactory` class. They are both Generic methods and make heavy use of constraints, and both are constraining the Generic parameter to implement the `IAggregateRoot` and `INumberedProjectChild` interfaces.

This method actually takes an instance of the `SqlCeRepositoryBase<T>` class, as well as a `Project` instance. The body of the method should look pretty familiar; it is just factoring out the code that would have been in the `ConstructionChangeDirectiveRepository` implementation. This method was made possible by the `SqlCeRepositoryBase<T>` instance, an argument of the method, and this pattern is known as inversion of control.

Unit of Work Implementation

Following the same steps that I have shown before to implement the Unit of Work pattern, I now need to override the `PersistNewItem(ConstructionChangeDirective item)` and `PersistUpdatedItem(ConstructionChangeDirective item)` methods.

The PersistNewItem Method

The first method override for the `ConstructionChangeDirective`'s Unit of Work implementation is the `PersistNewItem` method.

```
        protected override void PersistNewItem(ConstructionChangeDirective item)
        {
            StringBuilder builder = new StringBuilder(100);
            builder.Append(string.Format("INSERT INTO ConstructionChangeDirective
({0},{1},{2},{3},{4},{5},{6},{7},{8},{9},{10},{11},{12},{13},{14},{15},{16},{17},
{18},{19},{20},{21},{22},{23},{24},{25},{26},{27},{28},{29}) ",

ConstructionChangeDirectiveFactory.FieldNames.ConstructionChangeDirectiveId,
                ProjectFactory.FieldNames.ProjectId,
ConstructionChangeDirectiveFactory.FieldNames.ConstructionChangeDirectiveNumber,
                TransmittalFactory.FieldNames.TransmittalDate,
                ProjectFactory.FieldNames.ProjectContactId,
                EmployeeFactory.FieldNames.EmployeeId,
                TransmittalFactory.FieldNames.TotalPages,
                TransmittalFactory.FieldNames.DeliveryMethod,
                TransmittalFactory.FieldNames.OtherDeliveryMethod,
                TransmittalFactory.FieldNames.PhaseNumber,
                TransmittalFactory.FieldNames.Reimbursable,
                TransmittalFactory.FieldNames.Final,
                ConstructionChangeDirectiveFactory.FieldNames.IssueDate,
                CompanyFactory.FieldNames.CompanyId,
                ConstructionChangeDirectiveFactory.FieldNames.Description,
                ConstructionChangeDirectiveFactory.FieldNames.Attachment,
                ConstructionChangeDirectiveFactory.FieldNames.Reason,
                ConstructionChangeDirectiveFactory.FieldNames.Initiator,
                ConstructionChangeDirectiveFactory.FieldNames.Cause,
                ConstructionChangeDirectiveFactory.FieldNames.Origin,
                ConstructionChangeDirectiveFactory.FieldNames.Remarks,
                TransmittalFactory.FieldNames.TransmittalRemarks,
                ConstructionChangeDirectiveFactory.FieldNames.PriceChangeType,
ConstructionChangeDirectiveFactory.FieldNames.PriceChangeTypeDirection,
                ConstructionChangeDirectiveFactory.FieldNames.AmountChanged,
                ConstructionChangeDirectiveFactory.FieldNames.TimeChangeDirection,
                ConstructionChangeDirectiveFactory.FieldNames.TimeChangedDays,
                ConstructionChangeDirectiveFactory.FieldNames.OwnerSignatureDate,
ConstructionChangeDirectiveFactory.FieldNames.ArchitectSignatureDate,
ConstructionChangeDirectiveFactory.FieldNames.ContractorSignatureDate
                ));
            builder.Append(string.Format("VALUES
({0},{1},{2},{3},{4},{5},{6},{7},{8},{9},{10},{11},{12},{13},{14},{15},{16},{17},
{18},{19},{20},{21},{22},{23},{24},{25},{26},{27},{28},{29});",
                DataHelper.GetSqlValue(item.Key),
                DataHelper.GetSqlValue(item.ProjectKey),
                DataHelper.GetSqlValue(item.Number),
```

```
                DataHelper.GetSqlValue(item.TransmittalDate),
                DataHelper.GetSqlValue(item.To.Key),
                DataHelper.GetSqlValue(item.From.Key),
                DataHelper.GetSqlValue(item.TotalPages),
                DataHelper.GetSqlValue(item.DeliveryMethod),
                DataHelper.GetSqlValue(item.OtherDeliveryMethod),
                DataHelper.GetSqlValue(item.PhaseNumber),
                DataHelper.GetSqlValue(item.Reimbursable),
                DataHelper.GetSqlValue(item.Final),
                DataHelper.GetSqlValue(item.IssueDate),
                DataHelper.GetSqlValue(item.Contractor.Key),
                DataHelper.GetSqlValue(item.Description),
                DataHelper.GetSqlValue(item.Attachment),
                DataHelper.GetSqlValue(item.Reason),
                DataHelper.GetSqlValue(item.Initiator),
                DataHelper.GetSqlValue(item.Cause),
                DataHelper.GetSqlValue(item.Origin),
                DataHelper.GetSqlValue(item.Remarks),
                DataHelper.GetSqlValue(item.TransmittalRemarks),
                DataHelper.GetSqlValue(item.ChangeType),
                DataHelper.GetSqlValue(item.PriceChangeDirection),
                DataHelper.GetSqlValue(item.AmountChanged),
                DataHelper.GetSqlValue(item.TimeChangeDirection),
                DataHelper.GetSqlValue(item.TimeChanged),
                DataHelper.GetSqlValue(item.OwnerSignatureDate),
                DataHelper.GetSqlValue(item.ArchitectSignatureDate),
                DataHelper.GetSqlValue(item.ContractorSignatureDate)));

            this.Database.ExecuteNonQuery(
                this.Database.GetSqlStringCommand(builder.ToString()));

            // Now do the child objects
            this.InsertCopyToList(item);
        }
```

The code builds up a large insert statement composed of the values from the `ConstructionChangeDirective` instance and then executes the query using the Microsoft Enterprise Library's `Database` object. After the main insert statement has been executed, I then need to insert the `CopyTo` instances for the `ConstructionChangeDirective`.

PersistUpdatedItem

The `PersistUpdatedItem` method first does an update to the `ConstructionChangeDirective` table:

```
        protected override void PersistUpdatedItem(ConstructionChangeDirective item)
        {
            StringBuilder builder = new StringBuilder(100);
            builder.Append("UPDATE ConstructionChangeDirective SET ");

            builder.Append(string.Format("{0} = {1}",

    ConstructionChangeDirectiveFactory.FieldNames.ConstructionChangeDirectiveNumber,
                DataHelper.GetSqlValue(item.Number)));
```

(continued)

(continued)

```
            builder.Append(string.Format(",{0} = {1}",
                TransmittalFactory.FieldNames.TransmittalDate,
                DataHelper.GetSqlValue(item.TransmittalDate)));

            builder.Append(string.Format(",{0} = {1}",
                ProjectFactory.FieldNames.ProjectContactId,
                DataHelper.GetSqlValue(item.To.Key)));

            builder.Append(string.Format(",{0} = {1}",
                EmployeeFactory.FieldNames.EmployeeId,
                DataHelper.GetSqlValue(item.From.Key)));

            builder.Append(string.Format(",{0} = {1}",
                TransmittalFactory.FieldNames.TotalPages,
                DataHelper.GetSqlValue(item.TotalPages)));

            builder.Append(string.Format(",{0} = {1}",
                TransmittalFactory.FieldNames.DeliveryMethod,
                DataHelper.GetSqlValue(item.DeliveryMethod)));

            builder.Append(string.Format(",{0} = {1}",
                TransmittalFactory.FieldNames.OtherDeliveryMethod,
                DataHelper.GetSqlValue(item.OtherDeliveryMethod)));

            /*******************************************************/

            builder.Append(string.Format(",{0} = {1}",
                ConstructionChangeDirectiveFactory.FieldNames.PriceChangeType,
                DataHelper.GetSqlValue(item.ChangeType)));

            builder.Append(string.Format(",{0} = {1}",

ConstructionChangeDirectiveFactory.FieldNames.PriceChangeTypeDirection,
                DataHelper.GetSqlValue(item.PriceChangeDirection)));

            builder.Append(string.Format(",{0} = {1}",
                ConstructionChangeDirectiveFactory.FieldNames.AmountChanged,
                DataHelper.GetSqlValue(item.AmountChanged)));

            builder.Append(string.Format(",{0} = {1}",
                ConstructionChangeDirectiveFactory.FieldNames.TimeChangeDirection,
                DataHelper.GetSqlValue(item.TimeChangeDirection)));

            builder.Append(string.Format(",{0} = {1}",
                ConstructionChangeDirectiveFactory.FieldNames.TimeChangedDays,
                DataHelper.GetSqlValue(item.TimeChanged)));

            builder.Append(string.Format(",{0} = {1}",
                ConstructionChangeDirectiveFactory.FieldNames.OwnerSignatureDate,
                DataHelper.GetSqlValue(item.OwnerSignatureDate)));

            builder.Append(string.Format(",{0} = {1}",
```

```
ConstructionChangeDirectiveFactory.FieldNames.ArchitectSignatureDate,
                DataHelper.GetSqlValue(item.ArchitectSignatureDate)));

            builder.Append(string.Format(",{0} = {1}",

ConstructionChangeDirectiveFactory.FieldNames.ContractorSignatureDate,
                DataHelper.GetSqlValue(item.ContractorSignatureDate)));

            builder.Append(" ");
            builder.Append(this.BuildBaseWhereClause(item.Key));

            this.Database.ExecuteNonQuery(
                this.Database.GetSqlStringCommand(builder.ToString()));

            // Now do the child objects

            // First, delete the existing ones
            this.DeleteCopyToList(item);

            // Now, add the current ones
            this.InsertCopyToList(item);
        }
```

I have omitted several lines of repetitive code building the SQL update statement in the middle of the code in order to try to save you from the boring code.

The second part of the method then uses the `DeleteCopyToList` helper method to delete all of the `CopyTo` child objects of the Construction Change Directive, and then uses the `InsertCopyToList` helper method to add the existing `CopyTo` child objects from the Construction Change Directive to the database.

The Construction Change Directive Service Implementation

Like the other `Service` classes shown in the domain model so far, the `ConstructionChangeDirectiveService` class is responsible for retrieving and wrapping the methods of its associated Repository interface, in this case the `IConstructionChangeDirectiveRepository` instance.

```
using System;
using SmartCA.Infrastructure;
using SmartCA.Infrastructure.RepositoryFramework;
using System.Collections.Generic;
using SmartCA.Model.Projects;
using System.Linq;

namespace SmartCA.Model.ConstructionChangeDirectives
{
    public class ConstructionChangeDirectiveService
```

(continued)

(continued)

```
    {
        private static IConstructionChangeDirectiveRepository repository;
        private static IUnitOfWork unitOfWork;

        static ConstructionChangeDirectiveService()
        {
            ConstructionChangeDirectiveService.unitOfWork = new UnitOfWork();
            ConstructionChangeDirectiveService.repository =
                RepositoryFactory.GetRepository
                <IConstructionChangeDirectiveRepository,
                ConstructionChangeDirective>(
                ConstructionChangeDirectiveService.unitOfWork);
        }

        public static IList<ConstructionChangeDirective>
            GetConstructionChangeDirectives(Project project)
        {
            return
                ConstructionChangeDirectiveService.repository.FindBy(
                project);
        }

        public static void SaveConstructionChangeDirective(
            ConstructionChangeDirective ccd)
        {
            ConstructionChangeDirectiveService.repository[ccd.Key] = ccd;
            ConstructionChangeDirectiveService.unitOfWork.Commit();
        }
    }
}
```

These are the only methods needed for now, but others could easily be added later, such as a method for removing Construction Change Directives.

The Construction Change Directive ViewModel Class

Following the same patterns for all `ViewModel` classes as before, the `ConstructionChangeDirectiveViewModel` class adapts the Construction Change Directive Aggregate from the domain model to the UI. Just like the `ProposalRequestViewModel` class, it inherits from the `TransmittalViewModel<T>` class introduced previously:

```
using System;
using SmartCA.Model.ConstructionChangeDirectives;
using System.Collections.Generic;
using SmartCA.Model.Projects;
using SmartCA.Model.Employees;
using SmartCA.Model.Companies;
using SmartCA.Application;
using SmartCA.Infrastructure.UI;
using SmartCA.Infrastructure.DomainBase;
```

```
using SmartCA.Model.NumberedProjectChildren;

namespace SmartCA.Presentation.ViewModels
{
    public class ConstructionChangeDirectiveViewModel :
        TransmittalViewModel <ConstructionChangeDirective>
```

The Constructor

Here are the constructors for the `ConstructionChangeDirectiveViewModel` class:

```
        #region Constructors

        public ConstructionChangeDirectiveViewModel()
            : this(null)
        {
        }

        public ConstructionChangeDirectiveViewModel(IView view)
            : base(view)
        {
            this.toList = UserSession.CurrentProject.Contacts;
            this.fromList = EmployeeService.GetEmployees();
            this.contractors = CompanyService.GetAllCompanies();
        }

        #endregion
```

On the surface, this looks to be just like all of the other View Model implementations so far, but I have actually done some major refactoring to all of the `ViewModel` classes that I will show you shortly.

The Properties

All of the properties in the `ConstructionChangeDirectiveViewModel` class are read-only:

```
        #region Properties

        public IList<ProjectContact> ToList
        {
            get { return this.toList; }
        }

        public IList<Employee> FromList
        {
            get { return this.fromList; }
        }

        public IList<Company> Contractors
        {
            get { return this.contractors; }
        }

        #endregion
```

One thing you may have picked up on already is that there is no `CurrentConstructionChangeDirective` property in this class. That is due to the intense refactoring of the View Model base classes that I just did!

The ViewModel Class Refactoring

I have refactored a lot of the functionality out of the `ViewModel` class and into a new class called the `EditableViewModel<T>` class. Here is what the new `ViewModel` class looks like:

```
using System;

namespace SmartCA.Infrastructure.UI
{
    public abstract class ViewModel
    {
        private IView view;
        private DelegateCommand cancelCommand;

        protected ViewModel()
            : this(null)
        {
        }

        protected ViewModel(IView view)
        {
            this.view = view;
            this.cancelCommand = new DelegateCommand(this.CancelCommandHandler);
        }

        public DelegateCommand CancelCommand
        {
            get { return this.cancelCommand; }
        }

        protected virtual void CancelCommandHandler(object sender, EventArgs e)
        {
            this.CloseView();
        }

        protected void CloseView()
        {
            if (this.view != null)
            {
                this.view.Close();
            }
        }
    }
}
```

All I have really done here is pared this class down to what it used to be like back in Chapter 3, although it no longer implements the `INotifyPropertyChanged` interface. This is because the intent of this class is to serve only enough functionality for read-only user interfaces, such as dialog boxes. The `SelectProjectView` is a perfect example of the read-only user interface that I am talking about.

The EditableViewModel<T> Class

The next step was to put all of the functionality for editing objects into the `EditableViewModel<T>` class. It extends the `ViewModel` class, and adds a lot more functionality to it:

```
using System;
using SmartCA.Infrastructure.DomainBase;
using System.Collections.ObjectModel;
using System.Collections.Generic;
using System.Windows.Data;
using System.ComponentModel;

namespace SmartCA.Infrastructure.UI
{
    public abstract class EditableViewModel<T>
        : ViewModel, INotifyPropertyChanged where T : EntityBase
```

The first thing to note is that it is now a Generic class with a constraint on the type passed in. I had so much success with the Generic `TransmittalViewModel<T>` class that I decided to embrace that concept here!

The next thing to note about the `EditableViewModel<T>` class is that it is extending the `ViewModel` class and implementing the `INotifyPropertyChanged` interface. It is also responsible for maintaining the state of the current Entity that is being edited. This is done via the `ObjectState` enumeration:

```
        #region ObjectState Enum

        public enum ObjectState
        {
            New,
            Existing,
            Deleted
        }

        #endregion
```

The Constructors and Private Fields

Here are the private fields and constructors for the class:

```
        #region Private Fields

        private ObjectState currentObjectState;
        private IList<BrokenRule> brokenRules;
        private T currentEntity;
        private List<T> entitiesList;
        private CollectionView entitiesView;
        private DelegateCommand saveCommand;
        private DelegateCommand newCommand;

        #endregion

        #region Constructors

        protected EditableViewModel()
```

(continued)

(continued)

```
            : this(null)
        {
        }

        protected EditableViewModel(IView view)
            : base(view)
        {
            this.currentObjectState = ObjectState.Existing;
            this.brokenRules = new List<BrokenRule>();
            this.currentEntity = default(T);
            this.entitiesList = this.GetEntitiesList();
            this.entitiesView = new CollectionView(this.entitiesList);
            this.saveCommand = new DelegateCommand(this.SaveCommandHandler);
            this.newCommand = new DelegateCommand(this.NewCommandHandler);
        }

        #endregion
```

Notice is that I am fully embracing the concept of treating Broken Rules as a first-class citizen in this class. The derived `ViewModel` classes no longer have to worry about them as this class will take care of all of that infrastructure-type code. The next important concept that should jump out at you is that I have made the current object being edited and the list of available objects to edit generic enough to fit into this class. This really opens up a lot of possibilities for code reduction as you will see later in the derived classes. Also, since I know that every object I an editing is going to have a `Save` command and a `New` command, I have centralized them into this class as well.

The interesting thing to note about the constructor is how it initializes the `entitiesList` private field. It is calling the `GetEntitiesList` method, which is actually an abstract method:

```
    protected abstract List<T> GetEntitiesList();
```

This is great; I can now let the derived `ViewModel` class know how to get their list of Entities. I love the Template Method pattern; it just gives me so much flexibility, especially when combined with Generics!

The Properties

I will only show the read-write properties here. Suffice it to say that all private fields not shown here are exposed as read-only properties.

The CurrentObjectState Property

This property represents the state of the object currently being edited:

```
        public ObjectState CurrentObjectState
        {
            get { return this.currentObjectState; }
            set
            {
                if (this.currentObjectState != value)
                {
                    this.currentObjectState = value;
                    this.OnPropertyChanged(
```

```
                    EditableViewModel<T>.currentObjectStatePropertyName);
            }
        }
    }
```

The interesting part of this property is its setter. The setter is actually raising the `PropertyChanged` event if the state of the current object has changed. This is important for the WPF UI, as WPF is smart about knowing how to handle this event automatically.

The CurrentEntity Property

This property used to be in the derived classes, and you probably knew it before from such names as `CurrentCompany`, `CurrentTransmittal`, and so on. Now it has been made appropriately generic to eliminate that code in the derived classes:

```
        public T CurrentEntity
        {
            get { return this.currentEntity; }
            set
            {
                if (this.currentEntity != value)
                {
                    this.currentEntity = value;
                    this.SetCurrentEntity(value);
                    this.saveCommand.IsEnabled = (this.currentEntity != null);
                    this.OnPropertyChanged(
                        EditableViewModel<T>.currentEntityPropertyName);
                }
            }
        }
```

The property setter again makes use of another abstract method, the `SetCurrentEntity` method:

```
protected abstract void SetCurrentEntity(T entity);
```

This method is made abstract in order to give the derived class some freedom on what must happen when the `CurrentEntity` being edited changes. It may need to do things such as create new mutable objects based on the values of some of the Value objects in the `CurrentEntity`.

The last thing the property setter does is to raise the `PropertyChanged` event to let the UI know that it has a new object to display and edit now.

The ValidateCurrentObject Method

This method makes use of the previous refactoring on the `EntityBase` class to keep track of Broken Rules:

```
        #region ValidateCurrentObject

        protected bool ValidateCurrentObject()
        {
            this.brokenRules.Clear();
```

(continued)

(continued)

```
            ReadOnlyCollection<BrokenRule> currentObjectBrokenRules =
                this.currentEntity.GetBrokenRules();
            foreach (BrokenRule rule in currentObjectBrokenRules)
            {
                this.brokenRules.Add(rule);
            }
            return (this.brokenRules.Count == 0);
        }

        #endregion
```

The first thing it does is to clear the `brokenRules` private field. It then asks the `CurrentEntity` for all of its Broken Rules (via the functionality in the `EntityBase` class) and then adds the Broken Rules returned by the `CurrentEntity` to the `brokenRules` private field. Now, the UI can bind to the `BrokenRules` property and do whatever it wants with that property when the property changes. The last thing the method does is to return a `Boolean` value indicating whether there were any Broken Rules.

The Command Handler Methods

In order to separate `New` and `Save` algorithms from the derived classes, the `SaveCommandHandler` and `NewCommandHandler` methods have been placed into this class.

The NewCommandHandler method

Here is the code for the `NewCommandHandler` method:

```
        protected virtual void NewCommandHandler(object sender, EventArgs e)
        {
            this.CurrentObjectState = ObjectState.New;
            this.brokenRules.Clear();
            this.entitiesList.Add(this.BuildNewEntity());
            this.currentEntity = null;
            this.entitiesView.Refresh();
            this.entitiesView.MoveCurrentToLast();
        }
```

As you can see, this method does a lot of generic housekeeping duties, such as changing the state of the object being edited, clearing the Broken Rules, and resetting the `CurrentEntity`. It also uses another abstract class to build the new Entity that is being added:

```
    protected abstract T BuildNewEntity();
```

This lets the derived class do whatever it needs to do to build the Entity, as long as the Entity conforms to the constraints placed on the generic `T` parameter.

The last thing the method does is to refresh the `CollectionView` and make sure that the new Entity is the last item in the `CollectionView`.

The SaveCommandHandler Method

This method is responsible for validating and saving the `CurrentEntity` instance.

```
        protected void SaveCommandHandler(object sender, EventArgs e)
        {
            if (this.ValidateCurrentObject())
            {
                this.SaveCurrentEntity(sender, e);
                this.CurrentObjectState = ObjectState.Existing;
            }
        }
```

It begins by validating the `CurrentEntity` via the `ValidateCurrentObject` method. If that validation passes, it then calls another abstract method, `SaveCurrentEntity`, in order to save the Entity.

```
protected abstract void SaveCurrentEntity(object sender, EventArgs e);
```

Again, I am delegating down to the derived class here to figure out what it needs to do to save the Entity.

The last thing the method does is to change the state of `CurrentEntity` to that of Existing.

The Newly Refactored TransmittalViewModel Class

The signature of this class has changed a little bit; here is what it looks like now:

```
using System;
using SmartCA.Infrastructure.UI;
using SmartCA.Infrastructure.DomainBase;
using SmartCA.Model.Transmittals;
using SmartCA.Model.Submittals;
using System.Collections.Generic;
using SmartCA.Model;
using System.ComponentModel;
using System.Windows.Data;
using System.Collections.ObjectModel;

namespace SmartCA.Presentation.ViewModels
{
    public abstract class TransmittalViewModel<T> : EditableViewModel<T>
        where T : EntityBase, ITransmittal
```

Instead of inheriting from the `ViewModel` class, it now inherits from the `EditableViewModel<T>` class.

The Constructor and Private Fields

The number of private fields and the amount of code in the constructor have been significantly reduced:

```
        #region Private Fields

        private IList<SpecificationSection> specificationSections;
        private IList<ItemStatus> itemStatuses;
        private BindingList<MutableCopyTo> mutableCopyToList;
        private CollectionView deliveryMethods;
        private IList<Discipline> disciplines;
```

(continued)

(continued)

```
        private DelegateCommand deleteCopyToCommand;

        #endregion

        #region Constructors

        public TransmittalViewModel()
            : this(null)
        {
        }

        public TransmittalViewModel(IView view)
            : base(view)
        {
            this.specificationSections
                = SubmittalService.GetSpecificationSections();
            this.itemStatuses = SubmittalService.GetItemStatuses();
            this.mutableCopyToList = new BindingList<MutableCopyTo>();
            this.deliveryMethods = new CollectionView(
                                       Enum.GetNames(typeof(Delivery)));
            this.disciplines = SubmittalService.GetDisciplines();
            this.deleteCopyToCommand =
                new DelegateCommand(this.DeleteCopyToCommandHandler);
        }

        #endregion
```

As you can see, it is not doing anything really special. In fact, a lot of the code that would have been in this constructor is now handled by the constructor in the base class, the `EditableViewModel<T>` class.

The Properties

There is really nothing interesting to look at for the properties, they are all just read-only representations of their respective private fields.

The NewCommandHandler Method

This method has really been reduced:

```
        protected override void NewCommandHandler(object sender, EventArgs e)
        {
            this.mutableCopyToList.Clear();
            base.NewCommandHandler(sender, e);
        }
```

It simply clears the `mutableCopyToList` private field and then calls the base method for `NewCommandHandler`.

The SaveCurrentEntity Method Override

This method takes care of the Transmittal-specific action of clearing and resetting the `CopyTo` list:

```
protected override void SaveCurrentEntity(object sender, EventArgs e)
{
    this.CurrentEntity.CopyToList.Clear();
    foreach (MutableCopyTo copyTo in this.mutableCopyToList)
    {
        this.CurrentEntity.CopyToList.Add(copyTo.ToCopyTo());
    }
}
```

It does not need to do anything else, as the derived class will take care of actually saving the `Transmittal`.

The SetCurrentEntity Method Override

This method simply raises the `PropertyChanged` event for the `Status` property as well as calling down to the `PopulateTransmittalChildren` method.

```
protected override void SetCurrentEntity(T entity)
{
    this.OnPropertyChanged("Status");
    this.PopulateTransmittalChildren();
}
```

The ConstructionChangeDirectiveViewModel Class Method Overrides

Ok, it is time to get back to the `ConstructionChangeDirectiveViewModel` class! The last thing to look at in this class is the methods that it needs to override from the base classes.

The BuildNewEntity Method Override

This method makes use of the previously shown `NumberedProjectChildFactory` class to build a new `ConstructionChangeDirective` instance:

```
protected override ConstructionChangeDirective BuildNewEntity()
{
    return NumberedProjectChildFactory.CreateNumberedProjectChild
        <ConstructionChangeDirective>(UserSession.CurrentProject);
}
```

All it needs to do is to pass in the `Project` instance and specify that it wants a type of `ConstructionChangeDirective` returned.

The SaveCurrentEntity Method Override

This method just needs to call the base method first, and then it simply calls its associated `Service` class to save the `ConstructionChangeDirective`:

```
protected override void SaveCurrentEntity(object sender, EventArgs e)
{

    base.SaveCurrentEntity(sender, e);
    ConstructionChangeDirectiveService.SaveConstructionChangeDirective(
        this.CurrentEntity);
}
```

Notice how it is passing the `CurrentEntity` property value, and that value is coming from the base class, but is typed as a `ConstructionChangeDirective`. . . . Man, I love Generics!

The GetEntitiesList Method Override

The signature on this method is also typed properly, because of Generics again:

```
        protected override List<ConstructionChangeDirective> GetEntitiesList()
        {
            return new List<ConstructionChangeDirective>(

ConstructionChangeDirectiveService.GetConstructionChangeDirectives(
                    UserSession.CurrentProject));
        }
```

It simply delegates the `ConstructionChangeDirectiveService` class to get the list of `ConstructionChangeDirective` instances for the current Project.

The Construction Change Directive View

The View for Construction Change Directives is very similar to that seen in the past few chapters, where the list of Construction Change Directives is on the left, and the currently selected Construction Change Directive is on the right. Figure 9.5 shows what the form looks like at run time.

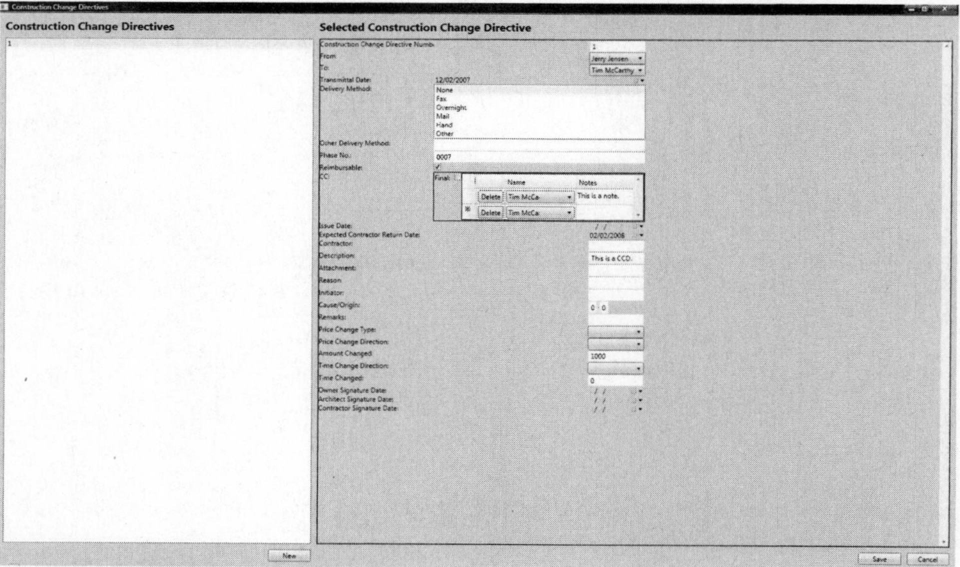

Figure 9.5: Construction Change Directive View.

One of the last things left to do in the UI is to hook up the `BrokenRules` property from the `EditableViewModel<T>` class to the UI. That could actually get pretty interesting, especially using WPF Triggers. Again, I am focusing on the domain model here, so I am not going to go into that; I am just going to suggest that the framework is there to do whatever you want to do with the `BrokenRule` instances in the UI.

Summary

In this chapter, I introduced the concept of a Construction Change Directive in the construction industry, and then I used that concept to model the Construction Change Directive Aggregate. As you may have noticed, I did a ton of refactoring in this chapter. Most of the refactoring was focused on the various `ViewModel` classes. A lot of the refactoring was made possible by using interfaces and Generics together. This proved to be quite a powerful combination in making the code base more maintainable, more robust, and also in making the domain model that much richer.

10

Synchronizing With the Server

In Chapter 1, Introducing the Project: The SmartCA Application, I stated that one of the requirements for the SmartCA application was that it must be offline capable. Now, when I say offline capable, the best example that comes to mind is Microsoft Outlook. In Microsoft Outlook versions 2003 and above, you can work connected to or disconnected from your email server and still have a good user experience. During this chapter, I would like you to keep in mind how Microsoft Outlook works in order to understand some of the design decisions presented later in the chapter.

The Problem

Thanks to using a local data store on the client, the SmartCA is definitely offline capable. Now, the challenge is to get it online and connected to the server. I am going to be calling this process of connecting to the server and transferring application data back and forth the Synchronization process.

What the SmartCA application needs is an intelligent, service-based way of synchronizing its data with the server. The user should not be bothered with any silly errors because they are not connected to the network or the Internet, they should be able to do their work, and the application should gracefully handle the transactions and pushing the data back and forth.

The Design

I also mentioned in Chapter 1 that I would be using Microsoft Synchronization Services for ADO.NET for this synchronization, but I have since changed my mind. After analyzing the problem domain further, I really feel that what the SmartCA application needs is a way to keep some type of running log of all of the transactions that the user performs on the client domain model, and then to send that in some message form to the server and have the server try to execute all of the messages on its own domain model.

Although Microsoft Synchronization Services for ADO.NET is a great piece of work, I did not feel it met the requirements that I had. I really do not want to get backed into a low-level database replication corner, and it seemed like that was really what Microsoft Synchronization Services for ADO.NET was doing, although it is doing it in an n-tier way.

Redesigning the Unit of Work

The more I thought about it, the more I liked the idea of encapsulating all of the client-side transactions into messages. I really want to make the synchronization a business-level process rather than a data-level process. As it turns out, I have already implemented a pattern in the SmartCA application that will lend itself very well to this type of architecture, and that is the Unit of Work pattern.

So after coming to this conclusion, I have decided to refactor my Unit of Work implementation a little bit in order to handle creating and storing transaction messages as it sends them to the various repositories for processing.

What is also needed is some type of process (or background thread) running that can take all of the messages created by the Unit of Work instances and send them to the server, as well as taking messages from the server and handing them to the SmartCA domain model.

The diagram in Figure 10.1 shows the modification to the Unit of Work implementation that allows me to use it for persisting transaction messages on the client:

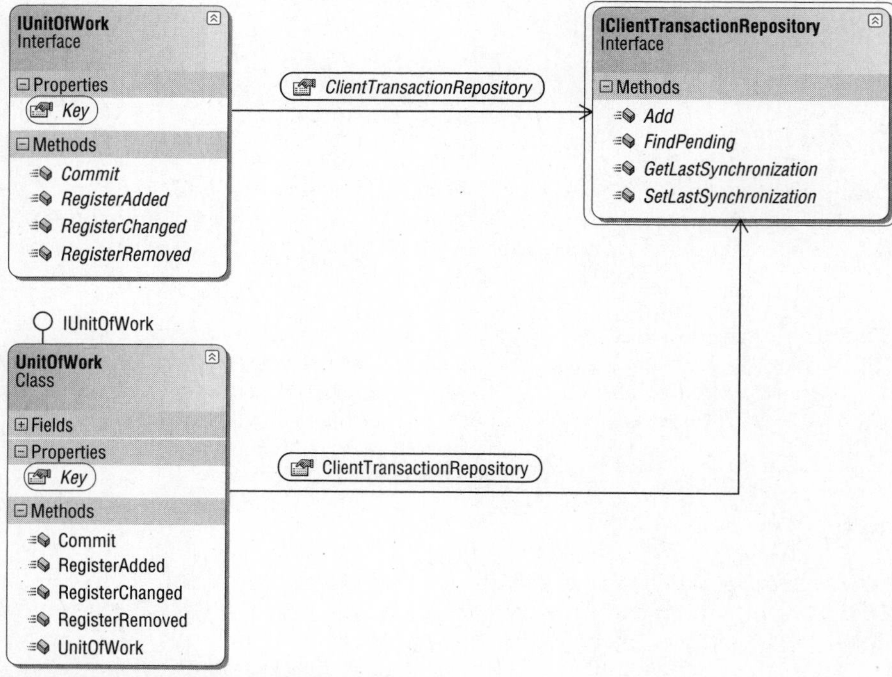

Figure 10.1: Unit of Work modifications.

What this diagram shows is that a `Key` property has been added to the `IUnitOfWork` interface, and that value represents a unique identifier for a Unit of Work. Also, the diagram shows a relationship to an `IClientTransactionRepository`, which implies that a Unit of Work message can be persisted. I will talk more about the Client Transaction Repository implementation later in this chapter.

The Refactored IUnitOfWork Interface

```
using System;
using SmartCA.Infrastructure.DomainBase;
using SmartCA.Infrastructure.RepositoryFramework;
using SmartCA.Infrastructure.Transactions;

namespace SmartCA.Infrastructure
{
    public interface IUnitOfWork
    {
        void RegisterAdded(EntityBase entity, IUnitOfWorkRepository repository);
        void RegisterChanged(EntityBase entity, IUnitOfWorkRepository repository);
        void RegisterRemoved(EntityBase entity, IUnitOfWorkRepository repository);
        void Commit();
        object Key { get; }
        IClientTransactionRepository ClientTransactionRepository { get; }
    }
}
```

The new IClientTransactionRepository Interface

Since I want to be flexible in how these messages are persisted, I have created an interface for the repository, called the `IClientTransactionRepository`. This Repository interface contains all of the methods necessary to save and retrieve client transactions.

```
using System;
using SmartCA.Infrastructure.DomainBase;
using System.Collections.Generic;

namespace SmartCA.Infrastructure.Transactions
{
    public interface IClientTransactionRepository
    {
        DateTime? GetLastSynchronization();
        void SetLastSynchronization(DateTime? lastSynchronization);
        void Add(ClientTransaction transaction);
        IList<ClientTransaction> FindPending();
    }
}
```

The Transaction Class Implementations

You may have noticed the reference to the `ClientTransaction` class in the `IClientTransactionRepository` interface in the above code sample. For the purposes of synchronization, there are two types of transactions, Client Transactions and Server Transactions (see Figure 10.2).

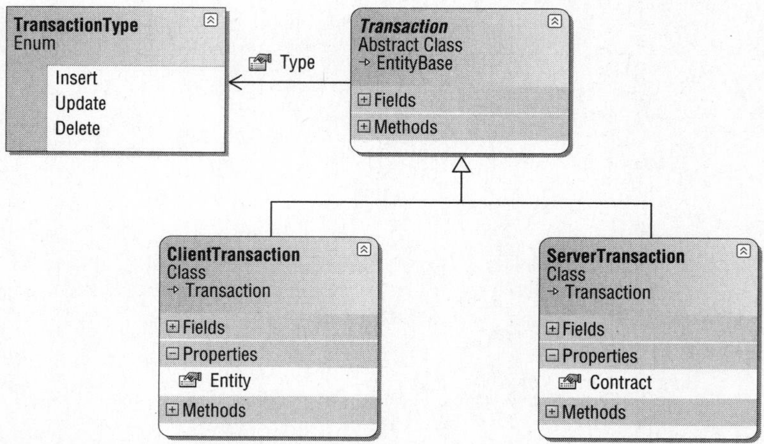

Figure 10.2: The Transaction classes.

Both of these types of Transactions inherit from the `Transaction` abstract class. Notice how the `Transaction` class only has to implement the `IEntity` interface and not inherit from the `EntityBase` class. This works out well because although a Transaction is an Entity, it does not need all of the functionality that the `EntityBase` class has, and therefore I can keep it lightweight.

Designing the Synchronization

Figure 10.3 is a drawing showing the different pieces involved in the SmartCA synchronization strategy.

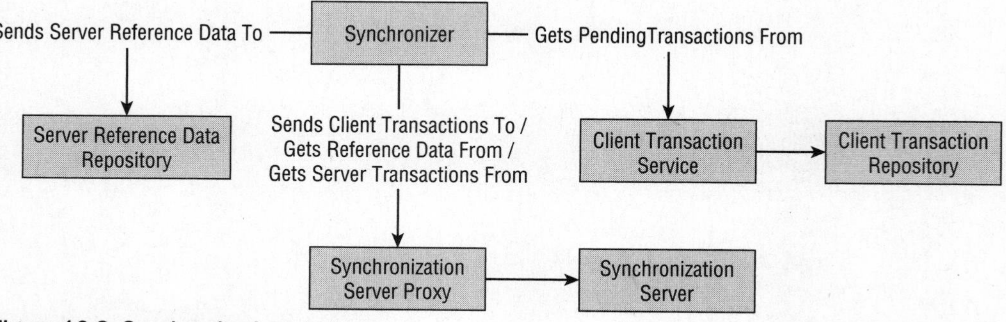

Figure 10.3: Synchronization strategy.

The diagram shows the pieces involved in getting transactions that happen on the client up to the server, as well as getting reference data and transactions from the server down to the client. There is a lot going on in this diagram, and many new classes will need to be added to support the new synchronization functionality.

Writing the Unit Tests

In this section, I am going to show the tests for the IClientTransactionRepository interface, mainly because it is this interface that is going to be called the most on the client whenever an IUnitOfWork instance is going to commit a transaction.

Very similarly to how I tested the other Repository interfaces, I have written a suite of unit tests that will test an instance of the IClientTransactionRepository interface that is returned from the ClientTransactionRepositoryFactory (which I have not shown yet, but I will later in this chapter).

The IClientTransactionRepositoryAddTest Method

This method tests the process of adding a new ClientTransaction to the IClientTransactionRepository instance.

```
/// <summary>
///A test for adding a Transaction
///</summary>
[DeploymentItem("SmartCA.sdf"), TestMethod()]
public void IClientTransactionRepositoryAddTest()
{
    IClientTransactionRepository target =
        ClientTransactionRepositoryFactory.GetTransactionRepository();
    TransactionType type = TransactionType.Insert;
    Company entity = new Company();
    entity.Name = "Test 123";
    object unitOfWorkKey = Guid.NewGuid();
    target.Add(new ClientTransaction(unitOfWorkKey, type, entity));
}
```

The method starts out by first getting an instance of the IClientTransactionRepository interface, and it then builds up a ClientTransaction instance filled with a new Company (which is an IEntity) instance, and then calls the Add method of the IClientTransactionRepository interface.

The FindPendingTransactionsTest Method

The purpose of this method is to test how the system finds all of the pending transactions on the client:

```
/// <summary>
/// A test for finding all of the pending transactions
/// </summary>
[DeploymentItem("SmartCA.sdf"), TestMethod()]
public void FindPendingTransactionsTest()
{
    // Make sure there is at least one pending transaction
    this.IClientTransactionRepositoryAddTest();

    // Get the pending transactions
    IClientTransactionRepository target =
        ClientTransactionRepositoryFactory.GetTransactionRepository();
    IList<ClientTransaction> transactions = target.FindPending();
    Assert.IsTrue(transactions.Count > 0);
}
```

This test starts out by first calling the `IClientTransactionRepositoryAddTest` method in order to make sure that there is at least one Transaction that needs to be synchronized on the client. Next, it makes the usual call to the factory to get the instance of the `IClientTransactionRepository`, and then it calls the `FindPending` method to get the list of all pending transactions on the client. Finally, it asserts that there is more than one pending transaction on the client.

The SetLastSynchronizationTest Method

This method is really simple; it tests how the system sets the last time that synchronization has occurred on the client:

```
/// <summary>
///A test for SetLastSynchronization
///</summary>
[DeploymentItem("SmartCA.sdf"), TestMethod()]
public void SetLastSynchronizationTest()
{
    IClientTransactionRepository target =
        ClientTransactionRepositoryFactory.GetTransactionRepository();
    target.SetLastSynchronization(DateTime.Now);
}
```

The first line is the familiar call of getting the instance of the `IClientTransactionRepository`. The next line simply calls the `SetLastSynchronization` method and passes in the current `DateTime` as the argument.

The GetLastSynchronizationTest Method

This test method exercises and tests the `GetLastSynchronization` method of the `IClientTransactionRepository` interface:

```
/// <summary>
///A test for GetLastSynchronization
///</summary>
[DeploymentItem("SmartCA.sdf"), TestMethod()]
public void GetLastSynchronizationTest()
{
    IClientTransactionRepository target =
        ClientTransactionRepositoryFactory.GetTransactionRepository();
    target.SetLastSynchronization(DateTime.Now);
    DateTime? lastSynchronization = target.GetLastSynchronization();
    Assert.IsTrue(lastSynchronization.HasValue);
    Assert.IsTrue(DateTime.Now > lastSynchronization.Value);
}
```

It starts out with the familiar, by getting an instance of the `IClientTransactionRepository` instance. It then calls the `SetLastSynchronization` method and passes in the current `DateTime` value to the method. Next, it calls the `GetLastSynchronization` method to get the `DateTime` value of the last time that the synchronization occurred, and then it makes sure that the synchronization `DateTime` value is in the past.

The Solution

There really are two main parts to the synchronization solution. The first part is all of the changes required to the Unit of Work implementation in order to support the saving of client transactions as messages. The second part is everything that is involved in getting the client transactions up to the server, and getting the server transactions and reference data from the server and into the client application.

I am splitting up the work in this fashion because the first part happens synchronously while a Unit of Work is committing the changes to Entities, and the second part does not need to happen right away; it can, and should, be an asynchronous operation. I say that it should be an asynchronous operation because I do not want the synchronization to freeze the application while it is running; again, think Microsoft Outlook here. This is why I chose to use a local database such as SQL Server CE in the first place. It allows me to work happily in my client domain and not have to worry about the server, since I can concern myself with the server during the synchronization process. Since the synchronization will be happening without blocking the main thread, the user experience is not impacted nearly as much as it would be if this synchronization were synchronous. The users can keep doing work with the application and not have their screen freeze up. This is exactly how Microsoft Outlook 2003 and above behaves when it synchronizes with a Microsoft Exchange mail server.

Unit of Work Refactoring

For the synchronization, I need to know what has changed on the client, without having to resort to doing a lot of low-level database queries and comparisons. As I was thinking about how to do this, I realized that I already have code that knows all about what changes are being persisted on the client, and that is my Unit of Work implementation.

The Commit Method

The code that knows about changes being persisted on the client is the `Commit` method. In that method, I already iterate through everything that has been changed, added, and deleted in the current Unit of Work transaction.

```
public void Commit()
{
    using (TransactionScope scope = new TransactionScope())
    {
        foreach (EntityBase entity in this.deletedEntities.Keys)
        {
            this.deletedEntities[entity].PersistDeletedItem(entity);
        }

        foreach (EntityBase entity in this.addedEntities.Keys)
        {
            this.addedEntities[entity].PersistDeletedItem(entity);
        }

        foreach (EntityBase entity in this.changedEntities.Keys)
        {
            this.changedEntities[entity].PersistDeletedItem(entity);
```

(continued)

(continued)

```
                }

                scope.Complete();
            }

            this.deletedEntities.Clear();
            this.addedEntities.Clear();
            this.changedEntities.Clear();
        }
```

I can simply add more code to this method to save these transactions as messages that need to be sent to the server for processing:

```
        public void Commit()
        {
            using (TransactionScope scope = new TransactionScope())
            {
                foreach (EntityBase entity in this.deletedEntities.Keys)
                {
                    this.deletedEntities[entity].PersistDeletedItem(entity);
                    this.clientTransactionRepository.Add(
                        new ClientTransaction(this.key,
                        TransactionType.Delete, entity));
                }

                foreach (EntityBase entity in this.addedEntities.Keys)
                {
                    this.addedEntities[entity].PersistNewItem(entity);
                    this.clientTransactionRepository.Add(
                        new ClientTransaction(this.key,
                        TransactionType.Insert, entity));
                }

                foreach (EntityBase entity in this.changedEntities.Keys)
                {
                    this.changedEntities[entity].PersistUpdatedItem(entity);
                    this.clientTransactionRepository.Add(
                        new ClientTransaction(this.key,
                        TransactionType.Update, entity));
                }

                scope.Complete();
            }

            this.deletedEntities.Clear();
            this.addedEntities.Clear();
            this.changedEntities.Clear();
            this.key = Guid.NewGuid();
        }
```

In the new code, you should notice a new Repository reference, the `clientTransactionRepository` class-level variable, and a new class-level variable, the `key` variable.

The UnitOfWork Key

The `key` variable is the primary identifier for the transaction, and it lets me know what operations in the transaction are tied together. The key variable is a `System.Guid` data type. Notice how when the transaction is committed and all of the dictionaries are emptied, I assign the `key` variable a new value. This signals that the `UnitOfWork` is cleared and ready to start up a new transaction.

New Properties and Changes to the Constructor

Here are the private variables in the `UnitOfWork` class:

```
        private Guid key;
        private IClientTransactionRepository clientTransactionRepository;
        private Dictionary<EntityBase, IUnitOfWorkRepository> addedEntities;
        private Dictionary<EntityBase, IUnitOfWorkRepository> changedEntities;
        private Dictionary<EntityBase, IUnitOfWorkRepository> deletedEntities;
```

Here are the new properties exposing the new private fields as read-only:

```
        public object Key
        {
            get { return this.key; }
        }

        public IClientTransactionRepository ClientTransactionRepository
        {
            get { return this.clientTransactionRepository; }
        }
```

If you remember from the design earlier in the chapter, these properties were already added to the `IUnitOfWork` interface, and they are just being implemented here.

The Transaction Class Implementations

In this section, I will take a look at the implementations for the `Transaction`, `ClientTransaction`, and `ServerTransaction` classes.

The Transaction Class

Both the `ClientTransaction` and `ServerTransaction` classes inherit from the `Transaction` abstract class, which itself only holds two properties, `Type` and `Key`. The `Type` property represents the three different types of transaction operations, Insert, Update, and Delete, and the `Key` property represents the unique identifier for the Transaction.

```
using System;
using SmartCA.Infrastructure.DomainBase;

namespace SmartCA.Infrastructure.Transactions
{
    public abstract class Transaction : IEntity
    {
        private object key;
        private TransactionType type;
```

(continued)

(continued)

```
protected Transaction(object key, TransactionType type)
{
    this.key = key;
    if (this.key == null)
    {
        this.key = Guid.NewGuid();
    }
    this.type = type;
}

public TransactionType Type
{
    get { return this.type; }
}

#region IEntity Members

public object Key
{
    get { return this.key; }
}

#endregion

#region Equality Tests

/// <summary>
/// Determines whether the specified transaction is equal to the
/// current instance.
/// </summary>
/// <param name="entity">An <see cref="System.Object"/> that
/// will be compared to the current instance.</param>
/// <returns>True if the passed in entity is equal to the
/// current instance.</returns>
public override bool Equals(object transaction)
{
    return transaction != null
        && transaction is Transaction
        && this == (Transaction)transaction;
}

/// <summary>
/// Operator overload for determining equality.
/// </summary>
/// <param name="base1">The first instance of an
/// <see cref="Transaction"/>.</param>
/// <param name="base2">The second instance of an
/// <see cref="Transaction"/>.</param>
/// <returns>True if equal.</returns>
public static bool operator ==(Transaction base1,
    Transaction base2)
{
    // check for both null (cast to object or recursive loop)
```

```
            if ((object)base1 == null && (object)base2 == null)
            {
                return true;
            }

            // check for either of them == to null
            if ((object)base1 == null || (object)base2 == null)
            {
                return false;
            }

            if (base1.Key != base2.Key)
            {
                return false;
            }

            return true;
        }

        /// <summary>
        /// Operator overload for determining inequality.
        /// </summary>
        /// <param name="base1">The first instance of an
        /// <see cref="Transaction"/>.</param>
        /// <param name="base2">The second instance of an
        /// <see cref="Transaction"/>.</param>
        /// <returns>True if not equal.</returns>
        public static bool operator !=(Transaction base1,
            Transaction base2)
        {
            return (!(base1 == base2));
        }

        /// <summary>
        /// Serves as a hash function for this type.
        /// </summary>
        /// <returns>A hash code for the current Key
        /// property.</returns>
        public override int GetHashCode()
        {
            return this.key.GetHashCode();
        }

        #endregion
    }
}
```

As mentioned in the design section, the `Transaction` class implements the `IEntity` interface, and, therefore, it has to expose a `Key` property. The rest of the class is equality logic tests and probably could be refactored out into some type of Generic class at a later time.

The ClientTransaction Class

As you might have expected by the name, the `ClientTransaction` class inherits from the `Transaction` class. It contains an instance of the `IEntity` that the current Transaction is acting upon.

```
using System;
using SmartCA.Infrastructure.DomainBase;

namespace SmartCA.Infrastructure.Transactions
{
    public class ClientTransaction : Transaction
    {
        private IEntity entity;

        public ClientTransaction(object key, TransactionType type,
            IEntity entity)
            : base(key, type)
        {
            this.entity = entity;
        }

        public IEntity Entity
        {
            get { return this.entity; }
        }
    }
}
```

The ServerTransaction Class

The `ServerTransaction` class is almost the same as the `ClientTransaction` class except that it holds an instance of a `ContractBase` class instead of an `IEntity` instance:

```
using System;
using SmartCA.Infrastructure.DomainBase;
using SmartCA.DataContracts;

namespace SmartCA.Infrastructure.Transactions
{
    public class ServerTransaction : Transaction
    {
        private ContractBase contract;

        public ServerTransaction(object key, TransactionType type,
            ContractBase contract)
            : base(key, type)
        {
            this.contract = contract;
        }

        public ContractBase Contract
```

```
        {
            get { return this.contract; }
        }
    }
}
```

Data Contracts

The `ContractBase` class is the Data Contract equivalent of the `EntityBase` class:

```
using System;

namespace SmartCA.DataContracts
{
    [Serializable]
    public abstract class ContractBase
    {
        private object key;

        /// <summary>
        /// An <see cref="System.Object"/> that represents the
        /// primary identifier value for the class.
        /// </summary>
        public object Key
        {
            get { return this.key; }
            set { this.key = value; }
        }
    }
}
```

So, the question you probably are asking now is what in the world is a Data Contract? It is basically a Data Transfer Object (DTO) used to get data back and forth from the client to the server. All of the Data Contract classes are nothing but data, that is, they contain just a bunch of property setters and getters. Their main purpose in life is to be serialized and sent across the wire and then deserialized on the receiving end of the wire. I will go into more detail on these classes in the section of this chapter that deals with the server.

The only Data Contract classes that inherit from the `ContractBase` class are those that represent the Entity Root classes in the domain model. An example would be a `CompanyContract` class, whose main purpose is to represent the data of the Company Domain Model class in a way that is easily serializable.

The Client Transaction Repository Implementation

Since I am going to be storing the client transactions as messages that will be sent later, I need a way to save them, and what better way than to use the existing Repository pattern already being used everywhere else in the domain model.

The ClientTransactionRepositoryFactory Class

In order to program against this interface, just like I have with the other Repository interfaces in this application, I need a Factory to give the correct instance of the interface. This is a little bit different from the Repository Framework that I developed earlier for the other Entity Repositories, so I have created a new Factory for this implementation, and I am calling it the `ClientTransactionRepositoryFactory` class. Here is what it looks like:

```
using System;
using SmartCA.Infrastructure.Transactions;
using SmartCA.Infrastructure.RepositoryFramework.Configuration;
using System.Configuration;

namespace SmartCA.Infrastructure.RepositoryFramework
{
    public static class ClientTransactionRepositoryFactory
    {
        private static IClientTransactionRepository transactionRepository;

        public static IClientTransactionRepository GetTransactionRepository()
        {
            // See if the ITransactionRepository instance was already created
            if (ClientTransactionRepositoryFactory.transactionRepository == null)
            {
                // It was not created, so build it now
                RepositorySettings settings =
                    (RepositorySettings)ConfigurationManager.GetSection(

RepositoryMappingConstants.RepositoryMappingsConfigurationSectionName);

                // Get the type to be created
                Type repositoryType =
                    Type.GetType(

settings.RepositoryMappings["IClientTransactionRepository"].RepositoryFullTypeName);

                // Create the repository, and cast it to the
                // ITransactionRepository interface
                ClientTransactionRepositoryFactory.transactionRepository =
                    Activator.CreateInstance(repositoryType)
                    as IClientTransactionRepository;

            }

            return ClientTransactionRepositoryFactory.transactionRepository;
        }
    }
}
```

I was not able to use the existing `RepositoryFactory` class because it has the `IRepository` constraint, and the `IClientTransactionRepository` interface does not extend that interface, nor does it make sense for it to extend it.

The ClientTransactionRepository Class

The `ClientTransactionRepository` class is an abstract class that is intended to abstract away the implementation of the `Add` method of the `IClientTransactionRepository` interface.

```
using System;
using SmartCA.Infrastructure.DomainBase;
using SmartCA.Infrastructure.Transactions;
using SmartCA.DataContracts.Helpers;
using System.Collections.Generic;

namespace SmartCA.Infrastructure.Repositories
{
    public abstract class ClientTransactionRepository :
        IClientTransactionRepository
    {
        #region IClientTransactionRepository Members

        public abstract DateTime? GetLastSynchronization();
        public abstract void SetLastSynchronization(DateTime? lastSynchronization);

        public void Add(ClientTransaction transaction)
        {
            // Convert the entity to one of the data contract types
            object contract = Converter.ToContract(transaction.Entity);

            // Serialize the data contract into an array of bytes
            byte[] serializedContractData = Serializer.Serialize(contract);

            // Persist the transaction (delegate to the derived class)
            this.PersistNewTransaction(transaction.Type,
                serializedContractData, transaction.Key);
        }

        public abstract IList<ClientTransaction> FindPending();

        #endregion

        protected abstract void PersistNewTransaction(TransactionType type,
            byte[] serializedContractData, object transactionKey);
    }
}
```

As you can see, it implements the `IClientTransactionRepository` interface methods by exposing all of them as abstract methods or properties, except for the `Add` method. In the `Add` method, it takes care of converting the `ClientTransaction`'s `IEntity` instance into a Data Contract, and then serializes the Data Contract to an array of bytes so that it can be persisted. By taking advantage of the Template Method pattern, it leaves the persistence of the data up to the derived class, via the `PersistNewTransaction` abstract method that it calls in its `Add` method.

The SqlCeClientTransactionRepository Class

As you might expect, this class inherits from the `ClientTransactionRepository` class. Its purpose is to persist `ClientTransaction` objects to and from the local SQL CE database.

Constructor

The constructor is similar to the SqlCeRepositoryBase<T> constructor, as it grabs an instance of the Enterprise Library's Database class for use in some of its methods:

```
using System.Data.Common;
using System.Data;
using System.Collections.Generic;
using SmartCA.Infrastructure.EntityFactoryFramework;
using System.Text;

namespace SmartCA.Infrastructure.Repositories
{
    public class SqlCeClientTransactionRepository : ClientTransactionRepository
    {
        private Database database;

        public SqlCeClientTransactionRepository()
        {
            this.database = DatabaseFactory.CreateDatabase();
        }
```

The PersistNewTransaction Method

This is the override of the abstract method on the base class, ClientTransactionRepository:

```
        protected override void PersistNewTransaction(TransactionType type,
            byte[] serializedContractData, object transactionKey)
        {
            // See if the parent transaction already exists

            // Perform a query to see if it exists
            StringBuilder builder = new StringBuilder(100);
            builder.Append("SELECT 1 FROM ClientTransaction ");
            builder.Append(string.Format("WHERE ClientTransactionID='{0}';",
                transactionKey));
            object result = this.database.ExecuteScalar(
                this.database.GetSqlStringCommand(builder.ToString()));

            // Test the result of the query to see if it exists
            if (result == null)
            {
                // It does not exist, so create a new parent transaction
                builder = new StringBuilder(100);
                builder.Append("INSERT INTO ClientTransaction ");
                builder.Append("(ClientTransactionID) ");
                builder.Append(string.Format("VALUES ('{0}');", transactionKey));
                this.database.ExecuteNonQuery(
                    this.database.GetSqlStringCommand(builder.ToString()));
            }

            // Insert the details of the transaction,
            // including the serialized object's byte array
```

```
            builder = new StringBuilder(100);
            builder.Append("INSERT INTO ClientTransactionDetail ");
            builder.Append("(ClientTransactionID,TransactionType,ObjectData) ");
            builder.Append(string.Format("VALUES ('{0}',{1},@data);",
                transactionKey, (int)type));
            using (DbCommand command =
                this.database.GetSqlStringCommand(builder.ToString()))
            {
                this.database.AddInParameter(command, "@data",
                    DbType.Binary, serializedContractData);
                this.database.ExecuteNonQuery(command);
            }
        }
```

This code first has to detect whether a parent transaction has already been started, based upon the value of the `transactionKey` (which is the new `Key` property I added to the `IUnitOfWork` interface). It does this by executing a query and seeing whether the query returned null. If the parent transaction does not exist, then the code creates it by executing a SQL insert statement. The last step is to insert the details of the transaction, which contains the main piece of data for the transaction, the serialized Data Contract's byte array.

The FindPending Method

The job of this method is to find all pending transactions in the repository:

```
        public override IList<ClientTransaction> FindPending()
        {
            List<ClientTransaction> transactions = new List<ClientTransaction>();
            StringBuilder builder = new StringBuilder(100);
            builder.Append("SELECT ctd.ClientTransactionID,");
            builder.Append("ctd.TransactionType,ctd.ObjectData ");
            builder.Append("FROM ClientTransaction ct ");
            builder.Append("INNER JOIN ClientTransactionDetail ctd ");
            builder.Append("ON ct.ClientTransactionID = ctd.ClientTransactionID ");
            builder.Append("WHERE ct.ReconciliationResult = 1;");
            using (DbCommand command =
this.database.GetSqlStringCommand(builder.ToString()))
            {
                using (IDataReader reader = this.database.ExecuteReader(command))
                {
                    IEntityFactory<ClientTransaction> entityFactory =
                        EntityFactoryBuilder.BuildFactory<ClientTransaction>();
                    while (reader.Read())
                    {
                        transactions.Add(entityFactory.BuildEntity(reader));
                    }
                }
            }
            return transactions;
        }
```

This method builds a query to pull all of the pending transaction data from the data store and then uses the `ClientTransactionFactory` to transform the results into `ClientTransaction` instances:

```
using System;
using SmartCA.Infrastructure.EntityFactoryFramework;
using SmartCA.Infrastructure.Transactions;
using System.Data;
using SmartCA.Infrastructure.DomainBase;
using SmartCA.DataContracts;
using SmartCA.DataContracts.Helpers;

namespace SmartCA.Infrastructure.Repositories
{
    public class ClientTransactionFactory : IEntityFactory<ClientTransaction>
    {

        internal static class FieldNames
        {
            public const string ClientTransactionId = "ClientTransactionID";
            public const string ReconciliationResult = "ReconciliationResult";
            public const string ReconciliationErrorMessage =
                "ReconciliationErrorMessage";
            public const string TransactionType = "TransactionType";
            public const string ObjectData = "ObjectData";
        }
        #region IEntityFactory<ClientTransaction> Members

        public ClientTransaction BuildEntity(IDataReader reader)
        {
            byte[] objectData =
                DataHelper.GetByteArrayValue(reader[FieldNames.ObjectData]);
            ContractBase contract =
                Serializer.Deserialize(objectData) as ContractBase;
            EntityBase entity = Converter.ToEntity(contract);
            return new ClientTransaction(reader[FieldNames.ClientTransactionId],

(TransactionType)DataHelper.GetInteger(reader[FieldNames.TransactionType]),
                    entity);
        }

        #endregion
    }
}
```

Most of the code in this method is the standard implementation of the Entity Factory Framework that I have been using in all of the chapters. There is an interesting aspect in the implementation, particularly where the byte array is retrieved from the `IDataReader` instance and deserialized into its proper

ContractBase instance via the Serializer class. As you might expect, the Serializer class contains two methods, Serialize and Deserialize. The job of the Serialize method is to take a ContractBase instance and turn it into an array of bytes using binary formatting:

```
public static byte[] Serialize(object graph)
{
    byte[] serializedData = null;
    using (MemoryStream stream = new MemoryStream())
    {
        BinaryFormatter formatter = new BinaryFormatter();
        formatter.Serialize(stream, graph);
        serializedData = stream.ToArray();
    }
    return serializedData;
}
```

This method takes an object instance and uses the BinaryFormatter class to serialize the object graph into an array of bytes.

The Deserialize method does just the opposite. It takes an array of bytes and deserializes it into an object.

```
public static object Deserialize(byte[] serializedData)
{
    object graph = null;
    if (serializedData != null)
    {
        using (MemoryStream stream = new MemoryStream())
        {
            for (int i = 0; i < serializedData.Length; i++)
            {
                stream.WriteByte(serializedData[i]);
            }
            stream.Position = 0;
            BinaryFormatter formatter = new BinaryFormatter();
            graph = formatter.Deserialize(stream);
        }
    }
    return graph;
}
```

It is nice to encapsulate this functionality because it guarantees that each time I serialize or deserialize an object I know that it will be done the same way in the same format.

The next interesting part of the BuildEntity method in the ClientTransactionFactory class is where it takes the array of bytes returned from the Serializer class and then uses a Converter helper class to convert the ContractBase instance into an IEntity instance. This magic is done in the Converter class using reflection.

Here is the code for the `Converter` class's `ToEntity` method:

```
public static IEntity ToEntity(ContractBase contract)
{
    // Do reflection to call the right method here
    string methodName = string.Format("To{0}",
        contract.GetType().Name.Replace("Contract", ""));
    MethodInfo method = typeof(Converter).GetMethod(methodName);
    return method.Invoke(null, new object[] { contract }) as IEntity;
}
```

I know this code may look a little funky, but it gets rid of a giant switch statement of method names to do this conversion. For every class in the domain model, there is an equivalent Data Contract class, and, for each set of classes, there is a `To[Entity Name]` method and a `To[Entity Name]Contract` method. For example, the Company Domain Model class has a `ToCompanyContract` method (from a Company Entity) and a `ToCompany` method (from a Company Data Contract).

To further illustrate the concept, here is the `ToCompanyContract` method:

```
public static CompanyContract ToCompanyContract(Company company)
{
    CompanyContract contract = new CompanyContract();
    contract.Key = company.Key;
    contract.Abbreviation = company.Abbreviation;
    foreach (Address address in company.Addresses)
    {
        contract.Addresses.Add(Converter.ToAddressContract(address));
    }
    contract.FaxNumber = company.FaxNumber;
    contract.HeadquartersAddress =
        Converter.ToAddressContract(company.HeadquartersAddress);
    contract.Name = company.Name;
    contract.PhoneNumber = company.PhoneNumber;
    contract.Remarks = company.Remarks;
    contract.Url = company.Url;
    return contract;
}
```

Here is the `ToCompany` method:

```
public static Company ToCompany(CompanyContract contract)
{
    Company company = new Company(contract.Key);
    company.Abbreviation = contract.Abbreviation;
    foreach (AddressContract address in contract.Addresses)
    {
        company.Addresses.Add(Converter.ToAddress(address));
    }
    company.FaxNumber = contract.FaxNumber;
    company.HeadquartersAddress =
        Converter.ToAddress(contract.HeadquartersAddress);
    company.Name = contract.Name;
```

```
        company.PhoneNumber = contract.PhoneNumber;
        company.Remarks = contract.Remarks;
        company.Url = contract.Url;
        return company;
    }
```

As you can see, these two methods are pretty straightforward and are just the inverse of each other.

The `ToEntity` method assumes that the naming is consistent in the `Converter` class, and uses reflection to call the right method to convert a `ContractBase` instance to an `IEntity` instance. I know that this is a lot of plumbing, but that's why it lives in the Infrastructure namespace; the domain model is still free from this clutter!

The GetLastSynchronization Method

This method is used to retrieve the last `DateTime` value a Synchronization with the server occurred:

```
public override DateTime? GetLastSynchronization()
{
    string query = "SELECT LastSynchronization FROM Synchronization";
    using (DbCommand command =
        this.database.GetSqlStringCommand(query))
    {
        return DataHelper.GetNullableDateTime(
            this.database.ExecuteScalar(command));
    }
}
```

This code is pretty simple; it performs a query on the `Synchronization` table (which is always a one-row table) in order get the `Nullable DateTime` value.

The SetLastSynchronization Method

This method is just the opposite of the `GetLastSynchronization` method; it updates the date that the last synchronization with the server took place:

```
public override void SetLastSynchronization(DateTime? lastSynchronization)
{
    if (lastSynchronization.HasValue)
    {
        string query = "SELECT COUNT(*) FROM Synchronization";
        bool synchronizationRecordExists = false;
        using (DbCommand command =
            this.database.GetSqlStringCommand(query))
        {
            synchronizationRecordExists =
                ((int)this.database.ExecuteScalar(command) > 0);
        }

        StringBuilder builder = new StringBuilder(50);

        if (synchronizationRecordExists)
```

(continued)

(continued)

```
                {
                    builder.Append("UPDATE Synchronization ");
                    builder.Append(
                        string.Format("SET LastSynchronization = '{0}'",
                        lastSynchronization.Value));
                }
                else
                {
                    builder.Append("INSERT INTO Synchronization ");
                    builder.Append("(LastSynchronization) ");
                    builder.Append(string.Format("VALUES ('{0}')",
                        lastSynchronization));
                }
                using (DbCommand command =
                    this.database.GetSqlStringCommand(builder.ToString()))
                {
                    this.database.ExecuteNonQuery(command);
                }
            }
        }
```

The ClientTransactionService Class

This class is similar to a lot of the other service classes in that it is acting as a façade to a Repository interface instance, in this case the `IClientTransactionRepository` interface:

```
using System;
using System.Collections.Generic;
using SmartCA.Infrastructure.RepositoryFramework;

namespace SmartCA.Infrastructure.Transactions
{
    public static class ClientTransactionService
    {
        private static IClientTransactionRepository repository =
            ClientTransactionRepositoryFactory.GetTransactionRepository();

        public static IList<ClientTransaction> GetPendingTransactions()
        {
            return ClientTransactionService.repository.FindPending();
        }

        public static DateTime? GetLastSynchronization()
        {
            return ClientTransactionService.repository.GetLastSynchronization();
        }

        public static void SetLastSynchronization(DateTime? lastSynchronization)
        {
ClientTransactionService.repository.SetLastSynchronization(lastSynchronization);
        }
    }
}
```

As you can see, it is delegating to the `IClientTransactionRepository` methods and then exposing them via its static methods. I do not necessarily have to have this class, but it does make it easy to call static methods.

Synchronizing with the Synchronizer Class

Now that I have covered persisting transactions on the client, it is time to cover how to send the transactions to the server, and also how to get the transactions and reference data from the server.

If you remember from the diagram at the beginning of the chapter, the `Synchronizer` class was the class that was controlling everything in the synchronization process. The `Synchronizer` class is a static `Service` class whose job is to orchestrate the process of getting the transaction messages processed back and forth from the server.

Constructor

This `static` class does have a static constructor, and it is used to initialize the last time that the client synchronized with the server.

```
using System;
using SmartCA.Infrastructure.Transactions;
using System.Collections.Generic;
using SmartCA.Infrastructure.DomainBase;
using SmartCA.DataContracts.Helpers;
using SmartCA.Infrastructure.RepositoryFramework;
using System.Reflection;
using SmartCA.Infrastructure.ReferenceData;

namespace SmartCA.Infrastructure.Synchronization
{
    public static class Synchronizer
    {
        private static DateTime? lastSynchronized;

        static Synchronizer()
        {
            Synchronizer.GetLastSynchronized();
        }
```

The last synchronized value is used later in the class when communicating with the server.

The GetLastSynchronized Method

This method uses the `ClientTransactionService` to get the last time the client has synchronized with the server:

```
        private static void GetLastSynchronized()
        {
            Synchronizer.lastSynchronized =
                ClientTransactionService.GetLastSynchronization();
        }
```

This code is really just a pass-through to the `Service` method, but it is still useful for it to be wrapped in this method, as it makes the code more readable. This method is only called from the constructor.

The SetLastSynchronized Method

This method is the inverse of the `GetLastSynchronization` method:

```
private static void SetLastSynchronized()
{
    // Persist the last synchronized datetime
    Synchronizer.lastSynchronized = DateTime.Now;
    ClientTransactionService.SetLastSynchronization(
        Synchronizer.lastSynchronized);
}
```

This method is always called at the end of the synchronization process. Besides the obvious job of setting the last synchronized value, this method also persists the value via the `ClientTransactionService`. Where it is persisted is up to the `IClientTransactionRepository` instance that the `ClientTransactionService` refers to at run time.

The ProcessReferenceData Method

The `ProcessReferenceData` method takes in a composite `DataContract` that contains all of the collections of reference data items from the server, and then proceeds to send this data to the `ReferenceDataRepository` for persistence on the client:

```
private static void ProcessReferenceData(
    ReferenceDataContract referenceData)
{
    if (referenceData != null)
    {
        IReferenceDataRepository repository =
            ReferenceDataRepositoryFactory.GetReferenceDataRepository();

        if (referenceData.Disciplines != null)
        {
            repository.Add(referenceData.Disciplines);
        }
        if (referenceData.ItemStatuses != null)
        {
            repository.Add(referenceData.ItemStatuses);
        }
        if (referenceData.Sectors != null)
        {
            repository.Add(referenceData.Sectors);
        }
        if (referenceData.Segments != null)
        {
            repository.Add(referenceData.Segments);
        }
        if (referenceData.SpecSections != null)
```

```
                {
                    repository.Add(referenceData.SpecSections);
                }
            }
        }
```

This code first gets a reference to the `IReferenceDataRepository` interface instance via the `ReferenceDataRepositoryFactory` and then calls the appropriate `Add` method overloads to persist each type of reference `DataContract` type.

The IReferenceDataRepository Interface

The `IReferenceDataRepository` interface is a very simple interface with one method, the `Add` method, but with an overload of the `Add` method consisting of an `IList` type for each type of reference `DataContract`:

```
using System;
using System.Collections.Generic;
using SmartCA.DataContracts;

namespace SmartCA.Infrastructure.ReferenceData
{
    public interface IReferenceDataRepository
    {
        void Add(IList<DisciplineContract> disciplines);
        void Add(IList<ItemStatusContract> itemStatuses);
        void Add(IList<MarketSectorContract> sectors);
        void Add(IList<MarketSegmentContract> segments);
        void Add(IList<SpecificationSectionContract> specSections);
    }
}
```

The ReferenceDataRepositoryFactory Class

Following the same pattern that I have used all along when programming to an interface, I created an instance of the `IReferenceDataRepository` interface via a Factory. In this case, the Factory, the `ReferenceDataRepositoryFactory`, is just like the `ClientTransactionRepositoryFactory`. Again, I was not able to reuse the Repository Factory Framework I used for all of the other Repository interfaces in the domain model. I probably should refactor the `ClientTransactionRepositoryFactory` and the `ReferenceDataRepositoryFactory` into one class, but I have not done that yet.

```
using System;
using SmartCA.Infrastructure.RepositoryFramework.Configuration;
using System.Configuration;
using SmartCA.Infrastructure.ReferenceData;

namespace SmartCA.Infrastructure.RepositoryFramework
{
    public static class ReferenceDataRepositoryFactory
    {
        private static IReferenceDataRepository referenceDataRepository;

        public static IReferenceDataRepository GetReferenceDataRepository()
```

(continued)

(continued)

```
        {
            // See if the IReferenceDataRepository instance was already created
            if (ReferenceDataRepositoryFactory.referenceDataRepository == null)
            {
                // It was not created, so build it now
                RepositorySettings settings =
                    (RepositorySettings)ConfigurationManager.GetSection(

RepositoryMappingConstants.RepositoryMappingsConfigurationSectionName);

                // Get the type to be created
                Type repositoryType =
                    Type.GetType(

settings.RepositoryMappings["IReferenceDataRepository"].RepositoryFullTypeName);

                // Create the repository, and cast it to the
                // IReferenceDataRepository interface
                ReferenceDataRepositoryFactory.referenceDataRepository =
                    Activator.CreateInstance(repositoryType) as
IReferenceDataRepository;

            }

            return ReferenceDataRepositoryFactory.referenceDataRepository;
        }
    }
}
```

As you can see, the only real difference between the two repositories is that the interface type instance is returned. The nice thing is that I have created unit tests for these factories, so I can refactor them as much as I like and just re-run my tests until they pass.

The IReferenceDataRepository Implementation – The SqlCeReferenceDataRepository Class

This class is very similar to the `SqlCeClientTransactionRepository` implementation. As you can probably guess from its name, its job is to persist reference data to the local SQL CE database. As you can see from the `IReferenceDataRepository` interface, it does not perform any searching operations; it is strictly adding and updating reference data on the client.

Its private field and constructor are pretty much identical to the `SqlCeClientTransactionRepository` constructor as well:

```
using System;
using System.Collections.Generic;
using SmartCA.Infrastructure.ReferenceData;
using Microsoft.Practices.EnterpriseLibrary.Data;
using SmartCA.DataContracts;
using System.Text;

namespace SmartCA.Infrastructure.Repositories
```

```
{
    public class SqlCeReferenceDataRepository : IReferenceDataRepository
    {
        private Database database;

        public SqlCeReferenceDataRepository()
        {
            this.database = DatabaseFactory.CreateDatabase();
        }
```

All of the interface methods that it implements delegate out to private helper methods, as shown here:

```
        #region IReferenceDataRepository Members

        public void Add(IList<DisciplineContract> disciplines)
        {
            foreach (DisciplineContract discipline in disciplines)
            {
                this.AddDiscipline(discipline);
            }
        }

        public void Add(IList<ItemStatusContract> itemStatuses)
        {
            foreach (ItemStatusContract itemStatus in itemStatuses)
            {
                this.AddItemStatus(itemStatus);
            }
        }

        public void Add(IList<MarketSectorContract> sectors)
        {
            foreach (MarketSectorContract sector in sectors)
            {
                this.AddMarketSector(sector);
            }
        }

        public void Add(IList<MarketSegmentContract> segments)
        {
            foreach (MarketSegmentContract segment in segments)
            {
                this.AddMarketSegment(segment);
            }
        }

        public void Add(IList<SpecificationSectionContract> specSections)
        {
            foreach (SpecificationSectionContract specSection in specSections)
            {
                this.AddSpecificationSection(specSection);
            }
        }

        #endregion
```

The private helper methods just execute basic insert SQL statements on the local database. I am not going to show all of them here, but this is what the first one looks like:

```
private void AddDiscipline(DisciplineContract discipline)
{
    StringBuilder builder = new StringBuilder(100);
    builder.Append("INSERT INTO Discipline ");
    builder.Append("(DisciplineID,DisciplineName,Description) ");
    builder.Append(string.Format("VALUES ({0},'{1}','{2}');",
        discipline.Key, discipline.Name, discipline.Description));
    this.database.ExecuteNonQuery(
            this.database.GetSqlStringCommand(builder.ToString()));
}
```

As you can see, this method takes in the `DataContract` for a Discipline and uses it to build an insert SQL statement, and then executes the SQL statement.

The ProcessServerTransactions Method

Now that I have covered `Synchronizer` class's `ProcessReferenceData` method, it is time to move on to the last method in the `Synchronizer` class, which is the `ProcessServerTransactions` method:

```
private static void ProcessServerTransactions(
    IList<ServerTransaction> serverTransactions)
{
    IEntity entity = null;
    Type serviceType = null;
    string saveMethodName = string.Empty;
    MethodInfo method = null;

    foreach (ServerTransaction transaction in serverTransactions)
    {
        // Convert the DataContract into an EntityBase
        // and use the right service class to save it

        // 1. Get the EntityBase from the DataContract
        entity = Converter.ToEntity(transaction.Contract);

        // 2. Get the right service class type for the entity
        serviceType = Type.GetType(string.Format("{0}Service",
            entity.GetType().Name));

        // 3. Use reflection to get the correct Save method
        saveMethodName = string.Format("Save{0}", entity.GetType().Name);
        method = serviceType.GetMethod("Save");

        // 4. Call the Save method
        method.Invoke(null, new object[] { entity });
    }
}
```

This method takes a collection of server transactions, iterates through them, converts each server transaction that is represented by the `DataContract` back into an Entity, and then uses the Entity's associated Repository to persist it. Remember, the `ServerTransaction` class was covered in the beginning of the chapter, but this is the first time that I am using it. It really is about the same as the `ClientTransaction` class, except that it holds a reference to a `DataContract` instance instead of an `IEntity` instance.

Iterating through the server transactions and persisting them sounds pretty simple, but the way this method has to do it is a little bit tricky. The first thing the method has to do is to convert the `DataContract` instance of the `ServerTransaction` into an `IEntity` instance. This is done via the `ToEntity` method of the `Converter` class, which we looked at earlier in the chapter. The next step is to figure out the type name of the Entity, that is, Company, and then use that type name to figure out the associated Service for that Entity's Repository. For the Company example, it knows to get the `System.Type` of the type name of `CompanyService`. Then, once it has the `System.Type` reference, it reflects on the type to get an instance of the `Save[Entity Name]` method; in the case of the `CompanyService`, it would be `SaveCompany`. When it has the reference to the reflected method, it invokes the method, which in turn saves the Company instance to its proper Repository.

The Main Method – the Synchronize Method

You may have noticed that all of the methods I have shown so far in the `Synchronizer` class are all private methods. I wanted to show them to you so you could understand how the class works. The main entry point to the class, however, is one public static method, and that is the `Synchronize` method. This method is a Controller method, that is, it coordinates calls to other methods in the class that enable it to perform the overall synchronization with the server.

```
public static void Synchronize()
{
    // Send pending transactions to the server
    SynchronizationServerProxy.SendTransactions(
        ClientTransactionService.GetPendingTransactions());

    // Get reference data from the server
    ReferenceDataContract referenceData =
        SynchronizationServerProxy.GetReferenceData(lastSynchronized);

    // Process the reference data
    Synchronizer.ProcessReferenceData(referenceData);

    // Get transactions from the server
    IList<ServerTransaction> serverTransactions =
        SynchronizationServerProxy.GetTransactions(lastSynchronized);

    // Process the server transactions
    Synchronizer.ProcessServerTransactions(serverTransactions);

    // If the synchronization was successful,
    // then record the timestamp
    Synchronizer.SetLastSynchronized();
}
```

As you can see, it coordinates all of the calls to the private methods that I have just shown, but it calls them in the proper order required for Synchronization. There are two calls in this controller method that are not calls to private methods, and those are the calls to the server to get the reference data and the server transactions. These calls are done with a class called `SynchronizationServerProxy`. This class is mocked up for now, but this is the class that will actually make the calls to the server. It is the application's proxy to the server. Here is what the class looks like now:

```
using System;
using System.Collections.Generic;
using SmartCA.Infrastructure.Transactions;

namespace SmartCA.Infrastructure.Synchronization
{
    public static class SynchronizationServerProxy
    {
        public static void SendTransactions(
            IList<ClientTransaction> transactions)
        {
        }

        public static IList<ServerTransaction> GetTransactions(
            DateTime? lastSynchronized)
        {
            return new List<ServerTransaction>();
        }

        public static ReferenceDataContract GetReferenceData(
            DateTime? lastSynchronized)
        {
            return null;
        }
    }
}
```

I probably will refactor this class into an interface and create a Factory to give me different instances of the interface. This will allow me to use a mocked up `SynchronizationServerProxy` class that does pretty much what this one is doing, which will make my unit tests fast. When it comes time for actual integration with the server, I will create the real implementation of the interface and have the application configured to use that one for the actual synchronizations with the server.

Summary

In this chapter, I tackled the concept of how to synchronize the client's offline data with the server. I came to the conclusion that it was better to make my synchronization process more business-driven than data-driven, and therefore I chose not to use database replication or to use the new ADO.NET Synchronization Services. Instead, I went with a message-based approach and ended up refactoring my Unit of Work implementation to store transaction messages on the client. I then came up with a strategy and implementation for synchronizing those messages stored on the client with the messages on the server. Overall, the solution feels fairly elegant to me, and how it works makes sense. What I did not do is figure out how to reconcile synchronization conflicts, but that can be done in a later iteration of the application. The important point is that the synchronization process has been brought back and tied into the domain model, so any logic that needs to be performed to reconcile synchronization conflicts can be easily refactored into the domain model, which is where it belongs.

11

The Client Membership System

In the last chapter, I talked about synchronizing data with the server and how important it was to be able to work offline. In this chapter, I am going to discuss how to implement membership features, such as authentication, in an offline scenario.

The Problem

Now that the application has a nice, service-based way of working offline and synchronizing all of its data with the server, there needs to be a way to enable authentication and authorization while offline as well.

Users should be able to authenticate (i.e., log in to the application) and be able to perform work based on their assigned role(s) in the system. This is easy to do in an online ASP.NET application using the ASP.NET Membership System, but it is a lot trickier in a smart client application. One way of implementing these features is to call web services on the server that will authenticate the user and provide authorization information. The web services could actually wrap methods on the ASP.NET Membership System. The problem with that approach in the SmartCA application is that it requires that the user has a network or Internet connection, and if you remember from Chapter 1, the users sometimes are out in the middle of nowhere with no access to any type of network connection.

The Design

Since I already have a nice data synchronization strategy in place, why not use that to help solve the problem of performing membership tasks offline? After thinking about it for a while, I thought, why not put the membership data that is normally on the server down on the client? This would allow the users to authenticate themselves locally and do things like change their passwords locally. If any changes were then made on the server, or if the user changed any of his or her membership data on the client, the changes could be synchronized using the existing framework from the last chapter.

Password Security

One of the key factors about trying something like that is how to secure stored passwords on the client. The ASP.NET Membership Service specifies three formats for storing a password — in clear text, encrypted, or hashed, as defined in the `PasswordFormat` enumeration.

Password Format Setting	Description	Password Retrieval
`PasswordFormat.Clear`	The password is stored in clear text.	Yes
`PasswordFormat.Hashed`	A one-way hash of the password is stored.	No
`PasswordFormat.Encrypted`	The password is stored in encrypted format.	Yes

It should be obvious, but for security reasons, the option of storing passwords in clear text is definitely out. That would essentially allow any user who could figure out how to open and read the SQL CE database file to see all of the other users' passwords!

Encryption is definitely a better option than clear text. In order to perform password comparisons when passwords are stored in the encrypted format, the stored password must be decrypted first. To me, this still presents a problem, because that means someone could possibly figure out the algorithm to decrypt the passwords.

The best option is hashing. To compare passwords when they are stored in the hashed format, a hash using the same key is calculated on the supplied password and then compared against the stored hash. This is one-way encryption, that is, the password can never be decrypted. This means that once the password is created, it can never be decrypted back into plain text again. Nobody can ever retrieve their password with this option. If a user forgets his or her password, a new one must be created.

Designing the Client Membership System

I have decided for this application that I will implement a Membership System very similar to the ASP .NET Membership System, but with a "Client Membership" type of API. What this means is that I want users to be able to authenticate locally when using the application offline. The users will not only be able to authenticate themselves, but it will also be able to change and reset their passwords and password questions and answers.

All other functions, such as creating and managing users will be handled by the server. The client will communicate its Membership changes via the Synchronization Framework from the last chapter. In addition to sending the server membership data, the client will also receive updates to its membership data from the server as well.

In order to make it easier to synchronize data, I have decided to make the Client Membership System behave as close as possible to the ASP.NET Membership System. What I mean by that is that I am going with a provider-based model for accessing the Client Membership data. I know, you might be thinking, why not a repository like the ones I have been using all along? Well, the reason why is because the user data that I am holding on the client does not really fit that pattern. I am not really going to need to access it like an in-memory collection. All I really need to be able to do is retrieve and update the current User from the Client Membership System.

One of the main differences between my Membership implementation on the client and Microsoft's ASP .NET Membership implementation is that I am keeping my membership-related logic in the domain model, whereas with the ASP.NET Membership there is logic scattered across several classes and even in stored procedures in the out of the box `SqlMembershipProvider` implementation that comes with the ASP.NET Provider Toolkit.

The diagram in Figure 11.1 shows how the Client Membership system interacts with the user data.

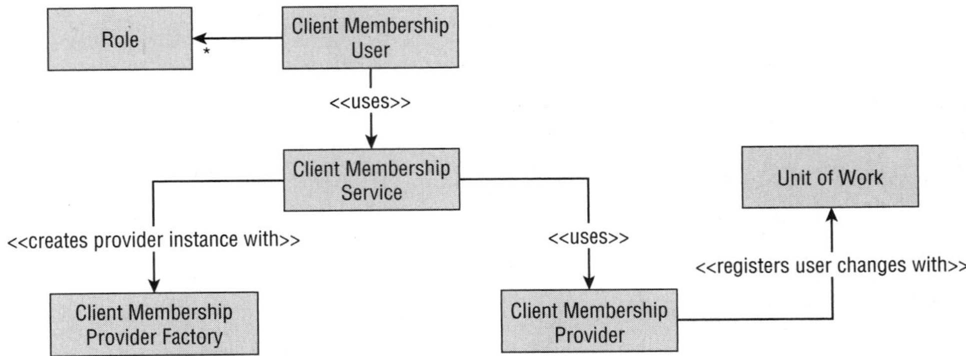

Figure 11.1: Client Membership System conceptual model.

In the diagram, you can see how this looks relatively similar to what I have been doing all along, except, instead of a repository behind the Service class, now there is a Provider behind it. The Provider is still kept abstract via an interface, and I still use a Factory to create an instance of the interface, thus allowing me to keep a dependency to only the interface of the Provider in my domain model.

An important item to note in the diagram is that the Client Membership provider is using a Unit of Work to register any changes to User instances, such as changed passwords, account lockouts, and so on. Since the Unit of Work implementation is tied into the synchronization strategy from the last chapter, this means that all of the User instance change transactions will be propagated to the server when the Synchronizer runs. Also, any relevant Membership transactions and refer to data from the server side will also be brought down to the client with the Synchronizer. I will go into more detail into how that works later in the chapter.

The Solution

The solution for the Client Membership System is mainly divided into two areas, the domain model and the Provider Framework.

The Client Membership System Domain Model Classes

Instead of just having one `User` class, I decided to try to split out some of the security-related data and behavior from the User class into a separate ClientMembershipUser class. Consumers of the Client Membership System should only ever have to work with the User class; the `ClientMembershipUser` class shields them from having to know all of the security-related details, such as keeping track of bad login attempts, locking users out, and so on. When I show the interface for the Client Membership Provider later in the chapter, you will see how this encapsulation is enforced by the interface.

The diagram in Figure 11.2 shows how the Client Membership System classes interrelate to each other.

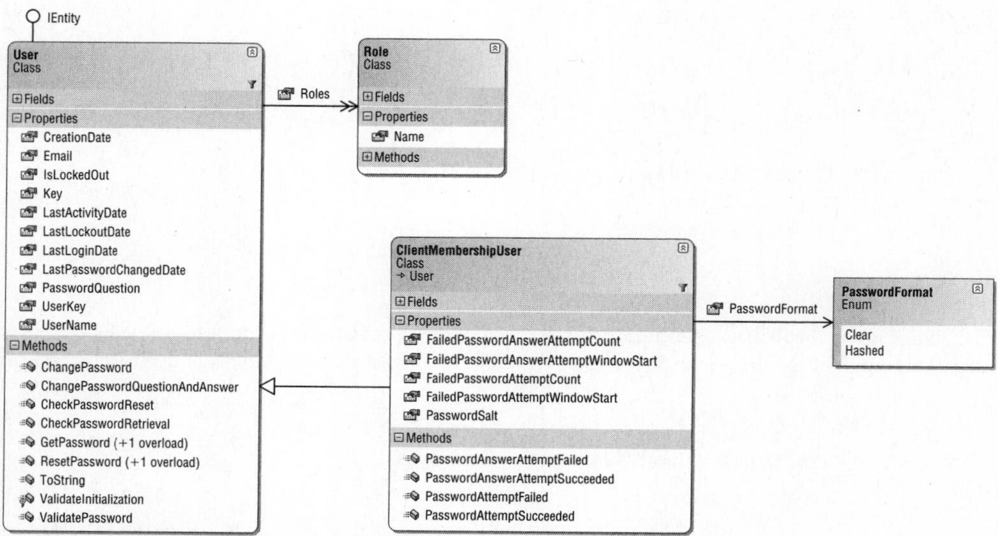

Figure 11.2: Client Membership System domain model classes.

The User Class

Since the `User` class is the main class that developers will be using to interact with the Client Membership System, I will cover it first.

Class Signature and Private Fields

Note that the `User` class implements the `IEntity` interface, which will prove to be very important later on when I need this class to participate in the Synchronization Framework:

```
using System;
using System.Collections.Generic;
using System.Text.RegularExpressions;
using SmartCA.Infrastructure;
using SmartCA.Infrastructure.DomainBase;

namespace SmartCA.Model.Membership
```

```
{
    public class User : IEntity
    {
        #region Private Fields

        private Guid userKey;
        private DateTime creationDate;
        private string email;
        private bool isLockedOut;
        private DateTime lastActivityDate;
        private DateTime lastLockoutDate;
        private DateTime lastLoginDate;
        private DateTime lastPasswordChangedDate;
        private string passwordQuestion;
        private string userName;
        private List<Role> roles;

        #endregion
```

As you can see, this class is not holding any security-sensitive information, such as the User's password or password answer. This data fields in this class are very similar to the ASP.NET `MembershipUser` class, but as you will see, there is much more logic in this class.

The Constructor

The constructor for this class essentially makes it mandatory for all of the data to be passed into the class in order to use it. This is similar to Value class functionality, but the `User` class is definitely an Entity.

```
        #region Constructors

        public User(Guid userKey, string name, string email,
            string passwordQuestion, bool isLockedOut,
            DateTime creationDate, DateTime lastLoginDate,
            DateTime lastActivityDate, DateTime lastPasswordChangedDate,
            DateTime lastLockoutDate)
        {
            this.userKey = userKey;
            if (name != null)
            {
                name = name.Trim();
            }
            if (email != null)
            {
                email = email.Trim();
            }
            if (passwordQuestion != null)
            {
                passwordQuestion = passwordQuestion.Trim();
            }
            this.userName = name;
            this.email = email;
            this.passwordQuestion = passwordQuestion;
            this.isLockedOut = isLockedOut;
```

(continued)

(continued)

```
        this.creationDate = creationDate.ToUniversalTime();
        this.lastLoginDate = lastLoginDate.ToUniversalTime();
        this.lastActivityDate = lastActivityDate.ToUniversalTime();
        this.lastPasswordChangedDate
            = lastPasswordChangedDate.ToUniversalTime();
        this.lastLockoutDate = lastLockoutDate.ToUniversalTime();
        this.roles = new List<Role>();
        this.ValidateInitialization();
    }

    #endregion
```

The constructor starts out by cleaning up the `name`, `email`, and `passwordQuestion` arguments before assigning them to their respective class fields. The next interesting bit of logic is the conversion of all of the `DateTime` argument values to Universal Time. Doing this allows the Client Membership system to standardize on one time zone for users who may be working around the country or the world.

The last task for the constructor is to validate the data passed in, and this is done via the `ValidateInitialization` method:

```
protected virtual void ValidateInitialization()
{
    SecurityHelper.CheckParameter(this.userName, true, true, true,
        ClientMembershipService.Application.MaxUsernameSize, "username");
    SecurityHelper.CheckParameter(this.email, true, true, true,
        0, "email");
    SecurityHelper.CheckParameter(this.passwordQuestion, true, true, true,
        ClientMembershipService.Application.MaxPasswordQuestionSize,
        "passwordQuestion");
}
```

This method validates the `username`, `email`, and `passwordQuestion` fields that were passed in from the constructor. To do this validation, the `SecurityHelper` class's `CheckParameter` method is used:

```
public static void CheckParameter(string param, bool checkForNull,
    bool checkIfEmpty, bool checkForCommas, int maxSize, string paramName)
{
    if (param == null)
    {
        if (checkForNull)
        {
            throw new ArgumentNullException(paramName);
        }
    }
    else
    {
        param = param.Trim();
        if (checkIfEmpty && (param.Length < 1))
        {
            throw new ArgumentException("Parameter cannot be empty",
                paramName);
        }
        if ((maxSize > 0) && (param.Length > maxSize))
```

```
                {
                    throw new ArgumentException("Parameter too long",
                        paramName);
                }
                if (checkForCommas && param.Contains(","))
                {
                    throw new ArgumentException("Parameter cannot contain commas",
                        paramName);
                }
            }
        }
```

This method is very flexible; it lets the caller specify, via its `Boolean` arguments, what types of checks should be made. The first check that is made, without giving the caller a choice, is whether the parameter is null. If it is null, then an `ArgumentNullException` is thrown.

The next check is for an empty parameter. If the call specified that it wanted this checked, then it is checked. If it turns out that the parameter is empty, then an `ArgumentException` is thrown. The checks for parameter length and commas perform the exact same pattern; that is, the method is only checking if instructed to do so, and then throwing exceptions if the check does not pass.

You can see in the `ValidateInitialization` method that everything is being checked for the `username`, `email`, and `passwordQuestion` fields.

The Properties

There really is not that much interesting about the properties of this class from a code and logic point of view; however, there is some nice encapsulation done with the private fields. Almost all of the properties are read-only, except for the `LastActivityDate`, `Email`, and `LastLoginDate` properties. For all of the `DateTime` properties, all of their getters return the `DateTime` value in the `LocalTime` format:

```
        public DateTime CreationDate
        {
            get { return this.creationDate.ToLocalTime(); }
        }
```

Some of the properties do have setters, but they are protected setters, meaning they needed to be opened up for changing to any classes that derive from the `User` class. This will make more sense when I show you the `ClientMembershipUser` class a little later. Here is an example of one of the properties with a protected setter:

```
        public bool IsLockedOut
        {
            get { return this.isLockedOut; }
            protected set { this.isLockedOut = value; }
        }
```

This is useful because it means that I could put some logic in a derived class that may need to change depending on whether the User is in a locked out state.

The Methods

Unlike some of the other classes in the SmartCA domain model, this class has a lot of behavior in it.

The ChangePassword Method

This is the first of several methods that will be delegating any heavy lifting to the `ClientMembershipService` class, which I will look at later in the chapter.

```
public void ChangePassword(string oldPassword, string newPassword)
{
    SecurityHelper.CheckPasswordParameter(oldPassword, 0, "oldPassword");
    SecurityHelper.CheckPasswordParameter(newPassword, 0, "newPassword");
    User.ValidatePassword(newPassword);
    ClientMembershipService.ChangePassword(this.UserName,
        oldPassword, newPassword);
}
```

This method starts out by first validating its arguments, and then calls the static `ValidateUser` method.

```
public static void ValidatePassword(string password)
{
    SecurityHelper.CheckParameter(password, true, false, false,
        0, "password");

    Application application = ClientMembershipService.Application;

    if (password.Length < application.MinRequiredPasswordLength)
    {
        throw new ArgumentException("Password too short",
                    "password");
    }

    int count = 0;

    for (int i = 0; i < password.Length; i++)
    {
        if (!char.IsLetterOrDigit(password, i))
        {
            count++;
        }
    }

    if (count < application.MinRequiredNonAlphanumericCharacters)
    {
        throw new ArgumentException
            ("Password needs more non alphanumeric chars",
            "password");
    }

    if (application.PasswordStrengthRegularExpression.Length > 0)
    {
        if (!Regex.IsMatch(password,
            application.PasswordStrengthRegularExpression))
        {
            throw new ArgumentException
                ("Password does not match regular expression",
                "password");
        }
```

```
            }

            if (password.Length > application.MaxPasswordSize)
            {
                throw new ArgumentException("Password too long",
                    "password");
            }
        }
```

I made this method static so I would be able to centralize this logic in the domain, in order for it to be reused from a Client Membership Provider. This method does a very exhaustive job of validating the password.

It ends up conducting five different tests on the password parameter:

1. It first checks to see whether the parameter is null via the `CheckParameter` method shown previously.
2. The next check is to make sure that the password meets the minimum length requirements of the Client Membership System. If it does not, then you guessed it, an `ArgumentException` is thrown.
3. The next check is a little bit more complicated. It iterates through all of the characters of the password and makes sure that it has the minimum number of non-alphanumeric characters in it.
4. The last test is to see whether the password meets the regular expression criteria of the Client Membership System. If that test passes, then the last test is to make sure that the password is not too long.

Now, let's go back to the `ChangePassword` method that I was originally showing. After performing all of the necessary checks, the last thing the `ChangePassword` method needs to do is to change the User's password! This is done by using the `ChangePassword` method of the `ClientMembershipService` class, and passing in the User's `UserName` property value, their old password, and their new password.

The ChangePasswordQuestionAndAnswer Method

This method is for changing the User's password question and password answer. It requires the password to be passed in, in order for the provider to authenticate the user before changing the User's password question and answer values.

```
    public void ChangePasswordQuestionAndAnswer(string password,
            string newPasswordQuestion, string newPasswordAnswer)
        {
            SecurityHelper.CheckPasswordParameter(password, 0, "password");
            SecurityHelper.CheckParameter(newPasswordQuestion, false, true,
                false, 0, "newPasswordQuestion");
            SecurityHelper.CheckParameter(newPasswordAnswer, false, true,
                false, 0, "newPasswordAnswer");
            ClientMembershipService.ChangePasswordQuestionAndAnswer(this.UserName,
                password, newPasswordQuestion, newPasswordAnswer);
            this.passwordQuestion = newPasswordQuestion;
        }
```

It starts out by validating all of the arguments with the SecurityHelper class. It then goes on to delegate to the ClientMembershipService class the changing of the User's password question and answer. The last thing it does is to update the passwordQuestion field of the User class to the value of the newPasswordQuestion argument passed in.

The ResetPassword Method

The ResetPassword method has two overloads; the first one takes no parameters:

```
public string ResetPassword()
{
    User.CheckPasswordReset(null);
    return ClientMembershipService.ResetPassword(this.UserName);
}
```

This method first calls the CheckPasswordReset static method to verify that the Client Membership System is configured to allow password resets:

```
public static void CheckPasswordReset(string passwordAnswer)
{
    Application application = ClientMembershipService.Application;

    if (!application.EnablePasswordReset)
    {
        throw new NotSupportedException
            ("Not configured to support password resets");
    }

    if (string.IsNullOrEmpty(passwordAnswer))
    {
        if (application.RequiresQuestionAndAnswer)
        {
            throw new NotSupportedException
                ("Must reset password with a password answer");
        }
    }
}
```

This method first checks to see whether the Client Membership System allows password resets. If no password answer was passed in, it checks to see whether the Client Membership System requires a password answer to be supplied before it resets the password. If any of those tests does not pass, it throws a NotSupportedException exception.

The ResetPassword method finishes by calling the ResetPassword method of the ClientMembershipService class.

The second overload of the ResetPassword method takes in a passwordAnswer argument, and passes the argument, along with the UserName property value to the ResetPassword method of the ClientMembershipService class.

```
        public string ResetPassword(string passwordAnswer)
        {
            User.CheckPasswordReset(passwordAnswer);
            return ClientMembershipService.ResetPassword(
                this.UserName, passwordAnswer);
        }
```

The ClientMembershipUser Class

The `ClientMembershipUser` class contains the logic and data for auditing and managing User authentication.

Class Signature and Private Fields

As previously mentioned, the `ClientMembershipUser` class derives from the `User` class, and its behavior affects some of the data in the `User` class:

```
using System;
using SmartCA.Model.Membership;

namespace SmartCA.Model.Membership
{
    public class ClientMembershipUser : User
    {
        #region Private Fields

        private string passwordSalt;
        private PasswordFormat passwordFormat;
        private int failedPasswordAttemptCount;
        private DateTime failedPasswordAttemptWindowStart;
        private int failedPasswordAnswerAttemptCount;
        private DateTime failedPasswordAnswerAttemptWindowStart;

        #endregion
```

This class holds password and password answer authentication auditing information. This class also has a lot of behavior in it that helps it manage its auditing information.

The Constructor

The Constructor for the `ClientMembershipUser` class is very similar to that of the `User` class; all of the data for its fields must be passed in:

```
        #region Constructor

        public ClientMembershipUser(User user, string passwordSalt,
            PasswordFormat passwordFormat, int failedPasswordAttemptCount,
            DateTime failedPasswordAttemptWindowStart,
            int failedPasswordAnswerAttemptCount,
            DateTime failedPasswordAnswerAttemptWindowStart)
            : base(user.UserKey,
            user.UserName, user.Email, user.PasswordQuestion,
            user.IsLockedOut, user.CreationDate, user.LastLoginDate,
```

(continued)

(continued)

```
        user.LastActivityDate, user.LastPasswordChangedDate,
        user.LastLockoutDate)
    {
        if (passwordSalt != null)
        {
            passwordSalt = passwordSalt.Trim();
        }
        this.passwordSalt = passwordSalt;
        this.passwordFormat = passwordFormat;
        this.failedPasswordAttemptCount = failedPasswordAttemptCount;
        this.failedPasswordAttemptWindowStart
            = failedPasswordAttemptWindowStart;
        this.failedPasswordAnswerAttemptCount
            = failedPasswordAnswerAttemptCount;
        this.failedPasswordAnswerAttemptWindowStart
            = failedPasswordAnswerAttemptWindowStart;
    }

    #endregion
```

Almost all of the arguments being passed in are `Integer` and `DateTime` data types, except for the `passwordSalt` argument, which is a string. Just like before, the string argument is trimmed before being assigned.

The Properties

I am not going to show any of the code for the properties here, since there is nothing special code-wise about them. All of the properties are read-only representations of the field data for the class.

The Methods

The only way the internal data in the class can be changed is through its methods. The methods contain all of the logic for successful logins, bad logins, successful password answer authentications, and failed password answer authentications.

The PasswordAttemptFailed Method

This method changes the state of the class appropriately whenever a failed password verification attempt occurs:

```
    public void PasswordAnswerAttemptFailed()
    {
        DateTime currentDateTime = DateTime.Now.ToUniversalTime();

        if (currentDateTime >
            this.failedPasswordAnswerAttemptWindowStart.AddMinutes(
            ClientMembershipService.Application.PasswordAttemptWindow))
        {
            this.failedPasswordAnswerAttemptWindowStart = currentDateTime;
            this.failedPasswordAnswerAttemptCount = 1;
        }
```

```
        else
        {
            this.failedPasswordAnswerAttemptCount++;
        }

        if (this.failedPasswordAnswerAttemptCount >
            ClientMembershipService.Application.MaxInvalidPasswordAttempts)
        {
            this.IsLockedOut = true;
            this.LastLockoutDate = currentDateTime;
        }

        this.LastActivityDate = currentDateTime;
    }
```

The logic in this method first captures the current timestamp in Universal Time (UTC) format. Next, a check is made to see if the timestamp is greater than the failed password attempt window plus the number of minutes configured for the window in the Client Membership System. The time window represents the `DateTime` from the last failed password. When this occurs, the failed password attempt time window starts ticking. If the current timestamp is greater than that time window plus the minutes from configuration, then the method knows that it is time to start the time window over again. This concept is probably best illustrated with an example. Take the case where a User has a bad login two days ago. Today he has another bad login. In this case, a new time window starts, and the failed password attempt count is set to 1 because it has been too long since the last bad login. This behavior is intended to prevent people from guessing passwords through some type of dictionary attack.

If it turns out that the bad password attempt did occur within the time window, then the failed password attempt counter is incremented by one. After that logic has completed, the next step is to see whether the User should be locked out. If the number of bad password attempts is greater than that allowed in the Client Membership System configuration, then the User is locked out of the account.

Notice how the method is setting the `IsLockedOut`, `LastLockedOut`, and `LastActivityDate` base class property values. This is made possible because they are marked with the protected keyword, which means that only classes that derive from the `User` class can set those values. Here is the `IsLockedOut` property of the `User` class again:

```
public bool IsLockedOut
{
    get { return this.isLockedOut; }
    protected set { this.isLockedOut = value; }
}
```

This is a nice little trick because the property is encapsulated from outside users of the class, but I am still able to change its values from the derived class.

The PasswordAttemptSucceeded Method

As you can probably infer by the name, this method is almost exactly the opposite of the previous method.

```
public void PasswordAttemptSucceeded()
{
    DateTime currentDateTime = DateTime.Now.ToUniversalTime();
    this.failedPasswordAttemptWindowStart = DateTime.MinValue;
    this.failedPasswordAttemptCount = 0;
    this.IsLockedOut = false;
    this.LastLockoutDate = DateTime.MinValue;
    this.LastActivityDate = currentDateTime;
}
```

This method starts out the same as the one before it, also by capturing the current timestamp. Since it represents a successful login, it resets the failed password attempt window to the lowest `DateTime` possible, and it resets the failed password attempt count to zero. Just to make sure, it sets the `IsLockedOut` property value of the `User` class to false, as well as setting the `LastLockoutDate` property value to the lowest `DateTime` value possible. Finally, it sets the `LastActivityDate` property for auditing purposes.

The PasswordAnswerAttemptFailed Method

This method is almost exactly the same as the `PasswordAttemptFailed` method, only instead of tracking bad password attempts, it is tracking bad password answer attempts.

```
public void PasswordAnswerAttemptFailed()
{
    DateTime currentDateTime = DateTime.Now.ToUniversalTime();

    if (currentDateTime >
        this.failedPasswordAnswerAttemptWindowStart.AddMinutes(
        ClientMembershipService.Application.PasswordAttemptWindow))
    {
        this.failedPasswordAnswerAttemptWindowStart = currentDateTime;
        this.failedPasswordAnswerAttemptCount = 1;
    }
    else
    {
        this.failedPasswordAnswerAttemptCount++;
    }

    if (this.failedPasswordAnswerAttemptCount >
        ClientMembershipService.Application.MaxInvalidPasswordAttempts)
    {
        this.IsLockedOut = true;
        this.LastLockoutDate = currentDateTime;
    }

    this.LastActivityDate = currentDateTime;
}
```

There really is not much different here from the `PasswordAttemptFailed` method—the logic is identical. The only difference is that I am tracking failed password answer attempts, but I still use the same logic as before for the time window and locking the User's account out if necessary.

The PasswordAnswerAttemptSucceeded Method

Again, the name of this method should give you a hint that it is very similar to the `PasswordAttemptSucceeded` method.

```
public void PasswordAnswerAttemptSucceeded()
{
    DateTime currentDateTime = DateTime.Now.ToUniversalTime();
    this.failedPasswordAnswerAttemptWindowStart = DateTime.MinValue;
    this.failedPasswordAnswerAttemptCount = 0;
    this.IsLockedOut = false;
    this.LastLockoutDate = DateTime.MinValue;
    this.LastActivityDate = currentDateTime;
}
```

The only thing different about this method is that it resets the values for the failed password answer attempt fields instead of the failed password attempt fields.

The Application Class

I have already shown parts of the `Application` class being used in the methods of the `User` and `ClientMembershipUser` classes. The `Application` class is a `Value` class that is only meant to store the configuration values of the Client Membership System. Here is the signature and data fields for the `Application` class:

```
using System;

namespace SmartCA.Model.Membership
{
    public class Application
    {
        #region Private Fields

        private string name;
        private bool enablePasswordReset;
        private bool enablePasswordRetrieval;
        private int maxInvalidPasswordAttempts;
        private int minRequiredNonAlphanumericCharacters;
        private int minRequiredPasswordLength;
        private int passwordAttemptWindow;
        private PasswordFormat passwordFormat;
        private string passwordStrengthRegularExpression;
        private bool requiresQuestionAndAnswer;
        private bool requiresUniqueEmail;
        private bool isDecryptionKeyAutogenerated;
        private bool isHashAlgorithmFromMembershipConfig;
        private string hashAlgorithmType;
        private int maxPasswordSize;
        private int maxPasswordAnswerSize;
        private int maxUsernameSize;
        private int maxPasswordQuestionSize;

        #endregion
```

I am not going to show the constructor and properties of the `Application` class here. Since it is a standard `Value` class, all of its properties are read-only and the constructor requires all of the field data to be passed in as arguments.

Its job is to represent the configuration from the Client Membership System, thus allowing me to not have to hard-code any values in the domain model or Providers.

The Client Membership System Provider Framework and Implementation

The Client Membership System Provider is very much like that of a repository, only it does not necessarily represent an in-memory collection of Aggregate Root Entities. In this case, the Client Membership provider's job is to provide the necessary data and persistence behavior for storing and retrieving Client Membership System data.

The IClientMembershipProvider Interface

Following the same pattern as with repositories, I am keeping the interface for the Client Membership System Provider in the domain model, along with its associated Service class. This way I can use it from my Domain Model classes but only be tied to the interface and not to the implementation.

The `IClientMembershipProvider` interface provides all of the functionality that my domain model needs in a nice, clean, well-encapsulated interface:

```
namespace SmartCA.Model.Membership
{
    public interface IClientMembershipProvider
    {
        #region Methods

        User GetUser(object userKey);
        User GetUser(string username);
        string GetPassword(string username);
        string GetPassword(string username, string answer);
        bool ChangePassword(string username, string oldPassword,
            string newPassword);
        bool ChangePasswordQuestionAndAnswer(string username, string password,
            string newPasswordQuestion, string newPasswordAnswer);
        string ResetPassword(string username);
        string ResetPassword(string username, string answer);
        void UpdateUser(User user);
        bool ValidateUser(string username, string password);

        #endregion

        #region Properties

        Application Application { get; }

        #endregion
    }
}
```

There are few things to notice on this interface; the first is that it has a property on it as well as methods. That property is the `Application` property, which represents an instance of the `Application` class that I just demonstrated.

The next important item to note is that it offers methods to change the User's password and password answer values, as well as for password retrieval. Since I have decided to use hashed passwords for the Client Membership System, these password retrieval methods probably should not be there, but I left them there in case, later, someone wanted to change to an encryption algorithm that would support retrieving passwords.

The last important piece of functionality this interface offers is the ability to get a `User` instance from a data store and also update that instance and have the changes persisted to a data store.

The ProviderFactory Class

Just like the `RepositoryFactory` class from the Repository Framework, the `ProviderFactory` class is used to create instances of the `IClientMembershipProvider` interface implementation class:

```
using System;
using System.Configuration;
using SmartCA.Infrastructure.RepositoryFramework.Configuration;

namespace SmartCA.Infrastructure.Membership
{
    public static class ProviderFactory
    {
        private static object provider;

        public static T GetProvider<T>() where T : class
        {
            // See if the provider instance was already created
            if (ProviderFactory.provider == null)
            {
                // It was not created, so build it now
                RepositorySettings settings =
                    (RepositorySettings)ConfigurationManager.GetSection(
RepositoryMappingConstants.RepositoryMappingsConfigurationSectionName);

                // Get the type to be created
                string interfaceTypeName = typeof(T).Name;
                Type repositoryType =
                    Type.GetType(
settings.RepositoryMappings[interfaceTypeName].RepositoryFullTypeName);

                // Create the provider
                ProviderFactory.provider =
                    Activator.CreateInstance(repositoryType);
            }

            return ProviderFactory.provider as T;
        }
    }
}
```

This code is very similar to the `RepositoryFactory` code from Chapter 2, but it is a little bit more scaled down. In order to make things easier, it actually uses the same configuration code as the `RepositoryFactory` class.

Again, just like with the Repository interfaces and the `RepositoryFactory`, by using the combination of interface and Factory, it allows me to implement the Separated Interface Pattern (Fowler). In other words, I can keep the interface separate from the implementation and yet still create instances of the interface and use those instances without even knowing what they are.

The ClientMembershipProvider Class

This is probably the most complicated class in the Client Membership System, or at least it was the hardest one for me to create. I wanted to make sure that I did not hide any domain logic in this class; I really wanted the domain logic to stay in the domain model where it is supposed to be.

This class kind of resembles the `MembershipProvider` class of the ASP.NET Membership system, but the main difference is that it implements the `IClientMembershipProvider` interface.

Class Signature and Private Fields

The first thing to notice about this class is that it is abstract and implements two different interfaces:

```
using System;
using System.Globalization;
using System.Security.Cryptography;
using System.Text;
using SmartCA.Infrastructure.DomainBase;
using SmartCA.Infrastructure.RepositoryFramework;
using SmartCA.Model.Membership;

namespace SmartCA.Infrastructure.Membership.Providers
{
    public abstract class ClientMembershipProvider
        : IClientMembershipProvider, IUnitOfWorkRepository
    {
        #region Constants

        private static class Constants
        {
            public const int SaltSizeInBytes = 0x10;
            public const string NoEncryptedPasswordsWithAutoGenKeys =
                "Cannot use encrypted passwords with autogenerated keys";
            public const string CannotDecodeHashedPassword =
                "Provider cannot decode hashed password";
            public const string NoPasswordRetrieval =
                "Password retrieval is not supported";
            public const int PasswordSize = 14;
        }

        #endregion

        #region Private Fields
```

```
        private IUnitOfWork unitOfWork;

        #endregion
```

The first interface that this class implements is the `IClientMembershipProvider` interface. This should not be a surprise, and makes total sense from what I have shown so far. The second one, the `IUnitOfWorkRepository` interface, is a little bit more intriguing. By implementing this interface, this allows me to let the Client Membership System take part in the Synchronization Framework introduced in the last chapter. This is very important, because this allows the Client Membership System to stay synchronized with the membership data on the server.

The next important thing about this class is that it is an abstract class. By being abstract, it can absorb and encapsulate any type of Client Membership Provider logic and make it easier to write the Client Membership Provider implementations. As you will later see, this class uses the Template Method pattern all over the place to make implementing a Client Membership provider as simple as storing and retrieving data from a data store.

The Constructor

The constructor for the class does not do much, except instantiate a `UnitOfWork` class and delegate for the Provider to initialize itself:

```
        #region Constructors

        protected ClientMembershipProvider()
        {
            this.unitOfWork = new UnitOfWork();
            this.Initialize();
        }

        #endregion
```

Note that it is protected, and that the `Initialize` method that it is calling is also abstract. This is the first occurrence of the Template Method pattern in the class.

Here is the `Initialize` method signature:

```
protected abstract void Initialize();
```

The method is protected, which helps encapsulate the provider implementation by not allowing other callers to initialize it except the `ClientMembershipProvider` class.

The Methods

Probably the easiest way to look at the methods in the `ClientMembershipProvider` class is to look at them from the perspective of the `IClientMembershipProvider` interface. The first two methods of the `IClientMembershipProvider` interface are implemented as pass-through methods to the derived Provider:

```
        public abstract User GetUser(object userKey);
        public abstract User GetUser(string username);
```

They are both marked as abstract, so it is up to the derived Provider to retrieve the `User` instances from the data store properly.

The next two methods of the interface implementation are the `GetPassword` overloaded methods. I will only show the code for one of the overloads here:

```
public virtual string GetPassword(string username, string answer)
{
    ClientMembershipUser user = this.GetClientMembershipUser(username);
    return this.GetPassword(user, answer);
}
```

Notice how this method is marked virtual. I made it virtual in case someone else writing a Client Membership Provider wanted to override the logic in this method. You will see this pattern repeated on all of the methods implemented for the `IClientMembershipProvider` interface in this class.

This method first gets a `ClientMembershipUser` instance from the `username` argument. This is something you will see a lot in this class, because the `ClientMembershipUser` class has all of the security-related data and behavior that the Provider needs. This happens with the `GetlClientMembershipUser` method:

```
private ClientMembershipUser GetClientMembershipUser(string username)
{
    return this.GetUser(this.GetUser(username));
}
```

This method is calling two methods in a nested fashion. Here is the outer method:

```
protected abstract ClientMembershipUser GetUser(User user);
```

This method is implemented in the derived Client Membership provider and is protected, which is good encapsulation. The purpose of the method is to take a `User` instance and decorate it with the necessary data to be a `ClientMembershipUser` instance. The inner `GetUser` method looks like this:

```
public abstract User GetUser(string username);
```

This method should look familiar, as I showed it earlier in this section. Finally, the `GetPassword` method finishes by calling the class's protected virtual `GetPassword` method:

```
protected virtual string GetPassword(ClientMembershipUser user,
    string passwordAnswer)
{
    // Make sure password retrievals are allowed
    User.CheckPasswordRetrieval();

    // Validate the user's password answer
    this.ValidateUserWithPasswordAnswer(user, passwordAnswer, true);

    // Get the user's password from persistence
    return this.GetPasswordFromPersistence(user);
}
```

This method first checks to see whether password retrievals are even allowed in the Client Membership System. Next, it authenticates the user with the User's supplied password answer via the `ValidateUserWithPasswordAnswer` method:

```
private void ValidateUserWithPasswordAnswer(ClientMembershipUser user,
    string passwordAnswer, bool throwIfFails)
{
    if (passwordAnswer != null)
    {
        passwordAnswer = passwordAnswer.Trim();
    }

    SecurityHelper.CheckParameter(passwordAnswer,
        this.Application.RequiresQuestionAndAnswer,
        this.Application.RequiresQuestionAndAnswer,
        false, this.Application.MaxPasswordAnswerSize,
        "passwordAnswer");

    string passwordAnswerFromPersistence =
        this.GetPasswordAnswerFromPersistence(user);

    try
    {
        if (!this.CheckPasswordAnswer(passwordAnswer,
            passwordAnswerFromPersistence,
            user.PasswordFormat, user.PasswordSalt))
        {
            user.PasswordAnswerAttemptFailed();
            if (throwIfFails)
            {
                throw new SecurityException
                    ("The password answer supplied was not correct");
            }
        }
        else
        {
            user.PasswordAnswerAttemptSucceeded();
        }
    }
    finally
    {
        this.PersistUser(user);
    }
}
```

This method first starts out by validating all of the arguments passed in. The next step it needs to perform is to get the User's password answer from the data store so that it can compare it to the password answer that the User supplied. It gets the User's password answer from the data store via the `GetPasswordAnswerFromPersistence` method, which is another protected, abstract method:

```
protected abstract string GetPasswordAnswerFromPersistence(
        ClientMembershipUser user);
```

Once the password answer is obtained, the next step is to check to see if the password answer supplied equals the password answer from the data store. This is where the `CheckPasswordAnswer` method comes in:

```
private bool CheckPasswordAnswer(string passwordAnswer,
    string passwordAnswerFromPersistence,
    PasswordFormat passwordFormat, string salt)
{
    return this.CheckPassword(
        passwordAnswer.ToLower(CultureInfo.InvariantCulture),
        passwordAnswerFromPersistence, passwordFormat, salt);
}
```

This method does a pass-through to the `CheckPassword` method. I did this, instead of just having one method, to make the code more readable. Here is the `CheckPassword` method:

```
private bool CheckPassword(string password, string passwordFromPersistence,
    PasswordFormat passwordFormat, string salt)
{
    string encodedPassword = this.EncodePassword(password,
        passwordFormat, salt);
    return passwordFromPersistence.Equals(encodedPassword);
}
```

The important thing to take away from this code is that the password answer from the data store is already hashed. I have to hash the password answer that is being passed in, so I can compare apples to apples. The way I hash the value is to call the `EncodePassword` method:

```
private string EncodePassword(string password,
    PasswordFormat passwordFormat, string salt)
{
    if (passwordFormat == PasswordFormat.Clear)
    {
        return password;
    }
    byte[] bytes = Encoding.Unicode.GetBytes(password);
    byte[] source = Convert.FromBase64String(salt);
    byte[] destination = new byte[source.Length + bytes.Length];
    byte[] passwordBytes = null;
    Buffer.BlockCopy(source, 0, destination, 0, source.Length);
    Buffer.BlockCopy(bytes, 0, destination, source.Length, bytes.Length);
    if (passwordFormat == PasswordFormat.Hashed)
    {
        HashAlgorithm algorithm = HashAlgorithm.Create(
            this.Application.HashAlgorithmType);
        if ((algorithm == null) &&
            this.Application.IsHashAlgorithmFromMembershipConfig)
        {
            this.ThrowHashAlgorithmException();
        }
        passwordBytes = algorithm.ComputeHash(destination);
    }
    return Convert.ToBase64String(passwordBytes);
}
```

This code essentially takes a password string and a password salt, and then encodes the password using the salt in the manner specified in the `passwordFormat` argument. In the case of the current configuration of the Client Membership System, it will be using a `PasswordFormat` enumeration value of `Hashed`.

The next `IClientMembershipProvider` interface method implementation is the `ChangePassword` method:

```
public virtual bool ChangePassword(string username, string oldPassword,
    string newPassword)
{
    ClientMembershipUser user = this.GetClientMembershipUser(username);
    this.ChangePassword(user, oldPassword, newPassword);
    return true;
}
```

This method is also marked virtual for flexibility reasons and starts out just like the `GetPassword` method by calling the `GetClientMembershipUser` method to get a `ClientMembershipUser` instance. It then passes that instance on to the protected `ChangePassword` method:

```
protected virtual void ChangePassword(ClientMembershipUser user,
    string oldPassword, string newPassword)
{
    SecurityHelper.CheckParameter(oldPassword, true, true, false,
        this.Application.MaxPasswordSize, "oldPassword");
    SecurityHelper.CheckParameter(newPassword, true, true, false,
        this.Application.MaxPasswordSize, "newPassword");

    // Validate the user before making any changes
    this.ValidateUserWithPassword(user, oldPassword, true);

    // Make sure the new password is ok
    User.ValidatePassword(newPassword);

    // encode the new password
    string encodedPassword = this.EncodePassword(newPassword,
        user.PasswordFormat, user.PasswordSalt);

    if (encodedPassword.Length > this.Application.MaxPasswordSize)
    {
        throw new ArgumentException("Membership password too long",
            "newPassword");
    }

    // Save the new password
    this.PersistChangedPassword(user, encodedPassword);
}
```

I marked this method as protected in order to encapsulate it and made it virtual, so the derived provider would have some flexibility in using it. This code starts out with very familiar methods for validating the password values passed in. It then authenticates the user with the `oldPassword` argument value that was passed in via the `ValidateUserWithPassword` method:

```
private void ValidateUserWithPassword(ClientMembershipUser user,
    string password, bool throwIfFails)
{
    if (password != null)
    {
        password = password.Trim();
    }

    SecurityHelper.CheckParameter(password,
        true, true, true,
        this.Application.MaxPasswordAnswerSize,
        "password");

    string passwordFromPersistence =
        this.GetPasswordFromPersistence(user);

    try
    {
        if (!this.CheckPassword(password,
            passwordFromPersistence,
            user.PasswordFormat, user.PasswordSalt))
        {
            user.PasswordAttemptFailed();
            if (throwIfFails)
            {
                throw new SecurityException
                    ("The password supplied was not correct");
            }
        }
        else
        {
            user.PasswordAttemptSucceeded();
        }
    }
    finally
    {
        this.PersistUser(user);
    }
}
```

Very similar to the `ValidateUserWithPasswordAnswer` method previously shown, this method's job is to authenticate a user based on their user password value. Its logic is almost identical to the `ValidateUserWithPasswordAnswer` method, except that it validates the user using their password instead of their password answer.

Okay, going back to the `ChangePassword` method, the next step after authenticating the user is to encode the new password via the previously shown `EncodePassword` method. Once the new password is encoded, it is then checked to make sure it is not too long.

```
if (password.Length > this.Application.MaxPasswordSize)
{
    throw new ArgumentException("Membership password too long",
        "newPassword");
}

this.PersistChangedPassword(user, password);
```

Once the check of the newly encoded password is done, then the User's new password is saved to the data store via the `PersistChangedPassword` method:

```
protected abstract void PersistChangedPassword(ClientMembershipUser user,
            string newPassword);
```

The `PersistChangedPassword` method is another protected abstract method that the derived Client Membership Provider must override. Its job is to save the User's data, including their new password, to the data store.

The next `IClientMembershipProvider` interface method implementation is the `ChangePasswordQuestionAndAnswer` method:

```
public virtual bool ChangePasswordQuestionAndAnswer(string username,
    string password, string newPasswordQuestion,
    string newPasswordAnswer)
{
    ClientMembershipUser user = this.GetClientMembershipUser(username);
    this.ChangePasswordQuestionAndAnswer(user, password,
        newPasswordQuestion, newPasswordAnswer);
    return true;
}
```

This method first obtains a `ClientMembershipUser` instance, and then passes that instance to the protected virtual `ChangePasswordQuestionAndAnswer` method:

```
protected virtual void ChangePasswordQuestionAndAnswer(
    ClientMembershipUser user, string password,
    string newPasswordQuestion, string newPasswordAnswer)
{
    SecurityHelper.CheckParameter(newPasswordQuestion,
        this.Application.RequiresQuestionAndAnswer,
        this.Application.RequiresQuestionAndAnswer, false,
        this.Application.MaxPasswordQuestionSize, "newPasswordQuestion");

    if (newPasswordAnswer != null)
    {
        newPasswordAnswer = newPasswordAnswer.Trim();
    }

    SecurityHelper.CheckParameter(newPasswordAnswer,
        this.Application.RequiresQuestionAndAnswer,
        this.Application.RequiresQuestionAndAnswer, false,
```

(continued)

(continued)

```
                this.Application.MaxPasswordAnswerSize, "newPasswordAnswer");

            // Validate the user before making any changes
            this.ValidateUserWithPassword(user, password, true);

            string encodedPasswordAnswer;

            if (!string.IsNullOrEmpty(newPasswordAnswer))
            {
                encodedPasswordAnswer = this.EncodePassword(
                    newPasswordAnswer.ToLower(CultureInfo.InvariantCulture),
                    user.PasswordFormat, user.PasswordSalt);
            }
            else
            {
                encodedPasswordAnswer = newPasswordAnswer;
            }

            SecurityHelper.CheckParameter(encodedPasswordAnswer,
                this.Application.RequiresQuestionAndAnswer,
                this.Application.RequiresQuestionAndAnswer, false,
                this.Application.MaxPasswordAnswerSize, "newPasswordAnswer");

            this.PersistChangedPasswordQuestionAndAnswer(user, password,
                newPasswordAnswer);
        }
```

This method starts out by validating all of the parameters passed into it, as well as authenticating the User based on the password argument passed in. Once all of those tests pass, it encodes the new password answer string using the familiar `EncodePassword` method. Once the password answer has been encoded, it must be validated again in order to make sure that it does not exceed the maximum password size limits of the Client Membership System. Once the encoded password answer has passed all of these tests, the password question and answer are then persisted to the data store via the `PersistChangedPasswordQuestionAndAnswer` method:

```
    protected abstract void PersistChangedPasswordQuestionAndAnswer(
            ClientMembershipUser user, string password,
            string newPasswordAnswer);
```

Since this method is abstract, it is implemented in the derived Client Membership Provider.

The next method in the `IClientMembershipProvider` interface is the `ResetPassword` method, which has one overload. I will just show the code for the `ResetPassword` method that requires a password answer to be passed in:

```
        public virtual string ResetPassword(string username, string answer)
        {
            ClientMembershipUser user = this.GetClientMembershipUser(username);
            return this.ResetPassword(user, answer);
        }
```

This method gets the `ClientMembershipUser` instance and then passes it to the protected virtual `ResetPassword` method:

```
protected virtual string ResetPassword(ClientMembershipUser user,
    string passwordAnswer)
{
    // Are password resets allowed?
    User.CheckPasswordReset(passwordAnswer);

    // Validate the user's password answer
    this.ValidateUserWithPasswordAnswer(user, passwordAnswer, true);

    int maxPasswordSize =
        (this.Application.MinRequiredPasswordLength <
            Constants.PasswordSize)
                ? Constants.PasswordSize :
                this.Application.MinRequiredPasswordLength;

    // Create the new password
    string newPassword = System.Web.Security.Membership.GeneratePassword(
        maxPasswordSize,
        this.Application.MinRequiredNonAlphanumericCharacters);

    // Encode the password
    string newEncodedPassword = this.EncodePassword(newPassword,
        user.PasswordFormat, user.PasswordSalt);

    // Save the user's new password
    this.PersistResetPassword(user, newEncodedPassword);

    // return the new password (not the encoded one!)
    return newPassword;
}
```

This method first checks to see whether password resets have been configured to be allowed in the Client Membership System. If that test passes, then the User is authenticated with his or her password answer. If that test passes, then the `Membership` class of the .NET Framework's `System.Web.Security` namespace is used to generate a new password via its `GeneratePassword` method. After getting the newly generated password, it is encoded via the `EncodePassword` method and then saved to the data store. Finally the new password value is returned in clear text to the caller.

The next `IClientMembershipProvider` interface method implementation is the `UpdateUser` method:

```
public virtual void UpdateUser(User user)
{
    ClientMembershipUser clientMembershipUser = this.GetUser(user);
    this.unitOfWork.RegisterChanged(clientMembershipUser, this);
    this.unitOfWork.Commit();
}
```

This method is interesting to me because instead of just delegating to the protected abstract method `PersistUser`, it instead calls the `RegisterChanged` method of the `IUnitOfWork` instance. Then it calls the `Commit` method on the `IUnitOfWork` instance. This is very significant because this is how the Provider is hooking in to the Synchronization Framework from the last chapter. When the `IUnitOfWork` instance's `Commit` method is called, it calls back into the `IUnitOfWorkRepository` interface passed in with the `RegisterChanged` method. This is better known as a double dispatch.

If you recall from earlier in the chapter, the `ClientMembershipProvider` class implements the `IUnitOfWorkRepository` interface, whose methods are called in the `IUnitOfWork`'s `Commit` implementation. Here is the `IUnitOfWorkRepository` interface implementation:

```
#region IUnitOfWorkRepository Members

public void PersistNewItem(IEntity item)
{
    throw new NotImplementedException();
}

public void PersistUpdatedItem(IEntity item)
{
    ClientMembershipUser user = (ClientMembershipUser)item;
    this.PersistUser(user);
}

public void PersistDeletedItem(IEntity item)
{
    throw new NotImplementedException();
}

#endregion
```

As you can see, the only method implemented on the interface is the `PersistUpdatedItem` method. This is because all I am doing in the `ClientMembershipProvider` with the User instances is updating them, I am not adding new users or deleting users—those types of activities are all done on the server.

The `PersistUpdatedItem` method is very simple; it casts the `IEntity` instance passed into it to a `ClientMembershipUser` instance, and then passes that to the protected abstract `PersistUser` method previously shown.

The SqlCeClientMembershipProvider Class

The `SqlCeClientMembershipProvider` class inherits from the `ClientMembershipProvider` abstract class. Its main purpose is to persist User data to and from the local SQL CE database.

Class Signature and Private Fields

The signature is similar to the SqlCeRepositoryBase<T> signature, as it contains a private field for the Enterprise Library's Database class for use in some of its methods:

```
using System.Data;
using System.Data.Common;
using System.Text;
using Microsoft.Practices.EnterpriseLibrary.Data;
using SmartCA.Infrastructure.EntityFactoryFramework;
using SmartCA.Infrastructure.Helpers;
using SmartCA.Model.Membership;

namespace SmartCA.Infrastructure.Membership.Providers
{
    public class SqlCeClientMembershipProvider : ClientMembershipProvider
    {
        private Database database;
        private Application application;
```

The Initialize Method Override

This is the method override that the constructor of the ClientMembershipProvider base class calls:

```
        protected override void Initialize()
        {
            this.database = DatabaseFactory.CreateDatabase();
            string sql = "SELECT * FROM Application;";
            using (DbCommand command = this.database.GetSqlStringCommand(sql))
            {
                using (IDataReader reader = this.database.ExecuteReader(command))
                {
                    if (reader.Read())
                    {
                        this.application =
                            ApplicationFactory.BuildApplication(reader);
                    }
                }
            }
        }
```

The main tasks that this method performs are to initialize the database field value and to populate the application field value with the Client Membership System configuration information from the database.

The GetUser Method Overrides

There are three method overrides for GetUser. Here are the first two:

```
        public override User GetUser(object userKey)
        {
            return this.GetUserFromSql(string.Format
                ("SELECT * FROM [User] WHERE UserId = '{0}'", userKey));
        }
```

(continued)

(continued)

```
public override User GetUser(string username)
{
    return this.GetUserFromSql(string.Format
        ("SELECT * FROM [User] WHERE UserName = '{0}'", username));
}
```

As you can see, they both only differ by their SQL statements and both of them use the `GetUserFromSql` helper method:

```
private User GetUserFromSql(string sql)
{
    User user = null;
    using (DbCommand command = this.database.GetSqlStringCommand(sql))
    {
        using (IDataReader reader = this.database.ExecuteReader(command))
        {
            IEntityFactory<User> entityFactory =
                EntityFactoryBuilder.BuildFactory<User>();
            if (reader.Read())
            {
                user = entityFactory.BuildEntity(reader);
            }
        }
    }
    return user;
}
```

This code in this method should look pretty familiar by now; it is following the standard pattern laid out for converting data from the database into `IEntity` instances.

The third method override for `GetUser` is a little bit different; it takes an existing `User` instance and adds the necessary data to it in order to make it a `ClientMembershipUser` instance:

```
protected override ClientMembershipUser GetUser(User user)
{
    ClientMembershipUser membershipUser = null;
    string sql = string.Format(
        "SELECT * FROM [User] WHERE UserId = '{0}'",
        user.UserKey.ToString());
    using (DbCommand command = this.database.GetSqlStringCommand(sql))
    {
        using (IDataReader reader = this.database.ExecuteReader(command))
        {
            if (reader.Read())
            {
                membershipUser =
                    ClientMembershipUserFactory.BuildClientMembershipUser(
                        user, reader);
            }
        }
    }
    return membershipUser;
}
```

This code follows almost the same pattern as the `GetUserFromSql` method, except that it does not use the `IEntityFactory<T>` class to build the `ClientMembershipUser` instance.

The Other Method Overrides of the SqlCeClientMembershipProvider Class

All of the other methods in this class are just performing simple read and update operations in the SQL CE database, so I do not think there is any point in boring you with that code here. The important thing to note about this class is that almost all of its methods are either protected or private, which is really good from an encapsulation standpoint. Almost all of the retrieval logic is stored in the `ClientMembershipProvider` base class. The only two public methods on this class are two of the `GetUser` methods, which simply take a parameter and return a `User` instance.

The ClientMembershipService Class

This class is very similar to the other service classes in that it acts as a façade to an interface, in this case the `IClientMembershipService` interface. Here is what its signature and constructor look like:

```
using SmartCA.Infrastructure.Membership;

namespace SmartCA.Model.Membership
{
    public static class ClientMembershipService
    {
        private static IClientMembershipProvider provider;

        static ClientMembershipService()
        {
            ClientMembershipService.provider =
                ProviderFactory.GetProvider<IClientMembershipProvider>()
                as IClientMembershipProvider;
        }
```

This should look pretty familiar by now; the constructor is using the `ProviderFactroy` to instantiate an instance of the `IClientMembershipProvider` interface for the class to use.

I am not going to show all of the methods from the `Service` class, since they are all simply wrapping the interface and passing the argument data through. Here is a sample so that you can see what I am talking about:

```
        public static User GetUser(object userKey)
        {
            return ClientMembershipService.provider.GetUser(userKey);
        }

        public static User GetUser(string username)
        {
            return ClientMembershipService.provider.GetUser(username);
        }
```

Both of these `GetUser` methods pass their call through to the interface instance held by the Service.

Client Membership System Unit Tests

Instead of showing UI code exercising the Client Membership System, I thought it might be better if I show some of the unit tests used to develop the Client Membership System. This way you can see the data going in and out and get a better feel for how to use the system. All of the following tests will be going against the `ClientMembershipService` class.

The Login Test

This test verifies the behavior of the `ValidateUser` method:

```
/// <summary>
///A test for logging in
///</summary>
[TestMethod()]
public void ValidateUserTest()
{
    string username = "timm";
    string password = "Password!23";
    bool expected = true;
    bool actual = ClientMembershipService.ValidateUser(username, password);
    Assert.AreEqual(expected, actual);
}
```

As you can see, all of the complexity of the back-end system is masked by the façade, and the call to authenticate a User is very easy to make. As long as the Assertion returns true, then the unit test will pass.

The Change Password Test

This test is for changing a User's password:

```
/// <summary>
///A test for ChangePassword
///</summary>
[TestMethod()]
public void ChangePasswordTest()
{
    string username = "timm";
    string oldPassword = "Password!23";
    string newPassword = "Password!24";
    bool expected = true;
    bool actual = ClientMembershipService.ChangePassword(username,
        oldPassword, newPassword);
    Assert.AreEqual(expected, actual);

    // Change it back so the other tests don't fail
    ClientMembershipService.ChangePassword(username,
        newPassword, oldPassword);
}
```

Notice how, at the end, I have to change the password again to what it was originally. This is so the rest of the Client Membership System unit tests will pass because they are expecting the data to be in the same state as it was at the beginning of this method.

The Change Password Question and Answer Test

This test is for changing a User's password question and answer:

```
/// <summary>
///A test for ChangePasswordQuestionAndAnswer
///</summary>
[TestMethod()]
public void ChangePasswordQuestionAndAnswerTest()
{
    string username = "timm";
    string password = "Password!23";
    string newPasswordQuestion = "What color is the sky?";
    string newPasswordAnswer = "Grey";
    bool expected = true;
    bool actual = ClientMembershipService.ChangePasswordQuestionAndAnswer(
        username, password, newPasswordQuestion, newPasswordAnswer);
    Assert.AreEqual(expected, actual);

    // Change it back so the other tests don't fail
    ClientMembershipService.ChangePasswordQuestionAndAnswer(
        username, password, newPasswordQuestion, "Blue");
}
```

Summary

In order to satisfy the requirement of allowing users to be able to perform Membership-related tasks in an offline scenario, I created the Client Membership System in this chapter. This involved a very rich domain model for representing the Users and their membership data, as well as a new concept of using a Provider instead of a repository for interacting with the data store. It also was able to piggyback on the Synchronization Framework from the last chapter, which meant that all local Membership transactions would be replayed on the server as well as all server Membership transactions being played back on the client.

This chapter was by the far the most difficult code to implement, but that is also why it was so much fun! Probably the one thing that made this chapter's code easier to correct and implement were my unit tests. I was able to do a lot of refactoring with the comfort of knowing that as long as my unit tests passed I was all right.

I sure have come a long way since the first chapter! If you remember, I started out with nothing more than a problem statement and some design ideas to build a smart client application. During the course of the book, I took you on a journey of building a pretty robust Repository Framework (that was refactored several times), introduced WPF and the Model-View-ViewModel pattern, implemented lot of business logic for the various functional areas of the application, built a Synchronization Framework, and finally concluded with a Client Membership System. If nothing else, I hope you at least got some great reusable code from all of these exercises that I took you on throughout the book! Finally, I want to thank you for being patient enough to read through this book, I appreciate the fact that you are reading it right now!

Index

A

AddProposalRequestTest method, 239–240
Address class
- creating headquarter address dropdown, 147
- defining Aggregate boundaries, 111–112
- designing domain model, 110

Address property, Project, 68–70
Addresses UserControl, 145–146
AddressesViewModel class, 148–151
AddressFactory class, 127
AddRfiTest method, RFI, 204–205, 207
AddSubmittalTest method, 162, 164
AddTest method, IClientTransaction Repository, 331
AddTest method, ICompanyRepository, 115–116
Aggregate boundaries
- Change Order, 268
- Company and Contact, 111–112
- Construction Change Directive Aggregate, 298
- Employee, 57–58
- Project, 57–58
- Proposal Request, 236–237
- Request for Information, 202
- Submittal, 159–160

Aggregates
- Change Order Aggregate, 266–268
- Company Aggregate, 57–58, 111–112
- Construction Change Directive Aggregate, 296–298
- Contact Aggregate, 110–112
- Employee Aggregate, 57–59
- overview of, 16–17
- Project Aggregate, 56–59, 111–112
- Proposal Request Aggregate, 234–237
- RFI Aggregate, 201–203, 213–219
- Submittal Aggregate, 158–161

Allowances property, Project, 75
AmountChanged property, ChangeOrder, 277
API (application programming interface), 14
AppendAddresses method, CompanyRepository, 125–126
AppendConstructionAdministrator method, ProjectRepository, 85
AppendContractor method
- ChangeOrderRepository class, 283
- ConstructionChangeDirective class, 308

AppendCopyToList method
- RequestForInformation class, 214, 217–218
- Submittal class, 180–181

AppendFrom method
- ProposalRequest class, 254
- RequestForInformation class, 214
- Submittal class, 179

AppendOwner method, ProjectRepository, 84
AppendPrincipal method, ProjectRepository, 85
AppendProjectAllowances method, ProjectRepository, 84, 85–86
AppendRoutingItems method
- ChangeOrderRepository class, 283–284
- RequestForInformation class, 214
- Submittal class, 182–183

AppendTo method
ConstructionChangeDirective class, 308
ProposalRequest class, 254
Submittal class, 179–180
AppendTrackingItems method, Submittal, 181–182
Application class, 371–372
application layer
defined, 7–9
designing, 14
services, 16
application programming interface (API), 14
Application property, IClientMembershipProvider, 373
***Applying Domain-Driven Design and Patterns, With Examples in C# and .NET* (Nilsson), 15, 30**
architectural layers. *See* layered architecture
Auto-update requirement, 5, 11
Availability requirement, 4, 6

B

BidPackageNumber property, Contract, 77
BindingList<MutableAddress> type, CompanyViewModel, 140–141
BindingList<T>, SubmittalViewModel constructors, 188–189
BrokenRule class, ProposalRequest, 249–250
BrokenRuleMessages class
ChangeOrder class, 282
ConstructionChangeDirective class, 304
ProposalRequest class, 250–251
BuildBaseWhereClause method, SqlCeRepositoryBase<T>, 79, 88
BuildChildCallbacks method
ChangeOrderRepository class, 283
CompanyRepository class, 125
ConstructionChangeDirective class, 307–308
ProjectRepository class, 83–86
ProposalRequest class, 254
RequestForInformation class, 213–214
SqlCeRepositoryBase<T> class, 39
SubmittalRepository class, 178–179
BuildEntitiesFromSql method, SqlCeRepositoryBase<T>, 41
BuildEntity method, IEntityFactory<T>, 42
BuildEntityFromReader method, SqlCeRepositoryBase<T>, 40–41
BuildEntityFromSql method, SqlCeRepositoryBase<T>, 40
BuildFactory method, EntityFactorBuilder class, 44–45
BuildNewEntity method, ConstructionChangeDirectiveViewModel, 323

C

C# 3.0 object initializer features, 100
CalculateDaysLapsed method, Submittal, 177
caller registration, Unit of Work, 30
CancelCommand property, ViewModel, 51, 94
Change Order Aggregate, 266–268
Change Orders, 265–293
design, 266–267, 267, 268, 268–271, 271
problem, 265
solution, 271–275, 275–280, 280–283, 283–285, 285–288, 288–289, 289–291, 292–293
ChangeOrderNumberSpecification class, 278
ChangeOrderRepository class, 283–285
ChangeOrderRuleMessages class, 282
ChangeOrderService class, 288–289, 305–306
ChangeOrderViewModel class, 289–291
ChangePassword method, IClientMembershipProvider, 364–365, 379–381

ChangePasswordQuestionAndAnswer method, IClientMembershipProvider, 365–366, 381–382
CheckParameter method, SecurityHelper class, 362–363
CheckPassword method, IClientMembershipProvider, 378
CheckPasswordAnswer method, IClientMembershipProvider, 378
ChildCallBacks property, 39, 84
class signature
- ClientMembershipProvider class, 374–375
- SqlCeClientMembershipProvider class, 384
- User class, 360–361

classes
- application layer design, 14
- Change Order Aggregate, 267
- Company and Contact Aggregates, 111
- Construction Change Directive, 296
- Construction Change Directive Aggregate, 298
- designing Repositories for, 58–59
- Project Aggregate, 56–57
- Repository base, 33–41
- Request for Information, 200
- RFI Aggregate, 201–202
- Submittal Aggregate, 159

ClickOnce technology, 11
Client Device requirement, 5–7
Client Membership System, 357–389
- designing, 358–359
- domain model classes, 360, 360–367, 367–371, 371–372, 387. *See* Client Membership System Provider
- Microsoft ASP.NET Membership vs., 359
- password security, 358
- problem, 357
- unit tests, 388–389

Client Membership System Provider, 372–387
- ClientMembershipProvider class, 374–384
- designing, 359
- IClientMembershipProvider, 372–373
- ProviderFactory class, 373–374
- SqlCeClientMembershipProvider class, 384–386

ClientMembershipProvider class, 374–384
- class signature and private fields, 374–375
- constructors, 375
- IUnitOfWorkRepository implementation, 384
- methods, 375–384

ClientMembershipUser class
- class signature and private fields, 367
- constructor, 367–368
- methods, 368–369, 369–370, 370, 371
- properties, 368

ClientTransaction class, 329, 338
ClientTransactionRepository class, 334, 341
ClientTransactionRepositoryFactory class, 340
ClientTransactionService class, 348–349
CollectionView class, 49
CollectionView variable, SubmittalViewModel, 189, 192
ComboBox control, headquarters address dropdown, 147
ComboBox declaration, ViewModel, 52–53
command handlers. *See* handlers
Command pattern, WPF, 47–53
Command property, Delete Button, 146
Commit method, Unit of Work
- AddProposalRequestTest method, 240
- AddRfiTest method, 205
- AddSubmittalTest method, 163
- AddTest method, Companies, 116
- CompanyService class, 135
- overview of, 33
- RepositoryBase<T> class, 132
- synchronizing with server, 333–334

Companies and Contacts, 109–155
- designing, 110, 110–111, 110–119, 111–112, 112–114, 114–119
- problem, 109

Companies and Contacts (continued)
solution, 119–121, 119–155, 121–123, 123–124, 124–130, 130–131, 131–134, 134–137, 137–143, 144–147, 148–154, 154–155
Company Aggregate, 57–58, 111–112
Company class, 70–71, 119–121
Company property, Contact, 111
CompanyRepository class, 124–130
AppendAddresses method, 125–126
AppendOwner method, 84
BuildChildCallbacks method, 125
GetBaseQuery method, 126
GetBaseWhereClause, 127
implementing, 124
overview of, 124–130
public constructors, 125
Unit of Work implementation, 127–130
CompanyRepositoryTest class, 114
CompanyService class, 134–135
CompanyView class
HeadquartersAddress dropdown, 147
overview of, 144–145
using Xceed DataGrid, 145–146
CompanyViewModel class, 137–143
constructors, 140–141
handlers, 143
implementing, 137–140
properties, 141–143
Configuration folder
EntityFactoryFramework, 44
RepositoryFramework, 24–28
configuration section, Entity Factory Framework, 42–44
configuration section, Repository Factory, 24–28
ConfigurationElementCollection class, 27
ConfigurationSection class, 25
Construction Administration Database
design requirement, 4–6
problems of legacy application, 1–3
solution, 6–11
Construction Administrator, Project Domain, 56–57
Construction Change Directive, 295–325
designing, 296, 297, 298, 299, 300
problem, 295
solution, 300–302, 302–304, 304–305, 305–306, 306–307, 307–309, 310–313, 313–314, 314–321, 321–323, 324–325
Construction Change Directive Aggregate, 296–298
ConstructionAdministrator property, Project class, 71–73
ConstructionChangeDirectiveRule Messages class, 304
ConstructionChangeDirectiveService class, 313–314
ConstructionChangeDirectiveView Model class
EditableViewModel<T> class, 317–319
handlers, 319–320
overview of, 314–316
refactoring ViewModel class, 316
constructors
ChangeOrder class, 271–275
ChangeOrderViewModel class, 289–290
ClientMembershipProvider class, 375
Company class, 121
CompanyRepository class, 125
Construction Change Directive, 300–302
ConstructionChangeDirectiveView Model class, 315
ContactRepository class, 130
EditableViewModel<T> class, 317–318
EmployeeRepository class, 88–89
Project class, 65–67
ProjectContactViewModel class, 152
ProjectInformationViewModel class, 98–101
ProjectRepository class, 80–83
ProposalRequest class, 242–245
ProposalRequestViewModel class, 258–259
RequestForInformation class, 207–209
RequestForInformationViewmodel class, 228–229

SqlCeClientTransactionRepository class, 342
Submittal class, 164–166
SubmittalViewModel class, 188–189
Synchronizer class, 349
TransmittalViewModel<T> class, RFI, 225–226
UnitOfWork class, new, 335
User class, 361–363
Contact Aggregate, 110–112
Contact class, 121–124
Contact instance, ProjectContact, 123–124
ContactRepository class, 130–131
Contacts. *See* Companies and Contacts
ContactService class, 135–137
ContingencyAllowanceAmount property, Project, 75
Contract price, ChangeOrder, 265
Contract time, Change Order, 265
ContractBase class, 339
Contracts, Project Domain, 56–57
Contracts property, Project, 76–77
controls, and Rich Client Applications, 11
Converter class, 345–346
CopyTo instances, RequestForInformation, 217–219
CopyToList property, Submittal, 171–172
CopyToList section, SubmittalView, 195–197
CreateNumberedProjectChild method, 307
CSLA Framework (CSLA Framework), 249
CurrentChangeOrder property, ChangeOrderViewModel, 290–291
CurrentCompany property
CompanyViewModel class, 141–143
Contact class, 111–112, 123
ProjectContactViewModel, 153
CurrentEntity property, EditableViewModel<T>, 319
CurrentObjectState property, EditableViewModel<T>, 318–319
CurrentObjectState property, ProjectInformationViewModel, 105
CurrentSubmittal property, SubmittalViewModel, 190–191
CurrentTransmittal property, TransmittalViewModel<T>, 226
customization, and Rich Client Applications, 11

D

Data Contracts, 339
Data Transfer Objects (DTOs), 15, 339
data transfer, requirement, 6
Database property, SqlCeRepositoryBase<T>, 39
data-binding, 47
DataGridControl, 145–146
DataHelper class, 40–41
DateOfSubstantialCompletion property, ChangeOrder, 277–278
DatePicker control, 194
DateReceived property, RequestForInformation, 206
DateSent property, RoutingItem, 177
DateToFieldSpecification property, RequestForInformation, 212
DaysLapsed property, RequestForInformation, 211
DDD rule, 270
declarative programming, WPF, 10
DeferredApproval property, Submittal, 174
DelegateCommand class, 49–51
DelegateCommand properties
CompanyViewModel class, 144
ProjectContactViewModel class, 153
SubmittalViewModel class, 191–192
Delete Button, Xceed DataGrid, 146
DeleteAddressCommandHandler method, CompanyViewModel, 143
DeleteCopyToCommandHandler method, SubmittalViewModel, 192
DeleteCopyToList method
PersistUpdatedItem method, 257
RequestForInformation class, 218, 222

DeleteCopyToList method (continued)
Submittal class, 186
DeleteRoutingItems method
RequestForInformation class, 222
Submittal class, 186
DeleteTrackingItems method, Submittal, 186
DeliveryMethod property, Submittal, 170–171
dependencies, implementing Visual Studio, 19
deployment, and Rich Client Applications, 11
DeploymentItem attribute, 63
Description property, Proposal Request, 240
DescriptionRuleMessageKeys class, 304
DescriptionSpecification property
ConstructionChangeDirective class, 302–303
ProposalRequest class, 248
Deserialize method, 345
Deserializer class, 345
***Design Patterns: Elements of Reusable Object-Oriented Software* (Gamma, Helm, Johnson and Vlissides), 110**
Discipline property, RoutingItem, 177
domain layer
designing, 15–18
fulfilling Maintainability requirement, 8–9
services, 16
domain model
Change Orders, 266–267
Client Membership System classes, 360, 360–367, 367–371, 371–372, 387. *See* Client Membership System Provider
Companies and Contacts, 110
Construction Change Directive, 296
Project, 56
Proposal Requests, 234–235
Request for Information, 200–201
Submittal Transmittal, 158
Domain-Driven Design, concepts of, 15–17
***Domain-Driven Design: Tackling Complexity in the Heart of Software* (Evans), 2, 15, 17, 69, 200**
double dispatch, 384
DTOs (Data Transfer Objects), 15, 339

E

EditableViewModel<T> class, 316, 317–319
Employee Aggregate, 57–59
Employee class, 71–73
Employee Repositories, 59, 88–90
EmployeeService class, 91–92
EncodePassword method, IClientMembershipProvider, 378, 380
encryption, password security, 358
Entities
Domain-Driven Design concept, 15
Value objects vs., 15
Entity Factory Framework
configuration section, 42–44
defined, 41
EntityFactorBuilder class, 44–45
IEntityFactory<T> interface, 42
IProjectRepository implementation, 82–83
EntityBase class
ChangeOrder class, 280–282
implementing architectural layers, 20–22
ProposalRequest class, 250–251
RequestForInformation class, 217–218
ValidateInitialization method, 275
EntityFactorBuilder class, 44–45
EntityName property, RequestForInformation, 217–219
ExecuteReader method, SqlCeRepositoryBase<T>, 40–41
expectedContractorReturnDays class variable, 244
Extensible Application Markup Language (XAML), 10, 144–147

F

Factories, Domain-Driven Design, 17
FieldNames static class, 83
Find methods, 23
FindAll methods, 78–79, 82

FindAllDisciplines method, ISubmittalRepository, 161
FindAllMarketSegmentsTest method, unit test, 64
FindAllSpecificationSections method, ISubmittalRepository, 161
FindAllSubmittalStatuses method, ISubmittalRepository, 161
FindAllTest method, ICompanyRepository, 115
FindBy method
- ChangeOrderRepository class, 284
- ConstructionChangeDirective class, 309
- FindSubmittalsByProjectTest method, 162
- ProjectRepository class, 79, 81–82, 132
- SubmittalRepository class, 161

FindByKeyTest method, ICompanyRepository, 114–115
FindByProjectNumberTest method, 63–64
FindBySegmentsAndNotCompletedTest method, 62–63
FindPending method, SqlCeClientTransactionRepository, 343–347
FindPendingTransactionsTest method, IClientTransactionRepository, 331–332
FindProposalRequestsByProjectTest method, 239
FindRfisByProjectTest method, 204
FindSubmittalsByProjectTest method, 161–162

G

Gang-of-Four (GoF), 110
GetBaseQuery method
- CompanyRepository class, 126
- ContactRepository class, 131
- Employee Repository class, 89
- ProjectRepository class, 86
- refactoring FindAll method, 78

GetBaseWhereClause method
- CompanyRepository class, 127
- ContactRepository class, 131
- ProjectRepository class, 86
- SqlCeRepositoryBase<T> class, 79

GetBrokenRulesMessages method, ChangeOrder, 282
GetClientMembershipUser method, IClientMembershipProvider, 379
GetConstructionAdministrators method, IEmployeeRepository, 65, 89, 91–92
GetCurrentProject method, ChangeOrder, 275
GetEmployee method, Proposal Request, 254
GetEntitiesList method, ConstructionChangeDirectiveView Model, 324
GetExpectedContractorReturnDays method, ProposalRequest, 243–244
GetLastSynchronization method, SqlCeClientTransaction Repository, 347
GetLastSynchronizationTest method, 332
GetLastSynchronized method, Synchronizer, 349–350
GetPassword method, IClientMembershipProvider, 376
GetPasswordAnswerFromPersistence method, IClientMembershipProvider, 377
GetPreviousAuthorizedAmountFrom method, ChangeOrder, 269, 276, 284–285
GetPreviousTimeChangedTotal method, ChangeOrder, 269, 277–278
GetPreviousTimeChangedTotalFrom method, ChangeOrder, 285
GetPrincipals method, IEmployeeRepository, 64, 89, 91–92
GetProjectContact method
- ProjectContactService, 180
- ProposalRequest c, 254

GetProjects method, ProjectService, 47
GetRepository method, RepositoryFactory, 28–30
GetRuleDescription method, ProposalRequest, 250
GetTransmittals method
ProposalRequestViewModel class, 260
RequestForInformationViewmodel class, 231
TransmittalViewModel<T> class, 226, 228
GetUser method
ClientMembershipService class, 387
IClientMembershipProvider, 376
SqlCeClientMembershipProvider class, 384–386
GoF (Gang-of-Four), 110
Gossman, John, 47

H

handlers
ChangeOrderViewModel class, 291–292
EditableViewModel<T> class, 319–320
ProjectContactViewModel class, 154
ProposalRequestViewModel class, 259–260
RequestForInformationViewmodel class, 230–231
SubmittalViewModel class, 191–192
TransmittalViewModel class, 321–323
TransmittalViewModel<T> class, 227–228
HasBeenTransformedToChangeOrder property, ConstructionChange Directive, 303–304
hashing, password security, 358
headquarter address dropdown, 147
HeadquartersAddress property, Company, 121, 142–143

I

IAggregateRoot interface, 270–271, 297
IBindingList<T> interface, 188–189
IChangeOrderRepository interface, 269–271, 283–285, 288–289
IClientMembershipProvider interface, 372–373, 375
IClientTransactionRepository interface, 329, 331–332
ICommand interface, 49
ICompanyRepository interface
designing Company Repository, 112–113
unit tests, 114–115, 115, 115–116, 116–117, 117
IConstructionChangeDirective Repository interface
ConstructionChangeDirective Service class, 313–314
implementing Repository, 307–309
overview of, 299
IContactRepository interface, 118
IDataReader interface, 38, 40–42
IDescribable interface, 297
IEmployeeRepository interface
EmployeeRepository class, 89–90
EmployeeService class, 91–92
overview of, 59
unit tests, 64–65
IEntity interface
Transaction class implementing, 330
User class implementing, 360
ValidateInitialization method, 274–275
IEntityFactory<T> interface, 39–40, 42
immutable Value objects, 15
indexer
CompanyService class, 135
UpdateSubmittalTest method, 163
infrastructure layer
designing, 18
fulfilling Maintainability requirement, 8–9
naming standards for, 14
services, 16
Initialize method
IClientMembershipProvider class, 375
SqlCeClientMembershipProvider class, 384

INotifyPropertyChanged interface, ViewModel class, 94
InsertCopyTo method, RequestForInformation, 218–219, 221–222
InsertCopyToList method
RequestForInformation class, 218–219, 221–222
Submittal class, 184–185
InsertRoutingItems method
ChangeOrder class, 287
Submittal class, 184–185
InsertTrackingItems method, Submittal, 184–185
Intelligent Installation requirement, 5, 11
INumberedProjectChild interface
Change Orders, 267, 269–270, 274, 280
Construction Change Directive, 297, 306–307
IProjectRepository interface
Companies and Contacts, 113–114, 118–119
managing projects, 61–64, 77, 81–83, 91
IProposalRequestRepository interface, 238, 253–257
IReferenceDataRepository, 351, 352–354
IRepository<T> interface
IEmployeeRepository implementing, 59
implementing Repository Framework, 22–23
INumberedProjectChild extending, 269
IProjectRepository implementing, 59
refactoring FindAll method, 78–79
RepositoryBase<T> class implementing, 33–35
TRepository parameter, 29–30
IRequestForInformationRepository interface, 203, 206
IRoutableTransmittal interface, 215, 221
ISubmittalRepository interface, 161, 178–187
ITransmittal interface
ProposalRequest class, 234
RequestForInformation class, 214–215, 217–218
IUnitOfWork interface
refactoring for synchronization with server, 329
RemoveProposalRequestTest method, 241
RepositoryBase<T> class implementing, 35, 132
Unit of Work implementation, 31–33
IUnitOfWorkRepository interface
ClientMembershipProvider class implementing, 384
RepositoryBase<T> class implementing, 35
Unit of Work implementation, 31–33

K

Key property, Transaction, 335–337
KeyFieldName property, RequestForInformation, 217–218
KPIs (key performance indicators), 5

L

layered architecture, 13–53
designing, 13–14, 14, 15–18, 18
problem, 13
solution, 19, 20–22, 41–45, 45–53. *See* Repository Framework
Layered Supertype, 18, 20–22
LINQ queries, RFIs, 212
login test, 388

M

Maintainability requirement, 5, 7–9
managing projects, 55–107
designing, 56, 56–57, 57–58, 58–59, 60–65
problem, 55
solution, 88–90, 90–92, 92–102, 102–106. *See* Project class; Project Repository

Market Segments (Sectors), Project Domain
defined, 56
Project Aggregate classes, 57
Segment property, Project class, 73–75
unit tests, 63–64
MarketSector class, 73–75
MarketSegment class, 74–75
Microsoft ASP.NET Membership, 359
Microsoft Synchronization Services for ADO .NET, 7, 327–328
Model-View-Controller (MVC) pattern, 47
Model-View-Presenter (MVP) pattern, 47
Model-View-ViewModel pattern, 45–53
defining ViewModel, 46
example, 47–53
overview of, 46
traditional presentation patterns, 45–46
MutableAddress class
CompanyViewModel class, 141, 142–143
creating headquarter address dropdown, 147
ProjectInformationViewModel class, 99
using C# 3.0 initializer features, 100
MutableCopyTo type, SubmittalViewModel, 189
MutableCopyToList property, SubmittalViewModel, 191–192
MVC (Model-View-Controller) pattern, 47
MVP (Model-View-Presenter) pattern, 47
MyTestInitialize method, unit test, 62

N

Name property, Project, 67–68
namespace pattern, Visual Studio, 14
.NET Generics, 23
.NET Reflection, 44–45
.NET Value types, 68
NewCommandHandler method
ChangeOrderViewModel class, 291
CompanyViewModel class, 143
EditableViewModel<T> class, 319–320
ProjectContactViewModel class, 154
ProposalRequestViewModel class, 259
RequestForInformationViewmodel class, 230–231
SubmittalViewModel class, 191–192
TransmittalViewModel<T> class, 227–228
NewConstructionCost property, ChangeOrder, 276–277
Number property, Project, 67–68
NumberedProjectChildFactory class, 306–307
NumberedProjectChildRepository-Helper class, 309
NumberedProjectChildValidator class, 273–274
NumberSpecification property
ChangeOrder class, 278–280
ProposalRequest class, 247–248
RequestForInformation class, 211–212

O

object registration, Unit of Work, 30
ObjectState property, ViewModel, 94
Offline capability requirement, 5, 6–7
OnFinalDistributionList property, ProjectContact, 124
OriginalConstructionCost property, ChangeOrder, 275–276
Owner, Project, 56, 57, 84
Owner property, Project class, 70–71

P

password security
ClientMembershipProvider class methods, 375–384
ClientMembershipUser class, 368–369, 369–370, 370, 371
designing, 358
IClientMembershipProvider and, 373
unit tests for, 388–389
User class, 364–365, 365–366, 366–367

PasswordAnswerAttemptFailed method, ClientMembershipUser, 370
PasswordAnswerAttemptSucceeded method, ClientMembershipUser, 371
PasswordAttemptFailed method, ClientMembershipUser, 368–369
PasswordAttemptSucceeded method, ClientMembershipUser, 369–370
PasswordFormat enumeration, 358
***Patterns of Enterprise Application Architecture* (Fowler), 15, 17–18, 30**
PersistChangedPassword method, IClientMembershipProvider, 381
PersistChangedPasswordQuestion andAnswer method, IClientMembershipProvider, 382
PersistDeletedItem method
- CompanyRepository class, 129–130
- ProjectRepository class, 88, 132–133
- RequestForInformationRepository class, 222–223
- SubmittalRepository class, 186–187

persistence ignorance, 7, 17
PersistNewItem method
- ChangeOrderRepository class, 285–287
- CompanyRepository class, 127–128
- ConstructionChangeDirective class, 310–311
- IProjectRepository, 88
- ProjectRepository class, 132–133
- ProposalRequest class, 255–256
- RequestForInformationRepository class, 220–221
- SubmittalRepository class, 183–185

PersistNewTransaction method, SqlCeClientTransaction Repository, 342–343
PersistUpdatedItem method
- ChangeOrderRepository class, 287–288
- CompanyRepository class, 128–129
- ConstructionChangeDirective class, 311–313
- IProjectRepository, 87–88
- IUnitOfWorkRepository, 384
- ProjectRepository class, 132–133
- ProposalRequest class, 256–257
- RequestForInformationRepository class, 221–222
- SubmittalRepository class, 185–186

Person class, 72–73
Plain-Old CLR Objects (POCO) approach, 15
POCO (Plain-Old CLR Objects) approach, 15
PopulateAddresses method, ProjectContactViewModel, 153
PopulateMutableCopyToList method
- SubmittalViewModel class, 190–191
- TransmittalViewModel<T> class, 227

PopulateRoutingItems method, SubmittalViewModel, 191
PopulateSubmittalChildren method
- SubmittalViewModel class, 190
- TransmittalViewModel<T> class, 226–227

presentation layer, designing, 18
PreviousAuthorizedAmount property, ChangeOrder, 276
PreviousTimeChangedTotal property, ChangeOrder, 277
PriceChangeDirection property, ChangeOrderViewModel, 290
Principal-in-Charge, Project Domain, 56–57
PrincipalInCharge property, Project, 71–73
private fields
- ChangeOrder class, 271–275
- ClientMembershipProvider class, 374–375
- ConstructionChangeDirective class, 300–302
- EditableViewModel<T> class, 317–318
- Project class, 65–67
- ProposalRequest class, 242–245
- RequestForInformation class, 207–209
- SqlCeClientMembershipProvider class, 384
- Submittal class, 164–166
- User class, 360–361

ProcessReferenceData method, Synchronizer, 350–351
ProcessServerTransactions method, Synchronizer, 354–355
Project Aggregate, 56–59, 111–112
Project class, 65–77
- Address property, 68–70
- ConstructionAdministrator property, 71–73
- ContingencyAllowanceAmount property, 75
- Contracts property, 76–77
- Name and Number properties, 67–68
- overview of, 65
- Owner property, 70–71
- PrincipalInCharge property, 71–73
- private fields and constructors, 65–67
- Segment property, 73–75
- TestingAllowanceAmount property, 75
- UtilityAllowanceAmount property, 75

Project Repository. *See also* IProjectRepository interface
- Companies and Contacts, implementing, 131–134
- managing projects, 77–88, 78–79, 80, 80–83, 83–86, 86, 87–88

ProjectAddress property, ProjectInformationViewModel, 106
ProjectContact class
- defining agggregates, 110–111
- designing domain model, 110
- designing Repositories, 113–114
- implementing, 123–124
- ProjectRepository class, 132

ProjectContactView class, 154–155
ProjectContactViewModel class
- constructors, 152
- handlers, 154
- overview of, 148–151
- properties, 153

ProjectInformationView class, 102–106
ProjectInformationViewModel class
- constructors, 98–101
- creating, 94–98
- properties, 101–102
- view implementation, 102–106

projectKey parameter, Submittal, 164
ProjectName property, ProjectInformationViewModel, 101–102
ProjectNumber property, ProjectInformationViewModel, 101–102
ProjectService class
- implementing, 90–91
- saving ProjectContact, 136–137
- ViewModel class, 47–53

properties
- ChangeOrder class, 275–280
- CompanyViewModel class, 141–143
- ConstructionChangeDirective class, 302–304
- ConstructionChangeDirectiveViewModel class, 315–316
- EditableViewModel<T> class, 318–319
- ProjectContactViewModel class, 153
- ProjectInformationViewModel class, 101–102
- ProposalRequest class, 245–248
- RequestForInformation class, 209–213. *See also* Submittal class, properties
- RequestForInformationViewmodel class, 230
- Submittal class. *See* Submittal class, properties
- SubmittalViewModel class, 190–191
- TransmittalViewModel<T> class, 226–227
- UnitOfWork class, new, 335
- User class, 363

Proposal Request Aggregate, 234–237
Proposal Requests, 233–263
- designing, 234–235, 235–236, 236–237, 237–238, 239–241
- problem, 233–234
- solution, 242–245, 245–248, 248–253, 253–257, 257–258, 258–260, 260–261, 261–262, 263

ProposalRequest class, 242–245
ProposalRequestViewModel class, 258–260

Provider Framework. *See* Client Membership System Provider
ProviderFactory class, 373–374

Q

QuestionAnswerSpecification property, RequestForInformation, 213

R

Recipient property, RoutingItem, 177
ReferenceDataRepositoryFactory class, 351–352
Reliability requirement, 4, 6–7
RemainderLocation property, Submittal, 178
RemoveProposalRequestTest method, 241
RemoveRfiTest method, 206–207
RemoveSubmittalTest method, 164
RemoveTest method, 117
Repositories
- designing, 58–59, 112–114, 160–161, 203, 237–238, 268–271, 299
- Domain-Driven Design concept, 17
- implementing, 88–90, 124–130, 130–131, 131–134, 213–219, 253–257, 283–285, 307–309. *See* Project Repository; Submittal Transmittals, Repository
- using in domain layer, 17–18

Repository Factory
- configuration section, 24
- configuration section handling, 24–28
- defined, 23
- RepositoryFactory class, 28–30

Repository Framework, 22–41
- in infrastructure layer, 18
- interfaces, 22–23
- Repository Factory, 23–30
- RepositoryBase<T> class, 33–35
- SqlCeRepositoryBase<T> class, 35–41
- Unit of Work, 30–33

RepositoryBase<T> class, 33–35, 38, 78
RepositoryFactory class, 28–30
RepositoryMappingCollection data type, 25–27
RepositoryMappingConstants class, 25
RepositoryMappingElement class, 27–28
RepositoryMappings element, 24–25
RepositoryMappingsConfiguration configuration section, 25
RepositorySettings class, 25, 27
Request for Information. *See* RFI (Request for Information)
RequestForInformation class
- defining Aggregate boundaries, 202–203
- defining RFI Aggregate, 201–202
- designing RFI Repository, 203
- private fields and constructors, 207–209
- refactoring RFI Repository, 215
- RFI domain model, 200–201
- writing unit tests, 204–207

RequestForInformationDateSpecification class, 212
RequestForInformationNumberSpecification class, 211
RequestForInformationQuestionAnswerSpecification class, 213
RequestForInformationRepository class, 203, 213–214
RequestForInformationService class, 224
RequestForInformationViewModel class, 224, 228–231
ResetPassword method, 366–367, 382–383
RFI (Request for Information), 199–232
- designing, 200–201, 201–202, 202, 203, 204–207
- private fields and constructors, 207–209
- problem, 199
- properties, 209–213. *See also* Submittal class, properties
- Repository implementation, 213–214, 214, 219–223
- RequestForInformation class, 213–219
- RequestForInformationService class, 223–224

RFI (Request for Information) (continued)
RequestForInformationViewModel class, 228–231
TransmittalViewModel<T> class, 224–228
View, 231–232
RFI Aggregate, 201–203, 213–219
Rich Client Application requirement, 5, 9–11
routable Transmittals, 219
RoutableTransmittal class, 235
RoutableTransmittal User Control, 263
RoutingItems class
RequestForInformation class, 201, 219
RoutingItems property, 175–176
SubmittalTransmittal class, 158
RoutingItems property
RoutingItems class, 177
Submittal class, 175–177
SubmittalViewModel class, 191–192

S

SaveCommandHandler method
ChangeOrderViewModel class, 291–292
ProjectContactViewModel class, 154
ProposalRequestViewModel class, 260
RequestForInformationViewmodel class, 230–231
TransmittalViewModel<T> class, 227
SaveContact method, IProjectRepository, 113–114, 118–119, 132
SaveCurrentEntity method
ConstructionChangeDirectiveViewModel class, 323–324
TransmittalViewModel class, 322–323
SaveProject method
CompanyService class, 135
ProjectService class, 91
SaveProjectContact method, ProjectService, 136–137
Scalability requirement, 5–7
SecurityHelper class, 362–363
Segment property, Project, 73–75
SelectCommand property, ViewModel, 51
SelectProjectView class, 47–49, 51, 102–103
SelectProjectViewModel class, 49–52
Separated Interface pattern
defined, 17
ProviderFactory class, 374
RepositoryFactory class, 23, 24
Serialize method, 345
Serializer class, 345
server
supporting requirement, 6
synchronizing data with. See synchronization with server
ServerTransaction class, 338–339
Service class implementations
ChangeOrderService class, 288–289
ClientMembershipService class, 387
CompanyService class, 134–135
ConstructionChangeDirectiveService class, 313–314
ContactService class, 135
EmployeeService class, 91–92
ProjectService class, 90–91, 136–137
ProposalRequestService class, 257–258
RequestForInformationService class, 223–224
SubmittalService class, 187–188
Services, Domain-Driven Design concept, 16
SetCurrentEntity method, TransmittalViewModel, 323
SetLastSynchronization method, SqlCeClientTransactionRepository, 347–348
SetLastSynchronizationTest method, 332
SetLastSynchronized method, Synchronizer, 350
Smart Client anti-pattern, 2
smart client applications, 9–11
Smart Design, defined, 1
SmartCA application. *See* Construction Administration Database
Specification class, 200

Specification Section
AddSubmittalTest method, 162–163
every Submittal associated with, 164
RFI vs. Submittal Transmittal, 201
Submittal Transmittals, 158
SpecSection property, Submittal, 170
SQL CE (SQL Server Compact Edition) 3.5, 6–7, 11
SQL Server, 6
SQL Server Express, 7
SqlCeClientMembershipProvider class, 384–386
SqlCeClientTransactionRepository class, 341–348
constructor, 342
defined, 341
FindPending method, 343–347
GetLastSynchronization method, 347
PersistNewTransaction method, 342–343
SetLastSynchronization method, 347–348
SqlCeReferenceDataRepository class, 352–354
SqlCeRepositoryBase<T> class
refactoring FindAll/FindBy methods, 78–79
Repository Framework and, 35–41
RequestForInformation class, 222–223
RFI Repository, 203, 215–216
SqlCeRoutableTransmittalRepository <T> class, 223
SqlCeTransmittalRepository<T> class, 215, 219
StackPanel elements, SubmittalView class, 193–194, 195
static methods, application layer design, 14
Status class, 200–201
Status property, Submittal, 175, 177–178
Submittal Aggregate, 158–161
Submittal class
private fields and constructors, 164–166
refactoring RFI Repository, 215
as root of Submittal Aggregate, 158
Submittal class, properties, 166–178
CopyToList property, 171–172
DeferredApproval property, 174
DeliveryMethod property, 170–171
overview of, 166–169
RemainderLocation property, 178
RoutingItems property, 175–177
SpecSection property, 170
Status property, 175, 177–178
TotalItemsReceived property, 174
TotalItemsSent property, 174
TrackingItems property, 173–174
Submittal Transmittals, 157–197
designing, 158, 159, 159–160, 160–161, 161–164
problem, 157
Repository, 178–179, 178–187, 179, 179–180, 180–181, 181–182, 182–183, 183–187
service implementation, 187–188
Submittal class private fields and constructors, 164–166
Submittal class properties. See Submittal class, properties
SubmittalView class, 192–197
SubmittalViewModel class, 188–192
SubmittalService class, 187–188
SubmittalStatus class, 177–178
SubmittalView class, 192–197
CopyToList section, 195–197
overview of, 192–193
using StackPanel element, 193–194
using Xceed DatePicker control, 194
SubmittalViewModel class, 188–192
synchronization with server, 327–356
design, 328–330, 330, 331–332
problem, 327
solution, 349–355, 355–356. See Unit of Work implementation
SynchronizationServerProxy class, 356
Synchronize method, Synchronizer class, 355–356
Synchronizer class, 349–355
constructor, 349
GetLastSynchronized method, 349–350

Synchronizer class (continued)
IReferenceDataRepository, 351–354
ProcessReferenceData method, 350–351
ProcessServerTransactions method, 354–355
ReferenceDataRepositoryFactory class, 351–352
SetLastSynchronized method, 350
Synchronize method, 355–356
System.String class, 69

T

TCandidate Generic parameter, 280
Template method pattern, 83–86, 89
TEntity parameter, 29
Test method attribute, 63
TestContext private field, 62
TestingAllowanceAmount property, Project class, 75
TimeChanged property, ChangeOrder, 278
TimeChangeDirection property, ChangeOrderViewModel, 290
ToAddress method, MutableAddress, 100
ToCompany method, 346
ToCompanyContract method, 346
ToEntity method, 347
TotalItemsReceived property, Submittal, 174
TotalItemsSent property, Submittal, 174
TrackingItems class, 173–174
TrackingItems property, Submittal, 173–174
Transaction class
ClientTransaction class, 338
ClientTransactionRepository class, 341
ClientTransactionRepository Factory class, 340
ClientTransactionService class, 348–349
Data Contracts, 339
overview of, 335–337
ServerTransaction class, 338–339
SqlCeClientTransactionRepository class, 341–348
TransactionScope class, 33
TransformToChangeOrder method, ConstructionChangeDirective, 305–306
Transmittal class
ConstructionChangeDirective class i, 297
designing Proposal Request Aggregate, 234–235
refactoring RFI Repository, 214–217
Transmittal User Control, 261–262
TransmittalDate property, Transmittal, 244
TransmittalViewModel class, 321–323
TransmittalViewModel<T> class, 225–228
TRepository parameter, 29–30
Type property, Transaction, 335–337

U

UI (user interface)
declarative programming for, 10
fulfilling Maintainability requirement, 7–9
legacy application, 2
Unit of Work implementation
ChangeOrder class, 285–288
Client Membership System, 359
CompanyRepository class, 127–130
ConstructionChangeDirective class, 310–313
ContactRepository class, 131
ProjectRepository class, 87–88
ProposalRequest class, 254–257
Repository Framework, 30–33
RequestForInformation class, 219–223
SubmittalRepository class, 183–187
synchronizing with server, 328–330, 333–334, 335, 335–339, 340, 341, 341–348, 348–349

unit tests
Change Orders, 271
Client Membership System, 388–389
Companies and Contacts, 114–117, 114–119, 118, 118–119
Construction Change Directive, 300
Projects and Employees, 60–65
Proposal Requests, 239–241
Request for Information, 204–207
Submittal Transmittals, 161–164
synchronizing with server and, 331–332
UnitOfWork class
synchronizing with server, 335
Unit of Work implementation, 31–33
unit tests, 62
Update requirement, 5, 11
UpdateProposalRequestTest method, 240–241
UpdateRfiTest method, 205–206
UpdateSubmittalTest method, 163
UpdateTest method, ICompanyRepository, 116–117
UpdateUser method, IClientMembershipProvider, 383–384
User class, 360–367
ChangePassword method, 363–364
ChangePasswordQuestionAndAnswer method, 365–366
constructors, 361–363
properties, 363
ResetPassword method, 366–367
signature and private fields, 360–361
user interface. *See* UI (user interface)
UtilityAllowanceAmount property, Project, 75

V

Validate method
ChangeOrder class, 280–283
ConstructionChangeDirective class, 304–305
ProposalRequest class, 248–253
ValidateCurrentObject method, EditableViewModel<T>, 319–320
ValidateInitialization method
ChangeOrder class, 273
ConstructionChangeDirective class, 302
ProposalRequest class, 245
User class, 362–363
ValidateInitialState method, NumberedProjectChildValidator, 273–274
ValidateUser method, 364
ValidateUserWithPasswordAnswer method, IClientMembershipProvider, 377, 380
ValidateWithUserPassword method, IClientMembershipProvider, 380
Value Objects
Address property of Project class as, 68
Domain-Driven Design concept, 15
.NET Value types vs., 68
View
ChangeOrder class, 292–293
ConstructionChangeDirective class, 324–325
ProposalRequest class, 260–261
RequestForInformation class, 231–232
SubmittalTransmittal class, 192–197
ViewModel classes
CompanyViewModel class, 137–140, 137–143, 140–141, 141–143, 143
Construction Change Directive, 314–321, 321–323
defining, 47
Model-View-ViewModel pattern, 45–46, 45–53, 46, 47–53
overview of, 92–94
ProjectContactViewModel class, 148–151, 148–154, 152, 153, 154
ProjectInformationViewModel class, 94–98, 94–102, 98–101, 101–102, 102–106
ProposalRequestViewModel class, 258–260

ViewModel classes (continued)
RequestForInformationViewmodel class, 224, 228–231
SelectProjectViewModel class, 49–52
SubmittalViewModel class, 188–192
TransmittalViewModel<T> class, 225–228
Visual Studio
designing, 13–14
implementing, 19
Visual Studio Team System (VSTS), unit test, 60
VSTS (Visual Studio Team System), unit test, 60

W

Web Access requirement, 5, 11
Web applications, benefits of, 10
Windows applications, benefits of, 10
WPF (Windows Presentation Foundation), 10–11, 47–53

X

XAML (Extensible Application Markup Language), 10, 144–147
Xceed DataGrid control, CompanyView class, 145–146
Xceed DatePicker control, SubmittalView class, 194

Y

YAGNI (You Ain't Gonna Need It) principle, 70

Professional C# 2008

Acknowledgments xiii
Introduction xlvii

Part I: The C# Language

Chapter 1: .NET Architecture 3
Chapter 2: C# Basics 25
Chapter 3: Objects and Types 75
Chapter 4: Inheritance 101
Chapter 5: Arrays 121
Chapter 6: Operators and Casts 141
Chapter 7: Delegates and Events 177
Chapter 8: Strings and Regular Expressions 203
Chapter 9: Generics 223
Chapter 10: Collections 247
Chapter 11: Language Integrated Query 297
Chapter 12: Memory Management and Pointers 329
Chapter 13: Reflection 357
Chapter 14: Errors and Exceptions 377

Part II: Visual Studio

Chapter 15: Visual Studio 2008 401
Chapter 16: Deployment 443

Part III: Base Class Libraries

Chapter 17: Assemblies 469
Chapter 18: Tracing and Events 509
Chapter 19: Threading and Synchronization 533
Chapter 20: Security 583
Chapter 21: Localization 639
Chapter 22: Transactions 679
Chapter 23: Windows Services 715
Chapter 24: Interoperability 749

(Continued)

Part IV: Data

Chapter 25: Manipulating Files and the Registry 791
Chapter 26: Data Access 845
Chapter 27: LINQ to SQL 895
Chapter 28: Manipulating XML 921
Chapter 29: LINQ to XML 967
Chapter 30:.NET Programming with SQLServer 985

Part V: Presentation

Chapter 31: Windows Forms 1017
Chapter 32: Data Binding 1061
Chapter 33: Graphics with GDI+ 1093
Chapter 34: Windows Presentation Foundation 1149
Chapter 35: Advanced WPF 1199
Chapter 36: Add-Ins 1251
Chapter 37: ASP.NET Pages 1273
Chapter 38: ASP.NET Development 1311
Chapter 39: ASP.NET AJAX 1355
Chapter 40: Visual Studio Tools for Office 1385

Part VI: Communication

Chapter 41: Accessing the Internet 1423
Chapter 42: Windows Communication Foundation 1455
Chapter 43: Windows Workflow Foundation 1487
Chapter 44: Enterprise Services 1527
Chapter 45: Message Queuing 1555
Chapter 46: Directory Services 1587
Chapter 47: Peer-to-Peer Networking 1625
Chapter 48: Syndication 1643

Part VII: Appendices

Appendix A: ADO.NET Entity Framework 1655
Appendix B: C#, Visual Basic, and C++/CLI 1681
Appendix C: Windows Vista and Windows Server 2008 1711

Index 1731

Professional
C# 2008

Professional C# 2008

Christian Nagel
Bill Evjen
Jay Glynn
Morgan Skinner
Karli Watson

Wiley Publishing, Inc.

Wrox Professional C# 2008

Published by
Wiley Publishing, Inc.
10475 Crosspoint Boulevard
Indianapolis, IN 46256
www.wiley.com

Published simultaneously in Canada

ISBN: 978-0-470-19137-8

Manufactured in the United States of America

10 9 8 7 6 5 4 3 2 1

Library of Congress Cataloging-in-Publication Data is available from the publisher.

To my brother George – moving strong from basketball to coding (they're practically the same thing, aren't they?). Congrats and keep moving forward in C# land!

—Bill Evjen

for Donna

—Karli Watson

To my parents, Joan and Donald Skinner, for their ever present love, support, and encouragement. The world was made a sweeter place by their being in it and their memory will be cherished forever. Thanks Mum & Dad — you were brilliant.

"Love is as strong as death.
Many waters cannot quench love,
neither can the floods drown it." (Song of Songs 8: 6 -7)

—Morgan Skinner

About the Authors

Christian Nagel of thinktecture is a software architect and developer who offers training and consulting on how to design and develop Microsoft .NET solutions. He looks back on more than 20 years of software development experience. Christian started his computing career with PDP 11 and VAX/VMS platforms, covering a variety of languages and platforms. Since the year 2000, when .NET was just a technology preview, he has been working with various .NET technologies to build numerous .NET solutions. With his profound knowledge of Microsoft technologies, he has written numerous .NET books, and is certified as a Microsoft Certified Trainer and Professional Developer for ASP.NET. Christian speaks at international conferences such as TechEd and Tech Days, and supports .NET user groups with INETA Europe. You can contact Christian via his Web sites, `www.christiannagel.com` and `www.thinktecture.com`.

Bill Evjen, Microsoft MVP is an active proponent of .NET Technologies and community-based learning initiatives for .NET. He has been actively involved with .NET since the first bits were released in 2000. In the same year, Bill founded the St. Louis .NET User Group (`www.stlnet.org`), one of the world's first such groups. Bill is also the founder and former executive director of the International .NET Association (`www.ineta.org`), which represents more than 450,000 members worldwide.

Based in St. Louis, Missouri, Bill is an acclaimed author (more than 15 books to date) and speaker on ASP.NET and SML Web services. In addition to writing and speaking at conferences such as DevConnections, VSLive, and TechEd, Bill works closely with Microsoft as a Microsoft regional director. Bill is the technical architect for Lipper (`www.lipperweb.com`), a wholly owned subsidiary of Reuters, the international news and financial services company. He graduated from Western Washington University in Bellingham, Washington with a Russian language degree. When he isn't tinkering on the computer, he can usually be found at his summer house in Toivakka, Finland. You can reach Bill at `evjen@yahoo.cpm`.

Morgan Skinner began his computing career at a young age on the Sinclair ZX80 at school, where he was underwhelmed by some code a teacher had written and so began programming in assembly language. Since then he's used all sorts of languages and platforms, including VAX Macro Assembler, Pascal, Modula2, Smalltalk, X86 assembly language, PowerBuilder, C/C++, VB, and currently C# (of course). He's been programming in .NET since the PDC release in 2000, and liked it so much he joined Microsoft in 2001. He now works in premier support for developers and spends most of his time assisting customers with C#. You can reach Morgan at `www.morganskinner.com`.

Jay Glynn started writing software nearly 20 years ago, writing applications for the PICK operating system using PICK basic. Since then, he has created software using Paradox PAL and Object PAL, Delphi, VBA, Visual Basic, C, C++, Java, and of course, C#. He is currently a project coordinator and architect for a large financial services company in Nashville, Tennessee, working on software for the TabletPC platform. You can contact Jay at `jlsglynn@hotmail.com`.

Karli Watson is a freelance author and a technical consultant of 3form Ltd (`www.3form.net`) and Boost .net, and an associate technologist at Content Master (`www.contentmaster.com`). He started out with the intention of becoming a world-famous nanotechnologist, so perhaps one day you might recognize his name as he receives a Nobel Prize. For now, though, Karli's main academic interest is the .NET Framework, and all the boxes of tricks it contains. A snowboarding enthusiast, Karli also loves cooking, spends far too much time playing Anarchy Online and EVE, and wishes he had a cat. As yet, nobody has seen fit to publish Karli's first novel, but the rejection letters make an attractive pile. If he ever puts anything up there, you can visit Karli online at `http://www.karliwatson.com`.

About the Authors

Credits

Acquisitions Editor
Katie Mohr

Development Editors
Ami Frank Sullivan
Lori Cerreto

Technical Editors
Michael Erickson
Doug Holland

Production Editor
Daniel Scribner

Copy Editor
Kim Cofer
Nancy Rapaport

Editorial Manager
Mary Beth Wakefield

Production Manager
Tim Tate

Vice President and Executive Group Publisher
Richard Swadley

Vice President and Executive Publisher
Joseph B. Wikert

Project Coordinator, Cover
Lynsey Stanford

Proofreaders
Word One:
Edward Moyer
Jen Larsen
Amy Rasmussen
Corina Copp
Scott Klemp
Joshua Chase

Indexer
Ron Strauss

Acknowledgments

Bill Evjen:

The .NET Framework 3.5 release came quickly for us writers and it wouldn't have been possible to produce this book as fast as they came out if it weren't for the dedication of the teams built for it. Tremendous thanks to Katie Mohr for being more than patient with me in getting this and some other .NET 3.5 books out the door. Also, big thanks go out to Ami Sullivan for getting at me and helping me be *somewhat* on schedule. Other big thanks go to all the editors of the book including Lori Cerreto, Daniel Scribner, and the copyeditors.

Finally, to the ones that paid the biggest price for this writing session — my wife, Tuija, and the three kids: Sofia, Henri, and Kalle. Thanks for all you do!

Karli Watson:

Thanks to all at Wiley for helping me through this project and reigning in my strange British stylings, to assorted clients for giving me the time to write, and to Donna for keeping me sane and coping with my temperamental back. Thanks also to friends and family for being patient with my deadline-laden lifestyle.

Contents

Acknowledgments **xiii**
Introduction **xlvii**

Part I: The C# Language 1

Chapter 1: .NET Architecture 3

The Relationship of C# to .NET **4**
The Common Language Runtime **4**
Platform Independence 4
Performance Improvement 4
Language Interoperability 5
A Closer Look at Intermediate Language **7**
Support for Object Orientation and Interfaces 7
Distinct Value and Reference Types 8
Strong Data Typing 8
Error Handling with Exceptions 14
Use of Attributes 15
Assemblies **15**
Private Assemblies 16
Shared Assemblies 16
Reflection 17
.NET Framework Classes **17**
Namespaces **18**
Creating .NET Applications Using C# **19**
Creating ASP.NET Applications 19
Creating Windows Forms 21
Using the Windows Presentation Foundation (WPF) 21
Windows Controls 21
Windows Services 21
Windows Communication Foundation (WCF) 22
The Role of C# in the .NET Enterprise Architecture **22**
Summary **23**

Chapter 2: C# Basics **25**

Before We Start **25**
Your First C# Program **26**
The Code 26
Compiling and Running the Program 26
A Closer Look 27
Variables **29**
Initialization of Variables 29
Type Inference 30
Variable Scope 31
Constants 34
Predefined Data Types **34**
Value Types and Reference Types 35
CTS Types 36
Predefined Value Types 36
Predefined Reference Types 40
Flow Control **42**
Conditional Statements 42
Loops 45
Jump Statements 49
Enumerations **50**
Arrays **51**
Namespaces **52**
The using Directive 53
Namespace Aliases 54
The Main() Method **55**
Multiple Main() Methods 55
Passing Arguments to Main() 56
More on Compiling C# Files **57**
Console I/O **58**
Using Comments **60**
Internal Comments within the Source Files 60
XML Documentation 61
The C# Preprocessor Directives **63**
#define and #undef 63
#if, #elif, #else, and #endif 64
#warning and #error 65
#region and #endregion 65
#line 65
#pragma 66
C# Programming Guidelines **66**

Rules for Identifiers 66
Usage Conventions 67
Summary **73**

Chapter 3: Objects and Types **75**

Classes and Structs **76**
Class Members **76**
Data Members 77
Function Members 77
Anonymous Types **91**
Structs **92**
Structs Are Value Types 93
Structs and Inheritance 94
Constructors for Structs 94
Partial Classes **95**
Static Classes **96**
The Object Class **97**
System.Object Methods 97
The ToString() Method 98
Extension Methods **99**
Summary **100**

Chapter 4: Inheritance **101**

Types of Inheritance **101**
Implementation versus Interface Inheritance 101
Multiple Inheritance 102
Structs and Classes 102
Implementation Inheritance **103**
Virtual Methods 104
Hiding Methods 104
Calling Base Versions of Functions 106
Abstract Classes and Functions 106
Sealed Classes and Methods 107
Constructors of Derived Classes 107
Modifiers **112**
Visibility Modifiers 112
Other Modifiers 113
Interfaces **114**
Defining and Implementing Interfaces 115
Derived Interfaces 118
Summary **120**

Chapter 5: Arrays 121

Simple Arrays 121
Array Declaration 121
Array Initialization 122
Accessing Array Elements 123
Using Reference Types 123
Multidimensional Arrays 125
Jagged Arrays 126
Array Class 127
Properties 127
Creating Arrays 127
Copying Arrays 128
Sorting 129
Array and Collection Interfaces 132
IEnumerable 132
ICollection 132
IList 132
Enumerations 133
IEnumerator Interface 134
foreach Statement 134
yield Statement 134
Summary 139

Chapter 6: Operators and Casts 141

Operators 141
Operator Shortcuts 143
The Conditional Operator 144
The checked and unchecked Operators 145
The is Operator 146
The as Operator 146
The sizeof Operator 146
The typeof Operator 146
Nullable Types and Operators 147
The Null Coalescing Operator 147
Operator Precedence 147
Type Safety 148
Type Conversions 149
Boxing and Unboxing 152
Comparing Objects for Equality 153
Comparing Reference Types for Equality 153
Comparing Value Types for Equality 154

Operator Overloading **155**
How Operators Work 156
Operator Overloading Example: The Vector Struct 157
Which Operators Can You Overload? 163
User-Defined Casts **164**
Implementing User-Defined Casts 165
Multiple Casting 171
Summary **175**

Chapter 7: Delegates and Events **177**

Delegates **177**
Declaring Delegates in C# 178
Using Delegates in C# 179
Simple Delegate Example 182
BubbleSorter Example 184
Multicast Delegates 187
Anonymous Methods 190
Lambda Expressions 191
Covariance and Contra-variance 193
Events **194**
The Receiver's View of Events 195
Defining Events 197
Summary **201**

Chapter 8: Strings and Regular Expressions **203**

System.String **204**
Building Strings 205
StringBuilder Members 208
Format Strings 209
Regular Expressions **214**
Introduction to Regular Expressions 215
The RegularExpressionsPlayground Example 216
Displaying Results 219
Matches, Groups, and Captures 220
Summary **222**

Chapter 9: Generics **223**

Overview **223**
Performance 224
Type Safety 225

Binary Code Reuse 225
Code Bloat 226
Naming Guidelines 226
Creating Generic Classes 226
Generic Classes' Features 231
Default Values 231
Constraints 232
Inheritance 234
Static Members 235
Generic Interfaces 235
Generic Methods 236
Generic Delegates 238
Implementing Methods Called by Delegates 238
Using Generic Delegates with the Array Class 240
Other Generic Framework Types 243
Nullable<T> 243
EventHandler<TEventArgs> 244
ArraySegment<T> 245
Summary 246

Chapter 10: Collections 247

Collection Interfaces and Types 247
Lists 250
Creating Lists 252
Read-Only Collections 261
Queues 261
Stacks 266
Linked Lists 268
Sorted Lists 275
Dictionaries 278
Key Type 278
Dictionary Example 280
Lookup 283
Other Dictionary Classes 284
HashSet 286
Bit Arrays 289
BitArray 289
BitVector32 291
Performance 294
Summary 296

Chapter 11: Language Integrated Query 297

LINQ Overview 297
Query using List<T> 298
Extension Methods 304
Lambda Expressions 306
LINQ Query 307
Deferred Query Execution 307
Standard Query Operators 309
Filtering 311
Filtering with Index 312
Type Filtering 312
Compound from 313
Sorting 314
Grouping 315
Grouping with Nested Objects 316
Join 317
Set Operations 318
Partitioning 319
Aggregate Operators 321
Conversion 322
Generation Operators 323
Expression Trees 324
LINQ Providers 327
Summary 328

Chapter 12: Memory Management and Pointers 329

Memory Management Under the Hood 329
Value Data Types 330
Reference Data Types 331
Garbage Collection 333
Freeing Unmanaged Resources 334
Destructors 335
The IDisposable Interface 336
Implementing IDisposable and a Destructor 337
Unsafe Code 339
Accessing Memory Directly with Pointers 339
Pointer Example: PointerPlayaround 347
Using Pointers to Optimize Performance 352
Summary 355

Chapter 13: Reflection 357

Custom Attributes **358**
Writing Custom Attributes 358
Custom Attribute Example: WhatsNewAttributes 362
Reflection **365**
The System.Type Class 365
The TypeView Example 367
The Assembly Class 370
Completing the WhatsNewAttributes Example 371
Summary **376**

Chapter 14: Errors and Exceptions 377

Exception Classes **378**
Catching Exceptions **379**
Implementing Multiple Catch Blocks 382
Catching Exceptions from Other Code 385
System.Exception Properties 386
What Happens If an Exception Isn't Handled? 386
Nested try Blocks 387
User-Defined Exception Classes **389**
Catching the User-Defined Exceptions 390
Throwing the User-Defined Exceptions 391
Defining the User-Defined Exception Classes 394
Summary **397**

Part II: Visual Studio 399

Chapter 15: Visual Studio 2008 401

Working with Visual Studio 2008 **401**
Creating a Project 406
Solutions and Projects 412
Windows Application Code 415
Reading in Visual Studio 6 Projects 416
Exploring and Coding a Project 416
Building a Project 427
Debugging 430
Refactoring **434**
Multi-Targeting **436**
WPF, WCF, WF, and More **438**

Building WPF Applications in Visual Studio 438
Building WF Applications in Visual Studio 439
Summary **441**

Chapter 16: Deployment **443**

Designing for Deployment **443**
Deployment Options **444**
Xcopy 444
Copy Web Tool 444
Publishing Web Sites 444
Deployment Projects 444
ClickOnce 444
Deployment Requirements **444**
Deploying the .NET Runtime **446**
Simple Deployment **446**
Xcopy 447
Xcopy and Web Applications 447
Copy Web Tool 447
Publishing a Web Site 447
Installer Projects **448**
What Is Windows Installer? 449
Creating Installers 449
ClickOnce **458**
ClickOnce Operation 458
Publishing an Application 459
ClickOnce Settings 459
Application Cache 460
Security 460
Advanced Options 460
Summary **466**

Part III: Base Class Libraries **467**

Chapter 17: Assemblies **469**

What Are Assemblies? **469**
Features of Assemblies 470
Assembly Structure 470
Assembly Manifests 472
Namespaces, Assemblies, and Components 472
Private and Shared Assemblies 472

Satellite Assemblies 473
Viewing Assemblies 473
Creating Assemblies 474
Creating Modules and Assemblies 474
Assembly Attributes 475
Dynamic Loading and Creating Assemblies 478
Application Domains 481
Shared Assemblies 485
Strong Names 486
Integrity Using Strong Names 486
Global Assembly Cache 487
Creating a Shared Assembly 489
Create a Strong Name 489
Install the Shared Assembly 491
Using the Shared Assembly 491
Delayed Signing of Assemblies 492
References 493
Native Image Generator 494
Configuring .NET Applications 495
Configuration Categories 496
Configuring Directories for Assembly Searches 497
Versioning 499
Version Numbers 499
Getting the Version Programmatically 500
Application Configuration Files 500
Publisher Policy Files 504
Runtime Version 506
Summary 507

Chapter 18: Tracing and Events 509

Tracing 509
Trace Sources 511
Trace Switches 512
Trace Listeners 512
Filters 515
Asserts 516
Event Logging 517
Event-Logging Architecture 518
Event-Logging Classes 519
Creating an Event Source 521

Writing Event Logs 522
Resource Files 522
Event Log Listener 526
Performance Monitoring **527**
Performance-Monitoring Classes 528
Performance Counter Builder 528
Adding PerformanceCounter Components 529
perfmon.exe 531
Summary **532**

Chapter 19: Threading and Synchronization **533**

Overview **534**
Asynchronous Delegates **535**
Polling 535
Wait Handle 536
Asynchronous Callback 537
The Thread Class **538**
Passing Data to Threads 540
Background Threads 541
Thread Priority 542
Controlling Threads 543
Thread Pools **543**
Threading Issues **545**
Race Condition 545
Deadlock 548
Synchronization **549**
lock Statement and Thread Safety 550
Interlocked 555
Monitor 557
Wait Handle 557
Mutex 559
Semaphore 560
Events 562
ReaderWriterLockSlim 564
Timers **568**
COM Apartments **569**
Event-Based Asynchronous Pattern **570**
BackgroundWorker 571
Creating an Event-Based Asynchronous Component 576
Summary **581**

Chapter 20: Security 583

Authentication and Authorization 583
Identity and Principal 583
Roles 585
Declarative Role-Based Security 585
Client Application Services 586
Encryption 591
Signature 594
Key Exchange and Secure Transfer 596
Access Control to Resources 599
Code Access Security 602
Permissions 603
Code Groups 613
Code Access Permissions and Permissions Sets 618
Policy Levels: Machine, User, and Enterprise 621
Managing Security Policies 622
Managing Code Groups and Permissions 626
Turning Security On and Off 626
Creating a Code Group 626
Deleting a Code Group 627
Changing a Code Group's Permissions 627
Creating and Applying Permissions Sets 628
Distributing Code Using a Strong Name 630
Distributing Code Using Certificates 631
Summary 637

Chapter 21: Localization 639

Namespace System.Globalization 639
Unicode Issues 640
Cultures and Regions 641
Cultures in Action 645
Sorting 650
Resources 651
Creating Resource Files 651
Resource File Generator 651
ResourceWriter 652
Using Resource Files 653
The System.Resources Namespace 659
Windows Forms Localization Using Visual Studio 659
Changing the Culture Programmatically 663
Using Custom Resource Messages 665

Automatic Fallback for Resources 666
Outsourcing Translations 666
Localization with ASP.NET 667
Localization with WPF 669
WPF Application 670
.NET Resources 670
Localization with XAML 671
A Custom Resource Reader 673
Creating a DatabaseResourceReader 674
Creating a DatabaseResourceSet 676
Creating a DatabaseResourceManager 676
Client Application for DatabaseResourceReader 677
Creating Custom Cultures 677
Summary 678

Chapter 22: Transactions 679

Overview 679
Transaction Phases 680
ACID Properties 681
Database and Entity Classes 681
Traditional Transactions 683
ADO.NET Transactions 683
System.EnterpriseServices 684
System.Transactions 685
Committable Transactions 687
Transaction Promotion 690
Dependent Transactions 692
Ambient Transactions 694
Isolation Level 701
Custom Resource Managers 703
Transactional Resources 704
Transactions with Windows Vista and Windows Server 2008 710
Summary 713

Chapter 23: Windows Services 715

What Is a Windows Service? 715
Windows Services Architecture 716
Service Program 717
Service Control Program 718
Service Configuration Program 718

System.ServiceProcess Namespace 718
Creating a Windows Service 719
A Class Library Using Sockets 719
TcpClient Example 722
Windows Service Project 725
Threading and Services 730
Service Installation 730
Installation Program 730
Monitoring and Controlling the Service 734
MMC Computer Management 735
net.exe 736
sc.exe 736
Visual Studio Server Explorer 737
ServiceController Class 737
Troubleshooting 745
Interactive Services 745
Event Logging 746
Power Events 746
Summary 748

Chapter 24: Interoperability 749

.NET and COM 750
Metadata 750
Freeing Memory 750
Interfaces 751
Method Binding 752
Data Types 753
Registration 753
Threading 753
Error Handling 754
Event Handling 754
Marshaling 755
Using a COM Component from a .NET Client 756
Creating a COM Component 756
Creating a Runtime Callable Wrapper 762
Using the RCW 763
Primary Interop Assemblies 764
Threading Issues 764
Adding Connection Points 765
Using ActiveX Controls in Windows Forms 768
Using COM Objects from within ASP.NET 771

Using a .NET Component from a COM Client **771**
COM Callable Wrapper 771
Creating a .NET Component 772
Creating a Type Library 772
COM Interop Attributes 774
COM Registration 777
Creating a COM Client 778
Adding Connection Points 780
Creating a Client with a Sink Object 781
Running Windows Forms Controls in Internet Explorer 782
Platform Invoke **783**
Summary **787**

Part IV: Data **789**

Chapter 25: Manipulating Files and the Registry **791**

Managing the File System **791**
.NET Classes That Represent Files and Folders 792
The Path Class 795
Example: A File Browser 796
Moving, Copying, and Deleting Files **800**
Example: FilePropertiesAndMovement 801
Looking at the Code for FilePropertiesAndMovement 802
Reading and Writing to Files **805**
Reading a File 805
Writing to a File 807
Streams 808
Buffered Streams 810
Reading and Writing to Binary Files Using FileStream 810
Reading and Writing to Text Files 815
Reading Drive Information **822**
File Security **824**
Reading ACLs from a File 824
Reading ACLs from a Directory 825
Adding and Removing ACLs from a File 827
Reading and Writing to the Registry **828**
The Registry 829
The .NET Registry Classes 830
Example: SelfPlacingWindow 833
Reading and Writing to Isolated Storage **839**
Summary **844**

Chapter 26: Data Access 845

ADO.NET Overview 846
Namespaces 846
Shared Classes 847
Database-Specific Classes 847
Using Database Connections 849
Managing Connection Strings 850
Using Connections Efficiently 852
Transactions 854
Commands 855
Executing Commands 856
Calling Stored Procedures 860
Fast Data Access: The Data Reader 863
Managing Data and Relationships: The DataSet Class 865
Data Tables 866
Data Relationships 873
Data Constraints 874
XML Schemas: Generating Code with XSD 877
Populating a DataSet 883
Populating a DataSet Class with a Data Adapter 883
Populating a DataSet from XML 884
Persisting DataSet Changes 884
Updating with Data Adapters 885
Writing XML Output 887
Working with ADO.NET 889
Tiered Development 889
Key Generation with SQL Server 890
Naming Conventions 892
Summary 894

Chapter 27: LINQ to SQL 895

LINQ to SQL and Visual Studio 2008 897
Calling the Products Table Using LINQ to SQL — Creating the Console Application 897
Adding a LINQ to SQL Class 898
Introducing the O/R Designer 899
Creating the Product Object 900
How Objects Map to LINQ Objects 902
The DataContext Object 903
The Table<TEntity> Object 907
Working Without the O/R Designer 907

Creating Your Own Custom Object 908
Querying with Your Custom Object and LINQ 908
Limiting the Columns Called with the Query 910
Working with Column Names 910
Creating Your Own DataContext Object 911
Custom Objects and the O/R Designer 912
Querying the Database 914
Using Query Expressions 914
Query Expressions in Detail 915
Filtering Using Expressions 916
Performing Joins 916
Grouping Items 918
Stored Procedures 919
Summary 920

Chapter 28: Manipulating XML 921

XML Standards Support in .NET 922
Introducing the System.Xml Namespace 922
Using System.Xml Classes 923
Reading and Writing Streamed XML 924
Using the XmlReader Class 924
Validating with XmlReader 928
Using the XmlWriter Class 930
Using the DOM in .NET 931
Using the XmlDocument Class 933
Using XPathNavigators 937
The System.Xml.XPath Namespace 937
The System.Xml.Xsl Namespace 942
XML and ADO.NET 948
Converting ADO.NET Data to XML 948
Converting XML to ADO.NET Data 954
Serializing Objects in XML 956
Serialization Without Source Code Access 963
Summary 965

Chapter 29: LINQ to XML 967

LINQ to XML and .NET 3.5 968
New Objects for Creating XML Documents 968
Visual Basic 2008 Ventures Down Another Path 968
Namespaces and Prefixes 968

New XML Objects from the .NET Framework 3.5 **969**
XDocument 969
XElement 969
XNamespace 971
XComment 973
XAttribute 974
Using LINQ to Query XML Documents **974**
Querying Static XML Documents 975
Querying Dynamic XML Documents 976
Working Around the XML Document **978**
Reading from an XML Document 978
Writing to an XML Document 979
Using LINQ to SQL with LINQ to XML **981**
Setting up the LINQ to SQL Components 981
Querying the Database and Outputting XML 982
Summary **983**

Chapter 30: .NET Programming with SQL Server **985**

.NET Runtime Host **986**
Microsoft.SqlServer.Server **987**
User-Defined Types **988**
Creating UDTs 988
Using UDTs 993
Using UDTs from Client-Side Code 994
Creating User-Defined Aggregates 996
Using User-Defined Aggregates 997
Stored Procedures **998**
Creating Stored Procedures 998
Using Stored Procedures 999
User-Defined Functions **1000**
Creating User-Defined Functions 1000
Using User-Defined Functions 1001
Triggers **1001**
Creating Triggers 1002
Using Triggers 1003
XML Data Type **1003**
Tables with XML Data 1003
Reading XML Values 1005
Query of Data 1008
XML Data Modification Language (XML DML) 1010

XML Indexes 1010
Strongly Typed XML 1011
Summary **1013**

Part V: Presentation **1015**

Chapter 31: Windows Forms **1017**

Creating a Windows Form Application **1018**
Class Hierarchy 1023
Control Class **1023**
Size and Location 1023
Appearance 1024
User Interaction 1024
Windows Functionality 1025
Miscellaneous Functionality 1026
Standard Controls and Components **1026**
Button 1026
CheckBox 1028
RadioButton 1028
ComboBox, ListBox, and CheckedListBox 1029
DateTimePicker 1031
ErrorProvider 1031
HelpProvider 1032
ImageList 1033
Label 1033
ListView 1033
PictureBox 1035
ProgressBar 1035
TextBox, RichTextBox, and MaskedTextBox 1036
Panel 1037
FlowLayoutPanel and TableLayoutPanel 1037
SplitContainer 1038
TabControl and TabPages 1038
ToolStrip 1039
MenuStrip 1041
ContextMenuStrip 1042
ToolStripMenuItem 1042
ToolStripManager 1042
ToolStripContainer 1042
Forms **1043**
Form Class 1043

Multiple Document Interface 1047
Custom Controls 1048
Summary **1059**

Chapter 32: Data Binding **1061**

The DataGridView Control **1061**
Displaying Tabular Data 1062
Data Sources 1063
DataGridView Class Hierarchy **1072**
Data Binding **1075**
Simple Binding 1075
Data-Binding Objects 1076
Visual Studio .NET and Data Access **1080**
Creating a Connection 1080
Selecting Data 1084
Updating the Data Source 1084
Other Common Requirements 1085
Summary **1092**

Chapter 33: Graphics with GDI+ **1093**

Understanding Drawing Principles **1094**
GDI and GDI+ 1094
Drawing Shapes 1096
Painting Shapes Using OnPaint() 1099
Using the Clipping Region 1100
Measuring Coordinates and Areas **1102**
Point and PointF 1102
Size and SizeF 1103
Rectangle and RectangleF 1105
Region 1106
A Note About Debugging **1106**
Drawing Scrollable Windows **1107**
World, Page, and Device Coordinates **1113**
Colors **1114**
Red-Green-Blue Values 1114
The Named Colors 1115
Graphics Display Modes and the Safety Palette 1115
The Safety Palette **1116**
Pens and Brushes **1116**
Brushes 1117
Pens 1117

Drawing Shapes and Lines **1118**
Displaying Images **1120**
Issues When Manipulating Images **1123**
Drawing Text **1123**
Simple Text Example **1124**
Fonts and Font Families **1125**
Example: Enumerating Font Families **1126**
Editing a Text Document: The CapsEditor Sample **1129**
The Invalidate() Method 1133
Calculating Item Sizes and Document Size 1134
OnPaint() 1135
Coordinate Transforms 1137
Responding to User Input 1138
Printing **1141**
Implementing Print and Print Preview 1143
Summary **1147**

Chapter 34: Windows Presentation Foundation **1149**

Overview **1149**
XAML 1150
Cooperation of Designers and Developers 1154
Class Hierarchy 1155
Namespaces 1156
Shapes **1159**
Transformation **1162**
Brushes **1163**
SolidColorBrush 1163
LinearGradientBrush 1164
RadialGradientBrush 1164
DrawingBrush 1165
ImageBrush 1165
VisualBrush 1166
Controls **1167**
Simple Controls 1167
Content Controls 1168
Headered Content Controls 1170
Items Controls 1171
Headered Items Controls 1171
Layout **1172**
StackPanel 1172
WrapPanel 1173

Canvas 1173
DockPanel 1174
Grid 1175
Event Handling 1176
Styles, Templates, and Resources 1177
Styles 1177
Resources 1178
Triggers 1182
Templates 1184
Styling a ListBox 1192
Summary 1198

Chapter 35: Advanced WPF 1199

Data Binding 1199
Overview 1200
Binding with XAML 1200
Simple Object Binding 1203
Object Data Provider 1206
List Binding 1208
Value Conversion 1212
Adding List Items Dynamically 1213
Data Templates 1214
Binding to XML 1217
Binding Validation 1219
Command Bindings 1224
Animations 1228
Timeline 1229
Triggers 1233
Storyboard 1235
Adding 3-D Features in WPF 1237
Triangle 1238
Windows Forms Integration 1245
WPF Controls Within Windows Forms 1245
Windows Forms Controls Within WPF Applications 1247
WPF Browser Application 1249
Summary 1249

Chapter 36: Add-Ins 1251

System.AddIn Architecture 1251
Issues with Add-ins 1252
Pipeline Architecture 1253

Discovery 1254
Activation and Isolation 1255
Contracts 1257
Lifetime 1258
Versioning 1259
Add-In Sample **1259**
Calculator Contract 1261
Calculator Add-In View 1261
Calculator Add-In Adapter 1262
Calculator Add-In 1264
Calculator Host View 1265
Calculator Host Adapter 1265
Calculator Host 1267
Additional Add-Ins 1271
Summary **1271**

Chapter 37: ASP.NET Pages **1273**

ASP.NET Introduction **1274**
State Management in ASP.NET 1274
ASP.NET Web Forms **1275**
The ASP.NET Code Model 1278
ASP.NET Server Controls 1279
ADO.NET and Data Binding **1295**
Updating the Event-Booking Application 1295
More on Data Binding 1302
Application Configuration **1308**
Summary **1309**

Chapter 38: ASP.NET Development **1311**

User and Custom Controls **1312**
User Controls 1312
Custom Controls 1318
Master Pages **1323**
Accessing Master Page Content from Web Pages 1325
Nested Master Pages 1326
Master Pages in PCSDemoSite 1326
Site Navigation **1328**
Navigation in PCSDemoSite 1330
Security **1331**
Adding Forms Authentication Using the Security Wizard 1332
Implementing a Login System 1334

Login Web Server Controls 1336
Securing Directories 1336
Security in PCSDemoSite 1337
Themes **1339**
Applying Themes to Pages 1339
Defining Themes 1340
Themes in PCSDemoSite 1340
Web Parts **1344**
Web Parts Application Components 1344
Web Parts Example 1346
Summary **1353**

Chapter 39: ASP.NET AJAX **1355**

What Is Ajax? **1356**
What Is ASP.NET AJAX? **1358**
Core Functionality 1359
ASP.NET AJAX Control Toolkit 1361
Using ASP.NET AJAX **1361**
ASP.NET AJAX Web Site Example 1362
ASP.NET AJAX-Enabled Web Site Configuration 1365
Adding ASP.NET AJAX Functionality 1368
Using the AJAX Library 1374
Summary **1383**

Chapter 40: Visual Studio Tools for Office **1385**

VSTO Overview **1386**
Project Types 1386
Project Features 1389
VSTO Fundamentals **1390**
Office Object Model 1391
VSTO Namespaces 1391
Host Items and Host Controls 1392
Basic VSTO Project Structure 1394
The Globals Class 1397
Event Handling 1397
Building VSTO Solutions **1398**
Managing Application-Level Add-Ins 1399
Interacting with Applications and Documents 1400
UI Customization 1401
Example Application **1405**

VBA Interoperability **1415**
Summary **1418**

Part VI: Communication **1421**

Chapter 41: Accessing the Internet **1423**

The WebClient Class **1424**
Downloading Files 1424
Basic Web Client Example 1424
Uploading Files 1426
WebRequest and WebResponse Classes **1426**
Other WebRequest and WebResponse Features 1427
Displaying Output as an HTML Page **1429**
Allowing Simple Web Browsing from Your Applications 1430
Launching Internet Explorer Instances 1432
Giving Your Application More IE-Type Features 1432
Printing Using the WebBrowser Control 1437
Displaying the Code of a Requested Page 1438
The Web Request and Web Response Hierarchy 1438
Utility Classes **1440**
URIs 1440
IP Addresses and DNS Names 1441
Lower-Level Protocols **1443**
Lower-Level Classes 1444
Summary **1453**

Chapter 42: Windows Communication Foundation **1455**

WCF Overview **1456**
SOAP 1457
WSDL 1457
JSON 1458
Simple Service and Client **1458**
Service Contract 1460
Service Implementation 1460
WCF Service Host and WCF Test Client 1461
Custom Service Host 1463
WCF Client 1464
Diagnostics 1466
Contracts **1467**
Data Contract 1468

Versioning 1468
Service Contract 1469
Message Contract 1470
Service Implementation 1471
Error Handling 1476
Binding 1477
Hosting 1480
Custom Hosting 1480
WAS Hosting 1481
Clients 1482
Duplex Communication 1484
Summary 1486

Chapter 43: Windows Workflow Foundation 1487

Hello World 1488
Activities 1489
IfElseActivity 1490
ParallelActivity 1491
CallExternalMethodActivity 1492
DelayActivity 1493
ListenActivity 1493
Activity Execution Model 1494
Custom Activities 1495
Activity Validation 1497
Themes and Designers 1498
ActivityToolboxItem and Icons 1500
Custom Composite Activities 1502
Workflows 1508
Sequential Workflows 1509
State Machine Workflows 1509
Passing Parameters to a Workflow 1511
Returning Results from a Workflow 1512
Binding Parameters to Activities 1513
The Workflow Runtime 1514
Workflow Services 1515
The Persistence Service 1517
The Tracking Service 1518
Custom Services 1520
Integration with Windows Communication Foundation 1521
Hosting Workflows 1524
The Workflow Designer 1526
Summary 1526

Chapter 44: Enterprise Services 1527

Overview 1527
History 1528
Where to Use Enterprise Services 1528
Contexts 1529
Automatic Transactions 1529
Distributed Transactions 1530
Object Pooling 1530
Role-Based Security 1530
Queued Components 1530
Loosely Coupled Events 1530
Creating a Simple COM+ Application 1531
The ServicedComponent Class 1531
Sign the Assembly 1532
Assembly Attributes 1532
Creating the Component 1533
Deployment 1534
Automatic Deployment 1534
Manual Deployment 1534
Creating an Installer Package 1535
Component Services Explorer 1536
Client Application 1538
Transactions 1539
Transaction Attributes 1539
Transaction Results 1540
Sample Application 1540
Entity Classes 1541
The OrderControl Component 1543
The OrderData Component 1544
The OrderLineData Component 1546
Client Application 1548
Integrating WCF and Enterprise Services 1549
WCF Service Façade 1549
Client Application 1553
Summary 1554

Chapter 45: Message Queuing 1555

Overview 1555
When to Use Message Queuing 1556
Message Queuing Features 1557
Message Queuing Products 1558

Message Queuing Architecture **1559**
Messages 1559
Message Queue 1559
Message Queuing Administrative Tools **1560**
Creating Message Queues 1560
Message Queue Properties 1561
Programming Message Queuing **1562**
Creating a Message Queue 1562
Finding a Queue 1563
Opening Known Queues 1563
Sending a Message 1565
Receiving Messages 1567
Course Order Application **1569**
Course Order Class Library 1570
Course Order Message Sender 1570
Sending Priority and Recoverable Messages 1571
Course Order Message Receiver 1573
Receiving Results **1576**
Acknowledgment Queues 1576
Response Queues 1577
Transactional Queues **1577**
Message Queuing with WCF **1579**
Entity Classes with a Data Contract 1579
WCF Service Contract 1580
WCF Message Receiver Application 1581
WCF Message Sender Application 1583
Message Queue Installation **1585**
Summary **1585**

Chapter 46: Directory Services **1587**

The Architecture of Active Directory **1588**
Features 1588
Active Directory Concepts 1588
Characteristics of Active Directory Data 1592
Schema 1592
Administration Tools for Active Directory **1594**
Active Directory Users and Computers 1594
ADSI Edit 1595
Programming Active Directory **1596**
Classes in System.DirectoryServices 1598
Binding 1598
Cache 1605

Creating New Objects 1605
Updating Directory Entries 1606
Accessing Native ADSI Objects 1607
Searching in Active Directory 1608
Searching for User Objects **1611**
User Interface 1611
Get the Schema Naming Context 1612
Get the Property Names of the User Class 1613
Search for User Objects 1614
Account Management **1616**
Display User Information 1618
Create a User 1618
Reset a Password 1618
Create a Group 1619
Add a User to a Group 1619
Finding Users 1619
DSML **1620**
Classes in System.DirectoryServices.Protocols 1621
Searching for Active Directory Objects with DSML 1621
Summary **1623**

Chapter 47: Peer-to-Peer Networking **1625**

Peer-to-Peer Networking Overview **1625**
Client-Server Architecture 1626
P2P Architecture 1627
P2P Architectural Challenges 1627
P2P Terminology 1628
P2P Solutions 1629
Microsoft Windows Peer-to-Peer Networking **1629**
Peer Name Resolution Protocol (PNRP) 1629
People Near Me 1632
Building P2P Applications **1632**
System.Net.PeerToPeer 1633
System.Net.PeerToPeer.Collaboration 1638
Summary **1642**

Chapter 48: Syndication **1643**

Overview of System.Servicemodel.Syndication **1643**
Syndication Reader **1645**
Offering Syndication Feeds **1647**
Summary **1652**

Part VII: Appendices 1653

Appendix A: ADO.NET Entity Framework 1655

Overview of the ADO.NET Entity Framework 1656
Entity Framework Layers 1657
Logical 1657
Conceptual 1659
Mapping 1660
Entities 1661
Object Context 1664
Relationships 1666
Table per Hierarchy 1666
Table per Type 1668
Object Query 1670
Updates 1674
Object Tracking 1674
Change Information 1675
Attaching and Detaching Entities 1677
Storing Entity Changes 1677
LINQ to Entities 1678
Summary 1679

Appendix B: C#, Visual Basic, and C++/CLI 1681

Namespaces 1682
Defining Types 1683
Reference Types 1683
Value Types 1684
Type Inference 1685
Interfaces 1685
Enumerations 1686
Methods 1687
Method Parameters and Return Types 1687
Parameter Modifiers 1688
Constructors 1689
Properties 1690
Object Initializers 1691
Extension Methods 1692
Static Members 1692
Arrays 1693
Control Statements 1694
if Statement 1694

Conditional Operator 1694
switch Statement 1694
Loops **1696**
for Statement 1696
while and do . . . while Statements 1696
foreach Statement 1697
Exception Handling **1697**
Inheritance **1699**
Access Modifiers 1699
Keywords 1699
Resource Management **1701**
IDisposable Interface Implementation 1701
Using Statement 1702
Override Finalize 1702
Delegates **1703**
Events **1705**
Generics **1707**
LINQ Queries **1708**
C++/CLI Mixing Native and Managed Code **1708**
C# Specifics **1709**
Summary **1710**

Appendix C: Windows Vista and Windows Server 2008 **1711**

Vista Bridge **1711**
User Account Control **1712**
Applications Requiring Admin Privileges 1712
Shield Icon 1713
Directory Structure **1715**
New Controls and Dialogs **1716**
Command Link 1717
Task Dialog 1718
File Dialogs 1721
Search **1722**
OLE DB Provider 1724
Advanced Query Syntax 1728
Summary **1729**

Index **1731**

Introduction

If we were to describe the C# language and its associated environment, the .NET Framework, as the most important new technology for developers for many years, we would not be exaggerating. .NET is designed to provide a new environment within which you can develop almost any application to run on Windows, whereas C# is a new programming language that has been designed specifically to work with .NET. Using C# you can, for example, write a dynamic Web page, an XML Web service, a component of a distributed application, a database access component, a classic Windows desktop application, or even a new smart client application that allows for online/offline capabilities. This book covers the .NET Framework 3.5. If you are coding using version 1.0, 1.1, 2.0, or even 3.0, there may be sections of the book that will not work for you. We try to notify you of items that are new to the .NET Framework 3.5 specifically.

Don't be fooled by the .NET label. The NET bit in the name is there to emphasize Microsoft's belief that distributed applications, in which the processing is distributed between client and server, are the way forward, but C# is not just a language for writing Internet or network-aware applications. It provides a means for you to code up almost any type of software or component that you might need to write for the Windows platform. Between them, C# and .NET are set both to revolutionize the way that you write programs, and to make programming on Windows much easier than it has ever been.

That's quite a substantial claim, and it needs to be justified. After all, we all know how quickly computer technology changes. Every year Microsoft brings out new software, programming tools, or versions of Windows, with the claim that these will be hugely beneficial to developers. So what's different about .NET and C#?

The Significance of .NET and C#

In order to understand the significance of .NET, it is useful to remind ourselves of the nature of many of the Windows technologies that have appeared in the past 10 years or so. Although they may look quite different on the surface, all of the Windows operating systems from Windows 3.1 (introduced in 1992) through Windows Server 2008 have the same familiar Windows API at their core. As we've progressed through new versions of Windows, huge numbers of new functions have been added to the API, but this has been a process of evolving and extending the API rather than replacing it.

The same can be said for many of the technologies and frameworks that we've used to develop software for Windows. For example, *COM* (*Component Object Model*) originated as *OLE* (*Object Linking and Embedding*). At the time, it was, to a large extent, simply a means by which different types of Office documents could be linked, so that, for example, you could place a small Excel spreadsheet in your Word document. From that it evolved into COM, *DCOM* (*Distributed COM*), and eventually *COM+* — a sophisticated technology that formed the basis of the way almost all components communicated, as well as implementing transactions, messaging services, and object pooling.

Microsoft chose this evolutionary approach to software for the obvious reason that it is concerned about backward compatibility. Over the years, a huge base of third-party software has been written for Windows, and Windows wouldn't have enjoyed the success it has had if every time Microsoft introduced a new technology it broke the existing code base!

Although backward compatibility has been a crucial feature of Windows technologies and one of the strengths of the Windows platform, it does have a big disadvantage. Every time some technology evolves and adds new features, it ends up a bit more complicated than it was before.

It was clear that something had to change. Microsoft couldn't go on forever extending the same development tools and languages, always making them more and more complex in order to satisfy the conflicting demands of keeping up with the newest hardware and maintaining backward compatibility with what was around when Windows first became popular in the early 1990s. There comes a point where you have to start with a clean slate if you want a simple yet sophisticated set of languages, environments, and developer tools, which makes it easy for developers to write state-of-the-art software.

This fresh start is what C# and .NET are all about. Roughly speaking, .NET is a framework — an API — for programming on the Windows platform. Along with the .NET Framework, C# is a language that has been designed from scratch to work with .NET, as well as to take advantage of all the progress in developer environments and in our understanding of object-oriented programming principles that have taken place over the past 20 years.

Before we continue, we should make it clear that backward compatibility has not been lost in the process. Existing programs will continue to work, and .NET was designed with the ability to work with existing software. Presently, communication between software components on Windows almost entirely takes place using COM. Taking account of this, .NET does have the ability to provide wrappers around existing COM components so that .NET components can talk to them.

It is true that you don't need to learn C# in order to write code for .NET. Microsoft has extended C++, provided another new language called J#, and made substantial changes to Visual Basic to turn it into the more powerful language Visual Basic .NET, in order to allow code written in either of these languages to target the .NET environment. These other languages, however, are hampered by the legacy of having evolved over the years rather than having been written from the start with today's technology in mind.

This book will equip you to program in C#, while at the same time provide the necessary background in how the .NET architecture works. We not only cover the fundamentals of the C# language but also go on to give examples of applications that use a variety of related technologies, including database access, dynamic Web pages, advanced graphics, and directory access. The only requirement is that you be familiar with at least one other high-level language used on Windows — either C++, Visual Basic, or J++.

Advantages of .NET

We've talked in general terms about how great .NET is, but we haven't said much about how it helps to make your life as a developer easier. In this section, we discuss some of the improved features of .NET in brief.

- **Object-oriented programming** — Both the .NET Framework and C# are entirely based on object-oriented principles right from the start.
- **Good design** — A base class library, which is designed from the ground up in a highly intuitive way.
- **Language independence** — With .NET, all of the languages — Visual Basic .NET, C#, J#, and managed C++ — compile to a common *Intermediate Language*. This means that languages are interoperable in a way that has not been seen before.
- **Better support for dynamic Web pages** — Though ASP offered a lot of flexibility, it was also inefficient because of its use of interpreted scripting languages, and the lack of object-oriented design often resulted in messy ASP code. .NET offers an integrated support for Web pages, using a new technology — ASP.NET. With ASP.NET, code in your pages is compiled, and may be written in a .NET-aware high-level language such as C# or Visual Basic 2008.
- **Efficient data access** — A set of .NET components, collectively known as ADO.NET, provides efficient access to relational databases and a variety of data sources. Components are also available to allow access to the file system, and to directories. In particular, XML support is built into .NET, allowing you to manipulate data, which may be imported from or exported to non-Windows platforms.

- **Code sharing** — .NET has completely revamped the way that code is shared between applications, introducing the concept of the *assembly*, which replaces the traditional DLL. Assemblies have formal facilities for versioning, and different versions of assemblies can exist side by side.
- **Improved security** — Each assembly can also contain built-in security information that can indicate precisely who or what category of user or process is allowed to call which methods on which classes. This gives you a very fine degree of control over how the assemblies that you deploy can be used.
- **Zero-impact installation** — There are two types of assemblies: shared and private. Shared assemblies are common libraries available to all software, whereas private assemblies are intended only for use with particular software. A private assembly is entirely self-contained, so the process of installing it is simple. There are no registry entries; the appropriate files are simply placed in the appropriate folder in the file system.
- **Support for Web services** — .NET has fully integrated support for developing Web services as easily as you'd develop any other type of application.
- **Visual Studio 2008** — .NET comes with a developer environment, Visual Studio 2008, which can cope equally well with C++, C#, and Visual Basic 2008, as well as with ASP.NET code. Visual Studio 2008 integrates all the best features of the respective language-specific environments of Visual Studio .NET 2002/2003/2005 and Visual Studio 6.
- C# — C# is a new object-oriented language intended for use with .NET.

We look more closely at the benefits of the .NET architecture in Chapter 1, ".NET Architecture."

Looking at What's New in the .NET Framework 3.5

The first version of the .NET Framework (1.0) was released in 2002 to much enthusiasm. The.NET Framework 2.0 was introduced in 2005 and was considered a major release of the Framework. The .NET Framework 3.5, though not as big a release as the 2.0 release, is still considered a rather major release of the product with many outstanding new features.

With each release of the Framework, Microsoft has always tried to ensure that there were minimal breaking changes to code developed. Thus far, Microsoft has been very successful at this goal.

> **Make sure that you create a staging server to completely test the upgrading of your applications to the .NET Framework 3.5 as opposed to just upgrading a live application.**

The following section details some of the changes that are new to C# 2008, the .NET Framework 3.5, as well as new additions to Visual Studio 2008 — the development environment for the .NET Framework 3.5.

Implicitly Typed Variables

Using C# 2008, you can now declare a variable and allow the compiler to determine the type of the item implicitly. You will find that LINQ uses this capability to work with the queries that are created. To work with this new capability, you use the `var` keyword:

```
var x = 5;
```

When you use this statement, the compiler will actually use the value of `5` to figure out the type that this needs to be. That means, in this case, that the statement will actually be as you would expect:

```
int x = 5;
```

Automatically Implemented Properties

A common task of declaring your properties just got easier with C# 2008. Prior to this release, you would declare your properties as such:

```
private int _myItem;

public int MyItem
{
    get {
        return myItem
    }

    set {
        myItem = value;
    }
}
```

Now you can let the compiler do the work for you on your behalf. Instead of constantly putting the preceding structure in your code over and over again, you are now able to use the shortcut of automatic implemented properties:

```
public int MyProperty { get; set; }
```

Using this syntax will produce the same results as the lengthy example. The compiler will perform the operation of converting this short form to the proper format on your behalf, making your code simpler to read and work with and allowing you to code your solutions faster than before.

Object and Collection Initializers

C# 2008 now allows you to assign values to an object's properties at the moment the property is initialized. For instance, suppose you have the following object in your code:

```
public class MyStructure
{
        public int MyProperty1 { get; set; }
        public int MyProperty2 { get; set; }
}
```

Using C# 2008, you can instantiate the `MyStructure` object as follows:

```
MyStructure myStructure = new MyStructure() { MyProperty1 = 5,
    MyProperty2 = 10 };
```

This same capability allows you to declare many items of a collection at once:

```
List<int> myInts = new List<int>() { 5, 10, 15, 20, 25 };
```

In this case, all the numbers are added to the `myInts` object as if you used the `Add()` method.

Built-In ASP.NET AJAX Support

Although you could build ASP.NET AJAX web pages using the .NET Framework 2.0, this required additional installs. You will find that ASP.NET AJAX support is now built into ASP.NET 3.5 and Visual Studio 2008.

Now, every page that you build using ASP.NET with the .NET Framework 3.5 is Ajax-enabled (you can see all the Ajax configuration in the `Web.config` file). You will also find some new server controls within the ASP.NET toolbox of controls that allow you to add Ajax capabilities to your Web sites. See Chapter 39 for more information on ASP.NET AJAX.

.NET Language Integrated Query Framework (LINQ)

One of the coolest features and most anticipated of the bunch, LINQ offers you the ability to easily access underlying data. Microsoft has provided LINQ as a lightweight façade that provides a strongly typed interface to the underlying data stores. LINQ provides the means for developers to stay within the coding environment that they are used to and access the underlying data as objects that work with the IDE, IntelliSense, and even debugging.

Using LINQ, you can query against objects, data sets, the SQL Server database, XML, and more. The nice thing is that regardless of the underlying data source, getting at the data is done in the same manner because LINQ provides a structured way to query the data.

An example of getting at a pseudo XML document and grabbing all the customer names within the XML file is presented here:

```
XDocument xdoc = XDocument.Load(@"C:\Customers.xml");

var query = from people in xdoc.Descendants("CustomerName")
            select people.Value;

Console.WriteLine("{0} Customers Found", query.Count());
Console.WriteLine();

foreach (var item in query)
{
   Console.WriteLine(item);
}
```

Chapters 11, 27, and 29 all cover various aspects of LINQ.

Multi-Targeting within Visual Studio

In many cases, .NET developers are now working with multiple .NET applications that are targeted at either of the .NET Frameworks of 2.0, 3.0, or now 3.5. It would be silly to have to continue to have multiple versions of Visual Studio on your development computer in order to work with multiple versions of the .NET Framework.

For this reason, you will find that the latest version of Visual Studio 2008 now supports the ability to target the version of the framework that you are interested in working with. Now when creating a new application, you are giving the option of creating an application that targets either the .NET Framework 2.0, 3.0, or 3.5.

Supporting the Latest Application Types

It wasn't that long ago that the .NET Framework 3.0 was released and with it came some dramatic new capabilities. Included in that version was the ability to build a new application type using the Windows Presentation Foundation (WPF) as well as applications and libraries based on the Windows Communication Foundation (WCF), and the Windows Workflow Foundation (WF).

With the release of Visual Studio 2008, you will find that you are now able to build these applications — they are all now available as project types with new controls and Visual Studio wizards and capabilities.

Where C# Fits In

In one sense, C# can be seen as being the same thing to programming languages as .NET is to the Windows environment. Just as Microsoft has been adding more and more features to Windows and the Windows API over the past decade, Visual Basic 2008 and C++ have undergone expansion. Although Visual Basic and C++ have ended up as hugely powerful languages as a result of this, both languages also suffer from problems due to the legacies from how they have evolved.

In the case of Visual Basic 6 and earlier versions, the main strength of the language was the fact that it was simple to understand and made many programming tasks easy, largely hiding the details of the Windows API and the COM component infrastructure from the developer. The downside to this was that Visual Basic was never truly object oriented, so that large applications quickly became disorganized and hard to maintain. As well, because Visual Basic's syntax was inherited from early versions of BASIC (which, in turn, was designed to be intuitively simple for beginning programmers to understand, rather than to write large commercial applications), it didn't really lend itself to well-structured or object-oriented programs.

C++, on the other hand, has its roots in the ANSI C++ language definition. It isn't completely ANSI-compliant for the simple reason that Microsoft first wrote its C++ compiler before the ANSI definition had become official, but it comes close. Unfortunately, this has led to two problems. First, ANSI C++ has its roots in a decade-old state of technology, and this shows up in a lack of support for modern concepts (such as Unicode strings and generating XML documentation) and for some archaic syntax structures designed for the compilers of yesteryear (such as the separation of declaration from definition of member functions). Second, Microsoft has been simultaneously trying to evolve C++ into a language that is designed for high-performance tasks on Windows, and in order to achieve that, it has been forced to add a huge number of Microsoft-specific keywords as well as various libraries to the language. The result is that on Windows, the language has become a complete mess. Just ask C++ developers how many definitions for a string they can think of: `char*`, `LPTSTR`, `string`, `CString` (MFC version), `CString` (WTL version), `wchar_t*`, `OLECHAR*`, and so on.

Now enter .NET — a completely new environment that is going to involve new extensions to both languages. Microsoft has gotten around this by adding yet more Microsoft-specific keywords to C++, and by completely revamping Visual Basic into Visual Basic .NET into Visual Basic 2008, a language that retains some of the basic VB syntax but that is so different in design that it can be considered, for all practical purposes, a new language.

It's in this context that Microsoft has decided to give developers an alternative — a language designed specifically for .NET, and designed with a clean slate. C# is the result. Officially, Microsoft describes C# as a "simple, modern, object-oriented, and type-safe programming language derived from C and C++." Most independent observers would probably change that to "derived from C, C++, and Java." Such descriptions are technically accurate but do little to convey the beauty or elegance of the language. Syntactically, C# is very similar to both C++ and Java, to such an extent that many keywords are the same, and C# also shares the same block structure with braces (`{}`) to mark blocks of code, and semicolons to separate statements. The first impression of a piece of C# code is that it looks quite like C++ or Java code. Beyond that initial similarity, however, C# is a lot easier to learn than C++, and of comparable difficulty to Java. Its design is more in tune with modern developer tools than both of those other languages, and it has been designed to provide, simultaneously, the ease of use of Visual Basic and the high-performance, low-level memory access of C++, if required. Some of the features of C# are:

- Full support for classes and object-oriented programming, including both interface and implementation inheritance, virtual functions, and operator overloading.
- A consistent and well-defined set of basic types.
- Built-in support for automatic generation of XML documentation.

- Automatic cleanup of dynamically allocated memory.
- The facility to mark classes or methods with user-defined attributes. This can be useful for documentation and can have some effects on compilation (for example, marking methods to be compiled only in debug builds).
- Full access to the .NET base class library, as well as easy access to the Windows API (if you really need it, which won't be all that often).
- Pointers and direct memory access are available if required, but the language has been designed in such a way that you can work without them in almost all cases.
- Support for properties and events in the style of Visual Basic.
- Just by changing the compiler options, you can compile either to an executable or to a library of .NET components that can be called up by other code in the same way as ActiveX controls (COM components).
- C# can be used to write ASP.NET dynamic Web pages and XML Web services.

Most of these statements, it should be pointed out, do also apply to Visual Basic 2008 and Managed C++. The fact that C# is designed from the start to work with .NET, however, means that its support for the features of .NET is both more complete, and offered within the context of a more suitable syntax than for those other languages. Though the C# language itself is very similar to Java, there are some improvements; in particular, Java is not designed to work with the .NET environment.

Before we leave the subject, we should point out a couple of limitations of C#. The one area the language is not designed for is time-critical or extremely high-performance code — the kind where you really are worried about whether a loop takes 1,000 or 1,050 machine cycles to run through, and you need to clean up your resources the millisecond they are no longer needed. C++ is likely to continue to reign supreme among low-level languages in this area. C# lacks certain key facilities needed for extremely high-performance apps, including the ability to specify inline functions and destructors that are guaranteed to run at particular points in the code. However, the proportions of applications that fall into this category are very low.

What You Need to Write and Run C# Code

The .NET Framework 3.5 will run on Windows XP, 2003, Vista, and the latest Windows Server 2008. In order to write code using .NET, you will need to install the .NET 3.5 SDK.

Also, unless you are intending to write your C# code using a text editor or some other third-party developer environment, you will almost certainly also want Visual Studio 2008. The full SDK isn't needed to run managed code, but the .NET runtime is needed. You may find you need to distribute the .NET runtime with your code for the benefit of those clients who do not have it already installed.

What This Book Covers

This book starts by reviewing the overall architecture of .NET in Chapter 1 in order to give you the background you need to be able to write managed code. After that the book is divided into a number of sections that cover both the C# language and its application in a variety of areas.

Part I: The C# Language

This section gives a good grounding in the C# language itself. This section doesn't presume knowledge of any particular language, although it does assume you are an experienced programmer. You start by looking at C#'s basic syntax and data types, and then explore the object-oriented features of C# before moving on to look at more advanced C# programming topics.

Part II: Visual Studio

This section looks at the main IDE utilized by C# developers world-wide: Visual Studio 2005. The two chapters in this section look at the best way to use the tool to build applications based upon either the .NET Framework 2.0 or 3.0. In addition to this, this section also focuses on the deployment of your projects.

Part III: Base Class Libraries

In this section, you look at the principles of programming in the .NET environment. In particular, you look at security, threading localization, transactions, how to build Windows services, and how to generate your own libraries as assemblies.

Part IV: Data

Here, you look at accessing databases with ADO.NET and LINQ, and at interacting with directories and files. This part also extensively covers support in .NET for XML and on the Windows operating system side, and the .NET features of SQL Server 2008. Within the large space of LINQ, particular focus is put on LINQ to SQL and LINQ to XML.

Part V: Presentation

This section focuses on building classic Windows applications, which are called Windows Forms in .NET. Windows Forms are the thick-client version of applications, and using .NET to build these types of applications is a quick and easy way of accomplishing this task. In addition to looking at Windows Forms, you take a look at GDI+, which is the technology you will use for building applications that include advanced graphics. This section also covers writing components that will run on Web sites, serving up Web pages. This covers the tremendous number of new features that ASP.NET 3.5 provides. Finally, this section also shows how to build applications based upon the Windows Presentation Foundation and VSTO.

Part VI: Communication

This section is all about communication. It covers Web services for platform-independent communication, .NET Remoting for communication between .NET clients and servers, Enterprise Services for the services in the background, and DCOM communication. With Message Queuing asynchronous, disconnected communication is shown. This section also looks at utilizing the Windows Communication Foundation and the Windows Workflow Foundation.

Part VII: Appendices (Online)

This section includes three appendices focused on how to build applications that take into account the new features and barriers found in Windows Vista. Also, this section looks at the upcoming ADO.NET Entities technology and how to use this new technology in your C# applications. You can find these three appendices online at `www.wrox.com`. See "Source Code and Appendices" later in this introduction for instructions.

Conventions

We have used a number of different styles of text and layout in the book to help differentiate between the different kinds of information. Here are examples of the styles we use and an explanation of what they mean.

Bullets appear indented, with each new bullet marked as follows:

- *Important Words* are in italics.
- Keys that you press on the keyboard take the form Ctrl + Enter.

Code appears in a number of different ways. If it's a word that we're talking about in the text — for example, when discussing the `if...else` loop — it's in `this font`. If it's a block of code that you can type in as a program and run, it appears like this:

```
public static void Main()
{
   AFunc(1,2,"abc");
}
```

```
      // If we haven't reached the end, return true, otherwise
      // set the position to invalid, and return false.
      pos++;
      if (pos < 4)
         return true;
      else {
         pos = -1;
         return false;
      }
```

Advice, hints, and background information come in an italicized, indented font like this.

Important pieces of information come in boxes like this.

We demonstrate the syntactical usage of methods, properties (and so on) using the following format:

```
Regsvcs BookDistributor.dll [COM+AppName] [TypeLibrary.tbl]
```

Here, italicized parts indicate object references, variables, or parameter values to be inserted; the square braces indicate optional parameters.

Source Code and Appendices

As you work through the examples in this book, you may choose either to type in all the code manually or to use the source code files that accompany the book. All of the source code used in this book is available for downloading at `www.wrox.com`. Once at the site, simply locate the book's title (either by using the Search box or by using one of the title lists) and click the Download Code link on the book's detail page to obtain all the source code for the book.

Because many books have similar titles, you may find it easiest to search by ISBN; this book's ISBN is 978-0-470-19137-8.

Once you download the code, just decompress it with your favorite compression tool. Alternatively, you can go to the main Wrox code download page at `www.wrox.com/dynamic/books/download.aspx` to see the code available for this book and all other Wrox books.

Errata

We make every effort to ensure that there are no errors in the text or in the code. However, no one is perfect, and mistakes do occur. If you find an error in one of our books, such as a spelling mistake or faulty piece of code, we would be very grateful for your feedback. By sending in errata you may save another reader hours of frustration, and at the same time you will be helping us provide even higher-quality information.

To find the errata page for this book, go to `www.wrox.com` and locate the title using the Search box or one of the title lists. Then, on the book details page, click the Book Errata link. On this page, you can view all errata that have been submitted for this book and posted by Wrox editors. A complete book list, including links to each book's errata, is also available at `www.wrox.com/misc-pages/booklist.shtml`.

If you don't spot "your" error already on the Book Errata page, go to `www.wrox.com/contact/techsupport.shtml` and complete the form there to send us the error you have found. We'll check the information and, if appropriate, post a message to the book's errata page and fix the problem in subsequent editions of the book.

p2p.wrox.com

For author and peer discussion, join the P2P forums at `p2p.wrox.com`. The forums are a Web-based-system for you to post messages relating to Wrox books and related technologies and interact with other readers and technology users. The forums offer a subscription feature to email you topics of interest of your choosing when new posts are made to the forums. Wrox authors, editors, other industry experts, and your fellow readers are present on these forums.

At `http://p2p.wrox.com` you will find a number of different forums that will help you not only as you read this book but also as you develop your own applications. To join the forums, just follow these steps:

1. Go to `p2p.wrox.com` and click the Register link.
2. Read the terms of use and click Agree.
3. Supply the required information to join as well as any optional information you wish to provide and click Submit.

You will receive an email with information describing how to verify your account and complete the joining process.

You can read messages in the forums without joining P2P, but you must join in order to post your own messages.

Once you join, you can post new messages and respond to other users' posts. You can read messages at any time on the Web. If you would like to have new messages from a particular forum emailed to you, click the Subscribe to this Forum icon by the forum name in the forum listing.

For more information about how to use the Wrox P2P, be sure to read the P2P FAQs for answers to questions about how the forum software works as well as many common questions specific to P2P and Wrox books. To read the FAQs, click the FAQ link on any P2P page.

Professional
C# 2008

Part I
The C# Language

Chapter 1: .NET Architecture

Chapter 2: C# Basics

Chapter 3: Objects and Types

Chapter 4: Inheritance

Chapter 5: Arrays

Chapter 6: Operators and Casts

Chapter 7: Delegates and Events

Chapter 8: Strings and Regular Expressions

Chapter 9: Generics

Chapter 10: Collections

Chapter 11: Language Integrated Query

Chapter 12: Memory Management and Pointers

Chapter 13: Reflection

Chapter 14: Errors and Exceptions

1

.NET Architecture

Throughout this book, we emphasize that the C# language must be considered in parallel with the .NET Framework, rather than viewed in isolation. The C# compiler specifically targets .NET, which means that all code written in C# will always run within the .NET Framework. This has two important consequences for the C# language:

1. The architecture and methodologies of C# reflect the underlying methodologies of .NET.
2. In many cases, specific language features of C# actually depend on features of .NET, or of the .NET base classes.

Because of this dependence, it is important to gain some understanding of the architecture and methodology of .NET before you begin C# programming. That is the purpose of this chapter. The following is an outline of what this chapter covers:

- This chapter begins by explaining what happens when all code (including C#) that targets .NET is compiled and run.
- Once you have this broad overview, you take a more detailed look at the *Microsoft Intermediate Language* (MSIL or simply IL); the assembly language that all compiled code ends up in on .NET. In particular, you see how IL, in partnership with the *Common Type System* (CTS) and *Common Language Specification* (CLS), works to give you interoperability between languages that target .NET. This chapter also discusses where common languages (including Visual Basic and C++) fit into .NET.
- Next, you move on to examine some of the other features of .NET, including assemblies, namespaces, and the .NET base classes.
- The chapter finishes with a brief look at the kinds of applications you can create as a C# developer.

The Relationship of C# to .NET

C# is a relatively new programming language and is significant in two respects:

- It is specifically designed and targeted for use with Microsoft's .NET Framework (a feature-rich platform for the development, deployment, and execution of distributed applications).
- It is a language based on the modern object-oriented design methodology, and, when designing it, Microsoft learned from the experience of all the other similar languages that have been around since object-oriented principles came to prominence some 20 years ago.

One important thing to make clear is that C# is a language in its own right. Although it is designed to generate code that targets the .NET environment, it is not itself part of .NET. Some features are supported by .NET but not by C#, and you might be surprised to learn that some features of the C# language are not supported by .NET (for example, some instances of operator overloading)!

However, because the C# language is intended for use with .NET, it is important for you to have an understanding of this Framework if you want to develop applications in C# effectively. Therefore, this chapter takes some time to peek underneath the surface of .NET. Let's get started.

The Common Language Runtime

Central to the .NET Framework is its runtime execution environment, known as the *Common Language Runtime* (CLR) or the *.NET runtime*. Code running under the control of the CLR is often termed *managed code*.

However, before it can be executed by the CLR, any source code that you develop (in C# or some other language) needs to be compiled. Compilation occurs in two steps in .NET:

1. Compilation of source code to IL.
2. Compilation of IL to platform-specific code by the CLR.

This two-stage compilation process is very important, because the existence of the IL (managed code) is the key to providing many of the benefits of .NET.

Microsoft Intermediate Language shares with Java byte code the idea that it is a low-level language with a simple syntax (based on numeric codes rather than text), which can be very quickly translated into native machine code. Having this well-defined universal syntax for code has significant advantages: platform independence, performance improvement, and language interoperability.

Platform Independence

First, platform independence means that the same file containing byte code instructions can be placed on any platform; at runtime, the final stage of compilation can then be easily accomplished so that the code will run on that particular platform. In other words, by compiling to IL you obtain platform independence for .NET, in much the same way as compiling to Java byte code gives Java platform independence.

Note that the platform independence of .NET is only theoretical at present because, at the time of writing, a complete implementation of .NET is available only for Windows. However, a partial implementation is available (see, for example, the Mono project, an effort to create an open source implementation of .NET, at `www.go-mono.com`).

Performance Improvement

Although we previously made comparisons with Java, IL is actually a bit more ambitious than Java byte code. IL is always *Just-in-Time* compiled (known as JIT compilation), whereas Java byte code was often interpreted. One of the disadvantages of Java was that, on execution, the process of translating from Java byte code to native executable resulted in a loss of performance (with the exception of more recent cases, where Java is JIT compiled on certain platforms).

Instead of compiling the entire application in one go (which could lead to a slow startup time), the JIT compiler simply compiles each portion of code as it is called (just in time). When code has been compiled once, the resultant native executable is stored until the application exits so that it does not need to be recompiled the next time that portion of code is run. Microsoft argues that this process is more efficient than compiling the entire application code at the start, because of the likelihood that large portions of any application code will not actually be executed in any given run. Using the JIT compiler, such code will never be compiled.

This explains why we can expect that execution of managed IL code will be almost as fast as executing native machine code. What it does not explain is why Microsoft expects that we will get a performance *improvement*. The reason given for this is that, because the final stage of compilation takes place at runtime, the JIT compiler will know exactly what processor type the program will run on. This means that it can optimize the final executable code to take advantage of any features or particular machine code instructions offered by that particular processor.

Traditional compilers will optimize the code, but they can only perform optimizations that are independent of the particular processor that the code will run on. This is because traditional compilers compile to native executable before the software is shipped. This means that the compiler does not know what type of processor the code will run on beyond basic generalities, such as that it will be an x86-compatible processor or an Alpha processor. The older Visual Studio 6, for example, optimizes for a generic Pentium machine, so the code that it generates cannot take advantage of hardware features of Pentium III processors. However, the JIT compiler can do all the optimizations that Visual Studio 6 can, and in addition, it will optimize for the particular processor that the code is running on.

Language Interoperability

The use of IL not only enables platform independence; it also facilitates *language interoperability*. Simply put, you can compile to IL from one language, and this compiled code should then be interoperable with code that has been compiled to IL from another language.

You are probably now wondering which languages aside from C# are interoperable with .NET; the following sections briefly discuss how some of the other common languages fit into .NET.

Visual Basic 2008

Visual Basic .NET 2002 underwent a complete revamp from Visual Basic 6 to bring it up to date with the first version of the .NET Framework. The Visual Basic language itself had dramatically evolved from VB6, and this meant that VB6 was not a suitable language for running .NET programs. For example, VB6 is heavily integrated into Component Object Model (COM) and works by exposing only event handlers as source code to the developer — most of the background code is not available as source code. Not only that; it does not support implementation inheritance, and the standard data types that Visual Basic 6 uses are incompatible with .NET.

Visual Basic 6 was upgraded to Visual Basic .NET in 2002, and the changes that were made to the language are so extensive you might as well regard Visual Basic as a new language. Existing Visual Basic 6 code does not compile to the present Visual Basic 2008 code (or to Visual Basic .NET 2002, 2003, and 2005 for that matter). Converting a Visual Basic 6 program to Visual Basic 2008 requires extensive changes to the code. However, Visual Studio 2008 (the upgrade of Visual Studio for use with .NET) can do most of the changes for you. If you attempt to read a Visual Basic 6 project into Visual Studio 2008, it will upgrade the project for you, which means that it will rewrite the Visual Basic 6 source code into Visual Basic 2008 source code. Although this means that the work involved for you is heavily cut down, you will need to check through the new Visual Basic 2008 code to make sure that the project still works as intended because the conversion might not be perfect.

One side effect of this language upgrade is that it is no longer possible to compile Visual Basic 2008 to native executable code. Visual Basic 2008 compiles only to IL, just as C# does. If you need to continue coding in Visual Basic 6, you can do so, but the executable code produced will completely ignore the .NET Framework, and you will need to keep Visual Studio 6 installed if you want to continue to work in this developer environment.

Visual C++ 2008

Visual C++ 6 already had a large number of Microsoft-specific extensions on Windows. With Visual C++ .NET, extensions have been added to support the .NET Framework. This means that existing C++ source code will continue to compile to native executable code without modification. It also means, however, that it will run independently of the .NET runtime. If you want your C++ code to run within the .NET Framework, you can simply add the following line to the beginning of your code:

```
#using <mscorlib.dll>
```

You can also pass the flag `/clr` to the compiler, which then assumes that you want to compile to managed code, and will hence emit IL instead of native machine code. The interesting thing about C++ is that when you compile to managed code, the compiler can emit IL that contains an embedded native executable. This means that you can mix managed types and unmanaged types in your C++ code. Thus the managed C++ code

```
class MyClass
{
```

defines a plain C++ class, whereas the code

```
ref class MyClass
{
```

gives you a managed class, just as if you had written the class in C# or Visual Basic 2008. The advantage of using managed C++ over C# code is that you can call unmanaged C++ classes from managed C++ code without having to resort to COM interop.

The compiler raises an error if you attempt to use features that are not supported by .NET on managed types (for example, templates or multiple inheritances of classes). You will also find that you will need to use nonstandard C++ features when using managed classes.

Because of the freedom that C++ allows in terms of low-level pointer manipulation and so on, the C++ compiler is not able to generate code that will pass the CLR's memory type-safety tests. If it is important that your code be recognized by the CLR as memory type-safe, you will need to write your source code in some other language (such as C# or Visual Basic 2008).

COM and COM+

Technically speaking, COM and COM+ are not technologies targeted at .NET, because components based on them cannot be compiled into IL (although it is possible to do so to some degree using managed C++, if the original COM component was written in C++). However, COM+ remains an important tool, because its features are not duplicated in .NET. Also, COM components will still work — and .NET incorporates COM interoperability features that make it possible for managed code to call up COM components and vice versa (this is discussed in Chapter 24, "Interoperability"). In general, however, you will probably find it more convenient for most purposes to code new components as .NET components, so that you can take advantage of the .NET base classes as well as the other benefits of running as managed code.

A Closer Look at Intermediate Language

From what you learned in the previous section, Microsoft Intermediate Language obviously plays a fundamental role in the .NET Framework. As C# developers, we now understand that our C# code will be compiled into IL before it is executed (indeed, the C# compiler compiles *only* to managed code). It makes sense, then, to now take a closer look at the main characteristics of IL, because any language that targets .NET will logically need to support the main characteristics of IL, too.

Here are the important features of IL:

- Object orientation and use of interfaces
- Strong distinction between value and reference types
- Strong data typing
- Error handling using exceptions
- Use of attributes

The following sections explore each of these characteristics.

Support for Object Orientation and Interfaces

The language independence of .NET does have some practical limitations. IL is inevitably going to implement some particular programming methodology, which means that languages targeting it need to be compatible with that methodology. The particular route that Microsoft has chosen to follow for IL is that of classic object-oriented programming, with single implementation inheritance of classes.

If you are unfamiliar with the concepts of object orientation, refer to Appendix B, "C#, Visual Basic, C++/CLI," for more information.

In addition to classic object-oriented programming, IL also brings in the idea of interfaces, which saw their first implementation under Windows with COM. Interfaces built using .NET produce interfaces that are not the same as COM interfaces. They do not need to support any of the COM infrastructure (for example, they are not derived from `IUnknown`, and they do not have associated globally unique identifiers, more commonly know as GUIDs). However, they do share with COM interfaces the idea that they provide a contract, and classes that implement a given interface must provide implementations of the methods and properties specified by that interface.

You have now seen that working with .NET means compiling to IL, and that in turn means that you will need to use traditional object-oriented methodologies. However, that alone is not sufficient to give you language interoperability. After all, C++ and Java both use the same object-oriented paradigms, but they are still not regarded as interoperable. We need to look a little more closely at the concept of language interoperability.

To start with, we need to consider exactly what we mean by language interoperability. After all, COM allowed components written in different languages to work together in the sense of calling each other's methods. What was inadequate about that? COM, by virtue of being a binary standard, did allow components to instantiate other components and call methods or properties against them, without worrying about the language in which the respective components were written. To achieve this, however, each object had to be instantiated through the COM runtime, and accessed through an interface. Depending on the threading models of the relative components, there may have been large performance losses associated with marshaling data between apartments or running components or both on different threads. In the extreme case of components hosted as an executable rather than DLL files, separate processes would need to be created to run them. The emphasis was very much that components could talk to each other but only via the COM runtime. In no way with COM did components written in different languages directly communicate with each other, or instantiate instances of each other — it was always done with COM as an intermediary. Not only that, but the COM architecture did not permit implementation inheritance, which meant that it lost many of the advantages of object-oriented programming.

An associated problem was that, when debugging, you would still need to debug components written in different languages independently. It was not possible to step between languages in the debugger. Therefore, what we *really* mean by language interoperability is that classes written in one language should be able to talk directly to classes written in another language. In particular:

- A class written in one language can inherit from a class written in another language.
- The class can contain an instance of another class, no matter what the languages of the two classes are.
- An object can directly call methods against another object written in another language.
- Objects (or references to objects) can be passed around between methods.
- When calling methods between languages you can step between the method calls in the debugger, even when this means stepping between source code written in different languages.

This is all quite an ambitious aim, but amazingly, .NET and IL have achieved it. In the case of stepping between methods in the debugger, this facility is really offered by the Visual Studio integrated development environment (IDE) rather than by the CLR itself.

Distinct Value and Reference Types

As with any programming language, IL provides a number of predefined primitive data types. One characteristic of IL, however, is that it makes a strong distinction between value and reference types. *Value types* are those for which a variable directly stores its data, whereas *reference types* are those for which a variable simply stores the address at which the corresponding data can be found.

In C++ terms, using reference types can be considered to be similar to accessing a variable through a pointer, whereas for Visual Basic, the best analogy for reference types are objects, which in Visual Basic 6 are always accessed through references. IL also lays down specifications about data storage: instances of reference types are always stored in an area of memory known as the *managed heap*, whereas value types are normally stored on the *stack* (although if value types are declared as fields within reference types, they will be stored inline on the heap). Chapter 2, "C# Basics," discusses the stack and the heap and how they work.

Strong Data Typing

One very important aspect of IL is that it is based on exceptionally *strong data typing*. That means that all variables are clearly marked as being of a particular, specific data type (there is no room in IL, for example, for the `Variant` data type recognized by Visual Basic and scripting languages). In particular, IL does not normally permit any operations that result in ambiguous data types.

For instance, Visual Basic 6 developers are used to being able to pass variables around without worrying too much about their types, because Visual Basic 6 automatically performs type conversion. C++ developers are used to routinely casting pointers between different types. Being able to perform this kind of operation can be great for performance, but it breaks type safety. Hence, it is permitted only under certain circumstances in some of the languages that compile to managed code. Indeed, pointers (as opposed to references) are permitted only in marked blocks of code in C#, and not at all in Visual Basic (although they are allowed in managed C++). Using pointers in your code causes it to fail the memory type-safety checks performed by the CLR.

You should note that some languages compatible with .NET, such as Visual Basic 2008, still allow some laxity in typing, but that is possible only because the compilers behind the scenes ensure that the type safety is enforced in the emitted IL.

Although enforcing type safety might initially appear to hurt performance, in many cases the benefits gained from the services provided by .NET that rely on type safety far outweigh this performance loss. Such services include:

- Language interoperability
- Garbage collection
- Security
- Application domains

The following sections take a closer look at why strong data typing is particularly important for these features of .NET.

The Importance of Strong Data Typing for Language Interoperability

If a class is to derive from or contains instances of other classes, it needs to know about all the data types used by the other classes. This is why strong data typing is so important. Indeed, it is the absence of any agreed-on system for specifying this information in the past that has always been the real barrier to inheritance and interoperability across languages. This kind of information is simply not present in a standard executable file or DLL.

Suppose that one of the methods of a Visual Basic 2008 class is defined to return an `Integer` — one of the standard data types available in Visual Basic 2008. C# simply does not have any data type of that name. Clearly, you will be able to derive from the class, use this method, and use the return type from C# code, only if the compiler knows how to map Visual Basic 2008's `Integer` type to some known type that is defined in C#. So, how is this problem circumvented in .NET?

Common Type System

This data type problem is solved in .NET using the *Common Type System* (CTS). The CTS defines the predefined data types that are available in IL, so that all languages that target the .NET Framework will produce compiled code that is ultimately based on these types.

For the previous example, Visual Basic 2008's `Integer` is actually a 32-bit signed integer, which maps exactly to the IL type known as `Int32`. This will therefore be the data type specified in the IL code. Because the C# compiler is aware of this type, there is no problem. At source code level, C# refers to `Int32` with the keyword `int`, so the compiler will simply treat the Visual Basic 2008 method as if it returned an `int`.

The CTS does not specify merely primitive data types but a rich hierarchy of types, which includes well-defined points in the hierarchy at which code is permitted to define its own types. The hierarchical structure of the CTS reflects the single-inheritance object-oriented methodology of IL, and resembles Figure 1-1.

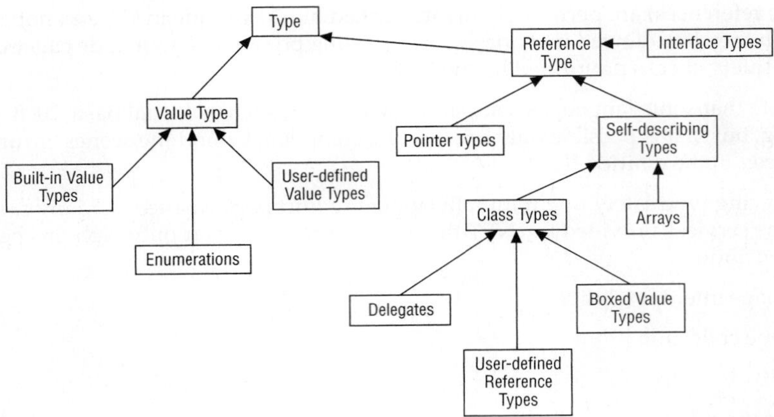

Figure 1-1

The following table explains the types shown in Figure 1-1.

Type	Meaning
`Type`	Base class that represents any type.
`Value Type`	Base class that represents any value type.
`Reference Types`	Any data types that are accessed through a reference and stored on the heap.
`Built-in Value Types`	Includes most of the standard primitive types, which represent numbers, Boolean values, or characters.
`Enumerations`	Sets of enumerated values.
`User-defined Value Types`	Types that have been defined in source code and are stored as value types. In C# terms, this means any struct.
`Interface Types`	Interfaces.
`Pointer Types`	Pointers.
`Self-describing Types`	Data types that provide information about themselves for the benefit of the garbage collector (see the next section).
`Arrays`	Any type that contains an array of objects.
`Class Types`	Types that are self-describing but are not arrays.
`Delegates`	Types that are designed to hold references to methods.
`User-defined Reference Types`	Types that have been defined in source code and are stored as reference types. In C# terms, this means any class.
`Boxed Value Types`	A value type that is temporarily wrapped in a reference so that it can be stored on the heap.

We will not list all of the built-in value types here, because they are covered in detail in Chapter 3, "Objects and Types." In C#, each predefined type recognized by the compiler maps onto one of the IL built-in types. The same is true in Visual Basic 2008.

Common Language Specification

The *Common Language Specification* (CLS) works with the CTS to ensure language interoperability. The CLS is a set of minimum standards that all compilers targeting .NET must support. Because IL is a very rich language, writers of most compilers will prefer to restrict the capabilities of a given compiler to support only a subset of the facilities offered by IL and the CTS. That is fine, as long as the compiler supports everything that is defined in the CLS.

It is perfectly acceptable to write non-CLS-compliant code. However, if you do, the compiled IL code is not guaranteed to be fully language interoperable.

For example, take case sensitivity. IL is case sensitive. Developers who work with case-sensitive languages regularly take advantage of the flexibility that this case sensitivity gives them when selecting variable names. Visual Basic 2008, however, is not case sensitive. The CLS works around this by indicating that CLS-compliant code should not expose any two names that differ only in their case. Therefore, Visual Basic 2008 code can work with CLS-compliant code.

This example shows that the CLS works in two ways. First, it means that individual compilers do not have to be powerful enough to support the full features of .NET — this should encourage the development of compilers for other programming languages that target .NET. Second, it provides a guarantee that, if you restrict your classes to exposing only CLS-compliant features, then code written in any other compliant language can use your classes.

The beauty of this idea is that the restriction to using CLS-compliant features applies only to public and protected members of classes and public classes. Within the private implementations of your classes, you can write whatever non-CLS code you want, because code in other assemblies (units of managed code; see later in this chapter) cannot access this part of your code anyway.

We will not go into the details of the CLS specifications here. In general, the CLS will not affect your C# code very much because there are very few non-CLS-compliant features of C# anyway.

Garbage Collection

The *garbage collector* is .NET's answer to memory management and in particular to the question of what to do about reclaiming memory that running applications ask for. Up until now, two techniques have been used on the Windows platform for de-allocating memory that processes have dynamically requested from the system:

- Make the application code do it all manually.
- Make objects maintain reference counts.

Having the application code responsible for deallocating memory is the technique used by lower-level, high-performance languages such as C++. It is efficient, and it has the advantage that (in general) resources are never occupied for longer than necessary. The big disadvantage, however, is the frequency of bugs. Code that requests memory also should explicitly inform the system when it no longer requires that memory. However, it is easy to overlook this, resulting in memory leaks.

Although modern developer environments do provide tools to assist in detecting memory leaks, they remain difficult bugs to track down. That's because they have no effect until so much memory has been leaked that Windows refuses to grant any more to the process. By this point, the entire computer may have appreciably slowed down due to the memory demands being made on it.

Maintaining reference counts is favored in COM. The idea is that each COM component maintains a count of how many clients are currently maintaining references to it. When this count falls to zero, the component can destroy itself and free up associated memory and resources. The problem with this is that it still relies on the good behavior of clients to notify the component that they have finished with it. It takes only one client not to do so, and the object sits in memory. In some ways, this is a potentially more serious problem than a simple C++-style memory leak because the COM object may exist in its own process, which means that it will never be removed by the system. (At least with C++ memory leaks, the system can reclaim all memory when the process terminates.)

The .NET runtime relies on the garbage collector instead. The purpose of this program is to clean up memory. The idea is that all dynamically requested memory is allocated on the heap (that is true for all languages, although in the case of .NET, the CLR maintains its own managed heap for .NET applications to use). Every so often, when .NET detects that the managed heap for a given process is becoming full and therefore needs tidying up, it calls the garbage collector. The garbage collector runs through variables currently in scope in your code, examining references to objects stored on the heap to identify which ones are accessible from your code — that is, which objects have references that refer to them. Any objects that are not referred to are deemed to be no longer accessible from your code and can therefore be removed. Java uses a system of garbage collection similar to this.

Garbage collection works in .NET because IL has been designed to facilitate the process. The principle requires that you cannot get references to existing objects other than by copying existing references and that IL be type safe. In this context, what we mean is that if any reference to an object exists, then there is sufficient information in the reference to exactly determine the type of the object.

It would not be possible to use the garbage collection mechanism with a language such as unmanaged C++, for example, because C++ allows pointers to be freely cast between types.

One important aspect of garbage collection is that it is not deterministic. In other words, you cannot guarantee when the garbage collector will be called; it will be called when the CLR decides that it is needed, though it is also possible to override this process and call up the garbage collector in your code.

Security

.NET can really excel in terms of complementing the security mechanisms provided by Windows because it can offer code-based security, whereas Windows really offers only role-based security.

Role-based security is based on the identity of the account under which the process is running (that is, who owns and is running the process). *Code-based security*, by contrast, is based on what the code actually does and on how much the code is trusted. Thanks to the strong type safety of IL, the CLR is able to inspect code before running it to determine required security permissions. .NET also offers a mechanism by which code can indicate in advance what security permissions it will require to run.

The importance of code-based security is that it reduces the risks associated with running code of dubious origin (such as code that you have downloaded from the Internet). For example, even if code is running under the administrator account, it is possible to use code-based security to indicate that that code should still not be permitted to perform certain types of operations that the administrator account would normally be allowed to do, such as read or write to environment variables, read or write to the registry, or access the .NET reflection features.

Security issues are covered in more depth in Chapter 20, "Security."

Application Domains

Application domains are an important innovation in .NET and are designed to ease the overhead involved when running applications that need to be isolated from each other but that also need to be able to communicate with each other. The classic example of this is a Web server application, which may be simultaneously responding to a number of browser requests. It will, therefore, probably have a number of instances of the component responsible for servicing those requests running simultaneously.

In pre-.NET days, the choice would be between allowing those instances to share a process (with the resultant risk of a problem in one running instance bringing the whole Web site down) or isolating those instances in separate processes (with the associated performance overhead).

Up until now, the only means of isolating code has been through processes. When you start a new application, it runs within the context of a process. Windows isolates processes from each other through address spaces. The idea is that each process has available 4GB of virtual memory in which to store its data and executable code (4GB is for 32-bit systems; 64-bit systems use more memory). Windows imposes an extra level of indirection by which this virtual memory maps into a particular area of actual physical memory or disk space. Each process gets a different mapping, with no overlap between the actual physical memories that the blocks of virtual address space map to (see Figure 1-2).

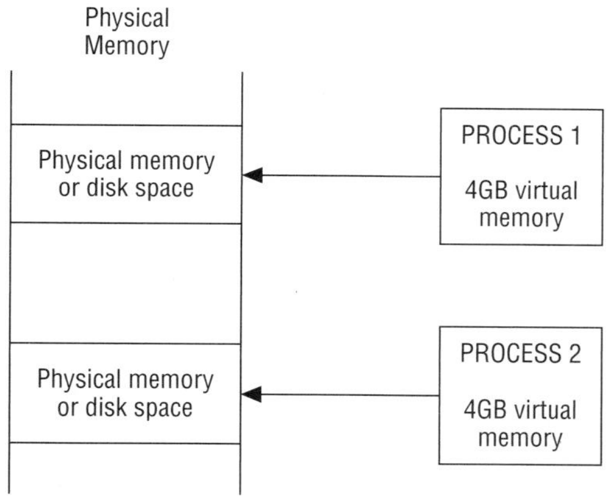

Figure 1-2

In general, any process is able to access memory only by specifying an address in virtual memory — processes do not have direct access to physical memory. Hence, it is simply impossible for one process to access the memory allocated to another process. This provides an excellent guarantee that any badly behaved code will not be able to damage anything outside of its own address space. (Note that on Windows 95/98, these safeguards are not quite as thorough as they are on Windows NT/2000/XP/2003/Vista, so the theoretical possibility exists of applications crashing Windows by writing to inappropriate memory.)

Processes do not just serve as a way to isolate instances of running code from each other. On Windows NT/2000/XP/2003/Vista systems, they also form the unit to which security privileges and permissions are assigned. Each process has its own security token, which indicates to Windows precisely what operations that process is permitted to do.

Although processes are great for security reasons, their big disadvantage is in the area of performance. Often, a number of processes will actually be working together, and therefore need to communicate with each other. The obvious example of this is where a process calls up a COM component, which is an executable and therefore is required to run in its own process. The same thing happens in COM when surrogates are used. Because processes cannot share any memory, a complex marshaling process must be used to copy data between the processes. This results in a very significant performance hit. If you need components to work together and do not want that performance hit, you must use DLL-based components and have everything running in the same address space — with the associated risk that a badly behaved component will bring everything else down.

Application domains are designed as a way of separating components without resulting in the performance problems associated with passing data between processes. The idea is that any one process is divided into a number of application domains. Each application domain roughly corresponds to a single application, and each thread of execution will be running in a particular application domain (see Figure 1-3).

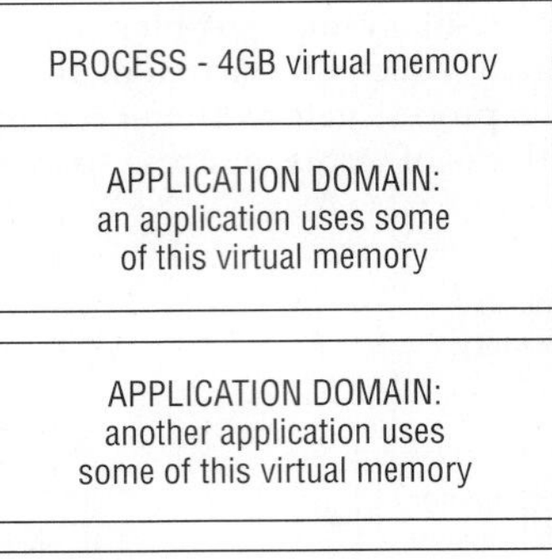
PROCESS - 4GB virtual memory
APPLICATION DOMAIN:
an application uses some
of this virtual memory
APPLICATION DOMAIN:
another application uses
some of this virtual memory

Figure 1-3

If different executables are running in the same process space, then they are clearly able to easily share data, because, theoretically, they can directly see each other's data. However, although this is possible in principle, the CLR makes sure that this does not happen in practice by inspecting the code for each running application to ensure that the code cannot stray outside of its own data areas. This looks, at first, like an almost impossible task to pull off — after all, how can you tell what the program is going to do without actually running it?

In fact, it is usually possible to do this because of the strong type safety of the IL. In most cases, unless code is using unsafe features such as pointers, the data types it is using will ensure that memory is not accessed inappropriately. For example, .NET array types perform bounds checking to ensure that no out-of-bounds array operations are permitted. If a running application does need to communicate or share data with other applications running in different application domains, it must do so by calling on .NET's remoting services.

Code that has been verified to check that it cannot access data outside its application domain (other than through the explicit remoting mechanism) is said to be *memory type safe*. Such code can safely be run alongside other type-safe code in different application domains within the same process.

Error Handling with Exceptions

The .NET Framework is designed to facilitate handling of error conditions using the same mechanism, based on exceptions, that is employed by Java and C++. C++ developers should note that because of IL's stronger typing system, there is no performance penalty associated with the use of exceptions with IL in the way that there is in C++. Also, the `finally` block, which has long been on many C++ developers' wish lists, is supported by .NET and by C#.

Exceptions are covered in detail in Chapter 14, "Errors and Exceptions." Briefly, the idea is that certain areas of code are designated as exception handler routines, with each one able to deal with a particular error condition (for example, a file not being found, or being denied permission to perform some operation). These conditions can be defined as narrowly or as widely as you want. The exception architecture ensures that when an error condition occurs, execution can immediately jump to the exception handler routine that is most specifically geared to handle the exception condition in question.

The architecture of exception handling also provides a convenient means to pass an object containing precise details of the exception condition to an exception handling routine. This object might include an appropriate message for the user and details of exactly where in the code the exception was detected.

Most exception-handling architecture, including the control of program flow when an exception occurs, is handled by the high-level languages (C#, Visual Basic 2008, C++), and is not supported by any special IL commands. C#, for example, handles exceptions using `try{}`, `catch{}`, and `finally{}` blocks of code. (For more details, see Chapter 14.)

What .NET does do, however, is provide the infrastructure to allow compilers that target .NET to support exception handling. In particular, it provides a set of .NET classes that can represent the exceptions, and the language interoperability to allow the thrown exception objects to be interpreted by the exception-handling code, regardless of what language the exception-handling code is written in. This language independence is absent from both the C++ and Java implementations of exception handling, although it is present to a limited extent in the COM mechanism for handling errors, which involves returning error codes from methods and passing error objects around. The fact that exceptions are handled consistently in different languages is a crucial aspect of facilitating multi-language development.

Use of Attributes

Attributes are familiar to developers who use C++ to write COM components (through their use in Microsoft's COM Interface Definition Language [IDL]). The initial idea of an attribute was that it provided extra information concerning some item in the program that could be used by the compiler.

Attributes are supported in .NET — and hence now by C++, C#, and Visual Basic 2008. What is, however, particularly innovative about attributes in .NET is that you can define your own custom attributes in your source code. These user-defined attributes will be placed with the metadata for the corresponding data types or methods. This can be useful for documentation purposes, in which they can be used in conjunction with reflection technology to perform programming tasks based on attributes. In addition, in common with the .NET philosophy of language independence, attributes can be defined in source code in one language and read by code that is written in another language.

Attributes are covered in Chapter 13, "Reflection."

Assemblies

An *assembly* is the logical unit that contains compiled code targeted at the .NET Framework. Assemblies are not covered in detail in this chapter because they are covered thoroughly in Chapter 17, "Assemblies," but we summarize the main points here.

An assembly is completely self-describing and is a logical rather than a physical unit, which means that it can be stored across more than one file (indeed, dynamic assemblies are stored in memory, not on file at all). If an assembly is stored in more than one file, there will be one main file that contains the entry point and describes the other files in the assembly.

Note that the same assembly structure is used for both executable code and library code. The only real difference is that an executable assembly contains a main program entry point, whereas a library assembly does not.

An important characteristic of assemblies is that they contain metadata that describes the types and methods defined in the corresponding code. An assembly, however, also contains assembly metadata that describes the assembly itself. This assembly metadata, contained in an area known as the *manifest*, allows checks to be made on the version of the assembly, and on its integrity.

> `ildasm`*, a Windows-based utility, can be used to inspect the contents of an assembly, including the manifest and metadata.* `ildasm` *is discussed in Chapter 17, "Assemblies."*

The fact that an assembly contains program metadata means that applications or other assemblies that call up code in a given assembly do not need to refer to the registry, or to any other data source, to find out how to use that assembly. This is a significant break from the old COM way of doing things, in which the GUIDs of the components and interfaces had to be obtained from the registry, and in some cases, the details of the methods and properties exposed would need to be read from a type library.

Having data spread out in up to three different locations meant there was the obvious risk of something getting out of synchronization, which would prevent other software from being able to use the component successfully. With assemblies, there is no risk of this happening, because all the metadata is stored with the program executable instructions. Note that even though assemblies are stored across several files, there are still no problems with data going out of synchronization. This is because the file that contains the assembly entry point also stores details of, and a hash of, the contents of the other files, which means that if one of the files gets replaced, or in any way tampered with, this will almost certainly be detected and the assembly will refuse to load.

Assemblies come in two types: *private* and *shared* assemblies.

Private Assemblies

Private assemblies are the simplest type. They normally ship with software and are intended to be used only with that software. The usual scenario in which you will ship private assemblies is when you are supplying an application in the form of an executable and a number of libraries, where the libraries contain code that should be used only with that application.

The system guarantees that private assemblies will not be used by other software because an application may load only private assemblies that are located in the same folder that the main executable is loaded in, or in a subfolder of it.

Because you would normally expect that commercial software would always be installed in its own directory, there is no risk of one software package overwriting, modifying, or accidentally loading private assemblies intended for another package. And, because private assemblies can be used only by the software package that they are intended for, you have much more control over what software uses them. There is, therefore, less need to take security precautions because there is no risk, for example, of some other commercial software overwriting one of your assemblies with some new version of it (apart from software that is designed specifically to perform malicious damage). There are also no problems with name collisions. If classes in your private assembly happen to have the same name as classes in someone else's private assembly, that does not matter, because any given application will be able to see only the one set of private assemblies.

Because a private assembly is entirely self-contained, the process of deploying it is simple. You simply place the appropriate file(s) in the appropriate folder in the file system (no registry entries need to be made). This process is known as *zero impact (xcopy) installation*.

Shared Assemblies

Shared assemblies are intended to be common libraries that any other application can use. Because any other software can access a shared assembly, more precautions need to be taken against the following risks:

- Name collisions, where another company's shared assembly implements types that have the same names as those in your shared assembly. Because client code can theoretically have access to both assemblies simultaneously, this could be a serious problem.
- The risk of an assembly being overwritten by a different version of the same assembly — the new version being incompatible with some existing client code.

The solution to these problems is placing shared assemblies in a special directory subtree in the file system, known as the *global assembly cache* (GAC). Unlike with private assemblies, this cannot be done by simply copying the assembly into the appropriate folder — it needs to be specifically installed into the cache. This process can be performed by a number of .NET utilities and requires certain checks on the assembly, as well as the set up of a small folder hierarchy within the assembly cache that is used to ensure assembly integrity.

To prevent name collisions, shared assemblies are given a name based on private key cryptography (private assemblies are simply given the same name as their main file name). This name is known as a *strong name*; it is guaranteed to be unique and must be quoted by applications that reference a shared assembly.

Problems associated with the risk of overwriting an assembly are addressed by specifying version information in the assembly manifest and by allowing side-by-side installations.

Reflection

Because assemblies store metadata, including details of all the types and members of these types that are defined in the assembly, it is possible to access this metadata programmatically. Full details of this are given in Chapter 13, "Reflection." This technique, known as *reflection*, raises interesting possibilities, because it means that managed code can actually examine other managed code, and can even examine itself, to determine information about that code. This is most commonly used to obtain the details of attributes, although you can also use reflection, among other purposes, as an indirect way of instantiating classes or calling methods, given the names of those classes or methods as strings. In this way, you could select classes to instantiate methods to call at runtime, rather than at compile time, based on user input (dynamic binding).

.NET Framework Classes

Perhaps one of the biggest benefits of writing managed code, at least from a developer's point of view, is that you get to use the .NET *base class library*.

The .NET base classes are a massive collection of managed code classes that allow you to do almost any of the tasks that were previously available through the Windows API. These classes follow the same object model that IL uses, based on single inheritance. This means that you can either instantiate objects of whichever .NET base class is appropriate or derive your own classes from them.

The great thing about the .NET base classes is that they have been designed to be very intuitive and easy to use. For example, to start a thread, you call the `Start()` method of the `Thread` class. To disable a `TextBox`, you set the `Enabled` property of a `TextBox` object to `false`. This approach — though familiar to Visual Basic and Java developers, whose respective libraries are just as easy to use — will be a welcome relief to C++ developers, who for years have had to cope with such API functions as `GetDIBits()`, `RegisterWndClassEx()`, and `IsEqualIID()`, as well as a whole plethora of functions that required Windows handles to be passed around.

However, C++ developers always had easy access to the entire Windows API, unlike Visual Basic 6 and Java developers who were more restricted in terms of the basic operating system functionality that they have access to from their respective languages. What is new about the .NET base classes is that they combine the ease of use that was typical of the Visual Basic and Java libraries with the relatively comprehensive coverage of the Windows API functions. Many features of Windows still are not available through the base classes, and for those you will need to call into the API functions, but in general, these are now confined to the more exotic features. For everyday use, you will probably find the base classes adequate. Moreover, if you do need to call into an API function, .NET offers a so-called *platform-invoke* that ensures data types are correctly converted, so the task is no harder than calling the function directly from C++ code would have been — regardless of whether you are coding in C#, C++, or Visual Basic 2008.

WinCV, a Windows-based utility, can be used to browse the classes, structs, interfaces, and enums in the base class library. WinCV is discussed in Chapter 15, "Visual Studio 2008."

Although Chapter 3 is nominally dedicated to the subject of base classes, once we have completed our coverage of the syntax of the C# language, most of the rest of this book shows you how to use various classes within the .NET base class library for the .NET Framework 3.5. That is how comprehensive base classes are. As a rough guide, the areas covered by the .NET 3.5 base classes include:

- Core features provided by IL (including the primitive data types in the CTS discussed in Chapter 3, "Objects and Types")
- Windows GUI support and controls (see Chapters 31, "Windows Forms," and 34, "Windows Presentation Foundation")
- Web Forms (ASP.NET, discussed in Chapters 37, "ASP.NET Pages" and 38, "ASP.NET Development")
- Data access (ADO.NET; see Chapters 26, "Data Access," 30, ".NET Programming with SQL Server," 27 and 29, "LINQ to SQL" and "LINQ to XML" and 28, "Manipulating XML")
- Directory access (see Chapter 46, "Directory Services")
- File system and registry access (see Chapter 25, "Manipulating Files and the Registry")
- Networking and Web browsing (see Chapter 41, "Accessing the Internet")
- .NET attributes and reflection (see Chapter 13, "Reflection")
- Access to aspects of the Windows OS (environment variables and so on; see Chapter 20, "Security")
- COM interoperability (see Chapters 44, "Enterprise Services" and 24, "Interoperability")

Incidentally, according to Microsoft sources, a large proportion of the .NET base classes have actually been written in C#!

Namespaces

Namespaces are the way that .NET avoids name clashes between classes. They are designed to prevent situations in which you define a class to represent a customer, name your class `Customer`, and then someone else does the same thing (a likely scenario — the proportion of businesses that have customers seems to be quite high).

A namespace is no more than a grouping of data types, but it has the effect that the names of all data types within a namespace are automatically prefixed with the name of the namespace. It is also possible to nest namespaces within each other. For example, most of the general-purpose .NET base classes are in a namespace called `System`. The base class `Array` is in this namespace, so its full name is `System.Array`.

.NET requires all types to be defined in a namespace; for example, you could place your `Customer` class in a namespace called `YourCompanyName`. This class would have the full name `YourCompanyName.Customer`.

If a namespace is not explicitly supplied, the type will be added to a nameless global namespace.

Microsoft recommends that for most purposes you supply at least two nested namespace names: the first one represents the name of your company, and the second one represents the name of the technology or software package of which the class is a member, such as `YourCompanyName.SalesServices.Customer`.

This protects, in most situations, the classes in your application from possible name clashes with classes written by other organizations.

Chapter 2, "C# Basics," looks more closely at namespaces.

Creating .NET Applications Using C#

C# can also be used to create console applications: text-only applications that run in a DOS window. You will probably use console applications when unit testing class libraries, and for creating UNIX or Linux daemon processes. More often, however, you will use C# to create applications that use many of the technologies associated with .NET. This section gives you an overview of the different types of applications that you can write in C#.

Creating ASP.NET Applications

Active Server Pages (ASP) is a Microsoft technology for creating Web pages with dynamic content. An ASP page is basically an HTML file with embedded chunks of server-side VBScript or JavaScript. When a client browser requests an ASP page, the Web server delivers the HTML portions of the page, processing the server-side scripts as it comes to them. Often these scripts query a database for data and mark up that data in HTML. ASP is an easy way for clients to build browser-based applications.

However, ASP is not without its shortcomings. First, ASP pages sometimes render slowly because the server-side code is interpreted instead of compiled. Second, ASP files can be difficult to maintain because they are unstructured; the server-side ASP code and plain HTML are all jumbled up together. Third, ASP sometimes makes development difficult because there is little support for error handling and type-checking. Specifically, if you are using VBScript and want to implement error handling in your pages, you must use the `On Error Resume Next` statement, and follow every component call with a check to `Err.Number` to make sure that the call has gone well.

ASP.NET is a complete revision of ASP that fixes many of its problems. It does not replace ASP; rather, ASP.NET pages can live side by side on the same server with legacy ASP applications. Of course, you can also program ASP.NET with C#!

The following section explores the key features of ASP.NET. For more details, refer to Chapters 37, "ASP.NET Pages," 38, "ASP.NET Development," and 39, "ASP.NET AJAX."

Features of ASP.NET

First, and perhaps most important, ASP.NET pages are *structured*. That is, each page is effectively a class that inherits from the .NET `System.Web.UI.Page` *class* and can override a set of methods that are evoked during the `Page` object's lifetime. (You can think of these events as page-specific cousins of the `OnApplication_Start` and `OnSession_Start` events that went in the `global.asa` files of plain old ASP.) Because you can factor a page's functionality into event handlers with explicit meanings, ASP.NET pages are easier to understand.

Another nice thing about ASP.NET pages is that you can create them in Visual Studio 2008, the same environment in which you create the business logic and data access components that those ASP.NET pages use. A Visual Studio 2008 project, or *solution*, contains all of the files associated with an application. Moreover, you can debug your classic ASP pages in the editor as well; in the old days of Visual InterDev, it was often a vexing challenge to configure InterDev and the project's Web server to turn debugging on.

For maximum clarity, the ASP.NET `code-behind` feature lets you take the structured approach even further. ASP.NET allows you to isolate the server-side functionality of a page to a class, compile that class into a DLL, and place that DLL into a directory below the HTML portion. A `code-behind` directive at the top of the page associates the file with its DLL. When a browser requests the page, the Web server fires the events in the class in the page's `code-behind` DLL.

Last, but not least, ASP.NET is remarkable for its increased performance. Whereas classic ASP pages are interpreted with each page request, the Web server caches ASP.NET pages after compilation. This means that subsequent requests of an ASP.NET page execute more quickly than the first.

ASP.NET also makes it easy to write pages that cause forms to be displayed by the browser, which you might use in an intranet environment. The traditional wisdom is that form-based applications offer a richer user interface but are harder to maintain because they run on so many different machines. For this reason, people have relied on form-based applications when rich user interfaces were a necessity and extensive support could be provided to the users.

Web Forms

To make Web page construction even easier, Visual Studio 2008 supplies *Web Forms*. They allow you to build ASP.NET pages graphically in the same way that Visual Basic 6 or C++ Builder windows are created; in other words, by dragging controls from a toolbox onto a form, then flipping over to the code aspect of that form and writing event handlers for the controls. When you use C# to create a Web Form, you are creating a C# class that inherits from the `Page` base class and an ASP.NET page that designates that class as its code behind. Of course, you do not have to use C# to create a Web Form; you can use Visual Basic 2008 or another .NET-compliant language just as well.

In the past, the difficulty of Web development discouraged some teams from attempting it. To succeed in Web development, you needed to know so many different technologies, such as VBScript, ASP, DHTML, JavaScript, and so on. By applying the Form concepts to Web pages, Web Forms have made Web development considerably easier.

Web Server Controls

The controls used to populate a Web Form are not controls in the same sense as ActiveX controls. Rather, they are XML tags in the ASP.NET namespace that the Web browser dynamically transforms into HTML and client-side script when a page is requested. Amazingly, the Web server is able to render the same server-side control in different ways, producing a transformation appropriate to the requestor's particular Web browser. This means that it is now easy to write fairly sophisticated user interfaces for Web pages, without worrying about how to ensure that your page will run on any of the available browsers — because Web Forms will take care of that for you.

You can use C# or Visual Basic 2008 to expand the Web Form toolbox. Creating a new server-side control is simply a matter of implementing .NET's `System.Web.UI.WebControls.WebControl` class.

XML Web Services

Today, HTML pages account for most of the traffic on the World Wide Web. With XML, however, computers have a device-independent format to use for communicating with each other on the Web. In the future, computers may use the Web and XML to communicate information rather than dedicated lines and proprietary formats such as *Electronic Data Interchange* (EDI). XML Web services are designed for a service-oriented Web, in which remote computers provide each other with dynamic information that can be analyzed and reformatted, before final presentation to a user. An XML Web service is an easy way for a computer to expose information to other computers on the Web in the form of XML.

In technical terms, an XML Web service on .NET is an ASP.NET page that returns XML instead of HTML to requesting clients. Such pages have a `code-behind` DLL containing a class that derives from the `WebService` class. The Visual Studio 2008 IDE provides an engine that facilitates Web service development.

An organization might choose to use XML Web services for two main reasons. The first reason is that they rely on HTTP; XML Web services can use existing networks (HTTP) as a medium for conveying information. The other is that because XML Web services use XML, the data format is self-describing, nonproprietary, and platform-independent.

Creating Windows Forms

Although C# and .NET are particularly suited to Web development, they still offer splendid support for so-called *fat-client* or *thick-client* apps — applications that must be installed on the end user's machine where most of the processing takes place. This support is from *Windows Forms*.

A Windows Form is the .NET answer to a Visual Basic 6 Form. To design a graphical window interface, you just drag controls from a toolbox onto a Windows Form. To determine the window's behavior, you write event-handling routines for the form's controls. A Windows Form project compiles to an executable that must be installed alongside the .NET runtime on the end user's computer. Like other .NET project types, Windows Form projects are supported by both Visual Basic 2008 and C#. Chapter 31, "Windows Forms," examines Windows Forms more closely.

Using the Windows Presentation Foundation (WPF)

One of the newest technologies to hit the block is the *Windows Presentation Foundation* (WPF). WPF makes use of XAML in building applications. XAML stands for Extensible Application Markup Language. This new way of creating applications within a Microsoft environment is something that was introduced in 2006 and is part of the .NET Framework 3.0 and 3.5. This means that to run any WPF application, you need to make sure that the .NET Framework 3.0 or 3.5 is installed on the client machine. WPF applications are available for Windows Vista, Windows XP, Windows Server 2003, and Windows Server 2008 (the only operating systems that allow for the installation of the .NET Framework 3.0 or 3.5).

XAML is the XML declaration that is used to create a form that represents all the visual aspects and behaviors of the WPF application. Though it is possible to work with a WPF application programmatically, WPF is a step in the direction of declarative programming, which the industry is moving to. Declarative programming means that instead of creating objects through programming in a compiled language such as C#, VB, or Java, you declare everything through XML-type programming. Chapter 34, "Windows Presentation Foundation" details how to build these new types of applications using XAML and C#.

Windows Controls

Although Web Forms and Windows Forms are developed in much the same way, you use different kinds of controls to populate them. Web Forms use Web server controls, and Windows Forms use *Windows Controls*.

A Windows Control is a lot like an ActiveX control. After a Windows Control is implemented, it compiles to a DLL that must be installed on the client's machine. In fact, the .NET SDK provides a utility that creates a wrapper for ActiveX controls, so that they can be placed on Windows Forms. As is the case with Web Controls, Windows Control creation involves deriving from a particular class, `System.Windows.Forms.Control`.

Windows Services

A Windows Service (originally called an NT Service) is a program designed to run in the background in Windows NT/2000/XP/2003/Vista (but not Windows 9*x*). Services are useful when you want a program to be running continuously and ready to respond to events without having been explicitly started by the user. A good example is the World Wide Web Service on Web servers, which listens for Web requests from clients.

It is very easy to write services in C#. .NET Framework base classes are available in the `System.ServiceProcess` namespace that handles many of the boilerplate tasks associated with services. In addition, Visual Studio .NET allows you to create a C# Windows Service project, which uses C# source code for a basic Windows Service. Chapter 23, "Windows Services," explores how to write C# Windows Services.

Windows Communication Foundation (WCF)

Looking at how you move data and services from one point to another using Microsoft-based technologies, you will find that there are a lot of choices at your disposal. For instance, you can use ASP.NET Web services, .NET Remoting, Enterprise Services, and MSMQ for starters. What technology should you use? Well, it really comes down to what you are trying to achieve, because each technology is better used in a particular situation.

With that in mind, Microsoft brought all of these technologies together, and with the release of the .NET Framework 3.0 as well as its inclusion in the .NET Framework 3.5, you now have a single way to move data — the *Windows Communication Foundation* (WCF). WCF provides you with the ability to build your service one time and then expose this service in a multitude of ways (under different protocols even) by just making changes within a configuration file. You will find that WCF is a powerful new way of connecting disparate systems. Chapter 42, "Windows Communication Foundation," covers this in detail.

The Role of C# in the .NET Enterprise Architecture

C# requires the presence of the .NET runtime, and it will probably be a few years before most clients — particularly most home computers — have .NET installed. In the meantime, installing a C# application is likely to mean also installing the .NET redistributable components. Because of that, it is likely that we will see many C# applications first in the enterprise environment. Indeed, C# arguably presents an outstanding opportunity for organizations that are interested in building robust, *n*-tiered client-server applications.

When combined with ADO.NET, C# has the ability to access quickly and generically data stores such as SQL Server and Oracle databases. The returned datasets can easily be manipulated using the ADO.NET object model or LINQ, and automatically render as XML for transport across an office intranet.

Once a database schema has been established for a new project, C# presents an excellent medium for implementing a layer of data access objects, each of which could provide insertion, updates, and deletion access to a different database table.

Because it's the first component-based C language, C# is a great language for implementing a business object tier, too. It encapsulates the messy plumbing for intercomponent communication, leaving developers free to focus on gluing their data access objects together in methods that accurately enforce their organizations' business rules. Moreover, with attributes, C# business objects can be outfitted for method-level security checks, object pooling, and JIT activation supplied by COM+ Services. Furthermore, .NET ships with utility programs that allow your new .NET business objects to interface with legacy COM components.

To create an enterprise application with C#, you create a Class Library project for the data access objects and another for the business objects. While developing, you can use Console projects to test the methods on your classes. Fans of extreme programming can build Console projects that can be executed automatically from batch files to unit test that working code has not been broken.

On a related note, C# and .NET will probably influence the way you physically package your reusable classes. In the past, many developers crammed a multitude of classes into a single physical component because this arrangement made deployment a lot easier; if there was a versioning problem, you knew just where to look. Because deploying .NET enterprise components involves simply copying files into directories, developers can now package their classes into more logical, discrete components without encountering "DLL Hell."

Last, but not least, ASP.NET pages coded in C# constitute an excellent medium for user interfaces. Because ASP.NET pages compile, they execute quickly. Because they can be debugged in the Visual Studio 2008 IDE, they are robust. Because they support full-scale language features such as early binding, inheritance, and modularization, ASP.NET pages coded in C# are tidy and easily maintained.

Seasoned developers acquire a healthy skepticism about strongly hyped new technologies and languages and are reluctant to use new platforms simply because they are urged to. If you are an enterprise developer in an IT department, though, or if you provide application services across the World Wide Web, let us assure you that C# and .NET offer at least four solid benefits, even if some of the more exotic features like XML Web services and server-side controls don't pan out:

- Component conflicts will become infrequent and deployment is easier because different versions of the same component can run side by side on the same machine without conflicting.
- Your ASP.NET code will not look like spaghetti code.
- You can leverage a lot of the functionality in the .NET base classes.
- For applications requiring a Windows Forms user interface, C# makes it very easy to write this kind of application.

Windows Forms have, to some extent, been downplayed due to the advent of Web Forms and Internet-based applications. However, if you or your colleagues lack expertise in JavaScript, ASP, or related technologies, Windows Forms are still a viable option for creating a user interface with speed and ease. Just remember to factor your code so that the user interface logic is separate from the business logic and the data access code. Doing so will allow you to migrate your application to the browser at some point in the future if you need to. In addition, it is likely that Windows Forms will remain the dominant user interface for applications for use in homes and small businesses for a long time to come. In addition to this, the new smart client features of Windows Forms (the ability to easily work in an online/offline mode) will bring a new round of exciting applications.

Summary

This chapter has covered a lot of ground, briefly reviewing important aspects of the .NET Framework and C#'s relationship to it. It started by discussing how all languages that target .NET are compiled into Microsoft Intermediate Language (IL) before this is compiled and executed by the Common Language Runtime (CLR). This chapter also discussed the roles of the following features of .NET in the compilation and execution process:

- Assemblies and .NET base classes
- COM components
- JIT compilation
- Application domains
- Garbage collection

Figure 1-4 provides an overview of how these features come into play during compilation and execution.

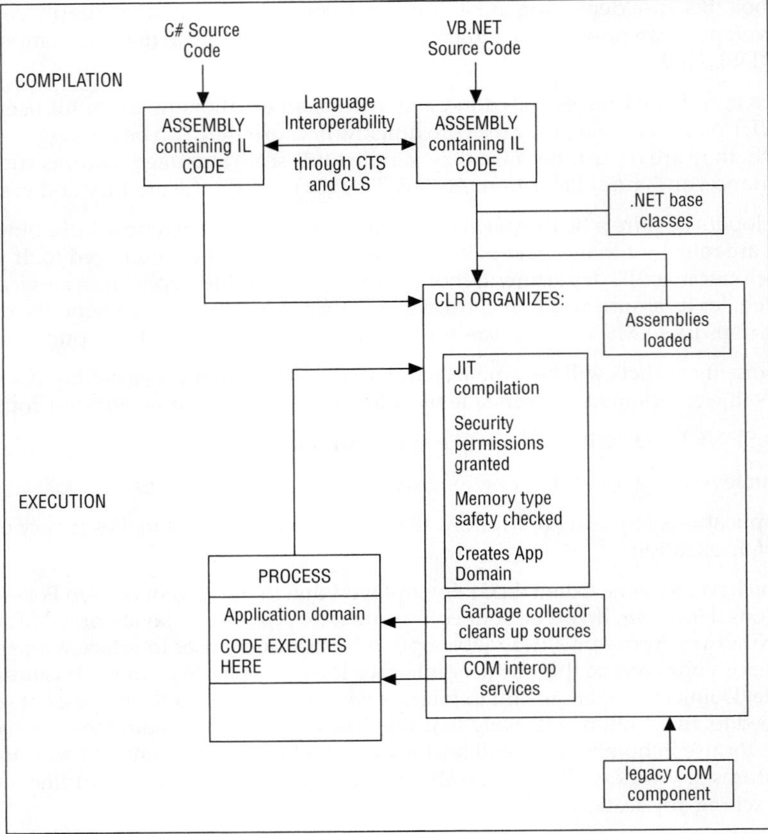

Figure 1-4

You learned about the characteristics of IL, particularly its strong data typing and object orientation, and how these characteristics influence the languages that target .NET, including C#. You also learned how the strongly typed nature of IL enables language interoperability, as well as CLR services such as garbage collection and security. There was also a focus on the Common Language Specification (CLS) and the Common Type System (CTS) to help deal with language interoperability.

Finally, you learned how C# could be used as the basis for applications that are built on several .NET technologies, including ASP.NET.

Chapter 2 discusses how to write code in C#.

2

C# Basics

Now that you understand more about what C# can do, you will want to learn how to use it. This chapter gives you a good start in that direction by providing you with a basic knowledge of the fundamentals of C# programming, which is built on in subsequent chapters. The main topics covered are:

- Declaring variables
- Initialization and scope of variables
- Predefined C# data types
- Dictating the flow of execution within a C# program using loops and conditional statements
- Enumerations
- Namespaces
- The `Main()` method
- Basic command-line C# compiler options
- Using `System.Console` to perform console I/O
- Using comments and documentation features
- Preprocessor directives
- Guidelines and conventions for good programming in C#

By the end of this chapter, you will know enough C# to write simple programs, though without using inheritance or other object-oriented features, which are covered in later chapters.

Before We Start

As already mentioned, C# is an object-oriented language. Throughout this chapter and later chapters, we assume that you have a good grasp of the concepts behind object-oriented (OO) programming. In other words, we expect that you understand what we mean by *classes*, *objects*, *interfaces*, and *inheritance*. If you have programmed in C++ or Java before, you should have a pretty good grounding in object-oriented programming (OOP). However, if you do not have a background in OOP, you may find it helpful to familiarize yourself with OOP basics before continuing.

In this chapter, we make many comparisons among C#, C++, Java, and Visual Basic 6 as we walk through the basics of C#. If you are an experienced developer in these programs, you might prefer to read a comparison between C# and your selected language before reading this chapter. If so, we have also made available separate documents for download on the Wrox Press Web site (`www.wrox.com`) that give introductions to C# from the point of view of each of these languages.

Your First C# Program

Let's start by compiling and running the simplest possible C# program — a simple class consisting of a console application that writes a message to the screen.

Later chapters present a number of code samples. The most common technique for writing C# programs is to use Visual Studio 2008 to generate a basic project and add your own code to it. However, because the aim of these early chapters is to teach the C# language, we are going to keep things simple and avoid relying on Visual Studio 2008 until Chapter 15, "Visual Studio 2008." Instead, we will present the code as simple files that you can type in using any text editor and compile from the command line.

The Code

Type the following into a text editor (such as Notepad), and save it with a `.cs` extension (for example, `First.cs`). The `Main()` method is shown here:

```
using System;

namespace Wrox.ProCSharp.Basics
{
   class MyFirstCSharpClass
   {
      static void Main()
      {
         Console.WriteLine("This isn't at all like Java!");
         Console.ReadLine();
         return;
      }
   }
}
```

Compiling and Running the Program

You can compile this program by simply running the C# command-line compiler (`csc.exe`) against the source file, like this:

```
csc First.cs
```

If you want to compile code from the command line using the `csc` command, you should be aware that the .NET command-line tools, including `csc`, are available only if certain environment variables have been set up. Depending on how you installed .NET (and Visual Studio 2008), this may or may not be the case on your machine.

If you do not have the environment variables set up, you have the following two options. The first is to run the batch file `%Microsoft Visual Studio 2008%\Common7\Tools\vsvars32.bat` *from the command prompt before running* `csc`*, where* `%Microsoft Visual Studio 2008` *is the folder to which Visual Studio 2008 has been installed. The second, and easier, way is to use the Visual Studio 2008 command prompt instead of the usual command prompt window. You will find the Visual Studio 2008 command prompt in the Start Menu, under Programs, Microsoft Visual Studio 2008, Microsoft Visual Studio Tools. It is simply a command prompt window that automatically runs* `vsvars32.bat` *when it opens.*

Compiling the code produces an executable file named `First.exe`, which you can run from the command line or from Windows Explorer like any other executable. Give it a try:

csc First.cs

```
Microsoft (R) Visual C# Compiler version 9.00.20404
for Microsoft (R) .NET Framework version 3.5
Copyright (C) Microsoft Corporation. All rights reserved.
```

First.exe

```
This isn't at all like Java!
```

Well, maybe that message isn't quite true! This program has some fairly fundamental similarities to Java, although there are one or two points (such as the capitalized `Main()` function) to catch the unwary Java or C++ developer. Let's look more closely at what's going on in the code.

A Closer Look

First, a few general comments about C# syntax. In C#, as in other C-style languages, most statements end in a semicolon (`;`) and can continue over multiple lines without needing a continuation character (such as the underscore in Visual Basic). Statements can be joined into blocks using curly braces (`{}`). Single-line comments begin with two forward slash characters (`//`), and multiline comments begin with a slash and an asterisk (`/*`) and end with the same combination reversed (`*/`). In these aspects, C# is identical to C++ and Java but different from Visual Basic. It is the semicolons and curly braces that give C# code such a different visual appearance from Visual Basic code. If your background is predominantly Visual Basic, take extra care to remember the semicolon at the end of every statement. Omitting this is usually the biggest single cause of compilation errors among developers new to C-style languages. Another thing to remember is that C# is case sensitive. That means that variables named `myVar` and `MyVar` are two different variables.

The first few lines in the previous code example have to do with *namespaces* (mentioned later in this chapter), which are a way to group together associated classes. This concept will be familiar to Java and C++ developers but may be new to Visual Basic 6 developers. C# namespaces are basically the same as C++ namespaces or, equivalently, Java packages, but there is no comparable concept in Visual Basic 6. The `namespace` keyword declares the namespace your class should be associated with. All code within the braces that follow it is regarded as being within that namespace. The `using` statement specifies a namespace that the compiler should look at to find any classes that are referenced in your code but that aren't defined in the current namespace. This serves the same purpose as the `import` statement in Java and the `using namespace` statement in C++.

```
using System;

namespace Wrox.ProCSharp.Basics
{
```

The reason for the presence of the `using` statement in the `First.cs` file is that you are going to use a library class, `System.Console`. The `using System` statement allows you to refer to this class simply as `Console` (and similarly for any other classes in the `System` namespace). The standard `System` namespace is where the most commonly used .NET types reside. It is important to realize that everything you do in C# depends on the .NET base classes. In this case, you are using the `Console` class within the `System` namespace in order to write to the console window. C# has no built-in keywords of its own for input or output; it is completely reliant on the .NET classes.

Because almost every C# program uses classes in the System namespace, we will assume that a `using System;` *statement is present in the file for all code snippets in this chapter.*

Next, you declare a class called `MyFirstClass`. However, because it has been placed in a namespace called `Wrox.ProCSharp.Basics`, the fully qualified name of this class is `Wrox.ProCSharp.Basics.MyFirstCSharpClass`:

```
class MyFirstCSharpClass
{
```

As in Java, all C# code must be contained within a class. Classes in C# are similar to classes in Java and C++, and very roughly comparable to class modules in Visual Basic 6. The class declaration consists of the `class` keyword, followed by the class name and a pair of curly braces. All code associated with the class should be placed between these braces.

Next, you declare a method called `Main()`. Every C# executable (such as console applications, Windows applications, and Windows services) must have an entry point — the `Main()` method (note the capital `M`):

```
static void Main()
{
```

The method is called when the program is started, like the `main()` function in C++ or Java, or `Sub Main()` in a Visual Basic 6 module. This method must return either nothing (`void`) or an integer (`int`). A C# method corresponds to a method in C++ and Java (sometimes referred to in C++ as a member function). It also corresponds to either a Visual Basic `Function` or a Visual Basic `Sub`, depending on whether the method returns anything (unlike Visual Basic, C# makes no conceptual distinction between functions and subroutines).

Note the format of method definitions in C#:

```
  [modifiers] return_type MethodName([parameters])
{
   // Method body. NB. This code block is pseudo-code.
}
```

Here, the first square brackets represent certain optional keywords. Modifiers are used to specify certain features of the method you are defining, such as where the method can be called from. In this case, you have two modifiers: `public` and `static`. The `public` modifier means that the method can be accessed from anywhere, so it can be called from outside your class. This is the same meaning as `public` in C++ and Java, and `Public` in Visual Basic. The `static` modifier indicates that the method does not operate on a specific instance of your class and therefore is called without first instantiating the class. This is important because you are creating an executable rather than a class library. Once again, this has the same meaning as the `static` keyword in C++ and Java, though in this case there is no Visual Basic equivalent (the `Static` keyword in Visual Basic has a different meaning). You set the return type to `void`, and in the example, you don't include any parameters.

Finally, we come to the code statements themselves:

```
Console.WriteLine("This isn't at all like Java!");
Console.ReadLine();
return;
```

In this case, you simply call the `WriteLine()` method of the `System.Console` class to write a line of text to the console window. `WriteLine()` is a `static` method, so you don't need to instantiate a `Console` object before calling it.

`Console.ReadLine()` reads user input. Adding this line forces the application to wait for the carriage return key to be pressed before the application exits, and, in the case of Visual Studio 2008, the console window disappears.

You then call `return` to exit from the method (also, because this is the `Main()` method, you exit the program as well.). You specified `void` in your method header, so you don't return any values. The `return` statement is equivalent to `return` in C++ and Java, and `Exit Sub` or `Exit Function` in Visual Basic.

Now that you have had a taste of basic C# syntax, you are ready for more detail. Because it is virtually impossible to write any nontrivial program without *variables*, we will start by looking at variables in C#.

Variables

You declare variables in C# using the following syntax:

```
datatype identifier;
```

For example:

```
int i;
```

This statement declares an `int` named `i`. The compiler won't actually let you use this variable in an expression until you have initialized it with a value.

Once it has been declared, you can assign a value to the variable using the assignment operator, =:

```
i = 10;
```

You can also declare the variable and initialize its value at the same time:

```
int i = 10;
```

This syntax is identical to C++ and Java syntax but very different from Visual Basic syntax for declaring variables. If you are coming from Visual Basic 6, you should also be aware that C# doesn't distinguish between objects and simple types, so there is no need for anything like the `Set` keyword, even if you want your variable to refer to an object. The C# syntax for declaring variables is the same no matter what the data type of the variable.

If you declare and initialize more than one variable in a single statement, all of the variables will be of the same data type:

```
int x = 10, y =20;    // x and y are both ints
```

To declare variables of different types, you need to use separate statements. You cannot assign different data types within a multiple variable declaration:

```
int x = 10;
bool y = true;                // Creates a variable that stores true or false
int x = 10, bool y = true;    // This won't compile!
```

Notice the `//` and the text after it in the preceding examples. These are comments. The `//` character sequence tells the compiler to ignore the text that follows on this line because it is for a human to better understand the program and not part of the program itself. We further explain comments in code later in this chapter.

Initialization of Variables

Variable initialization demonstrates an example of C#'s emphasis on safety. Briefly, the C# compiler requires that any variable be initialized with some starting value before you refer to that variable in an operation. Most modern compilers will flag violations of this as a warning, but the ever-vigilant C#

compiler treats such violations as errors. This prevents you from unintentionally retrieving junk values from memory that is left over from other programs.

C# has two methods for ensuring that variables are initialized before use:

- Variables that are fields in a class or struct, if not initialized explicitly, are by default zeroed out when they are created (classes and structs are discussed later).
- Variables that are local to a method must be explicitly initialized in your code prior to any statements in which their values are used. In this case, the initialization doesn't have to happen when the variable is declared, but the compiler will check all possible paths through the method and will flag an error if it detects any possibility of the value of a local variable being used before it is initialized.

C#'s approach contrasts with C++'s approach, in which the compiler leaves it up to the programmer to make sure that variables are initialized before use, and with Visual Basic's approach, in which all variables are zeroed out automatically.

For example, you can't do the following in C#:

```
public static int Main()
{
   int d;
   Console.WriteLine(d);    // Can't do this! Need to initialize d before use
   return 0;
}
```

Notice that this code snippet demonstrates defining `Main()` so that it returns an `int` instead of `void`.

When you attempt to compile these lines, you will receive this error message:

```
Use of unassigned local variable 'd'
```

Consider the following statement:

```
Something objSomething;
```

In C++, this line would create an instance of the `Something` class on the stack. In C#, this same line of code would create only a *reference* for a `Something` object, but this reference would not yet actually refer to any object. Any attempt to call a method or property against this variable would result in an error.

Instantiating a reference object in C# requires use of the `new` keyword. You create a reference as shown in the previous example and then point the reference at an object allocated on the heap using the `new` keyword:

```
objSomething = new Something();    // This creates a Something on the heap
```

Type Inference

Type inference makes use of the `var` keyword. The syntax for declaring the variable changes somewhat. The compiler "infers" what the type of the variable is by what the variable is initialized to. For example,

```
int someNumber = 0;
```

becomes

```
var someNumber = 0;
```

Even though `someNumber` is never declared as being an `int`, the compiler figures this out and `someNumber` is an `int` for as long as it is in scope. Once compiled, the two preceding statements are equal.

Here is a short program to demonstrate:

```
using System;

namespace Wrox.ProCSharp.Basics
{
  class Program
  {
    static void Main(string[] args)
    {
      var name = "Bugs Bunny";
      var age = 25;
      var isRabbit = true;

      Type nameType = name.GetType();
      Type ageType = age.GetType();
      Type isRabbitType = isRabbit.GetType();

      Console.WriteLine("name is type " + nameType.ToString());
      Console.WriteLine("age is type " + ageType.ToString());
      Console.WriteLine("isRabbit is type " + isRabbitType.ToString());
    }
  }
}
```

The output from this program is:

```
name is type System.String
age is type System.Int32
isRabbit is type System.Bool
```

There are a few rules that you need to follow. The variable must be initialized. Otherwise, the compiler doesn't have anything to infer the type from. The initializer cannot be null, and the initializer must be an expression. You can't set the initializer to an object unless you create a new object in the initializer. We examine this more closely in the discussion of anonymous types in Chapter 3, "Objects and Types."

Once the variable has been declared and the type inferred, the variable's type cannot be changed. This is unlike the `Variant` type used in Visual Basic. Once established, the variable's type follows all of the strong typing rules that any other variable type must follow.

Variable Scope

The *scope* of a variable is the region of code from which the variable can be accessed. In general, the scope is determined by the following rules:

- A *field* (also known as a member variable) of a class is in scope for as long as its containing class is in scope (this is the same as for C++, Java, and VB).
- A *local variable* is in scope until a closing brace indicates the end of the block statement or method in which it was declared.
- A local variable that is declared in a `for`, `while`, or similar statement is in scope in the body of that loop. (C++ developers will recognize that this is the same behavior as the ANSI standard for C++. Early versions of the Microsoft C++ compiler did not comply with this standard but scoped such variables to remain in scope after the loop terminated.)

Scope Clashes for Local Variables

It's common in a large program to use the same variable name for different variables in different parts of the program. This is fine as long as the variables are scoped to completely different parts of the program so that there is no possibility for ambiguity. However, bear in mind that local variables with the same name can't be declared twice in the same scope. For example, you can't do this:

```
int x = 20;
// some more code
int x = 30;
```

Consider the following code sample:

```
using System;

namespace Wrox.ProCSharp.Basics
{
   public class ScopeTest
   {
      public static int Main()
      {
         for (int i = 0; i < 10; i++)
         {
            Console.WriteLine(i);
         }   // i goes out of scope here

         // We can declare a variable named i again, because
         // there's no other variable with that name in scope


         for (int i = 9; i >= 0; i--)
         {
            Console.WriteLine(i);
         }   // i goes out of scope here.
         return 0;
      }
   }
}
```

This code simply prints out the numbers from 0 to 9, and then back again from 9 to 0, using two `for` loops. The important thing to note is that you declare the variable `i` twice in this code, within the same method. You can do this because `i` is declared in two separate loops, so each `i` variable is local to its own loop.

Here's another example:

```
public static int Main()
{
   int j = 20;
   for (int i = 0; i < 10; i++)
   {
      int j = 30;    // Can't do this - j is still in scope
      Console.WriteLine(j + i);
   }
   return 0;
}
```

If you try to compile this, you'll get an error:

```
ScopeTest.cs(12,14): error CS0136: A local variable named 'j' cannot be declared in
this scope because it would give a different meaning to 'j', which is already used
in a 'parent or current' scope to denote something else.
```

This occurs because the variable `j`, which is defined before the start of the `for` loop, is still in scope within the `for` loop, and won't go out of scope until the `Main()` method has finished executing. Although the second `j` (the illegal one) is in the loop's scope, that scope is nested within the `Main()` method's scope. The compiler has no way to distinguish between these two variables, so it won't allow the second one to be declared. This, again, is different from C++, where variable hiding is permitted.

Scope Clashes for Fields and Local Variables

In certain circumstances, however, you can distinguish between two identifiers with the same name (although not the same fully qualified name) and the same scope, and in this case the compiler will allow you to declare the second variable. The reason is that C# makes a fundamental distinction between variables that are declared at the type level (fields) and variables that are declared within methods (local variables).

Consider the following code snippet:

```
using System;

namespace Wrox.ProCSharp.Basics
{
   class ScopeTest2
   {
      static int j = 20;
      Console.WriteLine(j);

      public static void Main()
      {
         int j = 30;
         Console.WriteLine(j);
         return;
      }
   }
}
```

This code will compile, even though you have two variables named `j` in scope within the `Main()` method: the `j` that was defined at the class level, and doesn't go out of scope until the class is destroyed (when the `Main()` method terminates, and the program ends); and the `j` defined in `Main()`. In this case, the new variable named `j` that you declare in the `Main()` method *hides* the class-level variable with the same name, so when you run this code, the number `30` will be displayed.

However, what if you want to refer to the class-level variable? You can actually refer to fields of a class or struct from outside the object, using the syntax `object.fieldname`. In the previous example, you are accessing a static field (you look at what this means in the next section) from a static method, so you can't use an instance of the class; you just use the name of the class itself:

```
...
public static void Main()
{
   int j = 30;
   Console.WriteLine(j);
   Console.WriteLine(ScopeTest2.j);
}
...
```

If you were accessing an instance field (a field that belongs to a specific instance of the class), you would need to use the `this` keyword instead. This keyword performs the same role as `this` in C++ and Java, and `Me` in Visual Basic.

Constants

As the name implies, a constant is a variable whose value cannot be changed throughout its lifetime. Prefixing a variable with the `const` keyword when it is declared and initialized designates that variable as a constant:

```
const int a = 100;   // This value cannot be changed.
```

Constants will be familiar to Visual Basic and C++ developers. C++ developers should, however, note that C# does not permit all the subtleties of C++ constants. In C++, not only could variables be declared as constant, but depending on the declaration, you could have constant pointers, variable pointers to constants, constant methods (that don't change the contents of the containing object), constant parameters to methods, and so on. These subtleties have been discarded in C#, and all you can do is declare local variables and fields to be constant.

Constants have the following characteristics:

- They must be initialized when they are declared, and once a value has been assigned, it can never be overwritten.
- The value of a constant must be computable at compile time. Therefore, you can't initialize a constant with a value taken from a variable. If you need to do this, you will need to use a read-only field (this is explained in Chapter 3, "Objects and Types").
- Constants are always implicitly static. However, notice that you don't have to (and, in fact, are not permitted to) include the `static` modifier in the constant declaration.

At least three advantages exist to using constants in your programs:

- Constants make your programs easier to read by replacing magic numbers and strings with readable names whose values are easy to understand.
- Constants make your programs easier to modify. For example, assume that you have a `SalesTax` constant in one of your C# programs, and that constant is assigned a value of 6 percent. If the sales tax rate changes at a later point in time, you can modify the behavior of all tax calculations simply by assigning a new value to the constant; you don't have to hunt throughout your code for the value `.06` and change each one, hoping that you will find all of them.
- Constants help to prevent mistakes in your programs. If you attempt to assign another value to a constant somewhere in your program other than at the point where the constant is declared, the compiler will flag the error.

Predefined Data Types

Now that you have seen how to declare variables and constants, let's take a closer look at the data types available in C#. As you will see, C# is much stricter about the types available and their definitions than some other languages are.

Value Types and Reference Types

Before examining the data types in C#, it is important to understand that C# distinguishes between two categories of data type:

- Value types
- Reference types

The next few sections look in detail at the syntax for value and reference types. Conceptually, the difference is that a *value type* stores its value directly, whereas a *reference type* stores a reference to the value. Value types in C# are basically the same as simple types (integer, float, but not pointers or references) in Visual Basic or C++. Reference types are the same as reference types in Visual Basic and are similar to types accessed through pointers in C++.

These types are stored in different places in memory; value types are stored in an area known as the *stack*, and reference types are stored in an area known as the *managed heap*. It is important to be aware of whether a type is a value type or a reference type because of the different effect each assignment has. For example, `int` is a value type, which means that the following statement will result in two locations in memory storing the value 20:

```
// i and j are both of type int
i = 20;
j = i;
```

However, consider the following code. For this code, assume that you have defined a class called `Vector`. Assume that `Vector` is a reference type and has an `int` member variable called `Value`:

```
Vector x, y;
x = new Vector();
x.Value = 30;    // Value is a field defined in Vector class
y = x;
Console.WriteLine(y.Value);
y.Value = 50;
Console.WriteLine(x.Value);
```

The crucial point to understand is that after executing this code, there is only one `Vector` object around. `x` and `y` both point to the memory location that contains this object. Because `x` and `y` are variables of a reference type, declaring each variable simply reserves a reference—it doesn't instantiate an object of the given type. This is the same as declaring a pointer in C++ or an object reference in Visual Basic. In neither case is an object actually created. In order to create an object, you have to use the `new` keyword, as shown. Because `x` and `y` refer to the same object, changes made to `x` will affect `y` and vice versa. Hence the code will display `30` then `50`.

C++ developers should note that this syntax is like a reference, not a pointer. We use the `.` notation, not `->`, to access object members. Syntactically, C# references look more like C++ reference variables. However, behind the superficial syntax, the real similarity is with C++ pointers.

If a variable is a reference, it is possible to indicate that it does not refer to any object by setting its value to `null`:

```
y = null;
```

This is the same as setting a reference to `null` in Java, a pointer to `NULL` in C++, or an object reference in Visual Basic to `Nothing`. If a reference is set to `null`, then clearly it is not possible to call any nonstatic member functions or fields against it; doing so would cause an exception to be thrown at runtime.

In languages like C++, the developer can choose whether a given value is to be accessed directly or via a pointer. Visual Basic is more restrictive, taking the view that COM objects are reference types and simple types are always value types. C# is similar to Visual Basic in this regard: whether a variable is a value or reference is determined solely by its data type, so `int`, for example, is always a value type. It is not possible to declare an `int` variable as a reference (although in Chapter 6, "Operators and Casts," which covers *boxing*, you see it is possible to wrap value types in references of type `object`).

In C#, basic data types like `bool` and `long` are value types. This means that if you declare a `bool` variable and assign it the value of another `bool` variable, you will have two separate `bool` values in memory. Later, if you change the value of the original `bool` variable, the value of the second `bool` variable does not change. These types are copied by value.

In contrast, most of the more complex C# data types, including classes that you yourself declare, are reference types. They are allocated upon the heap, have lifetimes that can span multiple function calls, and can be accessed through one or several aliases. The Common Language Runtime (CLR) implements an elaborate algorithm to track which reference variables are still reachable and which have been orphaned. Periodically, the CLR will destroy orphaned objects and return the memory that they once occupied back to the operating system. This is done by the garbage collector.

C# has been designed this way because high performance is best served by keeping primitive types (like `int` and `bool`) as value types and larger types that contain many fields (as is usually the case with classes) as reference types. If you want to define your own type as a value type, you should declare it as a struct.

CTS Types

As mentioned in Chapter 1, ".NET Architecture," the basic predefined types recognized by C# are not intrinsic to the language but are part of the .NET Framework. For example, when you declare an `int` in C#, what you are actually declaring is an instance of a .NET struct, `System.Int32`. This may sound like a small point, but it has a profound significance: it means that you are able to treat all the primitive data types syntactically as if they were classes that supported certain methods. For example, to convert an `int i` to a `string`, you can write:

```
string s = i.ToString();
```

It should be emphasized that, behind this syntactical convenience, the types really are stored as primitive types, so there is absolutely no performance cost associated with the idea that the primitive types are notionally represented by .NET structs.

The following sections review the types that are recognized as built-in types in C#. Each type is listed, along with its definition and the name of the corresponding .NET type (CTS type). C# has 15 predefined types, 13 value types, and 2 (`string` and `object`) reference types.

Predefined Value Types

The built-in value types represent primitives, such as integer and floating-point numbers, character, and Boolean types.

Integer Types

C# supports eight predefined integer types, shown in the following table.

Name	CTS Type	Description	Range (min:max)
`sbyte`	`System.SByte`	8-bit signed integer	-128:127 ($-2^7:2^7-1$)
`short`	`System.Int16`	16-bit signed integer	-32,768:32,767 ($-2^{15}:2^{15}-1$)
`int`	`System.Int32`	32-bit signed integer	-2,147,483,648:2,147,483,647 ($-2^{31}:2^{31}-1$)
`long`	`System.Int64`	64-bit signed integer	-9,223,372,036,854,775,808: 9,223,372,036,854,775,807 ($-2^{63}:2^{63}-1$)
`byte`	`System.Byte`	8-bit unsigned integer	0:255 ($0:2^8-1$)
`ushort`	`System.UInt16`	16-bit unsigned integer	0:65,535 ($0:2^{16}-1$)
`uint`	`System.UInt32`	32-bit unsigned integer	0:4,294,967,295 ($0:2^{32}-1$)
`ulong`	`System.UInt64`	64-bit unsigned integer	0:18,446,744,073,709,551,615 ($0:2^{64}-1$)

Future versions of Windows will target 64-bit processors, which can move bits into and out of memory in larger chunks to achieve faster processing times. Consequently, C# supports a rich palette of signed and unsigned integer types ranging in size from 8 to 64 bits.

Many of these type names will be new to programmers experienced in Visual Basic. C++ and Java developers should be careful; some C# types have the same names as C++ and Java types but have different definitions. For example, in C#, an `int` is always a 32-bit signed integer. In C++ an `int` is a signed integer, but the number of bits is platform-dependent (32 bits on Windows). In C#, all data types have been defined in a platform-independent manner to allow for the possible future porting of C# and .NET to other platforms.

A `byte` is the standard 8-bit type for values in the range 0 to 255 inclusive. Be aware that, in keeping with its emphasis on type safety, C# regards the `byte` type and the `char` type as completely distinct, and any programmatic conversions between the two must be explicitly requested. Also be aware that unlike the other types in the integer family, a `byte` type is by default unsigned. Its signed version bears the special name `sbyte`.

With .NET, a `short` is no longer quite so short; it is now 16 bits long. The `int` type is 32 bits long. The `long` type reserves 64 bits for values. All integer-type variables can be assigned values in decimal or in hex notation. The latter require the `0x` prefix:

```
long x = 0x12ab;
```

If there is any ambiguity about whether an integer is `int`, `uint`, `long`, or `ulong`, it will default to an `int`. To specify which of the other integer types the value should take, you can append one of the following characters to the number:

```
uint ui = 1234U;
long l = 1234L;
ulong ul = 1234UL;
```

You can also use lowercase `u` and `l`, although the latter could be confused with the integer `1` (one).

Floating-Point Types

Although C# provides a plethora of integer data types, it supports floating-point types as well. They will be familiar to C and C++ programmers.

Name	CTS Type	Description	Significant Figures	Range (approximate)
`float`	`System.Single`	32-bit single-precision floating point	7	$\pm 1.5 \times 10^{-45}$ to $\pm 3.4 \times 10^{38}$
`double`	`System.Double`	64-bit double-precision floating point	15/16	$\pm 5.0 \times 10^{-324}$ to $\pm 1.7 \times 10^{308}$

The `float` data type is for smaller floating-point values, for which less precision is required. The `double` data type is bulkier than the `float` data type but offers twice the precision (15 digits).

If you hard-code a non-integer number (such as 12.3) in your code, the compiler will normally assume that you want the number interpreted as a `double`. If you want to specify that the value is a `float`, you append the character `F` (or `f`) to it:

```
float f = 12.3F;
```

The Decimal Type

The `decimal` type represents higher-precision floating-point numbers, as shown in the following table.

Name	CTS Type	Description	Significant Figures	Range (approximate)
`decimal`	`System.Decimal`	128-bit high-precision decimal notation	28	$\pm 1.0 \times 10^{-28}$ to $\pm 7.9 \times 10^{28}$

One of the great things about the CTS and C# is the provision of a dedicated `decimal` type for financial calculations. How you use the 28 digits that the decimal type provides is up to you. In other words, you can track smaller dollar amounts with greater accuracy for cents or larger dollar amounts with more rounding in the fractional area. Bear in mind, however, that `decimal` is not implemented under the hood as a primitive type, so using `decimal` will have a performance effect on your calculations.

To specify that your number is a `decimal` type rather than a `double`, `float`, or an integer, you can append the `M` (or `m`) character to the value, as shown in the following example:

```
decimal d = 12.30M;
```

The Boolean Type

The C# `bool` type is used to contain Boolean values of either `true` or `false`.

Name	CTS Type	Description	Significant Figures	Range (approximate)
`bool`	`System.Boolean`	Represents true or false	NA	true false

You cannot implicitly convert `bool` values to and from integer values. If a variable (or a function return type) is declared as a `bool`, you can only use values of `true` and `false`. You will get an error if you try to use zero for `false` and a non-zero value for `true`, as is possible to do in C++.

The Character Type

For storing the value of a single character, C# supports the `char` data type.

Name	CTS Type	Values
`char`	`System.Char`	Represents a single 16-bit (Unicode) character

Although this data type has a superficial resemblance to the `char` type provided by C and C++, there is a significant difference. A C++ `char` represents an 8-bit character, whereas a C# `char` contains 16 bits. This is part of the reason that implicit conversions between the `char` type and the 8-bit `byte` type are not permitted.

Although 8 bits may be enough to encode every character in the English language and the digits 0–9, they aren't enough to encode every character in more expansive symbol systems (such as Chinese). In a gesture toward universality, the computer industry is moving away from the 8-bit character set and toward the 16-bit Unicode scheme, of which the ASCII encoding is a subset.

Literals of type `char` are signified by being enclosed in single quotation marks, for example `'A'`. If you try to enclose a character in double quotation marks, the compiler will treat this as a string and throw an error.

As well as representing `char`s as character literals, you can represent them with four-digit hex Unicode values (for example `'\u0041'`), as integer values with a cast (for example, `(char)65`), or as hexadecimal values (`'\x0041'`). You can also represent them with an escape sequence, as shown in the following table.

Escape Sequence	Character
`\'`	Single quotation mark
`\"`	Double quotation mark
`\\`	Backslash
`\0`	Null
`\a`	Alert
`\b`	Backspace
`\f`	Form feed
`\n`	Newline
`\r`	Carriage return
`\t`	Tab character
`\v`	Vertical tab

C++ developers should note that because C# has a native string type, you don't need to represent strings as arrays of `char`s.

Predefined Reference Types

C# supports two predefined reference types, `object` and `string`, described in the following table.

Name	CTS Type	Description
`object`	`System.Object`	The root type. All other types in the CTS are derived (including value types) from `object`.
`string`	`System.String`	Unicode character string.

The object Type

Many programming languages and class hierarchies provide a root type, from which all other objects in the hierarchy are derived. C# and .NET are no exception. In C#, the `object` type is the ultimate parent type from which all other intrinsic and user-defined types are derived. This is a key feature of C# that distinguishes it from both Visual Basic 6.0 and C++, although its behavior here is very similar to Java. All types implicitly derive ultimately from the `System.Object` class. This means that you can use the `object` type for two purposes:

- You can use an `object` reference to bind to an object of any particular subtype. For example, in Chapter 6, "Operators and Casts," you will see how you can use the `object` type to box a value object on the stack to move it to the heap. `object` references are also useful in reflection, when code must manipulate objects whose specific types are unknown. This is similar to the role played by a void pointer in C++ or by a `Variant` data type in VB.
- The `object` type implements a number of basic, general-purpose methods, which include `Equals()`, `GetHashCode()`, `GetType()`, and `ToString()`. Responsible user-defined classes may need to provide replacement implementations of some of these methods using an object-oriented technique known as *overriding*, which is discussed in Chapter 4, "Inheritance." When you override `ToString()`, for example, you equip your class with a method for intelligently providing a string representation of itself. If you don't provide your own implementations for these methods in your classes, the compiler will pick up the implementations in `object`, which may or may not be correct or sensible in the context of your classes.

We examine the `object` type in more detail in subsequent chapters.

The string Type

Veterans of C and C++ probably have battle scars from wrestling with C-style strings. A C or C++ string is nothing more than an array of characters, so the client programmer has to do a lot of work just to copy one string to another or to concatenate two strings. In fact, for a generation of C++ programmers, implementing a string class that wraps up the messy details of these operations was a rite of passage requiring many hours of teeth gnashing and head scratching. Visual Basic programmers have a somewhat easier life, with a `string` type, and Java people have it even better, with a `String` class that is in many ways very similar to a C# string.

C# recognizes the `string` keyword, which under the hood is translated to the .NET class, `System.String`. With it, operations like string concatenation and string copying are a snap:

```
string str1 = "Hello ";
string str2 = "World";
string str3 = str1 + str2; // string concatenation
```

Despite this style of assignment, `string` is a reference type. Behind the scenes, a `string` object is allocated on the heap, not the stack, and when you assign one string variable to another string, you get two references to the same string in memory. However, with `string` there are some differences from the usual behavior for reference types. For example, should you make changes to one of these strings, this will create an entirely new `string` object, leaving the other string unchanged. Consider the following code:

```
using System;

class StringExample
{
   public static int Main()
   {
      string s1 = "a string";
      string s2 = s1;
      Console.WriteLine("s1 is " + s1);
      Console.WriteLine("s2 is " + s2);
      s1 = "another string";
      Console.WriteLine("s1 is now " + s1);
      Console.WriteLine("s2 is now " + s2);
      return 0;
   }
}
```

The output from this is:

```
s1 is a string
s2 is a string
s1 is now another string
s2 is now a string
```

Changing the value of `s1` had no effect on `s2`, contrary to what you'd expect with a reference type! What's happening here is that when `s1` is initialized with the value `a string`, a new string object is allocated on the heap. When `s2` is initialized, the reference points to this same object, so `s2` also has the value `a string`. However, when you now change the value of `s1`, instead of replacing the original value, a new object will be allocated on the heap for the new value. The `s2` variable will still point to the original object, so its value is unchanged. Under the hood, this happens as a result of operator overloading, a topic that is explored in Chapter 6, "Operators and Casts." In general, the `string` class has been implemented so that its semantics follow what you would normally intuitively expect for a string.

String literals are enclosed in double quotation marks (`". . ."`); if you attempt to enclose a string in single quotation marks, the compiler will take the value as a `char`, and throw an error. C# strings can contain the same Unicode and hexadecimal escape sequences as `char`s. Because these escape sequences start with a backslash, you can't use this character unescaped in a string. Instead, you need to escape it with two backslashes (`\\`):

```
string filepath = "C:\\ProCSharp\\First.cs";
```

Even if you are confident that you can remember to do this all the time, typing all of those double backslashes can prove annoying. Fortunately, C# gives you an alternative. You can prefix a string literal with the at character (`@`) and all the characters in it will be treated at face value; they won't be interpreted as escape sequences:

```
string filepath = @"C:\ProCSharp\First.cs";
```

This even allows you to include line breaks in your string literals:

```
string jabberwocky = @"'Twas brillig and the slithy toves
Did gyre and gimble in the wabe.";
```

Then the value of `jabberwocky` would be this:

```
'Twas brillig and the slithy toves
Did gyre and gimble in the wabe.
```

Flow Control

This section looks at the real nuts and bolts of the language: the statements that allow you to control the *flow* of your program rather than executing every line of code in the order it appears in the program.

Conditional Statements

Conditional statements allow you to branch your code depending on whether certain conditions are met or on the value of an expression. C# has two constructs for branching code — the `if` statement, which allows you to test whether a specific condition is met, and the `switch` statement, which allows you to compare an expression with a number of different values.

The if Statement

For conditional branching, C# inherits the C and C++ `if...else` construct. The syntax should be fairly intuitive for anyone who has done any programming with a procedural language:

```
if (condition)
   statement(s)
else
   statement(s)
```

If more than one statement is to be executed as part of either condition, these statements will need to be joined together into a block using curly braces (`{...}`). (This also applies to other C# constructs where statements can be joined into a block, such as the `for` and `while` loops):

```
bool isZero;
if (i == 0)
{
   isZero = true;
   Console.WriteLine("i is Zero");
}
else
{
   isZero = false;
   Console.WriteLine("i is Non-zero");
}
```

The syntax here is similar to C++ and Java but once again different from Visual Basic. Visual Basic developers should note that C# does not have any statement corresponding to Visual Basic's `EndIf`. Instead, the rule is that each clause of an `if` contains just one statement. If you need more than one statement, as in the preceding example, you should enclose the statements in braces, which will cause the whole group of statements to be treated as a single block statement.

If you want to, you can use an `if` statement without a final `else` statement. You can also combine `else if` clauses to test for multiple conditions:

```
using System;

namespace Wrox.ProCSharp.Basics
{
   class MainEntryPoint
```

```
        {
           static void Main(string[] args)
           {
              Console.WriteLine("Type in a string");
              string input;
              input = Console.ReadLine();
              if (input == "")
              {
                 Console.WriteLine("You typed in an empty string.");
              }
              else if (input.Length < 5)
              {
                 Console.WriteLine("The string had less than 5 characters.");
              }
              else if (input.Length < 10)
              {
                 Console.WriteLine("The string had at least 5 but less than 10
                    Characters.");
              }
              Console.WriteLine("The string was " + input);
           }
        }
     }
```

There is no limit to how many `else ifs` you can add to an `if` clause.

You'll notice that the previous example declares a string variable called `input`, gets the user to enter text at the command line, feeds this into `input`, and then tests the length of this string variable. The code also shows how easy string manipulation can be in C#. To find the length of `input`, for example, use `input.Length`.

One point to note about `if` is that you don't need to use the braces if there's only one statement in the conditional branch:

```
if (i == 0) Let's add some brackets here.
   Console.WriteLine("i is Zero");        // This will only execute if i == 0
Console.WriteLine("i can be anything");  // Will execute whatever the
                                          // value of i
```

However, for consistency, many programmers prefer to use curly braces whenever they use an `if` statement.

The `if` statements presented also illustrate some of the C# operators that compare values. Note in particular that, like C++ and Java, C# uses == to compare variables for equality. Do not use = for this purpose. A single = is used to assign values.

In C#, the expression in the `if` clause must evaluate to a Boolean. C++ programmers should be particularly aware of this; in C#, unlike in C++, it is not possible to test an integer (returned from a function, say) directly. In C#, you have to convert the integer that is returned to a Boolean `true` or `false`, for example, by comparing the value with zero or with `null`:

```
if (DoSomething() != 0)
{
   // Non-zero value returned
}
else
{
   // Returned zero
}
```

This restriction is there in order to prevent some common types of runtime bugs that occur in C++. In particular, in C++ it was common to mistype = when == was intended, resulting in unintentional assignments. In C# this will normally result in a compile-time error, because unless you are working with `bool` values, = will not return a `bool`.

The switch Statement

The `switch...case` statement is good for selecting one branch of execution from a set of mutually exclusive ones. It will be familiar to C++ and Java programmers and is similar to the `Select Case` statement in Visual Basic.

It takes the form of a `switch` argument followed by a series of `case` clauses. When the expression in the `switch` argument evaluates to one of the values beside a `case` clause, the code immediately following the `case` clause executes. This is one example where you don't need to use curly braces to join statements into blocks; instead, you mark the end of the code for each case using the `break` statement. You can also include a `default` case in the `switch` statement, which will execute if the expression evaluates to none of the other cases. The following `switch` statement tests the value of the `integerA` variable:

```
switch (integerA)
{
   case 1:
      Console.WriteLine("integerA =1");
      break;
   case 2:
      Console.WriteLine("integerA =2");
      break;
   case 3:
      Console.WriteLine("integerA =3");
      break;
   default:
      Console.WriteLine("integerA is not 1,2, or 3");
      break;
}
```

Note that the case values must be constant expressions; variables are not permitted.

Though the `switch...case` statement should be familiar to C and C++ programmers, C#'s `switch...case` is a bit safer than its C++ equivalent. Specifically, it prohibits fall-through conditions in almost all cases. This means that if a `case` clause is fired early on in the block, later clauses cannot be fired unless you use a `goto` statement to mark that you want them fired, too. The compiler enforces this restriction by flagging every `case` clause that is not equipped with a `break` statement as an error similar to this:

```
Control cannot fall through from one case label ('case 2:') to another
```

Although it is true that fall-through behavior is desirable in a limited number of situations, in the vast majority of cases, it is unintended and results in a logical error that's hard to spot. Isn't it better to code for the norm rather than for the exception?

By getting creative with `goto` statements, however, you can duplicate fall-through functionality in your `switch...cases`. But, if you find yourself really wanting to, you probably should reconsider your approach. The following code illustrates both how to use `goto` to simulate fall-through, and how messy the resultant code can get:

```
// assume country and language are of type string
switch(country)
{
   case "America":
      CallAmericanOnlyMethod();
```

```
        goto case "Britain";
    case "France":
        language = "French";
        break;
    case "Britain":
        language = "English";
        break;
}
```

There is one exception to the no-fall-through rule, however, in that you can fall through from one case to the next if that case is empty. This allows you to treat two or more cases in an identical way (without the need for `goto` statements):

```
switch(country)
{
    case "au":
    case "uk":
    case "us":
        language = "English";
        break;
    case "at":
    case "de":
        language = "German";
        break;
}
```

One intriguing point about the `switch` statement in C# is that the order of the cases doesn't matter — you can even put the `default` case first! As a result, no two cases can be the same. This includes different constants that have the same value, so you can't, for example, do this:

```
// assume country is of type string
const string england = "uk";
const string britain = "uk";
switch(country)
{
    case england:
    case britain:     // This will cause a compilation error.
        language = "English";
        break;
}
```

The previous code also shows another way in which the `switch` statement is different in C# compared to C++: In C#, you are allowed to use a string as the variable being tested.

Loops

C# provides four different loops (`for`, `while`, `do...while`, and `foreach`) that allow you to execute a block of code repeatedly until a certain condition is met. The `for`, `while`, and `do...while` loops are essentially identical to those encountered in C++.

The for Loop

C# `for` loops provide a mechanism for iterating through a loop where you test whether a particular condition holds before you perform another iteration. The syntax is

```
for (initializer; condition; iterator)
    statement(s)
```

where

- The initializer is the expression evaluated before the first loop is executed (usually initializing a local variable as a loop counter).
- The condition is the expression checked before each new iteration of the loop (this must evaluate to `true` for another iteration to be performed).
- The iterator is an expression evaluated after each iteration (usually incrementing the loop counter).

The iterations end when the condition evaluates to `false`.

The `for` loop is a so-called pretest loop because the loop condition is evaluated before the loop statements are executed, and so the contents of the loop won't be executed at all if the loop condition is `false`.

The `for` loop is excellent for repeating a statement or a block of statements for a predetermined number of times. The following example is typical of the use of a `for` loop. The following code will write out all the integers from 0 to 99:

```
for (int i = 0; i < 100; i=i+1)    // This is equivalent to
                                      // For i = 0 To 99 in VB.
{
   Console.WriteLine(i);
}
```

Here, you declare an `int` called `i` and initialize it to zero. This will be used as the loop counter. You then immediately test whether it is less than 100. Because this condition evaluates to `true`, you execute the code in the loop, displaying the value 0. You then increment the counter by one, and walk through the process again. Looping ends when `i` reaches 100.

Actually, the way the preceding loop is written isn't quite how you would normally write it. C# has a shorthand for adding 1 to a variable, so instead of `i = i + 1`, you can simply write `i++`:

```
for (int i = 0; i < 100; i++)
{
    // etc.
       }
```

C# `for` loop syntax is far more powerful than the Visual Basic `For...Next` loop because the iterator can be any statement. In Visual Basic, all you can do is add or subtract some number from the loop control variable. In C# you can do anything; for example, you can multiply the loop control variable by 2.

You can also make use of type inference for the iteration variable `i` in the preceding example. Using type inference the loop construct would be:

```
for (var i = 0; i < 100; i++)
...
```

It's not unusual to nest `for` loops so that an inner loop executes once completely for each iteration of an outer loop. This scheme is typically employed to loop through every element in a rectangular multidimensional array. The outermost loop loops through every row, and the inner loop loops through every column in a particular row. The following code displays rows of numbers. It also uses another `Console` method, `Console.Write()`, which does the same as `Console.WriteLine()` but doesn't send a carriage return to the output.

```
using System;

namespace Wrox.ProCSharp.Basics
{
   class MainEntryPoint
   {
      static void Main(string[] args)
      {
         // This loop iterates through rows...
         for (int i = 0; i < 100; i+=10)
         {
            // This loop iterates through columns...
            for (int j = i; j < i + 10; j++)
            {
               Console.Write("  " + j);
            }
            Console.WriteLine();
         }
      }
   }
}
```

Although `j` is an integer, it will be automatically converted to a string so that the concatenation can take place. C++ developers will note that this is far easier than string handling ever was in C++; for Visual Basic developers this is familiar ground.

C and C++ programmers should take note of one particular feature of the preceding example. The counter variable in the innermost loop is effectively redeclared with each successive iteration of the outer loop. This syntax is legal not only in C# but in C++ as well.

The preceding sample results in this output:

csc NumberTable.cs

```
Microsoft (R) Visual C# Compiler version 9.00.20404
for Microsoft (R) .NET Framework version 3.5
Copyright (C) Microsoft Corporation. All rights reserved.

  0   1   2   3   4   5   6   7   8   9
 10  11  12  13  14  15  16  17  18  19
 20  21  22  23  24  25  26  27  28  29
 30  31  32  33  34  35  36  37  38  39
 40  41  42  43  44  45  46  47  48  49
 50  51  52  53  54  55  56  57  58  59
 60  61  62  63  64  65  66  67  68  69
 70  71  72  73  74  75  76  77  78  79
 80  81  82  83  84  85  86  87  88  89
 90  91  92  93  94  95  96  97  98  99
```

Although it is technically possible to evaluate something other than a counter variable in a `for` loop's test condition, it is certainly not typical. It is also possible to omit one (or even all) of the expressions in the `for` loop. In such situations, however, you should consider using the `while` loop.

The while Loop

The `while` loop is identical to the `while` loop in C++ and Java, and the `While...Wend` loop in Visual Basic. Like the `for` loop, `while` is a pretest loop. The syntax is similar, but `while` loops take only one expression:

```
while(condition)
   statement(s);
```

Unlike the `for` loop, the `while` loop is most often used to repeat a statement or a block of statements for a number of times that is not known before the loop begins. Usually, a statement inside the `while` loop's body will set a Boolean flag to `false` on a certain iteration, triggering the end of the loop, as in the following example:

```
bool condition = false;
while (!condition)
{
   // This loop spins until the condition is true.
   DoSomeWork();
   condition = CheckCondition();    // assume CheckCondition() returns a bool
}
```

All of C#'s looping mechanisms, including the `while` loop, can forgo the curly braces that follow them if they intend to repeat just a single statement and not a block of statements. Again, many programmers consider it good practice to use braces all of the time.

The do . . . while Loop

The `do...while` loop is the post-test version of the `while` loop. It does the same thing with the same syntax as `do...while` in C++ and Java, and the same thing as `Loop...While` in Visual Basic. This means that the loop's test condition is evaluated after the body of the loop has been executed. Consequently, `do...while` loops are useful for situations in which a block of statements must be executed at least one time, as in this example:

```
bool condition;
do
{
   // This loop will at least execute once, even if Condition is false.
   MustBeCalledAtLeastOnce();
   condition = CheckCondition();
} while (condition);
```

The foreach Loop

The `foreach` loop is the final C# looping mechanism that we discuss. Whereas the other looping mechanisms were present in the earliest versions of C and C++, the `foreach` statement is a new addition (borrowed from Visual Basic), and a very welcome one at that.

The `foreach` loop allows you to iterate through each item in a collection. For now, we won't worry about exactly what a collection is (it is explained fully in Chapter 10, "Collections"); we will just say that it is an object that contains other objects. Technically, to count as a collection, it must support an interface called `IEnumerable`. Examples of collections include C# arrays, the collection classes in the `System.Collection` namespaces, and user-defined collection classes. You can get an idea of the syntax of `foreach` from the following code, if you assume that `arrayOfInts` is (unsurprisingly) an array of `int`s:

```
foreach (int temp in arrayOfInts)
{
   Console.WriteLine(temp);
}
```

Here, `foreach` steps through the array one element at a time. With each element, it places the value of the element in the `int` variable called `temp` and then performs an iteration of the loop.

Here is another situation where type inference can be used. The `foreach` loop would become:

```
foreach (var temp in arrayOfInts)
...
```

`temp` would be inferred to `int` because that is what the collection item type is.

An important point to note with `foreach` is that you can't change the value of the item in the collection (`temp` in the preceding code), so code such as the following will not compile:

```
foreach (int temp in arrayOfInts)
{
   temp++;
   Console.WriteLine(temp);
}
```

If you need to iterate through the items in a collection and change their values, you will need to use a `for` loop instead.

Jump Statements

C# provides a number of statements that allow you to jump immediately to another line in the program. The first of these is, of course, the notorious `goto` statement.

The goto Statement

The `goto` statement allows you to jump directly to another specified line in the program, indicated by a *label* (this is just an identifier followed by a colon):

```
goto Label1;
   Console.WriteLine("This won't be executed");
Label1:
   Console.WriteLine("Continuing execution from here");
```

A couple of restrictions are involved with `goto`. You can't jump into a block of code such as a `for` loop, you can't jump out of a class, and you can't exit a `finally` block after `try...catch` blocks (Chapter 14, "Errors and Exceptions," looks at exception handling with `try...catch...finally`).

The reputation of the `goto` statement probably precedes it, and in most circumstances, its use is sternly frowned upon. In general, it certainly doesn't conform to good object-oriented programming practice. However, there is one place where it is quite handy: jumping between cases in a `switch` statement, particularly because C#'s `switch` is so strict on fall-through. You saw the syntax for this earlier in this chapter.

The break Statement

You have already met the `break` statement briefly — when you used it to exit from a case in a `switch` statement. In fact, `break` can also be used to exit from `for`, `foreach`, `while`, or `do...while` loops. Control will switch to the statement immediately after the end of the loop.

If the statement occurs in a nested loop, control will switch to the end of the innermost loop. If the break occurs outside of a `switch` statement or a loop, a compile-time error will occur.

The continue Statement

The `continue` statement is similar to `break`, and must also be used within a `for`, `foreach`, `while`, or `do...while` loop. However, it exits only from the current iteration of the loop, meaning that execution will restart at the beginning of the next iteration of the loop, rather than outside the loop altogether.

The return Statement

The `return` statement is used to exit a method of a class, returning control to the caller of the method. If the method has a return type, `return` must return a value of this type; otherwise if the method returns `void`, you should use `return` without an expression.

Enumerations

An *enumeration* is a user-defined integer type. When you declare an enumeration, you specify a set of acceptable values that instances of that enumeration can contain. Not only that, but you can give the values user-friendly names. If, somewhere in your code, you attempt to assign a value that is not in the acceptable set of values to an instance of that enumeration, the compiler will flag an error. This concept may be new to Visual Basic programmers. C++ does support enumerations (or enums), but C# enumerations are far more powerful than their C++ counterparts.

Creating an enumeration can save you a lot of time and headaches in the long run. At least three benefits exist to using enumerations instead of plain integers:

- As mentioned, enumerations make your code easier to maintain by helping to ensure that your variables are assigned only legitimate, anticipated values.
- Enumerations make your code clearer by allowing you to refer to integer values by descriptive names rather than by obscure "magic" numbers.
- Enumerations make your code easier to type, too. When you go to assign a value to an instance of an enumerated type, the Visual Studio .NET IDE will, through IntelliSense, pop up a list box of acceptable values in order to save you some keystrokes and to remind you of what the possible options are.

You can define an enumeration as follows:

```
public enum TimeOfDay
{
   Morning = 0,
   Afternoon = 1,
   Evening = 2
}
```

In this case, you use an integer value to represent each period of the day in the enumeration. You can now access these values as members of the enumeration. For example, `TimeOfDay.Morning` will return the value `0`. You will typically use this enumeration to pass an appropriate value into a method and iterate through the possible values in a `switch` statement:

```
class EnumExample
{
   public static int Main()
   {
      WriteGreeting(TimeOfDay.Morning);
      return 0;
   }

   static void WriteGreeting(TimeOfDay timeOfDay)
   {
      switch(timeOfDay)
      {
         case TimeOfDay.Morning:
            Console.WriteLine("Good morning!");
```

```
               break;
            case TimeOfDay.Afternoon:
               Console.WriteLine("Good afternoon!");
               break;
            case TimeOfDay.Evening:
               Console.WriteLine("Good evening!");
               break;
            default:
               Console.WriteLine("Hello!");
               break;
         }
      }
   }
```

The real power of enums in C# is that behind the scenes they are instantiated as structs derived from the base class, `System.Enum`. This means it is possible to call methods against them to perform some useful tasks. Note that because of the way the .NET Framework is implemented there is no performance loss associated with treating the enums syntactically as structs. In practice, once your code is compiled, enums will exist as primitive types, just like `int` and `float`.

You can retrieve the string representation of an enum as in the following example, using the earlier `TimeOfDay` enum:

```
TimeOfDay time = TimeOfDay.Afternoon;
Console.WriteLine(time.ToString());
```

This will return the string `Afternoon`.

Alternatively, you can obtain an enum value from a string:

```
TimeOfDay time2 = (TimeOfDay) Enum.Parse(typeof(TimeOfDay), "afternoon", true);
Console.WriteLine((int)time2);
```

This code snippet illustrates both obtaining an enum value from a string and converting to an integer. To convert from a string, you need to use the static `Enum.Parse()` method, which, as shown, takes three parameters. The first is the type of enum you want to consider. The syntax is the keyword `typeof` followed by the name of the enum class in brackets. (Chapter 6, "Operators and Casts," explores the `typeof` operator in more detail.) The second parameter is the string to be converted, and the third parameter is a `bool` indicating whether you should ignore case when doing the conversion. Finally, note that `Enum.Parse()` actually returns an object reference — you need to explicitly convert this to the required enum type (this is an example of an unboxing operation). For the preceding code, this returns the value `1` as an object, corresponding to the enum value of `TimeOfDay.Afternoon`. On converting explicitly to an `int`, this produces the value `1` again.

Other methods on `System.Enum` do things such as return the number of values in an enum definition or list the names of the values. Full details are in the MSDN documentation.

Arrays

We won't say too much about arrays in this chapter because arrays are covered in detail in Chapter 5, "Arrays." However, we'll give you just enough syntax here that you can code one-dimensional arrays. Arrays in C# are declared by fixing a set of square brackets to the end of the variable type of the individual elements (note that all the elements in an array must be of the same data type).

A note to Visual Basic users: arrays in C# use square brackets, not parentheses. C++ users will be familiar with the square brackets but should carefully check the code presented here because C# syntax for actually declaring array variables is not the same as C++ syntax.

For example, whereas `int` represents a single integer, `int[]` represents an array of integers:

```
int[] integers;
```

To initialize the array with specific dimensions, you can use the `new` keyword, giving the size in the square brackets after the type name:

```
// Create a new array of 32 ints.
int[] integers = new int[32];
```

All arrays are reference types and follow reference semantics. Hence, in this code, even though the individual elements are primitive value types, the `integers` array is a reference type. So if you later write

```
int [] copy = integers;
```

this will simply assign the variable `copy` to refer to the same array — it won't create a new array.

To access an individual element within the array, you use the usual syntax, placing the index of the element in square brackets after the name of the array. All C# arrays use zero-based indexing, so you can reference the first variable with the index zero:

```
integers[0] = 35;
```

Similarly, you reference the 32 element value with an index value of 31:

```
integers[31] = 432;
```

C#'s array syntax is flexible. In fact, C# allows you to declare arrays without initializing them so that the array can be dynamically sized later in the program. With this technique, you are basically creating a `null` reference and later pointing that reference at a dynamically allocated stretch of memory locations requested with the `new` keyword:

```
int[] integers;
integers = new int[32];
```

You can find out how many elements are in any array by using this syntax:

```
int numElements = integers.Length;    // integers is any reference to an array.
```

Namespaces

As you have seen, namespaces provide a way of organizing related classes and other types. Unlike a file or a component, a namespace is a logical, rather than a physical, grouping. When you define a class in a C# file, you can include it within a namespace definition. Later, when you define another class that performs related work in another file, you can include it within the same namespace, creating a logical grouping that gives an indication to other developers using the classes how they are related and used:

```
namespace CustomerPhoneBookApp
{
   using System;

   public struct Subscriber
   {
      // Code for struct here...
   }
}
```

Placing a type in a namespace effectively gives that type a long name, consisting of the type's namespace as a series of names separated with periods (`.`), terminating with the name of the class. In the preceding example, the full name of the `Subscriber` struct is `CustomerPhoneBookApp.Subscriber`. This allows distinct classes with the same short name to be used within the same program without ambiguity. This full name is often called the fully qualified name.

You can also nest namespaces within other namespaces, creating a hierarchical structure for your types:

```
namespace Wrox
{
   namespace ProCSharp
   {
      namespace Basics
      {
         class NamespaceExample
         {
            // Code for the class here...
         }
      }
   }
}
```

Each namespace name is composed of the names of the namespaces it resides within, separated with periods, starting with the outermost namespace and ending with its own short name. So the full name for the `ProCSharp` namespace is `Wrox.ProCSharp`, and the full name of `NamespaceExample` class is `Wrox.ProCSharp.Basics.NamespaceExample`.

You can use this syntax to organize the namespaces in your namespace definitions too, so the previous code could also be written as follows:

```
namespace Wrox.ProCSharp.Basics
{
   class NamespaceExample
   {
      // Code for the class here...
   }
}
```

Note that you are not permitted to declare a multipart namespace nested within another namespace.

Namespaces are not related to assemblies. It is perfectly acceptable to have different namespaces in the same assembly or to define types in the same namespace in different assemblies.

The using Directive

Obviously, namespaces can grow rather long and tiresome to type, and the ability to indicate a particular class with such specificity may not always be necessary. Fortunately, as noted at the beginning of the chapter, C# allows you to abbreviate a class's full name. To do this, list the class's namespace at the top of the file, prefixed with the `using` keyword. Throughout the rest of the file, you can refer to the types in the namespace simply by their type names:

```
using System;
using Wrox.ProCSharp;
```

As remarked earlier, virtually all C# source code will have the statement `using System;` simply because so many useful classes supplied by Microsoft are contained in the `System` namespace.

If two namespaces referenced by `using` statements contain a type of the same name, you will need to use the full (or at least a longer) form of the name to ensure that the compiler knows which type is to be accessed. For example, say classes called `NamespaceExample` exist in both the `Wrox.ProCSharp.Basics` and `Wrox.ProCSharp.OOP` namespaces. If you then create a class called `Test` in the `Wrox.ProCSharp` namespace, and instantiate one of the `NamespaceExample` classes in this class, you need to specify which of these two classes you're talking about:

```
using Wrox.ProCSharp;

class Test
{
   public static int Main()
   {
      Basics.NamespaceExample nSEx = new Basics.NamespaceExample();
    // do something with the nSEx variable.
      return 0;
   }
}
```

Because `using` *statements occur at the top of C# files, in the same place that C and C++ list* `#include` *statements, it's easy for programmers moving from C++ to C# to confuse namespaces with C++-style header files. Don't make this mistake. The* `using` *statement does no physical linking between files, and C# has no equivalent to C++ header files.*

Your organization will probably want to spend some time developing a namespace schema so that its developers can quickly locate functionality that they need and so that the names of the organization's homegrown classes won't conflict with those in off-the-shelf class libraries. Guidelines on establishing your own namespace scheme along with other naming recommendations are discussed later in this chapter.

Namespace Aliases

Another use of the `using` keyword is to assign aliases to classes and namespaces. If you have a very long namespace name that you want to refer to several times in your code but don't want to include in a simple `using` statement (for example, to avoid type name conflicts), you can assign an alias to the namespace. The syntax for this is:

```
using alias = NamespaceName;
```

The following example (a modified version of the previous example) assigns the alias `Introduction` to the `Wrox.ProCSharp.Basics` namespace and uses this to instantiate a `NamespaceExample` object, which is defined in this namespace. Notice the use of the namespace alias qualifier (`::`). This forces the search to start with the `Introduction` namespace alias. If a class called `Introduction` had been introduced in the same scope, a conflict would happen. The `::` operator allows the alias to be referenced even if the conflict exists. The `NamespaceExample` class has one method, `GetNamespace()`, which uses the `GetType()` method exposed by every class to access a `Type` object representing the class's type. You use this object to return a name of the class's namespace:

```
using System;
using Introduction =  Wrox.ProCSharp.Basics;
class Test
{
   public static int Main()
   {
      Introduction::NamespaceExample NSEx =
         new Introduction::NamespaceExample();
```

```
            Console.WriteLine(NSEx.GetNamespace());
            return 0;
         }
      }

      namespace Wrox.ProCSharp.Basics
      {
         class NamespaceExample
         {
            public string GetNamespace()
            {
               return this.GetType().Namespace;
            }
         }
      }
```

The Main() Method

As you saw at the start of this chapter, C# programs start execution at a method named `Main()`. This must be a static method of a class (or struct), and must have a return type of either `int` or `void`.

Although it is common to specify the `public` modifier explicitly, because by definition the method must be called from outside the program, it doesn't actually matter what accessibility level you assign to the entry-point method — it will run even if you mark the method as `private`.

Multiple Main() Methods

When a C# console or Windows application is compiled, by default the compiler looks for exactly one `Main()` method in any class matching the signature that was just described and makes that class method the entry point for the program. If there is more than one `Main()` method, the compiler will return an error message. For example, consider the following code called `MainExample.cs`:

```
using System;

namespace Wrox.ProCSharp.Basics
{
   class Client
   {
      public static int Main()
      {
         MathExample.Main();
         return 0;
      }
   }

   class MathExample
   {
      static int Add(int x, int y)
      {
         return x + y;
      }

      public static int Main()
```

(continued)

(continued)

```
        {
            int i = Add(5,10);
            Console.WriteLine(i);
            return 0;
        }
    }
}
```

This contains two classes, both of which have a `Main()` method. If you try to compile this code in the usual way, you will get the following errors:

csc MainExample.cs

```
Microsoft (R) Visual C# Compiler version 9.00.20404
for Microsoft (R) .NET Framework version 3.5
Copyright (C) Microsoft Corporation. All rights reserved.

MainExample.cs(7,23): error CS0017: Program 'MainExample.exe' has more than
one entry point defined: 'Wrox.ProCSharp.Basics.Client.Main()'
MainExample.cs(21,23): error CS0017: Program 'MainExample.exe' has more than
one entry point defined: 'Wrox.ProCSharp.Basics.MathExample.Main()'
```

However, you can explicitly tell the compiler which of these methods to use as the entry point for the program by using the `/main` switch, together with the full name (including namespace) of the class to which the `Main()` method belongs:

```
csc MainExample.cs /main:Wrox.ProCSharp.Basics.MathExample
```

Passing Arguments to Main()

The examples so far have shown only the `Main()` method without any parameters. However, when the program is invoked, you can get the CLR to pass any command-line arguments to the program by including a parameter. This parameter is a string array, traditionally called `args` (although C# will accept any name). The program can use this array to access any options passed through the command line when the program is started.

The following sample, `ArgsExample.cs`, loops through the string array passed in to the `Main()` method and writes the value of each option to the console window:

```
using System;

namespace Wrox.ProCSharp.Basics
{
    class ArgsExample
    {
        public static int Main(string[] args)
        {
            for (int i = 0; i < args.Length; i++)
            {
                Console.WriteLine(args[i]);
            }
            return 0;
        }
    }
}
```

You can compile this as usual using the command line. When you run the compiled executable, you can pass in arguments after the name of the program, for example:

ArgsExample /a /b /c

```
/a
/b
/c
```

More on Compiling C# Files

You have seen how to compile console applications using `csc.exe`, but what about other types of applications? What if you want to reference a class library? The full set of compilation options for the C# compiler is of course detailed in the MSDN documentation, but we list here the most important options.

To answer the first question, you can specify what type of file you want to create using the `/target` switch, often abbreviated to `/t`. This can be one of those shown in the following table.

Option	Output
`/t:exe`	A console application (the default)
`/t:library`	A class library with a manifest
`/t:module`	A component without a manifest
`/t:winexe`	A Windows application (without a console window)

If you want a nonexecutable file (such as a DLL) to be loadable by the .NET runtime, you must compile it as a library. If you compile a C# file as a module, no assembly will be created. Although modules cannot be loaded by the runtime, they can be compiled into another manifest using the `/addmodule` switch.

Another option we need to mention is `/out`. This allows you to specify the name of the output file produced by the compiler. If the `/out` option isn't specified, the compiler will base the name of the output file on the name of the input C# file, adding an extension according to the target type (for example, `exe` for a Windows or console application or `dll` for a class library). Note that the `/out` and `/t`, or `/target`, options must precede the name of the file you want to compile.

If you want to reference types in assemblies that aren't referenced by default, you can use the `/reference` or `/r` switch, together with the path and file name of the assembly. The following example demonstrates how you can compile a class library and then reference that library in another assembly. It consists of two files:

- The class library
- A console application, which will call a class in the library

The first file is called `MathLibrary.cs` and contains the code for your DLL. To keep things simple, it contains just one (public) class, `MathLib`, with a single method that adds two `int`s:

```
namespace Wrox.ProCSharp.Basics
{
   public class MathLib
   {
      public int Add(int x, int y)
```

(continued)

(continued)

```
         {
            return x + y;
         }
      }
   }
```

You can compile this C# file into a .NET DLL using the following command:

```
csc /t:library MathLibrary.cs
```

The console application, `MathClient.cs`, will simply instantiate this object and call its `Add()` method, displaying the result in the console window:

```
using System;

namespace Wrox.ProCSharp.Basics
{
   class Client
   {
      public static void Main()
      {
         MathLib mathObj = new MathLib();
         Console.WriteLine(mathObj.Add(7,8));
      }
   }
}
```

You can compile this code using the `/r` switch to point at or reference the newly compiled DLL:

```
csc MathClient.cs /r:MathLibrary.dll
```

You can then run it as normal just by entering `MathClient` at the command prompt. This displays the number `15` — the result of your addition.

Console I/O

By this point, you should have a basic familiarity with C#'s data types, as well as some knowledge of how the thread-of-control moves through a program that manipulates those data types. In this chapter, you have also used several of the `Console` class's static methods used for reading and writing data. Because these methods are so useful when writing basic C# programs, this section quickly reviews them in more detail.

To read a line of text from the console window, you use the `Console.ReadLine()` method. This will read an input stream (terminated when the user presses the `Return` key) from the console window and return the input string. There are also two corresponding methods for writing to the console, which you have already used extensively:

- `Console.Write()`—Writes the specified value to the console window.
- `Console.WriteLine()`—This does the same, but adds a newline character at the end of the output.

Various forms (overloads) of these methods exist for all of the predefined types (including `object`), so in most cases you don't have to convert values to strings before you display them.

For example, the following code lets the user input a line of text and displays that text:

```
string s = Console.ReadLine();
Console.WriteLine(s);
```

`Console.WriteLine()` also allows you to display formatted output in a way comparable to C's `printf()` function. To use `WriteLine()` in this way, you pass in a number of parameters. The first is a string containing markers in curly braces where the subsequent parameters will be inserted into the text. Each marker contains a zero-based index for the number of the parameter in the following list. For example, `{0}` represents the first parameter in the list. Consider the following code:

```
int i = 10;
int j = 20;
Console.WriteLine("{0} plus {1} equals {2}", i, j, i + j);
```

This code displays:

```
10 plus 20 equals 30
```

You can also specify a width for the value, and justify the text within that width, using positive values for right-justification and negative values for left-justification. To do this, use the format `{n,w}`, where n is the parameter index and w is the width value:

```
int i = 940;
int j = 73;
Console.WriteLine(" {0,4}\n+{1,4}\n ---- \n {2,4}", i, j, i + j);
```

The result of this is:

```
  940
+  73
 ----
 1013
```

Finally, you can also add a format string, together with an optional precision value. It is not possible to give a complete list of potential format strings because, as you will see in Chapter 8, "Strings and Regular Expressions," you can define your own format strings. However, the main ones in use for the predefined types are shown in the following table.

String	Description
`C`	Local currency format.
`D`	Decimal format. Converts an integer to base 10, and pads with leading zeros if a precision specifier is given.
`E`	Scientific (exponential) format. The precision specifier sets the number of decimal places (6 by default). The case of the format string (`e` or `E`) determines the case of the exponential symbol.
`F`	Fixed-point format; the precision specifier controls the number of decimal places. Zero is acceptable.
`G`	General format. Uses `E` or `F` formatting, depending on which is more compact.
`N`	Number format. Formats the number with commas as thousands separators, for example 32,767.44.
`P`	Percent format.
`X`	Hexadecimal format. The precision specifier can be used to pad with leading zeros.

Note that the format strings are normally case insensitive, except for e/E.

If you want to use a format string, you should place it immediately after the marker that gives the parameter number and field width, and separate it with a colon. For example, to format a decimal value as currency for the computer's locale, with precision to two decimal places, you would use C2:

```
decimal i = 940.23m;
decimal j = 73.7m;
Console.WriteLine(" {0,9:C2}\n+{1,9:C2}\n ---------\n {2,9:C2}", i, j, i + j);
```

The output of this in U.S. currency is:

```
    $940.23
+    $73.70
  ---------
  $1,013.93
```

As a final trick, you can also use placeholder characters instead of these format strings to map out formatting. For example:

```
double d = 0.234;
Console.WriteLine("{0:#.00}", d);
```

This displays as .23, because the # symbol is ignored if there is no character in that place, and zeros will either be replaced by the character in that position if there is one or be printed as a zero.

Using Comments

The next topic — adding comments to your code — looks very simple on the surface but can be complex.

Internal Comments within the Source Files

As noted earlier in this chapter, C# uses the traditional C-type single-line (// ...) and multiline (/* ... */) comments:

```
// This is a single-line comment
/* This comment
   spans multiple lines. */
```

Everything in a single-line comment, from the // to the end of the line, will be ignored by the compiler, and everything from an opening /* to the next */ in a multiline comment combination will be ignored. Obviously, you can't include the combination */ in any multiline comments, because this will be treated as the end of the comment.

It is actually possible to put multiline comments within a line of code:

```
Console.WriteLine(/* Here's a comment! */ "This will compile.");
```

Use inline comments with care because they can make code hard to read. However, they can be useful when debugging if, say, you temporarily want to try running the code with a different value somewhere:

```
DoSomething(Width, /*Height*/ 100);
```

Comment characters included in string literals are, of course, treated like normal characters:

```
string s = "/* This is just a normal string .*/";
```

XML Documentation

In addition to the C-type comments, illustrated in the preceding section, C# has a very neat feature that we want to highlight: the ability to produce documentation in XML format automatically from special comments. These comments are single-line comments but begin with three slashes (///) instead of the usual two. Within these comments, you can place XML tags containing documentation of the types and type members in your code.

The tags in the following table are recognized by the compiler.

Tag	Description
<c>	Marks up text within a line as code, for example <c>int i = 10;</c>.
<code>	Marks multiple lines as code.
<example>	Marks up a code example.
<exception>	Documents an exception class. (Syntax is verified by the compiler.)
<include>	Includes comments from another documentation file. (Syntax is verified by the compiler.)
<list>	Inserts a list into the documentation.
<param>	Marks up a method parameter. (Syntax is verified by the compiler.)
<paramref>	Indicates that a word is a method parameter. (Syntax is verified by the compiler.)
<permission>	Documents access to a member. (Syntax is verified by the compiler.)
<remarks>	Adds a description for a member.
<returns>	Documents the return value for a method.
<see>	Provides a cross-reference to another parameter. (Syntax is verified by the compiler.)
<seealso>	Provides a "see also" section in a description. (Syntax is verified by the compiler.)
<summary>	Provides a short summary of a type or member.
<value>	Describes a property.

To see how this works, add some XML comments to the `MathLibrary.cs` file from the "More on Compiling C# Files" section, and call it `Math.cs`. You will add a <summary> element for the class and for its `Add()` method, and also a <returns> element and two <param> elements for the `Add()` method:

```
// Math.cs
namespace Wrox.ProCSharp.Basics
{

   ///<summary>
   ///   Wrox.ProCSharp.Basics.Math class.
   ///   Provides a method to add two integers.
   ///</summary>
   public class Math
```

(continued)

(continued)

```
      {
         ///<summary>
         ///   The Add method allows us to add two integers.
         ///</summary>
         ///<returns>Result of the addition (int)</returns>
         ///<param name="x">First number to add</param>
         ///<param name="y">Second number to add</param>
         public int Add(int x, int y)
         {
            return x + y;
         }
      }
   }
```

The C# compiler can extract the XML elements from the special comments and use them to generate an XML file. To get the compiler to generate the XML documentation for an assembly, you specify the `/doc` option when you compile, together with the name of the file you want to be created:

```
csc /t:library /doc:Math.xml Math.cs
```

The compiler will throw an error if the XML comments do not result in a well-formed XML document.

This will generate an XML file named `Math.xml`, which looks like this:

```
<?xml version="1.0"?>
<doc>
   <assembly>
      <name>Math</name>
   </assembly>
   <members>
      <member name="T:Wrox.ProCSharp.Basics.Math">
         <summary>
            Wrox.ProCSharp.Basics.Math class.
            Provides a method to add two integers.
         </summary>
      </member>
      <member name=
            "M:Wrox.ProCSharp.Basics.Math.Add(System.Int32,System.Int32)">
         <summary>
            The Add method allows us to add two integers.
         </summary>
         <returns>Result of the addition (int)</returns>
         <param name="x">First number to add</param>
         <param name="y">Second number to add</param>
      </member>
   </members>
</doc>
```

Notice how the compiler has actually done some work for you; it has created an `<assembly>` element and also added a `<member>` element for each type or member of a type in the file. Each `<member>` element has a `name` attribute with the full name of the member as its value, prefixed by a letter that indicates whether this is a type (`T:`), field (`F:`), or member (`M:`).

The C# Preprocessor Directives

Besides the usual keywords, most of which you have now encountered, C# also includes a number of commands that are known as *preprocessor directives*. These commands never actually get translated to any commands in your executable code, but instead they affect aspects of the compilation process. For example, you can use preprocessor directives to prevent the compiler from compiling certain portions of your code. You might do this if you are planning to release two versions of the code — a basic version and an enterprise version that will have more features. You could use preprocessor directives to prevent the compiler from compiling code related to the additional features when you are compiling the basic version of the software. Another scenario is that you might have written bits of code that are intended to provide you with debugging information. You probably don't want those portions of code compiled when you actually ship the software.

The preprocessor directives are all distinguished by beginning with the # symbol.

C++ developers will recognize the preprocessor directives as something that plays an important part in C and C++. However, there aren't as many preprocessor directives in C#, and they are not used as often. C# provides other mechanisms, such as custom attributes, that achieve some of the same effects as C++ directives. Also, note that C# doesn't actually have a separate preprocessor in the way that C++ does. The so-called preprocessor directives are actually handled by the compiler. Nevertheless, C# retains the name preprocessor directive because these commands give the impression of a preprocessor.

The next sections briefly cover the purposes of the preprocessor directives.

#define and #undef

`#define` is used like this:

```
#define DEBUG
```

What this does is tell the compiler that a symbol with the given name (in this case `DEBUG`) exists. It is a little bit like declaring a variable, except that this variable doesn't really have a value — it just exists. And this symbol isn't part of your actual code; it exists only for the benefit of the compiler, while the compiler is compiling the code, and has no meaning within the C# code itself.

`#undef` does the opposite, and removes the definition of a symbol:

```
#undef DEBUG
```

If the symbol doesn't exist in the first place, then `#undef` has no effect. Similarly, `#define` has no effect if a symbol already exists.

You need to place any `#define` and `#undef` directives at the beginning of the C# source file, before any code that declares any objects to be compiled.

`#define` isn't much use on its own, but when combined with other preprocessor directives, especially `#if`, it becomes very powerful.

Incidentally, you might notice some changes from the usual C# syntax. Preprocessor directives are not terminated by semicolons and normally constitute the only command on a line. That's because for the preprocessor directives, C# abandons its usual practice of requiring commands to be separated by semicolons. If it sees a preprocessor directive, it assumes that the next command is on the next line.

#if, #elif, #else, and #endif

These directives inform the compiler whether to compile a block of code. Consider this method:

```
int DoSomeWork(double x)
{
   // do something
   #if DEBUG
      Console.WriteLine("x is " + x);
   #endif
}
```

This code will compile as normal, except for the `Console.WriteLine()` method call that is contained inside the `#if` clause. This line will be executed only if the symbol `DEBUG` has been defined by a previous `#define` directive. When the compiler finds the `#if` directive, it checks to see if the symbol concerned exists and compiles the code inside the `#if` clause only if the symbol does exist. Otherwise, the compiler simply ignores all the code until it reaches the matching `#endif` directive. Typical practice is to define the symbol `DEBUG` while you are debugging and have various bits of debugging-related code inside `#if` clauses. Then, when you are close to shipping, you simply comment out the `#define` directive, and all the debugging code miraculously disappears, the size of the executable file gets smaller, and your end users don't get confused by being shown debugging information. (Obviously, you would do more testing to make sure your code still works without `DEBUG` defined.) This technique is very common in C and C++ programming and is known as *conditional compilation.*

The `#elif` (`=else if`) and `#else` directives can be used in `#if` blocks and have intuitively obvious meanings. It is also possible to nest `#if` blocks:

```
#define ENTERPRISE
#define W2K

// further on in the file

#if ENTERPRISE
   // do something
   #if W2K
      // some code that is only relevant to enterprise
      // edition running on W2K
   #endif
#elif PROFESSIONAL
   // do something else
#else
   // code for the leaner version
#endif
```

Note that, unlike the situation in C++, using `#if` *is not the only way to compile code conditionally. C# provides an alternative mechanism through the* `Conditional` *attribute, which is explored in Chapter 13, "Reflection."*

`#if` and `#elif` support a limited range of logical operators too, using the operators `!`, `==`, `!=`, and `||`. A symbol is considered to be `true` if it exists and `false` if it doesn't. For example:

```
#if W2K && (ENTERPRISE==false)   // if W2K is defined but ENTERPRISE isn't
```

#warning and #error

Two other very useful preprocessor directives are #warning and #error. These will respectively cause a warning or an error to be raised when the compiler encounters them. If the compiler sees a #warning directive, it will display whatever text appears after the #warning to the user, after which compilation continues. If it encounters a #error directive, it will display the subsequent text to the user as if it were a compilation error message and then immediately abandon the compilation, so no IL code will be generated.

You can use these directives as checks that you haven't done anything silly with your #define statements; you can also use the #warning statements to remind yourself to do something:

```
#if DEBUG && RELEASE
   #error "You've defined DEBUG and RELEASE simultaneously!"
#endif

#warning "Don't forget to remove this line before the boss tests the code!"
   Console.WriteLine("*I hate this job.*");
```

#region and #endregion

The #region and #endregion directives are used to indicate that a certain block of code is to be treated as a single block with a given name, like this:

```
#region Member Field Declarations
   int x;
   double d;
   Currency balance;
#endregion
```

This doesn't look that useful by itself; it doesn't affect the compilation process in any way. However, the real advantage is that these directives are recognized by some editors, including the Visual Studio .NET editor. These editors can use these directives to lay out your code better on the screen. You will see how this works in Chapter 15, "Visual Studio 2008."

#line

The #line directive can be used to alter the file name and line number information that is output by the compiler in warnings and error messages. You probably won't want to use this directive that often. It's most useful when you are coding in conjunction with some other package that alters the code you are typing in before sending it to the compiler. In this situation, line numbers, or perhaps the file names reported by the compiler, won't match up to the line numbers in the files or the file names you are editing. The #line directive can be used to restore the match. You can also use the syntax #line default to restore the line to the default line numbering:

```
#line 164 "Core.cs"    // We happen to know this is line 164 in the file
                       // Core.cs, before the intermediate
                       // package mangles it.

// later on

#line default      // restores default line numbering
```

#pragma

The `#pragma` directive can either suppress or restore specific compiler warnings. Unlike command-line options, the `#pragma` directive can be implemented on a class or method level, allowing a fine-grained control of what warnings are suppressed and when. The following example disables the "field not used" warning and then restores it after the `MyClass` class compiles:

```
#pragma warning disable 169
public class MyClass
{
  int neverUsedField;
}
#pragma warning restore 169
```

C# Programming Guidelines

The final section of this chapter supplies the guidelines you need to bear in mind when writing C# programs.

Rules for Identifiers

This section examines the rules governing what names you can use for variables, classes, methods, and so on. Note that the rules presented in this section are not merely guidelines: they are enforced by the C# compiler.

Identifiers are the names you give to variables, to user-defined types such as classes and structs, and to members of these types. Identifiers are case sensitive, so, for example, variables named `interestRate` and `InterestRate` would be recognized as different variables. Following are a few rules determining what identifiers you can use in C#:

- They must begin with a letter or underscore, although they can contain numeric characters.
- You can't use C# keywords as identifiers.

The following table lists the C# reserved keywords.

abstract	event	New	struct
as	explicit	Null	switch
base	extern	Object	this
bool	false	Operator	throw
break	finally	Out	true
byte	fixed	Override	try
case	float	Params	typeof
catch	for	Private	uint
char	foreach	Protected	ulong
checked	goto	Public	unchecked
class	if	Readonly	unsafe

const	implicit	Ref	ushort
continue	in	Return	using
decimal	int	Sbyte	virtual
default	interface	Sealed	volatile
delegate	internal	Short	void
do	is	Sizeof	while
double	lock	Stackalloc	
else	long	Static	
enum	namespace	String	

If you do need to use one of these words as an identifier (for example, if you are accessing a class written in a different language), you can prefix the identifier with the `@` symbol to indicate to the compiler that what follows is to be treated as an identifier, not as a C# keyword (so `abstract` is not a valid identifier, but `@abstract` is).

Finally, identifiers can also contain Unicode characters, specified using the syntax `\uXXXX`, where `XXXX` is the four-digit hex code for the Unicode character. The following are some examples of valid identifiers:

- `Name`
- `Überfluß`
- `_Identifier`
- `\u005fIdentifier`

The last two items in this list are identical and interchangeable (because `005f` is the Unicode code for the underscore character), so obviously these identifiers couldn't both be declared in the same scope. Note that although syntactically you are allowed to use the underscore character in identifiers, this isn't recommended in most situations. That's because it doesn't follow the guidelines for naming variables that Microsoft has written to ensure that developers use the same conventions, making it easier to read each other's code.

Usage Conventions

In any development language, there usually arise certain traditional programming styles. The styles are not part of the language itself but are conventions concerning, for example, how variables are named or how certain classes, methods, or functions are used. If most developers using that language follow the same conventions, it makes it easier for different developers to understand each other's code — which in turn generally helps program maintainability. For example, a common (though not universal) convention in Visual Basic 6 was that variables that represent strings have names beginning with lowercase `s` or lowercase `str`, as in the Visual Basic 6 statements `Dim sResult As String` or `Dim strMessage As String`. Conventions do, however, depend on the language and the environment. For example, C++ developers programming on the Windows platform have traditionally used the prefixes `psz` or `lpsz` to indicate strings—`char *pszResult; char *lpszMessage;`—but on Unix machines it's more common not to use any such prefixes: `char *Result; char *Message;`.

You'll notice from the sample code in this book that the convention in C# is to name variables without prefixes: `string Result; string Message;`.

The convention by which variable names are prefixed with letters that represent the data type is known as Hungarian notation. It means that other developers reading the code can immediately tell from the variable name what data type the variable represents. Hungarian notation is widely regarded as redundant in these days of smart editors and IntelliSense.

Whereas, with many languages, usage conventions simply evolved as the language was used, with C# and the whole of the .NET Framework, Microsoft has written very comprehensive usage guidelines, which are detailed in the .NET/C# MSDN documentation. This should mean that, right from the start, .NET programs will have a high degree of interoperability in terms of developers being able to understand code. The guidelines have also been developed with the benefit of some 20 years' hindsight in object-oriented programming, and as a result have been carefully thought out and appear to have been well received in the developer community, to judge by the relevant newsgroups. Hence the guidelines are well worth following.

It should be noted, however, that the guidelines are not the same as language specifications. You should try to follow the guidelines when you can. Nevertheless, you won't run into problems if you do have a good reason for not doing so — for example, you won't get a compilation error because you don't follow these guidelines. The general rule is that if you don't follow the usage guidelines you must have a convincing reason. Departing from the guidelines should be a positive decision rather than simply not bothering. Also, if you compare the guidelines with the samples in the remainder of this book, you'll notice that in numerous examples we have chosen not to follow the conventions. That's usually because the conventions are designed for much larger programs than our samples, and although they are great if you are writing a complete software package, they are not really so suitable for small 20-line standalone programs. In many cases, following the conventions would have made our samples harder, rather than easier, to follow.

The full guidelines for good programming style are quite extensive. This section is confined to describing some of the more important guidelines, as well as the ones most likely to surprise you. If you want to make absolutely certain that your code follows the usage guidelines completely, you will need to refer to the MSDN documentation.

Naming Conventions

One important aspect to making your programs understandable is how you choose to name your items — and that includes naming variables, methods, classes, enumerations, and namespaces.

It is intuitively obvious that your names should reflect the purpose of the item and should not clash with other names. The general philosophy in the .NET Framework is also that the name of a variable should reflect the purpose of that variable instance and not the data type. For example, `height` is a good name for a variable, whereas `integerValue` isn't. However, you will probably feel that that principle is an ideal that is hard to achieve. Particularly when you are dealing with controls, in most cases, you'll probably be happier sticking with variable names like `confirmationDialog` and `chooseEmployeeListBox`, which do indicate the data type in the name.

The following sections look at some of the things you need to think about when choosing names.

Casing of Names

In many cases you should use *Pascal casing* for names. Pascal casing means that the first letter of each word in a name is capitalized: `EmployeeSalary`, `ConfirmationDialog`, `PlainTextEncoding`. You will notice that essentially all of the names of namespaces, classes, and members in the base classes follow Pascal casing. In particular, the convention of joining words using the underscore character is discouraged. So, you should try not to use names like `employee_salary`. It has also been common in other languages to use all capitals for names of constants. This is not advised in C# because such names are harder to read—the convention is to use Pascal casing throughout:

```
const int MaximumLength;
```

The only other casing scheme that you are advised to use is *camel casing*. Camel casing is similar to Pascal casing, except that the first letter of the first word in the name is not capitalized: `employeeSalary`, `confirmationDialog`, `plainTextEncoding`. Following are three situations in which you are advised to use camel casing:

- For names of all private member fields in types:

```
public int subscriberId;
```

Note, however, that often it is conventional to prefix names of member fields with an underscore:

```
public int _subscriberId;
```

- For names of all parameters passed to methods:

```
public void RecordSale(string salesmanName, int quantity);
```

- To distinguish items that would otherwise have the same name. A common example is when a property wraps around a field:

```
private string employeeName;


public string EmployeeName
{
   get
   {
      return employeeName;

   }

}
```

If you are doing this, you should always use camel casing for the private member and Pascal casing for the public or protected member, so that other classes that use your code see only names in Pascal case (except for parameter names).

You should also be wary about case sensitivity. C# is case sensitive, so it is syntactically correct for names in C# to differ only by the case, as in the previous examples. However, you should bear in mind that your assemblies might at some point be called from Visual Basic .NET applications — and *Visual Basic .NET is not case sensitive*. Hence, if you do use names that differ only by case, it is important to do so only in situations in which both names will never be seen outside your assembly. (The previous example qualifies as okay because camel case is used with the name that is attached to a `private` variable.) Otherwise, you may prevent other code written in Visual Basic .NET from being able to use your assembly correctly.

Name Styles

You should be consistent about your style of names. For example, if one of the methods in a class is called `ShowConfirmationDialog()`, then you should not give another method a name like `ShowDialogWarning()` or `WarningDialogShow()`. The other method should be called `ShowWarningDialog()`.

Namespace Names

Namespace names are particularly important to design carefully to avoid risk of ending up with the same name for one of your namespaces as someone else uses. Remember, namespace names are the *only* way that .NET distinguishes names of objects in shared assemblies. So, if you use the same namespace name for your software package as another package, and both packages get installed on the same computer, there are going to be problems. Because of this, it's almost always a good idea to create a top-level namespace with the name of your company and then nest successive namespaces that narrow down the technology, group, or department you are working in or the name of the package your classes are intended for. Microsoft recommends namespace names that begin with `<CompanyName>.<TechnologyName>` as in these two examples:

```
WeaponsOfDestructionCorp.RayGunControllers
WeaponsOfDestructionCorp.Viruses
```

Names and Keywords

It is important that the names do not clash with any keywords. In fact, if you attempt to name an item in your code with a word that happens to be a C# keyword, you'll almost certainly get a syntax error because the compiler will assume that the name refers to a statement. However, because of the possibility that your classes will be accessed by code written in other languages, it is also important that you don't use names that are keywords in other .NET languages. Generally speaking, C++ keywords are similar to C# keywords, so confusion with C++ is unlikely, and those commonly encountered keywords that are unique to Visual C++ tend to start with two underscore characters. Like C#, C++ keywords are spelled in lowercase, so if you hold to the convention of naming your public classes and members with Pascal-style names, they will always have at least one uppercase letter in their names, and there will be no risk of clashes with C++ keywords. However, you are more likely to have problems with Visual Basic .NET, which has many more keywords than C# does, and being non-case-sensitive means that you cannot rely on Pascal-style names for your classes and methods.

The following table lists the keywords and standard function calls in Visual Basic .NET, which you should avoid, if possible, in whatever case combination, for your public C# classes.

Abs	Do	Loc	RGB
Add	Double	Local	Right
AddHandler	Each	Lock	RmDir
AddressOf	Else	LOF	Rnd
Alias	ElseIf	Log	RTrim
And	Empty	Long	SaveSettings
Ansi	End	Loop	Second
AppActivate	Enum	LTrim	Seek
Append	EOF	Me	Select
As	Erase	Mid	SetAttr
Asc	Err	Minute	SetException
Assembly	Error	MIRR	Shared
Atan	Event	MkDir	Shell

Auto
Beep
Binary
BitAnd
BitNot
BitOr
BitXor
Boolean
ByRef
Byte
ByVal
Call
Case
Catch
CBool
CByte
CDate
CDbl
CDec
ChDir
ChDrive
Choose
Chr
CInt
Class
Clear
CLng
Close
Collection
Command
Compare
Const
Exit
Exp
Explicit
ExternalSource
False
FileAttr
FileCopy
FileDateTime
FileLen
Filter
Finally
Fix
For
Format
FreeFile
Friend
Function
FV
Get
GetAllSettings
GetAttr
GetException
GetObject
GetSetting
GetType
GoTo
Handles
Hex
Hour
If
Iif
Implements
Module
Month
MustInherit
MustOverride
MyBase
MyClass
Namespace
New
Next
Not
Nothing
NotInheritable
NotOverridable
Now
NPer
NPV
Null
Object
Oct
Off
On
Open
Option
Optional
Or
Overloads
Overridable
Overrides
ParamArray
Pmt
PPmt
Preserve
Short
Sign
Sin
Single
SLN
Space
Spc
Split
Sqrt
Static
Step
Stop
Str
StrComp
StrConv
Strict
String
Structure
Sub
Switch
SYD
SyncLock
Tab
Tan
Text
Then
Throw
TimeOfDay
Timer
TimeSerial
TimeValue
To

Cos	Imports	Print	Today
CreateObject	In	Private	Trim
CShort	Inherits	Property	Try
CSng	Input	Public	TypeName
CStr	InStr	Put	TypeOf
CurDir	Int	PV	UBound
Date	Integer	QBColor	UCase
DateAdd	Interface	Raise	Unicode
DateDiff	Ipmt	RaiseEvent	Unlock
DatePart	IRR	Randomize	Until
DateSerial	Is	Rate	Val
DateValue	IsArray	Read	Weekday
Day	IsDate	ReadOnly	While
DDB	IsDbNull	ReDim	Width
Decimal	IsNumeric	Remove	With
Declare	Item	RemoveHandler	WithEvents
Default	Kill	Rename	Write
Delegate	Lcase	Replace	WriteOnly
DeleteSetting	Left	Reset	Xor
Dim	Lib	Resume	Year
Dir	Line	Return	

Use of Properties and Methods

One area that can cause confusion in a class is whether a particular quantity should be represented by a property or a method. The rules here are not hard and fast, but in general, you ought to use a property if something really should look and feel like a variable. (If you're not sure what a property is, see Chapter 3, "Objects and Types.") This means, among other things, that:

- Client code should be able to read its value. Write-only properties are not recommended, so, for example, use a `SetPassword()` method, not a write-only `Password` property.
- Reading the value should not take too long. The fact that something is a property usually suggests that reading it will be relatively quick.
- Reading the value should not have any observable and unexpected side effect. Further, setting the value of a property should not have any side effect that is not directly related to the property. Setting the width of a dialog box has the obvious effect of changing the appearance of the dialog box on the screen. That's fine, because that's obviously related to the property in question.

- It should be possible to set properties in any order. In particular, it is not good practice when setting a property to throw an exception because another related property has not yet been set. For example, if in order to use a class that accesses a database, you need to set `ConnectionString`, `UserName`, and `Password`, then the author of the class should make sure the class is implemented so that the user really can set them in any order.
- Successive reads of a property should give the same result. If the value of a property is likely to change unpredictably, you should code it up as a method instead. `Speed`, in a class that monitors the motion of an automobile, is not a good candidate for a property. Use a `GetSpeed()` method here; but, `Weight` and `EngineSize` are good candidates for properties because they will not change for a given object.

If the item you are coding satisfies all of the preceding criteria, it is probably a good candidate for a property. Otherwise, you should use a method.

Use of Fields

The guidelines are pretty simple here. Fields should almost always be private, except that in some cases it may be acceptable for constant or read-only fields to be public. The reason is that if you make a field public, you may hinder your ability to extend or modify the class in the future.

The previous guidelines should give you a foundation of good practices, and you should also use them in conjunction with good object-oriented programming style.

A final helpful note to keep in mind is that Microsoft has been fairly careful about being consistent and has followed its own guidelines when writing the .NET base classes. So a very good way to get an intuitive feel for the conventions to follow when writing .NET code is to simply look at the base classes — see how classes, members, and namespaces are named, and how the class hierarchy works. Consistency between the base classes and your classes will help in readability and maintainability.

Summary

This chapter examined some of the basic syntax of C#, covering the areas needed to write simple C# programs. We covered a lot of ground, but much of it will be instantly recognizable to developers who are familiar with any C-style language (or even JavaScript).

You have seen that although C# syntax is similar to C++ and Java syntax, there are many minor differences. You have also seen that in many areas this syntax is combined with facilities to write code very quickly, for example high-quality string handling facilities. C# also has a strongly defined type system, based on a distinction between value and reference types. Chapters 3 and 4 cover the C# object-oriented programming features.

3

Objects and Types

So far, you've been introduced to some of the building blocks of the C# language, including variables, data types, and program flow statements, and you have seen a few very short complete programs containing little more than the `Main()` method. What you haven't really seen yet is how to put all of these together to form a longer, complete program. The key to this lies in working with classes — the subject of this chapter. In particular, this chapter covers:

- The differences between classes and structs
- Class members
- Passing values by value and by reference
- Method overloading
- Constructors and static constructors
- Read-only fields
- Partial classes
- Static classes
- The `Object` class, from which all other types are derived

Note that we cover inheritance and features related to inheritance in Chapter 4, "Inheritance."

This chapter introduces the basic syntax associated with classes. However, we assume that you are already familiar with the underlying principles of using classes — for example, that you know what a constructor or a property is. This chapter is largely confined to applying those principles in C# code.

In this chapter, we introduce and explain those concepts that are not necessarily supported by most object-oriented languages. For example, although object constructors are a widely used concept that you should be familiar with, static constructors are something new to C#, so this chapter explains how static constructors work.

Classes and Structs

Classes and structs are essentially templates from which you can create objects. Each object contains data and has methods to manipulate and access that data. The class defines what data and functionality each particular object (called an *instance*) of that class can contain. For example, if you have a class that represents a customer, it might define fields such as `CustomerID`, `FirstName`, `LastName`, and `Address`, which you will use to hold information about a particular customer. It might also define functionality that acts upon the data stored in these fields. You can then instantiate an object of this class to represent one specific customer, set the field values for that instance, and use its functionality.

```
class PhoneCustomer
{
   public const string DayOfSendingBill = "Monday";
   public int CustomerID;
   public string FirstName;
   public string LastName;
}
```

Structs differ from classes in the way that they are stored in memory and accessed (classes are reference types stored in the heap; structs are value types stored on the stack), and in some of their features (for example, structs don't support inheritance). You will tend to use structs for smaller data types for performance reasons. In terms of syntax, however, structs look very similar to classes; the main difference is that you use the keyword `struct` instead of `class` to declare them. For example, if you wanted all `PhoneCustomer` instances to be allocated on the stack instead of the managed heap, you could write:

```
struct PhoneCustomerStruct
{
   public const string DayOfSendingBill = "Monday";
   public int CustomerID;
   public string FirstName;
   public string LastName;
}
```

For both classes and structs, you use the keyword `new` to declare an instance. This keyword creates the object and initializes it; in the following example, the default behavior is to zero out its fields:

```
PhoneCustomer myCustomer = new PhoneCustomer();       // works for a class
PhoneCustomerStruct myCustomer2 = new PhoneCustomerStruct();// works for a struct
```

In most cases, you'll use classes much more often than structs. Therefore, we discuss classes first and then the differences between classes and structs and the specific reasons why you might choose to use a struct instead of a class. Unless otherwise stated, however, you can assume that code presented for a class will work equally well for a struct.

Class Members

The data and functions within a class are known as the class's *members*. Microsoft's official terminology distinguishes between data members and function members. In addition to these members, classes can contain nested types (such as other classes). All members of a class can be declared as `public` (in which case they are directly accessible from outside the class) or as `private` (in which case they are visible only to other code within the class), just as in Visual Basic, C++, and Java. C# also has variants on this theme, such as `protected` (which indicates a member is visible only to the class in question and to any derived classes). Chapter 4 provides a comprehensive list of the different accessibilities.

Data Members

Data members are those members that contain the data for the class — fields, constants, and events. Data members can be either static (associated with the class as a whole) or instance (each instance of the class has its own copy of the data). As usual for object-oriented languages, a class member is always an instance member unless it is explicitly declared as `static`.

Fields are any variables associated with the class. You have already seen fields in use in the `PhoneCustomer` class in the previous example.

Once you have instantiated a `PhoneCustomer` object, you can then access these fields using the `Object.FieldName` syntax, as shown in this example:

```
PhoneCustomer Customer1 = new PhoneCustomer();
Customer1.FirstName = "Simon";
```

Constants can be associated with classes in the same way as variables. You declare a constant using the `const` keyword. Once again, if it is declared as `public`, it will be accessible from outside the class.

```
class PhoneCustomer
{
   public const string DayOfSendingBill = "Monday";
   public int CustomerID;
   public string FirstName;
   public string LastName;
}
```

Events are class members that allow an object to notify a caller whenever something noteworthy happens, such as a field or property of the class changing, or some form of user interaction occurring. The client can have code, known as an event handler, that reacts to the event. Chapter 7, "Delegates and Events," looks at events in detail.

Function Members

Function members are those members that provide some functionality for manipulating the data in the class. They include methods, properties, constructors, finalizers, operators, and indexers.

Methods are functions that are associated with a particular class. They can be either instance methods, which work on a particular instance of a class, or static methods, which provide more generic functionality that doesn't require you to instantiate a class (like the `Console.WriteLine()` method). Methods are discussed in the next section.

Properties are sets of functions that can be accessed from the client in a similar way to the public fields of the class. C# provides a specific syntax for implementing read and write properties on your classes, so you don't have to jury-rig methods whose names have the words `Get` or `Set` embedded in them. Because there's a dedicated syntax for properties that is distinct from that for normal functions, the illusion of objects as actual things is strengthened for client code.

Constructors are special functions that are called automatically when an object is instantiated. They must have the same name as the class to which they belong and cannot have a return type. Constructors are useful for initializing the values of fields.

Finalizers are similar to constructors but are called when the CLR detects that an object is no longer needed. They have the same name as the class, preceded by a tilde (~). C++ programmers should note that finalizers are used much less frequently in C# than their nearest C++ equivalent, destructors, because the CLR handles garbage collection automatically. Also, it is impossible to predict precisely when a finalizer will be called. Finalizers are discussed in Chapter 12, "Memory Management and Pointers."

Operators, at their simplest, are actions like + or –. When you add two integers, you are, strictly speaking, using the + operator for integers. However, C# also allows you to specify how existing operators will work with your own classes (*operator overloading*). Chapter 6, "Operators and Casts," looks at operators in detail.

Indexers allow your objects to be indexed in the same way as an array or collection. This topic is also covered in Chapter 6.

Methods

In Visual Basic, C, and C++, you could define global functions that were not associated with a particular class. This is not the case in C#. As noted earlier, in C# every function must be associated with a class or struct.

Note that official C# terminology does in fact make a distinction between functions and methods. In C# terminology, the term "function member" includes not only methods, but also other nondata members of a class or struct. This includes indexers, operators, constructors, destructors, and also — perhaps somewhat surprisingly — properties. These are contrasted with data members: fields, constants, and events.

Declaring Methods

The syntax for defining a method in C# is just what you'd expect from a C-style language and is virtually identical to the syntax in C++ and Java. The main syntactical difference from C++ is that, in C#, each method is separately declared as public or private. It is not possible to use `public:` blocks to group several method definitions. Also, all C# methods are declared and defined in the class definition. There is no facility in C# to separate the method implementation as there is in C++.

In C#, the definition of a method consists of any method modifiers (such as the method's accessibility), the type of the return value, followed by the name of the method, followed by a list of input arguments enclosed in parentheses, followed by the body of the method enclosed in curly braces:

```
[modifiers] return_type MethodName([parameters])
{
   // Method body
}
```

Each parameter consists of the name of the type of the parameter, and the name by which it can be referenced in the body of the method. Also, if the method returns a value, a return statement must be used with the return value to indicate each exit point. For example:

```
public bool IsSquare(Rectangle rect)
{
   return (rect.Height == rect.Width);
}
```

This code uses one of the .NET base classes, `System.Drawing.Rectangle`, which represents a rectangle.

If the method doesn't return anything, you specify a return type of void because you can't omit the return type altogether, and if it takes no arguments, you still need to include an empty set of parentheses after the method name (as with the `Main()` method). In this case, including a return statement is optional — the method returns automatically when the closing curly brace is reached. You should note that a method can contain as many return statements as required:

```
public bool IsPositive(int value)
{
   if (value < 0)
      return false;
   return true;
}
```

Invoking Methods

The syntax for invoking a method is exactly the same in C# as it is in C++ and Java. And, the only difference between C# and Visual Basic is that round brackets must always be used when invoking the method in C# — this is actually simpler than the Visual Basic 6 set of rules whereby brackets were sometimes necessary and at other times not allowed.

The following example, `MathTest`, illustrates the syntax for definition and instantiation of classes, and definition and invocation of methods. Besides the class that contains the `Main()` method, it defines a class named `MathTest`, which contains a couple of methods and a field.

```
using System;

namespace Wrox.ProCSharp.MathTestSample
{
   class MainEntryPoint
   {
      static void Main()
      {
         // Try calling some static functions.
         Console.WriteLine("Pi is " + MathTest.GetPi());
         int x = MathTest.GetSquareOf(5);
         Console.WriteLine("Square of 5 is " + x);

         // Instantiate at MathTest object
         MathTest math = new MathTest();   // this is C#'s way of
                                           // instantiating a reference type

         // Call non-static methods
         math.value = 30;
         Console.WriteLine(
            "Value field of math variable contains " + math.value);
         Console.WriteLine("Square of 30 is " + math.GetSquare());
      }
   }

   // Define a class named MathTest on which we will call a method
   class MathTest
   {
      public int value;

      public int GetSquare()
      {
         return value*value;
      }

      public static int GetSquareOf(int x)
      {
         return x*x;
      }

      public static double GetPi()
      {
         return 3.14159;
      }
   }
}
```

Running the `MathTest` example produces these results:

csc MathTest.cs

```
Microsoft (R) Visual C# Compiler version 9.00.20404
for Microsoft (R) .NET Framework version 3.5
Copyright (C) Microsoft Corporation. All rights reserved.

MathTest.exe
Pi is 3.14159
Square of 5 is 25
Value field of math variable contains 30
Square of 30 is 900
```

As you can see from the code, the `MathTest` class contains a field that contains a number, as well as a method to find the square of this number. It also contains two static methods, one to return the value of pi and one to find the square of the number passed in as a parameter.

Some features of this class are not really good examples of C# program design. For example, `GetPi()` would usually be implemented as a `const` field, but following good design here would mean using some concepts that we have not yet introduced.

Most of the syntax in the preceding example should be familiar to C++ and Java developers. If your background is in Visual Basic, just think of the `MathTest` class as being like a Visual Basic class module that implements fields and methods. There are a couple of points to watch out for though, whatever your language.

Passing Parameters to Methods

In general, parameters can be passed into methods by reference or by value. When a variable is passed by reference, the called method gets the actual variable — so any changes made to the variable inside the method persist when the method exits. But, when a variable is passed by value, the called method gets an identical copy of the variable — which means any changes made are lost when the method exits. For complex data types, passing by reference is more efficient because of the large amount of data that must be copied when passing by value.

In C#, all parameters are passed by value unless you specifically say otherwise. This is the same behavior as in C++ but the opposite of Visual Basic. However, you need to be careful in understanding the implications of this for reference types. Because reference type variables hold only a reference to an object, it is this reference that will be copied, not the object itself. Hence, changes made to the underlying object will persist. Value type variables, in contrast, hold the actual data, so a copy of the data itself will be passed into the method. An `int`, for instance, is passed by value to a method, and any changes that the method makes to the value of that `int` do not change the value of the original `int` object. Conversely, if an array or any other reference type, such as a class, is passed into a method, and the method uses the reference to change a value in that array, the new value is reflected in the original array object.

Here is an example, `ParameterTest.cs`, that demonstrates this:

```
using System;

namespace Wrox.ProCSharp.ParameterTestSample
{
   class ParameterTest
   {
      static void SomeFunction(int[] ints, int i)
      {
         ints[0] = 100;
         i = 100;
      }

      public static int Main()
```

```
        {
            int i = 0;
            int[] ints = { 0, 1, 2, 4, 8 };
            // Display the original values.
            Console.WriteLine("i = " + i);
            Console.WriteLine("ints[0] = " + ints[0]);
            Console.WriteLine("Calling SomeFunction...");

            // After this method returns, ints will be changed,
            // but i will not.
            SomeFunction(ints, i);
            Console.WriteLine("i = " + i);
            Console.WriteLine("ints[0] = " + ints[0]);
            return 0;
        }
    }
}
```

The output of this is:

csc ParameterTest.cs

```
Microsoft (R) Visual C# Compiler version 9.00.20404
for Microsoft (R) .NET Framework version 3.5
Copyright (C) Microsoft Corporation. All rights reserved.

ParameterTest.exe
i = 0
ints[0] = 0
Calling SomeFunction...
i = 0
ints[0] = 100
```

Notice how the value of `i` remains unchanged, but the value changed in `ints` is also changed in the original array.

The behavior of strings is different again. This is because strings are immutable (if you alter a string's value, you create an entirely new string), so strings don't display the typical reference-type behavior. Any changes made to a string within a method call won't affect the original string. This point is discussed in more detail in Chapter 8, "Strings and Regular Expressions."

ref Parameters

As mentioned, passing variables by value is the default, but you can force value parameters to be passed by reference. To do so, use the `ref` keyword. If a parameter is passed to a method, and if the input argument for that method is prefixed with the `ref` keyword, any changes that the method makes to the variable will affect the value of the original object:

```
static void SomeFunction(int[] ints, ref int i)
{
   ints[0] = 100;
   i = 100;      // The change to i will persist after SomeFunction() exits.
}
```

You will also need to add the `ref` keyword when you invoke the method:

```
SomeFunction(ints, ref i);
```

Adding the `ref` keyword in C# serves the same purpose as using the `&` syntax in C++ to specify passing by reference. However, C# makes the behavior more explicit (thus hopefully preventing bugs) by requiring the use of the `ref` keyword when invoking the method.

Finally, it is also important to understand that C# continues to apply initialization requirements to parameters passed to methods. Any variable must be initialized before it is passed into a method, whether it is passed in by value or by reference.

out Parameters

In C-style languages, it is common for functions to be able to output more than one value from a single routine. This is accomplished using output parameters, by assigning the output values to variables that have been passed to the method by reference. Often, the starting values of the variables that are passed by reference are unimportant. Those values will be overwritten by the function, which may never even look at any previous value.

It would be convenient if you could use the same convention in C#. However, C# requires that variables be initialized with a starting value before they are referenced. Although you could initialize your input variables with meaningless values before passing them into a function that will fill them with real, meaningful ones, this practice seems at best needless and at worst confusing. However, there is a way to short-circuit the C# compiler's insistence on initial values for input arguments.

You do this with the `out` keyword. When a method's input argument is prefixed with `out`, that method can be passed a variable that has not been initialized. The variable is passed by reference, so any changes that the method makes to the variable will persist when control returns from the called method. Again, you also need to use the `out` keyword when you call the method, as well as when you define it:

```
static void SomeFunction(out int i)
{
   i = 100;
}

public static int Main()
{
   int i; // note how i is declared but not initialized.
   SomeFunction(out i);
   Console.WriteLine(i);
   return 0;
}
```

The `out` keyword is an example of something new in C# that has no analogy in either Visual Basic or C++ and that has been introduced to make C# more secure against bugs. If an `out` parameter isn't assigned a value within the body of the function, the method won't compile.

Method Overloading

C# supports method overloading — several versions of the method that have different signatures (that is, the same name, but a different number of parameters and or different parameter data types). However, C# does not support default parameters in the way that, say, C++ or Visual Basic does. In order to overload methods, you simply declare the methods with the same name but different numbers or types of parameters:

```
class ResultDisplayer
{
   void DisplayResult(string result)
   {
      // implementation
   }
```

```
      void DisplayResult(int result)
      {
         // implementation
      }
   }
```

Because C# does not support optional parameters, you will need to use method overloading to achieve the same effect:

```
   class MyClass
   {
      int DoSomething(int x)    // want 2nd parameter with default value 10
      {
         DoSomething(x, 10);
      }

      int DoSomething(int x, int y)
      {
         // implementation
      }
   }
```

As in any language, method overloading carries with it the potential for subtle runtime bugs if the wrong overload is called. Chapter 4 discusses how to code defensively against these problems. For now, you should know that C# does place some minimum differences on the parameters of overloaded methods:

- It is not sufficient for two methods to differ only in their return type.
- It is not sufficient for two methods to differ only by virtue of a parameter having been declared as `ref` or `out`.

Properties

Properties are unusual in that they represent an idea that C# has taken from Visual Basic, not from C++ and Java. The idea of a property is that it is a method or pair of methods that are dressed to look like a field as far as any client code is concerned. A good example of this is the `Height` property of a Windows Form. Suppose that you have the following code:

```
// mainForm is of type System.Windows.Forms
mainForm.Height = 400;
```

On executing this code, the height of the window will be set to 400, and you will see the window resize on the screen. Syntactically, this code looks like you're setting a field, but in fact you are calling a property accessor that contains code to resize the form.

To define a property in C#, you use the following syntax:

```
public string SomeProperty
{
   get
   {
      return "This is the property value.";
   }
   set
   {
      // do whatever needs to be done to set the property.
   }
}
```

The get accessor takes no parameters and must return the same type as the declared property. You should not specify any explicit parameters for the set accessor either, but the compiler assumes it takes one parameter, which is of the same type again, and which is referred to as value. As an example, the following code contains a property called ForeName, which sets a field called foreName and applies a length limit:

```
private string foreName;

public string ForeName
{
   get
   {
      return foreName;
   }
   set
   {
      if (value.Length > 20)
         // code here to take error recovery action
         // (eg. throw an exception)
      else
         foreName = value;
   }
}
```

Note the naming convention used here. You take advantage of C#'s case sensitivity by using the same name, Pascal-cased for the public property, and camel-cased for the equivalent private field if there is one. Some developers prefer to use field names that are prefixed by an underscore: _foreName; this provides an extremely convenient way of identifying fields.

Visual Basic 6 programmers should remember that C# does not distinguish between Visual Basic 6 Set and Visual Basic 6 Let: In C#, the write accessor is always identified with the keyword set.

Read-Only and Write-Only Properties

It is possible to create a read-only property by simply omitting the set accessor from the property definition. Thus, to make ForeName read-only in the previous example:

```
private string foreName;

public string ForeName
{
   get
   {
      return foreName;
   }
}
```

It is similarly possible to create a write-only property by omitting the get accessor. However, this is regarded as poor programming practice because it could be confusing to authors of client code. In general, it is recommended that if you are tempted to do this, you should use a method instead.

Access Modifiers for Properties

C# does allow the set and get accessors to have differing access modifiers. This would allow a property to have a public get and a private or protected set. This can help control how or when a property can be set. In the following code example, notice that the set has a private access modifier and the get does not have any. In this case, the get takes on the access level of the property. One of the accessors must follow the access level of the property. A compile error will be generated if the `get` accessor has the `protected` access level associated with it because that would make both accessors have a different access level from the property.

```
public string Name
{
  get
  {
    return _name;
  }
  private set
  {
    _name = value;
  }
}
```

Auto-Implemented Properties

If there isn't going to be any logic in the properties `set` and `get`, then auto-implemented properties can be used. Auto-implemented properties implement the backing member variable automatically. The code for the previous example would look like this:

```
public string ForeName  {get; set;}
```

The declaration `private string foreName;` is not needed. The compiler will create this automatically.

By using auto-implemented properties, validation of the property cannot be done at the property set. So in the previous example we could not have checked to see if it is less than 20 characters. Also both accessors must be present. So an attempt to make a property read-only would cause an error:

```
public string ForeName  {get;}
```

However, the access level of each accessor can be different. So the following is acceptable:

```
public string ForeName  {get; private set;}
```

A Note About Inlining

Some developers may worry that the previous sections have presented a number of situations in which standard C# coding practices have led to very small functions — for example, accessing a field via a property instead of directly. Is this going to hurt performance because of the overhead of the extra function call? The answer is that there is no need to worry about performance loss from these kinds of programming methodologies in C#. Recall that C# code is compiled to IL, then JIT compiled at runtime to native executable code. The JIT compiler is designed to generate highly optimized code and will ruthlessly inline code as appropriate (in other words, it replaces function calls with inline code). A method or property whose implementation simply calls another method or returns a field will almost certainly be inlined. Note, however, that the decision of where to inline is made entirely by the CLR. There is no way for you to control which methods are inlined by using, for example, some keyword similar to the `inline` keyword of C++.

Constructors

The syntax for declaring basic constructors in C# is the same as in Java and C++. You declare a method that has the same name as the containing class and that does not have any return type:

```
public class MyClass
{
   public MyClass()
   {
   }
   // rest of class definition
```

As in C++ and Java, it's not necessary to provide a constructor for your class. We haven't supplied one for any of the examples so far in this book. In general, if you don't supply any constructor, the compiler will just make up a default one for you behind the scenes. It will be a very basic constructor that just initializes all the member fields by zeroing them out (`null` reference for reference types, zero for numeric data types, and false for `bool`s). Often, that will be adequate; if not, you'll need to write your own constructor.

> **For C++ programmers: Because primitive fields in C# are by default initialized by being zeroed out, whereas primitive fields in C++ are by default uninitialized, you may find that you don't need to write constructors in C# as often as you would in C++.**

Constructors follow the same rules for overloading as other methods (that is, you can provide as many overloads to the constructor as you want, provided they are clearly different in signature):

```
public MyClass()    // zero-parameter constructor
{
   // construction code
}
public MyClass(int number)    // another overload
{
   // construction code
}
```

Note, however, that if you supply any constructors that take parameters, the compiler will not automatically supply a default one. This is done only if you have not defined any constructors at all. In the following example, because a one-parameter constructor is defined, the compiler assumes that this is the only constructor you want to be available, so it will not implicitly supply any others:

```
public class MyNumber
{
   private int number;
   public MyNumber(int number)
   {
      this.number = number;
   }
}
```

This code also illustrates typical use of the `this` keyword to distinguish member fields from parameters of the same name. If you now try instantiating a `MyNumber` object using a no-parameter constructor, you will get a compilation error:

```
MyNumber numb = new MyNumber();    // causes compilation error
```

We should mention that it is possible to define constructors as private or protected, so that they are invisible to code in unrelated classes too:

```
public class MyNumber
{
   private int number;
   private MyNumber(int number)    // another overload
   {
      this.number = number;
   }
}
```

This example hasn't actually defined any public or even any protected constructors for `MyNumber`. This would actually make it impossible for `MyNumber` to be instantiated by outside code using the `new` operator (though you might write a public static property or method in `MyNumber` that can instantiate the class). This is useful in two situations:

- If your class serves only as a container for some static members or properties and therefore should never be instantiated
- If you want the class to only ever be instantiated by calling some static member function (this is the so-called class factory approach to object instantiation)

Static Constructors

One novel feature of C# is that it is also possible to write a static no-parameter constructor for a class. Such a constructor will be executed only once, as opposed to the constructors written so far, which are instance constructors that are executed whenever an object of that class is created. There is no equivalent to the static constructor in C++ or Visual Basic 6.

```
class MyClass
{
   static MyClass()
   {
      // initialization code
   }
   // rest of class definition
}
```

One reason for writing a static constructor is if your class has some static fields or properties that need to be initialized from an external source before the class is first used.

The .NET runtime makes no guarantees about when a static constructor will be executed, so you should not place any code in it that relies on it being executed at a particular time (for example, when an assembly is loaded). Nor is it possible to predict in what order static constructors of different classes will execute. However, what is guaranteed is that the static constructor will run at most once, and that it will be invoked before your code makes any reference to the class. In C#, the static constructor usually seems to be executed immediately before the first call to any member of the class.

Notice that the static constructor does not have any access modifiers. It's never called by any other C# code, but always by the .NET runtime when the class is loaded, so any access modifier like `public` or `private` would be meaningless. For this same reason, the static constructor can never take any parameters, and there can be only one static constructor for a class. It should also be obvious that a static constructor can access only static members, not instance members, of the class.

Note that it is possible to have a static constructor and a zero-parameter instance constructor defined in the same class. Although the parameter lists are identical, there is no conflict. That's because the static constructor is executed when the class is loaded, but the instance constructor is executed whenever an instance is created — so there won't be any confusion about which constructor gets executed when.

Note that if you have more than one class that has a static constructor, the static constructor that will be executed first is undefined. This means that you should not put any code in a static constructor that depends on other static constructors having been or not having been executed. However, if any static fields have been given default values, these will be allocated before the static constructor is called.

The next example illustrates the use of a static constructor and is based on the idea of a program that has user preferences (which are presumably stored in some configuration file). To keep things simple, we'll assume just one user preference — a quantity called `BackColor`, which might represent the background color to be used in an application. And because we don't want to get into the details of writing code to read data from an external source here, we'll make the assumption that the preference is to have a background color of red on weekdays and green on weekends. All the program will do is display the preference in a console window — but this is enough to see a static constructor at work.

```
namespace Wrox.ProCSharp.StaticConstructorSample
{
   public class UserPreferences
   {
      public static readonly Color BackColor;

      static UserPreferences()
      {
         DateTime now = DateTime.Now;
         if (now.DayOfWeek == DayOfWeek.Saturday
            || now.DayOfWeek == DayOfWeek.Sunday)
            BackColor = Color.Green;
         else
            BackColor = Color.Red;
      }

      private UserPreferences()
      {
      }
   }
}
```

This code shows how the color preference is stored in a static variable, which is initialized in the static constructor. This field is declared as read-only, which means that its value can only be set in a constructor. You learn about read-only fields in more detail later in this chapter. The code uses a few helpful structs that Microsoft has supplied as part of the Framework class library, `System.DateTime` and `System.Drawing.Color`. `DateTime` implements both a static property, `Now`, which returns the current time, and an instance property, `DayOfWeek`, which works out what day of the week a date-time represents. `Color` (which is discussed in Chapter 33, "Graphics with GDI+") is used to store colors. It implements various static properties, such as `Red` and `Green` as used in this example, which return commonly used colors. In order to use `Color`, you need to reference the `System.Drawing.dll` assembly when compiling, and you must add a `using` statement for the `System.Drawing` namespace:

```
using System;
using System.Drawing;
```

You test the static constructor with this code:

```
class MainEntryPoint
{
   static void Main(string[] args)
   {
      Console.WriteLine("User-preferences: BackColor is: " +
                        UserPreferences.BackColor.ToString());
   }
}
```

Compiling and running this code results in this output:

StaticConstructor.exe

```
User-preferences: BackColor is: Color [Red]
```

Of course if the code is executed during the weekend, your color preference would be `Green`.

Calling Constructors from Other Constructors

You may sometimes find yourself in the situation where you have several constructors in a class, perhaps to accommodate some optional parameters, for which the constructors have some code in common. For example, consider this:

```
class Car
{
   private string description;
   private uint nWheels;
   public Car(string description, uint nWheels)
   {
      this.description = description;
      this.nWheels = nWheels;
   }

   public Car(string description)
   {
      this.description = description;
      this.nWheels = 4;
   }
// etc.
```

Both constructors initialize the same fields. It would clearly be neater to place all the code in one place, and C# has a special syntax, known as a constructor initializer, to allow this:

```
class Car
{
   private string description;
   private uint nWheels;

   public Car(string description, uint nWheels)
   {
      this.description = description;
      this.nWheels = nWheels;
   }

   public Car(string description) : this(description, 4)
   {
   }
   // etc
```

In this context, the `this` keyword simply causes the constructor with the nearest matching parameters to be called. Note that any constructor initializer is executed before the body of the constructor. Say that the following code is run:

```
Car myCar = new Car("Proton Persona");
```

In this example, the two-parameter constructor executes before any code in the body of the one-parameter constructor (though in this particular case, because there is no code in the body of the one-parameter constructor, it makes no difference).

A C# constructor initializer may contain either one call to another constructor in the same class (using the syntax just presented) or one call to a constructor in the immediate base class (using the same syntax, but using the keyword `base` instead of `this`). It is not possible to put more than one call in the initializer.

The syntax for constructor initializers in C# is similar to that for constructor initialization lists in C++, but C++ developers should beware: Behind the similarity in syntax, C# initializers follow very different rules for what can be placed in them. Whereas you can use a C++ initialization list to indicate initial values of any member variables or to call a base constructor, the only thing you can put in a C# initializer is one call to one other constructor. This forces C# classes to follow a strict sequence for how they get constructed, whereas C++ allows some leniency. This issue is studied more in Chapter 4, where you see that the sequence enforced by C# arguably amounts to no more than good programming practice anyway.

readonly Fields

The concept of a constant as a variable that contains a value that cannot be changed is something that C# shares with most programming languages. However, constants don't necessarily meet all requirements. On occasion, you may have some variable whose value shouldn't be changed, but where the value is not known until runtime. C# provides another type of variable that is useful in this scenario: the `readonly` field.

The `readonly` keyword gives a bit more flexibility than `const`, allowing for situations in which you might want a field to be constant but also need to carry out some calculations to determine its initial value. The rule is that you can assign values to a `readonly` field inside a constructor, but not anywhere else. It's also possible for a `readonly` field to be an instance rather than a static field, having a different value for each instance of a class. This means that, unlike a `const` field, if you want a `readonly` field to be static, you have to declare it as such.

Suppose that you have an MDI program that edits documents, and, for licensing reasons, you want to restrict the number of documents that can be opened simultaneously. Now assume that you are selling different versions of the software, and it's possible that customers can upgrade their licenses to open more documents simultaneously. Clearly this means you can't hard-code the maximum number in the source code. You'd probably need a field to represent this maximum number. This field will have to be read in — perhaps from a registry key or some other file storage — each time the program is launched. So your code might look something like this:

```
public class DocumentEditor
{
   public static readonly uint MaxDocuments;

   static DocumentEditor()
   {
      MaxDocuments = DoSomethingToFindOutMaxNumber();
   }
```

In this case, the field is static, because the maximum number of documents needs to be stored only once per running instance of the program. This is why it is initialized in the static constructor. If you had an instance `readonly` field, you would initialize it in the instance constructor(s). For example, presumably each document you edit has a creation date, which you wouldn't want to allow the user to change (because that would be rewriting the past!). Note that the field is also public — you don't normally need to make `readonly` fields private, because by definition they cannot be modified externally (the same principle also applies to constants).

As noted earlier, date is represented by the class `System.DateTime`. The following code uses a `System.DateTime` constructor that takes three parameters (the year, month, and day of the month — you can find details of this and other `DateTime` constructors in the MSDN documentation):

```
public class Document
{
   public readonly DateTime CreationDate;

   public Document()
   {
      // Read in creation date from file. Assume result is 1 Jan 2002
      // but in general this can be different for different instances
      // of the class
      CreationDate = new DateTime(2002, 1, 1);
      }
   }
```

`CreationDate` and `MaxDocuments` in the previous code snippet are treated like any other field, except that because they are read-only, they cannot be assigned outside the constructors:

```
void SomeMethod()
{
   MaxDocuments = 10;     // compilation error here. MaxDocuments is readonly
}
```

It's also worth noting that you don't have to assign a value to a `readonly` field in a constructor. If you don't do so, it will be left with the default value for its particular data type or whatever value you initialized it to at its declaration. That applies to both static and instance `readonly` fields.

Anonymous Types

Chapter 2 discussed the `var` keyword in reference to implicitly typed variables. When used with the `new` keyword, anonymous types can be created. An anonymous type is simply a nameless class that inherits from `object`. The definition of the class is inferred from the initializer, just like in implicitly typed variables.

If you needed an object that contained a person's first, middle, and last name the declaration would look like this:

```
var captain = new {FirstName = "James", MiddleName = "T", LastName = "Kirk"};
```

This would produce an object with `FirstName`, `MiddleName`, and `LastName` properties. If you were to create another object that looked like this:

```
var doctor = new {FirstName = "Leonard", MiddleName = "", LastName = "McCoy"};
```

The types of `captain` and `doctor` are the same. You could set `captain = doctor`, for example.

If the values that are being set come from another object, then the initializer can be abbreviated. If you already have a class that contains the properties `FirstName`, `MiddleName`, and `LastName` and you have an instance of that class with the instance name `person`, then the `captain` object could be initialized like this:

```
var captain = new (person.FirstName, person.MidleName, person.LastName};
```

The property names from the `person` object would be projected to the new object named `captain`. So the object named `captain` would have the `FirstName`, `MiddleName`, and `LastName` properties.

The actual type name of these new objects is unknown. The compiler "makes up" a name for the type, but only the compiler will ever be able to make use of it. So you can't and shouldn't plan on using any type reflection on the new objects because you will not get consistent results.

Structs

So far, you have seen how classes offer a great way of encapsulating objects in your program. You have also seen how they are stored on the heap in a way that gives you much more flexibility in data lifetime, but with a slight cost in performance. This performance cost is small thanks to the optimizations of managed heaps. However, in some situations all you really need is a small data structure. In this case, a class provides more functionality than you need, and for performance reasons you will probably prefer to use a struct. Look at this example:

```
class Dimensions
{
   public double Length;
   public double Width;
}
```

This code defines a class called `Dimensions`, which simply stores the length and width of some item. Perhaps you're writing a furniture-arranging program to let people experiment with rearranging their furniture on the computer, and you want to store the dimensions of each item of furniture. It looks like you're breaking the rules of good program design by making the fields public, but the point is that you don't really need all the facilities of a class for this. All you have is two numbers, which you'll find convenient to treat as a pair rather than individually. There is no need for a lot of methods, or for you to be able to inherit from the class, and you certainly don't want to have the .NET runtime go to the trouble of bringing in the heap with all the performance implications, just to store two `double`s.

As mentioned earlier in this chapter, the only thing you need to change in the code to define a type as a struct instead of a class is to replace the keyword `class` with `struct`:

```
struct Dimensions
{
   public double Length;
   public double Width;
}
```

Defining functions for structs is also exactly the same as defining them for classes. The following code demonstrates a constructor and a property for a struct:

```
struct Dimensions
{
   public double Length;
   public double Width;

   Dimensions(double length, double width)
```

```
        {
            Length=length;
            Width=width;
        }

        public double Diagonal
        {
            get
            {
              return Math.Sqrt(Length*Length + Width*Width);
            }
        }
    }
```

In many ways, you can think of structs in C# as being like scaled-down classes. They are basically the same as classes but designed more for cases where you simply want to group some data together. They differ from classes in the following ways:

- Structs are value types, not reference types. This means they are stored either in the stack or in-line (if they are part of another object that is stored on the heap) and have the same lifetime restrictions as the simple data types.
- Structs do not support inheritance.
- There are some differences in the way constructors work for structs. In particular, the compiler always supplies a default no-parameter constructor, which you are not permitted to replace.
- With a struct, you can specify how the fields are to be laid out in memory (this is examined in Chapter 13, "Reflection," which covers attributes).

Because structs are really intended to group data items together, you'll sometimes find that most or all of their fields are declared as public. This is, strictly speaking, contrary to the guidelines for writing .NET code — according to Microsoft, fields (other than `const` fields) should always be private and wrapped by public properties. However, for simple structs, many developers would nevertheless consider public fields to be acceptable programming practice.

C++ developers beware — structs in C# are very different from classes in their implementation. This is unlike C++, in which classes and structs are virtually the same thing.

The following sections look at some of these differences between structs and classes in more detail.

Structs Are Value Types

Although structs are value types, you can often treat them syntactically in the same way as classes. For example, with the definition of the `Dimensions` class in the previous section, you could write:

```
Dimensions point = new Dimensions();
point.Length = 3;
point.Width = 6;
```

Note that because structs are value types, the `new` operator does not work in the same way as it does for classes and other reference types. Instead of allocating memory on the heap, the `new` operator simply calls the appropriate constructor, according to the parameters passed to it, initializing all fields. Indeed, for structs it is perfectly legal to write:

```
Dimensions point;
point.Length = 3;
point.Width = 6;
```

If `Dimensions` was a class, this would produce a compilation error, because `point` would contain an uninitialized reference — an address that points nowhere, so you could not start setting values to its fields. For a struct, however, the variable declaration actually allocates space on the stack for the entire struct, so it's ready to assign values to. Note, however, that the following code would cause a compilation error, with the compiler complaining that you are using an uninitialized variable:

```
Dimensions point;
Double D = point.Length;
```

Structs follow the same rules as any other data type — everything must be initialized before use. A struct is considered fully initialized either when the `new` operator has been called against it, or when values have been individually assigned to all its fields. And of course, a struct defined as a member field of a class is initialized by being zeroed-out automatically when the containing object is initialized.

The fact that structs are value types will affect performance, though depending on how you use your struct, this can be good or bad. On the positive side, allocating memory for structs is very fast because this takes place inline or on the stack. The same goes for removing structs when they go out of scope. On the negative side, whenever you pass a struct as a parameter or assign a struct to another struct (as in `A=B`, where `A` and `B` are structs), the full contents of the struct are copied, whereas for a class only the reference is copied. This will result in a performance loss that depends on the size of the struct, emphasizing the fact that structs are really intended for small data structures. Note, however, that when passing a struct as a parameter to a method, you can avoid this performance loss by passing it as a `ref` parameter — in this case, only the address in memory of the struct will be passed in, which is just as fast as passing in a class. If you do this, though, be aware that it means the called method can in principle change the value of the struct.

Structs and Inheritance

Structs are not designed for inheritance. This means that it is not possible to inherit from a struct. The only exception to this is that structs, in common with every other type in C#, derive ultimately from the class `System.Object`. Hence, structs also have access to the methods of `System.Object`, and it is even possible to override them in structs — an obvious example would be overriding the `ToString()` method. The actual inheritance chain for structs is that each struct derives from a class, `System.ValueType`, which in turn derives from `System.Object`. `ValueType` does not add any new members to `Object`, but provides implementations of some of them that are more suitable for structs. Note that you cannot supply a different base class for a struct: every struct is derived from `ValueType`.

Constructors for Structs

You can define constructors for structs in exactly the same way that you can for classes, except that you are not permitted to define a constructor that takes no parameters. This may seem nonsensical, and the reason is buried in the implementation of the .NET runtime. Some rare circumstances exist in which the .NET runtime would not be able to call a custom zero-parameter constructor that you have supplied. Microsoft has therefore taken the easy way out and banned zero-parameter constructors for structs in C#.

That said, the default constructor, which initializes all fields to zero values, is always present implicitly, even if you supply other constructors that take parameters. It's also impossible to circumvent the default constructor by supplying initial values for fields. The following code will cause a compile-time error:

```
struct Dimensions
{
   public double Length = 1;       // error. Initial values not allowed
   public double Width = 2;        // error. Initial values not allowed
}
```

Of course, if `Dimensions` had been declared as a class, this code would have compiled without any problems.

Incidentally, you can supply a `Close()` or `Dispose()` method for a struct in the same way you do for a class.

Partial Classes

The `partial` keyword allows the class, struct, or interface to span across multiple files. Typically, a class will reside entirely in a single file. However, in situations where multiple developers need access to the same class, or more likely in the situation where a code generator of some type is generating part of a class, then having the class in multiple files can be beneficial.

The way that the `partial` keyword is used is to simply place `partial` before `class`, `struct`, or `interface`. In the following example the class `TheBigClass` resides in two separate source files, `BigClassPart1.cs` and `BigClassPart2.cs`:

```
//BigClassPart1.cs
partial class TheBigClass
{
  public void MethodOne()
  {
  }
}

//BigClassPart2.cs
partial class TheBigClass
{
  public void MethodTwo()
  {
  }
}
```

When the project that these two source files are part of is compiled, a single type called `TheBigClass` will be created with two methods, `MethodOne()` and `MethodTwo()`.

If any of the following keywords are used in describing the class, the same must apply to all partials of the same type:

- `public`
- `private`
- `protected`
- `internal`
- `abstract`
- `sealed`
- `new`
- generic constraints

Nested partials are allowed as long as the `partial` keyword precedes the `class` keyword in the nested type. Attributes, XML comments, interfaces, generic-type parameter attributes, and members will be combined when the partial types are compiled into the type. Given the two source files:

```
//BigClassPart1.cs
[CustomAttribute]
partial class TheBigClass : TheBigBaseClass, IBigClass
{
  public void MethodOne()
  {
  }
}

//BigClassPart2.cs
[AnotherAttribute]
partial class TheBigClass : IOtherBigClass
{
  public void MethodTwo()
  {
  }
}
```

After the compile, the equivalent source file would be:

```
[CustomAttribute]
[AnotherAttribute]
partial class TheBigClass : TheBigBaseClass, IBigClass, IOtherBigClass
{
  public void MethodOne()
  {
  }

  public void MethodTwo()
  {
  }
}
```

Static Classes

Earlier, this chapter discussed static constructors and how they allowed the initialization of static member variables. If a class contains nothing but static methods and properties, the class itself can become static. A static class is functionally the same as creating a class with a private static constructor. An instance of the class can never be created. By using the `static` keyword, the compiler can help by checking that instance members are never accidentally added to the class. If they are, a compile error happens. This can help guarantee that an instance is never created. The syntax for a static class looks like this:

```
static class StaticUtilities
{
  public static void HelperMethod()
  {
  }
}
```

An object of type `StaticUtilities` is not needed to call the `HelperMethod()`. The type name is used to make the call:

```
StaticUtilities.HelperMethod();
```

The Object Class

As indicated earlier, all .NET classes are ultimately derived from `System.Object`. In fact, if you don't specify a base class when you define a class, the compiler will automatically assume that it derives from `Object`. Because inheritance has not been used in this chapter, every class you have seen here is actually derived from `System.Object`. (As noted earlier, for structs this derivation is indirect: A struct is always derived from `System.ValueType`, which in turn derives from `System.Object`.)

The practical significance of this is that, besides the methods and properties and so on that you define, you also have access to a number of public and protected member methods that have been defined for the `Object` class. These methods are available in all other classes that you define.

System.Object Methods

For the time being, we simply summarize the purpose of each method in the following list, and then, in the next section, we provide more detail about the `ToString()` method in particular.

- `ToString()` — This is intended as a fairly basic, quick-and-easy string representation; use it when you just want a quick idea of the contents of an object, perhaps for debugging purposes. It provides very little choice of how to format the data: For example, dates can in principle be expressed in a huge variety of different formats, but `DateTime.ToString()` does not offer you any choice in this regard. If you need a more sophisticated string representation that, for example, takes account of your formatting preferences or of the culture (the locale), then you should implement the `IFormattable` interface (see Chapter 8, "Strings and Regular Expressions").
- `GetHashCode()` — This is used if objects are placed in a data structure known as a map (also known as a hash table or dictionary). It is used by classes that manipulate these structures in order to determine where to place an object in the structure. If you intend your class to be used as a key for a dictionary, you will need to override `GetHashCode()`. Some fairly strict requirements exist for how you implement your overload, and you learn about those when you examine dictionaries in Chapter 10, "Collections."
- `Equals()` (both versions) and `ReferenceEquals()` — As you'll gather by the existence of three different methods aimed at comparing the equality of objects, the .NET Framework has quite a sophisticated scheme for measuring equality. Subtle differences exist between how these three methods, along with the comparison operator, ==, are intended to be used. Not only that, but restrictions also exist on how you should override the virtual, one-parameter version of `Equals()` if you choose to do so, because certain base classes in the `System.Collections` namespace call the method and expect it to behave in certain ways. You explore the use of these methods in Chapter 6, "Operators and Casts," when you examine operators.
- `Finalize()` — This method is covered in Chapter 12, "Memory Management and Pointers." It is intended as the nearest that C# has to C++-style destructors and is called when a reference object is garbage collected to clean up resources. The `Object` implementation of `Finalize()` actually does nothing and is ignored by the garbage collector. You will normally override `Finalize()` if an object owns references to unmanaged resources that need to be removed when the object is deleted. The garbage collector cannot do this directly because it only knows about managed resources, so it relies on any finalizers that you supply.

- `GetType()` — This method returns an instance of a class derived from `System.Type`. This object can provide an extensive range of information about the class of which your object is a member, including base type, methods, properties, and so on. `System.Type` also provides the entry point into .NET's reflection technology. Chapter 13, "Reflection," examines this topic.
- `MemberwiseClone()` — This is the only member of `System.Object` that isn't examined in detail anywhere in the book. There is no need to because it is fairly simple in concept. It simply makes a copy of the object and returns a reference (or in the case of a value type, a boxed reference) to the copy. Note that the copy made is a shallow copy — this means that it copies all the value types in the class. If the class contains any embedded references, then only the references will be copied, not the objects referred to. This method is protected and so cannot be called to copy external objects. It is also not virtual, so you cannot override its implementation.

The ToString() Method

You've already encountered `ToString()` in Chapter 2, "C# Basics." It provides the most convenient way to get a quick string representation of an object.

For example:

```
int i = -50;
string str = i.ToString();  // returns "-50"
```

Here's another example:

```
enum Colors {Red, Orange, Yellow};
// later on in code...
Colors favoriteColor = Colors.Orange;
string str = favoriteColor.ToString();     // returns "Orange"
```

`Object.ToString()` is actually declared as virtual, and all these examples are taking advantage of the fact that its implementation in the C# predefined data types has been overridden for us in order to return correct string representations of those types. You might not think that the `Colors` enum counts as a predefined data type. It actually gets implemented as a struct derived from `System.Enum`, and `System.Enum` has a rather clever override of `ToString()` that deals with all the enums you define.

If you don't override `ToString()` in classes that you define, your classes will simply inherit the `System.Object` implementation — which displays the name of the class. If you want `ToString()` to return a string that contains information about the value of objects of your class, you will need to override it. To illustrate this, the following example, `Money`, defines a very simple class, also called `Money`, which represents U.S. currency amounts. `Money` simply acts as a wrapper for the decimal class but supplies a `ToString()` method. Note that this method must be declared as `override` because it is replacing (overriding) the `ToString()` method supplied by `Object`. Chapter 4 discusses overriding in more detail. The complete code for this example is as follows. Note that it also illustrates use of properties to wrap fields:

```
using System;

namespace Wrox.ProCSharp.OOCSharp
{
   class MainEntryPoint
   {
      static void Main(string[] args)
      {
         Money cash1 = new Money();
         cash1.Amount = 40M;
```

```
            Console.WriteLine("cash1.ToString() returns: " + cash1.ToString());
            Console.ReadLine();
         }
      }
      class Money
      {
         private decimal amount;

         public decimal Amount
         {
            get
            {
               return amount;
            }
            set
            {
               amount = value;
            }
         }
         public override string ToString()
         {
            return "$" + Amount.ToString();
         }
      }

   }
```

This example is here just to illustrate syntactical features of C#. C# already has a predefined type to represent currency amounts, `decimal`, so in real life, you wouldn't write a class to duplicate this functionality unless you wanted to add various other methods to it. And in many cases, due to formatting requirements, you'd probably use the `String.Format()` method (which is covered in Chapter 8) rather than `ToString()` to display a currency string.

In the `Main()` method, you first instantiate a `Money` object. The `ToString()` method is then called, which actually executes the override version of the method. Running this code gives the following results:

```
StringRepresentations
cash1.ToString() returns: $40
```

Extension Methods

There are many ways to extend a class. If you have the source for the class, then inheritance, which is covered in Chapter 4, is a great way to add functionality to your objects. What if the source code isn't available? Extension methods can help by allowing you to change a class without requiring the source code for the class.

Extension methods are static methods that can appear to be part of a class without actually being in the source code for the class. Let's say that the `Money` class from the previous example needs to have a method `AddToAmount(decimal amountToAdd)`. However, for whatever reason the original source for the assembly cannot be changed directly. All that you have to do is create a static class and add the `AddToAmount` method as a static method. Here is what the code would look like:

```
namespace Chapter3.Extensions
{
  public static class MoneyExtension
```

(continued)

(continued)

```
    {
      public static void AddToAmount(this Money money, decimal amountToAdd)
      {
        money.Amount += amountToAdd;
      }
    }
  }
```

Notice the parameters for the AddToAmount method. For an extension method, the first parameter is the type that is being extended preceded by the this keyword. This is what tells the compiler that this method is part of the Money type. In this example Money is the type that is being extended. In the extension method you have access to all the public methods and properties of the type being extended.

In the main program the AddToAmount method appears just as another method. The first parameter doesn't appear, and you do not have to do anything with it. To use the new method, you make the call just like any other method:

```
cash1.AddToAmount(10M);
```

Even though the extension method is static, you use standard instance method syntax. Notice that we called AddToAmount using the cash1 instance variable and not using the type name.

If the extension method has the same name as a method in the class, the extension method will never be called. Any instance methods already in the class take precedence.

Summary

This chapter examined C# syntax for declaring and manipulating objects. You have seen how to declare static and instance fields, properties, methods, and constructors. You have also seen that C# adds some new features not present in the OOP model of some other languages — for example, static constructors provide a means of initializing static fields, whereas structs allow you to define types that do not require the use of the managed heap, which could lead to performance gains. You have also seen how all types in C# derive ultimately from the type System.Object, which means that all types start with a basic set of useful methods, including ToString().

We mentioned inheritance a few times throughout this chapter. We examine implementation and interface inheritance in C# in Chapter 4.

Inheritance

Chapter 3, "Objects and Types," examined how to use individual classes in C#. The focus in that chapter was how to define methods, constructors, properties, and other members of a single class (or a single struct). Although you did learn that all classes are ultimately derived from the class `System.Object`, you did not see how to create a hierarchy of inherited classes. Inheritance is the subject of this chapter. In this chapter, you will see how C# and the .NET Framework handle inheritance. Topics covered include:

- Types of inheritance
- Implementing inheritance
- Access modifiers
- Interfaces

Types of Inheritance

Let's start off by reviewing exactly what C# does and does not support as far as inheritance is concerned.

Implementation versus Interface Inheritance

In object-oriented programming, there are two distinct types of inheritance — implementation inheritance and interface inheritance:

- **Implementation inheritance** means that a type derives from a base type, taking all the base type's member fields and functions. With implementation inheritance, a derived type adopts the base type's implementation of each function, unless it is indicated in the definition of the derived type that a function implementation is to be overridden. This type of inheritance is most useful when you need to add functionality to an existing type, or when a number of related types share a significant amount of common functionality. A good example of this comes in the Windows Forms classes, which are discussed in Chapter 31, "Windows Forms." Specific examples are the base class `System.Windows.Forms.Control`, which provides a very sophisticated implementation of a generic Windows control, and numerous other classes such as `System.Windows.Forms.TextBox` and `System.Windows.Forms.ListBox` that are derived from `Control` and that override functions or provide new functions to implement specific types of control.

- **Interface inheritance** means that a type inherits only the signatures of the functions and does not inherit any implementations. This type of inheritance is most useful when you want to specify that a type makes certain features available. For example, certain types can indicate that they provide a resource cleanup method called `Dispose()` by deriving from an interface, `System.IDisposable` (see Chapter 12, "Memory Management and Pointers"). Because the way that one type cleans up resources is likely to be very different from the way that another type cleans up resources, there is no point in defining any common implementation, so interface inheritance is appropriate here. Interface inheritance is often regarded as providing a contract: By deriving from an interface, a type is guaranteed to provide certain functionality to clients.

Traditionally, languages such as C++ have been very strong on implementation inheritance. Indeed, implementation inheritance has been at the core of the C++ programming model. Although Visual Basic 6 did not support any implementation inheritance of classes, it did support interface inheritance thanks to its underlying COM foundations.

C# supports both implementation and interface inheritance. Both are baked into the framework and the language from the ground up, thereby allowing you to decide which to use based on the architecture of the application.

Multiple Inheritance

Some languages such as C++ support what is known as *multiple inheritance*, in which a class derives from more than one other class. The benefits of using multiple inheritance are debatable: On one hand, there is no doubt that it is possible to use multiple inheritance to write extremely sophisticated, yet compact, code, as demonstrated by the C++ ATL library. On the other hand, code that uses multiple implementation inheritance is often difficult to understand and debug (a point that is equally well demonstrated by the C++ ATL library). As mentioned, making it easy to write robust code was one of the crucial design goals behind the development of C#. Accordingly, C# does not support multiple implementation inheritance. It does, however, allow types to be derived from multiple interfaces — multiple interface inheritance. This means that a C# class can be derived from one other class, and any number of interfaces. Indeed, we can be more precise: Thanks to the presence of `System.Object` as a common base type, every C# class (except for `Object`) has exactly one base class, and may additionally have any number of base interfaces.

Structs and Classes

Chapter 3 distinguishes between structs (value types) and classes (reference types). One restriction of using a struct is that structs do not support inheritance, beyond the fact that every struct is automatically derived from `System.ValueType`. In fact, we should be more careful. It's true that it is not possible to code a type hierarchy of structs; however, it is possible for structs to implement interfaces. In other words, structs don't really support implementation inheritance, but they do support interface inheritance. We can summarize the situation for any types that you define as follows:

- **Structs** are always derived from `System.ValueType`. They can also be derived from any number of interfaces.
- **Classes** are always derived from one other class of your choosing. They can also be derived from any number of interfaces.

Implementation Inheritance

If you want to declare that a class derives from another class, use the following syntax:

```
class MyDerivedClass : MyBaseClass
{
   // functions and data members here
}
```

This syntax is very similar to C++ and Java syntax. However, C++ programmers, who will be used to the concepts of public and private inheritance, should note that C# does not support private inheritance, hence the absence of a public or private qualifier on the base class name. Supporting private inheritance would have complicated the language for very little gain. In practice, private inheritance is used extremely rarely in C++ anyway.

If a class (or a struct) also derives from interfaces, the list of base class and interfaces is separated by commas:

```
public class MyDerivedClass : MyBaseClass, IInterface1, IInterface2
{
         // etc.
 }
```

For a struct, the syntax is as follows:

```
public struct MyDerivedStruct : IInterface1, IInterface2
{
         // etc.
 }
```

If you do not specify a base class in a class definition, the C# compiler will assume that `System.Object` is the base class. Hence, the following two pieces of code yield the same result:

```
class MyClass : Object  // derives from System.Object
{
   // etc.
}
```

and

```
class MyClass   // derives from System.Object
{
   // etc.
}
```

For the sake of simplicity, the second form is more common.

Because C# supports the `object` keyword, which serves as a pseudonym for the `System.Object` class, you can also write:

```
class MyClass : object   // derives from System.Object
{
   // etc.
}
```

If you want to reference the `Object` class, use the `object` keyword, which is recognized by intelligent editors such as Visual Studio .NET and thus facilitates editing your code.

Virtual Methods

By declaring a base class function as `virtual`, you allow the function to be overridden in any derived classes:

```
class MyBaseClass
{
   public virtual string VirtualMethod()
   {
      return "This method is virtual and defined in MyBaseClass";
   }
}
```

It is also permitted to declare a property as `virtual`. For a virtual or overridden property, the syntax is the same as for a nonvirtual property, with the exception of the keyword `virtual`, which is added to the definition. The syntax looks like this:

```
public virtual string ForeName
{
   get { return fName;}
   set { fName = value;}
}
private string foreName;
```

For simplicity, the following discussion focuses mainly on methods, but it applies equally well to properties.

The concepts behind virtual functions in C# are identical to standard OOP concepts. You can override a virtual function in a derived class, and when the method is called, the appropriate method for the type of object is invoked. In C#, functions are not virtual by default but (aside from constructors) can be explicitly declared as `virtual`. This follows the C++ methodology: for performance reasons, functions are not virtual unless indicated. In Java, by contrast, all functions are virtual. C# does differ from C++ syntax, though, because it requires you to declare when a derived class's function overrides another function, using the `override` keyword:

```
class MyDerivedClass : MyBaseClass
{
   public override string VirtualMethod()
   {
      return "This method is an override defined in MyDerivedClass.";
   }
}
```

This syntax for method overriding removes potential runtime bugs that can easily occur in C++, when a method signature in a derived class unintentionally differs slightly from the base version, resulting in the method failing to override the base version. In C#, this is picked up as a compile-time error because the compiler would see a function marked as `override` but no base method for it to override.

Neither member fields nor static functions can be declared as virtual. The concept simply wouldn't make sense for any class member other than an instance function member.

Hiding Methods

If a method with the same signature is declared in both base and derived classes, but the methods are not declared as `virtual` and `override`, respectively, then the derived class version is said to *hide* the base class version.

In most cases, you would want to override methods rather than hide them; by hiding them you risk calling the wrong method for a given class instance. However, as shown in the following example,

C# syntax is designed to ensure that the developer is warned at compile time about this potential problem, thus making it safer to hide methods if that is your intention. This also has versioning benefits for developers of class libraries.

Suppose that you have a class called `HisBaseClass`:

```
class HisBaseClass
{
   // various members
}
```

At some point in the future you write a derived class that adds some functionality to `HisBaseClass`. In particular, you add a method called `MyGroovyMethod()`, which is not present in the base class:

```
class MyDerivedClass: HisBaseClass
{
   public int MyGroovyMethod()
   {
      // some groovy implementation
      return 0;
   }
}
```

One year later, you decide to extend the functionality of the base class. By coincidence, you add a method that is also called `MyGroovyMethod()` and that has the same name and signature as yours, but probably doesn't do the same thing. When you compile your code using the new version of the base class, you have a potential clash because your program won't know which method to call. It's all perfectly legal in C#, but because your `MyGroovyMethod()` is not intended to be related in any way to the base class `MyGroovyMethod()`, the result is that running this code does not yield the result you want. Fortunately, C# has been designed to cope very well with these types of conflicts.

In these situations, C# generates a compilation warning that reminds you to use the `new` keyword to declare that you intend to hide a method, like this:

```
class MyDerivedClass : HisBaseClass
{
   public new int MyGroovyMethod()
   {
      // some groovy implementation
      return 0;
   }
}
```

However, because your version of `MyGroovyMethod()` is not declared as `new`, the compiler will pick up on the fact that it's hiding a base class method without being instructed to do so and will generate a warning (this applies whether or not you declared `MyGroovyMethod()` as `virtual`). If you want, you can rename your version of the method. This is the recommended course of action because it will eliminate future confusion. However, if you decide not to rename your method for whatever reason (for example, if you've published your software as a library for other companies, so you can't change the names of methods), all your existing client code will still run correctly, picking up your version of `MyGroovyMethod()`. That's because any existing code that accesses this method must be doing so through a reference to `MyDerivedClass` (or a further derived class).

Your existing code cannot access this method through a reference to `HisBaseClass`; it would generate a compilation error when compiled against the earlier version of `HisBaseClass`. The problem can happen in only client code you have yet to write. C# arranges things so that you get a warning that a potential problem might occur in future code — you will need to pay attention to this warning and take care not to attempt to call your version of `MyGroovyMethod()` through any reference to `HisBaseClass` in any future code you add. However, all your existing code will still work fine. It may be a subtle point, but it's quite an impressive example of how C# is able to cope with different versions of classes.

Calling Base Versions of Functions

C# has a special syntax for calling base versions of a method from a derived class: `base.<MethodName>()`. For example, if you want a method in a derived class to return 90 percent of the value returned by the base class method, you can use the following syntax:

```
class CustomerAccount
{
   public virtual decimal CalculatePrice()
   {
      // implementation
      return 0.0M;
   }
}
class GoldAccount : CustomerAccount
{
   public override decimal CalculatePrice()
   {
      return base.CalculatePrice() * 0.9M;
   }
}
```

Java uses a similar syntax, with the exception that Java uses the keyword `super` rather than `base`. C++ has no similar keyword but instead requires specification of the class name (`CustomerAccount::CalculatePrice()`). Any equivalent to `base` in C++ would have been ambiguous because C++ supports multiple inheritance.

Note that you can use the `base.<MethodName>()` syntax to call any method in the base class — you don't have to call it from inside an override of the same method.

Abstract Classes and Functions

C# allows both classes and functions to be declared as abstract. An abstract class cannot be instantiated, whereas an abstract function does not have an implementation, and must be overridden in any non-abstract derived class. Obviously, an abstract function is automatically virtual (although you don't need to supply the `virtual` keyword; doing so results in a syntax error). If any class contains any abstract functions, that class is also abstract and must be declared as such:

```
abstract class Building
{
   public abstract decimal CalculateHeatingCost();    // abstract method
}
```

C++ developers will notice some syntactical differences in C# here. C# does not support the `=0` syntax to declare abstract functions. In C#, this syntax would be misleading because `=<value>` is allowed in member fields in class declarations to supply initial values:

```
abstract class Building
{
   private bool damaged = false;    // field
   public abstract decimal CalculateHeatingCost();    // abstract method
}
```

C++ developers should also note the slightly different terminology: In C++, abstract functions are often described as pure virtual; in the C# world, the only correct term to use is abstract.

Sealed Classes and Methods

C# allows classes and methods to be declared as `sealed`. In the case of a class, this means that you can't inherit from that class. In the case of a method, this means that you can't override that method.

```
sealed class FinalClass
{
   // etc
}
class DerivedClass : FinalClass       // wrong. Will give compilation error
{
   // etc
}
```

Java developers will recognize `sealed` *as the C# equivalent of Java's* `final`.

The most likely situation in which you'll mark a class or method as `sealed` will be if the class or method is internal to the operation of the library, class, or other classes that you are writing, so that you ensure that any attempt to override some of its functionality will lead to instability in the code. You might also mark a class or method as `sealed` for commercial reasons, in order to prevent a third party from extending your classes in a manner that is contrary to the licensing agreements. In general, however, you should be careful about marking a class or member as `sealed` because by doing so you are severely restricting how it can be used. Even if you don't think it would be useful to inherit from a class or override a particular member of it, it's still possible that at some point in the future someone will encounter a situation you hadn't anticipated in which it is useful to do so. The .NET base class library frequently uses sealed classes in order to make these classes inaccessible to third-party developers who might want to derive their own classes from them. For example, `string` is a sealed class.

Declaring a method as `sealed` serves a similar purpose as for a class:

```
class MyClass
{
   public sealed override void FinalMethod()
   {
      // etc.
   }
}
class DerivedClass : MyClass
{
   public override void FinalMethod()      // wrong. Will give compilation error
   {
   }
}
```

In order to use the `sealed` keyword on a method or property, it must have first been overridden from a base class. If you do not want a method or property in a base class overridden, then don't mark it as virtual.

Constructors of Derived Classes

Chapter 3 discusses how constructors can be applied to individual classes. An interesting question arises as to what happens when you start defining your own constructors for classes that are part of a hierarchy, inherited from other classes that may also have custom constructors.

Assume that you have not defined any explicit constructors for any of your classes. This means that the compiler supplies default zeroing-out constructors for all your classes. There is actually quite a lot going on under the hood when that happens, but the compiler is able to arrange it so that things work out nicely throughout the class hierarchy and every field in every class gets initialized to whatever its default value is. When you add a constructor of your own, however, you are effectively taking control of construction. This has implications right down through the hierarchy of derived classes, and you have to make sure that you don't inadvertently do anything to prevent construction through the hierarchy from taking place smoothly.

You might be wondering why there is any special problem with derived classes. The reason is that when you create an instance of a derived class, there is actually more than one constructor at work. The constructor of the class you instantiate isn't by itself sufficient to initialize the class — the constructors of the base classes must also be called. That's why we've been talking about construction through the hierarchy.

To see why base class constructors must be called, you're going to develop an example based on a cell phone company called MortimerPhones. The example contains an abstract base class, `GenericCustomer`, which represents any customer. There is also a (non-abstract) class, `Nevermore60Customer`, that represents any customer on a particular rate called the `Nevermore60` rate. All customers have a name, represented by a private field. Under the `Nevermore60` rate, the first few minutes of the customer's call time are charged at a higher rate, necessitating the need for the field `highCostMinutesUsed`, which details how many of these higher-cost minutes each customer has used up. The class definitions look like this:

```
abstract class GenericCustomer
{
   private string name;
   // lots of other methods etc.
}
class Nevermore60Customer : GenericCustomer
{
   private uint highCostMinutesUsed;
   // other methods etc.
}
```

We won't worry about what other methods might be implemented in these classes, because we are concentrating solely on the construction process here. And if you download the sample code for this chapter, you'll find that the class definitions include only the constructors.

Take a look at what happens when you use the `new` operator to instantiate a `Nevermore60Customer`:

```
GenericCustomer customer = new Nevermore60Customer();
```

Clearly, both of the member fields `name` and `highCostMinutesUsed` must be initialized when `customer` is instantiated. If you don't supply constructors of your own, but rely simply on the default constructors, then you'd expect `name` to be initialized to the `null` reference, and `highCostMinutesUsed` initialized to zero. Let's look in a bit more detail at how this actually happens.

The `highCostMinutesUsed` field presents no problem: the default `Nevermore60Customer` constructor supplied by the compiler will initialize this field to zero.

What about `name`? Looking at the class definitions, it's clear that the `Nevermore60Customer` constructor can't initialize this value. This field is declared as private, which means that derived classes don't have access to it. So, the default `Nevermore60Customer` constructor simply won't know that this field exists. The only code items that have that knowledge are other members of `GenericCustomer`. This means that if `name` is going to be initialized, that'll have to be done by some constructor in `GenericCustomer`. No matter how big your class hierarchy is, this same reasoning applies right down to the ultimate base class, `System.Object`.

Now that you have an understanding of the issues involved, you can look at what actually happens whenever a derived class is instantiated. Assuming that default constructors are used throughout, the compiler first grabs the constructor of the class it is trying to instantiate, in this case Nevermore60Customer. The first thing that the default Nevermore60Customer constructor does is attempt to run the default constructor for the immediate base class, GenericCustomer. The GenericCustomer constructor attempts to run the constructor for its immediate base class, System.Object. System.Object doesn't have any base classes, so its constructor just executes and returns control to the GenericCustomer constructor. That constructor now executes, initializing name to null, before returning control to the Nevermore60Customer constructor. That constructor in turn executes, initializing highCostMinutesUsed to zero, and exits. At this point, the Nevermore60Customer instance has been successfully constructed and initialized.

The net result of all this is that the constructors are called in order of System.Object first, then progressing down the hierarchy until the compiler reaches the class being instantiated. Notice also that in this process, each constructor handles initialization of the fields in its own class. That's how it should normally work, and when you start adding your own constructors you should try to stick to that principle.

Notice the order in which this happens. It's always the base class constructors that get called first. This means that there are no problems with a constructor for a derived class invoking any base class methods, properties, and any other members that it has access to, because it can be confident that the base class has already been constructed and its fields initialized. It also means that if the derived class doesn't like the way that the base class has been initialized, it can change the initial values of the data, provided that it has access to do so. However, good programming practice almost invariably means you'll try to prevent that situation from occurring if you can, and you will trust the base class constructor to deal with its own fields.

Now that you know how the process of construction works, you can start fiddling with it by adding your own constructors.

Adding a Constructor in a Hierarchy

We'll take the easiest case first and see what happens if you simply replace the default constructor somewhere in the hierarchy with another constructor that takes no parameters. Suppose that you decide that you want everyone's name to be initially set to the string "<no name>" instead of to the null reference. You'd modify the code in GenericCustomer like this:

```
public abstract class GenericCustomer
{
   private string name;
   public GenericCustomer()
      : base()  // We could omit this line without affecting the compiled code.
   {
      name = "<no name>";
   }
```

Adding this code will work fine. Nevermore60Customer still has its default constructor, so the sequence of events described earlier will proceed as before, except that the compiler will use the custom GenericCustomer constructor instead of generating a default one, so the name field will always be initialized to "<no name>" as required.

Notice that in your constructor you've added a call to the base class constructor before the GenericCustomer constructor is executed, using a syntax similar to that used earlier when we discussed how to get different overloads of constructors to call each other. The only difference is that this time you use the base keyword instead of this to indicate that it's a constructor to the base class rather than a constructor to the current class you want to call. There are no parameters in the brackets after the base keyword — that's important because it means you are not passing any parameters to the base constructor, so the compiler will have to look for a parameterless constructor to call. The result of all this is that the compiler will inject code to call the System.Object constructor, just as would happen by default anyway.

In fact, you can omit that line of code and write the following (as was done for most of the constructors so far in this chapter):

```
public GenericCustomer()
{
   name = "<no name>";
}
```

If the compiler doesn't see any reference to another constructor before the opening curly brace, it assumes that you intended to call the base class constructor; this fits in with the way that default constructors work.

The `base` and `this` keywords are the only keywords allowed in the line that calls another constructor. Anything else causes a compilation error. Also note that only one other constructor can be specified.

So far, this code works fine. One way to mess up the progression through the hierarchy of constructors, however, is to declare a constructor as `private`:

```
private GenericCustomer()
{
   name = "<no name>";
}
```

If you try this, you'll find you get an interesting compilation error, which could really throw you if you don't understand how construction down a hierarchy works:

```
'Wrox.ProCSharp.GenericCustomer()' is inaccessible due to its protection level
```

The interesting thing is that the error occurs not in the `GenericCustomer` class, but in the derived class, `Nevermore60Customer`. What's happened is that the compiler has tried to generate a default constructor for `Nevermore60Customer` but has not been able to because the default constructor is supposed to invoke the no-parameter `GenericCustomer` constructor. By declaring that constructor as `private`, you've made it inaccessible to the derived class. A similar error occurs if you supply a constructor to `GenericCustomer`, which takes parameters, but at the same time you fail to supply a no-parameter constructor. In this case, the compiler will not generate a default constructor for `GenericCustomer`, so when it tries to generate the default constructors for any derived class, it will again find that it can't because a no-parameter base class constructor is not available. A workaround would be to add your own constructors to the derived classes, even if you don't actually need to do anything in these constructors, so that the compiler doesn't try to generate any default constructors for them.

Now that you have all the theoretical background you need, you're ready to move on to an example of how you can neatly add constructors to a hierarchy of classes. In the next section, you start adding constructors that take parameters to the MortimerPhones example.

Adding Constructors with Parameters to a Hierarchy

You're going to start with a one-parameter constructor for `GenericCustomer`, which specifies that customers can be instantiated only when they supply their names:

```
abstract class GenericCustomer
{
   private string name;
   public GenericCustomer(string name)
   {
      this.name = name;
   }
```

So far, so good. However, as mentioned previously, this will cause a compilation error when the compiler tries to create a default constructor for any derived classes because the default compiler-generated constructors for `Nevermore60Customer` will try to call a no-parameter `GenericCustomer` constructor, and `GenericCustomer` does not possess such a constructor. Therefore, you'll need to supply your own constructors to the derived classes to avoid a compilation error:

```
class Nevermore60Customer : GenericCustomer
{
   private uint highCostMinutesUsed;
   public Nevermore60Customer(string name)
      :   base(name)
   {
   }
```

Now instantiation of `Nevermore60Customer` objects can occur only when a string containing the customer's name is supplied, which is what you want anyway. The interesting thing is what the `Nevermore60Customer` constructor does with this string. Remember that it can't initialize the `name` field itself because it has no access to private fields in its base class. Instead, it passes the name through to the base class for the `GenericCustomer` constructor to handle. It does this by specifying that the base class constructor to be executed first is the one that takes the name as a parameter. Other than that, it doesn't take any action of its own.

Next, you're going to investigate what happens if you have different overloads of the constructor as well as a class hierarchy to deal with. To this end, assume that Nevermore60 customers may have been referred to MortimerPhones by a friend as part of one of those sign-up-a-friend-and-get-a-discount offers. This means that when you construct a `Nevermore60Customer`, you may need to pass in the referrer's name as well. In real life, the constructor would have to do something complicated with the name, such as process the discount, but here you'll just store the referrer's name in another field.

The `Nevermore60Customer` definition will now look like this:

```
class Nevermore60Customer : GenericCustomer
{
   public Nevermore60Customer(string name, string referrerName)
      : base(name)
   {
      this.referrerName = referrerName;
   }

   private string referrerName;
   private uint highCostMinutesUsed;
```

The constructor takes the name and passes it to the `GenericCustomer` constructor for processing. `referrerName` is the variable that is your responsibility here, so the constructor deals with that parameter in its main body.

However, not all `Nevermore60Customers` will have a referrer, so you still need a constructor that doesn't require this parameter (or a constructor that gives you a default value for it). In fact, you will specify that if there is no referrer, then the `referrerName` field should be set to `"<None>"`, using the following one-parameter constructor:

```
public Nevermore60Customer(string name)
   : this(name, "<None>")
{
}
```

You now have all your constructors set up correctly. It's instructive to examine the chain of events that now occurs when you execute a line like this:

```
GenericCustomer customer = new Nevermore60Customer("Arabel Jones");
```

The compiler sees that it needs a one-parameter constructor that takes one string, so the constructor it will identify is the last one that you've defined:

```
public Nevermore60Customer(string Name)
   : this(Name, "<None>")
```

When you instantiate `customer`, this constructor will be called. It immediately transfers control to the corresponding `Nevermore60Customer` two-parameter constructor, passing it the values `"ArabelJones"`, and `"<None>"`. Looking at the code for this constructor, you see that it in turn immediately passes control to the one-parameter `GenericCustomer` constructor, giving it the string `"ArabelJones"`, and in turn that constructor passes control to the `System.Object` default constructor. Only now do the constructors execute. First, the `System.Object` constructor executes. Next comes the `GenericCustomer` constructor, which initializes the `name` field. Then the `Nevermore60Customer` two-parameter constructor gets control back, and sorts out initializing the `referrerName` to `"<None>"`. Finally, the `Nevermore60Customer` one-parameter constructor gets to execute; this constructor doesn't do anything else.

As you can see, this is a very neat and well-designed process. Each constructor handles initialization of the variables that are obviously its responsibility, and, in the process, your class is correctly instantiated and prepared for use. If you follow the same principles when you write your own constructors for your classes, you should find that even the most complex classes get initialized smoothly and without any problems.

Modifiers

You have already encountered quite a number of so-called modifiers — keywords that can be applied to a type or to a member. Modifiers can indicate the visibility of a method, such as `public` or `private`, or the nature of an item, such as whether a method is `virtual` or `abstract`. C# has a number of modifiers, and at this point it's worth taking a minute to provide the complete list.

Visibility Modifiers

Visibility modifiers indicate which other code items can view an item.

Modifier	Applies To	Description
`public`	Any types or members	The item is visible to any other code.
`protected`	Any member of a type, also any nested type	The item is visible only to any derived type.
`internal`	Any member of a type, also any nested type	The item is visible only within its containing assembly.
`private`	Any types or members	The item is visible only inside the type to which it belongs.
`protected internal`	Any member of a type, also any nested type	The item is visible to any code within its containing assembly and also to any code inside a derived type.

Note that type definitions can be internal or public, depending on whether you want the type to be visible outside its containing assembly.

```
public class MyClass
{
  // etc.
```

You cannot define types as protected, private, or protected internal because these visibility levels would be meaningless for a type contained in a namespace. Hence these visibilities can be applied only to members. However, you can define nested types (that is, types contained within other types) with these visibilities because in this case the type also has the status of a member. Hence, the following code is correct:

```
public class OuterClass
{
  protected class InnerClass
  {
         // etc.
  }
  // etc.
}
```

If you have a nested type, the inner type is always able to see all members of the outer type. Therefore, with the preceding code, any code inside `InnerClass` always has access to all members of `OuterClass`, even where those members are private.

Other Modifiers

The modifiers in the following table can be applied to members of types and have various uses. A few of these modifiers also make sense when applied to types.

Modifier	Applies To	Description
`new`	Function members	The member hides an inherited member with the same signature.
`static`	All members	The member does not operate on a specific instance of the class.
`virtual`	Classes and function members only	The member can be overridden by a derived class.
`abstract`	Function members only	A virtual member that defines the signature of the member, but doesn't provide an implementation.
`override`	Function members only	The member overrides an inherited virtual or abstract member.
`sealed`	Classes, methods, and properties	For classes, the class cannot be inherited from. For properties and methods, the member overrides an inherited virtual member, but cannot be overridden by any members in any derived classes. Must be used in conjunction with `override`.
`extern`	Static `[DllImport]` methods only	The member is implemented externally, in a different language.

Of these, internal and protected internal are the ones that are new to C# and the .NET Framework. internal acts in much the same way as public, but access is confined to other code in the same assembly — that is, code that is being compiled at the same time in the same program. You can use internal to ensure that all the other classes that you are writing have access to a particular member, while at the same time hiding it from other code written by other organizations. protected internal combines protected and internal, but in an OR sense, not an AND sense. A protected internal member can be seen by any code in the same assembly. It can also be seen by any derived classes, even those in other assemblies.

Interfaces

As mentioned earlier, by deriving from an interface, a class is declaring that it implements certain functions. Because not all object-oriented languages support interfaces, this section examines C#'s implementation of interfaces in detail.

Developers familiar with COM should be aware that, although, conceptually, C# interfaces are similar to COM interfaces, they are not the same thing. The underlying architecture is different. For example, C# interfaces are not derived from IUnknown. *A C# interface provides a contract stated in terms of .NET functions. Unlike a COM interface, a C# interface does not represent any kind of binary standard.*

This section illustrates interfaces by presenting the complete definition of one of the interfaces that has been predefined by Microsoft, System.IDisposable. IDisposable contains one method, Dispose(), which is intended to be implemented by classes to clean up code:

```
public interface IDisposable
{
   void Dispose();
}
```

This code shows that declaring an interface works syntactically in pretty much the same way as declaring an abstract class. You should be aware, however, that it is not permitted to supply implementations of any of the members of an interface. In general, an interface can only contain declarations of methods, properties, indexers, and events.

You can never instantiate an interface; it contains only the signatures of its members. An interface has neither constructors (how can you construct something that you can't instantiate?) nor fields (because that would imply some internal implementation). An interface definition is also not allowed to contain operator overloads, although that's not because there is any problem in principle with declaring them — there isn't; it is because interfaces are usually intended to be public contracts, and having operator overloads would cause some incompatibility problems with other .NET languages, such as Visual Basic .NET, which do not support operator overloading.

It is also not permitted to declare modifiers on the members in an interface definition. Interface members are always implicitly public, and cannot be declared as virtual or static. That's up to implementing classes to decide. It is therefore fine for implementing classes to declare access modifiers, as is done in the example in this section.

Take for example IDisposable. If a class wants to declare publicly that it implements the Dispose() method, it must implement IDisposable — which in C# terms means that the class derives from IDisposable.

```
class SomeClass : IDisposable
{
   // This class MUST contain an implementation of the
   // IDisposable.Dispose() method, otherwise
   // you get a compilation error.
```

```
        public void Dispose()
        {
            // implementation of Dispose() method
        }
        // rest of class
    }
```

In this example, if `SomeClass` derives from `IDisposable` but doesn't contain a `Dispose()` implementation with the exact same signature as defined in `IDisposable`, you get a compilation error because the class would be breaking its agreed-on contract to implement `IDisposable`. Of course, there's no problem for the compiler about a class having a `Dispose()` method but not deriving from `IDisposable`. The problem, then, would be that other code would have no way of recognizing that `SomeClass` has agreed to support the `IDisposable` features.

> `IDisposable` *is a relatively simple interface because it defines only one method. Most interfaces will contain more members.*

Another good example of an interface is provided by the `foreach` loop in C#. In principle, the `foreach` loop works internally by querying the object to find out whether it implements an interface called `System.Collections.IEnumerable`. If it does, the C# compiler will inject IL code, which uses the methods on this interface to iterate through the members of the collection. If it doesn't, `foreach` will raise an exception. The `IEnumerable` interface is examined in more detail in Chapter 10, "Collections." It's worth pointing out that both `IEnumerable` and `IDisposable` are somewhat special interfaces to the extent that they are actually recognized by the C# compiler, which takes account of these interfaces in the code that it generates. Obviously, any interfaces that you define yourself won't be so privileged!

Defining and Implementing Interfaces

This section illustrates how to define and use interfaces through developing a short program that follows the interface inheritance paradigm. The example is based on bank accounts. Assume that you are writing code that will ultimately allow computerized transfers between bank accounts. And assume for this example that there are many companies that may implement bank accounts, but they have all mutually agreed that any classes that represent bank accounts will implement an interface, `IBankAccount`, which exposes methods to deposit or withdraw money, and a property to return the balance. It is this interface that will allow outside code to recognize the various bank account classes implemented by different bank accounts. Although the aim is to allow the bank accounts to talk to each other to allow transfers of funds between accounts, we won't introduce that feature just yet.

To keep things simple, you will keep all the code for the example in the same source file. Of course, if something like the example were used in real life, you could surmise that the different bank account classes would not only be compiled to different assemblies, but would also be hosted on different machines owned by the different banks. That's all much too complicated for our purposes here. However, to maintain some attempt at realism, you will define different namespaces for the different companies.

To begin, you need to define the `IBankAccount` interface:

```
namespace Wrox.ProCSharp
{
   public interface IBankAccount
   {
      void PayIn(decimal amount);
      bool Withdraw(decimal amount);
      decimal Balance
```

(continued)

(continued)

```
         {
            get;
         }
      }
   }
```

Notice the name of the interface, `IBankAccount`. It's a convention that an interface name traditionally starts with the letter I, so that you know that it's an interface.

Chapter 2, "C# Basics," pointed out that, in most cases, .NET usage guidelines discourage the so-called Hungarian notation in which names are preceded by a letter that indicates the type of object being defined. Interfaces are one of the few exceptions in which Hungarian notation is recommended.

The idea is that you can now write classes that represent bank accounts. These classes don't have to be related to each other in any way; they can be completely different classes. They will, however, all declare that they represent bank accounts by the mere fact that they implement the `IBankAccount` interface.

Let's start off with the first class, a saver account run by the Royal Bank of Venus:

```
namespace Wrox.ProCSharp.VenusBank
{
   public class SaverAccount : IBankAccount
   {
      private decimal balance;
      public void PayIn(decimal amount)
      {
         balance += amount;
      }
      public bool Withdraw(decimal amount)
      {
         if (balance >= amount)
         {
            balance -= amount;
            return true;
         }
         Console.WriteLine("Withdrawal attempt failed.");
         return false;
      }
      public decimal Balance
      {
         get
         {
            return balance;
         }
      }
      public override string ToString()
      {
         return String.Format("Venus Bank Saver: Balance = {0,6:C}", balance);
      }
   }
}
```

It should be pretty obvious what the implementation of this class does. You maintain a private field, `balance`, and adjust this amount when money is deposited or withdrawn. You display an error message if an attempt to withdraw money fails because there is insufficient money in the account. Notice also that, because we want to keep the code as simple as possible, you are not implementing extra properties, such as the account holder's name! In real life that would be pretty essential information, but for this example it's unnecessarily complicated.

The only really interesting line in this code is the class declaration:

```
public class SaverAccount : IBankAccount
```

You've declared that `SaverAccount` is derived from one interface, `IBankAccount`, and you have not explicitly indicated any other base classes (which of course means that `SaverAccount` is derived directly from `System.Object`). By the way, derivation from interfaces acts completely independently from derivation from classes.

Being derived from `IBankAccount` means that `SaverAccount` gets all the members of `IBankAccount`. But because an interface doesn't actually implement any of its methods, `SaverAccount` must provide its own implementations of all of them. If any implementations are missing, you can rest assured that the compiler will complain. Recall also that the interface just indicates the presence of its members. It's up to the class to decide if it wants any of them to be `virtual` or `abstract` (though `abstract` functions are of course only allowed if the class itself is `abstract`). For this particular example, you don't have any reason to make any of the interface functions virtual.

To illustrate how different classes can implement the same interface, assume that the Planetary Bank of Jupiter also implements a class to represent one of its bank accounts — a Gold Account:

```
namespace Wrox.ProCSharp.JupiterBank
{
   public class GoldAccount : IBankAccount
   {
      // etc
   }
}
```

We won't present details of the `GoldAccount` class here; in the sample code, it's basically identical to the implementation of `SaverAccount`. We stress that `GoldAccount` has no connection with `SaverAccount`, other than that both happen to implement the same interface.

Now that you have your classes, you can test them out. You first need a couple of `using` statements:

```
using System;
using Wrox.ProCSharp;
using Wrox.ProCSharp.VenusBank;
using Wrox.ProCSharp.JupiterBank;
```

Now you need a `Main()` method:

```
namespace Wrox.ProCSharp
{
   class MainEntryPoint
   {
      static void Main()
      {
         IBankAccount venusAccount = new SaverAccount();
         IBankAccount jupiterAccount = new GoldAccount();
         venusAccount.PayIn(200);
         venusAccount.Withdraw(100);
         Console.WriteLine(venusAccount.ToString());
         jupiterAccount.PayIn(500);
```

(continued)

(continued)

```
            jupiterAccount.Withdraw(600);
            jupiterAccount.Withdraw(100);
            Console.WriteLine(jupiterAccount.ToString());
        }
    }
}
```

This code (which if you download the sample, you can find in the file `BankAccounts.cs`) produces this output:

```
C:> BankAccounts
Venus Bank Saver: Balance = £100.00
Withdrawal attempt failed.
Jupiter Bank Saver: Balance = £400.00
```

The main point to notice about this code is the way that you have declared both your reference variables as `IBankAccount` references. This means that they can point to any instance of any class that implements this interface. However, it also means that you can call only methods that are part of this interface through these references — if you want to call any methods implemented by a class that are not part of the interface, you need to cast the reference to the appropriate type. In the example code, you were able to call `ToString()` (not implemented by `IBankAccount`) without any explicit cast, purely because `ToString()` is a `System.Object` method, so the C# compiler knows that it will be supported by any class (put differently, the cast from any interface to `System.Object` is implicit). Chapter 6, "Operators and Casts," covers the syntax for how to perform casts.

Interface references can in all respects be treated like class references — but the power of an interface reference is that it can refer to any class that implements that interface. For example, this allows you to form arrays of interfaces, where each element of the array is a different class:

```
IBankAccount[] accounts = new IBankAccount[2];
accounts[0] = new SaverAccount();
accounts[1] = new GoldAccount();
```

Note, however, that we'd get a compiler error if we tried something like this:

```
accounts[1] = new SomeOtherClass();    // SomeOtherClass does NOT implement
                                              // IBankAccount: WRONG!!
```

This causes a compilation error similar to this:

```
Cannot implicitly convert type 'Wrox.ProCSharp. SomeOtherClass' to 'Wrox.ProCSharp.
IBankAccount'
```

Derived Interfaces

It's possible for interfaces to inherit from each other in the same way that classes do. This concept is illustrated by defining a new interface, `ITransferBankAccount`, which has the same features as `IBankAccount` but also defines a method to transfer money directly to a different account:

```
namespace Wrox.ProCSharp
{
   public interface ITransferBankAccount : IBankAccount
   {
      bool TransferTo(IBankAccount destination, decimal amount);
   }
}
```

Because ITransferBankAccount is derived from IBankAccount, it gets all the members of IBankAccount as well as its own. That means that any class that implements (derives from) ITransferBankAccount must implement all the methods of IBankAccount, as well as the new TransferTo() method defined in ITransferBankAccount. Failure to implement all of these methods will result in a compilation error.

Note that the TransferTo() method uses an IBankAccount interface reference for the destination account. This illustrates the usefulness of interfaces: when implementing and then invoking this method, you don't need to know anything about what type of object you are transferring money to — all you need to know is that this object implements IBankAccount.

To illustrate ITransferBankAccount, assume that the Planetary Bank of Jupiter also offers a current account. Most of the implementation of the CurrentAccount class is identical to the implementations of SaverAccount and GoldAccount (again, this is just to keep this example simple — that won't normally be the case), so in the following code just the differences are highlighted:

```
public class CurrentAccount : ITransferBankAccount
{
   private decimal balance;
   public void PayIn(decimal amount)
   {
      balance += amount;
   }
   public bool Withdraw(decimal amount)
   {
      if (balance >= amount)
      {
         balance -= amount;
         return true;
      }
      Console.WriteLine("Withdrawal attempt failed.");
      return false;
   }
   public decimal Balance
   {
      get
      {
         return balance;
      }
   }

   public bool TransferTo(IBankAccount destination, decimal amount)
   {
      bool result;
      if ((result == Withdraw(amount))
         destination.PayIn(amount);
      return result;
   }

   public override string ToString()
   {

      return String.Format("Jupiter Bank Current Account: Balance = {0,6:C}",
balance);
   }
}
```

The class can be demonstrated with this code:

```
static void Main()
{
    IBankAccount venusAccount = new SaverAccount();
    ITransferBankAccount jupiterAccount = new CurrentAccount();
    venusAccount.PayIn(200);
    jupiterAccount.PayIn(500);
    jupiterAccount.TransferTo(venusAccount, 100);
    Console.WriteLine(venusAccount.ToString());
    Console.WriteLine(jupiterAccount.ToString());
}
```

This code (`CurrentAccount.cs`) produces the following output, which, as you can verify, shows that the correct amounts have been transferred:

```
C:> CurrentAccount
Venus Bank Saver: Balance = £300.00
Jupiter Bank Current Account: Balance = £400.00
```

Summary

This chapter examined how to code inheritance in C#. You have seen that C# offers rich support for both multiple interface and single implementation inheritance. You have also learned that C# provides a number of useful syntactical constructs designed to assist in making code more robust, such as the `override` keyword, which indicates when a function should override a base function; the `new` keyword, which indicates when a function hides a base function; and rigid rules for constructor initializers that are designed to ensure that constructors are designed to interoperate in a robust manner.

5

Arrays

If you need to work with multiple objects of the same type, you can use collections and arrays. C# has a special notation to declare and use arrays. Behind the scenes, the `Array` class comes into play, which offers several methods to sort and filter the elements inside the array.

Using an enumerator, you can iterate through all the elements of an array.

This chapter discusses the following:

- Simple arrays
- Multidimensional arrays
- Jagged arrays
- The `Array` class
- Interfaces for arrays
- Enumerations

Simple Arrays

If you need to use multiple objects of the same type, you can use an array. An *array* is a data structure that contains a number of elements of the same type.

Array Declaration

An array is declared by defining the type of the elements inside the array followed by empty brackets and a variable name; for example, an array containing integer elements is declared like this:

```
int[] myArray;
```

Array Initialization

After declaring an array, memory must be allocated to hold all the elements of the array. An array is a reference type, so memory on the heap must be allocated. You do this by initializing the variable of the array using the `new` operator with the type and the number of elements inside the array. Here you specify the size of the array:

```
myArray = new int[4];
```

Value and reference types are covered in Chapter 3, "Objects and Types."

With this declaration and initialization, the variable `myArray` references four integer values that are allocated on the managed heap (see Figure 5-1).

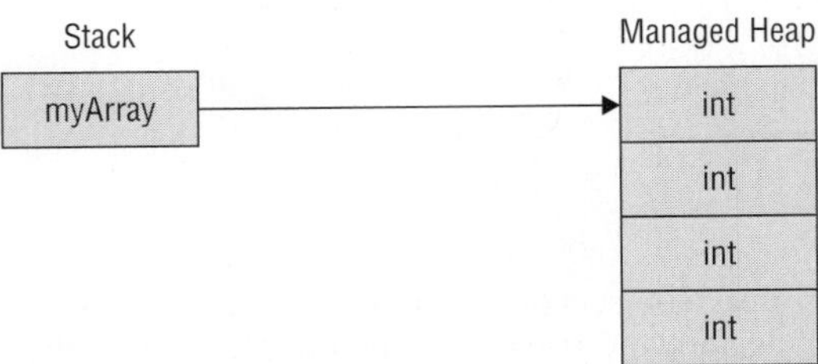

Figure 5-1

> **The array cannot be resized after the size was specified without copying all elements. If you don't know the number of elements that should be in the array in advance, you can use a collection. Collections are covered in Chapter 10, "Collections."**

Instead of using a separate line for the declaration and initialization, you can declare and initialize an array in a single line:

```
int[] myArray = new int[4];
```

You can also assign values to every array element using an array initializer. Array initializers can be used only while declaring an array variable, not after the array is declared.

```
int[] myArray = new int[4] {4, 7, 11, 2};
```

If you initialize the array using curly brackets, the size of the array can also be left out, because the compiler can count the number of elements itself:

```
int[] myArray = new int[] {4, 7, 11, 2};
```

There's even a shorter form using the C# compiler. Using curly brackets you can write the array declaration and initialization. The code generated from the compiler is the same as in the previous example.

```
int[] myArray = {4, 7, 11, 2};
```

Accessing Array Elements

After an array is declared and initialized, you can access the array elements using an indexer. Arrays only support indexers that have integer parameters.

With custom classes, you can also create indexers that support other types. You can read about creating custom indexers in Chapter 6, "Operators and Casts."

With the indexer, you pass the element number to access the array. The indexer always starts with a value of 0 for the first element. The highest number you can pass to the indexer is the number of elements minus one, because the index starts at zero. In the following example, the array `myArray` is declared and initialized with four integer values. The elements can be accessed with indexer values 0, 1, 2, and 3.

```
int[] myArray = new int[] {4, 7, 11, 2};
int v1 = myArray[0];   // read first element
int v2 = myArray[1];   // read second element
myArray[3] = 44;       // change fourth element
```

If you use a wrong indexer value where no element exists, an exception of type `IndexOutOfRangeException` is thrown.

If you don't know the number of elements in the array, you can use the `Length` property that is used in this `for` statement:

```
for (int i = 0; i < myArray.Length; i++)
{
   Console.WriteLine(myArray[i]);
}
```

Instead of using a `for` statement to iterate through all elements of the array, you can also use the `foreach` statement:

```
foreach (int val in myArray)
{
   Console.WriteLine(val);
}
```

The `foreach` statement makes use of the `IEnumerable` and `IEnumerator` interfaces, which are discussed later in this chapter.

Using Reference Types

In addition to being able to declare arrays of predefined types, you can also declare arrays of custom types. Let's start with this `Person` class with two constructors, the properties `FirstName` and `LastName` using auto-implemented properties, and an override of the `ToString()` method from the `Object` class:

```
public class Person
{
   public Person()
   {
   }

   public Person(string firstName, string lastName)
```

(continued)

(continued)

```
    {
      this.FirstName = firstName;
      this.LastName = lastName;
    }

    public string FirstName { get; set; }

    public string LastName { get; set; }

    public override string ToString()
    {
      return String.Format("{0} {1}",
            FirstName, LastName);
    }
  }
```

Declaring an array of two `Person` elements is similar to declaring an array of `int`:

```
Person[] myPersons = new Person[2];
```

However, you must be aware that if the elements in the array are reference types, memory must be allocated for every array element. In case you use an item in the array where no memory was allocated, a `NullReferenceException` is thrown.

Chapter 14, "Errors and Exceptions," gives you all the information you need about errors and exceptions.

You can allocate every element of the array by using an indexer starting from 0:

```
myPersons[0] = new Person("Ayrton", "Senna");
myPersons[1] = new Person("Michael", "Schumacher");
```

Figure 5-2 shows the objects in the managed heap with the `Person` array. `myPersons` is a variable that is stored on the stack. This variable references an array of `Person` elements that is stored on the managed heap. This array has enough space for two references. Every item in the array references a `Person` object that is also stored in the managed heap.

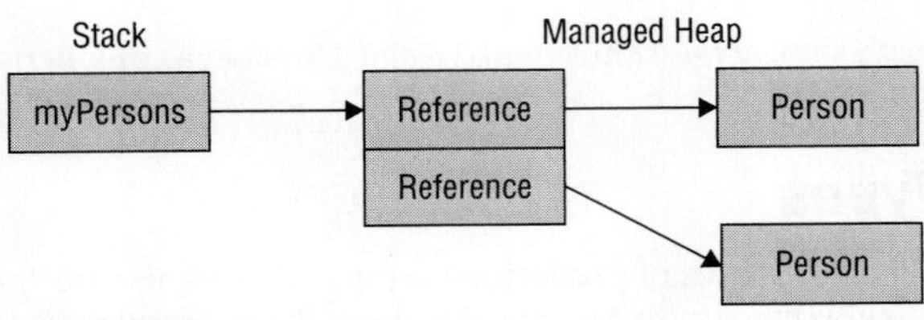

Figure 5-2

As with the `int` type, you can also use an array initializer with custom types:

```
Person[] myPersons = { new Person("Ayrton", "Senna"),
                      new Person("Michael",
                           "Schumacher") };
```

Multidimensional Arrays

Ordinary arrays (also known as 1-dimensional arrays) are indexed by a single integer. A multidimensional array is indexed by two or more integers.

Figure 5-3 shows the mathematical notation for a 2-dimensional array that has three rows and three columns. The first row has the values 1, 2, and 3, and the third row has the values 7, 8, and 9.

$$a = \begin{bmatrix} 1, & 2, & 3 \\ 4, & 5, & 6 \\ 7, & 8, & 9 \end{bmatrix}$$

Figure 5-3

Declaring this 2-dimensional array with C# is done by putting a comma inside the brackets. The array is initialized by specifying the size of every dimension (also known as rank). Then the array elements can be accessed by using two integers with the indexer:

```
int[,] twodim = new int[3, 3];
twodim[0, 0] = 1;
twodim[0, 1] = 2;
twodim[0, 2] = 3;
twodim[1, 0] = 4;
twodim[1, 1] = 5;
twodim[1, 2] = 6;
twodim[2, 0] = 7;
twodim[2, 1] = 8;
twodim[2, 2] = 9;
```

You cannot change the rank after declaring an array.

You can also initialize the 2-dimensional array by using an array indexer if you know the value for the elements in advance. For the initialization of the array, one outer curly bracket is used, and every row is initialized by using curly brackets inside the outer curly brackets.

```
int[,] twodim = {
                    {1, 2, 3},
                    {4, 5, 6},
                    {7, 8, 9}
                };
```

When using an array initializer, you must initialize every element of the array. It is not possible to leave the initialization for some values.

By using two commas inside the brackets, you can declare a 3-dimensional array:

```
int[,,] threedim = {
                      { { 1, 2 }, { 3, 4 } },
                      { { 5, 6 }, { 7, 8 } },
                      { { 9, 10 }, { 11, 12 } }
                   };

Console.WriteLine(threedim[0, 1, 1]);
```

Jagged Arrays

A 2-dimensional array has a rectangular size (for example, 3 × 3 elements). A jagged array is more flexible in sizing the array. With a jagged array every row can have a different size.

Figure 5-4 contrasts a 2-dimensional array that has 3 × 3 elements with a jagged array. The jagged array shown contains three rows where the first row has two elements, the second row has six elements, and the third row has three elements.

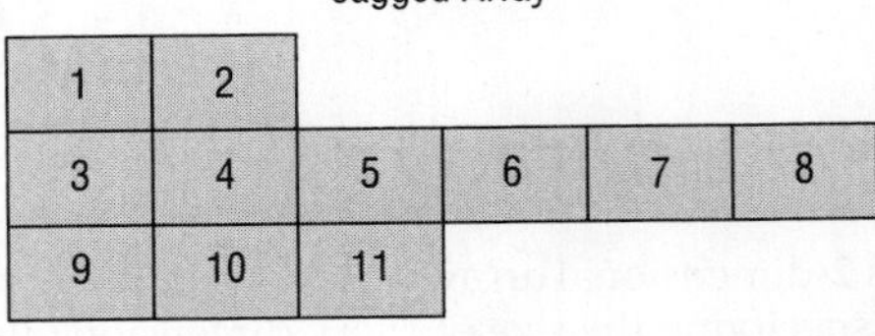

Figure 5-4

A jagged array is declared by placing one pair of opening and closing brackets after another. With the initialization of the jagged array, only the size that defines the number of rows in the first pair of brackets is set. The second brackets that define the number of elements inside the row are kept empty because every row has a different number of elements. Next, the element number of the rows can be set for every row:

```
int[][] jagged = new int[3][];
jagged[0] = new int[2] { 1, 2 };
jagged[1] = new int[6] { 3, 4, 5, 6, 7, 8 };
jagged[2] = new int[3] { 9, 10, 11 };
```

Iterating through all elements of a jagged array can be done with nested `for` loops. In the outer `for` loop every row is iterated, and the inner `for` loop iterates through every element inside a row.

```
for (int row = 0; row < jagged.Length; row++)
{
   for (int element = 0;
      element < jagged[row].Length; element++)
   {
      Console.WriteLine(
         "row: {0}, element: {1}, value: {2}",
         row, element, jagged[row][element]);
   }
}
```

The outcome of the iteration displays the rows and every element within the rows:

```
row: 0, element: 0, value: 1
row: 0, element: 1, value: 2
row: 1, element: 0, value: 3
row: 1, element: 1, value: 4
row: 1, element: 2, value: 5
row: 1, element: 3, value: 6
row: 1, element: 4, value: 7
row: 1, element: 5, value: 8
row: 2, element: 1, value: 9
row: 2, element: 2, value: 10
row: 2, element: 3, value: 11
```

Array Class

Declaring an array with brackets is a C# notation of using the `Array` class. Using the C# syntax behind the scenes creates a new class that derives from the abstract base class `Array`. It is possible, in this way, to use methods and properties that are defined with the `Array` class with every C# array. For example, you've already used the `Length` property or iterated through the array by using the `foreach` statement. By doing this, you are using the `GetEnumerator()` method of the `Array` class.

Properties

The `Array` class contains the properties listed in the following table that you can use with every array instance. More properties are available, which are discussed later in this chapter.

Property	Description
`Length`	The `Length` property returns the number of elements inside the array. If the array is a multidimensional array, you get the number of elements of all ranks. If you need to know the number of elements within a dimension, you can use the `GetLength()` method instead.
`LongLength`	The `Length` property returns an `int` value; the `LongLength` property returns the length in a `long` value. If the array contains more elements than fit into a 32-bit `int` value, you need to use the `LongLength` property to get the number of elements.
`Rank`	With the `Rank` property you get the number of dimensions of the array.

Creating Arrays

The `Array` class is abstract, so you cannot create an array by using a constructor. However, instead of using the C# syntax to create array instances, it is also possible to create arrays by using the static `CreateInstance()` method. This is extremely useful if you don't know the type of the elements in advance, because the type can be passed to the `CreateInstance()` method as a `Type` object.

The following example shows how to create an array of type `int` with a size of 5. The first argument of the `CreateInstance()` method requires the type of the elements, and the second argument defines the size. You can set values with the `SetValue()` method, and read values with the `GetValue()` method.

```
Array intArray1 = Array.CreateInstance(typeof(int), 5);
for (int i = 0; i < 5; i++)
{
   intArray1.SetValue(33, i);
}

for (int i = 0; i < 5; i++)
{
   Console.WriteLine(intArray1.GetValue(i));
}
```

You can also cast the created array to an array declared as `int[]`:

```
int[] intArray2 = (int[])intArray1;
```

The `CreateInstance()` method has many overloads to create multidimensional arrays and also to create arrays that are not 0-based. The following example creates a 2-dimensional array with 2 × 3 elements. The first dimension is 1-based; the second dimension is 10-based.

```
int[] lengths = { 2, 3 };
int[] lowerBounds = { 1, 10 };
Array racers = Array.CreateInstance(typeof(Person), lengths, lowerBounds);
```

Setting the elements of the array, the `SetValue()` method accepts indices for every dimension:

```
racers.SetValue(new Person("Alain", "Prost"), 1, 10);
racers.SetValue(new Person("Emerson", "Fittipaldi"), 1, 11);
racers.SetValue(new Person("Ayrton", "Senna"), 1, 12);
racers.SetValue(new Person("Ralf", "Schumacher"), 2, 10);
racers.SetValue(new Person("Fernando", "Alonso"), 2, 11);
racers.SetValue(new Person("Jenson", "Button"), 2, 12);
```

Although the array is not 0-based you can assign it to a variable with the normal C# notation. You just have to pay attention to not crossing the boundaries.

```
Person[,] racers2 = (Person[,])racers;
Person first = racers2[1, 10];
Person last = racers2[2, 12];
```

Copying Arrays

Because arrays are reference types, assigning an array variable to another one just gives you two variables referencing the same array. For copying arrays, the array implements the interface `ICloneable`. The `Clone()` method that is defined with this interface creates a shallow copy of the array.

If the elements of the array are value types, as in the following code segment, all values are copied, as you can see in Figure 5-5.

```
int[] intArray1 = {1, 2};
int[] intArray2 = (int[])intArray1.Clone();
```

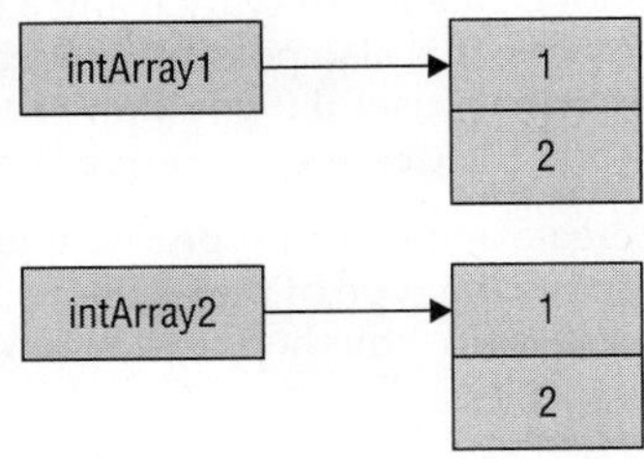

Figure 5-5

If the array contains reference types, only the references are copied; not the elements. Figure 5-6 shows the variables `beatles` and `beatlesClone`, where `beatlesClone` is created by calling the `Clone()` method from `beatles`. The `Person` objects that are referenced are the same with `beatles` and `beatlesClone`. If you change a property of an element of `beatlesClone`, you change the same object of `beatles`.

```
Person[] beatles = {
                     new Person("John", "Lennon"),
                     new Person("Paul", "McCartney")
                   };
Person[] beatlesClone = (Person[])beatles.Clone();
```

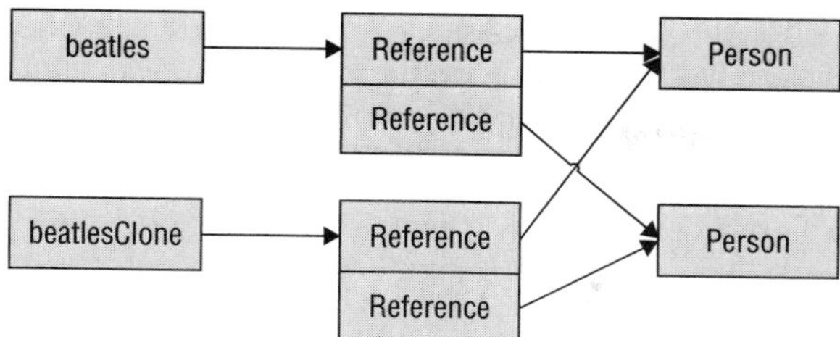

Figure 5-6

Instead of using the `Clone()` method, you can use the `Array.Copy()` method, which creates a shallow copy as well. But there's one important difference with `Clone()` and `Copy()`: `Clone()` creates a new array; with `Copy()` you have to pass an existing array with the same rank and enough elements.

If you need a deep copy of an array containing reference types, you have to iterate the array and create new objects.

Sorting

The `Array` class implements a bubble-sort for sorting the elements in the array. The `Sort()` method requires the interface `IComparable` to be implemented by the elements in the array. Simple types such as `System.String` and `System.Int32` implement `IComparable`, so you can sort elements containing these types.

With the sample program, the array name contains elements of type string, and this array can be sorted:

```
string[] names = {
                    "Christina Aguilera",
                    "Shakira",
                    "Beyonce",
                    "Gwen Stefani"
                 };

Array.Sort(names);

foreach (string name in names)
{
   Console.WriteLine(name);
}
```

The output of the application shows the sorted result of the array:

```
Beyonce
Christina Aguilera
Gwen Stefani
Shakira
```

If you are using custom classes with the array, you must implement the interface `IComparable`. This interface defines just one method, `CompareTo()`, that must return 0 if the objects to compare are equal, a value smaller than 0 if the instance should go before the object from the parameter, and a value larger than 0 if the instance should go after the object from the parameter.

Change the `Person` class to implement the interface `IComparable`. The comparison is done on the value of the `LastName`. Because the `LastName` is of type `string`, and the `String` class already implements the

IComparable interface, with the implementation you can rely on the CompareTo() method of the String class. If the LastName has the same value, the FirstName is compared:

```
public class Person : IComparable
{
   public int CompareTo(object obj)
   {
      Person other = obj as Person;
      int result = this.LastName.CompareTo(
                 other.LastName);
      if (result == 0)
      {
         result = this.FirstName.CompareTo(
               other.FirstName);
      }
      return result;
   }
//...
```

Now it is possible to sort an array of Person objects by the last name:

```
Person[] persons = {
   new Person("Emerson", "Fittipaldi"),
   new Person("Niki", "Lauda"),
   new Person("Ayrton", "Senna"),
   new Person("Michael", "Schumacher")
};

Array.Sort(persons);
foreach (Person p in persons)
{
   Console.WriteLine(p);
}
```

Using the sort of the Person class, the output returns the names sorted by the last name:

```
Emerson Fittipaldi
Niki Lauda
Michael Schumacher
Ayrton Senna
```

If the Person object should be sorted differently, or if you don't have the option to change the class that is used as an element in the array, you can implement the interface IComparer. This interface defines the method Compare(). The interface IComparable must be implemented by the class that should be compared. The IComparer interface is independent of the class to compare. That's why the Compare() method defines two arguments that should be compared. The return value is similar to the CompareTo() method of the IComparable interface.

The class PersonComparer implements the IComparer interface to sort Person objects either by firstName or by lastName. The enumeration PersonCompareType defines the different sorting options that are available with the PersonComparer: FirstName and LastName. How the compare should happen is defined with the constructor of the class PersonComparer where a PersonCompareType value is set. The Compare() method is implemented with a switch statement to compare either by LastName or by FirstName.

```
public class PersonComparer : IComparer
{
   public enum PersonCompareType
   {
      FirstName,
      LastName
   }

   private PersonCompareType compareType;

   public PersonComparer(
         PersonCompareType compareType)
   {
      this.compareType = compareType;
   }

   public int Compare(object x, object y)
   {
      Person p1 = x as Person;
      Person p2 = y as Person;
      switch (compareType)
      {
         case PersonCompareType.FirstName:
            return p1.FirstName.CompareTo(
                  p2.FirstName);
         case PersonCompareType.LastName:
            return p1.LastName.CompareTo(
                  p2.LastName);
         default:
            throw new ArgumentException(
                  "unexpected compare type");
      }
   }
}
```

Now you can pass a `PersonComparer` object to the second argument of the `Array.Sort()` method. Here the persons are sorted by first name:

```
Array.Sort(persons,
   new PersonComparer(
                  PersonComparer.PersonCompareType.
                  FirstName));
foreach (Person p in persons)
{
   Console.WriteLine(p);
}
```

The `persons` array is now sorted by the first name:

```
Ayrton Senna
Emerson Fittipaldi
Michael Schumacher
Niki Lauda
```

The `Array` class also offers `Sort` methods that require a delegate as an argument. Chapter 7, "Delegates and Events," discusses how to use delegates.

Array and Collection Interfaces

The `Array` class implements the interfaces `IEnumerable`, `ICollection`, and `IList` for accessing and enumerating the elements of the array. Because with a custom array a class is created that derives from the abstract class `Array`, you can use the methods and properties of the implemented interfaces with an array variable.

IEnumerable

`IEnumerable` is an interface that is used by the `foreach` statement to iterate through the array. Because this is a very special feature, it is discussed in the next section, "Enumerations."

ICollection

The interface `ICollection` derives from the interface `IEnumerable` and has additional properties and methods as shown in the following table. This interface is mainly used to get the number of elements in a collection and for synchronization.

ICollection Interface Properties and Methods	Description
`Count`	The `Count` property gives you the number of elements inside the collection. The `Count` property returns the same value as the `Length` property.
`IsSynchronized` `SyncRoot`	The property `IsSynchronized` defines whether the collection is thread-safe. For arrays, this property always returns `false`. For synchronized access, the `SyncRoot` property can be used for thread-safe access. Chapter 19, "Threading and Synchronization," explains threads and synchronization, and there you can read how to implement thread safety with collections.
`CopyTo()`	With the `CopyTo()` method you can copy the elements of an array to an existing array. This is similar to the static method `Array.Copy()`.

IList

The `IList` interface derives from the interface `ICollection` and defines additional properties and methods. The major reason why the `Array` class implements the `IList` interface is that the `IList` interface defines the `Item` property for accessing the elements using an indexer. Many of the other `IList` members are implemented by the `Array` class by throwing a `NotSupportedException`, because these do not apply to arrays. All the properties and methods of the `IList` interface are shown in the following table.

IList Interface	Description
`Add()`	The `Add()` method is used to add elements to a collection. With arrays, the method throws a `NotSupportedException`.
`Clear()`	The `Clear()` method empties all elements of the array. Value types are set to `0`, reference types to `null`.

IList Interface	Description
`Contains()`	With the `Contains()` method, you can find out if an element is within the array. The return value is `true` or `false`. This method does a linear search through all elements of the array until the element is found.
`IndexOf()`	The `IndexOf()` method does a linear search through all elements of the array similar to the `Contains()` method. What's different is that the `IndexOf()` method returns the index of the first element found.

`Insert()`
`Remove()`
`RemoveAt()`
	With collections, the `Insert()` method is used to insert elements; with `Remove()` and `RemoveAt()`, elements can be removed. With arrays, all these methods throw a `NotSupportedException`.

`IsFixedSize`	Because arrays are always fixed in size, this property always returns `true`.
`IsReadOnly`	Arrays are always read/write, so this property returns `false`. In Chapter 10, "Collections," you can read how to create a read-only collection from an array.
`Item`	The `Item` property allows accessing the array using an integer index.

Enumerations

By using the `foreach` statement you can iterate elements of a collection without the need to know the number of elements inside the collection. The `foreach` statement uses an enumerator. Figure 5-7 shows the relationship between the client invoking the `foreach` method and the collection. The array or collection implements the `IEnumerable` interface with the `GetEnumerator()` method. The `GetEnumerator()` method returns an enumerator implementing the `IEnumerable` interface. The interface `IEnumerable` then is used by the `foreach` statement to iterate through the collection.

The `GetEnumerator()` *method is defined with the interface* `IEnumerable`. *The* `foreach` *statement doesn't really need this interface implemented in the collection class. It's enough to have a method with the name* `GetEnumerator()` *that returns an object implementing the* `IEnumerator` *interface.*

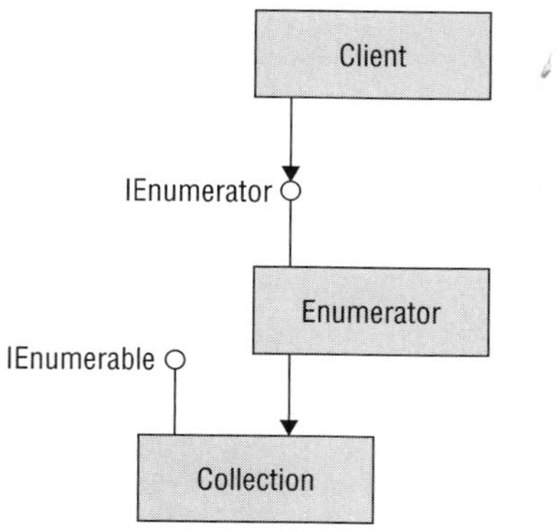

Figure 5-7

IEnumerator Interface

The `foreach` statement uses the methods and properties of the `IEnumerator` interface to iterate all elements in a collection. The properties and methods from this interface are defined in the following table.

IEnumerator Interface Properties and Methods	Description
`MoveNext()`	The `MoveNext()` method moves to the next element of the collection and returns `true` if there's an element. If the collection does not contain any more elements, the value `false` is returned.
`Current`	The property `Current` returns the element where the cursor is positioned.
`Reset()`	The method `Reset()` repositions the cursor to the beginning of the collection. Many enumerators throw a `NotSupportedException`.

foreach Statement

The C# `foreach` statement is not resolved to a `foreach` statement in the IL code. Instead, the C# compiler converts the `foreach` statement to methods and properties of the `IEnumerable` interface. Here's a simple `foreach` statement to iterate all elements in the `persons` array and to display them person by person:

```
foreach (Person p in persons)
{
   Console.WriteLine(p);
}
```

The `foreach` statement is resolved to the following code segment. First, the `GetEnumerator()` method is invoked to get an enumerator for the array. Inside a `while` loop — as long as `MoveNext()` returns `true` — the elements of the array are accessed using the `Current` property:

```
IEnumerator enumerator = persons.GetEnumerator();
while (enumerator.MoveNext())
{
   Person p = (Person)enumerator.Current;
   Console.WriteLine(p);
}
```

yield Statement

C# 1.0 made it easy to iterate through collections by using the `foreach` statement. With C# 1.0, it was still a lot of work to create an enumerator. C# 2.0 adds the `yield` statement for creating enumerators easily.

`yield return` returns one element of a collection and moves the position to the next element, and `yield break` stops the iteration.

The next example shows the implementation of a simple collection using the `yield return` statement. The class `HelloCollection` contains the method `GetEnumerator()`. The implementation of the `GetEnumerator()` method contains two `yield return` statements where the strings `Hello` and `World` are returned.

```
using System;
using System.Collections;

namespace Wrox.ProCSharp.Arrays
{
   public class HelloCollection
   {
      public IEnumerator GetEnumerator()
      {
         yield return "Hello";
         yield return "World";
      }
   }
```

A method or property that contains `yield` *statements is also known as an* iterator block. *An iterator block must be declared to return an* `IEnumerator` *or* `IEnumerable` *interface. This block may contain multiple* `yield return` *or* `yield break` *statements; a* `return` *statement is not allowed.*

Now it is possible to iterate through the collection using a `foreach` statement:

```
   public class Program
   {
      HelloCollection helloCollection =
            new HelloCollection();
      foreach (string s in helloCollection)
      {
         Console.WriteLine(s);
      }
   }
}
```

With an iterator block the compiler generates a yield type, including a state machine, as shown with the following code segment. The yield type implements the properties and methods of the interfaces `IEnumerator` and `IDisposable`. In the sample, you can see the yield type as the inner class `Enumerator`. The `GetEnumerator()` method of the outer class instantiates and returns a new yield type. Within the yield type, the variable `state` defines the current position of the iteration and is changed every time the method `MoveNext()` is invoked. `MoveNext()` encapsulates the code of the iterator block and sets the value of the `current` variable so that the `Current` property returns an object depending on the position.

```
public class HelloCollection
{
   public IEnumerator GetEnumerator()
   {
      Enumerator enumerator = new Enumerator();
      return enumerator;
   }

   public class Enumerator : IEnumerator, IDisposable
   {
      private int state;
      private object current;

      public Enumerator(int state)
```

(continued)

(continued)

```
        {
            this.state = state;
        }
        bool System.Collections.IEnumerator.MoveNext()
        {
            switch (state)
            {
                case 0:
                    current = "Hello";
                    state = 1;
                    return true;
                case 1:
                    current = "World";
                    state = 2;
                    return true;
                case 2:
                    break;
            }

            return false;
        }

        void System.Collections.IEnumerator.Reset()
        {
            throw new NotSupportedException();
        }

        object System.Collections.IEnumerator.Current
        {
            get
            {
                return current;
            }
        }

        void IDisposable.Dispose()
        {
        }
    }
}
```

Now, using the `yield return` statement makes it easy to implement a class that allows iterating through a collection in different ways. The class `MusicTitles` allows iterating the titles in a default way with the `GetEnumerator()` method, in reverse order with the `Reverse()` method, and to iterate through a subset with the `Subset()` method:

```
public class MusicTitles
{
    string[] names = {
            "Tubular Bells", "Hergest Ridge",
            "Ommadawn", "Platinum" };

    public IEnumerator GetEnumerator()
```

```
        {
            for (int i = 0; i < 4; i++)
            {
                yield return names[i];
            }
        }

        public IEnumerable Reverse()
        {
            for (int i = 3; i >= 0; i--)
            {
                yield return names[i];
            }
        }

        public IEnumerable Subset(int index,
              int length)
        {
            for (int i = index; i < index + length;
                      i++)
            {
                yield return names[i];
            }
        }
    }
```

The client code to iterate through the string array first uses the `GetEnumerator()` method, which you don't have to write in your code because this one is used by default. Then the titles are iterated in reverse, and finally a subset is iterated by passing the index and number of items to iterate to the `Subset()` method:

```
MusicTitles titles = new MusicTitles();
foreach (string title in titles)
{
    Console.WriteLine(title);
}
Console.WriteLine();

Console.WriteLine("reverse");
foreach (string title in titles.Reverse())
{
    Console.WriteLine(title);
}
Console.WriteLine();

Console.WriteLine("subset");
foreach (string title in
      titles.Subset(2, 2))
{
    Console.WriteLine(title);
}
```

With the yield statement you can also do more complex things, for example, returning an enumerator from `yield return`.

With the TicTacToe game, players alternate putting a cross or a circle in one of nine fields. These moves are simulated by the `GameMoves` class. The methods `Cross()` and `Circle()` are the iterator blocks for creating iterator types. The variables `cross` and `circle` are set to `Cross()` and `Circle()` inside the constructor of the `GameMoves` class. By setting these fields the methods are not invoked, but set to the iterator types that are defined with the iterator blocks. Within the `Cross()` iterator block, information about the move is written to the console and the move number is incremented. If the move number is higher than 9, the iteration ends with `yield break`; otherwise, the enumerator object of the cross yield type is returned with each iteration. The `Circle()` iterator block is very similar to the `Cross()` iterator block; it just returns the circle iterator type with each iteration.

```
public class GameMoves
{
    private IEnumerator cross;
    private IEnumerator circle;

    public GameMoves()
    {
        cross = Cross();
        circle = Circle();
    }

    private int move = 0;

    public IEnumerator Cross()
    {
        while (true)
        {
            Console.WriteLine("Cross, move {0}",
                  move);
            move++;
            if (move > 9)
                yield break;
            yield return circle;
        }
    }

    public IEnumerator Circle()
    {
        while (true)
        {
            Console.WriteLine("Circle, move {0}",
                  move);
            move++;
            if (move > 9)
                yield break;
            yield return cross;
        }
    }
}
```

From the client program you can use the class `GameMoves` as follows. The first move is set by setting enumerator to the enumerator type returned by `game.Cross()`. `enumerator.MoveNext` invokes one iteration defined with the iterator block that returns the other enumerator. The returned value can be accessed with the `Current` property and is set to the `enumerator` variable for the next loop:

```
GameMoves game = new GameMoves();
IEnumerator enumerator = game.Cross();
while (enumerator.MoveNext())
```

```
            {
               enumerator =
                     (IEnumerator)enumerator.Current;
            }
```

The outcome of this program shows alternating moves until the last move:

```
Cross, move 0
Circle, move 1
Cross, move 2
Circle, move 3
Cross, move 4
Circle, move 5
Cross, move 6
Circle, move 7
Cross, move 8
```

Summary

In this chapter, you've seen the C# notation to create and use simple, multidimensional, and jagged arrays. The `Array` class is used behind the scenes of C# arrays, and this way you can invoke properties and methods of this class with array variables.

You've seen how to sort elements in the array by using the `IComparable` and `IComparer` interfaces. The features of the `IEnumerable`, `ICollection`, and `IList` interfaces as implemented with the `Array` class were described, and finally, you've seen the advantages of the `yield` statement. Moving on, the next chapter focuses on operators and casts, in which you read about creating a custom indexer. Chapter 7 gives you information about delegates and events. Some methods of the `Array` class use delegates as parameters. Chapter 10 is about collection classes that already have been mentioned in this chapter. Collection classes give you more flexibility of the size, and there you can also read about other containers such as dictionaries and linked lists.

6

Operators and Casts

The preceding chapters have covered most of what you need to start writing useful programs using C#. This chapter completes the discussion of the essential language elements and begins to illustrate some powerful aspects of C# that allow you to extend the capabilities of the C# language. Specifically, this chapter discusses the following:

- The operators available in C#
- The idea of equality when dealing with reference and value types
- Data conversion between the primitive data types
- Converting value types to reference types using boxing
- Converting between reference types by casting
- Overloading the standard operators to support operations on the custom types you define
- Adding cast operators to the custom types you define to support seamless data type-conversions

Operators

Although most of C#'s operators should be familiar to C and C++ developers, this section discusses the most important operators for the benefit of new programmers and Visual Basic converts, as well as to shed light on some of the changes introduced with C#.

C# supports the operators listed in the following table.

Category	Operator
Arithmetic	`+ - * / %`
Logical	`& | ^ ~ && || !`
String concatenation	`+`
Increment and decrement	`++ --`
Bit shifting	`<< >>`
Comparison	`== != < ><= >=`
Assignment	`= += -= *= /= %= &= |= ^= <<= >>=`
Member access (for objects and structs)	`.`
Indexing (for arrays and indexers)	`[]`
Cast	`()`
Conditional (the ternary operator)	`?:`
Delegate concatenation and removal (discussed in Chapter 7, "Delegates and Events")	`+ -`
Object creation	`new`
Type information	`sizeof is typeof as`
Overflow exception control	`checked unchecked`
Indirection and address	`[]`
Namespace alias qualifier (discussed in Chapter 2, "C# Basics")	`::`
Null coalescing operator	`??`

Note that four specific operators (`sizeof`, `*`, `->`, and `&`, listed in the following table), however, are available only in unsafe code (code that bypasses C#'s type-safety checking), which is discussed in Chapter 12, "Memory Management and Pointers." It is also important to note that the `sizeof` operator keywords, when used with the .NET Framework 1.0 and 1.1, require the unsafe mode. This is not a requirement since the .NET Framework 2.0.

Category	Operator
Operator keywords	`sizeof` (for .NET Framework versions 1.0 and 1.1 only)
Operators	`* -> &`

One of the biggest pitfalls to watch out for when using C# operators is that, like other C-style languages, C# uses different operators for assignment (=) and comparison (==). For instance, the following statement means *let x equal three*:

```
x = 3;
```

If you now want to compare x to a value, you need to use the double equals sign ==:

```
if (x == 3)
{

}
```

Fortunately, C#'s strict type-safety rules prevent the very common C error where assignment is performed instead of comparison in logical statements. This means that in C# the following statement will generate a compiler error:

```
if (x = 3)
{

}
```

Visual Basic programmers who are accustomed to using the ampersand (&) character to concatenate strings will have to make an adjustment. In C#, the plus sign (+) is used instead for concatenation, whereas the & symbol denotes a bitwise AND between two different integer values. The symbol | allows you to perform a bitwise OR between two integers. Visual Basic programmers also might not recognize the modulus (%) arithmetic operator. This returns the remainder after division, so, for example, x % 5 returns 2 if x is equal to 7.

You will use few pointers in C#, and, therefore, few indirection operators. More specifically, the only place you will use them is within blocks of unsafe code, because that is the only place in C# where pointers are allowed. Pointers and unsafe code are discussed in Chapter 12, "Memory Management and Pointers."

Operator Shortcuts

The following table shows the full list of shortcut assignment operators available in C#.

Shortcut Operator	Equivalent To
x++, ++x	x = x + 1
x--, --x	x = x - 1
x += y	x = x + y
x -= y	x = x - y
x *= y	x = x * y
x /= y	x = x / y
x %= y	x = x % y
x >>= y	x = x >> y
x <<= y	x = x << y
x &= y	x = x & y
x |= y	x = x | y
x ^= y	x = x ^ y

You may be wondering why there are two examples each for the ++ increment and the -- decrement operators. Placing the operator *before* the expression is known as a *prefix*, placing the operator *after* the expression is known as a *postfix*, and it is important to note that there is a difference in the way they behave.

The increment and decrement operators can act both as whole expressions and within expressions. When used by themselves, the effect of both the prefix and postfix versions is identical and corresponds to the statement `x = x + 1`. When used within larger expressions, the prefix operator will increment the value of x *before* the expression is evaluated; in other words, x is incremented and the new value is used in the expression. In contrast, the postfix operator increments the value of x *after* the expression is evaluated — the expression is evaluated using the original value of x. The following example uses the increment operator (++) as an example to demonstrate the difference between the prefix and postfix behavior:

```
int x = 5;

if (++x == 6)  // true - x is incremented to 6 before the evaluation
{
   Console.WriteLine("This will execute");
}

if (x++ == 7) // false - x is incremented to 7 after the evaluation
{
   Console.WriteLine("This won't");
}
```

The first `if` condition evaluates to `true`, because x is incremented from 5 to 6 *before* the expression is evaluated. The condition in the second `if` statement is `false`, however, because x is incremented to 7 only after the entire expression has been evaluated (while `x = 6`).

The prefix and postfix operators `--x` and `x--` behave in the same way, but decrement rather than increment the operand.

The other shortcut operators, such as += and -=, require two operands, and are used to modify the value of the first operand by performing an arithmetic, logical, or bitwise operation on it. For example, the next two lines are equivalent:

```
x += 5;
x = x + 5;
```

The following sections look at some of the primary and cast operators that you will frequently use within your C# code.

The Conditional Operator

The conditional operator (`?:`), also known as the ternary operator, is a shorthand form of the `if...else` construction. It gets its name from the fact that it involves three operands. It allows you to evaluate a condition, returning one value if that condition is true, or another value if it is false. The syntax is:

```
condition ? true_value : false_value
```

Here, *condition* is the Boolean expression to be evaluated, *true_value* is the value that will be returned if *condition* is true, and *false_value* is the value that will be returned otherwise.

When used sparingly, the conditional operator can add a dash of terseness to your programs. It is especially handy for providing one of a couple of arguments to a function that is being invoked. You can use it to quickly convert a Boolean value to a string value of `true` or `false`. It is also handy for displaying the correct singular or plural form of a word, for example:

```
int x = 1;
string s = x + " ";
s += (x == 1 ? "man" : "men");
Console.WriteLine(s);
```

This code displays `1 man` if `x` is equal to one but will display the correct plural form for any other number. Note, however, that if your output needs to be localized to different languages, you will have to write more sophisticated routines to take into account the different grammatical rules of different languages.

The checked and unchecked Operators

Consider the following code:

```
byte b = 255;
b++;
Console.WriteLine(b.ToString());
```

The `byte` data type can hold values only in the range zero to 255, so incrementing the value of `b` causes an overflow. How the CLR handles this depends on a number of issues, including compiler options, so whenever there's a risk of an unintentional overflow, you need some way of making sure that you get the result you want.

To do this, C# provides the `checked` and `unchecked` operators. If you mark a block of code as `checked`, the CLR will enforce overflow checking, and throw an `OverflowException` if an overflow occurs. Let's change the code to include the `checked` operator:

```
byte b = 255;
checked
{
   b++;
}
Console.WriteLine(b.ToString());
```

When you try to run this code, you will get an error message like this:

```
Unhandled Exception: System.OverflowException: Arithmetic operation resulted in an
overflow.
   at Wrox.ProCSharp.Basics.OverflowTest.Main(String[] args)
```

You can enforce overflow checking for all unmarked code in your program by specifying the `/checked` *compiler option.*

If you want to suppress overflow checking, you can mark the code as `unchecked`:

```
byte b = 255;
unchecked
{
   b++;
}
Console.WriteLine(b.ToString());
```

In this case, no exception will be raised, but you will lose data — because the `byte` type cannot hold a value of 256, the overflowing bits will be discarded, and your `b` variable will hold a value of zero (0).

Note that `unchecked` is the default behavior. The only time you are likely to need to explicitly use the `unchecked` keyword is if you need a few unchecked lines of code inside a larger block that you have explicitly marked as `checked`.

The is Operator

The `is` operator allows you to check whether an object is compatible with a specific type. The phrase "is compatible" means that an object either is of that type or is derived from that type. For example, to check whether a variable is compatible with the `object` type, you could use the following bit of code:

```
int i = 10;
if (i is object)
{
   Console.WriteLine("i is an object");
}
```

`int`, like all C# data types, inherits from `object`; therefore the expression `i is object` will evaluate to `true` in this case, and the appropriate message will be displayed.

The as Operator

The `as` operator is used to perform explicit type conversions of reference types. If the type being converted is compatible with the specified type, conversion is performed successfully. However, if the types are incompatible, the `as` operator returns the value `null`. As shown in the following code, attempting to convert an `object` reference to a `string` will return `null` if the `object` reference does not actually refer to a `string` instance:

```
object o1 = "Some String";
object o2 = 5;

string s1 = o1 as string;    // s1 = "Some String"
string s2 = o2 as string;    // s2 = null
```

The `as` operator allows you to perform a safe type conversion in a single step without the need to first test the type using the `is` operator and then perform the conversion.

The sizeof Operator

You can determine the size (in bytes) required on the stack by a value type using the `sizeof` operator:

```
unsafe
{
   Console.WriteLine(sizeof(int));
}
```

This will display the number `4`, because an `int` is 4 bytes long.

Notice that you can use the `sizeof` operator only in unsafe code. Chapter 12, "Memory Management and Pointers," looks at unsafe code in more detail.

The typeof Operator

The `typeof` operator returns a `System.Type` object representing a specified type. For example, `typeof(string)` will return a `Type` object representing the `System.String` type. This is useful when you want to use reflection to find information about an object dynamically. Chapter 13, "Reflection," looks at reflection.

Nullable Types and Operators

Looking at the Boolean type, you have a true or false value that you can assign to this type. However, what if you wanted to define the value of the type as undefined? This is where using nullable types can have a distinct value to your applications. If you use nullable types in your programs, you must always consider the effect a `null` value can have when used in conjunction with the various operators. Usually, when using a unary or binary operator with nullable types, the result will be `null` if one or both of the operands is `null`. For example:

```
int? a = null;

int? b = a + 4;      // b = null
int? c = a * 5;      // c = null
```

However, when comparing nullable types, if only one of the operands is `null`, the comparison will always equate to `false`. This means that you cannot assume a condition is `true` just because its opposite is `false`, as often happens in programs using non-nullable types. For example:

```
int? a = null;
int? b = -5;

if (a >= b)
   Console.WriteLine("a >= b");
else
   Console.WriteLine("a < b");
```

The possibility of a `null` *value means that you cannot freely combine nullable and non-nullable types in an expression. This is discussed in the "Type Conversions" section later in this chapter.*

The Null Coalescing Operator

The null coalescing operator (`??`) provides a shorthand mechanism to cater to the possibility of `null` values when working with nullable and reference types. The operator is placed between two operands — the first operand must be a nullable type or reference type, and the second operand must be of the same type as the first or of a type that is implicitly convertible to the type of the first operand. The null coalescing operator evaluates as follows: If the first operand is not `null`, then the overall expression has the value of the first operand. However, if the first operand is `null`, then the overall expression has the value of the second operand. For example:

```
int? a = null;
int b;

b = a ?? 10;      // b has the value 10
a = 3;
b = a ?? 10;      // b has the value 3
```

If the second operand cannot be implicitly converted to the type of the first operand, a compile-time error is generated.

Operator Precedence

The following table shows the order of precedence of the C# operators. The operators at the top of the table are those with the highest precedence (that is, the ones evaluated first in an expression containing multiple operators).

Group	Operators
Primary	`() . [] x++ x-- new typeof sizeof checked unchecked`
Unary	`+ - ! ~ ++x --x` and casts
Multiplication/division	`* / %`
Group	Operators
Addition/subtraction	`+ -`
Bitwise shift operators	`<< >>`
Relational	`< ><= >= is as`
Comparison	`== !=`
Bitwise AND	`&`
Bitwise XOR	`^`
Bitwise OR	`|`
Boolean AND	`&&`
Boolean OR	`||`
Conditional operator	`?:`
Assignment	`= += -= *= /= %= &= |= ^= <<= >>= >>>=`

In complex expressions, you should avoid relying on operator precedence to produce the correct result. Using parentheses to specify the order in which you want operators applied clarifies your code and prevents potential confusion.

Type Safety

Chapter 1, ".NET Architecture," noted that the Intermediate Language (IL) enforces strong type safety upon its code. Strong typing enables many of the services provided by .NET, including security and language interoperability. As you would expect from a language compiled into IL, C# is also strongly typed. Among other things, this means that data types are not always seamlessly interchangeable. This section looks at conversions between primitive types.

C# also supports conversions between different reference types and allows you to define how data types that you create behave when converted to and from other types. Both of these topics are discussed later in this chapter.

Generics, a feature included in C#, allows you to avoid some of the most common situations in which you would need to perform type conversions. See Chapter 9, "Generics," for details.

Type Conversions

Often, you need to convert data from one type to another. Consider the following code:

```
byte value1 = 10;
byte value2 = 23;
byte total;
total = value1 + value2;
Console.WriteLine(total);
```

When you attempt to compile these lines, you get the following error message:

```
Cannot implicitly convert type 'int' to 'byte'
```

The problem here is that when you add 2 bytes together, the result will be returned as an `int`, not as another `byte`. This is because a `byte` can contain only 8 bits of data, so adding 2 bytes together could very easily result in a value that cannot be stored in a single `byte`. If you do want to store this result in a `byte` variable, you are going to have to convert it back to a `byte`. The following sections discuss two conversion mechanisms supported by C# — *implicit* and *explicit*.

Implicit Conversions

Conversion between types can normally be achieved automatically (implicitly) only if you can guarantee that the value is not changed in any way. This is why the previous code failed; by attempting a conversion from an `int` to a `byte`, you were potentially losing 3 bytes of data. The compiler is not going to let you do that unless you explicitly tell it that that's what you want to do. If you store the result in a `long` instead of a `byte`, however, you will have no problems:

```
byte value1 = 10;
byte value2 = 23;
long total;                // this will compile fine
total = value1 + value2;
Console.WriteLine(total);
```

Your program has compiled with no errors at this point because a `long` holds more bytes of data than a `byte`, so there is no risk of data being lost. In these circumstances, the compiler is happy to make the conversion for you, without your needing to ask for it explicitly.

The following table shows the implicit type conversions supported in C#.

From	To
`sbyte`	`short, int, long, float, double, decimal`
`byte`	`short, ushort, int, uint, long, ulong, float, double, decimal`
`short`	`int, long, float, double, decimal`
`ushort`	`int, uint, long, ulong, float, double, decimal`
`int`	`long, float, double, decimal`
`uint`	`long, ulong, float, double, decimal`
`long, ulong`	`float, double, decimal`
`float`	`Double`
`char`	`ushort, int, uint, long, ulong, float, double, decimal`

As you would expect, you can perform implicit conversions only from a smaller integer type to a larger one, not from larger to smaller. You can also convert between integers and floating-point values; however, the rules are slightly different here. Though you can convert between types of the same size, such as `int`/`uint` to `float` and `long`/`ulong` to `double`, you can also convert from `long`/`ulong` back to `float`. You might lose 4 bytes of data doing this, but this only means that the value of the `float` you receive will be less precise than if you had used a `double`; this is regarded by the compiler as an acceptable possible error because the magnitude of the value is not affected. You can also assign an unsigned variable to a signed variable as long as the limits of value of the unsigned type fit between the limits of the signed variable.

Nullable types introduce additional considerations when implicitly converting value types:

- Nullable types implicitly convert to other nullable types following the conversion rules described for non-nullable types in the previous table; that is, `int?` implicitly converts to `long?`, `float?`, `double?`, and `decimal?`.
- Non-nullable types implicitly convert to nullable types according to the conversion rules described in the preceding table; that is, `int` implicitly converts to `long?`, `float?`, `double?`, and `decimal?`.
- Nullable types *do not* implicitly convert to non-nullable types; you must perform an explicit conversion as described in the next section. This is because there is the chance a nullable type will have the value `null`, which cannot be represented by a non-nullable type.

Explicit Conversions

Many conversions cannot be implicitly made between types, and the compiler will give you an error if any are attempted. These are some of the conversions that cannot be made implicitly:

- `int` to `short` — Data loss is possible.
- `int` to `uint` — Data loss is possible.
- `uint` to `int` — Data loss is possible.
- `float` to `int` — You will lose everything after the decimal point.
- Any numeric type to `char` — Data loss is possible.
- `decimal` to any numeric type — The decimal type is internally structured differently from both integers and floating-point numbers.
- `int?` to `int` — The nullable type may have the value `null`.

However, you can explicitly carry out such conversions using *casts*. When you cast one type to another, you deliberately force the compiler to make the conversion. A cast looks like this:

```
long val = 30000;
int i = (int)val;   // A valid cast. The maximum int is 2147483647
```

You indicate the type to which you are casting by placing its name in parentheses before the value to be converted. If you are familiar with C, this is the typical syntax for casts. If you are familiar with the C++ special cast keywords such as `static_cast`, note that these do not exist in C# and that you have to use the older C-type syntax.

Casting can be a dangerous operation to undertake. Even a simple cast from a `long` to an `int` can cause problems if the value of the original `long` is greater than the maximum value of an `int`:

```
long val = 3000000000;
int i = (int)val;         // An invalid cast. The maximum int is 2147483647
```

In this case, you will not get an error, but you also will not get the result you expect. If you run this code and output the value stored in `i`, this is what you get:

```
-1294967296
```

It is good practice to assume that an explicit cast will not give the results you expect. As you saw earlier, C# provides a `checked` operator that you can use to test whether an operation causes an arithmetic overflow. You can use the `checked` operator to check that a cast is safe and to force the runtime to throw an overflow exception if it is not:

```
long val = 3000000000;
int i = checked((int)val);
```

Bearing in mind that all explicit casts are potentially unsafe, you should take care to include code in your application to deal with possible failures of the casts. Chapter 14, "Errors and Exceptions," introduces structured exception handling using the `try` and `catch` statements.

Using casts, you can convert most primitive data types from one type to another; for example, in this code, the value 0.5 is added to `price`, and the total is cast to an `int`:

```
double price = 25.30;
int approximatePrice = (int)(price + 0.5);
```

This will give the price rounded to the nearest dollar. However, in this conversion, data is lost — namely, everything after the decimal point. Therefore, such a conversion should never be used if you want to go on to do more calculations using this modified price value. However, it is useful if you want to output the approximate value of a completed or partially completed calculation — if you do not want to bother the user with lots of figures after the decimal point.

This example shows what happens if you convert an unsigned integer into a `char`:

```
ushort c = 43;
char symbol = (char)c;
Console.WriteLine(symbol);
```

The output is the character that has an ASCII number of 43, the + sign. You can try any kind of conversion you want between the numeric types (including `char`), and it will work, such as converting a `decimal` into a `char`, or vice versa.

Converting between value types is not restricted to isolated variables, as you have seen. You can convert an array element of type `double` to a struct member variable of type `int`:

```
struct ItemDetails
{
   public string Description;
   public int ApproxPrice;
}

//...

double[] Prices = { 25.30, 26.20, 27.40, 30.00 };

ItemDetails id;
id.Description = "Whatever";
id.ApproxPrice = (int)(Prices[0] + 0.5);
```

To convert a nullable type to a non-nullable type or another nullable type where data loss may occur, you must use an explicit cast. This is true even when converting between elements with the same basic underlying type, for example, `int?` to `int` or `float?` to `float`. This is because the nullable type may have the value `null`, which cannot be represented by the non-nullable type. As long as an explicit cast between two equivalent non-nullable types is possible, so is the explicit cast between nullable types. However, when casting from a nullable to non-nullable type and the variable has the value `null`, an `InvalidOperationException` is thrown. For example:

```
int? a = null;
int  b = (int)a;     // Will throw exception
```

Using explicit casts and a bit of care and attention, you can convert any instance of a simple value type to almost any other. However, there are limitations on what you can do with explicit type conversions — as far as value types are concerned, you can only convert to and from the numeric and `char` types and `enum` types. You cannot directly cast Booleans to any other type or vice versa.

If you need to convert between numeric and string, you can use methods provided in the .NET class library. The `Object` class implements a `ToString()` method, which has been overridden in all the .NET predefined types and which returns a string representation of the object:

```
int i = 10;
string s = i.ToString();
```

Similarly, if you need to parse a string to retrieve a numeric or Boolean value, you can use the `Parse()` method supported by all the predefined value types:

```
string s = "100";
int i = int.Parse(s);
Console.WriteLine(i + 50);   // Add 50 to prove it is really an int
```

Note that `Parse()` will register an error by throwing an exception if it is unable to convert the string (for example, if you try to convert the string `Hello` to an integer). Again, exceptions are covered in Chapter 14.

Boxing and Unboxing

In Chapter 2, "C# Basics," you learned that all types, both the simple predefined types such as `int` and `char`, and the complex types such as classes and structs, derive from the `object` type. This means that you can treat even literal values as though they were objects:

```
string s = 10.ToString();
```

However, you also saw that C# data types are divided into value types, which are allocated on the stack, and reference types, which are allocated on the heap. How does this square with the ability to call methods on an `int`, if the `int` is nothing more than a 4-byte value on the stack?

The way C# achieves this is through a bit of magic called *boxing*. Boxing and its counterpart, *unboxing*, allow you to convert value types to reference types and then back to value types. We include this in the section on casting because this is essentially what you are doing — you are casting your value to the `object` type. Boxing is the term used to describe the transformation of a value type to a reference type. Basically, the runtime creates a temporary reference-type box for the object on the heap.

This conversion can occur implicitly, as in the preceding example, but you can also perform it explicitly:

```
int myIntNumber = 20;
object myObject = myIntNumber;
```

Unboxing is the term used to describe the reverse process, where the value of a previously boxed value type is cast back to a value type. We use the term *cast* here, because this has to be done explicitly. The syntax is similar to explicit type conversions already described:

```
int myIntNumber = 20;
object myObject = myIntNumber;       // Box the int
int mySecondNumber = (int)myObject;   // Unbox it back into an int
```

You can only unbox a variable that has previously been boxed. If you execute the last line when myObject is not a boxed int, you will get an exception thrown at runtime.

One word of warning: when unboxing, you have to be careful that the receiving value variable has enough room to store all the bytes in the value being unboxed. C#'s ints, for example, are only 32 bits long, so unboxing a long value (64 bits) into an int as shown here will result in an InvalidCastException:

```
long myLongNumber = 333333423;
object myObject = (object)myLongNumber;
int myIntNumber = (int)myObject;
```

Comparing Objects for Equality

After discussing operators and briefly touching on the equality operator, it is worth considering for a moment what equality means when dealing with instances of classes and structs. Understanding the mechanics of object equality is essential for programming logical expressions and is important when implementing operator overloads and casts, which is the topic of the rest of this chapter.

The mechanisms of object equality are different depending on whether you are comparing reference types (instances of classes) or value types (the primitive data types, instances of structs or enums). The following sections present the equality of reference and value types independently.

Comparing Reference Types for Equality

You might be surprised to learn that System.Object defines three different methods for comparing objects for equality: ReferenceEquals() and two versions of Equals(). Add to this the comparison operator (==), and you actually have four ways of comparing for equality. Some subtle differences exist between the different methods, which are examined next.

The ReferenceEquals() Method

ReferenceEquals() is a static method that tests whether two references refer to the same instance of a class, specifically whether the two references contain the same address in memory. As a static method, it is not possible to override, so the System.Object implementation is what you always have. ReferenceEquals() will always return true if supplied with two references that refer to the same object instance, and false otherwise. It does, however, consider null to be equal to null:

```
SomeClass x, y;
x = new SomeClass();
y = new SomeClass();
bool B1 = ReferenceEquals(null, null);     // returns true
bool B2 = ReferenceEquals(null,x);         // returns false
bool B3 = ReferenceEquals(x, y);           // returns false because x and y
                                           // point to different objects
```

The virtual Equals() Method

The System.Object implementation of the virtual version of Equals() also works by comparing references. However, because this method is virtual, you can override it in your own classes in order to compare objects by value. In particular, if you intend instances of your class to be used as keys in a dictionary, you will need to override this method to compare values. Otherwise, depending on how you override Object.GetHashCode(), the dictionary class that contains your objects will either not work at all or will work very inefficiently. One point you should note when overriding Equals() is that your override should never throw exceptions. Once again, this is because doing so could cause problems for dictionary classes and possibly certain other .NET base classes that internally call this method.

The static Equals() Method

The `static` version of `Equals()` actually does the same thing as the virtual instance version. The difference is that the static version takes two parameters and compares them for equality. This method is able to cope when either of the objects is `null`, and, therefore, provides an extra safeguard against throwing exceptions if there is a risk that an object might be `null`. The `static` overload first checks whether the references it has been passed are `null`. If they are both `null`, it returns `true` (because `null` is considered to be equal to `null`). If just one of them is `null`, it returns `false`. If both references actually refer to something, it calls the virtual instance version of `Equals()`. This means that when you override the instance version of `Equals()`, the effect is as if you were overriding the static version as well.

Comparison Operator (==)

It is best to think of the comparison operator as an intermediate option between strict value comparison and strict reference comparison. In most cases, writing the following means that you are comparing references:

```
bool b = (x == y);    // x, y object references
```

However, it is accepted that there are some classes whose meanings are more intuitive if they are treated as values. In those cases, it is better to override the comparison operator to perform a value comparison. Overriding operators is discussed next, but the obvious example of this is the `System.String` class for which Microsoft has overridden this operator to compare the contents of the strings rather than their references.

Comparing Value Types for Equality

When comparing value types for equality, the same principles hold as for reference types: `ReferenceEquals()` is used to compare references, `Equals()` is intended for value comparisons, and the comparison operator is viewed as an intermediate case. However, the big difference is that value types need to be boxed in order to be converted to references so that methods can be executed on them. In addition, Microsoft has already overloaded the instance `Equals()` method in the `System.ValueType` class in order to test equality appropriate to value types. If you call `sA.Equals(sB)` where `sA` and `sB` are instances of some struct, the return value will be `true` or `false`, according to whether `sA` and `sB` contain the same values in all their fields. On the other hand, no overload of `==` is available by default for your own structs. Writing `(sA == sB)` in any expression will result in a compilation error unless you have provided an overload of `==` in your code for the struct in question.

Another point is that `ReferenceEquals()` always returns `false` when applied to value types because, to call this method, the value types will need to be boxed into objects. Even if you write the following, you will still get the answer of `false`:

```
bool b = ReferenceEquals(v,v);    // v is a variable of some value type
```

The reason for this is that `v` will be boxed separately when converting each parameter, which means you get different references. Because of this, there really is no reason to call `ReferenceEquals()` to compare value types because it doesn't make much sense.

Although the default override of `Equals()` supplied by `System.ValueType` will almost certainly be adequate for the vast majority of structs that you define, you might want to override it again for your own structs in order to improve performance. Also, if a value type contains reference types as fields, you might want to override `Equals()` to provide appropriate semantics for these fields because the default override of `Equals()` will simply compare their addresses.

Operator Overloading

This section looks at another type of member that you can define for a class or a struct: the *operator overload*.

Operator overloading is something that will be familiar to C++ developers. However, because the concept will be new to both Java and Visual Basic developers, we explain it here. C++ developers will probably prefer to skip ahead to the main operator overloading example.

The point of operator overloading is that you do not always just want to call methods or properties on objects. Often, you need to do things like adding quantities together, multiplying them, or performing logical operations such as comparing objects. Suppose that you had defined a class that represents a mathematical matrix. Now in the world of math, matrices can be added together and multiplied, just like numbers. Therefore, it is quite plausible that you would want to write code like this:

```
Matrix a, b, c;
// assume a, b and c have been initialized
Matrix d = c * (a + b);
```

By overloading the operators, you can tell the compiler what + and * do when used in conjunction with a `Matrix` object, allowing you to write code like the preceding. If you were coding in a language that did not support operator overloading, you would have to define methods to perform those operations. The result would certainly be less intuitive and would probably look something like this:

```
Matrix d = c.Multiply(a.Add(b));
```

With what you have learned so far, operators like + and * have been strictly for use with the predefined data types, and for good reason: The compiler knows what all the common operators mean for those data types. For example, it knows how to add two `long`s or how to divide one `double` by another `double`, and it can generate the appropriate intermediate language code. When you define your own classes or structs, however, you have to tell the compiler everything: what methods are available to call, what fields to store with each instance, and so on. Similarly, if you want to use operators with your own types, you will have to tell the compiler what the relevant operators mean in the context of that class. The way you do that is by defining overloads for the operators.

The other thing we should stress is that overloading is not concerned just with arithmetic operators. You also need to consider the comparison operators, ==, <, >, !=, >=, and <=. Take the statement `if (a==b)`. For classes, this statement will, by default, compare the references `a` and `b`. It tests to see if the references point to the same location in memory, rather than checking to see if the instances actually contain the same data. For the `string` class, this behavior is overridden so that comparing strings really does compare the contents of each string. You might want to do the same for your own classes. For structs, the == operator does not do anything at all by default. Trying to compare two structs to see if they are equal produces a compilation error unless you explicitly overload == to tell the compiler how to perform the comparison.

A large number of situations exist in which being able to overload operators will allow you to generate more readable and intuitive code, including:

- Almost any mathematical object such as coordinates, vectors, matrices, tensors, functions, and so on. If you are writing a program that does some mathematical or physical modeling, you will almost certainly use classes representing these objects.
- Graphics programs that use mathematical or coordinate-related objects when calculating positions onscreen.
- A class that represents an amount of money (for example, in a financial program).

- A word processing or text analysis program that uses classes representing sentences, clauses, and so on; you might want to use operators to combine sentences (a more sophisticated version of concatenation for strings).

However, there are also many types for which operator overloading would not be relevant. Using operator overloading inappropriately will make code that uses your types far more difficult to understand. For example, multiplying two `DateTime` objects just does not make any sense conceptually.

How Operators Work

To understand how to overload operators, it's quite useful to think about what happens when the compiler encounters an operator. Using the addition operator (+) as an example, suppose that the compiler processes the following lines of code:

```
int myInteger = 3;
uint myUnsignedInt = 2;
double myDouble = 4.0;
long myLong = myInteger + myUnsignedInt;
double myOtherDouble = myDouble + myInteger;
```

What happens when the compiler encounters the following line?

```
long myLong = myInteger + myUnsignedInt;
```

The compiler identifies that it needs to add two integers and assign the result to a `long`. However, the expression `myInteger + myUnsignedInt` is really just an intuitive and convenient syntax for calling a method that adds two numbers together. The method takes two parameters, `myInteger` and `myUnsignedInt`, and returns their sum. Therefore, the compiler does the same thing as it does for any method call — it looks for the best matching overload of the addition operator based on the parameter types — in this case, one that takes two integers. As with normal overloaded methods, the desired return type does not influence the compiler's choice as to which version of a method it calls. As it happens, the overload called in the example takes two `int` parameters and returns an `int`; this return value is subsequently converted to a `long`.

The next line causes the compiler to use a different overload of the addition operator:

```
double myOtherDouble = myDouble + myInteger;
```

In this instance, the parameters are a `double` and an `int`, but there is not an overload of the addition operator that takes this combination of parameters. Instead, the compiler identifies the best matching overload of the addition operator as being the version that takes two `double`s as its parameters, and it implicitly casts the `int` to a `double`. Adding two `double`s requires a different process from adding two integers. Floating-point numbers are stored as a mantissa and an exponent. Adding them involves bit-shifting the mantissa of one of the `double`s so that the two exponents have the same value, adding the mantissas, then shifting the mantissa of the result and adjusting its exponent to maintain the highest possible accuracy in the answer.

Now, you are in a position to see what happens if the compiler finds something like this:

```
Vector vect1, vect2, vect3;
// initialize vect1 and vect2
vect3 = vect1 + vect2;
vect1 = vect1*2;
```

Here, `Vector` is the struct, which is defined in the following section. The compiler will see that it needs to add two `Vector` instances, `vect1` and `vect2`, together. It will look for an overload of the addition operator, which takes two `Vector` instances as its parameters.

If the compiler finds an appropriate overload, it will call up the implementation of that operator. If it cannot find one, it will look to see if there is any other overload for + that it can use as a best match — perhaps something that has two parameters of other data types that can be implicitly converted to `Vector` instances. If the compiler cannot find a suitable overload, it will raise a compilation error, just as it would if it could not find an appropriate overload for any other method call.

Operator Overloading Example: The Vector Struct

This section demonstrates operator overloading through developing a struct named `Vector` that represents a 3-dimensional mathematical vector. Do not worry if mathematics is not your strong point — we will keep the vector example very simple. As far as you are concerned, a 3D-vector is just a set of three numbers (`doubles`) that tell you how far something is moving. The variables representing the numbers are called `x`, `y`, and `z`: `x` tells you how far something moves east, `y` tells you how far it moves north, and `z` tells you how far it moves upward (in height). Combine the three numbers and you get the total movement. For example, if `x=3.0`, `y=3.0`, and `z=1.0` (which you would normally write as `(3.0, 3.0, 1.0)`, you're moving 3 units east, 3 units north, and rising upward by 1 unit.

You can add or multiply vectors by other vectors or by numbers. Incidentally, in this context, we use the term *scalar*, which is math-speak for a simple number — in C# terms that is just a `double`. The significance of addition should be clear. If you move first by the vector `(3.0, 3.0, 1.0)` then you move by the vector `(2.0, -4.0, -4.0)`, the total amount you have moved can be worked out by adding the two vectors. Adding vectors means adding each component individually, so you get `(5.0, -1.0, -3.0)`. In this context, mathematicians write `c=a+b`, where `a` and `b` are the vectors and `c` is the resulting vector. You want to be able to use the `Vector` struct the same way.

The fact that this example will be developed as a struct rather than a class is not significant. Operator overloading works in the same way for both structs and classes.

The following is the definition for `Vector` — containing the member fields, constructors, a `ToString()` override so you can easily view the contents of a `Vector`, and, finally, that operator overload:

```
namespace Wrox.ProCSharp.OOCSharp
{
   struct Vector
   {
      public double x, y, z;

      public Vector(double x, double y, double z)
      {
         this.x = x;
         this.y = y;
         this.z = z;
      }

      public Vector(Vector rhs)
      {
         x = rhs.x;
         y = rhs.y;
         z = rhs.z;
      }

      public override string ToString()
      {
         return "( " + x + " , " + y + " , " + z + " )";
      }
```

This example has two constructors that require the initial value of the vector to be specified, either by passing in the values of each component or by supplying another `Vector` whose value can be copied. Constructors like the second one that takes a single `Vector` argument are often termed *copy constructors* because they effectively allow you to initialize a class or struct instance by copying another instance. Note that to keep things simple, the fields are left as `public`. We could have made them `private` and written corresponding properties to access them, but it would not have made any difference to the example, other than to make the code longer.

Here is the interesting part of the `Vector` struct — the operator overload that provides support for the addition operator:

```
        public static Vector operator + (Vector lhs, Vector rhs)
        {
            Vector result = new Vector(lhs);
            result.x += rhs.x;
            result.y += rhs.y;
            result.z += rhs.z;

            return result;
        }
    }
}
```

The operator overload is declared in much the same way as a method, except that the `operator` keyword tells the compiler it is actually an operator overload you are defining. The `operator` keyword is followed by the actual symbol for the relevant operator, in this case the addition operator (+). The return type is whatever type you get when you use this operator. Adding two vectors results in a vector, therefore, the return type is also a `Vector`. For this particular override of the addition operator, the return type is the same as the containing class, but that is not necessarily the case as you will see later in this example. The two parameters are the things you are operating on. For binary operators (those that take two parameters), like the addition and subtraction operators, the first parameter is the value on the left of the operator, and the second parameter is the value on the right.

Note that it is convention to name your left-hand parameters `lhs` *(for left-hand side) and your right-hand parameters* `rhs` *(for right-hand side).*

C# requires that all operator overloads be declared as `public` and `static`, which means that they are associated with their class or struct, not with a particular instance. Because of this, the body of the operator overload has no access to non-static class members and has no access to the `this` identifier. This is fine because the parameters provide all the input data the operator needs to know to perform its task.

Now that you understand the syntax for the addition operator declaration, you can look at what happens inside the operator:

```
{
    Vector result = new Vector(lhs);
    result.x += rhs.x;
    result.y += rhs.y;
    result.z += rhs.z;

    return result;
}
```

This part of the code is exactly the same as if you were declaring a method, and you should easily be able to convince yourself that this really will return a vector containing the sum of `lhs` and `rhs` as defined. You simply add the members `x`, `y`, and `z` together individually.

Now all you need to do is write some simple code to test the `Vector` struct. Here it is:

```
static void Main()
{
   Vector vect1, vect2, vect3;

   vect1 = new Vector(3.0, 3.0, 1.0);
   vect2 = new Vector(2.0, -4.0, -4.0);
   vect3 = vect1 + vect2;

   Console.WriteLine("vect1 = " + vect1.ToString());
   Console.WriteLine("vect2 = " + vect2.ToString());
   Console.WriteLine("vect3 = " + vect3.ToString());
}
```

Saving this code as `Vectors.cs` and compiling and running it returns this result:

Vectors

```
vect1 = ( 3 , 3 , 1 )
vect2 = ( 2 , -4 , -4 )
vect3 = ( 5 , -1 , -3 )
```

Adding More Overloads

In addition to adding vectors, you can multiply and subtract them and compare their values. In this section, you develop the `Vector` example further by adding a few more operator overloads. You will not develop the complete set that you'd probably need for a fully functional `Vector` type, but just enough to demonstrate some other aspects of operator overloading. First, you'll overload the multiplication operator to support multiplying vectors by a scalar and multiplying vectors by another vector.

Multiplying a vector by a scalar simply means multiplying each component individually by the scalar: for example, `2 * (1.0, 2.5, 2.0)` returns `(2.0, 5.0, 4.0)`. The relevant operator overload looks like this:

```
public static Vector operator * (double lhs, Vector rhs)
{
   return new Vector(lhs * rhs.x, lhs * rhs.y, lhs * rhs.z);
}
```

This by itself, however, is not sufficient. If `a` and `b` are declared as type `Vector`, it will allow you to write code like this:

```
b = 2 * a;
```

The compiler will implicitly convert the integer `2` to a `double` in order to match the operator overload signature. However, code like the following will not compile:

```
b = a * 2;
```

The thing is that the compiler treats operator overloads exactly as method overloads. It examines all the available overloads of a given operator to find the best match. The preceding statement requires the first parameter to be a `Vector` and the second parameter to be an integer, or something that an integer can be implicitly converted to. You have not provided such an overload. The compiler cannot start swapping the order of parameters, so the fact that you've provided an overload that takes a `double` followed by a `Vector` is not sufficient. You need to explicitly define an overload that takes a `Vector` followed by a `double` as well. There are two possible ways of implementing this. The first way involves breaking down the vector multiplication operation in the same way that you have done for all operators so far:

```
public static Vector operator * (Vector lhs, double rhs)
{
   return new Vector(rhs * lhs.x, rhs * lhs.y, rhs *lhs.z);
}
```

Given that you have already written code to implement essentially the same operation, however, you might prefer to reuse that code by writing:

```
public static Vector operator * (Vector lhs, double rhs)
{
   return rhs * lhs;
}
```

This code works by effectively telling the compiler that if it sees a multiplication of a `Vector` by a `double`, it can simply reverse the parameters and call the other operator overload. The sample code for this chapter uses the second version, because it looks neater and illustrates the idea in action. This version also makes for more maintainable code because it saves duplicating the code to perform the multiplication in two separate overloads.

Next, you need to overload the multiplication operator to support vector multiplication. Mathematics provides a couple of ways of multiplying vectors together, but the one we are interested in here is known as the *dot product* or *inner product*, which actually gives a scalar as a result. That's the reason for this example, to demonstrate that arithmetic operators don't have to return the same type as the class in which they are defined.

In mathematical terms, if you have two vectors `(x, y, z)` and `(X, Y, Z)`, then the inner product is defined to be the value of `x*X + y*Y + z*Z`. That might look like a strange way to multiply two things together, but it is actually very useful because it can be used to calculate various other quantities. Certainly, if you ever end up writing code that displays complex 3D graphics, for example using Direct3D or DirectDraw, you will almost certainly find your code needs to work out inner products of vectors quite often as an intermediate step in calculating where to place objects on the screen. What concerns us here is that we want people using your `Vector` to be able to write `double X = a*b` to calculate the inner product of two `Vector` objects (`a` and `b`). The relevant overload looks like this:

```
public static double operator * (Vector lhs, Vector rhs)
{
   return lhs.x * rhs.x + lhs.y * rhs.y + lhs.z * rhs.z;
}
```

Now that you understand the arithmetic operators, you can check that they work using a simple test method:

```
static void Main()
{
   // stuff to demonstrate arithmetic operations
   Vector vect1, vect2, vect3;
   vect1 = new Vector(1.0, 1.5, 2.0);
   vect2 = new Vector(0.0, 0.0, -10.0);

   vect3 = vect1 + vect2;

   Console.WriteLine("vect1 = " + vect1);
   Console.WriteLine("vect2 = " + vect2);
   Console.WriteLine("vect3 = vect1 + vect2 = " + vect3);
   Console.WriteLine("2*vect3 = " + 2*vect3);
```

```
        vect3 += vect2;

        Console.WriteLine("vect3+=vect2 gives " + vect3);

        vect3 = vect1*2;

        Console.WriteLine("Setting vect3=vect1*2 gives " + vect3);

        double dot = vect1*vect3;

        Console.WriteLine("vect1*vect3 = " + dot);
    }
```

Running this code (`Vectors2.cs`) produces the following result:

Vectors2

```
vect1 = ( 1 , 1.5 , 2 )
vect2 = ( 0 , 0 , -10 )
vect3 = vect1 + vect2 = ( 1 , 1.5 , -8 )
2*vect3 = ( 2 , 3 , -16 )
vect3+=vect2 gives ( 1 , 1.5 , -18 )
Setting vect3=vect1*2 gives ( 2 , 3 , 4 )
vect1*vect3 = 14.5
```

This shows that the operator overloads have given the correct results, but if you look at the test code closely, you might be surprised to notice that it actually used an operator that wasn't overloaded — the addition assignment operator, +=:

```
        vect3 += vect2;

        Console.WriteLine("vect3 += vect2 gives " + vect3);
```

Although += normally counts as a single operator, it can be broken down into two steps: the addition and the assignment. Unlike the C++ language, C# will not actually allow you to overload the = operator, but if you overload +, the compiler will automatically use your overload of + to work out how to perform a += operation. The same principle works for all of the assignment operators such as `-=`, `*=`, `/=`, `&=`, and so on.

Overloading the Comparison Operators

C# has six comparison operators, and they come in three pairs:

- == and !=
- > and <
- >= and <=

The C# language requires that you overload these operators in pairs. That is, if you overload `==`, you must overload `!=` too; otherwise, you get a compiler error. In addition, the comparison operators must return a `bool`. This is the fundamental difference between these operators and the arithmetic operators. The result of adding or subtracting two quantities, for example, can theoretically be any type depending on the quantities. You have already seen that multiplying two `Vector` objects can be implemented to give a scalar. Another example involves the .NET base class `System.DateTime`. It's possible to subtract two `DateTime` instances, but the result is not a `DateTime`; instead it is a `System.TimeSpan` instance. By contrast, it doesn't really make much sense for a comparison to return anything other than a `bool`.

If you overload == and `!=`*, you must also override the* `Equals()` *and* `GetHashCode()` *methods inherited from* `System.Object`*; otherwise, you'll get a compiler warning. The reasoning is that the* `Equals()` *method should implement the same kind of equality logic as the == operator.*

Apart from these differences, overloading the comparison operators follows the same principles as overloading the arithmetic operators. However, comparing quantities isn't always as simple as you might think. For example, if you simply compare two object references, you will compare the memory address where the objects are stored. This is rarely the desired behavior of a comparison operator, and so you must code the operator to compare the value of the objects and return the appropriate Boolean response. The following example overrides the == and `!=` operators for the `Vector` struct. Here is the implementation of ==:

```
public static bool operator == (Vector lhs, Vector rhs)
{
   if (lhs.x == rhs.x && lhs.y == rhs.y && lhs.z == rhs.z)
      return true;
   else
      return false;
}
```

This approach simply compares two `Vector` objects for equality based on the values of their components. For most structs, that is probably what you will want to do, though in some cases you may need to think carefully about what you mean by equality. For example, if there are embedded classes, should you simply compare whether the references point to the same object (*shallow comparison*) or whether the values of the objects are the same (*deep comparison*)?

A shallow comparison is where the objects point to the same point in memory, whereas deep comparisons are working with values and properties of the object to deem equality. You want to perform equality checks depending on the depth to help you decide what you will want to verify.

Don't be tempted to overload the comparison operator by calling the instance version of the `Equals()` *method inherited from* `System.Object`*. If you do and then an attempt is made to evaluate* `(objA == objB)`*, when* `objA` *happens to be* `null`*, you will get an exception as the .NET runtime tries to evaluate* `null.Equals(objB)`*. Working the other way around (overriding* `Equals()` *to call the comparison operator) should be safe.*

You also need to override the `!=` operator. The simple way to do this is:

```
public static bool operator != (Vector lhs, Vector rhs)
{
   return ! (lhs == rhs);
}
```

As usual, you should quickly check that your override works with some test code. This time you'll define three `Vector` objects and compare them:

```
static void Main()
{
   Vector vect1, vect2, vect3;

   vect1 = new Vector(3.0, 3.0, -10.0);
   vect2 = new Vector(3.0, 3.0, -10.0);
   vect3 = new Vector(2.0, 3.0, 6.0);

   Console.WriteLine("vect1==vect2 returns  " + (vect1==vect2));
   Console.WriteLine("vect1==vect3 returns  " + (vect1==vect3));
   Console.WriteLine("vect2==vect3 returns  " + (vect2==vect3));
```

```
        Console.WriteLine();

        Console.WriteLine("vect1!=vect2 returns  " + (vect1!=vect2));
        Console.WriteLine("vect1!=vect3 returns  " + (vect1!=vect3));
        Console.WriteLine("vect2!=vect3 returns  " + (vect2!=vect3));
    }
```

Compiling this code (the `Vectors3.cs` sample in the code download) generates the following compiler warning because you haven't overridden `Equals()` for your `Vector`. For our purposes here, that does not matter, so we will ignore it.

csc Vectors3.cs

```
Microsoft (R) Visual C# 2008 Compiler version 3.05.20706.1
for Microsoft (R) .NET Framework version 3.5
Copyright (C) Microsoft Corporation. All rights reserved.


Vectors3.cs(5,11): warning CS0660: 'Wrox.ProCSharp.OOCSharp.Vector' defines
        operator == or operator != but does not override Object.Equals(object o)
Vectors3.cs(5,11): warning CS0661: 'Wrox.ProCSharp.OOCSharp.Vector' defines
        operator == or operator != but does not override Object.GetHashCode()
```

Running the example produces these results at the command line:

Vectors3

```
vect1==vect2 returns  True
vect1==vect3 returns  False
vect2==vect3 returns  False

vect1!=vect2 returns  False
vect1!=vect3 returns  True
vect2!=vect3 returns  True
```

Which Operators Can You Overload?

It is not possible to overload all of the available operators. The operators that you can overload are listed in the following table.

Category	Operators	Restrictions
Arithmetic binary	`+, *, /, -, %`	None.
Arithmetic unary	`+, -, ++, --`	None.
Bitwise binary	`&, |, ^, <<, >>`	None.
Bitwise unary	`!, ~true, false`	The `true` and `false` operators must be overloaded as a pair.
Comparison	`==, !=, >=, <=>, <,`	Comparison operators must be overloaded in pairs.

Category	Operators	Restrictions
Assignment	`+=, -=, *=, /=, >>=, <<=, %=, &=, |=, ^=`	You cannot explicitly overload these operators; they are overridden implicitly when you override the individual operators such as +, -, %, and so on.
Index	`[]`	You cannot overload the index operator directly. The indexer member type, discussed in Chapter 2, "C# Basics," allows you to support the index operator on your classes and structs.
Cast	`()`	You cannot overload the cast operator directly. User-defined casts (discussed next) allow you to define custom cast behavior.

User-Defined Casts

Earlier in this chapter, you learned that you can convert values between predefined data types through a process of *casting*. You also saw that C# allows two different types of casts: implicit and explicit. This section looks at these types of casts.

For an explicit cast, you *explicitly* mark the cast in your code by writing the destination data type inside parentheses:

```
int I = 3;
long l = I;             // implicit
short s = (short)I;     // explicit
```

For the predefined data types, explicit casts are required where there is a risk that the cast might fail or some data might be lost. The following are some examples:

- When converting from an `int` to a `short`, the `short` might not be large enough to hold the value of the `int`.
- When converting from signed to unsigned data types, incorrect results will be returned if the signed variable holds a negative value.
- When converting from floating-point to integer data types, the fractional part of the number will be lost.
- When converting from a nullable type to a non-nullable type, a value of `null` will cause an exception.

By making the cast explicit in your code, C# forces you to affirm that you understand there is a risk of data loss, and therefore presumably you have written your code to take this into account.

Because C# allows you to define your own data types (structs and classes), it follows that you will need the facility to support casts to and from those data types. The mechanism is that you can define a cast as a member operator of one of the relevant classes. Your cast operator must be marked as either `implicit` or `explicit` to indicate how you are intending it to be used. The expectation is that you follow the same guidelines as for the predefined casts: If you know that the cast is always safe whatever the value held by the source variable, then you define it as `implicit`. If, however, you know there is a risk of something going wrong for certain values — perhaps some loss of data or an exception being thrown — then you should define the cast as `explicit`.

> **You should define any custom casts you write as explicit if there are any source data values for which the cast will fail or if there is any risk of an exception being thrown.**

The syntax for defining a cast is similar to that for overloading operators discussed earlier in this chapter. This is not a coincidence — a cast is regarded as an operator whose effect is to convert from the source type to the destination type. To illustrate the syntax, the following is taken from an example `struct` named `Currency`, which is introduced later in this section:

```
public static implicit operator float (Currency value)
{
   // processing
}
```

The return type of the operator defines the target type of the cast operation, and the single parameter is the source object for the conversion. The cast defined here allows you to implicitly convert the value of a `Currency` into a `float`. Note that if a conversion has been declared as `implicit`, the compiler will permit its use either implicitly or explicitly. If it has been declared as `explicit`, the compiler will only permit it to be used explicitly. In common with other operator overloads, casts must be declared as both `public` and `static`.

C++ developers will notice that this is different from what they are used to with C++, in which casts are instance members of classes.

Implementing User-Defined Casts

This section illustrates the use of implicit and explicit user-defined casts in an example called `SimpleCurrency` (which, as usual, is available in the code download). In this example, you define a struct, `Currency`, which holds a positive USD ($) monetary value. C# provides the `decimal` type for this purpose, but it is possible you will still want to write your own struct or class to represent monetary values if you want to perform sophisticated financial processing and therefore want to implement specific methods on such a class.

The syntax for casting is the same for structs and classes. This example happens to be for a struct, but would work just as well if you declared `Currency` as a class.

Initially, the definition of the `Currency` struct is:

```
struct Currency
{
   public uint Dollars;
   public ushort Cents;

   public Currency(uint dollars, ushort cents)
   {
      this.Dollars = dollars;
```

(continued)

(continued)

```
            this.Cents = cents;
        }

        public override string ToString()
        {
            return string.Format("${0}.{1,-2:00}", Dollars,Cents);
        }
    }
```

The use of unsigned data types for the `Dollar` and `Cents` fields ensures that a `Currency` instance can hold only positive values. It is restricted this way in order to illustrate some points about explicit casts later on. You might want to use a class like this to hold, for example, salary information for employees of a company (people's salaries tend not to be negative!). To keep the class simple, the fields are public, but usually you would make them `private` and define corresponding properties for the dollars and cents.

Start by assuming that you want to be able to convert `Currency` instances to `float` values, where the integer part of the `float` represents the dollars. In other words, you would like to be able to write code like this:

```
Currency balance = new Currency(10,50);
float f = balance; // We want f to be set to 10.5
```

To be able to do this, you need to define a cast. Hence, you add the following to your `Currency` definition:

```
public static implicit operator float (Currency value)
{
   return value.Dollars + (value.Cents/100.0f);
}
```

The preceding cast is implicit. It is a sensible choice in this case because, as should be clear from the definition of `Currency`, any value that can be stored in the currency can also be stored in a `float`. There is no way that anything should ever go wrong in this cast.

There is a slight cheat here — in fact, when converting a `uint` *to a* `float`*, there can be a loss in precision, but Microsoft has deemed this error sufficiently marginal to count the* `uint`*-to-*`float` *cast as implicit.*

However, if you have a `float` that you would like to be converted to a `Currency`, the conversion is not guaranteed to work. A `float` can store negative values, which `Currency` instances can't, and a `float` can store numbers of a far higher magnitude than can be stored in the (`uint`) `Dollar` field of `Currency`. Therefore, if a `float` contains an inappropriate value, converting it to a `Currency` could give unpredictable results. Because of this risk, the conversion from `float` to `Currency` should be defined as explicit. Here is the first attempt, which will not give quite the correct results, but it is instructive to examine why:

```
public static explicit operator Currency (float value)
{
   uint dollars = (uint)value;
   ushort cents = (ushort)((value-dollars)*100);
   return new Currency(dollars, cents);
}
```

The following code will now successfully compile:

```
float amount = 45.63f;
Currency amount2 = (Currency)amount;
```

However, the following code, if you tried it, would generate a compilation error, because it attempts to use an explicit cast implicitly:

```
float amount = 45.63f;
Currency amount2 = amount;    // wrong
```

By making the cast explicit, you warn the developer to be careful because data loss might occur. However, as you will soon see, this is not how you want your `Currency` struct to behave. Try writing a test harness and running the sample. Here is the `Main()` method, which instantiates a `Currency` struct and attempts a few conversions. At the start of this code, you write out the value of `balance` in two different ways (this will be needed to illustrate something later in the example):

```
static void Main()
{
   try
   {
      Currency balance = new Currency(50,35);

      Console.WriteLine(balance);
      Console.WriteLine("balance is " + balance);
      Console.WriteLine("balance is (using ToString()) " + balance.ToString());

      float balance2= balance;

      Console.WriteLine("After converting to float, = " + balance2);

      balance = (Currency) balance2;

      Console.WriteLine("After converting back to Currency, = " + balance);
      Console.WriteLine("Now attempt to convert out of range value of " +
                        "-$100.00 to a Currency:");

      checked
      {
         balance = (Currency) (-50.5);
         Console.WriteLine("Result is " + balance.ToString());
      }
   }
   catch(Exception e)
   {
      Console.WriteLine("Exception occurred: " + e.Message);
   }
}
```

Notice that the entire code is placed in a `try` block to catch any exceptions that occur during your casts. In addition, the lines that test converting an out-of-range value to `Currency` are placed in a `checked` block in an attempt to trap negative values. Running this code gives this output:

SimpleCurrency

```
50.35
Balance is $50.35
Balance is (using ToString()) $50.35
After converting to float, = 50.35
After converting back to Currency, = $50.34
Now attempt to convert out of range value of -$100.00 to a Currency:
Result is $4294967246.60486
```

This output shows that the code did not quite work as expected. First, converting back from `float` to `Currency` gave a wrong result of `$50.34` instead of `$50.35`. Second, no exception was generated when you tried to convert an obviously out-of-range value.

The first problem is caused by rounding errors. If a cast is used to convert from a `float` to a `uint`, the computer will *truncate* the number rather than *rounding* it. The computer stores numbers in binary rather than decimal, and the fraction 0.35 cannot be exactly represented as a binary fraction (just as 1/3 cannot be represented exactly as a decimal fraction; it comes out as 0.3333 recurring). The computer ends up storing a value very slightly lower than 0.35 that can be represented exactly in binary format. Multiply by 100 and you get a number fractionally less than 35, which is truncated to 34 cents. Clearly, in this situation, such errors caused by truncation are serious, and the way to avoid them is to ensure that some intelligent rounding is performed in numerical conversions instead. Luckily, Microsoft has written a class that will do this: `System.Convert`. The `System.Convert` object contains a large number of static methods to perform various numerical conversions, and the one that we want is `Convert.ToUInt16()`. Note that the extra care taken by the `System.Convert` methods does come at a performance cost. You should use them only when you need them.

Let's examine the second problem — why the expected overflow exception wasn't thrown. The issue here is this: The place where the overflow really occurs isn't actually in the `Main()` routine at all — it is inside the code for the cast operator, which is called from the `Main()` method. The code in this method was not marked as `checked`.

The solution is to ensure that the cast itself is computed in a `checked` context too. With both this change and the fix for the first problem, the revised code for the conversion looks like the following:

```
public static explicit operator Currency (float value)
{
   checked
   {
      uint dollars = (uint)value;
      ushort cents = Convert.ToUInt16((value-dollars)*100);
      return new Currency(dollars, cents);
   }
}
```

Note that you use `Convert.ToUInt16()` to calculate the cents, as described earlier, but you do not use it for calculating the dollar part of the amount. `System.Convert` is not needed when working out the dollar amount because truncating the `float` value is what you want there.

It is worth noting that the `System.Convert` *methods also carry out their own overflow checking. Hence, for the particular case we are considering, there is no need to place the call to* `Convert.ToUInt16()` *inside the checked context. The checked context is still required, however, for the explicit casting of* `value` *to dollars.*

You won't see a new set of results with this new `checked` cast just yet because you have some more modifications to make to the `SimpleCurrency` example later in this section.

If you are defining a cast that will be used very often, and for which performance is at an absolute premium, you may prefer not to do any error checking. That is also a legitimate solution, provided that the behavior of your cast and the lack of error checking are very clearly documented.

Casts Between Classes

The `Currency` example involves only classes that convert to or from `float` — one of the predefined data types. However, it is not necessary to involve any of the simple data types. It is perfectly legitimate to define casts to convert between instances of different structs or classes that you have defined. You need to be aware of a couple of restrictions, however:

- You cannot define a cast if one of the classes is derived from the other (these types of casts already exist, as you will see).
- The cast must be defined inside the definition of either the source or the destination data type.

To illustrate these requirements, suppose that you have the class hierarchy shown in Figure 6-1.

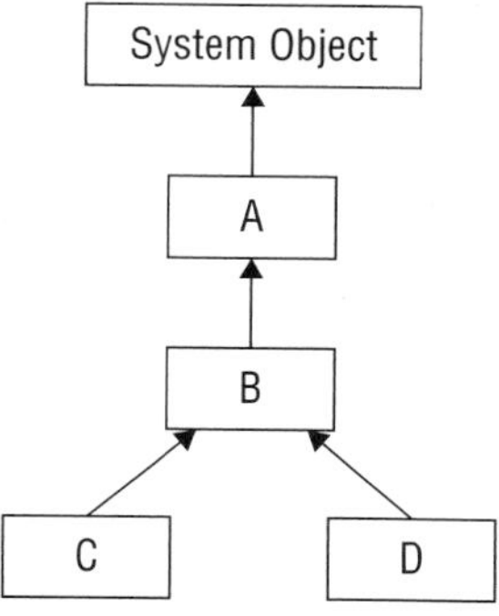

Figure 6-1

In other words, classes `C` and `D` are indirectly derived from `A`. In this case, the only legitimate user-defined cast between `A`, `B`, `C`, or `D` would be to convert between classes `C` and `D`, because these classes are not derived from each other. The code to do so might look like this (assuming that you want the casts to be explicit, which is usually the case when defining casts between user-defined casts):

```
public static explicit operator D(C value)
{
   // and so on
}
public static explicit operator C(D value)
{
   // and so on
}
```

For each of these casts, you have a choice of where you place the definitions — inside the class definition of `C` or inside the class definition of `D`, but not anywhere else. C# requires you to put the definition of a cast inside either the source class (or struct) or the destination class (or struct). A side effect of this is that you cannot define a cast between two classes unless you have access to edit the source code for at least one of them. This is sensible because it prevents third parties from introducing casts into your classes.

Once you have defined a cast inside one of the classes, you cannot also define the same cast inside the other class. Obviously, there should be only one cast for each conversion — otherwise, the compiler would not know which one to pick.

Casts Between Base and Derived Classes

To see how these casts work, start by considering the case where the source and destination are both reference types, and consider two classes, `MyBase` and `MyDerived`, where `MyDerived` is derived directly or indirectly from `MyBase`.

First, from `MyDerived` to `MyBase`, it is always possible (assuming the constructors are available) to write:

```
MyDerived derivedObject = new MyDerived();
MyBase baseCopy = derivedObject;
```

In this case, you are casting implicitly from `MyDerived` to `MyBase`. This works because of the rule that any reference to a type `MyBase` is allowed to refer to objects of class `MyBase` or to objects of anything derived from `MyBase`. In OO programming, instances of a derived class are, in a real sense, instances of the base class, plus something extra. All the functions and fields defined on the base class are defined in the derived class too.

Alternatively, you can write:

```
MyBase derivedObject = new MyDerived();
MyBase baseObject = new MyBase();
MyDerived derivedCopy1 = (MyDerived) derivedObject;   // OK
MyDerived derivedCopy2 = (MyDerived) baseObject;      // Throws exception
```

This code is perfectly legal C# (in a syntactic sense, that is) and illustrates casting from a base class to a derived class. However, the final statement will throw an exception when executed. When you perform the cast, the object being referred to is examined. Because a base class reference can in principle refer to a derived class instance, it is possible that this object is actually an instance of the derived class that you are attempting to cast to. If that is the case, the cast succeeds, and the derived reference is set to refer to the object. If, however, the object in question is not an instance of the derived class (or of any class derived from it), the cast fails and an exception is thrown.

Notice that the casts that the compiler has supplied, which convert between base and derived class, do not actually do any data conversion on the object in question. All they do is set the new reference to refer to the object if it is legal for that conversion to occur. To that extent, these casts are very different in nature from the ones that you will normally define yourself. For example, in the `SimpleCurrency` example earlier, you defined casts that convert between a `Currency` struct and a `float`. In the `float`-to-`Currency` cast, you actually instantiated a new `Currency` struct and initialized it with the required values. The predefined casts between base and derived classes do not do this. If you actually want to convert a `MyBase` instance into a real `MyDerived` object with values based on the contents of the `MyBase` instance, you would not be able to use the cast syntax to do this. The most sensible option is usually to define a derived class constructor that takes a base class instance as a parameter and have this constructor perform the relevant initializations:

```
class DerivedClass : BaseClass
{
   public DerivedClass(BaseClass rhs)
   {
      // initialize object from the Base instance
   }
   // etc.
```

Boxing and Unboxing Casts

The previous discussion focused on casting between base and derived classes where both participants were reference types. Similar principles apply when casting value types, although in this case it is not possible to simply copy references — some copying of data must take place.

It is not, of course, possible to derive from structs or primitive value types. Casting between base and derived structs invariably means casting between a primitive type or a struct and `System.Object`. (Theoretically, it is possible to cast between a struct and `System.ValueType`, though it is hard to see why you would want to do this.)

The cast from any struct (or primitive type) to `object` is always available as an implicit cast — because it is a cast from a derived to a base type — and is just the familiar process of *boxing*. For example, with the `Currency` struct:

```
Currency balance = new Currency(40,0);
object baseCopy = balance;
```

When this implicit cast is executed, the contents of `balance` are copied onto the heap into a boxed object, and the `baseCopy` object reference is set to this object. What actually happens behind the scenes is this: When you originally defined the `Currency` struct, the .NET Framework implicitly supplied another (hidden) class, a boxed `Currency` class, which contains all the same fields as the `Currency` struct, but it is a reference type, stored on the heap. This happens whenever you define a value type — whether it is a `struct` or `enum`, and similar boxed reference types exist corresponding to all the primitive value types of `int`, `double`, `uint`, and so on. It is not possible, or necessary, to gain direct programmatic access to any of these boxed classes in source code, but they are the objects that are working behind the scenes whenever a value type is cast to `object`. When you implicitly cast `Currency` to `object`, a boxed `Currency` instance gets instantiated and initialized with all the data from the `Currency` struct. In the preceding code, it is this boxed `Currency` instance that `baseCopy` will refer to. By these means, it is possible for casting from derived to base type to work syntactically in the same way for value types as for reference types.

Casting the other way is known as *unboxing*. Just as for casting between a base reference type and a derived reference type, it is an explicit cast because an exception will be thrown if the object being cast is not of the correct type:

```
object derivedObject = new Currency(40,0);
object baseObject = new object();
Currency derivedCopy1 = (Currency)derivedObject;    // OK
Currency derivedCopy2 = (Currency)baseObject;       // Exception thrown
```

This code works in a way similar to the code presented earlier for reference types. Casting `derivedObject` to `Currency` works fine because `derivedObject` actually refers to a boxed `Currency` instance — the cast will be performed by copying the fields out of the boxed `Currency` object into a new `Currency` struct. The second cast fails because `baseObject` does not refer to a boxed `Currency` object.

When using boxing and unboxing, it is important to understand that both processes actually copy the data into the new boxed or unboxed object. Hence, manipulations on the boxed object, for example, will not affect the contents of the original value type.

Multiple Casting

One thing you will have to watch for when you are defining casts is that if the C# compiler is presented with a situation in which no direct cast is available to perform a requested conversion, it will attempt to find a way of combining casts to do the conversion. For example, with the `Currency` struct, suppose the compiler encounters a few lines of code like this:

```
Currency balance = new Currency(10,50);
long amount = (long)balance;
double amountD = balance;
```

You first initialize a `Currency` instance, and then you attempt to convert it to a `long`. The trouble is that you haven't defined the cast to do that. However, this code will still compile successfully. What will happen is that the compiler will realize that you have defined an implicit cast to get from `Currency` to `float`, and the compiler already knows how to explicitly cast a `float` to a `long`. Hence, it will compile that line of code into IL code that converts `balance` first to a `float`, and then converts that result to a long. The same thing happens in the final line of the code, when you convert balance to a double. However, because the cast from Currency to float and the predefined cast from float to double are both implicit, you can write this conversion in your code as an implicit cast. If you had preferred, you could have specified the casting route explicitly:

```
Currency balance = new Currency(10,50);
long amount = (long)(float)balance;
double amountD = (double)(float)balance;
```

However, in most cases, this would be seen as needlessly complicating your code. The following code, by contrast, would produce a compilation error:

```
Currency balance = new Currency(10,50);
long amount = balance;
```

The reason is that the best match for the conversion that the compiler can find is still to convert first to float then to long. The conversion from float to long needs to be specified explicitly, though.

Not all of this by itself should give you too much trouble. The rules are, after all, fairly intuitive and designed to prevent any data loss from occurring without the developer knowing about it. However, the problem is that if you are not careful when you define your casts, it is possible for the compiler to figure out a path that leads to unexpected results. For example, suppose that it occurs to someone else in the group writing the Currency struct that it would be useful to be able to convert a uint containing the total number of cents in an amount into a Currency (cents, not dollars, because the idea is not to lose the fractions of a dollar). Therefore, this cast might be written to try to achieve this:

```
public static implicit operator Currency (uint value)
{
   return new Currency(value/100u, (ushort)(value%100));
} // Do not do this!
```

Note the u after the first 100 in this code to ensure that value/100u is interpreted as a uint. If you had written value/100, the compiler would have interpreted this as an int, not a uint.

The code comment Do not do this is clearly commented in this code, and here is why. Look at the following code snippet; all it does is convert a uint containing 350 into a Currency and back again. What do you think bal2 will contain after executing this?

```
uint bal = 350;
Currency balance = bal;
uint bal2 = (uint)balance;
```

The answer is not 350 but 3! Moreover, it all follows logically. You convert 350 implicitly to a Currency, giving the result balance.Dollars = 3, balance.Cents = 50. Then the compiler does its usual figuring out of the best path for the conversion back. Balance ends up being implicitly converted to a float (value 3.5), and this is converted explicitly to a uint with value 3.

Of course, other instances exist in which converting to another data type and back again causes data loss. For example, converting a float containing 5.8 to an int and back to a float again will lose the fractional part, giving you a result of 5, but there is a slight difference in principle between losing the fractional part of a number and dividing an integer by more than 100! Currency has suddenly become a rather dangerous class that does strange things to integers!

The problem is that there is a conflict between how your casts interpret integers. The casts between Currency and float interpret an integer value of 1 as corresponding to one dollar, but the latest uint-to-Currency cast interprets this value as one cent. This is an example of very poor design. If you want your classes to be easy to use, you should make sure that all of your casts behave in a way that is mutually compatible, in the sense that they intuitively give the same results. In this case, the solution is obviously to rewrite the `uint`-to-`Currency` cast so that it interprets an integer value of `1` as one dollar:

```
public static implicit operator Currency (uint value)
{
   return new Currency(value, 0);
}
```

Incidentally, you might wonder whether this new cast is necessary at all. The answer is that it could be useful. Without this cast, the only way for the compiler to carry out a `uint`-to-`Currency` conversion would be via a `float`. Converting directly is a lot more efficient in this case, so having this extra cast provides performance benefits, though you need to make sure it gives the same result as via a `float`, which you have now done. In other situations, you may also find that separately defining casts for different predefined data types allows more conversions to be implicit rather than explicit, though that is not the case here.

A good test of whether your casts are compatible is to ask whether a conversion will give the same results (other than perhaps a loss of accuracy as in `float`-to-`int` conversions), regardless of which path it takes. The `Currency` class provides a good example of this. Look at this code:

```
Currency balance = new Currency(50, 35);
ulong bal = (ulong) balance;
```

At present, there is only one way that the compiler can achieve this conversion: by converting the `Currency` to a `float` implicitly, then to a `ulong` explicitly. The `float`-to-`ulong` conversion requires an explicit conversion, but that is fine because you have specified one here.

Suppose, however, that you then added another cast, to convert implicitly from a `Currency` to a `uint`. You will actually do this by modifying the `Currency` struct by adding the casts both to and from `uint`. This code is available as the `SimpleCurrency2` example:

```
public static implicit operator Currency (uint value)
{
   return new Currency(value, 0);
}

public static implicit operator uint (Currency value)
{
   return value.Dollars;
}
```

Now the compiler has another possible route to convert from `Currency` to `ulong`: to convert from `Currency` to `uint` implicitly, then to `ulong` implicitly. Which of these two routes will it take? C# does have some precise rules to say how the compiler decides which is the best route if there are several possibilities. (The rules are not detailed in this book, but if you are interested, details are in the MSDN documentation.) The best answer is that you should design your casts so that all routes give the same answer (other than possible loss of precision), in which case it doesn't really matter which one the compiler picks. (As it happens in this case, the compiler picks the `Currency`-to-`uint`-to-`ulong` route in preference to `Currency`-to-`float`-to-`ulong`.)

To test the `SimpleCurrency2` sample, add this code to the test code for `SimpleCurrency`:

```
try
{
   Currency balance = new Currency(50,35);

   Console.WriteLine(balance);
   Console.WriteLine("balance is " + balance);
```

```
Console.WriteLine("balance is (using ToString()) " + balance.ToString());

uint balance3 = (uint) balance;

Console.WriteLine("Converting to uint gives " + balance3);
```

Running the sample now gives you these results:

SimpleCurrency2

```
50
balance is $50.35
balance is (using ToString()) $50.35
Converting to uint gives 50
After converting to float, = 50.35
After converting back to Currency, = $50.34
Now attempt to convert out of range value of -$100.00 to a Currency:
Exception occurred: Arithmetic operation resulted in an overflow.
```

The output shows that the conversion to `uint` has been successful, though as expected, you have lost the cents part of the `Currency` in making this conversion. Casting a negative `float` to `Currency` has also produced the expected overflow exception now that the `float`-to-`Currency` cast itself defines a `checked` context.

However, the output also demonstrates one last potential problem that you need to be aware of when working with casts. The very first line of output has not displayed the balance correctly, displaying `50` instead of `$50.35`. Consider these lines:

```
Console.WriteLine(balance);
Console.WriteLine("balance is " + balance);
Console.WriteLine("balance is (using ToString()) " + balance.ToString());
```

Only the last two lines correctly display the `Currency` as a string. So what is going on? The problem here is that when you combine casts with method overloads, you get another source of unpredictability. We will look at these lines in reverse order.

The third `Console.WriteLine()` statement explicitly calls the `Currency.ToString()` method, ensuring that the `Currency` is displayed as a string. The second does not do so. However, the string literal `"balance is"` passed to `Console.WriteLine()` makes it clear to the compiler that the parameter is to be interpreted as a string. Hence, the `Currency.ToString()` method will be called implicitly.

The very first `Console.WriteLine()` method, however, simply passes a raw `Currency` struct to `Console.WriteLine()`. Now, `Console.WriteLine()` has many overloads, but none of them takes a `Currency` struct. So the compiler will start fishing around to see what it can cast the `Currency` to in order to make it match up with one of the overloads of `Console.WriteLine()`. As it happens, one of the `Console.WriteLine()` overloads is designed to display `uint`s quickly and efficiently, and it takes a `uint` as a parameter — you have now supplied a cast that converts `Currency` implicitly to `uint`.

In fact, `Console.WriteLine()` has another overload that takes a `double` as a parameter and displays the value of that `double`. If you look closely at the output from the first `SimpleCurrency` example, you will find the very first line of output displayed `Currency` as a `double`, using this overload. In that example, there wasn't a direct cast from `Currency` to `uint`, so the compiler picked `Currency`-to-`float`-to-`double` as its preferred way of matching up the available casts to the available `Console.WriteLine()` overloads. However, now that there is a direct cast to `uint` available in `SimpleCurrency2`, the compiler has opted for this route.

The upshot of this is that if you have a method call that takes several overloads, and you attempt to pass it a parameter whose data type doesn't match any of the overloads exactly, then you are forcing the compiler to decide not only what casts to use to perform the data conversion, but which overload, and hence which data conversion, to pick. The compiler always works logically and according to strict rules, but the results may not be what you expected. If there is any doubt, you are better off specifying which cast to use explicitly.

Summary

This chapter looked at the standard operators provided by C#, described the mechanics of object equality, and examined how the compiler converts the standard data types from one to another. It also demonstrated how you can implement custom operator support on your data types using operator overloads. Finally, the chapter looked at a special type of operator overload, the cast operator, which allows you to specify how instances of your types are converted to other data types.

Chapter 7 focuses on two closely related member types that you can implement in your types to support very clean event-based object models: delegates and events.

7

Delegates and Events

Callback functions are an important part of programming in Windows. If you have a background in C or C++ programming, you have seen callbacks used in many of the Windows APIs. With the addition of the `AddressOf` keyword, Visual Basic developers are now able to take advantage of the API that once was off limits. Callback functions are really pointers to a method call. Also known as function pointers, they are a very powerful programming feature. .NET has implemented the concept of a function pointer in the form of delegates. What makes them special is that, unlike the C function pointer, the .NET delegate is type-safe. What this means is that a function pointer in C is nothing but a pointer to a memory location. You have no idea what that pointer is really pointing to. Things like parameters and return types are not known. As you see in this chapter, .NET has made delegates a type-safe operation. Later in the chapter, you see how .NET uses delegates as the means of implementing events.

The main topics of this chapter are:

- Delegates
- Anonymous methods
- Lambda expressions
- Events

Delegates

Delegates exist for situations in which you want to pass methods around to other methods. To see what that means, consider this line of code:

```
int i = int.Parse("99");
```

You are so used to passing data to methods as parameters, as in this example, that you don't consciously think about it, and for this reason the idea of passing methods around instead of data might sound a little strange. However, there are cases in which you have a method that does something, and rather than operating on data, the method might need to do something that involves invoking another method. To complicate things further, you do not know at compile time what this second method is. That information is available only at runtime and hence will need to be passed in as a parameter to the first method. That might sound confusing but should become clearer with a couple of examples:

- **Starting threads** — It is possible in C# to tell the computer to start some new sequence of execution in parallel with what it is currently doing. Such a sequence is known as a thread, and starting one up is done using the `Start()` method on an instance of one of the base classes, `System.Threading.Thread`. If you tell the computer to start a new sequence of execution, you have to tell it where to start that sequence. You have to supply it with the details of a method in which execution can start. In other words, the constructor of the `Thread` class takes a parameter that defines the method to be invoked by the thread.
- **Generic library classes** — Many libraries contain code to perform various standard tasks. It is usually possible for these libraries to be self-contained, in the sense that you know when you write to the library exactly how the task must be performed. However, sometimes the task contains some subtask, which only the individual client code that uses the library knows how to perform. For example, say that you want to write a class that takes an array of objects and sorts them into ascending order. Part of the sorting process involves repeatedly taking two of the objects in the array and comparing them in order to see which one should come first. If you want to make the class capable of sorting arrays of any object, there is no way that it can tell in advance how to do this comparison. The client code that hands your class the array of objects will also have to tell your class how to do this comparison for the particular objects it wants sorted. The client code will have to pass your class details of an appropriate method that can be called and does the comparison.
- **Events** — The general idea here is that often you have code that needs to be informed when some event takes place. GUI programming is full of situations like this. When the event is raised, the runtime will need to know what method should be executed. This is done by passing the method that handles the event as a parameter to a delegate. This is discussed later in the chapter.

In C and C++, you can just take the address of a function and pass this as a parameter. There's no type safety with C. You can pass any function to a method where a function pointer is required. Unfortunately, this direct approach not only causes some problems with type safety but also neglects the fact that when you are doing object-oriented programming, methods rarely exist in isolation, but usually need to be associated with a class instance before they can be called. As a result of these problems, the .NET Framework does not syntactically permit this direct approach. Instead, if you want to pass methods around, you have to wrap up the details of the method in a new kind of object, a delegate. Delegates quite simply are a special type of object — special in the sense that, whereas all the objects defined up to now contain data, a delegate contains the address of a method.

Declaring Delegates in C#

When you want to use a class in C#, you do so in two stages. First, you need to define the class — that is, you need to tell the compiler what fields and methods make up the class. Then (unless you are using only static methods), you instantiate an object of that class. With delegates it is the same thing. You have to start off by defining the delegates you want to use. In the case of delegates, defining them means telling the compiler what kind of method a delegate of that type will represent. Then, you have to create one or more instances of that delegate. Behind the scenes, the compiler creates a class that represents the delegate.

The syntax for defining delegates looks like this:

```
delegate void IntMethodInvoker(int x);
```

In this case, you have defined a delegate called `IntMethodInvoker`, and you have indicated that each instance of this delegate can hold a reference to a method that takes one `int` parameter and returns `void`. The crucial point to understand about delegates is that they are type-safe. When you define the delegate, you have to give full details of the signature and the return type of the method that it is going to represent.

> **One good way of understanding delegates is by thinking of a delegate as something that gives a name to a method signature and the return type.**

Suppose that you wanted to define a delegate called `TwoLongsOp` that will represent a method that takes two `longs` as its parameters and returns a `double`. You could do it like this:

```
delegate double TwoLongsOp(long first, long second);
```

Or, to define a delegate that will represent a method that takes no parameters and returns a `string`, you might write this:

```
delegate string GetAString();
```

The syntax is similar to that for a method definition, except that there is no method body and the definition is prefixed with the keyword `delegate`. Because what you are doing here is basically defining a new class, you can define a delegate in any of the same places that you would define a class — that is to say either inside another class or outside of any class and in a namespace as a top-level object. Depending on how visible you want your definition to be, you can apply any of the normal access modifiers to delegate definitions — `public`, `private`, `protected`, and so on:

```
public delegate string GetAString();
```

We really mean what we say when we describe defining a delegate as defining a new class. Delegates are implemented as classes derived from the class `System.MulticastDelegate`*, which is derived from the base class,* `System.Delegate`*. The C# compiler is aware of this class and uses its delegate syntax to shield you from the details of the operation of this class. This is another good example of how C# works in conjunction with the base classes to make programming as easy as possible.*

After you have defined a delegate, you can create an instance of it so that you can use it to store details of a particular method.

There is an unfortunate problem with terminology here. With classes there are two distinct terms — class, which indicates the broader definition, and object, which means an instance of the class. Unfortunately, with delegates there is only the one term. When you create an instance of a delegate, what you have created is also referred to as a delegate. You need to be aware of the context to know which meaning we are using when we talk about delegates.

Using Delegates in C#

The following code snippet demonstrates the use of a delegate. It is a rather long-winded way of calling the `ToString()` method on an `int`:

```
private delegate string GetAString();

static void Main()
{
   int x = 40;
   GetAString firstStringMethod = new GetAString(x.ToString);
   Console.WriteLine("String is {0}", firstStringMethod());
```

(continued)

(continued)

```
        // With firstStringMethod initialized to x.ToString(),
        // the above statement is equivalent to saying
        // Console.WriteLine("String is {0}", x.ToString());
    }
```

In this code, you instantiate a delegate of type `GetAString`, and you initialize it so it refers to the `ToString()` method of the integer variable `x`. Delegates in C# always syntactically take a one-parameter constructor, the parameter being the method to which the delegate will refer. This method must match the signature with which you originally defined the delegate. So in this case, you would get a compilation error if you tried to initialize the variable `firstStringMethod` with any method that did not take any parameters and return a string. Notice that, because `int.ToString()` is an instance method (as opposed to a static one), you need to specify the instance (`x`) as well as the name of the method to initialize the delegate properly.

The next line actually uses the delegate to display the string. In any code, supplying the name of a delegate instance, followed by brackets containing any parameters, has exactly the same effect as calling the method wrapped by the delegate. Hence, in the preceding code snippet, the `Console.WriteLine()` statement is completely equivalent to the commented-out line.

In fact, supplying brackets to the delegate instance is the same as invoking the `Invoke()` method of the delegate class. Because `firstStringMethod` is a variable of a delegate type, the C# compiler replaces `firstStringMethod()` with `firstStringMethod.Invoke()`:

```
firstStringMethod();
firstStringMethod.Invoke();
```

For less typing, at every place where a delegate instance is needed, you can just pass the name of the address. This is known by the term *delegate inference*. This C# feature works as long as the compiler can resolve the delegate instance to a specific type. The example initialized the variable `firstStringMethod` of type `GetAString` with a new instance of the delegate `GetAString`:

```
GetAString firstStringMethod = new GetAString(x.ToString);
```

You can write the same just by passing the method name with the variable `x` to the variable `firstStringMethod`:

```
GetAString firstStringMethod = x.ToString;
```

The code that is created by the C# compiler is the same. The compiler detects that a delegate type is required with `firstStringMethod`, so it creates an instance of the delegate type `GetAString` and passes the address of the method with the object `x` to the constructor.

Be aware that you can't type the `(` and `)` as `x.ToString()` and pass it to the delegate variable. This would be an invocation of the method. The invocation of `x.ToString()` returns a string object that can't be assigned to the delegate variable. You can only assign the address of a method to the delegate variable.

Delegate inference can be used any place a delegate instance is required. Delegate inference can also be used with events because events are based on delegates (as you can see later in this chapter).

One feature of delegates is that they are type-safe to the extent that they ensure the signature of the method being called is correct. However, interestingly, they do not care what type of object the method is being called against or even whether the method is a static method or an instance method.

An instance of a given delegate can refer to any instance or static method on any object of any type, provided that the signature of the method matches the signature of the delegate.

To demonstrate this, the following example expands the previous code snippet so that it uses the `firstStringMethod` delegate to call a couple of other methods on another object — an instance method and a static method. For this, you use the `Currency` struct, which is defined as follows. The `Currency` struct has its own overload of `ToString()` and a static method with the same signature to `GetCurrencyUnit()`. This way the same delegate variable can be used to invoke these methods.

```
struct Currency
{
   public uint Dollars;
   public ushort Cents;

   public Currency(uint dollars, ushort cents)
   {
      this.Dollars = dollars;
      this.Cents = cents;
   }

   public override string ToString()
   {
      return string.Format("${0}.{1,-2:00}", Dollars,Cents);
   }

   public static string GetCurrencyUnit()
   {
      return "Dollar";
   }

   public static explicit operator Currency (float value)
   {
      checked
      {
         uint dollars = (uint)value;
         ushort cents = (ushort)((value-dollars)*100);
         return new Currency(dollars, cents);
      }
   }

   public static implicit operator float (Currency value)
   {
      return value.Dollars + (value.Cents/100.0f);
   }

   public static implicit operator Currency (uint value)
   {
      return new Currency(value, 0);
   }

   public static implicit operator uint (Currency value)
   {
      return value.Dollars;
   }
}
```

Now you can use your `GetAString` instance as follows:

```
private delegate string GetAString();

static void Main()
{
   int x = 40;
   GetAString firstStringMethod = x.ToString;
   Console.WriteLine("String is {0}", firstStringMethod());

   Currency balance = new Currency(34, 50);

   // firstStringMethod references an instance method
   firstStringMethod = balance.ToString;
   Console.WriteLine("String is {0}", firstStringMethod());

   // firstStringMethod references a static method
   firstStringMethod = new GetAString(Currency.GetCurrencyUnit);
   Console.WriteLine("String is {0}", firstStringMethod());
}
```

This code shows how you can call a method via a delegate and subsequently reassign the delegate to refer to different methods on different instances of classes, even static methods or methods against instances of different types of class, provided that the signature of each method matches the delegate definition.

When you run the application, you get the output from the different methods that are referenced by the delegate:

```
String is 40
String is $34.50
String is Dollar
```

However, you still haven't seen the process of actually passing a delegate to another method. Nor have you actually achieved anything particularly useful yet. It is possible to call the `ToString()` method of `int` and `Currency` objects in a much more straightforward way than using delegates! Unfortunately, the nature of delegates requires a fairly complex example before you can really appreciate their usefulness. The next section presents two delegate examples. The first one simply uses delegates to call a couple of different operations. It illustrates how to pass delegates to methods and how you can use arrays of delegates — although arguably it still doesn't do much that you couldn't do a lot more simply without delegates. Then, a second, much more complex example of a `BubbleSorter` class is presented, which implements a method to sort out arrays of objects into increasing order. This class would be difficult to write without delegates.

Simple Delegate Example

This example defines a `MathOperations` class that has a couple of static methods to perform two operations on doubles. Then you use delegates to call up these methods. The math class looks like this:

```
class MathOperations
{
   public static double MultiplyByTwo(double value)
   {
      return value * 2;
   }
```

```
        public static double Square(double value)
        {
            return value * value;
        }
    }
```

You call up these methods like this:

```
using System;

namespace Wrox.ProCSharp.Delegates
{
    delegate double DoubleOp(double x);

    class Program
    {
        static void Main()
        {
            DoubleOp[] operations =
                {
                    MathOperations.MultiplyByTwo,
                    MathOperations.Square
                };

            for (int i=0 ; i < operations.Length ; i++)
            {
                Console.WriteLine("Using operations[{0}]:", i);
                ProcessAndDisplayNumber(operations[i], 2.0);
                ProcessAndDisplayNumber(operations[i], 7.94);
                ProcessAndDisplayNumber(operations[i], 1.414);
                Console.WriteLine();
            }
        }

        static void ProcessAndDisplayNumber(DoubleOp action, double value)
        {
            double result = action(value);
            Console.WriteLine(
                "Value is {0}, result of operation is {1}", value, result);
        }
    }
}
```

In this code, you instantiate an array of `DoubleOp` delegates (remember that once you have defined a delegate class, you can basically instantiate instances just like you can with normal classes, so putting some into an array is no problem). Each element of the array gets initialized to refer to a different operation implemented by the `MathOperations` class. Then, you loop through the array, applying each operation to three different values. This illustrates one way of using delegates — that you can group methods together into an array using them, so that you can call several methods in a loop.

The key lines in this code are the ones in which you actually pass each delegate to the `ProcessAndDisplayNumber()` method, for example:

```
                ProcessAndDisplayNumber(operations[i], 2.0);
```

Here, you are passing in the name of a delegate but without any parameters. Given that `operations[i]` is a delegate, syntactically:

- `operations[i]` means *the delegate* (that is, the method represented by the delegate).
- `operations[i](2.0)` means *actually call this method, passing in the value in parentheses.*

The `ProcessAndDisplayNumber()` method is defined to take a delegate as its first parameter:

```
static void ProcessAndDisplayNumber(DoubleOp action, double value)
```

Then, when in this method, you call:

```
double result = action(value);
```

This actually causes the method that is wrapped up by the `action` delegate instance to be called and its return result stored in `Result`.

Running this example gives you the following:

```
SimpleDelegate
Using operations[0]:
Value is 2, result of operation is 4
Value is 7.94, result of operation is 15.88
Value is 1.414, result of operation is 2.828

Using operations[1]:
Value is 2, result of operation is 4
Value is 7.94, result of operation is 63.0436
Value is 1.414, result of operation is 1.999396
```

BubbleSorter Example

You are now ready for an example that will show delegates working in a situation in which they are very useful. You are going to write a class called `BubbleSorter`. This class implements a static method, `Sort()`, which takes as its first parameter an array of objects, and rearranges this array into ascending order. For example, if you were to pass it this array of ints, `{0, 5, 6, 2, 1}`, it would rearrange this array into `{0, 1, 2, 5, 6}`.

The bubble-sorting algorithm is a well-known and very simple way of sorting numbers. It is best suited to small sets of numbers, because for larger sets of numbers (more than about 10) far more efficient algorithms are available). It works by repeatedly looping through the array, comparing each pair of numbers and, if necessary, swapping them, so that the largest numbers progressively move to the end of the array. For sorting `int`s, a method to do a bubble sort might look like this:

```
for (int i = 0; i < sortArray.Length; i++)
{
   for (int j = i + 1; j < sortArray.Length; j++)
   {
      if (sortArray[j] < sortArray[i])    // problem with this test
      {
         int temp = sortArray[i];    // swap ith and jth entries
         sortArray[i] = sortArray[j];
         sortArray[j] = temp;
      }
   }
}
```

This is all very well for `int`s, but you want your `Sort()` method to be able to sort any object. In other words, if some client code hands you an array of `Currency` structs or any other class or struct that it may have defined, you need to be able to sort the array. This presents a problem with the line `if(sortArray[j]<sortArray[i])` in the preceding code, because that requires you to compare two objects on the array to see which one is greater. You can do that for `int`s, but how are you to do it for some new class that is unknown or undecided until runtime? The answer is the client code that knows about the class will have to pass in a delegate wrapping a method that will do the comparison.

You define the delegate like this:

```
delegate bool Comparison(object x, object y);
```

And you give your `Sort` method this signature:

```
static public void Sort(object[] sortArray, Comparison comparison)
```

The documentation for this method states that `comparison` must refer to a static method that takes two arguments, and returns `true` if the value of the second argument is *greater than* (that is, should come later in the array than) the first one.

Now you are all set. Here is the definition for the `BubbleSorter` class:

```
class BubbleSorter
{
   static public void Sort(object[] sortArray, Comparison comparison)
   {
      for (int i = 0 ; i < sortArray.Length ; i++)
      {
         for (int j = i + 1 ; j < sortArray.Length ; j++)
         {
            if (comparison(sortArray[j], sortArray[i]))
            {
               object temp = sortArray[i];
               sortArray[i] = sortArray[j];
               sortArray[j] = temp;
            }
         }
      }
   }
}
```

To use this class, you need to define some other class, which you can use to set up an array that needs sorting. For this example, assume that the Mortimer Phones mobile phone company has a list of employees and wants them sorted according to salary. The employees are each represented by an instance of a class, `Employee`, which looks like this:

```
class Employee
{
   private string name;
   private decimal salary;

   public Employee(string name, decimal salary)
   {
      this.name = name;
      this.salary = salary;
   }
```

(continued)

(continued)

```
      public override string ToString()
      {
         return string.Format("{0}, {1:C}", name, salary);
      }

      public static bool CompareSalary(object x, object y)
      {
         Employee e1 = (Employee) x;
         Employee e2 = (Employee) y;
         return (e1.salary < e2.salary);
      }
   }
```

Notice that in order to match the signature of the `Comparison` delegate, you had to define `CompareSalary` in this class as taking two object references, rather than `Employee` references, as parameters. This means that you had to cast the parameters into `Employee` references in order to perform the comparison.

Instead of using objects as parameters here, strong typing generics can also be used. Chapter 9 explains generics and generic delegates.

Now you are ready to write some client code to request a sort:

```
using System;

namespace Wrox.ProCSharp.Delegates
{
   delegate bool Comparison(object x, object y);

   class Program
   {
      static void Main()
      {
         Employee[] employees =
            {
              new Employee("Bugs Bunny", 20000),
              new Employee("Elmer Fudd", 10000),
              new Employee("Daffy Duck", 25000),
              new Employee("Wiley Coyote", (decimal)1000000.38),
              new Employee("Foghorn Leghorn", 23000),
              new Employee("RoadRunner", 50000)};

         BubbleSorter.Sort(employees, Employee.CompareSalary);

         foreach (var employee in employees)
         {
            Console.WriteLine(employee);
         }
      }
   }
}
```

Running this code shows that the `Employees` are correctly sorted according to salary:

```
BubbleSorter
Elmer Fudd, $10,000.00
Bugs Bunny, $20,000.00
```

```
Foghorn Leghorn, $23,000.00
Daffy Duck, $25,000.00
RoadRunner, $50,000.00
Wiley Coyote, $1,000,000.38
```

Multicast Delegates

So far, each of the delegates you have used wraps just one single method call. Calling the delegate amounts to calling that method. If you want to call more than one method, you need to make an explicit call through a delegate more than once. However, it is possible for a delegate to wrap more than one method. Such a delegate is known as a *multicast delegate*. If a multicast delegate is called, it will successively call each method in order. For this to make sense, the delegate signature should return a `void`; otherwise, you would only get the result of the last method that is invoked by the delegate.

Consider the following code, which is adapted from the `SimpleDelegate` example. Although the syntax is the same as before, it is actually a multicast delegate, `Operations`, that gets instantiated:

```
   delegate void DoubleOp(double value);
//   delegate double DoubleOp(double value);    // can't do this now

   class MainEntryPoint
   {
      static void Main()
      {
         DoubleOp operations = MathOperations.MultiplyByTwo;
         operations += MathOperations.Square;
```

In the earlier example, you wanted to store references to two methods, so you instantiated an array of delegates. Here, you simply add both operations into the same multicast delegate. Multicast delegates recognize the operators + and +=. Alternatively, you can also expand the last two lines of the preceding code, as in this snippet:

```
DoubleOp operation1 = MathOperations.MultiplyByTwo;
DoubleOp operation2 = MathOperations.Square;
DoubleOp operations = operation1 + operation2;
```

Multicast delegates also recognize the operators - and -= to remove method calls from the delegate.

In terms of what's going on under the hood, a multicast delegate is a class derived from `System.MulticastDelegate`*, which in turn is derived from* `System.Delegate`*.* `System.MulticastDelegate`*, and has additional members to allow chaining of method calls together into a list.*

To illustrate the use of multicast delegates, the following code recasts the `SimpleDelegate` example into a new example, `MulticastDelegate`. Because you now need the delegate to refer to methods that return `void`, you have to rewrite the methods in the `MathOperations` class, so they display their results instead of returning them:

```
class MathOperations
{
   public static void MultiplyByTwo(double value)
   {
      double result = value * 2;
      Console.WriteLine(
         "Multiplying by 2: {0} gives {1}", value, result);
   }
```

(continued)

(continued)

```
        public static void Square(double value)
        {
            double result = value * value;
            Console.WriteLine("Squaring: {0} gives {1}", value, result);
        }
    }
```

To accommodate this change, you also have to rewrite `ProcessAndDisplayNumber`:

```
static void ProcessAndDisplayNumber(DoubleOp action, double valueToProcess)
{
    Console.WriteLine();
    Console.WriteLine("ProcessAndDisplayNumber called with value = {0}",
                      valueToProcess);
    action(valueToProcess);
}
```

Now you can try out your multicast delegate like this:

```
        static void Main()
        {
            DoubleOp operations = MathOperations.MultiplyByTwo;
            operations += MathOperations.Square;

            ProcessAndDisplayNumber(operations, 2.0);
            ProcessAndDisplayNumber(operations, 7.94);
            ProcessAndDisplayNumber(operations, 1.414);
            Console.WriteLine();
        }
```

Now, each time `ProcessAndDisplayNumber` is called, it will display a message to say that it has been called. Then the following statement will cause each of the method calls in the `action` delegate instance to be called in succession:

```
    action(value);
```

Running this code produces this result:

```
MulticastDelegate

ProcessAndDisplayNumber called with value = 2
Multiplying by 2: 2 gives 4
Squaring: 2 gives 4

ProcessAndDisplayNumber called with value = 7.94
Multiplying by 2: 7.94 gives 15.88
Squaring: 7.94 gives 63.0436

ProcessAndDisplayNumber called with value = 1.414
Multiplying by 2: 1.414 gives 2.828
Squaring: 1.414 gives 1.999396
```

If you are using multicast delegates, you should be aware that the order in which methods chained to the same delegate will be called is formally undefined. You should, therefore, avoid writing code that relies on such methods being called in any particular order.

Invoking multiple methods by one delegate might cause an even bigger problem. The multicast delegate contains a collection of delegates to invoke one after the other. If one of the methods invoked by a delegate throws an exception, the complete iteration stops. Have a look at the following `MulticastIteration` example. Here, a simple delegate named `DemoDelegate` that returns `void` without arguments is defined. This delegate is meant to invoke the methods `One()` and `Two()` that fulfill the parameter and return type requirements of the delegate. Be aware that method `One()` throws an exception.

```
using System;

namespace Wrox.ProCSharp.Delegates
{
   public delegate void DemoDelegate();

   class Program
   {
      static void One()
      {
         Console.WriteLine("One");
         throw new Exception("Error in one");
      }

      static void Two()
      {
         Console.WriteLine("Two");
      }
```

In the `Main()` method, delegate `d1` is created to reference method `One()`; next, the address of method `Two()` is added to the same delegate. `d1` is invoked to call both methods. The exception is caught in a `try/catch` block.

```
      static void Main()
      {
         DemoDelegate d1 = One;
         d1 += Two;

         try
         {
            d1();
         }
         catch (Exception)
         {
            Console.WriteLine("Exception caught");
         }
      }
   }
}
```

Only the first method is invoked by the delegate. Because the first method throws an exception, iterating the delegates stops here and method `Two()` is never invoked. The result might differ because the order of calling the methods is not defined.

```
One
Exception Caught
```

Errors and exceptions are explained in detail in Chapter 14, "Errors and Exceptions."

In such a scenario, you can avoid the problem by iterating the list on your own. The `Delegate` class defines the method `GetInvocationList()` that returns an array of `Delegate` objects. You can now use this delegate to invoke the methods associated with them directly, catch exceptions, and continue with the next iteration:

```
static void Main()
{
   DemoDelegate d1 = One;
   d1 += Two;

   Delegate[] delegates = d1.GetInvocationList();
   foreach (DemoDelegate d in delegates)
   {
      try
      {
         d();
      }
      catch (Exception)
      {
         Console.WriteLine("Exception caught");
      }
   }
}
```

When you run the application with the code changes, you can see that the iteration continues with the next method after the exception is caught:

```
One
Exception caught
Two
```

Anonymous Methods

Up to this point, a method must already exist in order for the delegate to work (that is, the delegate is defined with the same signature as the method(s) it will be used with). However, there is another way to use delegates — with anonymous methods. An anonymous method is a block of code that is used as the parameter for the delegate.

The syntax for defining a delegate with an anonymous method doesn't change. It's when the delegate is instantiated that things change. The following is a very simple console application that shows how using an anonymous method can work:

```
using System;

namespace Wrox.ProCSharp.Delegates
{
  class Program
  {
    delegate string DelegateTest(string val);

    static void Main()
    {
      string mid = ", middle part,";

      DelegateTest anonDel = delegate(string param)
      {
        param += mid;
        param += " and this was added to the string.";
        return param;
      };
```

```
        Console.WriteLine(anonDel("Start of string"));

      }
    }
  }
```

The delegate `DelegateTest` is defined inside the class `Program`. It takes a single string parameter. Where things become different is in the `Main` method. When `anonDel` is defined, instead of passing in a known method name, a simple block of code is used, prefixed by the delegate keyword, followed by a parameter:

```
delegate (string param)
{
  param += mid;
  param += " and this was added to the string.";
  return param;
};
```

As you can see, the block of code uses a method-level string variable, `mid`, which is defined outside of the anonymous method and adds it to the parameter that was passed in. The code then returns the string value. When the delegate is called, a string is passed in as the parameter and the returned string is output to the console.

The benefit of anonymous methods is to reduce the code you have to write. You don't have to define a method just to use it with a delegate. This becomes very evident when defining the delegate for an event. (Events are discussed later in this chapter.) This can help reduce the complexity of code, especially where there are several events defined. With anonymous methods, the code does not perform faster. The compiler still defines a method; the method just has an automatically assigned name that you don't need to know.

A couple of rules must be followed when using anonymous methods. You can't have a jump statement (`break`, `goto`, or `continue`) in an anonymous method that has a target outside of the anonymous method. The reverse is also true — a jump statement outside the anonymous method cannot have a target inside the anonymous method.

Unsafe code cannot be accessed inside an anonymous method. Also, `ref` and `out` parameters that are used outside of the anonymous method cannot be accessed. Other variables defined outside of the anonymous method can be used.

If you have to write the same functionality more than once, don't use anonymous methods. In this case, instead of duplicating the code, writing a named method is the preferred way. You only have to write it once and reference it by its name.

Lambda Expressions

C# 3.0 offers a new syntax for anonymous methods: Lambda expressions. Lambda expressions can be used with delegate types. The previous example using anonymous methods is changed to use a Lambda expression:

```
using System;

namespace Wrox.ProCSharp.Delegates
{
  class Program
  {
    delegate string DelegateTest(string val);

    static void Main()
```

(continued)

(continued)

```
        {
          string mid = ", middle part,";

          DelegateTest anonDel = param =>
              {
                param += mid;
                param += " and this was added to the string.";
                return param;
              };

          Console.WriteLine(anonDel("Start of string"));
        }
      }
    }
```

The left side of the Lambda operator => lists the parameters needed with the anonymous method. There are several ways to write this. For example, if a string parameter is needed as the delegate type defined in the sample code, one way to write this is by defining the type and variable name inside brackets:

```
(string param)
```

With Lambda expressions there's no need to add the variable type to the declaration because the compiler knows about the type:

```
(param)
```

If there's only one parameter, the brackets can be removed:

```
param
```

The right side of the Lambda expression lists the implementation. With the sample program the implementation was surrounded by curly brackets similar to the anonymous method earlier:

```
        {
          param += mid;
          param += " and this was added to the string.";
          return param;
        };
```

If the implementation consists of just a single line, you can also remove the curly brackets and the return statement because this is filled automatically by the compiler.

For example, with the following delegate that requires an `int` parameter and returns a `bool`:

```
public delegate bool Predicate(int obj)
```

you can declare a variable of the delegate and assign a Lambda expression. With the Lambda expression here, on the left side the variable `x` is defined. This variable is automatically of type `int` because this is as it is defined with the delegate. The implementation returns the Boolean result of comparing x > 5. If x is larger than 5, true is returned, otherwise false.

```
Predicate p1 = x => x > 5;
```

You can pass this Lambda expression to a method that requires a Predicate parameter:

```
list.FindAll(x => x > 5);
```

The same Lambda expression is shown here, without using variable type inference by defining the variable `x` of type `int`, and also adding the return statement to the implementation:

```
list.FindAll(int x) => { return x > 5; });
```

Using the older syntax, the same functionality is written by using an anonymous method:

```
list.FindAll(delegate(int x) { return x > 5; });
```

With all these different variants, the C# compiler always creates the same IL code.

Changing the `SimpleDelegate` sample shown earlier, you can eliminate the class `MathOperations` by using Lambda expressions. The `Main()` method would then look like this:

```
static void Main()
{
   DoubleOp multByTwo = val => val * 2;
   DoubleOp square = val => val * val;

   DoubleOp [] operations = {multByTwo, square};

   for (int i=0 ; i<operations.Length ; i++)
   {
      Console.WriteLine("Using operations[{0}]:", i);
      ProcessAndDisplayNumber(operations[i], 2.0);
      ProcessAndDisplayNumber(operations[i], 7.94);
      ProcessAndDisplayNumber(operations[i], 1.414);
      Console.WriteLine();
   }
}
```

Running this version will give you the same results as the previous example. The advantage is that it eliminated a class.

Lambda expressions can be used any place where the type is a delegate. Another use of Lambda expressions is when the type is `Expression` *or* `Expression<T>`*. Here the compiler creates an expression tree. This feature is discussed in Chapter 11, "Language Integrated Query."*

Covariance and Contra-variance

The method that is invoked by the delegate does not need the exact same types as defined by the delegate declaration. Covariance and contra-variance are possible.

Return Type Covariance

The return type of a method can derive from the type defined by the delegate. In the example the delegate `MyDelegate1` is defined to return the type `DelegateReturn`. The method that is assigned to the delegate instance `d1` returns the type `DelegateReturn2` that derives from the base class `DelegateReturn` and thus fulfills the requirements of the delegate. This behavior is known by the name *return type covariance*.

```
public class DelegateReturn
{
}

public class DelegateReturn2 : DelegateReturn
{
}

public delegate DelegateReturn MyDelegate1();

class Program
```

(continued)

(continued)

```
{
   static void Main()
   {
      MyDelegate1 d1 = Method1;
      d1();
   }

   static DelegateReturn2 Method1()
   {
      DelegateReturn2 d2 = new DelegateReturn2();
      return d2;
   }
}
```

Parameter Type Contra-variance

The term *parameter type contra-variance* means that the parameters defined by the delegate might differ in the method that is called by the delegate. Here it's different from the return type because the method might use a parameter type that derives from the type defined by the delegate. In the code sample the delegate uses the parameter type `DelegateParam2`, and the method that is assigned to the delegate instance `d2` uses the parameter type `DelegateParam` that is the base type of `DelegateParam2`.

```
public class DelegateParam
{
}
public class DelegateParam2 : DelegateParam
{
}

public delegate void MyDelegate2(DelegateParam2 p);

class Program
{
   static void Main()
   {
      MyDelegate2 d2 = Method2;
      DelegateParam2 p = new DelegateParam2();
      d2(p);
   }

   static void Method2(DelegateParam p)
   {
   }
}
```

Events

Windows-based applications are message-based. This means that the application is communicating with Windows and Windows is communicating with the application by using predefined messages. These messages are structures that contain various pieces of information that the application and Windows will use to determine what to do next. Prior to libraries such as MFC (Microsoft Foundation Classes) or to development environments such as Visual Basic, the developer would have to handle the message that Windows sends to the application. Visual Basic and now .NET wrap some of these incoming messages as something called events. If you need to react to a specific incoming message, you would handle the corresponding event. A common example of this is when the user clicks a button on a form. Windows is sending a `WM_MOUSECLICK` message to the button's message handler (sometimes referred to as the Windows Procedure or WndProc). To the .NET developer, this is exposed as the `Click` event of the button.

In developing object-based applications, another form of communication between objects is required. When something of interest happens in one of your objects, chances are that other objects will want to be informed. Again, events come to the rescue. Just as the .NET Framework wraps up Windows messages in events, you can also utilize events as the communications medium between your objects.

Delegates are used as the means of wiring up the event when the message is received by the application. Believe it or not, in the preceding section on delegates, you learned just about everything you need to know to understand how events work. However, one of the great things about how Microsoft has designed C# events is that you don't actually need to understand anything about the underlying delegates in order to use them. So, this section starts off with a short discussion of events from the point of view of the client software. It focuses on what code you need to write in order to receive notifications of events, without worrying too much about what is happening behind the scenes — just so you can see how easy handling events really is. After that, you write an example that generates events, and as you do so, you should see how the relationship between events and delegates works.

The discussion in this section will be of most use to C++ developers because C++ does not have any concept similar to events. C# events, on the other hand, are quite similar in concept to Visual Basic events, although the syntax and the underlying implementation are different in C#.

In this context, the term "event" is used in two different senses. First, as something interesting that happens, and second, as a precisely defined object in the C# language — the object that handles the notification process. When we mean the latter, we will usually refer to it either as a C# event or, when the meaning is obvious from the context, simply as an event.

The Receiver's View of Events

The event receiver is any application, object, or component that wants to be notified when something happens. To go along with the receiver, there will of course be the event sender. The sender's job will be to raise the event. The sender can be either another object or assembly in your application, or in the case of system events such as mouse clicks or keyboard entry, the sender will be the .NET runtime. It is important to note that the sender of the event will not have any knowledge of who or what the receiver is. This is what makes events so useful.

Now, somewhere inside the event receiver will be a method that is responsible for handling the event. This event handler will be executed each time the event that it is registered to is raised. This is where the delegate comes in. Because the sender has no idea who the receiver(s) will be, there cannot be any type of reference set between the two. So the delegate is used as the intermediary. The sender defines the delegate that will be used by the receiver. The receiver registers the event handler with the event. The process of hooking up the event handler is known as wiring up an event. A simple example of wiring up the `Click` event will help illustrate this process.

First, create a simple Windows Forms application. Drag over a button control from the toolbox and place it on the form. In the properties window rename the button to `buttonOne`. In the code editor, add the following line of code in the `Form1` constructor:

```
public Form1()
{
   InitializeComponent();
   buttonOne.Click += new EventHandler(Button_Click);
}
```

Now in Visual Studio, you should have noticed that after you typed in the += operator, all you had to do was press the Tab key a couple of times and the editor did the rest of the work for you. In most cases this is fine. However, in this example the default handler name is not being used, so you should just enter the text yourself.

What is happening is that you are telling the runtime that when the `Click` event of `buttonOne` is raised, that `Button_Click` method should be executed. `EventHandler` is the delegate that the event uses to assign the handler (`Button_Click`) to the event (`Click`). Notice that you used the += operator to add this new method to the delegate list. This is just like the multicast example that you looked at earlier in this chapter. This means that you can add more than one handler for any event. Because this is a multicast delegate, all of the rules about adding multiple methods apply; however, there is no guarantee as to the order in which the methods are called. Go ahead and drag another button onto the form and rename it to `buttonTwo`. Now connect the `buttonTwo Click` event to the same `Button_Click` method, as shown here:

```
buttonOne.Click += new EventHandler(Button_Click);
buttonTwo.Click += new EventHandler(Button_Click);
```

With delegate inference you can also write the code as follows, where the compiler generates the same code as in the previous version:

```
buttonOne.Click += Button_Click;
buttonTwo.Click += Button_Click;
```

The `EventHandler` delegate is defined for you in the .NET Framework. It is in the `System` namespace, and all of the events that are defined in the .NET Framework use it. As discussed earlier, a delegate requires that all of the methods that are added to the delegate list must have the same signature. This obviously holds true for event delegates as well. Here is the `Button_Click` method defined:

```
private void Button_Click(object sender, EventArgs e)
{

}
```

A few things are important about this method. First, it always returns `void`. Event handlers cannot return a value. Next are the parameters. As long as you use the `EventHandler` delegate, your parameters will be `object` and `EventArgs`. The first parameter is the object that raised the event. In this example it is either `buttonOne` or `buttonTwo`, depending on which button is clicked. By sending a reference to the object that raised the event you can assign the same event handler to more than one object. For example, you can define one button click handler for several buttons and then determine which button was clicked by asking the sender parameter.

The second parameter, `EventArgs`, is an object that contains other potentially useful information about the event. This parameter could actually be any type as long as it is derived from `EventArgs`. The `MouseDown` event uses `MouseDownEventArgs`. It contains properties for which button was used, the X and Y coordinates of the pointer, and other information related to the event. Notice the naming pattern of ending the type with `EventArgs`. Later in the chapter, you'll see how to create and use a custom `EventArgs`-based object.

The name of the method should also be mentioned. As a convention, event handlers follow a naming convention of `object_event`. `object` is the object that is raising the event, and `event` is the event being raised. There is a convention and, for readability's sake, it should be followed.

The last thing to do in this example is to add some code to actually do something in the handler. Now remember that two buttons are using the same handler. So, first you have to determine which button raises the event, and then you can call the action that should be performed. In this example, you can just output some text to a label control on the form. Drag a label control from the toolbox onto the form and name it `labelInfo`. Then write the following code on the `Button_Click` method:

```
if(((Button)sender).Name == "buttonOne")
   labelInfo.Text = "Button One was pressed";
else
   labelInfo.Text = "Button Two was pressed";
```

Notice that because the sender parameter is sent as `object`, you will have to cast it to whatever object is raising the event, in this case `Button`. In this example, you use the `Name` property to determine what button raised the event; however, you can also use another property. The `Tag` property is handy to use in this scenario, because it can contain anything that you want to place in it. To see how the multicast capability of the event delegate works, add another method to the `Click` event of `buttonTwo`. The constructor of the form should look something like this now:

```
buttonOne.Click += new EventHandler(Button_Click);
buttonTwo.Click += new EventHandler(Button_Click);
buttonTwo.Click += new EventHandler(Button2_Click);
```

If you let Visual Studio create the stub for you, you will have the following method at the end of the source file. However, you have to add the call to the `MessageBox.Show()` function:

```
private void Button2_Click(object sender, EventArgs e)
{
   MessageBox.Show("This only happens in Button 2 click event");
}
```

If you go back and make use of Lambda expressions, the methods `Button_Click` and `Button2_Click` would not be needed. The code for the events would like this:

```
buttonOne.Click += (sender, e) => labelInfo.Text = "Button One was pressed";
buttonTwo.Click += (sender, e) => labelInfo.Text = "Button Two was pressed";
buttonTwo.Click += (sender, e) =>
      {
         MessageBox.Show("This only happens in Button 2 click event");
      };
```

When you run this example, clicking `buttonOne` will change the text in the label. Clicking `buttonTwo` will not only change the text but also display the `MessageBox`. Again, the important thing to remember is that there is no guarantee that the label text will change before the `MessageBox` appears, so be careful not to write dependent code in the handlers.

You might have had to learn a lot of concepts to get this far, but the amount of coding you need to do in the receiver is fairly trivial. Also bear in mind that you will find yourself writing event receivers a lot more often than you write event senders. At least in the field of the Windows user interface, Microsoft has already written all the event senders you are likely to need (these are in the .NET base classes, in the `Windows.Forms` namespace).

Defining Events

Receiving events and responding to them is only one side of the story. For events to be really useful, you need the ability to define them and raise them in your code. The example in this section looks at creating, raising, receiving, and optionally canceling an event.

The example has a form raise an event that will be listened to by another class. When the event is raised, the receiving object will determine if the process should execute and then cancel the event if the process cannot continue. The goal in this case is to determine whether the number of seconds of the current time is greater than or less than 30. If the number of seconds is less than 30, a property is set with a string that represents the current time; if the number of seconds is greater than 30, the event is canceled and the time string is set to an empty string.

The form used to generate the event has a button and a label on it. In the example code to download the button is named `buttonRaise` and the label is `labelInfo`. After you have created the form and added the two controls, you will be able to create the event and the corresponding delegate. Add the following code in the class declaration section of the form class:

```
public delegate void ActionEventHandler(object sender,
      ActionCancelEventArgs ev);

public static event ActionEventHandler Action;
```

So, what exactly is going on with these two lines of code? First, you are declaring a new delegate type of `ActionEventHandler`. The reason that you have to create a new one and not use one of the predefined delegates in the .NET Framework is that there will be a custom `EventArgs` class used. Remember that the method signature must match the delegate. So, you now have a delegate to use; the next line actually defines the event. In this case the `Action` event is defined, and the syntax for defining the event requires that you specify the delegate that will be associated with the event. You can also use a delegate that is defined in the .NET Framework. Nearly 100 classes are derived from the `EventArgs` class, so you might find one that works for you. Again, because a custom `EventArgs` class is used in this example, a new delegate type has to be created that matches it.

Defining the event in one line is a C# shorthand notation to add methods that add and remove handler methods and to declare a variable of a delegate. Instead of writing one line you can do the same with the following lines. A variable of the event type as well as methods to add and remove event handlers are declared. The syntax for defining the methods to add and remove event handlers is very similar to properties. The variable value is also defined similarly to add and remove the event handler.

```
private static ActionEventHandler action;

public static event ActionEventHandler Action
{
   add
   {
      action += value;
   }
   remove
   {
      action -= value;
   }
}
```

The long notation for defining an event is useful if more needs to be done than just adding and removing the event handler: for example, to add synchronization for multiple thread access. The WPF controls make use of the long notation to add bubbling and tunneling functionality with the events. You can read more about bubbling and tunneling events in Chapter 34, "Windows Presentation Foundation."

The new `EventArgs`-based class, `ActionCancelEventArgs`, is actually derived from `CancelEventArgs`, which is derived from `EventArgs`. `CancelEventArgs` and adds the `Cancel` property. `Cancel` is a Boolean that informs the sender object that the receiver wants to cancel or stop the event processing. In the `ActionCancelEventArgs` class a `Message` property has been added. This is a string property that will contain textual information on the processing state of the event. Here is the code for the `ActionCancelEventArgs` class:

```
public class ActionCancelEventArgs : System.ComponentModel.CancelEventArgs
{
   public ActionCancelEventArgs() : this(false)  {}

   public ActionCancelEventArgs(bool cancel) : this(false, String.Empty)  {}
   public ActionCancelEventArgs(bool cancel, string message) : base(cancel)
```

```
        {
            this.Message = message;
        }

        public string Message { get; set; }
    }
```

You can see that all an `EventArgs`-based class does is carry information about an event to and from the sender and receiver. Most times the information used from the `EventArgs` class will be used by the receiver object in the event handler. However, sometimes the event handler can add information into the `EventArgs` class and it will be available to the sender. This is how the example uses the `EventArgs` class. Notice that a couple of constructors are available in the `EventArgs` class. This extra flexibility adds to the usability of the class by others.

At this point, an event has been declared, the delegate has been defined, and the `EventArgs` class has been created. The next thing that has to happen is that the event needs to be raised. The only thing that you really need to do is make a call to the event with the proper parameters as shown in this example:

```
ActionCancelEventArgs e = new ActionCancelEventArgs();
Action(this, e);
```

This sounds simple enough. Create the new `ActionCancelEventArgs` class and pass it in as one of the parameters to the event. However, there is one small problem. What if the event hasn't been used anywhere yet? What if an event handler has not yet been defined for the event? The `Action` event would actually be null. If you tried to raise the event, you would get a null reference exception. If you wanted to derive a new form class and use the form that has the `Action` event defined as the base, you would have to do something else whenever the `Action` event were raised. Currently, you would have to enable another event handler in the derived form in order to get access to it. To make this process a little easier and to catch the null reference error, you have to create a method with the name `OnEventName` where `EventName` is the name of the event. The example has a method named `OnAction()`. Here is the complete code for the `OnAction()` method:

```
protected void OnAction(object sender, ActionCancelEventArgs e)
{
   if (Action != null)
   {
      Action(sender, e);
   }
}
```

Not much to it, but it does accomplish what is needed. By making the method protected, only derived classes have access to it. You can also see that the event is tested against null before it is raised. If you were to derive a new class that contains this method and event, you would have to override the `OnAction` method and then you would be hooked into the event. To do this, you would have to call `base.OnAction()` in the override. Otherwise, the event would not be raised. This naming convention is used throughout the .NET Framework and is documented in the .NET SDK documentation.

Notice the two parameters that are passed into the `OnAction` method. They should look familiar to you because they are the same parameters that will need to be passed to the event. If the event needed to be raised from another object other than the one that the method is defined in, you would need to make the accessor internal or public and not protected. Sometimes it makes sense to have a class that consists of nothing but event declarations, and that these events are called from other classes. You would still want to create the `OnEventName` methods. However, in that case they might be static methods.

So, now that the event has been raised, something needs to handle it. Create a new class in the project and call it `BusEntity`. Remember that the goal of this project is to check the seconds property of the current time, and if it is less than 30, set a string value to the time, and if it is greater than 30, set the string to `::` and cancel the event. Here is the code:

```
using System;
using System.IO;
using System.ComponentModel;

namespace Wrox.ProCSharp.Delegates
{
   public class BusEntity
   {
      string time = String.Empty;

      public BusEntity()
      {
         Form1.Action += new Form1.ActionEventHandler(Form1_Action);
      }

      private void Form1_Action(object sender, ActionCancelEventArgs e)
      {
         e.Cancel = !DoActions();
         if(e.Cancel)
            e.Message = "Wasn't the right time.";
      }

      private bool DoActions()
      {
         bool retVal = false;
         DateTime tm = DateTime.Now;

         if(tm.Second < 30)
         {
            time = "The time is " + DateTime.Now.ToLongTimeString();
            retVal = true;
         }
         else
            time = "";

         return retVal;
      }

      public string TimeString
      {
         get {return time;}
      }
   }
}
```

In the constructor, the handler for the `Form1.Action` event is declared. Notice that the syntax is very similar to the `Click` event that you registered earlier. Because you used the same pattern for declaring the event, the usage syntax stays consistent as well. Something else worth mentioning at this point is how you were able to get a reference to the `Action` event without having a reference to `Form1` in the

BusEntity class. Remember that in the Form1 class the Action event is declared static. This isn't a requirement, but it does make it easier to create the handler. You could have declared the event public, but then an instance of Form1 would need to be referenced.

When you coded the event in the constructor, you called the method that was added to the delegate list Form1_Action, in keeping with the naming standards. In the handler a decision on whether or not to cancel the event needs to be made. The DoActions method returns a Boolean value based on the time criteria described earlier. DoAction also sets the time string to the proper value.

Next, the DoActions return value is set to the ActionCancelEventArgs Cancel property. Remember that EventArg classes generally do not do anything other than carry values to and from the event senders and receivers. If the event is canceled (e.Cancel = true), the Message property is also set with a string value that describes why the event was canceled.

Now if you look at the code in the buttonRaise_Click event handler again you will be able to see how the Cancel property is used:

```
private void buttonRaise_Click(object sender, EventArgs e)
{
   ActionCancelEventArgs cancelEvent = new ActionCancelEventArgs();
   OnAction(this, cancelEvent);
   if (cancelEvent.Cancel)
      labelInfo.Text = cancelEvent.Message;
   else
      labelInfo.Text = busEntity.TimeString;
}
```

Note that the ActionCancelEventArgs object is created. Next, the event Action is raised, passing in the newly created ActionCancelEventArgs object. When the OnAction method is called and the event is raised, the code in the Action event handler in the BusEntity object is executed. If there were other objects that had registered for the Action event, they too would execute. Something to keep in mind is that if there were other objects handling this event, they would all see the same ActionCancelEventArgs object. If you needed to keep up with which object canceled the event and whether more than one object canceled the event, you would need some type of list-based data structure in the ActionCancelEventArgs class.

After the handlers that have been registered with the event delegate have been executed, you can query the ActionCancelEventArgs object to see if it has been canceled. If it has been canceled, lblInfo will contain the Message property value. If the event has not been canceled, lblInfo will show the current time.

This should give you a basic idea of how you can utilize events and the EventArgs-based object in the events to pass information around in your applications.

Summary

This chapter gave you the basics of delegates and events. You learned how to declare a delegate and add methods to the delegate list. You also learned the process of declaring event handlers to respond to an event, as well as how to create a custom event and use the patterns for raising the event.

As a .NET developer, you will be using delegates and events extensively, especially when developing Windows Forms applications. Events are the means that the .NET developer has to monitor the various Windows messages that occur while the application is executing. Otherwise, you would have to monitor the WndProc and catch the WM_MOUSEDOWN message instead of getting the mouse Click event for a button.

The use of delegates and events in the design of a large application can reduce dependencies and the coupling of layers. This allows you to develop components that have a higher reusability factor.

Anonymous methods and Lambda expressions are C# language features on delegates. With these, you can reduce the amount of code you need to write. Lambda expressions are not only used with delegates, as you can see in Chapter 11, "Language Integrated Query."

The next chapter goes into the foundation of strings and regular expressions.

8

Strings and Regular Expressions

Since the beginning of this book, you have been using strings almost constantly and might not have realized that the stated mapping that the `string` keyword in C# actually refers to is the `System.String` .NET base class. `System.String` is a very powerful and versatile class, but it is by no means the only string-related class in the .NET armory. This chapter starts by reviewing the features of `System.String` and then looks at some nifty things you can do with strings using some of the other .NET classes — in particular those in the `System.Text` and `System.Text.RegularExpressions` namespaces. This chapter covers the following areas:

- **Building strings** — If you're performing repeated modifications on a string, for example, in order to build up a lengthy string prior to displaying it or passing it to some other method or application, the `String` class can be very inefficient. For this kind of situation, another class, `System.Text.StringBuilder`, is more suitable because it has been designed exactly for this situation.
- **Formatting expressions** — We also take a closer look at those formatting expressions that have been used in the `Console.WriteLine()` method throughout the past few chapters. These formatting expressions are processed using a couple of useful interfaces, `IFormatProvider` and `IFormattable`. By implementing these interfaces on your own classes, you can actually define your own formatting sequences so that `Console.WriteLine()` and similar classes will display the values of your classes in whatever way you specify.
- **Regular expressions** — .NET also offers some very sophisticated classes that deal with situations in which you need to identify or extract substrings that satisfy certain fairly sophisticated criteria; for example, finding all occurrences within a string where a character or set of characters is repeated, finding all words that begin with s and contain at least one n, or strings that adhere to employee ID or Social Security number constructions. Although you can write methods to perform this kind of processing using the `String` class, such methods are cumbersome to write. Instead, you can use some classes from `System.Text.RegularExpressions`, which are designed specifically to perform this kind of processing.

System.String

Before examining the other string classes, this section quickly reviews some of the available methods in the `String` class.

`System.String` is a class specifically designed to store a string and allow a large number of operations on the string. In addition, due to the importance of this data type, C# has its own keyword and associated syntax to make it particularly easy to manipulate strings using this class.

You can concatenate strings using operator overloads:

```
string message1 = "Hello";  // returns "Hello"
message1 += ", There"; // returns "Hello, There"
string message2 = message1 + "!"; // returns "Hello, There!"
```

C# also allows extraction of a particular character using an indexer-like syntax:

```
char char4 = message[4];    // returns 'a'. Note the char is zero-indexed
```

This enables you to perform such common tasks as replacing characters, removing whitespace, and capitalization. The following table introduces the key methods.

Method	Purpose
`Compare`	Compares the contents of strings, taking into account the culture (locale) in assessing equivalence between certain characters
`CompareOrdinal`	Same as `Compare` but doesn't take culture into account
`Concat`	Combines separate string instances into a single instance
`CopyTo`	Copies a specific number of characters from the selected index to an entirely new instance of an array
`Format`	Formats a string containing various values and specifiers for how each value should be formatted
`IndexOf`	Locates the first occurrence of a given substring or character in the string
`IndexOfAny`	Locates the first occurrence of any one of a set of characters in the string
`Insert`	Inserts a string instance into another string instance at a specified index
`Join`	Builds a new string by combining an array of strings
`LastIndexOf`	Same as `IndexOf` but finds the last occurrence
`LastIndexOfAny`	Same as `IndexOfAny` but finds the last occurrence
`PadLeft`	Pads out the string by adding a specified repeated character to the left side of the string
`PadRight`	Pads out the string by adding a specified repeated character to the right side of the string
`Replace`	Replaces occurrences of a given character or substring in the string with another character or substring

Method	Purpose
`Split`	Splits the string into an array of substrings, the breaks occurring wherever a given character occurs
`Substring`	Retrieves the substring starting at a specified position in the string
`ToLower`	Converts string to lowercase
`ToUpper`	Converts string to uppercase
`Trim`	Removes leading and trailing whitespace

Please note that this table is not comprehensive but is intended to give you an idea of the features offered by strings.

Building Strings

As you have seen, `String` is an extremely powerful class that implements a large number of very useful methods. However, the `String` class has a shortcoming that makes it very inefficient for making repeated modifications to a given string — it is actually an *immutable* data type, which means that once you initialize a string object, that string object can never change. The methods and operators that appear to modify the contents of a string actually create new strings, copying across the contents of the old string if necessary. For example, look at the following code:

```
string greetingText = "Hello from all the guys at Wrox Press. ";
greetingText += "We do hope you enjoy this book as much as we enjoyed writing it.";
```

What happens when this code executes is this: first, an object of type `System.String` is created and initialized to hold the text `Hello from all the guys at Wrox Press.`. Note the space *after* the period. When this happens, the .NET runtime allocates just enough memory in the string to hold this text (39 chars), and the variable `greetingText` is set to refer to this string instance.

In the next line, syntactically it looks like more text is being added onto the string — though it is not. Instead, what happens is that a new string instance is created with just enough memory allocated to store the combined text — that's 103 characters in total. The original text, `Hello from all the people at Wrox Press.`, is copied into this new string instance along with the extra text, `We do hope you enjoy this book as much as we enjoyed writing it.`. Then, the address stored in the variable `greetingText` is updated, so the variable correctly points to the new `String` object. The old `String` object is now unreferenced — there are no variables that refer to it — and so will be removed the next time the garbage collector comes along to clean out any unused objects in your application.

By itself, that does not look too bad, but suppose that you wanted to encode that string by replacing each letter (not the punctuation) with the character that has an ASCII code further on in the alphabet, as part of some extremely simple encryption scheme. This would change the string to `Ifmmp gspn bmm uif hvst bu Xspy Qsftt. Xf ep ipqf zpv fokpz uijt cppl bt nvdi bt xf fokpzfe xsjujoh ju.`. Several ways of doing this exist, but the simplest and (if you are restricting yourself to using the `String` class) almost certainly the most efficient way is to use the `String.Replace()` method, which replaces all occurrences of a given substring in a string with another substring. Using `Replace()`, the code to encode the text looks like this:

```
string greetingText = "Hello from all the guys at Wrox Press. ";
greetingText += "We do hope you enjoy this book as much as we enjoyed writing it.";

for(int i = 'z'; i>= 'a' ; i--)
{
   char old1 = (char)i;
   char new1 = (char)(i+1);
   greetingText = greetingText.Replace(old1, new1);
}

for(int i = 'Z'; i>='A' ; i--)
{
   char old1 = (char)i;
   char new1 = (char)(i+1);
   greetingText = greetingText.Replace(old1, new1);
}

Console.WriteLine("Encoded:\n" + greetingText);
```

For simplicity, this code does not wrap Z to A or z to a. These letters get encoded to [and {, respectively.

Here, the `Replace()` method works in a fairly intelligent way, to the extent that it won't actually create a new string unless it actually makes changes to the old string. The original string contained 23 different lowercase characters and 3 different uppercase ones. The `Replace` method will therefore have allocated a new string 26 times in total, with each new string storing 103 characters. That means that because of the encryption process, there will be string objects capable of storing a combined total of 2,678 characters now sitting on the heap waiting to be garbage-collected! Clearly, if you use strings to do text processing extensively, your applications will run into severe performance problems.

To address this kind of issue, Microsoft has supplied the `System.Text.StringBuilder` class. `StringBuilder` is not as powerful as `String` in terms of the number of methods it supports. The processing you can do on a `StringBuilder` is limited to substitutions and appending or removing text from strings. However, it works in a much more efficient way.

When you construct a string using the `String` class, just enough memory is allocated to hold the string. The `StringBuilder`, however, normally allocates more memory than is actually needed. You, as a developer, have the option to indicate how much memory the `StringBuilder` should allocate, but if you do not, the amount will default to some value that depends on the size of the string that the `StringBuilder` instance is initialized with. The `StringBuilder` class has two main properties:

- `Length`, which indicates the length of the string that it actually contains
- `Capacity`, which indicates the maximum length of the string in the memory allocation

Any modifications to the string take place within the block of memory assigned to the `StringBuilder` instance, which makes appending substrings and replacing individual characters within strings very efficient. Removing or inserting substrings is inevitably still inefficient because it means that the following part of the string has to be moved. Only if you perform some operation that exceeds the capacity of the string is it necessary to allocate new memory and possibly move the entire contained string. In adding extra capacity, based on our experiments the `StringBuilder` appears to double its capacity if it detects the capacity has been exceeded and no new value for the capacity has been set.

For example, if you use a `StringBuilder` object to construct the original greeting string, you might write this code:

```
StringBuilder greetingBuilder =
   new StringBuilder("Hello from all the guys at Wrox Press. ", 150);
greetingBuilder.AppendFormat("We do hope you enjoy this book as much as we enjoyed
                             writing it");
```

In order to use the `StringBuilder` *class, you will need a* `System.Text` *reference in your code.*

This code sets an initial capacity of `150` for the `StringBuilder`. It is always a good idea to set some capacity that covers the likely maximum length of a string, to ensure the `StringBuilder` does not need to relocate because its capacity was exceeded. Theoretically, you can set as large a number as you can pass in an `int`, although the system will probably complain that it does not have enough memory if you actually try to allocate the maximum of 2 billion characters (this is the theoretical maximum that a `StringBuilder` instance is in principle allowed to contain).

When the preceding code is executed, it first creates a `StringBuilder` object that looks like Figure 8-1.

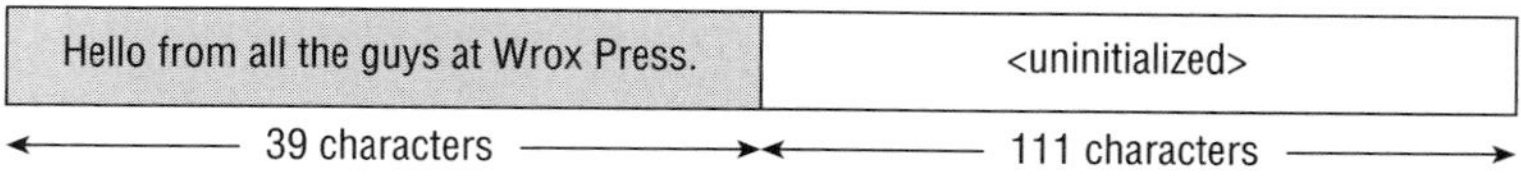

Figure 8-1

Then, on calling the `AppendFormat()` method, the remaining text is placed in the empty space, without the need for more memory allocation. However, the real efficiency gain from using a `StringBuilder` comes when you are making repeated text substitutions. For example, if you try to encrypt the text in the same way as before, you can perform the entire encryption without allocating any more memory whatsoever:

```
StringBuilder greetingBuilder =
   new StringBuilder("Hello from all the guys at Wrox Press. ", 150);
greetingBuilder.AppendFormat("We do hope you enjoy this book as much as we " +
   "enjoyed writing it");

Console.WriteLine("Not Encoded:\n" + greetingBuilder);

for(int i = 'z'; i>='a' ; i--)
{
   char old1 = (char)i;
   char new1 = (char)(i+1);
   greetingBuilder = greetingBuilder.Replace(old1, new1);
}

for(int i = 'Z'; i>='A' ; i--)
{
   char old1 = (char)i;
   char new1 = (char)(i+1);
   greetingBuilder = greetingBuilder.Replace(old1, new1);
}

Console.WriteLine("Encoded:\n" + greetingBuilder);
```

This code uses the `StringBuilder.Replace()` method, which does the same thing as `String.Replace()`, but without copying the string in the process. The total memory allocated to hold strings in the preceding code is 150 characters for the `StringBuilder` instance, as well as the memory allocated during the string operations performed internally in the final `Console.WriteLine()` statement.

Normally, you will want to use `StringBuilder` to perform any manipulation of strings and `String` to store or display the final result.

StringBuilder Members

You have seen a demonstration of one constructor of `StringBuilder`, which takes an initial string and capacity as its parameters. There are others. For example, you can supply only a string:

```
StringBuilder sb = new StringBuilder("Hello");
```

Or you can create an empty `StringBuilder` with a given capacity:

```
StringBuilder sb = new StringBuilder(20);
```

Apart from the `Length` and `Capacity` properties, there is a read-only `MaxCapacity` property that indicates the limit to which a given `StringBuilder` instance is allowed to grow. By default, this is given by `int.MaxValue` (roughly 2 billion, as noted earlier), but you can set this value to something lower when you construct the `StringBuilder` object:

```
// This will both set initial capacity to 100, but the max will be 500.
// Hence, this StringBuilder can never grow to more than 500 characters,
// otherwise it will raise exception if you try to do that.
StringBuilder sb = new StringBuilder(100, 500);
```

You can also explicitly set the capacity at any time, though an exception will be raised if you set it to a value less than the current length of the string or a value that exceeds the maximum capacity:

```
StringBuilder sb = new StringBuilder("Hello");
sb.Capacity = 100;
```

The following table lists the main `StringBuilder` methods.

Method	Purpose
`Append()`	Appends a string to the current string
`AppendFormat()`	Appends a string that has been worked out from a format specifier
`Insert()`	Inserts a substring into the current string
`Remove()`	Removes characters from the current string
`Replace()`	Replaces all occurrences of a character with another character or a substring with another substring in the current string
`ToString()`	Returns the current string cast to a `System.String` object (overridden from `System.Object`)

Several overloads of many of these methods exist.

> `AppendFormat()` *is actually the method that is ultimately called when you call* `Console.WriteLine()`, *which has responsibility for working out what all the format expressions like* `{0:D}` *should be replaced with. This method is examined in the next section.*

There is no cast (either implicit or explicit) from `StringBuilder` to `String`. If you want to output the contents of a `StringBuilder` as a `String`, you must use the `ToString()` method.

Now that you have been introduced to the `StringBuilder` class and have learned some of the ways in which you can use it to increase performance, you should be aware that this class will not always give you the increased performance that you are looking for. Basically, the `StringBuilder` class should be used when you are manipulating multiple strings. However, if you are just doing something as simple as concatenating two strings, you will find that `System.String` will be better-performing.

Format Strings

So far, a large number of classes and structs have been written for the code samples presented in this book, and they have normally implemented a `ToString()` method in order to be able to display the contents of a given variable. However, quite often users might want the contents of a variable to be displayed in different, often culture- and locale-dependent, ways. The .NET base class, `System.DateTime`, provides the most obvious example of this. For example, you might want to display the same date as 10 June 2008, 10 Jun 2008, 6/10/08 (USA), 10/6/08 (UK), or 10.06.2008 (Germany).

Similarly, the `Vector` struct in Chapter 6, "Operators and Casts" implements the `Vector.ToString()` method to display the vector in the format `(4, 56, 8)`. There is, however, another very common way of writing vectors, in which this vector would appear as `4i + 56j + 8k`. If you want the classes that you write to be user-friendly, they need to support the facility to display their string representations in any of the formats that users are likely to want to use. The .NET runtime defines a standard way in which this should be done: the `IFormattable` interface. Showing how to add this important feature to your classes and structs is the subject of this section.

As you probably know, you need to specify the format in which you want a variable displayed when you call `Console.WriteLine()`. Therefore, this section uses this method as an example, although most of the discussion applies to any situation in which you want to format a string. For example, if you want to display the value of a variable in a list box or text box, you will normally use the `String.Format()` method to obtain the appropriate string representation of the variable. However, the actual format specifiers you use to request a particular format are identical to those passed to `Console.WriteLine()`. Hence, you will focus on `Console.WriteLine()` as an example. You start by examining what actually happens when you supply a format string to a primitive type, and from this, you will see how you can plug format specifiers for your own classes and structs into the process.

Chapter 2, "C# Basics," uses format strings in `Console.Write()` and `Console.WriteLine()` like this:

```
double d = 13.45;
int i = 45;
Console.WriteLine("The double is {0,10:E} and the int contains {1}", d, i);
```

The format string itself consists mostly of the text to be displayed, but wherever there is a variable to be formatted, its index in the parameter list appears in braces. You might also include other information inside the braces concerning the format of that item. For example, you can include:

- The number of characters to be occupied by the representation of the item, prefixed by a comma. A negative number indicates that the item should be left-justified, whereas a positive number indicates that it should be right-justified. If the item actually occupies more characters than have been requested, it will still appear in full.
- A format specifier, preceded by a colon. This indicates how you want the item to be formatted. For example, you can indicate whether you want a number to be formatted as a currency or displayed in scientific notation.

The following table lists the common format specifiers for the numeric types, which were briefly discussed in Chapter 2.

Specifier	Applies To	Meaning	Example
C	Numeric types	Locale-specific monetary value	\$4834.50 (USA) £4834.50 (UK)
D	Integer types only	General integer	4834
E	Numeric types	Scientific notation	4.834E+003
F	Numeric types	Fixed-point decimal	4384.50
G	Numeric types	General number	4384.5
N	Numeric types	Common locale-specific format for numbers	4,384.50 (UK/USA) | 4 384,50 (continental Europe)
P	Numeric types	Percentage notation	432,000.00%
X	Integer types only	Hexadecimal format	1120 (If you want to display 0x1120, you will have to write out the 0x separately)

If you want an integer to be padded with zeros, you can use the format specifier `0` (zero) repeated as many times as the number length is required. For example, the format specifier `0000` will cause `3` to be displayed as `0003`, and `99` to be displayed as `0099`, and so on.

It is not possible to give a complete list because other data types can add their own specifiers. Showing how to define your own specifiers for your own classes is the aim of this section.

How the String Is Formatted

As an example of how strings are formatted, if you execute the following statement:

```
Console.WriteLine("The double is {0,10:E} and the int contains {1}", d, i);
```

`Console.WriteLine()` just passes the entire set of parameters to the static method, `String.Format()`. This is the same method that you would call if you wanted to format these values for use in a string to be displayed in a text box, for example. The implementation of the three-parameter overload of `WriteLine()` basically does this:

```
// Likely implementation of Console.WriteLine()

public void WriteLine(string format, object arg0, object arg1)
{
   Console.WriteLine(string.Format(format, arg0, arg1));
}
```

The one-parameter overload of this method, which is in turn called in the preceding code sample, simply writes out the contents of the string it has been passed, without doing any further formatting on it.

`String.Format()` now needs to construct the final string by replacing each format specifier with a suitable string representation of the corresponding object. However, as you saw earlier, for this process of building up a string, you need a `StringBuilder` instance rather than a `string` instance. In this example, a `StringBuilder` instance is created and initialized with the first known portion of the string, the text "`The double is`". Next, the `StringBuilder.AppendFormat()` method is called, passing in the first format specifier, {0,10:E}, as well as the associated object, double, in order to add the string representation of this object to the string object being constructed. This process continues with StringBuilder.Append() and StringBuilder.AppendFormat() being called repeatedly until the entire formatted string has been obtained.

Now comes the interesting part: StringBuilder.AppendFormat() has to figure out how to format the object. First, it probes the object to find out whether it implements an interface in the System namespace called IFormattable. You can determine this quite simply by trying to cast an object to this interface and seeing whether the cast succeeds, or by using the C# is keyword. If this test fails, AppendFormat() calls the object's ToString() method, which all objects either inherit from System.Object or override. This is exactly what happens here because none of the classes written so far has implemented this interface. That is why the overrides of Object.ToString() have been sufficient to allow the structs and classes from earlier chapters such as Vector to get displayed in Console.WriteLine() statements.

However, all of the predefined primitive numeric types do implement this interface, which means that for those types, and in particular for double and int in the example, the basic ToString() method inherited from System.Object will not be called. To understand what happens instead, you need to examine the IFormattable interface.

IFormattable defines just one method, which is also called ToString(). However, this method takes two parameters as opposed to the System.Object version, which doesn't take any parameters. The following code shows the definition of IFormattable:

```
interface IFormattable
{
   string ToString(string format, IFormatProvider formatProvider);
}
```

The first parameter that this overload of ToString() expects is a string that specifies the requested format. In other words, it is the specifier portion of the string that appears inside the braces ({}) in the string originally passed to Console.WriteLine() or String.Format(). For example, in the example the original statement was:

```
Console.WriteLine("The double is {0,10:E} and the int contains {1}", d, i);
```

Hence, when evaluating the first specifier, {0,10:E}, this overload will be called against the double variable, d, and the first parameter passed to it will be E. StringBuilder.AppendFormat() will pass in here the text that appears after the colon in the appropriate format specifier from the original string.

We won't worry about the second ToString() parameter in this book. It is a reference to an object that implements the IFormatProvider interface. This interface gives further information that ToString() might need to consider when formatting the object, such as culture-specific details (a .NET culture is similar to a Windows locale; if you are formatting currencies or dates, you need this information). If you are calling this ToString() overload directly from your source code, you might want to supply such an object. However, StringBuilder.AppendFormat() passes in null for this parameter. If formatProvider is null, then ToString() is expected to use the culture specified in the system settings.

Getting back to the example, the first item you want to format is a double, for which you are requesting exponential notation, with the format specifier E. The StringBuilder.AppendFormat() method establishes that the double does implement IFormattable, and will therefore call the two-parameter ToString() overload, passing it the string E for the first parameter and null for the second parameter. It is now up to the double's implementation of this method to return the string representation of the double in the appropriate format, taking into account the requested format and the current culture. StringBuilder.AppendFormat() will then sort out padding the returned string with spaces, if necessary, to fill the 10 characters the format string specified.

The next object to be formatted is an `int`, for which you are not requesting any particular format (the format specifier was simply `{1}`). With no format requested, `StringBuilder.AppendFormat()` passes in a null reference for the format string. The two-parameter overload of `int.ToString()` is expected to respond appropriately. No format has been specifically requested; therefore, it will call the no-parameter `ToString()` method.

This entire string formatting process is summarized in Figure 8-2.

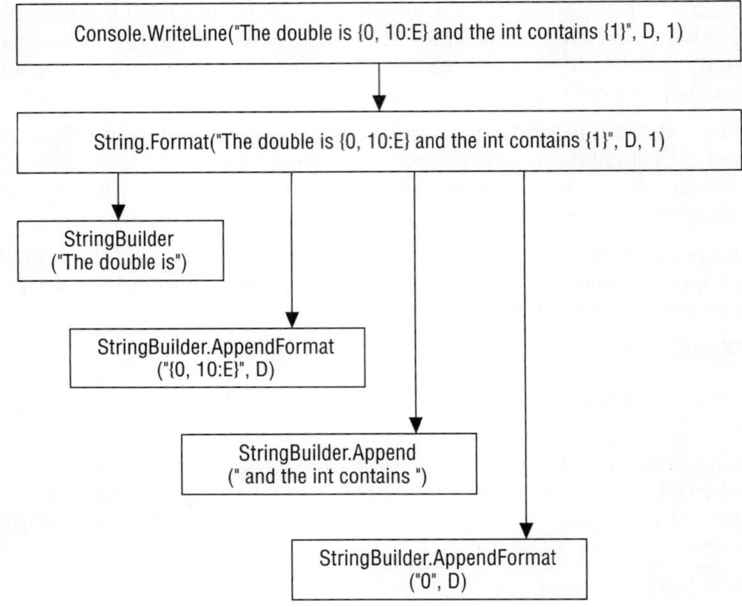

Figure 8-2

The FormattableVector Example

Now that you know how format strings are constructed, in this section you extend the `Vector` example from Chapter 6, so that you can format vectors in a variety of ways. You can download the code for this example from `www.wrox.com`. With your new knowledge of the principles involved now in hand, you will discover that the actual coding is quite simple. All you need to do is implement `IFormattable` and supply an implementation of the `ToString()` overload defined by that interface.

The format specifiers you are going to support are:

- `N` — Should be interpreted as a request to supply a quantity known as the `Norm` of the `Vector`. This is just the sum of squares of its components, which for mathematics buffs happens to be equal to the square of the length of the `Vector`, and is usually displayed between double vertical bars, like this: `||34.5||`.
- `VE` — Should be interpreted as a request to display each component in scientific format, just as the specifier `E` applied to a `double` indicates `(2.3E+01, 4.5E+02, 1.0E+00)`.

- `IJK` — Should be interpreted as a request to display the vector in the form `23i + 450j + 1k`.
- Anything else should simply return the default representation of the `Vector (23, 450, 1.0)`.

To keep things simple, you are not going to implement any option to display the vector in combined `IJK` and scientific format. You will, however, make sure you test the specifier in a case-insensitive way, so that you allow `ijk` instead of `IJK`. Note that it is entirely up to you which strings you use to indicate the format specifiers.

To achieve this, you first modify the declaration of `Vector` so it implements `IFormattable`:

```
struct Vector : IFormattable
{
   public double x, y, z;

   // Beginning part of Vector
```

Now you add your implementation of the two-parameter `ToString()` overload:

```
public string ToString(string format, IFormatProvider formatProvider)
{
   if (format == null)
   {
      return ToString();
   }

   string formatUpper = format.ToUpper();

   switch (formatUpper)
   {
      case "N":
         return "|| " + Norm().ToString() + " ||";
      case "VE":
         return String.Format("( {0:E}, {1:E}, {2:E} )", x, y, z);
      case "IJK":
         StringBuilder sb = new StringBuilder(x.ToString(), 30);
         sb.AppendFormat(" i + ");
         sb.AppendFormat(y.ToString());
         sb.AppendFormat(" j + ");
         sb.AppendFormat(z.ToString());
         sb.AppendFormat(" k");
         return sb.ToString();
      default:
         return ToString();
   }
}
```

That is all you have to do! Notice how you take the precaution of checking whether format is `null` before you call any methods against this parameter — you want this method to be as robust as reasonably possible. The format specifiers for all the primitive types are case-insensitive, so that is the behavior that other developers are going to expect from your class, too. For the format specifier `VE`, you need each component to be formatted in scientific notation, so you just use `String.Format()` again to achieve this. The fields `x`, `y`, and `z` are all `doubles`. For the case of the `IJK` format specifier, there are quite a few substrings to be added to the string, so you use a `StringBuilder` object to improve performance.

For completeness, you also reproduce the no-parameter `ToString()` overload developed earlier:

```
public override string ToString()
{
   return "( " + x + " , " + y + " , " + z + " )";
}
```

Finally, you need to add a `Norm()` method that computes the square (norm) of the vector because you didn't actually supply this method when you developed the `Vector` struct:

```
public double Norm()
{
   return x*x + y*y + z*z;
}
```

Now you can try your formattable vector with some suitable test code:

```
static void Main()
{
   Vector v1 = new Vector(1,32,5);
   Vector v2 = new Vector(845.4, 54.3, -7.8);
   Console.WriteLine("\nIn IJK format,\nv1 is {0,30:IJK}\nv2 is {1,30:IJK}",
                     v1, v2);
   Console.WriteLine("\nIn default format,\nv1 is {0,30}\nv2 is {1,30}", v1, v2);
   Console.WriteLine("\nIn VE format\nv1 is {0,30:VE}\nv2 is {1,30:VE}", v1, v2);
   Console.WriteLine("\nNorms are:\nv1 is {0,20:N}\nv2 is {1,20:N}", v1, v2);
}
```

The result of running this sample is this:

```
FormattableVector
In IJK format,
v1 is               1 i + 32 j + 5 k
v2 is      845.4 i + 54.3 j + -7.8 k

In default format,
v1 is                 ( 1 , 32 , 5 )
v2 is        ( 845.4 , 54.3 , -7.8 )

In VE format
v1 is ( 1.000000E+000, 3.200000E+001, 5.000000E+000 )
v2 is ( 8.454000E+002, 5.430000E+001, -7.800000E+000 )

Norms are:
v1 is           || 1050 ||
v2 is      || 717710.49 ||
```

This shows that your custom specifiers are being picked up correctly.

Regular Expressions

Regular expressions are part of those small technology areas that are incredibly useful in a wide range of programs, yet rarely used among developers. You can think of regular expressions as a mini-programming language with one specific purpose: to locate substrings within a large string expression. It is not a new technology; it originated in the Unix environment and is commonly used with the Perl programming language. Microsoft ported it onto Windows, where up until now it has been used mostly with scripting languages. Today, regular expressions are, however, supported by a number of .NET classes in the namespace `System.Text.RegularExpressions`. You can also find the use of regular expressions in various parts of the .NET Framework. For instance, you will find that they are used within the ASP.NET Validation server controls.

If you are not familiar with the regular expressions language, this section introduces both regular expressions and their related .NET classes. If you are already familiar with regular expressions, you will probably want to just skim through this section to pick out the references to the .NET base classes. You might like to know that the .NET regular expression engine is designed to be mostly compatible with Perl 5 regular expressions, although it has a few extra features.

Introduction to Regular Expressions

The regular expressions language is designed specifically for string processing. It contains two features:

- A set of *escape codes* for identifying specific types of characters. You will be familiar with the use of the `*` character to represent any substring in DOS expressions. (For example, the DOS command `Dir Re*` lists the files with names beginning with `Re`.) Regular expressions use many sequences like this to represent items such as *any one character, a word break, one optional character*, and so on.
- A system for grouping parts of substrings and intermediate results during a search operation.

With regular expressions, you can perform quite sophisticated and high-level operations on strings. For example, you can:

- Identify (and perhaps either flag or remove) all repeated words in a string (for example, "The computer books books" to "The computer books")
- Convert all words to title case (for example, "this is a Title" to "This Is A Title")
- Convert all words longer than three characters to title case (for example, "this is a Title" to "This is a Title")
- Ensure that sentences are properly capitalized
- Separate the various elements of a URI (for example, given `http://www.wrox.com`, extract the protocol, computer name, file name, and so on)

Of course, all of these tasks can be performed in C# using the various methods on `System.String` and `System.Text.StringBuilder`. However, in some cases, this would require writing a fair amount of C# code. If you use regular expressions, this code can normally be compressed to just a couple of lines. Essentially, you instantiate a `System.Text.RegularExpressions.RegEx` object (or, even simpler, invoke a static `RegEx()` method), pass it the string to be processed, and pass in a regular expression (a string containing the instructions in the regular expressions language), and you're done.

A regular expression string looks at first sight rather like a regular string, but interspersed with escape sequences and other characters that have a special meaning. For example, the sequence `\b` indicates the beginning or end of a word (a word boundary), so if you wanted to indicate you were looking for the characters `th` at the beginning of a word, you would search for the regular expression, `\bth` (that is, the sequence word boundary-`t`-`h`). If you wanted to search for all occurrences of `th` at the end of a word, you would write `th\b` (the sequence `t`-`h`-word boundary). However, regular expressions are much more sophisticated than that and include, for example, facilities to store portions of text that are found in a search operation. This section merely scratches the surface of the power of regular expressions.

> *For more on regular expressions, please review the book* Beginning Regular Expressions *(ISBN 978-0-7645-7489-4).*

Suppose your application needed to convert U.S. phone numbers to an international format. In the United States, the phone numbers have this format: 314-123-1234, which is often written as (314) 123-1234. When converting this national format to an international format you have to include +1 (the country code of the United States) and add brackets around the area code: +1 (314) 123-1234. As find-and-replace operations go, that's not too complicated. It would still require some coding effort if you were going to use the `String` class for this purpose (which would mean that you would have to write your code using the methods available from `System.String`). The regular expressions language allows you to construct a short string that achieves the same result.

This section is intended only as a very simple example, so it concentrates on searching strings to identify certain substrings, not on modifying them.

The RegularExpressionsPlayaround Example

For the rest of this section, you develop a short example, called RegularExpressionsPlayaround, that illustrates some of the features of regular expressions and how to use the .NET regular expressions engine in C# by performing and displaying the results of some searches. The text you are going to use as your sample document is an introduction to a Wrox Press book on ASP.NET (*Professional ASP.NET 3.5: in C# and VB*, ISBN 978-0-470-18757-9).

```
string Text =
@"This comprehensive compendium provides a broad and thorough investigation of all
aspects of programming with ASP.NET. Entirely revised and updated for the 3.5
Release of .NET, this book will give you the information you need to master ASP.NET
and build a dynamic, successful, enterprise Web application.";
```

This code is valid C# code, despite all the line breaks. It nicely illustrates the utility of verbatim strings that are prefixed by the @ symbol.

This text is referred to as the *input string*. To get your bearings and get used to the regular expressions .NET classes, you start with a basic plain text search that does not feature any escape sequences or regular expression commands. Suppose that you want to find all occurrences of the string `ion`. This search string is referred to as the *pattern*. Using regular expressions and the `Text` variable declared previously, you can write this:

```
string Pattern = "ion";
MatchCollection Matches = Regex.Matches(Text, Pattern,
                                        RegexOptions.IgnoreCase |
                                        RegexOptions.ExplicitCapture);
foreach (Match NextMatch in Matches)
{
   Console.WriteLine(NextMatch.Index);
}
```

This code uses the static method `Matches()` of the `Regex` class in the `System.Text.RegularExpressions` namespace. This method takes as parameters some input text, a pattern, and a set of optional flags taken from the `RegexOptions` enumeration. In this case, you have specified that all searching should be case insensitive. The other flag, `ExplicitCapture`, modifies the way that the match is collected in a way that, for your purposes, makes the search a bit more efficient — you see why this is later (although it does have other uses that we won't explore here). `Matches()` returns a reference to a `MatchCollection` object. A *match* is the technical term for the results of finding an instance of the pattern in the expression. It is represented by the class `System.Text.RegularExpressions.Match`. Therefore, you return a `MatchCollection` that contains all the matches, each represented by a `Match` object. In the preceding code, you simply iterate over the collection and use the `Index` property of the `Match` class, which returns the index in the input text of where the match was found. Running this code results in three matches. The following table details some of the `RegexOptions` enumerations.

Member Name	Description
`CultureInvariant`	Specifies that the culture of the string is ignored
`ExplicitCapture`	Modifies the way the match is collected by making sure that valid captures are the ones that are explicitly named
`IgnoreCase`	Ignores the case of the string that is input
`IgnorePatternWhitespace`	Removes unescaped whitespace from the string and enables comments that are specified with the pound or hash sign
`Multiline`	Changes the characters ^ and $ so that they are applied to the beginning and end of each line and not just to the beginning and end of the entire string
`RightToLeft`	Causes the inputted string to be read from right to left instead of the default left to right (ideal for some Asian and other languages that are read in this direction)
`Singleline`	Specifies a single-line mode where the meaning of the dot (.) is changed to match every character

So far, nothing is really new from the preceding example apart from some .NET base classes. However, the power of regular expressions really comes from that pattern string. The reason is that the pattern string does not have to contain only plain text. As hinted earlier, it can also contain what are known as *meta-characters*, which are special characters that give commands, as well as escape sequences, which work in much the same way as C# escape sequences. They are characters preceded by a backslash (\) and have special meanings.

For example, suppose that you wanted to find words beginning with `n`. You could use the escape sequence `\b`, which indicates a word boundary (a word boundary is just a point where an alphanumeric character precedes or follows a whitespace character or punctuation symbol). You would write this:

```
string Pattern = @"\bn";
MatchCollection Matches = Regex.Matches(Text, Pattern,
                                        RegexOptions.IgnoreCase |
                                        RegexOptions.ExplicitCapture);
```

Notice the `@` character in front of the string. You want the `\b` to be passed to the .NET regular expressions engine at runtime — you don't want the backslash intercepted by a well-meaning C# compiler that thinks it's an escape sequence intended for itself! If you want to find words ending with the sequence `ion`, you write this:

```
string Pattern = @"ion\b";
```

If you want to find all words beginning with the letter `a` and ending with the sequence `ion` (which has as its only match the word *application* in the example), you will have to put a bit more thought into your code. You clearly need a pattern that begins with `\ba` and ends with `ion\b`, but what goes in the middle? You need to somehow tell the application that between the a and the ion there can be any number of characters as long as none of them are whitespace. In fact, the correct pattern looks like this:

```
string Pattern = @"\ba\S*ion\b";
```

Eventually you will get used to seeing weird sequences of characters like this when working with regular expressions. It actually works quite logically. The escape sequence \S indicates any character that is not a whitespace character. The * is called a *quantifier*. It means that the preceding character can be repeated any number of times, including zero times. The sequence \S* means *any number of characters as long as they are not whitespace characters*. The preceding pattern will, therefore, match any single word that begins with a and ends with ion.

The following table lists some of the main special characters or escape sequences that you can use. It is not comprehensive, but a fuller list is available in the MSDN documentation.

Symbol	Meaning	Example	Matches
^	Beginning of input text	^B	B, but only if first character in text
$	End of input text	X$	X, but only if last character in text
.	Any single character except the newline character (\n)	i.ation	isation, ization
*	Preceding character may be repeated zero or more times	ra*t	rt, rat, raat, raaat, and so on
+	Preceding character may be repeated one or more times	ra+t	rat, raat, raaat and so on, but not rt
?	Preceding character may be repeated zero or one time	ra?t	rt and rat only
\s	Any whitespace character	\sa	[space]a, \ta, \na (\t and \n have the same meanings as in C#)
\S	Any character that isn't a whitespace	\SF	aF, rF, cF, but not \tf
\b	Word boundary	ion\b	Any word ending in ion
\B	Any position that isn't a word boundary	\BX\B	Any X in the middle of a word

If you want to search for one of the meta-characters, you can do so by escaping the corresponding character with a backslash. For example, . (a single period) means any single character other than the newline character, whereas \. means a dot.

You can request a match that contains alternative characters by enclosing them in square brackets. For example, [1|c] means one character that can be either 1 or c. If you wanted to search for any occurrence of the words map or man, you would use the sequence ma[n|p]. Within the square brackets, you can also indicate a range, for example [a-z] to indicate any single lowercase letter, [A-E] to indicate any uppercase letter between A and E (including the letters A and E themselves), or [0-9] to represent a single digit. If you want to search for an integer (that is, a sequence that contains only the characters 0 through 9), you could write [0-9]+ (note the use of the + character to indicate there must be at least one such digit, but there may be more than one — so this would match 9, 83, 854, and so on).

Displaying Results

In this section, you code the `RegularExpressionsPlayaround` example, so you can get a feel for how the regular expressions work.

The core of the example is a method called `WriteMatches()`, which writes out all the matches from a `MatchCollection` in a more detailed format. For each match, it displays the index of where the match was found in the input string, the string of the match, and a slightly longer string, which consists of the match plus up to ten surrounding characters from the input text — up to five characters before the match and up to five afterward. (It is fewer than five characters if the match occurred within five characters of the beginning or end of the input text.) In other words, a match on the word `messaging` that occurs near the end of the input text quoted earlier would display `and messaging of d` (five characters before and after the match), but a match on the final word `data` would display `g of data.` (only one character after the match), because after that you get to the end of the string. This longer string lets you see more clearly where the regular expression locates the match:

```
static void WriteMatches(string text, MatchCollection matches)
{
   Console.WriteLine("Original text was: \n\n" + text + "\n");
   Console.WriteLine("No. of matches: " + matches.Count);
   foreach (Match nextMatch in matches)
   {
      int Index = nextMatch.Index;
      string result = nextMatch.ToString();
      int charsBefore = (Index < 5) ? Index : 5;
      int fromEnd = text.Length - Index - result.Length;
      int charsAfter = (fromEnd < 5) ? fromEnd : 5;
      int charsToDisplay = charsBefore + charsAfter + result.Length;

      Console.WriteLine("Index: {0}, \tString: {1}, \t{2}",
         Index, result,
         text.Substring(Index - charsBefore, charsToDisplay));
   }
}
```

The bulk of the processing in this method is devoted to the logic of figuring out how many characters in the longer substring it can display without overrunning the beginning or end of the input text. Note that you use another property on the `Match` object, `Value`, which contains the string identified for the match. Other than that, `RegularExpressionsPlayaround` simply contains a number of methods with names like `Find1`, `Find2`, and so on, which perform some of the searches based on the examples in this section. For example, `Find2` looks for any string that contains `a` at the beginning of a word:

```
static void Find2()
{
   string text = @"This comprehensive compendium provides a broad and thorough
     investigation of all aspects of programming with ASP.NET. Entirely revised and
     updated for the 3.5 Release of .NET, this book will give you the information
     you need to master ASP.NET and build a dynamic, successful, enterprise Web
     application.";
   string pattern = @"\ba";
   MatchCollection matches = Regex.Matches(text, pattern,
     RegexOptions.IgnoreCase);
   WriteMatches(text, matches);
}
```

Along with this comes a simple `Main()` method that you can edit to select one of the `Find<n>()` methods:

```
static void Main()
{
   Find1();
   Console.ReadLine();
}
```

The code also needs to make use of the `RegularExpressions` namespace:

```
using System;
using System.Text.RegularExpressions;
```

Running the example with the `Find1()` method shown previously gives these results:

```
RegularExpressionsPlayaround
Original text was:

This comprehensive compendium provides a broad and thorough investigation of all
aspects of programming with ASP.NET. Entirely revised and updated for the 3.5
Release of .NET, this book will give you the information you need to master ASP.NET
and build a dynamic, successful, enterprise Web application.

No. of matches: 1
Index: 291,     String: application,     Web application.
```

Matches, Groups, and Captures

One nice feature of regular expressions is that you can group characters. It works the same way as compound statements in C#. In C#, you can group any number of statements by putting them in braces, and the result is treated as one compound statement. In regular expression patterns, you can group any characters (including meta-characters and escape sequences), and the result is treated as a single character. The only difference is that you use parentheses instead of braces. The resultant sequence is known as a *group*.

For example, the pattern `(an)+` locates any recurrences of the sequence `an`. The `+` quantifier applies only to the previous character, but because you have grouped the characters together, it now applies to repeats of `an` treated as a unit. This means that if you apply `(an)+` to the input text, `bananas came to Europe late in the annals of history`, the `anan` from `bananas` is identified. Yet, if you write `an+`, the program selects the `ann` from `annals`, as well as two separate sequences of `an` from `bananas`. The expression `(an)+` identifies occurrences of `an`, `anan`, `ananan`, and so on, whereas the expression `an+` identifies occurrences of `an`, `ann`, `annn`, and so on.

> *You might wonder why with the preceding example* `(an)+` *picks out* `anan` *from the word banana but doesn't identify either of the two occurrences of* `an` *from the same word. The rule is that matches must not overlap. If there are a couple of possibilities that would overlap, then by default the longest possible sequence will be matched.*

However, groups are actually more powerful than that. By default, when you form part of the pattern into a group, you are also asking the regular expression engine to remember any matches against just that group, as well as any matches against the entire pattern. In other words, you are treating that group as a pattern to be matched and returned in its own right. This can actually be extremely useful if you want to break up strings into component parts.

For example, URIs have the format `<protocol>://<address>:<port>`, where the port is optional. An example of this is `http://www.wrox.com:4355`. Suppose that you want to extract the protocol, the address, and the port from a URI, where you know that there may or may not be whitespace (but no punctuation) immediately following the URI. You could do so using this expression:

```
\b(\S+)://(\S+)(?::(\S+))?\b
```

Here is how this expression works: First, the leading and trailing `\b` sequences ensure that you consider only portions of text that are entire words. Within that, the first group, `(\S+)://`, identifies one or more characters that don't count as whitespace, and that are followed by `://` — the `http://` at the start of an HTTP URI. The brackets cause the `http` to be stored as a group. The subsequent `(\S+)` identifies the string `www.wrox.com` in the URI. This group will end either when it encounters the end of the word (the closing `\b`) or a colon (`:`) as marked by the next group.

The next group identifies the port (`:4355`). The following `?` indicates that this group is optional in the match — if there is no `:xxxx`, this won't prevent a match from being marked. This is very important because the port number is not always specified in a URI — in fact, it is absent most of the time. However, things are a bit more complicated than that. You want to indicate that the colon might or might not appear too, but you don't want to store this colon in the group. You've achieved this by having two nested groups. The inner `(\S+)` identifies anything that follows the colon (for example, `4355`). The outer group contains the inner group preceded by the colon, and this group in turn is preceded by the sequence `?:`. This sequence indicates that the group in question should not be saved (you only want to save `4355`; you don't need `:4355` as well!). Don't get confused by the two colons following each other — the first colon is part of the `?:` sequence that says "don't save this group," and the second is text to be searched for.

If you run this pattern on the following string, you'll get one match: `http://www.wrox.com`.

```
Hey I've just found this amazing URI at http:// what was it -- oh yes
http://www.wrox.com
```

Within this match, you will find the three groups just mentioned as well as a fourth group, which represents the match itself. Theoretically, it is possible that each group itself might return no, one, or more than one match. Each of these individual matches is known as a *capture*. So, the first group, (`\S+`), has one capture, `http`. The second group also has one capture (`www.wrox.com`). The third group, however, has no captures, because there is no port number on this URI.

Notice that the string contains a second `http://`. Although this does match up to the first group, it will not be captured by the search because the entire search expression does not match this part of the text.

There isn't space to show examples of C# code that uses groups and captures, but you should know that the .NET `RegularExpressions` classes support groups and captures, through classes known as `Group` and `Capture`. Also, the `GroupCollection` and `CaptureCollection` classes represent collections of groups and captures. The `Match` class exposes the `Groups()` method, which returns the corresponding `GroupCollection` object. The `Group` class correspondingly implements the `Captures()` method, which returns a `CaptureCollection`. The relationship between the objects is shown in Figure 8-3.

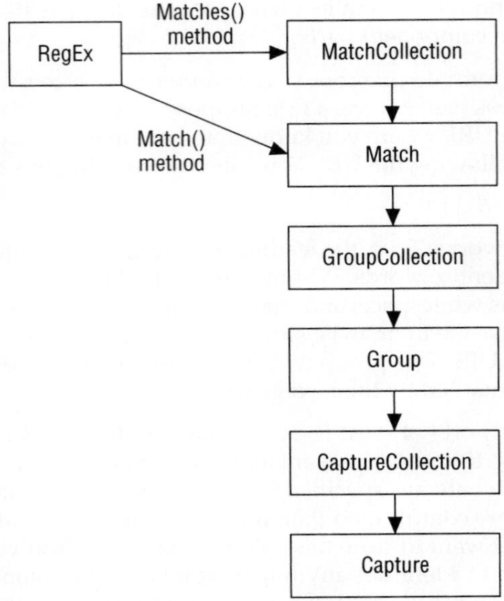

Figure 8-3

You might not want to return a `Group` object every time you just want to group some characters. A fair amount of overhead is involved in instantiating the object, which is not necessary if all you want is to group some characters as part of your search pattern. You can disable this by starting the group with the character sequence `?:` for an individual group, as was done for the URI example, or for all groups by specifying the `RegExOptions.ExplicitCaptures` flag on the `RegEx.Matches()` method, as was done in the earlier examples.

Summary

You have quite a number of available data types at your disposal when working with the .NET Framework. One of the most used types in your applications (especially applications that focus on the submission and retrieval of data) is the `string` data type. The importance of `string` is the reason that this book has a complete chapter focused on how to use the `string` data type and manipulate it in your applications.

When working with strings in the past, it was quite common to just slice and dice the strings as needed using concatenation. With the .NET Framework, you can use the `StringBuilder` class to accomplish a lot of this task with better performance than before.

Last, but hardly least, advanced string manipulation using regular expressions is an excellent tool to search through and validate your strings.

The next chapter takes a look at one of the more powerful features of C# — generics.

9

Generics

A new feature of the CLR 2.0 is the introduction of generics. With CLR 1.0, creating a flexible class or method that should use classes that are not known at compile time must be based on the `Object` class. With the `Object` class, there's no type safety during compile time. Casting is necessary. Also, using the `Object` class for value types has a performance impact.

CLR 2.0 (.NET 3.5 is based on the CLR 2.0) supports generics. With generics, the `Object` class is no longer necessary in such scenarios. Generic classes make use of generic types that are replaced with specific types as needed. This allows for type safety: the compiler complains if a specific type is not supported with the generic class.

Generics are a great feature, especially with collection classes. Most of the .NET 1.0 collection classes are based on the `Object` type. Starting with version 2.0, .NET offers collection classes that are implemented as generics.

Generics are not limited to classes; in this chapter, you also see generics with delegates, interfaces, and methods.

This chapter discusses the following:

- Generics overview
- Creating generic classes
- Features of generic classes
- Generic interfaces
- Generic methods
- Generic delegates
- Other generic framework types

Overview

Generics are not a completely new construct; similar concepts exist with other languages. For example, C++ templates can be compared to generics. However, there's a big difference between C++ templates and .NET generics. With C++ templates, the source code of the template is required when a template is instantiated with a specific type. Contrary to C++ templates, generics are not only a construct of the C# language; generics are defined with the CLR. This makes it possible to instantiate generics with a specific type in Visual Basic even though the generic class was defined with C#.

The following sections look into the advantages and disadvantages of generics, particularly:

- Performance
- Type safety
- Binary code reuse
- Code bloat
- Naming guidelines

Performance

One of the big advantages of generics is performance. In Chapter 10, you will see non-generic and generic collection classes from the namespaces `System.Collections` and `System.Collections.Generic`. Using value types with non-generic collection classes results in boxing and unboxing when the value type is converted to a reference type and vice versa.

Boxing and unboxing is discussed in Chapter 6, "Operators and Casts." Here is just a short refresher about these terms.

Value types are stored on the stack. Reference types are stored on the heap. C# classes are reference types; structs are value types. .NET makes it easy to convert value types to reference types, and so you can use a value type everywhere an object (which is a reference type) is needed. For example, an `int` can be assigned to an object. The conversion from a value type to a reference type is known as boxing. Boxing happens automatically if a method requires an object as a parameter, and a value type is passed. On the other side, a boxed value type can be converted to a value type by using unboxing. With unboxing, the cast operator is required.

The following example shows the `ArrayList` class from the namespace `System.Collections`. `ArrayList` stores objects, the `Add()` method is defined to require an object as a parameter, and so an integer type is boxed. When the values from an `ArrayList` are read, unboxing occurs when the object is converted to an integer type. This may be obvious with the cast operator that is used to assign the first element of the `ArrayList` collection to the variable `i1`, but also happens inside the `foreach` statement where the variable `i2` of type `int` is accessed:

```
ArrayList list = new ArrayList();
list.Add(44);   // boxing - convert a value type to a reference type

int i1 = (int)list[0];   // unboxing - convert a reference type to
                         // a value type

foreach (int i2 in list)
{
   Console.WriteLine(i2);   // unboxing
}
```

Boxing and unboxing are easy to use, but have a big performance impact, especially when iterating through many items.

Instead of using objects, the `List<T>` class from the namespace `System.Collections.Generic` allows you to define the type when it is used. In the example here, the generic type of the `List<T>` class is defined as `int`, so the `int` type is used inside the class that is generated dynamically from the JIT compiler. Boxing and unboxing no longer happens:

```
List<int> list = new List<int>();
list.Add(44);    // no boxing - value types are stored in the List<int>

int i1 = list[0];    // no unboxing, no cast needed

foreach (int i2 in list)
{
   Console.WriteLine(i2);
}
```

Type Safety

Another feature of generics is type safety. As with the `ArrayList` class, if objects are used, any type can be added to this collection. This example shows adding an integer, a string, and an object of type `MyClass` to the collection of type `ArrayList`:

```
ArrayList list = new ArrayList();
list.Add(44);
list.Add("mystring");
list.Add(new MyClass());
```

Now if this collection is iterated using the following `foreach` statement, which iterates using integer elements, the compiler accepts this code. However, because not all elements in the collection can be cast to an `int`, a runtime exception will occur:

```
foreach (int i in list)
{
   Console.WriteLine(i);
}
```

Errors should be detected as early as possible. With the generic class `List<T>`, the generic type `T` defines what types are allowed. With a definition of `List<int>`, only integer types can be added to the collection. The compiler doesn't compile this code because the `Add()` method has invalid arguments:

```
List<int> list = new List<int>();
list.Add(44);
list.Add("mystring");    // compile time error
list.Add(new MyClass());    // compile time error
```

Binary Code Reuse

Generics allow better binary code reuse. A generic class can be defined once and can be instantiated with many different types. Unlike C++ templates, it is not necessary to access the source code.

As an example, here the `List<T>` class from the namespace `System.Collections.Generic` is instantiated with an `int`, a `string`, and a `MyClass` type:

```
List<int> list = new List<int>();
list.Add(44);

List<string> stringList = new List<string>();
stringList.Add("mystring");

List<MyClass> myclassList = new List<MyClass>();
myClassList.Add(new MyClass());
```

Generic types can be defined in one language and used from any other .NET language.

Code Bloat

How much code is created with generics when instantiating them with different specific types?

Because a generic class definition goes into the assembly, instantiating generic classes with specific types doesn't duplicate these classes in the IL code. However, when the generic classes are compiled by the JIT compiler to native code, a new class for every specific value type is created. Reference types share all the same implementation of the same native class. This is because with reference types only a 4-byte memory address (with 32-bit systems) is needed within the generic instantiated class to reference a reference type. Value types are contained within the memory of the generic instantiated class, and because every value type can have different memory requirements, a new class for every value type is instantiated.

Naming Guidelines

If generics are used in the program, it helps when generic types can be distinguished from non-generic types. Here are naming guidelines for generic types:

- Generic type names should be prefixed with the letter T.
- If the generic type can be replaced by any class because there's no special requirement, and only one generic type is used, the character T is good as a generic type name:

```
public class List<T> { }

public class LinkedList<T> { }
```

- If there's a special requirement for a generic type (for example, it must implement an interface or derive from a base class), or if two or more generic types are used, descriptive names should be used for the type names:

```
public delegate void EventHandler<TEventArgs>(object sender, TEventArgs e);

public delegate TOutput Converter<TInput, TOutput>(TInput from);

public class SortedList<TKey, TValue> { }
```

Creating Generic Classes

First start with a normal, non-generic simplified linked list class that can contain objects of any kind, and later convert this class to a generic class.

With a linked list, one element references the next one. So, you must create a class that wraps the object inside the linked list and references the next object. The class `LinkedListNode` contains an object named `value` that is initialized with the constructor, and can be read with the `Value` property. In addition to that, the `LinkedListNode` class contains references to the next and previous elements in the list that can be accessed from properties.

```
public class LinkedListNode
{
   private object value;
   public LinkedListNode(object value)
   {
      this.value = value;
   }

   public object Value
```

```
      {
         get { return value; }
      }


      private LinkedListNode next;
      public LinkedListNode Next
      {
         get { return next; }
         internal set { next = value; }
      }

      private LinkedListNode prev;
      public LinkedListNode Prev
      {
         get { return prev; }
         internal set { prev = value; }
      }
   }
```

The `LinkedList` class includes `first` and `last` fields of type `LinkedListNode` that mark the beginning and end of the list. The method `AddLast()` adds a new element to the end of the list. First, an object of type `LinkedListNode` is created. If the list is empty, the `first` and `last` fields are set to the new element; otherwise, the new element is added as the last element to the list. By implementing the `GetEnumerator()` method, it is possible to iterate through the list with the `foreach` statement. The `GetEnumerator()` method makes use of the `yield` statement for creating an enumerator type.

The yield statement is explained in Chapter 5, "Arrays."

```
   public class LinkedList : IEnumerable
   {
      private LinkedListNode first;
      public LinkedListNode First
      {
         get { return first; }
      }

      private LinkedListNode last;
      public LinkedListNode Last
      {
         get { return last; }
      }

      public LinkedListNode AddLast(object node)
      {
         LinkedListNode newNode = new LinkedListNode(node);
         if (first == null)
         {
            first = newNode;
            last = first;
         }
         else
```

(continued)

(continued)

```
         {
            last.Next = newNode;
            last = newNode;
         }
         return newNode;
      }

      public IEnumerator GetEnumerator()
      {
         LinkedListNode current = first;
         while (current != null)
         {
            yield return current.Value;
            current = current.Next;
         }
      }
   }
```

Now you can use the `LinkedList` class with any type. The following code segment instantiates a new `LinkedList` object and adds two integer types and one string type. As the integer types are converted to an object, boxing occurs as was discussed earlier. With the `foreach` statement unboxing happens. In the `foreach` statement the elements from the list are cast to an integer, so with the third element in the list a runtime exception occurs as casting to an `int` fails.

```
LinkedList list1 = new LinkedList();
list1.AddLast(2);
list1.AddLast(4);
list1.AddLast("6");

foreach (int i in list1)
{
   Console.WriteLine(i);
}
```

Now let's make a generic version of the linked list. A generic class is defined similarly to a normal class with the generic type declaration. The generic type can then be used within the class as a field member, or with parameter types of methods. The class `LinkedListNode` is declared with a generic type `T`. The field `value` is now type `T` instead of `object`; the constructor and property `Value` are changed as well to accept and return an object of type `T`. A generic type can also be returned and set, so the properties `Next` and `Prev` are now of type `LinkedListNode<T>`:

```
public class LinkedListNode<T>
{
   private T value;
   public LinkedListNode(T value)
   {
      this.value = value;
   }

   public T Value
   {
      get { return value; }
   }

   private LinkedListNode<T> next;
```

```
        public LinkedListNode<T> Next
        {
           get { return next; }
           internal set { next = value; }
        }

        private LinkedListNode<T> prev;
        public LinkedListNode<T> Prev
        {
           get { return prev; }
           internal set { prev = value; }
        }
     }
```

In the following code the class `LinkedList` is changed to a generic class as well. `LinkedList<T>` contains `LinkedListNode<T>` elements. The type `T` from the `LinkedList` defines the type `T` of the containing fields `first` and `last`. The method `AddLast()` now accepts a parameter of type `T` and instantiates an object of `LinkedListNode<T>`.

Beside the interface `IEnumerable`, a generic version is also available: `IEnumerable<T>`. `IEnumerable<T>` derives from `IEnumerable` and adds the `GetEnumerator()` method that returns `IEnumerator<T>`. `LinkedList<T>` implements the generic interface `IEnumerable<T>`.

Enumerations and the interfaces `IEnumerable` and `IEnumerator` are discussed in Chapter 5, "Arrays."

```
     public class LinkedList<T> : IEnumerable<T>
     {
        private LinkedListNode<T> first;
        public LinkedListNode<T> First
        {
           get { return first; }
        }

        private LinkedListNode<T> last;
        public LinkedListNode<T> Last
        {
           get { return last; }
        }

        public LinkedListNode<T> AddLast(T node)
        {
           LinkedListNode<T> newNode = new LinkedListNode<T>(node);
           if (first == null)
           {
              first = newNode;
              last = first;
           }
           else
           {
              last.Next = newNode;
              last = newNode;
           }
```

(continued)

(continued)

```
         return newNode;
      }

      public IEnumerator<T> GetEnumerator()
      {
         LinkedListNode<T> current = first;

         while (current != null)
         {
            yield return current.Value;
            current = current.Next;
         }
      }

      IEnumerator IEnumerable.GetEnumerator()
      {
         return GetEnumerator();
      }
   }
```

Using the generic `LinkedList<T>`, you can instantiate it with an `int` type, and there's no boxing. Also, you get a compiler error if you don't pass an `int` with the method `AddLast()`. Using the generic `IEnumerable<T>`, the `foreach` statement is also type-safe, and you get a compiler error if that variable in the `foreach` statement is not an `int`.

```
LinkedList<int> list2 = new LinkedList<int>();
list2.AddLast(1);
list2.AddLast(3);
list2.AddLast(5);

foreach (int i in list2)
{
   Console.WriteLine(i);
}
```

Similarly, you can use the generic `LinkedList<T>` with a `string` type and pass strings to the `AddLast()` method:

```
LinkedList<string> list3 = new LinkedList<string>();
list3.AddLast("2");
list3.AddLast("four");
list3.AddLast("foo");

foreach (string s in list3)
{
   Console.WriteLine(s);
}
```

> **Every class that deals with the object type is a possible candidate for a generic implementation. Also, if classes make use of hierarchies, generics can be very helpful in making casting unnecessary.**

Generic Classes' Features

When creating generic classes, you might need some more C# keywords. For example, it is not possible to assign `null` to a generic type. In this case, the keyword `default` can be used. If the generic type does not require the features of the `Object` class, but you need to invoke some specific methods in the generic class, you can define constraints.

This section discusses the following topics:

- Default Values
- Constraints
- Inheritance
- Static members

Let's start this example with a generic document manager. The document manager is used to read and write documents from a queue. Start by creating a new Console project named `DocumentManager` and add the class `DocumentManager<T>`. The method `AddDocument()` adds a document to the queue. The read-only property `IsDocumentAvailable` returns true if the queue is not empty.

```
using System;
using System.Collections.Generic;

namespace Wrox.ProCSharp.Generics
{
   public class DocumentManager<T>
   {
      private readonly Queue<T> documentQueue = new Queue<T>();

      public void AddDocument(T doc)
      {
         lock (this)
         {
            documentQueue.Enqueue(doc);
         }
      }

      public bool IsDocumentAvailable
      {
         get { return documentQueue.Count > 0; }
      }
   }
}
```

Default Values

Now you add a `GetDocument()` method to the `DocumentManager<T>` class. Inside this method the type `T` should be assigned to `null`. However, it is not possible to assign `null` to generic types. The reason is that a generic type can also be instantiated as a value type, and `null` is allowed only with reference types. To circumvent this problem, you can use the `default` keyword. With the `default` keyword, `null` is assigned to reference types and `0` is assigned to value types.

```
public T GetDocument()
{
   T doc = default(T);
   lock (this)
   {
      doc = documentQueue.Dequeue();
   }
   return doc;
}
```

The `default` keyword has multiple meanings depending on the context where it is used. The switch statement uses a default for defining the default case, and with generics the default is used to initialize generic types either to null or 0 depending on if it is a reference or value type.

Constraints

If the generic class needs to invoke some methods from the generic type, you have to add constraints. With the `DocumentManager<T>`, all the titles of the documents should be displayed in the `DisplayAllDocuments()` method.

The `Document` class implements the interface `IDocument` with the properties `Title` and `Content`:

```
public interface IDocument
{
   string Title { get; set; }
   string Content { get; set; }
}

public class Document : IDocument
{
   public Document()
   {
   }

   public Document(string title, string content)
   {
      this.Title = title;
      this.Content = content;
   }

   public string Title { get; set; }
   public string Content { get; set; }
}
```

For displaying the documents with the `DocumentManager<T>` class, you can cast the type `T` to the interface `IDocument` to display the title:

```
public void DisplayAllDocuments()
{
   foreach (T doc in documentQueue)
   {
      Console.WriteLine(((IDocument)doc).Title);
   }
}
```

The problem is that doing a cast results in a runtime exception if the type `T` does not implement the interface `IDocument`. Instead, it would be better to define a constraint with the `DocumentManager<TDocument>` class that the type `TDocument` must implement the interface `IDocument`. To clarify the requirement in the name of the generic type, `T` is changed to `TDocument`. The `where` clause defines the requirement to implement the interface `IDocument`:

```
public class DocumentManager<TDocument>
    where TDocument : IDocument
{
```

This way you can write the `foreach` statement in such a way that the type `T` contains the property `Title`. You get support from Visual Studio IntelliSense and from the compiler:

```
public void DisplayAllDocuments()
{
    foreach (TDocument doc in documentQueue)
    {
        Console.WriteLine(doc.Title);
    }
}
```

In the `Main()` method the `DocumentManager<T>` class is instantiated with the type `Document` that implements the required interface `IDocument`. Then new documents are added and displayed, and one of the documents is retrieved:

```
static void Main()
{
   DocumentManager<Document> dm = new DocumentManager<Document>();
   dm.AddDocument(new Document("Title A", "Sample A"));
   dm.AddDocument(new Document("Title B", "Sample B"));

   dm.DisplayAllDocuments();

   if (dm.IsDocumentAvailable)
   {
      Document d = dm.GetDocument();
      Console.WriteLine(d.Content);
   }
}
```

The `DocumentManager` now works with any class that implements the interface `IDocument`.

In the sample application, you've seen an interface constraint. Generics support several constraint types:

Constraint	**Description**
`where T : struct`	With a struct constraint, type `T` must be a value type.
`where T : class`	The class constraint indicates that type `T` must be a reference type.
`where T : IFoo`	`where T : IFoo` specifies that type `T` is required to implement interface `IFoo`.
`where T : Foo`	`where T : Foo` specifies that type `T` is required to derive from base class `Foo`.
`where T : new()`	`where T : new()` is a constructor constraint and specifies that type `T` must have a default constructor.
`where T1 : T2`	With constraints it is also possible to specify that type `T1` derives from a generic type `T2`. This constraint is known as *naked type constraint*.

With CLR 2.0 only constructor constraints for the default constructor can be defined. It is not possible to define a constructor constraint for other constructors.

With a generic type, you can also combine multiple constraints. The constraint `where T : IFoo, new()` with the `MyClass<T>` declaration specifies that type `T` implements the interface `IFoo` and has a default constructor:

```
public class MyClass<T>
   where T : IFoo, new()
{
   //...
```

> **One important restriction of the `where` clause with C# is that it's not possible to define operators that must be implemented by the generic type. Operators cannot be defined in interfaces. With the `where` clause, it is only possible to define base classes, interfaces, and the default constructor.**

Inheritance

The `LinkedList<T>` class created earlier implements the interface `IEnumerable<T>`:

```
public class LinkedList<T> : IEnumerable<T>
{
   //...
```

A generic type can implement a generic interface. The same is possible by deriving from a class. A generic class can be derived from a generic base class:

```
public class Base<T>
{
}

public class Derived<T> : Base<T>
{
}
```

The requirement is that the generic types of the interface must be repeated, or the type of the base class must be specified, as in this case:

```
public class Base<T>
{
}

public class Derived<T> : Base<string>
{
}
```

This way, the derived class can be a generic or non-generic class. For example, you can define an abstract generic base class that is implemented with a concrete type in the derived class. This allows you to do specialization for specific types:

```
public abstract class Calc<T>
{
   public abstract T Add(T x, T y);
```

```
        public abstract T Sub(T x, T y);
    }

    public class SimpleCalc : Calc<int>
    {
        public override int Add(int x, int y)
        {
            return x + y;
        }

        public override int Sub(int x, int y)
        {
            return x - y;
        }
    }
```

Static Members

Static members of generic classes require special attention. Static members of a generic class are only shared with one instantiation of the class. Let's have a look at one example. The class `StaticDemo<T>` contains the static field `x`:

```
public class StaticDemo<T>
{
    public static int x;
}
```

Because of using the class `StaticDemo<T>` both with a `string` type and an `int` type, two sets of static fields exist:

```
StaticDemo<string>.x = 4;
StaticDemo<int>.x = 5;
Console.WriteLine(StaticDemo<string>.x);     // writes 4
```

Generic Interfaces

Using generics, you can define interfaces that define methods with generic parameters. In the linked list sample, you've already implemented the interface `IEnumerable<T>`, which defines a `GetEnumerator()` method to return `IEnumerator<T>`. For many non-generic interfaces of .NET 1.0, new generic versions have been defined since .NET 2.0, for example `IComparable<T>`:

```
public interface IComparable<T>
{
    int CompareTo(T other);
}
```

In Chapter 5, "Arrays," the non-generic interface `IComparable` that requires an object with the `CompareTo()` method is implemented with the `Person` class to sort persons by `LastName`:

```
    public class Person : IComparable
    {
        public int CompareTo(object obj)
        {
            Person other = obj as Person;
            return this.lastname.CompareTo(other.LastName);
        }
//...
```

When implementing the generic version, it is no longer necessary to cast the `object` to a `Person`:

```
public class Person : IComparable<Person>
{
   public int CompareTo(Person other)
   {
      return this.LastName.CompareTo(other.LastName);
   }
   //...
```

Generic Methods

In addition to defining generic classes, it is also possible to define generic methods. With a generic method, the generic type is defined with the method declaration.

The method `Swap<T>` defines `T` as a generic type that is used for two arguments and a variable `temp`:

```
void Swap<T>(ref T x, ref T y)
{
   T temp;
   temp = x;
   x = y;
   y = temp;
}
```

A generic method can be invoked by assigning the generic type with the method call:

```
int i = 4;
int j = 5;
Swap<int>(ref i, ref j);
```

However, because the C# compiler can get the type of the parameters by calling the `Swap` method, it is not required to assign the generic type with the method call. The generic method can be invoked as simply as non-generic methods:

```
int i = 4;
int j = 5;
Swap(ref i, ref j);
```

Here's an example where a generic method is used to accumulate all elements of a collection. To show the features of generic methods, the following `Account` class that contains a `name` and a `balance` is used:

```
public class Account
{
   private string name;
   public string Name
   {
      get
      {
         return name;
      }
   }

   private decimal balance;
   public decimal Balance
```

```
        {
           get
           {
              return balance;
           }
        }

        public Account(string name, Decimal balance)
        {
           this.name = name;
           this.balance = balance;
        }
    }
```

All the accounts where the balance should be accumulated are added to an accounts list of type `List<Account>`:

```
            List<Account> accounts = new List<Account>();
            accounts.Add(new Account("Christian", 1500));
            accounts.Add(new Account("Sharon", 2200));
            accounts.Add(new Account("Katie", 1800));
```

A traditional way to accumulate all `Account` objects is by looping through all `Account` objects with a `foreach` statement, as shown here. Because the `foreach` statement is using the `IEnumerable` interface to iterate the elements of a collection, the argument of the `AccumulateSimple()` method is of type `IEnumerable`. This way, the `AccumulateSimple()` method can be used with all collection classes that implement the interface `IEnumerable<Account>`. In the implementation of this method, the property `Balance` of the `Account` object is directly accessed:

```
    public static class Algorithm
    {
       public static decimal AccumulateSimple(IEnumerable<Account> e)
       {
          decimal sum = 0;
          foreach (Account a in e)
          {
             sum += a.Balance;
          }
          return sum;
       }
    }
```

The `AccumulateSimple()` method is invoked this way:

```
        decimal amount = Algorithm.AccumulateSimple(accounts);
```

The problem with the first implementation is that it works only with `Account` objects. This can be avoided by using a generic method.

The second version of the `Accumulate()` method accepts any type that implements the interface `IAccount`. As you've seen earlier with generic classes, generic types can be restricted with the `where` clause. The same clause that is used with generic classes can be used with generic methods. The parameter of the `Accumulate()` method is changed to `IEnumerable<T>`. `IEnumerable<T>` is a generic version of the interface `IEnumerable` that is implemented by the generic collection classes:

```
public static decimal Accumulate<TAccount>(IEnumerable<TAccount> coll)
      where TAccount : IAccount
{
   decimal sum = 0;

   foreach (TAccount a in coll)
   {
      sum += a.Balance;
   }
   return sum;
}
```

The `Account` class is now re-factored to implement the interface `IAccount`:

```
public class Account : IAccount
{
   //...
```

The `IAccount` interface defines the read-only properties `Balance` and `Name`:

```
public interface IAccount
{
   decimal Balance { get; }
   string Name { get; }
}
```

The new `Accumulate()` method can be invoked by defining the `Account` type as generic type parameter:

```
decimal amount = Algorithm.Accumulate<Account>(accounts);
```

Because the generic type parameter can be automatically inferred by the compiler from the parameter type of the method, it is valid to invoke the `Accumulate()` method this way:

```
decimal amount = Algorithm.Accumulate(accounts);
```

The requirement for the generic types to implement the interface `IAccount` may be too restrictive. This requirement can be changed by using generic delegates. In the next section, the `Accumulate()` method will be changed to be independent of any interface.

Generic Delegates

As discussed in Chapter 7, "Delegates and Events," delegates are type-safe references to methods. With generic delegates, the parameters of the delegate can be defined later.

The .NET Framework defines a generic `EventHandler` delegate with the second parameter of type `TEventArgs`, so it is no longer necessary to define a new delegate with every new parameter type:

```
public sealed delegate void EventHandler<TEventArgs>(object sender,
      TEventArgs e)
   where TEventArgs : EventArgs
```

Implementing Methods Called by Delegates

The method `Accumulate()` is changed to have two generic types. `TInput` is the type of the objects that are accumulated, and `TSummary` is the returned type. The first parameter of `Accumulate` is the interface

IEnumerable<T>, as it was before. The second parameter requires the Action delegate to reference a method that is invoked to accumulate all balances.

With the implementation, the method referenced by the Action delegate is now invoked for every element, and then the sum of the calculation is returned:

```
public delegate TSummary Action<TInput, TSummary>(TInput t, TSummary u);

public static TSummary Accumulate<TInput, TSummary>(
      IEnumerable<TInput> coll,
      Action<TInput, TSummary> action)
{
   TSummary sum = default(TSummary);

   foreach (TInput input in coll)
   {
      sum = action(input, sum);
   }
   return sum;
}
```

The method Accumulate() can be invoked using an anonymous method that specifies that the balance of the account should be added to the second parameter that is of type Action:

```
decimal amount = Algorithm.Accumulate<Account, decimal>(
      accounts,
      delegate(Account a, decimal d)
      { return a.Balance + d; });
```

Instead of using anonymous methods, you can use a Lambda expression to pass it to the second parameter:

```
decimal amount = Algorithm.Accumulate<Account, decimal>(
      accounts, (a, d) => a.Balance + d;);
```

Anonymous methods and Lambda expressions are explained in Chapter 7, "Delegates and Events."

If the addition of Account balances is needed more than once, it can be useful to move the functionality into a separate method, AccountAdder():

```
static decimal AccountAdder(Account a, decimal d)
{
   return a.Balance + d;
}
```

And use the address of the AccountAdder method with the Accumulate method:

```
decimal amount = Algorithm.Accumulate<Account, decimal>(
      accounts, AccountAdder);
```

The method referenced by the Action delegate can implement any logic; for example, a multiplication could be done instead of a summation.

The Accumulate() method is made more flexible with the AccumulateIf() method. With AccumulateIf(), an additional parameter of type Predicate<T> is used. The delegate Predicate<T> references the method that will be invoked to check whether the account should be part of the accumulation. In the `foreach` statement, the `action` method will be invoked only if the predicate `match` returns `true`:

```
public static TSummary AccumulateIf<TInput, TSummary>(
        IEnumerable<TInput> coll,
        Action<TInput, TSummary> action,
        Predicate<TInput> match)
{
    TSummary sum = default(TSummary);

    foreach (TInput a in coll)
    {
        if (match(a))
        {
            sum = action(a, sum);
        }
    }
    return sum;
}
```

Calling the method `AccumulateIf()` can have an implementation for the accumulation and an implementation for the predicate. Here, only the accounts with a balance higher than 2,000 are accumulated as defined by the second Lambda expression `a => a.Balance > 2000`:

```
decimal amount = Algorithm.AccumulateIf<Account, decimal>(
    accounts, (a, d) => a.Balance + d, a => a.Balance > 2000);
```

Using Generic Delegates with the Array Class

Chapter 5, "Arrays," demonstrated different sort techniques with the `Array` class by using the `IComparable` and `IComparer` interfaces. Starting with .NET 2.0, some methods of the `Array` class use generic delegate types as parameters. The following table shows these methods, the generic type, and the functionality.

Method	Generic Parameter Type	Description
`Sort()`	`int Comparison<T> (T x, T y)`	The `Sort()` method defines several overloads. One overload requires a parameter of type `Comparison<T>`. `Sort()` is using the method referenced by the delegate for ordering all elements in the collection.
`ForEach()`	`void Action<T> (T obj)`	The method `ForEach()` invokes the method referenced by the `Action<T>` delegate with every item in the collection.

`FindAll()`
`Find()`
`FindLast()`
`FindIndex()`
`FindLastIndex()`
	`bool Predicate<T> (T match)`	The `FindXXX()` methods accept the `Predicate<T>` delegate as parameter. The method referenced by the delegate is invoked multiple times, and the elements of the collection are passed one after the other. The `Find()` method stops a search until the predicate returns true the first time and returns this

Method	Generic Parameter Type	Description
		element. `FindIndex()` returns the index of the first element found. `FindLast()` and `FindLastIndex()` invoke the predicate in the reversed order of the elements in the collection, and thus either return the last item or the last index. `FindAll()` returns a new list with all items where the predicate was true.
`ConvertAll()`	`TOutput Converter<TInput, TOutput>(TInput input)`	The `ConvertAll()` method invokes the `Converter<TInput, TOutput>` delegate for every element in the collection and returns a list of converted elements.
`TrueForAll()`	`bool Predicate<T>(T match)`	The method `TrueForAll()` invokes the predicate delegate for every element. If the predicate returns true for every element, `TrueForAll()` returns true as well. If the predicate returns false just for one of the elements, `TrueForAll()` returns false.

Let's get into how these methods can be used.

The `Sort()` method accepts this delegate as parameter:

```
public delegate int Comparison<T>(T x, T y);
```

This way, it is possible to sort the array by using a Lambda expression passing two `Person` objects. With an array of `Person` objects, parameter `T` is of type `Person`:

```
Person[] persons = {
   new Person("Emerson", "Fittipaldi"),
   new Person("Niki", "Lauda"),
   new Person("Ayrton", "Senna"),
   new Person("Michael", "Schumacher")
};

Array.Sort(persons, (p1, p2) => p1.FirstName.CompareTo(p2.FirstName);
```

The `Array.ForEach()` method accepts an `Action<T>` delegate as parameter to invoke the action for every element of the array:

```
public delegate void Action<T>(T obj);
```

This way, you can write every person to the console by passing the address of the method `Console.WriteLine`. One overload of the `WriteLine()` method accepts the `Object` class as parameter type. Because `Person` derives from `Object`, this fits with a `Person` array:

```
Array.ForEach(persons, Console.WriteLine);
```

The result of the `ForEach()` statement writes every person of the collection referenced by the `persons` variable to the console:

```
Emerson Fittipaldi
Niki Lauda
Ayrton Senna
Michael Schumacher
```

If more control is needed, you can pass a Lambda expression that fits the parameter defined by the delegate:

```
Array.ForEach(persons, p => Console.WriteLine("{0}", p.LastName);
```

Here, the result is the last name written to the console:

```
Fittipaldi
Lauda
Senna
Schumacher
```

The `Array.FindAll()` method requires the `Predicate<T>` delegate:

```
public delegate bool Predicate<T>(T match);
```

The `Array.FindAll()` method invokes the predicate for every element in the array and returns a new array where the predicate returns `true` for the element. In the example, `true` is returned for all `Person` objects where the `LastName` starts with the string "S":

```
Person[] sPersons = Array.FindAll(persons, p => p.LastName.StartsWith("S");
```

Iterating through the returned collection `sPersons` to write it to the console gives this result:

```
Ayrton Senna
Michael Schumacher
```

The `Array.ConvertAll()` method used the generic delegate `Converter` with two generic types. The first generic type `TInput` is the input parameter, the second generic type `TOutput` is the return type:

```
public delegate TOutput Converter<TInput, TOutput>(TInput input);
```

The `ConvertAll()` method is very useful if an array of one type should be converted to an array of another type. Following is a `Racer` class that is unrelated to the `Person` class. The `Person` class contains the `FirstName` and `LastName` properties, while the `Racer` class defines for the name of the racer just one property `Name`:

```
public class Racer
{
   public Racer(string name)
   {
      this.Name = name;
   }

   public string Name { get; set; }
   public string Team { get; set; }
}
```

Using `Array.ConvertAll()` you can easily convert the person array `persons` to a `Racer` array. The delegate is invoked for every `Person` element. In the anonymous method implementation for every person, a new `Racer` object is created, and the `FirstName` and `LastName` are passed concatenated to the constructor, which accepts a string. The result is an array of `Racer` objects:

```
Racer[] racers =
      Array.ConvertAll<Person, Racer>(
            persons,
            p => new Racer(String.Format("{0} {1}", p.FirstName, p.LastName));
```

Other Generic Framework Types

In addition to the `System.Collections.Generic` namespace, the .NET Framework has other uses for generic types. The structs and delegates discussed here are all in the `System` namespace and serve different purposes.

This section discusses the following:

- The struct `Nullable<T>`
- The delegate `EventHandler<TEventArgs>`
- The struct `ArraySegment<T>`

Nullable<T>

A number in a database and a number in a programming language have an important difference in their characteristics, as a number in the database can be `null`. A number in C# cannot be `null`. `Int32` is a struct, and because structs are implemented as value types, they cannot be `null`.

The problem doesn't exist only with databases but also with mapping XML data to .NET types.

This difference often causes headaches and lot of additional work to map the data. One solution is to map numbers from databases and XML files to reference types, because reference types can have a `null` value. However, this also means additional overhead during runtime.

With the structure `Nullable<T>` this can be easily resolved. In the example, `Nullable<T>` is instantiated with `Nullable<int>`. The variable `x` can now be used like an `int`, assigning values and using operators to do some calculation. This behavior is made possible by casting operators of the `Nullable<T>` type. However, `x` can also be `null`. The `Nullable<T>` properties `HasValue` and `Value` can check if there is a value, and the value can be accessed:

```
Nullable<int> x;
x = 4;
x += 3;
if (x.HasValue)
{
   int y = x.Value;
}
x = null;
```

Because nullable types are used very often, C# has a special syntax for defining variables of this type. Instead of using the syntax with the generic structure, the `?` operator can be used. In the following example, the variables `x1` and `x2` both are instances of a nullable `int` type:

```
Nullable<int> x1;
int? x2;
```

A nullable type can be compared with `null` and numbers as shown. Here, the value of `x` is compared with `null`, and if it is not `null`, it is compared with a value smaller than `0`:

```
int? x = GetNullableType();if (x == null)
{
   Console.WriteLine("x is null");
}
else if (x < 0)
{
   Console.WriteLine("x is smaller than 0");
}
```

Nullable types can also be used with arithmetic operators. The variable `x3` is the sum of the variables `x1` and `x2`. If any of the nullable types has a `null` value, the result is `null`:

```
int? x1 = GetNullableType();
int? x2 = GetNullableType();
int? x3 = x1 + x2;
```

The method `GetNullableType()` *that is called here is just a placeholder for any method that returns a nullable* `int`*. For testing you can implement it as simple to return* `null` *or to return any integer value.*

Non-nullable types can be converted to nullable types. With the conversion from a non-nullable type to a nullable type, an implicit conversion is possible where casting is not required. This conversion always succeeds:

```
int y1 = 4;
int? x1 = y1;
```

The other way around, the conversion from a nullable type to a non-nullable type, can fail. If the nullable type has a `null` value and the `null` value is assigned to a non-nullable type, an exception of type `InvalidOperationException` is thrown. That's the reason the cast operator is required to do an explicit conversion:

```
int? x1 = GetNullableType();
int y1 = (int)x1;
```

Instead of doing an explicit cast, it is also possible to convert a nullable type to a non-nullable type with the coalescing operator. The coalescing operator has the syntax `??` to define a default value for the conversion in case the nullable type has a value of `null`. Here, `y1` gets the value `0` if `x1` is `null`:

```
int? x1 = GetNullableType();
int y1 = x1 ?? 0;
```

EventHandler<TEventArgs>

With Windows Forms and Web applications, delegates for many different event handlers are defined. Some of the event handlers are listed here:

```
public sealed delegate void EventHandler(object sender, EventArgs e);
public sealed delegate void PaintEventHandler(object sender,
      PaintEventArgs e);
public sealed delegate void MouseEventHandler(object sender,
      MouseEventArgs e);
```

These delegates have in common that the first argument is always the sender, who was the origin of the event, and the second argument is of a type to contain information specific to the event.

With the new `EventHandler<TEventArgs>`, it is not necessary to define a new delegate for every event handler. As you can see, the first parameter is defined the same way as before, but the second parameter is a generic type TEventArgs. The where clause specifies that the type for TEventArgs must be derived from the base class EventArgs:

```
public sealed delegate void EventHandler<TEventArgs>(object sender,
      TEventArgs e)
   where TEventArgs : EventArgs
```

ArraySegment<T>

The struct ArraySegment<T> represents a segment of an array. If parts of an array are needed, a segment can be used. With the struct ArraySegment<T>, the information about the segment (the offset and count) is contained within this structure.

In the example, the variable arr is defined as an int array with eight elements. The variable segment of type ArraySegment<int> is used to represent a segment of the integer array. The segment is initialized with the constructor, where the array is passed together with an offset and an item count. Here, the offset is set to 2, so you start with the third element, and the count is set to 3, so 6 is the last element of the segment.

The array behind the array segment can be accessed with the Array property. ArraySegment<T> also has the properties Offset and Count that indicate the initialized values to define the segment. The for loop is used to iterate through the array segment. The first expression of the for loop is initialized to the offset where the iteration should begin. With the second expression, the count of the element numbers in the segment is used to check if the iteration should stop. Within the for loop, the elements contained by the segment are accessed with the Array property:

```
int[] arr = {1, 2, 3, 4, 5, 6, 7, 8};
ArraySegment<int> segment = new ArraySegment<int>(arr, 2, 3);

for (int i = segment.Offset; i < segment.Offset + segment.Count; i++)
{
   Console.WriteLine(segment.Array[i]);
}
```

With the example so far, you might question the usefulness of the ArraySegment<T> structure. However, the ArraySegment<T> can also be passed as an argument to methods. This way, just a single argument is needed instead of three that define the offset and count in addition to the array.

The method WorkWithSegment() gets an ArraySegment<string> as a parameter. In the implementation of this method, the properties Offset, Count, and Array are used as before:

```
void WorkWithSegment(ArraySegment<string> segment)
{
   for (int i = segment.Offset; i < segment.Offset + segment.Count; i++)
   {
      Console.WriteLine(segment.Array[i]);
   }
}
```

It's important to note that array segments don't copy the elements of the originating array. Instead, the originating array can be accessed through ArraySegment<T>. If elements of the array segment are changed, the changes can be seen in the original array.

Summary

This chapter introduced a very important feature of the CLR 2.0: generics. With generic classes you can create type-independent classes, and generic methods allow type-independent methods. Interfaces, structs, and delegates can be created in a generic way as well. Generics make new programming styles possible. You've seen how algorithms, particularly actions and predicates, can be implemented to be used with different classes — and all type-safe. Generic delegates make it possible to decouple algorithms from -collections.

Other .NET Framework types include `Nullable<T>`, `EventHandler<TEventArgs>`, and `ArraySegment<T>`.

The next chapter makes use of generics showing collection classes.

10

Collections

In Chapter 5, "Arrays," you read information about arrays and the interfaces implemented by the `Array` class. The size of arrays is fixed. If the number of elements is dynamic, you should use a collection class.

`List<T>` and `ArrayList` are collection classes that can be compared to arrays. But there are also other kinds of collections: queues, stacks, linked lists, and dictionaries.

This chapter shows you how to work with groups of objects. It takes a close look at these topics:

- Collection interfaces and types
- Lists
- Queues
- Stacks
- Linked lists
- Sorted lists
- Dictionaries
- Lookups
- HashSets
- Bit arrays
- Performance

Collection Interfaces and Types

Collection classes can be grouped into collections that store elements of type `Object` and generic collection classes. Previous to CLR 2.0, generics didn't exist. Now the generic collection classes usually are the preferred type of collection. Generic collection classes are type-safe, and there is no boxing if value types are used. You need object-based collection classes only if you want to add objects of different types where the types are not based on each other, for example, adding `int` and string objects to one collection. Another group of collection classes is collections specialized for a specific type; for example, the StringCollection class is specialized for the string type.

You can read all about generics in Chapter 9, "Generics."

Object-type collections are located in the namespace System.Collections; generic collection classes are located in the namespace System.Collections.Generic. Collection classes that are specialized for a specific type are located in the namespace System.Collections.Specialized.

Of course, there are also other ways to group collection classes. Collections can be grouped into lists, collections, and dictionaries based on the interfaces that are implemented by the collection class. Interfaces and their functionalities are described in the following table. .NET 2.0 added new generic interfaces for collection classes, for example, IEnumerable<T> and IList<T>. Whereas the non-generic versions of these interfaces define an Object as a parameter of the methods, the generic versions of these interfaces use the generic type T.

You can read detailed information about the interfaces IEnumerable, ICollection, *and* IList *in Chapter 5, "Arrays."*

The following table describes interfaces implemented by collections and lists, and their methods and properties.

Interface	Methods and Properties	Description
IEnumerable, IEnumerable<T>	GetEnumerator()	The interface IEnumerable is required if a foreach statement is used with the collection. This interface defines the method GetEnumerator(), which returns an enumerator that implements IEnumerator. The generic interface IEnumerable<T> inherits from the non-generic interface IEnumerable, and defines a GetEnumerator method to return Enumerator<T>. Because of the inheritance with these two interfaces, with every method that requires a parameter of type IEnumerable, you can also pass IEnumerable<T> objects.
ICollection	Count, IsSynchronized, SyncRoot, CopyTo()	The interface ICollection is implemented by collection classes. With collections implementing this interface, you can get the number of elements and copy the collection to an array. The interface ICollection extends the functionality from the interface IEnumerable.
ICollection<T>	Count, IsReadOnly, Add(), Clear(), Contains(), CopyTo(), Remove()	ICollection<T> is the generic version of the ICollection interface. The generic version of this interface allows adding and removing elements as well as getting the element number.

Interface	Methods and Properties	Description
`IList`	`IsFixedSize, IsReadOnly, Item, Add(), Clear(), Contains(), IndexOf(), Insert(), Remove(), RemoveAt()`	The interface `IList` derives from the interface `ICollection`. `IList` allows you to access a collection using an indexer. It is also possible to insert or remove elements at any position of the collection.
`IList<T>`	`Item, IndexOf(), Insert(), RemoveAt()`	Similar to `IList`, the interface `IList<T>` inherits from `ICollection<T>`. In Chapter 5, "Arrays," you saw that the `Array` class implements this interface, but methods to add or remove elements throw a `NotSupportedException`. Collections that have a fixed size (for example, the `Array` class) and are read-only can throw a `NotSupportedException` with some of the methods defined in this interface. Comparing the non-generic and the generic version of the `IList` interfaces, the new generic interface just defines the methods and properties important for collections that offer an index. The other methods have been refactored to the `ICollection<T>` interface.
`IDictionary`	`IsFixedSize, IsReadOnly, Item, Keys, Values, Add(), Clear(), Contains(), GetEnumerator(), Remove()`	The interface `IDictionary` is implemented by non-generic collections whose elements have a key and a value.
`IDictionary<TKey, TValue>`	`Item, Keys, Values, Add(), ContainsKey(), Remove(), TryGetValue()`	`IDictionary<TKey, TValue>` is implemented by generic collection classes that have a key and a value. This interface is simpler compared to `IDictionary`.
`ILookup<TKey, TElement>`	`Count, Item, Contains()`	`ILookup<TKey, TElement>` is a new interface with .NET 3.5 that is used by collections that have multiple values for a key. The indexer returns an enumeration for a specified key.
`IComparer<T>`	`Compare()`	The interface `IComparer<T>` is implemented by a comparer and used to sort elements inside a collection with the `Compare()` method.
`IEquality Comparer<T>`	`Equals(), GetHashCode()`	`IEqualityComparer<T>` is implemented by a comparer that can be used for keys in a dictionary. With this interface the objects can be compared for equality.

The non-generic interface `ICollection` defines properties used to synchronize different threads accessing the same collection. These properties are no longer available with the new generic interfaces. The reason for this change was that these properties led to a false safety regarding synchronization, because the collection usually is not the only thing that must be synchronized. You can read information about synchronization with collections in Chapter 19, "Threading and Synchronization."

The following table lists the collection classes and the collection interfaces that are implemented by these classes.

Collection Class	Collection Interfaces
`ArrayList`	`IList, ICollection, IEnumerable`
`Queue`	`ICollection, IEnumerable`
`Stack`	`ICollection, IEnumerable`
`BitArray`	`ICollection, IEnumerable`
`Hashtable`	`IDictionary, ICollection, IEnumerable`
`SortedList`	`IDictionary, ICollection, IEnumerable`
`List<T>`	`IList<T>, ICollection<T>, IEnumerable<T>, IList, ICollection, IEnumerable`
`Queue<T>`	`IEnumerable<T>, ICollection, IEnumerable`
`Stack<T>`	`IEnumerable<T>, ICollection, IEnumerable`
`LinkedList<T>`	`ICollection<T>, IEnumerable<T>, ICollection, IEnumerable`
`HashSet<T>`	`ICollection<T>, IEnumerable<T>, IEnumerable`
`Dictionary<TKey, TValue>`	`IDictionary<TKey, TValue>, ICollection<KeyValuePair<TKey, TValue>>, IEnumerable<KeyValuePair<TKey, TValue>>, IDictionary, ICollection, IEnumerable`
`SortedDictionary<TKey, TValue>`	`IDictionary<TKey, TValue>, ICollection<KeyValuePair<TKey, TValue>>, IEnumerable<KeyValuePair<TKey, TValue>>, IDictionary, ICollection, IEnumerable`
`SortedList<TKey, TValue>`	`IDictionary<TKey, TValue>, ICollection<KeyValuePair<TKey, TValue>>, IEnumerable<KeyValuePair<TKey, TValue>>, IDictionary, ICollection, IEnumerable`
`Lookup<TKey, TElement>`	`ILookup<TKey, TElement>,IEnumerable<IGrouping<TKey, TElement>>,IEnumerable`

Lists

For dynamic lists, the .NET Framework offers the classes `ArrayList` and `List<T>`. The class `List<T>` in the namespace `System.Collections.Generic` is very similar in its usage to the `ArrayList` class from the namespace `System.Collections`. This class implements the `IList`, `ICollection`, and

IEnumerable interfaces. Because Chapter 9, "Generics," already discussed the methods of these interfaces, this section looks at how to use the List<T> class.

The following examples use the members of the class Racer as elements to be added to the collection to represent a Formula-1 racer. This class has four fields: firstName, lastName, country, and the number of wins. The fields can be accessed with properties. With the constructor of the class, the name of the racer and the number of wins can be passed to set the members. The method ToString() is overridden to return the name of the racer. The class Racer also implements the generic interface IComparer<T> for sorting racer elements.

```
[Serializable]
public class Racer : IComparable<Racer>, IFormattable
{
   public Racer()
      : this(String.Empty, String.Empty,
            String.Empty) {}

   public Racer(string firstName, string lastName,
               string country)
      : this(firstName, lastName, country, 0) {}

   public Racer(string firstName, string lastName,
               string country, int wins)
   {
      this.FirstName = firstName;
      this.LastName = lastName;
      this.Country = country;
      this.Wins = wins;
   }

   public string FirstName { get; set; }
   public string LastName { get; set; }
   public string Country { get; set; }
   public int Wins { get; set; }

   public override string ToString()
   {
      return String.Format("{0} {1}",
            FirstName, LastName);
   }

   public string ToString(string format,
         IFormatProvider formatProvider)
   {
      switch (format.ToUpper())
      {
         case null:
         case "N": // name
            return ToString();
         case "F": // first name
            return FirstName;
         case "L": // last name
            return LastName;
         case "W": // Wins
```

(continued)

(continued)

```
                    return String.Format("{0}, Wins: {1}",
                          ToString(), Wins);
                 case "C": // Country
                    return String.Format(
                          "{0}, Country: {1}",
                          ToString(), Country);
                 case "A": // All
                    return String.Format(
                          "{0}, {1} Wins: {2}",
                          ToString(), Country, Wins);
                 default:
                    throw new FormatException(String.Format(
                          formatProvider,
                          "Format {0} is not supported",
                          format));
              }
           }

           public string ToString(string format)
           {
              return ToString(format, null);
           }

           public int CompareTo(Racer other)
           {
              int compare = this.LastName.CompareTo(
                    other.LastName);
              if (compare == 0)
                 return this.FirstName.CompareTo(
                       other.FirstName);
              return compare;
           }
        }
```

Creating Lists

You can create list objects by invoking the default constructor. With the generic class `List<T>`, you must specify the type for the values of the list with the declaration. The code shows how to declare a `List<T>` with `int` and a list with `Racer` elements. `ArrayList` is a non-generic list that accepts any `Object` type for its elements.

Using the default constructor creates an empty list. As soon as elements are added to the list, the capacity of the list is extended to allow four elements. If the fifth element is added, the list is resized to allow eight elements. If eight elements are not enough, the list is resized again to contain 16 elements. With every resize the capacity of the list is doubled.

```
ArrayList objectList = new ArrayList();

List<int> intList = new List<int>();
List<Racer> racers = new List<Racer>();
```

If the capacity of the list changes, the complete collection is reallocated to a new memory block. With the implementation of `List<T>`, an array of type `T` is used. With reallocation, a new array is created, and `Array.Copy()` copies the elements from the old to the new array. To save time, if you know the number of elements in advance, that should be in the list; you can define the capacity with the constructor. Here a collection with a capacity of 10 elements is created. If the capacity is not large enough for the elements added, the capacity is resized to 20 and 40 elements — doubled again.

```
ArrayList objectList = new ArrayList(10);
List<int> intList = new List<int>(10);
```

You can get and set the capacity of a collection by using the `Capacity` property:

```
objectList.Capacity = 20;
intList.Capacity = 20;
```

The capacity is not the same as the number of elements in the collection. The number of elements in the collection can be read with the `Count` property. Of course, the capacity is always larger or equal to the number of items. As long as no element was added to the list, the count is 0.

```
Console.WriteLine(intList.Count);
```

If you are finished adding elements to the list and don't want to add any more elements, you can get rid of the unneeded capacity by invoking the `TrimExcess()` method. However, because the relocation takes time, `TrimExcess()` does nothing if the item count is more than 90 percent of capacity.

```
intList.TrimExcess();
```

Because with new applications usually you can use the generic `List<T>` *class instead of the non-generic* `ArrayList` *class, and also because the methods of* `ArrayList` *are very similar, the reminder of this section focuses just on* `List<T>`.

Collection Initializers

C# 3.0 allows you to assign values to collections using collection initializers. The syntax of collection initializers is similar to array initializers, which were explained in Chapter 5. With a collection initializer, values are assigned to the collection within curly brackets at the initialization of the collection:

```
List<int> intList = new List<int>() {1, 2};
List<string> stringList =
      new List<string>() {"one", "two"};
```

Collection initializers are a feature of the C# 3.0 programming language and are not reflected within the IL code of the compiled assembly. The compiler converts the collection initializer to invoking the `Add()` *method for every item from the initializer list.*

Adding Elements

You can add elements to the list with the `Add()` method as shown. The generic instantiated type defines the parameter type of the `Add()` method.

```
List<int> intList = new List<int>();
intList.Add(1);
intList.Add(2);

List<string> stringList = new List<string>();
stringList.Add("one");
stringList.Add("two");
```

The variable `racers` is defined as type `List<Racer>`. With the `new` operator, a new object of the same type is created. Because the class `List<T>` was instantiated with the concrete class `Racer`, now only `Racer` objects can be added with the `Add()` method. In the following sample code, five Formula-1 racers are created and added to the collection. The first three are added using the collection initializer, and the last two are added by invoking the `Add()` method explicitly.

```
Racer graham = new Racer("Graham", "Hill",
      "UK", 14);
Racer emerson = new Racer("Emerson",
      "Fittipaldi", "Brazil", 14);
Racer mario = new Racer("Mario", "Andretti",
      "USA", 12);
```

```
List<Racer> racers = new List<Racer>(20)
      {graham, emerson, mario};

racers.Add(new Racer("Michael", "Schumacher",
      "Germany", 91));
racers.Add(new Racer("Mika", "Hakkinen",
      "Finland", 20));
```

With the `AddRange()` method of the `List<T>` class, you can add multiple elements to the collection at once. The method `AddRange()` accepts an object of type `IEnumerable<T>`, so you can also pass an array as shown:

```
racers.AddRange(new Racer[] {
      new Racer("Niki", "Lauda", "Austria",
            25),
      new Racer("Alain", "Prost", "France",
            51)});
```

The collection initializer can be used only during declaration of the collection. The `AddRange()` *method can be invoked after the collection is initialized.*

If you know some elements of the collection when instantiating the list, you can also pass any object that implements `IEnumerable<T>` to the constructor of the class. This is very similar to the `AddRange()` method.

```
List<Racer> racers =
   new List<Racer>(new Racer[] {
      new Racer("Jochen", "Rindt", "Austria",
            6),
      new Racer("Ayrton", "Senna", "Brazil",
            41) });
```

Inserting Elements

You can insert elements at a specified position with the `Insert()` method:

```
racers.Insert(3, new Racer("Phil", "Hill",
      "USA", 3));
```

The method `InsertRange()` offers the capability to insert a number of elements, similarly to the `AddRange()` method shown earlier.

If the index set is larger than the number of elements in the collection, an exception of type `ArgumentOutOfRangeException` is thrown.

Accessing Elements

All classes that implement the `IList` and `IList<T>` interface offer an indexer, so you can access the elements by using an indexer and passing the item number. The first item can be accessed with an index value 0. By specifying `racers[3]`, you will access the fourth element of the list:

```
Racer r1 = racers[3];
```

Getting the number of elements with the `Count` property, you can do a `for` loop to iterate through every item in the collection, and use the indexer to access every item:

```
for (int i = 0; i < racers.Count; i++)
{
   Console.WriteLine(racers[i]);
}
```

> **Indexed access to collection classes is available with `ArrayList`, `StringCollection`, and `List<T>`.**

Because `List<T>` implements the interface `IEnumerable`, you can iterate through the items in the collection using the `foreach` statement as well:

```
foreach (Racer r in racers)
{
   Console.WriteLine(r);
}
```

How the `foreach` *statement is resolved by the compiler to make use of the* `IEnumerable` *and* `IEnumerator` *interfaces is explained in Chapter 5, "Arrays."*

Instead of using the `foreach` statement, the `List<T>` class also offers a `ForEach()` method that is declared with an `Action<T>` parameter:

```
public void ForEach(Action<T> action);
```

The implementation of `ForEach()` is shown next. `ForEach()` iterates through every item of the collection and invokes the method that is passed as parameter for every item.

```
public class List<T> : IList<T>
{
   private T[] items;

   //...

   public void ForEach(Action<T> action)
   {
      if (action == null) throw new ArgumentNullException("action");

      foreach (T item in items)
      {
         action(item);
      }
   }

   //...
}
```

For passing a method with `ForEach`, `Action<T>` is declared as a delegate that defines a method with `void` return type and parameter `T`:

```
public delegate void Action<T>(T obj);
```

With a list of `Racer` items, the handler for the `ForEach()` method must be declared with a `Racer` object as parameter and a `void` return type:

```
public void ActionHandler(Racer obj);
```

Because one overload of the `Console.WriteLine()` method accepts `Object` as parameter, you can pass the address of this method to the `ForEach()` method, and every racer of the collection is written to the console:

```
racers.ForEach(Console.WriteLine);
```

You can also write an anonymous method that accepts a `Racer` object as parameter. Here, the format `A` is used with the `ToString()` method of the `IFormattable` interface to display all information of the racer:

```
racers.ForEach(
   delegate(Racer r)
   {
      Console.WriteLine("{0:A}", r);
   });
```

With C# 3.0 you can also use Lambda expressions with methods accepting a delegate parameter. The same iteration that was implemented using an anonymous method is defined with a Lambda expression:

```
racers.ForEach(
      r => Console.WriteLine("{0:A}", r));
```

Anonymous methods and Lambda expressions are explained in Chapter 7, "Delegates and Events."

Removing Elements

You can remove elements by index or pass the item that should be removed. Here, the fourth element is removed by passing 3 to `RemoveAt()`:

```
racers.RemoveAt(3);
```

You can also directly pass a `Racer` object to the `Remove()` method to remove this element. Removing by index is faster, because here the collection must be searched for the item to remove. The `Remove()` method first searches in the collection to get the index of the item with the `IndexOf()` method, and then uses the index to remove the item. `IndexOf()` first checks if the item type implements the interface `IEquatable`. If it does, the `Equals()` method of this interface is invoked to find the item in the collection that is the same as the one passed to the method. If this interface is not implemented, the `Equals()` method of the `Object` class is used to compare the items. The default implementation of the `Equals()` method in the `Object` class does a bitwise compare with value types, but compares only references with reference types.

Chapter 6, "Operators and Casts," explains how you can override the `Equals()` *method.*

Here, the racer referenced by the variable `graham` is removed from the collection. The variable `graham` was created earlier when the collection was filled. Because the interface `IEquatable` and the `Object.Equals()` method are not overridden with the `Racer` class, you cannot create a new object with the same content as the item that should be removed and pass it to the `Remove()` method.

```
if (!racers.Remove(graham))
{
   Console.WriteLine(
         "object not found in collection");
}
```

The method `RemoveRange()` removes a number of items from the collection. The first parameter specifies the index where the removal of items should begin; the second parameter specifies the number of items to be removed.

```
int index = 3;
int count = 5;
racers.RemoveRange(index, count);
```

To remove all items with some specific characteristics from the collection, you can use the `RemoveAll()` method. This method uses the `Predicate<T>` parameter when searching for elements , which is discussed next. For removing all elements from the collection, use the `Clear()` method defined with the `ICollection<T>` interface.

Searching

There are different ways to search for elements in the collection. You can get the index to the found item, or the item itself. You can use methods such as `IndexOf()`, `LastIndexOf()`, `FindIndex()`, `FindLastIndex()`, `Find()`, and `FindLast()`. And for just checking if an item exists, the `List<T>` class offers the `Exists()` method.

The method `IndexOf()` requires an object as parameter and returns the index of the item if it is found inside the collection. If the item is not found, –1 is returned. Remember that `IndexOf()` is using the `IEquatable` interface for comparing the elements.

```
int index1 = racers.IndexOf(mario);
```

With the `IndexOf()` method, you can also specify that the complete collection should not be searched, but rather specify an index where the search should start and the number of elements that should be iterated for the comparison.

Instead of searching a specific item with the `IndexOf()` method, you can search for an item that has some specific characteristics that you can define with the `FindIndex()` method. `FindIndex()` requires a parameter of type `Predicate`:

```
public int FindIndex(Predicate<T> match);
```

The `Predicate<T>` type is a delegate that returns a Boolean value and requires type `T` as parameter. This delegate can be used similarly to the `Action` delegate shown earlier with the `ForEach()` method. If the predicate returns `true`, there's a match and the element is found. If it returns `false`, the element is not found and the search continues.

```
public delegate bool Predicate<T>(T obj);
```

With the `List<T>` class that is using `Racer` objects for type `T`, you can pass the address of a method that returns a `bool` and defines a parameter of type `Racer` to the `FindIndex()` method. Finding the first racer of a specific country, you can create the `FindCountry` class as shown. The `Find()` method has the signature and return type defined by the `Predicate<T>` delegate. The `Find()` method uses the variable `country` to search for a country that you can pass with the constructor of the class.

```
public class FindCountry
{
   public FindCountry(string country)
   {
      this.country = country;
   }
   private string country;

   public bool FindCountryPredicate(Racer racer)
   {
      if (racer == null)
         throw new ArgumentNullException("racer");
      return r.Country == country;
   }
}
```

With the FindIndex() method, you can create a new instance of the FindCountry() class, pass a country string to the constructor, and pass the address of the Find method. After FindIndex() completes successfully, index2 contains the index of the first item where the Country property of the racer is set to Finland.

```
int index2 = racers.FindIndex(
      new FindCountry("Finland").FindCountryPredicate);
```

Instead of creating a class with a handler method, you can use a Lambda expression here as well. The result is exactly the same as before. Now the Lambda expression defines the implementation to search for an item where the Country property is set to Finland.

```
int index3 = racers.FindIndex(
      r => r.Country == "Finland");
```

Similarly to the IndexOf() method, with the FindIndex() method, you can also specify the index where the search should start and the count of items that should be iterated through. To do a search for an index beginning from the last element in the collection, you can use the FindLastIndex() method.

The method FindIndex() returns the index of the found item. Instead of getting the index, you can also get directly to the item in the collection. The Find() method requires a parameter of type Predicate<T>, much like the FindIndex() method. The Find() method here is searching for the first racer in the list that has the FirstName property set to Niki. Of course, you can also do a FindLast() to find the last item that fulfills the predicate.

```
Racer r = racers.Find(
      r => r.FirstName == "Niki");
```

To get not only one, but all items that fulfill the requirements of a predicate, you can use the FindAll() method. The FindAll() method uses the same Predicate<T> delegate as the Find() and FindIndex() methods. The FindAll() method does not stop when the first item is found but instead iterates through every item in the collection and returns all items where the predicate returns true.

With the FindAll() method invoked here, all racer items are returned where the property Wins is set to more than 20. All racers that won more than 20 races are referenced from the bigWinners list.

```
List<Racer> bigWinners = racers.FindAll(
      r => r.Wins > 20);
```

Iterating through the variable bigWinners with a foreach statement gives the following result:

```
foreach (Racer r in bigWinners)
{
      Console.WriteLine("{0:A}", r);
}
```

```
Michael Schumacher, Germany Wins: 91
Niki Lauda, Austria Wins: 25
Alain Prost, France Wins: 51
```

The result is not sorted, but this is done next.

Sorting

The List<T> class allows sorting its elements by using the Sort() method. Sort() uses the quick sort algorithm where all elements are compared until the complete list is sorted.

You can use several overloads of the `Sort()` method. The arguments that can be passed are a generic delegate `Comparison<T>`, the generic interface `IComparer<T>`, and a range together with the generic interface `IComparer<T>`:

```
public void List<T>.Sort();
public void List<T>.Sort(Comparison<T>);
public void List<T>.Sort(IComparer<T>);
public void List<T>.Sort(Int32, Int32, IComparer<T>);
```

Using the `Sort()` method without arguments is possible only if the elements in the collection implement the interface `IComparable`.

The class `Racer` implements the interface `IComparable<T>` to sort racers by the last name:

```
racers.Sort();
racers.ForEach(Console.WriteLine);
```

If you need to do a sort other than the default supported by the item types, you need to use other techniques, for example passing an object that implements the `IComparer<T>` interface.

The class `RacerComparer` implements the interface `IComparer<T>` for `Racer` types. This class allows you to sort either by the first name, last name, country, or number of wins. The kind of sort that should be done is defined with the inner enumeration type `CompareType`. The `CompareType` is set with the constructor of the class `RacerComparer`. The interface `IComparer<Racer>` defines the method `Compare` that is required for sorting. In the implementation of this method, the `CompareTo()` method of the `string` and `int` types is used.

```
public class RacerComparer : IComparer<Racer>
{
   public enum CompareType
   {
      FirstName,
      LastName,
      Country,
      Wins
   }

   private CompareType compareType;
   public RacerComparer(CompareType compareType)
   {
      this.compareType = compareType;
   }

   public int Compare(Racer x, Racer y)
   {
      if (x == null)
         throw new ArgumentNullException("x");
      if (y == null)
         throw new ArgumentNullException("y");

      int result;
      switch (compareType)
      {
         case CompareType.FirstName:
            return
               x.FirstName.CompareTo(y.FirstName);
```

(continued)

(continued)

```
                case CompareType.LastName:
                    return x.LastName.CompareTo(y.LastName);
                case CompareType.Country:
                    if ((result =
                        x.Country.CompareTo(y.Country) == 0)
                        return x.LastName.CompareTo(
                                y.LastName);
                    else
                        return res;
                case CompareType.Wins:
                    return x.Wins.CompareTo(y.Wins);
                default:
                    throw new ArgumentException(
                            "Invalid Compare Type");
            }
        }
    }
```

An instance of the `RacerComparer` class can now be used with the `Sort()` method. Passing the enumeration `RacerComparer.CompareType.Country` sorts the collection by the property `Country`:

```
        racers.Sort(new RacerComparer(
                RacerComparer.CompareType.Country));
        racers.ForEach(Console.WriteLine);
```

Another way to do the sort is by using the overloaded `Sort()` method, which requires a `Comparison<T>` delegate:

```
    public void List<T>.Sort(Comparison<T>);
```

`Comparison<T>` is a delegate to a method that has two parameters of type `T` and a return type `int`. If the parameter values are equal, the method must return `0`. If the first parameter is less than the second, a value less than zero must be returned; otherwise, a value greater than zero is returned.

```
    public delegate int Comparison<T>(T x, T y);
```

Now you can pass a Lambda expression to the `Sort()` method to do a sort by the number of wins. The two parameters are of type `Racer`, and in the implementation the `Wins` properties are compared by using the `int` method `CompareTo()`. In the implementation, `r2` and `r1` are used in the reverse order, so the number of wins is sorted in descending order. After the method has been invoked, the complete racer list is sorted based on the number of wins of the racer.

```
        racers.Sort(
            (r1, r2) => r2.Wins.CompareTo(r1.Wins));
```

You can also reverse the order of a complete collection by invoking the `Reverse()` method.

Type Conversion

With the `List<T>` method `ConvertAll()`, all types of a collection can be converted to a different type. The `ConvertAll()` method uses a `Converter` delegate that is defined like this:

```
    public sealed delegate TOutput Converter<TInput, TOutput>(TInput from);
```

The generic types `TInput` and `TOutput` are used with the conversion. `TInput` is the argument of the delegate method, and `TOutput` is the return type.

In this example, all `Racer` types should be converted to `Person` types. Whereas the `Racer` type contains a `firstName`, `lastName`, `country`, and the number of `wins`, the `Person` type contains just a `name`. For the conversion, the country of the racer and race wins can be ignored, but the name must be converted:

```
[Serializable]
public class Person
{
   private string name;

   public Person(string name)
   {
      this.name = name;
   }

   public override string ToString()
   {
      return name;
   }
}
```

The conversion happens by invoking the `racers.ConvertAll<Person>()` method. The argument of this method is defined as a Lambda expression with an argument of type `Racer` and a `Person` type that is returned. In the implementation of the Lambda expression, a new `Person` object is created and returned. For the `Person` object, the `FirstName` and `LastName` are passed to the constructor:

```
List<Person> persons =
      racers.ConvertAll<Person>(
      r => new Person(r.FirstName + " " +
      r.LastName));
```

The result of the conversion is a list containing the converted `Person` objects: `persons` of type `List<Person>`.

Read-Only Collections

After collections are created they are read/write. Of course, they must be read/write; otherwise, you couldn't fill them with any values. However, after the collection is filled, you can create a read-only collection. The `List<T>` collection has the method `AsReadOnly()` that returns an object of type `ReadOnlyCollection<T>`. The class `ReadOnlyCollection<T>` implements the same interfaces as `List<T>`, but all methods and properties that change the collection throw a `NotSupportedException`.

Queues

A queue is a collection where elements are processed *first in, first out* (FIFO). The item that is put first in the queue is read first. Examples of queues are standing in the queue at the airport, a human resources queue to process employee applicants, print jobs waiting to be processed in a print queue, and a thread waiting for the CPU in a round-robin fashion. Often, there are queues where the elements processed differ in their priority. For example, in the queue at the airport, business passengers are processed before economy passengers. Here, multiple queues can be used, one queue for every priority. At the airport this can easily be found out, because there are separate check-in queues for business and economy passengers. The same is true for print queues and threads. You can have an array of a list of queues where one item in the array stands for a priority. Within every array item there's a queue, where processing happens with the FIFO principle.

Later in this chapter, a different implementation with a linked list is used to define a list of priorities.

With .NET you have the non-generic class `Queue` in the `System.Collections` namespace and the generic class `Queue<T>` in the `System.Collections.Generic` namespace. Both classes are very similar in their functionality with the exception that the generic class is strongly typed, defining type `T`, and the non-generic class is based on the `object` type.

Internally, the `Queue<T>` class is using an array of type `T` similar to the `List<T>` type. What's also similar is that the interfaces `ICollection` and `IEnumerable` are implemented. The `Queue` class implements the interfaces `ICollection`, `IEnumerable`, and `ICloneable`. The `Queue<T>` class implements the interfaces `IEnumerable<T>` and `ICollection`. The generic class `Queue<T>` does not implement the generic interface `ICollection<T>` because this interface defines methods to add and remove items to the collection with `Add()` and `Remove()` methods.

The big difference of the queue is that the interface `IList` is not implemented. You cannot access the queue using an indexer. The queue just allows you to add an item to the queue, where the item is put at the end of the queue (with the `Enqueue()` method), and to get items from the head of the queue (with the `Dequeue()` method).

Figure 10-1 shows the items of the queue. The `Enqueue()` method adds items to one end of the queue; the items are read and removed at the other end of the queue with the `Dequeue()` method. Reading items with the `Dequeue()` method also removes the items from the queue. Invoking the `Dequeue()` method once more removes the next item from the queue.

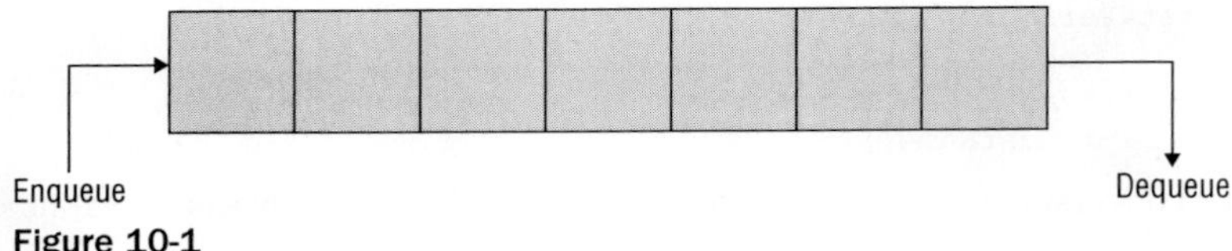

Figure 10-1

Methods of the `Queue` and `Queue<T>` classes are described in the following table.

Queue and Queue <T> Members	Description
`Enqueue()`	The `Enqueue()` method adds an item to the end of the queue.
`Dequeue()`	The `Dequeue()` method reads and removes an item from the head of the queue. If there are no more items in the queue when the `Dequeue()` method is invoked, an exception of type `InvalidOperationException` is thrown.
`Peek()`	The `Peek()` method reads an item from the head of the queue but does not remove the item.
`Count`	The property `Count` returns the number of items in the queue.
`TrimExcess()`	`TrimExcess()` resizes the capacity of the queue. The `Dequeue()` method removes items from the queue, but it doesn't resize the capacity of the queue. To get rid of the empty items at the beginning of the queue, use the `TrimExcess()` method.

Queue and Queue <T> Members	Description
`Contains()`	The `Contains()` method checks whether an item is in the queue and returns `true` if it is.
`CopyTo()`	With the `CopyTo()` method, you can copy the items from the queue to an existing array.
`ToArray()`	The method `ToArray()` returns a new array containing the elements of the queue.

When creating queues, you can use constructors similar to those used with the `List<T>` type. The default constructor creates an empty queue, but you can also use a constructor to specify the capacity. As items are added to the queue, the capacity is increased to hold 4, 8, 16, and 32 items if the capacity is not defined. Similarly to the `List<T>` class, the capacity is always doubled as required. The default constructor of the non-generic `Queue` class is different, because it creates an initial array of 32 empty items. With an overload of the constructor you can also pass any other collection that implements the `IEnumerable<T>` interface that is copied to the queue.

The sample application that demonstrates the use of the `Queue<T>` class is a document management application. One thread is used to add documents to the queue, and another thread reads documents from the queue and processes them.

The items stored in the queue are of type `Document`. The `Document` class defines a title and content:

```
public class Document
{
   private string title;
   public string Title
   {
      get
      {
         return title;
      }
   }

   private string content;
   public string Content
   {
      get
      {
         return content;
      }
   }

   public Document(string title, string content)
   {
      this.title = title;
      this.content = content;
   }
}
```

The DocumentManager class is a thin layer around the Queue<T> class. The class DocumentManager defines how to handle documents: adding documents to the queue with the AddDocument() method, and getting documents from the queue with the GetDocument() method.

Inside the AddDocument() method, the document is added to the end of the queue by using the Enqueue() method. The first document from the queue is read with the Dequeue() method inside GetDocument(). Because multiple threads can access the DocumentManager concurrently, access to the queue is locked with the lock statement.

Threading and the lock statement are discussed in Chapter 19, "Threading and Synchronization."

IsDocumentAvailable is a read-only Boolean property that returns true if there are documents in the queue, and false if not:

```
public class DocumentManager
{
   private readonly Queue<Document> documentQueue = new Queue<Document>();

   public void AddDocument(Document doc)
   {
      lock (this)
      {
         documentQueue.Enqueue(doc);
      }
   }

   public Document GetDocument()
   {
      Document doc = null;
      lock (this)
      {
         doc = documentQueue.Dequeue();
      }
      return doc;
   }

   public bool IsDocumentAvailable
   {
      get
      {
         return documentQueue.Count > 0;
      }
   }
}
```

The class ProcessDocuments processes documents from the queue in a separate thread. The only method that can be accessed from the outside is Start(). In the Start() method, a new thread is instantiated. A ProcessDocuments object is created for starting the thread, and the Run() method is defined as the start method of the thread. ThreadStart is a delegate that references the method to be started by the thread. After creating the Thread object, the thread is started by calling the method Thread.Start().

With the Run() method of the ProcessDocuments class, an endless loop is defined. Within this loop, the property IsDocumentAvailable is used to see if there is a document in the queue. If there is a document in the queue, the document is taken from the DocumentManager and processed. Processing here is writing information only to the console. In a real application, the document could be written to a file, written to the database, or sent across the network.

```
public class ProcessDocuments
{
   public static void Start(DocumentManager dm)
   {
      new Thread(new ProcessDocuments(dm).Run).Start();
   }

   protected ProcessDocuments(DocumentManager dm)
   {
      documentManager = dm;
   }

   private DocumentManager documentManager;

   protected void Run()
   {
      while (true)
      {
         if (documentManager.IsDocumentAvailable)
         {
            Document doc =
                  documentManager.GetDocument();
            Console.WriteLine(
                  "Processing document {0}",
                  doc.Title);
         }
         Thread.Sleep(new Random().Next(20));
      }
   }
}
```

In the `Main()` method of the application, a `DocumentManager` object is instantiated, and the document processing thread is started. Then 1,000 documents are created and added to the `DocumentManager`.

```
class Program
{
   static void Main()
   {
      DocumentManager dm = new DocumentManager();

      ProcessDocuments.Start(dm);

      // Create documents and add them to the
      // DocumentManager
      for (int i = 0; i < 1000; i++)
      {
         Document doc = new Document("Doc " +
               i.ToString(), "content");
         dm.AddDocument(doc);
         Console.WriteLine("Added document {0}",
               doc.Title);
         Thread.Sleep(new Random().Next(20));
      }
   }
}
```

When you start the application, the documents are added to and removed from the queue, and you get output similar to the following:

```
Added document Doc 279
Processing document Doc 236
Added document Doc 280
Processing document Doc 237
Added document Doc 281
Processing document Doc 238
Processing document Doc 239
Processing document Doc 240
Processing document Doc 241
Added document Doc 282
Processing document Doc 242
Added document Doc 283
Processing document Doc 243
```

A real-life scenario doing the task described with the sample application can be an application that processes documents received with a Web service.

Stacks

A stack is another container that is very similar to the queue. You just use different methods to access the stack. The item that is added last to the stack is read first. The stack is a *last in, first out* (LIFO) container.

Figure 10-2 shows the representation of a stack where the `Push()` method adds an item to the stack, and the `Pop()` method gets the item that was added last.

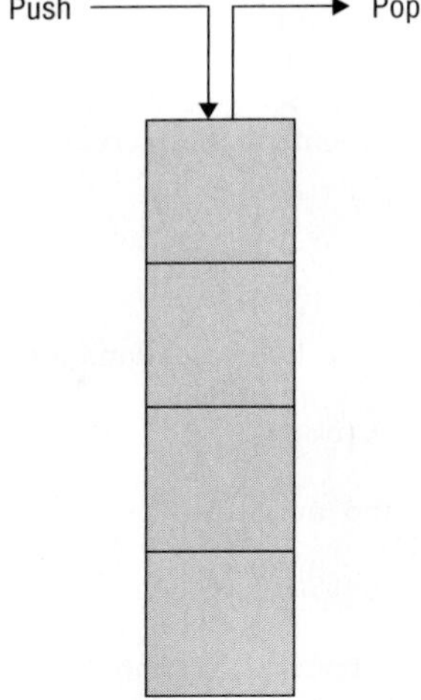

Figure 10-2

Similar to the queue classes, the non-generic `Stack` class implements the interfaces `ICollection`, `IEnumerable`, and `ICloneable`; the generic `Stack<T>` class implements the interfaces `IEnumerable<T>`, `ICollection`, and `IEnumerable`.

Members of the `Stack` and `Stack<T>` class are listed in the following table.

Stack and Stack<T> Members	Description
`Push()`	The `Push()` method adds an item on top of the stack.
`Pop()`	The `Pop()` method removes and returns an item from the top of the stack. If the stack is empty, an exception of type `InvalidOperationException` is thrown.
`Peek()`	The `Peek()` method returns an item from the top of the stack but does not remove the item.
`Count`	The property `Count` returns the number of items in the stack.
`Contains()`	The `Contains()` method checks whether an item is in the stack and returns `true` if it is.
`CopyTo()`	With the `CopyTo()` method, you can copy the items from the stack to an existing array.
`ToArray()`	The method `ToArray()` returns a new array containing the elements of the stack.

In this example, three items are added to the stack with the `Push()` method. With the `foreach` method, all items are iterated using the `IEnumerable` interface. The enumerator of the stack does not remove the items; it just returns item by item.

```
Stack<char> alphabet = new Stack<char>();
alphabet.Push('A');
alphabet.Push('B');
alphabet.Push('C');

foreach (char item in alphabet)
{
   Console.Write(item);
}
Console.WriteLine();
```

Because the items are read in the order from the last added to the first, the following result is produced:

```
CBA
```

Reading the items with the enumerator does not change the state of the items. With the `Pop()` method, every item that is read is also removed from the stack. This way you can iterate the collection using a `while` loop and verify the `Count` property if items are still existing:

```
Stack<char> alphabet = new Stack<char>();
alphabet.Push('A');
alphabet.Push('B');
alphabet.Push('C');

Console.Write("First iteration: ");
foreach (char item in alphabet)
{
   Console.Write(item);
}
```

(continued)

(continued)

```
            Console.WriteLine();

            Console.Write("Second iteration: ");
            while (alphabet.Count > 0)
            {
               Console.Write(alphabet.Pop());
            }
            Console.WriteLine();
```

The result gives CBA twice, once for each iteration. After the second iteration, the stack is empty because the second iteration used the `Pop()` method:

```
First iteration: CBA
Second iteration: CBA
```

Linked Lists

A collection class that has no similar version with a non-generic collection is `LinkedList<T>`. `LinkedList<T>` is a doubly linked list, where one element references the next and the previous one, as shown in Figure 10-3.

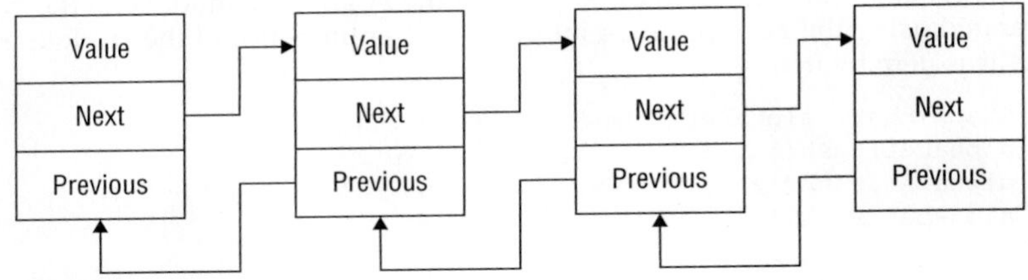

Figure 10-3

The advantage of a linked list is that if items are inserted in the middle of a list, the linked list is very fast. When an item is inserted, only the `Next` reference of the previous item and the `Previous` reference of the next item must be changed to reference the inserted item. With the `List<T>` and `ArrayList` classes, when an element is inserted all following elements must be moved.

Of course, there's also a disadvantage with linked lists. Items of linked lists can be accessed only one after the other. It takes a long time to find an item that's somewhere in the middle or at the end of the list.

A linked list cannot just store the items inside the list; together with every item, the linked list must have information about the next and previous items. That's why the `LinkedList<T>` contains items of type `LinkedListNode<T>`. With the class `LinkedListNode<T>`, you can get to the next and previous items in the list. The following table describes the properties of `LinkedListNode<T>`.

LinkedListNode<T> Properties	Description
`List`	The property `List` returns the `LinkedList<T>` that is associated with the node.
`Next`	The property `Next` returns the node that follows the current node. The return type is again of type `LinkedListNode<T>`.
`Previous`	The property `Previous` returns the node before the current node.
`Value`	The property `Value` returns the item that is associated with the node. `Value` is of type `T`.

The class `LinkedList<T>` implements the interfaces `ICollection<T>`, `IEnumerable<T>`, `ICollection`, `IEnumerable`, `ISerializable`, and `IDeserializationCallback`. Members of this class are explained in the following table.

LinkedList<T> Members	Description
`Count`	The property `Count` returns the number of items in the list.
`First`	The property `First` returns the first node in the list. The type returned is `LinkedListNode<T>`. Using this returned node, you can iterate through the other nodes of the collection.
`Last`	The property `Last` returns the last node in the list. Again, the type is `LinkedListNode<T>`. From here you can iterate through the list backwards.

`AddAfter()`
`AddBefore()`
`AddFirst()`
`AddLast()`
	With the `AddXXX` methods you can add items to the linked list. Use the corresponding `Add` method to add the item to a specific position inside the list. `AddAfter()` requires a `LinkedListNode<T>` object where you can specify the node after which the new item should be added. `AddBefore()` positions the new item before the node defined with the first parameter. `AddFirst()` and `AddLast()` just add the new item to the beginning or the end of the list.
	All these methods are overloaded to accept an object to add of either type `LinkedListNode<T>` or of type `T`. If you pass a `T` object, a new `LinkedListNode<T>` object is created.

`Remove()`
`RemoveFirst()`
`RemoveLast()`
	The `Remove()`, `RemoveFirst()`, and `RemoveLast()` methods remove nodes from the list. `RemoveFirst()` removes the first item, and `RemoveLast()` removes the last item. The `Remove()` method requires an object that is searched and removes the first occurrence of this item in the list.

`Clear()`	The `Clear()` method removes all nodes from the list.

LinkedList<T> Members	Description
`Contains()`	The method `Contains()` searches for an item and returns `true` if the item is found, and `false` otherwise.
`Find()`	The `Find()` method searches the list from the beginning to find the item passed. The `Find()` method then returns a `LinkedListNode<T>`.
`FindLast()`	The `FindLast()` method is similar to `Find()`, but the search starts from the end of the list.

The sample application uses a linked list, `LinkedList<T>`, together with a list, `List<T>`. The linked list contains documents as in the previous example, but the documents have an additional priority associated with them. The documents will be sorted inside the linked list depending on the priority. If multiple documents have the same priority, the elements are sorted according to the time the document was inserted.

Figure 10-4 describes the collections of the sample application. `LinkedList<Document>` is the linked list containing all the `Document` objects. The figure shows the title and the priority of the documents. The title indicates when the document was added to the list: The first document added has the title One, the second document has the title Two, and so on. You can see that the documents One and Four have the same priority, 8, but because One was added before Four, it is earlier in the list.

When new documents are added to the linked list, they should be added after the last document that has the same priority. A `LinkedList<Document>` collection contains elements of type `LinkedListNode<Document>`. The class `LinkedListNode<T>` adds `Next` and `Previous` properties to walk from one node to the next. For referencing such elements, the `List<T>` is defined as `List<LinkedListNode<Document>>`. For fast access to the last document of every priority, the collection `List<LinkedListNode>` contains up to 10 elements, each referencing the last document of every priority. In the upcoming discussion, the reference to the last document of every priority is called the *priority node*.

From the previous example, the `Document` class is extended to contain the priority. The priority is set with the constructor of the class:

```
public class Document
{
   private string title;
   public string Title
   {
      get
      {
         return title;
      }
   }

   private string content;
   public string Content
   {
      get
      {
         return content;
      }
   }
```

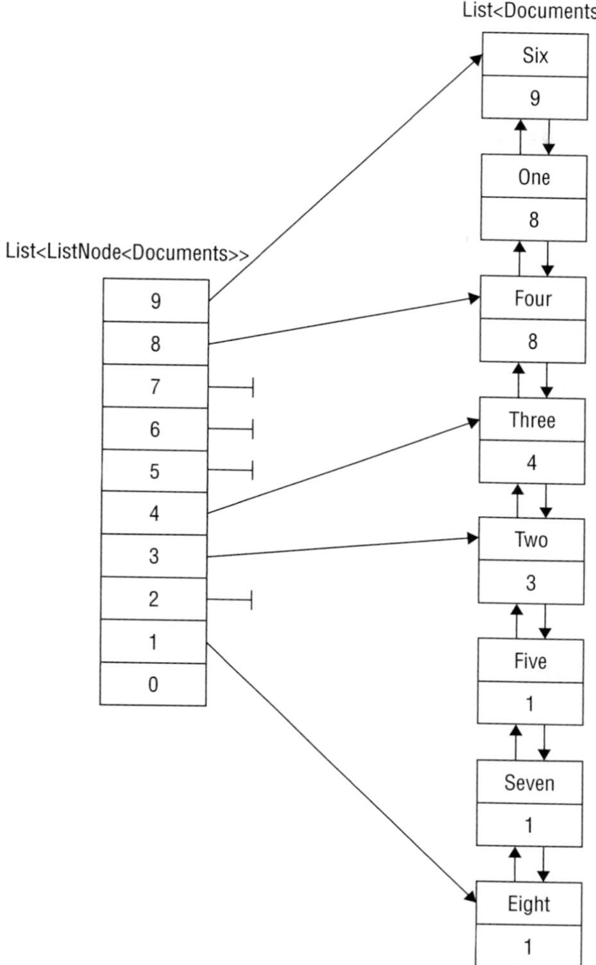

Figure 10-4

```
private byte priority;
public byte Priority
{
   get
   {
      return priority;
   }
}

public Document(string title, string content,
      byte priority)
```

(continued)

(continued)

```
        {
            this.title = title;
            this.content = content;
            this.priority = priority;
        }
    }
```

The heart of the solution is the `PriorityDocumentManager` class. This class is very easy to use. With the public interface of this class, new `Document` elements can be added to the linked list, the first document can be retrieved, and for testing purposes it also has a method to display all elements of the collection as they are linked in the list.

The class `PriorityDocumentManager` contains two collections. The collection of type `LinkedList<Document>` contains all documents. The collection of type `List<LinkedListNode<Document>>` contains references of up to 10 elements that are entry points for adding new documents with a specific priority. Both collection variables are initialized with the constructor of the class `PriorityDocumentManager`. The list collection is also initialized with `null`:

```
    public class PriorityDocumentManager
    {
        private readonly LinkedList<Document> documentList;

        // priorities 0..9
        private readonly List<LinkedListNode<Document>> priorityNodes;

        public PriorityDocumentManager()
        {
            documentList = new LinkedList<Document>();

            priorityNodes =
                  new List<LinkedListNode<Document>>(10);
            for (int i = 0; i < 10; i++)
            {
                priorityNodes.Add(
                      new LinkedListNode<Document>(null));
            }
        }
```

Part of the public interface of the class is the method `AddDocument()`. `AddDocument()` does nothing more than call the private method `AddDocumentToPriorityNode()`. The reason for having the implementation inside a different method is that `AddDocumentToPriorityNode()` may be called recursively, as you will see soon.

```
        public void AddDocument(Document d)
        {
            if (d == null)
                throw new ArgumentNullException("d");
            AddDocumentToPriorityNode(d, d.Priority);
        }
```

The first action that is done in the implementation of `AddDocumentToPriorityNode()` is a check to see if the priority fits in the allowed priority range. Here, the allowed range is between 0 and 9. If a wrong value is passed, an exception of type `ArgumentException` is thrown.

Next, you check if there's already a priority node with the same priority as the priority that was passed. If there's no such priority node in the list collection, `AddDocumentToPriorityNode()` is invoked recursively with the priority value decremented to check for a priority node with the next lower priority.

If there's no priority node with the same priority or any priority with a lower value, the document can be safely added to the end of the linked list by calling the method `AddLast()`. Also, the linked list node is referenced by the priority node that's responsible for the priority of the document.

If there's an existing priority node, you can get the position inside the linked list where the document should be inserted. Here, you must differentiate whether a priority node already exists with the correct priority, or if there's just a priority node that references a document with a lower priority. In the first case, you can just insert the new document after the position that's referenced by the priority node. Because the priority node always must reference the last document with a specific priority, the reference of the priority node must be set. It gets more complex if just a priority node referencing a document with a lower priority exists. Here, the document must be inserted before all documents with the same priority as the priority node. To get the first document of the same priority, a `while` loop iterates through all linked list nodes, using the `Previous` property, until a linked list node is reached that has a different priority. This way, you know the position where the document must be inserted, and the priority node can be set.

```
private void AddDocumentToPriorityNode(
      Document doc, int priority)
{
   if (priority > 9 || priority < 0)
      throw new ArgumentException(
            "Priority must be between 0 and 9");

   if (priorityNodes[priority].Value == null)
   {
      priority--;
      if (priority >= 0)
      {
         // check for the next lower priority
         AddDocumentToPriorityNode(doc,
               priority);
      }
      else // now no priority node exists with
           // the same priority or lower
           // add the new document to the end
      {
         documentList.AddLast(doc);
         priorityNodes[doc.Priority] =
               documentList.Last;
      }
      return;
   }
   else // a priority node exists
   {
      LinkedListNode<Document> prioNode =
            priorityNodes[priority];
      if (priority == doc.Priority)
            // priority node with the same
            // priority exists
```

(continued)

(continued)

```
            {
               documentList.AddAfter(prioNode, doc);

               // set the priority node to the last
               // document with the same priority
               priorityNodes[doc.Priority] =
                     prioNode.Next;
            }
            else // only priority node with a lower
                 // priority exists
            {
               // get the first node of the lower
               // priority
               LinkedListNode<Document>
                     firstPrioNode = prioNode;

               while (firstPrioNode.Previous != null &&
                  firstPrioNode.Previous.Value.Priority
                  == prioNode.Value.Priority)
               {
                  firstPrioNode =
                        prioNode.Previous;
               }

               documentList.AddBefore(firstPrioNode,
                     doc);

               // set the priority node to the
               // new value
               priorityNodes[doc.Priority] =
                     firstPrioNode.Previous;
            }
         }
      }
```

Now only simple methods are left for discussion. `DisplayAllNodes()` just does a `foreach` loop to display the priority and the title of every document to the console.

The method `GetDocument()` returns the first document (the document with the highest priority) from the linked list and removes it from the list:

```
      public void DisplayAllNodes()
      {
         foreach (Document doc in documentList)
         {
            Console.WriteLine(
                  "priority: {0}, title {1}",
                  doc.Priority, doc.Title);
         }
      }

      // returns the document with the highest priority
      // (that's first in the linked list)
      public Document GetDocument()
```

```
        {
            Document doc = documentList.First.Value;
            documentList.RemoveFirst();
            return doc;
        }
    }
```

In the `Main()` method, the `PriorityDocumentManager` is used to demonstrate its functionality. Eight new documents with different priorities are added to the linked list, and then the complete list is displayed:

```
        static void Main()
        {
            PriorityDocumentManager pdm =
                  new PriorityDocumentManager();
            pdm.AddDocument(new Document("one", "Sample",
                  8));
            pdm.AddDocument(new Document("two", "Sample",
                  3));
            pdm.AddDocument(new Document("three",
                  "Sample", 4));
            pdm.AddDocument(new Document("four", "Sample",
                  8));
            pdm.AddDocument(new Document("five", "Sample",
                  1));
            pdm.AddDocument(new Document("six", "Sample",
                  9));
            pdm.AddDocument(new Document("seven",
                  "Sample", 1));
            pdm.AddDocument(new Document("eight",
                  "Sample", 1));

            pdm.DisplayAllNodes();
        }
```

With the processed result, you can see that the documents are sorted first by the priority and second by when the document was added:

```
priority: 9, title six
priority: 8, title one
priority: 8, title four
priority: 4, title three
priority: 3, title two
priority: 1, title five
priority: 1, title seven
priority: 1, title eight
```

Sorted Lists

If you need a sorted list, you can use `SortedList<TKey, TValue>`. This class sorts the elements based on a key.

The example creates a sorted list where both the key and the value are of type `string`. The default constructor creates an empty list, and then two books are added with the `Add()` method. With overloaded constructors, you can define the capacity of the list and also pass an object that implements the interface `IComparer<TKey>`, which is used to sort the elements in the list.

The first parameter of the `Add()` method is the key (the book title); the second parameter is the value (the ISBN number). Instead of using the `Add()` method, you can use the indexer to add elements to the list. The indexer requires the key as index parameter. If a key already exists, the `Add()` method throws an exception of type `ArgumentException`. If the same key is used with the indexer, the new value replaces the old value.

```
SortedList<string, string> books =
      new SortedList<string, string>();
books.Add(".NET 2.0 Wrox Box",
      "978-0-470-04840-5");
books.Add(
      "Professional C# 2005 with .NET 3.0",
      "978-0-470-12472-7");

books["Beginning Visual C# 2005"] =
      "978-0-7645-4382-1";
books["Professional C# 2008"] =
      "978-0-470-19137-6";
```

You can iterate through the list by using a `foreach` statement. Elements that are returned by the enumerator are of type `KeyValuePair<TKey, TValue>`, which contains both the key and the value. The key can be accessed with the `Key` property, and the value can be accessed with the `Value` property.

```
foreach (KeyValuePair<string, string> book in
      books)
{
   Console.WriteLine("{0}, {1}", book.Key,
         book.Value);
}
```

The iteration displays book titles and ISBN numbers ordered by the key:

```
.NET 2.0 Wrox Box, 978-0-470-04840-5
Beginning Visual C# 2005, 978-0-7645-4382-1
Professional C# 2005 with .NET 3.0, 978-0-470-12472-7
Professional C# 2008, 978-0-470-19137-6
```

You can also access the values and keys by using the `Values` and `Keys` properties. The `Values` property returns `IList<TValue>` and the `Keys` property returns `IList<TKey>`, so you can use these properties with a `foreach`:

```
foreach (string isbn in books.Values)
{
   Console.WriteLine(isbn);
}

foreach (string title in books.Keys)
{
   Console.WriteLine(title);
}
```

The first loop displays the values, and next the keys:

```
978-0-470-04840-5
978-0-7645-4382-1
978-0-470-12472-7
978-0-470-19137-6
.NET 2.0 Wrox Box
Beginning Visual C# 2005
Professional C# 2005 with .NET 3.0
Professional C# 2008
```

Properties of the `SortedList<TKey, TValue>` class are described in the following table.

SortedList<TKey, TValue> Properties	Description
`Capacity`	With the property `Capacity` you can get and set the number of elements the list can contain. The capacity behaves as `List<T>`: the default constructor creates an empty list; adding the first item allocates a capacity of four items, and then the capacity is doubled as needed.
`Comparer`	The property `Comparer` returns the comparer that is associated with the list. You can pass the comparer in the constructor. The default comparer compares the key items by invoking the method `CompareTo` of the `IComparable<TKey>` interface. Either the key type implements this interface or you have to create a custom comparer.
`Count`	The property `Count` returns the number of elements in the list.
`Item`	With the indexer you can access the elements in the list. The parameter type of the indexer is defined by the key type.
`Keys`	The property `Keys` returns `IList<TKey>` containing all keys.
`Values`	The property `Values` returns `IList<TValue>` containing all values.

Methods of the `SortedList<T>` type are similar to the other collections you've learned about in this chapter. The difference is that `SortedList<T>` requires a key and a value.

SortedList<TKey, TValue> Methods	Description
`Add()`	The `Add()` method adds an element with key and value to the list.
`Remove()` `RemoveAt()`	The `Remove()` method requires the key of the element to be removed from the list. With `RemoveAt()`, you can remove an element at a specified index.
`Clear()`	The method `Clear()` removes all elements from the list.
`ContainsKey()` `ContainsValue()`	The `ContainsKey()` and `ContainsValue()` methods check if the list contains a specified key or value, and return `true` or `false`.
`IndexOfKey()` `IndexOfValue()`	The `IndexOfKey()` and `IndexOfValue()` methods check if the list contains a specified key or value and return the integer-based index.
`TrimExcess()`	The method `TrimExcess()` resizes the collection and changes the capacity to the required item count.
`TryGetValue()`	With the method `TryGetValue()`, you can try to get the value for a specified key. If the key does not exist, this method returns `false`. If the key exists, `true` is returned, and the value is returned as `out` parameter.

In addition to the generic `SortedList<TKey, TValue>`*, a corresponding non-generic list named* `SortedList` *is available.*

Dictionaries

Dictionaries represent a sophisticated data structure that allows you to access an element based on a key. Dictionaries are also known as hash tables or maps. The main feature of dictionaries is fast lookup based on keys. You can also add and remove items freely, a bit like a `List<T>`, but without the performance overhead of having to shift subsequent items in memory.

Figure 10-5 shows a simplified representation of a dictionary. Here `employee-ids` such as B4711 are the keys added to the dictionary. The key is transformed into a hash. With the hash a number is created to associate an index with the values. The index then contains a link to the value. The figure is simplified because it is possible that a single index entry can be associated with multiple values, and the index can be stored as a tree.

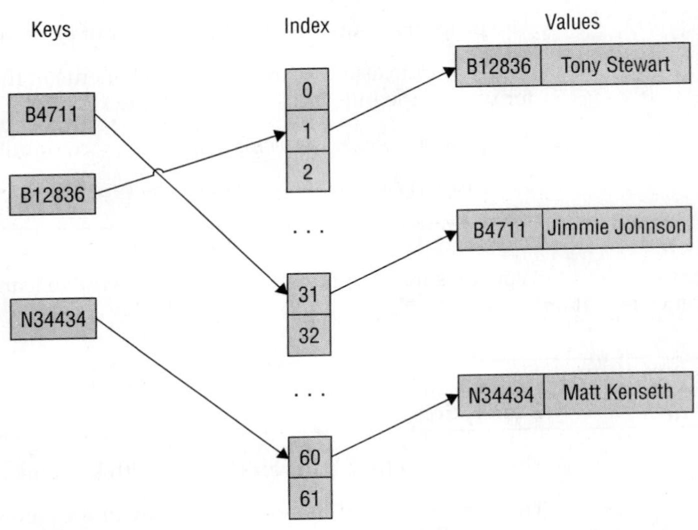

Figure 10-5

The .NET Framework offers several dictionary classes. The main class you can use is `Dictionary<TKey, TValue>`. This class offers nearly the same properties and methods as `SortedList<TKey, TValue>` discussed earlier; that's why they are not repeated here.

Key Type

A type that is used as a key in the dictionary must override the method `GetHashCode()` of the `Object` class. Whenever a dictionary class needs to work out where an item should be located, it calls the `GetHashCode()` method. The `int` that is returned by `GetHashCode()` is used by the dictionary to calculate an index of where to place the element. We don't go into this part of the algorithm. What you should know is that it involves prime numbers, so the capacity of a dictionary is a prime number.

The implementation of `GetHashCode()` must satisfy these requirements:

- The same object should always return the same value.
- Different objects can return the same value.
- It should execute as quickly as possible; it must be inexpensive to compute.
- It must not throw exceptions.
- It should use at least one instance field.
- The hash code value should be evenly distributed across the entire range of numbers that an `int` can store.
- At best, the hash code should not change during the lifetime of the object.

> **A good performance of the dictionary is based on a good implementation of the method `GetHashCode()`.**

What's the reason for having hash code values evenly distributed across the range of integers? If two keys return hashes that give the same index, the dictionary class needs to start looking for the nearest available free location to store the second item — and will have to do some searching in order to retrieve this item later on. This is obviously going to hurt performance, and clearly, if lots of your keys are tending to give the same indexes for where they should be stored, this kind of clash becomes more likely. However, because of the way that Microsoft's part of the algorithm works, this risk is minimized when the calculated hash values are evenly distributed between `int.MinValue` and `int.MaxValue`.

Besides having an implementation of `GetHashCode()`, the key type also must implement the `IEquality.Equals()` method or override the `Equals()` method from the `Object` class. Because different key objects may return the same hash code, the method `Equals()` is used by the dictionary comparing keys. The dictionary examines if two keys `A` and `B` are equal; it invokes `A.Equals(B)`. This means that you must ensure that the following is always true:

If `A.Equals(B)` is true, then `A.GetHashCode()` and `B.GetHashCode()` must always return the same hash code.

This probably seems a fairly subtle point, but it is crucial. If you contrived some way of overriding these methods so that the preceding statement was not always true, a dictionary that uses instances of this class as its keys would simply not work properly. Instead, you'd find funny things happening. For example, you might place an object in the dictionary and then discover that you could never retrieve it, or you might try to retrieve an entry and have the wrong entry returned.

> *For this reason, the C# compiler will display a compilation warning if you supply an override for* `Equals()` *but don't supply an override for* `GetHashCode()`.

For `System.Object` this condition is true, because `Equals()` simply compares references, and `GetHashCode()` actually returns a hash that is based solely on the address of the object. This means that hash tables based on a key that doesn't override these methods will work correctly. However, the problem with this way of doing things is that keys are regarded as equal only if they are the same object. That means that when you place an object in the dictionary, you then have to hang onto the reference to the key. You can't simply instantiate another key object later with the same value. If you don't override `Equals()` and `GetHashCode()`, the type is not very convenient to use in a dictionary.

Incidentally, `System.String` implements the interface `IEquatable` and overloads `GetHashCode()` appropriately. `Equals()` provides value comparison, and `GetHashCode()` returns a hash based on the value of the string. Strings can be used conveniently as keys in dictionaries.

Number types such as `Int32` also implement the interface `IEquatable` and overload `GetHashCode()`. However, the hash code returned by these types simply maps to the value. If the number you would like to use as a key is not itself distributed around the possible values of an integer, using integers as keys doesn't fulfill the rule of evenly distributing key values to get the best performance. `Int32` is not meant to be used in a dictionary.

If you need to use a key type that does not implement `IEquatable` and override `GetHashCode` according to the key values you store in the dictionary, you can create a comparer implementing the interface `IEqualityComparer<T>`. `IEqualityComparer<T>` defines the methods `GetHashCode()` and `Equals()` with an argument of the object passed, so you can offer an implementation different from the object type itself. An overload of the `Dictionary<TKey, TValue>` constructor allows passing an object implementing `IEqualityComparer<T>`. If such an object is assigned to the dictionary, this class is used to generate the hash codes and compare the keys.

Dictionary Example

The dictionary example is a program that sets up a dictionary of employees. The dictionary is indexed by `EmployeeId` objects, and each item stored in the dictionary is an `Employee` object that stores details of an employee.

The struct `EmployeeId` is implemented to define a key to be used in a dictionary. The members of the class are a prefix character and a number for the employee. Both of these variables are read-only and can be initialized only in the constructor. A key within the dictionary shouldn't change, and this way that is guaranteed. The fields are filled within the constructor. The `ToString()` method is overloaded to get a string representation of the employee ID. As required for a key type, `EmployeeId` implements the interface `IEquatable` and overloads the method `GetHashCode()`.

```
[Serializable]
public struct EmployeeId  : IEquatable<EmployeeId>
{
   private readonly char prefix;
   private readonly int number;

   public EmployeeId(string id)
   {
      if (id == null)
            throw new ArgumentNullException("id");

      prefix = (id.ToUpper())[0];
      int numLength = id.Length - 1;
      number = int.Parse(id.Substring(
            1, numLength > 6 ? 6 : numLength));
   }

   public override string ToString()
   {
      return prefix.ToString() +
            string.Format("{0,6:000000}", number);
   }

   public override int GetHashCode()
   {
      return (number ^ number << 16) * 0x15051505;
   }

   public bool Equals(EmployeeId other)
```

```
        {
            return (prefix == other.prefix &&
                  number == other.number);
        }
    }
```

The `Equals()` method that is defined by the `IEquatable<T>` interface compares the values of two `EmployeeId` objects and returns `true` if the both values are the same. Instead of implementing the `Equals()` method from the `IEquatable<T>` interface, you can also override the `Equals()` method from the `Object` class:

```
        public bool Equals(EmployeeId other)
        {
            if (other == null) return false;
            return (prefix == other.prefix &&
                  number == other.number);
        }
```

With the number variable, a value from 1 to around 190,000 is expected for the employees. This doesn't fill the range of an integer. The algorithm used by `GetHashCode()` shifts the number 16 bits to the left, then does an XOR with the original number, and finally multiplies the result by the hex value 15051505. The hash code is fairly distributed across the range of an integer.

```
        public override int GetHashCode()
        {
            return (number ^ number << 16) * 0x15051505;
        }
```

On the Internet, you can find a lot more complex algorithms that have a better distribution across the integer range. You can also use the `GetHashCode()` *method of a string to return a hash.*

The `Employee` class is a simple entity class containing the name, salary, and ID of the employee. The constructor initializes all values, and the method `ToString()` returns a string representation of an instance. The implementation of `ToString()` uses a format string to create the string representation for performance reasons.

```
    [Serializable]
    public class Employee
    {
        private string name;
        private decimal salary;
        private readonly EmployeeId id;

        public Employee(EmployeeId id, string name,
              decimal salary)
        {
            this.id = id;
            this.name = name;
            this.salary = salary;
        }

        public override string ToString()
        {
            return String.Format("{0}: {1, -20} {2:C}",
                  id.ToString(), name, salary);
        }
    }
```

In the `Main()` method of the sample application, a new `Dictionary<TKey, TValue>` instance is created, where the key is of type `EmployeeId` and the value is of type `Employee`. The constructor allocates a capacity of 31 elements. Remember, the capacity is based on prime numbers. However, when you assign a value that is not a prime number, you don't need to worry. The `Dictionary<TKey, TValue>` class itself takes the next prime number that follows the integer passed to the constructor to allocate the capacity. The employee objects and IDs are created and added to the dictionary with the `Add()` method. Instead of using the `Add()` method, you can also use the indexer to add keys and values to the dictionary, as shown with the employees Carl and Matt:

```
static void Main()
{
   Dictionary<EmployeeId, Employee> employees =
         new Dictionary<EmployeeId,
               Employee>(31);

   EmployeeId idJeff = new EmployeeId("C7102");
   Employee jeff = new Employee(idJeff,
         "Jeff Gordon", 5164580.00m);
   employees.Add(idJeff, jeff);
   Console.WriteLine(jeff);

   EmployeeId idTony = new EmployeeId("C7105");
   Employee tony = new Employee(idTony,
         "Tony Stewart", 4814200.00m);
   employees.Add(idTony, tony);
   Console.WriteLine(tony);

   EmployeeId idDenny = new EmployeeId("C8011");
   Employee denny = new Employee(idDenny,
         "Denny Hamlin", 3718710.00m);
   employees.Add(idDenny, denny);
   Console.WriteLine(denny);

   EmployeeId idCarl = new EmployeeId("F7908");
   Employee carl = new Employee(idCarl,
         "Carl Edwards", 3285710.00m);
   employees[idCarl] = carl;
   Console.WriteLine(carl);

   EmployeeId idMatt = new EmployeeId("F7203");
   Employee matt = new Employee(idMatt,
         "Matt Kenseth", 4520330.00m);
   employees[idMatt] = matt;
   Console.WriteLine(matt);
```

After the entries are added to the dictionary, inside a `while` loop employees are read from the dictionary. The user is asked to enter an employee number to store in the variable `userInput`. The user can exit the application by entering X. If the key is in the dictionary, it is examined with the `TryGetValue()` method of the `Dictionary<TKey, TValue>` class. `TryGetValue()` returns `true` if the key is found and `false` otherwise. If the value is found, the value associated with the key is stored in the employee variable. This value is written to the console.

You can also use an indexer of the `Dictionary<TKey, TValue>` *class instead of* `TryGetValue()` *to access a value stored in the dictionary. However, if the key is not found, the indexer throws an exception of type* `KeyNotFoundException`.

```
            while (true)
            {
               Console.Write(
                     "Enter employee id (X to exit)> ");
               string userInput = Console.ReadLine();
               userInput = userInput.ToUpper();
               if (userInput == "X") break;

               EmployeeId id = new EmployeeId(userInput);

               Employee employee;
               if (!employees.TryGetValue(id,
                     out employee))
               {
                  Console.WriteLine("Employee with id " +
                        "{0} does not exist", id);
               }
               else
               {
                  Console.WriteLine(employee);
               }
            }
         }
```

Running the application produces the following output:

```
Enter employee ID (format:A999999, X to exit)> C7102
C007102: Jeff Gordon          $5,164,580.00
Enter employee ID (format:A999999, X to exit)> F7908
F007908: Carl Edwards         $3,285,710.00
Enter employee ID (format:A999999, X to exit)> X
```

Lookup

`Dictionary<TKey, TValue>` supports only one value per key. The new class `Lookup<TKey, TElement>` that is part of .NET 3.5 resembles a `Dictionary<TKey, TValue>` but maps keys to a collection of values. This class is implemented in the assembly `System.Core` and defined with the namespace `System.Linq`.

Properties and methods of `Lookup<TKey, TElement>` are described in the following table.

Lookup<TKey, TElement> Properties and Methods	Description
`Count`	The property `Count` returns the number of elements in the collection.
`Item`	With the indexer you can access specific elements based on the key. Because multiple values can exist with the same key, this property returns an enumeration of all values.
`Contains()`	The method `Contains()` returns a Boolean result depending on whether there's an element passed with the key parameter.
`ApplyResultSelector()`	`ApplyResultSelector()` returns a collection by transforming every item based on the transformation function that is passed to this method.

`Lookup<TKey, TElement>` cannot be created like a normal dictionary. Instead, you have to invoke the method `ToLookup()` that returns a `Lookup<TKey, TElement>` object. The method `ToLookup()` is an extension method that is available with every class implementing `IEnumerable<T>`. In the following example, a list of `Racer` objects is filled. Because `List<T>` implements `IEnumerable<T>`, the `ToLookup()` method can be invoked on the racers list. This method requires a delegate of type `Func<TSource, TKey>` that defines the selector of the key. Here the racers are selected based on the country by using the Lambda expression `r => r.Country`. The `foreach` loop accesses only the racers from Australia by using the indexer.

You can read more about extension methods in Chapter 11, "Language Integrated Query." Lambda expressions are explained in Chapter 7, "Delegates and Events."

```
List<Racer> racers = new List<Racer>();
racers.Add(new Racer("Jacques", "Villeneuve",
      "Canada", 11));
racers.Add(new Racer("Alan", "Jones",
      "Australia", 12));
racers.Add(new Racer("Jackie", "Stewart",
      "United Kingdom", 27));
racers.Add(new Racer("James", "Hunt",
      "United Kingdom", 10));
racers.Add(new Racer("Jack", "Brabham",
      "Australia", 14));

Lookup<string, Racer> lookupRacers =
      (Lookup<string, Racer>)
      racers.ToLookup(r => r.Country);

foreach (Racer r in lookupRacers["Australia"])
{
   Console.WriteLine(r);
}
```

The output shows the racers from Australia:

```
Alan Jones
Jack Brabham
```

Other Dictionary Classes

`Dictionary<TKey, TValue>` is the major dictionary class from the framework. There are some more classes, and of course there are also some non-generic dictionary classes.

Dictionaries that are based on the `Object` type and are available since .NET 1.0 are described in the following table.

Non-generic dictionary	Description
`Hashtable`	`Hashtable` is the most-used dictionary implementation of .NET 1.0. Keys and values are based on the `Object` type.
`ListDictionary`	`ListDictionary` is located in the namespace `System.Collections.Specialized` and is faster than the `Hashtable` if 10 or fewer items are used. `ListDictionary` is implemented as a linked list.

Non-generic dictionary	Description
HybridDictionary	HybridDictionary uses a ListDictionary if the collection is small and switches to a Hashtable as the collection grows. If you don't know the number of items in advance, you can use the HybridDictionary.
NameObjectCollectionBase	NameObjectCollectionBase is an abstract base class to associate keys of type string to values of type object. This can be used as a base class for custom string/object collections.This class uses a Hashtable internally.
NameValueCollection	NameValueCollection derives from NameObjectCollection. Here, both the key and value are of type string. This class has another feature where multiple values can use the same key.

Since .NET 2.0, generic dictionaries are preferred over object-based dictionaries:

Generic Dictionary	Description
Dictionary<TKey, TValue>	Dictionary<TKey, TValue> is the general-purpose dictionary for mapping keys to values.
SortedDictionary<TKey, TValue>	SortedDictionary<TKey, TValue> is a binary search tree where the items are sorted based on the key. The key type must implement the interface IComparable<TKey>. If the key type is not sortable, you can also create a comparer implementing IComparer<TKey> and assign the comparer as a constructor argument of the sorted dictionary.

SortedDictionary<TKey, TValue> and SortedList<TKey, TValue> have similar functionality. But because SortedList<TKey, TValue> is implemented as a list that is based on an array and SortedDictionary<TKey, TValue> is implemented as a dictionary, the classes have different characteristics:

- SortedList<TKey, TValue> uses less memory than SortedDictionary<TKey, TValue>.
- SortedDictionary<TKey, TValue> has faster insertion and removal of elements.
- When populating the collection with already sorted data, SortedList<TKey, TValue> is faster, if capacity changes are not needed.

> SortedList **consumes less memory than** SortedDictionary**.** SortedDictionary **is faster for inserts and the removal of unsorted data.**

HashSet

.NET 3.5 includes a new collection class in the `System.Collections.Generic` namespace: `HashSet<T>`. This collection class contains an unordered list of distinct items. Such a collection is known by the term *set*. Because *set* is a reserved word, the class has a different name: `HashSet<T>`. The name was easily decided because this collection is based on hash values; inserting elements is fast. There's no need to rearrange the collection as is necessary with the `List<T>` class.

The `HashSet<T>` class offers methods to create a union, an intersection of sets. The following table describes the methods that change the values of the set.

HashSet<T> Modification Methods	Description
`Add()`	The `Add()` method adds elements to the collection if the element is not already in the collection. With the Boolean return value, the information is returned if the element was added.
`Clear()`	The method `Clear()` removes all elements from the collection.
`Remove()`	The `Remove()` method removes the element specified.
`RemoveWhere()`	The `RemoveWhere()` method requires a `Predicate<T>` delegate as argument. This method removes all elements where the predicate condition matches.
`CopyTo()`	The method `CopyTo()` copies the elements of the set to an array.
`ExceptWith()`	The `ExceptWith()` method receives a collection as argument and removes all the elements from this collection from the set.
`IntersectWith()`	`IntersectWith()` changes the set to include only elements that are part of both the collection that is passed and the set.
`UnionWith()`	The `UnionWith()` method adds all elements from the collection passed with the argument to the set.

The next table lists the methods that just return information about the set without changing the elements.

HashSet<T> Verification Methods	Description
`Contains()`	The method `Contains()` returns `true` if the passed element is within the collection.
`IsSubsetOf()`	The method `IsSubsetOf()` returns `true` if the collection that is passed with the argument is a subset of the set.
`IsSupersetOf()`	The method `IsSupersetOf()` returns `true` if the collection that is passed with the argument is a superset of the set.

HashSet<T> Verification Methods	Description
`Overlaps()`	If there's at least one element in common with the collection that is passed with the argument and the set, `true` is returned.
`SetEquals()`	The `SetEquals()` method returns `true` if both the collection passed with the argument and the set contain the same elements.

With the sample code, three new sets of type string are created and filled with Formula-1 cars. The `HashSet<T>` class implements the `ICollection<T>` interface. However, the `Add()` method is implemented explicitly and a different `Add()` method is offered by the class as you can see here. The `Add()` method differs by the return type; a Boolean value is returned to give the information if the element was added. If the element was already in the set, it is not added, and `false` is returned.

```
HashSet<string> companyTeams =
      new HashSet<string>()
      { "Ferrari", "McLaren", "Toyota", "BMW",
        "Renault", "Honda" };
HashSet<string> traditionalTeams =
      new HashSet<string>()
      { "Ferrari", "McLaren" };
HashSet<string> privateTeams =
      new HashSet<string>()
      { "Red Bull", "Toro Rosso", "Spyker",
        "Super Aguri" };

if (privateTeams.Add("Williams"))
   Console.WriteLine("Williams added");
if (!companyTeams.Add("McLaren"))
   Console.WriteLine(
         "McLaren was already in this set");
```

The result of these two `Add()` methods is written to the console:

```
Williams added
McLaren was already in this set
```

The methods `IsSubsetOf()` and `IsSupersetOf()` compare a set with a collection that implements the `IEnumerable<T>` interface and returns a Boolean result. Here, `IsSubsetOf()` verifies if every element in `traditionalTeams` is contained in `companyTeams`, which is the case; `IsSupersetOf()` verifies if `traditionalTeams` does not have any additional element compared to `companyTeams`.

```
if (traditionalTeams.IsSubsetOf(companyTeams))
{
   Console.WriteLine("traditionalTeams is " +
         "subset of companyTeams");
}

if (companyTeams.IsSupersetOf(traditionalTeams))
{
   Console.WriteLine(
         "companyTeams is a superset of " +
         "traditionalTeams");
}
```

The output of this verification is shown here:

```
traditionalTeams is a subset of companyTeams
companyTeams is a superset of traditionalTeams
```

Williams is a traditional team as well, and that's why this team is added to the `traditionalTeams` collection:

```
traditionalTeams.Add("Williams");
if (privateTeams.Overlaps(traditionalTeams))
{
   Console.WriteLine("At least one team is " +
         "the same with the traditional " +
         "and private teams");
}
```

Because there's an overlap, this is the result:

```
At least one team is the same with the traditional and private teams.
```

The variable `allTeams` is filled with a union of `companyTeams`, `privateTeams`, and `traditionalTeams` by calling the `UnionWith()` method:

```
HashSet<string> allTeams =
      new HashSet<string>(companyTeams);
allTeams.UnionWith(privateTeams);
allTeams.UnionWith(traditionalTeams);

Console.WriteLine();
Console.WriteLine("all teams");
foreach (var team in allTeams)
{
   Console.WriteLine(team);
}
```

Here all teams are returned, but every team is listed just once because the set contains only unique values:

```
Ferrari
McLaren
Toyota
BMW
Renault
Honda
Red Bull
Toro Rosso
Spyker
Super Aguri
Williams
```

The method `ExceptWith()` removes all private teams from the `allTeams` set:

```
allTeams.ExceptWith(privateTeams);
Console.WriteLine();
Console.WriteLine("no private team left");
foreach (var team in allTeams)
{
   Console.WriteLine(team);
}
```

The remaining elements in the collection do not contain any private team:

```
Ferrari
McLaren
Toyota
BMW
Renault
Honda
```

Bit Arrays

If you need to deal with a number of bits, you can use the class `BitArray` and the struct `BitVector32`. `BitArray` is located in the namespace `System.Collections`; `BitVector32` is in the namespace `System.Collections.Specialized`. The most important difference between these two types is that `BitArray` is resizable, which is useful if you don't know the number of bits needed in advance, and it can contain a large number of bits. `BitVector32` is stack-based and therefore faster. `BitVector32` contains only 32 bits, which are stored in an integer.

BitArray

The class `BitArray` is a reference type that contains an array of `int`s, where for every 32 bits a new integer is used. Members of this class are explained in the following table.

BitArray Members	Description
`Count` `Length`	The get accessor of both `Count` and `Length` return the number of bits in the array. With the `Length` property, you can also define a new size and resize the collection.
`Item`	You can use an indexer to read and write bits in the array. The indexer is of type `bool`.
`Get()` `Set()`	Instead of using the indexer, you can also use the `Get()` and `Set()` methods to access the bits in the array.
`SetAll()`	The method `SetAll()` sets the values of all bits according to the parameter passed to the method.
`Not()`	The method `Not()` generates the inverse of all bits of the array.

`And()`
`Or()`
`Xor()`
	With the methods `And()`, `Or()`, and `Xor()`, you can combine two `BitArray` objects. The `And()` method does a binary AND, where the result bits are set only if the bits from both input arrays are set. The `Or()` method does a binary OR, where the result bits are set if one or both of the input arrays are set. The `Xor()` method is an exclusive OR, where the result is set if only one of the input bits is set.

In Chapter 6, "Operators and Casts," you can read about the C# operators for working with bits.

The helper method `DisplayBits()` iterates through a `BitArray` and displays 1 or 0 to the console, depending on whether or not the bit is set:

```
static void DisplayBits(BitArray bits)
{
   foreach (bool bit in bits)
   {
      Console.Write(bit ? 1 : 0);
   }
}
```

The example to demonstrate the `BitArray` class creates a bit array with 8 bits, indexed from 0 to 7. The `SetAll()` method sets all 8 bits to `true`. Then the `Set()` method changes bit `1` to `false`. Instead of the `Set` method, you can also use an indexer, as shown with index `5` and `7`:

```
BitArray bits1 = new BitArray(8);
bits1.SetAll(true);
bits1.Set(1, false);
bits1[5] = false;
bits1[7] = false;
Console.Write("initialized: ");
DisplayBits(bits1);
Console.WriteLine();
```

This is the displayed result of the initialized bits:

```
initialized: 10111010
```

The `Not()` method generates the inverse of the bits of the `BitArray`:

```
Console.Write(" not ");
DisplayBits(bits1);
bits1.Not();
Console.Write(" = ");
DisplayBits(bits1);
Console.WriteLine();
```

The result of `Not()` is all bits inversed. If the bit was `true`, it is `false`, and if it was `false`, it is `true`:

```
not 10111010 = 01000101
```

Here, a new `BitArray` is created. With the constructor, the variable `bits1` is used to initialize the array, so the new array has the same values. Then the values for bits 0, 1, and 4 are set to different values. Before the `Or()` method is used, the bit arrays `bits1` and `bits2` are displayed. The `Or()` method changes the values of `bits1`.

```
BitArray bits2 = new BitArray(bits1);
bits2[0] = true;
bits2[1] = false;
bits2[4] = true;
DisplayBits(bits1);
Console.Write(" or ");
DisplayBits(bits2);
Console.Write(" = ");
bits1.Or(bits2);
DisplayBits(bits1);
Console.WriteLine();
```

With the `Or()` method, the set bits are taken from both input arrays. In the result, the bit is set if it was set with either the first or the second array:

```
01000101 or 10001101 = 11001101
```

Next, the `And()` method is used to operate on `bits2` and `bits1`:

```
DisplayBits(bits2);
Console.Write(" and ");
DisplayBits(bits1);
Console.Write(" = ");
bits2.And(bits1);
DisplayBits(bits2);
Console.WriteLine();
```

The result of the `And()` method only sets the bits where the bit was set in both input arrays:

```
10001101 and 11001101 = 10001101
```

Finally the `Xor()` method is used for an exclusive OR:

```
DisplayBits(bits1);
Console.Write(" xor ");
DisplayBits(bits2);
bits1.Xor(bits2);
Console.Write(" = ");
DisplayBits(bits1);
Console.WriteLine();
```

With the `Xor()` method, the resultant bits are set only if the bit was set either in the first or the second input, but not both:

```
11001101 xor 10001101 = 01000000
```

BitVector32

If you know the number of bits you need in advance, you can use the `BitVector32` structure instead of `BitArray`. `BitVector32` is more efficient, because it is a value type and stores the bits on the stack inside an integer. With a single integer you have a place for 32 bits. If you need more bits, you can use multiple `BitVector32` values or the `BitArray`. The `BitArray` can grow as needed; this is not an option with `BitVector32`.

The next table shows the members of `BitVector` that are very different from `BitArray`.

BitVector Members	Description
`Data`	The property `Data` returns the data behind the `BitVector32` as integer.
`Item`	The values for the `BitVector32` can be set using an indexer. The indexer is overloaded — you can get and set the values using a mask or a section of type `BitVector32.Section`.
`CreateMask()`	`CreateMask()` is a static method that you can use to create a mask for accessing specific bits in the `BitVector32`.
`CreateSection()`	`CreateSection()` is a static method that you can use to create several sections within the 32 bits.

The sample code creates a `BitVector32` with the default constructor, where all 32 bits are initialized to `false`. Then masks are created to access the bits inside the bit vector. The first call to `CreateMask()` creates a mask to access the first bit. After `CreateMask()` is invoked, `bit1` has a value of 1. Invoking `CreateMask()` once more and passing the first mask as a parameter to `CreateMask()` returns a mask to access the second bit, which is 2. `bit3` then has a value of 4 to access bit number 3. `bit4` has a value of 8 to access bit number 4.

Then the masks are used with the indexer to access the bits inside the bit vector and set fields accordingly:

```
BitVector32 bits1 = new BitVector32();
int bit1 = BitVector32.CreateMask();
int bit2 = BitVector32.CreateMask(bit1);
int bit3 = BitVector32.CreateMask(bit2);
int bit4 = BitVector32.CreateMask(bit3);
int bit5 = BitVector32.CreateMask(bit4);

bits1[bit1] = true;
bits1[bit2] = false;
bits1[bit3] = true;
bits1[bit4] = true;
bits1[bit5] = true;
Console.WriteLine(bits1);
```

The `BitVector32` has an overridden `ToString()` method that not only displays the name of the class but also 1 or 0 if the bits are set or not, respectively:

```
BitVector32{00000000000000000000000000011101}
```

Instead of creating a mask with the `CreateMask()` method, you can define the mask yourself; you can also set multiple bits at once. The hexadecimal value `abcdef` is the same as the binary value `1010 1011 1100 1101 1110 1111`. All the bits defined with this value are set:

```
bits1[0xabcdef] = true;
Console.WriteLine(bits1);
```

With the output shown you can verify the bits that are set:

```
BitVector32{00000000101010111100110111101111}
```

Separating the 32 bits to different sections can be extremely useful. For example, an IPv4 address is defined as a 4-byte number that is stored inside an integer. You can split the integer by defining four sections. With a multicast IP message, several 32-bit values are used. One of these 32-bit values is separated in these sections: 16 bits for the number of sources, 8 bits for a querier's query interval code, 3 bits for a querier's robustness variable, a 1-bit suppress flag, and 4 bits that are reserved. You can also define your own bit meanings to save memory.

The example simulates receiving the value `0x79abcdef` and passes this value to the constructor of `BitVector32`, so that the bits are set accordingly:

```
int received = 0x79abcdef;

BitVector32 bits2 = new BitVector32(received);
Console.WriteLine(bits2);
```

The bits are shown on the console as initialized:

```
BitVector32{01111001101010111100110111101111}
```

Then six sections are created. The first section requires 12 bits, as defined by the hexadecimal value `0xfff` (12 bits are set); section B requires 8 bits; section C, 4 bits; section D and E, 3 bits; and section F, 2 bits. The first call to `CreateSection()` just receives `0xfff` to allocate the first 12 bits. With the second call to `CreateSection()`, the first section is passed as an argument, so that the next section continues where the first section ended. `CreateSection()` returns a value of type `BitVector32.Section` that contains the offset and the mask for the section.

```
// sections: FF EEE DDD CCCC BBBBBBBB
// AAAAAAAAAAAA
BitVector32.Section sectionA =
      BitVector32.CreateSection(0xfff);
BitVector32.Section sectionB =
      BitVector32.CreateSection(0xff,
      sectionA);
BitVector32.Section sectionC =
      BitVector32.CreateSection(0xf,
      sectionB);
BitVector32.Section sectionD =
      BitVector32.CreateSection(0x7,
      sectionC);
BitVector32.Section sectionE =
      BitVector32.CreateSection(0x7,
      sectionD);
BitVector32.Section sectionF =
      BitVector32.CreateSection(0x3,
      sectionE);
```

Passing a `BitVector32.Section` to the indexer of the `BitVector32` returns an `int` just mapped to the section of the bit vector. Here, a helper method, `IntToBinaryString()`, retrieves a string representation of the `int` number:

```
Console.WriteLine("Section A: " +
      IntToBinaryString(bits2[sectionA],
      true));
Console.WriteLine("Section B: " +
      IntToBinaryString(bits2[sectionB],
      true));
Console.WriteLine("Section C: " +
      IntToBinaryString(bits2[sectionC],
      true));
Console.WriteLine("Section D: " +
      IntToBinaryString(bits2[sectionD],
      true));
Console.WriteLine("Section E: " +
      IntToBinaryString(bits2[sectionE],
      true));
Console.WriteLine("Section F: " +
      IntToBinaryString(bits2[sectionF],
      true));
```

The method `IntToBinaryString()` receives the bits in an integer and returns a string representation containing 0 and 1. With the implementation, 32 bits of the integer are iterated through. In the iteration, if the bit is set, 1 is appended to the `StringBuilder`; otherwise, 0 is appended. Within the loop, a bit shift happens to check if the next bit is set.

```
static string IntToBinaryString(int bits,
      bool removeTrailingZero)
   {
      StringBuilder sb = new StringBuilder(32);

      for (int i = 0; i < 32; i++)
      {
         if ((bits & 0x80000000) != 0)
         {
            sb.Append("1");
         }
         else
         {
            sb.Append("0");
         }
         bits = bits << 1;
      }
      string s = sb.ToString();
      if (removeTrailingZero)
      {
         return s.TrimStart('0');
      }
      else
      {
         return s;
      }
   }
```

The result displays the bit representation of sections A to F, which you can now verify with the value that was passed into the bit vector:

```
Section A: 110111101111
Section B: 10111100
Section C: 1010
Section D: 1
Section E: 111
Section F: 1
```

Performance

Many collection classes offer the same functionality as others; for example, `SortedList` offers nearly the same features as `SortedDictionary`. However, often there's a big difference in performance. Whereas one collection consumes less memory, the other collection class is faster with retrieval of elements. In the MSDN documentation, you often find performance hints with methods of the collection giving you information about the time the operation represents in *big-O* notation:

```
O(1)
O(log n)
O(n)
```

O(1) means that the time this operation needs is constant no matter how many items are in the collection. For example, the `ArrayList` has an `Add()` method with O(1) behavior. No matter how many elements are in the list, it always takes the same time when adding a new element to the end of the list. The `Count` property gives the number of items, so it is easy to find the end of the list.

O(n) means that for every element in the collection the same amount of additional time is needed. The `Add()` method of `ArrayList` can be an O(n) operation if a reallocation of the collection is required. Changing the capacity causes the copying of the list, and the time for the copy increases linearly with every element.

O(log n) means that the time needed for the operation increases with every element in the collection. But the increase of time for every element is not linear but logarithmic. `SortedDictionary<TKey,TValue>` has O(log n) behavior for inserting operations inside the collection; `SortedList<TKey,TValue>` has O(n) behavior for the same functionality. Here, `SortedDictionary<TKey,TValue>` is a lot faster because it is more efficient to insert elements into a tree structure than into a list.

The following table lists collection classes and their performance for different actions such as adding, inserting, and removing items. Using this table you can select the best collection class for the purpose of your use. The left column lists the collection class. The Add column gives timing information about adding items to the collection. The `List<T>` and the `HashSet<T>` classes define `Add` methods to add items to the collection. With other collection classes, there's a different method to add elements to the collection; for example, the `Stack<T>` class defines a `Push()` method, and the `Queue<T>` class defines an `Enqueue()` method. You can find this information in the table as well.

If there are multiple big-O values in a cell the reason is that if a collection needs to be resized, resizing takes a while. For example, with the `List<T>` class, adding items needs O(1). If the capacity of the collection is not large enough and the collection needs to be resized, the resize requires O(n) time. The larger the collection is, the longer the resize operation takes. It's best to avoid resizes by setting the capacity of the collection to a value that can hold all elements.

If the cell content is *na*, this means that this operation is *not applicable* with this collection type.

Collection	**Add**	**Insert**	**Remove**	**Item**	**Sort**	**Find**
`List<T>`	O(1) or O(n) if the collection must be resized	O(n)	O(n)	O(1)	O (n log n), worst case O(n ^ 2)	O(n)
`Stack<T>`	`Push()`, O(1) or O(n) if the stack must be resized	na	`Pop()`, O(1)	na	na	na
`Queue<T>`	`Enqueue()`, O(1) or O(n) if the queue must be resized	na	`Dequeue()`, O(1)	na	na	na
`HashSet<T>`	O(1) or O(n) if the set must be resized	`Add()` O(1) or O(n)	O(1)	na	na	na
`LinkedList<T>`	`AddLast()` O(1)	`AddAfter()` O(1)	O(1)	na	na	O(n)

Collection	Add	Insert	Remove	Item	Sort	Find
`Dictionary <TKey, TValue>`	O(1) or O(n)	na	O(1)	O(1)	na	na
`SortedDictionary <TKey, TValue>`	O(log n)	na	O(log n)	O(log n)	na	na
`SortedList <TKey, TValue>`	O(n) for unsorted data, O(log n) for end of list O(n) if resize is needed	na	O(n)	O(log n) to read, write O(log n) if the key is in the list, O(n) if the key is not in the list	na	na

Summary

This chapter took a look at working with different kinds of collections. Arrays are fixed in size, but you can use lists for dynamically growing collections. For accessing elements on a first-in, first-out basis, there's a queue, and there's a stack for last-in, first-out operations. Linked lists allow for fast inserting and removing of elements but are slow for searching. With keys and value, you can use dictionaries, which are fast for searching and inserting elements. A set (which has the name `HashSet<T>`) is for unique items that are not ordered.

In this chapter, you've seen a lot of interfaces and their use for accessing and sorting collections. You've also seen some specialized collections, such as `BitArray` and `BitVector32`, which are optimized for working with a collection of bits.

Chapter 11 gives you details about Language Integrated Query (LINQ), the major new language extensions of C# 3.0.

11

Language Integrated Query

LINQ (Language Integrated Query) is the most important new feature of C# 3.0 and .NET 3.5. LINQ integrates query syntax inside the C# programming language and makes it possible to access different data sources with the same syntax. LINQ makes this possible by offering an abstraction layer.

This chapter gives you the core foundation of LINQ and the language extensions for C# 3.0 that make the new features possible. The topics of this chapter are:

- Traditional queries across objects using `List<T>`
- Extension methods
- Lambda expressions
- LINQ query
- Standard query operators
- Expression trees
- LINQ providers

This chapter gives you the core foundation of LINQ. For using LINQ across the database you should read Chapter 27, "LINQ to SQL." To query XML data read Chapter 29, "LINQ to XML," after reading this chapter.

LINQ Overview

Before getting into the features of LINQ, this section uses an example to show how queries across objects were done before LINQ was available. As you read on, the query will evolve to show how the LINQ query is reached. By going through the steps you will know what's behind the LINQ query.

The example in this chapter is based on Formula-1 world champions. Queries are done across a list of `Racer` objects. The first query gets all Formula-1 champions from Brazil in the order of races won.

Query using List<T>

The first variant of a filter and sort is to search data in a list of type `List<T>`. Before the search can start, the object type and the list must be prepared.

For the object, the type `Racer` is defined. `Racer` defines several properties and an overloaded `ToString()` method to display a racer in a string format. This class implements the interface `IFormattable` to support different variants of format strings, and the interface `IComparable<Racer>`, which can be used to sort a list of racers based on the `LastName`. For doing more advanced queries, the class `Racer` contains not only single value properties such as `FirstName`, `LastName`, `Wins`, `Country`, and `Starts`, but also multivalue properties such as `Cars` and `Years`. The `Years` property lists all the years of the championship title. Some racers have won more than one title. The `Cars` property is used to list all the cars that have been used by the driver during the title years.

```
using System;
using System.Text;

namespace Wrox.ProCSharp.LINQ
{
   [Serializable]
   public class Racer : IComparable<Racer>, IFormattable
   {
      public string FirstName {get; set;}
      public string LastName {get; set;}
      public int Wins {get; set;}
      public string Country {get; set;}
      public int Starts {get; set;}
      public string[] Cars { get; set; }
      public int[] Years { get; set; }

      public override string ToString()
      {
         return String.Format("{0} {1}",
               FirstName, LastName);
      }

      public int CompareTo(Racer other)
      {
         return this.LastName.CompareTo(
               other.LastName);
      }

      public string ToString(string format)
      {
         return ToString(format, null);
      }

      public string ToString(string format,
            IFormatProvider formatProvider)
      {
         switch (format)
         {
            case null:
            case "N":
               return ToString();
```

```
                    case "F":
                        return FirstName;
                    case "L":
                        return LastName;
                    case "C":
                        return Country;
                    case "S":
                        return Starts.ToString();
                    case "W":
                        return Wins.ToString();
                    case "A":
                        return String.Format("{0} {1}, {2};" +
                              " starts: {3}, wins: {4}",
                              FirstName, LastName, Country,
                              Starts, Wins);
                    default:
                        throw new FormatException(String.Format(
                            "Format {0} not supported", format));
                }
            }
        }
    }
```

The class `Formula1` returns a list of racers in the method `GetChampions()`. The list is filled with all Formula-1 champions from the years 1950 to 2007:

```
using System;
using System.Collections.Generic;

namespace Wrox.ProCSharp.LINQ
{
    public static class Formula1
    {
        public static IList<Racer> GetChampions()
        {
            List<Racer> racers = new List<Racer>(40);
            racers.Add(new Racer() { FirstName = "Nino",
                  LastName = "Farina", Country = "Italy",
                                Starts = 33, Wins = 5,
                  Years = new int[] { 1950 },
                  Cars = new string[] { "Alfa Romeo" } });
            racers.Add(new Racer() {
                                FirstName = "Alberto",
                  LastName = "Ascari", Country = "Italy",
                  Starts = 32, Wins = 10,
                  Years = new int[] { 1952, 1953 },
                  Cars = new string[] { "Ferrari" } });
            racers.Add(new Racer() {
                  FirstName = "Juan Manuel",
                  LastName = "Fangio",
                  Country = "Argentina", Starts = 51,
                  Wins = 24, Years = new int[]
                        { 1951, 1954, 1955, 1956, 1957 },
                  Cars = new string[] { "Alfa Romeo",
```

(continued)

(continued)

```
                "Maserati", "Mercedes",
                "Ferrari" } });
racers.Add(new Racer() { FirstName = "Mike",
      LastName = "Hawthorn", Country = "UK",
      Starts = 45, Wins = 3,
      Years = new int[] { 1958 },
      Cars = new string[] { "Ferrari" } });
racers.Add(new Racer() { FirstName = "Phil",
      LastName = "Hill", Country = "USA",
      Starts = 48, Wins = 3,
      Years = new int[] { 1961 },
      Cars = new string[] { "Ferrari" } });
racers.Add(new Racer() { FirstName = "John",
      LastName = "Surtees", Country = "UK",
      Starts = 111, Wins = 6,
      Years = new int[] { 1964 },
      Cars = new string[] { "Ferrari" } });
racers.Add(new Racer() { FirstName = "Jim",
      LastName = "Clark", Country = "UK",
      Starts = 72, Wins = 25,
      Years = new int[] { 1963, 1965 },
      Cars = new string[] { "Lotus" } });
racers.Add(new Racer() { FirstName = "Jack",
      LastName = "Brabham",
               Country = "Australia", Starts = 125,
               Wins = 14,
      Years = new int[] { 1959, 1960, 1966 },
      Cars = new string[] { "Cooper",
            "Brabham" } });
racers.Add(new Racer() { FirstName = "Denny",
      LastName = "Hulme",
      Country = "New Zealand", Starts = 112,
      Wins = 8,
      Years = new int[] { 1967 },
      Cars = new string[] { "Brabham" } });
racers.Add(new Racer() { FirstName = "Graham",
      LastName = "Hill", Country = "UK",
      Starts = 176, Wins = 14,
      Years = new int[] { 1962, 1968 },
      Cars = new string[] { "BRM", "Lotus" }
      });
racers.Add(new Racer() { FirstName = "Jochen",
      LastName = "Rindt", Country = "Austria",
      Starts = 60, Wins = 6,
      Years = new int[] { 1970 },
      Cars = new string[] { "Lotus" } });
racers.Add(new Racer() { FirstName = "Jackie",
      LastName = "Stewart", Country = "UK",
      Starts = 99, Wins = 27,
      Years = new int[] { 1969, 1971, 1973 },
      Cars = new string[] { "Matra",
            "Tyrrell" } });
```

```
racers.Add(new Racer() {
      FirstName = "Emerson",
      LastName = "Fittipaldi",
      Country = "Brazil", Starts = 143,
      Wins = 14, Years = new int[] { 1972,
            1974 },
      Cars = new string[] { "Lotus",
            "McLaren" } });
racers.Add(new Racer() { FirstName = "James",
      LastName = "Hunt", Country = "UK",
      Starts = 91, Wins = 10,
      Years = new int[] { 1976 },
      Cars = new string[] { "McLaren" } });
racers.Add(new Racer() { FirstName = "Mario",
      LastName = "Andretti", Country = "USA",
      Starts = 128, Wins = 12,
      Years = new int[] { 1978 },
      Cars = new string[] { "Lotus" } });
racers.Add(new Racer() { FirstName = "Jody",
      LastName = "Scheckter",
      Country = "South Africa", Starts = 112,
      Wins = 10,
      Years = new int[] { 1979 },
      Cars = new string[] { "Ferrari" } });
racers.Add(new Racer() { FirstName = "Alan",
      LastName = "Jones",
      Country = "Australia", Starts = 115,
      Wins = 12,
      Years = new int[] { 1980 },
      Cars = new string[] { "Williams" } });
racers.Add(new Racer() { FirstName = "Keke",
      LastName = "Rosberg",
               Country = "Finland", Starts = 114,
               Wins = 5,
      Years = new int[] { 1982 },
      Cars = new string[] { "Williams" } });
racers.Add(new Racer() { FirstName = "Niki",
      LastName = "Lauda", Country = "Austria",
      Starts = 173, Wins = 25,
      Years = new int[] { 1975, 1977, 1984 },
      Cars = new string[] { "Ferrari",
      "McLaren" } });
racers.Add(new Racer() { FirstName = "Nelson",
      LastName = "Piquet", Country = "Brazil",
      Starts = 204, Wins = 23,
      Years = new int[] { 1981, 1983, 1987 },
      Cars = new string[] { "Brabham",
      "Williams" } });
racers.Add(new Racer() { FirstName = "Ayrton",
      LastName = "Senna", Country = "Brazil",
      Starts = 161, Wins = 41,
      Years = new int[] { 1988, 1990, 1991 },
      Cars = new string[] { "McLaren" } });
racers.Add(new Racer() { FirstName = "Nigel",
      LastName = "Mansell", Country = "UK",
```

(continued)

(continued)

```
            Starts = 187, Wins = 31,
            Years = new int[] { 1992 },
            Cars = new string[] { "Williams" } });
        racers.Add(new Racer() { FirstName = "Alain",
            LastName = "Prost", Country = "France",
            Starts = 197, Wins = 51,
            Years = new int[] { 1985, 1986, 1989,
            1993 },
            Cars = new string[] { "McLaren",
            "Williams" } });
        racers.Add(new Racer() { FirstName = "Damon",
            LastName = "Hill", Country = "UK",
            Starts = 114, Wins = 22,
            Years = new int[] { 1996 },
            Cars = new string[] { "Williams" } });
        racers.Add(new Racer() {
            FirstName = "Jacques",
            LastName = "Villeneuve",
            Country = "Canada", Starts = 165,
            Wins = 11, Years = new int[] { 1997 },
            Cars = new string[] { "Williams" } });
        racers.Add(new Racer() { FirstName = "Mika",
            LastName = "Hakkinen",
            Country = "Finland", Starts = 160,
            Wins = 20, Years = new int[] { 1998,
            1999 },
            Cars = new string[] { "McLaren" } });
        racers.Add(new Racer() {
            FirstName = "Michael",
            LastName = "Schumacher",
            Country = "Germany", Starts = 250,
            Wins = 91,
            Years = new int[] { 1994, 1995, 2000,
            2001, 2002, 2003, 2004 },
            Cars = new string[] { "Benetton",
            "Ferrari" } });
        racers.Add(new Racer() {
            FirstName = "Fernando",
            LastName = "Alonso", Country = "Spain",
            Starts = 105, Wins = 19,
            Years = new int[] { 2005, 2006 },
            Cars = new string[] { "Renault" } });
        racers.Add(new Racer() { FirstName = "Kimi",
            LastName = "Räikkönen",
            Country = "Finland", Starts = 122,
            Wins = 15, Years = new int[] { 2007 },
            Cars = new string[] { "Ferrari" } });
        return racers;
    }
  }
}
```

For later queries where queries are done across multiple lists, the `GetConstructorChampions()` method that follows returns the list of all constructor championships. Constructor championships have been around since 1958.

```
public static IList<Team>
      GetContructorChampions()
{
   List<Team> teams = new List<Team>(20);
   teams.Add(new Team() { Name = "Vanwall",
         Years = new int[] { 1958 } });
   teams.Add(new Team() { Name = "Cooper",
         Years = new int[] { 1959, 1960 } });
   teams.Add(new Team() { Name = "Ferrari",
         Years = new int[] { 1961, 1964, 1975,
         1976, 1977, 1979, 1982, 1983, 1999,
         2000, 2001, 2002, 2003, 2004, 2007 } });
   teams.Add(new Team() { Name = "BRM",
         Years = new int[] { 1962 } });
   teams.Add(new Team() { Name = "Lotus",
         Years = new int[] { 1963, 1965, 1968,
         1970, 1972, 1973, 1978 } });
   teams.Add(new Team() { Name = "Brabham",
         Years = new int[] { 1966, 1967 } });
   teams.Add(new Team() { Name = "Matra",
         Years = new int[] { 1969 } });
   teams.Add(new Team() { Name = "Tyrrell",
         Years = new int[] { 1971 } });
   teams.Add(new Team() { Name = "McLaren",
         Years = new int[] { 1974, 1984, 1985,
         1988, 1989, 1990, 1991, 1998 } });
   teams.Add(new Team() { Name = "Williams",
         Years = new int[] { 1980, 1981, 1986,
         1987, 1992, 1993, 1994, 1996, 1997 } });
   teams.Add(new Team() { Name = "Benetton",
         Years = new int[] { 1995 } });
   teams.Add(new Team() { Name = "Renault",
         Years = new int[] { 2005, 2006 } });
   return teams;
}
```

Now let's get into the heart of the object query. First, you need to get the list of objects with the static method `GetChampions()`. The list is filled into the generic class `List<T>`. The `FindAll()` method of this class accepts a `Predicate<T>` delegate that can be implemented as an anonymous method. Only the racers whose `Country` property is set to `Brazil` should be returned. Next, the resulting list is sorted with the `Sort()` method. The sort should not be done by the `LastName` property as is the default sort implementation of the `Racer` class, but you can pass a delegate of type `Comparison<T>`. It is again implemented as an anonymous method to compare the number of wins. Using the `r2` object and comparing it with `r1` does a descending sort as is required. The `foreach` statement finally iterates through all `Racer` objects in the resulting sorted collection.

```
private static void TraditionalQuery()
{
   List<Racer> racers =
         new List<Racer>(Formula1.GetChampions());
   List<Racer> brazilRacers = racers.FindAll(
      delegate(Racer r)
      {
         return r.Country == "Brazil";
      });
   brazilRacers.Sort(
      delegate(Racer r1, Racer r2)
      {
         return r2.Wins.CompareTo(r1.Wins);
      });
   foreach (Racer r in brazilRacers)
   {
      Console.WriteLine("{0:A}", r);
   }
}
```

The list displayed shows all champions from Brazil, sorted by the number of wins:

```
Ayrton Senna, Brazil; starts: 161, wins: 41
Nelson Piquet, Brazil; starts: 204, wins: 23
Emerson Fittipaldi, Brazil; starts: 143, wins: 14
```

Sorting and filtering object lists is discussed in Chapter 10, "Collections."

In the previous sample, methods from the `List<T>` class, `FindAll()` and `Sort()` have been used. It would be great to get the functionality of these methods with any collection and not just `List<T>`. This is where extension methods come into play. Extension methods are new to C# 3.0. This is the first change of the previous sample that will lead toward LINQ.

Extension Methods

Extension methods make it possible to write a method to a class that doesn't offer the method at first. You can also add a method to any class that implements a specific interface, so multiple classes can make use of the same implementation.

For example, wouldn't you like to have a `Foo()` method with the `String` class? The `String` class is sealed, so it is not possible to inherit from this class. You can do an extension method, as shown:

```
public static class StringExtension
{
   public static void Foo(this string s)
   {
      Console.WriteLine("Foo invoked for {0}", s);
   }
}
```

An extension method is declared in a static class. An extension method is defined as a static method where the first parameter defines the type it extends. The `Foo()` method extends the `string` class, as is defined with the first parameter. For differentiating extension methods from normal static methods, the extension method also requires the `this` keyword with the first parameter.

Indeed, it is now possible to use the `Foo()` method with the `string` type:

```
string s = "Hello";
s.Foo();
```

The result shows `Foo invoked for Hello` in the console, because `Hello` is the string passed to the `Foo()` method.

This might appear to be breaking object-oriented rules because a new method is defined for a type without changing the type. However, this is not the case. The extension method cannot access private members of the type it extends. Calling an extension method is just a new syntax of invoking a static method. With the string you can get the same result by calling the method `Foo()` this way:

```
string s = "Hello";
StringExtension.Foo(s);
```

To invoke the static method, write the class name followed by the method name. Extension methods are a different way to invoke static methods. You don't have to supply the name of the class where the static method is defined. Instead, the static method is taken because of the parameter type. You just have to import the namespace that contains the class to get the `Foo()` extension method in the scope of the `String` class.

One of the classes that define LINQ extension methods is `Enumerable` in the namespace `System.Linq`. You just have to import the namespace to open the scope of the extension methods of this class. A sample implementation of the `Where()` extension method is shown here. The first parameter of the `Where()` method that includes the `this` keyword is of type `IEnumerable<T>`. This way the `Where()` method can be used with every type that implements `IEnumerable<T>`. To mention just a few examples, arrays and `List<T>` implement `IEnumerable<T>`. The second parameter is a `Func<T, bool>` delegate that references a method that returns a Boolean value and requires a parameter of type `T`. This predicate is invoked within the implementation to examine if the item from the `IEnumerable<T>` source should go into the destination collection. If the method is referenced by the delegate, the `yield return` statement returns the item from the source to the destination.

```
public static IEnumerable<TSource> Where<TSource>(
      this IEnumerable<TSource> source,
      Func<TSource, bool> predicate)
{
   foreach (TSource item in source)
      if (predicate(item))
         yield return item;
}
```

Because `Where()` is implemented as a generic method, it works with any type that is contained in a collection. Any collection implementing `IEnumerable<T>` is supported.

The extension methods here are defined in the namespace `System.Linq` *in the assembly* `System.Core`.

Now it's possible to use the extension methods `Where()`, `OrderByDescending()`, and `Select()` from the class `Enumerable`. Because each of these methods returns `IEnumerable<TSource>`, it is possible to invoke one method after the other by using the previous result. With the arguments of the extension methods, anonymous methods that define the implementation for the delegate parameters are used.

```
private static void ExtensionMethods()
{
   List<Racer> champions =
      new List<Racer>(
         Formula1.GetChampions());
   IEnumerable<Racer> brazilChampions =
      champions.Where(
      delegate(Racer r)
```

(continued)

(continued)

```
        {
           return r.Country == "Brazil";
        }).OrderByDescending(
        delegate(Racer r)
        {
           return r.Wins;
        }).Select(
        delegate(Racer r)
        {
           return r;
        });

     foreach (Racer r in brazilChampions)
     {
        Console.WriteLine("{0:A}", r);
     }
  }
```

Lambda Expressions

C# 3.0 has a new syntax for anonymous methods — Lambda expressions. Instead of passing anonymous methods to the `Where()`, `OrderByDescending()`, and `Select()` methods, the same can be done using Lambda expressions.

Here the previous example is changed to make use of Lambda expressions. Now the syntax is shorter and also easier to understand due to the removal of the `return` statement, the parameter types, and the curly brackets.

Lambda expressions are covered in detail in Chapter 7, "Delegates and Events." Because of the importance of Lambda expressions with LINQ, here's a reminder about the syntax. For more details you should read Chapter 7.

By comparing Lambda expressions to anonymous delegates you can find many similarities. To the left of the Lambda operator => are parameters. It's ok not to add the parameter types because they are resolved by the compiler. The right side of the Lambda operator defines the implementation. With anonymous methods, curly brackets and the return statement are required. With Lambda expressions the syntax elements are not required because they are done by the compiler in any case. If you have more than one statement on the right side of the Lambda operator, curly brackets and the return statement are possible.

```
private static void LambdaExpressions()
{
   IEnumerable<Racer> brazilChampions =
      Formula1.GetChampions().
      Where(r => r.Country == "Brazil").
      OrderByDescending(r => r.Wins).
      Select(r => r);

   foreach (Racer r in brazilChampions)
   {
      Console.WriteLine("{0:A}", r);
   }
}
```

Return statements and curly brackets are optional when using Lambda expressions without parameter types. You can still use these language constructs with Lambda expressions. This is explained in Chapter 7, "Delegates and Events," where Lambda expressions are introduced.

LINQ Query

The last change that needs to be done is to define the query using the new LINQ query notation. The statement `from r in Formula1.GetChampions() where r.Country == "Brazil" orderby r .Wins descending select r;` is a LINQ query. The clauses `from`, `where`, `orderby`, `descending`, and `select` are predefined keywords in this query. The compiler maps these clauses to extension methods. The syntax used here is using the extension methods `Where()`, `OrderByDescending()`, and `Select()`. Lambda expressions are passed to the parameters.

`where r.Country == "Brazil"` is converted to `Where(r => r.Country == "Brazil")` `.orderby r.Wins descending` is converted to `OrderByDescending(r => r.Wins)`.

```
private static void LinqQuery()
{
   var query = from r in Formula1.GetChampions()
               where r.Country == "Brazil"
               orderby r.Wins descending
               select r;

   foreach (Racer r in query)
   {
      Console.WriteLine("{0:A}", r);
   }
}
```

The LINQ query is a simplified query notation inside the C# language. The compiler compiles the query expression to invoke extension methods. The query expression is just a nice syntax from C#, but changes to the underlying IL code are not needed.

The query expression must begin with a `from` clause and end with a `select` or `group` clause. In between you can optionally use `where`, `orderby`, `join`, `let`, and additional `from` clauses.

It is important to note that the variable `query` just has the LINQ query assigned to it. The query is not done by this assignment. The query is done as soon as the query is accessed using the `foreach` loop. This is discussed in more detail later.

With the samples so far you've seen new C# 3.0 language features and how they relate to the LINQ query. Now is the time to dig deeper into the features of LINQ.

Deferred Query Execution

When the query expression is defined during runtime, the query does not run. The query runs when the items are iterated.

Let's have a look once more at the extension method `Where()`. This extension method makes use of the `yield return` statement to return the elements where the predicate is true. Because the `yield return` statement is used, the compiler creates an enumerator and returns the items as soon as they are accessed from the enumeration.

```
public static IEnumerable<T> Where<T>(this IEnumerable<T> source,
Func<T, bool> predicate)
{
   foreach (T item in source)
      if (predicate(item))
         yield return item;
}
```

This has a very interesting and important effect. With the following example a collection of `String` elements is created and filled with the name `arr`. Next, a query is defined to get all names from the collection where the item starts with the letter `J`. The collection should also be sorted. The iteration does not happen when the query is defined. Instead, the iteration happens with the `foreach` statement, where all items are iterated. Only one element of the collection fulfills the requirements of the `where` expression by starting with the letter J: `Juan`. After the iteration is done and `Juan` is written to the console, four new names are added to the collection. Then the iteration is done once more.

```
List<string> names = new List<string>
      { "Nino", "Alberto", "Juan", "Mike",
        "Phil" };

var namesWithJ = from n in names
   where n.StartsWith("J")
   orderby n
   select n;

Console.WriteLine("First iteration");
foreach (string name in namesWithJ)
{
   Console.WriteLine(name);
}
Console.WriteLine();

names.Add("John");
names.Add("Jim");
names.Add("Jack");
names.Add("Denny");

Console.WriteLine("Second iteration");
foreach (string name in namesWithJ)
{
   Console.WriteLine(name);
}
```

Because the iteration does not happen when the query is defined, but it does happen with every `foreach`, changes can be seen, as the output from the application demonstrates:

```
First iteration
Juan

Second iteration
Jack
Jim
John
Juan
```

Of course, you also must be aware that the extension methods are invoked every time the query is used within an iteration. Most of the time this is very practical, because you can detect changes in the source data. However, there are situations where this is impractical. You can change this behavior by invoking the extension methods `ToArray()`, `ToEnumerable()`, `ToList()`, and the like. In the example, you can see that `ToList` iterates through the collection immediately and returns a collection implementing `IList<string>`. The returned list is then iterated through twice; in between iterations, the data source gets new names.

```
List<string> names = new List<string>
      { "Nino", "Alberto", "Juan", "Mike",
        "Phil" };
IList<string> namesWithJ = (from n in names
   where n.StartsWith("J")
   orderby n
   select n).ToList();

Console.WriteLine("First iteration");
foreach (string name in namesWithJ)
{
   Console.WriteLine(name);
}
Console.WriteLine();

names.Add("John");
names.Add("Jim");
names.Add("Jack");
names.Add("Denny");

Console.WriteLine("Second iteration");
foreach (string name in namesWithJ)
{
   Console.WriteLine(name);
}
```

In the result, you can see that in between the iterations the output stays the same although the collection values changed:

```
First iteration
Juan

Second iteration
Juan
```

Standard Query Operators

`Where`, `OrderByDescending`, and `Select` are only few of the query operators defined by LINQ. The LINQ query defines a declarative syntax for the most common operators. There are many more standard query operators available.

The following table lists the standard query operators defined by LINQ.

Standard Query Operators	Description
`Where OfType<TResult>`	*Filtering* operators define a restriction to the elements returned. With the `Where` query operator you can use a predicate, for example, defined by a Lambda expression that returns a bool. `OfType<TResult>` filters the elements based on the type and returns only the elements of the type `TResult`.
`Select SelectMany`	*Projection* operators are used to transform an object into a new object of a different type. `Select` and `SelectMany` define a projection to select values of the result based on a selector function.
`OrderBy ThenBy OrderByDescending ThenByDescending Reverse`	*Sorting* operators change the order of elements returned. `OrderBy` sorts values in ascending order; `OrderByDescending` sorts values in descending order. `ThenBy` and `ThenByDescending` operators are used for a secondary sort if the first sort gives similar results. `Reverse` reverses the elements in the collection.
`Join GroupJoin`	*Join* operators are used to combine collections that might not be directly related to each other. With the `Join` operator a join of two collections based on key selector functions can be done. This is similar to the JOIN you know from SQL. The `GroupJoin` operator joins two collections and groups the results.
`GroupBy`	*Grouping* operators put the data into groups. The `GroupBy` operator groups elements with a common key.
`Any All Contains`	*Quantifier* operators return a Boolean value if elements of the sequence satisfy a specific condition. `Any`, `All`, and `Contains` are quantifier operators. `Any` determines if any element in the collection satisfies a predicate function; `All` determines if all elements in the collection satisfy a predicate. `Contains` checks whether a specific element is in the collection. These operators return a Boolean value.
`Take Skip TakeWhile SkipWhile`	*Partitioning* operators return a subset of the collection. `Take`, `Skip`, `TakeWhile`, and `SkipWhile` are partitioning operators. With these, you get a partial result. With `Take`, you have to specify the number of elements to take from the collection; `Skip` ignores the specified number of elements and takes the rest. `TakeWhile` takes the elements as long as a condition is true.
`Distinct Union Intersect Except`	*Set* operators return a collection set. `Distinct` removes duplicates from a collection. With the exception of `Distinct`, the other set operators require two collections. `Union` returns unique elements that appear in either of the two collections. `Intersect` returns elements that appear in both collections. `Except` returns elements that appear in just one collection.

Standard Query Operators	Description
`First FirstOrDefault Last LastOrDefault ElementAt ElementAtOrDefault Single SingleOrDefault`	*Element* operators return just one element. `First` returns the first element that satisfies a condition. `FirstOrDefault` is similar to `First`, but it returns a default value of the type if the element is not found. `Last` returns the last element that satisfies a condition. With `ElementAt`, you specify the position of the element to return. `Single` returns only the one element that satisfies a condition. If more than one element satisfies the condition, an exception is thrown.
`Count Sum Min Max Average Aggregate`	*Aggregate* operators compute a single value from a collection. With aggregate operators, you can get the sum of all values, the number of all elements, the element with the lowest or highest value, an average number, and so on.
`ToArray AsEnumerable ToList ToDictionary Cast<TResult>`	*Conversion* operators convert the collection to an array: `IEnumerable`, `IList`, `IDictionary`, and so on.
`Empty Range Repeat`	*Generation* operators return a new sequence. The collection is empty using the `Empty` operator, `Range` returns a sequence of numbers, and `Repeat` returns a collection with one repeated value.

Following are examples of using these operators.

Filtering

Have a look at some examples for a query.

With the `where` clause, you can combine multiple expressions; for example, get only the racers from Brazil and Austria who won more than 15 races. The result type of the expression passed to the `where` clause just needs to be of type bool:

```
var racers = from r in Formula1.GetChampions()
             where r.Wins > 15 &&
                (r.Country == "Brazil" ||
                 r.Country == "Austria")
             select r;

foreach (var r in racers)
{
   Console.WriteLine("{0:A}", r);
}
```

Starting the program with this LINQ query returns Niki Lauda, Nelson Piquet, and Ayrton Senna as shown:

```
Niki Lauda, Austria, Starts: 173, Wins: 25
Nelson Piquet, Brazil, Starts: 204, Wins: 23
Ayrton Senna, Brazil, Starts: 161, Wins: 41
```

Not all queries can be done with the LINQ query. Not all extension methods are mapped to LINQ query clauses. Advanced queries require using extension methods. To better understand complex queries with extension methods it's good to see how simple queries are mapped. Using the extension methods `Where()` and `Select()` produces a query very similar to the LINQ query done before:

```
var racers = Formula1.GetChampions().
    Where(r => r.Wins > 15 &&
        (r.Country == "Brazil" ||
         r.Country == "Austria")).
    Select(r => r);
```

Filtering with Index

One example where you can't use the LINQ query is an overload of the `Where()` method. With an overload of the `Where()` method you can a pass a second parameter that is the index. The index is a counter for every result returned from the filter. You can use the index within the expression to do some calculation based on the index. Here the index is used within the code that is called by the `Where()` extension method to return only racers whose last name starts with A if the index is even:

```
var racers = Formula1.GetChampions().
   Where((r, index) =>
      r.LastName.StartsWith("A") &&
      index % 2 != 0);
foreach (var r in racers)
{
   Console.WriteLine("{0:A}", r);
}
```

All the racers with last names beginning with the letter A are Alberto Ascari, Mario Andretti, and Fernando Alonso. Because Mario Andretti is positioned within an index that is odd, he is not in the result:

```
Alberto Ascari, Italy; starts: 32, wins: 10
Fernando Alsonso, Spain; starts: 105, wins: 19
```

Type Filtering

For filtering based on a type you can use the `OfType()` extension method. Here the array data contains both `string` and `int` objects. Using the extension method `OfType()`, passing the string class to the generic parameter returns only the strings from the collection:

```
object[] data = { "one", 2, 3, "four", "five",
                  6 };
var query = data.OfType<string>();
foreach (var s in query)
{
   Console.WriteLine(s);
}
```

Running this code, the strings one, four, and five are displayed:

```
one
four
five
```

Compound from

If you need to do a filter based on a member of the object that itself is a sequence, you can use a compound `from`. The `Racer` class defines a property `Cars` where `Cars` is a string array. For a filter of all racers who were champions with a Ferrari, you can use the LINQ query as shown. The first `from` clause accesses the `Racer` objects returned from `Formula1.GetChampions()`. The second `from` clause accesses the `Cars` property of the `Racer` class to return all cars of type `string`. Next the cars are used with the `where` clause to filter only the racers who were champions with a Ferrari.

```
var ferrariDrivers = from r in
                     Formula1.GetChampions()
                     from c in r.Cars
                     where c == "Ferrari"
                     orderby r.LastName
                     select r.FirstName + " "
                        + r.LastName;
```

If you are curious about the result of this query, all Formula-1 champions driving a Ferrari are:

```
Alberto Ascari
Juan Manuel Fangio
Mike Hawthorn
Phil Hill
Niki Lauda
Jody Scheckter
Michael Schumacher
John Surtees
```

The C# compiler converts a compound `from` clause with a LINQ query to the `SelectMany()` extension method. `SelectMany()` can be used to iterate a sequence of a sequence. The overload of the `SelectMany` method that is used with the example is shown here:

```
public static IEnumerable<TResult> SelectMany<TSource, TCollection, TResult> (
      this IEnumerable<TSource> source,
      Func<TSource,
      IEnumerable<TCollection>> collectionSelector,
      Func<TSource, TCollection, TResult>
         resultSelector);
```

The first parameter is the implicit parameter that receives the sequence of `Racer` objects from the `GetChampions()` method. The second parameter is the `collectionSelector` delegate where the inner sequence is defined. With the Lambda expression `r => r.Cars` the collection of cars should be returned. The third parameter is a delegate that is now invoked for every car and receives the `Racer` and `Car` objects. The Lambda expression creates an anonymous type with a `Racer` and a `Car` property. As a result of this `SelectMany()` method the hierarchy of racers and cars is flattened and a collection of new objects of an anonymous type for every car is returned.

This new collection is passed to the `Where()` method so that only the racers driving a Ferrari are filtered. Finally, the `OrderBy()` and `Select()` methods are invoked.

```
var ferrariDrivers = Formula1.GetChampions().
    SelectMany(
      r => r.Cars,
      (r, c) => new { Racer = r, Car = c }).
      Where(r => r.Car == "Ferrari").
      OrderBy(r => r.Racer.LastName).
      Select(r => r.Racer.FirstName + " " +
         r.Racer.LastName);
```

Resolving the generic `SelectMany()` method to the types that are used here, the types are resolved as follows. In this case the source is of type `Racer`, the filtered collection is a `string` array, and of course the name of the anonymous type that is returned is not known and shown here as `TResult`:

```
public static IEnumerable<TResult> SelectMany<Racer, string, TResult> (
      this IEnumerable<Racer> source,
      Func<Racer, IEnumerable<string>> collectionSelector,
      Func<Racer, string, TResult> resultSelector);
```

Because the query was just converted from a LINQ query to extension methods, the result is the same as before.

Sorting

For sorting a sequence, the `orderby` clause was used already. Let's review the example from before with the `orderby descending` clause. Here the racers are sorted based on the number of wins as specified by the key selector in a descending order:

```
var racers = from r in Formula1.GetChampions()
             where r.Country == "Brazil"
             orderby r.Wins descending
             select r;
```

The `orderby` clause is resolved to the `OrderBy()` method, and the `orderby descending` clause is resolved to the `OrderBy Descending()` method:

```
var racers = Formula1.GetChampions().
   Where(r => r.Country == "Brazil").
   OrderByDescending(r => r.Wins).
   Select(r => r);
```

The `OrderBy()` and `OrderByDescending()` methods return `IOrderedEnumerable<TSource>`. This interface derives from the interface `IEnumerable<TSource>` but contains an additional method `CreateOrderedEnumerable<TSource>()`. This method is used for further ordering of the sequence. If two items are the same based on the key selector, ordering can continue with the `ThenBy()` and `ThenByDescending()` methods. These methods require an `IOrderedEnumerable<TSource>` to work on, but return this interface as well. So, you can add any number of `ThenBy()` and `ThenByDescending()` to sort the collection.

Using the LINQ query you just have to add all the different keys (with commas) for sorting to the `orderby` clause. Here the sort of all racers is done first based on the country, next on the last name, and finally on the first name. The `Take()` extension method that is added to the result of the LINQ query is used to take just the first 10 results.

```
var racers = (from r in
              Formula1.GetChampions()
              orderby r.Country, r.LastName,
                 r.FirstName
              select r).Take(10);
```

The sorted result is shown here:

```
Argentina: Fangio, Juan Manuel
Australia: Brabham, Jack
Australia: Jones, Alan
Austria: Lauda, Niki
Austria: Rindt, Jochen
Brazil: Fittipaldi, Emerson
```

```
Brazil: Piquet, Nelson
Brazil: Senna, Ayrton
Canada: Villeneuve, Jacques
Finland: Hakkinen, Mika
```

Doing the same with extension methods makes use of the `OrderBy()` and `ThenBy()` methods:

```
var racers = Formula1.GetChampions().
   OrderBy(r => r.Country).
   ThenBy(r => r.LastName).
   ThenBy(r => r.FirstName).
   Take(10);
```

Grouping

To group query results based on a key value, the `group` clause can be used. Now the Formula-1 champions should be grouped by the country, and the number of champions within a country should be listed. The clause `group r by r.Country into g` groups all the racers based on the `Country` property and defines a new identifier `g` that can be used later to access the group result information. The result from the `group` clause is ordered based on the extension method `Count()` that is applied on the group result, and if the count is the same the ordering is done based on the key, which is the country because this was the key used for grouping. The `where` clause filters the results based on groups that have at least two items, and the `select` clause creates an anonymous type with `Country` and `Count` properties.

```
var countries = from r in
      Formula1.GetChampions()
      group r by r.Country into g
      orderby g.Count() descending, g.Key
      where g.Count() >= 2
      select new { Country = g.Key,
                   Count = g.Count() };

foreach (var item in countries)
{
   Console.WriteLine("{0, -10} {1}",
      item.Country, item.Count);
}
```

The result displays the collection of objects with the `Country` and `Count` property:

```
UK         9
Brazil     3
Australia  2
Austria    2
Finland    2
Italy      2
USA        2
```

Doing the same with extension methods, the `groupby` clause is resolved to the `GroupBy()` method. What's interesting with the declaration of the `GroupBy()` method is that it returns an enumeration of objects implementing the `IGrouping` interface. The `IGrouping` interface defines the `Key` property, so you can access the key of the group after defining the call to this method:

```
public static IEnumerable<IGrouping<TKey, TSource>> GroupBy<TSource, TKey>(
      this IEnumerable<TSource> source,
      Func<TSource, TKey> keySelector);
```

The `group r by r.Country into g` clause is resolved to `GroupBy(r => r.Country)` and returns the group sequence. The group sequence is first ordered by the `OrderByDecending()` method, then by the `ThenBy()` method. Next the `Where()` and `Select()` methods that you already know are invoked.

```
var countries = Formula1.GetChampions().
    GroupBy(r => r.Country).
    OrderByDescending(g => g.Count()).
    ThenBy(g => g.Key).
    Where(g => g.Count() >= 2).
    Select(g => new { Country = g.Key,
                      Count = g.Count() });
```

Grouping with Nested Objects

If the grouped objects should contain nested sequences, you can do that by changing the anonymous type created by the `select` clause. With this example the returned countries should contain not only the properties for the name of the country and the number of racers, but also a sequence of the names of the racers. This sequence is assigned by using an inner `from/in` clause assigned to the `Racers` property. The inner `from` clause is using the group `g` to get all racers from the group, order them by the last name, and create a new string based on the first and last name.

```
var countries = from r in
                    Formula1.GetChampions()
                group r by r.Country into g
                orderby g.Count() descending, g.Key
                where g.Count() >= 2
                select new
                {
                   Country = g.Key,
                   Count = g.Count(),
                   Racers = from r1 in g
                            orderby r1.LastName
                            select r1.FirstName + " "
                            + r1.LastName
                };
foreach (var item in countries)
{
   Console.WriteLine("{0, -10} {1}",
      item.Country, item.Count);
   foreach (var name in item.Racers)
   {
      Console.Write("{0}; ", name);
   }
   Console.WriteLine();
}
```

The output now lists all champions from the specified countries:

```
UK         9
Jim Clark; Lewis Hamilton; Mike Hawthorn; Graham Hill; Damon Hill; James Hunt;
Nigel Mansell; Jackie Stewart; John Surtees;
Brazil     3
Emerson Fittipaldi; Nelson Piquet; Ayrton Senna;
Australia  2
```

```
Jack Brabham; Alan Jones;
Austria    2
Niki Lauda; Jochen Rindt;
Finland    2
Mika Hakkinen; Keke Rosberg;
Italy      2
Alberto Ascari; Nino Farina;
USA        2
Mario Andretti; Phil Hill;
```

Join

You can use the `join` clause to combine two sources based on specific criteria. But first, let's get two lists that should be joined. With Formula-1 there's a drivers and a constructors championship. The drivers are returned from the method `GetChampions()`, and the constructors are returned from the method `GetConstructorChampions()`. Now it would be interesting to get a list by the year where every year lists the driver and the constructor champion.

For doing this, first two queries for the racers and the teams are defined:

```
var racers = from r in Formula1.GetChampions()
             from y in r.Years
             where y > 2003
             select new
             {
                Year = y,
                Name = r.FirstName + " " +
                   r.LastName
             };

var teams = from t in
            Formula1.GetContructorChampions()
            from y in t.Years
            where y > 2003
            select new { Year = y,
                         Name = t.Name };
```

Using these two queries, a join is done based on the year of the driver champion and the year of the team champion with the clause `join t in teams on r.Year equals t.Year`. The `select` clause defines a new anonymous type containing `Year`, `Racer`, and `Team` properties.

```
var racersAndTeams =
      from r in racers
      join t in teams on r.Year equals t.Year
      select new
      {
         Year = r.Year,
         Racer = r.Name,
         Team = t.Name
      };
Console.WriteLine("Year  Champion " +
   "Constructor Title");
foreach (var item in racersAndTeams)
{
   Console.WriteLine("{0}: {1,-20} {2}",
      item.Year, item.Racer, item.Team);
}
```

Of course you can also combine this to one LINQ query, but that's a matter of taste:

```
int year = 2003;
var racersAndTeams =
    from r in
       from r1 in Formula1.GetChampions()
       from yr in r1.Years
       where yr > year
       select new
       {
          Year = yr,
          Name = r1.FirstName + " " +
             r1.LastName
       }
    join t in
       from t1 in
          Formula1.GetContructorChampions()
       from yt in t1.Years
       where yt > year
       select new { Year = yt,
                    Name = t1.Name }
    on r.Year equals t.Year
    select new
    {
       Year = r.Year,
       Racer = r.Name,
       Team = t.Name
    };
```

The output displays data from the anonymous type:

```
Year  Champion             Constructor Title
2004  Michael Schumacher   Ferrari
2005  Fernando Alonso      Renault
2006  Fernando Alonso      Renault
2007  Kimi Räikkönen       Ferrari
```

Set Operations

The extension methods `Distinct()`, `Union()`, `Intersect()`, and `Except()` are set operations. Let's create a sequence of Formula-1 champions driving a Ferrari and another sequence of Formula-1 champions driving a McLaren, and then let's find out if any driver has been a champion driving both of these cars. Of course, that's where the `Intersect()` extension method can help.

First get all champions driving a Ferrari. This is just using a simple LINQ query with a compound `from` to access the property `Cars` that's returning a sequence of string objects.

```
var ferrariDrivers = from r in
                     Formula1.GetChampions()
                     from c in r.Cars
                     where c == "Ferrari"
                     orderby r.LastName
                     select r;
```

Now the same query with a different parameter of the `where` clause would be needed to get all McLaren racers. It's not a good idea to write the same query another time. You have one option to create a method where you can pass the parameter `car`:

```
private static IEnumerable<Racer>
   GetRacersByCar(string car)
{
   return from r in Formula1.GetChampions()
          from c in r.Cars
          where c == car
          orderby r.LastName
          select r;
}
```

However, because the method wouldn't be needed in other places, defining a variable of a delegate type to hold the LINQ query is a good approach. The variable `racersByCar` needs to be of a delegate type that requires a string parameter and returns `IEnumerable<Racer>`, similar to the method that was implemented before. For doing this several generic `Func<>` delegates are defined, so you do not need to declare your own delegate. A Lambda expression is assigned to the variable `racersByCar`. The left side of the Lambda expression defines a `car` variable of the type that is the first generic parameter of the `Func` delegate (a string). The right side defines the LINQ query that uses the parameter with the `where` clause.

```
Func<string, IEnumerable<Racer>> racersByCar =
      Car => from r in Formula1.GetChampions()
             from c in r.Cars
             where c == car
             orderby r.LastName
             select r;
```

Now you can use the `Intersect()` extension method to get all racers that won the championship with a Ferrari and a McLaren:

```
Console.WriteLine("World champion with " +
   "Ferrari and McLaren");
foreach (var racer in racersByCar("Ferrari").
      Intersect(racersByCar("McLaren")))
{
   Console.WriteLine(racer);
}
```

The result is just one racer, Niki Lauda:

```
World champion with Ferrari and McLaren
Niki Lauda
```

Partitioning

Partitioning operations such as the extension methods `Take()` and `Skip()` can be used for easily paging, for example, to display 5 by 5 racers.

With the LINQ query shown here, the extension methods `Skip()` and `Take()` are added to the end of the query. The `Skip()` method first ignores a number of items calculated based on the page size and the actual page number; the `Take()` method then takes a number of items based on the page size:

```
int pageSize = 5;

int numberPages = (int)Math.Ceiling(
      Formula1.GetChampions().Count() /
      (double)pageSize);

for (int page = 0; page < numberPages; page++)
{
   Console.WriteLine("Page {0}", page);

   var racers =
      (from r in Formula1.GetChampions()
       orderby r.LastName
       select r.FirstName + " " + r.LastName).
      Skip(page * pageSize).Take(pageSize);

   foreach (var name in racers)
   {
      Console.WriteLine(name);
   }
   Console.WriteLine();
}
```

Here is the output of the first three pages:

```
Page 0
Fernando Alonso
Mario Andretti
Alberto Ascari
Jack Brabham
Jim Clark

Page 1
Juan Manuel Fangio
Nino Farina
Emerson Fittipaldi
Mika Hakkinen
Mike Hawthorn

Page 2
Phil Hill
Graham Hill
Damon Hill
Denny Hulme
James Hunt
```

Paging can be extremely useful with Windows or Web applications showing the user only a part of the data.

An important behavior of this paging mechanism that you will notice: because the query is done with every page, changing the underlying data affects the results. New objects are shown as paging continues. Depending on your scenario this can be advantageous to your application. If this behavior is not what you need you can do the paging not over the original data source, but by using a cache that maps to the original data.

With the `TakeWhile()` and `SkipWhile()` extension methods you can also pass a predicate to take or skip items based on the result of the predicate.

Aggregate Operators

The aggregate operators such as `Count()`, `Sum()`, `Min()`, `Max()`, `Average()`, and `Aggregate()` do not return a sequence but a single value instead.

The `Count()` extension method returns the number of items in the collection. Here the `Count()` method is applied to the `Years` property of a `Racer` to filter the racers and return only the ones who won more than three championships:

```
var query = from r in Formula1.GetChampions()
            where r.Years.Count() > 3
            orderby r.Years.Count() descending
            select new
            {
               Name = r.FirstName + " " +
                  r.LastName,
               TimesChampion = r.Years.Count()
            };
```

```
foreach (var r in query)
{
   Console.WriteLine("{0} {1}", r.Name,
      r.TimesChampion);
}
```

The result is shown here:

```
Michael Schumacher 7
Juan Manuel Fangio 5
Alain Prost 4
```

The `Sum()` method summarizes all numbers of a sequence and returns the result. Here, `Sum()` is used to calculate the sum of all race wins for a country. First the racers are grouped based on the country, then with the new anonymous type created the `Wins` property is assigned to the sum of all wins from a single country:

```
var countries =
   (from c in
       from r in Formula1.GetChampions()
       group r by r.Country into c
       select new
       {
          Country = c.Key,
          Wins = (from r1 in c
                  select r1.Wins).Sum()
       }
       orderby c.Wins descending, c.Country
       select c).Take(5);
```

(continued)

(continued)

```
foreach (var country in countries)
{
   Console.WriteLine("{0} {1}",
      country.Country, country.Wins);
}
```

The most successful countries based on the race wins by the Formula-1 champions are:

```
UK 138
Germany 91
Brazil 78
France 51
Finland 40
```

The methods `Min()`, `Max()`, `Average()`, and `Aggregate()` are used in the same way as `Count()` and `Sum()`. `Min()` returns the minimum number of the values in the collection, and `Max()` returns the maximum number. `Average()` calculates the average number. With the `Aggregate()` method you can pass a Lambda expression that should do an aggregation with all the values.

Conversion

In this chapter you've already seen that the query execution is deferred until the items are accessed. Using the query within an iteration, the query is executed. With conversion operator the query is executed immediately and you get the result in an array, a list, or a dictionary.

In this example the `ToList()` extension method is invoked to immediately execute the query and get the result into a `List<T>`:

```
List<Racer> racers =
   (from r in Formula1.GetChampions()
    where r.Starts > 150
    orderby r.Starts descending
    select r).ToList();

foreach (var racer in racers)
{
   Console.WriteLine("{0} {0:S}", racer);
}
```

It's not that simple to just get the returned objects to the list. For example, for a fast access from a car to a racer within a collection class, you can use the new class `Lookup<TKey, TElement>`.

The `Dictionary<TKey, TValue>` *supports only a single value for a key. With the class* `Lookup<TKey TElement>` *from the namespace* `System.Linq` *you can have multiple values for a single key. These classes are covered in detail in Chapter 10, "Collections."*

Using the compound `from` query, the sequence of racers and cars is flattened, and an anonymous type with the properties `Car` and `Racer` gets created. With the lookup that is returned, the key should be of type `string` referencing the car, and the value should be of type `Racer`. To make this selection, you can pass a key and an element selector to one overload of the `ToLookup()` method. The key selector references the `Car` property, and the element selector references the `Racer` property.

```
ILookup<string, Racer> racers =
    (from r in Formula1.GetChampions()
     from c in r.Cars
     select new
     {
        Car = c,
        Racer = r
     }).ToLookup(cr => cr.Car, cr => cr.Racer);
if (racers.Contains("Williams"))
{
   foreach (var williamsRacer in
      racers["Williams"])
   {
      Console.WriteLine(williamsRacer);
   }
}
```

The result of all "Williams" champions that are accessed using the indexer of the `Lookup` class is shown here:

```
Alan Jones
Keke Rosberg
Nigel Mansell
Alain Prost
Damon Hill
Jacques Villeneuve
```

In case you need to use a LINQ query over an untyped collection, for example the `ArrayList`, you can use the `Cast()` method. With the following sample an `ArrayList` collection that is based on the `Object` type is filled with `Racer` objects. To make it possible to define a strongly typed query, you can use the `Cast()` method:

```
System.Collections.ArrayList list =
      new System.Collections.ArrayList(
      Formula1.GetChampions() as
      System.Collections.ICollection);

var query = from r in list.Cast<Racer>()
            where r.Country == "USA"
            orderby r.Wins descending
            select r;
foreach (var racer in query)
{
   Console.WriteLine("{0:A}", racer);
}
```

Generation Operators

The generation operators `Range()`, `Empty()`, and `Repeat()` are not extension methods but normal static methods that return sequences. With LINQ to objects, these methods are available with the `Enumerable` class.

Have you ever needed a range of numbers filled? Nothing is easier than with the `Range()` method. This method receives the start value with the first parameter and the number of items with the second parameter:

```
var values = Enumerable.Range(1, 20);
foreach (var item in values)
{
   Console.Write("{0} ", item);
}
Console.WriteLine();
```

Of course the result now looks like this:

```
1 2 3 4 5 6 7 8 9 10 11 12 13 14 15 16 17 18 19 20
```

The `Range()` *method does not return a collection filled with the values as defined. This method does a deferred query execution similar to the other methods. The method returns a* `RangeEnumerator` *that just does a* `yield return` *with the values incremented.*

You can combine the result with other extension methods to get a different result, for example using the `Select()` extension method:

```
var values = Enumerable.Range(1, 20).
   Select(n => n * 3);
```

The `Empty()` method returns an iterator that does not return values. This can be used for parameters that require a collection where you can pass an empty collection.

The `Repeat()` method returns an iterator that returns the same value a specific number of times.

Expression Trees

With LINQ to objects, the extension methods require a delegate type as parameter; this way, a Lambda expression can be assigned to the parameter. Lambda expressions can also be assigned to parameters of type `Expression<T>`. The type `Expression<T>` specifies that an expression tree made from the Lambda expression is stored in the assembly. This way the expression can be analyzed during runtime and optimized for doing the query to the data source.

Let's turn to a query expression that was used previously:

```
var brazilRacers = from r in racers
                   where r.Country == "Brazil"
                   orderby r.Wins
                   select r;
```

This query expression is using the extension methods `Where`, `OrderBy`, and `Select`. The `Enumerable` class defines the `Where()` extension method with the delegate type `Func<T, bool>` as parameter predicate:

```
public static IEnumerable<TSource> Where<TSource> (
      this IEnumerable<TSource> source,
      Func<TSource, bool> predicate);
```

This way, the Lambda expression is assigned to the predicate. Here, the Lambda expression is similar to an anonymous method, as was explained earlier:

```
Func<Racer, bool> predicate = r => r.Country == "Brazil";
```

The `Enumerable` class is not the only class to define the `Where()` extension method. The `Where()` extension method is also defined by the class `Queryable<T>`. This class has a different definition of the `Where()` extension method:

```
public static IQueryable<TSource> Where<TSource> (
      this IQueryable<TSource> source,
      Expression<Func<TSource, bool>> predicate);
```

Here, the Lambda expression is assigned to the type `Expression<T>`, which behaves differently:

```
Expression<Func<Racer, bool>> predicate =
      r => r.Country == "Brazil";
```

Instead of using delegates, the compiler emits an expression tree to the assembly. The expression tree can be read during runtime. Expression trees are built from classes that are derived from the abstract base class `Expression`. The `Expression` class is not the same as `Expression<T>`. Some of the expression classes that inherit from `Expression` are `BinaryExpression`, `ConstantExpression`, `InvocationExpression`, `LambdaExpression`, `NewExpression`, `NewArrayExpression`, `TernaryExpression`, `UnaryExpression`, and so on. The compiler creates an expression tree resulting from the Lambda expression.

For example, the Lambda expression `r.Country == "Brazil"` makes use of `ParameterExpression`, `MemberExpression`, `ConstantExpression`, and `MethodCallExpression` to create a tree and store the tree in the assembly. This tree is then used during runtime to create an optimized query to the underlying data source.

The method `DisplayTree()` is implemented to display an expression tree graphically on the console. Here an `Expression` object can be passed, and depending on the expression type some information about the expression is written to the console. Depending on the type of the expression, `DisplayTree()` is called recursively.

With this method not all expression types are dealt with; only the types that are used with the next sample expression.

```
private static void DisplayTree(int indent,
      string message, Expression expression)
{
   string output = String.Format("{0} {1}" +
         "! NodeType: {2}; Expr: {3} ",
         "".PadLeft(indent, '>'), message,
         expression.NodeType, expression);

   indent++;
   switch (expression.NodeType)
   {
      case ExpressionType.Lambda:
         Console.WriteLine(output);
         LambdaExpression lambdaExpr =
            (LambdaExpression)expression;
         foreach (var parameter in
            lambdaExpr.Parameters)
         {
            DisplayTree(indent, "Parameter",
               parameter);
         }
         DisplayTree(indent, "Body",
            lambdaExpr.Body);
         break;
```

(continued)

(continued)

```
                case ExpressionType.Constant:
                   ConstantExpression constExpr =
                       (ConstantExpression)expression;
                   Console.WriteLine("{0} Const Value: " +
                       "{1}", output, constExpr.Value);
                   break;
                case ExpressionType.Parameter:
                   ParameterExpression paramExpr =
                         (ParameterExpression)expression;
                   Console.WriteLine("{0} Param Type: {1}",
                       output, paramExpr.Type.Name);
                   break;
                case ExpressionType.Equal:
                case ExpressionType.AndAlso:
                case ExpressionType.GreaterThan:
                   BinaryExpression binExpr =
                       (BinaryExpression)expression;
                   if (binExpr.Method != null)
                   {
                       Console.WriteLine("{0} Method: {1}",
                          output, binExpr.Method.Name);
                   }
                   else
                   {
                       Console.WriteLine(output);
                   }
                   DisplayTree(indent, "Left",
                       binExpr.Left);
                   DisplayTree(indent, "Right",
                       binExpr.Right);
                   break;
                case ExpressionType.MemberAccess:
                   MemberExpression memberExpr =
                       (MemberExpression)expression;
                   Console.WriteLine("{0} Member Name: " +
                       "{1}, Type: {2}", output,
                       memberExpr.Member.Name,
                       memberExpr.Type.Name);
                   DisplayTree(indent, "Member Expr",
                       memberExpr.Expression);
                   break;
                default:
                   Console.WriteLine();
                   Console.WriteLine("....{0} {1}",
                       expression.NodeType,
                       expression.Type.Name);
                   break;
             }
          }
```

The expression that is used for showing the tree is already well known. It's a Lambda expression with a `Racer` parameter, and the body of the expression takes racers from Brazil only if they have won more than six races:

```
Expression<Func<Racer, bool>> expression =
   r => r.Country == "Brazil" && r.Wins > 6;

DisplayTree(0, "Lambda", expression);
```

Let's look at the tree result. As you can see from the output, the Lambda expression consists of a `Parameter` and an `AndAlso` node type. The `AndAlso` node type has an `Equal` node type to the left and a `GreaterThan` node type to the right. The `Equal` node type to the left of the `AndAlso` node type has a `MemberAccess` node type to the left and a `Constant` node type to the right, and so on.

```
Lambda! NodeType: Lambda; Expr: r => ((r.Country = "Brazil") && (r.Wins > 6))
> Parameter! NodeType: Parameter; Expr: r  Param Type: Racer
> Body! NodeType: AndAlso; Expr: ((r.Country = "Brazil") && (r.Wins > 6))
>> Left! NodeType: Equal; Expr: (r.Country = "Brazil")  Method: op_Equality
>>> Left! NodeType: MemberAccess; Expr: r.Country  Member Name: Country, Type:
String
>>>> Member Expr! NodeType: Parameter; Expr: r  Param Type: Racer
>>> Right! NodeType: Constant; Expr: "Brazil"  Const Value: Brazil
>> Right! NodeType: GreaterThan; Expr: (r.Wins > 6)
>>> Left! NodeType: MemberAccess; Expr: r.Wins  Member Name: Wins, Type: Int32
>>>> Member Expr! NodeType: Parameter; Expr: r  Param Type: Racer
>>> Right! NodeType: Constant; Expr: 6  Const Value: 6
```

One example where the `Expression<T>` type is used is with LINQ to SQL. LINQ to SQL defines extension methods with `Expression<T>` parameters. This way the LINQ provider accessing the database can create a runtime-optimized query by reading the expressions to get the data from the database.

LINQ Providers

.NET 3.5 includes several LINQ providers. A LINQ provider implements the standard query operators for a specific data source. LINQ providers might implement more extension methods that are defined by LINQ, but the standard operators at least must be implemented. LINQ to XML implements more methods that are particularly useful with XML, for example the methods `Elements()`, `Descendants`, and `Ancestors` are defined by the class `Extensions` in the `System.Xml.Linq` namespace.

The implementation of the LINQ provider is selected based on the namespace and on the type of the first parameter. The namespace of the class that implements the extension methods must be opened, otherwise the extension class is not in scope. The parameter of the `Where()` method that is defined by LINQ to objects and the `Where()` method that is defined by LINQ to SQL is different.

The `Where()` method of LINQ to objects is defined with the `Enumerable` class:

```
public static IEnumerable<TSource> Where<TSource>(
      this IEnumerable<TSource> source,
      Func<TSource, bool> predicate);
```

Inside the `System.Linq` namespace there's another class that implements the operator `Where`. This implementation is used by LINQ to SQL. You can find the implementation in the class `Queryable`:

```
public static IQueryable<TSource> Where<TSource>(
      this IQueryable<TSource> source,
      Expression<Func<TSource, bool>> predicate);
```

Both of these classes are implemented in the `System.Core` assembly in the `System.Linq` namespace. How is it defined and what method is used? The Lambda expression is the same no matter whether it is passed with a `Func<TSource, bool>` parameter or with an `Expression<Func<TSource, bool>>` parameter. Just the compiler behaves differently. The selection is done based on the `source` parameter. The method that matches best based on its parameters is chosen by the compiler. The `GetTable()` method of the `DataContext` class that is defined by LINQ to SQL returns `IQueryable<TSource>`, and thus LINQ to SQL uses the `Where()` method of the `Queryable` class.

The LINQ to SQL provider is a provider that makes use of expression trees and implements the interfaces `IQueryable` and `IQueryProvider`.

Summary

In this chapter, you've probably seen the most important enhancements of the 3.0 version of C#. C# is continuously extended. With C# 2.0 the major new feature was generics, which provide the foundation for generic type-safe collection classes, as well as generic interfaces and delegates. The major feature of C# 3.0 is LINQ. You can use a syntax that is integrated with the language to query any data source, as long there's a provider for the data source.

You have now seen the LINQ query and the language constructs that the query is based on, such as extension methods and Lambda expressions. You've seen the various LINQ query operators not just for filtering and ordering of data sources, but also for partitioning, grouping, doing conversions, joins, and so on.

LINQ is a very in-depth topic, and you should see Chapters 27, 29, and Appendix A for more information. Other third-party providers are available for download; for example, LINQ to MySQL, LINQ to Amazon, LINQ to Flickr, and LINQ to SharePoint. No matter what data source you have, with LINQ you can use the same query syntax.

Another important concept not to be forgotten is the expression tree. Expression trees allow building the query to the data source at runtime because the tree is stored in the assembly. You can read about the great advantages of it in Chapter 27, "LINQ to SQL."

12

Memory Management and Pointers

This chapter presents various aspects of memory management and memory access. Although the runtime takes much of the responsibility for memory management away from the programmer, it is useful to understand how memory management works and important to know how to work with unmanaged resources efficiently.

A good understanding of memory management and knowledge of the pointer capabilities provided by C# will better enable you to integrate C# code with legacy code and perform efficient memory manipulation in performance-critical systems.

Specifically, this chapter discusses:

- How the runtime allocates space on the stack and the heap
- How garbage collection works
- How to use destructors and the `System.IDisposable` interface to ensure unmanaged resources are released correctly
- The syntax for using pointers in C#
- How to use pointers to implement high-performance stack-based arrays

Memory Management Under the Hood

One of the advantages of C# programming is that the programmer does not need to worry about detailed memory management; in particular, the garbage collector deals with the problem of memory cleanup on your behalf. The result is that you get something that approximates the efficiency of languages like C++ without the complexity of having to handle memory management yourself as you do in C++. However, although you do not have to manage memory manually, it still pays to understand what is going on behind the scenes. This section looks at what happens in the computer's memory when you allocate variables.

The precise details of much of the content of this section are undocumented. You should interpret this section as a simplified guide to the general processes rather than as a statement of exact implementation.

Value Data Types

Windows uses a system known as *virtual addressing*, in which the mapping from the memory address seen by your program to the actual location in hardware memory is entirely managed by Windows. The result of this is that each process on a 32-bit processor sees 4GB of available memory, regardless of how much hardware memory you actually have in your computer (on 64-bit processors this number will be greater). This 4GB of memory contains everything that is part of the program, including the executable code, any DLLs loaded by the code, and the contents of all variables used when the program runs. This 4GB of memory is known as the *virtual address space* or *virtual memory*. For convenience, in this chapter, we call it simply *memory*.

Each memory location in the available 4GB is numbered starting from zero. To access a value stored at a particular location in memory, you need to supply the number that represents that memory location. In any compiled high-level language, including C#, Visual Basic, C++, and Java, the compiler converts human-readable variable names into memory addresses that the processor understands.

Somewhere inside a processor's virtual memory is an area known as the *stack*. The stack stores value data types that are not members of objects. In addition, when you call a method, the stack is used to hold a copy of any parameters passed to the method. To understand how the stack works, you need to understand the importance of variable scope in C#. It is *always* the case that if a variable `a` goes into scope before variable `b`, then `b` will go out of scope first. Look at this code:

```
{
   int a;
   // do something
   {
      int b;
      // do something else
   }
}
```

First, `a` gets declared. Then, inside the inner code block, `b` gets declared. Then the inner code block terminates and `b` goes out of scope, then `a` goes out of scope. So, the lifetime of `b` is entirely contained within the lifetime of `a`. The idea that you always deallocate variables in the reverse order to how you allocate them is crucial to the way the stack works.

You do not know exactly where in the address space the stack is — you don't need to know for C# development. A *stack pointer* (a variable maintained by the operating system) identifies the next free location on the stack. When your program first starts running, the stack pointer will point to just past the end of the block of memory that is reserved for the stack. The stack actually fills downward, from high memory addresses to low addresses. As data is put on the stack, the stack pointer is adjusted accordingly, so it always points to just past the next free location. This is illustrated in Figure 12-1, which shows a stack pointer with a value of `800000` (`0xC3500` in hex); the next free location is the address `799999`.

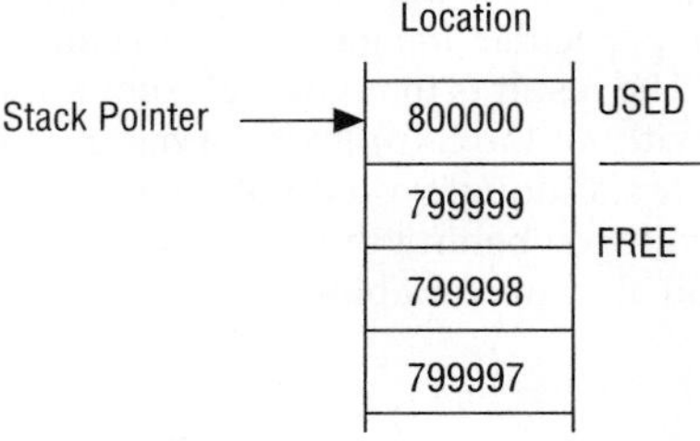

Figure 12-1

The following code instructs the compiler that you need space in memory to store an integer and a double, and these memory locations are referred to as nRacingCars and engineSize. The line that declares each variable indicates the point at which you will start requiring access to this variable. The closing curly brace of the block in which the variables are declared identifies the point at which both variables go out of scope.

```
{
    int nRacingCars = 10;
    double engineSize = 3000.0;
    // do calculations;
}
```

Assuming that you use the stack shown in Figure 12-1, when the variable nRacingCars comes into scope and is assigned the value 10, the value 10 is placed in locations 799996 through 799999, the 4 bytes just below the location pointed to by the stack pointer. (Four bytes because that's how much memory is needed to store an int.) To accommodate this, 4 is subtracted from the value of the stack pointer, so it now points to the location 799996, just after the new first free location (799995).

The next line of code declares the variable engineSize (a double) and initializes it to the value 3000.0. A double occupies 8 bytes, so the value 3000.0 will be placed in locations 799988 through 799995 on the stack, and the stack pointer is decremented by 8, so that once again, it points to the location just after the next free location on the stack.

When engineSize goes out of scope, the computer knows that it is no longer needed. Because of the way variable lifetimes are always nested, you can guarantee that, whatever has happened while engineSize was in scope, the stack pointer is now pointing to the location where engineSize is stored. To remove engineSize from the stack, the stack pointer is incremented by 8, so that it now points to the location immediately after the end of engineSize. At this point in the code, you are at the closing curly brace, so nRacingCars also goes out of scope. The stack pointer is incremented by 4. When another variable comes into scope after engineSize and nRacingCars have been removed from the stack, it will overwrite the memory descending from location 799999, where nRacingCars used to be stored.

If the compiler hits a line like int i, j, then the order of variables coming into scope looks indeterminate. Both variables are declared at the same time and go out of scope at the same time. In this situation, it does not matter in what order the two variables are removed from memory. The compiler internally always ensures that the one that was put in memory first is removed last, thus preserving the rule about no crossover of variable lifetimes.

Reference Data Types

Although the stack gives very high performance, it is not flexible enough to be used for all variables. The requirement that the lifetimes of variables must be nested is too restrictive for many purposes. Often, you will want to use a method to allocate memory to store some data and be able to keep that data available long after that method has exited. This possibility exists whenever storage space is requested with the new operator — as is the case for all reference types. That is where the *managed heap* comes in.

If you have done any C++ coding that required low-level memory management, you will be familiar with the heap. The managed heap is not quite the same as the heap C++ uses; the managed heap works under the control of the garbage collector and provides significant benefits when compared to traditional heaps.

The managed heap (or heap for short) is just another area of memory from the processor's available 4GB. The following code demonstrates how the heap works and how memory is allocated for reference data types:

```
void DoWork()
{
    Customer arabel;
    arabel = new Customer();
    Customer otherCustomer2 = new EnhancedCustomer();
}
```

This code assumes the existence of two classes, `Customer` and `EnhancedCustomer`. The `EnhancedCustomer` class extends the `Customer` class.

First, you declare a `Customer` reference called `arabel`. The space for this will be allocated on the stack, but remember that this is only a reference, not an actual `Customer` object. The `arabel` reference takes up 4 bytes, enough space to hold the address at which a `Customer` object will be stored. (You need 4 bytes to represent a memory address as an integer value between 0 and 4GB.)

The next line,

```
arabel = new Customer();
```

does several things. First, it allocates memory on the heap to store a `Customer` object (a real object, not just an address). Then it sets the value of the variable `arabel` to the address of the memory it has allocated to the new `Customer` object. (It also calls the appropriate `Customer()` constructor to initialize the fields in the class instance, but we won't worry about that here.)

The `Customer` instance is not placed on the stack — it is placed on the heap. In this example, you don't know precisely how many bytes a `Customer` object occupies, but assume for the sake of argument that it is 32. These 32 bytes contain the instance fields of `Customer` as well as some information that .NET uses to identify and manage its class instances.

To find a storage location on the heap for the new `Customer` object, the .NET runtime will look through the heap and grab the first adjacent, unused block of 32 bytes. Again for the sake of argument, assume that this happens to be at address `200000`, and that the `arabel` reference occupied locations `799996` through `799999` on the stack. This means that before instantiating the `arabel` object, the memory contents will look similar to Figure 12-2.

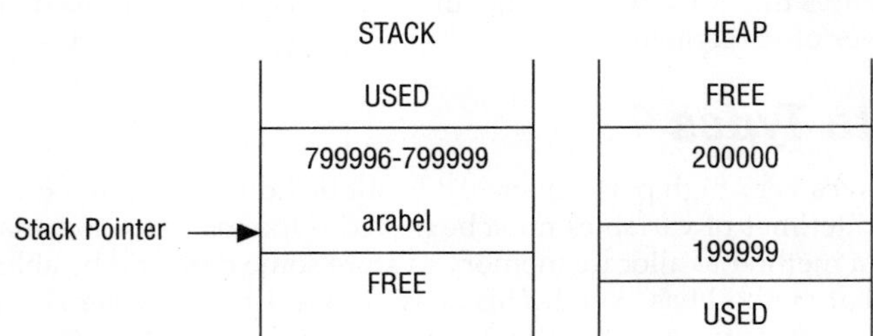

Figure 12-2

After allocating the new `Customer` object, the contents of memory will look like Figure 12-3. Note that unlike the stack, memory in the heap is allocated upward, so the free space can be found above the used space.

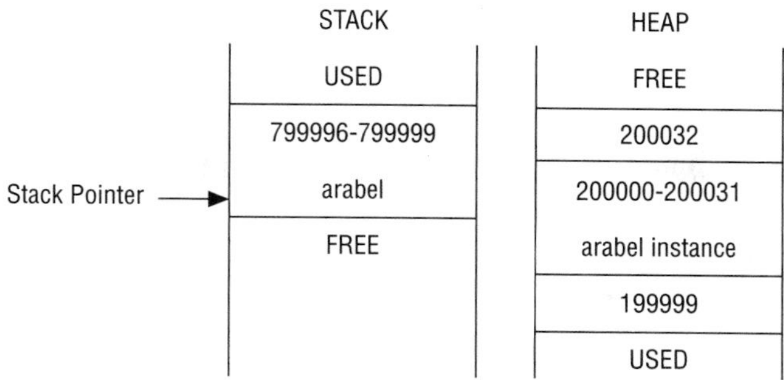

Figure 12-3

The next line of code both declares a `Customer` reference and instantiates a `Customer` object. In this instance, space on the stack for the `otherCustomer2` reference is allocated and space for the `mrJones` object is allocated on the heap in a single line of code:

```
Customer otherCustomer2 = new EnhancedCustomer();
```

This line allocates 4 bytes on the stack to hold the `otherCustomer2` reference, stored at locations `799992` through `799995`. The `otherCustomer2` object is allocated space on the heap starting at location `200032`.

It is clear from the example that the process of setting up a reference variable is more complex than that for setting up a value variable, and there is a performance overhead. In fact, the process is somewhat oversimplified here, because the .NET runtime needs to maintain information about the state of the heap, and this information needs to be updated whenever new data is added to the heap. Despite this overhead, you now have a mechanism for allocating variables that is not constrained by the limitations of the stack. By assigning the value of one reference variable to another of the same type, you have two variables that reference the same object in memory. When a reference variable goes out of scope, it is removed from the stack as described in the previous section, but the data for a referenced object is still sitting on the heap. The data will remain on the heap until either the program terminates or the garbage collector removes it, which will happen only when it is no longer referenced by any variables.

That is the power of reference data types, and you will see this feature used extensively in C# code. It means that you have a high degree of control over the lifetime of your data, because it is guaranteed to exist in the heap as long as you are maintaining some reference to it.

Garbage Collection

The previous discussion and diagrams show the managed heap working very much like the stack, to the extent that successive objects are placed next to each other in memory. This means that you can work out where to place the next object by using a heap pointer that indicates the next free memory location and that is adjusted as you add more objects to the heap. However, things are complicated because the lives of the heap-based objects are not coupled to the scope of the individual stack-based variables that reference them.

When the garbage collector runs, it will remove all those objects from the heap that are no longer referenced. Immediately after it has done this, the heap will have objects scattered on it, mixed up with memory that has just been freed (see Figure 12-4).

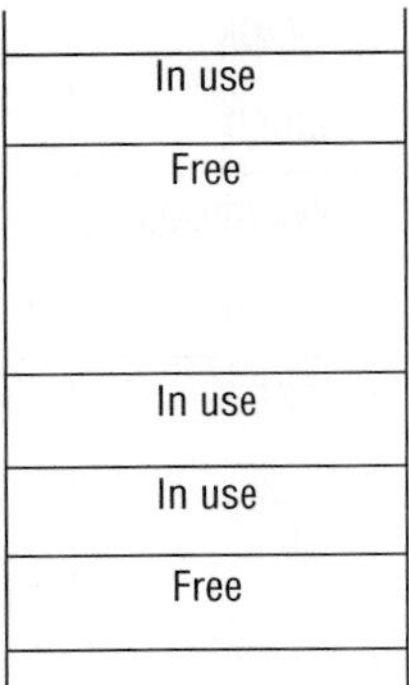

Figure 12-4

If the managed heap stayed like this, allocating space for new objects would be an awkward process, with the runtime having to search through the heap for a block of memory big enough to store each new object. However, the garbage collector does not leave the heap in this state. As soon as the garbage collector has freed up all the objects it can, it compacts the heap by moving all remaining objects to form one continuous block of memory. This means that the heap can continue working just like the stack as far as locating where to store new objects. Of course, when the objects are moved about, all the references to those objects need to be updated with the correct new addresses, but the garbage collector handles that too.

This action of compacting by the garbage collector is where the managed heap really works differently from old unmanaged heaps. With the managed heap, it is just a question of reading the value of the heap pointer, rather than iterating through a linked list of addresses to find somewhere to put the new data. For this reason, instantiating an object under .NET is much faster. Interestingly, accessing objects tends to be faster too, because the objects are compacted toward the same area of memory on the heap, resulting in less page swapping. Microsoft believes that these performance gains more than compensate for the performance penalty that you get whenever the garbage collector needs to do some work to compact the heap and change all those references to objects it has moved.

> *Generally, the garbage collector runs when the .NET runtime determines that garbage collection is required. You can force the garbage collector to run at a certain point in your code by calling* `System.GC.Collect()`*. The* `System.GC` *class is a .NET class that represents the garbage collector, and the* `Collect()` *method initiates a garbage collection. The* `GC` *class is intended for rare situations in which you know that it's a good time to call the garbage collector; for example, if you have just de-referenced a large number of objects in your code. However, the logic of the garbage collector does not guarantee that all unreferenced objects will be removed from the heap in a single garbage collection pass.*

Freeing Unmanaged Resources

The presence of the garbage collector means that you will usually not worry about objects that you no longer need; you will simply allow all references to those objects to go out of scope and allow the garbage collector to free memory as required. However, the garbage collector does not know how to free unmanaged resources (such as file handles, network connections, and database connections). When managed classes encapsulate direct or indirect references to unmanaged resources, you need to make special provision to ensure that the unmanaged resources are released when an instance of the class is garbage collected.

When defining a class, you can use two mechanisms to automate the freeing of unmanaged resources. These mechanisms are often implemented together because each provides a slightly different approach to the solution of the problem. The mechanisms are:

- Declaring a destructor (or finalizer) as a member of your class
- Implementing the `System.IDisposable` interface in your class

The following sections discuss each of these mechanisms in turn, and then look at how to implement them together for best effect.

Destructors

You have seen that constructors allow you to specify actions that must take place whenever an instance of a class is created. Conversely, destructors are called before an object is destroyed by the garbage collector. Given this behavior, a destructor would initially seem like a great place to put code to free unmanaged resources and perform a general cleanup. Unfortunately, things are not so straightforward.

Although we talk about destructors in C#, in the underlying .NET architecture these are known as finalizers. When you define a destructor in C#, what is emitted into the assembly by the compiler is actually a method called `Finalize()`. That is something that doesn't affect any of your source code, but you'll need to be aware of the fact if you need to examine the contents of an assembly.

The syntax for a destructor will be familiar to C++ developers. It looks like a method, with the same name as the containing class, but prefixed with a tilde (~). It has no return type, and takes no parameters and no access modifiers. Here is an example:

```
class MyClass
{
   ~MyClass()
   {
      // destructor implementation
   }
}
```

When the C# compiler compiles a destructor, it implicitly translates the destructor code to the equivalent of a `Finalize()` method, which ensures that the `Finalize()` method of the parent class is executed. The following example shows the C# code equivalent to the Intermediate Language (IL) that the compiler would generate for the `~MyClass` destructor:

```
protected override void Finalize()
{
   try
   {
      // destructor implementation
   }
   finally
   {
      base.Finalize();
   }
}
```

As shown, the code implemented in the `~MyClass` destructor is wrapped in a `try` block contained in the `Finalize()` method. A call to the parent's `Finalize()` method is ensured by placing the call in a `finally` block. We discuss `try` and `finally` blocks in Chapter 14, "Errors and Exceptions."

Experienced C++ developers make extensive use of destructors, sometimes not only to clean up resources but also to provide debugging information or perform other tasks. C# destructors are used far less than their C++ equivalents. The problem with C# destructors as compared to their C++ counterparts is that they are nondeterministic. When a C++ object is destroyed, its destructor runs immediately. However, because of the way the garbage collector works when using C#, there is no way to know when an object's destructor will actually execute. Hence, you cannot place any code in the destructor that relies on being run at a certain time, and you should not rely on the destructor being called for different class instances in any particular order. When your object is holding scarce and critical resources that need to be freed as soon as possible, you do not want to wait for garbage collection.

Another problem with C# destructors is that the implementation of a destructor delays the final removal of an object from memory. Objects that do not have a destructor are removed from memory in one pass of the garbage collector, but objects that have destructors require two passes to be destroyed: The first pass calls the destructor without removing the object, and the second pass actually deletes the object. In addition, the runtime uses a single thread to execute the `Finalize()` methods of all objects. If you use destructors frequently, and use them to execute lengthy cleanup tasks, the impact on performance can be noticeable.

The IDisposable Interface

In C#, the recommended alternative to using a destructor is using the `System.IDisposable` interface. The `IDisposable` interface defines a pattern (with language-level support) that provides a deterministic mechanism for freeing unmanaged resources and avoids the garbage collector–related problems inherent with destructors. The `IDisposable` interface declares a single method named `Dispose()`, which takes no parameters and returns `void`. Here is an implementation for `MyClass`:

```
class MyClass : IDisposable
{
   public void Dispose()
   {
      // implementation
   }
}
```

The implementation of `Dispose()` should explicitly free all unmanaged resources used directly by an object and call `Dispose()` on any encapsulated objects that also implement the `IDisposable` interface. In this way, the `Dispose()` method provides precise control over when unmanaged resources are freed.

Suppose that you have a class named `ResourceGobbler`, which relies on the use of some external resource and implements `IDisposable`. If you want to instantiate an instance of this class, use it, and then dispose of it, you could do it like this:

```
ResourceGobbler theInstance = new ResourceGobbler();

// do your processing

theInstance.Dispose();
```

Unfortunately, this code fails to free the resources consumed by `theInstance` if an exception occurs during processing, so you should write the code as follows using a `try` block (which is discussed fully in Chapter 14):

```
ResourceGobbler theInstance = null;

try
{
   theInstance = new ResourceGobbler();
```

```
      // do your processing
   }
   finally
   {
      if (theInstance != null)
      {
         theInstance.Dispose();
     }
   }
```

This version ensures that `Dispose()` is always called on `theInstance` and that any resources consumed by it are always freed, even if an exception occurs during processing. However, it would make for confusing code if you always had to repeat such a construct. C# offers a syntax that you can use to guarantee that `Dispose()` will automatically be called against an object that implements `IDisposable` when its reference goes out of scope. The syntax to do this involves the `using` keyword — though now in a very different context, which has nothing to do with namespaces. The following code generates IL code equivalent to the `try` block just shown:

```
using (ResourceGobbler theInstance = new ResourceGobbler())
{
   // do your processing
}
```

The `using` statement, followed in brackets by a reference variable declaration and instantiation, will cause that variable to be scoped to the accompanying statement block. In addition, when that variable goes out of scope, its `Dispose()` method will be called automatically, even if an exception occurs. However, if you are already using `try` blocks to catch other exceptions, it is cleaner and avoids additional code indentation if you avoid the `using` statement and simply call `Dispose()` in the `Finally` clause of the existing `try` block.

For some classes, the notion of a `Close()` *method is more logical than* `Dispose()`*; for example, when dealing with files or database connections. In these cases, it is common to implement the* `IDisposable` *interface and then implement a separate* `Close()` *method that simply calls* `Dispose()`*. This approach provides clarity in the use of your classes but also supports the* `using` *statement provided by C#.*

Implementing IDisposable and a Destructor

The previous sections discussed two alternatives for freeing unmanaged resources used by the classes you create:

- The execution of a destructor is enforced by the runtime but is nondeterministic and places an unacceptable overhead on the runtime because of the way garbage collection works.
- The `IDisposable` interface provides a mechanism that allows users of a class to control when resources are freed but requires discipline to ensure that `Dispose()` is called.

In general, the best approach is to implement both mechanisms in order to gain the benefits of both while overcoming their limitations. You implement `IDisposable` on the assumption that most programmers will call `Dispose()` correctly, but implement a destructor as a safety mechanism in case `Dispose()` is not called. Here is an example of a dual implementation:

```
using System;

public class ResourceHolder : IDisposable
```

(continued)

(continued)

```
{
   private bool isDisposed = false;

   public void Dispose()
   {
      Dispose(true);
      GC.SuppressFinalize(this);
   }

   protected virtual void Dispose(bool disposing)
   {
      if (!isDisposed)
      {
         if (disposing)
         {
            // Cleanup managed objects by calling their
            // Dispose() methods.
         }
         // Cleanup unmanaged objects
      }
      isDisposed = true;
   }

   ~ResourceHolder()
   {
      Dispose (false);
   }

   public void SomeMethod()
   {
      // Ensure object not already disposed before execution of any method
      if(isDisposed)
      {
         throw new ObjectDisposedException("ResourceHolder");
      }

      // method implementation…
   }
}
```

You can see from this code that there is a second `protected` overload of `Dispose()`, which takes one `bool` parameter — and this is the method that does all cleaning up. `Dispose(bool)` is called by both the destructor and by `IDisposable.Dispose()`. The point of this approach is to ensure that all cleanup code is in one place.

The parameter passed to `Dispose(bool)` indicates whether `Dispose(bool)` has been invoked by the destructor or by `IDisposable.Dispose()` — `Dispose(bool)` should not be invoked from anywhere else in your code. The idea is this:

- If a consumer calls `IDisposable.Dispose()`, that consumer is indicating that all managed and unmanaged resources associated with that object should be cleaned up.
- If a destructor has been invoked, all resources still need to be cleaned up. However, in this case, you know that the destructor must have been called by the garbage collector and you should not attempt to access other managed objects because you can no longer be certain of their state. In

this situation, the best you can do is clean up the known unmanaged resources and hope that any referenced managed objects also have destructors that will perform their own cleaning up.

The `isDisposed` member variable indicates whether the object has already been disposed of and allows you to ensure that you do not try to dispose of member variables more than once. It also allows you to test whether an object has been disposed of before executing any instance methods, as shown in `SomeMethod()`. This simplistic approach is not thread-safe and depends on the caller ensuring that only one thread is calling the method concurrently. Requiring a consumer to enforce synchronization is a reasonable assumption and one that is used repeatedly throughout the .NET class libraries (in the `Collection` classes, for example). Threading and synchronization are discussed in Chapter 19, "Threading and Synchronization."

Finally, `IDisposable.Dispose()` contains a call to the method `System.GC.SuppressFinalize()`. `GC` is the class that represents the garbage collector, and the `SuppressFinalize()` method tells the garbage collector that a class no longer needs to have its destructor called. Because your implementation of `Dispose()` has already done all the cleanup required, there's nothing left for the destructor to do. Calling `SuppressFinalize()` means that the garbage collector will treat that object as if it doesn't have a destructor at all.

Unsafe Code

As you have just seen, C# is very good at hiding much of the basic memory management from the developer, thanks to the garbage collector and the use of references. However, sometimes you will want direct access to memory. For example, you might want to access a function in an external (non-.NET) DLL that requires a pointer to be passed as a parameter (as many Windows API functions do), or possibly for performance reasons. This section examines C#'s facilities that provide direct access to the contents of memory.

Accessing Memory Directly with Pointers

Although we are introducing *pointers* as if they were a new topic, in reality pointers are not new at all. You have been using references freely in your code, and a reference is simply a type-safe pointer. You have already seen how variables that represent objects and arrays actually store the memory address of where the corresponding data (the *referent*) is stored. A pointer is simply a variable that stores the address of something else in the same way as a reference. The difference is that C# does not allow you direct access to the address contained in a reference variable. With a reference, the variable is treated syntactically as if it stores the actual contents of the referent.

C# references are designed to make the language simpler to use and to prevent you from inadvertently doing something that corrupts the contents of memory. With a pointer, however, the actual memory address is available to you. This gives you a lot of power to perform new kinds of operations. For example, you can add 4 bytes to the address, so that you can examine or even modify whatever data happens to be stored 4 bytes further on in memory.

The two main reasons for using pointers are:

- **Backward compatibility** — Despite all of the facilities provided by the .NET runtime, it is still possible to call native Windows API functions, and for some operations this may be the only way to accomplish your task. These API functions are generally written in C and often require pointers as parameters. However, in many cases it is possible to write the `DllImport` declaration in a way that avoids use of pointers; for example, by using the `System.IntPtr` class.
- **Performance** — On those occasions where speed is of the utmost importance, pointers can provide a route to optimized performance. If you know what you are doing, you can ensure that

data is accessed or manipulated in the most efficient way. However, be aware that, more often than not, there are other areas of your code where you can make the necessary performance improvements without resorting to using pointers. Try using a code profiler to look for the bottlenecks in your code — one comes with Visual Studio 2008.

Low-level memory access comes at a price. The syntax for using pointers is more complex than that for reference types, and pointers are unquestionably more difficult to use correctly. You need good programming skills and an excellent ability to think carefully and logically about what your code is doing in order to use pointers successfully. If you are not careful, it is very easy to introduce subtle, difficult-to-find bugs into your program when using pointers. For example, it is easy to overwrite other variables, cause stack overflows, access areas of memory that don't store any variables, or even overwrite information about your code that is needed by the .NET runtime, thereby crashing your program.

In addition, if you use pointers your code must be granted a high level of trust by the runtime's code access security mechanism or it will not be allowed to execute. Under the default code access security policy, this is only possible if your code is running on the local machine. If your code must be run from a remote location, such as the Internet, users must grant your code additional permissions for it to work. Unless the users trust you and your code, they are unlikely to grant these permissions. Code access security is discussed more in Chapter 20, "Security."

Despite these issues, pointers remain a very powerful and flexible tool in the writing of efficient code.

We strongly advise against using pointers unnecessarily because your code will not only be harder to write and debug, but it will also fail the memory type-safety checks imposed by the CLR, which is discussed in Chapter 1, ".NET Architecture."

Writing Unsafe Code with the unsafe Keyword

As a result of the risks associated with pointers, C# allows the use of pointers only in blocks of code that you have specifically marked for this purpose. The keyword to do this is `unsafe`. You can mark an individual method as being `unsafe` like this:

```
unsafe int GetSomeNumber()
{
   // code that can use pointers
}
```

Any method can be marked as `unsafe`, regardless of what other modifiers have been applied to it (for example, `static` methods or `virtual` methods). In the case of methods, the `unsafe` modifier applies to the method's parameters, allowing you to use pointers as parameters. You can also mark an entire class or struct as `unsafe`, which means that all of its members are assumed unsafe:

```
unsafe class MyClass
{
   // any method in this class can now use pointers
}
```

Similarly, you can mark a member as `unsafe`:

```
class MyClass
{
   unsafe int* pX;    // declaration of a pointer field in a class
}
```

Or you can mark a block of code within a method as `unsafe`:

```
void MyMethod()
{
   // code that doesn't use pointers
   unsafe
```

```
        {
           // unsafe code that uses pointers here
        }
        // more 'safe' code that doesn't use pointers
    }
```

Note, however, that you cannot mark a local variable by itself as `unsafe`:

```
int MyMethod()
{
   unsafe int *pX;    // WRONG
}
```

If you want to use an unsafe local variable, you will need to declare and use it inside a method or block that is unsafe. There is one more step before you can use pointers. The C# compiler rejects unsafe code unless you tell it that your code includes unsafe blocks. The flag to do this is `unsafe`. Hence, to compile a file named `MySource.cs` that contains unsafe blocks (assuming no other compiler options), the command is:

```
csc /unsafe MySource.cs
```

or:

```
csc -unsafe MySource.cs
```

If you are using Visual Studio 2005 or 2008, you will also find the option to compile unsafe code in the Build tab of the project properties window.

Pointer Syntax

Once you have marked a block of code as `unsafe`, you can declare a pointer using this syntax:

```
int* pWidth, pHeight;
double* pResult;
byte*[] pFlags;
```

This code declares four variables: `pWidth` and `pHeight` are pointers to integers, `pResult` is a pointer to a `double`, and `pFlags` is an array of pointers to bytes. It is common practice to use the prefix `p` in front of names of pointer variables to indicate that they are pointers. When used in a variable declaration, the symbol `*` indicates that you are declaring a pointer (that is, something that stores the address of a variable of the specified type).

C++ developers should be aware of the syntax difference between C++ and C#. The C# statement `int* pX, pY;` *corresponds to the C++ statement* `int *pX, *pY;`*. In C#, the* `*` *symbol is associated with the type rather than the variable name.*

Once you have declared variables of pointer types, you can use them in the same way as normal variables, but first you need to learn two more operators:

- `&` means *take the address of*, and converts a value data type to a pointer, for example `int` to `*int`. This operator is known as the *address operator*.
- `*` means *get the contents of this address*, and converts a pointer to a value data type (for example, `*float` to `float`). This operator is known as the *indirection operator* (or sometimes as the *dereference operator*).

You will see from these definitions that `&` and `*` have opposite effects.

You might be wondering how it is possible to use the symbols `&` *and* `*` *in this manner because these symbols also refer to the operators of bitwise AND (*`&`*) and multiplication (*`*`*). Actually, it is always possible for both you and the compiler to know what is meant in each case because with the new pointer* *meanings, these symbols always appear as unary operators — they act on only one variable and appear in front of that variable in your code. By contrast, bitwise AND and multiplication are binary operators — they require two operands.*

The following code shows examples of how to use these operators:

```
int x = 10;
int* pX, pY;
pX = &x;
pY = pX;
*pY = 20;
```

You start by declaring an integer, `x`, with the value 10 followed by two pointers to integers, `pX` and `pY`. You then set `pX` to point to `x` (that is, you set the contents of `pX` to be the address of `x`). Then you assign the value of `pX` to `pY`, so that `pY` also points to `x`. Finally, in the statement `*pY = 20`, you assign the value 20 as the contents of the location pointed to by `pY` — in effect changing `x` to `20` because `pY` happens to point to `x`. Note that there is no particular connection between the variables `pY` and `x`. It is just that at the present time, `pY` happens to point to the memory location at which `x` is held.

To get a better understanding of what is going on, consider that the integer `x` is stored at memory locations `0x12F8C4` through `0x12F8C7` (`1243332` to `1243335` in decimal) on the stack (there are four locations because an `int` occupies 4 bytes). Because the stack allocates memory downward, this means that the variables `pX` will be stored at locations `0x12F8C0` to `0x12F8C3`, and `pY` will end up at locations `0x12F8BC` to `0x12F8BF`. Note that `pX` and `pY` also occupy 4 bytes each. That is not because an `int` occupies 4 bytes. It is because on a 32-bit processor you need 4 bytes to store an address. With these addresses, after executing the previous code, the stack will look like Figure 12-5.

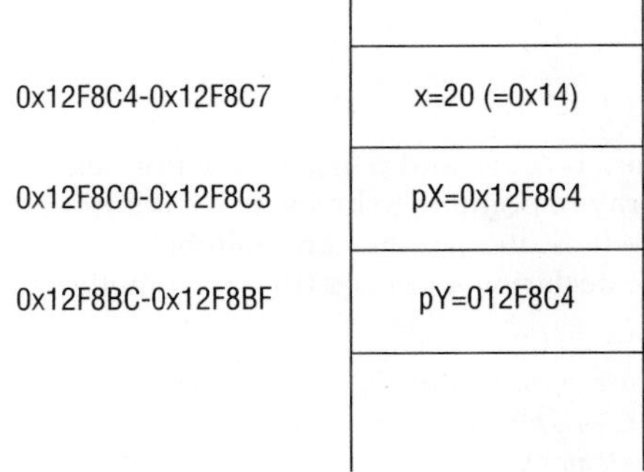

Figure 12-5

Although this process is illustrated with integers, which will be stored consecutively on the stack on a 32-bit processor, this does not happen for all data types. The reason is that 32-bit processors work best when retrieving data from memory in 4-byte chunks. Memory on such machines tends to be divided into 4-byte blocks, and each block is sometimes known under Windows as a DWORD because this was the name of a 32-bit unsigned int in pre-.NET days. It is most efficient to grab DWORDs from memory — storing data across DWORD boundaries normally results in a hardware performance hit. For this reason, the .NET runtime normally pads out data types so that the memory they occupy is a multiple of 4. For example, a short occupies 2 bytes, but if a short is placed on the stack, the stack pointer will still be decremented by 4, not 2, so that the next variable to go on the stack will still start at a DWORD boundary.

You can declare a pointer to any value type (that is, any of the predefined types `uint`, `int`, `byte`, and so on, or to a struct). However, it is not possible to declare a pointer to a class or an array; this is because doing so could cause problems for the garbage collector. In order to work properly, the garbage collector needs to know exactly what class instances have been created on the heap, and where they are, but if your code started manipulating classes using pointers, you could very easily corrupt the information on the heap concerning classes that the .NET runtime maintains for the garbage collector. In this context, any data type that the garbage collector can access is known as a *managed type*. Pointers can only be declared as *unmanaged types* because the garbage collector cannot deal with them.

Casting Pointers to Integer Types

Because a pointer really stores an integer that represents an address, you won't be surprised to know that the address in any pointer can be converted to or from any integer type. Pointer-to-integer-type conversions must be explicit. Implicit conversions are not available for such conversions. For example, it is perfectly legitimate to write the following:

```
int x = 10;
int* pX, pY;
pX = &x;
pY = pX;
*pY = 20;
uint y = (uint)pX;
int* pD = (int*)y;
```

The address held in the pointer `pX` is cast to a `uint` and stored in the variable `y`. You have then cast `y` back to an `int*` and stored it in the new variable `pD`. Hence, now `pD` also points to the value of `x`.

The primary reason for casting a pointer value to an integer type is to display it. The `Console.Write()` and `Console.WriteLine()` methods do not have any overloads that can take pointers, but will accept and display pointer values that have been cast to integer types:

```
Console.WriteLine("Address is " + pX);   // wrong -- will give a
                                         // compilation error
Console.WriteLine("Address is " + (uint)pX);   // OK
```

You can cast a pointer to any of the integer types. However, because an address occupies 4 bytes on 32-bit systems, casting a pointer to anything other than a `uint`, `long`, or `ulong` is almost certain to lead to overflow errors. (An `int` causes problems because its range is from roughly –2 billion to 2 billion, whereas an address runs from zero to about 4 billion.) When C# is released for 64-bit processors, an address will occupy 8 bytes. Hence, on such systems, casting a pointer to anything other than `ulong` is likely to lead to overflow errors. It is also important to be aware that the `checked` keyword does not apply to conversions involving pointers. For such conversions, exceptions will not be raised when overflows occur, even in a `checked` context. The .NET runtime assumes that if you are using pointers you know what you are doing and are not worried about possible overflows.

Casting Between Pointer Types

You can also explicitly convert between pointers pointing to different types. For example:

```
byte aByte = 8;
byte* pByte= &aByte;
double* pDouble = (double*)pByte;
```

This is perfectly legal code, though again, if you try something like this, be careful. In this example, if you look at the `double` value pointed to by `pDouble`, you will actually be looking up some memory that contains a `byte` (`aByte`), combined with some other memory, and treating it as if this area of memory contained a `double`, which will not give you a meaningful value. However, you might want to convert between types in order to implement the equivalent of a C union, or you might want to cast pointers from other types into pointers to sbyte in order to examine individual bytes of memory.

void Pointers

If you want to maintain a pointer, but do not want to specify what type of data it points to, you can declare it as a pointer to a void:

```
int* pointerToInt;
void* pointerToVoid;
pointerToVoid = (void*)pointerToInt;
```

The main use of this is if you need to call an API function that requires void* parameters. Within the C# language, there isn't a great deal that you can do using void pointers. In particular, the compiler will flag an error if you attempt to dereference a void pointer using the * operator.

Pointer Arithmetic

It is possible to add or subtract integers to and from pointers. However, the compiler is quite clever about how it arranges for this to be done. For example, suppose that you have a pointer to an int and you try to add 1 to its value. The compiler will assume that you actually mean you want to look at the memory location following the int, and hence it will increase the value by 4 bytes — the size of an int. If it is a pointer to a double, adding 1 will actually increase the value of the pointer by 8 bytes, the size of a double. Only if the pointer points to a byte or sbyte (1 byte each) will adding 1 to the value of the pointer actually change its value by 1.

You can use the operators +, -, +=, -=, ++, and -- with pointers, with the variable on the right-hand side of these operators being a long or ulong.

It is not permitted to carry out arithmetic operations on void pointers.

For example, assume these definitions:

```
uint u = 3;
byte b = 8;
double d = 10.0;
uint* pUint= &u;         // size of a uint is 4
byte* pByte = &b;        // size of a byte is 1
double* pDouble = &d;    // size of a double is 8
```

Next, assume the addresses to which these pointers point are:

- pUint: 1243332
- pByte: 1243328
- pDouble: 1243320

Then execute this code:

```
++pUint;              // adds (1*4) = 4 bytes to pUint
pByte -= 3;           // subtracts (3*1) = 3 bytes from pByte
double* pDouble2 = pDouble + 4; // pDouble2 = pDouble + 32 bytes (4*8 bytes)
```

The pointers now contain:

- pUint: 1243336
- pByte: 1243325
- pDouble2: 1243352

The general rule is that adding a number *X* to a pointer to type *T* with value *P* gives the result *P* + *X(sizeof(*T*)).**

You need to be aware of the previous rule. If successive values of a given type are stored in successive memory locations, pointer addition works very well to allow you to move pointers between memory locations. If you are dealing with types such as `byte` *or* `char`*, though, whose sizes are not multiples of 4, successive values will not, by default, be stored in successive memory locations.*

You can also subtract one pointer from another pointer, if both pointers point to the same data type. In this case, the result is a `long` whose value is given by the difference between the pointer values divided by the size of the type that they represent:

```
double* pD1 = (double*)1243324;    // note that it is perfectly valid to
                                   // initialize a pointer like this.
double* pD2 = (double*)1243300;
long L = pD1-pD2;                  // gives the result 3 (=24/sizeof(double))
```

The sizeof Operator

This section has been referring to the sizes of various data types. If you need to use the size of a type in your code, you can use the `sizeof` operator, which takes the name of a data type as a parameter and returns the number of bytes occupied by that type. For example:

```
int x = sizeof(double);
```

This will set `x` to the value `8`.

The advantage of using `sizeof` is that you don't have to hard-code data type sizes in your code, making your code more portable. For the predefined data types, `sizeof` returns the following values:

```
sizeof(sbyte) = 1;  sizeof(byte) = 1;
sizeof(short) = 2;  sizeof(ushort) = 2;
sizeof(int) = 4;    sizeof(uint) = 4;
sizeof(long) = 8;   sizeof(ulong) = 8;
sizeof(char) = 2;   sizeof(float) = 4;
sizeof(double) = 8; sizeof(bool) = 1;
```

You can also use `sizeof` for structs that you define yourself, although in that case, the result depends on what fields are in the struct. You cannot use `sizeof` for classes, and it can only be used in an `unsafe` code block.

Pointers to Structs: The Pointer Member Access Operator

Pointers to structs work in exactly the same way as pointers to the predefined value types. There is, however, one condition — the struct must not contain any reference types. This is due to the restriction mentioned earlier that pointers cannot point to any reference types. To avoid this, the compiler will flag an error if you create a pointer to any struct that contains any reference types.

Suppose that you had a struct defined like this:

```
struct MyStruct
{
   public long X;
   public float F;
}
```

You could define a pointer to it like this:

```
MyStruct* pStruct;
```

Then you could initialize it like this:

```
MyStruct Struct = new MyStruct();
pStruct = &Struct;
```

It is also possible to access member values of a struct through the pointer:

```
(*pStruct).X = 4;
(*pStruct).F = 3.4f;
```

However, this syntax is a bit complex. For this reason, C# defines another operator that allows you to access members of structs through pointers using a simpler syntax. It is known as the *pointer member access operator*, and the symbol is a dash followed by a greater-than sign, so it looks like an arrow: ->.

C++ developers will recognize the pointer member access operator because C++ uses the same symbol for the same purpose.

Using the pointer member access operator, the previous code can be rewritten:

```
pStruct->X = 4;
pStruct->F = 3.4f;
```

You can also directly set up pointers of the appropriate type to point to fields within a struct:

```
long* pL = &(Struct.X);
float* pF = &(Struct.F);
```

or

```
long* pL = &(pStruct->X);
float* pF = &(pStruct->F);
```

Pointers to Class Members

As indicated earlier, it is not possible to create pointers to classes. That is because the garbage collector does not maintain any information about pointers, only about references, so creating pointers to classes could cause garbage collection to not work properly.

However, most classes do contain value type members, and you might want to create pointers to them. This is possible but requires a special syntax. For example, suppose that you rewrite the struct from the previous example as a class:

```
class MyClass
{
   public long X;
   public float F;
}
```

Then you might want to create pointers to its fields, `X` and `F`, in the same way as you did earlier. Unfortunately, doing so will produce a compilation error:

```
MyClass myObject = new MyClass();
long* pL = &(myObject.X);   // wrong -- compilation error
float* pF = &(myObject.F);  // wrong -- compilation error
```

Although `X` and `F` are unmanaged types, they are embedded in an object, which sits on the heap. During garbage collection, the garbage collector might move `MyObject` to a new location, which would leave `pL` and `pF` pointing to the wrong memory addresses. Because of this, the compiler will not let you assign addresses of members of managed types to pointers in this manner.

The solution is to use the `fixed` keyword, which tells the garbage collector that there may be pointers referencing members of certain objects, so those objects must not be moved. The syntax for using `fixed` looks like this if you just want to declare one pointer:

```
MyClass myObject = new MyClass();
fixed (long* pObject = &(myObject.X))
{
   // do something
}
```

You define and initialize the pointer variable in the brackets following the keyword `fixed`. This pointer variable (`pObject` in the example) is scoped to the `fixed` block identified by the curly braces. As a result, the garbage collector knows not to move the `myObject` object while the code inside the `fixed` block is executing.

If you want to declare more than one pointer, you can place multiple `fixed` statements before the same code block:

```
MyClass myObject = new MyClass();
fixed (long* pX = &(myObject.X))
fixed (float* pF = &(myObject.F))
{
   // do something
}
```

You can nest entire `fixed` blocks if you want to fix several pointers for different periods:

```
MyClass myObject = new MyClass();
fixed (long* pX = &(myObject.X))
{
   // do something with pX
   fixed (float* pF = &(myObject.F))
   {
      // do something else with pF
   }
}
```

You can also initialize several variables within the same `fixed` block, if they are of the same type:

```
MyClass myObject = new MyClass();
MyClass myObject2 = new MyClass();
fixed (long* pX = &(myObject.X), pX2 = &(myObject2.X))
{
   // etc.
}
```

In all these cases, it is immaterial whether the various pointers you are declaring point to fields in the same or different objects or to static fields not associated with any class instance.

Pointer Example: PointerPlayaround

This section presents an example that uses pointers. The following code is an example named `PointerPlayaround`. It does some simple pointer manipulation and displays the results, allowing you to see what is happening in memory and where variables are stored:

```
using System;

namespace Wrox.ProCSharp.Memory
{
   class MainEntryPoint
   {
      static unsafe void Main()
```

(continued)

(continued)

```
      {
         int x=10;
         short y = -1;
         byte y2 = 4;
         double z = 1.5;
         int* pX = &x;
         short* pY = &y;
         double* pZ = &z;

         Console.WriteLine(
            "Address of x is 0x{0:X}, size is {1}, value is {2}",
            (uint)&x, sizeof(int), x);
         Console.WriteLine(
            "Address of y is 0x{0:X}, size is {1}, value is {2}",
            (uint)&y, sizeof(short), y);
         Console.WriteLine(
            "Address of y2 is 0x{0:X}, size is {1}, value is {2}",
            (uint)&y2, sizeof(byte), y2);
         Console.WriteLine(
            "Address of z is 0x{0:X}, size is {1}, value is {2}",
            (uint)&z, sizeof(double), z);
         Console.WriteLine(
            "Address of pX=&x is 0x{0:X}, size is {1}, value is 0x{2:X}",
            (uint)&pX, sizeof(int*), (uint)pX);
         Console.WriteLine(
            "Address of pY=&y is 0x{0:X}, size is {1}, value is 0x{2:X}",
            (uint)&pY, sizeof(short*), (uint)pY);
         Console.WriteLine(
            "Address of pZ=&z is 0x{0:X}, size is {1}, value is 0x{2:X}",
            (uint)&pZ, sizeof(double*), (uint)pZ);

         *pX = 20;
         Console.WriteLine("After setting *pX, x = {0}", x);
         Console.WriteLine("*pX = {0}", *pX);

         pZ = (double*)pX;
         Console.WriteLine("x treated as a double = {0}", *pZ);

         Console.ReadLine();
      }
   }
}
```

This code declares four value variables:

- An `int x`
- A `short y`
- A `byte y2`
- A `double z`

It also declares pointers to three of these values: `pX`, `pY`, and `pZ`.

Next, you display the values of these variables as well as their sizes and addresses. Note that in taking the address of `pX`, `pY`, and `pZ`, you are effectively looking at a pointer *to* a pointer — an address of an address of a value. Notice that, in accordance with the usual practice when displaying addresses, you have used the `{0:X}` format specifier in the `Console.WriteLine()` commands to ensure that memory addresses are displayed in hexadecimal format.

Finally, you use the pointer `pX` to change the value of `x` to `20` and do some pointer casting to see what happens if you try to treat the content of `x` as if it were a `double`.

Compiling and running this code results in the following output. This screen output demonstrates the effects of attempting to compile both with and without the `/unsafe` flag:

```
csc PointerPlayaround.cs
Microsoft (R) Visual C# 2008 Compiler version 3.05.20706.1
for Microsoft (R) .NET Framework version 3.5
Copyright (C) Microsoft Corporation. All rights reserved.

PointerPlayaround.cs(7,26): error CS0227: Unsafe code may only appear if
        compiling with /unsafe

csc /unsafe PointerPlayaround.cs
Microsoft (R) Visual C# 2008 Compiler version 3.05.20706.1
for Microsoft (R) .NET Framework version 3.5
Copyright (C) Microsoft Corporation. All rights reserved.

PointerPlayaround
Address of x is 0x12F4B0, size is 4, value is 10
Address of y is 0x12F4AC, size is 2, value is -1
Address of y2 is 0x12F4A8, size is 1, value is 4
Address of z is 0x12F4A0, size is 8, value is 1.5
Address of pX=&x is 0x12F49C, size is 4, value is 0x12F4B0
Address of pY=&y is 0x12F498, size is 4, value is 0x12F4AC
Address of pZ=&z is 0x12F494, size is 4, value is 0x12F4A0
After setting *pX, x = 20
*pX = 20
x treated as a double = 2.86965129997082E-308
```

Checking through these results confirms the description of how the stack operates that was given in the "Memory Management under the Hood" section earlier in this chapter. It allocates successive variables moving downward in memory. Notice how it also confirms that blocks of memory on the stack are always allocated in multiples of 4 bytes. For example, `y` is a `short` (of size 2), and has the (decimal) address `1242284`, indicating that the memory locations reserved for it are locations `1242284` through `1242287`. If the .NET runtime had been strictly packing up variables next to each other, `Y` would have occupied just two locations, `1242284` and `1242285`.

The next example illustrates pointer arithmetic, as well as pointers to structs and class members. This example is named `PointerPlayaround2`. To start, you define a struct named `CurrencyStruct`, which represents a currency value as dollars and cents. You also define an equivalent class named `CurrencyClass`:

```
internal struct CurrencyStruct
{
   public long Dollars;
   public byte Cents;

   public override string ToString()
   {
      return "$" + Dollars + "." + Cents;
```

(continued)

(continued)

```
      }
   }

   internal class CurrencyClass
   {
      public long Dollars;
      public byte Cents;

      public override string ToString()
      {
         return "$" + Dollars + "." + Cents;
      }
   }
```

Now that you have your struct and class defined, you can apply some pointers to them. Following is the code for the new example. Because the code is fairly long, we will go through it in detail. You start by displaying the size of `CurrencyStruct`, creating a couple of `CurrencyStruct` instances and creating some `CurrencyStruct` pointers. You use the `pAmount` pointer to initialize the members of the `amount1` `CurrencyStruct` and then display the addresses of your variables:

```
   public static unsafe void Main()
   {
      Console.WriteLine(
         "Size of CurrencyStruct struct is " + sizeof(CurrencyStruct));
      CurrencyStruct amount1, amount2;
      CurrencyStruct* pAmount = &amount1;
      long* pDollars = &(pAmount->Dollars);
      byte* pCents = &(pAmount->Cents);

      Console.WriteLine("Address of amount1 is 0x{0:X}", (uint)&amount1);
      Console.WriteLine("Address of amount2 is 0x{0:X}", (uint)&amount2);
      Console.WriteLine("Address of pAmount is 0x{0:X}", (uint)&pAmount);
      Console.WriteLine("Address of pDollars is 0x{0:X}", (uint)&pDollars);
      Console.WriteLine("Address of pCents is 0x{0:X}", (uint)&pCents);
      pAmount->Dollars = 20;
      *pCents = 50;
      Console.WriteLine("amount1 contains " + amount1);
```

Now you do some pointer manipulation that relies on your knowledge of how the stack works. Due to the order in which the variables were declared, you know that `amount2` will be stored at an address immediately below `amount1`. The `sizeof(CurrencyStruct)` operator returns 16 (as demonstrated in the screen output coming up), so `CurrencyStruct` occupies a multiple of 4 bytes. Therefore, after you decrement your currency pointer, it will point to `amount2`:

```
      --pAmount;   // this should get it to point to amount2
      Console.WriteLine("amount2 has address 0x{0:X} and contains {1}",
         (uint)pAmount, *pAmount);
```

Notice that when you call `Console.WriteLine()` you display the contents of `amount2`, but you haven't yet initialized it. What gets displayed will be random garbage — whatever happened to be stored at that location in memory before execution of the example. There is an important point here: Normally, the C# compiler would prevent you from using an uninitialized variable, but when you start using pointers, it is very easy to circumvent many of the usual compilation checks. In this case, you have done so because the compiler has no way of knowing that you are actually displaying the contents of `amount2`. Only you know that, because your knowledge of the stack means that you can tell what the effect of decrementing pAmount will be. Once you start doing pointer arithmetic, you will find that you can access all sorts of variables and memory locations that the compiler would usually stop you from accessing, hence the description of pointer arithmetic as unsafe.

Next, you do some pointer arithmetic on your pCents pointer. pCents currently points to amount1 .Cents, but the aim here is to get it to point to amount2.Cents, again using pointer operations instead of directly telling the compiler that's what you want to do. To do this, you need to decrement the address pCents contains by sizeof(Currency):

```
// do some clever casting to get pCents to point to cents
// inside amount2
CurrencyStruct* pTempCurrency = (CurrencyStruct*)pCents;
pCents = (byte*) ( --pTempCurrency );
Console.WriteLine("Address of pCents is now 0x{0:X}", (uint)&pCents);
```

Finally, you use the fixed keyword to create some pointers that point to the fields in a class instance and use these pointers to set the value of this instance. Notice that this is also the first time that you have been able to look at the address of an item stored on the heap rather than the stack:

```
Console.WriteLine("\nNow with classes");
// now try it out with classes
CurrencyClass amount3 = new CurrencyClass();

fixed(long* pDollars2 = &(amount3.Dollars))
fixed(byte* pCents2 = &(amount3.Cents))
{
   Console.WriteLine(
      "amount3.Dollars has address 0x{0:X}", (uint)pDollars2);
   Console.WriteLine(
      "amount3.Cents has address 0x{0:X}", (uint) pCents2);
   *pDollars2 = -100;
   Console.WriteLine("amount3 contains " + amount3);
}
```

Compiling and running this code gives output similar to this:

```
csc /unsafe PointerPlayaround2.cs
Microsoft (R) Visual C# 2008 Compiler version 3.05.20706.1
for Microsoft (R) .NET Framework version 3.5
Copyright (C) Microsoft Corporation. All rights reserved.

PointerPlayaround2
Size of CurrencyStruct struct is 16
Address of amount1 is 0x12F4A4
Address of amount2 is 0x12F494
Address of pAmount is 0x12F490
Address of pDollars is 0x12F48C
Address of pCents is 0x12F488
amount1 contains $20.50
amount2 has address 0x12F494 and contains $0.0
Address of pCents is now 0x12F488

Now with classes
amount3.Dollars has address 0xA64414
amount3.Cents has address 0xA6441C
amount3 contains $-100.0
```

Notice in this output the uninitialized value of `amount2` that is displayed, and notice that the size of the `CurrencyStruct` struct is `16` — somewhat larger than you would expect given the sizes of its fields (a `long` and a `byte` should total 9 bytes).

Using Pointers to Optimize Performance

Until now, all of the examples have been designed to demonstrate the various things that you can do with pointers. We have played around with memory in a way that is probably interesting only to people who like to know what's happening under the hood but that doesn't really help you to write better code. Here you're going to apply your understanding of pointers and see an example of how judicious use of pointers has a significant performance benefit.

Creating Stack-Based Arrays

This section explores one of the main areas in which pointers can be useful: creating high-performance, low-overhead arrays on the stack. As discussed in Chapter 2, "C# Basics," C# includes rich support for handling arrays. Although C# makes it very easy to use both 1-dimensional and rectangular or jagged multidimensional arrays, it suffers from the disadvantage that these arrays are actually objects; they are instances of `System.Array`. This means that the arrays are stored on the heap with all of the overhead that this involves. There may be occasions when you need to create a short-lived high-performance array and don't want the overhead of reference objects. You can do this using pointers, although as you see in this section, this is easy for only 1-dimensional arrays.

To create a high-performance array, you need to use a new keyword: `stackalloc`. The `stackalloc` command instructs the .NET runtime to allocate an amount of memory on the stack. When you call `stackalloc`, you need to supply it with two pieces of information:

- The type of data you want to store
- The number of these data items you need to store

For example, to allocate enough memory to store 10 `decimal` data items, you can write:

```
decimal* pDecimals = stackalloc decimal[10];
```

This command simply allocates the stack memory; it does not attempt to initialize the memory to any default value. This is fine for the purpose of this example because you are creating a high-performance array, and initializing values unnecessarily would hurt performance.

Similarly, to store 20 `double` data items, you write:

```
double* pDoubles = stackalloc double[20];
```

Although this line of code specifies the number of variables to store as a constant, this can equally be a quantity evaluated at runtime. So, you can write the previous example like this:

```
int size;
size = 20;   // or some other value calculated at run-time
double* pDoubles = stackalloc double[size];
```

You will see from these code snippets that the syntax of `stackalloc` is slightly unusual. It is followed immediately by the name of the data type you want to store (and this must be a value type) and then by the number of items you need space for in square brackets. The number of bytes allocated will be this number multiplied by `sizeof(data type)`. The use of square brackets in the preceding code sample suggests an array, which is not too surprising. If you have allocated space for 20 doubles, then what you have is an array of 20 doubles. The simplest type of array that you can have is a block of memory that stores one element after another (see Figure 12-6).

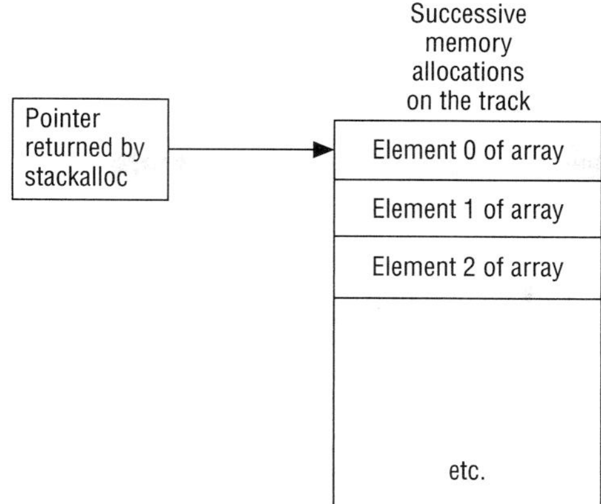

Figure 12-6

This diagram also shows the pointer returned by `stackalloc`, which is always a pointer to the allocated data type that points to the top of the newly allocated memory block. To use the memory block, you simply dereference the returned pointer. For example, to allocate space for 20 doubles and then set the first element (element 0 of the array) to the value `3.0`, write this:

```
double* pDoubles = stackalloc double [20];
*pDoubles = 3.0;
```

To access the next element of the array, you use pointer arithmetic. As described earlier, if you add 1 to a pointer, its value will be increased by the size of whatever data type it points to. In this case, this will be just enough to take you to the next free memory location in the block that you have allocated. So, you can set the second element of the array (element number `1`) to the value `8.4` like this:

```
double* pDoubles = stackalloc double [20];
*pDoubles = 3.0;
*(pDoubles+1) = 8.4;
```

By the same reasoning, you can access the element with index `X` of the array with the expression `*(pDoubles+X)`.

Effectively, you have a means by which you can access elements of your array, but for general-purpose use, this syntax is too complex. Fortunately, C# defines an alternative syntax using square brackets. C# gives a very precise meaning to square brackets when they are applied to pointers; if the variable `p` is any pointer type and `X` is an integer, then the expression `p[X]` is always interpreted by the compiler as meaning `*(p+X)`. This is true for all pointers, not only those initialized using `stackalloc`. With this shorthand notation, you now have a very convenient syntax for accessing your array. In fact, it means that you have exactly the same syntax for accessing 1-dimensional stack-based arrays as you do for accessing heap-based arrays that are represented by the `System.Array` class:

```
double* pDoubles = stackalloc double [20];
pDoubles[0] = 3.0;   // pDoubles[0] is the same as *pDoubles
pDoubles[1] = 8.4;   // pDoubles[1] is the same as *(pDoubles+1)
```

This idea of applying array syntax to pointers is not new. It has been a fundamental part of both the C and the C++ languages ever since those languages were invented. Indeed, C++ developers will recognize the stack-based arrays they can obtain using `stackalloc` *as being essentially identical to classic stack-based C and C++ arrays. It is this syntax and the way it links pointers and arrays that was one of the reasons why the C language became popular in the 1970s, and the main reason why the use of pointers became such a popular programming technique in C and C++.*

Although your high-performance array can be accessed in the same way as a normal C# array, a word of caution is in order. The following code in C# raises an exception:

```
double[] myDoubleArray = new double [20];
myDoubleArray[50] = 3.0;
```

The exception occurs because you are trying to access an array using an index that is out of bounds; the index is `50`, whereas the maximum allowed value is `19`. However, if you declare the equivalent array using `stackalloc`, there is no object wrapped around the array that can perform bounds checking. Hence, the following code will *not* raise an exception:

```
double* pDoubles = stackalloc double [20];
pDoubles[50] = 3.0;
```

In this code, you allocate enough memory to hold 20 doubles. Then you set `sizeof(double)` memory locations starting at the location given by the start of this memory + `50*sizeof(double)` to hold the double value `3.0`. Unfortunately, that memory location is way outside the area of memory that you have allocated for the doubles. There is no knowing what data might be stored at that address. At best, you may have used some currently unused memory, but it is equally possible that you may have just overwritten some locations in the stack that were being used to store other variables or even the return address from the method currently being executed. Once again, you see that the high performance to be gained from pointers comes at a cost; you need to be certain you know what you are doing, or you will get some very strange runtime bugs.

QuickArray Example

Our discussion of pointers ends with a `stackalloc` example called `QuickArray`. In this example, the program simply asks users how many elements they want to be allocated for an array. The code then uses `stackalloc` to allocate an array of `long`s that size. The elements of this array are populated with the squares of the integers starting with `0` and the results displayed on the console:

```
using System;

namespace QuickArray
{
    internal class Program
    {
        private static unsafe void Main()
        {
            Console.Write("How big an array do you want? \n> ");
            string userInput = Console.ReadLine();
            uint size = uint.Parse(userInput);

            long* pArray = stackalloc long[(int) size];
            for (int i = 0; i < size; i++)
            {
                pArray[i] = i*i;
            }

            for (int i = 0; i < size; i++)
            {
                Console.WriteLine("Element {0} = {1}", i, *(pArray + i));
            }

            Console.ReadLine();
        }
    }
}
```

Here is the output for the `QuickArray` example:

```
QuickArray
How big an array do you want?
> 15
Element 0 = 0
Element 1 = 1
Element 2 = 4
Element 3 = 9
Element 4 = 16
Element 5 = 25
Element 6 = 36
Element 7 = 49
Element 8 = 64
Element 9 = 81
Element 10 = 100
Element 11 = 121
Element 12 = 144
Element 13 = 169
Element 14 = 196
```

Summary

Remember, to become a truly proficient C# programmer, you must have a solid understanding of how memory allocation and garbage collection work. This chapter described how the CLR manages and allocates memory on the heap and the stack. It also illustrated how to write classes that free unmanaged resources correctly, and how to use pointers in C#. These are both advanced topics that are poorly understood and often implemented incorrectly by novice programmers.

This chapter should be treated as a companion to what you learn from Chapter 14 on error handling and in Chapter 19 when dealing with threading. The next chapter of this book looks at reflection in C#.

13

Reflection

Reflection is a generic term that describes the ability to inspect and manipulate program elements at runtime. For example, reflection allows you to:

- Enumerate the members of a type
- Instantiate a new object
- Execute the members of an object
- Find out information about a type
- Find out information about an assembly
- Inspect the custom attributes applied to a type
- Create and compile a new assembly

This list represents a great deal of functionality and encompasses some of the most powerful and complex capabilities provided by the .NET Framework class library. Although this chapter does not have the space to cover all the capabilities of reflection, it focuses on those elements that you are likely to use most frequently.

This chapter is about:

- Custom attributes, a mechanism that allows you to associate custom metadata with program elements. This metadata is created at compile time and embedded in an assembly.
- Inspecting the metadata at runtime using some of the capabilities of reflection.
- Some of the fundamental classes that enable reflection, including the `System.Type` and `System.Reflection.Assembly` classes, which provide the access points for much of what you can do with reflection.

To demonstrate custom attributes and reflection, you develop an example based on a company that regularly ships upgrades of its software and wants to have details of these upgrades documented automatically. In the example, you define custom attributes that indicate the date when program elements were last modified, and what changes were made. You then use reflection to develop an application that looks for these attributes in an assembly, and can automatically display all the details about what upgrades have been made to the software since a given date.

Another example in this chapter considers an application that reads from or writes to a database and uses custom attributes as a way of marking which classes and properties correspond to which database tables and columns. By reading these attributes from the assembly at runtime, the program is able to automatically retrieve or write data to the appropriate location in the database, without requiring specific logic for each table or column.

Custom Attributes

From this book, you have seen how you can define attributes on various items within your program. These attributes have been defined by Microsoft as part of the .NET Framework class library, and many of them receive special support from the C# compiler. This means that for those particular attributes, the compiler could customize the compilation process in specific ways; for example, laying out a struct in memory according to the details in the `StructLayout` attributes.

The .NET Framework also allows you to define your own attributes. Clearly, these attributes will not have any effect on the compilation process, because the compiler has no intrinsic awareness of them. However, these attributes will be emitted as metadata in the compiled assembly when they are applied to program elements.

By itself, this metadata might be useful for documentation purposes, but what makes attributes really powerful is that by using reflection, your code can read this metadata and use it to make decisions at runtime. This means that the custom attributes that you define can directly affect how your code runs. For example, custom attributes can be used to enable declarative code access security checks for custom permission classes, to associate information with program elements that can then be used by testing tools, or when developing extensible frameworks that allow the loading of plugins or modules.

Writing Custom Attributes

To understand how to write your own custom attributes, it is useful to know what the compiler does when it encounters an element in your code that has a custom attribute applied to it. To take the database example, suppose that you have a C# property declaration that looks like this:

```
[FieldName("SocialSecurityNumber")]
public string SocialSecurityNumber
{
   get {
      // etc.
```

When the C# compiler recognizes that this property has an attribute applied to it (`FieldName`), it will start by appending the string `Attribute` to this name, forming the combined name `FieldNameAttribute`. The compiler will then search all the namespaces in its search path (those namespaces that have been mentioned in a `using` statement) for a class with the specified name. Note that if you mark an item with an attribute whose name already ends in the string `Attribute`, the compiler will not add the string to the name a second time; it will leave the attribute name unchanged. Therefore, the preceding code is equivalent to this:

```
[FieldNameAttribute("SocialSecurityNumber")]
public string SocialSecurityNumber
{
   get {
   // etc.
```

The compiler expects to find a class with this name, and it expects this class to be derived directly or indirectly from `System.Attribute`. The compiler also expects that this class contains information that governs the use of the attribute. In particular, the attribute class needs to specify the following:

- The types of program elements to which the attribute can be applied (classes, structs, properties, methods, and so on)
- Whether it is legal for the attribute to be applied more than once to the same program element
- Whether the attribute, when applied to a class or interface, is inherited by derived classes and interfaces
- The mandatory and optional parameters the attribute takes

If the compiler cannot find a corresponding attribute class, or it finds one but the way that you have used that attribute does not match the information in the attribute class, the compiler will raise a compilation error. For example, if the attribute class indicates that the attribute can be applied only to classes, but you have applied it to a struct definition, a compilation error will occur.

To continue with the example, assume that you have defined the `FieldName` attribute like this:

```
[AttributeUsage(AttributeTargets.Property,
   AllowMultiple=false,
   Inherited=false)]
public class FieldNameAttribute : Attribute
{
   private string name;
   public FieldNameAttribute(string name)
   {
      this.name = name;
   }
}
```

The following sections discuss each element of this definition.

AttributeUsage Attribute

The first thing to note is that the attribute class itself is marked with an attribute — the `System.AttributeUsage` attribute. This is an attribute defined by Microsoft for which the C# compiler provides special support. (You could argue that `AttributeUsage` isn't an attribute at all; it is more like a meta-attribute, because it applies only to other attributes, not simply to any class.) The primary purpose of `AttributeUsage` is to identify the types of program elements to which your custom attribute can be applied. This information is given by the first parameter of the `AttributeUsage` attribute — this parameter is mandatory, and is of an enumerated type, `AttributeTargets`. In the previous example, you have indicated that the `FieldName` attribute can be applied only to properties, which is fine, because that is exactly what you have applied it to in the earlier code fragment. The members of the `AttributeTargets` enumeration are:

- All
- Assembly
- Class
- Constructor
- Delegate

- Enum
- Event
- Field
- GenericParameter (from .NET 2.0 on only)
- Interface
- Method
- Module
- Parameter
- Property
- ReturnValue
- Struct

This list identifies all of the program elements to which you can apply attributes. Note that when applying the attribute to a program element, you place the attribute in square brackets immediately before the element. However, two values in the preceding list do not correspond to any program element: `Assembly` and `Module`. An attribute can be applied to an assembly or module as a whole instead of to an element in your code; in this case the attribute can be placed anywhere in your source code, but needs to be prefixed with the `Assembly` or `Module` keyword:

```
[assembly:SomeAssemblyAttribute(Parameters)]
[module:SomeAssemblyAttribute(Parameters)]
```

When indicating the valid target elements of a custom attribute, you can combine these values using the bitwise OR operator. For example, if you wanted to indicate that your `FieldName` attribute can be applied to both properties and fields, you would write:

```
[AttributeUsage(AttributeTargets.Property | AttributeTargets.Field,
   AllowMultiple=false,
   Inherited=false)]
public class FieldNameAttribute : Attribute
```

You can also use `AttributeTargets.All` to indicate that your attribute can be applied to all types of program elements. The `AttributeUsage` attribute also contains two other parameters, `AllowMultiple` and `Inherited`. These are specified using the syntax of `<ParameterName>=<ParameterValue>`, instead of simply giving the values for these parameters. These parameters are optional — you can omit them if you want.

The `AllowMultiple` parameter indicates whether an attribute can be applied more than once to the same item. The fact that it is set to `false` here indicates that the compiler should raise an error if it sees something like this:

```
[FieldName("SocialSecurityNumber")]
[FieldName("NationalInsuranceNumber")]
public string SocialSecurityNumber
{

   // etc.
```

If the `Inherited` parameter is set to `true`, an attribute applied to a class or interface will also automatically be applied to all derived classes or interfaces. If the attribute is applied to a method or property, it will automatically apply to any overrides of that method or property, and so on.

Specifying Attribute Parameters

This section examines how you can specify the parameters that your custom attribute takes. The way it works is that when the compiler encounters a statement such as the following,

```
[FieldName("SocialSecurityNumber")]
public string SocialSecurityNumber
{

   // etc.
```

the compiler examines the parameters passed into the attribute — which is a string — and looks for a constructor for the attribute that takes exactly those parameters. If the compiler finds an appropriate constructor, the compiler will emit the specified metadata to the assembly. If the compiler does not find an appropriate constructor, a compilation error occurs. As discussed later in this chapter, reflection involves reading metadata (attributes) from assemblies and instantiating the attribute classes they represent. Because of this, the compiler must ensure that an appropriate constructor exists that will allow the runtime instantiation of the specified attribute.

In the example, you have supplied just one constructor for `FieldNameAttribute`, and this constructor takes one string parameter. Therefore, when applying the `FieldName` attribute to a property, you must supply one string as a parameter, as was done in the preceding sample code.

If you want to allow a choice of what types of parameters should be supplied with an attribute, you can provide different constructor overloads, although normal practice is to supply just one constructor and use properties to define any other optional parameters, as explained next.

Specifying Optional Attribute Parameters

As demonstrated with reference to the `AttributeUsage` attribute, an alternative syntax exists by which optional parameters can be added to an attribute. This syntax involves specifying the names and values of the optional parameters. It works through `public` properties or fields in the `attribute` class. For example, suppose that you modified the definition of the `SocialSecurityNumber` property as follows:

```
[FieldName("SocialSecurityNumber", Comment="This is the primary key field")]
public string SocialSecurityNumber
{

   // etc.
```

In this case, the compiler recognizes the `<ParameterName>=<ParameterValue>` syntax of the second parameter and does not attempt to match this parameter to a `FieldNameAttribute` constructor. Instead, it looks for a `public` property or field (although public fields are not considered good programming practice, so normally you will work with properties) of that name that it can use to set the value of this parameter. If you want the previous code to work, you have to add some code to `FieldNameAttribute`:

```
[AttributeUsage(AttributeTargets.Property,
   AllowMultiple=false,
   Inherited=false)]
public class FieldNameAttribute : Attribute
{
   private string comment;
   public string Comment
```

(continued)

(continued)

```
      {
         get
         {
            return comment;
         }
         set
         {
            comment = value;
         }
      }

         // etc
   }
```

Custom Attribute Example: WhatsNewAttributes

In this section, you start developing the example mentioned at the beginning of the chapter. `WhatsNewAttributes` provides for an attribute that indicates when a program element was last modified. This is a more ambitious code sample than many of the others in that it consists of three separate assemblies:

- The `WhatsNewAttributes` assembly, which contains the definitions of the attributes
- The `VectorClass` assembly, which contains the code to which the attributes have been applied
- The `LookUpWhatsNew` assembly, which contains the project that displays details of items that have changed

Of these, only `LookUpWhatsNew` is a console application of the type that you have used up until now. The remaining two assemblies are libraries — they each contain class definitions but no program entry point. For the `VectorClass` assembly, this means that the entry point and test harness class have been removed from the `VectorAsCollection` sample, leaving only the `Vector` class. These classes are represented later in this chapter.

Managing three related assemblies by compiling at the command line is tricky. Although the commands for compiling all these source files are provided separately, you might prefer to edit the code sample (which you can download from the Wrox Web site at `www.wrox.com`) as a combined Visual Studio solution, as discussed in Chapter 15, "Visual Studio 2008." The download includes the required Visual Studio 2008 solution files.

The WhatsNewAttributes Library Assembly

This section starts with the core `WhatsNewAttributes` assembly. The source code is contained in the file `WhatsNewAttributes.cs`, which is located in the WhatsNewAttributes project of the `WhatsNewAttributes` solution in the example code for this chapter. The syntax for doing this is quite simple. At the command line, you supply the flag `target:library` to the compiler. To compile `WhatsNewAttributes`, type the following:

```
csc /target:library WhatsNewAttributes.cs
```

The `WhatsNewAttributes.cs` file defines two attribute classes, `LastModifiedAttribute` and `SupportsWhatsNewAttribute`. The attribute, `LastModifiedAttribute`, is the attribute that you can use to mark when an item was last modified. It takes two mandatory parameters (parameters that are passed to the constructor): the date of the modification and a string containing a description of the changes. There is also one optional parameter named `issues` (for which a `public` property exists), which can be used to describe any outstanding issues for the item.

In practice, you would probably want this attribute to apply to anything. To keep the code simple, its usage is limited here to classes and methods. You will allow it to be applied more than once to the same item (`AllowMultiple=true`) because an item might be modified more than once, and each modification will have to be marked with a separate attribute instance.

`SupportsWhatsNew` is a smaller class representing an attribute that doesn't take any parameters. The idea of this attribute is that it is an assembly attribute that is used to mark an assembly for which you are maintaining documentation via the `LastModifiedAttribute`. This way, the program that will examine this assembly later on knows that the assembly it is reading is one on which you are actually using your automated documentation process. Here is the complete source code for this part of the example:

```
using System;

namespace Wrox.ProCSharp.WhatsNewAttributes
{
   [AttributeUsage(
      AttributeTargets.Class | AttributeTargets.Method,
      AllowMultiple=true, Inherited=false)]
   public class LastModifiedAttribute : Attribute
   {
        private readonly DateTime dateModified;
        private readonly string changes;
        private string issues;

        public LastModifiedAttribute(string dateModified, string changes)
        {
            this.dateModified = DateTime.Parse(dateModified);
            this.changes = changes;
        }

        public DateTime DateModified
        {
            get { return dateModified; }
        }

        public string Changes
        {
            get { return changes; }
        }

        public string Issues
        {
            get { return issues; }
            set { issues = value; }
        }    }

   [AttributeUsage(AttributeTargets.Assembly)]
   public class SupportsWhatsNewAttribute : Attribute
   {
   }
}
```

This code should be clear with reference to previous descriptions. Notice, however, that we have not bothered to supply `set` accessors to the `Changes` and `DateModified` properties. There is no need for these accessors because you are requiring these parameters to be set in the constructor as mandatory parameters. You need the `get` accessors so that you can read the values of these attributes.

The VectorClass Assembly

Next, you need to use these attributes. To this end, you use a modified version of the earlier `VectorAsCollection` sample. Note that you need to reference the `WhatsNewAttributes` library that you have just created. You also need to indicate the corresponding namespace with a `using` statement so that the compiler can recognize the attributes:

```
using System;
using System.Collections;
using System.Text;
using Wrox.ProCSharp.WhatsNewAttributes;

[assembly: SupportsWhatsNew]
```

In this code, you have also added the line that will mark the assembly itself with the `SupportsWhatsNew` attribute.

Now for the code for the `Vector` class. You are not making any major changes to this class; you only add a couple of `LastModified` attributes to mark out the work that you have done on this class in this chapter. Then `Vector` is defined as a class instead of a struct to simplify the code (of the next iteration of the sample) that displays the attributes. (In the `VectorAsCollection` sample, `Vector` is a struct, but its enumerator is a class. This means that the next iteration of the sample would have had to pick out both classes and structs when looking at the assembly, which would have made the example less straightforward.)

```
namespace Wrox.ProCSharp.VectorClass
{
   [LastModified("14 Feb 2008", "IEnumerable interface implemented " +
       "So Vector can now be treated as a collection")]
   [LastModified("10 Feb 2008", "IFormattable interface implemented " +
       "So Vector now responds to format specifiers N and VE")]
   class Vector : IFormattable, IEnumerable
   {
      public double x, y, z;

      public Vector(double x, double y, double z)
      {
         this.x = x;
         this.y = y;
         this.z = z;
      }

      [LastModified("10 Feb 2008",
                    "Method added in order to provide formatting support")]
      public string ToString(string format, IFormatProvider formatProvider)
      {
         if (format == null)
         {
            return ToString();
         }
```

You also mark the contained `VectorEnumerator` class as new:

```
   [LastModified("14 Feb 2008",
                 "Class created as part of collection support for Vector")]
   private class VectorEnumerator : IEnumerator
   {
```

To compile this code from the command line, type the following:

```
csc /target:library /reference:WhatsNewAttributes.dll VectorClass.cs
```

That's as far as you can get with this example for now. You are unable to run anything yet because all you have are two libraries. You will develop the final part of the example, in which you look up and display these attributes, as soon as you have had a look at how reflection works.

Reflection

In this section, we take a closer look at the `System.Type` class, which lets you access information concerning the definition of any data type. We then discuss the `System.Reflection.Assembly` class, which you can use to access information about an assembly or to load that assembly into your program. Finally, you will combine the code in this section with the code in the previous section to complete the `WhatsNewAttributes` sample.

The System.Type Class

So far you have used the `Type` class only to hold the reference to a type as follows:

```
Type t = typeof(double);
```

Although previously referred to as a class, `Type` is an abstract base class. Whenever you instantiate a `Type` object, you are actually instantiating a class derived from `Type`. `Type` has one derived class corresponding to each actual data type, though in general the derived classes simply provide different overloads of the various `Type` methods and properties that return the correct data for the corresponding data type. They do not generally add new methods or properties. In general, there are three common ways to obtain a `Type` reference that refers to any given type:

1. You can use the C# `typeof` operator as in the preceding code. This operator takes the name of the type (not in quotation marks, however) as a parameter.
2. You can use the `GetType()` method, which all classes inherit from `System.Object`:

```
double d = 10;
Type t = d.GetType();
```

   `GetType()` is called against a variable, rather than taking the name of a type. Note, however, that the `Type` object returned is still associated with only that data type. It does not contain any information that relates to that instance of the type. The `GetType()` method can be useful if you have a reference to an object but are not sure what class that object is actually an instance of.

3. You can call the `static` method of the `Type` class, `GetType()`:

```
Type t = Type.GetType("System.Double");
```

`Type` is really the gateway to much of the reflection functionality. It implements a huge number of methods and properties — far too many to provide a comprehensive list here. However, the following subsections should give you some idea of the kinds of things you can do with the `Type` class. Note that the available properties are all read-only; you use `Type` to find out about the data type — you cannot use it to make any modifications to the type!

Type Properties

You can split the properties implemented by `Type` into three categories:

- A number of properties retrieve the strings containing various names associated with the class, as shown in the following table:

Property	Returns
`Name`	The name of the data type
`FullName`	The fully qualified name of the data type (including the namespace name)
`Namespace`	The name of the namespace in which the data type is defined

- It is also possible to retrieve references to further type objects that represent related classes, as shown in the following table:

Property	Returns Type Reference Corresponding To
`BaseType`	Immediate base type of this type
`UnderlyingSystemType`	The type that this type maps to in the .NET runtime (recall that certain .NET base types actually map to specific predefined types recognized by IL)

- A number of Boolean properties indicate whether this type is, for example, a class, an `enum`, and so on. These properties include `IsAbstract`, `IsArray`, `IsClass`, `IsEnum`, `IsInterface`, `IsPointer`, `IsPrimitive` (one of the predefined primitive data types), `IsPublic`, `IsSealed`, and `IsValueType`.

For example, using a primitive data type:

```
Type intType = typeof(int);
Console.WriteLine(intType.IsAbstract);     // writes false
Console.WriteLine(intType.IsClass);        // writes false
Console.WriteLine(intType.IsEnum);         // writes false
Console.WriteLine(intType.IsPrimitive);    // writes true
Console.WriteLine(intType.IsValueType);    // writes true
```

Or using the `Vector` class:

```
Type vecType = typeof(Vector);
Console.WriteLine(vecType.IsAbstract);     // writes false
Console.WriteLine(vecType.IsClass);        // writes true
Console.WriteLine(vecType.IsEnum);         // writes false
Console.WriteLine(vecType.IsPrimitive);    // writes false
Console.WriteLine(vecType.IsValueType);    // writes false
```

You can also retrieve a reference to the assembly that the type is defined in. This is returned as a reference to an instance of the `System.Reflection.Assembly` class, which is examined shortly:

```
Type t = typeof (Vector);
Assembly containingAssembly = new Assembly(t);
```

Methods

Most of the methods of `System.Type` are used to obtain details of the members of the corresponding data type — the constructors, properties, methods, events, and so on. Quite a large number of methods exist, but they all follow the same pattern. For example, two methods retrieve details of the methods of the data type: `GetMethod()` and `GetMethods()`. `GetMethod()` returns a reference to a `System.Reflection.MethodInfo` object, which contains details of a method. `GetMethods()` returns an array of such references. The difference is that `GetMethods()` returns details of all the methods, whereas `GetMethod()` returns details of just one method with a specified parameter list. Both methods have overloads that take an extra parameter, a `BindingFlags` enumerated value that indicates which members should be returned — for example, whether to return public members, instance members, static members, and so on.

For example, the simplest overload of `GetMethods()` takes no parameters and returns details of all the public methods of the data type:

```
Type t = typeof(double);
MethodInfo[] methods = t.GetMethods();
foreach (MethodInfo nextMethod in methods)
{
   // etc.
       }
```

The member methods of `Type` that follow the same pattern are shown in the following table.

Type of Object Returned	Methods (The Method with the Plural Name Returns an Array)
`ConstructorInfo`	`GetConstructor(),GetConstructors()`
`EventInfo`	`GetEvent(),GetEvents()`
`FieldInfo`	`GetField(),GetFields()`
`InterfaceInfo`	`GetInterface(),GetInterfaces()`
`MemberInfo`	`GetMember(),GetMembers()`
`MethodInfo`	`GetMethod(),GetMethods()`
`PropertyInfo`	`GetProperty(),GetProperties()`

The `GetMember()` and `GetMembers()` methods return details of any or all members of the data type, regardless of whether these members are constructors, properties, methods, and so on. Finally, note that it is possible to invoke members either by calling the `InvokeMember()` method of `Type` or by calling the `Invoke()` method of the `MethodInfo`, `PropertyInfo`, and the other classes.

The TypeView Example

This section demonstrates some of the features of the `Type` class with a short example, `TypeView`, which you can use to list the members of a data type. The example demonstrates how to use `TypeView` for a `double`; however, you can swap this type with any other data type just by changing one line of the code in the sample. `TypeView` displays far more information than can be displayed in a console window, so we're going to take a break from our normal practice and display the output in a message box. Running `TypeView` for a `double` produces the results shown in Figure 13-1.

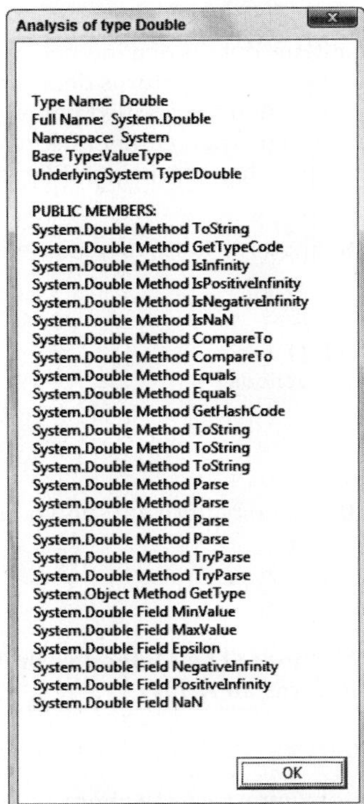

Figure 13-1

The message box displays the name, full name, and namespace of the data type as well as the name of the underlying type and the base type. Next, it simply iterates through all the public instance members of the data type, displaying for each member the declaring type, the type of member (method, field, and so on), and the name of the member. The *declaring type* is the name of the class that actually declares the type member (for example, `System.Double` if it is defined or overridden in `System.Double`, or the name of the relevant base type if the member is simply inherited from some base class).

`TypeView` does not display signatures of methods because you are retrieving details of all public instance members through `MemberInfo` objects, and information about parameters is not available through a `MemberInfo` object. In order to retrieve that information, you would need references to `MethodInfo` and other more specific objects, which means that you would need to obtain details of each type of member separately.

`TypeView` does display details of all public instance members, but for doubles, the only ones defined are fields and methods. For this example, you will compile `TypeView` as a console application — there is no problem with displaying a message box from a console application. However, the fact that you are using a message box means that you need to reference the base class assembly `System.Windows.Forms.dll`, which contains the classes in the `System.Windows.Forms` namespace in which the `MessageBox` class that you will need is defined. The code for `TypeView` is as follows. To begin, you need to add a few `using` statements:

```
using System;
using System.Text;
```

```
using System.Windows.Forms;
using System.Reflection;
```

You need `System.Text` because you will be using a `StringBuilder` object to build up the text to be displayed in the message box, and `System.Windows.Forms` for the message box itself. The entire code is in one class, `MainClass`, which has a couple of `static` methods and one `static` field, a `StringBuilder` instance called `OutputText`, which will be used to build up the text to be displayed in the message box. The main method and class declaration look like this:

```
class MainClass
{
   static StringBuilder OutputText = new StringBuilder();

   static void Main()
   {
      // modify this line to retrieve details of any
      // other data type
      Type t = typeof(double);

      AnalyzeType(t);
      MessageBox.Show(OutputText.ToString(), "Analysis of type "
                                              + t.Name);
      Console.ReadLine();
   }
```

The `Main()` method implementation starts by declaring a `Type` object to represent your chosen data type. You then call a method, `AnalyzeType()`, which extracts the information from the `Type` object and uses it to build up the output text. Finally, you show the output in a message box. Using the `MessageBox` class is fairly intuitive. You just call its `static Show()` method, passing it two strings, which will, respectively, be the text in the box and the caption. `AnalyzeType()` is where the bulk of the work is done:

```
   static void AnalyzeType(Type t)
   {
      AddToOutput("Type Name:   " + t.Name);
      AddToOutput("Full Name:   " + t.FullName);
      AddToOutput("Namespace:   " + t.Namespace);

      Type tBase = t.BaseType;

      if (tBase != null)
      {
         AddToOutput("Base Type:" + tBase.Name);
      }

      Type tUnderlyingSystem = t.UnderlyingSystemType;

      if (tUnderlyingSystem != null)
      {
         AddToOutput("UnderlyingSystem Type:" + tUnderlyingSystem.Name);
      }

      AddToOutput("\nPUBLIC MEMBERS:");
      MemberInfo [] Members = t.GetMembers();

      foreach (MemberInfo NextMember in Members)
```

(continued)

(continued)

```
            {
               AddToOutput(NextMember.DeclaringType + " " +
               NextMember.MemberType + " " + NextMember.Name);
            }
         }
```

You implement the `AnalyzeType()` method by calling various properties of the `Type` object to get the information you need concerning the type names, then call the `GetMembers()` method to get an array of `MemberInfo` objects that you can use to display the details of each member. Note that you use a helper method, `AddToOutput()`, to build up the text to be displayed in the message box:

```
static void AddToOutput(string Text)
{
   OutputText.Append("\n" + Text);
}
```

Compile the `TypeView` assembly using this command:

```
csc /reference:System.Windows.Forms.dll TypeView.cs
```

The Assembly Class

The `Assembly` class is defined in the `System.Reflection` namespace and provides access to the metadata for a given assembly. It also contains methods to allow you to load and even execute an assembly — assuming that the assembly is an executable. Like the `Type` class, `Assembly` contains a large number of methods and properties — too many to cover here. Instead, this section is confined to covering those methods and properties that you need to get started and that you will use to complete the `WhatsNewAttributes` example.

Before you can do anything with an `Assembly` instance, you need to load the corresponding assembly into the running process. You can do this with either the `static` members `Assembly.Load()` or `Assembly.LoadFrom()`. The difference between these methods is that `Load()` takes the name of the assembly, and the runtime searches in a variety of locations in an attempt to locate the assembly. These locations include the local directory and the global assembly cache. `LoadFrom()` takes the full path name of an assembly and does not attempt to find the assembly in any other location:

```
Assembly assembly1 = Assembly.Load("SomeAssembly");
Assembly assembly2 = Assembly.LoadFrom
   (@"C:\My Projects\Software\SomeOtherAssembly");
```

A number of other overloads of both methods exist, which supply additional security information. Once you have loaded an assembly, you can use various properties on it to find out, for example, its full name:

```
string name = assembly1.FullName;
```

Finding Out About Types Defined in an Assembly

One nice feature of the `Assembly` class is that it allows you to obtain details of all the types that are defined in the corresponding assembly. You simply call the `Assembly.GetTypes()` method, which returns an array of `System.Type` references containing details of all the types. You can then manipulate these `Type` references as explained in the previous section.

```
Type[] types = theAssembly.GetTypes();

foreach(Type definedType in types)
{
   DoSomethingWith(definedType);
}
```

Finding Out About Custom Attributes

The methods you use to find out which custom attributes are defined on an assembly or type depend on what type of object the attribute is attached to. If you want to find out what custom attributes are attached to an assembly as a whole, you need to call a `static` method of the `Attribute` class, `GetCustomAttributes()`, passing in a reference to the assembly:

```
Attribute[] definedAttributes =
            Attribute.GetCustomAttributes(assembly1);
            // assembly1 is an Assembly object
```

This is actually quite significant. You may have wondered why, when you defined custom attributes, you had to go to all the trouble of actually writing classes for them, and why Microsoft hadn't come up with some simpler syntax. Well, the answer is here. The custom attributes do genuinely exist as objects, and when an assembly is loaded you can read in these attribute objects, examine their properties, and call their methods.

`GetCustomAttributes()`, which is used to get assembly attributes, has a few overloads. If you call it without specifying any parameters other than an assembly reference, it will simply return all the custom attributes defined for that assembly. You can also call `GetCustomAttributes()` specifying a second parameter, which is a `Type` object that indicates the attribute class in which you are interested. In this case, `GetCustomAttributes()` returns an array consisting of all the attributes present that are of the specified type.

Note that all attributes are retrieved as plain `Attribute` references. If you want to call any of the methods or properties you defined for your custom attributes, you will need to cast these references explicitly to the relevant custom attribute classes. You can obtain details of custom attributes that are attached to a given data type by calling another overload of `Assembly.GetCustomAttributes()`, this time passing a `Type` reference that describes the type for which you want to retrieve any attached attributes. If you want to obtain attributes that are attached to methods, constructors, fields, and so on, however, you will need to call a `GetCustomAttributes()` method that is a member of one of the classes `MethodInfo`, `ConstructorInfo`, `FieldInfo`, and so on.

If you expect only a single attribute of a given type, you can call the `GetCustomAttribute()` method instead, which returns a single `Attribute` object. You will use `GetCustomAttribute()` in the `WhatsNewAttributes` example to find out whether the `SupportsWhatsNew` attribute is present in the assembly. To do this, you call `GetCustomAttribute()`, passing in a reference to the `WhatsNewAttributes` assembly, and the type of the `SupportsWhatsNewAttribute` attribute. If this attribute is present, you get an `Attribute` instance. If no instances of it are defined in the assembly, you get `null`. And if two or more instances are found, `GetCustomAttribute()` throws a `System.Reflection.AmbiguousMatchException`.

```
Attribute supportsAttribute =
          Attribute.GetCustomAttributes(assembly1,
          typeof(SupportsWhatsNewAttribute));
```

Completing the WhatsNewAttributes Example

You now have enough information to complete the `WhatsNewAttributes` example by writing the source code for the final assembly in the sample, the `LookUpWhatsNew` assembly. This part of the application is a console application. However, it needs to reference the other assemblies of `WhatsNewAttributes` and `VectorClass`. Although this is going to be a command-line application, you will follow the previous `TypeView` sample in actually displaying your results in a message box because there is a lot of text output — too much to show in a console window screenshot.

The file is called `LookUpWhatsNew.cs`, and the command to compile it is:

```
csc /reference:WhatsNewAttributes.dll /reference:VectorClass.dll LookUpWhatsNew.cs
```

In the source code of this file, you first indicate the namespaces you want to infer. `System.Text` is there because you need to use a `StringBuilder` object again:

```
using System;
using System.Reflection;
using System.Windows.Forms;
using System.Text;
using Wrox.ProCSharp.VectorClass;
using Wrox.ProCSharp.WhatsNewAttributes;

namespace Wrox.ProCSharp.LookUpWhatsNew
{
```

The class that contains the main program entry point as well as the other methods is `WhatsNewChecker`. All the methods you define are in this class, which also has two static fields: `outputText`, which contains the text as you build it up in preparation for writing it to the message box, and `backDateTo`, which stores the date you have selected. All modifications made since this date will be displayed. Normally, you would display a dialog box inviting the user to pick this date, but we don't want to get sidetracked into that kind of code. For this reason, `backDateTo` is hard-coded to a value of 1 Feb 2008. You can easily change this date if you want when you download the code:

```
   class WhatsNewChecker
   {
      static StringBuilder outputText = new StringBuilder(1000);
      static readonly DateTime backDateTo = new DateTime(2008, 2, 1);

      static void Main()
      {
         Assembly theAssembly = Assembly.Load("VectorClass");
         Attribute supportsAttribute =
            Attribute.GetCustomAttribute(
               theAssembly, typeof(SupportsWhatsNewAttribute));
         string Name = theAssembly.FullName;

         AddToMessage("Assembly: " + Name);

         if (supportsAttribute == null)
         {
            AddToMessage(
               "This assembly does not support WhatsNew attributes");
            return;
         }
         else
         {
            AddToMessage("Defined Types:");
         }

         Type[] types = theAssembly.GetTypes();

         foreach(Type definedType in types)
            DisplayTypeInfo(theAssembly, definedType);
```

```
        MessageBox.Show(outputText.ToString(),
            "What\'s New since " + backDateTo.ToLongDateString());
        Console.ReadLine();
    }
```

The `Main()` method first loads the `VectorClass` assembly, and verifies that it is marked with the `SupportsWhatsNew` attribute. You know `VectorClass` has the `SupportsWhatsNew` attribute applied to it because you have only recently compiled it, but this is a check that would be worth making if users were given a choice of what assembly they wanted to check.

Assuming that all is well, you use the `Assembly.GetTypes()` method to get an array of all the types defined in this assembly, and then loop through them. For each one, you call a method, `DisplayTypeInfo()`, which will add the relevant text, including details of any instances of `LastModifiedAttribute`, to the `outputText` field. Finally, you show the message box with the complete text. The `DisplayTypeInfo()` method looks like this:

```
    static void DisplayTypeInfo(Assembly theAssembly, Type type)
    {
        // make sure we only pick out classes
        if (!(type.IsClass))
        {
            return;
        }

        AddToMessage("\nclass " + type.Name);

        Attribute [] attribs = Attribute.GetCustomAttributes(type);

        if (attribs.Length == 0)
        {
            AddToMessage("No changes to this class\n");
        }
        else
        {
            foreach (Attribute attrib in attribs)
            {
                WriteAttributeInfo(attrib);
            }
        }

        MethodInfo [] methods = type.GetMethods();
        AddToMessage("CHANGES TO METHODS OF THIS CLASS:");

        foreach (MethodInfo nextMethod in methods)
        {
            object [] attribs2 =
                nextMethod.GetCustomAttributes(
                    typeof(LastModifiedAttribute), false);

            if (attribs2 != null)
            {
                AddToMessage(
                    nextMethod.ReturnType + " " + nextMethod.Name + "()");
                foreach (Attribute nextAttrib in attribs2)
```

(continued)

(continued)

```
                {
                    WriteAttributeInfo(nextAttrib);
                }
            }
        }
    }
```

Notice that the first thing you do in this method is check whether the `Type` reference you have been passed actually represents a class. Because, in order to keep things simple, you have specified that the `LastModified` attribute can be applied only to classes or member methods, you would be wasting your time doing any processing if the item is not a class (it could be a class, delegate, or enum).

Next, you use the `Attribute.GetCustomAttributes()` method to find out if this class does have any `LastModifiedAttribute` instances attached to it. If it does, you add their details to the output text, using a helper method, `WriteAttributeInfo()`.

Finally, you use the `Type.GetMethods()` method to iterate through all the member methods of this data type, and then do the same with each method as you did for the class — check if it has any `LastModifiedAttribute` instances attached to it and, if so, display them using `WriteAttributeInfo()`.

The next bit of code shows the `WriteAttributeInfo()` method, which is responsible for working out what text to display for a given `LastModifiedAttribute` instance. Note that this method is passed an `Attribute` reference, so it needs to cast this to a `LastModifiedAttribute` reference first. After it has done that, it uses the properties that you originally defined for this attribute to retrieve its parameters. It checks that the date of the attribute is sufficiently recent before actually adding it to the text for display:

```
static void WriteAttributeInfo(Attribute attrib)
{

   LastModifiedAttribute lastModifiedAttrib =
      attrib as LastModifiedAttribute;

   if (lastModifiedAttrib == null)
   {
      return;
   }

   // check that date is in range
   DateTime modifiedDate = lastModifiedAttrib.DateModified;

   if (modifiedDate < backDateTo)
   {
      return;
   }

   AddToMessage("  MODIFIED: " +
      modifiedDate.ToLongDateString() + ":");
   AddToMessage("    " + lastModifiedAttrib.Changes);

   if (lastModifiedAttrib.Issues != null)
   {
      AddToMessage("    Outstanding issues:" +
```

```
                        lastModifiedAttrib.Issues);
                }
            }
```

Finally, here is the helper AddToMessage() method:

```
            static void AddToMessage(string message)
            {
                outputText.Append("\n" + message);
            }
        }
    }
```

Running this code produces the results shown in Figure 13-2.

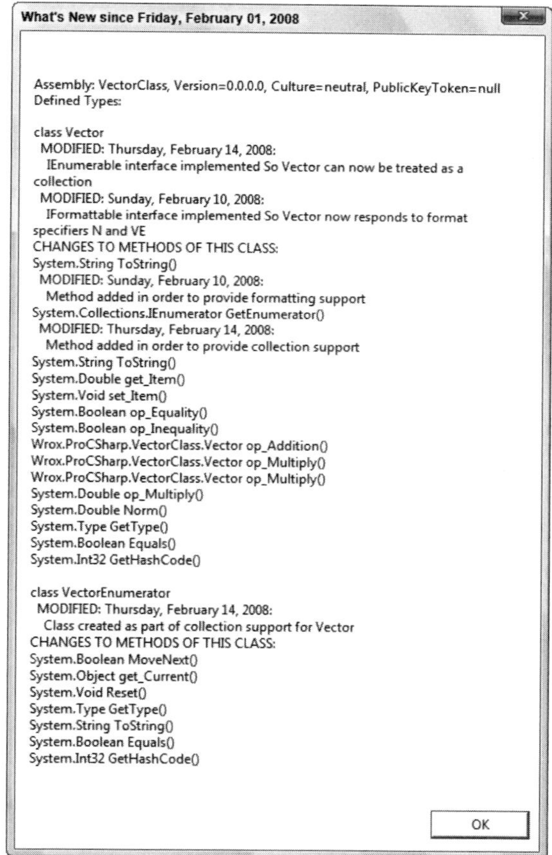

Figure 13-2

Notice that when you list the types defined in the VectorClass assembly, you actually pick up two classes: Vector and the embedded VectorEnumerator class. Also notice that because the backDateTo date of 1 Feb is hard-coded in this example, you actually pick up the attributes that are dated 14 Feb (when you added the collection support) but not those dated 14 Jan (when you added the IFormattable interface).

Summary

This chapter did not attempt to cover the entire topic of reflection. Reflection is an extensive subject worthy of a book of its own. Instead, it illustrated the `Type` and `Assembly` classes, which are the primary entry points through which you can access the extensive capabilities provided by reflection.

In addition, this chapter demonstrated a specific aspect of reflection that you are likely to use more often than any other — the inspection of custom attributes. You learned how to define and apply your own custom attributes, and how to retrieve information about custom attributes at runtime.

Chapter 14 explores exceptions and structured exception handling.

14

Errors and Exceptions

Errors happen, and they are not always caused by the person who coded the application. Sometimes your application will generate an error because of an action that was initiated by the end user of your application or it might be simply due to the environmental context in which your code is running. In any case, you should anticipate errors occurring in your applications and code accordingly.

The .NET Framework has enhanced the ways in which you deal with errors. C#'s mechanism for handling error conditions allows you to provide custom handling for each type of error condition as well as to separate code that identifies errors from the code that handles them.

The main topics covered in this chapter include:

- Looking at the exception classes
- Using `try - catch - finally` to capture exceptions
- Creating user-defined exceptions

By the end of the chapter, you will have a good grasp on advanced exception handling in your C# applications.

No matter how good your coding is, your programs should have the ability to handle any possible errors that may occur. For example, in the middle of some complex processing your code may discover that it doesn't have permission to read a file, or, while it is sending network requests, the network may go down. In such exceptional situations, it is not enough for a method to simply return an appropriate error code — there might be 15 or 20 nested method calls, so what you really want the program to do is jump back up through all those 15 or 20 calls in order to exit the task completely and take the appropriate counteractions. The C# language has very good facilities to handle this kind of situation, through the mechanism known as *exception handling*.

> *Error-handling facilities in Visual Basic 6 are very restricted and essentially limited to the* `On Error GoTo` *statement. If you are coming from a Visual Basic 6 background, you will find that C# exceptions open a completely new world of error handling in your programs. Java and C++ developers, however, will be familiar with the principle of exceptions because these languages handle errors in a similar way to C#. Developers using C++ are sometimes wary of exceptions because of possible C++ performance implications, but this is not the case in C#. Using exceptions in C# code in general does not adversely affect performance. Visual Basic developers will find that working with exceptions in C# is very similar to using exceptions in Visual Basic (except for the syntax differences).*

Exception Classes

In C#, an exception is an object created (or *thrown*) when a particular exceptional error condition occurs. This object contains information that should help track down the problem. Although you can create your own exception classes (and you will be doing so later), .NET provides you with many predefined exception classes.

This section provides a quick survey of some of the exceptions available in the .NET base class library. Microsoft has provided a large number of exception classes in .NET — too many to provide a comprehensive list here. This class hierarchy diagram in Figure 14-1 shows a few of these classes to give you a sense of the general pattern.

All the classes in Figure 14-1 are part of the `System` namespace, except for `IOException` and the classes derived from `IOException`, which are part of the namespace `System.IO`. The `System.IO` namespace deals with reading and writing data to files. In general, there is no specific namespace for exceptions. Exception classes should be placed in whatever namespace is appropriate to the classes that can generate them — hence IO-related exceptions are in the `System.IO` namespace. You will find exception classes in quite a few of the base class namespaces.

The generic exception class, `System.Exception`, is derived from `System.Object`, as you would expect for a .NET class. In general, you should not throw generic `System.Exception` objects in your code, because they provide no specifics about the error condition.

Two important classes in the hierarchy are derived from `System.Exception`:

- `System.SystemException` — This class is for exceptions that are usually thrown by the .NET runtime or that are considered to be of a generic nature and might be thrown by almost any application. For example, `StackOverflowException` will be thrown by the .NET runtime if it detects the stack is full. However, you might choose to throw `ArgumentException` or its subclasses in your own code, if you detect that a method has been called with inappropriate arguments. Subclasses of `System.SystemException` include classes that represent both fatal and nonfatal errors.
- `System.ApplicationException` — This class is important, because it is the intended base for any class of exception defined by third parties. If you define any exceptions covering error conditions unique to your application, you should derive these directly or indirectly from `System.ApplicationException`.

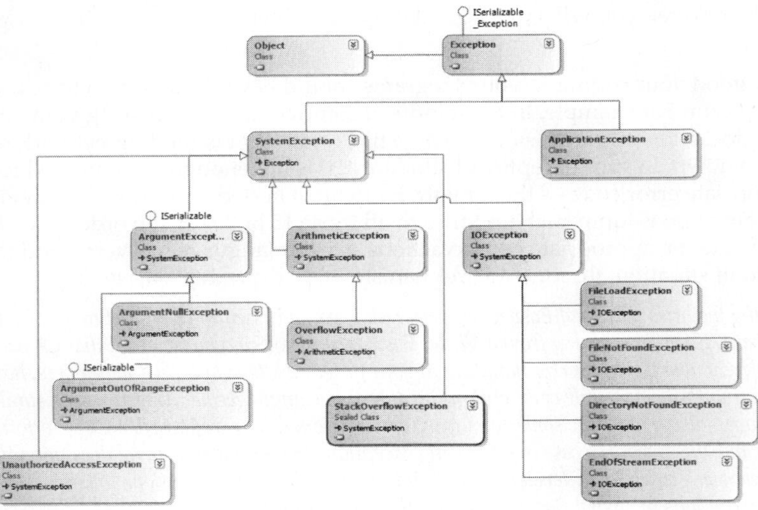

Figure 14-1

Other exception classes that might come in handy include the following:

- `StackOverflowException` — This exception is thrown when the area of memory allocated to the stack is full. A stack overflow can occur if a method continuously calls itself recursively. This is generally a fatal error, because it prevents your application from doing anything apart from terminating (in which case it is unlikely that even the `finally` block will execute). Trying to handle errors like this yourself is usually pointless; instead, you should get the application to gracefully exit.
- `EndOfStreamException` — The usual cause of an `EndOfStreamException` is an attempt to read past the end of a file. A *stream* represents a flow of data between data sources. Streams are covered in detail in Chapter 41, "Accessing the Internet."
- `OverflowException` — An `OverflowException` is what happens if you attempt to cast an `int` containing a value of `-40` to a `uint` in a `checked` context.

The other exception classes shown in Figure 14-1 are not discussed here.

The class hierarchy for exceptions is somewhat unusual in that most of these classes do not add any functionality to their respective base classes. However, in the case of exception handling, the common reason for adding inherited classes is to indicate more specific error conditions. There is often no need to override methods or add any new ones (although it is not uncommon to add extra properties that carry extra information about the error condition). For example, you might have a base `ArgumentException` class intended for method calls where inappropriate values are passed in, and an `ArgumentNullException` class derived from it, which is intended to handle a `null` argument if passed.

Catching Exceptions

Given that the .NET Framework includes a selection of predefined base class exception objects, how do you use them in your code to trap error conditions? To deal with possible error conditions in C# code, you will normally divide the relevant part of your program into blocks of three different types:

- `try` blocks encapsulate the code that forms part of the normal operation of your program and that might encounter some serious error conditions.
- `catch` blocks encapsulate the code that deals with the various error conditions that your code might have encountered by working through any of the code in the accompanying `try` block. This place could also be used for logging errors.
- `finally` blocks encapsulate the code that cleans up any resources or takes any other action that you will normally want done at the end of a `try` or `catch` block. It is important to understand that the `finally` block is executed whether or not an exception is thrown. Because the aim is that the `finally` block contains cleanup code that should always be executed, the compiler will flag an error if you place a `return` statement inside a `finally` block. For an example of using the `finally` block, you might close any connections that were opened in the `try` block. It is also important to understand that the `finally` block is completely optional. If you do not have a requirement for any cleanup code (such as disposing or closing any open objects), then there is no need for this block.

So how do these blocks fit together to trap error conditions? Here is how:

1. The execution flow first enters the `try` block.
2. If no errors occur in the `try` block, execution proceeds normally through the block, and when the end of the `try` block is reached, the flow of execution jumps to the `finally` block if one is present (Step 5). However, if an error does occur within the `try` block, execution jumps to a `catch` block (Step 3).

3. The error condition is handled in the `catch` block.
4. At the end of the `catch` block, execution automatically transfers to the `finally` block if one is present.
5. The `finally` block is executed (if present).

The C# syntax used to bring all of this about looks roughly like this:

```
try
{
   // code for normal execution
}
catch
{
   // error handling
}
finally
{
   // clean up
}
```

Actually, a few variations on this theme exist:

- You can omit the `finally` block because it is optional.
- You can also supply as many `catch` blocks as you want to handle specific types of errors. However, the idea is not to get too carried away and have a huge number of `catch` blocks, because this can hurt the performance of your application.
- You can omit the `catch` blocks altogether, in which case the syntax serves not to identify exceptions, but as a way of guaranteeing that code in the `finally` block will be executed when execution leaves the `try` block. This is useful if the `try` block contains several exit points.

So far so good, but the question that has yet to be answered is this: If the code is running in the `try` block, how does it know when to switch to the `catch` block if an error has occurred? If an error is detected, the code does something known as *throwing an exception*. In other words, it instantiates an exception object class and throws it:

```
throw new OverflowException();
```

Here, you have instantiated an exception object of the `OverflowException` class. As soon as the computer encounters a `throw` statement inside a `try` block, it immediately looks for the `catch` block associated with that `try` block. If there is more than one `catch` block associated with the `try` block, it identifies the correct `catch` block by checking which exception class the `catch` block is associated with. For example, when the `OverflowException` object is thrown, execution jumps to the following `catch` block:

```
catch (OverflowException ex)
{
   // exception handling here
}
```

In other words, the computer looks for the `catch` block that indicates a matching exception class instance of the same class (or of a base class).

With this extra information, you can expand the `try` block just demonstrated. Assume, for the sake of argument, that there are two possible serious errors that can occur in the `try` block: an overflow and an array out of bounds. Assume that your code contains two Boolean variables, `Overflow` and `OutOfBounds`, which indicate whether these conditions exist. You have already seen that a predefined exception class exists to indicate overflow (`OverflowException`); similarly, an `IndexOutOfRangeException` class exists to handle an array that is out of bounds.

Now your `try` block looks like this:

```
try
{
   // code for normal execution

   if (Overflow == true)
   {
      throw new OverflowException();
   }

   // more processing

   if (OutOfBounds == true)
   {
      throw new IndexOutOfRangeException();
   }

   // otherwise continue normal execution
}
catch (OverflowException ex)
{
   // error handling for the overflow error condition
}
catch (IndexOutOfRangeException ex)
{
   // error handling for the index out of range error condition
}
finally
{
   // clean up
}
```

So far, this might not look that much different from what you could have done with the Visual Basic 6 `On Error GoTo` statement (with the exception perhaps that the different parts in the code are separated). C#, however, provides a far more powerful and flexible mechanism for error handling.

This is because you can have `throw` statements that are nested in several method calls inside the `try` block, but the same `try` block continues to apply even as execution flow enters these other methods. If the computer encounters a `throw` statement, it immediately goes back up through all the method calls on the stack, looking for the end of the containing `try` block and the start of the appropriate `catch` block. During this process, all the local variables in the intermediate method calls will correctly go out of scope. This makes the `try...catch` architecture well suited to the situation described at the beginning of this section, where the error occurs inside a method call that is nested inside 15 or 20 method calls, and processing has to stop immediately.

As you can probably gather from this discussion, `try` blocks can play a very significant part in controlling the flow of execution of your code. However, it is important to understand that exceptions are intended for exceptional conditions, hence their name. You wouldn't want to use them as a way of controlling when to exit a `do...while` loop.

Implementing Multiple Catch Blocks

The easiest way to see how `try...catch...finally` blocks work in practice is with a couple of examples. The first example is called `SimpleExceptions`. It repeatedly asks the user to type in a number and then displays it. However, for the sake of this example, imagine that the number has to be between 0 and 5; otherwise, the program won't be able to process the number properly. Therefore, you will throw an exception if the user types in anything outside of this range.

The program then continues to ask for more numbers for processing until the user simply presses the Enter key without entering anything.

> *You should note that this code does not provide a good example of when to use exception handling. As already indicated, the idea of exceptions is that they are provided for exceptional circumstances. Users are always typing in silly things, so this situation doesn't really count. Normally, your program will handle incorrect user input by performing an instant check and asking the user to retype the input if there is a problem. However, generating exceptional situations is difficult in a small example that you can read through in a few minutes! So, we will tolerate this bad practice for now in order to demonstrate how exceptions work. The examples that follow present more realistic situations.*

The code for `SimpleExceptions` looks like this:

```
using System;

namespace Wrox.ProCSharp.AdvancedCSharp
{
   public class MainEntryPoint
   {
      public static void Main()
      {
         while (true)
         {
            try
            {
               string userInput;

               Console.Write("Input a number between 0 and 5 " +
                  "(or just hit return to exit)> ");
               userInput = Console.ReadLine();

               if (userInput == "")
               {
                  break;
               }

               int index = Convert.ToInt32(userInput);

               if (index < 0 || index > 5)
               {
                  throw new IndexOutOfRangeException(
                     "You typed in " + userInput);
               }

               Console.WriteLine("Your number was " + index);
            }
```

```
                catch (IndexOutOfRangeException ex)
                {
                   Console.WriteLine("Exception: " +
                      "Number should be between 0 and 5. {0}", ex.Message);
                }
                catch (Exception ex)
                {
                   Console.WriteLine(
                      "An exception was thrown. Message was: {0}", ex.Message);
                }
                catch
                {
                   Console.WriteLine("Some other exception has occurred");
                }
                finally
                {
                   Console.WriteLine("Thank you");
                }
            }
         }
      }
   }
```

The core of this code is a `while` loop, which continually uses `Console.ReadLine()` to ask for user input. `ReadLine()` returns a string, so your first task is to convert it to an `int` using the `System.Convert.ToInt32()` method. The `System.Convert` class contains various useful methods to perform data conversions and provides an alternative to the `int.Parse()` method. In general, `System.Convert` contains methods to perform various type conversions. Recall that the C# compiler resolves `int` to instances of the `System.Int32` base class.

> *It is also worth pointing out that the parameter passed to the* `catch` *block is scoped to that* `catch` *block — which is why you are able to use the same parameter name,* `ex`, *in successive* `catch` *blocks in the preceding code.*

In the preceding example, you also check for an empty string, because this is your condition for exiting the `while` loop. Notice how the `break` statement actually breaks right out of the enclosing `try` block as well as the `while` loop because this is valid behavior. Of course, once execution breaks out of the `try` block, the `Console.WriteLine()` statement in the `finally` block is executed. Although you just display a greeting here, more commonly, you will be doing tasks like closing file handles and calling the `Dispose()` method of various objects in order to perform any cleaning up. Once the computer leaves the `finally` block, it simply carries on executing unto the next statement that it would have executed had the `finally` block not been present. In the case of this example, though, you iterate back to the start of the `while` loop, and enter the `try` block once again (unless the `finally` block was entered as a result of executing the `break` statement in the `while` loop, in which case you simply exit the `while` loop).

Next, you check for your exception condition:

```
if (index < 0 || index > 5)
{
   throw new IndexOutOfRangeException("You typed in " + userInput);
}
```

When throwing an exception, you need to choose what type of exception to throw. Although the class `System.Exception` is available, it is intended only as a base class. It is considered bad programming practice to throw an instance of this class as an exception, because it conveys no information about the nature of the error condition. Instead, the .NET Framework contains many other exception classes that are derived from `System.Exception`. Each of these matches a particular type of exception condition, and you are free to define your own ones as well. The idea is that you give as much information as possible about the particular exception condition by throwing an instance of a class that matches the particular error condition. In the preceding example, `System.IndexOutOfRangeException` is the best choice for the circumstances. `IndexOutOfRangeException` has several constructor overloads. The one chosen in the example takes a string, which describes the error. Alternatively, you might choose to derive your own custom `Exception` object that describes the error condition in the context of your application.

Suppose that the user then types a number that is not between 0 and 5. This will be picked up by the `if` statement and an `IndexOutOfRangeException` object will be instantiated and thrown. At this point, the computer will immediately exit the `try` block and hunt for a `catch` block that handles `IndexOutOfRangeException`. The first `catch` block it encounters is this:

```
catch (IndexOutOfRangeException ex)
{
   Console.WriteLine(
      "Exception: Number should be between 0 and 5. {0}", ex.Message);
}
```

Because this `catch` block takes a parameter of the appropriate class, the `catch` block will be passed the exception instance and executed. In this case, you display an error message and the `Exception.Message` property (which corresponds to the string you passed to the `IndexOutOfRangeException`'s constructor). After executing this `catch` block, control then switches to the `finally` block, just as if no exception had occurred.

Notice that in the example, you have also provided another `catch` block:

```
catch (Exception ex)
{
   Console.WriteLine("An exception was thrown. Message was: {0}", ex.Message);
}
```

This `catch` block would also be capable of handling an `IndexOutOfRangeException` if it weren't for the fact that such exceptions will already have been caught by the previous `catch` block. A reference to a base class can also refer to any instances of classes derived from it, and all exceptions are derived from `System.Exception`. So why isn't this `catch` block executed? The answer is that the computer executes only the first suitable `catch` block it finds from the list of available `catch` blocks. So why is this second `catch` block even here? Well, it is not only your code that is covered by the `try` block. Inside the block, you actually make three separate calls to methods in the `System` namespace (`Console.ReadLine()`, `Console.Write()`, and `Convert.ToInt32()`), and any of these methods might throw an exception.

If you type in something that is not a number — say `a` or `hello` — the `Convert.ToInt32()` method will throw an exception of the class `System.FormatException` to indicate that the string passed into `ToInt32()` is not in a format that can be converted to an `int`. When this happens, the computer will trace back through the method calls, looking for a handler that can handle this exception. Your first `catch` block (the one that takes an `IndexOutOfRangeException`) will not do. The computer then looks at the second `catch` block. This one will do because `FormatException` is derived from `Exception`, so a `FormatException` instance can be passed in as a parameter here.

The structure of the example is actually fairly typical of a situation with multiple `catch` blocks. You start off with `catch` blocks that are designed to trap very specific error conditions. Then, you finish with more general blocks that will cover any errors for which you have not written specific error handlers. Indeed, the order of the `catch` blocks is important. If you had written the previous two blocks in the opposite order, the code would not have compiled, because the second `catch` block is unreachable (the `Exception catch` block would catch all exceptions). Therefore, the uppermost `catch` blocks should be the most granular options available and ending with the most general options.

However, in the previous example, you have a third `catch` block listed in the code:

```
catch
{
   Console.WriteLine("Some other exception has occurred");
}
```

This is the most general `catch` block of all — it does not take any parameter. The reason this `catch` block is here is to catch exceptions thrown by other code that is not written in C# or is not even managed code at all. You see, it is a requirement of the C# language that only instances of classes derived from `System.Exception` can be thrown as exceptions, but other languages might not have this restriction — C++, for example, allows any variable whatsoever to be thrown as an exception. If your code calls into libraries or assemblies that have been written in other languages, it might find that an exception has been thrown that is not derived from `System.Exception`, although in many cases, the .NET `PInvoke` mechanism will trap these exceptions and convert them into .NET `Exception` objects. However, there is not that much that this `catch` block can do, because you have no idea what class the exception might represent.

For this particular example, there is no point in adding this catch-all `catch` *handler. Doing this is useful if you are calling into some other libraries that are not .NET-aware and that might throw exceptions. However, it is included in the example to illustrate the principle.*

Now that you have analyzed the code for the example, you can run it. The following output illustrates what happens with different inputs and demonstrates both the `IndexOutOfRangeException` and the `FormatException` being thrown:

```
SimpleExceptions
Input a number between 0 and 5 (or just hit return to exit)>4
Your number was 4
Thank you
Input a number between 0 and 5 (or just hit return to exit)>0
Your number was 0
Thank you
Input a number between 0 and 5 (or just hit return to exit)>10
Exception: Number should be between 0 and 5. You typed in 10
Thank you
Input a number between 0 and 5 (or just hit return to exit)>hello
An exception was thrown. Message was: Input string was not in a correct format.
Thank you
Input a number between 0 and 5 (or just hit return to exit)>
Thank you
```

Catching Exceptions from Other Code

The previous example demonstrated the handling of two exceptions. One of them, `IndexOutOfRangeException`, was thrown by your own code. The other, `FormatException`, was thrown from inside one of the base classes. It is very common for code in a library to throw an exception if it detects that some problem has occurred, or if one of the methods has been called inappropriately by being passed the wrong parameters. However, library code rarely attempts to catch exceptions; this is regarded as the responsibility of the client code.

Often, you will find that exceptions are thrown from the base class libraries while you are debugging. The process of debugging to some extent involves determining why exceptions have been thrown and removing the causes. Your aim should be to ensure that by the time the code is actually shipped, exceptions do occur only in very exceptional circumstances, and if at all possible, are handled in some appropriate way in your code.

System.Exception Properties

The example has illustrated the use of only the `Message` property of the exception object. However, a number of other properties are available in `System.Exception`, as shown in the following table.

Property	Description
`Data`	This provides you with the ability to add key/value statements to the exception that can be used to supply extra information about the exception.
`HelpLink`	This is a link to a help file that provides more information about the exception.
`InnerException`	If this exception was thrown inside a `catch` block, then `InnerException` contains the exception object that sent the code into that `catch` block.
`Message`	This is text that describes the error condition.
`Source`	This is the name of the application or object that caused the exception.
`StackTrace`	This provides details of the method calls on the stack (to help track down the method that threw the exception).
`TargetSite`	This is a .NET reflection object that describes the method that threw the exception.

Of these properties, `StackTrace` and `TargetSite` are supplied automatically by the .NET runtime if a stack trace is available. `Source` will always be filled in by the .NET runtime as the name of the assembly in which the exception was raised (though you might want to modify the property in your code to give more specific information), whereas `Data`, `Message`, `HelpLink`, and `InnerException` must be filled in by the code that threw the exception, by setting these properties immediately before throwing the exception. For example, the code to throw an exception might look something like this:

```
if (ErrorCondition == true)
{
   Exception myException = new ClassMyException("Help!!!!");
   myException.Source = "My Application Name";
   myException.HelpLink = "MyHelpFile.txt";
   myException.Data["ErrorDate"] = DateTime.Now;
   myException.Data.Add("AdditionalInfo", "Contact Bill from the Blue Team");
   throw myException;
}
```

Here, `ClassMyException` is the name of the particular exception class you are throwing. Note that it is common practice for the names of all exception classes to end with `Exception`. Also note that the `Data` property is assigned in two possible ways.

What Happens If an Exception Isn't Handled?

Sometimes an exception might be thrown, but there might not be a `catch` block in your code that is able to handle that kind of exception. The `SimpleExceptions` example can serve to illustrate this. Suppose, for example, that you omitted the `FormatException` and catch-all `catch` blocks, and supplied only the block that traps an `IndexOutOfRangeException`. In that circumstance, what would happen if a `FormatException` were thrown?

The answer is that the .NET runtime would catch it. Later in this section, you learn how you can nest `try` blocks, and in fact, there is already a nested `try` block behind the scenes in the example. The .NET runtime has effectively placed the entire program inside another huge `try` block — it does this for every .NET program. This `try` block has a `catch` handler that can catch any type of exception. If an exception occurs that your code does not handle, the execution flow will simply pass right out of your program and be trapped by this `catch` block in the .NET runtime. However, the results of this probably will not be what you want. What happens is that the execution of your code will be terminated promptly; the user will see a dialog box that complains that your code has not handled the exception, and that provides any details about the exception the .NET runtime was able to retrieve. At least the exception will have been caught though! This is what actually happened earlier in Chapter 2, "C# Basics," in the `Vector` example when the program threw an exception.

In general, if you are writing an executable, try to catch as many exceptions as you reasonably can and handle them in a sensible way. If you are writing a library, it is normally best not to handle exceptions (unless a particular exception represents something wrong in your code that you can handle), but instead, assume that the calling code will handle any errors it encounters. However, you may nevertheless want to catch any Microsoft-defined exceptions, so that you can throw your own exception objects that give more specific information to the client code.

Nested try Blocks

One nice feature of exceptions is that you can nest `try` blocks inside each other, like this:

```
try
{
   // Point A
   try
   {
      // Point B
   }
   catch
   {
      // Point C
   }
   finally
   {
      // clean up
   }
   // Point D
}
catch
{
   // error handling
}
finally
{
   // clean up
}
```

Although each `try` block is accompanied by only one `catch` block in this example, you could string several `catch` blocks together, too. This section takes a closer look at how nested `try` blocks work.

If an exception is thrown inside the outer `try` block but outside the inner `try` block (points A and D), the situation is no different from any of the scenarios you have seen before: either the exception is caught by the outer `catch` block and the outer `finally` block is executed, or the `finally` block is executed and the .NET runtime handles the exception.

If an exception is thrown in the inner `try` block (point B), and there is a suitable inner `catch` block to handle the exception, then, again, you are in familiar territory: the exception is handled there, and the inner `finally` block is executed before execution resumes inside the outer `try` block (at point D).

Now suppose that an exception occurs in the inner `try` block, but there *isn't* a suitable inner `catch` block to handle it. This time, the inner `finally` block is executed as usual, but then the .NET runtime will have no choice but to leave the entire inner `try` block in order to search for a suitable exception handler. The next obvious place to look is in the outer `catch` block. If the system finds one here, then that handler will be executed and then the outer `finally` block will be executed after. If there is no suitable handler here, the search for one will go on. In this case, it means the outer `finally` block will be executed, and then, because there are no more `catch` blocks, control will be transferred to the .NET runtime. Note that at no point is the code beyond point D in the outer `try` block executed.

An even more interesting thing happens if an exception is thrown at point C. If the program is at point C, it must be already processing an exception that was thrown at point B. It is quite legitimate to throw another exception from inside a `catch` block. In this case, the exception is treated as if it had been thrown by the outer `try` block, so flow of execution will immediately leave the inner `catch` block, and execute the inner `finally` block, before the system searches the outer `catch` block for a handler. Similarly, if an exception is thrown in the inner `finally` block, control will immediately be transferred to the best appropriate handler, with the search starting at the outer `catch` block.

It is perfectly legitimate to throw exceptions from `catch` and `finally` blocks.

Although the situation has been shown with just two `try` blocks, the same principles hold no matter how many `try` blocks you nest inside each other. At each stage, the .NET runtime will smoothly transfer control up through the `try` blocks, looking for an appropriate handler. At each stage, as control leaves a `catch` block, any cleanup code in the corresponding `finally` block (if present) will be executed, but no code outside any `finally` block will be run until the correct `catch` handler has been found and run.

The nesting of `try` blocks can also occur between methods themselves. For example, if method A calls method B from within a `try` block, then method B itself has a `try` block within it as well.

You have now seen how having nested `try` blocks can work. The obvious next question is why would you want to do that? There are two reasons:

- To modify the type of exception thrown
- To enable different types of exception to be handled in different places in your code

Modifying the Type of Exception

Modifying the type of the exception can be useful when the original exception thrown does not adequately describe the problem. What typically happens is that something — possibly the .NET runtime — throws a fairly low-level exception that says something like an overflow occurred (`OverflowException`) or an argument passed to a method was incorrect (a class derived from `ArgumentException`). However, because of the context in which the exception occurred, you will know that this reveals some other underlying problem (for example, an overflow can only have happened at that point in your code because a file you have just read contained incorrect data). In that case, the most appropriate thing that your handler for the first exception can do is throw another exception that more accurately describes the problem, so that another `catch` block further along can deal with it more appropriately. In this case, it can also forward the original exception through a property implemented by `System.Exception` called `InnerException`. `InnerException` simply contains a reference to any other related exception that was thrown — in case the ultimate handler routine will need this extra information.

Of course, the situation also exists where an exception occurs inside a `catch` block. For example, you might normally read in some configuration file that contains detailed instructions for handling the error, and it might turn out that this file is not there.

Handling Different Exceptions in Different Places

The second reason for having nested `try` blocks is so that different types of exceptions can be handled at different locations in your code. A good example of this is if you have a loop where various exception conditions can occur. Some of these might be serious enough that you need to abandon the entire loop, whereas others might be less serious and simply require that you abandon that iteration and move on to the next iteration around the loop. You could achieve this by having one `try` block inside the loop, which handles the less serious error conditions, and an outer `try` block outside the loop, which handles the more serious error conditions. You will see how this works in the next exceptions example.

User-Defined Exception Classes

You are now ready to look at a second example that illustrates exceptions. This example, called `SolicitColdCall`, contains two nested `try` blocks and also illustrates the practice of defining your own custom exception classes and throwing another exception from inside a `try` block.

This example assumes that a sales company wants to have additional customers on its sales list. The company's sales team is going to phone a list of people to invite them to become customers, a practice known in sales jargon as *cold calling*. To this end, you have a text file available that contains the names of the people to be cold called. The file should be in a well-defined format in which the first line contains the number of people in the file and each subsequent line contains the name of the next person. In other words, a correctly formatted file of names might look like this:

```
4
George Washington
Benedict Arnold
John Adams
Thomas Jefferson
```

This version of cold calling is designed to display the name of the person on the screen (perhaps for the salesperson to read). That is why only names and not phone numbers of the individuals are contained in the file.

For this example, your program will ask the user for the name of the file and will then simply read it in and display the names of people. That sounds like a simple task, but even so, a couple of things can go wrong and require you to abandon the entire procedure:

- The user might type the name of a file that does not exist. This will be caught as a `FileNotFound` exception.
- The file might not be in the correct format. There are two possible problems here. First, the first line of the file might not be an integer. Second, there might not be as many names in the file as the first line of the file indicates. In both cases, you want to trap this oddity as a custom exception that has been written specially for this purpose, `ColdCallFileFormatException`.

There is something else that can go wrong that, while not causing you to abandon the entire process, will mean that you need to abandon that person and move on to the next person in the file (and therefore will need to be trapped by an inner `try` block). Some people are spies working for rival sales companies, and obviously, you would not want to let these people know what you are up to by accidentally phoning one of them. Your research has indicated that you can identify who the spies are because their names begin with B. Such people should have been screened out when the data file was first prepared, but just in case any have slipped through, you will need to check each name in the file and throw a `SalesSpyFoundException` if you detect a sales spy. This, of course, is another custom exception object.

Finally, you will implement this example by coding a class, `ColdCallFileReader`, which maintains the connection to the cold-call file and retrieves data from it. You will code this class in a very safe way, which means that its methods will all throw exceptions if they are called inappropriately; for example, if a method that will read a file is called before the file has even been opened. For this purpose, you will write another exception class, `UnexpectedException`.

Catching the User-Defined Exceptions

Let's start with the `Main()` method of the `SolicitColdCall` sample, which catches your user-defined exceptions. Note that you will need to call up file-handling classes in the `System.IO` namespace as well as the `System` namespace.

```
using System;
using System.IO;

namespace Wrox.ProCSharp.AdvancedCSharp
{
   class MainEntryPoint
   {
      static void Main()
      {
         string fileName;
         Console.Write("Please type in the name of the file " +
            "containing the names of the people to be cold called > ");
         fileName = Console.ReadLine();
         ColdCallFileReader peopleToRing = new ColdCallFileReader();

         try
         {
            peopleToRing.Open(fileName);
            for (int i=0 ; i<peopleToRing.NPeopleToRing; i++)
            {
               peopleToRing.ProcessNextPerson();
            }
            Console.WriteLine("All callers processed correctly");
         }
         catch(FileNotFoundException)
         {
            Console.WriteLine("The file {0} does not exist", fileName);
         }
         catch(ColdCallFileFormatException ex)
         {
            Console.WriteLine(
          "The file {0} appears to have been corrupted", fileName);
            Console.WriteLine("Details of problem are: {0}", ex.Message);
            if (ex.InnerException != null)
```

```
                {
                    Console.WriteLine(
                        "Inner exception was: {0}", ex.InnerException.Message);
                }
            }
            catch(Exception ex)
            {
                Console.WriteLine("Exception occurred:\n" + ex.Message);
            }
            finally
            {
                peopleToRing.Dispose();
            }
            Console.ReadLine();
        }
    }
```

This code is a little more than just a loop to process people from the file. You start by asking the user for the name of the file. Then you instantiate an object of a class called `ColdCallFileReader`, which is defined shortly. The `ColdCallFileReader` class is the class that handles the file reading. Notice that you do this outside the initial `try` block — that's because the variables that you instantiate here need to be available in the subsequent `catch` and `finally` blocks, and if you declared them inside the `try` block they would go out of scope at the closing curly brace of the `try` block, which would not be a good thing.

In the `try` block, you open the file (using the `ColdCallFileReader.Open()` method) and loop over all the people in it. The `ColdCallFileReader.ProcessNextPerson()` method reads in and displays the name of the next person in the file, and the `ColdCallFileReader.NPeopleToRing` property tells you how many people should be in the file (obtained by reading the first line of the file). There are three `catch` blocks: one for `FileNotFoundException`, one for `ColdCallFileFormatException`, and one to trap any other .NET exceptions.

In the case of a `FileNotFoundException`, you display a message to that effect. Notice that in this `catch` block, the exception instance is not actually used at all. This `catch` block is used to illustrate the user-friendliness of the application. Exception objects generally contain technical information that is useful for developers, but not the sort of stuff you want to show to your end users. So in this case, you create a simpler message of your own.

For the `ColdCallFileFormatException` handler, you have done the opposite, and illustrated how to give fuller technical information, including details of the inner exception, if one is present.

Finally, if you catch any other generic exceptions, you display a user-friendly message, instead of letting any such exceptions fall through to the .NET runtime. Note that you have chosen not to handle any other exceptions not derived from `System.Exception`, because you are not calling directly into non-.NET code.

The `finally` block is there to clean up resources. In this case, this means closing any open file — performed by the `ColdCallFileReader.Dispose()` method.

Throwing the User-Defined Exceptions

Now take a look at the definition of the class that handles the file reading and (potentially) throws your user-defined exceptions: `ColdCallFileReader`. Because this class maintains an external file connection, you will need to make sure that it is disposed of correctly in accordance with the principles laid down for the disposing of objects in Chapter 4, "Inheritance." Therefore, you derive this class from `IDisposable`.

First, you declare some variables:

```
class ColdCallFileReader : IDisposable
{
   FileStream fs;
   StreamReader sr;
   uint nPeopleToRing;
   bool isDisposed = false;
   bool isOpen = false;
```

`FileStream` and `StreamReader`, both in the `System.IO` namespace, are the base classes that you will use to read the file. `FileStream` allows you to connect to the file in the first place, whereas `StreamReader` is specially geared up to reading text files and implements a method, `ReadLine()`, which reads a line of text from a file. You look at `StreamReader` more closely in Chapter 25, "Manipulating Files and the Registry," which discusses file handling in depth.

The `isDisposed` field indicates whether the `Dispose()` method has been called. `ColdCallFileReader` is implemented so that once `Dispose()` has been called, it is not permitted to reopen connections and reuse the object. `isOpen` is also used for error checking — in this case, checking whether the `StreamReader` actually connects to an open file.

The process of opening the file and reading in that first line — the one that tells you how many people are in the file — is handled by the `Open()` method:

```
public void Open(string fileName)
{
   if (isDisposed)
      throw new ObjectDisposedException("peopleToRing");

   fs = new FileStream(fileName, FileMode.Open);
   sr = new StreamReader(fs);

   try
   {
      string firstLine = sr.ReadLine();
      nPeopleToRing = uint.Parse(firstLine);
      isOpen = true;
   }
   catch (FormatException ex)
   {
      throw new ColdCallFileFormatException(
         "First line isn\'t an integer", ex);
   }
}
```

The first thing you do in this method (as with all other `ColdCallFileReader` methods) is check whether the client code has inappropriately called it after the object has been disposed of, and if so, throw a predefined `ObjectDisposedException` object. The `Open()` method checks the `isDisposed` field to see whether `Dispose()` has already been called. Because calling `Dispose()` implies that the caller has now finished with this object, you regard it as an error to attempt to open a new file connection if `Dispose()` has been called.

Next, the method contains the first of two inner `try` blocks. The purpose of this one is to catch any errors resulting from the first line of the file not containing an integer. If that problem arises, the .NET runtime will throw a `FormatException`, which you trap and convert to a more meaningful exception that indicates there is actually a problem with the format of the cold-call file. Note that `System.FormatException` is there to indicate format problems with basic data types, not with files, and so is not a particularly useful exception to pass back to the calling routine in this case. The new exception thrown will be trapped by the outermost `try` block. Because no cleanup is needed here, there is no need for a `finally` block.

If everything is fine, you set the `isOpen` field to `true` to indicate that there is now a valid file connection from which data can be read.

The `ProcessNextPerson()` method also contains an inner `try` block:

```
public void ProcessNextPerson()
{
   if (isDisposed)
   {
      throw new ObjectDisposedException("peopleToRing");
   }

   if (!isOpen)
   {
      throw new UnexpectedException(
         "Attempted to access cold-call file that is not open");
   }

   try
   {
      string name;
      name = sr.ReadLine();
      if (name == null)
         throw new ColdCallFileFormatException("Not enough names");
      if (name[0] == 'B')
      {
         throw new SalesSpyFoundException(name);
      }
      Console.WriteLine(name);
   }
   catch(SalesSpyFoundException ex)
   {
      Console.WriteLine(ex.Message);
   }

   finally
   {
   }
}
```

Two possible problems exist with the file here (assuming that there actually is an open file connection; the `ProcessNextPerson()` method checks this first). First, you might read in the next name and discover that it is a sales spy. If that condition occurs, the exception is trapped by the first of the `catch` blocks in this method. Because that exception has been caught here, inside the loop, it means that execution can subsequently continue in the `Main()` method of the program, and the subsequent names in the file will continue to be processed.

A problem might also occur if you try to read the next name and discover that you have already reached the end of the file. The way that the `StreamReader` object's `ReadLine()` method works is if it has gone past the end of the file, it doesn't throw an exception, but simply returns `null`. Therefore, if you find a null string, you know that the format of the file was incorrect because the number in the first line of the file indicated a larger number of names than were actually present in the file. If that happens, you throw a `ColdCallFileFormatException`, which will be caught by the outer exception handler (which will cause execution to terminate).

Once again, you don't need a `finally` block here because there is no cleanup to do; however, this time an empty `finally` block is included, just to show that you can do so, if you want.

The example is nearly finished. You have just two more members of `ColdCallFileReader` to look at: the `NPeopleToRing` property, which returns the number of people supposed to be in the file, and the `Dispose()` method, which closes an open file. Notice that the `Dispose()` method just returns if it has already been called — this is the recommended way of implementing it. It also checks that there actually is a file stream to close before closing it. This example is shown here to illustrate defensive coding techniques, so that's what you are doing!

```
public uint NPeopleToRing
{
   get
   {
      if (isDisposed)
      {
         throw new ObjectDisposedException("peopleToRing");
      }

      if (!isOpen)
      {
         throw new UnexpectedException(
            "Attempted to access cold-call file that is not open");
      }

      return nPeopleToRing;
   }
}

public void Dispose()
{
   if (isDisposed)
   {
      return;
   }

   isDisposed = true;
   isOpen = false;

   if (fs != null)
   {
      fs.Close();
      fs = null;
   }
}
```

Defining the User-Defined Exception Classes

Finally, you need to define your own three exception classes. Defining your own exception is quite easy because there are rarely any extra methods to add. It is just a case of implementing a constructor to ensure that the base class constructor is called correctly. Here is the full implementation of `SalesSpyFoundException`:

```
class SalesSpyFoundException : ApplicationException
{
   public SalesSpyFoundException(string spyName)
      :   base("Sales spy found, with name " + spyName)
   {
   }

   public SalesSpyFoundException(
      string spyName, Exception innerException)
      :   base(
         "Sales spy found with name " + spyName, innerException)
   {
   }
}
```

Notice that it is derived from `ApplicationException`, as you would expect for a custom exception. In fact, in practice, you would probably have put in an intermediate class, something like `ColdCallFileException`, derived from `ApplicationException`, and derived both of your exception classes from this class. This would ensure that the handling code has that extra-fine degree of control over which exception handler handles which exception. However, to keep the example simple, you will not do that.

You have done one bit of processing in `SalesSpyFoundException`. You have assumed that the message passed into its constructor is just the name of the spy found, so you turn this string into a more meaningful error message. You have also provided two constructors, one that simply takes a message, and one that also takes an inner exception as a parameter. When defining your own exception classes, it is best to include, at a minimum, at least these two constructors (although you will not actually be using the second `SalesSpyFoundException` constructor in this example).

Now for the `ColdCallFileFormatException`. This follows the same principles as the previous exception, except that you don't do any processing on the message:

```
class ColdCallFileFormatException : ApplicationException
{
   public ColdCallFileFormatException(string message)
      :   base(message)
   {
   }

   public ColdCallFileFormatException(
      string message, Exception innerException)
      :   base(message, innerException)
   {
   }
}
```

And finally, `UnexpectedException`, which looks much the same as `ColdCallFileFormatException`:

```
class UnexpectedException : ApplicationException
{
   public UnexpectedException(string message)
      :   base(message)
```

(continued)

(continued)

```
        {
        }

        public UnexpectedException(string message, Exception innerException)
            :    base(message, innerException)
        {
        }
    }
```

Now you are ready to test the program. First, try the `people.txt` file whose contents are defined here.

```
4
George Washington
Benedict Arnold
John Adams
Thomas Jefferson
```

This has four names (which match the number given in the first line of the file), including one spy. Then try the following `people2.txt` file, which has an obvious formatting error:

```
49
George Washington
Benedict Arnold
John Adams
Thomas Jefferson
```

Finally, try the example but specify the name of a file that does not exist, say, `people3.txt`. Running the program three times for the three file names gives these results:

```
SolicitColdCall
Please type in the name of the file containing the names of the people to be cold
called > people.txt
George Washington
Sales spy found, with name Benedict Arnold
John Adams
Thomas Jefferson
All callers processed correctly


SolicitColdCall
Please type in the name of the file containing the names of the people to be cold
called > people2.txt
George Washington
Sales spy found, with name Benedict Arnold
John Adams
Thomas Jefferson
The file people2.txt appears to have been corrupted.
Details of the problem are: Not enough names


SolicitColdCall
Please type in the name of the file containing the names of the people to be cold
called > people3.txt
The file people3.txt does not exist.
```

In the end, this application shows you a number of different ways in which you can handle the errors and exceptions that you might find in your own applications.

Summary

This chapter examined the rich mechanism C# has for dealing with error conditions through exceptions. You are not limited to the generic error codes that could be output from your code; instead, you have the ability to go in and uniquely handle the most granular of error conditions. Sometimes these error conditions are provided to you through the .NET Framework itself, but at other times, you might want to go in and code your own error conditions as illustrated in this chapter. In either case, you have many ways of protecting the workflow of your applications from unnecessary and dangerous faults.

The next chapter allows you to take a lot of what you learned so far in this book and works at implementing these lessons within the .NET developers IDE — Visual Studio 2008.

Part II
Visual Studio

Chapter 15: Visual Studio 2008

Chapter 16: Deployment

15

Visual Studio 2008

At this point, you should be familiar with the C# language and almost ready to move on to the applied sections of the book, which cover how to use C# to program a variety of applications. Before doing that, however, you need to examine how you can use Visual Studio and some of the features provided by the .NET environment to get the best from your programs.

This chapter explains what programming in the .NET environment means in practice. It covers Visual Studio, the main development environment in which you will write, compile, debug, and optimize your C# programs, and provides guidelines for writing good applications. Visual Studio is the main IDE used for everything from writing Web Forms and Windows Forms to XML Web services, and more. For more details on Windows Forms and how to write user interface code, see Chapter 31, "Windows Forms." This chapter takes a strong look at the following:

- Using Visual Studio 2008
- Refactoring with Visual Studio
- Visual Studio 2008's multi-targeting capabilities
- Working with the new technologies WPF, WCF, WF, and more.

This chapter also explores what it takes to build applications that are targeted at the .NET Framework 3.0 or 3.5. The types of applications provided ever since the .NET Framework 3.0 class library include the Windows Presentation Foundation (WPF), the Windows Communication Foundation (WCF), and the Windows Workflow Foundation (WF). Working with Visual Studio 2008 will provide you the ability to work with these new application types directly.

Working with Visual Studio 2008

Visual Studio 2008 is a fully integrated development environment. It is designed to make the process of writing your code, debugging it, and compiling it to an assembly to be shipped as easy as possible. What this means is that Visual Studio gives you a very sophisticated multiple-document-interface application in which you can do just about everything related to developing your code. It offers these features:

- ❑ Text editor — Using this editor, you can write your C# (as well as Visual Basic 2008 and Visual C++) code. This text editor is quite sophisticated. For example, as you type, it automatically lays out your code by indenting lines, matching start and end brackets of code blocks, and color-coding keywords. It also performs some syntax checks as you type, and it underlines code that causes compilation errors, also known as design-time debugging. In addition, it features IntelliSense, which automatically displays the names of classes, fields, or methods as you begin to type them. As you start typing parameters to methods, it will also show you the parameter lists for the available overloads. Figure 15-1 shows the IntelliSense feature in action with one of the .NET base classes, `ListBox`.

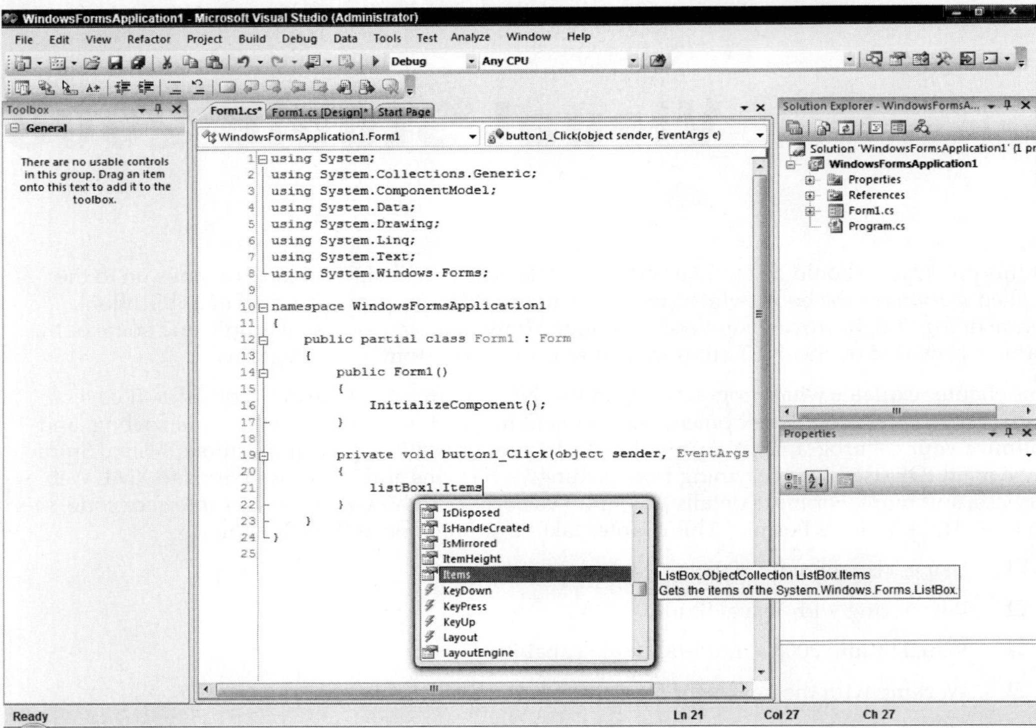

Figure 15-1

> **By pressing Ctrl+Space, you can bring back the IntelliSense list box if you need it and if for any reason it is not visible.**

- ❑ Design view editor — This editor enables you to place user-interface and data-access controls in your project; Visual Studio automatically adds the necessary C# code to your source files to instantiate these controls in your project. (This is possible because all .NET controls are instances of particular base classes.)
- ❑ Supporting windows — These windows allow you to view and modify aspects of your project, such as the classes in your source code, as well as the available properties (and their startup values) for Windows Forms and Web Forms classes. You can also use these windows to specify compilation options, such as which assemblies your code needs to reference.

- The ability to compile from within the environment — Instead of needing to run the C# compiler from the command line, you can simply select a menu option to compile the project, and Visual Studio will call the compiler for you and pass all the relevant command-line parameters to the compiler, detailing such things as which assemblies to reference and what type of assembly you want to be emitted (executable or library `.dll`, for example). If you want, it can also run the compiled executable for you so that you can see whether it runs satisfactorily. You can even choose between different build configurations (for example, a release or debug build).
- Integrated debugger — It is in the nature of programming that your code will not run correctly the first time you try it. Or the second time. Or the third time. Visual Studio seamlessly links up to a debugger for you, allowing you to set breakpoints and watches on variables from within the environment.
- Integrated MSDN help — Visual Studio enables you to access the MSDN documentation from within the IDE. For example, if you are not sure of the meaning of a keyword while using the text editor, simply select the keyword and press the F1 key, and Visual Studio will access MSDN to show you related topics. Similarly, if you are not sure what a certain compilation error means, you can bring up the documentation for that error by selecting the error message and pressing F1.
- Access to other programs — Visual Studio can also access a number of other utilities that allow you to examine and modify aspects of your computer or network, without your having to leave the developer environment. Among the tools available, you can check running services and database connections, look directly into your SQL Server tables, and even browse the Web using an Internet Explorer window.

If you have developed previously using C++ or Visual Basic, you will already be familiar with the relevant Visual Studio 6 version of the IDE, and many of the features in the preceding list will not be new to you. What is new in Visual Studio is that it combines all the features that were previously available across all Visual Studio 6 development environments. This means that whatever language you used in Visual Studio 6, you will find some new features in Visual Studio. For example, in the older Visual Basic environment, you could not compile separate debug and release builds. If you are coming to C# from a background of C++, though, then much of the support for data access and the ability to drop controls into your application with a click of the mouse, which has long been part of the Visual Basic developer's experience, will be new to you. In the C++ development environment, drag-and-drop support is limited to the most common user-interface controls.

C++ developers will miss two Visual Studio 6 features in Visual Studio 2008: edit-and-continue debugging and an integrated profiler. Visual Studio 2008 also does not include a full profiler application. Instead, you will find a number of .NET classes that assist with profiling in the `System.Diagnostics` *namespace. The perfmon profiling tool is available from the command line (just type perfmon) and has a number of new .NET-related performance monitors.*

Whatever your background, you will find that the overall look of the Visual Studio 2008 developer environment has changed since the days of Visual Studio 6 to accommodate the new features, the single cross-language IDE, and the integration with .NET. There are new menu and toolbar options, and many of the existing ones from Visual Studio 6 have been renamed. Therefore, you will need to spend some time familiarizing yourself with the layout and commands available in Visual Studio 2008.

The differences between Visual Studio 2005 and Visual Studio 2008 are a few nice additions that facilitate working in Visual Studio 2008. The biggest changes in Visual Studio 2008 include the ability to target specific versions of the .NET Framework (including the .NET Framework versions 2.0, 3.0, or 3.5), JavaScript IntelliSense support, and new abilities to work with CSS. You will also find new built-in features that allow you to build ASP.NET AJAX applications as well as applications using some of the newest technical capabilities coming out of Microsoft, including the Windows Communication Foundation, Windows Workflow Foundation, and the Windows Presentation Foundation.

One of the biggest items to notice with your installation of Visual Studio 2008 is that this new IDE works with the .NET Framework 3.5. In fact, when you install Visual Studio 2008, you will also be installing the .NET Framework 3.0 and 3.5 if they aren't already installed. Like Visual Studio 2005, this new IDE, Visual Studio 2008, is not built to work with version 1.0 or 1.1 of the .NET Framework, which means that if you still want to develop 1.0 or 1.1 applications, you will want to keep Visual Studio 2002 or 2003, respectively, installed on your machine. Installing Visual Studio 2008 installs a complete and new copy of Visual Studio and does not upgrade the previous Visual Studio 2002, 2003, or 2005 IDEs. The three copies of Visual Studio will then run side by side on your machine if required.

Note that if you attempt to open your Visual Studio 2002, 2003, or 2005 projects using Visual Studio 2008, the IDE will warn you that your solution will be upgraded to Visual Studio 2008 if you continue by popping up the Visual Studio Conversion Wizard (see Figure 15-2).

Figure 15-2

The upgrade wizard has been dramatically improved from Visual Studio 2003 to this newer one provided by Visual Studio 2008. This wizard can make backup copies of the solutions that are being backed up (see Figure 15-3), and it can also back up solutions that are contained within source control.

It is also possible to have Visual Studio generate a conversion report for you in the conversion process's final step. The report will then be viewable directly in the document window of Visual Studio. This report is illustrated (done with a simple conversion) in Figure 15-4.

Because this is a professional-level book, it does not look in detail at every feature or menu option available in Visual Studio 2008. Surely, you will be able to find your way around the IDE. The real aim of this Visual Studio coverage is to ensure that you are sufficiently familiar with the concepts involved when building and debugging a C# application that you can make the most of working with Visual Studio 2008. Figure 15-5 shows what your screen might look like when working in Visual Studio 2008. (Note that because the appearance of Visual Studio is highly customizable, the windows might not be in the same locations, or different windows might be visible when you launch this development environment.)

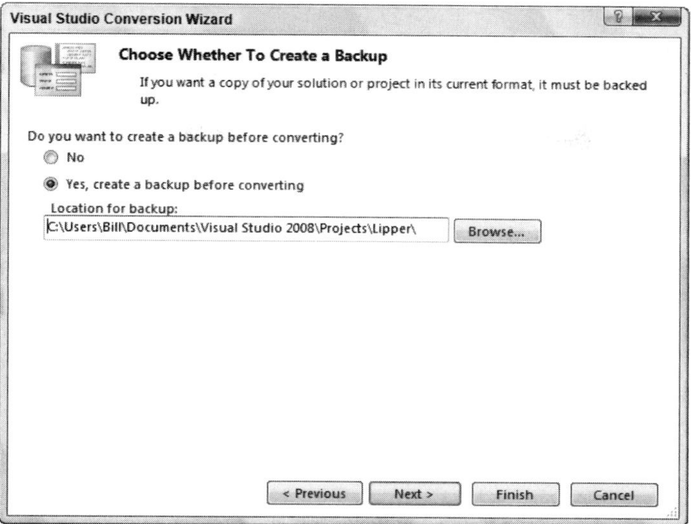

Figure 15-3

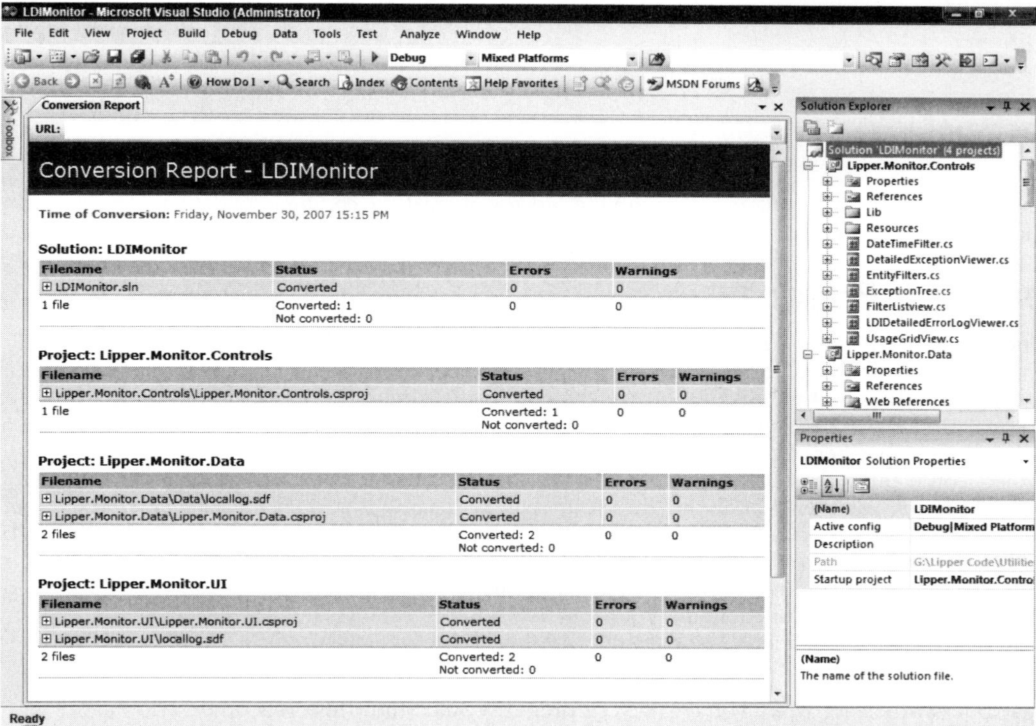

Figure 15-4

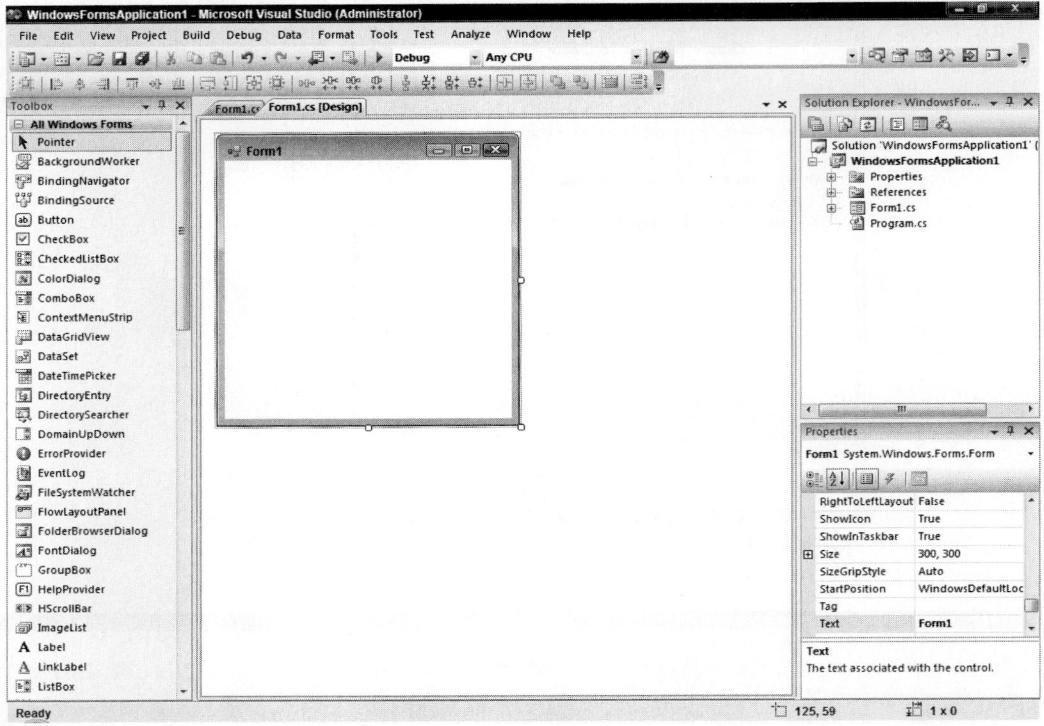

Figure 15-5

The following sections walk you through the process of creating, coding, and debugging a project, showing what Visual Studio can do to help you at each stage.

Creating a Project

Once you have installed Visual Studio 2008, you will want to start your first project. With Visual Studio, you rarely start with a blank file and then add C# code, in the way that you have been doing in the previous chapters in this book. (Of course, the option of asking for an empty application project is there if you really do want to start writing your code from scratch or if you are going to create a solution that will contain a number of projects.) Instead, the idea is that you tell Visual Studio roughly what type of project you want to create, and it will generate the files and C# code that provide a framework for that type of project. You then work by adding your code to this outline. For example, if you want to build a Windows GUI-interface-based application (or, in .NET terminology, a Windows Form), Visual Studio will start you off with a file containing C# source code that creates a basic form. This form is capable of talking to Windows and receiving events. It can be maximized, minimized, or resized; all you need to do is add the controls and functionality you want. If your application is intended to be a command-line utility (a console application), Visual Studio will give you a basic namespace, class, and a `Main()` method to start you off.

Last, but hardly least, when you create your project, Visual Studio also sets up the compilation options that you are likely to supply to the C# compiler — whether it is to compile to a command-line application, a library, or a Windows application. It will also tell the compiler which base class libraries you will need to reference (a Windows GUI application will need to reference many of the `Windows.Forms`-related libraries; a console application probably will not). You can, of course, modify all these settings as you are editing, if you need to.

The first time you start Visual Studio, you will be presented with a blank IDE (see Figure 15-6). The Start Page is an HTML page that contains various links to useful Web sites and enables you to open existing projects or start a new project altogether.

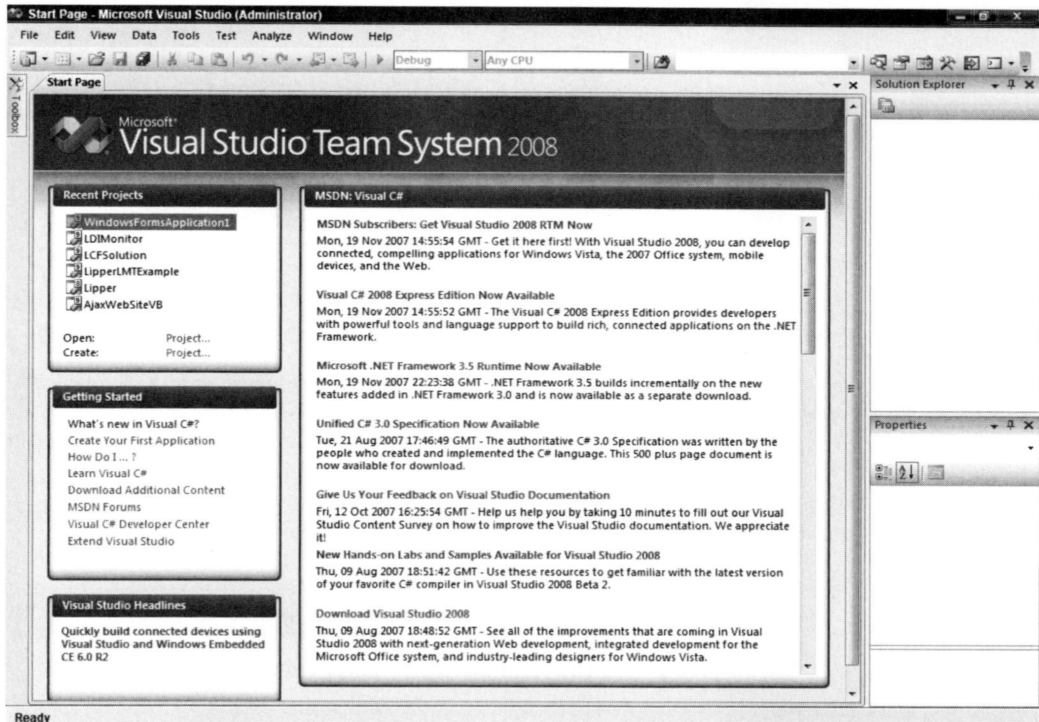

Figure 15-6

Figure 15-6 shows the type of Start Page you get after you have used Visual Studio 2008; it includes a list of the most recently edited projects. You can just click one of these projects to open it again.

Selecting a Project Type

You can create a new project by selecting File ⇨ New Project from the Visual Studio menu. From there you will get the New Project dialog box (see Figure 15-7) — and your first inkling of the variety of different projects you can create.

Using this dialog box, you effectively select the initial framework files and code you want Visual Studio to generate for you, the type of compilation options you want, and the compiler you want to compile your code with — either the Visual C#, Visual Basic 2008, or Visual C++ compiler. You can immediately see the language integration that Microsoft has promised for .NET at work here! This particular example uses a C# console application.

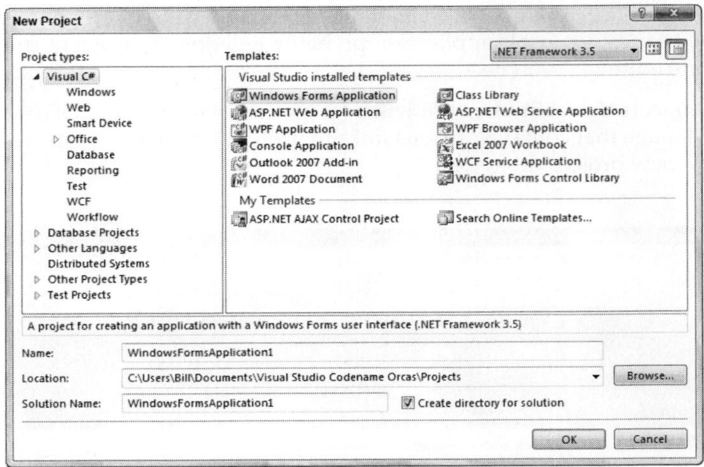

Figure 15-7

We do not have space to cover all the various options for different types of projects here. On the C++ side, all the old C++ project types are there — MFC application, ATL project, and so on. On the Visual Basic 2008 side, the options have changed somewhat. For example, you can create a Visual Basic 2008 command-line application (Console Application), a .NET component (Class Library), a .NET control (Windows Control Library), and more. However, you cannot create an old-style COM-based control (the .NET control is intended to replace such ActiveX controls).

The following table lists all the options that are available to you under Visual C# Projects. Note that some other, more specialized C# template projects are available under the Other Projects option.

If you choose . . .	You get the C# code and compilation options to generate . . .
Windows Forms Application	A basic empty form that responds to events.
Class Library	A .NET class that can be called up by other code.
WPF Application	A basic empty form that responds to events. Though the project type is similar to the Windows Forms Application project type (Windows Forms), this Windows Application project type allows you to build an XAML-based smart client solution.
WPF Browser Application	Quite similar to the Windows Application for WPF, this variant allows you to build an XAML-based application that is targeted at the browser.
ASP.NET Web Application	An ASP.NET-based Web site: ASP.NET pages and C# classes that generate the HTML response sent to browsers from those pages.
ASP.NET Web Service Application	A C# class that acts as a fully operational Web service.
ASP.NET AJAX Server Control	Allows you to build a custom server control for use within ASP.NET applications.

If you choose . . .	You get the C# code and compilation options to generate . . .
Web Control Library	A control that can be called up by ASP.NET pages, to generate the HTML code that gives the appearance of a control when displayed on a browser.
WPF Custom Control Library	A custom control that can be used in a Windows Presentation Foundation application.
WPF User Control Library	A user control library built using the Windows Presentation Foundation.
Windows Forms Control Library	A project for creating controls to use in Windows Forms applications.
Console Application	An application that runs at the command-line prompt, or in a console window.
WCF Service Application	A project type for Windows Communication Foundation services.
Windows Service	A service that runs in the background on a Windows operating system.
Reports Application	A project for creating an application with a Windows user interface and a Report.
Crystal Reports Windows Application	A project for creating a C# application with a Windows user interface and a sample Crystal Report.
SQL Server Project	A project for creating classes to use in SQL Server.
Smart Device	A project type that allows you to target a specific type of mobile device.
Sequential Workflow Service Library	A project that provides a sequential workflow exposed as a WCF service.
State Machine Workflow Service Library	A project that provides a state machine workflow exposed as a WCF service.
Syndication Service Library	A project that provides a syndication service exposed as a WCF service
WCF Service Library	A project that provides for creating a WCF service class library (`.dll`) that has endpoints controlled via XML configuration files.
Empty Workflow Project	A project that provides an empty project for creating a workflow.
Sequential Workflow Console Application	A project that provides for creating a sequential workflow console application.
Sequential Workflow Library	A project for creating a sequential workflow library.
SharePoint 2007 Sequential Workflow	A project that provides for creating a SharePoint sequential workflow.
SharePoint 2007 State Machine Workflow	A project that provides for creating a SharePoint state machine workflow.
State Machine Workflow Console Application	A project that provides for creating a state machine workflow console application.

If you choose . . .	You get the C# code and compilation options to generate . . .
State Machine Workflow Library	A project that provides for creating a state machine workflow library.
Workflow Activity Library	A project that provides for creating a library of activities that can later be reused as building blocks in workflows.
Office	A series of projects that are aimed at building applications or add-ins targeted at the Microsoft Office applications (Word, Excel, PowerPoint, InfoPath, Outlook, and SharePoint).

As mentioned, this is not a full list of the .NET Framework 3.5 projects, but it is a good start. The big additions to this project table are the new projects that are aimed at the Windows Presentation Foundation (WPF), the Windows Communication Foundation (WCF), and the Windows Workflow Foundation (WF). You will find chapters covering these new capabilities later in this book. Be sure to look at Chapter 34, "Windows Presentation Foundation," Chapter 42, "Windows Communication Foundation," and Chapter 43, "Windows Workflow Foundation."

The Newly Created Console Project

When you click OK after selecting the Console Application option, Visual Studio gives you a couple of files, including a source code file, `Program.cs`, which contains the initial framework code. Figure 15-8 shows what code Visual Studio has written for you.

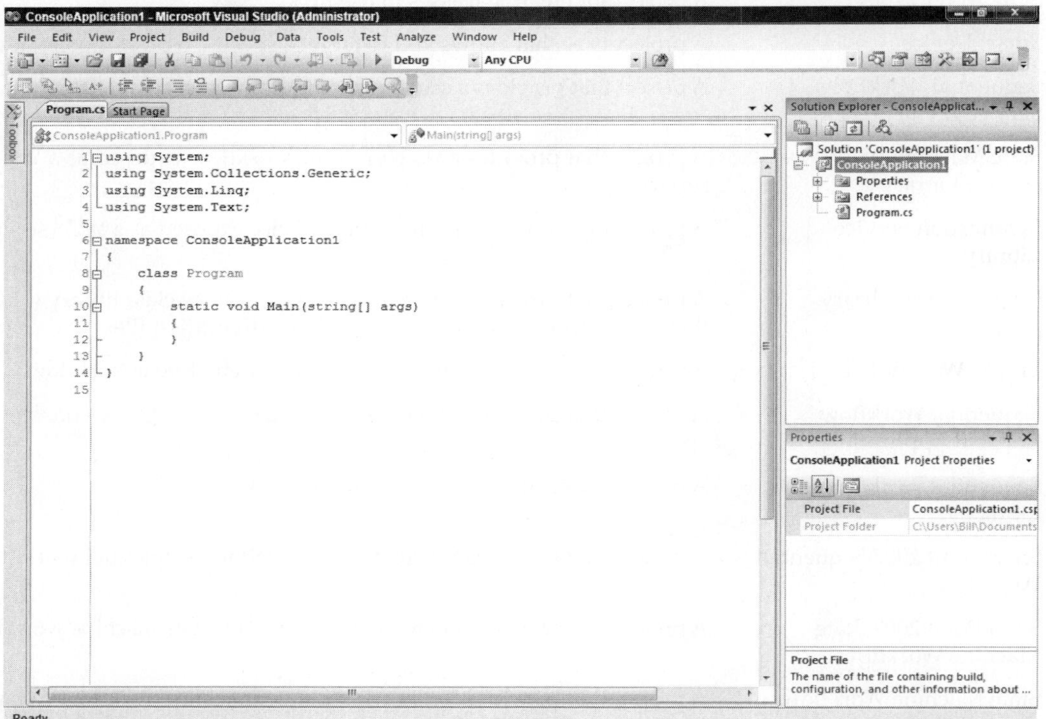

Figure 15-8

As you can see, you have a C# program that does not do anything yet but contains the basic items required in any C# executable program: a namespace and a class that contains the `Main()` method, which is the program's entry point. (Strictly speaking, the namespace is not necessary, but it would be very bad programming practice not to declare one.) This code is all ready to compile and run, which you can do immediately by pressing the F5 key or by selecting the Debug menu and choosing Start. However, before you do that, add the following line of code — to make your application actually do something!

```
static void Main(string[] args)
   {
      Console.WriteLine("Hello from all the authors of Professional C#");
   }
```

If you compile and run the project, you will see a console window that stays onscreen barely long enough to read the message. The reason this happens is that Visual Studio, remembering the settings you specified when you created the project, arranged for it to be compiled and run as a console application. Windows then realizes that it has to run a console application but does not have a console window to run it from. Therefore, Windows creates a console window and runs the program. As soon as the program exits, Windows recognizes that it does not need the console window anymore and promptly removes it. That is all very logical but does not help you very much if you actually want to look at the output from your project!

A good way to prevent this problem is to insert the following line just before the `Main()` method returns in your code:

```
static void Main(string[] args)
{
   Console.WriteLine("Hello from all the folks at Wrox Press");
   Console.ReadLine();
}
```

That way, your code will run, display its output, and come across the `Console.ReadLine()` statement, at which point it will wait for you to press the Return (or Enter) key before the program exits. This means that the console window will hang around until you press Return.

Note that all this is only an issue for console applications that you test-run from Visual Studio — if you are writing a Windows application, the window displayed by the application will automatically remain onscreen until you exit it. Similarly, if you run a console application from the command-line prompt, you will not have any problems with the window disappearing.

Other Files Created

The `Program.cs` source code file is not the only file that Visual Studio has created for you. Looking in the folder in which you asked Visual Studio to create your project, you will see not just the C# file, but a complete directory structure that looks like what is shown in Figure 15-9.

The two folders, `bin` and `obj`, store compiled and intermediate files. Subfolders of `obj` hold various temporary or intermediate files; subfolders of `bin` hold the compiled assemblies.

Traditionally, Visual Basic developers would simply write the code and then run it. Before shipping, the code would then need to be compiled into an executable; Visual Basic tended to hide the process of compilation when debugging. In C#, it is more explicit: to run the code, you have to compile (or build) it first, which means that an assembly must be created somewhere.

You will also find a `Properties` folder that holds the `AssemblyInfo.cs` file. The remaining files in the project's main folder, `ConsoleApplication1`, are there for Visual Studio's benefit. They contain information about the project (for example, the files it contains) so that Visual Studio knows how to have the project compiled and how to read it in the next time you open the project.

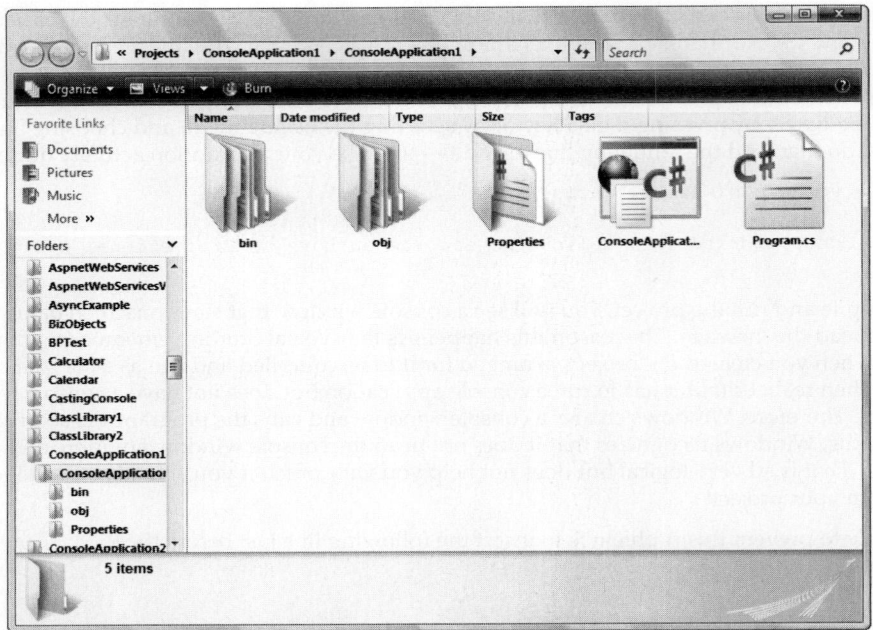

Figure 15-9

Solutions and Projects

One important distinction you must understand is that between a project and a solution:

- A *project* is a set of all the source code files and resources that will compile into a single assembly (or in some cases, a single module). For example, a project might be a class library or a Windows GUI application.
- A *solution* is the set of all the projects that make up a particular software package (application).

To understand this distinction, look at what happens when you ship a project — the project consists of more than one assembly. For example, you might have a user interface, custom controls, and other components that ship as libraries of the parts of the application. You might even have a different user interface for administrators. Each of these parts of the application might be contained in a separate assembly, and hence, they are regarded by Visual Studio as a separate project. However, it is quite likely that you will be coding these projects in parallel and in conjunction with each other. Thus, it is quite useful to be able to edit them all as one single unit in Visual Studio. Visual Studio allows this by regarding all the projects as forming one solution and by treating the solution as the unit that it reads in and allows you to work on.

Up until now, we have been loosely talking about creating a console project. In fact, in the example you are working on, Visual Studio has actually created a solution for you — though this particular solution contains just one project. You can see the situation in a window in Visual Studio known as the Solution Explorer (see Figure 15-10), which contains a tree structure that defines your solution.

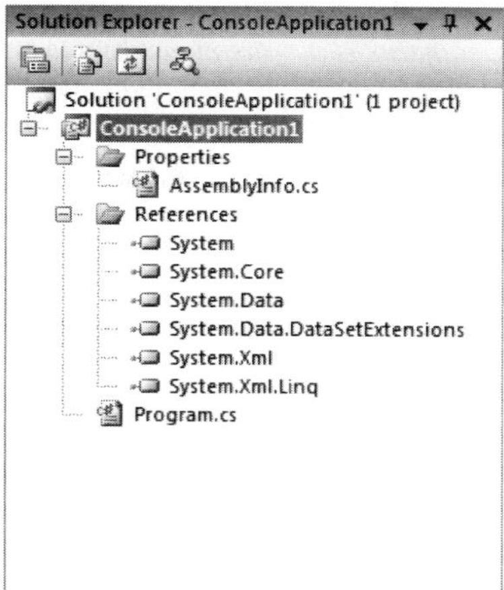

Figure 15-10

Figure 15-10 shows that the project contains your source file, `Program.cs`, as well as another C# source file, `AssemblyInfo.cs` (found in the `Properties` folder), which allows you to provide information that describes the assembly as well as the ability to specify versioning information. (You look at this file in detail in Chapter 17, "Assemblies.") The Solution Explorer also indicates the assemblies that your project references according to namespace. You can see this by expanding the `References` folder in the Solution Explorer.

If you have not changed any of the default settings in Visual Studio, you will probably find the Solution Explorer in the top-right corner of your screen. If you cannot see it, just go to the View menu and select Solution Explorer.

The solution is described by a file with the extension `.sln` — in this example, it is `ConsoleApplication1.sln`. The project is described by various other files in the project's main folder. If you attempt to edit these files using Notepad, you will find that they are mostly plain-text files, and, in accordance with the principle that .NET and .NET tools rely on open standards wherever possible, they are mostly in XML format.

C++ developers will recognize that a Visual Studio solution corresponds to an old Visual C++ project workspace (stored in a `.dsw` *file), and a Visual Studio project corresponds to an old C++ project (*`.dsp` *file). By contrast, Visual Basic developers will recognize that a solution corresponds to an old Visual Basic project group (*`.vbg` *file), and the .NET project corresponds to an old Visual Basic project (*`.vbp` *file). Visual Studio differs from the old Visual Basic IDE in that it always creates a solution for you automatically. In Visual Studio 6, Visual Basic developers would get a project; however, they would need to request a project group from the IDE separately.*

Adding Another Project to the Solution

As you work through the following sections, you will see how Visual Studio works with Windows applications as well as with console applications. To that end, you create a Windows project called `BasicForm` that you will add to your current solution, `ConsoleApplication1`.

This means that you will end up with a solution containing a Windows application and a console application. That is not a very common scenario — you are more likely to have one application and a number of libraries — but it allows you to see more code! You might, however, create a solution like this if, for example, you are writing a utility that you want to run either as a Windows application or as a command-line utility.

You can create the new project in two ways. You can select New Project from the File menu (as you have done already) or you can select Add ⇨ New Project from the File menu. If you select New Project from the File menu, this will bring up the familiar New Project dialog box; this time, however, you will notice that Visual Studio wants to create the new project in the preexisting `ConsoleApplication1` project location (see Figure 15-11).

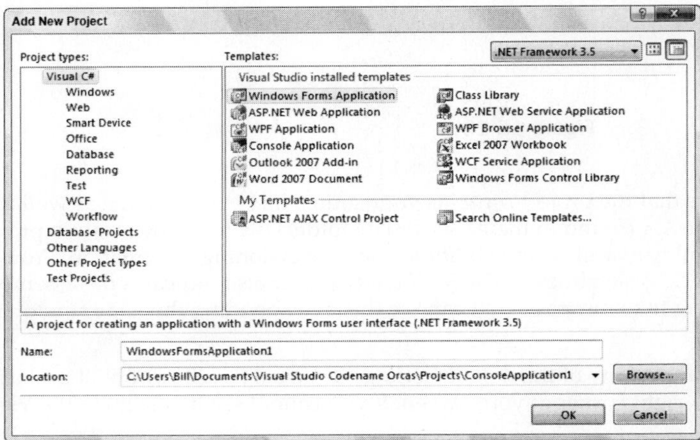

Figure 15-11

If you select this option, a new project is added so that the `ConsoleApplication1` solution now contains a console application and a Windows application.

In accordance with the language-independence of Visual Studio, the new project does not need to be a C# project. It is perfectly acceptable to put a C# project, a Visual Basic 2008 project, and a C++ project in the same solution. However, we will stick with C# here because this is a C# book!

Of course, this means that `ConsoleApplication1` is not really an appropriate name for the solution anymore! To change the name, you can right-click the name of the solution and select Rename from the context menu. Call the new solution `DemoSolution`. The Solution Explorer window now looks like Figure 15-12.

You can see from this that Visual Studio has made your newly added Windows project automatically reference some of the extra base classes that are important for Windows Forms functionality.

You will notice if you look in Windows Explorer that the name of the solution file has changed to `DemoSolution.sln`. In general, if you want to rename any files, the Solution Explorer window is the best place to do so, because Visual Studio will then automatically update any references to that file in the other project files. If you rename files using just Windows Explorer, you might break the solution because Visual Studio will not be able to locate all the files it needs to read in. You will then need to manually edit the project and solution files to update the file references.

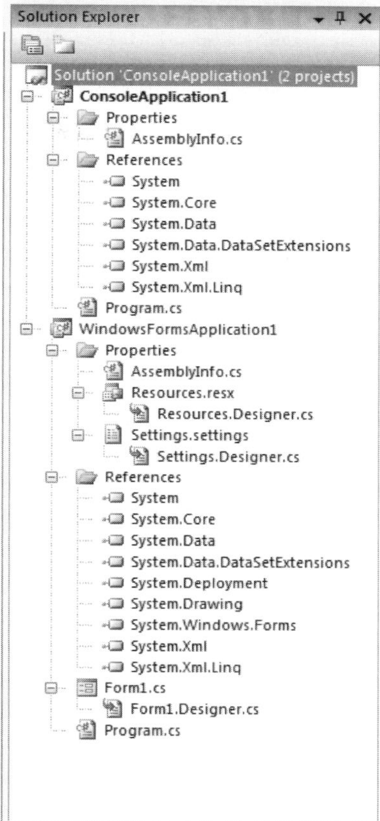

Figure 15-12

Setting the Startup Project

Bear in mind that if you have multiple projects in a solution only one of them can be run at a time! When you compile the solution, all the projects in it will be compiled. However, you must specify which one you want Visual Studio to start running when you press F5 or select Start. If you have one executable and several libraries that it calls, this will clearly be the executable. In this case, where you have two independent executables in the project, you would simply need to debug each in turn.

You can tell Visual Studio which project to run by right-clicking that project in the Solution Explorer window and selecting Set as Startup Project from the context menu. You can tell which one is the current startup project — it is the one that appears in bold in the Solution Explorer window (`WindowsFormsApplication1` in Figure 15-12).

Windows Application Code

A Windows application contains a lot more code right from the start than a console application when Visual Studio first creates it. That is because creating a window is an intrinsically more complex process. Chapter 31, "Windows Forms," discusses the code for a Windows application in detail. For now, look at the code in the `Form1` class in the `WindowsApplication1` project to see for yourself how much is auto-generated.

Reading in Visual Studio 6 Projects

If you are coding in C#, you will not need to read in any old Visual Studio 6 projects because C# does not exist in Visual Studio 6. However, language interoperability is a key part of the .NET Framework, so you might want your C# code to work alongside code written in Visual Basic or in C++. In that situation, you might need to edit projects that were created with Visual Studio 6.

Visual Studio has no problems reading in and upgrading Visual Studio 6 projects and workspaces. The situation is different for pre-Visual Studio C++ and Visual Basic projects:

- In Visual C++, no change to the source code is needed. All your old Visual C++ code still works fine with the new C++ compiler. Obviously, it is not managed code, but it will still compile to code that runs outside the .NET runtime; if you want your code to integrate with the .NET Framework, you will need to edit it. If you get Visual Studio to read in an old Visual C++ project, it will simply add a new solution file and updated project files. It will leave the old `.dsw` and `.dsp` files unchanged so that the project can still be edited by Visual Studio 6, if necessary.
- In Visual Basic, things are a bit more complicated. As mentioned in Chapter 1, ".NET Architecture," although Visual Basic 2008 has been designed very much around Visual Basic 6.0 and shares much of the same syntax, it is in many ways a new language. In Visual Basic 6.0, the source code largely consisted of the event handlers for the controls. In Visual Basic 2008, the code that actually instantiates the main window and many of its controls is not part of Visual Basic but is instead hidden behind the scenes as part of the configuration of your project. In contrast, Visual Basic 2008 works in the same way as C#, by putting the entire program out in the open as source code, so all the code that displays in the main window and all the controls on it need to be in the source file. Also, like C#, Visual Basic 2008 requires everything to be object oriented and part of a class, whereas VB did not even recognize the concept of classes in the .NET sense. If you try to read a Visual Basic project with Visual Studio, it will need to upgrade the entire source code to Visual Basic 2008 before it can handle it — and this involves making a lot of changes to the Visual Basic code. Visual Studio can largely make these changes automatically and will then create a new Visual Basic 2008 solution for you. You will find that the source code it gives you looks very different from the corresponding Visual Basic code, and you will still need to check carefully through the generated code to make sure that the project still works correctly. You might even find areas in the code where Visual Studio has left comments to the effect that it cannot figure out exactly what you wanted the code to do, and you might need to edit the code manually.

Exploring and Coding a Project

This section looks at the features that Visual Studio provides to help you add code to your project.

The Folding Editor

One really exciting feature of Visual Studio is its use of a folding editor as its default code editor (see Figure 15-13).

Figure 15-13 shows the code for the console application that you generated earlier. Notice those little minus signs on the left-hand side of the window. These signs mark the points where the editor assumes that a new block of code (or documentation comment) begins. You can click these icons to close up the view of the corresponding block of code just as you would close a node in a tree control (see Figure 15-14).

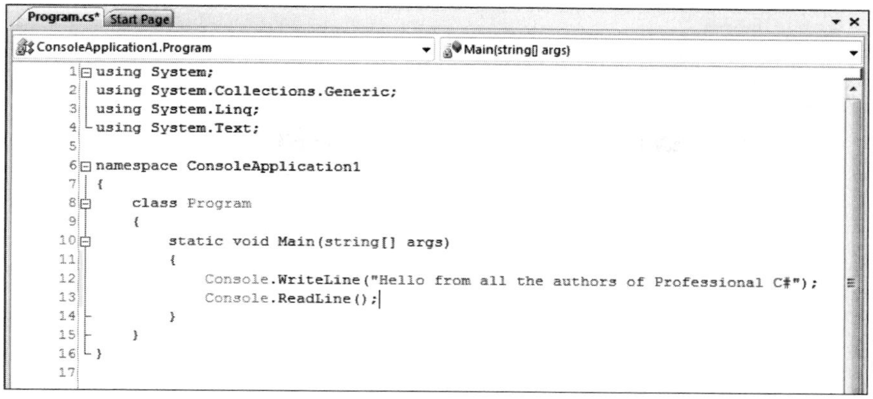

Program.cs* Start Page

ConsoleApplication1.Program | Main(string[] args)

```
using System;
using System.Collections.Generic;
using System.Linq;
using System.Text;

namespace ConsoleApplication1
{
    class Program
    {
        static void Main(string[] args)
        {
            Console.WriteLine("Hello from all the authors of Professional C#");
            Console.ReadLine();
        }
    }
}

```

Figure 15-13

This means that while you are editing you can focus on just the areas of code you want to look at, and you can hide the bits of code you are not interested in working with at that moment. If you do not like the way the editor has chosen to block off your code, you can indicate your own blocks of collapsing code with the C# preprocessor directives, `#region` and `#endregion`, which were examined earlier in the book. For example, to collapse the code inside the `Main()` method, you would add the code shown in Figure 15-15.

The code editor will automatically detect the `#region` block and place a new minus sign by the `#region` directive, as shown in Figure 15-15, allowing you to close the region. Enclosing this code in a region means that you can get the editor to close the block of code (see Figure 15-16), marking the area with the comment you specified in the `#region` directive. The compiler, however, ignores the directives and compiles the `Main()` method as normal.

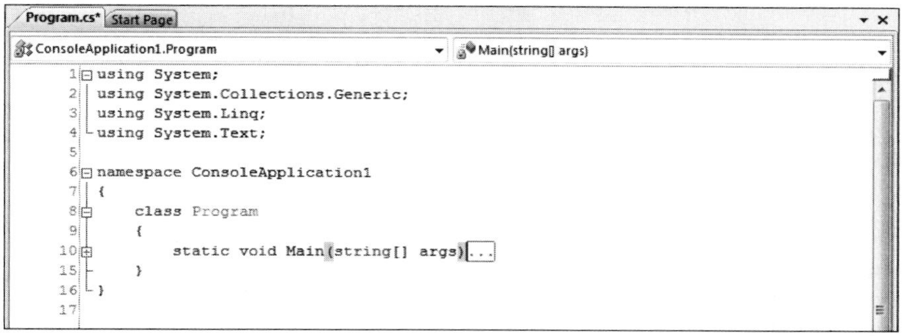

Program.cs* Start Page

ConsoleApplication1.Program | Main(string[] args)

```
using System;
using System.Collections.Generic;
using System.Linq;
using System.Text;

namespace ConsoleApplication1
{
    class Program
    {
        static void Main(string[] args)...
    }
}

```

Figure 15-14

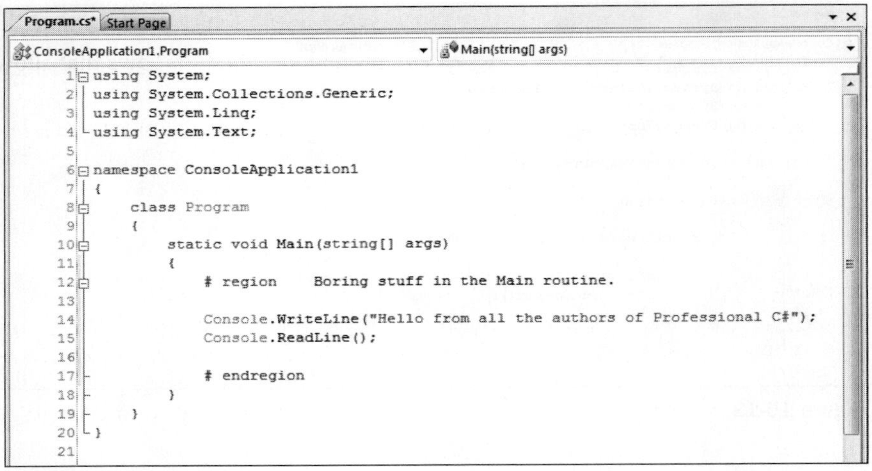

```
Program.cs*  Start Page
ConsoleApplication1.Program    Main(string[] args)
using System;
using System.Collections.Generic;
using System.Linq;
using System.Text;

namespace ConsoleApplication1
{
    class Program
    {
        static void Main(string[] args)
        {
            # region    Boring stuff in the Main routine.

            Console.WriteLine("Hello from all the authors of Professional C#");
            Console.ReadLine();

            # endregion
        }
    }
}
```

Figure 15-15

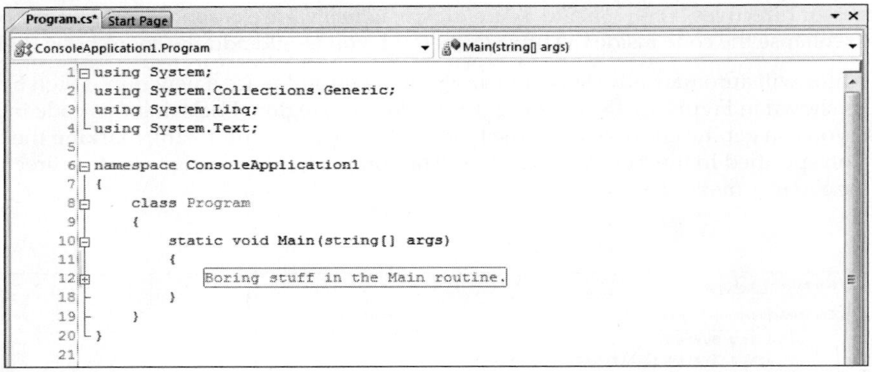

```
Program.cs*  Start Page
ConsoleApplication1.Program    Main(string[] args)
using System;
using System.Collections.Generic;
using System.Linq;
using System.Text;

namespace ConsoleApplication1
{
    class Program
    {
        static void Main(string[] args)
        {
            Boring stuff in the Main routine.
        }
    }
}
```

Figure 15-16

In addition to the folding editor feature, Visual Studio's code editor brings across all the familiar functionality from Visual Studio 6. In particular, it features IntelliSense, which not only saves you typing, but also ensures that you use the correct parameters. C++ developers will notice that the Visual Studio IntelliSense feature is a bit more robust than the Visual Studio 6 version and also works more quickly. You will also notice that IntelliSense has been improved in Visual Studio 2008. It is now smarter in that it remembers your preferred choices and starts with one of these choices instead of starting directly at the beginning of the sometimes rather lengthy lists that IntelliSense can now provide.

The code editor also performs some syntax checking on your code and underlines most syntax errors with a short wavy line, even before you compile the code. Hovering the mouse pointer over the underlined text brings up a small box telling you what the error is. Visual Basic developers have been familiar with this feature, known as *design-time debugging*, for years; now C# and C++ developers can benefit from it as well.

Other Windows

In addition to the code editor, Visual Studio provides a number of other windows that allow you to view your project from different points of view.

The rest of this section describes several other windows. If one of these windows is not visible on your screen, you can select it from the View menu. To show the design view and code editor, right-click the file name in the Solution Explorer and select View Designer or View Code from the context menu, or select the item from the toolbar at the top of the Solution Explorer. The design view and code editor share the same tabbed window.

The Design View Window

If you are designing a user interface application, such as a Windows application, Windows control library, or an ASP.NET application, you will use the Design View window. This window presents a visual overview of what your form will look like. You normally use the Design View window in conjunction with a window known as the toolbox. The toolbox contains a large number of .NET components that you can drag onto your program (see Figure 15-17).

Figure 15-17

The principle of the toolbox was applied in all development environments in Visual Studio 6, but with .NET, the number of components available from the toolbox has vastly increased. The categories of components available through the toolbox depend, to some extent, on the type of project you are editing — for example, you will get a far wider range when you are editing the `WindowsFormsApplication1` project in the `DemoSolution` solution than you will when you are editing the `ConsoleApplication1` project. The most important ranges of items available include the following:

- Data — Classes that allow you to connect to data sources and manage the data they contain. Here, you will find components for working with Microsoft SQL Server, Oracle, and any OleDb data source.
- Windows Forms Controls (labeled as Common Controls) — Classes that represent visual controls such as text boxes, list boxes, or tree views for working with thick-client applications.
- Web Forms Controls (labeled as Standard) — Classes that basically do the same thing as Windows controls, but that work in the context of Web browsers, and that work by sending HTML output to simulate the controls to the browser. (You will see this only when working with ASP.NET applications.)
- Components — Miscellaneous .NET classes that perform various useful tasks on your machine, such as connecting to directory services or to the event log.

You can also add your own custom categories to the toolbox by right-clicking any category and selecting Add Tab from the context menu. You can also place other tools in the toolbox by selecting Choose Items from the same context menu — this is particularly useful for adding your favorite COM components and ActiveX controls, which are not present in the toolbox by default. If you add a COM control, you can still click to place it in your project just as you would with a .NET control. Visual Studio automatically adds all the required COM interoperability code to allow your project to call up the control. In this case, what is actually added to your project is a .NET control that Visual Studio creates behind the scenes and that acts as a wrapper for your COM control.

C++ developers will recognize the toolbox as Visual Studio's (much-enhanced) version of the resource editor. Visual Basic developers might not be that impressed at first; after all, Visual Studio 6 also has a toolbox. However, the toolbox in Visual Studio has a dramatically different effect on your source code than its precursor.

To see how the toolbox works, place a text box in your basic form project. You simply click the `TextBox` control contained within the toolbox and then click again to place it in the form in the design view (or if you prefer, you can simply drag and drop the control directly onto the design surface). Now the design view looks like Figure 15-18, showing roughly what `WindowsFormsApplication1` will look like if you compile and run it.

If you look at the code view of your form, you see that Visual Studio 2008 does not add the code that instantiates a `TextBox` object to go on the form directly here as it did in the early versions of the IDE. Instead, you will need to expand the plus sign next to `Form1.cs` in the Visual Studio Solution Explorer. Here, you will find a file that is dedicated to the design of the form and the controls that are placed on the form — `Form1.Designer.cs`. In this class file, you will find a new member variable in the `Form1` class:

```
partial class Form1
{
    private System.Windows.Forms.TextBox textBox1;
```

There is also some code to initialize it in the method, `InitializeComponent()`, which is called from the `Form1` constructor:

```
/// <summary>
/// Required method for Designer support - do not modify
/// the contents of this method with the code editor.
/// </summary>
```

```
private void InitializeComponent()
{
            this.textBox1 = new System.Windows.Forms.TextBox();
            this.SuspendLayout();
            //
            // textBox1
            //
            this.textBox1.Location = new System.Drawing.Point(0, 0);
            this.textBox1.Name = "textBox1";
            this.textBox1.Size = new System.Drawing.Size(100, 20);
            this.textBox1.TabIndex = 0;
            //
            // Form1
            //
            this.AutoScaleDimensions = new System.Drawing.SizeF(6F, 13F);
            this.AutoScaleMode = System.Windows.Forms.AutoScaleMode.Font;
            this.ClientSize = new System.Drawing.Size(284, 264);
            this.Controls.Add(this.textBox1);
            this.Name = "Form1";
            this.Text = "Form1";
            this.ResumeLayout(false);
            this.PerformLayout();

}
```

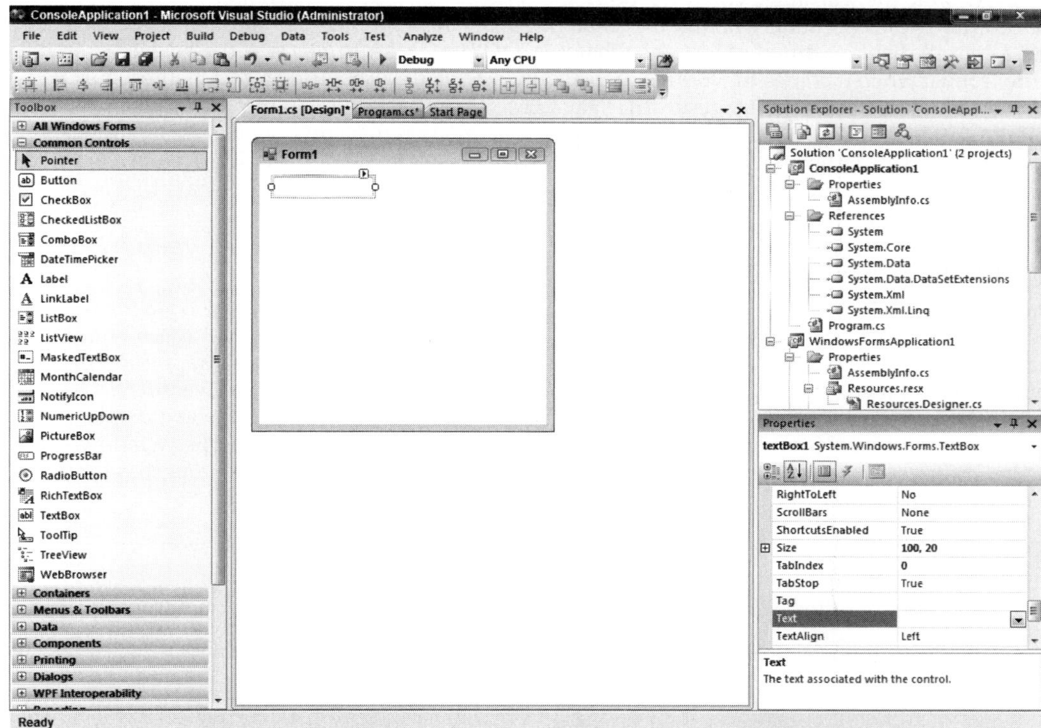

Figure 15-18

In one sense, there is no difference between the code editor and the design view; they simply present different views of the same code. What actually happened when you clicked to add the `TextBox` to the design view is that the editor placed the preceding extra code in your C# source file for you. The design view simply reflects this change because Visual Studio is able to read your source code and determine from it what controls should be around when the application starts up. This is a fundamental shift from the old Visual Basic way of looking at things, in which everything was based around the visual design. Now, your C# source code is what fundamentally controls your application, and the design view is just a different way of viewing the source code. Incidentally, if you do write any Visual Basic 2008 code with Visual Studio, you will find the same principles at work.

If you had wanted to, you could have worked the other way around. If you manually added the same code to your C# source files, Visual Studio would have automatically detected from the code that your application contained a `TextBox` control, and would have shown it in the design view at the designated position. It is best to add these controls visually, and let Visual Studio handle the initial code generation — it is a lot quicker and less error-prone to click the mouse button a couple of times than to type a few lines of code!

Another reason for adding these controls visually is that, to recognize that they are there, Visual Studio does need the relevant code to conform to certain criteria — and code that you write by hand might not do so. In particular, you will notice that the `InitializeComponent()` method that contains the code to initialize the `TextBox` is commented to warn you against modifying it. That is because this is the method that Visual Studio looks at to determine what controls are around when your application starts up. If you create and define a control somewhere else in your code, Visual Studio will not be aware of it, and you will not be able to edit it in the design view or in certain other useful windows.

In fact, despite the warnings, you can modify the code in `InitializeComponent()`, provided that you are careful. There is generally no harm in changing the values of some of the properties, for example, so that a control displays different text or so that it is a different size. In practice, the developer studio is pretty robust when it comes to working around any other code you place in this method. Just be aware that if you make too many changes to `InitializeComponent()`, you do run the risk that Visual Studio will not recognize some of your controls. We should stress that this will not affect your application in any way whatsoever when it is compiled, but it might disable some of the editing features of Visual Studio for those controls. Hence, if you want to add any other substantial initialization, it is probably better to do so in the `Form1` constructor or in some other method.

The Properties Window

This is another window that has its origins in the old Visual Basic IDE. You know from the first part of the book that .NET classes can implement properties. In fact, as you will discover when building Windows Forms (see Chapter 31, "Windows Forms"), the .NET base classes that represent forms and controls have a lot of properties that define their action or appearance — properties such as `Width`, `Height`, `Enabled` (whether the user can type input to the control), and `Text` (the text displayed by the control) — and Visual Studio knows about many of these properties. The Properties window, shown in Figure 15-19, displays and allows you to edit the initial values of most of these properties for the controls that Visual Studio has been able to detect by reading your source code.

> **The Properties window can also show events. You can view events for what you are focused on in the IDE or selected in the drop-down list box directly in the Properties window by clicking the icon that looks like a lightning bolt at the top of the window.**

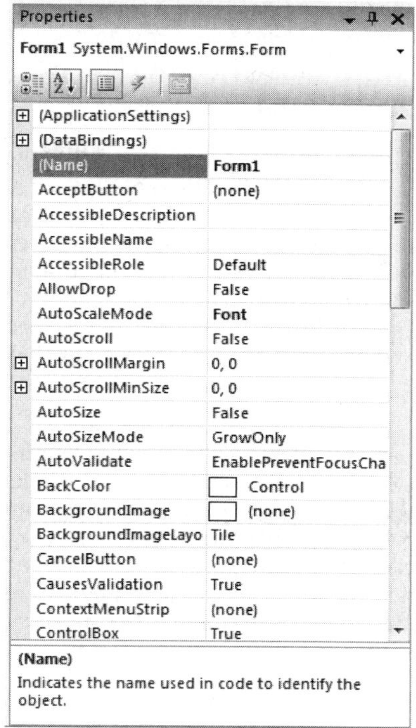

Figure 15-19

At the top of the Properties window is a list box that allows you to select which control you want to view. In the example in this chapter, you have selected `Form1`, the main form class for your `WindowsFormsApplication1` project, and have edited the text to "Basic Form — Hello!" If you now check the source code, you can see that what you have actually done is edit the source code — using a friendlier user interface:

```
this.AutoScaleDimensions = new System.Drawing.SizeF(6F, 13F);
this.AutoScaleMode = System.Windows.Forms.AutoScaleMode.Font;
this.ClientSize = new System.Drawing.Size(284, 264);
this.Controls.Add(this.textBox1);
this.Name = "Form1";
this.Text = "Basic Form - Hello";
this.ResumeLayout(false);
this.PerformLayout();
```

Not all the properties shown in the Properties window are explicitly mentioned in your source code. For those that are not, Visual Studio will display the default values that were set when the form was created and that are set when the form is actually initialized. Obviously, if you change a value for one of these properties in the Properties window, a statement explicitly setting that property will magically appear in your source code — and vice versa. It is interesting to note that if a property is changed from its original value, this property will then appear in bold type within the list box of the Properties window. Sometimes double-clicking the property in the Properties window returns the value to its original value.

The Properties window provides a convenient way to get a broad overview of the appearance and properties of a particular control or window.

It is interesting to note that the Properties window is implemented as a `System.Windows.Forms.PropertyGrid` *instance, which will internally use the reflection technology described in Chapter 13, "Reflection," to identify the properties and property values to display.*

The Class View Window

Unlike the Properties window, the Class View window, shown in Figure 15-20, owes its origins to the C++ (and J++) developer environments. This window will be new to Visual Basic developers because Visual Basic 6 did not even support the concept of the class, other than in the sense of a COM component. The class view is not actually treated by Visual Studio as a window in its own right — rather it is an additional tab to the Solution Explorer window. By default, the class view will not even appear in the Visual Studio Solution Explorer. To invoke the class view, select View ⇨ Class View. The class view (see Figure 15-20) shows the hierarchy of the namespaces and classes in your code. It gives you a tree view that you can expand to see what namespaces contain what classes and what classes contain what members.

A nice feature of the class view is that if you right-click the name of any item for which you have access to the source code, then the context menu features the Go To Definition option, which takes you to the definition of the item in the code editor. Alternatively, you can do this by double-clicking the item in class view (or, indeed, by right-clicking the item you want in the source code editor and choosing the same option from the resulting context menu). The context menu also gives you the option to add a field, method, property, or indexer to a class. This means that you specify the details of the relevant member in a dialog box, and the code is added for you. This might not be that useful for fields or methods, which can be quickly added to your code; however, you might find this feature helpful for properties and indexers, where it can save you quite a bit of typing.

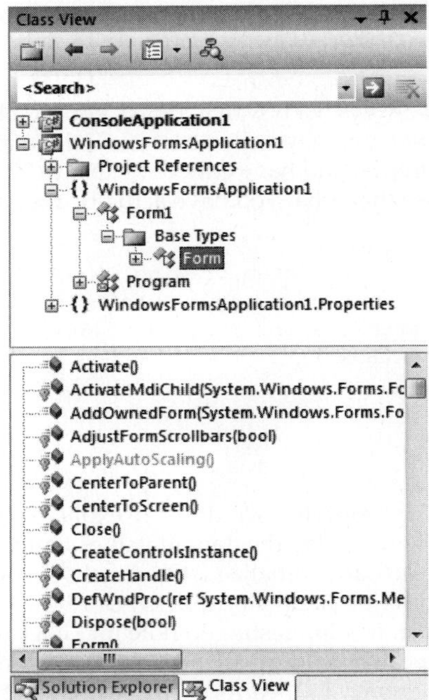

Figure 15-20

The Object Browser Window

One important aspect of programming in the .NET environment is being able to find out what methods and other code items are available in the base classes and any other libraries that you are referencing from your assembly. This feature is available through a window called the Object Browser. You can access this window by selecting Object Browser from the View menu in Visual Studio 2008.

The Object Browser window is quite similar to the Class View window in that it displays a tree view that gives the class structure of your application, allowing you to inspect the members of each class. The user interface is slightly different in that it displays class members in a separate pane rather than in the tree view itself. The real difference is that it lets you look at not just the namespaces and classes in your project but also the ones in all the assemblies referenced by the project. Figure 15-21 shows the Object Browser viewing the `SystemException` class from the .NET base classes.

One note of caution with the Object Browser is that it groups classes by the assembly in which they are located first and by namespace second. Unfortunately, because namespaces for the base classes are often spread across several assemblies, this means you might have trouble locating a particular class unless you know what assembly it is in.

The Object Browser is there to view .NET objects. If for any reason you want to investigate installed COM objects, you will find that the OLEView tool previously used in the C++ IDE is still available — it is located in the folder `C:\Program Files\Microsoft SDKs\Windows\v6.0A\bin` along with several other similar utilities.

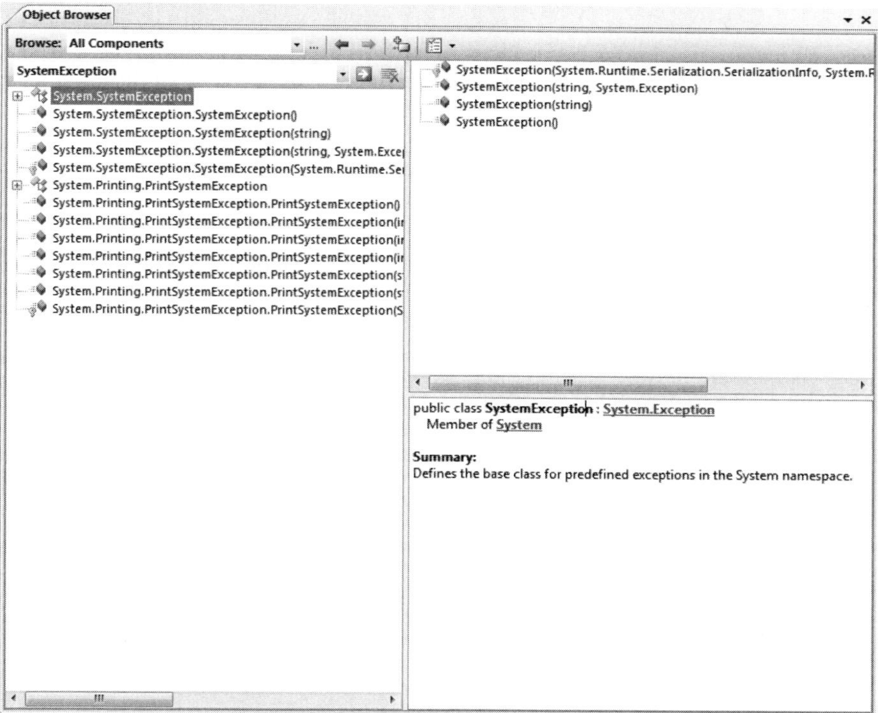

Figure 15-21

Visual Basic developers should not confuse the .NET Object Browser with the Object Browser of the Visual Basic 6 IDE. The .NET Object Browser is there to view .NET classes, whereas the tool of that name in Visual Basic 6 is used to view COM components. If you want the functionality of the old Object Browser, you should now use the OLEView tool.

The Server Explorer Window

You can use the Server Explorer window, shown in Figure 15-22, to find out about aspects of the computers in your network while coding.

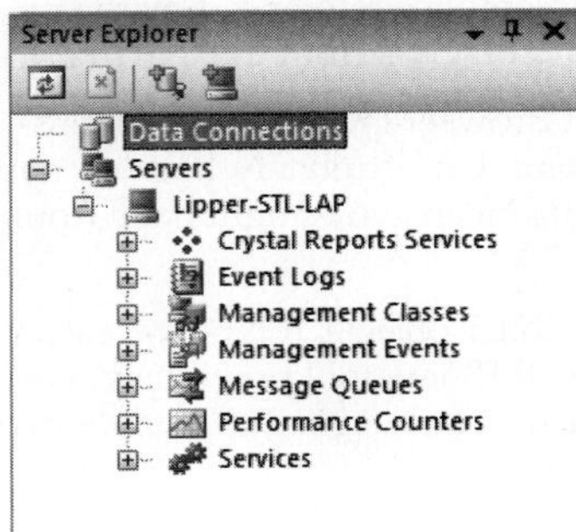

Figure 15-22

As you can see from the screenshot, among the things you can access through the Server Explorer are database connections, information about services, event logs, and more.

The Server Explorer is linked to the Properties window so that if you open the Services node, for example, and click a particular service, the properties of that service will be displayed in the Properties window.

Pin Buttons

While exploring Visual Studio, you might have noticed that many of the windows have some interesting functionality more reminiscent of toolbars. In particular, apart from the code editor, they can all be docked. Another feature of them is that when they are docked, they have an extra icon that looks like a pin next to the minimize button in the top-right corner of each window. This icon really does act like a pin — it can be used to pin the windows open. When they are pinned (the pin is displayed vertically), they behave just like the regular windows that you are used to. When they are unpinned, however (the pin is displayed horizontally), they remain open only as long as they have the focus. As soon as they lose the focus (because you clicked or moved your mouse somewhere else), they smoothly retreat into the main border around the entire Visual Studio application. (You can also feel the speed of your computer by how quickly or slowly they open and close.)

Pinning and unpinning windows provides another way of making the best use of the limited space on your screen. It has not really been seen a great deal in Windows before, though a few third-party applications, such as PaintShop Pro, have used similar concepts. Pinned windows have, however, been around on many Unix-based systems for quite a while.

Building a Project

This section examines the options that Visual Studio gives you for building your project.

Building, Compiling, and Making

Before examining the various build options, it is important to clarify some terminology. You will often see three different terms used in connection with the process of getting from your source code to some sort of executable code: compiling, building, and making. The origin of these various terms comes from the fact that until recently, the process of getting from source code to executable code involved more than one step (and this is still the case in C++). This was due in large part to the number of source files in a program. In C++, for example, each source file needs to be compiled individually. This leads to what are known as object files, each containing something like executable code, but where each object file relates to only one source file. To generate an executable, these object files need to be linked together, a process that is officially known as linking. The combined process was usually referred to — at least on the Windows platform — as building your code. However, in C# terms the compiler is more sophisticated and is able to read in and treat all your source files as one block. Hence, there is not really a separate linking stage, so in the context of C# the terms *compile* and *build* are used interchangeably.

In addition to this, the term *make* basically means the same as *build*, though it is not really used in the context of C#. The term originated on old mainframe systems on which, when a project was composed of many source files, a separate file would be written that contained instructions to the compiler on how to build a project — which files to include and what libraries to link to and so on. This file was generally known as a make file and is still quite standard on Unix systems. Make files are not normally needed on Windows, though you can still write them (or get Visual Studio to generate them) if you need to.

Debug and Release Builds

The idea of having separate builds is very familiar to C++ developers and less so to those with a Visual Basic background. The point here is that when you are debugging, you typically want your executable to behave differently from when you are ready to ship the software. When you are ready to ship your software, you want the size of the executable to be as small as possible and the executable itself to be as fast as possible. Unfortunately, these requirements are not really compatible with your needs when you are debugging code, as explained in the following sections.

Optimization

High performance is achieved partly by the compiler doing many optimizations on the code. This means that the compiler actively looks at your source code as it is compiling to identify places where it can modify the precise details of what you are doing in a way that does not change the overall effect but that makes things more efficient. For example, if the compiler encountered the following source code:

```
double InchesToCm(double Ins)
{
   return Ins*2.54;
}

// later on in the code

Y = InchesToCm(X);
```

it might replace it with this:

```
Y = X * 2.54;
```

Or it might replace this code:

```
{
   string Message = "Hi";
   Console.WriteLine(Message);
}
```

with this:

```
Console.WriteLine("Hi");
```

By doing so, it bypasses having to declare an unnecessary object reference in the process.

It is not possible to exactly pin down what optimizations the C# compiler does — nor whether the two previous examples actually would occur with any particular example — because those kinds of details are not documented. (Chances are that for managed languages such as C#, the previous optimizations would occur at JIT compilation time, not when the C# compiler compiles source code to assembly.) For obvious commercial reasons, companies that write compilers are usually quite reluctant to give too many details about the tricks that their compilers use. We should stress that optimizations do not affect your source code — they affect only the contents of the executable code. However, the previous examples should give you a good idea of what to expect from optimizations.

The problem is that although optimizations like the previous ones help a great deal in making your code run faster, they are not that helpful for debugging. Suppose with the first example that you want to set a breakpoint inside the `InchesToCm()` method to see what's going on in there. How can you possibly do that if the executable code does not actually have an `InchesToCm()` method because the compiler has removed it? Moreover, how can you set a watch on the `Message` variable when that does not exist in the compiled code either?

Debugger Symbols

When you are debugging, you often have to look at values of variables, and you will specify them by their source code names. The trouble is that executable code generally does not contain those names — the compiler replaces the names with memory addresses. .NET has modified this situation somewhat, to the extent that certain items in assemblies are stored with their names, but this is only true of a small minority of items — such as public classes and methods — and those names will still be removed when the assembly is JIT-compiled. Asking the debugger to tell you what the value is in the variable called `HeightInInches` is not going to get you very far if, when the debugger examines the executable code, it sees only addresses and no reference to the name `HeightInInches` anywhere. Therefore, to debug properly, you need to have extra debugging information made available in the executable. This information includes, among other things, names of variables and line information that allows the debugger to match up which executable machine assembly language instructions correspond to those of your original source code instructions. You will not, however, want that information in a release build, both for commercial reasons (debugging information makes it a lot easier for other people to disassemble your code) and because it increases the size of the executable.

Extra Source Code Debugging Commands

A related issue is that quite often while you are debugging there will be extra lines in your code to display crucial debugging-related information. Obviously, you want the relevant commands removed entirely from the executable before you ship the software. You could do this manually, but wouldn't it be so much easier if you could simply mark those statements in some way so that the compiler ignores them when it is compiling your code to be shipped? You've already seen in the first part of the book how this can be done in C# by defining a suitable processor symbol, and possibly using this in conjunction with the `Conditional` attribute, giving you what is known as *conditional compilation.*

What all these factors add up to is that you need to compile almost all commercial software in a slightly different way when debugging than in the final product that is shipped. Visual Studio is able to consider this because, as you have already seen, it stores details of all the options that it is supposed to pass to the compiler when it has your code compiled. All that Visual Studio has to do to support different types of builds is to store more than one set of such details. The different sets of build information are referred to as configurations. When you create a project, Visual Studio automatically gives you two configurations, called Debug and Release:

- The Debug configuration commonly specifies that no optimizations are to take place, extra debugging information is to be present in the executable, and the compiler is to assume that the debug preprocessor symbol `Debug` is present unless it is explicitly `#undefined` in the source code.
- The Release configuration specifies that the compiler should optimize, that there should be no extra debugging information in the executable, and that the compiler should not assume that any particular preprocessor symbol is present.

You can define your own configurations as well. You might want to do this, for example, if you want to set up professional-level builds and enterprise-level builds so that you can ship two versions of the software. In the past, because of issues concerning the Unicode character encodings being supported on Windows NT but not on Windows 95, it was common for C++ projects to feature a Unicode configuration and an MBCS (multi-byte character set) configuration.

Selecting a Configuration

One obvious question is that, because Visual Studio stores details of more than one configuration, how does it determine which one to use when arranging for a project to be built? The answer is that there is always an active configuration, which is the configuration that will be used when you ask Visual Studio to build a project. (Note that configurations are set for each project rather than for each solution.)

By default, when you create a project, the Debug configuration is the active configuration. You can change which configuration is the active one by clicking the Build menu option and selecting the Configuration Manager item. It is also available through a drop-down menu in the main Visual Studio toolbar.

Editing Configurations

In addition to choosing the active configuration, you can also examine and edit the configurations. To do this, you select the relevant project in the Solution Explorer and then select the Properties from the Project menu. This brings up a very sophisticated dialog box. (Alternatively, you can access the same dialog box by right-clicking the name of the project in the Solution Explorer and then selecting Properties from the context menu.)

This dialog contains a tree view, which allows you to select many different general areas to examine or edit. We do not have space to show all of these areas, but we will show a couple of the most important ones.

Figure 15-23 shows a tabbed view of the available properties for a particular application. This screenshot shows the general application settings for the `ConsoleApplication1` project that you created earlier in the chapter.

Among the points to note are that you can select the name of the assembly as well as the type of assembly to be generated. The options here are Console Application, Windows Application, and Class Library. You can, of course, change the assembly type if you want. (Though arguably, if you want, you might wonder why you did not pick the correct project type at the time that you asked Visual Studio to generate the project for you in the first place!)

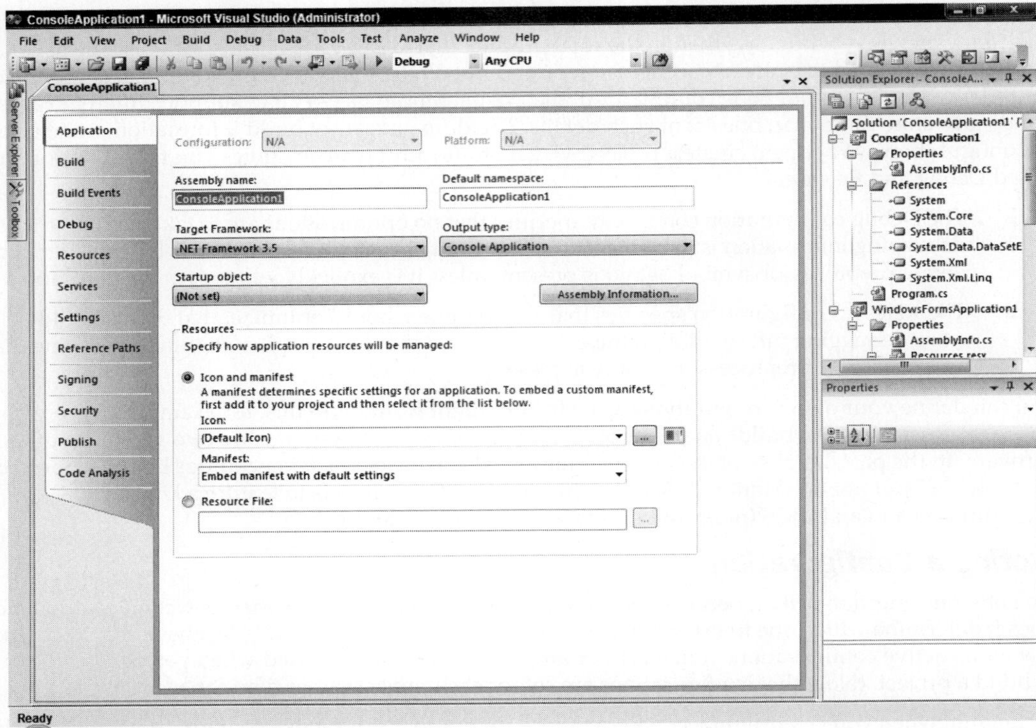

Figure 15-23

Figure 15-24 shows the build configuration properties. You will notice that a list box near the top of the dialog box allows you to specify which configuration you want to look at. You can see — in the case of the Debug configuration — that the compiler assumes that the `DEBUG` and `TRACE` preprocessor symbols have been defined. In addition, the code is not optimized and extra debugging information is generated.

In general, it is not that often that you will need to adjust the configuration settings. However, if you ever do need to use them, you now know the difference between the available configuration properties.

Debugging

After the long discussion about building and build configurations, you might be surprised to learn that this chapter is not going to spend a great deal of time discussing debugging itself. The reason for that is that the principles and the process of debugging — setting breakpoints and examining the values of variables — is not really significantly different in Visual Studio from any of the various Visual Studio 6 IDEs. Instead, this section briefly reviews the features offered by Visual Studio, focusing on those areas that might be new to some developers. It also discusses how to deal with exceptions, because these can cause problems during debugging.

In C#, as in pre-.NET languages, the main technique involved in debugging is simply setting breakpoints and using them to examine what is going on in your code at a certain point in its execution.

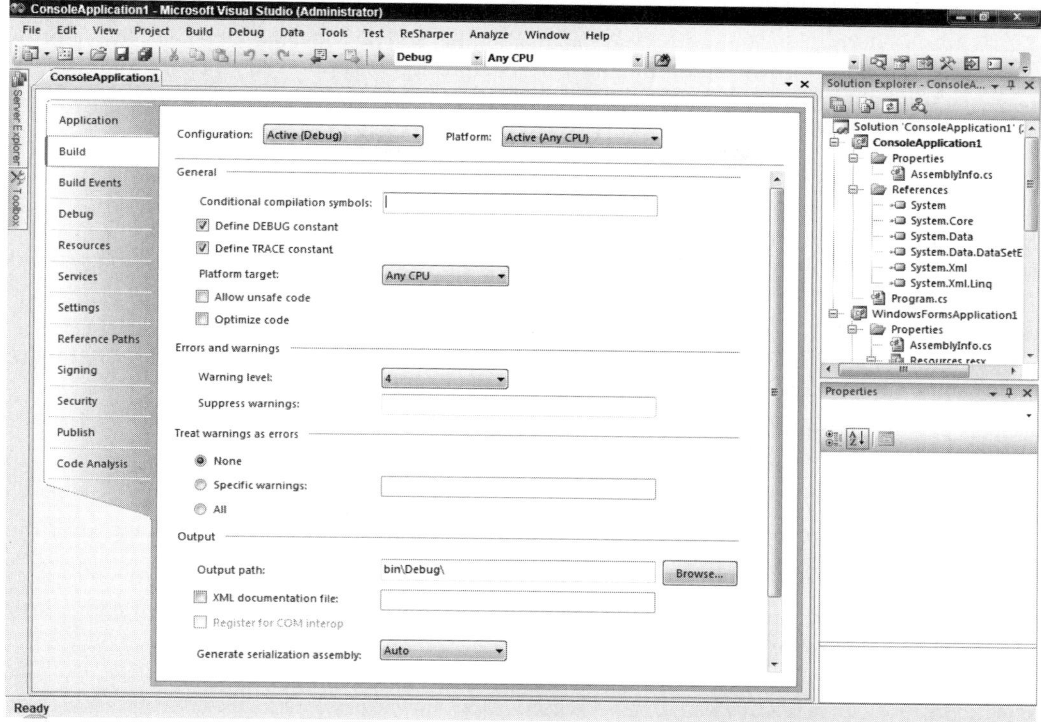

Figure 15-24

Breakpoints

You can set breakpoints from Visual Studio on any line of your code that is actually executed. The simplest way is to click the line in the code editor, within the shaded area toward the far left of the document window (or press the F9 key when the appropriate line is selected). This sets up a breakpoint on that particular line, which causes execution to break and control to be transferred to the debugger as soon as that line is reached in the execution process. As in previous versions of Visual Studio, a breakpoint is indicated by a large circle to the left of the line in the code editor. Visual Studio also highlights the line by displaying the text and background in a different color. Clicking the circle again removes the breakpoint.

If breaking every time at a particular line is not adequate for your particular problem, you can also set conditional breakpoints. To do this, select Debug ⇨ Windows ⇨ Breakpoints. This brings up a dialog box asking you for details of the breakpoint you want to set. Among the options available, you can:

- ❑ Specify that execution should break only after the breakpoint has been passed a certain number of times.
- ❑ Specify that the breakpoint should come into effect only every so many times that the line is reached, for example, every twentieth time that a line is executed. (This is useful when debugging large loops.)

- ❑ Set the breakpoints relative to a variable rather than to an instruction. In this case, the value of the variable will be monitored and the breakpoints will be triggered whenever the value of this variable changes. You might find, however, that using this option slows down your code considerably. Checking whether the value of a variable has changed after every instruction adds a lot of processor time.

Watches

After a breakpoint has been hit, you will usually want to investigate the values of variables. The simplest way to do this is to hover the mouse cursor over the name of the variable in the code editor. This causes a little box that shows the value of that variable to pop up, which can also be expanded to greater detail. This is shown in Figure 15-25.

However, you might also prefer to use the Autos window to examine the contents of variables. The Autos window (shown in Figure 15-26) is a tabbed window that appears only when the program is running under the debugger. If you do not see it, try selecting Debug ⇨ Windows ⇨ Autos.

Variables that are classes or structs are shown with a + icon next to them, which you can click to expand the variable and see the values of its fields.

The three tabs to this window are each designed to monitor different variables:

- ❑ **Autos** monitors the last few variables that have been accessed as the program was executing.
- ❑ **Locals** monitors variables that are accessible in the method currently being executed.
- ❑ **Watch** monitors any variables that you have explicitly specified by typing their names into the Watch window.

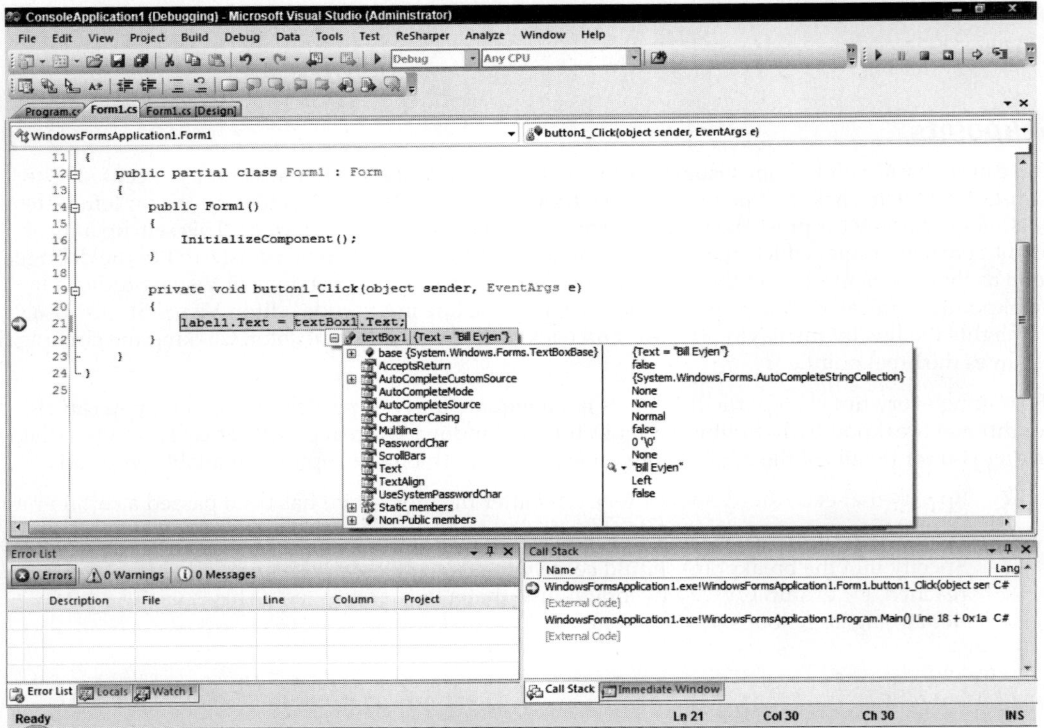

Figure 15-25

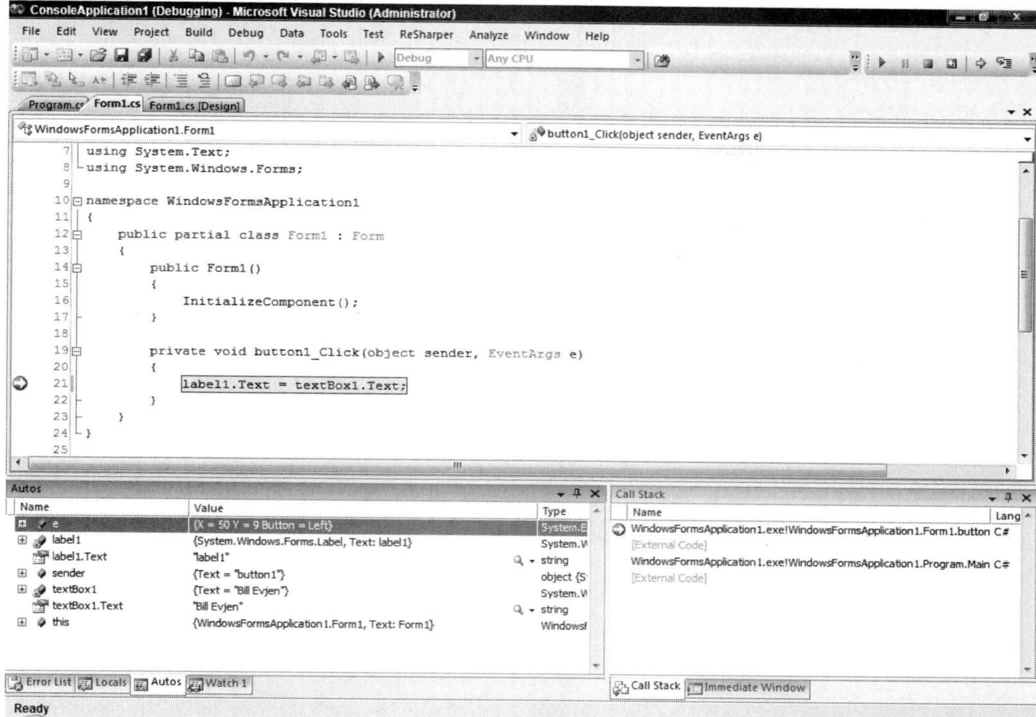

Figure 15-26

Exceptions

Exceptions are great when you ship your application and for making sure that error conditions are handled in an appropriate way within your application. Used well, they can ensure that your application copes with difficulties well and that the user is never presented with a technical dialog box. Unfortunately, exceptions are not so great when you are trying to debug your application. The problem is twofold:

- If an exception occurs when you are debugging, you often do not want it to be handled automatically — especially if automatically handling it means retiring gracefully and terminating execution! Rather, you want the debugger to help you find why the exception has occurred. Of course, the trouble is that if you have written good, robust, defensive code, your program will automatically handle almost anything — including the bugs that you want to detect!
- If an exception occurs that you have not written a handler for, the .NET runtime will still go off looking for a handler. However, by the time it discovers that there is not one, it will have terminated your program. There will not be a call stack left, and you will not be able to look at the values of any of your variables because they will all have gone out of scope.

Of course, you can set breakpoints in your catch blocks, but that often does not help very much because when the `catch` block is reached, flow of execution will, by definition, have exited the corresponding `try` block. That means that the variables you probably wanted to examine the values of to figure out what has gone wrong will have gone out of scope. You will not even be able to look at the stack trace to find what method was being executed when the `throw` statement occurred — because control will have left that method. Setting the breakpoints at the `throw` statement will of course solve this, except that if you are coding defensively, there will be many `throw` statements in your code. How can you tell which one is the one that threw the exception?

In fact, Visual Studio provides a very neat answer to all of this. If you look into the main Debug menu, you will find a menu item called Exceptions. This item opens the Exceptions dialog box (see Figure 15-27), which allows you to specify what happens when an exception is thrown. You can choose to continue execution or to stop and start debugging — in which case execution stops and the debugger steps in at the `throw` statement itself.

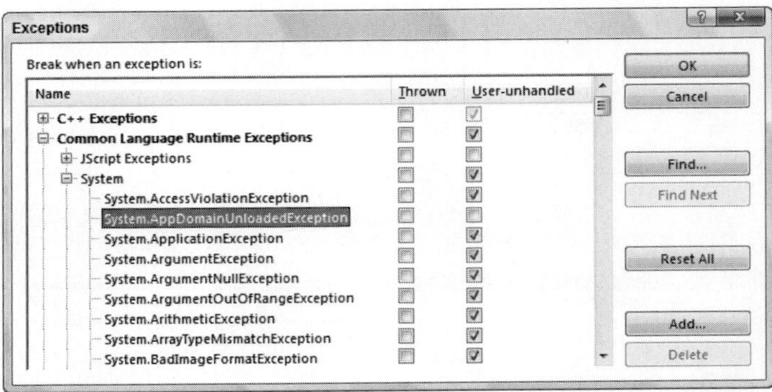

Figure 15-27

What makes this a really powerful tool is that you can customize the behavior according to which class of exception is thrown. For example, in Figure 15-27, we have told Visual Studio to break into the debugger whenever it encounters any exception thrown by a .NET base class, but not to break into the debugger if the exception is an `AppDomainUnloadedException`.

Visual Studio knows about all the exception classes available in the .NET base classes, and about quite a few exceptions that can be thrown outside the .NET environment. Visual Studio is not automatically aware of your own custom exception classes that you write, but you can manually add your exception classes to the list and thereby specify which of your exceptions should cause execution to stop immediately. To do this, just click the Add button (which is enabled when you have selected a top-level node from the tree) and type in the name of your exception class.

Refactoring

Many developers develop their applications first for functionality and then, once the functionality is in place, they *rework* their applications to make them more manageable and more readable. This is called *refactoring*. Refactoring is the process of reworking code for readability, performance, providing type safety, and lining applications up to better adhere to standard OO (object-oriented) programming practices.

For this reason, the C# environment of Visual Studio 2008 now includes a set of refactoring tools. You can find these tools under the Refactoring option in the Visual Studio menu. To show this in action, create a new class called `Car` in Visual Studio:

```
using System;
using System.Collections.Generic;
using System.Text;

namespace ConsoleApplication1
```

```
{
    public class Car
    {
        public string _color;
        public string _doors;

        public int Go()
        {
            int speedMph = 100;
            return speedMph;
        }
    }
}
```

Now, suppose that in the idea of refactoring, you want to change the code a bit so that the `color` and the `door` variables are encapsulated into public .NET properties. The refactoring capabilities of Visual Studio 2008 allow you to simply right-click either of these properties in the document window and select Refactor ➪ Encapsulate Field. This will pull up the Encapsulate Field dialog shown in Figure 15-28.

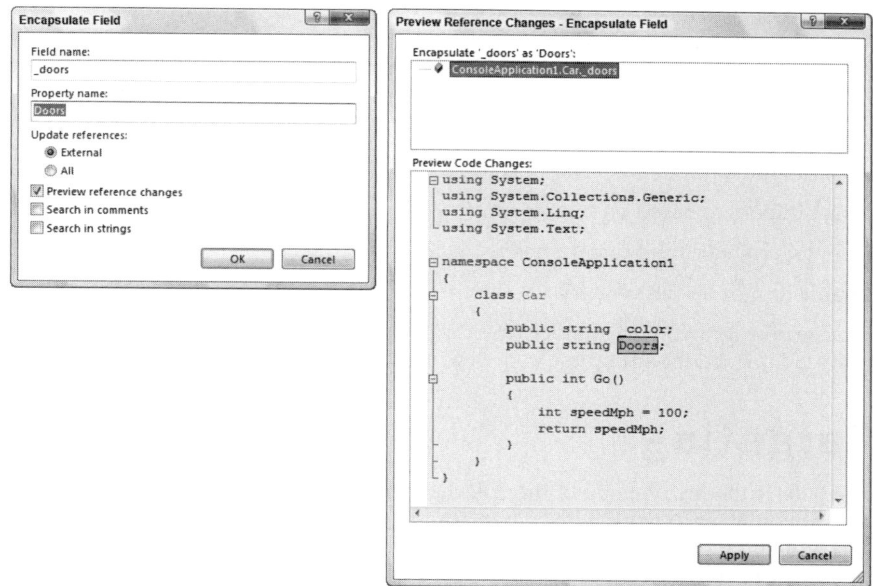

Figure 15-28

From this dialog, you can provide the name of the property and click the OK button. This will turn the selected public field into a private field, while also encapsulating the field into a public .NET property. After clicking OK, the code will have been reworked to the following (after redoing both fields):

```
namespace ConsoleApplication1
{
    public class Car
    {
        private string _color;

        public string Color
```

(continued)

(continued)

```
        {
            get { return _color; }
            set { _color = value; }
        }
        private string _doors;

        public string Doors
        {
            get { return _doors; }
            set { _doors = value; }
        }

        public int Go()
        {
            int speedMph = 100;
            return speedMph;
        }
    }
}
```

As you can see, these wizards make it quite simple to refactor your code not just on one page but for an entire application. Also included are abilities to do the following:

- Rename method names, local variables, fields, and more
- Extract methods from a selection of code
- Extract interfaces based on a set of existing type members
- Promote local variables to parameters
- Rename or reorder parameters

You will find the new refactoring abilities provided by Visual Studio 2008 a great way to get you the cleaner, more readable, better-structured code that you are looking for.

Multi-Targeting

Visual Studio 2008 is the first version of the IDE that allows you to target the version of the .NET Framework that you want to work with. When you open the New Project dialog and get ready to create a new project, you will notice that there is a drop-down list in the upper right-hand corner of the dialog that allows you to pick the version of the framework that you are interested in using. This dialog is presented in Figure 15-29.

From this figure, you can see that the drop-down list provides you the ability to target the .NET Framework 2.0, 3.0, or 3.5. This is possible only because the 3.0 and 3.5 versions of the framework are extensions of the .NET Framework 2.0. When you use the upgrade dialog to upgrade a Visual Studio 2005 solution to Visual Studio 2008, it is important that you are only upgrading the solution to *use* Visual Studio 2008 and that you are not upgrading your project to the .NET Framework 3.5. Your project will stay on the framework version you were using, but now, you will be able use the new Visual Studio 2008 to work on your project.

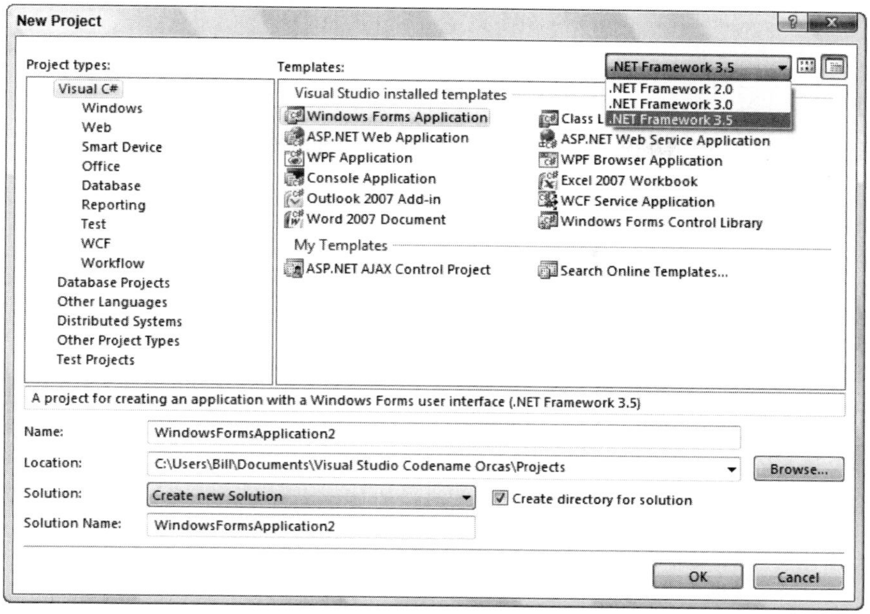

Figure 15-29

If you want to change the version of the framework the solution is using, right-click the solution and select the properties of the solution. If you are working with an ASP.NET project, you will get a dialog as shown in Figure 15-30.

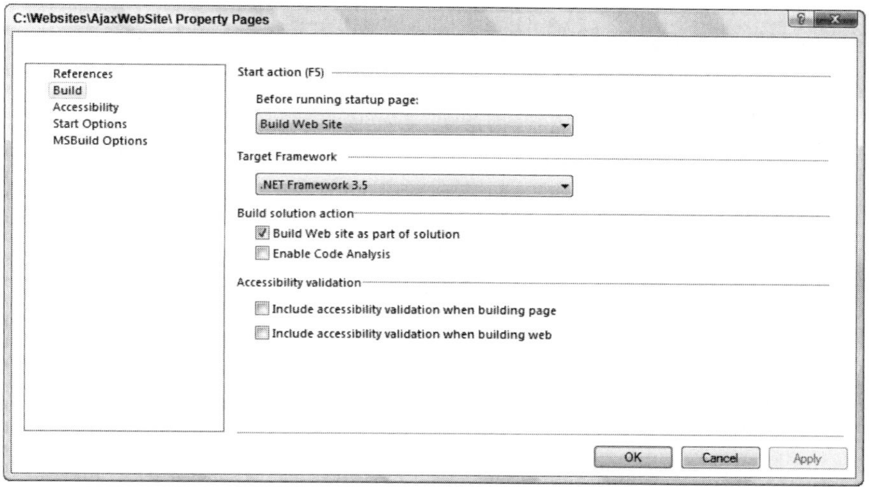

Figure 15-30

From this dialog, the Build tab will provide you the ability to change the version of the framework that the application is using. If you are working with a Windows Forms application's property pages, you will find the ability to target another version of the framework on the Application tab (the first tab). This is presented in Figure 15-31.

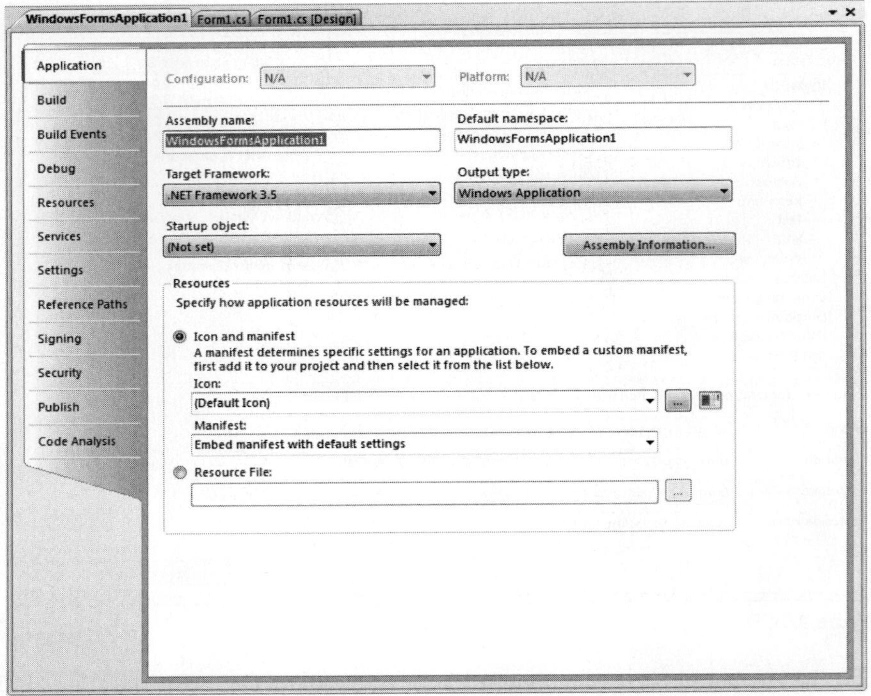

Figure 15-31

WPF, WCF, WF, and More

By default, Visual Studio 2005 did not allow you to build applications targeted at the .NET Framework 3.0, which was out during the VS2005 lifetime. The default install of Visual Studio 2005 was targeted only at the .NET Framework 2.0. To start working with the new technologies targeted at the .NET Framework 3.0, you had to do a few extra installs.

The .NET Framework 3.0 provided you with access to a class library for building application types such as applications that make use of the Windows Presentation Foundation (WPF), the Windows Communication Foundation (WCF), the Windows Workflow Foundation (WF), and Windows CardSpace.

The targeted framework capabilities of Visual Studio 2008 allow you to build these types of applications using either the .NET Framework 3.0 or 3.5.

Building WPF Applications in Visual Studio

One good example of some of the big changes that the .NET Framework 3.5 brings to Visual Studio is the WPF Application project type (found in the Windows category). Selecting this project type will create a `Window1.xaml` and `Window1.xaml.cs` file for you to work from. Everything that is created by default with this project type in the Solution Explorer is presented in Figure 15-32 (shown here with the new and searchable Properties dialog).

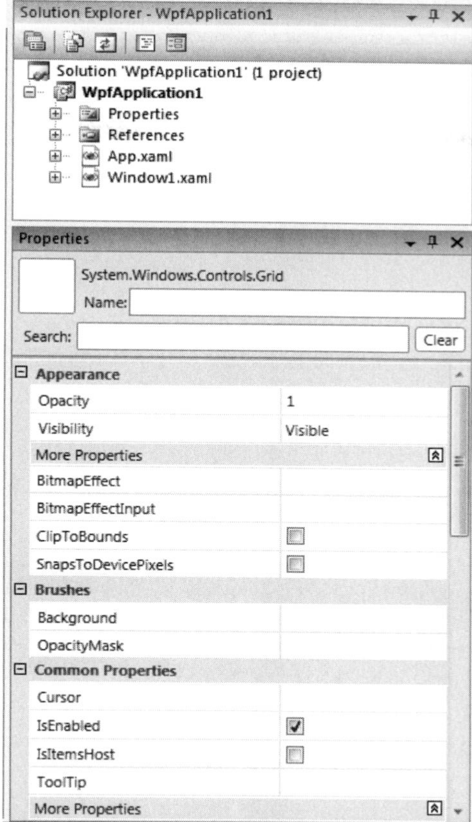

Figure 15-32

Right away, the biggest change you will notice in Visual Studio 2008 is contained within the document window. The default view of the document window after creating this project is presented in Figure 15-33.

The document window has two views — a design view and an XAML view. Making changes in the design view will make the appropriate changes in the XAML view, and vice versa. As with traditional Windows Forms applications, WPF applications also include the ability to use controls that are contained within Visual Studio's toolbox. This new toolbox of controls is presented in Figure 15-34.

Building WF Applications in Visual Studio

Another dramatically different application style (when it comes to building the application from within Visual Studio) is the Windows Workflow application type. For an example of this, select the Sequential Workflow Console Application project type from the Workflow section of the New Project dialog. This will create a console application as illustrated here with a view of the Solution Explorer (see Figure 15-35).

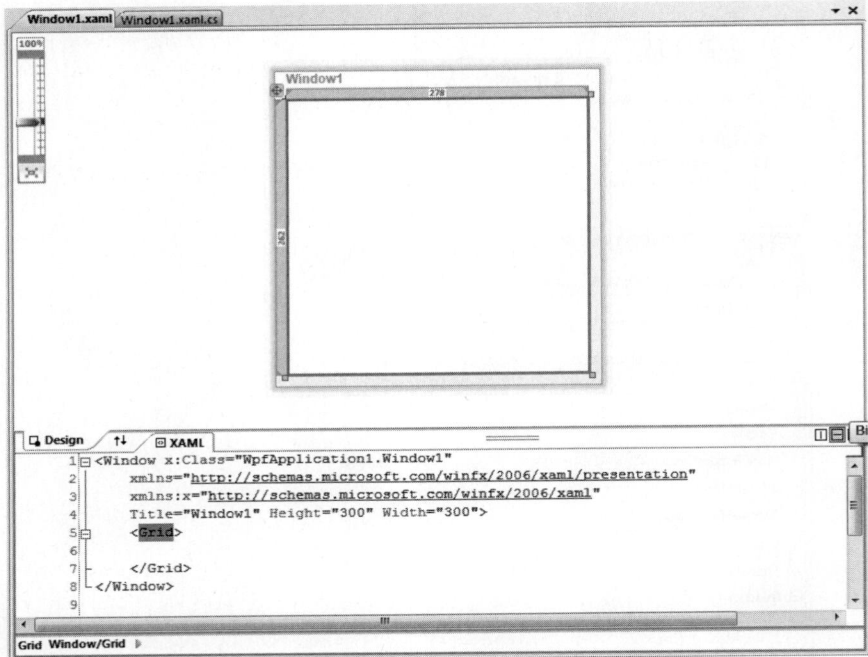

Figure 15-33

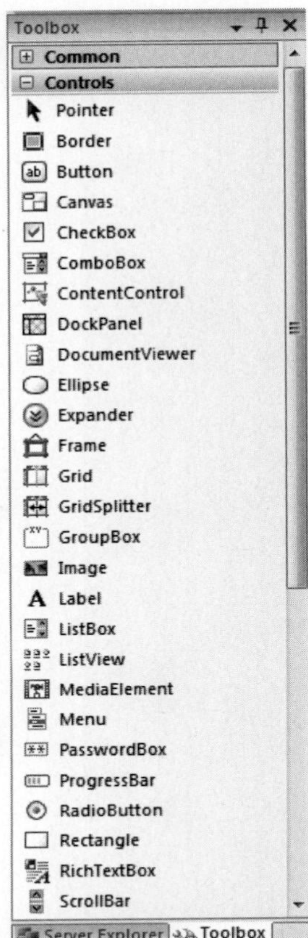

Figure 15-34

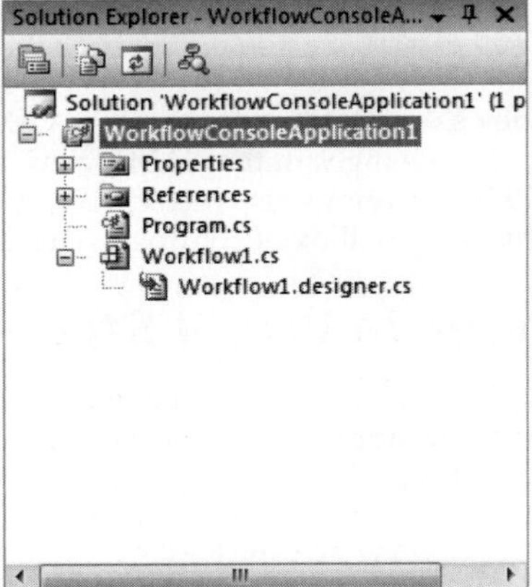

Figure 15-35

One big change you see when building applications that make use of the Windows Workflow Foundation is that there is a heavy dependency on the design view. Looking closely at the workflow (see Figure 15-36), you can see that it is made up of multiple sequential steps and even includes actions based on conditions (such as an `if-else` statement).

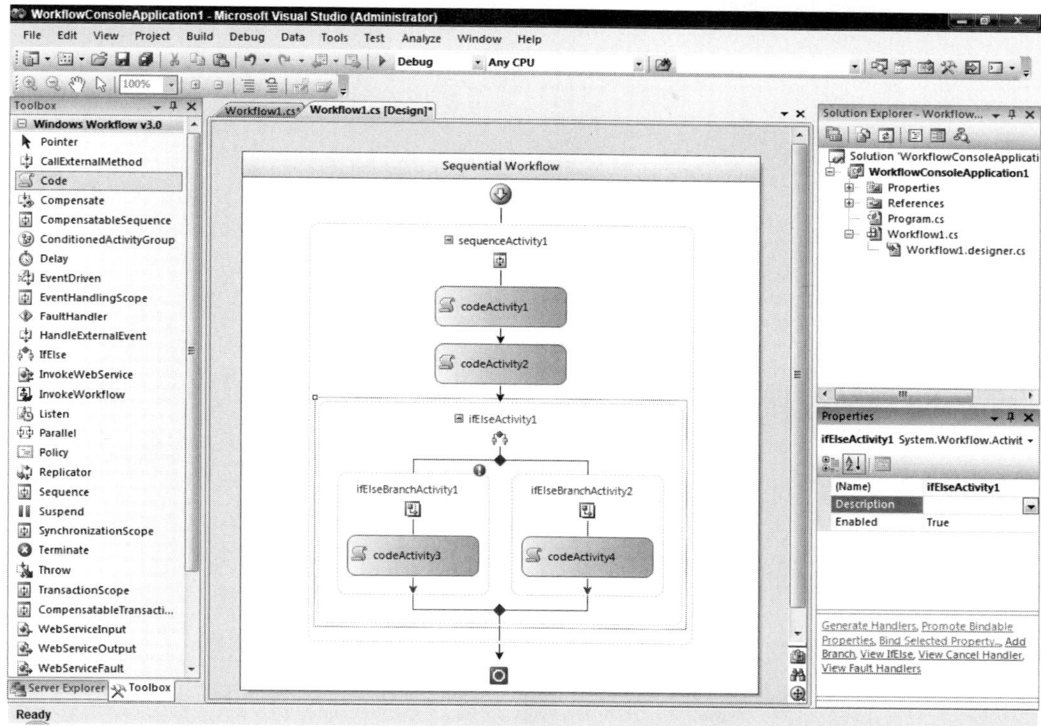

Figure 15-36

Summary

This chapter explored one of the most important programming tools in the .NET environment — Visual Studio 2008. The bulk of the chapter examined how this tool facilitates writing code in C# (and C++ and Visual Basic 2008).

Visual Studio 2008 is one of the easiest development environments to work with in the programming world. You will find that Visual Studio makes Rapid Application Development (RAD) easy to achieve, but at the same time, you can dig deep into the mechanics of how your applications are created. This chapter focused on using Visual Studio for everything from refactoring to multi-targeting to reading in Visual Studio 6 projects and to debugging. It also covered many of the windows available to Visual Studio.

This chapter also looked at the new projects available to you through the .NET Framework 3.5. These new project types focused on the Windows Presentation Foundation, the Windows Communication Foundation, and the Windows Workflow Foundation.

Chapter 16 presents the deployment situation in detail.

16

Deployment

The development process does not end when the source code is compiled and testing is complete. At that stage, the job of getting the application into the user's hands begins. Whether it's an ASP.NET application, a smart client application, or an application built using the Compact Framework, the software must be deployed to a target environment. The .NET Framework has made deployment much easier than it was in the past. The pains of registering COM components and writing new hives to the registry are all gone.

This chapter looks at the options that are available for application deployment, both from an ASP.NET perspective and from the smart client perspective. The following topics are discussed:

- Deployment requirements
- Simple deployment scenarios
- Windows Installer–based projects
- ClickOnce

Designing for Deployment

Often, deployment is an afterthought in the development process that can lead to nasty, if not costly, surprises. To avoid grief in deployment scenarios, the deployment process should be planned out during the initial design stage. Any special deployment considerations — such as server capacity, desktop security, or where assemblies will be loaded from — should be built into the design from the start, resulting in a much smoother deployment process.

Another issue that must be addressed early in the development process is the environment in which to test the deployment. Whereas unit testing of application code and of deployment options can be done on the developer's system, the deployment must be tested in an environment that resembles the target system. This is important to eliminate the dependencies that don't exist on a targeted computer. An example of this might be a third-party library that has been installed on the developer's computer early in the project. The target computer might not have this library on it. It can be easy to forget to include it in the deployment package. Testing on the developer's system would not uncover the error because the library already exists. Documenting dependencies can help in eliminating this potential problem.

Deployment processes can be very complex for a large application. Planning for the deployment can save time and effort when the deployment process is implemented.

Deployment Options

This section provides an overview of the deployment options that are available to .NET developers. Most of these options are discussed in greater detail later in this chapter.

Xcopy

The xcopy utility enables you to copy an assembly or group of assemblies to an application folder, cutting down on your development time. Because assemblies are self-discovering (that is, the metadata that describes the assembly is included in the assembly), there is no need to register anything in the registry. Each assembly keeps track of what other assemblies it requires to execute. By default, the assembly looks in the current application folder for the dependencies. The process of moving (or probing) assemblies to other folders is discussed later in this chapter.

Copy Web Tool

If you are developing a Web project, using the Copy Web tool option on the Web site menu will copy the components needed to run the application to the server.

Publishing Web Sites

When a Web site is published, the entire site is compiled and then copied to a specified location. As a result of precompiling, all source code is removed from the final output and all compile errors can be found and dealt with.

Deployment Projects

Visual Studio 2008 has the capability to create setup programs for an application. There are four options based on Microsoft Windows Installer technology: creating merge modules, creating a setup for client applications, creating a setup for Web applications, and creating a setup for Smart Device (Compact Framework) based applications. The ability to create cab files is also available. Deployment projects offer a great deal of flexibility and customization for the setup process. One of these deployment options will be useful for larger applications.

ClickOnce

ClickOnce is a way to build self-updating Windows-based applications. ClickOnce allows an application to be published to a Web site, file share, or even a CD. As updates and new builds are made to the application they can be published to the same location or site by the development team. As the application is used by the end user, it will check the location and see if an update is available. If there is, an update is attempted.

Deployment Requirements

It is instructive to look at the runtime requirements of a .NET-based application. The CLR does have certain requirements on the target platform before any managed application can execute.

The first requirement that must be met is the operating system. Currently, the following operating systems can run .NET-based applications:

- Windows 98
- Windows 98 Second Edition (SE)
- Windows Millennium Edition (ME)
- Windows NT 4.0 (Service Pack 6a)
- Windows 2000
- Windows XP Home
- Windows XP Professional
- Windows XP Professional TabletPC Edition
- Windows Vista

The following server platforms are supported:

- Windows 2000 Server and Advanced Server
- Windows 2003 Server Family

Other requirements are Windows Internet Explorer version 5.01 or later, MDAC version 2.6 or later (if the application is designed to access data), and Internet Information Services (IIS) for ASP.NET applications.

You also must consider hardware requirements when deploying .NET applications. The minimum requirements for hardware are as follows:

- **Client** — Pentium 90 MHz and 32 MB RAM
- **Server** — Pentium 133 MHz and 128 MB RAM

For best performance, increase the amount of RAM — the more RAM the better your .NET application runs. This is especially true for server applications.

If you want to run .NET 3.0 applications that make use of Windows Presentation Foundation (WPF), Windows Communication Foundation (WCF), or Windows Workflow Foundation (WF) the requirements are a little more strict. .NET 3.0 requires at least Windows XP SP2. The previous list is trimmed to the following:

- Windows XP Home (SP2)
- Windows XP Professional (SP2)
- Windows XP Professional TabletPC Edition (SP2)
- Windows Vista (not including IA64 platform)

The following server platforms are supported:

- Windows 2003 Server Family (SP1)
- Windows Server 2008 IA64 Edition

The minimum hardware requirements also change. They become Pentium 400 MHz and 96 MB RAM for both client and server.

Deploying the .NET Runtime

When an application is developed using .NET, there is a dependency on the .NET runtime. This may seem rather obvious, but sometimes the obvious can be overlooked. If the application does not use any .NET 3.0 features, then `dotnetfx.exe (netfx64.exe for 64 bit OS)` will be the only runtime installation required. If .NET 3.0 features are used, then `dotnetfx3.exe` will need to be used as well. If .NET 3.5 features are used, then `netfx35_x86.exe` will also have to be used.

In the following discussions on creating deployment packages, the inclusion of the runtime is optional. The installer can check to see if the proper runtime is installed, and if it isn't, the installer can then install the runtime from local media or even go to a specified download site and download and install the runtime.

Simple Deployment

If deployment is part of an application's original design considerations, deployment can be as simple as copying a set of files to the target computer. For a Web application, it can be a simple menu choice in Visual Studio 2008. This section discusses these simple deployment scenarios.

To see how the various deployment options are set up, you must have an application to deploy. The sample download at `www.wrox.com` contains three projects: `SampleClientApp`, `SampleWebApp`, and `AppSupport`. `SampleClientApp` is a smart client application. `SampleWebApp` is a simple Web app. `AppSupport` is a class library that contains one simple class that returns a string with the current date and time. `SampleClientApp` and `SampleWebApp` use `AppSupport` to fill a label with the output of `AppSupport`. To use the examples, first load and build `AppSupport`. Then, in each of the other applications, set a reference to the newly built `AppSupport.dll`.

Here is the code for the `AppSupport` assembly:

```
using System;

namespace AppSupport
  {
  /// <summary>
  /// Simple assembly to return date and time string.
  /// </summary>
  public class Support
  {
    private Support()
    {
    }

    public static string GetDateTimeInfo()
    {
      DateTime dt = DateTime.Now;
      return string.Concat(dt.ToLongDateString(), " ", dt.ToLongTimeString());
    }
  }
}
```

This simple assembly suffices to demonstrate the deployment options available to you.

Xcopy

Xcopy deployment is a term used for the process of copying a set of files to a folder on the target machine and then executing the application on the client. The term comes from the DOS command `xcopy.exe`. Regardless of the number of assemblies, if the files are copied into the same folder, the application will execute — rendering the task of editing the configuration settings or registry obsolete.

To see how an xcopy deployment works, execute the following steps:

1. Open the `SampleClientApp` solution (`SampleClientApp.sln`) that is part of the sample download file.
2. Change the target to Release and do a full compile.
3. Next, use either My Computer or File Explorer to navigate to the project folder `\SampleClientApp\bin\Release` and double-click `SampleClientApp.exe` to run the application.
4. Now, click the button to open another dialog. This verifies that the application functions properly. Of course, this folder is where Visual Studio placed the output, so you would expect the application to work.
5. Create a new folder and call it `ClientAppTest`. Copy the two files from the release folder to this new folder and then delete the release folder. Again, double-click the `SampleClientApp.exe` file to verify that it's working.

That's all there is to it; xcopy deployment provides the ability to deploy a fully functional application simply by copying the assemblies to the target machine. Just because the example that is used here is simple does not mean that this process cannot work for more complex applications. There really is no limit to the size or number of assemblies that can be deployed using this method. The reason that you might not want to use xcopy deployment is the ability to place assemblies in the global assembly cache (GAC) or the ability to add icons to the Start Menu. Also, if your application still relies on a COM library of some type, you will not be able to register the COM components easily.

Xcopy and Web Applications

Xcopy deployment can also work with Web applications with the exception of the folder structure. You must establish the virtual directory of your Web application and configure the proper user rights. This process is generally accomplished with the IIS administration tool. After the virtual directory is set up, the Web application files can be copied to the virtual directory. Copying a Web application's files can be a bit tricky. A couple of configuration files, as well as the images that the pages might be using, need to be accounted for.

Copy Web Tool

A better way would be to use the Copy Web tool. The Copy Web tool is accessed from the Website ⇨ Copy Web Site menu choice in Visual Studio 2008. It is basically an FTP client for transferring files to and from a remote location. The remote location can be any FTP or Web site including local Web sites, IIS Web sites, and Remote (FrontPage) Web sites. Another feature of the Copy Web tool is that it will synchronize files on the remote server with the source site. The source site will always be the site that is currently open in Visual Studio 2008. If the current project has multiple developers this tool can be used to keep changes in sync with the local development site. Changes can be synced back with a common server for testing.

Publishing a Web Site

Another deployment option for Web projects is to publish the Web site. Publishing a Web site will precompile the entire site and place the compiled version into a specified location. The location can be a file share, FTP location, or any other location that can be accessed via HTTP. The compilation process strips all source code from the assemblies and creates the DLLs for deployment. This also includes the markup contained in the `.ASPX` source files. Instead of containing the normal markup, the `.ASPX` files contain a pointer to an assembly. Each `.ASPX` file relates to an assembly. This process works regardless of the model: code behind or single file.

The advantages of publishing a Web site are speed and security. Speed is enhanced because all of the assemblies are already compiled. Otherwise, the first time a page is accessed there is a delay while the page and dependent code is compiled and cached. The security is enhanced because the source code is not deployed. Also, because everything is precompiled before deployment all compilation errors will be found.

You publish a Web site from the Website ⇨ Publish Web Site menu choice. You need to supply the location to publish to. Again, this can be a file share, FTP location, Web site, or local disk path. After the compilation is finished, the files are placed in the specified location. From there, they can be copied to a staging server, test server, or the production server.

Installer Projects

Xcopy deployment can be easy to use, but there are times when the lack of functionality becomes an issue. To overcome this shortcoming, Visual Studio 2008 has six installer project types. Four of these options are based on the Windows Installer technology. The following table lists the project types.

Project Type	Description
Setup Project	Used for the installation of client applications, middle-tier applications, and applications that run as a Windows Service.
Web Setup Project	Used for the installation of Web-based applications.
Merge Module Project	Creates `.msm` merge modules that can be used with other Windows Installer–based setup applications.
Cab Project	Creates `.cab` files for distribution through older deployment technologies.
Setup Wizard	Aids in the creation of a deployment project.
Smart Device CAB Project	CAB project for Pocket PC, Smartphone, and other CE-based applications.

Setup and Web Setup Projects are very similar. The key difference is that with Web Setup the project is deployed to a virtual directory on a Web server, whereas with Setup Project it is deployed to a folder structure. Both project types are based on Windows Installer and have all of the features of a Windows Installer–based setup program. Merge Module Project is generally used when you have created a component or library of functionality that is included in a number of deployment projects. By creating a merge module, you can set any configuration items specific to the component and without having to worry about them in the creation of the main deployment project. The Cab Project type simply creates cab files for the application. `.cab` files are used by older installation technologies as well as some Web-based installation processes. The Setup Wizard project type steps through the process of creating a deployment project, asking specific questions along the way. The following sections discuss how to create each of these deployment projects, what settings and properties can be changed, and what customization you can add.

What Is Windows Installer?

Windows Installer is a service that manages the installation, update, repair, and removal of applications on most Windows operating systems. It is part of Windows ME, Windows 2000, Windows XP, and Windows Vista and is available for Windows 95, Windows 98, and Windows NT 4.0. The current version of Windows Installer is 3.0.

Windows Installer tracks the installation of applications in a database. When an application has to be uninstalled, you can easily track and remove the registry settings that were added, the files that were copied to the hard drive, and the desktop and Start Menu icons that were added. If a particular file is still referenced by another application, the installer will leave it on the hard drive so that the other application doesn't break. The database also makes it possible to perform repairs. If a registry setting or a DLL associated with an application becomes corrupt or is accidentally deleted, you can repair the installation. During a repair, the installer reads the database from the last install and replicates that installation.

The deployment projects in Visual Studio 2008 give you the ability to create a Windows Installation package. The deployment projects give you access to most of what you will need to do in order to install a given application. However, if you need even more control, check out the Windows Installer SDK, which is part of the Platform SDK — it contains documentation on creating custom installation packages for your application. The following sections deal with creating these installation packages using the Visual Studio 2008 deployment projects.

Creating Installers

Creating installation packages for client applications or for Web applications is not that difficult. One of the first tasks is to identify all of the external resources your application requires, including configuration files, COM components, third-party libraries, and controls and images. Including a list of dependencies in the project documentation was discussed earlier. This is where having that documentation can prove to be very useful. Visual Studio 2008 can do a reasonable job of interrogating an assembly and retrieving the dependencies for it, but you still have to audit the findings to make sure that nothing is missing.

Another concern might be when in the overall process the install package is created. If you have an automated build process set up, you can include the building of the installation package upon a successful build of the project. Automating the process greatly reduces the chance for errors in what can be a time-consuming and complicated process for large projects. What you can do is to include the deployment project with the project solution. The Solution Property Pages dialog box has a setting for Configuration Properties. You can use this setting to select the projects that will be included for your various build configurations. If you select the Build check box under Release builds but not for the Debug builds, the installation package will be created only when you are creating a release build. This is the process used in the following examples. Figure 16-1 shows the Solution Property Pages dialog box of the `SampleClientApp` solution. Notice that the Debug configuration is displayed and that the Build check box is unchecked for the setup project.

Simple Client Application

In the following example, you create an installer for the `SimpleClientApp` solution (which is included in the sample download, together with the completed installer projects).

For the `SimpleClientApp` you create two deployment projects. One is done as a separate solution; the other is done in the same solution. This enables you to see the pros and cons of choosing each option.

The first example shows you how to create the deployment project in a separate solution. Before you get started on creating the deployment project, make sure that you have a release build of the application

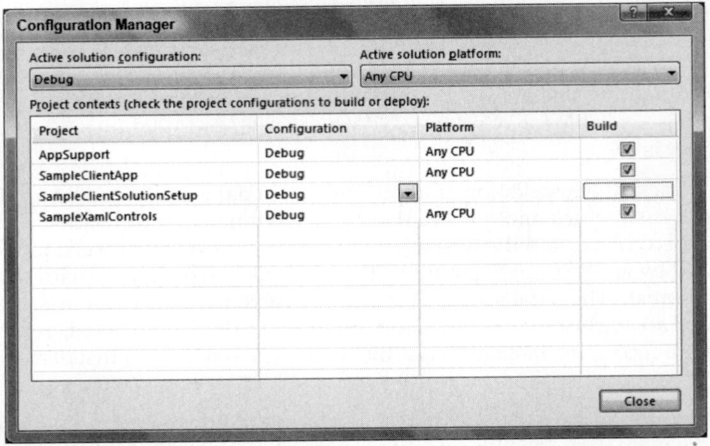

Figure 16-1

that will be deployed. Next, create a new project in Visual Studio 2008. In the New Project dialog box, select Setup and Deployment Projects on the left. On the right, select Setup Project and assign it a name of your choice (for example, `SampleClientStandaloneSetup`).

In the Solution Explorer window, click the project and then the Properties window. You will see a list of properties. These properties will be displayed during the setup of your application. Some of these properties are also displayed in the Add/Remove Programs Control Panel applet. Because most of these properties are visible to users during the installation process (or when they are looking at your installation in Add or Remove Programs), setting them correctly will add a professional touch to your application. The list of properties is important, especially if your application will be deployed commercially. The following table describes the properties and the values that you should enter.

Project Property	Description
`AddRemoveProgramsIcon`	The icon that appears in the Add/Remove dialog box.
`Author`	The author of the application. Generally this property setting is the same as the manufacturer. It is displayed on the Summary page of the Properties dialog of the `msi` package, as well as the Contact field of the SupportInfo page on the Add/Remove dialog box.
`Description`	A freeform text field that describes the application or component that is being installed. This information is displayed on the Summary page of the Properties dialog of the `msi` package, as well as the Comment field of the SupportInfo page on the Add/Remove dialog box.
`DetectNewerInstalled Version`	A Boolean value that, when set to `true`, will check to see if a newer version of the application is already installed. If so, the installation process will stop.
`InstallAllUsers`	Boolean value that, when set to `true`, will install that application for all users of the computer. If set to `false`, only the current user will have access.

Project Property	Description
`Keywords`	Keywords that can be used to search for the `.msi` file on the target computer. This information is displayed on the Summary page of the Properties dialog of the `msi` package.
`Localization`	The locale used for string resources and registry settings. This affects the user interface of the installer.
`Manufacturer`	Name of the company that manufactured the application or component. Typically, this is the same information as specified in the `Author` property. This information is displayed on the Summary page of the Properties dialog box of the `msi` package as well as the Publisher field of the SupportInfo page in the Add/Remove dialog box. It is used as part of the default installation path of the application.
`ManufacturerURL`	The URL for a Web site that relates to the application or component being installed.
`PostBuildEvent`	A command that is executed after the build ends.
`PreBuildEvent`	A command that is executed before the build begins.
`ProductCode`	A string GUID that is unique to this application or component. Windows Installer uses this property to identify the application for subsequent upgrades or installs.
`ProductName`	A name that describes the application. Used as the description of an application in the Add/Remove dialog box as well as part of the default install path: `C:\Program Files\Manufacturer\ProductName`.
`RemovePrevious-Versions`	Boolean value that, if set to `true`, will check for a previous version of the application. If yes, the uninstall function of the previous version is called before installation continues. This property uses `ProductCode` and `UpgradeCode` to determine if uninstall should occur. `UpgradeCode` should be the same; `ProductCode` should be different.
`RunPostBuildEvent`	When the `PostBuildEvent` should be run. Options are On successful build or Always.
`SearchPath`	A string that represents the search path for dependent assemblies, files, or merge modules. Used when the installer package is built on the development machine.
`Subject`	Additional information regarding the application. This information is displayed on the Summary page of the Properties dialog box of the `msi` package.
`SupportPhone`	A phone number for support of the application or component. This information is displayed in the Support Information field of the SupportInfo page on the Add/Remove dialog box.
`SupportURL`	A URL for support of the application or component. This information is displayed in the Support Information field of the SupportInfo page in the Add/Remove dialog box.
`TargetPlatform`	Supports the 32- or 64-bit versions of Windows.

Project Property	Description
`Title`	The title of the installer. This is displayed on the Summary page of the Properties dialog box of the `msi` package.
`UpgradeCode`	A string GUID that represents a shared identifier of different versions of the same application. The `UpgradeCode` should not change for different versions or different language versions of the application. Used by `DetectNewerInstalledVersion` and `RemovePreviousVersion`.
`Version`	The version number of the installer, `.cab` file, or merge module. Note that this is not the version of the application being installed.

After you have set the properties, you can start to add assemblies. In this example, the only assembly you have to add is the main executable (`SampleClientApp.exe`). To do this, you can either right-click the project in the Solution Explorer or select Add from the Project menu. You have four options:

- Project Output —You explore this option in the next example.
- File — This is used for adding a readme text file or any other file that is not part of the build process.
- Merge Module — A merge module that was created separately.
- Assembly — Use this option to select an assembly that is part of the installation.

Choose Assembly for this example. You will be presented with the Component Selector dialog box, which resembles the dialog box you use for adding references to a project. Browse to the `\bin\release` folder of your application. Select `SampleClientApp.exe` and click OK in the Component Selector dialog box. You can now see `SampleClientApp.exe` listed in the Solution Explorer of the deployment project. In the Detected Dependencies section, you can see that Visual Studio interrogated `SampleClientApp.exe` to find the assemblies on which it depends; in this case `AppSupport.dll` is included automatically. You would continue this process until all of the assemblies in your application are accounted for in the Solution Explorer of the deployment project.

Next, you have to determine where the assemblies will be deployed. By default, the File System editor is displayed in Visual Studio 2008. The File System editor is split into two panes: the left pane shows the hierarchical structure of the file system on the target machine; the right pane provides a detail view of the selected folder. The folder names might not be what you expect to see, but keep in mind that these are for the target machine. For example, the folder labeled User's Programs Menu maps to the `C:\Documents` and `Settings\User Name\Start Menu\Programs` folder on the target client.

You can add other folders at this point, either special folders or a custom folder. To add a special folder make sure that File System on Target Machine is highlighted in the left pane, and select Action menu on the main menu. The Add Special Folder menu choice provides a list of folders that can be added. For example, if you want to add a folder under the Application folder, you can select the Application Folder folder in the left pane of the editor and then select the Action menu. This time, there will be an Add menu that enables you to create the new folder. Rename the new folder and it will be created for you on the target machine.

One of the special folders that you might want to add is a folder for the GAC. `AppSupport.dll` can be installed to the GAC if it is used by several different applications. In order to add an assembly to the GAC, it does have to have a strong name. The process for adding the assembly to the GAC is to add the GAC from the Special Folder menu as described previously and then drag the assembly that you want in the GAC from the current folder to the Global Assembly Cache folder. If you try to do this with an assembly that is not strongly named, the deployment project will not compile.

If you select Application Folder, you will see on the right pane that the assemblies that you added are automatically added to the Application folder. You can move the assemblies to other folders, but keep in mind that the assemblies have to be able to find each other. (For more details on probing, see Chapter 17, "Assemblies.")

If you want to add a shortcut to the application on the user's desktop or to the Start Menu, drag the items to the appropriate folders. To create a desktop shortcut, go to the Application folder. On the right side of the editor select the application. Go to the Action menu, and select the Create Shortcut item to create a shortcut to the application. After the shortcut is created, drag it to the User's Desktop folder. Now when the application is installed, the shortcut will appear on the desktop. Typically, it is up to the user to decide if he or she wants a desktop shortcut to your application. The process of asking the user for input and taking conditional steps is explored later in this chapter. The same process can be followed to create an item in the Start Menu. Also, if you look at the properties for the shortcut that you just created, you will see that you can configure the basic shortcut properties such as Arguments and what icon to use. The application icon is the default icon.

Before you build the deployment project you might have to check some project properties. If you select Project menu, then SampleClientStandaloneSetup Properties, you will see the project Property Pages dialog box. These are properties that are specific to a current configuration. After selecting the configuration in the Configuration drop-down, you can change the properties listed in the following table.

Property	Description
Output file name	The name of the `.msi` or `.msm` file that is generated when the project is compiled.
Package files	This property enables you to specify how the files are packaged. Your options are: As loose uncompressed files — All of the deployment files are stored in the same directory as the `.msi` file. In setup file — Files are packaged in the `.msi` file (default setting). In cabinet file(s) — Files are in one or more `.cab` files in the same directory. When this is selected the CAB file size option becomes available.
Prerequisites URL	Allows you to specify where prerequisites such as the .NET Framework or Windows Installer 2.0 can be found. Clicking the Settings button will display a dialog that has the following technologies available to include in the setup: Windows Installer 2.0 .NET Framework Microsoft Visual J# .NET Redistributable Package 2.0 SQL Server 2008 Express Edition Microsoft Data Access Components 2.8 There is also an option to have the prerequisites downloaded from a predefined URL or to have them loaded from the same location as the setup.
Compression	This specifies the compression style for the files included. Your options are: Optimized for speed — Larger files but faster installation time (default setting). Optimized for size — Smaller files but slower installation time. None — No compression applied.
CAB size	This is enabled when the Package file setting is set to In cabinet files. Unlimited creates one single cabinet file; custom allows you to set the maximum size for each `.cab` file.

Property	Description
Authenticode signature	When this is checked, the deployment project output is signed using Authenticode; the default setting is unchecked.
Certificate file	The certificate used for signing.
Private key file	The private key that contains the digital encryption key for the signed files.
Timestamp server URL	URL for timestamp server. This is also used for Authenticode signing.

After you have set the project properties, you should be able to build the deployment project and create the setup for the `SampleClientApp` application. After you build the project, you can test the installation by right-clicking the project name in the Solution Explorer. This enables you to access an Install and Uninstall choice in the context menu. If you have done everything correctly, you should be able to install and uninstall `SampleClientApp` successfully.

Same Solution Project

The previous example works well for creating a deployment package, but it does have a couple of downsides. For example, what happens when a new assembly is added to the original application? The deployment project will not automatically recognize any changes; you will have to add the new assemblies and verify that any new dependencies are covered. In smaller applications (like the example), this isn't that big of a deal. However, when you're dealing with an application that contains dozens or maybe hundreds of assemblies, this can become quite tedious to maintain. Visual Studio 2008 has a simple way of resolving this potential headache. Include the deployment project in your application's solution. You can then capture the output of the main project as your deployment assemblies. You can look at the `SimpleClientApp` as an example.

Open the `SimpleClientApp` solution in Visual Studio 2008. Add a new project using Solution Explorer. Select Deployment and Setup Projects and then select Setup Project, following the steps outlined in the previous section. You can name this project `SimpleAppSolutionSetup`. In the previous example, you added the assemblies by selecting Add ⇨ Assemblies from the Project menu. This time, select Add ⇨ Project Output from the Project menu. This opens the Add Project Output Group dialog box (see Figure 16-2).

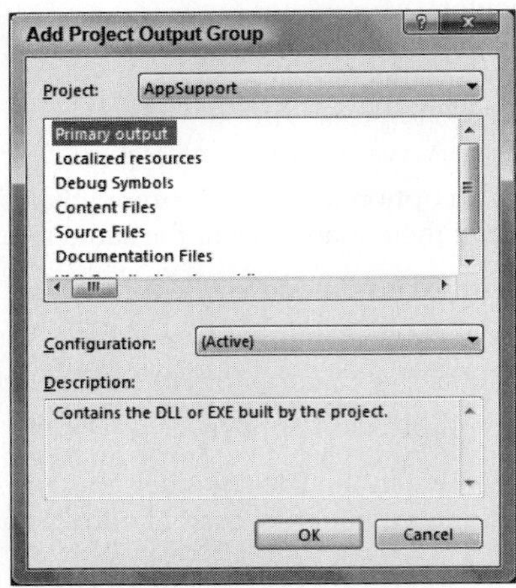

Figure 16-2

The top part of the dialog box has a drop-down list box that shows all projects in the current solution. Select the main startup project. Then select the items you want to include in your project from the list below. Your options are Documentation, Primary Output, Localized Resources, Debug Symbols, Content Files, and Source Files. First, select Primary Output. This includes the output and all dependencies when the application is built. Another drop-down list box lists the valid configurations: Debug and Release, plus any custom configurations you might have added. This also determines what outputs are picked up. For deployment, you will most likely want to use the Release configuration.

After you make these selections, a new item is added to your deployment project in Solution Explorer. The name of the item is Primary output from `SampleClientApp (Release .NET)`. You will also see the file `AppSupport.dll` listed under the dependencies. As before, no need to search for the dependent assemblies.

At this point, all of the various project properties discussed in the previous section still apply. You can change the Name, Manufacturer, `.cab` file size, and other properties. After setting the properties, do a release build of the solution and test the installation. Everything should work as expected.

To see the advantage of adding the deployment package to the applications solution, add a new project to the solution. In the example it is called `AppSupportII`. In it is a simple test method that returns the string Hello World. Set a reference in `SampleTestApp` to the newly added project, and do another release build of the solution. You should see that the deployment project picked up the new assembly without you having to do anything. If you go back and open up the standalone deployment project from the previous example, unless you specifically add the assembly, it will not be picked up.

Simple Web Application

Creating an installation package for a Web application is not that different than creating a client install package. The download examples include a `SimpleWebApp` that also utilizes the `AppSupport.dll` assembly. You can create the deployment project the same way that the client deployment projects are created, either standalone or in the same solution. In this example, the deployment project is built in the same solution.

Start the `SimpleWebApp` solution and add a new deployment and setup project. This time, be sure to choose Web Setup Project in the Templates window. If you look at the properties view for the project, you will see that all of the same properties exist for Web applications that existed for client applications. The only addition is `RestartWWWService`. This is a Boolean value that will restart IIS during the install. If you're using ASP.NET components and not replacing any ATL or ISAPI DLLs, you shouldn't have to do this.

If you look at the File System editor, you will notice that there is only one folder. The Web Application folder will be your virtual directory. By default, the name of the directory is the name of the deployment project, and it is located below the Web root directory. The following table explains the properties that can be set from the installer. The properties discussed in the previous section are not included.

Property	Description
`AllowDirectoryBrowsing`	A Boolean value that, if `true`, allows an HTML listing of the files and subfolders of the virtual directory. Maps to the Directory browsing property of IIS.
`AllowReadAccess`	A Boolean value that, if `true`, allows users to read or download files. Maps to the Read property of IIS.
`AllowScriptSourceAccess`	A Boolean value that, if `true`, allows users to access source code, including scripts. Maps to Script source access in IIS.

Property	Description
AllowWriteAccess	A Boolean value that, if `true`, allows users to change content in write-enabled files. Maps to the Write property of IIS.
ApplicationProtection	Determines the protection level of applications that are run on the server. The valid values are: Low — Applications run in the same process as Web services. Medium — Applications run in same process but not the same as Web services. High — Application runs in its own process. Maps to the Application Protection property in IIS. Has no effect if the `IsApplication` property is `false`.
AppMappings	A list of application names and document or data files that are associated with the applications. Maps to the Application Mappings property of IIS.
Condition	A Windows Installer condition that must be met in order for the item to be installed.
DefaultDocument	The default or startup document when the user first browses to the site.
ExecutePermissions	The level of permissions that a user has to execute applications. The valid values are: None — Only static content can be accessed. ScriptsOnly — Only scripts can be accessed. Includes ASP. ScriptsAndExecutables — Any files can be accessed. Maps to Execute Permissions in IIS.
Index	Boolean value that, if `true`, would allow indexing of the content for Microsoft Indexing Service. Maps to the Index this resource property of IIS.
IsApplication	Boolean value that, if `true`, instructs IIS to create the application root for the folder.
LogVisits	Boolean value that, if `true`, logs visits to the Web site in a log file. Maps to the Log visits property of IIS.
Property	The named property that can be accessed at installation time.
VirtualDirectory	The virtual directory for the application. This is relative to the Web server.

You might notice that most of these properties are properties of IIS and can be set in the IIS administrator tool. So, the logical assumption is that in order to set these properties in the installer, the installer will need to run with administrator privileges. The settings made here can compromise security, so the changes should be well documented.

Other than these properties, the process of creating the deployment package is very similar to the previous client example. The main difference between the two projects is the ability to modify IIS from the installation process. As you can see, you have a great deal of control over the IIS environment.

Client from Web Server

Another installation scenario is either running the install program from a Web site or actually running the application from a Web site. Both of these are attractive options if you must deploy an application to a large number of users. By deploying from a Web site, you eliminate the need for a distribution medium such as CD-ROM, DVD, or even floppy disks. By running the application from a Web site or even a network share, you eliminate the need to distribute a setup program at all.

Running an installer from a Web site is fairly simple. You use the Web Bootstrapper project compile option. You will be asked to provide the URL of the setup folder. This is the folder in which the setup program is going to look for the `.msi` and other files necessary for the setup to work. After you set this option and compile the deployment package you can copy it to the Web site that you specify in the Setup folder URL property. At this point, when the user navigates to the folder, she will be able to either run the setup or download it and then run it. In both instances, the user must be able to connect to the same site to finish the installation.

No-Touch Deployment

You can also run the application from a Web site or network share. This process becomes a little more involved and is a prime reason that you should design the application with deployment in mind. This is sometimes referred to as *no-touch deployment* (NTD).

To make this process work, the application code must be written in a way to support it. A couple of ways exist to architect the application to take advantage of NTD. One way is to write the majority of the application code into DLL assemblies. The DLLs will live on a Web server or file share on the network. Then you create a smaller application `.exe` that will be deployed to the client PC's. This stub program will start the application by calling into one of the DLL assemblies, using the `LoadFrom` method. The only thing that the stub program will see is the main entry point in the DLL. Once the DLL assembly has been loaded, the application will continue loading other assemblies from the same URL or network share. Remember that an assembly first looks for dependent assemblies in the application directory (that is, the URL that was used to start the application). Here is the code used in the stub application on the user's client. This example calls the `AppSupportII` DLL assembly and puts the output of the `TestMethod` call in `label1`:

```
Assembly testAssembly =

Assembly.LoadFrom("http://localhost/AppSupport/AppSupportII.dll");
Type type = testAssembly.GetType("AppSupportII.TestClass");
object testObject = Activator.CreateInstance(type);
label1.Text = (string)type.GetMethod("TestMethod").Invoke(testObject,null);
```

This process uses reflection to first load the assembly from the Web server. In this example, the Web site is a folder on the local machine (`localhost`). Next, the type of the class is retrieved (here: `TestClass`). Now that you have type information the object can be created using the `Activator.CreateInstance` method. The last step is to get a `MethodInfo` object (the output of `GetMethod`) and call the `Invoke` method. In a more complex application this is the main entry point of the application. From this point on, the stub is not needed anymore.

Alternatively, you can also deploy the entire application to a Web site. For this method, create a simple Web page that contains a link to the application's setup executable or perhaps a shortcut on the user's desktop that has the Web site link. When the link is clicked, the application will be downloaded to the user's assembly download cache, which is located in the global assembly cache. The application will run from the download cache. Each time a new assembly is requested, it will go to the download cache first to see if it exists; if not, it will go to the URL that the main application came from.

The advantage to deploying the application in this way is that when an update is made available for the application, it has to be deployed in only one place. You place the new assemblies in the Web folder and when the user starts the application, the runtime will actually look at the assemblies in the URL and the assemblies in the download cache to compare versions. If a new version is found at the URL, it is then downloaded to replace the current one in the download cache. This way, the user always has access to the most current version of the application. The downside is that security is difficult to set up. The assemblies have to have a wide set of permissions in order to operate. This has the effect of making the application very insecure.

For more control over the update process and over security, ClickOnce is probably a better choice.

ClickOnce

ClickOnce is a deployment technology that allows applications to be self-updating. Applications are published to a file share, Web site, or media such as a CD. Once published, ClickOnce apps can be automatically updated with minimal user input.

ClickOnce also solves the security permission problem. Normally, to install an application the user would need Administrative rights. With ClickOnce a user can install and run an application with only the absolute minimum permissions required to run the application.

ClickOnce Operation

ClickOnce applications have two XML-based manifest files associated with them. One is the application manifest, and the other is the deployment manifest. These two files describe everything that is required to know to deploy an application.

The application manifest contains information about the application such as permissions required, assemblies to include, and other dependencies. The deployment manifest is about the deployment of the app. Items such as the location of the application manifest are contained in the deployment manifest. The complete schemas for the manifests are in the .NET SDK documentation.

ClickOnce has some limitations. Assemblies cannot be added to the GAC, for example. The following table compares ClickOnce and Windows Installer.

	ClickOnce	**Windows Installer**
Application installation location	ClickOnce application cache	Program Files folder
Install for multiple users	No	Yes
Install Shared files	No	Yes
Install drivers	No	Yes
Install to the GAC	No	Yes
Add application to Startup group	No	Yes
Add application to the favorites menu	No	Yes
Register file types	No	Yes
Access registry	No. The HKLM can be accessed with Full Trust permissions.	Yes
Binary patching of files	Yes	No
Install assemblies on demand	Yes	No

Some situations certainly exist where using Windows Installer is clearly a better choice; however, ClickOnce can be used for a large number of applications.

Publishing an Application

Everything that ClickOnce needs to know is contained in the two manifest files. The process of publishing an application for ClickOnce deployment is simply generating the manifests and placing the files in the proper location. The manifest files can be generated in Visual Studio 2008. There is also a command-line tool (`mage.exe`) and a version with a GUI (`mageUI.exe`).

You can create the manifest files in Visual Studio 2008 in two ways. At the bottom of the Publish tab on the Project Properties dialog are two buttons. One is the Publish Wizard and the other is Publish Now. The Publish Wizard asks several questions about the deployment of the application and then generates the manifest files and copies all of the needed files to the deployment location. The Publish Now button uses the values that have been set in the Publish tab to create the manifest files and copies the files to the deployment location.

In order to use the command-line tool, `mage.exe`, the values for the various ClickOnce properties must be passed in. Manifest files can be both created and updated using `mage.exe`. Typing **mage.exe -help** at the command prompt will give the syntax for passing in the values required.

The GUI version of `mage.exe` (`mageUI.exe`) is similar in appearance to the Publish tab in Visual Studio 2008. An application and deployment manifest file can be created and updated using the GUI tool.

ClickOnce applications appear in the Add/Remove Control Panel applet just like any other installed application. One big difference is that the user is presented with the choice of either uninstalling the application or rolling back to the previous version. ClickOnce keeps the previous version in the ClickOnce application cache.

ClickOnce Settings

Several properties are available for both manifest files. The most important property is where the application should be deployed from. The dependencies for the application must be specified. The Publish tab has an Application Files button that shows a dialog for entering all of the assemblies required by the application. The Prerequisite button displays a list of common prerequisites that can be installed along with the application. You have the choice of installing the prerequisites from the same location that the application is being published to or optionally having the prerequisites installed from the vendor's Web site.

The Update button displays a dialog that has the information about how the application should be updated. As new versions of an application are made available, ClickOnce can be used to update the application. Options include to check for updates every time the application starts or to check in the background. If the background option is selected, a specified period of time between checks can be entered. Options for allowing the user to be able to decline or accept the update are available. This can be used to force an update in the background so that the user is never aware that the update is occurring. The next time the application is run, the new version will be used instead of the older version. A separate location for the update files can be used as well. This way the original installation package can be located in one location and installed for new users, and all of the updates can be staged in another location.

The application can be set up so that it will run in either online or offline mode. In offline mode the application can be run from the Start Menu and acts as if it were installed using the Windows Installer. Online mode means that the application will run only if the installation folder is available.

Application Cache

Applications distributed with ClickOnce are not installed in the Program Files folder. Instead, they are placed in an application cache that resides in the Local Settings folder under the current user's Documents and Settings folder. Controlling this aspect of the deployment means that multiple versions of an application can reside on the client PC at the same time. If the application is set to run online, every version that the user has accessed is retained. For applications that are set to run locally, the current and previous versions are retained.

Because of this, it is a very simple process to roll back a ClickOnce application to its previous version. If the user goes to the Add/Remove Programs Control Panel applet, the dialog presented will contain the choice of removing the ClickOnce application or rolling back to the previous version. An Administrator can change the manifest file to point to the previous version. If the administrator does this, the next time the user runs that application, a check will be made for an update. Instead of finding new assemblies to deploy, the application will restore the previous version without any interaction from the user.

Security

Applications deployed over the Internet or intranet have a lower security or trust setting than applications that have been installed to the local drive have. For example, by default if an application is launched or deployed from the Internet it is in the Internet Security Zone. This means that it cannot access the file system, among other things. If the application is installed from a file share, it will run in the Intranet Zone.

If the application requires a higher level of trust than the default, the user will be prompted to grant the permissions required for the application to run. These permissions are set in the `trustInfo` element of the application manifest. Only the permissions asked for in this setting will be granted. So, if an application asks for file access permissions, Full Trust will not be granted, only the specific permissions requested.

Another option is to use Trusted Application Deployment. Trusted Application Deployment is a way to grant permissions on an enterprise-wide basis without having to prompt the user. A trust license issuer is identified to each client machine. This is done with public key cryptography. Typically, an organization will have only one issuer. It is important to keep the private key for the issuer in a safe, secure location.

A trust license is requested from the issuer. The level of trust that is being requested is part of the trust license configuration. A public key used to sign the application must also be supplied to the license issuer. The license created contains the public key used to sign the application and the public key of the license issuer. This trust license is then embedded in the deployment manifest. The last step is to sign the deployment manifest with your own key pair. The application is now ready to deploy.

When the client opens the deployment manifest the Trust Manager will determine if the ClickOnce application has been given a higher trust. The issuer license is looked at first. If it is valid, the public key in the license is compared to the public key that was used to sign the application. If these match, the application is granted the requested permissions.

Advanced Options

The installation processes discussed so far are very powerful and can do quite a bit. But there is much more that you can control in the installation process. For example, you can use the various editors in Visual Studio 2008 to build conditional installations or add registry keys and custom dialog boxes. The `SampleClientSetupSolution` example has all of these advanced options enabled.

File System Editor

The File System editor enables you to specify where in the target the various files and assemblies that make up the application will be deployed. By default, a standard set of deployment folders is displayed.

You can add any number of custom and special folders with the editor. This is also where you would add desktop and Start Menu shortcuts to the application. Any file that must be part of the deployment must be referenced in the File System editor.

Registry Editor

The Registry editor allows you to add keys and data to the registry. When the editor is first displayed, a standard set of main keys is displayed:

- `HKEY_CLASSES_ROOT`
- `HKEY_CURRENT_USER`
- `HKEY_LOCAL_MACHINE`
- `HKEY_USERS`

`HKEY_CURRENT_USER` and `HKEY_LOCAL_MACHINE` contain additional entries in the Software/[Manufacturer] key where Manufacturer is the information you entered in the `Manufacturer` property of the deployment project.

To add additional keys and values, highlight one of the main keys on the left side of the editor. Select Action from the main menu and then select New. Select the key or the value type that you want to add. Repeat this step until you have all of the registry settings that you want. If you select the Registry on Target Machine item on the left pane and then select the Action menu, you will see an Import option, which enables you to import an already defined `*.reg` file.

To create a default value for a key you must first enter a value for the key, then select the value name in the right or value pane. Select Rename from the File menu and delete the name. Press Enter, and the value name is replaced with (Default).

You can also set some properties for the subkeys and values in the editor. The only one that hasn't been discussed already is the `DeleteAtUninstall` property. A well-designed application should remove all keys that have been added by the application at uninstall time. The default setting is not to delete the keys.

One thing to keep in mind is that the preferred method for maintaining application settings is to use XML-based configuration files. These files offer a great deal more flexibility and are much easier to restore and back up than registry entries.

File Types Editor

The File Types editor is used to establish associations between files and applications. For example, when you double-click a file with the `.doc` extension, the file is opened in Word. You can create these same associations for your application.

To add an association, execute the following steps:

1. Select File Types on Target Machine from the Action menu.
2. Then select Add File Type. In the properties window, you can now set the name of the association.
3. In the `Extension` property, add the file extension that should be associated with the application. Do not enter the periods; you can separate multiple extensions with a semicolon, like this: **ex1;ex2**.
4. In the Command property, select the ellipse button.
5. Now, select the file (typically an executable) that you want to associate with the specified file types. Keep in mind that any one extension should be associated with only one application.

By default, the editor shows &Open as the Document Action. You can add others. The order in which the actions appear in the editor is the order in which they will appear in the context menu when the user right-clicks the file type. Keep in mind that the first item is always the default action. You can set the `Arguments` property for the actions. This is the command-line argument used to start the application.

User Interface Editor

Sometimes you might want to ask the user for more information during the installation process. The User Interface editor is used to specify properties for a set of predefined dialog boxes. The editor is separated into two sections, Install and Admin. One is for the standard installation and the other is used for an administrator's installation. Each section is broken up into three subsections: Start, Progress, and End. These subsections represent the three basic stages of the installation process (see Figure 16-3).

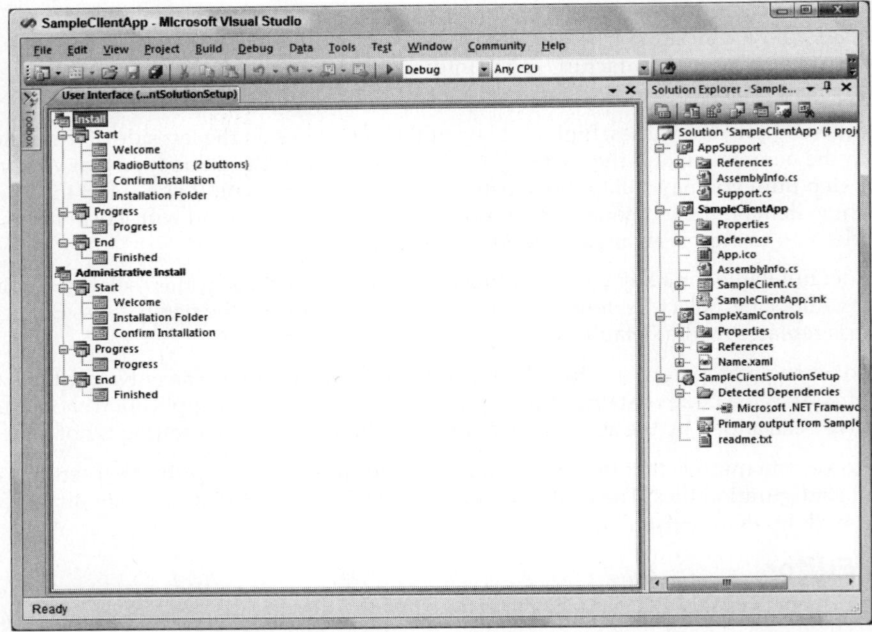

Figure 16-3

The following table lists the types of dialog boxes that you can add to the project.

Dialog Box	Description
Checkboxes	Contains up to four check boxes. Each check box has a `Label`, `Value`, and `Visible` property.
Confirm Installation	Gives the user the ability to confirm the various settings before installation takes place.
Customer Information	Has edit fields for the collection name, organization name, and serial number. Organization name and serial number are optional.
Finished	Displayed at the end of the setup process.

Dialog Box	Description
Installation Address	For Web applications, displays a dialog box so that users can choose an alternate installation URL.
Installation Folder	For client applications, displays a dialog box so that users can select an alternate installation folder.
License Agreement	Displays the license agreement that is located in a file specified by the `LicenseFile` property.
Progress	Displays a progress indicator during the installation process that shows the current installation status.
RadioButtons	Contains up to four radio buttons. Each radio button has a `Label` and `Value` property.
Read Me	Shows the readme information contained in the file specified by the `ReadMe` property.
Register User	Executes an application that will guide the user through the registration process. This application must be supplied in the setup project.
Splash	Displays a bitmap image.
TextBoxes	Contains up to four text box fields. Each text box has a `Label`, `Value`, and `Visible` property.
Welcome	Contains two properties: the `WelcomeText` property and the `CopyrightWarning`. Both are string properties.

Each of these dialog boxes also contains a property for setting the banner bitmap, and most have a property for banner text. You can also change the order in which the dialog boxes appear by dragging them up or down in the editor window.

Now that you can capture some of this information, the question is, how do you make use of it? This is where the `Condition` property that appears on most of the objects in the project comes in. The `Condition` property must evaluate to true for the installation step to proceed. For example, say the installation comes with three optional installation components. In this case, you would add a dialog box with three check boxes. The dialog should be somewhere after the Welcome and before the Confirm Installation dialog box. Change the `Label` property of each check box to describe the action. The first action could be "Install Component A," the second could be "Install Component B," and so on. In the File System editor select the file that represents Component A. Assuming that the name of the check box on the dialog box is CHECKBOXA1, the `Condition` property of the file would be `CHECKBOXA1=Checked` — that is, if CHECKBOXA1 is checked, install the file; otherwise, don't install it.

Custom Actions Editor

The Custom Actions editor allows you to define custom steps that will take place during certain phases of the installation. Custom actions are created beforehand and consist of a DLL, EXE, script, or Installer class. The action would contain special steps to perform that can't be defined in the standard deployment project. The actions will be performed at four specific points in the deployment. When the editor is first started, you will see the four points in the project (see Figure 16-4):

- Install — Actions will be executed at the end of the installation phase.
- Commit — Actions will be executed after the installation has finished and no errors have been recorded.
- Rollback — Actions occur after the rollback phase has completed.
- Uninstall — Actions occur after uninstall has completed.

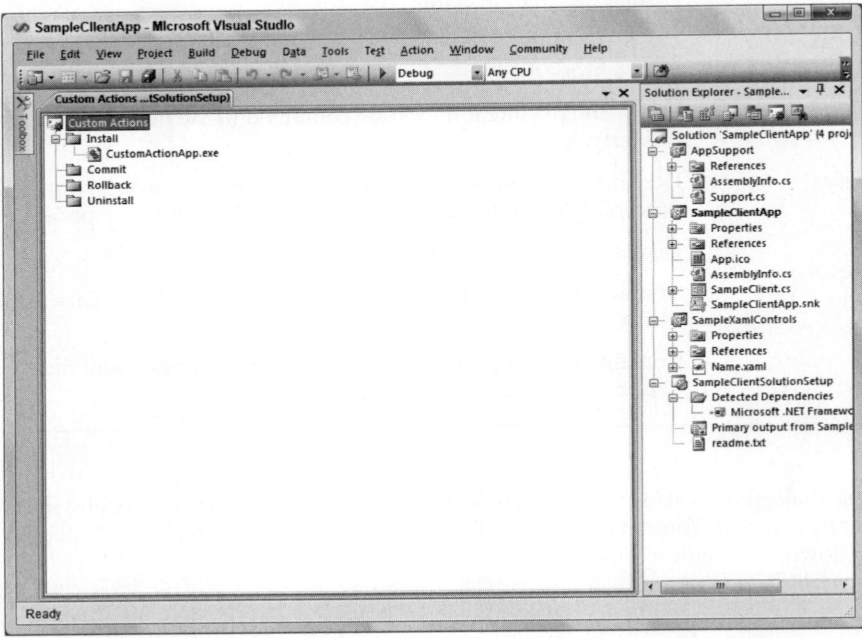

Figure 16-4

To add an action, you first select the phase of the installation in which you want the action to occur. Select the Add Custom Action menu option from the Action menu to open the file system dialog box. This means that the component that contains the action must be part of the deployment project. Because it will be executing on the target machine it has to be deployed; therefore, it should be listed in the File System editor.

After you have added the action, you can select one or more of the properties listed in the following table.

Arguments	Command-Line Arguments
Condition	A Windows Installer condition that must be evaluated and result in true for the action to execute.
CustomDataAction	Custom data that will be available to the action.
EntryPoint	The entry point for the custom DLL that contains the action. If the action is contained in an executable, this property does not apply.
InstallerClass	A Boolean value that, if true, specifies that the action is a .NET ProjectInstaller class.
Name	Name of the action. Defaults to the file name of the action.
SourcePath	The path to action on the development machine.

Because the action is code that you develop outside of the deployment project, you have the freedom to add just about anything that adds a professional touch to your application. The thing to remember is that such an action happens after the phase it is associated with is complete. If you select the Install phase, the action will not execute until after the install phase has completed. If you want to make determinations before the process, you will want to create a launch condition.

Launch Conditions Editor

The Launch Conditions editor allows you to specify that certain conditions must be met before installation can continue. Launch conditions are organized into types of conditions. The basic launch conditions are File Search, Registry Search, and Windows Installer Search. When the editor is first started you see two groups (see Figure 16-5): Search Target Machine and Launch Conditions. Typically, a search is conducted, and, based on the success or failure of that search, a condition is executed. This happens by setting the `Property` property of the search. The `Property` property can be accessed by the installation process. It can be checked in the `Condition` property of other actions, for example. You can also add a launch condition in the editor. In this condition, you set the `Condition` property to the value of the `Property` property in the search. In the condition, you can specify a URL that will download the file, registry key, or installer component that was being searched for. Notice in Figure 16-5 that a .NET Framework condition is added by default.

File Search will search for a file or type of file. You can set many different file-related properties that determine how files are searched, including file name, folder location, various date values, version information, and size. You can also set the number of subfolders that are searched.

Registry Search allows you to search for keys and values. It also allows you to set the root key for searching.

Windows Installer Search looks for the specified Installer component. The search is conducted by GUID.

The Launch Conditions editor provides two prepackaged launch conditions: the .NET Framework Launch Condition, which allows you to search for a specific version of the runtime, and a search for a specific version of MDAC, which uses the registry search to find the relevant MDAC registry entries.

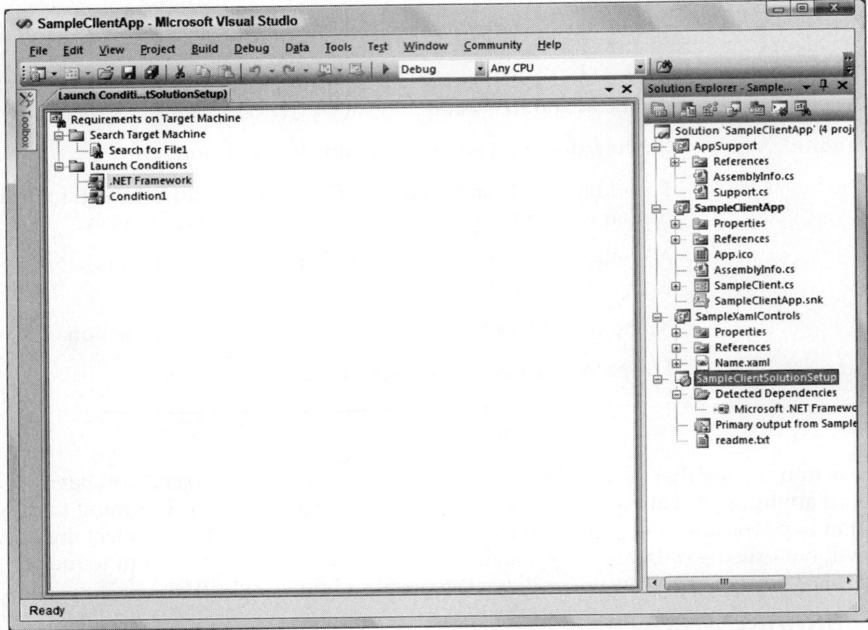

Figure 16-5

Summary

Deploying software has become difficult for developers of desktop software. As Web sites have grown more complex, the deployment of server-based software has become more difficult. This chapter looked at the options and capabilities that Visual Studio 2008 and version 3.5 of the .NET Framework provide to help make deployment easier and less error-prone.

After reading this chapter, you should be able to create a deployment package that resolves almost any deployment issue that you might have. Client applications can be deployed locally or via the Internet or an intranet. The extensive features of deployment projects and the ways that deployment projects can be configured were covered. You can also use no-touch deployment and ClickOnce to deploy applications. The security features of ClickOnce will make this a secure and efficient way of deploying client applications. Using deployment projects to install Web applications can make the process of configuring IIS much easier as well. Publishing a Web site provides the added benefit of precompiling the application.

Part III
Base Class Libraries

Chapter 17: Assemblies

Chapter 18: Tracing and Events

Chapter 19: Threading and Synchronization

Chapter 20: Security

Chapter 21: Localization

Chapter 22: Transactions

Chapter 23: Windows Services

Chapter 24: Interoperability

17

Assemblies

An *assembly* is the .NET term for a deployment and configuration unit. This chapter discusses exactly what assemblies are, how they can be applied, and why they are such a useful feature. In particular, this chapter covers the following topics:

- Overview
- Creating assemblies
- Application domains
- Shared assemblies
- Versioning

The chapter begins with an overview of assemblies.

What Are Assemblies?

Assemblies are the deployment units of .NET applications. .NET applications consist of one or more assemblies. .NET executables with the usual extension EXE or DLL are known by the term *assembly*. What's the difference between an assembly and a native DLL or EXE? Though they both have the same file extension, .NET assemblies include metadata that describe all the types that are defined in the assembly with information about its members — methods, properties, events, and fields.

The metadata of .NET assemblies also give information about the files that belong to the assembly, version information, and the exact information about assemblies that are used. .NET assemblies are the answer to the DLL hell we've seen previously with native DLLs.

Assemblies are self-describing installation units, consisting of one or more files. One assembly could be a single DLL or EXE that includes metadata, or it can be made of different files, for example, resource files, modules, and an EXE.

Assemblies can be private or shared. With simple .NET applications, using just private assemblies is the best way to work. No special management, registration, versioning, and so on is needed with private assemblies. The only application that could have version problems with private assemblies is your own application. Other applications are not influenced because they have their own copies of the assemblies. The private components you use within your application are installed at the same time as the application itself. Private assemblies are located in the same directory as the application or subdirectories thereof. This way you shouldn't have any versioning problems with the application. No other application will ever overwrite your private assemblies. Of course, it is still a good idea to use version numbers for private assemblies too. This helps a lot with code changes, but it's not a requirement of .NET.

With shared assemblies, several applications can use the same assembly and have a dependency on it. Shared assemblies reduce the need for disk and memory space. With shared assemblies, many rules must be fulfilled — a shared assembly must have a version number, a unique name, and usually it's installed in the *global assembly cache* (GAC).

Features of Assemblies

The features of assemblies can be summarized as follows:

- Assemblies are *self-describing*. It's no longer necessary to pay attention to registry keys for apartments, to get the type library from some other place, and so on. Assemblies include metadata that describes the assembly. The metadata includes the types exported from the assembly and a manifest; the next section describes the function of a manifest.
- *Version dependencies* are recorded inside an assembly manifest. Storing the version of any referenced assemblies in the manifest makes it possible to easily find deployment faults because of wrong versions available. The version of the referenced assembly that will be used can be configured by the developer and the system administrator. Later in this chapter, you learn which version policies are available and how they work.
- Assemblies can be loaded *side by side*. With Windows 2000 you already have a side-by-side feature where different versions of the same DLL can be used on a system. .NET extends this functionality of Windows 2000, allowing different versions of the same assembly to be used inside a single process! How is this useful? If assembly `A` references version 1 of the shared assembly `Shared`, and assembly `B` uses version 2 of the shared assembly `Shared`, and you are using both assembly `A` and `B`, you need both versions of the shared assembly `Shared` in your application — and with .NET both versions are loaded and used.
- Application isolation is ensured using *application domains*. With application domains a number of applications can run independently inside a single process. Faults in one application cannot directly affect other applications inside the same process.
- Installation can be as easy as copying the files that belong to an assembly. An xcopy can be enough. This feature is named *ClickOnce deployment*. However, there are cases in which ClickOnce deployment cannot be applied, and a normal Windows installation is required. Deployment of applications is discussed in Chapter 16, "Deployment."

Assembly Structure

An assembly consists of assembly metadata describing the complete assembly, type metadata describing the exported types and methods, MSIL code, and resources. All these parts can be inside of one file or spread across several files.

In the first example (see Figure 17-1), the assembly metadata, type metadata, MSIL code, and resources are all in one file — `Component.dll`. The assembly consists of a single file.

The second example shows a single assembly spread across three files (see Figure 17-2). `Component.dll` has assembly metadata, type metadata, and MSIL code, but no resources. The assembly uses a picture from picture.jpeg that is not embedded inside Component.dll, but is referenced from within the assembly metadata. The assembly metadata also references a module called util.netmodule, which itself includes only type metadata and MSIL code for a class. A module has no assembly metadata, thus the module itself has no version information; it also cannot be installed separately. All three files in this example make up a single assembly; the assembly is the installation unit. It would also be possible to put the manifest in a different file.

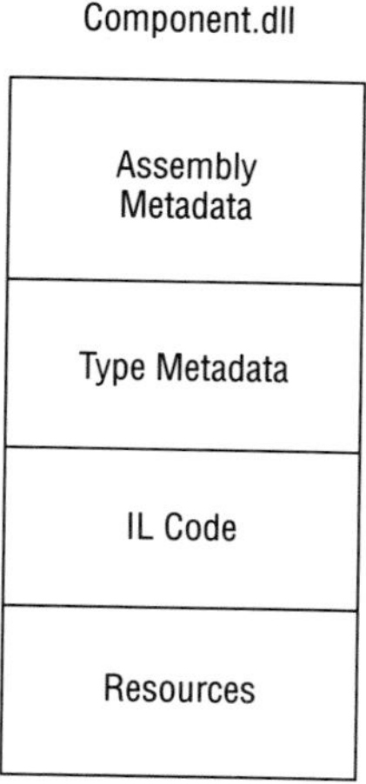

Figure 17-1

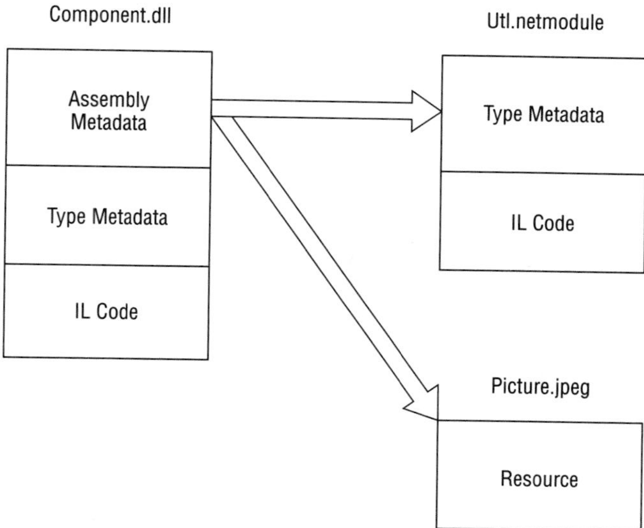

Figure 17-2

Assembly Manifests

An important part of an assembly is a *manifest*, which is part of the metadata. It describes the assembly with all the information that's needed to reference it and lists all its dependencies. The parts of the manifest are as follows:

- Identity — Name, version, culture, and public key.
- A list of files — Files belonging to this assembly. A single assembly must have at least one file but may contain a number of files.
- A list of referenced assemblies — All assemblies used from the assembly are documented inside the manifest. This reference information includes the version number and the public key, which is used to uniquely identify assemblies. The public key is discussed later in this chapter.
- A set of permission requests — These are the permissions needed to run this assembly. You can find more information about permissions in Chapter 20, " Security."
- Exported types — These are included if they are defined within a module and the module is referenced from the assembly; otherwise, they are not part of the manifest. A module is a unit of reuse. The type description is stored as metadata inside the assembly. You can get the structures and classes with the properties and methods from the metadata. This replaces the type library that was used with COM to describe the types. For the use of COM clients it's easy to generate a type library out of the manifest. The reflection mechanism uses the information about the exported types for late binding to classes. See Chapter 13, "Reflection," for more information about reflection.

Namespaces, Assemblies, and Components

You might be a little bit confused by the meanings of namespaces, types, assemblies, and components. How does a namespace fit into the assembly concept? The namespace is completely independent of an assembly. You can have different namespaces in a single assembly, but the same namespace can be spread across assemblies. The namespace is just an extension of the type name — it belongs to the name of the type.

For example, the assemblies mscorlib and system contain the namespace `System.Threading` among many other namespaces. Although the assemblies contain the same namespaces, you will not find the same class names.

Private and Shared Assemblies

Assemblies can be shared or private. A *private assembly* is found either in the same directory as the application, or within one of its subdirectories. With a private assembly, it's not necessary to think about naming conflicts with other classes or versioning problems. The assemblies that are referenced during the build process are copied to the application directory. Private assemblies are the usual way to build assemblies, especially when applications and components are built within the same company.

Although it is still possible to have naming conflicts with private assemblies (multiple private assemblies may be part of the application and they could have conflicts, or a name in a private assembly might conflict with a name in a shared assembly used by the application), naming conflicts are greatly reduced. If you find you'll be using multiple private assemblies or working with shared assemblies in other applications, it's a good idea to utilize well-named namespaces and types to minimize naming conflicts.

When using *shared assemblies*, you have to be aware of some rules. The assembly must be unique and therefore must also have a unique name called a *strong name*. Part of the strong name is a mandatory version number. Shared assemblies will mostly be used when a vendor, different from that of the application, builds the component, or when a large application is split into subprojects. Also, some technologies such as .NET Enterprise Services require shared assemblies in specific scenarios.

Satellite Assemblies

A satellite assembly is an assembly that only contains resources. This is extremely useful for localization. Because an assembly has a culture associated, the resource manager looks for satellite assemblies containing the resources of a specific culture.

You can read more about satellite assemblies in Chapter 21, "Localization."

Viewing Assemblies

Assemblies can be viewed using the command-line utility `ildasm`, the MSIL disassembler. You can open an assembly by starting `ildasm` from the command line with the assembly as an argument or by selecting the File ⇨ Open menu.

Figure 17-3 shows `ildasm` opening the example that you build a little later in the chapter, `SharedDemo.dll`. `ildasm` shows the manifest and the `SharedDemo` type in the `Wrox.ProCSharp.Assemblies.Sharing` namespace. When you open the manifest, you can see the version number and the assembly attributes, as well as the referenced assemblies and their versions. You can see the MSIL code by opening the methods of the class.

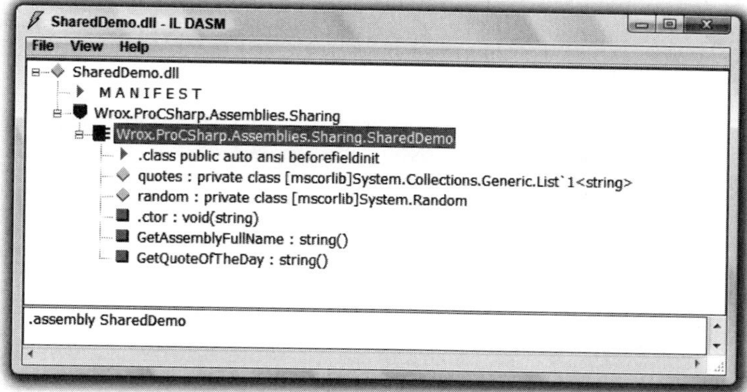

Figure 17-3

In addition to using `ildasm`, the .NET Reflector is another great tool to use to analyze assemblies. The .NET Reflector allows type and member search, and call and callee graphs, and decompiles IL code to C#, C++, or Visual Basic. You can download this tool from `www.aisto.com/roeder/dotnet`.

Creating Assemblies

Now that you know what assemblies are, it is time to build some. Of course, you have already built assemblies in previous chapters, because a .NET executable counts as an assembly. This section looks at special options for assemblies.

Creating Modules and Assemblies

All C# project types in Visual Studio create an assembly. Whether you choose a DLL or EXE project type, an assembly is always created. With the command-line C# compiler *csc*, it's also possible to create modules. A module is a DLL without assembly attributes (so it's not an assembly, but it can be added to assemblies at a later time). The command

```
csc /target:module hello.cs
```

creates a module `hello.netmodule`. You can view this module using `ildasm`.

A module also has a manifest, but there is no `.assembly` entry inside the manifest (except for the external assemblies that are referenced) because a module has no assembly attributes. It's not possible to configure versions or permissions with modules; that can be done only at the assembly scope. You can find references to assemblies in the manifest of the module. With the `/addmodule` option of `csc`, it's possible to add modules to existing assemblies.

To compare modules to assemblies, create a simple class `A` and compile it by using the following command:

```
csc /target:module A.cs
```

The compiler generates the file `A.netmodule`, which doesn't include assembly information (as you can see using `ildasm` to look at the manifest information). The manifest of the module shows the referenced assembly `mscorlib` and the `.module` entry in Figure 17-4.

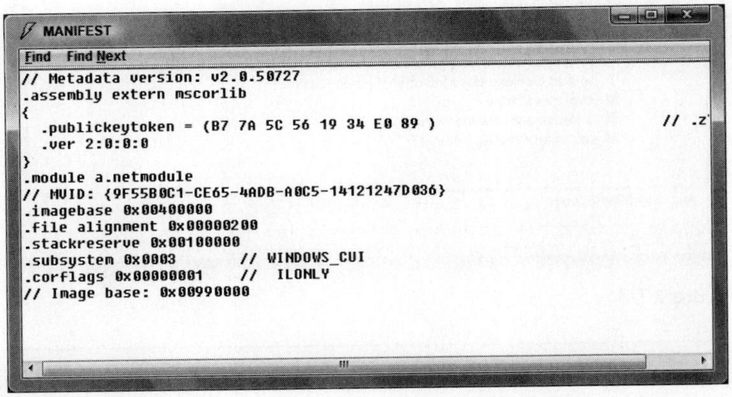

Figure 17-4

Next, create an assembly B, which includes the module `A.netmodule`. It's not necessary to have a source file to generate this assembly. The command to build the assembly is:

```
csc /target:library /addmodule:A.netmodule /out:B.dll
```

Looking at the assembly using `ildasm`, you can find only a manifest. In the manifest, the assembly `mscorlib` is referenced. Next, you see the assembly section with a hash algorithm and the version. The number of the algorithm defines the type of the algorithm that was used to create the hash code of the assembly. When creating an assembly programmatically it is possible to select the algorithm. Part of the manifest is a list of all modules belonging to the assembly. In Figure 17-5 you see `.module A.netmodule`, which belongs to the assembly. Classes exported from modules are part of the assembly manifest; classes exported from the assembly itself are not.

What's the purpose of modules? Modules can be used for faster startup of assemblies because not all types are inside a single file. The modules are loaded only when needed. Another reason to use modules is if you want to create an assembly with more than one programming language. One module could be written using Visual Basic, another module could be written using C#, and these two modules could be included in a single assembly.

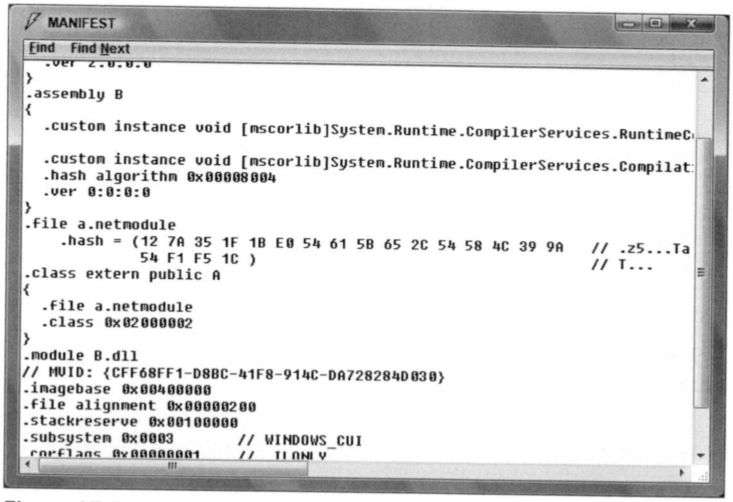

Figure 17-5

Assembly Attributes

When creating a Visual Studio project, the source file `AssemblyInfo.cs` is generated automatically. You can find this file below Properties in Solution Explorer. You can use the normal Source Code editor to configure the assembly attributes in this file. This is the file generated from the project template:

```
using System.Reflection;
using System.Runtime.CompilerServices;
using System.Runtime.InteropServices;
//
// General Information about an assembly is controlled through the
// following set of attributes. Change these attribute values to modify
// the information associated with an assembly.
//
[assembly: AssemblyTitle("DomainTest")]
[assembly: AssemblyDescription("")]
[assembly: AssemblyConfiguration("")]
```

(continued)

(continued)

```
[assembly: AssemblyCompany("")]
[assembly: AssemblyProduct("DomainTest")]
[assembly: AssemblyCopyright("Copyright @ Wrox Press 2007")]
[assembly: AssemblyTrademark("")]
[assembly: AssemblyCulture("")]

// Setting ComVisible to false makes the types in this assembly not visible
// to COM components.  If you need to access a type in this assembly from
// COM, set the ComVisible attribute to true on that type.
[assembly: ComVisible(false)]

// The following GUID is for the ID of the typelib if this project is exposed
// to COM
[assembly: Guid("ae0acc2c-0daf-4bb0-84a3-f9f6ac48bfe9")]

//
// Version information for an assembly consists of the following four
// values:
//
//      Major Version
//      Minor Version
//      Build Number
//      Revision
//
[assembly: AssemblyVersion("1.0.0.0")]
[assembly: AssemblyFileVersion("1.0.0.0")]
```

This file is used for configuration of the assembly manifest. The compiler reads the assembly attributes to inject the specific information into the manifest.

The `assembly:` prefix with the attribute marks an assembly-level attribute. Assembly-level attributes are, in contrast to the other attributes, not attached to a specific language element. The arguments that can be used for the assembly attribute are classes of the namespaces `System.Reflection`, `System.Runtime.CompilerServices`, and `System.Runtime.InteropServices`.

You can read more about attributes and how to create and use custom attributes in Chapter 13, "Reflection."

The following table contains a list of assembly attributes defined within the `System.Reflection` namespace.

Assembly Attribute	Description
`AssemblyCompany`	Specifies the company name.
`AssemblyConfiguration`	Specifies build information such as retail or debugging information.
`AssemblyCopyright` and `AssemblyTrademark`	Hold the copyright and trademark information.
`AssemblyDefaultAlias`	Can be used if the assembly name is not easily readable (such as a GUID when the assembly name is created dynamically). With this attribute an alias name can be specified.

Assembly Attribute	Description
`AssemblyDescription`	Describes the assembly or the product. Looking at the properties of the executable file this value shows up as Comments.
`AssemblyProduct`	Specifies the name of the product where the assembly belongs.
`AssemblyTitle`	Used to give the assembly a friendly name. The friendly name can include spaces. With the file properties you can see this value as Description.
`AssemblyCulture`	Defines the culture of the assembly. This attribute is important for satellite assemblies.
`AssemblyInformationalVersion`	This attribute isn't used for version checking when assemblies are referenced; it is for information only. It is very useful to specify the version of an application that uses multiple assemblies. Opening the properties of the executable you can see this value as the Product Version.
`AssemblyVersion`	This attribute gives the version number of the assembly. Versioning is discussed later in this chapter.
`AssemblyFileVersion`	This attribute defines the version of the file. The value shows up with the Windows file properties dialog, but it doesn't have any influence on the .NET behavior.

Here's an example of how these attributes might be configured:

```
[assembly: AssemblyTitle("Professional C#")]
[assembly: AssemblyDescription("Sample Application")]
[assembly: AssemblyConfiguration("Retail version")]
[assembly: AssemblyCompany("Wrox Press")]
[assembly: AssemblyProduct("Wrox Professional Series")]
[assembly: AssemblyCopyright("Copyright (C) Wrox Press 2008")]
[assembly: AssemblyTrademark("Wrox is a registered trademark of " +
     "John Wiley & Sons, Inc.")]
[assembly: AssemblyCulture("")]

[assembly: AssemblyVersion("1.0.0.0")]
[assembly: AssemblyFileVersion("1.0.0.0")]
```

With Visual Studio 2008 you can configure these attributes with the project properties, Application settings, and Assembly Information, as you can see in Figure 17-6.

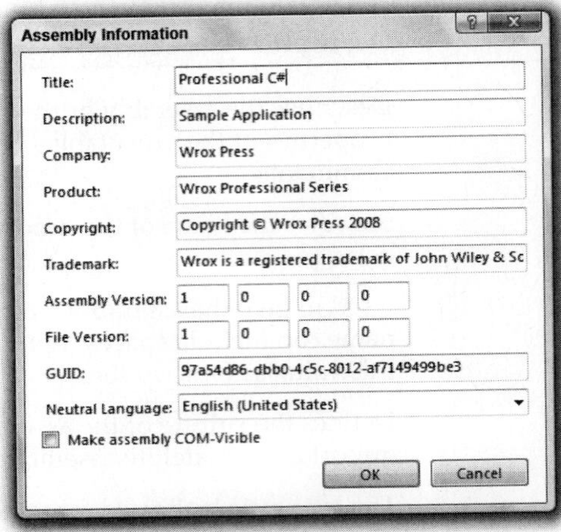

Figure 17-6

Dynamic Loading and Creating Assemblies

During development time you add a reference to an assembly so it gets included with the assembly references and the types of the assembly are available to the compiler. During runtime the referenced assembly gets loaded as soon as a type of the assembly is instantiated or a method of the type is used. Instead of using this automatic behavior, you can also load assemblies programmatically. To load assemblies programmatically you can use the class `Assembly` with the static method `Load()`. This method is overloaded where you can pass the name of the assembly using `AssemblyName`, the name of the assembly, or a byte array.

It is also possible to create an assembly on the fly as shown with the next example. This sample demonstrates how C# code can be entered in a text box, a new assembly is dynamically created by starting the C# compiler, and the compiled code is invoked.

To compile C# code dynamically you can use the class `CSharpCodeProvider` from the namespace `Microsoft.CSharp`. Using this class, you can compile code and generate assemblies from a DOM tree, from a file, and from source code.

The UI of the application is done using WPF. You can see the UI in Figure 17-7. The window is made up of a `TextBox` to enter C# code, a `Button`, and a `TextBlock` WPF control that spans all columns of the last row to display the result as shown in Figure 17-7.

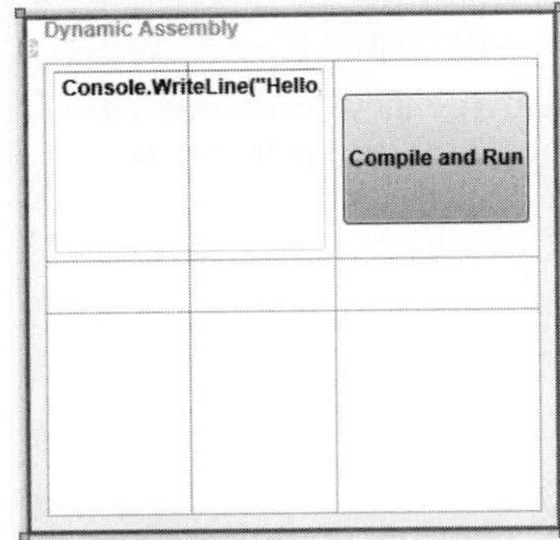

Figure 17-7

To dynamically compile and run C# code, the class `CodeDriver` defines the method `CompileAndRun()`. This method compiles the code from the text box and starts the generated method.

```
using System;
using System.CodeDom.Compiler;
using System.IO;
using System.Reflection;
using System.Text;
using Microsoft.CSharp;

namespace Wrox.ProCSharp.Assemblies
{

   public class CodeDriver
   {
      private string prefix =
         "using System;" +
         "public static class Driver" +
         "{" +
         "   public static void Run()" +
         "   {";

      private string postfix =
         "   }" +
         "}";


      public string CompileAndRun(string input, out bool hasError)
      {
         hasError = false;
         string returnData = null;

         CompilerResults results = null;
         using (CSharpCodeProvider provider = new CSharpCodeProvider())
         {
            CompilerParameters options = new CompilerParameters();
            options.GenerateInMemory = true;

            StringBuilder sb = new StringBuilder();
            sb.Append(prefix);
            sb.Append(input);
            sb.Append(postfix);

            results = provider.CompileAssemblyFromSource(
                  options, sb.ToString());
         }

         if (results.Errors.HasErrors)
         {
            hasError = true;
            StringBuilder errorMessage = new StringBuilder();
            foreach (CompilerError error in results.Errors)
```

(continued)

(continued)

```
            {
               errorMessage.AppendFormat("{0} {1}", error.Line,
                     error.ErrorText);
            }
            returnData = errorMessage.ToString();
         }
         else
         {
            TextWriter temp = Console.Out;
            StringWriter writer = new StringWriter();
            Console.SetOut(writer);
            Type driverType = results.CompiledAssembly.GetType("Driver");

            driverType.InvokeMember("Run", BindingFlags.InvokeMethod |
                  BindingFlags.Static | BindingFlags.Public,
                  null, null, null);
            Console.SetOut(temp);

            returnData = writer.ToString();
         }

         return returnData;
      }
   }
}
```

The method `CompileAndRun()` requires a string input parameter where one or multiple lines of C# code can be passed. Because every method that is called must be included in a method and a class, the variables `prefix` and `postfix` define the structure of the dynamically created class `Driver` and the method `Run()` that surround the code from the parameter. Using a `StringBuilder`, the `prefix`, `postfix`, and the code from the `input` variable are merged to create a complete class that can be compiled. Using this resultant string, the code is compiled with the `CSharpCodeProvider` class. The method `CompileAssemblyFromSource()` dynamically creates an assembly. Because this assembly is just needed in memory, the compiler parameter option `GenerateInMemory` is set.

If the source code that was passed contains some errors, these will show up in the `Errors` collection of `CompilerResults`. The errors are returned with the return data, and the variable `hasError` is set to `true`.

If the source code compiled successfully, the `Run()` method of the new `Driver` class is invoked. The invocation of this method is done using reflection. From the newly compiled assembly that can be accessed using `CompilerResults.CompiledType`, the new class `Driver` is referenced by the `driverType` variable. Then the `InvokeMember()` method of the `Type` class is used to invoke the method `Run()`. Because this method is defined as a public static method, the `BindingFlags` must be set accordingly. To see a result of the program that is written to the console, the console is redirected to a `StringWriter` to finally return the complete output of the program with the `returnData` variable.

Running the code with the `InvokeMember()` *method makes use of .NET reflection. Reflection is discussed in Chapter 13.*

The `Click` event of the WPF button is connected to the `Compile_Click()` method where the `CodeDriver` class is instantiated, and the `CompileAndRun()` method is invoked. The input is taken from the `TextBox` named `textCode`, and the result is written to the `TextBlock textOutput`.

```
private void Compile_Click(object sender, RoutedEventArgs e)
{
   CodeDriver driver = new CodeDriver ();
   bool isError;
   textOutput.Text = driver.CompileAndRun(textCode.Text, out isError);
   if (isError)
   {
      textOutput.Background = Brushes.Red;
   }
}
```

Now you can start the application, enter C# code in the `TextBox` as shown in Figure 17-8, and compile and run the code.

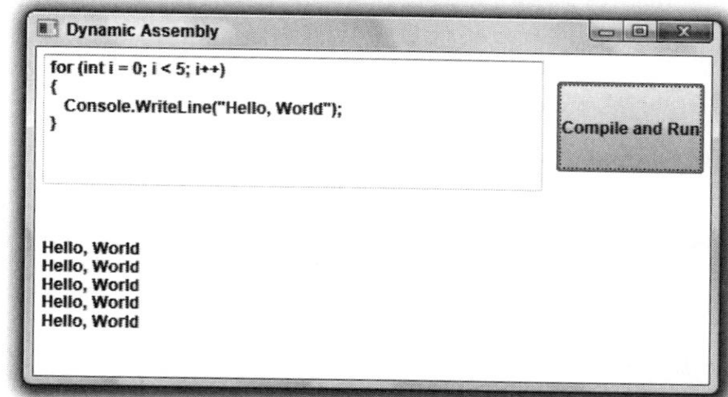

Figure 17-8

The program as written so far has the disadvantage that every time you click the `Compile and Run` button, a new assembly is created and loaded, and the program always needs more and more memory. You cannot unload an assembly from the application. To unload assemblies, application domains are needed.

Application Domains

Before .NET, processes were used as isolation boundaries, with every process having its private virtual memory; an application running in one process could not write to the memory of another application and thereby crash the other application. The process was used as an isolation and security boundary between applications. With the .NET architecture you have a new boundary for applications: *application domains*. With managed IL code, the runtime can ensure that access to the memory of another application inside a single process can't happen. Multiple applications can run in a single process within multiple application domains (see Figure 17-9).

An assembly is loaded into an application domain. In Figure 17-9 you can see process 4711 with two application domains. In application domain A, the objects one and two are instantiated, one in assembly One, and two in assembly Two. The second application domain in process 4711 has an instance one. To minimize memory consumption, the code of assemblies is only loaded once into an application domain. Instance and static members are not shared between application domains. It's not possible to directly access objects within another application domain; a proxy is needed instead. So in Figure 17-9,

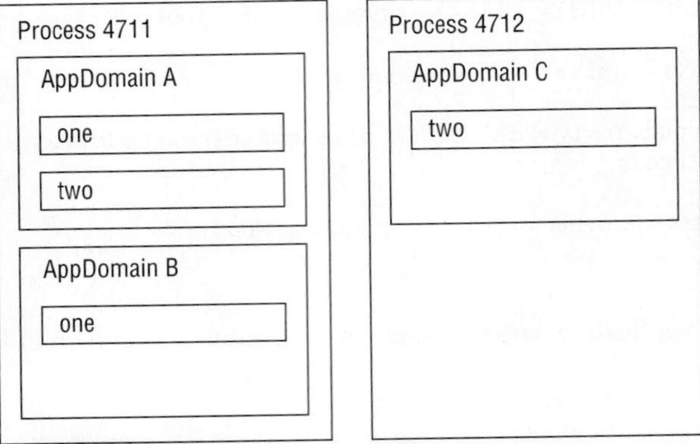

Figure 17-9

the object one in application domain B cannot directly access the objects one or two in application domain A without a proxy.

The `AppDomain` class is used to create and terminate application domains, load and unload assemblies and types, and enumerate assemblies and threads in a domain. In this section, you program a small example to see application domains in action.

First, create a C# console application called `AssemblyA`. In the `Main()` method add a `Console.WriteLine()` so that you can see when this method is called. In addition, add the class `Demo` with a constructor with two `int` values as arguments, which will be used to create instances with the `AppDomain` class. The `AssemblyA.exe` assembly will be loaded from the second application that will be created:

```
using System;

namespace Wrox.ProCSharp.Assemblies.AppDomains
{
   public class Demo
   {
      public Demo(int val1, int val2)
      {
         Console.WriteLine("Constructor with the values {0}, {1}" +
               " in domain {2} called", val1, val2,
               AppDomain.CurrentDomain.FriendlyName);
      }
   }

   class Program
   {
      static void Main()
      {
         Console.WriteLine("Main in domain {0} called",
               AppDomain.CurrentDomain.FriendlyName);
      }
   }
}
```

Running the application produces this output:

```
Main in domain AssemblyA.exe called.
Press any key to continue ...
```

The second project you create is again a C# console application: `DomainTest`. First, display the name of the current domain using the property `FriendlyName` of the `AppDomain` class. With the `CreateDomain()` method, a new application domain with the friendly name `New AppDomain` is created. Then load the assembly `AssemblyA` into the new domain and call the `Main()` method by calling `ExecuteAssembly()`:

```
using System;

namespace Wrox.ProCSharp.Assemblies.AppDomains
{
   class Program
   {
      static void Main()
      {
         AppDomain currentDomain = AppDomain.CurrentDomain;
         Console.WriteLine(currentDomain.FriendlyName);
         AppDomain secondDomain =
               AppDomain.CreateDomain("New AppDomain");
         secondDomain.ExecuteAssembly("AssemblyA.exe");
      }
   }
}
```

Before starting the program `DomainTest.exe`, reference the assembly `AssemblyA.exe` with the `DomainTest` project. Referencing the assembly with Visual Studio 2008 copies the assembly to the project directory, so that the assembly can be found. If the assembly cannot be found, a `System.IO.FileNotFoundException` exception is thrown.

When `DomainTest.exe` is run, you get the following console output. `DomainTest.exe` is the friendly name of the first application domain. The second line is the output of the newly loaded assembly in the `New AppDomain`. With a process viewer, you will not see the process `AssemblyA.exe` executing because there's no new process created. `AssemblyA` is loaded into the process `DomainTest.exe`.

```
DomainTest.exe
Main in domain New AppDomain called
Press any key to continue ...
```

Instead of calling the `Main()` method in the newly loaded assembly, you can also create a new instance. In the following example, replace the `ExecuteAssembly()` method with a `CreateInstance()`. The first argument is the name of the assembly, `AssemblyA`. The second argument defines the type that should be instantiated: `Wrox.ProCSharp.Assemblies.AppDomains.Demo`. The third argument, `true`, means that case is ignored. `System.Reflection.BindingFlags.CreateInstance` is a binding flag enumeration value to specify that the constructor should be called:

```
         AppDomain secondDomain =
            AppDomain.CreateDomain("New AppDomain");
         // secondDomain.ExecuteAssembly("AssemblyA.exe");
         secondDomain.CreateInstance("AssemblyA",
            "Wrox.ProCSharp.Assemblies.AppDomains.Demo", true,
            System.Reflection.BindingFlags.CreateInstance,
            null, new object[] {7, 3}, null, null, null);
```

The results of a successful run of the application are as follows:

```
DomainTest.exe
Constructor with the values 7, 3 in domain New AppDomain called
Press any key to continue ...
```

Now you have seen how to create and call application domains. In runtime hosts, application domains are created automatically. ASP.NET creates an application domain for each Web application that runs on a Web server. Internet Explorer creates application domains in which managed controls will run. For applications, it can be useful to create application domains if you want to unload an assembly. You can unload assemblies only by terminating an application domain.

Application domains are an extremely useful construct if assemblies are loaded dynamically, and the requirement exists to unload assemblies after use. Within the primary application domain it is not possible to get rid of loaded assemblies. However, it is possible to end application domains where all assemblies loaded just within the application domain are cleaned from the memory.

With this knowledge about application domains it is now possible to change the WPF program created earlier. The new class `CodeDriverInAppDomain` creates a new application domain using `AppDomain.CreateDomain`. Inside this new application domain the class `CodeDriver` is instantiated using `CreateInstanceAndUnwrap()`. Using the `CodeDriver` instance, the `CompileAndRun()` method is invoked before the new app-domain is unloaded again.

```
using System;
using System.Runtime.Remoting;

namespace Wrox.ProCSharp.Assemblies
{
   public class CodeDriverInAppDomain
   {
      public string CompileAndRun(string code, out bool hasError)
      {
         AppDomain codeDomain = AppDomain.CreateDomain("CodeDriver");

         CodeDriver codeDriver = (CodeDriver)
               codeDomain.CreateInstanceAndUnwrap("DynamicCompileWPF",
                     "Wrox.ProCSharp.Assemblies.CodeDriver");

         string result = codeDriver.CompileAndRun(code, out hasError);

         AppDomain.Unload(codeDomain);

         return result;
      }
   }
}
```

The class `CodeDriver` itself now is used both in the main app-domain and in the new app-domain, that's why it is not possible to get rid of the code that this class is using. If you would like to do that you can define an interface that is implemented by the `CodeDriver` and just use the interface in the main app-domain. However, here this is not an issue because there's only the need to get rid of the dynamically created assembly with the `Driver` class.

To access the class `CodeDriver` from a different app-domain, the class `CodeDriver` must derive from the base class `MarshalByRefObject`. Only classes that derive from this base type can be accessed across another app-domain. In the main app-domain a proxy is instantiated to invoke the methods of this class across an inter-appdomain channel.

```
using System;
using System.CodeDom.Compiler;
using System.IO;
using System.Reflection;
using System.Text;
using Microsoft.CSharp;

namespace Wrox.ProCSharp.Assemblies
{

   public class CodeDriver : MarshalByRefObject
   {
```

The `Compile_Click()` event handler can now be changed to use the `CodeDriverInAppDomain` class instead of the `CodeDriver` class:

```
      private void Compile_Click(object sender, RoutedEventArgs e)
      {
         CodeDriverInAppDomain driver = new CodeDriverInAppDomain();
         bool isError;
         textOutput.Text = driver.CompileAndRun(textCode.Text, out isError);
         if (isError)
         {
            textOutput.Background = Brushes.Red;
         }
      }
```

Now you can click the Compile and Run button of the application any number of times, and the generated assembly is always unloaded.

> *You can see the loaded assemblies in an app-domain with the* `GetAssemblies()` *method of the* `AppDomain` *class.*

Shared Assemblies

Assemblies can be isolated for use by a single application — not sharing an assembly is the default. When using shared assemblies there are specific requirements that must be followed.

This section explores the following:

- Strong names as a requirement for shared assemblies
- Global assembly cache
- Creating shared assemblies
- Installing shared assemblies in the GAC
- Delayed signing of shared assemblies

Strong Names

The goal of a shared assembly name is that it must be globally unique, and it must be possible to protect the name. At no time can any other person create an assembly using the same name.

COM solved the first problem by using a globally unique identifier (GUID). The second problem, however, still existed because anyone could steal the GUID and create a different object with the same identifier. Both problems are solved with *strong names* of .NET assemblies.

A strong name is made of these items:

- The *name* of the assembly itself.
- A *version number*. This allows it to use different versions of the same assembly at the same time. Different versions can also work side by side and can be loaded concurrently inside the same process.
- A *public key* guarantees that the strong name is unique. It also guarantees that a referenced assembly cannot be replaced from a different source.
- A *culture*. Cultures are discussed in Chapter 21, "Localization."

A shared assembly must have a strong name to uniquely identify the assembly.

A strong name is a simple text name accompanied by a version number, a public key, and a culture. You wouldn't create a new public key with every assembly, but you'd have one in your company, so the key uniquely identifies your company's assemblies.

However, this key cannot be used as a trust key. Assemblies can carry Authenticode signatures to build up a trust. The key for the Authenticode signature can be a different one from the key used for the strong name.

For development purposes, a different public key can be used and later be exchanged easily with the real key. This feature is discussed later in the section "Delayed Signing of Assemblies."

To uniquely identify the assemblies in your companies, a useful namespace hierarchy should be used to name your classes. Here is a simple example showing how to organize namespaces: Wrox Press can use the major namespace `Wrox` for its classes and namespaces. In the hierarchy below the namespace, the namespaces must be organized so that all classes are unique. Every chapter of this book uses a different namespace of the form `Wrox.ProCSharp.<Chapter>`; this chapter uses `Wrox.ProCSharp.Assemblies`. So, if there is a class `Hello` in two different chapters, there's no conflict because of different namespaces. Utility classes that are used across different books can go into the namespace `Wrox.Utilities`.

A company name commonly used as the first part of the namespace is not necessarily unique, so something more must be used to build a strong name. For this the public key is used. Because of the public/private key principle in strong names, no one without access to your private key can destructively create an assembly that could be unintentionally called by the client.

Integrity Using Strong Names

A public/private key pair must be used to create a shared component. The compiler writes the public key to the manifest, creates a hash of all files that belong to the assembly, and signs the hash with the private key, which is not stored within the assembly. It is then guaranteed that no one can change your assembly. The signature can be verified with the public key.

During development, the client assembly must reference the shared assembly. The compiler writes the public key of the referenced assembly to the manifest of the client assembly. To reduce storage, it is not the public key that is written to the manifest of the client assembly, but a public key token. The public key token consists of the last 8 bytes of a hash of the public key and is unique.

At runtime, during loading of the shared assembly (or at install time if the client is installed using the native image generator), the hash of the shared component assembly can be verified by using the public key stored inside the client assembly. Only the owner of the private key can change the shared component assembly. There is no way a component `Math` that was created by vendor `A` and referenced from a client can be replaced by a component from a hacker. Only the owner of the private key can replace the shared component with a new version. Integrity is guaranteed insofar as the shared assembly comes from the expected publisher.

Figure 17-10 shows a shared component with a public key referenced by a client assembly that has a public key token of the shared assembly inside the manifest.

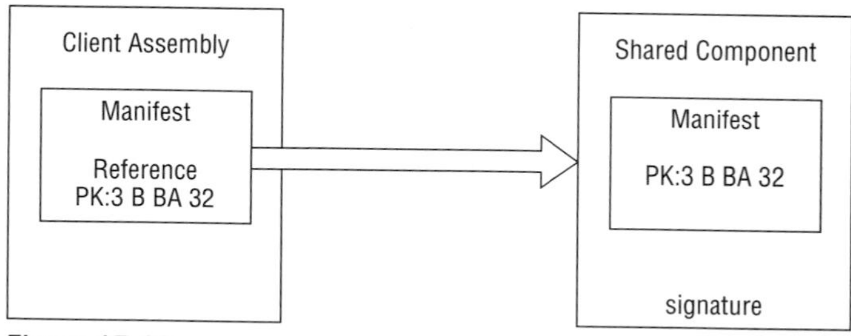

Figure 17-10

Global Assembly Cache

The *global assembly cache* (GAC) is, as the name implies, a cache for globally available assemblies. Most shared assemblies are installed inside this cache; otherwise a shared directory (also on a server) can be used.

The GAC can be displayed using `shfusion.dll`, which is a Windows shell extension to view and manipulate the contents of the cache. A Windows shell extension is a COM DLL that integrates with Windows Explorer. You just have to start Explorer and go to the `<windir>/assembly` directory.

With the Assembly Cache Viewer (see Figure 17-11), you can see the global assembly name, type, version, culture, and the public key token. Under Type you can see if the assembly was installed using the native image generator. When you select an assembly using the context menu, it's possible to delete an assembly and to view its properties (see Figure 17-12).

You can see the real files and directories behind the assembly cache by checking the directory from the command line. Inside the `<windir>\assembly` directory, you can find multiple `GACxxx` directories and a `NativeImages_<runtime version>` directory. The `GACxxx` directories contain shared assemblies. `GAC_MSIL` contains the assemblies with pure .NET code; `GAC_32` contains the assemblies that are specific to a 32-bit platform. On a 64-bit system, you can also find the directory `GAC_64` with assemblies specific for 64 bit. The directory `GAC` is for .NET 1.0 and 1.1. In the directory `NativeImages_<runtime version>`, you can find the assemblies compiled to native code. If you go deeper in the directory structure, you will find directory names that are similar to the assembly names, and below that a version directory and the assemblies themselves. This allows the installation of different versions of the same assembly.

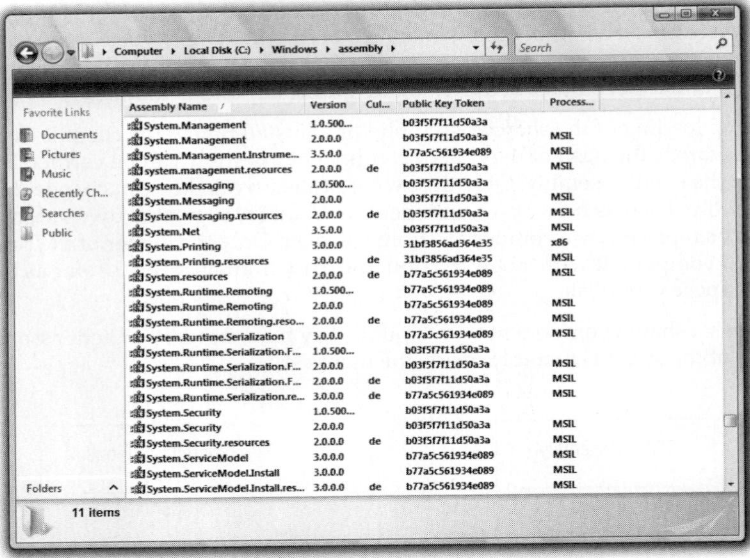

Figure 17-11

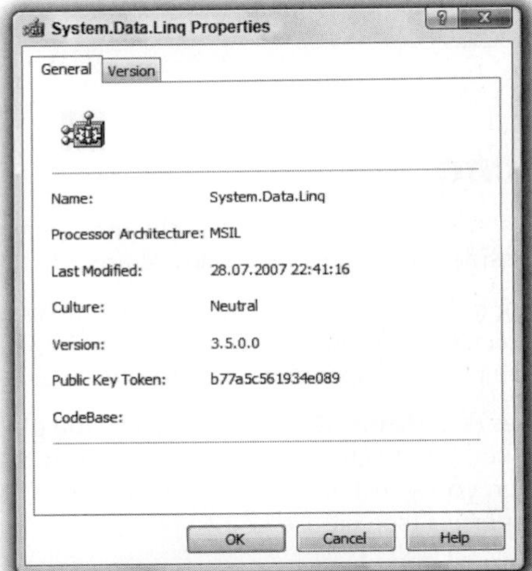

Figure 17-12

The assembly viewer can be used to view and delete assemblies with Windows Explorer. `gacutil.exe` is a utility to install, uninstall, and list assemblies using the command line.

The following list explains some of the `gacutil` options:

- `gacutil /l` lists all assemblies from the assembly cache.
- `gacutil /i mydll` installs the shared assembly `mydll` into the assembly cache.
- `gacutil /u mydll` uninstalls the assembly `mydll`.

For production you should use an installer program to install shared assemblies to the GAC. Deployment is covered in Chapter 16, "Deployment."

Creating a Shared Assembly

In the next example, you create a shared assembly and a client that uses it.

Creating shared assemblies is not much different from creating private assemblies. Create a simple Visual C# class library project with the name `SharedDemo`. Change the namespace to `Wrox.ProCSharp.Assemblies.Sharing` and the class name to `SharedDemo`. Enter the following code. In the constructor of the class, all lines of a file are read into a collection. The name of the file is passed as an argument to the constructor. The method `GetQuoteOfTheDay()` just returns a random string of the collection.

```
using System;
using System.Collections.Generic;
using System.IO;

namespace Wrox.ProCSharp.Assemblies.Sharing
{
   public class SharedDemo
   {
      private List<string> quotes;
      private Random random;

      public SharedDemo(string filename)
      {
         quotes = new List<string>();
         Stream stream = File.OpenRead(filename);
         StreamReader streamReader = new StreamReader(stream);
         string quote;
         while ((quote = streamReader.ReadLine()) != null)
         {
            quotes.Add(quote);
         }
         streamReader.Close();
         stream.Close();
         random = new Random();
      }

      public string GetQuoteOfTheDay()
      {
         int index = random.Next(1, quotes.Count);
         return quotes[index];
      }
   }
}
```

Create a Strong Name

A strong name is needed to share this assembly. You can create such a name with the *strong name tool* (`sn`):

```
sn -k mykey.snk
```

The strong name utility generates and writes a public/private key pair, and writes this pair to a file; here the file is `mykey.snk`.

With Visual Studio 2008, you can sign the assembly with the project properties by selecting the Signing tab, as shown in Figure 17-13. You can also create keys with this tool. However, you should not create a key file for every project. Just a few keys for the complete company can be used instead. It is useful to create different keys depending on security requirements (see Chapter 20, "Security").

Setting the signing option with Visual Studio adds the `/keyfile` option to the compiler setting. Visual Studio also allows you to create a keyfile that is secured with a password. Such a file has the file extension `.pfx` (see Figure 17-13).

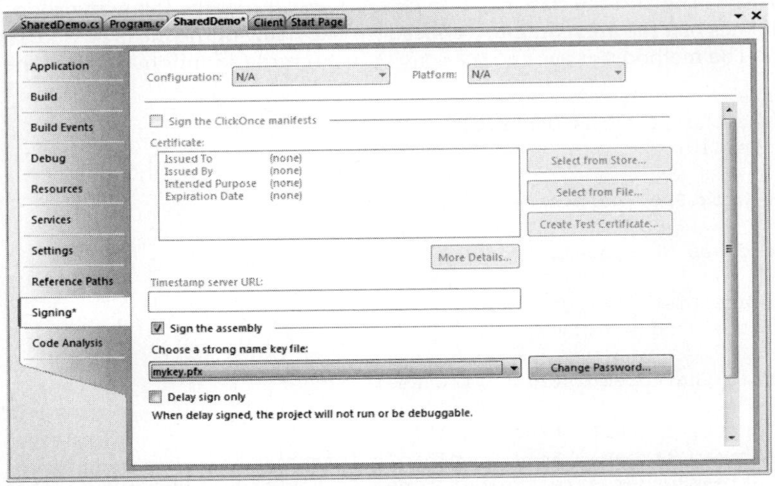

Figure 17-13

After rebuilding, the public key can be found inside the manifest. You can verify this using `ildasm`, as shown in Figure 17-14.

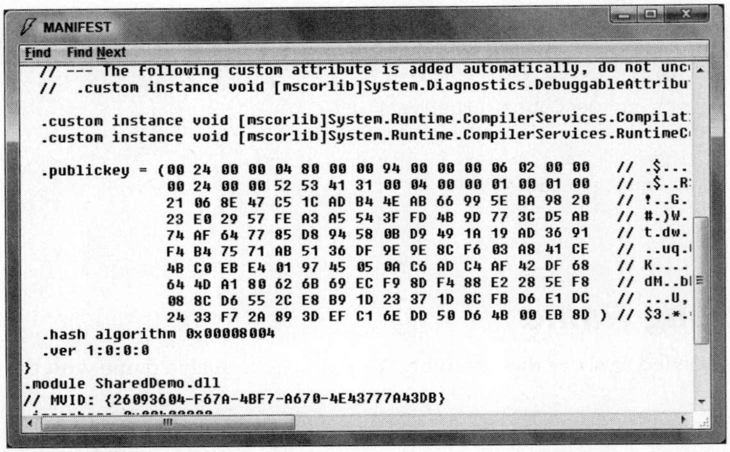

Figure 17-14

Install the Shared Assembly

With a public key in the assembly, you can now install it in the global assembly cache using the global assembly cache tool `gacutil` with the `/i` option:

```
gacutil /i SharedDemo.dll
```

By configuring a post-build event command line with Visual Studio (see Figure 17-15), the assembly can be installed in the GAC with each successful build.

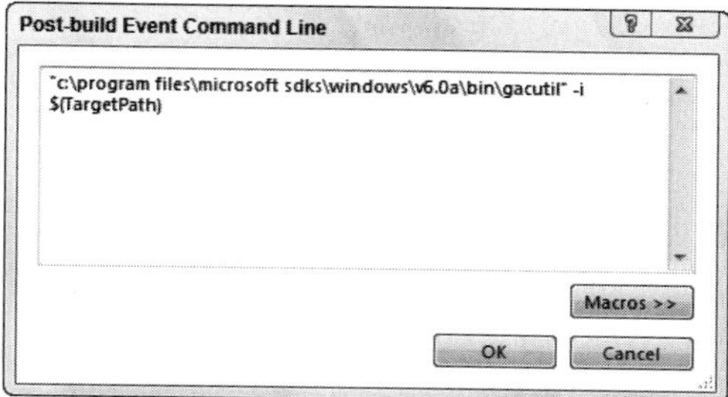

Figure 17-15

If you're using Windows Vista to install an assembly to the GAC from Visual Studio, Visual Studio must be started with elevated rights. Installing assemblies to the GAC requires admin privileges.

Then you can use the Global Assembly Cache Viewer to check the version of the shared assembly and see if it is successfully installed.

Using the Shared Assembly

To use the shared assembly, create a C# console application called `Client`. Change the name of the namespace to `Wrox.ProCSharp.Assemblies.Sharing`. The shared assembly can be referenced in the same way as a private assembly: by using the Project ⇨ Add Reference menu.

> **With shared assemblies the reference property `Copy Local` can be set to `false`. This way the assembly is not copied to the directory of the output files but will be loaded from the GAC instead.**

Here's the code for the `Client` application:

```
using System;
namespace Wrox.ProCSharp.Assemblies.Sharing
{
   class Program
   {
      static void Main()
      {
         SharedDemo quotes =
            new SharedDemo(@"C:\ProCSharp\Assemblies\Quotes.txt");
         for (int i=0; i < 3; i++)
```

(continued)

(continued)

```
                {
                    Console.WriteLine(quotes.GetQuoteOfTheDay());
                    Console.WriteLine();
                }
            }
        }
    }
```

Looking at the manifest in the client assembly using `ildasm` (see Figure 17-16), you can see the reference to the shared assembly `SharedDemo`: `.assembly extern SharedDemo`. Part of this referenced information is the version number, discussed next, and the token of the public key.

```
MANIFEST
Find  Find Next
// Metadata version: v2.0.50727
.assembly extern mscorlib
{
  .publickeytoken = (B7 7A 5C 56 19 34 E0 89 )                         //
  .ver 2:0:0:0
}
.assembly extern SharedDemo
{
  .publickeytoken = (7D 88 6A 6F 7B 9F 02 92 )                         //
  .ver 1:0:0:0
}
.assembly Client
{
  .custom instance void [mscorlib]System.Reflection.AssemblyFileVersionAtt
  .custom instance void [mscorlib]System.Runtime.InteropServices.GuidAttri

  .custom instance void [mscorlib]System.Runtime.InteropServices.ComVisibl
  .custom instance void [mscorlib]System.Reflection.AssemblyTrademarkAttri
```

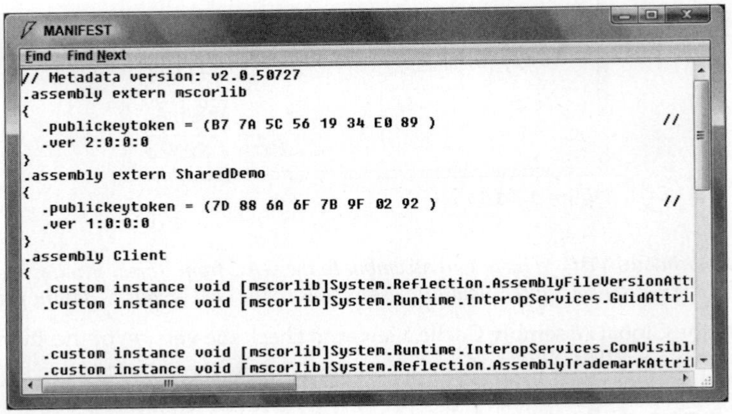

Figure 17-16

The token of the public key can also be seen within the shared assembly using the strong name utility: `sn -T` shows the token of the public key in the assembly, and `sn -Tp` shows the token and the public key. Pay attention to the use of the uppercase T!

The result of your program with a sample quotes file is shown here:

```
"We don't like their sound. And guitar music is on the way out." - Decca Recording,
Co., in rejecting the Beatles, 1962

"The ordinary 'horseless carriage' is at present a luxury for the wealthy; and
although its price will probably fall in the future, it will never come into as
common use as the bicycle."   —   The Literary Digest, 1889

"Landing and moving around the moon offer so many serious problems for human beings
that it may take science another 200 years to lick them", Lord Kelvin (1824-1907)

Press any key to continue ...
```

Delayed Signing of Assemblies

The private key of a company should be safely stored. Most companies don't give all developers access to the private key; only a few security people have it. That's why the signature of an assembly can be added at a later date, such as before distribution. When the assembly attribute `AssemblyDelaySign` is set to `true`, no signature is stored in the assembly, but enough free space is reserved so that it can be added later. Without using a key, you cannot test the assembly and install it in the GAC; however, you can use a temporary key for testing purposes, and replace this key with the real company key later.

The following steps are required to delay signing of assemblies:

1. Create a public/private key pair with the strong name utility `sn`. The generated file `mykey.snk` includes both the public and private key.

```
sn -k mykey.snk
```

2. Extract the public key to make it available to developers. The option `-p` extracts the public key of the keyfile. The file `mykeypub.snk` only holds the public key.

```
sn -p mykey.snk mykeypub.snk
```

All developers in the company can use this keyfile `mykeypub.snk` and compile the assembly with the `/delaysign+` option. This way the signature is not added to the assembly, but it can be added afterward. In Visual Studio 2008, the delay sign option can be set with a check box in the Signing settings.

3. Turn off the verification of the signature, because the assembly doesn't have a signature:

```
sn -Vr SharedDemo.dll
```

4. Before distribution the assembly can be re-signed with the `sn` utility. Use the `-R` option to re-sign previously signed or delayed signed assemblies. Resigning of the assembly can be done by the person doing the deployment package for the application and having access to the private key that is used for distribution.

```
sn -R MyAssembly.dll mykey.snk
```

The signature verification should be turned off only during the development process. Never distribute an assembly without verification, because it would be possible for this assembly to be replaced by a malicious one.

Re-signing of assemblies can be automated by defining the tasks in an MSBuild file. This is discussed in Chapter 15, "Visual Studio 2008."

References

Properties lists a reference count. This reference count is responsible for the fact that a cached assembly cannot be deleted if it is still needed by an application. For example, if a shared assembly is installed by a Microsoft installer package (`.msi` file), it can only be deleted by uninstalling the application, but not by deleting it from the GAC. Trying to delete the assembly from the GAC results in the error message "`Assembly <name> could not be uninstalled because it is required by other applications.`"

A reference to the assembly can be set using the `gacutil` utility with the option `/r`. The option `/r` requires a reference type, a reference ID, and a description. The type of the reference can be one of three options: `UNINSTALL_KEY`, `FILEPATH`, or `OPAQUE`. `UNINSTALL_KEY` is used by MSI where a registry key is defined that is also needed with the uninstallation. A directory can be specified with `FILEPATH`. A useful directory would be the root directory of the application. The `OPAQUE` reference type allows you to set any type of reference.

The command line

```
gacutil /i shareddemo.dll /r FILEPATH c:\ProCSharp\Assemblies\Client "Shared Demo"
```

installs the assembly `shareddemo` in the GAC with a reference to the directory of the client application. Another installation of the same assembly can happen with a different path, or an `OPAQUE` ID like in this command line:

```
gacutil /i shareddemo.dll /r OPAQUE 4711 "Opaque installation"
```

Now, the assembly is in the GAC only once, but it has two references. To delete the assembly from the GAC, both references must be removed:

```
gacutil /u shareddemo /r OPAQUE 4711 "Opaque installation"
gacutil /u shareddemo /r FILEPATH c:\ProCSharp\Assemblies\Client "Shared Demo"
```

To remove a shared assembly, the option `/u` requires the assembly name without the file extension DLL. On the contrary, the option `/i` to install a shared assembly requires the complete file name including the file extension.

Chapter 16, "Deployment," deals with deployment of assemblies, where the reference count is being dealt with in an MSI package.

Native Image Generator

With the native image generator, `Ngen.exe`, you can compile the IL code to native code at installation time. This way the program can start faster because the compilation during runtime is no longer necessary. Comparing precompiled assemblies to assemblies where the JIT compiler needs to run is not different from a performance view after the IL code is compiled. The only improvement you get with the native image generator is that the application starts faster because there's no need to run JIT. Reducing the startup time of the application might be enough reason for using the native image generator. In case you create a native image from the executable, you should also create native images from all the DLLs that are loaded by the executable. Otherwise the JIT compiler still needs to run.

The `ngen` utility installs the native image in the native image cache. The physical directory of the native image cache is `<windows>\assembly\NativeImages<RuntimeVersion>`.

With `ngen install myassembly`, you can compile the MSIL code to native code and install it into the native image cache. This should be done from an installation program if you would like to put the assembly in the native image cache.

With `ngen` you can also display all assemblies from the native image cache with the option `display`. If you add an assembly name to the `display` option you get the information about all installed versions of this assembly and the assemblies that are dependent on the native assembly:

```
C:\> ngen display System.Windows.Forms
Microsoft (R) CLR Native Image Generator - Version 2.0.50727.3178
Copyright (C) Microsoft Corporation. All rights reserved.

NGEN Roots:

System.Windows.Forms, Version=2.0.0.0, Culture=Neutral,
PublicKeyToken=b77a5c561934e089, processorArchitecture=msil

NGEN Roots that depend on "System.Windows.Forms":

ComSvcConfig, Version=3.0.0.0, Culture=Neutral,
```

```
PublicKeyToken=b03f5f7f11d50a3a, processorArchitecture=msil
ehepg, Version=6.0.6000.0, Culture=Neutral,
PublicKeyToken=31bf3856ad364e35, processorArchitecture=msil
ehepgdat, Version=6.0.6000.0, Culture=Neutral,
PublicKeyToken=31bf3856ad364e35, processorArchitecture=msil
ehExtCOM, Version=6.0.6000.0, Culture=Neutral,
PublicKeyToken=31bf3856ad364e35, processorArchitecture=msil
ehexthost, Version=6.0.6000.0, Culture=Neutral,
PublicKeyToken=31bf3856ad364e35,  processorArchitecture=msil
ehRecObj, Version=6.0.6000.0, Culture=Neutral,
PublicKeyToken=31bf3856ad364e35, processorArchitecture=msil
ehshell, Version=6.0.6000.0, Culture=Neutral,
PublicKeyToken=31bf3856ad364e35, processorArchitecture=msil
EventViewer, Version=6.0.0.0, Culture=Neutral,
PublicKeyToken=31bf3856ad364e35, processorArchitecture=msil
```

If the security of the system changes, it's not sure if the native image has the security requirements it needs for running the application. This is why the native images become invalid with a system configuration change. With the command `ngen update` all native images are rebuilt to include the new configurations.

Installing CLR 2.0 runtime also installs the Native Image Service (or the Window Service CLR Optimization Service), with the name Microsoft .NET Framework NGEN v2.0.50727_X86. This service can be used to defer compilation of native images and regenerates native images that have been invalidated.

The command `ngen install myassembly /queue` can be used by an installation program to defer compilation of `myassembly` to a native image using the Native Image Service. `ngen update /queue` regenerates all native images that have been invalidated. With the `ngen queue` options `pause`, `continue`, and `status` you can control the service and get status information.

> *You might ask why the native images cannot be created on the developer system, and you just distribute the native image to the production system. The reason is that the native image generator takes care of the CPU that is installed with the target system and compiles the code optimized for the CPU type. During installation of the application, the CPU is known.*

Configuring .NET Applications

COM components used the registry to configure components. Configuration of .NET applications is done by using configuration files. With registry configurations, an xcopy deployment is not possible. Configuration files can simply be copied. The configuration files use XML syntax to specify startup and runtime settings for applications.

This section explores the following:

- What you can configure using the XML base configuration files
- How you can redirect a strong named referenced assembly to a different version
- How you can specify the directory of assemblies to find private assemblies in subdirectories and shared assemblies in common directories or on a server

Configuration Categories

The configuration can be grouped into these categories:

- **Startup settings** enable you to specify the version of the required runtime. It's possible that different versions of the runtime could be installed on the same system. The version of the runtime can be specified with the `<startup>` element.
- **Runtime settings** enable you to specify how garbage collection is performed by the runtime, and how the binding to assemblies works. You can also specify the version policy and the code base with these settings. You take a more detailed look into the runtime settings later in this chapter.
- **WCF settings** are used to configure applications using WCF. You deal with these configurations in Chapter 42, "Windows Communication Foundation."
- **Security settings** are introduced in Chapter 20, " Security," and configuration for cryptography and permissions is done there.

These settings can be provided in three types of configuration files:

- **Application configuration files** include specific settings for an application, such as binding information to assemblies, configuration for remote objects, and so on. Such a configuration file is placed into the same directory as the executable; it has the same name as the executable with a `.config` extension appended. ASP.NET configuration files are named `web.config`.
- **Machine configuration files** are used for system-wide configurations. You can also specify assembly binding and remoting configurations here. During a binding process, the machine configuration file is consulted before the application configuration file. The application configuration can override settings from the machine configuration. The application configuration file should be the preferred place for application-specific settings so that the machine configuration file stays smaller and more manageable. A machine configuration file is located in `%runtime_install_path%\config\Machine.config`.
- **Publisher policy files** can be used by a component creator to specify that a shared assembly is compatible with older versions. If a new assembly version just fixes a bug of a shared component, it is not necessary to put application configuration files in every application directory that uses this component; the publisher can mark it as compatible by adding a publisher policy file instead. In case the component doesn't work with all applications, it is possible to override the publisher policy setting in an application configuration file. In contrast to the other configuration files, publisher policy files are stored in the GAC.

How are these configuration files used? How a client finds an assembly (also called *binding*) depends on whether the assembly is private or shared. Private assemblies must be in the directory of the application or in a subdirectory thereof. A process called *probing* is used to find such an assembly. If the assembly doesn't have a strong name, the version number is not used with probing.

Shared assemblies can be installed in the GAC or placed in a directory, on a network share, or on a Web site. You specify such a directory with the configuration of the `codeBase` shortly. The public key, version, and culture are all important aspects when binding to a shared assembly. The reference of the required assembly is recorded in the manifest of the client assembly, including the name, the version, and the public key token. All configuration files are checked to apply the correct version policy. The GAC and code bases specified in the configuration files are checked, followed by the application directories, and probing rules are then applied.

Configuring Directories for Assembly Searches

You've already seen how to install a shared assembly to the GAC. Instead of installing a shared assembly to the GAC, you can configure a specific shared directory by using configuration files. This feature can be used if you want to make the shared components available on a server. Another possible scenario arises if you want to share an assembly between your applications, but you don't want to make it publicly available in the GAC, so you put it into a shared directory instead.

There are two ways to find the correct directory for an assembly: the `codeBase` element in an XML configuration file, or through probing. The `codeBase` configuration is available only for shared assemblies, and probing is done for private assemblies.

<codeBase>

The `<codeBase>` can also be configured using the .NET Configuration utility. Code bases can be configured by selecting the properties of the configured application, `SimpleShared`, inside the Configured Assemblies in the Applications tree. Similarly to the Binding Policy, you can configure lists of versions with the Codebases tab. Figure 17-17 shows that the version 1.1 should be loaded from the Web server `http://www.christiannagel.com/WroxUtils`.

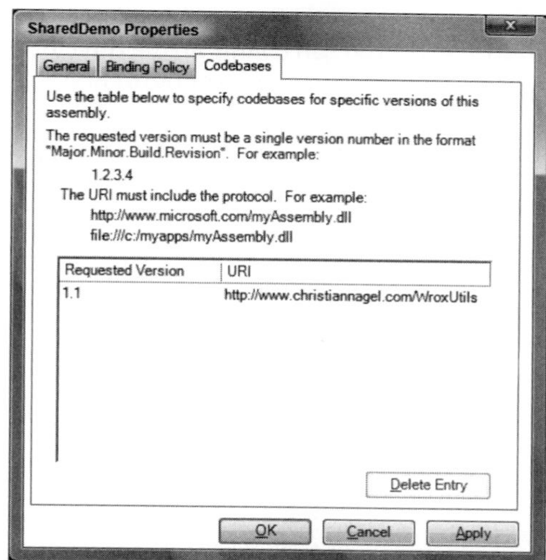

Figure 17-17

The .NET Configuration utility creates this application configuration file:

```
<?xml version="1.0"?>
<configuration>
  <runtime>
    <assemblyBinding xmlns="urn:schemas-microsoft-com:asm.v1">
      <dependentAssembly xmlns="">
        <assemblyIdentity name="SimpleShared"
                          publicKeyToken="7d886a6f7b9f0292" />
        <codeBase version="1.1"
              href="http://www.christiannagel.com/WroxUtils" />
```

(continued)

(continued)

```
        </dependentAssembly>
      </assemblyBinding>
    </runtime>
  </configuration>
```

The `<codeBase>` element has the attributes `version` and `href`. With `version`, the original referenced version of the assembly must be specified. With `href`, you can define the directory from where the assembly should be loaded. In the example, a path using the HTTP protocol is used. A directory on a local system or a share is specified using `href="file:C:/WroxUtils"`.

> *Using that assembly loaded from the network causes a* `System.Security.Permissions` *exception to occur. You must configure the required permissions for assemblies loaded from the network. In Chapter 20, "Security," you learn how to configure security for assemblies.*

<probing>

When the `<codeBase>` is not configured and the assembly is not stored in the GAC, the runtime tries to find an assembly through probing. The .NET runtime tries to find assemblies with either a `.dll` or an `.exe` file extension in the application directory, or in one of its subdirectories, that has the same name as the assembly searched for. If the assembly is not found here, the search continues. You can configure search directories with the `<probing>` element in the `<runtime>` section of application configuration files. This XML configuration can also be done easily by selecting the properties of the application with the .NET Framework Configuration tool. You can configure the directories where the probing should occur by using the search path in the .NET Framework configuration (see Figure 17-18).

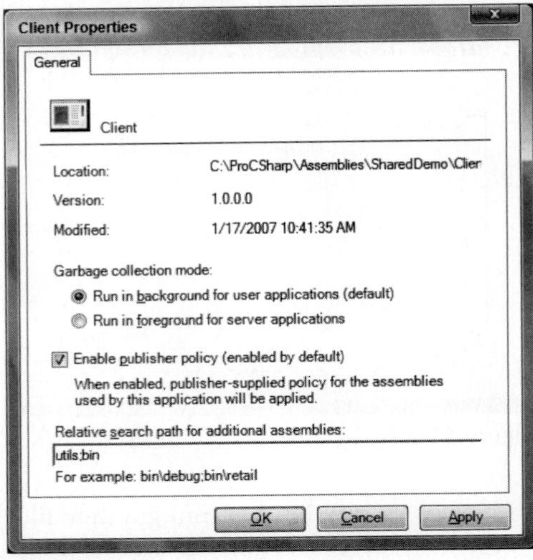

Figure 17-18

The XML file produced has these entries:

```
<?xml version="1.0"?>
<configuration>
   <runtime>
      <gcConcurrent enabled="true" />
      <assemblyBinding xmlns="urn:schemas-microsoft-com:asm.v1">
```

```
            <probing privatePath="bin;utils;" xmlns="" />
        </assemblyBinding>
    </runtime>
</configuration>
```

The <probing> element has just a single required attribute: privatePath. This application configuration file tells the runtime that assemblies should be searched for in the base directory of the application, followed by the bin and the util directory. Both directories are subdirectories of the application base directory. It's not possible to reference a private assembly outside the application base directory or a subdirectory thereof. An assembly outside of the application base directory must have a shared name and can be referenced using the <codeBase> element, as you saw earlier.

Versioning

For private assemblies, versioning is not important because the referenced assemblies are copied with the client. The client uses the assembly it has in its private directories.

This is, however, different for shared assemblies. This section looks at the traditional problems that can occur with sharing. With shared components, more than one client application can use the same component. The new version can break existing clients when updating a shared component with a newer version. You can't stop shipping new versions because new features are requested and introduced with new versions of existing components. You can try to program carefully to be backward compatible, but that's not always possible.

A solution to this dilemma could be an architecture that allows installation of different versions of shared components, with clients using the version that they referenced during the build process. This solves a lot of problems but not all of them. What happens if you detect a bug in a component that's referenced from the client? You would like to update this component and make sure that the client uses the new version instead of the version that was referenced during the build process.

Therefore, depending on the type in the fix of the new version, you sometimes want to use a newer version, and you also want to use the older referenced version as well. The .NET architecture enables both scenarios.

In .NET, the original referenced assembly is used by default. You can redirect the reference to a different version using configuration files. Versioning plays a key role in the binding architecture — how the client gets the right assembly where the components live.

Version Numbers

Assemblies have a four-part version number, for example, 1.1.400.3300. The parts are <Major>.<Minor>.<Build>.<Revision>.

How these numbers are used depends on your application configuration.

> **A good policy is to change the major or minor number on changes incompatible with the previous version, but just the build or revision number with compatible changes. This way, it can be assumed that redirecting an assembly to a new version where just the build and revision changed is safe.**

With Visual Studio 2008, you can define the version number of the assembly with the assembly information in the project settings. The project settings write the assembly attribute [AssemblyVersion] to the file AssemblyInfo.cs:

```
[assembly: AssemblyVersion("1.0.0.0")]
```

Instead of defining all four version numbers you can also place an asterisk in the third or fourth place:

```
[assembly: AssemblyVersion("1.0.*")]
```

With this setting, the first two numbers specify the major and minor version, and the asterisk (*) means that the build and revision numbers are auto-generated. The build number is the number of days since January 1, 2000, and the revision is the number of seconds since midnight divided by two. Though the automatic versioning might help during development time, before shipping it is a good practice to define a specific version number.

This version is stored in the `.assembly` section of the manifest.

Referencing the assembly in the client application stores the version of the referenced assembly in the manifest of the client application.

Getting the Version Programmatically

To make it possible to check the version of the assembly that is used from the client application, add the method `GetAssemblyFullName()` to the `SharedDemo` class created earlier to return the strong name of the assembly. For easy use of the `Assembly` class, you have to import the `System.Reflection` namespace:

```
public string GetAssemblyFullName()
{
   return Assembly.GetExecutingAssembly().FullName;
}
```

The `FullName` property of the `Assembly` class holds the name of the class, the version, the locality, and the public key token, as you see in the following output, when calling `GetAssemblyFullName()` in your client application.

In the client application, just add a call to `GetAssemblyFullName()` in the `Main()` method after creating the shared component:

```
static void Main()
{
   SharedDemo quotes = new
       SharedDemo(@"C:\ProCSharp\Assemblies\Quotes.txt");
   Console.WriteLine(quotes.GetAssemblyFullName());
```

Be sure to register the new version of the shared assembly `SharedDemo` again in the GAC using `gacutil`. If the referenced version cannot be found, you will get a `System.IO.FileLoadException`, because the binding to the correct assembly failed.

With a successful run, you can see the full name of the referenced assembly:

```
SharedDemo, Version=1.0.0.0, Culture=neutral, PublicKeyToken=7d886a6f7b9f0292
Press any key to continue ...
```

This client program can now be used to test different configurations of this shared component.

Application Configuration Files

With a configuration file, you can specify that the binding should happen to a different version of a shared assembly. Assume that you create a new version of the shared assembly `SharedDemo` with major and minor versions 1.1. Maybe you don't want to rebuild the client but just want the new version of the assembly to be used with the existing client instead. This is useful in cases where either a bug is fixed with the shared assembly or you just want to get rid of the old version because the new version is compatible.

Figure 17-19 shows the Global Assembly Cache Viewer, where the versions 1.0.0.0 and 1.0.3300.0 are installed for the `SharedDemo` assembly.

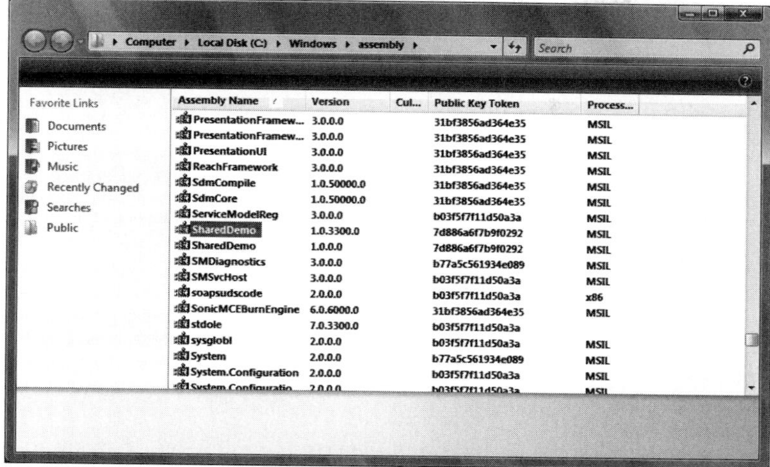

Figure 17-19

Figure 17-20 shows the manifest of the client application where the client references version 1.0.0.0 of the assembly `SharedDemo`.

```
MANIFEST
Find  Find Next
// Metadata version: v2.0.50727
.assembly extern mscorlib
{
  .publickeytoken = (B7 7A 5C 56 19 34 E0 89 )                         //
  .ver 2:0:0:0
}
.assembly extern SharedDemo
{
  .publickeytoken = (7D 88 6A 6F 7B 9F 02 92 )                         //
  .ver 1:0:0:0
}
.assembly Client
{
  .custom instance void [mscorlib]System.Reflection.AssemblyFileVersionAtt
  .custom instance void [mscorlib]System.Runtime.InteropServices.GuidAttri
```

Figure 17-20

Now an application configuration file is needed. It is not necessary to work directly with XML; the .NET Framework Configuration tool can create application and machine configuration files. Figure 17-21 shows the .NET Framework Configuration tool, which is an MMC Snap-in. You can start this tool from Administrative Tools in the Control Panel.

This tool is shipped with Framework SDK and not with the .NET runtime, so don't expect this tool to be available to system administrators.

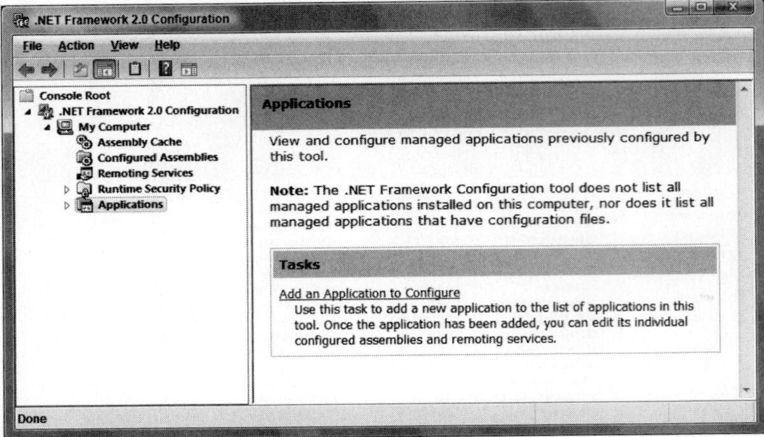

Figure 17-21

When you select Applications on the left side, and then select Action ➪ Add, you can choose a .NET application to configure. If the `Client.exe` application does not show up with the list, click the Other . . . button and browse to the executable. Select the application `Client.exe` to create an application configuration file for this application. After adding the client application to the .NET Configuration utility, the assembly dependencies can be listed, as shown in Figure 17-22.

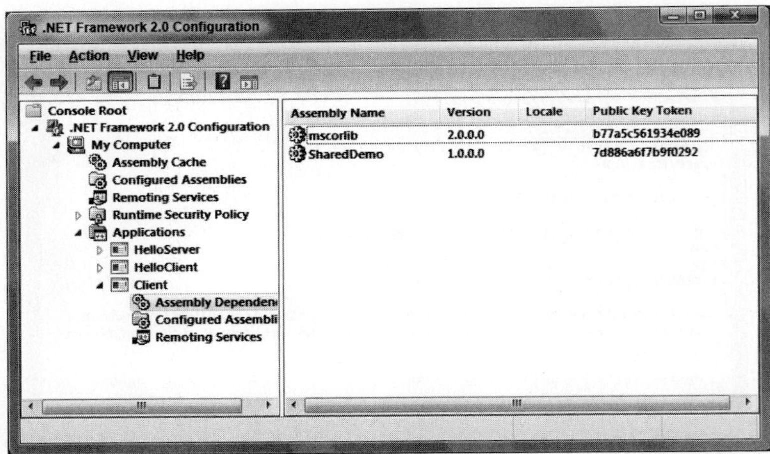

Figure 17-22

Select Configured Assemblies in the tree view and the menu Action ➪ Add . . . to configure the dependency of the assembly `SharedDemo` from the dependency list. Select the Binding Policy tab to define the version that should be used as shown in Figure 17-23.

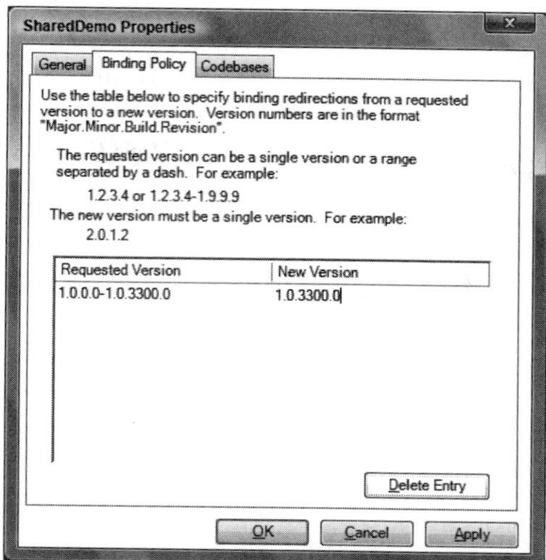

Figure 17-23

For the requested version, specify the version referenced in the manifest of the client assembly. `newVersion` specifies the new version of the shared assembly. In Figure 17-23, it is specified that the version 1.0.3300.0 should be used instead of any version in the range of 1.0.0.0 to 1.0.3300.0.

Now you can find the application configuration file `Client.exe.config` in the directory of the `Client.exe` application that includes this XML code:

```
<?xml version="1.0"?>
<configuration>
   <runtime>
      <assemblyBinding xmlns="urn:schemas-microsoft-com:asm.v1">
         <dependentAssembly>
            <assemblyIdentity name="SharedDemo"
                  publicKeyToken="7d886a6f7b9f0292" />
            <publisherPolicy apply="yes" />
            <bindingRedirect oldVersion="1.0.0.0-1.0.3300.0"
                  newVersion="1.0.3300.0" />
         </dependentAssembly>
      </assemblyBinding>
   </runtime>
</configuration>
```

Runtime settings can be configured with the `<runtime>` element. The subelement of `<runtime>` is `<assemblyBinding>`, which in turn has a subelement `<dependentAssembly>`. `<dependentAssembly>` has a required subelement `<assemblyIdentity>`. You specify the name of the referenced assembly with `<assemblyIdentity>`. `name` is the only mandatory attribute for `<assemblyIdentity>`. The optional attributes are `publicKeyToken` and `culture`. The other subelement of `<dependentAssembly>` that's needed for version redirection is `<bindingRedirect>`. The old and the new versions of the dependent assembly are specified with this element.

When you start the client with this configuration file, you will get the new version of the referenced shared assembly.

Publisher Policy Files

Using assemblies shared from the GAC allows you to use publisher policies to override versioning issues. Assume that you have an assembly used by some applications. What can be done if a critical bug is found in the shared assembly? You have seen that it is not necessary to rebuild all the applications that use this shared assembly, because you can use configuration files to redirect to the new version of this shared assembly. Maybe you don't know all the applications that use this shared assembly, but you want to get the bug fix to all of them. In that case, you can create publisher policy files to redirect all applications to the new version of the shared assembly.

> **Publisher policy files apply only to shared assemblies installed in the GAC.**

To set up publisher policies, you have to do the following:

- Create a publisher policy file
- Create a publisher policy assembly
- Add the publisher policy assembly to the GAC

Create a Publisher Policy File

A publisher policy file is an XML file that redirects an existing version or version range to a new version. The syntax used here is the same as for application configuration files, so you can use the same file you created earlier to redirect the old versions 1.0.0.0 through 1.0.3300.0 to the new version 1.0.3300.0.

Rename the previously created file to `mypolicy.config` to use it as a publisher policy file and remove the element `<publisherPolicy>`:

```
<?xml version="1.0"?>
<configuration>
   <runtime>
      <assemblyBinding xmlns="urn:schemas-microsoft-com:asm.v1">
         <dependentAssembly>
            <assemblyIdentity name="SharedDemo"
                                    publicKeyToken="7d886a6f7b9f0292" />
            <bindingRedirect oldVersion="1.0.0.0-1.0.3300.0"
                                    newVersion="1.0.3300.0" />
         </dependentAssembly>
      </assemblyBinding>
   </runtime>
</configuration>
```

Create a Publisher Policy Assembly

To associate the publisher policy file with the shared assembly, it is necessary to create a publisher policy assembly, and to put it into the GAC. The tool that can be used to create such files is the assembly linker `al`. The option `/linkresource` adds the publisher policy file to the generated assembly. The name of the generated assembly must start with policy, followed by the major and minor version number of the assembly that should be redirected, and the file name of the shared assembly. In this case the publisher policy assembly must be named `policy.1.0.SharedDemo.dll` to redirect the assemblies `SharedDemo` with the major version 1 and minor version 0. The key that must be added to this publisher key with the option `/keyfile` is the same key that was used to sign the shared assembly `SharedDemo` to guarantee that the version redirection is from the same publisher.

```
al /linkresource:mypolicy.config /out:policy.1.0.SharedDemo.dll
/keyfile:..\..\mykey.snk
```

Add the Publisher Policy Assembly to the GAC

The publisher policy assembly can now be added to the GAC with the utility `gacutil`:

```
gacutil -i policy.1.0.SharedDemo.dll
```

Now remove the application configuration file that was placed in the directory of the client application and start the client application. Although the client assembly references 1.0.0.0, you use the new version 1.0.3300.0 of the shared assembly because of the publisher policy.

Overriding Publisher Policies

With a publisher policy, the publisher of the shared assembly guarantees that a new version of the assembly is compatible with the old version. As you know, from changes of traditional DLLs, such guarantees don't always hold. Maybe all except one application is working with the new shared assembly. To fix the one application that has a problem with the new release, the publisher policy can be overridden by using an application configuration file.

With the .NET Framework Configuration tool you can override the publisher policy by deselecting the Enable Publisher Policy check box, as shown in Figure 17-24.

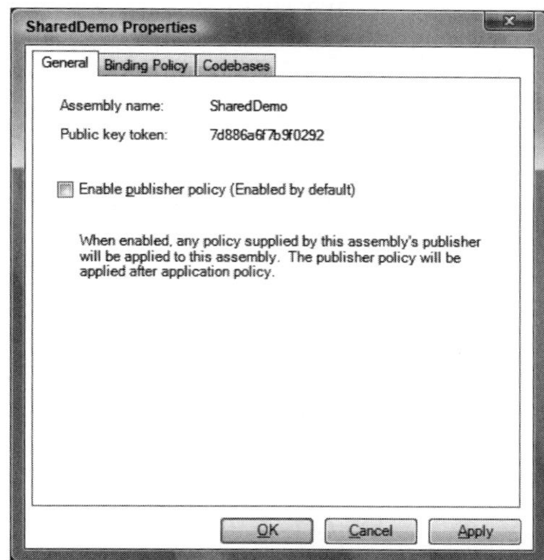

Figure 17-24

Disabling the publisher policy with the .NET Framework Configuration results in a configuration file with the XML element `<publisherPolicy>` and the attribute `apply="no"`.

```
<?xml version="1.0"?>
<configuration>
  <runtime>
    <assemblyBinding xmlns="urn:schemas-microsoft-com:asm.v1">
      <dependentAssembly>
        <assemblyIdentity name="SharedDemo"
              publicKeyToken="7d886a6f7b9f0292" />
```

(continued)

(continued)

```
            <publisherPolicy apply="no" />
         </dependentAssembly>
      </assemblyBinding>
   </runtime>
</configuration>
```

By disabling the publisher policy, you can configure different version redirection in the application configuration file.

Runtime Version

Installing and using multiple versions is not only possible with assemblies but also with the .NET runtime (CLR). The versions 1.0, 1.1, and 2.0 (and later versions) of the CLR can be installed on the same operating system side by side. Visual Studio 2008 targets applications running on CLR 2.0 with .NET 2.0, 3.0, and 3.5. With CLR 2.0 the assembly file format changed, so it is not possible to run CLR 2.0 applications with CLR 1.1.

If the application is built with CLR 1.1, it is possible to target systems that have only the CLR 1.0 runtime installed. The same can be expected about future minor releases in that they can target CLR 2.0 runtime versions.

An application that was built using CLR 1.0 may run without changes on CLR 1.1. If an operating system has both versions of the runtime installed, the application will use the version with which it was built. However, if only version 1.1 is installed with the operating system, and the application was built with version 1.0, it tries to run with the newer version. There's a good chance the application runs without problems. The registry key `HKEY_LOCAL_MACHINE\Software\Microsoft\.NETFramework\policy` lists the ranges of the versions that will be used for a specific runtime.

If an application was built using .NET 1.1, it may run without changes on .NET 1.0, in case no classes or methods are used that are available only with .NET 1.1. Here an application configuration file is needed to make this possible.

In an application configuration file, it's not only possible to redirect versions of referenced assemblies; you can also define the required version of the runtime. Different .NET runtime versions can be installed on a single machine. You can specify the version that's required for the application in an application configuration file. The element `<supportedVersion>` marks the runtime versions that are supported by the application:

```
<?xml version="1.0"?>
<configuration>
   <startup>
      <supportedRuntime version="v1.1.4322" />
      <supportedRuntime version="v1.0.3512" />
   </startup>
</configuration>
```

There is one major point in case you still have .NET 1.0 applications that should run on .NET 1.1 runtime versions. The element `<supportedVersion>` was new with .NET 1.1. .NET 1.0 used the element `<requiredRuntime>` to specify the needed runtime. So for .NET 1.0 applications, both configurations must be done as shown here:

```
<?xml version="1.0"?>
<configuration>
   <startup>
```

```
        <supportedRuntime version="v1.1.4322"/>
        <supportedRuntime version="v1.0.3705"/>
        <requiredRuntime version="v1.0.3512" safeMode="true" />
    </startup>
</configuration>
```

`<requiredRuntime>` does not overrule the configuration for `<supportedRuntime>` as it may look like, because `<requiredRuntime>` is used only with .NET 1.0, whereas `<supportedRuntime>` is used by .NET 1.1 and later versions.

> **You cannot configure a supported runtime for a library. The library always uses the runtime selected by the application process.**

Summary

Assemblies are the new installation unit for the .NET platform. Microsoft learned from problems with previous architectures and did a complete redesign to avoid the old problems. This chapter discussed the features of assemblies: they are self-describing, and no type library and registry information is needed. Version dependencies are exactly recorded so that with assemblies, the DLL hell with old DLLs no longer exists. Because of these features, both development and deployment and administration have become a lot easier.

You learned the differences between private and shared assemblies and saw how shared assemblies can be created. With private assemblies, you don't have to pay attention to uniqueness and versioning issues because these assemblies are copied and only used by a single application. Sharing assemblies requires you to use a key for uniqueness and to define the version. You looked at the GAC, which can be used as an intelligent store for shared assemblies.

You can have faster application startups by using the native image generator. With this the JIT compiler does not need to run because the native code is created during installation time.

You looked at overriding versioning issues to use a version of an assembly different from the one that was used during development; this is done through publisher policies and application configuration files. Finally, you learned how probing works with private assemblies.

The chapter also discussed loading assemblies dynamically and creating assemblies during runtime. If you want to get more information on this, you should read Chapter 36 about the Add-In model of .NET 3.5.

18

Tracing and Events

Chapter 14 covered errors and exception handling. Besides handling exceptional code, it might be really interesting to get some live information about your running application to find the reason for some issues that application might have during production, or to monitor resources needed to early adapt to higher user loads. This is where the namespace `System.Diagnostics` comes into play.

The application doesn't throw exceptions, but sometimes it doesn't behave as expected. The application might be running well on most systems but might have a problem on a few. On the live system, you change the log behavior by changing a configuration value and get detailed live information about what's going on in the application. This can be done with *tracing*.

If there are problems with applications, the system administrator needs to be informed. With the Event Viewer, the system administrator both interactively monitors problems with applications and gets informed about specific events that happen by adding subscriptions. The *event-logging* mechanism allows you to write information about the application.

To analyze resources needed from applications, monitor applications with specified time intervals, and plan for a different application distribution or extending of system resources, the system administrator uses the performance monitor. You can write live data of your application using *performance counts*.

This chapter explains these three facilities and demonstrates how you can use them from your applications:

- Tracing
- Event logging
- Performance monitoring

Tracing

With tracing you can see messages from the running application. To get some information about a running application, you can start the application in the debugger. During debugging, you can walk through the application step by step and set breakpoints at specific lines and when you reach specific conditions. The problem with debugging is that a released program can behave differently. For example, while the program is stopping at a breakpoint, other threads of the application are suspended as well. Also, with a release build, the compiler-generated output is optimized and thus different effects can occur. There is a need to have information from a release build as well. Trace messages are written both with debug and release code.

A scenario showing how tracing helps is described here. After an application is deployed, it runs on one system without problems, while on another system intermediate problems occur. Turning on verbose tracing on the system with the problems gives you detailed information about what's happening inside the application. The system that is running without problems has tracing configured just for error messages redirected to the Windows event log system. Critical errors are seen by the system administrator. The overhead of tracing is very small, because you configure a trace level only when needed.

The tracing architecture has four major parts:

- The *source* is the originator of the trace information. You use the source to send trace messages.
- The *switch* defines the level of information to log. For example, you can request just error information or detailed verbose information.
- Trace *listeners* define where the trace messages should be written.
- Listeners can have *filters* attached. The filter defines what trace messages should be written by the listener. This way, you can have different listeners for the same source that write different levels of information.

Figure 18-1 shows the major classes for tracing and how they are connected in a Visual Studio class diagram. The `TraceSource` uses a switch to define what information to log. The `TraceSource` has a `TraceListenerCollection` associated where trace messages are forwarded to. The collection consists of `TraceListener` objects, and every listener has a `TraceFilter` connected.

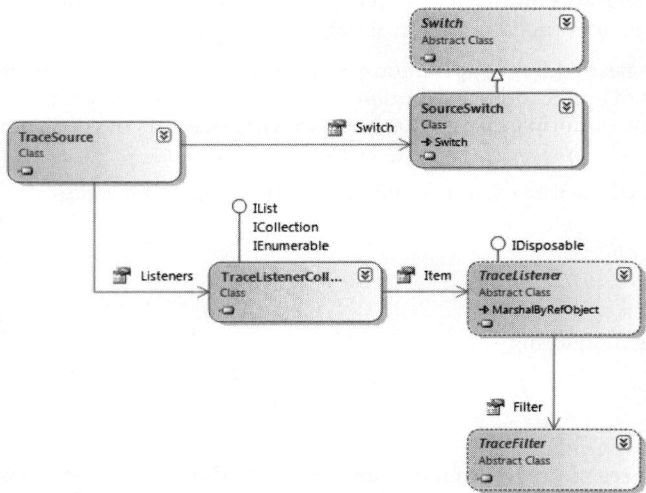

Figure 18-1

Trace Sources

You can write trace messages with the `TraceSource` class. Tracing requires the `Trace` flag of the compiler settings. With a Visual Studio project, the `Trace` flag is set by default with debug and release builds, but you can change it through the `Build` properties of the project.

The `TraceSource` *class is more difficult to use compared to the* `Trace` *class writing trace messages, but it provides more options.*

To write trace messages, you need to create a new `TraceSource` instance. In the constructor, the name of the trace source is defined. The method `TraceInformation()` writes an information message to the trace output. Instead of just writing informational messages, the `TraceEvent()` method requires an enumeration value of type `TraceEventType` to define the type of the trace message. `TraceEventType.Error` specifies the message as an error message. You can define it with a trace switch to see only error messages. The second argument of the `TraceEvent()` method requires an identifier. The ID can be used within the application itself. For example, you can use `id 1` for entering a method and `id 2` for exiting a method. The method `TraceEvent()` is overloaded, so the `TraceEventType` and the ID are the only required parameters. Using the third parameter of an overloaded method, you can pass the message written to the trace. `TraceEvent()` also supports passing a format string with any number of parameters in the same way as `Console.WriteLine()`. `TraceInformation()` does nothing more than invoke `TraceEvent()` with an identifier of 0. `TraceInformation()` is just a simplified version of `TraceEvent()`. With the `TraceData()` method, you can pass any object, for example an exception instance, instead of a message. To make sure that data is written by the listeners and does not stay in memory, you need to do a `Flush()`. If the source is no longer needed, you can invoke the `Close()` method that closes all listeners associated with the trace source. `Close()` does a `Flush()` as well.

```
TraceSource source1 = new TraceSource("Wrox.ProCSharp.Tracing");
source1.TraceInformation("Info message");
source1.TraceEvent(TraceEventType.Error, 3, "Error message");
source1.TraceData(TraceEventType.Information, 2,
                  new int[] { 1, 2, 3 });
source1.Flush();
source1.Close();
```

You can use different trace sources within your application. It makes sense to define different sources for different libraries, so that you can turn on different trace levels for different parts of your application. To use a trace source you need to know its name. A commonly used name for the trace source is the same name as the namespace.

The `TraceEventType` enumeration that is passed as an argument to the `TraceEvent()` method defines the following levels to specify the severity of the problem: `Verbose`, `Information`, `Warning`, `Error`, and `Critical`. `Critical` defines a fatal error or application crash; `Error` defines a recoverable error. Trace messages at the `Verbose` level give you detailed debugging information. `TraceEventType` also defines action levels `Start`, `Stop`, `Suspend`, and `Resume`. These levels define timely events inside a logical operation.

The code, as it is written now, does not display any trace message because the switch associated with the trace source is turned off.

Trace Switches

To enable or disable trace messages, you can configure a trace switch. Trace switches are classes that are derived from the abstract base class `Switch`. Derived classes are `BooleanSwitch`, `TraceSwitch`, and `SourceSwitch`. The class `BooleanSwitch` can be turned on and off, and the other two classes provide a range level that is defined by the `TraceLevel` enumeration. To configure trace switches, you must know the values associated with the `TraceLevel` enumeration. `TraceLevel` defines the values `Off`, `Error`, `Warning`, `Info`, and `Verbose`.

You can associate a trace switch programmatically by setting the `Switch` property of the `TraceSource`. Here the switch associated is of type `SourceSwitch`, has the name `MySwitch`, and has the level `Verbose`:

```
TraceSource source1 = new TraceSource("Wrox.ProCSharp.Tracing");
source1.Switch = new SourceSwitch("MySwitch", "Verbose");
```

Setting the level to `Verbose` means that all trace messages should be written. If you set the value to `Error`, only error messages should show up. Setting the value to `Information` means that error, warning, and info messages are shown. Writing the trace messages once more, you can see the messages while running the debugger in the Output window.

Usually, you would want to change the switch level not by recompiling the application, but instead by changing the configuration. The trace source can be configured in the application configuration file. Tracing is configured within the `<system.diagnostics>` element. The trace source is defined with the `<source>` element as a child element of `<sources>`. The name of the source in the configuration file must exactly match the name of the source in the program code. Here, the trace source has a switch of type `System.Diagnostics.SourceSwitch` associated with the name `MySourceSwitch`. The switch itself is defined within the `<switches>` section, and the level of the switch is set to `verbose`.

```
<?xml version="1.0" encoding="utf-8" ?>
<configuration>
  <system.diagnostics>
    <sources>
      <source name="Wrox.ProCSharp.Tracing" switchName="MySourceSwitch"
          switchType="System.Diagnostics.SourceSwitch" />
    </sources>
    <switches>
      <add name="MySourceSwitch" value="Verbose"/>
    </switches>
  </system.diagnostics>
</configuration>
```

Now, you can change the trace level just by changing the configuration file without the need to recompile the code. After the configuration file is changed, you must restart the application.

Currently, trace messages are written to just the Output window of Visual Studio while you are running it in a debug session. Adding trace listeners changes this.

Trace Listeners

By default, trace information is written to the Output window of the Visual Studio debugger. Just by changing the application configuration, you can redirect the trace output to different locations.

Where tracing should be written to is defined by trace listeners. A trace listener is derived from the abstract base class `TraceListener`.

Trace listeners defined by the .NET Framework are described in the following table.

Trace Listener	Description
`DefaultTraceListener`	A default trace listener is automatically added to the listeners collection of the `Trace` class. Default output goes to the attached debugger. In Visual Studio, this is shown in the Output window during a debugging session.
`EventLogTraceListener`	The `EventLogTraceListener` writes trace information to the event log. With the constructor of the `EventLogTraceListener`, you can specify an event log source or an object of type `EventLog`. Event logging is described later in this chapter.
`TextWriterTraceListener`	With the `TextWriterTraceListener` trace, output can be written to a file, a `TextWriter`, or a `Stream`. See Chapter 25, "Manipulating Files and the Registry," for file manipulation information. `Text WriterTraceListener` is the base class of `ConsoleTraceListener`, `DelimitedListTraceListener`, and `XmlWriterTraceListener`.
`ConsoleTraceListener`	`ConsoleTraceListener` writes trace messages to the console.
`DelimitedListTraceListener`	`DelimitedListTraceListener` writes trace messages to a delimited file. With trace output options, you can define a lot of separate tracing information such as process ID, time, and the like, which can be read more easily with a delimited file.
`XmlWriterTraceListener`	Instead of using a delimited file, you can redirect the trace information to an XML file with the `XmlWriterTraceListener`.
`IisTraceListener`	The `IisTraceListener` was added in .NET 3.0.
`WebPageTraceListener`	ASP.NET has another tracing option to get ASP.NET trace information about Web pages in a dynamically created output file `trace.axd`. If you configure the `WebPageTraceListener`, then `System.Diagnostics` trace information goes into `trace.axd` as well.

.NET Framework delivers many listeners to which trace information can be written. In case the listeners don't fulfill your requirements, you can create a custom listener by deriving a class from the base class `TraceListener`. With a custom listener, you can, for example, write trace information to a Web service, write messages to your mobile phone . . . I guess it's not that interesting to receive hundreds of messages to your phone in your spare time. And with verbose tracing this can become really expensive.

You can configure a trace listener programmatically by creating a listener object and assigning it to the `Listeners` property of the `TraceSource` class. However, usually it is more interesting to just change a configuration to define a different listener.

You can configure listeners as child elements of the `<source>` element. With the listener, you define the type of the listener class and use `initializeData` to specify where the output of the listener should go. The configuration here defines the `XmlWriterTraceListener` to write to the file `demotrace.xml` and the `DelimitedListTraceListener` to write to the file `demotrace.txt`:

```
<?xml version="1.0" encoding="utf-8" ?>
<configuration>
  <system.diagnostics>
    <sources>
      <source name="Wrox.ProCSharp.Tracing" switchName="MySourceSwitch"
          switchType="System.Diagnostics.SourceSwitch">
        <listeners>
          <add name="xmlListener"
              type="System.Diagnostics.XmlWriterTraceListener"
              traceOutputOptions="None"
              initializeData="c:/logs/demotrace.xml" />

          <add name="delimitedListener" delimiter=":"
              type="System.Diagnostics.DelimitedListTraceListener"
              traceOutputOptions="DateTime, ProcessId"
              initializeData="c:/logs/demotrace.txt" />
        </listeners>
      </source>
    </sources>
    <switches>
      <add name="MySourceSwitch" value="Verbose"/>
    </switches>
  </system.diagnostics>
</configuration>
```

You might get a warning from the XML schema regarding the delimiter attribute declaration. You can ignore it.

With the listener, you can also specify what additional information should be written to the trace log. This information is defined with the `traceOutputOptions` XML attribute and is defined by the `TraceOptions` enumeration. The enumeration defines `Callstack`, `DateTime`, `LogicalOperationStack`, `ProcessId`, `ThreadId`, and `None`. The information needed can be added with comma separation to the `traceOutputOptions` XML attribute, as shown with the delimited trace listener.

The delimited file output from the `DelimitedListTraceListener`, including the process ID and date/time, is shown here:

```
"Wrox.ProCSharp.Tracing":Information:0:"Info message"::4188:""::
"2007-01-23T12:38:31.3750000Z"::
"Wrox.ProCSharp.Tracing":Error:3:"Error message"::4188:""::
"2007-01-23T12:38:31.3810000Z"::
```

The XML output from the `XmlWriterTraceListener` always contains the name of the computer, the process ID, the thread ID, the message, the time created, the source, and the activity ID. Other fields, such as the call stack, logical operation stack, and timestamp, depend on the trace output options.

You can use the `XmlDocument` *and* `XPathNavigator` *classes to analyze the content from the XML file. These classes are covered in Chapter 28, "Manipulating XML."*

If a listener should be used by multiple trace sources, you can add the listener configuration to the element `<sharedListeners>`, which is independent of the trace source. The name of the listener that is configured with a shared listener must be referenced from the listeners of the trace source:

```
<?xml version="1.0" encoding="utf-8" ?>
<configuration>
  <system.diagnostics>
    <sources>
      <source name="Wrox.ProCSharp.Tracing" switchName="MySourceSwitch"
```

```
            switchType="System.Diagnostics.SourceSwitch">
          <listeners>
            <add name="xmlListener"
                type="System.Diagnostics.XmlWriterTraceListener"
                traceOutputOptions="None"
                initializeData="c:/logs/demotrace.xml" />
            <add name="delimitedListener" />
          </listeners>
        </source>
      </sources>
      <sharedListeners>
  <add name="delimitedListener" delimiter=":"
            type="System.Diagnostics.DelimitedListTraceListener"
            traceOutputOptions="DateTime, ProcessId"
            initializeData="c:/logs/demotrace.txt" />
      </sharedListeners>
      <switches>
        <add name="MySourceSwitch" value="Verbose"/>
      </switches>
    </system.diagnostics>
  </configuration>
```

Filters

Every listener has a `Filter` property that defines whether the listener should write the trace message. For example, multiple listeners can be used with the same trace source. One of the listeners writes verbose messages to a log file, and another listener writes error messages to the event log. Before a listener writes a trace message, it invokes the `ShouldTrace()` method of the associated filter object to decide if the trace message should be written.

A filter is a class that is derived from the abstract base class `TraceFilter`. .NET 3.0 offers two filter implementations: `SourceFilter` and `EventTypeFilter`. With the source filter, you can specify that trace messages are to be written only from specific sources. The event type filter is an extension to the switch functionality. With a switch, it is possible to define, according to the trace severity level, if the event source should forward the trace message to the listeners. If the trace message is forwarded, the listener now can use the filter to decide if the message should be written.

The changed configuration now defines that the delimited listener should write trace messages only if the severity level is of type warning or higher, because of the defined `EventTypeFilter`. The XML listener specifies a `SourceFilter` and accepts trace messages only from the source `Wrox.ProCSharp.Tracing`. In case you have a large number of sources defined to write trace messages to the same listener, you can change the configuration for the listener to concentrate on trace messages from a specific source.

```
<?xml version="1.0" encoding="utf-8" ?>
<configuration>
  <system.diagnostics>
    <sources>
      <source name="Wrox.ProCSharp.Tracing" switchName="MySourceSwitch"
          switchType="System.Diagnostics.SourceSwitch">
        <listeners>
          <add name="xmlListener" />
          <add name="delimitedListener" />
        </listeners>
      </source>
```

(continued)

(continued)

```
        </sources>
        <sharedListeners>
              <add name="delimitedListener" delimiter=":"
                  type="System.Diagnostics.DelimitedListTraceListener"
                  traceOutputOptions="DateTime, ProcessId"
                  initializeData="c:/logs/demotrace.txt">
                <filter type="System.Diagnostics.EventTypeFilter"
                    initializeData="Warning" />
              </add>
              <add name="xmlListener"
                  type="System.Diagnostics.XmlWriterTraceListener"
                  traceOutputOptions="None"
                  initializeData="c:/logs/demotrace.xml">
                <filter type="System.Diagnostics.SourceFilter"
                    initializeData="Wrox.ProCSharp.Tracing" />
              </add>
        </sharedListeners>
        <switches>
          <add name="MySourceSwitch" value="Verbose"/>
        </switches>
      </system.diagnostics>
    </configuration>
```

The tracing architecture can be extended. Just as you can write a custom listener derived from the base class `TraceListener`, you can also create a custom filter derived from `TraceFilter`. With that capability, you can create a filter that specifies to write trace messages, for example, depending on the time, depending on an exception that occurred lately, or depending on the weather.

Asserts

Another feature that belongs to tracing are asserts. Asserts are critical problems within the program path. With asserts, a message is displayed with the error, and you can abort or continue the application. Asserts are very helpful when you write a library that is used by another developer.

With the `Foo()` method, `Trace.Assert()` examines parameter `o` to see if it is not null. If the condition is `false`, the error message as shown in Figure 18-2 is issued. If the condition is `true`, the program

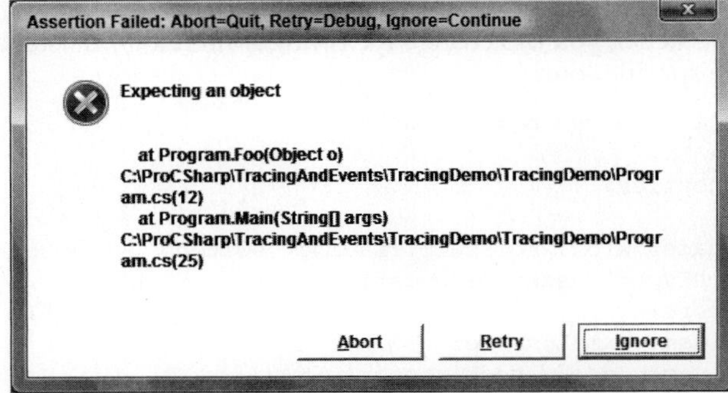

Figure 18-2

continues. The `Bar()` method includes a `Trace.Assert()` example where it is verified that the parameter is larger than 10 and smaller than 20. If the condition is `false`, an error message is shown again.

```
static void Foo(object o)
{
   Trace.Assert(o != null, "Expecting an object");
   Console.WriteLine(o);
}

static void Bar(int x)
{
   Trace.Assert(x > 10 && x < 20, "x should be between 10 and 20");
   Console.WriteLine(x);
}

static void Main()
{
   Foo(null);
   Bar(3);
}
```

You can create an application configuration file with the `<assert>` element to disable assert messages:

```
<?xml version="1.0" encoding="utf-8" ?>
<configuration>
  <system.diagnostics>
    <assert assertuienabled="false"/>
  </system.diagnostics>
</configuration>
```

Event Logging

The system administrator uses the Event Viewer to get critical and warning information about the system and applications. You should write error messages from your application to the event log so that the information can be read with the Event Viewer.

Trace messages can be written to the event log if you configure the `EventLogTraceListener` class. The `EventLogTraceListener` has an `EventLog` object associated with it to write the event log entry. You can also use the `EventLog` class directly to write and read event logs.

In this section, you explore the following:

- Event-logging architecture
- Classes for event logging from the `System.Diagnostics` namespace
- Adding event logging to services and to other application types
- Creating an event log listener with the `EnableRaisingEvents` property of the `EventLog` class

Figure 18-3 shows an example of a log entry from a modem.

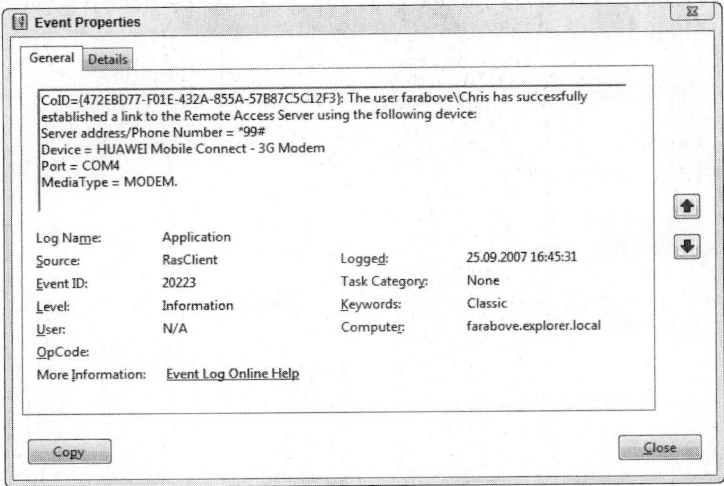

Figure 18-3

For custom event logging, you can use classes from the `System.Diagnostics` namespace.

Event-Logging Architecture

The event log information is stored in several log files. The most important ones are application, security, and system. Looking at the registry configuration of the event log service, you will notice several entries under `HKEY_LOCAL_MACHINE\System\CurrentControlSet\Services\Eventlog` with configurations pointing to the specific files. The system log file is used from the system and device drivers. Applications and services write to the application log. The security log is a read-only log for applications. The auditing feature of the operating system uses the security log. Every application can also create a custom category and log file to write event log entries there. For example, this is done by Windows OneCare and Media Center.

You can read these events by using the administrative tool Event Viewer. The Event Viewer can be started directly from the Server Explorer of Visual Studio by right-clicking the Event Logs item and selecting the Launch Event Viewer entry from the context menu. The Event Viewer is shown in Figure 18-4.

In the event log, you can see this information:

- **Type** — The type can be Information, Warning, or Error. Information is an infrequent successful operation; Warning is a problem that is not immediately significant; and Error is a major problem. Additional types are FailureAudit and SuccessAudit, but these types are used only for the security log.
- **Date** — Date and Time show the time when the event occurred.

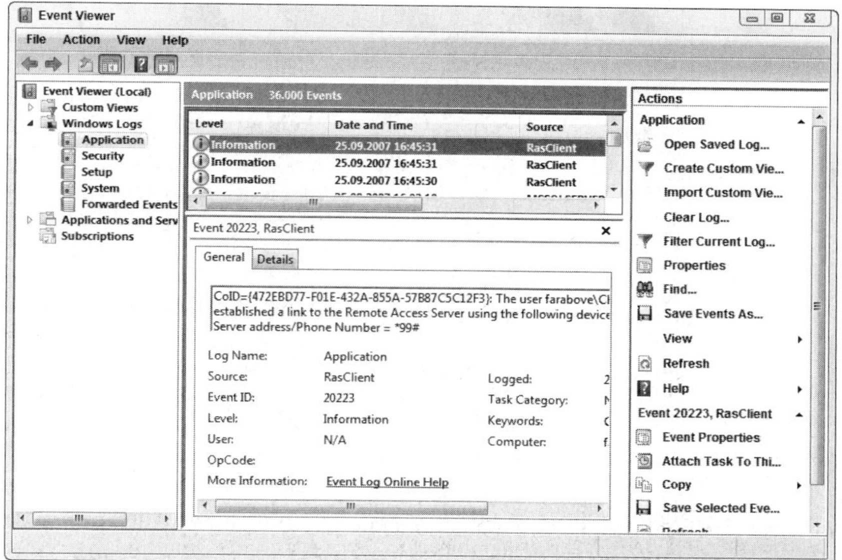

Figure 18-4

- **Source** — The Source is the name of the software that logs the event. The source for the application log is configured in:

```
HKEY_LOCAL_MACHINE\System\CurrentControlSet\Services\Eventlog\Application\
[ApplicationName]
```

  Below this key, the value `EventMessageFile` is configured to point to a resource DLL that holds error messages.

- **Category** — A Category can be defined so that event logs can be filtered when using the Event Viewer. Categories can be defined by an event source.
- **Event identifier** — The Event identifier specifies a particular event message.

Event-Logging Classes

The `System.Diagnostics` namespace has some classes for event logging, which are shown in the following table.

Class	Description
`EventLog`	With the `EventLog` class, you can read and write entries in the event log, and establish applications as event sources.
`EventLogEntry`	The `EventLogEntry` class represents a single entry in the event log. With the `EventLogEntryCollection`, you can iterate through `EventLogEntry` items.

Class	Description
EventLogInstaller	The EventLogInstaller class is the installer for an EventLog component. EventLogInstaller calls EventLog .CreateEventSource() to create an event source.
EventLogTraceListener	With the help of the EventLogTraceListener, traces can be written to the event log. This class implements the abstract class TraceListener.

The heart of event logging is in the EventLog class. The members of this class are explained in the following table.

EventLog Members	Description
Entries	With the Entries property, you can read event logs. Entries returns an EventLogEntryCollection that contains EventLogEntry objects holding information about the events. There is no need to invoke a Read() method. The collection is filled as soon as you access this property.
Log	Specify the log for reading or writing event logs with the Log property.
LogDisplayName	LogDisplayName is a read-only property that returns the display name of the log.
MachineName	With the MachineName, you can specify the system on which to read or write log entries.
Source	The Source property specifies the source of the event entries to write.
CreateEventSource()	The CreateEventSource() creates a new event source and a new log file, if a new log file is specified with this method.
DeleteEventSource()	To get rid of an event source, you can invoke DeleteEventSource().
SourceExists()	Before creating an event source, you can verify if the source already exists by using this element.
WriteEntry()WriteEvent()	Write event log entries with either the WriteEntry() or WriteEvent() method. WriteEntry() is simpler, because you just need to pass a string. WriteEvent() is more flexible, because you can use message files that are independent of the application and that support localization.
Clear()	The Clear() method removes all entries from an event log.
Delete()	The Delete() method deletes a complete event log.

Creating an Event Source

Before writing events, you must create an event source. You can use either the `CreateEventSource()` method of the `EventLog` class or the class `EventLogInstaller`. Because you need administrative privileges when creating an event source, an installation program would be best for defining the new source.

Chapter 16, "Deployment," explains how to create installation programs.

The following sample verifies that an event log source named `EventLogDemoApp` already exists. If it doesn't exist, an object of type `EventSourceCreationData` is instantiated that defines the source name `EventLogDemoApp` and the log name `ProCSharpLog`. Here, all events of this source are written to the `ProCSharpLog` event log. The default is the application log.

```
if (!EventLog.SourceExists("EventLogDemoApp"))
{
   EventSourceCreationData eventSourceData =
         new EventSourceCreationData("EventlogDemoApp",
         "ProCSharpLog");

   EventLog.CreateEventSource(eventSourceData);
}
```

The name of the event source is an identifier of the application that writes the events. For the system administrator reading the log, the information helps in identifying the event log entries to map them to application categories. Examples of names for event log sources are `LoadPerf` for the performance monitor, `MSSQLSERVER` for Microsoft SQL Server, `MsiInstaller` for the Windows Installer, `Winlogon`, `Tcpip`, `Time-Service`, and so on.

Setting the name Application for the event log writes event log entries to the application log. You can also create your own log by specifying a different application log name. Log files are located in the directory `<windows>\System32\WinEvt\Logs`.

With the `EventSourceCreationData`, you can also specify several more characteristics for the event log, as shown in the following table.

EventSourceCreationData	Description
`Source`	The property `Source` gets or sets the name of the event source.
`LogName`	`LogName` defines the log where event log entries are written. The default is the application log.
`MachineName`	With `MachineName`, you can define the system to read or write log entries.
`CategoryResourceFile`	With the `CategoryResourceFile` property, you can define a resource file for categories. Categories can be used for an easier filtering of event log entries within a single source.
`CategoryCount`	The `CategoryCount` property defines the number of categories in the category resource file.

EventSourceCreationData	Description
`MessageResourceFile`	Instead of specifying that the message should be written to the event log in the program that writes the events, messages can be defined in a resource file that is assigned to the `MessageResourceFile` property. Messages from the resource file are localizable.
`ParameterResourceFile`	Messages in a resource file can have parameters. The parameters can be replaced by strings defined in a resource file that is assigned to the `ParameterResourceFile` property.

Writing Event Logs

For writing event log entries, you can use the `WriteEntry()` or `WriteEvent()` methods of the `EventLog` class.

The `EventLog` class has both a static and an instance method `WriteEntry()`. The static method `WriteEntry()` requires a parameter of the source. The source can also be set with the constructor of the `EventLog` class. Here in the constructor, the log name, the local machine, and the event source name are defined. Next, three event log entries are written with the message as the first parameter of the `WriteEntry()` method. `WriteEntry()` is overloaded. The second parameter you can assign is an enumeration of type `EventLogEntryType`. With `EventLogEntryType`, you can define the severity of the event log entry. Possible values are `Information`, `Warning`, and `Error`, and for auditing `SuccessAudit` and `FailureAudit`. Depending on the type, different icons are shown in the Event Viewer. With the third parameter, you can specify an application-specific event ID that can be used by the application itself. In addition to that, you can also pass application-specific binary data and a category.

```
using (EventLog log = new EventLog("ProCSharpLog", ".",
        "EventLogDemoApp"))
{
    log.WriteEntry("Message 1");
    log.WriteEntry("Message 2", EventLogEntryType.Warning);
    log.WriteEntry("Message 3", EventLogEntryType.Information, 33);
}
```

Resource Files

Instead of defining the messages for the event log in the C# code and passing it to the `WriteEntry()` method, you can create a *message resource file*, define messages in the resource file, and pass message identifiers to the `WriteEvent()` method. Resource files also support localization.

Message resource files are native resource files that have nothing in common with .NET resource files. .NET resource files are covered in Chapter 21, "Localization."

A message file is a text file with the `mc` file extension. The syntax that this file uses to define messages is very strict. The sample file `EventLogMessages.mc` contains four categories followed by event messages. Every message has an ID that can be used by the application writing event entries. Parameters that can be passed from the application are defined with `%` syntax in the message text.

For the exact syntax of message files, check the MSDN documentation for Message Text Files.

```
; // EventLogDemoMessages.mc
; // *********************************************************

; // - Event categories -
; // Categories must be numbered consecutively starting at 1.
; // *********************************************************

MessageId=0x1
Severity=Success
SymbolicName=INSTALL_CATEGORY
Language=English
Installation
.

MessageId=0x2
Severity=Success
SymbolicName=DATA_CATEGORY
Language=English
Database Query
.

MessageId=0x3
Severity=Success
SymbolicName=UPDATE_CATEGORY
Language=English
Data Update
.

MessageId=0x4
Severity=Success
SymbolicName=NETWORK_CATEGORY
Language=English
Network Communication
.

; // - Event messages -
; // *********************************

MessageId = 1000
Severity = Success
Facility = Application
SymbolicName = MSG_CONNECT_1000
Language=English
Connection successful.
.

MessageId = 1001
Severity = Error
Facility = Application
SymbolicName = MSG_CONNECT_FAILED_1001
Language=English
Could not connect to server %1.
.
```

(continued)

(continued)

```
MessageId = 1002
Severity = Error
Facility = Application
SymbolicName = MSG_DB_UPDATE_1002
Language=English
Database update failed.
.

MessageId = 1003
Severity = Success
Facility = Application
SymbolicName = APP_UPDATE
Language=English
Application %%5002 updated.
.

; // - Event log display name -
; // ********************************************************

MessageId = 5001
Severity = Success
Facility = Application
SymbolicName = EVENT_LOG_DISPLAY_NAME_MSGID
Language=English
Professional C# Sample Event Log
.

; // - Event message parameters -
; //   Language independent insertion strings
; // ********************************************************


MessageId = 5002
Severity = Success
Facility = Application
SymbolicName = EVENT_LOG_SERVICE_NAME_MSGID
Language=English
EventLogDemo.EXE
.
```

Use the Messages Compiler, `mc.exe`, to create a binary message file. `mc -s EventLogDemoMessages.mc` compiles the source file containing the messages to a messages file with the `.bin` extension and the file `Messages.rc`, which contains a reference to the binary message file:

```
mc -s EventLogDemoMessages.mc
```

Next, you must use the Resource Compiler, `rc.exe`. `rc EventLogDemoMessages.rc` creates the resource file `EventLogDemoMessages.RES`:

```
rc EventLogDemoMessages.rc
```

With the linker, you can bind the binary message file `EventLogDemoMessages.RES` to a native DLL:

```
link /DLL /SUBSYSTEM:WINDOWS /NOENTRY /MACHINE:x86 EventLogDemoMessages.RES
```

Now, you can register an event source that defines the resource files as shown in the following code. First, a check is done if the event source named EventLogDemoApp exists. If the event log must be created because it does not exist, the next check verifies if the resource file is available. Some samples in the MSDN documentation demonstrate writing the message file to the <windows>\system32 directory, but you shouldn't do that. Copy the message DLL to a program-specific directory that you can get with the SpecialFolder enumeration value ProgramFiles. If you need to share the messages file among multiple applications, you can put it into Environment.SpecialFolder.CommonProgramFiles. If the file exists, a new object of type EventSourceCreationData is instantiated. In the constructor, the name of the source and the name of the log are defined. You use the properties CategoryResourceFile, MessageResourceFile, and ParameterResourceFile to define a reference to the resource file. After the event source is created, you can find the information on the resource files in the registry with the event source. The method CreateEventSource registers the new event source and log file. Finally, the method RegisterDisplayName() from the EventLog class specifies the name of the log as it is displayed in the Event Viewer. The ID 5001 is taken from the message file.

If you want to delete a previously created event source, you can do so with EventLog.DeleteEventSource(sourceName);. *To delete a log, you can invoke* EventLog.Delete(logName);.

```
string logName = "ProCSharpLog";
string sourceName = "EventLogDemoApp";
string resourceFile = Environment.GetFolderPath(
      Environment.SpecialFolder.ProgramFiles) +
      @"\procsharp\EventLogDemoMessages.dll";

if (!EventLog.SourceExists(sourceName))
{
   if (!File.Exists(resourceFile))
   {
      Console.WriteLine("Message resource file does not exist");
      return;
   }

   EventSourceCreationData eventSource =
         new EventSourceCreationData(sourceName, logName);

   eventSource.CategoryResourceFile = resourceFile;
   eventSource.CategoryCount = 4;
   eventSource.MessageResourceFile = resourceFile;
   eventSource.ParameterResourceFile = resourceFile;

   EventLog.CreateEventSource(eventSource);
}
else
{
   logName = EventLog.LogNameFromSourceName(sourceName, ".");
}

EventLog evLog = new EventLog(logName, ".", sourceName);
evLog.RegisterDisplayName(resourceFile, 5001);
```

Now, you can use the WriteEvent() method instead of WriteEntry() to write the event log entry. WriteEvent() requires an object of type EventInstance as parameter. With the EventInstance, you can assign the message ID, the category, and the severity of type EventLogEntryType. In addition to the EventInstance parameter, WriteEvent() accepts parameters for messages that have parameters and binary data as byte array.

```
EventLog log = new EventLog(logName, ".", sourceName);
EventInstance info1 = new EventInstance(1000, 4,
      EventLogEntryType.Information);

log.WriteEvent(info1);
EventInstance info2 = new EventInstance(1001, 4,
      EventLogEntryType.Error);
log.WriteEvent(info2, "avalon");

EventInstance info3 = new EventInstance(1002, 3,
      EventLogEntryType.Error);
byte[] addionalInfo = { 1, 2, 3 };
log.WriteEvent(info3, addionalInfo);

log.Dispose();
```

For the message identifiers, it is useful to define a class with const values that provide a more meaningful name for the identifiers in the application.

You can read the event log entries with the Event Viewer.

Event Log Listener

Instead of using the Event Viewer to read event log entries, you can create a custom event log reader that listens for events of specified types as needed. You can create a reader where important messages pop up to the screen, or send SMS to a system administrator.

Next, you write an application that receives an event when a service encounters a problem. Create a simple Windows application that monitors the events of your `Quote` service. This Windows application consists of a list box and an Exit button only, as shown in Figure 18-5.

Figure 18-5

Add an `EventLog` component to the design view by dragging and dropping it from the toolbox. Set the `Log` property to `Application`. You can set the `Source` property to a specific source to receive event log entries from only this source, for example the source `EventLogDemoApp` for receiving the event logs from the application created previously. If you leave the Source property empty, you will receive events from every source. You also need to change the property `EnableRaisingEvents`. The default value is `false`; setting it to `true` means that an event is generated each time this event occurs, and you can add an event handler for the `EntryWritten` event of the `EventLog` class. Add a handler with the name `OnEntryWritten()` to this event.

The `OnEntryWritten()` handler receives an `EntryWrittenEventArgs` object as argument, from which you can get the complete information about an event. With the `Entry` property, an `EventLogEntry` object with information about the time, event source, type, category, and so on is returned:

```
protected void OnEntryWritten (object sender,
   System.Diagnostics.EntryWrittenEventArgs e)
{
   StringBuilder sb = new StringBuilder();
   sb.AppendFormat("{0} {1} {2}",
         e.Entry.TimeGenerated.ToShortTimeString(),
         e.Entry.Source,
         e.Entry.Message);
   listBoxEvents.Items.Add(sb.ToString());
}
```

The running application displays event log information, as shown in Figure 18-6.

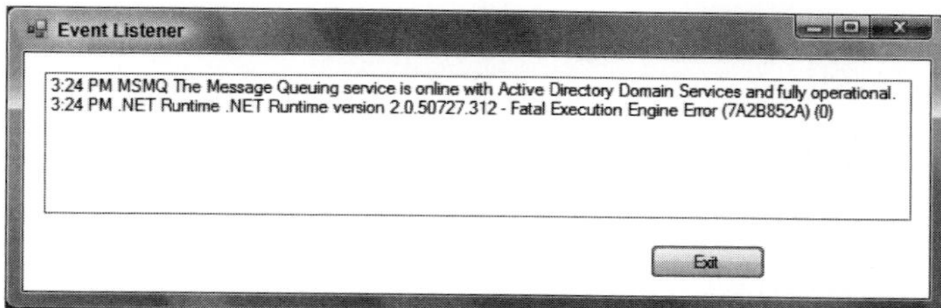

Figure 18-6

Performance Monitoring

Performance monitoring can be used to get information about the normal behavior of applications. Performance monitoring is a great tool that helps you understand the workload of the system and observe changes and trends, particularly in applications running on the server.

Microsoft Windows has many performance objects, such as `System`, `Memory`, `Objects`, `Process`, `Processor`, `Thread`, `Cache`, and so on. Each of these objects has many counts to monitor. For example, with the `Process` object, the user time, handle count, page faults, thread count, and so on can be monitored for all processes or for specific process instances. Some applications, such as SQL Server, also add application-specific objects.

For the quote service sample application, it might be interesting to get information about the number of client requests, the size of the data sent over the wire, and so on.

Performance-Monitoring Classes

The `System.Diagnostics` namespace provides these classes for performance monitoring:

- `PerformanceCounter` can be used both to monitor counts and to write counts. New performance categories can also be created with this class.
- `PerformanceCounterCategory` enables you to step through all existing categories as well as create new ones. You can programmatically get all the counters in a category.
- `PerformanceCounterInstaller` is used for the installation of performance counters. Its use is similar to that of the `EventLogInstaller` discussed previously.

Performance Counter Builder

The sample application is a simple Windows application with just one button so that you can see how to write performance counts. In a similar way, you can add performance counters to a Windows Service (see Chapter 23, "Windows Services"), to a network application (see Chapter 41, "Accessing the Internet"), or to any other application from which you would like to receive live counts.

Using Visual Studio, you can create a new performance counter category by selecting the performance counters in the Server Explorer and by selecting the menu entry Create New Category on the context menu. This launches the Performance Counter Builder (see Figure 18-7).

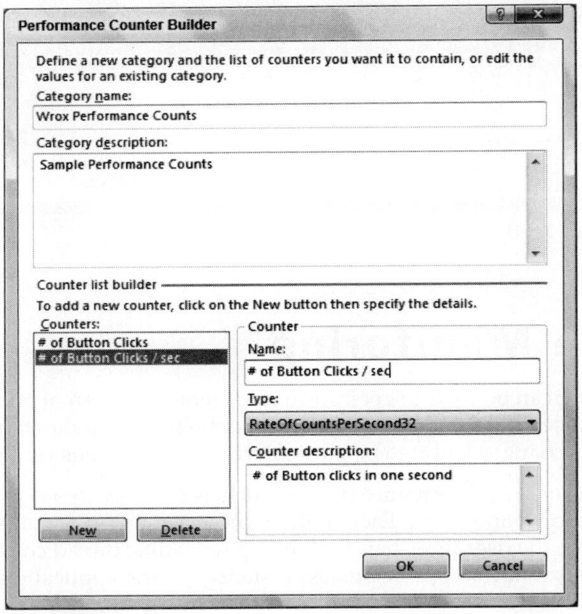

Figure 18-7

Set the name of the performance counter category to `Wrox Performance Counters`. The following table shows all performance counters of the quote service.

Name	Description	Type
# of Button clicks	Total # of button clicks	`NumberOfItems32`
# of Button clicks/sec	# of button clicks in one second	`RateOfCountsPerSecond32`
# of Mouse move events	Total # of mouse move events	`NumberOfItems32`
# of Mouse move events/sec	# of mouse move events in one second	`RateOfCountsPerSecond32`

The Performance Counter Builder writes the configuration to the performance database. This can also be done dynamically by using the `Create()` method of the `PerformanceCounterCategory` class in the `System.Diagnostics` namespace. An installer for other systems can easily be added later using Visual Studio.

Adding PerformanceCounter Components

Now you can add `PerformanceCounter` components from the toolbox. Instead of using the components from the toolbox category Components, you can directly drag and drop the previously created performance counters from the Server Explorer to the design view. This way, the instances are configured automatically; the `CategoryName` property is set to "Wrox Performance Counters" for all objects, and the `CounterName` property is set to one of the values available in the selected category. Because with this application the performance counts will not be read but written, you must set the `ReadOnly` property to `false`. Also, set the `MachineName` property to `.` so that the application writes performance counts locally.

Here is a part of the code generated into `InitalizeComponent()` by adding the `PerformanceCounter` components to the Designer and by setting the properties as indicated previously:

```
private void InitializeComponent()
{
   //...

   //
   // performanceCounterButtonClicks
   //
   this.performanceCounterButtonClicks.CategoryName =
         "Wrox Performance Counts";
   this.performanceCounterButtonClicks.CounterName =
         "# of Button Clicks";
   this.performanceCounterButtonClicks.ReadOnly = false;
   //
   // performanceCounterButtonClicksPerSec
   //
   this.performanceCounterButtonClicksPerSec.CategoryName =
         "Wrox Performance Counts";
   this.performanceCounterButtonClicksPerSec.CounterName =
         "# of Button Clicks / sec";
```

(continued)

(continued)

```
            this.performanceCounterButtonClicksPerSec.ReadOnly = false;
            //
            // performanceCounterMouseMoveEvents
            //
            this.performanceCounterMouseMoveEvents.CategoryName =
                  "Wrox Performance Counts";
            this.performanceCounterMouseMoveEvents.CounterName =
                  "# of Mouse Move Events";
            this.performanceCounterMouseMoveEvents.ReadOnly = false;
            //
            // performanceCounterMouseMoveEventsPerSec
            //
            this.performanceCounterMouseMoveEventsPerSec.CategoryName =
                  "Wrox Performance Counts";
            this.performanceCounterMouseMoveEventsPerSec.CounterName =
                  "# of Mouse Move Events / sec";
            this.performanceCounterMouseMoveEventsPerSec.ReadOnly = false;
            //...
         }
```

For the calculation of the performance values, you need to add the fields `clickCountPerSec` and `mouseMoveCountPerSec` to the class `Form1`:

```
   public partial class Form1 : Form
   {
      // Performance monitoring counter values
      private int clickCountPerSec = 0;
      private int mouseMoveCountPerSec = 0;
```

Add an event handler to the `Click` event of the button and an event handler to the `MouseMove` event to the form, and add the following code to the handlers:

```
      private void button1_Click(object sender, EventArgs e)
      {
         performanceCounterButtonClicks.Increment();
         clickCountPerSec++;
      }

      private void OnMouseMove(object sender, MouseEventArgs e)
      {
         performanceCounterMouseMoveEvents.Increment();
         mouseMoveCountPerSec++;
      }
```

The `Increment()` method of the `PerformanceCounter` object increments the counter by one. If you need to increment the counter by more than one, for example to add information about a byte count sent or received, you can use the `IncrementBy()` method. For the performance counts that show the value in seconds, just the two variables, `clickCountPerSec` and `mouseMovePerSec`, are incremented.

To show updated values every second, add a `Timer` component. Set the `OnTimer()` method to the `Elapsed` event of this component. The `OnTimer()` method is called once per second if you set the Interval property to 1000. In the implementation of this method, set the performance counts by using the `RawValue` property of the `PerformanceCounter` class:

```
protected void OnTimer (object sender, System.Timers.ElapsedEventArgs e)
{
   performanceCounterButtonClicksPerSec.RawValue = clickCountPerSec;
   clickCountPerSec = 0;

   performanceCounterMouseMoveEventsPerSec.RawValue =
         mouseMoveCountPerSec;
   mouseMoveCountPerSec = 0;
}
```

The timer must be started:

```
public Form1()
{
   InitializeComponent();

   this.timer1.Start();
}
```

perfmon.exe

Now you can monitor the application. You can start the Performance tool by selecting Administrative Tools ⇨ Performance with Windows XP or Reliability and Performance Monitor with Windows Vista. Select the Performance Monitor, and click the + button in the toolbar where you can add performance counts. The Quote Service shows up as a performance object. All the counters that have been configured show up in the counter list, as shown in Figure 18-8.

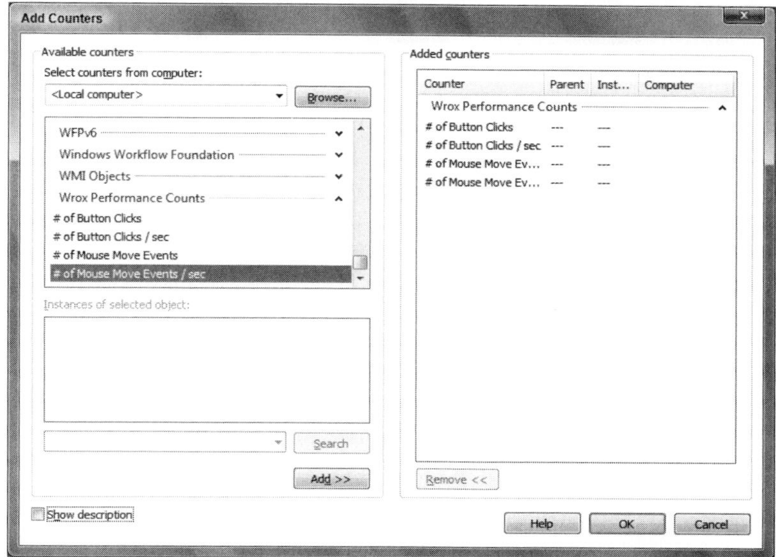

Figure 18-8

After you have added the counters to the performance monitor, you can see the actual values of the service over time (see Figure 18-9). Using this performance tool, you can also create log files to analyze the performance at a later time.

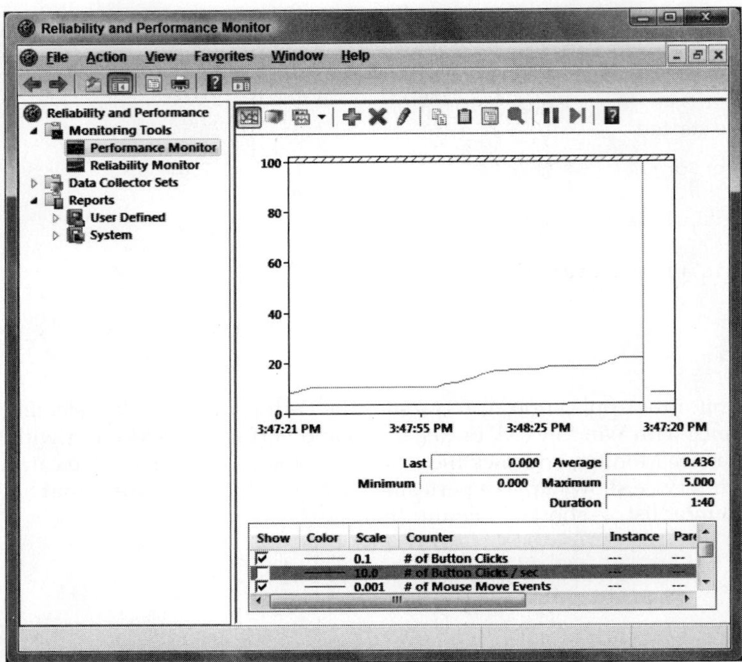

Figure 18-9

Summary

In this chapter, you have seen tracing and logging facilities that can help you find intermediate problems in your applications. You should plan early, building these features into your applications. This will help you avoid many troubleshooting problems later.

With tracing, you can write debugging messages to an application that can also be used for the final product delivered. In case there are problems, you can turn tracing on by changing configuration values, and find the issues.

Event logging provides information to the system administrator to help find some of the critical issues with the application. Performance monitoring helps in analyzing the load from applications and in planning in advance for resources that might be required in the future.

In the next chapter you learn all about writing multithreaded applications.

19

Threading and Synchronization

There are several reasons for using threading. Suppose that you are making a network call from an application that might take some time. You don't want to stall the user interface and just let the user wait until the response is returned from the server. The user could do some other actions in the meantime or even cancel the request that was sent to the server. Using threads can help.

For all activities that require a wait — for example, because of a file, database, or network access — a new thread can be started to fulfill other tasks at the same time. Even if you have only processing-intensive tasks to do, threading can help. Multiple threads of a single process can run on different CPUs, or, nowadays, on different cores of a multiple-core CPU, at the same time.

You must be aware of some issues when running multiple threads, however. Because they can run during the same time, you can easily get into problems if the threads access the same data. You must implement synchronization mechanisms.

This chapter provides the foundation you will need when programming applications with multiple threads, including:

- An overview of threading
- Lightweight threading using delegates
- Thread class
- Thread pools
- Threading issues
- Synchronization techniques
- Timers
- COM apartments
- Event-based asynchronous pattern

Overview

A thread is an independent stream of instructions in a program. All your C# programs up to this point have one entry point — the `Main()` method. Execution starts with the first statement in the `Main()` method and continues until that method returns.

This program structure is all very well for programs, in which there is one identifiable sequence of tasks, but often a program needs to do more than one thing at the same time. Threads are important both for client-side and for server-side applications. While you type C# code in the Visual Studio editor, the Dynamic Help window immediately shows the topics that fit to the code you type. A background thread is searching through help. The same thing is done by the spell checker in Microsoft Word. One thread is waiting for input from the user, while the other does some background research. A third thread can store the written data in an interim file, while another one downloads some additional data from the Internet.

In an application that is running on the server, one thread, the listener thread, waits for a request from a client. As soon as the request comes in, the request is forwarded to a separate worker thread, which continues the communication with the client. The listener thread immediately comes back to get the next request from the next client.

With the Windows Task Manager, you can turn on the column Threads from the menu View ➪ Select Columns and see the processes and the number of threads for every process. Only `cmd.exe` is running inside a single thread; all the other applications shown in Figure 19-1 use multiple threads. You can see one instance of Internet Explorer running 51 threads.

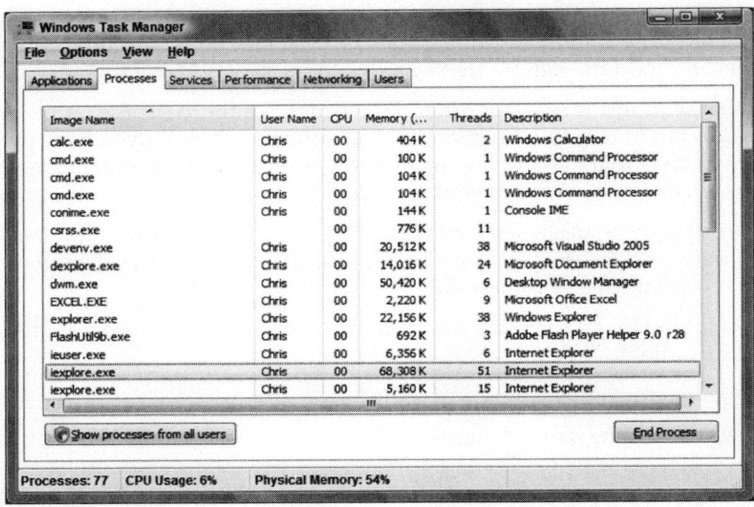

Figure 19-1

A process contains resources, such as Window handles, handles to the file system, or other kernel objects. Every process has virtual memory allocated. A process contains at least one thread. The operating system schedules threads. A thread has a priority, a program counter for the program location where it is actually processing, and a stack to store its local variables. Every thread has its own stack, but the memory for the program code and the heap are shared among all threads of a single process. This makes communication among threads of one process fast — the same virtual memory is addressed by all threads of a process. However, this also makes things difficult because multiple threads can change the same memory location.

A process manages resources that include virtual memory and Window handles, and contains at least one thread. A thread is required to run the program.

With .NET, a managed thread is defined by the `Thread` class. A managed thread does not necessarily map to one operating system thread. This can be the case, but it is the work of the .NET runtime host to map managed threads to the physical threads of the operating system. Here, the runtime host of SQL Server 2005 behaves very differently from the runtime host for Windows applications. You can get information about the native thread with the `ProcessThread` class, but with managed applications, it is usually just fine to use managed threads.

Asynchronous Delegates

A simple way to create a thread is by defining a delegate and invoking the delegate asynchronously. In Chapter 7, "Delegates and Events," you saw delegates as type-safe references to methods. The `Delegate` class also supports invoking the methods asynchronously. Behind the scenes, the `Delegate` class creates a thread that fulfills the task.

The delegate uses a thread pool for asynchronous tasks. Thread pools are discussed later.

To demonstrate the asynchronous features of delegates, start with a method that takes a while to complete. The method `TakesAWhile()` needs at least the number of milliseconds passed with the second argument to finish because of the `Thread.Sleep()` method:

```
static int TakesAWhile(int data, int ms)
{
   Console.WriteLine("TakesAWhile started");
   Thread.Sleep(ms);
   Console.WriteLine("TakesAWhile completed");
   return ++data;
}
```

To invoke this method from a delegate, a delegate with the same parameter and return types must be defined, as shown by the delegate `TakesAWhileDelegate`:

```
public delegate int TakesAWhileDelegate(int data, int ms);
```

Now you can use different techniques, invoking the delegate asynchronously and having the result returned.

Polling

One technique is to poll and check if the delegate has already finished its work. The created `delegate` class provides the method `BeginInvoke()`, where you can pass the input parameters defined with the delegate type. `BeginInvoke()` always has two additional parameters of type `AsyncCallback` and `object`, which are discussed later. What's important now is the return type of `BeginInvoke()`: `IAsyncResult`. With `IAsyncResult`, you can get information about the delegate, and also verify if the delegate already finished its work, as is done with the `IsCompleted` property. The main thread of the program continues the `while` loop as long as the delegate hasn't completed its work.

```
static void Main()
{
   // synchronous method call
   // TakesAWhile(1, 3000);

   // asynchronous by using a delegate
```

(continued)

(continued)

```
        TakesAWhileDelegate d1 = TakesAWhile;

        IAsyncResult ar = d1.BeginInvoke(1, 3000, null, null);
        while (!ar.IsCompleted)
        {
           // doing something else in the main thread
           Console.Write(".");
           Thread.Sleep(50);
        }
        int result = d1.EndInvoke(ar);
        Console.WriteLine("result: {0}", result);
     }
```

When you run the application, you can see the main thread and the thread of the delegate running concurrently, and the main thread stops looping after the delegate thread completes:

```
.TakesAWhile started
...........................................................TakesAWhile completed
result: 2
```

Instead of examining if the delegate is completed, you can also just invoke the `EndInvoke()` method of the delegate type after you are finished with the work that can be done by the main thread. `EndInvoke()` itself waits until the delegate has completed its work.

> **If you don't wait for the delegate to complete its work and end the main thread before the delegate is finished, the thread of the delegate will be stopped.**

Wait Handle

Another way to wait for the result from the asynchronous delegate is by using the wait handle that is associated with `IAsyncResult`. You can access the wait handle with the `AsyncWaitHandle` property. This property returns an object of type `WaitHandle`, where you can wait for the delegate thread to finish its work. The method `WaitOne()` accepts a timeout with the optional first parameter, where you can define the maximum time you want to wait; here it is set to 50 milliseconds. If a timeout occurs, `WaitOne()` returns with a `false` and the `while` loop continues. If the wait is successful, the `while` loop is exited with a break, and the result is received with the delegate `EndInvoke()` method.

```
     static void Main()
     {
        TakesAWhileDelegate d1 = TakesAWhile;

        IAsyncResult ar = d1.BeginInvoke(1, 3000, null, null);
        while (true)
        {
           Console.Write(".");
           if (ar.AsyncWaitHandle.WaitOne(50, false))
           {
              Console.WriteLine("Can get the result now");
              break;
           }
        }
```

```
    int result = d1.EndInvoke(ar);
    Console.WriteLine("result: {0}", result);
}
```

You can read more information about wait handles later in the synchronization section of this chapter.

Asynchronous Callback

The third version of waiting for the result from the delegate uses an asynchronous callback. With the third parameter of `BeginInvoke()`, you can pass a method that fulfills the requirements of the `AsyncCallback` delegate. The `AsyncCallback` delegate defines a parameter of `IAsnycResult` and a `void` return type. Here, the address of the method `TakesAWhileCompleted` is assigned to the third parameter that fulfills the requirements of the `AsyncCallback` delegate. With the last parameter, you can pass any object for accessing it from the callback method. It is useful to pass the delegate instance itself, so the callback method can use it to get the result of the asynchronous method.

Now the method `TakesAWhileCompleted()` is invoked as soon as the delegate `TakesAWhileDelegate` has completed its work. There is no need to wait for a result inside the main thread. However, you may not end the main thread before the work of the delegate threads is finished unless you don't have a problem with delegate threads stopping when the main thread ends.

```
static void Main()
{
    TakesAWhileDelegate d1 = TakesAWhile;

    d1.BeginInvoke(1, 3000, TakesAWhileCompleted, d1);
    for (int i = 0; i < 100; i++)
    {
        Console.Write(".");
        Thread.Sleep(50);
    }
}
```

The method `TakesAWhileCompleted()` is defined with the parameter and return type specified by the `AsyncCallback` delegate. The last parameter passed with the `BeginInvoke()` method can be read here using `ar.AsyncState`. With the `TakesAWhileDelegate` you can invoke the `EndInvoke` method to get the result.

```
static void TakesAWhileCompleted(IAsyncResult ar)
{
    if (ar == null) throw new ArgumentNullException("ar");

    TakesAWhileDelegate d1 = ar.AsyncState as TakesAWhileDelegate;
    Trace.Assert(d1 != null, "Invalid object type");

    int result = d1.EndInvoke(ar);
    Console.WriteLine("result: {0}", result);
}
```

With a callback method, you need to pay attention to the fact that this method is invoked from the thread of the delegate and not from the main thread.

Instead of defining a separate method and passing it to the BeginInvoke() method, Lambda expressions can be used. The parameter ar is of type IAsyncResult. With the implementation, there is no need to assign a value to the last parameter of the BeginInvoke() method because the Lambda expression can directly access variable d1 that is in the outer scope. However, the implementation block of the Lambda expression is still invoked from the thread of the delegate, which might not be clear immediately when defining the method this way.

```
static void Main()
{
   TakesAWhileDelegate d1 = TakesAWhile;

   d1.BeginInvoke(1, 3000,
      ar =>
         {
            int result = d1.EndInvoke(ar);
            Console.WriteLine("result: {0}", result);
         },
      null);
   for (int i = 0; i < 100; i++)
   {
      Console.Write(".");
      Thread.Sleep(50);
   }
}
```

You should use Lambda expressions only if the code within is not too big, and the implementation is not required in different places. In such cases, defining a separate method is preferred. Lambda expressions are explained in Chapter 7, "Delegates and Events."

The programming model and all of these options with asynchronous delegates — polling, wait handles, and asynchronous callbacks — are not only available with delegates. The same programming model — this is the asynchronous pattern — can be found in various places in the .NET Framework. For example, you can send an HTTP Web request asynchronously with the BeginGetResponse() method of the HttpWebRequest class. You can send an asynchronous request to the database with the BeginExecuteReader() of the SqlCommand class. The parameters are similar to those of the BeginInvoke() class of the delegate, and you can use the same mechanisms to get the result.

HttpWebRequest *is covered in Chapter 41, "Accessing the Internet," and* SqlCommand *is discussed in Chapter 26, "Data Access."*

Instead of using the delegate for creating threads, you can create threads with the Thread class, which is covered in the next section.

The Thread Class

With the Thread class you can create and control threads. The code here is a very simple example of creating and starting a new thread. The constructor of the Thread class accepts a delegate parameter of type ThreadStart and ParameterizedThreadStart. The ThreadStart delegate defines a method with a void return type and without arguments. After the Thread object is created, you can start the thread with the Start() method:

```
using System;
using System.Threading;

namespace Wrox.ProCSharp.Threading
```

```
{
   class Program
   {
      static void Main()
      {
         Thread t1 = new Thread(ThreadMain);
         t1.Start();
         Console.WriteLine("This is the main thread.");
      }

      static void ThreadMain()
      {
         Console.WriteLine("Running in a thread.");
      }
   }
}
```

When you run the application, you get the output of the two threads:

```
This is the main thread.
Running in a thread.
```

There is no guarantee as to what output comes first. Threads are scheduled by the operating system; which thread comes first can be different each time.

You have seen how a Lambda expression can be used with an asynchronous delegate. You can use it with the `Thread` class as well by passing the implementation of the thread method to the argument of the `Thread` constructor:

```
using System;
using System.Threading;

namespace Wrox.ProCSharp.Threading
{
   class Program
   {
      static void Main()
      {
         Thread t1 = new Thread(() => Console.WriteLine(
               "running in a thread"));
         t1.Start();
         Console.WriteLine("This is the main thread.");
      }
   }
}
```

If you don't need a variable referencing the thread to control the thread object after it was created, you can also write the code in a shorter way. Create a new `Thread` object with the constructor, pass a Lambda expression to the constructor, and with the `Thread` object returned, invoke the `Start()` method directly:

```
using System.Threading;

namespace Wrox.ProCSharp.Threading
{
   class Program
```

(continued)

(continued)

```
    {
        static void Main()
        {
            new Thread(() => Console.WriteLine("running in a thread")).Start();
            Console.WriteLine("This is the main thread.");
        }
    }
}
```

There are some good reasons for having a variable to reference the `Thread` object. One example, for better control of the threads, is that you can assign a name to the thread by setting the `Name` property before starting the thread. To get the name of the current thread, you can use the static property `Thread.CurrentThread` to get to the `Thread` instance of the current thread and access the `Name` property for read access. The thread also has a managed thread ID that you can read with the property `ManagedThreadId`.

```
static void Main()
{
    Thread t1 = new Thread(ThreadMain);
    t1.Name = "MyNewThread1";
    t1.Start();
    Console.WriteLine("This is the main thread.");
}

static void ThreadMain()
{
    Console.WriteLine("Running in the thread {0}, id: {1}.",
            Thread.CurrentThread.Name,
            Thread.CurrentThread.ManagedThreadId);
}
```

With the output of the application, now you can also see the thread name and ID:

```
This is the main thread.
Running in the thread MyNewThread1, id: 3.
```

Assigning a name to the thread helps a lot with debugging threads. During your debugging session with Visual Studio, you can turn on the Debug Location toolbar that shows the name of the thread.

Passing Data to Threads

There are two ways to pass some data to a thread. You can either use the `Thread` constructor with the `ParameterizedThreadStart` delegate, or you can create a custom class and define the method of the thread as an instance method so that you can initialize data of the instance before starting the thread.

For passing data to a thread, any class or struct that holds the data is needed. Here, the struct `Data` containing a string is defined, but you can pass any object you want:

```
public struct Data
{
    public string Message;
}
```

If the `ParameterizedThreadStart` delegate is used, the entry point of the thread must have a parameter of type object and a void return type. The object can be cast to what it is, and here the message is written to the console:

```
static void ThreadMainWithParameters(object o)
{
   Data d = (Data)o;
   Console.WriteLine("Running in a thread, received {0}", d.Message);
}
```

With the constructor of the `Thread` class, you can assign the new entry point `ThreadMainWithParameters` and invoke the `Start()` method passing the variable `d`:

```
static void Main()
{
   Data d = new Data();
   d.Message = "Info";
   Thread t2 = new Thread(ThreadMainWithParameters);
   t2.Start(d);
}
```

Another way to pass data to the new thread is to define a class (see the class `MyThread`), where you define the fields that are needed as well as the main method of the thread as an instance method of the class:

```
public class MyThread
{
   private string data;

   public MyThread(string data)
   {
      this.data = data;
   }

   public void ThreadMain()
   {
      Console.WriteLine("Running in a thread, data: {0}", data);
   }
}
```

This way, you can create an object of `MyThread`, and pass the object and the method `ThreadMain()` to the constructor of the `Thread` class. The thread can access the data.

```
MyThread obj = new MyThread("info");
Thread t3 = new Thread(obj.ThreadMain);
t3.Start();
```

Background Threads

The process of the application keeps running as long as at least one foreground thread is running. If more than one foreground thread is running and the `Main()` method ends, the process of the application keeps active until all foreground threads finish their work.

A thread you create with the `Thread` class, by default, is a foreground thread. Thread pool threads are always background threads.

When you create a thread with the `Thread` class, you can define whether it should be a foreground or background thread by setting the property `IsBackground`. The `Main()` method sets the `IsBackground` property of the thread `t1` to `false` (which is the default). After starting the new thread, the main thread just writes to the console an end message. The new thread writes a start and an end message, and in between it sleeps for 3 seconds. The 3 seconds provide a good chance for the main thread to finish before the new thread completes its work.

```
class Program
{
    static void Main()
    {
        Thread t1 = new Thread(ThreadMain);
        t1.Name = "MyNewThread1";
        t1.IsBackground = false;
        t1.Start();
        Console.WriteLine("Main thread ending now...");
    }

    static void ThreadMain()
    {
        Console.WriteLine("Thread {0} started", Thread.CurrentThread.Name);
        Thread.Sleep(3000);
        Console.WriteLine("Thread {0} completed", Thread.CurrentThread.Name);
    }
}
```

When you start the application, you will still see the completion message written to the console, although the main thread completed its work earlier. The reason is that the new thread is a foreground thread as well.

```
Main thread ending now...
Thread MyNewThread1 started
Thread MyNewThread1 completed
```

If you change the `IsBackground` property to start the new thread to `true`, the result shown at the console is different. You can have the same result as shown here — the start message of the new thread is shown but never the end message. You might not see the start message either, if the thread was prematurely ended before it had a chance to kick off.

```
Main thread ending now...
Thread MyNewThread1 started
```

Background threads are very useful for background tasks. For example, when you close the Word application, it doesn't make sense for the spell checker to keep its process running. The spell checker thread can be killed when the application is closed. However, the thread organizing the Outlook message store should remain active until it is finished even if Outlook is closed.

Thread Priority

You have learned that the operating system schedules threads. You have had a chance to influence the scheduling by assigning a priority to the thread.

Before changing the priority, you must understand the thread scheduler. The operating system schedules threads based on a priority, and the thread with the highest priority is scheduled to run in the CPU. A thread stops running and gives up the CPU if it waits for a resource. There are several reasons why a thread must wait; for example, in response to a sleep instruction, while waiting for disk I/O to complete, while waiting for a network packet to arrive, and so on. If the thread does not give up the CPU on its own, it is preempted by the thread scheduler. If a thread does have a *time quantum*, it can use the CPU continuously. If there are multiple threads running with the same priority waiting to get the CPU, the thread scheduler uses a *round-robin* scheduling principle to give the CPU to one thread after the other. If a thread is preempted, it goes last to the queue.

The time quantum and round-robin principles are used only if multiple threads are running at the same priority. The priority is dynamic. If a thread is CPU-intensive (requires the CPU continuously without waiting for resources), the priority is lowered to the level of the base priority that is defined with the thread. If a thread is waiting for a resource, the thread gets a priority boost and the priority is increased. Because of the boost, there is a good chance that the thread gets the CPU the next time that the wait ends.

With the `Thread` class, you can influence the base priority of the thread by setting the `Priority` property. The `Priority` property requires a value that is defined by the `ThreadPriority` enumeration. The levels defined are `Highest`, `AboveNormal`, `Normal`, `BelowNormal`, and `Lowest`.

Be careful when giving a thread a higher priority, because this may decrease the chance for other threads to run. You can change the priority for a short time if needed.

Controlling Threads

The thread is created by invoking the `Start()` method of a `Thread` object. However, after invoking the `Start()` method, the new thread is still not in the `Running` state, but in the `Unstarted` state instead. The thread changes to the `Running` state as soon as the operating system thread scheduler selects the thread to run. You can read the current state of a thread by reading the property `Thread.ThreadState`.

With the `Thread.Sleep()` method, a thread goes into the `WaitSleepJoin` state and waits until it is woken up again after the time span defined with the `Sleep()` method has elapsed.

To stop another thread, you can invoke the method `Thread.Abort()`. When this method is called, an exception of type `ThreadAbortException` is thrown in the thread that receives the abort. With a handler to catch this exception, the thread can do some cleanup before it ends. The thread also has a chance to continue running after receiving the `ThreadAbortException` as a result of invoking `Thread.ResetAbort()`. The state of the thread receiving the abort request changes from `AbortRequested` to the `Aborted` state if the thread does not reset the abort.

If you need to wait for a thread to end, you can invoke the `Thread.Join()` method. `Thread.Join()` blocks the current thread and sets it to the `WaitSleepJoin` state until the thread that is joined is completed.

.NET 1.0 also supported `Thread.Suspend()` and `Thread.Resume()` methods to pause and continue a thread, respectively. However, you don't know what the thread is doing when it gets the `Suspend` request, and the thread might be in a synchronized section holding locks. This can easily result in deadlocks. That's why these methods are now obsolete. Instead, you can signal a thread, using synchronization objects, so it can suspend itself. This way, the thread knows best when to go into a waiting state.

Thread Pools

Creating threads takes time. When you have different short tasks to do, you can create a number of threads in advance and send requests as they should be done. It would be nice if this number increased as more threads were needed and decreased as needed to release resources.

There is no need to create such a list on your own. The list is managed by the `ThreadPool` class. This class increases and decreases the number of threads in the pool as they are needed, up to the maximum number of threads. The maximum number of threads in a pool is configurable. With a dual-core CPU, the default number is set to 50 worker threads and 1,000 I/O threads. You can specify the minimum number of threads that should be started immediately when the pool is created and the maximum number of threads that are available in the pool. If there are more jobs to process, and the maximum number of threads in the pool has already been reached, the newest jobs are queued and must wait for a thread to complete its work.

The sample application first reads the maximum number of worker and I/O threads and writes this information to the console. Then in a `for` loop, the method `JobForAThread()` is assigned to a thread from the thread pool by invoking the method `ThreadPool.QueueUserWorkItem()` and passing a delegate of type `WaitCallback`. The thread pool receives this request and selects one of the threads from the pool to invoke the method. If the pool is not already running, the pool is created and the first thread is started. If the pool is already running and one thread is free to do the task, the job is forwarded to this thread.

```
using System;
using System.Threading;

namespace Wrox.ProCSharp.Threading
{
   class Program
   {
      static void Main()
      {
         int nWorkerThreads;
         int nCompletionPortThreads;
         ThreadPool.GetMaxThreads(out nWorkerThreads,
                                  out nCompletionPortThreads);
         Console.WriteLine("Max worker threads: {0}, " +
                           "I/O completion threads: {1}",
                           nWorkerThreads, nCompletionPortThreads);

         for (int i = 0; i < 5; i++)
         {
            ThreadPool.QueueUserWorkItem(JobForAThread);
         }
         Thread.Sleep(3000);
      }

      static void JobForAThread(object state)
      {
         for (int i = 0; i < 3; i++)
         {
            Console.WriteLine("loop {0}, running inside pooled thread {1}",
               i, Thread.CurrentThread.ManagedThreadId);
            Thread.Sleep(50);
         }
      }
   }
}
```

When you run the application, you can see that 50 worker threads are possible with the current settings. The five jobs are processed by just two pooled threads. Your experience may be different, and you can also change the sleep time with the job and the number of jobs to process to get very different results.

```
Max worker threads: 50, I/O completion threads: 1000
loop 0, running inside pooled thread 4
loop 0, running inside pooled thread 3
loop 1, running inside pooled thread 4
loop 1, running inside pooled thread 3
loop 2, running inside pooled thread 4
loop 2, running inside pooled thread 3
loop 0, running inside pooled thread 4
loop 0, running inside pooled thread 3
loop 1, running inside pooled thread 4
loop 1, running inside pooled thread 3
loop 2, running inside pooled thread 4
loop 2, running inside pooled thread 3
loop 0, running inside pooled thread 4
loop 1, running inside pooled thread 4
loop 2, running inside pooled thread 4
```

Thread pools are very easy to use. However, there are some restrictions:

- All thread pool threads are background threads. If all foreground threads of a process are finished, all background threads are stopped. You cannot change a pooled thread to a foreground thread.
- You cannot set the priority or name of a pooled thread.
- For COM objects, all pooled threads are multithreaded apartment (MTA) threads. Many COM objects require a single-threaded apartment (STA) thread.
- Use pooled threads only for a short task. If a thread should run all the time (for example, the spell-checker thread of Word), create a thread with the `Thread` class.

Threading Issues

Programming with multiple threads is not easy. When starting multiple threads that access the same data, you can get intermittent problems that are hard to find. To avoid getting into trouble, you must pay attention to synchronization issues and the problems that can happen with multiple threads. We discuss two in particular next: race conditions and deadlocks.

Race Condition

A race condition can occur if two or more threads access the same objects and access to the shared state is not synchronized.

To demonstrate a race condition, the class `StateObject` with an `int` field and the method `ChangeState` are defined. In the implementation of `ChangeState`, the state variable is verified if it contains 5; if it does, the value is incremented. `Trace.Assert` is the next statement that immediately verifies that state now contains the value 6. After incrementing a variable by 1 that contains the value 5, you might expect that the variable now has the value 6. But this is not necessarily the case. For example, if one thread has just completed the `if (state == 5)` statement, it might be preempted, and the scheduler will run another thread. The second thread now goes into the `if` body and, because the state still has the value 5, the state is incremented by 1 to 6. The first thread is now scheduled again, and in the next statement the state is incremented to 7. This is when the race condition occurs and the assert message is shown.

```
public class StateObject
{
   private int state = 5;

   public void ChangeState(int loop)
   {
      if (state == 5)
      {
         state++;
         Trace.Assert(state == 6, "Race condition occurred after " +
               loop + " loops");
      }
      state = 5;
   }
}
```

Let's verify this by defining a thread method. The method `RaceCondition()` of the class `SampleThread` gets a `StateObject` as a parameter. Inside an endless `while` loop, the `ChangeState()` method is invoked. The variable `i` is used just to show the loop number in the assert message:

```
public class SampleThread
{
   public void RaceCondition(object o)
   {
      Trace.Assert(o is StateObject, "o must be of type StateObject");
      StateObject state = o as StateObject;

      int i = 0;
      while (true)
      {
         state.ChangeState(i++);
      }
   }
}
```

In the `Main()` method of the program, a new `StateObject` is created that is shared between all the threads. `Thread` objects are created by passing the address of `RaceCondition` with an object of type `SampleThread` in the constructor of the `Thread` class. The thread is then started with the `Start()` method, passing the `state` object.

```
static void Main()
{
   StateObject state = new StateObject();
   for (int i = 0; i < 20; i++)
   {
      new Thread(new SampleThread().RaceCondition).Start(state);
   }
}
```

When you start the program, you will get race conditions. How long it takes until the first race condition happens depends on your system and whether you build the program as a release or debug build. With a release build, the problem will happen more often because the code is optimized. If you have multiple CPUs in your system or dual-core CPUs where multiple threads can run concurrently, the problem will also occur more often than with a single-core CPU. The problem will occur with a single-core CPU because thread scheduling is preemptive, but not that often.

Figure 19-2 shows an assert of the program where the race condition occurred after 3,816 loops. You can start the application multiple times, and you will always get different results.

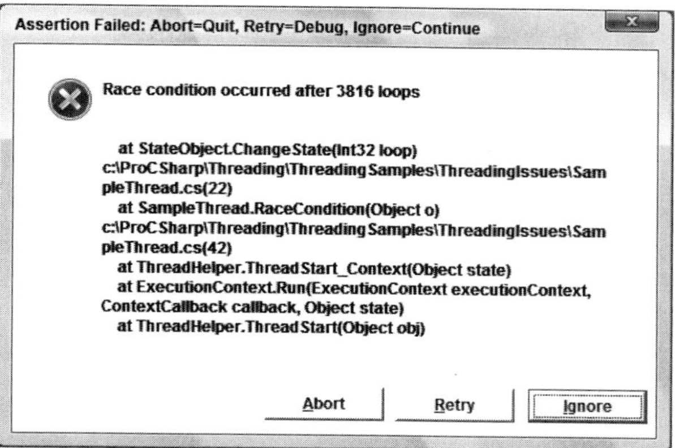

Figure 19-2

You can avoid the problem by locking the shared object. You can do this inside the thread by locking variable state that is shared between the threads with the `lock` statement as shown. Only one thread can be inside the lock block for the state object. Because this object is shared between all threads, a thread must wait at the lock if another thread has the lock for state. As soon as the lock is accepted, the thread owns the lock and gives it up with the end of the lock block. If every thread changing the object referenced with the state variable is using a lock, the race condition no longer occurs.

```
public class SampleThread
{
   public void RaceCondition(object o)
   {
      Trace.Assert(o is StateObject, "o must be of type StateObject");
      StateObject state = o as StateObject;

      int i = 0;
      while (true)
      {
         lock (state)  // no race condition with this lock
         {
            state.ChangeState(i++);
         }
      }
   }
}
```

Instead of doing the lock when using the shared object, you can make the shared object thread-safe. Here, the `ChangeState()` method contains a `lock` statement. Because you cannot lock the `state` variable itself (only reference types can be used for a lock), the variable `sync` of type `object` is defined and used with the `lock` statement. If a lock is done using the same synchronization object every time the value state is changed, race conditions no longer happen.

```
public class StateObject
{
   private int state = 5;
   private object sync = new object();

   public void ChangeState(int loop)
   {
      lock (sync)
      {
         if (state == 5)
         {
            state++;
            Trace.Assert(state == 6, "Race condition occurred after " +
                  loop + " loops");
         }
         state = 5;
      }
   }
}
```

Deadlock

Too much locking can get you in trouble as well. In a deadlock, at least two threads halt and wait for each other to release a lock. As both threads wait for each other, a deadlock occurs and the threads wait endlessly.

To demonstrate deadlocks, two objects of type `StateObject` are instantiated and passed with the constructor of the `SampleThread` class. Two threads are created: one thread running the method `Deadlock1()` and the other thread running the method `Deadlock2()`:

```
StateObject state1 = new StateObject();
StateObject state2 = new StateObject();
new Thread(new SampleThread(state1, state2).Deadlock1).Start();
new Thread(new SampleThread(state1, state2).Deadlock2).Start();
```

The methods `Deadlock1()` and `Deadlock2()` now change the state of two objects `s1` and `s2`. That's why two locks are done. The method `Deadlock1()` first does a lock for `s1` and next for `s2`. The method `Deadlock2()` first does a lock for `s2` and then for `s1`. Now it may happen from time to time that the lock for `s1` in `Deadlock1()` is resolved. Next, a thread switch occurs, and `Deadlock2()` starts to run and gets the lock for `s2`. The second thread now waits for the lock of `s1`. Because it needs to wait, the thread scheduler schedules the first thread again, which now waits for `s2`. Both threads now wait and don't release the lock as long as the lock block is not ended. This is a typical deadlock.

```
public class SampleThread
{
   public SampleThread(StateObject s1, StateObject s2)
   {
      this.s1 = s1;
      this.s2 = s2;
   }

   private StateObject s1;
   private StateObject s2;
```

```
      public void Deadlock1()
      {
         int i = 0;
         while (true)
         {
            lock (s1)
            {
               lock (s2)
               {
                  s1.ChangeState(i);
                  s2.ChangeState(i++);
                  Console.WriteLine("still running, {0}", i);
               }
            }
         }
      }

      public void Deadlock2()
      {
         int i = 0;
         while (true)
         {
            lock (s2)
            {
               lock (s1)
               {
                  s1.ChangeState(i);
                  s2.ChangeState(i++);
                  Console.WriteLine("still running, {0}", i);
               }
            }
         }
      }
   }
```

As a result, the program will run a number of loops and will soon be unresponsive. The message still running is just written a few times to the console. Again, how soon the problem happens depends on your system configuration. And the result will differ from time to time.

The problem of deadlocks is not always as obvious as it is here. One thread locks `s1` and then `s2`; the other thread locks `s2` and then `s1`. You just need to change the order so that both threads do the lock in the same order. However, the locks might be hidden deeply inside a method. You can prevent this problem by designing a good lock order from the beginning in the architecture of the application, and also by defining timeouts for the locks, which we show in the next section.

Synchronization

It is best to avoid synchronization issues by not sharing data between threads. Of course, this is not always possible. If data sharing is necessary, you must use synchronization techniques so that only one thread at a time accesses and changes shared state. Remember the synchronization issues with race conditions and deadlocks. If you don't pay attention to these issues, the reason for problems in applications is hard to find because threading issues occur just from time to time.

This section discusses synchronization technologies that you can use with multiple threads:

- `lock` statement
- `Interlocked` class
- `Monitor` class
- Wait handles
- Mutex
- Semaphore
- Events
- `ReaderWriterLockSlim`

`lock`, `Interlocked`, and `Monitor` can be used for synchronization within a process. The classes `Mutex`, `Event`, `Semaphore`, and `ReaderWriterLockSlim` also offer synchronization between threads of multiple processes.

lock Statement and Thread Safety

C# has its own keyword for the synchronization of multiple threads: the `lock` statement. The `lock` statement is an easy way to hold for a lock and release it.

Before adding `lock` statements, let's go into another race condition. The class `SharedState` just demonstrates using shared state between threads, and keeps an integer value:

```
public class SharedState
{
   public int State { get; set; }
}
```

The class `Task` contains the method `DoTheTask()`, which is the entry point for a new thread. With the implementation, the `State` of `SharedState` is incremented 50,000 times. The variable `sharedState` is initialized in the constructor of this class.

```
public class Task
{
   SharedState sharedState;
   public Task(SharedState sharedState)
   {
      this.sharedState = sharedState;
   }
   public void DoTheTask()
   {
      for (int i = 0; i < 50000; i++)
      {
         sharedState.State += 1;
      }
   }
}
```

In the `Main()` method, a `SharedState` object is created and passed to the constructor of 20 `Thread` objects. All threads are started. After starting the threads, the `Main()` method does another loop to join every one of the 20 threads to wait until all threads are completed. After the threads are completed, the summarized value of the shared state is written to the console. Having 50,000 loops and 20 threads, a value of 1,000,000 could be expected. Often, however, this is not the case.

```
    class Program
    {
        static void Main()
        {
            int numThreads = 20;
            SharedState state = new SharedState();
            Thread[] threads = new Thread[numThreads];

            for (int i = 0; i < numThreads; i++)
            {
                threads[i] = new Thread(new Task(state).DoTheTask);
                threads[i].Start();
            }

            for (int i = 0; i < numThreads; i++)
            {
                threads[i].Join();
            }
            Console.WriteLine("summarized {0}", state.State);
        }
    }
}
```

Results received from multiple runs of the application are as shown here:

```
summarized 939270
summarized 993799
summarized 998304
summarized 937630
```

The behavior is different every time, but none of the results is correct. You get big differences between debug and release builds, and on the types of CPUs you are using. If you change the loop count for smaller values, you will get correct values many times — but not every time. The application is small enough to see the problem easily; the reason for such a problem can be hard to find in a large application.

You must add synchronization to this program. This can be done with the `lock` keyword.

The object defined with the `lock` statement means you wait to get the lock for the specified object. You can pass only a reference type. Locking a value type would just lock a copy, and this wouldn't make any sense. Anyway, the C# compiler provides an error if value types are used with the `lock` statement. As soon as the lock is granted — only one thread gets the lock — the block of the `lock` statement can run. At the end of the `lock` statement block, the lock for the object is released, and another thread waiting for the lock can be granted.

```
lock (obj)
{
   // synchronized region
}
```

To lock static members, you can place the lock on the type object:

```
lock (typeof(StaticClass))
{
}
```

You can make the instance members of a class thread-safe by using the `lock` keyword. This way, only one thread at a time can access the methods `DoThis()` and `DoThat()` for the same instance.

```
public class Demo
{
   public void DoThis()
   {
      lock (this)
      {
         // only one thread at a time can access the DoThis and DoThat methods
      }
   }
   public void DoThat()
   {
      lock (this)
      {
      }
   }
}
```

However, because the object of the instance can also be used for synchronized access from the outside, and you can't control this from the class itself, you can apply the SyncRoot pattern. With the SyncRoot pattern, a private object named `syncRoot` is created, and this object is used with the `lock` statements:

```
public class Demo
{
   private object syncRoot = new object();

   public void DoThis()
   {
      lock (syncRoot)
      {
         // only one thread at a time can access the DoThis and DoThat methods
      }
   }
   public void DoThat()
   {
      lock (syncRoot)
      {
      }
   }
}
```

Using locks costs time and is not always needed. You can create two versions of a class: a synchronized and a nonsynchronized version. This is demonstrated here by changing the class `Demo`. The class `Demo` itself is not synchronized, as you can see in the implementation of the `DoThis()` and `DoThat()` methods. The class also defines the `IsSynchronized` property, where the client can get information about the synchronization option of the class. To make a synchronized variant of the class, the static method `Synchronized()` can be used to pass a nonsynchronized object, and this method returns an object of type `SynchronizedDemo`. `SynchronizedDemo` is implemented as an inner class that is derived from the base class `Demo` and overrides the virtual members of the base class. The overridden members make use of the SyncRoot pattern.

```
public class Demo
{
   private class SynchronizedDemo : Demo
   {
      private object syncRoot = new object();
      private Demo d;
```

```
         public SynchronizedDemo(Demo d)
         {
            this.d = d;
         }

         public override bool IsSynchronized
         {
            get { return true; }
         }

         public override void DoThis()
         {
            lock (syncRoot)
            {
               d.DoThis();
            }
         }

         public override void DoThat()
         {
            lock (syncRoot)
            {
               d.DoThat();
            }
         }
      }

      public virtual bool IsSynchronized
      {
         get { return false; }
      }

      public static Demo Synchronized(Demo d)
      {
         if (!d.IsSynchronized)
         {
            return new SynchronizedDemo(d);
         }
         return d;
      }

      public virtual void DoThis()
      {
      }

      public virtual void DoThat()
      {
      }
   }
```

You must bear in mind that when using the `SynchronizedDemo` class, only methods are synchronized. There is no synchronization for invoking two members of this class.

The SyncRoot pattern might lead to a false sense of thread safety. The .NET 1.0 collection classes implement the SyncRoot pattern; the .NET 2.0 generic collection classes don't implement this pattern anymore.

Let's compare this with the example shown earlier. If you try to make the `SharedState` class thread-safe by locking access to the properties with the SyncRoot pattern, you still get the race condition shown earlier.

```
public class SharedState
{
   private int state = 0;
   private object syncRoot = new object();

   public int State // there's still a race condition,
                    // don't do this!
   {
      get { lock (syncRoot) {return state; }}
      set { lock (syncRoot) {state = value; }}
   }
}
```

The thread invoking the `DoTheTask` method is accessing the get accessor of the `SharedState` class to get the current value of the state, and then the get accessor sets the new value for the state. In between calling the get and the set accessor the object is not locked, and another thread can be the interim value.

```
public void DoTheTask()
{
   for (int i = 0; i < 50000; i++)
   {
      sharedState.State += 1;
   }
}
```

So, it is better to leave the `SharedState` class as it was earlier without thread safety:

```
public class SharedState
{
   public int State { get; set; }
}
```

and to add the `lock` statement where it belongs, inside the method `DoTheTask()`:

```
public void DoTheTask()
{
   for (int i = 0; i < 50000; i++)
   {
      lock (sharedState)
      {
         sharedState.State += 1;
      }
   }
}
```

This way, the results of the application are always as expected:

```
summarized 1000000
```

> **Using the `lock` statement in one place does not mean that all other threads accessing the object are waiting. You have to explicitly use synchronization with every thread accessing the shared state.**

Of course, you can also change the design of the `SharedState` class and offer increment as an atomic operation. This is a design question — what should be an atomic functionality of the class?

```
public class SharedState
{
   private int state = 0;
   private object syncRoot = new object();

   public int State
   {
      get { return state; }
   }

   public int IncrementState()
   {
      lock (syncRoot)
      {
         return ++state;
      }
   }
}
```

There is, however, a faster way to lock the increment of the state, as shown next.

Interlocked

The `Interlocked` class is used to make simple statements for variables atomic. `i++` is not thread-safe. `i++` consists of getting a value from the memory, incrementing the value by 1, and storing the value back into memory. These operations can be interrupted by the thread scheduler. The `Interlocked` class provides methods for incrementing, decrementing, and exchanging values in a thread-safe manner.

The methods provided by the `Interlocked` class are described in the following table.

Interlocked Member	Description
`Increment()`	The `Increment()` method increments a variable and stores the result in an atomic operation.
`Decrement()`	`Decrement()` decrements a variable and stores the result.
`Exchange()`	`Exchange()` sets a variable to the specified value and returns the original value of the variable.

Interlocked Member	Description
`CompareExchange()`	`CompareExchange()` compares two variables for equality, and if they are the same, the specified value is set and the original value returned.
`Add()`	The `Add()` method adds two values and replaces the first variable with the result.
`Read()`	The `Read()` method is used to read 64-bit values from memory in an atomic operation. On a 32-bit system, reading 64 bits is not atomic; here, values from two memory addresses are read. On a 64-bit system, the `Read()` method is not required because accessing 64 bit values is an atomic operation.

Using the `Interlocked` class in contrast to other synchronization techniques is much faster. However, you can use it only for simple synchronization issues.

For example, instead of using the `lock` statement to lock access to the variable `someState` when setting it to a new value, in case it is null, you can use the `Interlocked` class, which is faster:

```
lock (this)
{
   if (someState == null)
   {
      someState = newState;
   }
}
```

The faster version with the same functionality uses the `Interlocked.CompareExchange()` method:

```
Interlocked.CompareExchange<SomeState>(ref someState, newState,
                                                      null);
```

And instead of doing an increment inside a `lock` statement:

```
public int State
{
   get
   {
      lock (this)
      {
         return ++state;
      }
   }
}
```

`Interlocked.Increment()` is faster:

```
public int State
{
   get
   {
      return Interlocked.Increment(ref state);
   }
}
```

Monitor

The C# compiler resolves the `lock` statement to use the `Monitor` class. The following `lock` statement

```
lock (obj)
{
   // synchronized region for obj
}
```

is resolved to invoking the `Enter()` method that waits until the thread gets the lock of the object. Only one thread at a time may be the owner of the object lock. As soon as the lock is resolved, the thread can enter the synchronized section. The `Exit()` method of the `Monitor` class releases the lock. The compiler puts the `Exit()` method into a finally handler of a try block so that the lock is also released if an exception is thrown.

`try/finally` *is covered in Chapter 14, "Errors and Exceptions."*

```
Monitor.Enter(obj);
try
{
   // synchronized region for obj
}
finally
{
   Monitor.Exit(obj);
}
```

The class `Monitor` has a big advantage compared to the `lock` statement of C#: you can add a timeout value waiting to get the lock. So instead of endlessly waiting to get the lock, you can use the `TryEnter()` method, where you can pass a timeout value that defines the maximum amount of time waiting to get the lock. If the lock for `obj` is acquired, `TryEnter()` returns `true` and performs synchronized access to the state guarded by the object `obj`. If `obj` is locked for more than 500 milliseconds by another thread, `TryEnter()` returns `false`, and the thread does not wait any longer but is used to do something else. Maybe at a later time, the thread can try to acquire the lock once more.

```
if (Monitor.TryEnter(obj, 500))
{
   try
   {
      // acquired the lock
      // synchronized region for obj
   }
   finally
   {
      Monitor.Exit(obj);
   }

}
else
{
   // didn't get the lock, do something else
}
```

Wait Handle

`WaitHandle` is an abstract base class that you can use to wait for a signal to be set. There are different things you can wait for, because `WaitHandle` is a base class and some classes are derived from it.

In the use of asynchronous delegates early in this chapter, the `WaitHandle` was already in use. The method `BeginInvoke()` of the asynchronous delegate returns an object that implements the interface `IAsyncResult`. Using `IAsyncResult`, you can access a `WaitHandle` with the property `AsyncWaitHandle`. When you invoke the method `WaitOne()`, the thread waits until a signal is received that is associated with the wait handle.

```
static void Main()
{
   TakesAWhileDelegate d1 = TakesAWhile;

   IAsyncResult ar = d1.BeginInvoke(1, 3000, null, null);
   while (true)
   {
      Console.Write(".");
      if (ar.AsyncWaitHandle.WaitOne(50, false))
      {
         Console.WriteLine("Can get the result now");
         break;
      }
   }
   int result = d1.EndInvoke(ar);
   Console.WriteLine("result: {0}", result);
}
```

The methods that are defined by the class `WaitHandle` to perform a wait are described in the following table.

WaitHandle Member	Description
`WaitOne()`	`WaitOne()` is an instance method where you can wait for a signal to occur. Optionally, you can specify a timeout value for the maximum amount of time to wait.
`WaitAll()`	`WaitAll()` is a static method used to pass an array of `WaitHandle` objects and wait until all of these handles are signaled.
`WaitAny()`	`WaitAny()` is a static method used to pass an array of `WaitHandle` objects and to wait until one of these handles is signaled. This method returns the index of the wait handle object that was signaled, so you know with what functionality you can continue in the program. If the timeout occurred before one handle was signaled, `WaitAny()` returns `WaitTimeout`.

With the `SafeWaitHandle` property, you can also assign a native handle to an operating system resource and wait for that handle. For example, you can assign a `SafeFileHandle` to wait for a file I/O operation to complete, or a custom `SafeTransactionHandle` as shown in Chapter 22, "Transactions."

The classes `Mutex`, `Event`, and `Semaphore` are derived from the base class `WaitHandle`, so you can use all of these with waits.

Mutex

`Mutex` (mutual exclusion) is one of the classes of the .NET Framework that offers synchronization across multiple processes. It is very similar to the `Monitor` class in that there is just one owner. Just one thread can get a lock of the mutex and access the synchronized code regions that are secured by the mutex.

With the constructor of the `Mutex` class, you can define if the mutex should initially be owned by the calling thread, define a name of the mutex, and get the information if the mutex already existed. In the sample code, the third parameter is defined as an out parameter to receive a Boolean value if the mutex was newly created. If the value returned is `false`, the mutex was already defined. The mutex might be defined in a different process, because a mutex with a name is known for the operating system and is shared between different processes. If there is not a name assigned to the mutex, the mutex is unnamed and not shared between different processes.

```
bool createdNew;
Mutex mutex = new Mutex(false, "ProCSharpMutex", out createdNew);
```

To open an existing mutex, you can also use the method `Mutex.OpenExisting()`, which doesn't require the same .NET privileges as creating the mutex with the constructor.

Because the `Mutex` class derives from the base class `WaitHandle`, you can do a `WaitOne()` to acquire the mutex lock and be the owner of the mutex during that time. The mutex is released by invoking the `ReleaseMutex()` method.

```
if (mutex.WaitOne())
{
   try
   {
      // synchronized region
   }
   finally
   {
      mutex.ReleaseMutex();
   }
}
else
{
   // some problem happened while waiting
}
```

Because a named mutex is known system-wide, you can use it to not allow an application to be started twice. In the following Windows Forms application, the constructor of the `Mutex` object is invoked. Then it is verified if the mutex with the name `SingletonWinAppMutex` exists already. If it does, the application exits.

```
static class Program
{
   [STAThread]
   static void Main()
   {
      bool createdNew;
      Mutex mutex = new Mutex(false, "SingletonWinAppMutex",
                              out createdNew);
      if (!createdNew)
      {
         MessageBox.Show("You can only start one instance " +
                         "of the application");
```

(continued)

(continued)

```
                Application.Exit();
                return;
            }

            Application.EnableVisualStyles();
            Application.SetCompatibleTextRenderingDefault(false);
            Application.Run(new Form1());
        }
    }
```

Semaphore

A semaphore is very similar to a mutex, but, in contrast, the semaphore can be used by multiple threads at once. A semaphore is a counting mutex, meaning that with a semaphore you can define the number of threads that are allowed to access the resource guarded by the semaphore simultaneously. This can be used if you have several of the resources available and can allow only a specific number of threads access to the resource. For example, say that you want to access physical I/O ports on the system and there are three ports available. So, three threads can access the I/O ports simultaneously, but the fourth thread needs to wait until the resource is released by one of the other threads.

In the sample application, in the `Main()` method six threads are created and one semaphore with a count of 4. In the constructor of the `Semaphore` class, you can define count for the number of locks that can be acquired with the semaphore (the second parameter) and the number of locks that are free initially (the first parameter). If the first parameter has a lower value than the second parameter, the difference between the values defines the already allocated semaphore count. As with the mutex, you can also assign a name to the semaphore to share it between different processes. Here, no name is defined with the semaphore, so it is used only within this process. After the `Semaphore` object is created, six threads are started, and they all get the same semaphore.

```
using System;
using System.Threading;
using System.Diagnostics;

namespace Wrox.ProCSharp.Threading
{
   class Program
   {
      static void Main()
      {
         int threadCount = 6;
         int semaphoreCount = 4;
         Semaphore semaphore = new Semaphore(semaphoreCount, semaphoreCount);
         Thread[] threads = new Thread[threadCount];

         for (int i = 0; i < threadCount; i++)
         {
            threads[i] = new Thread(ThreadMain);
            threads[i].Start(semaphore);
         }

         for (int i = 0; i < threadCount; i++)
```

```
            {
               threads[i].Join();
            }
            Console.WriteLine("All threads finished");
         }
```

In the thread's main method, `ThreadMain()`, the thread does a `WaitOne()` to lock the semaphore. Remember, the semaphore has a count of 4, so four threads can acquire the lock. Thread 5 must wait and, here, the timeout of 600 milliseconds is defined for a maximum wait time. If the lock cannot be acquired after the wait time, the thread writes a message to the console and repeats the wait in a loop. As soon as the lock is made, the thread writes a message to the console, sleeps for some time, and releases the lock. Again, with the release of the lock it is important that the resource be released in all cases. That's why the `Release()` method of the `Semaphore` class is invoked in a finally handler.

```
         static void ThreadMain(object o)
         {
            Semaphore semaphore = o as Semaphore;
            Trace.Assert(semaphore != null, "o must be a Semaphore type");
            bool isCompleted = false;
            while (!isCompleted)
            {
               if (semaphore.WaitOne(600, false))
               {
                  try
                  {
                     Console.WriteLine("Thread {0} locks the semaphore",
                           Thread.CurrentThread.ManagedThreadId);
                     Thread.Sleep(2000);
                  }
                  finally
                  {
                     semaphore.Release();
                     Console.WriteLine("Thread {0} releases the semaphore",
                        Thread.CurrentThread.ManagedThreadId);
                     isCompleted = true;
                  }
               }
               else
               {
                  Console.WriteLine("Timeout for thread {0}; wait again",
                     Thread.CurrentThread.ManagedThreadId);
               }
            }
         }
      }
   }
```

When you run the application, you can indeed see that with four threads the lock is made immediately. The threads with IDs 7 and 8 must wait. The wait continues in the loop until one of the other threads releases the semaphore.

```
Thread 3 locks the semaphore
Thread 4 locks the semaphore
Thread 5 locks the semaphore
Thread 6 locks the semaphore
```

(continued)

(continued)

```
Timeout for thread 8; wait again
Timeout for thread 7; wait again
Timeout for thread 8; wait again
Timeout for thread 7; wait again
Timeout for thread 7; wait again
Timeout for thread 8; wait again
Thread 3 releases the semaphore
Thread 8 locks the semaphore
Thread 4 releases the semaphore
Thread 7 locks the semaphore
Thread 5 releases the semaphore
Thread 6 releases the semaphore
Thread 8 releases the semaphore
Thread 7 releases the semaphore
All threads finished
```

Events

Events are the next of the system-wide synchronization resources. For using system events from managed code, the .NET Framework offers the classes `ManualResetEvent` and `AutoResetEvent` in the namespace `System.Threading`.

> *The* `event` *keyword from C# that was covered in Chapter 7 has nothing to do with the event classes from the namespace* `System.Threading`*. The* `event` *keyword is based on delegates, whereas both event classes are .NET wrappers to the system-wide native event resource for synchronization.*

You can use events to inform other threads that some data is here, something is completed, and so on. An event can be signaled or not signaled. A thread can wait for the event to be in a signaled state with the help of the `WaitHandle` class, which was already discussed.

A `ManualResetEvent` is signaled by invoking the `Set()` method and turned back to a non-signaled state with the `Reset()` method. If multiple threads are waiting for an event to be signaled, and the `Set()` method is invoked, then all threads waiting are released. Also, if a thread just invokes the `WaitOne()` method, but the event is already signaled, the waiting thread can continue immediately.

An `AutoResetEvent` is also signaled by invoking the `Set()` method. It is also possible to set it back to a non-signaled state with the `Reset()` method. However, if a thread is waiting for an auto-reset event to be signaled, the event is automatically changed into a non-signaled state when the wait state of the first thread is finished. The event changes automatically back into a non-signaled state. This way, if multiple threads are waiting for the event to be set, only one thread is released from its wait state. It is not the thread that has been waiting the longest for the event to be signaled but the thread waiting with the highest priority.

To demonstrate events with the `AutoResetEvent` class, the class `ThreadTask` defines the method `Calculation()`, which is the entry point for a thread. With this method, the thread receives input data for calculation (defined with the struct `InputData`) and writes the result to the variable result that can be accessed from the `Result` property. As soon as the result is completed (after a random amount of time), the event is signaled by invoking the `Set()` method of the `AutoResetEvent`.

```
public struct InputData
{
   public int X;
   public int Y;

   public InputData(int x, int y)
```

```
      {
         this.X = x;
         this.Y = y;
      }
   }

   public class ThreadTask
   {
      private AutoResetEvent autoEvent;

      public int Result { get; private set; }

      public ThreadTask(AutoResetEvent ev)
      {
         this.autoEvent = ev;
      }

      public void Calculation(object obj)
      {
         InputData data = (InputData)obj;
         Console.WriteLine("Thread {0} starts calculation",
            Thread.CurrentThread.ManagedThreadId);
         Thread.Sleep(new Random().Next(3000));
         Result = data.X + data.Y;

         // signal the event - completed!
         Console.WriteLine("Thread {0} is ready",
            Thread.CurrentThread.ManagedThreadId);
         autoEvent.Set();
      }
   }
```

The `Main()` method of the program defines arrays of four `AutoResetEvent` objects and four `ThreadTask` objects. Every `ThreadTask` is initialized in the constructor with an `AutoResetEvent` object, so that every thread gets its own event object to signal when it is completed. Now the `ThreadPool` class is used to have background threads running the calculation tasks by invoking the method `QueueUserWorkItem()`.

```
   class Program
   {
      static void Main()
      {
         int taskCount = 4;

         AutoResetEvent[] autoEvents = new AutoResetEvent[taskCount];
         ThreadTask[] tasks = new ThreadTask[taskCount];

         for (int i = 0; i < taskCount; i++)
         {
            autoEvents[i] = new AutoResetEvent(false);
            tasks[i] = new ThreadTask(mevents[i]);

            ThreadPool.QueueUserWorkItem(tasks[i].Calculation,
               new InputData(i + 1, i + 3));
         }
         //...
```

The `WaitHandle` class is now used to wait for any one of the events in the array. `WaitAny()` waits until any one of the events is signaled. `WaitAny()` returns an index value that provides information about the event that was signaled. The returned value matches the index of the event array that is passed to `WaitAny()`. Using this index the information from the signaled event can be read.

```
            for (int i = 0; i < taskCount; i++)
            {
               int index = WaitHandle.WaitAny(autoEvents);
               if (index == WaitHandle.WaitTimeout)
               {
                  Console.WriteLine("Timeout!!");
               }
               else
               {
                  Console.WriteLine("finished task for {0}, result: {1}",
                                    index, tasks[index].Result);
               }
            }
         }
      }
```

Starting the application, you can see the threads doing the calculation and setting the event to inform the main thread that it can read the result. Depending on random times, whether the build is a debug or release build, and your hardware, you might see different orders and also a different number of threads from the pool doing the tasks. Here, thread 4 was reused from the pool for doing two tasks because it was fast enough to finish the calculation first:

```
Thread 3 starts calculation
Thread 4 starts calculation
Thread 5 starts calculation
Thread 4 is ready
finished task for 1, result: 6
Thread 4 starts calculation
Thread 3 is ready
finished task for 0, result: 4
Thread 4 is ready
finished task for 3, result: 10
Thread 5 is ready
finished task for 2, result: 8
```

ReaderWriterLockSlim

For a locking mechanism to allow multiple readers, but just one writer, to a resource, the class `ReaderWriterLockSlim` can be used. This class offers a locking functionality in which multiple readers can access the resource if no writer locked it, and only a single writer can lock the resource.

`ReaderWriterLockSlim` *is new with .NET 3.0. The .NET 1.0 class with similar functionality is* `ReaderWriterLock`. `ReaderWriterLockSlim` *was redesigned to prevent deadlocks and to offer better performance.*

The methods and properties of `ReaderWriterLockSlim` are explained in the following tables.

ReaderWriterLockSlim Methods	Description

`TryEnterReadLock()`
`EnterReadLock()`
`ExitReadLock()`
	With `TryEnterReadLock()` and `EnterReadLock()` a read lock is done to access the resource. As long as there is no write lock, the read lock is successful. Multiple reads are allowed concurrently.
	With `TryEnterReadLock()` a time-out value can be specified for a maximum amount of time to wait for the lock to be acquired.
	`ExitReadLock()` releases the lock.

`TryEnterUpgradableReadLock()`
`EnterUpgradableReadLock()`
`ExitUpgradableReadLock()`
	If the read lock needs to be changed to a write lock after doing a read access to the resource, `TryEnterUpgradableReadLock()` and `EnterUpgradableReadLock()` can be used. The thread having a read lock can acquire a write lock without releasing the read lock.

`TryEnterWriteLock()`
`EnterWriteLock()`
`ExitWriteLock()`
	`TryEnterWriteLock()` and `EnterWriteLock()` are used to acquire a write lock to the resource. Only one thread acquiring the lock gets the lock. Also, there may not be any thread holding a read lock. When waiting for a write lock, it is also necessary that all read locks have been released.
	If one thread holding a write lock tries to get a write lock once again, the lock is acquired if the `ReaderWriterLockSlim` was created with the `RecursionPolicy` set to `LockRecursionPolicy.SupportsRecursion`.

Properties of the `ReaderWriterLockSlim` class give some status information about the current locks.

ReaderWriterLockSlim Properties	Description
`CurrentReadCount`	This returns the number of threads that acquired a read lock.

`IsReadLockHeld`
`IsUpgradableReadLockHeld`
`IsWriteLockHeld`
	These properties return a Boolean value about the corresponding lock type.

`WaitingReadCount`
`WaitingUpgradableReadCount`
`WaitingWriteCount`
	These properties return the number of threads that wait for the corresponding lock type.

`RecursionPolicy`
`RecursiveReadCount`
`RecursiveUpgradableReadCount`
`RecursiveWriteCount`
	With recursion, it is possible that one thread can acquire a lock again. The property `RecursionPolicy` is a read-only property to return the `LockRecursionPolicy`. The recursion policy can be configured with the `ReaderWriterLockSlim` constructor to `NoRecursion` or `SupportsRecursion`.

The sample program creates a collection containing six items and a `ReaderWriterLockSlim` object. The method `ReaderMethod()` acquired a read lock to read all items of the list and write it to the console. The method `WriterMethod()` tries to acquire a write lock to change all values of the collection. In the `Main()` method six threads are started that invoke either the method `ReaderMethod()` or the method `WriterMethod()`.

```
using System;
using System.Collections.Generic;
using System.Threading;

namespace Wrox.ProCSharp.Threading
{
   class Program
   {
      private static List<int> items = new List<int>()
            { 0, 1, 2, 3, 4, 5};
      private static ReaderWriterLockSlim rwl = new
            ReaderWriterLockSlim(LockRecursionPolicy.SupportsRecursion);

      static void ReaderMethod(object reader)
      {
         try
         {
            rwl.EnterReadLock();

            for (int i = 0; i < items.Count; i++)
            {
               Console.WriteLine("reader {0}, loop: {1}, item: {2}",
                     reader, i, items[i]);
               Thread.Sleep(40);
            }
         }
         finally
         {
            rwl.ExitReadLock();
         }
      }

      static void WriterMethod(object writer)
      {
         try
         {
            while (!rwl.TryEnterWriteLock(50))
            {
               Console.WriteLine("Writer {0} waiting for the write lock",
                     writer);
               Console.WriteLine("current reader count: {0}",
                     rwl.CurrentReadCount);
            }
            Console.WriteLine("Writer {0} acquired the lock", writer);
            for (int i = 0; i < items.Count; i++)
            {
               items[i]++;
               Thread.Sleep(50);
            }
```

```
                Console.WriteLine("Writer {0} finished", writer);
            }
            finally
            {
                rwl.ExitWriteLock();
            }
        }

        static void Main()
        {
            new Thread(WriterMethod).Start(1);
            new Thread(ReaderMethod).Start(1);
            new Thread(ReaderMethod).Start(2);
            new Thread(WriterMethod).Start(2);
            new Thread(ReaderMethod).Start(3);
            new Thread(ReaderMethod).Start(4);
        }
    }
}
```

With a run of the application here the first writer gets the lock first. The second writer and all readers need to wait. Next, the readers can work concurrently while the second writer still waits for the resource.

```
Writer 1 acquired the lock
Writer 2 waiting for the write lock
current reader count: 0
Writer 2 waiting for the write lock
current reader count: 0
Writer 2 waiting for the write lock
current reader count: 0
Writer 2 waiting for the write lock
current reader count: 0
Writer 1 finished
reader 4, loop: 0, item: 1
reader 1, loop: 0, item: 1
Writer 2 waiting for the write lock
current reader count: 4
reader 2, loop: 0, item: 1
reader 3, loop: 0, item: 1
reader 4, loop: 1, item: 2
reader 1, loop: 1, item: 2
reader 3, loop: 1, item: 2
reader 2, loop: 1, item: 2
Writer 2 waiting for the write lock
current reader count: 4
reader 4, loop: 2, item: 3
reader 1, loop: 2, item: 3
reader 2, loop: 2, item: 3
reader 3, loop: 2, item: 3
Writer 2 waiting for the write lock
current reader count: 4
reader 4, loop: 3, item: 4
reader 1, loop: 3, item: 4
reader 2, loop: 3, item: 4
```

(continued)

(continued)

```
reader 3, loop: 3, item: 4
reader 4, loop: 4, item: 5
reader 1, loop: 4, item: 5
Writer 2 waiting for the write lock
current reader count: 4
reader 2, loop: 4, item: 5
reader 3, loop: 4, item: 5
reader 4, loop: 5, item: 6
reader 1, loop: 5, item: 6
reader 2, loop: 5, item: 6
reader 3, loop: 5, item: 6
Writer 2 waiting for the write lock
current reader count: 4
Writer 2 acquired the lock
Writer 2 finished
```

Timers

The .NET Framework offers several `Timer` classes that can be used to invoke a method after some time interval. The following table lists the `Timer` classes and their namespaces, as well as their functionality.

Namespace	Description
`System.Threading`	The `Timer` class from the `System.Threading` namespace offers core functionality. In the constructor, you can pass a delegate that should be invoked at the time interval specified.
`System.Timers`	The `Timer` class from the `System.Timers` namespace is a component, because it derives from the `Component` base class. This way, you can drag and drop it from the Toolbox to the design surface of a server-application such as a Windows Service. This `Timer` class uses `System.Threading.Timer` but offers an event-based mechanism instead of a delegate.
`System.Windows.Forms`	With the `Timer` classes from the namespaces `System.Threading` and `System.Timers`, the callback or event methods are invoked from a different thread than the calling thread. Windows Forms controls are bound to the creator thread. Calling back into this thread is done by the `Timer` class from the `System.Windows.Forms` namespace.
`System.Web.UI`	The `Timer` from the `System.Web.UI` namespace is an Ajax extension that can be used with Web pages.

Using the `System.Threading.Timer` class, you can pass the method to be invoked as the first parameter in the constructor. This method must fulfill the requirements of the `TimerCallback` delegate that defines a void return type and an `object` parameter. With the second parameter, you can pass any object that is then received with the object argument in the callback method. For example, you can pass an `Event` object to signal the caller. The third parameter specifies the time span when the callback should be invoked the first time. With the last parameter, you specify the repeating interval for the callback. If the timer should fire only once, set parameter four to the value –1.

If the time interval should be changed after creating the `Timer` object, you can pass new values with the `Change()` method.

```
private static void ThreadingTimer()
{
   System.Threading.Timer t1 = new System.Threading.Timer(
      TimeAction, null, TimeSpan.FromSeconds(2),
      TimeSpan.FromSeconds(3));

   Thread.Sleep(15000);

   t1.Dispose();
}

static void TimeAction(object o)
{
   Console.WriteLine("System.Threading.Timer {0:T}", DateTime.Now);
}
```

The constructor of the `Timer` class from the `System.Timers` namespace requires just a time interval. The method that should be invoked after the interval is specified by the `Elapsed` event. This event requires a delegate of type `ElapsedEventHandler` that requires object and `ElapsedEventArgs` parameters as you can see with the `TimeAction` method. The `AutoReset` property specifies whether the timer should be fired repeatedly. Setting this property to `false`, the event is fired only once. Calling the `Start` method enables the timer to fire the events. Instead of calling the `Start` method you can set the `Enabled` property to `true`. Behind the scenes `Start()` does nothing else. The `Stop()` method sets the `Enabled` property to `false` to stop the timer.

```
private static void TimersTimer()
{
   System.Timers.Timer t1 = new System.Timers.Timer(1000);
   t1.AutoReset = true;
   t1.Elapsed += TimeAction;
   t1.Start();
   Thread.Sleep(10000);
   t1.Stop();

   t1.Dispose();
}

static void TimeAction(object sender, System.Timers.ElapsedEventArgs e)
{
   Console.WriteLine("System.Timers.Timer {0:T}", e.SignalTime );
}
```

COM Apartments

Threading has always been an important topic with COM objects. COM defines apartment models for synchronization. With a single-threaded apartment (STA), the COM runtime does the synchronization. A multithreaded apartment (MTA) means better performance but without synchronization by the COM runtime.

A COM component defines the apartment model it requires by setting a configuration value in the registry. A COM component that is developed in a thread-safe manner supports the MTA. Multiple threads can access this component at once, and the component must do synchronization on its own.

A COM component that doesn't deal with multiple threads requires an STA. Here, just one (and always the same) thread accesses the component. Another thread can access the component only by using a proxy that sends a Windows message to the thread that is connected to the COM object. STAs use Windows messages for synchronization.

Visual Basic 6 components supported only the STA model. A COM component that is configured with the option `both` supports both STA and MTA.

Whereas the COM component defines the requirements for the apartment, the thread that instantiates the COM object defines the apartment it is running in. This apartment should be the same one that the COM component requires.

A .NET thread, by default, runs in a MTA. You have probably already seen the attribute `[STAThread]` with the `Main()` method of a Windows application. This attribute specifies that the main thread joins an STA. Windows Forms applications require an STA thread.

```
[STAThread]
static void Main()
{
   //...
```

When creating a new thread, you can define the apartment model either by applying the attribute `[STAThread]` or `[MTAThread]` to the entry point method of the thread or by invoking the `SetApartmentState()` method of the `Thread` class before starting the thread:

```
Thread t1 = new Thread(DoSomeWork);
t1.SetApartmentState(ApartmentState.STA);
t1.Start();
```

You can get the apartment of the thread with the `GetApartmentThread()` method.

In Chapter 24, "Interoperability," you can read about .NET interop with COM components and more about COM apartment models.

Event-Based Asynchronous Pattern

Earlier in this chapter, you saw the asynchronous pattern based on the `IAsyncResult` interface. With an asynchronous callback, the callback thread is different from the calling thread. Using Windows Forms or WPF, this is a problem, because Windows Forms and WPF controls are bound to a single thread. With every control, you can invoke methods only from the thread that created the control. This also means that if you have a background thread, you cannot directly access the UI controls from this thread.

The only methods with Windows Forms controls that you can invoke from a different thread than the creator thread are `Invoke()`, `BeginInvoke()`, `EndInvoke()`, and the property `InvokeRequired`. `BeginInvoke()` and `EndInvoke()` are asynchronous variants of `Invoke()`. These methods switch to the creator thread to invoke the method that is assigned to a delegate parameter that you can pass to these methods. Using these methods is not that easy, which is why, since .NET 2.0, a new component together with a new asynchronous pattern was invented: the event-based asynchronous pattern.

With the event-based asynchronous pattern, the asynchronous component offers a method with the suffix `Async`; for example, the synchronous method `DoATask()` has the name `DoATaskAsync()` in the asynchronous version. To get the result information, the component also needs to define an event that has the suffix `Completed`, for example, `DoATaskCompleted`. While the action happening in the `DoATaskAsync()` method is running in a background thread, the event `DoATaskCompleted` is fired in the same thread as the caller.

With the event-based asynchronous pattern, the asynchronous component optionally can support cancellation and information about progress. For cancellation, the method should have the name `CancelAsync()`, and for progress information, an event with the suffix `ProgressChanged`, for example, `DoATaskProgressChanged`, is offered.

If you haven't written any Windows applications until now, you can skip this section of the chapter and keep it for later. Just remember, using threads from Windows applications adds another complexity, and you should come back here after reading the Windows Forms chapters (Chapters 31 to 33) or WPF chapters (Chapters 34 and 35). In any case, the Windows Forms application demonstrated here is very simple from a Windows Forms viewpoint.

BackgroundWorker

The `BackgroundWorker` class is one implementation of the asynchronous event pattern. This class implements methods, properties, and events, as described in the following table.

Another class that implements the asynchronous event pattern is the component `WebClient` in the `System.Net` namespace. This class uses the `WebRequest` and `WebResponse` classes but offers an easier-to-use interface. The `WebRequest` and `WebResponse` classes also offer asynchronous programming, but here it is based on the asynchronous pattern with the `IAsyncResult` interface.

BackgroundWorker Members	Description
`IsBusy`	The property `IsBusy` returns `true` while an asynchronous task is active.
`CancellationPending`	The property `CancellationPending` returns `true` after the `CancelAsync()` method is invoked. If this property is set to `true`, the asynchronous task should stop its work.
`RunWorkerAsync()` `DoWork`	The method `RunWorkerAsync()` fires the `DoWork` event to start the asynchronous task in a separate thread.
`CancelAsync()` `WorkerSupportsCancellation`	If cancellation is enabled (by setting the `WorkerSupportsCancellation` property to `true`), the asynchronous task can be canceled with the `CancelAsync()` method.

`ReportProgress()`
`ProgressChanged`
`WorkerReportsProgress`
	If the `WorkerReportsProgress` property is set to `true`, the `BackgroundWorker` can give interim feedback about the progress of the asynchronous task. The asynchronous task provides feedback about the percentage of work completed, by invoking the method `ReportProgress()`. This method then fires the `ProgressChanged` event.

`RunWorkerCompleted`	The `RunWorkerCompleted` event is fired as soon as the asynchronous task is completed, regardless of whether it was canceled.

The sample application demonstrates the use of the `BackgroundWorker` control in a Windows Forms application by doing a task that takes some time. Create a new Windows Forms application and add three `Label` controls, three `TextBox` controls, two `Button` controls, one `ProgressBar`, and one `BackgroundWorker` to the form, as shown in Figure 19-3.

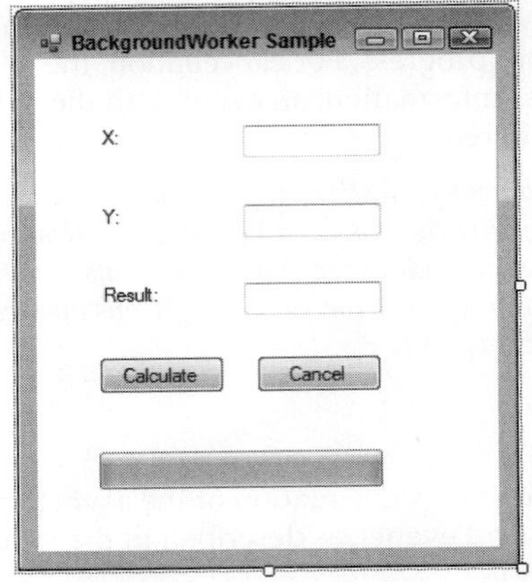

Figure 19-3

Configure the properties of the controls as listed in the following table.

Control	Property and Events	Value
Label	Text	X:
TextBox	Name	textbox
Label	Text	Y:
TextBox	Name	textBoxY
Label	Text	Result:
TextBox	Name	textBoxResult
Button	Name	buttonCalculate
Text	Calculate	
Click	OnCalculate	
Button	Name	buttonCancel
Text	Cancel	
Enabled	False	
Click	OnCancel	
ProgressBar	Name	progressBar
BackgroundWorker	Name	backgroundWorker
DoWork	OnDoWork	
RunWorkerCompleted	OnWorkCompleted	

Add the struct CalcInput to the project. This struct will be used to contain the input data from the TextBox controls.

```
public struct CalcInput
{
   public CalcInput(int x, int y)
   {
      this.x = x;
      this.y = y;
   }
   public int x;
   public int y;
}
```

The method OnCalculate() is the event handler for the Click event from the Button control named buttonCalculate. In the implementation buttonCalculate is disabled, so the user cannot click the button once more until the calculation is completed. To start the BackgroundWorker, invoke the method RunWorkerAsync(). The BackgroundWorker uses a thread pool thread to do the calculation. RunWorkerAsync() requires the input parameters that are passed to the handler that is assigned to the DoWork event.

```
private void OnCalculate(object sender, EventArgs e)
{
   this.buttonCalculate.Enabled = false;
   this.textBoxResult.Text = String.Empty;
   this.buttonCancel.Enabled = true;
   this.progressBar.Value = 0;

   backgroundWorker.RunWorkerAsync(new CalcInput(
      int.Parse(this.textBoxX.Text), int.Parse(this.textBoxY.Text)));
}
```

The method OnDoWork() is connected to the DoWork event of the BackgroundWorker control. With the DoWorkEventArgs, the input parameters are received with the property Argument. The implementation simulates functionality that takes some time with a sleep time of 5 seconds. After sleeping, the result of the calculation is written to the Result property of DoEventArgs. If you add the calculation and sleep to the OnCalculate() method instead, the Windows application is blocked from user input while this is active. However, here, a separate thread is used and the user interface is still active.

```
private void OnDoWork(object sender, DoWorkEventArgs e)
{
   CalcInput input = (CalcInput)e.Argument;

   Thread.Sleep(5000);
   e.Result = input.x + input.y;
}
```

After OnDoWork is completed, the background worker fires the RunWorkerCompleted event. The method OnWorkCompleted() is associated with this event. Here, the result is received from the Result property of the RunWorkerCompletedEventArgs parameter, and this result is written to the result TextBox control. When firing the event, the BackgroundWorker control changes control to the creator thread, so there is no need to use the Invoke methods of the Windows Forms controls, and you can invoke properties and methods of Windows Forms controls directly.

```
private void OnWorkCompleted(object sender,
                             RunWorkerCompletedEventArgs e)
{
   this.textBoxResult.Text = e.Result.ToString();

   this.buttonCalculate.Enabled = true;
   this.buttonCancel.Enabled = false;
   this.progressBar.Value = 100;
}
```

Now you can test the application and see that the calculation runs independently of the UI thread, the UI is still active, and the Form can be moved around. However, the cancel and progress bar functionality still needs implementation.

Enable Cancel

To enable the cancel functionality to stop the thread's progress while it is running, you must set the `BackgroundWorker` property `WorkerSupportsCancellation` to `True`. Next, you have to implement the `OnCancel` handler that is connected to the `Click` event of the control `buttonCancel`. The `BackGroundWorker` control has the `CancelAsync()` method to cancel an asynchronous task that is going on.

```
private void OnCancel(object sender, EventArgs e)
{
   backgroundWorker.CancelAsync();
}
```

The asynchronous task is not canceled automatically. In the `OnDoWork()` handler that does the asynchronous task, you must change the implementation to examine the `CancellationPending` property of the `BackgroundWorker` control. This property is set as soon as `CancelAsync()` is invoked. If a cancellation is pending, set the `Cancel` property of `DoWorkEventArgs` to true and exit the handler.

```
private void OnDoWork(object sender, DoWorkEventArgs e)
{
   CalcInput input = (CalcInput)e.Argument;

   for (int i = 0; i < 10; i++)
   {
      Thread.Sleep(500);

      if (backgroundWorker.CancellationPending)
      {
         e.Cancel = true;
         return;
      }
   }

   e.Result = input.x + input.y;
}
```

The completion handler `OnWorkCompleted()` is invoked if the asynchronous method has completed successfully or if it was canceled. If it was canceled, you cannot access the `Result` property, because this throws an `InvalidOperationException` with the information that the operation has been canceled. So, you have to check the `Cancelled` property of `RunWorkerCompletedEventArgs` and behave accordingly.

```
private void OnWorkCompleted(object sender,
                              RunWorkerCompletedEventArgs e)
{
   if (e.Cancelled)
   {
      this.textBoxResult.Text = "Cancelled";
   }
   else
   {
      this.textBoxResult.Text = e.Result.ToString();
   }
   this.buttonCalculate.Enabled = true;
   this.buttonCancel.Enabled = false;
}
```

Running the application once more, you can cancel the asynchronous progress from the user interface.

Enable Progress

To get progress information to the user interface, you must set the `BackgroundWorker` property `WorkerReportsProgress` to `True`.

With the `OnDoWork` method, you can report the progress to the `BackgroundWorker` control with the `ReportProgress()` method:

```
private void OnDoWork(object sender, DoWorkEventArgs e)
{
   CalcInput input = (CalcInput)e.Argument;

   for (int i = 0; i < 10; i++)
   {
      Thread.Sleep(500);
      backgroundWorker.ReportProgress(i * 10);
      if (backgroundWorker.CancellationPending)
      {
         e.Cancel = true;
         return;
      }
   }

   e.Result = input.x + input.y;
}
```

The method `ReportProgress()` fires the `ProgressChanged` event of the `BackgroundWorker` control. This event changes the control to the UI thread.

Add the method `OnProgressChanged()` to the `ProgressChanged` event, and in the implementation set a new value to the progress bar control that is received from the property `ProgressPercentage` of `ProgressChangedEventArgs`:

```
private void OnProgressChanged(object sender,
                               ProgressChangedEventArgs e)
{
   this.progressBar.Value = e.ProgressPercentage;
}
```

In the `OnWorkCompleted()` event handler, the progress bar finally is set to the 100% value:

```
private void OnWorkCompleted(object sender,
                              RunWorkerCompletedEventArgs e)
{
   if (e.Cancelled)
   {
      this.textBoxResult.Text = "Cancelled";
   }
   else
   {
      this.textBoxResult.Text = e.Result.ToString();
   }
   this.buttonCalculate.Enabled = true;
   this.buttonCancel.Enabled = false;
   this.progressBar.Value = 100;
}
```

Figure 19-4 shows the running application while the calculation is just active.

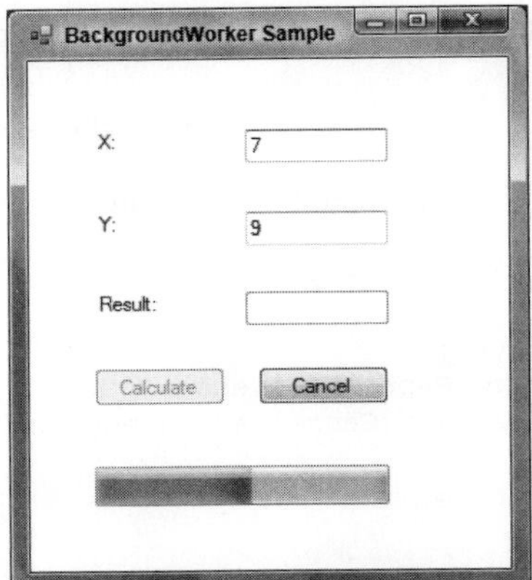

Figure 19-4

Creating an Event-Based Asynchronous Component

To create a custom component that supports the event-based asynchronous pattern, more work needs to be done. To demonstrate this with a simple scenario, the class `AsyncComponent` just returns a converted input string after a time span, as you can see with the synchronous method `LongTask()`. To offer asynchronous support, the public interface offers the asynchronous method `LongTaskAsync()` and the event `LongTaskCompleted`. This event is of type `LongTaskCompletedEventHandler` that defines the parameters `object sender` and `LongTaskCompletedEventArgs e`. `LongTaskCompletedEventArgs` is a new type where the caller can read the result of the asynchronous operation.

In addition, some helper methods such as `DoLongTask` and `CompletionMethod` are needed; these are discussed next.

```
using System;
using System.Collections.Generic;
using System.ComponentModel;
using System.Threading;

namespace Wrox.ProCSharp.Threading
{
   public delegate void LongTaskCompletedEventHandler(object sender,
         LongTaskCompletedEventArgs e);

   public partial class AsyncComponent : Component
   {
      private Dictionary<object, AsyncOperation> userStateDictionary =
            new Dictionary<object, AsyncOperation>();
      private SendOrPostCallback onCompletedDelegate;

      public AsyncComponent()
      {
         InitializeComponent();
         InitializeDelegates();
      }

      public AsyncComponent(IContainer container)
      {
         container.Add(this);

         InitializeComponent();
         InitializeDelegates();
      }

      private void InitializeDelegates()
      {
         onCompletedDelegate = LongTaskCompletion;
      }

      public string LongTask(string input)
      {
         Console.WriteLine("LongTask started");
         Thread.Sleep(5000);
         Console.WriteLine("LongTask finished");
         return input.ToUpper();
      }

      public void LongTaskAsync(string input, object taskId)
      {
         //...
      }

      public event LongTaskCompletedEventHandler LongTaskCompleted;

      private void LongTaskCompletion(object operationState)
      {
         //...
      }
```

(continued)

(continued)

```
        protected void OnLongTaskCompleted(LongTaskCompletedEventArgs e)
        {
           //...
        }

        private delegate void LongTaskWorkHandler(string input,
              AsyncOperation asyncOp);

        // running in a background thread
        private void DoLongTask(string input, AsyncOperation asyncOp)
        {
           //...
        }

        private void CompletionMethod(string output, Exception ex,
              bool cancelled, AsyncOperation asyncOp)
        {
           //...
        }
     }

     public class LongTaskCompletedEventArgs : AsyncCompletedEventArgs
     {
        //...
     }
  }
```

The method `LongTaskAsync` needs to start the synchronous operation asynchronously. If the component allows starting the asynchronous task several times concurrently, the client needs to have an option to map the different results to the tasks started. This is why the second parameter of `LongTaskAsync` requires a `taskId` that can be used by the client to map the results. Of course, inside the component itself the task ID needs to be remembered to map the results. .NET offers the class `AsyncOperationManager` to create `AsyncOperationObjects` to help keep track of the state of operations. The class `AsyncOperationManager` has one method, `CreateOperation`, where a task identifier can be passed, and an `AsyncOperation` object is returned. This operation is kept as an item in the dictionary `userStateDictionary` that was created earlier.

Then, a delegate of type `LongTaskWorkHandler` is created, and the method `DoLongTask` is assigned to that delegate instance. `BeginInvoke()` is the method of the delegate to start the method `DoLongTask()` asynchronously using a thread from the thread pool.

```
        public void LongTaskAsync(string input, object taskId)
        {
           AsyncOperation asyncOp =
                 AsyncOperationManager.CreateOperation(taskId);

           lock (userStateDictionary)
           {
              if (userStateDictionary.ContainsKey(taskId))
                 throw new ArgumentException("taskId must be unique", "taskId");

              userStateDictionary[taskId] = asyncOp;
           }
```

```
        LongTaskWorkHandler longTaskDelegate = DoLongTask;
        longTaskDelegate.BeginInvoke(input, asyncOp, null, null);
    }
```

The delegate type `LongTaskWorkHandler` is just defined within the class `AsyncComponent` with a private access modifier because it is not needed outside. The parameters needed with this delegate are all input parameters from the caller plus the `AsyncOperation` parameter for getting the status and mapping the result of the operation.

```
private delegate void LongTaskWorkHandler(string input,
      AsyncOperation asyncOp);
```

The method `DoLongTask()` is now called asynchronously by using the delegate. The synchronous method `LongTask()` can now be invoked to get the output value.

Because an exception that might happen inside the synchronous method should not just blow up the background thread, any exception is caught and remembered with the variable `e` of type `Exception`. Finally, the `CompletionMethod()` is invoked to inform the caller about the result.

```
// running in a background thread
private void DoLongTask(string input, AsyncOperation asyncOp)
{
   Exception e = null;
   string output = null;
   try
   {
      output = LongTask(input);
   }
   catch (Exception ex)
   {
      e = ex;
   }

   this.CompletionMethod(output, e, false, asyncOp);
}
```

With the implementation of the `CompletionMethod`, the `userStateDictionary` is cleaned up as the operation is removed. The `PostOperationCompleted()` method of the `AsyncOperation` object ends the lifetime of the asynchronous operation and informs the caller using the `onCompletedDelegate` method. This method ensures that the delegate is invoked on the thread as needed for the application type. To get information to the caller, an object of type `LongTaskCompletedEventArgs` is created and passed to the method `PostOperationCompleted()`.

```
   private void CompletionMethod(string output, Exception ex,
         bool cancelled, AsyncOperation asyncOp)
   {
      lock (userStateDictionary)
      {
         userStateDictionary.Remove(asyncOp.UserSuppliedState);
      }

      // results of the operation
      LongTaskCompletedEventArgs e = new LongTaskCompletedEventArgs(
            output, ex, cancelled, asyncOp.UserSuppliedState);

      asyncOp.PostOperationCompleted(onCompletedDelegate, e);
   }
}
```

For passing information to the caller, the class LongTaskCompletedEventArgs derives from the base class AsyncCompletedEventArgs and adds a property containing output information. In the constructor, the base constructor is invoked to pass exception, cancellation, and user state information.

```
public class LongTaskCompletedEventArgs : AsyncCompletedEventArgs
{
   public LongTaskCompletedEventArgs(string output, Exception e,
         bool cancelled, object state)
      : base(e, cancelled, state)
   {
      this.output = output;
   }

   private string output;

   public string Output
   {
      get
      {
         RaiseExceptionIfNecessary();

         return output;
      }
   }
}
```

The method asyncOp.PostOperationCompleted() uses the onCompletedDelegate. This delegate was initialized to reference the method LongTaskCompletion. LongTaskCompletion needs to fulfill the parameter requirements of the SendOrPostCallbackDelegate. The implementation just casts the parameter to LongTaskCompletedEventArgs, which was the type of the object that was passed to the PostOperationCompleted method, and calls the method OnLongTaskCompleted.

```
private void LongTaskCompletion(object operationState)
{
   LongTaskCompletedEventArgs e =
      operationState as LongTaskCompletedEventArgs;

   OnLongTaskCompleted(e);
}
```

OnLongTaskCompleted then just fires the event LongTaskCompleted to return the LongTaskCompletedEventArgs to the caller.

```
protected void OnLongTaskCompleted(LongTaskCompletedEventArgs e)
{
   if (LongTaskCompleted != null)
   {
      LongTaskCompleted(this, e);
   }
}
```

After creating the component, it is really easy to use it. The event LongTaskCompleted is assigned to the method Comp_LongTaskCompleted, and the method LongTaskAsync() is invoked. With a simple console application, you will see that the event handler `Comp_LongTaskCompleted` is called from a thread different from the main thread. (This is different from Windows Forms applications, as you will see next.)

```
static void Main()
{
   Console.WriteLine("Main thread: {0}",
         Thread.CurrentThread.ManagedThreadId);

   AsyncComponent comp = new AsyncComponent();
   comp.LongTaskCompleted += Comp_LongTaskCompleted;

   comp.LongTaskAsync("input", 33);

   Console.ReadLine();
}

static void Comp_LongTaskCompleted(object sender,
      LongTaskCompletedEventArgs e)
{
   Console.WriteLine("completed, result: {0}, thread: {1}", e.Output,
         Thread.CurrentThread.ManagedThreadId);
}
```

With a Windows Forms application the `SynchronizationContext` is set to `WindowsFormsSynchronizationContext` — that's why the event handler code is invoked in the same thread:

```
WindowsFormsSynchronizationContext syncContext =
      new WindowsFormsSynchronizationContext();
SynchronizationContext.SetSynchronizationContext(syncContext);
```

Summary

This chapter explored how to code applications that use multiple threads using the `System.Threading` namespace. Using multithreading in your applications takes careful planning. Too many threads can cause resource issues, and not enough threads can cause your application to seem sluggish and to perform poorly.

You've seen various ways to create multiple threads such as using the delegate, timers, a `ThreadPool`, and the `Thread` class. Various synchronization techniques have been explored such as a simple `lock` statement but also the `Monitor`, `Semaphore`, and `Event` classes. You've seen how to program the asynchronous pattern with the `IAsyncResult` interface, and the event-based asynchronous pattern.

The `System.Threading` namespace in the .NET Framework gives you multiple ways to manipulate threads; however, this does not mean that the .NET Framework handles all the difficult tasks of multithreading for you. You need to consider thread priority and synchronization issues. This chapter discussed these issues and how to code for them in your C# applications. It also looked at the problems associated with deadlocks and race conditions.

Just remember that if you are going to use multithreading in your C# applications, careful planning needs to be a major part of your efforts.

Some final guidelines regarding threading:

- Try to keep synchronization requirements to a minimum. Synchronization is complex and blocks threads. You can avoid it if you try to avoid sharing state. Of course, this is not always possible.
- Static members of a class should be thread-safe. Usually, this is the case with classes in the .NET Framework.
- Instance state does not need to be thread-safe. For best performance, synchronization is better used outside of the class where it is needed and not with every member of the class. Instance members of .NET Framework classes usually are not thread-safe. In the MSDN library you can find this information documented for every class of the Framework in the Thread Safety section.

The next chapter gives information on another core .NET topic: security.

20

Security

Security has several key aspects to consider. One is the user of the application. Is it really the user, or someone posing as the user, who is accessing the application? How can this user be trusted? As you will see in this chapter, the user first needs to be authenticated, and then authorization occurs to verify if the user is allowed to use the requested resources.

What about data that is stored or sent across the network? Is it possible that someone accesses this data, for example, by using a network sniffer? Encryption of data is important here.

Yet another aspect is the application itself. How can you trust the application? What is the origin or evidence from the application? This is extremely important, for example, in a Web hosting scenario. A Web hosting provider does not allow its customers to access all resources from the system. Depending on the evidence of the assembly, different permissions for the application apply.

This chapter explores the features available in .NET to help you manage security, including how .NET protects you from malicious code, how to administer security policies, and how to access the security subsystem programmatically. The topics of this chapter are:

- Authentication and authorization
- Cryptography
- Access control to resources
- Code access security
- Managing security policies

Authentication and Authorization

Authentication is the process of identifying the user, and authorization occurs afterward to verify if the identified user is allowed to access a specific resource.

Identity and Principal

You can identify the user running the application by using an identity. The `WindowsIdentity` class represents a Windows user. If you don't identify the user with a Windows account, you can use other classes that implement the interface IIdentity. With this interface you have access to the name of the user, information about whether the user is authenticated, and the authentication type.

A principal is an object that contains the identity of the user and the roles that the user belongs to. The interface IPrincipal defines the property Identity that returns an IIdentity object and the method IsInRole in which you can verify if the user is a member of a specific role. A role is a collection of users who have the same security permissions, and it is the unit of administration for users. Roles can be Windows groups or just a collection of strings that you define.

Principal classes available with .NET are WindowsPrincipal and GenericPrincipal. You can also create a custom principal class that implements the interface IPrincipal.

In the following example, you create a console application that provides access to the principal in an application that, in turn, enables you to access the underlying Windows account. You need to import the System.Security.Principal and System.Threading namespaces. First of all, you must specify that .NET automatically hooks up the principal with the underlying Windows account. This is because .NET does not automatically populate the thread's CurrentPrincipal property for security reasons. You can do it like this:

```
using System;
using System.Security.Principal;
using System.Threading;

namespace Wrox.ProCSharp.Security
{
   class Program
   {
      static void Main()
      {
         AppDomain.CurrentDomain.SetPrincipalPolicy(
            PrincipalPolicy.WindowsPrincipal);
```

It is possible to use WindowsIdentity.GetCurrent() to access the Windows account details; however, that method is best used when you are going to look at the principal only once. If you want to access the principal a number of times, it is more efficient to set the policy so that the current thread provides access to the principal for you. If you use the SetPrincipalPolicy method, it is specified that the principal in the current thread should hold a WindowsIdentity object. All identity classes, such as WindowsIdentity, implement the IIdentity interface. The interface contains three properties (AuthenticationType, IsAuthenticated, and Name) for all derived identity classes to implement.

Add code to access the principal's properties from the Thread object:

```
         WindowsPrincipal principal =
            (WindowsPrincipal)Thread.CurrentPrincipal;
         WindowsIdentity identity = (WindowsIdentity)principal.Identity;
         Console.WriteLine("IdentityType: " + identity.ToString());
         Console.WriteLine("Name: {0}", identity.Name);
         Console.WriteLine("'Users'?: {0} ",
               principal.IsInRole("BUILTIN\\Users"));
         Console.WriteLine("'Administrators'? {0}",
               principal.IsInRole(WindowsBuiltInRole.Administrator));
         Console.WriteLine("Authenticated: {0}", identity.IsAuthenticated);
         Console.WriteLine("AuthType: {0}", identity.AuthenticationType);
         Console.WriteLine("Anonymous? {0}", identity.IsAnonymous);
         Console.WriteLine("Token: {0}", identity.Token);
      }
   }
}
```

The output from this console application looks similar to the following lines; it will vary according to your machine's configuration and the roles associated with the account under which you are signed in:

```
IdentityType:System.Security.Principal.WindowsIdentity
Name: farabove\christian
'Users'? True
'Administrators'? True
Authenticated: True
AuthType: NTLM
Anonymous? False
Token: 368
```

It is enormously beneficial to be able to easily access details about the current users and their roles. With this information, you can make decisions about what actions should be permitted or denied. The ability to make use of roles and Windows user groups provides the added benefit that administration can be done by using standard user administration tools, and you can usually avoid altering the code when user roles change. The following section looks at roles in more detail.

Roles

Role-based security is especially useful in situations in which access to resources is an issue. A primary example is the finance industry, in which employees' roles define what information they can access and what actions they can perform.

Role-based security is also ideal for use in conjunction with Windows accounts, or a custom user directory to manage access to Web-based resources. For example, a Web site could restrict access to its content until a user registers with the site, and then additionally provide access to special content only, if the user is a paying subscriber. In many ways, ASP.NET makes role-based security easier because much of the code is based on the server.

For example, to implement a Web service that requires authentication, you could use the account subsystem of Windows and write the Web method in such a way that it ensures the user is a member of a specific Windows user group before allowing access to the method's functionality.

Imagine a scenario with an intranet application that relies on Windows accounts. The system has a group called `Manager` and one called `Assistant`; users are assigned to these groups according to their role within the organization. Say that the application contains a feature that displays information about employees that should be accessed only by users in the `Managers` group. You can easily use code that checks whether the current user is a member of the `Managers` group and whether he is permitted or denied access.

However, if you decide later to rearrange the account groups and to introduce a group called `Personnel` that also has access to employee details, you will have a problem. You will need to go through all the code and update it to include rules for this new group.

A better solution would be to create a permission called something like `ReadEmployeeDetails` and assign it to groups where necessary. If the code applies a check for the `ReadEmployeeDetails` permission, updating the application to allow those in the `Personnel` group access to employee details is simply a matter of creating the group, placing the users in it, and assigning the `ReadEmployeeDetails` permission.

Declarative Role-Based Security

Just as with code access security, you can implement role-based security requests ("the user must be in the Administrators group") using imperative requests by calling the `IsInRole()` method from the

IPrincipal class, or using attributes. You can state permission requirements declaratively at the class or method level using the [PrincipalPermission] attribute:

```
using System;
using System.Security;
using System.Security.Principal;
using System.Security.Permissions;

namespace Wrox.ProCSharp.Security
{
   class Program
   {
      static void Main()
      {
         AppDomain.CurrentDomain.SetPrincipalPolicy(
            PrincipalPolicy.WindowsPrincipal);
         try
         {
            ShowMessage();
         }
         catch (SecurityException exception)
         {
            Console.WriteLine("Security exception caught (" +
                                 exception.Message + ")");
            Console.WriteLine("The current principal must be in the local"
                                 + "Users group");
         }
         Console.ReadLine();
      }

      [PrincipalPermission(SecurityAction.Demand,
                                    Role = "BUILTIN\\Users")]
      static void ShowMessage()
      {
         Console.WriteLine("The current principal is logged in locally ");
         Console.WriteLine("(member of the local Users group)");
      }
   }
}
```

The ShowMessage() method will throw an exception unless you execute the application in the context of a user in the Windows local Users group. For a Web application, the account under which the ASP.NET code is running must be in the group, although in a "real-world" example you would certainly avoid adding this account to the administrators group!

If you run the preceding code using an account in the local Users group, the output will look like this:

```
The current principal is logged in locally
(member of the local Users group)
```

Client Application Services

Visual Studio 2008 makes it easy to use authentication services that previously have been built for ASP.NET Web applications. With this service, it is possible to use the same authentication mechanism both with Windows and Web applications. This is a provider model that is primarily based on the classes Membership and Roles in the namespace System.Web.Security. With the Membership class you can validate, create, delete, find users, change the password, and other various things related to users. With the `Roles` class you can add and delete roles, get the roles for a user, and change roles from a user. Where the roles and users are stored depends on the provider. The `ActiveDirectoryMembershipProvider` accesses users and roles in the Active Directory; the `SqlMembershipProvider` uses a SQL Server database. For client application services new providers exist with .NET 3.5: `ClientFormsAuthenticationMembershipProvider` and `ClientWindowsAuthenticationMembershipProvider`.

Next, you use client application services with Forms authentication. To do this, first you need to start an application server, and then you can use this service from Windows Forms or WPF.

Application Services

For using client application services, you can create an ASP.NET Web service project that offers application services.

With the project a membership provider is needed. The sample code here defines the class `SampleMembershipProvider` that derives from the base class `MembershipProvider`. You must override all abstract methods from the base class. For login, the only implementation needed is the method `ValidateUser`. All other methods can throw a `NotSupportedException` as shown with the property `ApplicationName`. The sample code here uses a `Dictionary<string, string>` that contains usernames and passwords. Of course, you can change it to your own implementation, for example, to read username and password from the database.

```
using System;
using System.Collections.Generic;
using System.Collections.Specialized;
using System.Web.Security;

namespace Wrox.ProCSharp.Security
{
   public class SampleMembershipProvider : MembershipProvider
   {
      private Dictionary<string, string> users = null;
      internal static string ManagerUserName = "Manager".ToLowerInvariant();
      internal static string EmployeeUserName = "Employee".ToLowerInvariant();


      public override void Initialize(string name, NameValueCollection config)
      {
         users = new Dictionary<string, string>();
         users.Add(ManagerUserName, "secret@Pa$$w0rd");
         users.Add(EmployeeUserName, "s0me@Secret");

         base.Initialize(name, config);
      }

      public override string ApplicationName
      {
         get
         {
            throw new NotImplementedException();
         }
```

(continued)

(continued)

```
            set
            {
               throw new NotImplementedException();
            }
         }

         // override abstract Membership members
         // ...

         public override bool ValidateUser(string username, string password)
         {
            if (users.ContainsKey(username.ToLowerInvariant()))
            {
               return password.Equals(users[username.ToLowerInvariant()]);
            }
            return false;
         }
      }
   }
```

For using roles, you also need to implement a role provider. The class `SampleRoleProvider` derives from the base class `RoleProvider` and implements the methods `GetRolesForUser()` and `IsUserInRole()`:

```
using System;
using System.Collections.Specialized;
using System.Web.Security;

namespace Wrox.ProCSharp.Security
{
   public class SampleRoleProvider : RoleProvider
   {
      internal static string ManagerRoleName =
          "Manager".ToLowerInvariant();
      internal static string EmployeeRoleName =
          "Employee".ToLowerInvariant();

      public override void Initialize(string name, NameValueCollection config)
      {
         base.Initialize(name, config);
      }

      public override void AddUsersToRoles(string[] usernames,
            string[] roleNames)
      {
         throw new NotImplementedException();
      }

      //... override abstract RoleProvider members

      public override string[] GetRolesForUser(string username)
      {
         if (string.Compare(username,
             SampleMembershipProvider.ManagerUserName, true) == 0)
```

```
            {
               return new string[] { ManagerRoleName };
            }
            else if (string.Compare(username,
                 SampleMembershipProvider.EmployeeUserName, true) == 0)
            {
               return new string[] { EmployeeRoleName };
            }
            else
            {
               return new string[0];
            }
         }

         public override bool IsUserInRole(string username, string roleName)
         {
            string[] roles = GetRolesForUser(username);
            foreach (string role in roles)
            {
               if (string.Compare(role, roleName, true) == 0)
               {
                  return true;
               }
            }
            return false;
         }
      }
   }
```

Authentication services must be configured in the `Web.config` file. On the production system, it would be useful from a security standpoint to configure SSL with the server hosting application services.

```
<system.web.extensions>
  <scripting>
    <webServices>
      <authenticationService enabled="true" requireSSL="false"/>
      <roleService enabled="true"/>
    </webServices>
  </scripting>
</system.web.extensions>
```

Within the `<system.web>` section, the `membership` and `roleManager` elements must be configured to reference the classes that implement the membership and role provider:

```
<system.web>
  <membership defaultProvider="SampleMembershipProvider">
    <providers>
      <add name="SampleMembershipProvider"
            type="Wrox.ProCSharp.Security.SampleMembershipProvider"/>
    </providers>
  </membership>
  <roleManager enabled="true" defaultProvider="SampleRoleProvider">
    <providers>
      <add name="SampleRoleProvider"
          type="Wrox.ProCSharp.Security.SampleRoleProvider"/>
    </providers>
  </roleManager>
```

For debugging, you can assign a port number and virtual path with the Web tab of project properties. The sample application uses the port 55555 and the virtual path `/AppServices`. If you use different values, you need to change the configuration of the client application accordingly.

Now the application service can be used from a client application.

Client Application

With the client application WPF is used. Windows Forms can be used in the same way. Visual Studio 2008 has a new project setting named Services that allows using client application services. Here you can set Forms authentication and the location of the authentication and roles service to the address defined previously: `http://localhost:55555/AppServices`. All that's done from this project configuration is referencing the assemblies `System.Web` and `System.Web.Extensions`, and changing the application configuration file to configure membership and role providers that use the classes `ClientFormsAuthenticationMembershipProvider` and `ClientRoleProvider` and the address of the Web service that is used by these providers.

```
<?xml version="1.0" encoding="utf-8"?>
<configuration>
  <system.web>
    <membership defaultProvider="ClientAuthenticationMembershipProvider">
      <providers>
        <add name="ClientAuthenticationMembershipProvider"
            type="System.Web.ClientServices.Providers.
            ClientFormsAuthenticationMembershipProvider,
            System.Web.Extensions, Version=3.5.0.0, Culture=neutral,
            PublicKeyToken=31bf3856ad364e35" serviceUri=
"http://localhost:55555/AppServices/Authentication_JSON_AppService.axd" />
      </providers>
    </membership>
    <roleManager defaultProvider="ClientRoleProvider" enabled="true">
      <providers>
        <add name="ClientRoleProvider"
            type="System.Web.ClientServices.Providers.ClientRoleProvider,
            System.Web.Extensions, Version=3.5.0.0, Culture=neutral,
            PublicKeyToken=31bf3856ad364e35" serviceUri=
            "http://localhost:55555/AppServices/Role_JSON_AppService.axd"
            cacheTimeout="86400" />
      </providers>
    </roleManager>
  </system.web>
</configuration>
```

The Windows application just uses `Label`, `TextBox`, `PasswordBox`, and `Button` controls as shown in Figure 20-1. The `Label` with the content User Validated shows up only when the logon is successful.

Figure 20-1

The handler of the `Button.Click` event invokes the `ValidateUser()` method of the `Membership` class. Because of the configured provider `ClientAuthenticationMembershipProvider`, the provider in turn invokes the Web service and calls the method `ValidateUser()` of the `SampleMembershipProvider` class to verify a successful logon. With success, the Label `labelValidatedInfo` is made visible; otherwise a message box pops up:

```
private void buttonLogin_Click(object sender, RoutedEventArgs e)
{
   try
   {
      if (Membership.ValidateUser(textUsername.Text,
            textPassword.Password))
      {
         // user validated!
         labelValidatedInfo.Visibility = Visibility.Visible;
      }
      else
      {
         MessageBox.Show("Username or password not valid",
               "Client Authentication Services", MessageBoxButton.OK,
               MessageBoxImage.Warning);
      }
   }
   catch (WebException ex)
   {
      MessageBox.Show(ex.Message, "Client Application Services",
            MessageBoxButton.OK, MessageBoxImage.Error);
   }
}
```

Encryption

Confidential data should be secured so that it cannot be read by unprivileged users. This is valid both for data that is sent across the network, or data that is stored somewhere. You can encrypt such data with symmetric or asymmetric encryption keys.

With a symmetric key, the same key can be used for encryption and decryption. With asymmetric encryption, different keys are used for encryption and decryption: a public and a private key. Something encrypted using a public key can be decrypted with the corresponding private key. This also works the other way around: something encrypted using a private key can be decrypted by using the corresponding public key but not the private key.

Public and private keys are always created as a pair. The public key can be made available to everybody, and it can even be put on a Web site, but the private key must be safely locked away. Following are some examples where these public and private keys are used to explain encryption.

If Alice sends a message to Bob (see Figure 20-2), and Alice wants to make sure that no one else but Bob can read the message, she uses Bob's public key. The message is encrypted using Bob's public key. Bob opens the message and can decrypt it using his secretly stored private key. This key exchange guarantees that no one but Bob can read Alice's message.

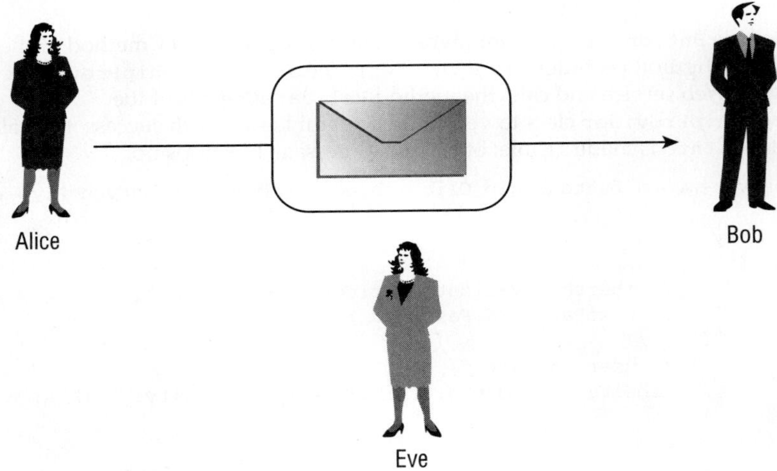

Figure 20-2

There is one problem left: Bob can't be sure that the mail comes from Alice. Eve can use Bob's public key to encrypt messages sent to Bob and pretend to be Alice. We can extend this principle using public/private keys. Let's start again with Alice sending a message to Bob. Before Alice encrypts the message using Bob's public key, she adds her signature and encrypts the signature using her own private key. Then she encrypts the mail using Bob's public key. Therefore, it is guaranteed that no one else but Bob can read the mail. When Bob decrypts the message, he detects an encrypted signature. The signature can be decrypted using Alice's public key. For Bob, it is not a problem to access Alice's public key because the key is public. After decrypting the signature, Bob can be sure that it was Alice who sent the message.

The encryption and decryption algorithms using symmetric keys are a lot faster than using asymmetric keys. The problem with symmetric keys is that the keys must be exchanged in a safe manner. With network communication, one way to do this is by using asymmetric keys first for the key exchange, and then symmetric keys for encryption of the data that is sent across the wire.

With the .NET Framework, you find classes for encryption in the namespace `System.Security.Cryptography`. Several symmetric and asymmetric algorithms are implemented. You can find different algorithm classes for many different purposes. Some of the new classes with .NET 3.5 have a `Cng` prefix or suffix. Cng is short for *Cryptography Next Generation*, which can be used with Windows Vista and Windows Server 2008. This API makes it possible to write a program independent of the algorithm by using a provider-based model. If you are targeting Windows Server 2003 as well, you need to pay attention to what encryption classes to use.

The following table lists encryption classes from the namespace `System.Security.Cryptography` and their purposes. The classes without a `Cng`, `Managed`, or `CryptoServiceProvider` suffix are abstract base classes, such as `MD5`. The `Managed` suffix means this algorithm is implemented with managed code; other classes might wrap native Windows API calls. The suffix `CryptoServiceProvider` is used with classes that implement the abstract base class. The `Cng` suffix is used with classes that make use of the new Cryptography CNG API that is available only with Windows Vista and Windows Server 2008.

Category	Classes	Description

Hash	`MD5`, `MD5Cng`
	`SHA1`, `SHA1Managed`,
	`SHA1Cng`
	`SHA256`, `SHA256Managed`, `SHA256Cng`
	`SHA384`, `SHA384Managed`, `SHA384Cng`
	`SHA512`, `SHA512Managed`, `SHA512Cng`
		Hash algorithms have the purpose of creating a fixed-length hash value from binary strings of arbitrary length. These algorithms are used with digital signatures and for data integrity. If the same binary string is hashed again, the same hash result is returned.
		
		MD5 (Message Digest Algorithm 5) was developed at RSA Laboratories and is faster than SHA1. SHA1 is stronger against brute force attacks. The SHA algorithms have been designed by the National Security Agency (NSA). MD5 uses a 128-bit hash size; SHA1 uses 160 bit. The other SHA algorithms contain the hash size in the name. SHA512 is the strongest of these algorithms; with a hash size of 512 bits, it is also the slowest.

Symmetric	`DES`, `DESCryptoServiceProvider`
	`TripleDES`,
	`TripleDESCryptoServiceProvider`
	`Aes`, `AesCryptoServiceProvider`,
	`AesManaged`
	`RC2`, `RC2CryptoServiceProvider`
	`Rijandel`, `RijandelManaged`
		Symmetric key algorithms use the same key for encryption and decryption of data. DES (Data Encryption Standard) is now considered insecure because it uses just 56 bits for the key size and can be broken in less than 24 hours. Triple-DES is the successor of DES and has a key length of 168 bits, but the effective security it provides is only 112 bit. AES (Advanced Encryption Standard) has a key size of 128, 192, or 256 bits. Rijandel is very similar to AES; it just has more options with the key size. AES is an encryption standard adopted by the U.S. government.

Category	Classes	Description

Asymmetric	`DSA, DSACryptoServiceProvider`
	`ECDsa, ECDsaCng`
	`ECDiffieHellman,`
	`ECDiffieHellmanCng`
	`RSA, RSACryptoServiceProvider`
		Asymmetric algorithms use different keys for encryption and decryption. RSA (Rivest, Shamir, Adleman) was the first algorithm used for signing as well as encryption. This algorithm is widely used in e-commerce protocols.
		
		DSA (Digital Signature Algorithm) is a United States Federal Government standard for digital signatures.
		
		ECDSA (Elliptic Curve DSA) and ECDiffieHellman use algorithms based on elliptic curve groups. These algorithms are more secure with shorter key sizes. For example, having a key size of 1024 bits for DSA is similar in security with 160 bits for ECDSA. As a result, ECDSA is much faster.
		
		ECDiffieHellman is an algorithm used to exchange private keys in a secure way over a public channel.

Let's get into examples of how these algorithms can be used programmatically.

Signature

The first example demonstrates a signature using the ECDSA algorithm for signing. Alice creates a signature that is encrypted with her private key and can be accessed using her public key. This way, it is guaranteed that the signature is from Alice.

First, take a look at the major steps in the `Main()` method: Alice's keys are created, and the string Alice is signed and finally verified if the signature is really from Alice by using the public key. The message that is signed is converted to a byte array by using the `Encoding` class. To write the encrypted signature to the console, the byte array that contains the signature is converted to a string with the method `Convert.ToBase64String()`.

Never convert encrypted data to a string using the `Encoding` class. The `Encoding` class verifies and converts invalid values that are not allowed with Unicode, and thus converting the string back to a byte array yields a different result.

```
using System;
using System.Security.Cryptography;
using System.Text;

namespace Wrox.ProCSharp.Security
{
   class Program
   {
      internal static CngKey aliceKeySignature;
```

```
internal static byte[] alicePubKeyBlob;

static void Main()
{
   CreateKeys();

   byte[] aliceData = Encoding.UTF8.GetBytes("Alice");
   byte[] aliceSignature = CreateSignature(aliceData,
         aliceKeySignature);
   Console.WriteLine("Alice created signature: {0}",
         Convert.ToBase64String(aliceSignature));

   if (VerifySignature(aliceData, aliceSignature, alicePubKeyBlob))
   {
      Console.WriteLine("Alice signature verified successfully");
   }
}
```

`CreateKeys()` is the method that creates a new key pair for Alice. This key pair is stored in a static field so it can be accessed from the other methods. The `Create()` method of `CngKey` gets the algorithm as an argument to define a key pair for the algorithm. With the `Export()` method, the public key of the key pair is exported. This public key can be given to Bob for the verification of the signature. Alice keeps the private key. Instead of creating a key pair with the `CngKey` class, you can open existing keys that are stored in the key store. Usually Alice would have a certificate containing a key pair in her private store, and the store could be accessed with `CngKey.Open()`.

```
static void CreateKeys()
{
   aliceKeySignature = CngKey.Create(CngAlgorithm.ECDsaP256);
   alicePubKeyBlob = aliceKeySignature.Export(
                           CngKeyBlobFormat.GenericPublicBlob);
}
```

With the key pair, Alice can create the signature using the `ECDsaCng` class. The constructor of this class receives the `CngKey` from Alice that contains both the public and private key. The private key is used, signing the data with the `SignData()` method.

```
static byte[] CreateSignature(byte[] data, CngKey key)
{
   ECDsaCng signingAlg = new ECDsaCng(key);
   byte[] signature = signingAlg.SignData(data);
   signingAlg.Clear();

   return signature;
}
```

For verification if the signature was really from Alice, Bob checks the signature by using the public key from Alice. The byte array containing the public key blob can be imported to a `CngKey` object with the static `Import()` method. The `ECDsaCng` class is then used to verify the signature by invoking `VerifyData()`.

```
static bool VerifySignature(byte[] data, byte[] signature,
      byte[] pubKey)
{
   bool retValue = false;
```

(continued)

(continued)

```
            using (CngKey key = CngKey.Import(pubKey,
                  CngKeyBlobFormat.GenericPublicBlob))
            {
               ECDsaCng signingAlg = new ECDsaCng(key);
               retValue = signingAlg.VerifyData(data, signature);
               signingAlg.Clear();
            }
            return retValue;
         }
      }
   }
```

Key Exchange and Secure Transfer

Let's get into a more complex example to exchange a symmetric key for a secure transfer by using the Diffie Hellman algorithm. In the `Main()` method, you can see the main functionality. Alice creates an encrypted message and sends the encrypted message to Bob. Before that, key pairs are created for Alice and Bob. Bob gets access only to Alice's public key, and Alice gets access only to Bob's public key.

```
using System;
using System.IO;
using System.Security.Cryptography;
using System.Text;

namespace Wrox.ProCSharp.Security
{
   class Program
   {
      static CngKey aliceKey;
      static CngKey bobKey;
      static byte[] alicePubKeyBlob;
      static byte[] bobPubKeyBlob;

      static void Main()
      {
         CreateKeys();
         byte[] encrytpedData = AliceSendsData("secret message");
         BobReceivesData(encrytpedData);

      }
```

In the implementation of the `CreateKeys()` method, keys are created to be used with the EC Diffie Hellman 256 algorithm.

```
      private static void CreateKeys()
      {
         aliceKey = CngKey.Create(CngAlgorithm.ECDiffieHellmanP256);
         bobKey = CngKey.Create(CngAlgorithm.ECDiffieHellmanP256);
         alicePubKeyBlob = aliceKey.Export(CngKeyBlobFormat.EccPublicBlob);
         bobPubKeyBlob = bobKey.Export(CngKeyBlobFormat.EccPublicBlob);
      }
```

In the method `AliceSendsData()`, the string that contains text characters is converted to a byte array by using the `Encoding` class. An `ECDiffieHellmanCng` object is created and initialized with the key pair from Alice. Alice creates a symmetric key by using her key pair and the public key from Bob calling the method `DeriveKeyMaterial()`. The returned symmetric key is used with the symmetric algorithm AES to encrypt the data. `AesCryptoServiceProvider` requires the key and an initialization vector (IV). The IV is generated dynamically from the method `GenerateIV()`. The symmetric key is exchanged with the help of the EC Diffie Hellman algorithm, but the IV must also be exchanged. From the security standpoint, it is okay to transfer the IV unencrypted across the network — just the key exchange must be secured. The IV is stored as first content in the memory stream followed by the encrypted data where the `CryptoStream` class uses the `encryptor` created by the `AesCryptoServiceProvider` class. Before the encrypted data is accessed from the memory stream, the crypto stream must be closed. Otherwise, end bits would be missing from the encrypted data.

```
private static byte[] AliceSendsData(string message)
{
   Console.WriteLine("Alice sends message: {0}", message);
   byte[] rawData = Encoding.UTF8.GetBytes(message);
   byte[] encryptedData = null;

   ECDiffieHellmanCng aliceAlgorithm = new ECDiffieHellmanCng(aliceKey);
   using (CngKey bobPubKey = CngKey.Import(bobPubKeyBlob,
         CngKeyBlobFormat.EccPublicBlob))
   {
      byte[] symmKey = aliceAlgorithm.DeriveKeyMaterial(bobPubKey);
      Console.WriteLine("Alice creates this symmetric key with " +
            "Bobs public key information: {0}",
            Convert.ToBase64String(symmKey));

      AesCryptoServiceProvider aes = new AesCryptoServiceProvider();
      aes.Key = symmKey;
      aes.GenerateIV();
      using (ICryptoTransform encryptor = aes.CreateEncryptor())
      using (MemoryStream ms = new MemoryStream())
      {
         // create CryptoStream and encrypt data to send
         CryptoStream cs = new CryptoStream(ms, encryptor,
               CryptoStreamMode.Write);

         // write initialization vector not encrypted
         ms.Write(aes.IV, 0, aes.IV.Length);
         cs.Write(rawData, 0, rawData.Length);
         cs.Close();
         encryptedData = ms.ToArray();
      }
      aes.Clear();
   }
   Console.WriteLine("Alice: message is encrypted: {0}",
         Convert.ToBase64String(encryptedData)); ;
   Console.WriteLine();
   return encryptedData;
}
```

Bob receives encrypted data in the argument of the method `BobReceivesData()`. First, the unencrypted initialization vector must be read. The `BlockSize` property of the class `AesCryptoServiceProvider` returns the number of bits for a block. The number of bytes can be calculated by doing a divide by 8, and the fastest way to do this is by doing a bit shift of 3 bits. Shifting by 1 bit is a division by 2, 2 bits by 4, and 3 bits by 8. With the `for` loop, the first bytes of the raw bytes that contain the IV unencrypted are written to the array `iv`. Next, an `ECDiffieHellmanCng` object is instantiated with the key pair from Bob. Using the public key from Alice, the symmetric key is returned from the method `DeriveKeyMaterial()`. Comparing the symmetric keys created from Alice and Bob shows that the same key value gets created. Using this symmetric key and the initialization vector, the message from Alice can be decrypted with the `AesCryptoServiceProvider` class.

```
private static void BobReceivesData(byte[] encryptedData)
{
   Console.WriteLine("Bob receives encrypted data");
   byte[] rawData = null;

   AesCryptoServiceProvider aes = new AesCryptoServiceProvider();

   int nBytes = aes.BlockSize >> 3;
   byte[] iv = new byte[nBytes];
   for (int i = 0; i < iv.Length; i++)
      iv[i] = encryptedData[i];

   ECDiffieHellmanCng bobAlgorithm = new ECDiffieHellmanCng(bobKey);

   using (CngKey alicePubKey = CngKey.Import(alicePubKeyBlob,
         CngKeyBlobFormat.EccPublicBlob))
   {
      byte[] symmKey = bobAlgorithm.DeriveKeyMaterial(alicePubKey);
      Console.WriteLine("Bob creates this symmetric key with " +
            "Alices public key information: {0}",
            Convert.ToBase64String(symmKey));

      aes.Key = symmKey;
      aes.IV = iv;

      using (ICryptoTransform decryptor = aes.CreateDecryptor())
      using (MemoryStream ms = new MemoryStream())
      {
         CryptoStream cs = new CryptoStream(ms, decryptor,
               CryptoStreamMode.Write);
         cs.Write(encryptedData, nBytes, encryptedData.Length - nBytes);
         cs.Close();

         rawData = ms.ToArray();

         Console.WriteLine("Bob decrypts message to: {0}",
               Encoding.UTF8.GetString(rawData));
      }
      aes.Clear();
   }
}
```

When you run the application you can see similar output on the console. The message from Alice is encrypted, and decrypted by Bob with the securely exchanged symmetric key.

```
Alice sends message: secret message
Alice creates this symmetric key with Bobs public key information:
5NWat8AemzFCYo1IIae9S3Vn4AXyai4aL8ATFo41vbw=
Alice: message is encrypted: 3C5U9CpYxnoFTk3Ew2V0T5Po0Jgryc5R7Te8ztau5N0=

Bob receives encrypted message
Bob creates this symmetric key with Alices public key information:
5NWat8AemzFCYo1IIae9S3Vn4AXyai4aL8ATFo41vbw=
Bob decrypts message to: secret message
```

Access Control to Resources

With the operating system, resources such as files and registry keys, as well as handles of a named pipe, are secured by using an access control list. Figure 20-3 shows the structure of how this maps. The resource has a security descriptor associated. The security descriptor contains information about the owner of the resource and references two access control lists: a discretionary access-control list (DACL) and a system access-control list (SACL). The DACL defines who has access or no access; the SACL defines audit rules for security event logging. An ACL contains a list of access-control entries (ACE). The ACE contains a type, a security identifier, and rights. With the DACL, the ACE can be of type access allowed or access denied. Some of the rights that you can set and get with a file are create, read, write, delete, modify, change permissions, and take ownership.

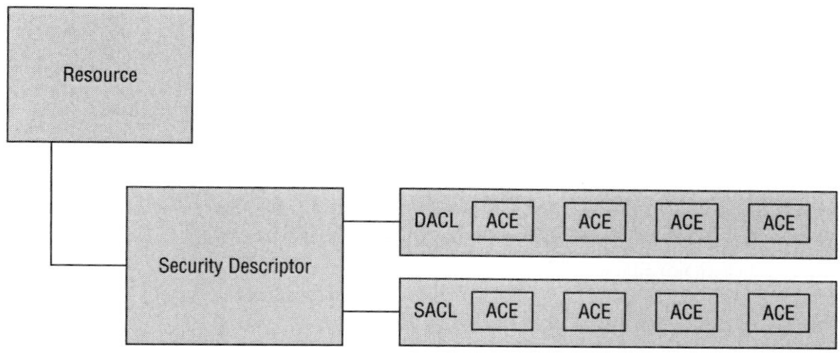

Figure 20-3

Classes to read and modify access control are in the namespace `System.Security.AccessControl`.

The following program demonstrates reading the access control list from a file.

The `FileStream` class defines the `GetAccessControl()` method that returns a `FileSecurity` object. `FileSecurity` is the .NET class that represents a security descriptor for files. `FileSecurity` derives from the base classes `ObjectSecurity`, `CommonObjectSecurity`, `NativeObjectSecurity`, and `FileSystemSecurity`. Other classes that represent a security descriptor are `CryptoKeySecurity`, `EventWaitHandleSecurity`, `MutexSecurity`, `RegistrySecurity`, `SemaphoreSecurity`, `PipeSecurity`, and `ActiveDirectorySecurity`. All of these objects can be secured using an access control list. In general, the corresponding .NET class defines the method `GetAccessControl` to return the corresponding security class; for example, the `Mutex.GetAccessControl()` method returns a `MutexSecurity`, and the `PipeStream.GetAccessControl()` method returns a `PipeSecurity`.

The `FileSecurity` class defines methods to read and change the DACL and SACL. The method `GetAccessRules()` returns the DACL in the form of the class `AuthorizationRuleCollection`. To access the SACL, you can use the method `GetAuditRules()`.

With the method `GetAccessRules()`, you can define if inherited access rules, and not only access rules directly defined with the object, should be used. The last parameter defines the type of the security identifier that should be returned. This type must derive from the base class `IdentityReference`. Possible types are `NTAccount` and `SecurityIdentifier`. Both of these classes represent users or groups; the `NTAccount` class finds the security object by its name and the `SecurityIdentifier` class finds the security object by a unique security identifier.

The returned `AuthorizationRuleCollection` contains `AuthorizationRule` objects. The `AuthorizationRule` is the .NET representation of an ACE. With the sample here, a file is accessed, so the `AuthorizationRule` can be cast to a `FileSystemAccessRule`. With ACEs of other resources, different .NET representations exist, such as `MutexAccessRule` and `PipeAccessRule`. With the `FileSystemAccessRule` class, the properties `AccessControlType`, `FileSystemRights`, and `IdentityReference` return information about the ACE.

```
using System;
using System.IO;
using System.Security.AccessControl;
using System.Security.Principal;

namespace Wrox.ProCSharp.Security
{
   class Program
   {
      static void Main(string[] args)
      {
         string filename = null;
         if (args.Length == 0)
            return;

         filename = args[0];

         FileStream stream = File.Open(filename, FileMode.Open);
         FileSecurity securityDescriptor = stream.GetAccessControl();
         AuthorizationRuleCollection rules =
               securityDescriptor.GetAccessRules(true, true,
                     typeof(NTAccount));

         foreach (AuthorizationRule rule in rules)
         {
            FileSystemAccessRule fileRule = rule as FileSystemAccessRule;
            Console.WriteLine("Access type: {0}", fileRule.AccessControlType);
            Console.WriteLine("Rights: {0}", fileRule.FileSystemRights);
            Console.WriteLine("Identity: {0}",
                  fileRule.IdentityReference.Value);
            Console.WriteLine();
         }
      }
   }
}
```

By running the application and passing a filename, you can see the access control list for the file. The output shown here lists full control to Administrators and System, modification rights to authenticated users, and read and execute rights to all users belonging to the group Users:

```
Access type: Allow
Rights: FullControl
Identity: BUILTIN\Administrators

Access type: Allow
Rights: FullControl
Identity: NT AUTHORITY\SYSTEM

Access type: Allow
Rights: Modify, Synchronize
Identity: NT AUTHORITY\Authenticated Users

Access type: Allow
Rights: ReadAndExecute, Synchronize
Identity: BUILTIN\Users
```

Setting access rights is very similar to reading access rights. To set access rights, several resource classes that can be secured offer the `SetAccessControl()` and `ModifyAccessControl()` methods. The sample code here modifies the access control list of a file by invoking the `SetAccessControl()` method from the `File` class. To this method a `FileSecurity` object is passed. The `FileSecurity` object is filled with `FileSystemAccessRule` objects. The access rules listed here deny write access to the Sales group, give read access to the Everyone group, and give full control to the Developers group.

This program runs on your system only if the Windows groups Sales and Developers are defined. You can change the program to use groups that are available in your environment.

```
private static void WriteAcl(string filename)
{
   NTAccount salesIdentity = new NTAccount("Sales");
   NTAccount developersIdentity = new NTAccount("Developers");
   NTAccount everyOneIdentity = new NTAccount("Everyone");

   FileSystemAccessRule salesAce = new FileSystemAccessRule(
         salesIdentity, FileSystemRights.Write, AccessControlType.Deny);
   FileSystemAccessRule everyoneAce = new FileSystemAccessRule(
         everyOneIdentity, FileSystemRights.Read,
         AccessControlType.Allow);
   FileSystemAccessRule developersAce = new FileSystemAccessRule(
         developersIdentity, FileSystemRights.FullControl,
         AccessControlType.Allow);

   FileSecurity securityDescriptor = new FileSecurity();
   securityDescriptor.SetAccessRule(everyoneAce);
   securityDescriptor.SetAccessRule(developersAce);
   securityDescriptor.SetAccessRule(salesAce);

   File.SetAccessControl(filename, securityDescriptor);
}
```

You can verify the access rules by opening the Properties and selecting a file in the Windows Explorer. Selecting the Security tab lists the access control list.

Code Access Security

What is the importance of code access security? With role-based security, you can define what the user is allowed to do. Code access security defines what the code is allowed to do. It depends on the evidence of the code — where is the code coming from? Depending on the origin of the code, different permissions apply. Of course, role-based security still applies. The code cannot do more than the user is allowed to do.

Code access security is a feature of the runtime that manages code, according to your level of trust. If the CLR trusts the code enough to allow it to run, it will begin executing the code. Depending on the permissions given to the assembly, however, it might run within a restricted environment. If the code is not trusted enough to run, or if it runs but then attempts to perform an action for which it does not have the relevant permissions, a security exception (of type `SecurityException` or a subclass of it) is thrown. The code access security system means that you can stop malicious code from running, but you can also allow code to run within a protected environment where you are confident that it cannot do any damage.

There are different scenarios in which code access security becomes important. With ClickOnce deployment, in many scenarios it is okay to use full trust, meaning the code is allowed to do anything that the user is allowed to do. If the ClickOnce deployed application is installed within the company, then maybe you trust your own application. An application certificate that is coming with the application can also give enough information about a vendor that you trust, so you can deploy the vendor's application using ClickOnce with full rights to your own system. Of course, restricted rights are also possible with ClickOnce. Scenarios in which code access security becomes more important than with ClickOnce are in hosting environments and with add-ins. If you create an add-in host, you might not want to give all your rights to the add-ins that are loaded from your application. You can restrict the permissions for assemblies that are called. A Web site hosting company does not want Web applications from different customers running on the server to have full rights to the system. They could break a server that might run hundreds or thousands of Web applications. Restricting permissions for Web applications is a good option.

> *Chapter 16, "Deployment," explains ClickOnce in detail. Creating add-ins is discussed in Chapter 36, "Add-Ins."*

Code access security is based on these concepts: permissions, permission sets, code groups, and policies. Take a look at them now, because they form the foundations of the sections that follow:

- **Permissions** are the actions that you allow each code group to perform. For example, permissions include "read files from the file system," "write to the Active Directory," and "use sockets to open network connections." Several predefined permissions exist, but you can also create your own permissions.
- **Permission sets** are collections of permissions. With permission sets, it is not necessary to apply every single permission to code; permissions are grouped to permission sets. Some examples of permission sets are FullTrust, LocalIntranet, and Internet. You can create a permission set that includes required permissions. An assembly that has FullTrust permissions has full access to all resources. With LocalIntranet, the assembly is restricted, that is, it is not allowed to write to the file system other than using the isolated storage.
- **Code groups** bring together code with similar characteristics. A code group defines the origin of the code. Examples for existing code groups are Internet and Intranet. The group Internet defines code that is sourced from the Internet, and the group Intranet defines code sourced from the LAN. The information used to place assemblies into code groups is called *evidence*. Other evidence is collected by the CLR, including the publisher of the code, the strong name, and (where applicable) the URI from which it was downloaded. Code groups are arranged in a

hierarchy, and assemblies are nearly always matched to several code groups. The code group at the root of the hierarchy is called All Code and contains all other code groups. The hierarchy is used for deciding which code groups an assembly belongs to; if an assembly does not provide evidence that matches it to a group in the tree, no attempt is made to match it to code groups below.

- **Policies** allow the system administrator to define different levels of permissions for the complete company, machines, and users. Code groups are defined within all of these policies, and the permissions are combined.

Permissions

.NET permissions are independent of operating system permissions. .NET permissions are just verified by the CLR. An assembly demands a permission for a specific operation (for example, the `File` class demands the `FileIOPermission`), and the CLR verifies if the assembly has the permission granted so that it can continue.

There is a very fine-grained list of permissions that you can apply to an assembly or request from code. The following list shows a few of the code access permissions provided by the CLR; as you can see, you have great control of what code is or is not permitted to do:

- **DirectoryServicesPermission** controls the ability to access Active Directory through the `System.DirectoryServices` classes.
- **DnsPermission** controls the ability to use the TCP/IP Domain Name System (DNS).
- **EnvironmentPermission** controls the ability to read and write environment variables.
- **EventLogPermission** controls the ability to read and write to the event log.
- **FileDialogPermission** controls the ability to access files that have been selected by the user in the Open dialog box. This permission is commonly used when `FileIOPermission` is not granted to allow limited access to files.
- **FileIOPermission** controls the ability to work with files (reading, writing, and appending to files, as well as creating, altering, and accessing folders).
- **IsolatedStorageFilePermission** controls the ability to access private virtual file systems.
- **IsolatedStoragePermission** controls the ability to access isolated storage; storage that is associated with an individual user and with some aspect of the code's identity. Isolated storage is discussed in Chapter 25, "Manipulating Files and the Registry."
- **MessageQueuePermission** controls the ability to use message queues through the Microsoft Message Queue.
- **PerformanceCounterPermission** controls the ability to make use of performance counters.
- **PrintingPermission** controls the ability to print.
- **ReflectionPermission** controls the ability to discover information about a type at runtime by using `System.Reflection`.
- **RegistryPermission** controls the ability to read, write, create, or delete registry keys and values.
- **SecurityPermission** controls the ability to execute, assert permissions, call into unmanaged code, skip verification, and other rights.
- **ServiceControllerPermission** controls the ability to control Windows services.

- **SocketPermission** controls the ability to make or accept TCP/IP connections on a network transport address.
- **SQLClientPermission** controls the ability to access SQL Server databases with the .NET data provider for SQL Server.
- **UIPermission** controls the ability to access the user interface.
- **WebPermission** controls the ability to make or accept connections to or from the Web.

With each of these permission classes, it is often possible to specify an even deeper level of granularity; for example, the `DirectoryServicesPermission` allows you to differentiate between read and write access, and also allows you to define which entries in the directory services are allowed or denied access.

In terms of best practice, you should ensure that any attempts to use resources require permissions to be enclosed within `try/catch` error-handling blocks, so that your application degrades gracefully, should it be running under restricted permissions. The design of your application should specify how your application should act under these circumstances. Do not assume that it will be running under the same security policy under which it has been developed. For example, if your application cannot access the local drive, should it exit or operate in an alternative fashion?

Another set of permissions is assigned by the CLR on the basis of the identity of the code, which cannot be granted. These permissions relate to the evidence the CLR has collated about the assembly and are called *identity permissions*. Here are the names of the classes for the identity permissions:

- **PublisherIdentityPermission** refers to the software publisher's digital signature.
- **SiteIdentityPermission** refers to the name of the Web site from which the code originated.
- **StrongNameIdentityPermission** refers to the assembly's strong name.
- **URLIdentityPermission** refers to the URL from which the code came (including the protocol, for example, `https://`).
- **ZoneIdentityPermission** refers to the zone from which the assembly originates.

By assigning the permission to code groups, there is no need to deal with every single permission. Instead, the permissions are applied in blocks, which is why .NET has the concept of permission sets. These are lists of code access permissions grouped into a named set. The following list explains the named permission sets you get out of the box:

- **FullTrust** means no permission restrictions.
- **SkipVerification** means that verification is not done.
- **Execution** grants the ability to run, but not to access any protected resources.
- **Nothing** grants no permissions and prevents the code from executing.
- **LocalIntranet** specifies the default policy for the local intranet, a subset of the full set of permissions. For example, file IO is restricted to read access on the share where the assembly originates.
- **Internet** specifies the default policy for code of unknown origin. This is the most restrictive policy listed. For example, code executing in this permission set has no file IO capability, cannot read or write event logs, and cannot read or write environment variables.
- **Everything** grants all the permissions that are listed under this set, except the permission to skip code verification. The administrator can alter any of the permissions in this permission set. This is useful when the default policy needs to be tighter.

Note that of these you can change the definitions of only the Everything permission set — the other sets are fixed and cannot be changed. Of course, you can also create your own permission set.

Identity permissions cannot be included in permission sets because the CLR is the only body able to grant identity permissions to code. For example, if a piece of code is from a specific publisher, it would make little sense for the administrator to assign the identity permissions associated with another publisher. The CLR grants identity permissions where necessary, and if you want, you can use them.

Demanding Permissions Programmatically

An assembly can demand permissions declaratively or programmatically. To see how demanding permissions works, create a Windows Forms application that contains just a button. When the button is clicked, a file on the local file system is accessed. If the application does not have the relevant permission to access the local drive (`FileIOPermission`), the button will be marked as disabled (dimmed).

If you import the namespace `System.Security.Permissions`, you can change the constructor of the class `Form1` to check for permissions by creating a `FileIOPermission` object, calling its `Demand()` method, and then acting on the result:

```
public Form1()
{
   InitializeComponent();

   try
   {
      FileIOPermission fileIOPermission = new
         FileIOPermission(FileIOPermissionAccess.AllAccess,@"c:\");
      fileIOPermission.Demand();
   }
   catch (SecurityException)
   {
      button1.Enabled = false;
   }
}
```

`FileIOPermission` is contained within the `System.Security.Permissions` namespace, which is home to the full set of permissions and also provides classes for declarative permission attributes and enumerations for the parameters that are used to create permissions objects (for example, creating a `FileIOPermission` specifying whether read-only or full access is needed).

If you run the application from the local drive where the default security policy allows access to local storage, you will see a dialog box with a button that is enabled. However, if you copy the executable to a network share and run it again, you are operating within the `LocalIntranet` permission set, which blocks access to local storage, and the button will be disabled.

Within the implementation of the click event handler, there is no need to check the required security because the relevant class in the .NET Framework already demands the file permission, and the CLR ensures that each caller up the stack has those permissions before proceeding. If you run the application from the intranet, and it attempts to open a file on the local disk, you will see an exception unless the security policy has been altered to grant access to the local drive.

To catch exceptions thrown by the CLR when code attempts to act contrary to its granted permissions, you can catch the exception of the type `SecurityException`, which provides access to a number of useful pieces of information, including a human-readable stack trace (`SecurityException.StackTrace`) and a reference to the method that threw the exception (`SecurityException.TargetSite`). `SecurityException` even provides you with the `SecurityException.PermissionType` property, which returns the type of `Permission` object that caused the security exception to occur. If you have problems with security exceptions, this should be one of your first parts to diagnose. Simply remove the `try` and `catch` blocks from the previous code to see the security exception.

Declarative Permissions

You can deny, demand, and assert permissions by invoking permission classes programmatically. However, you can also use attributes and specify permission requirements declaratively.

The main benefit of using declarative security is that the settings are accessible through reflection. This can be of enormous benefit to system administrators, who often will want to view the security requirements of applications.

For example, you can specify that a method must have permission to read from `C:\` to execute:

```
using System;
using System.Security.Permissions;

namespace Wrox.ProCSharp.Security
{
   class Program
   {
      static void Main()
      {
         MyClass.Method();
      }
   }

   class MyClass
   {
      [FileIOPermission(SecurityAction.Demand, Read="C:/")]
      public static void Method()
      {
         // implementation goes here
      }
   }
}
```

Be aware that if you use attributes to assert or demand permissions, you cannot catch any exceptions that are raised if the action fails, because there is no imperative code around in which you can place a `try-catch-finally` clause.

Requesting Permissions

As discussed in the previous section, demanding permissions (either by code or declaratively) is where you state clearly what you need at runtime; however, you can configure an assembly so it makes a softer request for permissions right at the start of execution. The assembly can specify the required permissions before it begins executing.

You can request permissions in three ways:

- **Minimum** permissions specify the permissions your code must run.
- **Optional** permissions specify the permissions your code can use but is able to run effectively without.
- **Refused** permissions specify the permissions that you want to ensure are not granted to your code.

Why would you want to request permissions when your assembly starts? There are several reasons:

- If your assembly needs certain permissions to run, it makes sense to state this at the start of execution rather than during execution to ensure that the user does not experience a road block after beginning to work in your program.
- You will be granted only the permissions you request and nothing more. Without explicitly requesting permissions your assembly might be granted more permissions than it needs to execute. This increases the risk of your assembly being used for malicious purposes by other code.
- If you request only a minimum set of permissions, you are increasing the probability that your assembly will run, because you cannot predict the security policies that are effective at the user's location.

Requesting permissions is likely to be most useful if you are doing more complex deployment, and there is a higher risk that your application will be installed on a machine that does not grant the required permissions. It is usually preferable for the application to know right at the start if it will not be granted permissions, rather than halfway through execution.

With Visual Studio, you can get help to calculate the required permissions of an application by selecting the Security tab with the properties (see Figure 20-4). Clicking the Calculate Permissions button checks the code of the assembly and lists all required permissions.

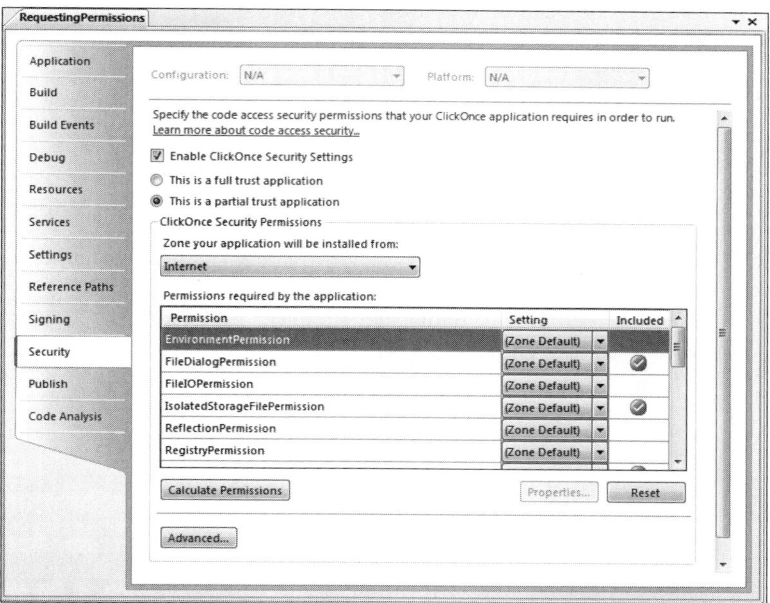

Figure 20-4

Instead of using Visual Studio, you can use the command-line tool `permcalc.exe` to calculate the required permissions of an assembly.

The command line

```
permcalc.exe -show -stacks -cleancache DemandingPermissions.exe
```

creates an XML file that contains all required permissions. With the option `-show`, the XML file is opened immediately. The option `-stacks` adds the stack information to the XML file for you to see where the permissions demand originated from.

The required permissions can be added as attributes to the assembly. Following are three examples that demonstrate using attributes to request permissions. If you are following this with the code download, you can find these examples in the `RequestingPermissions` project. The first attribute requests that the assembly have `UIPermission` granted, which will allow the application access to the user interface. The request is for the minimum permissions, so if this permission is not granted, the assembly will fail to start:

```
using System.Security.Permissions;
[assembly:UIPermission(SecurityAction.RequestMinimum, Unrestricted=true)]
```

Next, there is a request that the assembly be refused access to the `C:\` drive. This attribute's setting means that the entire assembly will be blocked from accessing this drive:

```
[assembly:FileIOPermission(SecurityAction.RequestRefuse, Read="C:/")]
```

Finally, here is an attribute that requests that the assembly be optionally granted the permission to access unmanaged code:

```
[assembly:SecurityPermission(SecurityAction.RequestOptional,
    Flags = SecurityPermissionFlag.UnmanagedCode)]
```

In this scenario, you want to add this attribute to an application that accesses unmanaged code in at least one place. In this case, it is specified that this permission is optional, which means that the application can run without the permission to access unmanaged code. If the assembly is not granted permission to access unmanaged code and attempts to do so, a `SecurityException` will be raised, which the application should expect and handle accordingly. The following table shows the full list of available `SecurityAction` enumeration values; some of these values are covered in more detail later in this chapter.

SecurityAction Enumeration	Description
`Assert`	Allows code to access resources not available to the caller.
`Demand`	Requires all callers in the call stack to have the specified permission.
`DemandChoice`	Requires all callers in the stack to have one of the specified permissions.
`Deny`	Denies a permission by forcing any subsequent demand for the permission to fail.
`InheritanceDemand`	Requires derived classes to have the specified permission granted.
`LinkDemand`	Requires the immediate caller to have the specified permission.
`LinkDemandChoice`	Requires the immediate caller to have one of the specified permissions.
`PermitOnly`	Similar to `Deny`; subsequent demands for resources not explicitly listed by `PermitOnly` are refused.

SecurityAction Enumeration	Description
`RequestMinimum`	Applied at assembly scope; this contains a permission required for an assembly to operate correctly.
`RequestOptional`	Applied at assembly scope; this asks for permissions the assembly can use, if available, to provide additional features and functionality.
`RequestRefuse`	Applied at assembly scope when there is a permission you do not want your assembly to have.

When you consider the permission requirements of your application, you need to decide between two options:

- Request all the permissions you need at the start of execution, and degrade gracefully or exit if those permissions are not granted.
- Avoid requesting permissions at the start of execution, but be prepared to handle security exceptions throughout your application.

After an assembly has been configured using permission attributes in this way, you can use the `permcalc.exe` utility to show the required permissions by aiming at the assembly file that contains the assembly manifest using the `-assembly` option of the `permcalc.exe` utility:

```
>permcalc.exe -show -assembly RequestingPermissions.exe
```

The output for an application using the three previously discussed attributes looks like this:

```
Microsoft (R) .NET Framework Permissions Calculator.
Copyright (C) Microsoft Corporation 2005. All rights reserved.

Analyzing...
|--------------------------------|
................................................................................

RequestingPermissions.exe
Minimal permission set:
<PermissionSet class="System.Security.PermissionSet"
version="1">
<IPermission class="System.Security.Permissions.UIPermission, mscorlib,
Version=2.0.0.0, Culture=neutral, PublicKeyToken=b77a5c561934e089" version="1"
Unrestricted="true"/>
</PermissionSet>

Optional permission set:
<PermissionSet class="System.Security.PermissionSet"
version="1">
<IPermission class="System.Security.Permissions.SecurityPermission, mscorlib,
Version=2.0.0.0, Culture=neutral, PublicKeyToken=b77a5c561934e089" version="1" Flag
s="SecurityPermissionFlag.UnmanagedCode" />
</PermissionSet>
```

(continued)

(continued)

```
Refused permission set:
<PermissionSet class="System.Security.PermissionSet"
version="1">
<IPermission class="System.Security.Permissions.FileIOPermission, mscorlib,
Version=2.0.0.0, Culture=neutral, PublicKeyToken=b77a5c561934e089" version="1"
Read="C:"/>
</PermissionSet>

Generating output...
Writing file: RequestingPermissions.exe.PermCalc.xml...
```

In addition to requesting permissions, you can also request a complete permissions set; the advantage is that you don't have to deal with every single permission. However, you can only request permission sets that cannot be altered. The Everything permission set can be altered through the security policy while an assembly is running, so it cannot be requested.

Here is an example of how to request a built-in permission set:

```
[assembly:PermissionSet(SecurityAction.RequestMinimum,
                               Name = "FullTrust")]
```

In this example, the assembly requests that as a minimum it needs the FullTrust built-in permission set granted. If this set of permissions is not granted, the assembly will throw a security exception at runtime.

Implicit Permissions

When permissions are granted, there is often an implicit statement that you are also granted other permissions. For example, if you assign the `FileIOPermission` for `C:\`, there is an implicit assumption that there is also access to its subdirectories.

To check whether a granted permission implicitly brings another permission as a subset, you can do this:

```
class Program
{
   static void Main()
   {
      CodeAccessPermission permissionA =
         new FileIOPermission(FileIOPermissionAccess.AllAccess, @"C:\");
      CodeAccessPermission permissionB =
         new FileIOPermission(FileIOPermissionAccess.Read, @"C:\temp");
      if (permissionB.IsSubsetOf(permissionA))
      {
         Console.WriteLine("PermissionB is a subset of PermissionA");
      }
   }
}
```

The output looks like this:

```
PermissionB is a subset of PermissionA
```

Denying Permissions

Under certain circumstances, you might want to perform an action and be absolutely sure that the method that is called is acting within a protected environment. An assembly shouldn't be allowed to do anything unexpected. For example, say that you want to make a call to an add-in component in a way that it will not access the local disk. Create an instance of the permission you want to ensure that the method is not granted, and then call its `Deny()` method before making the call to the class:

```
using System;
using System.IO;
using System.Security;
using System.Security.Permissions;

namespace Wrox.ProCSharp.Security
{
   class Program
   {
      static void Main()
      {
         CodeAccessPermission permission =
            new FileIOPermission(FileIOPermissionAccess.AllAccess,@"C:\");
         permission.Deny();
         UntrustworthyClass.Method();
         CodeAccessPermission.RevertDeny();
      }
   }

   class UntrustworthyClass
   {
      public static void Method()
      {
         try
         {
            using (StreamReader reader = File.OpenText(@"C:\textfile.txt"))
            {
            }
         }
         catch
         {
            Console.WriteLine("Failed to open file");
         }
      }
   }
}
```

If you build this code, the output will state *Failed to open file,* because the untrustworthy class does not have access to the local disk.

Note that the `Deny()` call is made on an instance of the `permission` object, whereas the `RevertDeny()` call is made statically. The reason for this is that the `RevertDeny()` call reverts all deny requests within the current stack frame; if you have made several calls to `Deny()`, you need to make only one follow-up call to `RevertDeny()`.

Asserting Permissions

Imagine that an assembly has been installed with full trust on a user's system. Within that assembly there is a method that saves auditing information to a text file on the local disk. If, later, an application is installed that wants to make use of the auditing feature, it will be necessary for the application to have the relevant `FileIOPermission` permissions to save the data to disk.

This seems excessive, however, because all you really want to do is perform a highly restricted action on the local disk. In these situations, it would be useful if assemblies with limiting permissions could make calls to more trusted assemblies that can temporarily increase the scope of the permissions on the stack, and perform operations on behalf of the caller. The caller, itself, doesn't need to have the permissions.

Another example in which asserts become important is when you create assemblies that invoke native code using platform invoke. The assembly invoking native methods requires full trust. But is it really necessary that all callers of this assembly require full trust as well? Take a look at how this is done with the .NET Framework assemblies. The `File` class invokes the native Windows API `CreateFile()` and thus needs full trust. The `File` class itself asserts the permission it requires by itself so that the caller does not require having this permission itself, but demands the `FileIOPermission`. (Platform invoke is discussed in Chapter 24, "Interoperability.")

Assemblies with a high enough level of trust can assert permissions that they require. If the assembly has the permissions it needs to assert additional permissions, it removes the need for callers up the stack to have such wide-ranging permissions.

The code that follows contains a class called `AuditClass` that implements a method called `Save()`, which takes a string and saves audit data to `C:\audit.txt`. The `AuditClass` method asserts the permissions it needs to add the audit lines to the file. For testing it, the `Main()` method for the application explicitly denies the file permission that the `Audit` method needs:

```
using System;
using System.IO;
using System.Security;
using System.Security.Permissions;

namespace Wrox.ProCSharp.Security
{
   class Program
   {
      static void Main()
      {
         CodeAccessPermission permission =
            new FileIOPermission(FileIOPermissionAccess.Append,
                                 @"C:\audit.txt");
         permission.Deny();
         AuditClass.Save("some data to audit");
         CodeAccessPermission.RevertDeny();
      }
   }
   class AuditClass
   {
      public static void Save(string value)
      {
         try
         {
            FileIOPermission permission =
               new FileIOPermission(FileIOPermissionAccess.Append,
                                    @"C:\audit.txt");
            permission.Assert();
            FileStream stream = new FileStream(@"C:\audit.txt",
               FileMode.Append, FileAccess.Write);

            // code to write to audit file here...
```

```
                CodeAccessPermission.RevertAssert();
                Console.WriteLine("Data written to audit file");
            }
            catch
            {
                Console.WriteLine("Failed to write data to audit file");
            }
        }
    }
}
```

When this code is executed, you will find that the call to the `AuditClass` method does not cause a security exception, even though when it was called it did not have the required permissions to carry out the disk access.

Like `RevertDeny()`, `RevertAssert()` is a static method, and it reverts all assertions within the current frame.

It is important to be very careful when using assertions. You are explicitly assigning permissions to a method that has been called by code that might not have those permissions, and this could open a security hole. For example, in the auditing example, even if the security policy dictated that an installed application cannot write to the local disk, your assembly would be able to write to the disk when the auditing assembly asserts `FileIOPermissions` for writing.

However, to perform the assertion, the auditing assembly must have been installed with permission for `FileIOAccess` and `SecurityPermission`. The `SecurityPermission` allows an assembly to perform an assert, and the assembly will need both the `SecurityPermission` and the permission being asserted to complete successfully.

Code Groups

This section gets into management of assemblies and their permissions. Instead of managing every assembly on its own, code groups are defined. Code groups have an entry requirement called *membership condition*. For an assembly to be filed in a code group, it must match the group's membership condition. Membership conditions include "the assembly is from the site `www.microsoft.com`" or "the publisher of this software is Microsoft Corporation."

Each code group has one, and only one, membership condition. Assemblies can be within multiple code groups. The following list provides the types of code group membership conditions available in .NET:

- **Zone** — The region from which the code originated.
- **Site** — The Web site from which the code originated.
- **Strong name** — A unique, verifiable name for the code. Strong names are discussed in Chapter 17, "Assemblies."
- **Publisher** — The publisher of the code.
- **URL** — The specific location from which the code originated.
- **Hash value** — The hash value for the assembly.
- **Skip verification** — This condition requests that it bypass code verification checks. Code verification ensures that the code accesses types in a well-defined and acceptable way. The runtime cannot enforce security on code that is not type-safe.
- **Application directory** — The location of the assembly within the application.
- **All code** — All code fulfills this condition.
- **Custom** — A user-specified condition.

The first, and most commonly used, type of membership condition is the *Zone* condition. A zone is the region of origin of a piece of code and refers to one of the following: MyComputer, Internet, Intranet, Trusted, or Untrusted. These zones can be managed by using the Internet Options in Windows Security Center.

Code groups are arranged hierarchically with the All Code membership condition at the root (see Figure 20-5). You can see that each code group has a single membership condition and specifies the permissions that the code group has been granted. Note that if an assembly does not match the membership condition in a code group, the CLR does not attempt to match code groups below it.

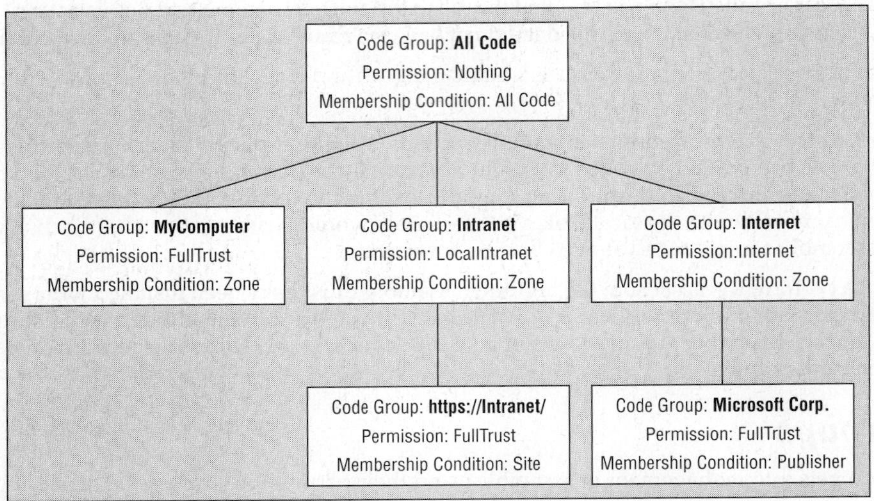

Figure 20-5

caspol.exe — The Code Access Security Policy Tool

This section spends a good deal of time looking at the command-line Code Access Security Policy tool. To get a list of options for the tool, just type the following at the command prompt:

```
caspol.exe -?
```

To send the output to a text file, use:

```
caspol.exe > output.txt
```

Take a look at the code groups on a machine using `caspol.exe`. The output of the command lists the hierarchical structure of the code groups on the machine, and next to each group there is a description of the code group. Type this command:

```
caspol.exe -listdescription
```

Alternatively, the `-listdescription` parameter has a shortcut: `-ld`. A part of the output is shown here:

```
Microsoft (R) .NET Framework CasPol 2.0.50727.1426
Copyright (c) Microsoft Corporation. All rights reserved.

Security is ON
```

```
Execution checking is ON
Policy change prompt is ON

Level = Machine

Full Trust Assemblies:

1. All_Code: Code group grants no permissions and forms the root of the code
group tree.
   1.1. My_Computer_Zone: Code group grants full trust to all code originating
        on the local computer
      1.1.1. Microsoft_Strong_Name: Code group grants full trust to code
             signed with the Microsoft strong name.
      1.1.2. ECMA_Strong_Name: Code group grants full trust to code signed
             with the ECMA strong name.
   1.2. LocalIntranet_Zone: Code group grants the intranet permission set to
        code from the intranet zone. This permission set grants intranet code
        the right to use isolated storage, full UI access, some capability to
        do reflection, and limited access to environment variables.
      1.2.1. Intranet_Same_Site_Access: All intranet code gets the right to
             connect back to the site of its origin.
      1.2.2. Intranet_Same_Directory_Access: All intranet code gets the right
             to read from its install directory.
   1.3. Internet_Zone: Code group grants code from the Internet zone the
        Internet permission set. This permission set grants Internet code the
        right to use isolated storage and limited UI access.
```

The .NET security subsystem ensures that code from each code group is allowed to do only certain things. For example, code from the Internet zone will, by default, have much stricter limits than code from the local drive. Code from the local drive is normally granted access to data stored on the local drive, but assemblies from the Internet are not granted this permission by default.

Using caspol and its equivalent in the Microsoft Management Console, you can specify what level of trust you have for each code access group, as well as managing code groups and permissions in a more granular fashion.

Take another look at the code access groups, but this time in a slightly more compact view. Make sure that you are logged in as a local administrator, go to a command prompt, and type this command:

```
caspol.exe -listgroups
```

You will see something like this:

```
Microsoft (R) .NET Framework CasPol 2.0.50727.1426
Copyright (c) Microsoft Corporation. All rights reserved.

Security is ON
Execution checking is ON
Policy change prompt is ON

Level = Machine

Code Groups:
```

(continued)

(continued)

```
1.  All code: Nothing
   1.1.  Zone - MyComputer: FullTrust
      1.1.1.  StrongName -
002400000480000094000000060200000024000052534131000400
000100010007D1FA57C4AED9F0A32E84AA0FAEFD0DE9E8FD6AEC8F87FB03766C834C99921EB23
BE79AD9D5DCC1DD9AD236132102900B723CF980957FC4E177108FC607774F29E8320E92EA05ECE
4E821C0A5EFE8F1645C4C0C93C1AB99285D622CAA652C1DFAD63D745D6F2DE5F17E5EAF0FC4963
D261C8A12436518206DC093344D5AD293: FullTrust
      1.1.2.  StrongName - 00000000000000000400000000000000: FullTrust
   1.2.  Zone - Intranet: LocalIntranet
      1.2.1.  All code: Same site Web.
      1.2.2.  All code: Same directory FileIO - 'Read, PathDiscovery'
   1.3.  Zone - Internet: Internet
      1.3.1.  All code: Same site Web.
   1.4.  Zone - Untrusted: Nothing
   1.5.  Zone - Trusted: Internet
      1.5.1.  All code: Same site Web.
Success
```

You will notice that near the start of the output it says `Security is ON`. Later in the chapter you will see that it can be turned off and then turned on again.

The Execution Checking setting is on by default, which means that all assemblies must be granted the permission to execute before they can run. If execution checking is turned off using caspol (`caspol.exe -execution on|off`), assemblies that do not have the permission to run can execute, although they might cause security exceptions if they attempt to act contrary to the security policy later in their execution.

The Policy Change Prompt option specifies whether you see an "Are you sure" warning message when you attempt to alter the security policy.

As code is broken down into these groups, you can manage security at a more granular level, and apply full trust to a much smaller percentage of code. Note that each group has a label (for example, 1.2). These labels are auto-generated by .NET, and can differ between machines. Generally, security is not managed for each assembly, but for a code group instead.

When a machine has several side-by-side installations of CLR, the copy of `caspol.exe` that you run will alter the security policy only for the installation of .NET with which it is associated.

Viewing an Assembly's Code Groups

Assemblies are matched to code groups according to the membership conditions they match. If you were to go back to the code groups example and load an assembly from the `https://intranet/` Web site, it would match the code groups shown in Figure 20-6. The assembly is a member of the root code group (All Code); because it came from the local network, it is also a member of the Intranet code group. However, because it was loaded from the specific site `https://intranet`, it is also granted *FullTrust*, which means that it can run unrestricted.

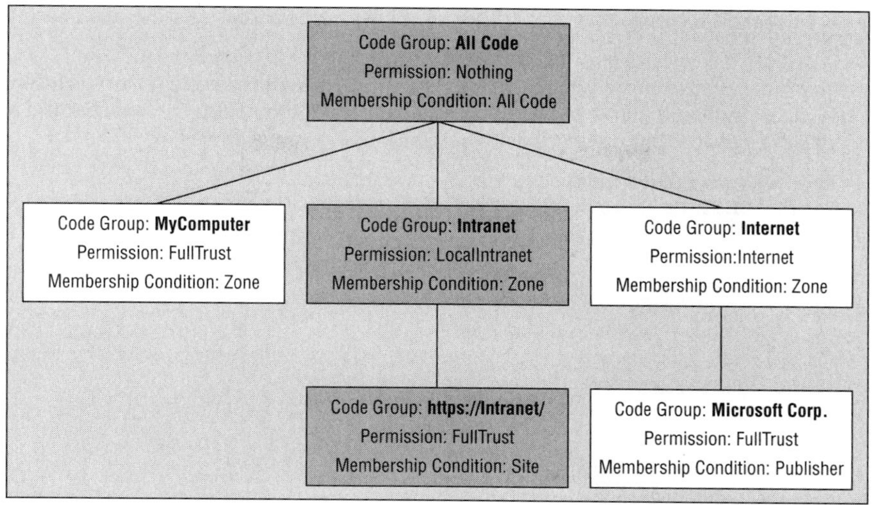

Figure 20-6

You can easily view the code groups that an assembly is a member of using this command:

```
caspol.exe -resolvegroup assembly.dll
```

Running this command on an assembly on the local drive produces the following output:

```
Microsoft (R) .NET Framework CasPol 2.0.50727.1426
Copyright (c) Microsoft Corporation. All rights reserved.

Level = Enterprise

Code Groups:

1.  All code: FullTrust

Level = Machine

Code Groups:

1.  All code: Nothing
   1.1.  Zone - MyComputer: FullTrust

Level = User

Code Groups:

1.  All code: FullTrust

Success
```

You will notice that code groups are listed on three levels — Enterprise, Machine, and User. For now, stay focused on the machine level. In case you are curious about the relationship among the three, the effective permission given to an assembly is the intersection of the permissions from the three levels. For example, if you remove the FullTrust permission from the Internet zone at the enterprise-level policy, all permissions are revoked for code from the Internet zone, and the settings of the other two levels become irrelevant.

Now use this command once more with the same assembly to read the code groups. However, this time, the assembly is accessed from a Web server using the HTTP protocol. You can see that the assembly is a member of different groups that have much more restrictive permissions:

```
caspol.exe -resolvegroup http://server/assembly.dll
Microsoft (R) .NET Framework CasPol 2.0.50727.1426
Copyright (c) Microsoft Corporation. All rights reserved.

Level = Enterprise

Code Groups:

1.  All code: FullTrust
Level = Machine

Code Groups:

1.  All code: Nothing
   1.1.  Zone - Internet: Internet
      1.1.1.  All code: Same site Web.


Level = User

Code Groups:

1.  All code: FullTrust

Success
```

The assembly grants the Internet and the Same Site Web permissions. The intersection of the permissions allows the code limited UI access. It also permits the code to establish connections to the site it originated from.

Code Access Permissions and Permissions Sets

Imagine yourself administering security policy on a network of desktop machines in a large enterprise scenario. In this environment, it is immensely useful for the CLR to collect evidence information on code before the code is allowed to execute. Likewise, you, as the administrator, must have the opportunity to control what code is allowed on the several hundred machines you manage once the CLR has identified its origin. This is where permissions start to act.

After an assembly has been matched to code groups, the CLR looks at the security policy to calculate the permissions it grants to an assembly. When managing permissions in Windows, you generally don't want to apply permissions to users, but you apply permissions to user groups instead. This is also true with assemblies; permissions are applied to code groups rather than to individual assemblies, which makes the management of security policy in .NET a much easier task.

Look more closely at viewing an assembly's permissions. Imagine using a Microsoft application in which you use a feature that you have not used before. The application does not have a copy of the code stored locally, so the code is requested from the Internet and downloaded into the Download Assembly Cache. Figure 20-7 illustrates what an assembly's code group membership might look like with code from the Internet published by a named organization that has signed the assembly with a certificate.

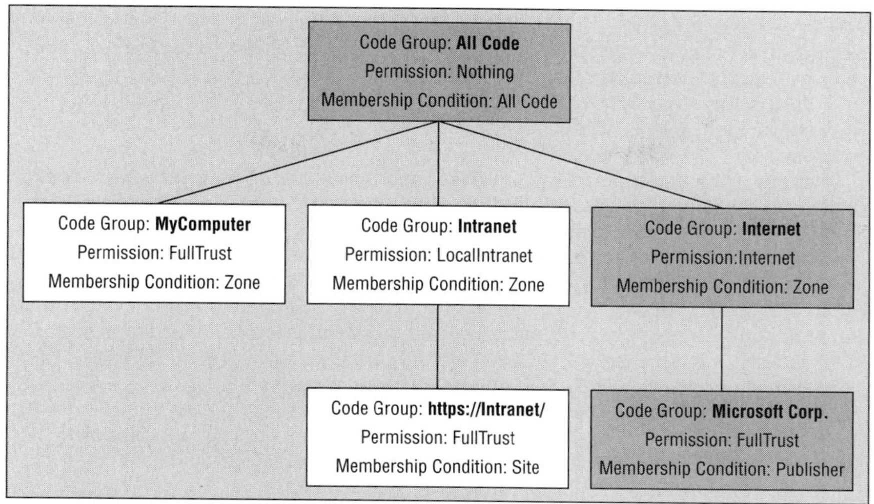

Figure 20-7

Although the All Code and Internet code groups have only limited permissions according to the policy in this example, membership of the code group in the bottom right-hand corner grants the assembly the FullTrust permission. The overall effective permission is the *union* of permissions across the matching code groups. When the permissions are merged this way, the effective permission is that of all permissions granted, that is, each code group to which an assembly belongs brings additional permissions.

Just as you can check what code groups an assembly belongs to, it is also possible to look at the permissions assigned to the code groups. By doing this you will see not only the code access permissions (what the code is allowed to do), but also the code identity permissions that will give you access to the evidence the code presented to the runtime. To see the permissions for an assembly's code groups, use a command like this:

```
caspol.exe -resolveperm assembly.dll
```

Try this on an assembly and look at the granted code access and identity permissions when the assembly is accessed over a local intranet. When you type the following command, you will see the code access permissions and then the three identity permissions at the end:

```
caspol.exe -resolveperm http://somehost/assembly.dll
Microsoft (R) .NET Framework CasPol 2.0.50727.1426
Copyright (c) Microsoft Corporation. All rights reserved.

Resolving permissions for level = Enterprise
Resolving permissions for level = Machine
Resolving permissions for level = User

Grant =
<PermissionSet class="System.Security.PermissionSet"
      version="1">
   <IPermission class="System.Security.Permissions.EnvironmentPermission,
         mscorlib, Version=2.0.0.0, Culture=neutral,
         PublicKeyToken=b77a5c561934e089" Version="1" Read="USERNAME"/>
```

(continued)

(continued)

```
    <IPermission class="System.Security.Permissions.FileDialogPermission,
          mscorlib, Version=2.0.0.0, Culture=neutral,
          PublicKeyToken=b77a5c561934e089"
          version="1" Unrestricted="true"/>
    <IPermission
          class="System.Security.Permissions.IsolatedStorageFilePermission,
          mscorlib, Version=2.0.0.0, Culture=neutral,
          PublicKeyToken=b77a5c561934e089" version="1"
          Allowed="AssemblyIsolationByUser"
          UserQuota="9223372036854775807" Expiry="9223372036854775807"
          Permanent="True"/>
    <IPermission class="System.Security.Permissions.ReflectionPermission,
          mscorlib, Version="2.0.0.0, Culture=neutral,
          PublicKeyToken= b77a5c561934e089" Version="1"
          Flags="ReflectionEmit" />
    <IPermission class="System.Security.Permissions.SecurityPermission,
          mscorlib, Version=2.0.0.0, Culture=neutral,
          PublicKeyToken=b77a5c561934e089" version="1"
          Flags="Assertion, Execution, BindingRedirects"/>
    <IPermission class="System.Security.Permissions.UIPermission,
          mscorlib, Version=2.0.0.0, Culture=neutral,
          PublicKeyToken=b77a5c561934e089" version="1"
          Unrestricted="true" />
    <IPermission class="System.Security.Permissions.SiteIdentityPermission,
          mscorlib, Version=2.0.0.0, Culture=neutral,
          PublicKeyToken=b77a5c561934e089" version="1"
          Site="somehost" />
    <IPermission class="System.Security.Permissions.UrlIdentityPermission,
          mscorlib, Version=2.0.0.0, Culture=neutral,
          PublicKeyToken=b77a5c561934e089" version="1"
          Url="http://somehost/assembly.dll" />
    <IPermission class="System.Security.Permissions.ZoneIdentityPermission,
          mscorlib, Version=2.0.0.0, Culture=neutral,
          PublicKeyToken=b77a5c561934e089" version="1"
          Zone="Intranet" />
    <IPermission class="System.Net.DnsPermission,
          System, Version=2.0.0.0, Culture=neutral,
          PublicKeyToken=b77a5c561934e089" version="1"
          Unrestricted="true" />
    <IPermission class="System.Drawing.Printing.PrintingPermission,
          System.Drawing, Version=2.0.0.0, Culture=neutral,
          PublicKeyToken=b03f5f7f11d50a3a" version="1"
          Level="DefaultPrinting" />
    <IPermission class="System.Net.WebPermission,
          System, Version=2.0.0.0, Culture=neutral,
          PublicKeyToken=b77a5c561934e089" version="1">
       <ConnectAccess>
          <URI uri="(https|http)://somehost/.*"/>
       </ConnectAccess>
    </IPermission>
</PermissionSet>

Success
```

The output shows each of the permissions in XML, including the class defining the permission, the assembly containing the class, the permission version, and an encryption token. The output suggests that it is possible for you to create your own permissions. You can also see that each of the identity permissions includes more detailed information on, for example, the `UrlIdentityPermission` class, which provides access to the URL from which the code originated.

Note how at the start of the output, `caspol.exe` resolved the permissions at the enterprise, machine, and user levels and then listed the effective granted permissions, which is worth a closer look.

Policy Levels: Machine, User, and Enterprise

Up to now, you have dealt with security in the context of a single machine. It's often necessary to specify security policies for specific users or for an entire organization, and that is why .NET provides not one but three policy levels:

- Machine
- Enterprise
- User

The code group levels are independently managed and exist in parallel, as shown in Figure 20-8.

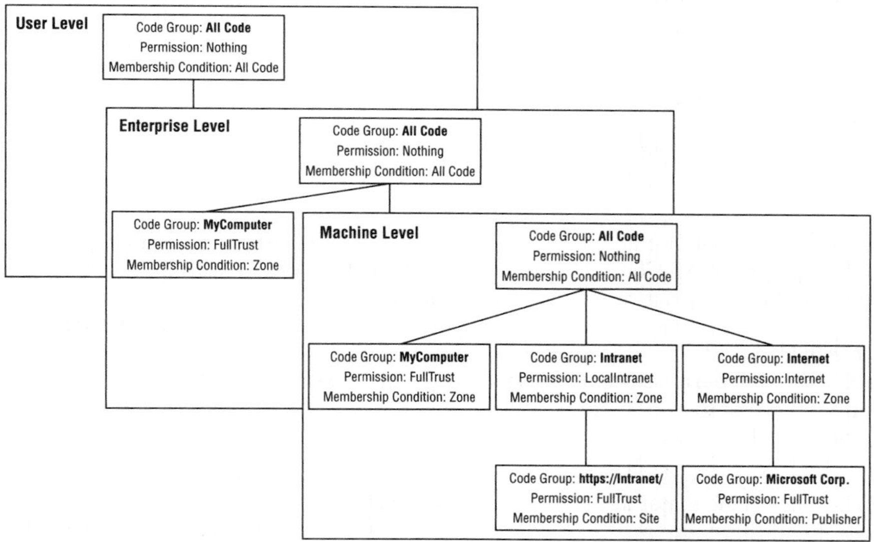

Figure 20-8

If there are three security policies, how do you know which one applies? The effective permission is the *intersection* of the permissions from these three levels. Each of the three levels has the ability to veto the permissions allowed by another — this is really good news for administrators because their settings will override user settings.

To work with code groups and permissions on the user or enterprise levels using `caspol.exe`, add either the `-enterprise` or `-user` argument to change the command's mode. `caspol.exe` works at the machine level by default and that's how you've been using it until now. Use the following command to see the code groups listing at the user level:

```
caspol.exe -user -listgroups
```

The output of the command on a default installation looks like this:

```
Security is ON
Execution checking is ON
Policy change prompt is ON

Level = User

Code Groups:

1.  All code: FullTrust
Success
```

Now run the same command, but this time with the code groups at the enterprise level:

```
caspol.exe -enterprise -listgroups
```

The output of the command looks like this:

```
Security is ON
Execution checking is ON
Policy change prompt is ON

Level = Enterprise

Code Groups:

1.  All code: FullTrust
Success
```

As you can see, by default, both the user level and the enterprise level are configured to allow FullTrust for the single code group All Code. The result of this is that the default setting for .NET security places no restrictions at the enterprise or user levels, and the enforced policy is dictated solely by the machine-level policy. For example, if you were to assign a more restrictive permission or permission set than FullTrust to either the enterprise or user levels, those restrictions would restrict the overall permissions, and probably override permissions at the machine level. The effective permissions are intersected. If you want to apply FullTrust to a code group, this permission must be assigned to the code group on each of the three policy levels.

When you run `caspol.exe` as an administrator, it defaults to the machine level, but if you log out and log back in as a user who is not in the Administrator user group, `caspol.exe` will default to the user level instead. In addition, `caspol.exe` will not allow you to alter the security policy in a way that renders the `caspol.exe` utility itself inoperable.

Managing Security Policies

As you have already seen, the glue that connects code groups, permissions, and permission sets consists of three levels of security policy (enterprise, machine, and user). Security configuration information in .NET is stored in XML configuration files that are protected by Windows security. For example, the machine-level security policy is writable only by users in the Administrators and `SYSTEM` Windows groups.

The files that store the security policy are located in the following paths:

- **Enterprise policy configuration** — <windows>\Microsoft.NET\Framework\<version>\Config\enterprise.config
- **Machine policy configuration** — <windows>\Microsoft.NET\Framework\<version>\Config\security.config
- **User policy configuration** — %USERPROFILE%\application data\Microsoft\CLR Security Config\<version>\security.config

The subdirectory <version> varies, depending on the version of the CLR you have on your machine. Because .NET 2.0, 3.0, and .NET 3.5 are based on the same version of the runtime, you find just one configuration for all these Framework versions. If necessary, it's possible to edit these configuration files manually, for example, if an administrator needs to configure policy for a user without logging in to his account. However, in general it's recommended to use caspol.exe or other administrator tools.

Given everything you have read so far, you are ready for a simple application that accesses the local drive — the kind of behavior you are likely to want to manage carefully. The application is a C# Windows Forms application with a list box and a button (see Figure 20-9). When you click the button, the list box is populated from a file called animals.txt from your local user folder. Before starting the application, you need to copy the file to this folder. In Windows Vista, the file is c:\users\<username>\Documents\animals.txt.

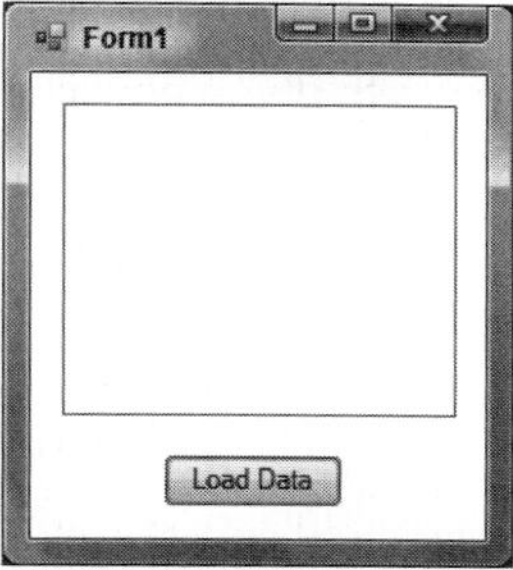

Figure 20-9

The application was created by using Visual Studio, and the only changes were to add the list box and Load Data button to the form and to add an event to the button that looks like this:

```
// Example from SimpleExample

private void OnLoadData(object sender, System.EventArgs e)
{
   string filename = Path.Combine(Environment.GetFolderPath(
         Environment.SpecialFolder.MyDocuments), "animals.txt");
   using (StreamReader stream = File.OpenText(filename))
   {
      string str;
      while ((str=stream.ReadLine()) != null)
      {
         listAnimals.Items.Add(str);
      }
   }
}
```

It opens a simple text file animals.txt from the user folder, which contains a list of animals on separate lines, and loads each line into a string, which it then uses to create each item in the list box.

If you run the application from your local machine and click the button, you will see the data loaded and displayed in the list box (see Figure 20-10). Behind the scenes the runtime has granted the assembly the permission it needs to execute, access the user interface, and read data from the local disk.

Figure 20-10

As mentioned earlier, the permissions on the Intranet zone code group are more restrictive than on the local machine; in particular, they do not allow access to the local disk. If you run the application again, but this time from a network share, it will run just as before because it is granted the permissions to execute and access the user interface; however, if you now click the Load Data button on the form, a security exception is thrown (see Figure 20-11). You'll see in the exception message text that it mentions the `System.Security.Permissions.FileIOPermission` object; this is the permission that the application was not granted and that was demanded by the class in the Framework that was used to load the data from the file on the local disk.

By default, the Intranet code group is granted the LocalIntranet permission set; change the permission set to FullTrust so that any code from the Intranet zone can run completely unrestricted.

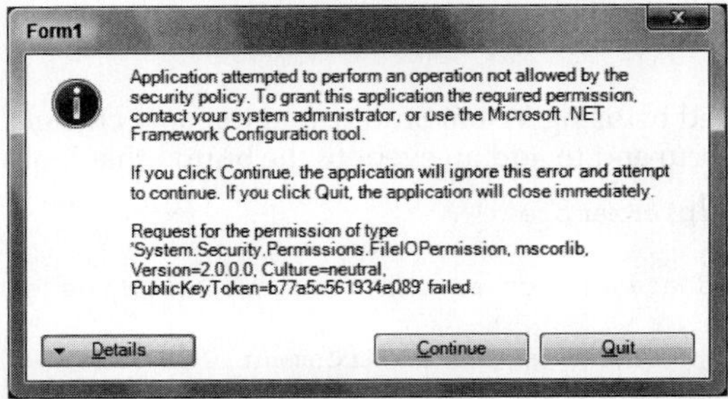

Figure 20-11

First, you need to get the numeric label of the LocalIntranet code group. You can do this with the following command:

```
>caspol.exe -listgroups
```

This will output something like this:

```
Code Groups:

1.  All code: Nothing
   1.1.  Zone - MyComputer: FullTrust
      1.1.1.  StrongName -
002400000480000094000000060200000024000052534131000400000100010007D1FA57C4AED9
F0A32E84AA0FAEFD0DE9E8FD6AEC8F87FB03766C834C99921EB23BE79AD9D5DCC1DD9AD2361321
02900B723CF980957FC4E177108FC607774F29E8320E92EA05ECE4E821C0A5EFE8F1645C4C0C93
C1AB99285D622CAA652C1DFAD63D745D6F2DE5F17E5EAF0FC4963D261C8A12436518206DC09334
4D5AD293: FullTrust
      1.1.2.  StrongName - 00000000000000000400000000000000: FullTrust
   1.2.  Zone - Intranet: LocalIntranet
      1.2.1.  All code: Same site Web.
      1.2.2.  All code: Same directory FileIO - 'Read, PathDiscovery'
   1.3.  Zone - Internet: Internet
      1.3.1.  All code: Same site Web.
   1.4.  Zone - Untrusted: Nothing
   1.5.  Zone - Trusted: Internet
      1.5.1.  All code: Same site Web.
```

Notice that the LocalIntranet group is listed as 1.2. You can use the following command to apply full trust:

```
>caspol.exe -chggroup 1.2 FullTrust
```

If you run the application from the network share again and click the button, you will see that the list box is populated with the content of the file in the root of the `C:\` drive and no exception occurs.

In scenarios like these, in which you are making use of resources governed by permissions, it is advisable to extend the code so that security exceptions are caught and the application can degrade gracefully. For example, in the sample application, you can add a `try/catch` block around the file access code, and if a `SecurityException` is thrown, you can display a line in the list box saying "Permission denied accessing file":

```
private void OnLoadData(object sender, System.EventArgs e)
{
   try
   {
      string filename = Environment.GetFolderPath(
            Environment.SpecialFolder.MyDocuments) + @"\animals.txt";
      StreamReader din = File.OpenText(filename);
      string str;
      while ((str=din.ReadLine()) != null)
      {
         listAnimals.Items.Add(str);
      }
   }
   catch (SecurityException ex)
   {
      MessageBox.Show(ex.Message);
   }
}
```

In reality, if you wanted to run a specific application from a network share, you would most likely opt for a solution that didn't open up the client machine to all code on the intranet. Instead, code groups and membership conditions can be used to tightly control the requirements of the application — perhaps using its location on the intranet, a strong name, or a certificate proving the identity of the publisher.

Managing Code Groups and Permissions

In managing security on .NET, if you find that an assembly is failing with a security exception, you usually have three choices:

- **Ease the policy permissions** — You can change the permissions for the Machine policy to allow more permissions for specific code groups. However, it is not a good practice to give more permissions to the assemblies from an intranet or the Internet, because this can lead to Trojan horses gaining access to your system. Instead, you can add new code groups that have specific permissions as required.
- **Move the assembly** — Assemblies from a network share are not trusted as much as assemblies installed on the local system. Instead of creating a new code group, you can move the assembly to the local system so that it gets more permissions.
- **Apply a strong name to the assembly** — A good practice is to apply a strong name to the assembly and create a code group that trusts the strong name.

To make these kinds of decisions, you must take into account your level of trust of the assembly.

Turning Security On and Off

By default, .NET security is enabled. If, for any reason, you need to turn it off, you can do so like this:

```
>caspol.exe -security off
```

As a new security feature, running this command from the command prompt turns security off only temporarily. As soon as you press the Enter key, security is turned on again. You can keep this command prompt open as long as required and continue working with another command prompt. When you are finished doing the security related tasks, press the Enter key and security is turned on again. You can also explicitly turn it on again:

```
>caspol.exe -security on
```

To return the security configuration to its original state, you can type this command:

```
>caspol.exe -reset
```

This command resets the security policy to the installation's default.

Creating a Code Group

You can create your own code groups and then apply specific permissions to them. For example, you could specify that you want to trust all code from the Web site `www.wrox.com` and to give it full access to the system (without trusting code from any other Web site).

Earlier, the tool caspol was used to display a list with the available group and number assignments. The zone Internet is labeled 1.3, so now type this command:

```
>caspol.exe -addgroup 1.3 -site www.wrox.com FullTrust
```

Note that this command will ask for confirmation because this is an attempt to alter the security policy on the machine. If the command `caspol.exe -listgroups` is now run again, you will see that the new code group has been added and assigned FullTrust:

```
...
1.2.  Zone - Intranet: LocalIntranet
   1.2.1.  All code: Same site Web.
   1.2.2.  All code: Same directory FileIO - Read, PathDiscovery
 1.3.  Zone - Internet: Internet
   1.3.1.  All code: Same site Web.
   1.3.2.  Site - www.wrox.com: FullTrust
 1.4.  Zone - Untrusted: Nothing
 1.5.  Zone - Trusted: Internet
   1.5.1.  All code: Same site Web.
```

Here's another example. Say that you want to create a code group under the Intranet code group (1.2) that grants FullTrust to all applications running from a specific network share. To do so, you run the following command:

```
>caspol.exe -addgroup 1.2 -url file:\\intranetserver/sharename/* FullTrust
```

Deleting a Code Group

To remove a code group that has been created, you can type a command like this:

```
>caspol.exe -remgroup 1.3.2
```

It will ask for confirmation that you want to alter the security policy, and if you give it positive confirmation, it will state that the group has been removed.

Be aware that although you cannot delete the code group All Code, you can delete code groups at the level below it, including the Internet, MyComputer, and LocalIntranet groups.

Changing a Code Group's Permissions

To ease or restrict the permissions assigned to a code group, you use `caspol.exe` again. Suppose that you want to apply FullTrust to the Intranet zone; first, you need to get the label that represents the Intranet code group:

```
>caspol.exe -listgroups
```

The output shows the Intranet code group:

```
Code Groups:

1.  All code: Nothing
   1.1.  Zone - MyComputer: FullTrust
      1.1.1.  StrongName -
0024000004800000940000000602000000240000525341310004000001000100007D1FA57C4AED9
F0A32E84AA0FAEFD0DE9E8FD6AEC8F87FB03766C834C99921EB23BE79AD9D5DCC1DD9AD2361321
02900B72
3CF980957FC4E177108FC607774F29E8320E92EA05ECE4E821C0A5EFE8F1645C4C0C93C1AB9928
5D622CAA652C1DFAD63D745D6F2DE5F17E5EAF0FC4963D261C8A12436518206DC093344D5AD293
: FullTrust
      1.1.2.  StrongName - 00000000000000000400000000000000: FullTrust
   1.2.  Zone - Intranet: LocalIntranet
      1.2.1.  All code: Same site Web.
      1.2.2.  All code: Same directory FileIO - Read, PathDiscovery
```

(continued)

(continued)

```
      1.3.  Zone - Internet: Internet
         1.3.1.  All code: Same site Web.
      1.4.  Zone - Untrusted: Nothing
      1.5.  Zone - Trusted: Internet
         1.5.1.  All code: Same site Web.
```

Once you have the Intranet code group's label, 1.2, you can enter a second command to alter the code group's permissions:

```
>caspol.exe -chggroup 1.2 FullTrust
```

The command asks you to confirm the change to the security policy, and if you run the `caspol.exe -listgroups` command again, you can see that the permission on the end of the Intranet line has changed to FullTrust:

```
Code Groups:

1.  All code: Nothing
   1.1.  Zone - MyComputer: FullTrust
      1.1.1.  StrongName -
002400000480000094000000060200000024000052534131000400000100010007D1FA57C4AED9
F0A32E84AA0FAEFD0DE9E8FD6AEC8F87FB03766C834C99921EB23BE79AD9D5DCC1DD9AD2361321
02900B723CF980957FC4E177108FC607774F29E8320E92EA05ECE4E821C0A5EFE8F1645C4C0C93
C1AB99285D622CAA652C1DFAD63D745D6F2DE5F17E5EAF0FC4963D261C8A12436518206DC09334
4D5AD293: FullTrust
      1.1.2.  StrongName - 00000000000000000400000000000000: FullTrust
   1.2.  Zone - Intranet: FullTrust
      1.2.1.  All code: Same site Web.
      1.2.2.  All code: Same directory FileIO - Read, PathDiscovery
   1.3.  Zone - Internet: Internet
      1.3.1.  All code: Same site Web.
   1.4.  Zone - Untrusted: Nothing
   1.5.  Zone - Trusted: Internet
      1.5.1.  All code: Same site Web.
```

Creating and Applying Permissions Sets

You can create new permission sets using a command like this:

```
>caspol.exe -addpset MyCustomPermissionSet permissionset.xml
```

This command specifies that you are creating a new permission set called MyCustomPermissionSet, which is configured with the contents of the specified XML file. The XML file must contain a standard format that specifies a `PermissionSet`. For reference, here is the permission set file for the Everything permission set, which you can trim down to the permission set you want to create:

```
<PermissionSet class="System.Security.NamedPermissionSet" version="1"
    Name="Everything"
    Description="Allows unrestricted access to all resources covered by
           built-in permissions">
  <IPermission class="System.Security.Permissions.EnvironmentPermission,
      mscorlib, Version=2.0.0.0, Culture=neutral,
      PublicKeyToken=b77a5c561934e089" version="1" Unrestricted="true" />
  <IPermission class="System.Security.Permissions.FileDialogPermission,
      mscorlib, Version=2.0.0.0, Culture=neutral,
      PublicKeyToken=b77a5c561934e089" version="1" Unrestricted="true" />
```

```
    <IPermission class="System.Security.Permissions.FileIOPermission,
        mscorlib, Version=2.0.0.0, Culture=neutral,
        PublicKeyToken=b77a5c561934e089" version="1" Unrestricted="true" />
    <IPermission class="System.Security.Permissions.IsolatedStorageFilePermission,
        mscorlib, Version=2.0.0.0, Culture=neutral,
        PublicKeyToken=b77a5c561934e089" version="1" Unrestricted="true" />
    <IPermission class="System.Security.Permissions.ReflectionPermission,
        mscorlib, Version=2.0.0.0, Culture=neutral,
        PublicKeyToken=b77a5c561934e089" version="1" Unrestricted="true" />
    <IPermission class="System.Security.Permissions.RegistryPermission,
        mscorlib, Version=2.0.0.0, Culture=neutral,
        PublicKeyToken=b77a5c561934e089" version="1" Unrestricted="true" />
    <IPermission class="System.Security.Permissions.SecurityPermission,
        mscorlib, Version=2.0.0.0, Culture=neutral,
        PublicKeyToken=b77a5c561934e089" version="1"
        Flags="Assertion, UnmanagedCode, Execution, ControlThread,
            ControlEvidence, ControlPolicy, SerializationFormatter,
            ControlDomainPolicy, ControlPrincipal, ControlAppDomain,
            RemotingConfiguration, Infrastructure, BindingRedirects" />
    <IPermission class="System.Security.Permissions.UIPermission,
        mscorlib, Version=2.0.0.0, Culture=neutral,
        PublicKeyToken=b77a5c561934e089" version="1" Unrestricted="true" />
    <IPermission class="System.Security.Permissions.KeyContainerPermission,
        mscorlib, Version=2.0.0.0, Culture=neutral,
        PublicKeyToken=b77a5c561934e089" version="1" Unrestricted="true" />
    <IPermission class="System.Net.DnsPermission, System, Version=2.0.3600.0,
        Culture=neutral, PublicKeyToken=b77a5c561934e089" version="1"
        Unrestricted="true" />
    <IPermission class="System.Net.SocketPermission, System,
        Version=2.0.0.0, Culture=neutral,
        PublicKeyToken=b77a5c561934e089" version="1" Unrestricted="true" />
    <IPermission class="System.Net.WebPermission, System,
        Version=2.0.0.0, Culture=neutral, PublicKeyToken=b77a5c561934e089"
        version="1" Unrestricted="true" />
    <IPermission class="System.Security.Permissions.StorePermission, System,
        Version=2.0.0.0, Culture=neutral,
        PublicKeyToken=b77a5c561934e089" version="1" Unrestricted="true" />
    <IPermission class="System.Diagnostics.PerformanceCounterPermission,
        System, Version=2.0.0.0, Culture=neutral,
        PublicKeyToken=b77a5c561934e089" version="1" Unrestricted="true" />
    <IPermission class="System.Data.OleDb.OleDbPermission,
        System.Data, Version=2.0.0.0, Culture=neutral,
        PublicKeyToken=b77a5c561934e089" version="1" Unrestricted="true" />
    <IPermission class="System.Data.SqlClient.SqlClientPermission,
        System.Data, Version=2.0.0.0, Culture=neutral,
        PublicKeyToken=b77a5c561934e089" version="1" Unrestricted="true" />
    <IPermission class="System.Security.Permissions.DataProtectionPermission,
        System.Security, Version=2.0.0.0, Culture=neutral,
        PublicKeyToken=b03f5f7f11d50a3a" version="1" Unrestricted="true" />
</PermissionSet>
```

To view all permission sets in XML format, you can use this command:

```
>caspol.exe -listpset
```

To give a new definition to an existing permission set by applying an XML `PermissionSet` configuration file, you can use this command:

```
>caspol.exe -chgpset permissionset.xml MyCustomPermissionSet
```

Distributing Code Using a Strong Name

.NET provides the ability to match an assembly to a code group when the assembly's identity and integrity have been confirmed using a strong name. This scenario is very common when assemblies are being deployed across networks (for example, when distributing software over the Internet).

If you are a software company and you want to provide code to your customers via the Internet, you build an assembly and give it a strong name. The strong name ensures that the assembly can be uniquely identified, and also provides protection against tampering. Your customers can incorporate this strong name into their code access security policy; an assembly that matches this unique strong name can then be assigned permissions explicitly. As discussed in Chapter 17, "Assemblies," the strong name includes checksums for hashes of all the files within an assembly, so you have strong evidence that the assembly has not been altered since the publisher created the strong name.

Note that if your application uses an installer, the installer will install assemblies that have already been given a strong name. The strong name is generated once for each distribution before being sent to customers; the installer does not run these commands. The reason for this is that the strong name provides an assurance that the assembly has not been modified since it left your company. A common way to achieve this is to give your customer not only the application code but also, separately, a copy of the strong name for the assembly. You might find it beneficial to pass the strong name to your customer using a secure form (perhaps a fax or an encrypted email) to guard against the assembly being tampered with in the process.

Consider an example in which an assembly with a strong name is created to distribute it in such a way that the recipient of the assembly can use the strong name to grant the `FullTrust` permission to the assembly.

First, a key pair is needed. Creating strong names has already been discussed in Chapter 17, so there is no need to repeat it here. Rebuilding the assembly with the key ensures that the hash is recalculated and the assembly is protected against malicious modifications. Also, the assembly can be uniquely identified with the strong name. This identification can be used with membership conditions of code groups. A membership condition can be based on the requirement to match a specific strong name.

The following command states that a new code group is created using the strong name from the specified assembly manifest file, that the code group is independent of the version number of the assembly, and that the code group has granted the FullTrust permissions:

```
>caspol.exe -addgroup 1 -strong -file SimpleExample.exe -noname -noversion
FullTrust
```

In this example, the application will now run from any zone, even the Internet zone, because the strong name provides powerful evidence that the assembly can be trusted. Look at your code groups using `caspol.exe -listgroups`, and you will see the new code group (1.6 and its associated public key in hexadecimal):

```
Code Groups:

1.  All code: Nothing
   1.1.  Zone - MyComputer: FullTrust
      1.1.1.  StrongName -
002400000480000094000000060200000024000052534131000400000100010007D1FA57C4AED9
F0A32E84AA0FAEFD0DE9E8FD6AEC8F87FB03766C834C99921EB23BE79AD9D5DCC1DD9AD2361321
```

```
02900B723CF980957FC4E177108FC607774F29E8320E92EA05ECE4E821C0A5EFE8F1645C4C0C93
C1AB99285D622CAA652C1DFAD63D745D6F2DE5F17E5EAF0FC4963D261C8A12436518206DC09334
4D5AD293: FullTrust
      1.1.2.  StrongName - 00000000000000000400000000000000: FullTrust
   1.2.  Zone - Intranet: LocalIntranet
      1.2.1.  All code: Same site Web
      1.2.2.  All code: Same directory FileIO - 'Read, PathDiscovery'
   1.3.  Zone - Internet: Internet
      1.3.1.  All code: Same site Web
   1.4.  Zone - Untrusted: Nothing
   1.5.  Zone - Trusted: Internet
      1.5.1.  All code: Same site Web
   1.6.  StrongName -
002400000480000094000000060200000024000052534131000400000100010047008BB48DA2FA
B8C17E6277D76D0E8867273B5BB7962C155A03F118D8C6289CA3F05C08174EE2A933ABF8D3E9E4
24D2635399B9A7B0C7CD45742A3770694456776087AABB92041CB0783CDD9E4AAD04AA8D43488A
C599469ABD2E891DB2B5BDAD5C62EB5AFF23CEEA3EFED03539AC9FFEA8D3165EEBD67B246AB4C3
D6B31EB3: FullTrust
Success
```

To access the strong name in an assembly, you can use the `secutil.exe` tool against the assembly manifest file. Using the `-hex` option, the public key is shown in hexadecimal (like `caspol.exe`); the argument `-strongname` specifies that the strong name should be shown. Type this command, and you will see a listing containing the strong name public key, the assembly name, and the assembly version:

```
>secutil.exe -hex -strongname SimpleExample.exe
Microsoft (R) .NET Framework SecUtil 3.5.21004.1
Copyright (c) Microsoft Corporation. All rights reserved.

Public Key =
0x002400000480000094000000060200000024000052534131000400000100010047008BB48DA2
FAB8C17E6277D76D0E8867273B5BB7962C155A03F118D8C6289CA3F05C08174EE2A933ABF8D3E9
E424D2635399B9A7B0C7CD45742A3770694456776087AABB92041CB0783CDD9E4AAD04AA8D4348
8AC599469ABD2E891DB2B5BDAD5C62EB5AFF23CEEA3EFED03539AC9FFEA8D3165EEBD67B246AB4
C3D6B31EB3
Name =
SimpleExample
Version =
1.0.0.0
Success
```

You may be surprised about the two strong name code groups that are installed by default and what they refer to. One is a strong name key for Microsoft code; the other strong name key is for the parts of .NET that have been submitted to the ECMA for standardization, which will give Microsoft much less control.

Distributing Code Using Certificates

The preceding section discussed how a strong name can be applied to an assembly so that system administrators can explicitly grant permissions to assemblies that match that strong name, using a code access group. Although this method of security policy management can be very effective, it is sometimes necessary to work at a higher level, where the administrator of the security policy grants permissions on the basis of the publisher of the software, rather than to each individual software component. You probably have seen a similar method used before when you have downloaded executables from the Internet that have been Authenticode signed.

To provide information about the software publisher, you can make use of digital certificates and sign assemblies so that consumers of the software can verify the identity of the software publisher. In a commercial environment, you would obtain a certificate from a company such as Verisign or Thawte.

The advantage of buying a certificate from a supplier instead of creating your own is that it provides a high level of trust in its authenticity; the supplier acts as a trusted third party. For test purposes, however, .NET includes a command-line utility you can use to create a test certificate. The process of creating certificates and using them for publishing software is complex, but we walk through a simple example in this section.

The example code will be made for the fictitious company called ABC Corporation. In this company, the software product ABC Suite should be trusted. First, create a test certificate by typing the following command:

```
>makecert -sv abckey.pvk -r -n "CN=ABC Corporation" abccorptest.cer
```

The command creates a test certificate under the name ABC Corporation and saves it to a file called `abccorptest.cer`. The `-sv abckey.pvk` argument creates a key file to store the private key. When creating the key file, you are asked for a password that you should remember.

After creating the certificate, you can create a software publisher test certificate with the Software Publisher Certificate Test tool (`Cert2spc.exe`):

```
>cert2spc abccorptest.cer abccorptest.spc
```

To sign the assembly with the certificate, use the `signcode.exe` utility on the assembly file containing the assembly manifest. Often, the easiest way to sign an assembly is to use the `signtool.exe` in its wizard mode; to start the wizard, just type `signtool.exe` with the parameter `signwizard`.

When you click Next, the program asks you to specify where the file is that should be signed. For an assembly, select the file containing the manifest, for example `SimpleExample.exe`, and click the Next button. On the Signing Options page, you must select the Custom option to define the previously created certificate file.

In the next dialog box, you are asked to specify the certificate that should be used to sign the assembly. Click Select from File and browse to the file `abccorptest.spc`. You will now see the screen shown in Figure 20-12.

The next screen that appears asks for your private key. The key file `abckey.pvk` was created by the `makecert` utility, so you can select the options as shown in Figure 20-13. The cryptographic service provider is an application that implements the cryptographic standards.

Next you are asked a series of questions about the encryption algorithm that should be used for signing the assembly (`md5` or `sha1`) and the name and URL of the application, and you are shown a final confirmation dialog.

Because the executable is now signed with the certificate, a recipient of the assembly has access to strong evidence as to who published the software. The runtime can examine the certificate and match the publisher of the assembly to a code group with high levels of confidence about the identity of the code because the trusted third-party certifies the publisher's identity.

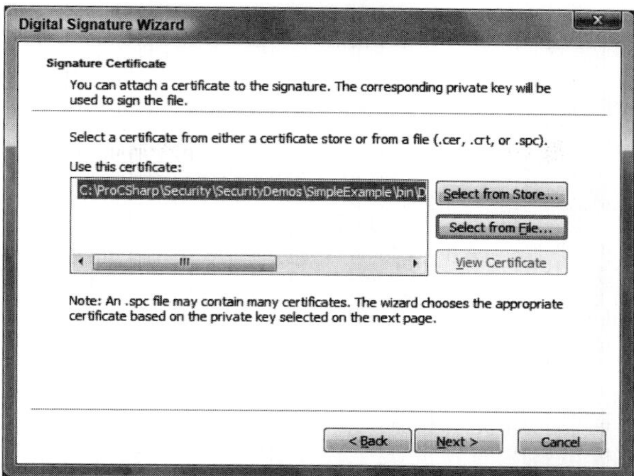

Figure 20-12

Figure 20-13

The test certificate must now be installed with the trusted certificates. Start the Certificate Manager `certmgr`:

```
>certmgr
```

Select the Trusted Root Certification Authorities tab and Certificates below in the tree. Select Action ⇨ All Task ⇨ Import . . . to import the certificate file. With the Certificate Import, select the certificate file `abccorptest.cer`.

After clicking the Next button, verify that the certificate store listed is Trusted Root Certification Authorities, which is the case when you have chosen this selection in the tree view (see Figure 20-14).

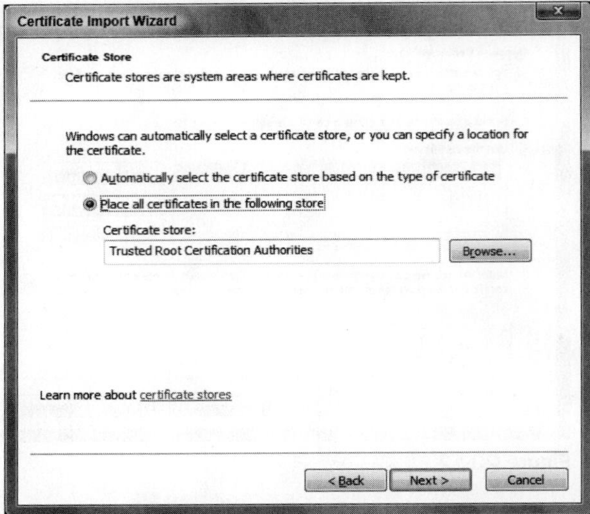

Figure 20-14

Before the import is completed, you will get a warning dialog, as shown in Figure 20-15, because the test certificate cannot be validated. Click Yes to install the certificate.

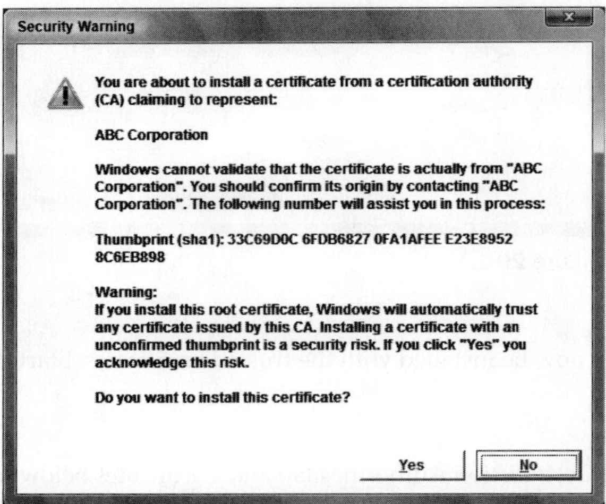

Figure 20-15

After the certificate is installed as a trusted root authority, you can see it in the certificates list, as shown in Figure 20-16.

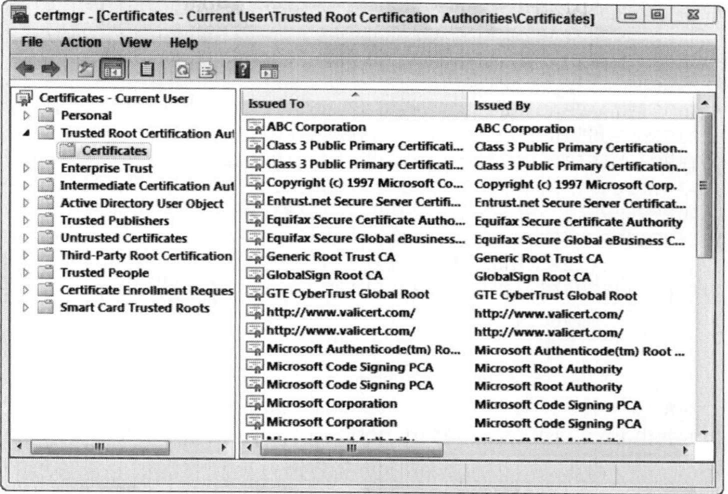

Figure 20-16

Now turn your attention to a machine that you want to configure to trust software from the ABC Corporation. You can create a new code access group that matches this software from ABC Corporation. You just have to grab a hexadecimal representation of the certificate from the assembly using the `secutil.exe` tool:

```
>secutil.exe -hex -x SimpleExample.exe
```

This command results in the following output:

```
Microsoft (R) .NET Framework SecUtil 2.0.50727.42
Copyright (c) Microsoft Corp. All rights reserved.

X.509 Certificate =
0x3082020830820171A0030201020210229DECFA1C01E89D46E23F35B6284691300D06092A8648
86F70D0101040500301A311830160603550403130F41424320436F72706F726174696F6E301E17
0D3037303132323130323334395A170D3339313233313233353935395A301A3118301606035504
03130F41424320436F72706F726174696F6E30819F300D06092A864886F70D010101050003818D
0030818902818100B7AE9EC301F76CC661EBF7F9C23E2B4A92F6B4BE318F50B7CB0DA36D4BFECC
69E390384AC33717779A0EAD683536A18B98FC8CA67D10CA05B9FF5AEAA42BCA01D85F95E79442
7915B9AAA8CC5C55E9855F5F5D7A5FEEBDF788E2B574E9CBB11B30BC424260415B28A73509048A
DDC9BEF28C07E9C8CE166CB92074D07D17798F0203010001A34F304D304B0603551D0104443042
80101BA15BEAA3E3B66F2497401512C79799A11C301A311830160603550403130F41424320436F
72706F726174696F6E8210229DECFA1C01E89D46E23F35B6284691300D06092A864886F70D0101
0405000381810074 6FFF169DE478C34684FAABDBF326A8CEB4588B96C0948BA14D5C73ACF174E5
608CBAE8C7BB77B2A38622E7662BA75F9D0E2A328C8A7E3A28790DC05A7E32557150F8F549E2B3
F36F8A609248AF094387784048A7A4B0FFA505A7105A4DDDAAF12DC622B4E7956247BEF3D95F18
7DAEF1A92A34DE83880174ADCFF93A97BBA8
Success
```

Now create the new code group and apply the FullTrust permission to assemblies published by the ABC Corporation using this (rather long) command:

```
>caspol -addgroup 1 -pub -hex
"0x3082020830820171A0030201020210229DECFA1C01E89D46E23F35B6284691300D06092A864
886F70D0101040500301A311830160603550403130F41424320436F72706F726174696F6E301E1
70D303730313232313032333439 5A170D3339313233313233353935395A301A311830160603550
403130F41424320436F72706F726174696F6E30819F300D06092A864886F70D010101050003818
D0030818902818100B7AE9EC301F76CC661EBF7F9C23E2B4A92F6B4BE318F50B7CB0DA36D4BFEC
C69E390384AC33717779A0EAD683536A18B98FC8CA67D10CA05B9FF5AEAA42BCA01D85F95E7944
27915B9AAA8CC5C55E9855F5F5D7A5FEEBDF788E2B574E9CBB11B30BC424260415B28A73509048
ADDC9BEF28C07E9C8CE166CB92074D07D17798F0203010001A34F304D304B0603551D010444304
280101BA15BEAA3E3B66F2497401512C79799A11C301A311830160603550403130F41424320436
F72706F726174696F6E8210229DECFA1C01E89D46E23F35B6284691300D06092A864886F70D010
104050003818100746FFF169DE478C34684FAABDBF326A8CEB4588B96C0948BA14D5C73ACF174E
5608CBAE8C7BB77B2A38622E7662BA75F9D0E2A328C8A7E3A28790DC05A7E32557150F8F549E2B
3F36F8A609248AF094387784048A7A4B0FFA505A7105A4DDDAAF12DC622B4E7956247BEF3D95F1
87DAEF1A92A34DE83880174ADCFF93A97BBA8"
FullTrust
```

The parameters specify that the code group should be added at the top level (1) and that the code group membership condition is of the type `Publisher`; the last parameter specifies the permission set to grant (FullTrust). The command will ask for confirmation:

```
Microsoft (R) .NET Framework CasPol 2.0.50727.1426
Copyright (c) Microsoft Corporation. All rights reserved.

The operation you are performing will alter security policy.
Are you sure you want to perform this operation? (yes/no)
y
Added union code group with "-pub" membership condition to the Machine level.
Success
```

The machine is now configured to fully trust all assemblies that have been signed with the certificate from ABC Corporation. To confirm that, you can run a `caspol.exe -lg` command, which lists the new code access group.

As another check, ask `caspol.exe` to tell you what code groups your assembly matches:

```
>caspol.exe -resolvegroup SimpleExample.exe
Level = Enterprise

Code Groups:

1.  All code: FullTrust

Level = Machine

Code Groups:
1.  All code: Nothing
   1.1.  Zone - MyComputer: FullTrust
   1.7.  Publisher -
30818902818100B7AE9EC301F76CC661EBF7F9C23E2B4A92F6B4BE318F50B7CB0DA36D4BFECC69
E390384AC33717779A0EAD683536A18B98FC8CA67D10CA05B9FF5AEAA42BCA01D85F95E7944279
15B9AAA8CC5C55E9855F5F5D7A5FEEBDF788E2B574E9CBB11B30BC424260415B28A73509048ADD
C9BEF28C07E9C8CE166CB92074D07D17798F0203010001: FullTrust
```

```
Level = User

Code Groups:

1.  All code: FullTrust

Success
```

In the center of the results, you can see that the assembly has been successfully matched to your new code group and granted the FullTrust permission set.

Summary

This chapter covered several security aspects with .NET applications. Code-access security adds a security layer to an application in that it gives different permissions to applications based on the evidence of the application. How much can you trust the application? It depends on what .NET permissions apply. Permissions are grouped in permission sets and managed with using user, machine, and enterprise policies.

Authentication and authorization with role-based security allow you to decide in the application which users are allowed to access application features. Users are represented by identities and principals, classes that implement the interface `IIdentity` and `IPrincipal`. Role verification can be done within the code but also in a simple way using attributes.

Cryptography was shown to demonstrate signing and encrypting of data, to exchange keys in a secure way. .NET offers several cryptography algorithms offering both symmetric and asymmetric algorithms. .NET 3.5 also supports Cryptography Next Generation, which is available with Windows Vista and Windows Server 2008.

With access control lists, you have also seen how to read and modify access to operating system resources such as files. Programming ACLs is done in ways similar to the programming of secure pipes, registry keys, Active Directory entries, and many other operating system resources.

You've seen how to use tools to manage security policies such as caspol, and how to distribute code with a certificate.

If your applications are used in different regions and with different languages, in the next chapter you can read about globalization and localization features of .NET.

21

Localization

NASA's Mars Climate Orbiter was lost on September 23, 1999, at a cost of $125 million, because one engineering team used metric units, while another one used inches for a key spacecraft operation. When writing applications for international distribution, different cultures and regions must be kept in mind.

Different cultures have diverging calendars and use different number and date formats. Also, sorting strings may lead to various results because the order of A–Z is defined differently based on the culture. To make applications fit for global markets, you have to globalize and localize them.

Globalization is about internationalizing applications: preparing applications for international markets. With globalization, the application supports number and date formats that vary depending on the culture, different calendars, and so on. *Localization* is about translating applications for specific cultures. For translations of strings, you can use resources.

.NET supports globalization and localization of Windows and Web applications. To globalize an application, you can use classes from the namespace `System.Globalization`; to localize an application, you can use resources that are supported by the namespace `System.Resources`.

This chapter covers the globalization and localization of .NET applications; more specifically, it discusses the following:

- Using classes that represent cultures and regions
- Globalization of applications
- Localization of applications

Namespace System.Globalization

The `System.Globalization` namespace holds all culture and region classes to support different date formats, different number formats, and even different calendars that are represented in classes such as `GregorianCalendar`, `HebrewCalendar`, `JapaneseCalendar`, and so on. By using these classes, you can display different representations depending on the user's locale.

This section looks at the following issues and considerations with using the `System.Globalization` namespace:

- Unicode issues
- Cultures and regions
- An example showing all cultures and their characteristics
- Sorting

Unicode Issues

A Unicode character has 16 bits, so there is room for 65,536 characters. Is this enough for all languages currently used in information technology? In the case of the Chinese language, for example, more than 80,000 characters are needed. However, Unicode has been designed to deal with this issue. With Unicode you have to differentiate between base characters and combining characters. You can add multiple combining characters to a base character to build up a single display character or a text element.

Take, for example, the Icelandic character Ogonek. Ogonek can be combined by using the base character 0x006F (Latin small letter o) and the combining characters 0x0328 (combining Ogonek) and 0x0304 (combining Macron) as shown in Figure 21-1. Combining characters are defined within ranges from 0x0300 to 0x0345. For American and European markets, predefined characters exist to facilitate dealing with special characters. The character Ogonek is also defined with the predefined character 0x01ED.

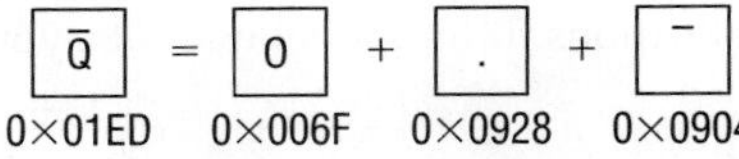

Figure 21-1

For Asian markets, where more than 80,000 characters are necessary for Chinese alone, such predefined characters do not exist. In Asian languages, you always have to deal with combining characters. The problem is getting the right number of display characters or text elements, and getting to the base characters instead of the combined characters. The namespace `System.Globalization` offers the class `StringInfo`, which you can use to deal with this issue.

The following table lists the static methods of the class `StringInfo` that help in dealing with combined characters.

Method	Description
`GetNextTextElement`	Returns the first text element (base character and all combining characters) of a specified string.
`GetTextElementEnumerator`	Returns a `TextElementEnumerator` object that allows iterating all text elements of a string.
`ParseCombiningCharacters`	Returns an integer array referencing all base characters of a string.

> **A single display character can contain multiple Unicode characters. To address this issue, when you write applications that support international markets, don't use the data type `char`; use `string` instead. A string can hold a text element that contains both base characters and combining characters, whereas a `char` cannot.**

Cultures and Regions

The world is divided into multiple cultures and regions, and applications have to be aware of these cultural and regional differences. A culture is a set of preferences based on a user's language and cultural habits. RFC 1766 (`www.ietf.org/rfc/rfc1766.txt`) defines culture names that are used worldwide depending on a language and a country or region. Some examples are en-AU, en-CA, en-GB, and en-US for the English language in Australia, Canada, the United Kingdom, and the United States, respectively.

Possibly the most important class in the `System.Globalization` namespace is `CultureInfo`. `CultureInfo` represents a culture and defines calendars, formatting of numbers and dates, and sorting strings used with the culture.

The class `RegionInfo` represents regional settings (such as the currency) and shows whether the region is using the metric system. Some regions can use multiple languages. One example is the region of Spain, which has Basque (eu-ES), Catalan (ca-ES), Spanish (es-ES), and Galician (gl-ES) cultures. Similar to one region having multiple languages, one language can be spoken in different regions; for example, Spanish is spoken in Mexico, Spain, Guatemala, Argentina, and Peru, to name only a few countries.

Later in this chapter, you see a sample application that demonstrates these characteristics of cultures and regions.

Specific, Neutral, and Invariant Cultures

With the use of cultures in the .NET Framework, you have to differentiate between three types: *specific*, *neutral*, and *invariant* cultures.

A specific culture is associated with a real, existing culture defined with RFC 1766, as you saw in the preceding section. A specific culture can be mapped to a neutral culture. For example, de is the neutral culture of the specific cultures de-AT, de-DE, de-CH, and others. de is shorthand for the German language; AT, DE, and CH are shorthand for the countries Austria, Germany, and Switzerland, respectively.

When translating applications, it is typically not necessary to do translations for every region; not much difference exists between the German language in the countries Austria and Germany. Instead of using specific cultures, you can use a neutral culture for localizing applications.

The invariant culture is independent of a real culture. When storing formatted numbers or dates in files, or sending them across a network to a server, using a culture that is independent of any user settings is the best option.

Figure 21-2 shows how the culture types relate to each other.

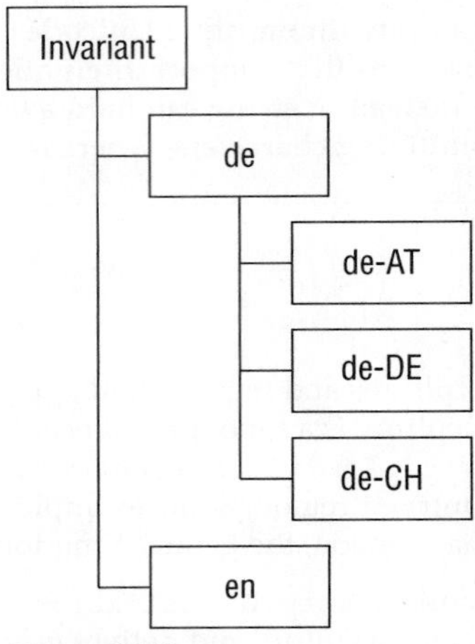

Figure 21-2

CurrentCulture and CurrentUICulture

When you set cultures, you need to differentiate between a culture for the user interface and a culture for the number and date formats. Cultures are associated with a thread, and with these two culture types, two culture settings can be applied to a thread. The `Thread` class has the properties `CurrentCulture` and `CurrentUICulture`. The property `CurrentCulture` is for setting the culture that is used with formatting and sort options, whereas the property `CurrentUICulture` is used for the language of the user interface.

Users can change the default setting of the `CurrentCulture` by using the Regional and Language options in the Windows Control Panel (see Figure 21-3). With this configuration, it is also possible to change the default number, the time, and the date format for the culture.

The `CurrentUICulture` does not depend on this configuration. The `CurrentUICulture` setting depends on the language of the operating system. There is one exception, though: If a multi-language user interface (MUI) is installed with Windows Vista or Windows XP, it is possible to change the language of the user interface with the regional configuration, and this influences the property `CurrentUICulture`.

These settings make a very good default, and in many cases, there is no need to change the default behavior. If the culture should be changed, you can easily do this by changing both cultures of the thread to, say, the Spanish culture, as shown in this code snippet:

```
System.Globalization.CultureInfo ci = new
   System.Globalization.CultureInfo("es-ES");
System.Threading.Thread.CurrentThread.CurrentCulture = ci;
System.Threading.Thread.CurrentThread.CurrentUICulture = ci;
```

Now that you know about setting the culture, the following sections discuss number and date formatting, which are influenced by the `CurrentCulture` setting.

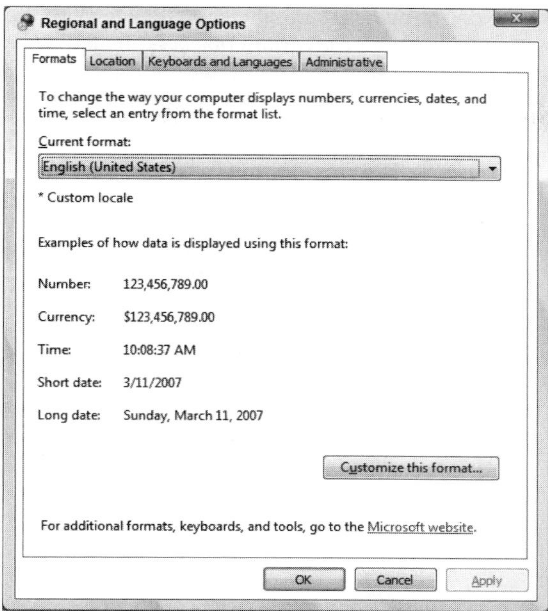

Figure 21-3

Number Formatting

The number structures `Int16`, `Int32`, `Int64`, and so on in the `System` namespace have an overloaded `ToString()` method. This method can be used to create a different representation of the number depending on the locale. For the `Int32` structure, `ToString()` is overloaded with these four versions:

```
public string ToString();
public string ToString(IFormatProvider);
public string ToString(string);
public string ToString(string, IFormatProvider);
```

`ToString()` without arguments returns a string without format options. You can also pass a string and a class that implements `IFormatProvider`.

The string specifies the format of the representation. The format can be a standard numeric formatting string or a picture numeric formatting string. For standard numeric formatting, strings are predefined, where `C` specifies the currency notation, `D` creates a decimal output, `E` creates scientific output, `F` creates fixed-point output, `G` creates general output, `N` creates number output, and `X` creates hexadecimal output. With a picture numeric format string, it is possible to specify the number of digits, section and group separators, percent notation, and so on. The picture numeric format string `###,###` means two three-digit blocks separated by a group separator.

The `IFormatProvider` interface is implemented by the `NumberFormatInfo`, `DateTimeFormatInfo`, and `CultureInfo` classes. This interface defines a single method, `GetFormat()`, that returns a format object.

`NumberFormatInfo` can be used to define custom formats for numbers. With the default constructor of `NumberFormatInfo`, a culture-independent or invariant object is created. Using the properties of `NumberFormatInfo`, it is possible to change all the formatting options, such as a positive sign, a percent symbol, a number group separator, a currency symbol, and a lot more. A read-only culture-independent `NumberFormatInfo` object is returned from the static property `InvariantInfo`. A `NumberFormatInfo` object in which the format values are based on the `CultureInfo` of the current thread is returned from the static property `CurrentInfo`.

To create the next example, you can start with a simple console project. In this code, the first example shows a number displayed in the format of the culture of the thread (here: English-US, the setting of the operating system). The second example uses the `ToString()` method with the `IFormatProvider` argument. `CultureInfo` implements `IFormatProvider`, so create a `CultureInfo` object using the French culture. The third example changes the culture of the thread. The culture is changed to German using the property `CurrentCulture` of the `Thread` instance:

```
using System;
using System.Globalization;
using System.Threading;

namespace Wrox.ProCSharp.Localization
{
   class Program
   {
      static void Main()
      {
         int val = 1234567890;

         // culture of the current thread
         Console.WriteLine(val.ToString("N"));

         // use IFormatProvider
         Console.WriteLine(val.ToString("N",
                           new CultureInfo("fr-FR")));

         // change the culture of the thread
         Thread.CurrentThread.CurrentCulture =
                           new CultureInfo("de-DE");
         Console.WriteLine(val.ToString("N"));
      }
   }
}
```

The output is shown here. You can compare the outputs with the previously listed differences for U.S. English, French, and German.

```
1,234,567,890.00
1 234 567 890,00
1.234.567.890,00
```

Date Formatting

The same support for numbers is available for dates. The `DateTime` structure has some methods for date-to-string conversions. The public instance methods `ToLongDateString()`, `ToLongTimeString()`, `ToShortDateString()`, and `ToShortTimeString()` create string representations using the current culture. You can use the `ToString()` method to assign a different culture:

```
public string ToString();
public string ToString(IFormatProvider);
public string ToString(string);
public string ToString(string, IFormatProvider);
```

With the string argument of the `ToString()` method, you can specify a predefined format character or a custom format string for converting the date to a string. The class `DateTimeFormatInfo` specifies the possible values. With `DateTimeFormatInfo`, the case of the format strings has a different meaning. `D` defines a long date format, `d` a short date format. Other examples of possible formats are `ddd` for the abbreviated day of the week, `dddd` for the full day of the week, `yyyy` for the year, `T` for a long time, and `t` for a short time format. With the `IFormatProvider` argument, you can specify the culture. Using an overloaded method without the `IFormatProvider` argument implies that the culture of the current thread is used:

```
DateTime d = new DateTime(2008, 02, 14);

// current culture
Console.WriteLine(d.ToLongDateString());

// use IFormatProvider
Console.WriteLine(d.ToString("D", new CultureInfo("fr-FR")));

// use culture of thread
CultureInfo ci = Thread.CurrentThread.CurrentCulture;
Console.WriteLine("{0}: {1}", ci.ToString(), d.ToString("D"));

ci = new CultureInfo("es-ES");
Thread.CurrentThread.CurrentCulture = ci;
Console.WriteLine("{0}: {1}", ci.ToString(), d.ToString("D"));
```

The output of this example program shows `ToLongDateString()` with the current culture of the thread, a French version where a `CultureInfo` instance is passed to the `ToString()` method, and a Spanish version where the `CurrentCulture` property of the thread is changed to es-ES:

```
Thursday, February 14, 2008
jeudi 14 février 2008
en-US: Thursday, February 14, 2008
es-ES: jeuves, 14 de febrero de 2008
```

Cultures in Action

To see all cultures in action, you can use a sample WPF application that lists all cultures and demonstrates different characteristics of culture properties. Figure 21-4 shows the user interface of the application in the Visual Studio 2008 WPF Designer.

During initialization of the application, all available cultures are added to the tree view control that is placed on the left side of the application. This initialization happens in the method `AddCulturesToTree()` that is called in the constructor of the `Window` class `CultureDemoWindow`:

```
public CultureDemoWindow()
{
   InitializeComponent();

   AddCulturesToTree();
}
```

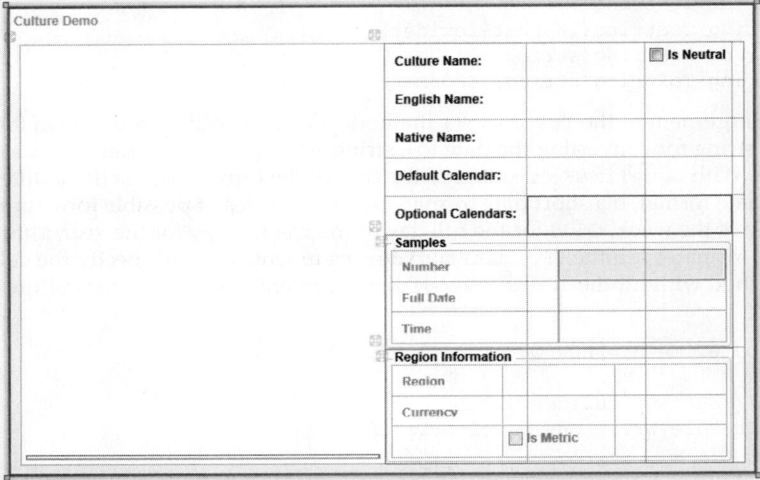

Figure 21-4

In the method `AddCulturesToTree()`, you get all cultures from the static method `CultureInfo.GetCultures()`. Passing `CultureTypes.AllCultures` to this method returns an unsorted array of all available cultures. The array is sorted using a Lambda expression that is passed to the `Comparison` delegate of the second argument of the `Array.Sort()` method. Next, in the `foreach` loop, every single culture is added to the tree view. A `TreeViewItem` object is created for every single culture because the WPF `TreeView` class uses `TreeViewItem` objects for display. The `Tag` property of the `TreeViewItem` object is set to the `CultureInfo` object, so that you can access the `CultureInfo` object at a later time from within the tree.

Where the `TreeViewItem` is added inside the tree depends on the culture type. If the culture does not have a parent culture, it is added to the root nodes of the tree. To find parent cultures, all cultures are remembered inside a dictionary. Recall Chapter 10, "Collections," for more information about dictionaries and Chapter 7, "Delegates and Events" for Lambda expressions.

```
// add all cultures to the tree view
public void AddCulturesToTree()
{
   Dictionary<string, TreeViewItem> culturesByName =
         new Dictionary<string, TreeViewItem>();

   // get all cultures
   var cultures =
      CultureInfo.GetCultures(CultureTypes.AllCultures);
   Array.Sort(cultures, (c1, c2) => c1.Name.CompareTo(c2.Name));

   TreeViewItem[] nodes = new TreeViewItem[cultures.Length];

   int i = 0;
   foreach (var ci in cultures)
   {
      nodes[i] = new TreeViewItem();
      nodes[i].Header = ci.DisplayName;
```

```
            nodes[i].Tag = ci;
            culturesByName.Add(ci.Name, nodes[i]);

            TreeViewItem parent;
            if (String.IsNullOrEmpty(ci.Parent.Name) &&
                  culturesByName.TryGetValue(ci.Parent.Name, out parent)
            {
               parent.Items.Add(nodes[i]);
            }
            else
            {
               treeCultures.Items.Add(nodes[i]);
            }
            i++;
         }
      }
```

When the user selects a node inside the tree, the handler of the `SelectedItemChanged` event of the `TreeView` will be called. Here the handler is implemented in the method `TreeCultures_SelectedItemChanged()`. Within this method, all fields are cleared by calling the method `ClearTextFields()` before you get the `CultureInfo` object from the tree by selecting the `Tag` property of the `TreeViewItem`. Then some text fields are set using the properties `Name`, `NativeName`, and `EnglishName` of the `CultureInfo` object. If the `CultureInfo` is a neutral culture that can be queried with the `IsNeutralCulture` property, the corresponding check box will be set:

```
      private void TreeCultures_SelectedItemChanged(object sender,
                     RoutedPropertyChangedEventArgs<object> e)
      {
         ClearTextFields();

         // get CultureInfo object from tree
         CultureInfo ci = (CultureInfo)((TreeViewItem)e.NewValue).Tag;

         textCultureName.Text = ci.Name;
         textNativeName.Text = ci.NativeName;
         textEnglishName.Text = ci.EnglishName;

         checkIsNeutral.IsChecked = ci.IsNeutralCulture;
```

Then you get the calendar information about the culture. The `Calendar` property of the `CultureInfo` class returns the default `Calendar` object for the specific culture. Because the `Calendar` class doesn't have a property to tell its name, you use the `ToString()` method of the base class to get the name of the class, and remove the namespace of this string to be displayed in the text field `textCalendar`.

Because a single culture might support multiple calendars, the `OptionalCalendars` property returns an array of additional supported `Calendar` objects. These optional calendars are displayed in the list box `listCalendars`. The `GregorianCalendar` class that derives from `Calendar` has an additional property called `CalendarType` that lists the type of the Gregorian calendar. This type can be a value of the enumeration `GregorianCalendarTypes: Arabic, MiddleEastFrench, TransliteratedFrench, USEnglish`, or `Localized` depending on the culture. With Gregorian calendars, the type is also displayed in the list box:

```
         // default calendar
         textCalendar.Text = ci.Calendar.ToString().
               Remove(0, 21).Replace("Calendar", "");
```

(continued)

(continued)

```
        // fill optional calendars
        listCalendars.Items.Clear();
        foreach (Calendar optCal in ci.OptionalCalendars)
        {
           StringBuilder calName = new StringBuilder(50);
           calName.Append(optCal.ToString());
           calName.Remove(0, 21);
           calName.Replace("Calendar", "");

           // for GregorianCalendar add type information
           GregorianCalendar gregCal = optCal as GregorianCalendar;
           if (gregCal != null)
           {
              calName.AppendFormat(" {0}", gregCal.CalendarType.ToString());
           }
           listCalendars.Items.Add(calName.ToString());
        }
```

Next, you check whether the culture is a specific culture (not a neutral culture) by using `!ci.IsNeutralCulture` in an `if` statement. The method `ShowSamples()` displays number and date samples. This method is implemented in the next code section. The method `ShowRegionInformation()` is used to display some information about the region. With the invariant culture, you can display only number and date samples, but no region information. The invariant culture is not related to any real language, and therefore it is not associated with a region:

```
        // display number and date samples
        if (!ci.IsNeutralCulture)
        {
           groupSamples.IsEnabled = true;
           ShowSamples(ci);

           // invariant culture doesn't have a region
           if (ci.ThreeLetterISOLanguageName == "IVL")
           {
              groupRegion.IsEnabled = false;
           }
           else
           {
              groupRegion.IsEnabled = true;
              ShowRegionInformation(ci.Name);
           }
        }
        else // neutral culture: no region, no number/date formatting
        {
           groupSamples.IsEnabled = false;
           groupRegion.IsEnabled = false;
        }
     }
```

To show some localized sample numbers and dates, the selected object of type `CultureInfo` is passed with the `IFormatProvider` argument of the `ToString()` method:

```
private void ShowSamples(CultureInfo ci)
{
   double number = 9876543.21;
   textSampleNumber.Text = number.ToString("N", ci);

   DateTime today = DateTime.Today;
   textSampleDate.Text = today.ToString("D", ci);

   DateTime now = DateTime.Now;
   textSampleTime.Text = now.ToString("T", ci);
}
```

To display the information associated with a `RegionInfo` object, in the method `ShowRegionInformation()` a `RegionInfo` object is constructed passing the selected culture identifier. Then you access the properties `DisplayName`, `CurrencySymbol`, `ISOCurrencySymbol`, and `IsMetric` properties to display this information:

```
private void ShowRegionInformation(string culture)
{
   RegionInfo ri = new RegionInfo(culture);
   textRegion.Text = ri.DisplayName;
   textCurrency.Text = ri.CurrencySymbol;
   textCurrencyISO.Text = ri.ISOCurrencySymbol;
   checkIsMetric.IsChecked = ri.IsMetric;
}
```

When you start the application, you can see all available cultures in the tree view, and selecting a culture lists the cultural characteristics, as shown in Figure 21-5.

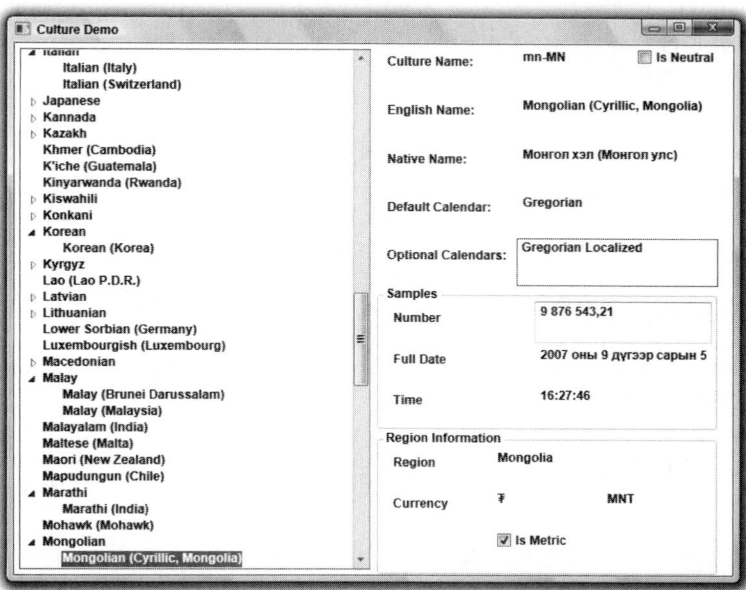

Figure 21-5

Sorting

Sorting strings is dependent on the culture. Some cultures have different sorting orders. One example is Finnish, where the characters V and W are treated the same. The algorithms that compare strings for sorting by default use a culture-sensitive sort, in which the sort is dependent on the culture.

To demonstrate this behavior with a Finnish sort, the following code creates a small sample console application where some U.S. states are stored unsorted inside an array. You are going to use classes from the namespaces `System.Collections.Generic`, `System.Threading`, and `System.Globalization`, so these namespaces must be declared. The method `DisplayNames()` shown here is used to display all elements of an array or of a collection on the console:

```
static void DisplayNames(string title, IEnumerable<string> e)
{
   Console.WriteLine(title);
   foreach (string s in e)
      Console.Write(s + " - ");
   Console.WriteLine();
   Console.WriteLine();
}
```

In the `Main()` method, after creating the array with some of the U.S. states, the thread property `CurrentCulture` is set to the Finnish culture, so that the following `Array.Sort()` uses the Finnish sort order. Calling the method `DisplayNames()` displays all the states on the console:

```
static void Main()
{
   string[] names = {"Alabama", "Texas", "Washington",
                     "Virginia", "Wisconsin", "Wyoming",
                     "Kentucky", "Missouri", "Utah", "Hawaii",
                     "Kansas", "Louisiana", "Alaska", "Arizona"};

   Thread.CurrentThread.CurrentCulture =
      new CultureInfo("fi-FI");

   Array.Sort(names);
   DisplayNames("Sorted using the Finnish culture", names);
```

After the first display of some U.S. states in the Finnish sort order, the array is sorted once again. If you want to have a sort that is independent of the users' culture, which would be useful when the sorted array is sent to a server or stored somewhere, you can use the invariant culture.

You can do this by passing a second argument to `Array.Sort()`. The `Sort()` method expects an object implementing `IComparer` with the second argument. The `Comparer` class from the `System.Collections` namespace implements `IComparer`. `Comparer.DefaultInvariant` returns a `Comparer` object that uses the invariant culture for comparing the array values for a culture-independent sort:

```
   // sort using the invariant culture
   Array.Sort(names, System.Collections.Comparer.DefaultInvariant);
   DisplayNames("Sorted using the invariant culture", names);
}
```

The program output shows different sorts with the Finnish and the culture-independent cultures: Virginia goes before Washington when using the invariant sort order and vice versa using Finnish.

```
Sorted using the Finnish culture
Alabama - Alaska - Arizona - Hawaii - Kansas - Kentucky - Louisiana - Missouri
- Texas - Utah - Washington - Virginia - Wisconsin - Wyoming -

Sorted using the invariant culture
Alabama - Alaska - Arizona - Hawaii - Kansas - Kentucky - Louisiana - Missouri
- Texas - Utah - Virginia - Washington - Wisconsin - Wyoming -
```

If sorting a collection should be independent of a culture, the collection must be sorted with the invariant culture. This can be particularly useful when sending the sort result to a server or storing it inside a file.

In addition to a locale-dependent formatting and measurement system, text and pictures may differ depending on the culture. This is where resources come into play.

Resources

Resources such as pictures or string tables can be put into resource files or satellite assemblies. Such resources can be very helpful when localizing applications, and .NET has built-in support to search for localized resources.

Before you see how to use resources to localize applications, the next sections discuss how resources can be created and read without looking at language aspects.

Creating Resource Files

Resource files can contain such things as pictures and string tables. A resource file is created by using either a normal text file or a `.resX` file that uses XML. This section starts with a simple text file.

A resource that embeds a string table can be created by using a normal text file. The text file just assigns strings to keys. The key is the name that can be used from a program to get the value. Spaces are allowed in both keys and values.

This example shows a simple string table in the file `strings.txt`:

```
Title = Professional C#
Chapter = Localization
Author = Christian Nagel
Publisher = Wrox Press
```

When saving text files with Unicode characters, you must save the file with the proper encoding. Select the Unicode encoding with the Save dialog.

Resource File Generator

The Resource File Generator (`Resgen.exe`) utility can be used to create a resource file out of `strings.txt`. Typing

```
resgen strings.txt
```

creates the file `strings.resources`. The resulting resource file can either be added to an assembly as an external file or embedded into the DLL or EXE. Resgen also supports the creation of XML-based `.resX` resource files. One easy way to build an XML file is by using Resgen itself:

```
resgen strings.txt strings.resX
```

This command creates the XML resource file `strings.resX`. You see how to work with XML resource files in the section "Windows Forms Localization Using Visual Studio" later in this chapter.

Since .NET 2.0, Resgen supports strongly typed resources. A strongly typed resource is represented by a class that accesses the resource. The class can be created with the `/str` option of the Resgen utility:

```
resgen /str:C#,DemoNamespace,DemoResource,DemoResource.cs strings.resX
```

With the option `/str`, the language, namespace, class name, and the file name for the source code are defined in that order.

The Resgen utility does not support adding pictures. With the .NET Framework SDK samples, you get a ResXGen sample with the tutorials. With ResXGen it is possible to reference pictures in a `.resX` file. Adding pictures can also be done programmatically by using the `ResourceWriter` or `ResXResourceWriter` classes, as you see next.

ResourceWriter

Instead of using the Resgen utility to build resource files, it's a simple task to write a program to create resources. The class `ResourceWriter` from the namespace `System.Resources` can be used to write binary resource files; `ResXResourceWriter` writes XML-based resource files. Both of these classes support pictures and any other object that is serializable. When you use the class `ResXResourceWriter`, the assembly `System.Windows.Forms` must be referenced.

In the following code example, you create a `ResXResourceWriter` object, `rw`, using a constructor with the file name `Demo.resx`. After creating an instance, you can add a number of resources of up to 2GB in total size using the `AddResource()` method of the `ResXResourceWriter` class. The first argument of `AddResource()` specifies the name of the resource and the second argument specifies the value. A picture resource can be added using an instance of the `Image` class. To use the `Image` class, you have to reference the assembly `System.Drawing`. You also add the `using` directive to open the namespace `System.Drawing`.

Create an `Image` object by opening the file `logo.gif`. You will have to copy the picture to the directory of the executable or specify the full path to the picture in the method argument of `Image.ToFile()`. The `using` statement specifies that the image resource should automatically be disposed at the end of the using block. Additional simple string resources are added to the `ResXResourceWriter` object. The `Close()` method of the `ResXResourceWriter` class automatically calls `ResXResourceWriter.Generate()` to finally write the resources to the file `Demo.resx`:

```
using System;
using System.Resources;
using System.Drawing;

class Program
{
   static void Main()
   {
      ResXResourceWriter rw = new ResXResourceWriter("Demo.resx");
      using (Image image = Image.FromFile("logo.gif"))
      {
         rw.AddResource("WroxLogo", image);
```

```
                rw.AddResource("Title", "Professional C#");
                rw.AddResource("Chapter", "Localization");
                rw.AddResource("Author", "Christian Nagel");
                rw.AddResource("Publisher", "Wrox Press");
                rw.Close();
            }
        }
    }
```

Starting this small program creates the resource file `Demo.resx` that embeds the image `logo.gif`. The resources will now be used in the next example with a Windows application.

Using Resource Files

You can add resource files to assemblies with the command-line C# compiler `csc.exe` using the `/resource` option, or directly with Visual Studio 2008. To see how resource files can be used with Visual Studio 2008, create a C# Windows application and name it `ResourceDemo`.

Use the context menu of the Solution Explorer (Add ⇨ Add Existing Item) to add the previously created resource file `Demo.resx` to this project. By default, Build Action of this resource is set to Embedded Resource so that this resource is embedded into the output assembly (see Figure 21-6).

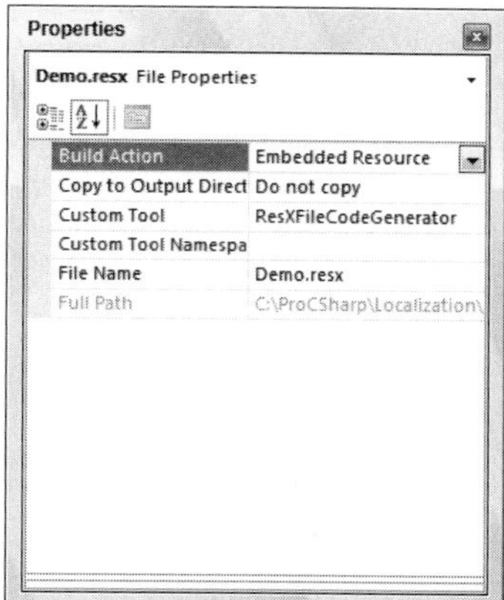

Figure 21-6

Set the Neutral Language setting of the application to the main language, for example, English (United States), as shown in Figure 21-7.

Changing this setting adds the attribute `[NeutralResourceLanguageAttribute]` to the file `assemblyinfo.cs` as you can see here:

```
[assembly: NeutralResourcesLanguageAttribute("en-US")]
```

Figure 21-7

Setting this option gives a performance improvement with the `ResourceManager` because it more quickly finds the resources for en-US that are also used as a default fallback. With this attribute you can also specify the location of the default resource using the second parameter with the constructor. With the enumeration `UltimateResourceFallbackLocation` you can specify the default resource to be stored in the main assembly or in a satellite assembly (values `MainAssembly` and `Satellite`).

After building the project, you can check the generated assembly with `ildasm` to see the attribute `.mresource` in the manifest (see Figure 21-8). `.mresource` declares the name for the resource in the assembly. If `.mresource` is declared as `public` (as in the example), the resource is exported from the assembly and can be used from classes in other assemblies. `.mresource private` means that the resource is not exported and is available only within the assembly.

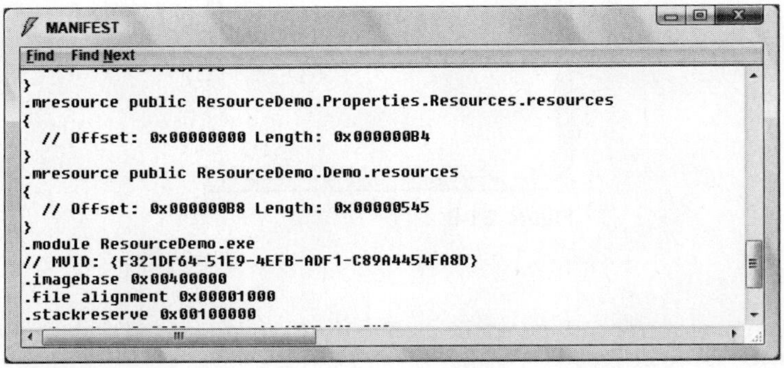

Figure 21-8

When you add resources to the assembly using Visual Studio 2008, the resource is always public, as shown in Figure 21-8. If the assembly generation tool is used to create assemblies, you can use command-line options to differentiate between adding public and private resources. The option `/embed:demo.resources,Y` adds the resource as public, whereas `/embed:demo.resources,N` adds the resource as private.

> **If the assembly was generated using Visual Studio 2008, you can change the visibility of the resources later. Use `ilasm` and select File ⇨ Dump to open the assembly and generate an MSIL source file. You can change the MSIL code with a text editor. Using the text editor, you can change `.mresource public` to `.mresource private`. Using the tool `ilasm`, you can then regenerate the assembly with the MSIL source code: `ilasm /exe ResourceDemo.il`.**

In your Windows application, you add some text boxes and a picture by dropping Windows Forms elements from the toolbox into the Designer. The values from the resources will be displayed in these Windows Forms elements. Change the `Text` and `Name` properties of the text boxes and the labels to the values that you can see in the following code. The name property of the `PictureBox` control is changed to logo. Figure 21-9 shows the final form in the Forms Designer. The `PictureBox` control is shown as a rectangle without a grid in the upper-left corner.

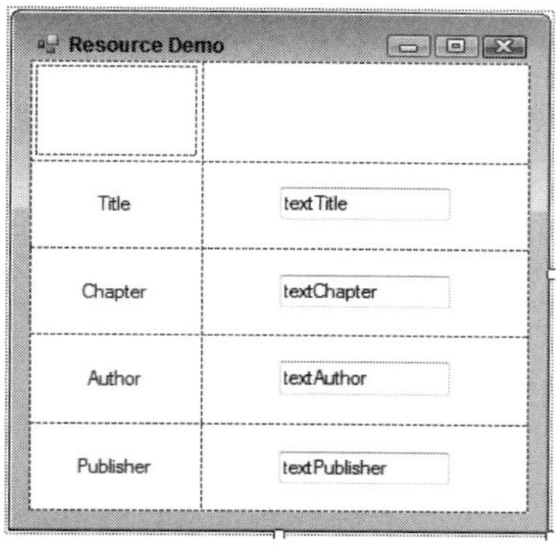

Figure 21-9

To access the embedded resource, use the `ResourceManager` class from the `System.Resources` namespace. You can pass the assembly that has the resources as an argument to the constructor of the `ResourceManager` class. In this example, the resources are embedded in the executing assembly, so pass the result of `Assembly.GetExecutingAssembly()` as the second argument. The first argument is the root name of the resources. The root name consists of the namespace, with the name of the resource file but without the resources extension. As you saw earlier, `ildasm` shows the name. All you have to do is remove the file extension `resources` from the name shown. You can also get the name programmatically using the `GetManifestResourceNames()` method of the `System.Reflection.Assembly` class:

```
using System.Reflection;
using System.Resources;

//...

   partial class ResourceDemoForm : Form
   {
      private System.Resources.ResourceManager rm;
```

(continued)

(continued)

```
public ResourceDemoForm()
{
   InitializeComponent();

   Assembly assembly = Assembly.GetExecutingAssembly();

   rm = new ResourceManager("ResourceDemo.Demo", assembly);
```

Using the `ResourceManager` instance `rm`, you can get all the resources by specifying the key to the methods `GetObject()` and `GetString()`:

```
   logo.Image = (Image)rm.GetObject("WroxLogo");
   textTitle.Text = rm.GetString("Title");
   textChapter.Text = rm.GetString("Chapter");
   textAuthor.Text = rm.GetString("Author");
   textPublisher.Text = rm.GetString("Publisher");
}
```

When you run the code, you can see the string and picture resources (see Figure 21-10).

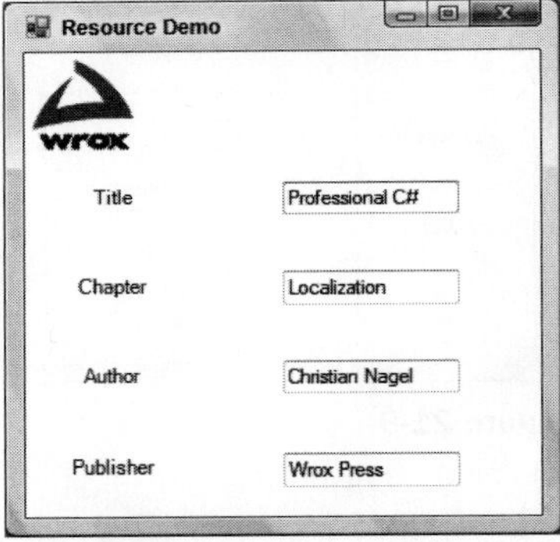

Figure 21-10

With strongly typed resources, the code written earlier in the constructor of the class `ResourceDemoForm` can be simplified; there is no need to instantiate the `ResourceManager` and access the resources using indexers. Instead, the names of the resources are accessed with properties:

```
public ResourceDemoForm()
{
   InitializeComponent();

   pictureLogo.Image = Demo.WroxLogo;
   textTitle.Text = Demo.Title;
   textChapter.Text = Demo.Chapter;
   textAuthor.Text = Demo.Author;
   textPublisher.Text = Demo.Publisher;
}
```

To create a strongly typed resource, the `Custom Tool` property of the XML-based resource file must be set to `ResXFileCodeGenerator`. By setting this option, the class `Demo` (it has the same name as the resource) is created. This class has static properties for all the resources to offer a strongly typed resource name. With the implementation of the static properties, a `ResourceManager` object is used that is instantiated on first access and then cached:

```
/// <summary>
///    A strongly-typed resource class, for looking up localized strings,
///    etc.
/// </summary>
// This class was auto-generated by the StronglyTypedResourceBuilder
// class via a tool like ResGen or Visual Studio.
// To add or remove a member, edit your .ResX file then rerun ResGen
// with the /str option, or rebuild your VS project.
[global::System.CodeDom.Compiler.GeneratedCodeAttribute(
      "System.Resources.Tools.StronglyTypedResourceBuilder",
      "2.0.0.0")]
[global::System.Diagnostics.DebuggerNonUserCodeAttribute()]
[global::System.Runtime.CompilerServices.CompilerGeneratedAttribute()]
internal class Demo {

   private static global::System.Resources.ResourceManager resourceMan;

   private static global::System.Globalization.CultureInfo resourceCulture;

   [global::System.Diagnostics.CodeAnalysis.SuppressMessageAttribute(
         "Microsoft.Performance", "CA1811:AvoidUncalledPrivateCode")]
   internal Demo() {
   }

   /// <summary>
   ///    Returns the cached ResourceManager instance used by this class.
   /// </summary>
   [global::System.ComponentModel.EditorBrowsableAttribute(
         global::System.ComponentModel.EditorBrowsableState.Advanced)]
   internal static global::System.Resources.ResourceManager
         ResourceManager {
      get {
         if (object.ReferenceEquals(resourceMan, null)) {
            global::System.Resources.ResourceManager temp =
                  new global::System.Resources.ResourceManager(
                  "ResourceDemo.Demo", typeof(Demo).Assembly);
            resourceMan = temp;
         }
         return resourceMan;
      }
   }

   /// <summary>
   ///    Overrides the current thread's CurrentUICulture property for all
   ///    resource lookups using this strongly typed resource class.
```

(continued)

(continued)

```
    /// </summary>
    [global::System.ComponentModel.EditorBrowsableAttribute(
        global::System.ComponentModel.EditorBrowsableState.Advanced)]
    internal static System.Globalization.CultureInfo Culture {
        get {
            return resourceCulture;
        }
        set {
            resourceCulture = value;
        }
    }

    /// <summary>
    ///    Looks up a localized string similar to "Christian Nagel".
    /// </summary>
    internal static string Author {
        get {
            return ResourceManager.GetString("Author", resourceCulture);
        }
    }

    /// <summary>
    ///    Looks up a localized string similar to "Localization".
    /// </summary>
    internal static string Chapter {
        get {
            return ResourceManager.GetString("Chapter", resourceCulture);
        }
    }

    /// <summary>
    ///    Looks up a localized string similar to "Wrox Press".
    /// </summary>
    internal static string Publisher {
        get {
            return ResourceManager.GetString("Publisher", resourceCulture);
        }
    }

    /// <summary>
    ///    Looks up a localized string similar to "Professional C#".
    /// </summary>
    internal static string Title {
        get {
            return ResourceManager.GetString("Title", resourceCulture);
        }
    }

    internal static System.Drawing.Bitmap WroxLogo {
        get {
            return ((System.Drawing.Bitmap)(ResourceManager.GetObject(
                    "WroxLogo", resourceCulture)));
        }
    }
}
```

The System.Resources Namespace

Before moving on to the next example, this section concludes with a review of the classes contained in the `System.Resources` namespace that deal with resources:

- The `ResourceManager` class can be used to get resources for the current culture from assemblies or resource files. Using the `ResourceManager`, you can also get a `ResourceSet` for a particular culture.
- A `ResourceSet` represents the resources for a particular culture. When a `ResourceSet` instance is created, it enumerates over a class, implementing the interface `IResourceReader`, and it stores all resources in a `Hashtable`.
- The interface `IResourceReader` is used from the `ResourceSet` to enumerate resources. The class `ResourceReader` implements this interface.
- The class `ResourceWriter` is used to create a resource file. `ResourceWriter` implements the interface `IResourceWriter`.
- `ResXResourceSet`, `ResXResourceReader`, and `ResXResourceWriter` are similar to `ResourceSet`, `ResourceReader`, and `ResourceWriter`; however, they are used to create an XML-based resource file `.resX` instead of a binary file. You can use `ResXFileRef` to make a link to a resource instead of embedding it inside an XML file.

Windows Forms Localization Using Visual Studio

In this section, you create a simple Windows application that shows how to use Visual Studio 2008 for localization. This application does not use complex Windows Forms and does not have any real inner functionality because the key feature it is intended to demonstrate here is localization. In the automatically generated source code, change the namespace to `Wrox.ProCSharp.Localization` and the class name to `BookOfTheDayForm`. The namespace is not only changed in the source file `BookOfTheDayForm.cs` but also in the project settings, so that all generated resource files will get this namespace, too. You can change the namespace for all new items that are created by selecting Common Properties from the Project ⇨ Properties menu.

Windows Forms applications are covered in more detail in Chapter 31, "Windows Forms," Chapter 32, "Data Binding," and Chapter 33, "Graphics with GDI+."

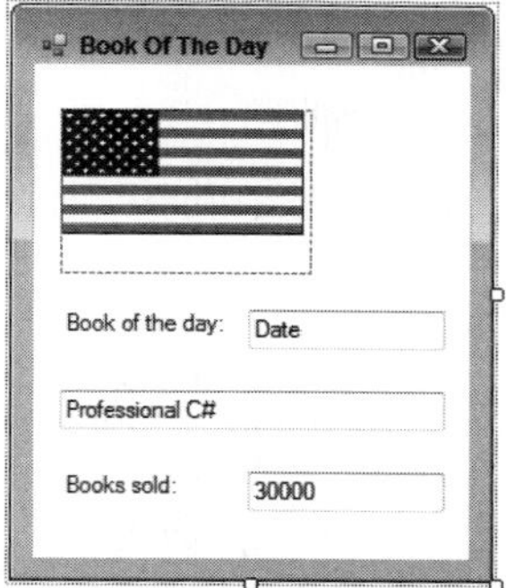

Figure 21-11

To show some issues with localization, this program has a picture, some text, a date, and a number. The picture shows a flag that is also localized. Figure 21-11 shows this form of the application as seen in the Windows Forms Designer.

The following table lists the values for the `Name` and `Text` properties of the Windows Forms elements.

Name	Text
`labelBookOfTheDay`	Book of the day
`labelItemsSold`	Books sold
`textDate`	Date
`textTitle`	Professional C#
`textItemsSold`	30000
`pictureFlag`	

In addition to this form, you might want a message box that displays a welcome message; this message might change depending on the current time of day. This example demonstrates that the localization for dynamically created dialogs must be done differently. In the method `WelcomeMessage()`, display a message box using `MessageBox.Show()`. Call the method `WelcomeMessage()` in the constructor of the form class `BookOfTheDayForm`, before the call to `InitializeComponent()`.

Here is the code for the method `WelcomeMessage()`:

```
public void WelcomeMessage()
{
   DateTime now = DateTime.Now;
   string message;
   if (now.Hour <= 12)
   {
      message = "Good Morning";
   }
   else if (now.Hour <= 19)
   {
      message = "Good Afternoon";
   }
   else
   {
      message = "Good Evening";
   }
   MessageBox.Show(String.Format("{0}\nThis is a localization sample",
         message);
}
```

The number and date in the form should be set by using formatting options. Add a new method, `SetDateAndNumber()`, to set the values with the format option. In a real application, these values could be received from a Web service or a database, but this example is just concentrating on localization. The date is formatted using the `D` option (to display the long date name). The number is displayed using the picture number format string `###,###,###`, where `#` represents a digit and "`,`" is the group separator.

```
public void SetDateAndNumber()
{
   DateTime today = DateTime.Today;
   textDate.Text = today.ToString("D");
   int itemsSold = 327444;
   textItemsSold.Text = itemsSold.ToString("###,###,###");
}
```

In the constructor of the `BookOfTheDayForm` class, both the `WelcomeMessage()` and `SetDateAndNumber()` methods are called:

```
public BookOfTheDayForm()
{
   WelcomeMessage();

   InitializeComponent();

   SetDateAndNumber();
}
```

A magic feature of the Windows Forms Designer is started when you set the `Localizable` property of the form from `false` to `true`. This results in the creation of an XML-based resource file for the dialog box that stores all resource strings, properties (including the location and size of Windows Forms elements), embedded pictures, and so on. In addition, the implementation of the `InitializeComponent()` method is changed; an instance of the class `System.Resources.ResourceManager` is created, and to get to the values and positions of the text fields and pictures, the `GetObject()` method is used instead of writing the values directly into the code. `GetObject()` uses the `CurrentUICulture` property of the current thread for finding the correct localization of the resources.

Here is part of `InitializeComponent()` from the file `BookOfTheDayForm.Designer.cs` before the `Localizable` property is set to `true`, where all properties of `textboxTitle` are set:

```
private void InitializeComponent()
{
   //...
   this.textTitle = new System.Windows.Forms.TextBox();
   //...
   //
   // textTitle
   //
   this.textTitle.Location = new System.Drawing.Point(24, 152);
   this.textTitle.Name = "textTitle";
   this.textTitle.Size = new System.Drawing.Size(256, 20);
   this.textTitle.TabIndex = 2;
   this.textTitle.Text = "Professional C#";
```

The code for the `IntializeComponent()` method is automatically changed by setting the `Localizable` property to `true`:

```
private void InitializeComponent()
{
   System.ComponentModel.ComponentResourceManager resources =
      new System.ComponentModel.ComponentResourceManager(
      typeof(BookOfTheDayForm));
   //...
   this.textTitle = new System.Windows.Forms.TextBox();
   //...
   resources.ApplyResources(this.textTitle, "textTitle");
```

Where does the resource manager get the data from? When the `Localizable` property is set to `true`, the resource file `BookOfTheDay.resX` is generated. In this file, you can find the scheme of the XML resource, followed by all elements in the form: `Type`, `Text`, `Location`, `TabIndex`, and so on.

The class `ComponentResourceManager` is derived from `ResourceManager` and offers the method `ApplyResources()`. With `ApplyResources()`, the resources that are defined with the second argument are applied to the object in the first argument.

The following XML segment shows a few of the properties of `textBoxTitle`: the `Location` property has a value of `13, 133`; the `TabIndex` property has a value of `2`; the `Text` property is set to `Professional C#`; and so on. For every value, the type of the value is stored as well. For example, the `Location` property is of type `System.Drawing.Point`, and this class can be found in the assembly `System.Drawing`.

Why are the locations and sizes stored in this XML file? With translations, many strings have completely different sizes and no longer fit into the original positions. When the locations and sizes are all stored inside the resource file, everything that is needed for localizations is stored in these files, separate from the C# code:

```
<data name="textTitle.Anchor" type="System.Windows.Forms.AnchorStyles,
    System.Windows.Forms">
    <value>Bottom, Left, Right</value>
</data>
<data name="textTitle.Location" type="System.Drawing.Point, System.Drawing>
    <value>13, 133</value>
</data>
<data name="textTitle.Size" type="System.Drawing.Size, System.Drawing>
    <value>196, 20</value>
</data>
<data name="textTitle.TabIndex" type="System.Int32, mscorlib>
    <value>2</value>
</data>
<data name="textTitle.Text">
    <value xml:space="preserve">Professional C#</value>
</data>
```

When changing some of these resource values, it is not necessary to work directly with the XML code. You can change these resources directly in the Visual Studio 2008 Designer. Whenever you change the `Language` property of the form and the properties of some form elements, a new resource file is generated for the specified language. Create a German version of the form by setting the `Language` property to German, and a French version by setting the `Language` property to French. For every language, you get a resource file with the changed properties: in this case, `BookOfTheDayForm.de.resX` and `BookOfTheDayForm.fr.resX`.

The following table shows the changes needed for the German version.

German Name	Value
`$this.Text` (title of the form)	Buch des Tages
`labelItemsSold.Text`	Bücher verkauft:
`labelBookOfTheDay.Text`	Buch des Tages:

The following table lists the changes for the French version.

French Name	Value
`$this.Text` (title of the form)	Le livre du jour
`labelItemsSold.Text`	Des livres vendus:
`labelBookOfTheDay.Text`	Le livre du jour:

By default, images are not moved to satellite assemblies. However, in the sample application, the flag should be different depending on the country. To do this, you have to add the image of the American flag to the file `Resources.resx`. You can find this file in the Properties section of the Visual Studio Solution Explorer. With the resource editor, select the Images categories as shown in Figure 21-12, and add the file `americanflag.bmp`. To make localization with images possible, the image must have the same name in all languages. Here the image in the file `Resources.resx` has the name Flag. You can rename the image in the properties editor. Within the properties editor, you can also change whether the image should be linked or embedded. For best performance with resources, images are linked by default. With linked images, the image file must be delivered together with the application. If you want to embed the image within the assembly, you can change the `Persistence` property to `Embedded`.

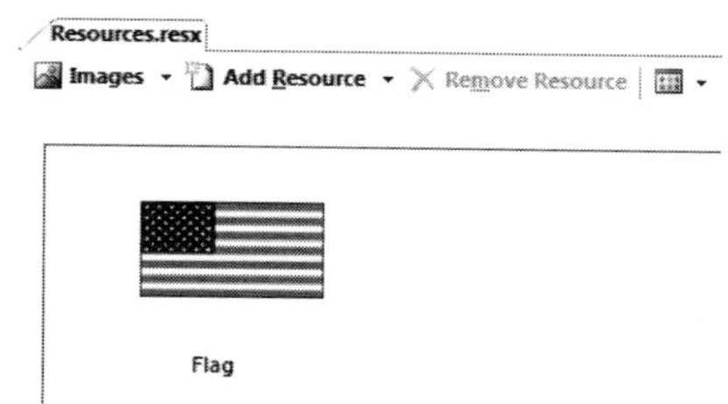

Figure 21-12

The localized versions of the flags can be added by copying the file `Resource.resx` to `Resource.de.resx` and `Resource.fr.resx` and replacing the flags with `GermanFlag.bmp` and `FranceFlag.bmp`. Because a strongly typed resource class is needed only with the neutral resource, the property `CustomTool` can be cleared with the resource files of all specific languages.

Compiling the project now creates a *satellite assembly* for each language. Inside the debug directory (or the release, depending on your active configuration), language subdirectories like `de` and `fr` are created. In such a subdirectory, you will find the file `BookOfTheDay.resources.dll`. Such a file is a satellite assembly that includes only localized resources. Opening this assembly with `ildasm`, you see a manifest with the embedded resources and a defined locale. The assembly has the locale `de` in the assembly attributes, so it can be found in the `de` subdirectory. You can also see the name of the resource with `.mresource`; it is prefixed with the namespace name `Wrox.ProCSharp.Localization`, followed by the class name `BookOfTheDayForm` and the language code `de`.

Changing the Culture Programmatically

After translating the resources and building the satellite assemblies, you will get the correct translations depending on the configured culture for the user. The welcome message is not translated at this time. This needs to be done in a different way, as you'll see shortly.

In addition to the system configuration, it should be possible to send the language code as a command-line argument to your application for testing purposes. The `BookOfTheDayForm` constructor is changed to allow passing a culture string, and setting the culture depending on this string. A `CultureInfo` instance is created to pass it to the `CurrentCulture` and `CurrentUICulture` properties of the current thread. Remember that the `CurrentCulture` is used for formatting, and the `CurrentUICulture` is used for loading of resources.

```
public BookOfTheDayForm(string culture)
{
    if (!String.IsNullOrEmpty(culture))
    {
        CultureInfo ci = new CultureInfo(culture);
        // set culture for formatting
        Thread.CurrentThread.CurrentCulture = ci;
        // set culture for resources
        Thread.CurrentThread.CurrentUICulture = ci;
    }

    WelcomeMessage();

    InitializeComponent();
    SetDateAndNumber();
}
```

The `BookOfTheDayForm` is instantiated in the `Main()` method, which can be found in the file `Program.cs`. In this method, you pass the culture string to the `BookOfTheDayForm` constructor:

```
[STAThread]
static void Main(string[] args)
{
    string culture = "";
    if (args.Length == 1)
    {
        culture = args[0];
    }

    Application.EnableVisualStyles();
    Application.SetCompatibleTextRenderingDefault(false);
    Application.Run(new BookOfTheDayForm(culture));
}
```

Now you can start the application by using command-line options. With the running application, you can see that the formatting options and the resources that were generated from the Windows Forms Designer show up. Figures 21-13 and 21-14 show two localizations in which the application is started with the command-line options `de-DE` and `fr-FR`.

There is still a problem with the welcome message box: the strings are hard-coded inside the program. Because these strings are not properties of elements inside the form, the Forms Designer does not extract XML resources as it does from the properties for Windows controls when changing the `Localizable` property of the form. You have to change this code yourself.

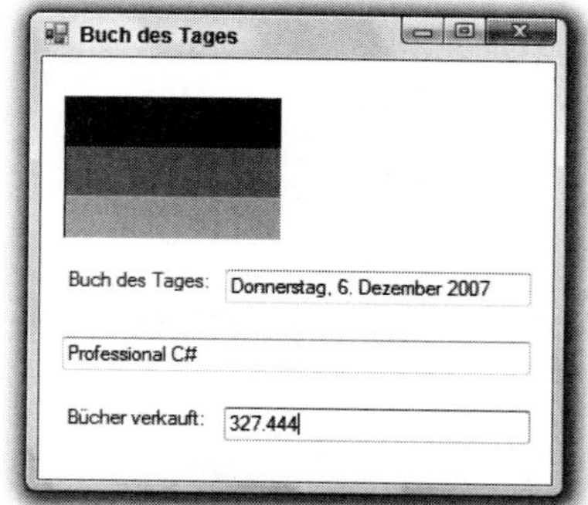

Figure 21-13

Figure 21-14

Using Custom Resource Messages

For the welcome message, you have to translate the hard-coded strings. The following table shows the translations for German and French. You can write custom resource messages directly in the file `Resources.resx` and the language-specific derivations. Of course, you can also create a new resource file.

Name	English	German	French
GoodMorning	Good Morning	Guten Morgen	Bonjour
GoodAfternoon	Good Afternoon	Guten Tag	Bonjour
GoodEvening	Good Evening	Guten Abend	Bonsoir
Message1	This is a localization sample.	Das ist ein Beispiel mit Lokalisierung.	C'est un exemple avec la localisation.

The source code of the method `WelcomeMessage()` must also be changed to use the resources. With strongly typed resources, there is no need to instantiate the `ResourceManager` class. Instead, the properties of the strongly typed resource can be used:

```
public static void WelcomeMessage()
{
   DateTime now = DateTime.Now;
   string message;
   if (now.Hour <= 12)
   {
      message = Properties.Resources.GoodMorning;
   }
   else if (now.Hour <= 19)
   {
      message = Properties.Resources.GoodAfternoon;
   }
   else
```

(continued)

(continued)

```
        {
           message = Properties.Resources.GoodEvening;
        }
        MessageBox.Show(message + "\n" +
           Properties.Resources.Message1);
     }
```

When the program is started using English, German, or French, you will get the message boxes shown in Figures 21-15, 21-16, and 21-17, respectively.

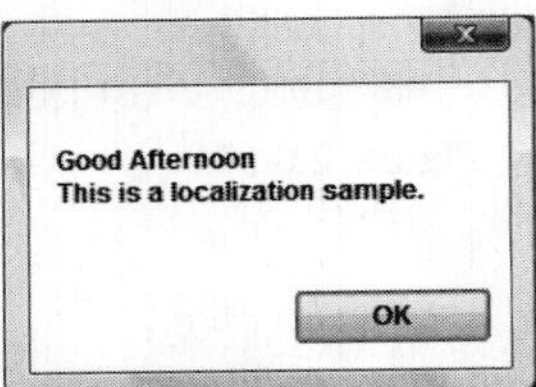

Figure 21-15

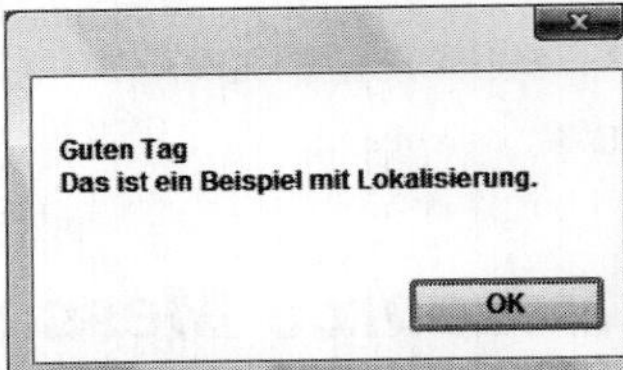

Figure 21-16

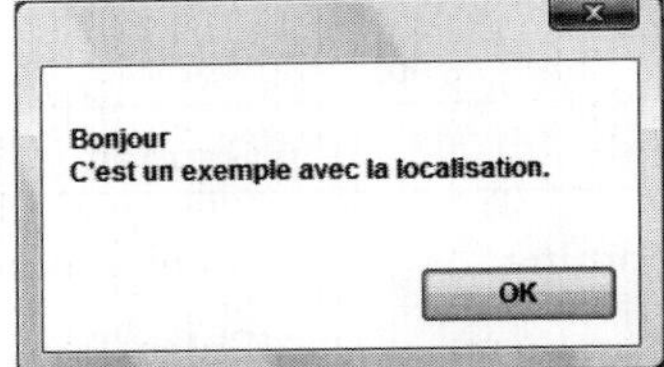

Figure 21-17

Automatic Fallback for Resources

For the French and German versions in the example, all the resources are inside the satellite assemblies. If not, then all the values of labels or text boxes are changed; this is not a problem at all. You must have only the values that will change in the satellite assembly; the other values will be taken from the parent assembly. For example, for `de-at` (Austria), you could change the value for the *Good Afternoon* resource to *Grüß Gott* while leaving the other values intact. During runtime, when looking for the value of the resource *Good Morning*, which is not located in the `de-at` satellite assembly, the parent assembly would be searched. The parent for `de-at` is `de`. In cases where the `de` assembly does not have this resource either, the value would be searched for in the parent assembly of `de`, the neutral assembly. The neutral assembly does not have a culture code.

> **Keep in mind that with the culture code of the main assembly, you shouldn't define any culture!**

Outsourcing Translations

It is an easy task to outsource translations using resource files. It is not necessary to install Visual Studio for translating resource files; a simple XML editor will suffice. The disadvantage of using an XML editor is that there is no real chance to rearrange Windows Forms elements and change the sizes if the translated text does not fit into the original borders of a label or button. Using a Windows Forms Designer to do translations is a natural choice.

Microsoft provides a tool as part of the .NET Framework SDK that fulfills all these requirements: the Windows Resource Localization Editor `winres.exe` (see Figure 21-18). Users working with this tool do not need access to the C# source files; only binary or XML-based resource files are needed for translations. After these translations are completed, you can import the resource files to the Visual Studio project to build satellite assemblies.

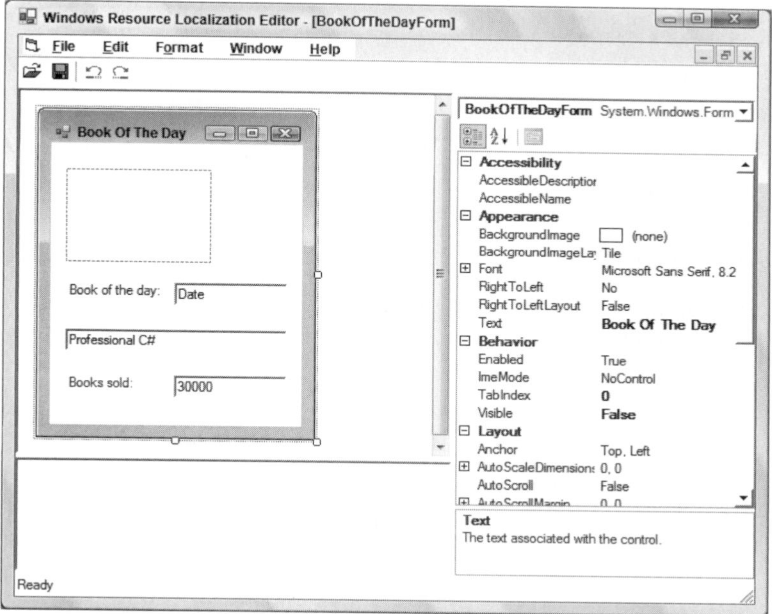

Figure 21-18

If you don't want your translation bureau to change the sizes and locations of labels and buttons, and they cannot deal with XML files, you can send a simple text-based file. With the command-line utility `resgen.exe`, you can create a text file from an XML file:

```
resgen myresource.resX myresource.txt
```

And after you have received the translation from the translation bureau, you can create an XML file from the returned text file. Remember to add the culture name to the file name:

```
resgen myresource.es.txt myresource.es.resX
```

Localization with ASP.NET

With ASP.NET applications, localization happens in a similar way to Windows applications. Chapter 37, "ASP.NET Pages," discusses the functionality of ASP.NET applications; this section discusses the localization issues of ASP.NET applications. ASP.NET 2.0 and Visual Studio 2008 have many new features to support localization. The basic concepts of localization and globalization are the same as discussed before. However, some specific issues are associated with ASP.NET.

As you have already learned, with ASP.NET you have to differentiate between the user interface culture and the culture used for formatting. Both of these cultures can be defined on a web and page level, as well as programmatically.

To be independent of the web server's operating system, the culture and user interface culture can be defined with the `<globalization>` element in the configuration file `web.config`:

```
<configuration>
   <system.web>
      <globalization culture="en-US" uiCulture="en-US" />
   </system.web>
</configuration>
```

If the configuration should be different for specific web pages, the `Page` directive allows assigning the culture:

```
<%Page Language="C#" Culture="en-US" UICulture="en-US" %>
```

The user can configure the language with the browser. With Internet Explorer, this setting is defined with the Language Preference options (see Figure 21-19).

If the page language should be set depending on the language setting of the client, the culture of the thread can be set programmatically to the language setting that is received from the client. ASP.NET 2.0 has an automatic setting that does just that. Setting the culture to the value `Auto` sets the culture of the thread depending on the client's settings.

```
<%Page Language="C#" Culture="Auto" UICulture="Auto" %>
```

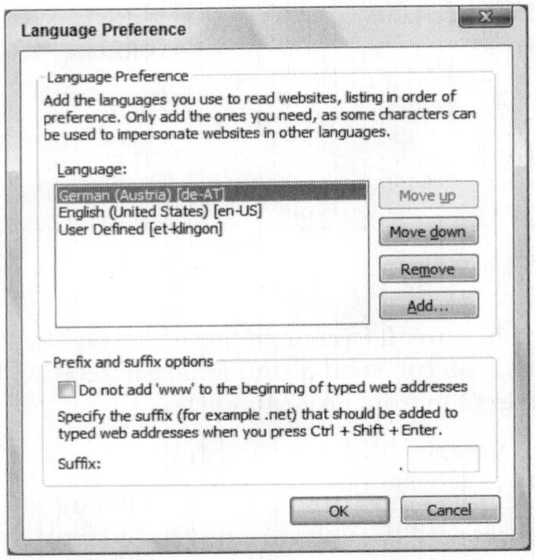

Figure 21-19

In dealing with resources, ASP.NET differentiates resources that are used for the complete web site and resources that are needed only within a page.

If a resource is used within a page, you can create resources for the page by selecting the Visual Studio 2008 menu Tools ⇨ Generate Local Resource in the design view. This way, the subdirectory `App_LocalResources` is created where a resource file for every page is stored. These resources can be localized similarly to Windows applications. The association between the web controls and the local resource files happens with a `meta:resourcekey` attribute as shown here with the ASP.NET `Label` control. `LabelResource1` is the name of the resource that can be changed in the local resource file:

```
<asp:Label ID="Label1" Runat="server" Text="Label"
    meta:resourcekey="LabelResource1"></asp:Label>
```

For the resources that should be shared between multiple pages, you have to create a subdirectory, `Appl_GlobalResources`. In this directory, you can add resource files, for example, `Messages.resx` with its resources. To associate the web controls with these resources, you can use Expressions in the property editor. Clicking the Expressions button opens the Expressions dialog (see Figure 21-20). Here, you can select the expression type Resources, set the name of the `ClassKey` (which is the name of the resource file — here, a strongly typed resource file is generated), and the name of the `ResourceKey`, which is the name of the resource.

In the ASPX file, you can see the association to the resource with the binding expressions syntax `<%$`:

```
<asp:Label ID="Label1" Runat="server"
    Text="<%$ Resources:Messages, String1 %>">
</asp:Label>
```

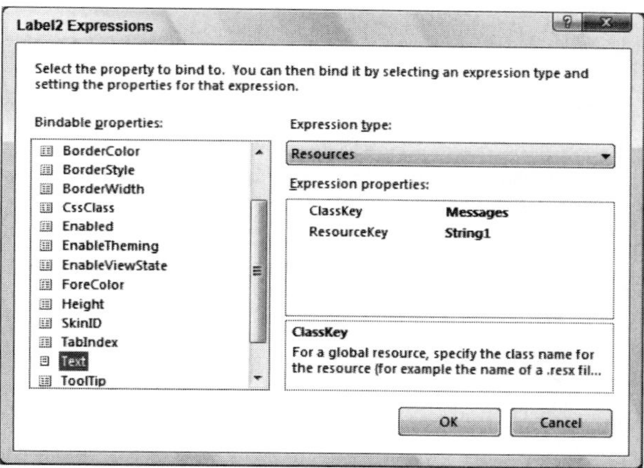

Figure 21-20

Localization with WPF

Visual Studio 2008 does not have great support for localization of WPF (Windows Presentation Foundation) applications. However, you do not have to wait until the next version to localize your WPF application. WPF has localization support built-in from the beginning, and you have several options to localize your applications. You can use .NET resources similar to what you've done with Windows Forms and ASP.NET applications, but you can also use an XAML (XML for Applications Markup Language) resource dictionary.

These options are discussed next. You can read more about WPF and XAML in Chapters 34, "Windows Presentation Foundation," and 35, "Advanced WPF."

WPF Application

To demonstrate the use of resources with a WPF application, create a simple WPF application containing just one button, as shown in Figure 21-21.

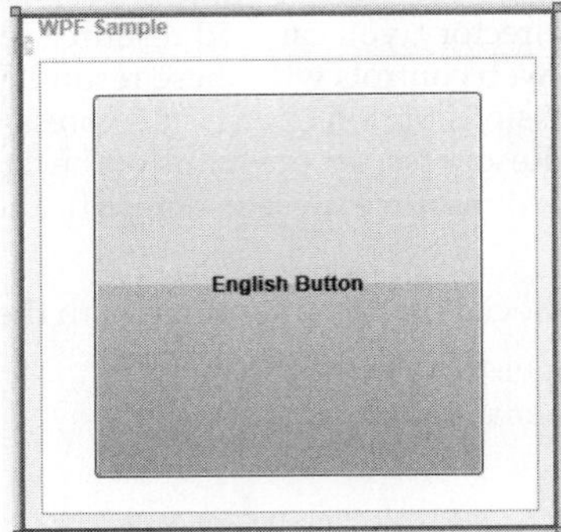

Figure 21-21

The XAML code for this application is shown here:

```
<Window x:Class="Wrox.ProCSharp.Localization.Window1"
      xmlns="http://schemas.microsoft.com/winfx/2006/xaml/presentation"
      xmlns:x="http://schemas.microsoft.com/winfx/2006/xaml"
      Title="WPF Sample" Height="300" Width="300">
   <Grid>
      <Button Name="button1" Margin="30,20,30,20" Click="Button_Click"
            Content="English Button" />
   </Grid>
</Window>
```

With the handler code for the click event of the button, just a message box containing a sample message pops up:

```
private void Button_Click(object sender, RoutedEventArgs e)
{
   MessageBox.Show("English Message");
}
```

.NET Resources

You can add .NET resources to a WPF application similar to the way you have with other applications. Define the resources named `Button1Text` and `Button1Message` in the file `Resources.resx`.

To use the generated resource class, you need to change the XAML code. Add an XML namespace alias to reference the .NET namespace `Wrox.ProCSharp.Localization.Properties` as shown. Here, the alias is set to the value `props`. From XAML elements, properties of this class can be used with the `x:Static` markup extension. The `Content` property of the `Button` is set to the `Button1Text` property of the `Resources` class.

```
<Window x:Class="Wrox.ProCSharp.Localization.Window1"
      xmlns="http://schemas.microsoft.com/winfx/2006/xaml/presentation"
      xmlns:x="http://schemas.microsoft.com/winfx/2006/xaml"
```

```
        xmlns:props="clr-namespace:Wrox.ProCSharp.Localization.Properties"
        Title="WPF Sample" Height="300" Width="300">
    <Grid>
        <Button Name="button1" Margin="30,20,30,20" Click="Button_Click"
                Content="{x:Static props:Resources.Button1Text}" />
    </Grid>
</Window>
```

Because resources added in a Visual Studio Solution have the `internal` *access modifier with the resource class and its members, and there is not an option to change this, you should add a custom build step to use the Resgen utility with the* `/publicClass` *option and add the generated class to the project. Otherwise, the WPF project won't compile.*

To use the .NET resource from code-behind, you can just access the `Button1Message` property directly in the same way you did with Windows Forms applications:

```
private void Button_Click(object sender, RoutedEventArgs e)
{
    MessageBox.Show(Properties.Resources.Button1Message);
}
```

Localization with XAML

Instead of using .NET resources for localization of WPF applications, you can work directly with XAML to create localized content. The steps for a localization process can be described by these actions:

- Create a satellite assembly from the main content
- Use resource dictionaries for localizable content
- Add `x:Uid` attributes to elements that should be localized
- Extract localization content from an assembly
- Translate the content
- Create satellite assemblies for every language

When compiling a WPF application, the XAML code is compiled to a binary format BAML that is stored into an assembly. To move the BAML code from the main assembly to a separate satellite assembly, you can change the `.csproj` build file and add a `<UICulture>` element as shown as a child to the `<PropertyGroup>` element. The culture, here `en-US`, defines the default culture of the project. Building the project with this build-setting creates a subdirectory en-US and creates a satellite assembly containing BAML code for the default language.

```
<UICulture>en-US</UICulture>
```

Separating the BAML into a satellite assembly, you should also apply the `NeutralResourcesLanguage` attribute and supply the resource fallback location to a satellite assembly. If you decide to keep BAML in the main assembly (by not defining the `<UICulture>` to the `.csproj` file), the `UltimateResourceFallbackLocation` should be set to `MainAssembly`.

```
[assembly: NeutralResourcesLanguage("en-US",
      UltimateResourceFallbackLocation.Satellite)]
```

For code-behind content that needs to be localized, a resource dictionary can be added. Using XAML, you can define resources within the `<ResourceDictionary>` element as shown. With Visual Studio, you can create a new resource dictionary by adding a new resource dictionary item and defining the file name. In the example here, the resource dictionary contains one string item. To get access to the `String` type from the `System` namespace, an XML namespace alias needs to be defined. Here, the alias `system` is set to the clr-namespace `System` in the assembly `mscorlib`. The string that is defined can be accessed with the key `message1`. This resource dictionary is defined in the file `LocalizedStrings.xaml`.

```
<ResourceDictionary
      xmlns="http://schemas.microsoft.com/winfx/2006/xaml/presentation"
      xmlns:x="http://schemas.microsoft.com/winfx/2006/xaml"
      xmlns:system="clr-namespace:System;assembly=mscorlib"
      >
   <system:String x:Key="message1">English Message</system:String>
</ResourceDictionary>
```

To have the resource dictionary available with the application, it must be added to the resources. If the resource dictionary would be required only within a window or just within a specific WPF element, it can be added to the resources collection of the specific window or WPF element. Here, the resource dictionary is added to the file `App.xaml` within the `<Application>` element, and thus is available to the complete application.

```
<Application x:Class="Wrox.ProCSharp.Localization.App"
      xmlns="http://schemas.microsoft.com/winfx/2006/xaml/presentation"
      xmlns:x="http://schemas.microsoft.com/winfx/2006/xaml"
      StartupUri="Window1.xaml">
   <Application.Resources>
      <ResourceDictionary>
         <ResourceDictionary.MergedDictionaries>
            <ResourceDictionary Source="LocalizationStrings.xaml" />
         </ResourceDictionary.MergedDictionaries>
      </ResourceDictionary>
   </Application.Resources>
</Application>
```

To use the XAML resource dictionary from code behind, you can use the `FindResource()` method. Because the resource is defined with the application, here an object of the `Application` class is used to find the resource. You can also use the `FindResource()` method from a WPF element, because the resources are searched in a hierarchical way. With the simple application here, if you use the `FindResource()` method of the `Button`, and if it is not found with the `Button` resources, then resources are searched in the `Grid`. If the resource is not there, a lookup to the `Window` resources is done before the `Application` resources are consulted.

```
      private void Button_Click(object sender, RoutedEventArgs e)
      {
         string message1 =
              (string)Application.Current.FindResource("message1");
         MessageBox.Show(message1);
      }
```

With WPF elements, the `x:Uid` attribute is used as a unique identifier for elements that need localization. You don't have to apply this attribute manually to the XAML content; instead you can use the `msbuild` command with this option:

```
msbuild /t:updateuid
```

When you call this command in the directory where the project file is located, the XAML files of the project are modified to add an `x:Uid` attribute with a unique identifier to every element. The same XAML as shown before now has the new attributes applied:

```
<Window x:Uid="Window_1" x:Class="Wrox.ProCSharp.Localization.Window1"
      xmlns="http://schemas.microsoft.com/winfx/2006/xaml/presentation"
      xmlns:x="http://schemas.microsoft.com/winfx/2006/xaml"
```

```
        Title="WPF Sample" Height="300" Width="300">
    <Grid x:Uid="Grid_1">
        <Button x:Uid="button1" Name="button1" Margin="30,20,30,20"
                Click="Button_Click" Content="English Button" />
    </Grid>
</Window>
```

If you change the XAML file after `x:Uid` attributes have been added, you can verify correctness of the `x:Uid` attributes with the option `/t:checkuid`.

Compiling the project creates a satellite assembly containing the BAML code. From this satellite assembly, you can extract the content that needs to be localized with classes from the `System.Windows.Markup.Localizer` namespace. With the Windows SDK you will find the sample program LocBaml. This program can be used to extract localization content from BAML. You need to copy the executable, the satellite assembly with the default content, and `LocBaml.exe` to one directory and start the sample program to produce a `.csv` file with the localization content:

```
LocBaml /parse WPFandXAMLresources.resources.dll /out: trans.csv
```

You can use Microsoft Excel to open the `.csv` file and translate its content. An extract from the `.csv` file that lists the content of the button and the message from the resource dictionary is shown here:

```
WPFandXAMLResources.g.en-US.resources:localizationstrings.baml,
system:String_1:System.String.$Content,None,True,True,,English Message
WPFandXAMLResources.g.en-US.resources:window1.baml,
button1:System.Windows.Controls.ContentControl.Content,Button,True,True,,
English Button
```

This file contains these fields:

- Name of the BAML
- The identifier of the resource
- The category of the resource that gives the type of the content
- A Boolean value if the resource is visible for translation (readable)
- A Boolean value if the resource can be modified for the translation (modifiable)
- Localization comments
- The value of the resource

After localization of the resource, you can create a new directory for the new language (for example, de for German). The directory structure follows the same convention as shown earlier in this chapter with satellite assemblies. With the LocBaml tool, you can create satellite assemblies with the translated content:

```
LocBaml /generate WPFandXAMLResources.resources.dll /trans:trans_de.csv /out: ../de
/cul:de-DE
```

Now the same rules for setting the culture of the thread and finding satellite assemblies as shown with Windows Forms applications apply here.

A Custom Resource Reader

With the resource readers that are part of .NET Framework 3.5, you can read resources from resource files and satellite assemblies. If you want to put the resources into a different store (such as a database), you can use a custom resource reader to read these resources.

To use a custom resource reader, you also need to create a custom resource set and a custom resource manager. Doing this is not a difficult task, however, because you can derive the custom classes from existing classes.

For the sample application, you need to create a simple database with just one table for storing messages that has one column for every supported language. The following table lists the columns and their corresponding values.

Key	Default	de	es	fr	it
Welcome	Welcome	Willkommen	Recepción	Bienvenue	Benvenuto
GoodMorning	Good morning	Guten Morgen	Buonas díaz	Bonjour	Buona mattina
GoodEvening	Good evening	Guten Abend	Buonas noches	Bonsoir	Buona sera
ThankYou	Thank you	Danke	Gracias	Merçi	Grazie
Goodbye	Goodbye	Auf Wiedersehen	Adiós	Au revoir	Arrivederci

For the custom resource reader, you create a component library with three classes. The classes are `DatabaseResourceReader`, `DatabaseResourceSet`, and `DatabaseResourceManager`.

Creating a DatabaseResourceReader

With the class `DatabaseResourceReader`, you define two fields: the connection string that is needed to access the database and the language that should be returned by the reader. These fields are filled inside the constructor of this class. The field `language` is set to the name of the culture that is passed with the `CultureInfo` object to the constructor:

```
public class DatabaseResourceReader : IResourceReader
{
   private string connectionString;
   private string language;

   public DatabaseResourceReader(string connectionString,
         CultureInfo culture)
   {
      this.connectionString = connectionString;
      this.language = culture.Name;
   }
```

A resource reader has to implement the interface `IResourceReader`. This interface defines the methods `Close()` and `GetEnumerator()` to return an `IDictionaryEnumerator` that returns keys and values for the resources. In the implementation of `GetEnumerator()`, create a `Hashtable` where all keys and values for a specific language are stored. Next, you can use the `SqlConnection` class in the namespace `System.Data.SqlClient` to access the database in SQL Server. `Connection.CreateCommand()` creates a `SqlCommand()` object that you use to specify the SQL `SELECT` statement to access the data in the database. If the language is set to `de`, the `SELECT` statement is `SELECT [key], [de] FROM Messages`. Then you use a `SqlDataReader` object to read all values from the database, and put it into a `Hashtable`. Finally, the enumerator of the `Hashtable` is returned.

For more information about accessing data with ADO.NET, see Chapter 26, "Data Access."

```
public System.Collections.IDictionaryEnumerator GetEnumerator()
{
   Dictionary<string, string> dict = new Dictionary<string, string>();

   SqlConnection connection = new SqlConnection(connectionString);
   SqlCommand command = connection.CreateCommand();
   if (String.IsNullOrEmpty(language))
      language = "Default";

   command.CommandText = "SELECT [key], [" + language + "] " +
                         "FROM Messages";

   try
   {
      connection.Open();

      SqlDataReader reader = command.ExecuteReader();
      while (reader.Read())
      {
         if (reader.GetValue(1) != System.DBNull.Value)
         {
            dict.Add(reader.GetString(0).Trim(), reader.GetString(1));
         }
      }

      reader.Close();
   }
   catch (SqlException ex)
   {
      if (ex.Number != 207)  // ignore missing columns in the database
         throw;              // rethrow all other exceptions
   }
   finally
   {
      connection.Close();
   }
   return dict.GetEnumerator();
}

public void Close()
{
}
```

Because the interface `IResourceReader` is derived from `IEnumerable` and `IDisposable`, the methods `GetEnumerator()`, which returns an `IEnumerator` interface, and `Dispose()` must be implemented, too:

```
   IEnumerator IEnumerable.GetEnumerator()
   {
      return this.GetEnumerator();
   }

   void IDisposable.Dispose()
   {
   }
}
```

Creating a DatabaseResourceSet

The class `DatabaseResourceSet` can use nearly all implementations of the base class `ResourceSet`. You just need a different constructor that initializes the base class with your own resource reader, `DatabaseResourceReader`. The constructor of `ResourceSet` allows passing an object by implementing `IResourceReader`; this requirement is fulfilled by `DatabaseResourceReader`:

```
public class DatabaseResourceSet : ResourceSet
{
   internal DatabaseResourceSet(string connectionString,
         CultureInfo culture)
      : base(new DatabaseResourceReader(connectionString, culture))
   {
   }

   public override Type GetDefaultReader()
   {
      return typeof(DatabaseResourceReader);
   }
}
```

Creating a DatabaseResourceManager

The third class you have to create is the custom resource manager. `DatabaseResourceManager` is derived from the class `ResourceManager`, and you only have to implement a new constructor and override the method `InternalGetResourceSet()`.

In the constructor, create a new `Hashtable` to store all queried resource sets and set it into the field `ResourceSets` defined by the base class:

```
public class DatabaseResourceManager : ResourceManager
{
   private string connectionString;

   public DatabaseResourceManager(string connectionString)
   {
      this.connectionString = connectionString;
      ResourceSets = new Hashtable();
   }
```

The methods of the `ResourceManager` class that you can use to access resources (such as `GetString()` and `GetObject()`) invoke the method `InternalGetResourceSet()` to access a resource set where the appropriate values can be returned.

In the implementation of `InternalGetResourceSet()`, check first if the resource set for the culture queried for a resource is already in the hash table; if it already exists, return it to the caller. If the resource set is not available, create a new `DatabaseResourceSet` object with the queried culture, add it to the hash table, and return it to the caller:

```
   protected override ResourceSet InternalGetResourceSet(
         CultureInfo culture, bool createIfNotExists, bool tryParents)
   {
      DatabaseResourceSet rs = null;

      if (ResourceSets.Contains(culture.Name))
      {
         rs = ResourceSets[culture.Name] as DatabaseResourceSet;
      }
```

```
            else
            {
               rs = new DatabaseResourceSet(connectionString, culture);
               ResourceSets.Add(culture.Name, rs);
            }
            return rs;
         }
      }
```

Client Application for DatabaseResourceReader

How the class ResourceManager is used from the client application here does not differ much from the previous use of the ResourceManager class. The only difference is that the custom class DatabaseResourceManager is used instead of the class ResourceManager. The following code snippet demonstrates how you can use your own resource manager.

A new DatabaseResourceManager object is created by passing the database connection string to the constructor. Then, you can invoke the GetString() method that is implemented in the base class as you did earlier, passing the key and an optional object of type CultureInfo to specify a culture. In turn, you get a resource value from the database because this resource manager is using the classes DatabaseResourceSet and DatabaseResourceReader.

```
DatabaseResourceManager rm = new DatabaseResourceManager(
      "server=(local);database=LocalizationDemo;trusted_connection=true");

string spanishWelcome = rm.GetString("Welcome",
                                      new CultureInfo("es-ES"));
string italianThankyou = rm.GetString("ThankYou",
                                      new CultureInfo("it"));
string threadDefaultGoodMorning = rm.GetString("GoodMorning");
```

Creating Custom Cultures

Over time, more and more languages are supported with the .NET Framework. However, not all languages of the world are available with .NET. You can create a custom culture. Some examples of when creating custom cultures can be useful are to support a minority within a region or to create subcultures for different dialects.

Custom cultures and regions can be created with the class CultureAndRegionInfoBuilder in the namespace System.Globalization. This class is located in the assembly sysglobl in the file sysglobl.dll.

With the constructor of the class CultureAndRegionInfoBuilder, you can pass the culture's name. The second argument of the constructor requires an enumeration of type CultureAndRegionModifiers. This enumeration allows one of three values: Neutral for a neutral culture, Replacement if an existing Framework-culture should be replaced, or None.

After the CultureAndRegionInfoBuilder object is instantiated, you can configure the culture by setting properties. With the properties of this class, you can define all the cultural and regional information such as name, calendar, number format, metric information, and so on. If the culture should be based on existing cultures and regions, you can set the properties of the instance using the methods LoadDataFromCultureInfo() and LoadDataFromRegionInfo(), and change the values that are different by setting the properties afterward.

Calling the method Register() registers the new culture with the operating system. Indeed, you can find the file that describes the culture in the directory <windows>\Globalization. Look for files with the extension .nlp.

```
// Create a Styria culture
CultureAndRegionInfoBuilder styria = new CultureAndRegionInfoBuilder(
      "de-AT-ST", CultureAndRegionModifiers.None);
CultureInfo parent = new CultureInfo("de-AT");
styria.LoadDataFromCultureInfo(parent);
styria.LoadDataFromRegionInfo(new RegionInfo("AT"));
styria.Parent = parent;
styria.RegionNativeName = "Steiermark";
styria.RegionEnglishName = "Styria";
styria.CultureEnglishName = "Styria (Austria)";
styria.CultureNativeName = "Steirisch";

styria.Register();
```

The newly created culture can now be used like other cultures:

```
CultureInfo ci = new CultureInfo("de-AT-ST");
Thread.CurrentThread.CurrentCulture = ci;
Thread.CurrentThread.CurrentUICulture = ci;
```

You can use the culture for formatting and also for resources. If you start the Cultures in Action application that was written earlier in this chapter again, you can see the custom culture as well.

Summary

This chapter discussed the globalization and localization of .NET applications.

In the context of globalization of applications, you learned about using the namespace System.Globalization to format culture-dependent numbers and dates. Furthermore, you learned that sorting strings by default depends on the culture, and you used the invariant culture for a culture-independent sort. Using the CultureAndRegionInfoBuilder class, you've learned how to create a custom culture.

Localization of applications is accomplished by using resources. Resources can be packed into files, satellite assemblies, or a custom store such as a database. The classes used with localization are in the namespace System.Resources. For reading resources from other places such as satellite assemblies or resource files, you can create a custom resource reader.

You have seen how to localize Windows Forms, WPF, and ASP.NET applications.

The next chapter provides information about a completely different topic — transactions. Don't expect that transactions are only useful with databases. In addition to database transactions, the chapter also gives you information on memory-based transactional resources and a transactional file system.

22

Transactions

All or nothing — this is the main characteristic of a transaction. When writing a few records, either all are written, or everything will be undone. If there is even one failure when writing one record, all the other things that are done within the transaction will be rolled back.

Transactions are commonly used with databases, but with classes from the namespace `System.Transactions`, you can also perform transactions on volatile or in-memory-based objects such as a list of objects. With a list that supports transactions, if an object is added or removed and the transaction fails, the list action is automatically undone. Writing to a memory-based list can be done in the same transaction as writing to a database.

In Windows Vista, the file system and registry also get transactional support. Writing a file and making changes within the registry supports transactions.

In this chapter, the following topics are covered:

- Overview of transaction phases and ACID properties
- Traditional transactions
- Committable transactions
- Transaction promotions
- Dependent transactions
- Ambient transactions
- Transaction isolation level
- Custom resource managers
- Transactions with Windows Vista and Windows Server 2008

Overview

What are transactions? Think about ordering a book from a web site. The book-ordering process removes the book you want to buy from stock and puts it in your order box, and the cost of your book is charged to your credit card. With these two actions, either both actions should complete successfully or neither of these actions should happen. If there is a failure when getting the book from stock, the credit card should not be charged. Transactions address such scenarios.

The most common use of transactions is writing or updating data within the database. Transactions can also be performed when writing a message to a message queue, or writing data to a file or the registry. Multiple actions can be part of a single transaction.

`System.Messaging` *is discussed in Chapter 45, "Message Queuing."*

Figure 22-1 shows the main actors in a transaction. Transactions are managed and coordinated by the transaction manager, and a resource manager manages every resource that influences the outcome of the transaction. The transaction manager communicates with resource managers to define the outcome of the transaction.

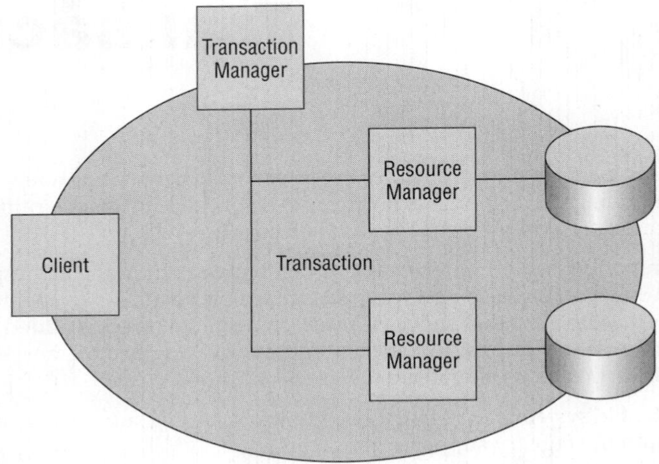

Figure 22-1

Transaction Phases

The timely phases of a transaction are the *active*, *preparing*, and *committing* phases:

- **Active phase** — During the active phase, the transaction is created. Resource managers that manage the transaction for resources can enlist with the transaction.
- **Preparing phase** — During the preparing phase, every resource manager can define the outcome of the transaction. This phase starts when the creator of the transaction sends a commit to end the transaction. The transaction manager sends a *Prepare* message to all resource managers. If the resource manager can produce the transaction outcome successfully, it sends a *Prepared* message to the transaction manager. Resource managers can abort the transaction if they fail to prepare by forcing a rollback with the transaction manager by sending a *Rollback* message. After the Prepared message is sent, the resource managers must guarantee to finish the work successfully in the committing phase. To make this possible, durable resource managers must write a log with the information from the prepared state, so that they can continue from there in case of, for example, a power failure between prepared and committing.
- **Committing phase** — The committing phase begins when all resource managers have prepared successfully. This is when the *Prepared* message is received from all resource managers. Then the

transaction manager can complete the work by sending a *Commit* message to all participants. The resource managers can now finish the work on the transaction and return a *Committed* message.

ACID Properties

A transaction has specific requirements; for example, a transaction must result in a valid state, even if the server has a power failure. The characteristics of transactions can be defined by the term ACID. ACID is a four-letter acronym for *atomicity*, *consistency*, *isolation*, and *durability*:

- **Atomicity** — Atomicity represents one unit of work. With a transaction, either the complete unit of work succeeds or nothing is changed.
- **Consistency** — The state before the transaction was started and after the transaction is completed must be valid. During the transaction, the state may have interim values.
- **Isolation** — Isolation means that transactions that happen concurrently are isolated from the state, which is changed during a transaction. Transaction A cannot see the interim state of transaction B until the transaction is completed.
- **Durability** — After the transaction is completed, it must be stored in a durable way. This means that if the power goes down or the server crashes, the state must be recovered at reboot.

Not every transaction requires all four ACID properties. For example, a memory-based transaction (for example, writing an entry into a list) does not need to be durable. Also, a complete isolation from the outside is not always required, as we discuss later with transaction isolation levels.

Database and Entity Classes

The sample database `CourseManagement` that is used with the transactions in this chapter is defined by the structure from Figure 22-2. The table `Courses` contains information about courses: course numbers and titles; for example, the course number 2124 with the title Programming C#. The table `CourseDates` contains the date of specific courses and is linked to the `Courses` table. The table `Students` contains information about persons attending a course. The table `CourseAttendees` is the link between `Students` and `CourseDates`. It defines which student is attending what course.

You can download the database along with the source code for this chapter from the Wrox web site.

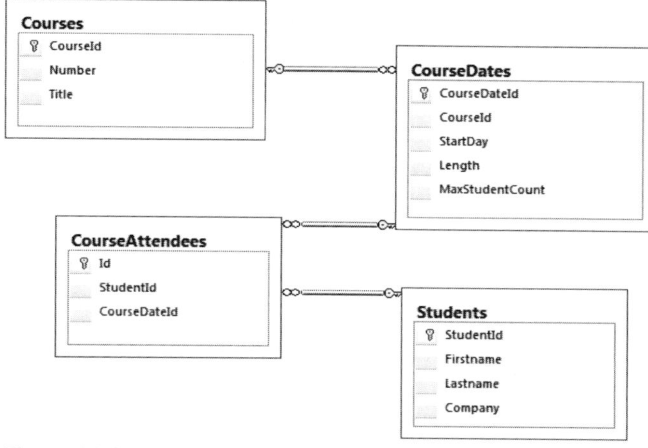

Figure 22-2

The sample applications in this chapter use a library with entity and data access classes. The class `Student` contains properties to define a student; for example, `FirstName`, `LastName`, and `Company`:

```
using System;

namespace Wrox.ProCSharp.Transactions
{
   [Serializable]
   public class Student
   {
      public Student() { }

      public Student(string firstName, string lastName)
      {
         this.FirstName = firstName;
         this.LastName = lastName;
      }

      public string FirstName { get; set; }
      public string LastName { get; set; }
      public string Company { get; set; }
      public int Id { get; set; }

      public override string ToString()
      {
         return String.Format("{0} {1}", FirstName, LastName);
      }
   }
}
```

Adding student information to the database is done in the method `AddStudent()` of the class `StudentData`. Here, an ADO.NET connection is created to connect to the SQL Server database, the `SqlCommand` object defines the SQL statement, and the command is executed by invoking `ExecuteNonQuery()`:

```
using System;
using System.Collections.Generic;
using System.Data;
using System.Data.SqlClient;
using System.Transactions;

namespace Wrox.ProCSharp.Transactions
{
   public class StudentData
   {
      public void AddStudent(Student student)
      {
         SqlConnection connection = new SqlConnection(
             Properties.Settings.Default.CourseManagementConnectionString);
         connection.Open();
         try
         {
            SqlCommand command = connection.CreateCommand();

            command.CommandText = "INSERT INTO Students " +
                  "(FirstName, LastName, Company) VALUES " +
```

```
                  "(@FirstName, @LastName, @Company)";
            command.Parameters.AddWithValue("@FirstName", student.FirstName);
            command.Parameters.AddWithValue("@LastName", student.LastName);
            command.Parameters.AddWithValue("@Company", student.Company);

            command.ExecuteNonQuery();
         }
         finally
         {
            connection.Close();
         }
      }
   }
}
```

ADO.NET is covered in detail in Chapter 26, "Data Access"

Traditional Transactions

Before `System.Transaction` was released, you could create transactions directly with ADO.NET, or you could do transactions with the help of components, attributes, and the COM+ runtime, which is covered in the namespace `System.EnterpriseServices`. To show you how the new transaction model compares to the traditional ways of working with transactions, we present a short look at how ADO.NET transactions and transactions with Enterprise Services are done.

ADO.NET Transactions

Let's start with traditional ADO.NET transactions. If you don't create transactions manually, there is a single transaction with every SQL statement. If multiple statements need to participate with the same transaction, however, you must create a transaction manually to achieve this.

The following code segment shows how to work with ADO.NET transactions. The `SqlConnection` class defines the method `BeginTransaction()`, which returns an object of type `SqlTransaction`. This transaction object must then be associated with every command that participates with the transaction. To associate a command with a transaction, set the `Transaction` property of the `SqlCommand` class to the `SqlTransaction` instance. For the transaction to be successful, you must invoke the `Commit()` method of the `SqlTransaction` object. If there is an error, you have to invoke the `Rollback()` method, and every change is undone. You can check for an error with the help of a `try/catch` and do the rollback inside the catch.

```
using System;
using System.Data.SqlClient;
using System.Diagnostics;

namespace Wrox.ProCSharp.Transactions
{
   public class CourseData
   {
      public void AddCourse(Course course)
      {
         SqlConnection connection = new SqlConnection(
               Properties.Settings.Default.CourseManagementConnectionString);
         SqlCommand courseCommand = connection.CreateCommand();
```

(continued)

(continued)

```
            courseCommand.CommandText =
                  "INSERT INTO Courses (Number, Title) VALUES (@Number, @Title)";
            connection.Open();
            SqlTransaction tx = connection.BeginTransaction();

            try
            {
               courseCommand.Transaction = tx;

               courseCommand.Parameters.AddWithValue("@Number", course.Number);
               courseCommand.Parameters.AddWithValue("@Title", course.Title);
               courseCommand.ExecuteNonQuery();

               tx.Commit();
            }
            catch (Exception ex)
            {
               Trace.WriteLine("Error: " + ex.Message);
               tx.Rollback();
            }
            finally
            {
               connection.Close();
            }
         }
      }
   }
```

If you have multiple commands that should run in the same transaction, every command must be associated with the transaction. Because the transaction is associated with a connection, every one of these commands must also be associated with the same connection instance. ADO.NET transactions do not support transactions across multiple connections; it is always a local transaction associated with one connection.

When you create an object persistence model using multiple objects, for example, classes `Course` and `CourseDate`, which should be persisted inside one transaction, it gets very difficult using ADO.NET transactions. Here, it is necessary to pass the transaction to all of the objects participating in the same transaction.

> **ADO.NET transactions are not distributed transactions. In ADO.NET transactions, it is difficult to have multiple objects working on the same transaction.**

System.EnterpriseServices

With Enterprise Services you get a lot of services for free. One of them is automatic transactions. Using transactions with `System.EnterpriseServices` has the advantage that it is not necessary to deal with transactions explicitly; transactions are automatically created by the runtime. You just have to add the attribute `[Transaction]` with the transactional requirements to the class. The `[AutoComplete]` attribute marks the method to automatically set the status bit for the transaction: if the method succeeds, the success bit is set, so the transaction can commit. If an exception happens, the transaction is aborted.

```
using System;
using System.Data.SqlClient;
using System.EnterpriseServices;
using System.Diagnostics;

namespace Wrox.ProCSharp.Transactions
{
   [Transaction(TransactionOption.Required)]
   public class CourseData : ServicedComponent
   {
      [AutoComplete]
      public void AddCourse(Course course)
      {
         SqlConnection connection = new SqlConnection(
               Properties.Settings.Default.CourseManagementConnectionString);
         SqlCommand courseCommand = connection.CreateCommand();
         courseCommand.CommandText =
               "INSERT INTO Courses (Number, Title) VALUES (@Number, @Title)";
         connection.Open();
         try
         {
            courseCommand.Parameters.AddWithValue("@Number", course.Number);
            courseCommand.Parameters.AddWithValue("@Title", course.Title);
            courseCommand.ExecuteNonQuery();
         }
         finally
         {
            connection.Close();
         }
      }
   }
}
```

A big advantage of creating transactions with `System.EnterpriseServices` is that multiple objects can easily run within the same transaction, and transactions are automatically enlisted. The disadvantages are that it requires the COM+ hosting model, and the class using the features of this technology must be derived from the base class `ServicedComponent`.

Enterprise Services and using COM+ transactional services are covered in Chapter 44, "Enterprise Services."

System.Transactions

The namespace `System.Transactions` has been available since .NET 2.0 and brings a new transaction programming model to .NET applications. Figure 22-3 shows a Visual Studio class diagram with the transaction classes, and their relationships, from the `System.Transactions` namespace: `Transaction`, `CommittableTransaction`, `DependentTransaction`, and `SubordinateTransaction`.

`Transaction` is the base class of all transaction classes and defines properties, methods, and events available with all transaction classes. `CommittableTransaction` is the only transaction class that supports committing. This class has a `Commit()` method; all other transaction classes can do only a rollback. The class `DependentTransaction` is used with transactions that are dependent on another transaction. A dependent transaction can depend on a transaction created from the committable transaction. Then the dependent transaction adds to the outcome of the committable transaction whether or not it is successful.

The class SubordinateTransaction is used in conjunction with the Distributed Transaction Coordinator (DTC). This class represents a transaction that is not a root transaction but can be managed by the DTC.

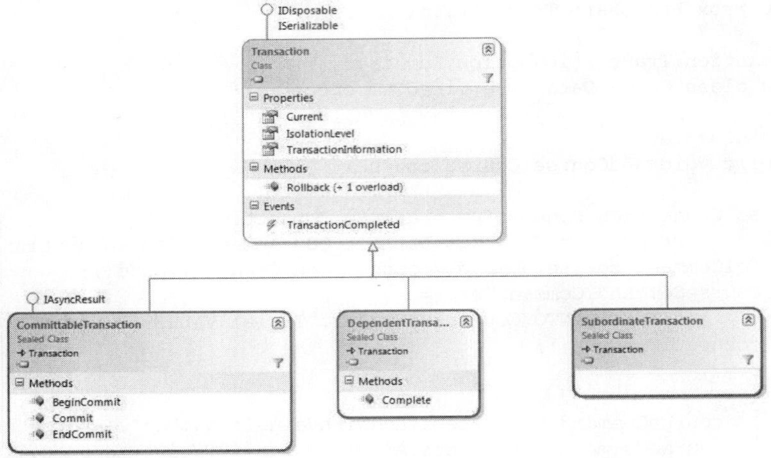

Figure 22-3

The following table describes the properties and methods of the Transaction class.

Transaction Class Members	Description
Current	The property Current is a static property without the need to have an instance. Transaction.Current returns an ambient transaction if one exists. Ambient transactions are discussed later in this chapter.
IsolationLevel	The IsolationLevel property returns an object of type IsolationLevel. IsolationLevel is an enumeration that defines what access other transactions have to the interim results of the transaction. This affects the I of ACID; not all transactions are isolated.
TransactionInformation	The TransactionInformation property returns a TransactionInformation object. TransactionInformation gives you information about the current state of the transaction, the time when the transaction was created, and transaction identifiers.
EnlistVolatile() EnlistDurable() EnlistPromotableSinglePhase()	With the enlist methods EnlistVolatile(), EnlistDurable(), and EnlistPromotableSinglePhase(), you can enlist custom resource managers that participate with the transaction.

Transaction Class Members	Description
`Rollback()`	With the `Rollback()` method, you can abort a transaction and undo everything to set all results to the state before the transaction.
`DependentClone()`	With the `DependentClone()` method, you can create a transaction that depends on the current transaction.
`TransactionCompleted`	`TransactionCompleted` is an event that is fired when the transaction is completed — either successfully or unsuccessfully. With an event handler object of type `Transaction CompletedEventHandler`, you get access to the `Transaction` object and can read its status.

For demonstrating the features of `System.Transaction`, the class `Utilities` inside a separate assembly offers some static methods. The method `AbortTx()` returns `true` or `false` depending on the input from the user. The method `DisplayTransactionInformation()` gets a `TransactionInformation` object as parameter and displays all the information from the transaction: creation time, status, local, and distributed identifiers:

```
public static class Utilities
{
   public static bool AbortTx()
   {
      Console.Write("Abort the Transaction (y/n)?");
      return Console.ReadLine() == "y";
   }

   public static void DisplayTransactionInformation(string title,
         TransactionInformation ti)
   {
      if (ti != null)
      {
         Console.WriteLine(title);

         Console.WriteLine("Creation Time: {0:T}", ti.CreationTime);
         Console.WriteLine("Status: {0}", ti.Status);
         Console.WriteLine("Local ID: {0}", ti.LocalIdentifier);
         Console.WriteLine("Distributed ID: {0}",
                           ti.DistributedIdentifier);
         Console.WriteLine();
      }
   }
}
```

Committable Transactions

The `Transaction` class cannot be committed programmatically; it does not have a method to commit the transaction. The base class `Transaction` just supports aborting the transaction. The only transaction class that supports a commit is the class `CommittableTransaction`.

With ADO.NET, a transaction can be enlisted with the connection. To make this possible, an `AddStudent()` method is added to the class `StudentData` that accepts a `System.Transactions.Transaction` object as second parameter. The object `tx` is enlisted with the connection by calling the method `EnlistTransaction` of the `SqlConnection` class. This way, the ADO.NET connection is associated with the transaction.

```
public void AddStudent(Student student, Transaction tx)
{
   SqlConnection connection = new SqlConnection(
         Properties.Settings.Default.CourseManagementConnectionString);
   connection.Open();
   try
   {
      if (tx != null)
         connection.EnlistTransaction(tx);
      SqlCommand command = connection.CreateCommand();

      command.CommandText = "INSERT INTO Students (FirstName, " +
            "LastName, Company)" +
            "VALUES (@FirstName, @LastName, @Company)";
      command.Parameters.AddWithValue("@FirstName", student.FirstName);
      command.Parameters.AddWithValue("@LastName", student.LastName);
      command.Parameters.AddWithValue("@Company", student.Company);

      command.ExecuteNonQuery();
   }
   finally
   {
      connection.Close();
   }
}
```

In the `Main()` method of the console application `CommittableTransaction`, first a transaction of type `CommittableTransaction` is created, and information is shown on the console. Then a `Student` object is created, and this object is written to the database from the `AddStudent()` method. If you verify the record in the database from outside of the transaction, you cannot see the student added until the transaction is completed. In case the transaction fails, there is a rollback, and the student is not written to the database.

After the `AddStudent()` method is invoked, the helper method `Utilities.AbortTx()` is called to ask if the transaction should be aborted. If the user aborts, an exception of type `ApplicationException` is thrown and, in the catch block, a rollback with the transaction is done by calling the method `Rollback()` of the `Transaction` class. The record is not written to the database. If the user does not abort, the `Commit()` method commits the transaction, and the final state of the transaction is committed.

```
static void Main()
{
   CommittableTransaction tx = new CommittableTransaction();
   Utilities.DisplayTransactionInformation("TX created",
         tx.TransactionInformation);

   try
   {
      Student s1 = new Student();
```

```
            s1.FirstName = "Neno";
            s1.LastName = "Loye";
            s1.Company = "thinktecture";
            StudentData db = new StudentData();
            db.AddStudent(s1, tx);

            if (Utilities.AbortTx())
            {
               throw new ApplicationException("transaction abort");
            }

            tx.Commit();
         }
         catch (Exception ex)
         {
            Console.WriteLine(ex.Message);
            Console.WriteLine();
            tx.Rollback();
         }

         Utilities.DisplayTransactionInformation("TX completed",
               tx.TransactionInformation);

      }
```

Here, you can see the output of the application where the transaction is active and has a local identifier. The output of the application that follows shows the result with the user choice to abort the transaction. After the transaction is finished, you can see the aborted state.

```
TX created
Creation Time: 7:30:49 PM
Status: Active
Local ID: bdcf1cdc-a67e-4ccc-9a5c-cbdfe0fe9177:1
Distributed ID: 00000000-0000-0000-0000-000000000000

Abort the Transaction (y/n)? y
Transaction abort

TX completed
Creation Time: 7:30:49 PM
Status: Aborted
Local ID: bdcf1cdc-a67e-4ccc-9a5c-cbdfe0fe9177:1
Distributed ID: 00000000-0000-0000-0000-000000000000
Press any key to continue ...
```

With the second output of the application that you can see here, the transaction is not aborted by the user. The transaction has the status committed, and the data is written to the database.

```
TX Created
Creation Time: 7:33:04 PM
Status: Active
Local ID: 708bda71-fa24-46a9-86b4-18b83120f6af:1
```

(continued)

(continued)

```
Distributed ID: 00000000-0000-0000-0000-000000000000

Abort the Transaction (y/n)? n

TX completed
Creation Time: 7:33:04 PM
Status: Committed
Local ID: 708bda71-fa24-46a9-86b4-18b83120f6af:1
Distributed ID: 00000000-0000-0000-0000-000000000000

Press any key to continue ...
```

Transaction Promotion

`System.Transactions` supports promotable transactions. Depending on the resources that participate with the transaction, either a local or a distributed transaction is created. SQL Server 2005 and 2008 support promotable transactions. So far you have seen only local transactions. With the samples until now, the distributed transaction ID was always set to 0, and only the local ID was assigned. With a resource that does not support promotable transactions, a distributed transaction is created. If multiple resources are added to the transaction, the transaction may start with a local transaction and promote to a distributed transaction as required. Such a promotion happens when multiple SQL Server database connections are added to the transaction. The transaction starts as a local transaction and then is promoted to a distributed transaction.

The console application is now changed in that a second student is added by using the same transaction object `tx`. Because every `AddStudent()` method opens a new connection, two connections are associated with the transaction after the second student is added.

```
static void Main()
{
   CommittableTransaction tx = new CommittableTransaction();
   Utilities.DisplayTransactionInformation("TX created",
         tx.TransactionInformation);

   try
   {
      Student s1 = new Student();
      s1.FirstName = "Neno";
      s1.LastName = "Loye";
      s1.Company = "thinktecture";
      StudentData db = new StudentData();
      db.AddStudent(s1, tx);

      Student s2 = new Student();
      s2.FirstName = "Dominick";
      s2.LastName = "Baier";
      s2.Company = "thinktecture";
      db.AddStudent(s2, tx);

      Utilities.DisplayTransactionInformation("2nd connection enlisted",
            tx.TransactionInformation);

      if (Utilities.AbortTx())
```

```
            {
               throw new ApplicationException("transaction abort");
            }

            tx.Commit();
         }
         catch (Exception ex)
         {
            Console.WriteLine(ex.Message);
            Console.WriteLine();
            tx.Rollback();
         }

         Utilities.DisplayTransactionInformation("TX finished",
               tx.TransactionInformation);

      }
```

Running the application now, you can see that with the first student added the distributed identifier is 0, but with the second student added the transaction was promoted, so a distributed identifier is associated with the transaction.

```
TX created
Creation Time: 7:56:24 PM
Status: Active
Local ID: 0d2f5ada-32aa-40eb-b9d7-cc6aa9a2a554:1
Distributed ID: 00000000-0000-0000-0000-0000000000

2nd connection enlisted
Creation Time: 7:56:24 PM
Status: Active
Local ID: 0d2f5ada-32aa-40eb-b9d7-cc6aa9a2a554:1
Distributed ID: 70762617-2ee8-4d23-aa87-6ac8c1418bdfd

Abort the Transaction (y/n)?
```

Transaction promotion requires the Distributed Transaction Coordinator (DTC) to be started. If promoting transactions fails with your system, verify that the DTC service is started. Starting the Component Services MMC snap-in, you can see the actual status of all DTC transactions running on your system. By selecting Transaction List on the tree view, you can see all active transactions. In Figure 22-4, you can see that there is a transaction active with the same distributed identifier as was shown with the console output earlier. If you verify the output on your system, make sure that the transaction has a timeout and aborts in case the timeout is reached. After the timeout, you cannot see the transaction in the transaction list anymore. You can also verify the transaction statistics with the same tool. Transaction Statistics shows the number of committed and aborted transactions.

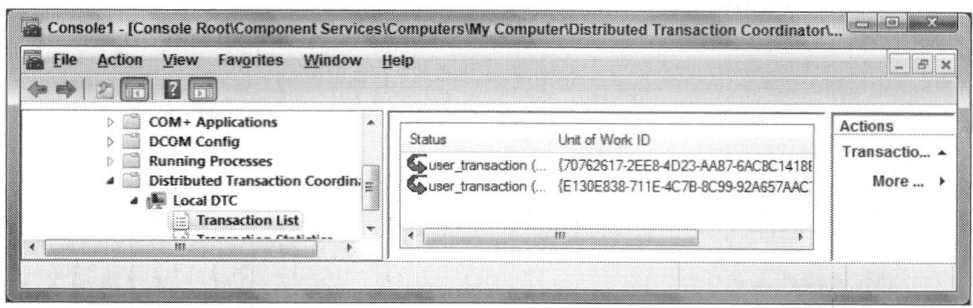

Figure 22-4

You can start the Component Services MMC snap-in by starting the Microsoft Management Console (`mmc.exe`) application, selecting the menu File ⇨ Add/Remove Snap-In, and selecting Component Services from the list of snap-ins.

Dependent Transactions

With dependent transactions, you can influence one transaction from multiple threads. A dependent transaction depends on another transaction and influences the outcome of the transaction.

The sample application `DependentTransactions` creates a dependent transaction for a new thread. The method `TxThread()` is the method of the new thread where a `DependentTransaction` object is passed as a parameter. Information about the dependent transaction is shown with the helper method `DisplayTransactionInformation()`. Before the thread exits, the `Complete()` method of the dependent transaction is invoked to define the outcome of the transaction. A dependent transaction can define the outcome of the transaction by calling either the `Complete()` or `Rollback()` method. The `Complete()` method sets the success bit. If the root transaction finishes, and if all dependent transactions have set the success bit to `true`, the transaction commits. If any of the dependent transactions set the abort bit by invoking the `Rollback()` method, the complete transaction aborts.

```
static void TxThread(object obj)
{
   DependentTransaction tx = obj as DependentTransaction;
   Utilities.DisplayTransactionInformation("Dependent Transaction",
         tx.TransactionInformation);

   Thread.Sleep(3000);

   tx.Complete();

   Utilities.DisplayTransactionInformation("Dependent TX Complete",
         tx.TransactionInformation);
}
```

With the `Main()` method, first a root transaction is created by instantiating the class `CommittableTransaction`, and the transaction information is shown. Next, the method `tx.DependentClone()` creates a dependent transaction. This dependent transaction is passed to the method `TxThread()` that is defined as the entry point of a new thread.

The method `DependentClone()` requires an argument of type `DependentCloneOption`, which is an enumeration with the values `BlockCommitUntilComplete` and `RollbackIfNotComplete`. This option is important if the root transaction completes before the dependent transaction. Setting the option to `RollbackIfNotComplete`, the transaction aborts if the dependent transaction didn't invoke the `Complete()` method before the `Commit()` method of the root transaction. Setting the option to `BlockCommitUntilComplete`, the method `Commit()` waits until the outcome is defined by all dependent transactions.

Next, the `Commit()` method of the `CommittableTransaction` class is invoked if the user does not abort the transaction.

Chapter 19, "Threading and Synchronization," covers threading.

```
static void Main()
{
   CommittableTransaction tx = new CommittableTransaction();
   Utilities.DisplayTransactionInformation("Root TX created",
         tx.TransactionInformation);
```

```
            try
            {
               new Thread(TxThread).Start(
                     tx.DependentClone(
                     DependentCloneOption.BlockCommitUntilComplete));

               if (Utilities.AbortTx())
               {
                  throw new ApplicationException("transaction abort");
               }

               tx.Commit();
            }
            catch (Exception ex)
            {
               Console.WriteLine(ex.Message);
               tx.Rollback();
            }

            Utilities.DisplayTransactionInformation("TX finished",
                  tx.TransactionInformation);
         }
```

With the output of the application, you can see the root transaction with its identifier. Because of the option `DependentCloneOption.BlockCommitUntilComplete`, the root transaction waits in the `Commit()` method until the outcome of the dependent transaction is defined. As soon as the dependent transaction is finished, the transaction is committed.

```
Root TX created
Creation Time: 8:35:25 PM
Status: Active
Local ID: 50126e07-cd28-4e0f-a21f-a81a8e14a1a8:1
Distributed ID: 00000000-0000-0000-0000-0000000000

Abort the Transaction (y/n)? n

Dependent Transaction
Creation Time: 8:35:25 PM
Status: Active
Local ID: 50126e07-cd28-4e0f-a21f-a81a8e14a1a8:1
Distributed ID: 00000000-0000-0000-0000-0000000000

Dependent TX Complete
Root TX finished
Creation Time: 8:35:25 PM
Status: Committed
Local ID: 50126e07-cd28-4e0f-a21f-a81a8e14a1a8:1
Distributed ID: 00000000-0000-0000-0000-0000000000

Creation Time: 8:35:25 PM
Status: Committed
Local ID: 50126e07-cd28-4e0f-a21f-a81a8e14a1a8:1
Distributed ID: 00000000-0000-0000-0000-0000000000

Press any key to continue ...
```

Ambient Transactions

The really big advantage of `System.Transactions` is the ambient transactions feature. With ambient transactions, there is no need to manually enlist a connection with a transaction; this is done automatically from the resources supporting ambient transactions.

An ambient transaction is associated with the current thread. You can get and set the ambient transaction with the static property `Transaction.Current`. APIs supporting ambient transactions check this property to get an ambient transaction, and enlist with the transaction. ADO.NET connections support ambient transactions.

You can create a `CommittableTransaction` object and assign it to the property `Transaction.Current` to initialize the ambient transaction. Another way to create ambient transactions is with the `TransactionScope` class. The constructor of the `TransactionScope` creates an ambient transaction. Because of the implemented interface `IDisposable`, you can use a transaction scope easily with the `using` statement.

The members of `TransactionScope` are listed in the following table.

TransactionScope Members	Description
`Constructor`	With the constructor of `TransactionScope`, you can define the transactional requirements. You can also pass an existing transaction and define the transaction timeout.
`Complete()`	Invoking the `Complete()` method, you set the success bit of the transaction scope.
`Dispose()`	The `Dispose()` method completes the scope and commits or aborts the transaction if the scope is associated with the root transaction. If the success bit is set with all dependent transactions, the `Dispose()` method commits; otherwise, a rollback is done.

Because the `TransactionScope` class implements the `IDisposable` interface, you can define the scope with the `using` statement. The default constructor creates a new transaction. Immediately after creating the `TransactionScope` instance, the transaction is accessed with the get accessor of the property `Transaction.Current` to display the transaction information on the console.

To get the information when the transaction is completed, the method `OnTransactionCompleted()` is set to the `TransactionCompleted` event of the ambient transaction.

Then a new `Student` object is created and written to the database by calling the `StudentData.AddStudent()` method. With ambient transactions, it is no longer necessary to pass a `Transaction` object to this method because the `SqlConnection` class supports ambient transactions and automatically enlists it with the connection. Then the `Complete()` method of the `TransactionScope` class sets the success bit. With the end of the `using` statement, the `TransactionScope` is disposed, and a commit is done. If the `Complete()` method is not invoked, the `Dispose()` method aborts the transaction.

If an ADO.NET connection should not enlist with an ambient transaction, you can set the value `Enlist=false` *with the connection string.*

```
static void Main()
{
   using (TransactionScope scope = new TransactionScope())
   {
      Transaction.Current.TransactionCompleted +=
            OnTransactionCompleted;

      Utilities.DisplayTransactionInformation("Ambient TX created",
            Transaction.Current.TransactionInformation);

      Student s1 = new Student();
      s1.FirstName = "Ingo";
      s1.LastName = "Rammer";
      s1.Company = "thinktecture";
      StudentData db = new StudentData();
      db.AddStudent(s1);

      if (!Utilities.AbortTx())
         scope.Complete();
      else
         Console.WriteLine("transaction will be aborted");

   } // scope.Dispose()
}

static void OnTransactionCompleted(object sender,
                                   TransactionEventArgs e)
{
   Utilities.DisplayTransactionInformation("TX completed",
         e.Transaction.TransactionInformation);
}
```

Running the application, you can see an active ambient transaction after an instance of the `TransactionScope` class is created. The last output of the application is the output from the `TransactionCompleted` event handler to display the finished transaction state.

```
Ambient TX created
Creation Time: 9:55:40 PM
Status: Active
Local ID: a06df6fb-7266-435e-b90e-f024f1d6966e:1
Distributed ID: 00000000-0000-0000-0000-0000000000

Abort the Transaction (y/n)? n

TX completed
Creation Time: 9:55:40 PM
Status: Committed
Local ID: a06df6fb-7266-435e-b90e-f024f1d6966e:1
Distributed ID: 00000000-0000-0000-0000-0000000000

Press any key to continue ...
```

Nested Scopes with Ambient Transactions

With the `TransactionScope` class you can also nest scopes. The nested scope can be directly inside the scope or within a method that is invoked from a scope. A nested scope can use the same transaction as the outer scope, suppress the transaction, or create a new transaction that is independent from the outer scope. The requirement for the scope is defined with a `TransactionScopeOption` enumeration that is passed to the constructor of the `TransactionScope` class.

The values available with the `TransactionScopeOption` enumeration and their functionality are described in the following table.

TransactionScopeOption Member	Description
`Required`	`Required` defines that the scope requires a transaction. If the outer scope already contains an ambient transaction, the inner scope uses the existing transaction. If an ambient transaction does not exist, a new transaction is created. If both scopes share the same transaction, every scope influences the outcome of the transaction. Only if all scopes set the success bit can the transaction commit. If one scope does not invoke the `Complete()` method before the root scope is disposed of, the transaction is aborted.
`RequiresNew`	`RequiresNew` always creates a new transaction. If the outer scope already defines a transaction, the transaction from the inner scope is completely independent. Both transactions can commit or abort independently.
`Suppress`	With `Suppress`, the scope does not contain an ambient transaction, whether or not the outer scope contains a transaction.

The next sample defines two scopes, in which the inner scope is configured to require a new transaction with the option `TransactionScopeOption.RequiresNew`:

```
using (TransactionScope scope = new TransactionScope())
{
   Transaction.Current.TransactionCompleted +=
         OnTransactionCompleted;

   Utilities.DisplayTransactionInformation("Ambient TX created",
         Transaction.Current.TransactionInformation);

   using (TransactionScope scope2 =
         new TransactionScope(TransactionScopeOption.RequiresNew))
   {
      Transaction.Current.TransactionCompleted +=
            OnTransactionCompleted;

      Utilities.DisplayTransactionInformation(
             "Inner Transaction Scope",
             Transaction.Current.TransactionInformation);

      scope2.Complete();
   }
   scope.Complete();
}
```

Running the application, you can see that both scopes have different transaction identifiers, although the same thread is used. Having one thread with different ambient transactions because of different scopes, the transaction identifier differs in the last number following the GUID.

A GUID is a globally unique identifier consisting of a 128-bit unique value.

```
Ambient TX created
Creation Time: 11:01:09 PM
Status: Active
Local ID: 54ac1276-5c2d-4159-84ab-36b0217c9c84:1
Distributed ID: 00000000-0000-0000-0000-0000000000

Inner Transaction Scope
Creation Time: 11:01:09 PM
Status: Active
Local ID: 54ac1276-5c2d-4159-84ab-36b0217c9c84:2
Distributed ID: 00000000-0000-0000-0000-0000000000

TX completed
Creation Time: 11:01:09 PM
Status: Committed
Local ID: 54ac1276-5c2d-4159-84ab-36b0217c9c84:2
Distributed ID: 00000000-0000-0000-0000-0000000000

TX completed
Creation Time: 11:01:09 PM
Status: Committed
Local ID: 54ac1276-5c2d-4159-84ab-36b0217c9c84:1
Distributed ID: 00000000-0000-0000-0000-0000000000
```

If you change the inner scope to the setting `TransactionScopeOption.Required`, you will find that both scopes are using the same transaction, and both scopes influence the outcome of the transaction.

Multithreading with Ambient Transactions

If multiple threads should use the same ambient transaction, you need to do some extra work. An ambient transaction is bound to a thread, so if a new thread is created, it does not have the ambient transaction from the starter thread.

This behavior is demonstrated in the next example. In the `Main()` method, a `TransactionScope` is created. Within this transaction scope, a new thread is started. The main method of the new thread `ThreadMethod()` creates a new transaction scope. With the creation of the scope, no parameters are passed, and therefore, the default option `TransactionScopeOption.Required` gets into play. If an ambient transaction exists, the existing transaction is used. If there is no ambient transaction, a new transaction is created.

```
using System;
using System.Threading;
using System.Transactions;

namespace Wrox.ProCSharp.Transactions
{
   class Program
   {
      static void Main()
```

(continued)

(continued)

```
      {
         try
         {
            using (TransactionScope scope = new TransactionScope())
            {
               Transaction.Current.TransactionCompleted +=
                     TransactionCompleted;

               Utilities.DisplayTransactionInformation("Main thread TX",
                     Transaction.Current.TransactionInformation);

               new Thread(ThreadMethod).Start(null);

               scope.Complete();
            }
         }
         catch (TransactionAbortedException ex)
         {
            Console.WriteLine("Main - Transaction was aborted, {0}",
                     ex.Message);
         }
      }

      static void TransactionCompleted(object sender, TransactionEventArgs e)
      {
         Utilities.DisplayTransactionInformation("TX completed",
               e.Transaction.TransactionInformation);
      }

      static void ThreadMethod(object dependentTx)
      {
         try
         {
            using (TransactionScope scope = new TransactionScope())
            {
               Transaction.Current.TransactionCompleted +=
                     Current_TransactionCompleted;

               Utilities.DisplayTransactionInformation("Thread TX",
                     Transaction.Current.TransactionInformation);
               scope.Complete();
            }
         }
         catch (TransactionAbortedException ex)
         {
             Console.WriteLine("ThreadMethod - Transaction was aborted, {0}",
                   ex.Message);
         }
      }
   }
}
```

As you start the application, you can see that the transactions from the two threads are completely independent. The transaction from the new thread has a different transaction ID. The transaction ID differs by the last number after the GUID in the same way as you have seen with nested scopes when the nested scope required a new transaction.

```
Main thread TX
Creation Time: 21:41:25
Status: Active
Local ID: f1e736ae-84ab-4540-b71e-3de272ffc476:1
Distributed ID: 00000000-0000-0000-0000-000000000000

TX completed
Creation Time: 21:41:25
Status: Committed
Local ID: f1e736ae-84ab-4540-b71e-3de272ffc476:1
Distributed ID: 00000000-0000-0000-0000-000000000000

Thread TX
Creation Time: 21:41:25
Status: Active
Local ID: f1e736ae-84ab-4540-b71e-3de272ffc476:2
Distributed ID: 00000000-0000-0000-0000-000000000000

TX completed
Creation Time: 21:41:25
Status: Committed
Local ID: f1e736ae-84ab-4540-b71e-3de272ffc476:2
Distributed ID: 00000000-0000-0000-0000-000000000000
```

To use the same ambient transaction in another thread, you need the help of dependent transactions. Now the sample is changed to pass a dependent transaction to the new thread. The dependent transaction is created from the ambient transaction by calling the `DependentClone()` method on the ambient transaction. With this method, the setting `DependentCloneOption.BlockCommitUntilComplete` is set so that the calling thread waits until the new thread is completed before committing the transaction.

```
class Program
{
   static void Main()
   {
      try
      {
         using (TransactionScope scope = new TransactionScope())
         {
            Transaction.Current.TransactionCompleted +=
                  TransactionCompleted;

            Utilities.DisplayTransactionInformation("Main thread TX",
                  Transaction.Current.TransactionInformation);

            new Thread(ThreadMethod).Start(
                  Transaction.Current.DependentClone(
                  DependentCloneOption.BlockCommitUntilComplete));

            scope.Complete();
         }
```

(continued)

(continued)

```
        }
        catch (TransactionAbortedException ex)
        {
            Console.WriteLine("Main - Transaction was aborted, {0}",
                        ex.Message);
        }
    }
```

In the method of the thread, the dependent transaction that is passed is assigned to the ambient transaction by using the set accessor of the `Transaction.Current` property. Now the transaction scope is using the same transaction by using the dependent transaction. When you are finished using the dependent transaction, you need to invoke the `Complete()` method of the `DependentTransaction` object.

```
    static void ThreadMethod(object dependentTx)
    {
        DependentTransaction dTx = dependentTx as DependentTransaction;

        try
        {
            Transaction.Current = dTx;

            using (TransactionScope scope = new TransactionScope())
            {
                Transaction.Current.TransactionCompleted +=
                        Current_TransactionCompleted;

                Utilities.DisplayTransactionInformation("Thread TX",
                        Transaction.Current.TransactionInformation);
                scope.Complete();
            }
        }
        catch (TransactionAbortedException ex)
        {
            Console.WriteLine("ThreadMethod - Transaction was aborted, {0}",
                    ex.Message);
        }
        finally
        {
            if (dTx != null)
            {
                dTx.Complete();
            }
        }
    }
}
```

Running the application now, you can see that the main thread and the newly created thread are using, and influencing, the same transaction. The transaction listed by the threads has the same identifier. If with one thread the success bit is not set by calling the `Complete()` method, the complete transaction aborts.

```
Main thread TX
Creation Time: 23:00:57
Status: Active
Local ID: 2fb1b54d-61f5-4d4e-a55e-f4a9e04778be:1
Distributed ID: 00000000-0000-0000-0000-000000000000

Thread TX
Creation Time: 23:00:57
Status: Active
Local ID: 2fb1b54d-61f5-4d4e-a55e-f4a9e04778be:1
Distributed ID: 00000000-0000-0000-0000-000000000000

TX completed
Creation Time: 23:00:57
Status: Committed
Local ID: 2fb1b54d-61f5-4d4e-a55e-f4a9e04778be:1
Distributed ID: 00000000-0000-0000-0000-000000000000

TX completed
Creation Time: 23:00:57
Status: Committed
Local ID: 2fb1b54d-61f5-4d4e-a55e-f4a9e04778be:1
Distributed ID: 00000000-0000-0000-0000-000000000000
```

Isolation Level

At the beginning of this chapter, you saw the ACID properties used to describe transactions. The letter *I* (Isolation) of *ACID* is not always fully required. For performance reasons, you might reduce isolation requirements, but you must be aware of the issues that you will encounter if you change the isolation level.

The problems that you can encounter if you don't completely isolate the scope outside the transaction can be divided into three categories:

- **Dirty reads** — With a *dirty read*, another transaction can read records that are changed within the transaction. Because the data that is changed within the transaction might roll back to its original state, reading this intermediate state from another transaction is considered "dirty" — the data has not been committed. You can avoid this by locking the records to be changed.
- **Nonrepeatable reads** — *Nonrepeatable reads* occur when data is read inside a transaction, and while the transaction is running, another transaction changes the same records. If the record is read once more inside the transaction, the result is different — nonrepeatable. You can avoid this by locking the read records.
- **Phantom reads** — *Phantom reads* happen when a range of data is read, for example, with a `WHERE` clause. Another transaction can add a new record that belongs to the range that is read within the transaction. A new read with the same `WHERE` clause returns a different number of rows. Phantom reads can be a specific problem when doing an `UPDATE` of a range of rows. For example, `UPDATE Addresses SET Zip=4711 WHERE (Zip=2315)` updates the ZIP code of all records from 2315 to 4711. After doing the update, there may still be records with a ZIP code of 2315 if another user added a new record with ZIP 2315 while the update was running. You can avoid this by doing a range lock.

When defining the isolation requirements, you can set the isolation level. This is set with an `IsolationLevel` enumeration that is configured when the transaction is created (either with the constructor of the `CommittableTransaction` class or with the constructor of the `TransactionScope` class). The `IsolationLevel` defines the locking behavior. The next table lists the values of the `IsolationLevel` enumeration.

Isolation Level	Description
`ReadUncommitted`	With `ReadUncommitted`, transactions are not isolated from each other. With this level, there is no wait for locked records from other transactions. This way, uncommitted data can be read from other transactions — dirty reads. This level is usually used just for reading records where it does not matter if you read interim changes (for example, reports).
`ReadCommitted`	`ReadCommitted` waits for records with a write-lock from other transactions. This way, a dirty read cannot happen. This level sets a read-lock for the current record read and a write-lock for the records being written until the transaction is completed. Reading a sequence of records, with every new record that is read, the prior record is unlocked. That's why nonrepeatable reads can happen.
`RepeatableRead`	`RepeatableRead` holds the lock for the records read until the transaction is completed. This way, the problem of nonrepeatable reads is avoided. Phantom reads can still occur.
`Serializable`	`Serializable` holds a range lock. While the transaction is running, it is not possible to add a new record that belongs to the same range from which the data is being read.
`Snapshot`	The isolation level `Snapshot` is possible only with SQL Server 2005 and later versions. This level reduces the locks as modified rows are copied. This way, other transactions can still read the old data without the need to wait for an unlock.
`Unspecified`	The level `Unspecified` indicates that the provider is using an isolation level value that is different from the values defined by the `IsolationLevel` enumeration.
`Chaos`	The level `Chaos` is similar to `ReadUncommitted`, but in addition to performing the actions of the `ReadUncommitted` value, `Chaos` does not lock updated records.

The next table gives you a summary of the problems that can occur as a result of setting the most commonly used transaction isolation levels.

Isolation Level	Dirty Reads	Nonrepeatable Reads	Phantom Reads
Read Uncommitted	Y	Y	Y
Read Committed	N	Y	Y
Repeatable Read	N	N	Y
Serializable	N	N	N

The following code segment shows how the isolation level can be set with the `TransactionScope` class. With the constructor of `TransactionScope`, you can set the `TransactionScopeOption` that was discussed earlier and the `TransactionOptions`. The `TransactionOptions` class allows you to define the `IsolationLevel` and the `Timeout`.

```
TransactionOptions options = new TransactionOptions();
options.IsolationLevel = IsolationLevel.ReadUncommitted;
options.Timeout = TimeSpan.FromSeconds(90);
using (TransactionScope scope =
      new TransactionScope(TransactionScopeOption.Required,
      options))
{
   // Read data without waiting for locks from other transactions,
   // dirty reads are possible.
}
```

Custom Resource Managers

One of the biggest advantages of the new transaction model is that it is relatively easy to create custom resource managers that participate in the transaction. A resource manager does not manage only durable resources but can also manage volatile or in-memory resources — for example, a simple `int` and a generic list.

Figure 22-5 shows the relationship between a resource manager and transaction classes. The resource manager implements the interface `IEnlistmentNotification` that defines the methods `Prepare()`, `InDoubt()`, `Commit()`, and `Rollback()`. The resource manager implements this interface to manage transactions for a resource. To be part of a transaction, the resource manager must enlist with the `Transaction` class. Volatile resource managers invoke the method `EnlistVolatile()`; durable resource managers invoke `EnlistDurable()`. Depending on the transaction's outcome, the transaction manager invokes the methods from the interface `IEnlistmentNotification` with the resource manager.

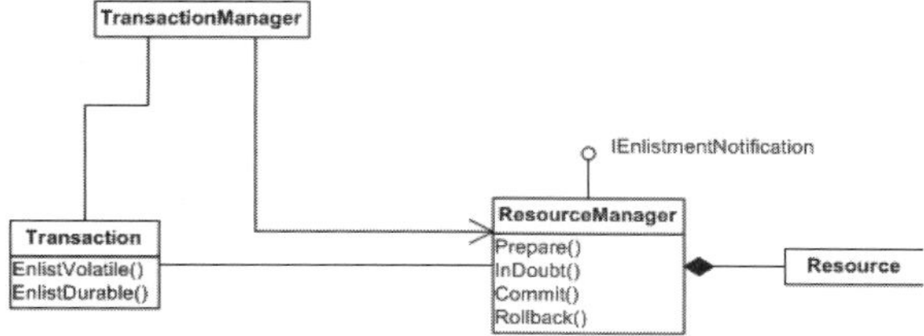

Figure 22-5

The next table explains the methods of the `IEnlistmentNotification` interface that you must implement with resource managers. As you review the table, recall the active, prepared, and committing phases explained earlier in this chapter.

IEnlistmentNotification Members	Description
`Prepare()`	The transaction manager invokes the `Prepare()` method for preparation of the transaction. The resource manager completes the preparation by invoking the `Prepared()` method of the `PreparingEnlistment` parameter, which is passed to the `Prepare()` method. If the work cannot be done successfully, the resource manager informs the transaction manager by invoking the method `ForceRollback()`. A durable resource manager must write a log so that it can finish the transaction successfully after the prepare phase.
`Commit()`	When all resource managers have successfully prepared for the transaction, the transaction manager invokes the `Commit()` method. The resource manager can now complete the work to make it visible outside the transaction and invoke the `Done()` method of the `Enlistment` parameter.
`Rollback()`	If one of the resources could not successfully prepare for the transaction, the transaction manager invokes the `Rollback()` method with all resource managers. After the state is returned to the state prior to the transaction, the resource manager invokes the `Done()` method of the `Enlistment` parameter.
`InDoubt()`	If there is a problem after the transaction manager invokes the `Commit()` method (and the resources don't return completion information with the `Done()` method), the transaction manager invokes the `InDoubt()` method.

Transactional Resources

A transactional resource must keep the live value and a temporary value. The live value is read from outside the transaction and defines the valid state when the transaction rolls back. The temporary value defines the valid state of the transaction when the transaction commits.

To make non-transactional types transactional, the generic sample class `Transactional<T>` wraps a non-generic type, so you can use it like this:

```
Transactional<int> txInt = new Transactional<int>();
Transactional<string> txString = new Transactional<string>();
```

Let's look at the implementation of the class `Transactional<T>`. The live value of the managed resource has the variable `liveValue`; the temporary value that is associated with a transaction is stored within the `ResourceManager<T>`. The variable `enlistedTransaction` is associated with the ambient transaction if there is one.

```
using System.Diagnostics;
using System.Transactions;

namespace Wrox.ProCSharp.Transactions
{

   public partial class Transactional<T>
   {
      private T liveValue;
      private ResourceManager<T> enlistment;
      private Transaction enlistedTransaction;
```

With the `Transactional` constructor, the live value is set to the variable `liveValue`. If the constructor is invoked from within an ambient transaction, the `GetEnlistment()` helper method is invoked. `GetEnlistment()` first checks if there is an ambient transaction and asserts if there is none. If the transaction is not already enlisted, the `ResourceManager<T>` helper class is instantiated, and the resource manager is enlisted with the transaction by invoking the method `EnlistVolatile()`. Also, the variable `enlistedTransaction` is set to the ambient transaction.

If the ambient transaction is different from the enlisted transaction, an exception is thrown. The implementation does not support changing the same value from within two different transactions. If you have this requirement, you can create a lock and wait for the lock to be released from one transaction before changing it within another transaction.

```
      public Transactional(T value)
      {
         if (Transaction.Current == null)
         {
            this.liveValue = value;
         }
         else
         {
            this.liveValue = default(T);
            GetEnlistment().Value = value;
         }
      }

      public Transactional()
            : this(default(T)) {}

      private ResourceManager<T> GetEnlistment()
      {
         Transaction tx = Transaction.Current;
         Trace.Assert(tx != null, "Must be invoked with ambient transaction");

         if (enlistedTransaction == null)
         {
            enlistment = new ResourceManager<T>(this, tx);
            tx.EnlistVolatile(enlistment, EnlistmentOptions.None);
            enlistedTransaction = tx;
            return enlistment;
         }
         else if (enlistedTransaction == Transaction.Current)
```

(continued)

(continued)

```
        {
           return enlistment;
        }
        else
        {
           throw new TransactionException(
                 "This class only supports enlisting with one transaction");
        }
     }
```

The property `Value` returns the value of the contained class and sets it. However, with transactions, you cannot just set and return the `liveValue` variable. This would be the case only if the object were outside a transaction. To make the code more readable, the property `Value` uses the methods `GetValue()` and `SetValue()` in the implementation:

```
     public T Value
     {
        get { return GetValue(); }
        set { SetValue(value); }
     }
```

The method `GetValue()` checks if an ambient transaction exists. If one doesn't exist, the `liveValue` is returned. If there is an ambient transaction, the `GetEnlistment()` method shown earlier returns the resource manager, and with the `Value` property, the temporary value for the contained object within the transaction is returned.

The method `SetValue()` is very similar to `GetValue()`; the difference is that it changes the live or temporary value.

```
     protected virtual T GetValue()
     {
        if (Transaction.Current == null)
        {
           return liveValue;
        }
        else
        {
           return GetEnlistment().Value;
        }
     }

     protected virtual void SetValue(T value)
     {
        if (Transaction.Current == null)
        {
           liveValue = value;
        }
        else
        {
           GetEnlistment().Value = value;
        }
     }
```

The `Commit()` and `Rollback()` methods that are implemented in the class `Transactional<T>` are invoked from the resource manager. The `Commit()` method sets the live value from the temporary value received with the first argument and nullifies the variable `enlistedTransaction` as the transaction is completed. With the `Rollback()` method, the transaction is completed as well, but here the temporary value is ignored, and the live value is kept in use.

```
        internal void Commit(T value, Transaction tx)
        {
           liveValue = value;
           enlistedTransaction = null;
        }

        internal void Rollback(Transaction tx)
        {
           enlistedTransaction = null;
        }
     }
```

Because the resource manager that is used by the class `Transactional<T>` is used only within the `Transactional<T>` class itself, it is implemented as an inner class. With the constructor, the parent variable is set to have an association with the transactional wrapper class. The temporary value used within the transaction is copied from the live value. Remember the isolation requirements with transactions.

```
using System;
using System.Diagnostics;
using System.IO;
using System.Runtime.Serialization.Formatters.Binary;
using System.Transactions;

namespace Wrox.ProCSharp.Transactions
{
   public partial class Transactional<T>
   {
      internal class ResourceManager<T1> : IEnlistmentNotification
      {
         private Transactional<T1> parent;
         private Transaction currentTransaction;

         internal ResourceManager(Transactional<T1> parent, Transaction tx)
         {
            this.parent = parent;
            Value = DeepCopy(parent.liveValue);
            currentTransaction = tx;
         }

         public T1 Value { get; set; }
```

Because the temporary value may change within the transaction, the live value of the wrapper class may not be changed within the transaction. When creating a copy with some classes, it is possible to invoke the `Clone()` method that is defined with the `ICloneable` interface. However, as the `Clone()` method is defined, it allows implementations to create either a shallow or a deep copy. If type `T` contains reference types and implements a shallow copy, changing the temporary value would also change the original value. This would be in conflict with the isolation and consistency features of transactions. Here, a deep copy is required.

To do a deep copy, the method `DeepCopy()` serializes and deserializes the object to and from a stream. Because in C# 3.0 it is not possible to define a constraint to the type `T` indicating that serialization is required, the static constructor of the class `Transactional<T>` checks if the type is serializable by checking the property `IsSerializable` of the `Type` object.

```
        static ResourceManager()
        {
           Type t = typeof(T1);
           Trace.Assert(t.IsSerializable, "Type " + t.Name +
                 " is not serializable");
        }

        private T1 DeepCopy(T1 value)
        {
           using (MemoryStream stream = new MemoryStream())
           {
              BinaryFormatter formatter = new BinaryFormatter();
              formatter.Serialize(stream, value);
              stream.Flush();
              stream.Seek(0, SeekOrigin.Begin);

              return (T1)formatter.Deserialize(stream);
           }
        }
```

The interface `IEnlistmentNotification` is implemented by the class `ResourceManager<T>`. This is the requirement for enlisting with transactions.

The implementation of the `Prepare()` method just answers by invoking `Prepared()` with `preparingEnlistment`. There should not be a problem assigning the temporary value to the live value, so the `Prepare()` method succeeds. With the implementation of the `Commit()` method, the `Commit()` method of the parent is invoked, where the variable `liveValue` is set to the value of the `ResourceManager` that is used within the transaction. The `Rollback()` method just completes the work and leaves the live value where it was. With a volatile resource, there is not a lot you can do in the `InDoubt()` method. Writing a log entry could be useful.

```
        public void Prepare(PreparingEnlistment preparingEnlistment)
        {
           preparingEnlistment.Prepared();
        }

        public void Commit(Enlistment enlistment)
        {
           parent.Commit(Value, currentTransaction);
           enlistment.Done();
        }

        public void Rollback(Enlistment enlistment)
        {
           parent.Rollback(currentTransaction);
           enlistment.Done();
        }

        public void InDoubt(Enlistment enlistment)
        {
           enlistment.Done();
        }
     }
  }
}
```

The class `Transactional<T>` can now be used to make non-transactional classes transactional — for example, `int` and `string` but also more complex classes such as `Student` — as long as the type is serializable:

```
using System;
using System.Transactions;

namespace Wrox.ProCSharp.Transactions
{
   class Program
   {
      static void Main()
      {
         Transactional<int> intVal = new Transactional<int>(1);
         Transactional<Student> student1 = new Transactional<Student>(
               new Student());
         student1.Value.FirstName = "Andrew";
         student1.Value.LastName = "Wilson";

         Console.WriteLine("before the transaction, value: {0}",
               intVal.Value);
         Console.WriteLine("before the transaction, student: {0}",
               student1.Value);

         using (TransactionScope scope = new TransactionScope())
         {
            intVal.Value = 2;
            Console.WriteLine("inside transaction, value: {0}", intVal.Value);

            student1.Value.FirstName = "Ten";
            student1.Value.LastName = "Sixty-Nine";

            if (!Utilities.AbortTx())
               scope.Complete();
         }
         Console.WriteLine("outside of transaction, value: {0}",
               intVal.Value);
         Console.WriteLine("outside of transaction, student: {0}",
               student1.Value);
      }
   }
}
```

The following console output shows a run of the application with a committed transaction:

```
before the transaction, value: 1
before the transaction: student: Andrew Wilson
inside transaction, value: 2

Abort the Transaction (y/n)? n

outside of transaction, value: 2
outside of transaction, student: Ten Sixty-Nine

Press any key to continue . . .
```

Transactions with Windows Vista and Windows Server 2008

You can write a custom durable resource manager that works with the `File` and `Registry` classes. A file-based durable resource manager can copy the original file and write changes to the temporary file inside a temporary directory to make the changes persistent. When committing the transaction, the original file is replaced by the temporary file. Writing custom durable resource managers for files and the registry is no longer necessary with Windows Vista and Windows Server 2008. With these operating systems, native transactions with the file system and with the registry are supported. For this, there are new API calls such as `CreateFileTransacted()`, `CreateHardLinkTransacted()`, `CreateSymbolicLinkTransacted()`, `CopyFileTransacted()`, and so on. What these API calls have in common is that they require a handle to a transaction passed as an argument; they do not support ambient transactions. The transactional API calls are not available from .NET 3.5, but you can create a custom wrapper by using `Platform Invoke`.

> `Platform Invoke` *is discussed in more detail in Chapter 24, " Interoperability."*

The sample application wraps the native method `CreateFileTransacted()` for creating transactional file streams from .NET applications.

When invoking native methods, the parameters of the native methods must be mapped to .NET data types. Because of security issues, .NET 2.0 introduced the class `SafeHandle` to map a native `HANDLE` type. `SafeHandle` is an abstract type that wraps operating system handles and supports critical finalization of handle resources. Depending on the allowed values of a handle, the derived classes `SafeHandleMinusOneIsInvalid` and `SafeHandleZeroOrMinusOneIsInvalid` can be used to wrap native handles. `SafeFileHandle` itself derives from `SafeHandleZeroOrMinusOneIsInvalid`. To map a handle to a transaction, the class `SafeTransactionHandle` is defined.

```
using System;
using System.Runtime.Versioning;
using System.Security.Permissions;
using Microsoft.Win32.SafeHandles;

namespace Wrox.ProCSharp.Transactions
{
   [SecurityPermission(SecurityAction.LinkDemand, UnmanagedCode = true)]
   public sealed class SafeTransactionHandle :
         SafeHandleZeroOrMinusOneIsInvalid
   {
      private SafeTransactionHandle()
            : base(true) { }

      public SafeTransactionHandle(IntPtr preexistingHandle, bool ownsHandle)
            : base(ownsHandle)
      {
         SetHandle(preexistingHandle);
      }

      [ResourceExposure(ResourceScope.Machine)]
      [ResourceConsumption(ResourceScope.Machine)]
      protected override bool ReleaseHandle()
      {
         return NativeMethods.CloseHandle(handle);
      }
   }
}
```

All native methods used from .NET are defined with the class `NativeMethods` shown here. With the sample, the native APIs needed are `CreateFileTransacted()` and `CloseHandle()`, which are defined as static members of the class. The methods are declared extern because there is no C# implementation. Instead, the implementation is found in the native DLL as defined by the attribute `DllImport`. Both of these methods can be found in the native DLL `Kernel32.dll`. With the method declaration, the parameters defined with the Windows API call are mapped to .NET data types. The parameter `txHandle` represents a handle to a transaction and is of the previously defined type `SafeTransactionHandle`.

```
using System;
using System.Runtime.ConstrainedExecution;
using System.Runtime.InteropServices;
using System.Runtime.Versioning;
using Microsoft.Win32.SafeHandles;

namespace Wrox.ProCSharp.Transactions
{
   internal static class NativeMethods
   {
      [DllImport("Kernel32.dll",
                 CallingConvention = CallingConvention.StdCall,
                 CharSet = CharSet.Unicode)]
      internal static extern SafeFileHandle CreateFileTransacted(
          String lpFileName,
          uint dwDesiredAccess,
          uint dwShareMode,
          IntPtr lpSecurityAttributes,
          uint dwCreationDisposition,
          int dwFlagsAndAttributes,
          IntPtr hTemplateFile,
          SafeTransactionHandle txHandle,
          IntPtr miniVersion,
          IntPtr extendedParameter);

      [DllImport("Kernel32.dll", SetLastError = true)]
      [ResourceExposure(ResourceScope.Machine)]
      [ReliabilityContract(Consistency.WillNotCorruptState, Cer.Success)]
      [return: MarshalAs(UnmanagedType.Bool)]
      internal static extern bool CloseHandle(IntPtr handle);

   }
}
```

The interface `IKernelTransaction` is used to get a transaction handle and pass it to the transacted Windows API calls. This is a COM interface and must be wrapped to .NET by using COM Interop attributes as shown. The attribute GUID must have exactly the identifier as it is used here with the interface definition, because this is the identifier used with the definition of the COM interface.

```
using System;
using System.Runtime.InteropServices;

namespace Wrox.ProCSharp.Transactions
{
   [ComImport]
   [Guid("79427A2B-F895-40e0-BE79-B57DC82ED231")]
   [InterfaceType(ComInterfaceType.InterfaceIsIUnknown)]
   public interface IKernelTransaction
```

(continued)

(continued)

```
    {
        void GetHandle(out SafeTransactionHandle ktmHandle);
    }
}
```

Finally, the class `TransactedFile` is the class that will be used by .NET applications. This class defines the method `GetTransactedFileStream()` that requires a file name as parameter and returns a `System.IO.FileStream`. The returned stream is a normal .NET stream; it just references a transacted file.

With the implementation, `TransactionInterop.GetDtcTransaction()` creates an interface pointer of the `IKernelTransaction` to the ambient transaction that is passed as an argument to `GetDtcTransaction()`. Using the interface `IKernelTransaction`, the handle of type `SafeTransactionHandle` is created. This handle is then passed to the wrapped API call `NativeMethods.CreateFileTransacted()`. With the returned file handle, a new `FileStream` instance is created and returned to the caller.

```
using System;
using System.IO;
using System.Transactions;
using Microsoft.Win32.SafeHandles;
using System.Runtime.InteropServices;

namespace Wrox.ProCSharp.Transactions
{
   public static class TransactedFile
   {
      internal const short FILE_ATTRIBUTE_NORMAL = 0x80;
      internal const short INVALID_HANDLE_VALUE = -1;
      internal const uint GENERIC_READ = 0x80000000;
      internal const uint GENERIC_WRITE = 0x40000000;
      internal const uint CREATE_NEW = 1;
      internal const uint CREATE_ALWAYS = 2;
      internal const uint OPEN_EXISTING = 3;

      [FileIOPermission(SecurityAction.Demand, Unrestricted=true)]
      public static FileStream GetTransactedFileStream(string fileName)
      {
         IKernelTransaction ktx = (IKernelTransaction)
               TransactionInterop.GetDtcTransaction(Transaction.Current);

         SafeTransactionHandle txHandle;
         ktx.GetHandle(out txHandle);

         SafeFileHandle fileHandle = NativeMethods.CreateFileTransacted(
               fileName, GENERIC_WRITE, 0,
               IntPtr.Zero, CREATE_ALWAYS, FILE_ATTRIBUTE_NORMAL,
               null,
               txHandle, IntPtr.Zero, IntPtr.Zero);

         return new FileStream(fileHandle, FileAccess.Write);
      }
   }
}
```

Now it is very easy to use the transactional API from .NET code. You can create an ambient transaction with the `TransactionScope` class and use the `TransactedFile` class within the context of the ambient transaction scope. If the transaction is aborted, the file is not written. If the transaction is committed, you can find the file in the temp directory.

```
using System;
using System.IO;
using System.Transactions;

namespace Wrox.ProCSharp.Transactions
{
   class Program
   {
      static void Main()
      {
         using (TransactionScope scope = new TransactionScope())
         {
            FileStream stream =
                  TransactedFile.GetTransactedFileStream(
                  "c:/temp/sample.txt");

            StreamWriter writer = new StreamWriter(stream);
            writer.WriteLine("Write a transactional file");
            writer.Close();

            if (!Utilities.AbortTx())
               scope.Complete();
         }
      }
   }
}
```

Now you can use databases, volatile resources, and files within the same transaction.

Summary

In this chapter, you learned the attributes of transactions and how you can create and manage transactions with the classes from the `System.Transactions` namespace.

Transactions are described with ACID properties: atomicity, consistency, isolation, and durability. Not all of these properties are always required, as you have seen with volatile resources that don't support durability and with isolation options.

The easiest way to deal with transactions is by creating ambient transactions and using the `TransactionScope` class. Ambient transactions are very useful working with the ADO.NET data adapter and LINQ to SQL where usually you do not open and close database connections explicitly. ADO.NET is covered in Chapter 26. LINQ to SQL is explained in Chapter 27.

Using the same transaction across multiple threads, you can use the `DependentTransaction` class to create a dependency on another transaction. By enlisting a resource manager that implements the interface `IEnlistmentNotification`, you can create custom resources that participate with transactions.

Finally, you have seen how to use Windows Vista and Windows Server 2008 transactions with the .NET Framework and C#.

With .NET Enterprise Services, you can create automatic transactions that make use of `System.Transactions`. You can read about this technology in Chapter 44, "Enterprise Services."

In the next chapter, you can read how to create a Windows service that can be automatically started when the operating system boots. Transactions can be useful within a service as well.

23

Windows Services

Windows Services are programs that can be started automatically at boot time without the need for anyone to log on to the machine.

In this chapter, you learn:

- The architecture of Windows Services, including the functionality of a service program, a service control program, and a service configuration program
- How to implement a Windows Service with the classes found in the `System.ServiceProcess` namespace
- Installation programs to configure the Windows Service in the registry
- How to write a program to control the Windows Service using the `ServiceController` class
- How to troubleshoot Windows Service programs
- How to react to power events from the operating system

The first section explains the architecture of Windows Services. You can download the code for this chapter from the Wrox Web site at `www.wrox.com`.

What Is a Windows Service?

Windows Services are applications that can be automatically started when the operating system boots. They can run without having an interactive user logged on to the system and do some processing in the background. For example, on a Windows Server, system networking services should be accessible from the client without a user logging on to the server. On the client system, services are useful as well; for example, to get a new software version from the Internet or to do some file cleanup on the local disk. You can configure a Windows Service to be run from a specially configured user account or from the system user account — a user account that has even more privileges than that of the system administrator.

Unless otherwise noted, when we refer to a service, we are referring to a Windows Service.

Here are a few examples of services:

- Simple TCP/IP Services is a service program that hosts some small TCP/IP servers: echo, daytime, quote, and others.
- World Wide Publishing Service is the service of the Internet Information Server (IIS).
- Event Log is a service to log messages to the event log system.
- Windows Search is a service that creates indexes of data on the disk.

You can use the Services administration tool, shown in Figure 23-1, to see all of the services on a system. On a Windows 2003 server, this program can be accessed by selecting Start ⇨ Programs ⇨ Administrative Tools ⇨ Services; on Windows Vista and Windows XP, the program is accessible through Settings ⇨ Control Panel ⇨ Administrative Tools ⇨ Services.

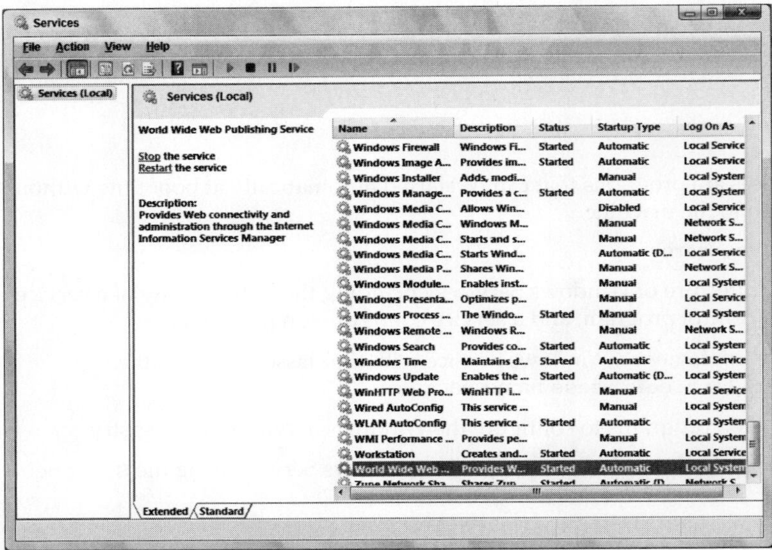

Figure 23-1

Windows Services Architecture

Three program types are necessary to operate a Windows Service:

- A service program
- A service control program
- A service configuration program

The *service program* itself provides the actual functionality you are looking for. With a *service control* program, it is possible to send control requests to a service, such as start, stop, pause, and continue. With a *service configuration* program, a service can be installed; it is copied to the file system, written into the registry, and configured as a service. Although .NET components can be installed simply with an xcopy, because they don't need to write information to the registry, installation for services requires registry configuration. A service configuration program can also be used to change the configuration of that service at a later point.

These three ingredients of a Windows Service are discussed in the following subsections.

Service Program

Before looking at the .NET implementation of a service, let's explore, from an independent point of view, what the Windows architecture of services looks like and what the inner functionality of a service is.

The service program implements the functionality of the service. It needs three parts:

- A main function
- A service-main function
- A handler

Before discussing these parts, we need to quickly introduce you to the *Service Control Manager* (SCM). The SCM plays an important role for services — sending requests to your service to start and to stop it.

Service Control Manager

The SCM is the part of the operating system that communicates with the service. Figure 23-2 illustrates how this communication works with a Unified Modeling Language (UML) sequence diagram.

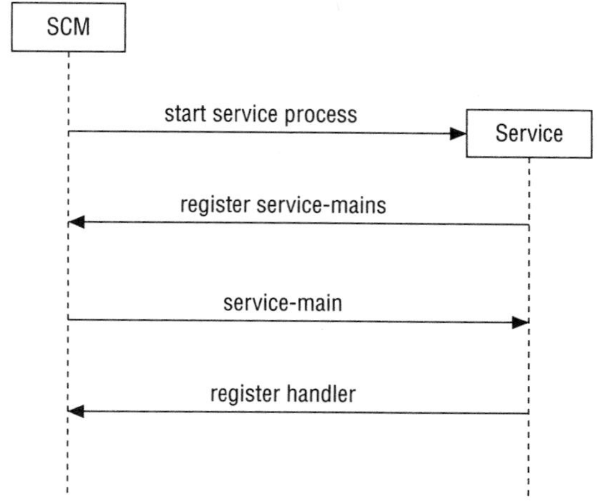

Figure 23-2

At boot time, each process for which a service is set to start automatically is started, and so the main function of this process is called. The service has the responsibility of registering the service-main function for each of its services. The main function is the entry point of the service program, and in this function the entry points for the service-main functions must be registered with the SCM.

Main Function, Service-Main, and Handlers

The main function of the service is the normal entry point of a program, the `Main()` method. The main function of the service might register more than one service-main function. The *service-main* function contains the actual functionality of the service. The service must register a service-main function for each service it provides. A service program can provide a lot of services in a single program; for example, `<windows>\system32\services.exe` is the service program that includes Alerter, Application Management, Computer Browser, and DHCP Client, among other items.

The SCM now calls the service-main function for each service that should be started. One important task of the service-main function is to register a handler with the SCM.

The *handler* function is the third part of a service program. The handler must respond to events from the SCM. Services can be stopped, suspended, and resumed, and the handler must react to these events.

Once a handler has been registered with the SCM, the service control program can post requests to the SCM to stop, suspend, and resume the service. The service control program is independent of the SCM and the service itself. The operating system contains many service control programs, for example, the MMC Services snap-in that you saw earlier. You can also write your own service control program; a good example of this is the SQL Server Configuration Manager shown in Figure 23-3.

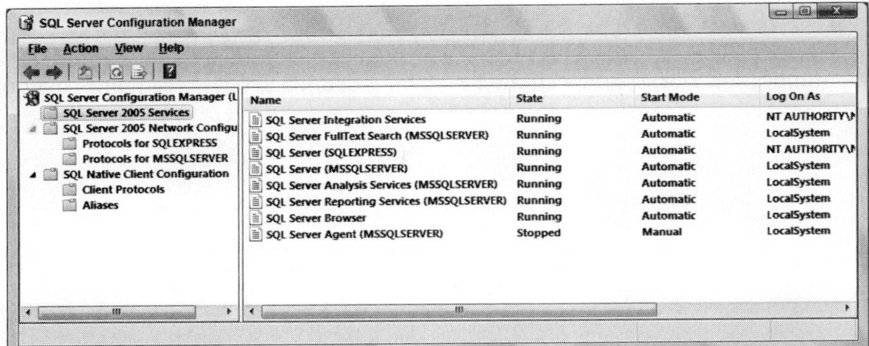

Figure 23-3

Service Control Program

As the name suggests, with a service control program, you can control the service. For stopping, suspending, and resuming the service, you can send control codes to the service, and the handler should react to these events. It is also possible to ask the service about the actual status and to implement a custom handler that responds to custom control codes.

Service Configuration Program

Because services must be configured in the registry, you can't use Xcopy installation with services. The registry contains the startup type of the service which can be set to automatic, manual, or disabled. You also need to configure the user of the service program and dependencies of the service — for example, the services that must be started before this one can start. All of these configurations are made within a service configuration program. The installation program can use the service configuration program to configure the service, but this program can also be used at a later time to change service configuration parameters.

System.ServiceProcess Namespace

In the .NET Framework, you can find service classes in the `System.ServiceProcess` namespace that implement the three parts of a service:

- You must inherit from the `ServiceBase` class to implement a service. The `ServiceBase` class is used to register the service and to answer start and stop requests.
- The `ServiceController` class is used to implement a service control program. With this class, you can send requests to services.
- The `ServiceProcessInstaller` and `ServiceInstaller` classes are, as their names suggest, classes to install and configure service programs.

Now you are ready to create a new service.

Creating a Windows Service

The service that you create will host a quote server. With every request that is made from a client, the quote server returns a random quote from a quote file. The first part of the solution uses three assemblies, one for the client and two for the server. Figure 23-4 gives an overview of the solution. The assembly `QuoteServer` holds the actual functionality. The service reads the quote file in a memory cache, and answers requests for quotes with the help of a socket server. The `QuoteClient` is a Windows Forms rich-client application. This application creates a client socket to communicate with the `QuoteServer`. The third assembly is the actual service. The `QuoteService` starts and stops the `QuoteServer`; the service controls the server:

Before creating the service part of your program, create a simple socket server in an extra C# class library that will be used from your service process.

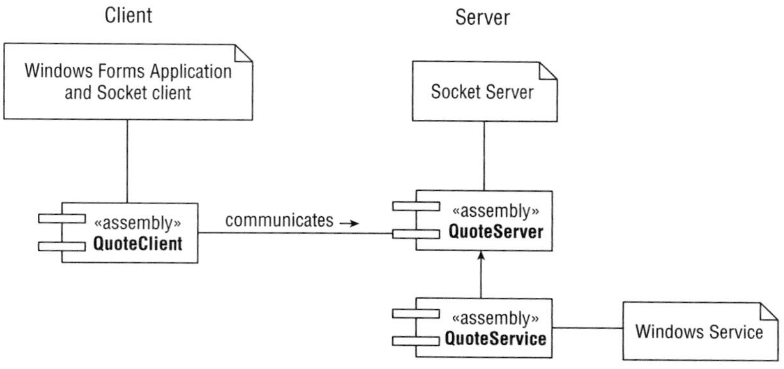

Figure 23-4

A Class Library Using Sockets

You can build any functionality in the service, for example, scanning for files to do a backup or a virus check, or starting a WCF server. However, all service programs share some similarities. The program must be able to start (and to return to the caller), stop, and suspend. This section looks at such an implementation using a socket server.

With Windows Vista, the Simple TCP/IP Services can be installed as part of the Windows components. Part of the Simple TCP/IP Services is a "quote of the day," or qotd, TCP/IP server. This simple service listens to port 17 and answers every request with a random message from the file `<windir>\system32\drivers\etc\quotes`. With the sample service, a similar server will be built. The sample server returns a Unicode string, in contrast to the good-old qotd server that returns an ASCII string.

First, create a Class Library called `QuoteServer` and implement the code for the server. The following walks through the source code of your `QuoteServer` class in the file `QuoteServer.cs`:

```
using System;
using System.Collections.Generic;
using System.IO;
using System.Net;
using System.Net.Sockets;
using System.Text;
using System.Threading;

namespace Wrox.ProCSharp.WinServices
{
   public class QuoteServer
   {
      private TcpListener listener;
      private int port;
      private string filename;
      private List<string> quotes;
      private Random random;
      private Thread listenerThread;
```

The constructor `QuoteServer()` is overloaded so that a file name and a port can be passed to the call. The constructor where just the file name is passed uses the default port 7890 for the server. The default constructor defines the default file name for the quotes as `quotes.txt`:

```
      public QuoteServer() : this ("quotes.txt"")
      {
      }
      public QuoteServer(string filename) : this(filename, 7890)
      {
      }
      public QuoteServer(string filename, int port)
      {
         this.filename = filename;
         this.port = port;
      }
```

`ReadQuotes()` is a helper method that reads all the quotes from a file that was specified in the constructor. All the quotes are added to the `StringCollection` quotes. In addition, you are creating an instance of the `Random` class that will be used to return random quotes:

```
      protected void ReadQuotes()
      {
         quotes = new List<string>();
         Stream stream = File.OpenRead(filename);
         StreamReader streamReader = new StreamReader(stream);
         string quote;
         while ((quote = streamReader.ReadLine()) != null)
         {
            quotes.Add(quote);
         }
         streamReader.Close();
         stream.Close();
         random = new Random();
      }
```

Another helper method is `GetRandomQuoteOfTheDay()`. This method returns a random quote from the `StringCollection` quotes:

```
protected string GetRandomQuoteOfTheDay()
{
   int index = random.Next(0, quotes.Count);
   return quotes[index];
}
```

In the `Start()` method, the complete file containing the quotes is read in the `StringCollection` quotes by using the helper method `ReadQuotes()`. After this, a new thread is started, which immediately calls the `Listener()` method — similarly to the `TcpReceive` example in Chapter 41, "Accessing the Internet."

Here a thread is used because the `Start()` method cannot block and wait for a client; it must return immediately to the caller (SCM). The SCM would assume that the start failed if the method didn't return to the caller in a timely fashion (30 seconds). The listener thread is set as a background thread so that the application can exit without stopping this thread. The `Name` property of the thread is set because this helps with debugging, as the name will show up in the debugger:

```
public void Start()
{
   ReadQuotes();
   listenerThread = new Thread(ListenerThread);
   listenerThread.IsBackground = true;
   listenerThread.Name = "Listener";
   listenerThread.Start();
}
```

The thread function `ListenerThread()` creates a `TcpListener` instance. The `AcceptSocket()` method waits for a client to connect. As soon as a client connects, `AcceptSocket()` returns with a socket associated with the client. Next, `GetRandomQuoteOfTheDay()` is called to send the returned random quote to the client using `socket.Send()`:

```
protected void ListenerThread()
{
   try
   {
      IPAddress ipAddress = IPAddress.Parse("127.0.0.1");
      listener = new TcpListener(ipAddress, port);
      listener.Start();
      while (true)
      {
         Socket clientSocket = listener.AcceptSocket();
         string message = GetRandomQuoteOfTheDay();
         UnicodeEncoding encoder = new UnicodeEncoding();
         byte[] buffer = encoder.GetBytes(message);
         clientSocket.Send(buffer, buffer.Length, 0);
         clientSocket.Close();
      }
   }
   catch (SocketException ex)
   {
      Console.WriteLine(ex.Message);
   }
}
```

In addition to the `Start()` method, the following methods are needed to control the service: `Stop()`, `Suspend()`, and `Resume()`:

```
        public void Stop()
        {
           listener.Stop();
        }
        public void Suspend()
        {
           listener.Stop();
        }
        public void Resume()
        {
           Start();
        }
```

Another method that will be publicly available is `RefreshQuotes()`. If the file containing the quotes changes, the file is re-read with this method:

```
        public void RefreshQuotes()
        {
           ReadQuotes();
        }
     }
  }
```

Before building a service around the server, it is useful to build a test program that creates just an instance of the `QuoteServer` and calls `Start()`. This way, you can test the functionality without the need to handle service-specific issues. This test server must be started manually, and you can easily walk through the code with a debugger.

The test program is a C# console application, `TestQuoteServer`. You need to reference the assembly of the `QuoteServer` class. The file containing the quotes must be copied to the directory `c:\ProCSharp\Services` (or you must change the argument in the constructor to specify where you have copied the file). After calling the constructor, the `Start()` method of the `QuoteServer` instance is called. `Start()` returns immediately after having created a thread, so the console application keeps running until `Return` is pressed:

```
        static void Main()
        {
           QuoteServer qs = new QuoteServer(
                 @"c:\ProCSharp\WindowsServices\quotes.txt", 4567);
           qs.Start();
           Console.WriteLine("Hit return to exit");
           Console.ReadLine();
           qs.Stop();
        }
```

Note that `QuoteServer` will be running on port 4567 on localhost using this program — you will have to use these settings in the client later.

TcpClient Example

The client is a simple WPF Windows application in which you can request quotes from the server. This application uses the `TcpClient` class to connect to the running server, and receives the returned message, displaying it in a text box (see Figure 23-5).

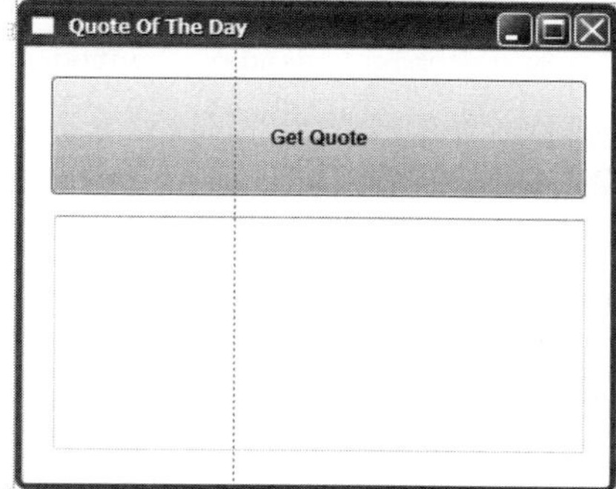

Figure 23-5

Server and port information to connect to the server is configured with settings of the application. You can add settings with the Settings tab inside the properties of the project (see Figure 23-6). Here, you can define the `ServerName` and `PortNumber` settings, and define some default values. From here, with the Scope set to User, the settings go into a user-specific configuration file, and every user of the application can have different settings. This Settings feature of Visual Studio also creates a `Settings` class so that the settings can be read and written with a strongly typed class.

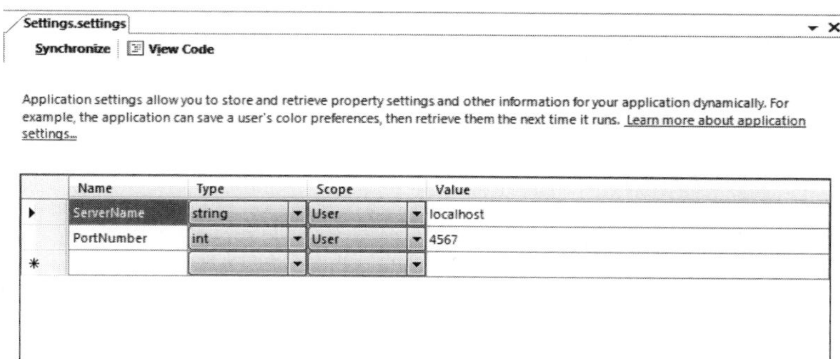

Figure 23-6

You need to add the following `using` directives to your code:

```
using System;
using System.Net.Sockets;
using System.Text;
using System.Windows;
using System.Windows.Input;
```

Within the constructor of the class `QuoteOfTheDayWindow`, you can define a handler method to the `Click` event of the button `buttonGetQuote`:

```
public QuoteOfTheDayWindow()
{
   InitializeComponent();
   this.buttonGetQuote.Click += new RoutedEventHandler(OnGetQuote);
}
```

The major functionality of the client lies in the handler for the click event of the Get Quote button:

```
protected void OnGetQuote(object sender, RoutedEventArgs e)
{
   Cursor currentCursor = this.Cursor;
   this.Cursor = Cursors.Wait;

   string serverName = Properties.Settings.Default.ServerName;
   int port = Properties.Settings.Default.PortNumber;

   TcpClient client = new TcpClient();
   NetworkStream stream = null;
   try
   {
      client.Connect(serverName, port);
      stream = client.GetStream();
      byte[] buffer = new Byte[1024];
      int received = stream.Read(buffer, 0, 1024);
      if (received <= 0)
      {
         return;
      }
     textQuote.Text = Encoding.Unicode.GetString(buffer).Trim('\0');
   }
   catch (SocketException ex)
   {
      MessageBox.Show(ex.Message, "Error Quote of the day"",
            MessageBoxButton.OK, MessageBoxImage.Error);
   }
   finally
   {
      if (stream != null)
      {
         stream.Close();
      }

      if (client.Connected)
      {
         client.Close();
      }
   }
   this.Cursor = currentCursor;
}
```

After starting the test server and this Windows application client, you can test the functionality. Figure 23-7 shows a successful run of this application.

Next, you implement the service functionality in the server. The program is already running, so what else do you need? Well, the server program should be automatically started at boot time without anyone logged on to the system. You want to control this by using service control programs.

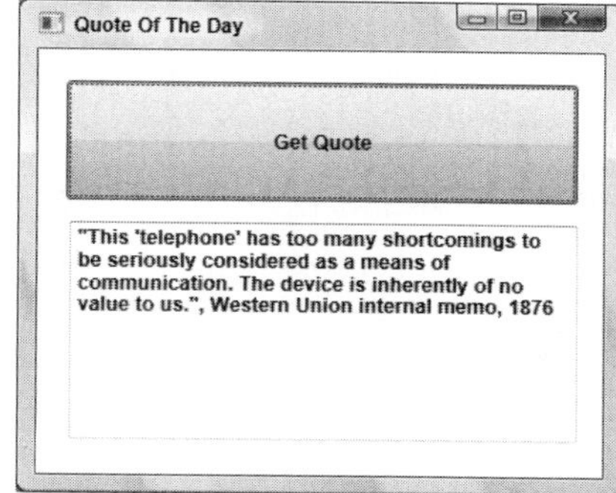

Figure 23-7

Windows Service Project

Using the new project wizard for C# Windows Services, you can now start to create a Windows Service. For the new service, use the name `QuoteService` (see Figure 23-8).

After you click the OK button to create the Windows Service application, you will see the Designer surface (just as with Windows Forms applications). However, you can't insert any Windows Forms components because the application cannot directly display anything on the screen. The Designer surface is used later in this chapter to add other components, such as performance counters and event logging.

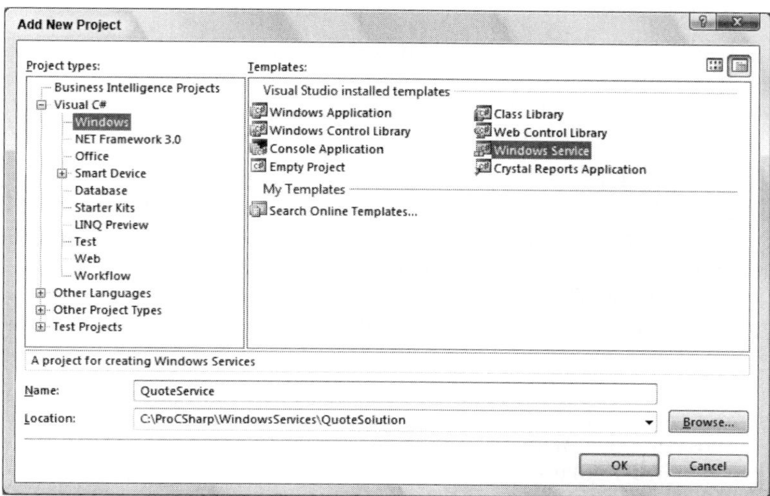

Figure 23-8

Selecting the properties of this service opens up the Properties editor window (see Figure 23-9).

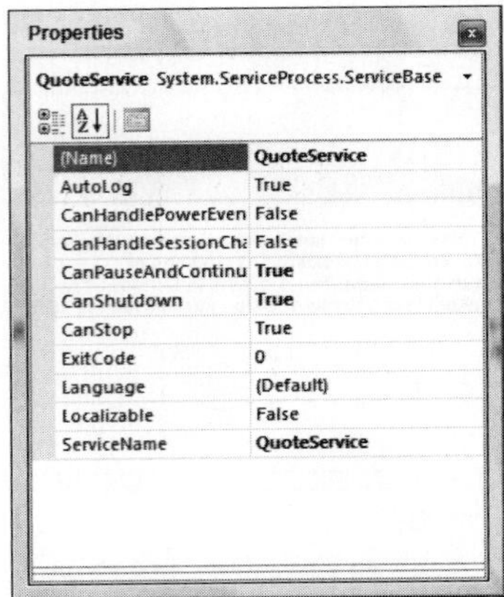

Figure 23-9

With the service properties, you can configure the following values:

- `AutoLog` specifies that events are automatically written to the event log for starting and stopping the service.
- `CanPauseAndContinue`, `CanShutdown`, and `CanStop` specify pause, continue, shut down, and stop requests.
- `ServiceName` is the name of the service written to the registry and is used to control the service.
- `CanHandleSessionChangeEvent` defines if the service can handle change events from a terminal server session.
- `CanHandlePowerEvent` is a very useful option for services running on a laptop or mobile devices. If this option is enabled, the service can react to low-power events, and change the behavior of the service accordingly.

> **The default service name is `WinService1`, regardless of what the project is called. You can install only one WinService1 service. If you get installation errors during your testing process, you might already have installed one WinService1 service. Therefore, make sure that you change the name of the service with the Properties editor to a more suitable name at the beginning of the service development.**

Changing these properties with the Properties editor sets the values of your `ServiceBase`-derived class in the `InitalizeComponent()` method. You already know this method from Windows Forms applications. It is used in a similar way with services.

A wizard generates the code, but change the file name to `QuoteService.cs`, the name of the namespace to `Wrox.ProCSharp.WinServices`, and the class name to `QuoteService`. The code of the service is discussed in detail shortly.

The ServiceBase Class

The `ServiceBase` class is the base class for all Windows Services developed with the .NET Framework. The class `QuoteService` is derived from `ServiceBase`; this class communicates with the SCM using an undocumented helper class, `System.ServiceProcess.NativeMethods`, which is just a wrapper class to the Win32 API calls. The class is private, so it cannot be used in your code.

The sequence diagram in Figure 23-10 shows the interaction of the SCM, the class `QuoteService`, and the classes from the `System.ServiceProcess` namespace. In the sequence diagram, you can see the lifelines of objects vertically and the communication going on horizontally. The communication is time-ordered from top to bottom.

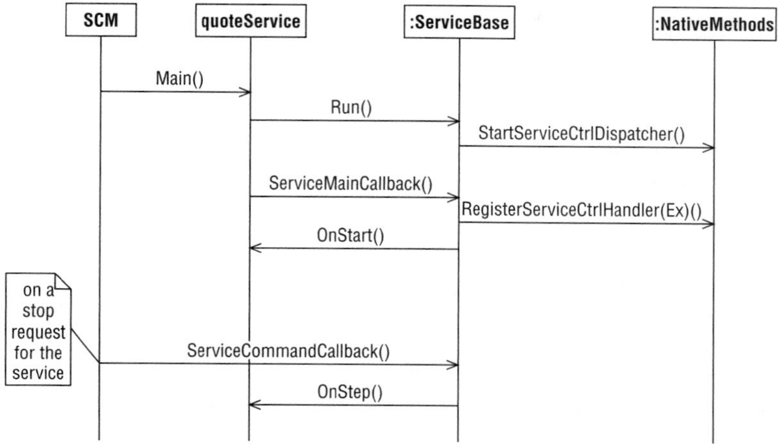

Figure 23-10

The SCM starts the process of a service that should be started. At startup, the `Main()` method is called. In the `Main()` method of the sample service, the `Run()` method of the base class `ServiceBase` is called. `Run()` registers the method `ServiceMainCallback()` using `NativeMethods.StartServiceCtrlDispatcher()` in the SCM and writes an entry to the event log.

Next, the SCM calls the registered method `ServiceMainCallback()` in the service program. `ServiceMainCallback()` itself registers the handler in the SCM using `NativeMethods.RegisterServiceCtrlHandler[Ex]()` and sets the status of the service in the SCM. Then the `OnStart()` method is called. In `OnStart()`, you need to implement the startup code. If `OnStart()` is successful, the string "Service started successfully" is written to the event log.

The handler is implemented in the `ServiceCommandCallback()` method. The SCM calls this method when changes are requested from the service. The `ServiceCommandCallback()` method routes the requests further to `OnPause()`, `OnContinue()`, `OnStop()`, `OnCustomCommand()`, and `OnPowerEvent()`.

Main Function

This section looks into the application wizard–generated main function of the service process. In the main function, an array of `ServiceBase` classes, `ServicesToRun`, is declared. One instance of the `QuoteService` class is created and passed as the first element to the `ServicesToRun` array. If more than one service should run inside this service process, it is necessary to add more instances of the specific service classes to the array. This array is then passed to the static `Run()` method of the `ServiceBase` class. With the `Run()` method of `ServiceBase`, you are giving the SCM references to the entry points of your services. The main thread of your service process is now blocked and waits for the service to terminate.

Here is the automatically generated code:

```
/// <summary>
/// The main entry point for the process
/// </summary>
static void Main()
{
   ServiceBase[] ServicesToRun;
   ServicesToRun = new ServiceBase[]
   {
      new QuoteService()
   };
   ServiceBase.Run(ServicesToRun);
}
```

If there is only a single service in the process, the array can be removed; the `Run()` method accepts a single object derived from the class `ServiceBase`, so the `Main()` method can be reduced to this:

```
System.ServiceProcess.ServiceBase.Run(new QuoteService());
```

The service program `Services.exe` includes multiple services. If you have a similar service, where more than one service is running in a single process in which you must initialize some shared state for multiple services, the shared initialization must be done before the `Run()` method. With the `Run()` method, the main thread is blocked until the service process is stopped, and any following instructions would not be reached before the end of the service.

The initialization shouldn't take longer than 30 seconds. If the initialization code were to take longer than this, the SCM would assume that the service startup failed. You need to take into account the slowest machines where this service should run within the 30-second limit. If the initialization takes longer, you could start the initialization in a different thread so that the main thread calls `Run()` in time. An event object can then be used to signal that the thread has completed its work.

Service Start

At service start, the `OnStart()` method is called. In this method, you can start the previously created socket server. You must reference the `QuoteServer` assembly for the use of the `QuoteService`. The thread calling `OnStart()` cannot be blocked; this method must return to the caller, which is the `ServiceMainCallback()` method of the `ServiceBase` class. The `ServiceBase` class registers the handler and informs the SCM that the service started successfully after calling `OnStart()`:

```
protected override void OnStart(string[] args)
{
   quoteServer = new QuoteServer(
         @"c:\ProCSharp\WindowsServices\quotes.txt", 5678);
   quoteServer.Start();
}
```

The `quoteServer` variable is declared as a private member in the class:

```
namespace Wrox.ProCSharp.WinServices
{
   public partial class QuoteService : ServiceBase
   {
      private QuoteServer quoteServer;
```

Handler Methods

When the service is stopped, the `OnStop()` method is called. You should stop the service functionality in this method:

```
protected override void OnStop()
{
   quoteServer.Stop();
}
```

In addition to `OnStart()` and `OnStop()`, you can override the following handlers in the service class:

- `OnPause()` is called when the service should be paused.
- `OnContinue()` is called when the service should return to normal operation after being paused. To make it possible for the overridden methods `OnPause()` and `OnContinue()` to be called, the `CanPauseAndContinue` property must be set to `true`.
- `OnShutdown()` is called when Windows is undergoing system shutdown. Normally, the behavior of this method should be similar to the `OnStop()` implementation; if more time is needed for a shutdown, you can request additional time. Similarly to `OnPause()` and `OnContinue()`, a property must be set to enable this behavior: `CanShutdown` must be set to `true`.
- `OnPowerEvent()` is called when the power status of the system changes. The information about the change of the power status is in the argument of type `PowerBroadcastStatus`. `PowerBroadcastStatus` is an enumeration with values such as `Battery Low` and `PowerStatusChange`. Here, you will also get information if the system would like to suspend (`QuerySuspend`), where you can approve or deny the suspend. You can read more about power events later in this chapter.
- `OnCustomCommand()` is a handler that can serve custom commands that are sent by a service control program. The method signature of `OnCustomCommand()` has an `int` argument where you get the custom command number. The value can be in the range from 128 to 256; values below 128 are system-reserved values. In your service, you are re-reading the quotes file with the custom command 128:

```
protected override void OnPause()
{
   quoteServer.Suspend();
}

protected override void OnContinue()
{
   quoteServer.Resume();
}

protected override void OnShutdown()
{
   OnStop();
}

public const int commandRefresh = 128;
protected override void OnCustomCommand(int command)
{
   switch (command)
   {
      case commandRefresh:
         quoteServer.RefreshQuotes();
         break;

      default:
         break;
   }
}
```

Threading and Services

As stated earlier, the SCM will assume that the service failed if the initialization takes too long. To deal with this, you need to create a thread.

The `OnStart()` method in your service class must return in time. If you call a blocking method like `AcceptSocket()` from the `TcpListener` class, you need to start a thread for doing this. With a networking server that deals with multiple clients, a thread pool is also very useful. `AcceptSocket()` should receive the call and hand the processing off to another thread from the pool. This way, no one waits for the execution of code and the system seems responsive.

Service Installation

A service must be configured in the registry. All services can be found in `HKEY_LOCAL_MACHINE\System\CurrentControlSet\Services`. You can view the registry entries by using `regedit`. The type of the service, display name, path to the executable, startup configuration, and so on are all found here. Figure 23-11 shows the registry configuration of the W3SVC service.

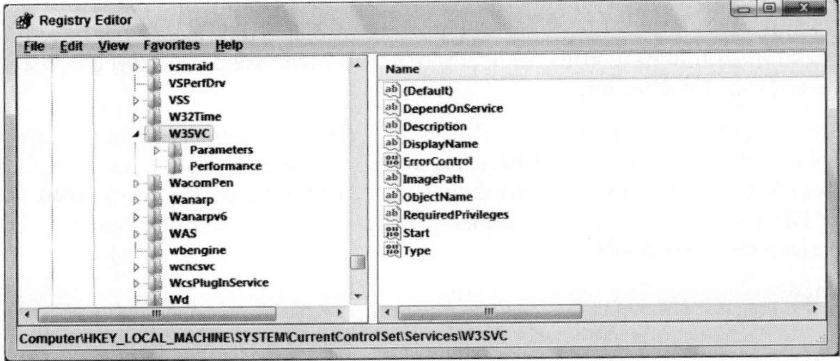

Figure 23-11

This configuration can be done by using the installer classes from the `System.ServiceProcess` namespace, as discussed in the following section.

Installation Program

You can add an installation program to the service by switching to the design view with Visual Studio and then selecting the Add Installer option from the context menu. With this option, a new `ProjectInstaller` class is created, and a `ServiceInstaller` and a `ServiceProcessInstaller` instance are created.

Figure 23-12 shows the class diagram of the installer classes for services.

With this diagram in mind, let's go through the source code in the file `ProjectInstaller.cs` that was created with the Add Installer option.

The Installer Class

The class `ProjectInstaller` is derived from `System.Configuration.Install.Installer`. This is the base class for all custom installers. With the `Installer` class, it is possible to build transaction-based installations. With a transaction-based installation, it is possible to roll back to the previous state if the installation fails, and any changes made by this installation up to that point will be undone. As you can see in Figure 23-12, the `Installer` class has `Install()`, `Uninstall()`, `Commit()`, and `Rollback()` methods, and they are called from installation programs.

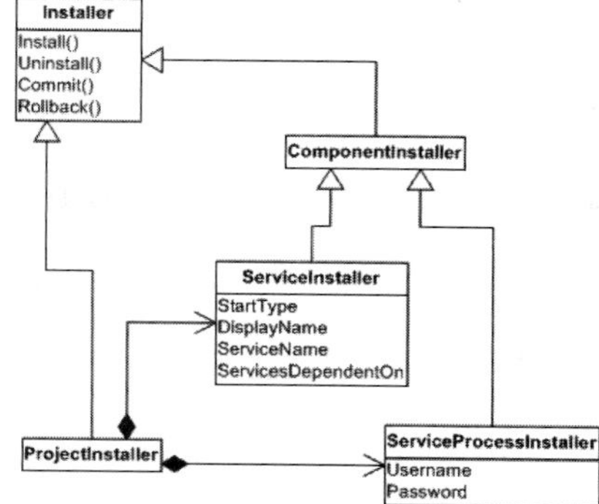

Figure 23-12

The attribute `[RunInstaller(true)]` means that the class `ProjectInstaller` should be invoked when installing an assembly. Custom action installers, as well as `installutil.exe` (which is used later in this chapter), check for this attribute.

Similarly to Windows Forms applications, `InitializeComponent()` is called inside the constructor of the `ProjectInstaller` class:

```
using System.ComponentModel;
using System.Configuration.Install;

namespace Wrox.ProCSharp.WinServices
{
   [RunInstaller(true)]
   public partial class ProjectInstaller : Installer
   {
      public ProjectInstaller()
      {
         InitializeComponent();
      }
   }
```

The ServiceProcessInstaller and ServiceInstaller Classes

Within the implementation of `InitializeComponent()`, instances of the `ServiceProcessInstaller` class and the `ServiceInstaller` class are created. Both of these classes derive from the `ComponentInstaller` class, which itself derives from `Installer`.

Classes derived from `ComponentInstaller` can be used with an installation process. Remember that a service process can include more than one service. The `ServiceProcessInstaller` class is used for the configuration of the process that defines values for all services in this process, and the `ServiceInstaller` class is for the configuration of the service, so one instance of `ServiceInstaller` is required for each service. If three services are inside the process, you need to add `ServiceInstaller` objects — three `ServiceInstaller` instances are needed in that case:

```
partial class ProjectInstaller
{
   /// <summary>
   /// Required designer variable.
   /// </summary>
```

(continued)

(continued)

```
        private System.ComponentModel.Container components = null;

        /// <summary>
        /// Required method for Designer support - do not modify
        /// the contents of this method with the code editor.
        /// </summary>
        private void InitializeComponent()
        {
           this.serviceProcessInstaller1 =
                       new System.ServiceProcess.ServiceProcessInstaller();
           this.serviceInstaller1 =
                       new System.ServiceProcess.ServiceInstaller();
           //
           // serviceProcessInstaller1
           //
           this.serviceProcessInstaller1.Password = null;
           this.serviceProcessInstaller1.Username = null;
           //
           // serviceInstaller1
           //
           this.serviceInstaller1.ServiceName = "QuoteService";
           //
           // ProjectInstaller
           //
           this.Installers.AddRange(
              new System.Configuration.Install.Installer[]
                 {this.serviceProcessInstaller1,
                  this.serviceInstaller1});
        }

        private System.ServiceProcess.ServiceProcessInstaller
                       serviceProcessInstaller1;
        private System.ServiceProcess.ServiceInstaller serviceInstaller1;

    }
```

`ServiceProcessInstaller` installs an executable that implements the class `ServiceBase`. `ServiceProcessInstaller` has properties for the complete process. The following table explains the properties shared by all the services inside the process.

Property	Description
`Username, Password`	Indicates the user account under which the service runs if the `Account` property is set to `ServiceAccount.User`.
`Account`	With this property, you can specify the account type of the service.
`HelpText`	`HelpText` is a read-only property that returns the help text for setting the username and password.

The process that is used to run the service can be specified with the `Account` property of the `ServiceProcessInstaller` class using the `ServiceAccount` enumeration. The following table explains the different values of the `Account` property.

Value	Meaning
`LocalSystem`	Setting this value specifies that the service uses a highly privileged user account on the local system, but this account presents an anonymous user to the network. Thus, it doesn't have rights on the network.
`LocalService`	This account type presents the computer's credentials to any remote server.
`NetworkService`	Similarly to `LocalService`, this value specifies that the computer's credentials are passed to remote servers, but unlike `LocalService`, such a service acts as a nonprivileged user on the local system. As the name implies, this account should be used only for services that need resources from the network.
`User`	Setting the `Account` property to `ServiceAccount.User` means that you can define the account that should be used from the service.

`ServiceInstaller` is the class needed for every service; it has the following properties for each service inside a process: `StartType`, `DisplayName`, `ServiceName`, and `ServicesDependentOn`, as described in the following table.

Property	Description
`StartType`	The `StartType` property indicates whether the service is manually or automatically started. Possible values are `ServiceStartMode.Automatic`, `ServiceStartMode.Manual`, and `ServiceStartMode.Disabled`. With `ServiceStartMode.Disabled`, the service cannot be started. This option is useful for services that shouldn't be started on a system. You might want to set the option to `Disabled` if, for example, a required hardware controller is not available.
`DisplayName`	`DisplayName` is the friendly name of the service that is displayed to the user. This name is also used by management tools that control and monitor the service.
`ServiceName`	`ServiceName` is the name of the service. This value must be identical to the `ServiceName` property of the `ServiceBase` class in the service program. This name associates the configuration of the `ServiceInstaller` to the required service program.
`ServicesDependentOn`	Specifies an array of services that must be started before this service can be started. When the service is started, all these dependent services are started automatically, and then your service will start.

If you change the name of the service in the `ServiceBase`-derived class, be sure to also change the `ServiceName` property in the `ServiceInstaller` object!

In the testing phases, set `StartType` *to* `Manual`*. This way, if you can't stop the service (for example, when it has a bug), you still have the possibility to reboot the system. But if you have* `StartType` *set to* `Automatic`*, the service would be started automatically with the reboot! You can change this configuration at a later time when you are sure that it works.*

The ServiceInstallerDialog Class

Another installer class in the `System.ServiceProcess.Design` namespace is `ServiceInstallerDialog`. This class can be used if you want the System Administrator to enter the username and password during the installation.

If you set the `Account` property of the class `ServiceProcessInstaller` to `ServiceAccount.User` and the `Username` and `Password` properties to `null`, you will see the Set Service Login dialog box at installation time (see Figure 23-13). You can also cancel the installation at this point.

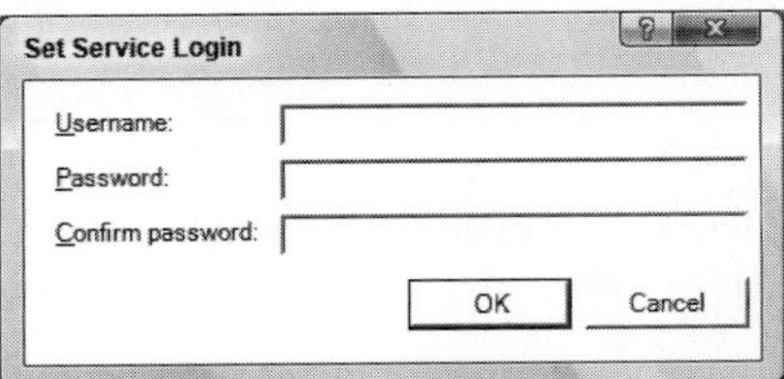

Figure 23-13

installutil

After adding the installer classes to the project, you can use the `installutil.exe` utility to install and uninstall the service. This utility can be used to install any assembly that has an `Installer` class. The `installutil.exe` utility calls the method `Install()` of the class that derives from the `Installer` class for installation, and `Uninstall()` for the *uninstallation*.

The command-line inputs for the installation and uninstallation of our service are:

```
installutil quoteservice.exe
installutil /u quoteservice.exe
```

If the installation fails, be sure to check the installation log files, `InstallUtil.InstallLog` and `<servicename>.InstallLog`. Often, you can find very useful information, such as "The specified service already exists."

Client

After the service has been successfully installed, you can start the service manually from the Services MMC (see the next section for further details), and then you can start the client application. Figure 23-14 shows the client accessing the service.

Monitoring and Controlling the Service

To monitor and control services, you can use the Services MMC snap-in that is part of the Computer Management administration tool. Every Windows system also has a command-line utility, `net.exe`, which allows you to control services. Another command-line utility is `sc.exe`. This utility has much

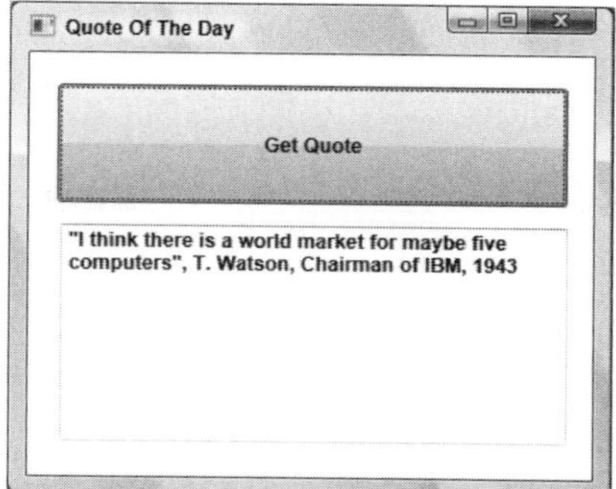

Figure 23-14

more functionality than `net.exe`, which is part of the Platform SDK. In this section, you create a small Windows application that makes use of the `System.ServiceProcess.ServiceController` class to monitor and control services.

MMC Computer Management

Using the Services snap-in to the Microsoft Management Console (MMC), you can view the status of all services (see Figure 23-15). It is also possible to send control requests to services to stop, enable, or disable them, as well as to change their configuration. The Services snap-in is a service control program as well as a service configuration program.

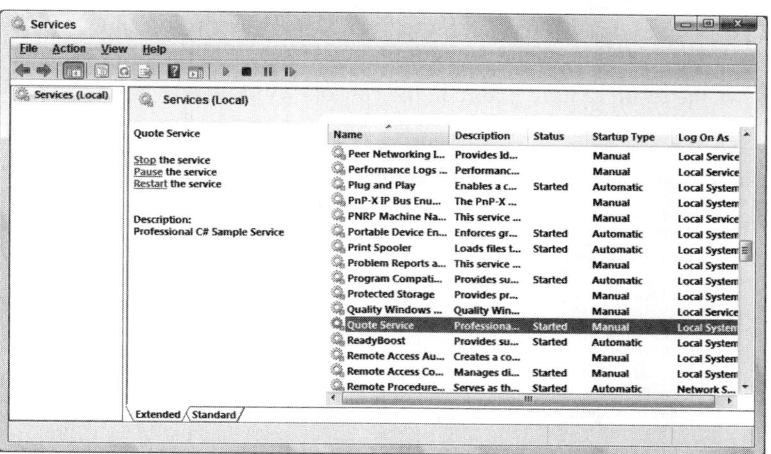

Figure 23-15

When you double-click QuoteService, you will get the Properties dialog box shown in Figure 23-16. This dialog box enables you to view the service name, the description, the path to the executable, the startup type, and the status. The service is currently started. The account for the service process can be changed with the Log On tab in this dialog.

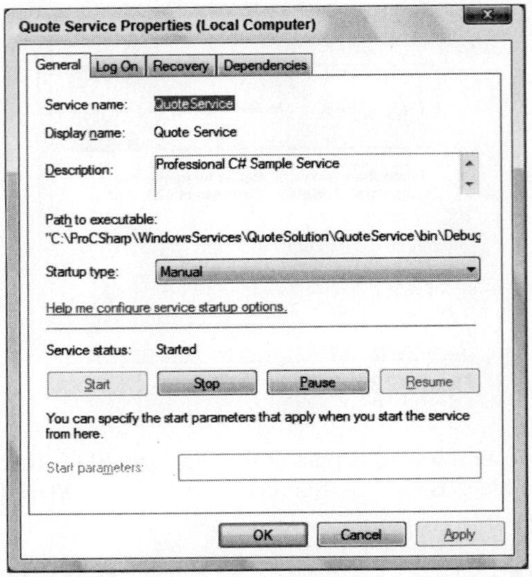

Figure 23-16

net.exe

The Services snap-in is easy to use, but the system administrator cannot automate it because it is not usable within an administrative script. To control services, you can use the command-line utility `net.exe`: `net start` shows all running services, `net start servicename` starts a service, and `net stop servicename` sends a stop request to the service. It is also possible to pause and to continue a service with `net pause` and `net continue` (only if the service allows it, of course).

Figure 23-17 shows the result of `net start` in the console window.

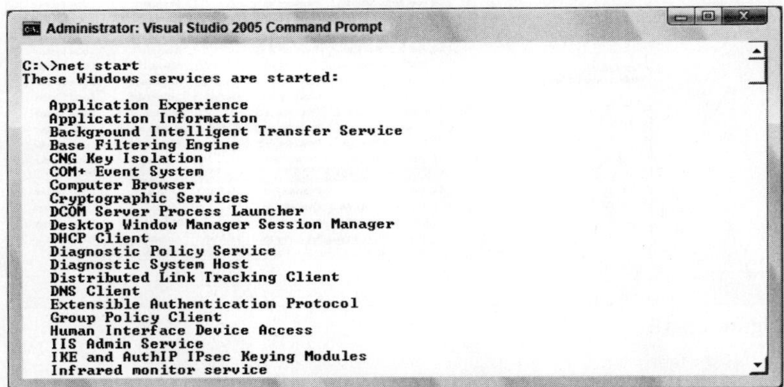
Administrator: Visual Studio 2005 Command Prompt
C:\>net start
These Windows services are started:
Application Experience
Application Information
Background Intelligent Transfer Service
Base Filtering Engine
CNG Key Isolation
COM+ Event System
Computer Browser
Cryptographic Services
DCOM Server Process Launcher
Desktop Window Manager Session Manager
DHCP Client
Diagnostic Policy Service
Diagnostic System Host
Distributed Link Tracking Client
DNS Client
Extensible Authentication Protocol
Group Policy Client
Human Interface Device Access
IIS Admin Service
IKE and AuthIP IPsec Keying Modules
Infrared monitor service

Figure 23-17

sc.exe

There is a little-known utility delivered as part of the operating system: `sc.exe`.

sc.exe is a great tool to play with services. Much more can be done with sc.exe than with the net.exe utility. With sc.exe, it is possible to check the actual status of a service, or configure, remove, and add services, as Figure 23-18 shows. This tool also facilitates the deinstallation of the service, if it fails to function correctly.

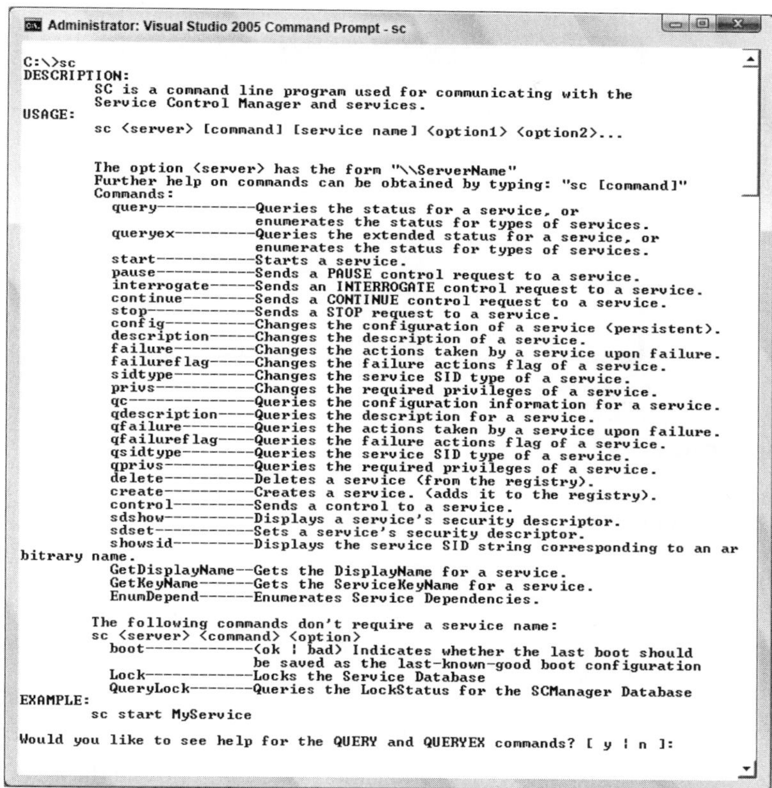

Figure 23-18

Visual Studio Server Explorer

It is also possible to control services using the Server Explorer within Visual Studio; Services is below Servers and the name of your computer. By selecting a service and opening the context menu, a service can be started and stopped. This context menu can also be used to add a ServiceController class to the project. To control a specific service in your application, drag and drop a service from the Server Explorer to the Designer: a ServiceController instance is added to the application. The properties of this object are automatically set to access the selected service, and the assembly System.ServiceProcess is referenced. You can use this instance to control a service in the same way you can with the application that you develop in the next section.

ServiceController Class

In this section, you create a small Windows application that uses the ServiceController class to monitor and control Windows Services.

Create a WPF application with a user interface as shown in Figure 23-19. The main window of this application has a list box to show all services, four text boxes to display the display name, status, type, and name of the service, and six buttons. Four buttons are used to send control events, one button for a refresh of the list, and one button to exit the application.

You can read more about WPF in Chapter 34, "Windows Presentation Foundation."

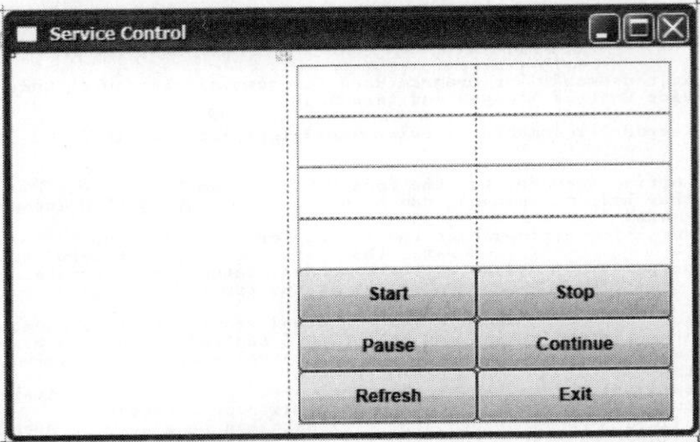

Figure 23-19

Monitoring the Service

With the `ServiceController` class, you can get the information about each service. The following table shows the properties of the `ServiceController` class.

Property	Description
`CanPauseAndContinue`	Returns `true` if pause and continue requests can be sent to the service.
`CanShutdown`	Returns `true` if the service has a handler for a system shutdown.
`CanStop`	Returns `true` if the service is stoppable.
`DependentServices`	Returns a collection of dependent services. If the service is stopped, then all dependent services are stopped beforehand.
`ServicesDependentOn`	Returns a collection of the services that this service depends on.
`DisplayName`	Specifies the name that should be displayed for this service.
`MachineName`	Specifies the name of the machine that the service runs on.
`ServiceName`	Specifies the name of the service.
`ServiceType`	Specifies the type of the service. The service can be run inside a shared process where more than one service uses the same process (`Win32ShareProcess`), or run in such a way that there is just one service in a process (`Win32OwnProcess`). If the service can interact with the desktop, the type is `InteractiveProcess`.
`Status`	Specifies the status of the service. The status can be running, stopped, paused, or in some intermediate mode like start pending, stop pending, and so on. The status values are defined in the enumeration `ServiceControllerStatus`.

In the sample application, the properties DisplayName, ServiceName, ServiceType, and Status are used to display the service information. Also, CanPauseAndContinue and CanStop are used to enable or disable the Pause, Continue, and Stop buttons.

To get all the needed information for the user interface, the class ServiceControllerInfo is created. This class can be used for data binding and offers status information, the name of the service, the service type, and the information about which buttons to control the service should be enabled or disabled.

> *Because the class* System.ServiceProcess.ServiceController *is used, you must reference the assembly* System.ServiceProcess.

ServiceControllerInfo contains an embedded ServiceController that is set with the constructor of the ServiceControllerInfo class. There is also a read-only property Controller to access the embedded ServiceController.

```
public class ServiceControllerInfo
{
   private ServiceController controller;

   public ServiceControllerInfo(ServiceController controller)
   {
      this.controller = controller;
   }

   public ServiceController Controller
   {
      get { return controller; }
   }
```

To display current information about the service, the ServiceControllerInfo class has the read-only properties DisplayName, ServiceName, ServiceTypeName, and ServiceStatusName. The implementation of the properties DisplayName and ServiceName just accesses the properties DisplayName and ServiceName of the underlying ServiceController class. With the implementation of the properties ServiceTypeName and ServiceStatusName, more work is done: The status and type of the service cannot be returned that easily because a string should be displayed instead of a number, which is what the ServiceController class returns. The property ServiceTypeName returns a string that represents the type of the service. The ServiceType you get from the property ServiceController.ServiceType represents a set of flags that can be combined by using the bitwise OR operator. The InteractiveProcess bit can be set together with Win32OwnProcess and Win32ShareProcess. So, first it is checked if the InteractiveProcess bit is set before continuing to check for the other values. With services, the string returned will be "Win32 Service Process" or "Win32 Shared Process":

```
   public string ServiceTypeName
   {
      get
      {
         ServiceType type = controller.ServiceType;
         string serviceTypeName = "";
         if ((type & ServiceType.InteractiveProcess) != 0)
         {
            serviceTypeName = "Interactive ";
            type -= ServiceType.InteractiveProcess;
         }
         switch (type)
```

(continued)

(continued)

```
            {
               case ServiceType.Adapter:
                  serviceTypeName += "Adapter";
                  break;

               case ServiceType.FileSystemDriver:
               case ServiceType.KernelDriver:
               case ServiceType.RecognizerDriver:
                  serviceTypeName += "Driver";
                  break;

               case ServiceType.Win32OwnProcess:
                  serviceTypeName += "Win32 Service Process";
                  break;

               case ServiceType.Win32ShareProcess:
                  serviceTypeName += "Win32 Shared Process";
                  break;

               default:
                  serviceTypeName += "unknown type " + type.ToString();
                  break;
            }
            return serviceTypeName;
         }
      }

      public string ServiceStatusName
      {
         get
         {
            switch (controller.Status)
            {
               case ServiceControllerStatus.ContinuePending:
                  return "Continue Pending";
               case ServiceControllerStatus.Paused:
                  return "Paused";
               case ServiceControllerStatus.PausePending:
                  return "Pause Pending";
               case ServiceControllerStatus.StartPending:
                  return "Start Pending";
               case ServiceControllerStatus.Running:
                  return "Running";
               case ServiceControllerStatus.Stopped:
                  return "Stopped";
               case ServiceControllerStatus.StopPending:
                  return "Stop Pending";
               default:
                  return "Unknown status";
            }
         }
      }

      public string DisplayName
```

```
{
   get { return controller.DisplayName; }
}

public string ServiceName
{
   get { return controller.ServiceName; }
}
```

The ServiceControllerInfo class has some more properties to enable the Start, Stop, Pause, and Continue buttons: EnableStart, EnableStop, EnablePause, and EnableContinue. These properties return a Boolean value according to the current status of the service:

```
public bool EnableStart
{
   get
   {
      return controller.Status == ServiceControllerStatus.Stopped;
   }
}

public bool EnableStop
{
   get
   {
      return controller.Status == ServiceControllerStatus.Running;
   }
}

public bool EnablePause
{
   get
   {
      return controller.Status == ServiceControllerStatus.Running &&
            controller.CanPauseAndContinue;
   }
}

public bool EnableContinue
{
   get
   {
      return controller.Status == ServiceControllerStatus.Paused;
   }
 }
}
```

In the ServiceControlWindow class, the method RefreshServiceList() gets all the services using ServiceController.GetServices() for display in the list box. The GetServices() method returns an array of ServiceController instances representing all Windows Services installed on the operating system. The ServiceController class also has the static method GetDevices() that returns a ServiceController array representing all device drivers. The returned array is sorted with the help of the generic Array.Sort() method. The sort is done by the DisplayName as is defined with the anonymous method that is passed to the Sort() method. Using Array.ConvertAll(), the ServiceController instances are converted to the type ServiceControllerInfo. Here, an anonymous method is passed that invokes the `ServiceControllerInfo` constructor for every `ServiceController` object. Last, the `ServiceControllerInfo` array is assigned to the `DataContext` property of the window for data binding.

```
protected void RefreshServiceList()
{
   ServiceController[] services = ServiceController.GetServices();

   Array.Sort<ServiceController>(services,
      delegate(ServiceController s1, ServiceController s2)
      {
         return s1.DisplayName.CompareTo(s2.DisplayName);
      });
   ServiceControllerInfo[] serviceInfo =
      Array.ConvertAll<ServiceController, ServiceControllerInfo>(
      services,
      delegate(ServiceController controller)
      {
         return new ServiceControllerInfo(controller);
      });

  this.DataContext = serviceInfo;
}
```

The method `RefreshServiceList()` to get all the services in the list box is called within the constructor of the class `ServiceControlWindow`. The constructor also defines the event handler for the `Click` event of the buttons:

```
public ServiceControlWindow()
{
   InitializeComponent();

   buttonStart.Click += OnServiceCommand;
   buttonStop.Click += OnServiceCommand;
   buttonPause.Click += OnServiceCommand;
   buttonContinue.Click += OnServiceCommand;
   buttonRefresh.Click += OnRefresh;
   buttonExit.Click += OnExit;

   RefreshServiceList();
}
```

Now, you can define the XAML code to bind the information to the controls.

First, a `DataTemplate` is defined for the information that is shown inside the `ListBox`. The `ListBox` will contain a `Label` where the `Content` is bound to the `DisplayName` property of the data source. As you bind an array of `ServiceControllerInfo` objects, the property `DisplayName` is defined with the `ServiceControllerInfo` class:

```
<Window.Resources>
  <DataTemplate x:Key="listTemplate">
    <Label Content="{Binding Path=DisplayName}"/>
  </DataTemplate>
</Window.Resources>
```

The `ListBox` that is placed in the left side of the Window sets the `ItemsSource` property to `{Binding}`. This way, the data that is shown in the list is received from the `DataContext` property that was set in the `RefreshServiceList()` method. The `ItemTemplate` property references the resource `listTemplate` that is defined with the `DataTemplate` shown earlier. The property `IsSynchronizedWithCurrentItem` is set to `True` so that the `TextBox` and `Button` controls that are inside the same Window are bound to the current item that is selected with the `ListBox`.

```
<ListBox Grid.Row="0" Grid.Column="0" HorizontalAlignment="Left"
      Name="listBoxServices" VerticalAlignment="Top"
      ItemsSource="{Binding}"
      ItemTemplate="{StaticResource listTemplate}"
      IsSynchronizedWithCurrentItem="True">
</ListBox>
```

With the `TextBox` controls, the `Text` property is bound to the corresponding property of the `ServiceControllerInfo` instance. Whether the `Button` controls are enabled or disabled is also defined from the data binding by binding the `IsEnabled` property to the corresponding properties of the `ServiceControllerInfo` instance that return a Boolean value:

```
<TextBox Grid.Row="0" Grid.ColumnSpan="2" Name="textDisplayName"
    Text="{Binding Path=DisplayName, Mode=OneTime}" />
<TextBox Grid.Row="1" Grid.ColumnSpan="2" Name="textStatus"
    Text="{Binding Path=ServiceStatusName, Mode=OneTime}" />
<TextBox Grid.Row="2" Grid.ColumnSpan="2" Name="textType"
    Text="{Binding Path=ServiceTypeName, Mode=OneTime}" />
<TextBox Grid.Row="3" Grid.ColumnSpan="2" Name="textName"
    Text="{Binding Path=ServiceName, Mode=OneTime}" />
<Button Grid.Row="4" Grid.Column="0" Name="buttonStart" Content="Start"
    IsEnabled="{Binding Path=EnableStart, Mode=OneTime}" />
<Button Grid.Row="4" Grid.Column="1" Name="buttonStop" Content="Stop"
    IsEnabled="{Binding Path=EnableStop, Mode=OneTime}" />
<Button Grid.Row="5" Grid.Column="0" Name="buttonPause" Content="Pause"
    IsEnabled="{Binding Path=EnablePause, Mode=OneTime}" />
<Button Grid.Row="5" Grid.Column="1" Name="buttonContinue"
    Content="Continue" IsEnabled="{Binding Path=EnableContinue,
    Mode=OneTime}" />
```

Controlling the Service

With the `ServiceController` class, you can also send control requests to the service. The following table explains the methods that can be applied.

Method	Description
`Start()`	`Start()` tells the SCM that the service should be started. In the example service program, `OnStart()` is called.
`Stop()`	`Stop()` calls `OnStop()` in the example service program with the help of the SCM if the property `CanStop` is `true` in the service class.
`Pause()`	`Pause()` calls `OnPause()` if the property `CanPauseAndContinue` is `true`.
`Continue()`	`Continue()` calls `OnContinue()` if the property `CanPauseAndContinue` is `true`.
`ExecuteCommand()`	With `ExecuteCommand()`, it is possible to send a custom command to the service.

The following code controls the services. Because the code for starting, stopping, suspending, and pausing is similar, only one handler is used for the four buttons:

```
protected void OnServiceCommand(object sender, RoutedEventArgs e)
{
   Cursor oldCursor = Cursor.Current;
   Cursor.Current = Cursors.Wait;
   ServiceControllerInfo si =
         (ServiceControllerInfo)listBoxServices.SelectedItem;
   if (sender == this.buttonStart)
   {
      si.Controller.Start();
      si.Controller.WaitForStatus(ServiceControllerStatus.Running);
   }
   else if (sender == this.buttonStop)
   {
      si.Controller.Stop();
      si.Controller.WaitForStatus(ServiceControllerStatus.Stopped);
   }
   else if (sender == this.buttonPause)
   {
      si.Controller.Pause();
      si.Controller.WaitForStatus(ServiceControllerStatus.Paused);
   }
   else if (sender == this.buttonContinue)
   {
      si.Controller.Continue();
      si.Controller.WaitForStatus(ServiceControllerStatus.Running);
   }
   int index =listBoxServices.SelectedIndex;
   RefreshServiceList();
   listBoxServices.SelectedIndex = index;
   Cursor.Current = oldCursor;
}

protected void OnExit(object sender, RoutedEventArgs e)
{
   Application.Current.Shutdown();
}

protected void OnRefresh_Click(object sender, RoutedEventArgs e)
{
   RefreshServiceList();
}
```

Because the action of controlling the services can take some time, the cursor is switched to the wait cursor in the first statement. Then a `ServiceController` method is called depending on the pressed button. With the `WaitForStatus()` method, you are waiting to check that the service changes the status to the requested value, but you only wait 10 seconds maximum. After this time, the information in the `ListBox` is refreshed, and the same service as before is selected, and the new status of this service is displayed. Figure 23-20 shows the completed, running application.

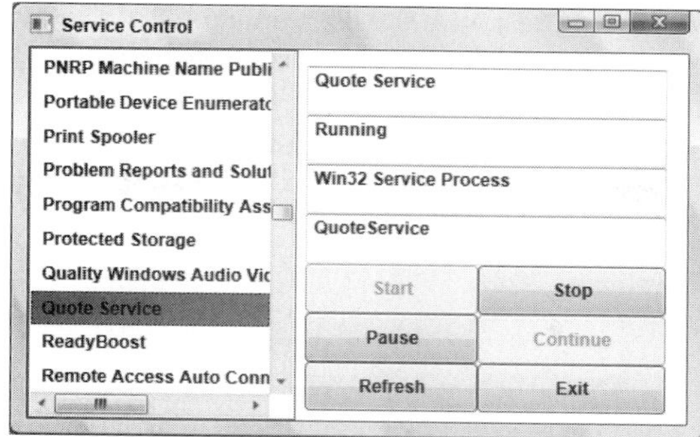

Figure 23-20

Troubleshooting

Troubleshooting services is different from troubleshooting normal applications. This section touches on some service issues, problems specific to interactive services, and event logging.

The best way to start building a service is to create an assembly with the functionality you want and a test client, before the service is actually created. Here, you can do normal debugging and error handling. As soon as the application is running, you can build a service by using this assembly. Of course, there might still be problems with the service:

- Don't display errors in a message box from the service (except for interactive services that are running on the client system). Instead, use the event logging service to write errors to the event log. Of course, in the client application that uses the service, you can display a message box to inform the user about errors.
- The service cannot be started from within a debugger, but a debugger can be attached to the running service process. Open the solution with the source code of the service and set breakpoints. From the Visual Studio Debug menu, select Processes and attach the running process of the service.
- The Performance Monitor can be used to monitor the activity of services. You can add your own performance objects to the service. This can add some useful information for debugging. For example, with the Quote service, you could set up an object to give the total number of quotes returned, the time it takes to initialize, and so on.

Interactive Services

When an interactive service runs with a logged-on user, it can be helpful to display message boxes to the user. If the service should run on a server that is locked inside a computer room, the service should never display a message box. When you open a message box to wait for some user input, the user input probably won't happen for some days because nobody is looking at the server in the computer room. Even worse, if the service isn't configured as an interactive service, the message box opens up on a different, hidden, window station. In this case, no one can respond to that message box because it is hidden, and the service is blocked.

> **Never open dialog boxes for services running on a server system. Nobody will respond to them.**

In cases when you really want to interact with the user, an interactive service can be configured. Some examples of such interactive services are the Print Spooler, which displays paper-out messages to the user, and the NetMeeting Remote Desktop Sharing service.

To configure an interactive service, you must set the option "Allow service to interact with desktop" in the Services configuration tool (see Figure 23-21). This changes the type of the service by adding the `SERVICE_INTERACTIVE_PROCESS` flag to the type.

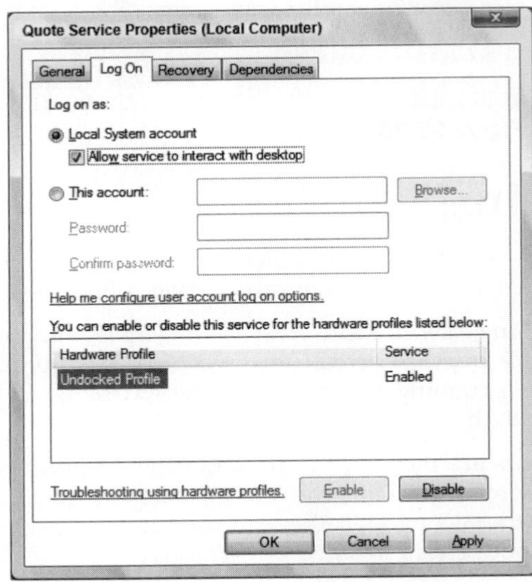

Figure 23-21

Event Logging

Services can report errors and other information by adding events to the event log. A service class derived from `ServiceBase` automatically logs events when the `AutoLog` property is set to `true`. The `ServiceBase` class checks this property and writes a log entry at start, stop, pause, and continue requests.

Figure 23-22 shows an example of a log entry from a service.

You can read more about event logging and how to write custom events in Chapter 18, "Tracing and Events."

Power Events

The Windows Service can react when the power status changes. One example of a power event is when the system hibernates — all the memory content is written to the disk, so a faster boot is possible. It is also possible to suspend the system to reduce the power consumption, but it can be awakened automatically on demand.

For all power events, the service can receive the control code `SERVICE_CONTROL_POWEREVENT` with additional parameters. The reason for the event is passed through these parameters. The reason could be

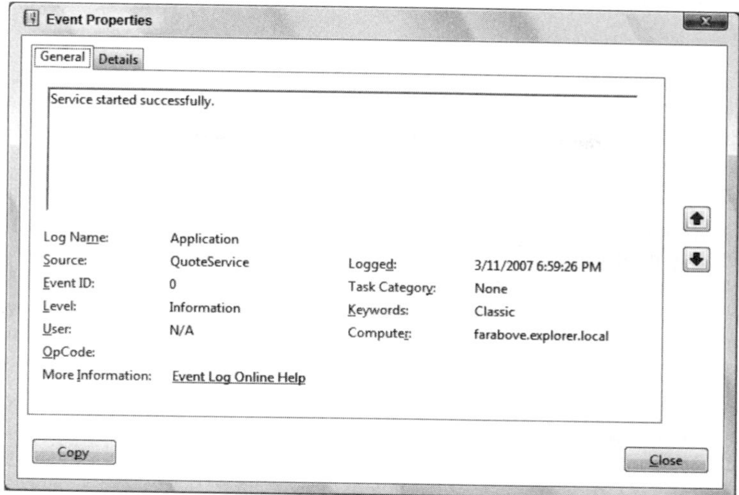

Figure 23-22

low battery power, a power status change, or the system is going to a suspended state. Depending on the circumstances, the service should slow down, suspend background threads, close network connections, close files, and so on.

The classes in the `System.ServiceProcess` namespace have support for power events. In the same way that you can configure a service so that it reacts to pause and continue events with the `CanPauseAndContinue` property, you can also set a property for power management: `CanHandlePowerEvent`. Windows Services that handle power events are registered in the SCM with the Win32 API method `RegisterServiceCtrlHandlerEx()`.

If you set the property `CanHandlePowerEvent` to `true`, the method `OnPowerEvent()` of the class `ServiceBase` is called. You can override this method to receive power events and to react with your service implementation accordingly. The reason for the power event is passed in an argument of type `PowerBroadcastStatus`. The possible values of this enumeration are listed in the following table.

Value	Description
`BatteryLow`	The battery power is low. You should reduce the functionality of the service to a minimum.
`PowerStatusChange`	A switch from battery power to A/C happened, or the battery power slipped below a threshold, and so on.
`QuerySuspend`	The system requests permission to go into a suspended mode. You could deny the permission, or prepare to go into the suspended mode by closing files, disconnecting network connections, and so on.
`QuerySuspendFailed`	The change into the suspended mode was denied for the system. You can go on with the functionality as before.
`Suspend`	Nobody denied the request to go into the suspended mode. The system will be suspended soon.

Summary

In this chapter, you have seen the architecture of Windows Services and how you can create them with the .NET Framework. Applications can start automatically at boot time with Windows Services, and you can use a privileged system account as the user of the service. Windows Services are built from a main function, a service-main function, and a handler, and you've seen other relevant programs in regard to Windows Services, such as a service control program and a service installation program.

The .NET Framework has great support for Windows Services. All the plumbing code that is necessary for building, controlling, and installing services is built into the .NET Framework classes in the `System.ServiceProcess` namespace. By deriving a class from `ServiceBase`, you can override methods that are invoked when the service is paused, resumed, or stopped. For installation of services, the classes `ServiceProcessInstaller` and `ServiceInstaller` deal with all registry configurations needed for services. You can also control and monitor services by using `ServiceController`.

The next chapter gives you information about interop with native code. Behind the scenes, many .NET classes make use of native code. For example, the `ServiceBase` class wraps the Windows API `CreateService()`. With the next chapter, you learn how to use native methods and COM objects from your own classes.

24

Interoperability

If you have Windows programs written prior to .NET, you probably don't have the time and resources to rewrite everything for .NET. Sometimes rewriting code is useful for refactoring or rethinking the application architecture. A rewrite can also help with productivity in the long-term, when adding new features is easier to do with the new technology. However, there should not be a reason to rewrite old code just because a new technology is available. You might have thousands of lines of existing, running code, which would require too much effort to rewrite just to move it into the managed environment.

The same applies to Microsoft. With the namespace `System.DirectoryServices`, Microsoft hasn't rewritten the COM objects accessing the hierarchical data store; the classes inside this namespace are wrappers accessing the ADSI COM objects instead. The same thing happens with `System.Data.OleDb`, where the OLE DB providers that are used by classes from this namespace do have quite complex COM interfaces.

The same issue may apply for your own solutions. If you have existing COM objects that should be used from .NET applications, or the other way around, if you want to write .NET components that should be used in old COM clients, this chapter will be a starter for using COM interoperability.

If you don't have existing COM components you want to integrate with your application, or old COM clients that should use some .NET components, you can skip this chapter.

This chapter discusses the following:

- COM and .NET technologies
- Using COM objects from within .NET applications
- Using .NET components from within COM clients
- Platform invoke for invoking native methods

Like all other chapters, you can download the sample code for this chapter from the Wrox web site at `www.wrox.com`.

.NET and COM

COM is the predecessor technology to .NET. COM defines a component model where components can be written in different programming languages. A component written with C++ can be used from a Visual Basic client. Components can also be used locally inside a process, across processes, or across the network. Does this sound familiar? Of course, .NET has similar goals. However, the way in which these goals are achieved is different. The COM concepts became more and more complex to use and turned out not to be extensible enough. .NET fulfills goals similar to those of COM, but introduces new concepts to make your job easier.

Even today, when using COM interop the prerequisite is to know COM. It doesn't matter if .NET components are used by COM clients or COM components are used by .NET applications, you must know COM. So, this section compares COM and .NET functionality.

If you already have a good grasp of COM technologies, this section may be a refresher to your COM knowledge. Otherwise, it introduces you to the concepts of COM — now using .NET — that you can be happy not to deal with anymore in your daily business. However, all the problems that came with COM still apply when COM technology is integrated in .NET applications.

COM and .NET do have many similar concepts with very different solutions, including the following:

- Metadata
- Freeing memory
- Interfaces
- Method binding
- Data types
- Registration
- Threading
- Error handling
- Event handling

Metadata

With COM, all information about the component is stored inside the type library. The type library includes information such as names and IDs of interfaces, methods, and arguments. With .NET, all this information can be found inside the assembly itself, as you saw in Chapter 13, "Reflection," and Chapter 17, "Assemblies." The problem with COM is that the type library is not extensible. With C++, IDL (interface definition language) files have been used to describe the interfaces and methods. Some of the IDL modifiers cannot be found inside the type library, because Visual Basic (and the Visual Basic team was responsible for the type library) couldn't use these IDL modifiers. With .NET, this problem doesn't exist because the .NET metadata is extensible using custom attributes.

As a result of this behavior, some COM components have a type library and others don't. Where no type library is available, a C++ header file can be used that describes the interfaces and methods. With .NET, it is easier using COM components that do have a type library, but it is also possible to use COM components without a type library. In that case, it is necessary to redefine the COM interface by using C# code.

Freeing Memory

With .NET, memory is released by the garbage collector. This is completely different with COM. COM relies on reference counts.

The interface `IUnknown`, which is the interface that is required to be implemented by every COM object, offers three methods. Two of these methods are related to reference counts. The method `AddRef()` must be called by the client if another interface pointer is needed; this method increments the reference count. The method `Release()` decrements the reference count, and if the resulting reference count is 0, the object destroys itself to free memory.

Interfaces

Interfaces are the heart of COM. They distinguish between a contract used between the client and the object, and the implementation. The interface (the contract) defines the methods that are offered by the component and that can be used by the client. With .NET, interfaces play an important part, too.

COM distinguishes among three interface types: *custom*, *dispatch*, and *dual* interfaces.

Custom Interfaces

Custom interfaces derive from the interface `IUnknown`. A custom interface defines the order of the methods in a *virtual table* (*vtable*), so that the client can access the methods of the interface directly. This also means that the client needs to know the vtable during development time, because binding to the methods happens by using memory addresses. As a conclusion, custom interfaces cannot be used by scripting clients. Figure 24-1 shows the vtable of the custom interface `IMath` that offers the methods `Add()` and `Sub()` in addition to the methods of the `IUnknown` interface.

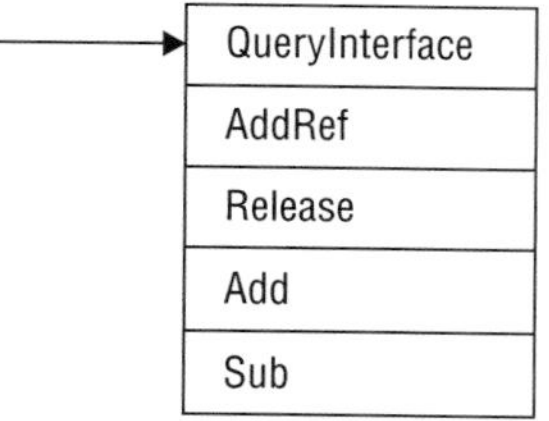

Figure 24-1

Dispatch Interfaces

Because a scripting client (and earlier Visual Basic clients) doesn't support custom interfaces, a different interface type is needed. With dispatch interfaces, the interface available for the client is always the `IDispatch` interface. `IDispatch` derives from `IUnknown` and offers four methods in addition to the `IUnknown` methods. The two most important methods are `GetIDsOfNames()` and `Invoke()`. As shown in Figure 24-2, with a dispatch interface two tables are needed. The first one maps the method or property name to a dispatch ID; the second one maps the dispatch ID to the implementation of the method or property.

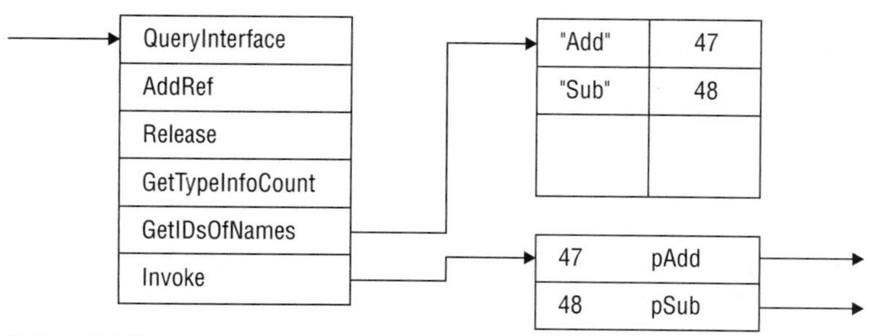

Figure 24-2

When the client invokes a method in the component, at first it calls the method `GetIDsOfNames()`, passing the name of the method it wants to call. `GetIDsOfNames()` makes a lookup into the name-to-ID table to return the dispatch ID. This ID is used by the client to call the `Invoke()` method.

Usually, the two tables for the `IDispatch` *interface are stored inside the type library, but this is not a requirement, and some components have the tables in other places.*

Dual Interfaces

As you can imagine, dispatch interfaces are a lot slower than custom interfaces. On the other hand, custom interfaces cannot be used by scripting clients. A dual interface can solve this dilemma. As you can see in Figure 24-3, a dual interface is derived from `IDispatch` but offers the additional methods of the interface directly in the vtable. Scripting clients can use the `IDispatch` interface to invoke the methods, whereas clients aware of the vtable can call the methods directly.

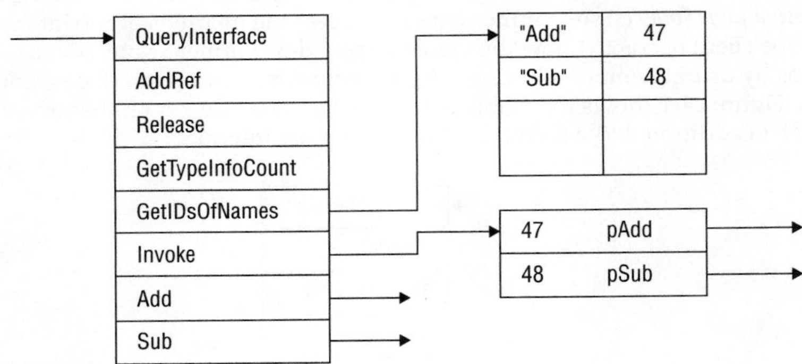

Figure 24-3

Casting and QueryInterface

If a .NET class implements multiple interfaces, casts can be done to get one interface or another. With COM, the interface `IUnknown` offers a similar mechanism with the method `QueryInterface()`. As discussed in the previous section, the interface `IUnknown` is the base interface of every interface, so `QueryInterface()` is available anyway.

Method Binding

How a client maps to a method is defined with the terms *early* and *late binding*. Late binding means that the method to invoke is looked for during runtime. .NET uses the `System.Reflection` namespace to make this possible (see Chapter 13, "Reflection").

COM uses the `IDispatch` interface discussed earlier for late binding. Late binding is possible with dispatch and dual interfaces.

With COM, early binding has two different options. One way of early binding, also known as vtable binding, is to use the vtable directly — this is possible with custom and dual interfaces. The second option for early binding is also known as ID binding. Here the dispatch ID is stored inside the client code, so during runtime only a call to `Invoke()` is necessary. `GetIdsOfNames()` is called during design time. With such clients, it is important to remember that the dispatch ID must not be changed.

Data Types

For dual and dispatch interfaces, the data types that can be used with COM are restricted to a list of automation-compatible data types. The `Invoke()` method of the `IDispatch` interface accepts an array of `VARIANT` data types. The `VARIANT` is a union of many different data types, such as `BYTE`, `SHORT`, `LONG`, `FLOAT`, `DOUBLE`, `BSTR`, `IUnknown*`, `IDispatch*`, and so on. `VARIANT`s have been easy to use from Visual Basic, but it was complex to use them from C++. .NET has the `Object` class instead of `VARIANT`s.

With custom interfaces, all data types available with C++ can be used with COM. However, this also restricts the clients that can use this component to certain programming languages.

Registration

.NET distinguishes between private and shared assemblies, as discussed in Chapter 17, "Assemblies." With COM, all components are globally available by a registry configuration.

All COM objects have a unique identifier that consists of a 128-bit number and is also known as class ID (CLSID). The COM API call to create COM objects, `CoCreateInstance()`, just looks into the registry to find the CLSID and the path to the DLL or EXE to load the DLL or launch the EXE and instantiate the component.

Because such a 128-bit number cannot be easily remembered, many COM objects also have a ProgID. The ProgID is an easy-to-remember name, such as `Excel.Application`, that just maps to the CLSID.

In addition to the CLSID, COM objects also have a unique identifier for each interface (IID) and for the type library (typelib ID).

Information in the registry is discussed in more detail later in the chapter.

Threading

COM uses apartment models to relieve the programmer of having to deal with threading issues. However, this also adds some more complexity. Different apartment types have been added with different releases of the operating system. This section discusses the single-threaded apartment and the multithreaded apartment.

Threading with .NET is discussed in Chapter 19, "Threading and Synchronization."

Single-threaded Apartment

The single-threaded apartment (STA) was introduced with Windows NT 3.51. With an STA, only one thread (the thread that created the instance) is allowed to access the component. However, it is legal to have multiple STAs inside one process, as shown in Figure 24-4.

In this figure, the inner rectangles with the lollipop represent COM components. Components and threads (curved arrows) are surrounded by apartments. The outer rectangle represents a process.

With STAs, there's no need to protect instance variables from multiple thread access, because this protection is provided by a COM facility, and only one thread accesses the component.

A COM object that is not programmed with thread safety marks the requirements for an STA in the registry with the registry key `ThreadingModel` set to `Apartment`.

Multithreaded Apartment

Windows NT 4.0 introduced the concept of a *multithreaded apartment* (*MTA*). With an MTA, multiple threads can access the component simultaneously. Figure 24-5 shows a process with one MTA and two STAs.

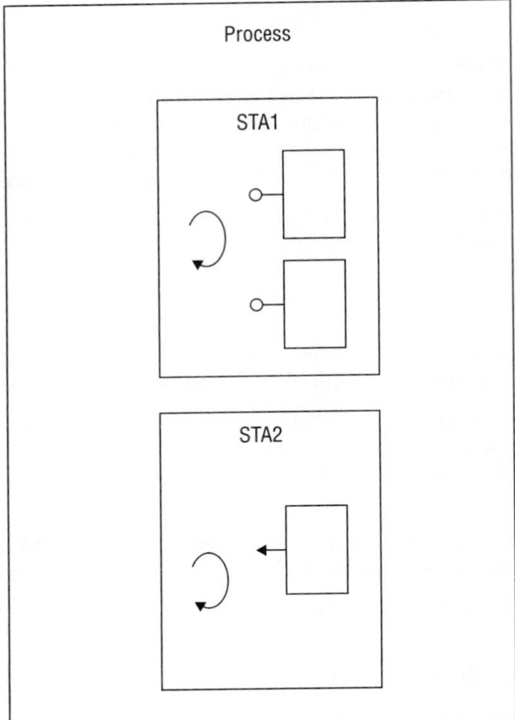

Figure 24-4

A COM object programmed with thread safety in mind marks the requirement for an MTA in the registry with the key `ThreadingModel` set to `Free`. The value `Both` is used for thread-safe COM objects that don't mind the apartment type.

Visual Basic 6.0 didn't offer support for multithreaded apartments. If you're using COM objects that have been developed with VB6 that's an important issue to know.

Error Handling

With .NET, errors are generated by throwing exceptions. With the older COM technology, errors are defined by returning `HRESULT` values with the methods. An `HRESULT` value of `S_OK` means that the method was successful.

If a more detailed error message is offered by the COM component, the COM component implements the interface `ISupportErrorInfo`, where not only an error message but also a link to a help file and the source of the error is returned with an error information object on the return of the method. Objects that implement `ISupportErrorInfo` are automatically mapped to more detailed error information with an exception in .NET.

How to trace and log errors is discussed in Chapter 18, "Tracing and Events."

Event Handling

.NET offers an event-handling mechanism with the C# keywords `event` and `delegate` (see Chapter 7, "Delegates and Events").

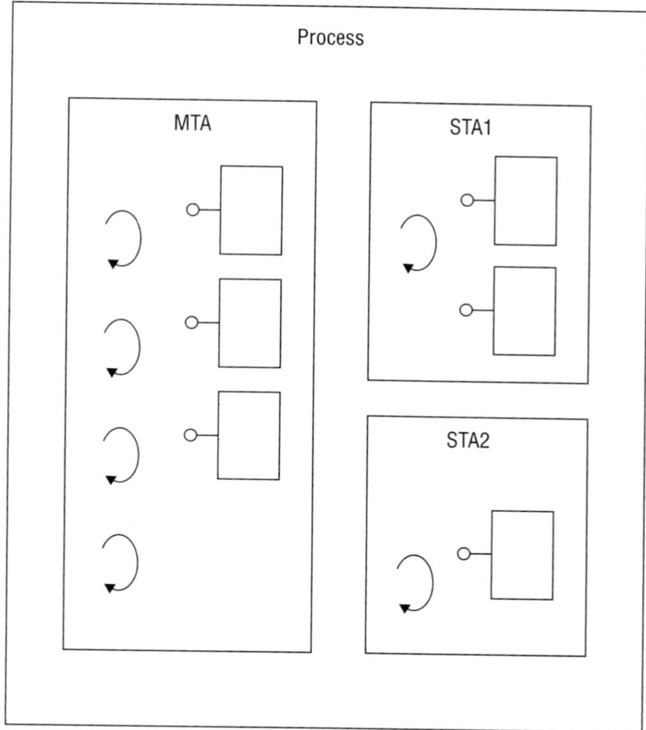

Figure 24-5

Figure 24-6 shows the COM event-handling architecture. With COM events, the component has to implement the interface `IConnectionPointContainer` and one or more connection point objects (CPOs) that implement the interface `IConnectionPoint`. The component also defines an outgoing interface — `ICompletedEvents` in Figure 24-6 — that is invoked by the CPO. The client must implement this out-going interface in the sink object, which itself is a COM object. During runtime, the client queries the server for the interface `IConnectionPointContainer`. With the help of this interface, the client asks for a CPO with the method `FindConnectionPoint()` to get a pointer to `IConnectionPoint` returned. This interface pointer is used by the client to call the `Advise()` method, where a pointer to the sink object is passed to the server. In turn, the component can invoke methods inside the sink object of the client.

Later in this chapter, you learn how the .NET events and the COM events can be mapped so that COM events can be handled by a .NET client and vice versa.

Marshaling

Data passed from .NET to the COM component and the other way around must be converted to the corresponding representation. This mechanism is also known as *marshaling*. What happens here depends on the data type of the data that is passed: You have to differentiate between blittable and nonblittable data types.

Blittable data types have a common representation with both .NET and COM, and no conversion is needed. Simple data types such as `byte`, `short`, `int`, `long`, and classes and arrays that only contain these simple data types belong to the blittable data types. Arrays must be one-dimensional to be blittable.

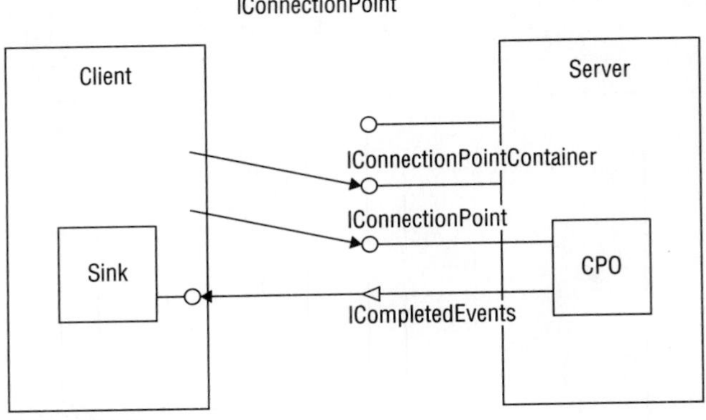

Figure 24-6

A conversion is needed with *nonblittable* data types. The following table lists some of the nonblittable COM data types with their .NET-related data types. Nonblittable types have a higher overhead because of the conversion.

COM Data Type	.NET Data Type
`SAFEARRAY`	`Array`
`VARIANT`	`Object`
`BSTR`	`String`
`IUnknown*, IDispatch*`	`Object`

Using a COM Component from a .NET Client

To see how a .NET application can use a COM component, you first have to create a COM component. Creating COM components is not possible with C# or Visual Basic 2005; you need either Visual Basic 6.0 or C++ (or any other language that supports COM). This chapter uses the Active Template Library (ATL) and C++.

A short note about building COM components with Visual Basic 9.0 and C#: With Visual Basic 9.0 and C# it is possible to build .NET components that can be used as COM objects by using a wrapper that is the real COM component. It would make no sense for a .NET component that is wrapped from a COM component to be used by a .NET client with a COM interop.

Because this is not a COM book, it does not discuss all aspects of the code but only what you need to build the sample.

Creating a COM Component

To create a COM component with ATL and C++, create a new ATL Project. You can find the ATL Project Wizard within the Visual C++ Projects group when you select File ⇨ New ⇨ Project. Set the name to COMServer. With the Application Settings, select Dynamic Link Library and click Finish.

The ATL Project Wizard just creates the foundation for the server. A COM object is still needed. Add a class in Solution Explorer and select ATL Simple Object. In the dialog that starts up, enter **COMDemo** in the field for the Short name. The other fields will be filled automatically, but change the interface name to **IWelcome** (see Figure 24-7). Click Finish to create the stub code for the class and the interface.

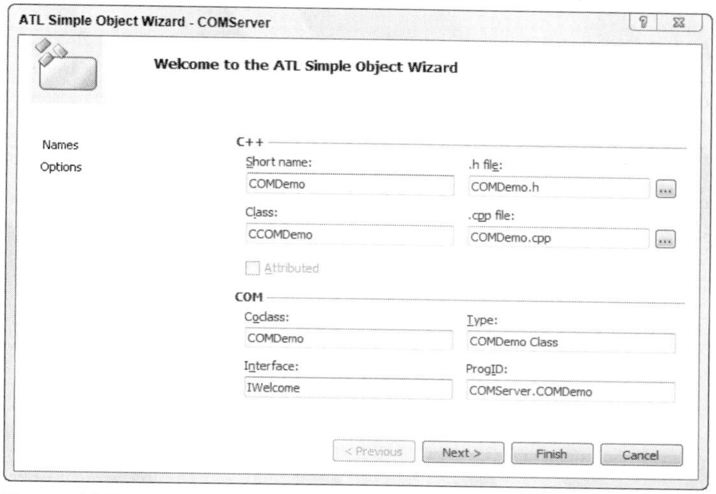

Figure 24-7

The COM component offers two interfaces, so that you can see how `QueryInterface()` is mapped from .NET, and just three simple methods, so that you can see how the interaction takes place. In class view, select the interface `IWelcome` and add the method `Greeting()` (see Figure 24-8) with these parameters:

```
HRESULT Greeting([in] BSTR name, [out, retval] BSTR* message);
```

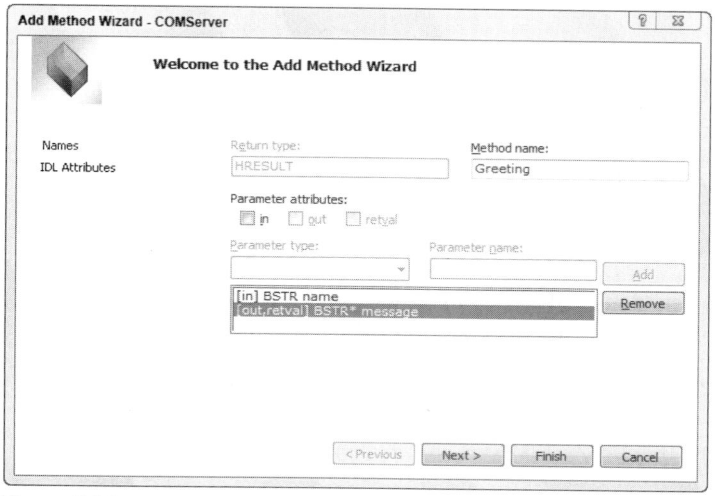

Figure 24-8

The IDL file `COMDemo.idl` defines the interface for COM. Your wizard-generated code from the file `COMDemo.idl` should look similar to the following code. The unique identifiers (`uuids`) will differ. The interface `IWelcome` defines the `Greeting()` method. The brackets before the keyword `_interface` define some attributes for the interface. `uuid` defines the interface ID and `dual` marks the type of the interface:

```
[
   object,
   uuid(615B801E-3A5C-44EA-913B-8C8F53BBFB3F),
   dual,
   nonextensible,
   helpstring("IWelcome Interface"),
   pointer_default(unique)
]
interface IWelcome : IDispatch{
   [id(1), helpstring("method Greeting")] HRESULT Greeting(
      [in] BSTR name, [out,retval] BSTR* message);
};
```

The IDL file also defines the content of the type library, which is the COM object (`coclass`) that implements the interface `IWelcome`:

```
[
   uuid(1CE0DFFF-ADA8-47DD-BA06-DDD89C584242),
   version(1.0),
   helpstring("COMServer 1.0 Type Library")
]
library COMServerLib
{
   importlib("stdole2.tlb");
   [
      uuid(AB13E0B8-F8E1-497E-985F-FA30C5F449AA),
      helpstring("COMDemo Class")
   ]
   coclass COMDemo
   {
      [default] interface IWelcome;
   };
};
```

With custom attributes, it is possible to change the name of the class and interfaces that are generated by a .NET wrapper class. You just have to add the attribute `custom` with the identifier `0F21F359-AB84-41e8-9A78-36D110E6D2F9`, and the name under which it should appear within .NET.

Add the custom attribute with the same identifier and the name `Wrox.ProCSharp.COMInterop.Server.IWelcome` to the header section of the `IWelcome` interface. Add the same attribute with a corresponding name to the class `CCOMDemo`:

```
[
   object,
   uuid(615B801E-3A5C-44EA-913B-8C8F53BBFB3F),
   dual,
   nonextensible,
   helpstring("IWelcome Interface"),
```

```
    pointer_default(unique),
    custom(0F21F359-AB84-41e8-9A78-36D110E6D2F9,
       "Wrox.ProCSharp.COMInterop.Server.IWelcome")
]
interface IWelcome : IDispatch{
    [id(1), helpstring("method Greeting")] HRESULT Greeting([in] BSTR name,
[out,retval] BSTR* message);
};

library COMServerLib
{
    importlib("stdole2.tlb");
    [
       uuid(AB13E0B8-F8E1-497E-985F-FA30C5F449AA),
       helpstring("COMDemo Class")
       custom(0F21F359-AB84-41e8-9A78-36D110E6D2F9,
          "Wrox.ProCSharp.COMInterop.Server.COMDemo"),
    ]
    coclass COMDemo
    {
       [default] interface IWelcome;
    };
```

Now add a second interface to the file `COMDemo.idl`. You can copy the header section of the `IWelcome` interface to the header section of the new `IMath` interface, but be sure to change the unique identifier that is defined with the `uuid` keyword. You can generate such an ID with the `guidgen` utility. The interface `IMath` offers the methods `Add()` and `Sub()`:

```
// IMath
[
    object,
    uuid("2158751B-896E-461d-9012-EF1680BE0628"),
    dual,
    nonextensible,
    helpstring("IMath Interface"),
    pointer_default(unique),
    custom(0F21F359-AB84-41e8-9A78-36D110E6D2F9,
       "Wrox.ProCSharp.COMInterop.Server.IMath")
]
interface IMath : IDispatch
{
    [id(1)] HRESULT Add([in] LONG val1, [in] LONG val2,
                        [out, retval] LONG* result);
    [id(2)] HRESULT Sub([in] LONG val1, [in] LONG val2,
                        [out, retval] LONG* result);
};
```

The coclass `COMDemo` must also be changed so that it implements both the interfaces `IWelcome` and `IMath`. The `IWelcome` interface is the default interface:

```
    [
       uuid(AB13E0B8-F8E1-497E-985F-FA30C5F449AA),
       helpstring("COMDemo Class"),
       custom(0F21F359-AB84-41e8-9A78-36D110E6D2F9,
          "Wrox.ProCSharp.COMInterop.Server.COMDemo")
    ]
```

(continued)

(continued)

```
coclass COMDemo
{
   [default] interface IWelcome;
   interface IMath;
};
```

Now, you can set the focus away from the IDL file toward the C++ code. In the file `COMDemo.h`, you can find the class definition of the COM object. The class `CCOMDemo` uses multiple inheritances to derive from the template classes `CComObjectRootEx`, `CComCoClass`, and `IDisplatchImpl`. `CComObjectRootEx` offers an implementation of the `IUnknown` interface functionality such as `AddRef` and `Release`, `CComCoClass` creates a factory that instantiates objects of the template argument, which here is `CComDemo`, and `IDispatchImpl` offers an implementation of the methods from the `IDispatch` interface.

With the macros that are surrounded by `BEGIN_COM_MAP` and `END_COM_MAP`, a map is created to define all the COM interfaces that are implemented by the COM class. This map is used by the implementation of the `QueryInterface` method.

```
class ATL_NO_VTABLE CCOMDemo :
   public CComObjectRootEx<CComSingleThreadModel>,
   public CComCoClass<CCOMDemo, &CLSID_COMDemo>,
   public IDispatchImpl<IWelcome, &IID_IWelcome, &LIBID_COMServerLib,
      /*wMajor =*/ 1, /*wMinor =*/ 0>
{
public:
   CCOMDemo()
   {
   }

DECLARE_REGISTRY_RESOURCEID(IDR_COMDEMO)


BEGIN_COM_MAP(CCOMDemo)
   COM_INTERFACE_ENTRY(IWelcome)
   COM_INTERFACE_ENTRY(IDispatch)
END_COM_MAP()


   DECLARE_PROTECT_FINAL_CONSTRUCT()

   HRESULT FinalConstruct()
   {
      return S_OK;
   }

   void FinalRelease()
   {
   }

public:
   STDMETHOD(Greeting)(BSTR name, BSTR* message);
};

OBJECT_ENTRY_AUTO(__uuidof(COMDemo), CCOMDemo)
```

With this class definition, you have to add the second interface, `IMath`, as well as the methods that are defined with the `IMath` interface:

```
class ATL_NO_VTABLE CCOMDemo :
   public CComObjectRootEx<CComSingleThreadModel>,
   public CComCoClass<CCOMDemo, &CLSID_COMDemo>,
   public IDispatchImpl<IWelcome, &IID_IWelcome, &LIBID_COMServerLib,
      /*wMajor =*/ 1, /*wMinor =*/ 0>
   public IDispatchImpl<IMath, &IID_IMath, &LIBID_COMServerLib, 1, 0>
{
public:
   CCOMDemo()
   {
   }

DECLARE_REGISTRY_RESOURCEID(IDR_COMDEMO)


BEGIN_COM_MAP(CCOMDemo)
   COM_INTERFACE_ENTRY(IWelcome)
   COM_INTERFACE_ENTRY(IMath)
   COM_INTERFACE_ENTRY2(IDispatch, IWelcome)
END_COM_MAP()


   DECLARE_PROTECT_FINAL_CONSTRUCT()

   HRESULT FinalConstruct()
   {
      return S_OK;
   }

   void FinalRelease()
   {
   }

public:
   STDMETHOD(Greeting)(BSTR name, BSTR* message);
   STDMETHOD(Add)(long val1, long val2, long* result);
   STDMETHOD(Sub)(long val1, long val2, long* result);
};

OBJECT_ENTRY_AUTO(__uuidof(COMDemo), CCOMDemo)
```

Now, you can implement the three methods in the file `COMDemo.cpp` with the following code. The `CComBSTR` is an ATL class that makes it easier to deal with `BSTR`s. In the `Greeting()` method, only a welcome message is returned, which adds the name passed in the first argument to the message that is returned. The `Add()` method just does a simple addition of two values, and the `Sub()` method does a subtraction and returns the result:

```
STDMETHODIMP CCOMDemo::Greeting(BSTR name, BSTR* message)
{
   CComBSTR tmp("Welcome, ");
   tmp.Append(name);
   *message = tmp;
   return S_OK;
}
```

(continued)

(continued)

```
STDMETHODIMP CCOMDemo::Add(LONG val1, LONG val2, LONG* result)
{
   *result = val1 + val2;
   return S_OK;
}

STDMETHODIMP CCOMDemo::Sub(LONG val1, LONG val2, LONG* result)
{
   *result = val1 - val2;
   return S_OK;
}
```

Now, you can build the component. The build process also configures the component in the registry.

Creating a Runtime Callable Wrapper

You can now use the COM component from within .NET. To make this possible, you must create a runtime callable wrapper (RCW). Using the RCW, the .NET client sees a .NET object instead of the COM component; there is no need to deal with the COM characteristics because this is done by the wrapper. An RCW hides the `IUnknown` and `IDispatch` interfaces (see Figure 24-9) and deals itself with the reference counts of the COM object.

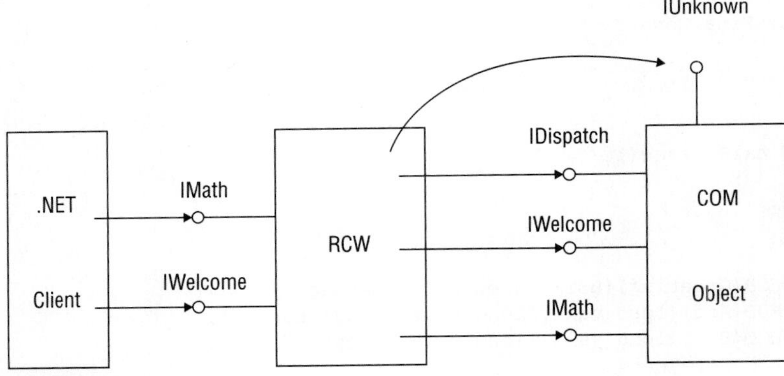

Figure 24-9

The RCW can be created by using the command-line utility `tlbimp` or by using Visual Studio. Starting the command

```
tlbimp COMServer.dll /out:Interop.COMServer.dll
```

creates the file `Interop.COMServer.dll` that contains a .NET assembly with the wrapper class. In this generated assembly, you can find the namespace `COMWrapper` with the class `CCOMDemoClass` and the interfaces `CCOMDemo`, `IMath`, and `IWelcome`. The name of the namespace can be changed by using options of the `tlbimp` utility. The option `/namespace` allows you to specify a different namespace, and with `/asmversion` you can define the version number of the assembly.

Another important option of this command-line utility is `/keyfile`, which is used for assigning a strong name to the generated assembly. Strong names are discussed in Chapter 17, "Assemblies."

An RCW can also be created by using Visual Studio. To create a simple sample application, create a C# console project. In Solution Explorer, add a reference to the COM server by selecting the COM tab in the Add Reference dialog, and scroll down to the entry `COMServer 1.0 Type Library` (see Figure 24-10).

Here, all COM objects are listed that are configured in the registry. Selecting a COM component from the list creates an assembly with an RCW class.

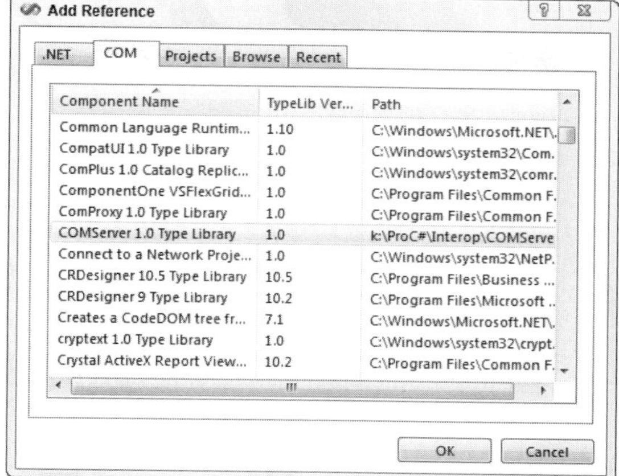

Figure 24-10

Using the RCW

After creating the wrapper class, you can write the code for the application to instantiate and access the component. Because of the custom attributes in the C++ file, the generated namespace of the RCW class is `Wrox.ProCSharp.COMInterop.Server`. Add this namespace as well as the namespace `System.Runtime.InteropServices` to the declarations. From the namespace `System.Runtime.InteropServices`, the `Marshal` class will be used to release the COM object:

```
using System;
using System.Runtime.InteropServices;
using Wrox.ProCSharp.COMInteorp.Server

namespace Wrox.ProCSharp.COMInterop.Client
{
   class Program
   {
      [STAThread]
      static void Main()
      {
```

Now, the COM component can be used similarly to a .NET class. `obj` is a variable of type `COMDemo`. `COMDemo` is a .NET interface that offers the methods of both the `IWelcome` and `IMath` interfaces. However, it is also possible to cast to a specific interface such as `IWelcome`. With a variable that is declared as type `IWelcome`, the method `Greeting()` can be called.

```
         COMDemo obj = new COMDemo();
         IWelcome welcome = obj;
         Console.WriteLine(welcome.Greeting("Christian"));
```

Although `COMDemo` is an interface, you can instantiate new objects of type `COMDemo`. Contrary to normal interfaces, you can do this with wrapped COM interfaces.

If the object — as in this case — offers multiple interfaces, a variable of the other interface can be declared, and by using a simple assignment with the cast operator, the wrapper class does a `QueryInterface()` with the COM object to return the second interface pointer. With the `math` variable, the methods of the `IMath` interface can be called.

```
            IMath math;
            math = (IMath)welcome;
            int x = math.Add(4, 5);
            Console.WriteLine(x);
```

If the COM object should be released before the garbage collector cleans up the object, the static method `Marshal.ReleaseComObject()` invokes the `Release()` method of the component, so that the component can destroy itself and free up memory:

```
            Marshal.ReleaseComObject(math);
        }
    }
}
```

Earlier you learned that the COM object is released as soon as the reference count is 0. `Marshal.ReleaseComObject()` *decrements the reference count by 1 by invoking the* `Release()` *method. Because the RCW does just one call to* `AddRef()` *to increment the reference count, a single call to* `Marshal.ReleaseComObject()` *is enough to release the object no matter how many references to the RCW you keep.*

After releasing the COM object using `Marshal.ReleaseComObject()`, you may not use any variable that references the object. In the example, the COM object is released by using the variable `math`. The variable `welcome`, which references the same object, cannot be used after releasing the object. Otherwise, you will get an exception of type `InvalidComObjectException`.

Releasing COM objects when they are no longer needed is extremely important. COM objects make use of the native memory heap, whereas .NET objects make use of the managed memory heap. The garbage collector only deals with managed memory.

As you can see, with a runtime callable wrapper, a COM component can be used similarly to a .NET object.

A special case of a runtime callable wrapper is a primary interop assembly, which is discussed next.

Primary Interop Assemblies

A *primary interop assembly* is an assembly that is already prepared by the vendor of the COM component. This makes it easier to use the COM component. A primary interop assembly is a runtime-callable wrapper that might differ from an automatically generated RCW.

You can find primary interop assemblies in the directory `<program files>\Microsoft.NET\Primary Interop Assemblies`. A primary interop assembly already exists for the use of ADO from within .NET. If you add a reference to the COM library Microsoft ActiveX Data Objects 2.7 Library, no wrapper class is created because a primary interop assembly already exists; the primary interop assembly is referenced instead.

Threading Issues

As discussed earlier in this chapter, a COM component marks the apartment (STA or MTA) it wants to live in, based on whether or not it is implemented as thread-safe. However, the thread has to join an apartment. What apartment the thread should join can be defined with the `[STAThread]` and `[MTAThread]` attributes, which can be applied to the `Main()` method of an application. The attribute `[STAThread]` means that the thread joins an STA, whereas the attribute `[MTAThread]` means that the thread joins an MTA. Joining an MTA is the default if no attribute is applied.

It is also possible to set the apartment state programmatically with the `ApartmentState` property of the `Thread` class. The `ApartmentState` property allows you to set a value from the `ApartmentState` enumeration. `ApartmentState` has the possible values `STA` and `MTA` (and `Unknown` if it wasn't set). Be aware that the apartment state of a thread can be set only once. If it is set a second time, the second setting is ignored.

> **What happens if the thread chooses a different apartment from the apartments supported by the component? The correct apartment for the COM component is created automatically by the COM runtime. However, the performance decreases if the apartment boundaries are crossed while calling the methods of a component.**

Adding Connection Points

To see how COM events can be handled in a .NET application, first the COM component must be extended. Implementing a COM event in an ATL class using attributes looks very similar to the events in .NET, although the functionality is different.

First, you have to add another interface to the interface definition file `COMDemo.idl`. The interface `_ICompletedEvents` is implemented by the client, which is the .NET application, and called by the component. In this example, the method `Completed()` is called by the component when the calculation is ready. Such an interface is also known as an outgoing interface. An outgoing interface must either be a dispatch or a custom interface. Dispatch interfaces are supported by all clients. The custom attribute with the `ID 0F21F359-AB84-41e8-9A78-36D110E6D2F9` defines the name of this interface that will be created in the RCW. The outgoing interface must also be written to the interfaces supported by the component inside the `coclass` section, and marked as a `source` interface:

```
library COMServerLib
{
   importlib("stdole2.tlb");

   [
      uuid(5CFF102B-0961-4EC6-8BB4-759A3AB6EF48),
      helpstring("_ICompletedEvents Interface"),
      custom(0F21F359-AB84-41e8-9A78-36D110E6D2F9,
         "Wrox.ProCSharp.COMInterop.Server.ICompletedEvents"),
   ]
   dispinterface _ICompletedEvents
   {
      properties:
      methods:
         [id(1)] void Completed(void);
   };

   [
      uuid(AB13E0B8-F8E1-497E-985F-FA30C5F449AA),
      helpstring("COMDemo Class")
      custom(0F21F359-AB84-41e8-9A78-36D110E6D2F9,
         "Wrox.ProCSharp.COMInterop.Server.COMDemo"),
   ]
   coclass COMDemo
```

(continued)

(continued)

```
{
    [default] interface IWelcome;
    interface IMath;
    [default, source] dispinterface _ICompletedEvents;
};
```

You can use a wizard to create an implementation that fires the event back to the client. Open the class view, select the class CComDemo, open the context menu, and start the Implement Connection Point Wizard (see Figure 24-11). Select the source interface ICompletedEvents for implementation with the connection point.

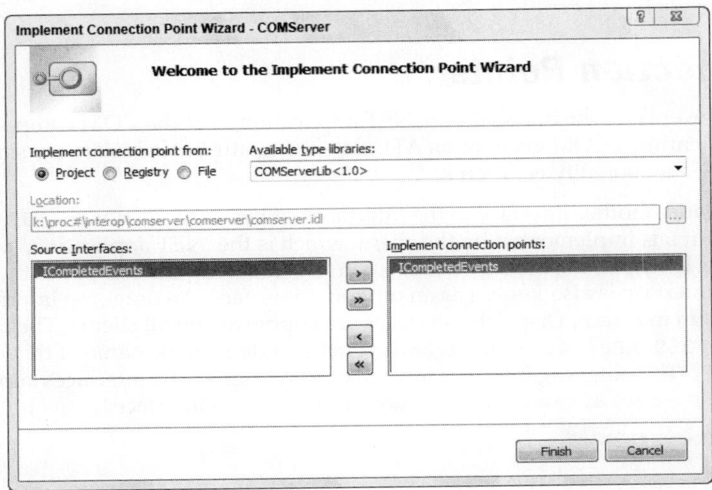

Figure 24-11

The wizard creates the proxy class CProxy_ICompletedEvents to fire the events to the client. Also, the class CCOMDemo is changed. The class now inherits from IConnectionPointContainerImpl and the proxy class. The interface IConnectionPointContainer is added to the interface map, and a connection point map is added to the source interface _ICompletedEvents.

```
class ATL_NO_VTABLE CCOMDemo :
    public CComObjectRootEx<CComSingleThreadModel>,
    public CComCoClass<CCOMDemo, &CLSID_COMDemo>,
    public IDispatchImpl<IWelcome, &IID_IWelcome, &LIBID_COMServerLib,
        /*wMajor =*/ 1, /*wMinor =*/ 0>,
    public IDispatchImpl<IMath, &IID_IMath, &LIBID_COMServerLib, 1, 0>,
    public IConnectionPointContainerImpl<CCOMDemo>,
    public CProxy_ICompletedEvents<CCOMDemo>
{
public:

//...

BEGIN_COM_MAP(CCOMDemo)
    COM_INTERFACE_ENTRY(IWelcome)
    COM_INTERFACE_ENTRY(IMath)
```

```
      COM_INTERFACE_ENTRY2(IDispatch, IWelcome)
      COM_INTERFACE_ENTRY(IConnectionPointContainer)
   END_COM_MAP()

   //...

   public:
      BEGIN_CONNECTION_POINT_MAP(CCOMDemo)
         CONNECTION_POINT_ENTRY(__uuidof(_ICompletedEvents))
      END_CONNECTION_POINT_MAP()
};
```

Finally, the method `Fire_Completed()` from the proxy class can be called inside the methods `Add()` and `Sub()` in the file `COMDemo.cpp`:

```
STDMETHODIMP CCOMDemo::Add(LONG val1, LONG val2, LONG* result)
{
   *result = val1 + val2;
   Fire_Completed();
   return S_OK;
}

STDMETHODIMP CCOMDemo::Sub(LONG val1, LONG val2, LONG* result)
{
   *result = val1 - val2;
   Fire_Completed();
   return S_OK;
}
```

After rebuilding the COM DLL, you can change the .NET client to use these COM events just like a normal .NET event:

```
      static void Main()
      {
         COMDemo obj = new COMDemo();

         IWelcome welcome = obj;
         Console.WriteLine(welcome.Greeting("Christian"));

         obj.Completed +=
               delegate
               {
                  Console.WriteLine("Calculation completed");
               });

         IMath math = (IMath)welcome;
         int result = math.Add(3, 5);
         Console.WriteLine(result);

         Marshal.ReleaseComObject(math);
   }
```

As you can see, the RCW offers automatic mapping from COM events to .NET events. COM events can be used similarly to .NET events in a .NET client.

Using ActiveX Controls in Windows Forms

ActiveX controls are COM objects with a user interface and many optional COM interfaces to deal with the user interface and the interaction with the container. ActiveX controls can be used by many different containers, such as Internet Explorer, Word, Excel, and applications written using Visual Basic 6.0, MFC (Microsoft Foundation Classes), or ATL (Active Template Library). A Windows Forms application is another container that can manage ActiveX controls. ActiveX controls can be used similarly to Windows Forms controls as you'll see shortly.

ActiveX Control Importer

Similar to runtime callable wrappers, you can also create a wrapper for ActiveX controls. A wrapper for an ActiveX control is created by using the command-line utility *Windows Forms ActiveX Control Importer*, `aximp.exe`. This utility creates a class that derives from the base class `System.Windows.Forms.AxHost` that acts as a wrapper to use the ActiveX control.

You can enter this command to create a wrapper class from the Web Forms control:

```
aximp c:\windows\system32\shdocvw.dll
```

ActiveX controls can also be imported directly using Visual Studio. If the ActiveX control is configured within the toolbox, it can be dragged and dropped onto a Windows Forms control that creates the wrapper.

Creating a Windows Forms Application

To see ActiveX controls running inside a Windows Forms application, create a simple Windows Forms application project. With this application, you will build a simple Internet browser that uses the Web Browser control, which comes as part of the operating system.

Create a form as shown in Figure 24-12. The form should include a toolstrip with a text box and three buttons. The text box with the name `toolStripTextUrl` is used to enter a URL, three buttons with the names `toolStripButtonNavigate`, `toolStripButtonBack`, and `toolStripButtonForward` to navigate web pages, and a status strip with the name `statusStrip`. The status strip also needs a label to display status messages.

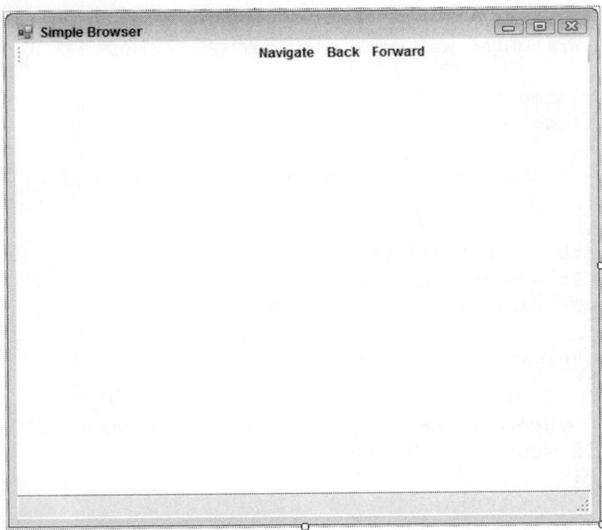

Figure 24-12

Using Visual Studio, you can add ActiveX controls to the toolbar to use it in the same way as a Windows Forms control. On the Customize Toolbox context menu, select the Add/Remove Items menu entry and select the Microsoft Web Browser control in the COM Components category (see Figure 24-13).

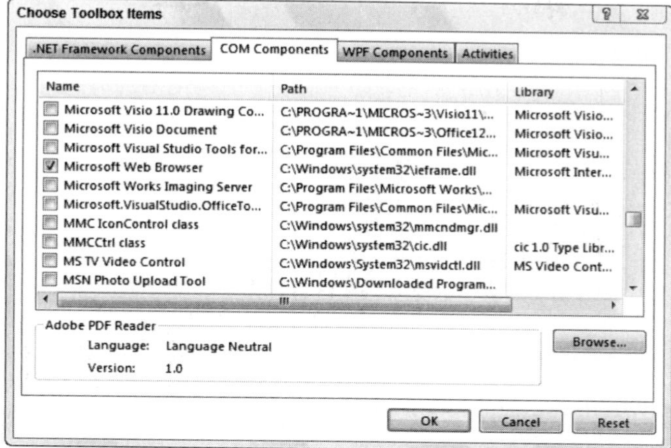

Figure 24-13

This way, an icon will show up in the toolbox. Similarly to other Windows controls, you can drag and drop this icon to the Windows Forms designer to create (with the `aximp` utility) a wrapper assembly hosting the ActiveX control. You can see the wrapper assemblies with the references in the project: `AxSHDocVw` and `SHDocVw`. Now you can invoke methods of the control by using the generated variable `axWebBrowser1`, as shown in the following code. Add a `Click` event handler to the button `toolStripButtonNavigate` in order to navigate the browser to a web page. The method `Navigate()` used for this purpose requires a URL string with the first argument that you get by accessing the `Text` property of the text box control `toolStripTextUrl`:

```
private void OnNavigate(object sender, System.EventArgs e)
{
   try
   {
      axWebBrowser1.Navigate(toolStripTextUrl.Text);
   }
   catch (COMException ex)
   {
      statusStrip.Items[0].Text = ex.Message;
   }
}
```

With the `Click` event handler of the `Back` and `Forward` buttons, call the `GoBack()` and `GoForward()` methods of the browser control:

```
private void OnGoBack(object sender, System.EventArgs e)
{
   try
   {
      axWebBrowser1.GoBack();
   }
   catch (COMException ex)
```

(continued)

(continued)

```
        {
           statusStrip.Items[0].Text = ex.Message;
        }
     }

     private void OnGoForward(object sender, System.EventArgs e)
     {
        try
        {
           axWebBrowser1.GoForward();
        }
        catch (COMException ex)
        {
           statusStrip.Items[0].Text = ex.Message;
        }
     }
```

The web control also offers some events that can be used just like a .NET event. Add the event handler `OnStatusChange()` to the event `StatusTextChange` to set the status that is returned by the control to the status strip in the Windows Forms application:

```
     private void OnStatusChange(object sender,
                     AxSHDocVw.DWebBrowserEvents2_StatusTextChangeEvent e)
     {
        statusStrip.Items[0].Text = e.text;
     }
```

Now, you have a simple browser that you can use to navigate to web pages (see Figure 24-14).

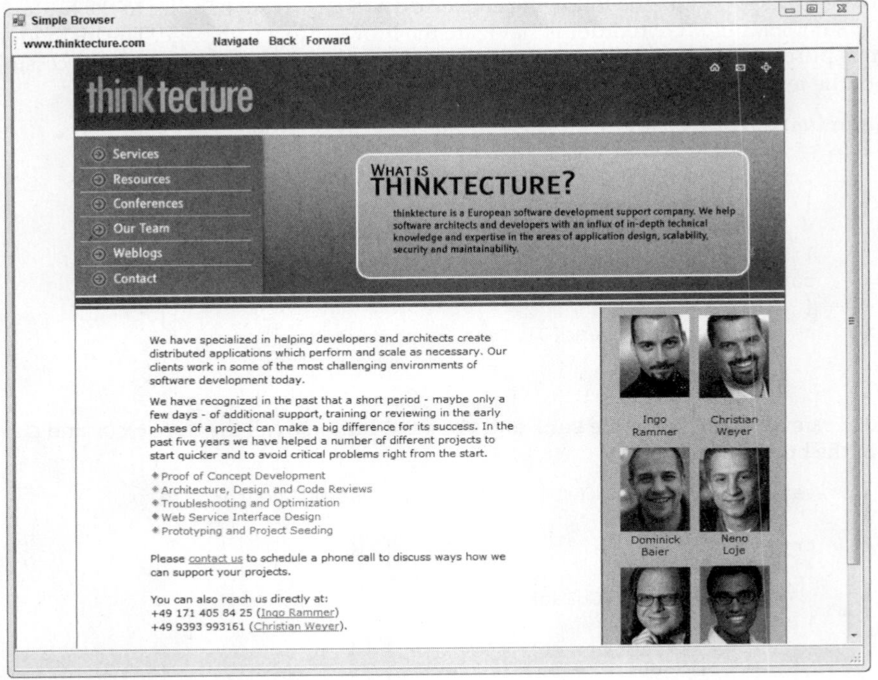

Figure 24-14

Using COM Objects from Within ASP.NET

COM objects can be used in a similar way to what you have seen before from within ASP.NET. However, there is one important distinction. The ASP.NET runtime by default runs in an MTA. If the COM object is configured with the threading model value `Apartment` (as all COM objects that have been written with Visual Basic 6.0 are), an exception is thrown. For performance and scalability reasons, it is best to avoid STA objects within ASP.NET. If you really want to use an STA object with ASP.NET, you can set the `AspCompat` attribute with the `Page` directive as shown in the following snippet. Be aware that the web site performance might suffer when you are using this option:

```
<%@ Page AspCompat="true" Language="C#" %>
```

> **Using STA COM objects with ASP.NET can lead to scalability problems. It's best to avoid using STA COM objects with ASP.NET.**

Using a .NET Component from a COM Client

So far, you have seen how to access a COM component from a .NET client. Equally interesting is to find a solution for accessing .NET components in an old COM client that is using Visual Basic 6.0, or C++ with MFC, or ATL.

COM Callable Wrapper

If you want to access a COM component with a .NET client, you have to work with an RCW. To access a .NET component from a COM client application, you must use a COM callable wrapper (CCW). Figure 24-15 shows a CCW that wraps a .NET class, and offers COM interfaces that a COM client expects to use. The CCW offers interfaces such as `IUnknown`, `IDispatch`, `ISupportErrorInfo`, and others. It also offers interfaces such as `IConnectionPointContainer` and `IConnectionPoint` for events. A COM client gets what it expects from a COM object — although a .NET component is behind the scenes. The wrapper deals with methods such as `AddRef()`, `Release()`, and `QueryInterface()` from the `IUnknown` interface, whereas in the .NET object you can count on the garbage collector without the need to deal with reference counts.

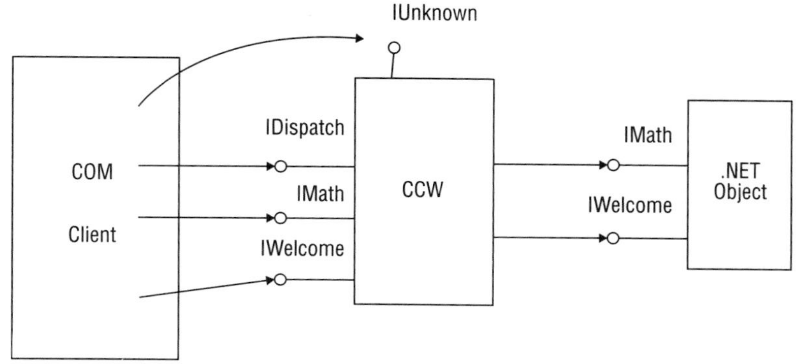

Figure 24-15

Creating a .NET Component

In the following example, you build the same functionality into a .NET class that you have previously built into a COM component. Start by creating a C# class library, and name it `DotNetComponent`. Then add the interfaces `IWelcome` and `IMath`, and the class `DotNetComponent` that implements these interfaces. The attribute `[ComVisible(true)]` makes the class and interfaces available for COM:

```
using System;
using System.Runtime.InteropServices;

namespace Wrox.ProCSharp.COMInterop.Server
{
   [ComVisible(true)]
   public interface IWelcome
   {
      string Greeting(string name);
   }

   [ComVisible(true)]
   public interface IMath
   {
      int Add(int val1, int val2);
      int Sub(int val1, int val2);
   }

   [ComVisible(true)]
   public class DotnetComponent : IWelcome, IMath
   {
      public DotnetComponent()
      {
      }

      public string Greeting(string name)
      {
         return "Hello " + name;
      }

      public int Add(int val1, int val2)
      {
         return val1 + val2;
      }

      public int Sub(int val1, int val2)
      {
         return val1 - val2;
      }
   }
}
```

After building the project, you can create a type library.

Creating a Type Library

A type library can be created by using the command-line utility `tlbexp`. The command

```
tlbexp DotnetComponent.dll
```

creates the type library `DotnetComponent.tlb`. You can view the type library with the utility *OLE/COM Object Viewer*`oleview32.exe`. This tool is part of the Microsoft SDK, and you can start it from the Visual Studio 2008 Command Prompt. Select File ⇨ View TypeLib to open the type library. Now you can see the interface definition shown in the following code. The unique IDs will differ.

The name of the type library is created from the name of the assembly. The header of the type library also defines the full name of the assembly in a custom attribute, and all the interfaces are forward-declared before they are defined:

```
// Generated .IDL file (by the OLE/COM Object Viewer)
//
// typelib filename: dotnetcomponent.dll

[
  uuid(0AA0953A-B2A0-32CB-A5AC-5DA0DF698EB8),
  version(1.0),
  custom(90883F05-3D28-11D2-8F17-00A0C9A6186D, DotNetComponent,
         Version=1.0.0.0., Culture=neutral, PublicKeyToken=null)
]
library DotnetComponent
{
   // TLib : Common Language Runtime Library :
   // {BED7F4EA-1A96-11D2-8F08-00A0C9A6186D}
   importlib("mscorlib.tlb");
   // TLib : OLE Automation : {00020430-0000-0000-c000-000000000046}
   importlib("stdole2.tlb");

   // Forward declare all types defined in this typelib
   interface IWelcome;
   interface IMath;
   interface _DotnetComponent;
```

In the following generated code, you can see that the interfaces `IWelcome` and `IMath` are defined as COM dual interfaces. You can see all methods that have been declared in the C# code are listed here in the type library definition. The parameters changed; the .NET types are mapped to COM types (for example, from the `String` class to the `BSTR` type), and the signature is changed, so that a `HRESULT` is returned. Because the interfaces are dual, dispatch IDs are also generated:

```
   [
     odl,
     uuid(F39A4143-F88D-321E-9A33-8208E256A2DF),
     version(1.0),
     dual,
     oleautomation,
     custom(0F21F359-AB84-41E8-9A78-36D110E6D2F9,
            Wrox.ProCSharp.COMInterop.Server.IWelcome)
   ]
   interface IWelcome : IDispatch {
      [id(0x60020000)]
      HRESULT Greeting([in] BSTR name, [out, retval] BSTR* pRetVal);
   };

   [
     odl,
     uuid(EF596F3F-B69B-3657-9D48-C906CBF12565),
     version(1.0),
     dual,
```

(continued)

(continued)

```
      oleautomation,
      custom(0F21F359-AB84-41E8-9A78-36D110E6D2F9,
             Wrox.ProCSharp.COMInterop.Server.IMath)
    ]
    interface IMath : IDispatch {
       [id(0x60020000)] HRESULT Add([in] long val1, [in] long val2,
                                    [out, retval] long* pRetVal);
       [id(0x60020001)] HRESULT Sub([in] long val1, [in] long val2,
                                    [out, retval] long* pRetVal);
    };
```

The `coclass` section marks the COM object itself. The `uuid` in the header is the CLSID used to instantiate the object. The class `DotnetComponent` supports the interfaces `_DotnetComponent`, `_Object`, `IWelcome`, and `IMath`. `_Object` is defined in the file `mscorlib.tlb` included in an earlier code section and offers the methods of the base class `Object`. The default interface of the component is `_DotnetComponent`, which is defined after the `coclass` section as a dispatch interface. In the interface declaration it is marked as dual, but because no methods are included, it is a dispatch interface. With this interface, it is possible to access all methods of the component using late binding:

```
    [
      uuid(5BCD9C26-D68D-38C2-92E3-DA0C1741A8CD),
      version(1.0),
      custom(0F21F359-AB84-41E8-9A78-36D110E6D2F9,
             Wrox.ProCSharp.COMInterop.Server.DotnetComponent)
    ]
    coclass DotnetComponent {
       [default] interface _DotnetComponent;
       interface _Object;
       interface IWelcome;
       interface IMath;
    };

    [
      odl,
      uuid(884C59C6-B3C2-3455-BB74-52753C409097),
      hidden,
      dual,
      oleautomation,
      custom(0F21F359-AB84-41E8-9A78-36D110E6D2F9,
             Wrox.ProCSharp.COMInterop.Server.DotnetComponent)
    ]
    interface _DotnetComponent : IDispatch {
    };
};
```

There are quite a few defaults for generating the type library. However, often it is advantageous to change some of the default .NET to COM mappings. This can be done with several attributes in the `System.Runtime.InteropServices` namespaces.

COM Interop Attributes

Applying attributes from the namespace `System.Runtime.InteropServices` to classes, interfaces, or methods allows you to change the implementation of the CCW. The following table lists these attributes and a description.

Attribute	Description
Guid	This attribute can be assigned to the assembly, interfaces, and classes. Using the `Guid` as an assembly attribute defines the type-library ID, applying it to interfaces defines the interface ID (IID), and setting the attribute to a class defines the class ID (CLSID). The unique IDs needed to be defined with this attribute can be created with the utility `guidgen`. The CLSID and type-library IDs are changed automatically with every build. If you don't want to change it with every build, you can fix it by using this attribute. The IID is only changed if the signature of the interface changes; for example, a method is added or removed, or some parameters changed. Because with COM the IID should change with every new version of this interface, this is a very good default behavior, and usually there's no need to apply the IID with the `Guid` attribute. The only time you want to apply a fixed IID for an interface is when the .NET interface is an exact representation of an existing COM interface, and the COM client already expects this identifier.
ProgId	This attribute can be applied to a class to specify what name should be used when the object is configured in the registry.
ComVisible	This attribute enables you to hide classes, interfaces, and delegates from COM when set to `false`. This prevents a COM representation from being created.
InterfaceType	This attribute, if set to a `ComInterfaceType enumeration value`, enables you to modify the default dual interface type that is created for .NET interfaces. `ComInterfaceType` has the values `InterfaceIsDual`, `InterfaceIsIDispatch`, and `InterfaceIsIUnknown`. If you want to apply a custom interface type to a .NET interface, set the attribute like this: `[InterfaceType(ComInterfaceType.InterfaceIsIUnknown)]`
ClassInterface	This attribute enables you to modify the default dispatch interface that is created for a class. `ClassInterface` accepts an argument of a `ClassInterfaceType` enumeration. The possible values are `AutoDispatch`, `AutoDual`, and `None`. In the previous example, you have seen that the default is `AutoDispatch`, because a dispatch interface is created. If the class should only be accessible by the defined interfaces, apply the attribute `[ClassInterface(ClassInterfaceType.None)]` to the class.
DispId	This attribute can be used with dual and dispatch interfaces to define the `DispId` of methods and properties.
InOut	COM allows specifying attributes to parameter types if the parameter should be sent to the component `[In]`, from the component to the client `[Out]`, or in both directions `[In, Out]`.
Optional	Parameters of COM methods may be optional. Parameters that should be optional can be marked with the `Optional` attribute.

Now, you can change the C# code to specify a dual interface type for the `IWelcome` interface and a custom interface type for the `IMath` interface. With the class `DotnetComponent`, the attribute `ClassInterface` with the argument `ClassInterfaceType.None` specifies that no separate COM interface will be generated. The attributes `ProgId` and `Guid` specify a ProgID and a GUID:

```
[InterfaceType(ComInterfaceType.InterfaceIsDual)]
[ComVisible(true)]
public interface IWelcome
{
   [DispId(60040)] string Greeting(string name);
}

[InterfaceType(ComInterfaceType.InterfaceIsIUnknown)]
[ComVisible(true)]
public interface IMath
{
 int Add(int val1, int val2);
 int Sub(int val1, int val2);
}

[ClassInterface(ClassInterfaceType.None)]
[ProgId("Wrox.DotnetComponent")]
[Guid("77839717-40DD-4876-8297-35B98A8402C7")]
[ComVisible(true)]
public class DotnetComponent : IWelcome, IMath
{
   public DotnetComponent()
   {
   }
```

Rebuilding the class library and the type library changes the interface definition. You can verify this with `OleView.exe`. As you can see in the following IDL code, the interface `IWelcome` is still a dual interface, whereas the `IMath` interface now is a custom interface that is derived from `IUnknown` instead of `IDispatch`. In the `coclass` section, the interface `_DotnetComponent` is removed, and now `IWelcome` is the new default interface, because it was the first interface in the inheritance list of the class `DotnetComponent`:

```
// Generated .IDL file (by the OLE/COM Object Viewer)
//
// typelib filename: <could not determine filename>

[
 uuid(11E86506-EA54-3611-A55C-6830C48A554B),
 version(1.0),
 custom(90883F05-3D28-11D2-8F17-00A0C9A6186D, DotNetComponent,
      Version=1.0.1321.28677, Culture=neutral, PublicKeyToken=null)
]
library DotnetComponent
{
   // TLib : Common Language Runtime Library :
   // {BED7F4EA-1A96-11D2-8F08-00A0C9A6186D}
   importlib("mscorlib.tlb");
   // TLib : OLE Automation : {00020430-0000-0000-c000-000000000046}
   importlib("stdole2.tlb");

   // Forward declare all types defined in this typelib
```

```
    interface IWelcome;
    interface IMath;

    [
      odl,
      uuid(F39A4143-F88D-321E-9A33-8208E256A2DF),
      version(1.0),
      dual,
      oleautomation,
      custom(0F21F359-AB84-41E8-9A78-36D110E6D2F9,
             Wrox.ProCSharp.COMInterop.Server.IWelcome)
    ]
    interface IWelcome : IDispatch {
        [id(0x0000ea88)]
        HRESULT Greeting([in] BSTR name, [out, retval] BSTR* pRetVal);
    };

    [
      odl,
      uuid(EF596F3F-B69B-3657-9D48-C906CBF12565),
      version(1.0),
      oleautomation,
      custom(0F21F359-AB84-41E8-9A78-36D110E6D2F9,
             Wrox.ProCSharp.COMInterop.Server.IMath)
    ]
    interface IMath : IUnknown {
        HRESULT _stdcall Add([in] long val1, [in] long val2,
                             [out, retval] long* pRetVal);
        HRESULT _stdcall Sub([in] long val1, [in] long val2,
                             [out, retval] long* pRetVal);
    };

    [
      uuid(77839717-40DD-4876-8297-35B98A8402C7),
      version(1.0),
      custom(0F21F359-AB84-41E8-9A78-36D110E6D2F9,
             Wrox.ProCSharp.COMInterop.Server.DotnetComponent)
    ]
    coclass DotnetComponent {
       interface _Object;
       [default] interface IWelcome;
       interface IMath;
    };
};
```

COM Registration

Before the .NET component can be used as a COM object, it is necessary to configure it in the registry. Also, if you don't want to copy the assembly into the same directory as the client application, it is necessary to install the assembly in the global assembly cache. The global assembly cache itself is discussed in Chapter 17, "Assemblies."

To install the assembly in the global assembly cache, you must sign it with a strong name (using Visual Studio 2008, you can define a strong name in properties of the solution). Then you can register the assembly in the global assembly cache:

```
gacutil -i dotnetcomponent.dll
```

Now, you can use the regasm utility to configure the component inside the registry. The option /tlb extracts the type library and also configures the type library in the registry:

```
regasm dotnetcomponent.dll /tlb
```

The information for the .NET component that is written to the registry is as follows. The All COM configuration is in the hive HKEY_CLASSES_ROOT (HKCR). The key of the ProgID (in this example, it is Wrox.DotnetComponent) is written directly to this hive, along with the CLSID.

The key HKCR\CLSID\{CLSID}\InProcServer32 has the following entries:

- mscoree.dll — mscoree.dll represents the CCW. This is a real COM object that is responsible for hosting the .NET component. This COM object accesses the .NET component to offer COM behavior for the client. The file mscoree.dll is loaded and instantiated from the client via the normal COM instantiation mechanism.
- ThreadingModel=Both — This is an attribute of the mscoree.dll COM object. This component is programmed in a way to offer support both for STA and MTA.
- Assembly=DotnetComponent, Version=1.0.0.0, Culture=neutral, PublicKeyToken= 5cd57c93b4d9c41a — The value of the Assembly stores the assembly full name, including the version number and the public key token, so that the assembly can be uniquely identified. The assembly registered here will be loaded by mscoree.dll.
- Class=Wrox.ProCSharp.COMInterop.Server.DotnetComponent — The name of the class will also be used by mscoree.dll. This is the class that will be instantiated.
- RuntimeVersion=v2.0.50727 — The registry entry RuntimeVersion specifies the version of the .NET runtime that will be used to host the .NET assembly.

In addition to the configurations shown here, all the interfaces and the type library are configured with their identifiers, too.

Creating a COM Client

Now, it's time to create a COM client. Start by creating a simple C++ Win32 Console application project, and name it COMClient. You can leave the default options selected, and click Finish in the project wizard.

At the beginning of the file COMClient.cpp, add a preprocessor command to include the <iostream> header file and to import the type library that you created for the .NET component. The import statement creates a "smart pointer" class that makes it easier to deal with COM objects. During a build process, the import statement creates .tlh and .tli files that you can find in the debug directory of your project, which includes the smart pointer class. Then add using namespace directives to open the namespace std that will be used for writing output messages to the console, and the namespace DotnetComponent that is created inside the smart pointer class:

```
// COMClient.cpp : Defines the entry point for the console application.
//

#include "stdafx.h"
#include <iostream>
#import "../DotNetComponent/bin/debug/DotnetComponent.tlb" named_guids

using namespace std;
using namespace DotnetComponent;
```

In the _tmain() method, the first thing to do before any other COM call is the initialization of COM with the API call CoInitialize(). CoInitialize() creates and enters an STA for the thread. The variable spWelcome is of type IWelcomePtr, which is a smart pointer. The smart pointer method

`CreateInstance()` accepts the ProgID as an argument to create the COM object by using the COM API `CoCreateInstance()`. The operator `->` is overridden with the smart pointer, so that you can invoke the methods of the COM object such as `Greeting()`:

```
int _tmain(int argc, _TCHAR* argv[])
{
  HRESULT hr;
  hr = CoInitialize(NULL);

  try
  {
    IWelcomePtr spWelcome;

    // CoCreateInstance()
    hr = spWelcome.CreateInstance("Wrox.DotnetComponent");

    cout << spWelcome->Greeting("Bill") << endl;
```

The second interface supported by your .NET component is `IMath`, and there is also a smart pointer that wraps the COM interface: `IMathPtr`. You can directly assign one smart pointer to another as in `spMath = spWelcome;`. In the implementation of the smart pointer (the = operator is overridden), the `QueryInterface()` method is called. With a reference to the `IMath` interface, you can call the `Add()` method.

```
    IMathPtr spMath;
    spMath = spWelcome;    // QueryInterface()

    long result = spMath->Add(4, 5);
    cout << "result:" << result << endl;
  }
```

If an `HRESULT` error value is returned by the COM object (this is done by the CCW that returns `HRESULT` errors if the .NET component generates exceptions), the smart pointer wraps the `HRESULT` errors and generates `_com_error` exceptions instead. Errors are handled in the `catch` block. At the end of the program, the COM DLLs are closed and unloaded using `CoUninitialize()`:

```
  catch (_com_error& e)
  {
    cout << e.ErrorMessage() << endl;
  }

  CoUninitialize();
  return 0;
}
```

Now you can run the application, and you will get outputs from the `Greeting()` and the `Add()` methods to the console. You can also try to debug into the smart pointer class, where you can see the COM API calls directly.

> **If you get an exception that the component cannot be found, check if the same version of the assembly that is configured in the registry is installed in the global assembly cache.**

Adding Connection Points

Adding support for COM events to the .NET components requires some changes to the implementation of your .NET class. Offering COM events is not a simple matter of using the `event` and `delegate` keywords; it is necessary to add some more COM interop attributes.

First, you have to add an interface to the .NET project: `IMathEvents`. This interface is the source or outgoing interface for the component, and will be implemented by the `sink` object in the client. A source interface must be either a dispatch or a custom interface. A scripting client supports only dispatch interfaces. Dispatch interfaces are usually preferred as source interfaces:

```
[InterfaceType(ComInterfaceType.InterfaceIsIDispatch)]
[ComVisible(true)]
public interface IMathEvents
{
   [DispId(46200)] void CalculationCompleted();
}
```

Next, you have to add a delegate. The delegate must have the same signature and return type as the method in the outgoing interface. If you have multiple methods in your source interface, for each one that differs in its arguments, you have to specify a separate delegate. Because the COM client does not have to access this delegate directly, the delegate can be marked with the attribute `[ComVisible(false)]`:

```
[ComVisible(false)]
public delegate void CalculationCompletedEventHandler();
```

With the class `DotnetComponent`, a source interface must be specified. This can be done with the attribute `[ComSourceInterfaces]`. Add the attribute `[ComSourceInterfaces]`, and specify the outgoing interface declared earlier. You can add more than one source interface with different constructors of the attribute class; however, the only client language that supports more than one source interface is C++. Visual Basic 6.0 clients support only one source interface.

```
[ClassInterface(ClassInterfaceType.None)]
[ProgId("Wrox.DotnetComponent")]
[Guid("77839717-40DD-4876-8297-35B98A8402C7")]
[ComSourceInterfaces(typeof(IMathEvents))]
[ComVisible(true)]
public class DotnetComponent : IWelcome, IMath
{
   public DotnetComponent()
   {
   }
```

Inside the class `DotnetComponent`, you have to declare an event for every method of the source interface. The type of the method must be the name of the delegate, and the name of the event must be exactly the same as the name of the method inside the source interface. You can add the event calls to the `Add()` and `Sub()` methods. This step is the normal .NET way to invoke events, as discussed in Chapter 7, "Delegates and Events."

```
   public event CalculationCompletedEventHandler CalculationCompleted;

   public int Add(int val1, int val2)
   {
      int result = val1 + val2;
      if (CalculationCompleted != null)
         CalculationCompleted();
      return result;
   }
```

```
        public int Sub(int val1, int val2)
        {
            int result = val1 - val2;
            if (CalculationCompleted != null)
                CalculationCompleted();
            return result;
        }
    }
```

The name of the event must be the same as the name of the method inside the source interface. Otherwise, the events cannot be mapped for COM clients.

Creating a Client with a Sink Object

After you've built and registered the .NET assembly, and installed it into the global assembly cache, you can build a client application by using the event sources. Implementing a callback or sink object that implements the `IDispatch` interface was — using Visual Basic 6.0 — just a matter of adding the `With Events` keyword, very similar to how Visual Basic deals with .NET events today. It's more work with C++, but here the Active Template Library helps.

Open the C++ Console application created previously and add the following includes to the file `stdafx.h`:

```
#include <atlbase.h>
extern CComModule _Module;
#include <atlcom.h>
```

The file `stdafx.cpp` requires an include of the ATL implementation file `atlimpl.cpp`:

```
#include <atlimpl.cpp>
```

Add the new class `CEventHandler` to the file `COMClient.cpp`. This class contains the implementation of the `IDispatch` interface to be called by the component. The implementation of the `IDispatch` interface is done by the base class `IDispEventImpl`. This class reads the type library to match the dispatch IDs of the methods and the parameters to the methods of the class. The template parameters of the class `IDispatchEventImpl` requires an ID of the sink object (here the ID 4 is used), the class that implements the callback methods (`CEventHandler`), the interface ID of the callback interface (`DIID_IMathEvents`), the ID of the type library (`LIBID_DotnetComponent`), and the version number of the type library. You can find the named IDs `DIID_IMathEvents` and `LIBID_DotnetComponent` in the file `dotnetcomponent.tlh` that was created from the `#import` statement.

The sink map that is surrounded by `BEGIN_SINK_MAP` and `END_SINK_MAP` defines the methods that are implemented by the sink object. `SINK_ENTRY_EX` maps the method `OnCalcCompleted` to the dispatch ID 46200. This dispatch ID was defined with the method `CalculationCompleted` of the `IMathEvents` interface in the .NET component.

```
class CEventHandler : public IDispEventImpl<4, CEventHandler,
        &DIID_IMathEvents, &LIBID_DotnetComponent, 1, 0>
{
public:
    BEGIN_SINK_MAP(CEventHandler)
        SINK_ENTRY_EX(4, DIID_IMathEvents, 46200, OnCalcCompleted)
    END_SINK_MAP()
```

(continued)

(continued)

```
        HRESULT __stdcall OnCalcCompleted()
        {
            cout << "calculation completed" << endl;
            return S_OK;
        }
    };
```

The main method now needs a change to advise the event sink object to the component, so that the component can call back into the sink. This can be done with the method `DispEventAdvise()` of the `CEventHandler` class by passing an `IUnknown` interface pointer. The method `DispEventUnadvise()` unregisters the sink object again.

```
int _tmain(int argc, _TCHAR* argv[])
{
    HRESULT hr;
    hr = CoInitialize(NULL);

    try
    {
        IWelcomePtr spWelcome;
        hr = spWelcome.CreateInstance("Wrox.DotnetComponent");

        IUnknownPtr spUnknown = spWelcome;


        cout << spWelcome->Greeting("Isabella") << endl;

        CEventHandler* eventHandler = new CEventHandler();
        hr = eventHandler->DispEventAdvise(spUnknown);


        IMathPtr spMath;
        spMath = spWelcome;   // QueryInterface()

        long result = spMath->Add(4, 5);
        cout << "result:" << result << endl;

        eventHandler->DispEventUnadvise(spWelcome.GetInterfacePtr());
        delete eventHandler;
    }
    catch (_com_error& e)
    {
        cout << e.ErrorMessage() << endl;
    }

    CoUninitialize();
    return 0;
}
```

Running Windows Forms Controls in Internet Explorer

Windows Forms controls can be hosted in Internet Explorer as ActiveX controls. Because there are many different ActiveX control containers, and all these containers do have different requirements on the ActiveX controls, hosting Windows Forms controls in any container is not supported by Microsoft.

Supported containers are Internet Explorer and MFC containers (MFC containers were supported first in Visual Studio .NET 2003). With MFC containers, however, you have to manually change the code to host ActiveX controls from an MFC application.

To host a Windows Forms control inside Internet Explorer, you have to copy the assembly file to your web server and add some information about the control inside the HTML page. For the support of Windows Forms controls, the syntax of the `<object>` tag has been extended. With the attribute `classid`, you can add the assembly file and the name of the class separated by a `#` sign: `classid="<assembly file>#class name"`.

With the assembly file `ControlDemo.dll` and the class `UserControl1` in the namespace `Wrox.ProCSharp.COMInterop`, the syntax looks like this:

```
<object id="myControl"
  classid="ControlDemo.dll#Wrox.ProCSharp.COMInterop.UserControl1"
  height="400" width="400">
</object>
```

As soon as a user opens the HTML page, the assembly is downloaded to the client system. The assembly is stored in the download assembly cache, and every time the user accesses the page, the version numbers are rechecked. If the version numbers haven't changed, the assembly will be used from the local cache.

> **A requirement for using a Windows Forms control in a web page is that the client must have the .NET runtime installed. Internet Explorer 5.5 or higher must be used, and the security setting must allow the downloading of assemblies.**

Platform Invoke

Not all the features of Windows API calls are available from the .NET Framework. This is not only true for old Windows API calls but also for very new features from Windows Vista or Windows Server 2008. Maybe you've written some DLLs that export unmanaged methods, and you would like to use them from C# as well.

You can read about some Windows Vista — and Windows Server 2008–specific features in Appendix C, "Windows Vista and Windows Server 2008."

To reuse an unmanaged library that doesn't contain COM objects but just exported functions, platform invoke can be used. With platform invoke services, the CLR loads the DLL that includes the function that should be called and marshals the parameters.

To use the unmanaged function, first you have to find out the name of the function as it is exported. You can do this by using the `dumpbin` tool with the `/exports` option.

For example, the command

```
dumpbin /exports c:\windows\system32\kernel32.dll | more
```

lists all exported functions from the DLL `kernel32.dll`. In the example, you use the `CreateHardLink()` Windows API function to create a hard link to an existing file. With this API call, you can have several file names that reference the same file as long as the file names are on just one hard disk. This API call is not available from .NET Framework 3.5, so platform invoke must be used.

To call a native function, you have to define a C# external method with the same number of arguments, and the argument types that are defined with the unmanaged method must have mapped types with managed code.

The Windows API call `CreateHardLink()` has this definition in C++:

```
BOOL CreateHardLink(
    LPCTSTR lpFileName,
    LPCTSTR lpExistingFileName,
    LPSECURITY_ATTRIBUTES lpSecurityAttributes);
```

Now, this definition must be mapped to .NET data types. The return type is a `BOOL` with unmanaged code; this simply maps to the `bool` data type. `LPCTSTR` defines a `long` pointer to a `const` string. The Windows API uses the Hungarian naming convention for the data type. `LP` is a `long` pointer, `C` a const, and `STR` is a null-terminated string. The `T` marks the type as a generic type, and the type is either resolved to `LPCSTR` (an ANSI string) or `LPWSTR` (a wide Unicode string), depending on compiler settings. C strings map to the .NET type `String`. `LPSECURITY_ATTRIBUTES`, which is a long pointer to a struct of type `SECURITY_ATTRIBUTES`. Because you can pass `NULL` to this argument, mapping this type to `IntPtr` is okay. The C# declaration of this method must be marked with the `extern` modifier, because there's no implementation of this method within the C# code. Instead, the implementation of this method is found in the DLL `kernel32.dll`, which is referenced with the attribute `[DllImport]`. Because the return type of the .NET declaration `CreateHardLink()` is of type `bool`, and the native method `CreateHardLink()` returns a `BOOL`, some additional clarification is useful. Because there are different Boolean data types with C++, for example the native `bool` and the Windows-defined `BOOL`, which have different values, the attribute `[MarshalAs]` specifies to what native type the .NET type `bool` should map.

```
[DllImport("kernel32.dll", SetLastError="true",
      EntryPoint="CreateHardLink", CharSet=CharSet.Unicode)]
[return: MarshalAs(UnmanagedType.Bool)]
public static extern bool CreateHardLink(string newFileName,
      string existingFilename, IntPtr securityAttributes);
```

The settings that you can specify with the attribute `[DllImport]` are listed in the following table.

DllImport Property or Field	Description
`EntryPoint`	You can give the C# declaration of the function a different name than it has with the unmanaged library. The name of the method in the unmanaged library is defined in the field `EntryPoint`.
`CallingConvention`	Depending on the compiler or compiler settings that were used to compile the unmanaged function, different calling conventions can be used. The calling convention defines how the parameters are dealt with and where to put them on the stack. You can define the calling convention by setting an enumerable value. The Windows API usually uses the `StdCall` calling convention on the Windows operating system, and it uses the `Cdecl` calling convention on Windows CE. Setting the value to `CallingConvention.Winapi` works for the Windows API both in the Windows and the Windows CE environments.

DllImport Property or Field	Description
CharSet	String parameters can be either ANSI or Unicode. With the CharSet setting, you can define how strings are managed. Possible values that are defined with the CharSet enumeration are Ansi, Unicode, and Auto. CharSet.Auto uses Unicode on the Windows NT platform, and ANSI on Windows 98 and Windows ME.
SetLastError	If the unmanaged function sets an error by using the Windows API SetLastError, you can set the SetLastError field to true. This way, you can read the error number afterward by using Marshal.GetLastWin32Error().

To make the CreateHardLink() method easier to use from a .NET environment, you should follow these guidelines:

- Create an internal class named NativeMethods that wraps the platform invoke method calls
- Create a public class to offer the native method functionality to .NET applications
- Use security attributes to mark the required security

In the sample code, the public method CreateHardLink() in the class FileUtility is the method that can be used by .NET applications. This method has the file name arguments reversed compared to the native Windows API method CreateHardLink(). The first argument is the name of the existing file, and the second argument is the name of the new file. This is similar to other classes in the Framework; for example, File.Copy(). Because the third argument to pass the security attributes for the new file name is not used with this implementation, the public method has just two parameters. The return type is changed as well. Instead of returning an error by returning the value false, an exception is thrown. In case of an error, the unmanaged method CreateHardLink() sets the error number with the unmanaged API SetLastError(). To read this value from .NET, the [DllImport] field SetLastError is set to true. Within the managed method CreateHardLink(), the error number is read by calling Marshal.GetLastWin32Error(). To create an error message from this number, the Win32Exception class from the namespace System.ComponentModel is used. This class accepts an error number with the constructor, and returns a localized error message. In case of an error, an exception of type IOException is thrown, which has an inner exception of type Win32Exception. The public method CreateHardLink() has the FileIOPermission attribute applied to check if the caller has the necessary permission. You can read more information about .NET security in Chapter 20.

```
using System;
using System.Runtime.InteropServices;
using System.ComponentModel;
using System.IO;

namespace Wrox.ProCSharp.Interop
{
   internal static class NativeMethods
   {
      [DllImport("kernel32.dll", SetLastError=true,
         EntryPoint="CreateHardLink", CharSet=CharSet.Unicode)]
      [return: MarshalAs(UnmanagedType.Bool)]
```

(continued)

(continued)

```
        private static extern bool CreateHardLink(
            string newFileName, string existingFileName,
            IntPtr securityAttributes);

        internal static void CreateHardLink(string oldFileName,
                                             string newFileName)
        {
            if (!CreateHardLink(newFileName, oldFileName, IntPtr.Zero))
            {
                Win32Exception ex = new Win32Exception(
                        Marshal.GetLastWin32Error());
                    throw new IOException(ex.Message, ex);
            }
        }
    }

    public static class FileUtility
    {
        [FileIOPermission(SecurityAction.LinkDemand, Unrestricted=true)]
        public static void CreateHardLink(string oldFileName,
                                           string newFileName)
        {
            NativeMethods.CreateHardLink(oldFileName, newFileName);
        }
    }
}
```

This class can now be used to create hard links very easily. If the file `file1.txt` does not exist, you will get an exception with the message "The system cannot find the file specified." If the file exists, you get a new file name referencing the original file. You can easily verify this by changing text in one file; it will show up in the other file as well.

```
        static void Main()
        {
            try
            {
                FileUtility.CreateHardLink("file1.txt", "file2.txt");
            }
            catch (IOException ex)
            {
                Console.WriteLine(ex.Message);
            }
        }
```

With native method calls, often you have to use Window handles. A Window handle is a 32-bit value where depending on the handle types some values are not allowed. With .NET 1.0 for handles, usually the `IntPtr` structure was used because you can set every possible 32-bit value with this structure. However, with some handle types, this led to security problems and possible threading race conditions and leaked handles with the finalization phase. That's why .NET 2.0 introduced the `SafeHandle` class. The class `SafeHandle` is an abstract base class for every Windows handle. Derived classes inside the `Microsoft.Win32.SafeHandles` namespace are `SafeHandleZeroOrMinusOneIsInvalid` and `SafeHandleMinusOneIsInvalid`. As the name tells, these classes do not accept invalid 0 or –1 values. Further derived handle types are `SafeFileHandle`, `SafeWaitHandle`, `SafeNCryptHandle`, and `SafePipeHandle` that can be used by the specific Windows API calls.

For example, to map the Windows API `CreateFile()`, you can use this declaration to return a `SafeFileHandle`. Of course, usually you could use the .NET classes `File` and `FileInfo` instead.

```
[DllImport("Kernel32.dll", SetLastError = true,
           CharSet = CharSet.Unicode)]
internal static extern SafeFileHandle CreateFile(
   string fileName,
   [MarshalAs(UnmanagedType.U4)] FileAccess fileAccess,
   [MarshalAs(UnmanagedType.U4)] FileShare fileShare,
   IntPtr securityAttributes,
   [MarshalAs(UnmanagedType.U4)] FileMode creationDisposition,
   int flags,
   SafeFileHandle template);
```

In Chapter 22, "Transactions," you see how to create a custom `SafeHandle` *class to work with the transacted file API from Windows Vista.*

Summary

In this chapter, you have seen how the different generations of COM and .NET applications can interact. Instead of rewriting applications and components, a COM component can be used from a .NET application just like a .NET class. The tool that makes this possible is `tlbimp`, which creates a runtime callable wrapper (RCW) that hides the COM object behind a .NET façade.

Likewise, `tlbexp` creates a type library from a .NET component that is used by the COM callable wrapper (CCW). The CCW hides the .NET component behind a COM façade. Using .NET classes as COM components makes it necessary to use some attributes from the namespace `System.Runtime.InteropServices` to define specific COM characteristics that are needed by the COM client.

With platform invoke, you've seen how native methods can be invoked using C#. Platform invoke requires redefining the native method with C# and .NET data types. After defining the mapping, you can invoke the native method as if it would be a C# method. Another option for doing interop would be to use the technology It Just Works (IJW) with C++/CLI. You can read information about C++/CLI in Appendix B.

The next part of this book is all about data. The next chapter gives information on how to access the file system, followed by chapters on how to read and write from the database and manipulate XML.

Part IV
Data

Chapter 25: Manipulating Files and the Registry

Chapter 26: Data Access

Chapter 27: LINQ to SQL

Chapter 28: Manipulating XML

Chapter 29: LINQ to XML

Chapter 30: .NET Programming with SQL Server

25

Manipulating Files and the Registry

This chapter examines how to perform tasks involving reading from and writing to files and the system registry in C#. In particular, it covers the following:

- Exploring the directory structure, finding out what files and folders are present, and checking their properties
- Moving, copying, and deleting files and folders
- Reading and writing text in files
- Reading and writing keys in the registry
- Reading and writing to isolated storage

Microsoft has provided very intuitive object models covering these areas, and in this chapter, you learn how to use .NET base classes to perform the listed tasks. In the case of file system operations, the relevant classes are almost all found in the `System.IO` namespace, whereas registry operations are dealt with by classes in the `Microsoft.Win32` namespace.

> *The .NET base classes also include a number of classes and interfaces in the* `System.Runtime.Serialization` *namespace concerned with serialization — that is, the process of converting data (for example, the contents of a document) into a stream of bytes for storage. This chapter does not focus on these classes; it focuses on the classes that give you direct access to files.*

Note that security is particularly important when modifying files or registry entries. The whole area of security is covered separately in Chapter 20, "Security." In this chapter, however, we assume that you have sufficient access rights to run all of the examples that modify files or registry entries, which should be the case if you are running from an account with administrator privileges.

Managing the File System

The classes that are used to browse around the file system and perform operations such as moving, copying, and deleting files are shown in Figure 25-1.

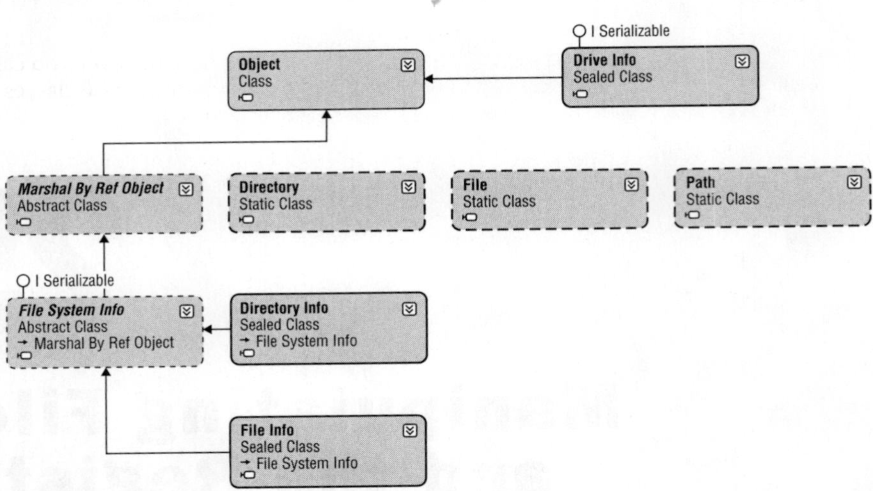

Figure 25-1

The following list explains the function of these classes:

- `System.MarshalByRefObject` — This is the base object class for .NET classes that are remotable; permits marshaling of data between application domains.
- `FileSystemInfo` — This is the base class that represents any file system object.
- `FileInfo` and `File` — These classes represent a file on the file system.
- `DirectoryInfo` and `Directory` — These classes represent a folder on the file system.
- `Path` — This class contains static members that you can use to manipulate path names.
- `DriveInfo` — This class provides properties and methods that provide information on a selected drive.

On Windows, the objects that contain files and that are used to organize the file system are termed folders. For example, in the path `C:\My Documents\ReadMe.txt`, `ReadMe.txt` *is a file and* `My Documents` *is a folder. Folder is a very Windows-specific term: on virtually every other operating system the term directory is used in place of folder, and in accordance with Microsoft's goal to design .NET as a platform-independent technology, the corresponding .NET base classes are called* `Directory` *and* `DirectoryInfo`*. However, due to the potential for confusion with LDAP directories (as discussed in Chapter 46, "Directory Services"), and because this is a Windows book, we'll stick to the term folder in this discussion.*

.NET Classes That Represent Files and Folders

You will notice from the previous list that two classes are used to represent a folder and two classes are used to represent a file. Which one of these classes you use depends largely on how many times you need to access that folder or file:

- `Directory` and `File` contain only static methods and are never instantiated. You use these classes by supplying the path to the appropriate file system object whenever you call a member method. If you want to do only one operation on a folder or file, using these classes is more efficient because it saves the overhead of instantiating a .NET class.
- `DirectoryInfo` and `FileInfo` implement roughly the same public methods as `Directory` and `File`, as well as some public properties and constructors, but they are stateful and the members of these classes are not static. You need to instantiate these classes before each instance is associated with a particular folder or file. This means that these classes are more efficient if you are performing multiple operations using the same object. That's because they read in the authentication and other information for the appropriate file system object on construction, and then do not need to read that information again, no matter how many methods and so on you call against each object (class instance). In comparison, the corresponding stateless classes need to check the details of the file or folder again with every method you call.

In this section, you will be mostly using the `FileInfo` and `DirectoryInfo` classes, but it so happens that many (though not all) of the methods called are also implemented by `File` and `Directory` (although in those cases these methods require an extra parameter — the path name of the file system object; also, a couple of the methods have slightly different names). For example:

```
FileInfo myFile = new FileInfo(@"C:\Program Files\My Program\ReadMe.txt");
myFile.CopyTo(@"D:\Copies\ReadMe.txt");
```

has the same effect as:

```
File.Copy(@"C:\Program Files\My Program\ReadMe.txt", @"D:\Copies\ReadMe.txt");
```

The first code snippet will take slightly longer to execute because of the need to instantiate a `FileInfo` object, `myFile`, but it leaves `myFile` ready for you to perform further actions on the same file. By using the second example, there is no need to instantiate an object to copy the file.

You can instantiate a `FileInfo` or `DirectoryInfo` class by passing to the constructor a string containing the path to the corresponding file system object. You have just seen the process for a file. For a folder, the code looks similar:

```
DirectoryInfo myFolder = new DirectoryInfo(@"C:\Program Files");
```

If the path represents an object that does not exist, an exception will not be thrown at construction, but will instead be thrown the first time that you call a method that actually requires the corresponding file system object to be there. You can find out whether the object exists and is of the appropriate type by checking the `Exists` property, which is implemented by both of these classes:

```
FileInfo test = new FileInfo(@"C:\Windows");
Console.WriteLine(test.Exists.ToString());
```

Note that for this property to return `true`, the corresponding file system object must be of the appropriate type. In other words, if you instantiate a `FileInfo` object supplying the path of a folder, or you instantiate a `DirectoryInfo` object, giving it the path of a file, `Exists` will have the value `false`. Most of the properties and methods of these objects will return a value if possible — they won't necessarily throw an exception just because the wrong type of object has been called, unless they are asked to do something that really is impossible. For example, the preceding code snippet might first display `false` (because `C:\Windows` is a folder). However, it still displays the time the folder was created because a folder still has that information. But if you tried to open the folder as if it were a file, using the `FileInfo.Open()` method, you'd get an exception.

After you have established whether the corresponding file system object exists, you can (if you are using the `FileInfo` or `DirectoryInfo` class) find out information about it using the properties in the following table.

Name	Description
`CreationTime`	Time file or folder was created
`DirectoryName` (`FileInfo` only)	Full path name of the containing folder
`Parent` (`DirectoryInfo` only)	The parent directory of a specified subdirectory
`Exists`	Whether file or folder exists
`Extension`	Extension of the file; returns blank for folders
`FullName`	Full path name of the file or folder
`LastAccessTime`	Time file or folder was last accessed
`LastWriteTime`	Time file or folder was last modified
`Name`	Name of the file or folder
`Root` (`DirectoryInfo` only)	The root portion of the path
`Length` (`FileInfo` only)	The size of the file in bytes

You can also perform actions on the file system object using the methods in the following table.

Name	Purpose
`Create()`	Creates a folder or empty file of the given name. For a `FileInfo` this also returns a stream object to let you write to the file. (Streams are covered later in the chapter.)
`Delete()`	Deletes the file or folder. For folders, there is an option for the `Delete` to be recursive.
`MoveTo()`	Moves and/or renames the file or folder.
`CopyTo()`	(`FileInfo` only) Copies the file. Note that there is no copy method for folders. If you are copying complete directory trees you will need to individually copy each file and create new folders corresponding to the old folders.
`GetDirectories()`	(`DirectoryInfo` only) Returns an array of `DirectoryInfo` objects representing all folders contained in this folder.
`GetFiles()`	(`DirectoryInfo` only) Returns an array of `FileInfo` objects representing all files contained in this folder.
`GetFileSystemInfos()`	(`DirectoryInfo` only) Returns `FileInfo` and `DirectoryInfo` objects representing all objects contained in this folder, as an array of `FileSystemInfo` references.

Note that these tables list the main properties and methods and are not intended to be exhaustive.

The preceding tables do not list most of the properties or methods that allow you to write to or read the data in files. This is actually done using stream objects, which are covered later in this chapter. `FileInfo` *also implements a number of methods,* `Open()`, `OpenRead()`, `OpenText()`, `OpenWrite()`, `Create()`, *and* `CreateText()`, *that return stream objects for this purpose.*

Interestingly, the creation time, last access time, and last write time are all writable:

```
// displays the creation time of a file,
// then changes it and displays it again
FileInfo test = new FileInfo(@"C:\MyFile.txt");
Console.WriteLine(test.Exists.ToString());
Console.WriteLine(test.CreationTime.ToString());
test.CreationTime = new DateTime(2008, 1, 1, 7, 30, 0);
Console.WriteLine(test.CreationTime.ToString());
```

Running this application produces results similar to the following:

```
True
2/5/2007 2:59:32 PM
1/1/2008 7:30:00 AM
```

Being able to manually modify these properties might seem strange at first, but it can be quite useful. For example, if you have a program that effectively modifies a file by simply reading it in, deleting it, and creating a new file with the new contents, you would probably want to modify the creation date to match the original creation date of the old file.

The Path Class

The `Path` class is not a class that you would instantiate. Rather, it exposes some static methods that make operations on path names easier. For example, suppose that you want to display the full path name for a file, `ReadMe.txt` in the folder `C:\My Documents`. You could find the path to the file using the following code:

```
Console.WriteLine(Path.Combine(@"C:\My Documents", "ReadMe.txt"));
```

Using the `Path` class is a lot easier than using separation symbols manually, especially because the `Path` class is aware of different formats for path names on different operating systems. At the time of writing, Windows is the only operating system supported by .NET. However, if .NET were later ported to Unix, `Path` would be able to cope with Unix paths, in which `/`, rather than `\`, is used as a separator in path names. `Path.Combine()` is the method of this class that you are likely to use most often, but `Path` also implements other methods that supply information about the path or the required format for it.

Some of the properties available to the `Path` class include the following:

Property	Description
`AltDirectorySeparatorChar`	Provides a platform-agnostic way to specify an alternative character to separate directory levels. On Windows, a `/` symbol is used, whereas on UNIX, a `\` symbol is used.
`DirectorySeparatorChar`	Provides a platform-agnostic way to specify a character to separate directory levels. On Windows, a `/` symbol is used, whereas on UNIX, a `\` symbol is used.
`PathSeparator`	Provides a platform-agnostic way to specify path strings which divide environmental variables. The default value of this setting is a semicolon.
`VolumeSeparatorChar`	Provides a platform-agnostic way to specify a volume separator. The default value of this setting is a colon.

The following example illustrates how to browse directories and view the properties of files.

Example: A File Browser

This section presents a sample C# application called `FileProperties`. This application presents a simple user interface that allows you to browse the file system and view the creation time, last access time, last write time, and size of files. (You can download the sample code for this application from the Wrox web site at `www.wrox.com`.)

The `FileProperties` application works like this. You type in the name of a folder or file in the main text box at the top of the window and click the Display button. If you type in the path to a folder, its contents are listed in the list boxes. If you type in the path to a file, its details are displayed in the text boxes at the bottom of the form and the contents of its parent folder are displayed in the list boxes. Figure 25-2 shows the `FileProperties` sample application in action.

The user can very easily navigate around the file system by clicking any folder in the right-hand list box to move down to that folder or by clicking the Up button to move up to the parent folder. Figure 25-2 shows the contents of the My Documents folder. The user can also select a file by clicking its name in the list box. This displays the file's properties in the text boxes at the bottom of the application (see Figure 25-3).

Note that if you wanted to, you could also display the creation time, last access time, and last modification time for folders using the `DirectoryInfo` property. You are going to display these properties only for a selected file to keep things simple.

You create the project as a standard C# Windows application in Visual Studio 2008, and add the various text boxes and the list box from the Windows Forms area of the toolbox. You have also renamed the controls with the more intuitive names of `textBoxInput`, `textBoxFolder`, `buttonDisplay`, `buttonUp`, `listBoxFiles`, `listBoxFolders`, `textBoxFileName`, `textBoxCreationTime`, `textBoxLastAccessTime`, `textBoxLastWriteTime`, and `textBoxFileSize`.

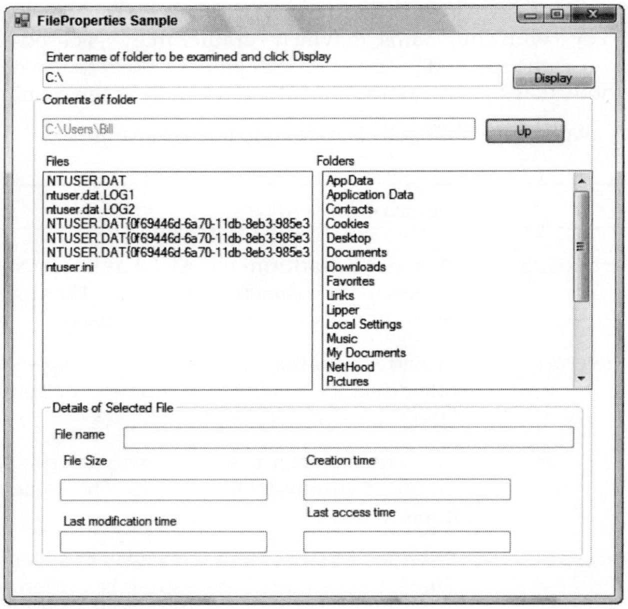

Figure 25-2

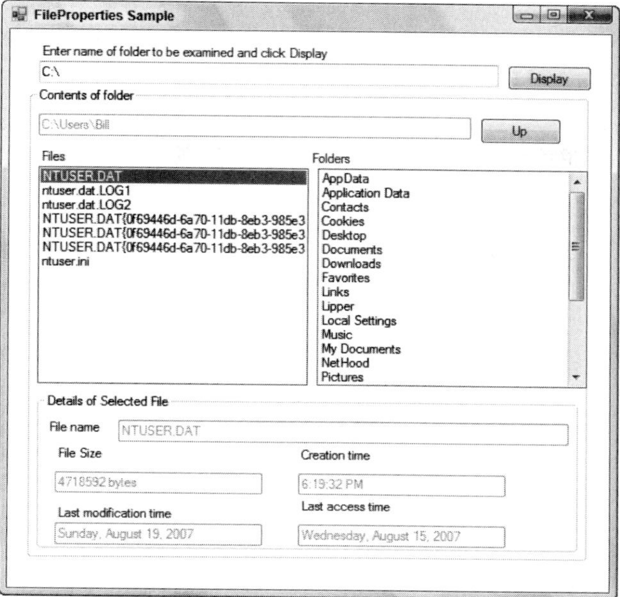

Figure 25-3

Next, you need to indicate that you will be using the `System.IO` namespace:

```
using System;
using System.IO;
using System.Windows.Forms;
```

You need to do this for all of the file-system–related examples in this chapter, but this part of the code will not be explicitly shown in the remaining examples. You then add a member field to the main form:

```
   public partial class Form1 : Form
   {
      private string currentFolderPath;
```

`currentFolderPath` stores the path of the folder whose contents are displayed in the list boxes.

Next, you need to add event handlers for the user-generated events. The possible user inputs are:

- User clicks the Display button — In this case, you need to determine whether what the user has typed in the main text box is the path to a file or folder. If it is a folder, you list the files and subfolders of this folder in the list boxes. If it is a file, you still do this for the folder containing that file, but you also display the file properties in the lower text boxes.
- User clicks a file name in the Files list box — In this case, you display the properties of this file in the lower text boxes.
- User clicks a folder name in the Folders list box — In this case, you clear all the controls and then display the contents of this subfolder in the list boxes.
- User clicks the Up button — In this case, you clear all the controls and then display the contents of the parent of the currently selected folder.

Before you see the code for the event handlers, here is the code for the methods that do all the work. First, you need to clear the contents of all the controls. This method is fairly self-explanatory:

```
protected void ClearAllFields()
{
   listBoxFolders.Items.Clear();
   listBoxFiles.Items.Clear();
   textBoxFolder.Text = "";
   textBoxFileName.Text = "";
   textBoxCreationTime.Text = "";
   textBoxLastAccessTime.Text = "";
   textBoxLastWriteTime.Text = "";
   textBoxFileSize.Text = "";
}
```

Next, you define a method, `DisplayFileInfo()`, that handles the process of displaying the information for a given file in the text boxes. This method takes one parameter, the full path name of the file as a `String`, and works by creating a `FileInfo` object based on this path:

```
protected void DisplayFileInfo(string fileFullName)
{
   FileInfo theFile = new FileInfo(fileFullName);

   if (!theFile.Exists)
   {
      throw new FileNotFoundException("File not found: " + fileFullName);
   }

   textBoxFileName.Text = theFile.Name;
   textBoxCreationTime.Text = theFile.CreationTime.ToLongTimeString();
   textBoxLastAccessTime.Text = theFile.LastAccessTime.ToLongDateString();
   textBoxLastWriteTime.Text = theFile.LastWriteTime.ToLongDateString();
   textBoxFileSize.Text = theFile.Length.ToString() + " bytes";
}
```

Note that you take the precaution of throwing an exception if there are any problems locating a file at the specified location. The exception itself will be handled in the calling routine (one of the event handlers). Finally, you define a method, `DisplayFolderList()`, which displays the contents of a given folder in the two list boxes. The full path name of the folder is passed in as a parameter to this method:

```
protected void DisplayFolderList(string folderFullName)
{
   DirectoryInfo theFolder = new DirectoryInfo(folderFullName);

   if (!theFolder.Exists)
   {
      throw new DirectoryNotFoundException("Folder not found: " + folderFullName);
   }

   ClearAllFields();
   textBoxFolder.Text = theFolder.FullName;
   currentFolderPath = theFolder.FullName;
```

```
      // list all subfolders in folder
      foreach(DirectoryInfo nextFolder in theFolder.GetDirectories())
         listBoxFolders.Items.Add(nextFolder.Name);

      // list all files in folder
      foreach(FileInfo nextFile in theFolder.GetFiles())
         listBoxFiles.Items.Add(nextFile.Name);
   }
```

Next, you examine the event handlers. The event handler that manages the event that is triggered when the user clicks the Display button is the most complex because it needs to handle three different possibilities for the text the user enters in the text box. For instance, it could be the path name of a folder, the path name of a file, or neither of these:

```
protected void OnDisplayButtonClick(object sender, EventArgs e)
{
   try
   {
      string folderPath = textBoxInput.Text;
      DirectoryInfo theFolder = new DirectoryInfo(folderPath);
      if (theFolder.Exists)
      {
         DisplayFolderList(theFolder.FullName);
         return;
      }
      FileInfo theFile = new FileInfo(folderPath);
      if (theFile.Exists)
      {
         DisplayFolderList(theFile.Directory.FullName);
         int index = listBoxFiles.Items.IndexOf(theFile.Name);
         listBoxFiles.SetSelected(index, true);
         return;
      }
      throw new FileNotFoundException("There is no file or folder with "
                                       + "this name: " + textBoxInput.Text);
   }
   catch(Exception ex)
   {
      MessageBox.Show(ex.Message);
   }
}
```

In this code, you establish if the supplied text represents a folder or file by instantiating `DirectoryInfo` and `FileInfo` instances and examining the `Exists` property of each object. If neither exists, you throw an exception. If it's a folder, you call `DisplayFolderList()` to populate the list boxes. If it's a file, you need to populate the list boxes and sort out the text boxes that display the file properties. You handle this case by first populating the list boxes. You then programmatically select the appropriate file name in the Files list box. This has exactly the same effect as if the user had selected that item — it raises the item-selected event. You can then simply exit the current event handler, knowing that the selected item event handler will immediately be called to display the file properties.

The following code is the event handler that is called when an item in the Files list box is selected, either by the user or, as indicated previously, programmatically. It simply constructs the full path name of the selected file, and passes this to the `DisplayFileInfo()` method presented earlier:

```
protected void OnListBoxFilesSelected(object sender, EventArgs e)
{
   try
   {
      string selectedString = listBoxFiles.SelectedItem.ToString();
      string fullFileName = Path.Combine(currentFolderPath, selectedString);
      DisplayFileInfo(fullFileName);
   }
   catch(Exception ex)
   {
      MessageBox.Show(ex.Message);
   }
}
```

The event handler for the selection of a folder in the Folders list box is implemented in a very similar way, except that in this case you call `DisplayFolderList()` to update the contents of the list boxes:

```
protected void OnListBoxFoldersSelected(object sender, EventArgs e)
{
   try
   {
      string selectedString = listBoxFolders.SelectedItem.ToString();
      string fullPathName = Path.Combine(currentFolderPath, selectedString);
      DisplayFolderList(fullPathName);
   }
   catch(Exception ex)
   {
      MessageBox.Show(ex.Message);
   }
}
```

Finally, when the Up button is clicked, `DisplayFolderList()` must also be called, except that this time you need to obtain the path of the parent of the folder currently being displayed. This is done with the `FileInfo.DirectoryName` property, which returns the parent folder path:

```
protected void OnUpButtonClick(object sender, EventArgs e)
{
   try
   {
      string folderPath = new FileInfo(currentFolderPath).DirectoryName;
      DisplayFolderList(folderPath);
   }
   catch(Exception ex)
   {
      MessageBox.Show(ex.Message);
   }
}
```

Moving, Copying, and Deleting Files

As mentioned, moving and deleting files or folders is done by the `MoveTo()` and `Delete()` methods of the `FileInfo` and `DirectoryInfo` classes. The equivalent methods on the `File` and `Directory` classes are `Move()` and `Delete()`. The `FileInfo` and `File` classes also implement the methods `CopyTo()` and

`Copy()`, respectively. However, no methods exist to copy complete folders — you need to do that by copying each file in the folder.

Using all of these methods is quite intuitive — you can find detailed descriptions in the SDK documentation. This section illustrates their use for the particular cases of calling the static `Move()`, `Copy()`, and `Delete()` methods on the `File` class. To do this, you will build on the previous `FileProperties` example and call its iteration `FilePropertiesAndMovement`. This example will have the extra feature that whenever the properties of a file are displayed, the application gives you the option of deleting that file or moving or copying the file to another location.

Example: FilePropertiesAndMovement

Figure 25-4 shows the user interface of the new sample application.

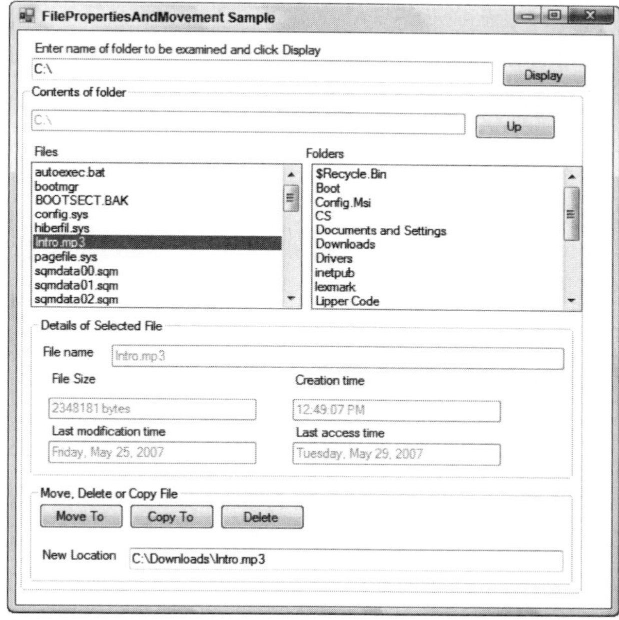

Figure 25-4

As you can see, `FilePropertiesAndMovement` is similar in appearance to `FileProperties`, except for the group of three buttons and a text box at the bottom of the window. These controls are enabled only when the example is actually displaying the properties of a file; at all other times, they are disabled. The existing controls are also squashed up a bit to stop the main form from getting too big. When the properties of a selected file are displayed, `FilePropertiesAndMovement` automatically places the full path name of that file in the bottom text box for the user to edit. Users can then click any of the buttons to perform the appropriate operation. When they do, a message box is displayed that confirms the action taken by the user (see Figure 25-5).

When the user clicks the Yes button, the action will be initiated. There are some actions in the form that the user can take that will then cause the display to be incorrect. For instance, if the user moves or deletes a file, you obviously cannot continue to display the contents of that file in the same location. In addition, if you change the name of a file in the same folder, your display will also be out of date. In these cases, `FilePropertiesAndMovement` resets its controls to display only the folder where the file resides after the file operation.

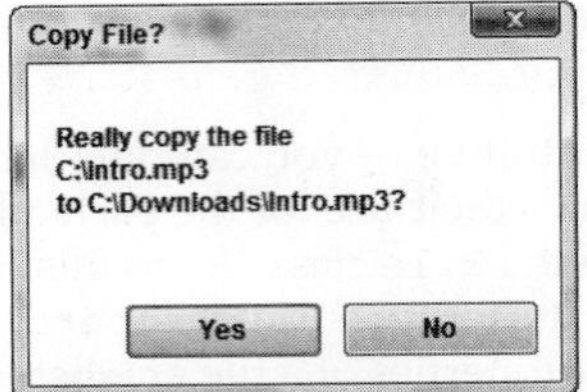

Figure 25-5

Looking at the Code for FilePropertiesAndMovement

To code this process, you need to add the relevant controls, as well as their event handlers, to the code for the `FileProperties` example. The new controls are given the names `buttonDelete`, `buttonCopyTo`, `buttonMoveTo`, and `textBoxNewPath`.

First, look at the event handler that is called when the user clicks the Delete button:

```
protected void OnDeleteButtonClick(object sender, EventArgs e)
{
   try
   {
      string filePath = Path.Combine(currentFolderPath,
                                     textBoxFileName.Text);
      string query = "Really delete the file\n" + filePath + "?";
      if (MessageBox.Show(query,
         "Delete File?", MessageBoxButtons.YesNo) == DialogResult.Yes)
      {
         File.Delete(filePath);
         DisplayFolderList(currentFolderPath);
      }
   }
   catch(Exception ex)
   {
      MessageBox.Show("Unable to delete file. The following exception"
                     + " occurred:\n" + ex.Message, "Failed");
   }
}
```

The code for this method is contained in a `try` block because of the obvious risk of an exception being thrown if, for example, you don't have permission to delete the file, or the file is moved by another process after it has been displayed but before the user presses the Delete button. You construct the path of the file to be deleted from the `CurrentParentPath` field, which contains the path of the parent folder, and the text in the `textBoxFileName` text box, which contains the name of the file.

The methods to move and copy the file are structured in a very similar manner:

```
protected void OnMoveButtonClick(object sender, EventArgs e)
{
   try
   {
      string filePath = Path.Combine(currentFolderPath,
                                     textBoxFileName.Text);
      string query = "Really move the file\n" + filePath + "\nto "
                   + textBoxNewPath.Text + "?";
```

```
            if (MessageBox.Show(query,
               "Move File?", MessageBoxButtons.YesNo) == DialogResult.Yes)
            {
               File.Move(filePath, textBoxNewPath.Text);
               DisplayFolderList(currentFolderPath);
            }
         }
         catch(Exception ex)
         {
            MessageBox.Show("Unable to move file. The following exception"
                              + " occurred:\n" + ex.Message, "Failed");
         }
      }

      protected void OnCopyButtonClick(object sender, EventArgs e)
      {
         try
         {
            string filePath = Path.Combine(currentFolderPath,
                                           textBoxFileName.Text);
            string query = "Really copy the file\n" + filePath + "\nto "
                            + textBoxNewPath.Text + "?";
            if (MessageBox.Show(query,
               "Copy File?", MessageBoxButtons.YesNo) == DialogResult.Yes)
            {
               File.Copy(filePath, textBoxNewPath.Text);
               DisplayFolderList(currentFolderPath);
            }
         }
         catch(Exception ex)
         {
            MessageBox.Show("Unable to copy file. The following exception"
                              + " occurred:\n" + ex.Message, "Failed");
         }
      }
```

You are not quite done yet. You also need to make sure that the new buttons and text box are enabled and disabled at the appropriate times. To enable them when you are displaying the contents of a file, you add the following code to `DisplayFileInfo()`:

```
      protected void DisplayFileInfo(string fileFullName)
      {
         FileInfo theFile = new FileInfo(fileFullName);

         if (!theFile.Exists)
         {
            throw new FileNotFoundException("File not found: " + fileFullName);
         }

         textBoxFileName.Text = theFile.Name;
         textBoxCreationTime.Text = theFile.CreationTime.ToLongTimeString();
         textBoxLastAccessTime.Text = theFile.LastAccessTime.ToLongDateString();
         textBoxLastWriteTime.Text = theFile.LastWriteTime.ToLongDateString();
         textBoxFileSize.Text = theFile.Length.ToString() + " bytes";
```

(continued)

(continued)

```
        // enable move, copy, delete buttons
        textBoxNewPath.Text = theFile.FullName;
        textBoxNewPath.Enabled = true;
        buttonCopyTo.Enabled = true;
        buttonDelete.Enabled = true;
        buttonMoveTo.Enabled = true;
    }
```

You also need to make one change to `DisplayFolderList`:

```
    protected void DisplayFolderList(string folderFullName)
    {
        DirectoryInfo theFolder = new DirectoryInfo(folderFullName);

        if (!theFolder.Exists)
        {
            throw new DirectoryNotFoundException("Folder not found: " + folderFullName);
        }

        ClearAllFields();
        DisableMoveFeatures();
        textBoxFolder.Text = theFolder.FullName;
        currentFolderPath = theFolder.FullName;

        // list all subfolders in folder
        foreach(DirectoryInfo nextFolder in theFolder.GetDirectories())
            listBoxFolders.Items.Add(NextFolder.Name);

        // list all files in folder
        foreach(FileInfo nextFile in theFolder.GetFiles())
            listBoxFiles.Items.Add(NextFile.Name);
    }
```

`DisableMoveFeatures` is a small utility function that disables the new controls:

```
        void DisableMoveFeatures()
        {
            textBoxNewPath.Text = "";
            textBoxNewPath.Enabled = false;
            buttonCopyTo.Enabled = false;
            buttonDelete.Enabled = false;
            buttonMoveTo.Enabled = false;
        }
```

You also need to add extra code to `ClearAllFields()` to clear the extra text box:

```
        protected void ClearAllFields()
        {
            listBoxFolders.Items.Clear();
            listBoxFiles.Items.Clear();
            textBoxFolder.Text = "";
            textBoxFileName.Text = "";
            textBoxCreationTime.Text = "";
```

```
            textBoxLastAccessTime.Text = "";
            textBoxLastWriteTime.Text = "";
            textBoxFileSize.Text = "";
            textBoxNewPath.Text = "";
        }
```

The next section takes a look at reading and writing to files.

Reading and Writing to Files

Reading and writing to files is in principle very simple; however, it is not done through the `DirectoryInfo` or `FileInfo` objects. Instead, using the .NET Framework 3.5, you can do it through the `File` object. Later in this chapter, you see how to accomplish this using a number of other classes that represent a generic concept called a *stream*.

Before the .NET Framework 2.0, it took a bit of wrangling to read and write to files. It was possible using the available classes from the framework, but it was not that straightforward. The .NET Framework 2.0 has expanded the `File` class to make it as simple as just one line of code to read or write to a file. This same functionality is also available in version 3.5 of the .NET Framework.

Reading a File

For an example of reading a file, create a Windows Form application that contains a regular text box, a button, and a multiline text box. In the end, your form should appear something like Figure 25-6.

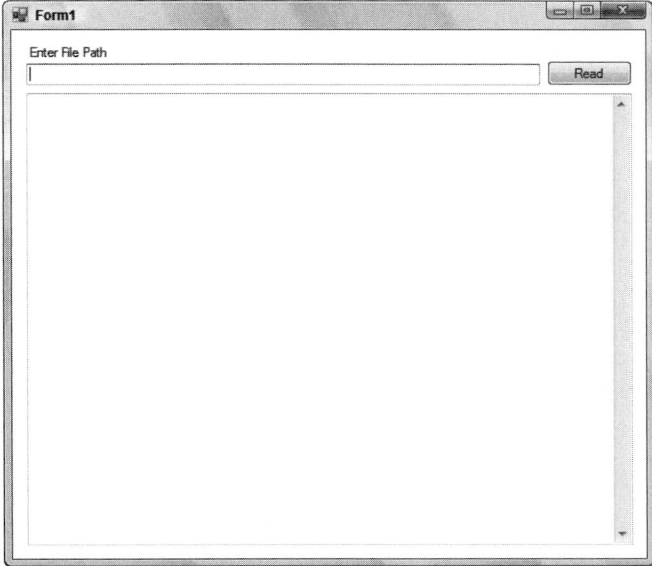

Figure 25-6

The idea of this form is that the end user will enter in the path of a specific file in the first text box and click the Read button. From here, the application will read the specified file and display the file's contents in the multiline text box. This is illustrated in the following code example:

```
using System;
using System.IO;
using System.Windows.Forms;

namespace ReadingFiles
{
    public partial class Form1 : Form
    {
        public Form1()
        {
            InitializeComponent();
        }

        private void button1_Click(object sender, EventArgs e)
        {
            textBox2.Text = File.ReadAllText(textBox1.Text);
        }
    }
}
```

In building this example, the first step is to add the `using` statement to bring in the `System.IO` namespace. From there, simply use the `button1_Click` event for the Send button on the form to populate the text box with what comes back from the file. You can now access the file's contents by using the `File.ReadAllText()` method. As you can see, you can read files with a single statement. The `ReadAllText()` method opens the specified file, reads the contents, and then closes the file. The return value of the `ReadAllText()` method is a string array containing the entire contents of the file specified. The result would be something similar to what is shown in Figure 25-7.

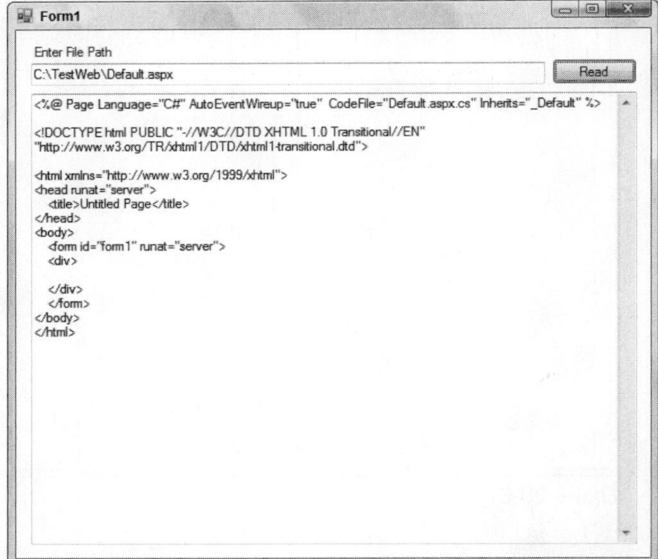

Figure 25-7

The `File.ReadAllText()` signature shown in the preceding example is of the following construction:

```
File.ReadAllText(FilePath);
```

The other option is to also specify the encoding of the file being read:

```
File.ReadAllText(FilePath, Encoding);
```

Using this signature allows you to specify the encoding to use when opening and reading the contents of the file. Therefore, this means that you could do something like the following:

```
File.ReadAllText(textBox1.Text, Encoding.ASCII);
```

Some of the other options for opening and working with files include using the `ReadAllBytes()` and the `ReadAllLines()` methods. The `ReadAllBytes()` method allows you to open a binary file and read the contents into a byte array. The `ReadAllText()` method shown earlier gives you the entire contents of the specified file in a single string array instance. This might not be something that you are interested in. You might instead be interested in working with what comes back from the file in a line-by-line fashion. In this case, you will want to use the `ReadAllLines()` method because it will allow for this kind of functionality.

Writing to a File

Besides making reading from files an extremely simple process under the .NET Framework umbrella, the base class library has made writing to files just as easy. Just as the base class library (BCL) gives you the `ReadAllText()`, `ReadAllLines()`, and `ReadAllBytes()` methods to read files in a few different ways, it gives you the `WriteAllText()`, `WriteAllBytes()`, and `WriteAllLines()` methods to write files.

For an example of how to write to a file, use the same Windows Form application, but use the multiline text box in the form to input data into a file. The code for the `button1_Click` event handler should appear as shown here:

```
private void button1_Click(object sender, EventArgs e)
{
   File.WriteAllText(textBox1.Text, textBox2.Text);
}
```

Build and start the form, type `C:\Testing.txt` in the first text box, type some random content in the second text box, and then click the button. Nothing will happen visually, but if you look in your root C drive, you will see the `Testing.txt` file with the content you specified.

The `WriteAllText()` method went to the specified location, created a new text file, and provided the specified contents to the file before saving and closing the file. Not bad for just one line of code!

If you run the application again, and specify the same file (`Testing.txt`) but with some new content, pressing the button again will cause the application to perform the same task. This time though, the new content is not added to the previous content you specified — instead, the new content completely overrides the previous content. In fact, `WriteAllText()`, `WriteAllBytes()`, and `WriteAllLines()` all override any previous files, so you must be careful when using these methods.

The `WriteAllText()` method in the previous example uses the following signature:

```
File.WriteAllText(FilePath, Contents)
```

You can also specify the encoding of the new file:

```
File.WriteAllText(FilePath, Contents, Encoding)
```

The `WriteAllBytes()` method allows you to write content to a file using a byte array, and the `WriteAllLines()` method allows you to write a string array to a file. An example of this is illustrated in the following event handler:

```
private void button1_Click(object sender, EventArgs e)
{
   string[] movies =
      {"Grease",
       "Close Encounters of the Third Kind",
       "The Day After Tomorrow"};

   File.WriteAllLines(@"C:\Testing.txt", movies);
}
```

Now clicking the button for such an application will give you a `Testing.txt` file with the following contents:

```
Grease
Close Encounters of the Third Kind
The Day After Tomorrow
```

The `WriteAllLines()` method writes out the string array with each array item taking its own line in the file.

Because data may be written not only to disk but to other places as well (such as to named pipes or to memory), it is also important to understand how to deal with file I/O in .NET using streams as a means of moving file contents around. This is shown in the following section.

Streams

The idea of a stream has been around for a very long time. A stream is an object used to transfer data. The data can be transferred in one of two directions:

- If the data is being transferred from some outside source into your program, it is called *reading* from the stream.
- If the data is being transferred from your program to some outside source, it is called *writing* to the stream.

Very often, the outside source will be a file, but that is not always the case. Other possibilities include:

- Reading or writing data on the network using some network protocol, where the intention is for this data to be picked up by or sent from another computer
- Reading or writing to a named pipe
- Reading or writing to an area of memory

Of these examples, Microsoft has supplied a .NET base class for writing to or reading from memory, the `System.IO.MemoryStream` object. The `System.Net.Sockets.NetworkStream` object handles network data. There are no base stream classes for writing to or reading from pipes, but there is a generic stream class, `System.IO.Stream`, from which you would inherit if you wanted to write such a class. `Stream` does not make any assumptions about the nature of the external data source.

The outside source might even be a variable within your own code. This might sound paradoxical, but the technique of using streams to transmit data between variables can be a useful trick for converting data between data types. The C language used something similar — the function, `sprintf` — to convert between integer data types and strings or to format strings.

The advantage of having a separate object for the transfer of data, rather than using the `FileInfo` or `DirectoryInfo` classes to do this, is that separating the concept of transferring data from the particular data source makes it easier to swap data sources. Stream objects themselves contain a lot of generic code that concerns the movement of data between outside sources and variables in your code. By keeping this code separate from any concept of a particular data source, you make it easier for this code to be reused (through inheritance) in different circumstances. For example, the `StringReader` and `StringWriter` classes are part of the same inheritance tree as two classes that you will be using later on to read and write text files. The classes will almost certainly share a substantial amount of code behind the scenes.

Figure 25-8 illustrates the actual hierarchy of stream-related classes in the `System.IO` namespace.

As far as reading and writing files, the classes that concern us most are:

- `FileStream` — This class is intended for reading and writing binary data in a binary file. However, you can also use it to read from or write to any file.
- `StreamReader` and `StreamWriter` — These classes are designed specifically for reading from and writing to text files.

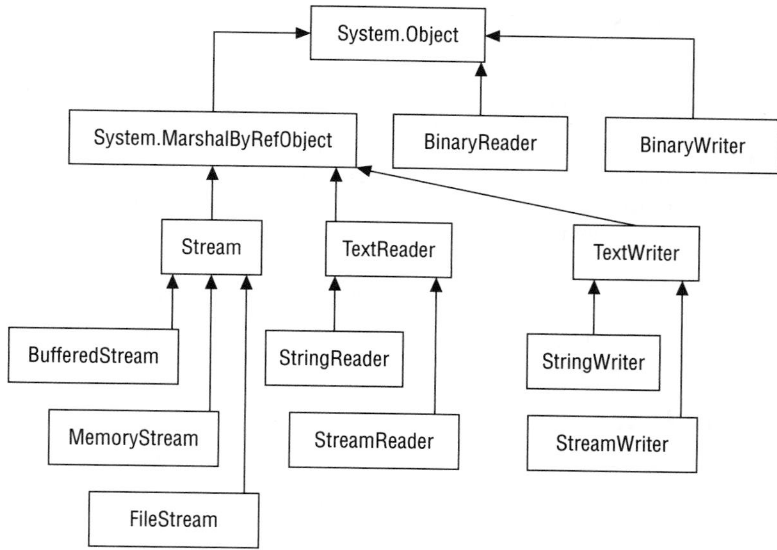

Figure 25-8

You might also find the `BinaryReader` and `BinaryWriter` classes useful, although they are not used in the examples here. These classes do not actually implement streams themselves, but they are able to provide wrappers around other stream objects. `BinaryReader` and `BinaryWriter` provide extra formatting of binary data, which allows you to directly read or write the contents of C# variables to or from the relevant stream. Think of the `BinaryReader` and `BinaryWriter` as sitting between the stream and your code, providing extra formatting (see Figure 25-9).

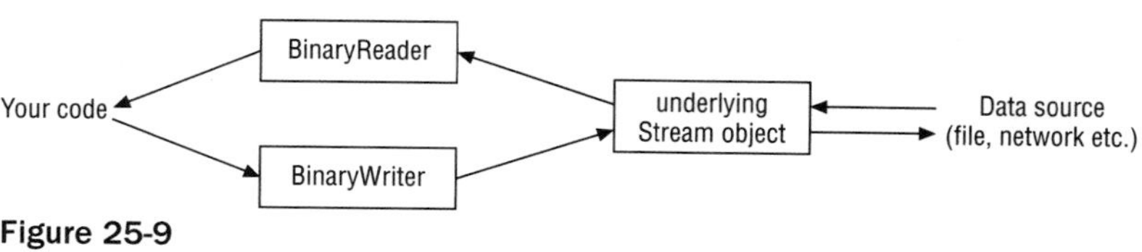

Figure 25-9

The difference between using these classes and directly using the underlying stream objects is that a basic stream works in bytes. For example, suppose that as part of the process of saving some document you want to write the contents of a variable of type `long` to a binary file. Each `long` occupies 8 bytes, and if you used an ordinary binary stream, you would have to explicitly write each of those 8 bytes of memory. In C# code, that would mean you would have to perform some bitwise operations to extract each of those 8 bytes from the `long` value. Using a `BinaryWriter` instance, you can encapsulate the entire operation in an overload of the `BinaryWriter.Write()` method, which takes a `long` as a parameter, and which will place those 8 bytes into the stream (and if the stream is directed to a file, into the file). A corresponding `BinaryReader.Read()` method will extract 8 bytes from the stream and recover the value of the `long`. For more information on the `BinaryReader` and `BinaryWriter` classes, refer to the SDK documentation.

Buffered Streams

For performance reasons, when you read or write to or from a file, the output is buffered. This means that if your program asks for the next 2 bytes of a file stream, and the stream passes the request on to Windows, then Windows will not go through the trouble of connecting to the file system and then locating and reading the file off the disk, just to get 2 bytes. Instead, Windows will retrieve a large block of the file at one time and store this block in an area of memory known as a *buffer*. Subsequent requests for data from the stream are satisfied from the buffer until the buffer runs out, at which point, Windows grabs another block of data from the file. Writing to files works in the same way. For files, this is done automatically by the operating system, but you might have to write a stream class to read from some other device that is not buffered. If so, you can derive your class from `BufferedStream`, which implements a buffer itself. (Note, however, that `BufferedStream` is not designed for the situation in which an application frequently alternates between reading and writing data.)

Reading and Writing to Binary Files Using FileStream

Reading and writing to and from binary files can be done using the `FileStream` class. (Note that if you are working with the .NET Framework 1.x, this will most likely be the case.)

The FileStream Class

A `FileStream` instance is used to read or write data to or from a file. In order to construct a `FileStream`, you need four pieces of information:

1. The **file** you want to access.
2. The **mode**, which indicates how you want to open the file. For example, are you intending to create a new file or open an existing file? And if you are opening an existing file, should any write operations be interpreted as overwriting the contents of the file or appending to the file?
3. The **access**, which indicates how you want to access the file. For example, do you want to read from or write to the file or do both?
4. The **share** access, which specifies whether you want exclusive access to the file. Or, are you willing to have other streams access the file simultaneously? If so, should other streams have access to read the file, to write to it, or to do both?

The first of these pieces of information is usually represented by a string that contains the full path name of the file, and this chapter considers only those constructors that require a string here. Besides those constructors, however, some additional ones take an old Windows-API–style Windows handle to a file instead. The remaining three pieces of information are represented by three .NET enumerations called

`FileMode`, `FileAccess`, and `FileShare`. The values of these enumerations are listed in the following table; they should be self-explanatory.

Enumeration	Values
`FileMode`	`Append`, `Create`, `CreateNew`, `Open`, `OpenOrCreate`, or `Truncate`
`FileAccess`	`Read`, `ReadWrite`, or `Write`
`FileShare`	`Delete`, `Inheritable`, `None`, `Read`, `ReadWrite`, or `Write`

Note that in the case of `FileMode`, exceptions can be thrown if you request a mode that is inconsistent with the existing status of the file. `Append`, `Open`, and `Truncate` will throw an exception if the file does not already exist, and `CreateNew` will throw an exception if it does. `Create` and `OpenOrCreate` will cope with either scenario, but `Create` will delete any existing file to replace it with a new, initially empty, one. The `FileAccess` and `FileShare` enumerations are bitwise flags, so values can be combined with the C# bitwise OR operator, `|`.

There are a large number of constructors for the `FileStream`. The three simplest ones work as follows:

```
// creates file with read-write access and allows other streams read access
FileStream fs = new FileStream(@"C:\C# Projects\Project.doc",
                    FileMode.Create);
// as above, but we only get write access to the file
FileStream fs2 = new FileStream(@"C:\C# Projects\Project2.doc",
                    FileMode.Create, FileAccess.Write);
// as above but other streams don't get access to the file while
// fs3 is open
FileStream fs3 = new FileStream(@"C:\C# Projects\Project3.doc",
                    FileMode.Create, FileAccess.Write, FileShare.None);
```

As this code reveals, the overloads of these constructors have the effect of providing default values of `FileAccess.ReadWrite` and `FileShare.Read` to the third and fourth parameters. It is also possible to create a file stream from a `FileInfo` instance in various ways:

```
FileInfo myFile4 = new FileInfo(@"C:\C# Projects\Project4.doc");
FileStream fs4 = myFile4.OpenRead();
FileInfo myFile5= new FileInfo(@"C:\C# Projects\Project5doc");
FileStream fs5 = myFile5.OpenWrite();
FileInfo myFile6= new FileInfo(@"C:\C# Projects\Project6doc");
FileStream fs6 = myFile6.Open(FileMode.Append, FileAccess.Write,
                 FileShare.None);
FileInfo myFile7 = new FileInfo(@"C:\C# Projects\Project7.doc");
FileStream fs7 = myFile7.Create();
```

`FileInfo.OpenRead()` supplies a stream that gives you read-only access to an existing file, whereas `FileInfo.OpenWrite()` gives you read-write access. `FileInfo.Open()` allows you to specify the mode, access, and file share parameters explicitly.

Of course, after you have finished with a stream, you should close it:

```
fs.Close();
```

Closing the stream frees up the resources associated with it and allows other applications to set up streams to the same file. This action also flushes the buffer. In between opening and closing the stream, you will want to read data from it and/or write data to it. `FileStream` implements a number of methods to do this.

`ReadByte()` is the simplest way of reading data. It grabs 1 byte from the stream and casts the result to an `int` that has a value between 0 and 255. If you have reached the end of the stream, it returns `-1`:

```
int NextByte = fs.ReadByte();
```

If you prefer to read a number of bytes at a time, you can call the `Read()` method, which reads a specified number of bytes into an array. `Read()` returns the number of bytes actually read — if this value is zero, you know that you are at the end of the stream. Here is an example where you read into a byte array called `ByteArray`:

```
int nBytesRead = fs.Read(ByteArray, 0, nBytes);
```

The second parameter to `Read()` is an offset, which you can use to request that the `Read` operation start populating the array at some element other than the first. The third parameter is the number of bytes to read into the array.

If you want to write data to a file, two parallel methods are available, `WriteByte()` and `Write()`. `WriteByte()` writes a single byte to the stream:

```
byte NextByte = 100;
fs.WriteByte(NextByte);
```

`Write()`, however, writes out an array of bytes. For instance, if you initialized the `ByteArray` mentioned before with some values, you could use the following code to write out the first `nBytes` of the array:

```
fs.Write(ByteArray, 0, nBytes);
```

As with `Read()`, the second parameter allows you to start writing from some point other than the beginning of the array. Both `WriteByte()` and `Write()` return `void`.

In addition to these methods, `FileStream` implements various other methods and properties related to bookkeeping tasks such as determining how many bytes are in the stream, locking the stream, or flushing the buffer. These other methods are not usually required for basic reading and writing, but if you need them, full details are in the SDK documentation.

Example: BinaryFileReader

The use of the `FileStream` class is illustrated by writing an example, `BinaryFileReader`, which reads in and displays any file. Create the project in Visual Studio 2008 as a Windows application. It has one menu item, which brings up a standard `OpenFileDialog` asking what file to read in and then displays the file as binary code. As you are reading in binary files, you need to be able to display nonprintable characters. You will do this by displaying each byte of the file individually, showing 16 bytes on each line of a multiline text box. If the byte represents a printable ASCII character, you will display that character; otherwise, you will display the value of the byte in a hexadecimal format. In either case, you pad out the displayed text with spaces so that each byte displayed occupies four columns; this way, the bytes line up nicely under each other.

Figure 25-10 shows what the `BinaryFileReader` application looks like when viewing a text file. (Because `BinaryFileReader` can view any file, it is quite possible to use it on text files as well as binary ones.) In this case, the application has read in a basic ASP.NET page (`.aspx`).

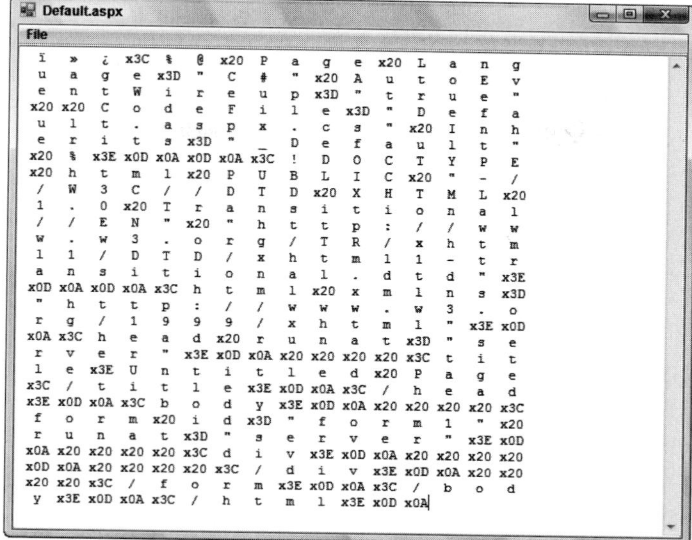

Figure 25-10

Clearly, this format is more suited to looking at the values of individual bytes than to displaying text! Later in this chapter, when you develop an example that is specifically designed to read text files, you will be able to see what this file really says. The advantage of this example is that you can look at the contents of any file.

This example will not demonstrate writing to files because you don't want to get bogged down in the complexities of trying to translate the contents of a text box like the one shown in Figure 25-10 into a binary stream! You see how to write to files later when you develop an example that can read or write, but only to and from text files.

Here is the code used to get these results. First, you need to make sure that you have brought in the `System.IO` namespace through the use of the `using` statement:

```
using System.IO;
```

Next, you add a couple of fields to the main form class — one representing the file dialog and a string that gives the path of the file currently being viewed:

```
partial class Form1 : Form
{
   private readonly OpenFileDialog chooseOpenFileDialog =
      new OpenFileDialog();
   private string chosenFile;
```

You also need to add some standard Windows Forms code to deal with the handlers for the menu and the file dialog:

```
   public Form1()
   {
      InitializeComponent();
```

(continued)

(continued)

```
        menuFileOpen.Click += OnFileOpen;
        chooseOpenFileDialog.FileOk += OnOpenFileDialogOK;
    }

    void OnFileOpen(object Sender, EventArgs e)
    {
        chooseOpenFileDialog.ShowDialog();
    }

    void OnOpenFileDialogOK(object Sender, CancelEventArgs e)
    {
        chosenFile = chooseOpenFileDialog.FileName;
        this.Text = Path.GetFileName(chosenFile);
        DisplayFile();
    }
```

As this code demonstrates, when the user clicks OK to select a file in the file dialog, you call the `DisplayFile()` method, which does the work of reading in the selected file:

```
    void DisplayFile()
    {
        int nCols = 16;
        FileStream inStream = new FileStream(chosenFile, FileMode.Open,
                                                         FileAccess.Read);
        long nBytesToRead = inStream.Length;
        if (nBytesToRead > 65536/4)
            nBytesToRead = 65536/4;

        int nLines = (int)(nBytesToRead/nCols) + 1;
        string [] lines = new string[nLines];
        int nBytesRead = 0;

        for (int i=0 ; i<nLines ; i++)
        {
            StringBuilder nextLine = new StringBuilder();
            nextLine.Capacity = 4*nCols;

            for (int j = 0 ; j<nCols ; j++)
            {
                int nextByte = inStream.ReadByte();
                nBytesRead++;
                if (nextByte < 0 || nBytesRead > 65536)
                    break;
                char nextChar = (char)nextByte;
                if (nextChar < 16)
                    nextLine.Append(" x0" + string.Format("{0,1:X}",
                                                 (int)nextChar));
                else if
                    (char.IsLetterOrDigit(nextChar) ||
                                         char.IsPunctuation(nextChar))
                    nextLine.Append("  " + nextChar + " ");
                else
                    nextLine.Append(" x" + string.Format("{0,2:X}",
                                         (int)nextChar));
            }
```

```
            lines[i] = nextLine.ToString();
        }
        inStream.Close();
        this.textBoxContents.Lines = lines;
    }
```

There is quite a lot going on in this method, so here is a breakdown. You instantiate a `FileStream` object for the selected file, which specifies that you want to open an existing file for reading. You then work out how many bytes there are to read in and how many lines should be displayed. The number of bytes will normally be the number of bytes in the file. However, text boxes can display a maximum of only 65,536 characters and with the chosen display format, you are displaying four characters for every byte in the file. Therefore, you will need to cap the number of bytes shown in the text box if the selected file is longer than 65,536/4 = 16,384 bytes.

> *If you want to display longer files in this sort of environment, you might want to look up the* `RichTextBox` *class in the* `System.Windows.Forms` *namespace.* `RichTextBox` *is similar to a text box, but has many more advanced formatting facilities and does not have a limit on how much text it can display.* `TextBox` *is used here to keep the example simple and focused on the process of reading in files.*

The bulk of the method is given over to two nested `for` loops that construct each line of text to be displayed. You use a `StringBuilder` class to construct each line for performance reasons: you are appending suitable text for each byte to the string that represents each line 16 times. If on each occasion you allocate a new string and take a copy of the half-constructed line, you are not only going to be spending a lot of time allocating strings but will also be wasting a lot of memory on the heap. Notice that the definition of *printable* characters is anything that is a letter, digit, or punctuation, as indicated by the relevant static `System.Char` methods. You exclude any character with a value less than 16 from the printable list, however; this means that you will trap the carriage return (13) and line feed (10) as binary characters (a multiline text box isn't able to display these characters properly if they occur individually within a line).

Furthermore, using the Properties window, you change the Font property for the text box to a fixed-width font. In this case, you choose `Courier New 9pt regular`, and set the text box to have vertical and horizontal scroll bars.

Upon completion, you close the stream and set the contents of the text box to the array of strings that you have built up.

Reading and Writing to Text Files

Theoretically, it is perfectly possible to use the `FileStream` class to read in and display text files. You have, after all, just done that. The format in which the `Default.aspx` file is displayed in the preceding example is not particularly user-friendly, but that has nothing to do with any intrinsic problem with the `FileStream` class, only with how you chose to display the results in the text box.

Having said that, if you know that a particular file contains text, you will usually find it more convenient to read and write it using the `StreamReader` and `StreamWriter` classes instead of the `FileStream` class. That is because these classes work at a slightly higher level and are specifically geared to reading and writing text. The methods that they implement are able to automatically detect convenient points to stop reading text, based on the contents of the stream. In particular:

- These classes implement methods to read or write one line of text at a time, `StreamReader.ReadLine()` and `StreamWriter.WriteLine()`. In the case of reading, this means that the stream will automatically determine for you where the next carriage return is and stop reading at that point. In the case of writing, it means that the stream will automatically append the carriage return–line feed combination to the text that it writes out.

- By using the `StreamReader` and `StreamWriter` classes, you don't need to worry about the encoding (the text format) used in the file. Possible encodings include ASCII (1 byte for each character), or any of the Unicode-based formats, Unicode, UTF7, UTF8, and UTF32. Text files on Windows 9x systems are always in ASCII because Windows 9x does not support Unicode; however, because Windows NT, 2000, XP, 2003, Vista, and Windows Server 2008 all do support Unicode, text files might theoretically contain Unicode, UTF7, UTF8, or UTF32 data instead of ASCII data. The convention is that if the file is in ASCII format, it will simply contain the text. If it is in any Unicode format, this will be indicated by the first 2 or 3 bytes of the file, which are set to particular combinations of values to indicate the format used in the file.

These bytes are known as the *byte code markers*. When you open a file using any of the standard Windows applications, such as Notepad or WordPad, you do not need to worry about this because these applications are aware of the different encoding methods and will automatically read the file correctly. This is also true for the `StreamReader` class, which will correctly read in a file in any of these formats, and the `StreamWriter` class is capable of formatting the text it writes out using whatever encoding technique you request. If you wanted to read in and display a text file using the `FileStream` class, however, you would have to handle all of this yourself.

The StreamReader Class

`StreamReader` is used to read text files. Constructing a `StreamReader` is in some ways easier than constructing a `FileStream` instance because some of the `FileStream` options are not required when using `StreamReader`. In particular, the mode and access types are not relevant to `StreamReader` because the only thing you can do with a `StreamReader` is read! Furthermore, there is no direct option to specify the sharing permissions. However, there are a couple of new options:

- You need to specify what to do about the different encoding methods. You can instruct the `StreamReader` to examine the byte code markers in the beginning of the file to determine the encoding method, or you can simply tell the `StreamReader` to assume that the file uses a specified encoding method.
- Instead of supplying a file name to be read from, you can supply a reference to another stream.

This last option deserves a bit more discussion because it illustrates another advantage of basing the model for reading and writing data on the concept of streams. Because the `StreamReader` works at a relatively high level, you might find it useful if you have another stream that is there to read data from some other source, but you would like to use the facilities provided by `StreamReader` to process that other stream as if it contained text. You can do so by simply passing the output from this stream to a `StreamReader`. In this way, `StreamReader` can be used to read and process data from any data source — not only files. This is essentially the situation discussed earlier with regard to the `BinaryReader` class. However, in this book you will only use `StreamReader` to connect directly to files.

The result of these possibilities is that `StreamReader` has a large number of constructors. Not only that, but there are a couple of `FileInfo` methods that return `StreamReader` references, too: `OpenText()` and `CreateText()`. The following just illustrates some of the constructors.

The simplest constructor takes just a file name. This `StreamReader` will examine the byte order marks to determine the encoding:

```
StreamReader sr = new StreamReader(@"C:\My Documents\ReadMe.txt");
```

Alternatively, if you prefer to specify that UTF8 encoding should be assumed:

```
StreamReader sr = new StreamReader(@"C:\My Documents\ReadMe.txt",
                                   Encoding.UTF8);
```

You specify the encoding by using one of several properties on a class, `System.Text.Encoding`. This class is an abstract base class, from which a number of classes are derived and which implements methods that actually perform the text encoding. Each property returns an instance of the appropriate class, and the possible properties you can use here are:

- `ASCII`
- `Unicode`
- `UTF7`
- `UTF8`
- `UTF32`
- `BigEndianUnicode`

The following example demonstrates hooking up a `StreamReader` to a `FileStream`. The advantage of this is that you can specify whether to create the file and the share permissions, which you cannot do if you directly attach a `StreamReader` to the file:

```
FileStream fs = new FileStream(@"C:\My Documents\ReadMe.txt",
                    FileMode.Open, FileAccess.Read, FileShare.None);
StreamReader sr = new StreamReader(fs);
```

For this example, you specify that the `StreamReader` will look for byte code markers to determine the encoding method used, as it will do in the following examples, in which the `StreamReader` is obtained from a `FileInfo` instance:

```
FileInfo myFile = new FileInfo(@"C:\My Documents\ReadMe.txt");
StreamReader sr = myFile.OpenText();
```

Just as with a `FileStream`, you should always close a `StreamReader` after use. Failure to do so will result in the file remaining locked to other processes (unless you used a `FileStream` to construct the `StreamReader` and specified `FileShare.ShareReadWrite`):

```
sr.Close();
```

Now that you have gone to the trouble of instantiating a `StreamReader`, you can do something with it. As with the `FileStream`, you will simply see the various ways to read data, and the other, less commonly used `StreamReader` methods are left to the SDK documentation.

Possibly the easiest method to use is `ReadLine()`, which keeps reading until it gets to the end of a line. It does not include the carriage return–line feed combination that marks the end of the line in the returned string:

```
string nextLine = sr.ReadLine();
```

Alternatively, you can grab the entire remainder of the file (or strictly, the remainder of the stream) in one string:

```
string restOfStream = sr.ReadToEnd();
```

You can read a single character:

```
int nextChar = sr.Read();
```

This overload of `Read()` casts the returned character to an `int`. This is so that it has the option of returning a value of `-1` if the end of the stream has been reached.

Finally, you can read a given number of characters into an array, with an offset:

```
// to read 100 characters in.

int nChars = 100;
char [] charArray = new char[nChars];
int nCharsRead = sr.Read(charArray, 0, nChars);
```

`nCharsRead` will be less than `nChars` if you have requested to read more characters than are left in the file.

The StreamWriter Class

This works in the same way as the `StreamReader`, except that you can use `StreamWriter` only to write to a file (or to another stream). Possibilities for constructing a `StreamWriter` include:

```
StreamWriter sw = new StreamWriter(@"C:\My Documents\ReadMe.txt");
```

This will use UTF8 encoding, which is regarded by .NET as the default encoding method. If you want, you can specify an alternative encoding:

```
StreamWriter sw = new StreamWriter(@"C:\My Documents\ReadMe.txt", true,
   Encoding.ASCII);
```

In this constructor, the second parameter is a `Boolean` that indicates whether the file should be opened for appending. There is, oddly, no constructor that takes only a file name and an encoding class.

Of course, you may want to hook up `StreamWriter` to a file stream to give you more control over the options for opening the file:

```
FileStream fs = new FileStream(@"C:\My Documents\ReadMe.txt",
   FileMode.CreateNew, FileAccess.Write, FileShare.Read);
StreamWriter sw = new StreamWriter(fs);
```

`FileStream` does not implement any methods that return a `StreamWriter` class.

Alternatively, if you want to create a new file and start writing data to it, you will find this sequence useful:

```
FileInfo myFile = new FileInfo(@"C:\My Documents\NewFile.txt");
StreamWriter sw = myFile.CreateText();
```

Just as with all other stream classes, it is important to close a `StreamWriter` class when you have finished with it:

```
sw.Close();
```

Writing to the stream is done using any of four overloads of `StreamWriter.Write()`. The simplest writes out a string and appends it with a carriage return–line feed combination:

```
string nextLine = "Groovy Line";
sw.Write(nextLine);
```

It is also possible to write out a single character:

```
char nextChar = 'a';
sw.Write(nextChar);
```

And an array of characters:

```
char [] charArray = new char[100];

// initialize these characters

sw.Write(charArray);
```

It is even possible to write out a portion of an array of characters:

```
int nCharsToWrite = 50;
int startAtLocation = 25;
char [] charArray = new char[100];

// initialize these characters

sw.Write(charArray, startAtLocation, nCharsToWrite);
```

Example: ReadWriteText

The `ReadWriteText` example displays the use of the `StreamReader` and `StreamWriter` classes. It is similar to the earlier `ReadBinaryFile` example, but it assumes that the file to be read in is a text file and displays it as such. It is also capable of saving the file (with any modifications you have made to the text in the text box). It will save any file in Unicode format.

The screenshot in Figure 25-11 shows `ReadWriteText` displaying the same `Default.aspx` file that you used earlier. This time, however, you are able to read the contents a bit more easily!

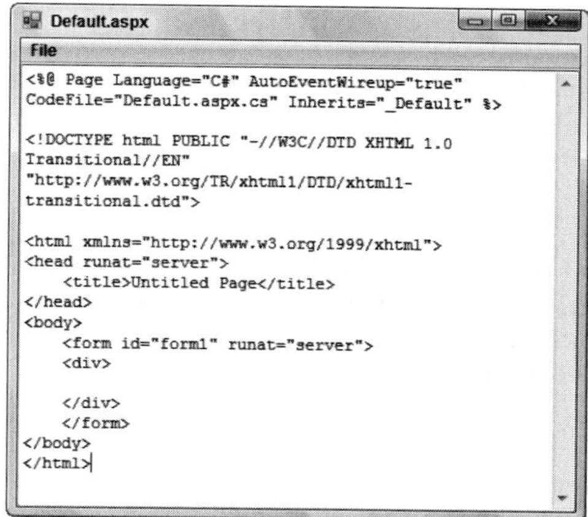

Figure 25-11

We won't cover the details of adding the event handlers for the Open File dialog box, because they are basically the same as in the earlier `BinaryFileReader` example. As with that example, opening a new file causes the `DisplayFile()` method to be called. The only real difference between this example and the previous one is the implementation of `DisplayFile` as well as that you now have the option to save a file. This is represented by another menu option, Save. The handler for this option calls another method you have added to the code, `SaveFile()`. (Note that the new file always overwrites the original file; this example does not have an option to write to a different file.)

You will look at `SaveFile()` first because that is the simplest function. You simply write each line of the text box, in turn, to a `StreamWriter` stream, relying on the `StreamReader.WriteLine()` method to append the trailing carriage return and line feed to the end of each line:

```
void SaveFile()
{
   StreamWriter sw = new StreamWriter(chosenFile, false, Encoding.Unicode);

   foreach (string line in textBoxContents.Lines)
      sw.WriteLine(line);
   sw.Close();
}
```

`chosenFile` is a string field of the main form, which contains the name of the file you have read in (just as for the previous example). Notice that you specify Unicode encoding when you open the stream. If you wanted to write files in some other format, you would simply need to change the value of this parameter. The second parameter to this constructor would be set to `true` if you wanted to append to a file, but you do not in this case. The encoding must be set at construction time for a `StreamWriter`. It is subsequently available as a read-only property, `Encoding`.

Now you examine how files are read in. The process of reading in is complicated by the fact that you don't know how many lines it is going to contain until you have read in the file. For example, you don't know how many `(char)13(char)10` sequences are in the file because `char(13)char(10)` is the carriage return–line feed combination that occurs at the end of a line. You solve this problem by initially reading the file into an instance of the `StringCollection` class, which is in the `System.Collections.Specialized` namespace. This class is designed to hold a set of strings that can be dynamically expanded. It implements two methods that you will be interested in: `Add()`, which adds a string to the collection, and `CopyTo()`, which copies the string collection into a normal array (a `System.Array` instance). Each element of the `StringCollection` object will hold one line of the file.

The `DisplayFile()` method calls another method, `ReadFileIntoStringCollection()`, which actually reads in the file. After doing this, you now know how many lines there are, so you are in a position to copy the `StringCollection` into a normal, fixed-size array and feed this array into the text box. Because only the references to the strings, not the strings themselves, are copied when you actually make the copy, the process is reasonably efficient:

```
void DisplayFile()
{
   StringCollection linesCollection = ReadFileIntoStringCollection();
   string [] linesArray = new string[linesCollection.Count];
   linesCollection.CopyTo(linesArray, 0);
   this.textBoxContents.Lines = linesArray;
}
```

The second parameter of `StringCollection.CopyTo()` indicates the index within the destination array of where you want the collection to start.

Now you examine the `ReadFileIntoStringCollection()` method. You use a `StreamReader` to read in each line. The main complication here is the need to count the characters read in to make sure that you do not exceed the capacity of the text box:

```
StringCollection ReadFileIntoStringCollection()
{
   const int MaxBytes = 65536;
   StreamReader sr = new StreamReader(chosenFile);
   StringCollection result = new StringCollection();
```

```
        int nBytesRead = 0;
        string nextLine;
        while ( (nextLine = sr.ReadLine()) != null)
        {
           nBytesRead += nextLine.Length;
           if (nBytesRead > MaxBytes)
              break;
           result.Add(nextLine);
        }
        sr.Close();
        return result;
    }
```

That completes the code for this example.

If you run `ReadWriteText`, read in the `Default.aspx` file, and then save it, the file will be in Unicode format. You would not be able to tell this from any of the usual Windows applications. Notepad, WordPad, and even the `ReadWriteText` example will still read the file in and display it correctly under Windows NT/2000/XP/2003/Vista/2008, although, because Windows 9x doesn't support Unicode, applications like Notepad won't be able to understand the Unicode file on those platforms. (If you download the example from the Wrox Press web site at `www.wrox.com`, you can try this!) However, if you try to display the file again using the earlier `BinaryFileReader` example, you can see the difference immediately, as shown in Figure 25-12. The two initial bytes that indicate the file is in Unicode format are visible, and thereafter you see that every character is represented by 2 bytes. This last fact is obvious because the high-order byte of every character in this particular file is zero, so every second byte in this file now displays `x00`.

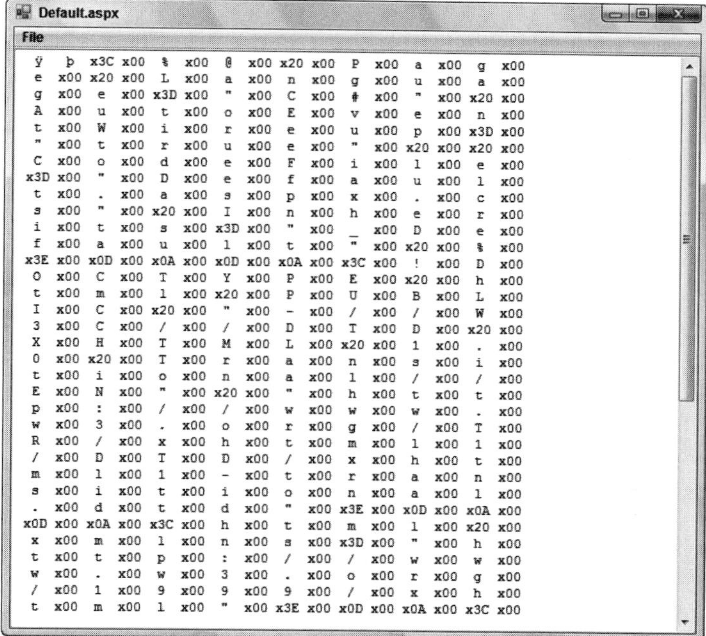

Figure 25-12

Reading Drive Information

In addition to working with files and directories, the .NET Framework includes the ability to read information from a specified drive. This is done using the `DriveInfo` class. The `DriveInfo` class can perform a scan of a system to provide a list of available drives and then can dig in deeper, providing you with tons of details about any of the drives.

For an example of using the `DriveInfo` class, create a simple Windows Form that will list out all the available drives on a computer and then will provide details on a user-selected drive. Your Windows Form will consist of a simple `ListBox` and should look as illustrated in Figure 25-13.

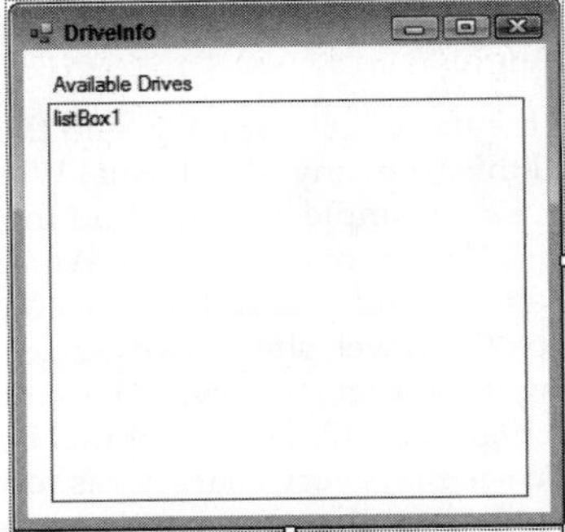

Figure 25-13

Once you have the form all set, the code will consist of two events — one for when the form loads and another for when the end user makes a drive selection in the list box. The code for this form is shown here:

```
using System;
using System.IO;
using System.Windows.Forms;

namespace DriveInfo
{
    public partial class Form1 : Form
    {
        public Form1()
        {
            InitializeComponent();
        }

        private void Form1_Load(object sender, EventArgs e)
        {
            DriveInfo[] di = DriveInfo.GetDrives();

            foreach (DriveInfo itemDrive in di)
            {
                listBox1.Items.Add(itemDrive.Name);
            }
        }

        private void listBox1_SelectedIndexChanged(object sender, EventArgs e)
        {
            DriveInfo di = new DriveInfo(listBox1.SelectedItem.ToString());
```

```
                MessageBox.Show("Available Free Space: "
                   + di.AvailableFreeSpace + "\n" +
                   "Drive Format: " + di.DriveFormat + "\n" +
                   "Drive Type: " + di.DriveType + "\n" +
                   "Is Ready: " + di.IsReady + "\n" +
                   "Name: " + di.Name + "\n" +
                   "Root Directory: " + di.RootDirectory + "\n" +
                   "ToString() Value: " + di + "\n" +
                   "Total Free Space: " + di.TotalFreeSpace + "\n" +
                   "Total Size: " + di.TotalSize + "\n" +
                   "Volume Label: " + di.VolumeLabel, di.Name +
                   " DRIVE INFO");
            }
        }
    }
```

The first step is to bring in the `System.IO` namespace with the `using` keyword. Within the `Form1_Load` event, you use the `DriveInfo` class to get a list of all the available drives on the system. This is done using an array of `DriveInfo` objects and populating this array with the `DriveInfo.GetDrives()` method. Then using a `foreach` loop, you are able to iterate through each drive found and populate the list box with the results. This produces something similar to what is shown in Figure 25-14.

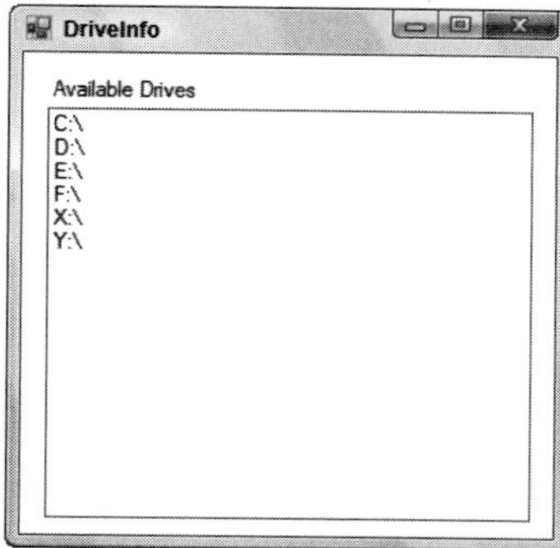

Figure 25-14

This form allows the end user to select one of the drives in the list. Once a drive is selected, a message box appears that contains details about that drive. As you can see in Figure 25-14, I have six drives on my current computer. Selecting a couple of these drives produces the message boxes collectively shown in Figure 25-15.

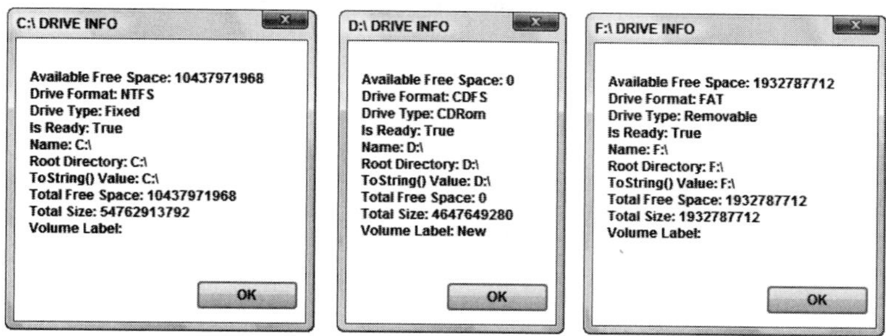

Figure 25-15

From here, you can see that these message boxes provide details about three entirely different drives. The first, drive `C:\`, is my hard drive, as the message box shows its drive type as `Fixed`. The second drive, drive `D:\`, is my CD/DVD drive. The third drive, drive `F:\`, is my USB pen and is labeled with a drive type of `Removable`.

File Security

When the .NET Framework 1.0/1.1 was first introduced, it didn't come with a way to easily access and work access control lists (ACLs) for files, directories, and registry keys. To do such things at that time usually meant some work with COM interop, thus also requiring a more advanced programming knowledge of working with ACLs.

This has considerably changed since the release of the .NET Framework 2.0, which made the process of working with ACLs considerably easier with a namespace — `System.Security.AccessControl`. With this namespace, it is now possible to manipulate security settings for files, registry keys, network shares, Active Directory objects, and more.

Reading ACLs from a File

For an example of working with `System.Security.AccessControl`, this section looks at working with the ACLs for both files and directories. It starts by looking at how you would review the ACLs for a particular file. This example is accomplished in a console application and illustrated here:

```
using System;
using System.IO;
using System.Security.AccessControl;
using System.Security.Principal;

namespace ConsoleApplication1
{
    internal class Program
    {
        private static string myFilePath;

        private static void Main()
        {
            Console.Write("Provide full file path: ");
            myFilePath = Console.ReadLine();

            try
            {
                using (FileStream myFile =
                   new FileStream(myFilePath, FileMode.Open, FileAccess.Read))
                {
                    FileSecurity fileSec = myFile.GetAccessControl();

                    foreach (FileSystemAccessRule fileRule in
                        fileSec.GetAccessRules(true, true,
                           typeof (NTAccount)))
                    {
                        Console.WriteLine("{0} {1} {2} access for {3}",
                           myFilePath,
                           fileRule.AccessControlType ==
```

```
                                AccessControlType.Allow
                                    ? "provides" : "denies",
                                    fileRule.FileSystemRights,
                                    fileRule.IdentityReference);
                        }
                    }
                }
                catch
                {
                    Console.WriteLine("Incorrect file path given!");
                }

                Console.ReadLine();
            }
        }
    }
```

For this example to work, the first step is to refer to the `System.Security.AccessControl` namespace. This will give you access to the `FileSecurity` and the `FileSystemAccessRule` classes later in the program.

After the specified file is retrieved and placed in a `FileStream` object, the ACLs of the file are grabbed using the `GetAccessControl()` method now found on the `File` object. This information from the `GetAccessControl()` method is then placed in a `FileSecurity` class. This class has access rights to the referenced item. Each individual access right is then in turn represented by a `FileSystemAccessRule` object. That is why a `foreach` loop is used to iterate through all the access rights found in the created `FileSecurity` object.

Running this example with a simple text file in the root directory produces something similar to the following results:

```
Provide full file path: C:\Sample.txt
C:\Sample.txt provides FullControl access for BUILTIN\Administrators
C:\Sample.txt provides FullControl access for NT AUTHORITY\SYSTEM
C:\Sample.txt provides FullControl access for PUSHKIN\Bill
C:\Sample.txt provides ReadAndExecute, Synchronize access for BUILTIN\Users
```

The next section presents reading ACLs from a directory instead of a file.

Reading ACLs from a Directory

Reading ACL information about a directory instead of an actual file is not much different from the preceding example. The code for this is illustrated in the following sample:

```
using System;
using System.IO;
using System.Security.AccessControl;
using System.Security.Principal;

namespace ConsoleApplication1
{
    internal class Program
    {
        private static string mentionedDir;

        private static void Main()
```

(continued)

(continued)

```
        {
            Console.Write("Provide full directory path: ");
            mentionedDir = Console.ReadLine();

            try
            {
                DirectoryInfo myDir = new DirectoryInfo(mentionedDir);

                if (myDir.Exists)
                {
                    DirectorySecurity myDirSec = myDir.GetAccessControl();

                    foreach (FileSystemAccessRule fileRule in
                        myDirSec.GetAccessRules(true, true,
                                                typeof (NTAccount)))
                    {
                        Console.WriteLine("{0} {1} {2} access for {3}",
                           mentionedDir, fileRule.AccessControlType ==
                              AccessControlType.Allow
                              ? "provides" : "denies",
                              fileRule.FileSystemRights,
                              fileRule.IdentityReference);
                    }
                }
            }
            catch
            {
                Console.WriteLine("Incorrect directory provided!");
            }

            Console.ReadLine();
        }
    }
}
```

The big difference with this example is that it uses the `DirectoryInfo` class, which now also includes the `GetAccessControl()` method to pull information about the directory's ACLs. Running this example produces the following results:

```
Provide full directory path: C:\Test
C:\Test provides FullControl access for BUILTIN\Administrators
C:\Test provides FullControl access for NT AUTHORITY\SYSTEM
C:\Test provides FullControl access for PUSHKIN\Bill
C:\Test provides 268435456 access for CREATOR OWNER
C:\Test provides ReadAndExecute, Synchronize access for BUILTIN\Users
C:\Test provides AppendData access for BUILTIN\Users
C:\Test provides CreateFiles access for BUILTIN\Users
```

The final thing you will look at in working with ACLs is using the new `System.Security.AccessControl` namespace to add and remove items to and from a file's ACL.

Adding and Removing ACLs from a File

It is also possible to manipulate the ACLs of a resource using the same objects that were used in the previous examples. The following code example changes a previous code example where a file's ACL information was read. Here, the ACLs are read for a specified file, changed, and then read again:

```
try
{
   using (FileStream myFile = new FileStream(myFilePath,
      FileMode.Open, FileAccess.ReadWrite))
   {
      FileSecurity fileSec = myFile.GetAccessControl();

      Console.WriteLine("ACL list before modification:");

      foreach (FileSystemAccessRule fileRule in
         fileSec.GetAccessRules(true, true,
          typeof(System.Security.Principal.NTAccount)))
      {
         Console.WriteLine("{0} {1} {2} access for {3}", myFilePath,
            fileRule.AccessControlType == AccessControlType.Allow ?
            "provides" : "denies",
            fileRule.FileSystemRights,
            fileRule.IdentityReference);
      }

      Console.WriteLine();
      Console.WriteLine("ACL list after modification:");

      FileSystemAccessRule newRule = new FileSystemAccessRule(
         new System.Security.Principal.NTAccount(@"PUSHKIN\Tuija"),
         FileSystemRights.FullControl,
         AccessControlType.Allow);

      fileSec.AddAccessRule(newRule);
      File.SetAccessControl(myFilePath, fileSec);

      foreach (FileSystemAccessRule fileRule in
         fileSec.GetAccessRules(true, true,
         typeof(System.Security.Principal.NTAccount)))
      {
         Console.WriteLine("{0} {1} {2} access for {3}", myFilePath,
            fileRule.AccessControlType == AccessControlType.Allow ?
            "provides" : "denies",
            fileRule.FileSystemRights,
            fileRule.IdentityReference);
      }
   }
}
```

In this case, a new access rule is added to the file's ACL. This is done by using the `FileSystemAccessRule` object. The `FileSystemAccessRule` class is an abstraction access control entry (ACE) instance. The ACE defines the user account to use, the type of access that this user account can deal with, and whether or not to allow or deny this access. In creating a new instance of this object, a new `NTAccount` is created and given `Full Control` to the file. Even though a new `NTAccount` is created, it must still reference an existing user. Then the `AddAccessRule` method of the `FileSecurity` class is used to assign the new rule. From there, the `FileSecurity` object reference is used to set the access control to the file in question using the `SetAccessControl()` method of the `File` class.

Next, the file's ACL is listed again. The following is an example of what the preceding code could produce:

```
Provide full file path: C:\Sample.txt
ACL list before modification:
C:\Sample.txt provides FullControl access for BUILTIN\Administrators
C:\Sample.txt provides FullControl access for NT AUTHORITY\SYSTEM
C:\Sample.txt provides FullControl access for PUSHKIN\Bill
C:\Sample.txt provides ReadAndExecute, Synchronize access for BUILTIN\Users

ACL list after modification:
C:\Sample.txt provides FullControl access for PUSHKIN\Tuija
C:\Sample.txt provides FullControl access for BUILTIN\Administrators
C:\Sample.txt provides FullControl access for NT AUTHORITY\SYSTEM
C:\Sample.txt provides FullControl access for PUSHKIN\Bill
C:\Sample.txt provides ReadAndExecute, Synchronize access for BUILTIN\Users
```

To remove a rule from the ACL list, there is really not much that needs to be done to the code. From the previous code example, you simply need to change the line

```
fileSec.AddAccessRule(newRule);
```

to the following to remove the rule that was just added:

```
fileSec.RemoveAccessRule(newRule);
```

Reading and Writing to the Registry

In all versions of Windows since Windows 95, the registry has been the central repository for all configuration information relating to Windows setup, user preferences, and installed software and devices. Almost all commercial software these days uses the registry to store information about itself, and COM components must place information about themselves in the registry in order to be called by clients. The .NET Framework and its accompanying concept of zero-impact installation has slightly reduced the significance of the registry for applications in the sense that assemblies are entirely self-contained; no information about particular assemblies needs to be placed in the registry, even for shared assemblies. In addition, the .NET Framework has brought the concept of isolated storage, by which applications can store information that is particular to each user in files; the .NET Framework ensures that data is stored separately for each user registered on a machine.

The fact that applications can now be installed using the Windows Installer also frees developers from some of the direct manipulation of the registry that used to be involved in installing applications. However, despite this, the possibility exists that if you distribute any complete application, your application will use the registry to store information about its configuration. For instance, if you want your application to show up in the Add/Remove Programs dialog box in the Control Panel, this will involve appropriate registry entries. You may also need to use the registry for backward compatibility with legacy code.

As you would expect from a library as comprehensive as the .NET library, it includes classes that give you access to the registry. Two classes are concerned with the registry, and both are in the `Microsoft.Win32` namespace. The classes are `Registry` and `RegistryKey`. Before you examine these classes, the following section briefly reviews the structure of the registry itself.

The Registry

The registry has a hierarchical structure much like that of the file system. The usual way to view or modify the contents of the registry is with one of two utilities: `regedit` or `regedt32`. Of these, `regedit` comes standard with all versions of Windows since Windows 95. `regedt32` comes with Windows NT and Windows 2000; it is less user-friendly than `regedit`, but allows access to security information that `regedit` is unable to view. Windows Server 2003 has merged `regedit` and `regedt32` into a single new editor simply called `regedit`. For the discussion here, you will use `regedit` from Windows XP Professional, which you can launch by typing in **regedit** in the Run dialog or at the command prompt.

Figure 25-16 shows what you get when you launch `regedit` for the first time.

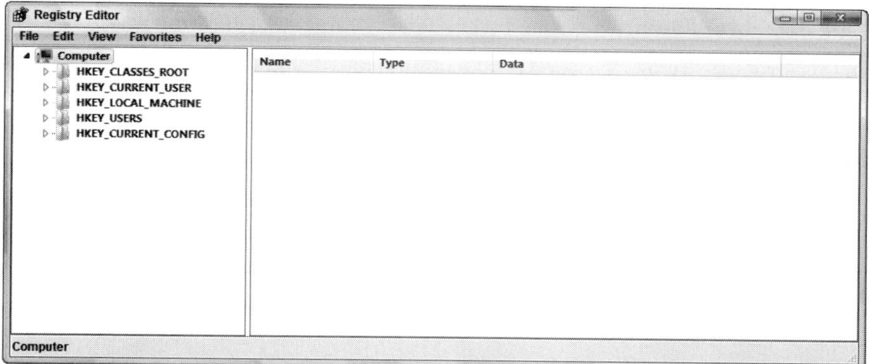

Figure 25-16

`regedit` has a tree view/list view–style user interface similar to Windows Explorer, which matches the hierarchical structure of the registry itself. However, you will see some key differences shortly.

In a file system, the topmost-level nodes can be thought of as being the partitions on your disks, `C:\`, `D:\`, and so on. In the registry, the equivalent to a partition is the *registry hive*. It is not possible to change the existing hives — they are fixed, and there are seven of them, although only five are actually visible through `regedit`:

- `HKEY_CLASSES_ROOT` (HKCR) contains details of types of files on the system (`.txt`, `.doc`, and so on) and which applications are able to open files of each type. It also contains registration information for all COM components (this latter area is usually the largest single area of the registry because Windows, these days, comes with a huge number of COM components).
- `HKEY_CURRENT_USER` (HKCU) contains details of user preferences for the user currently logged on to the machine locally. These settings include desktop settings, environment variables, network and printer connections, and other settings that define the user operating environment of the user.
- `HKEY_LOCAL_MACHINE` (HKLM) is a huge hive that contains details of all software and hardware installed on the machine. These settings are not user-specific but are for all users that log on to the machine. This hive also includes the HKCR hive; HKCR is actually not really an independent hive in its own right but is simply a convenient mapping onto the registry key `HKLM/SOFTWARE/Classes`.
- `HKEY_USERS` (HKUSR) contains details of user preferences for all users. As you might guess, it also contains the HKCU hive, which is simply a mapping onto one of the keys in `HKEY_USERS`.
- `HKEY_CURRENT_CONFIG` (HKCF) contains details of hardware on the machine.

The remaining two keys contain information that is temporary and that changes frequently

- `HKEY_DYN_DATA` is a general container for any volatile data that needs to be stored somewhere in the registry.
- `HKEY_PERFORMANCE_DATA` contains information concerning the performance of running applications.

Within the hives is a tree structure of registry *keys*. Each key is in many ways analogous to a folder or file on the file system. However, there is one very important difference. The file system distinguishes between files (which are there to contain data) and folders (which are primarily there to contain other files or folders), but in the registry there are only keys. A key may contain both data and other keys.

If a key contains data, it will be presented as a series of values. Each value will have an associated name, data type, and data. In addition, a key can have a default value, which is unnamed.

You can see this structure by using `regedit` to examine registry keys. Figure 25-17 shows the contents of the key `HKCU\Control Panel\Appearance`, which contains the details of the chosen color scheme of the currently logged-in user. `regedit` shows which key is being examined by displaying it with an open folder icon in the tree view.

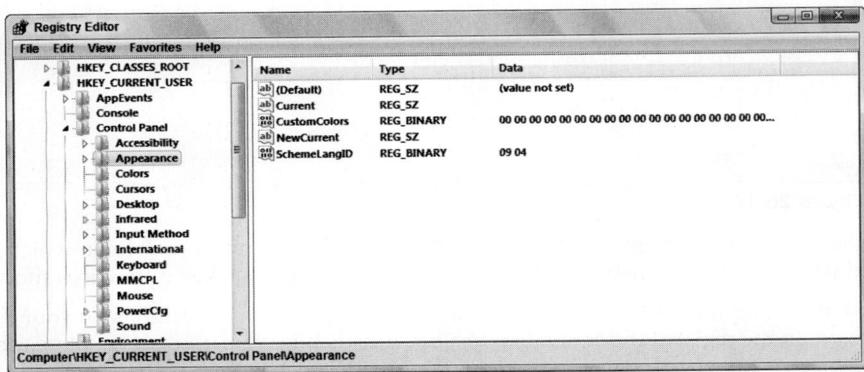

Figure 25-17

The `HKCU\Control Panel\Appearance` key has three named values set, although the default value does not contain any data. The column in the screenshot marked Type details the data type of each value. Registry entries can be formatted as one of three data types:

- `REG_SZ` (which roughly corresponds to a .NET string instance; the matching is not exact because the registry data types are not .NET data types)
- `REG_DWORD` (corresponds roughly to `uint`)
- `REG_BINARY` (array of bytes)

An application that stores data in the registry will do so by creating a number of registry keys, usually under the key `HKLM\Software\<CompanyName>`. Note that it is not necessary for these keys to contain any data. Sometimes the very fact that a key exists provides the data that an application needs.

The .NET Registry Classes

Access to the registry is available through two classes in the `Microsoft.Win32` namespace: `Registry` and `RegistryKey`. A `RegistryKey` instance represents a registry key. This class implements methods to browse child keys, to create new keys, or to read or modify the values in the key — in other words, to do everything you would normally want to do with a registry key, including setting the security levels for the key. RegistryKey will be the class you use for much of your work with the registry. Registry, by contrast, is a class that allows for singular access to registry keys for simple operations. Another role of the Registry class is simply to provide you with RegistryKey instances that represent the top-level keys, the different hives, in order to enable you to navigate the registry. Registry provides these instances through static properties, and there are seven of them called, respectively, ClassesRoot, CurrentConfig, CurrentUser, DynData, LocalMachine, PerformanceData, and Users. It should be obvious which property corresponds to which hive.

So, for example, to obtain a RegistryKey instance that represents the HKLM key, you would write:

```
RegistryKey hklm = Registry.LocalMachine;
```

The process of obtaining a reference to a RegistryKey object is known as opening the key.

Although you might expect that the methods exposed by RegistryKey would be similar to those implemented by DirectoryInfo, given that the registry has a similar hierarchical structure to the file system, this actually isn't the case. Often, the way that you access the registry is different from the way that you would use files and folders, and RegistryKey implements methods that reflect this.

The most obvious difference is in how you open a registry key at a given location in the registry. The Registry class does not have any public constructor that you can use, nor does it have any methods that let you go directly to a key, given its name. Instead, you are expected to browse down to that key from the top of the relevant hive. If you want to instantiate a RegistryKey object, the only way is to start off with the appropriate static property of Registry, and work down from there. So, for example, if you want to read some data in the HKLM/Software/Microsoft key, you would get a reference to it like this:

```
RegistryKey hklm = Registry.LocalMachine;
RegistryKey hkSoftware = hklm.OpenSubKey("Software");
RegistryKey hkMicrosoft = hkSoftware.OpenSubKey("Microsoft");
```

A registry key accessed in this way will give you read-only access. If you want to be able to write to the key (that includes writing to its values or creating or deleting direct children of it), you need to use another override to OpenSubKey, which takes a second parameter, of type bool, that indicates whether you want read-write access to the key. For example, if you want to be able to modify the Microsoft key (and assuming that you are a system administrator with permission to do this), you would write this:

```
RegistryKey hklm = Registry.LocalMachine;
RegistryKey hkSoftware = hklm.OpenSubKey("Software");
RegistryKey hkMicrosoft = hkSoftware.OpenSubKey("Microsoft", true);
```

Incidentally, because this key contains information used by Microsoft's applications, in most cases you probably shouldn't be modifying this particular key.

The OpenSubKey() method is the one you will call if you are expecting the key to be present. If the key isn't there, it will return a null reference. If you want to create a key, you should use the CreateSubKey() method (which automatically gives you read-write access to the key through the reference returned):

```
RegistryKey hklm = Registry.LocalMachine;
RegistryKey hkSoftware = hklm.OpenSubKey("Software");
RegistryKey hkMine = hkSoftware.CreateSubKey("MyOwnSoftware");
```

The way that CreateSubKey() works is quite interesting. It will create the key if it does not already exist, but if it does already exist, it will quietly return a RegistryKey instance that represents the existing key. The reason for the method behaving in this manner has to do with how you will normally use the registry. The registry, overall, contains long-term data such as configuration information for

Windows and for various applications. It is not very common, therefore, that you find yourself in a situation where you need to explicitly create a key.

What is much more common is that your application needs to make sure that some data is present in the registry — in other words, create the relevant keys if they do not already exist, but do nothing if they do. `CreateSubKey()` fills that need perfectly. Unlike the situation with `FileInfo.Open()`, for example, there is no chance with `CreateSubKey()` of accidentally removing any data. If deleting registry keys is your intention, you will need to call the `RegistryKey.DeleteSubKey()` method. This makes sense given the importance of the registry to Windows. The last thing you want is to completely break Windows accidentally by deleting a couple of important keys while you are debugging your C# registry calls!

Once you have located the registry key you want to read or modify, you can use the `SetValue()` or `GetValue()` methods to set or get at the data in it. Both of these methods take a string giving the name of the value as a parameter, and `SetValue()` requires an additional object reference containing details of the value. Because the parameter is defined as an object reference, it can actually be a reference to any class you want. `SetValue()` will decide from the type of class actually supplied whether to set the value as a `REG_SZ`, `REG_DWORD`, or `REG_BINARY` value. For example:

```
RegistryKey hkMine = HkSoftware.CreateSubKey("MyOwnSoftware");
hkMine.SetValue("MyStringValue", "Hello World");
hkMine.SetValue("MyIntValue", 20);
```

This code will set the key to have two values: `MyStringValue` will be of type `REG_SZ`, and `MyIntValue` will be of type `REG_DWORD`. These are the only two types you will consider here, and use in the example presented later.

`RegistryKey.GetValue()` works in much the same way. It is defined to return an object reference, which means that it is free to actually return a `string` reference if it detects the value is of type `REG_SZ`, and an `int` if that value is of type `REG_DWORD`:

```
string stringValue = (string)hkMine.GetValue("MyStringValue");
int intValue = (int)hkMine.GetValue("MyIntValue");
```

Finally, after you have finished reading or modifying the data, close the key:

```
hkMine.Close();
```

`RegistryKey` implements a large number of methods and properties. The following table lists the most useful properties.

Property Name	Description
`Name`	Name of the key (read-only)
`SubKeyCount`	The number of children of this key
`ValueCount`	How many values the key contains

The following table lists the most useful methods.

Method Name	Purpose
`Close()`	Closes the key.
`CreateSubKey()`	Creates a subkey of a given name (or opens it if it already exists).
`DeleteSubKey()`	Deletes a given subkey.
`DeleteSubKeyTree()`	Recursively deletes a subkey and all its children.
`DeleteValue()`	Removes a named value from a key.
`GetAccessControl()`	Returns the access control list (ACL) for a specified registry key. This method is new to the .NET Framework 2.0.
`GetSubKeyNames()`	Returns an array of strings containing the names of the subkeys.
`GetValue()`	Returns a named value.
`GetValueKind()`	Returns a named value whose registry data type is to be retrieved. This method is new to the .NET Framework 2.0.
`GetValueNames()`	Returns an array of strings containing the names of all the values of the key.
`OpenSubKey()`	Returns a reference to a `RegistryKey` instance that represents a given subkey.
`SetAccessControl()`	Allows you to apply an access control list (ACL) to a specified registry key.
`SetValue()`	Sets a named value.

Example: SelfPlacingWindow

The use of the registry classes is illustrated with an application called `SelfPlacingWindow`. This example is a simple C# Windows application that has almost no features. The only thing you can do with it is click a button, which brings up a standard Windows color dialog box (represented by the `System.Windows.Forms.ColorDialog` class) to let you choose a color, which will become the background color of the form.

Despite its lack of features, the self-placing window scores higher than just about every other application that you have developed in this book in one important and very user-friendly way. If you drag the window around the screen, change its size, or maximize or minimize it before you exit the application, it will remember the new position, as well as the background color, so that the next time it is launched it automatically reappears the way you chose last time. It remembers this information because it writes it to the registry whenever it shuts down. In this way, it demonstrates not only the .NET registry classes themselves but also a very typical use for them, which you will almost certainly want to replicate in any serious commercial Windows Forms application that you write.

The location in which `SelfPlacingWindow` stores its information in the registry is the key `HKLM\Software\WroxPress\SelfPlacingWindow`. HKLM is the usual place for application configuration information, but note that it is not user-specific. If you wanted to be more sophisticated in a real application, you would probably want to replicate the information inside the `HK_Users` hive as well, so that each user can have his or her own profile.

It is also worth noting that, if you are implementing this in a real .NET application, you may want to consider using isolated storage instead of the registry to store this information. However, because isolated storage is available only in .NET, you will need to use the registry if you need any interoperability with non-.NET apps.

The very first time that you run the example, it will look for this key and not find it (obviously). Therefore, it is forced to use a default size, color, and position that you set in the developer environment. The example also features a list box in which it displays any information read in from the registry. On its first run, it will look similar to Figure 25-18.

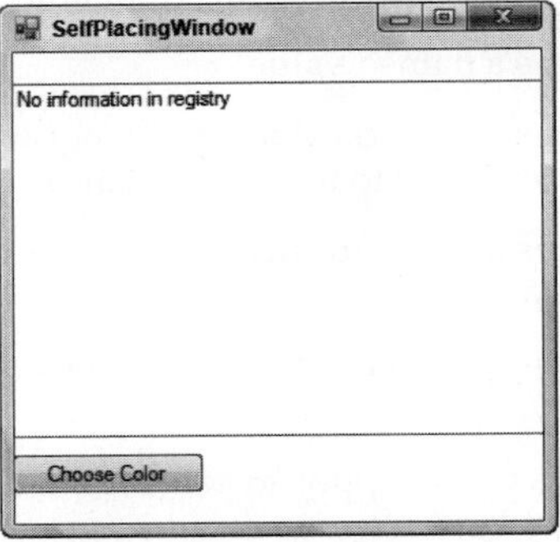

Figure 25-18

If you now modify the background color and resize `SelfPlacingWindow` or move it around on the screen a bit before exiting, it will create the `HKLM\Software\WroxPress\SelfPlacingWindow` key and write its new configuration information into it. You can examine the information using `regedit`. The details are shown in Figure 25-19.

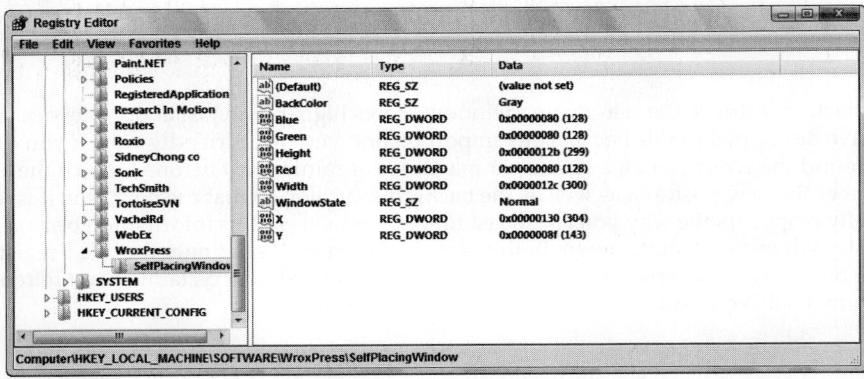

Figure 25-19

As this figure shows, `SelfPlacingWindow` has placed a number of values in the registry key.

The values Red, Green, and Blue give the color components that make up the selected background color (see Chapter 33, "Graphics with GDI+"). For now, just know that any color display on the system can be completely described by these three components, which are each represented by a number between 0 and 255 (or 0x00 and 0xff in hexadecimal). The values given here make up a bright green color. There are also four more `REG_DWORD` values, which represent the position and size of the window: X and Y are the coordinates of the top left of the window on the desktop — that is to say the numbers of pixels across from the top left of the screen and the numbers of pixels down. And, Width and Height give the size of the window. `WindowsState` is the only value for which you have used a string data type (`REG_SZ`), and it can contain one of the strings `Normal`, `Maximized`, or `Minimized`, depending on the final state of the window when you exited the application.

When you launch `SelfPlacingWindow` again, it will read this registry key and automatically position itself accordingly (see Figure 25-20).

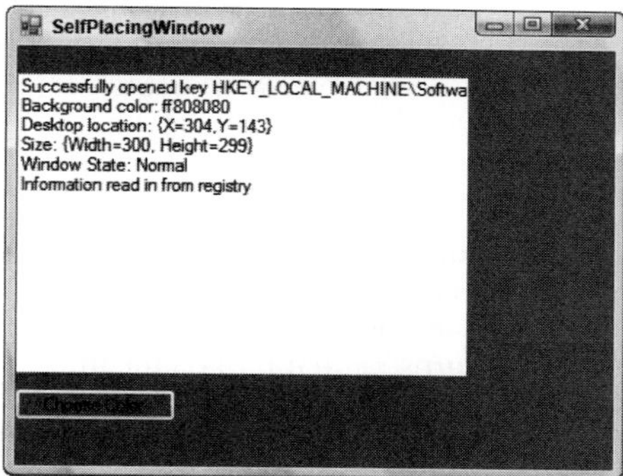

Figure 25-20

This time when you exit `SelfPlacingWindow`, it will overwrite the previous registry settings with whatever new values are relevant at the time that you exit it. To code the example, you create the usual Windows Forms project in Visual Studio .NET and add the list box and button, using the developer environment's toolbox. You will change the names of these controls, respectively, to `listBoxMessages` and `buttonChooseColor`. You also need to ensure that you use the `Microsoft.Win32` namespace:

```
using System;
using System.Drawing;
using System.Windows.Forms;
using Microsoft.Win32;
```

You need to add one field (`chooseColorDialog`) to the main `Form1` class, which will represent the color dialog box:

```
public partial class Form1 : Form
{
   private readonly ColorDialog chooseColorDialog = new ColorDialog();
```

Quite a lot of action takes place in the `Form1` constructor:

```
public Form1()
{
   InitializeComponent();

   buttonChooseColor.Click += OnClickChooseColor;
```

(continued)

(continued)

```
         try
         {
            if (ReadSettings() == false)
            {
               listBoxMessages.Items.Add("No information in registry");
            }
            else
            {
               listBoxMessages.Items.Add("Information read in from registry");
            }

            StartPosition = FormStartPosition.Manual;
         }
         catch (Exception e)
         {
            listBoxMessages.Items.Add("A problem occurred reading in data
                                       from registry:");
            listBoxMessages.Items.Add(e.Message);
         }
      }
```

In this constructor, you begin by setting up the event handler for when the user clicks the button. The handler is a method called `OnClickChooseColor()`, which is covered shortly. Reading in the configuration information is done using another method that you have to write, called `ReadSettings()`. `ReadSettings()` returns `true` if it finds the information in the registry, and `false` if it does not (which it should be because this is the first time you have run the application). You place this part of the constructor in a `try` block, just in case any exceptions are generated while reading in the registry values (this might happen if some user has come in and played around with the registry using `regedit`).

The `StartPosition = FormStartPosition.Manual;` statement tells the form to take its initial starting position from the `DeskTopLocation` property instead of using the Windows default location (the default behavior). Possible values are taken from the `FormStartPosition` enumeration.

`SelfPlacingWindow` is also one of the few applications in this book in which you have a serious use for adding code to the `Dispose()` method. Remember that `Dispose()` is called whenever the application terminates normally, so this is the ideal place from which to save the configuration information to the registry. You will find the `Dispose()` method in the `Form1.Designer.cs` file. Within this method, you will place another method that you have to write, `SaveSettings()`:

```
protected override void Dispose(bool disposing)
{
    if (disposing && (components != null))
    {
        components.Dispose();
    }
    SaveSettings();
    base.Dispose(disposing);
}
```

The `SaveSettings()` and `ReadSettings()` methods are the ones that contain the registry code you are interested in, but before you examine them, you have one more piece of housekeeping to do: handle the event of the user clicking that button. This involves displaying the color dialog and setting the background color to whatever color the user chose:

```
void OnClickChooseColor(object Sender, EventArgs e)
{
   if(chooseColorDialog.ShowDialog() == DialogResult.OK)
      BackColor = chooseColorDialog.Color;
}
```

Now, look at how you save the settings:

```
void SaveSettings()
{
   RegistryKey softwareKey =
               Registry.LocalMachine.OpenSubKey("Software", true);
   RegistryKey wroxKey = softwareKey.CreateSubKey("WroxPress");
   RegistryKey selfPlacingWindowKey =
               wroxKey.CreateSubKey("SelfPlacingWindow");
   selfPlacingWindowKey.SetValue("BackColor",
               BackColor.ToKnownColor());
   selfPlacingWindowKey.SetValue("Red", (int)BackColor.R);
   selfPlacingWindowKey.SetValue("Green", (int)BackColor.G);
   selfPlacingWindowKey.SetValue("Blue", (int)BackColor.B);
   selfPlacingWindowKey.SetValue("Width", Width);
   selfPlacingWindowKey.SetValue("Height", Height);
   selfPlacingWindowKey.SetValue("X", DesktopLocation.X);
   selfPlacingWindowKey.SetValue("Y", DesktopLocation.Y);
   selfPlacingWindowKey.SetValue("WindowState",
               WindowState.ToString());
}
```

There is a lot going on here. You start by navigating through the registry to get to the `HKLM\Software\WroxPress\SelfPlacingWindow` registry key using the technique demonstrated earlier, starting with the `Registry.LocalMachine` static property that represents the HKLM hive.

Then you use the `RegistryKey.OpenSubKey()` method, rather than `RegistryKey.CreateSubKey()`, to get to the `HKLM/Software` key. That is because you can be very confident that this key already exists. If it does not, then there is something seriously wrong with your computer, because this key contains settings for a lot of system software! You also indicate that you need write access to this key. That is because if the `WroxPress` key does not already exist, you will need to create it, which involves writing to the parent key.

The next key to navigate to is `HKLM\Software\WroxPress` — and here you are not certain whether the key already exists, so you use `CreateSubKey()` to automatically create it if it does not. Note that `CreateSubKey()` automatically gives you write access to the key in question. Once you have reached `HKLM\Software\WroxPress\SelfPlacingWindow`, it is simply a matter of calling the `RegistryKey.SetValue()` method a number of times to either create or set the appropriate values. There are, however, a couple of complications.

First, you might notice that you are using a couple of classes that you have not encountered before. The `DeskTopLocation` property of the `Form` class indicates the position of the top-left corner of the screen and is of type `Point`. (The `Point` is discussed in Chapter 33, "Graphics with GDI+".) What you need to know here is that it contains two `int` values, `X` and `Y`, which represent the horizontal and vertical position on the screen. You also look up three member properties of the `Form.BackColor` property, which is an instance of the `Color` class: `R`, `G`, and `B`: `Color`, which represents a color. These properties on it give the red, green, and blue components that make up the color, and they are all of type `byte`. You also use the `Form.WindowState` property, which contains an enumeration that gives the current state of the window: `Minimized`, `Maximized`, or `Normal`.

The other complication here is that you need to be a little careful about your casts. SetValue() takes two parameters: a string that gives the name of the key and a System.Object instance, which contains the value. SetValue() has a choice of format for storing the value — it can store it as REG_SZ, REG_BINARY, or REG_DWORD — and it is actually pretty intelligent about making a sensible choice depending on the data type that has been given. Hence for the WindowState, you pass it a string, and SetValue() determines that this should be translated to REG_SZ. Similarly, for the various positions and dimensions, you supply ints, which will be converted into REG_DWORD. However, the color components are more complicated, as you want these to be stored as REG_DWORD too because they are numeric types. However, if SetValue() sees that the data is of type byte, it will store it as a string — as REG_SZ in the registry. To prevent this, you cast the color components to ints.

You have also explicitly cast all the values to the type object. You don't really need to do this because the cast from any other data type to object is implicit, but you are doing this to make it clear what is going on and to remind yourself that SetValue() is defined to take just an object reference as its second parameter.

The ReadSettings() method is a little longer because for each value read in, you also need to interpret it, display the value in the list box, and make the appropriate adjustments to the relevant property of the main form. ReadSettings() looks like this:

```
bool ReadSettings()
{
   RegistryKey softwareKey =
      Registry.LocalMachine.OpenSubKey("Software");
   RegistryKey wroxKey = softwareKey.OpenSubKey("WroxPress");

   if (wroxKey == null)
   {
      return false;
   }

   RegistryKey selfPlacingWindowKey =
      wroxKey.OpenSubKey("SelfPlacingWindow");

   if (selfPlacingWindowKey == null)
   {
      return false;
   }
   else
   {
      listBoxMessages.Items.Add("Successfully opened key " +
                                        selfPlacingWindowKey);
   }

   int redComponent = (int) selfPlacingWindowKey.GetValue("Red");
   int greenComponent = (int) selfPlacingWindowKey.GetValue("Green");
   int blueComponent = (int) selfPlacingWindowKey.GetValue("Blue");
   BackColor = Color.FromArgb(redComponent, greenComponent,
                                    blueComponent);
   listBoxMessages.Items.Add("Background color: " + BackColor.Name);
   int X = (int) selfPlacingWindowKey.GetValue("X");
   int Y = (int) selfPlacingWindowKey.GetValue("Y");
```

```
            DesktopLocation = new Point(X, Y);
            listBoxMessages.Items.Add("Desktop location: " +
               DesktopLocation);
            Height = (int) selfPlacingWindowKey.GetValue("Height");
            Width = (int) selfPlacingWindowKey.GetValue("Width");
            listBoxMessages.Items.Add("Size: " + new Size(Width, Height));
            string initialWindowState =
              (string) selfPlacingWindowKey.GetValue("WindowState");
            listBoxMessages.Items.Add("Window State: " + initialWindowState);
            WindowState = (FormWindowState) FormWindowState.Parse
              (WindowState.GetType(), initialWindowState);
               return true;
        }
```

In `ReadSettings()` you first have to navigate to the `HKLM/Software/WroxPress/SelfPlacingWindow` registry key. In this case, however, you are hoping to find the key there so that you can read it. If it is not there, it is probably the first time you have run the example. In this case, you just want to abort reading the keys, and you certainly don't want to create any keys. Now you use the `RegistryKey.OpenSubKey()` method all the way down. If at any stage `OpenSubkey()` returns a `null` reference, then you know that the registry key is not there, and you can simply return the value `false` to the calling code.

When it comes to actually reading the keys, you use the `RegistryKey.GetValue()` method, which is defined as returning an object reference (meaning that this method can actually return an instance of literally any class it chooses). Like `SetValue()`, it will return a class of object appropriate to the type of data it found in the key. Therefore, you can usually assume that the `REG_SZ` keys will give you a string, and the other keys will give you an `int`. You also cast the return reference from `SetValue()` accordingly. If there is an exception, say someone has fiddled with the registry and mangled the value types, your cast will cause an exception to be thrown — which will be caught by the handler in the `Form1` constructor.

The rest of this code uses one more data type, the `Size` structure. This is similar to a `Point` structure but is used to represent sizes rather than coordinates. It has two member properties, `Width` and `Height`, and you use the `Size` structure here simply as a convenient way of packaging the size of the form for displaying in the list box.

Reading and Writing to Isolated Storage

In addition to being able to read and write to and from the registry, another option is reading and writing values to and from what is called *isolated storage*. If you are having issues writing to the registry or to disk in general, then isolated storage is where you should turn. You can use isolated storage to store application state or user settings quite easily.

Think of isolated storage as a virtual disk where you can save items that can be shared only by the application that created them, or with other application instances. There are two types of access types for isolated storage. The first is user and assembly.

When accessing isolated storage by user and assembly, there is a single storage location on the machine, which is accessible via multiple application instances. Access is guaranteed through the user identity and the application (or assembly) identity. Figure 25-21 shows this in a diagram.

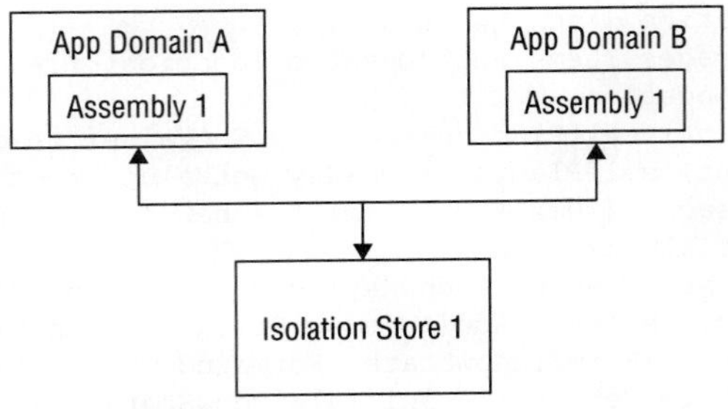

Figure 25-21

This means that you can have multiple instances of the same application all working from the same store.

The second type of access for isolated storage is user, assembly, and domain. In this case, each application instance will work off its own isolation store. This is detailed in Figure 25-22.

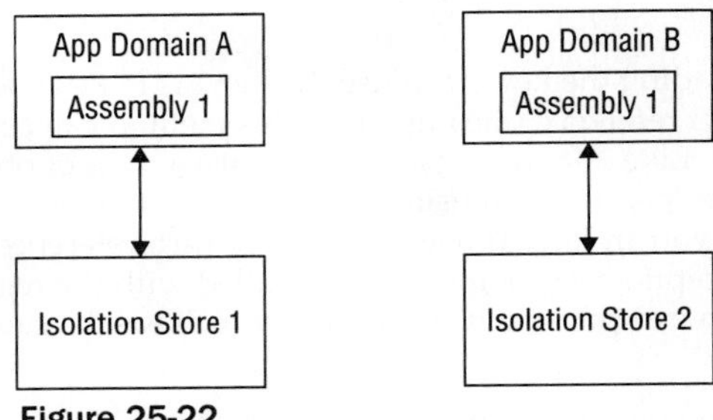

Figure 25-22

In this case, each application instance works off its own store, and the settings that each application instance records are related only to itself. This is a more fine-grained approach to isolated storage.

For an example of using isolated storage from a Windows Forms application (although you can use this from an ASP.NET application just as well), change the `SelfPlacingWindow` example that was previously used in this chapter to illustrate how to record information to the registry. Through a new `ReadSettings()` and `SaveSettings()` method, you read and write values to isolated storage as opposed to doing the same to the registry.

> *It is important to note that the only code shown here is for the* `ReadSettings()` *and* `SaveSettings()` *methods. There is more code to the application, and you can see the rest of the code in the previous example titled "Example: SelfPlacingWindow."*

To start, you need to rework the `SaveSettings()` method. For this next bit of code to work, you need to add the following using directives:

```
using System.IO;
using System.IO.IsolatedStorage;
using System.Text;
```

The `SaveSettings()` method is detailed in the following code example:

```
void SaveSettings()
{
   IsolatedStorageFile storFile = IsolatedStorageFile.GetUserStoreForDomain();
   IsolatedStorageFileStream storStream = new
      IsolatedStorageFileStream("SelfPlacingWindow.xml",

      FileMode.Create, FileAccess.Write);

   System.Xml.XmlTextWriter writer = new
      System.Xml.XmlTextWriter(storStream, Encoding.UTF8);
   writer.Formatting = System.Xml.Formatting.Indented;

   writer.WriteStartDocument();
   writer.WriteStartElement("Settings");

   writer.WriteStartElement("BackColor");
   writer.WriteValue(BackColor.ToKnownColor().ToString());
   writer.WriteEndElement();

   writer.WriteStartElement("Red");
   writer.WriteValue(BackColor.R);
   writer.WriteEndElement();

   writer.WriteStartElement("Green");
   writer.WriteValue(BackColor.G);
   writer.WriteEndElement();

   writer.WriteStartElement("Blue");
   writer.WriteValue(BackColor.B);
   writer.WriteEndElement();

   writer.WriteStartElement("Width");
   writer.WriteValue(Width);
   writer.WriteEndElement();

   writer.WriteStartElement("Height");
   writer.WriteValue(Height);
   writer.WriteEndElement();

   writer.WriteStartElement("X");
   writer.WriteValue(DesktopLocation.X);
   writer.WriteEndElement();

   writer.WriteStartElement("Y");
   writer.WriteValue(DesktopLocation.Y);
   writer.WriteEndElement();

   writer.WriteStartElement("WindowState");
   writer.WriteValue(WindowState.ToString());
   writer.WriteEndElement();

   writer.WriteEndElement();
```

(continued)

```
        writer.Flush();
        writer.Close();

        storStream.Close();
        storFile.Close();
    }
```

It is a bit more code than working with the registry example, but that is mainly due to the code required to build the XML document placed in isolated storage. The first important thing happening with this code is presented here:

```
IsolatedStorageFile storFile = IsolatedStorageFile.GetUserStoreForDomain();
IsolatedStorageFileStream storStream = new
   IsolatedStorageFileStream("SelfPlacingWindow.xml",
   FileMode.Create, FileAccess.Write);
```

Here, an instance of an `IsolatedStorageFile` is created using a user, assembly, and domain type of access. A stream is created using the `IsolatedStorageFileStream` object, which will create the virtual `SelfPlacingWindow.xml` file.

From there, an `XmlTextWriter` object is created to build the XML document and the XML contents are written to the `IsolatedStorageFileStream` object instance:

```
System.Xml.XmlTextWriter writer = new
   System.Xml.XmlTextWriter(storStream, Encoding.UTF8);
```

After the `XmlTextWriter` object is created, all the values are written to the XML document node by node. Once everything is written to the XML document, everything is closed and will now be stored in the isolated storage.

Reading from the storage is done through the `ReadSettings()` method. This method is presented in the following code sample:

```
bool ReadSettings()
{
   IsolatedStorageFile storFile = IsolatedStorageFile.GetUserStoreForDomain();
   string[] userFiles = storFile.GetFileNames("SelfPlacingWindow.xml");

   foreach (string userFile in userFiles)
   {
      if(userFile == "SelfPlacingWindow.xml")
      {
         listBoxMessages.Items.Add("Successfully opened file " +
                                   userFile.ToString());

         StreamReader storStream =
            new StreamReader(new IsolatedStorageFileStream("SelfPlacingWindow.xml",
            FileMode.Open, storFile));
         System.Xml.XmlTextReader reader = new
            System.Xml.XmlTextReader(storStream);

         int redComponent = 0;
         int greenComponent = 0;
         int blueComponent = 0;
```

```
            int X = 0;
            int Y = 0;

            while (reader.Read())
            {
               switch (reader.Name)
               {
                  case "Red":
                     redComponent = int.Parse(reader.ReadString());
                     break;
                  case "Green":
                     greenComponent = int.Parse(reader.ReadString());
                     break;
                  case "Blue":
                     blueComponent = int.Parse(reader.ReadString());
                     break;
                  case "X":
                     X = int.Parse(reader.ReadString());
                     break;
                  case "Y":
                     Y = int.Parse(reader.ReadString());
                     break;
                  case "Width":
                     this.Width = int.Parse(reader.ReadString());
                     break;
                  case "Height":
                     this.Height = int.Parse(reader.ReadString());
                     break;
                  case "WindowState":
                     this.WindowState = (FormWindowState)FormWindowState.Parse
                       (WindowState.GetType(), reader.ReadString());
                     break;
                  default:
                     break;
               }
            }

            this.BackColor =
               Color.FromArgb(redComponent, greenComponent, blueComponent);
            this.DesktopLocation = new Point(X, Y);

            listBoxMessages.Items.Add("Background color: " + BackColor.Name);
            listBoxMessages.Items.Add("Desktop location: " +
               DesktopLocation.ToString());
            listBoxMessages.Items.Add("Size: " + new Size(Width, Height).ToString());
            listBoxMessages.Items.Add("Window State: " + WindowState.ToString());

            storStream.Close();
            storFile.Close();
         }
      }
      return true;
   }
```

Using the `GetFileNames()` method, the `SelfPlacingWindow.xml` document is pulled from the isolated storage and then placed into a stream and parsed using the `XmlTextReader` object:

```
IsolatedStorageFile storFile = IsolatedStorageFile.GetUserStoreForDomain();
string[] userFiles = storFile.GetFileNames("SelfPlacingWindow.xml");

foreach (string userFile in userFiles)
{
   if(userFile == "SelfPlacingWindow.xml")
   {
      listBoxMessages.Items.Add("Successfully opened file " +
                                userFile.ToString());

      StreamReader storStream =
         new StreamReader(new IsolatedStorageFileStream("SelfPlacingWindow.xml",
         FileMode.Open, storFile));
```

Once the XML document is contained within the `IsolatedStorageFileStream` object, it is parsed using the `XmlTextReader` object:

```
      System.Xml.XmlTextReader reader = new
         System.Xml.XmlTextReader(storStream);
```

After, it is pulled from the stream via the `XmlTextReader`. The element values are then pushed back into the application. You will now find — just as was accomplished in the `SelfPlacingWindow` example that used the registry to record and retrieve application state values — using isolated storage is just as effective as working with the registry. The application will remember the color, size, and position just as before.

Summary

In this chapter, you have examined how to use the .NET base classes to access the file system and registry from your C# code. You have seen that in both cases the base classes expose simple, but powerful, object models that make it very simple to perform almost any kind of action in these areas. For the file system, these actions are copying files; moving, creating, and deleting files and folders; and reading and writing both binary and text files. For the registry, these are creating, modifying, or reading keys.

This chapter also reviewed isolated storage and how to use this from your applications to store them in the application state.

This chapter assumed that you are running your code from an account that has sufficient access rights to do whatever the code needs to do. Obviously, the question of security is an important one, and it is discussed in Chapter 20, "Security."

The next chapter walks you through data access and ADO.NET, XML, and XML Schemas.

26

Data Access

This chapter discusses how to access data from your C# programs using ADO.NET. The following details are covered:

- **Connecting to the database** — You learn how to use the `SqlConnection` and `OleDbConnection` classes to connect to and disconnect from the database.
- **Executing commands** — ADO.NET has command objects that can execute SQL commands or issue a call to a stored procedure with optional return values. You learn the various command object options and see how commands can be used for each of the options presented by the `Sql` and `OleDB` classes.
- **Stored procedures** — You learn how to call stored procedures with command objects and how the results of those stored procedures can be integrated into the data cached on the client.
- **The ADO.NET object model** — This is significantly different from the objects available with ADO. The `DataSet`, `DataTable`, `DataRow`, and `DataColumn` classes are discussed as well as the relationships between tables and constraints that are part of `DataSet`. The class hierarchy has changed significantly with version 2 of the .NET Framework, and some of these changes are also described.
- **Using XML and XML schemas** — You examine the XML framework on which ADO.NET is built.

Microsoft has also added support for Language Integrated Query (LINQ) in C# for the 3.0 release. Although this topic largely supersedes the information in this chapter, it is included here for completeness. See Chapters 28, "Manipulating XML,"29, "LINQ to XML," and 31, "Windows Forms," for some details on new data access capabilities in .NET.

As is the case with the other chapters, you can download the code for the examples used in this chapter from the Wrox Web site at `www.wrox.com`. The chapter begins with a brief tour of ADO.NET.

ADO.NET Overview

ADO.NET is more than just a thin veneer over some existing API. The similarity to ADO is fairly minimal — the classes and methods of accessing data are completely different.

ADO (ActiveX Data Objects) is a library of COM components that has had many incarnations over the past few years. Currently at version 2.8, ADO consists primarily of the `Connection`, `Command`, `Recordset`, and `Field` objects. Using ADO, a connection is opened to the database, some data is selected into a record set consisting of fields, that data is then manipulated and updated on the server, and the connection is closed. ADO also introduced a so-called disconnected record set, which is used when keeping the connection open for long periods of time is not desirable.

There were several problems that ADO did not address satisfactorily, most notably the unwieldiness (in physical size) of a disconnected record set. This support was more necessary than ever with the evolution of Web-centric computing, so a fresh approach was required. Upgrading to ADO.NET from ADO shouldn't be too difficult because there are some similarities between the two. What's more, if you are using SQL Server, there is a fantastic new set of managed classes that are tuned to squeeze maximum performance out of the database. This alone should be reason enough to migrate to ADO.NET.

ADO.NET ships with four database client namespaces: one for SQL Server, another for Oracle, the third for ODBC data sources, and the fourth for any database exposed through OLE DB. If your database of choice is not SQL Server or Oracle, use the OLE DB route unless you have no other choice than to use ODBC.

Namespaces

All of the examples in this chapter access data in one way or another. The following namespaces expose the classes and interfaces used in .NET data access.

Namespace	Brief Description
`System.Data`	All generic data access classes
`System.Data.Common`	Classes shared (or overridden) by individual data providers
`System.Data.Odbc`	ODBC provider classes
`System.Data.OleDb`	OLE DB provider classes
`System.Data.ProviderBase`	New base classes and connection factory classes
`System.Data.Oracle`	Oracle provider classes
`System.Data.Sql`	New generic interfaces and classes for SQL Server data access
`System.Data.SqlClient`	SQL Server provider classes
`System.Data.SqlTypes`	SQL Server data types

The main classes in ADO.NET are listed in the following subsections.

Shared Classes

ADO.NET contains a number of classes that are used regardless of whether you are using the SQL Server classes or the OLE DB classes.

The following classes are contained in the `System.Data` namespace.

Class	Description
`DataSet`	This object is designed for disconnected use and can contain a set of `DataTables` and relationships between these tables.
`DataTable`	A container of data that consists of one or more `DataColumns` and, when populated, will have one or more `DataRows` containing data.
`DataRow`	A number of values, akin to a row from a database table or a row from a spreadsheet.
`DataColumn`	This object contains the definition of a column, such as the name and data type.
`DataRelation`	A link between two `DataTable` classes within a `DataSet` class; used for foreign key and master/detail relationships.
`Constraint`	This class defines a rule for a `DataColumn` class (or set of data columns), such as unique values.

The following classes are found in the `System.Data.Common` namespace:

Class	Description
`DataColumnMapping`	Maps the name of a column from the database with the name of a column within a `DataTable`.
`DataTableMapping`	Maps a table name from the database to a `DataTable` within a `DataSet`.

Database-Specific Classes

In addition to the shared classes introduced in the previous section, ADO.NET contains a number of database-specific classes. These classes implement a set of standard interfaces defined within the `System.Data` namespace, allowing the classes to be used in a generic manner if necessary. For example, both the `SqlConnection` and `OleDbConnection` classes derive from the `DbConnection` class, which implements the `IDbConnection` interface.

Classes	Description
SqlCommand, OleDbCommand, OracleCommand, and ODBCCommand	Used as wrappers for SQL statements or stored procedure calls. Examples for the SqlCommand class are shown later in the chapter.
SqlCommandBuilder, OleDbCommandBuilder, OracleCommandBuilder, and ODBCCommandBuilder	Used to generate SQL commands (such as INSERT, UPDATE, and DELETE statements) from a SELECT statement.
SqlConnection, OleDbConnection, OracleConnection, and ODBCConnection	Used to connect to the database and is similar to an ADO connection. Examples are shown later in the chapter.
SqlDataAdapter, OleDbDataAdapter, OracleDataAdapter, and ODBCDataAdapter	Used to hold select, insert, update, and delete commands, which are then used to populate a DataSet and update the database. Examples of the SqlDataAdapter are presented in this chapter.
SqlDataReader, OleDbDataReader, OracleDataReader, and ODBCDataReader	Used as a forward only, connected data reader. Some examples of the SqlDataReader are shown in this chapter.
SqlParameter, OleDbParameter, OracleParameter, and ODBCParameter	Used to define a parameter to a stored procedure. Examples of how to use the SqlParameter class are shown in this chapter.
SqlTransaction, OleDbTransaction, OracleTransaction, and ODBCTransaction	Used for a database transaction, wrapped in an object.

As you can see from the previous list, there are four classes for each type of object — one for each of the providers that are part of .NET version 1.1. In the rest of this chapter, unless otherwise stated, the prefix <provider> is used to indicate that the particular class used is dependent on the database provider in use. With version 2.0 of .NET, the designers have updated the class hierarchy for these classes significantly. In 1.1, all that was common between the various connection classes was the implementation of the IConnection interface. This has changed in .NET 2.0 because now both share a common base class. Similarly the other classes such as Commands, DataAdapters, DataReaders, and so on also share common base classes.

The most important feature of the ADO.NET classes is that they are designed to work in a disconnected manner, which is important in today's highly Web-centric world. It is now common practice to architect a service (such as an online bookshop) to connect to a server, retrieve some data, and then work on that data on the client before reconnecting and passing the data back for processing. The disconnected nature of ADO.NET enables this type of behavior.

ADO 2.1 introduced the disconnected record set, which would permit data to be retrieved from a database, passed to the client for processing, and then reattached to the server. This used to be cumbersome to use because disconnected behavior was not part of the original design. The ADO.NET classes are different — in all but one case (the `<provider>DataReader`) they are designed for use offline from the database.

The classes and interfaces used for data access in the .NET Framework are introduced in the course of this chapter. The focus is mainly on the SQL classes used when connecting to the database because the Framework SDK samples install an MSDE database (SQL Server). In most cases, the OLE DB, Oracle, and ODBC classes mimic the SQL code exactly.

Using Database Connections

To access the database, you need to provide connection parameters, such as the machine that the database is running on and possibly your login credentials. Anyone who has worked with ADO will be familiar with the .NET connection classes: `OleDbConnection` and `SqlConnection`. Figure 26-1 shows two of the connection classes and includes the class hierarchy.

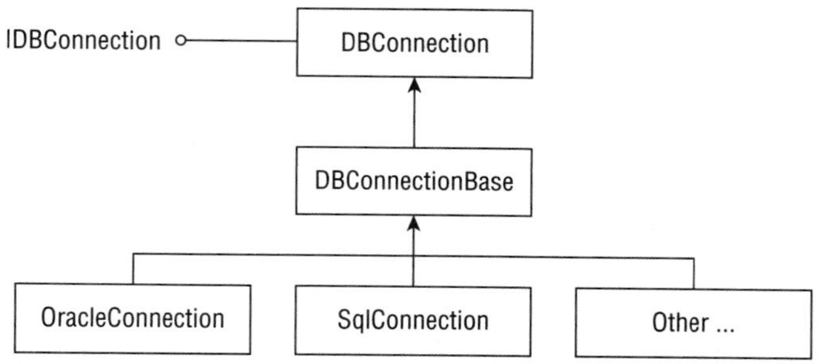

Figure 26-1

This is a significant change from .NET versions 1.0 and 1.1; however, in practice, using the connection class (and other classes in ADO.NET) is backward compatible.

The examples in this chapter use the Northwind database, which is installed with the .NET Framework SDK samples. The following code snippet illustrates how to create, open, and close a connection to the Northwind database:

```
using System.Data.SqlClient;

string source = "server=(local);" +
                "integrated security=SSPI;" +
                "database=Northwind";
SqlConnection conn = new SqlConnection(source);
conn.Open();

// Do something useful

conn.Close();
```

The connection string should be very familiar to you if you have used ADO or OLE DB before — indeed, you should be able to cut and paste from your old code if you use the `OleDb` provider. In the example connection string, the parameters used are as follows (the parameters are delimited by a semicolon in the connection string):

- `server=(local)` — This denotes the database server to connect to. SQL Server permits a number of separate database server instances to be running on the same machine, and here you are connecting to the default SQL Server instance. If you are using SQL Express, change the server part to `server=./sqlexpress`.
- `integrated security=SSPI` — This uses Windows Authentication to connect to the database, which is highly recommended over using a username and password within the source code.
- `database=Northwind` — This describes the database instance to connect to; each SQL Server process can expose several database instances.

> **In case you forget the format of database connection strings (as many of us do now and then), the following URL is very handy:** `www.connectionstrings.com`.

The example opens a database connection using the defined connection string and then closes that connection. Once the connection has been opened, you can issue commands against the data source, and when you are finished, the connection can be closed.

SQL Server has another mode of authentication — it can use Windows-integrated security, so that the credentials supplied at logon are passed to SQL Server. This is accomplished by removing the `uid` and `pwd` portions of the connection string, and adding in `Integrated Security=SSPI`.

In the download code available for this chapter, you will find the file `Login.cs`, which simplifies the examples in this chapter. It is linked to all the example code and includes database connection information used for the examples; you can alter this to supply your own server name, user, and password as appropriate. This by default uses Windows-integrated security; however, you can change the username and password as appropriate.

Managing Connection Strings

In the initial release of .NET, it was up to the developer to manage the database connection strings, often done by storing a connection string in the application configuration file or, more commonly, hard-coded somewhere within the application itself.

With .NET 2.0, you now have a predefined way to store connection strings, and even use database connections in a type-agnostic manner — for example, it would now be possible to write an application and then plug in various database providers, all without altering the main application.

To define a database connection string, you should use the `<connectionStrings>` section of the configuration file. Here, you can specify a name for the connection and the actual database connection string parameters; in addition, you can also specify the provider for this connection type. Here is an example:

```
<configuration>
  ...
  <connectionStrings>
    <add name="Northwind"
         providerName="System.Data.SqlClient"
         connectionString="server=(local);integrated security=SSPI;
                           database=Northwind" />
  </connectionStrings>
</configuration>
```

You use this same connection string in the other examples in this chapter.

Once the database connection information has been defined within the configuration file, you then need to utilize this within the application. You will most likely want to create a method such as the following to retrieve a database connection based on the name of the connection:

```
private DbConnection GetDatabaseConnection ( string name )
{
  ConnectionStringSettings settings =
    ConfigurationManager.ConnectionStrings[name];

  DbProviderFactory factory = DbProviderFactories.GetFactory
    ( settings.ProviderName ) ;

  DbConnection conn = factory.CreateConnection ( ) ;
  conn.ConnectionString = settings.ConnectionString ;

  return conn ;
}
```

This code reads the named connection string section (using the `ConnectionStringSettings` class), and then requests a provider factory from the base `DbProviderFactories` class. This uses the `ProviderName` property, which was set to `"System.Data.SqlClient"` in the application configuration file. You might be wondering how this maps to the actual factory class used to generate a database connection for SQL Server — in this case, it should utilize the `SqlClientFactory` class from `System.Data.SqlClient`. You will need to add a reference to the `System.Configuration` assembly in order to resolve the `ConfigurationManager` class used in the preceding code.

If you look into the `machine.config` file for .NET 2.0, you may notice the `DbProviderFactories` section — this maps the alias names (such as `'System.Data.SqlClient'`) to the factory object for that type of database. The following shows an abridged copy of the information within that file:

```
<system.data>
  <DbProviderFactories>
    ...
    <add name="SqlClient Data Provider"
         invariant="System.Data.SqlClient" support="FF"
         description=".Net Framework Data Provider for SqlServer"
         type="System.Data.SqlClient.SqlClientFactory, System.Data,
           Version=2.0.0.0, Culture=neutral,
           PublicKeyToken=b77a5c561934e089" />
    ...
  </DbProviderFactories>
</system.data>
```

This just shows the entry for the `SqlClient` provider — there are other entries for `Odbc`, `OleDb`, `Oracle`, and also `SqlCE`.

So, in the example, the `DbProviderFactory` class just looks up the factory class from the machine configuration settings, and uses that concrete factory class to instantiate the connection object. In the case of the `SqlClientFactory` class, all this does is construct an instance of `SqlConnection` and return this to the caller.

This may seem like a lot of unnecessary work to obtain a database connection, and indeed it is if your application is never going to run on any other database than the one it was designed for. If, however, you use the preceding factory method and also use the generic `Db*` classes (such as `DbConnection`, `DbCommand`, and `DbDataReader`), you will future-proof the application, and any move in the future to another database system will be fairly simple.

Using Connections Efficiently

In general, when using *scarce* resources in .NET, such as database connections, windows, or graphics objects, it is good practice to ensure that each resource is closed after use. Although the designers of .NET have implemented automatic garbage collection, which will tidy up eventually, it is necessary to release resources as early as possible to avoid starvation of resources.

This is all too apparent when writing code that accesses a database because keeping a connection open for slightly longer than necessary can affect other sessions. In extreme circumstances, not closing a connection can lock other users out of an entire set of tables, hurting application performance considerably. Closing database connections should be considered mandatory, so this section shows how to structure your code to minimize the risk of leaving a resource open.

You have two main ways to ensure that database connections and the like are released after use.

Option One: try . . . catch . . . finally

The first option to ensure that resources are cleaned up is to use `try...catch...finally` blocks, and ensure that you close any open connections within the `finally` block. Here is a short example:

```
try
{
   // Open the connection
   conn.Open();
   // Do something useful
}
catch ( SqlException ex )
{
   // Log the exception
}
finally
{
   // Ensure that the connection is freed
   conn.Close ( ) ;
}
```

Within the `finally` block, you can release any resources you have used. The only trouble with this method is that you have to ensure that you close the connection — it is all too easy to forget to add the `finally` clause, so something less prone to vagaries in coding style might be worthwhile.

Also, you might find that you open a number of resources (say two database connections and a file) within a given method, so the cascading of `try...catch...finally` blocks can sometimes become less easy to read. There is, however, another way to guarantee resource cleanup — the `using` statement.

Option Two: The using Block Statement

During development of C#, the debate on how .NET uses nondeterministic destruction became very heated.

In C++, as soon as an object went out of scope, its destructor would be automatically called. This was great news for designers of resource-based classes because the destructor was the ideal place to close the resource if the user had forgotten to do so. A C++ destructor is called whenever an object goes out of scope — so, for instance, if an exception was raised and not caught, all destructors would be called.

With C# and the other managed languages, there is no concept of automatic, deterministic destruction. Instead, there is the garbage collector, which disposes of resources at some point in the future. What makes this nondeterministic is that you have little say over when this process actually happens. Forgetting to close a database connection could cause all sorts of problems for a .NET executable. Luckily, help is at hand. The following code demonstrates how to use the `using` clause to ensure that objects that implement the `IDisposable` interface (see Chapter 12, "Memory Management and Pointers") are cleared up immediately after the block exits:

```
string source = "server=(local);" +
                "integrated security=SSPI;" +
                "database=Northwind";

using ( SqlConnection conn = new SqlConnection ( source ) )
{
   // Open the connection
   conn.Open ( ) ;

   // Do something useful
}
```

In this instance, the `using` clause ensures that the database connection is closed, regardless of how the block is exited.

Looking at the IL code for the `Dispose()` method of the connection classes, all of them check the current state of the connection object, and if open will call the `Close()` method. A great tool for browsing .NET assemblies is Reflector (available at `www.aisto.com/roeder/dotnet`). This tool permits you to view the IL code for any .NET method and will also reverse-engineer the IL into C# source code, so you can easily see what a given method is doing.

When programming, you should use at least one of these methods, and probably both. Wherever you acquire resources, it is good practice to use the `using` statement; even though we all mean to write the `Close()` statement, sometimes we forget, and in the face of exceptions the `using` clause does the right thing. There is no substitute for good exception handling either, so in most instances, it is best to use both methods together, as in the following example:

```
try
{
   using (SqlConnection conn = new SqlConnection ( source ))
   {
      // Open the connection
      conn.Open ( ) ;

      // Do something useful

      // Close it myself
      conn.Close ( ) ;
   }
}
catch (SqlException e)
{
   // Log the exception
}
```

Note that this example called `Close()`, which isn't strictly necessary, because the `using` clause will ensure that this is done anyway. However, you should ensure that any resources such as this are released as soon as possible — you might have more code in the rest of the block, and there is no point locking a resource unnecessarily.

In addition, if an exception is raised within the `using` block, the `IDisposable.Dispose` method will be called on the resource guarded by the `using` clause, which in this example ensures that the database connection is always closed. This produces easier-to-read code than having to ensure you close a connection within an exception clause. You might also note that the exception is defined as a `SqlException` rather than the catch-all `Exception` type — always try to catch as specific an exception as possible and let all others that are not explicitly handled rise up the execution stack.

In conclusion, if you are writing a class that wraps a resource, whatever that resource may be, always implement the `IDisposable` interface to close the resource. That way anyone coding with your class can use the `using()` statement and guarantee that the resource will be cleared up.

Transactions

Often when there is more than one update to be made to the database, these updates must be performed within the scope of a transaction. It is common in code to find a transaction object being passed around to many methods that update the database, however in .NET 2.0 and above the `TransactionScope` class has been added which is defined within the `System.Transactions` assembly. This can vastly simplify writing transactional code because you can compose several transactional methods within a transaction scope, and the transaction will be flowed to each of these methods as necessary.

The following sequence of code initiates a transaction on a SQL Server connection:

```
string source = "server=(local);" +
                "integrated security=SSPI;" +
                "database=Northwind";

using (TransactionScope scope = new TransactionScope(TransactionScopeOption
.Required))
{
    using (SqlConnection conn = new SqlConnection(source))
    {
        // Do something in SQL
        ...

        // Then mark complete
        scope.Complete();
    }
}
```

Here the transaction is explicitly marked as complete by using the `scope.Complete()` method. In the absence of this call, the transaction will be rolled back so that no changes are made to the database.

When you use a transaction scope you can optionally choose the isolation level for commands executed within that transaction. The level determines how changes made in one database session are viewed by another. Not all database engines support all of the four levels presented in the following table.

Isolation Level	Description
`ReadCommitted`	The default for SQL Server. This level ensures that data written by one transaction will be accessible in a second transaction only after the first transaction is committed.
`ReadUncommitted`	This permits your transaction to read data within the database, even data that has not yet been committed by another transaction. For example, if two users were accessing the same database, and the first inserted some data without concluding the transaction (by means of a `Commit` or `Rollback`), the second user with his or her isolation level set to `ReadUncommitted` could read the data.
`RepeatableRead`	This level, which extends the `ReadCommitted` level, ensures that if the same statement is issued within the transaction, regardless of other potential updates made to the database, the same data will always be returned. This level does require extra locks to be held on the data, which could adversely affect performance. This level guarantees that, for each row in the initial query, no changes can be made to that data. It does, however, permit "phantom" rows to show up — these are completely new rows that another transaction might have inserted while your transaction was running.
`Serializable`	This is the most "exclusive" transaction level, which in effect serializes access to data within the database. With this isolation level, phantom rows can never show up, so a SQL statement issued within a serializable transaction will always retrieve the same data. The negative performance impact of a `Serializable` transaction should not be underestimated — if you don't absolutely need to use this level of isolation, stay away from it.

The SQL Server default isolation level, `ReadCommitted`, is a good compromise between data coherence and data availability because fewer locks are required on data than in `RepeatableRead` or `Serializable` modes. However, situations exist where the isolation level should be increased, and so within .NET you can simply begin a transaction with a different level from the default. There are no hard-and-fast rules as to which levels to pick — that comes with experience.

If you are currently using a database that does not support transactions, it is well worth changing to a database that does. Once I was working as a trusted employee and had been given complete access to the bug database. I typed what I thought was `delete from bug where id=99999`*, but in fact had typed a < rather than an =. I deleted the entire database of bugs (except the one I wanted to!). Luckily for me, our IS team backed up the database on a nightly basis and we could restore this, but a rollback command would have been much easier.*

Commands

The "Using Database Connections" section briefly touched on the idea of issuing commands against a database. A command is, in its simplest form, a string of text containing SQL statements that is to be issued to the database. A command could also be a stored procedure, or the name of a table that will return all columns and all rows from that table (in other words, a `SELECT *`-style clause).

A command can be constructed by passing the SQL clause as a parameter to the constructor of the `Command` class, as shown in this example:

```
string source = "server=(local);" +
                "integrated security=SSPI;" +
                "database=Northwind";
string select = "SELECT ContactName,CompanyName FROM Customers";
SqlConnection conn = new SqlConnection(source);
conn.Open();
SqlCommand cmd = new SqlCommand(select, conn);
```

The `<provider>Command` classes have a property called `CommandType`, which is used to define whether the command is a SQL clause, a call to a stored procedure, or a full table statement (which simply selects all columns and rows from a given table). The following table summarizes the `CommandType` enumeration.

CommandType	Example
`Text` (default)	`String select = "SELECT ContactName FROM Customers"; SqlCommand cmd = new SqlCommand(select , conn);`
`StoredProcedure`	`SqlCommand cmd = new SqlCommand("CustOrderHist", conn); cmd.CommandType = CommandType.StoredProcedure; cmd.Parameters.AddWithValue("@CustomerID", "QUICK");`
`TableDirect`	`OleDbCommand cmd = new OleDbCommand("Categories", conn); cmd.CommandType = CommandType.TableDirect;`

When executing a stored procedure, it might be necessary to pass parameters to that procedure. The previous example sets the `@CustomerID` parameter directly, although there are other ways of setting the parameter value, which you look at later in this chapter. Note that in .NET 2.0, the `AddWithValue()` method was added to the command parameters collection — and the `Add ( name, value)` member was attributed as `Obsolete`. If you have used this original method of constructing parameters for calling a stored procedure, you will receive compiler warnings when you recompile your code. We suggest altering your code now because Microsoft will most likely remove the older method in a subsequent release of .NET.

The `TableDirect` command type is valid only for the `OleDb` provider; other providers will throw an exception if you attempt to use this command type with them.

Executing Commands

After you have defined the command, you need to execute it. A number of ways exist to issue the statement, depending on what you expect to be returned (if anything) from that command. The `<provider>Command` classes provide the following execute methods:

- `ExecuteNonQuery()` — Executes the command but does not return any output
- `ExecuteReader()` — Executes the command and returns a typed `IDataReader`
- `ExecuteScalar()` — Executes the command and returns a single value

In addition to these methods, the `SqlCommand` class exposes the following method:

- `ExecuteXmlReader()` — Executes the command and returns an `XmlReader` object, which can be used to traverse the XML fragment returned from the database

As with the other chapters, you can download the sample code from the Wrox Web site at `www.wrox.com`.

ExecuteNonQuery()

This method is commonly used for `UPDATE`, `INSERT`, or `DELETE` statements, where the only returned value is the number of records affected. This method can, however, return results if you call a stored procedure that has output parameters:

```
using System;
using System.Data.SqlClient;
public class ExecuteNonQueryExample
{
   public static void Main(string[] args)
   {
      string source = "server=(local);" +
                      "integrated security=SSPI;" +
                      "database=Northwind";
      string select = "UPDATE Customers " +
                      "SET ContactName = 'Bob' " +
                      "WHERE ContactName = 'Bill'";
      SqlConnection  conn = new SqlConnection(source);
      conn.Open();
      SqlCommand cmd = new SqlCommand(select, conn);
      int rowsReturned = cmd.ExecuteNonQuery();
      Console.WriteLine("{0} rows returned.", rowsReturned);
      conn.Close();
   }
}
```

`ExecuteNonQuery()` returns the number of rows affected by the command as an `int`.

ExecuteReader()

This method executes the command and returns a typed data reader object, depending on the provider in use. The object returned can be used to iterate through the record(s) returned, as shown in the following code:

```
using System;
using System.Data.SqlClient;
public class ExecuteReaderExample
{
   public static void Main(string[] args)
   {
      string source = "server=(local);" +
                      "integrated security=SSPI;" +
                      "database=Northwind";
      string select = "SELECT ContactName,CompanyName FROM Customers";
      SqlConnection conn = new SqlConnection(source);
      conn.Open();
      SqlCommand cmd = new SqlCommand(select, conn);
```

(continued)

(continued)

```
        SqlDataReader reader = cmd.ExecuteReader();
        while(reader.Read())
        {
           Console.WriteLine("Contact : {0,-20} Company : {1}" ,
                               reader[0] , reader[1]);
        }
     }
  }
```

Figure 26-2 shows the output of this code.

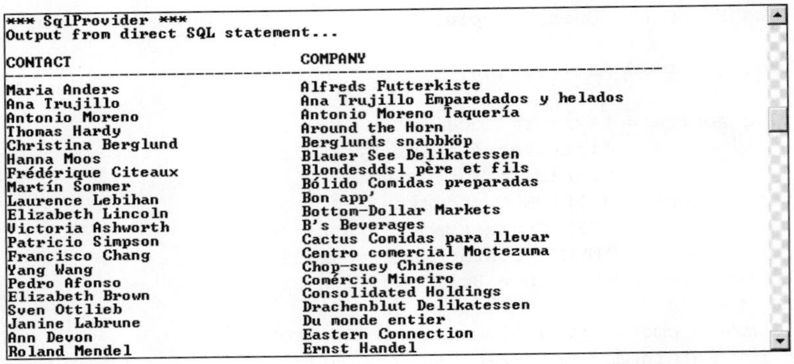

```
*** SqlProvider ***
Output from direct SQL statement...
CONTACT                          COMPANY
---------------------------------------------------------------------
Maria Anders                     Alfreds Futterkiste
Ana Trujillo                     Ana Trujillo Emparedados y helados
Antonio Moreno                   Antonio Moreno Taquería
Thomas Hardy                     Around the Horn
Christina Berglund               Berglunds snabbköp
Hanna Moos                       Blauer See Delikatessen
Frédérique Citeaux               Blondesddsl père et fils
Martín Sommer                    Bólido Comidas preparadas
Laurence Lebihan                 Bon app'
Elizabeth Lincoln                Bottom-Dollar Markets
Victoria Ashworth                B's Beverages
Patricio Simpson                 Cactus Comidas para llevar
Francisco Chang                  Centro comercial Moctezuma
Yang Wang                        Chop-suey Chinese
Pedro Afonso                     Comércio Mineiro
Elizabeth Brown                  Consolidated Holdings
Sven Ottlieb                     Drachenblut Delikatessen
Janine Labrune                   Du monde entier
Ann Devon                        Eastern Connection
Roland Mendel                    Ernst Handel
```

Figure 26-2

The <provider>DataReader objects are discussed later in this chapter.

ExecuteScalar()

On many occasions, it is necessary to return a single result from a SQL statement, such as the count of records in a given table, or the current date/time on the server. The `ExecuteScalar` method can be used in such situations:

```
using System;
using System.Data.SqlClient;
public class ExecuteScalarExample
{
   public static void Main(string[] args)
   {
      string source = "server=(local);" +
                      "integrated security=SSPI;" +
                      "database=Northwind";
      string select = "SELECT COUNT(*) FROM Customers";
      SqlConnection conn = new SqlConnection(source);
      conn.Open();
      SqlCommand cmd = new SqlCommand(select, conn);
      object o = cmd.ExecuteScalar();
      Console.WriteLine ( o ) ;
   }
}
```

The method returns an object, which you can cast to the appropriate type if required. If the SQL you are calling returns only one column, it is preferable to use ExecuteScalar over any other method of retrieving that column. That also applies to stored procedures that return a single value.

ExecuteXmlReader() (SqlClient Provider Only)

As its name implies, this method executes the command and returns an XmlReader object to the caller. SQL Server permits a SQL SELECT statement to be extended with a FOR XML clause. This clause can take one of three options:

- FOR XML AUTO — Builds a tree based on the tables in the FROM clause
- FOR XML RAW — Maps result set rows to elements, with columns mapped to attributes
- FOR XML EXPLICIT — Requires that you specify the shape of the XML tree to be returned

Professional SQL Server 2000 XML (Wrox Press, ISBN 1-861005-46-6) includes a complete description of these options. For this example, use AUTO:

```
using System;
using System.Data.SqlClient;
using System.Xml;
public class ExecuteXmlReaderExample
{
   public static void Main(string[] args)
   {
      string source = "server=(local);" +
                      "integrated security=SSPI;" +
                      "database=Northwind";
      string select = "SELECT ContactName,CompanyName " +
                      "FROM Customers FOR XML AUTO";
      SqlConnection conn = new SqlConnection(source);
      conn.Open();
      SqlCommand cmd = new SqlCommand(select, conn);
      XmlReader xr = cmd.ExecuteXmlReader();
      xr.Read();
      string data;
      do
      {
         data = xr.ReadOuterXml();
         if (!string.IsNullOrEmpty(data))
            Console.WriteLine(data);
      } while (!string.IsNullOrEmpty(data));
      conn.Close();
   }
}
```

Note that you have to import the System.Xml namespace in order to output the returned XML. This namespace and further XML capabilities of .NET Framework are explored in more detail in Chapter 28, "Manipulating XML." Here, you include the FOR XML AUTO clause in the SQL statement, then call the ExecuteXmlReader() method. Figure 26-3 shows the output of this code.

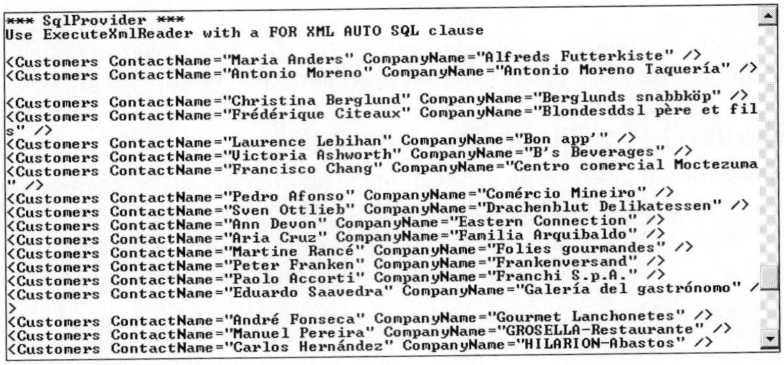

```
*** SqlProvider ***
Use ExecuteXmlReader with a FOR XML AUTO SQL clause

<Customers ContactName="Maria Anders" CompanyName="Alfreds Futterkiste" />
<Customers ContactName="Antonio Moreno" CompanyName="Antonio Moreno Taquería" />

<Customers ContactName="Christina Berglund" CompanyName="Berglunds snabbköp" />
<Customers ContactName="Frédérique Citeaux" CompanyName="Blondesddsl père et fil
s" />
<Customers ContactName="Laurence Lebihan" CompanyName="Bon app'" />
<Customers ContactName="Victoria Ashworth" CompanyName="B's Beverages" />
<Customers ContactName="Francisco Chang" CompanyName="Centro comercial Moctezuma
" />
<Customers ContactName="Pedro Afonso" CompanyName="Comércio Mineiro" />
<Customers ContactName="Sven Ottlieb" CompanyName="Drachenblut Delikatessen" />
<Customers ContactName="Ann Devon" CompanyName="Eastern Connection" />
<Customers ContactName="Aria Cruz" CompanyName="Familia Arquibaldo" />
<Customers ContactName="Martine Rancé" CompanyName="Folies gourmandes" />
<Customers ContactName="Peter Franken" CompanyName="Frankenversand" />
<Customers ContactName="Paolo Accorti" CompanyName="Franchi S.p.A." />
<Customers ContactName="Eduardo Saavedra" CompanyName="Galería del gastrónomo" /
>
<Customers ContactName="André Fonseca" CompanyName="Gourmet Lanchonetes" />
<Customers ContactName="Manuel Pereira" CompanyName="GROSELLA-Restaurante" />
<Customers ContactName="Carlos Hernández" CompanyName="HILARION-Abastos" />
```

Figure 26-3

In the SQL clause, you specified `FROM Customers`, so an element of type `Customers` is shown in the output. To this are added attributes, one for each column selected from the database. This builds up an XML fragment for each row selected from the database.

Calling Stored Procedures

Calling a stored procedure with a command object is just a matter of defining the name of the stored procedure, adding a definition for each parameter of the procedure, and then executing the command with one of the methods presented in the previous section.

To make the examples in this section more useful, a set of stored procedures has been defined that can be used to insert, update, and delete records from the `Region` table in the Northwind sample database. Despite its small size, this is a good candidate to choose for the example because it can be used to define examples for each of the types of stored procedures you will commonly write.

Calling a Stored Procedure That Returns Nothing

The simplest example of calling a stored procedure is one that returns nothing to the caller. Two such procedures are defined in the following two subsections: one for updating a preexisting `Region` record and one for deleting a given `Region` record.

Record Update

Updating a `Region` record is fairly trivial because there is only one column that can be modified (assuming primary keys cannot be updated). You can type these examples directly into the SQL Server Query Analyzer, or run the `StoredProcs.sql` file that is part of the downloadable code for this chapter. This file installs each of the stored procedures in this section:

```
CREATE PROCEDURE RegionUpdate (@RegionID INTEGER,
                              @RegionDescription NCHAR(50)) AS
   SET NOCOUNT OFF
   UPDATE Region
      SET RegionDescription = @RegionDescription
      WHERE RegionID = @RegionID
GO
```

An update command on a more real-world table might need to reselect and return the updated record in its entirety. This stored procedure takes two input parameters (`@RegionID` and `@RegionDescription`), and issues an `UPDATE` statement against the database.

To run this stored procedure from within .NET code, you need to define a SQL command and execute it:

```
SqlCommand cmd = new SqlCommand("RegionUpdate", conn);

cmd.CommandType = CommandType.StoredProcedure;
cmd.Parameters.AddWithValue ( "@RegionID", 23 );
cmd.Parameters.AddWithValue ( "@RegionDescription", "Something" );
```

This code creates a new `SqlCommand` object named `aCommand`, and defines it as a stored procedure. You then add each parameter in turn using the `AddWithValue` method. This constructs a parameter and also sets its value — you can also manually construct `SqlParameter` instances and add these to the `Parameters` collection if appropriate.

The stored procedure takes two parameters: the unique primary key of the `Region` record being updated and the new description to be given to this record. After the command has been created, it can be executed by issuing the following command:

```
cmd.ExecuteNonQuery();
```

Because the procedure returns nothing, `ExecuteNonQuery()` will suffice. Command parameters can be set directly using the `AddWithValue` method, or by constructing `SqlParameter` instances. Note that the parameter collection is indexable by position or parameter name.

Record Deletion

The next stored procedure required is one that can be used to delete a `Region` record from the database:

```
CREATE PROCEDURE RegionDelete (@RegionID INTEGER) AS
   SET NOCOUNT OFF
   DELETE FROM Region
   WHERE       RegionID = @RegionID
GO
```

This procedure requires only the primary key value of the record. The code uses a `SqlCommand` object to call this stored procedure as follows:

```
SqlCommand cmd = new SqlCommand("RegionDelete" , conn);
cmd.CommandType = CommandType.StoredProcedure;
cmd.Parameters.Add(new SqlParameter("@RegionID" , SqlDbType.Int , 0 ,
                                    "RegionID"));
cmd.UpdatedRowSource = UpdateRowSource.None;
```

This command accepts only a single parameter, as shown in the following code, which will execute the `RegionDelete` stored procedure; here, you see an example of setting the parameter by name. If you have many similar calls to make to the same stored procedure, then constructing `SqlParameter` instances and setting the values as in the following may lead to better performance than re-constructing the entire `SqlCommand` for each call.

```
cmd.Parameters["@RegionID"].Value= 999;
cmd.ExecuteNonQuery();
```

Calling a Stored Procedure That Returns Output Parameters

Both of the previous examples execute stored procedures that return nothing. If a stored procedure includes output parameters, these need to be defined within the .NET client so that they can be filled when the procedure returns. The following example shows how to insert a record into the database and return the primary key of that record to the caller.

Record Insertion

The `Region` table consists of only a primary key (`RegionID`) and description field (`RegionDescription`). To insert a record, this numeric primary key must be generated, and then a new row needs to be inserted into the database. The primary key generation in this example has been simplified by creating one within the stored procedure. The method used is exceedingly crude, which is why there is a section on key generation later in this chapter. For now, this primitive example suffices:

```
CREATE PROCEDURE RegionInsert(@RegionDescription NCHAR(50),
                              @RegionID INTEGER OUTPUT)AS
   SET NOCOUNT OFF
   SELECT @RegionID = MAX(RegionID)+ 1
   FROM Region
   INSERT INTO Region(RegionID, RegionDescription)
   VALUES(@RegionID, @RegionDescription)
GO
```

The insert procedure creates a new `Region` record. Because the primary key value is generated by the database itself, this value is returned as an output parameter from the procedure (`@RegionID`). This is sufficient for this simple example, but for a more complex table (especially one with default values), it is more common not to use output parameters, and instead select the entire inserted row and return this to the caller. The .NET classes can cope with either scenario.

```
SqlCommand  cmd = new SqlCommand("RegionInsert" , conn);
cmd.CommandType = CommandType.StoredProcedure;
cmd.Parameters.Add(new SqlParameter("@RegionDescription" ,
                                    SqlDbType.NChar ,
                                    50 ,
                                    "RegionDescription"));
cmd.Parameters.Add(new SqlParameter("@RegionID" ,
                                    SqlDbType.Int,
                                    0 ,
                                    ParameterDirection.Output ,
                                    false ,
                                    0 ,
                                    0 ,
                                    "RegionID" ,
                                    DataRowVersion.Default ,
                                    null));
cmd.UpdatedRowSource = UpdateRowSource.OutputParameters;
```

Here, the definition of the parameters is much more complex. The second parameter, `@RegionID`, is defined to include its parameter direction, which in this example is `Output`. In addition to this flag, on the last line of the code, the `UpdateRowSource` enumeration is used to indicate that data will be returned from this stored procedure via output parameters. This flag is mainly used when issuing stored procedure calls from a `DataTable` (which is discussed later in this chapter).

Calling this stored procedure is similar to the previous examples, except in this instance the output parameter is read after executing the procedure:

```
cmd.Parameters["@RegionDescription"].Value = "South West";
cmd.ExecuteNonQuery();
int newRegionID = (int) cmd.Parameters["@RegionID"].Value;
```

After executing the command, the value of the `@RegionID` parameter is read and cast to an integer. A shorthand version of the preceding is the `ExecuteScalar()` method, which will return (as an object) the first value returned from the stored procedure.

You might be wondering what to do if the stored procedure you call returns output parameters and a set of rows. In this instance, define the parameters as appropriate, and rather than calling `ExecuteNonQuery()`, call one of the other methods (such as `ExecuteReader()`) that will permit you to traverse any record(s) returned.

Fast Data Access: The Data Reader

A data reader is the simplest and fastest way of selecting some data from a data source, but it is also the least capable. You cannot directly instantiate a data reader object — an instance is returned from the appropriate database's command object (such as `SqlCommand`) after having called the `ExecuteReader()` method.

The following code demonstrates how to select data from the `Customers` table in the Northwind database. The example connects to the database, selects a number of records, loops through these selected records, and outputs them to the console.

This example uses the OLE DB provider as a brief respite from the SQL provider. In most cases, the classes have a one-to-one correspondence with their `SqlClient` cousins; for example, there is the `OleDbConnection` object, which is similar to the `SqlConnection` object used in the previous examples.

To execute commands against an OLE DB data source, the `OleDbCommand` class is used. The following code shows an example of executing a simple SQL statement and reading the records by returning an `OleDbDataReader` object.

Note the second `using` directive that makes available the `OleDb` classes:

```
using System;
using System.Data.OleDb;
```

Most of the data providers currently available are shipped within the same assembly, so it is only necessary to reference the `System.Data.dll` assembly to import all classes used in this section. The only exceptions are the Oracle classes, which reside in `System.Data.Oracle.dll`.

```
public class DataReaderExample
{
   public static void Main(string[] args)
   {
      string source = "Provider=SQLOLEDB;" +
                      "server=(local);" +
                      "integrated security=SSPI;" +
                      "database=northwind";
      string select = "SELECT ContactName,CompanyName FROM Customers";
      OleDbConnection conn = new OleDbConnection(source);
      conn.Open();
      OleDbCommand cmd = new OleDbCommand(select , conn);
      OleDbDataReader aReader = cmd.ExecuteReader();
      while(aReader.Read())
         Console.WriteLine("'{0}' from {1}" ,
                           aReader.GetString(0) , aReader.GetString(1));
      aReader.Close();
      conn.Close();
   }
}
```

The preceding code includes many familiar aspects of C# already covered in this chapter. To compile the example, issue the following command:

```
csc /t:exe /debug+ DataReaderExample.cs /r:System.Data.dll
```

The following code from the previous example creates a new OLE DB .NET database connection, based on the source connection string:

```
OleDbConnection conn = new OleDbConnection(source);
   conn.Open();
   OleDbCommand cmd = new OleDbCommand(select, conn);
```

The third line creates a new `OleDbCommand` object, based on a particular `SELECT` statement, and the database connection to be used when the command is executed. When you have a valid command, you need to execute it, which returns an initialized `OleDbDataReader`:

```
OleDbDataReader aReader = cmd.ExecuteReader();
```

An `OleDbDataReader` is a forward-only "connected" cursor. In other words, you can only traverse the records returned in one direction, and the database connection used is kept open until the data reader has been closed.

An `OleDbDataReader` keeps the database connection open until it is explicitly closed.

The `OleDbDataReader` class cannot be instantiated directly — it is always returned by a call to the `ExecuteReader()` method of the `OleDbCommand` class. Once you have an open data reader, there are various ways to access the data contained within the reader.

When the `OleDbDataReader` object is closed (via an explicit call to `Close()`, or the object being garbage collected), the underlying connection may also be closed, depending on which of the `ExecuteReader()` methods is called. If you call `ExecuteReader()` and pass `CommandBehavior.CloseConnection`, you can force the connection to be closed when the reader is closed.

The `OleDbDataReader` class has an indexer that permits access (although not type-safe access) to any field using the familiar array style syntax:

```
   object o = aReader[0];
or
   object o = aReader["CategoryID"];
```

Assuming that the `CategoryID` field was the first in the `SELECT` statement used to populate the reader, these two lines are functionally equivalent, although the second is slower than the first; to verify this, a test application was written that performed a million iterations of accessing the same column from an open data reader, just to get some numbers that were big enough to read. You probably don't read the same column a million times in a tight loop, but every (micro) second counts, so you should write code that is as optimal as possible.

As an aside, the numeric indexer took on average 0.09 seconds for the million accesses, and the textual one 0.63 seconds. The reason for this difference is that the textual method looks up the column number internally from the schema and then accesses it using its ordinal. If you know this information beforehand you can do a better job of accessing the data.

So, should you use the numeric indexer? Maybe, but there is a better way.

In addition to the indexers just presented, `OleDbDataReader` has a set of type-safe methods that can be used to read columns. These are fairly self-explanatory, and all begin with `Get`. There are methods to read most types of data, such as `GetInt32`, `GetFloat`, `GetGuid`, and so on.

The million iterations using `GetInt32` took 0.06 seconds. The overhead in the numeric indexer is incurred while getting the data type, calling the same code as `GetInt32`, then boxing (and in this instance unboxing) an integer. So, if you know the schema beforehand, are willing to use cryptic numbers instead of column names, and can be bothered to use a type-safe function for each and every column access, you stand to gain somewhere in the region of a tenfold speed increase over using a textual column name (when selecting those million copies of the same column).

Needless to say, there is a tradeoff between maintainability and speed. If you must use numeric indexers, define constants within class scope for each of the columns that you will be accessing. The preceding code can be used to select data from any OLE DB database; however, there are a number of SQL Server–specific classes that can be used with the obvious portability tradeoff.

The following example is the same as the previous one, except that in this instance the OLE DB provider and all references to OLE DB classes have been replaced with their SQL counterparts. The example is in the `04_DataReaderSql` directory:

```
using System;
using System.Data.SqlClient;
public class DataReaderSql
{
   public static int Main(string[] args)
   {
      string source = "server=(local);" +
                      "integrated security=SSPI;" +
                      "database=northwind";
      string select = "SELECT ContactName,CompanyName FROM Customers";
      SqlConnection conn = new SqlConnection(source);
      conn.Open();
      SqlCommand cmd = new SqlCommand(select , conn);
      SqlDataReader aReader = cmd.ExecuteReader();
      while(aReader.Read())
         Console.WriteLine("'{0}' from {1}" , aReader.GetString(0) ,
                           aReader.GetString(1));
      aReader.Close();
      conn.Close();
      return 0;
   }
}
```

Notice the difference? If you're typing this, do a global replace on `OleDb` with `Sql`, change the data source string, and recompile. It's that easy!

The same performance tests were run on the indexers for the SQL provider, and this time the numeric indexers were both exactly the same at 0.13 seconds for the million accesses, and the string-based indexer ran at about 0.65 seconds.

Managing Data and Relationships: The DataSet Class

The `DataSet` class has been designed as an offline container of data. It has no notion of database connections. In fact, the data held within a `DataSet` does not necessarily need to have come from a database — it could just as easily be records from a CSV file, or points read from a measuring device.

A DataSet class consists of a set of data tables, each of which will have a set of data columns and data rows (see Figure 26-4). In addition to defining the data, you can also define *links* between tables within the DataSet class. One common scenario would be when defining a parent-child relationship (commonly known as master/detail). One record in a table (say Order) links to many records in another table (say Order_Details). This relationship can be defined and navigated within the DataSet.

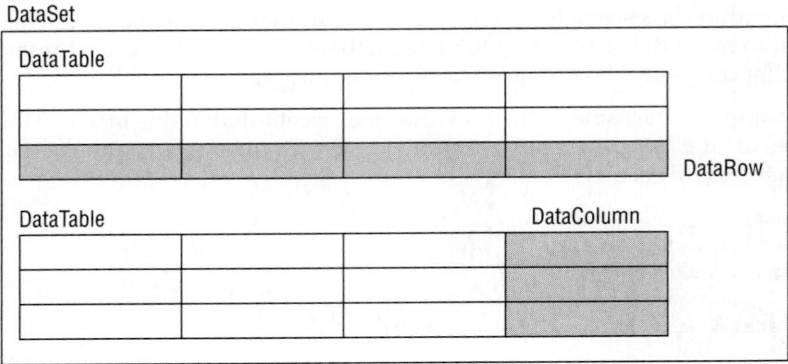

Figure 26-4

The following sections describe the classes that are used with a DataSet class.

Data Tables

A data table is very similar to a physical database table — it consists of a set of columns with particular properties and might have zero or more rows of data. A data table might also define a primary key, which can be one or more columns, and might also contain constraints on columns. The generic term for this information used throughout the rest of the chapter is *schema*.

Several ways exist to define the schema for a particular data table (and indeed the DataSet class as a whole). These are discussed after introducing data columns and data rows. Figure 26-5 shows some of the objects that are accessible through the data table.

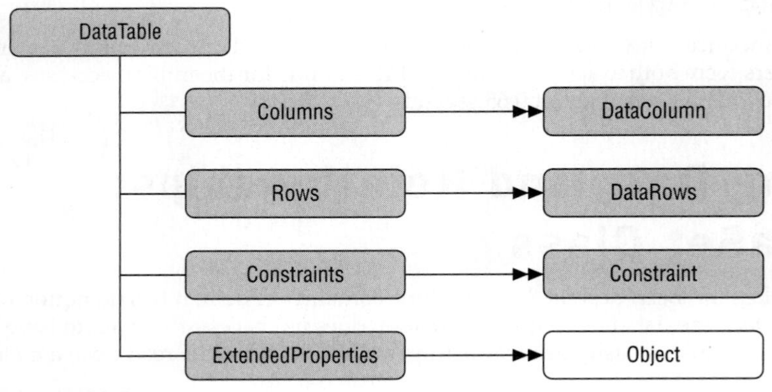

Figure 26-5

A DataTable object (and also a DataColumn) can have an arbitrary number of extended properties associated with it. This collection can be populated with any user-defined information pertaining to the object. For example, a given column might have an input mask used to validate the contents of that column — a typical example is the U.S. Social Security number. Extended properties are especially useful when the data is constructed within a middle tier and returned to the client for some processing. You could, for example, store validation criteria (such as min and max) for numeric columns in extended properties and use this in the UI tier when validating user input.

When a data table has been populated — by selecting data from a database, reading data from a file, or manually populating within code — the Rows collection will contain this retrieved data.

The Columns collection contains DataColumn instances that have been added to this table. These define the schema of the data, such as the data type, nullability, default values, and so on.
The Constraints collection can be populated with either unique or primary key constraints.

One example of where the schema information for a data table is used is when displaying that data in a DataGrid (which is discussed in Chapter 32, "Data Binding"). The DataGrid control uses properties such as the data type of the column to decide what control to use for that column. A bit field within the database will be displayed as a check box within the DataGrid. If a column is defined within the database schema as NOT NULL, this fact will be stored within the DataColumn so that it can be tested when the user attempts to move off a row.

Data Columns

A DataColumn object defines properties of a column within the DataTable, such as the data type of that column, whether the column is read-only, and various other facts. A column can be created in code, or it can be automatically generated by the runtime.

When creating a column, it is also useful to give it a name; otherwise, the runtime will generate a name for you in the form Columnn where n is an incrementing number.

The data type of the column can be set either by supplying it in the constructor or by setting the DataType property. Once you have loaded data into a data table you cannot alter the type of a column — you will just receive an ArgumentException.

Data columns can be created to hold the following .NET Framework data types:

Boolean	Decimal
Int64	TimeSpan
Byte	Double
Sbyte	UInt16
Char	Int16
Single	UInt32
DateTime	Int32
String	UInt64

Once created, the next thing to do with a `DataColumn` object is to set up other properties, such as the nullability of the column or the default value. The following code fragment shows a few of the more common options to set on a `DataColumn` object:

```
DataColumn customerID = new DataColumn("CustomerID" , typeof(int));
customerID.AllowDBNull = false;
customerID.ReadOnly = false;
customerID.AutoIncrement = true;
customerID.AutoIncrementSeed = 1000;
DataColumn name = new DataColumn("Name" , typeof(string));
name.AllowDBNull = false;
name.Unique = true;
```

The following table shows the properties that can be set on a `DataColumn` object.

Property	Description
`AllowDBNull`	If `true`, permits the column to be set to `DBNull`.
`AutoIncrement`	Defines that this column value is automatically generated as an incrementing number.
`AutoIncrementSeed`	Defines the initial seed value for an `AutoIncrement` column.
`AutoIncrementStep`	Defines the step between automatically generated column values, with a default of one.
`Caption`	Can be used for displaying the name of the column onscreen.
`ColumnMapping`	Defines how a column is mapped into XML when a `DataSet` class is saved by calling `DataSet.WriteXml`.
`ColumnName`	The name of the column; this is auto-generated by the runtime if not set in the constructor.
`DataType`	Defines the `System.Type` value of the column.
`DefaultValue`	Can define a default value for a column.
`Expression`	Defines the expression to be used in a computed column.

Data Rows

This class makes up the other part of the `DataTable` class. The columns within a data table are defined in terms of the `DataColumn` class. The actual data within the table is accessed using the `DataRow` object. The following example shows how to access rows within a data table. First, the connection details:

```
string source = "server=(local);" +
                " integrated security=SSPI;" +
                "database=northwind";
string select = "SELECT ContactName,CompanyName FROM Customers";
SqlConnection  conn = new SqlConnection(source);
```

The following code introduces the `SqlDataAdapter` class, which is used to place data into a `DataSet` class. `SqlDataAdapter` issues the SQL clause and fills a table in the `DataSet` class called `Customers` with the output of the following query. (For more details on the SqlDataAdapter class, see the section "Populating a DataSet" later in this chapter.)

```
SqlDataAdapter da = new SqlDataAdapter(select, conn);
DataSet ds = new DataSet();
da.Fill(ds , "Customers");
```

In the following code, you might notice the use of the DataRow indexer to access values from within that row. The value for a given column can be retrieved using one of the several overloaded indexers. These permit you to retrieve a value knowing the column number, name, or DataColumn:

```
foreach(DataRow row in ds.Tables["Customers"].Rows)
   Console.WriteLine("'{0}' from {1}" , row[0] ,row[1]);
```

One of the most appealing aspects of DataRow is that it is versioned. This permits you to receive various values for a given column in a particular row. The versions are described in the following table.

DataRow Version Value	Description
Current	The value existing at present within the column. If no edit has occurred, this will be the same as the original value. If an edit (or edits) has occurred, the value will be the last valid value entered.
Default	The default value (in other words, any default set up for the column).
Original	The value of the column when originally selected from the database. If the DataRow's AcceptChanges() method is called, this value will update to the Current value.
Proposed	When changes are in progress for a row, it is possible to retrieve this modified value. If you call BeginEdit() on the row and make changes, each column will have a proposed value until either EndEdit() or CancelEdit() is called.

The version of a given column could be used in many ways. One example is when updating rows within the database, in which instance it is common to issue a SQL statement such as the following:

```
UPDATE Products
SET    Name = Column.Current
WHERE  ProductID = xxx
AND    Name = Column.Original;
```

Obviously, this code would never compile, but it shows one use for original and current values of a column within a row.

To retrieve a versioned value from the DataRow indexer, use one of the indexer methods that accepts a DataRowVersion value as a parameter. The following snippet shows how to obtain all values of each column in a DataTable object:

```
foreach (DataRow row in ds.Tables["Customers"].Rows )
{
  foreach ( DataColumn dc in ds.Tables["Customers"].Columns )
  {
```

(continued)

(continued)

```
        Console.WriteLine ("{0} Current  = {1}" , dc.ColumnName ,
                                                  row[dc,DataRowVersion.Current]);
        Console.WriteLine ("    Default  = {0}" , row[dc,DataRowVersion.Default]);
        Console.WriteLine ("    Original = {0}" ,
                         row[dc,DataRowVersion.Original]);
    }
  }
```

The whole row has a state flag called `RowState`, which can be used to determine what operation is needed on the row when it is persisted back to the database. The `RowState` property is set to keep track of all the changes made to the `DataTable`, such as adding new rows, deleting existing rows, and changing columns within the table. When the data is reconciled with the database, the row state flag is used to determine what SQL operations should occur. The following table provides an overview of the flags that are defined by the `DataRowState` enumeration.

DataRowState Value	Description
`Added`	Indicates that the row has been newly added to a `DataTable`'s `Rows` collection. All rows created on the client are set to this value and will ultimately issue SQL `INSERT` statements when reconciled with the database.
`Deleted`	Indicates that the row has been marked as deleted from the `DataTable` by means of the `DataRow.Delete()` method. The row still exists within the `DataTable` but will not normally be viewable onscreen (unless a `DataView` has been explicitly set up). `DataViews` are discussed in the next chapter. Rows marked as deleted in the `DataTable` will be deleted from the database when reconciled.
`Detached`	Indicates that a row is in this state immediately after it is created, and can also be returned to this state by calling `DataRow.Remove()`. A detached row is not considered to be part of any data table, and, as such, no SQL for rows in this state will be issued.
`Modified`	Indicates that a row will be `Modified` if the value in any column has been changed.
`Unchanged`	Indicates that the row has not been changed since the last call to `AcceptChanges()`.

The state of the row depends also on what methods have been called on the row. The `AcceptChanges()` method is generally called after successfully updating the data source (that is, after persisting changes to the database).

The most common way to alter data in a `DataRow` is to use the indexer; however, if you have a number of changes to make, you also need to consider the `BeginEdit()` and `EndEdit()` methods.

When an alteration is made to a column within a `DataRow`, the `ColumnChanging` event is raised on the row's `DataTable`. This permits you to override the `ProposedValue` property of the `DataColumnChangeEventArgs` class, and change it as required. This is one way of performing some data validation on column values. If you call `BeginEdit()` before making changes, the `ColumnChanging` event will not be raised. This permits you to make multiple changes and then call `EndEdit()` to persist these changes. If you want to revert to the original values, call `CancelEdit()`.

A `DataRow` can be linked in some way to other rows of data. This permits the creation of navigable links between rows, which is common in master/detail scenarios. The `DataRow` contains a `GetChildRows()` method that will return an array of associated rows from another table in the same `DataSet` as the current row. These are discussed in the "Data Relationships" section later in this chapter.

Schema Generation

You can create the schema for a `DataTable` in three ways:

- Let the runtime do it for you.
- Write code to create the table(s).
- Use the XML schema generator.

Runtime Schema Generation

The `DataRow` example shown earlier presented the following code for selecting data from a database and populating a `DataSet` class:

```
SqlDataAdapter da = new SqlDataAdapter(select , conn);
DataSet ds = new DataSet();
da.Fill(ds , "Customers");
```

This is obviously easy to use, but it has a few drawbacks as well. For example, you have to make do with the default column names, which might work for you, but in certain instances, you might want to rename a physical database column (say `PKID`) to something more user-friendly.

You could naturally alias columns within your SQL clause, as in `SELECT PID AS PersonID FROM PersonTable`; it's best to not rename columns within SQL, though, because a column only really needs to have a "pretty" name onscreen.

Another potential problem with automated `DataTable`/`DataColumn` generation is that you have no control over the column types that the runtime chooses for your data. It does a fairly good job of deciding the correct data type for you, but as usual there are instances where you need more control. For example, you might have defined an enumerated type for a given column to simplify user code written against your class. If you accept the default column types that the runtime generates, the column will likely be an integer with a 32-bit range, as opposed to an `enum` with your predefined options.

Last, and probably most problematic, is that when using automated table generation, you have no type-safe access to the data within the `DataTable` — you are at the mercy of indexers, which return instances of `object` rather than derived data types. If you like sprinkling your code with typecast expressions, skip the following sections.

Hand-Coded Schema

Generating the code to create a `DataTable`, replete with associated `DataColumns`, is fairly easy. The examples within this section access the `Products` table from the Northwind database shown in Figure 26-6.

Column Name	Data Type	Allow Nulls
ProductID	int	☐
ProductName	nvarchar(40)	☐
SupplierID	int	☑
CategoryID	int	☑
QuantityPerUnit	nvarchar(20)	☑
UnitPrice	money	☑
UnitsInStock	smallint	☑
UnitsOnOrder	smallint	☑
ReorderLevel	smallint	☑
Discontinued	bit	☐

Figure 26-6

The following code manufactures a DataTable, which corresponds to the schema shown in Figure 26-6 (but does not cover the nullability of columns):

```
public static void ManufactureProductDataTable(DataSet ds)
{
   DataTable   products = new DataTable("Products");
   products.Columns.Add(new DataColumn("ProductID", typeof(int)));
   products.Columns.Add(new DataColumn("ProductName", typeof(string)));
   products.Columns.Add(new DataColumn("SupplierID", typeof(int)));
   products.Columns.Add(new DataColumn("CategoryID", typeof(int)));
   products.Columns.Add(new DataColumn("QuantityPerUnit", typeof(string)));
   products.Columns.Add(new DataColumn("UnitPrice", typeof(decimal)));
   products.Columns.Add(new DataColumn("UnitsInStock", typeof(short)));
   products.Columns.Add(new DataColumn("UnitsOnOrder", typeof(short)));
   products.Columns.Add(new DataColumn("ReorderLevel", typeof(short)));
   products.Columns.Add(new DataColumn("Discontinued", typeof(bool)));
   ds.Tables.Add(products);
}
```

You can alter the code in the DataRow example to use this newly generated table definition as follows:

```
string source = "server=(local);" +
                "integrated security=sspi;" +
                "database=Northwind";
string select = "SELECT * FROM Products";
SqlConnection conn = new SqlConnection(source);
SqlDataAdapter cmd = new SqlDataAdapter(select, conn);
DataSet ds = new DataSet();
ManufactureProductDataTable(ds);
cmd.Fill(ds, "Products");
foreach(DataRow row in ds.Tables["Products"].Rows)
   Console.WriteLine("'{0}' from {1}", row[0], row[1]);
```

The ManufactureProductDataTable() method creates a new DataTable, adds each column in turn, and finally appends this to the list of tables within the DataSet. The DataSet has an indexer that takes the name of the table and returns that DataTable to the caller.

The previous example is still not really type-safe because indexers are being used on columns to retrieve the data. What would be better is a class (or set of classes) derived from DataSet, DataTable, and DataRow that defines type-safe accessors for tables, rows, and columns. You can generate this code yourself; it is not particularly tedious and you end up with truly type-safe data access classes.

If you don't like generating these type-safe classes yourself, help is at hand. The .NET Framework includes support for the third method listed at the start of this section: using XML schemas to define a `DataSet` class, a `DataTable` class, and the other classes that we have described here. (For more details on this method, see the section "XML Schemas: Generating Code with XSD" later in this chapter.)

Data Relationships

When writing an application, it is often necessary to obtain and cache various tables of information. The `DataSet` class is the container for this information. With regular OLE DB, it was necessary to provide a strange SQL dialect to enforce hierarchical data relationships, and the provider itself was not without its own subtle quirks.

The `DataSet` class, however, has been designed from the start to establish relationships between data tables with ease. The code in this section shows how to generate manually and populate two tables with data. So, if you don't have access to SQL Server or the Northwind database, you can run this example anyway:

```
DataSet ds = new DataSet("Relationships");
ds.Tables.Add(CreateBuildingTable());
ds.Tables.Add(CreateRoomTable());
ds.Relations.Add("Rooms",
                 ds.Tables["Building"].Columns["BuildingID"],
                 ds.Tables["Room"].Columns["BuildingID"]);
```

The tables used in this example are shown in Figure 26-7. They contain a primary key and name field, with the `Room` table having `BuildingID` as a foreign key.

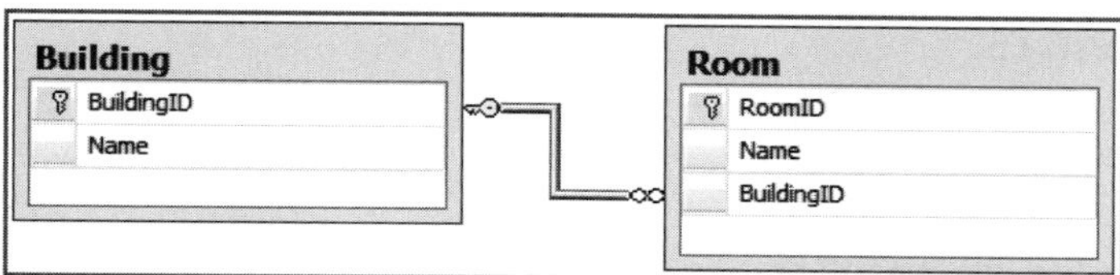

Figure 26-7

These tables have been kept deliberately simple. The following code shows how to iterate through the rows in the `Building` table and traverse the relationship to list all of the child rows from the `Room` table:

```
foreach(DataRow theBuilding in ds.Tables["Building"].Rows)
{
   DataRow[] children = theBuilding.GetChildRows("Rooms");
   int roomCount = children.Length;
   Console.WriteLine("Building {0} contains {1} room{2}",
                     theBuilding["Name"],
                     roomCount,
                     roomCount > 1 ? "s" : "");
   // Loop through the rooms
   foreach(DataRow theRoom in children)
      Console.WriteLine("Room: {0}", theRoom["Name"]);
}
```

The key difference between the `DataSet` class and the old-style hierarchical `Recordset` object is in the way the relationship is presented. In a hierarchical `Recordset` object, the relationship was presented as a pseudo-column within the row. This column itself was a `Recordset` object that could be iterated through. Under ADO.NET, however, a relationship is traversed simply by calling the `GetChildRows()` method:

```
DataRow[] children = theBuilding.GetChildRows("Rooms");
```

This method has a number of forms, but the preceding simple example uses just the name of the relationship to traverse between parent and child rows. It returns an array of rows that can be updated as appropriate by using the indexers, as shown in earlier examples.

What's more interesting with data relationships is that they can be traversed both ways. Not only can you go from a parent to the child rows, but you can also find a parent row (or rows) from a child record simply by using the `ParentRelations` property on the `DataTable` class. This property returns a `DataRelationCollection`, which can be indexed using the `[]` array syntax (for example, `ParentRelations["Rooms"]`), or as an alternative, the `GetParentRows()` method can be called, as shown here:

```
foreach(DataRow theRoom in ds.Tables["Room"].Rows)
{
   DataRow[] parents = theRoom.GetParentRows("Rooms");
   foreach(DataRow theBuilding in parents)
      Console.WriteLine("Room {0} is contained in building {1}",
                        theRoom["Name"],
                        theBuilding["Name"]);
}
```

Two methods with various overrides are available for retrieving the parent row(s): `GetParentRows()` (which returns an array of zero or more rows) and `GetParentRow()` (which retrieves a single parent row given a relationship).

Data Constraints

Changing the data type of columns created on the client is not the only thing a `DataTable` is good for. ADO.NET permits you to create a set of constraints on a column (or columns), which are then used to enforce rules within the data.

The following table lists the constraint types that are currently supported by the runtime, embodied as classes in the `System.Data` namespace.

Constraint	Description
`ForeignKeyConstraint`	Enforces a link between two `DataTable`s within a `DataSet`.
`UniqueConstraint`	Ensures that entries in a given column are unique.

Setting a Primary Key

As is common with a table in a relational database, you can supply a primary key, which can be based on one or more columns from the `DataTable`.

The following code creates a primary key for the `Products` table, whose schema was constructed by hand earlier.

Note that a primary key on a table is just one form of constraint. When a primary key is added to a `DataTable`, the runtime also generates a unique constraint over the key column(s). This is because there isn't actually a constraint type of PrimaryKey — a primary key is simply a unique constraint over one or more columns.

```
public static void ManufacturePrimaryKey(DataTable dt)
{
   DataColumn[] pk = new DataColumn[1];
   pk[0] = dt.Columns["ProductID"];
   dt.PrimaryKey = pk;
}
```

Because a primary key can contain several columns, it is typed as an array of DataColumns. A table's primary key can be set to those columns simply by assigning an array of columns to the property.

To check the constraints for a table, you can iterate through the ConstraintCollection. For the auto-generated constraint produced by the preceding code, the name of the constraint is Constraint1. That's not a very useful name, so to avoid this problem it is always best to create the constraint in code first, then define which column(s) make up the primary key.

The following code names the constraint before creating the primary key:

```
DataColumn[] pk = new DataColumn[1];
pk[0] = dt.Columns["ProductID"];
dt.Constraints.Add(new UniqueConstraint("PK_Products", pk[0]));
dt.PrimaryKey = pk;
```

Unique constraints can be applied to as many columns as you want.

Setting a Foreign Key

In addition to unique constraints, a DataTable class can also contain foreign key constraints. These are primarily used to enforce master/detail relationships but can also be used to replicate columns between tables if you set up the constraint correctly. A master/detail relationship is one where there is commonly one parent record (say an order) and many child records (order lines), linked by the primary key of the parent record.

A foreign key constraint can operate only over tables within the same DataSet, so the following example uses the Categories table from the Northwind database (shown in Figure 26-8), and assigns a constraint between it and the Products table.

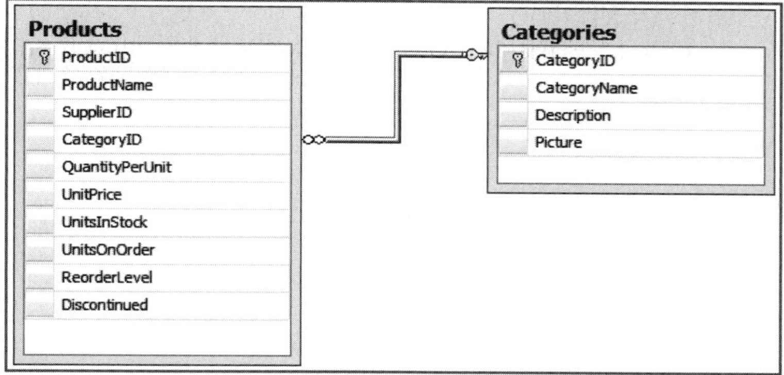

Figure 26-8

The first step is to generate a new data table for the `Categories` table:

```
DataTable categories = new DataTable("Categories");
categories.Columns.Add(new DataColumn("CategoryID", typeof(int)));
categories.Columns.Add(new DataColumn("CategoryName", typeof(string)));
categories.Columns.Add(new DataColumn("Description", typeof(string)));
categories.Constraints.Add(new UniqueConstraint("PK_Categories",
                               categories.Columns["CategoryID"]));
categories.PrimaryKey = new DataColumn[1]
                              {categories.Columns["CategoryID"]};
```

The last line of this code creates the primary key for the `Categories` table. The primary key in this instance is a single column; however, it is possible to generate a key over multiple columns using the array syntax shown.

Then the constraint can be created between the two tables:

```
DataColumn parent = ds.Tables["Categories"].Columns["CategoryID"];
DataColumn child = ds.Tables["Products"].Columns["CategoryID"];
ForeignKeyConstraint fk =
   new ForeignKeyConstraint("FK_Product_CategoryID", parent, child);
fk.UpdateRule = Rule.Cascade;
fk.DeleteRule = Rule.SetNull;
ds.Tables["Products"].Constraints.Add(fk);
```

This constraint applies to the link between `Categories.CategoryID` and `Products.CategoryID`. There are four different `ForeignKeyConstraints` — use those that permit you to name the constraint.

Setting Update and Delete Constraints

In addition to defining that there is some type of constraint between parent and child tables, you can define what should happen when a column in the constraint is updated.

The previous example sets the update rule and the delete rule. These rules are used when an action occurs to a column (or row) within the parent table, and the rule is used to decide what should happen to the row(s) within the child table that could be affected. Four different rules can be applied through the `Rule` enumeration:

- `Cascade` — If the parent key has been updated, copy the new key value to all child records. If the parent record has been deleted, delete the child records also. This is the default option.
- `None` — No action whatsoever. This option leaves orphaned rows within the child data table.
- `SetDefault` — Each child record affected has the foreign key column(s) set to its default value, if one has been defined.
- `SetNull` — All child rows have the key column(s) set to `DBNull`. (Following the naming convention that Microsoft uses, this should really be `SetDBNull`.)

> **Constraints are enforced only within a `DataSet` class if the `EnforceConstraints` property of the `DataSet` is `true`.**

This section has covered the main classes that make up the constituent parts of the `DataSet` class and has shown how to manually generate each of these classes in code. You can also define a `DataTable`, `DataRow`, `DataColumn`, `DataRelation`, and `Constraint` using the XML schema file(s) and the XSD tool that ships with .NET. The following section describes how to set up a simple schema and generate type-safe classes to access your data.

XML Schemas: Generating Code with XSD

XML is firmly entrenched in ADO.NET — indeed, the remoting format for passing data between objects is now XML. With the .NET runtime, it is possible to describe a `DataTable` class within an XML schema definition file (XSD). What's more, you can define an entire `DataSet` class, with a number of `DataTable` classes, and a set of relationships between these tables, and you can include various other details to fully describe the data.

When you have defined an XSD file, there is a tool in the runtime that will convert this schema to the corresponding data access class(es), such as the type-safe product `DataTable` class shown earlier. Let's start with a simple XSD file (`Products.xsd`) that describes the same information as the `Products` sample discussed earlier and then extend it to include some extra functionality:

```
<?xml version="1.0" encoding="utf-8" ?>
<xs:schema id="Products" targetNamespace="http://tempuri.org/XMLSchema1.xsd"
 xmlns:mstns="http://tempuri.org/XMLSchema1.xsd"
  xmlns:xs="http://www.w3.org/2001/XMLSchema"
  xmlns:msdata="urn:schemas-microsoft-com:xml-msdata">
  <xs:element name="Product">
    <xs:complexType>
      <xs:sequence>
        <xs:element name="ProductID" msdata:ReadOnly="true"
          msdata:AutoIncrement="true" type="xs:int" />
        <xs:element name="ProductName" type="xs:string" />
        <xs:element name="SupplierID" type="xs:int" minOccurs="0" />
        <xs:element name="CategoryID" type="xs:int" minOccurs="0" />
        <xs:element name="QuantityPerUnit" type="xs:string" minOccurs="0" />
        <xs:element name="UnitPrice" type="xs:decimal" minOccurs="0" />
        <xs:element name="UnitsInStock" type="xs:short" minOccurs="0" />
        <xs:element name="UnitsOnOrder" type="xs:short" minOccurs="0" />
        <xs:element name="ReorderLevel" type="xs:short" minOccurs="0" />
        <xs:element name="Discontinued" type="xs:boolean" />
      </xs:sequence>
    </xs:complexType>
  </xs:element>
</xs:schema>
```

These options are covered in detail in Chapter 28, "Manipulating XML"; for now, this file basically defines a schema with the `id` attribute set to `Products`. A complex type called `Product` is defined, which contains a number of elements, one for each of the fields within the `Products` table.

These items map to data classes as follows. The `Products` schema maps to a class derived from `DataSet`. The `Product` complex type maps to a class derived from `DataTable`. Each sub-element maps to a class derived from `DataColumn`. The collection of all columns maps to a class derived from `DataRow`.

Thankfully, there is a tool within the .NET Framework that produces the code for these classes with the help of the input XSD file. Because its sole job is to perform various functions on XSD files, the tool itself is called `XSD.EXE`.

Assuming that you saved the preceding file as `Product.xsd`, you would convert the file into code by issuing the following command in a command prompt:

```
xsd Product.xsd /d
```

This creates the file `Product.cs`.

Various switches can be used with XSD to alter the output generated. Some of the more commonly used switches are shown in the following table.

Switch	Description
`/dataset (/d)`	Enables you to generate classes derived from `DataSet`, `DataTable`, and `DataRow`.
`/language:<language>`	Permits you to choose which language the output file will be written in. C# is the default, but you can choose `VB` for a Visual Basic .NET file.
`/namespace:<namespace>`	Enables you to define the namespace that the generated code should reside within. The default is no namespace.

The following is an abridged version of the output from XSD for the `Products` schema. The output has been altered slightly to fit into a format appropriate for this book. To see the complete output, run `XSD.EXE` on the `Products` schema (or one of your own making) and take a look at the `.cs` file generated. The example includes the entire source code plus the `Product.xsd` file (note that this output is part of the downloadable code file available at `www.wrox.com`):

```
//------------------------------------------------------------------------------
// <autogenerated>
//     This code was generated by a tool.
//     Runtime Version:2.0.50727.312
//
//     Changes to this file may cause incorrect behavior and will be lost if
//     the code is regenerated.
// </autogenerated>
//------------------------------------------------------------------------------

using System;

//
// This source code was auto-generated by xsd, Version=2.0.40426.16.
//


[Serializable()]
[System.ComponentModel.DesignerCategoryAttribute("code")]
[System.Diagnostics.DebuggerStepThrough()]
[System.ComponentModel.ToolboxItem(true)]
[System.Xml.Serialization.XmlSchemaProviderAttribute("GetTypedDataSetSchema")]
[System.Xml.Serialization.XmlRootAttribute("Products")]
public partial class Products : System.Data.DataSet {
{
   private ProductDataTable tableProduct;
   public Products()
   public ProductDataTable Product
```

```
    public override DataSet Clone()
    public delegate void ProductRowChangeEventHandler ( object sender,
                                                        ProductRowChangeEvent e);

    [System.Diagnostics.DebuggerStepThrough()]
    public partial class ProductDataTable : DataTable, IEnumerable

    [System.Diagnostics.DebuggerStepThrough()]
    public class ProductRow : DataRow
}
```

All private and protected members have been removed to concentrate on the public interface. The ProductDataTable and ProductRow definitions show the positions of two nested classes, which will be implemented next. You review the code for these classes after a brief explanation of the DataSet-derived class.

The Products() constructor calls a private method, InitClass(), which constructs an instance of the DataTable-derived class ProductDataTable, and adds the table to the Tables collection of the DataSet class. The Products data table can be accessed by the following code:

```
DataSet ds = new Products();
DataTable products = ds.Tables["Products"];
```

Or, more simply by using the property Product, available on the derived DataSet object:

```
DataTable products = ds.Product;
```

Because the Product property is strongly typed, you could naturally use ProductDataTable rather than the DataTable reference shown in the previous code.

The ProductDataTable class includes far more code (note this is an abridged version of the code):

```
 [System.Serializable()]
[System.Diagnostics.DebuggerStepThrough()]
[System.Xml.Serialization.XmlSchemaProviderAttribute("GetTypedTableSchema")]
public partial class ProductDataTable : DataTable, System.Collections.IEnumerable
{
   private DataColumn columnProductID;
   private DataColumn columnProductName;
   private DataColumn columnSupplierID;
   private DataColumn columnCategoryID;
   private DataColumn columnQuantityPerUnit;
   private DataColumn columnUnitPrice;
   private DataColumn columnUnitsInStock;
   private DataColumn columnUnitsOnOrder;
   private DataColumn columnReorderLevel;
   private DataColumn columnDiscontinued;

   public ProductDataTable()   {
        this.TableName = "Product";
        this.BeginInit();
        this.InitClass();
        this.EndInit();   }
```

The ProductDataTable class, derived from DataTable and implementing the IEnumerable interface, defines a private DataColumn instance for each of the columns within the table. These are initialized again from the constructor by calling the private InitClass() member. Each column is given an internal accessor, which is used by the DataRow class (which is described shortly):

```
 [System.ComponentModel.Browsable(false)]
public int Count
{
   get { return this.Rows.Count; }
}
internal DataColumn ProductIDColumn
{
   get { return this.columnProductID; }
}
// Other row accessors removed for clarity -- there is one for each  column
```

Adding rows to the table is taken care of by the two overloaded (and significantly different) AddProductRow() methods. The first takes an already constructed DataRow and returns a void. The second takes a set of values, one for each of the columns in the DataTable, constructs a new row, sets the values within this new row, adds the row to the DataTable object, and returns the row to the caller. Such widely different functions shouldn't really have the same name!

```
public void AddProductRow(ProductRow row)
{
   this.Rows.Add(row);
}

public ProductRow AddProductRow ( string ProductName , int SupplierID ,
                                  int CategoryID , string QuantityPerUnit ,
                                  System.Decimal UnitPrice , short UnitsInStock ,
                                  short UnitsOnOrder , short ReorderLevel ,
                                  bool Discontinued )
{
   ProductRow rowProductRow = ((ProductRow)(this.NewRow()));
   rowProductRow.ItemArray = new object[]
   {
      null,
      ProductName,
      SupplierID,
      CategoryID,
      QuantityPerUnit,
      UnitPrice,
      UnitsInStock,
      UnitsOnOrder,
      ReorderLevel,
      Discontinued
   };
   this.Rows.Add(rowProductRow);
   return rowProductRow;
}
```

Just like the InitClass() member in the DataSet-derived class, which added the table into the DataSet class, the InitClass() member in ProductDataTable adds columns to the DataTable class.

Each column's properties are set as appropriate, and the column is then appended to the columns collection:

```
private void InitClass()
{
   this.columnProductID = new DataColumn ( "ProductID",
                                           typeof(int),
                                           null,
                                           System.Data.MappingType.Element);
    this.columnProductID.ExtendedProperties.Add
         ("Generator_ChangedEventName", "ProductIDChanged");
    this.columnProductID.ExtendedProperties.Add
         ("Generator_ChangingEventName", "ProductIDChanging");
    this.columnProductID.ExtendedProperties.Add
         ("Generator_ColumnPropNameInRow", "ProductID");
    this.columnProductID.ExtendedProperties.Add
         ("Generator_ColumnPropNameInTable", "ProductIDColumn");
    this.columnProductID.ExtendedProperties.Add
         ("Generator_ColumnVarNameInTable", "columnProductID");
    this.columnProductID.ExtendedProperties.Add
         ("Generator_DelegateName", "ProductIDChangeEventHandler");
    this.columnProductID.ExtendedProperties.Add
         ("Generator_EventArgName", "ProductIDChangeEventArg");
   this.Columns.Add(this.columnProductID);
   // Other columns removed for clarity

   this.columnProductID.AutoIncrement = true;
   this.columnProductID.AllowDBNull = false;
   this.columnProductID.ReadOnly = true;
   this.columnProductName.AllowDBNull = false;
   this.columnDiscontinued.AllowDBNull = false;
}

public ProductRow NewProductRow()
{
    return ((ProductRow)(this.NewRow()));
}
```

`NewRowFromBuilder()` is called internally from the `DataTable` class's `NewRow()` method. Here, it creates a new strongly typed row. The `DataRowBuilder` instance is created by the `DataTable` class, and its members are accessible only within the `System.Data` assembly:

```
protected override DataRow NewRowFromBuilder(DataRowBuilder builder)
{
   return new ProductRow(builder);
}
```

The last class to discuss is the `ProductRow` class, derived from `DataRow`. This class is used to provide type-safe access to all fields in the data table. It wraps the storage for a particular row, and provides members to read (and write) each of the fields in the table.

In addition, for each nullable field, there are functions to set the field to `null`, and to check if the field is `null`. The following example shows the functions for the `SupplierID` column:

```
 [System.Diagnostics.DebuggerStepThrough()]
public class ProductRow : DataRow
{
   private ProductDataTable tableProduct;

   internal ProductRow(DataRowBuilder rb) : base(rb)
   {
      this.tableProduct = ((ProductDataTable)(this.Table));
   }

   public int ProductID
   {
      get { return ((int)(this[this.tableProduct.ProductIDColumn])); }
      set { this[this.tableProduct.ProductIDColumn] = value; }
   }
  // Other column accessors/mutators removed for clarity

   public bool IsSupplierIDNull()
   {
      return this.IsNull(this.tableProduct.SupplierIDColumn);
   }

   public void SetSupplierIDNull()
   {
      this[this.tableProduct.SupplierIDColumn] = System.Convert.DBNull;
   }
}
```

The following code uses the classes ouptut from the XSD tool to retrieve data from the `Products` table and display that data to the console:

```
using System;
using System.Data;
using System.Data.SqlClient;

public class XSD_DataSet
{
   public static void Main()
   {
      string source = "server=(local);" +
                      " integrated security=SSPI;" +
                      "database=northwind";
      string select = "SELECT * FROM Products";
      SqlConnection conn = new SqlConnection(source);
      SqlDataAdapter da = new SqlDataAdapter(select , conn);
      Products ds = new Products();
      da.Fill(ds , "Product");
      foreach(Products.ProductRow row in ds.Product )
      Console.WriteLine("'{0}' from {1}" ,
                        row.ProductID ,
                        row.ProductName);
   }
}
```

The output of the XSD file contains a class derived from `DataSet`, `Products`, which is created and then filled by the use of the data adapter. The `foreach` statement uses the strongly typed `ProductRow` and also the `Product` property, which returns the `Product` data table.

To compile this example, issue the following commands:

```
xsd product.xsd /d
```

and

```
csc /recurse:*.cs
```

The first generates the `Products.cs` file from the `Products.XSD` schema, and then the `csc` command uses the `/recurse:*.cs` parameter to go through all files with the extension `.cs` and add these to the resulting assembly.

Populating a DataSet

After you have defined the schema of your data set, replete with `DataTable`, `DataColumn`, and `Constraint` classes, and whatever else is necessary, you need to be able to populate the `DataSet` class with some information. You have two main ways to read data from an external source and insert it into the `DataSet` class:

- Use a data adapter.
- Read XML into the `DataSet` class.

Populating a DataSet Class with a Data Adapter

The section on data rows briefly introduced the `SqlDataAdapter` class, as shown in the following code:

```
string select = "SELECT ContactName,CompanyName FROM Customers";
SqlConnection conn = new SqlConnection(source);
SqlDataAdapter da = new SqlDataAdapter(select , conn);
DataSet ds = new DataSet();
da.Fill(ds , "Customers");
```

The bold line shows the `SqlDataAdapter` class in use; the other data adapter classes are again virtually identical in functionality to the `Sql` equivalent.

To retrieve data into a `DataSet`, it is necessary to have some form of command that is executed to select that data. The command in question could be a SQL `SELECT` statement, a call to a stored procedure, or for the OLE DB provider, a `TableDirect` command. The preceding example uses one of the constructors available on `SqlDataAdapter` that converts the passed SQL `SELECT` statement into a `SqlCommand`, and issues this when the `Fill()` method is called on the adapter.

In the stored procedures example earlier in this chapter, the `INSERT`, `UPDATE`, and `DELETE` procedures were defined but the `SELECT` procedure was not. That gap is filled in the next section, which also shows how to call a stored procedure from a `SqlDataAdapter` class to populate data in a `DataSet` class.

Using a Stored Procedure in a Data Adapter

The first step in this example is to define the stored procedure. The stored procedure to `SELECT` data is:

```
CREATE PROCEDURE RegionSelect AS
  SET NOCOUNT OFF
  SELECT * FROM Region
GO
```

You can type this stored procedure directly into the SQL Server Query Analyzer, or you can run the `StoredProc.sql` file that is provided for use by this example.

Next, you need to define the `SqlCommand` that executes this stored procedure. Again the code is very simple, and most of it was already presented in the earlier section on issuing commands:

```
private static SqlCommand GenerateSelectCommand(SqlConnection conn )
{
   SqlCommand  aCommand = new SqlCommand("RegionSelect" , conn);
   aCommand.CommandType = CommandType.StoredProcedure;
   aCommand.UpdatedRowSource = UpdateRowSource.None;
   return aCommand;
}
```

This method generates the `SqlCommand` that calls the `RegionSelect` procedure when executed. All that remains is to hook up this command to a `SqlDataAdapter` class, and call the `Fill()` method:

```
DataSet ds = new DataSet();
// Create a data adapter to fill the DataSet
SqlDataAdapter da = new SqlDataAdapter();
// Set the data adapter's select command
da.SelectCommand = GenerateSelectCommand (conn);
da.Fill(ds , "Region");
```

Here, the `SqlDataAdapter` class is created, and the generated `SqlCommand` is then assigned to the `SelectCommand` property of the data adapter. Subsequently, `Fill()` is called, which will execute the stored procedure and insert all rows returned into the `Region DataTable` (which in this instance is generated by the runtime).

There's more to a data adapter than just selecting data by issuing a command, as discussed shortly in the "Persisting DataSet Changes" section.

Populating a DataSet from XML

In addition to generating the schema for a given `DataSet`, associated tables, and so on, a `DataSet` class can read and write data in native XML, such as a file on disk, a stream, or a text reader.

To load XML into a `DataSet` class, simply call one of the `ReadXML()` methods to read data from a disk file, as shown in this example:

```
DataSet ds = new DataSet();
ds.ReadXml(".\\MyData.xml");
```

The `ReadXml()` method attempts to load any inline schema information from the input XML, and if found, uses this schema in the validation of any data loaded from that file. If no inline schema is found, the `DataSet` will extend its internal structure as data is loaded. This is similar to the behavior of `Fill()` in the previous example, which retrieves the data and constructs a `DataTable` based on the data selected.

Persisting DataSet Changes

After editing data within a `DataSet`, it is usually necessary to persist these changes. The most common example is selecting data from a database, displaying it to the user, and returning those updates to the database.

In a less "connected" application, changes might be persisted to an XML file, transported to a middle-tier application server, and then processed to update several data sources.

A `DataSet` class can be used for either of these examples; what's more, it's really easy to do.

Updating with Data Adapters

In addition to the SelectCommand that a SqlDataAdapter most likely includes, you can also define an InsertCommand, UpdateCommand, and DeleteCommand. As these names imply, these objects are instances of the command object appropriate for your provider such as SqlCommand and OleDbCommand.

With this level of flexibility, you are free to tune the application by judicious use of stored procedures for frequently used commands (say SELECT and INSERT), and use straight SQL for less commonly used commands such as DELETE. In general, it is recommended to provide stored procedures for all database interaction because it is faster and easier to tune.

This example uses the stored procedure code from the "Calling Stored Procedures" section for inserting, updating, and deleting Region records, coupled with the RegionSelect procedure written previously, which produces an example that uses each of these commands to retrieve and update data in a DataSet class. The main body of code is shown in the following section.

Inserting a New Row

You can add a new row to a DataTable in two ways. The first way is to call the NewRow() method, which returns a blank row that you then populate and add to the Rows collection, as follows:

```
DataRow r = ds.Tables["Region"].NewRow();
r["RegionID"]=999;
r["RegionDescription"]="North West";
ds.Tables["Region"].Rows.Add(r);
```

The second way to add a new row would be to pass an array of data to the Rows.Add() method as shown in the following code:

```
DataRow r = ds.Tables["Region"].Rows.Add
             (new object [] { 999 , "North West" });
```

Each new row within the DataTable will have its RowState set to Added. The example dumps out the records before each change is made to the database, so after adding a row (either way) to the DataTable, the rows will look something like the following. Note that the right-hand column shows the row state:

```
New row pending inserting into database
  1    Eastern                                             Unchanged
  2    Western                                             Unchanged
  3    Northern                                            Unchanged
  4    Southern                                            Unchanged
  999  North West                                          Added
```

To update the database from the DataAdapter, call one of the Update() methods as shown here:

```
da.Update(ds , "Region");
```

For the new row within the DataTable, this executes the stored procedure (in this instance RegionInsert). The example then dumps the state of the data so you can see that changes have been made to the database.

```
New row updated and new RegionID assigned by database
  1    Eastern                                             Unchanged
  2    Western                                             Unchanged
  3    Northern                                            Unchanged
  4    Southern                                            Unchanged
  5    North West                                          Unchanged
```

Look at the last row in the `DataTable`. The `RegionID` had been set in code to `999`, but after executing the `RegionInsert` stored procedure the value has been changed to `5`. This is intentional — the database will often generate primary keys for you, and the updated data in the `DataTable` is due to the fact that the `SqlCommand` definition within the source code has the `UpdatedRowSource` property set to `UpdateRowSource.OutputParameters`:

```
SqlCommand aCommand = new SqlCommand("RegionInsert" , conn);

aCommand.CommandType = CommandType.StoredProcedure;
aCommand.Parameters.Add(new SqlParameter("@RegionDescription" ,
                            SqlDbType.NChar ,
                            50 ,
                            "RegionDescription"));
aCommand.Parameters.Add(new SqlParameter("@RegionID" ,
                            SqlDbType.Int,
                            0 ,
                            ParameterDirection.Output ,
                            false ,
                            0 ,
                            0 ,
                            "RegionID" ,    // Defines the SOURCE column
                            DataRowVersion.Default ,
                            null));
aCommand.UpdatedRowSource = UpdateRowSource.OutputParameters;
```

What this means is that whenever a data adapter issues this command, the output parameters should be mapped to the source of the row, which in this instance was a row in a `DataTable`. The flag states what data should be updated — the stored procedure has an output parameter that is mapped to the `DataRow`. The column it applies to is `RegionID` because this is defined within the command definition.

The following table shows the values for `UpdateRowSource`.

UpdateRowSource Value	Description
`Both`	A stored procedure might return output parameters and also a complete database record. Both of these data sources are used to update the source row.
`FirstReturnedRecord`	This infers that the command returns a single record, and that the contents of that record should be merged into the original source `DataRow`. This is useful where a given table has a number of default (or computed) columns because after an `INSERT` statement these need to be synchronized with the `DataRow` on the client. An example might be `'INSERT` (columns) `INTO` (table) `WITH` (primarykey)`'`, then `'SELECT` (columns) `FROM` (table) `WHERE` (primarykey)`'`. The returned record would then be merged into the original row.
`None`	All data returned from the command is discarded.
`OutputParameters`	Any output parameters from the command are mapped onto the appropriate column(s) in the `DataRow`.

Updating an Existing Row

Updating an existing row within the `DataTable` is just a case of using the `DataRow` class's indexer with either a column name or column number, as shown in the following code:

```
r["RegionDescription"]="North West England";
r[1] = "North Wast England";
```

Both of these statements are equivalent (in this example):

```
Changed RegionID 5 description
  1    Eastern                                         Unchanged
  2    Western                                         Unchanged
  3    Northern                                        Unchanged
  4    Southern                                        Unchanged
  5    North West England                              Modified
```

Prior to updating the database, the row updated has its state set to `Modified` as shown.

Deleting a Row

Deleting a row is a matter of calling the `Delete()` method:

```
r.Delete();
```

A deleted row has its row state set to `Deleted`, but you cannot read columns from the deleted `DataRow` because they are no longer valid. When the adaptor's `Update()` method is called, all deleted rows will use the `DeleteCommand`, which in this instance executes the `RegionDelete` stored procedure.

Writing XML Output

As you have seen already, the `DataSet` class has great support for defining its schema in XML, and just as you can read data from an XML document, you can also write data to an XML document.

The `DataSet.WriteXml()` method enables you to output various parts of the data stored within the `DataSet`. You can elect to output just the data, or the data and the schema. The following code shows an example of both for the `Region` example shown earlier:

```
ds.WriteXml(".\\WithoutSchema.xml");
ds.WriteXml(".\\WithSchema.xml" , XmlWriteMode.WriteSchema);
```

The first file, `WithoutSchema.xml`, is shown here:

```
<?xml version="1.0" standalone="yes"?>
<NewDataSet>
   <Region>
      <RegionID>1</RegionID>
      <RegionDescription>Eastern                        </RegionDescription>
   </Region>
   <Region>
      <RegionID>2</RegionID>
      <RegionDescription>Western                        </RegionDescription>
   </Region>
   <Region>
      <RegionID>3</RegionID>
      <RegionDescription>Northern                       </RegionDescription>
```

(continued)

(continued)

```
    </Region>
    <Region>
      <RegionID>4</RegionID>
      <RegionDescription>Southern                                          </RegionDescription>
    </Region>
  </NewDataSet>
```

The closing tag on `RegionDescription` is over to the right of the page because the database column is defined as `NCHAR(50)`, which is a 50-character string padded with spaces.

The output produced in the `WithSchema.xml` file includes the XML schema for the `DataSet` as well as the data itself:

```
<?xml version="1.0" standalone="yes"?>
<NewDataSet>
  <xs:schema id="NewDataSet" xmlns=""
           xmlns:xs="http://www.w3.org/2001/XMLSchema"
           xmlns:msdata="urn:schemas-microsoft-com:xml-msdata">
    <xs:element name="NewDataSet" msdata:IsDataSet="true">
      <xs:complexType>
        <xs:choice maxOccurs="unbounded">
          <xs:element name="Region">
            <xs:complexType>
              <xs:sequence>
                <xs:element name="RegionID"
                            msdata:AutoIncrement="true"
                            msdata:AutoIncrementSeed="1"
                            type="xs:int" />
                <xs:element name="RegionDescription"
                            type="xs:string" />
              </xs:sequence>
            </xs:complexType>
          </xs:element>
        </xs:choice>
      </xs:complexType>
    </xs:element>
  </xs:schema>
  <Region>
    <RegionID>1</RegionID>
    <RegionDescription>Eastern                                           </RegionDescription>
  </Region>
  <Region>
    <RegionID>2</RegionID>
    <RegionDescription>Western                                           </RegionDescription>
  </Region>
  <Region>
    <RegionID>3</RegionID>
    <RegionDescription>Northern                                          </RegionDescription>
  </Region>
  <Region>
    <RegionID>4</RegionID>
    <RegionDescription>Southern                                          </RegionDescription>
  </Region>
</NewDataSet>
```

Note the use in this file of the `msdata` schema, which defines extra attributes for columns within a `DataSet`, such as `AutoIncrement` and `AutoIncrementSeed` — these attributes correspond directly with the properties definable on a `DataColumn` class.

Working with ADO.NET

This section addresses some common scenarios when developing data access applications with ADO.NET.

Tiered Development

Producing an application that interacts with data is often done by splitting up the application into tiers. A common model is to have an application tier (the front end), a data services tier, and the database itself.

One of the difficulties with this model is deciding what data to transport between tiers, and the format that it should be transported in. With ADO.NET you will be pleased to learn that these wrinkles have been ironed out, and support for this style of architecture is part of the design.

One of the things that is much better in ADO.NET than OLE DB is the support for copying an entire record set. In .NET it is easy to copy a `DataSet`:

```
DataSet source = {some dataset};
DataSet dest = source.Copy();
```

This creates an exact copy of the source `DataSet` — each `DataTable`, `DataColumn`, `DataRow`, and `Relation` will be copied, and all data will be in exactly the same state as it was in the source. If all you want to copy is the schema of the `DataSet`, you can use the following code:

```
DataSet source = {some dataset};
DataSet dest = source.Clone();
```

This again copies all tables, relations, and so on. However, each copied `DataTable` will be empty. This process really couldn't be more straightforward.

A common requirement when writing a tiered system, whether based on a Windows client application or the Web, is to be able to ship as little data as possible between tiers. This reduces the amount of resources consumed.

To cope with this requirement, the `DataSet` class has the `GetChanges()` method. This simple method performs a huge amount of work, and returns a `DataSet` with only the changed rows from the source data set. This is ideal for passing data between tiers because only a minimal set of data has to be passed along.

The following example shows how to generate a "changes" `DataSet`:

```
DataSet source = {some dataset};
DataSet dest = source.GetChanges();
```

Again, this is trivial. Under the hood, things are a little more interesting. There are two overloads of the `GetChanges()` method. One overload takes a value of the `DataRowState` enumeration, and returns only rows that correspond to that state (or states). `GetChanges()` simply calls `GetChanges(Deleted | Modified | Added)`, and first checks to ensure that there are some changes by calling `HasChanges()`. If no changes have been made, `null` is returned to the caller immediately.

The next operation is to clone the current `DataSet`. Once done, the new `DataSet` is set up to ignore constraint violations (`EnforceConstraints = false`), and then each changed row for every table is copied into the new `DataSet`.

When you have a `DataSet` that just contains changes, you can then move these off to the data services tier for processing. After the data has been updated in the database, the "changes" `DataSet` can be returned to the caller (for example, there might be some output parameters from the stored procedures that have updated values in the columns). These changes can then be merged into the original `DataSet` using the `Merge()` method. Figure 26-9 depicts this sequence of operations.

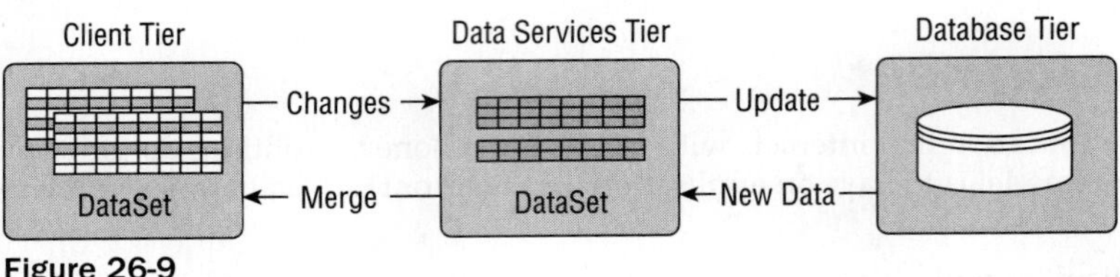

Figure 26-9

Key Generation with SQL Server

The `RegionInsert` stored procedure presented earlier in this chapter is one example of generating a primary key value on insertion into the database. The method for generating the key in this particular example is fairly crude and wouldn't scale well, so for a real application you should use some other strategy for generating keys.

Your first instinct might be to define an identity column, and return the `@@IDENTITY` value from the stored procedure. The following stored procedure shows how this might be defined for the `Categories` table in the Northwind example database. Type this stored procedure into SQL Query Analyzer, or run the `StoredProcs.sql` file that is part of the code download:

```
CREATE PROCEDURE CategoryInsert(@CategoryName NVARCHAR(15),
                                @Description NTEXT,
                                @CategoryID INTEGER OUTPUT) AS
   SET NOCOUNT OFF
   INSERT INTO Categories (CategoryName, Description)
      VALUES(@CategoryName, @Description)
   SELECT @CategoryID = @@IDENTITY
GO
```

This inserts a new row into the `Category` table and returns the generated primary key to the caller (the value of the `CategoryID` column). You can test the procedure by typing the following in SQL Query Analyzer:

```
DECLARE @CatID int;
EXECUTE CategoryInsert 'Pasties' , 'Heaven Sent Food' , @CatID OUTPUT;
PRINT @CatID;
```

When executed as a batch of commands, this inserts a new row into the `Categories` table, and returns the identity of the new record, which is then displayed to the user.

Suppose that some months down the line, someone decides to add a simple audit trail, which will record all insertions and modifications made to the category name. In that case, you define a table similar to the one shown in Figure 26-10, which will record the old and new value of the category.

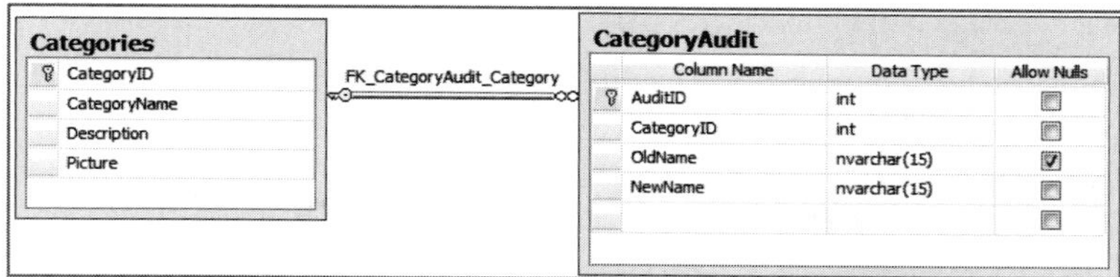

Figure 26-10

The script for this table is included in the `StoredProcs.sql` file. The `AuditID` column is defined as an `IDENTITY` column. You then construct a couple of database triggers that will record changes to the `CategoryName` field:

```
CREATE TRIGGER CategoryInsertTrigger
   ON Categories
   AFTER UPDATE
AS
   INSERT INTO CategoryAudit(CategoryID , OldName , NewName )
      SELECT old.CategoryID, old.CategoryName, new.CategoryName
      FROM Deleted AS old,
           Categories AS new
      WHERE old.CategoryID = new.CategoryID;
GO
```

If you are used to Oracle stored procedures, SQL Server doesn't exactly have the concept of `OLD` and `NEW` rows; instead, for an insert trigger there is an in-memory table called `Inserted`, and for deletes and updates the old rows are available within the `Deleted` table.

This trigger retrieves the `CategoryID` of the record(s) affected and stores this together with the old and new value of the `CategoryName` column.

Now, when you call your original stored procedure to insert a new `CategoryID`, you receive an identity value; however, this is no longer the identity value from the row inserted into the `Categories` table — it is now the new value generated for the row in the `CategoryAudit` table. Ouch!

To view the problem first-hand, open a copy of SQL Server Enterprise Manager, and view the contents of the `Categories` table (see Figure 26-11).

CategoryID	CategoryName	Description	Picture
1	Beverages	Soft drinks, coffees, teas, beers, and ales	<Binary data>
2	Condiments	Sweet and savory sauces, relishes, spreads, and seasonings	<Binary data>
3	Confections	Desserts, candies, and sweet breads	<Binary data>
4	Dairy Products	Cheeses	<Binary data>
5	Grains/Cereals	Breads, crackers, pasta, and cereal	<Binary data>
6	Meat/Poultry	Prepared meats	<Binary data>
7	Produce	Dried fruit and bean curd	<Binary data>
8	Seafood	Seaweed and fish	<Binary data>
NULL	NULL	NULL	NULL

Figure 26-11

This lists all the categories in the Northwind database.

The next identity value for the Categories table should be 9, so a new row can be inserted by executing the following code, to see what ID is returned:

```
DECLARE @CatID int;
EXECUTE CategoryInsert 'Pasties' , 'Heaven Sent Food' , @CatID OUTPUT;
PRINT @CatID;
```

The output value of this on a test PC was 1. If you look at the CategoryAudit table shown in Figure 26-12, you will find that this is the identity of the newly inserted audit record, not the identity of the category record created.

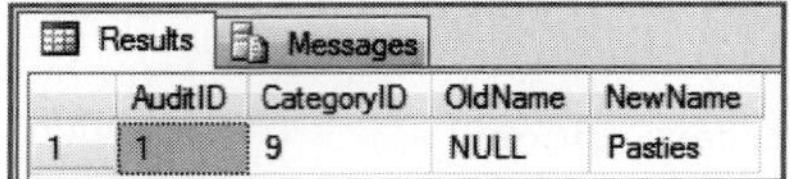

	AuditID	CategoryID	OldName	NewName
1	1	9	NULL	Pasties

Figure 26-12

The problem lies in the way that @@IDENTITY actually works. It returns the LAST identity value created by your session, so as shown in Figure 26-12, it isn't completely reliable.

Two other identity functions can be used instead of @@IDENTITY, but neither is free from possible problems. The first, SCOPE_IDENTITY(), returns the last identity value created within the current *scope*. SQL Server defines scope as a stored procedure, trigger, or function. This may work most of the time, but if for some reason someone adds another INSERT statement into the stored procedure, you can receive this value rather than the one you expected.

The other identity function, IDENT_CURRENT(), returns the last identity value generated for a given table in any scope. For example, if two users were accessing SQL Server at exactly the same time, it might be possible to receive the other user's generated identity value.

As you might imagine, tracking down a problem of this nature isn't easy. The moral of the story is to beware when using IDENTITY columns in SQL Server.

Naming Conventions

The following tips and conventions are not directly .NET-related. However, they are worth sharing and following, especially when naming constraints. Feel free to skip this section if you already have your own views on this subject.

Conventions for Database Tables

- Always use singular names — Product rather than Products. This one is largely due to having to explain a database schema to customers; it is much better grammatically to say "The Product table contains products" than "The Products table contains products." Check out the Northwind database to see an example of how not to do this.
- Adopt some form of naming convention for the fields that go into a table — Ours is <Table>_Id for the primary key of a table (assuming that the primary key is a single column), Name for the field considered to be the user-friendly name of the record, and Description for any textual information about the record itself. Having a good table convention means you can look at virtually any table in the database and instinctively know what the fields are used for.

Conventions for Database Columns

- Use singular rather than plural names.
- Any columns that link to another table should be named the same as the primary key of that table. For example, a link to the `Product` table would be `Product_Id`, and to the `Sample` table `Sample_Id`. This isn't always possible, especially if one table has multiple references to another. In that case, use your own judgment.
- Date fields should have a suffix of `_On`, as in `Modified_On` and `Created_On`. Then it is easy to read some SQL output and infer what a column means just by its name.
- Fields that record the user should be suffixed with `_By`, as in `Modified_By` and `Created_By`. Again, this aids legibility.

Conventions for Constraints

- If possible, include in the name of the constraint the table and column name, as in `CK_<Table>_<Field>`. For example, `CK_Person_Sex` for a check constraint on the `Sex` column of the `Person` table. A foreign key example would be `FK_Product_Supplier_Id`, for the foreign key relationship between product and supplier.
- Show the type of constraint with a prefix, such as `CK` for a check constraint and `FK` for a foreign key constraint. Feel free to be more specific, as in `CK_Person_Age_GT0` for a constraint on the age column indicating that the age should be greater than zero.
- If you have to trim the length of the constraint, do it on the table name part rather than the column name. When you get a constraint violation, it is usually easy to infer which table was in error, but sometimes not so easy to check which column caused the problem. Oracle has a 30-character limit on names, which is easy to surpass.

Stored Procedures

Just like the obsession many have fallen into over the past few years of putting a `C` in front of each and every class they declare (you know you have!), many SQL Server developers feel compelled to prefix every stored procedure with `sp_` or something similar. This is not a good idea.

SQL Server uses the `sp_` prefix for all (well, most) system stored procedures. So, you risk confusing your users into thinking that `sp_widget` is something that comes as standard with SQL Server. In addition, when looking for a stored procedure, SQL Server treats procedures with the `sp_` prefix differently from those without it.

If you use this prefix and do not qualify the database/owner of the stored procedure, SQL Server will look in the current scope and then jump into the master database and look up the stored procedure there. Without the `sp_` prefix, your users would get an error a little earlier. What's worse, and also possible to do, is to create a local stored procedure (one within your database) that has the same name and parameters as a system stored procedure. Avoid this at all costs — if in doubt, don't prefix.

When calling stored procedures, always prefix them with the owner of the procedure, as in `dbo.selectWidgets`. This is slightly faster than not using the prefix, because SQL Server has less work to do to find the stored procedure. Something like this is not likely to have a huge impact on the execution speed of your application, but it is a tuning trick that is essentially available for free.

Above all, when naming entities, whether within the database or within code, *be consistent*.

Summary

The subject of data access is a large one, especially in .NET, because there is an abundance of new material to cover. This chapter has provided an outline of the main classes in the ADO.NET namespaces and has shown how to use the classes when manipulating data from a data source.

First, the `Connection` object was explored, through the use of both `SqlConnection` (SQL Server–specific) and `OleDbConnection` (for any OLE DB data sources). The programming model for these two classes is so similar that one can normally be substituted for the other, and the code will continue to run. With the advent of .NET version 1.1, you can use an Oracle provider and also an ODBC provider.

This chapter also discussed how to use connections properly, so that these scarce resources could be closed as early as possible. All of the connection classes implement the `IDisposable` interface, called when the object is placed within a `using` clause. If there is one thing you should take away from this chapter, it is the importance of closing database connections as early as possible.

In addition, this chapter discussed database commands by way of examples that executed with no returned data to calling stored procedures with input and output parameters. It described various execute methods, including the `ExecuteXmlReader` method available only on the SQL Server provider. This vastly simplifies the selection and manipulation of XML-based data.

The generic classes within the `System.Data` namespace were all described in detail, from the `DataSet` class through `DataTable`, `DataColumn`, `DataRow`, and on to relationships and constraints. The `DataSet` class is an excellent container of data, and various methods make it ideal for cross-tier data flow. The data within a `DataSet` is represented in XML for transport, and in addition, methods are available that pass a minimal amount of data between tiers. The ability to have many tables of data within a single `DataSet` can greatly increase its usability; being able to maintain relationships automatically between master/details rows is explored further in the next chapter, "LINQ to SQL."

Having the schema stored within a `DataSet` is one thing, but .NET also includes the data adapter that, next to various `Command` objects, can be used to select data for a `DataSet` and subsequently update data in the data store. One of the beneficial aspects of a data adapter is that a distinct command can be defined for each of the four actions: `SELECT`, `INSERT`, `UPDATE`, and `DELETE`. The system can create a default set of commands based on database schema information and a `SELECT` statement, but for the best performance, a set of stored procedures can be used, with the `DataAdapter`'s commands defined appropriately to pass only the necessary information to these stored procedures.

The XSD tool (`XSD.EXE`) was described, using an example that shows how to work with classes based on an XML schema from within .NET. The classes produced are ready to be used within an application, and their automatic generation can save many hours of laborious typing.

Finally, this chapter discussed some best practices and naming conventions for database development.

Further information about accessing SQL Server databases is provided in Chapter 30, ".NET Programming with SQL Server."

27

LINQ to SQL

Probably the biggest and most exciting addition to the .NET Framework 3.5 is the addition of the .NET Language Integrated Query Framework (LINQ) into C# 2008. Basically, what LINQ provides is a lightweight façade over programmatic data integration. This is such a big deal because *data is king*.

Pretty much every application deals with data in some manner, whether that data comes from memory (in-memory data), databases, XML files, text files, or something else. Many developers find it very difficult to move from the strongly typed object-oriented world of C# to the data tier where objects are second-class citizens. The transition from the one world to the next was a kludge at best and was full of error-prone actions.

In C#, programming with objects means a wonderful strongly typed ability to work with code. You can navigate very easily through the namespaces, work with a debugger in the Visual Studio IDE, and more. However, when you have to access data, you will notice that things are dramatically different.

You end up in a world that is not strongly typed, where debugging is a pain or even non-existent, and you end up spending most of the time sending strings to the database as commands. As a developer, you also have to be aware of the underlying data and how it is structured or how all the data points relate.

Microsoft has provided LINQ as a lightweight façade that provides a strongly typed interface to the underlying data stores. LINQ provides the means for developers to stay within the coding environment they are used to and access the underlying data as objects that work with the IDE, IntelliSense, and even debugging.

With LINQ, the queries that you create now become first-class citizens within the .NET Framework alongside everything else you are used to. When you work with queries for the data store you are working with, you will quickly realize that they now work and behave as if they are types in the system. This means that you can now use any .NET-compliant language and query the underlying data store as you never have before.

Chapter 11, "Language Integrated Query," provides an introduction to LINQ.

Figure 27-1 shows LINQ's place in querying data.

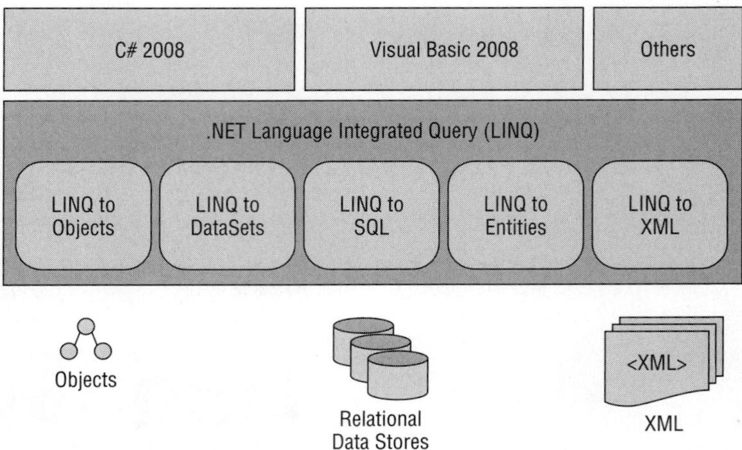

Figure 27-1

Looking at the figure, you can see that there are different types of LINQ capabilities depending on the underlying data that you are going to be working with in your application. From the list, you will find the following LINQ technologies:

- LINQ to Objects
- LINQ to DataSets
- LINQ to SQL
- LINQ to Entities
- LINQ to XML

As a developer, you are given class libraries that provide objects that, using LINQ, can be queried as any other data store can. Objects are really nothing more than data that is stored in memory. In fact, your objects themselves might be querying data. This is where LINQ to Objects comes into play.

LINQ to SQL (the focus of this chapter), LINQ to Entities, and LINQ to DataSets provide the means to query relational data. Using LINQ, you can query directly against your database and even against the stored procedures that your database exposes. The last item from the diagram is the ability to query against your XML using LINQ to XML (this topic is covered in Chapter 29). The big thing that makes LINQ exciting is that it matters very little what you are querying against, because your queries will be quite similar.

This chapter looks at the following:

- Working with LINQ to SQL along with Visual Studio 2008
- Looking at how LINQ to SQL objects map to database entities
- Building LINQ to SQL operations without the O/R Designer
- Using the O/R Designer with custom objects
- Querying the SQL Server database using LINQ
- Stored procedures and LINQ to SQL

LINQ to SQL and Visual Studio 2008

LINQ to SQL in particular is a means to have a strongly typed interface against a SQL Server database. You will find the approach that LINQ to SQL provides is by far the easiest approach to querying SQL Server available at the moment. It is not just simply about querying single tables within the database, but, for instance, if you call the `Customers` table of the Northwind database and want to pull a customer's specific orders from the `Orders` table in the same database, LINQ will use the relations of the tables and make the query on your behalf. LINQ will query the database and load up the data for you to work with from your code (again, strongly typed).

It is important to remember that LINQ to SQL is not only about querying data, but you also are able to perform the Insert/Update/Delete statements that you need to perform.

You can also interact with the entire process and customize the operations performed to add your own business logic to any of the CRUD operations (Create/Read/Update/Delete).

Visual Studio 2008 comes into strong play with LINQ to SQL in that you will find an extensive user interface that allows you to design the LINQ to SQL classes you will work with.

The next section of the chapter focuses on showing you how to set up your first LINQ to SQL instance and pull items from the `Products` table of the Northwind database.

Calling the Products Table Using LINQ to SQL — Creating the Console Application

For an example of using LINQ to SQL, this chapter starts by calling a single table from the Northwind database and using this table to populate some results to the screen.

To start off, create a console application (using the .NET Framework 3.5) and add the Northwind database file to this project (`Northwind.MDF`).

The following example makes use of the `Northwind.mdf` *SQL Server Express Database file. To get this database, please search for "Northwind and pubs Sample Databases for SQL Server 2000." You can find this link at* `http://www.microsoft.com/downloads/details.aspx?familyid=06616212-0356-46a0-8da2-eebc53a68034&displaylang=en`. *Once installed, you will find the* `Northwind.mdf` *file in the* `C:\SQL Server 2000 Sample Databases` *directory. To add this database to your application, right-click the solution you are working with and select Add Existing Item. From the provided dialog, you are then able to browse to the location of the* `Northwind.mdf` *file that you just installed. If you are having trouble getting permissions to work with the database, make a data connection to the file from the Visual Studio Server Explorer and you will be asked to be made the appropriate user of the database. VS will make the appropriate changes on your behalf for this to occur.*

By default now, when creating many of the application types provided in the .NET Framework 3.5 within Visual Studio 2008, you will notice that you already have the proper references in place to work with LINQ. When creating a console application, you will get the following `using` statements in your code:

```
using System;
using System.Collections.Generic;
using System.Linq;
using System.Net;
using System.Net.Sockets;
using System.Runtime.Remoting.Messaging;
using System.Text;
```

From this, you can see that the LINQ reference that will be required is already in place. The next step is to add a LINQ to SQL class.

Adding a LINQ to SQL Class

When working with LINQ to SQL, one of the big advantages you will find is that Visual Studio 2008 does an outstanding job of making it as easy as possible. VS2008 provides an object-relational mapping designer, called the O/R Designer, which allows you to visually design the object to database mapping.

To start this task, right-click your solution and select Add New Item from the provided menu. From the items in the Add New Item dialog, you will find LINQ to SQL Classes as an option. This is presented in Figure 27-2.

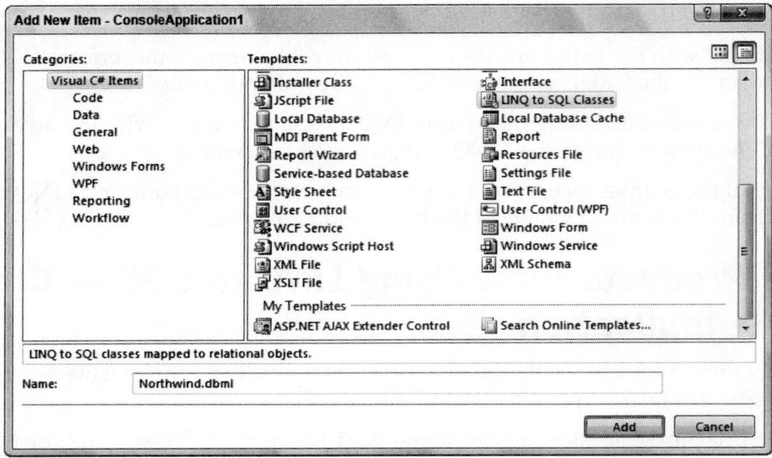

Figure 27-2

Because this example is using the Northwind database, name the file `Northwind.dbml`. Click the Add button, and you will see that this operation creates a couple of files for you. Figure 27-3 presents the Solution Explorer after adding the `Northwind.dbml` file.

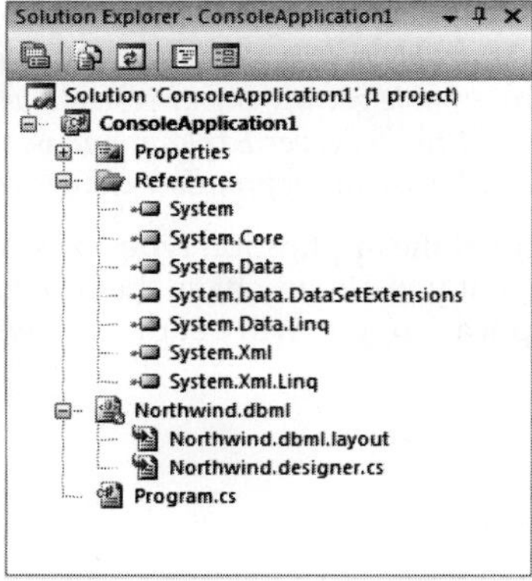

Figure 27-3

A number of things were added to your project with this action. The `Northwind.dbml` file was added and it contains two components. Because the LINQ to SQL class that was added works with LINQ, the following references were also added on your behalf: `System.Core`, `System.Data.DataSetExtensions`, `System.Data.Linq`, and `System.Xml.Linq`.

Introducing the O/R Designer

Another big addition to the IDE that appeared when you added the LINQ to SQL class to your project (the `Northwind.dbml` file), was a visual representation of the `.dbml` file. The new O/R Designer will appear as a tab within the document window directly in the IDE. Figure 27-4 shows a view of the O/R Designer when it is first initiated.

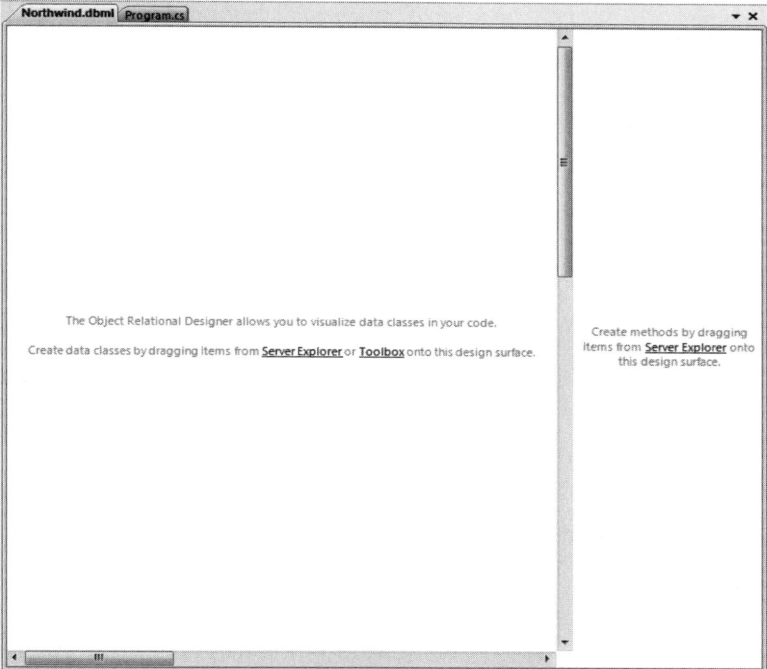

Figure 27-4

The O/R Designer is made up of two parts. The first part is for data classes, which can be tables, classes, associations, and inheritances. Dragging such items on this design surface will give you a visual representation of the object that can be worked with. The second part (on the right) is for methods, which map to the stored procedures within a database.

When viewing your `.dbml` file within the O/R Designer, you will also have an Object Relational Designer set of controls in the Visual Studio toolbox. The toolbox is presented in Figure 27-5.

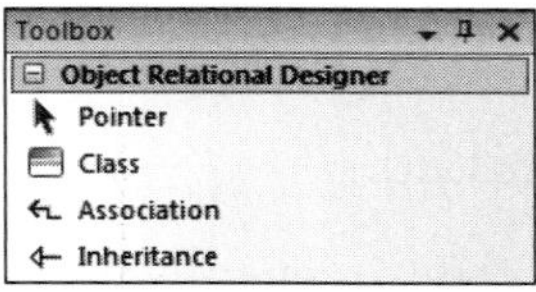

Figure 27-5

Creating the Product Object

For this example, you want to work with the `Products` table from the Northwind database, which means that you are going to have to create a `Products` table that will use LINQ to SQL to map to this table. Accomplishing this task is simply a matter of opening up a view of the tables contained within the database from the Server Explorer dialog within Visual Studio and dragging and dropping the `Products` table onto the design surface of the O/R Designer. This action's results are illustrated in Figure 27-6.

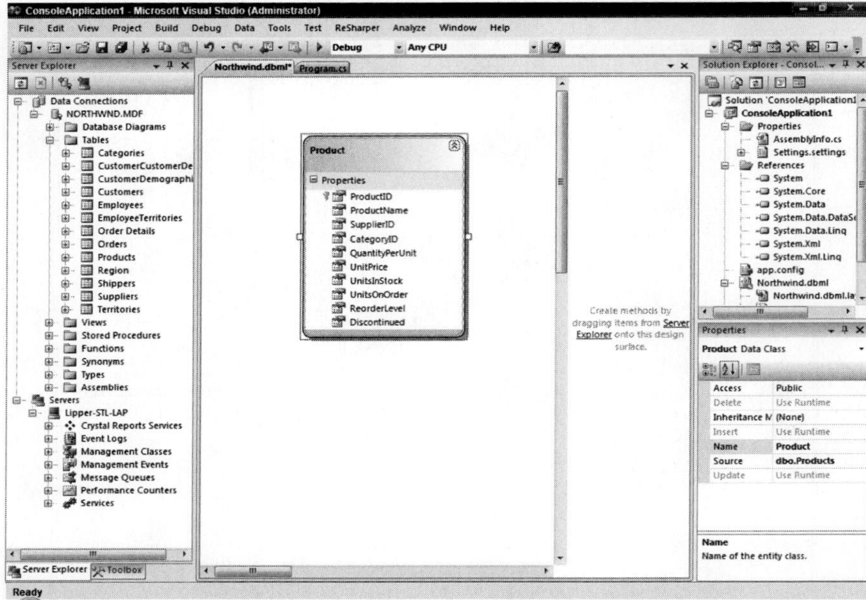

Figure 27-6

With this action, a bunch of code is added to the designer files of the `.dbml` file on your behalf. These classes will give you a strongly typed access to the `Products` table. For a demonstration of this, turn your attention to the console application's `Program.cs` file. The following shows the code that is required for this example:

```
using System;
using System.Linq;

namespace ConsoleApplication1
{
    class Class1
    {
        static void Main(string[] args)
        {
            NorthwindDataContext dc = new NorthwindDataContext();

            var query = dc.Products;

            foreach (Product item in query)
```

```
                {
                    Console.WriteLine("{0} | {1} | {2}",
                       item.ProductID, item.ProductName, item.UnitsInStock);
                }

                Console.ReadLine();
            }
        }
    }
```

This bit of code does not have many lines to it, but it is querying the `Products` table within the Northwind database and pulling out the data to display. It is important to step through this code starting with the first line in the `Main()` method:

```
NorthwindDataContext dc = new NorthwindDataContext();
```

The `NorthwindDataContext` object is an object of type `DataContext`. Basically, you can view this as something that maps to a `Connection` type object. This object works with the connection string and connects to the database for any required operations.

The next line is quite interesting:

```
var query = dc.Products;
```

Here, you are using the new `var` keyword, which is an implicitly typed variable. If you are unsure of the output type, you can use `var` instead of defining a type and the type will be set into place at compile time. Actually, the code `dc.Products;` returns a `System.Data.Linq.Table<ConsoleApplication1.Product>` object and this is what `var` is set as when the application is compiled. Therefore, this means that you could have also just as easily written the statement as such:

```
Table<Product> query = dc.Products;
```

This approach is actually better because programmers coming to look at the code of the application will find it easier to understand what is happening. Using the `var` keyword has so much of a hidden aspect to it that programmers might find it problematic. To use `Table<Product>`, which is basically a generic list of `Product` objects, you should make a reference to the `System.Data.Linq` namespace.

The value assigned to the `query` object is the value of the `Products` property, which is of type `Table<Product>`. From there, the next bit of code iterates through the collection of `Product` objects found in `Table<Product>`:

```
foreach (Product item in query)
{
   Console.WriteLine("{0} | {1} | {2}",
      item.ProductID, item.ProductName, item.UnitsInStock);
}
```

The iteration, in this case, pulls out the `ProductID`, `ProductName`, and `UnitsInStock` properties from the `Product` object and writes them out to the program. Because you are using only a few of the items from the table, you also have the option from the O/R Designer to delete the columns that you are not interested in pulling from the database. The results coming out from the program are presented here:

```
1 | Chai | 39
2 | Chang | 17
3 | Aniseed Syrup | 13
4 | Chef Anton's Cajun Seasoning | 53
5 | Chef Anton's Gumbo Mix | 0

** Results removed for space reasons **

73 | Röd Kaviar | 101
74 | Longlife Tofu | 4
75 | Rhönbräu Klosterbier | 125
76 | Lakkalikööri | 57
77 | Original Frankfurter grüne Soße | 32
```

From this example, you can see just how easy it is to query a SQL Server database using LINQ to SQL.

How Objects Map to LINQ Objects

The great thing about LINQ is that it gives you strongly typed objects to use in your code (with IntelliSense) and these objects map to existing database objects. Again, LINQ is nothing more than a thin façade over these pre-existing database objects. The following table shows the mappings that are between the database objects and the LINQ objects.

Database Object	LINQ Object
Database	DataContext
Table	Class and Collection
View	Class and Collection
Column	Property
Relationship	Nested Collection
Stored Procedure	Method

On the left side, you are dealing with your database. The database is the entire entity — the tables, views, triggers, stored procedures — everything that makes up the database. On the LINQ side of this, you have an object called the `DataContext` object. A `DataContext` object is bound to the database. For the required interaction with the database, it contains a connection string, it will manage all of the transactions that occur, it will take care of any logging, and it will manage the output of the data. The `DataContext` object completely manages the transactions with the database on your behalf.

Tables, as you saw in the example, are converted to classes. This means that if you have a `Products` table, you will have a `Product` class. You will notice that LINQ is name-friendly in that it changes plural tables to singular to give the proper name to the class that you are using in your code. In addition to database tables being treated as classes, you will find that database views are also treated as the same. Columns, on the other hand, are treated as properties. This gives you the ability to manage the attributes (names and type definitions) of the column directly.

Relationships are nested collections that map between these various objects. This gives you the ability to define relationships that are mapped to multiple items.

It is also important to understand the mapping of stored procedures. These actually map to methods within your code from the `DataContext` instance. The next section takes a closer look at the `DataContext` and the table objects within LINQ.

When dealing with the architecture of LINQ to SQL, you will notice that there are really three layers to this — your application, the LINQ to SQL layer, and the SQL Server database. As you saw from the previous examples, you can create a strongly typed query in your application's code:

```
dc.Products;
```

This in turn gets translated to a SQL query by the LINQ to SQL layer, which is then supplied to the database on your behalf:

```
SELECT [t0].[ProductID], [t0].[ProductName], [t0].[SupplierID],
[t0].[CategoryID], [t0].[QuantityPerUnit], [t0].[UnitPrice],
[t0].[UnitsInStock], [t0].[UnitsOnOrder], [t0].[ReorderLevel],
[t0].[Discontinued]
FROM [dbo].[Products] AS [t0]
```

In return, the LINQ to SQL layer takes the rows coming out of the database from this query and turns the returned data into a collection of strongly typed objects that you can easily work with.

The DataContext Object

Again, the `DataContext` object manages the transactions that occur with the database that you are working with when working with LINQ to SQL. There is actually a lot that you can do with the `DataContext` object.

In instantiating one of these objects, you will notice that it takes a couple of optional parameters. These options include:

- A string that represents the location of the SQL Server Express database file or the name of the SQL Server that is used
- A connection string
- Another `DataContext` object

The first two string options also have the option of including your own database mapping file. Once you have instantiated this object, you are then able to programmatically use it for many types of operations.

Using ExecuteQuery

One of the simpler things that you can accomplish with the `DataContext` object is to run quick commands that you write yourself using the `ExecuteQuery<T>()` method. For instance, if you are going to pull all the products from the `Products` table using the `ExecuteQuery<T>()` method, your code would be similar to the following:

```
using System;
using System.Collections.Generic;
using System.Data.Linq;

namespace ConsoleApplication1
{
    class Class1
    {
        static void Main(string[] args)
        {
            DataContext dc = new DataContext(@"Data Source=.\SQLEXPRESS;
               AttachDbFilename=|DataDirectory|\NORTHWND.MDF;
               Integrated Security=True;User Instance=True");

            IEnumerable<Product> myProducts =
               dc.ExecuteQuery<Product>("SELECT * FROM PRODUCTS", "");

            foreach (Product item in myProducts)
            {
              Console.WriteLine(item.ProductID + " | " + item.ProductName);
            }

            Console.ReadLine();
        }
    }
}
```

In this case, the `ExecuteQuery<T>()` method is called passing in a query string and returning a collection of `Product` objects. The query utilized in the method call is a simple `Select` statement that doesn't require any additional parameters to be passed in. Because there are no parameters passed in with the query, you will instead need to use the double quotes as the second required parameter to the method call. If you were going to optionally substitute any values in the query, you would construct your `ExecuteQuery<T>()` call as such:

```
IEnumerable<Product> myProducts =
   dc.ExecuteQuery<Product>("SELECT * FROM PRODUCTS WHERE UnitsInStock > {0}",
   50);
```

In this case, the `{0}` is a placeholder for the substituted parameter value that you are going to pass in, and the second parameter of the `ExecuteQuery<T>()` method is the parameter that will be used in the substitution.

Using Connection

The `Connection` property actually returns an instance of the `System.Data.SqlClient.SqlConnection` that is used by the `DataContext` object. This is ideal if you need to share this connection with other ADO.NET code that you might be using in your application, or if you need to get at any of the `SqlConnection` properties or methods that it exposes. For instance, getting at the connection string is a simple affair:

```
NorthwindDataContext dc = new NorthwindDataContext();

Console.WriteLine(dc.Connection.ConnectionString);
```

Using Transaction

If you have an ADO.NET transaction that you can use, you are able to assign that transaction to the `DataContext` object instance using the `Transaction` property. You can also make use of transactions using the `TransactionScope` object that is from the .NET 2.0 Framework:

```
using System;
using System.Collections.Generic;
using System.Data.Linq;
using System.Transactions;

namespace ConsoleApplication1
{
    class Class1
    {
        static void Main(string[] args)
        {
            NorthwindDataContext dc = new NorthwindDataContext();

            using (TransactionScope myScope = new TransactionScope())
            {
               Product p1 = new Product() { ProductName = "Bill's Product" };
               dc.Products.InsertOnSubmit(p1);

               Product p2 = new Product() { ProductName = "Another Product" };
               dc.Products.InsertOnSubmit(p2);

               try
               {
                   dc.SubmitChanges();

                   Console.WriteLine(p1.ProductID);
                   Console.WriteLine(p2.ProductID);
               }
               catch (Exception ex)
               {
                   Console.WriteLine(ex.ToString());
               }

               myScope.Complete();
            }

            Console.ReadLine();
        }
    }
}
```

In this case, the `TransactionScope` object is used and if one of the operations on the database fails, everything will be rolled back to the original state.

Other Methods and Properties of the DataContext Object

In addition to the items just described, a number of other methods and properties are available from the `DataContext` object. The following table shows some of the available methods from `DataContext`.

Method	Description
`CreateDatabase`	Allows you to create a database on the server.
`DatabaseExists`	Allows you to determine whether a database exists and can be opened.
`DeleteDatabase`	Deletes the associated database.
`ExecuteCommand`	Allows you to pass in a command to the database to be executed.
`ExecuteQuery`	Allows you to pass queries directly to the database.
`GetChangeSet`	The `DataContext` object keeps track of changes occurring in the database on your behalf and this method allows you access to these changes.
`GetCommand`	Gives you access to the commands that are performed.
`GetTable`	Provides access to a collection of tables from the database.
`Refresh`	Allows you to refresh your objects from the data that is stored within the database.
`SubmitChanges`	Executes your CRUD commands in the database that have been established in your code.
`Translate`	Converts an `IDataReader` to objects.

In addition to these methods, the `DataContext` object exposes some of the properties shown in the following table.

Property	Description
`ChangeConflicts`	Provides a collection of objects that cause concurrency conflicts when the `SubmitChanges()` method is called.
`CommandTimeout`	Allows you to set the timeout period in which a command against the database is allowed to run. You should set this to a higher value if your query needs more time to execute.
`Connection`	Allows you to work with the `System.Data.SqlClient.SqlConnection` object used by the client.
`DeferredLoadingEnabled`	Allows you to specify whether or not to delay the loading of one-to-many or one-to-one relationships.
`LoadOptions`	Allows you to specify or retrieve the value of the `DataLoadOptions` object.
`Log`	Allows you to specify the location of the output of the command that was used in the query.
`Mapping`	Provides the `MetaModel` on which the mapping is based.
`ObjectTrackingEnabled`	Specifies whether or not to track changes to the objects within the database for transactional purposes. If you are dealing with a read-only database, you should set this property to `false`.
`Transaction`	Allows you to specify the local transaction used with the database.

The Table<TEntity> Object

The `Table<TEntity>` object is a representation of the tables that you are working with from the database. For instance, you saw the use of the `Product` class, which is a `Table<Product>` instance. As you will see throughout this chapter, a number of methods are available from the `Table<TEntity>` object. Some of these methods are defined in the following table.

Method	Description
`Attach`	Allows you to attach an entity to the `DataContext` instance.
`AttachAll`	Allows you to attach a collection of entities to the `DataContext` instance.
`DeleteAllOnSubmit<TSubEntity>`	Allows you to put all the pending actions into a state of being ready for deletion. Everything here is enacted when the `SubmitChanges()` method is called from the `DataContext` object.
`DeleteOnSubmit`	Allows you to put a pending action into a state of being ready for deletion. Everything here is enacted when the `SubmitChanges()` method is called from the `DataContext` object.
`GetModifiedMembers`	Provides an array of modified objects. You will be able to access their current and changed values.
`GetNewBindingList`	Provides a new list for binding to the data store.
`GetOriginalEntityState`	Provides you an instance of the object as it appeared in its original state.
`InsertAllOnSubmit<TSubEntity>`	Allows you to put all the pending actions into a state of being ready for insertion. Everything here is enacted with the `SubmitChanges()` method called off of the `DataContext` object.
`InsertOnSubmit`	Allows you to put a pending action into a state of being ready for insertion. Everything here is enacted when the `SubmitChanges()` method is called from the `DataContext` object.

Working Without the O/R Designer

Although the new O/R Designer in Visual Studio 2008 makes the creation of everything you need for LINQ to SQL quite easy, it is important to note that the underlying framework upon which this all rests allows you to do everything from the ground up yourself. This provides the most control over the situation and what is actually happening.

Creating Your Own Custom Object

To accomplish the same task as was accomplished earlier with the `Customer` table, you will need to expose the `Customer` table yourself via a class. The first step is to create a new class in your project called `Customer.cs`. The code for this class is presented here:

```
using System.Data.Linq.Mapping;

namespace ConsoleApplication1
{
    [Table(Name = "Customers")]
    public class Customer
    {
        [Column(IsPrimaryKey = true)]
        public string CustomerID { get; set; }
        [Column]
        public string CompanyName { get; set; }
        [Column]
        public string ContactName { get; set; }
        [Column]
        public string ContactTitle { get; set; }
        [Column]
        public string Address { get; set; }
        [Column]
        public string City { get; set; }
        [Column]
        public string Region { get; set; }
        [Column]
        public string PostalCode { get; set; }
        [Column]
        public string Country { get; set; }
        [Column]
        public string Phone { get; set; }
        [Column]
        public string Fax { get; set; }
    }
}
```

Here, the `Customer.cs` file defines the `Customer` object that you want to use with LINQ to SQL. The class has the `Table` attribute assigned to it in order to signify the table class. The `Table` class attribute includes a property called `Name`, which defines the name of the table to use within the database that is referenced with the connection string. Using the `Table` attribute also means that you need to make a reference to the `System.Data.Linq.Mapping` namespace in your code.

In addition to the `Table` attribute, each of the defined properties in the class makes use of the `Column` attribute. As stated earlier, columns from the SQL Server database will map to properties in your code.

Querying with Your Custom Object and LINQ

With only the `Customer` class in place, you are then able to query the Northwind database for the `Customers` table. The code to accomplish this task is illustrated in the following example:

```
using System;
using System.Data.Linq;
```

```
namespace ConsoleApplication1
{
    class Program
    {
        static void Main()
        {
            DataContext dc = new DataContext(@"Data Source=.\SQLEXPRESS;
               AttachDbFilename=|DataDirectory|\NORTHWND.MDF;
               Integrated Security=True;User Instance=True");

            dc.Log = Console.Out; // Used for outputting the SQL used

            Table<Customer> myCustomers = dc.GetTable<Customer>();

            foreach (Customer item in myCustomers)
            {
                Console.WriteLine("{0} | {1}",
                   item.CompanyName, item.Country);
            }

            Console.ReadLine();
        }
    }
}
```

In this case, the default `DataContext` object is used and the connection string to the Northwind SQL Server Express database is passed in as a parameter. A `Table` class of type `Customer` is then populated using the `GetTable<TEntity>()` method. For this example, the `GetTable<TEntity>()` operation uses your custom-defined `Customer` class:

```
dc.GetTable<Customer>();
```

What happens is that LINQ to SQL will use the `DataContext` object to make the query to the SQL Server database on your behalf and will get the returned rows as strongly typed `Customer` objects. This will allow you to then iterate through each of the `Customer` objects in the `Table` object's collection and get at the information that you need, as is done with the `Console.WriteLine()` statements here:

```
foreach (Customer item in myCustomers)
{
   Console.WriteLine("{0} | {1}",
      item.CompanyName, item.Country);
}
```

Running this code produces the following results in your console application:

```
SELECT [t0].[CustomerID], [t0].[CompanyName], [t0].[ContactName],
[t0].[ContactTitle], [t0].[Address], [t0].[City], [t0].[Region],
[t0].[PostalCode], [t0].[Country], [t0].[Phone], [t0].[Fax]
FROM [Customers] AS [t0]
-- Context: SqlProvider(Sql2005) Model: AttributedMetaModel Build: 3.5.21022.8

Alfreds Futterkiste | Germany
Ana Trujillo Emparedados y helados | Mexico
Antonio Moreno Taquería | Mexico
```

(continued)

(continued)

```
Around the Horn | UK
Berglunds snabbköp | Sweden

// Output removed for clarity

Wartian Herkku | Finland
Wellington Importadora | Brazil
White Clover Markets | USA
Wilman Kala | Finland
Wolski  Zajazd | Poland
```

Limiting the Columns Called with the Query

You will notice that the query retrieved every single column that was specified in your `Customer` class file. If you remove the columns that you are not going to need, you can then have a new `Customer` class file as shown here:

```
using System.Data.Linq.Mapping;

namespace ConsoleApplication1
{
    [Table(Name = "Customers")]
    public class Customer
    {
        [Column(IsPrimaryKey = true)]
        public string CustomerID { get; set; }
        [Column]
        public string CompanyName { get; set; }
        [Column]
        public string Country { get; set; }
    }
}
```

In this case, I removed all the columns that are not utilized by the application. Now if you run the console application and look at the SQL query that is produced, you will see the following results:

```
SELECT [t0].[CustomerID], [t0].[CompanyName], [t0].[Country]
FROM [Customers] AS [t0]
```

You can see that only the three columns that are defined within the `Customer` class are utilized in the query to the `Customers` table.

The property `CustomerID` is interesting in that you are able to signify that this column is a primary key for the table through the use of the `IsPrimaryKey` setting in the `Column` attribute. This setting takes a `Boolean` value and in this case, it is set to `true`.

Working with Column Names

The other important point of the columns is that the name of the property that you define in the `Customer` class needs to be the same name as what is used in the database. For instance, if you change the name of the CustomerID property to MyCustomerID, you will get the following exception when you try to run your console application:

```
System.Data.SqlClient.SqlException was unhandled
  Message="Invalid column name 'MyCustomerID'."
  Source=".Net SqlClient Data Provider"
  ErrorCode=-2146232060
  Class=16
  LineNumber=1
  Number=207
  Procedure=""
  Server="\\\\.\\pipe\\F5E22E37-1AF9-44\\tsql\\query"
```

To get around this, you need to define the name of the column in the custom Customer class that you have created. You can do this by using the Column attribute as illustrated here:

```
[Column(IsPrimaryKey = true, Name = "CustomerID")]
public string MyCustomerID { get; set; }
```

Like the Table attribute, the Column attribute includes a Name property that allows you to specify the name of the column as it appears in the Customers table.

Doing this will generate a query as shown here:

```
SELECT [t0].[CustomerID] AS [MyCustomerID], [t0].[CompanyName], [t0].[Country]
FROM [Customers] AS [t0]
```

This also means that you will need to now reference the column using the new name of MyCustomerID (for example, item.MyCustomerID).

Creating Your Own DataContext Object

Now it is probably not the best approach to use the plain-vanilla DataContext object, but instead, you will find that you have more control by creating your own DataContext class. To accomplish this task, create a new class called MyNorthwindDataContext.cs and have the class inherit from DataContext. Your class in its simplest form is illustrated here:

```
using System.Data.Linq;

namespace ConsoleApplication1
{
    public class MyNorthwindDataContext : DataContext
    {
        public Table<Customer> Customers;

        public MyNorthwindDataContext()
            : base(@"Data Source=.\SQLEXPRESS;
                     AttachDbFilename=|DataDirectory|\NORTHWND.MDF;
                     Integrated Security=True;User Instance=True")
        {
        }
    }
}
```

Here, the class MyNorthwindDataContext inherits from DataContext and provides an instance of the Table<Customer> object from the Customer class that you created earlier. The constructor is the other requirement of this class. This constructor uses a base to initialize a new instance of the object referencing a file (in this case a connection to a SQL database file).

Using your own DataContext object now allows you to change the code in your application to the following:

```
using System;
using System.Data.Linq;

namespace ConsoleApplication1
{
    class Program
    {
        static void Main()
        {
            MyNorthwindDataContext dc = new MyNorthwindDataContext();
            Table<Customer> myCustomers = dc.Customers;

            foreach (Customer item in myCustomers)
            {
                Console.WriteLine("{0} | {1}",
                   item.CompanyName, item.Country);
            }

            Console.ReadLine();
        }
    }
}
```

By creating an instance of the MyNorthwindDataContext object, you are now allowing the class to manage the connection to the database. You will also notice that now you have direct access to the Customer class through the dc.Customers statement.

Note that the examples provided in this chapter are considered bare-bones examples in that they don't include all the error handling and logging that would generally go into building your applications. This is done to illustrate the points being discussed in the chapter and nothing more.

Custom Objects and the O/R Designer

In addition to building your custom object in your own .cs file and then tying that class to the DataContext that you have built, you can also use the O/R Designer in Visual Studio 2008 to build your class files. When you use Visual Studio in this manner, it will create the appropriate .cs file on your behalf, but by using the O/R Designer, you will also have a visual representation of the class file and any possible relationships that you have established.

When viewing the Designer view of your .dbml file, you will notice that there are three items present in the toolbox. These items are Class, Association, and Inheritance.

For an example of this, take the Class object from the toolbox and drop it onto the design surface. You will be presented with an image of the generic class as shown in Figure 27-7.

Figure 27-7

From here, you can now click the `Class1` name and rename this class to `Customer`. Right-clicking next to the name enables you to add properties to the class file by selecting Add ⇨ Property from the provided menu. For this example, give the `Customer` class three properties — `CustomerID`, `CompanyName`, and `Country`. If you highlight the `CustomerID` property, you will be able to configure the property from the Properties dialog in Visual Studio and change the Primary Key setting from `False` to `True`. You also want to highlight the entire class and go to the Properties dialog and change the `Source` property to `Customers` because this is the name of the table from which this `Customer` object needs to work. After this is all done, you will have a visual representation of the class as shown in Figure 27-8.

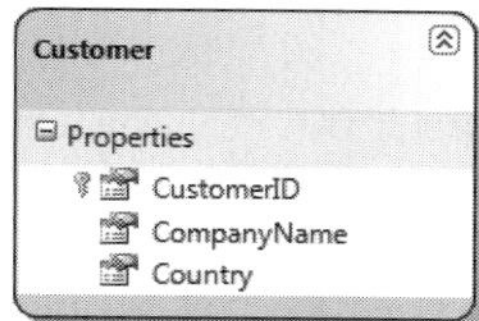

Figure 27-8

As you can see from this image, the `CustomerID` property is properly represented with a primary key icon next to the name. With this in place, you can expand the plus sign next to the `Northwind.dbml` file and you will find two files here — `Northwind.dbml.layout` and `Northwind.designer.cs`. The `Northwind.dbml.layout` file is an XML file that helps Visual Studio with the visual representation shown in the O/R Designer. The file that is the most important is the `Northwind.designer.cs` file. This is the `Customer` class file that was created on your behalf. When you open this file, you are able to see what Visual Studio created for you.

First, you will find the `Customer` class file within the code of the page:

```
[Table(Name="Customers")]
public partial class Customer : INotifyPropertyChanging,
                                INotifyPropertyChanged
{

   // Code removed for clarity

}
```

The `Customer` class is the name of the class according to what you provided in the designer. The class comes with the `Table` attribute and provides a name value of `Customers` because this is the name of the database that this object will need to work with when connecting to the Northwind database.

Within the `Customer` class, you will find the three properties that you defined. Presented here is just one of the properties — `CustomerID`:

```
[Column(Storage="_CustomerID", CanBeNull=false, IsPrimaryKey=true)]
public string CustomerID
{
   get
   {
      return this._CustomerID;
   }
   set
```

(continued)

(continued)

```
        {
            if ((this._CustomerID != value))
            {
                this.OnCustomerIDChanging(value);
                this.SendPropertyChanging();
                this._CustomerID = value;
                this.SendPropertyChanged("CustomerID");
                this.OnCustomerIDChanged();
            }
        }
    }
```

Similar to when you built a class for yourself from the earlier example, the properties defined use the `Column` attribute and some of the properties available to this attribute. You can see that the primary key setting is set using the `IsPrimaryKey` item.

In addition to the `Customer` class, you will find that a class inheriting from the `DataContext` object is also within the created file:

```
[System.Data.Linq.Mapping.DatabaseAttribute(Name="NORTHWND")]
public partial class NorthwindDataContext : System.Data.Linq.DataContext
{

    // Code removed for clarity

}
```

This `DataContext` object, `NorthwindDataContext`, allows you to connect to the Northwind database and class the `Customers` table as was accomplished in the previous examples.

You will find that using the O/R Designer is a process that can make the creation of your database object class files simple and straightforward. However, at the same time, if you want complete control, you can code up everything yourself and get the results you are after.

Querying the Database

As you've seen, there are a number of ways in which you can query the database from the code of your application. In some of the simplest forms, your queries looked like the following:

```
Table<Product> query = dc.Products;
```

This command was pulling down the entire `Products` table to your `query` object instance.

Using Query Expressions

In addition to a pulling a table straight out of the database using `dc.Products`, you also can use a query expression directly in your code that is strongly typed. An example of this is shown in the following code:

```
using System;
using System.Linq;
```

```
namespace ConsoleApplication1
{
    class Class1
    {
        static void Main(string[] args)
        {
            NorthwindDataContext dc = new NorthwindDataContext();

            var query = from p in dc.Products
                        select p;

            foreach (Product item in query)
            {
                Console.WriteLine(item.ProductID + " | " + item.ProductName);
            }

            Console.ReadLine();
        }
    }
}
```

In this case, a query object (again, a Table<Product> object) is populated with the query value of from p in dc.Products select p;. This command, though shown on two lines for readability purposes, can also be presented on a single line if you wish.

Query Expressions in Detail

You will find that there are a number of query expressions that you can use from your code. The previous example is a simple select statement that returns the entire table. The following list of items are some of the other query expressions that you have at your disposal.

Segmentation	Syntax
Project	select <*expression*>
Filter	where <*expression*>, distinct
Test	any(<*expression*>), all(<*expression*>)
Join	<*expression*> join <*expression*> on <*expression*> equals <*expression*>
Group	group by <*expression*>, into <*expression*>, <*expression*> group join <*decision*> on <*expression*> equals <*expression*> into <*expression*>
Aggregate	count([<*expression*>]), sum(<*expression*>), min(<*expression*>), max(<*expression*>), avg(<*expression*>)
Partition	skip [while] <*expression*>, take [while] <*expression*>
Set	union, intersect, except
Order	order by <*expression*>, <*expression*> [ascending | descending]

Filtering Using Expressions

In addition to straight queries for the entire table, you can filter items using the `where` and `distinct` options. The following provides an example of querying the `Products` table for a specific type of record:

```
var query = from p in dc.Products
            where p.ProductName.StartsWith("L")
            select p;
```

In this case, this query is selecting all the records from the `Products` table that start with the letter `L`. This is done via the `where p.ProductName.StartsWith("L")` expression. You will find a large selection of methods available from the `ProductName` property that allows you to fine-tune the filtering you need. This operation produces the following results:

```
65 | Louisiana Fiery Hot Pepper Sauce
66 | Louisiana Hot Spiced Okra
67 | Laughing Lumberjack Lager
74 | Longlife Tofu
76 | Lakkalikööri
```

You can also add as many of these expressions to the list as you need. For instance, here is an example of adding two `where` statements to your query:

```
var query = from p in dc.Products
            where p.ProductName.StartsWith("L")
            where p.ProductName.EndsWith("i")
            select p;
```

In this case, there is a filter expression that looks for items with a product name starting with the letter `L` and then a second expression is done to make sure that the second criteria is also applied, which states that the items must also end with the letter `i`. This would give you the following results:

```
76 | Lakkalikööri
```

Performing Joins

In addition to working with one table, you can work with multiple tables and perform joins with your queries. If you drag and drop both the `Customers` table and the `Orders` table onto the `Northwind.dbml` design surface, you will get the result presented in Figure 27-9.

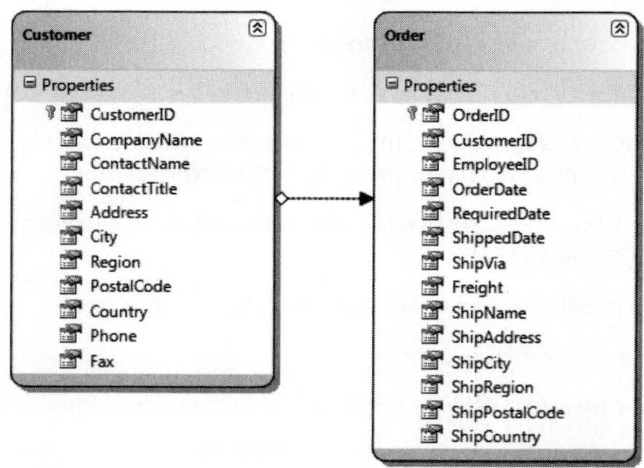

Figure 27-9

From this figure, you can see that after you drag and drop both of these elements onto the design surface, Visual Studio will know that there is a relationship between these items and will create this relationship for you in the code and represent it with the black arrow.

From here, you can use a `join` statement in your query to work with both of the tables as presented in the following example:

```
using System;
using System.Linq;

namespace ConsoleApplication1
{
    class Class1
    {
        static void Main(string[] args)
        {
            NorthwindDataContext dc = new NorthwindDataContext();
            dc.Log = Console.Out;

            var query = from c in dc.Customers
                  join o in dc.Orders on c.CustomerID equals o.CustomerID
                  orderby c.CustomerID
                  select new { c.CustomerID, c.CompanyName,
                     c.Country, o.OrderID, o.OrderDate };

            foreach (var item in query)
            {
                Console.WriteLine(item.CustomerID + " | " + item.CompanyName
                     + " | " + item.Country  + " | " + item.OrderID
                      + " | " + item.OrderDate);
            }

            Console.ReadLine();
        }
    }
}
```

This example is pulling from the `Customers` table and joining on the `Orders` table where the `CustomerID` columns match. This is done through the `join` statement:

```
join o in dc.Orders on c.CustomerID equals o.CustomerID
```

From here, a new object is created with the `select new` statement and this new object comprises of the `CustomerID`, `CompanyName`, and `Country` columns from the `Customer` table as well as the `OrderID` and `OrderDate` columns from the `Orders` table.

When it comes to iterating through the collection of this new object, the interesting part is that the `foreach` statement also uses the `var` keyword because the type is not known at this point in time:

```
foreach (var item in query)
{
   Console.WriteLine(item.CustomerID + " | " + item.CompanyName
      + " | " + item.Country  + " | " + item.OrderID
      + " | " + item.OrderDate);
}
```

Regardless, the `item` object here has access to all the properties that you specified. When you run this example, you will get results similar to what is presented in this partial result:

```
WILMK | Wilman Kala | Finland | 10695 | 10/7/1997 12:00:00 AM
WILMK | Wilman Kala | Finland | 10615 | 7/30/1997 12:00:00 AM
WILMK | Wilman Kala | Finland | 10673 | 9/18/1997 12:00:00 AM
WILMK | Wilman Kala | Finland | 11005 | 4/7/1998 12:00:00 AM
WILMK | Wilman Kala | Finland | 10879 | 2/10/1998 12:00:00 AM
WILMK | Wilman Kala | Finland | 10873 | 2/6/1998 12:00:00 AM
WILMK | Wilman Kala | Finland | 10910 | 2/26/1998 12:00:00 AM
```

Grouping Items

You are also easily able to group items with your queries. In the `Northwind.dbml` example that you are working with, drag and drop the `Categories` table onto the design surface and you will see that there is a relation with this table and the `Products` table from earlier. The following example shows you how to group products by categories:

```
using System;
using System.Linq;

namespace ConsoleApplication1
{
    class Class1
    {
        static void Main(string[] args)
        {
            NorthwindDataContext dc = new NorthwindDataContext();

            var query = from p in dc.Products
                        orderby p.Category.CategoryName ascending
                        group p by p.Category.CategoryName into g
                        select new { Category = g.Key, Products = g};

            foreach (var item in query)
            {
                Console.WriteLine(item.Category);

                foreach (var innerItem in item.Products)
                {
                    Console.WriteLine("      " + innerItem.ProductName);
                }

                Console.WriteLine();
            }

            Console.ReadLine();
        }
    }
}
```

This example creates a new object, which is a group of categories, and packages the entire `Product` table into this new table called `g`. Before that, the categories are ordered by name using the `orderby` statement because the order provided is an `ascending` order (the other option being `descending`). The output is the `Category` (passed in through the `Key` property) and the `Product` instance. The iteration with the `foreach` statements is done once for the categories and another for each of the products that are found in the category.

A partial output of this program is presented here:

```
Beverages
      Chai
      Chang
      Guaraná Fantástica
      Sasquatch Ale
      Steeleye Stout
      Côte de Blaye
      Chartreuse verte
      Ipoh Coffee
      Laughing Lumberjack Lager
      Outback Lager
      Rhönbräu Klosterbier
      Lakkalikööri

Condiments
      Aniseed Syrup
      Chef Anton's Cajun Seasoning
      Chef Anton's Gumbo Mix
      Grandma's Boysenberry Spread
      Northwoods Cranberry Sauce
      Genen Shouyu
      Gula Malacca
      Sirop d'érable
      Vegie-spread
      Louisiana Fiery Hot Pepper Sauce
      Louisiana Hot Spiced Okra
      Original Frankfurter grüne Sobe
```

You will find that there a lot more commands and expressions available to you beyond what are presented in this short chapter.

Stored Procedures

So far, you have been querying the tables directly and leaving it up to LINQ to create the appropriate SQL statement for the operation. When working with pre-existing databases that make heavy use of stored procedures and for those that want to follow the best practice of using stored procedures within a database, you will find that LINQ is still a viable option.

LINQ to SQL treats working with stored procedures as a method call. As you saw in Figure 27-4, there is a design surface called the O/R Designer that allows you to drag and drop tables onto it so that you can then programmatically work with the table. On the right side of the O/R Designer, you will find a spot where you are able to drag and drop stored procedures.

Any stored procedures that you drag and drop onto this part of the O/R Designer will now become available methods to you from `DataContext` object. For this example, drag and drop the `TenMostExpensiveProducts` stored procedure onto this part of the O/R Designer.

The following example shows how you would call this stored procedure within the Northwind database:

```
using System;
using System.Collections.Generic;
using System.Data.Linq;
using System.Linq;

namespace ConsoleApplication1
{
    class Class1
    {
        static void Main(string[] args)
        {
            NorthwindDataContext dc = new NorthwindDataContext();

            ISingleResult<Ten_Most_Expensive_ProductsResult> result =
                dc.Ten_Most_Expensive_Products();

            foreach (Ten_Most_Expensive_ProductsResult item in result)
            {
                Console.WriteLine(item.TenMostExpensiveProducts + " | " +
                   item.UnitPrice);
            }

            Console.ReadLine();
        }
    }
}
```

From this example, you can see that the rows coming out of the stored procedure are collected into an `ISingleResult<Ten_Most_Expensive_ProductsResult>` object. From here, iteration through this object is as simple as all the rest.

As you can see from this example, calling your stored procedures is a simple process.

Summary

One of the more exciting features of the .NET Framework 3.5 release is the LINQ capabilities that the platform provides. This chapter focused on using LINQ to SQL and some of the options available to you in querying your SQL Server databases.

Using LINQ to SQL enables to have a strongly typed set of operations for performing CRUD operations against your database. With that said, though, you are still able to use pre-existing access capabilities whether that is interacting with ADO.NET or working with your stored procedures.

The next chapter takes a look manipulating XML, in preparation for Chapter 29, "LINQ to XML."

28

Manipulating XML

XML plays a significant role in the .NET Framework. Not only does the .NET Framework allow you to use XML in your application, but the .NET Framework itself uses XML for configuration files and source code documentation, as do SOAP, Web services, and ADO.NET, to name just a few.

To accommodate this extensive use of XML, the .NET Framework includes the `System.Xml` namespace. This namespace is loaded with classes that can be used for the processing of XML, and many of these classes are discussed in this chapter.

This chapter discusses how to use the `XmlDocument` class, which is the implementation of the Document Object Model (DOM), as well as what .NET offers as a replacement for SAX (the `XmlReader` and `XmlWriter` classes). It also discusses the class implementations of XPath and XSLT and demonstrates how XML and ADO.NET work together, as well as how easy it is to transform one to the other. You also learn how you can serialize your objects to XML and create an object from (or deserialize) an XML document using classes in the `System.Xml.Serialization` namespace. More to the point, you learn how you can incorporate XML into your C# applications.

You should note that the XML namespace allows you to get similar results in a number of different ways. It is impossible to include all these variations in one chapter, so while exploring one possible way of doing things we'll try our best to mention alternative routes that will yield the same or similar results.

Because it's beyond the scope of this book to teach you XML from scratch, we assume that you are already somewhat familiar with XML technology. For example, you should be familiar with elements, attributes, and nodes, and you should also know what we mean when we refer to a well-formed document. You should also be familiar with SAX and DOM. If you want to find out more about XML, Wrox's *Beginning XML* (Wiley Publishing, Inc., ISBN 0-7645-7077-3) is a great place to start.

This chapter covers the following:

- XML standards
- `XmlReader` and `XmlWriter`
- `XmlDocument`

- `XPathDocument`
- `XmlNavigator`

The discussion begins with a brief overview of the current status of XML standards.

XML Standards Support in .NET

The World Wide Web Consortium (W3C) has developed a set of standards that give XML its power and potential. Without these standards, XML would not have the impact on the development world that it does. The W3C Web site (`www.w3.org`) is a valuable source for all things XML.

The .NET Framework supports the following W3C standards:

- XML 1.0 (`www.w3.org/TR/1998/REC-xml-19980210`), including DTD support
- XML namespaces (`www.w3.org/TR/REC-xml-names`), both stream level and DOM
- XML schemas (`www.w3.org/2001/XMLSchema`)
- XPath expressions (`www.w3.org/TR/xpath`)
- XSLT transformations (`www.w3.org/TR/xslt`)
- DOM Level 1 Core (`www.w3.org/TR/REC-DOM-Level-1`)
- DOM Level 2 Core (`www.w3.org/TR/DOM-Level-2-Core`)
- SOAP 1.1 (`www.w3.org/TR/SOAP`)

The level of standards support will change as the framework matures and the W3C updates the recommended standards. Because of this, you need to make sure you stay up-to-date with the standards and the level of support provided by Microsoft.

Introducing the System.Xml Namespace

Support for processing XML is provided by the classes in the `System.Xml` namespace in .NET. This section looks (in no particular order) at some of the more important classes that the `System.Xml` namespace provides. The following table lists the main XML reader and writer classes.

Class Name	Description
`XmlReader`	An abstract reader class that provides fast, non-cached XML data. `XmlReader` is forward-only, like the SAX parser.
`XmlWriter`	An abstract writer class that provides fast, non-cached XML data in stream or file format.
`XmlTextReader`	Extends `XmlReader`. Provides fast forward-only stream access to XML data.
`XmlTextWriter`	Extends `XmlWriter`. Fast forward-only generation of XML streams.

The following table lists some other useful classes for handling XML.

Class Name	Description
`XmlNode`	An abstract class that represents a single node in an XML document. Base class for several classes in the XML namespace.
`XmlDocument`	Extends `XmlNode`. This is the W3C DOM implementation. It provides a tree representation in memory of an XML document, enabling navigation and editing.
`XmlDataDocument`	Extends `XmlDocument`. This is a document that can be loaded from XML data or from relational data in an ADO.NET `DataSet`. Allows the mixing of XML and relational data in the same view.
`XmlResolver`	An abstract class that resolves external XML-based resources such as DTD and schema references. Also used to process `<xsl:include>` and `<xsl:import>` elements.
`XmlNodeList`	A list of `XmlNodes` that can be iterated through.
`XmlUrlResolver`	Extends `XmlResolver`. Resolves external resources named by a uniform resource identifier (URI).

Many of the classes in the `System.Xml` namespace provide a means to manage XML documents and streams, whereas others (such as the `XmlDataDocument` class) provide a bridge between XML data stores and the relational data stored in `DataSets`.

It is worth noting that the XML namespace is available to any language that is part of the .NET family. This means that all of the examples in this chapter could also be written in Visual Basic .NET, managed C++, and so on.

Using System.Xml Classes

The following examples use `books.xml` as the source of data. You can download this file from the Wrox Web site (`www.wrox.com`), but it is also included in several examples in the .NET SDK. The `books.xml` file is a book catalog for an imaginary bookstore. It includes book information such as genre, author name, price, and ISBN number. As with the other chapters, you can download all code examples in this chapter from the Wrox Web site (`www.wrox.com`).

This is what the `books.xml` file looks like:

```
<?xml version='1.0'?>
<!-- This file represents a fragment of a book store inventory database -->
<bookstore>
   <book genre="autobiography" publicationdate="1991" ISBN="1-861003-11-0">
      <title>The Autobiography of Benjamin Franklin</title>
      <author>
         <first-name>Benjamin</first-name>
         <last-name>Franklin</last-name>
      </author>
```

(continued)

(continued)

```
      <price>8.99</price>
   </book>
   <book genre="novel" publicationdate="1967" ISBN="0-201-63361-2">
      <title>The Confidence Man</title>
      <author>
         <first-name>Herman</first-name>
         <last-name>Melville</last-name>
      </author>
      <price>11.99</price>
   </book>
   <book genre="philosophy" publicationdate="1991" ISBN="1-861001-57-6">
      <title>The Gorgias</title>
      <author>
         <name>Plato</name>
      </author>
      <price>9.99</price>
   </book></bookstore>
```

Reading and Writing Streamed XML

The `XmlReader` and `XmlWriter` classes will feel familiar if you have ever used SAX. `XmlReader`-based classes provide a very fast, forward-only, read-only cursor that streams the XML data for processing. Because it is a streaming model, the memory requirements are not very demanding. However, you don't have the navigation flexibility and the read or write capabilities that would be available from a DOM-based model. `XmlWriter`-based classes produce an XML document that conforms to the W3C's XML 1.0 Namespace Recommendations.

`XmlReader` and `XmlWriter` are both abstract classes. The following classes are derived from `XmlReader`:

- `XmlNodeReader`
- `XmlTextReader`
- `XmlValidatingReader`

The following classes are derived from `XmlWriter`:

- `XmlTextWriter`
- `XmlQueryOutput`

`XmlTextReader` and `XmlTextWriter` work with either a stream-based object from the `System.IO` namespace or `TextReader`/`TextWriter` objects. `XmlNodeReader` uses an `XmlNode` as its source instead of a stream. The `XmlValidatingReader` adds DTD and schema validation and therefore offers data validation. You look at these a bit more closely later in this chapter.

Using the XmlReader Class

`XmlReader` is a lot like SAX in the MSXML SDK. One of the biggest differences, however, is that whereas SAX is a *push* type of model (that is, it pushes data out to the application, and the developer has to be ready to accept it), the `XmlReader` has a *pull* model, where data is pulled into an application requesting it. This provides an easier and more intuitive programming model. Another advantage to this is that a pull model can be selective about the data that is sent to the application: if you don't want all of the data, you don't need to process it. In a push model, all of the XML data has to be processed by the application, whether it is needed or not.

The following is a very simple example of reading XML data, and later you take a closer look at the `XmlReader` class. You'll find the code in the XmlReaderSample folder. Here is the code for reading in the `books.xml` document. As each node is read, the `NodeType` property is checked. If the node is a text node, the value is appended to the text box:

```
using System.Xml;
private void button3_Click(object sender, EventArgs e)
{
  richTextBox1.Clear();
  XmlReader rdr = XmlReader.Create("books.xml");
  while (rdr.Read())
  {
    if (rdr.NodeType == XmlNodeType.Text)
      richTextBox1.AppendText(rdr.Value + "\r\n");
  }
}
```

As previously discussed, `XmlReader` is an abstract class. So in order to use the `XmlReader` class directly, a `Create` static method has been added. The create method returns an `XmlReader` object. The overload list for the `Create` method contains nine entries. In the preceding example, a string that represents the file name of the `XmlDocument` is passed in as a parameter. Stream-based objects and `TextReader`-based objects can also be passed in.

An `XmlReaderSettings` object can also be used. `XmlReaderSettings` specifies the features of the reader. For example, a schema can be used to validate the stream. Set the `Schemas` property to a valid `XmlSchemaSet` object, which is a cache of XSD schemas. Then the `XsdValidate` property on the `XmlReaderSettings` object can be set to `true`.

Several `Ignore` properties exist that can be used to control the way the reader processes certain nodes and values. These properties include `IgnoreComments`, `IgnoreIdentityConstraints`, `IgnoreInlineSchema`, `IgnoreProcessingInstructions`, `IgnoreSchemaLocation`, and `IgnoreWhitespace`. These properties can be used to strip certain items from the document.

Read Methods

Several ways exist to move through the document. As shown in the previous example, `Read()` takes you to the next node. You can then verify whether the node has a value (`HasValue()`) or, as you see shortly, whether the node has any attributes (`HasAttributes()`). You can also use the `ReadStartElement()` method, which verifies whether the current node is the start element and then positions you on to the next node. If you are not on the start element, an `XmlException` is raised. Calling this method is the same as calling the `IsStartElement()` method followed by a `Read()` method.

`ReadElementString()` is similar to `ReadString()`, except that you can optionally pass in the name of an element. If the next content node is not a start tag, or if the `Name` parameter does not match the current node `Name`, an exception is raised.

Here is an example of how `ReadElementString()` can be used. Notice that this example uses `FileStreams`, so you will need to make sure that you include the `System.IO` namespace via a `using` statement:

```
private void button6_Click(object sender, EventArgs e)
{
  richTextBox1.Clear();
        XmlReader rdr = XmlReader.Create("books.xml");
  while (!rdr.EOF)
```

(continued)

(continued)

```
    {
      //if we hit an element type, try and load it in the listbox
      if (rdr.MoveToContent() == XmlNodeType.Element && rdr.Name == "title")
      {
        richTextBox1.AppendText(rdr.ReadElementString() + "\r\n");
      }
      else
      {
        //otherwise move on
        rdr.Read();
      }
    }
  }
```

In the `while` loop, you use `MoveToContent()` to find each node of type `XmlNodeType.Element` with the name `title`. You use the `EOF` property of the `XmlTextReader` as the loop condition. If the node is not of type `Element` or not named `title`, the `else` clause will issue a `Read()` method to move to the next node. When you find a node that matches the criteria, you add the result of a `ReadElementString()` to the list box. This should leave you with just the book titles in the list box. Note that you don't have to issue a `Read()` call after a successful `ReadElementString()` because `ReadElementString()` consumes the entire `Element` and positions you on the next node.

If you remove `&& rdr.Name=="title"` from the `if` clause, you will have to catch the `XmlException` when it is thrown. If you look at the data file, you will see that the first element that `MoveToContent()` will find is the `<bookstore>` element. Because it is an element, it will pass the check in the `if` statement. However, because it does not contain a simple text type, it will cause `ReadElementString()` to raise an `XmlException`. One way to work around this is to put the `ReadElementString()` call in a function of its own. Then, if the call to `ReadElementString()` fails inside this function, you can deal with the error and return to the calling function.

Go ahead and do this; call this new method `LoadTextBox()` and pass in the `XmlTextReader` as a parameter. This is what the `LoadTextBox()` method looks like with these changes:

```
private void LoadTextBox(XmlReader reader)
{
   try
   {
      richTextBox1.AppendText (reader.ReadElementString() + "\r\n");
   }
   // if an XmlException is raised, ignore it.
   catch(XmlException er){}
}
```

This section from the previous example:

```
if (tr.MoveToContent() == XmlNodeType.Element && tr.Name == "title")
{
  richTextBox1.AppendText(tr.ReadElementString() + "\r\n");
}
else
{
  //otherwise move on
  tr.Read();
}
```

will have to change to the following:

```
if (tr.MoveToContent() == XmlNodeType.Element)
{
  LoadTextBox(tr);
}
else
{
  //otherwise move on
  tr.Read();
}
```

After running this example, the results should be the same as before. What you are seeing is that there is more than one way to accomplish the same goal. This is where the flexibility of the classes in the `System.Xml` namespace starts to become apparent.

The `XmlReader` can also read strongly typed data. There are several `ReadElementContentAs` methods, such as `ReadElementContentAsDouble`, `ReadElementContentAsBoolean`, and so on. The following example shows how to read in the values as a decimal and do some math on the value. In this case, the value from the price element is increased by 25 percent:

```
private void button5_Click(object sender, EventArgs e)
{
  richTextBox1.Clear();
  XmlReader rdr = XmlReader.Create("books.xml");
  while (rdr.Read())
  {
    if (rdr.NodeType == XmlNodeType.Element)
    {
      if (rdr.Name == "price")
      {
        decimal price = rdr.ReadElementContentAsDecimal();
        richTextBox1.AppendText("Current Price = " + price + "\r\n");
        price += price * (decimal).25;
        richTextBox1.AppendText("New Price = " + price + "\r\n\r\n");
      }
      else if(rdr.Name== "title")
        richTextBox1.AppendText(rdr.ReadElementContentAsString() + "\r\n");
    }
  }
}
```

If the value cannot be converted to a decimal value, a `FormatException` is raised. This is a much more efficient method than reading the value as a string and casting it to the proper data type.

Retrieving Attribute Data

As you play with the sample code, you might notice that when the nodes are read in, you don't see any attributes. This is because attributes are not considered part of a document's structure. When you are on an element node, you can check for the existence of attributes and optionally retrieve the attribute values.

For example, the `HasAttributes` property returns `true` if there are any attributes; otherwise, it returns `false`. The `AttributeCount` property tells you how many attributes there are, and the `GetAttribute()` method gets an attribute by name or by index. If you want to iterate through the attributes one at a time, you can use the `MoveToFirstAttribute()` and `MoveToNextAttribute()` methods.

The following is an example of iterating through the attributes of the `books.xml` document:

```
private void button7_Click(object sender, EventArgs e)
{
  richTextBox1.Clear();
  XmlReader tr = XmlReader.Create("books.xml");
  //Read in node at a time
  while (tr.Read())
  {
    //check to see if it's a NodeType element
    if (tr.NodeType == XmlNodeType.Element)
    {
      //if it's an element, then let's look at the attributes.
      for (int i = 0; i < tr.AttributeCount; i++)
      {
        richTextBox1.AppendText(tr.GetAttribute(i) + "\r\n");
      }
    }
  }
}
```

This time you are looking for element nodes. When you find one, you loop through all of the attributes and, using the `GetAttribute()` method, you load the value of the attribute into the list box. In this example, those attributes would be `genre`, `publicationdate`, and `ISBN`.

Validating with XmlReader

Sometimes it's important to know not only that the document is well formed but also that the document is valid. An `XmlReader` can validate the XML according to an XSD schema by using the `XmlReaderSettings` class. The XSD schema is added to the `XmlSchemaSet` that is exposed through the `Schemas` property. The `XsdValidate` property must also be set to `true`; the default for this property is `false`.

The following example demonstrates the use of the `XmlReaderSettings` class. The following is the XSD schema that will be used to validate the `books.xml` document:

```
<?xml version="1.0" encoding="utf-8"?>
<xs:schema attributeFormDefault="unqualified"
        elementFormDefault="qualified" xmlns:xs="http://www.w3.org/2001/XMLSchema">
  <xs:element name="bookstore">
    <xs:complexType>
      <xs:sequence>
        <xs:element maxOccurs="unbounded" name="book">
          <xs:complexType>
            <xs:sequence>
              <xs:element name="title" type="xs:string" />
              <xs:element name="author">
                <xs:complexType>
                  <xs:sequence>
                    <xs:element minOccurs="0" name="name"
                                             type="xs:string" />
                    <xs:element minOccurs="0" name="first-name"
                                             type="xs:string" />
                    <xs:element minOccurs="0" name="last-name"
                                             type="xs:string" />
                  </xs:sequence>
```

```
                    </xs:complexType>
                  </xs:element>
                  <xs:element name="price" type="xs:decimal" />
                </xs:sequence>
                <xs:attribute name="genre" type="xs:string" use="required" />
                <!-- <xs:attribute name="publicationdate"
                                     type="xs:unsignedShort" use="required" /> -->
                <xs:attribute name="ISBN" type="xs:string" use="required" />
              </xs:complexType>
            </xs:element>
          </xs:sequence>
        </xs:complexType>
      </xs:element>
    </xs:schema>
```

This schema was generated from the `books.xml` in Visual Studio. Notice that the `publicationdate` attribute has been commented out. This will cause the validation to fail.

The following is the code that uses the schema to validate the `books.xml` document:

```
private void button8_Click(object sender, EventArgs e)
{

 richTextBox1.Clear();
  XmlReaderSettings settings = new XmlReaderSettings();
  settings.Schemas.Add(null, "books.xsd");
  settings.ValidationType = ValidationType.Schema;
  settings.ValidationEventHandler +=
new System.Xml.Schema.ValidationEventHandler(settings_ValidationEventHandler);
  XmlReader rdr = XmlReader.Create("books.xml", settings);
  while (rdr.Read())
  {
    if (rdr.NodeType == XmlNodeType.Text)
      richTextBox1.AppendText(rdr.Value + "\r\n");
  }
}
```

After the `XmlReaderSettings` object setting is created, the schema `books.xsd` is added to the `XmlSchemaSet` object. The `Add` method for `XmlSchemaSet` has four overloads. One takes an `XmlSchema` object. The `XmlSchema` object can be used to create a schema on-the-fly without having to create the schema file on disk. Another overload takes another `XmlSchemaSet` object as a parameter. Another takes two string values: the first is the target namespace and the other is the URL for the XSD document. If the target namespace parameter is null, the `targetNamespace` of the schema will be used. The last overload takes the `targetNamespace` as the first parameter as well, but it used an `XmlReader`-based object to read in the schema. The `XmlSchemaSet` preprocesses the schema before the document to be validated is processed.

After the schema is referenced, the `XsdValidate` property is set to one of the `ValidationType` enumeration values. These valid values are `DTD`, `Schema`, or `None`. If the value selected is set to `None`, then no validation will occur.

Because the `XmlReader` object is being used, if there is a validation problem with the document, it will not be found until that attribute or element is read by the reader. When the validation failure does occur, an `XmlSchemaValidationException` is raised. This exception can be handled in a `catch` block; however, handling exceptions can make controlling the flow of the data difficult. To help with this, a ValidationEvent is available in the XmlReaderSettings class. This way, the validation failure can be handled without your having to use exception handling. The event is also raised by validation warnings, which do not raise an exception. The ValidationEvent passes in a ValidationEventArgs object that contains a Severity property. This property determines whether the event was raised by an error or a warning. If the event was raised by an error, the exception that caused the event to be raised is passed in as well. There is also a message property. In the example, the message is displayed in a MessageBox.

Using the XmlWriter Class

The XmlWriter class allows you write XML to a stream, a file, a StringBuilder, a TextWriter, or another XmlWriter object. Like XmlTextReader, it does so in a forward-only, non-cached manner. XmlWriter is highly configurable, allowing you to specify such things as whether or not to indent content, the amount to indent, what quote character to use in attribute values, and whether namespaces are supported. Like the XmlReader, this configuration is done using an XmlWriterSettings object.

Here's a simple example that shows how the XmlTextWriter class can be used:

```
private void button9_Click(object sender, EventArgs e)
{
  XmlWriterSettings settings = new XmlWriterSettings();
  settings.Indent = true;
  settings.NewLineOnAttributes = true;
  XmlWriter writer = XmlWriter.Create("newbook.xml", settings);
  writer.WriteStartDocument();
  //Start creating elements and attributes
  writer.WriteStartElement("book");
  writer.WriteAttributeString("genre", "Mystery");
  writer.WriteAttributeString("publicationdate", "2001");
  writer.WriteAttributeString("ISBN", "123456789");
  writer.WriteElementString("title", "Case of the Missing Cookie");
  writer.WriteStartElement("author");
  writer.WriteElementString("name", "Cookie Monster");
  writer.WriteEndElement();
  writer.WriteElementString("price", "9.99");
  writer.WriteEndElement();
  writer.WriteEndDocument();
  //clean up
  writer.Flush();
  writer.Close();
}
```

Here, you are writing to a new XML file called newbook.xml, adding the data for a new book. Note that XmlWriter will overwrite an existing file with a new one. You look at inserting a new element or node into an existing document later in this chapter. You are instantiating the XmlWriter object using the Create static method. In this example, a string representing a file name is passed as a parameter along with an instance of an XmlWriterSetting class.

The XmlWriterSettings class has properties that control the way that the XML is generated. The CheckedCharacters property is a Boolean that will raise an exception if a character in the XML does not conform to the W3C XML 1.0 recommendation. The Encoding class sets the encoding used for the XML being generated; the default is Encoding.UTF8. The Indent property is a Boolean value that determines if elements should be indented. The IndentChars property is set to the character string that it is used to indent. The default is two spaces. The `NewLine` property is used to determine the characters for line breaks. In the preceding example, the `NewLineOnAttribute` is set to `true`. This will put each attribute in a separate line, which can make the XML generated a little easier to read.

`WriteStartDocument()` adds the document declaration. Now you start writing data. First comes the `book` element; then you add the `genre`, `publicationdate`, and `ISBN` attributes. Then you write the `title`, `author`, and `price` elements. Note that the `author` element has a child element name.

When you click the button, you produce the `booknew.xml` file, which looks like this:

```
<?xml version="1.0" encoding="utf-8"?>
<book
  genre="Mystery"
  publicationdate="2001"
  ISBN="123456789">
  <title>Case of the Missing Cookie</title>
  <author>
    <name>Cookie Monster</name>
  </author>
  <price>9.99</price>
</book>
```

The nesting of elements is controlled by paying attention to when you start and finish writing elements and attributes. You can see this when you add the `name` child element to the `authors` element. Note how the `WriteStartElement()` and `WriteEndElement()` method calls are arranged and how that arrangement produces the nested elements in the output file.

To go along with the `WriteElementString()` and `WriteAttributeString()` methods, there are several other specialized write methods. `WriteCData()` outputs a `CData` section (`<!CDATA[...]]>`), writing out the text it takes as a parameter. `WriteComment()` writes out a comment in proper XML format. `WriteChars()` writes out the contents of a `char` buffer. This works in a similar fashion to the `ReadChars()` method that you looked at earlier; they both use the same type of parameters. `WriteChars()` needs a buffer (an array of characters), the starting position for writing (an integer), and the number of characters to write (an integer).

Reading and writing XML using the `XmlReader`- and `XmlWriter`-based classes are surprisingly flexible and simple to do. Next you'll learn how the DOM is implemented in the `System.Xml` namespace through the `XmlDocument` and `XmlNode` classes.

Using the DOM in .NET

The DOM implementation in .NET supports the W3C DOM Level 1 and Core DOM Level 2 specifications. The DOM is implemented through the `XmlNode` class, which is an abstract class that represents a node of an XML document.

There is also an `XmlNodeList` class, which is an ordered list of nodes. This is a live list of nodes, and any changes to any node are immediately reflected in the list. `XmlNodeList` supports indexed access or iterative access.

The `XmlNode` and `XmlNodeList` classes make up the core of the DOM implementation in the .NET Framework. The following table lists some of the classes that are based on `XmlNode`.

Class Name	Description
XmlLinkedNode	Returns the node immediately before or after the current node. Adds NextSibling and PreviousSibling properties to XmlNode.
XmlDocument	Represents the entire document. Implements the DOM Level 1 and Level 2 specifications.
XmlDocumentFragment	Represents a fragment of the document tree.
XmlAttribute	Represents an attribute object of an XmlElement object.
XmlEntity	Represents a parsed or unparsed entity node.
XmlNotation	Contains a notation declared in a DTD or schema.

The following table lists classes that extend XmlCharacterData.

Class Name	Description
XmlCDataSection	Represents a CData section of a document.
XmlComment	Represents an XML comment object.
XmlSignificantWhitespace	Represents a node with whitespace. Nodes are created only if the PreserveWhiteSpace flag is true.
XmlWhitespace	Represents whitespace in element content. Nodes are created only if the PreserveWhiteSpace flag is true.
XmlText	Represents the textual content of an element or attribute.

The following table lists classes that extend the XmlLinkedNode.

Class Name	Description
XmlDeclaration	Represents the declaration node (<?xml version='1.0'...>).
XmlDocumentType	Represents data relating to the document type declaration.
XmlElement	Represents an XML element object.
XmlEntityReferenceNode	Represents an entity reference node.
XmlProcessingInstruction	Contains an XML processing instruction.

As you can see, .NET makes available a class to fit just about any XML type that you might encounter. Because of this, you end up with a very flexible and powerful tool set. This section won't look at every class in detail, but you will see several examples to give you an idea of what you can accomplish.

Using the XmlDocument Class

`XmlDocument` and its derived class `XmlDataDocument` (discussed later in this chapter) are the classes that you will be using to represent the DOM in .NET. Unlike `XmlReader` and `XmlWriter`, `XmlDocument` gives you read and write capabilities as well as random access to the DOM tree. `XmlDocument` resembles the DOM implementation in MSXML. If you have experience programming with MSXML, you will feel comfortable using `XmlDocument`.

This section introduces an example that creates an `XmlDocument` object, loads a document from disk, and loads a text box with data from the title elements. This is similar to one of the examples that you constructed in the "Using the XmlReader Class" section. The difference here is that you will be selecting the nodes you want to work with, instead of going through the entire document as in the `XmlReader`-based example.

Here is the code to create an `XmlDocument` object. Notice how simple it looks in comparison to the `XmlReader` example:

```
private void button1_Click(object sender, System.EventArgs e)
{
//doc is declared at the module level
      //change path to math your path structure
      _doc.Load("books.xml");
      //get only the nodes that we want.
      XmlNodeList nodeLst = _doc.GetElementsByTagName("title");
      //iterate through the XmlNodeList
      textBox1.Text = "";
      foreach (XmlNode node in nodeLst)
      {
          textBox1.Text += node.OuterXml + "\r\n";
      }
}
```

Note that you also add the following declaration at the module level for the examples in this section:

```
private XmlDocument doc=new XmlDocument();
```

If this is all that you wanted to do, using the `XmlReader` would have been a much more efficient way to load the text box, because you just go through the document once and then you are finished with it. This is exactly the type of work that `XmlReader` was designed for. However, if you wanted to revisit a node, using `XmlDocument` is a better way.

Here is an example of using the XPath syntax to retrieve a set of nodes from the document.

```
private void button2_Click(object sender, EventArgs e)
{
  //doc is declared at the module level
  //change path to math your path structure
  doc.Load("books.xml");
  //get only the nodes that we want.
  XmlNodeList nodeLst = _doc.SelectNodes("/bookstore/book/title");
  textBox1.Text = "";
  //iterate through the XmlNodeList
  foreach (XmlNode node in nodeLst)
  {
      textBox1.Text += node.OuterXml + "\r\n";
  }
}
```

SelectNodes() returns a NodeList, or a collection of XmlNodes. The list contains only nodes that match the XPath statement passed in as the parameter SelectNodes. In this example, all you want to see are the title nodes. If you would have made the call to SelectSingleNode, then you would have received a single node object that contained the first node in the XmlDocument that matched the XPath criteria.

A quick comment regarding the SelectSingleNode() method: This is an XPath implementation in the XmlDocument class. Both the SelectSingleNode() and SelectNodes() methods are defined in XmlNode, which XmlDocument is based on. SelectSingleNode() returns an XmlNode and SelectNodes() returns an XmlNodeList. However, the System.Xml.XPath namespace contains a richer XPath implementation, and you look at that in a later section.

Inserting Nodes

Earlier, you looked at an example using XmlTextWriter that created a new document. The limitation was that it would not insert a node into a current document. With the XmlDocument class, you can do just that. Change the button1_Click() event handler from the last example to the following (DOMSample3 in the download code):

```
private void button4_Click(object sender, System.EventArgs e)
{
//change path to match your structure
      _doc.Load("books.xml");
      //create a new 'book' element
      XmlElement newBook = _doc.CreateElement("book");
      //set some attributes
      newBook.SetAttribute("genre", "Mystery");
      newBook.SetAttribute("publicationdate", "2001");
      newBook.SetAttribute("ISBN", "123456789");
      //create a new 'title' element
      XmlElement newTitle = _doc.CreateElement("title");
      newTitle.InnerText = "Case of the Missing Cookie";
      newBook.AppendChild(newTitle);
      //create new author element
      XmlElement newAuthor = _doc.CreateElement("author");
      newBook.AppendChild(newAuthor);
      //create new name element
      XmlElement newName = _doc.CreateElement("name");
      newName.InnerText = "Cookie Monster";
      newAuthor.AppendChild(newName);
      //create new price element
      XmlElement newPrice = _doc.CreateElement("price");
      newPrice.InnerText = "9.95";
      newBook.AppendChild(newPrice);
      //add to the current document
      _doc.DocumentElement.AppendChild(newBook);
      //write out the doc to disk
      XmlTextWriter tr = new XmlTextWriter("booksEdit.xml", null);
      tr.Formatting = Formatting.Indented;
      _doc.WriteContentTo(tr);
      tr.Close();
      //load listBox1 with all of the titles, including new one
      XmlNodeList nodeLst = _doc.GetElementsByTagName("title");
```

```
            textBox1.Text = "";
            foreach (XmlNode node in nodeLst)
            {
                textBox1.Text += node.OuterXml + "\r\n";
            }
    }
```

After executing this code, you end up with the same functionality as in the previous example, but there is one additional book in the text box, *The Case of the Missing Cookie* (a soon-to-be classic). If you look closely at the code, you can see that this is actually a fairly simple process. The first thing that you do is create a new `book` element:

```
XmlElement newBook = doc.CreateElement("book");
```

`CreateElement()` has three overloads that allow you to specify the following:

- The element name
- The name and namespace URI
- The prefix, localname, and namespace

Once the element is created you need to add attributes:

```
newBook.SetAttribute("genre","Mystery");
newBook.SetAttribute("publicationdate","2001");
newBook.SetAttribute("ISBN","123456789");
```

Now that you have the attributes created, you need to add the other elements of a book:

```
XmlElement newTitle = doc.CreateElement("title");
newTitle.InnerText = "The Case of the Missing Cookie";
newBook.AppendChild(newTitle);
```

Once again, you create a new `XmlElement`-based object (`newTitle`). Then you set the `InnerText` property to the title of our new classic, and append the element as a child to the `book` element. You repeat this for the rest of the elements in this `book` element. Note that you add the `name` element as a child to the `author` element. This will give you the proper nesting relationship, as in the other `book` elements.

Finally, you append the `newBook` element to the `doc.DocumentElement` node. This is the same level as all of the other `book` elements. You have now updated an existing document with a new element.

The last thing to do is to write the new XML document to disk. In this example, you create a new `XmlTextWriter` and pass it to the `WriteContentTo()` method. `WriteContentTo()` and `WriteTo()` both take an `XmlTextWriter` as a parameter. `WriteContentTo()` saves the current node and all of its children to the `XmlTextWriter`, whereas `WriteTo()` just saves the current node. Because `doc` is an `XmlDocument`-based object, it represents the entire document and so that is what is saved. You could also use the `Save()` method. It will always save the entire document. `Save()` has four overloads. You can specify a string with the file name and path, a `Stream`-based object, a `TextWriter`-based object, or an `XmlWriter`-based object.

You also call the `Close()` method on `XmlTextWriter` to flush the internal buffers and close the file.

Figure 28-1 shows what you get when you run this example. Notice the new entry at the bottom of the list.

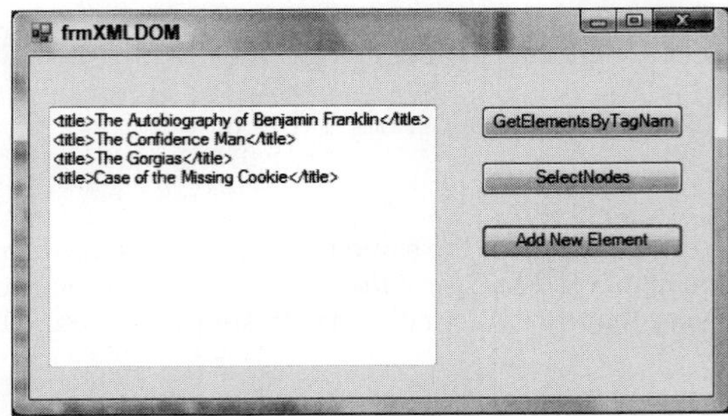

Figure 28-1

Earlier in the chapter, you saw how to create a document using the `XmlTextWriter` class. You can also use `XmlDocument`. Why would you use one in preference to the other? If the data that you want streamed to XML is available and ready to write, then the `XmlTextWriter` class is the best choice. However, if you need to build the XML document a little at a time, inserting nodes into various places, then creating the document with `XmlDocument` might be the better choice. You can accomplish this by changing the following line:

```
doc.Load("books.xml");
```

to this:

```
//create the declaration section
XmlDeclaration newDec = doc.CreateXmlDeclaration("1.0",null,null);
doc.AppendChild(newDec);
//create the new root element
XmlElement newRoot = doc.CreateElement("newBookstore");
doc.AppendChild(newRoot);
```

First, you create a new `XmlDeclaration`. The parameters are the version (always `1.0` for now), the encoding, and the standalone flag. The encoding parameter should be set to a string that is part of the `System.Text.Encoding` class if `null` isn't used (`null` defaults to UTF-8). The standalone flag can be either `yes`, `no`, or `null`. If it is `null`, the attribute is not used and will not be included in the document.

The next element that is created will become the `DocumentElement`. In this case, it is called `newBookstore` so that you can see the difference. The rest of the code is the same as in the previous example and works in the same way. This is `booksEdit.xml`, which is generated from the following code:

```
<?xml version="1.0"?>
<newBookstore>
   <book genre="Mystery" publicationdate="2001" ISBN="123456789">
      <title>The Case of the Missing Cookie</title>
      <author>
         <name>C. Monster</name>
      </author>
      <price>9.95</price>
   </book>
</newBookstore>
```

You will want to use the `XmlDocument` class when you want to have random access to the document, or the `XmlReader`-based classes when you want a streaming-type model instead. Remember that there is a cost for the flexibility of the `XmlNode`-based `XmlDocument` class — memory requirements are higher and the performance of reading the document is not as good as when using `XmlReader`. There is another way to traverse an XML document: the `XPathNavigator`.

Using XPathNavigators

An XPathNavigator is used to select, iterate, and sometimes edit data from an XML document. An XPathNavigator can be created from an XmlDocument to allow editing capabilities or from an XPathDocument for read-only use. Because the XPathDocument is read-only, it performs very well. Unlike the XmlReader, the XPathNavigator isn't a streaming model, so the same document can be used without having to re-read and parse.

The XPathNavigaor is part of the System.Xml.XPath namespace. XPath is a query language used to select specific nodes or elements from an XML document for processing.

The System.Xml.XPath Namespace

The System.Xml.XPath namespace is built for speed. It provides a read-only view of your XML documents, so there are no editing capabilities. Classes in this namespace are built to do fast iteration and selections on the XML document in a cursory fashion.

The following table lists the key classes in System.Xml.XPath and gives a short description of the purpose of each class.

Class Name	Description
XPathDocument	Provides a view of the entire XML document. Read-only.
XPathNavigator	Provides the navigational capabilities to an XPathDocument.
XPathNodeIterator	Provides iteration capabilities to a node set.
XPathExpression	Represents a compiled XPath expression. Used by SelectNodes, SelectSingleNodes, Evaluate, and Matches.
XPathException	An XPath exception class.

XPathDocument

XPathDocument doesn't offer any of the functionality of the XmlDocument class. Its sole purpose is to create XPathNavigators. As a matter of fact, that is the only method available on the XPathDocument class (other then those provided by Object).

An XPathDocument can be created in a number of different ways. You can pass in an XmlReader, a file name of an XML document or a Stream-based object to the constructor. This allows a great deal of flexibility. For example, you can use the XmlValidatingReader to validate the XML and then use that same object to create the XPathDocument.

XPathNavigator

XPathNavigator contains all of the methods for moving and selecting elements that you need. The following table lists some of the "move" methods defined in this class.

Method Name	Description
`MoveTo()`	Takes `XPathNavigator` as a parameter. Moves the current position to be the same as that passed in to `XPathNavigator`.
`MoveToAttribute()`	Moves to the named attribute. Takes the attribute name and namespace as parameters.
`MoveToFirstAttribute()`	Moves to the first attribute in the current element. Returns `true` if successful.
`MoveToNextAttribute()`	Moves to the next attribute in the current element. Returns `true` if successful.
`MoveToFirst()`	Moves to the first sibling in the current node. Returns `true` if successful; otherwise it returns `false`.
`MoveToLast()`	Moves to the last sibling in the current node. Returns `true` if successful.
`MoveToNext()`	Moves to the next sibling in the current node. Returns `true` if successful.
`MoveToPrevious()`	Moves to the previous sibling in the current node. Returns `true` if successful.
`MoveToFirstChild()`	Moves to the first child of the current element. Returns `true` if successful.
`MoveToId()`	Moves to the element with the ID supplied as a parameter. There needs to be a schema for the document, and the data type for the element must be of type `ID`.
`MoveToParent()`	Moves to the parent of the current node. Returns `true` if successful.
`MoveToRoot()`	Moves to the root node of the document.

In order to select a subset of the document you can use one of the Select methods listed in the following table.

Method Name	Description
`Select()`	Selects a node set using an XPath expression.
`SelectAncestors()`	Selects all of the ancestors of the current node based on an XPath expression.
`SelectChildren()`	Selects all of the children of the current node based on an XPath expression.
`SelectDescendants()`	Selects all of the descendants of the current node based on an XPath expression.
`SelectSingleNode()`	Selects one node based on an XPath expression.

If the XPathNavigator was created from an XPathDocument, it is read-only. If it is created from an XmlDocument, the XPathNavigator can be used to edit the document. This can be verified by checking the CanEdit property. If it is true, you can use one of the Insert methods. InsertBefore and InsertAfter will create a new node either before or after the current node. The source of the new node can be from an XmlReader or a string. Optionally, an XmlWriter can be returned and used to write the new node information.

Strongly typed values can be read from the nodes using the ValueAs properties. Notice that this is different from XmlReader, which used ReadValue methods.

XPathNodeIterator

XPathNodeIterator can be thought of as the equivalent of a NodeList or a NodeSet in XPath. This object has three properties and two methods:

- Clone — Creates a new copy of itself
- Count — Number of nodes in the XPathNodeIterator object
- Current — Returns an XPathNavigator pointing to the current node
- CurrentPosition() — Returns an integer with the current position
- MoveNext() — Moves to the next node that matches the XPath expression that created the XPathNodeIterator

The XPathNodeIterator is returned by the XPathNavigator Select methods. You use it to iterate over the set of nodes returned by a Select method of the XPathNavigator. Using the MoveNext method of the XPathNodeIterator does not change the location of the XPathNavigator that created it.

Using Classes from the XPath Namespace

The best way to see how these classes are used is to look at some code that iterates through the books.xml document. This will allow you to see how the navigation works. In order to use the examples, you first add a reference to the System.Xml.Xsl and System.Xml.XPath namespaces:

```
using System.Xml.XPath;
using System.Xml.Xsl;
```

For this example, you use the file booksxpath.xml. It is similar to the books.xml file that you have been using, except that there are a couple of extra books added. Here's the form code, which is part of the XmlSample project:

```
private void button1_Click(object sender, EventArgs e)
{
  //modify to match your path structure
  XPathDocument doc = new XPathDocument("books.xml");
  //create the XPath navigator
  XPathNavigator nav = ((IXPathNavigable)doc).CreateNavigator();
  //create the XPathNodeIterator of book nodes
  // that have genre attribute value of novel
  XPathNodeIterator iter = nav.Select("/bookstore/book[@genre='novel']");
  textBox1.Text = "";
  while (iter.MoveNext())
  {
    XPathNodeIterator newIter =
 iter.Current.SelectDescendants(XPathNodeType.Element, false);
```

(continued)

(continued)

```
        while (newIter.MoveNext())
        {
            textBox1.Text += newIter.Current.Name + ": " +
                newIter.Current.Value + "\r\n";
        }
    }
}
```

The first thing you do in the `button1_Click()` method is create the `XPathDocument` (called `doc`), passing in the file and path string of the document you want opened. The next line is where the `XPathNavigator` is created:

```
XPathNavigator nav = doc.CreateNavigator();
```

In the example, you can see that you use the `Select()` method to retrieve a set of nodes that all have `novel` as the value of the `genre` attribute. You then use the `MoveNext()` method to iterate through all of the novels in the book list.

To load the data into the list box, you use the `XPathNodeIterator.Current` property. This creates a new `XPathNavigator` object based on just the node that the `XPathNodeIterator` is pointing to. In this case, you are creating an `XPathNavigator` for one `book` node in the document.

The next loop takes this `XPathNavigator` and creates another `XPathNodeIterator` by issuing another type of select method, the `SelectDescendants()` method. This gives you an `XPathNodeIterator` of all of the child nodes and children of the child nodes of the `book` node.

Then you do another `MoveNext()` loop on the `XPathNodeIterator` and load the text box with the element names and element values.

Figure 28-2 shows what the screen looks like after running the code. Note that novels are the only books listed now.

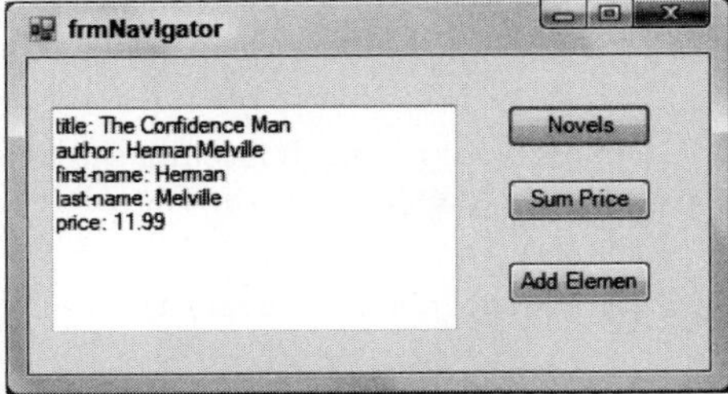

Figure 28-2

What if you wanted to add up the cost of these books? `XPathNavigator` includes the `Evaluate()` method for just this reason. `Evaluate()` has three overloads. The first one contains a string that is the XPath function call. The second overload uses the `XPathExpression` object as a parameter, and the third uses `XPathExpression` and an `XPathNodeIterator` as parameters. The following code is similar to the previous example, except this time all of the nodes in the document are iterated. The `Evaluate` method call at the end totals up the cost of all of the books:

```
private void button2_Click(object sender, EventArgs e)
{
  //modify to match your path structure
  XPathDocument doc = new XPathDocument("books.xml");
  //create the XPath navigator
  XPathNavigator nav = ((IXPathNavigable)doc).CreateNavigator();
```

```
    //create the XPathNodeIterator of book nodes
    XPathNodeIterator iter = nav.Select("/bookstore/book");
    textBox1.Text = "";
    while (iter.MoveNext())
    {
      XPathNodeIterator newIter =
  iter.Current.SelectDescendants(XPathNodeType.Element, false);
      while (newIter.MoveNext())
      {
        textBox1.Text += newIter.Current.Name + ": " + newIter.Current.Value +
  "\r\n";
      }
    }
    textBox1.Text += "=========================" + "\r\n";
    textBox1.Text += "Total Cost = " + nav.Evaluate("sum(/bookstore/book/price)");
  }
```

This time, you see the total cost of the books evaluated in the text box (see Figure 28-3).

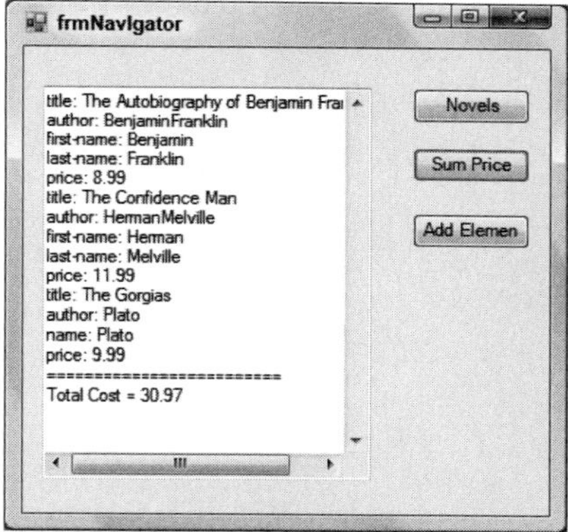

Figure 28-3

Now let's say that you need to add a node for discount. You can use the `InsertAfter` method to get this done fairly easily. Here is the code:

```
private void button3_Click(object sender, EventArgs e)
{
  XmlDocument doc = new XmlDocument();
  doc.Load("books.xml");
  XPathNavigator nav = doc.CreateNavigator();

  if (nav.CanEdit)
  {
    XPathNodeIterator iter = nav.Select("/bookstore/book/price");
    while (iter.MoveNext())
    {
      iter.Current.InsertAfter("<disc>5</disc>");
    }
  }
  doc.Save("newbooks.xml");
}
```

Here, you add the <disc>5</disc> element after the price elements. First, all of the price nodes are selected. The XPathNodeIterator is used to iterate over the nodes and the new node is inserted. The modified document is saved with a new name, newbooks.xml. The new version looks like the following:

```
<?xml version="1.0"?>
<!-- This file represents a fragment of a book store inventory database -->
<bookstore>
  <book genre="autobiography" publicationdate="1991" ISBN="1-861003-11-0">
    <title>The Autobiography of Benjamin Franklin</title>
    <author>
      <first-name>Benjamin</first-name>
      <last-name>Franklin</last-name>
    </author>
    <price>8.99</price>
    <disc>5</disc>
  </book>
  <book genre="novel" publicationdate="1967" ISBN="0-201-63361-2">
    <title>The Confidence Man</title>
    <author>
      <first-name>Herman</first-name>
      <last-name>Melville</last-name>
    </author>
    <price>11.99</price>
    <disc>5</disc>
  </book>
  <book genre="philosophy" publicationdate="1991" ISBN="1-861001-57-6">
    <title>The Gorgias</title>
    <author>
      <name>Plato</name>
    </author>
    <price>9.99</price>
    <disc>5</disc>
  </book>
</bookstore>
```

Nodes can be inserted before or after a selected node. The nodes can also be changed, and they can be deleted. If you have changes that have to be done to large numbers of nodes, using the XPathNavigator created from an XmlDocument may be your best choice.

The System.Xml.Xsl Namespace

The System.Xml.Xsl namespace contains the classes that the .NET Framework uses to support XSL transforms. The contents of this namespace are available to any store whose classes implement the IXPathNavigable interface. In the .NET Framework, that would currently include XmlDocument, XmlDataDocument, and XPathDocument. Again, just as with XPath, use the store that makes the most sense. If you plan to create a custom store, such as one using the file system and you want to be able to do transforms, be sure to implement the IXPathNavigable interface in your class.

XSLT is based on a streaming pull model. Because of this, you can chain several transforms together. You could even apply a custom reader between transforms if needed. This allows a great deal of flexibility in design.

Transforming XML

The first example you look at takes the `books.xml` document and transforms it into a simple HTML document for display using the XSLT file `books.xsl`. (This code is in the `XSLSample` folder.) You will need to add the following `using` statements:

```
using System.IO;
using System.Xml.Xsl;
using System.Xml.XPath;
```

The following is the code to perform the transform:

```
private void button1_Click(object sender, EventArgs e)
{
  XslCompiledTransform trans = new XslCompiledTransform();
  trans.Load("books.xsl");
  trans.Transform("books.xml", "out.html");
  webBrowser1.Navigate(AppDomain.CurrentDomain.BaseDirectory + "out.html");
}
```

A transform doesn't get any simpler than this. First, a new `XmlCompiledTransform` object is created. It loads the `books.xsl` transform document and then performs the transform. In this example, a string with the file name is used as the input. The output is `out.html`. This file is then loaded into the Web browser control used on the form. Instead of the file name `books.xml` as the input document, you can also use an `IXPathNavigable`-based object. This would be any object that can create an `XPathNavigator`.

After the `XmlCompiledTransform` object is created and the stylesheet is loaded, the transform is performed. The `Transform` method can take just about any combination of `IXPathNavigable objects`, `Streams`, `TextWriters`, `XmlWriters`, and URIs as parameters. This allows a great deal of flexibility on transform flow. You can pass the output of one transform in as the input to the next transform.

`XsltArgumentLists` and `XmlResolver` objects are also included in the parameter options. We look at the `XsltArgumentList` object in the next section. `XmlResolver`-based objects are used to resolve items that are external to the current document. This could be things such as schemas, credentials and, of course, stylesheets.

The `books.xsl` document is a fairly straightforward stylesheet. The document looks like this:

```
<xsl:stylesheet version="1.0"
                      xmlns:xsl="http://www.w3.org/1999/XSL/Transform">
<xsl:template match="/">
   <html>
      <head>
         <title>Price List</title>
      </head>
      <body>
         <table>
            <xsl:apply-templates/>
         </table>
      </body>
   </html>
    </xsl:template>
   <xsl:template match="bookstore">
      <xsl:apply-templates select="book"/>
```

(continued)

(continued)

```
    </xsl:template>
    <xsl:template match="book">
        <tr><td>
            <xsl:value-of select="title"/>
        </td><td>
            <xsl:value-of select="price"/>
        </td></tr>
    </xsl:template>
</xsl:stylesheet>
```

Using XsltArgumentList

`XsltArgumentList` is a way that you can bind an object with methods to a namespace. Once this is done, you can invoke the methods during the transform. Here's an example:

```
private void button3_Click(object sender, EventArgs e)
{
  //new XPathDocument
  XPathDocument doc = new XPathDocument("books.xml");
  //new XslTransform
  XslCompiledTransform trans = new XslCompiledTransform();
  trans.Load("booksarg.xsl");
  //new XmlTextWriter since we are creating a new xml document
  XmlWriter xw = new XmlTextWriter("argSample.xml", null);
  //create the XslArgumentList and new BookUtils object
  XsltArgumentList argBook = new XsltArgumentList();
  BookUtils bu = new BookUtils();
  //this tells the argumentlist about BookUtils
  argBook.AddExtensionObject("urn:XslSample", bu);
  //new XPathNavigator
  XPathNavigator nav = doc.CreateNavigator();
  //do the transform
  trans.Transform(nav, argBook, xw);
  xw.Close();
  webBrowser1.Navigate(AppDomain.CurrentDomain.BaseDirectory + "argSample.xml");
}
```

The following is the code for the `BooksUtil` class. This is the class that will be called from the transform:

```
class BookUtils
{
  public BookUtils() { }

  public string ShowText()
  {
    return "This came from the ShowText method!";
  }
}
```

The following is what the output of the transform looks like; the output has been formatted for easier viewing (`argSample.xml`):

```
<books>
    <discbook>
        <booktitle>The Autobiography of Benjamin Franklin</booktitle>
        <showtext>This came from the ShowText method!</showtext>
```

```
    </discbook>
    <discbook>
       <booktitle>The Confidence Man</booktitle>
       <showtext>This came from the ShowText method!</showtext>
    </discbook>
    <discbook>
       <booktitle>The Gorgias</booktitle>
       <showtext>This came from the ShowText method!</showtext>
    </discbook>
    <discbook>
       <booktitle>The Great Cookie Caper</booktitle>
       <showtext>This came from the ShowText method!</showtext>
    </discbook>
    <discbook>
       <booktitle>A Really Great Book</booktitle>
       <showtext>This came from the ShowText method!</showtext>
    </discbook>
</books>
```

In this example, you define a new class, BookUtils. In this class, you have one rather useless method that returns the string This came from the ShowText method! In the button3_Click() event, you create the XPathDocument and XslTransform objects. In a previous example, you loaded the XML document and the transform document directly into the XslCompiledTransform object. This time, you will use the XPathNavigator to load the documents.

Next, you need to do the following:

```
XsltArgumentList argBook=new XsltArgumentList();
BookUtils bu=new BookUtils();
argBook.AddExtensionObject("urn:XslSample",bu);
```

This is where you create the XsltArgumentList object. You create an instance of the BookUtils object, and when you call the AddExtensionObject() method, you pass in a namespace for your extension and the object that you want to be able to call methods from. When you make the Transform() call, you pass in the XsltArgumentList (argBook) along with the XPathNavigator and the XmlWriter object you made.

The following is the booksarg.xsl document (based on books.xsl):

```
<xsl:stylesheet version="1.0" xmlns:xsl="http://www.w3.org/1999/XSL/Transform"
   xmlns:bookUtil="urn:XslSample">
   <xsl:output method="xml" indent="yes"/>

   <xsl:template match="/">
      <xsl:element name="books">
         <xsl:apply-templates/>
      </xsl:element>
   </xsl:template>
   <xsl:template match="bookstore">
      <xsl:apply-templates select="book"/>
   </xsl:template>
   <xsl:template match="book">
      <xsl:element name="discbook">
         <xsl:element name="booktitle">
```

(continued)

(continued)

```
                <xsl:value-of select="title"/>
            </xsl:element>
            <xsl:element name="showtext">
                <xsl:value-of select="bookUtil:ShowText()"/>
            </xsl:element>
        </xsl:element>
    </xsl:template>
</xsl:stylesheet>
```

The two important new lines are highlighted. First, you add the namespace that you created when you added the object to `XsltArgumentList`. Then when you want to make the method call, you use standard XSLT namespace prefixing syntax and make the method call.

Another way you could have accomplished this is with XSLT scripting. You can include C#, Visual Basic, and JavaScript code in the stylesheet. The great thing about this is that unlike current non-.NET implementations, the script is compiled at the `XslTransform.Load()` call; this way, you are executing already compiled scripts.

Go ahead and modify the previous XSLT file in this way. First, you add the script to the stylesheet. You can see the following changes in `booksscript.xsl`:

```
<xsl:stylesheet version="1.0" xmlns:xsl="http://www.w3.org/1999/XSL/Transform"
                              xmlns:msxsl="urn:schemas-microsoft-com:xslt"
                              xmlns:user="http://wrox.com">

   <msxsl:script language="C#" implements-prefix="user">

      string ShowText()
         {
            return "This came from the ShowText method!";

         }
   </msxsl:script>
   <xsl:output method="xml" indent="yes"/>
      <xsl:template match="/">
   <xsl:element name="books">
      <xsl:apply-templates/>
   </xsl:element>
      </xsl:template>
   <xsl:template match="bookstore">
      <xsl:apply-templates select="book"/>
   </xsl:template>
      <xsl:template match="book">
      <xsl:element name="discbook">
      <xsl:element name="booktitle">
         <xsl:value-of select="title"/>
      </xsl:element>
      <xsl:element name="showtext">
        <xsl:value-of select="user:ShowText()"/>
      </xsl:element>
    </xsl:element>
   </xsl:template>
</xsl:stylesheet>
```

Once again, the changes are highlighted. You set the scripting namespace, add the code (which was copied and pasted in from the Visual Studio .NET IDE), and make the call in the stylesheet. The output looks the same as that of the previous example.

Debugging XSLT

Visual Studio 2008 has the capability to debug transforms. You can actually step through a transform line by line, inspect variables, access the call stack, and set break points just like you were debugging C# source code. You can debug a transform in two ways: by just using the stylesheet and input XML file or by running the application that the transform belongs to.

Debugging Without the Application

When you first start creating the transforms, sometimes you don't really want to run through the entire application. You just want to get a stylesheet working. Visual Studio 2008 allows you to do this using the XSLT editor.

Load the `books.xsl` stylesheet into the Visual Studio 2008 XSLT editor. Set a break point on the following line:

```
<xsl:value-of select="title"/>
```

Now select the XML menu and then Debug XSLT. You will be asked for the input XML document. This is the XML that you will want transformed. Now under the default configuration the next thing you will see is in Figure 28-4.

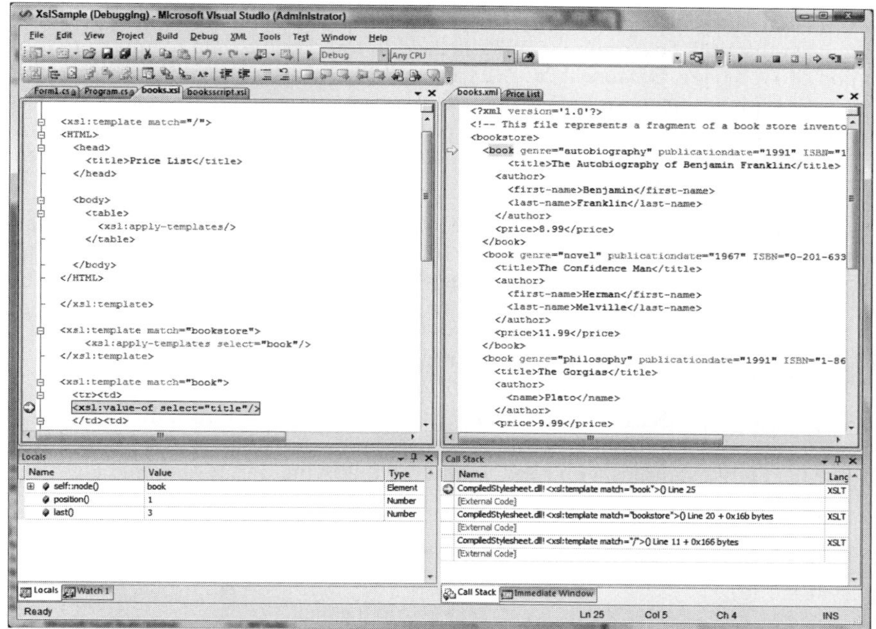

Figure 28-4

Now that the transform has been paused, you can explore almost all of the same debug information you can when debugging source code. Notice that the debugger is showing you the XSLT, the input document with the current element highlighted and the output of the transform. Now you can step through the transform line by line. If your XSLT had any scripting, you could also set breakpoints in the scripts and have the same debugging experience.

Debugging with the Application

If you want to debug a transform and the application at the same time, then you will have to make one small change when you create the `XslCompiledTransform` object. The constructor has an overload that takes a Boolean as a parameter. This parameter is `enableDebug`. The default is false, which means that even if you have a breakpoint set in the transform, if you run the application code that calls the transform, it will not break. If you set the parameter to true, the debug information for the CSLT is generated and the break point will be hit. So in the previous example, the line of code that created the `XlsCompiledTransform` would change to this:

```
XslCompiledTransform trans = new XslCompiledTransform(true);
```

Now when the application is run in debug mode, even the XSLT will have debug information and you will again have the full Visual Studio debugging experience in your stylesheets.

To summarize, the key thing to keep in mind when performing transforms is to remember to use the proper XML data store. Use `XPathDocument` if you don't need editing capabilities, `XmlDataDocument` if you're getting your data from ADO.NET, and `XmlDocument` if you need to be able to edit the data. In each case, you are dealing with the same process.

XML and ADO.NET

XML is the glue that binds ADO.NET to the rest of the world. ADO.NET was designed from the ground up to work within the XML environment. XML is used to transfer the data to and from the data store and the application or Web page. Because ADO.NET uses XML as the transport in remoting scenarios, data can be exchanged with applications and systems that are not even aware of ADO.NET. Because of the importance of XML in ADO.NET, there are some powerful features in ADO.NET that allow the reading and writing of XML documents. The `System.Xml` namespace also contains classes that can consume or utilize ADO.NET relational data.

The database that is used for the examples is from the AdventureWorksLT sample application. The sample database can be downloaded from `codeplex.com/SqlServerSamples`. Note that there are several versions of the AdventureWorks database. Most will work, but the LT version is the simplified version and is more than adequate for the purposes of this chapter.

Converting ADO.NET Data to XML

The first example uses ADO.NET, streams, and XML to pull some data from the database into a `DataSet`, load an `XmlDocument` object with the XML from the `DataSet`, and load the XML into a text box. To run the next few examples, you need to add the following `using` statements:

```
using System.Data;
using System.Xml;
using System.Data.SqlClient;
using System.IO;
```

The connection string is defined as a module-level variable.

```
string _connectString = "Server=.\\SQLExpress;
                            Database=adventureworkslt;Trusted_Connection=Yes";
```

The ADO.NET samples have a `DataGrid` object added to the forms. This will allow you to see the data in the ADO.NET `DataSet` because it is bound to the grid, as well as the data from the generated XML documents that you load in the text box. Here is the code for the first example. The first step in the examples is to create the standard ADO.NET objects to create a dataset. After the dataset has been created, it is bound to the grid.

```
private void button1_Click(object sender, EventArgs e)
{
  XmlDocument doc = new XmlDocument();
  DataSet ds = new DataSet("XMLProducts");
  SqlConnection conn = new SqlConnection(_connectString);
  SqlDataAdapter da = new SqlDataAdapter
                   ("SELECT Name, StandardCost FROM SalesLT.Product", conn);
  //fill the dataset
  da.Fill(ds, "Products");
  //load data into grid
  dataGridView1.DataSource = ds.Tables["Products"];
```

After you create the ADO.Net objects and bind to the grid, you instantiate a `MemoryStream` object, a `StreamReader` object, and a `StreamWriter` object. The `StreamReader` and `StreamWriter` objects will use the `MemoryStream` to move the XML around:

```
MemoryStream memStrm=new MemoryStream();
StreamReader strmRead=new StreamReader(memStrm);
StreamWriter strmWrite=new StreamWriter(memStrm);
```

You use a `MemoryStream` so that you don't have to write anything to disk; however, you could have used any object that was based on the `Stream` class, such as `FileStream`.

This next step is where the XML is generated. You call the `WriteXml()` method from the `DataSet` class. This method generates an XML document. `WriteXml()` has two overloads: one takes a string with the file path and name, and the other adds a mode parameter. This mode is an `XmlWriteMode` enumeration, with the following possible values:

- `IgnoreSchema`
- `WriteSchema`
- `DiffGram`

`IgnoreSchema` is used if you don't want `WriteXml()` to write an inline schema at the start of your XML file; use the `WriteSchema` parameter if you do want one. A DiffGram shows the data before and after an edit in a DataSet.

```
    //write the xml from the dataset to the memory stream
  ds.WriteXml(strmWrite, XmlWriteMode.IgnoreSchema);
  memStrm.Seek(0, SeekOrigin.Begin);
  //read from the memory stream to a XmlDocument object
  doc.Load(strmRead);
  //get all of the products elements
  XmlNodeList nodeLst = doc.SelectNodes("//XMLProducts/Products");
  textBox1.Text = "";

  foreach (XmlNode node in nodeLst)
  {
    textBox1.Text += node.InnerXml + "\r\n";
  }
```

Figure 28-5 shows the data in the list as well as the bound data grid.

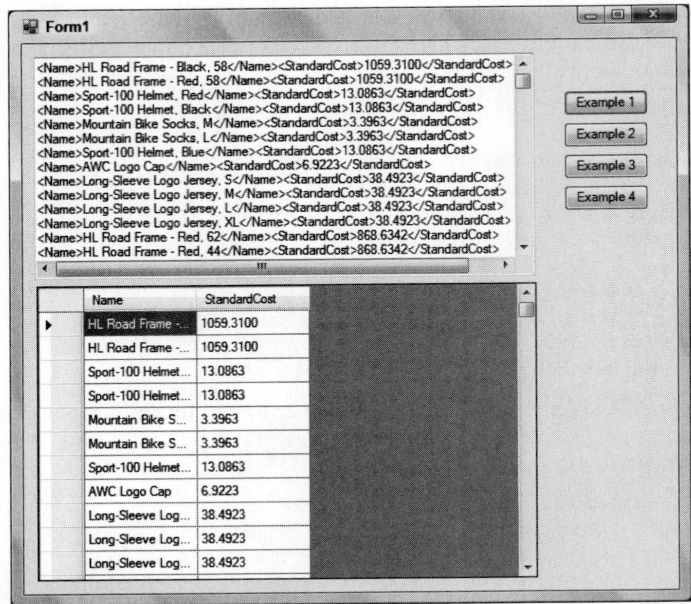

Figure 28-5

If you had wanted only the schema, you could have called `WriteXmlSchema()` instead of `WriteXml()`. This method has four overloads. One takes a string, which is the path and file name of where to write the XML document. The second overload uses an object that is based on the `XmlWriter` class. The third overload uses an object based on the `TextWriter` class. The fourth overload is derived from the `Stream` class.

Also, if you wanted to persist the XML document to disk, you would have used something like this:

```
string file = "c:\\test\\product.xml";
ds.WriteXml(file);
```

This would give you a well-formed XML document on disk that could be read in by another stream, or by `DataSet`, or used by another application or Web site. Because no `XmlMode` parameter is specified, this `XmlDocument` would have the schema included. In this example, you use the stream as a parameter to the `XmlDocument.Load()` method.

You now have two views of the data, but more important, you can manipulate the data using two different models. You can use the `System.Data` namespace to use the data, or you can use the `System.Xml` namespace on the data. This can lead to some very flexible designs in your applications, because now you are not tied to just one object model to program with. This is the real power to the ADO.NET and `System.Xml` combination. You have multiple views of the same data and multiple ways to access the data.

The following example simplifies the process by eliminating the three streams and by using some of the ADO capabilities built into the `System.Xml` namespace. You will need to change the module-level line of code:

```
private XmlDocument doc = new XmlDocument();
```

to:

```
private XmlDataDocument doc;
```

You need this because you are now using the `XmlDataDocument`. Here is the code (which you can find in the `ADOSample2` folder):

```
private void button3_Click(object sender, EventArgs e)
{
  XmlDataDocument doc;
  //create a dataset
  DataSet ds = new DataSet("XMLProducts");
  //connect to the northwind database and
  //select all of the rows from products table
  SqlConnection conn = new SqlConnection(_connectString);
  SqlDataAdapter da = new SqlDataAdapter
                   ("SELECT Name, StandardCost FROM SalesLT.Product", conn);
  //fill the dataset
  da.Fill(ds, "Products");
  ds.WriteXml("sample.xml", XmlWriteMode.WriteSchema);
  //load data into grid
  dataGridView1.DataSource = ds.Tables[0];
  doc = new XmlDataDocument(ds);
  //get all of the products elements
  XmlNodeList nodeLst = doc.GetElementsByTagName("Products");
  textBox1.Text = "";
  foreach (XmlNode node in nodeLst)
  {
    textBox1.Text += node.InnerXml + "\r\n";
  }
}
```

As you can see, the code to load the `DataSet` object into the XML document has been simplified. Instead of using the `XmlDocument` class, you are using the `XmlDataDocument` class. This class was built specifically for using data with a `DataSet` object.

The `XmlDataDocument` is based on the `XmlDocument` class, so it has all of the functionality that the `XmlDocument` class has. One of the main differences is the overloaded constructor that the `XmlDataDocument` has. Note the line of code that instantiates `XmlDataDocument` (`doc`):

```
doc = new XmlDataDocument(ds);
```

It passes in the `DataSet` object that you created, `ds`, as a parameter. This creates the XML document from the `DataSet`, and you don't have to use the `Load()` method. In fact, if you instantiate a new `XmlDataDocument` object without passing in a `DataSet` as the parameter, it will contain a `DataSet` with the name `NewDataSet` that has no `DataTables` in the `tables` collection. There is also a `DataSet` property, which you can set after an `XmlDataDocument`-based object is created.

Suppose that you add the following line of code after the `DataSet.Fill()` call:

```
ds.WriteXml("c:\\test\\sample.xml", XmlWriteMode.WriteSchema);
```

In this case, the following XML file, `sample.xml`, is produced in the folder `c:\test`:

```
<?xml version="1.0" standalone="yes"?>
<XMLProducts>
  <xs:schema id="XMLProducts" xmlns="" xmlns:xs="http://www.w3.org/2001/XMLSchema"
xmlns:msdata="urn:schemas-microsoft-com:xml-msdata">
    <xs:element name="XMLProducts" msdata:IsDataSet="true" msdata:
UseCurrentLocale="true">
      <xs:complexType>
```

(continued)

(continued)

```
        <xs:choice minOccurs="0" maxOccurs="unbounded">
          <xs:element name="Products">
            <xs:complexType>
              <xs:sequence>
                <xs:element name="Name" type="xs:string" minOccurs="0" />
                <xs:element name="StandardCost" type="xs:decimal" minOccurs="0" />
              </xs:sequence>
            </xs:complexType>
          </xs:element>
        </xs:choice>
      </xs:complexType>
    </xs:element>
  </xs:schema>
  <Products>
    <Name>HL Road Frame - Black, 58</Name>
    <StandardCost>1059.3100</StandardCost>
  </Products>
  <Products>
    <Name>HL Road Frame - Red, 58</Name>
    <StandardCost>1059.3100</StandardCost>
  </Products>
  <Products>
    <Name>Sport-100 Helmet, Red</Name>
    <StandardCost>13.0863</StandardCost>
  </Products>
</XMLProducts>
```

Only the first couple of `Products` elements are shown. The actual XML file would contain all of the products in the Products table of Northwind database.

Converting Relational Data

This looks simple enough for a single table, but what about relational data, such as multiple `DataTables` and `Relations` in the `DataSet`? It all still works the same way. Here is an example using two related tables:

```
private void button5_Click(object sender, EventArgs e)
{
  XmlDocument doc = new XmlDocument();
  DataSet ds = new DataSet("XMLProducts");
  SqlConnection conn = new SqlConnection(_connectString);
  SqlDataAdapter daProduct = new SqlDataAdapter
  ("SELECT Name, StandardCost, ProductCategoryID FROM SalesLT.Product", conn);
  SqlDataAdapter daCategory = new SqlDataAdapter
        ("SELECT ProductCategoryID, Name from SalesLT.ProductCategory", conn);
  //Fill DataSet from both SqlAdapters
  daProduct.Fill(ds, "Products");
  daCategory.Fill(ds, "Categories");
  //Add the relation
  ds.Relations.Add(ds.Tables["Categories"].Columns["ProductCategoryID"],
  ds.Tables["Products"].Columns["ProductCategoryID"]);
  //Write the Xml to a file so we can look at it later
  ds.WriteXml("Products.xml", XmlWriteMode.WriteSchema);
  //load data into grid
  dataGridView1.DataSource = ds.Tables[0];
```

```
        //create the XmlDataDocument
        doc = new XmlDataDocument(ds);
        //Select the productname elements and load them in the grid
        XmlNodeList nodeLst = doc.SelectNodes("//XMLProducts/Products");
        textBox1.Text = "";
        foreach (XmlNode node in nodeLst)
        {
          textBox1.Text += node.InnerXml + "\r\n";
        }
    }
```

In this sample you are creating, two `DataTables` in the `XMLProducts` `DataSet`: `Products` and `Categories`. You create a new relation on the `ProductCategoryID` column in both tables.

By making the same `WriteXml()` method call that you did in the previous example, you will get the following XML file (`SuppProd.xml`):

```
<?xml version="1.0" standalone="yes"?>
<XMLProducts>
  <xs:schema id="XMLProducts" xmlns="" xmlns:xs="http://www.w3.org/2001/XMLSchema"
xmlns:msdata="urn:schemas-microsoft-com:xml-msdata">
    <xs:element name="XMLProducts" msdata:IsDataSet="true"
msdata:UseCurrentLocale="true">
      <xs:complexType>
        <xs:choice minOccurs="0" maxOccurs="unbounded">
          <xs:element name="Products">
            <xs:complexType>
              <xs:sequence>
                <xs:element name="Name" type="xs:string" minOccurs="0" />
                <xs:element name="StandardCost" type="xs:decimal" minOccurs="0" />
                <xs:element name="ProductCategoryID" type="xs:int" minOccurs="0" />
              </xs:sequence>
            </xs:complexType>
          </xs:element>
          <xs:element name="Categories">
            <xs:complexType>
              <xs:sequence>
                <xs:element name="ProductCategoryID" type="xs:int" minOccurs="0" />
                <xs:element name="Name" type="xs:string" minOccurs="0" />
              </xs:sequence>
            </xs:complexType>
          </xs:element>
        </xs:choice>
      </xs:complexType>
      <xs:unique name="Constraint1">
        <xs:selector xpath=".//Categories" />
        <xs:field xpath="ProductCategoryID" />
      </xs:unique>
      <xs:keyref name="Relation1" refer="Constraint1">
        <xs:selector xpath=".//Products" />
        <xs:field xpath="ProductCategoryID" />
      </xs:keyref>
    </xs:element>
```

(continued)

(continued)

```
    </xs:schema>
    <Products>
      <Name>HL Road Frame - Black, 58</Name>
      <StandardCost>1059.3100</StandardCost>
      <ProductCategoryID>18</ProductCategoryID>
    </Products>
    <Products>
      <Name>HL Road Frame - Red, 58</Name>
      <StandardCost>1059.3100</StandardCost>
      <ProductCategoryID>18</ProductCategoryID>
    </Products>
  </XMLProducts>
```

The schema includes both `DataTables` that were in the `DataSet`. In addition, the data includes all of the data from both tables. For the sake of brevity, only the first `Products` and `ProductCategory` records are shown here. As before, you could have saved just the schema or just the data by passing in the correct `XmlWriteMode` parameter.

Converting XML to ADO.NET Data

Suppose that you have an XML document that you would like to get into an ADO.NET `DataSet`. You would want to do this so that you could load the XML into a database, or perhaps bind the data to a .NET data control such as a `DataGrid`. This way, you could actually use the XML document as your data store and eliminate the overhead of the database altogether. If your data is reasonably small in size, this is an attractive possibility. Here is some code to get you started (`ADOSample5`):

```
private void button7_Click(object sender, EventArgs e)
{
//create the DataSet
DataSet ds = new DataSet("XMLProducts");
//read in the xml document
ds.ReadXml("Products.xml");
//load data into grid
dataGridView1.DataSource = ds.Tables[0];
        textBox1.Text = "";
foreach (DataTable dt in ds.Tables)
{
            textBox1.Text += dt.TableName + "\r\n";
foreach (DataColumn col in dt.Columns)
{
textBox1.Text += "\t" + col.ColumnName + " - " + col.DataType.FullName + "\r\n";
}
}
}
```

It is that easy. You instantiate a new `DataSet` object. Then you call the `ReadXml()` method, and you have XML in a `DataTable` in your `DataSet`. As with the `WriteXml()` methods, `ReadXml()` has an `XmlReadMode` parameter. `ReadXml()` has a few more options in the `XmlReadMode`, as shown in the following table.

Value	Description
Auto	Sets the XmlReadMode to the most appropriate setting. If the data is in DiffGram format, DiffGram is selected. If a schema has already been read, or an inline schema is detected, then ReadSchema is selected. If no schema has been assigned to the DataSet, and none is detected inline, then IgnoreSchema is selected.
DiffGram	Reads in the DiffGram and applies the changes to the DataSet.
Fragment	Reads documents that contain XDR schema fragments, such as the type created by SQL Server.
IgnoreSchema	Ignores any inline schema that may be found. Reads data into the current DataSet schema. If data does not match DataSet schema, it is discarded.
InferSchema	Ignores any inline schema. Creates the schema based on data in the XML document. If a schema exists in the DataSet, that schema is used, and extended with additional columns and tables if needed. An exception is thrown if a column exists but is of a different data type.
ReadSchema	Reads the inline schema and loads the data. Will not overwrite a schema in the DataSet but will throw an exception if a table in the inline schema already exists in the DataSet.

There is also the ReadXmlSchema() method. This reads in a standalone schema and creates the tables, columns, and relations. You use this if your schema is not inline with your data. ReadXmlSchema() has the same four overloads: a string with file and path name, a Stream-based object, a TextReader-based object, and an XmlReader-based object.

To show that the data tables are getting created properly we iterate through the tables and columns and display the names in the text box. You can compare this to the database and see that all is well. The last foreach loops perform this task.

Figure 28-6 shows the output.

Looking at the list box, you can check that the data tables were created with the columns all having the correct names and data types.

Something else you might want to note is that because the previous two examples didn't transfer any data to or from a database, no SqlDataAdapter or SqlConnection was defined. This shows the real flexibility of both the System.Xml namespace and ADO.NET: You can look at the same data in multiple formats. If you need to do a transform and show the data in HTML format, or if you need to bind the data to a grid, you can take the same data and, with just a method call, have it in the required format.

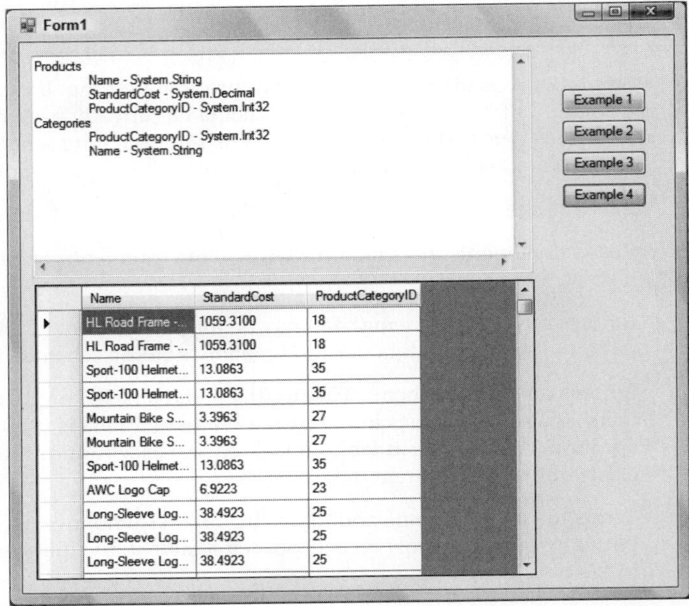

Figure 28-6

Serializing Objects in XML

Serializing is the process of persisting an object to disk. Another part of your application, or even a separate application, can deserialize the object and it will be in the same state it was in prior to serialization. The .NET Framework includes a couple of ways to do this.

This section looks at the `System.Xml.Serialization` namespace, which contains classes used to serialize objects into XML documents or streams. This means that an object's public properties and public fields are converted into XML elements or attributes or both.

The most important class in the `System.Xml.Serialization` namespace is `XmlSerializer`. To serialize an object, you first need to instantiate an `XmlSerializer` object, specifying the type of the object to serialize. Then you need to instantiate a stream/writer object to write the file to a stream/document. The final step is to call the `Serialize()` method on the `XMLSerializer`, passing it the stream/writer object and the object to serialize.

Data that can be serialized can be primitive types, fields, arrays, and embedded XML in the form of `XmlElement` and `XmlAttribute` objects.

To deserialize an object from an XML document, you reverse the process in the previous example. You create a stream/reader and an `XmlSerializer` object and then pass the stream/reader to the `Deserialize()` method. This method returns the deserialized object, although it needs to be cast to the correct type.

The XML serializer cannot convert private data, only public data, and it cannot serialize object graphs.

However, these should not be serious limitations; by carefully designing your classes, they should be easily avoided. If you do need to be able to serialize public and private data as well as an object graph containing many nested objects, you will want to use the `System.Runtime.Serialization.Formatters.Binary` namespace.

Some of the other tasks that you can accomplish with `System.Xml.Serialization` classes are:

- Determine if the data should be an attribute or element
- Specify the namespace
- Change the attribute or element name

The links between your object and the XML document are the custom C# attributes that annotate your classes. These attributes are what are used to inform the serializer how to write out the data. The `xsd.exe` tool, which is included with the .NET Framework, can help create these attributes for you. `xsd.exe` can do the following:

- Generate an XML schema from an XDR schema file
- Generate an XML schema from an XML file
- Generate `DataSet` classes from an XSD schema file
- Generate runtime classes that have the custom attributes for `XmlSerialization`
- Generate an XSD file from classes that you have already developed
- Limit which elements are created in code
- Determine which programming language the generated code should be in (C#, Visual Basic .NET, or JScript .NET)
- Create schemas from types in compiled assemblies

You should refer to the framework documentation for details of command-line options for `xsd.exe`.

Despite these capabilities, you don't *have* to use `xsd.exe` to create the classes for serialization. The process is quite simple. The following is a simple application that serializes a class. At the beginning of the example, you have very simple code that creates a new `Product` object, `pd`, and fills it with some data:

```
private void button1_Click(object sender, EventArgs e)
{
  //new products object
  Product pd = new Product();
  //set some properties
  pd.ProductID = 200;
  pd.CategoryID = 100;
  pd.Discontinued = false;
  pd.ProductName = "Serialize Objects";
  pd.QuantityPerUnit = "6";
  pd.ReorderLevel = 1;
  pd.SupplierID = 1;
  pd.UnitPrice = 1000;
  pd.UnitsInStock = 10;
  pd.UnitsOnOrder = 0;

}
```

The `Serialize()` method of the `XmlSerializer` class actually performs the serialization, and it has nine overloads. One of the parameters required is a stream to write the data to. It can be a `Stream`, `TextWriter`, or an `XmlWriter` parameter. In the example, you create a `TextWriter`-based object, `tr`. The next thing to do is to create the `XmlSerializer`-based object, `sr`. The `XmlSerializer` needs to know type information for the object that it is serializing, so you use the `typeof` keyword with the type that is to be serialized. After the `sr` object is created, you call the `Serialize()` method, passing in the tr (Stream-based object) and the object that you want serialized, in this case pd. Be sure to close the stream when you are finished with it:

```
//new TextWriter and XmlSerializer
TextWriter tr = new StreamWriter("serialprod.xml");
XmlSerializer sr = new XmlSerializer(typeof(Product));
//serialize object
sr.Serialize(tr, pd);
tr.Close();
webBrowser1.Navigate(AppDomain.CurrentDomain.BaseDirectory + "serialprod.xml");
```

Next is the Product class, the class to be serialized. The only differences between this and any other class that you may write are the C# attributes that have been added. The XmlRootAttribute and XmlElementAttribute classes in the attributes inherit from the System.Attribute class. Don't confuse these attributes with the attributes in an XML document. A C# attribute is simply some declarative information that can be retrieved at runtime by the CLR (see Chapter 7, "Delegates and Events," for more details). In this case, the attributes describe how the object should be serialized:

```
//class that will be serialized.
//attributes determine how object is serialized
[System.Xml.Serialization.XmlRootAttribute()]
  public class Product {
    private int prodId;
    private string prodName;
    private int suppId;
    private int catId;
    private string qtyPerUnit;
    private Decimal unitPrice;
    private short unitsInStock;
    private short unitsOnOrder;
    private short reorderLvl;
    private bool discont;
    private int disc;
    //added the Discount attribute
    [XmlAttributeAttribute(AttributeName="Discount")]
    public int Discount {
      get {return disc;}
      set {disc=value;}
    }
    [XmlElementAttribute()]
    public int  ProductID {
      get {return prodId;}
      set {prodId=value;}
    }
    [XmlElementAttribute()]
    public string ProductName {
      get {return prodName;}
      set {prodName=value;}
    }
    [XmlElementAttribute()]
    public int SupplierID {
      get {return suppId;}
      set {suppId=value;}
    }
    [XmlElementAttribute()]
```

```
    public int CategoryID {
      get {return catId;}
      set {catId=value;}
    }
    [XmlElementAttribute()]
    public string QuantityPerUnit {
      get {return qtyPerUnit;}
      set {qtyPerUnit=value;}
    }
    [XmlElementAttribute()]
    public Decimal UnitPrice {
      get {return unitPrice;}
      set {unitPrice=value;}
    }
    [XmlElementAttribute()]
    public short UnitsInStock {
      get {return unitsInStock;}
      set {unitsInStock=value;}
    }
    [XmlElementAttribute()]
    public short UnitsOnOrder {
      get {return unitsOnOrder;}
      set {unitsOnOrder=value;}
    }
    [XmlElementAttribute()]
    public short ReorderLevel {
      get {return reorderLvl;}
      set {reorderLvl=value;}
    }
    [XmlElementAttribute()]
    public bool Discontinued {
      get {return discont;}
      set {discont=value;}
    }
    public override string ToString()
    {
      StringBuilder outText = new StringBuilder();
      outText.Append(prodId);
      outText.Append(" ");
      outText.Append(prodName);
      outText.Append(" ");
      outText.Append(unitPrice);
      return outText.ToString();
    }
  }
```

The `XmlRootAttribute()` invocation in the attribute above the `Products` class definition identifies this class as a root element (in the XML file produced upon serialization). The attribute containing `XmlElementAttribute()` identifies that the member below the attribute represents an XML element.

You will also notice that the `ToString()` method has been overridden. This provides the string that the message box will show when you run the deserialize example.

If you take a look at the XML document created during serialization, you will see that it looks like any other XML document that you might have created, which is the point of the exercise:

```
<?xml version="1.0" encoding="utf-8"?>
<Products xmlns:xsi=http://www.w3.org/2001/XMLSchema-instance
                         xmlns:xsd="http://www.w3.org/2001/XMLSchema"
Discount="0">
  <ProductID>200</ProductID>
  <ProductName>Serialize Objects</ProductName>
  <SupplierID>1</SupplierID>
  <CategoryID>100</CategoryID>
  <QuantityPerUnit>6</QuantityPerUnit>
  <UnitPrice>1000</UnitPrice>
  <UnitsInStock>10</UnitsInStock>
  <UnitsOnOrder>0</UnitsOnOrder>
  <ReorderLevel>1</ReorderLevel>
  <Discontinued>false</Discontinued>
</Products>
```

There is nothing out of the ordinary here. You could use this any way that you would use an XML document. You could transform it and display it as HTML, load it into a `DataSet` using ADO.NET, load an `XmlDocument` with it, or, as you can see in the example, deserialize it and create an object in the same state that `pd` was in prior to serializing it (which is exactly what you're doing with the second button).

Next, you add another button event handler to deserialize a new `Products`-based object, `newPd`. This time you use a `FileStream` object to read in the XML:

```
private void button2_Click(object sender, EventArgs e)
    {
      //create a reference to producst type
      Product newPd;
      //new filestream to open serialized object
      FileStream f = new FileStream("serialprod.xml", FileMode.Open);
```

Once again, you create a new `XmlSerializer`, passing in the type information of `Product`. You can then make the call to the `Deserialize()` method. Note that you still need to do an explicit cast when you create the `newPd` object. At this point, `newPd` is in exactly the same state that `pd` was:

```
    //new serializer
      XmlSerializer newSr = new XmlSerializer(typeof(Product));
      //deserialize the object
      newPd = (Product)newSr.Deserialize(f);
      f.Close();
      MessageBox.Show(newPd.ToString());
    }
```

The message box should show you the product ID, product name, and the unit price of the object you just deserialized. This comes from the `ToString()` override that you implemented in the `Product` class.

What about situations where you have derived classes and possibly properties that return an array? `XmlSerializer` has that covered as well. Here's a slightly more complex example that deals with these issues.

First, you define three new classes, `Product`, `BookProduct` (derived from `Product`), and `Inventory` (which contains both of the other classes). Notice that once again you have overridden the `ToString()` method. This time you're just going to list the items in the `Inventory` class:

```
public class BookProduct : Product
{
   private string isbnNum;
```

```
        public BookProduct() {}
        public string ISBN
        {
           get {return isbnNum;}
           set {isbnNum=value;}
        }
    }
    public class Inventory
    {
        private Product[] stuff;
        public Inventory() {}
        //need to have an attribute entry for each data type
        [XmlArrayItem("Prod",typeof(Product)),
        XmlArrayItem("Book",typeof(BookProduct))]
        public Product[] InventoryItems
        {
           get {return stuff;}
           set {stuff=value;}
        }
        public override string ToString()
        {
          StringBuilder outText = new StringBuilder();
          foreach (Product prod in stuff)
          {
            outText.Append(prod.ProductName);
            outText.Append("\r\n");
          }
          return outText.ToString();
        }
    }
```

The `Inventory` class is the one of interest here. If you are to serialize this class, you need to insert an attribute containing `XmlArrayItem` constructors for each type that can be added to the array. You should note that `XmlArrayItem` is the name of the .NET attribute represented by the `XmlArrayItemAttribute` class.

The first parameter supplied to these constructors is what you would like the element name to be in the XML document that is created during serialization. If you leave off the `ElementName` parameter, the elements will be given the same name as the object type (`Product` and `BookProduct` in this case). The second parameter that must be specified is the type of the object.

There is also an `XmlArrayAttribute` class that you would use if the property were returning an array of objects or primitive types. Because you are returning different types in the array, you use `XmlArrayItemAttribute`, which allows the higher level of control.

In the `button4_Click()` event handler, you create a new `Product` object and a new `BookProduct` object (`newProd` and `newBook`). You add data to the various properties of each object, and add the objects to a `Product` array. You then create a new `Inventory` object and pass in the array as a parameter. You can then serialize the `Inventory` object to recreate it at a later time:

```
    private void button4_Click(object sender, EventArgs e)
    {
      //create the XmlAttributes boject
      XmlAttributes attrs = new XmlAttributes();
      //add the types of the objects that will be serialized
      attrs.XmlElements.Add(new XmlElementAttribute("Book", typeof(BookProduct)));
```

(continued)

(continued)

```
        attrs.XmlElements.Add(new XmlElementAttribute("Product", typeof(Product)));
        XmlAttributeOverrides attrOver = new XmlAttributeOverrides();
        //add to the attributes collection
        attrOver.Add(typeof(Inventory), "InventoryItems", attrs);
        //create the Product and Book objects
        Product newProd = new Product();
        BookProduct newBook = new BookProduct();
        newProd.ProductID = 100;
        newProd.ProductName = "Product Thing";
        newProd.SupplierID = 10;
        newBook.ProductID = 101;
        newBook.ProductName = "How to Use Your New Product Thing";
        newBook.SupplierID = 10;
        newBook.ISBN = "123456789";
        Product[] addProd ={ newProd, newBook };
        Inventory inv = new Inventory();
        inv.InventoryItems = addProd;
        TextWriter tr = new StreamWriter("inventory.xml");
        XmlSerializer sr = new XmlSerializer(typeof(Inventory), attrOver);
        sr.Serialize(tr, inv);
        tr.Close();
        webBrowser1.Navigate(AppDomain.CurrentDomain.BaseDirectory + "inventory.xml");
    }
    }
```

The XML document looks like this:

```
<?xml version="1.0" encoding="utf-8"?>
<Inventory xmlns:xsi="http://www.w3.org/2001/XMLSchema-instance"
xmlns:xsd="http://www.w3.org/2001/XMLSchema">
  <Product Discount="0">
    <ProductID>100</ProductID>
    <ProductName>Product Thing</ProductName>
    <SupplierID>10</SupplierID>
    <CategoryID>0</CategoryID>
    <UnitPrice>0</UnitPrice>
    <UnitsInStock>0</UnitsInStock>
    <UnitsOnOrder>0</UnitsOnOrder>
    <ReorderLevel>0</ReorderLevel>
    <Discontinued>false</Discontinued>
  </Product>
  <Book Discount="0">
    <ProductID>101</ProductID>
    <ProductName>How to Use Your New Product Thing</ProductName>
    <SupplierID>10</SupplierID>
    <CategoryID>0</CategoryID>
    <UnitPrice>0</UnitPrice>
    <UnitsInStock>0</UnitsInStock>
    <UnitsOnOrder>0</UnitsOnOrder>
    <ReorderLevel>0</ReorderLevel>
    <Discontinued>false</Discontinued>
    <ISBN>123456789</ISBN>
  </Book>
</Inventory>
```

The `button2_Click()` event handler implements deserialization of the `Inventory` object. Note that you iterate through the array in the newly created `newInv` object to show that it is the same data:

```
private void button2_Click(object sender, System.EventArgs e)
{
   Inventory newInv;
   FileStream f=new FileStream("order.xml",FileMode.Open);
   XmlSerializer newSr=new XmlSerializer(typeof(Inventory));
   newInv=(Inventory)newSr.Deserialize(f);
   foreach(Product prod in newInv.InventoryItems)
      listBox1.Items.Add(prod.ProductName);
   f.Close();
}
```

Serialization Without Source Code Access

Well, this all works great, but what if you don't have access to the source code for the types that are being serialized? You can't add the attribute if you don't have the source. There is another way. You can use the `XmlAttributes` class and the `XmlAttributeOverrides` class. Together these classes enable you to accomplish exactly what you have just done, but without adding the attributes. This section looks at an example of how this works.

For this example, imagine that the `Inventory`, `Product`, and derived `BookProduct` classes are in a separate DLL and that you don't have the source. The `Product` and `BookProduct` classes are the same as in the previous example, but you should note that there are now no attributes added to the `Inventory` class:

```
public class Inventory
{
   private Product[] stuff;
   public Inventory() {}
   public Product[] InventoryItems
   {
      get {return stuff;}
      set {stuff=value;}
   }
}
```

Next, you deal with the serialization in the `button1_Click()` event handler:

```
private void button1_Click(object sender, System.EventArgs e)
{
```

The first step in the serialization process is to create an `XmlAttributes` object and an `XmlElementAttribute` object for each data type that you will be overriding:

```
   XmlAttributes attrs=new XmlAttributes();
   attrs.XmlElements.Add(new XmlElementAttribute("Book",typeof(BookProduct)));
   attrs.XmlElements.Add(new XmlElementAttribute("Product",typeof(Product)));
```

Here you can see that you are adding new `XmlElementAttribute` objects to the `XmlElements` collection of the `XmlAttributes` class. The `XmlAttributes` class has properties that correspond to the attributes that can be applied; `XmlArray` and `XmlArrayItems`, which you looked at in the previous example, are just a couple of these. You now have an `XmlAttributes` object with two `XmlElementAttribute`-based objects added to the `XmlElements` collection.

The next thing you have to do is create an `XmlAttributeOverrides` object:

```
XmlAttributeOverrides attrOver=new XmlAttributeOverrides();
attrOver.Add(typeof(Inventory),"InventoryItems",attrs);
```

The `Add()` method of this class has two overloads. The first one takes the type information of the object to override and the `XmlAttributes` object that you created earlier. The other overload, which is the one you are using, also takes a string value that is the member in the overridden object. In this case, you want to override the `InventoryItems` member in the `Inventory` class.

When you create the `XmlSerializer` object, you add the `XmlAttributeOverrides` object as a parameter. Now the `XmlSerializer` knows which types you want to override and what you need to return for those types:

```
    //create the Product and Book objects
    Product newProd=new Product();
    BookProduct newBook=new BookProduct();
    newProd.ProductID=100;
    newProd.ProductName="Product Thing";
    newProd.SupplierID=10;
    newBook.ProductID=101;
    newBook.ProductName="How to Use Your New Product Thing";
    newBook.SupplierID=10;
    newBook.ISBN="123456789";
    Product[] addProd={newProd,newBook};

    Inventory inv=new Inventory();
    inv.InventoryItems=addProd;
    TextWriter tr=new StreamWriter("inventory.xml");
    XmlSerializer sr=new XmlSerializer(typeof(Inventory),attrOver);
    sr.Serialize(tr,inv);
    tr.Close();
}
```

If you execute the `Serialize()` method, you get this XML output:

```
<?xml version="1.0" encoding="utf-8"?>
<Inventory xmlns:xsi="http://www.w3.org/2001/XMLSchema-instance"
xmlns:xsd="http://www.w3.org/2001/XMLSchema">
  <Product Discount="0">
    <ProductID>100</ProductID>
    <ProductName>Product Thing</ProductName>
    <SupplierID>10</SupplierID>
    <CategoryID>0</CategoryID>
    <UnitPrice>0</UnitPrice>
    <UnitsInStock>0</UnitsInStock>
    <UnitsOnOrder>0</UnitsOnOrder>
    <ReorderLevel>0</ReorderLevel>
    <Discontinued>false</Discontinued>
  </Product>
  <Book Discount="0">
    <ProductID>101</ProductID>
    <ProductName>How to Use Your New Product Thing</ProductName>
    <SupplierID>10</SupplierID>
    <CategoryID>0</CategoryID>
    <UnitPrice>0</UnitPrice>
    <UnitsInStock>0</UnitsInStock>
```

```
        <UnitsOnOrder>0</UnitsOnOrder>
        <ReorderLevel>0</ReorderLevel>
        <Discontinued>false</Discontinued>
        <ISBN>123456789</ISBN>
    </Book>
</Inventory>
```

As you can see, you get the same XML as you did with the earlier example. To deserialize this object and recreate the `Inventory`-based object that you started out with, you need to create all of the same `XmlAttributes`, `XmlElementAttribute`, and `XmlAttributeOverrides` objects that you created when you serialized the object. Once you do that, you can read in the XML and recreate the `Inventory` object just as you did before. Here is the code to deserialize the `Inventory` object:

```
private void button2_Click(object sender, System.EventArgs e)
{
   //create the new XmlAttributes collection
   XmlAttributes attrs=new XmlAttributes();
   //add the type information to the elements collection
   attrs.XmlElements.Add(new XmlElementAttribute("Book",typeof(BookProduct)));
   attrs.XmlElements.Add(new XmlElementAttribute("Product",typeof(Product)));

   XmlAttributeOverrides attrOver=new XmlAttributeOverrides();
   //add to the Attributes collection
   attrOver.Add(typeof(Inventory),"InventoryItems",attrs);

   //need a new Inventory object to deserialize to
   Inventory newInv;

   //deserialize and load data into the listbox from deserialized object
   FileStream f=new FileStream("..\\..\\..\\inventory.xml",FileMode.Open);
   XmlSerializer newSr=new XmlSerializer(typeof(Inventory),attrOver);

   newInv=(Inventory)newSr.Deserialize(f);
   if(newInv!=null)
   {
      foreach(Product prod in newInv.InventoryItems)
      {
         listBox1.Items.Add(prod.ProductName);
      }
   }
   f.Close();
}
```

Note that the first few lines of code are identical to the code you used to serialize the object.

The `System.Xml.XmlSerialization` namespace provides a very powerful tool set for serializing objects to XML. By serializing and deserializing objects to XML instead of to binary format, you are given the option of doing something else with this XML, greatly adding to the flexibility of your designs.

Summary

In this chapter, you explored many aspects of the `System.Xml` namespace of the .NET Framework. You looked at how to read and write XML documents using the very fast `XmlReader`- and `XmlWriter`-based classes. You looked at how the DOM is implemented in .NET and how to use the power of DOM. You saw that XML and ADO.NET are indeed very closely related. A `DataSet` and an XML document are just two different views of the same underlying architecture. And, of course, you visited XPath and XSL transforms and the debugging features added to Visual Studio.

Finally, you serialized objects to XML and were able to bring them back with just a couple of method calls.

XML will be an important part of your application development for years to come. The .NET Framework has made available a very rich and powerful toolset for working with XML. The next chapter will delve into using LINQ with XML.

29

LINQ to XML

As stated in Chapter 27, "LINQ to SQL," probably the biggest and most exciting addition to the .NET Framework 3.5 is the addition of the .NET Language Integrated Query framework (LINQ) into C# 2008. LINQ comes in many flavors depending on the final data store that you are working with in querying your data. Chapter 27 took a look at using LINQ to SQL to query SQL Server databases; this chapter takes a quick look at using LINQ to query your XML data sources instead.

You read about the following in this chapter:

- What LINQ to XML brings to the table
- The new objects available in the `System.Xml.Linq` namespace
- How to query your XML documents using LINQ
- Moving around your XML documents using LINQ
- Using LINQ to SQL and LINQ to XML together

Extensible Markup Language (XML) is now in widespread use. Many applications on the Internet or residing on individual computers use some form of XML to run or manage the processes of an application. Earlier books about XML commented that XML was to be the "next big thing." Now, it *is* "the big thing." In fact, there really isn't anything bigger.

Microsoft has been working for years to make using XML in the .NET world as easy as possible. You can't help but notice the additional capability and the enhancements to XML usage introduced in each new version of the .NET Framework. In fact, Bill Gates highlighted Microsoft's faith in XML in his keynote address at the Microsoft Professional Developers Conference in 2005 in Los Angeles. He stated that XML is being pushed deeper and deeper into the Windows core each year. If you look around the .NET Framework, you will probably agree.

For this reason, this chapter focuses on using LINQ to XML to query your XML documents. Figure 29-1 shows LINQ's place in querying XML data.

Much of what you learned in the chapter on using LINQ to SQL can be applied here when working with LINQ to XML.

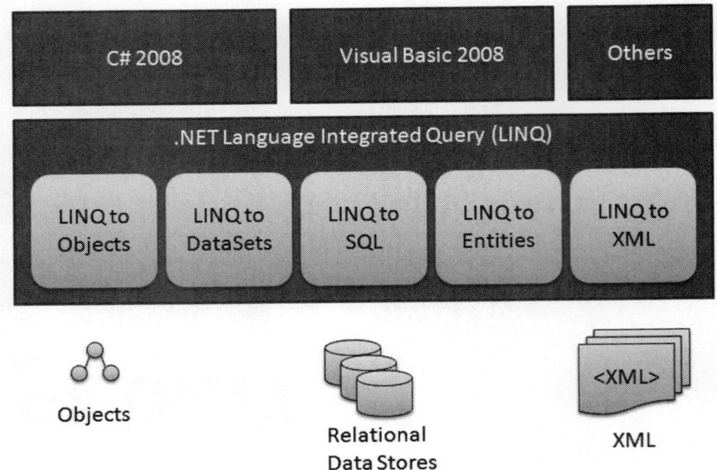

Figure 29-1

LINQ to XML and .NET 3.5

With the introduction of LINQ to the .NET Framework 3.5, the focus was on easy access to the data that you want to work with in your applications. One of the main data stores in the application space is XML and, therefore, it really was considered a no-brainer to create the LINQ to XML implementation.

Prior to the LINQ to XML release, working with XML using `System.Xml` was really not the easiest thing in the world to achieve. With the inclusion of `System.Xml.Linq`, you now find a series of capabilities that make the process of working with XML in your code that much easier.

New Objects for Creating XML Documents

In creating XML within application code, many developers turned to the `XmlDocument` object to do this job. This object allows you to create XML documents that enable you to append elements, attributes, and other items in a hierarchical fashion. With LINQ to XML and the inclusion of the new `System.Xml.Linq` namespace, you will now find some new objects that make the creation of XML documents a much simpler process.

Visual Basic 2008 Ventures Down Another Path

An interesting side note to the LINQ to XML feature set is that the Visual Basic 2008 team at Microsoft actually took the LINQ to XML capabilities a little further in some areas. For instance, something you are unable to accomplish in C# 2008 that you can do in Visual Basic 2008 is include XML as a core part of the language. XML literals are now a true part of the Visual Basic language and you are able to paste XML fragments directly in your code for inclusion, and the XML included is not treated as a string.

Namespaces and Prefixes

One issue that was somewhat ignored in parts of the .NET Framework 2.0 was how the items in the framework dealt with the inclusion of XML namespaces and prefixes in documents. LINQ to XML makes this an important part of the XML story, and you will find the capabilities to work with these types of objects to be quite simple.

New XML Objects from the .NET Framework 3.5

Even if the LINQ querying ability wasn't available in this release of the .NET Framework, the new XML objects provided by the .NET Framework 3.5 to work with the XML that are available in place of working directly with the DOM in this release are so good, that they even can stand on their own outside of LINQ. Within the new `System.Xml.Linq` namespace you will find a series of new LINQ to XML helper objects that make working with an XML document in memory that much easier.

The following sections work through the new objects that are available to you within this new namespace.

> *Many of the examples in this chapter use a file called* `Hamlet.xml`*. This is a file you can find at* `http://metalab.unc.edu/bosak/xml/eg/shaks200.zip` *that includes all of Shakespeare's plays as XML files.*

XDocument

The `XDocument` is a replacement of the `XmlDocument` object from the pre-.NET 3.5 world. You will find the `XDocument` object easier to work with in dealing with XML documents. The `XDocument` object works with the other new objects in this space, such as the `XNamespace`, `XComment`, `XElement`, and `XAttribute` objects.

One of the more important members of the `XDocument` object is the `Load()` method:

```
XDocument xdoc = XDocument.Load(@"C:\Hamlet.xml");
```

This operation will load up the `Hamlet.xml` contents as an in-memory `XDocument` object. You are also able to pass a `TextReader` or `XmlReader` object into the `Load()` method. From here, you are able to programmatically work with the XML:

```
XDocument xdoc = XDocument.Load(@"C:\Hamlet.xml");
Console.WriteLine(xdoc.Root.Name.ToString());
Console.WriteLine(xdoc.Root.HasAttributes.ToString());
```

This produces the following results:

```
PLAY
False
```

Another important member to be aware of is the `Save()` method, which, similar to the `Load()` method, allows you to save to a physical disk location or to a `TextWriter` or `XmlWriter` object:

```
XDocument xdoc = XDocument.Load(@"C:\Hamlet.xml");

xdoc.Save(@"C:\CopyOfHamlet.xml");
```

XElement

One of the more common objects that you will work with is the `XElement` object. With these objects, you are easily able to create just single-element objects that are XML documents themselves and even just fragments of XML. For instance, here is an example of writing an XML element with a corresponding value:

```
XElement xe = new XElement("Company", "Lipper");
Console.WriteLine(xe.ToString());
```

In the creation of a new `XElement` object, you are able to define the name of the element as well as the value used in the element. In this case, the name of the element will be `<Company>`, and the value of the `<Company>` element will be `Lipper`. Running this in a console application with a `System.Xml.Linq` reference produces the following result:

```
<Company>Lipper</Company>
```

You are able to create an even more complete XML document using multiple `XElement` objects, as illustrated in the following example:

```
using System;
using System.Linq;
using System.Xml.Linq;

namespace ConsoleApplication1
{
    class Class1
    {
        static void Main()
        {
            XElement xe = new XElement("Company",
                new XElement("CompanyName", "Lipper"),
                new XElement("CompanyAddress",
                    new XElement("Address", "123 Main Street"),
                    new XElement("City", "St. Louis"),
                    new XElement("State", "MO"),
                    new XElement("Country", "USA")));

            Console.WriteLine(xe.ToString());

            Console.ReadLine();
        }
    }
}
```

Running this application produces the results illustrated in Figure 29-2.

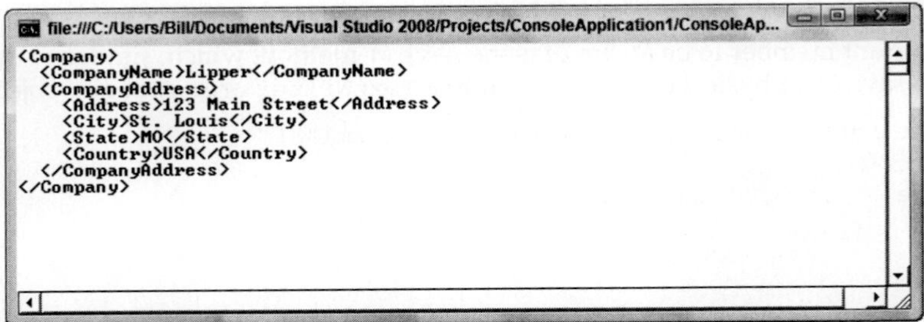

Figure 29-2

XNamespace

The `XNamespace` is an object that represents an XML namespace and is easily applied to elements within your document. For example, you can take the previous example and easily apply a namespace to the root element:

```
using System;
using System.Linq;
using System.Xml.Linq;

namespace ConsoleApplication1
{
    class Class1
    {
        static void Main()
        {
            XNamespace ns = "http://www.lipperweb.com/ns/1";

            XElement xe = new XElement(ns + "Company",
                new XElement("CompanyName", "Lipper"),
                new XElement("CompanyAddress",
                    new XElement("Address", "123 Main Street"),
                    new XElement("City", "St. Louis"),
                    new XElement("State", "MO"),
                    new XElement("Country", "USA")));

            Console.WriteLine(xe.ToString());

            Console.ReadLine();
        }
    }
}
```

In this case, an `XNamespace` object is created by assigning it a value of `http://www.lipperweb.com/ns/1`. From there, it is actually used in the root element `<Company>` with the instantiation of the `XElement` object:

```
XElement xe = new XElement(ns + "Company", // ...
```

This produces the results illustrated in Figure 29-3.

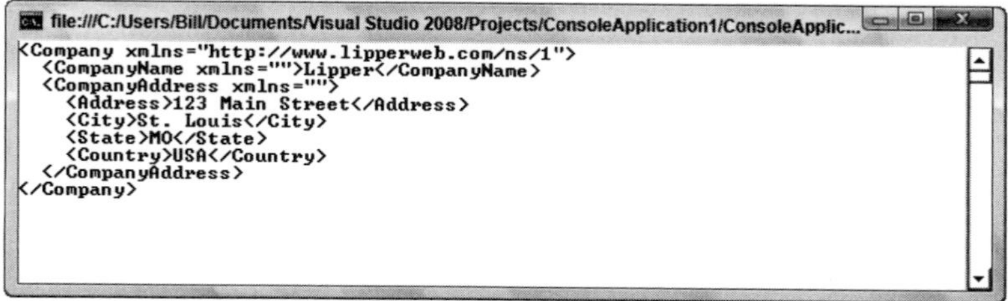

Figure 29-3

In addition to dealing with only the root element, you can also apply namespaces to all your elements as shown in the following example:

```
using System;
using System.Linq;
using System.Xml.Linq;

namespace ConsoleApplication1
{
    class Class1
    {
        static void Main()
        {
            XNamespace ns1 = "http://www.lipperweb.com/ns/root";
            XNamespace ns2 = "http://www.lipperweb.com/ns/sub";

            XElement xe = new XElement(ns1 + "Company",
                new XElement(ns2 + "CompanyName", "Lipper"),
                new XElement(ns2 + "CompanyAddress",
                    new XElement(ns2 + "Address", "123 Main Street"),
                    new XElement(ns2 + "City", "St. Louis"),
                    new XElement(ns2 + "State", "MO"),
                    new XElement(ns2 + "Country", "USA")));

            Console.WriteLine(xe.ToString());

            Console.ReadLine();
        }
    }
}
```

This produces the results shown in Figure 29-4.

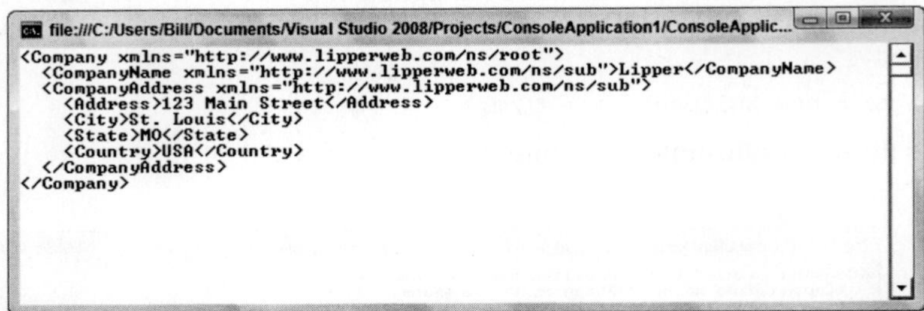

Figure 29-4

In this case, you can see that the sub-namespace was applied to everything you specified except for the <Address>, <City>, <State>, and the <Country> elements because they inherit from their parent, <CompanyAddress>, which has the namespace declaration.

XComment

The `XComment` object allows you to easily add XML comments to your XML documents. The following example shows adding a comment to the top of the document:

```
using System;
using System.Linq;
using System.Xml.Linq;

namespace ConsoleApplication1
{
    class Class1
    {
        static void Main(string[] args)
        {
            XDocument xdoc = new XDocument();

            XComment xc = new XComment("Here is a comment.");
            xdoc.Add(xc);

            XElement xe = new XElement("Company",
                new XElement("CompanyName", "Lipper"),
                new XElement("CompanyAddress",
                    new XComment("Here is another comment."),
                    new XElement("Address", "123 Main Street"),
                    new XElement("City", "St. Louis"),
                    new XElement("State", "MO"),
                    new XElement("Country", "USA")));
            xdoc.Add(xe);

            Console.WriteLine(xdoc.ToString());

            Console.ReadLine();
        }
    }
}
```

Here, an `XDocument` object that contains two XML comments is written to the console, one at the top of the document and another within the `<CompanyAddress>` element. The output of this is presented in Figure 29-5.

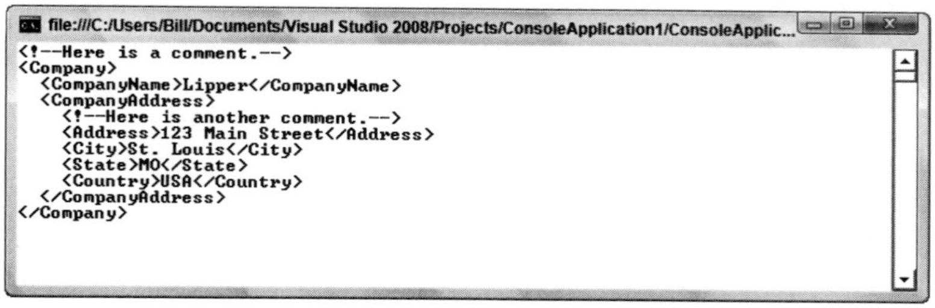

file:///C:/Users/Bill/Documents/Visual Studio 2008/Projects/ConsoleApplication1/ConsoleApplic...

```
<!--Here is a comment.-->
<Company>
  <CompanyName>Lipper</CompanyName>
  <CompanyAddress>
    <!--Here is another comment.-->
    <Address>123 Main Street</Address>
    <City>St. Louis</City>
    <State>MO</State>
    <Country>USA</Country>
  </CompanyAddress>
</Company>
```

Figure 29-5

XAttribute

In addition to elements, another important factor of XML is attributes. Adding and working with attributes is done through the use of the `XAttribute` object. The following example shows adding an attribute to the root `<Customers>` node:

```
using System;
using System.Linq;
using System.Xml.Linq;

namespace ConsoleApplication1
{
    class Class1
    {
        static void Main()
        {
            XElement xe = new XElement("Company",
                new XAttribute("MyAttribute", "MyAttributeValue"),
                new XElement("CompanyName", "Lipper"),
                new XElement("CompanyAddress",
                    new XElement("Address", "123 Main Street"),
                    new XElement("City", "St. Louis"),
                    new XElement("State", "MO"),
                    new XElement("Country", "USA")));

            Console.WriteLine(xe.ToString());

            Console.ReadLine();
        }
    }
}
```

Here, the attribute `MyAttribute` with a value of `MyAttributeValue` is added to the root element of the XML document, producing the results shown in Figure 29-6.

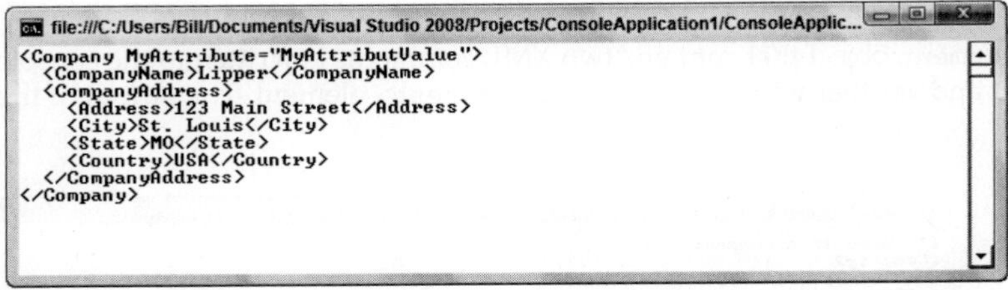

Figure 29-6

Using LINQ to Query XML Documents

Now that you can get your XML documents into an `XDocument` object and work with the various parts of this document, you can also use LINQ to XML to query your XML documents and work with the results.

Querying Static XML Documents

You will notice that querying a static XML document using LINQ to XML takes almost no work at all. The following example makes use of the `hamlet.xml` file and queries to get all the players (actors) that appear in the play. Each one of these players is defined in the XML document with the `<PERSONA>` element:

```
using System;
using System.Linq;
using System.Xml.Linq;

namespace ConsoleApplication1
{
    class Class1
    {
        static void Main(string[] args)
        {
            XDocument xdoc = XDocument.Load(@"C:\hamlet.xml");

            var query = from people in xdoc.Descendants("PERSONA")
                        select people.Value;

            Console.WriteLine("{0} Players Found", query.Count());
            Console.WriteLine();

            foreach (var item in query)
            {
                Console.WriteLine(item);
            }

            Console.ReadLine();
        }
    }
}
```

In this case, an `XDocument` object loads up a physical XML file (`hamlet.xml`) and then performs a LINQ query over the contents of the document:

```
var query = from people in xdoc.Descendants("PERSONA")
            select people.Value;
```

The `people` object is an object that is a representation of all the `<PERSONA>` elements found in the document. Then the `select` statement gets at the values of these elements. From there, a `Console.WriteLine()` method is used to write out a count of all the players found using `query.Count()`. Then, each of the items is written to the screen in a `foreach` loop. The results you should see are presented here:

```
26 Players Found

CLAUDIUS, king of Denmark.
HAMLET, son to the late king, and nephew to the present king.
POLONIUS, lord chamberlain.
HORATIO, friend to Hamlet.
LAERTES, son to Polonius.
LUCIANUS, nephew to the king.
```

(continued)

(continued)

```
VOLTIMAND
CORNELIUS
ROSENCRANTZ
GUILDENSTERN
OSRIC
A Gentleman
A Priest.
MARCELLUS
BERNARDO
FRANCISCO, a soldier.
REYNALDO, servant to Polonius.
Players.
Two Clowns, grave-diggers.
FORTINBRAS, prince of Norway.
A Captain.
English Ambassadors.
GERTRUDE, queen of Denmark, and mother to Hamlet.
OPHELIA, daughter to Polonius.
Lords, Ladies, Officers, Soldiers, Sailors, Messengers, and other Attendants.
Ghost of Hamlet's Father.
```

Querying Dynamic XML Documents

A lot of dynamic XML documents are available on the Internet these days. You will find blog feeds, podcast feeds, and more that provide an XML document by sending a request to a specific URL endpoint. These feeds can be viewed either in the browser, through an RSS-aggregator, or as pure XML.

```
using System;
using System.Linq;
using System.Xml.Linq;

namespace ConsoleApplication1
{
    class Class1
    {
        static void Main()
        {
            XDocument xdoc =
               XDocument.Load(@"http://geekswithblogs.net/evjen/Rss.aspx");

            var query = from rssFeed in xdoc.Descendants("channel")
                        select new
                        {
                          Title = rssFeed.Element("title").Value,
                          Description = rssFeed.Element("description").Value,
                          Link = rssFeed.Element("link").Value,
                        };

            foreach (var item in query)
            {
                Console.WriteLine("TITLE: " + item.Title);
                Console.WriteLine("DESCRIPTION: " + item.Description);
                Console.WriteLine("LINK: " + item.Link);
            }
```

```
            Console.WriteLine();

            var queryPosts = from myPosts in xdoc.Descendants("item")
                             select new
                             {
                                Title = myPosts.Element("title").Value,
                                Published =
                                   DateTime.Parse(
                                     myPosts.Element("pubDate").Value),
                                Description =
                                   myPosts.Element("description").Value,
                                Url = myPosts.Element("link").Value,
                                Comments = myPosts.Element("comments").Value
                             };

            foreach (var item in queryPosts)
            {
                Console.WriteLine(item.Title);
            }

            Console.ReadLine();
        }
    }
}
```

Looking at this code, you can see that the `Load()` method off of the `XDocument` object points to a URL where the XML is retrieved. The first query pulls out all the main sub-elements of the `<channel>` element in the feed and creates new objects called `Title`, `Description`, and `Link` to get at the values of these sub-elements.

From there, a `foreach` statement is run to iterate through all the items found in this query. The results are as follows:

```
TITLE: Bill Evjen's Blog
DESCRIPTION: Code, Life and Community
LINK: http://geekswithblogs.net/evjen/Default.aspx
```

The second query works through all the `<item>` elements and the various sub-elements it has (these are all the blog entries found in the blog). Though a lot of the items found are rolled up into properties, in the `foreach` loop, only the `Title` property is used. You will see something similar to the following results from this query:

```
AJAX Control Toolkit Controls Grayed Out - HOW TO FIX
Welcome .NET 3.5!
Visual Studio 2008 Released
IIS 7.0 Rocks the House!
Word Issue - Couldn't Select Text
Microsoft Releases XML Schema Designer CTP1
Silverlight Book
Microsoft Tafiti as a beta
ReSharper on Visual Studio 2008
Windows Vista Updates for Performance and Reliability Issues
New Version of ODP.NET for .NET 2.0 Released as Beta Today
First Review of Professional XML
Go to MIX07 for free!
```

(continued)

(continued)

```
Microsoft Surface and the Future of Home Computing?
Alas my friends - I'm *not* TechEd bound
New Book - Professional VB 2005 with .NET 3.0!
An article showing Oracle and .NET working together
My Latest Book - Professional XML
CISCO VPN Client Software on Windows Vista
Server-Side Excel Generation
Scott Guthrie Gives Short Review of Professional ASP.NET 2.0 SE
Windows Forms Additions in the Next Version of .NET
Tag, I'm It
```

Working Around the XML Document

If you have been working with the XML document, `hamlet.xml`, you will notice that it is quite large. Querying into the XML document was shown in a couple of ways throughout this chapter, but this next section takes a look at reading and writing to the XML document.

Reading from an XML Document

Earlier you saw just how easy it was to query into an XML document using the LINQ query statements as shown here:

```
var query = from people in xdoc.Descendants("PERSONA")
            select people.Value;
```

This query returned all the players that were found in the document. Using the `Element()` method of the `XDocument` object, you can also get at specific values of the XML document that you are working with. For instance, continuing to work with the `hamlet.xml` document, the following XML fragment shows you how the title is represented in the XML document:

```
<?xml version="1.0"?>

<PLAY>
   <TITLE>The Tragedy of Hamlet, Prince of Denmark</TITLE>

   <!-- XML removed for clarity -->

</PLAY>
```

As you can see, the `<TITLE>` element is a nested element of the `<PLAY>` element. You can easily get at the title by using the following bit of code in your console application:

```
XDocument xdoc = XDocument.Load(@"C:\hamlet.xml");

Console.WriteLine(xdoc.Element("PLAY").Element("TITLE").Value);
```

This bit of code will write out the title, `The Tragedy of Hamlet, Prince of Denmark`, to the console screen. In the code, you were able to work down the hierarchy of the XML document by using two `Element()` method calls — first calling the `<PLAY>` element and then the `<TITLE>` element found nested within the `<PLAY>` element.

Looking more at the `hamlet.xml` document, you will see a large list of players that are defined with the use of the `<PERSONA>` element:

```
<?xml version="1.0"?>

<PLAY>
   <TITLE>The Tragedy of Hamlet, Prince of Denmark</TITLE>

   <!-- XML removed for clarity -->

   <PERSONAE>
      <TITLE>Dramatis Personae</TITLE>

      <PERSONA>CLAUDIUS, king of Denmark. </PERSONA>
      <PERSONA>HAMLET, son to the late king,
       and nephew to the present king.</PERSONA>
      <PERSONA>POLONIUS, lord chamberlain. </PERSONA>
      <PERSONA>HORATIO, friend to Hamlet.</PERSONA>
      <PERSONA>LAERTES, son to Polonius.</PERSONA>
      <PERSONA>LUCIANUS, nephew to the king.</PERSONA>

      <!-- XML removed for clarity -->

   </PERSONAE>

</PLAY>
```

Using this XML document, review the following bit of C# code's use of this XML:

```
XDocument xdoc = XDocument.Load(@"C:\hamlet.xml");

Console.WriteLine(
   xdoc.Element("PLAY").Element("PERSONAE").Element("PERSONA").Value);
```

This bit of code starts at `<PLAY>`, works down to the `<PERSONAE>` element, and then makes use of the `<PERSONA>` element. However, using this will produce the following results:

```
CLAUDIUS, king of Denmark
```

The reason for this is that, although there is a collection of `<PERSONA>` elements, you are dealing only with the first one that is encountered using the `Element().Value` call.

Writing to an XML Document

In addition to reading from an XML document, you can also write to the document just as easily. For instance, if you wanted to change the name of the first player of the Hamlet play file, you could make use of the following code to accomplish this task:

```
using System;
using System.Linq;
using System.Xml.Linq;

namespace ConsoleApplication1
{
    class Class1
    {
        static void Main()
```

(continued)

(continued)

```
        {
            XDocument xdoc = XDocument.Load(@"C:\hamlet.xml");

            xdoc.Element("PLAY").Element("PERSONAE").
               Element("PERSONA").SetValue("Bill Evjen, king of Denmark");

            Console.WriteLine(xdoc.Element("PLAY").
               Element("PERSONAE").Element("PERSONA").Value);

            Console.ReadLine();
        }
    }
}
```

In this case, the first instance of the `<PERSONA>` element is overwritten with the value of `Bill Evjen, king of Denmark` using the `SetValue()` method of the `Element()` object. After the `SetValue()` is called and the value is applied to the XML document, the value is then retrieved using the same approach as before. When you run this bit of code, you can indeed see that the value of the first `<PERSONA>` element has been changed.

Another way to change the document (by adding items to it in this example) is to create the element you want as `XElement` objects and then add them to the document:

```
using System;
using System.Linq;
using System.Xml.Linq;

namespace ConsoleApplication1
{
    class Class1
    {
        static void Main()
        {
            XDocument xdoc = XDocument.Load(@"C:\hamlet.xml");

            XElement xe = new XElement("PERSONA",
               "Bill Evjen, king of Denmark");

            xdoc.Element("PLAY").Element("PERSONAE").Add(xe);

            var query = from people in xdoc.Descendants("PERSONA")
                        select people.Value;

            Console.WriteLine("{0} Players Found", query.Count());
            Console.WriteLine();

            foreach (var item in query)
            {
                Console.WriteLine(item);
            }

            Console.ReadLine();
        }
    }
}
```

In this case, an `XElement` document is created called `xe`. The construction of `xe` will give you the following XML output:

```
<PERSONA>Bill Evjen, king of Denmark</PERSONA>
```

Then using the `Element().Add()` method from the `XDocument` object, you are able to add the created element:

```
xdoc.Element("PLAY").Element("PERSONAE").Add(xe);
```

Now when you query all the players, you will find that instead of 26 as before, you now have 27 with the new one at the bottom of the list. In addition to `Add()`, you can also use `AddFirst()`, which will do what it says — add it to the beginning of the list instead of the end as is the default.

Using LINQ to SQL with LINQ to XML

When working with LINQ to SQL or LINQ to XML, you are limited to working with the specific data source for which it was designed. In fact, you are able to mix multiple data sources together when working with LINQ. For an example of this, this section uses LINQ to SQL to query the customers in the Northwind database and turn the results pulled into an XML document.

You can find instructions on how to get the Northwind sample database file as well as information on working with LINQ to SQL in Chapter 27.

Setting up the LINQ to SQL Components

The first step for this to work is to add the Northwind SQL Server Express Edition database file to your project. From there, right-click the project to add a new LINQ to SQL class file to your project. Name the file `Northwind.dbml`.

This operation will give you a design surface that you are able to work with. From the Server Explorer, drag and drop tables from the database onto this design surface. You want to drag and drop both the `Customers` and the `Orders` tables onto the design surface. By doing this, you will notice that there is then a relationship established between these two tables. Once to this point, your view in the IDE should look as is illustrated in Figure 29-7.

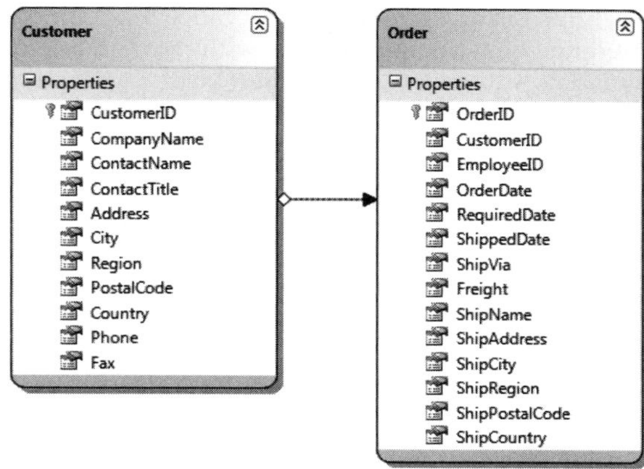

Figure 29-7

Now that you have your `Northwind.dbml` in place, you are ready to query this database structure and output the results as an XML file.

Querying the Database and Outputting XML

The next step in your console application is to put the following code in your `Program.cs` file:

```
using System;
using System.Linq;
using System.Xml.Linq;

namespace ConsoleApplication1
{
    class Class1
    {
        static void Main()
        {
            NorthwindDataContext dc = new NorthwindDataContext();

            XElement xe = new XElement("Customer",
                from c in dc.Customers
                select new XElement("Customer",
                    new XElement("CustomerId", c.CustomerID),
                    new XElement("CompanyName", c.CompanyName),
                    new XElement("Country", c.Country),
                    new XElement("OrderNum", c.Orders.Count)));

            xe.Save(@"C:\myCustomers.xml");
            Console.WriteLine("File created");
            Console.ReadLine();
        }
    }
}
```

This example creates a new instance of the `NorthwindDataContext` object that is created for you automatically with the LINQ to SQL class you created. Then instead of doing the normal

```
var query = [query]
```

you populate the query performed in an `XElement` object called `xe`. Within the select statement of the query, you also create an iteration of `Customers` objects with the nested elements of `<Customer>`, `<CustomerId>`, `<CompanyName>`, `<Country>`, and `<OrderNum>`. Once queried, the `xe` instance is then saved to disk using `xe.Save()`. When you go to disk and look at the `myCustomers.xml` file, you will see the following results (shown only partially here):

```
<?xml version="1.0" encoding="utf-8"?>
<Customer>
  <Customer>
    <CustomerId>ALFKI</CustomerId>
    <CompanyName>Alfreds Futterkiste</CompanyName>
    <Country>Germany</Country>
    <OrderNum>6</OrderNum>
  </Customer>
  <Customer>
    <CustomerId>ANATR</CustomerId>
    <CompanyName>Ana Trujillo Emparedados y helados</CompanyName>
```

```
      <Country>Mexico</Country>
      <OrderNum>4</OrderNum>
    </Customer>

    <!-- XML removed for clarity -->

    <Customer>
      <CustomerId>WILMK</CustomerId>
      <CompanyName>Wilman Kala</CompanyName>
      <Country>Finland</Country>
      <OrderNum>7</OrderNum>
    </Customer>
    <Customer>
      <CustomerId>WOLZA</CustomerId>
      <CompanyName>Wolski  Zajazd</CompanyName>
      <Country>Poland</Country>
      <OrderNum>7</OrderNum>
    </Customer>
  </Customer>
```

From this, you can see just how easy it is to mix the two data sources using LINQ. Using LINQ to SQL, the customers were pulled from the database, and then using LINQ to XML, an XML file was created and output to disk.

Summary

This chapter focused on using LINQ to XML and some of the options available to you in reading and writing from XML files and XML sources, whether the source is static or dynamic.

Using LINQ to XML, you are able to have a strongly typed set of operations for performing CRUD operations against your XML files and sources. However, with that said, you can still use your `XmlReader` and `XmlWriter` code along with the new LINQ to XML capabilities.

This chapter also introduced the new LINQ to XML helper objects of `XDocument`, `XElement`, `XNamespace`, `XAttribute`, and `XComment`. You will find these are outstanding new objects that make working with XML easier than ever before.

The next chapter looks at programming with Microsoft's SQL Server.

30

.NET Programming with SQL Server

SQL Server 2005 was the first version of this database product to host the .NET runtime. In fact, it was the first new version of Microsoft's SQL Server product in nearly six years. It allows running .NET assemblies in the SQL Server process. Furthermore, it enables you to create stored procedures, functions, and data types with .NET programming languages such as C# and Visual Basic.

In this chapter, you learn about the following:

- Hosting the .NET runtime with SQL Server
- Classes from the namespace `System.Data.SqlServer`
- Creating user-defined types
- Creating user-defined aggregates
- Stored procedures
- User-defined functions
- Triggers
- XML data types

This chapter requires SQL Server 2005 or a later version of this database product.

SQL Server has many features that are not directly associated with the CLR, such as many T-SQL improvements, but they are not covered in this book. To get more information about these features you can read Wrox's SQL Server 2005 Express Edition Starter Kit *(Wiley Publishing, Inc., ISBN 0-7645-8923-7).*

The samples in this chapter make use of a ProCSharp database that you can download with the code samples, and the AdventureWorks database. The AdventureWorks database is a sample database from Microsoft that you can install as an optional component with SQL Server.

.NET Runtime Host

SQL Server is a host of the .NET runtime. In versions prior to CLR 2.0, multiple hosts already existed to run .NET applications; for example, a host for Windows Forms and a host for ASP.NET. Internet Explorer is another runtime host that allows running Windows Forms controls.

SQL Server allows running a .NET assembly inside the SQL Server process, where it is possible to create stored procedures, functions, data types, and triggers with CLR code.

Every database that makes use of CLR code creates its own *application domain*. This guarantees that CLR code from one database doesn't have any influence on any other database.

You can read more about application domains in Chapter 17, "Assemblies."

.NET 1.0 already had a well-thought-out security environment with evidence-based security. However, this security environment was not enough for mission-critical databases — .NET needed some extensions. SQL Server as a .NET runtime host defines additional permission levels: *safe*, *external*, and *unsafe*.

You can read more about evidence-based security in Chapter 20, "Security."

- **Safe** — With the safety level *safe*, only computational CLR classes can be used. The assembly is able to perform only local data access. The functionality of these classes is similar to a T-SQL stored procedure. The code access security defines that the only .NET permission is execution of CLR code.
- **External** — With the safety level *external* it is possible to access the network, file system, registry, or other databases with client-side ADO.NET.
- **Unsafe** — The safety level *unsafe* means that everything can happen, because this safety level allows you to invoke native code. Assemblies with the unsafe permission level can be installed only by a database administrator.

To enable custom .NET code to be run within SQL Server, the CLR must be enabled with the `sp_configure` stored procedure:

```
sp_configure [clr enabled], 1
reconfigure
```

With .NET 2.0, the attribute class `HostProtectionAttribute` in the namespace `System.Security.Permissions` was invented for better protection of the hosting environment. With this attribute, it is possible to define if a method uses shared state, exposes synchronization, or controls the hosting environment. Because such behavior is usually not needed within SQL Server code (and could influence the performance of the SQL Server), assemblies that have these settings applied are not allowed to be loaded in SQL Server with safe and external safety levels.

For using assemblies with SQL Server, the assembly can be installed with the `CREATE ASSEMBLY` command. With this command, the name of the assembly used in SQL Server, the path to the assembly, and the safety level can be applied:

```
CREATE ASSEMBLY mylibrary FROM c:/ProCSharp/SqlServer/Demo.dll
   WITH PERMISSION SET = SAFE
```

With Visual Studio 2008, the permission level of the generated assembly can be defined with the Database properties of the project, as shown in Figure 30-1.

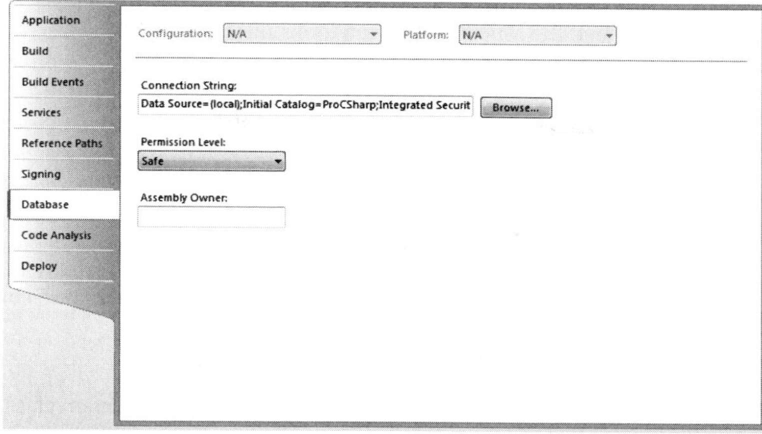

Figure 30-1

Microsoft.SqlServer.Server

Chapter 26, "Data Access," discussed classes from the namespace `System.Data.SqlClient`. This section discusses another namespace, the `Microsoft.SqlServer.Server` namespace. The `Microsoft.SqlServer.Server` namespace includes classes, interfaces, and enumerations specific to the .NET Framework. However, many of the `System.Data.SqlClient` classes are also needed within server-side code as you will see.

The following table lists the major classes from the `Microsoft.SqlServer.Server` namespace and their functionality.

Class	Description
`SqlContext`	Like an HTTP context, the SQL context is associated with the request of a client. With static members of the `SqlContext` class, `SqlPipe`, `SqlTriggerContext`, and `WindowsIdentity` can be accessed.
`SqlPipe`	With the `SqlPipe` class results or information can be sent to the client. This class offers the methods `ExecuteAndSend()`, `Send()`, and `SendResultsRow()`. The `Send()` method has different overloads to either send a `SqlDataReader`, `SqlDataRecord`, or `string`.
`SqlDataRecord`	The `SqlDataRecord` represents a single row of data. This class is used in conjunction with `SqlPipe` to send or receive information from the client.
`SqlTriggerContext`	The `SqlTriggerContext` class is used within triggers. This class provides information about the trigger that was fired.

This namespace also includes several attribute classes: `SqlProcedureAttribute`, `SqlFunctionAttribute`, `SqlUserDefinedAttribute`, and `SqlTriggerAttribute`. These classes are used for deployment of stored procedures, functions, user-defined types, and triggers in SQL Server. When deploying from Visual Studio, it is required that you apply these attributes. When deploying the database objects using SQL statements, these attributes are not needed but they help, because some properties of these attributes influence the characteristics of the database objects.

You see these classes in action later in this chapter when writing stored procedures and user-defined functions is discussed, but first, the following section looks into creating user-defined types with C#.

User-Defined Types

User-defined types (UDTs) can be used similarly to normal SQL Server data types to define the type of a column in a table. With older versions of SQL Server, it was already possible to define UDTs. Of course, these UDTs could be based only on SQL types, such as the `ZIP` type shown in the following code. The stored procedure `sp_addtype` allows you to create user-defined types. Here the user-defined type `ZIP` is based on the `CHAR` data type with a length of `5`. `NOT NULL` specifies that `NULL` is not allowed with the `ZIP` data type. By using `ZIP` as a data type, it is no longer necessary to remember that it should be 5 char long and not null:

```
EXEC sp_addtype ZIP 'CHAR(5)', 'NOT NULL'
```

With SQL Server 2005 and later, UDTs can be defined with CLR classes. However, this feature is not meant to add object orientation to the database; for example, to create a `Person` class to have a `Person` data type. SQL Server is a relational data store, and this is still true with UDTs. You cannot create a class hierarchy of UDTs, and it is not possible to reference fields or properties of a UDT type with a `SELECT` statement. If properties of a person (for example, `Firstname` or `Lastname`) must be accessed or a list of `Person` objects must be sorted (for example, by `Firstname` or `Lastname`), it is still better to define columns for first name or last name inside a `Persons` table or to use the XML data type.

UDTs are meant for very simple data types. Before .NET, it was also possible to create custom data types; for example, the `ZIP` data type. With UDTs it is not possible to create a class hierarchy, and they are not meant to get complex data types to the database. One requirement of a UDT is that it must be convertible to a string, because the string representation is used to display the value.

How the data is stored within SQL Server can be defined: either an automatic mechanism can be used to store the data in a native format, or you can convert the data to a byte stream to define how the data should be stored.

Creating UDTs

Next, you look at how to create a user-defined type. You create a `SqlCoordinate` type representing the world coordinates longitude and latitude for easily defining the location of places, cities, and the like. To create CLR objects with Visual Studio you can use the Visual Studio 2008 SQL Server Project (in the category Visual C# ⇨ Database). Select the Solution Explorer and add a UDT by using the User-Defined Type template. Name the type `SqlCoordinate`. With the template, the base functionality of a custom type is already defined:

```
using System;
using System.Data;
using System.Data.Sql;
using System.Data.SqlTypes;
using Microsoft.SqlServer.Server;

[Serializable]
[Microsoft.SqlServer.Server.SqlUserDefinedType(Format.Native)]
public struct SqlCoordinate : INullable
{
   public override string ToString()
   {
      // Replace the following code with your code
      return "";
   }

   public bool IsNull
```

```
    {
       get
       {
          // Put your code here
          return m_Null;
       }
    }

    public static SqlCoordinate Null
    {
       get
       {
          SqlCoordinate h = new SqlCoordinate();
          h.m_Null = true;
          return h;
       }
    }

    public static SqlCoordinate Parse(SqlString s)
    {
       if (s.IsNull)
          return Null;
       SqlCoordinate u = new SqlCoordinate();
       // Put your code here
       return u;
    }

    // This is a place-holder method
    public string Method1()
    {
       //Insert method code here
       return "Hello";
    }

    // This is a place-holder static method
    public static SqlString Method2()
    {
       // Insert method code here
       return new SqlString("Hello");
    }

    // This is a placeholder field member
    public int var1;
    // Private member
    private bool m_Null;
}
```

Because this type can also be used directly from client code, it is a good idea to add a namespace, which is not done automatically.

The struct `SqlCoordinate` implements the interface `INullable`. The interface `INullable` is required for UDTs because database types can also be null. The attribute `[SqlUserDefinedType]` is used for automatic deployment with Visual Studio for UDTs. The argument `Format.Native` defines the serialization format to be used. Two serialization formats are possible: `Format.Native` and `Format.UserDefined`. `Format.Native` is the simple serialization format where the engine performs serialization and deserialization of instances. This serialization allows only blittable data types (*blittable data types* have the same memory representation in managed and native code). With the `Coordinate` class, the data types to serialize are of type `int` and `bool`, which are blittable data types. A `string` is not a blittable data type. Using `Format.UserDefined` requires the interface `IBinarySerialize` to be implemented. The `IBinarySerialize` interface provides custom implementation for user-defined types. `Read()` and `Write()` methods must be implemented for serialization of the data to a `BinaryReader` and a `BinaryWriter`.

Blittable data types have the same memory representation in both managed and unmanaged memory. Conversion is not needed with blittable data types. Blittable data types are `byte`, `sbyte`, `short`, `ushort`, `int`, `uint`, `long`, `ulong`, *and combinations of these data types such as arrays and structs that contain only these data types.*

```
namespace Wrox.ProCSharp.SqlServer
{

   [Serializable]
   [SqlUserDefinedType(Format.Native)]
   public struct SqlCoordinate : INullable
   {
      private int longitude;
      private int latitude;
      private bool isNull;
```

The attribute `[SqlUserDefinedType]` allows setting several properties, which are shown in the following table.

SqlUserDefinedTypeAttribute Property	Description
`Format`	The property `Format` defines how the data type is stored within SQL Server. Currently supported formats are `Format.Native` and `Format.UserDefined`.
`IsByteOrdered`	If the property `IsByteOrdered` is set to `true`, it is possible to create an index for the data type, and it can be used with `GROUP BY` and `ORDER BY` SQL statements. The disk representation will be used for binary comparisons. Each instance can have only one serialized representation, so binary comparisons can succeed. The default is `false`.
`IsFixedLength`	If the disk representation of all instances is of the same size, `IsFixedLength` can be set to `true`.
`MaxByteSize`	The maximum number of bytes needed to store the data is set with `MaxByteSize`. This property is specified only with a user-defined serialization.
`Name`	With the `Name` property, a different name of the type can be set. By default the name of the class is used.
`ValidationMethodName`	With the `ValidationMethodName` property a method name can be defined to validate instances when the deserialization takes place.

To represent the direction of the coordinate, the enumeration `Orientation` is defined:

```
public enum Orientation
{
   NorthEast,
   NorthWest,
   SouthEast,
   SouthWest
}
```

This enumeration can be used only within methods of the struct `Coordinate`, not as a member field because enumerations are not blittable. Future versions may support enums with the native format in SQL Server.

The struct `Coordinate` specifies some constructors to initialize the `longitude`, `latitude`, and `isNull` variables. The variable `isNull` is set to `true` if no values are assigned to `longitude` and `latitude`, which is the case in the default constructor. A default constructor is needed with UDTs.

With the worldwide coordination system, longitude and latitude are defined with degrees, minutes, and seconds. Vienna, Austria has the coordinates 48° 14' longitude and 16° 20' latitude. The symbols °, ', and " represent degrees, minutes, and seconds, respectively.

With the variables `longitude` and `latitude`, the longitude and latitude values are stored using seconds. The constructor with seven integer parameters converts degrees, minutes, and seconds to seconds, and sets the longitude and latitude to negative values if the coordinate is based in the South or West:

```
public SqlCoordinate(int longitude, int latitude)
{
   isNull = false;
   this.longitude = longitude;
   this.latitude = latitude;
}


public SqlCoordinate(int longitudeDegrees, int longitudeMinutes,
      int longitudeSeconds, int latitudeDegrees, int latitudeMinutes,
      int latitudeSeconds, Orientation orientation)
{
   isNull = false;
   this.longitude = longitudeSeconds + 60 * longitudeMinutes + 3600 *
         longitudeDegrees;
   this.latitude = latitudeSeconds + 60 * latitudeMinutes + 3600 *
         latitudeDegrees;
   switch (orientation)
   {
      case Orientation.SouthWest:
         longitude = -longitude;
         latitude = -latitude;
         break;
      case Orientation.SouthEast:
         longitude = -longitude;
         break;
      case Orientation.NorthWest:
         latitude = -latitude;
         break;
   }
}
```

The `INullable` interface defines the property `IsNull`, which must be implemented to support nullability. The static property `Null` is used to create an object that represents a null value. In the `get` accessor a `Coordinate` object is created, and the `isNull` field is set to `true`:

```
public bool IsNull
{
   get
   {
      return isNull;
   }
}

public static SqlCoordinate Null
{
   get
   {
      SqlCoordinate c = new SqlCoordinate();
      c.isNull = true;
      return c;
   }
}
```

A UDT must be converted from and to a string. For conversion to a string, the `ToString()` method of the `Object` class must be overridden. The variables `longitude` and `latitude` are converted in the following code for a string representation to show the degrees, minutes, and seconds notation:

```
public override string ToString()
{
   if (this.isNull)
      return null;

   char northSouth = longitude > 0 ? 'N' : 'S';
   char eastWest = latitude > 0 ? 'E' : 'W';

   int longitudeDegrees = Math.Abs(longitude) / 3600;
   int remainingSeconds = Math.Abs(longitude) % 3600;
   int longitudeMinutes = remainingSeconds / 60;
   int longitudeSeconds = remainingSeconds % 60;

   int latitudeDegrees = Math.Abs(latitude) / 3600;
   remainingSeconds = Math.Abs(latitude) % 3600;
   int latitudeMinutes = remainingSeconds / 60;
   int latitudeSeconds = remainingSeconds % 60;

   return String.Format("{0}˚{1}'{2}\"{3},{4}˚{5}'{6}\"{7}",
         longitudeDegrees, longitudeMinutes, longitudeSeconds,
         northSouth, latitudeDegrees, latitudeMinutes,
         latitudeSeconds, eastWest);
}
```

The string that is entered from the user is represented in the `SqlString` parameter of the static method `Parse()`. First, the `Parse()` method checks if the string represents a null value, in which case the `Null` property is invoked to return an empty `Coordinate` object. If the `SqlString s` does not represent a null value, the text of the string is converted to pass the longitude and latitude values to the `Coordinate` constructor:

```
      public static SqlCoordinate Parse(SqlString s)
      {
         if (s.IsNull)
            return SqlCoordinate.Null;

         try
         {
            string[] coordinates = s.Value.Split(',');
            char[] separators = { '°', '\'', '\"' };
            string[] longitudeVals = coordinates[0].Split(separators);
            string[] latitudeVals = coordinates[1].Split(separators);

            Orientation orientation;
            if (longitudeVals[3] == "N" && latitudeVals[3] == "E")
               orientation = Orientation.NorthEast;
            else if (longitudeVals[3] == "S" && latitudeVals[3] == "W")
               orientation = Orientation.SouthWest;
            else if (longitudeVals[3] == "S" && latitudeVals[3] == "E")
               orientation = Orientation.SouthEast;
            else
               orientation = Orientation.NorthWest;

            return new SqlCoordinate(
                  int.Parse(longitudeVals[0]), int.Parse(longitudeVals[1]),
                  int.Parse(longitudeVals[2]),
                  int.Parse(latitudeVals[0]), int.Parse(latitudeVals[1]),
                  int.Parse(latitudeVals[2]), orientation);
         }
         catch (Exception ex)
         {
            throw new ArgumentException(
                  "Argument has a wrong syntax. " +
                  "This syntax is required: 37°47\'0\"N,122°26\'0\"W",
                  ex.Message);
         }
      }
   }
```

Using UDTs

After building the assembly, it can be deployed with SQL Server. Configuration of the UDT in SQL Server can either be done with Visual Studio 2008 using the Build ⇨ Deploy Project menu or using these SQL commands:

```
CREATE ASSEMBLY SampleTypes FROM
'c:\ProCSharp\SqlServer\PropCSharp.SqlTypes.dll'
CREATE TYPE Coordinate EXTERNAL NAME
[ProCSharp.SqlTypes].[ProCSharp.SqlTypes.SqlCoordinate]
```

With `EXTERNAL NAME`, the name of the assembly as well as the name of the class, including the namespace, must be set.

Now, it is possible to create a table called `Cities` that contains the data type `SqlCoordinate`, as shown in Figure 30-2. Fill the table with data as shown in Figure 30-3.

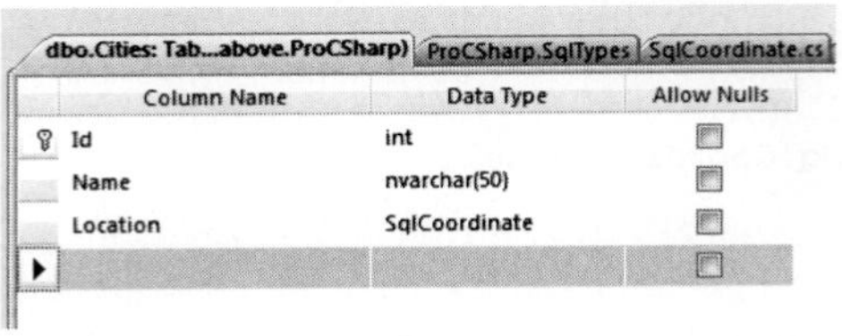

dbo.Cities: Tab...above.ProCSharp) | ProCSharp.SqlTypes | SqlCoordinate.cs

Column Name	Data Type	Allow Nulls
Id	int	☐
Name	nvarchar(50)	☐
Location	SqlCoordinate	☐
		☐

Figure 30-2

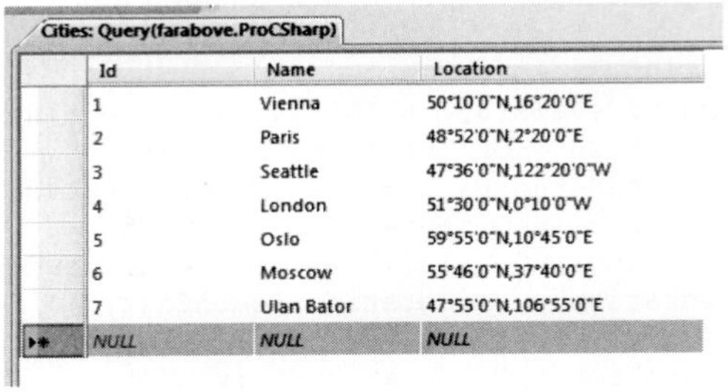

Cities: Query(farabove.ProCSharp)

Id	Name	Location
1	Vienna	50°10'0"N,16°20'0"E
2	Paris	48°52'0"N,2°20'0"E
3	Seattle	47°36'0"N,122°20'0"W
4	London	51°30'0"N,0°10'0"W
5	Oslo	59°55'0"N,10°45'0"E
6	Moscow	55°46'0"N,37°40'0"E
7	Ulan Bator	47°55'0"N,106°55'0"E
NULL	*NULL*	*NULL*

Figure 30-3

Using UDTs from Client-Side Code

The assembly of the UDT must be referenced to use the UDT from client-side code. Then it can be used like any other type on the client.

> **Because the assembly containing the UDTs is used both from the client and from the SQL Server, it is a good idea to put UDTs in a separate assembly from the other SQL Server extensions such as stored procedures and functions.**

In the sample code, the `SELECT` statement of the `SqlCommand` object references the columns of the `Cities` table that contains the `Location` column, which is of type `SqlCoordinate`. Calling the method `ToString()` invokes the `ToString()` method of the `SqlCoordinate` class to display the coordinate value in a string format:

```
// UDTClient
using System;
using System.Data;
using System.Data.SqlClient;
using Wrox.ProCSharp.SqlServer;

class Program
{
   static void Main()
   {
      string connectionString =
         @"server=(local);database=ProCSharp;trusted_connection=true";
      SqlConnection connection = new SqlConnection(connectionString);
      SqlCommand command = connection.CreateCommand();
```

```
            command.CommandText = "SELECT Id, Name, Location FROM Cities";
            connection.Open();

            SqlDataReader reader =
                  command.ExecuteReader(CommandBehavior.CloseConnection);
            while (reader.Read())
            {

               Console.WriteLine("{0,-10}: {1}", reader[1].ToString(),
                     reader[2].ToString());
            }
            reader.Close();
      }
   }
```

Of course, it is also possible to cast the returned object from the `SqlDataReader` to a `SqlCoordinate` type for using any other implemented methods of the `Coordinate` type:

```
SqlCoordinate coordinate = (SqlCoordinate)reader[2];
```

Running the application produces the following output:

```
Vienna     50°10'0"N,16°20'0"E
Paris      48°52'0"N,2°20'0"E
Seattle    47°36'0"N,122°20'0"W
London     51°30'0"N,0°10'0"W
Oslo       59°55'0"N,10°45'0"E
Moscow     55°46'0"N,37°40'0"E
Ulan Bator 47°55'0"N,106°55'0"E
```

With all the great functionality of UDTs, you have to be aware of an important restriction. Before deploying a new version of a UDT, the existing version must be dropped. This is possible only if all columns using the type are removed. Don't plan on using UDTs for types that you change frequently.

User-Defined Aggregates

An aggregate is a function that returns a single value based on multiple rows. Examples of built-in aggregates are `COUNT`, `AVG`, and `SUM`. `COUNT` returns the record count of all selected records, `AVG` returns the average of values from a column of selected rows, and `SUM` returns the sum of all values of a column. All built-in aggregates work only with built-in value types.

A simple usage of the built-in aggregate `AVG` is shown here to return the average unit price of all products from the AdventureWorks sample database by passing the `ListPrice` column to the `AVG` aggregate in the `SELECT` statement:

```
SELECT AVG(ListPrice) AS 'average list price'
FROM Production.Product
```

The result from the `SELECT` gives the average list price of all products:

```
average list price
438,6662
```

The `SELECT` statement returns just a single value that represents the average of all `ListPrice` column values. Aggregates can also work with groups. In the next example, the `AVG` aggregate is combined with the `GROUP BY` clause to return the average list price of every product line:

```
SELECT ProductLine, AVG(ListPrice) AS 'average list price'
FROM Production.Product
GROUP BY ProductLine
```

The average list price is now grouped by the product line:

```
ProductLine      average list price
NULL             16,8429
M                827,0639
R                965,3488
S                50,3988
T                840,7621
```

For custom value types, and if you want to do a specific calculation based on a selection of rows, you can create a user-defined aggregate.

Creating User-Defined Aggregates

To write a user-defined aggregate with CLR code, a simple class with the methods `Init()`, `Accumulate()`, `Merge()`, and `Terminate()` must be implemented. The functionality of these methods is shown in the following table.

UDT Method	Description
`Init()`	The `Init()` method is invoked for every group of rows to be processed. In this method, initialization can be done for calculation of every row group.
`Accumulate()`	The `Accumulate()` method is invoked for every value in all groups. The parameter of this method must be of the correct type that is accumulated; this can also be the class of a user-defined type.
`Merge()`	The `Merge()` method is invoked when the result of one aggregation must be combined with another aggregation.
`Terminate()`	After the last row of every group is processed, the `Terminate()` method is invoked. Here, the result of the aggregate must be returned with the correct data type.

The code sample shows how to implement a simple user-defined aggregate to calculate the sum of all rows in every group. For deployment with Visual Studio, the attribute `[SqlUserDefinedAggregate]` is applied to the class `SampleSum`. As with the user-defined type, with user-defined aggregates the format for storing the aggregate must be defined with a value from the `Format` enumeration. Again, `Format.Native` is for using automatic serialization with blittable data types.

In the code sample the variable `sum` is used for accumulation of all values of a group. In the `Init()` method, the variable `sum` is initialized for every new group to accumulate. The method `Accumulate()`, which is invoked for every value, adds the value of the parameter to the `sum` variable. With the `Merge()` method, one aggregated group is added to the current group. Finally, the method `Terminate()` returns the result of a group:

```
[Serializable]
[SqlUserDefinedAggregate(Format.Native)]
public struct SampleSum
{
   private int sum;

   public void Init()
   {
      sum = 0;
   }
```

```
        public void Accumulate(SqlInt32 Value)
        {
           sum += Value.Value;
        }

        public void Merge(SampleSum Group)
        {
           sum += Group.sum;
        }

        public SqlInt32 Terminate()
        {
           return new SqlInt32(sum);
        }
    }
```

You can use the Aggregate template from Visual Studio to create the core code for building the user-defined aggregate. The template from Visual Studio creates a struct that uses the `SqlString` *type as a parameter and return type with the* `Accumulate` *and* `Terminate` *methods. You can change the type to a type that represents the requirement of your aggregate. In the example, the* `SqlInt32` *type is used.*

Using User-Defined Aggregates

The user-defined aggregate can be deployed either with Visual Studio or with the `CREATE AGGREGATE` statement. Following the `CREATE AGGREGATE` is the name of the aggregate, the parameter `(@value int)`, and the return type. `EXTERNAL NAME` requires the name of the assembly and the .NET type including the namespace.

```
CREATE AGGREGATE [SampleSum] (@value int) RETURNS [int] EXTERNAL NAME
[Demo].[SampleSum]
```

After the user-defined aggregate has been installed, it can be used as shown in the following `SELECT` statement, where the number of ordered products is returned by joining the `Product` and `PurchaseOrderDetail` tables. For the user-defined aggregate, the `OrderQty` column of the `Order PurchaseOrderDetail` table is defined as an argument:

```
SELECT Purchasing.PurchaseOrderDetail.ProductID AS Id,
   Production.Product.Name AS Product,
   dbo.SampleSum(Purchasing.PurchaseOrderDetail.OrderQty) AS Sum
FROM Production.Product INNER JOIN
   Purchasing.PurchaseOrderDetail ON
   Purchasing.PurchaseOrderDetail.ProductID = Production.Product.ProductID
GROUP BY Purchasing.PurchaseOrderDetail.ProductID, Production.Product.Name
ORDER BY Id
```

An extract of the returned result that shows the number of orders for products by using the aggregate function `SampleSum` is presented here:

```
Id      Product                Sum
1       Adjustable Race        154
2       Bearing Ball           150
4       Headset Ball Bearings  153
317     LL Crankarm            44000
318     ML Crankarm            44000
319     HL Crankarm            71500
320     Chainring Bolts        375
321     Chainring Nut          375
322     Chainring              7440
```

Stored Procedures

SQL Server allows the creation of stored procedures with C#. A stored procedure is a subroutine, and they are physically stored in the database. They definitely are not to be considered a replacement for T-SQL. T-SQL still has an advantage when the procedure is mainly data-driven.

Take a look at the T-SQL stored procedure `GetCustomerOrders`, which returns information from customer orders from the AdventureWorks database. This stored procedure returns orders from the customer that is specified with the parameter `CustomerID`:

```
CREATE PROCEDURE GetCustomerOrders
   (
   @CustomerID int
   )
AS
SELECT SalesOrderID, OrderDate, DueDate, ShipDate FROM Sales.SalesOrderHeader
   WHERE (CustomerID = @CustomerID)
   ORDER BY SalesOrderID
```

Creating Stored Procedures

As you can see in the following code listing, implementing the same stored procedure with C# has more complexity. The attribute `[SqlProcedure]` is used to mark a stored procedure for deployment. With the implementation, a `SqlCommand` object is created. With the constructor of the `SqlConnection` object, the string `"Context Connection=true"` is passed to use the connection that was already opened by the client calling the stored procedure. Very similarly to the code you saw in Chapter 26, the SQL `SELECT` statement is set and one parameter is added. The `ExecuteReader()` method returns a `SqlDataReader` object. This reader object is returned to the client by invoking the `Send()` method of the `SqlPipe`:

```
using System.Data;
using System.Data.SqlClient;
using Microsoft.SqlServer.Server;

public partial class StoredProcedures
{
   [SqlProcedure]
   public static void GetCustomerOrdersCLR(int customerId)
   {
      SqlConnection connection = new SqlConnection("Context Connection=true");
      connection.Open();
      SqlCommand command = new SqlCommand();
      command.Connection = connection;
      command.CommandText = "SELECT SalesOrderID, OrderDate, DueDate, " +
            "ShipDate " +
            "FROM Sales.SalesOrderHeader " +
            "WHERE (CustomerID = @CustomerID)" +
            "ORDER BY SalesOrderID";

      command.Parameters.Add("@CustomerID", SqlDbType.Int);
      command.Parameters["@CustomerID"].Value = customerId;
```

```
            SqlDataReader reader = command.ExecuteReader();
            SqlPipe pipe = SqlContext.Pipe;
            pipe.Send(reader);
            connection.Close();
        }
    };
```

CLR stored procedures are deployed to SQL Server either using Visual Studio or with the `CREATE PROCEDURE` statement. With this SQL statement the parameters of the stored procedure are defined, as well as the name of the assembly, class, and method:

```
CREATE PROCEDURE GetCustomerOrdersCLR
(
   @CustomerID nchar(5)
)
AS EXTERNAL NAME Demo.StoredProcedures.GetCustomerOrdersCLR
```

Using Stored Procedures

The CLR stored procedure can be invoked just like a T-SQL stored procedure by using classes from the namespace `System.Data.SqlClient`. First, a `SqlConnection` object is created. The `CreateCommand()` method returns a `SqlCommand` object. With the command object, the name of the stored procedure `GetCustomerOrdersCLR` is set to the `CommandText` property. As with all stored procedures, the `CommandType` property must be set to `CommandType.StoredProcedure`. The method `ExecuteReader()` returns a `SqlDataReader` object to read record by record:

```
using System;
using System.Data;
using System.Data.SqlClient;

//...

      string connectionString =
         @"server=(local);database=AdventureWorks;trusted_connection=true";
      SqlConnection connection = new SqlConnection(connectionString);
      SqlCommand command = connection.CreateCommand();
      command.CommandText = "GetCustomerOrdersCLR";
      command.CommandType = CommandType.StoredProcedure;
      SqlParameter param = new SqlParameter("@customerId", 3);
      command.Parameters.Add(param);
      connection.Open();
      SqlDataReader reader =
            command.ExecuteReader(CommandBehavior.CloseConnection);
      while (reader.Read())
      {
         Console.WriteLine("{0} {1:d}", reader["SalesOrderID"],
            reader["OrderDate"]);
      }
      reader.Close();
```

The classes from the namespace `System.Data.SqlClient` *are discussed in Chapter 26, "Data Access."*

Invoking the stored procedure written with T-SQL or with C# is not different at all. The code for calling stored procedures is completely identical; from the caller code you don't know if the stored procedure is implemented with T-SQL or the CLR. An extract of the result shows the order dates for the customer with ID 3:

```
44124 9/1/2001
44791 12/1/2001
45568 3/1/2002
46377 6/1/2002
47439 9/1/2002
48378 12/1/2002
```

As you have seen, mainly data-driven stored procedures are better done with T-SQL. The code is a lot shorter. Writing stored procedures with the CLR has the advantage if you need some specific data-processing, for example, by using the .NET cryptography classes.

User-Defined Functions

User-defined functions are somewhat similar to stored procedures. The big difference is that user-defined functions can be invoked within SQL statements.

Creating User-Defined Functions

A CLR user-defined function can be defined with the attribute `[SqlFunction]`. The sample function `CalcHash()` converts the string that is passed to a hashed string. The MD5 algorithm that is used for hashing the string is implemented with the class `MD5CryptoServiceProvider` from the namespace `System.Security.Cryptography`. The `ComputeHash()` method computes the hash from the byte array input and returns a computed hash byte array. The hashed byte array is converted back to a `string` by using the `StringBuilder` class:

```
using System.Data.SqlTypes;
using System.Security.Cryptography;
using System.Text;
using Microsoft.SqlServer.Server;

public partial class UserDefinedFunctions
{
   [SqlFunction]
   public static SqlString CalcHash(SqlString value)
   {
      byte[] source;
      byte[] hash;

      source = ASCIIEncoding.ASCII.GetBytes(value.ToString());
      hash = new MD5CryptoServiceProvider().ComputeHash(source);

      StringBuilder output = new StringBuilder(hash.Length);

      for (int i = 0; i < hash.Length - 1; i++)
      {
         output.Append(hash[i].ToString("X2"));
      }

      return new SqlString(output.ToString());
   }
}
```

Using User-Defined Functions

A user-defined function can be deployed with SQL Server very similarly to the other .NET extensions: either with Visual Studio 2008 or with the `CREATE FUNCTION` statement:

```
CREATE FUNCTION CalcHash
(
   @value nvarchar
)
RETURNS nvarchar
AS EXTERNAL NAME Demo.UserDefinedFunctions.CalcHash
```

A sample usage of the `CalcHash()` function is shown with this `SELECT` statement where the credit card number is accessed from the `CreditCard` table in the AdventureWorks database by returning just the hash code from the credit card number:

```
SELECT Sales.CreditCard.CardType AS [Card Type],
   dbo.CalcHash(Sales.CreditCard.CardNumber) AS [Hashed Card]
FROM Sales.CreditCard INNER JOIN Sales.ContactCreditCard ON
   Sales.CreditCard.CreditCardID = Sales.ContactCreditCard.CreditCardID
WHERE Sales.ContactCreditCard.ContactID = 11
```

The result returned shows the hashed credit card number for contact ID 11:

```
Card Type     Hashed Card
ColonialVoice 7482F7B4E613F71144A9B336A3B9F6
```

Triggers

A *trigger* is a special kind of stored procedure invoked when a table is modified (for example, when a row is inserted, updated, or deleted). Triggers are associated with tables and the action that should activate them (for example, on insert/update/delete of rows).

With triggers, changes of rows can be cascaded through related tables or more complex data integrity can be enforced.

Within a trigger you have access to the current data of a row and the original data, so it is possible to reset the change to the earlier state. Triggers are automatically associated with the same transaction as the command that fires the trigger, so you get a correct transactional behavior.

The trigger `uCreditCard` that follows is part of the AdventureWorks sample database. This trigger is fired when a row in the `CreditCard` table is updated. With this trigger the `ModifiedDate` column of the `CreditCard` table is updated to the current date. For accessing the data that is changed, the temporary table inserted is used.

```
CREATE TRIGGER [Sales].[uCreditCard] ON [Sales].[CreditCard]
AFTER UPDATE NOT FOR REPLICATION AS
BEGIN
    SET NOCOUNT ON;

    UPDATE [Sales].[CreditCard]
    SET [Sales].[CreditCard].[ModifiedDate] = GETDATE()
    FROM inserted
    WHERE inserted.[CreditCardID] = [Sales].[CreditCard].[CreditCardID];
END;
```

Creating Triggers

The example shown here demonstrates implementing data integrity with triggers when new records are inserted into the `Users` table. To create a trigger with the CLR, a simple class must be defined that includes static methods that have the attribute `[SqlTrigger]` applied. The attribute `[SqlTrigger]` defines the table that is associated with the trigger and the event when the trigger should occur. In the example, the associated table is `Person.Contact`, which is indicated by the `Target` property. The `Event` property defines when the trigger should occur; here, the event string is set to `FOR INSERT`, which means the trigger is started when a new row is inserted in the `Users` table.

The property `SqlContext.TriggerContext` returns the trigger context in an object of type `SqlTriggerContext`. The `SqlTriggerContext` class offers three properties: `ColumnsUpdated` returns a Boolean array to flag every column that was changed, `EventData` contains the new and the original data of an update in XML format, and `TriggerAction` returns an enumeration of type `TriggerAction` to mark the reason for the trigger. The example compares whether the `TriggerAction` of the trigger context is set to `TriggerAction.Insert` before continuing.

Triggers can access temporary tables; for example, in the following code listing the `INSERTED` table is accessed. With `INSERT`, `UPDATE`, and `DELETE` SQL statements, temporary tables are created. The `INSERT` statement creates an `INSERTED` table; the `DELETE` statement creates a `DELETED` table. With the `UPDATE` statement both `INSERTED` and `DELETED` tables are used. The temporary tables have the same columns as the table that is associated with the trigger. The SQL statement `SELECT Username, Email FROM INSERTED` is used to access username and email, and to check the email address for correct syntax. `SqlCommand.ExecuteRow()` returns a row represented in a `SqlDataRecord`. Username and email are read from the data record. Using the regular expression class, `RegEx`, the expression used with the `IsMatch()` method checks if the email address conforms to valid email syntax. If it does not conform, an exception is thrown and the record is not inserted, because a rollback occurs with the transaction:

```
using System;
using System.Data.SqlClient;
using System.Text.RegularExpressions;
using Microsoft.SqlServer.Server;

public partial class Triggers
{
   [SqlTrigger(Name ="InsertContact", Target="Person.Contact",
         Event="FOR INSERT")]
   public static void InsertContact()
   {
      SqlTriggerContext triggerContext = SqlContext.TriggerContext;

      if (triggerContext.TriggerAction == TriggerAction.Insert)
      {
         SqlConnection connection = new SqlConnection(
               "Context Connection=true");
         SqlCommand command = new SqlCommand();
         command.Connection = connection;
         command.CommandText = "SELECT EmailAddress FROM INSERTED";
         connection.Open();
         string email = (string)command.ExecuteScalar();
         connection.Close();

         if (!Regex.IsMatch(email,
               @"([\w-]+\.)*?[\w-]+@[\w-]+\.([\w-]+\.)*?[\w]+$"))
```

```
                {
                    throw new FormatException("Invalid email");
                }
            }
        }
    }
```

Using Triggers

Using deployment of Visual Studio 2008, the trigger can be deployed to the database. You can use the CREATE TRIGGER command to create the trigger manually:

```
CREATE TRIGGER InsertContact ON Person.Contact
FOR INSERT
AS EXTERNAL NAME Demo.Triggers.InsertContact
```

Trying to insert rows into the Users table with an incorrect email throws an exception, and the insert is not done.

XML Data Type

One of the major programming features of SQL Server is the XML data type. With older versions of SQL Server, XML data is stored inside a string or a blob. Now XML is a supported data type that allows you to combine SQL queries with XQuery expressions to search within XML data. An XML data type can be used as a variable, a parameter, a column, or a return value from a UDF.

With Office 2007, it is possible to store Word and Excel documents as XML. Word and Excel also support using custom XML schemas, where only the content (and not the presentation) is stored with XML. The output of Office applications can be stored directly in SQL Server, where it is possible to search within this data. Of course, custom XML data can also be stored in SQL Server.

> **Don't use XML types for relational data. If you do a search for some of the elements and if the schema is clearly defined for the data, storing these elements in a relational fashion allows the data to be accessed faster. If the data is hierarchical and some elements are optional and may change over time, storing XML data has many advantages.**

Tables with XML Data

Creating tables with XML data is as simple as selecting the Xml data type with a column. The following CREATE TABLE SQL command creates the Exams table with a column ID that is also the primary key, the column Number, and the column Info, which is of type xml:

```
CREATE TABLE [dbo].[Exams](
    [Id] [int] IDENTITY(1,1) NOT NULL,
    [Number] [nchar] (10) NOT NULL,
    [Info] [xml] NOT NULL,
    CONSTRAINT [PK_Exams] PRIMARY KEY CLUSTERED
    (
        [Id] ASC
    ) ON [PRIMARY]
) ON [PRIMARY]
```

For a simple test, the table is filled with this data:

```
INSERT INTO Exams values('70-536',
 '<Exam Number="70-536">
    <Title>TS: Microsoft .NET Framework 2.0 - Application Development Foundation
    </Title>
    <Certification Name="MCTS Windows Applications" Status="Core" />
    <Certification Name="MCTS Web Applications" Status="Core" />
    <Certification Name="MCTS Distributed Applications" Status="Core" />
    <Course>2956</Course>
    <Course>2957</Course>
    <Topic>Developing applications that use system types and collections
    </Topic>
    <Topic>Implementing service processes, threading, and application domains
    </Topic>
    <Topic>Embedding configuration, diagnostics, management, and installation
features
    </Topic>
    <Topic>Implementing serialization and input/output functionality</Topic>
    <Topic>Improving the security</Topic>
    <Topic>Implementing interoperability, reflection, and mailing functionality
    </Topic>
    <Topic>Implementing globalization, drawing, and text manipulation functionality
    </Topic>
  </Exam>')

INSERT INTO Exams values('70-528',
 '<Exam Number="70-528">
    <Title>TS: Microsoft .NET Framework - Web-Based Client Development</Title>
    <Certification Name="MCTS Web Applications" Status="Core" />
    <Course>2541</Course>
    <Course>2542</Course>
    <Course>2543</Course>
    <Course>2544</Course>
    <Topic>Creating and Programming a Web Application</Topic>
    <Topic>Integrating Data in a Web Application by using ADO.NET, XML, and
    Data-Bound Controls</Topic>
    <Topic>Creating Custom Web Controls</Topic>
    <Topic>Tracing, Configuring, and Deploying Applications</Topic>
    <Topic>Customizing and Personalizing a Web Application</Topic>
    <Topic>Implementing Authentication and Authorization</Topic>
    <Topic>Creating ASP.NET Mobile Web Applications</Topic>
  </Exam>')

INSERT INTO Exams values('70-526',
 '<Exam Number="70-526">
    <Title>TS: Microsoft .NET Framework 2.0 - Windows-Based Client Development
    </Title>
    <Certification Name="MCTS Windows Applications" Status="Core" />
    <Course>2541</Course>
    <Course>2542</Course>
    <Course>2546</Course>
    <Course>2547</Course>
    <Topic>Creating a UI for a Windows Forms Application by Using Standard Controls
    </Topic>
    <Topic>Integrating Data in a Windows Forms Application</Topic>
```

```
    <Topic>Implementing Printing and Reporting Functionality</Topic>
    <Topic>Enhancing Usability</Topic>
    <Topic>Implementing Asynchronous Programming Techniques to Improve the User
    Experience</Topic>
    <Topic>Developing Windows Forms Controls</Topic>
    <Topic>Configuring and Deploying Applications</Topic>
  </Exam>')
```

Reading XML Values

You can read the XML data with ADO.NET using a `SqlDataReader` object. The `SqlDataReader` method `GetSqlXml()` returns a `SqlXml` object. The `SqlXml` class has a property `Value` that returns the complete XML representation and a `CreateReader()` method that returns an `XmlReader` object.

The `Read()` method of the `XmlReader` is repeated in a `while` loop to read node by node. With the output there's interest only in information about the value of the attribute `Number`, and the values of the elements `Title` and `Course`. The node to which the reader is positioned is compared with the corresponding XML element names, and the corresponding values are written to the console.

```
using System;
using System.Data;
using System.Data.SqlClient;
using System.Data.SqlTypes;
using System.Text;
using System.Xml;

   class Program
   {
      static void Main()
      {
         string connectionString =
            @"server=(local);database=ProCSharp;trusted_connection=true";
         SqlConnection connection = new SqlConnection(connectionString);
         SqlCommand command = connection.CreateCommand();
         command.CommandText = "SELECT Id, Number, Info FROM Exams";
         connection.Open();
         SqlDataReader reader = command.ExecuteReader(
               CommandBehavior.CloseConnection);
         while (reader.Read())
         {
            SqlXml xml = reader.GetSqlXml(2);

            XmlReader xmlReader = xml.CreateReader();

            StringBuilder courses = new StringBuilder("Course(s): ", 40);
            while (xmlReader.Read())
            {
               if (xmlReader.Name == "Exam" && xmlReaderIsStartElement)
               {
                  Console.WriteLine("Exam: {0}",
                        xmlReader.GetAttribute("Number"));
               }
               else if (xmlReader.Name == "Title" && xmlReader.IsStartElement)
```

(continued)

```
            {
               Console.WriteLine("Title: {0}", xmlReader.ReadString());
            }
            else if (xmlReader.Name == "Course" &&
                  xmlReader.IsStartElement)
            {
               courses.AppendFormat("{0} ", xmlReader.ReadString());
            }
         }
         xmlReader.Close();
         Console.WriteLine(courses.ToString());
         Console.WriteLine();
      }
      reader.Close();
   }
}
```

Running the application you will get the output as shown:

```
Exam: 70-536
Title: TS: Microsoft .NET Framework 2.0 - Application Development Foundation
Course(s): 2956 2957

Exam: 70-528
Title: TS: Microsoft .NET Framework 2.0 - Web-Based Client Development
Course(s): 2541 2542 2543 2544

Exam: 70-526
Title: TS: Microsoft .NET Framework 2.0 - Windows-Based Client Development
Course(s): 2541 2542 2546 2547
```

Instead of using the `XmlReader` class you can read the complete XML content into the `XmlDocument` class and parse the elements by using the DOM model. The method `SelectSingleNode()` requires an XPath expression and returns an `XmlNode` object. The XPath expression `//Exam` looks for the `Exam` XML element inside the complete XML tree. The `XmlNode` object returned can be used to read the children of the represented element. The value of the `Number` attribute is accessed to write the exam number to the console, then the `Title` element is accessed and the content of the `Title` element is written to the console, and the content of all `Course` elements is written to the console as well.

```
string connectionString =
      @"server=(local);database=ProCSharp;trusted_connection=true";
SqlConnection connection = new SqlConnection(connectionString);
SqlCommand command = connection.CreateCommand();
command.CommandText = "SELECT Id, Number, Info FROM Exams";
connection.Open();
SqlDataReader reader = command.ExecuteReader(
      CommandBehavior.CloseConnection);
while (reader.Read())
{
   SqlXml xml = reader.GetSqlXml(2);
   XmlDocument doc = new XmlDocument();
   doc.LoadXml(xml.Value);

   XmlNode examNode = doc.SelectSingleNode("//Exam");
   Console.WriteLine("Exam: {0}",
         examNode.Attributes["Number"].Value);
```

```
            XmlNode titleNode = examNode.SelectSingleNode("./Title");
            Console.WriteLine("Title: {0}", titleNode.InnerText);
            Console.Write("Course(s): ");
            foreach (XmlNode courseNode in examNode.SelectNodes("./Course"))
            {
               Console.Write("{0} ", courseNode.InnerText);
            }
            Console.WriteLine();

         }
         reader.Close();
```

The `XmlReader` *and* `XmlDocument` *classes are discussed in Chapter 28, "Manipulating XML."*

With .NET 3.5 there's another option to access the XML column from the database. You can combine LINQ to SQL and LINQ to XML, which makes the programming code smaller.

You can use the LINQ to SQL designer by selecting the LINQ to SQL Classes template from the Data templates category. Name the file `ProCSharp.dbml` to create a mapping for the database `ProCSharp`. Create the mapping by dragging and dropping the `Exams` table from the Solution Explorer to the design surface as shown in Figure 30-4.

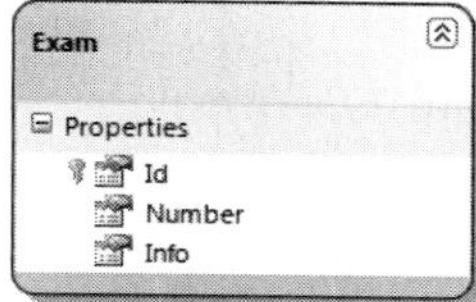

Figure 30-4

The mapping class that is created by the designer has the name `ProCSharpDataContext` and defines a property `Exams` to return all exam rows. Here a `foreach` statement is used to iterate through all records. Of course you can also define a LINQ query with a `where` expression if not all records are required. The `Exam` class defines the properties `Id`, `Number`, and `Info` accordingly to the columns in the database table. The `Info` property is of type `XDocument` and thus can be accessed by using the new LINQ to XML classes from the namespace `System.Xml.Linq`. Invoking the method `Element()` passing the name of the XML element `Exam` returns an `XElement` object that is then used to access the values of the attribute `Number` and the elements `Title` and `Course` in a much simpler way, as was done earlier with the `XmlDocument` class.

```
using System;
using System.Xml.Linq;

namespace Wrox.ProCSharp.SqlServer
{
   class Program
   {
      static void Main()
      {
         ProCSharpDataContext db = new ProCSharpDataContext();

         foreach (Exam item in db.Exams)
```

(continued)

(continued)

```
            {
               XElement exam = item.Info.Element("Exam");
               Console.WriteLine("Exam: {0}", exam.Attribute("Number").Value);
               Console.WriteLine("Title: {0}", exam.Element("Title").Value);
               Console.Write("Course(s): ");
               foreach (var course in exam.Elements("Course"))
               {
                  Console.Write("{0} ", course.Value);
               }
               Console.WriteLine();
            }
         }
      }
   }
```

LINQ to SQL and LINQ to XML are explained in Chapters 27 and 29, respectively.

Query of Data

Up until now, you haven't seen the really great features of the XML data type. SQL `SELECT` statements can be combined with XML XQuery.

A `SELECT` statement combined with an XQuery expression to read into the XML value is shown here:

```
SELECT [Id], [Number], [Info].query('/Exam/Course') AS Course FROM [Exams]
```

The XQuery expression `/Exam/Course` accesses the `Course` elements that are children of the `Exam` element. The result of this query returns the IDs, exam numbers, and courses:

```
1 70-536 <Course>2956</Course><Course>2957</Course>
2 70-528 <Course>2541</Course><Course>2542</Course><Course>2543</Course>
         <Course>2544</Course>
3 70-526 <Course>2541</Course><Course>2542</Course><Course>2546</Course>
         <Course>2547</Course>
```

With an XQuery expression, you can create more complex statements to query data within the XML content of a cell. The next example converts the XML from the exam information to XML that lists information about courses:

```
SELECT [Info].query('
   for $course in /Exam/Course
   return
<Course>
   <Exam>{ data(/Exam[1]/@Number) }</Exam>
   <Number>{ data($course) }</Number>
</Course>')
AS Course
FROM [Exams]
WHERE Id=2
```

Here, just a single row is selected with `SELECT [Info]... FROM Exams WHERE Id = 2`. With the result of this SQL query, the `for` and `return` statements of an XQuery expression are used. `for $course in /Exam/Course` iterates through all `Course` elements. `$course` declares a variable that is set with every iteration (similar to a C# `foreach` statement). Following the `return` statement, the result of the query for every row is defined. The result for every course element is surrounded by the `<Course>` element. Embedded inside the `<Course>` element are `<Exam>` and `<Number>`. The text within the <Exam> element is defined with data(/Exam[1]/@Number). data() is an XQuery function that returns the value of the node specified with the argument. The node /Exam[1] is used to access the first <Exam> element; @Number specifies the XML attribute Number. The text within the element <Number> is defined from the variable $course.

Contrary to C#, where the first element in a collection is accessed with an index of 0, with XPath the first element in a collection is accessed with an index of 1.

The result of this query is shown here:

```
<Course>
  <Exam>70-528</Exam>
  <Number>2541</Number>
</Course>
<Course>
  <Exam>70-528</Exam>
  <Number>2542</Number>
</Course>
<Course
  <Exam>70-528</Exam>
  <Number>2543</Number>
</Course>
<Course>
  <Exam>70-528</Exam>
  <Number>2544</Number>
</Course>
```

You can change the XQuery statement to also include a where clause for filtering XML elements. The following example only returns courses from the XML column if the course number has a value higher than 2542:

```
SELECT [Info].query('
   for $course in /Exam/Course
   where ($course > 2542)
   return
<Course>
   <Exam>{ data(/Exam[1]/@Number) }</Exam>
   <Number>{ data($course) }</Number>
</Course>')
AS Course
FROM [Exams]
WHERE Id=2
```

The result is reduced to just two course numbers:

```
<Course>
  <Exam>70-528</Exam>
  <Number>2543</Number>
</Course>
<Course>
  <Exam>70-528</Exam>
  <Number>2544</Number>
</Course>
```

XQuery in SQL Server allows using several other XQuery functions for getting minimum, maximum, or summary values, working with strings, numbers, checking for positions within collections, and so on.

The next example shows the use of the `count()` function to get the number of `/Exam/Course` elements:

```
SELECT [Id], [Number], [Info].query('
   count(/Exam/Course)')
   AS "Course Count"
FROM [Exams]
```

The data returned displays the number of courses for the exams:

```
Id          Number          Course Count
1           70-536          2
2           70-528          4
3           70-526          4
```

XML Data Modification Language (XML DML)

XQuery as it is defined by the W3C (`http://www.w3c.org`) allows only querying of data. Because of this XQuery restriction, Microsoft defined an extension to XQuery that has the name XML Data Modification Language (XML DML). XML DML makes it possible to modify XML data with the following XQuery extensions: `insert`, `delete`, and `replace value of`.

This section looks at some examples to insert, delete, and modify XML contents within a cell.

You can use the `insert` keyword to insert some XML content within an XML column without replacing the complete XML cell. Here, `<Course>2555</Course>` is inserted as the last child element of the first `Exam` element:

```
UPDATE [Exams]
SET [Info].modify('
   insert <Course>2555</Course> as last into Exam[1]')
WHERE [Id]=3
```

XML content can be deleted with the `delete` keyword. Within the first `Exam` element, the last `Course` element is deleted. The last element is selected by using the `last()` function.

```
UPDATE [Exams]
SET [Info].modify('
   delete /Exam[1]/Course[last()]')
FROM [Exams] WHERE [Id]=3
```

It is also possible to change XML content. Here, the keyword `replace value of` is used. The expression `/Exam/Course[text() = 2543]` accesses only the child elements `Course` where the text content contains the string `2543`. From these elements, only the text content is accessed for replacement with the `text()` function. If only a single element is returned from the query, it is still required that you specify just one element for replacement. This is why explicitly the first text element returned is specified with `[1]`. `2599` specifies that the new course number is `2599`:

```
UPDATE [Exams]
SET [Info].modify('
   replace value of (/Exam/Course[text() = 2543]/text())[1] with 2599')
FROM [Exams]
```

XML Indexes

If some specific elements are often searched within the XML data, you can specify indexes within the XML data type. XML indexes must be distinguished as being a primary or a secondary XML index type. A primary XML index is created for the complete persisted representation of the XML value.

The following SQL command, `CREATE PRIMARY XML INDEX`, creates the index `idx_exams` on the `Info` column:

```
CREATE PRIMARY XML INDEX idx_exams on Exams (Info)
```

Primary indexes don't help if the query contains an XPath expression to directly access XML elements of the XML type. For XPath and XQuery expressions, XML secondary indexes can be used. If an XML secondary index is created, the primary index must already exist. With secondary indexes, these index types must be distinguished:

- `PATH` index
- `VALUE` index
- `PROPERTY` index

A `PATH` index is used if `exists()` or `query()` functions are used and XML elements are accessed with an XPath expression. Using the XPath expression `/Exam/Course`, it might be useful to do a `PATH` index:

```
CREATE XML INDEX idx_examNumbers on [Exams] (Info)
   USING XML INDEX idx_exams FOR PATH
```

The `PROPERTY` index is used if properties are fetched from elements with the `value()` function. The `FOR PROPERTY` statement with the index creation defines a `PROPERTY` index:

```
CREATE XML INDEX idx_examNumbers on [Exams] (Info)
   USING XML INDEX idx_exams FOR PROPERTY
```

If elements are searched through the tree with an XPath descendant-or-self axis expression, the best performance might be achieved with a `VALUE` index. The XPath expression `//Certification` searches all `Certification` elements with the descendant-or-self axis. The expression `[@Name="MCTS Web Applications"]` returns only the elements where the attribute `Name` has the value `MCTS Web Applications`:

```
SELECT [Info].query('/Exam/Title/text()') FROM [Exams]
   WHERE [Info].exist('//Certification[@Name="MCTS Web Applications"]') = 1
```

The result returned lists the titles of the exams that contain the requested certification:

```
TS: Microsoft .NET Framework 2.0 - Application Development Foundation
TS: Microsoft .NET Framework - Web-Based Client Development
```

The `VALUE` index is created with the `FOR VALUE` statement:

```
CREATE XML INDEX idx_examNumbers on [Exams] (Info)
   USING XML INDEX idx_exams FOR VALUE
```

Strongly Typed XML

The XML data type in SQL Server can also be strongly typed with XML schemas. With a strongly typed XML column, it is verified if the data conforms to the schema when XML data is inserted.

A XML schema can be created with the `CREATE XML SCHEMA COLLECTION` statement. The statement shown here creates a simple XML schema, `CourseSchema`. The schema defines the type `CourseElt` that contains a sequence of `Number` and `Title`, which are both of type `string`, and an element `Any`, which can be any type. `Number` and `Title` may occur only once. Because `Any` has the `minOccurs` attribute set to `0`, and the `maxOccurs` attribute set to `unbounded`, this element is optional. This allows you to add any additional information to the `CourseElt` type in future versions, while the schema still remains valid. Finally, the element name `Course` is of type `CourseElt`.

```
CREATE XML SCHEMA COLLECTION CourseSchema AS
'<?xml version="1.0" encoding="UTF-8"?>
<xs:schema id="Courses" targetNamespace="http://thinktecture.com/Courses.xsd"
  elementFormDefault="qualified" xmlns="http://thinktecture.com/Courses.xsd"
  xmlns:mstns="http://thinktecture.com/Courses.xsd"
  xmlns:xs="http://www.w3.org/2001/XMLSchema">
    <xs:complexType name="CourseElt">
      <xs:sequence>
        <xs:element name="Number" type="xs:string" maxOccurs="1"
              minOccurs="1" />
        <xs:element name="Title" type="xs:string" maxOccurs="1"
              minOccurs="1" />
        <xs:element name="Any" type="xs:anyType"
            maxOccurs="unbounded" minOccurs="0" />
      </xs:sequence>
    </xs:complexType>
    <xs:element name="Course" type="CourseElt">
    </xs:element>
</xs:schema>'
```

With this schema, a valid XML looks like this:

```
<Course xmlns="http://thinktecture.com/Courses.xsd">
  <Number>2549</Number>
  <Title>Advanced Distributed Application Development with Visual Studio 2008</
Title>
</Course>
```

With the Visual Studio Database project type, there's no support to add a schema to the database. This feature is not available from the GUI by Visual Studio 2008 but must be created manually. To create an XML schema with Visual Studio 2008, create a new Visual Studio project by using the Empty Project template. Add a new XML schema to the project. Then copy the XML syntax of the schema into the `CREATE XML SCHEMA` statement.

Besides using Visual Studio, you can copy the XML syntax into SQL Server Management Studio to create and view the XML schemas (see Figure 30-5). The Object Explorer lists the XML schemas under the Types entry.

The XML schema can be assigned to a column by setting it with the `xml` data type:

```
CREATE TABLE [Courses]
(
   [Id] [int] IDENTITY(1,1) NOT NULL,
   [Course] [xml]([dbo].[CourseSchema]) NOT NULL
)
```

By creating the table with Visual Studio 2008 or with SQL Server Management Studio, the XML schema can be assigned to a column by setting the property `XML schema namespace`.

Now as you add data to the XML column, the schema is verified. If the XML does not satisfy the schema definition, a `SqlException` is thrown with an XML Validation error.

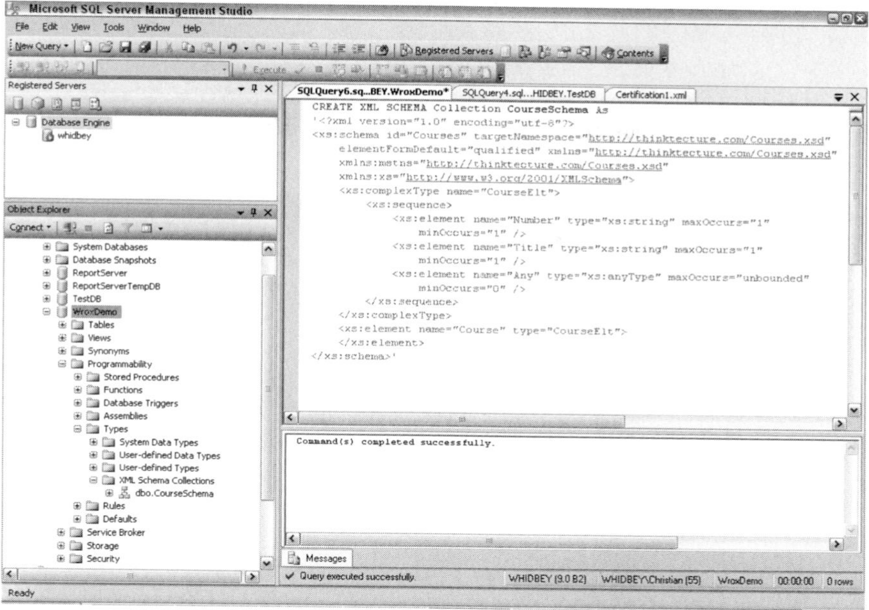

Figure 30-5

Summary

This chapter discussed the new features of SQL Server as they relate to CLR functionality. The CLR is hosted by SQL Server, so it is possible to create user-defined types, aggregates, stored procedures, functions, and triggers with C#.

User-defined types have some strict requirements in the .NET class for conversion to and from a string. How the data is stored internally in SQL Server depends on the format that is defined in the type. User-defined aggregates make it possible to do a custom accumulation using .NET classes. With stored procedures and functions, it is possible to make use of CLR classes for server-side code.

Using CLR with SQL Server doesn't mean that T-SQL is obsolete. You've seen that T-SQL has advantages because it requires less code if only data-intensive queries are done. CLR classes can have advantages in data-processing if .NET features such as cryptography come into play.

You've also had a glance into the XML data type of SQL Server to combine XQuery expressions with T-SQL statements.

This chapter concludes Part IV, "Data." Part V, "Presentation," gives details about defining the user interface of applications. With the user interface you have the options of working with Windows Forms, WPF, and ASP.NET.

Part V
Presentation

Chapter 31: Windows Forms

Chapter 32: Data Binding

Chapter 33: Graphics with GDI+

Chapter 34: Windows Presentation Foundation

Chapter 35: Advanced WPF

Chapter 36: Add-Ins

Chapter 37: ASP.NET Pages

Chapter 38: ASP.NET Development

Chapter 39: ASP.NET AJAX

Chapter 40: Visual Studio Tools for Office

31

Windows Forms

Web-based applications have become very popular over the past several years. The ability to have all of your application logic reside on a centralized server is very appealing from an administrator's viewpoint. Deploying client-based software can be very difficult, especially COM-based client software. The downside of Web-based applications is that they cannot provide that rich user experience. The .NET Framework has given developers the ability to create rich, smart client applications and eliminate the deployment problems and "DLL Hell" that existed before. Whether Windows Forms or Windows Presentation Foundation (see Chapter 34, "Windows Presentation Foundation") is chosen, client applications are no longer difficult to develop or deploy.

Windows Forms had quite an impact on Windows development. Now when an application is in the initial design phase, the decision between building a Web-based application or a client application has become a little more difficult. Windows client applications can be developed quickly and efficiently, and they can provide users with the rich experience that they expect.

Windows Forms will seem somewhat familiar if you are a Visual Basic developer. You create new forms (also known as windows or dialogs) in much the same way that you drag and drop controls from a toolbox onto the Form Designer. However, if your background is in the classic C style of Windows programming where you create the message pump and monitor messages, or if you're an MFC programmer, you will find that you're able to get to the lower-level internals if you need to. You can override the wndproc and catch those messages, but you might be surprised that you really won't need to very often.

This chapter looks at the following aspects of Windows Forms:

- The `Form` class
- The class hierarchy of Windows Forms
- The controls and components that are part of the `System.Windows.Forms` namespace
- Menus and toolbars
- Creating controls
- Creating user controls

Creating a Windows Form Application

First, you need to create a Windows Forms application. For the following example, create a blank form and show it on the screen. This example does not use Visual Studio .NET. It has been entered in a text editor and compiled using the command-line compiler.

```
using System;
using System.Windows.Forms;
namespace NotepadForms
{
  public class MyForm : System.Windows.Forms.Form
  {
    public MyForm()
    {
    }
    [STAThread]
    static void Main()
    {
      Application.Run(new MyForm());
    }
  }
}
```

When you compile and run this example, you will get a small blank form without a caption. Not real functional, but it is a Windows Form.

As you look at the code, two items deserve attention. The first is the fact that you have used inheritance to create the `MyForm` class. The following line declares that `MyForm` is derived from `System.Windows.Forms`:

```
public class MyForm : System.Windows.Forms.Form
```

The `Form` class is one of the main classes in the `System.Windows.Forms` namespace. The other section of code that you want to look at is:

```
[STAThread]
static void Main()
{
  Application.Run(new MyForm());
}
```

`Main` is the default entry point into any C# client application. Typically in larger applications, the `Main()` method would not be in a form, but in a class that is responsible for any startup processing that needs to be done. In this case, you would set the startup class name in the project properties dialog box. Notice the attribute `[STAThread]`. This sets the COM threading model to single-threaded apartment (STA). The STA threading model is required for COM interop and is added by default to a Windows Form project.

The `Application.Run()` method is responsible for starting the standard application message loop. `ApplicationRun()` has three overloads: the first takes no parameter, the second takes an `ApplicationContext` object as a parameter, and the one you see in the example takes a form object as a parameter. In the example, the `MyForm` object will become the main form of the application. This means that when this form is closed, the application ends. By using the `ApplicationContext` class, you can gain a little more control over when the main message loop ends and the application exits.

The `Application` class contains some very useful functionality. It provides a handful of static methods and properties for controlling the application's starting and stopping process and to gain access to the Windows messages that are being processed by the application. The following table lists some of the more useful of these methods and properties.

Method/Property	Description
CommonAppDataPath	The path for the data that is common for all users of the application. Typically this is BasePath\Company Name\Product Name\Version, where BasePath is C:\Documents and Settings\username\ApplicationData. If it does not exist, the path will be created.
ExecutablePath	This is the path and file name of the executable file that starts the application.
LocalUserAppDataPath	Similar to CommonAppDataPath with the exception that this property supports roaming.
MessageLoop	True or false if a message loop exists on the current thread.
StartupPath	Similar to ExecutablePath, except that the file name is not returned.
AddMessageFilter	Used to preprocess messages. By implementing an IMessageFilter-based object, the messages can be filtered from the message loop, or special processing can take place prior to the message being passed to the loop.
DoEvents	Similar to the Visual Basic DoEvents statement. Allows messages in the queue to be processed.
EnableVisualStyles	Enables XP visual styles for the various visual elements of the application. There are two overloads that will accept manifest information. One is a stream of the manifest, and the other is the full name and path of where the manifest exists.
Exit and ExitThread	Exit ends all currently running message loops and exits the application. ExitThread ends the message loop and closes all windows on the current thread.

Now, what does this sample application look like when it is generated in Visual Studio 2005? The first thing to notice is that two files are created because Visual Studio 2008 takes advantage of the partial class feature of the framework and separates all of the Designer-generated code into a separate file. Using the default name of Form1, the two files are Form1.cs and Form1.Designer.cs. Unless you have the Show All Files option checked on the Project menu you won't see Form1.Designer.cs in Solution Explorer. Following is the code that Visual Studio generates for the two files. First is Form1.cs:

```
using System;
using System.Collections.Generic;
using System.ComponentModel;
using System.Data;
using System.Drawing;
using System.Linq;
using System.Text;
using System.Windows.Forms;
namespace VisualStudioForm
{
public partial class Form1 : Form
{
public Form1()
```

(continued)

(continued)

```
{
InitializeComponent();
}
}
}
This is pretty simple, a handful of using statements and a simple constructor. Here
is the code in Form1.Designer.cs:
namespace VisualStudioForm
{
partial class Form1
{
/// <summary>
/// Required designer variable.
/// </summary>
private System.ComponentModel.IContainer components = null;
/// <summary>
/// Clean up any resources being used.
/// </summary>
/// <param name="disposing">true if managed resources should be disposed;
otherwise, false.</param>
protected override void Dispose(bool disposing)
{
if (disposing && (components != null))
{
 components.Dispose();
}
base.Dispose(disposing);
}
#region Windows Form Designer generated code
/// <summary>
/// Required method for Designer support - do not modify
/// the contents of this method with the code editor.
/// </summary>
private void InitializeComponent()
{
this.components = new System.ComponentModel.Container();
this.AutoScaleMode = System.Windows.Forms.AutoScaleMode.Font;
this.Text = "Form1";
}
#endregion
}
}
```

The Designer file of a form should rarely be edited directly. The only exception would be if there is any special processing that needs to take place in the `Dispose` method. The `InitializeComponent` method is discussed later in this chapter.

Looking at the code as a whole for this sample application, you can see it is much longer than the simple command-line example. There are several `using` statements at the start of the class; most are not necessary for this example. There is no penalty for keeping them there. The class `Form1` is derived from `System.Windows.Forms` just like the earlier Notepad example, but things start to get different at this point. First, there is this line in the `Form1.Designer` file:

```
private System.ComponentModel.IContainer components = null;
```

In the example, this line of code doesn't really do anything. When you add a component to a form, you can also add it to the components object, which is a container. The reason for adding to this container has to do with disposing of the form. The form class supports the `IDisposable` interface because it is implemented in the `Component` class. When a component is added to the components container, the container will make sure that the components are tracked properly and disposed of when the form is disposed of. You can see this if you look at the `Dispose` method in the code:

```
protected override void Dispose(bool disposing)
{
  if (disposing && (components != null))
  {
    components.Dispose();
  }
  base.Dispose(disposing);
}
```

Here you can see that when the `Dispose` method is called, the `Dispose` method of the components object is also called, and because the component object contains the other components, they are also disposed of.

The constructor of the `Form1` class, which is in the `Form1.cs` file, looks like this:

```
public Form1()
{
  InitializeComponent();
}
```

Notice the call to `InitializeComponent()`. `InitializeComponent()` is located in `Form1.Designer.cs` and does pretty much what it describes, and that is to initialize any controls that might have been added to the form. It also initializes the form properties. For this example, `InitializeComponent()` looks like the following:

```
private void InitializeComponent()
{
this.components = new System.ComponentModel.Container();
this.AutoScaleMode = System.Windows.Forms.AutoScaleMode.Font;
this.Text = "Form1";
}
```

As you can see, it is basic initialization code. This method is tied to the Designer in Visual Studio. When you make changes to the form by using the Designer, the changes are reflected in `InitializeComponent()`. If you make any type of code change in `InitializeComponent()`, the next time you make a change in the Designer, your changes will be lost. `InitializeComponent()` gets regenerated after each change in the Designer. If you need to add additional initialization code for the form or controls and components on the form, be sure to add it after `InitializeComponent()` is called. `InitializeComponent()` is also responsible for instantiating the controls so any call that references a control prior to `InitializeComponent()` will fail with a null reference exception.

To add a control or component to the form, press Ctrl+Alt+X or select Toolbox from the View menu in Visual Studio .NET. `Form1` should be in design mode. Right-click `Form1.cs` in Solution Explorer and select View Designer from the context menu. Select the Button control and drag it to the form in the Designer. You can also double-click the control, and it will be added to the form. Do the same with the `TextBox` control.

Now that you have added a `TextBox` control and a `Button` control to the form, `InitializeComponent()` expands to include the following code:

```
private void InitializeComponent()
{
  this.button1 = new System.Windows.Forms.Button();
  this.textBox1 = new System.Windows.Forms.TextBox();
  this.SuspendLayout();
  //
  // button1
  //
  this.button1.Location = new System.Drawing.Point(77, 137);
  this.button1.Name = "button1";
  this.button1.Size = new System.Drawing.Size(75, 23);
  this.button1.TabIndex = 0;
  this.button1.Text = "button1";
  this.button1.UseVisualStyleBackColor = true;
  //
  // textBox1
  //
  this.textBox1.Location = new System.Drawing.Point(67, 75);
  this.textBox1.Name = "textBox1";
  this.textBox1.Size = new System.Drawing.Size(100, 20);
  this.textBox1.TabIndex = 1;
  //
  // Form1
  //
  this.AutoScaleDimensions = new System.Drawing.SizeF(6F, 13F);
  this.AutoScaleMode = System.Windows.Forms.AutoScaleMode.Font;
  this.ClientSize = new System.Drawing.Size(284, 264);
  this.Controls.Add(this.textBox1);
  this.Controls.Add(this.button1);
  this.Name = "Form1";
  this.Text = "Form1";
  this.ResumeLayout(false);
  this.PerformLayout();
}
```

If you look at the first three lines of code in the method, you can see the `Button` and `TextBox` controls are instantiated. Notice the names given to the controls, `textBox1` and `button1`. By default, the Designer uses the name of the control and adds an integer value to the name. When you add another button, the Designer adds the name `button2`, and so on. The next line is part of the `SuspendLayout` and `ResumeLayout` pair. `SuspendLayout()` temporarily suspends the layout events that take place when a control is first initialized. At the end of the method the `ResumeLayout()` method is called to set things back to normal. In a complex form with many controls, the `InitializeComponent()` method can get quite large.

To change a property value of a control, either press F4 or select Properties Window from the View menu. The properties window enables you to modify most of the properties for a control or component. When a change is made in the properties window, the `InitializeComponent()` method is rewritten to reflect the new property value. For example, if the `Text` property is changed to `My Button` in the properties window, `InitializeComponent()` will contain this code:

```
//
// button1
//
this.button1.Location = new System.Drawing.Point(77, 137);
this.button1.Name = "button1";
```

```
this.button1.Size = new System.Drawing.Size(75, 23);
this.button1.TabIndex = 0;
this.button1.Text = "My Button";
this.button1.UseVisualStyleBackColor = true;
```

If you are using an editor other than Visual Studio .NET, you will want to include an `InitializeComponent()` type function in your designs. Keeping all of this initialization code in one spot will help keep the constructor cleaner, not to mention that if you have multiple constructors you can make sure that the initialization code is called from each constructor.

Class Hierarchy

The importance of understanding the hierarchy becomes apparent during the design and construction of custom controls. If your custom control is a derivative of a current control — for example, a text box with some added properties and methods — you will want to inherit from the text box control and then override and add the properties and methods to suit your needs. However, if you are creating a control that doesn't match up to any of the controls included with the .NET Framework, you will have to inherit from one of the three base control classes — `Control` or `ScrollableControl` if you need autoscrolling capabilities, and `ContainerControl` if your control needs to be a container of other controls.

The rest of this chapter is devoted to looking at many of these classes — how they work together and how they can be used to build professional-looking client applications.

Control Class

The `System.Windows.Forms` namespace has one particular class that is the base class for virtually every control and form that is created. This class is the `System.Windows.Forms.Control` class. The `Control` class implements the core functionality to create the display that the user sees. The `Control` class is derived from the `System.ComponentModel.Component` class. The `Component` class provides the `Control` class with the necessary infrastructure that is required to be dropped on a design surface and to be contained by another object. The `Control` class provides a large list of functionality to the classes that are derived from it. The list is too long to itemize here, so this section looks at the more important items that are provided by the `Control` class. Later in the chapter, when you look at the specific controls based on the `Control` class, you will see the properties and methods in some example code. The following subsections group the methods and properties by functionality, so related items can be looked at together.

Size and Location

The size and location of a control are determined by the properties `Height`, `Width`, `Top`, `Bottom`, `Left`, and `Right` along with the complementary properties `Size` and `Location`. The difference is that `Height`, `Width`, `Top`, `Bottom`, `Left`, and `Right` all take single integers as their value. `Size` takes a `Size` structure and `Location` takes a `Point` structure as their values. The `Size` and `Point` structures are a contained version of X,Y coordinates. `Point` generally relates to a location and `Size` is the height and width of an object. `Size` and `Point` are in the `System.Drawing` namespace. Both are very similar in that they provide an X,Y coordinate pair but also have overridden operators for easy comparison and conversion. You can, for example, add two `Size` structures together. In the case of the `Point` structure, the `Addition` operator is overridden so that you can add a `Size` structure to a `Point` and get a new `Point` in return. This has the effect of adding distance to a location and getting a new location. This is very handy if you have to dynamically create forms or controls.

The `Bounds` property returns a `Rectangle` object that represents the area of a control. This area includes scroll bars and title bars. `Rectangle` is also part of the `System.Drawing` namespace. The `ClientSize` property is a `Size` structure that represents the client area of the control, minus the scroll bars and title bar.

The PointToClient and PointToScreen methods are handy conversion methods that take a Point and return a Point. PointToClient takes a Point that represents screen coordinates and translates it to coordinates based on the current client object. This is handy for drag-and-drop actions. PointToScreen does just the opposite — it takes coordinates of a client object and translates them to screen coordinates. The RectangleToScreen and ScreenToRectangle methods perform the same functionality with Rectangle structures instead of Points.

The Dock property determines which edge of the parent control the control will be docked to. A DockStyle enumeration value is used as the property's value. This value can be Top, Bottom, Right, Left, Fill, or None. Fill sets the control's size to match the client area of the parent control.

The Anchor property anchors an edge of the control to the edge of the parent control. This is different from docking in that it does not set the edge to the parent control, but sets the current distance from the edge to be constant. For example, if you anchor the right edge of the control to the right edge of the parent and the parent is resized, the right edge of the control will maintain the same distance from the parent's right edge. The Anchor property takes a value of the AnchorStyles enumeration. The values are Top, Bottom, Left, Right, and None. By setting the values, you can make the control resize dynamically with the parent as the parent is resized. This way, buttons and text boxes will not be cut off or hidden as the form is resized by the user.

The Dock and Anchor properties used in conjunction with the Flow and Table layout controls (discussed later in this chapter) enable you to create very sophisticated user windows. Window resizing can be difficult with complex forms with many controls. These tools help make that process much easier.

Appearance

Properties that relate to the appearance of the control are BackColor and ForeColor, which take a System.Drawing.Color object as a value. The BackGroundImage property takes an Image-based object as a value. The System.Drawing.Image class is an abstract class that is used as the base for the Bitmap and Metafile classes. The BackgroundImageLayout property uses the ImageLayout enumeration to set how the image is displayed on the control. Valid values are Center, Tile, Stretch, Zoom, and None.

The Font and Text properties deal with displaying the written word. In order to change the Font you will need to create a Font object. When you create the Font object, you specify the font name, size, and style.

User Interaction

User interaction is best described as the various events that a control creates and responds to. Some of the more common events are Click, DoubleClick, KeyDown, KeyPress, Validating, and Paint.

The Mouse events — Click, DoubleClick, MouseDown, MouseUp, MouseEnter, MouseLeave, and MouseHover — deal with the interaction of the mouse and the control. If you are handling both the Click and the DoubleClick events, every time you catch a DoubleClick event, the Click event is raised as well. This can result in undesired results if not handled properly. Also, Click and DoubleClick receive EventArgs as an argument, whereas the MouseDown and MouseUp events receive MouseEventArgs. The MouseEventArgs contain several pieces of useful information such as the button that was clicked, the number of times the button was clicked, the number of mouse wheel detents (notches in the mouse wheel), and the current X and Y coordinates of the mouse. If you have access to any of this information, you will have to handle either the MouseDown or MouseUp events, not the Click or DoubleClick events.

The keyboard events work in a similar fashion: the amount of information needed determines the event that is handled. For simple situations, the KeyPress event receives KeyPressEventArgs. This contains KeyChar, which is a char value that represents the key pressed. The Handled property is used to determine whether or not the event was handled. If you set the `Handled` property to `true`, the event is not passed on for default handling by the operating system. If you need more information about the key that was pressed, the `KeyDown` or `KeyUp` event is more appropriate to handle this. They both receive `KeyEventArgs`. Properties in `KeyEventArgs` include whether the Ctrl, Alt, or Shift key was pressed. The `KeyCode` property returns a `Keys` enumeration value that identifies the key that was pressed. Unlike the `KeyPressEventArgs.KeyChar` property, the `KeyCode` property tells you about every key on the keyboard, not just the alphanumeric keys. The `KeyData` property returns a `Keys` value and will also set the modifier. The modifiers are OR'd with the value. This tells you that the Shift key or the Ctrl key was pressed as well. The `KeyValue` property is the `int` value of the `Keys` enumeration. The `Modifiers` property contains a `Keys` value that represents the modifier keys that were pressed. If more than one has been selected, the values are OR'd together. The key events are raised in the following order:

1. `KeyDown`
2. `KeyPress`
3. `KeyUp`

The `Validating`, `Validated`, `Enter`, `Leave`, `GotFocus`, and `LostFocus` events all deal with a control gaining focus (or becoming active) or losing focus. This happens when the user tabs into a control or selects the control with the mouse. `Enter`, `Leave`, `GotFocus`, and `LostFocus` seem to be very similar in what they do. The `GotFocus` and `LostFocus` events are lower-level events that are tied to the `WM_SETFOCUS` and the `WM_KILLFOCUS` Windows messages. Generally, you should use the `Enter` and `Leave` events if possible. The `Validating` and `Validated` events are raised when the control is validating. These events receive `CancelEventArgs`. With this, you can cancel the following events by setting the `Cancel` property to `true`. If you have custom validation code, and validation fails, you can set `Cancel` to `true` and the control will not lose focus. `Validating` occurs during validation; `Validated` occurs after validation. The order in which these events are raised is:

1. `Enter`
2. `GotFocus`
3. `Leave`
4. `Validating`
5. `Validated`
6. `LostFocus`

Understanding the order of these events is important so that you don't inadvertently create a recursive situation. For example, trying to set the focus of a control from the control's `LostFocus` event creates a message deadlock and the application stops responding.

Windows Functionality

The `System.Windows.Forms` namespace is one of the few namespaces that relies on Windows functionality. The `Control` class is a good example of that. If you were to do a disassembly of the `System.Windows.Forms.dll`, you would see a list of references to the `UnsafeNativeMethods` class. The .NET Framework uses this class to wrap all of the standard Win32 API calls. By using interop to the Win32 API, the look and feel of a standard Windows application can still be achieved with the `System.Windows.Forms` namespace.

Functionality that supports the interaction with Windows includes the `Handle` and `IsHandleCreated` properties. `Handle` returns an `IntPtr` that contains the HWND (windows handle) for the control. The window handle is an HWND that uniquely identifies the window. A control can be considered a window, so it has a corresponding HWND. You can use the `Handle` property to call any number of Win32 API calls.

To gain access to the Windows messages, you can override the WndProc method. The WndProc method takes a Message object as a parameter. The Message object is a simple wrapper for a windows message. It contains the HWnd, LParam, WParam, Msg, and Result properties. If you want to have the message processed by the system, you must make sure that you pass the message to the base.WndProc(msg) method. If you want to handle the message, you don't want to pass the message on.

Miscellaneous Functionality

Some items that are a little more difficult to classify are the data-binding capabilities. The BindingContext property returns a BindingManagerBase object. The DataBindings collection maintains a ControlBindingsCollection, which is a collection of binding objects for the control. Data binding is discussed in Chapter 32, "Data Binding."

The CompanyName, ProductName, and Product versions provide data on the origination of the control and its current version.

The Invalidate method allows you to invalidate a region of the control for repainting. You can invalidate the entire control or specify a region or rectangle to invalidate. This causes a paint message to be sent to the control's WndProc. You also have the option to invalidate any child controls at the same time.

Dozens of other properties, methods, and events make up the Control class. This list represents some of the more commonly used ones and is meant to give you an idea of the functionality available.

Standard Controls and Components

The previous section covered some of the common methods and properties for controls. This section looks at the various controls that ship with the .NET Framework, and explains what each of them offers in added functionality. The sample download (www.wrox.com) includes a sample application called FormExample. This sample application is an MDI application (discussed later in the chapter) and includes a form named frmControls that contains many controls with basic functionality enabled. Figure 31-1 shows what frmControls looks like.

Button

The Button class represents the simple command button and is derived from the ButtonBase class. The most common thing to do is to write code to handle the Click event of the button. The following code snippet implements an event handler for the Click event. When the button is clicked, a message box pops up that displays the button's name:

```
private void btnTest_Click(object sender, System.EventArgs e)
{
   MessageBox.Show(((Button)sender).Name + " was clicked.");
}
```

With the PerformClick method, you can simulate the Click event on a button without the user actually clicking the button. The NotifyDefault method takes a Boolean value as a parameter and tells the button to draw itself as the default button. Typically, the default button on a form has a slightly thicker border. To identify the button as default, you set the AcceptButton property on the form to the button. Then, when the user presses the Enter key, the button Click event for the default button is raised. Figure 31-2 shows that the button with the caption Default is the default button (notice the dark border).

Buttons can have images as well as text. Images are supplied by way of an ImageList object or the Image property. ImageList objects are exactly what they sound like: a list of images managed by a component placed on a form. They are explained in detail later in this chapter.

Both `Text` and `Image` have an `Align` property to align the text or image on the `Button`. The `Align` property takes a `ContentAlignment` enumeration value. The text or image can be aligned in combinations of left and right and top and bottom.

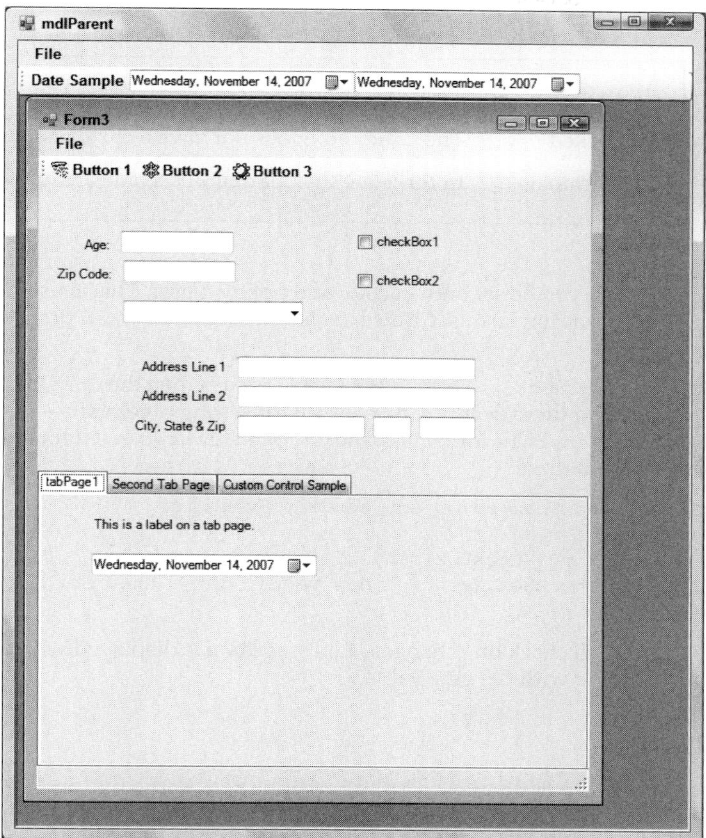

Figure 31-1

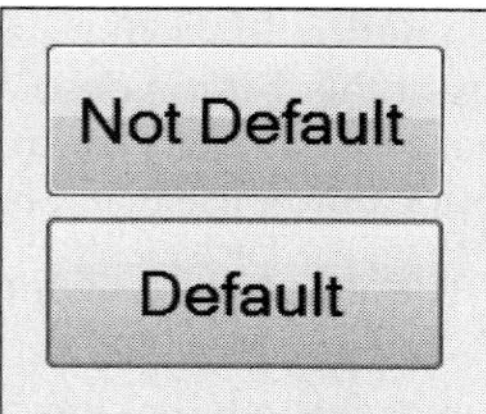

Figure 31-2

CheckBox

The CheckBox control is also derived from ButtonBase and is used to accept a two-state or three-state response from the user. If you set the ThreeState property to true, the CheckBox's CheckState property can be one of the three CheckState enum values in the following table.

Checked	The CheckBox has a check mark.
Unchecked	The CheckBox does not have a check mark.
Indeterminate	In this state the CheckBox becomes gray.

The Indeterminate value can be set only in code and not by a user. This is useful if you need to convey to the user that an option has not been set. You can also check the Checked property if you want a Boolean value.

The CheckedChanged and CheckStateChanged events occur when the CheckState or Checked properties change. Catching these events can be useful for setting other values based on the new state of the CheckBox. In the frmControls form class, the CheckedChanged event for several CheckBoxes is handled by the following method:

```
private void checkBoxChanged(object sender, EventArgs e)
{
  CheckBox checkBox = (CheckBox)sender;
  MessageBox.Show(checkBox.Name + " new value is " + checkBox.Checked.ToString());
}
```

As the checked state of each check box changes, a message box is displayed with the name of the check box that was changed along with the new value.

RadioButton

The last control derived from ButtonBase is the radio button. Radio buttons are generally used as a group. Sometimes referred to as option buttons, radio buttons allow the user to choose one of several options. When you have multiple RadioButton controls in the same container, only one at a time may be selected. So, if you have three options — for example, Red, Green, and Blue — if the Red option is selected and the user clicks the Blue option, the Red is automatically deselected.

The Appearance property takes an Appearance enumeration value. This can be either Button or Normal. When you choose Normal, the radio button looks like a small circle with a label beside it. Selecting the button fills the circle; selecting another button deselects the currently selected button and makes the circle look empty. When you choose Button, the control looks like a standard button, but it works like a toggle — selected is the in position, and deselected is the normal, or out, position.

The CheckedAlign property determines where the circle is in relation to the label text. It could be on top of the label, on either side, or below.

The CheckedChanged event is raised whenever the value of the Checked property changes. This way, you can perform other actions based on the new value of the control.

ComboBox, ListBox, and CheckedListBox

ComboBox, ListBox, and CheckedListBox are all derived from the ListControl class. This class provides some of the basic list management functionality. The most important aspects of using list controls are adding data to and selecting data from the list. Which list is used is generally determined by how the list is used and the type of data that is going to be in the list. If there is a need to have multiple selections or if the user needs to be able to see several items in the list at any time, the ListBox or CheckedListBox is going to be the best choice. If only a single item is ever selected in the list at any time, a ComboBox may be a good choice.

Data must be added to a list box before it can be useful. This is done by adding objects to the ListBox.ObjectCollection. This collection is exposed by the list's Items property. Because the collection stores objects, any valid .NET type can be added to the list. In order to identify the items, two important properties need to be set. The first is the DisplayMember property. This setting tells the ListControl what property of your object should be displayed in the list. The other is ValueMember, which is the property of your object that you want to return as the value. If strings have been added to the list, by default the string value is used for both of these properties. The frmLists form in the sample application shows how both objects and strings (which are of course objects) can be loaded into a list box. The example uses Vendor objects for the list data. The Vendor object contains just two properties: Name and PhoneNo. The DisplayMember property is set to the Name property. This tells the list control to display the value from the Name property in the list to the user.

You can access the data in the list control in a couple of ways, as shown in the following code example. The list is loaded with the Vendor objects. The DisplayMember and ValueMember properties are set. You can find this code in the frmLists form class in the sample application.

First is the LoadList method. This method loads the list with either Vendor objects or a simple string containing the vendor name. An option button is checked to see which values should be loaded in the list:

```
private void LoadList(Control ctrlToLoad)
    {
      ListBox tmpCtrl = null;
      if (ctrlToLoad is ListBox)
        tmpCtrl = (ListBox)ctrlToLoad;
      tmpCtrl.Items.Clear();
      tmpCtrl.DataSource = null;
      if (radioButton1.Checked)
      {
        //load objects
        tmpCtrl.Items.Add(new Vendor("XYZ Company", "555-555-1234"));
        tmpCtrl.Items.Add(new Vendor("ABC Company", "555-555-2345"));
        tmpCtrl.Items.Add(new Vendor("Other Company", "555-555-3456"));
        tmpCtrl.Items.Add(new Vendor("Another Company", "555-555-4567"));
        tmpCtrl.Items.Add(new Vendor("More Company", "555-555-6789"));
        tmpCtrl.Items.Add(new Vendor("Last Company", "555-555-7890"));
        tmpCtrl.DisplayMember = "Name";
      }
      else
      {
        tmpCtrl.Items.Clear();
        tmpCtrl.Items.Add("XYZ Company");
        tmpCtrl.Items.Add("ABC Company");
        tmpCtrl.Items.Add("Other Company");
        tmpCtrl.Items.Add("Another Company");
        tmpCtrl.Items.Add("More Company");
        tmpCtrl.Items.Add("Last Company");
      }
    }
```

Once the data is loaded in the list the SelectedItem and SelectedIndex properties can be used to get at the data. The SelectedItem property returns the object that is currently selected. If the list is set to allow multiple selections, there is no guarantee which of the selected items will be returned. In this case, the SelectObject collection should be used. This contains a list of all of the currently selected items in the list.

If the item at a specific index is needed, the Items property can be used to access the ListBox.ObjectCollection. Because this is a standard .NET collection class, the items in the collection can be accessed in the same way as any other collection class.

If DataBinding is used to populate the list, the SelectedValue property will return the property value of the selected object that was set to the ValueMember property. If Phone is set to ValueMember, the SelectedValue will return the Phone value from the selected item. In order to use ValueMember and SelectValue the list must be loaded by way of the DataSource property. An ArrayList or any other IList-based collection must be loaded with the objects first, then the list can be assigned to the DataSource property. This short example demonstrates this:

```
listBox1.DataSource = null;
System.Collections.ArrayList lst = new System.Collections.ArrayList();
lst.Add(new Vendor("XYZ Company", "555-555-1234"));
lst.Add(new Vendor("ABC Company", "555-555-2345"));
lst.Add(new Vendor("Other Company", "555-555-3456"));
lst.Add(new Vendor("Another Company", "555-555-4567"));
lst.Add(new Vendor("More Company", "555-555-6789"));
lst.Add(new Vendor("Last Company", "555-555-7890"));
listBox1.Items.Clear();
listBox1.DataSource = lst;
listBox1.DisplayMember = "Name";
listBox1.ValueMember = "Phone";
```

Using SelectedValue without using DataBinding will result in a NullException error.

The following lines of code show the syntax of accessing the data in the list:

```
//obj is set to the selected Vendor object
obj = listBox1.SelectedItem;
//obj is set to the Vendor object with index of 3 (4th object).
//obj is set to the values of the Phone property of the selected vendor object.
//This example assumes that databinding was used to populate the list.
listBox1.ValuesMember = "Phone";
obj = listBox1.SelectValue;
```

The thing to remember is that all of these methods return object as the type. A cast to the proper data type will need to be done in order to use the value of obj.

The Items property of the ComboBox returns ComboBox.ObjectCollection. A ComboBox is a combination of an edit control and a list box. You set the style of the ComboBox by passing a DropDownStyle enumeration value to the DropDownStyle property. The following table lists the various DropDownStyle values.

value	Description
DropDown	The text portion of the combo box is editable, and users can enter a value. They also must click the arrow button to show the list.
DropDownList	The text portion is not editable. Users must make a selection from the list.
Simple	This is similar to DropDown except that the list is always visible.

If the values in the list are wide, you can change the width of the drop-down portion of the control with the `DropDownWidth` property. The `MaxDropDownItems` property sets the number of items to show when the drop-down portion of the list is displayed.

The `FindString` and `FindStringExact` methods are two other useful methods of the list controls. `FindString` finds the first string in the list that starts with the passed-in string. `FindStringExact` finds the first string that matches the passed-in string. Both return the index of the value that is found or `-1` if the value is not found. They can also take an integer that is the starting index to search from.

DateTimePicker

The `DateTimePicker` allows users to select a date or time value (or both) in a number of different formats. You can display the `DateTime`-based value in any of the standard time and date formats. The Format property takes a `DateTimePickerFormat` enumeration that sets the format to `Long`, `Short`, `Time`, or `Custom`. If the Format property is set to `DateTiemePickerFormat.Custom`, you can set the `CustomFormat` property to a string that represents the format.

There is both a `Text` property and a `Value` property. The `Text` property returns a text representation of the `DateTime` value, whereas the `Value` property returns the `DateTime` object. You can also set the maximum and minimum allowable date values with the `MinDate` and `MaxDate` properties.

When users click the down arrow, a calendar is displayed allowing the users to select a date in the calendar. Properties are available that allow you to change the appearance of the calendar by setting the title and month background colors as well as the foreground colors.

The `ShowUpDown` property determines whether an `UpDown` arrow is displayed on the control. The currently highlighted value can be changed by clicking the up or down arrow.

ErrorProvider

`ErrorProvider` is actually not a control but a component. When you drag a component to the Designer, it shows in the component tray under the Designer. The `ErrorProvider` flashes an icon next to a control when an error condition or validation failure exists. Suppose that you have a `TextBox` entry for an age. Your business rules say that the age value cannot be greater than 65. If users try to enter an age greater than that, you must inform them that the age is greater than the allowable value and that they need to change the entered value. The check for a valid value takes place in the `Validated` event of the text box. If the validation fails, you call the `SetError` method, passing in the control that caused the error and a string that informs the user what the error is. An icon starts flashing, indicating that an error has occurred, and when the user hovers over the icon the error text is displayed. Figure 31-3 shows the icon that is displayed when an invalid entry is made in the text box.

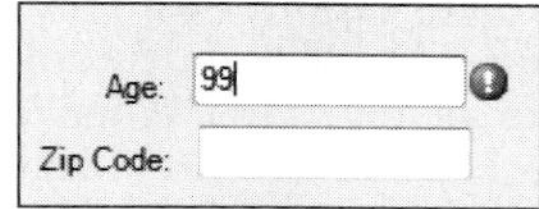

Figure 31-3

You can create an `ErrorProvider` for each control that produces errors on a form, but if you have a large number of controls this can become unwieldy. Another option is to use one error provider and, in the validate event, to call the `IconLocation` method with the control that is causing the validation and one of the `ErrorIconAlignment` enumeration values. This value sets where the icon is aligned near the control. Then you call the `SetError` method. If no error condition exists, you can clear the `ErrorProvider` by calling `SetError` with an empty string as the error string. The following example shows how this works:

```
private void txtAge_Validating(object sender,
System.ComponentModel.CancelEventArgs e)
{
  if(txtAge.TextLength > 0 && Convert.ToInt32(txtAge.Text) > 65)
  {
    errMain.SetIconAlignment((Control)sender,
                                          ErrorIconAlignment.MiddleRight);
    errMain.SetError((Control)sender, "Value must be less then 65.");
    e.Cancel = true;
  }
  else
  {
    errMain.SetError((Control)sender, "");
  }
}
private void txtZipCode_Validating(object sender, CancelEventArgs e)
    {
      if(txtZipCode.Text.Length != 5)
      {
        errMain.SetIconAlignment((Control)sender,
                   ErrorIconAlignment.MiddleRight);
        errMain.SetError((Control)sender, "Must be 5 charactors..");
        e.Cancel = true;
      }
      else
      {
        errMain.SetError((Control)sender, "");
      }
    }
```

If the validation fails (the age is over 65 in `txtAge`, for example), then the `SetIcon` method of the `ErrorProvider errMain` is called. It will set the icon next to the control that failed validation. The error is set next so that when users hover over the icon, the message informs them of what is responsible for the failed validation.

HelpProvider

`HelpProvider`, like `ErrorProvider`, is a component and not a control. `HelpProvider` allows you to hook up controls to help topics. To associate a control with the help provider, you call the `SetShowHelp` method, passing the control and a `Boolean` value that determines whether help will be shown. The `HelpNamespace` property allows you to set a help file. When the `HelpNamespace` property is set, the help file is displayed any time you select F1 and a control that you have registered with the `HelpProvider` is in focus. You can set a keyword to the help file with the `SetHelpKeyword` method. `SetHelpNavigator` takes a `HelpNavigator` enumeration value to determine which element in the help file should be displayed. You can set it for a specific topic, the index, the table of contents, or the search page. `SetHelpString` associates a string value of help-related text to a control. If the `HelpNamespace` property has not been set, pressing F1 will show this text in a pop-up window. Go ahead and add a `HelpProvider` to the previous example:

```
helpProvider1.SetHelpString(txtAge,"Enter an age that is less than 65."
helpProvider1.SetHelpString(txtZipCode,"Enter a 5-digit zip code."
```

ImageList

An ImageList component is exactly what the name implies — a list of images. Typically, this component is used for holding a collection of images that are used as toolbar icons or icons in a TreeView control. Many controls have an ImageList property. The ImageList property typically comes with an ImageIndex property. The ImageList property is set to an instance of the ImageList component, and the ImageIndex property is set to the index in the ImageList that represents the image that should be displayed on the control. You add images to the ImageList component by using the Add method of the ImageList.Images property. The Images property returns an ImageCollection.

The two most commonly used properties are ImageSize and ColorDepth. ImageSize uses a Size structure as its value. The default value is 16 × 16 but it can be any value from 1 to 256. The ColorDepth uses a ColorDepth enumeration as its value. The color depth values go from 4-bit to 32-bit. For .NET Framework 1.1, the default is ColorDepth.Depth8Bit.

Label

Labels are generally used to provide descriptive text to the user. The text might be related to other controls or the current system state. You usually see a label together with a text box. The label provides the user with a description of the type of data to be entered in the text box. The Label control is always read-only — the user cannot change the string value of the Text property. However, you can change the Text property in your code. The UseMnemonic property allows you to enable the access key functionality. When you precede a character in the Text property with the ampersand (&), that letter will appear underlined in the label control. Pressing the Alt key in combination with the underlined letter puts the focus on the next control in the tab order. If the Text property contains an ampersand in the text, add a second one and it will not underline the next letter. For example, if the label text is "Nuts & Bolts," set the property to "Nuts && Bolts." Because the Label control is read-only, it cannot gain focus; that's why focus is sent to the next control. Because of this, it is important to remember that if you enable mnemonics, you must be certain to set the tab order properly on your form.

The AutoSize property is a Boolean value that specifies whether the Label will resize itself based on the contents of the Label. This can be useful for multi-language applications where the length of the Text property can change based on the current language.

ListView

The ListView control enables you to display items in one of four different ways. You can display text with an optional large icon, text with an optional small icon, or text and small icons in a vertical list or in detail view, which allows you to display the item text plus any subitems in columns. If this sounds familiar, it should, because this is what the right side of File Explorer uses to display the contents of folders. ListView contains a collection of ListViewItems. ListViewItems allow you to set a Text property used for the display. ListViewItem has a property called SubItems that contains the text that appears in detail view.

The following example demonstrates how you might use ListView. This example includes a short list of countries. Each CountryList object contains a property for the country name, country abbreviation, and currency. Here is the code for the CountryList class:

```
using System;
namespace FormsSample
{

  public class CountryItem  : System.Windows.Forms.ListViewItem
  {
```

(continued)

(continued)

```
        string _cntryName = "";
        string _cntryAbbrev = "";
        public CountryItem(string countryName,
                                string countryAbbreviation, string currency)
        {
          _cntryName = countryName;
          _cntryAbbrev = countryAbbreviation;
          base.Text = _cntryName;
          base.SubItems.Add(currency);
        }
        public string CountryName
        {
          get {return _cntryName;}
        }
        public string CountryAbbreviation
        {
          get {return _cntryAbbrev;}
        }
      }
    }
```

Notice that you are deriving the `CountryList` class from `ListViewItem`. This is because you can add only `ListViewItem`-based objects to the `ListView` control. In the constructor, you pass the country name to the `base.Text` property and add the currency value to the `base.SubItems` property. This displays the country name in the list and the currency in a separate column when in details view.

Next, you need to add a couple of the `CountryItem` objects to the `ListView` control in the code of the form:

```
lvCountries.Items.Add(new CountryItem("United States","US","Dollar"));
lvCountries.Items[0].ImageIndex = 0;
lvCountries.Items.Add(new CountryItem("Great Britain", "GB", "Pound"));
lvCountries.Items[1].ImageIndex = 1;
lvCountries.Items.Add(new CountryItem("Canada", "CA", "Dollar"));
lvCountries.Items[2].ImageIndex = 2;
lvCountries.Items.Add(new CountryItem("Japan", "JP", "Yen"));
lvCountries.Items[3].ImageIndex = 3;
lvCountries.Items.Add(new CountryItem("Germany", "GM"", "Deutch Mark"));
lvCountries.Items[4].ImageIndex = 4;
```

Here you add a new `CountryItem` to the `Items` collection of the `ListView` control (`lvCountries`). Notice that you set the `ImageIndex` property of the item after you add it to the control. There are two `ImageIndex` objects, one for large icons and one for small icons (`SmallImageList` and `LargeImageList` properties). The trick to having two `ImageLists` with differing image sizes is to make sure you add the items to the `ImageList` in the same order. This way, the index of each `ImageList` represents the same image, just different sizes. In the example, the `ImageLists` contain icons of the flags for each country added.

On top of the form, there is a `ComboBox` (`cbView`) that lists the four different `View` enumeration values. You add the items to the `cbView` like this:

```
cbView.Items.Add(View.LargeIcon);
cbView.Items.Add(View.SmallIcon);
cbView.Items.Add(View.List);
cbView.Items.Add(View.Details);
cbView.SelectedIndex = 0;
```

In the `SelectedIndexChanged` event of `cbView`, you add the single line of code:

```
lvCountries.View = (View)cbView.SelectedItem;
```

This sets the View property of lvCountries to the new value selected in the ComboBox control. Notice that you need to cast to the View type because object is returned from the SelectedItem property of the cbView.

Last, but hardly least, you have to add columns to the Columns collection. The columns are for details view. In this case, you are adding two columns: Country Name and Currency. The order of the columns is as follows: the Text of the ListViewItem, then each item in the ListViewItem.SubItem collection, in the order it appears in the collection. You can add columns either by creating a ColumnHeader object and setting the Text property and optionally the Width and Alignment properties. After creating the ColumnHeader object, you can add it to the Columns property. The other way to add columns is to use an override of the Columns.Add method. It allows you to pass in the Text, Width, and Alignment values. Here is an example:

```
lvCountries.Columns.Add("Country",100, HorizontalAlignment.Left);
lvCountries.Columns.Add("Currency"",100, HorizontalAlignment.Left);
```

If you set the AllowColumnReorder property to true, the user can drag the column headers around and rearrange the column order.

The CheckBoxes property on the ListView shows check boxes next to the items in the ListView. This allows the user to easily select multiple items in the ListView control. You can check which items are selected by checking the CheckedItems collection.

The Alignment property sets the alignment of icons in Large and Small icon view. The value can be any of the ListViewAlignment enumeration values. They are Default, Left, Top, and SnapToGrid. The Default value allows users to arrange the icons in any position that they want. When choosing Left or Top, the items are aligned with the left or top of the ListView control. When choosing SnapToGrid, the items snap to an invisible grid on the ListView control. The AutoArrange property can be set to a Boolean value and will automatically align the icons based on the Alignment property.

PictureBox

The PictureBox control is used to display an image. The image can be a BMP, JPEG, GIF, PNG, metafile, or icon. The SizeMode property uses the PictureBoxSizeMode enumeration to determine how the image is sized and positioned in the control. The SizeMode property can be AutoSize, CenterImage, Normal, and StretchImage.

You can change the size of the display of the PictureBox by setting the ClientSize property. You load the PictureBox by first creating an Image-based object. For example, to load a JPEG file into a PictureBox you would do the following:

```
Bitmap myJpeg = new Bitmap("mypic.jpg");
pictureBox1.Image = (Image)myJpeg;
```

Notice that you will need to cast back to an Image type because that is what the Image property expects.

ProgressBar

The ProgressBar control is a visual clue to the status of a lengthy operation. It indicates to users that there is something going on and that they should wait. The ProgressBar control works by setting the Minimum and Maximum properties, which correspond to the progress indicator being all the way to the left (Minimum) or all the way to the right (Maximum). You set the Step property to determine the number that the value is incremented each time the PerformStep method is called. You can also use the Increment method and increment the value by the value passed in the method call. The Value property returns the current value of the ProgressBar.

You can use the `Text` property to inform the user of the percentage of the operation that has been completed or the number of items left to process. There is also a `BackgroundImage` property to customize the look of the progress bar.

TextBox, RichTextBox, and MaskedTextBox

The `TextBox` control is one of the most used controls in the toolbox. The `TextBox`, `RichTextBox`, and `MaskedTextBox` controls are all derived from `TextBoxBase`. `TextBoxBase` provides properties such as `MultiLine` and `Lines`. `MultiLine` is a `Boolean` value that allows the `TextBox` control to display text in more than one line. Each line in a text box is a part of an array of strings. This array is exposed through the `Lines` property. The `Text` property returns the entire text box contents as a single string. `TextLength` is the total length of the string that text would return. The `MaxLength` property will limit the length of the text to the specified amount.

`SelectedText`, `SelectionLength`, and `SelectionStart` all deal with the currently selected text in the text box. The selected text is highlighted when the control has focus.

The `TextBox` control adds a couple of interesting properties. `AcceptsReturn` is a Boolean value that will allow the `TextBox` to accept the Enter key as a new line or whether it activates the default button on the form. When set to `true`, pressing the Enter key creates a new line in the `TextBox`. `CharacterCasing` determines the casing of the text in the text box. The `CharacterCasing` enumeration contains three values, `Lower`, `Normal`, and `Upper`. `Lower` lowercases all text regardless of how it is entered, `Upper` renders all text in uppercase letters, and `Normal` displays the text as it is entered. The `PasswordChar` property takes a `char` that represents what is displayed to the users when they type text in the text box. This is typically used for entering passwords and PINs. The `text` property will return the actual text that was entered; only the display is affected by this property.

The `RichTextBox` is a text editing control that can handle special formatting features. As the name implies, the `RichTextBox` control uses Rich Text Format (RTF) to handle the special formatting. You can make formatting changes by using the `Selection` properties: `SelectionFont`, `SelectionColor`, and `SelectionBullet`, and paragraph formatting with `SelectionIndent`, `SelectionRightIndent`, and `SelectionHangingIndent`. All of the `Selection` properties work in the same way. If a section of text is highlighted, a change to a `Selection` property affects the selected text. If no text is selected, the change takes effect with any text that is inserted to the right of the current insertion point.

The text of the control can be retrieved by using the `Text` property or the `Rtf` property. The `Text` property returns just the text of the control, whereas the `Rtf` property returns the formatted text.

The `LoadFile` method can load text from a file in a couple of different ways. It can use either a string that represents the path and file name or it can use a stream object. You can also specify the `RichTextBoxStreamType`. The following table lists the values of `RichTextBoxStreamType`.

Value	Description
`PlainText`	No formatting information. In places that contained OLE objects, spaces are used.
`RichNoOleObjs`	Rich text formatting, but spaces where the OLE objects would have been.
`RichText`	Formatted RTF with OLE objects in place.
`TextTextOleObjs`	Plain text with text replacing the OLE objects.
`UnicodePlainText`	Same as `PlainText` but Unicode encoded.

The SaveFile method works with the same parameters, saving the data from the control to a specified file. If a file by that name already exists, it will be overwritten.

The MaskedTextBox supplies the ability to limit what the user may input into the control. It also allows for automatic formatting of the data entered. Several properties are used in order to validate or format the user's input. Mask is the property that contains the mask string, which is similar to a format string. The number of characters allowed, the data type of allowed characters, and the format of the data are all set using the Mask string. A MaskedTextProvider-based class can also provide the formatting and validation information needed. The MaskedTextProvider can only be set by passing it in on one of the constrictors.

Three different properties will return the text of the MaskedTextControl. The Text property returns the text of the control at the current moment. This could be different depending on whether or not the control has focus, which depends on the value of the HidePromptOnLeave property. The prompt is a string that users see to guide them on what should be entered. The InputText property always returns just the text that the user entered. The OutputText property returns the text-formatted based on the IncludeLiterals and IncludePrompt properties. If, for example, the mask is for a phone number, the Mask string would possibly include parentheses and a couple of dashes. These would be the literal characters and would be included in the OutputText property if the IncludeLiteral property were set to true.

A couple of extra events also exist for the MaskedTextBox control. OutputTextChanged and InputTextChanged are raised when InputText or OutputText changes.

Panel

A Panel is simply a control that contains other controls. By grouping controls together and placing them in a panel, it is a little easier to manage the controls. For example, you can disable all of the controls in the panel by disabling the panel. Because the Panel control is derived from ScrollableControl, you also can get the advantage of the AutoScroll property. If you have too many controls to display in the available area, place them in a Panel and set AutoScroll to true — now you can scroll through all of the controls.

Panels do not show a border by default, but by setting the BorderStyle property to something other than none, you can use the Panel to visually group related controls using borders. This makes the user interface more user-friendly.

Panel is the base class for the FlowLayoutPanel, TableLayoutPanel, TabPage, and SplitterPanel. By using these controls, a very sophisticated and professional-looking form or window can be created. The FlowLayoutPanel and TableLayoutPanel are especially useful for creating forms that resize properly.

FlowLayoutPanel and TableLayoutPanel

FlowLayoutPanel and TableLayoutPanel are new additions to the .NET Framework. As the names might suggest, the panels offer the capability to lay out a form using the same paradigm as a Web Form. FlowLayoutPanel is a container that allows the contained controls to flow in either the horizontal or vertical directions. Instead of flowing, it allows for the clipping of the controls. Flow direction is set using the FlowDirection property and the FlowDirection enumeration. The WrapContents property determines if controls flow to the next row or column when the form is resized or if the control is clipped.

TableLayoutPanel uses a grid structure to control the layout of controls. Any Windows Forms control can be a child of the TableLayoutPanel, including another TableLayoutPanel. This allows for a very flexible and dynamic window design. When a control is added to a TableLayoutPanel, four additional properties are added to the Layout category of the property page. They are Column, ColumnSpan, Row, and RowSpan. Much like an HTML table on a Web page, column and row spans can be set for each control. By default, the control will be centered in the cell of the table, but this can be changed by using the Anchor and Dock properties.

The default style of the rows and columns can be changed using RowStyles and ColumnsStyles collections. These collections contain RowStyle and ColumnsStyle objects, respectively. The Style objects have a common property, SizeType. SizeType uses the SizeType enumeration to determine how the column width or row height should be sized. Values include AutoSize, Absolute, and Percent. AutoSize shares the space with other peer controls. Absolute allows a set number of pixels for the size and Percent tells the control to size the column or width as a percentage of the parent control.

Rows, columns, and child controls can be added or removed at runtime. The GrowStyle property takes a TableLayoutPanelGrowStyle enumeration value that sets the table to add a column or a row, or stay a fixed size when a new control is added to a full table. If the value is FixedSized, an ArgumentException is thrown when there is an attempt to add another control. If a cell in the table is empty, the control will be placed in the empty cell. This property has an effect only when the table is full and a control is added.

The formPanel form in the sample application has FlowLayoutPanels and TableLayoutPanels with a variety of controls set in them. Experimenting with the controls, especially the Dock and Anchor properties of the controls placed in the layout panels, is the best way to understand how they work.

SplitContainer

The SplitContainer control is really three controls in one. It has two panel controls with a bar or splitter between them. The user is able to move the bar and resize the panels. As the panels resize, the controls in the panels also can be resized. The best example of a SplitContainer is File Explorer. The left panel contains a TreeView of folders and the right side contains a ListView of folder contents. When the user moves the mouse over the splitter bar, the cursor changes, showing that the bar can be moved. The SplitContainer can contain any control, including layout panels and other SplitContainers. This allows the creation of very complex and sophisticated forms.

The movement and position of the splitter bar can be controlled with the SplitterDistance and SplitterIncrement properties. The SplitterDistance property determines where the splitter starts in relation to the left or top of the control. The SplitterIncrement determines the number of pixels the splitter moves when being dragged. The panels can have their minimum size set with the Panel1MinSize and Panel2MinSize properties. These properties are also in pixels.

The Splitter control raises two events that relate to moving: the SplitterMoving event and the SplitterMoved event. One takes place during the move and the other takes place after the move has happened. They both receive SplitterEventArgs. SplitterEventArgs contains properties for the X and Y coordinates of the upper-left corner of the Splitter (SplitX and SplitY) and the X and Y coordinates of the mouse pointer (X and Y).

TabControl and TabPages

TabControl allows you to group related controls onto a series of tab pages. TabControl manages the collection of TabPages. Several properties control the appearance of TabControl. The Appearance property uses the TabAppearance enumeration to determine what the tabs look like. The values are FlatButtons, Buttons, or Normal. The Multiline property is a Boolean that determines if more than one row of tabs is shown. If the Multiline property is set to false and there are more tabs than can fit in the display, arrows appear that allow the user to scroll and see the rest of the tabs.

The TabPage Text property is what is displayed on the tab. The Text property is a parameter in a constructor override as well.

Once you create a `TabPage` control, it is basically a container control for you to place other controls. The Designer in Visual Studio .NET makes it easy to add `TabPage` controls to a `TabControl` control by using the collection editor. You can set the various properties as you add each page. Then you can drag the other child controls to each `TabPage` control.

You can determine the current tab by looking at the `SelectedTab` property. The `SelectedIndex` event is raised each time a new tab is selected. By listening to the `SelectedIndex` property and then confirming the current tab with `SelectedTab`, you can do special processing based on each tab. You could, for example, manage the data displayed for each tab.

ToolStrip

The `ToolStrip` control is a container control used to create toolbars, menu structures, and status bars. The `ToolStrip` is used directly for toolbars, and serves as the base class for the `MenuStrip` and `StatusStrip` controls.

When used as a toolbar, the `ToolStrip` control uses a set of controls based on the abstract `ToolStripItem` class. `ToolStripItem` adds the common display and layout functionality as well as managing most of the events used by the controls. `ToolStripItem` is derived from the `System.ComponentModel.Component` class and not from the `Control` class. `ToolStripItem`-based classes must be contained in a `ToolStrip`-based container.

`Image` and `Text` are probably the most common properties that will be set. Images can be set with either the `Image` property or by using the `ImageList` control and setting it to the `ImageList` property of the `ToolStrip` control. The `ImageIndex` property of the individual controls can then be set.

Formatting of the text on a `ToolStripItem` is handled with the `Font`, `TextAlign`, and `TextDirection` properties. `TextAlign` sets the alignment of the text in relation to the control. This can be any of the `ControlAlignment` enumeration values. The default is `MiddleRight`. The `TextDirection` property sets the orientation of the text. Values can be any of the `ToolStripTextDirection` enumeration values, which include `Horizontal`, `Inherit`, `Vertical270`, and `Vertical90`. `Vertical270` rotates the text 270 degrees and `Vertical90` rotates the text 90 degrees.

The `DisplayStyle` property controls whether text, image, text and image, or nothing is displayed on the control. When `AutoSize` is set to `true`, the `ToolStripItem` will resize itself so only the minimum amount of space is used.

The controls that are derived directly from `ToolStripItem` are listed in the following table.

Tool Strip Items	Description
`ToolStripButton`	Represents a button that the user can select.
`ToolStripLabel`	Displays nonselectable text or images on the `ToolStrip`. The `ToolStripLabel` can also display one or more hyperlinks.
`ToolStripSeparator`	Used to separate and group other `ToolStripItems`. Items can be grouped according to functionality.
`ToolStripDropDownItem`	Displays drop-down items. Base class for `ToolStripDropDownButton`, `ToolStripMenuItem`, and `ToolStripSplitButton`.
`ToolStripControlHost`	Hosts other non–`ToolStripItem`-derived controls on a `ToolStrip`. Base class for `ToolStripComboBox`, `ToolStripProgressBar`, and `ToolStripTextBox`.

The first two items in the list, ToolStripDropDownItem and ToolStripControlHost, deserve a little more discussion. ToolStripDropDownItem is the base class for ToolStripMenuItems, which are used to build the menu structure. ToolStripMenuItems are added to MenuStrip controls. As mentioned earlier, MenuStrips are derived from ToolStrip controls. This is important when it comes time to manipulate or extend menu items. Because toolbars and menus are derived from the same classes, creating a framework for managing and executing commands becomes much easier.

ToolStripControlHost can be used to host other controls that do not derive from ToolStripItem. Remember that the only controls that can be directly hosted by a ToolStrip are those that derive from ToolStripItem. The following example shows how to host a DateTimePicker control on a ToolStrip:

```
public mdiParent()
{
  InitializeComponent();
  ToolStripControlHost _dateTimeCtl;
 _dateTimeCtl = new ToolStripControlHost(new DateTimePicker());
  ((DateTimePicker)_dateTimeCtl.Control).ValueChanged +=
        delegate {
                  toolStripLabel1.Text =
((DateTimePicker)_dateTimeCtl.Control).Value.Subtract(DateTime.Now).ToString();
                  };
 _
  _dateTimeCtl.Width = 200;
  _dateTimeCtl.DisplayStyle = ToolStripItemDisplayStyle.Text;
  toolStrip1.Items.Add(_dateTimeCtl);
}
```

This is the constructor from the frmMain form in the code sample. First, a ToolStripControlHost is declared and instantiated. Notice that when the control is instantiated, the control that is to be hosted is passed in on the constructor. The next line sets up the ValueChanged event of the DateTimePicker control. The control can be accessed through the Control property of the ToolStripHostControl. This returns a Control object, so it will need to be cast back to the proper type of control. Once that is done, the properties and methods of the hosted control are available to use.

Another way to do this that would perhaps enforce encapsulation a little better is to create a new class derived from ToolStripControlHost. The following code is another version of the toolstrip version of the DateTimePicker called ToolStripDateTimePicker:

```
namespace FormsSample.SampleControls
{
  public class DTPickerToolStrip  : System.Windows.Forms.ToolStripControlHost
  {
    public event EventHandler ValueChanged;
    public DTPickerToolStrip()  : base(new DateTimePicker())
    {
    }
    public new DateTimePicker Control
    {
      get{return (DateTimePicker)base.Control;}
    }
    public DateTime Value
    {
      get { return Control.Value; }
    }

    protected override void OnSubscribeControlEvents(Control control)
```

```
    {
      base.OnSubscribeControlEvents(control);
      ((DateTimePicker)control).ValueChanged +=
new EventHandler(ValueChangedHandler);
    }

    protected override void OnUnsubscribeControlEvents(Control control)
    {
      base.OnSubscribeControlEvents(control);
      ((DateTimePicker)control).ValueChanged -=
new EventHandler(ValueChanged);
    }

    private void ValueChangedHandler(object sender, EventArgs e)
    {
      if (ValueChanged != null)
        ValueChanged(this, e);
    }
  }
}
```

Most of what this class is doing is exposing selected properties, methods, and events of the `DateTimePicker`. This way, a reference to the underlying control doesn't have to be maintained by the hosting application. The process of exposing events is a bit involved. The `OnSubscribeControlEvents` method is used to synchronize the events of the hosted control, in this case `DateTimePicker`, to the `ToolStripControlHost`-based class, which is `DTPickerToolStrip` in the example. In this example, the `ValueChanged` event is being passed up to the `DTPickerToolStrip`. What this effectively does is allow the user of the control to set up the event in the host application as if `DTPickerToolStrip` were derived from `DateTimePicker` instead of `ToolStripControlHost`. The following code example shows this. This is the code to use `DTPickerToolStrip`:

```
public mdiParent()
{
  DTPickerToolStrip otherDateTimePicker = new DTPickerToolStrip();
  otherDateTimePicker.Width = 200;
  otherDateTimePicker.ValueChanged +=
new EventHandler(otherDateTimePicker_ValueChanged);
  toolStrip1.Items.Add(otherDateTimePicker);
}
```

Notice that when the `ValueChanged` event handler is set up that the reference is to the `DTPickerToolStrip` class and not to the `DateTimePicker` control as in the previous example. Also notice how much cleaner the code in this example looks as compared to the first example. In addition, because the `DateTimePicker` is wrapped in another class, encapsulation has improved dramatically and `DTPickerToolStrip` is now much easier to use in other parts of the application or in other projects.

MenuStrip

The `MenuStrip` control is the container for the menu structure of an application. As mentioned earlier, `MenuStrip` is derived from the `ToolStrip` class. The menu system is built by adding `ToolStripMenu` objects to the `MenuStrip`. You can do this in code or in the Designer of Visual Studio. Drag a `MenuStrip` control onto a form in the Designer and the `MenuStrip` will allow the entry of the menu text directly on the menu items.

The `MenuStrip` control has only a couple of additional properties. `GripStyle` uses the `ToolStripGripStyle` enumeration to set the grip as visible or hidden. The `MdiWindowListItem` property takes or returns a ToolStripMenuItem. This ToolStripMenuItem is the menu that shows all open windows in an MDI application.

ContextMenuStrip

To show a context menu, or a menu displayed when the user right-clicks the mouse, the ContextMenuStrip class is used. Like MenuStrip, ContextMenuStrip is a container for ToolStripMenuItems objects. However, it is derived from ToolStripDropDownMenu. A ContextMenu is created the same way as a MenuStrip. ToolStripMenuItems are added, and the Click event of each item is defined to perform a specific task. Context menus are assigned to specific controls. This is done by setting the ContextMenuStrip property of the control. When the user right-clicks the control, the menu is displayed.

ToolStripMenuItem

ToolStripMenuItem is the class that builds the menu structures. Each ToolStripMenuItem object represents a single menu choice on the menu system. Each ToolStripMenuItem has a ToolStripItemCollection that maintains the child menus. This functionality is inherited from ToolStripDropDownItem.

Because ToolStripMenuItem is derived from ToolStripItem, all of the same formatting properties apply. Images appear as small icons to the right of the menu text. Menu items can have check marks show up next to them with the Checked and CheckState properties.

Shortcut keys can be assigned to each menu item. They are generally two key chords such as Ctrl+C (common shortcut for Copy). When a shortcut key is assigned, it can optionally be displayed on the menu by setting the ShowShortCutKey property to true.

To be useful, the menu item has to do something when the user clicks it or uses the defined shortcut keys. The most common way is to handle the Click event. If the Checked property is being used, the CheckStateChanged and CheckedChanged events can be used to determine a change in the checked state.

ToolStripManager

Menu and toolbar structures can become large and cumbersome to manage. The ToolStripManager class provides the ability to create smaller, more manageable pieces of a menu or toolbar structure and then combine them when needed. An example of this is a form that has several different controls on it. Each control must display a context menu. Several menu choices will be available for all of the controls, but each control will also have a couple of unique menu choices. The common choices can be defined on one ContextMenuStrip. Each of the unique menu items can be predefined or created at runtime. For each control that needs a context menu assigned to it, the common menu is cloned and the unique choices are merged with the common menu using the ToolStripManager.Merge method. The resulting menu is assigned to the ContextMenuStrip property of the control.

ToolStripContainer

The ToolStripContainer control is used for docking of ToolStrip-based controls. When you add a ToolStripContainer and set the Docked property to Fill, a ToolStripPanel is added to each side of the form, and a ToolStripContainerPanel is added to middle of the form. Any ToolStrip (ToolStrip, MenuStrip, or StatusStrip) can be added to any of the ToolStripPanels. The user can move the ToolStrips by grabbing the ToolStrip and dragging it to either side or bottom of the form. If you set the Visible property to false on any of the ToolStripPanels, a ToolStrip can no longer be placed in the panel. The ToolStripContainerPanel in the center of the form can be used to place the other controls the form may need.

Forms

Earlier in this chapter, you learned how to create a simple Windows application. The example contained one class derived from the `System.Windows.Forms.Form` class. According to the .NET Framework documentation, "a Form is a representation of any window in your application." If you come from a Visual Basic background, the term "form" will seem familiar. If your background is C++ using MFC, you're probably used to calling a form a window, dialog box, or maybe a frame. Regardless, the form is the basic means of interacting with the user. Earlier, the chapter covered some of the more common and useful properties, methods, and events of the `Control` class, and because the `Form` class is a descendant of the `Control class`, all of the same properties, methods, and events exist in the `Form` class. The `Form` class adds considerable functionality to what the `Control` class provides, and that's what this section discusses.

Form Class

A Windows client application can contain one form or hundreds of forms. The forms can be an SDI-based (Single Document Interface) or MDI-based (Multiple Document Interface) application. Regardless, the `System.Windows.Forms.Form` class is the heart of the Windows client. The `Form` class is derived from `ContainerControl`, which is derived from `ScrollableControl`, which is derived from `Control`. Because of this, you can assume that a form is capable of being a container for other controls, capable of scrolling when the contained controls do not fit the client area, and has many of the same properties, methods, and events that other controls have. This also makes the `Form` class rather complex. This section looks at much of that functionality.

Form Instantiation and Destruction

The process of form creation is important to understand. What you want to do depends on where you write the initialization code. For instantiation, the events occur in the following order:

- `Constructor`
- `Load`
- `Activated`
- `Closing`
- `Closed`
- `Deactivate`

The first three events are of concern during initialization. The type of initialization you want to do could determine which event you hook into. The constructor of a class occurs during the object instantiation. The `Load` event occurs after object instantiation, but just before the form becomes visible. The difference between this and the constructor is the viability of the form. When the `Load` event is raised, the form exists but isn't visible. During constructor execution, the form is in the process of coming into existence. The `Activated` event occurs when the form becomes visible and current.

This order can be altered slightly in one particular situation. If during the constructor execution of the form, the `Visible` property is set to `true` or the `Show` method is called (which sets the `Visible` property to `true`), the `Load` event fires immediately. Because this also makes the form visible and current, the `Activate` event is also raised. If there is code after the `Visible` property has been set, it will execute. So, the startup event might look something like this:

- `Constructor`, up to `Visible = true`
- `Load`
- `Activate`
- `Constructor`, after `Visible = true`

This could potentially lead to some unexpected results. From a best practices standpoint, it would seem that doing as much initialization as possible in the constructor might be a good idea.

Now what happens when the form is closed? The `Closing` event gives you the opportunity to cancel the process. The `Closing` event receives `CancelEventArgs` as a parameter. This has a `Cancel` property that, if set to `true`, cancels the event and the form remains open. The `Closing` event happens as the form is being closed, whereas the `Closed` event happens after the form has been closed. Both allow you to do any cleanup that might have to be done. Notice that the `Deactivate` event occurs after the form has been closed. This is another potential source of difficult-to-find bugs. Be sure that you don't have anything in `Deactivate` that could keep the form from being properly garbage collected. For example, setting a reference to another object would cause the form to remain alive.

If you call the `Application.Exit()` method and you have one or more forms currently open, the `Closing` and `Closed` events will not be raised. This is an important consideration if you have open files or database connections that you were going to clean up. The `Dispose` method is called, so perhaps another best practice would be to put most of your cleanup code in the `Dispose` method.

Some properties that relate to the startup of a form are `StartPosition`, `ShowInTaskbar`, and `TopMost`. `StartPosition` can be any of the `FormStartPosition` enumeration values. They are:

- `CenterParent` — The form is centered in the client area of the parent form.
- `CenterScreen` — The form is centered in the current display.
- `Manual` — The form's location is based on the values in the `Location` property.
- `WindowsDefaultBounds` — The form is located at the default Windows position and uses the default size.
- `WindowsDefaultLocation` — The Windows default location is used, but the size is based on the `Size` property.

The `ShowInTaskbar` property determines if the form should be available in the taskbar. This is relevant only if the form is a child form and you only want the parent form to show in the taskbar. The `TopMost` property tells the form to start in the topmost position in the Z-order of the application. This is true even if the form does not immediately have focus.

In order for users to interact with the application, they must be able to see the form. The `Show` and `ShowDialog` methods accomplish this. The `Show` method just makes the form visible to the user. The following code segment demonstrates how to create a form and show it to the user. Assume that the form you want to display is called `MyFormClass`.

```
MyFormClass myForm = new MyFormClass();
myForm.Show();
```

That's the simple way. The one drawback to this is that there isn't any notification back to the calling code that `myForm` is finished and has been exited. Sometimes this isn't a big deal, and the `Show` method will work fine. If you do need some type of notification, `ShowDialog` is a better option.

When the `Show` method is called, the code that follows the `Show` method is executed immediately. When `ShowDialog` is called, the calling code is blocked and will wait until the form that `ShowDialog` called is closed. Not only will the calling code be blocked, but the form will optionally return a `DialogResult` value. The `DialogResult` enumeration is a list of identifiers that describe the reason the dialog is closed. These include `OK`, `Cancel`, `Yes`, `No`, and several others. In order for the form to return a `DialogResult`, the form's `DialogResult` property must be set or the `DialogResult` property on one of the form's buttons must be set.

For example, suppose that part of application asks for the phone number of a client. The form has a text box for the phone number and two buttons; one is labeled `OK` and the other is labeled `Cancel`. If you set the `DialogResult` of the `OK` button to `DialogResult.OK` and the `DialogResult` property on the `Cancel` button to `DialogResult.Cancel`, then when either of these buttons is selected, the form becomes invisible and returns to the calling form the appropriate `DialogResult` value. Now notice that the form is not destroyed; the `Visible` property is just set to `false`. That's because you still must get values from the form. For this example, you need to get a phone number. By creating a property on the form for the phone number, the parent form can now get the value and call the `Close` method on the form. This is what the code for the child form looks like:

```
namespace FormsSample.DialogSample
{
  partial class Phone : Form
  {
    public Phone()
    {
      InitializeComponent();
      btnOK.DialogResult = DialogResult.OK;
      btnCancel.DialogResult = DialogResult.Cancel;
    }

    public string PhoneNumber
    {
      get { return textBox1.Text; }
      set { textBox1.Text = value; }
    }
  }
}
```

The first thing to notice is that there is no code to handle the `click` events of the buttons. Because the `DialogResult` property is set for each of the buttons, the form disappears after either the `OK` or `Cancel` button is clicked. The only property added is the `PhoneNumber` property. The following code shows the method in the parent form that calls the `Phone` dialog:

```
Phone frm = new Phone();
frm.ShowDialog();
if (frm.DialogResult == DialogResult.OK)
{
  label1.Text = "Phone number is " + frm.PhoneNumber;
}
else if (frm.DialogResult == DialogResult.Cancel)
{
  label1.Text = "Form was canceled. ";
}
frm.Close();
```

This looks simple enough. Create the new `Phone` object (`frm`). When the `frm.ShowDialog()` method is called, the code in this method will stop and wait for the `Phone` form to return. You can then check the `DialogResult` property of the `Phone` form. Because it has not been destroyed yet, just made invisible, you can still access the public properties, one of them being the `PhoneNumber` property. Once you get the data you need, you can call the `Close` method on the form.

This works well, but what if the returned phone number is not formatted correctly? If you put the `ShowDialog` inside of the loop, you can just recall it and have the user reenter the value. This way, you get a proper value. Remember that you must also handle the `DialogResult.Cancel` if the user clicks the `Cancel` button.

```
Phone frm = new Phone();
while (true)
{
  frm.ShowDialog();
```

(continued)

(continued)

```
    if (frm.DialogResult == DialogResult.OK)
    {
      label1.Text = "Phone number is " + frm.PhoneNumber;
      if (frm.PhoneNumber.Length == 8 || frm.PhoneNumber.Length == 12)
      {
        break;
      }
      else
      {
        MessageBox.Show("Phone number was not formatted correctly.
                                                   Please correct entry. ");
      }
    }
    else if (frm.DialogResult == DialogResult.Cancel)
    {
      label1.Text = "Form was canceled. ";
      break;
    }
  }
  frm.Close();
```

Now if the phone number does not pass a simple test for length, the `Phone` form appears so the user can correct the error. The `ShowDialog` box does not create a new instance of the form. Any text entered on the form will still be there, so if the form has to be reset, it will be up to you to do that.

Appearance

The first thing that the user sees is the form for the application. It should be first and foremost functional. If the application doesn't solve a business problem, it really doesn't matter how it looks. This is not to say that the form and application's overall GUI design should not be pleasing to the eye. Simple things like color combinations, font sizing, and window sizing can make an application much easier for the user.

Sometimes you don't want the user to have access to the system menu. This is the menu that appears when you click the icon on the top-left corner of a window. Generally, it has such items as `Restore`, `Minimize`, `Maximize`, and `Close`. The `ControlBox` property allows you to set the visibility of the system menu. You can also set the visibility of the `Maximize` and `Minimize` buttons with the `MaximizeBox` and `MinimizeBox` properties. If you remove all of the buttons and then set the `Text` property to an empty string (`""`), the title bar disappears completely.

If you set the `Icon` property of a form and you don't set the `ControlBox` property to `false`, the icon will appear in the top-left corner of the form. It's common to set this to the `app.ico`. This makes each form's icon the same as the application icon.

The `FormBorderStyle` property sets the type of border that appears around the form. This uses the `FormBorderStyle` enumeration. The values can be as follows:

- `Fixed3D`
- `FixedDialog`
- `FixedSingle`
- `FixedToolWindow`
- `None`
- `Sizable`
- `SizableToolWindow`

Most of these are self-explanatory, with the exception of the two tool window borders. A `Tool` window will not appear in the taskbar, regardless of how `ShowInTaskBar` is set. Also a `Tool` window will not show in the list of windows when the user presses Alt+Tab. The default setting is `Sizable`.

Unless a requirement dictates otherwise, colors for most GUI elements should be set to system colors and not to specific colors. This way, if some users like to have all of their buttons green with purple text, the application will follow along with the same colors. To set a control to use a specific system color, you must call the `FromKnownColor` method of the `System.Drawing.Color` class. The `FromKnownColor` method takes a `KnownColor` enumeration value. Many colors are defined in the enumeration, as well as the various GUI element colors, such as `Control`, `ActiveBorder`, and `Desktop`. So, for example, if the `Background` color of the form should always match the `Desktop` color, the code would look like this:

```
myForm.BackColor = Color.FromKnownColor(KnownColor.Desktop);
```

Now if users change the color of their desktops, the background of the form changes as well. This is a nice, friendly touch to add to an application. Users might pick out some strange color combinations for their desktops, but it is their choice.

Windows XP introduced a feature called visual styles. Visual styles change the way buttons, text boxes, menus, and other controls look and react when the mouse pointer is either hovering or clicking. You can enable visual styles for your application by calling the `Application.EnableVisualStyles` method. This method has to be called before any type of GUI is instantiated. Because of this, it is generally called in the `Main` method, as demonstrated in this example:

```
 [STAThread]
static void Main()
{
  Application.EnableVisualStyles();
  Application.Run(new Form1());
}
```

This code allows the various controls that support visual styles to take advantage of them. Because of an issue with the `EnableVisualStyles` method, you might have to add an `Application.DoEvents()` method right after the call to `EnableVisualStyles`. This should resolve the problem if icons on toolbars begin to disappear at runtime. Also, `EnableVisualStyles` is available in .NET Framework 1.1 only.

You have to accomplish one more task pertaining to the controls. Most controls expose the `FlatStyle` property, which takes a `FlatStyle` enumeration as its value. This property can take one of four different values:

- `Flat` — Similar to flat, except that when the mouse pointer hovers over the control, it appears in 3D.
- `Standard` — The control appears in 3D.
- `System` — The look of the control is controlled by the operating system.

To enable visual styles, the control's `FlatStyle` property should be set to `FlatStyle.System`. The application will now take on the XP look and feel and will support XP themes.

Multiple Document Interface

MDI-type applications are used when you have an application that can show either multiple instances of the same type of form or different forms that must be contained in some way — for example, a text editor that can show multiple edit windows at the same time or Microsoft Access, respectively. You can have query windows, design windows, and table windows all open at the same time. The windows never leave the boundaries of the main Access application.

The project that contains the examples for this chapter is an MDI application. The form `mdiParent` in the project is the MDI parent form. Setting the `IsMdiContainer` to `true` will make any form an MDI parent form. If you have the form in the Designer you'll notice that the background turns a dark gray color. This is to let you know that this is an MDI parent form. You can still add controls to the form, but it is generally not recommended.

For the child forms to behave like MDI children, the child form needs to know what form the parent is. This is done by setting the `MdiParent` property to the parent form. In the example, all children forms are created using the `ShowMdiChild` method. It takes a reference to the child form that is to be shown. After setting the `MdiParent` property to this, which is referencing the `mdiParent` form, the form is shown. Here is the code for the `ShowMdiParent` method:

```
private void ShowMdiChild(Form childForm)
{
  childForm.MdiParent = this;
  childForm.Show();
}
```

One of the issues with MDI applications is that there may be several child forms open at any given time. A reference to the current active child can be retrieved by using the `ActiveMdiChild` property on the parent form. This is demonstrated on the `Current Active` menu choice on the Window menu. This choice will show a message box with the form's name and text value.

The child forms can be arranged by calling the `LayoutMdi` method. The `LayoutMdi` method takes an `MdiLayout` enumeration value as a parameter. The possible values include `Cascade`, `TileHorizontal`, and `TileVertical`.

Custom Controls

Using controls and components is a big part of what makes developing with a forms package such as Windows Forms so productive. The ability to create your own controls, components, and user controls makes it even more productive. By creating controls, functionality can be encapsulated into packages that can be reused over and over.

You can create a control in a number of ways. You can start from scratch, deriving your class from either `Control`, `ScrollableControl`, or `ContainerControl`. You will have to override the `Paint` event and do all of your drawing, not to mention adding the functionality that your control is supposed to provide. If the control is supposed to be an enhanced version of a current control, the thing to do is to derive from the control that is being enhanced. For example, if a `TextBox` control is needed that changes background color if the `ReadOnly` property is set, creating a completely new `TextBox` control would be a waste of time. Derive from the `TextBox` control and override the `ReadOnly` property. Because the `ReadOnly` property of the `TextBox` control is not marked override, you have to use the new clause. The following code shows the new `ReadOnly` property:

```
public new bool ReadOnly
{
  get  { return base.ReadOnly;}
  set  {
    if(value)
      this.BackgroundColor = Color.Red;
    else
      this.BackgroundColor = Color.FromKnowColor(KnownColor.Window);

     base.ReadOnly = value;
  }
}
```

For the property `get`, you return what the base object is set to. The way that the property handles the process of making a text box read-only is not relevant here, so you just pass that functionality to the base object. In the property set, check to see if the passed-in value is `true` or `false`. If it is `true`, change the color to the read-only color (`Red` in this case); if it is `false`, set the `BackgroundColor` to the default. Finally, pass the value down to the base object so that the text box actually does become read-only. As you can see, you can add new functionality to a control by overriding one simple property.

Control Attributes

You can add attributes to the custom control that will enhance the design-time capabilities of the control. The following table describes some of the more useful attributes.

Attribute Name	Description
`BindableAttribute`	Used at design time to determine if the property supports two-way data binding.
`BrowsableAttribute`	Determines if the property is shown in the visual Designer.
`CategoryAttribute`	Determines under what category the property is displayed in the Property window. Use on predefined categories or create new ones. Default is `Misc`.
`DefaultEventAttribute`	Specifies the default event for a class.
`DefaultPropertyAttribute`	Specifies the default property for a class.
`DefaultValueAttribute`	Specifies the default value for a property. Typically, this is the initial value.
`DecriptionAttribute`	This is the text that appears at the bottom of the Designer window when the property is selected.
`DesignOnlyAttribute`	This marks the property as being editable in design mode only.

Other attributes are available that relate to the editor that the property uses in design time and other advanced design-time capabilities. The `Category` and `Description` attributes should almost always be added. This helps other developers who use the control to better understand the property's purpose. To add IntelliSense support, you should add XML comments for each property, method, and event. When the control is compiled with the `/doc` option, the XML file of comments that is generated will provide IntelliSense for the control.

TreeView-Based Custom Control

This section shows you how to develop a custom control based on the `TreeView` control. This control displays the file structure of a drive. You'll add properties that set the base or root folder and determine whether files and folders will be displayed. You also use the various attributes discussed in the previous section.

As with any new project, requirements for the control have to be defined. Here is a list of basic requirements that have to be implemented:

- Read folders and files and display to user.
- Display folder structure in a treelike hierarchical view.
- Optionally hide files from view.

- ❑ Define what folder should be the base or root folder.
- ❑ Return the currently selected folder.
- ❑ Provide the ability to delay loading of the file structure.

This should be a good starting point. One requirement has been satisfied by the fact that the `TreeView` control will be the base of the new control.

The `TreeView` control displays data in a hierarchical format. It displays text describing the object in the list and optionally an icon. This list can be expanded and contracted by clicking an object or using the arrow keys.

Create a new Windows Control Library project in Visual Studio .NET named `FolderTree`, and delete the class `UserControl1`. Add a new class and call it `FolderTree`. Because `FolderTree` will be derived from `TreeView`, change the class declaration from:

```
public class FolderTree
```

to:

```
public class FolderTree   :   System.Windows.Forms.TreeView
```

At this point, you actually have a fully functional and working `FolderTree` control. It will do everything that the `TreeView` can do, and nothing more.

The `TreeView` control maintains a collection of `TreeNode` objects. You can't load files and folders directly into the control. You have a couple of ways to map the `TreeNode` that is loaded into the `Nodes` collection of the `TreeView` and the file or folder that it represents.

For example, when each folder is processed, a new `TreeNode` object is created, and the text property is set to the name of the file or folder. If at some point additional information about the file or folder is needed, you have to make another trip to the disk to gather that information or store additional data regarding the file or folder in the `Tag` property.

Another method is to create a new class that is derived from `TreeNode`. New properties and methods can be added and the base functionality of the `TreeNode` is still there. This is the path that you use in this example. It allows for a more flexible design. If you need new properties, you can add them easily without breaking the existing code.

You must load two types of objects into the control: folders and files. Each has its own characteristics. For example, folders have a `DirectoryInfo` object that contains additional information, and files have a `FileInfo` object. Because of these differences, you use two separate classes to load the `TreeView` control: `FileNode` and `FolderNode`. You add these two classes to the project; each is derived from `TreeNode`. This is the listing for `FileNode`:

```
namespace FormsSample.SampleControls
{
  public class FileNode : System.Windows.Forms.TreeNode
  {
    string _fileName = "";
    FileInfo _info;
    public FileNode(string fileName)
    {
      _fileName = fileName;
      _info = new FileInfo(_fileName);
      base.Text = _info.Name;
      if (_info.Extension.ToLower() == ".exe")
        this.ForeColor = System.Drawing.Color.Red;
    }
    public string FileName
```

```
      {
        get { return _fileName; }
        set { _fileName = value; }
      }

      public FileInfo FileNodeInfo
      {
        get { return _info; }
      }
    }
  }
```

The name of the file being processed is passed into the constructor of `FileNode`. In the constructor, the `FileInfo` object for the file is created and set to the member variable `_info`. The `base.Text` property is set to the name of the file. Because you are deriving from `TreeNode`, this sets the `TreeNode`'s `Text` property. This is the text displayed in the `TreeView` control.

Two properties are added to retrieve the data. `FileName` returns the name of the file and `FileNodeInfo` returns the `FileInfo` object for the file.

The following is the code for the `FolderNode` class. It is very similar in structure to the `FileNode` class, but you have a `DirectoryInfo` property instead of `FileInfo`, and instead of `FileName` you have `FolderPath`:

```
namespace FormsSample.SampleControls
{
  public class FolderNode : System.Windows.Forms.TreeNode
  {
    string _folderPath = "";
    DirectoryInfo _info;
    public FolderNode(string folderPath)
    {
      _folderPath = folderPath;
      _info = new DirectoryInfo(folderPath);
      this.Text = _info.Name;
    }
    public string FolderPath
    {
      get { return _folderPath; }
      set { _folderPath = value; }
    }
    public DirectoryInfo FolderNodeInfo
    {
      get { return _info; }
    }
  }
}
```

Now you can construct the `FolderTree` control. Based on the requirements, you need a property to read and set the `RootFolder`. You also need a `ShowFiles` property for determining if files should be shown in the tree. A `SelectedFolder` property returns the currently highlighted folder in the tree. This is what the code looks like so far for the `FolderTree` control:

```
using System;
using System.Windows.Forms;
using System.IO;
using System.ComponentModel;
```

(continued)

(continued)

```
namespace FolderTree
{
  /// <summary>
  /// Summary description for FolderTreeCtrl.
  /// </summary>
  public class FolderTree :  System.Windows.Forms.TreeView
  {
    string _rootFolder = "";
    bool _showFiles = true;
    bool _inInit = false;
    public FolderTree()
    {

    }

    [Category("Behavior"),
       Description("Gets or sets the base or root folder of the tree"),
       DefaultValue("C:\\ ")]
    public string RootFolder
    {
      get {return _rootFolder;}
      set
      {
        _rootFolder = value;
        if(!_inInit)
          InitializeTree();

      }
    }

    [Category("Behavior"),
       Description("Indicates whether files will be seen in the list. "),
       DefaultValue(true)]
    public bool ShowFiles
    {
      get {return _showFiles;}
      set {_showFiles = value;}
    }

    [Browsable(false)]
    public string SelectedFolder
    {
      get
      {
        if(this.SelectedNode is FolderNode)
          return ((FolderNode)this.SelectedNode).FolderPath;

        return "";
      }
    }
  }
}
```

Three properties were added: `ShowFiles`, `SelectedFolder`, and `RootFolder`. Notice the attributes that have been added. You set `Category`, `Description`, and `DefaultValues` for the `ShowFiles` and

RootFolder. These two properties will appear in the property browser in design mode. The SelectedFolder really has no meaning at design time, so you select the Browsable=false attribute. SelectedFolder does not appear in the property browser. However, because it is a public property, it will appear in IntelliSense and is accessible in code.

Next, you have to initialize the loading of the file system. Initializing a control can be tricky. Both design-time and runtime initializing must be well thought out. When a control is sitting on a Designer, it is actually running. If there is a call to a database in the constructor, for example, this call will execute when you drop the control on the Designer. In the case of the FolderTree control, this can be an issue.

Here's a look at the method that is actually going to load the files:

```
private void LoadTree(FolderNode folder)
{
  string[] dirs = Directory.GetDirectories(folder.FolderPath);
  foreach(string dir in dirs)
  {
    FolderNode tmpfolder = new FolderNode(dir);
    folder.Nodes.Add(tmpfolder);
    LoadTree(tmpfolder);
  }
  if(_showFiles)
  {
    string[] files = Directory.GetFiles(folder.FolderPath);
    foreach(string file in files)
    {
      FileNode fnode = new FileNode(file);
      folder.Nodes.Add(fnode);
    }
  }
}
```

showFiles is a Boolean member variable that is set from the ShowFiles property. If true, files are also shown in the tree. The only question now is when LoadTree should be called. You have several options. It can be called when the RootFolder property is set. That is desirable in some situations, but not at design time. Remember that the control is "live" on the Designer, so when the RootNode property is set, the control will attempt to load the file system.

To solve this, check the DesignMode property, which returns true if the control is in the Designer. Now you can write the code to initialize the control:

```
private void InitializeTree()
{
  if (!this.DesignMode)
  {
    FolderNode rootNode = new FolderNode(_rootFolder);
    LoadTree(rootNode);
    this.Nodes.Clear();
    this.Nodes.Add(rootNode);
  }
}
```

If the control is not in design mode and _rootFolder is not an empty string, the loading of the tree will begin. The Root node is created first and this is passed into the LoadTree method.

Another option is to implement a public Init method. In the Init method, the call to LoadTree can happen. The problem with this option is that the developer who uses your control is required to make the Init call. Depending on the situation, this might be an acceptable solution.

For added flexibility, implement the `ISupportInitialize` interface. `ISupportInitialize` has two methods, `BeginInit` and `EndInit`. When a control implements `ISupportInitialize`, the `BeginInit` and `EndInit` methods are called automatically in the generated code in `InitializeComponent`. This allows the initialization process to be delayed until all of the properties are set. `ISupportInitialize` allows the code in the parent form to delay initialization as well. If the `RootNode` property is being set in code, a call to `BeginInit` first will allow the `RootNode` property as well as other properties to be set or actions to be performed before the control loads the file system. When `EndInit` is called, the control initializes. This is what `BeginInit` and `EndInit` code looks like:

```
#region ISupportInitialize Members
public void ISupportInitialize.BeginInit()
{
  _inInit = true;
}
public void ISupportInitialize.EndInit()
{

  if(_rootFolder != "")
  {
    InitializeTree();
  }

  _inInit = false;
}
#endregion
```

In the `BeginInit` method, all that is done is that a member variable `_inInit` is set to `true`. This flag is used to determine if the control is in the initialization process and is used in the `RootFolder` property. If the `RootFolder` property is set outside of the `InitializeComponent` class, the tree will need to be reinitialized. In the `RootFolder` property you check to see if `_inInit` is `true` or `false`. If it is `true`, then you don't want to go through the initialization process. If `inInit` is `false`, you call `InitializeTree`. You can also have a public `Init` method and accomplish the same task.

In the `EndInit` method, you check to see if the control is in design mode and if `_rootFolder` has a valid path assigned to it. Only then is `InitializeTree` called.

To add a final professional-looking touch, you have to add a bitmap image. This is the icon that shows up in the Toolbox when the control is added to a project. The bitmap image should be 16 × 6 pixels and 16 colors. You can create this image file with any graphics editor as long as the size and color depth are set properly. You can even create this file in Visual Studio .NET: Right-click the project and select Add New Item. From the list, select Bitmap File to open the graphics editor. After you have created the bitmap file, add it to the project, making sure that it is in the same namespace and has the same name as the control. Finally, set the Build Action of the bitmap to Embedded Resource: Right-click the bitmap file in the Solution Explorer and select Properties. Select Embedded Resource from the `Build Action` property.

To test the control, create a `TestHarness` project in the same solution. The `TestHarness` is a simple Windows Forms application with a single form. In the references section, add a reference to the `FolderTreeCtl` project. In the Toolbox window, add a reference to the `FolderTreeCtl.DLL` `.FolderTreeCtl` should now show up in the toolbox with the bitmap added as the icon. Click the icon and drag it to the `TestHarness` form. Set the `RootFolder` to an available folder and run the solution.

This is by no means a complete control. Several things could be enhanced to make this a full-featured, production-ready control. For example, you could add the following:

- **Exceptions** — If the control tries to load a folder that the user does not have access to, an exception is raised.

- **Background loading** — Loading a large folder tree can take a long time. Enhancing the initialization process to take advantage of a background thread for loading is a good idea.
- **Color codes** — You can make the text of certain file types a different color.
- **Icons** — You can add an `ImageList` control and add an icon to each file or folder as it is loaded.

User Control

User controls are one of the more powerful features of Windows Forms. They enable you to encapsulate user interface designs into nice reusable packages that can be plugged into project after project. It is not uncommon for an organization to have a couple of libraries of frequently used user controls. Not only can user interface functionality be contained in user controls, but common data validation can be incorporated in them as well, such as formatting phone numbers or ID numbers. A predefined list of items can be in the user control for fast loading of a list box or combo box. State codes or country codes fit into this category. Incorporating as much functionality that does not depend on the current application as possible into a user control makes the control that much more useful in the organization.

In this section, you create a simple address user control. You also will add the various events that make the control ready for data binding. The address control will have text entry for two address lines: city, state, and zip code.

To create a user control in a current project, just right-click the project in Solution Explorer and select Add; then select Add New User Control. You can also create a new Control Library project and add user controls to it. After a new user control has been started, you will see a form without any borders on the Designer. This is where you drop the controls that make up the user control. Remember that a user control is actually one or more controls added to a container control, so it is somewhat like creating a form. For the address control there are five `TextBox` controls and three `Label` controls. The controls can be arranged any way that seems appropriate (see Figure 31-4).

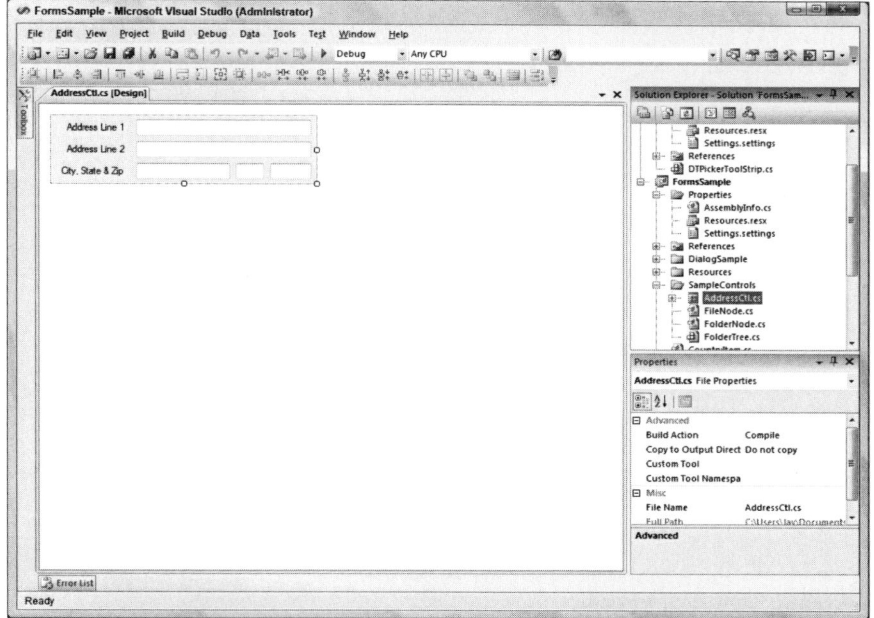

Figure 31-4

The TextBox controls in this example are named as follows:

- txtAddress1
- txtAddress2
- txtCity
- txtState
- txtZip

After the TextBox controls are in place and have valid names, add the public properties. You might be tempted to set the visibility of the TextBox controls to public instead of private. However, this is not a good idea because it defeats the purpose of encapsulating the functionality that you might want to add to the properties. The following is a listing of the properties that must be added:

```
public string AddressLine1
{
  get{return txtAddress1.Text;}
  set{
    if(txtAddress1.Text != value)
    {
      txtAddress1.Text = value;
      if(AddressLine1Changed != null)
        AddressLine1Changed(this, EventArgs.Empty);
    }
  }
}

public string AddressLine2
{
  get{return txtAddress2.Text;}
  set{
    if(txtAddress2.Text != value)
    {
      txtAddress2.Text = value;
      if(AddressLine2Changed != null)
        AddressLine2Changed(this, EventArgs.Empty);
    }
  }
}

public string City
{
  get{return txtCity.Text;}
  set{
    if(txtCity.Text != value)
    {
      txtCity.Text = value;
      if(CityChanged != null)
        CityChanged(this, EventArgs.Empty);
    }
  }
}

public string State
```

```
{
  get{return txtState.Text;}
  set{
    if(txtState.Text != value)
    {
      txtState.Text = value;
      if(StateChanged != null)
        StateChanged(this, EventArgs.Empty);
    }
  }
}

public string Zip
{
  get{return txtZip.Text;}
  set{
    if(txtZip.Text != value)
    {
      txtZip.Text = value;
      if(ZipChanged != null)
        ZipChanged(this, EventArgs.Empty);
    }
  }
}
```

The instances of the `get` property are fairly straightforward. They return the value of the corresponding `TextBox` control's text property. The instances of the `set` property, however, are doing a bit more work. All of the `set`s work the same way. A check is made to see whether or not the value of the property is actually changing. If the new value is the same as the current value, then a quick escape can be made. If there is a new value sent in, set the text property of the `TextBox` to the new value and test to see if an event has been instantiated. The event to look for is the changed event for the property. It has a specific naming format, `propertynameChanged`, where `propertyname` is the name of the property. In the case of the `AddressLine1` property, this event is called `AddressLine1Changed`. The properties are declared as follows:

```
public event EventHandler AddressLine1Changed;
public event EventHandler AddressLine2Changed;
public event EventHandler CityChanged;
public event EventHandler StateChanged;
public event EventHandler ZipChanged;
```

The purpose of the events is to notify binding that the property has changed. Once validation occurs, binding will make sure that the new value makes its way back to the object that the control is bound to. One other step should be done to support binding. A change to the text box by the user will not set the property directly. So, the `propertynameChanged` event must be raised when the text box changes as well. The easiest way to do this is to monitor the `TextChanged` event of the `TextBox` control. This example has only one `TextChanged` event handler and all of the text boxes use it. The control name is checked to see which control raised the event and the appropriate `propertynameChanged` event is raised. The following is the code for the event handler:

```
private void controls_TextChanged (object sender, System.EventArgs e)
{
  switch(((TextBox)sender).Name)
  {
    case "txtAddress1" :
      if(AddressLine1Changed != null)
```

(continued)

(continued)

```
          AddressLine1Changed(this, EventArgs.Empty);
        break;

      case "txtAddress2" :
        if(AddressLine2Changed != null)
          AddressLine2Changed(this, EventArgs.Empty);
        break;
      case "txtCity" :
        if(CityChanged != null)
          CityChanged(this, EventArgs.Empty);
        break;
      case "txtState" :
          if(StateChanged != null)
            StateChanged(this, EventArgs.Empty);
          break;
      case "txtZip" :
          if(ZipChanged != null)
            ZipChanged(this, EventArgs.Empty);
          break;
    }
  }
```

This example uses a simple `switch` statement to determine which text box raised the `TextChanged` event. Then a check is made to verify that the event is valid and not equal to null. Then the `Changed` event is raised. One thing to note is that an empty `EventArgs` is sent (`EventArgs.Empty`). The fact that these events have been added to the properties to support data binding does not mean that the only way to use the control is with data binding. The properties can be set in and read from code without using data binding. They have been added so that the user control is able to use binding if it is available. This is just one way of making the user control as flexible as possible so that it might be used in as many situations as possible.

Because a user control is essentially a control with some added features, all of the design-time issues discussed in the previous section apply here as well. Initializing user controls can bring on the same issues that you saw in the `FolderTree` example. Care must be taken in the design of user controls so that you avoid giving access to data stores that might not be available to other developers using your control.

Also similar to the control creation are the attributes that can be applied to user controls. The public properties and methods of the user control are displayed in the properties window when the control is placed on the Designer. In the example of the address user control it is a good idea to add `Category`, `Description`, and `DefaultValue` attributes to the address properties. A new `AddressData` category can be created and the default values would all be `""`. The following is an example of these attributes applied to the `AddressLine1` property:

```
  [Category("AddressData"),
        Description("Gets or sets the AddressLine1 value"),
        DefaultValue("")]
  public string AddressLine1
  {
    get{return txtAddress1.Text;}
    set{
      if(txtAddress1.Text != value)
      {
```

```
          txtAddress1.Text = value;
          if(AddressLine1Changed != null)
            AddressLine1Changed(this, EventArgs.Empty);
        }
      }
    }
```

As you can see, all that needs to be done to add a new category is to set the text in the `Category` attribute. The new category is automatically added.

There is still a lot of room for improvement. For example, you could include a list of state names and abbreviations in the control. Instead of just the state property, the user control could expose both the state name and state abbreviation properties. Exception handling should also be added. You could also add validation for the address lines. Making sure that the casing is correct, you might ask yourself whether `AddressLine1` could be optional or whether apartment and suite numbers should be entered on `AddressLine2` and not on `AddressLine1`.

Summary

This chapter has given you the basics for building Windows client-based applications. It explained each of the basic controls by discussing the hierarchy of the `Windows.Forms` namespace and examining the various properties and methods of the controls.

The chapter also showed you how to create a basic custom control as well as a basic user control. The power and flexibility of creating your own controls cannot be emphasized enough. By creating your own toolbox of custom controls, Windows-based client applications will become easier to develop and to test because you will be reusing the same tested components over and over again.

The next chapter, "Data Binding," covers how to link a data source to controls on a form. This will allow you to create forms that automatically update the data and keep the data on the form in sync.

32

Data Binding

This chapter builds on the content of Chapter 26, "Data Access," which covered various ways of selecting and changing data, by showing you how to present data to the user by binding to various Windows controls. More specifically, this chapter discusses:

- Displaying data using the `DataGridView` control
- The .NET data-binding capabilities and how they work
- How to use the Server Explorer to create a connection and generate a `DataSet` class (all without writing a line of code)
- How to use hit testing and reflection on rows in the `DataGrid`

You can download the source code for the examples in this chapter from the Wrox Web site at `www.wrox.com`.

The DataGridView Control

The `DataGrid` control that has been available from the initial release of .NET was functional, but had many areas that made it unsuitable for use in a commercial application — such as an inability to display images, drop-down controls, or lock columns, to name but a few. The control always felt half-completed, so many control vendors provided custom grid controls that overcame these deficiencies and also provided much more functionality.

.NET 2.0 introduced an additional `Grid` control — the `DataGridView`. This addresses many of the deficiencies of the original control, and adds significant functionality that previously was available only with add-on products.

The `DataGridView` control has binding capabilities similar to the old `DataGrid`, so it can bind to an `Array`, `DataTable`, `DataView`, or `DataSet` class, or a component that implements either the `IListSource` or `IList` interface. It gives you a variety of views of the same data. In its simplest guise, data can be displayed (as in a `DataSet` class) by setting the `DataSource` and `DataMember` properties — note that this control is not a plugin replacement for the `DataGrid`, so the programmatic interface to it is entirely different from that of the `DataGrid`. This control also provides more complex capabilities, which are discussed in the course of this chapter.

Displaying Tabular Data

Chapter 19, "Threading and Synchronization," introduced numerous ways of selecting data and reading it into a data table, although the data was displayed in a very basic fashion using `Console.WriteLine()`.

The following example demonstrates how to retrieve some data and display it in a `DataGridView` control. For this purpose, you will build a new application, `DisplayTabularData`, shown in Figure 32-1.

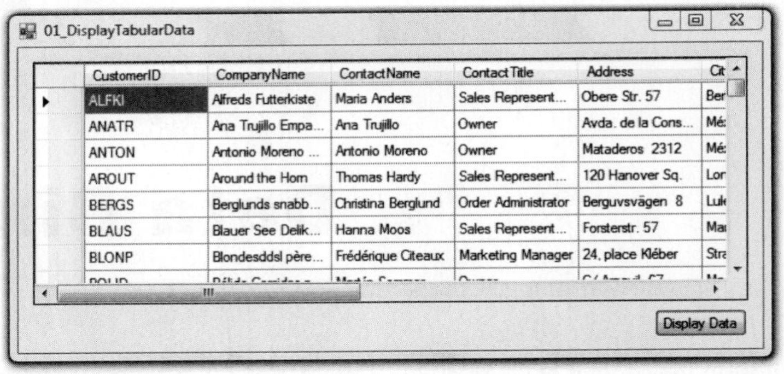

Figure 32-1

This simple application selects every record from the `Customer` table in the Northwind database and displays these records to the user in the `DataGridView` control. The following snippet shows the code for this example (excluding the form and control definition code):

```
using System;
using System.Configuration;
using System.Data;
using System.Data.Common;
using System.Data.SqlClient;
using System.Windows.Forms;

namespace DisplayTabularData
{
  partial class Form1: Form
  {
    public Form1()
    {
      InitializeComponent();
    }

    private void getData_Click(object sender, EventArgs e)
    {
      string customers = "SELECT * FROM Customers";

      using (SqlConnection con =
               new SqlConnection (ConfigurationManager.
                 ConnectionStrings["northwind"].ConnectionString))
      {
        DataSet ds = new DataSet();

        SqlDataAdapter da = new SqlDataAdapter(customers, con);
```

```
            da.Fill(ds, "Customers");

            dataGridView.AutoGenerateColumns = true;
            dataGridView.DataSource = ds;
            dataGridView.DataMember = "Customers";
         }
      }
   }
}
```

The form consists of the getData button, which when clicked calls the getData_Click() method shown in the example code.

This constructs a SqlConnection object, using the ConnectionStrings property of the ConfigurationManager class. Subsequently a data set is constructed and filled from the database table, using a DataAdapter object. The data is then displayed by the DataGridView control by setting the DataSource and DataMember properties. Note that the AutoGenerateColumns property is also set to true because this ensures that something is displayed to the user. If this flag is not specified, you need to create all columns yourself.

Data Sources

The DataGridView control provides a flexible way to display data; in addition to setting the DataSource to a DataSet and the DataMember to the name of the table to display, the DataSource property can be set to any of the following sources:

- An array (the grid can bind to any one-dimensional array)
- DataTable
- DataView
- DataSet or DataViewManager
- Components that implement the IListSource interface
- Components that implement the IList interface
- Any generic collection class or object derived from a generic collection class

The following sections give an example of each of these data sources.

Displaying Data from an Array

At first glance this seems to be easy. Create an array, fill it with some data, and set the DataSource property on the DataGridView control. Here's some example code:

```
string[] stuff = new string[] {"One", "Two", "Three"};
dataGridView.DataSource = stuff;
```

If the data source contains multiple possible candidate tables (such as when using a DataSet or DataViewManager), you need to also set the DataMember property.

You could replace the code in the previous example's getData_Click event handler with the preceding array code. The problem with this code is the resulting display (see Figure 32-2).

Instead of displaying the strings defined within the array, the grid displays the length of those strings. That's because when using an array as the source of data for a DataGridView control, the grid looks for the first public property of the object within the array and displays this value rather than the string value. The first (and only) public property of a string is its length, so that is what is displayed. The list of properties for any class can be obtained by using the GetProperties method of the TypeDescriptor class. This returns a collection of `PropertyDescriptor` objects, which can then be used when displaying data. The .NET `PropertyGrid` control uses this method when displaying arbitrary objects.

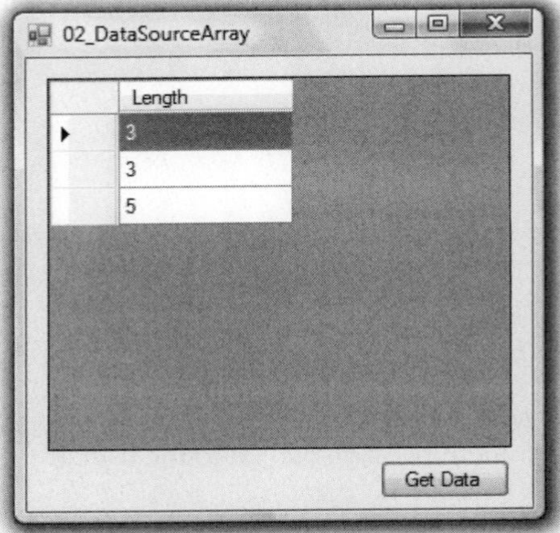

Figure 32-2

One way to rectify the problem with displaying strings in the `DataGridView` is to create a wrapper class:

```
protected class Item
{
   public Item(string text)
   {
      _text = text;
   }
   public string Text
   {
      get{return _text;}
   }
   private string _text;
}
```

Figure 32-3 shows the output when an array of this `Item` class (which could just as well be a `struct` for all the processing that it does) is added to your data source array code.

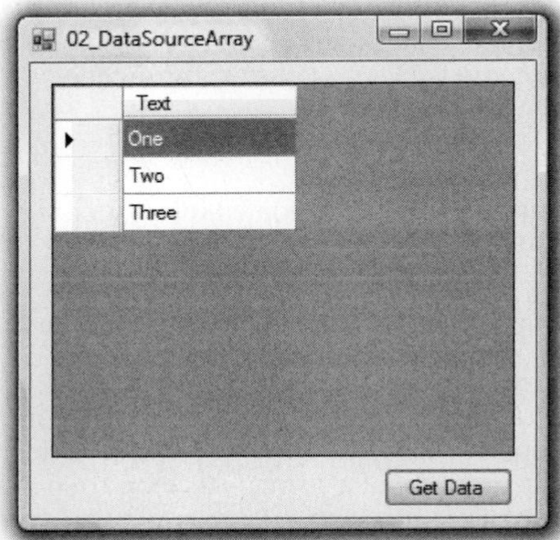

Figure 32-3

DataTable

You can display a DataTable within a DataGridView control in two ways:

- If you have a standalone DataTable, simply set the DataSource property of the control to the table.
- If your DataTable is contained within a DataSet, you need to set the DataSource to the data set and the DataMember property should be set to the name of the DataTable within the data set.

Figure 32-4 shows the result of running the DataSourceDataTable sample code.

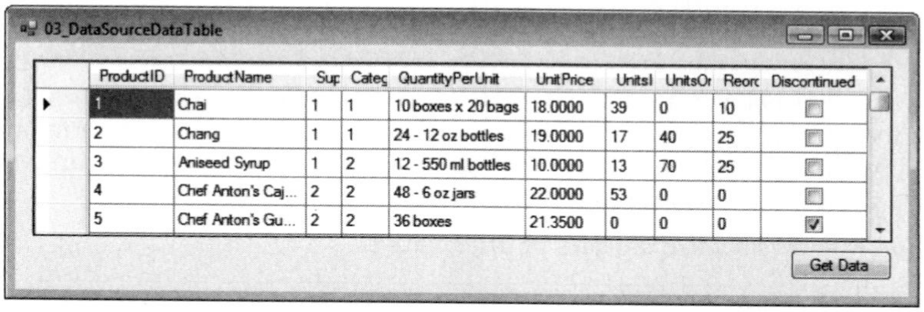

Figure 32-4

Note the display of the last column; it shows a check box instead of the more common edit control. The DataGridView control, in the absence of any other information, will read the schema from the data source (which in this case is the Products table), and infer from the column types what control is to be displayed. Unlike the original DataGrid control, the DataGridView control has built-in support for image columns, buttons, and combo boxes.

The data in the database does not change when fields are altered in the data grid because the data is stored only locally on the client computer — there is no active connection to the database. Updating data in the database is discussed later in this chapter.

Displaying Data from a DataView

A DataView provides a means to filter and sort data within a DataTable. When data has been selected from the database, it is common to permit the user to sort that data, for example, by clicking on column headings. In addition, the user might want to filter the data to show only certain rows, such as all those that have been altered. A DataView can be filtered so that only selected rows are shown to the user; however, you cannot filter the columns from the DataTable.

> **A DataView does not permit the filtering of columns, only rows.**

To create a DataView based on an existing DataTable, use the following code:

```
DataView dv = new DataView(dataTable);
```

Once created, further settings can be altered on the DataView, which affect the data and operations permitted on that data when it is displayed within the data grid. For example:

- Setting AllowEdit = false disables all column edit functionality for rows.
- Setting AllowNew = false disables the new row functionality.
- Setting AllowDelete = false disables the delete row capability.
- Setting the RowStateFilter displays only rows of a given state.
- Setting the RowFilter enables you to filter rows.

The next section explains how to use the RowStateFilter setting; the other options are fairly self-explanatory.

Filtering Rows by Data

After the DataView has been created, the data displayed by that view can be altered by setting the RowFilter property. This property, typed as a string, is used as a means of filtering based on certain criteria defined by the value of the string. Its syntax is similar to a WHERE clause in regular SQL, but it is issued against data already selected from the database.

The following table shows some examples of filter clauses.

Clause	Description
UnitsInStock > 50	Shows only those rows where the UnitsInStock column is greater than 50.
Client = 'Smith'	Returns only the records for a given client.
County LIKE 'C*'	Returns all records where the County field begins with a C — in this example, the rows for Cornwall, Cumbria, Cheshire, and Cambridgeshire would be returned. The % character can be used as a single-character wildcard, whereas the * denotes a general wildcard that will match zero or more characters.

The runtime will do its best to coerce the data types used within the filter expression into the appropriate types for the source columns. For instance, it is perfectly legal to write "UnitsInStock > '50'" in the earlier example, even though the column is an integer. If an invalid filter string is provided, an EvaluateException will be thrown.

Filtering Rows on State

Each row within a DataView has a defined row state, which has one of the values shown in the following table. This state can also be used to filter the rows viewed by the user.

DataViewRowState	Description
Added	Lists all rows that have been newly created.
CurrentRows	Lists all rows except those that have been deleted.
Deleted	Lists all rows that were originally selected and have been deleted; does not show newly created rows that have been deleted.

DataViewRowState	Description
`ModifiedCurrent`	Lists all rows that have been modified and shows the current value of each column.
`ModifiedOriginal`	Lists all rows that have been modified but shows the original value of the column and not the current value.
`OriginalRows`	Lists all rows that were originally selected from a data source. Does not include new rows. Shows the original values of the columns (that is, not the current values if changes have been made).
`Unchanged`	Lists all rows that have not changed in any way.

Figure 32-5 shows a grid that can have rows added, deleted, or amended, and a second grid that lists rows in one of the preceding states.

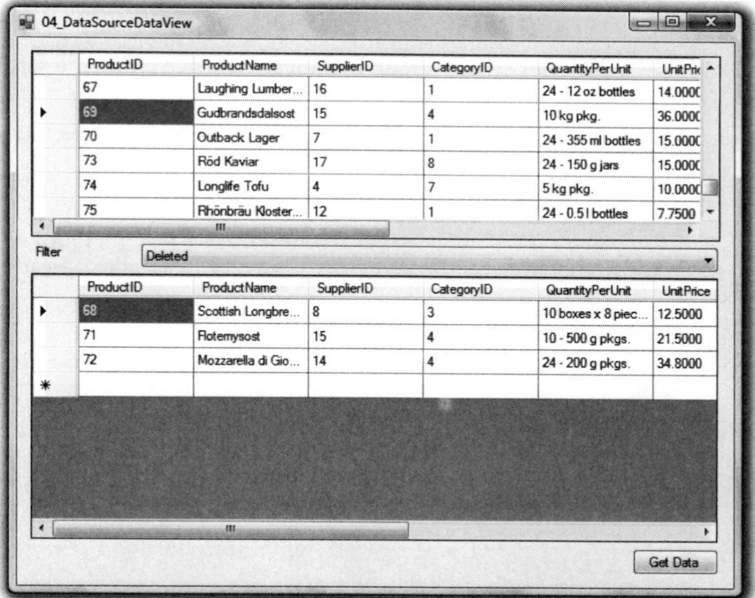

Figure 32-5

The filter not only applies to the visible rows but also to the state of the columns within those rows. This is evident when choosing the `ModifiedOriginal` or `ModifiedCurrent` selections. These states are described in Chapter 20, "Security," and are based on the `DataRowVersion` enumeration. For example, when the user has updated a column in the row, the row will be displayed when either `ModifiedOriginal` or `ModifiedCurrent` is chosen; however, the actual value will be either the `Original` value selected from the database (if `ModifiedOriginal` is chosen) or the current value in the `DataColumn` (if `ModifiedCurrent` is chosen).

Sorting Rows

Apart from filtering data, you might also have to sort the data within a `DataView`. To sort data in ascending or descending order, simply click the column header in the `DataGridView` control (see Figure 32-6). The only trouble is that the control can sort by only one column, whereas the underlying `DataView` control can sort by multiple columns.

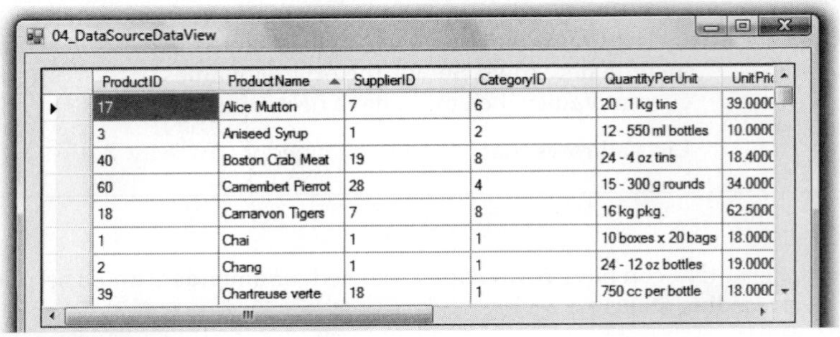

04_DataSourceDataView

ProductID	ProductName	SupplierID	CategoryID	QuantityPerUnit	UnitPric
17	Alice Mutton	7	6	20 - 1 kg tins	39.000C
3	Aniseed Syrup	1	2	12 - 550 ml bottles	10.000C
40	Boston Crab Meat	19	8	24 - 4 oz tins	18.400C
60	Camembert Pierrot	28	4	15 - 300 g rounds	34.000C
18	Carnarvon Tigers	7	8	16 kg pkg.	62.500C
1	Chai	1	1	10 boxes x 20 bags	18.000C
2	Chang	1	1	24 - 12 oz bottles	19.000C
39	Chartreuse verte	18	1	750 cc per bottle	18.000C

Figure 32-6

When a column is sorted, either by clicking the header (as shown on the `ProductName` column) or in code, the `DataGrid` displays an arrow bitmap to indicate which column the sort has been applied to.

To set the sort order on a column programmatically, use the `Sort` property of the `DataView`:

```
dataView.Sort = "ProductName";
dataView.Sort = "ProductName ASC, ProductID DESC";
```

The first line sorts the data based on the `ProductName` column, as shown in Figure 32-6. The second line sorts the data in ascending order, based on the `ProductName` column, then in descending order of `ProductID`.

The `DataView` supports both ascending (default) and descending sort orders on columns. If more than one column is sorted in code in the `DataView`, the `DataGridView` will cease to display any sort arrows.

Each column in the grid can be strongly typed, so its sort order is not based on the string representation of the column but instead is based on the data within that column. The upshot is that if there is a date column in the `DataGrid`, the user can sort numerically on the date rather than on the date string representation.

Displaying Data from a DataSet Class

There is one feature of `DataSets` that the `DataGridView` cannot match the `DataGrid` in — this is when a `DataSet` is defined that includes relationships between tables. As with the preceding `DataGridView` examples, the `DataGrid` can display only a single `DataTable` at a time. However, as shown in the following example, `DataSourceDataSet`, it is possible to navigate relationships within the `DataSet` onscreen. The following code can be used to generate such a `DataSet` based on the `Customers` and `Orders` tables in the Northwind database. This example loads data from these two `DataTables` and then creates a relationship between these tables called `CustomerOrders`:

```
string orders = "SELECT * FROM Orders";
string customers = "SELECT * FROM Customers";
SqlConnection conn = new SqlConnection(source);
SqlDataAdapter da = new SqlDataAdapter(orders, conn);
DataSet ds = new DataSet();
da.Fill(ds, "Orders");
da = new SqlDataAdapter(customers , conn);
da.Fill(ds, "Customers");
ds.Relations.Add("CustomerOrders",
                 ds.Tables["Customers"].Columns["CustomerID"],
                 ds.Tables["Orders"].Columns["CustomerID"]);
```

Once created, the data in the `DataSet` is bound to the `DataGrid` simply by calling `SetDataBinding()`:

```
dataGrid1.SetDataBinding(ds, "Customers");
```

This produces the output shown in Figure 32-7.

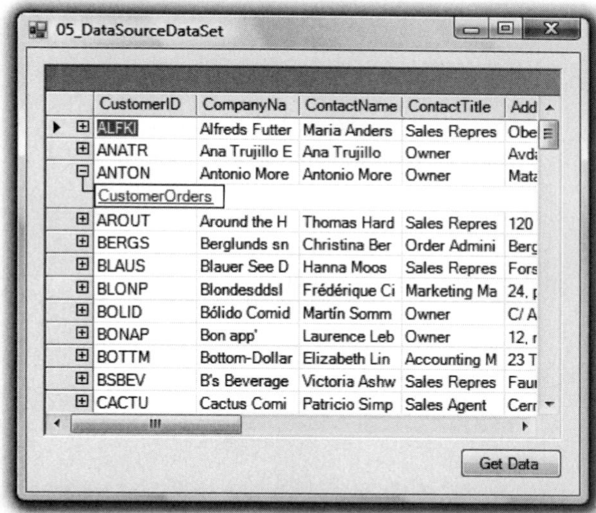

Figure 32-7

Unlike the `DataGridView` examples shown in this chapter, there is now a + sign to the left of each record. This reflects the fact that the `DataSet` has a navigable relationship between customers and orders. Any number of such relationships can be defined in code.

When the user clicks the + sign, the list of relationships is shown (or hidden if already visible). Clicking the name of the relationship enables you to navigate to the linked records (see Figure 32-8), in this example, listing all orders placed by the selected customer.

The `DataGrid` control also includes a couple of new icons in the top-right corner. The arrow permits the user to navigate to the parent row, and will change the display to that on the previous page. The header row showing details of the parent record can be shown or hidden by clicking the other button.

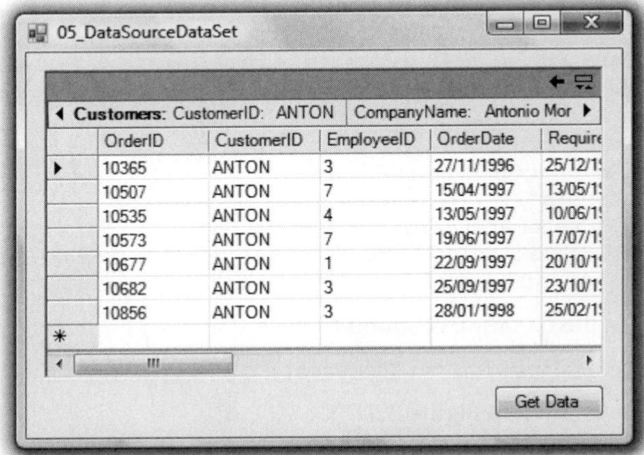

Figure 32-8

Displaying Data in a DataViewManager

The display of data in a `DataViewManager` is the same as that for the `DataSet` shown in the previous section. However, when a `DataViewManager` is created for a `DataSet`, an individual `DataView` is created for each `DataTable`, which then permits the code to alter the displayed rows based on a filter or the row state, as shown in the `DataView` example. Even if the code doesn't need to filter data, it is good practice to wrap the `DataSet` in a `DataViewManager` for display because it provides more options when revising the source code.

The following creates a `DataViewManager` based on the `DataSet` from the previous example and then alters the `DataView` for the `Customer` table to show only customers from the United Kingdom:

```
DataViewManager dvm = new DataViewManager(ds);
dvm.DataViewSettings["Customers"].RowFilter = "Country='UK'";
dataGrid.SetDataBinding(dvm, "Customers");
```

Figure 32-9 shows the output of the `DataSourceDataViewManager` sample code.

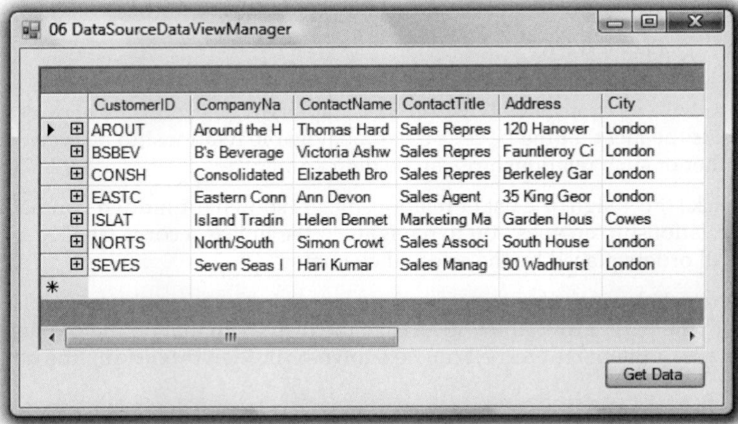

Figure 32-9

IListSource and IList Interfaces

The DataGridView also supports any object that exposes one of the interfaces IListSource or IList. IListSource has only one method, GetList(), which returns an IList interface. IList, however, is somewhat more interesting and is implemented by a large number of classes in the runtime. Some of the classes that implement this interface are Array, ArrayList, and StringCollection.

When using IList, the same caveat for the object within the collection holds true as for the Array implementation shown earlier — if a StringCollection is used as the data source for the DataGrid, the length of the strings is displayed within the grid, not within the text of the item as expected.

Displaying Generic Collections

In addition to the types already described, the DataGridView also supports binding to generic collections. The syntax is just as in the other examples already provided in this chapter — simply set the DataSource property to the collection, and the control will generate an appropriate display.

Once again, the columns displayed are based on the properties of the object — all public readable fields are displayed in the DataGridView. The following example shows the display for a list class defined as follows:

```
class PersonList : List < Person >
{
}

class Person
{
    public Person( string name, Sex sex, DateTime dob )
    {
        _name = name;
        _sex = sex;
        _dateOfBirth = dob;
    }

    public string Name
    {
        get { return _name; }
        set { _name = value; }
    }

    public Sex Sex
    {
        get { return _sex; }
        set { _sex = value; }
    }

    public DateTime DateOfBirth
    {
        get { return _dateOfBirth; }
        set { _dateOfBirth = value; }
    }

    private string _name;
    private Sex _sex;
    private DateTime _dateOfBirth;
}

enum Sex
```

(continued)

(continued)

```
{
    Male,
    Female
}
```

The display shows several instances of the `Person` class that were constructed within the `PersonList` class. See Figure 32-10.

In some circumstances, it might be necessary to hide certain properties from the grid display — for this you can use the `Browsable` attribute as shown in the following code snippet. Any properties marked as non-browsable are not displayed in the property grid.

```
  [Browsable(false)]
public bool IsEmployed
{
    ...
}
```

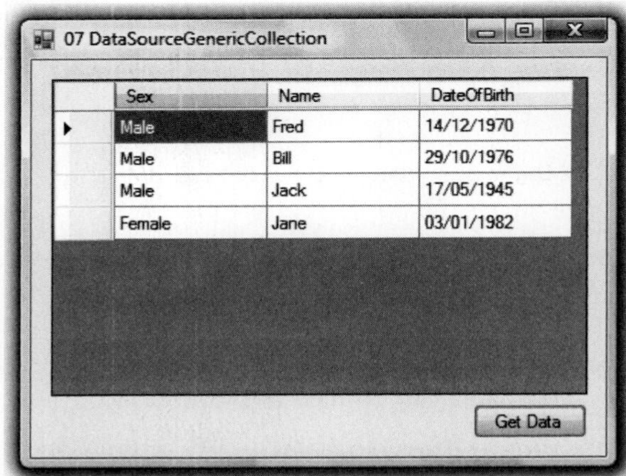

Figure 32-10

The `DataGridView` uses this property to determine whether to display the property or hide it. In the absence of the attribute, the default is to display the property. If a property is read-only, the grid control will display the values from the object, but it will be read-only within the grid.

Any changes made in the grid view are reflected in the underlying objects — so, for example, if in the previous code the name of a person was changed within the user interface, the setter method for that property would be called.

DataGridView Class Hierarchy

The class hierarchy for the main parts of the `DataGridView` control is shown in Figure 32-11.

The control uses objects derived from `DataGridViewColumn` when displaying data. As you can see from Figure 32-11, there are now far more options for displaying data than there were with the original `DataGrid`. One major omission was the display of drop-down columns within the `DataGrid` — this functionality is now provided for the `DataGridView` in the form of the `DataGridViewComboBoxColumn`.

When you specify a data source for the `DataGridView`, by default it will construct columns for you automatically. These will be created based on the data types in the data source, so, for example, any Boolean field will be mapped to the `DataGridViewCheckBoxColumn`. If you would rather handle the creation of columns yourself, you can set the `AutoGenerateColumns` property to `false` and construct the columns yourself.

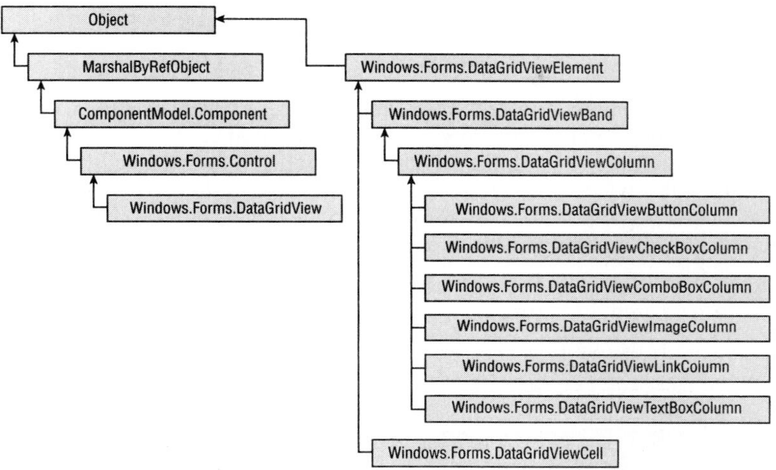

Figure 32-11

The following example shows how to construct columns and includes an image and a `ComboBox` column. The code uses a `DataSet` and retrieves data into two data tables. The first `DataTable` contains the employee information from the Northwind database. The second table consists of the `EmployeeID` column and a generated `Name` column, which is used when rendering the `ComboBox`:

```
using (SqlConnection con =
  new SqlConnection (
    ConfigurationSettings.ConnectionStrings["northwind"].ConnectionString ) )
{
    string select = "SELECT EmployeeID, FirstName, LastName, Photo,
                       IsNull(ReportsTo,0) as ReportsTo FROM Employees";

    SqlDataAdapter da = new SqlDataAdapter(select, con);

    DataSet ds = new DataSet();

    da.Fill(ds, "Employees");

    select = "SELECT EmployeeID, FirstName + ' ' + LastName as Name
                FROM Employees UNION SELECT 0,'(None)'";

    da = new SqlDataAdapter(select, con);
    da.Fill(ds, "Managers");

    // Construct the columns in the grid view
    SetupColumns(ds);
```

(continued)

(continued)

```
        // Set the default height for a row
        dataGridView.RowTemplate.Height = 100 ;

        // Then set up the datasource
        dataGridView.AutoGenerateColumns = false;
        dataGridView.DataSource = ds.Tables["Employees"];

    }
```

Here there are two things to note. The first select statement replaces `null` values in the `ReportsTo` column with the value zero. There is one row in the database that contains a `null` value in this field, indicating that the individual has no manager. However, when data binding, the `ComboBox` needs a value in this column; otherwise, an exception will be raised when the grid is displayed. In the example, the value zero is chosen because it does not exist within the table — this is commonly termed a *sentinel value* because it has special meaning to the application.

The second SQL clause selects data for the `ComboBox` and includes a manufactured row where the values `Zero` and `(None)` are created. In Figure 32-12, the second row displays the `(None)` entry.

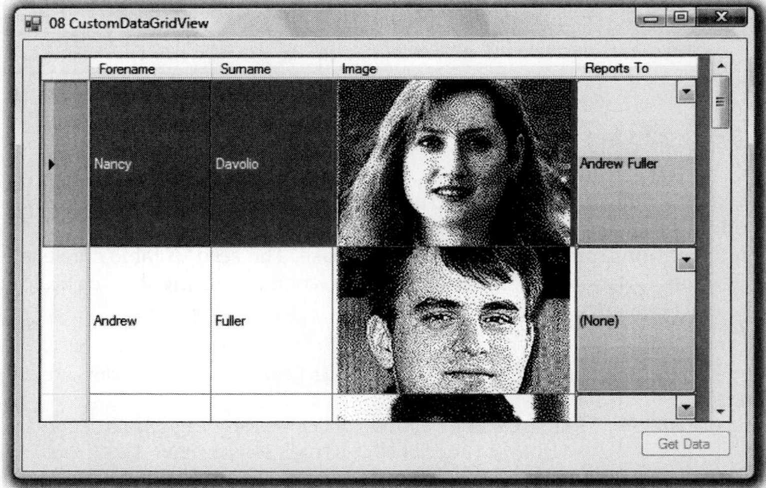

Figure 32-12

The custom columns are created by the following function:

```
    private void SetupColumns(DataSet ds)
    {
        DataGridViewTextBoxColumn forenameColumn = new DataGridViewTextBoxColumn();
        forenameColumn.DataPropertyName = "FirstName";
        forenameColumn.HeaderText = "Forename";
        forenameColumn.ValueType = typeof(string);
        forenameColumn.Frozen = true;
        dataGridView.Columns.Add(forenameColumn);

        DataGridViewTextBoxColumn surnameColumn = new DataGridViewTextBoxColumn();
        surnameColumn.DataPropertyName = "LastName";
        surnameColumn.HeaderText = "Surname";
```

```
        surnameColumn.Frozen = true;
        surnameColumn.ValueType = typeof(string);
        dataGridView.Columns.Add(surnameColumn);

        DataGridViewImageColumn photoColumn = new DataGridViewImageColumn();
        photoColumn.DataPropertyName = "Photo";
        photoColumn.Width = 100;
        photoColumn.HeaderText = "Image";
        photoColumn.ReadOnly = true;
        photoColumn.ImageLayout = DataGridViewImageCellLayout.Normal;
        dataGridView.Columns.Add(photoColumn);

        DataGridViewComboBoxColumn reportsToColumn = new DataGridViewComboBoxColumn();
        reportsToColumn.HeaderText = "Reports To";
        reportsToColumn.DataSource = ds.Tables["Managers"];
        reportsToColumn.DisplayMember = "Name";
        reportsToColumn.ValueMember = "EmployeeID";
        reportsToColumn.DataPropertyName = "ReportsTo";
        dataGridView.Columns.Add(reportsToColumn);
    }
```

The `ComboBox` is created last in this example — and uses the `Managers` table in the passed data set as its data source. This contains `Name` and `EmployeeID` columns, and these are assigned to the `DisplayMember` and `ValueMember` properties, respectively. These properties define where the data is coming from for the `ComboBox`.

The `DataPropertyName` is set to the column in the main data table that the combo box links to — this provides the initial value for the column, and if the user chooses another entry from the combo box, this value is updated.

The only other thing this example needs to do is handle `null` values correctly when updating the database. At present, it will attempt to write the value zero into any row if you choose the (None) item onscreen. This will cause an exception from SQL Server because this violates the foreign key constraint on the `ReportsTo` column. To overcome this, you need to preprocess the data before sending it back to SQL Server, and set to `null` the `ReportsTo` column for any rows where this value was zero.

Data Binding

The previous examples have used the `DataGrid` and `DataGridView` controls, which form only a small part of the controls in the .NET runtime that can be used to display data. The process of linking a control to a data source is called *data binding*.

In the Microsoft Foundation Class library, the process of linking data from class variables to a set of controls was termed *Dialog Data Exchange* (DDX). The facilities available within .NET for binding data to controls are substantially easier to use and also more capable. For example, in .NET you can bind data to most properties of a control, not just the text property. You can also bind data in a similar manner to ASP.NET controls (see Chapter 37, "ASP.NET Pages").

Simple Binding

A control that supports single binding typically displays only a single value at once, such as a text box or radio button. The following example shows how to bind a column from a `DataTable` to a `TextBox`:

```
DataSet ds = CreateDataSet();
textBox.DataBindings.Add("Text", ds , "Products.ProductName");
```

After retrieving some data from the `Products` table and storing it in the returned `DataSet` with the `CreateDataSet()` method as shown here, the second line binds the `Text` property of the control (`textBox1`) to the `Products.ProductName` column. Figure 32-13 shows the result of this type of data binding.

Figure 32-13

The text box displays a string from the database. Figure 32-14 shows how the SQL Server Management Studio tool could be used to verify the contents of the `Products` table to check that it is the right column and value.

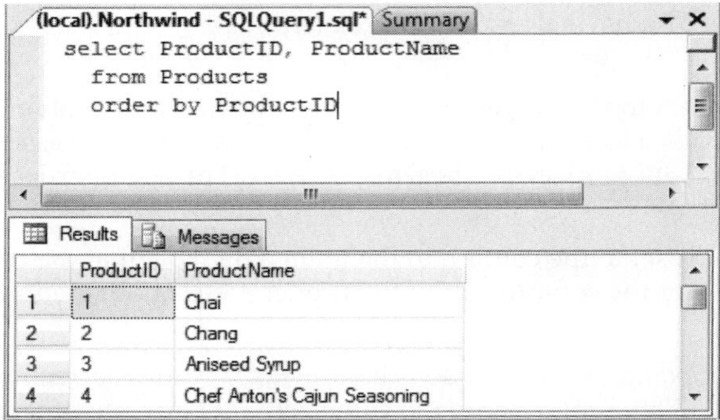

Figure 32-14

Having a single text box onscreen with no way to scroll to the next or the previous record and no way to update the database is not very useful. The following section shows a more realistic example and introduces the other objects that are necessary for data binding to work.

Data-Binding Objects

Figure 32-15 shows a class hierarchy for the objects that are used in data binding. This section discusses the `BindingContext`, `CurrencyManager`, and `PropertyManager` classes of the `System.Windows.Forms` namespace and shows how they interact when data is bound to one or more controls on a form. The shaded objects are those used in binding.

In the previous example, the `DataBindings` property of the `TextBox` control was used to bind a column from a `DataSet` to the `Text` property of the control. The `DataBindings` property is an instance of the `ControlBindingsCollection` shown in Figure 32-15:

```
textBox1.DataBindings.Add("Text", ds, "Products.ProductName");
```

This line adds a `Binding` object to the `ControlBindingsCollection`.

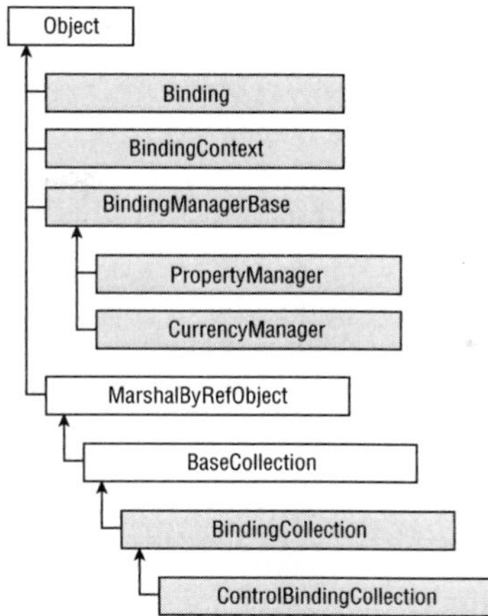

Figure 32-15

BindingContext

Each Windows Form has a `BindingContext` property. Incidentally, `Form` is derived from `Control`, which is where this property is actually defined, so most controls have this property. A `BindingContext` object has a collection of `BindingManagerBase` instances (see Figure 32-16). These instances are created and added to the binding manager object when a control is data-bound.

The `BindingContext` might contain several data sources, wrapped in either a `CurrencyManager` or a `PropertyManager`. The decision of which class is used is based on the data source itself.

If the data source contains a list of items, such as a `DataTable`, `DataView`, or any object that implements the `IList` interface, a `CurrencyManager` will be used. A `CurrencyManager` can maintain the current position within that data source. If the data source returns only a single value, a `PropertyManager` will be stored within the `BindingContext`.

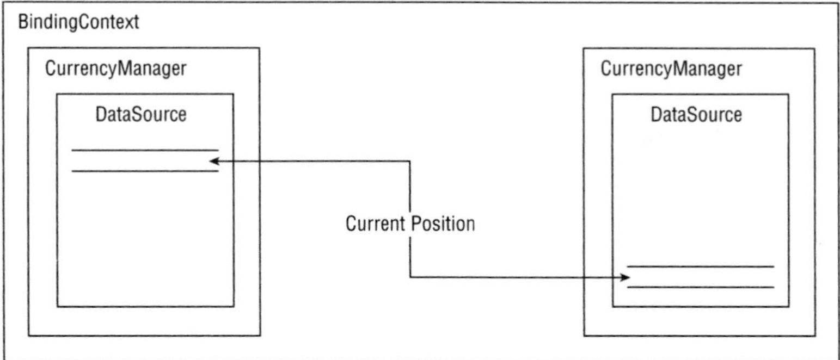

Figure 32-16

A `CurrencyManager` or `PropertyManager` is created only once for a given data source. If two text boxes are bound to a row from a `DataTable`, only one `CurrencyManager` will be created within the binding context.

Each control added to a form is linked to the form's binding manager, so all controls share the same instance. When a control is initially created, its `BindingContext` property is `null`. When the control is added to the `Controls` collection of the form, the `BindingContext` is set to that of the form.

To bind a control to a form, an entry needs to be added to its `DataBindings` property, which is an instance of `ControlBindingsCollection`. The following code creates a new binding:

```
textBox.DataBindings.Add("Text", ds, "Products.ProductName");
```

Internally, the `Add()` method of `ControlBindingsCollection` creates a new instance of a `Binding` object from the parameters passed to this method and adds this to the bindings collection represented in Figure 32-17.

Figure 32-17 illustrates roughly what is going on when a `Binding` object is added to a `Control`. The binding links the control to a data source, which is maintained within the `BindingContext` of the `Form` (or control itself). Changes within the data source are reflected into the control, as are changes in the control.

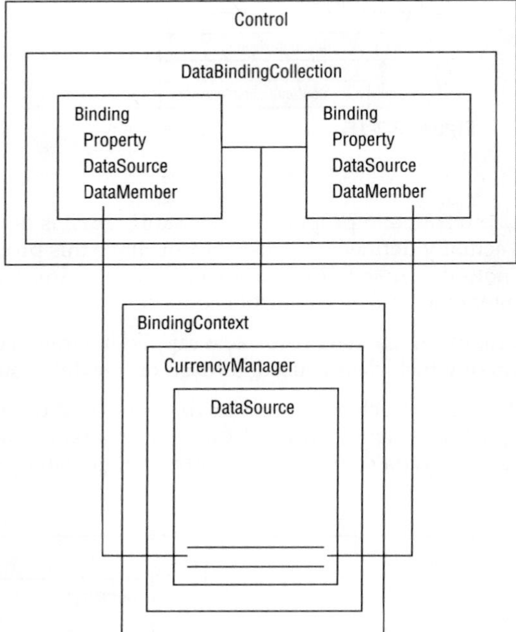

Figure 32-17

Binding

This class links a property of the control to a member of the data source. When that member changes, the control's property is updated to reflect this change. The opposite is also true — if the text in the text box is updated, this change is reflected in the data source.

Bindings can be set up from any column to any property of the control. For example, you can bind not only the text of a text box but also the color of that text box. It is possible to bind properties of a control to completely different data sources; for example, the color of the cell might be defined in a colors table, and the actual data might be defined in another table.

CurrencyManager and PropertyManager

When a `Binding` object is created, a corresponding `CurrencyManager` or `PropertyManager` object is also created, provided that this is the first time that data from the given source has been bound. The purpose of this class is to define the position of the current record within the data source and to coordinate all list bindings when the current record is changed. Figure 32-18 displays two fields from the `Products` table and includes a way to move between records by means of a `TrackBar` control.

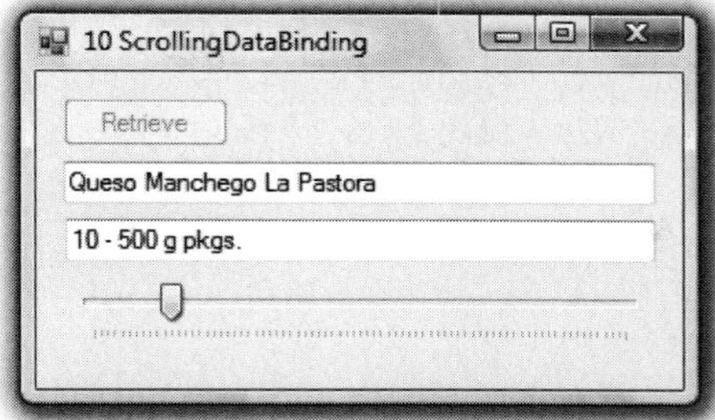

Figure 32-18

The following example shows the main `ScrollingDataBinding` code:

```
namespace ScrollingDataBinding
{
  partial class Form1: Form
  {
    public Form1()
    {
      InitializeComponent();
    }

    private DataSet CreateDataSet()
    {
      string customers = "SELECT * FROM Products";
      DataSet ds = new DataSet();

      using (SqlConnection con = new SqlConnection (
               ConfigurationSettings.
               ConnectionStrings["northwind"].ConnectionString))
      {
        SqlDataAdapter da = new SqlDataAdapter(customers, con);

        da.Fill(ds, "Products");
      }

      return ds;
    }

    private void trackBar_Scroll(object sender, EventArgs e)
    {
        this.BindingContext[ds, "Products"].Position = trackBar.Value;
    }

    private void retrieveButton_Click(object sender, EventArgs e)
    {
```

(continued)

(continued)

```
        retrieveButton.Enabled = false;

        ds = CreateDataSet();

        textName.DataBindings.Add("Text", ds, "Products.ProductName");
        textQuan.DataBindings.Add("Text", ds, "Products.QuantityPerUnit");

        trackBar.Minimum = 0;
        trackBar.Maximum = this.BindingContext[ds, "Products"].Count - 1;

        textName.Enabled = true;
        textQuan.Enabled = true;
        trackBar.Enabled = true;

      }

      private DataSet ds;
    }
  }
```

The scrolling mechanism is provided by the `trackBar_Scroll` event handler, which sets the position of the `BindingContext` to the current position of the track bar thumb. Altering the binding context here updates the data displayed on the screen.

Data is bound to the two text boxes in the `retrieveButton_Click` event by adding a data binding expression. Here the `Text` properties of the controls are set to fields from the data source. It is possible to bind any simple property of a control to an item from the data source; for example, you could bind the text color, enabled, or other properties as appropriate.

When the data is originally retrieved, the maximum position on the track bar is set to be the number of records. Then, in the scroll method, the position of the `BindingContext` for the products `DataTable` is set to the position of the scroll bar thumb. This changes the current record from the `DataTable`, so all controls bound to the current row (in this example, the two text boxes) are updated.

Now that you know how to bind to various data sources, such as arrays, data tables, data views, and various other containers of data, and how to sort and filter that data, the next section discusses how Visual Studio has been extended to permit data access to be better integrated with the application.

Visual Studio .NET and Data Access

This section discusses some of the ways that Visual Studio allows data to be integrated into the GUI, including how to create a connection, select some data, generate a `DataSet`, and use all of the generated objects to produce a simple application. The available tools enable you to create a database connection with the `OleDbConnection` or `SqlConnection` classes. The class you use depends on the type of database you are using. After a connection has been defined, you can create a `DataSet` and populate it from within Visual Studio .NET. This generates an XSD file for the `DataSet` and the `.cs` code. The result is a type-safe `DataSet`.

Creating a Connection

First, create a new Windows application, and then create a new database connection. Using the Server Explorer (see Figure 32-19), you can manage various aspects of data access.

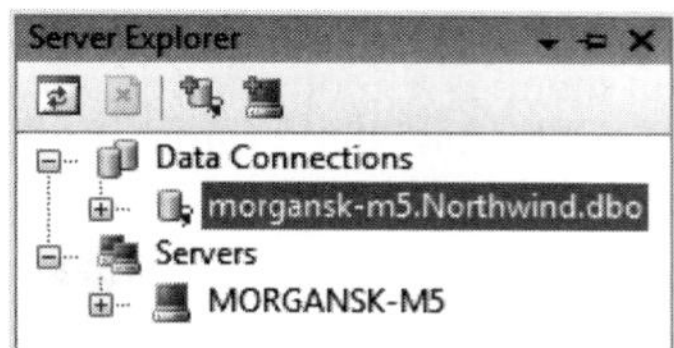

Figure 32-19

For this example, create a connection to the Northwind database. Select the Add Connection option from the context menu available on the Data Connections item to launch a wizard that enables you to choose a database provider. Select the .NET Framework Provider for SQL Server. Figure 32-20 shows the Add Connection dialog box.

Figure 32-20

Depending on your .NET Framework installation, the sample databases might be located in SQL Server, MSDE (Microsoft SQL Server Data Engine), or both.

To connect to the local MSDE database, if it exists, type **(local)\\sqlexpress** for the name of the server. To connect to a regular SQL Server instance, type **(local)** or '**.**' to select a database on the current machine, or the name of the desired server on the network. You may need to enter a user name and password to access the database.

Select the Northwind database from the drop-down list of databases, and to ensure that everything is set up correctly, click the Test Connection button. If everything is set up properly, you should see a message box with a confirmation message.

Visual Studio 2005 had numerous changes when accessing data, and these are available from several places in the user interface. The Data menu is a good choice because it permits you to view any data sources already added to the project, add a new data source, and preview data from the underlying database (or other data source).

The following example uses the Northwind database connection to generate a user interface for selecting data from the `Employees` table. The first step is to choose Add New Data Source from the Data menu, which begins a wizard that walks you through the process. The dialog shown in Figure 32-21 shows part of the Data Source Configuration Wizard, in this case where you can select appropriate tables for the data source.

As you progress through the wizard, you can choose the data source, which can be a database, local database file (such as an `.mdb` file), a Web service, or an object. You will then be prompted for further information based on the type of data source you choose. For a database connection, this includes the name of the connection (which is subsequently stored in the application configuration file shown in the following code), and you can then select the table, view, or stored procedure that supplies the data. Ultimately, this generates a strongly typed `DataSet` within your application.

```
<?xml version="1.0" encoding="utf-8"?>
<configuration>
  <connectionStrings>
    <add name="SimpleApp.Properties.Settings.NorthwindConnection"
       connectionString="Data Source=.;Integrated Security=True;Initial
Catalog=Northwind"
       providerName="System.Data.SqlClient" />
  </connectionStrings>
</configuration>
```

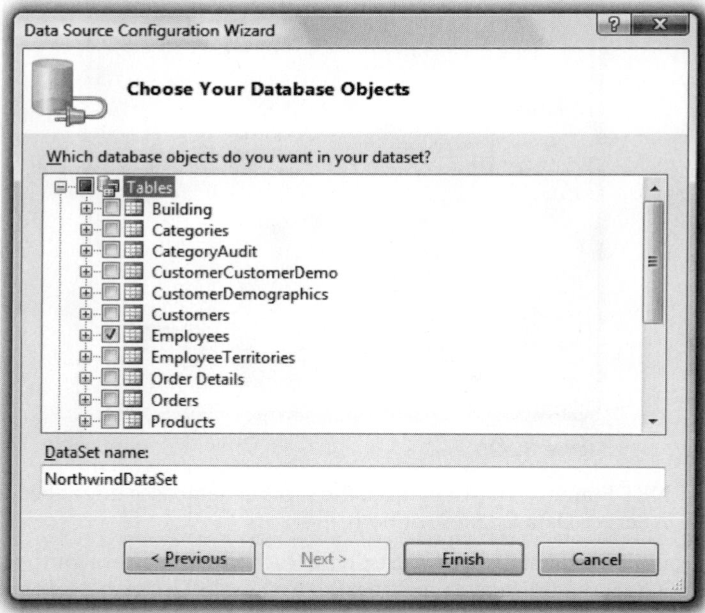

Figure 32-21

This includes the name of the connection, the connection string itself, and a provider name, which is used when generating the connection object. You can manually edit this information as necessary. To display a user interface for the employee data, you can simply drag the chosen data from the Data Sources window onto your form. This will generate one of two styles of user interface for you — a grid-style UI that utilizes the `DataGridView` control described earlier or a details view that presents just the data for a single record at a time. Figure 32-22 shows the details view.

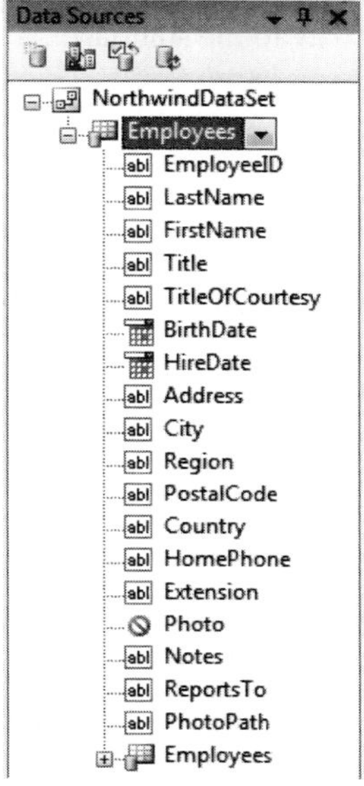

Figure 32-22

Dragging the data source onto the form generates a number of objects, both visual and nonvisual. The nonvisual objects are created within the tray area of the form and comprise a `DataConnector`, a strongly typed `DataSet`, and a `TableAdapter`, which contains the SQL used to select/update the data. The visual objects created depend on whether you have chosen the `DataGridView` or the details view. Both include a `DataNavigator` control that can be used to page through the data. Figure 32-23 shows the user interface generated using the `DataGridView` control — one of the goals of Visual Studio 2005 was to simplify data access to the point where you could generate functional forms without writing a single line of code.

11 SimpleApp

1 of 9

EmployeeID	LastName	FirstName	Title	TitleOfCourtesy	Birth
1	Davolio	Nancy	Sales Represent...	Ms.	08/1
2	Fuller	Andrew	Vice President, S...	Dr.	19/0
3	Leverling	Janet	Sales Represent...	Ms.	30/0
4	Peacock	Margaret	Sales Represent...	Mrs.	19/0
5	Buchanan	Steven	Sales Manager	Mr.	04/0
6	Suyama	Michael	Sales Represent...	Mr.	02/0
7	King	Robert	Sales Represent...	Mr.	29/0
8	Callahan	Laura	Inside Sales Coor...	Ms.	09/0
9	Dodsworth	Anne	Sales Represent...	Ms.	27/0

Figure 32-23

When the data source is created, it adds a number of files to your solution. To view these, click the Show All Files button in the Solution Explorer. You will then be able to expand the data set node and view the extra files added. The main one of interest is the `.Designer.cs` file, which includes the C# source code used to populate the data set.

You will find several classes defined within the `.Designer.cs` file. The classes represent the strongly typed data set, which acts in a similar way to the standard `DataAdapter` class. This class internally uses the `DataAdapter` to fill the `DataSet`.

Selecting Data

The table adapter generated contains commands for `SELECT`, `INSERT`, `UPDATE`, and `DELETE`. Needless to say, these can (and probably should) be tailored to call stored procedures rather than using straight SQL. The wizard-generated code will do for now, however. Visual Studio .NET adds the following code to the `.Designer` file:

```
private System.Data.SqlClient.SqlCommand m_DeleteCommand;
private System.Data.SqlClient.SqlCommand m_InsertCommand;
private System.Data.SqlClient.SqlCommand m_UpdateCommand;
private System.Data.SqlClient.SqlDataAdapter m_adapter;
```

An object is defined for each of the SQL commands, with the exception of the `Select` command, and also a `SqlDataAdapter`. Further down the file, in the `InitializeComponent()` method, the wizard has generated code to create each one of these commands as well as the data adapter.

In previous versions of Visual Studio .NET, the commands generated for `Insert` and `Update` also included a select clause — this was used as a way to resynchronize the data with that on the server, just in case any fields within the database were calculated (such as identity columns and/or computed fields).

The wizard-generated code works but is less than optimal. For a production system, all the generated SQL should probably be replaced with calls to stored procedures. If the `INSERT` or `UPDATE` clauses didn't have to resynchronize the data, the removal of the redundant SQL clause would speed up the application a little.

Updating the Data Source

So far, the applications have selected data from the database. This section discusses how to persist changes to the database. If you followed the steps in the previous section, you should have an application that contains everything needed for a rudimentary application. The one change necessary is to enable the Save button on the generated toolbar and write an event handler that will update the database.

From the IDE, select the Save button from the data navigator control, and change the `Enabled` property to `true`. Then, double-click the button to generate an event handler. Within this handler, save the changes made onscreen to the database:

```
private void dataNavigatorSaveItem_Click(object sender, EventArgs e)
{
    employeesTableAdapter.Update(employeesDataset.Employees);
}
```

Because Visual Studio has done the hard work for you, all that's needed is to use the `Update` method of the table adapter class that was generated. Six `Update` methods are available on the table adapter — this example uses the override that takes a `DataTable` as the parameter.

Other Common Requirements

A common requirement when displaying data is to provide a pop-up menu for a given row. You can do this in numerous ways. The example in this section focuses on one approach that can simplify the code required, especially if the display context is a `DataGrid`, where a `DataSet` with some relations is displayed. The problem here is that the context menu depends on the row that is selected, and that row could be part of any source `DataTable` in the `DataSet`.

Because the context menu functionality is likely to be general-purpose in nature, the implementation here uses a base class (`ContextDataRow`) that supports the menu-building code, and each data row class that supports a pop-up menu derives from this base class.

When the user right-clicks any part of a row in the `DataGrid`, the row is looked up to check if it derives from `ContextDataRow`, and if so, `PopupMenu()` can be called. This could be implemented using an interface; however, in this instance, a base class provides a simpler solution.

This example demonstrates how to generate `DataRow` and `DataTable` classes that can be used to provide type-safe access to data in much the same way as the previous XSD sample. However, this time you write the code yourself to show how to use custom attributes and reflection in this context.

Figure 32-24 illustrates the class hierarchy for this example.

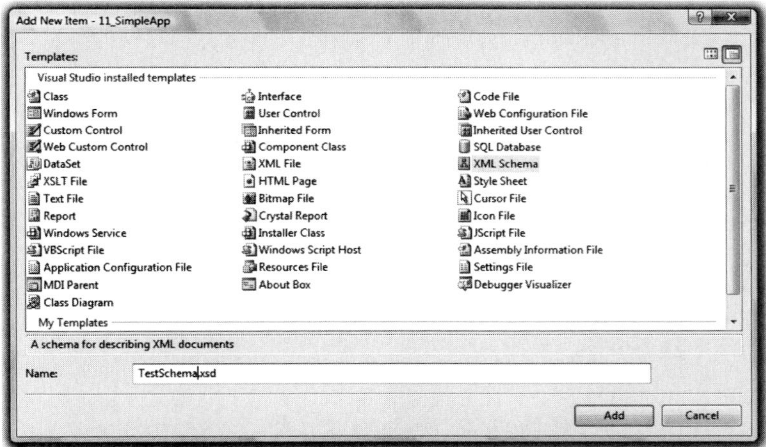

Figure 32-24

Here is the code for this example:

```
using System;
using System.Windows.Forms;
using System.Data;
using System.Data.SqlClient;
using System.Reflection;

public class ContextDataRow : DataRow
{
   public ContextDataRow(DataRowBuilder builder) : base(builder)
   {
   }
```

(continued)

(continued)

```
public void PopupMenu(System.Windows.Forms.Control parent, int x, int y)
{

   // Use reflection to get the list of popup menu commands.
   MemberInfo[] members = this.GetType().FindMembers (MemberTypes.Method,
                          BindingFlags.Public | BindingFlags.Instance ,
                          new System.Reflection.MemberFilter(Filter),
                          null);
   if (members.Length > 0)
   {

      // Create a context menu

      ContextMenu menu = new ContextMenu();

      // Now loop through those members and generate the popup menu.
      // Note the cast to MethodInfo in the foreach
      foreach (MethodInfo meth in members)
      {

         // Get the caption for the operation from the
         // ContextMenuAttribute

         ContextMenuAttribute[] ctx = (ContextMenuAttribute[])
            meth.GetCustomAttributes(typeof(ContextMenuAttribute), true);
         MenuCommand callback = new MenuCommand(this, meth);
         MenuItem item = new MenuItem(ctx[0].Caption, new
                         EventHandler(callback.Execute));
         item.DefaultItem = ctx[0].Default;
         menu.MenuItems.Add(item);
      }
      System.Drawing.Point pt = new System.Drawing.Point(x,y);
      menu.Show(parent, pt);
   }
}

private bool Filter(MemberInfo member, object criteria)
{
   bool bInclude = false;

   // Cast MemberInfo to MethodInfo

   MethodInfo meth = member as MethodInfo;
   if (meth != null)
   {
      if (meth.ReturnType == typeof(void))
      {
         ParameterInfo[] parms = meth.GetParameters();
         if (parms.Length == 0)
         {

            // Lastly check if there is a ContextMenuAttribute on the
```

```
                    // method...

                    object[] atts = meth.GetCustomAttributes
                              (typeof(ContextMenuAttribute), true);
                    bInclude = (atts.Length == 1);
                 }
              }
           }
           return bInclude;
        }
     }
```

The ContextDataRow class is derived from DataRow and contains just two member functions: PopupMenu and Filter(). PopupMenu uses reflection to look for methods that correspond to a particular signature, and it displays a pop-up menu of these options to the user. Filter() is used as a delegate by PopupMenu when enumerating methods. It simply returns true if the member function does correspond to the appropriate calling convention:

```
MemberInfo[] members = this.GetType().FindMembers(MemberTypes.Method,
             BindingFlags.Public | BindingFlags.Instance,
             new System.Reflection.MemberFilter(Filter),
             null);
```

This single statement is used to filter all methods on the current object and return only those that match the following criteria:

- The member must be a method.
- The member must be a public instance method.
- The member must return void.
- The member must accept zero parameters.
- The member must include the ContextMenuAttribute.

The last of these criteria refers to a custom attribute, written specifically for this example. (It's discussed after discussing the PopupMenu method.)

```
ContextMenu menu = new ContextMenu();
foreach (MethodInfo meth in members)
{
   // ... Add the menu item
}
System.Drawing.Point pt = new System.Drawing.Point(x,y);
menu.Show(parent, pt);
```

A context menu instance is created, and a pop-up menu item is added for each method that matches the preceding criteria. The menu is subsequently displayed as shown in Figure 32-25.

The main area of difficulty with this example is the following section of code, repeated once for each member function to be displayed on the pop-up menu:

```
System.Type ctxtype = typeof(ContextMenuAttribute);
ContextMenuAttribute[] ctx = (ContextMenuAttribute[])
                         meth.GetCustomAttributes(ctxtype, true);
MenuCommand callback = new MenuCommand(this, meth);
MenuItem item = new MenuItem(ctx[0].Caption,
                new EventHandler(callback.Execute));
item.DefaultItem = ctx[0].Default;
menu.MenuItems.Add(item);
```

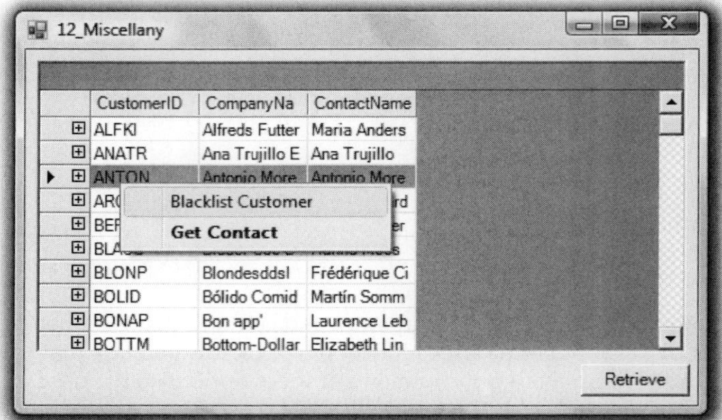

Figure 32-25

Each method that should be displayed on the context menu is attributed with the `ContextMenuAttribute`. This defines a user-friendly name for the menu option because a C# method name cannot include spaces, and it's wise to use real English on pop-up menus rather than some internal code. The attribute is retrieved from the method, and a new menu item is created and added to the menu items collection of the pop-up menu.

This sample code also shows the use of a simplified `Command` class (a common design pattern). The `MenuCommand` class used in this instance is triggered by the user choosing an item on the context menu, and it forwards the call to the receiver of the method — in this case, the object and method that was attributed. This also helps keep the code in the receiver object more isolated from the user interface code. This code is explained in the following sections.

Manufactured Tables and Rows

The XSD example earlier in the chapter showed the code produced when the Visual Studio .NET editor is used to generate a set of data access classes. The following class shows the required methods for a `DataTable`, which are fairly minimal (and they all have been generated manually):

```
public class CustomerTable : DataTable
{
   public CustomerTable() : base("Customers")
   {
      this.Columns.Add("CustomerID", typeof(string));
      this.Columns.Add("CompanyName", typeof(string));
      this.Columns.Add("ContactName", typeof(string));
   }
   protected override System.Type GetRowType()
   {
      return typeof(CustomerRow);
   }
   protected override DataRow NewRowFromBuilder(DataRowBuilder builder)
   {
      return(DataRow) new CustomerRow(builder);
   }
}
```

The first prerequisite of a `DataTable` is to override the `GetRowType()` method. This is used by the .NET internals when generating new rows for the table. The type used to represent each row should be returned from this method.

The next prerequisite is to implement `NewRowFromBuilder()`, which is called by the runtime when creating new rows for the table. That's enough for a minimal implementation. The corresponding `CustomerRow` class is fairly simple. It implements properties for each of the columns within the row and then implements the methods that ultimately are displayed on the context menu:

```
public class CustomerRow : ContextDataRow
{
   public CustomerRow(DataRowBuilder builder) : base(builder)
   {
   }
   public string CustomerID
   {
      get { return (string)this["CustomerID"];}
      set { this["CustomerID"] = value;}
   }

   // Other properties omitted for clarity

   [ContextMenu("Blacklist Customer")]
   public void Blacklist()
   {
      // Do something
   }
   [ContextMenu("Get Contact",Default=true)]
   public void GetContact()
   {
      // Do something else
   }
}
```

The class simply derives from `ContextDataRow`, including the appropriate getter/setter methods on properties that are named the same as each field, and then a set of methods may be added that are used when reflecting on the class:

```
[ContextMenu("Blacklist Customer")]
public void Blacklist()
{

   // Do something
}
```

Each method that is to be displayed on the context menu has the same signature and includes the custom ContextMenu attribute.

Using an Attribute

The idea behind writing the `ContextMenu` attribute is to be able to supply a free text name for a given menu option. The following example also adds a `Default` flag, which is used to indicate the default menu choice. The entire attribute class is presented here:

```
 [AttributeUsage(AttributeTargets.Method,AllowMultiple=false,Inherited=true)]
public class ContextMenuAttribute : System.Attribute
{
   public ContextMenuAttribute(string caption)
   {
      Caption = caption;
```

(continued)

(continued)

```
            Default = false;
        }
        public readonly string Caption;
    }
```

The `AttributeUsage` attribute on the class marks `ContextMenuAttribute` as being usable on only a method, and it also defines that there can only be one instance of this object on any given method. The `Inherited=true` clause defines whether the attribute can be placed on a superclass method and still reflected on by a subclass.

A number of other members could be added to this attribute, including the following:

- A hotkey for the menu option
- An image to be displayed
- Some text to be displayed in the toolbar as the mouse pointer rolls over the menu option
- A help context ID

Dispatching Methods

When a menu is displayed in .NET, each menu option is linked to the processing code for that option by means of a delegate. In implementing the mechanism for connecting menu choices to code, you have two options:

- Implement a method with the same signature as the `System.EventHandler`. This is defined as shown in this snippet:

```
public delegate void EventHandler(object sender, EventArgs e);
```

- Define a proxy class, which implements the preceding delegate and forwards calls to the received class. This is known as the Command pattern and is what has been chosen for this example.

The Command pattern separates the sender and the receiver of the call by means of a simple intermediate class. This may be overkill for such an example, but it makes the methods on each `DataRow` simpler (because they don't need the parameters passed to the delegate), and it is more extensible:

```
public class MenuCommand
{
   public MenuCommand(object receiver, MethodInfo method)
   {
      Receiver = receiver;
      Method = method;
   }
   public void Execute(object sender, EventArgs e)
   {
      Method.Invoke(Receiver, new object[] {} );
   }
   public readonly object Receiver;
   public readonly MethodInfo Method;
}
```

The class simply provides an `EventHandler` delegate (the `Execute` method), which invokes the desired method on the receiver object. This example handles two different types of row: rows from the `Customers` table and rows from the `Orders` table. Naturally, the processing options for each of these types of data are likely to differ. Figure 32-25 showed the operations available for a `Customer` row, whereas Figure 32-26 shows the options available for an `Order` row.

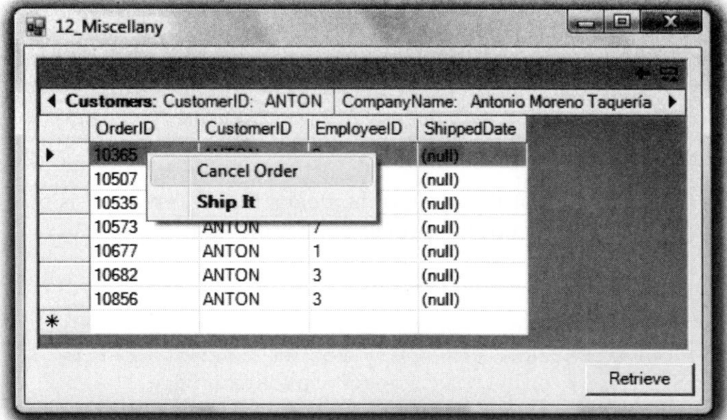

Figure 32-26

Getting the Selected Row

The last piece of the puzzle for this example is how to work out which row within the `DataSet` the user has selected. You might think that it must be a property on the `DataGrid`. However, this control is not available in this context. The hit test information obtained from within the `MouseUp()` event handler might also be a likely candidate to look at, but that only helps if the data displayed is from a single `DataTable`.

Remember how the grid is filled:

```
dataGrid.SetDataBinding(ds,"Customers");
```

This method adds a new `CurrencyManager` to the `BindingContext`, which represents the current `DataTable` and the `DataSet`. Now, the `DataGrid` has two properties, `DataSource` and `DataMember`, which are set when the `SetDataBinding()` is called. `DataSource` in this instance refers to a `DataSet` and the `DataMember` property refers to `Customers`.

Given the data source, a data member, and the binding context of the form, the current row can be located with the following code:

```
protected void dataGrid_MouseUp(object sender, MouseEventArgs e)
{
   // Perform a hit test
   if(e.Button == MouseButtons.Right)
   {
      // Find which row the user clicked on, if any
      DataGrid.HitTestInfo hti = dataGrid.HitTest(e.X, e.Y);

      // Check if the user hit a cell
      if(hti.Type == DataGrid.HitTestType.Cell)
      {
         // Find the DataRow that corresponds to the cell
         //the user has clicked upon
```

After calling `dataGrid.HitTest()` to calculate where the user has clicked the mouse, the `BindingManagerBase` instance for the data grid is retrieved:

```
         BindingManagerBase bmb = this.BindingContext[ dataGrid.DataSource,
                                                       dataGrid.DataMember];
```

This uses the DataGrid's DataSource and DataMember to name the object to be returned. All that is left now is to find the row the user clicked and display the context menu. With a right-click on a row, the current row indicator doesn't normally move, but that's not good enough. The row indicator should be moved and then the pop-up menu should be displayed. The HitTestInfo object includes the row number, so the BindingManagerBase object's current position can be changed as follows:

```
bmb.Position = hti.Row;
```

This changes the cell indicator, and at the same time means that when a call is made into the class to get the Row, the current row is returned, not the previous one selected:

```
                DataRowView drv = bmb.Current as DataRowView;
                if(drv != null)
                {
                   ContextDataRow ctx = drv.Row as ContextDataRow;
                   if(ctx != null) ctx.PopupMenu(dataGrid,e.X,e.Y);
                }
             }
          }
       }
```

Because the DataGrid is displaying items from a DataSet, the Current object within the BindingManagerBase collection is a DataRowView, which is tested by an explicit cast in the previous code. If this succeeds, the actual row that the DataRowView wraps can be retrieved by performing another cast to check if it is indeed a ContextDataRow, and finally pop up a menu.

In this example, you will notice that two data tables, Customers and Orders, have been created, and a relationship has been defined between these tables, so that when users click CustomerOrders they see a filtered list of orders. When the user clicks, the DataGrid changes the DataMember from Customers to Customers.CustomerOrders, which just so happens to be the correct object that the BindingContext indexer uses to retrieve the data being shown.

Summary

This chapter introduced some of the methods of displaying data under .NET. System.Windows.Forms includes a large number of classes to be explored, and this chapter used the DataGridView and DataGrid controls to display data from many different data sources, such as an Array, DataTable, or DataSet.

Because it is not always appropriate to display data in a grid, this chapter also discussed how to link a column of data to a single control in the user interface. The binding capabilities of .NET make this type of user interface very easy to support because it's generally just a case of binding a control to a column and letting .NET do the rest of the work.

Moving on, the next chapter covers presentation in the form of Graphics with GDI+.

33

Graphics with GDI+

This is the third of the eight chapters that deal with user interaction and the .NET Framework. Chapter 31, "Windows Forms," focused on how to display a dialog box or SDI or MDI window, and how to place various controls such as buttons, text boxes, and list boxes. Chapter 32, "Data Binding," looked at how to work with data in Windows Forms using a number of the Windows Forms controls that work with the disparate data sources that you might encounter.

Although these standard controls are powerful and, by themselves, quite adequate for the complete user interface for many applications, some situations require more flexibility. For example, you might want to draw text in a given font in a precise position in a window, or display images without using a picture box control, or draw simple shapes or other graphics. None of this can be done with the controls discussed in Chapter 31. To display that kind of output, the application must instruct the operating system what to display and where in its window to display it.

Therefore, this chapter shows you how to draw a variety of items including:

- Principles of drawing
- Lines and simple shapes
- BMP images and other image files
- Text
- Dealing with printing

In the process, you will need to use a variety of helper objects, including pens (to define the characteristics of lines), brushes (to define how areas are filled in), and fonts (to define the shape of the characters of text). This chapter also goes into some detail on how devices interpret and display different colors.

The chapter starts, however, by discussing a technology called *GDI+*. GDI+ consists of the set of .NET base classes that are available to control custom drawing on the screen. These classes arrange for the appropriate instructions to be sent to graphics device drivers to ensure the correct output is placed on the screen (or printed to a hard copy).

Understanding Drawing Principles

This section examines the basic principles that you need to understand to start drawing to the screen. It starts by giving an overview of GDI and the underlying technology on which GDI+ is based. It also shows how GDI and GDI+ are related. Then, we will move on to a couple of simple examples.

GDI and GDI+

In general, one of the strengths of Windows — and indeed of modern operating systems in general — lies in its ability to abstract the details of particular devices without input from the developer. For example, you do not need to understand anything about your hard drive device driver to programmatically read and write files to and from disk. You simply call the appropriate methods in the relevant .NET classes (or in pre-.NET days, the equivalent Windows API functions). This principle is also true when it comes to drawing. When the computer draws anything to the screen, it does so by sending instructions to the video card. However, many hundreds of different video cards are on the market, most of which have different instruction sets and capabilities. If you had to take that into account and write specific code for each video driver, writing any such application would be an almost impossible task. The Windows graphical device interface (GDI) has been around since the earliest versions of Windows because of these reasons.

GDI provides a layer of abstraction, hiding the differences between the different video cards. You simply call the Windows API function to do the specific task, and internally the GDI figures out how to get the client's particular video card to do whatever it is you want when the client runs your particular piece of code. Not only does GDI accomplish this, but if the client has several display devices — for example, monitors and printers — GDI achieves the remarkable feat of making the printer look the same as the screen, as far as the application is concerned. If the client wants to print something instead of displaying it, your application will simply inform the system that the output device is the printer, and then call the same API functions in exactly the same way.

As you can see, the device-context (DC) object (covered shortly) is a very powerful object, and you won't be surprised to learn that under GDI *all* drawing had to be done through a device context. The DC was even used for operations that do not involve drawing to the screen or to any hardware device, such as modifying images in memory.

Although GDI exposes a relatively high-level API to developers, it is still an API that is based on the old Windows API, with C-style functions. GDI+, to a large extent, sits as a layer between GDI and your application, providing a more intuitive, inheritance-based object model. Although GDI+ is basically a wrapper around GDI, Microsoft has been able, through GDI+, to provide new features and performance improvements to some of the older features of GDI as well.

The GDI+ part of the .NET base class library is huge, and this chapter barely scratches the surface of its features because trying to cover more than a tiny fraction of the library would have turned this chapter into a huge reference guide that simply listed classes and methods. It is more important to understand the fundamental principles involved in drawing so that you are in a good position to explore the available classes. Full lists of all the classes and methods available in GDI+ are, of course, available in the SDK documentation.

Visual Basic 6 developers are likely to find the concepts involved in drawing quite unfamiliar because Visual Basic 6 focuses on controls that handle their own painting. C++/MFC developers are likely to be in more familiar territory because MFC does require developers to take control of more of the drawing process, using GDI. However, even if you have a strong background in the classic GDI, you will find that a lot of the material presented in this chapter is new.

GDI+ Namespaces

The following table provides an overview of the main namespaces you will need to explore to find the GDI+ base classes.

You should note that almost all of the classes and structs used in this chapter are taken from the `System.Drawing` namespace.

Namespace	Description
`System.Drawing`	Contains most of the classes, structs, enums, and delegates concerned with the basic functionality of drawing
`System.Drawing.Drawing2D`	Provides most of the support for advanced 2D and vector drawing, including anti-aliasing, geometric transformations, and graphics paths
`System.Drawing.Imaging`	Contains various classes that assist in the manipulation of images (bitmaps, GIF files, and so on)
`System.Drawing.Printing`	Contains classes to assist when specifically targeting a printer or print preview window as the "output device"
`System.Drawing.Design`	Contains some predefined dialog boxes, property sheets, and other user interface elements concerned with extending the design-time user interface
`System.Drawing.Text`	Contains classes to perform more advanced manipulation of fonts and font families

Device Contexts and the Graphics Object

In GDI, you identify which device you want your output to go to through an object known as the *device context* (DC). The DC stores information about a particular device and is able to translate calls to the GDI API functions into whatever instructions need to be sent to that device. You can also query the device context to find out what the capabilities of the corresponding device are (for example, whether a printer prints in color or only in black and white), so the output can be adjusted accordingly. If you ask the device to do something it is not capable of, the DC will normally detect this and take appropriate action (which, depending on the situation, might mean throwing an exception or modifying the request to get the closest match that the device is actually capable of using).

However, the DC does not deal only with the hardware device. It acts as a bridge to Windows and is able to take account of any requirements or restrictions placed on the drawing by Windows. For example, if Windows knows that only a portion of your application's window needs to be redrawn, the DC can trap and nullify attempts to draw outside that area. Because of the DC's relationship with Windows, working through the device context can simplify your code in other ways.

For example, hardware devices need to be told where to draw objects, and they usually want coordinates relative to the top-left corner of the screen (or output device). Usually, however, your application will be thinking of drawing something at a certain position within the client area (the area reserved for drawing) of its own window, possibly using its own coordinate system. Because the window might be positioned anywhere on the screen, and a user might move it at any time, translating between the two coordinate systems is potentially a difficult task. However, the DC always knows where your window is and is able to perform this translation automatically.

With GDI+, the device context is wrapped up in the .NET base class `System.Drawing.Graphics`. Most drawing is done by calling methods on an instance of `Graphics`. In fact, because the `Graphics` class is the class that is responsible for handling most drawing operations, very little gets done in GDI+ that does not involve a `Graphics` instance somewhere, so understanding how to manipulate this object is the key to understanding how to draw to display devices with GDI+.

Drawing Shapes

This section starts with a short example, `DisplayAtStartup`, to illustrate drawing to an application's main window. The examples in this chapter are all created in Visual Studio 2008 as C# Windows Applications. Recall that for this type of project the code wizard gives you a class called `Form1`, derived from `System.Windows.Form`, which represents the application's main window. Also generated for you is a class called `Program` (found in the `Program.cs` file), which represents the application's main starting point. Unless otherwise stated, in all code samples, new or modified code means code that you have added to the wizard-generated code. (You can download the sample code from the Wrox Web site at `www.wrox.com`.)

In .NET usage, when we are talking about applications that display various controls, the terminology "form" has largely replaced "window" to represent the rectangular object that occupies an area of the screen on behalf of an application. In this chapter, we have tended to stick to the term window because in the context of manually drawing items it is more meaningful. We will also talk about the form when we are referring to the .NET class used to instantiate the form/window. Finally, we will use the terms "drawing" and "painting" interchangeably to describe the process of displaying some item on the screen or other display device.

The first example simply creates a form and draws to it in the constructor when the form starts up. Note that this is not actually the best or the correct way to draw to the screen — you will quickly find that this example has a problem because it is unable to redraw anything after starting up. However, this example illustrates quite a few points about drawing without your having to do very much work.

For this example, start Visual Studio 2008 and create a Windows Application. First, set the background color of the form to white. In the example, this line comes after the `InitializeComponent()` method so that Visual Studio 2008 recognizes the line and is able to alter the design view appearance of the form. You can find the `InitializeComponent()` method by first clicking the Show All Files button in the Visual Studio Solution Explorer and then clicking the plus sign next to the `Form1.cs` file. Here, you will find the `Form1.Designer.cs` file. It is in this file that you will find the `InitializeComponent()` method. You could have used the design view to set the background color, but this would have resulted in pretty much the same line being added automatically:

```
private void InitializeComponent()
{
    this.components = new System.ComponentModel.Container();
    this.AutoScaleMode = System.Windows.Forms.AutoScaleMode.Font;
    this.Text = "Form1";
    this.BackColor = System.Drawing.Color.White;
}
```

Then you add code to the `Form1` constructor. You create a `Graphics` object using the form's `CreateGraphics()` method. This `Graphics` object contains the Windows DC that you need to draw with. The device context created is associated with the display device and also with this window:

```
public Form1()
{
   InitializeComponent();
   Graphics dc = CreateGraphics();
   Show();
   Pen bluePen = new Pen(Color.Blue, 3);
   dc.DrawRectangle(bluePen, 0,0,50,50);
   Pen redPen = new Pen(Color.Red, 2);
   dc.DrawEllipse(redPen, 0, 50, 80, 60);
}
```

As you can see, you then call the `Show()` method to display the window. This is really done to force the window to display immediately because you cannot actually do any drawing until the window has been displayed. If the window is not displayed, there's nothing for you to draw onto.

Finally, you display a rectangle at coordinates (0,0) and with width and height 50, and an ellipse with coordinates (0,50) and with width 80 and height 50. Note that coordinates (x,y) translate to x pixels to the right and y pixels down from the top-left corner of the client area of the window — and these coordinates start from the top-left corner of the shape to be displayed.

The overloads that you are using of the `DrawRectangle()` and `DrawEllipse()` methods each take five parameters. The first parameter of each is an instance of the class `System.Drawing.Pen`. A `Pen` is one of a number of supporting objects to help with drawing — it contains information about how lines are to be drawn. Your first pen instructs the system that lines should be the color blue with a width of 3 pixels; the second pen instructs the system that the lines should be red and have a width of 2 pixels. The final four parameters are coordinates and size. For the rectangle, they represent the (x,y) coordinates of the top-left corner of the rectangle in addition to its width and height. For the ellipse, these numbers represent the same thing, except that you are talking about a hypothetical rectangle that the ellipse just fits into, rather than the ellipse itself. Figure 33-1 shows the result of running this code. Of course, because this book is not in color, you cannot see the colors.

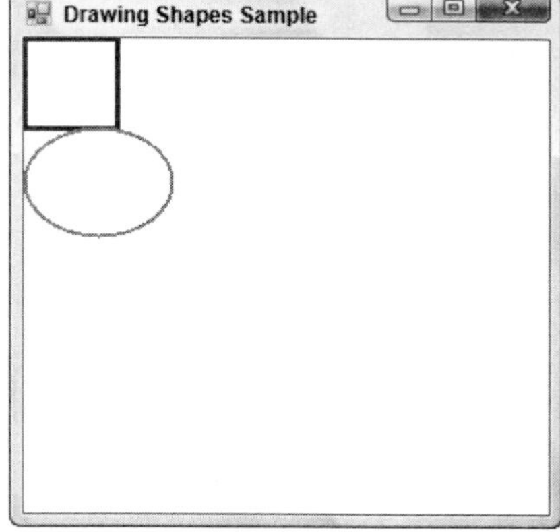

Figure 33-1

Figure 33-1 demonstrates a couple of points. First, you can see clearly where the client area of the window is located. It's the white area — the area that has been affected by setting the `BackColor` property. Notice that the rectangle nestles up in the corner of this area, as you would expect when you specify the coordinates of (0,0) for it. Second, notice that the top of the ellipse overlaps the rectangle slightly, which you would not expect from the coordinates given in the code. The culprit here is Windows itself and where it places the lines that border the rectangle and ellipse. By default, Windows will try to center the line on the border of the shape — that is not always possible to do exactly because the line has to be drawn on pixels (obviously). Normally, the border of each shape theoretically lies between two pixels. The result is that lines that are 1 pixel thick will get drawn just *inside* the top and left sides of a shape, but just *outside* the bottom and right sides — which means that shapes that are next to each other have their borders overlapping by one pixel. You have specified wider lines; therefore, the overlap is greater. It is possible to change the default behavior by setting the `Pen.Alignment` property, as detailed in the SDK documentation, but for these purposes, the default behavior is adequate.

Unfortunately, if you actually run the sample, you will notice that the form behaves a bit strangely. It is fine if you just leave it there. It is also fine if you drag it around the screen with the mouse. However, if you try minimizing the window and then restoring it, then your carefully drawn shapes just vanish! The same thing happens if you drag another window across the sample so that it only obscures a portion of your shapes. When you drag the other window away again, you will find that the temporarily obscured portion has disappeared and you are left with half an ellipse or half a rectangle!

So what's going on? The problem arises when part of a window is hidden because Windows usually discards immediately all the information concerning exactly what has been displayed. This is something Windows has to do or else the memory usage for storing screen data would be astronomical. A typical computer might be running with the video card set to display 1024 × 768 pixels, perhaps in a 24-bit color mode, which implies that each pixel on the screen occupies 3 bytes — 2.25MB to display the screen. (24-bit color is covered later in this chapter.) However, it is not uncommon for a user to work with 10 or 20 minimized windows in the taskbar. In a worst-case scenario, you might have 20 windows, each of which would occupy the whole screen if it was not minimized. If Windows actually stored the visual information those windows contained, ready for when the user restored them, then that would amount to some 45MB! These days, a good graphics card might have 64MB of memory and be able to cope with that, but it was only a few years ago that 4MB was considered generous in a graphics card — and the excess would need to be stored in the computer's main memory. Many people still have old machines, some of them with only 4MB graphic cards. Clearly, it would not be practical for Windows to manage its user interface like that.

The moment any part of a window is hidden, the "hidden" pixels get lost because Windows frees the memory that was holding those pixels. It does, however, note that a portion of the window is hidden, and when it detects that it is no longer hidden, it asks the application that owns the window to redraw its contents. There are a couple of exceptions to this rule — generally for cases in which a small portion of a window is hidden very temporarily (a good example is when you select an item from the main menu and that menu item drops down, temporarily obscuring part of the window below). In general, however, you can expect that if part of your window is hidden, your application will need to redraw it later.

That is the source of the problem for the sample application. You placed your drawing code in the `Form1` constructor, which is called just once when the application starts up, and you cannot call the constructor again to redraw the shapes when required later on.

When working with Windows Forms server controls, there is no need to know anything about how to accomplish this task. This is because the standard controls are pretty sophisticated, and they are able to redraw themselves correctly whenever Windows asks them to. That is one reason why, when programming controls, you do not need to worry about the actual drawing process at all. If you are taking responsibility for drawing to the screen in your application, you also need to make sure that your application will respond correctly whenever Windows asks it to redraw all or part of its window. In the next section, you modify the sample to do just that.

Painting Shapes Using OnPaint()

If the preceding explanation has made you worried that drawing your own user interface is going to be terribly complicated, do not worry. Getting your application to redraw itself when necessary is actually quite easy.

Windows notifies an application that some repainting needs to be done by raising a `Paint` event. Interestingly, the `Form` class has already implemented a handler for this event, so you do not need to add one yourself. The `Form1` handler for the `Paint` event will at some point in its processing call up a virtual method, `OnPaint()`, passing to it a single `PaintEventArgs` parameter. This means that all you need to do is override `OnPaint()` to perform your painting.

Although for this example you work by overriding `OnPaint()`, it is equally possible to achieve the same results by simply adding your own event handler for the `Paint` event (a `Form1_Paint()` method, say) — in much the same way as you would for any other Windows Forms event. This other approach is arguably more convenient because you can add a new event handler through the Visual Studio 2008 properties window, saving yourself from typing some code. However, the approach of overriding `OnPaint()` is slightly more flexible in terms of letting you control when the call to the base class window processing occurs, and it is the approach recommended in the documentation.

In this section, you create a new Windows Application called `DrawShapes` to do this. As before, you set the background color to white, using the properties window. You will also change the form's text to `DrawShapes Sample`. Then you add the following code to the generated code for the `Form1` class:

```
protected override void OnPaint( PaintEventArgs e )
{
   base.OnPaint(e);
   Graphics dc = e.Graphics;
   Pen bluePen = new Pen(Color.Blue, 3);
   dc.DrawRectangle(bluePen, 0,0,50,50);
   Pen redPen = new Pen(Color.Red, 2);
   dc.DrawEllipse(redPen, 0, 50, 80, 60);
}
```

Notice that `OnPaint()` is declared as `protected`, because it is normally used internally within the class, so there is no reason for any other code outside the class to know about its existence.

`PaintEventArgs` is a class that is derived from the `EventArgs` class normally used to pass in information about events. `PaintEventArgs` has two additional properties, of which the more important one is a `Graphics` instance, already primed and optimized to paint the required portion of the window. This means that you do not have to call `CreateGraphics()` to get a DC in the `OnPaint()` method — you have already been provided with one. You will look at the other additional property soon. This property contains more detailed information about which area of the window actually needs repainting.

In your implementation of `OnPaint()`, you first get a reference to the `Graphics` object from `PaintEventArgs`, and then you draw your shapes exactly as you did before. When you start this, you call the base class's `OnPaint()` method. This step is important. You have overridden `OnPaint()` to do your own painting, but it is possible that Windows may have some additional work of its own to do in the painting process — any such work will be dealt with in an `OnPaint()` method in one of the .NET base classes.

> *For this example, you will find that removing the call to* `base.OnPaint()` *does not seem to have any effect. Do not, however, be tempted to leave this call out. You might be stopping Windows from doing its work properly, and the results could be unpredictable.*

`OnPaint()` will also be called when the application first starts up and your window is displayed for the first time. Thus, there is no need to duplicate the drawing code in the constructor.

Running this code gives the same results initially as in the previous example, except that now your application behaves properly when you minimize it or hide parts of the window.

Using the Clipping Region

The `DrawShapes` sample from the previous section illustrates the main principles involved with drawing to a window, although the sample is not very efficient. The reason is that it attempts to draw everything in the window, regardless of how much needs to be drawn. Figure 33-2 shows the result of running the `DrawShapes` example and opening another window and moving it over the `DrawShapes` form so part of it is hidden.

However, when you move the overlapping window so that the `DrawShapes` window is fully visible again, Windows will, as usual, send a `Paint` event to the form, asking it to repaint itself. The rectangle and ellipse both lie in the top-left corner of the client area, and so were visible all the time. Therefore, there is actually nothing that needs to be done in this case apart from repainting the white background area. However, Windows does not know that, so it thinks it should raise the `Paint` event, resulting in your `OnPaint()` implementation being called. `OnPaint()` will then unnecessarily attempt to redraw the rectangle and ellipse.

Actually, in this case, the shapes will not be repainted because of the device context. Windows has preinitialized the device context with information concerning what area actually needed repainting. In the days of GDI, the region marked for repainting was known as the *invalidated region*, but with GDI+ the terminology has largely changed to *clipping region*. The device context recognizes this region. Therefore, it will intercept any attempts to draw outside this region and not pass the relevant drawing commands on to the graphics card. That sounds good, but there is still a potential performance hit here. You do not know how much processing the device context had to do before it figured out that the drawing was outside the invalidated region. In some cases, it might be quite a lot because calculating which pixels need to be changed to what color can be very processor-intensive (although a good graphics card will provide hardware acceleration to help with some of this).

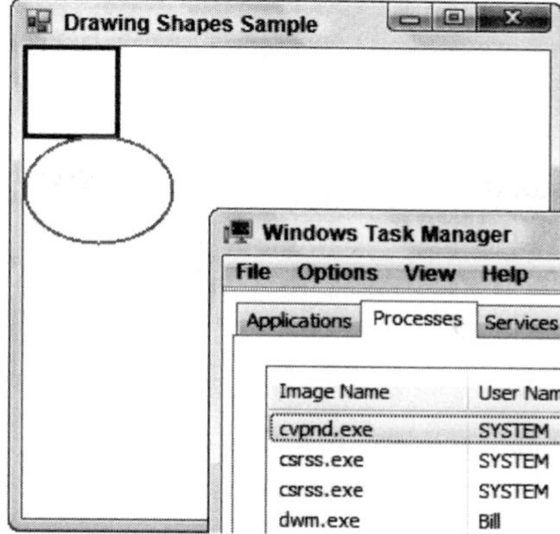

Figure 33-2

The bottom line to this is that asking the `Graphics` instance to do some drawing outside the invalidated region is almost certainly wasting processor time and slowing your application down. In a well-designed application, your code will help the device context by carrying out a few simple checks to see if the proposed drawing work is likely to be needed before it calls the relevant `Graphics` instance methods. In this section, you code a new example, `DrawShapesWithClipping`, by modifying the `DisplayShapes` example to do just that. In your `OnPaint()` code, you will do a simple test to see whether the invalidated region intersects the area you need to draw in, and you will call the drawing methods only if it does.

First, you need to obtain the details of the clipping region. This is where an extra property, `ClipRectangle`, on `PaintEventArgs` comes in. `ClipRectangle` contains the coordinates of the region to be repainted, wrapped up in an instance of a struct, `System.Drawing.Rectangle`. `Rectangle` is quite a simple struct — it contains four properties of interest: `Top`, `Bottom`, `Left`, and `Right`. These respectively contain the vertical coordinates of the top and bottom of the rectangle and the horizontal coordinates of the left and right edges.

Next, you need to decide what test you will use to determine whether drawing should take place. You will go for a simple test here. Notice that in your drawing, the rectangle and ellipse are both entirely contained within the rectangle that stretches from point (0,0) to point (80,130) of the client area. Actually, use point (82,132) to be on the safe side because you know that the lines might stray a pixel or so outside this area. So, you will check whether the top-left corner of the clipping region is inside this rectangle. If it is, then you will go ahead and redraw. If it is not, then you won't bother.

The following is the code to do this:

```
protected override void OnPaint( PaintEventArgs e )
{
   base.OnPaint(e);
   Graphics dc = e.Graphics;
   if (e.ClipRectangle.Top < 132 && e.ClipRectangle.Left < 82)
   {
      Pen bluePen = new Pen(Color.Blue, 3);
      dc.DrawRectangle(bluePen, 0,0,50,50);
      Pen redPen = new Pen(Color.Red, 2);
      dc.DrawEllipse(redPen, 0, 50, 80, 60);
   }
}
```

Note that what is displayed is exactly the same as before. However, performance is improved now by the early detection of some cases in which nothing needs to be drawn. Notice also that the example uses a fairly crude test for whether to proceed with the drawing. A more refined test might be to check separately whether the rectangle or the ellipse needs to be redrawn. However, there is a balance here. You can make your tests in `OnPaint()` more sophisticated, improving performance, but you will also make your own `OnPaint()` code more complex. It is almost always worth putting some test in — because you have written the code, you understand far more about what is being drawn than the `Graphics` instance, which just blindly follows drawing commands.

Measuring Coordinates and Areas

In the previous example, you encountered the base struct, `Rectangle`, which is used to represent the coordinates of a rectangle. GDI+ actually uses several similar structures to represent coordinates or areas. The following table lists the structs that are defined in the `System.Drawing` namespace.

Struct	Main Public Properties
`Point` and `PointF`	`X`, `Y`
`Size` and `SizeF`	`Width`, `Height`
`Rectangle` and `RectangleF`	`Left`, `Right`, `Top`, `Bottom`, `Width`, `Height`, `X`, `Y`, `Location`, `Size`

Note that many of these objects have a number of other properties, methods, or operator overloads not listed here. This section just discusses some of the most important ones.

Point and PointF

`Point` is conceptually the simplest of these structs. Mathematically, it is equivalent to a 2D vector. It contains two public integer properties, which represent how far you move horizontally and vertically from a particular location (perhaps on the screen), as shown in Figure 33-3.

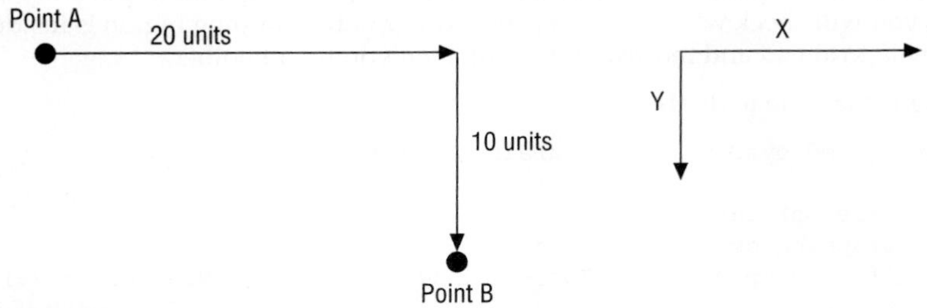

Figure 33-3

To get from point A to point B, you move 20 units across and 10 units down, marked as x and y on the diagram because this is how they are commonly referred to. The following `Point` struct represents that line:

```
Point ab = new Point(20, 10);
Console.WriteLine("Moved {0} across, {1} down", ab.X, ab.Y);
```

X and Y are read-write properties, which means that you can also set the values in a Point, like this:

```
Point ab = new Point();
ab.X = 20;
ab.Y = 10;
Console.WriteLine("Moved {0} across, {1} down", ab.X, ab.Y);
```

Note that although conventionally horizontal and vertical coordinates are referred to as x and y coordinates (lowercase), the corresponding Point properties are X and Y (uppercase) because the usual convention in C# is for public properties to have names that start with an uppercase letter.

PointF is essentially identical to Point, except that X and Y are of type float instead of int. PointF is used when the coordinates are not necessarily integer values. A cast has been defined so that you can implicitly convert from Point to PointF. (Note that because Point and PointF are structs, this cast involves actually making a copy of the data.) There is no corresponding reverse case — to convert from PointF to Point you have to copy the values across, or use one of three conversion methods, Round(), Truncate(), and Ceiling():

```
PointF abFloat = new PointF(20.5F, 10.9F);
// converting to Point
Point ab = new Point();
ab.X = (int)abFloat.X;
ab.Y = (int)abFloat.Y;
Point ab1 = Point.Round(abFloat);
Point ab2 = Point.Truncate(abFloat);
Point ab3 = Point.Ceiling(abFloat);
// but conversion back to PointF is implicit
PointF abFloat2 = ab;
```

You might be wondering what a unit is measured in. By default, GDI+ interprets units as pixels along the screen (or printer, whatever the graphics device is); that is how the Graphics object methods will view any coordinates that they are passed as parameters. For example, the point new Point(20,10) represents 20 pixels across the screen and 10 pixels down. Usually these pixels are measured from the top-left corner of the client area of the window, as has been the case in the previous examples. However, that will not always be the case. For example, on some occasions you might want to draw relative to the top-left corner of the whole window (including its border), or even to the top-left corner of the screen. In most cases, however, unless the documentation tells you otherwise, you can assume that you are talking about pixels relative to the top-left corner of the client area.

You will learn more on this subject later, after scrolling is examined, when we discuss the three different coordinate systems in use — world, page, and device coordinates.

Size and SizeF

As with Point and PointF, sizes come in two varieties. The Size struct is for int types. SizeF is available if you need to use float types. Otherwise, Size and SizeF are identical. This section focuses on the Size struct.

In many ways, the Size struct is identical to the Point struct. It has two integer properties that represent a distance horizontally and a distance vertically. The main difference is that instead of X and Y, these properties are named Width and Height. You can represent the earlier diagram using this code:

```
Size ab = new Size(20,10);
Console.WriteLine("Moved {0} across, {1} down", ab.Width, ab.Height);
```

Although Size mathematically represents exactly the same thing as Point, conceptually, it is intended to be used in a slightly different way. Point is used when you are talking about where something is, and

Size is used when you are talking about how big it is. However, because Size and Point are so closely related, there are even supported conversions between these two:

```
Point point = new Point(20, 10);
Size size = (Size) point;
Point anotherPoint = (Point) size;
```

As an example, think about the rectangle you drew earlier, with top-left coordinate (0,0) and size (50,50). The size of this rectangle is (50,50) and might be represented by a Size instance. The bottom-right corner is also at (50,50), but that would be represented by a Point instance. To see the difference, suppose that you draw the rectangle in a different location, so that its top-left coordinate is at (10,10):

```
dc.DrawRectangle(bluePen, 10,10,50,50);
```

Now the bottom-right corner is at coordinate (60,60), but the size is unchanged at (50,50).

The addition operator has been overloaded for Point and Size structs so that it is possible to add a Size to a Point struct, resulting in another Point struct:

```
static void Main(string[] args)
{
   Point topLeft = new Point(10,10);
   Size rectangleSize = new Size(50,50);
   Point bottomRight = topLeft + rectangleSize;
   Console.WriteLine("topLeft = " + topLeft);
   Console.WriteLine("bottomRight = " + bottomRight);
   Console.WriteLine("Size = " + rectangleSize);
}
```

This code, running as a simple console application called PointsAndSizes, produces the output shown in Figure 33-4.

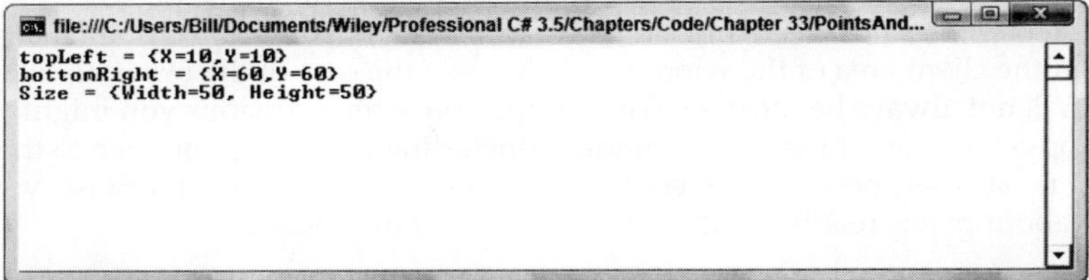

Figure 33-4

Note that this output also shows how the ToString() method has been overridden in both Point and Size to display the value in {X,Y} format.

It is also possible to subtract a Size from a Point struct to produce a Point struct, and you can add two Size structs together, producing another Size. It is not possible, however, to add a Point struct to another Point. Microsoft decided that adding Point structs does not conceptually make sense, and so it chose not to supply any overload to the + operator that would have allowed that.

You can also explicitly cast a Point to a Size struct and vice versa:

```
Point topLeft = new Point(10,10);
Size s1 = (Size)topLeft;
Point p1 = (Point)s1;
```

With this cast, s1.Width is assigned the value of topLeft.X, and s1.Height is assigned the value of topLeft.Y. Hence, s1 contains (10,10). p1 will end up storing the same values as topLeft.

Rectangle and RectangleF

These structures represent a rectangular region (usually of the screen). Just as with `Point` and `Size`, only the `Rectangle` struct is considered here. `RectangleF` is basically identical except that its properties that represent dimensions all use `float`, whereas those of `Rectangle` use `int`.

A `Rectangle` struct can be thought of as composed of a point, representing the top-left corner of the rectangle, and a `Size` struct, representing how large it is. One of its constructors actually takes a `Point` struct and a `Size` struct as its parameters. You can see this by rewriting the earlier code from the `DrawShapes` sample that draws a rectangle:

```
Graphics dc = e.Graphics;
Pen bluePen = new Pen(Color.Blue, 3);
Point topLeft = new Point(0,0);
Size howBig = new Size(50,50);
Rectangle rectangleArea = new Rectangle(topLeft, howBig);
dc.DrawRectangle(bluePen, rectangleArea);
```

This code also uses an alternative override of `Graphics.DrawRectangle()`, which takes a `Pen` and a `Rectangle` struct as its parameters.

You can also construct a `Rectangle` struct by supplying the top-left horizontal coordinate, top-left vertical coordinate, width, and height separately, and in that order, as individual numbers:

```
Rectangle rectangleArea = new Rectangle(0, 0, 50, 50)
```

`Rectangle` makes quite a few read-write properties available to set or extract its dimensions in different combinations. See the following table for details.

Property	Description
`int Left`	x-coordinate of left-hand edge
`int Right`	x-coordinate of right-hand edge
`int Top`	y-coordinate of top
`int Bottom`	y-coordinate of bottom
`int X`	Same as `Left`
`int Y`	Same as `Top`
`int Width`	Width of rectangle
`int Height`	Height of rectangle
`Point Location`	Top-left corner
`Size Size`	Size of rectangle

Note that these properties are not all independent. For example, setting `Width` also affects the value of `Right`.

Region

`Region` represents an area of the screen that has some complex shape. For example, the shaded area in Figure 33-5 could be represented by `Region`.

Figure 33-5

As you can imagine, the process of initializing a `Region` instance is itself quite complex. Broadly speaking, you can do it by indicating either what component simple shapes make up the region or what path you take as you trace around the edge of the region. If you do need to start working with areas like this, it is worth looking up the `Region` class in the SDK documentation.

A Note About Debugging

You are just about ready to do some more advanced types of drawing now. First, however, we just want to say a few things about debugging. If you have tried setting break points in the examples of this chapter, then you have noticed that debugging drawing routines is not quite as simple as debugging other parts of your program because entering and leaving the debugger often causes `Paint` messages to be sent to your application. As a result, setting a break point in your `OnPaint()` override can simply cause your application to keep painting itself over and over again, so it is basically unable to do anything else.

A typical scenario is as follows: You want to find out why your application is displaying something incorrectly, so you set a break point within the `OnPaint()` event. As expected, the application hits your break point and the debugger comes in, at which point your developer environment MDI window comes to the foreground. You more than likely have the developer environments set to full-screen display so that you can more easily view all the debugging information, which means it always completely hides the application you are debugging.

Moving on, you examine the values of some variables and hopefully discover something useful. Then you press F5 to tell the application to continue, so that you can go on to see what happens when the application displays something else after some processing. Unfortunately, the first thing that happens is that the application comes to the foreground, and Windows efficiently detects that the form is visible again and promptly sends it a `Paint` event. This means, of course, that your break point is hit again. If that is what you want, fine. More commonly, what you really want is to hit the break point *later*, when the application is drawing something more interesting, perhaps after you have selected some menu option to read in a file or in some other way changed what gets displayed. It looks like you are stuck. Either you do not have a break point in `OnPaint()` at all, or your application can never get beyond the point where it is displaying its initial startup window.

There is a workaround to this problem.

With a big screen, the easiest way is simply to keep your developer environment window tiled rather than maximized. Also, you want to keep it well away from your application window, so that your application is never hidden in the first place. Unfortunately, in most cases that is not a practical solution because that would make your developer environment window too small (you can also get a second monitor). An alternative that uses the same principle is to have your application declare itself as the topmost application while you are debugging. You do this by setting a property in the `Form` class, `TopMost`, which you can easily do in the `InitializeComponent()` method:

```
private void InitializeComponent()
{
   this.TopMost = true;
```

You can also set this property through the properties window in Visual Studio 2008.

Being a `TopMost` window means your application can never be hidden by other windows (except other topmost windows). It always remains above other windows even when another application has the focus. This is how the Task Manager behaves.

Even with this technique, you have to be careful because you can never be certain when Windows might decide for some reason to raise a `Paint` event. If you really want to trap some problem that occurs in `OnPaint()` in some specific circumstance (for example, the application draws something after you select a certain menu option, and something goes wrong at that point), then the best way to do this is to place some dummy code in `OnPaint()` that tests some condition, which will only be `true` in the specified circumstances. Then place the break point inside the `if` block, like this:

```
protected override void OnPaint( PaintEventArgs e )
{
   // Condition() evaluates to true when we want to break
   if (Condition())
   {
      int ii = 0;   // <-- SET BREAKPOINT HERE!!!
   }
```

This is a quick-and-easy way of setting a conditional break point.

Drawing Scrollable Windows

The earlier `DrawShapes` example worked very well because everything you needed to draw fit into the initial window size. This section covers what you need to do if that is not the case.

For this example, you expand the `DrawShapes` sample to demonstrate scrolling. To make things a bit more realistic, you start by creating an example, `BigShapes`, in which you make the rectangle and ellipse a bit bigger. Also, while you are at it, you will see how to use the `Point`, `Size`, and `Rectangle` structs by using them to assist in defining the drawing areas. With these changes, the relevant part of the `Form1` class looks like this:

```
// member fields
private readonly Point rectangleTopLeft = new Point(0, 0);
private readonly Size rectangleSize = new Size(200,200);
private readonly Point ellipseTopLeft = new Point(50, 200);
private readonly Size ellipseSize = new Size(200, 150);
private readonly Pen bluePen = new Pen(Color.Blue, 3);
private readonly Pen redPen = new Pen(Color.Red, 2);
```

(continued)

(continued)

```
      protected override void OnPaint( PaintEventArgs e )
      {
         base.OnPaint(e);
         Graphics dc = e.Graphics;
         if (e.ClipRectangle.Top < 350 || e.ClipRectangle.Left < 250)
         {
            Rectangle rectangleArea =
               new Rectangle (rectangleTopLeft, rectangleSize);
            Rectangle ellipseArea =
               new Rectangle (ellipseTopLeft, ellipseSize);
            dc.DrawRectangle(bluePen, rectangleArea);
            dc.DrawEllipse(redPen, ellipseArea);
         }
      }
```

Note that you have also turned the `Pen`, `Size`, and `Point` objects into member fields. This is more efficient than creating a new `Pen` every time you need to draw anything, as you have been doing so far.

The result of running this example looks like Figure 33-6.

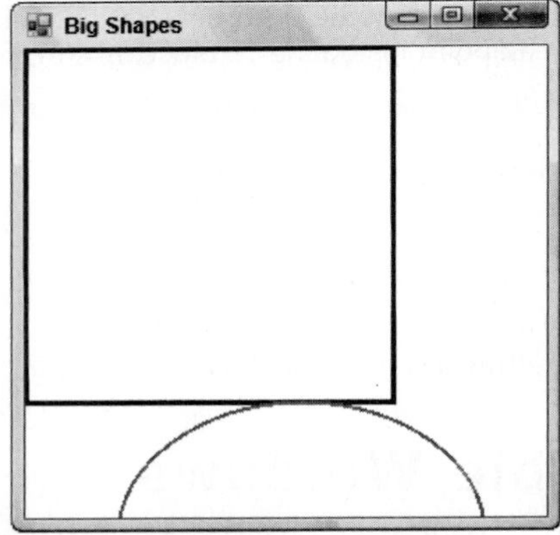

Figure 33-6

You can see a problem instantly. The shapes do not fit in your 300 × 300 pixel drawing area.

Normally, if a document is too large to display, an application will add scroll bars to let you scroll the window and look at a chosen part of it. This is another area in which if you were building Windows Forms using standard controls, you would simply allow the .NET runtime and the base classes to handle everything for you. If your form has various controls attached to it, then the `Form` instance will normally know where these controls are, and it will therefore know if its window becomes so small that scroll bars are necessary. The `Form` instance automatically adds the scroll bars for you. It is also able to draw correctly the portion of the screen you have scrolled to. In that case, there is nothing you need to do in your code. In this chapter, however, you are taking responsibility for drawing to the screen. Therefore, you need to help the `Form` instance out when it comes to scrolling.

Adding the scroll bars is actually very easy. The `Form` can still handle all that for you because the `Form` does not know how big an area you will want to draw in. (The reason it didn't do so in the earlier `BigShapes` example is that Windows does not know they are needed.) You need to determine whether the size of a rectangle that stretches from the top-left corner of the document (or equivalently, the top-left corner of the client area before you have done any scrolling) is big enough to contain the entire document. In this chapter, this area is called the document area. As shown in Figure 33-7, the document area for this example is (250 × 350) pixels.

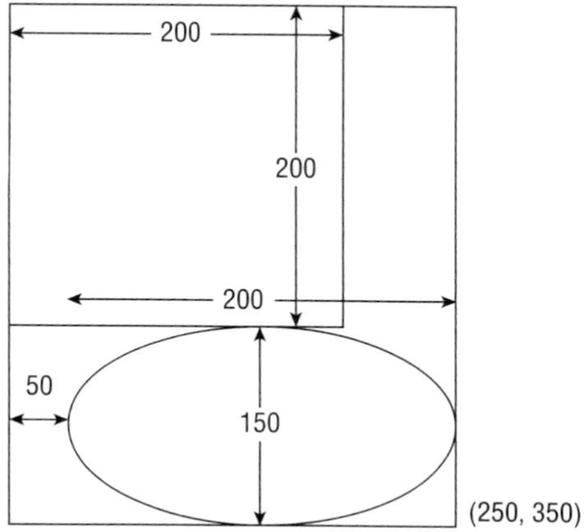

Figure 33-7

It is easy to tell the form how big the document is. You use the relevant property, `Form.AutoScrollMinSize`. Therefore, you can add this code to either the `InitializeComponent()` method or the `Form1` constructor:

```
private void InitializeComponent()
{
   this.components = new System.ComponentModel.Container();
   this.AutoScaleMode = System.Windows.Forms.AutoScaleMode.Font;
   this.Text = "Form1";
   this.BackColor = System.Drawing.Color.White;
   this.AutoScrollMinSize = new Size(250, 350);
}
```

Alternatively, the `AutoScrollMinSize` property can be set using the Visual Studio 2008 properties window. Note that to gain access to the `Size` class, you need to add the following `using` statement:

```
using System.Drawing;
```

Setting the minimum size at application startup and leaving it thereafter is fine in this particular example because you know that is how big the screen area will always be. Your document never changes size while this particular application is running. Keep in mind, however, that if your application does things like display contents of files or something else for which the area of the screen might change, you will need to set this property at other times (and in that case you will have to sort out the code manually — the Visual Studio 2008 properties window can help you only with the initial value that a property has when the form is constructed).

Setting `AutoScrollMinSize` is a start, but it is not yet quite enough. Figure 33-8 shows what the sample application looks like now — initially you get the screen that correctly displays the shapes.

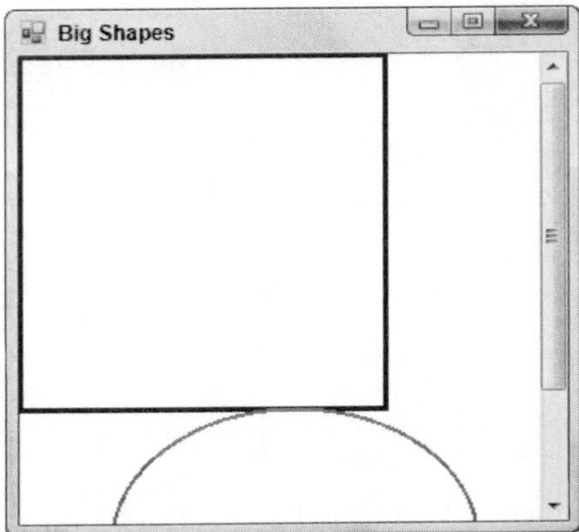

Figure 33-8

Notice that not only has the form correctly set the scroll bars, but also it has correctly sized them to indicate what proportion of the document is currently displayed. You can try resizing the window while the sample is running — you will find the scroll bars respond properly, and even disappear if you make the window big enough so that they are no longer needed.

However, look at what happens when you actually use one of the scroll bars to scroll down a bit (see Figure 33-9). Clearly, something has gone wrong!

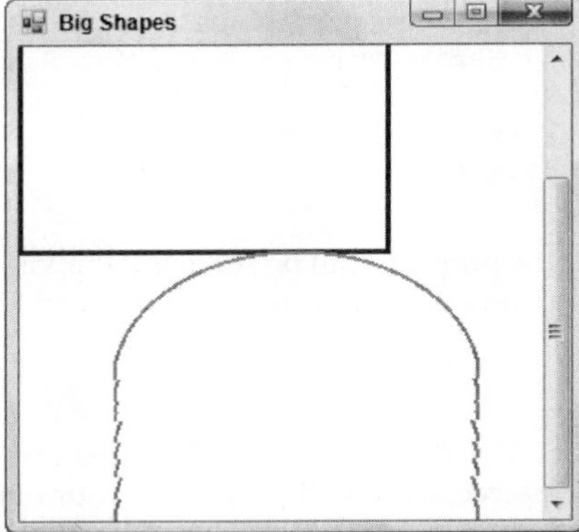

Figure 33-9

What's wrong is that you haven't taken into account the position of the scroll bars in the code in your `OnPaint()` override. You can see this very clearly if you force the window to repaint itself completely by minimizing and restoring it (see Figure 33-10).

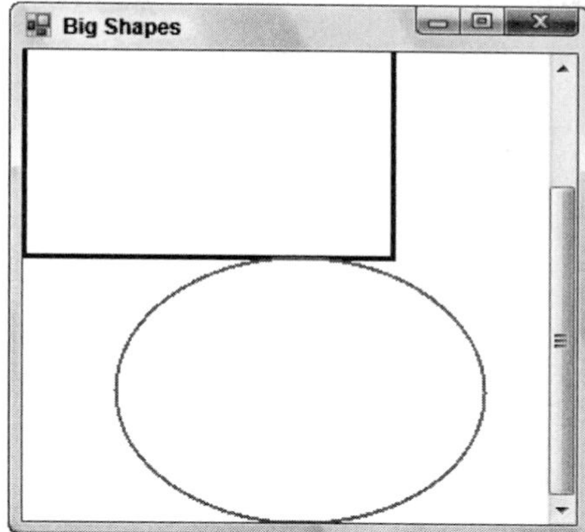

Figure 33-10

The shapes have been painted, just as before, with the top-left corner of the rectangle nestled into the top-left corner of the client area — as if you hadn't moved the scroll bars at all.

Before you see how to correct this problem, take a closer look at precisely what is happening in these screenshots.

Start with the `BigShapes` sample, shown in Figure 33-8. In this example, the entire window has just been repainted. Reviewing your code, you learn that it instructs the graphics instance to draw a rectangle with top-left coordinates (0,0) — relative to the top-left corner of the client area of the window — which is what has been drawn. The problem is that the graphics instance by default interprets coordinates as relative to the client window and is unaware of the scroll bars. Your code, as yet, does not attempt to adjust the coordinates for the scroll bar positions. The same goes for the ellipse.

Now, you can tackle the screenshot in Figure 33-9. After you scroll down, you notice that the top half of the window looks fine because it was drawn when the application first started up. When you scroll windows, Windows does not ask the application to redraw what was already on the screen. Windows is smart enough to determine which currently displayed bits can be smoothly moved around to match where the scroll bars now are located. This is a much more efficient process because it may be able to use some hardware acceleration to do that, too. The bit in this screenshot that is wrong is the bottom third of the window. This part of the window was not drawn when the application first appeared because before you started scrolling, it was outside the client area.This means that Windows asks your `BigShapes` application to draw this area. It will raise a `Paint` event passing in just this area as the clipping rectangle. And that is exactly what your `OnPaint()` override has done.

One way to look at the problem is that you are, at the moment, expressing your coordinates relative to the top-left corner of the start of the document — you need to convert them to express them relative to the top-left corner of the client area instead (see Figure 33-11).

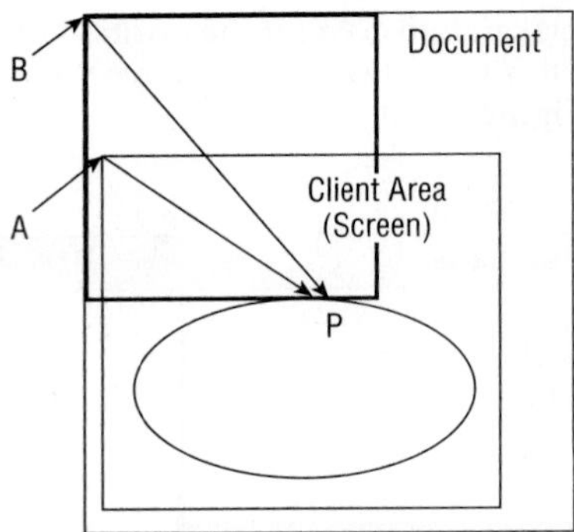

Figure 33-11

To make the diagram clearer, the document is actually extended further downward and to the right, beyond the boundaries of the screen, but this does not change our reasoning. It also assumes a small horizontal scroll as well as a vertical one.

In Figure 33-11, the thin rectangles mark the borders of the screen area and of the entire document. The thick lines mark the rectangle and ellipse that you are trying to draw. P marks some arbitrary point that you are drawing and that is being used as an example. When calling the drawing methods, the graphics instance was supplied with the vector from point B to (say) point P, expressed as a `Point` instance. You actually need to give it the vector from point A to point P.

The problem is that you do not know what the vector from A to P is. You know what B to P is; that is just the coordinates of P relative to the top-left corner of the document — the position where you want to draw point P in the document. You also know that the vector from B to A is just the amount you have scrolled by. This is stored in a property of the `Form` class called `AutoScrollPosition`. However, you do not know the vector from A to P.

To solve this problem, you subtract the one vector from the other. Say, for example, to get from B to P you move 150 pixels across and 200 pixels down, whereas to get from B to A you move 10 pixels across and 57 pixels down. That means to get from A to P you have to move 140 (150 minus 10) pixels across and 143 (200 minus 57) pixels down. To make it even simpler, the `Graphics` class actually implements a method that will do these calculations for you. It is called `TranslateTransform()`. You pass it the horizontal and vertical coordinates that say where the top left of the client area is relative to the top-left corner of the document (your `AutoScrollPosition` property, that is, the vector from B to A in the diagram). The `Graphics` device will now work out all its coordinates, taking into account where the client area is relative to the document.

If we translate this long explanation into code, all you typically need to do is add the following line to your drawing code:

```
dc.TranslateTransform(this.AutoScrollPosition.X, this.AutoScrollPosition.Y);
```

However, in this example, it is a little more complicated because you are also separately testing whether you need to do any drawing by looking at the clipping region. You need to adjust this test to take the scroll position into account, too. When you have done that, the full drawing code for the sample looks like this:

```
protected override void OnPaint( PaintEventArgs e )
{
   base.OnPaint(e);
```

```
        Graphics dc = e.Graphics;
        Size scrollOffset = new Size(this.AutoScrollPosition);
        if (e.ClipRectangle.Top+scrollOffset.Width < 350 ||
           e.ClipRectangle.Left+scrollOffset.Height < 250)
        {
           Rectangle rectangleArea = new Rectangle
              (rectangleTopLeft+scrollOffset, rectangleSize);
           Rectangle ellipseArea = new Rectangle
              (ellipseTopLeft+scrollOffset, ellipseSize);
           dc.DrawRectangle(bluePen, rectangleArea);
           dc.DrawEllipse(redPen, ellipseArea);
        }
    }
```

Now you have your scroll code working perfectly. You can at last obtain a correctly scrolled screenshot (see Figure 33-12).

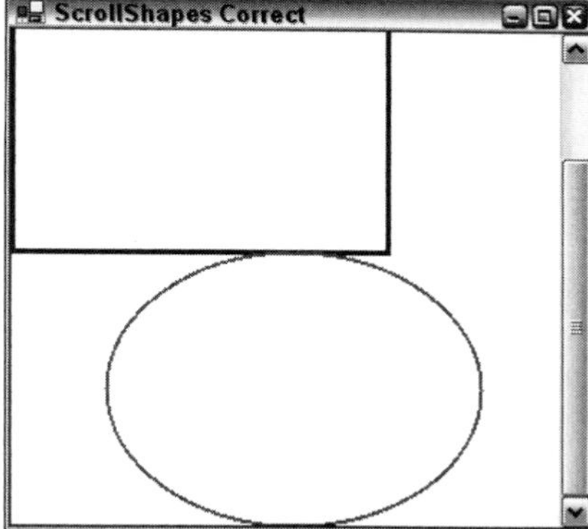

Figure 33-12

World, Page, and Device Coordinates

The distinction between measuring position relative to the top-left corner of the document and measuring it relative to the top-left corner of the screen (desktop) is so important that GDI+ has special names for these coordinate systems:

- **World coordinates** specify the position of a point measured in pixels from the top-left corner of the document.
- **Page coordinates** specify the position of a point measured in pixels from the top-left corner of the client area.

Developers familiar with GDI will note that world coordinates correspond to what in GDI were known as logical coordinates. Page coordinates correspond to what were known as device coordinates. As a developer familiar with GDI, you should also note that the way you code conversion between logical and device coordinates has changed in GDI+. In GDI, conversions took place via the device context, using the `LPtoDP()` *and* `DPtoLP()` *Windows API functions. In GDI+, it is the* `Control` *class, from which both* `Form` *and all the various Windows Forms controls derive, that maintains the information needed to carry out the conversion.*

GDI+ also distinguishes a third coordinate system, which is now known as *device coordinates*. Device coordinates are similar to page coordinates, except that you do not use pixels as the unit of measurement. Instead, you use some other unit that can be specified by the user by calling the `Graphics.PageUnit` property. Possible units, besides the default of pixels, include inches and millimeters. Although you will not use the `PageUnit` property in this chapter, you might find it useful as a way of getting around the different pixel densities of devices. For example, 100 pixels on most monitors will occupy approximately an inch. However, laser printers can have 1,200 or more dpi (dots per inch), which means that a shape specified to be 100 pixels wide will look a lot smaller when printed. By setting the units to, say, inches and specifying that the shape should be 1 inch wide, you can ensure that the shape will look the same size on the different devices. This is illustrated in the following:

```
Graphics dc = this.CreateGraphics();
dc.PageUnit = GraphicsUnit.Inch;
```

Possible units available via the `GraphicsUnit` enumeration include the following:

- **Display** — Defines the display's unit measure
- **Document** — Defines the document unit (1/300 inch) as the unit of measure
- **Inch** — Defines the inch measurement as the unit of measure
- **Millimeter** — Defines the millimeter measurement as the unit of measure
- **Pixel** — Defines the pixel measurement as the unit of measure
- **Point** — Defines the printer point (1/72 inch) as the unit of measure
- **World** — Defines the world coordinate system as the unit of measure

Colors

This section discusses the ways that you can specify what color you want something to be drawn in.

Colors in GDI+ are represented by instances of the `System.Drawing.Color` struct. Generally, once you have instantiated this struct, you won't do much with the corresponding `Color` instance — you just pass it to whatever other method you are calling that requires a `Color`. You have encountered this struct before, when you set the background color of the client area of the window in each of the examples, as well as when you set the colors of the various shapes you were displaying. The `Form.BackColor` property actually returns a `Color` instance. This section looks at this struct in more detail. In particular, it examines several different ways that you can construct a `Color`.

Red-Green-Blue Values

The total number of colors that can be displayed by a monitor is huge — more than 16 million. To be exact, the number is 2 to the power 24, which works out to 16,777,216. Obviously, you need some way of indexing those colors so that you can indicate which one is the color you want to display at any given pixel.

The most common way of indexing colors is by dividing them into the red, green, and blue components. This idea is based on the theory that any color that the human eye can distinguish can be constructed from a certain amount of red light, a certain amount of green light, and a certain amount of blue light. These colors are known as *components*. In practice, dividing the amount of each component light into 256 possible intensities yields a sufficiently fine gradation to be able to display images that are perceived by the human eye to be of photographic quality. You, therefore, specify colors by giving the amounts of these components on a scale of 0 to 255 where 0 means that the component is not present and 255 means that it is at its maximum intensity.

This gives you your first way of telling GDI+ about a color. You can indicate a color's red, green, and blue values by calling the static function `Color.FromArgb()`. Microsoft has chosen not to supply a constructor to do this task. The reason is that there are other ways, besides the usual RGB components, to indicate a color. Because of this, Microsoft felt that the meaning of parameters passed to any constructor they defined would be open to misinterpretation:

```
Color redColor = Color.FromArgb(255,0,0);
Color funnyOrangyBrownColor = Color.FromArgb(255,155,100);
Color blackColor = Color.FromArgb(0,0,0);
Color whiteColor = Color.FromArgb(255,255,255);
```

The three parameters are, respectively, the quantities of red, green, and blue. This function has a number of other overloads, some of which also allow you to specify something called an alpha-blend (that is the `A` in the name of the method, `FromArgb()`). Alpha blending is beyond the scope of this chapter, but it allows you to paint a color semitransparently by combining it with whatever color was already on the screen. This can give some beautiful effects and is often used in games.

The Named Colors

Constructing a `Color` using `FromArgb()` is the most flexible technique because it literally means you can specify any color that the human eye can see. However, if you want a simple, standard, well-known color such as red or blue, it is a lot easier to just be able to name the color you want. Hence, Microsoft has also provided a large number of static properties in `Color`, each of which returns a named color. It was one of these properties that you used when you set the background color of your windows to white in the examples:

```
this.BackColor = Color.White;
// has the same effect as:
// this.BackColor = Color.FromArgb(255, 255 , 255);
```

Several hundred such colors exist. The full list is given in the SDK documentation. They include all the simple colors: `Red`, `White`, `Blue`, `Green`, `Black`, and so on, as well as such delights as `MediumAquamarine`, `LightCoral`, and `DarkOrchid`. There is also a `KnownColor` enumeration, which lists the named colors.

Each of these named colors represents a precise set of RGB values. They were originally chosen many years ago for use on the Internet. The idea was to provide a useful set of colors right across the spectrum whose names would be recognized by Web browsers, thus saving you from having to write explicit RGB values in your HTML code. A few years ago, these colors were also important because early browsers could not necessarily display very many colors accurately, and the named colors were supposed to provide a set of colors that would be displayed correctly by most browsers. These days, that aspect is less important because modern Web browsers are quite capable of displaying any RGB value correctly. Web-safe color palettes are also available that provide developers with a comprehensive list of colors that work with most browsers.

Graphics Display Modes and the Safety Palette

Although in principle monitors can display any of the more than 16 million RGB colors, in practice this depends on how you have set the display properties on your computer. In Windows, there are traditionally three main color options (although some machines might provide other options depending on the hardware): true color (24 bit), high color (16 bit), and 256 colors. (On some graphics cards these days, true color is actually marked as 32 bit. This has to do with optimizing the hardware, though in that case only 24 bits of the 32 bits are used for the color itself.)

Only true color mode allows you to display all of the RGB colors simultaneously. This sounds like the best option, but it comes at a cost: 3 bytes are needed to hold a full RGB value, which means that 3 bytes of graphics card memory are needed to hold each pixel that is displayed. If graphics card memory is at a premium (a restriction that is less common now than it used to be), then you might want to choose one of the other modes. High color mode gives you 2 bytes per pixel, which is enough to give 5 bits for each RGB component. Therefore, instead of 256 gradations of red intensity, you get just 32 gradations. The same applies to blue and green,which produce a total of 65,536 colors. That is just about enough to give apparent photographic quality on a casual inspection, although areas of subtle shading tend to be broken up a bit.

The 256-color mode gives you even fewer colors. However, in this mode, you get to choose the colors. The system sets up something known as a *palette*. This is a list of 256 colors chosen from the 16 million RGB colors. Once you have specified the colors in the palette, the graphics device will be able to display just those colors. The palette can be changed at any time, but the graphics device can only display 256 different colors on the screen at any one time. The 256-color mode is used only when high performance is necessary and video memory is at a premium. Most computer games use this mode. They can still achieve decent-looking graphics because of a very careful choice of palette.

In general, if a display device is in high-color or 256-color mode and a particular RGB color is requested, then it will pick the nearest mathematical match from the pool of colors that it is able to display. It is for this reason that it is important to be aware of the color modes. If you are drawing something that involves subtle shading or photographic-quality images, and the user does not have 24-bit color mode selected, she might not see the image the same way you intended it. So if you are doing that kind of work with GDI+, then you should test your application in different color modes. (It is also possible for your application to programmatically set a given color mode, although that is not discussed in this chapter for lack of space.)

The Safety Palette

For reference, this section quickly mentions the safety palette, which is a very commonly used default palette. To use the safety palette, you set six equally spaced possible values for each color component: 0, 51, 102, 153, 204, and 255. In other words, the red component can have any of these values. The green component can have any of these values and so can the blue component. Possible colors from the safety palette include (0,0,0), black; (153,0,0), a fairly dark shade of red; (0, 255,102), green with a smattering of blue added; and so on. This gives you a total of 6 cubed = 216 colors. The idea is that this provides an easy way of creating a palette that contains colors from right across the spectrum and of all degrees of brightness. In practice, however, this does not actually work that well because equal mathematical spacing of color components does not mean equal perception of color differences by the human eye.

If you set Windows to 256-color mode, you will find that the default palette is the safety palette, with 20 Windows-standard colors added to it, and 20 spare colors.

Pens and Brushes

This section reviews two helper classes that are needed to draw shapes. You have already encountered the `Pen` class, which you used to instruct the graphics instance how to draw lines. A related class is `System.Drawing.Brush`, which instructs the graphics instance how to fill regions. For example, the `Pen` is needed to draw the outlines of the rectangle and ellipse in the previous examples. If you had needed to draw these shapes as solid, you would have used a brush to specify how to fill them. One aspect of both of these classes is that you will hardly ever call any methods on them. You simply construct a `Pen` or `Brush` instance with the required color and other properties, and then pass it to drawing methods that require a `Pen` or `Brush`.

If you have programmed using GDI before, you may have noticed from the first few examples that pens are used in a different way in GDI+. In GDI, the normal practice was to call a Windows API function, `SelectObject()`, *which actually associated a pen with the device context. That pen was then used in all drawing operations that required a pen until you informed the device context otherwise, by calling* `SelectObject()` *again. The same principle held for brushes and other objects such as fonts or bitmaps. With GDI+, Microsoft has opted for a stateless model in which there is no default pen or other helper object. Rather, you simply specify with each method call the appropriate helper object to be used for that particular method.*

Brushes

GDI+ has several different kinds of brushes — more than there is space to go into in this chapter, so this section just explains the simpler ones to give you an idea of the principles. Each type of brush is represented by an instance of a class derived from the abstract class `System.Drawing.Brush`. The simplest brush, `System.Drawing.SolidBrush`, indicates that a region is to be filled with solid color:

```
Brush solidBeigeBrush = new SolidBrush(Color.Beige);
Brush solidFunnyOrangyBrownBrush = new SolidBrush(Color.FromArgb(255,155,100));
```

Alternatively, if the brush is one of the Web-safe colors, then you can construct the brush using another class, `System.Drawing.Brushes`. `Brushes` is one of those classes that you never actually instantiate (it has a private constructor to stop you from doing that). It simply has a large number of static properties, each of which returns a brush of a specified color. You can use `Brushes` like this:

```
Brush solidAzureBrush = Brushes.Azure;
Brush solidChocolateBrush = Brushes.Chocolate;
```

The next level of complexity is a hatch brush, which fills a region by drawing a pattern. This type of brush is considered more advanced, so it is in the `Drawing2D` namespace, represented by the class `System.Drawing.Drawing2D.HatchBrush`. The `Brushes` class cannot help you with hatch brushes; you will need to construct one explicitly by supplying the hatch style and two colors — the foreground color followed by the background color. (Note, you can omit the background color, in which case it defaults to black). The hatch style comes from an enumeration, `System.Drawing.Drawing2D .HatchStyle`. You can choose from a large number of `HatchStyle` values (see the SDK documentation for the full list). To give you an idea, typical styles include `ForwardDiagonal`, `Cross`, `DiagonalCross`, `SmallConfetti`, and `ZigZag`. Examples of constructing a hatch brush include:

```
Brush crossBrush = new HatchBrush(HatchStyle.Cross, Color.Azure);
// background color of CrossBrush is black
Brush brickBrush = new HatchBrush(HatchStyle.DiagonalBrick,
                                  Color.DarkGoldenrod, Color.Cyan);
```

Solid and hatch brushes are the only brushes available under GDI. GDI+ has added a couple of new styles of brushes:

- `System.Drawing.Drawing2D.LinearGradientBrush` fills in an area with a color that varies across the screen.
- `System.Drawing.Drawing2D.PathGradientBrush` is similar, but in this case, the color varies along a path around the region to be filled.

Note that both brushes can render some spectacular effects if used carefully.

Pens

Unlike brushes, pens are represented by just one class: `System.Drawing.Pen`. However, the pen is slightly more complex than the brush because it needs to indicate how thick lines should be (how many pixels wide) and, for a wide line, how to fill the area inside the line. Pens can also specify a number of other properties, which are beyond the scope of this chapter, but which include the `Alignment` property mentioned earlier. This property indicates where in relation to the border of a shape a line should be drawn, as well as what shape to draw at the end of a line (whether to round off the shape).

The area inside a thick line can be filled with solid color or by using a brush. Hence, a `Pen` instance might contain a reference to a `Brush` instance. This is quite powerful because it means that you can draw lines that are colored in by using, say, hatching or linear shading. There are four different ways to construct a `Pen` instance that you have designed yourself. One is by passing a color; a second is by passing in a brush. Both of these constructors will produce a pen with a width of one pixel. Alternatively, a third way is to pass in a color or a brush, and additionally a `float`, which represents the width of the pen. (It needs to be a `float` in case you are using non-default units such as millimeters or inches for the `Graphics` object that will do the drawing, so you can, for example, specify fractions of an inch.) For example, you can construct pens like this:

```
Brush brickBrush = new HatchBrush(HatchStyle.DiagonalBrick,
                                   Color.DarkGoldenrod, Color.Cyan);
Pen solidBluePen = new Pen(Color.FromArgb(0,0,255));
Pen solidWideBluePen = new Pen(Color.Blue, 4);
Pen brickPen = new Pen(brickBrush);
Pen brickWidePen = new Pen(brickBrush, 10);
```

Additionally, a fourth way offers the quick construction of pens by using the class `System.Drawing.Pens`, which, like the `Brushes` class, contains a number of stock pens. These pens all have a 1-pixel width and come in the usual sets of Web-safe colors. This allows you to construct pens in this way:

```
Pen solidYellowPen = Pens.Yellow;
```

Drawing Shapes and Lines

You have almost finished the first part of the chapter, and you have seen all the basic classes and objects required to draw specified shapes and so on to the screen. This section starts by reviewing some of the drawing methods the `Graphics` class makes available and presents a short example that illustrates the use of several brushes and pens.

`System.Drawing.Graphics` has a large number of methods that allow you to draw various lines, outline shapes, and solid shapes. Once again, there are too many to provide a comprehensive list here, but the following table lists the main ones and should give you some idea of the variety of shapes you can draw.

Method	Typical Parameters	What It Draws
`DrawLine`	Pen, start and end points	A single straight line
`DrawRectangle`	Pen, position, and size	Outline of a rectangle
`DrawEllipse`	Pen, position, and size	Outline of an ellipse
`FillRectangle`	Brush, position, and size	Solid rectangle
`FillEllipse`	Brush, position, and size	Solid ellipse
`DrawLines`	Pen, array of points	Series of lines, connecting each point to the next one in the array
`DrawBezier`	Pen, four points	A smooth curve through the two end points, with the remaining two points used to control the shape of the curve

Method	Typical Parameters	What It Draws
`DrawCurve`	Pen, array of points	A smooth curve through the points
`DrawArc`	Pen, rectangle, two angles	Portion of circle within the rectangle defined by the angles
`DrawClosedCurve`	Pen, array of points	Like `DrawCurve` but also draws a straight line to close the curve
`DrawPie`	Pen, rectangle, two angles	Wedge-shaped outline within the rectangle
`FillPie`	Brush, rectangle, two angles	Solid wedge-shaped area within the rectangle
`DrawPolygon`	Pen, array of points	Like `DrawLines` but also connects first and last points to close the figure drawn

Before we leave the subject of drawing simple objects, this section rounds off with a simple example that demonstrates the kinds of visual effects you can achieve using brushes. The example is called `ScrollMoreShapes`, and it is essentially a revision of `ScrollShapes`. Besides the rectangle and ellipse, you will add a thick line and fill in the shapes with various custom brushes. You have already learned the principles of drawing, so the code speaks for itself. First, because of your new brushes, you need to indicate that you are using the `System.Drawing.Drawing2D` namespace:

```
using System;
using System.Collections.Generic;
using System.ComponentModel;
using System.Data;
using System.Drawing;
using System.Drawing.Drawing2D;
using System.Text;
using System.Windows.Forms;
```

Next are some extra fields in your `Form1` class, which contain details of the locations where the shapes are to be drawn, as well as various pens and brushes you will use:

```
private Rectangle rectangleBounds = new Rectangle(new Point(0,0),
                                                  new Size(200,200));
private Rectangle ellipseBounds = new Rectangle(new Point(50,200),
                                                new Size(200,150));
private readonly Pen bluePen = new Pen(Color.Blue, 3);
private readonly Pen redPen = new Pen(Color.Red, 2);
private readonly Brush solidAzureBrush = Brushes.Azure;
private readonly Brush solidYellowBrush = new SolidBrush(Color.Yellow);
private static readonly Brush brickBrush = new
   HatchBrush(HatchStyle.DiagonalBrick, Color.DarkGoldenrod, Color.Cyan);
private readonly Pen brickWidePen = new Pen(brickBrush, 10);
```

The `brickBrush` field has been declared as static so that you can use its value to initialize the `brickWidePen` field. C# will not let you use one instance field to initialize another instance field because it has not defined which one will be initialized first. However, declaring the field as static solves the problem. Because only one instance of the `Form1` class will be instantiated, it is immaterial whether the fields are static or instance fields.

The following is the `OnPaint()` override:

```
protected override void OnPaint( PaintEventArgs e )
{
   base.OnPaint(e);
   Graphics dc = e.Graphics;
   Point scrollOffset = AutoScrollPosition;
   dc.TranslateTransform(scrollOffset.X, scrollOffset.Y);
   if (e.ClipRectangle.Top+scrollOffset.X < 350 ||
       e.ClipRectangle.Left+scrollOffset.Y < 250)
   {
      dc.DrawRectangle(bluePen, rectangleBounds);
      dc.FillRectangle(solidYellowBrush, rectangleBounds);
      dc.DrawEllipse(redPen, ellipseBounds);
      dc.FillEllipse(solidAzureBrush, ellipseBounds);
      dc.DrawLine(brickWidePen, rectangleBounds.Location,
                                    ellipseBounds.Location+ellipseBounds.Size);
   }
}
```

As before, you also set the `AutoScrollMinSize` to (250,350). Figure 33-13 shows the new results.

Notice that the thick diagonal line has been drawn on top of the rectangle and ellipse because it was the last item to be painted.

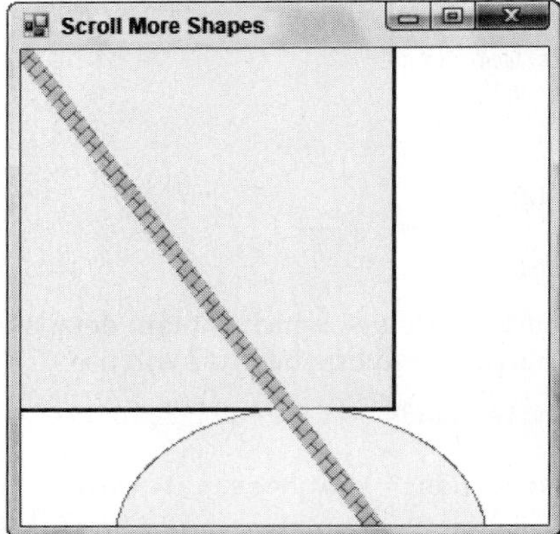

Figure 33-13

Displaying Images

One of the most common things you might want to do with GDI+ is display an image that already exists in a file. This is actually a lot simpler than drawing your own user interface because the image is already pre-drawn. Effectively, all you have to do is load the file and instruct GDI+ to display it. The image can be a simple line drawing, an icon, or a complex image such as a photograph. You can also manipulate the image by stretching or rotating it, or simply displaying only a portion of it.

This section, just for a change, presents the sample first. Then it discusses some of the issues you need to be aware of when displaying images. Presenting it this way is possible because the code needed to display an image is so simple.

The class you need is the .NET base class, `System.Drawing.Image`. An instance of `Image` represents one image. Reading in an image simply takes one line of code:

```
Image myImage = Image.FromFile("FileName");
```

`FromFile()` is a static member of `Image` and is the usual way of instantiating an image. The file can be any of the commonly supported graphics file formats, including `.bmp`, `.jpg`, `.gif`, and `.png`.

Displaying an image is also very simple, assuming that you have a suitable `Graphics` instance at hand — a call to either `Graphics.DrawImageUnscaled()` or `Graphics.DrawImage()` suffices. There are quite a few overloads of these methods, allowing you a lot of flexibility in the information you supply in terms of where the image is located and how big it is to be drawn. But this example uses `DrawImage()`, like this:

```
dc.DrawImage(myImage, points);
```

In this line of code, `dc` is assumed to be a `Graphics` instance, and `myImage` is the `Image` to be displayed. `points` is an array of `Point` structs, where `points[0]`, `points[1]`, and `points[2]` are the coordinates of the top-left, top-right, and bottom-left corner of the image.

Images are probably the area in which developers familiar with GDI will notice the biggest difference between GDI and GDI+. In GDI, displaying an image involved several nontrivial steps. If the image was a bitmap, then loading it was reasonably simple. Nevertheless, if it was any other file type, then loading it would involve a sequence of calls to OLE objects. Actually, getting a loaded image onto the screen required getting a handle to it, selecting it into a memory device context, and then performing a block transfer between device contexts. Although the device contexts and handles are still there behind the scenes and will be needed if you want to start doing sophisticated editing of the images from your code, simple tasks have now been extremely well wrapped up in the GDI+ object model.

The process of displaying an image is illustrated with an example called `DisplayImage`. The example simply displays a `.jpg` file in the application's main window. To keep things simple, the path of the `.jpg` file is hard-coded into the application (so if you run the example, then you will need to change it to reflect the location of the file in your system). The `.jpg` file you will display is a sunset picture in St. Petersburg.

As with the other examples, the `DisplayImage` project is a standard C# Visual Studio 2008–generated Windows application. You add the following fields to your `Form1` class:

```
readonly Image piccy;
private readonly Point [] piccyBounds;
```

You then load the file in the `Form1()` constructor:

```
public Form1()
{
   InitializeComponent();
   piccy =
      Image.FromFile(@"C:\ProCSharp\GdiPlus\Images\London.jpg");
   AutoScrollMinSize = piccy.Size;
   piccyBounds = new Point[3];
   piccyBounds[0] = new Point(0,0);       // top left
   piccyBounds[1] = new Point(piccy.Width,0);   // top right
   piccyBounds[2] = new Point(0,piccy.Height);   // bottom left
}
```

Note that the size in pixels of the image is obtained as its `Size` property, which you use to set the document area. You also set up the `piccyBounds` array, which is used to identify the position of the image on the screen. You have chosen the coordinates of the three corners to draw the image in its actual size and shape here, but if you had wanted the image to be resized, stretched, or even sheared into a nonrectangular parallelogram, then you could do so simply by changing the values of the `Points` in the `piccyBounds` array.

The image is displayed in the `OnPaint()` override:

```
protected override void OnPaint(PaintEventArgs e)
{
   base.OnPaint(e);
   Graphics dc = e.Graphics;
   dc.ScaleTransform(1.0f, 1.0f);
   dc.TranslateTransform(AutoScrollPosition.X, AutoScrollPosition.Y);
   dc.DrawImage(piccy, piccyBounds);
}
```

Finally, note the modification made to the IDE-generated `Form1.Dispose()` method:

```
protected override void Dispose(bool disposing)
{
   piccy.Dispose();
   if (disposing && (components != null))
   {
      components.Dispose();
   }
   base.Dispose(disposing);
}
```

Disposing of the image as soon as possible when it is no longer needed is important because images generally take up a lot of memory while in use. After `Image.Dispose()` has been called, the `Image` instance no longer refers to any actual image, and so it can no longer be displayed (unless you load a new image).

Figure 33-14 shows the result of running this code.

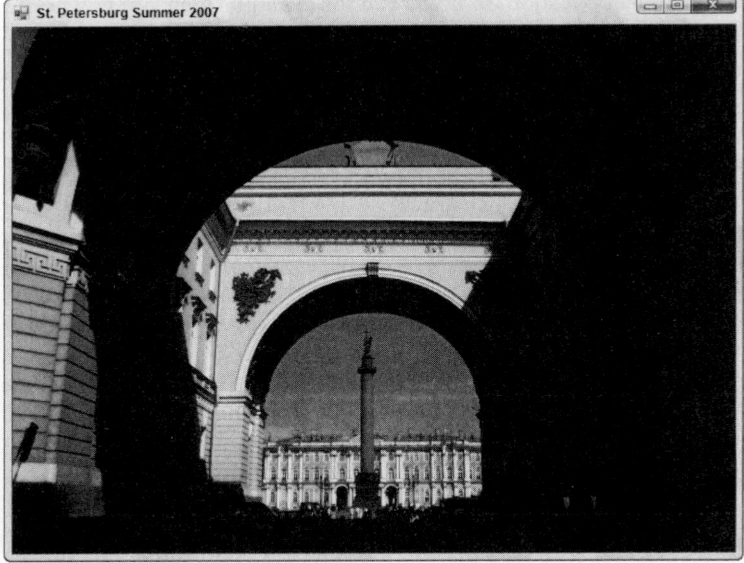

Figure 33-14

Issues When Manipulating Images

Although displaying images is very simple, it still pays to have some understanding of what is going on behind the scenes.

The most important point to understand about images is that they are always rectangular. That is not just a convenience; it is because of the underlying technology. All modern graphics cards have hardware built in that can efficiently copy blocks of pixels from one area of memory to another area of memory, provided that the block of pixels represents a rectangular region. This hardware-accelerated operation can occur virtually as one single operation, and as such, is extremely fast. Indeed, it is the key to modern high-performance graphics. This operation is known as a *bitmap block transfer* (or *BitBlt*). `Graphics.DrawImageUnscaled()` internally uses a `BitBlt`, which is why you can see a huge image, perhaps containing as many as a million pixels, appearing almost instantly. If the computer had to copy the image to the screen pixel by pixel, you would see the image gradually being drawn over a period of up to several seconds.

`BitBlts` are very efficient; therefore, almost all drawing and manipulation of images is carried out using them. Even some editing of images will be done by manipulating portions of images with `BitBlts` between DCs that represent areas of memory. In the days of GDI, the Windows 32 API function `BitBlt()` was arguably the most important and widely used function for image manipulation, although with GDI+, the `BitBlt` operations are largely hidden by the GDI+ object model.

It's not possible to `BitBlt` areas of images that are not rectangular, although similar effects can be easily simulated. One way is to mark a certain color as transparent for the purposes of a `BitBlt`, so that areas of that color in the source image will not overwrite the existing color of the corresponding pixel in the destination device. It is also possible to specify that in the process of a `BitBlt`, each pixel of the resultant image will be formed by some logical operation (such as a bitwise AND) on the colors of that pixel in the source image and in the destination device before the `BitBlt`. Such operations are supported by hardware acceleration and can be used to give a variety of subtle effects. Note that the `Graphics` object implements another method, `DrawImage()`. This is similar to `DrawImageUnscaled()` but comes in a large number of overloads that allow you to specify more complex forms of `BitBlt` to be used in the drawing process. `DrawImage()` also allows you to draw (using `BitBlt`) only a specified part of the image, or to perform certain other operations on it such as scaling it (expanding or reducing it in size) as it is drawn.

Drawing Text

We have chosen to cover the very important topic of displaying text late in this chapter because drawing text to the screen is (in general) more complex than drawing simple graphics. Although displaying a line or two of text when you don't care about the appearance is extremely easy (it takes one single call to the `Graphics.DrawString()` method), if you are trying to display a document that has a fair amount of text in it, then you will rapidly find that things become a lot more complex. This is for two reasons:

- If you are concerned about getting the appearance just right, then you must understand fonts. Whereas shape drawing requires brushes and pens as helper objects, the process of drawing text requires fonts as helper objects. Moreover, understanding fonts is not a trivial undertaking.
- Text needs to be very carefully laid out in the window. Users generally expect words to follow naturally from one word to another and to be lined up with clear spaces in between. Doing that is harder than you might think. For starters, you do not usually know in advance how much space on the screen a word is going to take up. That has to be calculated (using the `Graphics.MeasureString()` method). In addition, the space a word occupies on the screen affects where in the document every subsequent word is placed. If your application does any line wrapping, then it will need to assess word sizes carefully before deciding where to place the line break. The

next time you run Microsoft Word, look carefully at the way Word is continually repositioning text as you do your work; there is a lot of complex processing going on there. Chances are that any GDI+ application you work on will not be nearly as complex as Word. However, if you need to display any text, many of the same considerations apply.

In short, high-quality text processing is tricky to get right. However, putting a line of text on the screen, assuming that you know the font and where you want it to go, is actually very simple. Therefore, the next section presents a quick example that shows you how to display some text, followed by a short review of the principles of fonts and font families and a more realistic (and involved) text-processing example, `CapsEditor`.

Simple Text Example

This example, `DisplayText`, is your usual Windows Forms effort. This time you override `OnPaint()` and add member fields as follows:

```
private readonly Brush blackBrush = Brushes.Black;
private readonly Brush blueBrush = Brushes.Blue;
private readonly Font haettenschweilerFont = new Font("Haettenschweiler", 12);
private readonly Font boldTimesFont = new Font("Times New Roman", 10,
   FontStyle.Bold);
private readonly Font italicCourierFont = new Font("Courier", 11,
   FontStyle.Italic | FontStyle.Underline);
protected override void OnPaint(PaintEventArgs e)
{
   base.OnPaint(e);
   Graphics dc = e.Graphics;
   dc.DrawString("This is a groovy string", haettenschweilerFont, blackBrush,
                 10, 10);
   dc.DrawString("This is a groovy string " +
                 "with some very long text that will never fit in the box",
                 boldTimesFont, blueBrush,
                 new Rectangle(new Point(10, 40), new Size(100, 40)));
   dc.DrawString("This is a groovy string", italicCourierFont, blackBrush,
                 new Point(10, 100));
}
```

Figure 33-15 shows the result of running this example.

Figure 33-15

The example demonstrates the use of the `Graphics.DrawString()` method to draw items of text. The method `DrawString()` comes in a number of overloads, three of which are demonstrated here. The different overloads require parameters that indicate the text to be displayed, the font that the string should be drawn in, and the brush that should be used to construct the various lines and curves that make up each character of text. A few alternatives exist for the remaining parameters. In general, however, it is possible to specify either a `Point` (or equivalently, two numbers) or a `Rectangle`.

If you specify a `Point`, then the text will start with its top-left corner at that `Point` and simply stretch out to the right. If you specify a `Rectangle`, then the `Graphics` instance will lay out the string inside that rectangle. If the text does not fit within the boundaries of the rectangle, it will be cut off (see the fourth line of text in Figure 33-15). Passing a rectangle to `DrawString()` means that the drawing process will take longer because `DrawString()` will need to figure out where to put line breaks, but the result may look nicer — provided the string fits in the rectangle!

This example also shows a few ways to construct fonts. You always need to include the name of the font and its size (height). You can also optionally pass in various styles that modify how the text is to be drawn (bold, underline, and so on).

Fonts and Font Families

A font describes exactly how each letter should be displayed. Selection of the appropriate font and providing a reasonable variety of fonts within a document are important factors in improving readability.

Most people, if asked to name a font, might mention Arial or Times New Roman (if they are Windows users) or Times or Helvetica (if they are Mac OS users). In fact, these are not fonts at all — they are *font families*. The font family tells you, in generic terms, the visual style of the text and is a key factor in the overall appearance of your application. Most of us recognize the styles of the most common font families, even if we are not consciously aware of it.

An actual *font* would be something like Arial 9-point italic. In other words, the size and other modifications to the text are specified as well as the font family. These modifications might include whether text is **bold**, *italic*, underlined, or displayed in SMALL CAPS or as a $_{\text{subscript}}$; this is technically referred to as the *style*, although in some ways, the term is misleading because the visual appearance is determined as much by the font family.

The size of the text is measured by specifying its height. The height is measured in *points* — a traditional unit that represents 1⁄72 of an inch (0.351 mm). So letters in a 10-point font are roughly 1⁄7", or 3.5 mm high. However, you will not get seven lines of 10-point text into one inch of vertical screen or paper space, as you need to allow for the spacing between the lines as well.

Strictly speaking, measuring the height is not quite as simple as that because there are several different heights that you must consider. For example, there is the height of tall letters such as the A or F (this is the measurement that we are referring to when we talk about the height), the additional height occupied by any accents on letters such as Å or Ñ (the internal leading), and the extra height below the baseline needed for the tails of letters such as y and g (the descent). However, for this chapter we will not worry about that. Once you specify the font family and the main height, these subsidiary heights are determined automatically.

When you are dealing with fonts, you might also encounter some other terms commonly used to describe certain font families:

- **Serif** font families have feet at the ends of many of the lines that make up the characters (these ticks are known as serifs). Times New Roman is a classic example of this.

- **Sans serif** font families, by contrast, do not have these feet. Good examples of sans serif fonts are Arial and Verdana. The lack of feet often gives text a blunt, in-your-face appearance, so sans serif fonts are often used for important text.
- A **True Type** font family is one that is defined by expressing the shapes of the curves that make up the characters in a precise mathematical manner. This means that the same definition can be used to calculate how to draw fonts of any size within the family. These days, virtually all the fonts you might use are TrueType fonts. Some older font families from the days of Windows 3.1 were defined by individually specifying the bitmap for each character separately for each font size, but the use of these fonts is now discouraged.

Microsoft has provided two main classes that you need to deal with when selecting or manipulating fonts:

- `System.Drawing.Font`
- `System.Drawing.FontFamily`

You have already seen the main use of the `Font` class. When you want to draw text, you instantiate an instance of `Font` and pass it to the `DrawString()` method to indicate how the text should be drawn. A `FontFamily` instance is used to represent a family of fonts.

You can use the `FontFamily` class, for example, if you know you want a font of a particular type (serif, sans serif, or true type), but do not have a preference for which font. The static properties `GenericSerif`, `GenericSansSerif`, and `GenericMonospace` return default fonts that satisfy these criteria:

```
FontFamily sansSerifFont = FontFamily.GenericSansSerif;
```

However, if you are writing a professional application, then you will want to choose your font in a more sophisticated way. Most likely, you will implement your drawing code so that it checks the font families available and selects the appropriate one, perhaps by taking the first available one on a list of preferred fonts. Moreover, if you want your application to be very user-friendly, then the first choice on the list will probably be the one that users selected the last time they ran your software. Usually, if you are dealing with the most popular font families, such as Arial and Times New Roman, you will be safe. However, if you do try to display text using a font that does not exist, the results aren't always predictable. You are quite likely to find that Windows just substitutes the standard system font, which is very easy for the system to draw, but that it does not look very pleasant — and if it does appear in your document, then it is likely to give the impression of software that is of poor quality.

You can find out what fonts are available on your system using a class called `InstalledFontCollection`, which is in the `System.Drawing.Text` namespace. This class implements a property, `Families`, which is an array of all the fonts that are available to use on your system:

```
InstalledFontCollection insFont = new InstalledFontCollection();
FontFamily [] families = insFont.Families;
foreach (FontFamily family in families)
{
   // do processing with this font family
}
```

Example: Enumerating Font Families

In this section, you work through a quick example, `EnumFontFamilies`, which lists all the font families available on the system and illustrates them by displaying the name of each family using an appropriate font (the 12-point regular version of that font family). Figure 33-16 shows the result of running `EnumFontFamilies`.

Of course, the results that you get will depend on the fonts you have installed on your computer.

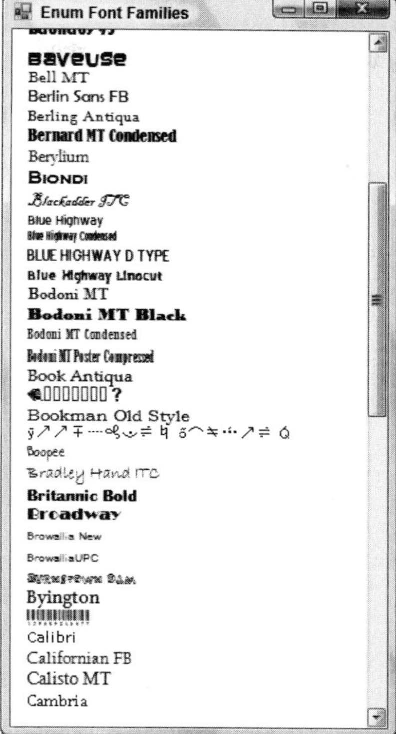

Figure 33-16

For this example, you create a standard C# Windows application, `EnumFontFamilies`. You start by adding an extra namespace to be searched. You will be using the `InstalledFontCollection` class, which is defined in `System.Drawing.Text`.

```
using System.Drawing;
using System.Drawing.Text;
using System.Windows.Forms;
```

You then add the following constant to the `Form1` class:

```
private const int margin = 10;
```

`margin` is the size of the left and top margin between the text and the edge of the document — it stops the text from appearing right at the edge of the client area.

This is designed as a quick-and-easy way of showing off font families; therefore, the code is crude and in many instances does not do things the way you ought to in a real application. For example, here you hard-code an estimated value for the document size of (200, 1500) and set the `AutoScrollMinSize` property to this value using the Visual Studio 2008 properties window. Typically, you would have to examine the text to be displayed to work out the document size. You do that in the next section.

Here is the `OnPaint()` method:

```
protected override void OnPaint(PaintEventArgs e)
{
   base.OnPaint(e);
   int verticalCoordinate = margin;
   InstalledFontCollection insFont = new InstalledFontCollection();
   FontFamily [] families = insFont.Families;
   e.Graphics.TranslateTransform(AutoScrollPosition.X,
                                 AutoScrollPosition.Y);
   foreach (FontFamily family in families)
   {
      if (family.IsStyleAvailable(FontStyle.Regular))
      {
         Font f = new Font(family.Name, 12);
         Point topLeftCorner = new Point(margin, verticalCoordinate);
         verticalCoordinate += f.Height;
         e.Graphics.DrawString (family.Name, f,
                                Brushes.Black,topLeftCorner);
         f.Dispose();
      }
   }
}
```

In this code, you start by using an `InstalledFontCollection` object to obtain an array that contains details of all the available font families. For each family, you instantiate a 12-point `Font`. You use a simple constructor for `Font` — there are many more that allow additional options to be specified. The constructor takes two parameters, the name of the family and the size of the font:

```
Font f = new Font(family.Name, 12);
```

This constructor builds a font that has the regular style. To be on the safe side, however, you first check that this style is available for each font family before attempting to display anything using that font. This is done using the `FontFamily.IsStyleAvailable()` method. This check is important because not all fonts are available in all styles:

```
if (family.IsStyleAvailable(FontStyle.Regular))
```

`FontFamily.IsStyleAvailable()` takes one parameter, a `FontStyle` enumeration. This enumeration contains a number of flags that might be combined with the bitwise `OR` operator. The possible flags are `Bold`, `Italic`, `Regular`, `Strikeout`, and `Underline`.

Finally, note that you use a property of the `Font` class, `Height`, which returns the height needed to display text of that font, to work out the line spacing:

```
Font f =  new Font(family.Name, 12);
Point topLeftCorner = new Point(margin, verticalCoordinate);
verticalCoordinate += f.Height;
```

Again, to keep things simple, this version of `OnPaint()` reveals some bad programming practices. For example, you have not bothered to check what area of the document actually needs drawing — you just tried to display everything. Also, instantiating a `Font` is, as remarked earlier, a computationally intensive process, so you really ought to save the fonts rather than instantiating new copies every time `OnPaint()` is called. Because of the way the code has been designed, you might note that this example actually takes a noticeable amount of time to paint itself. To try to conserve memory and help the garbage collector you do, however, call `Dispose()` on each font instance after you have finished with it. If you did not, after 10 or 20 paint operations, there would be a lot of wasted memory storing fonts that are no longer needed.

Editing a Text Document: The CapsEditor Sample

You now come to the extended example in this chapter. The `CapsEditor` example is designed to demonstrate how the principles of drawing that you have learned so far have to be applied in a more realistic context. The `CapsEditor` example does not require any new material, apart from responding to user input via the mouse, but it shows how to manage the drawing of text so that the application maintains performance while ensuring that the contents of the client area of the main window are always kept up-to-date.

The `CapsEditor` program allows the user to read in a text file, which is then displayed line by line in the client area. If the user double-clicks any line, then that line will be changed to all uppercase. That is literally all the example does. Even with this limited set of features, you will find that the work involved in making sure everything is displayed in the right place while considering performance issues is quite complex. In particular, you have a new element here: The contents of the document can change — either when the user selects the menu option to read a new file, or when she double-clicks to capitalize a line. In the first case, you need to update the document size so the scroll bars still work correctly, and you have to redisplay everything. In the second case, you need to check carefully whether the document size has changed, and what text needs to be redisplayed.

This section starts by reviewing the appearance of `CapsEditor`. When the application is first run, it has no document loaded and resembles Figure 33-17.

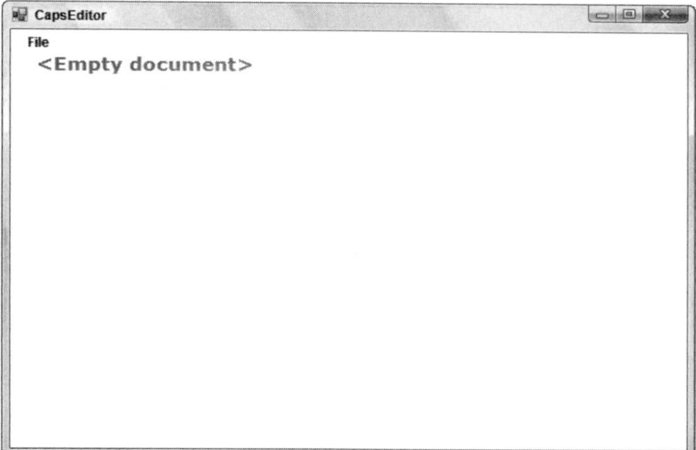

Figure 33-17

The File menu has two options: Open, which evokes `OpenFileDialog` when selected and reads in whatever file the user clicks, and Exit, which closes the application when clicked. Figure 33-18 shows `CapsEditor` displaying its own source file, `Form1.cs`. (A few lines have been double-clicked in this image to convert them to uppercase.)

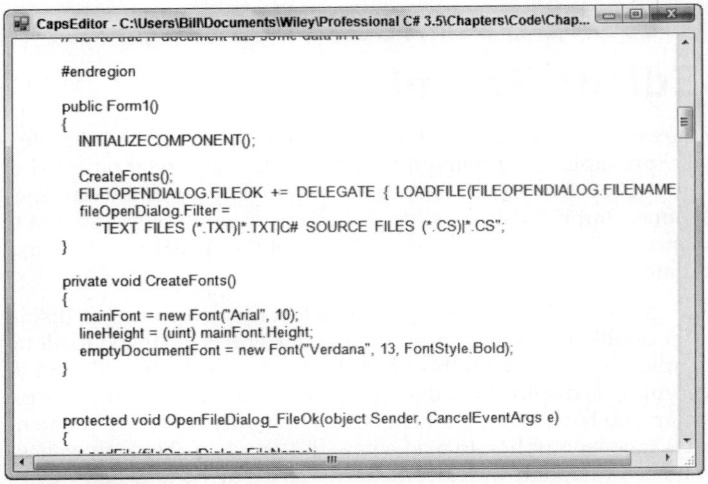

Figure 33-18

The sizes of the horizontal and vertical scroll bars are correct. The client area will scroll just enough to view the entire document. `CapsEditor` does not try to wrap lines of text — the example is already complicated enough as is. It just displays each line of the file exactly as it is read in. There are no limits to the size of the file, but you are assuming that it is a text file and does not contain any nonprintable characters.

Begin by adding a `using` command:

```
using System;
using System.Collections;
using System.ComponentModel;
using System.Drawing;
using System.IO;
using System.Windows.Forms;
```

You will be using the `StreamReader` class, which is in the `System.IO` namespace. Next, you add some fields to the `Form1` class:

```
      #region Constant fields
      private const string standardTitle = "CapsEditor";
                                                  // default text in titlebar
      private const uint margin = 10;
                                  // horizontal and vertical margin in client area
      #endregion
      #region Member fields
      // The 'document'
      private readonly List<TextLineInformation> documentLines =
         new List<TextLineInformation>();
      private uint lineHeight;        // height in pixels of one line
      private Size documentSize;      // how big a client area is needed to
                                      // display document
      private uint nLines;            // number of lines in document
      private Font mainFont;          // font used to display all lines
      private Font emptyDocumentFont; // font used to display empty message
```

```
private readonly Brush mainBrush = Brushes.Blue;
                              // brush used to display document text
private readonly Brush emptyDocumentBrush = Brushes.Red;
                        // brush used to display empty document message
private Point mouseDoubleClickPosition;
    // location mouse is pointing to when double-clicked
private readonly OpenFileDialog fileOpenDialog = new OpenFileDialog();
    // standard open file dialog
private bool documentHasData = false;
    // set to true if document has some data in it
#endregion
```

Most of these fields should be self-explanatory. The `documentLines` field is a `List<TextLineInformation>` that contains the actual text of the file that has been read in. Actually, this is the field that contains the data in the document. Each element of `documentLines` contains information for one line of text that has been read in. Because it is a `List<TextLineInformation>` rather than a plain array, you can dynamically add elements to it as you read in a file.

As previously mentioned, each `documentLines` element contains information about a line of text. This information is actually an instance of another class, `TextLineInformation`:

```
class TextLineInformation
{
   public string Text;
   public uint Width;
}
```

`TextLineInformation` looks like a classic case where you would normally use a struct rather than a class because it is just there to group a couple of fields. However, its instances are always accessed as elements of a `List<TextLineInformation>`, which expects its elements to be stored as reference types.

Each `TextLineInformation` instance stores a line of text — and that can be thought of as the smallest item that is displayed as a single item. In general, for each similar item in a GDI+ application, you would probably want to store the text of the item, as well as the world coordinates of where it should be displayed and its size. (The page coordinates will change frequently, whenever the user scrolls, whereas world coordinates will normally change only when other parts of the document are modified in some way.) In this case, you have stored only the `Width` of the item because the height in this case is just the height of whatever your selected font is. It is the same for all lines of text so there is no point storing the height separately for each one; you store it once, in the `Form1.lineHeight` field. As for the position, well, in this case, the x coordinate is just equal to the margin, and the y coordinate is easily calculated as:

```
margin + lineHeight*(however many lines are above this one)
```

If you had been trying to display and manipulate, say, individual words instead of complete lines, then the x position of each word would have to be calculated using the widths of all the previous words on that line of text, but the intent is to keep it simple here, which is why you are treating each line of text as one single item.

Let's turn to the main menu now. This part of the application is more the realm of Windows Forms (see Chapter 31, "Windows Forms") than of GDI+. Add the menu options using the design view in Visual Studio 2008, but rename them `menuFile`, `menuFileOpen`, and `menuFileExit`. Next, add event handlers for the File Open and File Exit menu options using the Visual Studio 2008 properties window. The event handlers have their Visual Studio 2008–generated names of `menuFileOpen_Click()` and `menuFileExit_Click()`.

Add some extra initialization code in the `Form1()` constructor:

```
public Form1()
{
   InitializeComponent();
   CreateFonts();
   fileOpenDialog.FileOk += delegate { LoadFile(fileOpenDialog.FileName); };
   fileOpenDialog.Filter =
      "Text files (*.txt)|*.txt|C# source files (*.cs)|*.cs";

}
```

You add the event handler here for instances when the user clicks OK in the File Open dialog box. You have also set the filter for the Open File dialog box, so that you can load text files only. The example in this case only uses `.txt` files, in addition to the C# source files, so you can use the application to examine the source code for the samples.

`CreateFonts()` is a helper method that sorts out the fonts you intend to use:

```
private void CreateFonts()
{
   mainFont = new Font("Arial", 10);
   lineHeight = (uint)mainFont.Height;
   emptyDocumentFont = new Font("Verdana", 13, FontStyle.Bold);
}
```

The actual definitions of the handlers are pretty standard:

```
protected void OpenFileDialog_FileOk(object Sender, CancelEventArgs e)
{
   LoadFile(fileOpenDialog.FileName);
}
protected void menuFileOpen_Click(object sender, EventArgs e)
{
   fileOpenDialog.ShowDialog();
}
protected void menuFileExit_Click(object sender, EventArgs e)
{
   Close();
}
```

Next, take a look at the `LoadFile()` method. It handles the opening and reading of a file (as well as ensuring a `Paint` event is raised to force a repaint with the new file):

```
private void LoadFile(string FileName)
{
   StreamReader sr = new StreamReader(FileName);
   string nextLine;
   documentLines.Clear();
   nLines = 0;
   TextLineInformation nextLineInfo;
   while ( (nextLine = sr.ReadLine()) != null)
   {
      nextLineInfo = new TextLineInformation();
      nextLineInfo.Text = nextLine;
      documentLines.Add(nextLineInfo);
      ++nLines;
   }
```

```
        sr.Close();
        documentHasData = (nLines>0) ? true : false;
        CalculateLineWidths();
        CalculateDocumentSize();
        Text = standardTitle + " - " + FileName;
        Invalidate();
    }
```

Most of this function is just standard file-reading (see Chapter 25, "Manipulating Files and the Registry"). Note that as the file is read, you progressively add lines to `documentLines ArrayList`, so this array ends up containing information for each of the lines in order. After you have read in the file, you set the `documentHasData` flag, which indicates whether there is actually anything to display. Your next task is to work out where everything is to be displayed, and, having done that, how much client area you need to display the file as well as the document size that will be used to set the scroll bars. Finally, you set the title bar text and call `Invalidate()`. `Invalidate()` is an important method supplied by Microsoft, so the next section discusses its use first, before examining the code for the `CalculateLineWidths()` and `CalculateDocumentSize()` methods.

The Invalidate() Method

`Invalidate()` is a member of `System.Windows.Forms.Form`. It marks an area of the client window as invalid and, therefore, in need of repainting, and then makes sure a `Paint` event is raised. `Invalidate()` has a couple of overrides: You can pass it a rectangle that specifies (in page coordinates) precisely which area of the window needs repainting. If you do not pass any parameters, it will just mark the entire client area as invalid.

If you know that something needs painting, why don't you just call `OnPaint()` or some other method to do the painting directly? The answer is that, in general, calling painting routines directly is regarded as bad programming practice — if your code decides it wants some painting done, you should call `Invalidate()`. Here is why:

- Drawing is almost always the most processor-intensive task a GDI+ application will carry out, so doing it in the middle of other work holds up the other work. With the example, if you had directly called a method to do the drawing from the `LoadFile()` method, then the `LoadFile()` method would not return until that drawing task was complete. During that time, your application cannot respond to any other events. However, by calling `Invalidate()`, you are simply getting Windows to raise a `Paint` event before immediately returning from `LoadFile()`. Windows is then free to examine the events that are in line to be handled. How this works internally is that the events sit as what are known as *messages* in a *message queue*. Windows periodically examines the queue, and if there are events in it, then it picks one and calls the corresponding event handler. Although the `Paint` event might be the only one sitting in the queue (so `OnPaint()` is called immediately anyway), in a more complex application there might be other events that ought to get priority over your `Paint` event. In particular, when the user has decided to quit the application, this will be marked by a message known as `WM_QUIT`.
- If you have a more complicated, multithreaded application, then you will probably want just one thread to handle all the drawing. Using `Invalidate()` to route all drawing through the message queue provides a good way of ensuring that the same thread does all the drawing, no matter what other thread requested the drawing operation. (Whatever thread is responsible for the message queue will be the thread that called `Application.Run()`.)
- There is an additional performance-related reason. Suppose that a couple of different requests to draw part of the screen come in at about the same time. Maybe your code has just modified the document and wants to ensure the updated document is displayed, while at the same time the user has just moved another window that was covering part of the client area out of the way.

By calling `Invalidate()`, you are giving Windows a chance to notice that this has occurred. Windows can then merge the `Paint` events if appropriate, combining the invalidated areas, so that the painting is only done once.

- The code to do the painting is probably going to be one of the most complex parts of the code in your application, especially if you have a very sophisticated user interface. The people who have to maintain your code in a couple of years time will thank you for having kept your painting code all in one place and as simple as you reasonably can — something that is easier to do if you do not have too many pathways into it from other parts of the program.

The bottom line from all of this is that it is good practice to keep all of your painting in the `OnPaint()` routine, or in other methods called from that method. However, you have to strike a balance; if you want to replace just one character on the screen and you know perfectly well that it won't affect anything else that you have drawn, then you might decide that it's not worth the overhead of going through `Invalidate()` and just write a separate drawing routine.

In a very complicated application, you might even write a full class that takes responsibility for drawing to the screen. A few years ago when MFC was the standard technology for GDI-intensive applications, MFC followed this model, with a C++ class, `C<ApplicationName>View`*, that was responsible for painting. However, even in this case, this class had one member function,* `OnDraw()`*, which was designed to be the entry point for most drawing requests.*

Calculating Item Sizes and Document Size

This section returns to the `CapsEditor` example and examines the `CalculateLineWidths()` and `CalculateDocumentSize()` methods called from `LoadFile()`:

```
private void CalculateLineWidths()
{
   Graphics dc = this.CreateGraphics();
   foreach (TextLineInformation nextLine in documentLines)
   {
      nextLine.Width = (uint)dc.MeasureString(nextLine.Text,
         mainFont).Width;
   }
}
```

This method simply runs through each line that has been read in and uses the `Graphics.MeasureString()` method to work out and store how much horizontal screen space the string requires. You store the value because `MeasureString()` is computationally intensive. If the `CapsEditor` sample had not been simple enough to easily work out the height and location of each item, then this method would almost certainly have needed to be implemented in such a way as to compute all those quantities, too.

Now that you know how big each item on the screen is and you can calculate where each item goes, you are in a position to work out the actual document size. The height is the number of lines multiplied by the height of each line. The width will need to be worked out by iterating through the lines to find the longest. For both height and width, you will also want to make an allowance for a small margin around the displayed document to make the application look more attractive.

The following is the method that calculates the document size:

```
private void CalculateDocumentSize()
{
   if (!documentHasData)
```

```
      {
         documentSize = new Size(100, 200);
      }
      else
      {
         documentSize.Height = (int)(nLines*lineHeight) + 2*(int)margin;
         uint maxLineLength = 0;
         foreach (TextLineInformation nextWord in documentLines)
         {
            uint tempLineLength = nextWord.Width;
            if (tempLineLength > maxLineLength)
            {
               maxLineLength = tempLineLength;
            }
         }
         maxLineLength += 2*margin;
         documentSize.Width = (int)maxLineLength;
      }
      AutoScrollMinSize = documentSize;
   }
```

This method first checks whether there is any data to be displayed. If there is not, then you cheat a bit and use a hard-coded document size, which is big enough to display the big red `<Empty Document>` warning. If you had wanted to really do it properly, you would have used `MeasureString()` to check how big that warning actually is.

Once you have worked out the document size, you tell the `Form` instance what the size is by setting the `Form.AutoScrollMinSize` property. When you do this, something interesting happens behind the scenes. In the process of setting this property, the client area is invalidated and a `Paint` event is raised, for the very sensible reason that changing the size of the document means scroll bars will need to be added or modified and the entire client area will almost certainly be repainted. Why is that interesting? If you look back at the code for `LoadFile()`, you will realize that the call to `Invalidate()` in that method is actually redundant. The client area will be invalidated anyway when you set the document size. The explicit call to `Invalidate()` was left in the `LoadFile()` implementation to illustrate how you should normally do things. In fact, in this case, calling `Invalidate()` again will only needlessly request a duplicate `Paint` event. However, this in turn illustrates how `Invalidate()` gives Windows the chance to optimize performance. The second `Paint` event will not, in fact, get raised: Windows will see that there is a `Paint` event already sitting in the queue and will compare the requested invalidated regions to see if it needs to do anything to merge them. In this case, both `Paint` events will specify the entire client area, so nothing needs to be done, and Windows will quietly drop the second `Paint` request. Of course, going through that process will take up a little bit of processor time, but it will be a negligible amount of time compared to how long it takes to actually do some painting.

OnPaint()

Now that you have seen how `CapsEditor` loads the file, it's time to look at how the painting is done:

```
protected override void OnPaint(PaintEventArgs e)
{
   base.OnPaint(e);
   Graphics dc = e.Graphics;
   int scrollPositionX = AutoScrollPosition.X;
   int scrollPositionY = AutoScrollPosition.Y;
   dc.TranslateTransform(scrollPositionX, scrollPositionY);
```

(continued)

(continued)

```
      if (!documentHasData)
      {
         dc.DrawString("<Empty document>", emptyDocumentFont,
            emptyDocumentBrush, new Point(20,20));
         base.OnPaint(e);
         return;
      }
      // work out which lines are in clipping rectangle
      int minLineInClipRegion =
                  WorldYCoordinateToLineIndex(e.ClipRectangle.Top -
                                                scrollPositionY);
      if (minLineInClipRegion == -1)
      {
         minLineInClipRegion = 0;
      }
      int maxLineInClipRegion =
                  WorldYCoordinateToLineIndex(e.ClipRectangle.Bottom -
                                                scrollPositionY);
      if (maxLineInClipRegion >= documentLines.Count ||
         maxLineInClipRegion == -1)
      {
         maxLineInClipRegion = documentLines.Count-1;
      }
      TextLineInformation nextLine;
      for (int i=minLineInClipRegion; i<=maxLineInClipRegion ; i++)
      {
         nextLine = (TextLineInformation)documentLines[i];
         dc.DrawString(nextLine.Text, mainFont, mainBrush,
                  LineIndexToWorldCoordinates(i));
      }
   }
```

At the heart of this `OnPaint()` override is a loop that goes through each line of the document, calling `Graphics.DrawString()` to paint each one. The rest of this code is mostly concerned with optimizing the painting — figuring out what exactly needs painting instead of rushing in and telling the graphics instance to redraw everything.

You begin by checking if there is any data in the document. If there is not, then you draw a quick message saying so, call the base class's `OnPaint()` implementation, and exit. If there is data, then you start looking at the clipping rectangle by calling another method, `WorldYCoordinateToLineIndex()`. This method is examined next, but essentially it takes a given y position relative to the top of the document, and works out what line of the document is being displayed at that point.

The first time you call the `WorldYCoordinateToLineIndex()` method, you pass it the coordinate value `(e.ClipRectangle.Top - scrollPositionY)`. This is just the top of the clipping region, converted to world coordinates. If the return value is `-1`, you play it safe and assume that you need to start at the beginning of the document (this is the case if the top of the clipping region is within the top margin).

Once you have done all that, you essentially repeat the same process for the bottom of the clipping rectangle to find the last line of the document that is inside the clipping region. The indices of the first and last lines are respectively stored in `minLineInClipRegion` and `maxLineInClipRegion`, so then you can just run a `for` loop between these values to do your painting. Inside the painting loop, you actually need to do roughly the reverse transformation to the one performed by `WorldYCoordinateToLineIndex()`. You are given the index of a line of text, and you need to check where it should be drawn. This calculation is actually quite simple, but you have wrapped it up in another method, `LineIndexToWorldCoordinates()`, which returns the required coordinates of the top-left corner of the item. The returned coordinates are world coordinates, but that is fine because you have already called `TranslateTransform()` on the `Graphics` object so that you need to pass it world, rather than page, coordinates when asking it to display items.

Coordinate Transforms

This section examines the implementation of the helper methods that are written in the `CapsEditor` sample to help you with coordinate transforms. These are the `WorldYCoordinateToLineIndex()` and `LineIndexToWorldCoordinates()` methods referred to in the previous section, as well as a couple of other methods.

First, `LineIndexToWorldCoordinates()` takes a given line index, and works out the world coordinates of the top-left corner of that line, using the known margin and line height:

```
private Point LineIndexToWorldCoordinates(int index)
{
   Point TopLeftCorner = new Point(
      (int)margin, (int)(lineHeight*index + margin));
   return TopLeftCorner;
}
```

You also use a method that roughly does the reverse transform in `OnPaint()`. `WorldYCoordinateToLineIndex()` works out the line index, but it takes into account only a vertical world coordinate because it is used to work out the line index corresponding to the top and bottom of the clip region:

```
private int WorldYCoordinateToLineIndex(int y)
{
   if (y < margin)
   {
      return -1;
   }
   return (int)((y-margin)/lineHeight);
}
```

There are three more methods, which will be called from the handler routine that responds to the user double-clicking the mouse. First, you have a method that works out the index of the line being displayed at given world coordinates. Unlike `WorldYCoordinateToLineIndex()`, this method takes into account the x and y positions of the coordinates. It returns `-1` if there is no line of text covering the coordinates passed in:

```
private int WorldCoordinatesToLineIndex(Point position)
{
   if (!documentHasData)
   {
      return -1;
   }
   if (position.Y < margin || position.X < margin)
   {
      return -1;
   }
   int index = (int)(position.Y-margin)/(int)this.lineHeight;
   // check position is not below document
```

(continued)

(continued)

```
      if (index >= documentLines.Count)
      {
         return -1;
      }
      // now check that horizontal position is within this line
      TextLineInformation theLine =
                              (TextLineInformation)documentLines[index];
      if (position.X > margin + theLine.Width)
      {
         return -1;
      }
      // all is OK. We can return answer
      return index;
   }
```

Finally, on occasion, you also need to convert between line index and page, rather than world, coordinates. The following methods achieve this:

```
   private Point LineIndexToPageCoordinates(int index)
   {
      return LineIndexToWorldCoordinates(index) +
                                          new Size(AutoScrollPosition);
   }
   private int PageCoordinatesToLineIndex(Point position)
   {
      return WorldCoordinatesToLineIndex(position - new
                                          Size(AutoScrollPosition));
   }
```

Note that when converting *to* page coordinates, you add the `AutoScrollPosition`, which is negative.

Although these methods by themselves do not look particularly interesting, they do illustrate a general technique that you will probably need to use often. With GDI+, you will often find yourself in a situation where you have been given specific coordinates (for example the coordinates of where the user has clicked the mouse), and you will need to figure out what item is being displayed at that point. Or it could happen the other way around — given a particular display item, where should it be displayed? Hence, if you are writing a GDI+ application, you will probably find it useful to write methods that do the equivalent of the coordinate transformation methods illustrated here.

Responding to User Input

So far, with the exception of the File menu in the `CapsEditor` sample, everything you have done in this chapter has been one way: The application has talked to the user by displaying information on the screen. Almost all software of course works both ways: the user can talk to the software as well. You are now going to add that functionality to `CapsEditor`.

Getting a GDI+ application to respond to user input is actually a lot simpler than writing the code to draw to the screen. (Chapter 31, "Windows Forms," covers how to handle user input.) Essentially, you override methods from the `Form` class that are called from the relevant event handler, in much the same way that `OnPaint()` is called when a `Paint` event is raised.

The following table lists the methods you might want to override when the user clicks or moves the mouse.

Method	Called When . . .
`OnClick(EventArgs e)`	Mouse is clicked.
`OnDoubleClick(EventArgs e)`	Mouse is double-clicked.
`OnMouseDown(MouseEventArgs e)`	Left mouse button is pressed.
`OnMouseHover(MouseEventArgs e)`	Mouse stays still somewhere after moving.
`OnMouseMove(MouseEventArgs e)`	Mouse is moved.
`OnMouseUp(MouseEventArgs e)`	Left mouse button is released.

If you want to detect when the user types in any text, then you will probably want to override the methods listed in the following table.

Method	Called When . . .
`OnKeyDown(KeyEventArgs e)`	A key is pressed.
`OnKeyPress(KeyPressEventArgs e)`	A key is pressed and released.
`OnKeyUp(KeyEventArgs e)`	A pressed key is released.

Note that some of these events overlap. For example, when the user presses a mouse button, the `MouseDown` event is raised. If the button is immediately released again, then this will raise the `MouseUp` event and the `Click` event. In addition, some of these methods take an argument that is derived from `EventArgs` rather than an instance of `EventArgs` itself. These instances of derived classes can be used to give more information about a particular event. `MouseEventArgs` has two properties, `X` and `Y`, which give the device coordinates of the mouse at the time it was pressed. Both `KeyEventArgs` and `KeyPressEventArgs` have properties that indicate which key or keys the event concerns.

That is all there is to it. It is up to you to think about the logic of precisely what you want to do. The only point to note is that you will probably find yourself doing a bit more logic work with a GDI+ application than you would have with a `Windows.Forms` application. That is because in a `Windows.Forms` application you are typically responding to high-level events (`TextChanged` for a text box, for example). By contrast, with GDI+, the events tend to be more elementary — user clicks the mouse or presses the H key. The action your application takes is likely to depend on a sequence of events rather than on a single event. For example, say your application works like Microsoft Word for Windows: to select some text, the user clicks the left mouse button, and then moves the mouse and releases the left mouse button. Your application receives the `MouseDown` event, but there is not much you can do with this event except record that the mouse was clicked with the cursor in a certain position. Then, when the `MouseMove` event is received, you will want to check from the record whether the left button is currently down, and if so, highlight text as the user selects it. When the user releases the left mouse button, your corresponding action (in the `OnMouseUp()` method) will need to check whether any dragging took place while the mouse button was down and act accordingly within the method. Only at this point is the sequence complete.

Another point to consider is that, because certain events overlap, you will often have a choice of which event you want your code to respond to.

The golden rule is to think carefully about the logic of every combination of mouse movement or click and keyboard event that the user might initiate, and ensure that your application responds in a way that is intuitive and in accordance with the expected behavior of applications in *every* case. Most of your work here will be in thinking rather than in coding, although the coding you do will be tricky because you might need to take into account many combinations of user input. For example, what should your application do if the user starts typing in text while one of the mouse buttons is held down? It might sound like an improbable combination, but eventually some user is going to try it!

The `CapsEditor` example keeps things very simple, so you do not really have any combinations to think about. The only thing you are going to respond to in the example is when the user double-clicks, in which case you capitalize whatever line of text the mouse pointer is hovering over.

This should be a simple task, but there is one snag. You need to trap the `DoubleClick` event, but the previous table shows that this event takes an `EventArgs` parameter, not a `MouseEventArgs` parameter. The trouble is that you need to know where the mouse is when the user double-clicks if you are to identify correctly the line of text to be capitalized — and you need a `MouseEventArgs` parameter to do that. There are two workarounds. One is to use a static method implemented by the `Form1` object `Control.MousePosition` to find the mouse position:

```
protected override void OnDoubleClick(EventArgs e)
{
   Point MouseLocation = Control.MousePosition;
   // handle double click
}
```

In most cases, this will work. However, there could be a problem if your application (or even some other application with a high priority) is doing some computationally intensive work at the moment the user double-clicks. It just might happen in that case that the `OnDoubleClick()` event handler does not get called until perhaps half a second or so *after* the user has double-clicked. You do not want such delays because they usually annoy users intensely, but even so, occasionally it does happen and sometimes for reasons beyond the control of your application (a slow computer, for instance). The trouble is that half a second is easily enough time for the mouse to be moved halfway across the screen, in which case your call to `Control.MousePosition` will return the completely wrong location!

A better approach here is to rely on one of the many overlaps between mouse event meanings. The first part of double-clicking a mouse involves pressing the left button down. This means that if `OnDoubleClick()` is called, you know that `OnMouseDown()` has also just been called, with the mouse at the same location. You can use the `OnMouseDown()` override to record the position of the mouse, ready for `OnDoubleClick()`. This is the approach taken in `CapsEditor`:

```
      protected override void OnMouseDown(MouseEventArgs e)
      {
         base.OnMouseDown(e);
         mouseDoubleClickPosition = new Point(e.X, e.Y);
      }
```

Now look at the `OnDoubleClick()` override. There is quite a bit more work to do here:

```
      protected override void OnDoubleClick(EventArgs e)
      {
         int i = PageCoordinatesToLineIndex(mouseDoubleClickPosition);
         if (i >= 0)
         {
            TextLineInformation lineToBeChanged =
                                (TextLineInformation)documentLines[i];
            lineToBeChanged.Text = lineToBeChanged.Text.ToUpper();
            Graphics dc = this.CreateGraphics();
            uint newWidth =(uint)dc.MeasureString(lineToBeChanged.Text,
                                                   mainFont).Width;
```

```
            if (newWidth > lineToBeChanged.Width)
               lineToBeChanged.Width = newWidth;
            if (newWidth+2*margin > this.documentSize.Width)
            {
               documentSize.Width = (int)newWidth;
               AutoScrollMinSize = this.documentSize;
            }
            Rectangle changedRectangle = new Rectangle(
                                        LineIndexToPageCoordinates(i),
                                        new Size((int)newWidth,
                                        (int)this.lineHeight));
            Invalidate(changedRectangle);
         }
         base.OnDoubleClick(e);
      }
```

You start off by calling `PageCoordinatesToLineIndex()` to work out which line of text the mouse pointer was hovering over when the user double-clicked. If this call returns `-1`, then you weren't over any text, so there is nothing to do — except, of course, call the base class version of `OnDoubleClick()` to let Windows do any default processing.

Assuming that you have identified a line of text, you can use the `string.ToUpper()` method to convert it to uppercase. That was the easy part. The hard part is figuring out what needs to be redrawn where. Fortunately, because this example is simple, there are not too many combinations. You can assume that converting to uppercase will always either leave the width of the line on the screen unchanged or increase it. Capital letters are bigger than lowercase letters; therefore, the width will never go down. You also know that because you are not wrapping lines, your line of text will not overflow to the next line and push out other text below. Your action of converting the line to uppercase will not, therefore, actually change the locations of any of the other items being displayed. That is a big simplification!

The next thing the code does is use `Graphics.MeasureString()` to work out the new width of the text. There are now just two possibilities:

- The new width might make your line the longest line and cause the width of the entire document to increase. If that is the case, then you will need to set `AutoScrollMinSize` to the new size so that the scroll bars are correctly placed.
- The size of the document might be unchanged.

In either case, you need to get the screen redrawn by calling `Invalidate()`. Only one line has changed; therefore, you do not want to have the entire document repainted. Rather, you need to work out the bounds of a rectangle that contains just the modified line, so that you can pass this rectangle to `Invalidate()`, ensuring that just that line of text will be repainted. That is precisely what the previous code does. Your call to `Invalidate()` initiates a call to `OnPaint()` when the mouse event handler finally returns. Keeping in mind the earlier comments about the difficulty in setting a break point in `OnPaint()`, if you run the sample and set a break point in `OnPaint()` to trap the resultant painting action, then you will find that the `PaintEventArgs` parameter to `OnPaint()` does indeed contain a clipping region that matches the specified rectangle. And because you have overloaded `OnPaint()` to take careful account of the clipping region, only the one required line of text will be repainted.

Printing

So far, the chapter has focused exclusively on drawing to the screen. However, at some point you will probably also want to be able to produce a hard copy of the data. That is the topic of this section. You are going to extend the `CapsEditor` sample so that it is able to print preview and print the document that is being edited.

Unfortunately, there is not enough space to go into too much detail about printing here, so the printing functionality you will implement is very basic. Typically, when you are implementing the ability for an application to print data, you will need to add three items to the application's main File menu:

- **Page Setup**, which allows the user to choose options such as which pages to print, which printer to use, and so on.
- **Print Preview**, which opens a new Form that displays a mock-up of what the printed copy should look like.
- **Print**, which prints the document.

In this case, to keep things simple, you will not implement a Page Setup menu option. Printing will only be possible using default settings. Note, however, that if you do want to implement Page Setup, Microsoft has already written a page setup dialog class for you to use `System.Windows.Forms.PrintDialog`. You will normally want to write an event handler that displays this form and saves the settings chosen by the user.

In many ways, printing is just the same as displaying to a screen. You will be supplied with a device context (`Graphics` instance) and call all the usual display commands against that instance. Microsoft has written a number of classes to assist you in doing this; the two main ones that you need to use are `System.Drawing.Printing.PrintDocument` and `System.Drawing.Printing.PrintPreviewDialog`. These two classes handle the process of making sure that drawing instructions passed to a device context are handled appropriately for printing, leaving you to think about the logic of what to print where.

Some important differences exist between printing or print previewing on the one hand, and displaying to the screen on the other hand. Printers cannot scroll; instead, they turn out pages. Therefore, you will need to make sure that you find a sensible way of dividing your document into pages and draw each page as requested. Among other things, that means calculating how much of your document will fit onto a single page and, therefore, how many pages you will need and which page each part of the document needs to be written to.

Despite these complications, the process of printing is quite simple. Programmatically, the steps you need to go through look roughly like this:

- **Printing** — You instantiate a `PrintDocument` object and call its `Print()` method. This method signals the `PrintPage` event to print the first page. `PrintPage` takes a `PrintPageEventArgs` parameter, which supplies information concerning paper size and setup, as well as a `Graphics` object used for the drawing commands. You should therefore have written an event handler for this event, and have implemented this handler to print a page. This event handler should also set a Boolean property of the `PrintPageEventArgs` called `HasMorePages` to either `true` or `false` to indicate whether there are more pages to be printed. The `PrintDocument.Print()` method will repeatedly raise the `PrintPage` event until it sees that `HasMorePages` has been set to `false`.
- **Print Previewing** — In this case, you instantiate both a `PrintDocument` object and a `PrintPreviewDialog` object. You attach the `PrintDocument` to the `PrintPreviewDialog` (using the property `PrintPreviewDialog.Document`) and then call the dialog's `ShowDialog()` method. This method modally displays the dialog, which turns out to be a standard Windows print preview form and which displays pages of the document. Internally, the pages are displayed once again by repeatedly raising the `PrintPage` event until the `HasMorePages` property is `false`. There is no need to write a separate event handler for this; you can use the same event handler as used for printing each page because the drawing code ought to be identical in both cases. (After all, whatever is print previewed ought to look identical to the printed version!)

Implementing Print and Print Preview

Now that this process has been outlined in broad strokes, in this section you see how this works in code terms. You can download the code as the `PrintingCapsEdit` project at `www.wrox.com`; it consists of the `CapsEditor` project with the changes displayed in the following snippet.

You begin by using the Visual Studio 2008 design view to add two new items to the File menu: Print and Print Preview. You also use the properties window to name these items `menuFilePrint` and `menuFilePrintPreview`, and to set them to be disabled when the application starts up (you cannot print anything until a document has been opened!). You arrange for these menu items to be enabled by adding the following code to the main form's `LoadFile()` method, which is responsible for loading a file into the `CapsEditor` application:

```
private void LoadFile(string FileName)
{
   StreamReader sr = new StreamReader(FileName);
   string nextLine;
   documentLines.Clear();
   nLines = 0;
   TextLineInformation nextLineInfo;
   while ( (nextLine = sr.ReadLine()) != null)
   {
      nextLineInfo = new TextLineInformation();
      nextLineInfo.Text = nextLine;
      documentLines.Add(nextLineInfo);
      ++nLines;
   }
   sr.Close();
   if (nLines > 0)
   {
      documentHasData = true;
      menuFilePrint.Enabled = true;
      menuFilePrintPreview.Enabled = true;
   }
   else
   {
      documentHasData = false;
      menuFilePrint.Enabled = false;
      menuFilePrintPreview.Enabled = false;
   }
   CalculateLineWidths();
   CalculateDocumentSize();
   Text = standardTitle + " - " + FileName;
   Invalidate();
}
```

The above code is the new code added to this method. Next, you add a member field to the `Form1` class:

```
public partial class Form1 : Form
{
   private int pagesPrinted = 0;
```

This field will be used to indicate which page you are currently printing. You are making it a member field because you will need to remember this information between calls to the `PrintPage` event handler.

Next, you will find the event handlers that handle the selection of the Print or Print Preview menu options:

```
private void menuFilePrintPreview_Click(object sender, System.EventArgs e)
{
   this.pagesPrinted = 0;
   PrintPreviewDialog ppd = new PrintPreviewDialog();
   PrintDocument pd = new PrintDocument();
   pd.PrintPage += this.pd_PrintPage;
   ppd.Document = pd;
   ppd.ShowDialog();
}
private void menuFilePrint_Click(object sender, System.EventArgs e)
{
   this.pagesPrinted = 0;
   PrintDocument pd = new PrintDocument();
   pd.PrintPage += new PrintPageEventHandler
      (this.pd_PrintPage);
   pd.Print();
}
```

You have already seen the steps involved in printing, and you can see that these event handlers are simply implementing that procedure. In both cases, you are instantiating a `PrintDocument` object and attaching an event handler to its `PrintPage` event. In the case of printing, you call `PrintDocument.Print()`, whereas for print previewing, you attach the `PrintDocument` object to a `PrintPreviewDialog` and call the preview dialog box object's `ShowDialog()` method. The real work to the `PrintPage` event is done in the event handler. Here is what this handler looks like:

```
private void pd_PrintPage(object sender, PrintPageEventArgs e)
{
   float yPos = 0;
   float leftMargin = e.MarginBounds.Left;
   float topMargin = e.MarginBounds.Top;
   string line = null;
   // Calculate the number of lines per page.
   int linesPerPage = (int)(e.MarginBounds.Height /
      mainFont.GetHeight(e.Graphics));
   int lineNo = pagesPrinted * linesPerPage;
   // Print each line of the file.
   int count = 0;
   while(count < linesPerPage && lineNo < this.nLines)
   {
      line = ((TextLineInformation)this.documentLines[lineNo]).Text;
      yPos = topMargin + (count * mainFont.GetHeight(e.Graphics));
      e.Graphics.DrawString(line, mainFont, Brushes.Blue,
         leftMargin, yPos, new StringFormat());
      lineNo++;
      count++;
   }
   // If more lines exist, print another page.
   if(this.nLines > lineNo)
      e.HasMorePages = true;
   else
      e.HasMorePages = false;
   pagesPrinted++;
}
```

After declaring a couple of local variables, the first thing you do is work out how many lines of text can be displayed on one page, which will be the height of a page divided by the height of a line and rounded down. The height of the page can be obtained from the `PrintPageEventArgs.MarginBounds` property. This property is a `RectangleF` struct that has been initialized to give the bounds of the page. The height of a line is obtained from the `Form1.mainFont` field, which is the font used for displaying the text. There is no reason here for not using the same font for printing too. Note that for the `PrintingCapsEditor` sample, the number of lines per page is always the same, so you arguably could have cached the value the first time you calculated it. However, the calculation is not too hard, and in a more sophisticated application the value might change, so it is not bad practice to recalculate it every time you print a page.

You also initialize a variable called `lineNo`. This gives the zero-based index of the line of the document that will be the first line of this page. This information is important because, in principle, the `pd_PrintPage()` method could have been called to print any page, not just the first page. `lineNo` is computed as the number of lines per page times the number of pages that have so far been printed.

Next, you run through a loop, printing each line. This loop will terminate either when you find that you have printed all the lines of text in the document, or when you find that you have printed all the lines that will fit on this page, whichever condition occurs first. Finally, you check whether there is any more of the document to be printed, and set the `HasMorePages` property of your `PrintPageEventArgs` accordingly. You also increment the `pagesPrinted` field so that you know to print the correct page the next time the `PrintPage` event handler is invoked.

One point to note about this event handler is that you do not worry about where the drawing commands are being sent. You simply use the `Graphics` object that was supplied with the `PrintPageEventArgs`. The `PrintDocument` class that Microsoft has written will internally take care of making sure that, if you are printing, the `Graphics` object has been hooked up to the printer; if you are print previewing, then the `Graphics` object has been hooked up to the print preview form on the screen.

Finally, you need to ensure that the `System.Drawing.Printing` namespace is searched for type definitions:

```
using System;
using System.Collections.Generic;
using System.ComponentModel;
using System.Data;
using System.Drawing;
using System.Drawing.Printing;
using System.Text;
using System.Windows.Forms;
using System.IO;
```

All that remains is to compile the project and check that the code works. Figure 33-19 shows what happens when you run `CapsEdit`, load a text document (as before, you have picked the C# source file for the project), and select Print Preview.

In Figure 33-19, the document is scrolled to page 5 and the preview is set to display normal size. The `PrintPreviewDialog` has supplied quite a lot of features, as you can see by looking at the toolbar at the top of the form. The options available include printing the document, zooming in or out, and displaying two, three, four, or six pages together. These options are all fully functional, without your having to do any work. Figure 33-20 shows the result of changing the zoom to auto and clicking to display four pages (third toolbar button from the right).

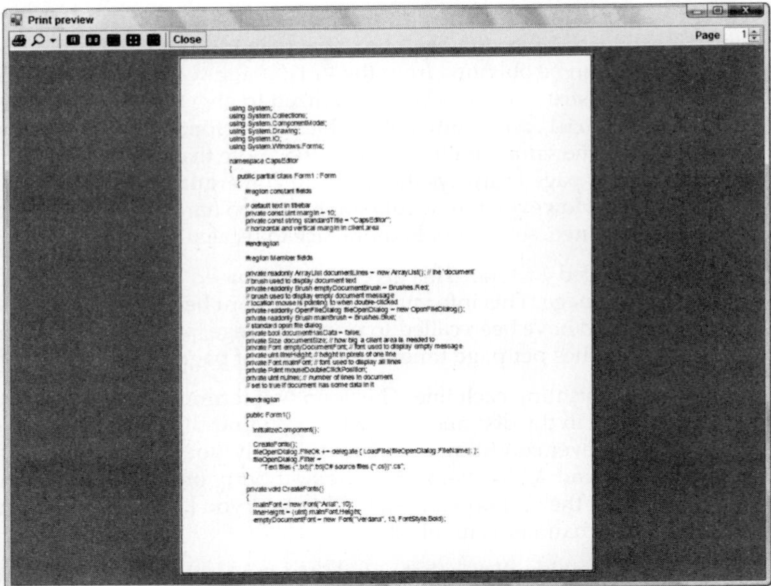

Figure 33-19

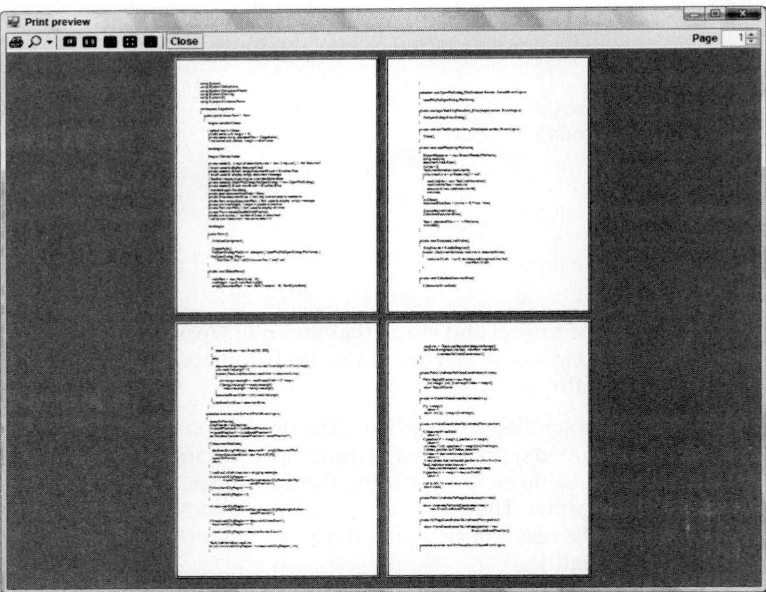

Figure 33-20

Summary

This chapter covered the realm of GDI+ — the area of drawing to a display device, where the drawing is done by your code rather than by some predefined control or dialog box. GDI+ is a powerful tool, and there are many .NET base classes available to help you draw to a device. You have seen that the process of drawing is actually relatively simple. In most cases you can draw text or sophisticated figures or display images with just a couple of C# statements. However, managing your drawing — the behind-the-scenes work involving working out what to draw, where to draw it, and what does or does not need repainting in any given situation — is far more complex and requires careful algorithm design. For this reason, it is also important to have a good understanding of how GDI+ works and what actions Windows takes to get something drawn. In particular, because of the architecture of Windows, it is important that, where possible, drawing should be done by invalidating areas of the window and relying on Windows to respond by issuing a `Paint` event.

Many more .NET classes can be used for drawing than there is space to cover in this chapter. However, if you have worked through it and understood the principles involved in drawing, then you will be in an excellent position to explore these classes by looking at their lists of methods in the SDK documentation and instantiating instances of them to see what they do. In the end, drawing, as with almost any other aspect of programming, requires logic, careful thought, and clear algorithms if you want to go beyond the standard controls. Your software will benefit in both user-friendliness and visual appearance if it is well thought out. Many applications out there rely entirely on controls for their user interface. Although this can be effective, such applications very quickly end up resembling each other. By adding some GDI+ code to do some custom drawing you can mark out your software as distinct and make it appear more original, which can only help increase your sales!

The next chapter takes a look at the latest thick-client presentation technology — Windows Presentation Foundation (WPF).

34

Windows Presentation Foundation

Windows Presentation Foundation (WPF) is one of the major extensions of .NET Framework 3.0. WPF is a new library to create the UI for smart client applications. While the Windows Forms controls are native Windows controls that use Window handles that are based on screen pixels, WPF is based on DirectX. The application does not use Window handles. It is easy to resize the UI, and it supports sound and video.

The main topics of this chapter are, as follows:

- An overview of WPF
- Shapes as the base drawing elements
- Scaling, rotating, and skewing with transformations
- Different kind of brushes to fill elements
- WPF controls and their features
- How to define a layout with WPF panels
- The WPF event-handling mechanism
- Styles, templates, and resources

Overview

One of the big features of WPF is that work can be easily separated between designers and developers. The outcome from the designer's work can directly be used by the developer. To make this possible, you need to understand XAML. The first topic of this chapter gives you an overview of WPF, including enough information to understand the principles of XAML. It also covers information on how designers and developers can cooperate. WPF consists of several assemblies containing thousands of classes. So that you can navigate within this vast number of classes and find what you need, the overview explains the class hierarchy and namespaces in WPF.

XAML

XML for Applications Markup Language (XAML) is an XML syntax used to define the hierarchical structure of the user interface. In the following line, you can see the declaration of a button named `button1` with the content `Click Me!`. The `<Button>` element specifies the use of the `Button` class:

```
<Button Name="button1">Click Me!</Button>
```

There's always a .NET class behind an XAML element. With attributes and child elements, you set the value of properties and define handler methods for events.

To test simple XAML code, you can start the utility XAMLPad.exe (see Figure 34-1) and enter the XAML code in the edit field. You can write the `<Button>` element within the `<Page>` and `<Grid>` elements that are already prepared from XAMLPad. With XAMLPad, you can see the XAML outcome immediately.

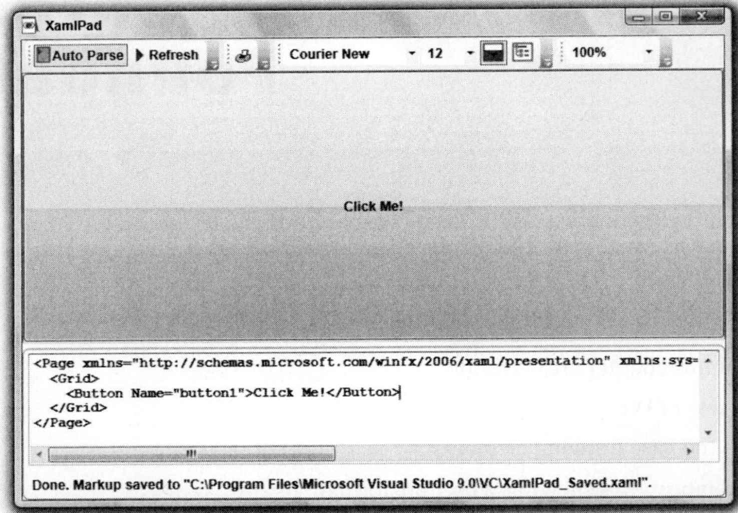

Figure 34-1

XAML code can be interpreted by the WPF runtime, but it can also be compiled to BAML (Binary Application Markup Language), which is done by default by Visual Studio WPF projects. BAML is added as a resource to the executable.

Instead of writing XAML, you can also create a button with C# code. You can create a normal C# console application, add references to the assemblies `WindowsBase`, `PresentationCore`, and `PresentationFramework`, and write the following code. In the `Main()` method, a `Window` object from the namespace `System.Windows` is created, and the property `Title` is set. Then a `Button` object from the namespace `System.Windows.Controls` is created, the `Content` is set, and the `Content` of the window is set to the button. The `Run()` method of the `Application` class is responsible for processing Windows messages:

```
using System;
using System.Windows;
using System.Windows.Controls;
namespace Wrox.ProCSharp.WPF
```

```
{
   class Program
   {
      [STAThread]
      static void Main()
      {
         Window mainWindow = new Window();
         mainWindow.Title = "WPF Application";
         Button button1 = new Button();
         button1.Content = "Click Me!";
         mainWindow.Content = button1;
         button1.Click +=
            (sender, e) => MessageBox.Show("Button clicked");
         Application app = new Application();
         app.Run(mainWindow);
      }
   }
}
```

The `Application` *class can also be defined by using XAML. With a Visual Studio WPF project, open the file* `App.xaml` *that includes the properties and* `StartupUri` *of the* `Application` *class.*

Running the application, you get a Window containing the button, as shown in Figure 34-2.

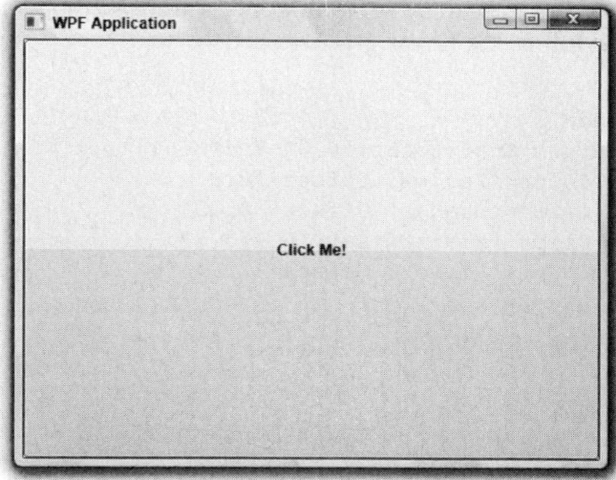

Figure 34-2

As you can see, programming WPF is very similar to Windows Forms programming — with the small difference that the `Button` has a `Content` instead of a `Text` property. However, compared to creating the UI forms with code, XAML has some great advantages. With XAML, the designer and developer can cooperate much better. The designer can work on the XAML code and design a stylish UI, while the developer adds functionality from the code behind using C#. It's much easier to separate the UI from the functionality by using XAML.

You can directly interact with the elements that are defined with XAML from the C# code using code behind and XAML. You just need to define a name for the element and use the same name as a variable to change properties and invoke methods.

The button has a `Content` property instead of a `Text` property because the button can show anything. You can add text to the content, but also a graphic, a list box, a video — whatever you can think of.

Properties as Attributes

Before working with XAML, you need to know important characteristics of the XAML syntax. You can use XML attributes to specify the properties of classes. The example shows the setting of the `Content` and `Background` properties of the `Button` class:

```
<Button Content="Click Me!" Background="LightGreen" />
```

Properties as Elements

Instead of using XML attributes, the properties can also be specified as child elements. The value for the content can be directly set by specifying the child elements of the `Button` element. For all other properties of the `Button`, the name of the child element is defined by the name of the outer element, followed by the property name:

```
<Button>
  <Button.Background>
    LightGreen
  </Button.Background>
  Click Me!
</Button>
```

In the previous example, it is not necessary to use child elements. By using XML attributes, the same result was achieved. However, using attributes is no longer possible if the value is more complex than a string. For example, the background can be set to not only a simple color but also to a brush. For example, you can define the following linear gradient brush:

```
<Button>
   <Button.Background>
    <LinearGradientBrush StartPoint="0,0" EndPoint="1,1">
      <GradientStop Color="Yellow" Offset="0.0" />
      <GradientStop Color="Orange" Offset="0.25" />
      <GradientStop Color="Red" Offset="0.75" />
      <GradientStop Color="Violet" Offset="1.0" />
    </LinearGradientBrush>
  </Button.Background>
  Click Me!
</Button>
```

Dependency Property

When programming WPF, you often come across the term *dependency property*. WPF elements are classes with methods, properties, and events. Nearly every property of a WPF element is a dependency property. What does this mean? A dependency property can be dependent on other inputs; for example, themes and user preferences. Dependency properties are used with data binding, animation, resources, and styles.

From the programmatic viewpoint, a dependency property can be read and written not only by invoking the strongly typed property but also by methods passing a dependency property object.

Only a class that derives from the base class `DependencyObject` can include dependency properties. The following class, `MyDependencyObject`, defines the dependency property `SomeState`. `SomeStateProperty` is a static field of type `DependencyProperty` that backs the dependency property. The dependency property is registered with the WPF dependency property system using the `Register()` method. The `Register()` method gets the name of the dependency property, the type of the dependency property, and the owner type. You can set the value of the dependency property by using the `SetValue()` method of the `DependencyObject` base class, and get the value by using the method `GetValue()`. Dependency properties usually have a strongly typed access as well. Instead of using the methods of the `DependencyObject` base class, the class `MyDependencyObject` includes the property `SomeState`, which invokes the methods of the base class from the implementation of the set and get accessors. You shouldn't do something else in the implementation of the set and get accessors as these property accessors might not be invoked.

```
public class MyDependencyObject : DependencyObject
{
   public static readonly DependencyProperty SomeStateProperty =
      DependencyProperty.Register("SomeState", typeof(String),
         typeof(MyDependencyObject));

   public string SomeState
   {
      get { return (string)this.GetValue(SomeStateProperty); }
      set { this.SetValue(SomeStateProperty, value); }
   }
}
```

With WPF, the class `DependencyObject` *is very high in the hierarchy. Every WPF element is derived from this base class.*

Attached Property

A WPF element can also get features from the parent element. For example, if the `Button` element is located inside a `Canvas` element, the button has `Top` and `Left` properties that are prefixed with the parent element's name. Such a property is known as *attached property:*

```
<Canvas>
  <Button Canvas.Top="30" Canvas.Left="40">
    Click Me!
  </Button>
</Canvas>
```

Writing the same functionality from the code behind is a bit different because the `Button` class doesn't have a `Canvas.Top` and `Canvas.Left` property, even if it is contained within the `Canvas` class. There is a naming pattern for setting attached properties that is common with all classes. The class supporting attached properties has static methods with the names `Set<Property>` and `Get<Property>`, where the first parameter is the object that the property value is applied to. The `Canvas` class defines the static methods `SetLeft()` and `SetTop()` to get the same result as in the XAML code shown earlier.

```
[STAThread]
static void Main()
{
   Window mainWindow = new Window();
   Canvas canvas = new Canvas();
   mainWindow.Content = canvas;
   Button button1 = new Button();
   canvas.Children.Add(button1);
   button1.Content = "Click Me!";
   Canvas.SetLeft(button1, 40);
   Canvas.SetTop(button1, 30);
   Application app = new Application();
   app.Run(mainWindow);
}
```

An attached property can be implemented as a dependency object. The method `DependencyProperty.RegisterAttached()` *registers an attached property.*

Markup Extensions

When setting values for elements, you can set the value directly. However, sometimes markup extensions are very helpful. Markup extensions consist of curly brackets followed by a string token that defines the type of the markup extension. Here is an example of a `StaticResource` markup extension:

```
<Button Name="button1" Style="{StaticResource key}" Content="Click Me" />
```

Instead of using the markup extension, you can write the same thing using child elements:

```
<Button Name="button1">
  <Button.Style>
    <StaticResource ResourceKey="key" />
  </Button.Style>
  Click Me!
</Button>
```

Markup extensions are mainly used for accessing resources and for data binding. Both of these topics are discussed later in this chapter.

Cooperation of Designers and Developers

Very often, developers not only implement Windows applications, but are also responsible for the design. This is especially true if the application was built just for in-house use. If someone with UI design skills was hired to design the UI, usually the developer is given a JPG file of the designer's vision of how the UI should look. The developer then has the problem of trying to match the designer's plans. Even simple changes by the designer, such as a different look for list boxes or buttons, can lead to a huge investment using owner-drawn controls. As a result, the UI done by the developer looks very different from the UI that was originally designed.

With WPF, this changes. The designer and developer can work on the same XAML code. The designer can use a tool such as Expression Blend, while the developer uses Visual Studio 2008. Both can work using the same project files. In the typical progression of this cooperative process, the designer starts a project with Expression Blend, using the same project files as in Visual Studio. Then the developer takes over to work on the code behind, while the designer enhances the UI. As the developer enhances the functionality, the designer can also add new UI features that take advantage of the functionality provided by the developer.

Of course, it is also possible to start the application with Visual Studio and enhance the UI later with Expression Blend. You just need to be careful not to do a UI as you used to do with Windows Forms because this doesn't take full advantage of WPF.

Figure 34-3 shows Expression Blend that was created by using WPF.

Comparing Expression Blend to Visual Studio extensions, the Expression Blend has great features for defining styles, creating animations, using graphics, and the like. To work cooperatively, the Expression Blend can use code-behind classes done by the developer, and the designer can specify the data binding from the WPF elements to the .NET classes. The designer can also test the complete application by starting it from Expression Blend. Because Expression Blend uses the same MS-Build files as Visual Studio does, the code-behind C# code is compiled to run the application.

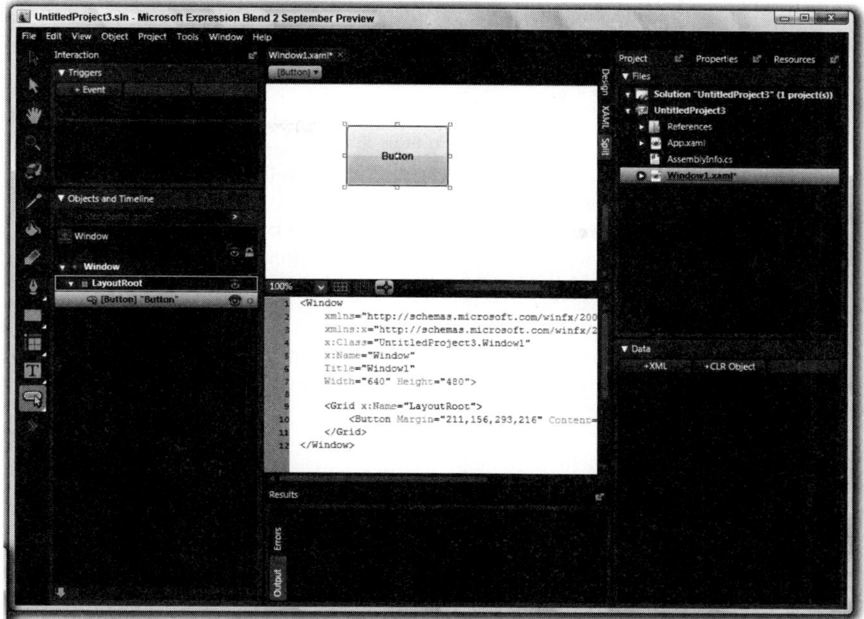

Figure 34-3

Class Hierarchy

WPF consists of thousands of classes with a deep hierarchy. To help in understanding the relationship among the classes, Figure 34-4 shows some of the WPF classes in a class diagram. Some classes and their functionality are described in the following table.

Class	Description
`DispatcherObject`	`DispatcherObject` is an abstract base class for classes that are bound to one thread. Similar to Windows Forms, WPF requires that methods and properties be invoked only from the creator thread. Classes that are derived from `DispatcherObject` have an associated `Dispatcher` object that can be used to switch the thread.
`Application`	In a WPF application, one instance of the `Application` class is created. This class implements a Singleton pattern for access to the windows of the application, resources, and properties.
`DependencyObject`	`DependencyObject` is the base class for all classes that support dependency properties. Dependency properties were discussed earlier.

Class	Description
Visual	The base class for all visual elements is Visual. This class includes features for hit testing and transformation.
UIElement	The abstract base class for all WPF elements that need basic presentation features is UIElement. This class provides tunneling and bubbling events for mouse moves, drag and drop, and key clicks. It exposes virtual methods for rendering that can be overridden by derived classes, and it provides methods for layout. You already know that WPF no longer uses Window handles. You can consider this class equivalent to a Windows handle.
FrameworkElement	FrameworkElement is derived from the base class UIElement and implements the default behavior of the methods defined by the base class.
Shape	Shape is the base class for all shape elements, for example, Line, Ellipse, Polygon, Rectangle.
Control	Control derives from FrameworkElement and is the base class for all user-interactive elements.
Panel	The class Panel derives from FrameworkElement and is the abstract base class for all panels. This class has a Children property for all UI elements within the panel and defines methods for arranging the child controls. Classes that are derived from Panel define different behavior for how the children are organized, for example, WrapPanel, StackPanel, Canvas, Grid.
ContentControl	ContentControl is the base class for all controls that have a single content (for example, Label, Button). The default style of a content control may be limited, but it is possible to change the look by using templates.

As you can see, WPF classes have a really deep hierarchy. In this and the next chapter, you will see classes of the core functionality, but it is not possible to cover all the features of WPF with two chapters.

Namespaces

Classes from Windows Forms and WPF can easily be confused. The Windows Forms classes are located in the namespace System.Windows.Forms, while the WPF classes are located inside the namespace System.Windows and subnamespaces thereof, with the exception of System.Windows.Forms. The Button class for Windows Forms has the full name System.Windows.Forms.Button, and the Button class for WPF has the full name System.Windows.Controls.Button. Windows Forms is covered in Chapters 31 and 32.

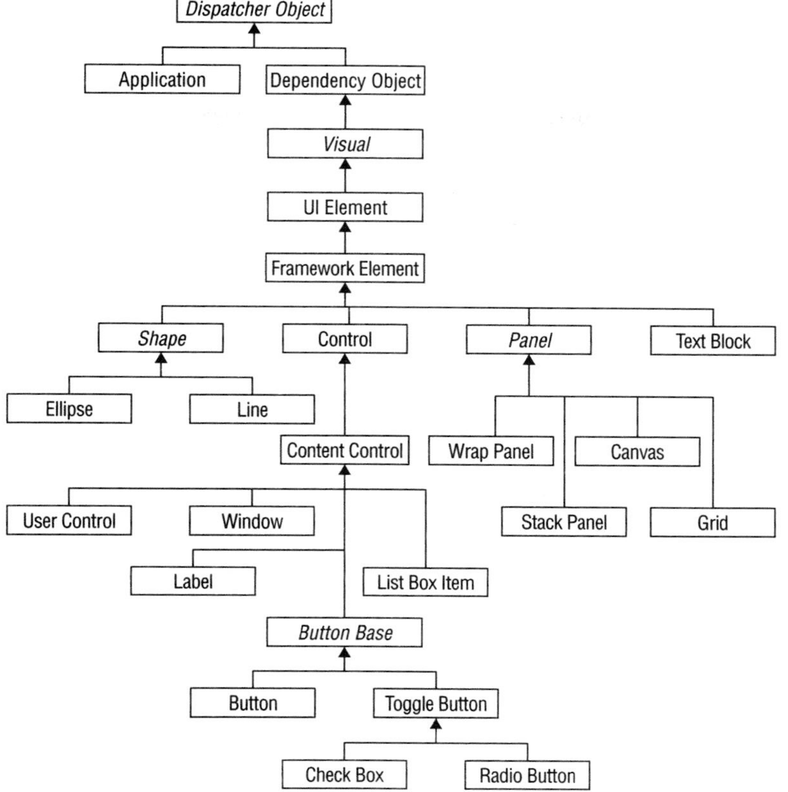

Figure 34-4

Namespaces and their functionality with WPF are described in the following table.

Namespace	Description
`System.Windows`	This is the core namespace of WPF. Here you can find core classes from WPF such as the `Application` class; classes for dependency objects, `DependencyObject` and `DependencyProperty`; and the base class for all WPF elements, `FrameworkElement`.
`System.Windows.Annotations`	The classes from this namespace are used for user-created annotations and notes on application data that are stored separately from the document. The namespace `System.Windows.Annotations.Storage` contains classes for storing annotations.

Namespace	Description
`System.Windows.Automation`	This namespace can be used for automation of WPF applications. Several subnamespaces are available. `System.Windows.Automation.Peers` exposes WPF elements to automation — for example, `ButtonAutomationPeer` and `CheckBoxAutomationPeer`. The namespace `System.Windows.Automation.Provider` is needed if you create a custom automation provider.
`System.Windows.Controls`	This is the namespace where you can find all the WPF controls, such as `Button`, `Border`, `Canvas`, `ComboBox`, `Expander`, `Slider`, `ToolTip`, `TreeView`, and the like. In the namespace `System.Windows.Controls.Primitives`, you can find classes to be used within complex controls — for example, `Popup`, `ScrollBar`, `StatusBar`, `TabPanel`, and so on.
`System.Windows.Converters`	This namespace contains classes for data conversion. Don't expect to find all converter classes in this namespace; core converter classes are defined in the namespace `System.Windows`.
`System.Windows.Data`	This namespace is used by WPF data binding. An important class in this namespace is the `Binding` class, which is used to define the binding between a WPF target element and a CLR source.
`System.Windows.Documents`	When working with documents, you can find many helpful classes in this namespace. `FixedDocument` and `FlowDocument` are content elements that can contain other elements from this namespace. With classes from the namespace `System.Windows.Documents.Serialization` you can write documents to disk.
`System.Windows.Ink`	The Windows Tablet PC and Ultra Mobile PCs are being used more and more. With these PCs, ink can be used for user input. The namespace `System.Windows.Ink` contains classes to deal with ink input.
`System.Windows.Input`	This namespace contains several classes for command handling, keyboard inputs, working with a stylus, and so on.
`System.Windows.Interop`	For integration with Win32 and WPF, you can find classes in this namespace.
`System.Windows.Markup`	Helper classes for XAML markup code are located in this namespace.
`System.Windows.Media`	To work with images, audio, and video content, you can use classes in this namespace.
`System.Windows.Navigation`	This namespace contains classes for navigation between windows.
`System.Windows.Resources`	This namespace contains supporting classes for resources.

Namespace	Description
`System.Windows.Shapes`	The core classes for the UI are located in the namespace `System.Windows.Shapes`: `Line`, `Ellipse`, `Rectangle`, and the like.
`System.Windows.Threading`	WPF elements are similar to Windows Forms controls bound to a single thread. In the namespace `System.Windows.Threading`, you can find classes to deal with multiple threads — for example, the `Dispatcher` class belongs to this namespace.
`System.Windows.Xps`	XML Paper Specification (XPS) is a new document specification that is also supported by Microsoft Word. In the namespaces `System.Windows.Xps`, `System.Windows.Xps.Packaging`, and `System.Windows.Xps.Serialization`, you can find classes to create and stream XPS documents.

Shapes

Shapes are the core elements of WPF. With shapes you can draw 2D graphics using rectangles, lines, ellipses, paths, polygons, and polylines that are represented by classes derived from the abstract base class `Shape`. Shapes are defined in the namespace `System.Windows.Shapes`.

The following XAML example draws a yellow face with blue legs, consisting of an ellipse for the face, two ellipses for the eyes, a path for the mouth, and four lines for the legs:

```
<Window x:Class="ProCSharp.WPF.Window1"
xmlns="http://schemas.microsoft.com/winfx/2006/xaml/presentation"
    xmlns:x="http://schemas.microsoft.com/winfx/2006/xaml"
    Title="WPF Samples" Height="260" Width="230">
  <Canvas>
    <Ellipse Canvas.Left="50" Canvas.Top="50" Width="100" Height="100"
        Stroke="Blue" StrokeThickness="4" Fill="Yellow" />
    <Ellipse Canvas.Left="60" Canvas.Top="65" Width="25" Height="25"
        Stroke="Blue" StrokeThickness="3" Fill="White" />
    <Ellipse Canvas.Left="70" Canvas.Top="75" Width="5" Height="5"
        Fill="Black" />
    <Path Stroke="Blue" StrokeThickness="4"
        Data="M 62,125 Q 95,122 102,108" />
    <Line X1="124" X2="132" Y1="144" Y2="166" Stroke="Blue"
        StrokeThickness="4" />
    <Line X1="114" X2="133" Y1="169" Y2="166" Stroke="Blue"
        StrokeThickness="4" />
    <Line X1="92" X2="82" Y1="146" Y2="168" Stroke="Blue"
        StrokeThickness="4" />
    <Line X1="68" X2="83" Y1="160" Y2="168" Stroke="Blue"
        StrokeThickness="4" />
  </Canvas>
</Window>
```

Figure 34-5 shows the result from the XAML code.

Figure 34-5

All of these WPF elements can be accessed programmatically, even if they are buttons or shapes such as lines or rectangles. Setting the Name property with the Path element to mouth allows you to access this element programmatically with the variable name mouth:

```
<Path Name="mouth" Stroke="Blue" StrokeThickness="4"
   Data="M 62,125 Q 95,122 102,108" />
```

In the code-behind Data property of the Path element, mouth is set to a new geometry. For setting the path, the Path class supports PathGeometry with path markup syntax. The letter M defines the starting point for the path; the letter Q specifies a control point and an endpoint for a quadratic Bézier curve. Running the application, you see the window shown in Figure 34-6.

```
public Window1()
{
   InitializeComponent();
   mouth.Data = Geometry.Parse(
       "M 62,125 Q 95,122 102,128");
}
```

Figure 34-6

Earlier in this chapter, you learned that a button can have content. Making a small change to the XAML code and adding the `Button` element as content to the window causes the graphic to be displayed inside a button (see Figure 34-7).

```
<Window x:Class="ShapesDemo.Window1"
xmlns="http://schemas.microsoft.com/winfx/2006/xaml/presentation"
    xmlns:x="http://schemas.microsoft.com/winfx/2006/xaml"
    Title="ShapesDemo" Height="260" Width="230">
  <Button Margin="5">
    <Canvas Height="250" Width="220">
      <Ellipse Canvas.Left="50" Canvas.Top="50" Width="100"
          Height="100" Stroke="Blue" StrokeThickness="4"
          Fill="Yellow" />
      <Ellipse Canvas.Left="60" Canvas.Top="65" Width="25"
          Height="25" Stroke="Blue" StrokeThickness="3"
          Fill="White" />
      <Ellipse Canvas.Left="70" Canvas.Top="75" Width="5"
          Height="5" Fill="Black" />
      <Path Name="mouth" Stroke="Blue" StrokeThickness="4"
          Data="M 62,125 Q 95,122 102,108" />
      <Line X1="124" X2="132" Y1="144" Y2="166" Stroke="Blue"
          StrokeThickness="4" />
      <Line X1="114" X2="133" Y1="169" Y2="166" Stroke="Blue"
          StrokeThickness="4" />
      <Line X1="92" X2="82" Y1="146" Y2="168" Stroke="Blue"
          StrokeThickness="4" />
      <Line X1="68" X2="83" Y1="160" Y2="168" Stroke="Blue"
          StrokeThickness="4" />
    </Canvas>
  </Button>
</Window>
```

Figure 34-7

Following are the shapes available in the namespace `System.Windows.Shapes`.

Shape Class	Description
Line	You can draw a line from the coordinates X1.Y1 to X2.Y2.
Rectangle	With the Rectangle class, you can draw a rectangle by specifying Width and Height.
Ellipse	With the Ellipse class, you can draw an ellipse.
Path	You can use the Path class to draw a series of lines and curves. The Data property is of type Geometry. You can do the drawing by using classes that derive from the base class Geometry, or you can use the path markup syntax to define geometry.
Polygon	You can draw a closed shape formed by connected lines with the Polygon class. The polygon is defined by a series of Point objects assigned to the Points property.
Polyline	Similarly to the Polygon class, you can draw connected lines with the Polyline. The difference is that the poly-line does not need to be a closed shape.

Transformation

Because WPF is based on DirectX, which is vector-based, you can resize every element. The vector-based graphics are now scaled, rotated, and skewed. Hit testing (for example with mouse moves and mouse clicks) is still working without the need for manual position calculation.

Adding the ScaleTransform element to the LayoutTransform property of the Canvas element, as shown, resizes the content of the complete canvas by 2 in X and Y direction.

```
<Canvas.LayoutTransform>
  <ScaleTransform ScaleX="2" ScaleY="2" />
</Canvas.LayoutTransform>
```

Rotation can be done in a similar way as scaling. Using the RotateTransform element you can define the Angle for the rotation.

```
<Canvas.LayoutTransform>
   <RotateTransform Angle="40" />
</Canvas.LayoutTransform>
```

For skewing, you can use the SkewTransform element. With skewing you can assign angles for the X and the Y direction.

```
<Canvas.LayoutTransform>
   <SkewTransform AngleX="20" AngleY="25" />
</Canvas.LayoutTransform>
```

Figure 34-8 shows the results of all the transformations. The figures are placed inside a StackPanel. Starting from the left side, the first figure is resized, the second figure rotated, and the third figure skewed. To more easily see the difference, the Background property of the Canvas elements are set to different colors.

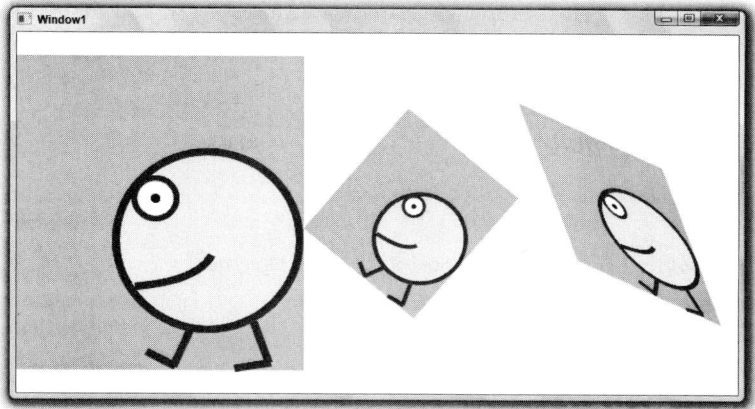

Figure 34-8

Brushes

This section illustrates how to use the brushes that WPF offers for drawing backgrounds and foregrounds. Throughout this section, we will reference Figure 34-9, which shows the effects of using various brushes within the `Background` of `Button` elements.

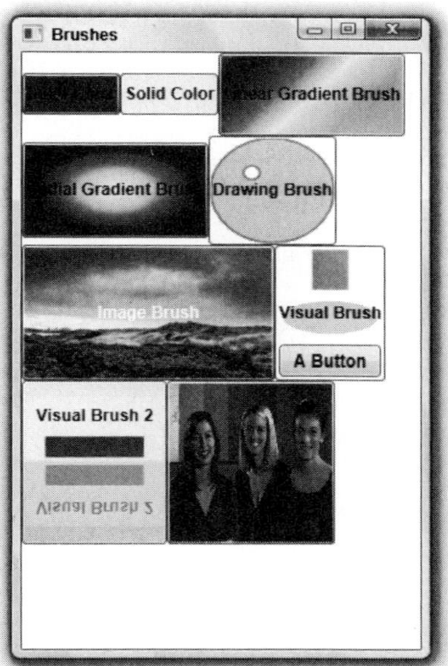

Figure 34-9

SolidColorBrush

The first button in Figure 34-9 uses the `SolidColorBrush`, which, by name, uses a solid color. The complete area is drawn with the same color.

You can define a solid color just by setting the `Background` attribute to a string that defines a solid color. The string is converted to a `SolidColorBrush` element.

```
<Button Height="30" Background="Purple">Solid Color</Button>
```

Of course, you will get the same effect by setting the `Background` child element and adding a `SolidColorBrush` element as its content. The second button in the application is using the solid color `Yellow` for the background.

```
<Button Height="30" >
   <Button.Background>
      <SolidColorBrush>Yellow</SolidColorBrush>
   </Button.Background>
   Solid Color
</Button>
```

LinearGradientBrush

For a smooth color change, you can use the `LinearGradientBrush`, as shown with the third button. This brush defines the `StartPoint` and `EndPoint` properties. With this, you can assign two-dimensional coordinates for the linear gradient. The default gradient is diagonal linear from `0,0` to `1,1`. By defining different values, the gradient can take different directions. For example, with a `StartPoint` of `0,0` and an `EndPoint` of `0,1` you get a vertical gradient. The same `StartPoint` and an `EndPoint` value of `1,0` creates a horizontal gradient.

With the content of this brush, you can define the color values at the specified offsets with the `GradientStop` element. Between the stops, the colors are smoothed.

```
<Button Height="60">
  <Button.Background>
    <LinearGradientBrush StartPoint="0,0"
        EndPoint="0.5,1.2">
      <GradientStop Color="Red" Offset="0"></GradientStop>
      <GradientStop Color="Blue" Offset="0.2">
      </GradientStop>
      <GradientStop Color="BlanchedAlmond" Offset="0.7">
      </GradientStop>
      <GradientStop Color="DarkOrange" Offset="1">
      </GradientStop>
    </LinearGradientBrush>
  </Button.Background>
  Linear Gradient Brush
</Button>
```

RadialGradientBrush

With the `RadialGradientBrush` you can smooth the color in a radiant way. In Figure 34-9, the fourth button is using the `RadialGradientBrush`. This brush defines the color start with the `GradientOrigin` point.

```
<Button Height="70" >
   <Button.Background>
      <RadialGradientBrush Center="0.5,0.5"
          GradientOrigin="0.5,0.5"
          RadiusX="0.5" RadiusY="0.5" SpreadMethod="Pad">
```

```
        <GradientStop Color="White" Offset="0" />
        <GradientStop Color="LightBlue" Offset="0.4" />
        <GradientStop Color="DarkBlue" Offset="1" />
      </RadialGradientBrush>
   </Button.Background>
   Radial Gradient Brush
</Button>
```

DrawingBrush

The `DrawingBrush` allows you to define a drawing that is painted with the brush. The drawing that is shown with the brush is defined within a `GeometryDrawing` element. The `GeometryGroup`, which you can see within the `Geometry` property, consists of `Geometry` elements such as `EllipseGeometry`, `LineGeometry`, `RectangleGeometry`, and `CombinedGeometry`.

```
<Button Height="80">
  <Button.Background>
    <DrawingBrush>
      <DrawingBrush.Drawing>
        <GeometryDrawing Brush="LightBlue">
          <GeometryDrawing.Geometry>
            <GeometryGroup>
              <EllipseGeometry RadiusX="30" RadiusY="30"
                  Center="20,20" />
              <EllipseGeometry RadiusX="4" RadiusY="4"
                  Center="10,10" />
            </GeometryGroup>
          </GeometryDrawing.Geometry>
          <GeometryDrawing.Pen>
            <Pen>
              <Pen.Brush>Red
              </Pen.Brush>
            </Pen>
          </GeometryDrawing.Pen>
        </GeometryDrawing>
      </DrawingBrush.Drawing>
    </DrawingBrush>
  </Button.Background>
  Drawing Brush
</Button>
```

ImageBrush

To load an image into a brush, you can use the `ImageBrush` element. With this element, the image defined by the `ImageSource` property is displayed.

```
<Button Height="100">
  <Button.Background>
    <ImageBrush
        ImageSource=" C:\Windows\Web\Wallpaper\img21.bmp"
    />
  </Button.Background>
  <Button.Foreground>White</Button.Foreground>
  Image Brush
</Button>
```

VisualBrush

The `VisualBrush` allows you to use other WPF elements in a brush. Here, you can add a WPF element to the `Visual` property. The seventh button in Figure 34-9 contains a `Rectangle`, an `Ellipse`, and a `Button`.

```
<Button Height="100">
   <Button.Background>
      <VisualBrush >
         <VisualBrush.Visual>
            <StackPanel Background="White">
               <Rectangle Width="25" Height="25"
                   Fill="LightCoral" Margin="2" />
               <Ellipse Width="65" Height="20"
                   Fill="Aqua" Margin="5" />
               <Button Margin="2">A Button</Button>
            </StackPanel>
         </VisualBrush.Visual>
      </VisualBrush>
   </Button.Background>
   Visual Brush
</Button>
```

With the `VisualBrush`, you can also create effects such as reflection. The button shown here contains a `StackPanel` that itself contains a `Border` and a `Rectangle`. The `Border` contains a `StackPanel` with a `Label` and a `Rectangle`. But that's not the real point here. The second `Rectangle` is filled with a `VisualBrush`. This brush defines an opacity value and a transformation. The `Visual` property is bound to the `Border` element. The transformation is done by setting the `RelativeTransform` property of the `VisualBrush`. This transformation is using relative coordinates. By setting `ScaleY` to -1, a reflection in Y direction is done. `TranslateTransform` moves the transformation in Y direction so that the reflection is below the original object. You can see the result in the eighth button ("Visual Brush 2") in Figure 34-9.

Data Binding and the Binding element that is used here are explained in detail in the next chapter, "Advanced WPF."

```
<Button Height="120">
   <StackPanel>
      <Border x:Name="reflected">
         <Border.Background>Yellow</Border.Background>
         <StackPanel>
            <Label>Visual Brush 2</Label>
            <Rectangle Width="70" Height="15" Margin="2"
                  Fill="BlueViolet" />
         </StackPanel>
      </Border>
      <Rectangle Height="30">
         <Rectangle.Fill>
            <VisualBrush Opacity="0.35" Stretch="None"
                  Visual="{Binding ElementName=reflected}">
               <VisualBrush.RelativeTransform>
                  <TransformGroup>
                     <ScaleTransform ScaleX="1" ScaleY="-1"
                     />
                     <TranslateTransform Y="1" />
                  </TransformGroup>
               </VisualBrush.RelativeTransform>
            </VisualBrush>
         </Rectangle.Fill>
```

```
            </Rectangle>
        </StackPanel>
    </Button>
```

You can also use the `VisualBrush` to display a video, simply by setting the `Visual` property to a `MediaElement`. With the `MediaControl`, the `Source` property is set to a WMV file. In Figure 34-9, the ninth button showing the three women meant to serve as an example of displaying a video. However, in a print media it is difficult to show a video. You can try that on your own — and if you've the Ultimate edition of Windows Vista you will find the same video on your hard disk. Otherwise just select a different video file.

```
<Button Height="120">
    <Button.Background>
        <VisualBrush>
            <VisualBrush.Visual>
                <MediaElement x:Name="video"
                     Source="C:\Windows\ehome\ColorTint.wmv" />
            </VisualBrush.Visual>
        </VisualBrush>
    </Button.Background>
</Button>
```

Controls

You can use hundreds of controls with WPF. For a better understanding, the controls are categorized into these groups:

- Simple controls
- Content controls
- Headered content controls
- Items controls
- Headered items controls

Simple Controls

Simple controls are controls that don't have a `Content` property. With the `Button` class, you have seen that the `Button` can contain any shape, or any element you like. This is not possible with simple controls. The following table shows simple controls and their functionality.

Simple Control	Description
`PasswordBox`	This control is used to enter a password and has specific properties for password input, for example, `PasswordChar` to define the character that should show up as the user enters the password, or `Password` to access the password entered. The `PasswordChanged` event is invoked as soon as the password is changed.
`ScrollBar`	This control contains a `Thumb` where the user can select a value. A scroll bar can be used, for example, if a document doesn't fit on the screen. Some controls contain scroll bars that show up if the content is too big.

Simple Control	Description
ProgressBar	With this control, you can indicate the progress of a lengthy operation.
Slider	With this control, the user can select a range of values by moving a Thumb. ScrollBar, ProgressBar, and Slider are derived from the same base class, RangeBase.
TextBox	Used to display simple unformatted text.
RichTextBox	Supports rich text with the help of the FlowDocument class. RichTextBox and TextBox are derived from the same base class, TextBoxBase.

Although simple controls do not have a Content *property, you can completely customize the look of the control by defining a template. Templates are discussed later in this chapter.*

Content Controls

A ContentControl has a Content property, with which you can add any content to the control. The Button class derives from the base class ContentControl, so you can add any content to this control. In a previous example, you saw a Canvas control within the Button. Content controls are described in the following table.

ContentControl Controls	Description
Button RepeatButton ToggleButton CheckBox RadioButton	The classes Button, RepeatButton, ToggleButton, and GridViewColumnHeader are derived from the same base class, ButtonBase. All buttons react to the Click event. The RepeatButton raises the Click event repeatedly until the button is released. ToggleButton is the base class for CheckBox and RadioButton. These buttons have an on and off state. The CheckBox can be selected and cleared by the user; the RadioButton can be selected by the user. Clearing the RadioButton must be done programmatically.
Label	The Label class represents the text label for a control. This class also has support for access keys, for example, a menu command.
Frame	The Frame control supports navigation. You can navigate to a page content with the Navigate() method. If the content is a Web page, then a browser control is used for display.
ListBoxItem	ListBoxItem is an item inside a ListBox control.
StatusBarItem	StatusBarItem is an item inside a StatusBar control.
ScrollViewer	The ScrollViewer control is a content control that includes scroll bars. You can put any content in this control; the scroll bars will show up as needed.
ToolTip	ToolTip creates a pop-up Window to display additional information for a control.

ContentControl Controls	Description
`UserControl`	Using the class `UserControl` as a base class provides a simple way to create custom controls. However, the base class `UserControl` does not support templates.
`Window`	The `Window` class allows you to create windows and dialog boxes. With the `Window` class, you get a frame with minimize/maximize/close buttons and a system menu. When showing a dialog box, you can use the method `ShowDialog();` the method `Show()` opens a window.
`NavigationWindow`	The class `NavigationWindow` derives from the `Window` class and supports content navigation.

Only a `Frame` control is contained within the `Window` of the following XAML code. The `Source` property is set to `http://www.wrox.com`, so the `Frame` control navigates to this Web site, as you can see in Figure 34-10.

```
<Window x:Class="FrameSample.Window1"
xmlns="http://schemas.microsoft.com/winfx/2006/xaml/presentation"
    xmlns:x="http://schemas.microsoft.com/winfx/2006/xaml"
    Title="Frame Sample" Height="400" Width="400">
  <Frame Source="http://www.wrox.com" />
</Window>
```

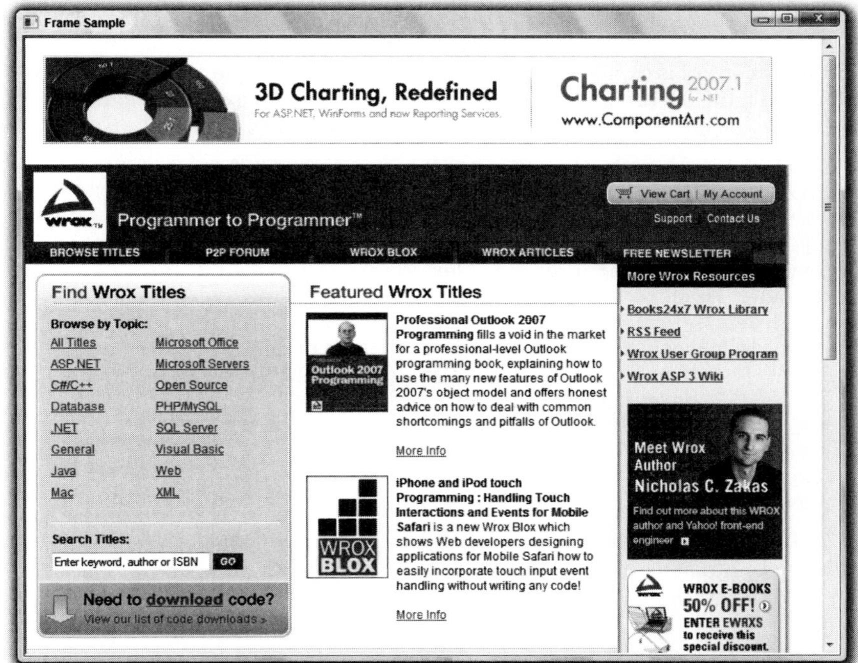

Figure 34-10

Headered Content Controls

Content controls with a header are derived from the base class `HeaderedContentControl`, which itself is derived from the base class `ContentControl`. The class `HeaderedContentControl` has a property `Header` to define the content of the header and `HeaderTemplate` for complete customization of the header. The controls that are derived from the base class `HeaderedContentControl` are listed in the following table.

HeaderedContentControl	Description
`Expander`	With the `Expander` control, you can create an "advanced" mode with a dialog box that, by default, does not show all information but that can be expanded by the user to show more information. In the unexpanded mode, header information is shown. In expanded mode, the content is visible.
`GroupBox`	The `GroupBox` control provides a border and a header to group controls.
`TabItem`	`TabItem` controls are items within the class `TabControl`. The `Header` property of the `TabItem` defines the content of the header shown with the tabs of the `TabControl`.

A simple use of the `Expander` control is shown in the next example. The `Expander` control has the property `Header` set to `Click for more`. This text is displayed for expansion. The content of this control is shown only if the control is expanded. Figure 34-11 shows the sample application with a collapsed `Expander` control. Figure 34-12 shows the same application with an expanded `Expander` control.

```
<Window x:Class="ExpanderSample.Window1"
        xmlns="http://schemas.microsoft.com/winfx/2006/xaml/presentation"
    xmlns:x="http://schemas.microsoft.com/winfx/2006/xaml"
    Title="Expander Sample" Height="300" Width="300">
    <StackPanel>
      <TextBlock>Short information</TextBlock>
      <Expander Header="Click for more">
         <Border Height="200" Width="200" Background="Yellow">
            <TextBlock HorizontalAlignment="Center"
                  VerticalAlignment="Center">
                  More information here!
            </TextBlock>
         </Border>
      </Expander>
    </StackPanel>
</Window>
```

To make the header text of the `Expander` *control change when the control is expanded, you can create a trigger. Triggers are explained later in this chapter.*

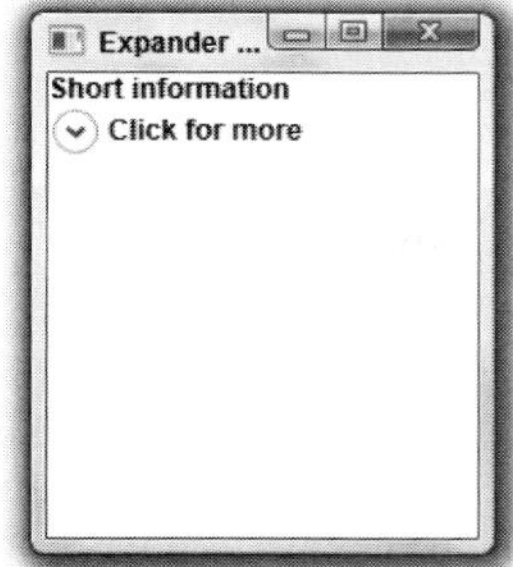

Figure 34-11

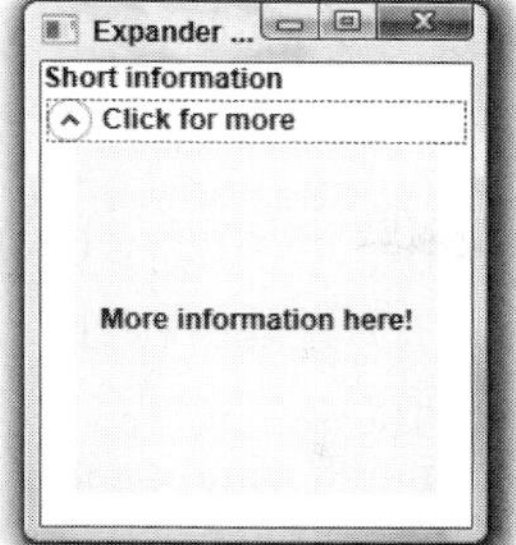

Figure 34-12

Items Controls

The class `ItemsControl` contains a list of items that can be accessed with the `Items` property. Classes that are derived from `ItemsControl` are shown in the following table.

ItemsControl	Description
`Menu` `ContextMenu`	The classes `Menu` and `ContextMenu` are derived from the abstract base class `MenuBase`. You can offer menus to the user by placing `MenuItem` elements in the items list and associating commands.
`StatusBar`	The `StatusBar` control is usually shown at the bottom of an application to give status information to the user. You can put `StatusBarItem` elements inside a `StatusBar` list.
`TreeView`	For a hierarchical display of items, you can use the `TreeView` control.

`ListBox`
`ComboBox`
`TabControl`
	`ListBox`, `ComboBox`, and `TabControl` have the same abstract base class, `Selector`. This base class makes it possible to select items from a list. The `ListBox` displays the items from a list. The `ComboBox` has an additional `Button` control to display the items only if the button is clicked. With the `TabControl`, content can be arranged in tabular form.

Headered Items Controls

`HeaderedItemsControl` is the base class of controls that include items but also has a header. The class `HeaderedItemsControl` is derived from `ItemsControl`.

Classes that are derived from `HeaderedItemsControl` are listed in the following table.

HeaderedItemsControl	Description
MenuItem	The menu classes Menu and ContextMenu include items of type MenuItem. Menu items can be connected to commands, as the MenuItem class implements the interface ICommandSource.
TreeViewItem	The TreeView class can include items of type TreeViewItem.
ToolBar	The ToolBar control is a container for a group of controls, usually Button and Separator elements. You can place the ToolBar inside a ToolBarTray that handles rearranging of ToolBar controls.

Layout

To define the layout of the application, you can use a class that derives from the Panel base class. Several layout containers are available that are discussed here. A layout container needs to do two main tasks: measure and arrange. With measuring, the container asks its children for the preferred sizes. Because the complete size answered by the controls might not be available, the container next decides and arranges the size and positions of its children.

StackPanel

The Window can contain just a single element as content. If you want to have more than one element inside there, then you can use a StackPanel as a child of the Window, and add elements to the content of the StackPanel. The StackPanel is a simple container control that just shows one element after the other. The orientation of the StackPanel can be horizontal or vertical. The class ToolBarPanel is derived from StackPanel.

```
<Window x:Class="LayoutSamples.Window1"
xmlns="http://schemas.microsoft.com/winfx/2006/xaml/presentation"
    xmlns:x="http://schemas.microsoft.com/winfx/2006/xaml"
    Title="Layout Samples" Height="300" Width="283">
  <StackPanel Orientation="Vertical">
    <Label>Label</Label>
    <TextBox>TextBox</TextBox>
    <CheckBox>Checkbox</CheckBox>
    <CheckBox>Checkbox</CheckBox>
    <ListBox>
      <ListBoxItem>ListBoxItem One</ListBoxItem>
      <ListBoxItem>ListBoxItem Two</ListBoxItem>
    </ListBox>
    <Button>Button</Button>
  </StackPanel>
</Window>
```

You can see the child controls of the StackPanel organized vertically in Figure 34-13.

For data-binding items to a StackPanel, if there is not enough space for all items to display, then you can use the VirtualizingStackPanel instead. With this panel, only the items shown are generated.

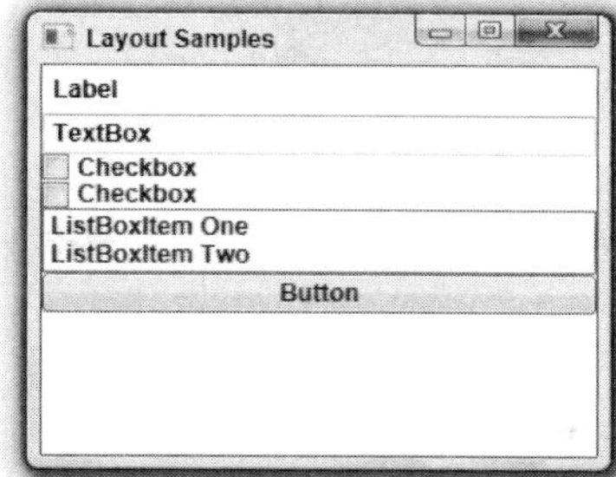

Figure 34-13

WrapPanel

The `Wrap Panel` positions the children from left to right, one after the other, as long as they fit into the line, and then continues with the next line. The orientation of the panel can be horizontal or vertical.

```
<Window x:Class="LayoutSamples.WrapPanelDemo"
xmlns="http://schemas.microsoft.com/winfx/2006/xaml/presentation"
    xmlns:x="http://schemas.microsoft.com/winfx/2006/xaml"
    Title="Layout Samples" Height="160" Width="250">
  <WrapPanel>
    <Button Width="100">Button</Button>
    <Button Width="100">Button</Button>
    <Button Width="100">Button</Button>
    <Button Width="100">Button</Button>
    <Button Width="100">Button</Button>
    <Button Width="100">Button</Button>
    <Button Width="100">Button</Button>
    <Button Width="100">Button</Button>
  </WrapPanel>
</Window>
```

Figure 34-14 shows the output of the panel. If you resize the application, then the buttons will be rearranged so that they fit into a line.

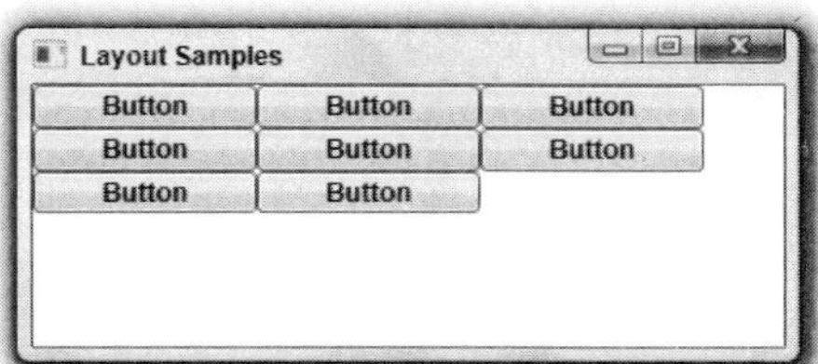

Figure 34-14

Canvas

`Canvas` is a panel that allows you to explicitly position controls. `Canvas` defines the attached properties `Left`, `Right`, `Top`, and `Bottom` that can be used by the children for positioning within the panel.

```
<Window x:Class="LayoutSamples.CanvasDemo"
xmlns="http://schemas.microsoft.com/winfx/2006/xaml/presentation"
    xmlns:x="http://schemas.microsoft.com/winfx/2006/xaml"
    Title="Layout Samples" Height="300" Width="300">
  <Canvas Background="LightBlue">
    <Label Canvas.Top="30" Canvas.Left="20">Enter here:</Label>
    <TextBox Canvas.Top="30" Canvas.Left="130" Width="100"></TextBox>
    <Button Canvas.Top="70" Canvas.Left="130">Click Me!</Button>
  </Canvas>
</Window>
```

Figure 34-15 shows the output of the `Canvas` panel with the positioned children `Label`, `TextBox`, and `Button`.

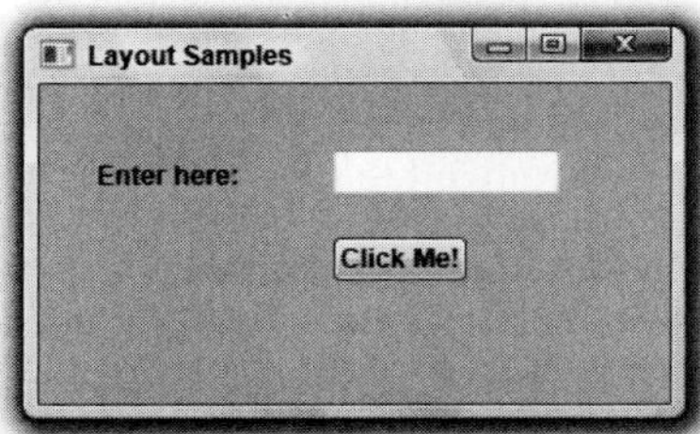

Figure 34-15

DockPanel

The `DockPanel` is very similar to the Windows Forms docking functionality. Here, you can specify the area where child controls should be arranged. `DockPanel` defines the attached property `Dock`, which you can set in the children of the controls to the values `Left`, `Right`, `Top`, and `Bottom`. Figure 34-16 shows the outcome of text blocks with borders that are arranged in the dock panel. For easier differentiation, different colors are specified for the various areas.

```
<Window x:Class="LayoutSamples.DockPanelDemo"
xmlns="http://schemas.microsoft.com/winfx/2006/xaml/presentation"
    xmlns:x="http://schemas.microsoft.com/winfx/2006/xaml"
    Title="Layout Samples" Height="300" Width="300">
  <DockPanel Background="LightBlue">
    <Border Height="25" Background="AliceBlue" DockPanel.Dock="Top">
      <TextBlock>Menu</TextBlock>
    </Border>
    <Border Height="25" Background="Aqua" DockPanel.Dock="Top">
      <TextBlock>Toolbar</TextBlock>
    </Border>
    <Border Height="30" Background="LightSteelBlue" DockPanel.Dock="Bottom">
      <TextBlock>Status</TextBlock>
    </Border>
    <Border Width="80" Background="Azure" DockPanel.Dock="Left">
      <TextBlock>Left Side</TextBlock>
    </Border>
    <Border Background="HotPink">
      <TextBlock>Remaining Part</TextBlock>
    </Border>
  </DockPanel>
</Window>
```

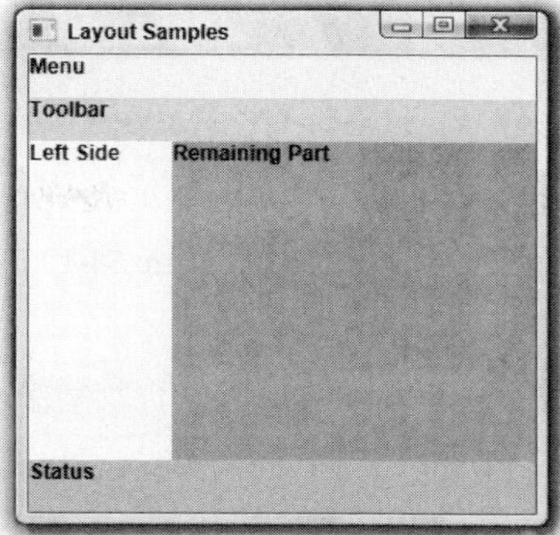

Figure 34-16

Grid

Using the Grid, you can arrange your controls with rows and columns. For every column, you can specify a ColumnDefinition. For every row, you can specify a RowDefinition. The sample code lists two columns and three rows. With each column and row, you can specify the width or height. ColumnDefinition has a Width dependency property; RowDefinition has a Height dependency property. You can define the height and width in pixels, centimeters, inches, or points, or by setting it to Auto to determine the size depending on the content. The grid also allows star sizing, whereby the space for the rows and columns is calculated according to the available space and relative to other rows and columns. When providing the available space for a column, you can set the Width property to *. To have the size doubled for another column, you specify 2*. The sample code, which defines two columns and three rows, doesn't define additional settings with the column and row definitions; the default is the star setting.

The grid contains several Label and TextBox controls. Because the parent of these controls is a grid, you can set the attached properties Column, ColumnSpan, Row, and RowSpan.

```
<Window x:Class="LayoutSamples.GridDemo"
xmlns="http://schemas.microsoft.com/winfx/2006/xaml/presentation"
    xmlns:x="http://schemas.microsoft.com/winfx/2006/xaml"
    Title="Layout Samples" Height="300" Width="283">
  <Grid ShowGridLines="True">
    <Grid.ColumnDefinitions>
      <ColumnDefinition />
      <ColumnDefinition />
    </Grid.ColumnDefinitions>
    <Grid.RowDefinitions>
      <RowDefinition />
      <RowDefinition />
      <RowDefinition />
    </Grid.RowDefinitions>
    <Label Grid.Column="0" Grid.ColumnSpan="2" Grid.Row="0"
        VerticalAlignment="Center" HorizontalAlignment="Center">Title</Label>
    <Label Grid.Column="0" Grid.Row ="1" VerticalAlignment="Center">
        Firstname:</Label>
    <TextBox Grid.Column="1" Grid.Row="1" Width="100" Height="30"></TextBox>
```

(continued)

(continued)

```
      <Label Grid.Column="0" Grid.Row ="2" VerticalAlignment="Center">
          Lastname:</Label>
      <TextBox Grid.Column="1" Grid.Row="2" Width="100" Height="30"></TextBox>
    </Grid>
  </Window>
```

The outcome arranging controls in a grid is shown in Figure 34-17. For easier viewing of the columns and rows, the property `ShowGridLines` is set to `true`.

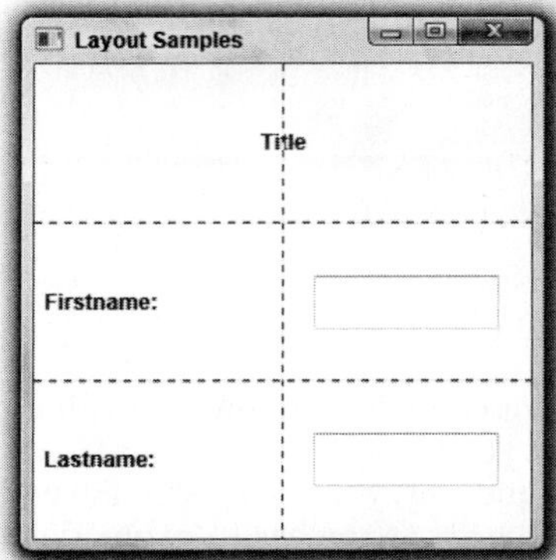

Figure 34-17

For a grid where every cell has the same size, you can use the `UniformGrid` *class.*

Event Handling

WPF classes define events where you can add your handlers. For example, you can add `MouseEnter`, `MouseLeave`, `MouseMove`, `Click`, and the like. This is based on the events and delegates mechanism on .NET. Chapter 7, "Delegates and Events," covers the event and delegate architecture of .NET.

With WPF, you can assign the event handler either with XAML or in the code behind. With `button1`, the XML attribute `Click` is used to assign the method `button_Click` to the click event. `button2` has no event handler assigned in XAML:

```
<Button Name="button1" Click="button_Click">Button 1</Button>
<Button Name="button2"> Button 2</Button>
```

The `Click` event for `button2` is assigned in the code behind by creating an instance of the delegate `RoutedEventHandler` and passing the method `button_Click` to the delegate. The method `button_Click()` that is invoked from both buttons has arguments as defined by the `RoutedEventHandler` delegate:

```
public Window1()
{
   InitializeComponent();
   button2.Click += button_Click;
}
void button_Click(object sender, RoutedEventArgs e)
{
   MessageBox.Show("Click Event");
}
```

The event-handling mechanism for WPF is based on .NET events but extended with bubbling and tunneling features. As you have already learned, a `Button` can contain graphics, list boxes, another button, and so on. What happens if a `CheckBox` is contained inside a `Button` and you click the `CheckBox`? Where should the event arrive? The answer is that the event is bubbled. First, the `Click` event arrives with the `CheckBox`, and then it bubbles up to the `Button`. This way, you can handle the `Click` event for all elements that are inside the `Button` with the `Button`.

Some events are tunneling events; others are bubbling events. A tunneling event first arrives with the outer element and tunnels to the inner elements. Bubbling events start with the inner element and bubble to the outer elements. Tunneling and bubbling events are usually paired. Tunneling events are prefixed with `Preview`, for example, `PreviewMouseMove`. This event tunnels from the outer controls to the inner controls. After the `PreviewMouseMove` event, the `MouseMove` event occurs. This event is a bubbling event that goes from the inner to the outer controls.

You can stop tunneling and bubbling by setting the `Handled` property of the event argument to `true`. The `Handled` property is a member of the `RoutedEventArgs` class. All event handlers that participate with the tunneling and bubbling facility have an event argument of type `RoutedEventArgs` or a type that derives from `RoutedEventArgs`.

> *If you stop the tunneling of an event by setting the* `Handled` *property to* `true`*, then the bubbling event that follows the tunneling event will not happen anymore.*

Styles, Templates, and Resources

You can define the look and feel of the WPF elements by setting properties, such as `FontSize` and `Background`, with the `Button` element as shown:

```
<StackPanel>
   <Button Name="button1" Width="150" FontSize="12" Background="AliceBlue">
      Click Me!
   </Button>
</StackPanel>
```

Instead of defining the look and feel with every element, you can define styles that are stored with resources. To completely customize the look for controls, you can use templates and store them into resources.

Styles

To define styles, you can use a `Style` element containing `Setter` elements. With the `Setter`, you specify the `Property` and the `Value` of the style, for example, the property `Button.Background` and the value `AliceBlue`.

To assign the styles to specific elements, you can assign a style to all elements of a type or use a key for the style. To assign a style to all elements of a type, use the `TargetType` property of the `Style` and assign it to a `Button` by specifying the `x:Type` markup extension `{x:Type Button}`.

```
<Window.Resources>
  <Style TargetType="{x:Type Button}">
    <Setter Property="Button.Background" Value="LemonChiffon"
    />
    <Setter Property="Button.FontSize" Value="18" />
  </Style>
  <Style x:Key="ButtonStyle">
    <Setter Property="Button.Background" Value="AliceBlue" />
```

(continued)

(continued)

```
        <Setter Property="Button.FontSize" Value="18" />
      </Style>
    </Window.Resources>
```

In the following XAML code, `button2`, which doesn't have a style defined with the element properties, gets the style that is defined for the `Button` type. For `button3`, the `Style` property is set with the `StaticResource` markup extension to `{StaticResource ButtonStyle}`, whereas `ButtonStyle` specifies the key value of the style resource defined earlier, so `button3` has an aliceblue background.

```
<Button Name="button2" Width="150">Click Me!</Button>
<Button Name="button3" Width="150" Style="{StaticResource ButtonStyle}">
  Click Me, Too!
</Button>
```

Instead of setting the `Background` of a button to just a single value, you can also do more. You can set the `Background` property to a `LinearGradientBrush` with a gradient color definition as shown:

```
    <Style x:Key="FancyButtonStyle">
       <Setter Property="Button.FontSize" Value="22" />
       <Setter Property="Button.Foreground" Value="White" />
       <Setter Property="Button.Background">
         <Setter.Value>
           <LinearGradientBrush StartPoint="0.5,0"
               EndPoint="0.5,1">
             <GradientStop Offset="0.0" Color="LightCyan" />
             <GradientStop Offset="0.14" Color="Cyan" />
             <GradientStop Offset="0.7" Color="DarkCyan" />
           </LinearGradientBrush>
         </Setter.Value>
       </Setter>
     </Style>
```

`button4` has the fancy style with the linear gradient cyan color applied:

```
<Button Name="button4" Width="200" Style="{StaticResource FancyButtonStyle}">
  Fancy!
</Button>
```

You can see the results of all these buttons styled in Figure 34-18.

Figure 34-18

Resources

As you have seen with the styles sample, usually styles are stored within resources. You can define any element within a resource. For example, the brush created earlier for the background style of the button can itself be defined as a resource, so you can use it everywhere a brush is required.

The following example defines a `LinearGradientBrush` with the key name `MyGradientBrush` inside the `StackPanel` resources. `button1` assigns the `Background` property by using a `StaticResource` markup extension to the resource `MyGradientBrush`. Figure 34-19 shows the output from this XAML code:

```
<Window x:Class="ResourcesSample.Window1"
            xmlns="http://schemas.microsoft.com/winfx/2006/xaml/presentation"
    xmlns:x="http://schemas.microsoft.com/winfx/2006/xaml"
    Title="Resources" Height="100" Width="300">
  <Window.Resources>
  </Window.Resources>
  <StackPanel>
    <StackPanel.Resources>
      <LinearGradientBrush x:Key="MyGradientBrush"
          StartPoint="0.5,0" EndPoint="0.5,1">
        <GradientStop Offset="0.0" Color="LightCyan" />
        <GradientStop Offset="0.14" Color="Cyan" />
        <GradientStop Offset="0.7" Color="DarkCyan" />
      </LinearGradientBrush>
    </StackPanel.Resources>
    <Button Name="button1" Width="200" Height="50"
      Foreground="White"
      Background="{StaticResource MyGradientBrush}">
      Click Me!
    </Button>
  </StackPanel>
</Window>
```

Figure 34-19

Here, the resources have been defined with the `StackPanel`. In the previous example, the resources were defined with the `Window` element. The base class `FrameworkElement` defines the property `Resources` of type `ResourceDictionary`. That's why resources can be defined with every class that is derived from the `FrameworkElement`—any WPF element.

Resources are searched hierarchically. If you define the resource with the window, it applies to every child element of the window. If the `Window` contains a `Grid`, and the `Grid` contains a `StackPanel`, and if you define the resource with the `StackPanel`, then the resource applies to every control within the `StackPanel`. If the `StackPanel` contains a `Button`, and you define the resource just with the `Button`, then this style is valid just for the button.

In regard to hierarchies, you need to pay attention if you use the `TargetType` *without a* `Key` *for styles. If you define a resource with the* `Canvas` *element and set the* `TargetType` *for the style to apply to* `TextBox` *elements, then the style applies to all* `TextBox` *elements within the* `Canvas`. *The style even applies to* `TextBox` *elements that are contained in a* `ListBox` *when the* `ListBox` *is in the* `Canvas`.

If you need the same style for more than one Window, then you can define the style with the application. In a Visual Studio WPF project, the file `App.xaml` is created for defining global resources of the application. The application styles are valid for every window of the application. Every element can access resources that are defined with the application. If resources are not found with the parent window, then the search for resources continues with the `Application`.

```
<Application x:Class="ResourcesSample.App"
xmlns="http://schemas.microsoft.com/winfx/2006/xaml/presentation"
    xmlns:x="http://schemas.microsoft.com/winfx/2006/xaml"
    StartupUri="Window1.xaml">
    <Application.Resources>

    </Application.Resources>
</Application>
```

System Resources

There are also some system-wide resources for colors and fonts that are available for all applications. These resources are defined with the classes `SystemColors`, `SystemFonts`, and `SystemParameters`:

- With `SystemColors` you get the color settings for borders, controls, the desktop, and windows, such as `ActiveBorderColor`, `ControlBrush`, `DesktopColor`, `WindowColor`, `WindowBrush`, and so on.
- The class `SystemFonts` returns the settings for the fonts of the menu, status bar, and message box. These include `CaptionFont`, `DialogFont`, `MenuFont`, `MessageBoxFont`, `StatusFont`, and so on.
- The class `SystemParameters` gives you settings for sizes of menu buttons, cursors, icons, borders, captions, timing information, and keyboard settings, such as `BorderWidth`, `CaptionHeight`, `CaptionWidth`, `MenuButtonWidth`, `MenuPopupAnimation`, `MenuShowDelay`, `SmallIconHeight`, `SmallIconWidth`, and so on.

Figure 34-20 shows the dialog box where the user can configure these settings. You can find the Appearance dialog box with the Personalization settings in the Control Panel.

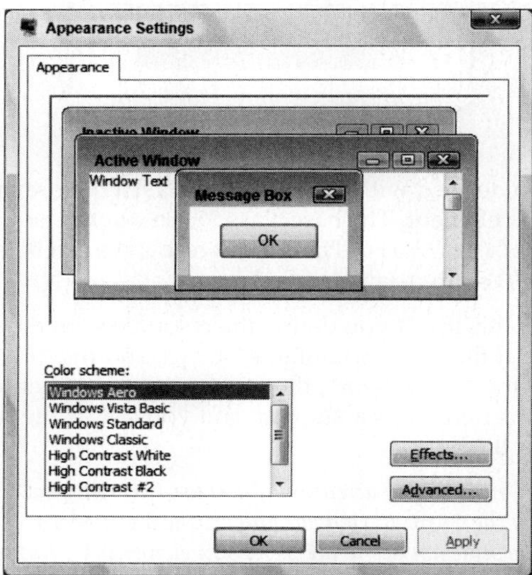

Figure 34-20

Accessing Resources from Code

To access resources from code behind, the base class `FrameworkElement` implements the method `FindResource()`, so you can invoke the `FindResource()` method with every WPF object.

To do this, `button1` doesn't have a background specified, but the `Click` event is assigned to the method `button1_Click`.

```
<StackPanel Name="myContainer">
  <StackPanel.Resources>
    <LinearGradientBrush x:Key="MyGradientBrush"
        StartPoint="0.5,0" EndPoint="0.5,1">
      <GradientStop Offset="0.0" Color="LightCyan" />
      <GradientStop Offset="0.14" Color="Cyan" />
      <GradientStop Offset="0.7" Color="DarkCyan" />
    </LinearGradientBrush>
  </StackPanel.Resources>
  <Button Name="button1" Width="200" Height="50"
      Click="button1_Click">
      Apply Resource Programmatically
  </Button>
```

With the implementation of `button1_Click()`, the `FindResource()` method is used on the `Button` that was clicked. Then a search for the resource `MyGradientBrush` happens hierarchically, and the brush is applied to the `Background` property of the control.

```
public void button1_Click(object sender, RoutedEventArgs e)
{
   Control ctrl = sender as Control;
   ctrl.Background =
       ctrl.FindResource("MyGradientBrush") as Brush;
}
```

If `FindResource()` does not find the resource key, then an exception is thrown. If you don't know for sure if the resource is available, then you can use the method `TryFindResource()` instead. `TryFindResource()` returns `null` if the resource is not found.

Dynamic Resources

With the `StaticResource` markup extension, resources are searched at load time. If the resource changes while the program is running, then you should use the `DynamicResource` markup extension instead.

The next example is using the same resource as defined previously. `button1` uses the resource as a `StaticResource`, and `button3` uses the resource as a `DynamicResource` with the `DynamicResource` markup extension. `button2` is used to change the resource programmatically. It has the `Click` event handler method `button2_Click` assigned.

```
<Button Name="button1" Width="200" Height="50"
      Background="{StaticResource MyGradientBrush}">
      Static Resource
</Button>
<Button Name="button2" Width="200" Height="50"
    Click="button2_Click">
    Change Resource
</Button>
<Button Name="button3" Width="200" Height="50"
    Background="{DynamicResource MyGradientBrush}">
    Dynamic Resource
</Button>
```

The implementation of `button2_Click()` clears the resources of the `StackPanel` and adds a new resource with the same name, `MyGradientBrush`. This new resource is very similar to the resource that is defined in XAML code; it just defines different colors.

```
public void button2_Click(object sender, RoutedEventArgs e)
{
   myContainer.Resources.Clear();
   LinearGradientBrush brush = new LinearGradientBrush();
   brush.StartPoint = new Point(0.5, 0);
   brush.EndPoint = new Point(0.5, 1);
   GradientStopCollection stops =
       new GradientStopCollection();
   stops.Add(new GradientStop(Colors.White, 0.0));
   stops.Add(new GradientStop(Colors.Yellow, 0.14));
   stops.Add(new GradientStop(Colors.YellowGreen, 0.7));
   brush.GradientStops = stops;
   myContainer.Resources.Add("MyGradientBrush", brush);
}
```

If you run the application and change the resource dynamically by clicking the third button, then `button4` immediately gets the new resource. `button1`, which was defined with the `StaticResource`, keeps the old resource that was loaded.

> **The `DynamicResource` requires more performance than the `StaticResource` because the resource is always loaded when needed. Use `DynamicResource` only with resources where you expect changes during runtime.**

Triggers

With triggers you can change the look and feel of your controls dynamically because of some events or some property value changes. For example, when the user moves with the mouse over a button, the button can change its look. Usually, you need to do this with the C# code. With WPF, you can also do this with XAML, as long as only the UI is influenced.

The `Style` class has a `Triggers` property where you can assign property triggers. The following example includes two `TextBox` elements inside a `Canvas` panel. With the `Window` resources, a style `TextBoxStyle` is defined that is referenced by the `TextBox` elements using the `Style` property. The `TextBoxStyle` specifies that the `Background` is set to `LightBlue` and the `FontSize` to `17`. This is the style of the `TextBox` elements when the application is started. Using triggers, the style of the controls change. The triggers are defined within the `Style.Triggers` element, using the `Trigger` element. One trigger is assigned to the property `IsMouseOver`; the other trigger is assigned to the property `IsKeyboardFocused`. Both of these properties are defined with the `TextBox` class that the style applies to. If `IsMouseOver` has a value of `true`, then the trigger fires and sets the `Background` property to `Red` and the `FontSize` property to `22`. If the `TextBox` has a keyboard focus, then the property `IsKeyboardFocused` is `true`, and the second trigger fires and sets the `Background` property of the `TextBox` to `Yellow`.

```
<Window x:Class="TriggerSample.Window1"
xmlns="http://schemas.microsoft.com/winfx/2006/xaml/presentation"
    xmlns:x="http://schemas.microsoft.com/winfx/2006/xaml"
    Title="Triggers" Height="200" Width="400">
  <Window.Resources>
    <Style x:Key="TextBoxStyle" TargetType="{x:Type TextBox}">
```

```
        <Setter Property="Background" Value="LightBlue" />
        <Setter Property="FontSize" Value="17" />
        <Style.Triggers>
          <Trigger Property="IsMouseOver" Value="True">
            <Setter Property="Background" Value="Red" />
            <Setter Property="FontSize" Value="22" />
          </Trigger>
          <Trigger Property="IsKeyboardFocused" Value="True">
            <Setter Property="Background" Value="Yellow" />
            <Setter Property="FontSize" Value="22" />
          </Trigger>
        </Style.Triggers>
      </Style>
    </Window.Resources>
    <Canvas>
      <TextBox Canvas.Top="80" Canvas.Left="30" Width="300"
          Style="{StaticResource TextBoxStyle}" />
      <TextBox Canvas.Top="120" Canvas.Left="30" Width="300"
          Style="{StaticResource TextBoxStyle}" />
    </Canvas>
  </Window>
```

You don't need to reset the property values to the original values when the reason for the trigger is not valid anymore. For example, you don't need to define a trigger for `IsMouseOver=true` and `IsMouseOver=false`. As soon as the reason for the trigger is no longer valid, the changes made by the trigger action are reset to the original values automatically.

Figure 34-21 shows the trigger sample application, where the first text box has the keyboard input focus, and the second text box has the default values of the style for the background and font size.

Figure 34-21

> **When using property triggers, it is extremely easy to change the look of controls, fonts, colors, opacity, and the like. When the mouse moves over them, the keyboard sets the focus — not a single line of programming code is required.**

The `Trigger` class defines the following properties to specify the trigger action.

Trigger Property	Description
`PropertyValue`	With property triggers, the `Property` and `Value` properties are used to specify when the trigger should fire, for example, `Property="IsMouseOver" Value="True"`.
`Setters`	As soon as the trigger fires, you can use `Setters` to define a collection of `Setter` elements to change values for properties. The `Setter` class defines the properties `Property`, `TargetName`, and `Value` for the object properties to change.
`EnterActions` `ExitActions`	Instead of defining setters, you can define `EnterActions` and `ExitActions`. With both of these properties, you can define a collection of `TriggerAction` elements. `EnterActions` fires when the trigger starts (with a property trigger, when the `Property/Value` combination applies); `ExitActions` fires before it ends (just at the moment when the `Property/Value` combination no longer applies). Trigger actions that you can specify with these actions are derived from the base class `TriggerAction`, such as, `SoundPlayerAction` and `BeginStoryboard`. With `SoundPlayerAction`, you can start the playing of sound. `BeginStoryboard` is used with animation, which will be shown later in this chapter.

Property triggers are just one type of trigger possible in WPF. Another trigger type is event triggers. Event triggers are discussed later in this chapter along with animations.

Templates

In this chapter, you have already seen that a `Button` control can have any content. The content can be a simple text, but you can also add a `Canvas` element, which can contain shapes. You can add a `Grid`, or a video to the button. However, there is even more than that you can do with a button!

In WPF, the functionality of controls is completely separate from their look and feel. A button has a default look, but you can completely customize that look as you like with templates.

WPF gives you several template types that derive from the base class `FrameworkTemplate`.

Template Type	Description
`ControlTemplate`	With a `ControlTemplate` you can specify the visual structure of a control and override the look.
`ItemsPanelTemplate`	For an `ItemsControl` you can specify the layout of its items by assigning an `ItemsPanelTemplate`. Each `ItemsControl` has a default `ItemsPanelTemplate`. For the `MenuItem`, it is a `WrapPanel`. The `StatusBar` uses a `DockPanel`, and the `ListBox` uses a `VirtualizingStackPanel`.
`DataTemplate`	`DataTemplates` are very useful for graphical representations of objects. Styling a `ListBox`, you will see that, by default, the items of the `ListBox` are shown according to the output of the `ToString()` method. By applying a `DataTemplate` you can override this behavior and define a custom presentation of the items.
`HierarchicalData` `Template`	The `HierarchicalDataTemplate` is used for arranging a tree of objects. This control supports `HeaderedItemsControls`, such as `TreeViewItem` and `MenuItem`.

The next sample shows several buttons, and later, list boxes are customized step by step, so you can see the intermediate results of the changes. First, start with two very simple buttons, in which the first button doesn't have a style at all. The second button references the style `ButtonStyle1` with changes to the `Background` and the `FontSize`. You can see this first result in Figure 34-22.

```
<Window x:Class="TemplateSample.Window1"
            xmlns="http://schemas.microsoft.com/winfx/2006/xaml/presentation"
    xmlns:x="http://schemas.microsoft.com/winfx/2006/xaml"
    Title="Template" Height="300" Width="300">
  <Window.Resources>
    <Style x:Key="ButtonStyle1" TargetType="{x:Type Button}">
      <Setter Property="Background" Value="Yellow" />
      <Setter Property="FontSize" Value="18" />
    </Style>
  </Window.Resources>
  <StackPanel>
    <Button Name="button1" Height="50" Width="150">Default Button</Button>
    <Button Name="button2" Height="50" Width="150"
        Style="{StaticResource ButtonStyle1}">Styled Button
    </Button>
  </StackPanel>
</Window>
```

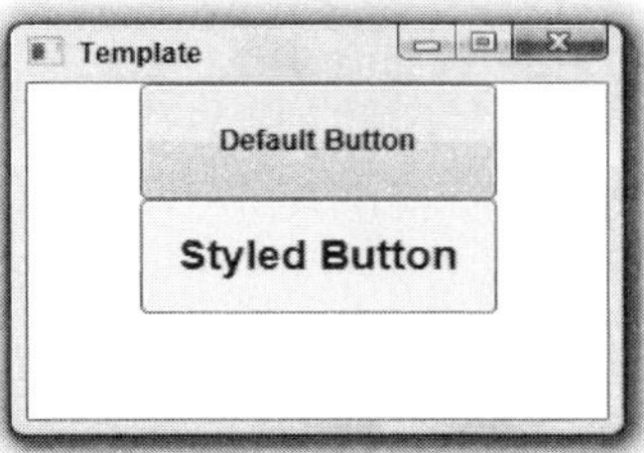

Figure 34-22

Now, add the new style `ButtonStyle2` to the resources. This style again sets the `TargetType` to the `Button` type. The `Setter` now specifies the `Template` property. By specifying the `Template` property, you can replace the look of the button completely. The value for the `Template` property is defined by a `ControlTemplate` element. A `ControlTemplate` defines the content of a control and allows the accessing of content from the control itself, as you will see soon. Here, the `ControlTemplate` defines a `Grid` with two rows. The rows use star sizing where the height of the first row is twice the height of the second row. Then two `Rectangle` elements are defined. The first rectangle spans both rows, and sets the `Stroke` property to `Green` for a green outline, and `RadiusX` and `RadiusY` values for rounded corners. The second rectangle, which is only within the first row, has its `Fill` property set to a linear gradient brush. `button3`, with the content `Template Button`, references style `ButtonStyle2`. Figure 34-23 shows `button3` with the new style, but the content is missing.

```
<Window x:Class="TemplateSample.Window1"
xmlns="http://schemas.microsoft.com/winfx/2006/xaml/presentation"
    xmlns:x="http://schemas.microsoft.com/winfx/2006/xaml"
    Title="Template" Height="300" Width="300"
    >
  <Window.Resources>
    <!-- other styles -->
    <Style x:Key="ButtonStyle2" TargetType="{x:Type Button}">
```

(continued)

(continued)

```
        <Setter Property="Template">
          <Setter.Value>
            <ControlTemplate>
              <Grid>
                <Grid.RowDefinitions>
                  <RowDefinition Height="2*" />
                  <RowDefinition Height="*" />
                </Grid.RowDefinitions>
                <Rectangle Grid.RowSpan="2" RadiusX="4" RadiusY="8"
                    Stroke="Green" />
                <Rectangle RadiusX="4" RadiusY="8" Margin="2">
                  <Rectangle.Fill>
                    <LinearGradientBrush StartPoint="0,0"
                        EndPoint="0,1">
                      <GradientStop Offset="0" Color="LightBlue" />
                      <GradientStop Offset="0.5" Color="#afff" />
                      <GradientStop Offset="1" Color="#6faa" />
                    </LinearGradientBrush>
                  </Rectangle.Fill>
                </Rectangle>
              </Grid>
            </ControlTemplate>
          </Setter.Value>
        </Setter>
      </Style>
    </Window.Resources>
    <StackPanel>
      <!-- other buttons -->
      <Button Name="button3" Background="Yellow" Height="100"
          Width="220" FontSize="24"
          Style="{StaticResource ButtonStyle2}">
          Template Button
      </Button>
    </StackPanel>
  </Window>
```

Figure 34-23

The button now has a completely different look. However, the content that is defined with the button itself is missing in Figure 34-23. The template created previously must be extended. The first rectangle in the template now has its `Fill` property set to `{TemplateBinding Background}`. The `TemplateBinding` markup extension enables a control template to use content from the templated control. Here, the rectangle is filled with the background that is defined with the button. `button3` defines a yellow background, which is combined with the background from the second rectangle of the control template. After the definition of the second rectangle, the element `ContentPresenter` is used. This element takes the content from the templated control and places it as defined — here on both rows, as `Grid.RowSpan` is set to `2`. If a `ContentPresenter` is defined, then the `TargetType` with the `ControlTemplate` must also be set. The content is positioned by setting the `HorizontalAlignment`, `VerticalAlignment`, and `Margin` properties to values defined by the button itself by using `TemplateBinding` markup extensions. With the `ControlTemplate` you can also define triggers, as previously shown within resources. Figure 34-24 shows the new outcome of the button, including the content and the background combined with the template.

```
<Style x:Key="ButtonStyle2" TargetType="{x:Type Button}">
  <Setter Property="Template">
    <Setter.Value>
      <ControlTemplate TargetType="{x:Type Button}" >
        <Grid>
          <Grid.RowDefinitions>
            <RowDefinition Height="2*" />
            <RowDefinition Height="*" />
          </Grid.RowDefinitions>
          <Rectangle Grid.RowSpan="2" RadiusX="4" RadiusY="8"
               Stroke="Green"
               Fill="{TemplateBinding Background}" />
          <Rectangle RadiusX="4" RadiusY="8" Margin="2">
            <Rectangle.Fill>
              <LinearGradientBrush StartPoint="0,0"
                  EndPoint="0,1">
                <GradientStop Offset="0" Color="LightBlue" />
                <GradientStop Offset="0.5" Color="#afff" />
                <GradientStop Offset="1" Color="#6faa" />
              </LinearGradientBrush>
            </Rectangle.Fill>
          </Rectangle>
          <ContentPresenter Grid.RowSpan="2"
              HorizontalAlignment="{TemplateBinding
              HorizontalContentAlignment}"
              VerticalAlignment="{TemplateBinding
              VerticalContentAlignment}"
              Margin="{TemplateBinding Padding}" />
        </Grid>
        <ControlTemplate.Triggers>
          <Trigger Property="IsMouseOver" Value="True">
            <Setter Property="Foreground" Value="Aqua" />
          </Trigger>
          <Trigger Property="IsPressed" Value="True">
            <Setter Property="Foreground" Value="Black" />
          </Trigger>
        </ControlTemplate.Triggers>
      </ControlTemplate>
```

(continued)

(continued)

```
            </Setter.Value>
          </Setter>
        </Style>
      </Window.Resources>
```

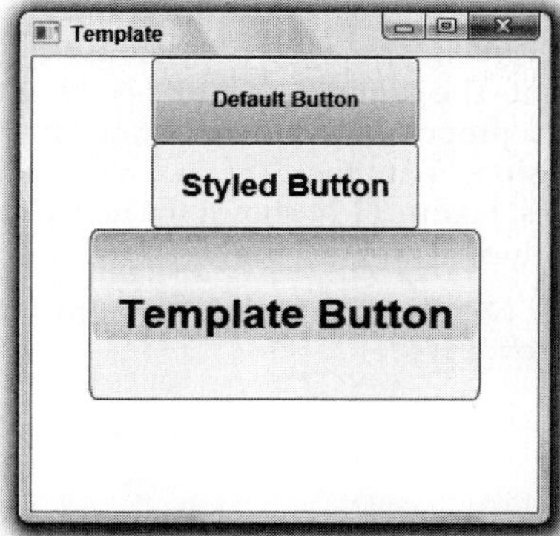

Figure 34-24

Let's make an even fancier button by using transparent features. The style `GelButton` sets the properties `Background`, `Height`, `Foreground` and `Margin`, and the `Template`. The template is the most interesting aspect with this style. The template specifies a `Grid` with just one row and one column.

Inside this cell, you can find a rectangle with the name `GelBackground`. This rectangle has rounded corners and a linear gradient brush for the stroke. The rounded corners are defined by the `RadiusX` and `RadiusY` settings. The stroke that surrounds the rectangle is very thin because the `StrokeThickness` is set to 0.35.

The second rectangle, `GelShine`, is just a small rectangle with a height of 15 pixels, and because of the `Margin` settings, it is visible within the first rectangle. The stroke is transparent, so there is no line surrounding the rectangle. This rectangle just uses a linear gradient fill brush, which goes from a light, partly transparent color to full transparency. This gives the rectangle a shimmering effect.

After the two rectangles, there is a `ContentPresenter` element that defines alignment for the content and takes the content from the button to display.

Such a styled button now looks very fancy on the screen. However, there is no action if the mouse is clicked or the mouse moves over the button. With a template-styled button, you must have triggers for the button to appear differently in response to mouse clicks. The property trigger, `IsMouseOver`, defines a new value for the `Rectangle.Fill` property with a different color for the radial gradient brush. The rectangle that gets the new fill is referenced with the `TargetName` property. The property trigger, `IsPressed`, is very similar; here, simply other radial gradient brush colors are used to fill the rectangle. You can see a button that references the style `GelButton` in Figure 34-25. Figure 34-26 shows the same button while the mouse moved over it where you can see the effect of the radial gradient brush.

```
<Style x:Key="GelButton" TargetType="{x:Type Button}">
  <Setter Property="Background" Value="Black" />
  <Setter Property="Height" Value="40" />
  <Setter Property="Foreground" Value="White" />
  <Setter Property="Margin" Value="3" />
  <Setter Property="Template">
    <Setter.Value>
      <ControlTemplate TargetType="{x:Type Button}">
        <Grid>
          <Rectangle Name="GelBackground" RadiusX="9"
              RadiusY="9"
              Fill="{TemplateBinding Background}"
              StrokeThickness="0.35">
            <Rectangle.Stroke>
              <LinearGradientBrush StartPoint="0,0"
                  EndPoint="0,1">
                <GradientStop Offset="0" Color="White" />
                <GradientStop Offset="1" Color="#666666" />
              </LinearGradientBrush>
            </Rectangle.Stroke>
          </Rectangle>
          <Rectangle Name="GelShine" Margin="2,2,2,0"
              VerticalAlignment="Top" RadiusX="6" RadiusY="6"
              Stroke="Transparent" Height="15px">
            <Rectangle.Fill>
              <LinearGradientBrush StartPoint="0,0"
                  EndPoint="0,1">
                <GradientStop Offset="0" Color="#ccffffff" />
                <GradientStop Offset="1" Color="Transparent"
                />
              </LinearGradientBrush>
            </Rectangle.Fill>
          </Rectangle>
          <ContentPresenter Name="GelButtonContent"
              VerticalAlignment="Center"
              HorizontalAlignment="Center"
              Content="{TemplateBinding Content}" />
        </Grid>
        <ControlTemplate.Triggers>
          <Trigger Property="IsMouseOver" Value="True">
            <Setter Property="Rectangle.Fill"
                TargetName="GelBackground">
              <Setter.Value>
                <RadialGradientBrush>
                  <GradientStop Offset="0" Color="Lime" />
                  <GradientStop Offset="1" Color="DarkGreen"
                  />
                </RadialGradientBrush>
              </Setter.Value>
            </Setter>
            <Setter Property="Foreground" Value="Black" />
          </Trigger>
          <Trigger Property="IsPressed" Value="True">
            <Setter Property="Rectangle.Fill"
```

(continued)

(continued)

```
                    TargetName="GelBackground">
                  <Setter.Value>
                    <RadialGradientBrush>
                      <GradientStop Offset="0" Color="#ffcc34" />
                      <GradientStop Offset="1" Color="#cc9900" />
                    </RadialGradientBrush>
                  </Setter.Value>
                </Setter>
              </Trigger>
            </ControlTemplate.Triggers>
          </ControlTemplate>
        </Setter.Value>
      </Setter>
    </Style>
```

Figure 34-25

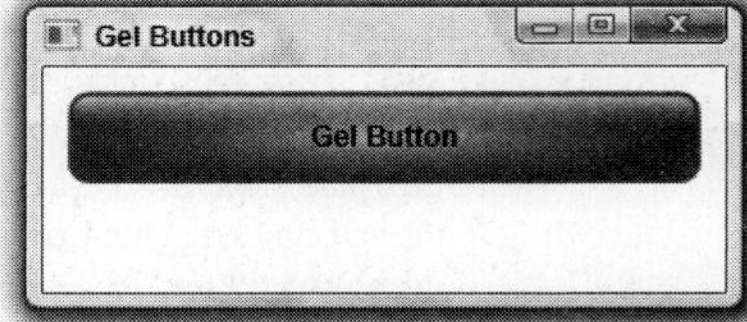

Figure 34-26

Instead of having a rectangular button, an ellipse can be used as a button. In the next example, you can also see how one style can be based on another style.

The style `RoundedGelButton` can be based on the style `GelButton` by setting the `BasedOn` property with the `Style` element. If one style is based on another style, then the new style gets all settings from the base style unless the settings are redefined. For example, the `RoundedGelButtonStyle` gets the `Foreground` and `Margin` settings from the `GelButton` because these settings are not redefined. If you change a setting in a base style, then all styles that are based on the style automatically get the new values.

The `Height` and `Template` properties are redefined with the new style. Here, the template defines two `Ellipse` elements instead of rectangles. The outer ellipse `GelBackground` defines a black ellipse with a gradient stroke around it. The second ellipse is smaller with a small margin (`5`) at the top and a large margin (`50`) at the bottom. This ellipse again has a linear gradient brush that goes from a light color to transparent and specifies the shine effect. Again, there are triggers for `IsMouseOver` and `IsPressed` that change the value of the `Fill` property for the first ellipse.

You can see the new button based on the `RoundedGelButton` style — and it is still a button — in Figure 34-27.

```
<Style x:Key="RoundedGelButton"
    BasedOn="{StaticResource GelButton}"
    TargetType="Button">
  <Setter Property="Width" Value="100" />
  <Setter Property="Height" Value="100" />
  <Setter Property="Grid.Row" Value="2" />
  <Setter Property="Template">
    <Setter.Value>
```

```
<ControlTemplate TargetType="{x:Type Button}">
  <Grid>
    <Ellipse Name="GelBackground" StrokeThickness="0.5"
        Fill="Black">
      <Ellipse.Stroke>
        <LinearGradientBrush StartPoint="0,0"
            EndPoint="0,1">
          <GradientStop Offset="0" Color="#ff7e7e7e" />
          <GradientStop Offset="1" Color="Black" />
        </LinearGradientBrush>
      </Ellipse.Stroke>
    </Ellipse>
    <Ellipse Margin="15,5,15,50">
      <Ellipse.Fill>
        <LinearGradientBrush StartPoint="0,0"
            EndPoint="0,1">
          <GradientStop Offset="0" Color="#aaffffff" />
          <GradientStop Offset="1" Color="Transparent"
          />
        </LinearGradientBrush>
      </Ellipse.Fill>
    </Ellipse>
    <ContentPresenter Name="GelButtonContent"
        VerticalAlignment="Center"
        HorizontalAlignment="Center"
        Content="{TemplateBinding Content}" />
  </Grid>
  <ControlTemplate.Triggers>
    <Trigger Property="IsMouseOver" Value="True">
      <Setter Property="Rectangle.Fill"
          TargetName="GelBackground">
        <Setter.Value>
          <RadialGradientBrush>
            <GradientStop Offset="0" Color="Lime" />
            <GradientStop Offset="1" Color="DarkGreen"
            />
          </RadialGradientBrush>
        </Setter.Value>
      </Setter>
      <Setter Property="Foreground" Value="Black" />
    </Trigger>
    <Trigger Property="IsPressed" Value="True">
      <Setter Property="Rectangle.Fill"
          TargetName="GelBackground">
        <Setter.Value>
          <RadialGradientBrush>
            <GradientStop Offset="0" Color="#ffcc34" />
            <GradientStop Offset="1" Color="#cc9900" />
          </RadialGradientBrush>
        </Setter.Value>
      </Setter>
      <Setter Property="Foreground" Value="Black" />
```

(continued)

(continued)

```
                </Trigger>
              </ControlTemplate.Triggers>
            </ControlTemplate>

          </Setter.Value>
        </Setter>
      </Style>
```

Figure 34-27

Styling a ListBox

Changing a style of a button or a label is a simple task. How about changing the style of an element that contains a list of elements. For example, how about changing a `ListBox`? Again, a list box has behavior and a look. It can display a list of elements, and you can select one or more elements from the list. For the behavior, the `ListBox` class defines methods, properties, and events. The look of the `ListBox` is separate from its behavior. The `ListBox` element has a default look, but you can change this look by creating a template.

To display some items in the list, the `Country` class has been created to represent the name and flag with a path to an image. The class `Country` defines the `Name` and `ImagePath` properties, and it has an overridden `ToString()` method for a default string representation:

```
public class Country
{
   public Country(string name)
      : this(name, null)
   {
   }
   public Country(string name, string imagePath)
   {
      this.Name = name;
      this.ImagePath = imagePath;
   }
   public string Name { get; set; }
   public string ImagePath { get; set; }
   public override string ToString()
   {
      return Name;
   }
}
```

The static class `Countries` returns a list of a few countries that will be displayed:

```
public static class Countries
{
   public static IEnumerable<Country> GetCountries()
   {
      List<Country> countries = new List<Country>();
      countries.Add(new Country("Austria",
          "Images/Austria.bmp"));
      countries.Add(new Country("Germany",
          "Images/Germany.bmp"));
      countries.Add(new Country("Norway",
          "Images/Norway.bmp"));
      countries.Add(new Country("USA", "Images/USA.bmp"));
      return countries;
   }
}
```

Inside the code-behind file in the constructor of the `Window1` class, the `DataContext` property of the Window1 instance is set to the list of countries that is returned from the method `Countries.GetCountries()`. (The `DataContext` property is a feature for data binding that we will discuss in the next chapter.)

```
public partial class Window1 : System.Windows.Window
{
   public Window1()
   {
      InitializeComponent();
      this.DataContext = Countries.GetCountries();
   }
}
```

Within the XAML code, the `ListBox` named `countryList1` is defined. `countryList1` doesn't have a different style. It uses the default look from the `ListBox` element. The property `ItemsSource` is set to the `Binding` markup extension, which is used by data binding. From the code behind, you have seen that the binding is done to an array of `Country` objects. Figure 34-28 shows the default look of the `ListBox`. By default, just the names of the countries returned by the `ToString()` method are displayed in a simple list.

```
<Window x:Class="ListboxStyling.Window1"
xmlns="http://schemas.microsoft.com/winfx/2006/xaml/presentation"
    xmlns:x="http://schemas.microsoft.com/winfx/2006/xaml"
    Title="ListBox Styling" Height="300" Width="300">
  <StackPanel>
    <ListBox Name="countryList1" ItemsSource="{Binding}" />
  </StackPanel>
</Window>
```

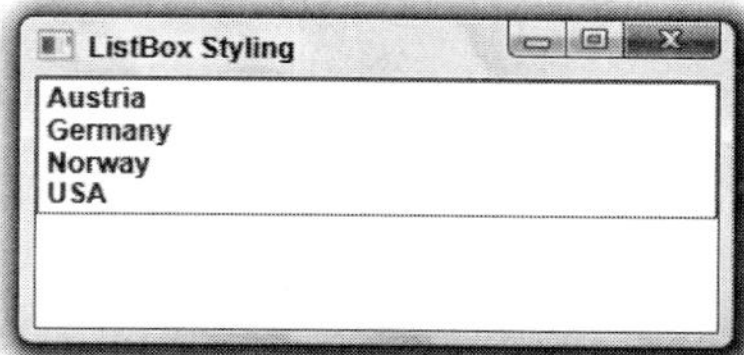

Figure 34-28

The `Country` objects do have both the name and the flag in the object. Of course, you can also display both values in the list box. To do this, you need to define a template.

The `ListBox` element contains `ListBoxItem` elements. You can define the content for an item with the `ItemTemplate`. The style `listBoxStyle1` defines an `ItemTemplate` with a value of a `DataTemplate`. A `DataTemplate` is used to bind data to elements. You can use the `Binding` markup extension with `DataTemplate` elements.

The `DataTemplate` contains a grid with three columns. The first column contains the string `Country:`. The second column contains the name of the country. The third column contains the flag for the country. Because the country names have different lengths, but the view should be the same size for every country name, the `SharedSizeGroup` property is set with the second column definition. This shared size information for the column is used only because the property `Grid.IsSharedSizeScope` is also set.

After the column and row definitions, you can see two `TextBlock` elements. The first `TextBlock` element contains the text `Country:`. The second `TextBlock` element binds to the `Name` property that is defined in the `Country` class.

The content for the third column is a `Border` element containing a `Grid`. The `Grid` contains a `Rectangle` with a linear gradient brush and an `Image` element that is bound to the `ImagePath` property of the `Country` class. Figure 34-29 shows the countries in a `ListBox` with completely different output than before.

```
<Window.Resources>
  <Style x:Key="listBoxStyle1" TargetType="{x:Type ListBox}" >
    <Setter Property="ItemTemplate">
      <Setter.Value>
        <DataTemplate>
          <Grid>
            <Grid.ColumnDefinitions>
              <ColumnDefinition Width="Auto" />
              <ColumnDefinition Width="*"
                  SharedSizeGroup="MiddleColumn" />
              <ColumnDefinition Width="Auto" />
            </Grid.ColumnDefinitions>
            <Grid.RowDefinitions>
              <RowDefinition Height="60" />
            </Grid.RowDefinitions>
            <TextBlock FontSize="16" VerticalAlignment="Center"
                Margin="5" FontStyle="Italic"
                Grid.Column="0">Country:</TextBlock>
            <TextBlock FontSize="16" VerticalAlignment="Center"
                Margin="5" Text="{Binding Name}"
                FontWeight="Bold" Grid.Column="1" />
            <Border Margin="4,0" Grid.Column="2"
                BorderThickness="2" CornerRadius="4">
              <Border.BorderBrush>
                <LinearGradientBrush StartPoint="0,0"
                    EndPoint="0,1">
                  <GradientStop Offset="0" Color="#aaa" />
                  <GradientStop Offset="1" Color="#222" />
                </LinearGradientBrush>
              </Border.BorderBrush>
              <Grid>
                <Rectangle>
```

```
                        <Rectangle.Fill>
                          <LinearGradientBrush StartPoint="0,0"
                              EndPoint="0,1">
                            <GradientStop Offset="0" Color="#444" />
                            <GradientStop Offset="1" Color="#fff" />
                          </LinearGradientBrush>
                        </Rectangle.Fill>
                      </Rectangle>
                      <Image Width="48" Margin="2,2,2,1"
                          Source="{Binding ImagePath}" />
                    </Grid>
                  </Border>
                </Grid>
              </DataTemplate>
            </Setter.Value>
          </Setter>
          <Setter Property="Grid.IsSharedSizeScope" Value="True" />
        </Style>
      </Window.Resources>
```

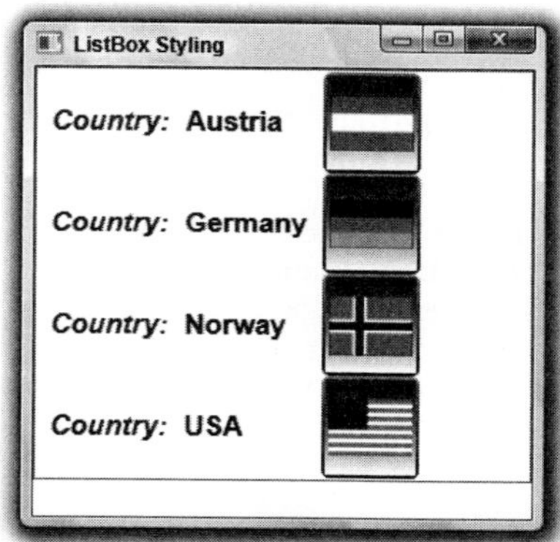

Figure 34-29

It is not necessary that a ListBox have items that follow vertically, one after the other. You can give the user a different view with the same functionality. The next style, listBoxStyle2, defines a template in which the items are shown horizontally with a scroll bar.

In the previous example, only an ItemTemplate was created to define how the items should look in the default ListBox. Now, a template is created to define a different ListBox. The template contains a ControlTemplate element to define the elements of the ListBox. The element is now a ScrollViewer — a view with a scroll bar — that contains a StackPanel. As the items should now be listed horizontally, the Orientation of the StackPanel is set to Horizontal. The stack panel will contain the items that are defined with the ItemsTemplate. As a result, the IsItemsHost of the StackPanel element is set to true. IsItemsHost is a property that is available with every Panel element that can contain a list of items.

The ItemTemplate defines the look for the items in the stack panel. Here, a grid with two rows is created. The first row contains Image elements that are bound to the ImagePath property. The second row contains TextBlock elements that are bound to the Name property.

Figure 34-30 shows the `ListBox` styled with `listBoxStyle2` where the scroll bar appears automatically when the view is too small to display all items in the list.

```
<Style x:Key="listBoxStyle2" TargetType="{x:Type ListBox}">
  <Setter Property="Template">
    <Setter.Value>
      <ControlTemplate TargetType="{x:Type ListBox}">
        <ScrollViewer HorizontalScrollBarVisibility="Auto">
          <StackPanel Name="StackPanel1" IsItemsHost="True"
              Orientation="Horizontal" />
        </ScrollViewer>
      </ControlTemplate>
    </Setter.Value>
  </Setter>
  <Setter Property="VerticalAlignment" Value="Center" />
  <Setter Property="ItemTemplate">
    <Setter.Value>
      <DataTemplate>
        <Grid>
          <Grid.ColumnDefinitions>
            <ColumnDefinition Width="Auto" />

          </Grid.ColumnDefinitions>
          <Grid.RowDefinitions>
            <RowDefinition Height="60" />
            <RowDefinition Height="30" />
          </Grid.RowDefinitions>
          <Image Grid.Row="0" Width="48" Margin="2,2,2,1"
              Source="{Binding ImagePath}" />
          <TextBlock Grid.Row="1" FontSize="14"
              HorizontalAlignment="Center" Margin="5"
              Text="{Binding Name}" FontWeight="Bold" />
        </Grid>
      </DataTemplate>
    </Setter.Value>
  </Setter>
</Style>
```

Figure 34-30

Certainly you see the advantages of separating the look of the controls from their behavior. You may already have many ideas about how you can display your items in a list that best fits the requirements of your application. Perhaps you just want to display as many items as will fit in the window, position them horizontally, and then continue to the next line vertically. That's where a `WrapPanel` comes in. And, of course, you can have a `WrapPanel` inside a template for a `ListBox`, as shown in `listBoxStyle3`. Figure 34-31 shows the result of using the `WrapPanel`.

```
<Style x:Key="listBoxStyle3" TargetType="{x:Type ListBox}">
  <Setter Property="Template">
    <Setter.Value>
      <ControlTemplate TargetType="{x:Type ListBox}">
        <ScrollViewer VerticalScrollBarVisibility="Auto"
              HorizontalScrollBarVisibility="Disabled">
          <WrapPanel IsItemsHost="True" />
        </ScrollViewer>
      </ControlTemplate>
    </Setter.Value>
  </Setter>
  <Setter Property="ItemTemplate">
    <Setter.Value>
      <DataTemplate>
        <Grid>
          <Grid.ColumnDefinitions>
            <ColumnDefinition Width="140" />
          </Grid.ColumnDefinitions>
          <Grid.RowDefinitions>
            <RowDefinition Height="60" />
            <RowDefinition Height="30" />
          </Grid.RowDefinitions>
          <Image Grid.Row="0" Width="48" Margin="2,2,2,1"
              Source="{Binding ImagePath}" />
          <TextBlock Grid.Row="1" FontSize="14"
              HorizontalAlignment="Center"
              Margin="5" Text="{Binding Name}" />

        </Grid>
      </DataTemplate>
    </Setter.Value>
  </Setter>
</Style>
```

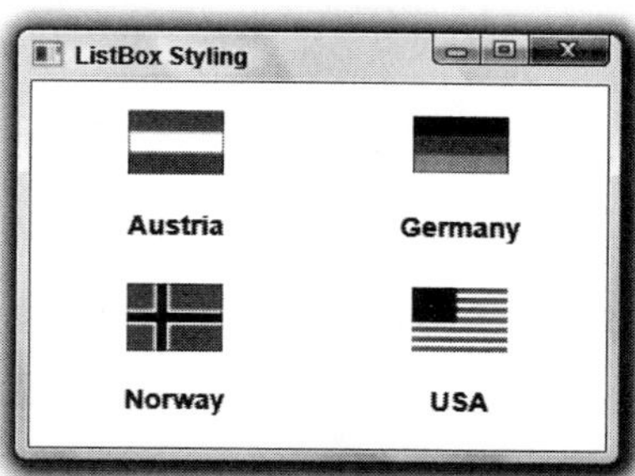

Figure 34-31

In the next chapter, you can read more about the `DataTemplate` *with data binding functionality.*

Summary

In this chapter, you have taken a first tour through the many features of WPF. WPF makes it easy to separate work between developers and designers. Both Microsoft Expression Blend and Visual Studio make it possible to work with XAML code. Compared to prior Windows Forms applications, XAML code does a better separation of the UI from the functionality behind it. All UI features can be created with XAML, and the functionality by using code behind.

You have seen many controls and containers that are all based on vector-graphics. Because of the vector-graphics, WPF elements can be scaled, sheared, and rotated. Because of the content flexibility of content controls, the event handling mechanism is based on bubbling and tunneling events.

Different kinds of brushes are available to paint background and foreground of elements. You can use solid brushes, linear or radial gradient brushes, but also visual brushes to do reflections or show videos.

Styling and templates allow you to customize the look of controls. Triggers allow you to change properties of WPF elements dynamically. Animations can be done easily by animating a property value from a WPF control.

The next chapter continues with WPF showing animations, 3D, data binding, and several more features.

35

Advanced WPF

In the previous chapter you read about some of the core functionality of WPF. In this chapter programming with WPF continues. Here you read about some important aspects for creating complete applications such as data binding and command handling, and you also get an introduction to animations and 3-D programming.

The main topics of this chapter are:

- Data binding
- Commands
- Animations
- 3-D
- Windows Forms integration

Data Binding

In the previous chapter you saw a few features of data binding when styling the `ListBox`. But of course there is a lot more. WPF data binding takes another huge step forward compared to Windows Forms. This section gives you a good start in data binding with WPF and discusses these topics:

- Overview
- Binding with XAML
- Simple object binding
- Object data provider
- List binding
- Binding to XML

Overview

With WPF data binding, the target can be any dependency property of a WPF element, and every property of a CLR object can be the source. Because a WPF element is implemented as a .NET class, every WPF element can be the source as well. See Figure 35-1 for the connection between the source and the target. The `Binding` object defines the connection.

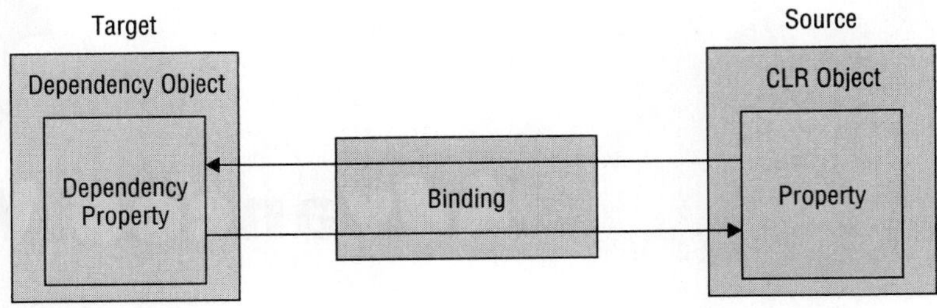

Figure 35-1

Binding supports several binding modes between the target and source. Binding can be *one-way*, where the source information goes to the target, but if the user changes information in the user interface, the source does not get updated. For updates to the source, *two-way* binding is required.

The following table shows the binding modes and their requirements.

Binding Mode	Description
One-time	Binding goes from the source to the target and occurs only once when the application is started or the data context changes. Here, you get a snapshot of the data.
One-way	Binding goes from the source to the target. This is useful for read-only data, because it is not possible to change the data from the user interface. To get updates to the user interface, the source must implement the interface `INotifyPropertyChanged`.
Two-way	With a two-way binding, the user can make changes to the data from the UI. Binding occurs in both directions — from the source to the target and from the target to the source. The source needs to implement read/write properties so that changes can be updated from the UI to the source.
One-way-to-source	With one-way-to-source binding, if the target property changes, the source object gets updated.

Binding with XAML

A WPF element can not only be the target for data binding, it can also be the source. You can bind the source property of one WPF element to the target of another WPF element.

The following code example uses the funny face created earlier, which is built up from WPF shapes and binds it to a slider, so you can move it across the window. The `Slider` is the source element with the name `slider`. The property `Value` gives the actual value of the slider position. The target for data binding is the inner `Canvas` element. The inner `Canvas` element with the name `FunnyFace` contains all the shapes needed to draw the funny face. This canvas is contained within an outer `Canvas` element, so it is possible to position this canvas within the outer canvas by setting the attached properties. The attached property `Canvas.Left` is set to the `Binding` markup extension. In the `Binding` markup extension, the `ElementName` is set to `slider` to reference the WPF slider element, and the `Path` is set to `Value` to get the value from the `Value` property.

```
<Window x:Class="DataBindingSample.Window1"
    xmlns="http://schemas.microsoft.com/winfx/2006/xaml/presentation"
    xmlns:x="http://schemas.microsoft.com/winfx/2006/xaml"
    Title="Data Binding" Height="345" Width="310">
    <StackPanel>
      <Canvas Height="210" Width="280">
        <Canvas Canvas.Top="0"
            Canvas.Left="{Binding Path=Value, ElementName=slider}"
            Name="FunnyFace" Height="210" Width="230">
          <Ellipse Canvas.Left="20" Canvas.Top="50" Width="100" Height="100"
              Stroke="Blue" StrokeThickness="4" Fill="Yellow" />
          <Ellipse Canvas.Left="40" Canvas.Top="65" Width="25" Height="25"
              Stroke="Blue" StrokeThickness="3" Fill="White" />
          <Ellipse Canvas.Left="50" Canvas.Top="75" Width="5" Height="5"
              Fill="Black" />
          <Path Name="mouth" Stroke="Blue" StrokeThickness="4"
              Data="M 32,125 Q 65,122 72,108" />

          <Line X1="94" X2="102" Y1="144" Y2="166" Stroke="Blue"
              StrokeThickness="4" />
          <Line X1="84" X2="103" Y1="169" Y2="166" Stroke="Blue"
              StrokeThickness="4" />

          <Line X1="62" X2="52" Y1="146" Y2="168" Stroke="Blue"
              StrokeThickness="4" />
          <Line X1="38" X2="53" Y1="160" Y2="168" Stroke="Blue"
              StrokeThickness="4" />
        </Canvas>
      </Canvas>

      <Slider Name="slider" Orientation="Horizontal" Value="10"
          Maximum="100" />

    </StackPanel>
</Window>
```

When running the application, you can move the slider and make the funny face move, as you can see in Figures 35-2 and 35-3.

Instead of defining the binding information with XAML code, as was done in the preceding code with the `Binding` metadata extension, you can do it with code behind. Have one more look at the XAML version of binding:

```
<Canvas Canvas.Top="0"
    Canvas.Left="{Binding Path=Value, ElementName=slider}"
    Name="FunnyFace" Height="210" Width="230">
```

With code behind you have to create a new `Binding` object and set the `Path` and `Source` properties. The `Source` property must be set to the source object; here, it is the WPF object `slider`. The `Path` is set to a `PropertyPath` instance that is initialized with the name of the property of the source object, `Value`.

Figure 35-2

Figure 35-3

With the target, you can invoke the method `SetBinding()` to define the binding. Here, the target is the `Canvas` object with the name `FunnyFace`. The method `SetBinding()` requires two parameters: the first one is a dependency property and the second one is the binding object. The `Canvas.Left` property should be bound, so the dependency property of type `DependencyProperty` can be accessed with the `Canvas.LeftProperty` field:

```
Binding binding = new Binding();
binding.Path = new PropertyPath("Value");
binding.Source = slider;

FunnyFace.SetBinding(Canvas.LeftProperty, binding);
```

You can configure a number of binding options with the `Binding` class, as described in the following table.

Binding Class Members	Description
`Source`	With the `Source` property, you define the source object for data binding.
`RelativeSource`	With `RelativeSource`, you can specify the source in relation to the target object. This is useful to display error messages when the source of the error comes from the same control.
`ElementName`	If the source is a WPF element, you can specify the source with the `ElementName` property.
`Path`	With the `Path` property, you specify the path to the source object. This can be the property of the source object, but indexers and properties of child elements are also supported.

Binding Class Members	Description
`XPath`	With an XML data source, you can define an XPath query expression to get the data for binding.
`Mode`	The mode defines the direction for the binding. The `Mode` property is of type `BindingMode`. `BindingMode` is an enumeration with the following values: `Default`, `OneTime`, `OneWay`, `TwoWay`, `OneWayToSource`. The default mode depends on the target: with a `TextBox`, two-way binding is the default; with a `Label` that is read-only, the default is one-way. `OneTime` means that the data is only `init` loaded from the source; `OneWay` also does updates from the source to the target. With `TwoWay` binding changes from the WPF elements are written back to the source. `OneWayToSource` means that the data is never read but always written from the target to the source.
`Converter`	With the `Converter` property, you can specify a converter class that converts the data for the UI and back. The converter class must implement the interface `IValueConverter`, which defines the methods `Convert()` and `ConvertBack()`. You can pass parameters to the converter methods with the `ConverterParameter` property. The converter can be culture-sensitive; the culture can be set with the `ConverterCulture` property.
`FallbackValue`	With the `FallbackValue` property, you can define a default value that is used if binding doesn't return a value.
`ValidationRules`	With the `ValidationRules` property, you can define a collection of `ValiationRule` objects that are checked before the source is updated from the WPF target elements. The class `ExceptionValidationRule` is derived from the class `ValidationRule` and checks for exceptions.

Simple Object Binding

For binding to CLR objects, with the .NET classes you just have to define properties, as shown in this example with the class `Book` and the properties `Title`, `Publisher`, `Isbn`, and `Authors`:

```
public class Book
{
   public Book(string title, string publisher, string isbn,
         params string[] authors)
   {
      this.Title = title;
      this.Publisher = publisher;
      this.Isbn = isbn;
      foreach (string author in authors)
      {
         this.authors.Add(author);
      }
   }
```

(continued)

(continued)

```
        public Book()
            : this("unknown", "unknown", "unknown")
        {
        }

        public string Title { get; set; }
        public string Publisher { get; set; }
        public string Isbn { get; set; }

        public override string ToString()
        {
            return Title;
        }

        private readonly List<string> authors = new List<string>();
        public string[] Authors
        {
            get { return authors.ToArray(); }
        }
    }
```

In the user interface, several labels and `TextBox` controls are defined to display book information. Using `Binding` markup extensions, the `TextBox` controls are bound to the properties of the `Book` class. With the `Binding` markup extension nothing more than the `Path` property is defined to bind it to the property of the `Book` class. There's no need to define a source because the source is defined by assigning the `DataContext`, as you can see in the code behind that follows. The mode is defined by its default with the `TextBox` element, and this is two-way binding.

```
<Window x:Class="ObjectBindingSample.Window1"
    xmlns="http://schemas.microsoft.com/winfx/2006/xaml/presentation"
    xmlns:x="http://schemas.microsoft.com/winfx/2006/xaml"
    Title="Object Binding Sample" Height="300" Width="340"
    >
    <Grid Name="bookGrid" Margin="5" >
      <Grid.ColumnDefinitions>
        <ColumnDefinition Width="30*" />
        <ColumnDefinition Width="70*" />
      </Grid.ColumnDefinitions>
      <Grid.RowDefinitions>
        <RowDefinition Height="50" />
        <RowDefinition Height="50" />
        <RowDefinition Height="50" />
        <RowDefinition Height="50" />
        <RowDefinition Height="50" />
       </Grid.RowDefinitions>
      <Label Grid.Column="0" Grid.Row="0">Title:</Label>
      <TextBox Margin="5" Height="30" Grid.Column="1" Grid.Row="0"
            Text="{Binding Title}" />
      <Label Grid.Column="0" Grid.Row="1">Publisher:</Label>
      <TextBox Margin="5" Height="30" Grid.Column="1" Grid.Row="1"
            Text="{Binding Publisher}" />
      <Label Grid.Column="0" Grid.Row="2">ISBN:</Label>
```

```
        <TextBox Margin="5" Height="30" Grid.Column="1" Grid.Row="2"
              Text="{Binding Isbn}" />

        <Button Margin="5" Grid.Column="1" Grid.Row="4"
            Click="bookButton_Click" Name="bookButton">Open Dialog</Button>

      </Grid>
  </Window>
```

With the code behind, a new `Book` object is created, and the book is assigned to the `DataContext` property of the `Grid` control. `DataContext` is a dependency property that is defined with the base class `FrameworkElement`. Assigning the `DataContext` with the `Grid` control means that every element in the `Grid` control has a default binding to the same data context.

```
public partial class Window1 : System.Windows.Window
{
   private Book book1 = new Book();

   public Window1()
   {
      InitializeComponent();

      book1.Title = "Professional C# 2005 with .NET 3.0";
      book1.Publisher = "Wrox Press";
      book1.Isbn = "978-0470124727";

      bookGrid.DataContext = book1;
   }
}
```

After starting the application, you can see the bound data, as shown in Figure 35-4.

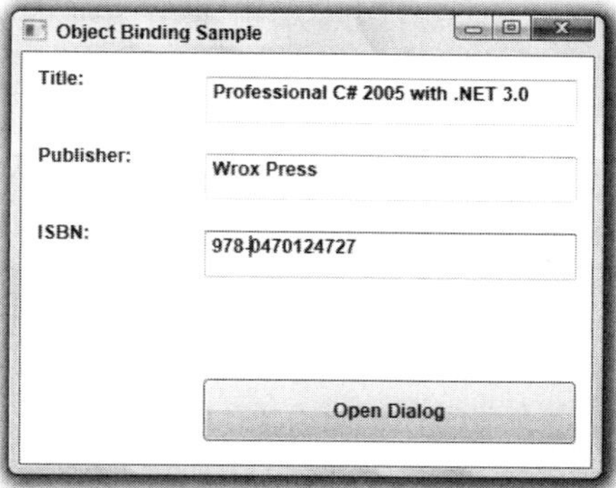

Figure 35-4

To demonstrate the two-way binding (changes to the input of the WPF element are reflected inside the CLR object), the `OnOpenBookDialog()` method is implemented. This method is assigned to the `Click` event of the `bookButton`, as you can see in the XAML code. When implemented a message box pops up to show the current title and ISBN number of the `book1` object. Figure 35-5 shows the output from the message box after a change to the input was made during runtime.

```
void bookButton_Click(object sender, RoutedEventArgs e)
{
   string message = book1.Title;
   string caption = book1.Isbn;
   MessageBox.Show(message, caption);
}
```

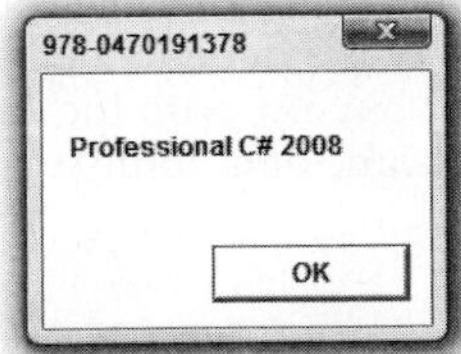

Figure 35-5

Object Data Provider

Instead of defining the object in code behind, you can define an object instance with XAML. To make this possible, you have to reference the namespace with the namespace declarations in the XML root element. The XML attribute `xmlns:src="clr-namespace:Wrox.ProCsharp.WPF"` assigns the .NET namespace `Wrox.ProCSharp.WPF` to the XML namespace alias `src`.

One object of the `Book` class is now defined with the `Book` element inside the `Window` resources. By assigning values to the XML attributes `Title` and `Publisher`, you set the values of the properties from the `Book` class. `x:Key="theBook"` defines the identifier for the resource so that you can reference the book object. In the `TextBox` element, now the `Source` is defined with the `Binding` markup extension to reference the `theBook` resource.

XAML markup extensions can be combined. In the following sample, the `StaticResource` markup extension used to reference the book resource is contained within the `Binding` markup extension.

```
<Window x:Class="Wrox.ProCSharp.WPF.Window1"
    xmlns="http://schemas.microsoft.com/winfx/2006/xaml/presentation"
    xmlns:x="http://schemas.microsoft.com/winfx/2006/xaml"
    xmlns:src="clr-namespace:Wrox.ProCSharp.WPF"
    Title="Object Binding Sample" Height="300" Width="340">
  <Window.Resources>
    <src:Book x:Key="theBook" Title="Professional C# 2008"
          Publisher="Wrox Press" />
  </Window.Resources>

<!-- ... -->
      <TextBox Margin="5" Height="30" Grid.Column="1" Grid.Row="0"
            Text="{Binding Source={StaticResource theBook}, Path=Title}" />
<!-- ... -->
```

If the .NET namespace to reference is in a different assembly, you have to add the assembly as well to the XML declaration:

```
xmlns:system="clr-namespace:System;assembly=mscorlib"
```

Instead of defining the object instance directly within XAML code, you can define an object data provider that references a class to invoke a method. For use by the `ObjectDataProvider`, it's best to create a factory class that returns the object to display, as shown with the `BookFactory` class:

```
public class BookFactory
{
   private List<Book> books = new List<Book>();

   public BookFactory()
   {
      books.Add(new Book("Professional C# 2008",
            "Wrox Press", "978-0470191378"));
   }

   public Book GetTheBook()
   {
      return books[0];
   }
}
```

The `ObjectDataProvider` element can be defined in the resources section. The XML attribute `ObjectType` defines the name of the class; with `MethodName` you specify the name of the method that is invoked to get the book object:

```
<Window.Resources>
  <ObjectDataProvider ObjectType="src:BookFactory" MethodName="GetTheBook"
      x:Key="theBook">
  </ObjectDataProvider>
</Window.Resources>
```

The properties you can specify with the `ObjectDataProvider` class are listed in the following table.

ObjectDataProvider	Description
`ObjectType`	The `ObjectType` property defines the type to create an instance of.
`ConstructorParameters`	Using the `ConstructorParameters` collection, you can add parameters to the class to create an instance.
`MethodName`	The `MethodName` property defines the name of the method that is invoked by the object data provider.
`MethodParameters`	With the `MethodParameters` property, you can assign parameters to the method defined with the `MethodName` property.
`ObjectInstance`	With the `ObjectInstance` property, you can get and set the object that is used by the `ObjectDataProvider` class. For example, you can assign an existing object programmatically instead of defining the `ObjectType` so that an object is instantiated by the `ObjectDataProvider`.
`Data`	With the `Data` property you can access the underlying object that is used for data binding. If the `MethodName` is defined, with the `Data` property you can access the object that is returned from the method defined.

List Binding

Binding to a list is more frequently done than binding to simple objects. Binding to a list is very similar to binding to a simple object. You can assign the complete list to the `DataContext` from code behind, or you can use an `ObjectDataProvider` that accesses an object factory that returns a list. With elements that support binding to a list (for example, a `ListBox`), the complete list is bound. With elements that support binding to just one object (for example, a `TextBox`), the current item is bound.

With the `BookFactory` class, now a list of `Book` objects is returned:

```
public class BookFactory
{
   private List<Book> books = new List<Book>();

   public BookFactory()
   {
      books.Add(new Book("Professional C# 2008", "Wrox Press",
            "978-0470191378", "Christian Nagel", "Bill Evjen",
            "Jay Glynn", "Karli Watson", "Morgan Skinner"));
      books.Add(new Book("Professional C# 2005 with .NET 3.0",
            "Wrox Press", "978-0-470-12472-7", "Christian Nagel",
            "Bill Evjen", "Jay Glynn", "Karli Watson", "Morgan Skinner"));
      books.Add(new Book("Professional C# 2005",
            "Wrox Press", "978-0-7645-7534-1", "Christian Nagel",
            "Bill Evjen","Jay Glynn", "Karli Watson", "Morgan Skinner",
            "Allen Jones"));
      books.Add(new Book("Beginning Visual C#",
            "Wrox Press", "978-0-7645-4382-1", "Karli Watson",
            "David Espinosa", "Zach Greenvoss", "Jacob Hammer Pedersen",
            "Christian Nagel", "John D. Reid", "Matthew Reynolds",
            "Morgan Skinner", "Eric White"));
      books.Add(new Book("ASP.NET Professional Secrets",
            "Wiley", "978-0-7645-2628-2", "Bill Evjen",
            "Thiru Thangarathinam", "Bill Hatfield", "Doug Seven",
            "S. Srinivasa Sivakumar", "Dave Wanta", "Jason T. Roff"));
      books.Add(new Book("Design and Analysis of Distributed Algorithms",
            "Wiley", "978-0-471-71997-7", "Nicolo Santoro"));
   }

   public IEnumerable<Book> GetBooks()
   {
      return books;
   }
}
```

In the WPF code-behind constructor of the class `Window1` a `BookFactory` is instantiated and the method `GetBooks()` is invoked to assign the `Book` array with the `DataContext` of the `Window1` instance:

```
public partial class Window1 : System.Windows.Window
{
   private BookFactory factory = new BookFactory();

   public Window1()
```

```
        {
            InitializeComponent();

            this.DataContext = factory.GetBooks();
        }
    }
```

In XAML you just need a control that supports lists, such as the `ListBox`, and to bind the `ItemsSource` property as shown:

```
<Window x:Class=" Wrox.ProCSharp.WPF.Window1"
    xmlns="http://schemas.microsoft.com/winfx/2006/xaml/presentation"
    xmlns:x="http://schemas.microsoft.com/winfx/2006/xaml"
    Title="List Binding Sample" Height="300" Width="518"
    >
  <DockPanel>
    <Grid >
      <Grid.ColumnDefinitions>
        <ColumnDefinition />
      </Grid.ColumnDefinitions>
      <Grid.RowDefinitions>
        <RowDefinition />
        <RowDefinition />
        <RowDefinition />
        <RowDefinition />
      </Grid.RowDefinitions>
      <ListBox HorizontalAlignment="Left" Margin="5" Grid.RowSpan="4"
          Grid.Row="0" Grid.Column="0" Name="booksList"
          ItemsSource="{Binding}" />
    </Grid>
  </DockPanel>
</Window>
```

Because the `Window` has the `Book` array assigned to the `DataContext`, and the `ListBox` is placed within the `Window`, the `ListBox` shows all books with the default template, as illustrated in Figure 35-6.

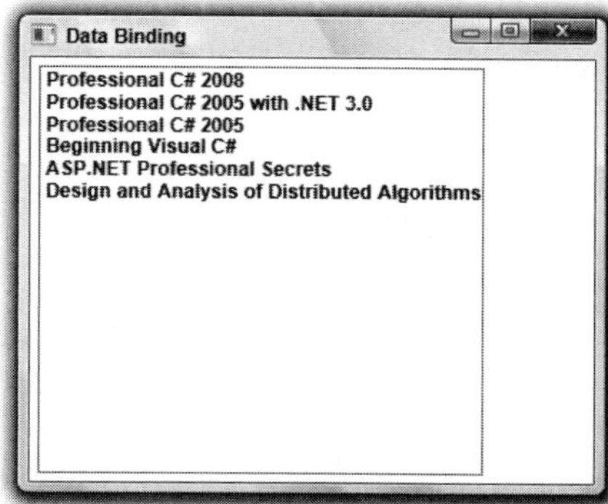

Figure 35-6

For a more flexible layout of the `ListBox`, you have to define a template, as was discussed in the previous chapter for `ListBox` styling. The `ItemTemplate` contained in the style `listBoxStyle` defines a `DataTemplate` with a `Label` element. The content of the label is bound to the `Title`. The item template is repeated for every item in the list.

The `ListBox` element has the `Style` property assigned. `ItemsSource` is, as before, set to the default binding. Figure 35-7 shows the output of the application with the new `ListBox` style.

```
<Window.Resources>
  <Style x:Key="listBoxStyle" TargetType="{x:Type ListBox}" >
    <Setter Property="ItemTemplate">
      <Setter.Value>
        <DataTemplate>
          <Label Content="{Binding Title}" />
        </DataTemplate>
      </Setter.Value>
    </Setter>
  </Style>
</Window.Resources>

<!-- ... -->

    <ListBox HorizontalAlignment="Left" Margin="5"
        Style="{StaticResource listBoxStyle}" Grid.RowSpan="4"
        ItemsSource="{Binding}" />
```

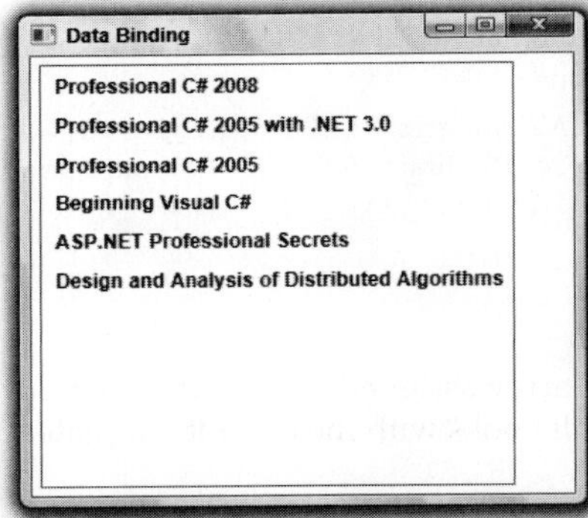

Figure 35-7

Master-Details Binding

Instead of just showing all the elements inside a list, you might want or need to show detail information about the selected item. It doesn't require a lot of work to do this. You just have to define the elements to display the current selection. In the sample application, three `Label` elements are defined with the `Binding` markup extension set to the `Book` properties `Title`, `Publisher`, and `Isbn`. There's one important change you have to make to the `ListBox`. By default, the labels are bound to just the first element of the list. By setting the `ListBox` property `IsSynchronizedWithCurrentItem="True"`, the selection of the list box is set to the current item. In Figure 35-8 you can see the result; the selected item is shown in the detail section labels.

```
<Window x:Class=" Wrox.ProCSharp.WPF.Window1"
    xmlns="http://schemas.microsoft.com/winfx/2006/xaml/presentation"
    xmlns:x="http://schemas.microsoft.com/winfx/2006/xaml"
    Title="List Binding Sample" Height="300" Width="518"
    >
```

```
  <Window.Resources>
    <Style x:Key="listBoxStyle" TargetType="{x:Type ListBox}" >
      <Setter Property="ItemTemplate">
        <Setter.Value>
          <DataTemplate>
            <Label Content="{Binding Title}" />
          </DataTemplate>
        </Setter.Value>
      </Setter>
    </Style>
    <Style x:Key="labelStyle" TargetType="{x:Type Label}">
      <Setter Property="Width" Value="190" />
      <Setter Property="Height" Value="40" />
      <Setter Property="Margin" Value="5,5,5,5" />
    </Style>
  </Window.Resources>
  <DockPanel>
    <Grid >
      <Grid.ColumnDefinitions>
        <ColumnDefinition />
        <ColumnDefinition />
      </Grid.ColumnDefinitions>
      <Grid.RowDefinitions>
        <RowDefinition />
        <RowDefinition />
        <RowDefinition />
        <RowDefinition />
      </Grid.RowDefinitions>
      <ListBox IsSynchronizedWithCurrentItem="True" HorizontalAlignment="Left"
          Margin="5" Style="{StaticResource listBoxStyle}"
          Grid.RowSpan="4" ItemsSource="{Binding}" />
      <Label Style="{StaticResource labelStyle}" Content="{Binding Title}"
          Grid.Row="0" Grid.Column="1" />
      <Label Style="{StaticResource labelStyle}" Content="{Binding Publisher}"
          Grid.Row="1" Grid.Column="1" />
      <Label Style="{StaticResource labelStyle}" Content="{Binding Isbn}"
          Grid.Row="2" Grid.Column="1" />

    </Grid>
  </DockPanel>
</Window>
```

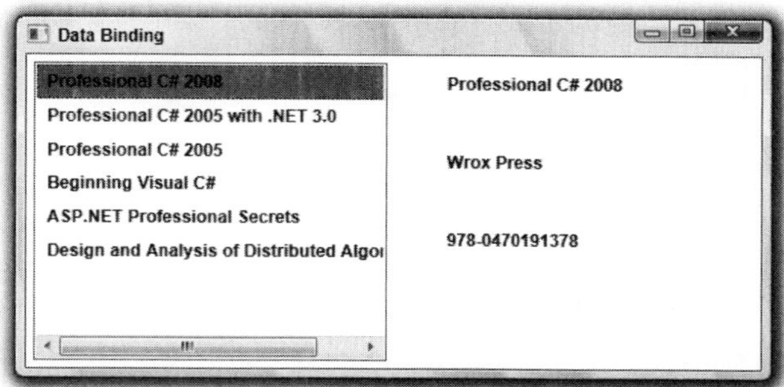

Figure 35-8

Value Conversion

The authors of the book are still missing in the output. If you bind the `Authors` property to a `Label` element, the `ToString()` method of the `Array` class is invoked, which just returns the name of the type. One solution to this is to bind the `Authors` property to a `ListBox`. For the `ListBox`, you can define a template for a specific view. Another solution is to convert the string array returned by the `Authors` property to a string and use the string for binding.

The class `StringArrayConverter` converts a string array to a string. WPF converter classes must implement the interface `IValueConverter` from the namespace `System.Windows.Data`. This interface defines the methods `Convert()` and `ConvertBack()`. With the `StringArrayConverter`, the `Convert()` method converts the string array from the variable `value` to a string by using the `String.Join()` method. The separator parameter of the `Join()` is taken from the variable `parameter` received with the `Convert()` method.

You can read more about the methods of the String classes in Chapter 8, "Strings and Regular Expressions."

```
public class StringArrayConverter : IValueConverter
{
   public object Convert(object value, Type targetType, object parameter,
         System.Globalization.CultureInfo culture)
   {
      string[] stringCollection = (string[])value;
      string separator = (string)parameter;

      return String.Join(separator, stringCollection);
   }

   public object ConvertBack(object value, Type targetType,
         object parameter, System.Globalization.CultureInfo culture)
   {
      string s = (string)value;
      char separator = (char)parameter;

      return s.Split(separator);
   }
}
```

In the XAML code, the `StringArrayConverter` class can be declared as a resource for referencing it from the `Binding` markup extension:

```
<Window x:Class=" Wrox.ProCSharp.WPF.Window1"
    xmlns="http://schemas.microsoft.com/winfx/2006/xaml/presentation"
    xmlns:x="http://schemas.microsoft.com/winfx/2006/xaml"
    xmlns:src="clr-namespace:Wrox.ProCSharp.WPF"
    Title="List Binding Sample" Height="300" Width="518"
    >
  <Window.Resources>
    <src:StringArrayConverter x:Key="stringArrayConverter" />
    <!-- ... -->
```

For multiline output, a `TextBlock` element is declared with the `TextWrapping` property set to `Wrap` to make it possible to display multiple authors. In the `Binding` markup extension the `Path` is set to `Authors`, which is defined as a property returning a string array. The string array is converted from the resource `stringArrayConverter` as defined by the `Converter` property. The `Convert` method of the converter implementation receives the `ConverterParameter', '` as input to separate the authors:

```
<TextBlock Width="190" Height="50" Margin="5" TextWrapping="Wrap"
      Text="{Binding Path=Authors,
      Converter={StaticResource stringArrayConverter},
      ConverterParameter=', ' }"
      Grid.Row="3" Grid.Column="1" />
```

Figure 35-9 shows the book details, including authors.

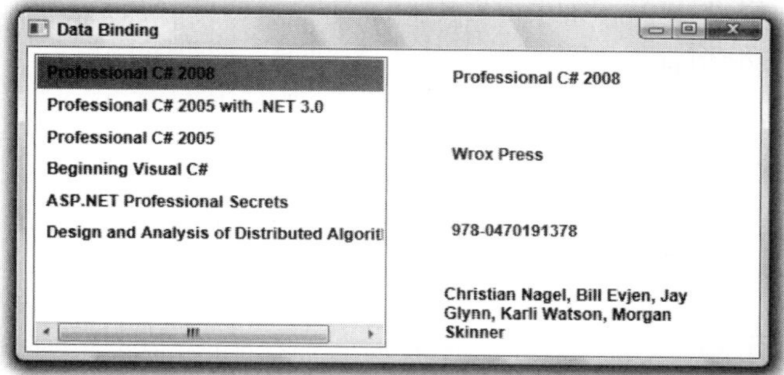

Figure 35-9

Adding List Items Dynamically

What if list items are added dynamically? The WPF element must be notified of elements added to the list.

In the XAML code of the WPF application, a `Button` element is added inside a `StackPanel`. The `Click` event is assigned to the method `OnAddBook()`:

```
<!-- ... -->
<DockPanel>
  <StackPanel Orientation="Horizontal" DockPanel.Dock="Bottom" Height="60">
    <Button Click="addBookButton_Click" Name="addBookButton" Margin="5"
        Width="80" Height="40">Add Book</Button>
  </StackPanel>
  <Grid >
    <!-- ... -->
```

In the method `OnAddBook()`, which implements the event handler code for the `addBookButton`, a new `Book` object is added to the list. If you test the application with the `BookFactory` as it is implemented now, there's no notification to the WPF elements that a new object has been added to the list.

```
void addBookButton_Click(object sender, RoutedEventArgs e)
{
   factory.AddBook(new Book(".NET 2.0 Wrox Box", "Wrox Press",
       "978-0-470-04840-5"));
}
```

The object that is assigned to the `DataContext` must implement the interface `INotifyCollectionChanged`. This interface defines the `CollectionChanged` event that is used by the WPF application. Instead of implementing this interface on your own with a custom collection class, you can use the generic collection class `ObservableCollection<T>` that is defined with the namespace `System.Collections.ObjectModel` in the assembly `WindowsBase`. Now, as a new item is added to the collection, the new item immediately shows up in the `ListBox`:

```
public class BookFactory
{
   private ObservableCollection<Book> books =
         new ObservableCollection<Book>();

   // ...

   public void AddBook(Book book)
   {
      books.Add(book);
   }

   public IEnumerable<Book> GetBooks()
   {
      return books;
   }
}
```

Data Templates

In the previous chapter, you saw how controls can be customized with templates. You can also define a template for a data type, for example, the `Book` class. No matter where the `Book` class is used, the template defines the default look.

In the example, the `DataTemplate` is defined within the `Window` resources. The `DataType` property references the class `Book` from the namespace `Wrox.ProCSharp.WPF`. The template defines a border with two label elements contained in a stack panel. With the `ListBox` element you can see there's no template referenced. The only property that is defined by the `ListBox` is `ItemsSource` with a value for the default `Binding` markup extension. Because the `DataTemplate` does not define a key, it is used by all lists containing `Book` objects. Figure 35-10 shows the output of the application with the data template.

```
<Window x:Class=" Wrox.ProCSharp.WPF.DataTemplateDemo"
    xmlns="http://schemas.microsoft.com/winfx/2006/xaml/presentation"
    xmlns:x="http://schemas.microsoft.com/winfx/2006/xaml"
    xmlns:src="clr-namespace:Wrox.ProCSharp.WPF"
    Title="Data Binding" Height="300" Width="300"
    >
  <Window.Resources>
    <DataTemplate DataType="{x:Type src:Book}">
      <Border BorderBrush="Blue" BorderThickness="2" Background="LightBlue"
          Margin="10" Padding="15">
        <StackPanel>
          <Label Content="{Binding Path=Title}" />
          <Label Content="{Binding Path=Publisher}" />
        </StackPanel>
      </Border>
    </DataTemplate>
  </Window.Resources>
    <Grid>
      <ListBox ItemsSource="{Binding}" />
    </Grid>
</Window>
```

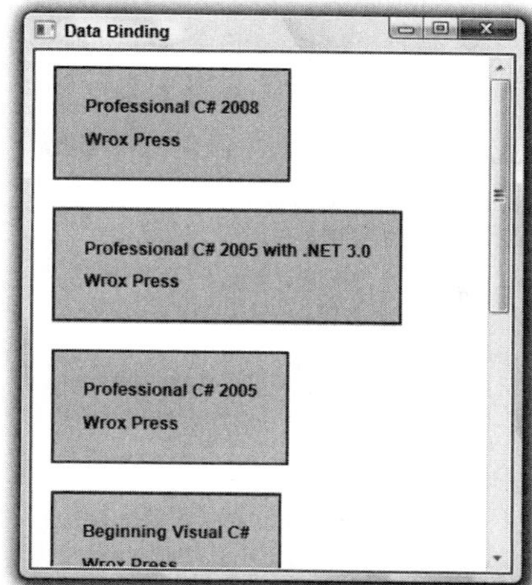

Figure 35-10

In case you want to use a different data template with the same data type, you can create a data template selector. A data template selector is implemented in a class that derives from the base class `DataTemplateSelector`.

Here a data template selector is implemented by selecting a different template based on the publisher. Within the `Window` resources these templates are defined. One template can be accessed by the key name `WroxBookTemplate`; the other template has the key name `WileyBookTemplate`:

```
<DataTemplate x:Key="WroxBookTemplate" DataType="{x:Type src:Book}">
   <Border BorderBrush="Blue" BorderThickness="2" Background="LightBlue"
         Margin="10" Padding="15">
      <StackPanel>
         <Label Content="{Binding Path=Title}" />
         <Label Content="{Binding Path=Publisher}" />
      </StackPanel>
   </Border>
</DataTemplate>

<DataTemplate x:Key="WileyBookTemplate" DataType="{x:Type src:Book}">
   <Border BorderBrush="Yellow" BorderThickness="2"
         Background="LightGreen" Margin="10" Padding="15">
      <StackPanel>
         <Label Content="{Binding Path=Title}" />
         <Label Content="{Binding Path=Publisher}" />
      </StackPanel>
   </Border>
</DataTemplate>
```

For selecting the template the class `BookDataTemplateSelector` overrides the method `SelectTemplate` from the base class `DataTemplateSelector`. The implementation selects the template based on the `Publisher` property from the `Book` class:

```
using System.Windows;
using System.Windows.Controls;

namespace Wrox.ProCSharp.WPF
{
   public class BookDataTemplateSelector : DataTemplateSelector
   {
      public override DataTemplate SelectTemplate(object item,
            DependencyObject container)
      {
         if (item != null && item is Book)
         {
            Window window = Application.Current.MainWindow;

            Book book = item as Book;
            switch (book.Publisher)
            {
               case "Wrox Press":
                  return window.FindResource("WroxBookTemplate")
                        as DataTemplate;
               case "Wiley":
                  return window.FindResource("WileyBookTemplate")
                        as DataTemplate;
               default:
                  return window.FindResource("BookTemplate") as DataTemplate;
            }
         }
         return null;
      }
   }
}
```

For accessing the class `BookDataTemplateSelector` from XAML code, the class is defined within the `Window` resources:

```
<src:BookDataTemplateSelector x:Key="bookTemplateSelector" />
```

Now the selector class can be assigned to the `ItemTemplateSelector` property of the `ListBox`:

```
<ListBox ItemsSource="{Binding}"
      ItemTemplateSelector="{StaticResource bookTemplateSelector}" />
```

When running the application, you can see different data templates based on the publisher, as shown in Figure 35-11.

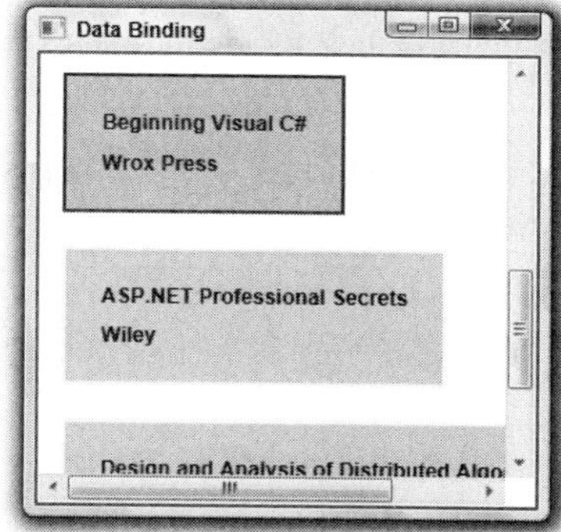

Figure 35-11

Binding to XML

WPF data binding has special support for binding to XML data. You can use `XmlDataProvider` as a data source and bind the elements by using XPath expressions. For a hierarchical display, you can use the `TreeView` control and create the view for the items by using the `HierarchicalDataTemplate`.

The following XML file containing `Book` elements is used as a source in the next examples:

```
<?xml version="1.0" encoding="utf-8" ?>
<Books>
  <Book isbn="978-0-470-12472-7">
    <Title>Professional C# 2008</Title>
    <Publisher>Wrox Press</Publisher>
    <Author>Christian Nagel</Author>
    <Author>Bill Evjen</Author>
    <Author>Jay Glynn</Author>
    <Author>Karli Watson</Author>
    <Author>Morgan Skinner</Author>
  </Book>
  <Book isbn="978-0-7645-4382-1">
    <Title>Beginning Visual C# 2008</Title>
    <Publisher>Wrox Press</Publisher>
    <Author>Karli Watson</Author>
    <Author>David Espinosa</Author>
    <Author>Zach Greenvoss</Author>
    <Author>Jacob Hammer Pedersen</Author>
    <Author>Christian Nagel</Author>
    <Author>John D. Reid</Author>
    <Author>Matthew Reynolds</Author>
    <Author>Morgan Skinner</Author>
    <Author>Eric White</Author>
  </Book>
</Books>
```

Similarly to defining an object data provider, you can define an XML data provider. Both `ObjectDataProvider` and `XmlDataProvider` are derived from the same base class, `DataSourceProvider`. With the `XmlDataProvider` in the example, the `Source` property is set to reference the XML file `books.xml`. The `XPath` property defines an XPath expression to reference the

XML root element `Books`. The `Grid` element references the XML data source with the `DataContext` property. With the data context for the grid, all `Book` elements are required for a list binding, so the XPath expression is set to `Book`. Inside the grid, you can find the `ListBox` element that binds to the default data context and uses the `DataTemplate` to include the title in `TextBlock` elements as items of the `ListBox`. Inside the grid, you can also see three `Label` elements with data binding set to XPath expressions to display the title, publisher, and ISBN numbers.

```
<Window x:Class="Wrox.ProCSharp.WPF.Window1"
    xmlns="http://schemas.microsoft.com/winfx/2006/xaml/presentation"
    xmlns:x="http://schemas.microsoft.com/winfx/2006/xaml"
    Title="XML Binding" Height="348" Width="498"
    >
  <Window.Resources>
    <XmlDataProvider x:Key="books" Source="Books.xml" XPath="Books" />

    <DataTemplate x:Key="listTemplate">
      <TextBlock Text="{Binding XPath=Title}" />
    </DataTemplate>

    <Style x:Key="labelStyle" TargetType="{x:Type Label}">
      <Setter Property="Width" Value="190" />
      <Setter Property="Height" Value="40" />
      <Setter Property="Margin" Value="5" />
    </Style>

  </Window.Resources>
    <Grid DataContext="{Binding Source={StaticResource books}, XPath=Book}">
      <Grid.ColumnDefinitions>
        <ColumnDefinition />
        <ColumnDefinition />
      </Grid.ColumnDefinitions>
      <Grid.RowDefinitions>
        <RowDefinition />
        <RowDefinition />
        <RowDefinition />
        <RowDefinition />
      </Grid.RowDefinitions>
      <ListBox IsSynchronizedWithCurrentItem="True" Margin="5"
          Grid.Column="0" Grid.RowSpan="4" ItemsSource="{Binding}"
          ItemTemplate="{StaticResource listTemplate}" />

      <Label Style="{StaticResource labelStyle}"
          Content="{Binding XPath=Title}"
          Grid.Row="0" Grid.Column="1" />
      <Label Style="{StaticResource labelStyle}"
          Content="{Binding XPath=Publisher}"
          Grid.Row="1" Grid.Column="1" />
      <Label Style="{StaticResource labelStyle}"
          Content="{Binding XPath=@isbn}"
          Grid.Row="2" Grid.Column="1" />
  </Grid>
</Window>
```

Figure 35-12 shows the result of the XML binding.

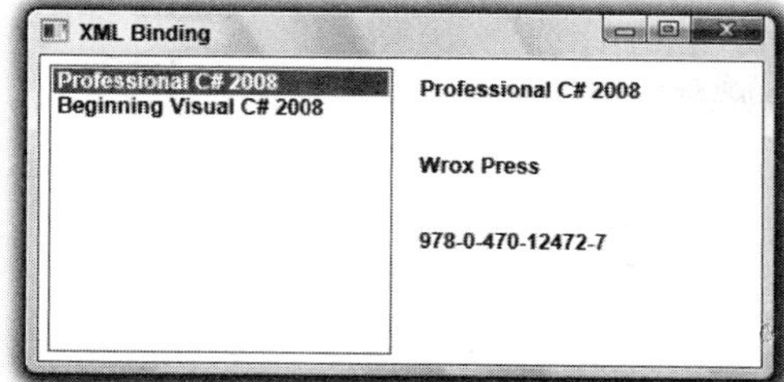

Figure 35-12

> **If XML data should be shown hierarchically, you can use the `TreeView` control.**

Binding Validation

Several options are available to validate data from the user before it is used with the .NET objects. These options are:

- Handling exceptions
- Data error information
- Custom validation rules

Handling Exceptions

One of the options demonstrated here is that the .NET class throws an exception if an invalid value is set as shown in the class `SomeData`. The property `Value1` accepts only values larger or equal to 5 and smaller than 12:

```
public class SomeData
{
   private int value1;
   public int Value1 {
      get
      {
         return value1;
      }
      set
      {
         if (value < 5 || value > 12)
            throw new ArgumentException(
                  "value must not be less than 5 or greater than 12");
         value1 = value;
      }
   }
}
```

In the constructor of the `Window1` class, a new object of the class `SomeData` is initialized and passed to the `DataContext` for data binding:

```
public partial class Window1 : Window
{
   SomeData p1 = new SomeData() { Value1 = 11 };

   public Window1()
   {
      InitializeComponent();
      this.DataContext = p1;

   }
```

The event handler method `buttonSubmit_Click` displays a message box to show the actual value of the `SomeData` instance:

```
   private void buttonSubmit_Click(object sender, RoutedEventArgs e)
   {
      MessageBox.Show(p1.Value1.ToString());
   }
}
```

With simple data binding, here the `Text` property of a `TextBox` is bound to the `Value1` property. If you run the application now and try to change the value to one that is not valid, you can verify that the value never changed by clicking the Submit button. WPF catches and ignores the exception thrown by the set accessor of the property `Value1`.

```
<Label Margin="5" Grid.Row="0" Grid.Column="0" >Value1:</Label>
<TextBox Margin="5" Grid.Row="0" Grid.Column="1"
      Text="{Binding Path=Value1}" />
```

To display an error as soon as the context of the input field changes, you can set the `ValidatesOnException` property of the `Binding` markup extension to `True`. With an invalid value (as soon as the exception is thrown when the value should be set), the `TextBox` is surrounded by a red colored line as shown in Figure 35-13.

```
<Label Margin="5" Grid.Row="0" Grid.Column="0" >Value1:</Label>
<TextBox Margin="5" Grid.Row="0" Grid.Column="1"
      Text="{Binding Path=Value1, ValidatesOnExceptions=True}" />
```

Figure 35-13

To return the error information in a different way to the user, you can assign the attached property `ErrorTemplate` that is defined by the `Validation` class to a template defining the UI for errors. The new template to mark the error is shown here with the key `validationTemplate`. The `ControlTemplate` puts a red exclamation point in front of the existing control content.

```
<ControlTemplate x:Key="validationTemplate">
   <DockPanel>
      <TextBlock Foreground="Red" FontSize="20">!</TextBlock>
      <AdornedElementPlaceholder/>
   </DockPanel>
</ControlTemplate>
```

Setting the `validationTemplate` with the `Validation.ErrorTemplate` attached property activates the template with the `TextBox`:

```
<Label Margin="5" Grid.Row="0" Grid.Column="0" >Value1:</Label>
<TextBox Margin="5" Grid.Row="0" Grid.Column="1"
      Text="{Binding Path=Value1, ValidatesOnExceptions=True}"
      Validation.ErrorTemplate="{StaticResource validationTemplate}" />
```

The new look of the application is shown in Figure 35-14.

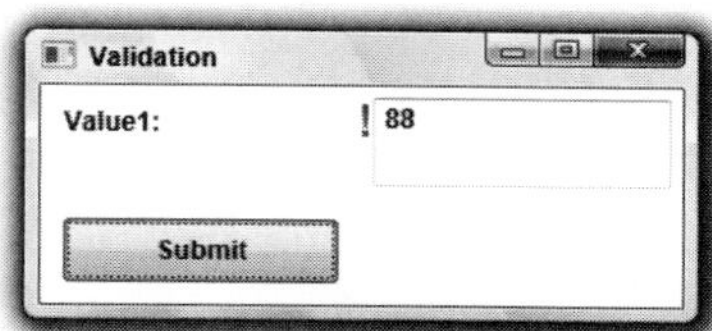

Figure 35-14

Another option for a custom error message is to register to the `Error` *event of the* `Validation` *class. Here the property* `NotifyOnValidationError` *must be set to true.*

The error information itself can be accessed from the `Errors` collection of the `Validation` class. To display the error information in the `ToolTip` of the `TextBox` you can create a property trigger as shown. The trigger is activated as soon as the `HasError` property of the `Validation` class is set to `True`. The trigger sets the `ToolTip` property of the `TextBox`.

```
<Style TargetType="{x:Type TextBox}">
   <Style.Triggers>
      <Trigger Property="Validation.HasError" Value="True">
         <Setter Property="ToolTip"
               Value="{Binding RelativeSource=
                     {x:Static RelativeSource.Self},
               Path=(Validation.Errors)[0].ErrorContent}" />
      </Trigger>
   </Style.Triggers>
</Style>
```

Data Error Information

Another way to deal with errors is if the .NET object implements the interface `IDataErrorInfo`.

The class `SomeData` is now changed to implement the interface `IDataErrorInfo`. This interface defines the property `Error` and an indexer with a string argument. With WPF validation during data binding, the indexer is called and the name of the property to validate is passed as the `columnName` argument. With the implementation the value is verified if it is valid, and an error string is passed otherwise.

Here the validation is done on the property `Value2` that is implemented by using the C# 3.0 simple property notation:

```
public class SomeData : IDataErrorInfo
{
   private int value1;
   public int Value1 {
      get
      {
         return value1;
      }
      set
      {
         if (value < 5 || value > 12)
            throw new ArgumentException(
                  "value must not be less than 5 or greater than 12");
         value1 = value;
      }
   }

   public int Value2 { get; set; }

   string IDataErrorInfo.Error
   {
      get
      {
         return null;
      }
   }

   string IDataErrorInfo.this[string columnName]
   {
      get
      {
         if (columnName == "Value2")
         {
            if (this.Value2 < 0 || this.Value2 > 80)
               return "age must not be less than 0 or greater than 80";

         }
         return null;
      }
   }
}
```

With a .NET entity class it would not be clear what an indexer would return; for example, what would you expect from an object of type `Person` *calling an indexer? That's why it is best to do an explicit implementation of the interface* `IDataErrorInfo`*. This way this indexer can be accessed only by using the interface, and the .NET class could do a different implementation for other purposes.*

If you set the property `ValidatesOnDataErrors` of the `Binding` class to `true`, the interface `IDataErrorInfo` is used during binding. Here, when the `TextBox` is changed, the binding mechanism invokes the indexer of the interface and passes `Value2` to the `columnName` variable:

```
<Label Margin="5" Grid.Row="1" Grid.Column="0" >Value2:</Label>
<TextBox Margin="5" Grid.Row="1" Grid.Column="1"
      Text="{Binding Path=Value2, ValidatesOnDataErrors=True}" />
```

Custom Validation Rules

To get more control of the validation you can implement a custom validation rule. A class implementing a custom validation rule needs to derive from the base class `ValidationRule`. With the previous two examples, validation rules have been used as well. Two classes that derive from the abstract base class `ValidationRule` are `DataErrorValidationRule` and `ExceptionValidationRule`. `DataErrorValidationRule` is activated by setting the property `ValidatesOnDataErrors` and uses the interface `IDataErrorInfo`; `ExceptionValidationRule` deals with exceptions and is activated by setting the property `ValidatesOnException`.

Here a validation rule is implemented to verify for a regular expression. The class `RegularExpressionValidationRule` derives from the base class `ValidationRule` and overrides the abstract method `Validate()` that is defined by the base class. With the implementation, the `RegEx` class from the namespace `System.Text.RegularExpressions` is used to validate the expression defined by the `Expression` property.

```
public class RegularExpressionValidationRule : ValidationRule
{
   public string Expression { get; set; }
   public string ErrorMessage { get; set; }

   public override ValidationResult Validate(object value,
         CultureInfo cultureInfo)
   {
      ValidationResult result = null;
      if (value != null)
      {
         Regex regEx = new Regex(Expression);
         bool isMatch = regEx.IsMatch(value.ToString());
         result = new ValidationResult(isMatch, isMatch ?
               null : ErrorMessage);
      }
      return result;
   }
}
```

Instead of using the `Binding` markup extension, now the binding is done as a child of the `TextBox.Text` element. The bound object now defines an `Email` property that is implemented with the simple property syntax. The `UpdateSourceTrigger` property defines when the source should be updated. Possible options for updating the source are:

- When the property value changes, which would be every character that is typed by the user
- When the focus is lost
- Explicitly

`ValidationRules` is a property of the `Binding` class that contains `ValidationRule` elements. Here the validation rule used is the custom class `RegularExpressionValidationRule`, where the `Expression` property is set to a regular expression that verifies if the input is a valid e-mail, and the `ErrorMessage` property that gives the error message in case the data entered to the `TextBox` is not valid:

```
<Label Margin="5" Grid.Row="2" Grid.Column="0">Email:</Label>
<TextBox Margin="5" Grid.Row="2" Grid.Column="1">
   <TextBox.Text>
      <Binding Path="Email" UpdateSourceTrigger="LostFocus">
         <Binding.ValidationRules>
```

(continued)

(continued)

```
                <src:RegularExpressionValidationRule
                      Expression="^([\w-\.]+)@((\[[0-9]{1,3}\.[0-9]{1,3}\.[0-9]{1,3}\.)
    |(([\w-]+\.)+))([a-zA-Z]{2,4}|[0-9]{1,3})(\]?)$"
                      ErrorMessage="Email is not valid" />
            </Binding.ValidationRules>
        </Binding>
    </TextBox.Text>
</TextBox>
```

Command Bindings

WPF has `Menu` and `ToolBar` controls that serve the same purpose as the controls you know from Windows Forms: to start commands. With these controls you could add event handlers to fulfill the functionality of the commands. However, you can start commands by selecting menus, clicking toolbar buttons, or by pressing some special keys on the keyboard. To handle all these different input gestures, WPF supplies another feature: commands.

Some of the WPF controls offer an implementation for predefined commands that make it extremely easy to get to some functionality.

WPF offers some predefined commands with the commands classes `ApplicationCommands`, `EditingCommands`, `ComponentCommands`, and `NavigationCommands`. All these commands classes are static classes with static properties that return `RoutedUICommand` objects. For example, some of the `ApplicationCommands` properties are `New`, `Open`, `Save`, `SaveAs`, `Print`, and `Close` — commands you know from many applications.

To get started with commands, create a simple WPF project and add a `Menu` control with items for undo and redo and cut, copy, and paste. The `TextBox` named `textContent` takes the remaining space of the `Window` and allows for multiline user input. Within the window a `DockPanel` is created to define the layout. Docked on top you can find the `Menu` control with `MenuItem` elements. The header is set to define the text of the menu. The _ (underscore) defines the letter that can be accessed directly with the keyboard without using the mouse. When you press the Alt key, the underscore is shown below the letter that follows in the header text. The `Command` property defines the command associated with the menu item.

```
<Window x:Class="Wrox.ProCSharp.WPF.WPFEditorWindow"
    xmlns="http://schemas.microsoft.com/winfx/2006/xaml/presentation"
    xmlns:x="http://schemas.microsoft.com/winfx/2006/xaml"
    Title="WPF Editor" Height="300" Width="300">

    <DockPanel>
        <Menu DockPanel.Dock="Top">
            <MenuItem Header="_Edit">
                <MenuItem Name="editUndoMenu" Header="_Undo"
                      Command="ApplicationCommands.Undo" />
                <MenuItem Name="editRedoMenu" Header="_Redo"
                      Command="ApplicationCommands.Redo" />
                <Separator />
                <MenuItem Name="editCutMenu" Header="Cu_t"
                      Command="ApplicationCommands.Cut" />
                <MenuItem Name="editCopyMenu" Header="_Copy"
```

```
                Command="ApplicationCommands.Copy" />
        <MenuItem Name="editPasteMenu" Header="_Paste"
                Command="ApplicationCommands.Paste" />
    </MenuItem>
</Menu>

<TextBox Name="textContent" TextWrapping="Wrap" AcceptsReturn="True"
        AcceptsTab="True" />
</DockPanel>

</Window>
```

That's all you need to do for clipboard functionality. The TextBox class already includes functionality for these predefined command bindings. Starting the application, when you enter text in the text box you can see possible menu items enabled. Selecting text in the text box makes the cut and copy menu items available. Figure 35-15 shows the running application.

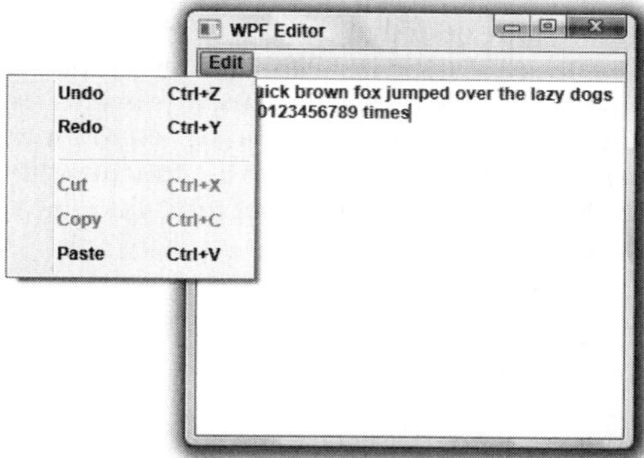

Figure 35-15

Now the application is going to be changed to add command bindings that are not previously defined with the controls. Commands to open and save a file are added to the editor.

To make the commands accessible, more MenuItem elements are added to the Menu element as shown:

```
<MenuItem Header="_File">
    <MenuItem Name="fileNewMenu" Header="_New"
          Command="ApplicationCommands.New" />
    <MenuItem Name="fileOpenMenu" Header="_Open"
          Command="ApplicationCommands.Open" />
    <Separator />
    <MenuItem Name="fileSave" Header="_Save"
          Command="ApplicationCommands.Save" />
    <MenuItem Name="fileSaveAs" Header="Save _As"
          Command="ApplicationCommands.SaveAs" />
 </MenuItem>
```

The commands can also be accessed from a toolbar. With the `ToolBar` element the same commands that are available from the menu are defined. For arranging the toolbar, the `ToolBar` element is placed within a `ToolBarTray`:

```
<ToolBarTray DockPanel.Dock="Top">
   <ToolBar>
      <Button Command="ApplicationCommands.New">
         <Image Source="toolbargraphics/New.bmp" />
      </Button>
      <Button Command="ApplicationCommands.Open">
         <Image Source="toolbargraphics/Open.bmp" />
      </Button>
      <Button Command="ApplicationCommands.Save">
         <Image Source="toolbargraphics/Save.bmp" />
      </Button>
   </ToolBar>
</ToolBarTray>
```

Now command bindings must be defined to associate the commands to event handlers. Command bindings can be assigned to any WPF class that derives from the base class `UIElement` that is very high in the hierarchy. Command bindings are added to the `CommandBindings` property by defining `CommandBinding` elements. The `CommandBinding` class has the property `Command` where you can specify an object implementing the `ICommand` interface, and the events `CanExecute` and `Executed` to specify event handlers. Here the command bindings are assigned to the `Window` class. The `Executed` event is set to the event handler methods that implement the functionality behind the commands. If a command should not be available at all times, you can set the `CanExecute` event to a handler that decides if the command should be available.

```
<Window.CommandBindings>
   <CommandBinding Command="ApplicationCommands.New"
         Executed="NewFileExecuted" />
   <CommandBinding Command="ApplicationCommands.Open"
         Executed="OpenFileExecuted" />
   <CommandBinding Command="ApplicationCommands.Save"
         Executed="SaveFileExecuted"
         CanExecute="SaveFileCanExecute" />
   <CommandBinding Command="ApplicationCommands.SaveAs"
         Executed="SaveAsFileExecuted" CanExecute="SaveFileCanExecute" />
</Window.CommandBindings>
```

In the code behind the handler method, `NewFileExecuted()` empties the text box and writes the file name `untitled.txt` to the `Title` property of the `Window` class. In `OpenFileExecuted()` the `Microsoft.Win32.OpenFileDialog` is created and shown as a dialog. With a successful exit of the dialog, the selected file is opened and its content is written to the `TextBox` control.

> **A dialog for opening a file is not predefined in WPF. You can either create a custom window for selecting files and folders, or you can use the `OpenFileDialog` class from the `Microsoft.Win32` namespace that is a wrapper around the new Windows dialog.**

```
public partial class Window1 : System.Windows.Window
    {
       private string fileName;
       private readonly string defaultFileName;
       private const string appName = "WPF Editor";
       private bool isChanged = false;

       public Window1()
       {
          defaultFileName = System.IO.Path.Combine(
             Environment.GetFolderPath(
                Environment.SpecialFolder.MyDocuments),
             @"untitled.txt");
          InitializeComponent();
          NewFile();
       }

       private void NewFileExecuted(object sender, ExecutedRoutedEventArgs e)
       {
          NewFile();
       }

       private void NewFile()
       {
          textContent.Clear();
          filename = defaultFilename;
          SetTitle();
          isChanged = false;
       }

       private void SetTitle()
       {
          Title = String.Format("{0} {1}",
                         System.IO.Path.GetFileName(filename), appName;
       }

       private void OpenFileExecuted(object sender, ExecutedRoutedEventArgs e)
       {
          try
          {
             OpenFileDialog dlg = new OpenFileDialog();
             bool? dialogResult = dlg.ShowDialog();
             if (dialogResult == true)
             {
                filename = dlg.FileName;
                SetTitle();
                textContent.Text = File.ReadAllText(filename);
             }
          }
          catch (IOException ex)
          {
             MessageBox.Show(ex.Message, "Error WPF Editor",
                  MessageBoxButton.OK, MessageBoxImage.Error);
          }
       }
```

The handler `SaveFileCanExecute()` returns the decision as to whether the command to save the file should be available depending on if the content has been changed:

```
private void SaveFileCanExecute(object sender,
      CanExecuteRoutedEventArgs e)
{
   if (isChanged)
   {
      e.CanExecute = true;
   }
   else
   {
      e.CanExecute = false;
   }
}
```

The application with the opened file `sample.txt` is shown in Figure 35-16.

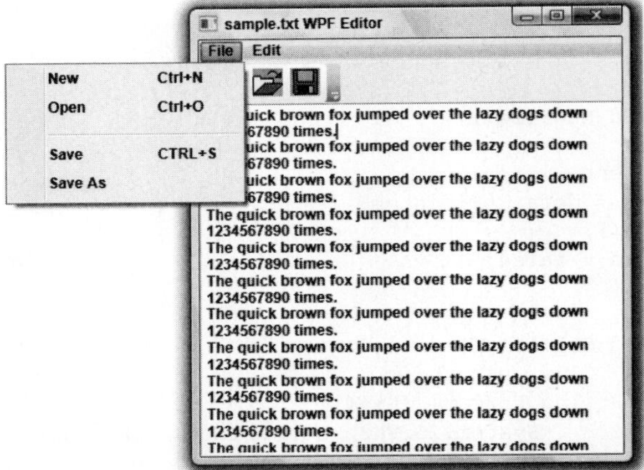

Figure 35-16

Animations

With animations you can make a smooth transition using moving elements, color changes, transforms, and so on. WPF makes it easy to create animations. You can animate the value of any dependency property. Different animation classes exist to animate the values of different properties, depending on their type.

The major elements of animations are as follows:

- **Timeline** — The timeline defines how a value changes over time. Different kinds of timelines are available for changing different types of values. The base class for all timelines is `Timeline`. To animate a `double`, the class `DoubleAnimation` can be used. `Int32Animation` is the animation class for `int` values.

- **Storyboard** — A storyboard is used to combine animations. The `Storyboard` class itself is derived from the base class `TimelineGroup`, which derives from `Timeline`. With `DoubleAnimation` you can animate a `double` value; with a `Storyboard` you combine all the animations that belong together.
- **Triggers** — With triggers you can start and stop animations. You've seen property triggers previously. Property triggers fire when a property value changes. You can also create an event trigger. An event trigger fires when an event occurs.

The namespace for animation classes is `System.Windows.Media.Animation`.

Timeline

A `Timeline` defines how a value changes over time. The first sample animates the size of an ellipse. Here a `DoubleAnimation` that is a timeline that changes a `double` value is used. The `Triggers` property of the `Ellipse` class is set to an `EventTrigger`. The event trigger is fired when the ellipse is loaded as defined with the `RoutedEvent` property of the `EventTrigger`. `BeginStoryboard` is a trigger action that begins the `Storyboard`. With the storyboard, a `DoubleAnimation` element is used to animate the `Width` property of the `Ellipse` class. The animation changes the width of the ellipse from 100 to 300 within 3 seconds, and reverses the animation after the 3 seconds.

```
<Window x:Class="EllipseAnimation.Window1"
    xmlns="http://schemas.microsoft.com/winfx/2006/xaml/presentation"
    xmlns:x="http://schemas.microsoft.com/winfx/2006/xaml"
    Title="Ellipse Animation" Height="300" Width="300">
    <Grid>
      <Ellipse Height="50" Width="100" Fill="SteelBlue">
         <Ellipse.Triggers>
            <EventTrigger RoutedEvent="Ellipse.Loaded" >
               <EventTrigger.Actions>
                  <BeginStoryboard>
                     <Storyboard Duration="00:00:06" RepeatBehavior="Forever">
                        <DoubleAnimation
                              Storyboard.TargetProperty="(Ellipse.Width)"
                              Duration="0:0:3" AutoReverse="True"
                              FillBehavior="Stop" RepeatBehavior="Forever"
                              AccelerationRatio="0.9" DecelerationRatio="0.1"
                              From="100" To="300" />
                     </Storyboard>
                  </BeginStoryboard>
               </EventTrigger.Actions>
            </EventTrigger>
         </Ellipse.Triggers>
      </Ellipse>
   </Grid>
</Window>
```

Figures 35-17 and 35-18 show two states from the animated ellipse.

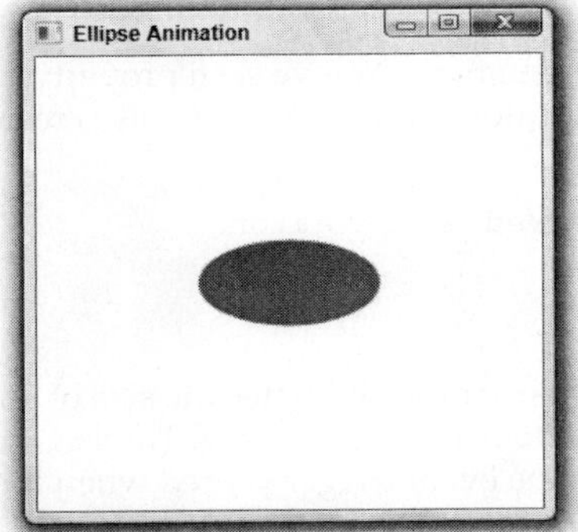

Figure 35-17

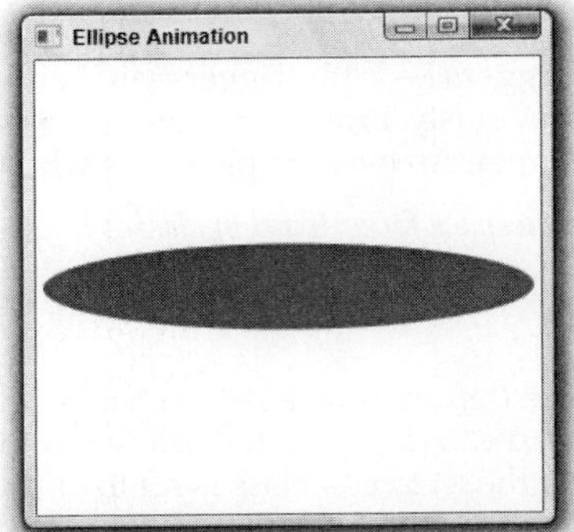

Figure 35-18

Animations are far more than typical window-dressing animation that appears onscreen constantly and immediately. You can add animation to business applications that make the user interface more responsive.

The following example demonstrates a decent animation and also shows how the animation can be defined in a style. Within the `Window` resources you can see the style `AnimatedButtonStyle` for buttons. In the template a rectangle named `outline` is defined. This template has a thin stroke with the thickness set to `0.4`.

The template has a property trigger for the `IsMouseOver` property defined. The `EnterActions` property of this trigger applies as soon as the mouse is moved over the button. The action to start is `BeginStoryboard`. `BeginStoryboard` is a trigger action that can contain and thus start `Storyboard` elements. The `Storyboard` element defines a `DoubleAnimation` to animate a `double` value. The property value that is changed in this animation is the `Rectangle.StrokeThickness` of the `Rectangle` element with the name `outline`. The value is changed in a smooth way by `1.2`, as the `By` property specifies, for a time length of `0.3` seconds as specified by the `Duration` property. At the end of the animation, the stroke thickness is reset to its original value because `AutoReverse="True"`. To summarize: as soon as the mouse moves over the button, the thickness of the outline is incremented by 1.2 for 0.3 seconds. Figure 35-19 shows the button without animation, and Figure 35-20 shows the button at the moment 0.3 seconds after the mouse moved over it. It's just not possible to show the smooth animation and intermediate looks in a print medium.

```
<Window x:Class="AnimationSample.ButtonAnimation"
    xmlns="http://schemas.microsoft.com/winfx/2006/xaml/presentation"
    xmlns:x="http://schemas.microsoft.com/winfx/2006/xaml"
    Title="Button Animation" Height="300" Width="300">
  <Window.Resources>
    <Style x:Key="AnimatedButtonStyle" TargetType="{x:Type Button}">
      <Setter Property="Template">
        <Setter.Value>
          <ControlTemplate TargetType="{x:Type Button}">
            <Grid>
              <Rectangle Name="outline" RadiusX="9" RadiusY="9" Stroke="Black"
                  Fill="{TemplateBinding Background}" StrokeThickness="0.4">
              </Rectangle>
```

```
                <ContentPresenter VerticalAlignment="Center"
                      HorizontalAlignment="Center"
                       />
              </Grid>
              <ControlTemplate.Triggers>
                <Trigger Property="IsMouseOver" Value="True">
                  <Trigger.EnterActions>
                    <BeginStoryboard>
                      <Storyboard>
                        <DoubleAnimation Duration="0:0:0.3" AutoReverse="True"
                            Storyboard.TargetProperty=
                                "(Rectangle.StrokeThickness)"
                            Storyboard.TargetName="outline" By="1.2" />
                      </Storyboard>
                    </BeginStoryboard>
                  </Trigger.EnterActions>
                </Trigger>
              </ControlTemplate.Triggers>

            </ControlTemplate>
          </Setter.Value>
        </Setter>
      </Style>
    </Window.Resources>
    <Grid>

      <Button Style="{StaticResource AnimatedButtonStyle}" Width="200"
            Height="100">
            Click Me!
      </Button>
    </Grid>
  </Window>
```

Figure 35-19

Figure 35-20

Things you can do with a `Timeline` are listed in the following table.

Timeline Properties	Description
`AutoReverse`	With the `AutoReverse` property, you can specify if the value that is animated should return to the original value after the animation.
`SpeedRatio`	With `SpeedRatio`, you can transform the speed at which an animation moves. With this property, you can define the relation in regard to the parent. The default value is `1`; setting the ratio to a smaller value makes the animation move slower; setting the value to a value higher than `1` makes it move faster.
`BeginTime`	With `BeginTime` you can specify the time span from the start of the trigger event until the moment the animation should start. You can specify days, hours, minutes, seconds, and fractions of seconds. This might not be the real time, depending on the speed ratio. For example, if the speed ratio is set to 2, and the beginning time is set to 6 seconds, the animation will start after 3 seconds.
`AccelerationRatio` `DecelerationRatio`	With an animation the values need not be changed in a linear way. You can specify an `AccelerationRatio` and `DecelerationRatio` to define the impact of acceleration and deceleration. The sum of both values set must not be greater than `1`.
`Duration`	With the `Duration` property, you specify the time length for one iteration of the animation.
`RepeatBehavior`	Assigning a `RepeatBehavior` struct to the `RepeatBehavior` property lets you define how many times or how long the animation should be repeated.
`FillBehavior`	The `FillBehavior` property is important if the parent timeline has a different duration. For example, if the parent timeline is shorter than the duration of the actual animation, setting the `FillBehavior` to `Stop` means that the actual animation stops. If the parent timeline is longer than the duration of the actual animation, `HoldEnd` keeps the actual animation active before resetting it to its original value (if `AutoReverse` is set).

Depending on the type of the `Timeline` class, some more properties may be available. For example, with `DoubleAnimation` you can specify the following additional properties.

DoubleAnimation Properties	Description
`From` `To`	By setting the `From` and `To` properties, you can specify the values to start and end the animation.
`By`	Instead of defining the start value for the animation, by setting the `By` property the animation starts with the current value of the bound property and is incremented with the value specified by the `By` property for the animation's end.

Triggers

Instead of having a property trigger, you can define an event trigger to start the animation. The next example creates an animation for the funny face you know from the previous chapter, where the eye moves as soon as a `Click` event from a button is fired. This example also demonstrates that you can start the animation both from XAML and code behind.

Figure 35-21 shows the running application of the animated face example.

Figure 35-21

Inside the `Window` element a `DockPanel` element is defined to arrange the funny face and the buttons. A `Grid` containing the `Canvas` element is docked on top. Bottom-docking is configured with a `StackPanel` element that contains four buttons. The first two buttons are used to animate the eye from code behind; the last two buttons are used to animate the eye from XAML.

The animation is defined within the `<DockPanel.Triggers>` section. Instead of a property trigger, an event trigger is used. The first event trigger is fired as soon as the `Click` event occurs with the button `startButtonXAML` defined by the `RoutedEvent` and `SourceName` properties. The trigger action is defined by the `BeginStoryboard` element that starts the containing `Storyboard`. `BeginStoryboard` has a name defined, because this is needed to control the storyboard with pause, continue, and stop actions. The `Storyboard` element contains two animations. The first animation changes the `Canvas.Left` position value of the eye; the second animation changes the `Canvas.Top` value. Both animations have different time values that make the eye movement very interesting using the defined repeated behavior.

The second event trigger is fired as soon as the `Click` event of the `stopButtonXAML` button occurs. Here, the storyboard is stopped with the `StopStoryboard` element, which references the started storyboard `beginMoveEye`:

```
<Window x:Class="AnimatedFace.Window1"
    xmlns="http://schemas.microsoft.com/winfx/2006/xaml/presentation"
    xmlns:x="http://schemas.microsoft.com/winfx/2006/xaml"
    Title="Face Animation" Height="300" Width="406">
  <DockPanel>

    <Grid DockPanel.Dock="Top">
      <!-- Funny Face -->
```

(continued)

(continued)

```
      <Canvas Width="200" Height="200">
        <Ellipse Canvas.Left="50" Canvas.Top="50" Width="100" Height="100"
            Stroke="Blue" StrokeThickness="4" Fill="Yellow" />
        <Ellipse Canvas.Left="60" Canvas.Top="65" Width="25" Height="25"
            Stroke="Blue" StrokeThickness="3" Fill="White" />
        <Ellipse Name="eye" Canvas.Left="67" Canvas.Top="72" Width="5"
            Height="5" Fill="Black" />
        <Path Name="mouth" Stroke="Blue" StrokeThickness="4"
            Data="M 62,125 Q 95,122 102,108" />

        <Line Name="LeftLeg" X1="92" X2="82" Y1="146" Y2="168" Stroke="Blue"
            StrokeThickness="4" />
        <Line Name="LeftFoot" X1="68" X2="83" Y1="160" Y2="169" Stroke="Blue"
            StrokeThickness="4" />

        <Line Name="RightLeg" X1="124" X2="132" Y1="144" Y2="166"
            Stroke="Blue" StrokeThickness="4" />
        <Line Name="RightFoot" X1="114" X2="133" Y1="169" Y2="166"
            Stroke="Blue" StrokeThickness="4" />
      </Canvas>
    </Grid>

    <StackPanel DockPanel.Dock="Bottom" Orientation="Horizontal">
      <Button Width="80" Height="40" Margin="20,5,5,5"
          Name="startAnimationButton">Start</Button>
      <Button Width="80" Height="40" Margin="5,5,5,5"
          Name="stopAnimationButton">Stop</Button>
      <Button Width="80" Height="40" Margin="5,5,5,5"
          Name="startButtonXAML">Start</Button>
      <Button Width="80" Height="40" Margin="5,5,5,5"
          Name="stopButtonXAML">Stop
      </Button>
    </StackPanel>

    <DockPanel.Triggers>

      <EventTrigger RoutedEvent="Button.Click" SourceName="startButtonXAML">
        <BeginStoryboard Name="beginMoveEye">
          <Storyboard Name="moveEye">
            <DoubleAnimation RepeatBehavior="Forever" DecelerationRatio=".8"
                AutoReverse="True" By="8" Duration="0:0:1"
                Storyboard.TargetName="eye"
                Storyboard.TargetProperty="(Canvas.Left)" />
            <DoubleAnimation RepeatBehavior="Forever" AutoReverse="True"
                By="8" Duration="0:0:5" Storyboard.TargetName="eye"
                Storyboard.TargetProperty="(Canvas.Top)" />
          </Storyboard>
        </BeginStoryboard>
      </EventTrigger>

      <EventTrigger RoutedEvent="Button.Click" SourceName="stopButtonXAML">
```

```
        <StopStoryboard BeginStoryboardName="beginMoveEye" />
      </EventTrigger>

    </DockPanel.Triggers>
  </DockPanel>

</Window>
```

Instead of starting and stopping the animation directly from event triggers in XAML, you can easily control the animation from code behind. The buttons `startAnimationButton` and `stopAnimationButton` have the event handlers `OnStartAnimation` and `OnStopAnimation` associated with them. Within the event handlers, the animation is started with the `Begin()` method and stopped with the `Stop()` method. With the `Begin()` method the second parameter is set to `true` to allow you to control the animation with a stop request.

```
public partial class Window1 : System.Windows.Window
{
   public Window1()
   {
      InitializeComponent();
      startAnimationButton.Click += OnStartAnimation;
      stopAnimationButton.Click += OnStopAnimation;
   }

   void OnStartAnimation(object sender, RoutedEventArgs e)
   {
      moveEye.Begin(eye, true);
   }
   void OnStopAnimation(object sender, RoutedEventArgs e)
   {
      moveEye.Stop(eye);
   }
}
```

Now, you can start the application and watch the eye move as soon as one of the Start buttons is clicked.

Storyboard

The `Storyboard` class inherits from the base class `Timeline` but can contain multiple timelines. The `Storyboard` class can be used to control timelines. The following table describes the methods of the `Storyboard` class.

Storyboard Methods	Description
`Begin()`	The `Begin()` method starts the animations associated with the storyboard.
`BeginAnimation()`	With `BeginAnimation()`, you can start a single animation for a dependency property.
`CreateClock()`	The `CreateClock()` method returns a `Clock` object that you can use to control the animations.

Storyboard Methods	Description
`Pause()Resume()`	With `Pause()` and `Resume()`, you can pause and resume animations.
`Seek()`	With the `Seek()` method, you can jump in time and move the animation to a specified time interval.
`Stop()`	The `Stop()` method halts the clock and stops the animation.

The `EventTrigger` class makes it possible to define actions when events occur. The following table describes the properties of this class.

EventTrigger Properties	Description
`RoutedEvent`	With the `RoutedEvent` property, you can define the event when the trigger should start; for example, a `Click` event of a `Button`.
`SourceName`	The `SourceName` property defines to what WPF element the event should connect.

Trigger actions that you can put within an `EventTrigger` are listed in the following table. You've seen the `BeginStoryboard` and `StopStoryboard` actions in the example, but the following table shows some others.

TriggerAction Classes	Description
`SoundPlayerAction`	With `SoundPlayerAction`, you can play a `.wav` file.
`BeginStoryboard`	`BeginStoryboard` starts an animation defined by a `Storyboard`.
`PauseStoryboard`	`PauseStoryboard` pauses an animation.
`ResumeStoryboard`	`ResumeStoryboard` resumes an animation that was paused.
`StopStoryboard`	`StopStoryboard` stops a running animation.
`SeekStoryboard`	With `SeekStoryboard`, you can change the current time of an animation.
`SkipStoryboardToFill`	`SkipStoryboardToFill` advances an animation to the fill period at the end.
`SetStoryboardSpeedRatio`	With `SetStoryboardSpeedRatio`, you can change the speed of an animation.

Adding 3-D Features in WPF

This section gives you an introduction to the 3-D features of WPF. Here you'll find the information to get started.

The namespace for 3-D with WPF is `System.Windows.Media.Media3D`.

To understand 3-D with WPF it is important to know the difference of the coordination system. Figure 35-22 shows the coordination system of WPF 3-D. The origin is placed in the center. The x-axis has positive values to the right and negative values to the left. The y-axis is vertical with positive values up and negative values down. The z-axis defines positive values in direction to the viewer.

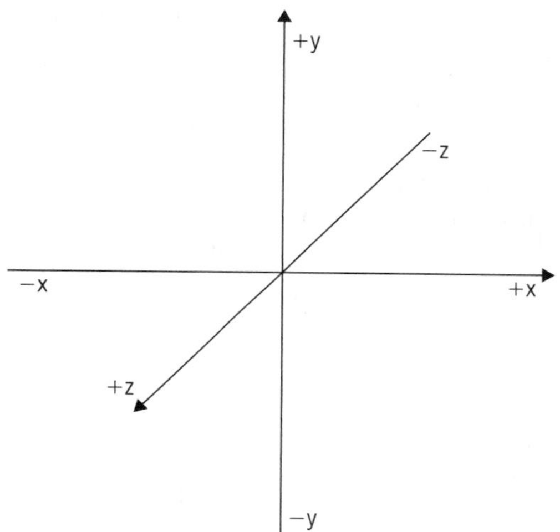

Figure 35-22

The most important classes and their functionality are described in the following table.

Class	Description
`ViewPort3D`	`ViewPort3D` defines the rendering surface for 3-D objects. This element contains all the visual elements for 3-D drawing.
`ModelVisual3D`	`ModelVisual3D` is contained in a `ViewPort3D` and contains all the visual elements. You can assign a transformation to a complete model.
`GeometryModel3D`	`GeometryModel3D` is contained within a `ModelVisual3D` and consists of a mesh and a material.
`Geometry3D`	`Geometry3D` is an abstract base class to define geometric shapes. The concrete class that derives from `Geometry3D` is `MeshGeometry3D`. With `MeshGeometry3D` you can define positions of triangles to build a 3-D model.

Class	Description
Material	Material is an abstract base class to define the front and back side from the triangles defined with the MeshGeometry3D. Material is contained within a GeometryModel3D. .NET 3.5 defines several material classes, such as DiffuseMaterial, EmissiveMaterial, and SpecularMaterial. Depending on the material type, the light calculates differently. EmissiveMaterial behaves with lighting calculations that the material emits the light equal to the color of the brush. DiffuseMaterial lights with a diffuse light, and SpecularMaterial defines a specularly lit model. With the MaterialGroup class you can create a combination consisting of other materials.
Light	Light is the abstract base class for lighting. Concrete implementations are AmbientLight, DirectionalLight, PointLight and SpotLight. AmbientLight is an unnatural light that lights the complete scene similarly. You will not see edges using that light. DirectionalLight defines a directed light. Sunlight is a example of directed light. The light comes from one side and here you can see edges and shadows. PointLight is a light with a specified position and lights in all directions. SpotLight lights in a specified direction. This light defines a cone so you can get a very intensive illuminated area.
Camera	Camera is the abstract base class for the camera that is used to map the 3-D scene to a 2-D display. Concrete implementations are PerspectiveCamera, OrthographicCamera, and MatrixCamera. With the PerspectiveCamera the 3-D objects are smaller the further away they are. This is different with the OrthographicCamera. Here the distance of the camera doesn't influence the size. With the MatrixCamera you can define the view and transformation in a matrix.
Transform3D	Transform3D is the abstract base class for 3-D transformations. Concrete implementations are RotateTransform3D, ScaleTransform3D, TranslateTransform3D, MatrixTransform3D, and Transform3DGroup. TranslateTransform3D allows transforming an object in the x, y, and z direction. ScaleTransform3D allows for an object resize. With the RotateTransform3D class you can rotate the object defined by an angle in the x, y, and z direction. With Transform3DGroup you can combine other transformations.

Triangle

This section starts with a simple 3-D sample. A 3-D model is made up of triangles, so a simple model is just one triangle. The triangle is defined by the Positions property of the MeshGeometry3D. The three points all use the same z coordinate, –4, and x/y coordinates –1 –1, 1 –1, and 0 1. The property TriangleIndices indicates the order of the positions in a counterclockwise way. With this property you define which side of the triangle is visible. One side of the triangle shows the color defined with the Material property of the GeometryModel3D class, and the other side shows the BackMaterial property.

The camera that is used to show the scenario is positioned at the coordinates 0, 0, 0, and looks into the direction 0, 0, –8. Changing the camera position to the left side, the rectangle moves to the right and vice versa. Changing the y position of the camera, the rectangle appears larger or smaller.

The light that is used in this scene is an `AmbientLight` to light up the complete scene with a white light. Figure 35-23 shows the result of the triangle.

```
<Window x:Class="Triangle3D.Window1"
    xmlns="http://schemas.microsoft.com/winfx/2006/xaml/presentation"
    xmlns:x="http://schemas.microsoft.com/winfx/2006/xaml"
    Title="3D" Height="300" Width="300">
   <Grid>
      <Viewport3D>
         <Viewport3D.Camera>
            <PerspectiveCamera Position="0 0 0" LookDirection="0 0 -8" />
         </Viewport3D.Camera>

         <ModelVisual3D>
            <ModelVisual3D.Content>
               <AmbientLight Color="White" />
            </ModelVisual3D.Content>
         </ModelVisual3D>

         <ModelVisual3D>
            <ModelVisual3D.Content>
               <GeometryModel3D>
                  <GeometryModel3D.Geometry>
                     <MeshGeometry3D
                           Positions="-1 -1 -4, 1 -1 -4, 0 1 -4"
                           TriangleIndices="0, 1, 2" />
                  </GeometryModel3D.Geometry>
                  <GeometryModel3D.Material>
                     <MaterialGroup>
                        <DiffuseMaterial>
                           <DiffuseMaterial.Brush>
                              <SolidColorBrush Color="Red" />
                           </DiffuseMaterial.Brush>
                        </DiffuseMaterial>
                     </MaterialGroup>
                  </GeometryModel3D.Material>
               </GeometryModel3D>
            </ModelVisual3D.Content>
         </ModelVisual3D>
      </Viewport3D>
   </Grid>
</Window>
```

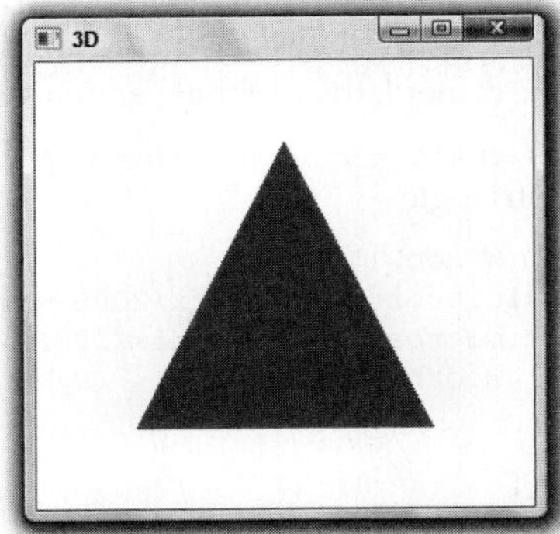

Figure 35-23

Changing Lights

Figure 35-23 just shows a simple triangle where you can get the same result with less effort using 2-D. However, from here you can continue getting into 3-D features. For example, by changing the light from an ambient light to a spotlight with the element `SpotLight` you can immediately see a different appearance of the triangle. With the spotlight you define a position where the light is placed, and the position to which the light is directed. Specifying `-1 1 2` for the position, the light is placed at the left corner of the triangle and the y coordinate to the height of the triangle. From there the light is directed down and to the left. You can see the new appearance of the triangle in Figure 35-24.

```
<ModelVisual3D>
   <ModelVisual3D.Content>
      <SpotLight Position="-1 1 -2" Color="White"
            Direction="-1.5, -1, -5" />
   </ModelVisual3D.Content>
</ModelVisual3D>
```

Figure 35-24

Adding Textures

Instead of using a solid color brush with the materials of the triangle, you can use a different brush such as the `LinearGradientBrush` as shown with the following XAML code. The `LinearGradientBrush` element defined with `DiffuseMaterial` defines gradient stops with the colors yellow, orange, red, blue, and violet. To map a 2-D surface from an object such as the brush to a 3-D geometry, the `TextCoordinates` property must be set. `TextCoordinates` defines a collection of 2-D points that map to the 3-D positions. Figure 35-25 shows the 2-D coordinates of the brush from the sample application. The first position in the triangle, –1 –1, maps to the brush coordinates 0 1; the position 1 –1, which is the lower corner on the right, maps to 1 1 of the brush, which is violet; and 0 1 maps to 0.5 0. Figure 35-26 shows the triangle with the material of the gradient brush, again with the ambient light.

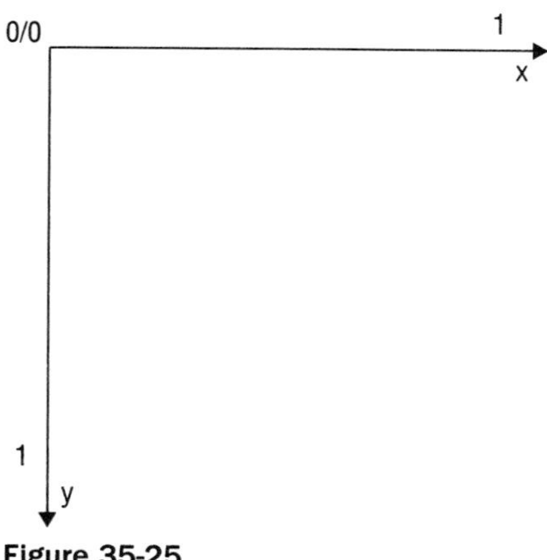

Figure 35-25

```
<ModelVisual3D>
   <ModelVisual3D.Content>
      <GeometryModel3D>
         <GeometryModel3D.Geometry>
            <MeshGeometry3D
            Positions="-1 -1 -4, 1 -1 -4, 0 1 -4"
            TriangleIndices="0, 1, 2"
            TextureCoordinates="0 1, 1 1, 0.5 0" />
         </GeometryModel3D.Geometry>

         <GeometryModel3D.Material>
            <MaterialGroup>
               <DiffuseMaterial>
                  <DiffuseMaterial.Brush>
                     <LinearGradientBrush StartPoint="0,0"
                           EndPoint="1,1">
                        <GradientStop Color="Yellow" Offset="0" />
                        <GradientStop Color="Orange" Offset="0.25" />
                        <GradientStop Color="Red" Offset="0.50" />
                        <GradientStop Color="Blue" Offset="0.75" />
```

(continued)

(continued)

```
                                        <GradientStop Color="Violet" Offset="1" />
                                    </LinearGradientBrush>
                                </DiffuseMaterial.Brush>
                            </DiffuseMaterial>
                        </MaterialGroup>
                    </GeometryModel3D.Material>
                </GeometryModel3D>
            </ModelVisual3D.Content>
        </ModelVisual3D>
```

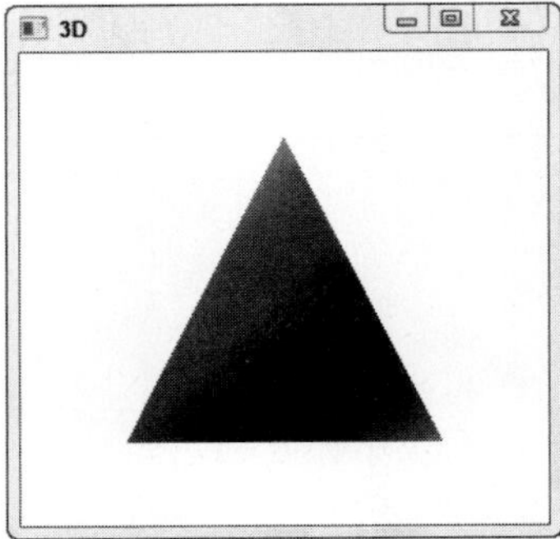

Figure 35-26

You can add text or other controls in a similar way to the materials. To do this you just need to create a `VisualBrush` *with the elements that should be painted. The* `VisualBrush` *is discussed in Chapter 34, "Windows Presentation Foundation."*

3-Dimensional Object

Now let's get into a real three-dimensional object: a box. The box is made up of five rectangles: the back, front, left, right, and bottom sides. Each rectangle is made up of two triangles because this is the core of a mesh. With WPF and 3-D the term *mesh* is used to describe the triangle primitive for building 3-D shapes.

Here is the code of the rectangle for the front side of the box that consists of two triangles. The positions of the triangles are set in a counterclockwise order as defined by the `TriangleIndices`. The front side of the rectangle is done with a red brush; the back side with a gray brush. Both of these brushes are of type `SolidColorBrush` and defined with the resources of the `Window`.

```
<!-- Front -->
<GeometryModel3D>
   <GeometryModel3D.Geometry>
      <MeshGeometry3D
            Positions="-1 -1 1, 1 -1 1, 1 1 1, 1 1 1,
                       -1 1 1, -1 -1 1"
            TriangleIndices="0 1 2, 3 4 5" />
   </GeometryModel3D.Geometry>
   <GeometryModel3D.Material>
      <DiffuseMaterial Brush="{StaticResource redBrush}" />
```

```
      </GeometryModel3D.Material>
      <GeometryModel3D.BackMaterial>
         <DiffuseMaterial Brush="{StaticResource grayBrush}" />
      </GeometryModel3D.BackMaterial>
   </GeometryModel3D>
```

The other rectangles look very similar, just with different positions. Here you can see the XAML code of the left side of the box:

```
   <!-- Left side -->
   <GeometryModel3D>
      <GeometryModel3D.Geometry>
         <MeshGeometry3D
      Positions="-1 -1 1, -1 1 1, -1 -1 -1, -1 -1 -1, -1 1 1,
                 -1 1 -1"
      TriangleIndices="0 1 2, 3 4 5" />
      </GeometryModel3D.Geometry>
      <GeometryModel3D.Material>
         <DiffuseMaterial Brush="{StaticResource redBrush}" />
      </GeometryModel3D.Material>
      <GeometryModel3D.BackMaterial>
         <DiffuseMaterial Brush="{StaticResource grayBrush}" />
      </GeometryModel3D.BackMaterial>
   </GeometryModel3D>
```

The sample code defines a separate `GeometryModel3D` *with every side of the box. This is just for better understanding of the code. As long as the same material is used with every side, it's also possible to define a mesh containing all 10 triangles from all sides of the box.*

All the rectangles are combined within a `Model3DGroup`, so one transformation can be done with all the sides of the box:

```
<!-- the model -->
<ModelVisual3D>
   <ModelVisual3D.Content>
      <Model3DGroup>

      <!—GeometryModel3D elements for every side of the box -->

      </Model3DGroup>
```

With the `Transform` property of the `Model3DGroup` element, all the geometries inside this group can be transformed. Here a `RotateTransform3D` is used that defines an `AxisAngleRotation3D`. To rotate the box during runtime, the `Angle` property is bound to the value of a `Slider` control.

```
   <!-- Transformation of the complete model -->
   <Model3DGroup.Transform>
      <RotateTransform3D CenterX="0" CenterY="0" CenterZ="0">
         <RotateTransform3D.Rotation>
            <AxisAngleRotation3D x:Name="axisRotation"
                  Axis="0, 0, 0"
                  Angle="{Binding Path=Value,
                        ElementName=axisAngle}" />
         </RotateTransform3D.Rotation>
      </RotateTransform3D>
   </Model3DGroup.Transform>
```

To see the box, a camera is needed. Here the `PerspectiveCamera` is used so that the box gets smaller the further the camera is. The position and direction of the camera can be set during runtime.

```
<!-- Camera -->
<Viewport3D.Camera>
   <PerspectiveCamera x:Name="camera"
         Position="{Binding Path=Text,
               ElementName=textCameraPosition}"
         LookDirection="{Binding Path=Text,
               ElementName=textCameraDirection}" />
</Viewport3D.Camera>
```

The application uses two different light sources. One light source is a `DirectionalLight`:

```
<!-- directional light -->
<ModelVisual3D>
   <ModelVisual3D.Content>
      <DirectionalLight Color="White" x:Name="directionalLight">
         <DirectionalLight.Direction>
            <Vector3D X="1" Y="2" Z="3" />
         </DirectionalLight.Direction>
      </DirectionalLight>
   </ModelVisual3D.Content>
</ModelVisual3D>
```

The other light source is a `SpotLight`. With this light source it is possible to highlight a specific area on the box. The `SpotLight` defines the properties `InnerConeAngle` and `OuterConeAngle` to define the area of the full illumination:

```
<!-- spot light -->
<ModelVisual3D>
   <ModelVisual3D.Content>
      <SpotLight x:Name="spotLight"
      InnerConeAngle="{Binding Path=Value,
                        ElementName=spotInnerCone}"
      OuterConeAngle="{Binding Path=Value,
                        ElementName=spotOuterCone}"
      Color="#FFFFFF"
      Direction="{Binding Path=Text, ElementName=spotDirection}"
      Position="{Binding Path=Text, ElementName=spotPosition}"
      Range="{Binding Path=Value, ElementName=spotRange}" />
   </ModelVisual3D.Content>
</ModelVisual3D>
```

When running the application you can change the rotation of the box, the camera, and lights as shown in Figure 35-27.

Creating a 3-D model that consists of just rectangles or triangles is easy to do. You would not manually create more complex models; instead you would use one of several tools. You can find 3-D tools for WPF at `www.codeplex/3DTools`.

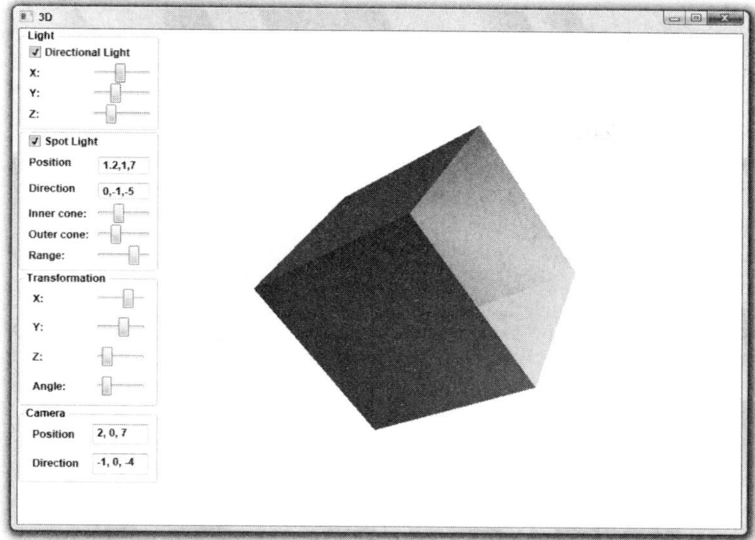

Figure 35-27

Windows Forms Integration

Instead of rewriting your user interface completely from scratch for WPF, you can use existing Windows Forms controls within WPF applications, and create new WPF controls to be used within Windows Forms applications. The best way of integrating Windows Forms and WPF is by creating controls and integrating the controls in the application types of the other technology.

The integration of Windows Forms and WPF has a big drawback. If you integrate Windows Forms with WPF, the Windows Forms controls still look like they looked in the old days. Windows Forms controls and applications don't get the new look of WPF. From a user interface standpoint, it would be better to rewrite the UI completely.

> **To integrate Windows Forms and WPF, you need classes from the namespace** `System.Windows.Forms.Integration` **in the assembly** `WindowsFormsIntegration`**.**

WPF Controls Within Windows Forms

You can use WPF controls within a Windows Forms application. A WPF element is a normal .NET class. However, you cannot use it directly from the Windows Forms code; a WPF control is not a Windows Forms control. The integration can be done by the wrapper class `ElementHost` from the namespace `System.Windows.Forms.Integration`. `ElementHost` is a Windows Forms control, because it derives from `System.Windows.Forms.Control`, and can be used like any other Windows Forms control in a Windows Forms application. `ElementHost` hosts and manages WPF controls.

Let's start with a simple WPF control. With Visual Studio 2008, you can create a WPF User Control Library. The sample control is derived from the base class `UserControl` and contains a grid and a button with a custom content:

```
<UserControl x:Class="WPFControl.UserControl1"
    xmlns="http://schemas.microsoft.com/winfx/2006/xaml/presentation"
    xmlns:x="http://schemas.microsoft.com/winfx/2006/xaml" >
    <Grid>
      <Button>
        <Canvas Height="230" Width="230">
          <Ellipse Canvas.Left="50" Canvas.Top="50" Width="100" Height="100"
              Stroke="Blue" StrokeThickness="4" Fill="Yellow" />
          <Ellipse Canvas.Left="60" Canvas.Top="65" Width="25" Height="25"
              Stroke="Blue" StrokeThickness="3" Fill="White" />
          <Ellipse Canvas.Left="70" Canvas.Top="75" Width="5" Height="5"
              Fill="Black" />
          <Path Name="mouth" Stroke="Blue" StrokeThickness="4"
              Data="M 62,125 Q 95,122 102,108" />

          <Line X1="124" X2="132" Y1="144" Y2="166" Stroke="Blue"
              StrokeThickness="4" />
          <Line X1="114" X2="133" Y1="169" Y2="166" Stroke="Blue"
              StrokeThickness="4" />

          <Line X1="92" X2="82" Y1="146" Y2="168" Stroke="Blue"
              StrokeThickness="4" />
          <Line X1="68" X2="83" Y1="160" Y2="168" Stroke="Blue"
              StrokeThickness="4" />
        </Canvas>
      </Button>
    </Grid>
</UserControl>
```

You can create a Windows Forms application by selecting the Windows Forms Application template. Because the WPF user control project is in the same solution as the Windows Forms application, you can drag and drop the WPF user control from the toolbox to the designer surface of the Windows Forms application. This adds references to the assemblies `PresentationCore`, `PresentationFramework`, `WindowsBase`, `WindowsFormsIntegration`, and of course, the assembly containing the WPF control.

Within the designer-generated code you will find a variable referencing the WPF user control and an object of type `ElementHost` that wraps the control:

```
private System.Windows.Forms.Integration.ElementHost elementHost1;
private WPFControl.UserControl1 userControl11;
```

In the method `InitializeComponent` you can see object initializations and the assigning of the WPF control instance to the `Child` property of the `ElementHost` class:

```
private void InitializeComponent()
{
   this.elementHost1 = new
         System.Windows.Forms.Integration.ElementHost();
   this.userControl11 = new WPFControl.UserControl1();
   this.SuspendLayout();
   //
   // elementHost1
   //
```

```
        this.elementHost1.Location = new System.Drawing.Point(39, 44);
        this.elementHost1.Name = "elementHost1";
        this.elementHost1.Size = new System.Drawing.Size(259, 229);
        this.elementHost1.TabIndex = 0;
        this.elementHost1.Text = "elementHost1";
        this.elementHost1.Child = this.userControl11;

        //...
    }
```

Starting the Windows Forms application, you can see both the WPF control as well the Windows Forms control inside one form, as shown in Figure 35-28.

Of course, you can add methods, properties, and events to the WPF control and use them the same way as other controls.

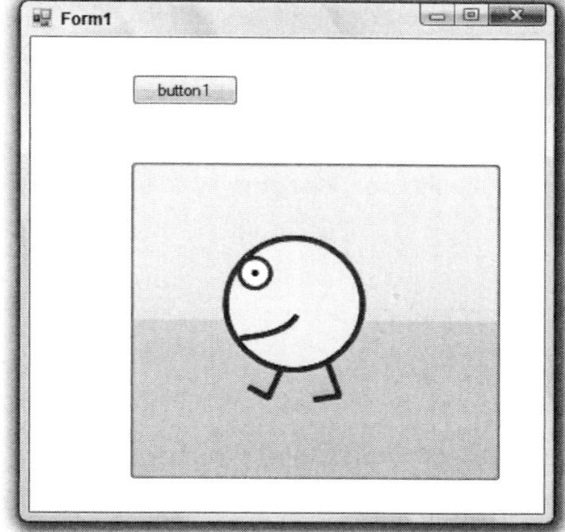

Figure 35-28

Windows Forms Controls Within WPF Applications

You can integrate Windows Forms and WPF in the other direction as well by placing a Windows Forms control within a WPF application. As with the `ElementHost` class used to host a WPF control inside Windows Forms, now you need a wrapper that is a WPF control to host a Windows Forms control. This class has the name `WindowsFormsHost` and is in the same assembly, `WindowsFormsIntegration`. The class `WindowsFormsHost` is derived from the base classes `HwndHost` and `FrameworkElement`, and thus can be used as a WPF element.

For this integration, a Windows Control Library is created first. Add a `TextBox` and `Button` control to the form by using the Designer. To change the `Text` property of the button, the property `ButtonText` is added to the code behind:

```
public partial class UserControl1 : UserControl
{
   public UserControl1()
   {
      InitializeComponent();
   }
```

(continued)

(continued)

```
        public string ButtonText
        {
            get { return button1.Text; }
            set { button1.Text = value; }
        }
    }
```

In the WPF application, you can add a `WindowsFormsHost` object from the toolbox to the Designer. This adds a reference to the assemblies `WindowsFormsIntegration`, `System.Windows.Forms`, and the assembly of the Windows Forms control. To use the Windows Forms control from XAML, you must add an XML namespace alias to reference the .NET namespace. Because the assembly containing the Windows Forms control is in a different assembly than the WPF application, you also must add the assembly name to the namespace alias. The Windows Forms control can now be contained within the `WindowsFormsHost` element as shown. You can assign a value for the property `ButtonText` directly from XAML similarly to .NET Framework elements.

```
<Window x:Class="WPFApplication.Window1"
    xmlns="http://schemas.microsoft.com/winfx/2006/xaml/presentation"
    xmlns:x="http://schemas.microsoft.com/winfx/2006/xaml"
    xmlns:winforms=
          "clr-namespace:Wrox.ProCSharp.WPF;assembly=WindowsFormsControl"
    Title="WPF Interop Application" Height="300" Width="300"
    >
    <Grid>
      <Grid.RowDefinitions>
        <RowDefinition />
        <RowDefinition />
      </Grid.RowDefinitions>
      <WindowsFormsHost Grid.Row="0" Height="180">
        <winforms:UserControl1 x:Name="myControl" ButtonText="Click Me!" />
      </WindowsFormsHost>
      <StackPanel Grid.Row="1">
        <TextBox Margin="5,5,5,5" Width="140" Height="30"></TextBox>
        <Button Margin="5,5,5,5" Width="80" Height="40">WPF Button</Button>
      </StackPanel>
    </Grid>
</Window>
```

You can see a view of the WPF application in Figure 35-29. Of course, the Windows Forms control still looks like a Windows Forms control and does not have all the resizing and styling features you get with WPF.

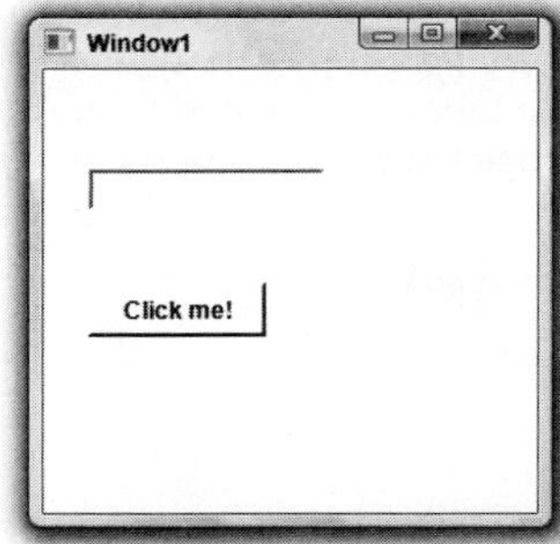

Figure 35-29

WPF Browser Application

Visual Studio 2008 has another WPF project template: a WPF Browser Application. Such an application can run within Internet Explorer, but still the .NET Framework version that you use must be installed with the client system. Here you get the features of the rich client to the browser. However, with WPF Browser Applications, the .NET Framework is required to be available on the client system, and only Internet Explorer is supported.

Creating such a project type, an XBAP (XAML Browser Application) file is created. XBAP is an XML file that defines the application and the assemblies it consists of for ClickOnce deployment.

An XBAP application is a partial-trust application. You can use only .NET code that is available with the Internet permissions.

> *ClickOnce is explained in Chapter 16, "Deployment."*

> *WPF Browser Applications are different from Silverlight. Silverlight defines a subset of WPF that does not require the .NET Framework to be installed with the client system. Silverlight requires an add-in with the browser but supports different browsers and different operating systems. Silverlight 1.0 cannot be programmed using .NET; you can use only JavaScript for accessing the XAML elements programmatically. Silverlight 1.1 will support the .NET Microframework.*

Summary

This chapter covered some more features of WPF.

WPF data binding gives a leap forward compared to Windows Forms. You can bind any property of a .NET class to a property of a WPF element. The binding mode defines the direction of the binding. You can bind .NET objects and lists, and define a data template to create a default look for a .NET class with a data template.

Command binding makes it possible to map handler code to menus and toolbars. You've also seen how easy it is to do copy and paste with WPF because a command handler for this technology is already included in the `TextBox` control.

Animation allows the user to dynamically change every property of a WPF element. Animations can be very decent and not annoying and make the UI more responsive and attractive for the user.

WPF also allows for an easy 3-D mapping to the 2-D surface of a screen. You've seen how to create a 3-D model and view it with the help of different light sources and cameras.

> *This and the previous chapter gave you an overview of WPF and enough information to get started with this technology. For more information on WPF, you should read a book that focuses on WPF; for example,* Professional WPF Programming: .NET Development with the Windows Presentation Foundation *by Chris Andrade et al. (Wiley Publishing, 2007).*

36

Add-Ins

Add-ins allow you to add functionality to an application at a later time. You can create a hosting application that gains more and more functionality over time — functionality that might be written by your developer team but also different vendors can extend your application by creating add-ins.

Today, add-ins are used with many different applications, such as Internet Explorer and Visual Studio. Internet Explorer is a hosting application that offers an add-in framework that is used by many companies to offer extensions when viewing Web pages. The Shockwave Flash Object allows you to view Web pages with Flash content. The Google toolbar offers specific Google features that can be accessed quickly from Internet Explorer. Visual Studio also has an add-in model that allows you to extend Visual Studio with different levels of extensions.

For your custom applications it has always been possible to create an add-in model to dynamically load and use functionality from assemblies. With an add-in model many issues need to be thought about. How can new assemblies be detected? How can versioning issues be resolved? Can the add-in change the stability of the hosting application?

The .NET Framework 3.5 offers a framework for hosting and creating add-ins with the assembly System.AddIn. This framework is also known by the name Managed AddIn Framework (MAF).

Add-ins are also known by different terms such as "add-on" or "plug-in."

Topics covered in this chapter are

- System.AddIn architecture
- Creating a simple add-in

System.AddIn Architecture

When you create an application that allows you to add add-ins during runtime, you will need to deal with certain issues — for example, how to find the add-ins, and how to solve versioning issues so that the hosting application and the add-in can progress independently. There are several ways to resolve these issues. In this section, you read about the issues of add-ins and how the architecture of MAF solves them:

- Issues with add-ins
- Pipeline architecture
- Discovery
- Activation
- Isolation
- Lifetime
- Versioning

Issues with Add-ins

Creating a hosted application that dynamically loads assemblies that are added at a later time has several issues that must be dealt with, as shown in the table that follows.

Add-Ins Issues	Description
Discovery	How can new add-ins be found for the hosting application? There are several different options. One way is to add information about add-ins to a configuration file. This has the disadvantage that the installation of new add-ins needs to change an existing configuration file. Another option is to just copy the assembly containing the add-in to a predefined directory and read information about the assembly with reflection. You can read more about reflection in Chapter 13, "Reflection."
Activation	With assemblies that are dynamically loaded it is not possible to just use the `new` operator to create an instance. You can create such assemblies with the `Activator` class. Also, different activation options might apply if the add-in is loaded within a different application domain or a new process.Assemblies and application domains are described in Chapter 17, "Assemblies."
Isolation	An add-in can break the hosting application as you've probably already seen with Internet Explorer crashes caused by various add-ins. Depending on the type of the hosting application and how the add-ins are integrated, the add-in can be loaded within a different application domain or also within a different process.
Lifetime	Cleaning up objects is a job of the garbage collector. However, the garbage collector cannot help here because add-ins might be active in a different application domain or a different process. Other ways to keep the object in memory are reference count or leasing and sponsoring mechanisms.
Versioning	Versioning is a big issue with add-ins. Usually it should be possible that a new version of the host still can load old add-ins, and an old host should have the option to load newer add-ins.

Now let's look at the architecture of MAF and how this framework solves these issues. The design of MAF was influenced by these goals:

- It should be easy to develop add-ins.
- Finding add-ins during runtime should be performant.
- Developing hosts should be an easy process as well, but not as easy as developing add-ins.
- The add-in and the host application should progress independently.

Pipeline Architecture

The MAF architecture is based on a pipeline of seven assemblies. This pipeline solves the versioning issues with add-ins. Because the assemblies from the pipeline have a very light dependency, it is possible that the contract, the hosting, and the add-in applications progress with new versions completely independent of one another.

Figure 36-1 shows the pipeline of the MAF architecture. In the center is the contract assembly. This assembly contains a contract interface that lists methods and properties that must be implemented by the add-in and can be called by the host. Left of the contract is the host side, and on the right, the add-in side. In the figure you can see the dependencies between the assemblies. The host assembly shown leftmost does not have a real dependency to the contract assembly; the same is true of the add-in assembly. Both do not really implement the interface that is defined by the contract. Instead, they just have a reference to a view assembly. The host application references the host view; the add-in references the add-in view. The views contain abstract view classes that define methods and properties as defined by the contract.

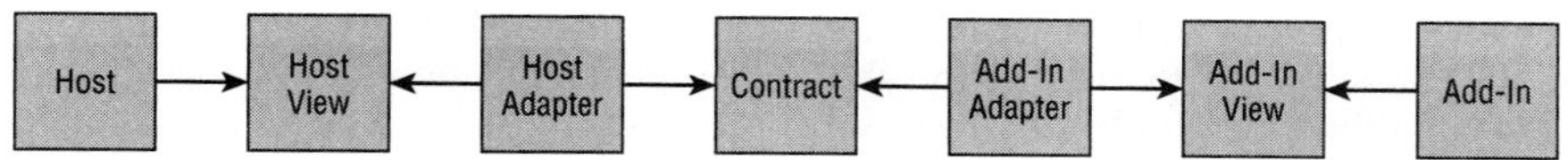

Figure 36-1

Figure 36-2 shows the relationship of the classes from the pipeline. The host class has an association with the abstract host view class and invokes its methods. The abstract host view class is implemented by the host adapter. Adapters make the connection between the views and the contract. The add-in adapter implements the methods and properties of the contract. This adapter contains a reference to the add-in view and forwards calls from the host side to the add-in view. The host adapter class defines a concrete class that derives from the abstract base class of the host view to implement the methods and properties. This adapter includes a reference to the contract to forward calls from the view to the contract.

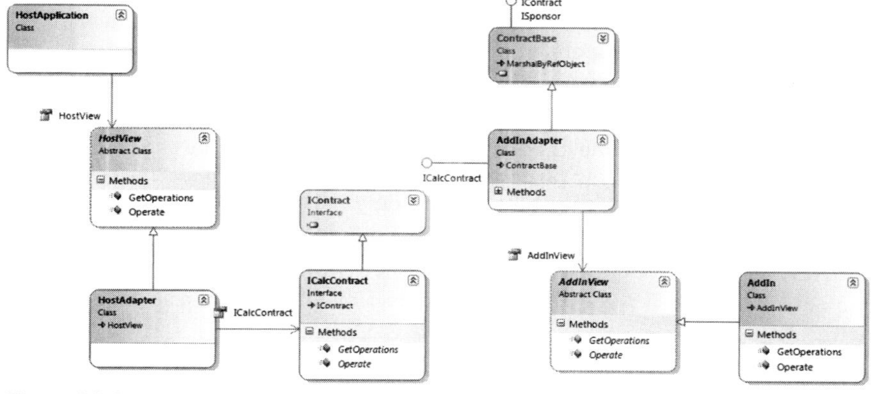

Figure 36-2

With this model it is possible that the add-in side and the host side emerge completely independent. Just the mapping layer needs to adapt. For example, if a new version of the host is done that uses completely new methods and properties, the contract can still stay the same and only the adapter needs to change. It is also possible that a new contract is defined. Adapters can change, or several contracts can be used in parallel.

Discovery

How can new add-ins be found for the hosting application? The MAF architecture uses a predefined directory structure to find add-ins and the other assemblies of the pipeline. The components of the pipeline must be stored in these subdirectories:

- `HostSideAdapters`
- `Contracts`
- `AddInSideAdapters`
- `AddInViews`
- `AddIns`

All these directories with the exception of the `AddIns` directory directly contain the assembly of the specific part of the pipeline. The `AddIns` directory contains subdirectories for every add-in assembly. With add-ins, it is also possible to store them in directories that are completely independent of the other pipeline components.

The assemblies of the pipeline are not just loaded dynamically to get all the information about the add-in using reflection. With many add-ins, this would increase the startup time of the hosting application. Instead, MAF uses a cache with information about the pipeline components. The cache is created by the program installing the add-in or by the hosting application if the hosting application has write access to the directory of the pipeline.

The cache information about the pipeline components is created by invoking methods of the `AddInStore` class. The method `Update()` finds new add-ins that are not already listed with the store files. The `Rebuild()` method rebuilds the complete binary store file with information about the add-ins.

The following table lists the members of the `AddInStore` class.

AddInStore Members	Description
`Rebuild()` `RebuildAddIns()`	The `Rebuild()` method rebuilds the cache for all components of the pipeline. If the add-ins are stored in a different directory, the method `RebuildAddIns()` can be used to rebuild the cache of the add-ins.
`Update()` `UpdateAddIns()`	While the `Rebuild()` method rebuilds the complete cache of the pipeline, the `Update` method just updates the cache with information about new pipeline components. The `UpdateAddIns()` method updates the cache of the add-ins only.
`FindAddIn()` `FindAddIns()`	These methods are used to find add-ins by using the cache. The method `FindAddIns()` returns a collection of all add-ins that match the host view. The `FindAddIn()` method returns a specific add-in.

Activation and Isolation

The FindAddIns() method of the AddInStore class returns a collection of AddInToken objects that represent an add-in. With the AddInToken class, you can access information about the add-in such as name, description, publisher, and version. You can activate the add-in by using the Activate() method. The following table lists properties and methods of the AddInToken class.

AddInToken Members	Description
Name Publisher Version Description	The Name, Publisher, Version and Description properties of the AddInToken class return information about an add-in that was assigned to the add-in with the attribute AddInAttribute.
AssemblyName	AssemblyName returns the name of the assembly that contains the add-in.
EnableDirectConnect	With the property EnableDirectConnect you can set a value that the host should directly connect to the add-in instead of using the components of the pipeline. This is only possible if the add-in and the host are running in the same application domain, and the types of the add-in view and the host view are the same. With this it is still required that all components of the pipeline exist.
QualificationData	The add-in can mark appdomain and security requirements with the attribute QualificationDataAttribute. The add-in can list requirements for security and isolation requirements. For example, [QualificationData("Isolation", "NewAppDomain")] means that the add-in requires to be hosted in a new process. You can read this information from the AddInToken to activate the add-in with the specified requirements. In addition to appdomain and security requirements, you can use this attribute to pass custom information through the pipeline.
Activate()	The add-in is activated with the Activate() method. With parameters of this method, you can define if the add-in should be loaded inside a new application domain or a new process. You can also define what permissions the add-in gets.

One add-in can break the complete application. You may have seen Internet Explorer crash because of a failing add-in. Depending on the application type and the add-in type, you can avoid this by letting the add-in run within a different application domain or within a different process. MAF gives you several options here. You can activate the add-in in a new application domain or a new process. The new application domain might also have restricted permissions.

The Activate() method of the AddInToken class has several overloads where you can pass the environment into which the add-in should be loaded. The different options are listed in the following table.

Parameters of AddInToken.Activate()	Description
`AppDomain`	You can pass a new application domain into which the add-in should be loaded. This way you can make it independent of the host application, and it can also be unloaded with the application domain.
`AddInSecurityLevel`	If the add-in should run with different security levels you can pass a value of the `AddInSecurityLevel` enumeration. Possible values are `Internet`, `Intranet`, `FullTrust`, and `Host`.
`PermissionSet`	If the predefined security levels are not specific enough, you can also assign a `PermissionSet` to the appdomain of the add-in.
`AddInProcess`	Add-ins can also run within a different process from the hosting application. You can pass a new `AddInProcess` to the `Activate()` method. The new process can shut down if all add-ins are unloaded, or it can keep running. This is an option that can be set with the property `KeepAlive`.
`AddInEnvironment`	Passing an `AddInEnvironment` object is another option to define the application domain where the add-in should be loaded. With the constructor of `AddInEnvironment`, you can pass an `AppDomain` object. You can also get an existing `AddInEnvironment` of an add-in with the `AddInEnvironment` property of the `AddInController` class.

Application domains are explained in Chapter 17, "Assemblies."

The type of application may restrict the choices you have. WPF add-ins currently do not support crossing processes. With Windows Forms, it is not possible to have Windows controls connected across different application domains.

Let's get into the steps of the pipeline when the `Activate()` method of an `AddInToken` is invoked:

1. The application domain is created with the permissions specified.
2. The assembly of the add-in is loaded into the new application domain with the `Assembly.LoadFrom()` method
3. The default constructor of the add-in is invoked by using reflection. Because the add-in derives from the base class that is defined with the add-in view, the assembly of the view is loaded as well.
4. Next, an instance of the add-in side adapter is constructed. The instance of the add-in is passed to the constructor of the adapter, so the adapter can connect the contract to the add-in. The add-in adapter derives from the base class `MarshalByRefObject`, so it can be invoked across application domains.
5. The activation code returns a proxy to the add-in side adapter to the application domain of the hosting application. Because the add-in adapter implements the contract interface, the proxy contains methods and properties of the contract interface.
6. An instance of the host side adapter is constructed in the application domain of the hosting application. The proxy of the add-in side adapter is passed to the constructor. The activation finds the type of the host-side adapter from the add-in token.

The host side adapter is returned to the hosting application.

Contracts

Contracts define the boundary between the host side and the add-in side. Contracts are defined with an interface that needs to derive from the base interface `IContract`. The contract should be well-thought in that it supports flexible add-in scenarios as needed.

Contracts are not versionable and may not be changed so that previous add-in implementations can still run in newer hosts. New versions are created by defining a new contract.

There's some restriction on the types you can use with the contract. The restriction exists because of versioning issues and also because application domains are crossed from the hosting application to the add-in. The types need to be safe and versionable, and able to pass it across the boundaries (application domain or cross-process) to pass it between hosts and add-ins.

Possible types that can be passed with a contract are:

- Primitive types
- Other contracts
- Serializable system types
- Simple serializable custom types that consists of primitive types, contracts, and do not have an implementation

The members of the `IContract` interface are explained in the following table.

IContract Members	Description
`QueryContract()`	With `QueryContract()` it is possible to query a contract to verify if another contract is implemented as well. An add-in can support several contracts.
`RemoteToString()`	The parameter of `QueryContract()` requires a string representation of the contract. `RemoteToString()` returns a string representation of the current contract.
`AcquireLifetimeToken()` `RevokeLifetimeToken()`	The client invokes `AcquireLifetimeToken()` to keep a reference to the contract. `AcquireLifetimeToken()` increments a reference count. `RevokeLifetimeToken()` decrements a reference count.
`RemoteEquals()`	`RemoteEquals()` can be used to compare two contract references.

Contract interfaces are defined in the namespaces `System.AddIn.Contract`, `System.AddIn.Contract.Collections`, and `System.AddIn.Contract.Automation`. The following table lists contract interfaces that you can use with a contract:

Contract	Description
IListContract<T>	The IListContract<T> can be used to return a list of contracts.
IEnumeratorContract<T>	IEnumeratorContract<T> is used to enumerate the elements of a IListContract<T>.
IServiceProviderContract	An add-in can offer services for other add-ins. Add-ins that offer services are known as service provider and implement the interface IServiceProviderContract. With the method QueryService() an add-in implementing this interface can be queried for services offered.
IProfferServiceContract	IProfferServiceContract is the interface offered by a service provider in conjunction with IServiceProviderContract. IProfferServiceContract defines the methods ProfferService() and RevokeService(). ProfferService() adds an IServiceProviderContract to the services offered, RevokeService() removes it.
INativeHandleContract	This interface provides access to native Window handles with the GetHandle() method. This contract is used with WPF hosts to use WPF add-ins.

Lifetime

How long does an add-in need to be loaded? How long is it used? When is it possible to unload the application domain? There are several options to resolve this. One option is to use reference counts. Every use of the add-in increments the reference count. If the reference count decrements to zero, the add-in can be unloaded. Another option is to use the garbage collector. If the garbage collector runs, and there's no more reference to an object, the object is the target of garbage collection. .NET Remoting is using a leasing mechanism and a sponsor to keep objects alive. As soon as the leasing time ends, sponsors are asked if the object should stay alive.

With add-ins, there's a specific issue for unloading add-ins because they can run in different application domains and also in different processes. The garbage collector cannot work across different processes. MAF is using a mixed model for lifetime management. Within a single application domain, garbage collection is used. Within the pipeline an implicit sponsorship is used, but reference counting is available from the outside to control the sponsor.

Let's consider a scenario where the add-in is loaded into a different application domain. Within the host application, the garbage collector cleans up the host view and the host side adapter when the reference is not needed anymore. For the add-in side, the contract defines the methods AcquireLifetimeToken() and RevokeLifetimeToken() to increment and decrement the reference count of the sponsor. These methods do not just increment and decrement a value which could lead to release an object too early if one party would call the revoke method too often. Instead, AcquireLifetimeToken() returns an identifier for the lifetime token, and this identifier must be used to invoke the RevokeLifetimeToken() method. So these methods are always called in pairs.

Usually you do not have to deal with invoking the `AcquireLifetimeToken()` and `RevokeLifetimeToken()` methods. Instead you can use the `ContractHandle` class that invokes `AcquireLifetimeToken()` in the constructor and `RevokeLifetimeToken()` in the finalizer.

The finalizer is explained in Chapter 12, "Memory Management and Pointers."

In scenarios where the add-in is loaded in a new application domain, it is possible to get rid of the loaded code when the add-in is not needed anymore. MAF uses a simple model to define one add-in as the owner of the application domain to unload the application domain if this add-in is not needed anymore. An add-in is the owner of the application domain if the application domain is created when the add-in is activated. The application domain is not unloaded automatically if it was created previously.

The class `ContractHandle` is used in the host side adapter to add a reference count to the add-in. The members of this class are explained in the following table.

ContractHandle Members	Description
`Contract`	In the construction of the `ContractHandle` class, an object implementing `IContract` can be assigned to keep a reference to it. The `Contract` property returns this object.
`Dispose()`	The `Dispose()` method can be called instead of waiting for the garbage collector to do the finalization to revoke the lifetime token.
`AppDomainOwner()`	`AppDomainOwner()` is a static method of the `ContractHandle` class that returns the add-in adapter if it owns the application domain that is passed with the method.
`ContractOwnsAppDomain()`	With the static method `ContractOwnsAppDomain()` you can verify if the specified contract is an owner of the application domain. Thus, the application domain gets unloaded when the contract is disposed.

Versioning

Versioning is a very big issue with add-ins. The host application is developed further as are the add-ins. One requirement for an add-in is that it should be possible that a new version of the host application can still load old versions of add-ins. The other direction should work as well: older hosts should run newer versions of add-ins. But what if the contract changes?

System.AddIn is completely independent from the implementation of the host application and add-ins. This is done with a pipeline concept that consists of seven parts.

Add-In Sample

Let's start a simple sample of a hosting application that can load calculator add-ins. The add-ins can support different calculation operations that are offered by add-ins.

You need to create a solution with six library projects and one console application. The projects of the sample application are listed in the following table. The table lists the assemblies that need to be referenced. With the references to the other projects within the solution you need to set the property

Copy Local to False, so that the assembly does not get copied. One exception is the HostApp console project that needs a reference to the HostView project. This assembly needs to be copied so it can be found from the host application. Also you need to change the output path of the generated assemblies so that the assemblies are copied to the correct directories of the pipeline.

Project	References	Output Path	Description
CalcContract	`System.AddIn.Contract`	`..\Pipeline\Contracts\`	This assembly contains the contract for communication with the add-in. The contract is defined with an interface.
CalcView	`System.AddIn`	`..\Pipeline\AddInViews\`	The CalcView assembly contains an abstract class that is referenced by the add-in. This is the add-in side of the contract.
CalcAddIn	`System.AddIn` `CalcView`	`..\Pipeline\AddIns\CalcAddIn\`	CalcAddIn is the add-in project that references the add-in view assembly. This assembly contains the implementation of the add-in.

CalcAddIn Adapter	`System.AddIn`
	`System.AddIn.Contract`
	`CalcView`
	`CalcContract`
		`..\Pipeline\AddInSideAdapters\`	CalcAddInAdapter connects the add-in view and the contract assembly and maps the contract to the add-in view.

HostView			The assembly containing the abstract class of the host view does not need to reference any Add-In assembly and also does not have a reference to another project in the solution.

HostAdapter	`System.AddIn`
	`System.AddIn.Contract`
	`HostView`
	`CalcContract`
		`..\Pipeline\HostSideAdapters\`	The host adapter maps the host view to the contract. Thus, it needs to reference both of these projects.

HostApp	`System.AddIn` `HostView`		The hosting application activates the add-in.

Calculator Contract

Let's start by implementing the contract assembly. Contract assemblies contain a contract interface that defines the protocol for communication between the host and the add-in.

With the following code you can see the contract defined for the calculator sample application. The application defines a contract with the methods `GetOperations()` and `Operate()`. `GetOperations()` returns a list of mathematical operations supported by the calculator add-in. An operation is defined by the interface `IOperationContract` that is a contract by itself. `IOperationContract` defines the read-only properties `Name` and `NumberOperands`.

The `Operate()` method invokes the operation within the add-in and requires an operation defined by the `IOperation` interface and the operands with a `double` array.

With this contract it is possible that the add-in supports any operations that require any number of `double` operands and returns one `double`.

The attribute `AddInContract` is used by the `AddInStore` to build the cache. The `AddInContract` attribute marks the class as an add-in contract interface.

```
using System.AddIn.Contract;
using System.AddIn.Pipeline;
namespace Wrox.ProCSharp.AddIns
{
   [AddInContract]
   public interface ICalculatorContract : IContract
   {
      IListContract<IOperationContract> GetOperations();
      double Operate(IOperationContract operation, double[] operands);
   }
   public interface IOperationContract : IContract
   {
      string Name { get; }
      int NumberOperands { get; }
   }
}
```

Calculator Add-In View

The add-in view redefines the contract as it is seen by the add-in. The contract defined the interfaces `ICalculatorContract` and `IOperationContract`. For this, the add-in view defines the abstract class `Calculator` and the concrete class `Operation`.

With `Operation` there's not a specific implementation required by every add-in. Instead, the class is already implemented with the add-in view assembly. This class describes an operation for mathematical calculations with the `Name` and `NumberOperands` properties.

The abstract class `Calculator` defines the methods that need to be implemented by the add-ins. While the contract defines parameters and return types that need to be passed across appdomain- and process-boundaries, that's not the case with the add-in view. Here you can use types, which make it easy to write add-ins for the add-in developer. The `GetOperations()` method returns `IList<Operation>` instead of `IListOperation<IOperationContract>`, as you've seen with the contract assembly.

The `AddInBase` attribute identifies the class as an add-in view for the store.

```
using System.AddIn.Pipeline;
using System.Collections.Generic;
```

(continued)

(continued)

```
namespace Wrox.ProCSharp.AddIns
{
   [AddInBase]
   public abstract class Calculator
   {
      public abstract IList<Operation> GetOperations();
      public abstract double Operate(Operation operation, double[] operand);
   }
   public class Operation
   {
       public string Name { get; set; }
       public int NumberOperands { get; set; }
   }
}
```

Calculator Add-In Adapter

The add-in adapter maps the contract to the add-in view. This assembly has references to both the contract and the add-in view assemblies. The implementation of the adapter needs to map the method `IListContract<IOperationContract> GetOperations()` from the contract to the view method `IList<Operation> GetOperations()`.

The assembly includes the classes `OperationViewToContractAddInAdapter` and `CalculatorViewToContractAddInAdapter`. These classes implement the interfaces `IOperationContract` and `ICalculatorContract`. The methods of the base interface `IContract` can be implemented by deriving from the base class `ContractBase`. This class offers a default implementation. `OperationViewToContractAddInAdapter` implements the other members of the `IOperationContract` interface and just forwards the calls to the `Operation view` that is assigned in the constructor.

The class `OperationViewToContractAddInAdapter` also contains static helper methods `ViewToContractAdapter()` and `ContractToViewAdapter()` that map `Operation` to `IOperationContract` and the other way around.

```
using System.AddIn.Pipeline;
namespace Wrox.ProCSharp.AddIns
{
   internal class OperationViewToContractAddInAdapter : ContractBase,
         IOperationContract
   {
      private Operation view;
      public OperationViewToContractAddInAdapter(Operation view)
      {
         this.view = view;
      }
      public string Name
      {
         get { return view.Name; }
      }
      public int NumberOperands
      {
         get { return view.NumberOperands; }
      }
      public static IOperationContract ViewToContractAdapter(Operation view)
```

```
        {
           return new OperationViewToContractAddInAdapter(view);
        }
        public static Operation ContractToViewAdapter(
              IOperationContract contract)
        {
           return (contract as OperationViewToContractAddInAdapter).view;
        }
     }
  }
```

The class `CalculatorViewToContractAddInAdapter` is very similar to `OperationViewToContractAddInAdapter`: It derives from `ContractBase` to inherit a default implementation of the `IContract` interface, and it implements a contract interface. This time the `ICalculatorContract` interface is implemented with the `GetOperations()` and `Operate()` methods.

The `Operate()` method of the adapter invokes the `Operate()` method of the view class `Calculator` where `IOperationContract` needs to be converted to `Operation`. This is done with the static helper method `ContractToViewAdapter()` that is defined with the `OperationViewToContractAddInAdapter` class.

The implementation of the `GetOperations` method needs to convert the collection `IListContract<IOperationContract>` to `IList<Operation>`. For such collection conversions, the class `CollectionAdapters` defines conversion methods `ToIList()` and `ToIListContract()`. Here, the method `ToIListContract()` is used for the conversion.

The attribute `AddInAdapter` identifies the class as an add-in side adapter for the add-in store.

```
using System.AddIn.Contract;
using System.AddIn.Pipeline;
namespace Wrox.ProCSharp.AddIns
{
   [AddInAdapter]
   internal class CalculatorViewToContractAddInAdapter : ContractBase,
         ICalculatorContract
   {
      private Calculator view;
      public CalculatorViewToContractAddInAdapter(Calculator view)
      {
         this.view = view;
      }
      public IListContract<IOperationContract> GetOperations()
      {
         return CollectionAdapters.ToIListContract<Operation,
               IOperationContract>(view.GetOperations(),
               OperationViewToContractAddInAdapter.ViewToContractAdapter,
               OperationViewToContractAddInAdapter.ContractToViewAdapter);
      }
      public double Operate(IOperationContract operation, double[] operands)
      {
         return view.Operate(
               OperationViewToContractAddInAdapter.ContractToViewAdapter(
                     operation), operands);
      }
   }
}
```

> **Because the adapter classes are invoked by .NET reflection, it is possible that the internal access modifier is used with these classes. As these classes are an implementation detail, it's a good idea to use the `internal` access modifier.**

Calculator Add-In

The add-in now contains the real implementation of the add-in. The add-in is implemented by the class `CalculatorV1`. The add-in assembly has a dependency on the add-in view assembly as it needs to implement the abstract `Calculator` class.

The attribute `AddIn` marks the class as an add-in for the add-in store, and adds publisher, version, and description information. On the host side, this information can be accessed from the `AddInToken`.

`CalculatorV1` returns a list of supported operations in the method `GetOperations()`. `Operate()` calculates the operands based on the operation.

```
using System;
using System.AddIn;
using System.Collections.Generic;
namespace Wrox.ProCSharp.AddIns
{
   [AddIn("CalculatorAddIn", Publisher="Wrox Press", Version="1.0.0.0",
      Description="Sample AddIn")]
   public class CalculatorV1 : Calculator
   {
      private List<Operation> operations;
      public CalculatorV1()
      {
         operations = new List<Operation>();
         operations.Add(new Operation() { Name = "+", NumberOperands = 2 });
         operations.Add(new Operation() { Name = "-", NumberOperands = 2 });
         operations.Add(new Operation() { Name = "/", NumberOperands = 2 });
         operations.Add(new Operation() { Name = "*", NumberOperands = 2 });
      }
      public override IList<Operation> GetOperations()
      {
         return operations;
      }
      public override double Operate(Operation operation, double[] operand)
      {
         switch (operation.Name)
         {
            case "+":
               return operand[0] + operand[1];
            case "-":
               return operand[0] - operand[1];
            case "/":
               return operand[0] / operand[1];
            case "*":
               return operand[0] * operand[1];
```

```
                default:
                   throw new InvalidOperationException(
                       String.Format("invalid operation {0}", operation.Name));
            }
        }
    }
}
```

Calculator Host View

Let's continue with the host view of the host side. Similar to the add-in view, the host view defines an abstract class with methods similar to the contract. However, the methods defined here are invoked by the host application.

Both the class `Calculator` and `Operation` are abstract as the members are implemented by the host adapter. The classes here just need to define the interface to be used by the host application.

```
using System.Collections.Generic;
namespace Wrox.ProCSharp.AddIns
{
   public abstract class Calculator
   {
       public abstract IList<Operation> GetOperations();
       public abstract double Operate(Operation operation,
             params double[] operand);
   }
   public abstract class Operation
   {
       public abstract string Name { get; }
       public abstract int NumberOperands { get; }
   }
}
```

Calculator Host Adapter

The host adapter assembly references the host view and the contract to map the view to the contract. The class `OperationContractToViewHostAdapter` implements the members of the abstract `Operation` class. The class `CalculatorContractToViewHostAdapter` implements the members of the abstract `Calculator` class.

With `OperationContractToViewHostAdapter`, the reference to the contract is assigned in the constructor. The adapter class also contains a `ContractHandle` instance that adds a lifetime reference to the `contract`, so that add-in stays loaded as long it is needed by the hosting application.

```
using System.AddIn.Pipeline;
namespace Wrox.ProCSharp.AddIns
{
   internal class OperationContractToViewHostAdapter : Operation
   {
      private ContractHandle handle;
      public IOperationContract Contract { get; private set; }
      public OperationContractToViewHostAdapter(IOperationContract contract)
```

(continued)

(continued)

```
        {
           this.Contract = contract;
           handle = new ContractHandle(contract);
        }
        public override string Name
        {
           get
           {
              return Contract.Name;
           }
        }
        public override int NumberOperands
        {
           get
           {
              return Contract.NumberOperands;
           }
        }
     }
     internal static class OperationHostAdapters
     {
        internal static IOperationContract ViewToContractAdapter(Operation view)
        {
           return ((OperationContractToViewHostAdapter)view).Contract;
        }
        internal static Operation ContractToViewAdapter(
              IOperationContract contract)
        {
           return new OperationContractToViewHostAdapter(contract);
        }
     }
  }
```

The class `CalculatorContractToViewHostAdapter` implements the methods of the abstract host view `Calculator` class and forwards the call to the contract. Again, you can see the `ContractHandle` holding the reference to the contract, which is similar to the adapter from the add-in side type conversions. This time the type conversions are just in the other direction from the add-in adapters.

The attribute `HostAdapter` marks the class as an adapter that needs to be installed in the HostSideAdapters directory.

```
  using System.Collections.Generic;
  using System.AddIn.Pipeline;
  namespace Wrox.ProCSharp.AddIns
  {
     [HostAdapter]
     internal class CalculatorContractToViewHostAdapter : Calculator
     {
        private ICalculatorContract contract;
        private ContractHandle handle;
        public CalculatorContractToViewHostAdapter(ICalculatorContract contract)
```

```
        {
            this.contract = contract;
            handle = new ContractHandle(contract);
        }
        public override IList<Operation> GetOperations()
        {
            return CollectionAdapters.ToIList<IOperationContract, Operation>(
                contract.GetOperations(),
                OperationHostAdapters.ContractToViewAdapter,
                OperationHostAdapters.ViewToContractAdapter);
        }
        public override double Operate(Operation operation, double[] operands)
        {
            return contract.Operate(OperationHostAdapters.ViewToContractAdapter(
                operation), operands);
        }
    }
}
```

Calculator Host

The sample host application uses the WPF technology. You can see the user interface of this application in Figure 36-3. On top is the list of available add-ins. On the left, the operations of the active add-in are shown. As you select the operation that should be invoked, operands are shown. After entering the values for the operands, the operation of the add-in can be invoked.

The buttons on the bottom row are used to rebuild and update the add-in store, and to exit the application.

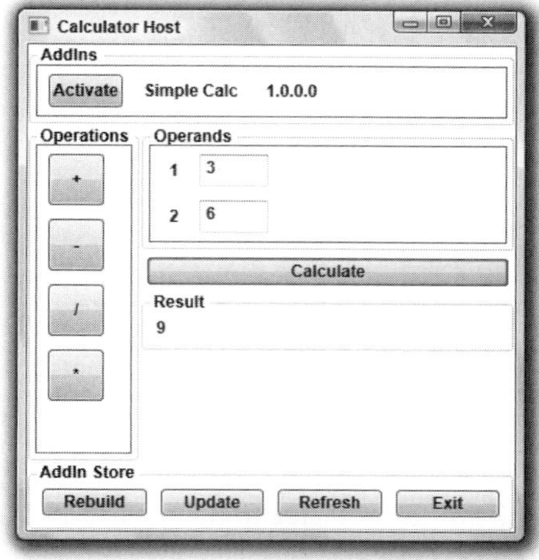

Figure 36-3

The XAML code that follows shows the tree of the user interface. With the ListBox elements, different styles with item templates are used to give a specific representation of the list of add-ins, the list of operations, and the list of operands.

You can read information about item templates in Chapter 35, "Advanced WPF."

```
<DockPanel>
   <GroupBox Header="AddIn Store" DockPanel.Dock="Bottom">
      <UniformGrid Columns="4">
         <Button x:Name="rebuildStore" Click="RebuildStore"
               Margin="5">Rebuild</Button>
         <Button x:Name="updateStore" Click="UpdateStore"
               Margin="5">Update</Button>
         <Button x:Name="refresh" Click="RefreshAddIns"
               Margin="5">Refresh</Button>
         <Button x:Name="exit" Click="App_Exit" Margin="5">Exit</Button>
      </UniformGrid>
   </GroupBox>
   <GroupBox Header="AddIns" DockPanel.Dock="Top">
      <ListBox x:Name="listAddIns" ItemsSource="{Binding}"
           Style="{StaticResource listAddInsStyle}" />
   </GroupBox>
   <GroupBox DockPanel.Dock="Left" Header="Operations">
      <ListBox x:Name="listOperations" ItemsSource="{Binding}"
            Style="{StaticResource listOperationsStyle}" />
   </GroupBox>
   <StackPanel DockPanel.Dock="Right" Orientation="Vertical">
      <GroupBox Header="Operands">
         <ListBox x:Name="listOperands" ItemsSource="{Binding}"
               Style="{StaticResource listOperandsStyle}">
         </ListBox>
      </GroupBox>
      <Button x:Name="buttonCalculate" Click="Calculate" IsEnabled="False"
            Margin="5">Calculate</Button>
      <GroupBox DockPanel.Dock="Bottom" Header="Result">
         <Label x:Name="labelResult" />
      </GroupBox>
   </StackPanel>
</DockPanel>
```

In the code behind, the FindAddIns() method is invoked in the constructor of the Window. FindAddIns() uses the AddInStore class to get a collection of AddInToken objects and pass them to the DataContext property of the ListBox listAddIns for display. The first parameter of the AddInStore.FindAddIns() method passes the abstract Calculator class that is defined by the host view to find all add-ins from the store that apply to the contract. The second parameter passes the directory of the pipeline that is read from the application configuration file. When you run the sample application from the Wrox download site you have to change the directory in the application configuration file to match your directory structure.

```
using System;
using System.AddIn.Hosting;
using System.AddIn.Pipeline;
using System.IO;
using System.Linq;
using System.Windows;
```

```
using System.Windows.Controls;
using Wrox.ProCSharp.AddIns.Properties;
namespace Wrox.ProCSharp.AddIns
{
   public partial class CalculatorHostWindow : Window
   {
      private Calculator activeAddIn = null;
      private Operation currentOperation = null;
      public CalculatorHostWindow()
      {
         InitializeComponent();
         FindAddIns();
      }
      void FindAddIns()
      {
         try
         {
            this.listAddIns.DataContext =
                  AddInStore.FindAddIns(typeof(Calculator),
                  Settings.Default.PipelinePath);
         }
         catch (DirectoryNotFoundException ex)
         {
            MessageBox.Show("Verify the pipeline directory in the " +
                  "config file");
            Application.Current.Shutdown();
         }
      }
      //...
```

To update the cache of the Add-In store, the `UpdateStore()` and `RebuildStore()` methods are mapped to the `Click` events of the Update and Rebuild buttons. Within the implementation of these methods, the `Rebuild()` or `Update()` methods of the `AddInStore` class are used. These methods return a string array of warnings if assemblies are stored in the wrong directories. Because of the complexity of the pipeline structure, there's a good chance that the first time you may not get the project configuration completely right for copying the assemblies to the correct directories. Reading the returned information from these methods, you will get a clear explanation about what's wrong. For example, the message "No usable AddInAdapter parts could be found in assembly Pipeline\AddInSideAdapters\CalcView .dll" gives a hint that the assembly CalcView is stored inside the wrong directory.

```
      private void UpdateStore(object sender, RoutedEventArgs e)
      {
         string[] messages = AddInStore.Update(Settings.Default.PipelinePath);
         if (messages.Length != 0)
         {
            MessageBox.Show(string.Join("\n", messages),
                  "AddInStore Warnings", MessageBoxButton.OK,
                  MessageBoxImage.Warning);
         }
      }
      private void RebuildStore(object sender, RoutedEventArgs e)
```

(continued)

(continued)

```
{
   string[] messages =
         AddInStore.Rebuild(Settings.Default.PipelinePath);
   if (messages.Length != 0)
   {
      MessageBox.Show(string.Join("\n", messages),
            "AddInStore Warnings", MessageBoxButton.OK,
            MessageBoxImage.Warning);
   }
}
```

In Figure 36-2 you can see an Activate button beside the available add-in. Clicking this button invokes the handler method `ActivateAddIn()`. With this implementation, the add-in is activated by using the `Activate()` method of the `AddInToken` class. Here the add-in is loaded inside a new process that is created with the `AddInProcess` class. This class starts the process AddInProcess32.exe. Setting the `KeepAlive` property of the process to `false`, the process is stopped as soon as the last add-in reference is garbage collected. The parameter `AddInSecurityLevel.Internet` leads to an add-in running with restricted permissions. The last statement of `ActivateAddIn()` invokes the `ListOperations()` method, which in turn invokes the `GetOperations()` method of the add-in. `GetOperations()` assigns the returned list to the data context of the `ListBox listOperations` for displaying all operations.

```
private void ActivateAddIn(object sender, RoutedEventArgs e)
{
   FrameworkElement el = sender as FrameworkElement;
   Trace.Assert(el != null, "ActivateAddIn invoked from the wrong " +
         "control type");

   AddInToken addIn = el.Tag as AddInToken;
   Trace.Assert(el.Tag != null, String.Format(
         "An AddInToken must be assigned to the Tag property " +
         "of the control {0}", el.Name);
   AddInProcess process = new AddInProcess();
   process.KeepAlive = false;

   activeAddIn = addIn.Activate<Calculator>(process,
         AddInSecurityLevel.Internet);
   ListOperations();
}
void ListOperations()
{
   this.listOperations.DataContext = activeAddIn.GetOperations();
}
```

After the add-in is activated and the list of operations displays in the UI, the user can select an operation. The `Click` event of the `Button` shown in the Operations category is assigned to the handler method `OperationSelected()`. In the implementation, the `Operation` object that is assigned to the `Tag` property of the `Button` is retrieved to get the number of operands needed with the operation. To allow the user adding values to the operands, an array of `OperandUI` objects is bound to the `ListBox listOperands`.

```
private void OperationSelected(object sender, RoutedEventArgs e)
{
   FrameworkElement el = sender as FrameworkElement;
   Trace.Assert(el != null, "OperationSelected invoked from " +
         "the wrong control type");
```

```
        Operation op = el.Tag as Operation;
        Trace.Assert(el.Tag != null, String.Format(
              "An AddInToken must be assigned to the Tag property " +
              "of the control {0}", el.Name);
        currentOperation = op;
        ListOperands(new double[op.NumberOperands]);
    }
    private class OperandUI
    {
        public int Index { get; set; }
        public double Value { get; set; }
    }
    void ListOperands(double[] operands)
    {
        this.listOperands.DataContext =
           operands.Select((operand, index) =>
                 new OperandUI()
                 { Index = index + 1, Value = operand }).ToArray();
    }
```

The `Calculate()` method is invoked with the `Click` event of the Calculate button. Here, the operands are retrieved from the UI, the operation and operands are passed to the `Operate()` method of the add-in, and the result is shown with the content of a label.

```
    private void Calculate(object sender, RoutedEventArgs e)
    {
        OperandUI[] operandsUI = (OperandUI[])this.listOperands.DataContext;
        double[] operands = operandsUI.Select(opui => opui.Value).ToArray();
        labelResult.Content = activeAddIn.Operate(currentOperation,
              operands);
    }
```

Additional Add-Ins

The hard work is now done. The pipeline components and the host application are created. The pipeline is now working, yet it's an easy task to add other add-ins such as the Advanced Calculator add-in shown in the following code segment into the host application.

```
[AddIn("Advanced Calc", Publisher = "Wrox Press", Version = "1.1.0.0",
     Description = "Another AddIn Sample")]
public class AdvancedCalculatorV1 : Calculator
```

Summary

In this chapter you've learned the concepts of a new .NET 3.5 technology: the Managed Add-In Framework.

MAF uses a pipeline concept to create a complete independence between the hosting and add-in assemblies. A clearly defined contract separates the host view from the add-in view. Adapters make it possible for both sides to change independently of each other.

The next chapter starts a sequence of three chapters for developing the UI with ASP.NET.

37

ASP.NET Pages

If you are new to the world of C# and .NET, you might wonder why a chapter on ASP.NET has been included in this book. It's a whole new language, right? Well, not really. In fact, as you will see, you can use C# to create ASP.NET pages.

ASP.NET is part of the .NET Framework and is a technology that allows for the dynamic creation of documents on a Web server when they are requested via HTTP. This mostly means HTML and XHTML documents, although it is equally possible to create XML documents, CSS files, images, PDF documents, or anything else that supports MIME types.

In some ways, ASP.NET is similar to many other technologies — such as PHP, ASP, or ColdFusion. There is, however, one key difference: ASP.NET, as its name suggests, has been designed to be fully integrated with the .NET Framework, part of which includes support for C#.

Perhaps you are familiar with Active Server Pages (ASP) technology, which enables you to create dynamic content. If you are, you will probably know that programming in this technology used scripting languages such as VBScript or JScript. The result was not always perfect, at least not for those of us used to "proper," compiled programming languages, and it certainly resulted in a loss of performance.

One major difference related to the use of more advanced programming languages is the provision of a complete server-side object model for use at runtime. ASP.NET provides access to all of the controls on a page as objects, in a rich environment. On the server side, you also have access to other .NET classes, allowing for the integration of many useful services. Controls used on a page expose a lot of functionality; in fact, you can do almost as much as with Windows Forms classes, which provide plenty of flexibility. For this reason, ASP.NET pages that generate HTML content are often called *Web Forms*.

This chapter takes a more detailed look at ASP.NET, including how it works, what you can do with it, and how C# fits in. The following is a brief outline of what is covered:

- An introduction to ASP.NET
- How to create ASP.NET Web Forms with server controls
- How to bind data to ASP.NET controls with ADO.NET
- Application configuration

ASP.NET Introduction

ASP.NET works with Internet Information Server (IIS) to deliver content in response to HTTP requests. ASP.NET pages are found in `.aspx` files. Figure 37-1 illustrates the technology's basic architecture.

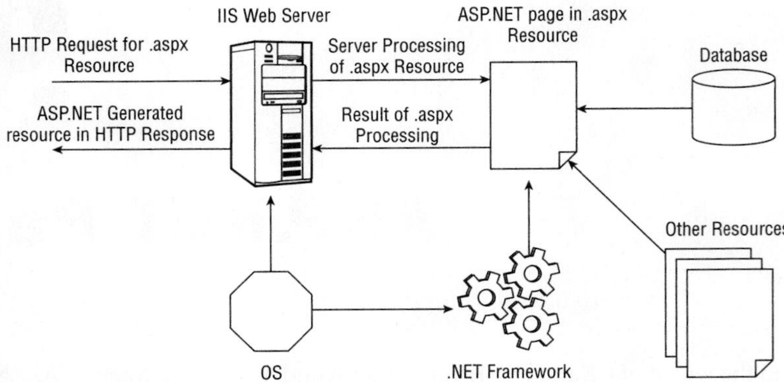

Figure 37-1

During ASP.NET processing, you have access to all .NET classes, custom components created in C# or other languages, databases, and so on. In fact, you have as much power as you would have running a C# application; using C# in ASP.NET is, in effect, running a C# application.

An ASP.NET file can contain any of the following:

- Processing instructions for the server
- Code in C#, Visual Basic .NET, JScript .NET, or any other language that the .NET Framework supports
- Content in whatever form is appropriate for the generated resource, such as HTML
- Client-side script code, such as JavaScript
- Embedded ASP.NET server controls

So, in fact, you could have an ASP.NET file as simple as this:

```
Hello!
```

This would simply result in an HTML page being returned (as HTML is the default output of ASP.NET pages) containing just this text.

As you will see later in this chapter, it is also possible to split certain portions of the code into other files, which can provide a more logical structure.

State Management in ASP.NET

One of the key properties of ASP.NET pages is that they are effectively stateless. By default, no information is stored on the server between user requests (although there are methods for doing this, as you will see later in this chapter). At first glance, this seems a little strange because state management is something that seems essential for user-friendly interactive sessions. However, ASP.NET provides a workaround to this problem, such that session management becomes almost transparent.

In short, information such as the state of controls on a Web Form (including data entered in text boxes or selections from drop-down lists) is stored in a hidden *viewstate* field that is part of the page generated by the server and passed to the user. Subsequent actions, such as triggering events that require server-side processing, like submitting form data, result in this information being sent back to the server; this is known as a *postback* operation. On the server, this information is used to repopulate the page object model allowing you to operate on it as if the changes had been made locally.

You will see this in action shortly and examine the details.

ASP.NET Web Forms

As mentioned earlier, much of the functionality in ASP.NET is achieved using Web Forms. Before long, you will dive in and create a simple Web Form to give you a starting point to explore this technology. First, however, this section reviews some key points pertinent to Web Form design. Note that some ASP.NET developers simply use a text editor such as Notepad to create files. We wouldn't advocate this ourselves because the benefits you get via an IDE such as Visual Studio or Web Developer Express are substantial, but it's worth mentioning because it is a possibility. If you do take this route, you have a great deal of flexibility as to which parts of a Web application you put where. This enables you, for example, to combine all of your code in one file. You can achieve this by enclosing code in `<script>` elements, using two attributes on the opening `<script>` tag:

```
<script language="c#" runat="server">
   // Server-side code goes here.
</script>
```

The `runat="server"` attribute here is crucial because it instructs the ASP.NET engine to execute this code on the server rather than sending it to the client, thus giving you access to the rich environment hinted at earlier. You can place your functions, event handlers, and so on in server-side script blocks.

If you omit the `runat="server"` attribute, you are effectively providing client-side code, which will fail if it uses any of the server-side style coding that is discussed in this chapter. You can, however, use `<script>` elements to supply client-side script in languages such as JavaScript. For example:

```
<script language="JavaScript" type="text/JavaScript">
   // Client-side code goes here; you can also use "vbscript".
</script>
```

Note that the `type` *attribute here is optional, but necessary if you want XHTML compliance.*

It may seem strange that the facility to add JavaScript code to your pages is included with ASP.NET. However, JavaScript allows you to add dynamic client-side behavior to your Web pages and can be very useful. This is especially true for Ajax programming, as you will see in Chapter 39, "ASP.NET AJAX."

It is possible to create ASP.NET files in Visual Studio, which is great for you, as you are already familiar with this environment for C# programming. However, the default project setup for Web applications in this environment has a slightly more complex structure than a single `.aspx` file. This isn't a problem for you, however, and does make things a bit more logical (more programmer-like and less Web developer–like). For this reason, you will use Visual Studio throughout this chapter for your ASP.NET programming (instead of Notepad).

The `.aspx` files can also include code in blocks enclosed by `<%` and `%>` tags. However, function definitions and variable declarations cannot go here. Instead, you can insert code that is executed as soon as the block is reached, which is useful when outputting simple HTML content. This behavior is similar to that of old-style ASP pages, with one important difference: The code is compiled, not interpreted. This results in far better performance.

Now it's time for an example. In Visual Studio, you create a new Web application by using the File ⇨ New ⇨ Web Site menu option. From the dialog box that appears, select the Visual C# language type and the ASP.NET Web Site template. At this point, you have a choice to make. Visual Studio can create Web sites in a number of different locations:

- On your local IIS Web server
- On your local disk, configured to use the built-in Visual Web Developer Web server
- At any location accessible via FTP
- On a remote Web server that supports Front Page Server Extensions

The latter two choices use remote servers so you are left with the first two choices. In general, IIS is the best place to install ASP.NET Web sites because it is likely to be closest to the configuration required when you deploy a Web site. The alternative, using the built-in Web server, is fine for testing but has certain limitations:

- Only the local computer can see the Web site.
- Access to services such as SMTP is restricted.
- The security model is different from IIS — the application runs in the context of the current user rather than in an ASP.NET-specific account.

This last point requires clarification because security is very important when it comes to accessing databases or anything else that requires authentication. By default, Web applications running on IIS do so in an account called ASPNET on Windows XP, 2000, and Vista Web servers, or in an account called NETWORK SERVICES on Windows Server 2003. This is configurable if you are using IIS, but not if you use the built-in Web server.

For the purposes of illustration, however, and because you may not have IIS installed on your computer, you can use the built-in Web server. You aren't worried about security at this stage, so you can go with simplicity.

Create a new ASP.NET Web site called `PCSWebApp1` using the File System option, at `C:\ProCSharp\Chapter37`, as shown in Figure 37-2.

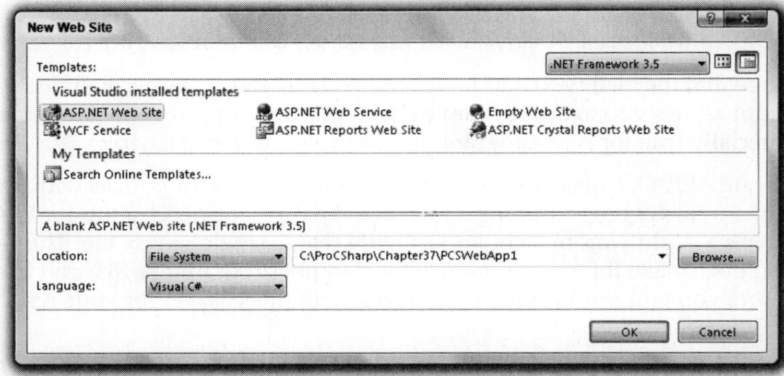

Figure 37-2

After a few moments, Visual Studio .NET should have set up the following:

- `PCSWebApp1`, a new solution containing the C# Web application PCSWebApp1
- A reserved folder called `App_Data` for containing data files, such as XML files or database files
- `Default.aspx`, the first ASP.NET page in the Web application
- `Default.aspx.cs`, a "code-behind" class file for `Default.aspx`
- `Web.config`, a configuration file for the Web application

You can see all of this in the Solution Explorer, as shown in Figure 37-3.

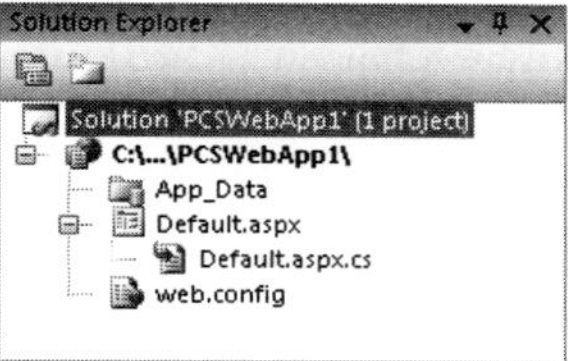

Figure 37-3

You can view `.aspx` files in design or source (HTML) view. This is the same as for Windows Forms (as discussed in Chapter 31, "Windows Forms"). The initial view in Visual Studio is either the design or source view for `Default.aspx` (you can toggle between the views or view them together in a split view using the buttons in the bottom left). The design view is shown in Figure 37-4.

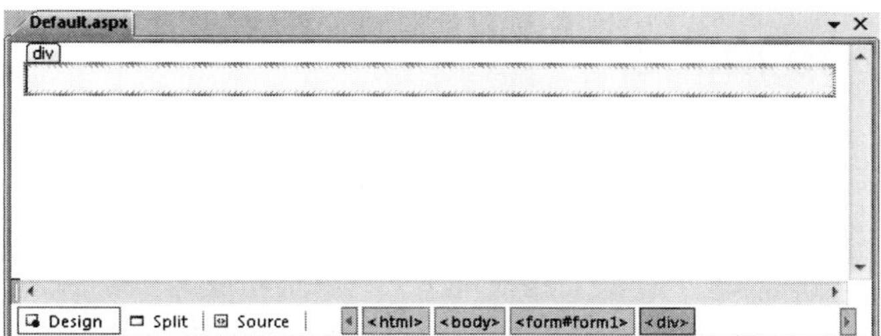

Figure 37-4

Underneath the (currently empty) form, you can see where in the HTML for the form the cursor is currently positioned. Here the cursor is in a `<div>` element inside a `<form>` element inside the `<body>` element of the page. The `<form>` element is displayed as `<form#form1>` to identify the element by its `id` attribute, which you will see shortly. The `<div>` element is also labeled in the design view.

The source view for the page shows you the code generated inside the `.aspx` file:

```
<%@ Page Language="C#" AutoEventWireup="true" CodeFile="Default.aspx.cs"
  Inherits="_Default" %>
<!DOCTYPE html PUBLIC "-//W3C//DTD XHTML 1.0 Transitional//EN"
  "http://www.w3.org/TR/xhtml1/DTD/xhtml1-transitional.dtd">
<html xmlns="http://www.w3.org/1999/xhtml">
<head runat="server">
```

(continued)

(continued)

```
    <title>Untitled Page</title>
  </head>
  <body>
    <form id="form1" runat="server">
      <div>
      </div>
    </form>
  </body>
  </html>
```

If you know any HTML syntax, then this will look familiar to you. You are presented with the basic code required for an HTML page following the XHTML schema, with a few extra bits of code. The most important extra is the `<form>` element, which has an `id` attribute of `form1`. This element will contain your ASP.NET code. The most important thing to note here is the `runat` attribute. Just as with the server-side code blocks you saw at the start of this section, this is set to `server`, meaning that the processing of the form will take place on the server. If you don't include this reference, then no server-side processing will be performed, and the form won't do anything. There can be only one server-side `<form>` element in an ASP.NET page.

The other interesting thing about this code is the `<%@ Page %>` tag at the top. This tag defines page characteristics that are important to you as a C# Web application developer. There is a `Language` attribute that specifies that you will use C# throughout your page, as you saw earlier with `<script>` blocks. (The default for Web applications is Visual Basic .NET, although this can be changed using a `Web.config` file, which you will see later in this chapter.) The other three attributes — `AutoEventWireup`, `CodeFile`, and `Inherits` — are used to associate the Web Form with a class in a code-behind code file, in this case the partial class `_Default` in the file `Default.aspx.cs`. This leads straight into a necessary discussion about the ASP.NET code model.

The ASP.NET Code Model

In ASP.NET, a combination of layout (HTML) code, ASP.NET controls, and C# code is used to generate the HTML that users see. The layout and ASP.NET code are stored in an `.aspx` file, such as the one you looked at in the preceding section. The C# code that you add to customize the behavior of the form is contained either in the `.aspx` file or, as in the preceding example, in a separate `.aspx.cs` file, which is usually referred to as the "code-behind" file.

When an ASP.NET Web Form is processed — typically when a user requests the page, although sites can be precompiled — several things happen:

- The ASP.NET process examines the page, and determines what objects must be created to instantiate the page object model.
- A base class for the page is dynamically created, including members for the controls on the page as well as event handlers for these controls (such as button click events).
- Additional code contained in the `.aspx` page is combined with this base class to complete the object model.
- The complete code is compiled and cached ready to process subsequent requests.
- HTML is generated and returned to the user.

The code-behind file generated for you in the PCSWebApp1 Web site for `Default.aspx` is initially very sparse. First, you see the default set of namespace references that you are likely to use in ASP.NET Web pages:

```
using System;
using System.Data;
using System.Configuration;
using System.Linq;
using System.Web;
using System.Web.Security;
using System.Web.UI;
using System.Web.UI.WebControls;
using System.Web.UI.WebControls.WebParts;
using System.Web.UI.HtmlControls;
using System.Xml.Linq;
```

Below these references, you see an almost completely empty partial class definition for `Default_aspx`:

```
public partial class _Default : System.Web.UI.Page
{
   protected void Page_Load(object sender, EventArgs e)
   {
   }
}
```

Here, the `Page_Load()` event handler can be used to add any code that is required when the page is loaded. As you add more event handlers, and so on, this class file will become increasingly full of code. Note that you don't see the code that wires up this event handler to the page — event handlers are inferred by the ASP.NET runtime, as noted earlier. This is due to the `AutoEventWireUp` attribute — setting this to `false` will mean that you will need to associate the event handlers in your code with events on your own.

This class is a partial class definition because the process outlined earlier requires it. When the page is precompiled, a separate partial class definition is created from the ASP.NET code for your page. This includes all the controls you have added to the page. At design time, the compiler infers this partial class definition, which allows you to use IntelliSense in your code behind to reference controls on your page.

ASP.NET Server Controls

Your generated code doesn't do very much yet, so next you need to add some content. You can do this in Visual Studio using the Web Form designer, which supports drag-and-drop in just the same way as the Windows Forms designer.

You can add three types of controls to your ASP.NET pages:

- **HTML server controls** — These controls mimic HTML elements, which will be familiar to HTML developers.
- **Web server controls** — This is a new set of controls, some of which have the same functionality as HTML controls. These controls have a common naming scheme for properties and other elements to ease development, and provide consistency with analogous Windows Forms controls. There are also some completely new and very powerful controls, as you will see later. Several types of Web server controls exist, including the standard ones such as buttons, validation controls for validating user input, login controls to simplify user management, and more complicated controls for dealing with data sources.
- **Custom and user controls** — These controls are defined by the developer and can be created in a number of ways, as discussed in Chapter 38, "ASP.NET Development."

The next section provides a list of many of the frequently used Web server controls, along with usage notes. Some additional controls are examined in the next chapter. HTML controls will not be covered in this book. These controls don't do anything more than the Web server controls, and the Web server controls provide a richer environment for developers more familiar with programming than with HTML design. If you learn how to use the Web server controls, then you will have all the information you require to use HTML server controls. For more information, check out Professional ASP.NET 2.0 (Wiley Publishing, Inc., ISBN 0-7645-7610-0).

Now you add a couple of Web server controls to the PCSWebApp1 Web site you created in the last section. All Web server controls are used in the following XML element-type form:

```
<asp:controlName runat="server" attribute="value">Contents</asp:controlName>
```

In the preceding code, `controlName` is the name of the ASP.NET server control, `attribute="value"` is one or more attribute specifications, and `Contents` specifies the control content, if any. Some controls allow properties to be set using attributes and control element content, such as `Label` (used for simple text display), where `Text` can be specified in either way. Other controls might use an element containment scheme to define their hierarchy — for example `Table` (which defines a table), which can contain `TableRow` elements in order to specify table rows declaratively.

Because the syntax for controls is based on XML (although the controls may be used embedded in non-XML code such as HTML), it is an error to omit the closing tags and `/>` for empty elements, or to overlap controls.

Finally, you once again see the `runat="server"` attribute on the Web server controls. It is just as essential here as it is elsewhere, and it is a common mistake to skip this attribute. If you do, your Web Forms won't work.

This first example is simple. Change the HTML design view for `Default.aspx` as follows:

```
<%@ Page Language="C#" AutoEventWireup="true" CodeFile="Default.aspx.cs"
Inherits="_Default" %>
<!DOCTYPE html PUBLIC "-//W3C//DTD XHTML 1.1//EN"
"http://www.w3.org/TR/xhtml11/DTD/xhtml11.dtd">
<html xmlns="http://www.w3.org/1999/xhtml">
<head runat="server">
  <title>Untitled Page</title>
</head>
<body>
  <form id="form1" runat="server">
    <div>
      <asp:Label runat="server" ID="resultLabel" /><br />
      <asp:Button runat="server" ID="triggerButton" Text="Click Me" />
    </div>
  </form>
</body>
</html>
```

Here you have added two Web Form controls: a label and a button.

Note that as you do this, Visual Studio .NET IntelliSense predicts your code entry, just as in the C# code editor. Also, if you edit your code in split view and synchronize the views, the element that you are editing in the source pane will be highlighted in the design pane.

Going back to the design screen, you can see that your controls have been added, and named using their `ID` attributes (the `ID` attribute is often known as the *identifier* of a control). As with Windows Forms, you have full access to properties, events, and so on through the Properties window and get instant feedback in code or design whenever you make changes.

You can also use the CSS Properties window and other style windows to style your controls. However, unless you are familiar with CSS, you will probably want to leave this technique alone for now and concentrate on the functionality of the controls.

Any server controls you add will automatically become part of the object model for the form that you are building. This is an instant bonus for Windows Forms developers — the similarities are beginning to emerge!

To make this application do something, you can add an event handler for clicking the button. Here you can either enter a method name in the Properties window for the button or just double-click the button to get the default event handler. If you double-click the button, you will automatically add an event-handling method as follows:

```
protected void triggerButton_Click(object sender, EventArgs e)
{
}
```

This is hooked up to the button by some code added to the source of `Default.aspx`:

```
<div>
  <asp:Label Runat="server" ID="resultLabel" /><br />
  <asp:Button Runat="server" ID="triggerButton" Text="Click Me"
    onclick="triggerButton_Click" />
</div>
```

Here, the `onclick` attribute lets the ASP.NET runtime know to wire up the click event of the button to the `triggerButton_Click()` method when it generates the code model for the form.

Modify the code in `triggerButton_Click()` as follows (note that the label control type is inferred from the ASP.NET code so that you can use it directly from the code behind):

```
void triggerButton_Click(object sender, EventArgs e)
{
   resultLabel.Text = "Button clicked!";
}
```

Now you're ready to make it go. There is no need to build the project; you simply need to make sure everything is saved and then point a Web browser at the location of the Web site. If you had used IIS, this would be simple because you would know the URL to point at. However, because you are using the built-in Web server for this example, you need to start things running. The quickest way to do this is to press Ctrl+F5, which will start the server and open a browser pointing at the required URL.

When the built-in Web server is running, an icon will appear in your system tray. By double-clicking this icon, you can see what the Web server is doing, and stop it if required (see Figure 37-5).

In Figure 37-5, you can see the port that the Web server is running on and the URL required to see the Web site you have created.

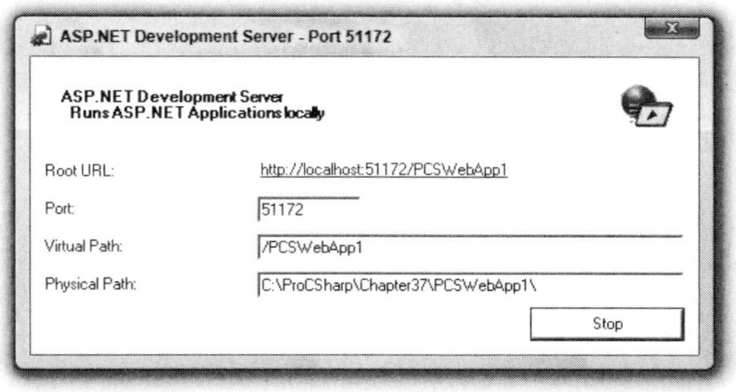

Figure 37-5

The browser that has opened should display the Click Me button on a Web page. Before you press the button, take a quick look at the code received by the browser by selecting Page ➪ View Source (in IE7). The <form> section should look something like this:

```
<form method="post" action="Default.aspx" id="form1">
  <div>
    <input type="hidden" name="__VIEWSTATE" id="__VIEWSTATE"
       value="/wEPDwUKLTE2MjY5MTY1NWRkzNjRYstd1OK5KcJ9a8/X3pYTHvM=" />
  </div>
  <div>
    <span id="resultLabel"></span><br />
    <input type="submit" name="triggerButton" value="Click Me"
      id="triggerButton" />
  </div>
  <div>
    <input type="hidden" name="__EVENTVALIDATION" id="__EVENTVALIDATION"
      value="/wEWAgK39qTFBwLHpP+yC4rCCl22/GGMaFwD0l7nokvyFZ8Q" />
  </div>
</form>
```

The Web server controls have generated straight HTML: <span> and <input> for <asp:Label> and <asp:Button>, respectively. There is also an <input type="hidden"> field with the name VIEWSTATE. This encapsulates the state of the form, as mentioned earlier. This information is used when the form is posted back to the server to re-create the user interface, so that the server can keep track of changes and so on. Note that the <form> element has been configured for this; it will post data back to Default.aspx (specified in action) via an HTTP POST operation (specified in method). It has also been assigned the name form1.

After clicking the button and seeing the text appear, check out the source HTML again (spacing has been added for clarity):

```
<form method="post" action="Default.aspx" id="form1">
  <div>
    <input type="hidden" name="__VIEWSTATE" id="__VIEWSTATE"
      value="/wEPDwUKLTE2MjY5MTY1NQ9kFgICAw9kFgICAQ8PFgIeBFRleHQFD0J1dHR
             vbiBjbGlja2VkIWRkZExUtMwuSlVTrzMtG7wrmj98tVn7" />
  </div>
  <div>
    <span id="resultLabel">Button clicked!</span><br />
    <input type="submit" name="triggerButton" value="Click Me"
      id="triggerButton" />
  </div>
  <div>
    <input type="hidden" name="__EVENTVALIDATION" id="__EVENTVALIDATION"
      value="/wEWAgKTpL7LBALHpP+yC0Ymqe9SgScfB2yHTGjnlQKtbudV" />
  </div>
</form>
```

This time, the value of the view state contains more information because the HTML result relies on more than the default output from the ASP.NET page. In complex forms this can be a very long string indeed, but you shouldn't complain because so much is done for you behind the scenes. You can almost forget about state management, keeping field values between posts, and so on. Where the length of the view state string becomes a problem, you can disable the view state for controls that do not need to retain state information. You can also do this for entire pages if you want, which can be useful if the page does not ever need to retain state between postbacks to improve performance.

For more on view state, see Chapter 38, "ASP.NET Development."

To convince yourself that you don't need to perform any compilation manually, try changing the text "Button clicked!" in `Default.aspx.cs` to something else, saving the file, and clicking the button again. The text on the Web page should change appropriately.

The Control Palette

This section takes a quick look at some of the available controls before you put more of them together into a full, and more interesting, application. Figure 37-6 shows the toolbox that you see when editing ASP.NET pages.

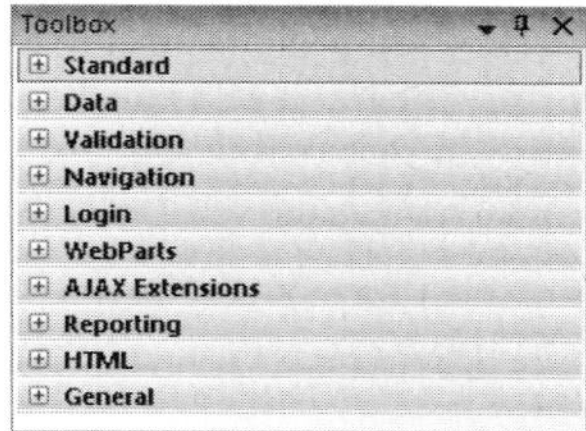

Figure 37-6

Note that the following control descriptions discuss properties — in all cases, the corresponding attribute for use in ASP.NET code is identically named. This section isn't an attempt to provide a complete reference, so instead, we will focus on only the most frequently used controls and properties. The controls you will see in this chapter are in the Standard, Data, and Validation categories. The Navigation and Login and WebParts categories are covered in Chapter 38, "ASP.NET Development," and the AJAX Extensions controls in Chapter 39, "ASP.NET AJAX." The Reporting controls to be presented on Web pages, which enable reporting information, including Crystal Reports, are not covered in this book.

Standard Web Server Controls

Almost all the Web server controls (in this and other categories) inherit from `System.Web.UI.WebControls.WebControl`, which in turn inherits from `System.Web.UI.Control`. Those that don't use this inheritance instead derive either directly from `Control` or from a more specialized base class that derives (eventually) from `Control`. As a result, the Web server controls have many common properties and events that you can use as required. There are quite a few of these, so we won't attempt to cover them all, just as with the properties and events of the Web server controls themselves.

Many of the frequently used inherited properties are those that deal with display style. This can be controlled simply, using properties such as `ForeColor`, `BackColor`, `Font`, and so on, but can also be controlled using cascading style sheet (CSS) classes. To use CSS styling you set the string property `CssClass` to the name of a CSS class in a separate file. You can use the CSS Properties window along with the style management windows to assist you with CSS control styling. Other notable properties include `Width` and `Height` to size a control, `AccessKey` and `TabIndex` to ease user interaction, and `Enabled` to set whether the control's functionality is activated in the Web Form.

Some controls can contain other controls, building up a control hierarchy on a page. You can get access to the controls contained by a given control using its `Controls` property, or to the container of a control via the `Parent` property.

You are likely to use the inherited `Load` event most often, to perform initialization on a control, and `PreRender` to perform last-minute modifications before HTML is output by the control.

Plenty more events and properties exist, and you will see many of these in more detail in the next chapter. In particular, the next chapter deals with more advanced styling and skinning techniques. The following table describes the standard Web server controls in more detail.

Control	Description
`Label`	Simple text display; use the `Text` property to set and programmatically modify displayed text.
`TextBox`	Provides a text box that users can edit. Use the `Text` property to access the entered data, and the `TextChanged` event to act on selection changes on postback. If automatic postback is required (as opposed to using a button), then set the `AutoPostBack` property to `true`.
`Button`	Adds a standard button for the user to click. Use the `Text` property for text on the button, and the `Click` event to respond to clicks (server postback is automatic). You can also use the `Command` event to respond to clicks, which gives access to additional `CommandName` and `CommandArgument` properties on receipt.
`LinkButton`	Is identical to `Button`, but displays button as a hyperlink.
`ImageButton`	Displays an image that doubles as a clickable button. Properties and events are inherited from `Button` and `Image`.
`HyperLink`	Adds an HTML hyperlink. Set the destination with `NavigateUrl` and the text to display with `Text`. You can also use `ImageUrl` to specify an image for the link and `Target` to specify the browser window to use. This control has no nonstandard events, so use a `LinkButton` instead if additional processing is required when the link is followed.
`DropDownList`	Allows the user to select one of a list of choices, either by choosing it directly from a list or by typing the first letter or two. Use the `Items` property to set the item list (this is a `ListItemCollection` class containing `ListItem` objects) and the `SelectedItem` and `SelectedIndex` properties to determine what is selected. The `SelectedIndexChanged` event can be used to determine whether the selection has changed, and this control also has an `AutoPostBack` property so that this selection change will trigger a postback operation.
`ListBox`	Allows the user to make one or more selections from a list. Set `SelectionMode` to `Multiple` or `Single` to specify if only one, or multiple items can be selected at the same time, and `Rows` to determine how many items to display. Other properties and events are the same as for `DropDownList`.
`CheckBox`	Displays a box that can be checked or unchecked. The state is stored in the Boolean property `Checked`, and the text associated with the check box in `Text`. The `AutoPostBack` property can be used to initiate automatic postback and the `CheckedChanged` event to act on changes.

Control	Description
CheckBoxList	Creates a group of check boxes. Properties and events are identical to other list controls, such as DropDownList.
RadioButton	Displays a button that can be turned on or off. Generally, these are grouped such that only one in the group is active at any time. Use the GroupName property to link RadioButton controls into a group. Other properties and events are as per CheckBox.
RadioButtonList	Creates a group of radio buttons where only one button in the group can be selected at a time. Properties and events are the same for other list controls, such as DropDownList.
Image	Displays an image. Use ImageUrl for the image reference, and AlternateText to provide text if the image fails to load.
ImageMap	Like Image, but it allows you to specify specific actions to trigger if users click one or more hotspots in the image. The action to take can either be a postback or a redirection to another URL. Hotspots are supplied by embedded controls that derive from HotSpot, such as RectangleHotSpot and CircleHotSpot.
Table	Specifies a table. Use this in conjunction with TableRow and TableCell at design time, or programmatically assign rows using the Rows property of type TableRowCollection. You can also use this property for runtime modifications. This control has several styling properties unique to tables, as do TableRow and TableCell.
BulletedList	Formats a list of items as a bulleted list. Unlike the other list controls, this one has a Click event that you can use to determine what item a user has clicked during a postback. Other properties and events are the same as for DropDownList.
HiddenField	Used to provide a hidden field, to store nondisplayed values for any reason. These can be very useful to store settings that would otherwise need an alternative storage mechanism to function. Use the Value property to access the stored value.
Literal	Performs the same function as Label, but has no styling properties because it derives from Control, not WebControl. You set the text to display for this control with the Text property.
Calendar	Allows the user to select a date from a graphical calendar display. This control has many style-related properties, but essential functionality can be achieved using the SelectedDate and VisibleDate properties (of type System.DateTime) to get access to the date selected by the user and the month to display (which will always contain VisibleDate). The key event to hook up to is SelectionChanged. Postback from this control is automatic.

Control	Description
AdRotator	Displays several images in succession, with a different one displayed after each server round trip. Use the AdvertisementFile property to specify the XML file describing the possible images, and the AdCreated event to perform processing before each image is sent back. You can also use the Target property to name a window to open when an image is clicked.
FileUpload	This control presents the user with a text box and a Browse button, such that a file to be uploaded can be selected. Once the user has done this, you can look at the HasFile property to determine if a file has been selected, and then use the SaveAs() method from code behind to perform the file upload.
Wizard	An advanced control used to simplify the common task of getting several pages of user input in one go. You can add multiple steps to a wizard, which can be presented to a user sequentially or nonsequentially, and rely on this control to maintain state and so on.
Xml	A more complicated text display control, used for displaying XML content, which may be transformed using an XSLT style sheet. The XML content is set using one of the Document, DocumentContent, or DocumentSource properties (depending on the format of the original XML), and the XSLT style sheet (optional) using either Transform or TransformSource.
MultiView	A control that contains one or more View controls, where only one View is rendered at a time. The currently displayed view is specified using ActiveViewIndex, and you can detect if the view changes (perhaps because a Next link on the currently displayed view is clicked) with the ActiveViewChanged event.
Panel	Adds a container for other controls. You can use HorizontalAlign and Wrap to specify how the contents are arranged.
PlaceHolder	This control doesn't render any output but can be handy for grouping other controls together, or for adding controls programmatically to a given location. Contained controls can be accessed using the Controls property.
View	A container for controls, much like PlaceHolder, but designed for use as a child of MultiView. You can tell if a given View is being displayed using Visible, or use the Activate and Deactivate events to detect changes in activation state.
Substitution	Specifies a section of a Web page that isn't cached along with other output. This is an advanced topic related to ASP.NET caching behavior, which you won't be looking at in this book.
Localize	Exactly like Literal, but enables text to be localized by using project resources to specify the text to display for various locales.

Data Web Server Controls

The data Web server controls are divided into two types:

- Data source controls (`SqlDataSource`, `AccessDataSource`, `LinqDataSource`, `ObjectDataSource`, `XmlDataSource`, and `SiteMapDataSource`)
- Data display controls (`GridView`, `DataList`, `DetailsView`, `FormView`, `ListView`, `Repeater`, and `DataPager`)

In general, you will place one of the (nonvisual) data source controls on a page to link to a data source; then you will add a data display control that binds to a data source control to display that data. Some of the more advanced data display controls, such as `GridView`, also allow you to edit data.

All the data source controls derive from either `System.Web.UI.DataSource` or `System.Web.UI.HierarchicalDataSource`. These classes expose methods such as `GetView()` (or `GetHierarchicalView()`) to give access to internal data views and skinning capabilities.

The following table describes the various data source controls. Note that there is less detail about properties in this section than in others — mainly because configuration of these controls is best done graphically or through wizards. Later in this chapter, you will see some of these controls in action.

Control	Description
`SqlDataSource`	Acts as a conduit for data stored in an SQL Server database. By placing this control on a page, you can manipulate SQL Server data using a data display control. You will see this control in action later in the chapter.
`AccessDataSource`	Like `SqlDataSource`, but it works with data stored in a Microsoft Access database.
`LinqDataSource`	This control allows you to manipulate objects in a LINQ-enabled data model.
`ObjectDataSource`	This control allows you to manipulate data stored in objects that you have created, which may be grouped in a collection class. This can be a very quick way to expose custom object models to an ASP.NET page.
`XmlDataSource`	Enables you to bind to XML data. This works well in binding to, for example, a `TreeView` control (one of the Navigation controls). You can also transform XML data using an XSL style sheet using this control if desired.
`SiteMapDataSource`	Allows binding to hierarchical site map data. See the section on navigation Web server controls in Chapter 38 for more information.

Next, you have the data display controls, shown in the following table. Several of these are available to suit various needs. Some are more fully functional than others, but often you can go with simplicity (for example, when you don't need to be able to edit data items).

Control	Description
`GridView`	Displays multiple data items (such as rows in a database) in the form of rows, where each row has columns reflecting data fields. By manipulating the properties of this control, you can select, sort, and edit data items.
`DataList`	Displays multiple data items where you can supply templates for each item to display data fields in any way you choose. As with `GridView`, you can select, sort, and edit data items.
`DetailsView`	Displays a single data item in tabular form, with each row of the table relating to a data field. This control enables you to add, edit, and delete data items.
`FormView`	Displays a single data item using a template. As with `DetailsView`, this control enables you to add, edit, and delete data items.
`ListView`	Like `DataList`, but with support for pagination using `DataPager` and more template capabilities.
`Repeater`	Like `DataList`, but without selecting or editing capabilities.
`DataPager`	Allows pagination of `ListView` controls.

Validation Web Server Controls

Validation controls provide a method of validating user input without (in most cases) your having to write any code at all. Whenever postback is initiated, each validation control checks the control it is validating and changes its `IsValid` property accordingly. If this property is `false`, then the user input for the validated control has failed validation. The page containing all the controls also has an `IsValid` property — if any of the validation controls has its version of this property set to `false`, then this will be `false` also. You can check this property from your server-side code and act on it.

Validation controls also have another function. Not only do they validate controls at runtime; they can also output helpful hints to users. Simply setting the `ErrorMessage` property to the text you want means users will see it when they attempt to postback invalid data.

The text stored in `ErrorMessage` may be output at the point where the validation control is located, or at a separate point, along with the messages from all other validation controls on a page. This latter behavior is achieved using the `ValidationSummary` control, which displays all error messages along with additional text as required.

On browsers that support it, these controls even generate client-side JavaScript functions to streamline their validation behavior. This means that in some cases postback won't even occur, because the validation controls can prevent this under certain circumstances and output error messages without involving the server.

All validation controls inherit from `BaseValidator` and thus share several important properties. Perhaps the most important is the `ErrorMessage` property discussed earlier, with the `ControlToValidate` property coming in a close second. This property specifies the programmatic `ID` of the control that is being validated. Another important property is `Display`, which determines whether to place text at the validation summary position (if set to `none`), or at the validator position. You also have the choice to make space for the error message even when it is not being displayed (set `Display` to `Static`) or to dynamically allocate space when required, which might shift page contents around slightly (set `Display` to `Dynamic`). The following table describes the validation controls.

Control	Description
RequiredFieldValidator	Used to check if the user has entered data in a control such as TextBox.
CompareValidator	Used to check that data entered fulfills simple requirements, by use of an operator set using the Operator property and a ValueToCompare property to validate against. Operator can be Equal, GreaterThan, GreaterThanEqual, LessThan, LessThanEqual, NotEqual, and DataTypeCheck. DataTypeCheck simply compares the data type of ValueToCompare with the data in the control to be validated. ValueToCompare is a string property but is interpreted as different data types based on its contents. To further control the comparison, you can set the Type property to Currency, Date, Double, Integer, or String.
RangeValidator	Validates that data in the control falls between MaximumValue and MinimumValue property values. Has a Type property like that of CompareValidator.
RegularExpressionValidator	Validates the contents of a field based on a regular expression stored in ValidationExpression. This can be useful for known sequences such as zip codes, phone numbers, IP numbers, and so on.
CustomValidator	Used to validate data in a control using a custom function. ClientValidationFunction is used to specify a client-side function used to validate a control (which means, unfortunately, that you can't use C#). This function should return a Boolean value indicating whether validation was successful. Alternatively, you can use the ServerValidate event to specify a server-side function to use for validation. This function is a bool type event handler that receives a string containing the data to validate, instead of an EventArgs parameter. Returns true if validation succeeds, otherwise false.
ValidationSummary	Displays validation errors for all validation controls that have an ErrorMessage set. The display can be formatted by setting the DisplayMode (BulletList, List, or SingleParagraph) and HeaderText properties. The display can be disabled by setting ShowSummary to false, and displayed in a pop-up message box by setting ShowMessageBox to true.

Server Control Example

In this example, you create the framework for a Web application, a meeting room booking tool. (As with the other examples in this book, you can download the sample application and code from the Wrox Web site at www.wrox.com.) At first, you will include only the front end and simple event processing; later, you will extend this example with ADO.NET and data binding to include server-side business logic.

The Web Form you are going to create contains fields for user name, event name, meeting room, and attendees, along with a calendar to select a date (you are assuming for the purposes of this example that you are dealing with all-day events). You will include validation controls for all fields except the calendar, which you will validate on the server side, and provide a default date in case none has been entered.

For user interface (UI) testing, you will also have a `Label` control on the form that you can use to display submission results.

For starters, create a new Web site in Visual Studio .NET in the `C:\ProCSharp\Chapter37\` directory, and call it PCSWebApp2. Next, modify the code in `Default.aspx` as follows:

```
<%@ Page Language="C#" AutoEventWireup="true" CodeFile="Default.aspx.cs"
  Inherits="_Default" %>
<!DOCTYPE html PUBLIC "-//W3C//DTD XHTML 1.1//EN"
  "http://www.w3.org/TR/xhtml11/DTD/xhtml11.dtd">
<html xmlns="http://www.w3.org/1999/xhtml">
<head runat="server">
  <title>Meeting Room Booker</title>
</head>
<body>
  <form id="form1" runat="server">
    <div>
      <h1 style="text-align: center;">
        Enter details and set a day to initiate an event.
      </h1>
    </div>
```

After the title of the page (which is enclosed in HTML `<h1>` tags to get large, title-style text), the main body of the form is enclosed in an HTML `<table>`. You could use a Web server control table, but this introduces unnecessary complexity because you are using a table purely for formatting the display, not to be a dynamic UI element. This is an important point to bear in mind when designing Web Forms — don't add Web server controls unnecessarily. The table is divided into three columns: the first column holds simple text labels; the second column holds UI fields corresponding to the text labels (along with validation controls for these); and the third column contains a calendar control for date selection, which spans four rows. The fifth row contains a submission button spanning all columns, and the sixth row contains a `ValidationSummary` control to display error messages, when required (all the other validation controls have `Display="None"`, because they will use this summary for display). Beneath the table is a simple label that you can use to display results for now, before you add database access later:

```
    <div style="text-align: center;">
      <table style="text-align: left; border-color: #000000;
        border-width: 2px; background-color: #fff99e;" cellspacing="0"
        cellpadding="8" rules="none" width="540">
        <tr>
          <td valign="top">
            Your Name:</td>
          <td valign="top">
            <asp:TextBox ID="nameBox" Runat="server" Width="160px" />
            <asp:RequiredFieldValidator ID="validateName" Runat="server"
              ErrorMessage="You must enter a name."
              ControlToValidate="nameBox" Display="None" />
          </td>
          <td valign="middle" rowspan="4">
            <asp:Calendar ID="calendar" Runat="server" BackColor="White" />
          </td>
        </tr>
```

```
<tr>
  <td valign="top">
    Event Name:</td>
  <td valign="top">
    <asp:TextBox ID="eventBox" Runat="server" Width="160px" />
    <asp:RequiredFieldValidator ID="validateEvent" Runat="server"
      ErrorMessage="You must enter an event name."
      ControlToValidate="eventBox" Display="None" />
  </td>
</tr>
```

Most of the ASP.NET code in this file is remarkably simple, and much can be learned simply by reading through it. Of particular note in this code is the way in which list items are attached to the controls for selecting a meeting room and multiple attendees for the event:

```
<tr>
  <td valign="top">
    Meeting Room:</td>
  <td valign="top">
    <asp:DropDownList ID="roomList" Runat="server" Width="160px">
      <asp:ListItem Value="1">The Happy Room</asp:ListItem>
      <asp:ListItem Value="2">The Angry Room</asp:ListItem>
      <asp:ListItem Value="3">The Depressing
       Room</asp:ListItem>
      <asp:ListItem Value="4">The Funked Out
       Room</asp:ListItem>
    </asp:DropDownList>
    <asp:RequiredFieldValidator ID="validateRoom" Runat="server"
      ErrorMessage="You must select a room."
      ControlToValidate="roomList" Display="None" />
  </td>
</tr>
<tr>
  <td valign="top">
    Attendees:</td>
  <td valign="top">
    <asp:ListBox ID="attendeeList" Runat="server" Width="160px"
      SelectionMode="Multiple" Rows="6">
      <asp:ListItem Value="1">Bill Gates</asp:ListItem>
      <asp:ListItem Value="2">Monica Lewinsky</asp:ListItem>
      <asp:ListItem Value="3">Vincent Price</asp:ListItem>
      <asp:ListItem Value="4">Vlad the Impaler</asp:ListItem>
      <asp:ListItem Value="5">Iggy Pop</asp:ListItem>
      <asp:ListItem Value="6">William
       Shakespeare</asp:ListItem>
    </asp:ListBox>
```

Here you are associating `ListItem` objects with the two Web server controls. These objects are not Web server controls in their own right (they simply inherit from `System.Object`), which is why you don't need to use `Runat="server"` on them. When the page is processed, the `<asp:ListItem>` entries are used to create `ListItem` objects, which are added to the `Items` collection of their parent list control. This makes it easier for you to initialize lists than to write code for this yourself (you would need to create a `ListItemCollection` object, add `ListItem` objects, and then pass the collection to the list control). Of course, you can still do all of this programmatically if you want.

```
                <asp:RequiredFieldValidator ID="validateAttendees" Runat="server"
                  ErrorMessage="You must have at least one attendee."
                  ControlToValidate="attendeeList" Display="None" />
              </td>
            </tr>
            <tr>
              <td align="center" colspan="3">
                <asp:Button ID="submitButton" Runat="server" Width="100%"
                  Text="Submit meeting room request" />
              </td>
            </tr>
            <tr>
              <td align="center" colspan="3">
                <asp:ValidationSummary ID="validationSummary" Runat="server"
                  HeaderText="Before submitting your request:" />
              </td>
            </tr>
          </table>
        </div>
        <div>
          <p>
            Results:
            <asp:Label Runat="server" ID="resultLabel" Text="None." />
          </p>
        </div>
      </form>
    </body>
    </html>
```

In design view, the form you have created looks like Figure 37-7. This is a fully functioning UI, which maintains its own state between server requests, and validates user input. Considering the brevity of the preceding code, this is quite something. In fact, it leaves you with very little to do, at least for this example; you just need to specify the button click event for the submission button.

Actually, that's not quite true. So far, you have no validation for the calendar control. All you need to do is give it an initial value. You can do this in the `Page_Load()` event handler for your page in the code-behind file:

```
private void Page_Load(object sender, EventArgs e)
{
   if (!this.IsPostBack)
   {
      calendar.SelectedDate = DateTime.Now;
   }
}
```

Here you just select today's date as a starting point. Note that you first check to see if `Page_Load()` is being called as the result of a postback operation, by checking the `IsPostBack` property of the page. If a postback is in progress, this property will be `true` and you leave the selected date alone (you don't want to lose the user's selection, after all).

To add the button click handler, simply double-click the button and add the following code:

```
private void submitButton_Click(object sender, EventArgs e)
{
   if (this.IsValid)
```

```
        {
            resultLabel.Text = roomList.SelectedItem.Text +
                " has been booked on " +
                calendar.SelectedDate.ToLongDateString() +
                " by " + nameBox.Text + " for " +
                eventBox.Text + " event. ";
            foreach (ListItem attendee in attendeeList.Items)
            {
                if (attendee.Selected)
                {
                    resultLabel.Text += attendee.Text + ", ";
                }
            }
            resultLabel.Text += " and " + nameBox.Text +
                " will be attending.";
        }
    }
```

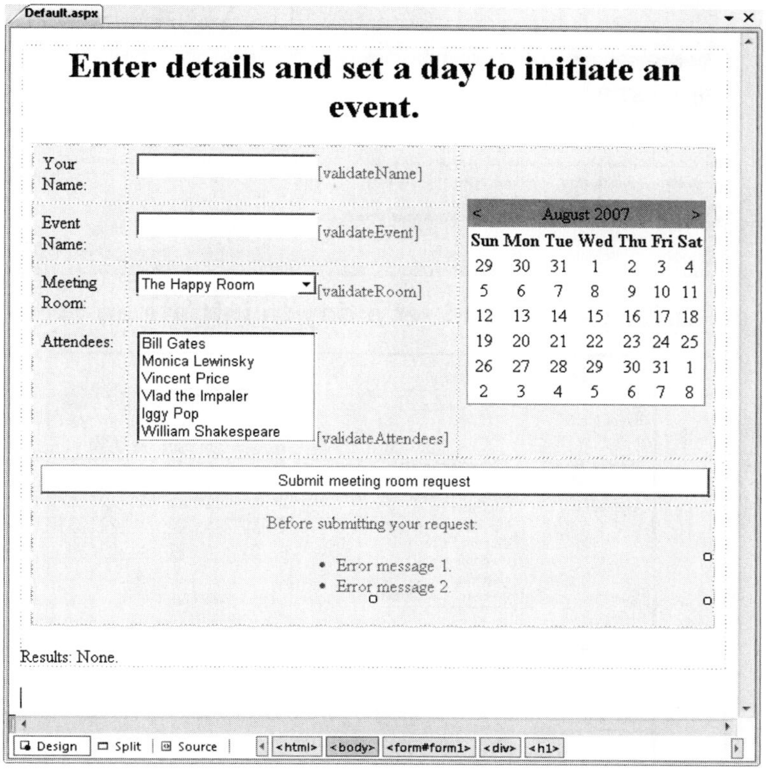

Figure 37-7

Here you just set the `resultLabel` control `Text` property to a result string, which will then appear below the main table. In IE, the result of such a submission might look something like Figure 37-8, unless there are errors, in which case the `ValidationSummary` will activate instead, as shown in Figure 37-9.

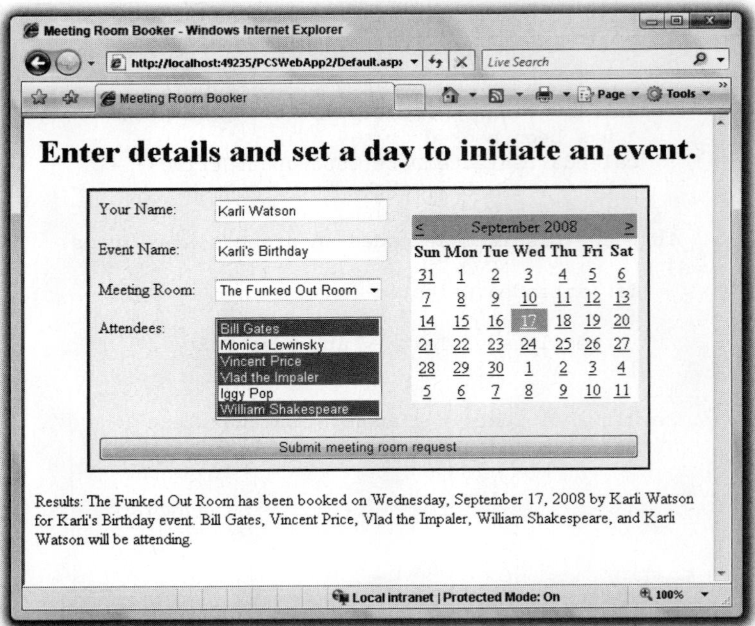

Figure 37-8

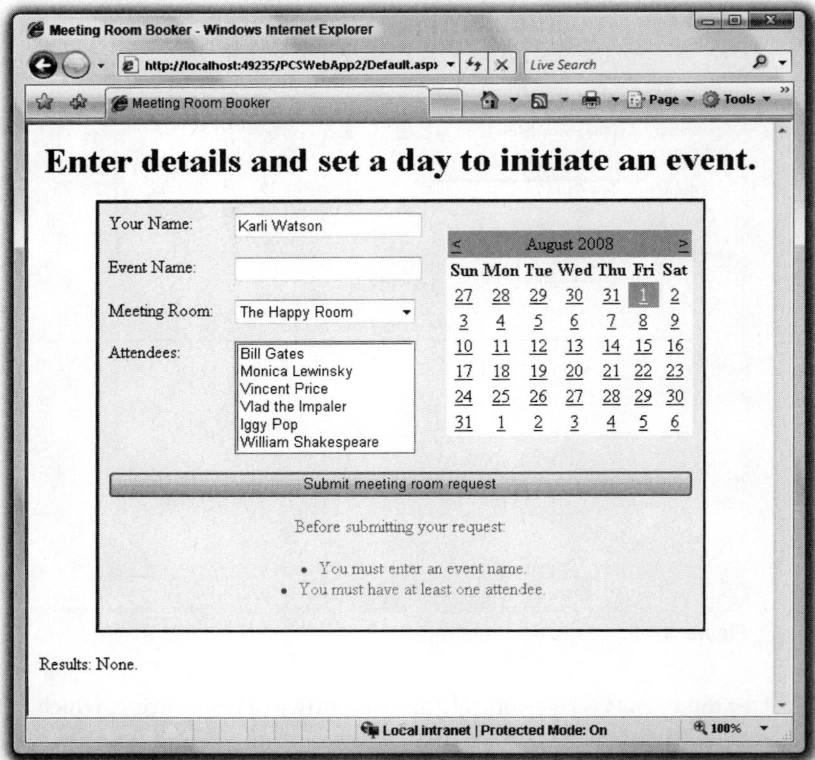

Figure 37-9

ADO.NET and Data Binding

The Web Form application you created in the previous section is perfectly functional, but it contains only static data. In addition, the event-booking process does not include persisting event data. To solve both of these problems, you can make use of ADO.NET to access data stored in a database, so that you can store and retrieve event data along with the lists of rooms and attendees.

Data binding makes the process of retrieving data even easier. Controls such as list boxes (and some of the more specialized controls you'll look at a bit later) come enabled for this technique. They can be bound to any object that exposes an `IEnumerable`, `ICollection`, or `IListSource` interface, as well as any of the data source Web server controls.

In this section, you start by updating your event-booking application to be data-aware, and then move on to take a look at some of the other results you can achieve with data binding, using some of the other data-aware Web controls.

Updating the Event-Booking Application

To keep things separate from the last example, create a new Web site called `PCSWebApp3` in the directory `C:\ProCSharp\Chapter37\` and copy the code from the `PCSWebApp2` application created earlier into the new application. Before you start on your new code, take a look at the database you will be accessing.

The Database

For the purposes of this example, you will use a Microsoft SQL Server Express database called `MeetingRoomBooker.mdf`, which is part of the downloadable code for this book. For an enterprise-scale application, it makes more sense to use a full SQL Server database, but the techniques involved are practically identical, and SQL Server Express makes life a bit easier for testing. The code will also be identical.

If you are adding your own version of this database, you will need to add a new database to the App_Data folder in the Solution Explorer. You can do this by right-clicking on the App_Data folder, selecting Add New Item, selecting a database, naming it MeetingRoomBooker, and clicking Add. This will also configure a data connection in the Server Explorer window ready for you to use. Next, you can add the tables required as shown in the next sections and supply your own data. Alternatively, to use the downloadable database with your own code, simply copy it to the `App_Data` *directory for your Web site.*

The database provided contains three tables:

- `Attendees`, which contains a list of possible event attendees
- `Rooms`, which contains a list of possible rooms for events
- `Events`, which contains a list of booked events

Attendees

The `Attendees` table contains the columns shown in the following table.

Column	Type	Notes
`ID`	Identity, primary key	Attendee identification number
`Name`	varchar, required, 50 chars	Name of attendee
`Email`	varchar, optional, 50 chars	E-mail address of attendee

The supplied database includes entries for 20 attendees, all with their own (fictional) e-mail addresses. You can envision that in a more developed application, e-mails could automatically be sent to attendees when a booking is made, but this is left to you as an optional exercise using techniques found elsewhere in this book.

Rooms

The `Rooms` table contains the columns shown in the following table.

Column	Type	Notes
`ID`	Identity, primary key	Room identification number
`Room`	varchar, required, 50 chars	Name of room

Twenty records are supplied in the database.

Events

The `Events` table contains the columns shown in the following table.

Column	Type	Notes
`ID`	Identity, primary key	Event identification number
`Name`	varchar, required, 255 chars	Name of event
`Room`	int, required	ID of room for event
`AttendeeList`	text, required	List of attendee names
`EventDate`	datetime, required	Date of event

A few events are supplied in the downloadable database.

Binding to the Database

The two controls you are going to bind to data are `attendeeList` and `roomList`. Before you do this, you need to add `SqlDataSource` Web server controls that map to the tables you want to access in the `MeetingRoomBooker.mdf` database. The quickest way to do this is to drag them from the toolbox onto the `Default.aspx` Web Form and configure them via the Configuration Wizard. Figure 37-10 shows how to access this wizard for a `SqlDataSource` control.

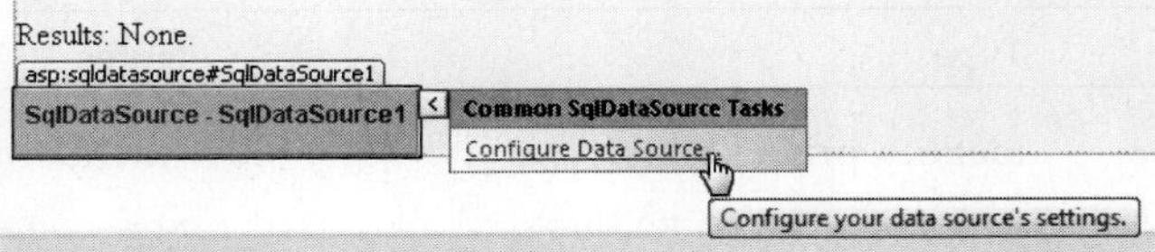

Figure 37-10

From the first page of the data source Configuration Wizard, you need to select the connection to the database created earlier. Next, choose to save the connection string as `MRBConnectionString`; then choose to select * (all fields) from the `Attendees` table in the database.

After completing the wizard, change the `ID` of the `SqlDataSource` control to `MRBAttendeeData`. You also need to add and configure two more `SqlDataSource` controls to obtain data from the `Rooms` and `Events` tables, with `ID` values of `MRBRoomData` and `MRBEventData` respectively. For these subsequent controls, you can use the saved `MRBConnectionString` for your connection.

Once you've added these data sources, you will see in the code for the form that the syntax is very simple:

```
<asp:SqlDataSource ID="MRBAttendeeData" runat="server"
  ConnectionString="<%$ ConnectionStrings:MRBConnectionString %>"
  SelectCommand="SELECT * FROM [Attendees]"></asp:SqlDataSource>
<asp:SqlDataSource ID="MRBRoomData" runat="server"
  ConnectionString="<%$ ConnectionStrings:MRBConnectionString %>"
  SelectCommand="SELECT * FROM [Rooms]"></asp:SqlDataSource>
<asp:SqlDataSource ID="MRBEventData" runat="server"
  ConnectionString="<%$ ConnectionStrings:MRBConnectionString %>"
  SelectCommand="SELECT * FROM [Events]"></asp:SqlDataSource>
```

The definition of the connection string in use is found in the `web.config` file, which we will look at in more detail later in this chapter.

Next, you need to set the data-binding properties of the `roomList` and `attendeeList` controls. For `roomList` the settings required are as follows:

- `DataSourceID` — `MRBRoomData`
- `DataTextField` — `Room`
- `DataValueField` — `ID`

And, similarly, for `attendeeList`:

- `DataSourceID` — `MRBAttendeeData`
- `DataTextField` — `Name`
- `DataValueField` — `ID`

You can also remove the existing hard-coded list items from the code for these controls.

Running the application now will result in the full attendee and room data being available from your data-bound controls. You will use the `MRBEventData` control shortly.

Customizing the Calendar Control

Before adding events to the database, you need to modify your calendar display. It would be nice to display all days where a booking has previously been made in a different color, and prevent such days from being selectable. This requires that you modify the way you set dates in the calendar and the way day cells are displayed.

You will start with date selection. You need to check three places for dates where events are booked and modify the selection accordingly: when you set the initial date in `Page_Load()`, when the user attempts to select a date from the calendar, and when an event is booked and you want to set a new date to prevent the user from booking two events on the same day before selecting a new date. Because this is going to be a common feature, you might as well create a private method to perform this calculation. This method should accept a trial date as a parameter and return the date to use, which will either be the same date as the trial date, or the next available day after the trial date.

Before adding this method, you need to give your code access to data in the `Events` table. You can use the `MRBEventData` control to do this because this control is capable of populating a `DataView`. To facilitate this, add the following private member and property:

```
private DataView eventData;
private DataView EventData
{
   get
   {
      if (eventData == null)
      {
         eventData =
           MRBEventData.Select(new DataSourceSelectArguments())
           as DataView;
      }
      return eventData;
   }
   set
   {
      eventData = value;
   }
}
```

The `EventData` property populated the `eventData` member with data as it is required, with the results cached for subsequent use. Here you use the `SqlDataSource.Select()` method to obtain a `DataView`.

Next, add this method, `GetFreeDate()`, to the code-behind file:

```
private DateTime GetFreeDate(DateTime trialDate)
{
   if (EventData.Count > 0)
   {
      DateTime testDate;
      bool trialDateOK = false;
      while (!trialDateOK)
      {
         trialDateOK = true;
         foreach (DataRowView testRow in EventData)
         {
            testDate = (DateTime)testRow["EventDate"];
            if (testDate.Date == trialDate.Date)
            {
               trialDateOK = false;
               trialDate = trialDate.AddDays(1);
            }
         }
      }
   }
   return trialDate;
}
```

This simple code uses the `EventData DataView` to extract event data. First, you check for the trivial case where no events have been booked, in which case you can just confirm the trial date by returning it. Next, you iterate through the dates in the `Event` table, comparing them with the trial date. If you find a match, add one day to the trial date and perform another search.

Extracting the date from the `DataTable` is remarkably simple:

```
testDate = (System.DateTime)testRow["EventDate"];
```

Casting the column data into `System.DateTime` works fine.

The first place you will use `getFreeDate()`, then, is back in `Page_Load()`. This simply means making a minor modification to the code that sets the calendar `SelectedDate` property:

```
if (!this.IsPostBack)
{
   DateTime trialDate = DateTime.Now;
   calendar.SelectedDate = GetFreeDate(trialDate);
}
```

Next, you need to respond to date selection on the calendar. To do this, simply add an event handler for the `SelectionChanged` event of the calendar, and force the date to be checked against existing events. Double-click the calendar in the Designer and add this code:

```
void calendar_SelectionChanged(object sender, EventArgs e)
{
   DateTime trialDate = calendar.SelectedDate;
   calendar.SelectedDate = GetFreeDate(trialDate);
}
```

The code here is practically identical to that in `Page_Load()`.

The third place that you must perform this check is in response to the pressed booking button. We will come back to this shortly, as you have several changes to make here.

Next, you need to color the day cells of the calendar to signify existing events. To do this, you add an event handler for the `DayRender` event of the `calendar` object. This event is raised each time an individual day is rendered, and gives you access to the `cell` object being displayed and the date of this cell through the `Cell` and `Date` properties of the `DayRenderEventArgs` parameter you receive in the handler function. You simply compare the date of the cell being rendered to the dates in the `eventTable` object and color the cell using the `Cell.BackColor` property if there is a match:

```
void calendar_DayRender(object sender, DayRenderEventArgs e)
{
   if (EventData.Count > 0)
   {
      DateTime testDate;
      foreach (DataRowView testRow in EventData)
      {
         testDate = (DateTime)testRow["EventDate"];
         if (testDate.Date == e.Day.Date)
         {
            e.Cell.BackColor = System.Drawing.Color.Red;
         }
      }
   }
}
```

Here you are using red, which will give you a display along the lines of Figure 37-11, in which June 12, 15, and 22 (2008) all contain events, and the user has selected June 24.

With the addition of the date-selection logic, it is now impossible to select a day that is shown in red. If you attempt it, a later date is selected instead (for example, selecting June 15 results in the selection of June 16).

<			June 2008			>
Sun	Mon	Tue	Wed	Thu	Fri	Sat
25	26	27	28	29	30	31
1	2	3	4	5	6	7
8	9	10	11	12	13	14
15	16	17	18	19	20	21
22	23	24	25	26	27	28
29	30	1	2	3	4	5

Figure 37-11

Adding Events to the Database

The `submitButton_Click()` event handler currently assembles a string from the event characteristics and displays it in the `resultLabel` control. To add an event to the database, you simply reformat the string created into a SQL `INSERT` query and execute it.

Note that in the development environment that you are using you don't have to worry too much about security. Adding a SQL Server 2005 Express database via a Web site solution and configuring `SqlDataSource` *controls to use it will automatically give you a connection string that you can use to write to the database. In more advanced situations, you might want to access resources using other accounts — for example, a domain account used to access a SQL Server instance elsewhere on a network. The capability to do this (via impersonation, COM+ Services, or other means) exists in ASP.NET, but is beyond the scope of this chapter. In most cases, configuring the connection string appropriately is as complicated as things need to get.*

Much of the following code will therefore look familiar:

```
void submitButton_Click(object sender, EventArgs e)
{
   if (this.IsValid)
   {
      System.Text.StringBuilder sb = new System.Text.StringBuilder();
      foreach (ListItem attendee in attendeeList.Items)
      {
         if (attendee.Selected)
         {
            sb.AppendFormat("{0} ({1}), ", attendee.Text, attendee.Value);
         }
      }
      sb.AppendFormat(" and {0}", nameBox.Text);
      string attendees = sb.ToString();
      try
      {
         System.Data.SqlClient.SqlConnection conn =
            new System.Data.SqlClient.SqlConnection(
               ConfigurationManager.ConnectionStrings[
               "MRBConnectionString"].ConnectionString);
         System.Data.SqlClient.SqlCommand insertCommand =
            new System.Data.SqlClient.SqlCommand("INSERT INTO [Events] "
               + "(Name, Room, AttendeeList, EventDate) VALUES (@Name, "
               + "@Room, @AttendeeList, @EventDate)", conn);
         insertCommand.Parameters.Add(
            "Name", SqlDbType.VarChar, 255).Value = eventBox.Text;
         insertCommand.Parameters.Add(
```

```
      "Room", SqlDbType.Int, 4).Value = roomList.SelectedValue;
   insertCommand.Parameters.Add(
      "AttendeeList", SqlDbType.Text, 16).Value = attendees;
   insertCommand.Parameters.Add(
      "EventDate", SqlDbType.DateTime, 8).Value =
      calendar.SelectedDate;
```

The most interesting thing here is how you access the connection string you created earlier, using the following syntax:

```
ConfigurationManager.ConnectionStrings["MRBConnectionString"].ConnectionString
```

The `ConfigurationManager` class gives you access to all assorted configuration information, all stored in the `Web.config` configuration file for your Web application. You will look at this in more detail later in this chapter.

After you have created your SQL command, you can use it to insert the new event:

```
   conn.Open();
   int queryResult = insertCommand.ExecuteNonQuery();
   conn.Close();
```

`ExecuteNonQuery()` returns an integer representing how many table rows were affected by the query. If this is equal to 1, your insertion was successful. If so, put a success message in `resultLabel`, clear `EventData` because it is now out of date, and change the calendar selection to a new, free date. Because `GetFreeDate()` involves using `EventData`, and the `EventData` property automatically refreshes itself if it has no data, the stored event data will be refreshed:

```
   if (queryResult == 1)
   {
      resultLabel.Text = "Event Added.";
      EventData = null;
      calendar.SelectedDate =
         GetFreeDate(calendar.SelectedDate.AddDays(1));
   }
```

If `ExecuteNonQuery()` returns a number other than 1, you know that there has been a problem. The code in this example throws an exception if a number other than 1 is returned. This exception is caught by the general catch block for the database access code.

This catch block simply displays a general failure notification in `resultLabel`:

```
            else
            {
               throw new System.Data.DataException("Unknown data error.");
            }
         }
         catch
         {
            resultLabel.Text = "Event not added due to DB access "
                                 + "problem.";
         }
      }
   }
```

This completes your data-aware version of the event-booking application.

More on Data Binding

As mentioned earlier in this chapter, the available Web server controls include several that deal with data display (`GridView`, `DataList`, `DetailsView`, `FormView`, and `Repeater`). These are all extremely useful when it comes to outputting data to a Web page because they perform many tasks automatically that would otherwise require a fair amount of coding.

First, you will look at how easy using these controls can be, by adding an event list display to the bottom of the display of `PCSWebApp3`.

Drag a `GridView` control from the toolbox to the bottom of `Default.aspx`, and select the `MRBEventData` data source you added earlier for it, as shown in Figure 37-12.

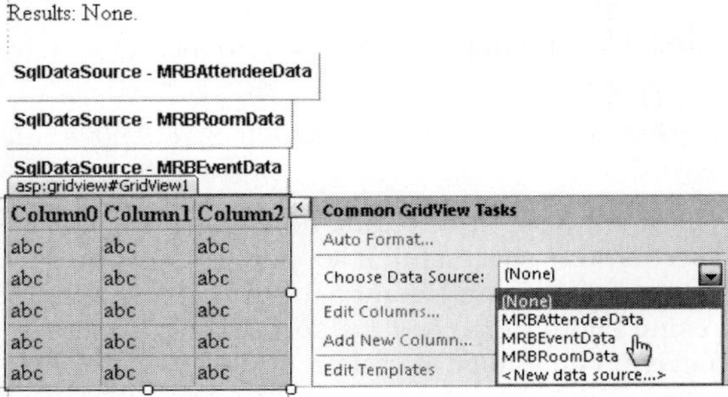

Figure 37-12

Next, click Refresh Schema, and that's all you need to do to display a list of events under the form — try viewing the Web site now and you should see the events, as shown in Figure 37-13.

ID	Name	Room	AttendeeList	EventDate
1	My Birthday	4	Iggy Pop (5), Sean Connery (7), Albert Einstein (10), George Clooney (14), Jules Verne (18), Robin Hood (20), and Karli Watson	9/17/2008 12:00:00 AM
2	Dinner	1	Bill Gates (1), Monika Lewinsky (2), and Bruce Lee	8/5/2008 12:00:00 AM
3	Discussion of darkness	6	Vlad the Impaler (4), Myra Hindley (13), and Beelzebub	10/29/2008 12:00:00 AM
4	Christmas with Pals	9	Dr Frank N Furter (11), Bobby Davro (15), John F Kennedy (16), Stephen King (19), and Karli Watson	12/25/2008 12:00:00 AM
5	Escape	17	Monika Lewinsky (2), Stephen King (19), and Spartacus	5/10/2008 12:00:00 AM
6	Planetary Conquest	14	Bill Gates (1), Albert Einstein (10), Dr Frank N Furter (11), Bobby Davro (15), and Darth Vader	6/15/2008 12:00:00 AM
7	Homecoming Celebration	7	William Shakespeare (6), Christopher Columbus (12), Robin Hood (20), and Ulysses	6/22/2008 12:00:00 AM
8	Dalek Reunion Ball	12	Roger Moore (8), George Clooney (14), Bobby Davro (15), and Davros	6/12/2008 12:00:00 AM
9	Romantic meal for two	13	George Clooney (14), and Donna Watson	3/29/2008 12:00:00 AM

Figure 37-13

You can also make one further modification in `submitButton_Click()` to ensure that this data is updated when new records are added:

```
if (queryResult == 1)
{
   resultLabel.Text = "Event Added.";
   EventData = null;
   calendar.SelectedDate =
      GetFreeDate(calendar.SelectedDate.AddDays(1));
   GridView1.DataBind();
}
```

All data-bindable controls support this method, which is normally called by the form if you call the top-level (`this`) `DataBind()` method.

You probably noticed in Figure 37-13 that the date/time display for the `EventDate` field is a little messy. Because you are looking at dates only, the time is always `12:00:00 AM` — information that it isn't really necessary to display. In the next sections, you will see how this date information can be displayed in a more user-friendly fashion in the context of a `ListView` control. As you might expect, the `DataGrid` control contains many properties that you can use to format the displayed data, but I'll leave these for you to discover.

Data Display with Templates

Many of the data display controls allow you to use templates to format data for display. Templates, in an ASP.NET sense, are parameterized sections of HTML that are used as elements of output in certain controls. They enable you to customize exactly how data is output to the browser, and can result in professional-looking displays without too much effort.

Several templates are available to customize various aspects of list behavior. One of the most important templates is `<ItemTemplate>`, which is used in the display of each data item in a list for `Repeater`, `DataList`, and `ListView` controls. You declare this template (and all the others) inside the control declaration. For example:

```
<asp:DataList Runat="server" ... >
  <ItemTemplate>
    ...
  </ItemTemplate>
</asp:DataList>
```

Within template declarations, you will normally want to output sections of HTML along with parameters from the data that is bound to the control. You can use a special syntax to output such parameters:

```
<%# expression %>
```

The *expression* placeholder might be simply an expression binding the parameter to a page or control property, but is more likely to consist of an `Eval()` or `Bind()` expression. These functions can be used to output data from a table bound to a control simply by specifying the column. The following syntax is used for `Eval()`:

```
<%# Eval("ColumnName") %>
```

An optional second parameter allows you to format the data returned, which has syntax identical to string formatting expressions used elsewhere. This can be used, for example, to format date strings into a more readable format — something that was lacking in the earlier example.

The `Bind()` expression is identical but allows you to insert data into attributes of server controls. For example:

```
<asp:Label RunAt="server" ID="ColumnDisplay" Text='<%# Bind("ColumnName") %>' />
```

Note that because double quotes are used in the `Bind()` parameter, single quotes are required to enclose the attribute value.

The following table provides a list of available templates and when they are used.

Template	Applies To	Description
`<ItemTemplate>`	`DataList, Repeater, ListView`	Used for list items
`<HeaderTemplate>`	`DataList, DetailsView, FormView, Repeater`	Used for output before item(s)
`<FooterTemplate>`	`DataList, DetailsView, FormView, Repeater`	Used for output after item(s)
`<LayoutTemplate>`	`ListView`	Used to specify output surrounding items
`<SeparatorTemplate>`	`DataList, Repeater`	Used between items in list
`<ItemSeparatorTemplate>`	`ListView`	Used between items in list
`<AlternatingItemTemplate>`	`DataList, ListView`	Used for alternate items; can aid visibility
`<SelectedItemTemplate>`	`DataList, ListView`	Used for selected items in the list
`<EditItemTemplate>`	`DataList, FormView, ListView`	Used for items being edited
`<InsertItemTemplate>`	`FormView, ListView`	Used for items being inserted
`<EmptyDataTemplate>`	`GridView, DetailsView, FormView, ListView`	Used to display empty items — for example, when no records are available in a `GridView`
`<PagerTemplate>`	`GridView, DetailsView, FormView`	Used to format pagination
`<GroupTemplate>`	`ListView`	Used to specify the output surrounding groups of items
`<GroupSeparatorTemplate>`	`ListView`	Used between groups of items
`<EmptyItemTemplate>`	`ListView`	When using item groups, used to supply output for empty items in a group. This template is used when there are not enough items in a group to fill the group.

The easiest way to understand how to use these is through an example.

Using Templates

You will extend the table at the top of the Default.aspx page of PCSWebApp3 to contain a ListView displaying each of the events stored in the database. You will make these events selectable such that details of any event can be displayed by clicking on its name, in a FormView control.

First, you need to create new data sources for the data-bound controls. It is good practice (and strongly recommended) to have a separate data source for each data-bound control.

The SqlDataSource control required for the ListView control, MRBEventData2, is much like MRBEventData, except that it needs to return only Name and ID data. The required code is as follows:

```
<asp:SqlDataSource ID="MRBEventData2" Runat="server"
  SelectCommand="SELECT [ID], [Name] FROM [Events]"
  ConnectionString="<%$ ConnectionStrings:MRBConnectionString %>">
</asp:SqlDataSource>
```

The data source for the FormView control, MRBEventDetailData, is more complicated, although you can build it easily enough through the data source Configuration Wizard. This data source uses the selected item of the ListView control, which you will call EventList, to get only the selected item data. This is achieved using a parameter in the SQL query, as follows:

```
<asp:SqlDataSource ID="MRBEventDetailData" Runat="server"
  SelectCommand="SELECT dbo.Events.Name, dbo.Rooms.Room,
                 dbo.Events.AttendeeList, dbo.Events.EventDate
                 FROM dbo.Events INNER JOIN dbo.Rooms
                 ON dbo.Events.ID = dbo.Rooms.ID WHERE dbo.Events.ID = @ID"
  ConnectionString="<%$ ConnectionStrings:MRBConnectionString %>">
  <SelectParameters>
    <asp:ControlParameter Name="ID" DefaultValue="-1" ControlID="EventList"
      PropertyName="SelectedValue" />
  </SelectParameters>
</asp:SqlDataSource>
```

Here, the ID parameter results in a value being inserted in place of @ID in the select query. The ControlParameter entry takes this value from the SelectedValue property of EventList, or uses –1 if there is no selected item. At first glance, this syntax seems a little odd, but it is very flexible, and once you've generated a few of these using the wizard, you won't have any trouble assembling your own.

Next, you need to add the ListView and FormView controls. The changes to the code in Default.aspx in the PCSWebApp3 project are shown in the following code:

```
        <tr>
          <td align="center" colspan="3">
            <asp:ValidationSummary ID="validationSummary" Runat="server"
              HeaderText="Before submitting your request:" />
          </td>
        </tr>
        <tr>
          <td align="left" colspan="3" style="width: 40%;">
            <table cellspacing="4" style="width: 100%;">
              <tr>
                <td colspan="2" style="text-align: center;">
                  <h2>Event details</h2>
                </td>
```

(continued)

(continued)

```
          </tr>
          <tr>
            <td style="width: 40%; background-color: #ccffcc;"
              valign="top">
              <asp:ListView ID="EventList" runat="server"
                DataSourceID="MRBEventData2" DataKeyNames="ID"
                OnSelectedIndexChanged="EventList_SelectedIndexChanged">
                <LayoutTemplate>
                  <ul>
                    <asp:PlaceHolder ID="itemPlaceholder"
                      runat="server" />
                  </ul>
                </LayoutTemplate>
                <ItemTemplate>
                  <li>
                    <asp:LinkButton Text='<%# Bind("Name") %>'
                      runat="server" ID="NameLink" CommandName="Select"
                      CommandArgument='<%# Bind("ID") %>'
                      CausesValidation="false" />
                  </li>
                </ItemTemplate>
                <SelectedItemTemplate>
                  <li>
                    <b><%# Eval("Name") %></b>
                  </li>
                </SelectedItemTemplate>
              </asp:ListView>
            </td>
            <td valign="top">
              <asp:FormView ID="FormView1" Runat="server"
                DataSourceID="MRBEventDetailData">
                <ItemTemplate>
                  <h3><%# Eval("Name") %></h3>
                  <b>Date:</b>
                  <%# Eval("EventDate", "{0:D}") %>
                  <br />
                  <b>Room:</b>
                  <%# Eval("Room") %>
                  <br />
                  <b>Attendees:</b>
                  <%# Eval("AttendeeList") %>
                </ItemTemplate>
              </asp:FormView>
            </td>
          </tr>
        </table>
      </td>
    </tr>
  </table>
```

Here you have added a new table row containing a table with a `ListView` control in one column and a `FormView` control in the other.

The `ListView` uses `<LayoutTemplate>` to output a bulleted list and `<ItemTemplate>` and `<SelectedItemTemplate>` to display event details as list items. In `<LayoutTemplate>`, a container element for items is specified with a `PlaceHolder` control that has the `ID="itemPlaceholder"` attribute. To facilitate selection, you raise a `Select` command from the event name link rendered in `<ItemTemplate>`, which automatically changes the selection. You also use the `OnSelectedIndexChanged` event, triggered when the `Select` command changes the selection, to ensure that the list display updates itself to display the selected item in a different style. The event handler for this is shown in the following code:

```
protected void EventList_SelectedIndexChanged(object sender, EventArgs e)
{
   EventList.DataBind();
}
```

You also need to ensure new events are added to the list:

```
         if (queryResult == 1)
         {
            resultLabel.Text = "Event Added.";
            EventData = null;
            calendar.SelectedDate =
               GetFreeDate(calendar.SelectedDate.AddDays(1));
            GridView1.DataBind();
            EventList.DataBind();
         }
```

Now selectable event details are available in the table, as shown in Figure 37-14.

There is *much* more that you can do with templates and data-bound controls in general, enough in fact to fill a whole book. However, this should be enough to get you started with your experimentation.

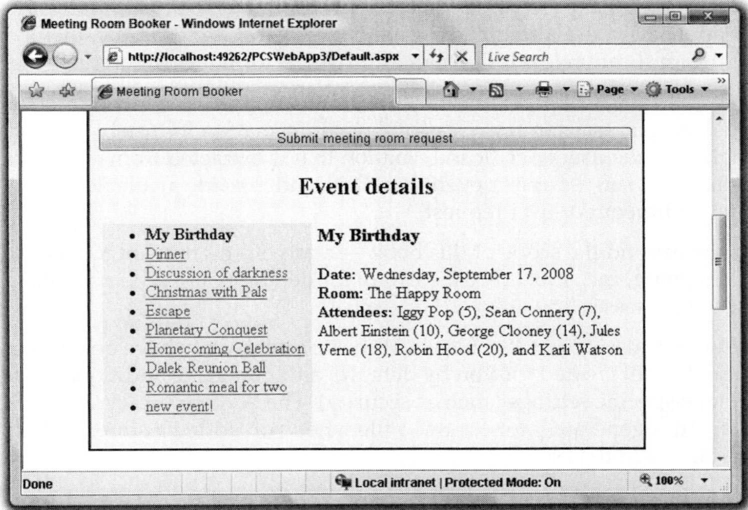

Figure 37-14

Application Configuration

Throughout this chapter, we have alluded to the existence of a conceptual application containing Web pages and configuration settings. This is an important concept to grasp, especially when configuring your Web site for multiple concurrent users.

A few notes on terminology and application lifetime are necessary here. An *application* is defined as all files in your project, and is configured by the `Web.config` file. An `Application` object is created when an application is started for the first time, which will be when the first HTTP request arrives. Also at this time, the `Application_Start` event is triggered and a pool of `HttpApplication` instances is created. Each incoming request receives one of these instances, which performs request processing. Note that this means `HttpApplication` objects do not need to cope with concurrent access, unlike the global `Application` object. When all `HttpApplication` instances finish their work, the `Application_End` event fires and the application terminates, destroying the `Application` object.

The event handlers for the events mentioned earlier (along with handlers for all other events discussed in this chapter) can be defined in a `Global.asax` file, which you can add to any Web site project. The generated file contains blanks for you to fill in; for example:

```
protected void Application_Start(Object sender, EventArgs e)
{
}
```

When an individual user accesses the Web application, a *session* is started. Similar to the application, this involves the creation of a user-specific `Session` object, along with the triggering of a `Session_Start` event. Within a session, individual *requests* trigger `Application_BeginRequest` and `Application_EndRequest` events. These can occur several times over the scope of a session as different resources within the application are accessed. Individual sessions can be terminated manually, or will time out if no further requests are received. Session termination triggers a `Session_End` event and the destruction of the `Session` object.

Against the background of this process, you can do several things to streamline your application. If all instances of your application use a single, resource-heavy object, for example, then you might consider instantiating it at the application level. This can improve performance and reduce memory usage with multiple users because in most requests no such instantiation will be required.

Another technique you can use is to store session-level information for use by individual users across requests. This might include user-specific information that is extracted from a data store when the user first connects (in the `Session_Start()` event handler), and is made available until the session is terminated (through a timeout or user request).

These techniques are beyond the scope of this book — and you might want to consult *Professional ASP.NET 2.0* (Wiley Publishing, Inc., ISBN 0-7645-7610-0) for details — but it helps to have a broad understanding of the processes.

Finally, you need to look at `Web.config` files. A Web site will usually have one of these in its root directory (although it is not created for you by default), and may have additional ones in subdirectories to configure directory-specific settings (such as security). The `PCSWebApp3` Web site developed in this chapter received an auto-generated `Web.config` file when you added a stored database connection string, which you can see in the file:

```
<connectionStrings>
  <add name="MRBConnectionString"
     connectionString="Data Source=.\SQLEXPRESS;
     AttachDbFilename=|DataDirectory|\MeetingRoomBooker.mdf;
     Integrated Security=True;User Instance=True"
     providerName="System.Data.SqlClient" />
</connectionStrings>
```

If you ran the project in debug mode, then you will also see some additional settings in the `Web.config` file.

You can edit `Web.config` files manually, but you can also configure Web sites (and their underlying configuration files) using a tool that is accessible on the Web site menu in Visual Studio, under ASP.NET Configuration. The display for this tool is shown in Figure 37-15.

As you can see from the text, this tool lets you configure a number of settings, including security. You will see much more of this tool in the next chapter.

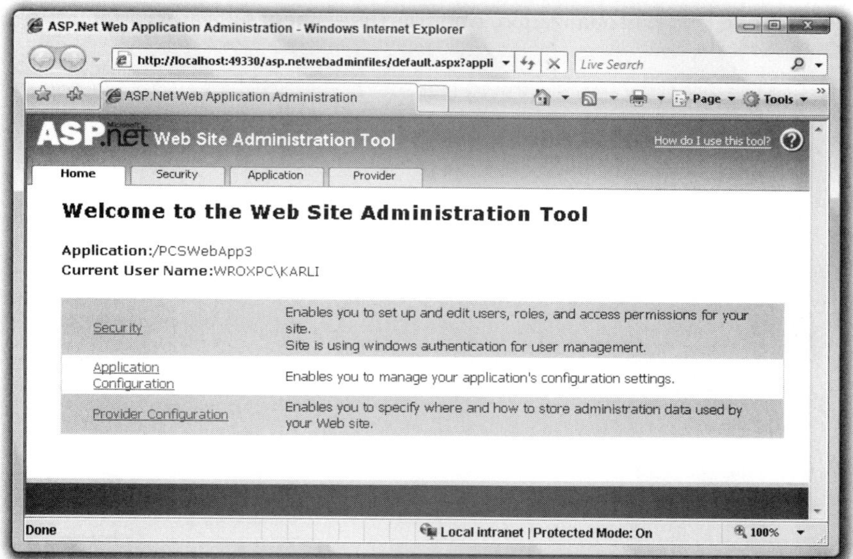

Figure 37-15

Summary

This chapter has provided an overview of Web application creation with ASP.NET. You have seen how you can use C# in combination with Web server controls to provide a truly rich development environment. You have developed an event-booking sample application to which illustrates many of the techniques available, such as the variety of server controls that exist, and data binding with ADO.NET.

Specifically, you have seen the following:

- An introduction to ASP.NET and how it fits in with .NET development in general
- How the basic syntax of ASP.NET works, how state management is achieved, and how to integrate C# code with ASP.NET pages
- How to create an ASP.NET Web application using Visual Studio, and what options exist for hosting and testing of Web sites
- A summary of the Web controls available to ASP.NET developers, and how they work together to deliver dynamic and/or data-driven content

- ❑ How to work with event handlers to both detect and act on user interaction with controls and customize controls via page and rendering events
- ❑ How to bind data to Web controls, and format the data displayed using templates and data binding expressions
- ❑ How to put all this together to build a meeting room booker application

With this information, you are already at a point where you could assemble powerful Web applications of your own. However, we've only scratched the surface of what's possible. So, before you put down this book and dive into your own Web development, we recommend that you keep reading. In Chapter 38, you will expand your knowledge of ASP.NET by looking at some more important Web topics, including master pages, skinning, and personalization. And trust us — the results are worth it!

38

ASP.NET Development

Sometimes the tools available for Web development, however powerful, don't quite match up with your requirements for a specific project. Perhaps a given control doesn't quite work as you would like it to, or perhaps one section of code, intended for reuse on several pages, is too complex in the hands of multiple developers. In such cases, there is a strong argument for building your own controls. Such controls can, at their simplest, wrap multiple existing controls together, perhaps with additional properties specifying layout. They can also be completely unlike any existing control. Using a control you have built yourself can be as simple as using any other control in ASP.NET (if you have written it well), which can certainly ease Web site coding.

In the first part of this chapter, you examine the options available to control developers, and assemble some simple user controls of your own. You also look at the basics of more advanced control construction, although you won't see these in any great depth; whole books are devoted to the subject.

Next, you look at master pages, a technique new to ASP.NET 2.0 that enables you to provide templates for your Web sites. Using master pages, you can implement complex layouts on Web pages throughout a Web site with a great deal of code reuse. You also see how you can use the navigation Web server controls in combination with a master page to provide consistent navigation across a Web site.

Site navigation can be made user-specific, such that only certain users (those that are registered with the site, or site administrators, say) can access certain sections. You also look at site security and how to log in to Web sites — something that is made extremely easy via the login Web server controls.

After that, you look at some more advanced styling techniques, namely, providing and choosing themes for Web sites, which separate the presentation of your Web pages from their functionality. You can supply alternative cascading style sheets for your sites, as well as different skins for Web server controls.

Finally, you will see how to use Web Parts to enable your users to dynamically personalize Web pages by positioning and customizing controls on a page.

To summarize, in this chapter you look at:

- User and custom controls
- Master pages
- Site navigation
- Security
- Themes
- Web Parts

Throughout this chapter, you will refer to one large example application that includes all the techniques that you have seen in this and the previous chapter. This application, `PCSDemoSite`, is available in the downloadable code for this chapter. It is a little too large to include all the code here, but you don't need to have it running in front of you to learn about the techniques it illustrates. The relevant sections of code are examined as and when necessary, and the additional code (mostly dummy content or simple code you have already seen) is left for you to examine at your convenience.

User and Custom Controls

In the past, implementing custom-built controls was tricky, especially on large-scale systems where complex registration procedures might be required to use them. Even on simple systems, the coding required to create a custom control could become a very involved process. The scripting capabilities of older Web languages also suffered by not giving you complete access to your cunningly crafted object models, which resulted in poor performance.

The .NET Framework provides an ideal setting for the creation of custom controls, using simple programming techniques. Every aspect of ASP.NET server controls is exposed for you to customize, including such capabilities as templating and client-side scripting. However, there is no need to write code for all of these eventualities; simpler controls can be a lot easier to create.

In addition, the dynamic discovery of assemblies that is inherent in a .NET system makes installation of Web applications on a new Web server as simple as copying the directory structure containing your code. To make use of the controls you have created, you simply copy the assemblies containing those controls along with the rest of the code. You can even place frequently used controls in an assembly located in the global assembly cache (GAC) on the Web server, so that all Web applications on the server have access to them.

This chapter discusses two different kinds of controls:

- **User controls** (and how to convert existing ASP.NET pages into controls)
- **Custom controls** (and how to group the functionality of several controls, extend existing controls, and create new controls from scratch)

User controls are illustrated with a simple control that displays a card suit (club, diamond, heart, or spade), so that you can embed it in other ASP.NET pages with ease. We won't go into too much depth for custom controls, although we will show you the basic principles and direct you to more information beyond this book.

User Controls

User controls are controls that you create using ASP.NET code, just as you use in standard ASP.NET Web pages. The difference is that after you have created a user control you can reuse it in multiple ASP.NET pages.

For example, say that you have created a page that displays some information from a database, perhaps information about an order. Instead of creating a fixed page that does this, it is possible to place the relevant code into a user control, and then insert that control into as many different Web pages as you want.

In addition, it is possible to define properties and methods for user controls. For example, you can specify a property for the background color for displaying your database table in a Web page, or a method to re-run a database query to check for changes.

To start, you create a simple user control. As is the case with the other chapters, you can download the code for the sample projects in this chapter from the Wrox Web site at `www.wrox.com`.

A Simple User Control

In Visual Studio .NET, create a new Web site called `PCSUserCWebApp1` in the directory `C:\ProCSharp\Chapter38`. After the standard files have been generated, select the Website ⇨ Add New Item . . . menu option and add a Web User Control called `PCSUserC1.ascx`, as shown in Figure 38-1.

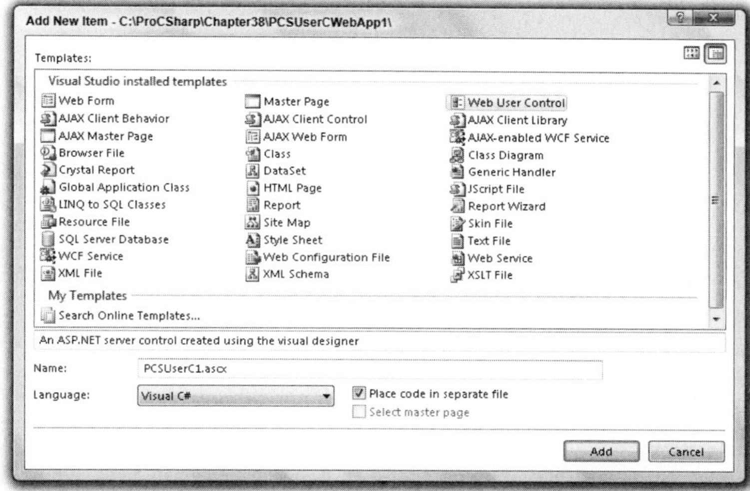

Figure 38-1

The files added to your project, with the extensions `.ascx` and `.ascx.cs`, work in a very similar way to the `.aspx` files that you have seen already. The `.ascx` file contains your ASP.NET code and looks very similar to a normal `.aspx` file. The `.ascx.cs` file is your code-behind file, which defines custom code for the user control, much in the same way that forms are extended by `.aspx.cs` files.

The `.ascx` files can be viewed in Design or Source view, just like `.aspx` files. Looking at the file in Source view reveals an important difference: there is no HTML code present, and in particular no `<form>` element. This is because user controls are inserted inside ASP.NET forms in other files and so don't need a `<form>` tag of their own. The generated code is as follows:

```
<%@ Control Language="C#" AutoEventWireup="true" CodeFile="PCSUserC1.ascx.cs"
    Inherits="PCSUserC1" %>
```

This is very similar to the `<%@ Page %>` directive generated in `.aspx` files, except that `Control` is specified rather than `Page`. The `CodeFile` attribute specifies the code-behind file and `Inherits` specifies the class defined in the code-behind file from which the page inherits. The code in the `.ascx.cs` file contains, as in auto-generated `.aspx.cs` files, a class definition that is empty apart from a `Page_Load()` event handler method.

Your simple control will be one that displays a graphic corresponding to one of the four standard suits in cards (club, diamond, heart, or spade). The graphics required for this were shipped as part of a previous version of Visual Studio .NET; you can find them in the downloadable code for this chapter, in the `CardSuitImages` directory, with the file names `CLUB.BMP`, `DIAMOND.BMP`, `HEART.BMP`, and `SPADE.BMP`. Copy these files into a new `Images` subdirectory of your project's directory, so that you can use them in a moment. If you do not have access to this download, you can use any images you like for this example because they are not important to the functionality of the code.

Note that unlike earlier versions of Visual Studio, changes you make to the Web site structure outside of Visual Studio are automatically reflected in the IDE. You have to hit the refresh button in the Solution Explorer window, but you should see the new `Images` *directory and bitmap files appear automatically.*

Now add some code to your new control. In the HTML view of `PCSUserC1.ascx`, add the following:

```
<%@ Control Language="C#" AutoEventWireup="true" CodeFile="PCSUserC1.ascx.cs"
    Inherits="PCSUserC1" %>
<table cellspacing="4">
  <tr valign="middle">
    <td>
      <asp:Image Runat="server" ID="suitPic" ImageURL="~/Images/club.bmp"/>
    </td>
    <td>
      <asp:Label Runat="server" ID="suitLabel">Club</asp:Label>
    </td>
  </tr>
</table>
```

This defines a default state for your control, which is a picture of a club along with a label. The ~ in the path to the image means "start at the root directory of the Web site." Before you add functionality, you will test this default by adding this control to your project Web page `webForm1.aspx`.

To use a custom control in an `.aspx` file, you first need to specify how you will refer to it, that is, the name of the tag that will represent the control in your HTML. To do this, you use the `<%@ Register %>` directive at the top of the code in `Default.aspx`, as follows:

```
<%@ Register TagPrefix="pcs" TagName="UserC1" Src="PCSUserC1.ascx" %>
```

The `TagPrefix` and `TagName` attributes specify the tag name to use (in the form `<TagPrefix: TagName>`), and you use the `Src` attribute to point to the file containing your user control. Now you can use the control by adding the following element:

```
  <form id="Form1" method="post" runat="server">
    <div>
      <pcs:UserC1 Runat="server" ID="myUserControl"/>
    </div>
  </form>
```

This is all you need to do to test your user control. Figure 38-2 shows the results of running this code.

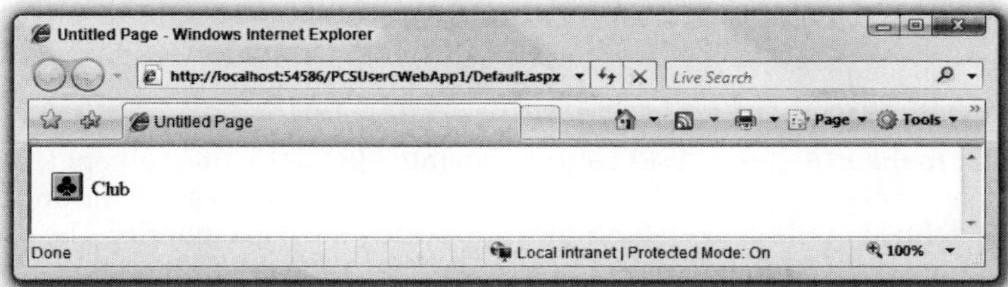

Figure 38-2

As it stands, this control groups two existing controls, an image and a label, in a table layout. Therefore, it falls into the category of a composite control.

To gain control over the displayed suit, you can use an attribute on the `<PCS:UserC1>` element. Attributes on user control elements are automatically mapped to properties on user controls, so all you have to do to make this work is add a property to the code behind your control, `PCSUserC1.ascx.cs`. Call this property `Suit`, and let it take any suit value. To make it easier for you to represent the state of the control, you define an enumeration to hold the four suit names. The best way to do this is to add an `App_Code` directory to your Web site, and then add a `.cs` file called `Suit.cs` in this directory. `App_Code` is another "special" directory, like `App_Data`, whose functionality is defined for you — in this case it holds additional code files for your Web application. You can add this directory by right-clicking the Web site in Solution Explorer and clicking Add ASP.NET Folder ⇨ App_Code. When you have done this, add `Suit.cs` with code as follows:

```
using System;

public enum suit
{
   club, diamond, heart, spade
}
```

The `PCSUserC1` class needs a member variable to hold the suit type, `currentSuit`:

```
public partial class PCSUserC1 : System.Web.UI.UserControl
{
   protected suit currentSuit;
```

And a property to access this member variable, `Suit`:

```
   public suit Suit
   {
      get
      {
         return currentSuit;
      }
      set
      {
         currentSuit = value;
         suitPic.ImageUrl = "~/Images/" + currentSuit.ToString() + ".bmp";
         suitLabel.Text = currentSuit.ToString();
      }
   }
```

The `set` accessor here sets the URL of the image to one of the files you copied earlier, and the text displayed to the suit name.

Next, you must add code to `Default.aspx` so that you can access this new property. You could simply specify the suit using the property you have just added:

```
<PCS:UserC1 Runat="server" id="myUserControl" Suit="diamond"/>
```

The ASP.NET processor is intelligent enough to get the correct enumeration item from the string provided. To make things a bit more interesting and interactive, though, you will use a radio button list to select a suit:

```
  <form id="form1" runat="server">
    <div>
      <pcs:UserC1 id="myUserControl" runat="server" />
      <asp:RadioButtonList Runat="server" ID="suitList" AutoPostBack="True">
```

(continued)

(continued)

```
        <asp:ListItem Value="club" Selected="True">Club</asp:ListItem>
        <asp:ListItem Value="diamond">Diamond</asp:ListItem>
        <asp:ListItem Value="heart">Heart</asp:ListItem>
        <asp:ListItem Value="spade">Spade</asp:ListItem>
      </asp:RadioButtonList>
    </div>
  </form>
```

You also need to add an event handler for the `SelectedIndexChanged` event of the list, which you can do simply by double-clicking the radio button list control in Design view.

Note that you have set the `AutoPostBack` property of this list to `True`, because the `suitList_SelectedIndexChanged()` event handler won't be executed on the server unless a postback is in operation, and this control doesn't trigger a postback by default.

The `suitList_SelectedIndexChanged()` method requires the following code in `Default.aspx.cs`:

```
public partial class Default
{
   protected void suitList_SelectedIndexChanged(object sender, EventArgs e)
   {
      myUserControl.Suit = (suit)Enum.Parse(typeof(suit),
                                            suitList.SelectedItem.Value);
   }
}
```

You know that the `Value` attributes on the `<ListItem>` elements represent valid values for the suit enumeration you defined earlier, so you simply parse these as enumeration types and use them as values of the `Suit` property of your user control. You cast the returned object type to `suit` using simple casing syntax, because this cannot be achieved implicitly.

Now you can change the suit when you run your Web application (see Figure 38-3).

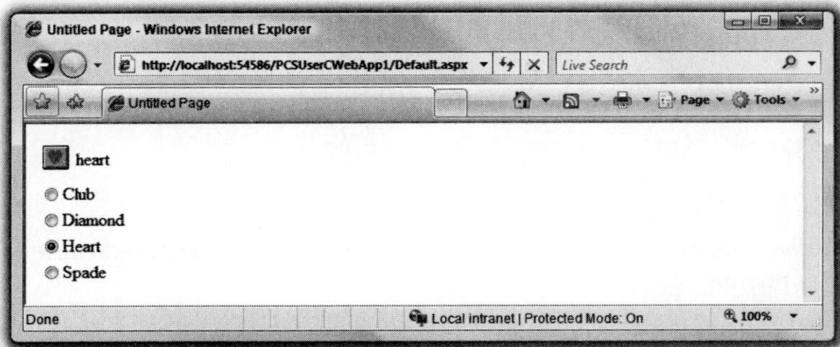

Figure 38-3

Next, you give your control some methods. Again, this is very simple; you just add methods to the `PCSUserC1` class:

```
   public void Club()
   {
      Suit = suit.club;
   }

   public void Diamond()
```

```
{
   Suit = suit.diamond;
}

public void Heart()
{
   Suit = suit.heart;
}

public void Spade()
{
   Suit = suit.spade;
}
```

These four methods — `Club()`, `Diamond()`, `Heart()`, and `Spade()` — change the suit displayed on the screen to the respective suit clicked.

You call these functions from four `ImageButton` controls in your `.aspx` page:

```
      </asp:RadioButtonList>
      <asp:ImageButton Runat="server" ID="clubButton"
        ImageUrl="~/Images/CLUB.BMP" OnClick="clubButton_Click" />
      <asp:ImageButton Runat="server" ID="diamondButton"
        ImageUrl="~/Images/DIAMOND.BMP" OnClick="diamondButton_Click" />
      <asp:ImageButton Runat="server" ID="heartButton"
        ImageUrl="~/Images/HEART.BMP" OnClick="heartButton_Click" />
      <asp:ImageButton Runat="server" ID="spadeButton"
        ImageUrl="~/Images/SPADE.BMP" OnClick="spadeButton_Click" />
    </div>
  </form>
```

You use the following event handlers:

```
protected void clubButton_Click(object sender, ImageClickEventArgs e)
{
   myUserControl.Club();
   suitList.SelectedIndex = 0;
}

protected void diamondButton_Click(object sender, ImageClickEventArgs e)
{
   myUserControl.Diamond();
   suitList.SelectedIndex = 1;
}

protected void heartButton_Click(object sender, ImageClickEventArgs e)
{
   myUserControl.Heart();
   suitList.SelectedIndex = 2;
}

protected void spadeButton_Click(object sender, ImageClickEventArgs e)
{
   myUserControl.Spade();
   suitList.SelectedIndex = 3;
}
```

Note that you could use a single event handler for all four buttons, because they have identical method signatures. You could detect which button has been pressed by the value passed to `sender`*, and thus determine which method of* `myUserControl` *to call and which index to set dynamically. In this case, though, there wouldn't be a huge difference in the amount of code required, so, for simplicity, things are kept separate.*

Now you have four new buttons you can use to change the suit, as shown in Figure 38-4.

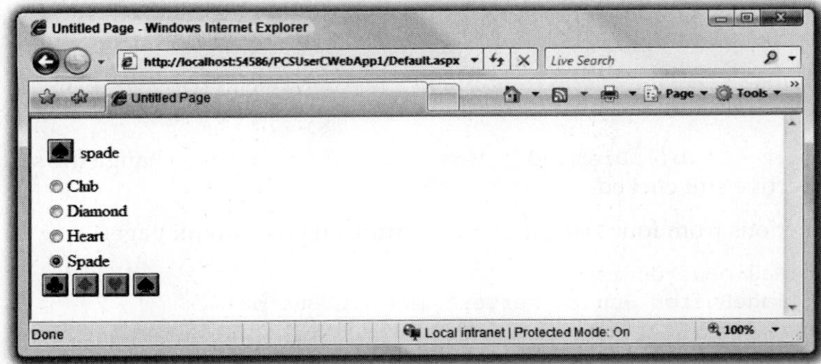

Figure 38-4

Now that you have created your user control, you can use it in any other Web page simply by using the `<%@ Register %>` directive and the two source code files (`PCSUserC1.ascx` and `PCSUserC1.ascx.cs`) you have created for the control.

User Controls in PCSDemoSite

In the PCSDemoSite, the meeting room booker application from the previous chapter has been converted into a user control for ease of reuse. To see the control, you have to log in to the site as User1, with password User1!!, and navigate to the Meeting Room Booker page, as shown in Figure 38-5. (You learn how the logging-in system works later in the chapter.)

Apart from the obvious change in style, which is achieved by themes, as you see later in this chapter, the major modifications are as follows:

- The username is automatically taken from user details.
- There is no extra data display at the bottom of the page, and corresponding `DataBind()` calls are removed from the code behind.
- There is no result label beneath the control — the user gets enough feedback by seeing events added to the calendar and event list, without being told that event addition was successful.
- The page containing the user control uses a master page.

The code modifications to achieve all of this are remarkably simple. You won't look at them here, but you will come back to this control later in the chapter, when you look at logging in.

Custom Controls

Custom controls go a step beyond user controls in that they are entirely self-contained in C# assemblies, requiring no separate ASP.NET code. This means that you don't need to go through the process of assembling a user interface (UI) in an `.ascx` file. Instead, you have complete control over what is written to the output stream, that is, the exact HTML generated by your control.

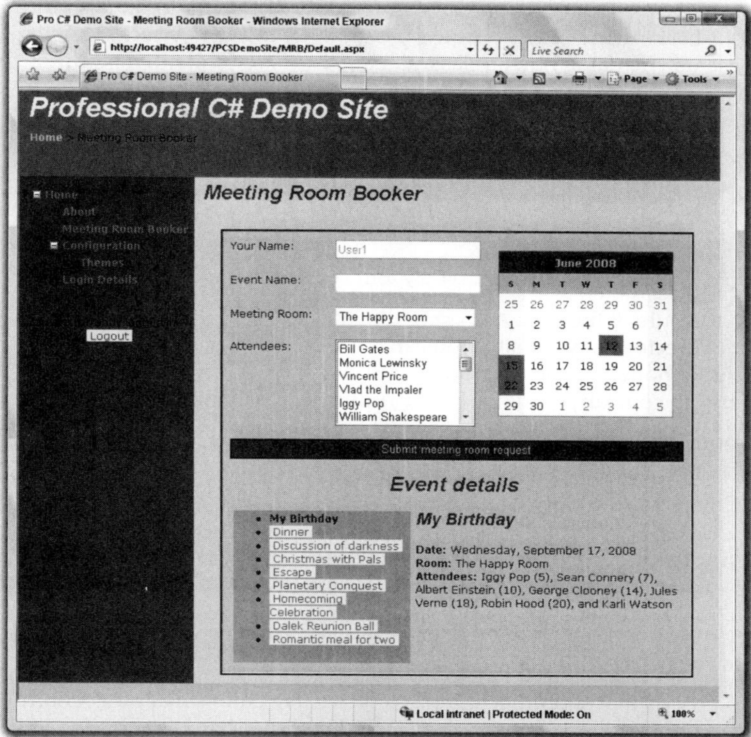

Figure 38-5

In general, it will take longer to develop custom controls than user controls because the syntax is more complex, and you often have to write significantly more code to get results. A user control may be as simple as a few other controls grouped together, as you have seen, whereas a custom control can do just about anything short of making you a cup of coffee.

To get the most customizable behavior for your custom controls, you can derive a class from `System.Web.UI.WebControls.WebControl`. If you do this, you are creating a full custom control. Alternatively, you can extend the functionality of an existing control, creating a derived custom control. Finally, you can group existing controls together, much as you did in the last section but with a more logical structure, to create a composite custom control.

Whatever you create can be used in ASP.NET pages in pretty much the same way. All you need to do is place the generated assembly in a location where the Web application that will use it can find it, and register the element names to use with the `<%@ Register %>` directive. For this location, you have two options: you can either put the assembly in the bin directory of the Web application, or place it in the GAC if you want all Web applications on the server to have access to it. Alternatively, if you are just using a user control on a single Web site, you can just put the `.cs` file for the control in the `App_Code` directory for the site.

The `<%@ Register %>` directive takes a slightly different syntax for custom controls:

```
<%@ Register TagPrefix="PCS" Namespace="PCSCustomWebControls"
             Assembly="PCSCustomWebControls"%>
```

You use the `TagPrefix` option in the same way as before, but you don't use the `TagName` or `Src` attributes. This is because the custom control assembly you use may contain several custom controls, and each of these will be named by its class, so `TagName` is redundant. In addition, because you can use the dynamic discovery capabilities of the .NET Framework to find your assembly, you simply have to name it and the namespace in it that contains your controls.

In the previous line of code, you are instructing the program to use an assembly called `PCSCustomWebControls.dll` with controls in the `PCSCustomWebControls` namespace, and use the tag prefix `PCS`. If you have a control called `Control1` in this namespace, you could use it with the ASP.NET code:

```
<PCS:Control1 Runat="server" ID="MyControl1"/>
```

The `Assembly` attribute of the `<%@ Register %>` directive is optional — if you have custom controls in the `App_Code` directory of your site, you can omit this, and the Web site will look at code here for controls. One thing though — the `Namespace` attribute is *not* optional. You must include a namespace in code files for custom controls, or the ASP.NET runtime will not be able to find them.

With custom controls, it is also possible to reproduce some of the control nesting behavior that exists in list controls, for example the way that you can nest `<asp:ListItem>` controls inside a list control to populate the list control:

```
<asp:DropDownList ID="roomList" Runat="server" Width="160px">
   <asp:ListItem Value="1">The Happy Room</asp:ListItem>
   <asp:ListItem Value="2">The Angry Room</asp:ListItem>
   <asp:ListItem Value="3">The Depressing Room</asp:ListItem>
   <asp:ListItem Value="4">The Funked Out Room</asp:ListItem>
</asp:DropDownList>
```

You can create controls that should be interpreted as being children of other controls in a very similar way to this. This is one of the more advanced techniques that you won't be looking at in this book.

Custom Control Sample

Now it's time to put some of this theory into practice. You will use a single Web site called `PCSCustomCWebApp1` in the `C:\ProCSharp\Chapter38\` directory, with a custom control in its `App_Code` directory to illustrate a simple custom control. The control here will be a multicolored version of the existing `Label` control, with the ability to cycle through a set of colors for each letter in its text.

The code for the control, `RainbowLabel`, in the file `App_Code\Rainbow.cs`, starts with the following `using` statements:

```
using System;
using System.Data;
using System.Configuration;
using System.Linq;
using System.Web;
using System.Web.Security;
using System.Web.UI;
using System.Web.UI.WebControls;
using System.Web.UI.WebControls.WebParts;
using System.Web.UI.HtmlControls;
using System.Xml.Linq;
using System.Drawing;
```

Apart from `System.Drawing`, these are the default namespaces that are added when you add a class file to a Web site. The `System.Drawing` namespace is required for the `Color` enumeration. The class maintains an array of colors to use for letters in its text in a private `Color` array called `colors`:

```
namespace PCSCustomWebControls
{
   public class RainbowLabel : Label
   {
      private Color[] colors = new Color[] {Color.Red,
                                            Color.Orange,
                                            Color.Yellow,
                                            Color.GreenYellow,
                                            Color.Blue,
                                            Color.Indigo,
                                            Color.Violet};
```

Also notice that the namespace `PCSCustomWebControls` is used to contain the control. As discussed earlier, this is necessary so that Web pages can reference the control correctly.

To enable color cycling, you also store an integer offset value in a private `offset` property:

```
      private int offset
      {
         get
         {
            object rawOffset = ViewState["_offset"];
            if (rawOffset != null)
            {
               return (int)rawOffset;
            }
            else
            {
               ViewState["_offset"] = 0;
               return 0;
            }
         }
         set
         {
            ViewState["_offset"] = value;
         }
      }
```

Note that this property isn't as simple as just storing a value in a member field. This is due to the way ASP.NET maintains state, as discussed in the previous chapter. Controls are instantiated on each postback operation, so to store values you must make use of view state. This is easy to access — you simply use the `ViewState` collection, which can store any object that is serializable. Otherwise, `offset` would revert to its initial value between each postback.

To modify `offset`, you use a method called `Cycle()`:

```
      public void Cycle()
      {
         offset = ++offset;
      }
```

This simply increments the value stored in the view state for `offset`.

Finally, you come to perhaps the most important method override for any custom control — `Render()`. This is where you output HTML, and as such it can be a very complicated method to implement. If you were to take into account all the browsers that may view your controls, and all the variables that could affect rendering, this method could get very big. Fortunately, for this example, it's quite simple:

```
         protected override void Render(HtmlTextWriter output)
         {
            string text = Text;
            for (int pos = 0; pos < text.Length; pos++)
            {
               int rgb = colors[(pos + offset) % colors.Length].ToArgb()
                                                             & 0xFFFFFF;
               output.Write(string.Format(
                  "<font color=\"#{0:X6}\">{1}</font>", rgb, text[pos]));
            }
         }
      }
   }
```

This method gives you access to the output stream to display your control content. There are only two cases where you don't need to implement this method:

- When you are designing a control that has no visual representation (usually known as a component)
- When you are deriving from an existing control and don't need to change its display characteristics

Custom controls can also expose custom methods, raise custom events, and respond to child controls (if any). In the case of `RainbowLabel`, you don't have to worry about any of this.

Next, you need to modify `Default.aspx` to view the control and provide access to `Cycle()`, as follows:

```
<%@ Page Language="C#" AutoEventWireup="true" CodeFile="Default.aspx.cs"
  Inherits="_Default" %>

<%@ Register TagPrefix="pcs" Namespace="PCSCustomWebControls" %>
<!DOCTYPE html PUBLIC "-//W3C//DTD XHTML 1.1//EN"
  "http://www.w3.org/TR/xhtml11/DTD/xhtml11.dtd">
<html xmlns="http://www.w3.org/1999/xhtml">
<head runat="server">
  <title>Untitled Page</title>
</head>
<body>
  <form id="form1" runat="server">
    <div>
      <pcs:RainbowLabel runat="server" ID="rainbowLabel1"
        Text="Multicolored label!" />
      <asp:Button Runat="server" ID="cycleButton" Text="Cycle colors"
        OnClick="cycleButton_Click" />
    </div>
  </form>
</body>
</html>
```

The required code in `Default.aspx.cs` is simply:

```
public partial class _Default : System.Web.UI.Page
{
   protected void Page_Load(object sender, EventArgs e)
```

```
        {

        }

        protected void cycleButton_Click(object sender, EventArgs e)
        {
            rainbowLabel1.Cycle();
        }
    }
```

Now you can view the sample and cycle the colors in the sample text, as shown in Figure 38-6.

Figure 38-6

You can do a lot more with custom controls; indeed, the possibilities are practically limitless, but you will have to experiment with these possibilities on your own.

Master Pages

Master pages provide an excellent way to make your Web sites easier to design. Putting all (or at least most) of your page layout in a single file allows you to concentrate on the more important things for the individual Web pages of your site.

Master pages are created in files with the extension `.master`, and can be added via the Web site ⇨ Add New Item . . . menu item, like any other site content. At first glance, the code generated for a master page is much like that for a standard `.aspx` page:

```
<%@ Master Language="C#" AutoEventWireup="true"
  CodeFile="MyMasterPage.master.cs" Inherits="MyMasterPage" %>
<!DOCTYPE html PUBLIC "-//W3C//DTD XHTML 1.0 Transitional//EN"
  "http://www.w3.org/TR/xhtml1/DTD/xhtml1-transitional.dtd">
<html xmlns="http://www.w3.org/1999/xhtml">
<head runat="server">
  <title>Untitled Page</title>
  <asp:ContentPlaceHolder id="head" runat="server">
  </asp:ContentPlaceHolder>
</head>
<body>
  <form id="form1" runat="server">
    <div>
      <asp:ContentPlaceHolder ID="ContentPlaceHolder1" Runat="server">
      </asp:ContentPlaceHolder>
    </div>
  </form>
</body>
</html>
```

The differences are:

- A `<%@ Master %>` directive is used instead of a `<%@ Page %>` directive, although the attributes are the same.
- A `ContentPlaceHolder` control with an `ID` of `head` is placed in the page header.
- A `ContentPlaceHolder` control with an `ID` of `ContentPlaceHolder1` is placed in the page body.

The `ContentPlaceHolder` controls are what make master pages so useful. You can have any number of these on a page, and they are used by `.aspx` pages using the master page to "plug in" content. You can put default content inside a `ContentPlaceHolder` control, but `.aspx` pages can override this content.

For an `.aspx` page to use a master page, you need to modify the `<%@ Page %>` directive as follows:

```
<%@ Page Language="C#" AutoEventWireup="true" CodeFile="Default.aspx.cs"
  Inherits="_Default" MasterPageFile="~/MyMasterPage.master"
  Title="Page Title" %>
```

Here you have added two new attributes: a `MasterPageFile` attribute saying which master page to use and a `Title` attribute that sets the content of the `<title>` element in the master page.

When you add an `.aspx` page to a Web site, you can choose to select a master page, as shown in Figure 38-7.

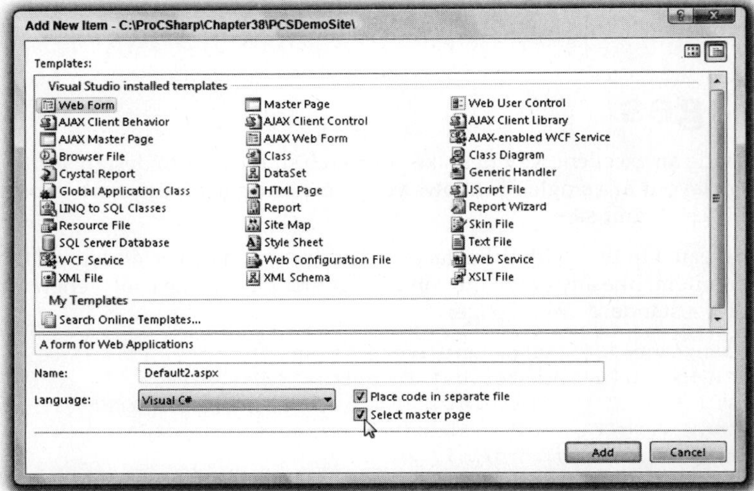

Figure 38-7

If you do this, you can navigate through your site structure to find the master page you want, as shown in Figure 38-8.

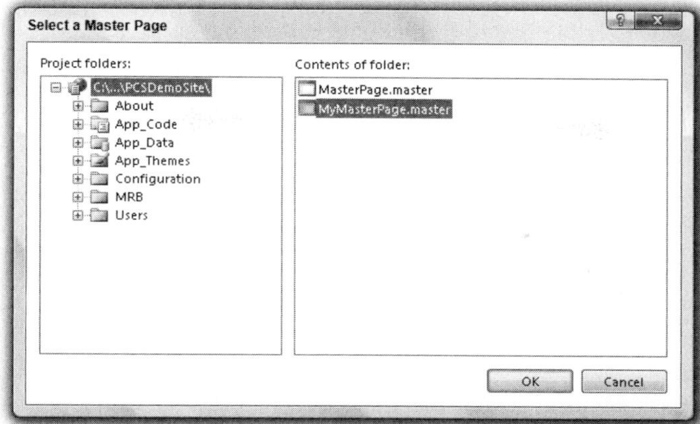

Figure 38-8

The .aspx page doesn't have to contain any other code, if you want to use the default master page content. In fact, it is an error to include a `Form` control, because a page may only have one of these and there is one in the master page.

.aspx pages that use a master page can contain no root-level content other than directives, script elements, and `Content` controls. You can have as many `Content` controls as you like, where each one inserts content into one of the `ContentPlaceHolder` controls in the master page. The only thing to look out for is to make sure that the `ContentPlaceHolderID` attribute of the `Content` control matches the `ID` of the `ContentPlaceHolder` control where you want to insert content. So, to add content into the master page shown earlier, you would simply need the following in the .aspx file:

```
<%@ Page Language="C#" MasterPageFile="~/MyMasterPage.master"
  AutoEventWireup="true" CodeFile="Default2.aspx.cs" Inherits="Default2"
  Title="Untitled Page" %>

<asp:Content ID="Content1" ContentPlaceHolderID="head" Runat="Server">
</asp:Content>
<asp:Content ID="Content2" ContentPlaceHolderID="ContentPlaceHolder1"
  runat="Server">
  Custom content!
</asp:Content>
```

The true power of master pages comes when you surround the `ContentPlaceHolder` controls in your master pages with other content, such as navigation controls, site logos, and HTML. You can supply multiple `ContentPlaceHolder` controls for main content, sidebar content, footer text, and so on.

You can omit `Content` controls on a page if you do not wish to supply content for a specific `ContentPlaceHolder`. For example, you could remove the `Content1` control from the preceding code without affecting the resultant display.

Accessing Master Page Content from Web Pages

When you add a master page to a Web page, you will sometimes need to access the master page from code in your Web page. To do this, you can use the `Page.Master` property, which will return a reference to the master page in the form of a `MasterPage` object. You can cast this to the type of the master page as defined by the master page file (for the example in the previous section, this class would be called `MyMasterPage`). Once you have this reference, you can access any public members of the master page class.

Also, you can use the `MasterPage.FindControl()` method to locate controls on the master page by their identifier. This enables you to manipulate content on the master page that is outside of content placeholders.

One typical use of this might be if you define a master page that is used for a standard form, with a submit button. You can locate the submit button in the child page and add an event handler for the submit button in the master page. In this way, you can provide, for example, custom validation logic in response to a form submission.

Nested Master Pages

The Select master page option is also available when you create a new master page. By using this option, you can create a *nested* master page that is based on a parent master page. For example, you can create a master page called `MyNestedMasterPage` that uses `MyMasterPage` as follows:

```
<%@ Master Language="C#" MasterPageFile="~/MyMasterPage.master"
  AutoEventWireup="false" CodeFile="MyNestedMasterPage.master.cs"
  Inherits="MyNestedMasterPage" %>

<asp:Content ID="Content1" ContentPlaceHolderID="head" Runat="Server">
  <!-- Disabled for child controls. -->
</asp:Content>
<asp:Content ID="Content2" ContentPlaceHolderID="ContentPlaceHolder1"
  Runat="Server">
  First nested place holder:
  <asp:ContentPlaceHolder ID="NestedContentPlaceHolder1" runat="server">

  </asp:ContentPlaceHolder>
  <br />
  <br />
  Second nested place holder:
  <asp:ContentPlaceHolder ID="NestedContentPlaceHolder2" runat="server">

  </asp:ContentPlaceHolder>
</asp:Content>
```

Pages that use this master page would supply content for `NestedContentPlaceHolder1` and `NestedContentPlaceHolder2`, but would not have direct access to the `ContentPlaceHolder` controls specified in `MyMasterPage`. In this example, `MyNestedMasterPage` fixes the content for the `head` control and supplies a template for the `ContentPlaceHolder1` control.

By creating a family of nested master pages, you can provide alternate layouts for pages while leaving some aspects of the base master pages untouched. For example, the root master page might include navigation and basic layout, and nested master pages could provide layouts with different amounts of columns. You could then use the nested master pages in the pages of your site and quickly switch between these alternate layouts on different pages.

Master Pages in PCSDemoSite

In PCSDemoSite, the single master page `MasterPage.master` (the default name for a master page) is used, with code as follows:

```
<%@ Master Language="C#" AutoEventWireup="true"
CodeFile="MasterPage.master.cs"
  Inherits="MasterPage" %>
<!DOCTYPE html PUBLIC "-//W3C//DTD XHTML 1.1//EN"
  "http://www.w3.org/TR/xhtml11/DTD/xhtml11.dtd">
```

```
<html xmlns="http://www.w3.org/1999/xhtml">
<head runat="server">
  <link rel="stylesheet" href="StyleSheet.css" type="text/css" />
  <title></title>
</head>
<body>
  <form id="form1" runat="server">
    <div id="header">
      <h1><asp:literal ID="Literal1" runat="server"
        text="<%$ AppSettings:SiteTitle %>" /></h1>
      <asp:SiteMapPath ID="SiteMapPath1" Runat="server"
        CssClass="breadcrumb" />
    </div>
    <div id="nav">
      <div class="navTree">
        <asp:TreeView ID="TreeView1" runat="server"
          DataSourceID="SiteMapDataSource1" ShowLines="True" />
      </div>
      <br />
      <br />
      <asp:LoginView ID="LoginView1" Runat="server">
        <LoggedInTemplate>
          You are currently logged in as
          <b><asp:LoginName ID="LoginName1" Runat="server" /></b>.
          <asp:LoginStatus ID="LoginStatus1" Runat="server" />
        </LoggedInTemplate>
      </asp:LoginView>
    </div>
    <div id="body">
      <asp:ContentPlaceHolder ID="ContentPlaceHolder1" Runat="server" />
    </div>
  </form>
  <asp:SiteMapDataSource ID="SiteMapDataSource1" Runat="server" />
</body>
</html>
```

Many of the controls here are ones that you haven't looked at yet, and you will come back to those shortly. The important things to note here are the `<div>` elements that hold the various content sections (header, navigation bar, and body), and the use of `<%$ AppSettings:SiteTitle %>` to obtain the site title from the `Web.config` file:

```
<appSettings>
  <add key="SiteTitle" value="Professional C# Demo Site"/>
</appSettings>
```

There is also a style sheet link to `StyleSheet.css`:

```
<link rel="stylesheet" href="StyleSheet.css" type="text/css" />
```

This CSS style sheet contains the basic layout information for the `<div>` elements on this page, as well as for a section of the meeting room booker control:

```
div#header
{
    position: absolute;
    top: 0px;
    left: 0px;
```

(continued)

(continued)

```
        height: 80px;
        width: 780px;
        padding: 10px;
    }

    div#nav
    {
        position: absolute;
        left: 0px;
        top: 100px;
        width: 180px;
        height: 580px;
        padding: 10px;
    }

    div#body
    {
        position: absolute;
        left: 200px;
        top: 100px;
        width: 580px;
        height: 580px;
        padding: 10px;
    }

    .mrbEventList
    {
        width: 40%;
    }
```

Note that none of this style information includes colors, fonts, and so on. This is achieved by style sheets within themes, which you will see later in this chapter. The only information here is layout information, such as `<div>` sizes.

> *Note that Web site best practices have been adhered to in this chapter whenever possible. Using CSS for layout rather than tables is fast becoming the industry standard for Web site layout and is well worth learning about. In the preceding code,* `#` *symbols are used to format* `<div>` *elements with specific* `id` *attributes, whereas* `.mrbEventList` *will format an HTML element with a specific* `class` *attribute.*

Site Navigation

The three navigation Web server controls, `SiteMapPath`, `Menu`, and `TreeView`, can work with an XML site map that you provide for your Web site, or a site map provided in a different format if you implement an alternative site map provider. Once you have created such a data source, these navigation Web server controls are able to automatically generate location and navigation information for users.

> *You see an example XML site map shortly.*

You can also use a `TreeView` control to display other structured data, but it really comes into its own with site maps, and gives you an alternative view of navigation information.

The navigation Web server controls are shown in the following table.

Control	Description
`SiteMapPath`	Displays breadcrumb-style information, allowing users to see where they are in the structure of a site and navigate to parent areas. You can supply various templates, such as `NodeStyle` and `CurrentNodeStyle` to customize the appearance of the breadcrumb trail.
`Menu`	Links to site map information via a `SiteMapDataSource` control, and enables a view of the complete site structure. The appearance of this control can be customized by templates.
`TreeView`	Allows the display of hierarchical data, such as a table of contents, in a tree structure. Tree nodes are stored in a `Nodes` property, with the selected node stored in `SelectedNode`. Several events allow for server-side processing of user interaction, including `SelectedNodeChanged` and `TreeNodeCollapsed`. This control is typically data-bound.

To provide a site map XML file for your site, you can add a site map file (`.sitemap`) using the Web site ⇨ Add New Item . . . menu item. You link to site maps via providers. The default XML provider looks for a file called `Web.sitemap` in the root of your site, so unless you are going to use a different provider, you should accept the default file name supplied.

A site map XML file contains a root `<siteMap>` element containing a single `<siteMapNode>` element, which in turn can contain any number of nested `<siteMapNode>` elements.

Each `<siteMapNode>` element uses the attributes shown in the following table.

Attribute	Description
`Title`	Page title, used as the text for links in site map displays
`url`	Page location, used as the hyperlink location in site map displays
`Roles`	The user roles that are allowed to see this site map entry in menus and so on
`description`	Optional text used for tooltip pop-ups for site map displays

Once a site has a `Web.sitemap` file, adding a breadcrumb trail is as simple as putting the following code on your page:

```
<asp:SiteMapPath ID="SiteMapPath1" Runat="server" />
```

This will use the default provider and the current URL location to format a list of links to parent pages.

Adding a menu or tree view menu requires a `SiteMapDataSource` control, but again this can be very simple:

```
<asp:SiteMapDataSource ID="SiteMapDataSource1" Runat="server" />
```

When using a custom provider, the only difference is that you can supply the provider ID via a `SiteMapProvider` attribute. You can also remove upper levels of the menu data (such as the root `Home` item) using `StartingNodeOffset`; remove just the top-level link using `ShowStartingNode="False"`;

start from the current location using `StartFromCurrentNode="True"`; and override the root node using `StartingNodeUrl`.

The data from this data source is consumed by `Menu` and `TreeView` controls simply by setting their `DataSourceID` to the ID of the `SiteMapDataSource`. Both controls include numerous styling properties and can be themed, as you see later in this chapter.

Navigation in PCSDemoSite

The site map for PCSDemoSite is as follows:

```
<?xml version="1.0" encoding="utf-8" ?>
<siteMap>
  <siteMapNode url="~/Default.aspx" title="Home">
    <siteMapNode url="~/About/Default.aspx" title="About" />
    <siteMapNode url="~/MRB/Default.aspx" title="Meeting Room Booker"
      roles="RegisteredUser,SiteAdministrator" />
    <siteMapNode url="~/Configuration/Default.aspx" title="Configuration"
      roles="RegisteredUser,SiteAdministrator">
      <siteMapNode url="~/Configuration/Themes/Default.aspx" title="Themes"
        roles="RegisteredUser,SiteAdministrator"/>
    </siteMapNode>
    <siteMapNode url="~/Users/Default.aspx" title="User Area"
      roles="SiteAdministrator" />
    <siteMapNode url="~/Login.aspx" title="Login Details" />
  </siteMapNode>
</siteMap>
```

The PCSDemoSite Web site uses a custom provider to obtain information from `Web.sitemap` — which is necessary because the default provider ignores the `roles` attributes. The provider is defined in the `Web.config` file for the Web site as follows:

```
<configuration xmlns="http://schemas.microsoft.com/.NetConfiguration/v2.0">
  ...
  <system.Web>
    ...
    <siteMap defaultProvider="CustomProvider">
      <providers>
        <add name="CustomProvider"
          description="SiteMap provider which reads in .sitemap XML files."
          type="System.Web.XmlSiteMapProvider, System.Web, Version=2.0.3600.0,
              Culture=neutral, PublicKeyToken=b03f5f7f11d50a3a"
          siteMapFile="Web.sitemap" securityTrimmingEnabled="true" />
      </providers>
    </siteMap>
    ...
```

The only difference between this and the default provider is the addition of `securityTrimmingEnabled="true"`, which instructs the provider to supply data for just those nodes that this current user is allowed to see. This visibility is determined by the role membership of the user, as you see in the next section.

The `MasterPage.master` page in PCSDemoSite includes `SiteMapPath` and `TreeView` navigation displays along with a data source, as follows:

```
<div id="header">
  <h1><asp:literal ID="Literal1" runat="server"
    text="<%$ AppSettings:SiteTitle %>" /></h1>
```

```
        <asp:SiteMapPath ID="SiteMapPath1" Runat="server"
          CssClass="breadcrumb" />
      </div>
      <div id="nav">
        <div class="navTree">
          <asp:TreeView ID="TreeView1" runat="server"
            DataSourceID="SiteMapDataSource1" ShowLines="True" />
        </div>
        <br />
        <br />
        <asp:LoginView ID="LoginView1" Runat="server">
          <LoggedInTemplate>
            You are currently logged in as
            <b><asp:LoginName ID="LoginName1" Runat="server" /></b>.
            <asp:LoginStatus ID="LoginStatus1" Runat="server" />
          </LoggedInTemplate>
        </asp:LoginView>
      </div>
      <div id="body">
        <asp:ContentPlaceHolder ID="ContentPlaceHolder1" Runat="server" />
      </div>
    </form>
    <asp:SiteMapDataSource ID="SiteMapDataSource1" Runat="server" />
```

The only point to note here is that CSS classes are supplied for both `SiteMapPath` and `TreeView`, to facilitate theming (discussed later in this chapter).

Security

Security and user management have often been seen as quite complicated to implement in Web sites, and with good reason. You have to consider a number of factors, including:

- What sort of user management system will I implement? Will users map to Windows user accounts, or will I implement something independent?
- How do I implement a login system?
- Do I let users register on the site, and if so, how?
- How do I let some users see and do only some things, while supplying other users with additional privileges?
- What happens in the case of forgotten passwords?

With ASP.NET 2.0, you have a whole suite of tools at your disposal for dealing with questions such as these, and it can in fact take only a matter of minutes to implement a user system on your site. You have three types of authentication at your disposal:

- Windows Authentication, whereby users have Windows accounts, typically used with intranet sites or WAN portals
- Forms Authentication, whereby the Web site maintains its own list of users and handles its own authentication
- Passport Authentication, whereby Microsoft provides a centralized authentication service for you to use

A full discussion of security in ASP.NET would take up at least a full chapter, but we provide a brief look in this section to give you an idea of how things work. You will concentrate on Forms Authentication here, because it is the most versatile system and very quick to get up and running.

The quickest way to implement Forms Authentication is via the Website ⇨ ASP.NET Configuration tool, which you saw briefly in the previous chapter. This tool has a Security tab, and on it a security wizard. This wizard lets you choose an authentication type, add roles, add users, and secure areas of your site.

Adding Forms Authentication Using the Security Wizard

For the purposes of this explanation, create a new Web site called `PCSAuthenticationDemo` in the directory `C:\ProCSharp\Chapter38\`. Once you create the site, open the Web site ⇨ ASP.NET Configuration tool. Navigate to the Security tab and click the "Use the security Setup Wizard to configure security step by step." link. Click Next on the first step after reading the information there. On the second step, select "From the internet," as shown in Figure 38-9.

Click Next, and then Next again after confirming that you will be using the default "Advanced provider settings" provider to store security information. This provider information is configurable via the Provider tab, where you can choose to store information elsewhere, such as in an SQL Server database, but an Access database is fine for illustrative purposes.

Check the "Enable roles for this Web site." option, as shown in Figure 38-10, and click Next.

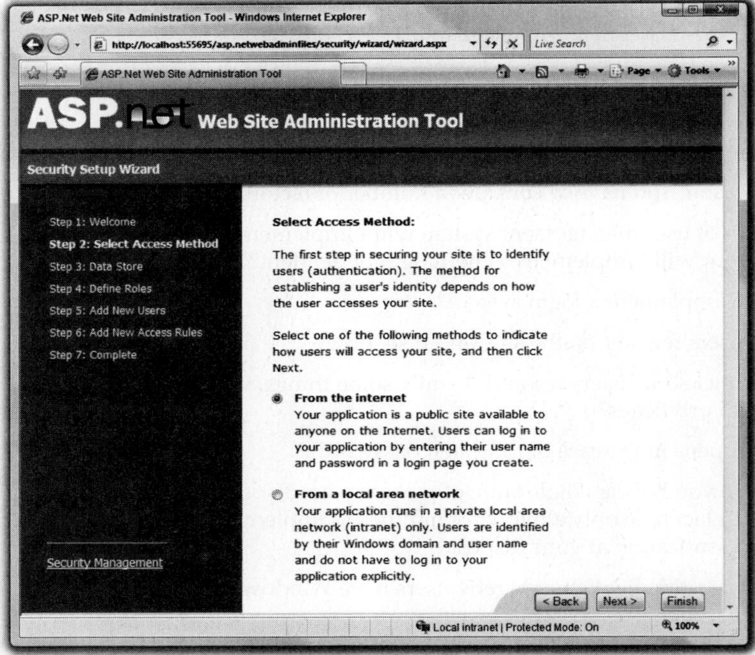

Figure 38-9

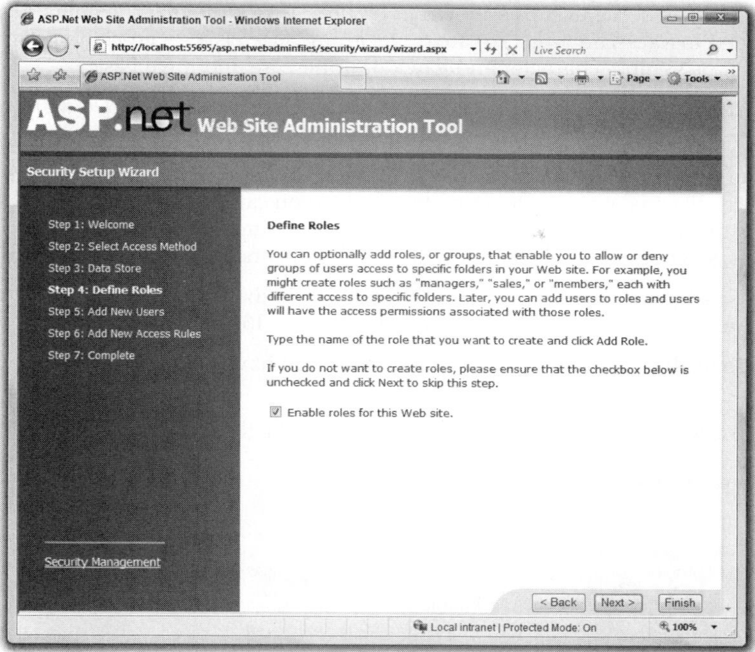

Figure 38-10

Then, add some roles, as shown in Figure 38-11.

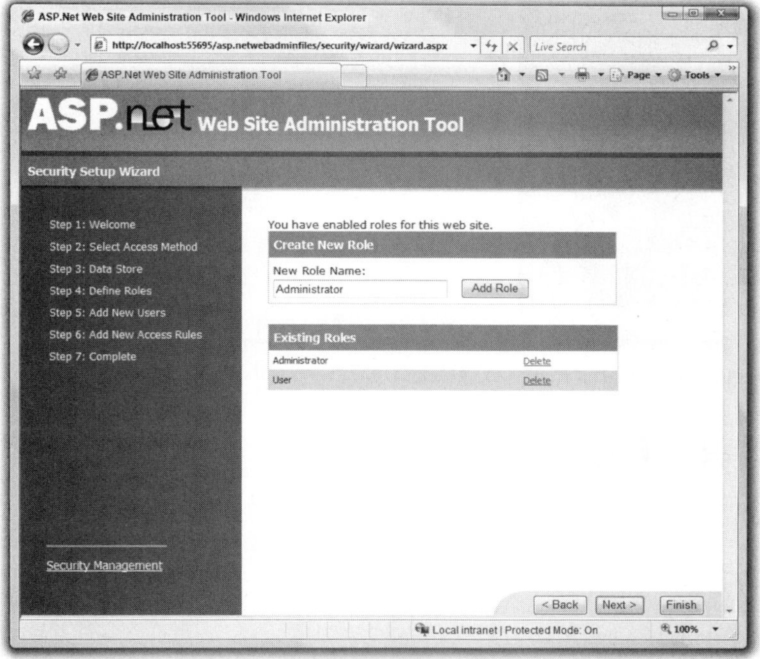

Figure 38-11

Click Next and then add some users, as shown in Figure 38-12. Note that the default security rules for passwords (defined in `machine.config`) are quite strong; there is a seven-character minimum, including at least one symbol character and a mix of uppercase and lowercase.

In the downloadable code for this chapter, two users are added in this example. The usernames are User and Administrator, and the password for both users is Pa$$w0rd.

After clicking Next again, you can define access rules for your site. By default, all users and roles will have access to all areas of your site. From this dialog you can restrict areas by role, by user, or for anonymous users. You can do this for each directory in your site because this is achieved via `Web.config` files in directories, as you see shortly. For now, skip this step, and complete authentication setup.

The last step is to assign users to roles, which you can do via the "Manage users" link on the Security tab. From here you can edit user roles, as shown in Figure 38-13.

Once you have done all this, you are pretty much there. You have a user system in place, as well as roles and users.

Now you have to add a few controls to your Web site to make things work.

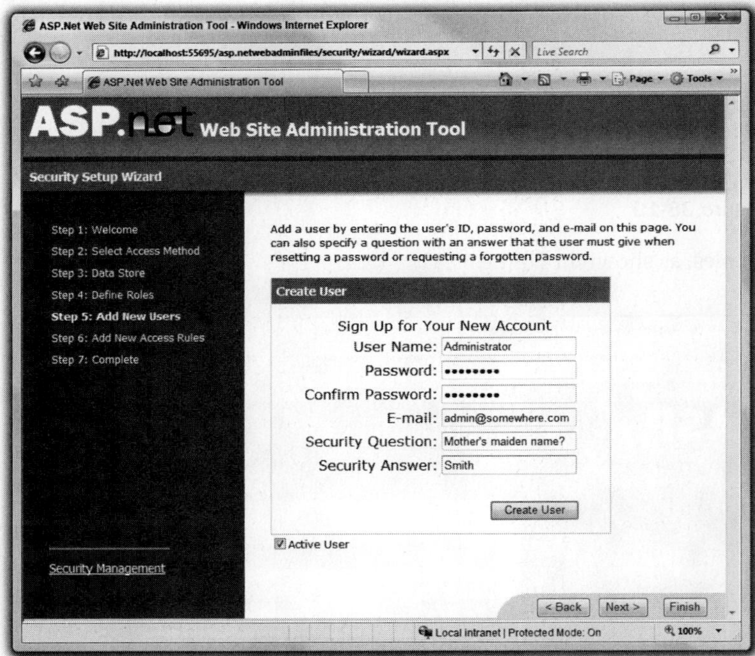

Figure 38-12

Implementing a Login System

If you open `Web.config` after running the security wizard you will see that it has been modified with the following content:

```
<roleManager enabled="true" />
```

and:

```
<authentication mode="Forms" />
```

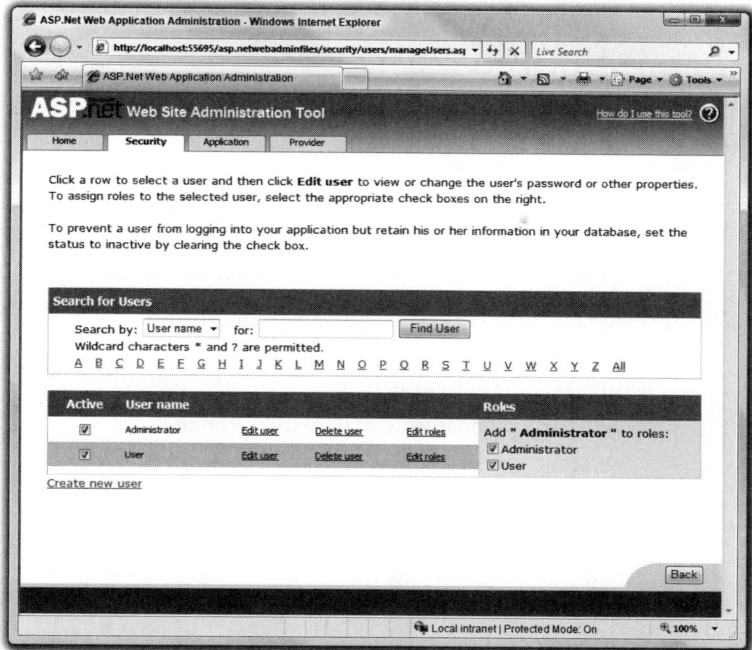

Figure 38-13

This doesn't seem like a lot for the work that you have put in, but remember that a lot of information is stored in an SQL Express database, which you can see in the `App_Data` directory, called `ASPNETDB.MDF`. You can inspect the data that has been stored in this file using any standard database management tool, including Visual Studio. You can even add users and roles directly to this database, if you are careful.

By default, logging in is achieved via a page called `Login.aspx` in the root of your Web site. If users attempt to navigate to a location that they don't have permission to access, they will automatically be redirected to this page and returned to the desired location after successfully logging in.

Add a Web Form called `Login.aspx` to the PCSAuthenticationDemo site and drag a `Login` control onto the form from the toolbox.

This is all you need to do to enable users to log in to your Web site. Open the site in a browser, and navigate to `Login.aspx`; then enter the details for a user you added in the wizard, as shown in Figure 38-14.

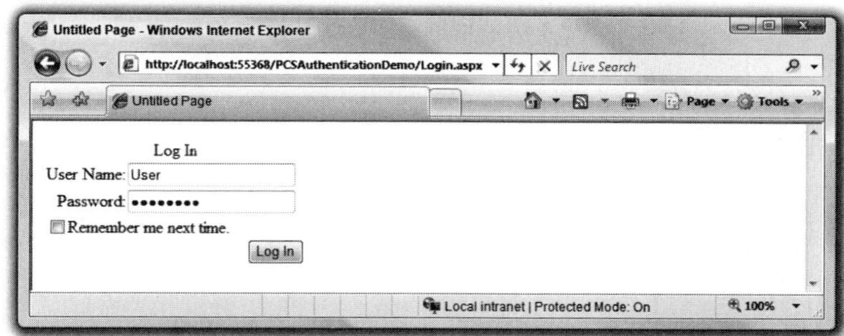

Figure 38-14

Once you have logged in, you will be sent back to `Default.aspx`, currently a blank page.

Login Web Server Controls

The Login section of the toolbox contains several controls, as shown in the following table.

Control	Description
`Login`	As you have seen, this control allows users to log in to your Web site. Most of the properties of this control are for styling the supplied template. You can also use `DestinationPageUrl` to force redirection to a specific location on logging in, and `VisibleWhenLoggedIn` to determine whether the control is visible to logged-in users. And, you can use various text properties such as `CreateUserText` to output helpful messages to users.
`LoginView`	This control enables you to display content that varies depending on whether users are logged in, or what roles users are in. You can put content in `<AnonymousTemplate>` and `<LoggedInTemplate>`, as well as `<RoleGroups>` to control the output of this control.
`PasswordRecovery`	This control enables users to have their password mailed to them, and it can use the password recovery question defined for a user. Again, most properties are for display formatting, but there are properties such as `MailDefinition-Subject` for configuring the email to be sent to the user's address, and `SuccessPageUrl` to redirect the users after they have requested a password.
`LoginStatus`	This control displays a Login or Logout link, with customizable text and images, to users depending on whether they are logged in.
`LoginName`	This control outputs the username for the currently logged-in user.
`CreateUserWizard`	This control displays a form that users can use to register with your site and to be added to the user list. As with other login controls, there are a large number of properties relating to layout formatting, but the default is perfectly serviceable.
`ChangePassword`	This control enables users to change their passwords. There are three fields, for the old password, the new password, and the confirmation. There are many styling properties.

You see some of these in action in PCSDemoSite shortly.

Securing Directories

One final thing to discuss is how to restrict access to directories. You can do this via the Site Configuration tool, as noted earlier, but it's actually quite easy to do this yourself.

Add a directory to PCSAuthenticationDemo called `SecureDirectory`, as well as a `Default.aspx` Web page in this directory, and a new `Web.config` file. Replace the contents of `Web.config` with the following:

```
<?xml version="1.0" ?>
<configuration>
  <system.web>
    <authorization>
      <deny users="?" />
      <allow roles="Administrator" />
      <deny roles="User" />
    </authorization>
  </system.web>
</configuration>
```

The <authorization> element can contain one or more <deny> or <allow> elements representing permission rules, each of which can have a users or roles attribute saying what the rule applies to. The rules are applied from top to bottom, so more specific rules should generally be near the top if the membership of rules overlaps. In this example, ? refers to anonymous users, who will be denied access to this directory, along with users in the User role. Note that users in both the User and Administrator roles will be allowed access only if the <allow> rule shown here comes before the <deny> rule for the User role — all of a user's roles are taken into account, but the rule order still applies.

Now when you log in to the Web site and try to navigate to SecureDirectory/Default.aspx, you will be permitted only if you are in the Admin role. Other users, or users that are not authenticated, will be redirected to the login page.

Security in PCSDemoSite

The PCSDemoSite site uses the Login control that you have already seen, as well as a LoginView control, a LoginStatus control, a LoginName control, a PasswordRecovery control, and a ChangePassword control.

One difference is that a Guest role is included, and one consequence of this is that guest users should not be able to change their password — an ideal use for LoginView, as illustrated by Login.aspx:

```
<asp:Content ID="Content1" ContentPlaceHolderID="ContentPlaceHolder1"
  Runat="server">
  <h2>Login Page</h2>
  <asp:LoginView ID="LoginView1" Runat="server">
    <RoleGroups>
      <asp:RoleGroup Roles="Guest">
        <ContentTemplate>
          You are currently logged in as <b>
          <asp:LoginName ID="LoginName1" Runat="server" /></b>.
          <br />
          <br />
          <asp:LoginStatus ID="LoginStatus1" Runat="server" />
        </ContentTemplate>
      </asp:RoleGroup>
      <asp:RoleGroup Roles="RegisteredUser,SiteAdministrator">
        <ContentTemplate>
          You are currently logged in as <b>
          <asp:LoginName ID="LoginName2" Runat="server" /></b>.
          <br />
          <br />
          <asp:ChangePassword ID="ChangePassword1" Runat="server">
          </asp:ChangePassword>
          <br />
```

(continued)

(continued)

```
          <br />
          <asp:LoginStatus ID="LoginStatus2" Runat="server" />
        </ContentTemplate>
      </asp:RoleGroup>
    </RoleGroups>
    <AnonymousTemplate>
      <asp:Login ID="Login1" Runat="server">
      </asp:Login>
      <asp:PasswordRecovery ID="PasswordRecovery1" Runat="Server" />
    </AnonymousTemplate>
  </asp:LoginView>
</asp:Content>
```

The view here displays one of several pages:

- For anonymous users a `Login` and a `PasswordRecovery` control are shown.
- For `Guest` users `LoginName` and `LoginStatus` controls are shown, giving the logged-in username and the facility to log out if required.
- For `RegisteredUser` and `SiteAdministrator` users `LoginName`, `LoginStatus`, and `ChangePassword` controls are shown.

The site also includes various `Web.config` files in various directories to limit access, and the navigation is also restricted by role.

Note that the configured users for the site are shown on the About page, or you can add your own. The users in the base site (and their passwords) are User1 (User1!!), Admin (Admin!!), and Guest (Guest!!).

One point to note here is that while the root of the site denies anonymous users, the Themes directory (described in the next section) overrides this setting by permitting anonymous users. This is necessary because without this, anonymous users would see a themeless site, because the theme files would not be accessible. In addition, the full security specification in the root `Web.config` file is as follows:

```
<configuration xmlns="http://schemas.microsoft.com/.NetConfiguration/v2.0">
  ...
  <location path="StyleSheet.css">
    <system.web>
      <authorization>
        <allow users="?"/>
      </authorization>
    </system.web>
  </location>
  <system.web>
    <authorization>
      <deny users="?" />
    </authorization>
    ...
  </system.web>
</configuration>
```

Here a `<location>` element is used to override the default setting for a specific file specified using a `path` attribute, in this case for the file `StyleSheet.css`. `<location>` elements can be used to apply any `<system.web>` settings to specific files or directories, and can be used to centralize all directory-specific settings in one place, if desired (as an alternative to multiple `Web.config` files). In the preceding code, permission is given for anonymous users to access the root style sheet for the Web site, which is necessary because this file defines the layout of the `<div>` elements in the master page. Without this, the HTML shown on the login page for anonymous users would be difficult to read.

Another point to note is in the code-behind file for the meeting room booker user control, in the `Page_Load()` event handler:

```
void Page_Load(object sender, EventArgs e)
{
   if (!this.IsPostBack)
   {
      nameBox.Text = Context.User.Identity.Name;
      DateTime trialDate = DateTime.Now;
      calendar.SelectedDate = GetFreeDate(trialDate);
   }
}
```

Here the username is extracted from the current context. Note that in your code-behind files you will probably also use `Context.User.IsInRole()` frequently to check access.

Themes

By combining ASP.NET pages with master pages and CSS style sheets, you can go a long way in separating form and function, whereby the look and feel of your pages are defined separately from their operation. With themes you can take this a step further and dynamically apply this look and feel from one of several themes that you supply yourself.

A theme consists of the following:

- A name for the theme
- An optional CSS style sheet
- Skin (`.skin`) files allowing individual control types to be styled

These can be applied to pages in two different ways — as a `Theme` or as a `StyleSheetTheme`:

- **Theme** — All skin properties are applied to controls, overriding any properties that the controls on the page may already have.
- **StyleSheetTheme** — Existing control properties take precedence over properties defined in skin files.

CSS style sheets work in the same way whichever method is used because they are applied in the standard CSS way.

Applying Themes to Pages

You can apply a theme to a page in several ways, declaratively or programmatically. The simplest declarative way to apply a theme is via the `<%@ Page %>` directive, using the `Theme` or `StyleSheetTheme` attribute:

```
<%@ Page Theme="myTheme" ... %>
```

or:

```
<%@ Page StyleSheetTheme="myTheme" ... %>
```

Here `myTheme` is the name defined for the theme.

Alternatively, you can specify a theme to use for all pages in a site, using an entry in the `Web.config` file for your Web site:

```
<configuration xmlns="http://schemas.microsoft.com/.NetConfiguration/v2.0">
  <system.web>
    <pages Theme="myTheme" />
  </system.web>
</configuration>
```

Again, you can use `Theme` or `StyleSheetTheme` here. You can also be more specific by using `<location>` elements to override this setting for individual pages or directories, in the same way as this element was used in the previous section for security information.

Programmatically, you can apply themes in the code-behind file for a page. There is only one place where you are allowed to do this — in the `Page_PreInit()` event handler, which is triggered very early on in the life cycle of the page. In this event, you simply have to set the `Page.Theme` or `Page.StyleSheetTheme` property to the name of the theme you want to apply, for example:

```
protected override void OnPreInit(EventArgs e)
{
  Page.Theme = "myTheme";
}
```

Because you are using code to do this, you can dynamically apply a theme file from a selection of themes. This technique is used in PCSDemoSite, as you see shortly.

Defining Themes

Themes are defined in yet another of the "special" directories in ASP.NET — in this case `App_Themes`. The `App_Themes` directory can contain any number of subdirectories, one per theme, where the name of the subdirectory defines the name of the theme.

Defining a theme involves putting the required files for the theme in the theme subdirectory. For CSS style sheets, you don't have to worry about the file name; the theme system simply looks for a file with a `.css` extension. Similarly, `.skin` files can have any file name, although it is recommended that you use multiple `.skin` files, one for each control type you want to skin, and each named after the control it skins.

Skin files contain server control definitions in exactly the same format as you would use in standard ASP.NET pages. The difference is that the controls in skin files are never added to your page; they are simply used to extract properties. A definition for a button skin, typically placed in a file called `Button.skin`, might be as follows:

```
<asp:Button Runat="server" BackColor="#444499" BorderColor="#000000"
  ForeColor="#ccccff" />
```

This skin is actually taken from the `DefaultTheme` theme in PCSDemoSite, and is responsible for the look of the button on the Meeting Room Booker page you saw earlier in this chapter.

When you create a skin for a control type in this way you don't use an `ID` property.

Themes in PCSDemoSite

The PCSDemoSite Web site includes three themes that you can select on the `/Configuration/Themes/Default.aspx` page — as long as you are logged in as a member of the `RegisteredUser` or `SiteAdministrator` role. This page is shown in Figure 38-15.

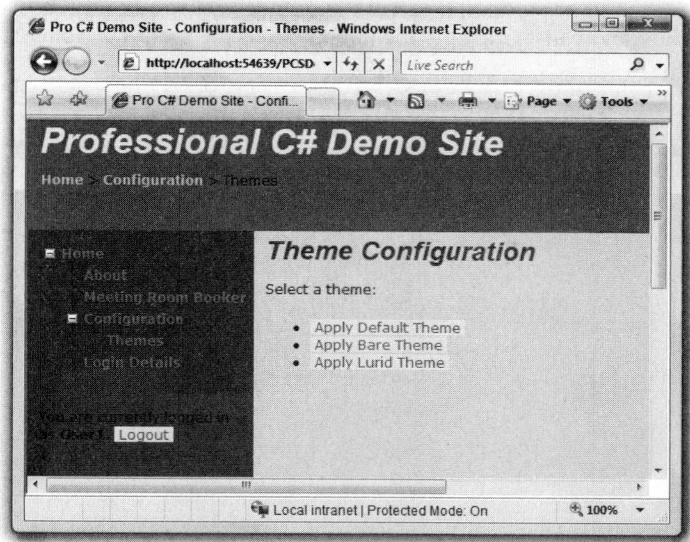

Figure 38-15

The theme in use here is `DefaultTheme`, but you can select from the other options on this page. Figure 38-16 shows the `BareTheme` theme.

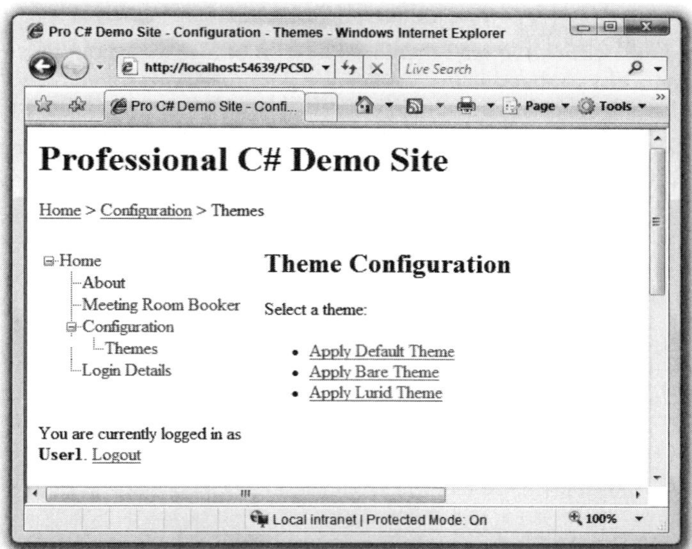

Figure 38-16

This sort of theme is useful in, for example, printable versions of Web pages. The `BareTheme` directory actually consists of no files at all — the only file in use here is the root `StyleSheet.css` style sheet.

Figure 38-17 shows the `LuridTheme` theme.

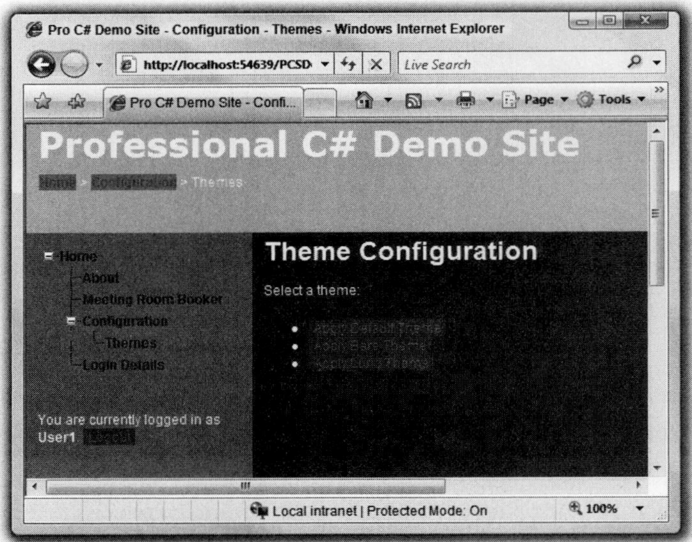

Figure 38-17

This brightly colored and difficult to read theme is just a bit of fun, really, but it does show how the look of a site can be dramatically changed using themes. On a more serious note, themes similar to this can be used to provide high-contrast or large-text versions of Web sites for accessibility purposes.

In PCSDemoSite, the currently selected theme is stored in session state, so the theme is maintained when you navigate around the site. The code-behind file for `/Configuration/Themes/Default.aspx` is as follows:

```
public partial class _Default : MyPageBase
{
   private void ApplyTheme(string themeName)
   {
      if (Session["SessionTheme"] != null)
      {
         Session.Remove("SessionTheme");
      }
      Session.Add("SessionTheme", themeName);
      Response.Redirect("~/Configuration/Themes", true);
   }

   void applyDefaultTheme_Click(object sender, EventArgs e)
```

```
      {
         ApplyTheme("DefaultTheme");
      }

      void applyBareTheme_Click(object sender, EventArgs e)
      {
         ApplyTheme("BareTheme");
      }

      void applyLuridTheme_Click(object sender, EventArgs e)
      {
         ApplyTheme("LuridTheme");
      }
   }
```

The key functionality here is in `ApplyTheme()`, which puts the name of the selected theme into session state, using the key `SessionTheme`. It also checks to see if there is already an entry here, and if so, removes it.

As mentioned earlier, themes must be applied in the `Page_PreInit()` event handler. This isn't accessible from the master page that all pages use, so if you want to apply a selected theme to all pages, you are left with two options:

- Override the `Page_PreInit()` event handler in all pages where you want themes to be applied.
- Provide a common base class for all pages where you want themes to be applied, and override the `Page_PreInit()` event handler in this base class.

PCSDemoSite uses the second option, with a common page base class provided in `Code/MyPageBase.cs`:

```
public class MyPageBase : Page
{
   protected override void OnPreInit(EventArgs e)
   {
      // theming
      if (Session["SessionTheme"] != null)
      {
         Page.Theme = Session["SessionTheme"] as string;
      }
      else
      {
         Page.Theme = "DefaultTheme";
      }

      // base call
      base.OnPreInit(e);
   }
}
```

This event handler checks the session state for an entry in `SessionTheme` and applies the selected theme if there is one; otherwise `DefaultTheme` is used.

Note also that this class inherits from the usual page base class `Page`. This is necessary because, otherwise, the page wouldn't function as an ASP.NET Web page.

For this to work, it is also necessary to specify this base class for all Web pages. There are several ways of doing this, the most obvious being either in the `<@ Page %>` directive for a page or in the code behind a page. The former strategy is fine for simple pages but precludes the use of custom code behind for a page, as the page will no longer use the code in its own code-behind file. The other alternative is to change the class that the page inherits from in the code-behind file. By default, new pages inherit from `Page`, but you can change this. In the code-behind file for the theme selection page shown earlier, you may have noticed the following code:

```
public partial class _Default : MyPageBase
{
    ...
}
```

Here `MyPageBase` is specified as the base of the `Default` class, and thus the method override in `MyPageBase.cs` is used.

Web Parts

ASP.NET contains a group of server controls known as Web Parts, which are designed to enable users to personalize Web pages. You may have seen this in action in, for example, SharePoint-based Web sites and the MSN home page `http://www.msn.com/`. When you use Web Parts, the resultant functionality is as follows:

- Users are presented with a default page layout that you supply. This layout consists of a number of component Web Parts, each of which has a title and content.
- Users can change the position of the Web Parts on a page.
- Users can customize the appearance of Web Parts on a page or remove them from the page completely.
- Users can be supplied with a catalog of Web Parts that they can add to the page.
- Users can export Web Parts from a page, and then import them on a different page or site.
- Connections can exist between Web Parts. For example, the content displayed in a Web Part could be a graphical representation of the content displayed in another Web Part.
- Any changes that users make persist between site visits.

ASP.NET supplies a complete framework for implanting Web Parts functionality, including management and editing controls.

The use of Web Parts is a complex topic, and this section does not describe all available functionality or list all of the properties and methods that the Web Part components supply. However, you do see enough to get a flavor of Web Parts and to understand the basic functionality that is possible.

Web Parts Application Components

The Web Parts section of the toolbox contains 13 controls, as shown in Figure 38-18 (note that `Pointer` is not a control).

These controls are described in the following table. The table also introduces some of the key concepts for Web Parts pages.

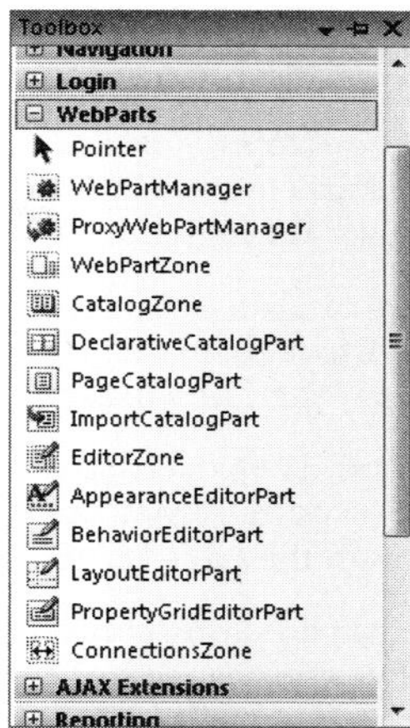

Figure 38-18

Control	Description
`WebPartManager`	Every page that uses Web Parts must have one (and only one) instance of the `WebPartManager` control. You can place it on a master page if you wish, although if you do you should use the master page only when you want to use Web Parts on a page. This control is responsible for the majority of Web Parts functionality, which it supplies without much intervention. You may not need to do much more than place it on a Web page, depending on the functionality you require. For more advanced functionality, you can use the large number of properties and events that this control exposes.
`ProxyWebPartManager`	If you place the `WebPartManager` control on a master page, it can be difficult to configure it on individual pages — and impossible to do so declaratively. This is particularly relevant for the definition of static connections between Web Parts. The `ProxyWebPartManager` control enables you to define static connections declaratively on a Web page, which circumvents the problem of not being able to have two `WebPartManager` controls on the same page.
`WebPartZone`	The `WebPartZone` control is used to define a region of a page that can contain Web Parts. You will typically use more than one of these controls on a page. For example, you might use three of them in a three-column layout on a page. Users can move Web Parts between `WebPartZone` regions or reposition them within a single `WebPartZone`.
`CatalogZone`	The `CatalogZone` control enables users to add Web Parts to a page. This control contains controls that derive from `CatalogPart`, of which three are supplied for you — the next three entries in this table describe these controls. Whether the `CatalogZone` control and the controls it contains are visible depends on the current display mode set by `WebPartManager`.

Control	Description
DeclarativeCatalogPart	The DeclarativeCatalogPart control enables you to define Web Part controls inline. These controls will then be available to the user through the CatalogZone control.
PageCatalogPart	Users can remove (close) Web Parts that are displayed on a page. To retrieve them, the PageCatalogPart control provides a list of closed Web Parts that can be replaced on the page.
ImportCatalogPart	The ImportCatalogPart control enables Web Parts that have been exported from a page to be imported to another page through the CatalogPart interface.
EditorZone	The EditorZone control contains controls that enable users to edit various aspects of Web Part display and behavior, depending on what controls it contains. It can contain controls that derive from EditorPart, including the four that are listed in the next four rows of this table. As with CatalogZone, the display of this control depends on the current display mode.
AppearanceEditorPart	This control enables users to modify the look and size of Web Part controls, as well as to hide them.
BehaviorEditorPart	This control enables users to configure the behavior of Web Parts by using a variety of properties that control, for example, whether a Web Part can be closed or what URL the title of a Web Part links to.
LayoutEditorPart	This control enables users to change layout properties of a Web Part, such as what zone it is contained in and whether it is displayed in a minimized state.
PropertyGridEditorPart	This is the most general Web Part editor control and enables you to define properties that can be edited for custom Web Part controls. Users can then edit these properties.
ConnectionsZone	This control enables users to create connections between Web Parts that expose connection functionality. Unlike CatalogZone and EditorZone, there are no controls to place inside this control. The user interface that this control generates depends on the controls on the page that are available for connections. The visibility of this control is dependant on the display mode.

You may notice that this list of controls does not include any Web Parts. This is because you create these yourself. Any control that you put into a WebPartZone region automatically becomes a Web Part — including (most important) user controls. By using user controls, you can group together other controls to provide the user interface and functionality of a Web Part control.

Web Parts Example

To illustrate the functionality of Web Parts, you can look at the example in the downloadable code for this chapter, PCSWebParts. This example uses the same security database as the PCSAuthenticationDemo example. It has two users with usernames of User and Administrator and a password of Pa$$w0rd for both. You can log in as a user, manipulate the Web Parts on the page, log out, log in as the other user, and manipulate the Web Parts in a completely different way. The personalization for both users is retained between site visits.

Once you have logged in to the site, the initial display (with User logged in) is as shown in Figure 38-19.

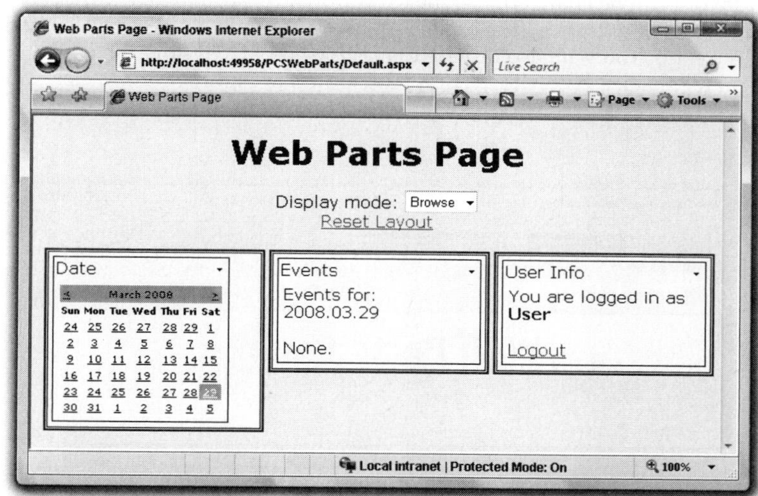

Figure 38-19

This page contains the following controls:

- A `WebPartManager` control (which doesn't have a visual component).
- Three `WebPartZone` controls.
- Three Web Parts (Date, Events, and User Info), one in each `WebPartZone`. Two of the Web Parts are connected by a static connection — if you change the date in Date, the date displayed in Events updates.
- A drop-down list for changing the display mode. This list doesn't contain all of the possible display modes, just the available ones. The available modes are obtained from the `WebPartManager` control, as you see shortly. The modes listed are:
  - **Browse** — This mode is the default and allows you to view and use Web Parts. In this mode, each Web Part can be minimized or closed by using the drop-down menu accessible in the top right of each Web Part.
  - **Design** — In this mode, you can reposition Web Parts.
  - **Edit** — In this mode, you can edit Web Part properties. An additional item in the drop-down menu for each Web Part becomes available: Edit.
  - **Catalog** — In this mode, you can add new Web Parts to the page.
- A link to reset the Web Part layout to the default (for the current user only).

- ❑ An `EditorZone` control (visible only in Edit mode).
- ❑ A `CatalogZone` control (visible only in Catalog mode).
- ❑ One additional Web Part in the catalog that you can add to the page.

Each of the Web Parts is defined in a user control.

To illustrate how layout can be changed, use the drop-down list to change the display mode to Design. You will notice that each `WebPartZone` is then labeled with an `ID` value (`LeftZone`, `CenterZone`, and `RightZone`, respectively). You will also be able to move Web Parts simply by dragging their titles — and will even see visual feedback as you drag. This is illustrated in Figure 38-20, which shows the Date Web Part being moved.

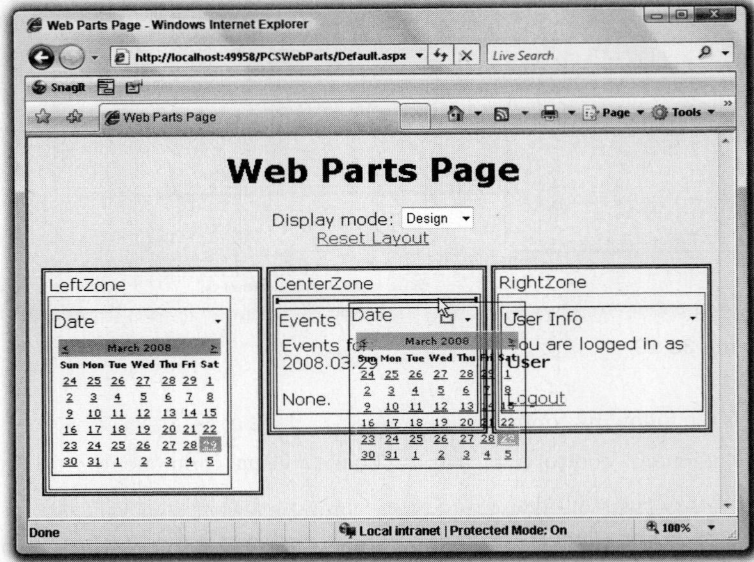

Figure 38-20

Next, try adding a new Web Part from the catalog. Change the display mode to Catalog, and you will notice that the `CatalogZone` control becomes visible at the bottom of the page. Click the Declarative Catalog link, and you will be able to add a `Links` control to the page, as shown in Figure 38-21.

Notice that there is also a Page Catalog link here. If you close a Web Part by using the drop-down menu for the part, you will find it here — it's not completely deleted, merely hidden.

Next, change the display mode to Edit and select the Edit item from the drop-down list for a Web Part, as shown in Figure 38-22.

When you select this menu option, you will open the `EditorZone` control. In the example, this control contains an `AppearanceEditorPart` control, as shown in Figure 38-23.

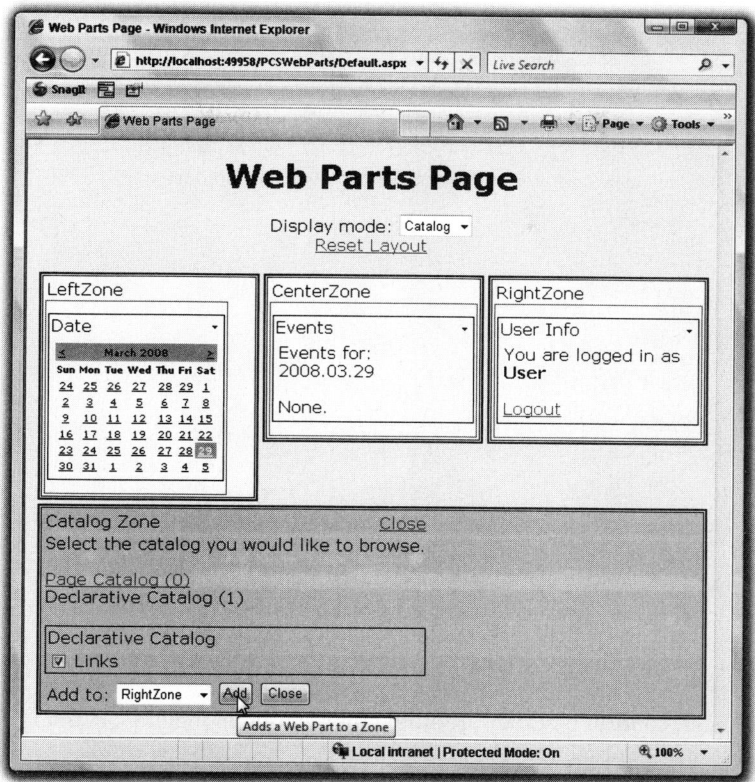

Figure 38-21

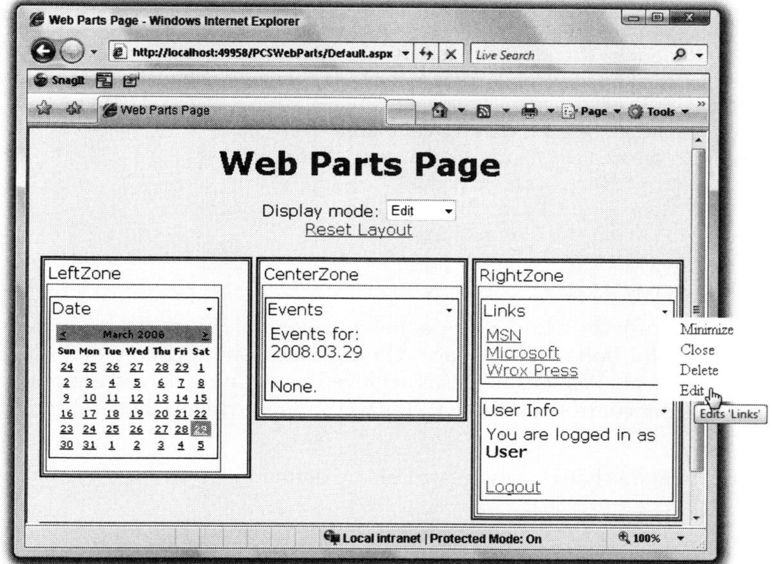

Figure 38-22

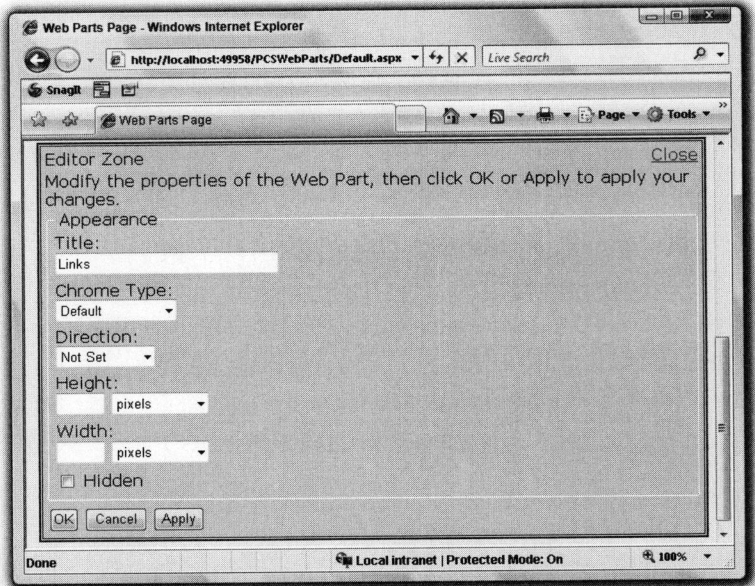

Figure 38-23

You can edit and apply property values for Web Parts by using this interface.

After making changes, confirm that they are stored for the user by logging off and logging in as a different user, and then switching back to the first user.

Now, you might think that this functionality requires quite a lot of code. In fact, the code in this example is remarkably simple. Look at the code for the Web Parts page. The `<form>` element starts with a `WebPartManager` control:

```
<form id="form1" runat="server">
  <asp:WebPartManager ID="WebPartManager1" runat="server"
    OnDisplayModeChanged="WebPartManager1_DisplayModeChanged">
    <StaticConnections>
      <asp:WebPartConnection ID="dateConnection"
        ConsumerConnectionPointID="DateConsumer"
        ConsumerID="EventListControl1"
        ProviderConnectionPointID="DateProvider"
        ProviderID="DateSelectorControl1" />
    </StaticConnections>
  </asp:WebPartManager>
```

There is an event handler for the `DisplayModeChanged` event of this control, which is used to show or hide the editor `<div>` at the bottom of the page. There is also a specification for a static connection between the Date and Events Web Parts. This is achieved by defining named endpoints for the connection in the two user controls for these Web Parts and referring to those endpoints here. You see the code for this shortly.

Next, the title, display mode changer, and reset link are defined:

```
<div class="mainDiv">
  <h1>Web Parts Page</h1>
  Display mode:
```

```
<asp:DropDownList ID="displayMode" runat="server" AutoPostBack="True"
  OnSelectedIndexChanged="displayMode_SelectedIndexChanged" />
<br />
<asp:LinkButton runat="server" ID="resetButton" Text="Reset Layout"
  OnClick="resetButton_Click" />
<br />
<br />
```

The display mode drop-down list is populated in the `Page_Load()` event handler, by using the `WebPartManager1.SupportedDisplayModes` property. The reset button uses the `WebPartManager1.Personalization.ResetPersonalizationState()` method to reset the personalization state for the current user.

Next come the three `WebPartZone` controls, each of which contains a user control that is loaded as a Web Part:

```
<div class="innerDiv">
  <div class="zoneDiv">
    <asp:WebPartZone ID="LeftZone" runat="server">
      <ZoneTemplate>
        <uc1:DateSelectorControl ID="DateSelectorControl1" runat="server"
          title="Date" />
      </ZoneTemplate>
    </asp:WebPartZone>
  </div>
  <div class="zoneDiv">
    <asp:WebPartZone ID="CenterZone" runat="server">
      <ZoneTemplate>
        <uc2:EventListControl ID="EventListControl1" runat="server"
          title="Events" />
      </ZoneTemplate>
    </asp:WebPartZone>
  </div>
  <div class="zoneDiv">
    <asp:WebPartZone ID="RightZone" runat="server">
      <ZoneTemplate>
        <uc4:UserInfo ID="UserInfo1" runat="server" title="User Info" />
      </ZoneTemplate>
    </asp:WebPartZone>
  </div>
```

And, finally you have the `EditorZone` and `CatalogZone` controls, containing an `AppearanceEditor` control and `PageCatalogPart` and `DeclarativeCatalogPart` controls, respectively:

```
<asp:PlaceHolder runat="server" ID="editorPH" Visible="false">
  <div class="footerDiv">
    <asp:EditorZone ID="EditorZone1" runat="server">
      <ZoneTemplate>
        <asp:AppearanceEditorPart ID="AppearanceEditorPart1"
          runat="server" />
      </ZoneTemplate>
    </asp:EditorZone>
    <asp:CatalogZone ID="CatalogZone1" runat="server">
      <ZoneTemplate>
        <asp:PageCatalogPart ID="PageCatalogPart1" runat="server" />
```

(continued)

(continued)

```
                <asp:DeclarativeCatalogPart ID="DeclarativeCatalogPart1"
                  runat="server">
                  <WebPartsTemplate>
                    <uc3:LinksControl ID="LinksControl1" runat="server"
                      title="Links" />
                  </WebPartsTemplate>
                </asp:DeclarativeCatalogPart>
              </ZoneTemplate>
            </asp:CatalogZone>
          </div>
        </asp:PlaceHolder>
      </div>
    </div>
  </form>
```

The `DeclarativeCatalogPart` control contains a fourth user control, which is the `Links` control that users can add to the page.

The code for the Web Parts is equally simple. The Links Web part, for example, simply contains the following code:

```
<%@ Control Language="C#" AutoEventWireup="true"
CodeFile="LinksControl.ascx.cs"
  Inherits="LinksControl" %>
<a href="http://www.msn.com/">MSN</a>
<br />
<a href="http://www.microsoft.com/">Microsoft</a>
<br />
<a href="http://www.wrox.com/">Wrox Press</a>
```

No additional markup is required to make this user control work as a Web Part. The only point to note here is that the `<uc3:LinksControl>` element for the user control has a `title` attribute — even though the user control doesn't have a `Title` property. This attribute is used by the `DeclarativeCatalogPart` control to infer a title to display for the Web Part (which you can edit at runtime with the `AppearanceEditorPart`).

The connection between the Date and Events controls is achieved by passing an interface reference from `DateSelectorControl` to `EventListControl` (the two user control classes used by these Web Parts):

```
public interface IDateProvider
{
   SelectedDatesCollection SelectedDates
   {
      get;
   }
}
```

`DateSelectorControl` supports this interface, and so can pass an instance of `IDateProvider` by using `this`. The reference is passed by an endpoint method in `DateSelectorControl`, which is decorated with the `ConnectionProvider` attribute:

```
[ConnectionProvider("Date Provider", "DateProvider")]
public IDateProvider ProvideDate()
{
   return this;
}
```

This is all that is required to mark a Web Part as a provider control. You can then reference the provider by its endpoint ID, in this case `DateProvider`.

To consume a provider, you use the `ConnectionConsumer` attribute to decorate a consumer method in `EventListControl`:

```
[ConnectionConsumer("Date Consumer", "DateConsumer")]
public void GetDate(IDateProvider provider)
{
   this.provider = provider;
   IsConnected = true;
   SetDateLabel();
}
```

This method stores a reference to the `IDateProvider` interface passed, sets a flag, and changes the label text in the control.

There is not a lot more to look at in this example. There are a few minor cosmetic sections of code, and details for the event handlers in `Page_Load()`, but nothing that you really need to see here. You can investigate further by examining the downloadable code for this chapter.

There is, however, a whole lot more to Web Parts than this. The Web Parts framework is extremely powerful and richly featured. Whole books are devoted to the subject. Hopefully, though, this section has enabled you to get an insight into Web Parts and has demystified some of their functionality.

Summary

In this chapter you looked at several more advanced techniques for creating ASP.NET pages and Web sites, and you saw these techniques in action in a demonstration Web site called PCSDemoSite.

First, you learned how to create reusable ASP.NET server controls by using C#. You saw how to create simple user controls from existing ASP.NET pages, as well as how to create custom controls from scratch. You also saw how the meeting room booker sample from the previous chapter can be reformatted as a user control.

Next, you looked at master pages, and how to provide a template for the pages of your Web site, which is another way to reuse code and simplify development. In PCSDemoSite, in the downloadable code for this chapter, you saw a master page that included navigation Web server controls to enable users to move around the site. The PCSDemoSite sample also laid the framework for themes, which are an excellent way to separate functionality from design and can be a powerful accessibility technique.

You also took a brief look at security and how you can implement forms-based authentication on your Web sites with minimal effort.

Finally, you investigated Web Parts and how to use the Web Parts server controls to put together a basic application that illustrated some of the possibilities that this technology offers.

You have only scratched the surface of what is possible in ASP.NET 2.0. For example, you can do a whole lot more with custom controls. It would have been interesting to discuss templates and data-binding, and how to create controls with this in mind. However, with the information in this chapter, you should be able to start building (and experimenting with) your own custom controls, as well as all the other techniques discussed.

In the next chapter you look at a way to make ASP.NET applications more dynamic by using Ajax techniques.

39

ASP.NET AJAX

Web application programming is subject to continuous change and improvement. In the previous two chapters, you learned how to use ASP.NET to create fully functional Web applications, and you may think that you have seen all the tools that you need to create your own Web applications. However, if you spend much time on the Internet, you may have noticed that more recent Web sites are significantly better, in terms of usability, than older Web sites. Many of today's best Web sites provide rich user interfaces that feel almost as responsive as Windows applications. They achieve this by using client-side processing, primarily through JavaScript code, and increasingly through a technology known as Ajax.

This change of direction is possible because the browsers that clients use to browse Web sites, and the computers that clients use to run browsers, have become more powerful. The current generation of Web browsers, such as Internet Explorer 7 and Firefox, also support a wide variety of standards. These standards, which include JavaScript, enable Web applications to provide functionality far in advance of what was previously possible using plain HTML. You have already seen some of this in previous chapters — for example the use of cascading style sheets (CSS) to style Web applications.

Ajax — as you will discover shortly — is not a new technology. Rather, it is a combination of standards that makes it possible to realize the rich potential functionality of current Web browsers.

Perhaps the key defining feature of Ajax-enabled Web applications is the ability for the Web browser to communicate with the Web server in out-of-band operations; this is known as asynchronous, or partial-page, postbacks. In practice, this means that the user can interact with server-side functionality and data without needing a full-page refresh. For example, when a link is followed to move to the second page of data in a table, Ajax makes it possible to refresh just the table's content rather than the entire Web page. This means that there is less traffic required across the Internet, which leads to a more responsive Web application. You will see this example in practice later in this chapter, as well as many more examples that illustrate the power of Ajax in Web applications.

You will be using Microsoft's implementation of Ajax in the code in this chapter, known as ASP.NET AJAX. This implementation takes the Ajax model and applies it to the ASP.NET framework. ASP.NET AJAX provides a number of server controls and client-side techniques that are specifically targeted at ASP.NET developers and that enable you to add Ajax functionality to your Web applications with surprisingly little effort.

This chapter is organized as follows:

- First, you learn more about Ajax and the technologies that make Ajax possible.
- Next, you learn about ASP.NET AJAX and its component parts, as well as the functionality that ASP.NET AJAX offers.
- Last, you see how to use ASP.NET AJAX in your Web applications, by using both server-side and client-side code. This coverage forms the largest part of this chapter.

What Is Ajax?

Ajax enables you to enhance the user interfaces of Web applications by means of asynchronous postbacks and dynamic client-side Web page manipulation. The term Ajax was invented by Jesse James Garrett and is shorthand for "Asynchronous JavaScript and XML."

Note that Ajax is not an acronym, which is why it is not capitalized as AJAX. However, it is capitalized in the product name ASP.NET AJAX, which is Microsoft's implementation of Ajax, as you will see in the next section of this chapter.

By definition, Ajax involves both JavaScript and XML. However, the Ajax programming requires the use of other technologies as well, which are described in the following table.

Technology	Description
HTML/XHTML	HTML (Hypertext Markup Language) is the presentation and layout language used by Web browsers to render information in a graphical user interface. In the previous two chapters, you have seen how HTML achieves this functionality and how ASP.NET generates HTML code. Extensible HTML (XHTML) is a stricter definition of HTML that uses XML structure.
CSS	CSS (cascading style sheets) is a means by which HTML elements can be styled according to rules defined in a separate style sheet. This enables you to apply styles simultaneously to multiple HTML elements and to swap styles to change the way a Web page looks without HTML modifications. CSS includes both layout and style information, so you can also use CSS to position HTML elements on a page. You have seen how to do this in the examples in previous chapters.
DOM	The DOM (Document Object Model) is a means of representing and manipulating (X)HTML code in a hierarchical structure. This enables you to access, for example, "the second column of the third row in table x" in a Web page, rather than having to locate this element using more primitive text processing.
JavaScript	JavaScript is a client-side scripting technology that enables you to execute code inside a Web browser. The syntax of JavaScript is similar to other C-based languages, including C#, and provides variables, functions, branching code, looping statements, event handlers, and other familiar programming elements. However, unlike C#, JavaScript is not strongly typed, and debugging JavaScript code can be notoriously difficult. In terms of Ajax programming, JavaScript is a key technology because it allows dynamic modifications to Web pages by way of DOM manipulation — among other functionality.

Technology	Description
XML	XML, as you have seen throughout this book, is a platform-neutral way to mark up data and is crucial to Ajax both as a way to manipulate data and as a language for communication between the client and the server.
`XMLHttpRequest`	Since Internet Explorer 5, browsers have supported the `XMLHttpRequest` API as a means of performing asynchronous communication between the client and server. This was originally introduced by Microsoft as a technology to access email stored in an Exchange server over the Internet, in a product known as Outlook Web Access. Since then, it has become the standard way to perform asynchronous communications in Web applications, and is a core technology of Ajax-enabled Web applications. Microsoft's implementation of this API is known as XMLHTTP, which communicates over what is often called the XMLHTTP protocol.

Ajax also requires server-side code to handle partial-page postbacks as well as full-page postbacks. This can include both event handlers for server-control events and Web services. Figure 39-1 shows how these technologies fit together in the Ajax Web browser model, in contrast to the "traditional" Web browser model.

Prior to Ajax, the first four technologies listed in the preceding table (HTML, CSS, the DOM, and JavaScript) were used to create what was known as Dynamic HTML (DHTML) Web applications. These applications were notable for two reasons: they provided a much better user interface, and they generally worked on only one type of Web browser.

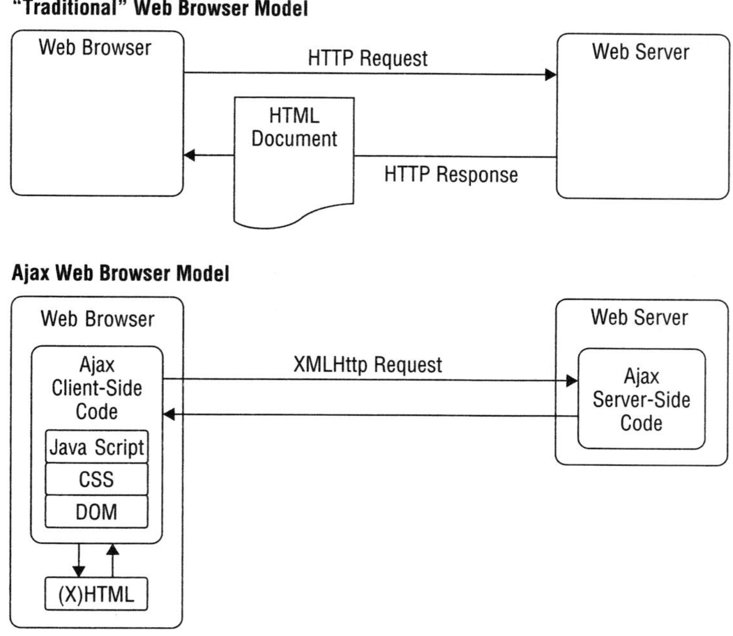

Figure 39-1

Since DHTML, standards have improved, along with the level of adherence to standards in Web browsers. However, there are still differences, and an Ajax solution must take these differences into account. This has meant that most developers have been quite slow to implement Ajax solutions. Only with the advent of more abstracted Ajax frameworks (such as ASP.NET AJAX) has Ajax-enabled Web site creation really become a viable option for enterprise-level development.

What Is ASP.NET AJAX?

ASP.NET AJAX is Microsoft's implementation of the Ajax framework and is specifically targeted at ASP.NET developers. With the latest release of ASP.NET, ASP.NET AJAX is part of the core ASP.NET functionality. It is also available for use with previous versions of ASP.NET from the Web site `http://ajax.asp.net`. This Web site also has documentation, forums, and sample code that you may find useful for whichever version of ASP.NET you are using.

ASP.NET AJAX provides the following functionality:

- A server-side framework that enables ASP.NET Web pages to respond to partial-page postback operations
- ASP.NET server controls that make the implementation of Ajax functionality easy
- An HTTP handler that enables ASP.NET Web services to communicate with client-side code by using JavaScript Object Notation (JSON) serialization in partial-page postback operations
- Web services that enable client-side code to gain access to ASP.NET application services, including authentication and personalization services
- A Web site template for creating ASP.NET AJAX-enabled Web applications
- A client-side JavaScript library that provides a number of enhancements to JavaScript syntax as well as code to simplify the implementation of Ajax functionality

These server controls and the server-side framework that makes them possible are collectively known as the ASP.NET Extensions. The client-side part of ASP.NET AJAX is known as the AJAX Library.

There are several additional downloads that you can obtain from `http://ajax.asp.net`, including the following important ones:

- **ASP.NET AJAX Control Toolkit** — This download contains additional server controls that have been created by the developer community. These controls are shared-source controls that you can inspect and modify as you see fit.
- **Microsoft AJAX Library 3.5** — This download contains the JavaScript client-side framework that is used by ASP.NET AJAX to implement Ajax functionality. You will not need this if you are developing ASP.NET AJAX applications. Instead, this download is intended to be used with other languages, for example PHP, to implement Ajax functionality using the same codebase as ASP.NET AJAX. This is beyond the scope of this chapter.

There is also a download known as Futures, which in the past has been used to add additional, pre-release, or legacy functionality to ASP.NET AJAX applications. However, at the time of writing it is unclear whether this download will be supported with the RTM release of VS 2008, and so it is not covered in this chapter.

Together these downloads provide you with a richly featured framework that you can use to add Ajax functionality to your ASP.NET Web applications. In the following sections, you learn more about what is contained in the various component parts of ASP.NET AJAX.

Core Functionality

The core functionality of ASP.NET AJAX is divided into two parts, the AJAX Extensions and the AJAX Library.

AJAX Extensions

ASP.NET AJAX functionality is contained in two assemblies that are installed in the GAC:

- `System.Web.Extensions.dll` — This assembly contains the ASP.NET AJAX functionality, including the AJAX Extensions and the AJAX Library JavaScript files, which are available through the `ScriptManager` component (which is described shortly).
- `System.Web.Extensions.Design.dll` — This assembly contains ASP.NET Designer components for the AJAX Extensions server controls. This is used by the ASP.NET Designer in Visual Studio or Visual Web developer.

Much of the AJAX Extensions component of ASP.NET AJAX is concerned with enabling partial-page postbacks and JSON serialization for Web services. This includes various HTTP handler components and extensions to the existing ASP.NET framework. All of this functionality can be configured through the `Web.config` file for a Web site. There are also classes and attributes that you can use for additional configuration. However, most of this configuration is transparent, and you will rarely need to change what is supplied in, for example, the ASP.NET Web Site template.

Your main interaction with AJAX Extensions will be using server controls to add Ajax functionality to your Web applications. There are several of these, which you can use to enhance your applications in various ways. The following table shows a selection of the server-side components. You see these components in action later in this chapter.

Control	Description
`ScriptManager`	This control is central to ASP.NET AJAX functionality and is required on every page that uses partial-page postbacks. Its main purpose is to manage client-side references to the AJAX Library JavaScript files, which are served from the ASP.NET AJAX assembly. The AJAX Library is used extensively by the AJAX Extensions server controls, which all generate their own client-side code. This control is also responsible for the configuration of Web services that you intend to access from client-side code. By supplying Web service information to the `ScriptManager` control, you can generate client-side and server-side classes to manage asynchronous communication with Web services transparently. You can also use the `ScriptManager` control to maintain references to your own JavaScript files.
`UpdatePanel`	The `UpdatePanel` control is an extremely useful one and is perhaps the ASP.NET AJAX control that you will use most often. This control acts like a standard ASP.NET placeholder and can contain any other controls. More important, it also marks a section of a page as a region that can be updated independently of the rest of the page, in a partial-page postback. Any controls contained by an `UpdatePanel` control that cause a postback (a `Button` control, for example) will not cause full-page postbacks. Instead, they cause partial-page postbacks that will update only the contents of the `UpdatePanel`.

Control	Description
	In many situations, this control is all you need to implement Ajax functionality. For example, you can place a `GridView` control in an `UpdatePanel` control, and any pagination, sorting, and other postback functionality of the control will take place in a partial-page postback.
`UpdateProgress`	This control enables you to provide feedback to users when a partial page postback is in progress. You can supply a template for this control that will be displayed when an `UpdatePanel` is updating. For example, you could use a floating `<div>` control to display a message such as "`Updating...`" so that the user is aware that the application is busy. Note that partial-page postbacks do not interfere with the rest of a Web page, which will remain responsive.
`Timer`	The ASP.NET AJAX `Timer` control is a useful way to cause an `UpdatePanel` to update periodically. You can configure this control to trigger postbacks at regular intervals. If this control is contained in an `UpdatePanel` control, then the `UpdatePanel` will be updated every time the `Timer` control is triggered. This control also has an associated event so that you can carry out periodic server-side processing.
`AsyncPostBackTrigger`	You can use this control to trigger `UpdatePanel` updates from controls that aren't contained in the `UpdatePanel`. For example, you can enable a drop-down list elsewhere on a Web page to cause an `UpdatePanel` containing a `GridView` control to update.

The AJAX Extensions also include the `ExtenderControl` abstract base class for extending existing ASP.NET server controls. This is used, for example, by various classes in the ASP.NET AJAX Control Toolkit, as you will see shortly.

AJAX Library

The AJAX Library consists of JavaScript files that are used by client-side code in ASP.NET AJAX-enabled Web applications. There is a lot of functionality included in these JavaScript files, some of which is general code that enhances the JavaScript language and some of which is specific to Ajax functionality. The AJAX Library contains layers of functionality that are built on top of each other, as shown in the following table.

Layer	Description
Browser compatibility	The lowest-level code in the AJAX Library consists of code that maps various JavaScript functionality according to the client Web browser. This is necessary because there are differences in the implementation of JavaScript in different browsers. By providing this layer, JavaScript code in other layers does not have to worry about browser compatibility, and you can write browser-neutral code that will work in all client environments.
Core services	This layer contains the enhancements to the JavaScript language, in particular OOP functionality. By using the code in this layer you can define namespaces, classes, derived classes, and interfaces using JavaScript script files. This is of particular interest to C# developers, because it makes writing JavaScript code much more like writing .NET code with using C# and encourages reusability.

Layer	Description
Base class library	The client base class library (BCL) includes many JavaScript classes that provide low-level functionality to classes further down the AJAX Library hierarchy. Most of these classes are not intended to be used directly.
Networking	Classes in the networking layer enable client-side code to call server-side code asynchronously. This layer includes the basic framework for making a call to a URL and responding to the result in a callback function. For the most part, this is also functionality that you will not use directly; instead, you will use classes that wrap this functionality. This layer also contains classes for JSON serialization and deserialization. You will find most of the networking classes on the client-side `Sys.Net` namespace.
User interface	This layer contains classes that abstract user interface elements such as HTML elements and DOM events. You can use the properties and methods of this layer to write language-neutral JavaScript code to manipulate Web pages from the client. User interface classes are contained in the `Sys.UI` namespace.
Controls	The final layer of the AJAX Library contains the highest-level code, which provides Ajax behaviors and server control functionality. This includes dynamically generated code that you can use, for example, to call Web services from client-side JavaScript code.

You can use the AJAX Library to extend and customize the behavior of ASP.NET AJAX-enabled Web applications, but it is important to note that you don't have to. You can go a long way without using any additional JavaScript in your applications — it becomes a requirement only when you require more advanced functionality. If you do write additional client-side code, however, you will find that it is much easier with the functionality that the AJAX Library offers.

ASP.NET AJAX Control Toolkit

The AJAX Control Toolkit is a collection of additional server controls, including extender controls, that have been written by the ASP.NET AJAX community. Extender controls are controls that enable you to add functionality to an existing ASP.NET server control, typically by associating a client-side behavior with it. For example, one of the extenders in the AJAX Control Toolkit extends the `TextBox` control by placing "watermark" text in the `TextBox`, which appears when the user hasn't yet added any content to the text box. This extender control is implemented in a server control called `TextBoxWatermark`.

You can use the AJAX Control Toolkit to add quite a lot more functionality to your sites, beyond what is in the core download. These controls are also interesting simply to browse and will probably give you plenty of ideas about enhancing your Web applications. However, because the AJAX Control Toolkit is separate from the core download, you should not expect the same level of support for these controls.

Using ASP.NET AJAX

Now that you have seen the component parts of ASP.NET AJAX, it is time to start looking at how to use them to enhance your Web sites. In this section, you see how Web applications that use ASP.NET AJAX work, and how to use the various aspects of functionality that ASP.NET AJAX includes. You start by examining and dissecting a simple application, and then add additional functionality in subsequent sections.

ASP.NET AJAX Web Site Example

The ASP.NET Web Site template includes all the ASP.NET AJAX core functionality. You can also use the AJAX Control Toolkit Web Site template (once installed) to include controls from the AJAX Control Toolkit. For the purposes of this example, you can create a new Web site that uses the default ASP.NET Web Site template in the `C:\ProCSharp\Chapter39` directory, called `PCSAjaxWebApp1`.

Modify the code in `Default.aspx` as follows:

```
<%@ Page Language="C#" AutoEventWireup="true" CodeFile="Default.aspx.cs"
  Inherits="_Default" %>

<!DOCTYPE html PUBLIC "-//W3C//DTD XHTML 1.0 Transitional//EN"
 "http://www.w3.org/TR/xhtml1/DTD/xhtml1-transitional.dtd">
<html xmlns="http://www.w3.org/1999/xhtml">
<head runat="server">
  <title>Pro C# ASP.NET AJAX Sample</title>
</head>
<body>
  <form id="form1" runat="server">
    <asp:ScriptManager ID="ScriptManager1" runat="server" />
    <div>
      <h1>Pro C# ASP.NET AJAX Sample</h1>
      This sample obtains a list of primes up to a maximum value.
      <br />
      Maximum:
      <asp:TextBox runat="server" id="MaxValue" Text="2500" />
      <br />
      Result:
      <asp:UpdatePanel runat="server" ID="ResultPanel">
        <ContentTemplate>
          <asp:Button runat="server" ID="GoButton" Text="Calculate " />
          <br />
          <asp:Label runat="server" ID="ResultLabel" />
          <br />
          <small>
            Panel render time: <% =DateTime.Now.ToLongTimeString() %>
          </small>
        </ContentTemplate>
      </asp:UpdatePanel>
      <asp:UpdateProgress runat="server" ID="UpdateProgress1">
        <ProgressTemplate>
          <div style="position: absolute; left: 100px; top: 200px;
              padding: 40px 60px 40px 60px; background-color: lightyellow;
              border: black 1px solid; font-weight: bold; font-size: larger;
              filter: alpha(opacity=80);">Updating...</div>
        </ProgressTemplate>
      </asp:UpdateProgress>
      <small>Page render time: <% =DateTime.Now.ToLongTimeString() %></small>
    </div>
  </form>
</body>
</html>
```

Switch to design view (note that the ASP.NET AJAX controls such as `UpdatePanel` and `UpdateProgress` have visual designer components), and double-click the Calculate button to add an event handler. Modify the code as follows:

```
protected void GoButton_Click(object sender, EventArgs e)
{
   int maxValue = 0;
   System.Text.StringBuilder resultText = new System.Text.StringBuilder();
   if (int.TryParse(MaxValue.Text, out maxValue))
   {
      for (int trial = 2; trial <= maxValue; trial++)
      {
         bool isPrime = true;
         for (int divisor = 2; divisor <= Math.Sqrt(trial); divisor++)
         {
            if (trial % divisor == 0)
            {
               isPrime = false;
               break;
            }
         }
         if (isPrime)
         {
            resultText.AppendFormat("{0} ", trial);
         }
      }
   }
   else
   {
      resultText.Append("Unable to parse maximum value.");
   }
   ResultLabel.Text = resultText.ToString();
}
```

Save your modifications and press F5 to run the project. If prompted, enable debugging in `Web.config`. When the Web page appears as shown in Figure 39-2, note that the two render times shown are the same.

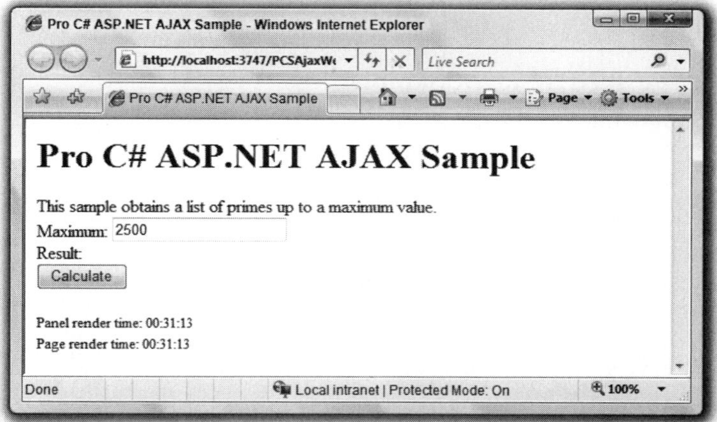

Figure 39-2

Click the Calculate button to display prime numbers less than or equal to 2500. Unless you are running on a slow machine, this should be almost instantaneous. Note that the render times are now different — only the one in the `UpdatePanel` has changed. This is shown in Figure 39-3.

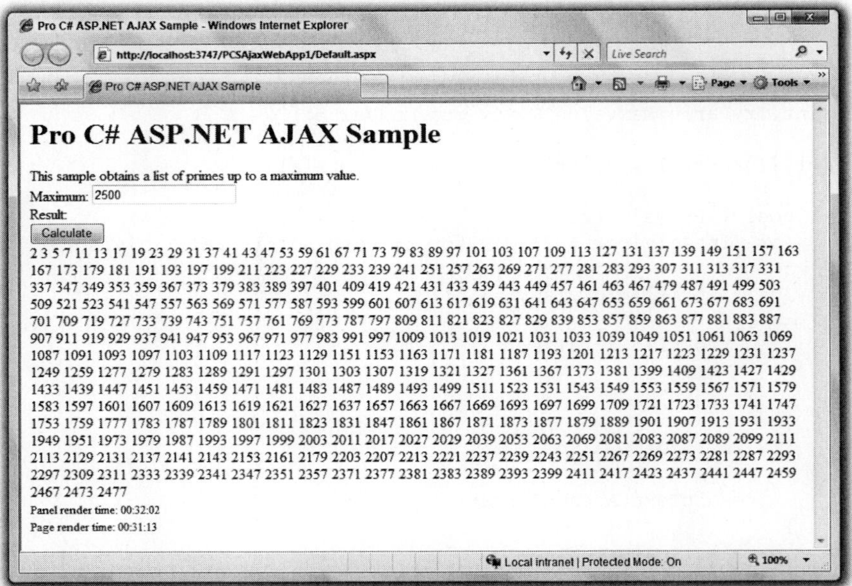

Figure 39-3

Finally, add some zeros to the maximum value to introduce a processing delay (about three more should be enough on a fast PC) and click the Calculate button again. This time, before the result is displayed, note that the `UpdateProgress` control displays a partially transparent feedback message, as shown in Figure 39-4.

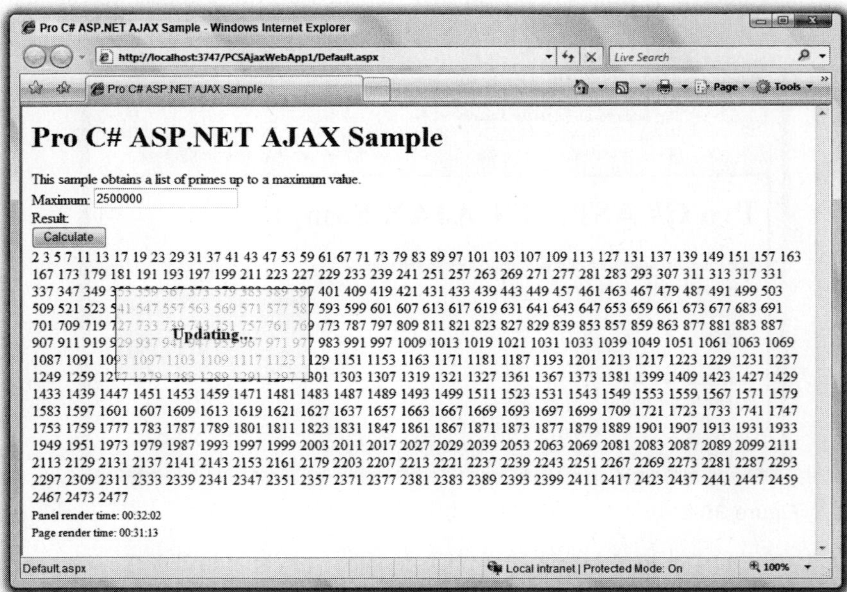

Figure 39-4

While the application updates, the page remains responsive. You can, for example, scroll through the page.

Note that when the update completes, the scroll position of the browser is set to the point it was at before you clicked Calculate. In most cases, when partial-page updates are quick to execute, this is great for usability.

Close the browser to return to Visual Studio.

ASP.NET AJAX-Enabled Web Site Configuration

Now that you have seen a simple ASP.NET AJAX-enabled Web application, you can examine it more closely to see how it works. The first thing to look at is the `Web.config` file for the application, in particular the following two blocks of code in the `<system.web>` configuration section of `<configuration>`:

```
<?xml version="1.0"?>
<configuration>
  ...
  <system.web>
    <compilation debug="true">
      <assemblies>
        <add assembly="System.Core, Version=3.5.0.0, Culture=neutral,
          PublicKeyToken=B77A5C561934E089"/>
        <add assembly="System.Web.Extensions, Version=3.5.0.0,
          Culture=neutral, PublicKeyToken=31BF3856AD364E35"/>
        <add assembly="System.Data.DataSetExtensions, Version=3.5.0.0,
          Culture=neutral, PublicKeyToken=B77A5C561934E089"/>
        <add assembly="System.Xml.Linq, Version=3.5.0.0, Culture=neutral,
          PublicKeyToken=B77A5C561934E089"/>
      </assemblies>
    </compilation>
    ...
    <compilation debug="true">
      <pages>
        <controls>
          <add tagPrefix="asp" namespace="System.Web.UI"
            assembly="System.Web.Extensions, Version=3.5.0.0, Culture=neutral,
            PublicKeyToken=31BF3856AD364E35"/>
          <add tagPrefix="asp" namespace="System.Web.UI.WebControls"
            assembly="System.Web.Extensions, Version=3.5.0.0, Culture=neutral,
            PublicKeyToken=31BF3856AD364E35"/>
        </controls>
      </pages>
    </compilation>
    ...
  </system.web>
  ...
</configuration>
```

The code in the `<assemblies>` configuration section in `<compilation>` ensures that the ASP.NET AJAX `System.Web.Extensions.dll` assembly is loaded from the GAC. The code in the `<controls>` configuration element in `<pages>` references this assembly and associates the controls it contains (in both the `System.Web.UI` and `System.Web.UI.WebControls` namespaces) with the tag prefix `asp`. These two sections are essential for all ASP.NET AJAX-enabled Web applications.

The next two sections, `<httpHandlers>` and `<httpModules>`, are also required for ASP.NET AJAX functionality. The `<httpHandlers>` section defines three things. First, the handler for `.asmx` Web services is replaced with a new class from the `System.Web.Extensions` namespace. This new class is capable of handling requests from client-side calls from the AJAX Library, including JSON serialization and deserialization. Second, a handler is added to enable the use of ASP.NET application services. Third, a new handler is added for the `ScriptResource.axd` resource. This resource serves the AJAX Library JavaScript files from the ASP.NET AJAX assembly, so that these files do not need to be included directly in your applications.

```
<system.web>
  ...
  <httpHandlers>
    <remove verb="*" path="*.asmx"/>
    <add verb="*" path="*.asmx" validate="false"
      type="System.Web.Script.Services.ScriptHandlerFactory,
      System.Web.Extensions, Version=3.5.0.0, Culture=neutral,
      PublicKeyToken=31BF3856AD364E35"/>
    <add verb="*" path="*_AppService.axd" validate="false"
      type="System.Web.Script.Services.ScriptHandlerFactory,
      System.Web.Extensions, Version=3.5.0.0, Culture=neutral,
      PublicKeyToken=31BF3856AD364E35"/>
    <add verb="GET,HEAD" path="ScriptResource.axd"
      type="System.Web.Handlers.ScriptResourceHandler,
      System.Web.Extensions, Version=3.5.0.0, Culture=neutral,
      PublicKeyToken=31BF3856AD364E35" validate="false"/>
  </httpHandlers>
  ...
</system.web>
```

The `<httpModules>` section adds a new HTTP module that adds additional processing for HTTP requests in the Web application. This enables partial-page postbacks.

```
<system.web>
  ...
  <httpModules>
    <add name="ScriptModule" type="System.Web.Handlers.ScriptModule,
      System.Web.Extensions, Version=3.5.0.0, Culture=neutral,
      PublicKeyToken=31BF3856AD364E35"/>
  </httpModules>
</system.web>
```

The remaining configuration settings are configured by the `<configSections>` settings, which are included as the first child element of `<configuration>`. This section, which is not listed here, must be included so that you can use the `<system.web.extensions>` and `<system.webServer>` sections.

The `<system.web.extensions>` *section is not included in the default ASP.NET Web Site configuration file; you look at it in the next section.*

The next configuration element, `<system.webServer>`, contains settings that relate to the IIS 7 Web server; this element is not required if you are using an earlier version of IIS. This configuration section is not listed here.

Finally, there is a `<runtime>` section as follows:

```
<runtime>
  <assemblyBinding xmlns="urn:schemas-microsoft-com:asm.v1">
    <dependentAssembly>
      <assemblyIdentity name="System.Web.Extensions"
```

```
        publicKeyToken="31bf3856ad364e35"/>
      <bindingRedirect oldVersion="1.0.0.0-1.1.0.0" newVersion="3.5.0.0"/>
    </dependentAssembly>
    <dependentAssembly>
      <assemblyIdentity name="System.Web.Extensions.Design"
        publicKeyToken="31bf3856ad364e35"/>
      <bindingRedirect oldVersion="1.0.0.0-1.1.0.0" newVersion="3.5.0.0"/>
    </dependentAssembly>
  </assemblyBinding>
</runtime>
```

This section is included to ensure backward compatibility with older versions of ASP.NET AJAX and will have no effect unless you have version 1.0 of ASP.NET AJAX installed. If you do have this version installed, this section enables third-party controls to bind to the latest version of ASP.NET AJAX.

Additional Configuration Options

The `<system.web.extensions>` section contains settings that provide additional configuration for ASP.NET AJAX, all of which is optional. This section is not included in the default ASP.NET Web application template, but you can add it if you need its functionality. Most of the configuration that you can add with this section concerns Web services and is contained in an element called `<webServices>`, which in turn is placed in a `<scripting>` element. First, you can add a section to enable access to the ASP.NET authentication service through a Web service (you can choose to enforce SSL here if you wish):

```
<system.web.extensions>
  <scripting>
    <webServices>
      <authenticationService enabled="true" requireSSL = "true|false"/>
```

Next, you can enable and configure access to ASP.NET personalization functionality through the profile Web service:

```
      <profileService enabled="true"
        readAccessProperties="propertyname1,propertyname2"
        writeAccessProperties="propertyname1,propertyname2" />
```

The last Web service-related setting is for enabling and configuring access to ASP.NET role functionality through the role Web service:

```
      <roleService enabled="true"/>
    </webServices>
```

Finally, the `<system.web.extensions>` section can contain an element that enables you to configure compression and caching for asynchronous communications:

```
    <scriptResourceHandler enableCompression="true" enableCaching="true" />
  </scripting>
</system.web.extensions>
```

Additional Configuration for the AJAX Control Toolkit

To use the controls in the AJAX Control Toolkit, you can add the following configuration to `Web.config`:

```
<controls>
  ...
  <add namespace="AjaxControlToolkit" assembly="AjaxControlToolkit"
    tagPrefix="ajaxToolkit"/>
</controls>
```

This maps the toolkit controls to the `ajaxToolkit` tag prefix. These controls are contained in the `AjaxControlToolkit.dll` assembly, which should be in the `/bin` directory for the Web application.

Alternatively, you could register the controls individually on Web pages using the `<%@ Register %>` directive:

```
<%@ Register Assembly="AjaxControlToolkit" Namespace="AjaxControlToolkit"
  TagPrefix="ajaxToolkit" %>
```

Adding ASP.NET AJAX Functionality

The first step in adding Ajax functionality to a Web site is to add a `ScriptManager` control to your Web pages. Next, you add server controls such as `UpdatePanel` controls to enable partial-page rendering and dynamic controls such as those supplied in the AJAX Control Toolkit to add usability and glitz to your application. You may also add client-side code, and you can use the AJAX Library for further assistance in customizing and enhancing the functionality of your application.

In this section, you learn about the functionality you can add using server controls. Later in the chapter you look at client-side techniques.

The ScriptManager Control

As mentioned earlier in the chapter, the `ScriptManager` control must be included on all pages that use partial-page postbacks and several other aspects of ASP.NET AJAX functionality.

> *A great way to ensure that all the pages in your Web application contain the* `ScriptManager` *control is to add this control to the master page (or master pages) that your application uses.*

As well as enabling ASP.NET AJAX functionality, you can also use properties to configure this control. The simplest of these properties is `EnablePartialRendering`, which is true by default. If you set this property to `false`, you will disable all asynchronous postback processing, such as that provided by `UpdatePanel` controls. This can be useful, for example, if you want to compare your AJAX-enabled Web site with a traditional Web site, perhaps if you are giving a demonstration to a manager.

You can use the `ScriptManager` control for several reasons, such as in the following common situations:

- ❑ To determine whether server-side code is being called as a result of a partial-page postback
- ❑ To add references to additional client-side JavaScript files
- ❑ To reference Web services
- ❑ To return error messages to the client

These configuration options are covered in the following sections.

Detect Partial-Page Postbacks

The `ScriptManager` control includes a Boolean property called `IsInAsyncPostBack`. You can use this property in server-side code to detect whether a partial-page postback is in progress. Note that the `ScriptManager` for a page may actually be on a master page. Rather than accessing this control through the master page, you can obtain a reference to the current `ScriptManager` instance by using the static `GetCurrent()` method, for example:

```
ScriptManager scriptManager = ScriptManager.GetCurrent(this);
if (scriptManager != null && scriptManager.IsInAsyncPostBack)
{
   // Code to execute for partial-page postbacks.
}
```

You must pass a reference to a Page control to the GetCurrent() method. For example, if you use this method in a Page_Load() event handler for an ASP.NET Web page, you can use this as your Page reference. Also, remember to check for a null reference to avoid exceptions.

Client-Side JavaScript References

Rather than adding code to the HTML page header, or in <script> elements on the page, you can use the Scripts property of the ScriptManager class. This centralizes your script references and makes it easier to maintain them. You can do this declaratively by adding a child <Scripts> element to the <UpdatePanel> control element, and then adding <asp:ScriptReference> child control elements to <Scripts>. You use the Path property of a ScriptReference control to reference a custom script.

The following sample shows how to add references to a custom script file called MyScript.js in the root folder of the Web application:

```
<asp:ScriptManager runat="server" ID="ScriptManager1">
  <Scripts>
    <asp:ScriptReference Path="~/MyScript.js" />
  </Scripts>
</asp:ScriptManager>
```

Web Service References

To access Web services from client-side JavaScript code, ASP.NET AJAX must generate a proxy class. To control this behavior, you use the Services property of the ScriptManager class. As with Scripts, you can specify this property declaratively, this time with a <Services> element. You add <asp:ServiceReference> controls to this element. For each ServiceReference object in the Services property, you specify the path to the Web service by using the Path property.

The ServiceReference class also has a property called InlineScript, which defaults to false. When this property is false, client-side code obtains a proxy class to call the Web service by requesting it from the server. To enhance performance (particularly if you use a lot of Web services on a page), you can set InlineScript to true. This causes the proxy class to be defined in the client-script for the page.

ASP.NET Web services use a file extension of .asmx. Without wanting to get into too much detail in this chapter, to add a reference to a Web service called MyService.asmx in the root folder of a Web application, you would use code as follows:

```
<asp:ScriptManager runat="server" ID="ScriptManager1">
  <Services>
    <asp:ServiceReference Path="~/MyService.asmx" />
  </Services>
</asp:ScriptManager>
```

You can only add references to local Web services (that is, Web services in the same Web application as the calling code) in this way. You can call remote Web services indirectly via local Web methods.

Later in this chapter you see how to make asynchronous Web method calls from client-side JavaScript code that uses proxy classes generated in this way.

Client-Side Error Messages

If an exception is thrown as part of a partial-page postback, the default behavior is to place the error message contained in the exception into a client-side JavaScript alert message box. You can customize the message that is displayed by handling the AsyncPostBackError event of the ScriptManager instance. In the event handler, you can use the AsyncPostBackErrorEventArgs.Exception property to access the exception that is thrown and the ScriptManager.AsyncPostBackErrorMessage property to set the message that is displayed to the client. You might do this to hide the exception details from users.

If you want to override the default behavior and display a message in a different way, you must handle the `endRequest` event of the client-side `PageRequestManager` object by using JavaScript. This is described later in this chapter.

Using UpdatePanel Controls

The `UpdatePanel` control is perhaps the control that you will use most often when you write ASP.NET AJAX-enabled Web applications. This control, as you have seen in the simple example earlier in the chapter, enables you to wrap a portion of a Web page so that it is capable of participating in a partial-page postback operation. To do this, you add an `UpdatePanel` control to the page and fill its child `<ContentTemplate>` element with the controls that you want it to contain.

```
<asp:UpdatePanel runat="Server" ID="UpdatePanel1">
  <ContentTemplate>
    ...
  </ContentTemplate>
</asp:UpdatePanel>
```

The contents of the `<ContentTemplate>` template are rendered in either a `<div>` or `<span>` element according to the value of the `RenderMode` property of the `UpdatePanel`. The default value of this property is `Block`, which will result in a `<div>` element. To use a `<span>` element, set `RenderMode` to `Inline`.

Multiple UpdatePanel Controls on a Single Web Page

You can include any number of `UpdatePanel` controls on a page. If a postback is caused by a control that is contained in the `<ContentTemplate>` of any `UpdatePanel` on the page, a partial-page postback will occur instead of a full-page postback. This will cause all the `UpdatePanel` controls to update according to the value of their `UpdateMode` property. The default value of this property is `Always`, which means that the `UpdatePanel` will update for a partial-page postback operation on the page, even if this operation occurs in a different `UpdatePanel` control. If you set this property to `Conditional`, the `UpdatePanel` updates only when a control that it contains causes a partial-page postback or when a trigger that you have defined occurs. Triggers are covered shortly.

If you have set `UpdateMode` to `Conditional`, you can also set the `ChildrenAsTriggers` property to `false` to prevent controls that are contained by the `UpdatePanel` from triggering an update of the panel. Note, though, that in this case these controls still trigger a partial-page update, which may result in other `UpdatePanel` controls on the page being updated. For example, this will update controls that have an `UpdateMode` property value of `Always`. This is illustrated in the following code:

```
<asp:UpdatePanel runat="Server" ID="UpdatePanel1" UpdateMode="Conditional"
  ChildrenAsTriggers="false">
  <ContentTemplate>
    <asp:Button runat="Server" ID="Button1" Text="Click Me" />
    <small>Panel 1 render time: <% =DateTime.Now.ToLongTimeString() %></small>
  </ContentTemplate>
</asp:UpdatePanel>
<asp:UpdatePanel runat="Server" ID="UpdatePanel2">
  <ContentTemplate>
    <small>Panel 2 render time: <% =DateTime.Now.ToLongTimeString() %></small>
  </ContentTemplate>
</asp:UpdatePanel>
<small>Page render time: <% =DateTime.Now.ToLongTimeString() %></small>
```

In this code, the `UpdatePanel2` control has an `UpdateMode` property of `Always`; the default value. When the button is clicked, it will cause a partial-page postback, but only `UpdatePanel2` will be updated. Visually, you will notice that only the "Panel 2 render time" label is updated.

Server-Side UpdatePanel Updates

Sometimes when you have multiple UpdatePanel controls on a page, you might decide not to update one of them unless certain conditions are met. In this case, you would configure the UpdateMode property of the panel to Conditional as shown in the previous section and possibly also set the ChildrenAsTriggers property to false. Then, in your server-side event-handler code for one of the controls on the page that causes a partial-page update, you would (conditionally) call the Update() method of the UpdatePanel. For example:

```
protected void Button1_Click(object sender, EventArgs e)
{
   if (TestSomeCondition())
   {
      UpdatePanel1.Update();
   }
}
```

UpdatePanel Triggers

You can cause an UpdatePanel control to be updated by a control elsewhere on the Web page by adding triggers to the Triggers property of the control. A trigger is an association between an event of a control elsewhere on the page and the UpdatePanel control. All controls have default events (for example, the default event of a Button control is Click), so specifying the name of an event is optional. There are two types of triggers that you can add, represented by the following two classes:

- AsyncPostBackTrigger — This class causes the UpdatePanel to update when the specified event of the specified control is triggered.
- PostBackTrigger — This class causes a full-page update to be triggered when the specified event of the specified control is triggered.

You will mostly use AsyncPostBackTrigger, but PostBackTrigger can be useful if you want a control inside an UpdatePanel to trigger a full-page postback.

Both of these trigger classes have two properties: ControlID, which specifies the control that causes the trigger by its identifier, and EventName, which specifies the name of the event for the control that is linked to the trigger.

To extend an earlier example, consider the following code:

```
<asp:UpdatePanel runat="Server" ID="UpdatePanel1" UpdateMode="Conditional"
  ChildrenAsTriggers="false">
  <Triggers>
    <asp:AsyncPostBackTrigger ControlID="Button2" />
  </Triggers>
  <ContentTemplate>
    <asp:Button runat="Server" ID="Button1" Text="Click Me" />
    <small>Panel 1 render time: <% =DateTime.Now.ToLongTimeString() %></small>
  </ContentTemplate>
</asp:UpdatePanel>
<asp:UpdatePanel runat="Server" ID="UpdatePanel2">
  <ContentTemplate>
    <asp:Button runat="Server" ID="Button2" Text="Click Me" />
    <small>Panel 2 render time: <% =DateTime.Now.ToLongTimeString() %></small>
  </ContentTemplate>
</asp:UpdatePanel>
<small>Page render time: <% =DateTime.Now.ToLongTimeString() %></small>
```

The new Button control, Button2, is specified as a trigger in the UpdatePanel1. When this button is clicked, both UpdatePanel1 and UpdatePanel2 will be updated: UpdatePanel1 because of the trigger, and UpdatePanel2 because it uses the default UpdateMode value of Always.

Using UpdateProgress

The UpdateProgress control, as you saw in the earlier example, enables you to display a progress message to the user while a partial-page postback is in operation. You use the ProgressTemplate property to supply an ITemplate for the progress display. You will typically use the <ProgressTemplate> child element of the control to do this.

You can place multiple UpdateProgress controls on a page by using the AssociatedUpdatePanelID property to associate the control with a specific UpdatePanel. If this is not set (the default), the UpdateProgress template will be displayed for any partial-page postback, regardless of which UpdatePanel causes it.

When a partial-page postback occurs, there is a delay before the UpdateProgress template is displayed. This delay is configurable through the DisplayAfter property, which is an int property that specifies the delay in milliseconds. The default is 500 milliseconds.

Finally, you can use the Boolean DynamicLayout property to specify whether space is allocated for the template before it is displayed. For the default value of true for this property, space on the page is dynamically allocated, which may result in other controls being moved out of the way for an inline progress template display. If you set this property to false, space will be allocated for the template before it is displayed, so the layout of other controls on the page will not change. You will set this property according to the effect you want to achieve when displaying progress. For a progress template that is positioned by using absolute coordinates, as in the earlier example, you should leave this property set to the default value.

Using Extender Controls

The core ASP.NET AJAX download includes a class called ExtenderControl. The purpose of this control is to enable you to extend (that is, add functionality to) other ASP.NET server controls. This is used extensively in the AJAX Control Toolkit to great effect, and you can use the ASP.NET AJAX Server Control Extender project template to create your own extended controls. ExtenderControl controls all work in a similar way — you place them on a page, associate them with target controls, and add further configuration. The extender then emits client-side code to add functionality.

To see this in action in a simple example, create a new Web site called PCSExtenderDemo in the C:\ProCSharp\Chapter39 directory, add the AJAX Control Toolkit assembly to the bin directory of the Web Site, and then add the following code to Default.aspx:

```
<%@ Page Language="C#" AutoEventWireup="true" CodeFile="Default.aspx.cs"
  Inherits="_Default" %>
<%@ Register Assembly="AjaxControlToolkit" Namespace="AjaxControlToolkit"
  TagPrefix="ajaxToolkit" %>

<!DOCTYPE html PUBLIC "-//W3C//DTD XHTML 1.0 Transitional//EN"
 "http://www.w3.org/TR/xhtml1/DTD/xhtml1-transitional.dtd">
<html xmlns="http://www.w3.org/1999/xhtml">
<head runat="server">
  <title>Color Selector</title>
</head>
<body>
  <form id="form1" runat="server">
    <asp:ScriptManager ID="ScriptManager1" runat="server" />
    <div>
      <asp:UpdatePanel runat="server" ID="updatePanel1">
```

```
        <ContentTemplate>
          <span style="display: inline-block; padding: 2px;">
            My favorite color is:
          </span>
          <asp:Label runat="server" ID="favoriteColorLabel" Text="green"
            style="color: #00dd00; display: inline-block; padding: 2px;
                   width: 70px; font-weight: bold;" />
          <ajaxToolkit:DropDownExtender runat="server" ID="dropDownExtender1"
            TargetControlID="favoriteColorLabel"
            DropDownControlID="colDropDown" />
          <asp:Panel ID="colDropDown" runat="server"
            Style="display: none; visibility: hidden; width: 60px;
                   padding: 8px; border: double 4px black;
                   background-color: #ffffdd; font-weight: bold;">
            <asp:LinkButton runat="server" ID="OptionRed" Text="red"
              OnClick="OnSelect" style="color: #ff0000;" /><br />
            <asp:LinkButton runat="server" ID="OptionOrange" Text="orange"
              OnClick="OnSelect" style="color: #dd7700;" /><br />
            <asp:LinkButton runat="server" ID="OptionYellow" Text="yellow"
              OnClick="OnSelect" style="color: #dddd00;" /><br />
            <asp:LinkButton runat="server" ID="OptionGreen" Text="green"
              OnClick="OnSelect" style="color: #00dd00;" /><br />
            <asp:LinkButton runat="server" ID="OptionBlue" Text="blue"
              OnClick="OnSelect" style="color: #0000dd;" /><br />
            <asp:LinkButton runat="server" ID="OptionPurple" Text="purple"
              OnClick="OnSelect" style="color: #dd00ff;" />
          </asp:Panel>
        </ContentTemplate>
      </asp:UpdatePanel>
    </div>
  </form>
</body>
</html>
```

You also need to add the following event handler to the code behind this file:

```
protected void OnSelect(object sender, EventArgs e)
{
   favoriteColorLabel.Text = ((LinkButton)sender).Text;
   favoriteColorLabel.Style["color"] = ((LinkButton)sender).Style["color"];
}
```

In the browser, not very much is visible at first, and the extender seems to have no effect. This is shown in Figure 39-5.

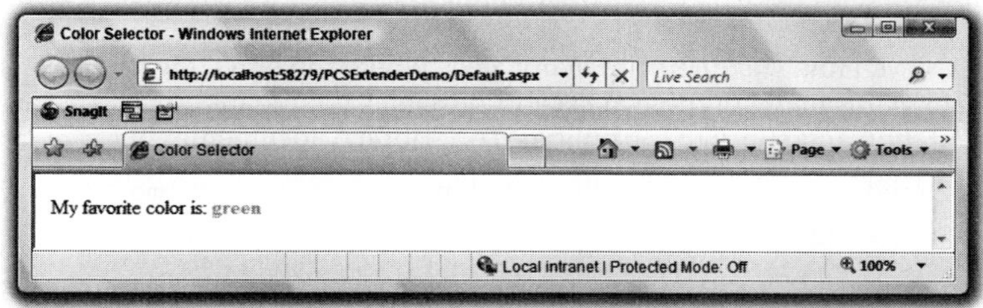

Figure 39-5

However, when you hover over the text that reads "green," a drop-down dynamically appears. If you click this drop-down, a list appears, as shown in Figure 39-6.

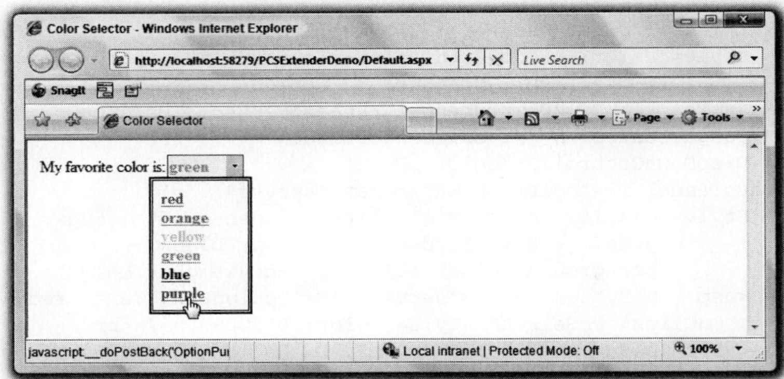

Figure 39-6

When you click one of the links in the drop-down list, the text changes accordingly (after a partial-page postback operation).

There are two important points to note about this simple example. First, it was extremely easy to associate the extender with target controls. Second, the drop-down list was styled using custom code — meaning that you can place whatever content you like in the list. This simple extender is a great way to add functionality to your Web applications, and it is very simple to use.

The extenders that are contained in the AJAX Control Toolkit are continually being added to and updated, so check `http://ajax.asp.net/ajaxtoolkit` regularly. This Web page includes live demonstrations of all the current extenders so that you can see them in action.

In addition to the extender controls that are supplied by the AJAX Control Toolkit, you can create your own. To make this process as simple as possible, you can use the ASP.NET AJAX Control project template. This project includes all the basic functionality that you require for an extender, including the server-side class for the extender and the client-side JavaScript behavior file that the extender uses. To create an effective extender, you must use the AJAX Library.

Using the AJAX Library

There is a great deal of functionality available in the AJAX Library that you can use to further enhance your Web applications. However, to do this you need at least a working knowledge of JavaScript. In this section, you see some of this functionality, although this is not an exhaustive tutorial.

The basic principles behind the use of the AJAX Library are much the same as for adding any type of client-side script to a Web application. You will still use the core JavaScript language, and you will still interact with the DOM. However, there are many areas where the AJAX Library makes things easier for you. This section explains many of these areas and provides a foundation that you can build on with further experimentation and study of the online AJAX Library documentation.

The techniques covered in this section are illustrated in the `PCSLibraryDemo` project, which is referred to throughout the rest of this chapter.

Adding JavaScript to a Web Page

The first thing you need to know is how to add client-side JavaScript to a Web Page. You have three options here:

- Add JavaScript inline in ASP.NET Web pages, by using the `<script>` element.
- Add JavaScript to separate JavaScript files with the extension `.js` and reference these files from `<script>` elements or (preferably) by using the `<Scripts>` child element of the `ScriptManager` control.
- Generate JavaScript from server-side code, such as code behind or custom extender controls.

Each of these techniques has its own benefits. For prototyping code, there is no substitute for inline code because it is so quick and easy to use. You will also find it easy to associate client-side event handlers of HTML elements and server controls with client-side functions, because everything is in the same file.

Having separate files is good for reusability, because you may create your own library of classes much like the existing AJAX Library JavaScript files.

Generating code from code behind can be tricky to implement because you will not usually have access to IntelliSense for JavaScript programming when you use C# code. However, you will be able to generate code dynamically in response to application state, and sometimes this is the only way to do things.

The extenders that you can create with the AJAX Control Toolkit include a separate JavaScript file that you use to define behaviors, which gets around some of the problems of exposing client-side code from the server.

In this chapter, you use the inline code technique, because it is simplest and allows you to concentrate on the JavaScript functionality.

Global Utility Functions

One of the features supplied by the AJAX Library that you will use most often is the set of global functions that wrap other functionality. These include the following:

- `$get()` — This function enables you to get a reference to a DOM element by supplying its client-side `id` value as a parameter, with an optional second parameter to specify the parent element to search in.
- `$create()` — This function enables you to create objects of a specific JavaScript type and perform initialization at the same time. You can supply between one and five parameters to this function. The first parameter is the type you want to instantiate, which will typically be a type defined by the AJAX Library. The other parameters enable you to specify initial property values, event handlers, references to other components, and the DOM element that the object is attached to, respectively.
- `$addHandler()` — This function provides a shorthand for adding an event handler to an object.

There are more global functions, but these are the ones you will use most often. `$create()` in particular is a very useful way to reduce the amount of code required to create and initialize an object.

Using the AJAX Library JavaScript OOP Extensions

The AJAX Library includes an enhanced framework for defining types that uses an OOP-based system that maps closely to .NET Framework techniques. You can create namespaces, add types to namespaces, add constructors, methods, properties, and events to types, and even use inheritance and interfaces in type definitions.

In this section, you see how to implement the basics of this functionality, but you won't look at events and interfaces here. These constructs are beyond the scope of this chapter.

Defining Namespaces

To define a namespace, you use the `Type.registerNamespace()` function, for example:

```
Type.registerNamespace("ProCSharp");
```

Once you have registered a namespace you can add types to it.

Defining Classes

Defining a class is a three-stage process. First, you define the constructor. Next, you add properties and methods. Finally, you register the class.

To define a constructor, you define a function using a namespace and class name, for example:

```
ProCSharp.Shape = function(color, scaleFactor) {
  this._color = color;
  this._scaleFactor = scaleFactor;
}
```

This constructor takes two parameters and uses them to set local fields (note that you do not have to explicitly define these fields — you just have to set their values).

To add properties and methods, you assign them to the `prototype` property of the class as follows:

```
ProCSharp.Shape.prototype = {

  getColor : function() {
    return this._color;
  },

  setColor : function(color) {
    this._color = color;
  },

  getScaleFactor : function() {
    return this._scaleFactor;
  },

  setScaleFactor : function(scaleFactor) {
    this._scaleFactor = scaleFactor;
  }

}
```

This code defines two properties by their get and set accessors.

To resister a class, you call its `registerClass()` function:

```
ProCSharp.Shape.registerClass('ProCSharp.Shape');
```

Inheritance

You derive a class in much the same way as creating a class but with some slight differences. You use the `initializeBase()` function to initialize the base class in the constructor, passing parameters in the form of an array:

```
ProCSharp.Circle = function(color, scaleFactor, diameter) {
  ProCSharp.Circle.initializeBase(this, [color, scaleFactor]);
  this._diameter = diameter;
}
```

You define properties and methods in the same way as before:

```
ProCSharp.Circle.prototype = {

  getDiameter : function() {
    return this._diameter;
  },

  setDiameter : function(diameter) {
    this._diameter = diameter;
  },

  getArea : function() {
    return Math.PI * Math.pow((this._diameter * this._scaleFactor) / 2, 2);
  },

  describe : function() {
    var description = "This is a " + this._color + " circle with an area of "
      + this.getArea();
    alert(description);
  }
}
```

When you register the class, you provide the base class type as a second parameter:

```
ProCSharp.Circle.registerClass('ProCSharp.Circle', ProCSharp.Shape);
```

You can implement interfaces by passing them as additional parameters, although, to keep things simple, you won't see details of that here.

Using User-Defined Types

Once you have defined classes in this way, you can instantiate and use them with simple syntax. For example:

```
var myCircle = new ProCSharp.Circle('red', 1.0, 4.4);
myCircle.describe();
```

This code would result in a JavaScript alert box, as shown in Figure 39-7.

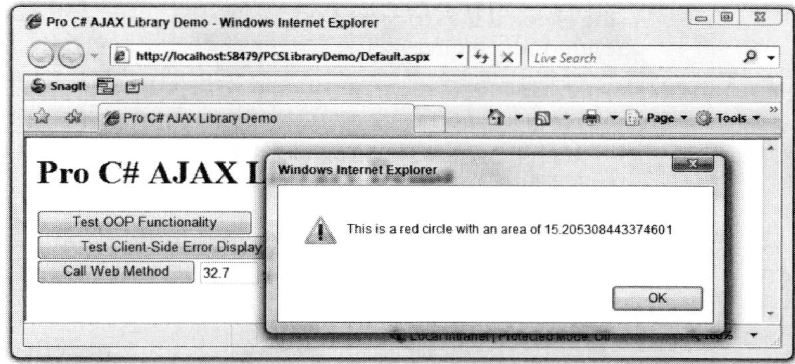

Figure 39-7

If you want to test this, run the PCSLibraryDemo project and click the Test OOP Functionality button.

The PageRequestManager and Application Objects

Among the most useful classes that the AJAX Library provides are the PageRequestManager and Application classes. You will find PageRequestManager in the Sys.WebForms namespace and Application in the Sys namespace. The important thing about these classes is that they expose several events that you can attach JavaScript event handlers to. These events occur at particularly interesting points in the life cycle of a page (for Application) or partial-page postback (for PageRequestManager) and enable you to perform operations at these critical times.

The AJAX Library defines event handlers in a similar way to event handlers in the .NET Framework. Every event handler has a similar signature, with two parameters. The first parameter is a reference to the object that generated the event. The second parameter is an instance of the Sys.EventArgs class or an instance of a class that derives from this class. Many of the events exposed by PageRequestManager and Application include specialized event argument classes that you can use to determine more information about the event. The following table lists these events in the order they will occur in a page that is loaded, triggers a partial-page postback, and is then closed.

Event	Description
Application.init	This event is the first to occur in the life cycle of a page. It is raised after all the JavaScript files have been loaded but before any objects in the application have been created.
Application.load	This event fires after the objects in the application have loaded and been initialized. You will often use an event handler attached to this event to perform actions when the page is first loaded. You can also provide an implementation for a function called pageLoad() on a page, which is automatically defined as an event handler for this event. It sends event arguments by using a Sys.ApplicationLoadEventArgs object, which includes the isPartialLoad property that you can use to determine if a partial-page postback has occurred. Access this property with the get_isPartialLoad() accessor.
PageRequestManager .initializeRequest	This event occurs before a partial-page postback, before the request object is created. You can use the Sys.WebForms .InitializeRequestEventArgs event argument properties to access the element that triggered the postback (postBackElement) and the underlying request object (request).
PageRequestManager .beginRequest	This event occurs before a partial-page postback, after the request object is created. You can use the Sys.WebForms. BeginRequestEventArgs event argument properties to access the element that triggered the postback (postBackElement) and the underlying request object (request).

Event	Description
PageRequestManager .pageLoading	This event is raised after a partial-page postback, before any subsequent processing occurs. This processing can include `<div>` elements that will be deleted or updated, which you can reference through the `Sys.WebForms.PageLoadingEventArgs` object by using the `panelsDeleting` and `panelsUpdating` properties.
PageRequestManager .pageLoaded	This event is raised after a partial-page postback, after `UpdatePanel` controls have been processed. This processing can include `<div>` elements that have been created or updated, which you can reference through the `Sys.WebForms.PageLoadedEventArgs` object by using the `panelsCreated` and `panelsUpdated` properties.
PageRequestManager .endRequest	This event occurs after processing of a partial-page postback has completed. The `Sys.WebForms.EndRequestEventArgs` object passed to the event handler enables you to detect and process server-side errors (by using the `error` and `errorHandled` properties) as well as to access the response object through `response`.
Application.unload	This event is raised just before the objects in the application are disposed, which gives you a chance to perform final actions or cleanup if necessary.

You can add an event handler to an event of the `Application` object by using the static `add_xxx()` functions, for example:

```
Sys.Application.add_load(LoadHandler);

function LoadHandler(sender, args)
{
  // Event handler code.
}
```

The process is similar for `PageRequestManager`, but you must use the `get_instance()` function to obtain an instance of the current object, for example:

```
Sys.WebForms.PageRequestManager.getInstance().add_beginRequest(
  BeginRequestHandler);

function BeginRequestHandler(sender, args)
{
  // Event handler code.
}
```

In the `PCSLibraryDemo` application, an event handler is added to the `PageRequestManager.endRequest` event. This event handler responds to server-side processing errors and displays an error message in a `<span>` element with an `id` of `errorDisplay`. To test this method, click the Test Client-Side Error Display button, as shown in Figure 39-8.

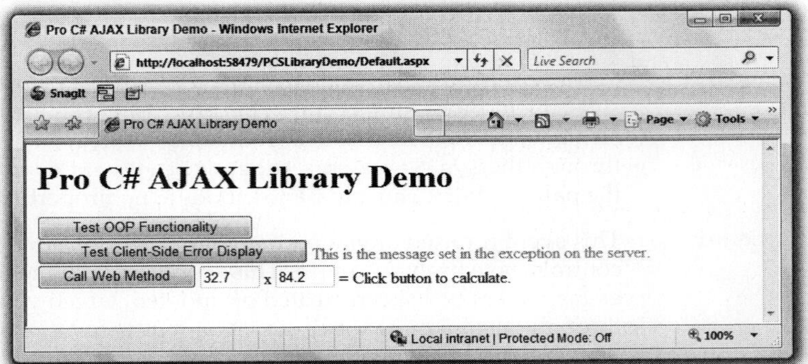

Figure 39-8

The code that achieves this is:

```
Sys.WebForms.PageRequestManager.getInstance().add_endRequest(
  EndRequestHandler);

function EndRequestHandler(sender, args)
{
  if (args.get_error() != undefined)
  {
    var errorMessage = args.get_error().message;
    args.set_errorHandled(true);
    $get('errorDisplay').innerHTML = errorMessage;
  }
}
```

Note that the `errorHandled` property of the `EndRequestEventArgs` object is set to `true`. This prevents the default behavior, which is to display the error message in a dialog box by using the JavaScript `alert()` function.

The error itself is generated by throwing an exception on the server as follows:

```
protected void testErrorDisplay_Click(object sender, EventArgs e)
{
   throw new ApplicationException(
 "This is the message set in the exception on the server.");
}
```

There are many other situations when you will want to use event handling techniques to act on the `Application` and `PageRequestManager` events.

JavaScript Debugging

In the past, JavaScript has had a reputation of being difficult to debug. However, this has been addressed in the latest version of Visual Studio. You can now add breakpoints and step through JavaScript code just like C# code. You can also interrogate object state in break mode, change property values, and so on. The IntelliSense that is available when you write JavaScript code is also vastly improved in the latest version of Visual Studio.

However, there will still be times when you will want to add debug and trace code to report information as code is executed. For example, you might want to use the JavaScript `alert()` function to show information in dialog boxes.

There are also some third-party tools that you can use to add a client-side UI for debugging. These include:

- **Fiddler** — This tool, which you can obtain from `www.fiddlertool.com`, enables you to log all HTTP traffic between your computer and a Web application — including partial-page postbacks. There are also additional tools that you can use to look at what occurs during the processing of Web pages in more detail.
- **Nikhil's Web Development Helper** — This tool, available at `http://projects.nikhilk.net/Projects/WebDevHelper.aspx`, can also log HTTP traffic. In addition, this tool contains a number of utilities specifically aimed at ASP.NET and ASP.NET AJAX development, for example, the ability to examine view state and to execute immediate JavaScript code. This latter feature is particularly useful to test objects that you may have created on the client. The Web Development Helper also displays extended error information when JavaScript errors occur, which makes it easier to track down bugs in JavaScript code.

The AJAX Library also provides the `Sys.Debug` class, which you can use to add some extra debugging features to your application. One of the most useful features of this class is the `Sys.Debug.traceDump()` function, which enables you to analyze objects. One way to use this function is to place a `textarea` control on your Web page with an `id` attribute of `TraceConsole`. Then, all output from `Debug` will be sent to this control. For example, you can use the `traceDump()` method to output information about the `Application` object to the console:

```
Sys.Application.add_load(LoadHandler);

function LoadHandler(sender, args)
{
  Sys.Debug.traceDump(sender);
}
```

This results in output along the lines of the following:

```
traceDump {Sys._Application}
    _updating: false
    _id: null
    _disposing: false
    _creatingComponents: false
    _disposableObjects {Array}
    _components {Object}
    _createdComponents {Array}
    _secondPassComponents {Array}
    _loadHandlerDelegate: null
    _events {Sys.EventHandlerList}
        _list {Object}
            load {Array}
                [0] {Function}
    _initialized: true
    _initializing: true
```

You can see all the properties of this object in this output. This technique can be extremely useful for ASP.NET AJAX development.

Making Asynchronous Web Method Calls

One of the most powerful features of ASP.NET AJAX is the ability to call Web methods from client-side script. This gives you access to data, server-side processing, and all manner of other functionality.

You will not be looking at Web methods in this book until Chapter 42, "Windows Communication Foundation," so we will save the details until then and cover the basics here. Put simply, a Web method is a method that you can expose from a Web service that enables you to access remote resources over the Internet. In ASP.NET AJAX, you can also expose Web methods as static methods of server-side Web page code-behind code. You can use parameters and return values in Web methods just as you do in other method types.

In ASP.NET AJAX, Web methods are called asynchronously. You pass parameters to a Web method and define a callback function, which is called when the Web method call completes. You use this callback function to process the Web method response. You can also provide an alternative callback function to call in the event of a call failure.

In the `PCSLibraryDemo` application, you can see a Web method call being performed by clicking the Call Web Method button, as shown in Figure 39-9.

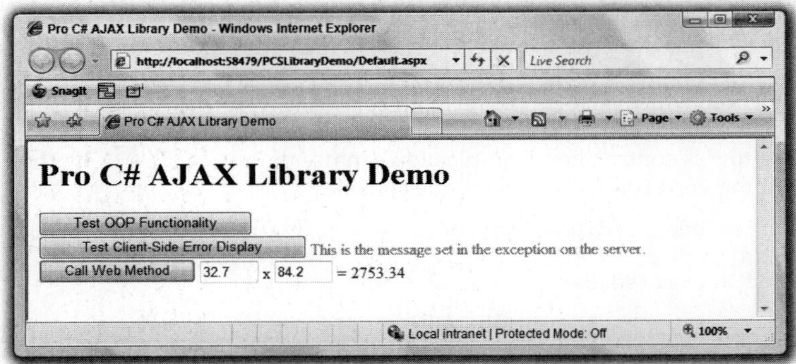

Figure 39-9

Before you can use a Web method from client-side script, you must generate a client-side proxy class to perform the communication. The easiest way to do this is simply to reference the URL of the Web service that contains the Web method in the `ScriptManager` control:

```
<asp:ScriptManager ID="ScriptManager1" runat="server">
  <Services>
    <asp:ServiceReference Path="~/SimpleService.asmx" />
  </Services>
</asp:ScriptManager>
```

ASP.NET Web services use the extension `.asmx`, as shown in this code. To use a client-side proxy to access a Web method in a Web service, you must apply the `System.Web.Script.Services.ScriptService` attribute to the Web service.

For Web methods in the code behind for the Web page, you do not need this attribute, or this reference in `ScriptManager`, but you must use static methods and apply the `System.Web.Services.WebMethod` attribute to the methods.

Once you have generated a client-side stub, you can access the Web method by its name, which is defined as a function of a class with the same name as the Web service. In `PCSLibraryDemo`, the `SimpleService.asmx` Web service has a Web method called `Multiply()`, which multiplies two double parameters. When you call this method from client-side code, you pass the two parameters required by the method (obtained from HTML `<input>` elements in the example) and can pass one or two callback function references. If you pass one reference, this is the callback function that is used when the call returns a success result. If you pass two references, the second one is the callback function that is used for Web method failure.

In `PCSLibraryDemo`, a single callback function is used, which takes the result of the Web method call and assigns it to the `<span>` with the `id` of `webMethodResult`:

```
function callWebMethod()
{
  SimpleService.Multiply(parseFloat($get('xParam').value),
    parseFloat($get('yParam').value), multiplyCallBack);
}

function multiplyCallBack(result)
{
  $get('webMethodResult').innerHTML = result;
}
```

This method is a very simple one but illustrates the ease with which you can call Web services asynchronously from client-side code.

ASP.NET Application Services

ASP.NET AJAX includes three specialized Web services that you can use to access ASP.NET application services. These services are accessed through the following client-side classes:

- `Sys.Services.AuthenticationService` — This service includes methods to log in or log out a user or determine whether a user is logged in.
- `Sys.Services.ProfileService` — This service enables you to get and set profile properties for the currently logged-on user. The profile properties are configured in the `Web.config` file for the application.
- `Sys.Services.RoleService` — This service enables you to determine role membership for the currently logged-on user.

Used properly, these classes enable you to implement extremely responsive user interfaces that include authorization, profile, and membership functionality.

These services are beyond the scope of this chapter, but you should be aware of them, and they are well worth investigating.

Summary

In this chapter, you have seen how you can use ASP.NET AJAX to enhance ASP.NET Web applications. ASP.NET AJAX contains a wealth of functionality that makes Web applications far more responsive and dynamic and can provide a much better user experience.

First, you learned what Ajax is, and about the separate components of ASP.NET AJAX that are available and what they offer. You saw the difference between AJAX Extensions and the AJAX Library and how these components work together to provide the core ASP.NET AJAX functionality. You also looked at the AJAX Control Toolkit, which adds to this core functionality.

Next, you looked at server-side techniques for creating ASP.NET AJAX-enabled Web applications. You saw how ASP.NET AJAX is configured in the `Web.config` file of your ASP.NET Web applications and how to use the various server controls that are part of the AJAX Extensions. Specifically, you learned about `ScriptManager`, `UpdatePanel` (and triggers), `UpdateProgress`, and extender controls. You saw how easy it is to use these controls to add a great deal of functionality to a Web application very quickly.

You then examined the AJAX Library, which extends and enhances JavaScript and provides you with additional functionality that you can add to applications. It does, however, require at least a working knowledge of JavaScript programming.

You learned about the global functions that the AJAX Library adds to JavaScript and how to define namespaces and classes by using the OOP extensions that the AJAX Library adds to JavaScript. You learned how to interact with events that occur on the client during the life cycle of a page and partial-page postbacks. You saw how to use one of these events, `PageRequestManager.endRequest`, to customize how server errors that occur during a partial-page postback are displayed in the Web browser.

Finally, you looked at client-side Web method calls. You saw how an asynchronous model is used for these and how to write the required code to call a simple Web method. You also learned about accessing the ASP.NET application services (authorization, profile, and membership) through Web services.

We hope that this chapter has given you an appetite for this exciting new technology. Ajax is blossoming across the Web, and ASP.NET AJAX is an excellent way to integrate Ajax functionality with ASP.NET applications. This product is also very well supported, and the community-based releases, such as the AJAX Control Toolkit, provide you with even more great functionality that you are free to use in your applications.

Even though you may find yourself having to learn the JavaScript language you never thought you would need, the end result is well worth the effort. By using ASP.NET AJAX you will make far better, more functional, and more dynamic Web applications than you could with ASP.NET alone. And with the latest release of Visual Studio you have tools that make ASP.NET AJAX much easier to use.

In the next chapter you move away from Web development and look at how you can extend Microsoft Office applications such as Word, Excel, and Outlook with code written in Visual Studio.

40

Visual Studio Tools for Office

Visual Studio Tools for Office (VSTO) is a technology that enables you to customize and extend Microsoft Office applications and documents by using the .NET Framework. It also includes tools that you can use to make this customization easier in Visual Studio — for example, a visual designer for office ribbon controls.

VSTO is the latest in a long line of products that Microsoft has released to allow the customization of Office applications. The object model that you use to access Office applications has evolved over time. If you have used it in the past, then parts of it will be familiar to you. If you have programmed VBA add-ins for Office applications, then you will be well prepared for the techniques discussed in this chapter (and, as you will see, VSTO is capable of interoperability with VBA). However, the classes that VSTO makes available so that you can interact with Office through the Office Primary Interop Assemblies (PIAs) have been extended beyond the Office object model. For example, the VSTO classes include .NET data binding functionality.

Up until Visual Studio 2008, VSTO was a separate download that you could obtain if you wanted to develop Office solutions. With Visual Studio 2008, VSTO is integrated with the VS IDE. This version of VSTO, which is also known as VSTO 3, includes full support for Office 2007 and has many new features. This includes the ability to interact with Word content controls, the visual ribbon designer mentioned previously, VBA integration, and more.

This chapter does not assume any prior knowledge of VSTO or its predecessors. In this chapter, you learn the following:

- What types of projects you can create with VSTO and what capabilities you can include in these projects
- Fundamental techniques that apply to all types of VSTO solutions
- How to build VSTO solutions with a custom UI, VBA interoperability, and ClickOnce deployment

VSTO Overview

VSTO consists of the following components:

- A selection of project templates that you can use to create various types of Office solutions
- Designer support for visual layout of ribbons, action panes, and custom task panels
- Classes built on top of the Office Primary Interop Assemblies (PIAs) that provide extensive capabilities

VSTO supports both 2003 and 2007 versions of Office. The VSTO class library comes in two flavors, one for each of these Office versions, which use different sets of assemblies. For simplicity (and because of its richer feature set), this chapter focuses on the 2007 version.

The general architecture of VSTO solutions is shown in Figure 40-1.

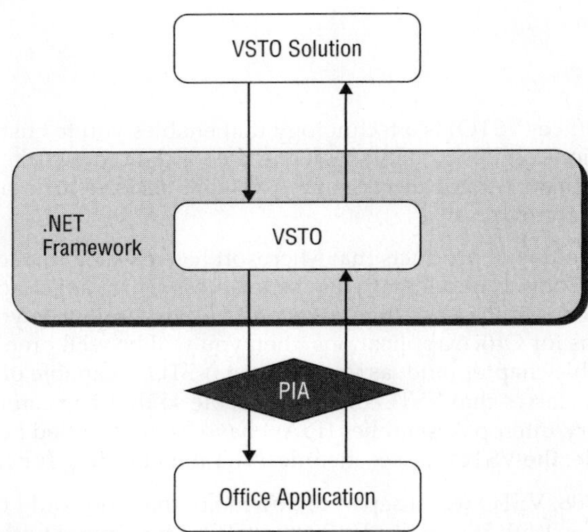

Figure 40-1

Project Types

Figure 40-2 shows the project templates that are available in VS.

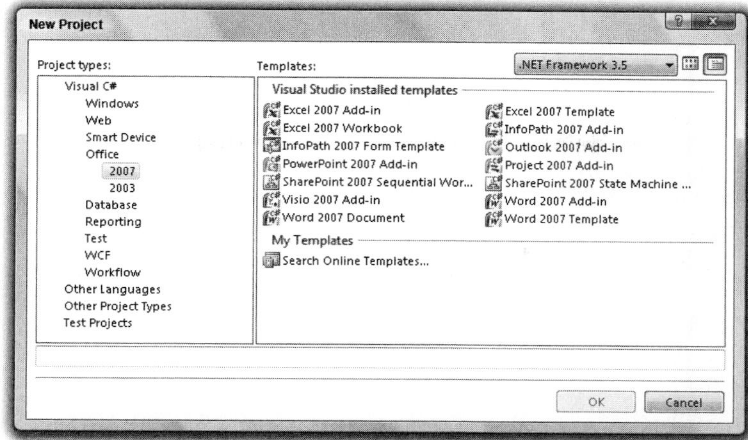

Figure 40-2

Note that when you create a project using one of the VSTO templates you may be asked to enable access to the VBA project system. This is necessary for VBA interoperability.

The VSTO project templates can be divided into the following categories:

- Document-level customizations
- Application-level add-ins
- SharePoint workflow templates
- InfoPath form templates

There are 2003 and 2007 versions of some of the project types, but as discussed earlier, you will look at only the 2007 versions here.

This chapter concentrates on the most commonly used project types, which are document-level customizations and application-level add-ins.

Document-Level Customizations

When you create a project of this type, you will generate an assembly that will be linked to an individual document — for example a Word document, Word template, or Excel workbook. When you load the document, the associated Office application will detect the customization, load the assembly, and make the VSTO customization available.

You might use a project of this type to provide additional functionality to a particular line-of-business document, or to a whole class of documents by adding customizations to a document template. You can include code that manipulates the document and the content of the document, including any embedded objects. You can also provide custom menus, including ribbon menus that you can create using the VS Ribbon Designer.

When you create a document-level project, you can choose to create a new document or to copy an existing document as a starting point for your development. You can also choose the type of document to create. For a Word document, for example, you can choose to create `.docx` (the default), `.doc`, or `.docm` documents (`.docm` is a macro-enabled document). The dialog box for this is shown in Figure 40-3.

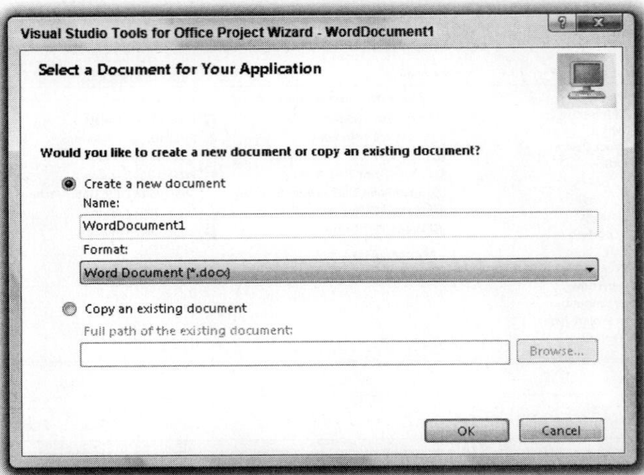

Figure 40-3

Application-Level Add-Ins

Application-level add-ins are different from document-level customizations in that they are available throughout their targeted Office application. You can access add-in code, which might include menus, document manipulations and so on, regardless of what documents are loaded.

When you start an Office application such as Word, it will look for associated add-ins that have entries in the registry and will load any assemblies that it needs to.

SharePoint Workflow Templates

These projects provide a template to create SharePoint workflow applications. These are used to manage the flow of documents within SharePoint processes. By creating a project of this type, you can execute custom code at key times during the document lifecycle.

InfoPath Form Templates

These are a form of document-level customization for InfoPath forms, although they use a slightly different methodology for Word and Excel document customizations and, so, are usually classified differently. You can create templates for InfoPath forms that extend the functionality of the InfoPath designer and that provide additional functionality and business logic for designers and end-users of InfoPath forms.

When you create an InfoPath Form template, you are presented with a wizard to specify exactly the sort of project you want to create, as shown in Figure 40-4.

As you can see in Figure 40-4, this wizard gives you quite a lot of flexibility in the source for the form you are creating — you can choose a variety of starting points (including forms on a SharePoint site). You can also create complete forms or template parts and limit functionality to browser-compatible features if desired.

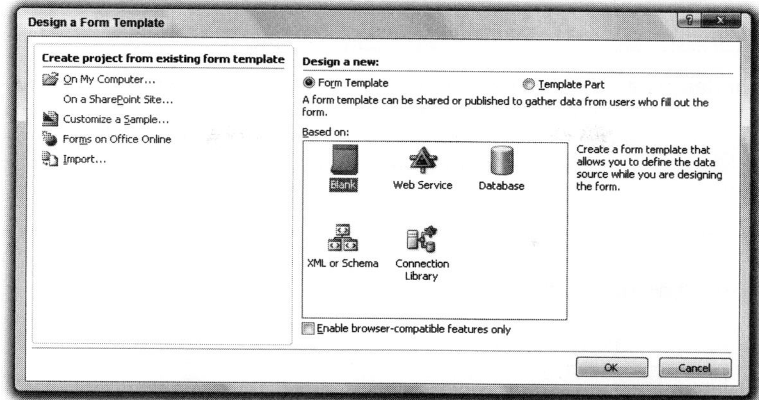

Figure 40-4

Project Features

There are several features that you can use in the various VSTO project types, such as interactive panes and controls. The project type you use determines the features that are available to you. The following tables list these features according to the projects in which they are available.

Document-Level Customization Features

Feature	Description
Actions pane	Actions panes are dialog boxes that are hosted inside the action pane of Word or Excel. You can display whatever controls you like here, which makes this an extremely versatile way of extending documents and applications.
Data cache	Data caching enables you to store data that is used in your documents externally to those documents in cached data islands. These data islands can be updated from data sources or manually, and enable the Office documents to access data when data sources are offline or unavailable.
Endpoints for VBA code	As discussed earlier, VSTO enables VBA interoperability. In document-level customizations, you can provide endpoint methods that can be called from VBA code.
Host controls	Host controls are extended wrappers around existing controls in the Office object model. You can manipulate and data-bind to these objects.
Smart tags	Smart tags are objects that are embedded in Office documents and that have typed content. They are automatically detected within the content of Office documents; for example, a stock quote smart tag is added automatically when the application detects appropriate text. You can create your own smart tag types and define operations that can be performed on them.

Feature	Description
Visual document designer	When you work with document customization projects, the Office object model is used to create a visual design surface that you can use to lay out controls interactively. The toolbars and menus shown in the designer are, as you will see later in this chapter, fully functional.

Application-Level Add-In Features

Feature	Description
Custom task pane	Task panes are typically docked to one edge of an Office application and provide a variety of functionality. For example, Word has a task pane used for manipulating styles. As with action panes, these give you a great deal of flexibility.
Cross-application communication	Once you have created an add-in for one Office application, you can expose that functionality to other add-ins. You could, for example, create a financial calculating service in Excel and then use that service from Word — without creating a separate add-in.
Outlook form regions	You can create form regions that can be used in Outlook.

Features Usable In All Project Types

Feature	Description
ClickOnce deployment	You can distribute any VSTO project that you create to end users through ClickOnce deployment methods. This enables users to stay up-to-date with updates to your document- and application-level solutions by detecting changes to the application manifest.
Ribbon menus	Ribbon menus are used in all Office applications, and VSTO includes two ways to create your own ribbon menus. You can either use XML to define a ribbon or use the Ribbon Designer. Typically, you will use the Ribbon Designer as it is much easier to use, although you may want the XML version for backwards compatibility.

VSTO Fundamentals

Now that you have seen what is included in VSTO, it is time to look at the more practical side of things, and how you can build VSTO projects. The techniques demonstrated in this section are general ones that apply to all types of VSTO projects.

In this section, you will look at the following:

- Office object model
- VSTO namespaces
- Host items and host controls
- Basic VSTO project structure
- The Globals class
- Event handling

Office Object Model

The Office 2007 suite of applications exposes its functionality through a COM object model. You can use this object model directly from VBA to control just about any aspect of Office functionality. The Office object model was introduced in Office 97, and has evolved since then as functionality in Office has changed.

There are a huge number of classes in the Office object model, some of which are used across the suite of Office applications and some of which are specific to individual applications. For example, the Word 2007 object model includes a `Documents` collection representing the currently loaded objects, each of which is represented by a `Document` object. In VBA code, you can access documents by name or index and call methods to perform operations on them. For example, the following VBA code closes the document with the name `My Document` without saving changes:

```
Documents("My Document").Close SaveChanges:=wdDoNotSaveChanges
```

The Office object model includes named constants (such as `wdDoNotSaveChanges` in the preceding code) and enumerations to make it easier to use.

VSTO Namespaces

VSTO contains a collection of namespaces, which contain types that you can use to program against the Office object model. Many of the classes and enumerations in these namespaces map directly to objects and enumerations in the Office object model. These are accessed through Office PIAs. However, VSTO also contains types that do not map directly, or are unrelated to the Office object model. For example, there are a lot of classes that are used for designer support in VS.

The types that do wrap or communicate with objects in the Office object model are divided into namespaces containing types for use with Office 2003 and those for use with Office 2007. The namespaces that you will use for Office 2007 development are summarized in the following table.

Namespace	Description
`Microsoft.Office.Core`, `Microsoft.Office.Interop.*`	These namespaces contain thin wrappers around the PIA classes and, so, provide the base functionality for working with the Office classes. There are several nested namespaces in the `Microsoft.Office.Interop` namespace for each of the Office products.

Namespace	Description
`Microsoft.Office.Tools`	This namespace contains general types that provide VSTO functionality and base classes for many of the classes in nested namespaces. For example, this namespace includes the classes required to implement action panes in document-level customizations and the base class for application-level add-ins.
`Microsoft.Office.Tools.Excel`, `Microsoft.Office.Tools.Excel.*`	These namespaces contain the types required to interact with the Excel application and Excel documents.
`Microsoft.Office.Tools.Outlook`	These namespaces contain the types required to interact with the Outlook application.
`Microsoft.Office.Tools.Ribbon`	This namespace includes the types required to work with and create your own ribbon menus.
`Microsoft.Office.Tools.Word`, `Microsoft.Office.Tools.Word.*`	These namespaces contain the types required to interact with the Word application and Word documents.
`Microsoft.VisualStudio.Tools.*`	These namespaces provide the VSTO infrastructure that you work with when you develop VSTO solutions in VS.

Host Items and Host Controls

Host items and host controls are classes that have been extended to make it easier for document-level customizations to interact with Office documents. These classes simplify your code as they expose .NET-style events and are fully managed. The "host" part of the name of host items and host classes references the fact that these classes wrap and extend the native Office objects that are accessed through PIAs.

Often when you use host items and host controls, you will find that it is necessary to use the underlying PIA interop types as well. For example, if you create a new Word document, then you receive a reference to the interop Word document type rather than the Word document host item. You need to be aware of this and write your code accordingly.

There are host items and host controls for both Word and Excel document-level customizations.

Word

There is a single host item for Word, `Microsoft.Office.Tools.Word.Document`. This represents a Word document. As you might expect, this class has an enormous number of methods and properties that you can use to interact with Word documents.

There are 12 host controls for Word, as shown in the following table, all of which are found in the `Microsoft.Office.Tools.Word` namespace.

Control	Description
Bookmark	This control represents a location within the Word document. This might be a single location or a range of characters.
XMLNode, XmlNodes	These controls are used when the document has an attached XML schema. They allow you to reference document content by the XML node location of that content. You can also manipulate the XML structure of a document with these controls.
ContentControl	This class is the base class for the remaining eight controls in this table, and enables you to deal with Word content controls. A content control is a control that presents content as a control or that enables functionality above and beyond that offered by plain text in a document.
BuildingBlockGalleryContentControl	This control enables you to add and manipulate document building blocks, such as formatted tables, cover pages, and so on.
ComboBoxContentControl	This control represents content formatted as a combo box.
DatePickerContentControl	This control represents content formatted in a date picker.
DropDownListContentControl	This control represents content formatted as a drop-down list.
GroupContentControl	This control represents content that is a grouped collection of other content items, including text and other content controls.
PictureContentControl	This control represents an image.
RichTextContentControl	This control represents a block of rich text content.
PlainTextContentControl	This control represents a block of plain text content.

Excel

There are three host items and four host controls for Excel, all of which are contained in the `Microsoft.Office.Tools.Excel` namespace.

The Excel host items are shown in the following table.

Host Item	Description
`Workbook`	This host item represents an entire Excel workbook, which may contain multiple worksheets and chartsheets.
`Worksheet`	This host item is used for individual worksheets within a workbook.
`Chartsheet`	This host item is used for individual chartsheets within a workbook.

The Excel host controls are shown in the following table.

Control	Description
`Chart`	This control represents a chart that is embedded in a worksheet.
`ListObject`	This control represents a list in a worksheet.
`NamedRange`	This control represents a named range in a worksheet.
`XmlMappedRange`	This control is used when an Excel spreadsheet has an attached schema, and is used to manipulate ranges that are mapped to XML schema elements.

Basic VSTO Project Structure

When you first create a VSTO project, the files you start with vary according to the project type, but there are some common features. In this section, you will see what constitutes a VSTO project.

Document-Level Customization Project Structure

When you create a document-level customization project, you will see an entry in Solution Explorer that represents the document type. This may be:

- A `.docx` file for a Word document
- A `.dotx` file for a Word template
- A `.xlsx` file for an Excel workbook
- A `.xltx` file for an Excel template

Each of these has a designer view and a code file, which you will see if you expand the item in Solution Explorer. The Excel templates also include sub-items representing the workbook as a whole and each spreadsheet in the workbook. This structure enables you to provide custom functionality on a per-sheet or per-workbook basis.

If you view the hidden files in one of these projects, you will see several designer files that you can look at to see the template-generated code. Each Office document item has an associated class from the VSTO namespaces, and the classes in the code files derive from these classes. These classes are defined as partial class definitions so that your custom code is separated from the code generated by the visual designer, similar to the structure of Windows Forms applications.

For example, the Word document template provides a class that derives from the host item `Microsoft.Office.Tools.Word.Document`. This code is contained in `ThisDocument.cs`, as follows:

```
using System;
using System.Collections.Generic;
using System.Data;
using System.Linq;
using System.Text;
using System.Windows.Forms;
using System.Xml.Linq;
using Microsoft.VisualStudio.Tools.Applications.Runtime;
using Office = Microsoft.Office.Core;
using Word = Microsoft.Office.Interop.Word;
namespace WordDocument1
{
    public partial class ThisDocument
    {
        private void ThisDocument_Startup(object sender, System.EventArgs e)
        {
        }
        private void ThisDocument_Shutdown(object sender, System.EventArgs e)
        {
        }
        #region VSTO Designer generated code
        /// <summary>
        /// Required method for Designer support - do not modify
        /// the contents of this method with the code editor.
        /// </summary>
        private void InternalStartup()
        {
            this.Startup += new System.EventHandler(ThisDocument_Startup);
            this.Shutdown += new System.EventHandler(ThisDocument_Shutdown);
        }
        #endregion
    }
}
```

This template-generated code includes aliases for the two main namespaces that you will use when creating a document-level customization for Word, `Microsoft.Office.Core` for the main VSTO Office classes and `Microsoft.Office.Interop.Word` for Word-specific classes. Note that if you want to use Word host controls, then you would also add a `using` statement for the `Microsoft.Office.Tools.Word` namespace. The template-generated code also defines two event handler hooks that you can use to execute code when the document is loaded or unloaded, `ThisDocument_Startup()` and `ThisDocument_Shutdown()`.

Every one of the document-level customization project types has a similar structure in its code file (or, in the case of Excel, code files). There are namespace aliases defined for you and handlers for the various `Startup` and `Shutdown` events that the VSTO classes define. From this starting point, you add dialog boxes, action panes, ribbon controls, event handlers, and custom code to define the behavior of your customization.

With document-level customizations, you can also customize the document or documents through the document designer. Depending on the type of solution you are creating, this might involve adding boilerplate content to templates, interactive content to documents, or something else. The designers are effectively hosted versions of Office applications, and you can use them to enter content just as you can in the applications themselves. However, you can also add controls such as host controls and Windows Forms controls to documents, and code around these controls.

Application-Level Add-In Project Structure

When you create an application-level add-in, there will be no document or documents in Solution Explorer. Instead, you will see an item representing the application that you are creating an add-in for, and if you expand this item, you will see a file called `ThisAddIn.cs`. This file contains a partial class definition for a class called `ThisAddIn`, which provides the entry point for your add-in. This class derives from `Microsoft.Office.Tools.AddIn`, which provides code add-in functionality, and implements the `Microsoft.VisualStudio.Tools.Office.IOfficeEntryPoint` interface, which is an infrastructure interface.

For example, the code generated by the Word add-in template is as follows:

```
using System;
using System.Collections.Generic;
using System.Linq;
using System.Text;
using System.Xml.Linq;
using Word = Microsoft.Office.Interop.Word;
using Office = Microsoft.Office.Core;
namespace WordAddIn1
{
    public partial class ThisAddIn
    {
        private void ThisAddIn_Startup(object sender, System.EventArgs e)
        {
        }
        private void ThisAddIn_Shutdown(object sender, System.EventArgs e)
        {
        }
        #region VSTO generated code
        /// <summary>
        /// Required method for Designer support - do not modify
        /// the contents of this method with the code editor.
        /// </summary>
        private void InternalStartup()
        {
            this.Startup += new System.EventHandler(ThisAddIn_Startup);
            this.Shutdown += new System.EventHandler(ThisAddIn_Shutdown);
        }

        #endregion
    }
}
```

As you can see, this structure is very similar to the structure used in document-level customizations. It includes aliases for the same `Microsoft.Office.Core` and `Microsoft.Office.Interop.Word` namespaces, and gives you event handlers for `Startup` and `Shutdown` events (`ThisAddIn_Startup()` and `ThisAddIn_Shutdown()`). These events are slightly different from the document ones, as they are raised when the add-in is loaded or unloaded rather than when individual documents are opened or closed.

You proceed to customize application-level add-ins much as you do document-level customizations: by adding ribbon controls, task panes, and additional code.

The Globals Class

All VSTO project types define a class called `Globals` that gives you global access to the following:

- For document-level customizations, all documents in the solution. These are exposed through members with names that match the document class names — for example, `Globals.ThisWorkbook` and `Globals.Sheet1`.
- For application-level add-ins, the add-in object. This is exposed through `Globals.ThisAddIn`.
- For Outlook add-in projects, all Outlook form regions.
- All ribbons in the solution, through the `Globals.Ribbons` property.

Behind the scenes, the `Globals` class is created through a series of partial definitions in the various designer-maintained code files in your solution. For example, the default `Sheet1` worksheet in an Excel Workbook project includes the following designer-generated code:

```
internal sealed partial class Globals
{
   private static Sheet1 _Sheet1;
   internal static Sheet1 Sheet1
   {
      get
      {
         return _Sheet1;
      }
      set
      {
         if ((_Sheet1 == null))
         {
            _Sheet1 = value;
         }
         else
         {
            throw new System.NotSupportedException();
         }
      }
   }
}
```

This code adds the `Sheet1` member to the `Globals` class.

Event Handling

Earlier in this chapter, you saw how the host item and host control classes expose events that you can handle. Unfortunately, this is not the case for the interop classes. There are a few events that you can use, but for the most part, you will find it difficult to create event-driven solutions by using these events. Most often, to respond to events you should focus on the events exposed by host items and host controls.

The obvious problem here is that there are no host items or host controls for application-level add-in projects. Sadly, this is a problem that you must learn to live with when you use VSTO. However, the most common events that you are likely to listen for in add-ins are those associated with ribbon menu and task pane interaction. You design ribbons with the integrated ribbon designer, and you can respond to any events generated by the ribbon to make the control interactive. Task panes are usually implemented as Windows Forms user controls (although you can use WPF), and you can use Windows Forms events here rather than PIA interop events. This means that you will not often encounter situations in which there is no event available for the functionality you require.

When you do need to use a PIA-exposed event, you will find that events are exposed through interfaces on the PIA objects. Consider a Word Add-In project. The `ThisAddIn` class in this project exposes a property called `Application` through which you can obtain a reference to the Office application. This property is of type `Microsoft.Office.Interop.Word.Application`, and exposes events through the `Microsoft.Office.Interop.Word.ApplicationEvents4_Event` interface. This interface exposes a total of 29 events (which really doesn't seem to be a lot for an application as complex as Word, does it?). You can handle, for example, the `DocumentBeforeClose` event to respond to Word document close requests.

Building VSTO Solutions

The previous sections explained what VSTO projects are, how they are structured, and the features that you can use in the various project types. In this section, you look at implementing VSTO solutions.

Figure 40-5 outlines the structure of document-level customization solutions.

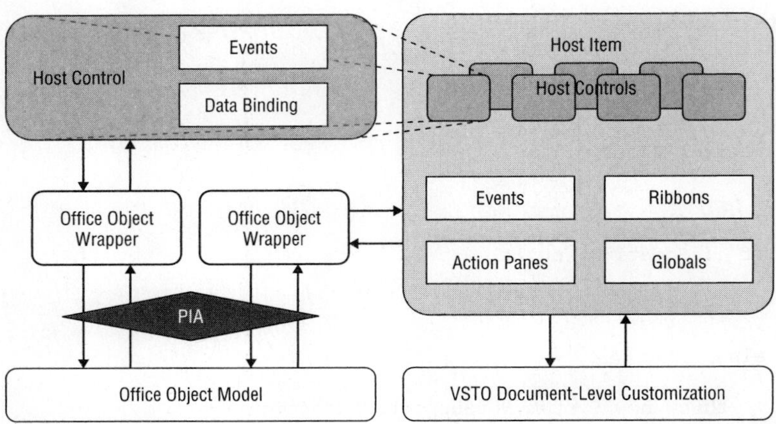

Figure 40-5

For document-level customizations you will interact with at least one host item, which will typically contain multiple host controls. You may use Office object wrappers directly, but for the most part, you will access the Office object model and its functionality through host items and host controls.

You will make use of host item and host control events, data binding, ribbon menus, action panes, and global objects in your code.

Figure 40-6 outlines the structure of application-level add-in solutions.

In this slightly simpler model, you are more likely to use the thinner wrappers around Office objects directly, or at least through the add-in class that encapsulates your solution. You will also use events exposed by the add-in class, ribbon menus, task panes, and global objects in your code.

In this section, you will look at both of these types of applications as appropriate, as well as the following topics:

- Managing application-level add-ins
- Interacting with applications and documents
- UI customization

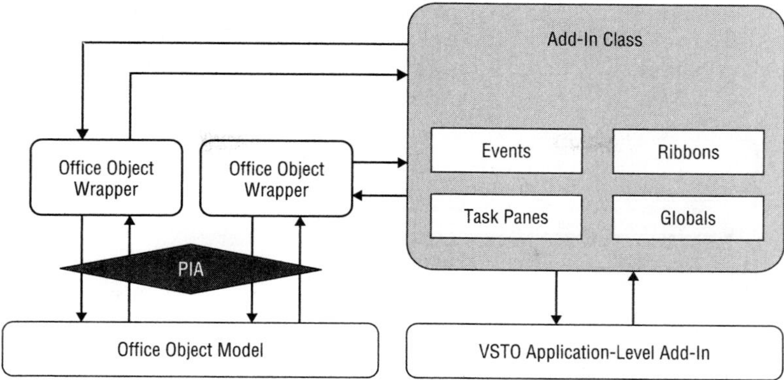

Figure 40-6

Managing Application-Level Add-Ins

One of the first things you will find when you create an application-level add-in is that VS carries out all the steps necessary to register the add-in with the Office application. This means that registry entries are added so that when the Office application starts, it will automatically locate and load your assembly. If you subsequently want to add or remove add-ins, then you must either navigate through Office application settings or manipulate the registry manually.

For example, in Word, you must open the Office Button menu, click Word Options, and select the Add-Ins tab, as shown in Figure 40-7.

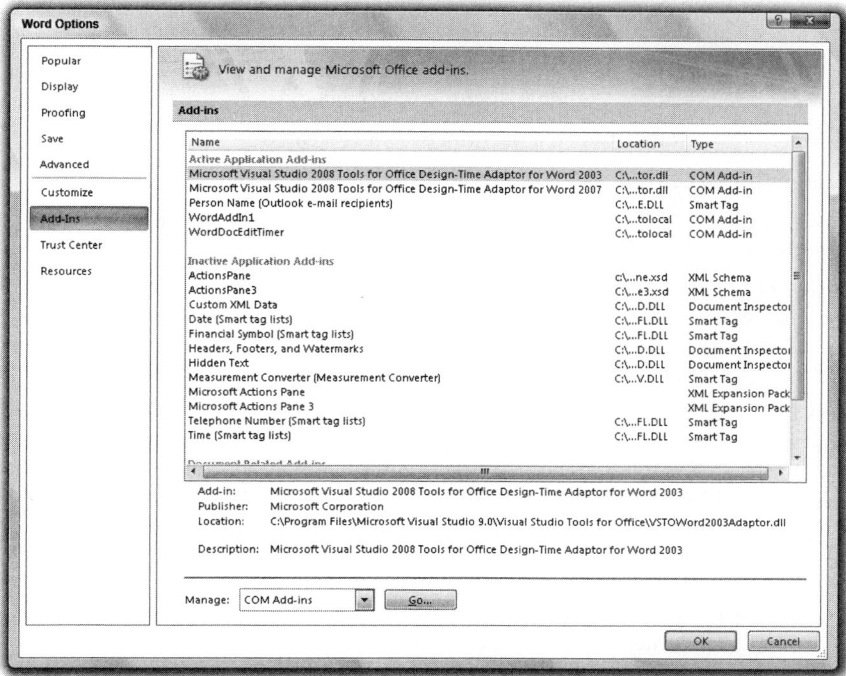

Figure 40-7

Figure 40-7 shows two add-ins that have been created with VSTO: `WordAddIn1` and `WordDocEditTimer`. To add or remove add-ins, you must select COM Add-Ins in the Manage drop-down (the default option) and click the Go button. The dialog box that appears is shown in Figure 40-8.

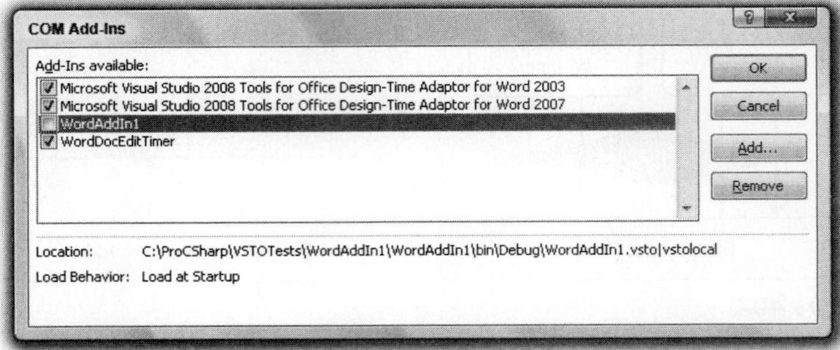

Figure 40-8

You can unload add-ins by deselecting them in the COM Add-Ins dialog box (as shown in Figure 40-8), and you can add new add-ins or remove old ones with the Add and Remove buttons.

Interacting with Applications and Documents

Whatever type of application you are creating, you will want to interact with the host application and/or documents in the host operation. In part, this includes using UI customizations, which you learn about in the next section. However, you may also need to monitor documents within an application, which means that you must handle some Office object model events. For example, to monitor documents in Word, you require event handlers for the following events of the `Microsoft.Office.Interop.Word.ApplicationEvents4_Event` interface:

- `DocumentOpen` — Raised when a document is opened.
- `NewDocument` — Raised when a new document is created.
- `DocumentBeforeClose` — Raised when a document is saved.

Also, when Word first starts, it will have a document loaded, which will either be a blank new document or a document that was loaded.

The downloadable code for this chapter includes an example called `WordDocEditTimer`*, which maintains a list of edit times for Word documents. Part of the functionality of this application is to monitor the documents that are loaded, for reasons that are explained later. Because this example also uses a custom task pane and ribbon menu, you will look at it after covering those topics.*

You can access the currently active document in Word through `ThisAddIn.Application.ActiveDocument` property, and the collection of open documents through `ThisAddIn.Application.Documents`. Similar properties exist for the other Office applications with a Multiple Document Interface (MDI). You can manipulate various properties of documents through the properties exposed by, for example, the `Microsoft.Office.Interop.Word.Document` class.

One point to note here is that the amount of classes and class members you must deal with when developing VSTO solutions is, frankly, enormous. Until you get used to it, it can be difficult to locate the features you are after. For example, it is not obvious why in Word the current active selection is available not through the active document, but through the application (through the `ThisAddIn.Application.Selection` property).

The selection is useful for inserting, reading, or replacing text through the `Range` property. For example:

```
ThisAddIn.Application.Selection.Range.Text = "Inserted text";
```

Unfortunately, there is not enough space in this chapter to cover the object libraries in great depth. Instead, you will learn about the object libraries as they are relevant to the ongoing discussion.

UI Customization

Perhaps the most important aspect of the latest release of VSTO is the flexibility that is available for customizing the UI of your customizations and add-ins. You can add content to any of the existing ribbon menus, add completely new ribbon menus, customize task panes by adding action panes, add completely new task panes, and integrate Windows Forms and WPF forms and controls.

In this section, we look at each of these subjects.

Ribbon Menus

You can add ribbon menus to any of the VSTO projects that you are looking at in this chapter. When you add a ribbon, you will see the designer window shown in Figure 40-9.

Figure 40-9

The designer allows you to customize this ribbon by adding controls to the Office button menu (shown in the top left of Figure 40-9) and to groups on the ribbon. You can also add additional groups.

The classes used in ribbons are found in the `Microsoft.Office.Tools.Ribbon` namespace. This includes the ribbon class that you derive from to create a ribbon, `OfficeRibbon`. This class can contain `RibbonTab` objects, each of which includes content for a single tab. Tabs contain `RibbonGroup` objects, like the `group1` group in Figure 40-9. These tabs can contain a variety of controls.

It is possible for the groups on a tab to be positioned on a completely new tab, or on one of the existing tabs in the Office application that you are targeting. Where the groups appear is determined by the `RibbonTab.ControlId` property. This property has a `ControlIdType` property, which you can set to `RibbonControlIdType.Custom` or `RibbonControlIdType.Office`. If you use `Custom`, then you must also set `RibbonTab.ControlId.CustomId` to a `string` value, which is the tab identifier. You can use any identifier you like here. However, if you use `Office` for `ControlIdType`, then you must set `RibbonTab.ControlId.OfficeId` to a `string` value that matches one of the identifiers used in the Office product you are using. For example, in Excel you could set this property to `TabHome` to add groups to the Home tab, `TabInsert` for the Insert tab, and so on. The default for add-ins is `TabAddIns`, which will be shared by all add-ins.

Many tabs are available, especially in Outlook; you can download a series of spreadsheets containing the full list from: `www.microsoft.com/downloads/details.aspx?FamilyID=4329D9E9-4D11-46A5-898D-23E4F331E9AE&displaylang=en.`

Once you have decided where to put your ribbon groups, you can add any of the controls shown in the following table.

Control	Description
`RibbonBox`	This is a container control that you can use to lay out other controls in a group. You can lay out controls in a `RibbonBox` horizontally or vertically by changing the `BoxStyle` property to `RibbonBoxStyle.Horizontal` or `RibbonBoxStyle.Vertical`.
`RibbonButton`	You can use this control to add a small or large button with or without a text label to a group. Set the `ControlSize` property to `RibbonControlSize.RibbonControlSizeLarge` or `RibbonControlSize.RibbonControlSizeRegular` to control the size. The button has a `Click` event handler that you can use to respond to interaction. You can also set the image to a custom image or to one of the images stored in the Office system (described following this table).
`RibbonButtonGroup`	This is a container control that represents a group of buttons. It can contain `RibbonButton`, `RibbonGallery`, `RibbonMenu`, `RibbonSplitButton`, and `RibbonToggleButton` controls.
`RibbonCheckBox`	A check box control with a `Click` event and a `Checked` property.
`RibbonComboBox`	A combo box (combined text entry with drop-down list of items). Use the `Items` property for items, the `Text` property for the entered text, and the `TextChanged` event to respond to changed.
`RibbonDropDown`	A container that can contain `RibbonDropDownItem` and `RibbonButton` items, in `Items` and `Buttons` properties respectively. The buttons and items are formatted into a drop-down list. You use the `SelectionChanged` event to respond to interaction.
`RibbonEditBox`	A text box that users can use to enter or edit text in the `Text` property. This control has a `TextChanged` event.
`RibbonGallery`	As with `RibbonDropDown`, this control can contain `RibbonDropDownItem` and `RibbonButton` items, in `Items` and `Buttons` properties respectively. This control uses `Click` and `ButtonClick` events rather than the `SelectionChanged` event that `RibbonDropDown` has.
`RibbonLabel`	Simple text display, set with the `Label` property.
`RibbonMenu`	A pop-up menu that you can populate with other controls, such as `RibbonButton` and nested `RibbonMenu` controls, when it is open in design view. Handle events for the items on the menu.
`RibbonSeparator`	A simple separator used to customize control layout in groups.

Control	Description
RibbonSplitButton	Control that combines a RibbonButton or RibbonToggleButton with a RibbonMenu. Set the button style with ButtonType, which can be RibbonButtonType.Button or RibbonButtonType.ToggleButton. Use the Click event for the main button or individual button Click events in the menu to respond to interaction.
RibbonToggleButton	A button that can be in a selected or unselected state, as indicated by the Checked property. This control also has a Click event.

You can also set the DialogBoxLauncher property of a group so that an icon appears in the bottom right of the group. You can use this to display a dialog box as its name suggests, or to open a task pane, or to perform any other action you want. You add or remove this icon through the GroupView Tasks menu, as shown in Figure 40-10, which also shows some of the other controls in the previous table as they appear on a ribbon in design view.

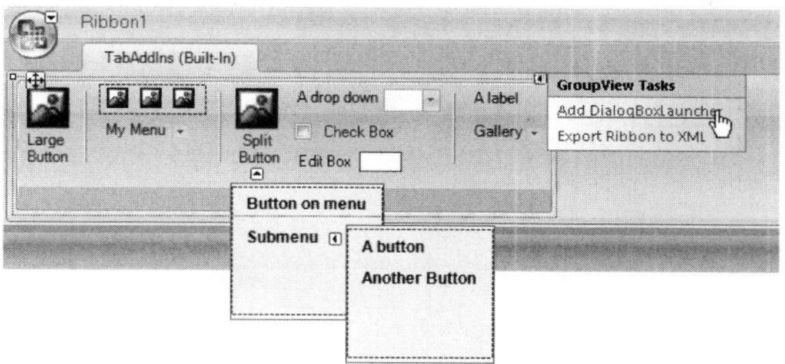

Figure 40-10

To set the image for a control, for example a RibbonButton control, you can either set the Image property to a custom image and ImageName to a name for the image (so that you can optimize image loading in an OfficeRibbon.LoadImage event hander), or you can use one of the built-in Office images. To do this, you set the OfficeImageId property to the ID of the image.

There are many images that you can use; you can download a spreadsheet that lists them from www.microsoft.com/downloads/details.aspx?familyid=12b99325-93e8-4ed4-8385-74d0f7661318&displaylang=en. Figure 40-11 shows a sample.

Figure 40-11 shows the Developer ribbon tab, which you can enable through the Office button, in the Excel Options dialog box, on the Popular tab.

When you click on an image, a dialog box appears to tell you what the image ID is, as shown in Figure 40-12.

The ribbon designer is extremely flexible, and you can provide pretty much any functionality that you would expect to find on an Office ribbon. However, if you want to customize your UI further, then you will want to use action and task panes, as you can create any UI and functionality you like there.

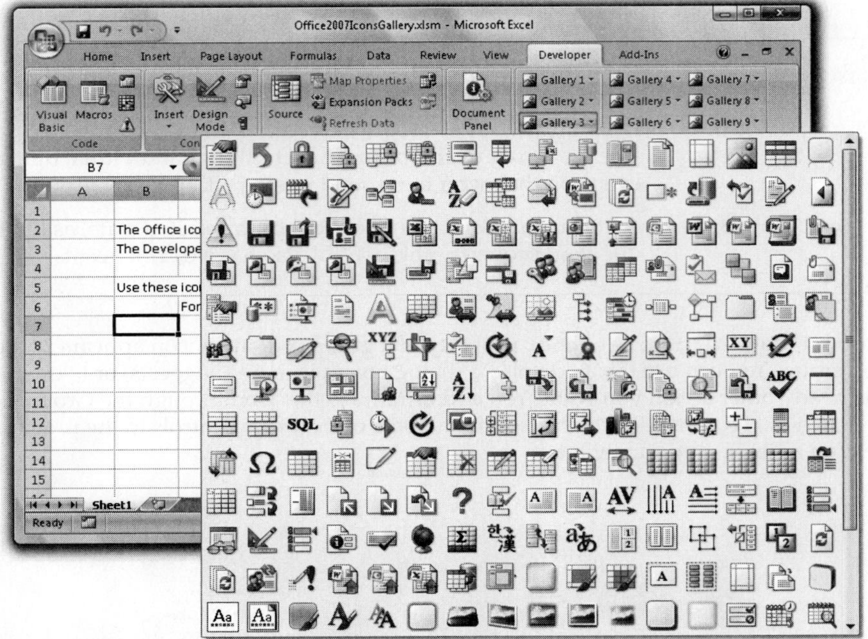

Figure 40-11

Figure 40-12

Action Panes and Custom Task Panes

You can use action and task panes to display content that is docked in the task pane area of the Office application interface. Task panes are used in application-level add-ins, and action panes are used in document-level customizations. Both task and action panes must inherit from `UserControl` objects, which means that you create a UI by using Windows Forms. You can also use a WPF UI if you host a WPF form in an `ElementHost` control on the `UserControl`. One difference between these controls is that you can add action panes to a document-level customization through the Action Pane Template item in the New Item Wizard or with a simple user control. Task panes must be added as plain user controls.

To add an action pane to a document in a document-level customization, you add an instance of the action pane class to the `Controls` collection of the `ActionsPane` property of the document. For example:

```
public partial class ThisWorkbook
{
   Private ActionsPaneControl1 actionsPane;
   private void ThisWorkbook_Startup(object sender, System.EventArgs e)
   {
      actionsPane = new ActionsPaneControl1();
      this.ActionsPane.Controls.Add(actionsPane);
   }
   ...
}
```

This code adds the actions pane when the document (in this case an Excel workbook) is loaded. You can also do this in, for example, a ribbon button event handler.

Custom task panes are added through the `ThisAddIn.CustomTaskPanes.Add()` method property in application-level add-in projects. This method also allows you to name the task window. For example:

```
public partial class ThisAddIn
{
   Microsoft.Office.Tools.CustomTaskPane taskPane;
   private void ThisAddIn_Startup(object sender, System.EventArgs e)
   {
      taskPane = this.CustomTaskPanes.Add(new UserControl1(), "My Task Pane");
      taskPane.Visible = true;
   }
   ...
}
```

Note that the `Add()` method returns an object of type `Microsoft.Office.Tools.CustomTaskPane`. You can access the user control itself through the `Control` property of this object. You can also use other properties exposed by this type — for example, the `Visible` property as shown in the previous code — to control the task pane.

At this point, it is worth mentioning a slightly unusual feature of Office applications, and in particular, a difference between Word and Excel. For historical reasons, although both Word and Excel are MDI applications, the way in which these applications host documents is different. In Word, every document has a unique parent window. In Excel, every document shares the same parent window.

When you call the `CustomTaskPanes.Add()` method, the default behavior is to add the task pane to the currently active window. In Excel, this means that every document will display the task pane, as the same parent window is used for all of them. In Word, the situation is different. If you want the task pane to appear for every document, then you must add it to every window that contains a document.

To add the task pane to a specific document, you pass an instance of the `Microsoft.Office.Interop.Word.Window` class to the `Add()` method as a third parameter. You can obtain the window associated with a document through the `Microsoft.Office.Interop.Word.Document.ActiveWindow` property.

In the next section, you will see how to do this in practice.

Example Application

As mentioned in previous sections, the example code for this chapter includes an application called `WordDocEditTimer`, which maintains a list of edit times for Word documents. In this section, we examine the code for this application in detail, as it illustrates everything you've read about so far and includes some useful tips.

The general operation of this application is that whenever a document is created or loaded, a timer is started, linked to the document name. If you close a document, then the timer for that document pauses. If you open a document that has previously been timed, then the timer resumes. Also, if you use Save As to save a document with a different filename, then the timer is updated to use the new filename.

This application is a Word application-level add-in, and uses a custom task pane and a ribbon menu. The ribbon menu contains a button that you can use to turn the task pane on and off and a check box that enables you to pause the timer for the currently active document. The group containing these controls is appended to the Home ribbon tab. The task pane displays a list of active timers.

This user interface is shown in Figure 40-13.

Figure 40-13

Timers are maintained through the `DocumentTimer` class:

```
public class DocumentTimer
{
   public Word.Document Document { get; set; }
   public DateTime LastActive { get; set; }
   public bool IsActive { get; set; }
   public TimeSpan EditTime { get; set; }
}
```

This keeps a reference to a `Microsoft.Office.Interop.Word.Document` object as well as the total edit time, whether the timer is active, and the time it last became active. The `ThisAddIn` class maintains a collection of these objects, associated with document names:

```
public partial class ThisAddIn
{
   private Dictionary<string, DocumentTimer> documentEditTimes;
```

Each timer can therefore be located by document reference or document name. This is necessary because document references allow you to keep track of document name changes (there is no event that you can use to monitor this), and document names allow you to keep track of closed and reopened documents.

The `ThisAddIn` class also maintains a list of `CustomTaskPane` objects (as noted earlier, one is required for each window in Word):

```
   private List<Tools.CustomTaskPane> timerDisplayPanes;
```

When the add-in starts, the `ThisAddIn_Startup()` method performs several tasks. First, it initializes the two collections:

```
   private void ThisAddIn_Startup(object sender, System.EventArgs e)
   {
      // Initialize timers and display panels
      documentEditTimes = new Dictionary<string, DocumentTimer>();
      timerDisplayPanes = new List<Microsoft.Office.Tools.CustomTaskPane>();
```

Next, it adds several event handlers through the `ApplicationEvents4_Event` interface:

```
      // Add event handlers
      Word.ApplicationEvents4_Event eventInterface = this.Application;
      eventInterface.DocumentOpen += new Microsoft.Office.Interop.Word
         .ApplicationEvents4_DocumentOpenEventHandler(
            eventInterface_DocumentOpen);
      eventInterface.NewDocument += new Microsoft.Office.Interop.Word
         .ApplicationEvents4_NewDocumentEventHandler(
            eventInterface_NewDocument);
      eventInterface.DocumentBeforeClose += new Microsoft.Office.Interop.Word
         .ApplicationEvents4_DocumentBeforeCloseEventHandler(
            eventInterface_DocumentBeforeClose);
      eventInterface.WindowActivate += new Microsoft.Office.Interop.Word
         .ApplicationEvents4_WindowActivateEventHandler(
            eventInterface_WindowActivate);
```

These event handlers are used to monitor documents as they are opened, created, and closed, and also to ensure that the Pause check box is kept up-to-date on the ribbon. This latter functionality is achieved by keeping track of window activations with the `WindowActivate` event.

The last task performed in this event handler is to start monitoring the current document and add the custom task panel to the window containing the document:

```
      // Start monitoring active document
      MonitorDocument(this.Application.ActiveDocument);
      AddTaskPaneToWindow(this.Application.ActiveDocument.ActiveWindow);
   }
```

The `MonitorDocument()` utility method adds a timer for a document:

```
   internal void MonitorDocument(Word.Document Doc)
   {
      // Monitor doc
      documentEditTimes.Add(Doc.Name, new DocumentTimer
```

(continued)

(continued)

```
        {
            Document = Doc,
            EditTime = new TimeSpan(0),
            IsActive = true,
            LastActive = DateTime.Now
        });
    }
```

This method simply creates a new `DocumentTimer` for the document. The `DocumentTimer` references the document, has zero edit time, is active, and was made active at the current time. It then adds this timer to the `documentEditTimes` collection and associates it with the document name.

The `AddTaskPaneToWindow()` method adds the custom task pane to a window. This method starts by checking the existing task panes to ensure that there isn't one in the window already. Also, one other strange feature of Word is that if you immediately open an old document after loading the application, the default Document1 document vanishes, without raising a close event. This can lead to an exception being raised when the window for the task pane that was in the document is accessed, so the method also checks for the `ArgumentNullException` that indicates this:

```
private void AddTaskPaneToWindow(Word.Window Wn)
{
    // Check for task pane in window
    Tools.CustomTaskPane docPane = null;
    Tools.CustomTaskPane paneToRemove = null;
    foreach (Tools.CustomTaskPane pane in timerDisplayPanes)
    {
        try
        {
            if (pane.Window == Wn)
            {
                docPane = pane;
                break;
            }
        }
        catch (ArgumentNullException)
        {
            // pane.Window is null, so document1 has been unloaded.
            paneToRemove = pane;
        }
    }
```

If an exception is thrown, then the offending task pane is removed from the collection:

```
    // Remove pane if necessary
    timerDisplayPanes.Remove(paneToRemove);
```

If no task pane was found for the window, then the method finishes by adding one:

```
    // Add task pane to doc
    if (docPane == null)
    {
        Tools.CustomTaskPane pane = this.CustomTaskPanes.Add(
            new TimerDisplayPane(documentEditTimes),
            "Document Edit Timer",
            Wn);
```

```
            timerDisplayPanes.Add(pane);
            pane.VisibleChanged +=
                new EventHandler(timerDisplayPane_VisibleChanged);
        }
    }
```

The added task pane is an instance of the `TimerDisplayPane` class. You will look at this class shortly. It is added with the name "Document Edit Timer." Also, an event handler is added for the `VisibleChanged` event of the `CustomTaskPane` that you obtain after calling the `CustomTaskPanes.Add()` method. This enables you to refresh the display when it first appears:

```
private void timerDisplayPane_VisibleChanged(object sender, EventArgs e)
{
    // Get task pane and toggle visibility
    Tools.CustomTaskPane taskPane = (Tools.CustomTaskPane)sender;
    if (taskPane.Visible)
    {
        TimerDisplayPane timerControl = (TimerDisplayPane)taskPane.Control;
        timerControl.RefreshDisplay();
    }
}
```

The `TimerDisplayPane` class exposes a `RefreshDisplay()` method that is called in the preceding code. This method, as its name suggests, refreshes the display of the `timerControl` object.

Next, there is the code that ensures that all documents are monitored. First, when a new document is created, the `eventInterface_NewDocument()` event handler is called, and the document is monitored by calling the `MonitorDocument()` and `AddTaskPaneToWindow()` methods, which you've already seen.

```
private void eventInterface_NewDocument(Word.Document Doc)
{
    // Monitor new doc
    MonitorDocument(Doc);
    AddTaskPaneToWindow(Doc.ActiveWindow);
```

This method also clears the Pause check box in the ribbon menu as new documents start with the time running. This is achieved through a utility method, `SetPauseStatus()`, which is defined on the ribbon:

```
    // Set checkbox
    Globals.Ribbons.TimerRibbon.SetPauseStatus(false);
}
```

Just before a document is closed, the `eventInterface_DocumentBeforeClose()` event handler is called. This method freezes the timer for the document, updates the total edit time, clears the `Document` reference, and removes the task pane from the document window (with `RemoveTaskPaneFromWindow()`, detailed shortly) before the document is closed.

```
private void eventInterface_DocumentBeforeClose(Word.Document Doc,
    ref bool Cancel)
{
    // Freeze timer
    documentEditTimes[Doc.Name].EditTime += DateTime.Now
        - documentEditTimes[Doc.Name].LastActive;
    documentEditTimes[Doc.Name].IsActive = false;
    documentEditTimes[Doc.Name].Document = null;
    // Remove task pane
    RemoveTaskPaneFromWindow(Doc.ActiveWindow);
}
```

When a document is opened, the `eventInterface_DocumentOpen()` method is called. There is a little more work to be done here, as before monitoring the document, the method must determine whether a timer already exists for the document by looking at its name:

```
private void eventInterface_DocumentOpen(Word.Document Doc)
{
    if (documentEditTimes.ContainsKey(Doc.Name))
    {
        // Monitor old doc
        documentEditTimes[Doc.Name].LastActive = DateTime.Now;
        documentEditTimes[Doc.Name].IsActive = true;
        documentEditTimes[Doc.Name].Document = Doc;
        AddTaskPaneToWindow(Doc.ActiveWindow);
    }
```

If the document isn't already being monitored, then a new monitor is configured as for a new document:

```
    else
    {
        // Monitor new doc
        MonitorDocument(Doc);
        AddTaskPaneToWindow(Doc.ActiveWindow);
    }
}
```

The `RemoveTaskPaneFromWindow()` method is used to remove the task pane from a window. The code for this method first checks that a task pane exists for the specified window:

```
private void RemoveTaskPaneFromWindow(Word.Window Wn)
{
    // Check for task pane in window
    Tools.CustomTaskPane docPane = null;
    foreach (Tools.CustomTaskPane pane in timerDisplayPanes)
    {
        if (pane.Window == Wn)
        {
            docPane = pane;
            break;
        }
    }
```

If a task window is found, then it is removed by calling the `CustomTaskPanes.Remove()` method. It is also removed from the local collection of task pane references.

```
    // Remove document task pane
    if (docPane != null)
    {
        this.CustomTaskPanes.Remove(docPane);
        timerDisplayPanes.Remove(docPane);
    }
}
```

The last event handler in this class is `eventInterface_WindowActivate()`, called when a window is activated. This method gets the timer for the active document and sets the check box on the ribbon menu so that the check box is kept updated for the document:

```
    private void eventInterface_WindowActivate(Word.Document Doc,
       Word.Window Wn)
    {
       // Ensure pause checkbox in ribbon is accurate, start by getting timer
       DocumentTimer documentTimer =
          documentEditTimes[this.Application.ActiveDocument.Name];
       // Set checkbox
       Globals.Ribbons.TimerRibbon.SetPauseStatus(!documentTimer.IsActive);
    }
```

The code for `ThisAddIn` also includes two utility methods. The first of these, `ToggleTaskPaneDisplay()`, is used to show or hide the display of the task pane for the currently active document by setting the `CustomTaskPane.Visible` property.

```
    internal void ToggleTaskPaneDisplay()
    {
       // Ensure window has task window
       AddTaskPaneToWindow(this.Application.ActiveDocument.ActiveWindow);
       // toggle document task pane
       Tools.CustomTaskPane docPane = null;
       foreach (Tools.CustomTaskPane pane in timerDisplayPanes)
       {
          if (pane.Window == this.Application.ActiveDocument.ActiveWindow)
          {
             docPane = pane;
             break;
          }
       }
       docPane.Visible = !docPane.Visible;
    }
```

The `ToggleTaskPaneDisplay()` method shown in the preceding code is called by event handlers on the ribbon control, as you will see shortly.

Finally, the class has another method that is called from the ribbon menu, which enables ribbon controls to pause or resume the timer for a document:

```
    internal void PauseOrResumeTimer(bool pause)
    {
       // Get timer
       DocumentTimer documentTimer =
          documentEditTimes[this.Application.ActiveDocument.Name];
       if (pause && documentTimer.IsActive)
       {
          // Freeze timer
          documentTimer.EditTime += DateTime.Now - documentTimer.LastActive;
          documentTimer.IsActive = false;
       }
       else if (!pause && !documentTimer.IsActive)
       {
          // Resume timer
          documentTimer.IsActive = true;
          documentTimer.LastActive = DateTime.Now;
       }
    }
 }
```

The only other code in this class definition is an empty event handler for `Shutdown`, and the VSTO-generated code to hook up the `Startup` and `Shutdown` event handlers.

Next, the ribbon in the project, `TimerRibbon`, is laid out, as shown in Figure 40-14.

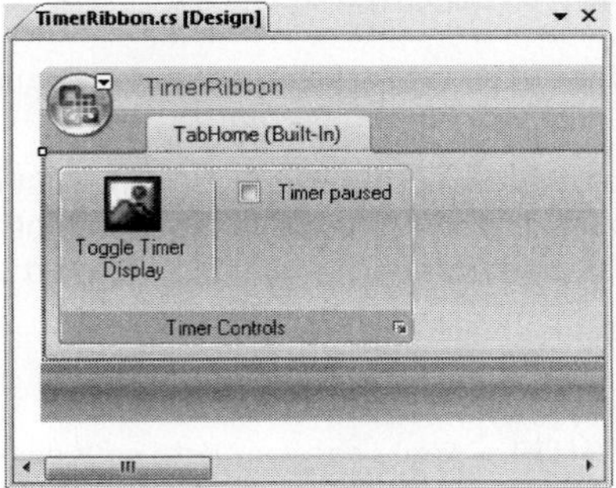

Figure 40-14

This ribbon contains a `RibbonButton`, a `RibbonSeparator`, a `RibbonCheckBox`, and a `DialogBoxLauncher`. The button uses the large display style, and has an `OfficeImageId` of `StartAfterPrevious`, which displays the clock face shown in Figure 40-13. (These images are not visible at design time.) The ribbon uses the TabHome tab type, which causes its contents to be appended to the Home tab.

The ribbon has three event handlers, each of which calls on one of the utility methods in `ThisAddIn` described earlier:

```
private void group1_DialogLauncherClick(object sender,
   RibbonControlEventArgs e)
{
   // Show or hide task pane
   Globals.ThisAddIn.ToggleTaskPaneDisplay();
}
private void pauseCheckBox_Click(object sender, RibbonControlEventArgs e)
{
   // Pause timer
   Globals.ThisAddIn.PauseOrResumeTimer(pauseCheckBox.Checked);
}
private void toggleDisplayButton_Click(object sender,
   RibbonControlEventArgs e)
{
   // Show or hide task pane
   Globals.ThisAddIn.ToggleTaskPaneDisplay();
}
```

The ribbon also includes its own utility method, `SetPauseStatus()`, which as you saw earlier is called by code in `ThisAddIn` to select or clear the check box:

```
internal void SetPauseStatus(bool isPaused)
{
   // Ensure checkbox is accurate
   pauseCheckBox.Checked = isPaused;
}
```

The other component in this solution is the `TimerDisplayPane` user control that is used in the task pane. The layout of this control is shown in Figure 40-15.

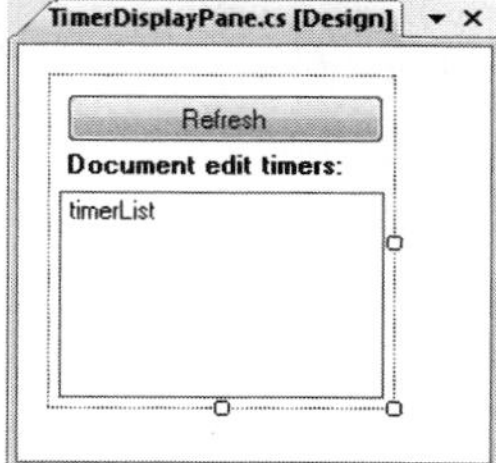

Figure 40-15

This control includes a button, a label, and a list box — not the most exciting of displays, although it would be simple enough to replace it with, for example, a prettier WPF control.

The code for the control keeps a local reference to the document timers, which is set in the constructor:

```
public partial class TimerDisplayPane : UserControl
{
   private Dictionary<string, DocumentTimer> documentEditTimes;
   public TimerDisplayPane()
   {
      InitializeComponent();
   }
   public TimerDisplayPane(Dictionary<string, DocumentTimer>
      documentEditTimes) : this()
   {
      // Store reference to edit times
      this.documentEditTimes = documentEditTimes;
   }
```

The button event handler calls the `RefreshDisplay()` method to refresh the timer display:

```
   private void refreshButton_Click(object sender, EventArgs e)
   {
      RefreshDisplay();
   }
```

The `RefreshDisplay()` method is also called from `ThisAddIn`, as you saw earlier. It is a surprisingly complicated method considering what it does. It also checks the list of monitored documents against the list of loaded documents and corrects any problems. This sort of code is often necessary in VSTO applications, as the interface with the COM Office object model occasionally doesn't work quite as it should. The rule of thumb here is to code defensively.

The method starts by clearing the current list of timers in the `timerList` list box:

```
   internal void RefreshDisplay()
   {
      // Clear existing list
      this.timerList.Items.Clear();
```

Next, the monitors are checked. The method iterates through each document in the `Globals.ThisAddIn.Application.Documents` collection and determines if the document is monitored, unmonitored, or monitored but has had a name change since the last refresh.

Finding monitored documents simply involves checking the document name against the document names in the `documentEditTimes` collection of keys:

```
// Ensure all docs are monitored
foreach (Word.Document doc in Globals.ThisAddIn.Application.Documents)
{
   bool isMonitored = false;
   bool requiresNameChange = false;
   DocumentTimer oldNameTimer = null;
   string oldName = null;
   foreach (string documentName in documentEditTimes.Keys)
   {
      if (doc.Name == documentName)
      {
         isMonitored = true;
         break;
      }
```

If the names don't match, then the document references are compared, which enables you to detect name changes to documents, as shown in the following code:

```
      else
      {
         if (documentEditTimes[documentName].Document == doc)
         {
            // Monitored, but name changed!
            oldName = documentName;
            oldNameTimer = documentEditTimes[documentName];
            isMonitored = true;
            requiresNameChange = true;
            break;
         }
      }
   }
```

For unmonitored documents, a new monitor is created:

```
   // Add monitor if not monitored
   if (!isMonitored)
   {
      Globals.ThisAddIn.MonitorDocument(doc);
   }
```

Whereas documents with name changes are re-associated with the monitor used for the old named document:

```
   // Rename if necessary
   if (requiresNameChange)
   {
      documentEditTimes.Remove(oldName);
      documentEditTimes.Add(doc.Name, oldNameTimer);
   }
}
```

After reconciling the document edit timers, a list is generated. This code also detects whether referenced documents are still loaded, and pauses the timer for documents that aren't by setting the `IsActive` property to `false`. Again, this is defensive programming.

```
         // Create new list
         foreach (string documentName in documentEditTimes.Keys)
         {
            // Check to see if doc is still loaded
            bool isLoaded = false;
            foreach (Word.Document doc in
               Globals.ThisAddIn.Application.Documents)
            {
               if (doc.Name == documentName)
               {
                  isLoaded = true;
                  break;
               }
            }
            if (!isLoaded)
            {
               documentEditTimes[documentName].IsActive = false;
               documentEditTimes[documentName].Document = null;
            }
```

For each monitor, a list item is added to the list box that includes the document name and its total edit time:

```
            // Add item
            this.timerList.Items.Add(string.Format("{0}: {1}", documentName,
               documentEditTimes[documentName].EditTime +
               (documentEditTimes[documentName].IsActive ?
               (DateTime.Now - documentEditTimes[documentName].LastActive) :
               new TimeSpan(0))));
         }
      }
   }
```

This completes the code in this example. This example has shown you how to use ribbon and task pane controls and how to maintain task panes in multiple Word documents. It has also illustrated many of the techniques covered earlier in the chapter.

VBA Interoperability

Because the Office system has existed for some years now, you may well be familiar with VBA code, and you may well have some in your existing applications. It is possible to rewrite VBA code in VSTO solutions, but this isn't always practical. However, having seen what is possible with VSTO you may want to replace existing VBA functionality, or add new functionality, with managed VSTO code.

VSTO makes it possible to expose VSTO functionality to VBA code to achieve just this. To do this, however, there are a few steps that you must perform to provide VBA code with a COM interface. These nine steps are shown here, along with example code and screenshots from the ExcelVBAInterop project in the downloadable code:

1. Before you start to expose VSTO code to VBA, you must have a document that includes a VBA project. For ease of development, it is also a good idea to have macros enabled in the document before you start. Then, when you create a document-level customization in VSTO, you use that document as the starting point for the document in your solution.

2. Once you have this starting point, you can proceed to write code that accesses the application and/or document in the usual way. This code needn't be accessible through the VSTO project, as you will provide a VBA interface later. Instead, create methods that you want VBA to be capable of calling. For example:

```
public partial class ThisWorkbook : ExcelVBAInterop.IThisWorkbook
{
   ...
   public void NameSheet()
   {
      NamingDialog dlg = new NamingDialog();
      if (dlg.ShowDialog() == DialogResult.OK)
      {
         ((Excel.Worksheet)this.ActiveSheet).Name = dlg.SheetName;
      }
   }
}
```

This code uses a simple custom dialog box that you will see shortly. This dialog box enables users to enter a string and select whether to include the current date in the sheet name.

3. You must override the `GetAutomationObject()` method to return the correct object for automation for VBA code as follows:

```
public partial class ThisWorkbook : ExcelVBAInterop.IThisWorkbook
{
   ...
   protected override object GetAutomationObject()
   {
      return this;
   }
}
```

4. Because the COM system works through interfaces, you must expose the method you want to call through an interface. The easiest way to do this is to right-click in your code and select Refactor ⇨ Extract Interface. You then select the method you want to be exposed on the interface, and the wizard (shown in Figure 40-16) does the rest.

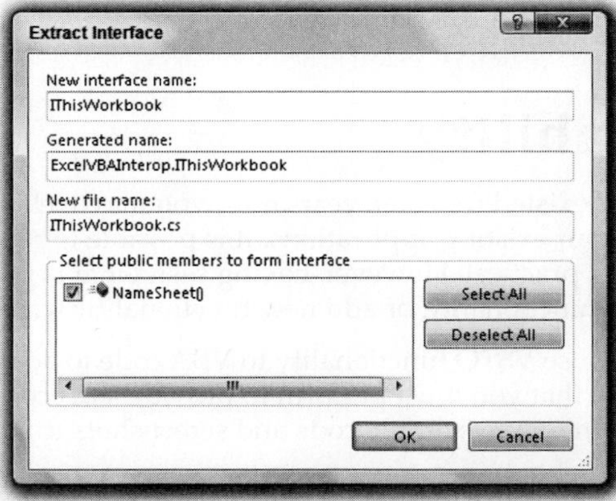

Figure 40-16

5. You must also add attributes from the `System.Runtime.InteropServices` namespace to the class to expose the class to COM (see Chapter 24, "Interoperability"):

```
using System.Runtime.InteropServices;
namespace ExcelVBAInterop
{
   [ComVisible(true)]
   [ClassInterface(ClassInterfaceType.None)]
   public partial class ThisWorkbook : ExcelVBAInterop.IThisWorkbook
   {
      ...
   }
}
```

6. The generated interface also needs the `ComVisible` attribute, and the interface must be made public:

```
using System.Runtime.InteropServices;
namespace ExcelVBAInterop
{
   [ComVisible(true)]
   public interface IThisWorkbook
   {
      void NameSheet();
   }
}
```

7. You must change the `ReferenceAssemblyFromVbaProject` property of the document to `true`, as shown in Figure 40-17. If the document doesn't contain VBA code, then you will not be able to change this property. When you change it, you will receive a warning that any VBA code you add to the project when it is running will be lost, so you should keep a copy of any VB code you change.

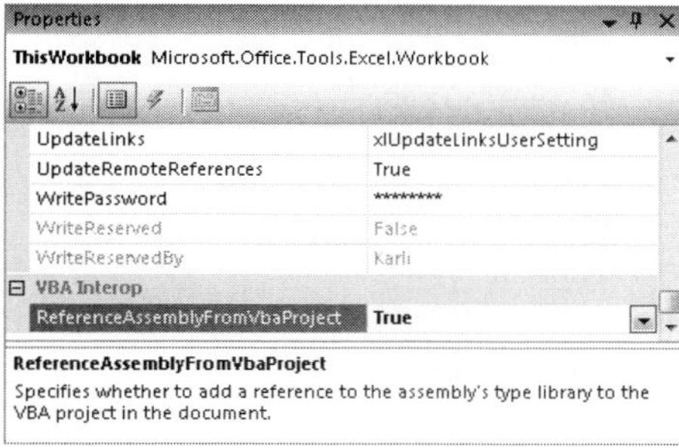

Figure 40-17

8. The remaining changes must be made to the VBA code in the document. You can run the project at this point, and when it is running you can access the VBA code through the Developer tab or by pressing Alt+F11. The first thing you need to add is a property that enables VBA to access your VSTO code, as follows (you reference the class that you have exposed by name, qualified by namespace):

```
Property Get VSTOAssembly() As ExcelVBAInterop.ThisWorkbook
   Set VSTOAssembly = GetManagedClass(Me)
End Property
```

9. You can then call the VSTO method through this property:

```
Public Sub RenameSheet()
   VSTOAssembly.NameSheet
End Sub
```

Once you have performed these steps, you can add code that calls the method on the interface, or just call it manually, as shown in Figure 40-18.

Figure 40-18

If your code includes a UI, as in this example, then it will display and be available to use. The UI in the sample project is shown in Figure 40-19.

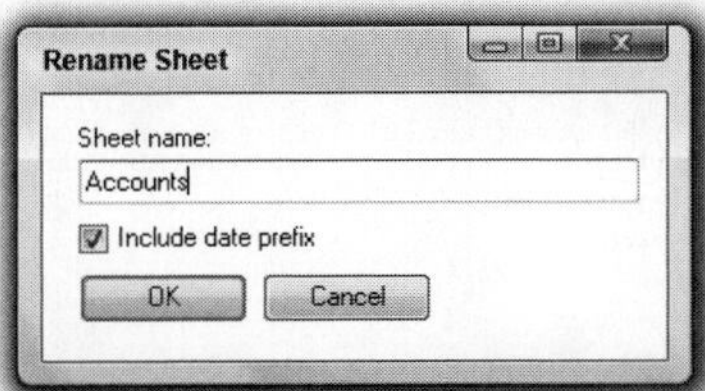

Figure 40-19

In this way, you can make any VSTO code you want available to VBA code.

Summary

In this chapter you have learned how to use VSTO to create managed solutions for Office products.

In the first part of this chapter, you learned about the general structure of VSTO projects and the project types that you can create. You also saw the features that you can use to make VSTO programming easier.

In the next section, you looked, in great depth, at some of the features available in VSTO solutions and you saw how communication with the Office object model is achieved. You also looked at the namespaces and types available in VSTO and learned how to use those types to implement a variety of functionality. Then, you explored some of the code features of VSTO projects and how to use these features to get the effect you want.

After this, you moved on to the more practical side of things. You learned how add-ins are managed in Office applications and how to interact with the Office object model. You also saw how to customize the UI of your applications with ribbon menus, task panes, and action panes.

Next, you explored a sample application that illustrated the UI and interaction techniques that you learned earlier. The example contained a lot of code, but it included useful techniques, including how to manage task panes in multiple Word document windows.

Finally, you looked at interoperability with VBA code. You saw how to expose your managed code to VBA through COM interop, and you looked at another example to illustrate the techniques.

This is the last chapter in Part V, "Presentation." In the first chapter in Part VI, "Communication," you will learn how to access the Internet from your applications with classes in the `System.Net` namespace.

Part VI
Communication

Chapter 41: Accessing the Internet

Chapter 42: Windows Communication Foundation

Chapter 43: Windows Workflow Foundation

Chapter 44: Enterprise Services

Chapter 45: Message Queuing

Chapter 46: Directory Services

Chapter 47: Peer to Peer Networking

Chapter 48: Syndication

41

Accessing the Internet

Chapters 37 through 39 discuss how you can use C# to write powerful, efficient, and dynamic Web pages using ASP.NET. For the most part, the clients accessing ASP.NET pages will be users running Internet Explorer or other Web browsers such as Opera or Firefox. However, you might want to add Web-browsing features to your own application, or you might need your applications to programmatically obtain information from a Web site. In this latter case, it is usually better for the site to implement a Web service. However, when you are accessing public Internet sites, you might not have any control over how the site is implemented.

This chapter covers facilities provided through the .NET base classes for using various network protocols, particularly HTTP and TCP, to access networks and the Internet as a client. In particular, this chapter covers:

- Downloading files from the World Wide Web
- Using the Web Browser control in a Windows Forms application
- Manipulating IP addresses and performing DNS lookups
- Socket programming with TCP, UDP, and socket classes

This chapter covers some of the lower-level means of getting at these protocols through the .NET Framework. You will also find other means of communicating via these items using technologies, such as the Windows Communication Foundation (WCF), which is covered in the next chapter.

The two namespaces of most interest for networking are `System.Net` and `System.Net.Sockets`. The `System.Net` namespace is generally concerned with higher-level operations, for example, downloading and uploading files, and making Web requests using HTTP and other protocols, whereas `System.Net.Sockets` contains classes to perform lower-level operations. You will find these classes useful when you want to work directly with sockets or protocols, such as TCP/IP. The methods in these classes closely mimic the Windows socket (Winsock) API functions derived from the Berkeley sockets interface. You will also find that some of the objects that this chapter works with are found in the `System.IO` namespace.

This chapter takes a fairly practical approach, mixing examples with a discussion of the relevant theory and networking concepts as appropriate. This chapter is not a guide to computer networking but an introduction to using the .NET Framework for network communication.

You will learn how to use the WebBrowser control in a Windows Forms environment. You will also learn how the WebBrowser control can make some specific Internet access tasks easier to accomplish.

However, the chapter starts with the simplest case, sending a request to a server and storing the information sent back in the response. (As with other chapters, you can download the sample code for this chapter from the Wrox Web site at www.wrox.com.)

The WebClient Class

If you only want to request a file from a particular URI, then you will find that the easiest .NET class to use is System.Net.WebClient. This is an extremely high-level class designed to perform basic operations with only one or two commands. The .NET Framework currently supports URIs beginning with the http:, https:, and file: identifiers.

It is worth noting that the term URL (Uniform Resource Locator) is no longer in use in new technical specifications, and URI (Uniform Resource Identifier) is now preferred. URI has roughly the same meaning as URL, but is a bit more general because URI does not imply you are using one of the familiar protocols, such as HTTP or FTP.

Downloading Files

Two methods are available for downloading a file using WebClient. The method you choose depends on how you want to process the file's contents. If you simply want to save the file to disk, then you use the DownloadFile() method. This method takes two parameters: the URI of the file and a location (path and file name) to save the requested data:

```
WebClient Client = new WebClient();
Client.DownloadFile("http://www.reuters.com/", "ReutersHomepage.htm");
```

More commonly, your application will want to process the data retrieved from the Web site. To do this, you use the OpenRead() method, which returns a Stream reference that you can then use to retrieve the data into memory:

```
WebClient Client = new WebClient();
Stream strm = Client.OpenRead("http://www.reuters.com/");
```

Basic Web Client Example

The first example demonstrates the WebClient.OpenRead() method. You will display the contents of the downloaded page in a ListBox control. To begin, create a new project as a standard C# Windows Forms application and add a ListBox called listBox1 with the docking property set to DockStyle.Fill. At the beginning of the file, you will need to add the System.Net and System.IO namespaces references to your list of using directives. You then make the following changes to the constructor of the main form:

```
public Form1()
{
   InitializeComponent();
   WebClient Client = new WebClient();
   Stream strm = Client.OpenRead("http://www.reuters.com");
   StreamReader sr = new StreamReader(strm);
   string line;
   while ( (line=sr.ReadLine()) != null )
```

```
        {
            listBox1.Items.Add(line);
        }

        strm.Close();
    }
```

In this example, you connect a `StreamReader` class from the `System.IO` namespace to the network stream. This allows you to obtain data from the stream as text through the use of higher-level methods, such as `ReadLine()`. This is an excellent example of the point made in Chapter 25, "Manipulating Files and the Registry," about the benefits of abstracting data movement into the concept of a stream.

Figure 41-1 shows the results of running this sample code.

Figure 41-1

The `WebClient` class also has an `OpenWrite()` method. This method returns a writable stream for you to send data to a URI. You can also specify the method used to send the data to the host; the default method is `POST`. The following code snippet assumes a writable directory named `accept` on the local machine. The code will create a file in the directory with the name `newfile.txt` and the contents `Hello World`:

```
WebClient webClient = new WebClient();
Stream stream = webClient.OpenWrite("http://localhost/accept/newfile.txt", "PUT");
StreamWriter streamWriter = new StreamWriter(stream);
streamWriter.WriteLine("Hello World");
streamWriter.Close();
```

Uploading Files

The `WebClient` class also features `UploadFile()` and `UploadData()` methods. You use these methods when you need to post an HTML form or to upload an entire file. `UploadFile()` uploads a file to a specified location given the local file name, whereas `UploadData()` uploads binary data supplied as an array of bytes to the specified URI (there is also a `DownloadData()` method for retrieving an array of bytes from a URI):

```
WebClient client = new WebClient();
client.UploadFile("http://www.ourwebsite.com/NewFile.htm",
                  "C:\\WebSiteFiles\\NewFile.htm");
byte[] image;
// code to initialize image so it contains all the binary data for
// some jpg file
client.UploadData("http://www.ourwebsite.com/NewFile.jpg", image);
```

WebRequest and WebResponse Classes

Although the `WebClient` class is very simple to use, it has very limited features. In particular, you cannot use it to supply authentication credentials — a particular problem with uploading data is that not many sites will accept uploaded files without authentication! It is possible to add header information to requests and to examine any headers in the response, but only in a very generic sense — there is no specific support for any one protocol. This is because `WebClient` is a very general-purpose class designed to work with any protocol for sending a request and receiving a response (such as HTTP or FTP). It cannot handle any features specific to any one protocol, such as cookies, which are specific to HTTP. To take advantage of these features, you need to use a family of classes based on two other classes in the `System.Net` namespace: `WebRequest` and `WebResponse`.

You start off by seeing how to download a Web page using these classes. This is the same example as before, but using `WebRequest` and `WebResponse`. In the process, you will uncover the class hierarchy involved, and then see how to take advantage of extra HTTP features supported by this hierarchy.

The following code shows the modifications you need to make to the `BasicWebClient` sample to use the `WebRequest` and `WebResponse` classes:

```
public Form1()
{
   InitializeComponent();

   WebRequest wrq = WebRequest.Create("http://www.reuters.com");
   WebResponse wrs = wrq.GetResponse();
   Stream strm = wrs.GetResponseStream();
   StreamReader sr = new StreamReader(strm);
   string line;
   while ( (line = sr.ReadLine()) != null)
   {
      listBox1.Items.Add(line);
   }
   strm.Close();
}
```

In the code example, you start by instantiating an object representing a Web request. You don't do this using a constructor, but instead call the static method `WebRequest.Create()`. As you will learn in more detail later in this chapter, the `WebRequest` class is part of a hierarchy of classes supporting different network protocols. In order to receive a reference to the correct object for the request type, a factory mechanism is in place. The `WebRequest.Create()` method will create the appropriate object for the given protocol.

The `WebRequest` class represents the request for information to send to a particular URI. The URI is passed as a parameter to the `Create()` method. A `WebResponse` represents the data you retrieve from the server. By calling the `WebRequest.GetResponse()` method, you actually send the request to the Web server and create a `WebResponse` object to examine the return data. As with the `WebClient` object, you can obtain a stream to represent the data, but in this case you use the `WebResponse.GetResponseStream()` method.

Other WebRequest and WebResponse Features

This section briefly discusses a few of the other areas supported by `WebRequest`, `WebResponse`, and other related classes.

HTTP Header Information

An important part of the HTTP protocol is the ability to send extensive header information with both request and response streams. This information can include cookies and the details of the particular browser sending the request (the user agent). As you would expect, the .NET Framework provides full support for accessing the most significant data. The `WebRequest` and `WebResponse` classes provide some support for reading the header information. However, two derived classes provide additional HTTP-specific information: `HttpWebRequest` and `HttpWebResponse`. As you will see in more detail later, creating a `WebRequest` with an HTTP URI results in an `HttpWebRequest` object instance. Because `HttpWebRequest` is derived from `WebRequest`, you can use the new instance whenever a `WebRequest` is required. In addition, you can cast the instance to an `HttpWebRequest` reference and access properties specific to the HTTP protocol. Likewise, the `GetResponse()` method call will actually return an `HttpWebResponse` instance as a `WebResponse` reference when dealing with HTTP. Again, you can perform a simple cast to access the HTTP-specific features.

You can examine a few of the header properties by adding the following code before the `GetResponse()` method call:

```
WebRequest wrq = WebRequest.Create("http://www.reuters.com");
HttpWebRequest hwrq = (HttpWebRequest)wrq;
listBox1.Items.Add("Request Timeout (ms) = " + wrq.Timeout);
listBox1.Items.Add("Request Keep Alive = " + hwrq.KeepAlive);
listBox1.Items.Add("Request AllowAutoRedirect = " + hwrq.AllowAutoRedirect);
```

The `Timeout` property is specified in milliseconds, and the default value is `100,000`. You can set the `Timeout` property to control how long the `WebRequest` object will wait for the response before throwing a `WebException`. You can check the `WebException.Status` property to view the reason for an exception. This enumeration includes status codes for timeouts, connection failures, protocol errors, and more.

The `KeepAlive` property is a specific extension to the HTTP protocol, so you access this property through an `HttpWebRequest` reference. `KeepAlive` allows multiple requests to use the same connection, saving time in closing and reopening connections on subsequent requests. The default value for this property is `true`.

The `AllowAutoRedirect` property is also specific to the `HttpWebRequest` class. Use this property to control whether the Web request should automatically follow redirection responses from the Web server. Again, the default value is `true`. If you want to allow only a limited number of redirections, then set the `MaximumAutomaticRedirections` property of the `HttpWebRequest` to the desired number.

Although the request and response classes expose most of the important headers as properties, you can also use the `Headers` property itself to view the entire collection of headers. Add the following code after the `GetResponse()` method call to place all of the headers in the `ListBox` control:

```
WebRequest wrq = WebRequest.Create("http://www.reuters.com");
WebResponse wrs = wrq.GetResponse();
WebHeaderCollection whc = wrs.Headers;
for(int i = 0; i < whc.Count; i++)
{
     listBox1.Items.Add(string.Format("Header {0} : {1}",
        whc.GetKey(i), whc[i]));
}
```

This example code produces the list of headers shown in Figure 41-2.

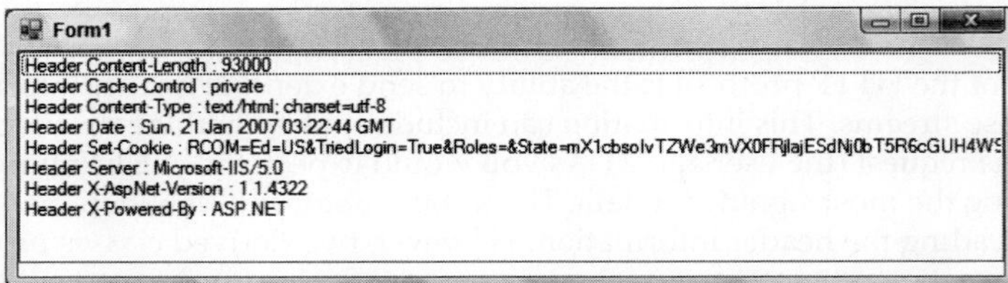

Figure 41-2

Authentication

Another property in the `WebRequest` class is the `Credentials` property. If you need authentication credentials to accompany your request, then you can create an instance of the `NetworkCredential` class (also from the `System.Net` namespace) with a username and password. You can place the following code *before* the call to `GetResponse()`.

```
NetworkCredential myCred = new NetworkCredential("myusername", "mypassword");
wrq.Credentials = myCred;
```

Working with Proxies

You will find in enterprises that many firms must deal with a proxy server to make any type of HTTP or FTP request. Many times, the proxy server, which routes all of the organization's requests and responses, uses some form of security (usually a username and a password). For your applications that use the `WebClient` or the `WebRequest` objects, you might need to take these proxy servers into account. As with the preceding `NetworkCredential` object, you are going to want to use the `WebProxy` object *before* you make a call to make the actual request.

```
WebProxy wp = new WebProxy("192.168.1.100", true);
wp.Credentials = new NetworkCredential("user1", "user1Password");
WebRequest wrq = WebRequest.Create("http://www.reuters.com");
wrq.Proxy = wp;
WebResponse wrs = wrq.GetResponse();
```

If you also require a designation of the user's domain in addition to its credentials, then you would use a different signature on the `NetworkCredential` instantiation:

```
WebProxy wp = new WebProxy("192.168.1.100", true);
wp.Credentials = new NetworkCredential("user1", "user1Password", "myDomain");
WebRequest wrq = WebRequest.Create("http://www.reuters.com");
wrq.Proxy = wp;
WebResponse wrs = wrq.GetResponse();
```

Asynchronous Page Requests

An additional feature of the `WebRequest` class is the ability to request pages asynchronously. This feature is significant because there can be quite a long delay between sending a request to a host and receiving the response. Methods such as `WebClient.DownloadData()` and `WebRequest.GetResponse()` will not return until the response from the server is complete. You might not want your application frozen due to a long period of inactivity, and in such scenarios it is better to use the `BeginGetResponse()` and `EndGetResponse()` methods. `BeginGetResponse()` works asynchronously and returns almost immediately. Under the covers, the runtime will asynchronously manage a background thread to retrieve the response from the server. Instead of returning a `WebResponse` object, `BeginGetResponse()` returns an object implementing the `IAsyncResult` interface. With this interface, you can poll or wait for the response to become available and then invoke `EndGetResponse()` to gather the results.

You can also pass a callback delegate into the `BeginGetResponse()` method. The target of a callback delegate is a method returning `void` and accepting an `IAsyncResult` reference as a parameter. When the worker thread is finished gathering the response, the runtime invokes the callback delegate to inform you of the completed work. As shown in the following code, calling `EndGetResponse()` in the callback method allows you to retrieve the `WebResponse` object:

```
public Form1()
{
   InitializeComponent();
   WebRequest wrq = WebRequest.Create("http://www.reuters.com");
   wrq.BeginGetResponse(new AsyncCallback(OnResponse), wrq);
}
protected static void OnResponse(IAsyncResult ar)
{
   WebRequest wrq = (WebRequest)ar.AsyncState;
   WebResponse wrs = wrq.EndGetResponse(ar);
   // read the response ...
}
```

Notice that you can retrieve the original `WebRequest` object by passing the object as the second parameter to `BeginGetResponse()`. The third parameter is an object reference known as the state parameter. During the callback method, you can retrieve the same state object using the `AsyncState` property of `IAsyncResult`.

Displaying Output as an HTML Page

The examples show how the .NET base classes make it very easy to download and process data from the Internet. However, so far, you have displayed files only as plain text. Quite often, you will want to view an HTML file in an Internet Explorer–style interface in which the rendered HTML allows you to see what the Web document actually looks like. Unfortunately, there is no .NET version of Microsoft's Internet Explorer, but that does not mean that you cannot easily accomplish this task. Before the release of the .NET Framework 2.0, you could make reference to a COM object that was an encapsulation of Internet Explorer and use the .NET-interop capabilities to have aspects of your application work as a browser. Now, in the .NET Framework 2.0, as well as the .NET Framework 3.5, you can use the built-in `WebBrowser` control available for your Windows Forms applications.

The `WebBrowser` control encapsulates the COM object even further for you making tasks that were once more complicated even easier. In addition to the `WebBrowser` control, another option is to use the programmatic ability to call up Internet Explorer instances from your code.

When not using the new `WebBrowser` control, you can programmatically start an Internet Explorer process and navigate to a Web page using the `Process` class in the `System.Diagnostics` namespace:

```
Process myProcess = new Process();
myProcess.StartInfo.FileName = "iexplore.exe";
myProcess.StartInfo.Arguments = "http://www.wrox.com";
myProcess.Start();
```

However, the preceding code launches Internet Explorer as a separate window. Your application has no connection to the new window and therefore cannot control the browser.

Using the new `WebBrowser` control, however, allows you to display and control the browser as an integrated part of your application. The new `WebBrowser` control is quite sophisticated, featuring a large number of methods, properties, and events.

Allowing Simple Web Browsing from Your Applications

For the sake of simplicity, start by creating a Windows Form application that simply has a `TextBox` control and a `WebBrowser` control. You will build the application so that the end user will simply enter a URL into the text box and press Enter, and the `WebBrowser` control will do all the work of fetching the Web page and displaying the resulting document.

In Visual Studio 2008 Designer, your application should look as shown in Figure 41-3.

With this application, when the end user types a URL and presses Enter, this key press will register with the application. Then the `WebBrowser` control will go off to retrieve the requested page, subsequently displaying it in the control itself.

Figure 41-3

The code behind this application is illustrated here:

```
using System;
using System.Windows.Forms;
namespace CSharpInternet
{
    partial class Form1 : Form
    {
        public Form1()
        {
            InitializeComponent();
        }
        private void textBox1_KeyPress(object sender, KeyPressEventArgs e)
        {
            if (e.KeyChar == (char)13)
            {
                webBrowser1.Navigate(textBox1.Text);
            }
        }
    }
}
```

From this example, you can see that each key press that the end user makes in the text box is captured by the `textBox1_KeyPress` event. If the character input is a carriage return (a press of the Enter key, which is `(char)13`), then you take action with the `WebBrowser` control. Using the `WebBrowser` control's `Navigate` method, you specify the URL (as a `string`) using the `textBox1.Text` property. The end result is shown in Figure 41-4.

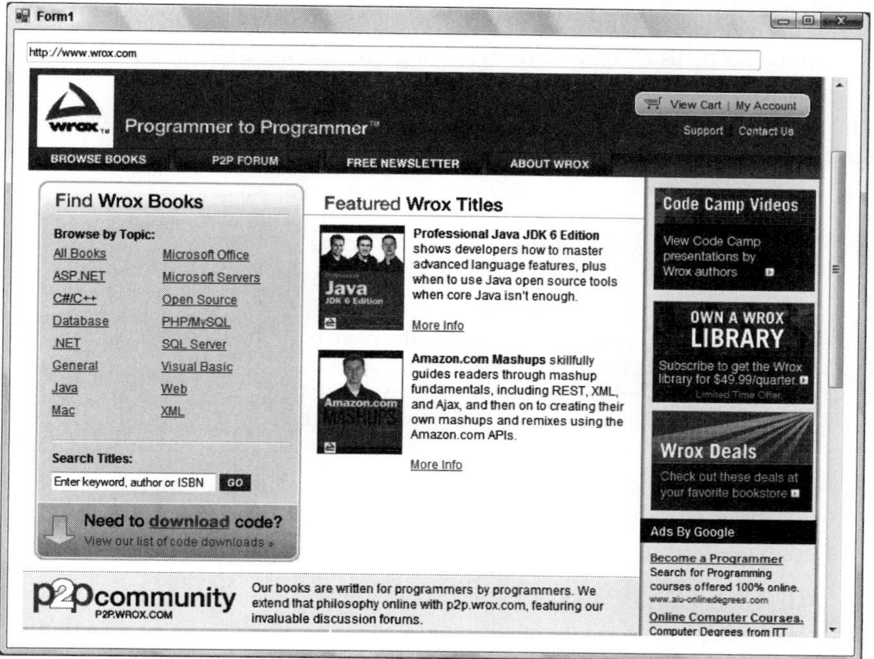

Figure 41-4

Launching Internet Explorer Instances

It might be that you are not interested in hosting a browser inside of your application, as shown in the previous section, but instead are only interested in allowing the user to find your Web site in a typical browser (for example, by clicking a link inside of your application). For an example of this task, create a Windows Form application that has a LinkLabel control on it. For instance, you can have a form that has a LinkLabel control on it that states "Visit our company Web site!"

Once you have this control in place, use the following code to launch your company's Web site in an independent browser as opposed to directly being in the form of your application:

```
private void linkLabel1_LinkClicked(object sender, LinkLabelLinkClickedEventArgs e)
{
   WebBrowser wb = new WebBrowser();
   wb.Navigate("http://www.wrox.com", true);
}
```

In this example, when the LinkLabel control is clicked by the user, a new instance of the WebBrowser class is created. Then, using the WebBrowser class's Navigate() method, the code specifies the location of the Web page as well as a Boolean value that specifies whether this endpoint should be opened within the Windows Form application (a false value) or from within an independent browser (using a true value). By default, this is set to false. With the preceding construct, when the end user clicks the link found in the Windows application, a browser instance will be instantiated, and the Wrox Web site at www.wrox.com will be immediately launched.

Giving Your Application More IE-Type Features

In the previous example, in which you used the WebBrowser control directly in the Windows Form application, you will notice that when you clicked on the links contained in the page, the text within the TextBox control was not updated to show the URL of the exact location where you were in the browsing process. You can fix this by listening for events coming from the WebBrowser control and adding handlers to the control.

Updating the form's title with the title of the HTML page is easy. You just need to use the Navigated event and update the Text property of the form:

```
private void webBrowser1_Navigated(object sender, EventArgs e)
{
   this.Text = webBrowser1.DocumentTitle.ToString();
}
```

In this case, when the WebBrowser control moves onto another page, the Navigated event will fire, and this will cause the form's title to change to the title of the page being viewed. In some instances when working with pages on the Web, even though you have typed in a specific address, you are going to be redirected to another page altogether. You are most likely going to want to reflect this in the textbox (address bar) of the form; to do this, you change the form's text box based on the complete URL of the page being viewed. To accomplish this task, you can use the WebBrowser control's Navigated event as well:

```
private void webBrowser1_Navigated(object sender, WebBrowserNavigatedEventArgs e)
{
   textBox1.Text = webBrowser1.Url.ToString();
   this.Text = webBrowser1.DocumentTitle.ToString();
}
```

In this case, when the requested page has finished downloading in the WebBrowser control, the Navigated event is fired. In your case, you simply update the Text value of the textBox1 control to the

URL of the page. This means that once a page is loaded in the `WebBrowser` control's HTML container, and if the URL changes in this process (for instance, if there is a redirect), then the new URL will be shown in the text box. If you employ these steps and navigate to the Wrox Web site (`www.wrox.com`), then you will notice that the page's URL will immediately change to `www.wrox.com/WileyCDA/`. This process also means that if the end user clicks one of the links contained within the HTML view, then the URL of the newly requested page will also be shown in the text box.

Now if you run the application with the preceding changes in place, you will find that the form's title and address bar work as they do in Microsoft's Internet Explorer, as demonstrated in Figure 41-5.

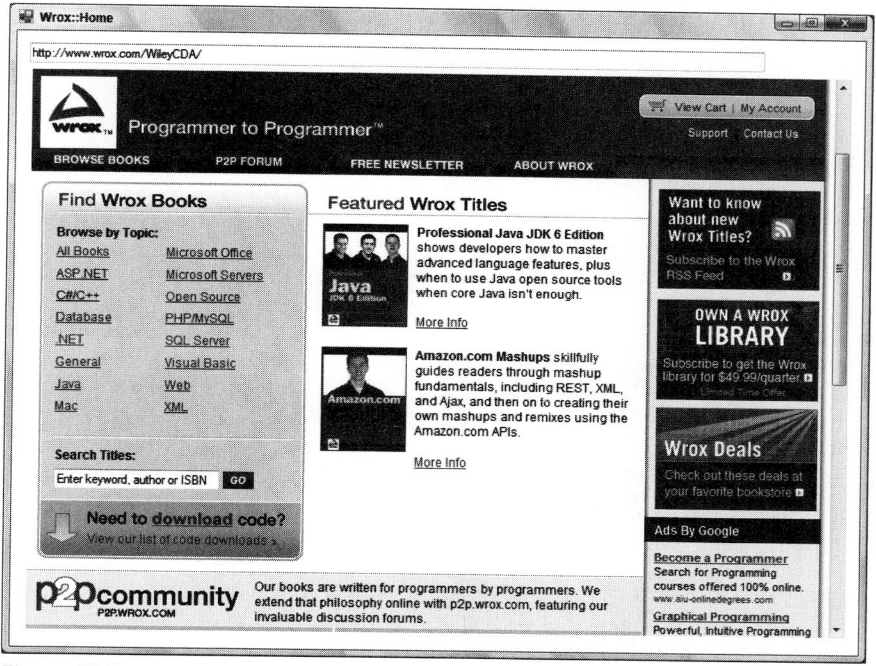

Figure 41-5

The next step is to create an IE-like toolbar that will allow the end user to control the `WebBrowser` control a little better. This means that you will incorporate buttons such as Back, Forward, Stop, Refresh, and Home.

Rather than using the `ToolBar` control, you will just add a set of `Button` controls at the top of the form where you currently have the address bar. Add five buttons to the top of the control, as illustrated in Figure 41-6.

In this example, the text on the button face is changed to indicate the function of the button. Of course, you can even go as far as to use a screen capture utility to "borrow" button images from IE and use those. The buttons should be named `buttonBack`, `buttonForward`, `buttonStop`, `buttonRefresh`, and `buttonHome`. To get the resizing to work properly, make sure that you set the `Anchor` property of the three buttons on the right to `Top, Right`.

On startup, `buttonBack`, `buttonForward`, and `buttonStop` should be disabled because there is no point to the buttons if there is no initial page loaded in the `WebBrowser` control. You will later tell the application when to enable and disable the Back and Forward buttons yourself, depending on where the user is in the page stack. In addition, when a page is being loaded, you will need to enable the Stop button — but also, you will need to disable the Stop button once the page has finished being loaded. You will also have a Submit button on the page that will allow for the submission of the URL being requested.

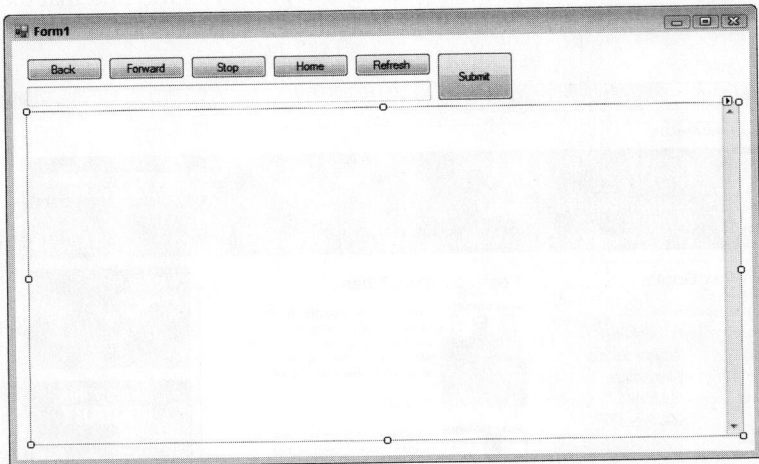

Figure 41-6

First, however, you will add the functionality behind the buttons. The `WebBrowser` class itself has all of the methods that you need, so this is all very straightforward:

```
using System;
using System.Windows.Forms;
namespace CSharpInternet
{
    partial class Form1 : Form
    {
        public Form1()
        {
            InitializeComponent();
        }
        private void textBox1_KeyPress(object sender, KeyPressEventArgs e)
        {
            if (e.KeyChar == (char)13)
            {
                webBrowser1.Navigate(textBox1.Text);
            }
        }
        private void webBrowser1_Navigated(object sender,
           WebBrowserNavigatedEventArgs e)
        {
            textBox1.Text = webBrowser1.Url.ToString();
            this.Text = webBrowser1.DocumentTitle.ToString();
        }
```

```
private void Form1_Load(object sender, EventArgs e)
{
    buttonBack.Enabled = false;
    buttonForward.Enabled = false;
    buttonStop.Enabled = false;
}
private void buttonBack_Click(object sender, EventArgs e)
{
    webBrowser1.GoBack();
    textBox1.Text = webBrowser1.Url.ToString();
}
private void buttonForward_Click(object sender, EventArgs e)
{
    webBrowser1.GoForward();
    textBox1.Text = webBrowser1.Url.ToString();
}
private void buttonStop_Click(object sender, EventArgs e)
{
    webBrowser1.Stop();
}
private void buttonHome_Click(object sender, EventArgs e)
{
    webBrowser1.GoHome();
    textBox1.Text = webBrowser1.Url.ToString();
}
private void buttonRefresh_Click(object sender, EventArgs e)
{
    webBrowser1.Refresh();
}
private void buttonSubmit_Click(object sender, EventArgs e)
{
    webBrowser1.Navigate(textBox1.Text);
}
private void webBrowser1_Navigating(object sender,
   WebBrowserNavigatingEventArgs e)
{
    buttonStop.Enabled = true;
}
private void webBrowser1_DocumentCompleted(object sender,
   WebBrowserDocumentCompletedEventArgs e)
{
    buttonStop.Enabled = false;
    if (webBrowser1.CanGoBack)
    {
        buttonBack.Enabled = true;
    }
    else
    {
        buttonBack.Enabled = false;
    }
    if (webBrowser1.CanGoForward)
    {
        buttonForward.Enabled = true;
    }
```

(continued)

(continued)

```
            else
            {
                buttonForward.Enabled = false;
            }
        }
    }
}
```

Many different activities are going on in this example because there are so many options for the end user when using this application. For each of the button-click events, there is a specific `WebBrowser` class method assigned as the action to initiate. For instance, for the Back button on the form, you simply use the `WebBrowser` control's `GoBack()` method; for the Forward button you have the `GoForward()` method; and for the others, you have methods such as `Stop()`, `Refresh()`, and `GoHome()`. This makes it fairly simple and straightforward to create a toolbar that will give you action similar to that of Microsoft's Internet Explorer.

When the form is first loaded, the `Form1_Load` event disables the appropriate buttons. From there, the end user can enter a URL into the text box and click the Submit button to have the application retrieve the desired page.

To manage the enabling and disabling of the buttons, you must key into a couple of events. As mentioned before, whenever downloading begins, you need to enable the Stop button. For this, you simply added an event handler for the `Navigating` event to enable the Stop button:

```
private void webBrowser1_Navigating(object sender,
   WebBrowserNavigatingEventArgs e)
{
    buttonStop.Enabled = true;
}
```

Then, the Stop button is again disabled when the document has finished loading:

```
private void webBrowser1_DocumentCompleted(object sender,
   WebBrowserDocumentCompletedEventArgs e)
{
    buttonStop.Enabled = false;
}
```

Enabling and disabling the appropriate Back and Forward buttons really depends on the ability to go backward or forward in the page stack. This is achieved by using both the `CanGoForwardChanged()` and the `CanGoBackChanged()` events:

```
private void webBrowser1_CanGoBackChanged(object sender, EventArgs e)
{
    if (webBrowser1.CanGoBack == true)
    {
        buttonBack.Enabled = true;
    }
    else
    {
        buttonBack.Enabled = false;
    }
}
private void webBrowser1_CanGoForwardChanged(object sender, EventArgs e)
{
    if (webBrowser1.CanGoForward == true)
```

```
            {
                buttonForward.Enabled = true;
            }
            else
            {
                buttonForward.Enabled = false;
            }
        }
```

Run the project now, visit a Web page, and click through a few links. You should also be able to use the toolbar to enhance your browsing experience. The end product is shown in Figure 41-7.

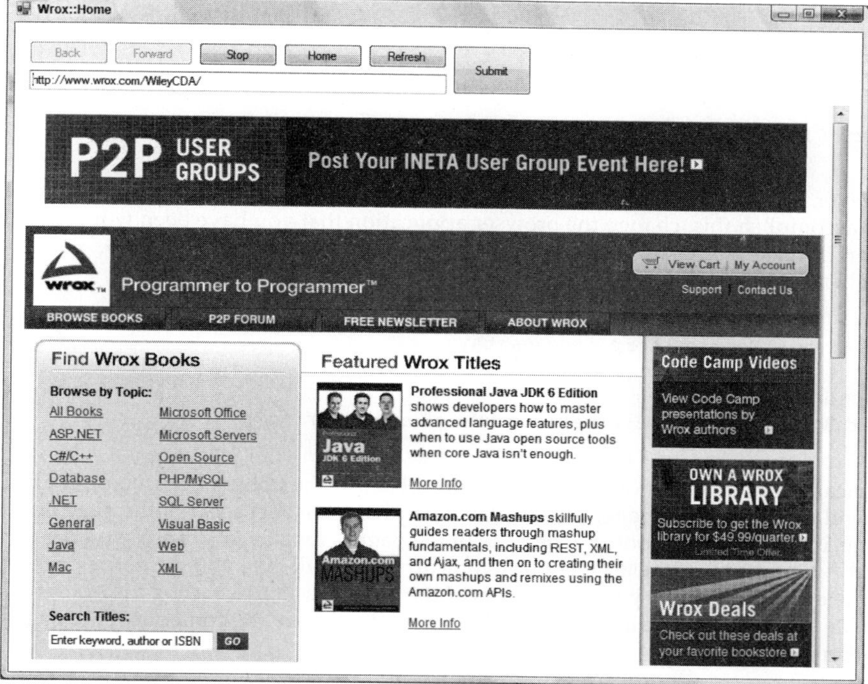

Figure 41-7

Printing Using the WebBrowser Control

Not only can users use the `WebBrowser` control to view pages and documents, but they can also use the control to send these pages and documents to the printer for printing. To print the page or document being viewed in the control, simply use the following construct:

```
webBrowser1.Print();
```

As before, you do not need to view the page or document to print it. For instance, you can use the `WebBrowser` class to load an HTML document and print it without even displaying the loaded document. This can be accomplished as shown here:

```
WebBrowser wb = new WebBrowser();
wb.Navigate("http://www.wrox.com");
wb.Print();
```

Displaying the Code of a Requested Page

In the beginning of this chapter, you used the `WebRequest` and the `Stream` classes to get at a remote page to display the code of the requested page. You used this code to accomplish this task:

```
public Form1()
{
   InitializeComponent();
   System.Net.WebClient Client = new WebClient();
   Stream strm = Client.OpenRead("http://www.reuters.com");
   StreamReader sr = new StreamReader(strm);
   string line;
   while ( (line=sr.ReadLine()) != null )
   {
      listBox1.Items.Add(line);
   }

   strm.Close();
}
```

Now, however, with the introduction of the `WebBrowser` control, it is quite easy to accomplish the same results. To accomplish this, change the browser application that you have been working on thus far in this chapter. To make this change, simply add a single line to the `Document_Completed` event, as illustrated here:

```
private void webBrowser1_DocumentCompleted(object sender,
   WebBrowserDocumentCompletedEventArgs e)
{
   buttonStop.Enabled = false;
   textBox2.Text = webBrowser1.DocumentText.ToString();
}
```

In the application itself, add another `TextBox` control below the `WebBrowser` control. The idea is that when the end user requests a page, you display not only the visual aspect of the page but also the code for the page, in the `TextBox` control. The code of the page is displayed simply by using the `DocumentText` property of the `WebBrowser` control, which will give you the entire page's content as a `String`. The other option is to get the contents of the page as a `Stream` using the `DocumentStream` property. The end result of adding the second `TextBox` to display the contents of the page as a `String` is shown in Figure 41-8.

The Web Request and Web Response Hierarchy

In this section, you will take a closer look at the underlying architecture of the `WebRequest` and `WebResponse` classes.

Figure 41-9 illustrates the inheritance hierarchy of the classes involved.

The hierarchy contains more than just the two classes you have used in your code. You should also know that the `WebRequest` and `WebResponse` classes are both abstract and cannot be instantiated. These base classes provide general functionality for dealing with Web requests and responses independent of the protocol used for a given operation. Requests are made using a particular protocol (HTTP, FTP, SMTP, and so on), and a derived class written for the given protocol will handle the request. Microsoft refers to this scheme as *pluggable protocols*. Remember in the code you examined earlier, your variables are defined as references to the base classes. However, `WebRequest.Create()` actually gives you an `HttpWebRequest` object, and the `GetResponse()` method actually returns an `HttpWebResponse` object. This factory-based mechanism hides many of the details from the client code, allowing support for a wide variety of protocols from the same code base.

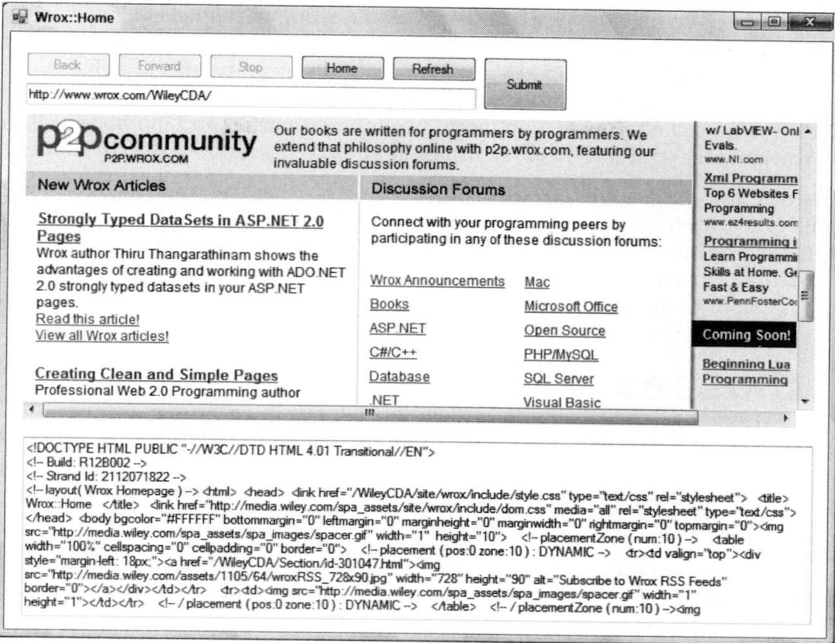

Figure 41-8

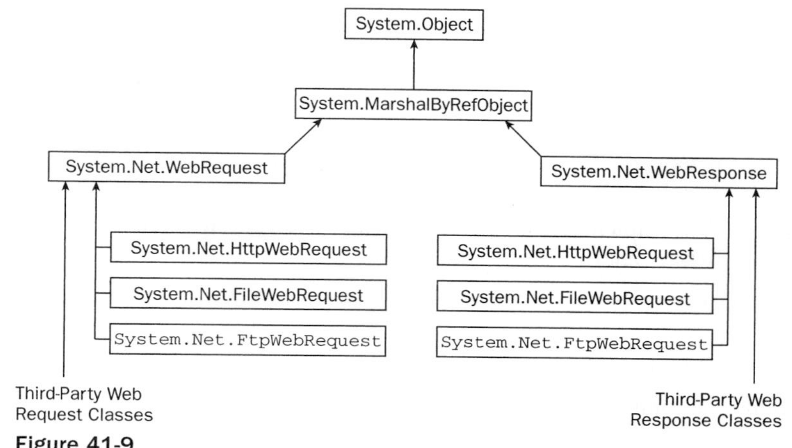

Figure 41-9

The fact that you need an object specifically capable of dealing with the HTTP protocol is clear from the URI that you supply to `WebRequest.Create()`. `WebRequest.Create()` examines the protocol specifier in the URI to instantiate and return an object of the appropriate class. This keeps your code free from having to know anything about the derived classes or specific protocol used. When you need to access specific features of a protocol, you might need the properties and methods of the derived class, in which case you can cast your `WebRequest` or `WebResponse` reference to the derived class.

With this architecture, you should be able to send requests using any of the common protocols. However, Microsoft currently provides derived classes to cover only the HTTP, HTTPS, FTP, and FILE protocols. The FTP option is the latest option provided by the .NET Framework (since the .NET Framework 2.0). If you want to utilize other protocols, for example, SMTP, then you will need to turn to using the Windows Communication Foundation, revert to using the Windows API, or use the `SmtpClient` object.

Utility Classes

This section covers a couple of utility classes to make Web programming easier when dealing with URIs and IP addresses.

URIs

`Uri` and `UriBuilder` are two classes in the `System` (not `System.Net`) namespace, and they are both intended to represent a URI. `UriBuilder` allows you to build a URI given the strings for the component parts, and the `Uri` class allows you to parse, combine, and compare URIs.

For the `Uri` class, the constructor requires a completed URI string:

```
Uri MSPage = new

Uri("http://www.Microsoft.com/SomeFolder/SomeFile.htm?Order=true");
```

The class exposes a large number of read-only properties. A `Uri` object is not intended to be modified once it has been constructed:

```
string Query = MSPage.Query;                          // Order=true;
string AbsolutePath = MSPage.AbsolutePath;            // SomeFolder/SomeFile.htm
string Scheme = MSPage.Scheme;                        // http
int Port = MSPage.Port;                               // 80 (the default for http)
string Host = MSPage.Host;                            // www.Microsoft.com
bool IsDefaultPort = MSPage.IsDefaultPort;            // true since 80 is default
```

`URIBuilder`, however, implements fewer properties, just enough to allow you to build up a complete URI. These properties are read-write.

You can supply the components to build up a URI to the constructor:

```
Uri MSPage = new
   UriBuilder("http", "www.Microsoft.com", 80, "SomeFolder/SomeFile.htm");
```

Or, you can build the components by assigning values to the properties:

```
UriBuilder MSPage = new UriBuilder();
MSPage.Scheme ="http";
MSPage.Host = "www.Microsoft.com";
MSPage.Port = 80;
MSPage.Path = "SomeFolder/SomeFile.htm";
```

Once you have completed initializing the `UriBuilder`, you can obtain the corresponding `Uri` object with the `Uri` property:

```
Uri CompletedUri = MSPage.Uri;
```

IP Addresses and DNS Names

On the Internet, you identify servers as well as clients by IP address or host name (also referred to as a DNS name). Generally speaking, the host name is the human-friendly name that you type in a Web browser window, such as `www.wrox.com` or `www.microsoft.com`. An IP address is the identifier computers use to identify each other. IP addresses are the identifiers used to ensure that Web requests and responses reach the appropriate machines. It is even possible for a computer to have more than one IP address.

Today, IP addresses are typically a 32-bit value. An example of a 32-bit IP address is 192.168.1.100. This format of IP address is referred to as Internet Protocol version 4. Because there are now so many computers and other devices vying for a spot on the Internet, a newer type of address was developed — Internet Protocol version 6. IPv6 provides a 64-bit IP address. IPv6 can potentially provide a maximum number of about 3×10^{28} unique addresses. You will find that the .NET Framework allows your applications to work with both IPv4 and IPv6.

For host names to work, you must first send a network request to translate the host name into an IP address, a task carried out by one or more DNS servers.

A DNS server stores a table mapping host names to IP addresses for all the computers it knows about, as well as the IP addresses of other DNS servers to look up the host names it does not know about. Your local computer should always know about at least one DNS server. Network administrators configure this information when a computer is set up.

Before sending out a request, your computer will first ask the DNS server to tell it the IP address corresponding to the host name you have typed in. Once armed with the correct IP address, the computer can address the request and send it over the network. All of this work normally happens behind the scenes while the user is browsing the Web.

.NET Classes for IP Addresses

The .NET Framework supplies a number of classes that are able to assist with the process of looking up IP addresses and finding information about host computers.

IPAddress

`IPAddress` represents an IP address. The address itself is available as the `GetAddressBytes` property and may be converted to a dotted decimal format with the `ToString()` method. `IPAddress` also implements a static `Parse()` method, which effectively performs the reverse conversion of `ToString()` — converting from a dotted decimal string to an `IPAddress`:

```
IPAddress ipAddress = IPAddress.Parse("234.56.78.9");
byte[] address = ipAddress.GetAddressBytes();
string ipString = ipAddress.ToString();
```

In this example, the `byte` integer `address` is assigned a binary representation of the IP address, and the string `ipString` is assigned the text `"234.56.78.9"`.

`IPAddress` also provides a number of constant static fields to return special addresses. For example, the `Loopback` address allows a machine to send messages to itself, whereas the `Broadcast` address allows multicasting to the local network:

```
// The following line will set loopback to "127.0.0.1".
// the loopback address indicates the local host.
string loopback = IPAddress.Loopback.ToString();
// The following line will set broadcast address to "255.255.255.255".
// the broadcast address is used to send a message to all machines on
// the local network.
string broadcast = IPAddress.Broadcast.ToString();
```

IPHostEntry

The `IPHostEntry` class encapsulates information relating to a particular host computer. This class makes the host name available via the `HostName` property (which returns a string), and the `AddressList` property returns an array of `IPAddress` objects. You are going to use the `IPHostEntry` class in the next example: `DNSLookupResolver`.

Dns

The `Dns` class is able to communicate with your default DNS server to retrieve IP addresses. The two important (static) methods are `Resolve()`, which uses the DNS server to obtain the details of a host with a given host name, and `GetHostByAddress()`, which also returns details of the host but this time using the IP address. Both methods return an `IPHostEntry` object:

```
IPHostEntry wroxHost = Dns.Resolve("www.wrox.com");
IPHostEntry wroxHostCopy = Dns.GetHostByAddress("208.215.179.178");
```

In this code, both `IPHostEntry` objects will contain details of the Wrox.com servers.

The `Dns` class differs from the `IPAddress` and `IPHostEntry` classes because it has the ability to actually communicate with servers to obtain information. In contrast, `IPAddress` and `IPHostEntry` are more along the lines of simple data structures with convenient properties to allow access to the underlying data.

The DnsLookup Example

The DNS and IP-related classes are illustrated with an example that looks up DNS names: `DnsLookup` (see Figure 41-10).

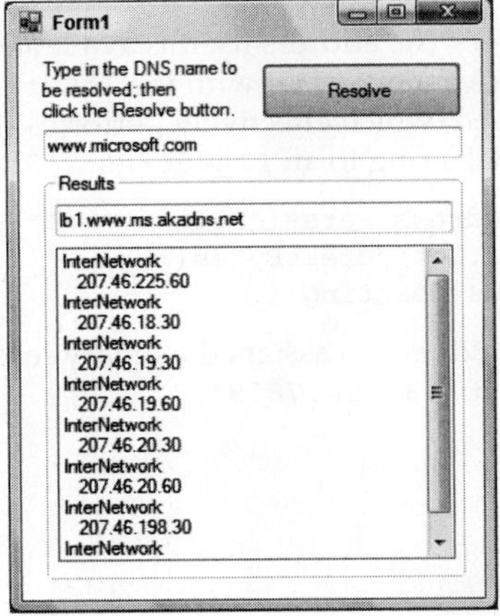

Figure 41-10

This sample application simply invites the user to type in a DNS name using the main text box. When the user clicks the Resolve button, the sample uses the `Dns.Resolve()` method to retrieve an `IPHostEntry` reference and display the host name and IP addresses. Note how the host name displayed may be different from the name typed in. This can occur if one DNS name (`www.microsoft.com`) simply acts as a proxy for another DNS name (`lb1.www.ms.akadns.net`).

The `DnsLookup` application is a standard C# Windows application. The controls are added as shown in Figure 41-10, giving them the names `txtBoxInput`, `btnResolve`, `txtBoxHostName`, and `listBoxIPs`, respectively. Then, you simply add the following method to the `Form1` class as the event handler for the `buttonResolve Click` event:

```
void btnResolve_Click (object sender, EventArgs e)
{
   try
   {
      IPHostEntry iphost = Dns.GetHostEntry(txtBoxInput.Text);
      foreach (IPAddress ip in iphost.AddressList)
      {
         string ipaddress = ip.AddressFamily.ToString();
         listBoxIPs.Items.Add(ipaddress);
         listBoxIPs.Items.Add("    " + ip.ToString());
      }
      txtBoxHostName.Text = iphost.HostName;
   }
   catch(Exception ex)
   {
      MessageBox.Show("Unable to process the request because " +
         "the following problem occurred:\n" +
          ex.Message, "Exception occurred");
   }
}
```

Notice that in this code you are careful to trap any exceptions. An exception might occur if the user types an invalid DNS name or if the network is down.

After retrieving the `IPHostEntry` instance, you use the `AddressList` property to obtain an array containing the IP addresses, which you then iterate through with a `foreach` loop. For each entry, you display the IP address as an integer and as a string, using the `IPAddress.AddressFamily.ToString()` method.

Lower-Level Protocols

This section briefly discusses some of the .NET classes used to communicate at a lower level.

Network communications work on several different levels. The classes you have seen in this chapter so far work at the highest level: the level at which specific commands are processed. It is probably easiest to understand this concept if you think of file transfer using FTP. Although today's GUI applications hide many of the FTP details, it was not so long ago when you executed FTP from a command-line prompt. In this environment, you explicitly typed commands to send to the server for downloading, uploading, and listing files.

FTP is not the only high-level protocol relying on textual commands. HTTP, SMTP, POP, and other protocols are based on a similar type of behavior. Again, many of the modern graphical tools hide the transmission of commands from the user, so you are generally not aware of them. For example, when you type a URL into a Web browser, and the Web request goes off to a server, the browser is actually sending a (plain-text) `GET` command to the server, which fulfills a similar purpose as the FTP `get` command. It can also send a `POST` command, which indicates that the browser has attached other data to the request.

These protocols, however, are not sufficient by themselves to achieve communication between computers. Even if both the client and the server understand, for example, the HTTP protocol, it will still not be possible for them to understand each other unless there is also agreement on exactly how to transmit the characters: What binary format will be used? Moreover, getting down to the lowest level, what voltages will be used to represent 0s and 1s in the binary data? Because there are so many items to configure and agree upon, developers and hardware engineers in the networking field often refer to a *protocol stack*. When you list all of the various protocols and mechanisms required for communication between two hosts, you create a protocol stack with high-level protocols on the top and low-level protocols on the bottom. This approach results in a modular and layered approach to achieving efficient communication.

Luckily, for most development work, you do not need to go far down the stack or work with voltage levels. If you are writing code that requires efficient communication between computers, then it's not unusual to write code that works directly at the level of sending binary data packets between computers. This is the realm of protocols such as TCP, and Microsoft has supplied a number of classes that allow you to conveniently work with binary data at this level.

Lower-Level Classes

The `System.Net.Sockets` namespace contains the relevant classes. These classes, for example, allow you to directly send out TCP network requests or to listen to TCP network requests on a particular port. The following table explains the main classes.

Class	Purpose
`Socket`	Deals with managing connections. Classes such as `WebRequest`, `TcpClient`, and `UdpClient` use this class internally.
`NetworkStream`	Derived from `Stream`. Represents a stream of data from the network.
`SmtpClient`	Enables you to send messages (mail) through the Simple Mail Transfer Protocol.
`TcpClient`	Enables you to create and use TCP connections.
`TcpListener`	Enables you to listen for incoming TCP connection requests.
`UdpClient`	Enables you to create connections for UDP clients. (UDP is an alternative protocol to TCP but is much less widely used, mostly on local networks.)

Using SmtpClient

The `SmtpClient` object allows you to send mail messages through the Simple Mail Transfer Protocol. A simple sample of using the `SmtpClient` object is illustrated here:

```
SmtpClient sc = new SmtpClient("mail.mySmtpHost.com");
sc.Send("evjen@yahoo.com", "editor@wrox.com",
   "The latest chapter", "Here is the latest.");
```

In its simplest form, you work from an instance of the `SmtpClient` object. In this case, the instantiation also provided the host of the SMTP server that is used to send the mail messages over the Internet. You could have also achieved the same task by using the `Host` property.

```
SmtpClient sc = new SmtpClient();
sc.Host = "mail.mySmtpHost.com";
sc.Send("evjen@yahoo.com", "editor@wrox.com",
   "The latest chapter", "Here is the latest.");
```

Once you have the `SmtpClient` in place, it is simply a matter of calling the `Send()` method and providing the From address, the To address, and the Subject, followed by the Body of the mail message.

In many cases, you will have mail messages that are more complex than this. To work with this possibility, you can also pass in a `MailMessage` object into the `Send()` method.

```
SmtpClient sc = new SmtpClient();
sc.Host = "mail.mySmtpHost.com";
MailMessage mm = new MailMessage();
mm.Sender = new MailAddress("evjen@yahoo.com", "Bill Evjen");
mm.To.Add(new MailAddress("editor@wrox.com", "Katie Mohr"));
mm.To.Add(new MailAddress("marketing@wrox.com", "Wrox Marketing"));
mm.CC.Add(new MailAddress("publisher@wrox.com", "Joe Wikert"));
mm.Subject = "The latest chapter";
mm.Body = "<b>Here you can put a long message</b>";
mm.IsBodyHtml = true;
mm.Priority = MailPriority.High;
sc.Send(mm);
```

Using `MailMessage` allows you to really fine-tune how you build your mail messages. You are able to send HTML messages, add as many To and CC recipients as you wish, change the message priority, work with the message encodings, and add attachments. The ability to add attachments is defined here in the following code snippet.

```
SmtpClient sc = new SmtpClient();
sc.Host = "mail.mySmtpHost.com";
MailMessage mm = new MailMessage();
mm.Sender = new MailAddress("evjen@yahoo.com", "Bill Evjen");
mm.To.Add(new MailAddress("editor@wrox.com", "Katie Mohr"));
mm.To.Add(new MailAddress("marketing@wrox.com", "Wrox Marketing"));
mm.CC.Add(new MailAddress("publisher@wrox.com", "Joe Wikert"));
mm.Subject = "The latest chapter";
mm.Body = "<b>Here you can put a long message</b>";
mm.IsBodyHtml = true;
mm.Priority = MailPriority.High;
Attachment att = new Attachment("myExcelResults.zip",
   MediaTypeNames.Application.Zip);
mm.Attachments.Add(att);
sc.Send(mm);
```

In this case, an `Attachment` object is created and added, using the `Add()` method, to the `MailMessage` object before the `Send()` method is called.

Using the TCP Classes

The Transmission Control Protocol (TCP) classes offer simple methods for connecting and sending data between two endpoints. An endpoint is the combination of an IP address and a port number. Existing protocols have well-defined port numbers, for example, HTTP uses port 80, whereas SMTP uses port 25. The Internet Assigned Number Authority, IANA, (`www.iana.org`) assigns port numbers to these well-known services. Unless you are implementing a well-known service, you will want to select a port number above 1,024.

TCP traffic makes up the majority of traffic on the Internet today. TCP is often the protocol of choice because it offers guaranteed delivery, error correction, and buffering. The `TcpClient` class encapsulates a TCP connection and provides a number of properties to regulate the connection, including buffering, buffer size, and timeouts. Reading and writing is accomplished by requesting a `NetworkStream` object via the `GetStream()` method.

The `TcpListener` class listens for incoming TCP connections with the `Start()` method. When a connection request arrives, you can use the `AcceptSocket()` method to return a socket for communication with the remote machine, or use the `AcceptTcpClient()` method to use a higher-level `TcpClient` object for communication. The easiest way to see how the `TcpListener` and `TcpClient` classes work together is to work through an example.

The TcpSend and TcpReceive Examples

To demonstrate how these classes work, you need to build two applications. Figure 41-11 shows the first application, `TcpSend`. This application opens a TCP connection to a server and sends the C# source code for itself.

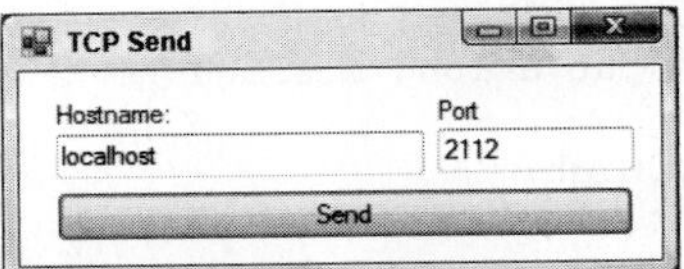

Figure 41-11

Once again, you create a C# Windows application. The form consists of two text boxes (`txtHost` and `txtPort`) for the host name and port, respectively, as well as a button (`btnSend`) to click and start a connection. First, you ensure that you include the relevant namespaces:

```
using System;
using System.IO;
using System.Net.Sockets;
using System.Windows.Forms;
```

The following code shows the event handler for the button's `Click` event:

```
private void btnSend_Click(object sender, System.EventArgs e)
{
    TcpClient tcpClient = new TcpClient(txtHost.Text, Int32.Parse(txtPort.Text));
    NetworkStream ns = tcpClient.GetStream();
    FileStream fs = File.Open(Server.MapPath("form1.cs"), FileMode.Open);

    int data = fs.ReadByte();
    while(data != -1)
    {
        ns.WriteByte((byte)data);
        data = fs.ReadByte();
    }
    fs.Close();
    ns.Close();
    tcpClient.Close();
}
```

This example creates the `TcpClient` using a host name and a port number. Alternatively, if you have an instance of the `IPEndPoint` class, then you can pass the instance to the `TcpClient` constructor. After retrieving an instance of the `NetworkStream` class, you open the source code file and begin to read bytes. As with many of the binary streams, you need to check for the end of the stream by comparing the return value of the `ReadByte()` method to `-1`. After your loop has read all of the bytes and sent them along to the network stream, you must close all of the open files, connections, and streams.

On the other side of the connection, the `TcpReceive` application displays the received file after the transmission is finished (see Figure 41-12).

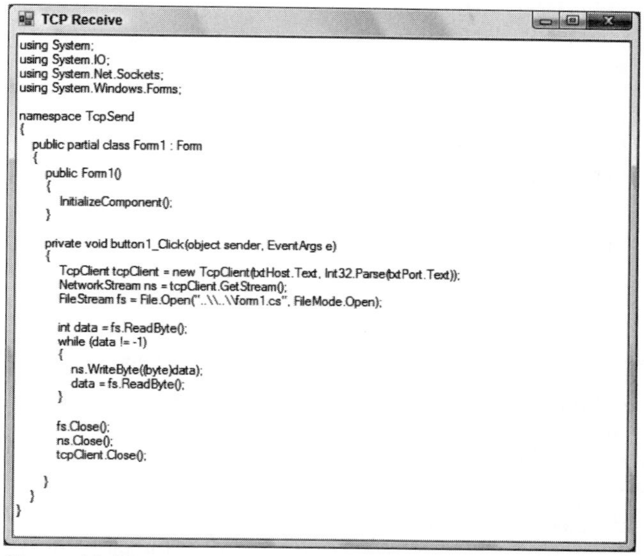

```
TCP Receive
using System;
using System.IO;
using System.Net.Sockets;
using System.Windows.Forms;

namespace TcpSend
{
    public partial class Form1 : Form
    {
        public Form1()
        {
            InitializeComponent();
        }

        private void button1_Click(object sender, EventArgs e)
        {
            TcpClient tcpClient = new TcpClient(txtHost.Text, Int32.Parse(txtPort.Text));
            NetworkStream ns = tcpClient.GetStream();
            FileStream fs = File.Open("..\\..\\form1.cs", FileMode.Open);

            int data = fs.ReadByte();
            while (data != -1)
            {
                ns.WriteByte((byte)data);
                data = fs.ReadByte();
            }

            fs.Close();
            ns.Close();
            tcpClient.Close();
        }
    }
}
```

Figure 41-12

The form consists of a single `TextBox` control, named `txtDisplay`. The `TcpReceive` application uses a `TcpListener` to wait for the incoming connection. To prevent freezing the application interface, you use a background thread to wait for and then read from the connection. Thus, you need to include the `System.Threading` namespace as well these other namespaces:

```
using System;
using System.IO;
using System.Net;
using System.Net.Sockets;
using System.Threading;
using System.Windows.Forms;
```

Inside the form's constructor, you spin up a background thread:

```
public Form1()
{
   InitializeComponent();
   Thread thread = new Thread(new ThreadStart(Listen));
   thread.Start();
}
```

The remaining important code is this:

```
public void Listen()
{
   IPAddress localAddr = IPAddress.Parse("127.0.0.1");
   Int32 port = 2112;
   TcpListener tcpListener = new TcpListener(localAddr, port);
   tcpListener.Start();

   TcpClient tcpClient = tcpListener.AcceptTcpClient();

   NetworkStream ns = tcpClient.GetStream();
   StreamReader sr = new StreamReader(ns);
   string result = sr.ReadToEnd();
   Invoke(new UpdateDisplayDelegate(UpdateDisplay),new object[] {result} );
   tcpClient.Close();
   tcpListener.Stop();
}
public void UpdateDisplay(string text)
{
   txtDisplay.Text= text;
}

protected delegate void UpdateDisplayDelegate(string text);
```

The thread begins execution in the `Listen()` method and allows you to make the blocking call to `AcceptTcpClient()` without halting the interface. Notice that the IP address (`127.0.0.1`) and the port number (`2112`) are hard-coded into the application, so you will need to enter the same port number from the client application.

You use the `TcpClient` object returned by `AcceptTcpClient()` to open a new stream for reading. As with the earlier example, you create a `StreamReader` to convert the incoming network data into a string. Before you close the client and stop the listener, you update the form's text box. You do not want to access the text box directly from your background thread, so you use the form's `Invoke()` method with a delegate and pass the result string as the first element in an array of `object` parameters. `Invoke()` ensures that your call is correctly marshaled into the thread that owns the control handles in the user interface.

TCP versus UDP

The other protocol covered in this section is UDP (User Datagram Protocol). UDP is a simple protocol with few features and little overhead. Developers often use UDP in applications where the speed and performance requirements outweigh the reliability needs, for example, video streaming. In contrast, TCP offers a number of features to confirm the delivery of data. TCP provides error correction and retransmission in the case of lost or corrupted packets. Last, but hardly least, TCP buffers incoming and outgoing data and also guarantees that a sequence of packets scrambled in transmission is reassembled before delivery to the application. Even with the extra overhead, TCP is the most widely used protocol across the Internet because of its high reliability.

The UDP Class

As you might expect, the `UdpClient` class features a smaller and simpler interface than `TcpClient`. This reflects the relatively simpler nature of the protocol. Although both TCP and UDP classes use a socket underneath the covers, the `UdpClient` class does not contain a method to return a network stream for reading and writing. Instead, the member function `Send()` accepts an array of bytes as a parameter, and the `Receive()` function returns an array of bytes. Also, because UDP is a connectionless protocol, you can wait to specify the endpoint for the communication as a parameter to the `Send()` and `Receive()`

methods, instead of specifying it earlier in a constructor or `Connect()` method. You can also change the endpoint on each subsequent send or receive.

The following code fragment uses the `UdpClient` class to send a message to an echo service. A server with an echo service running accepts TCP or UDP connections on port 7. The echo service simply echoes any data sent to the server back to the client. This service is useful for diagnostics and testing, although many system administrators disable echo services for security reasons:

```
using System;
using System.Text;
using System.Net;
using System.Net.Sockets;
namespace Wrox.ProCSharp.InternetAccess.UdpExample
{

   class Class1
   {
      [STAThread]
      static void Main(string[] args)
      {
         UdpClient udpClient = new UdpClient();
         string sendMsg = "Hello Echo Server";
         byte [] sendBytes = Encoding.ASCII.GetBytes(sendMsg);
         udpClient.Send(sendBytes, sendBytes.Length, "SomeEchoServer.net", 7);
         IPEndPoint endPoint = new IPEndPoint(0,0);
         byte [] rcvBytes = udpClient.Receive(ref endPoint);
         string rcvMessage = Encoding.ASCII.GetString(rcvBytes,
                                                      0,
                                                      rcvBytes.Length);
         // should print out "Hello Echo Server"
         Console.WriteLine(rcvMessage);
      }
   }
}
```

You make heavy use of the `Encoding.ASCII` class to translate strings into arrays of `byte` and vice versa. Also note that you pass an `IPEndPoint` by reference into the `Receive()` method. Because UDP is not a connection-oriented protocol, each call to `Receive()` might pick up data from a different endpoint, so `Receive()` populates this parameter with the IP address and port of the sending host.

Both `UdpClient` and `TcpClient` offer a layer of abstraction over the lowest of the low-level classes: the `Socket`.

The Socket Class

The `Socket` class offers the highest level of control in network programming. One of the easiest ways to demonstrate the class is to rewrite the `TcpReceive` application with the `Socket` class. The updated `Listen()` method is listed in this example:

```
public void Listen()
{
   Socket listener = new Socket(AddressFamily.InterNetwork,
                                SocketType.Stream,
                                ProtocolType.Tcp);
   listener.Bind(new IPEndPoint(IPAddress.Any, 2112));
   listener.Listen(0);
   Socket socket = listener.Accept();
```

(continued)

(continued)

```
        Stream netStream = new NetworkStream(socket);
        StreamReader reader = new StreamReader(netStream);

        string result = reader.ReadToEnd();
        Invoke(new UpdateDisplayDelegate(UpdateDisplay),
               new object[] {result} );
        socket.Close();
        listener.Close();
    }
```

The `Socket` class requires a few more lines of code to complete the same task. For starters, the constructor arguments need to specify an IP addressing scheme for a streaming socket with the TCP protocol. These arguments are just one of the many combinations available to the `Socket` class. The `TcpClient` class can configure these settings for you. You then bind the listener socket to a port and begin to listen for incoming connections. When an incoming request arrives, you can use the `Accept()` method to create a new socket to handle the connection. You ultimately attach a `StreamReader` instance to the socket to read the incoming data, in much the same fashion as before.

The `Socket` class also contains a number of methods for asynchronously accepting, connecting, sending, and receiving. You can use these methods with callback delegates in the same way you used the asynchronous page requests with the `WebRequest` class. If you really need to dig into the internals of the socket, the `GetSocketOption()` and `SetSocketOption()` methods are available. These methods allow you to see and configure options, including timeout, time-to-live, and other low-level options. Next, this chapter looks at another example of using sockets.

Building a Server Console Application

Looking further into the `Socket` class, this next example will create a console application that acts as a server for incoming socket requests. From there, a second example will be created in parallel (another console application), which sends a message to the server console application.

The first application you will build is the console application that acts as a server. This application will open a socket on a specific TCP port and listen for any incoming messages. The code for this console application is presented in its entirety here:

```
using System;
using System.Net;
using System.Net.Sockets;
using System.Text;
namespace SocketConsole
{
    class Program
    {
        static void Main()
        {
            Console.WriteLine("Starting: Creating Socket object");
            Socket listener = new Socket(AddressFamily.InterNetwork,
                                         SocketType.Stream,
                                         ProtocolType.Tcp);
            listener.Bind(new IPEndPoint(IPAddress.Any, 2112));
            listener.Listen(10);
            while (true)
            {
                Console.WriteLine("Waiting for connection on port 2112");
                Socket socket = listener.Accept();
                string receivedValue = string.Empty;
```

```
                    while (true)
                    {
                        byte[] receivedBytes = new byte[1024];
                        int numBytes = socket.Receive(receivedBytes);
                        Console.WriteLine("Receiving ...");
                        receivedValue += Encoding.ASCII.GetString(receivedBytes,
                                             0, numBytes);
                        if (receivedValue.IndexOf("[FINAL]") > -1)
                        {
                            break;
                        }
                    }
                    Console.WriteLine("Received value: {0}", receivedValue);
                    string replyValue = "Message successfully received.";
                    byte[] replyMessage = Encoding.ASCII.GetBytes(replyValue);
                    socket.Send(replyMessage);
                    socket.Shutdown(SocketShutdown.Both);
                    socket.Close();
                }
                listener.Close();
            }
        }
    }
```

This example sets up a socket using the `Socket` class. The socket created uses the TCP protocol and is set up to receive incoming messages from any IP address using port 2112. Values that come in through the open socket are written to the console screen. This consuming application will continue to receive bytes until the `[FINAL]` string is received. This `[FINAL]` string signifies the end of the incoming message, and the message can then be interpreted.

After the end of the message is received from a client, a reply message is sent to the same client. From there, the socket is closed using the `Close()` method, and the console application will continue to stay up until a new message is received.

Building the Client Application

The next step is to build a client application that will send a message to the first console application. The client will be able to send any message that it wants to the server console application as long as it follows some rules that were established by this application. The first of these rules is that the server console application is listening only on a particular protocol. In the case of this server application, it is listening using the TCP protocol. The other rule is that the server application is listening only on a particular port — in this case, port 2112. The last rule is that in any message that is being sent, the last bits of the message need to end with the string `[FINAL]`.

The following client console application follows all of these rules:

```
using System;
using System.Net;
using System.Net.Sockets;
using System.Text;
namespace SocketConsoleClient
{
    class Program
    {
        static void Main()
        {
            byte[] receivedBytes = new byte[1024];
```

(continued)

(continued)

```
            IPHostEntry ipHost = Dns.Resolve("127.0.0.1");
            IPAddress ipAddress = ipHost.AddressList[0];
            IPEndPoint ipEndPoint = new IPEndPoint(ipAddress, 2112);
            Console.WriteLine("Starting: Creating Socket object");

            Socket sender = new Socket(AddressFamily.InterNetwork,
                                       SocketType.Stream,
                                       ProtocolType.Tcp);
            sender.Connect(ipEndPoint);
            Console.WriteLine("Successfully connected to {0}",
                 sender.RemoteEndPoint);
            string sendingMessage = "Hello World Socket Test";
            Console.WriteLine("Creating message: Hello World Socket Test");
            byte[] forwardMessage = Encoding.ASCII.GetBytes(sendingMessage
               + "[FINAL]");
            sender.Send(forwardMessage);
            int totalBytesReceived = sender.Receive(receivedBytes);
            Console.WriteLine("Message provided from server: {0}",
                              Encoding.ASCII.GetString(receivedBytes,
                              0, totalBytesReceived));
            sender.Shutdown(SocketShutdown.Both);
            sender.Close();
            Console.ReadLine();
        }
    }
}
```

In this example, an `IPEndPoint` object is created using the IP address of *localhost* as well as using port 2112 as required by the server console application. In this case, a socket is created and the `Connect()` method is called. After the socket is opened and connected to the server console application socket instance, a string of text is sent to the server application using the `Send()` method. Because the server application is going to return a message, the `Receive()` method is used to grab this message (placing it in a byte array). From there, the byte array is converted into a string and displayed in the console application before the socket is shut down.

Running this application will produce the results presented in Figure 41-13.

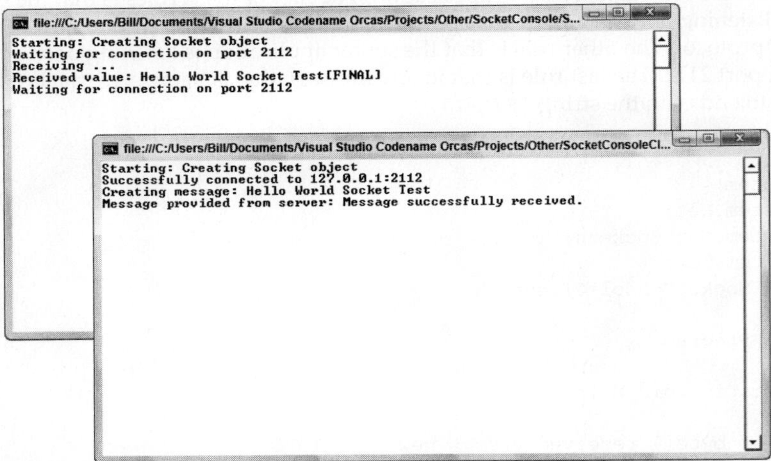

Figure 41-13

Reviewing the two console applications in the figure, you can see that the server application opens and awaits incoming messages. The incoming message is sent from the client application, and the string sent is then displayed by the server application. The server application waits for other messages to come in, even after the first message is received and displayed. You can see this for yourself by shutting down the client application and re-running the application. You will then see that the server application again displays the message received.

Summary

In this chapter, you reviewed the .NET Framework classes available in the `System.Net` namespace for communication across networks. You have seen some of the .NET base classes that deal with opening client connections on the network and Internet, and how to send requests to and receive responses from servers (the most obvious use of this being to receive HTML pages). By taking advantage of the `WebBrowser` control in .NET 3.5, you can easily make use of Internet Explorer from your desktop applications.

As a rule of thumb, when programming with classes in the `System.Net` namespace, you should always try to use the most generic class possible. For instance, using the `TCPClient` class instead of the `Socket` class isolates your code from many of the lower-level socket details. Moving one-step higher, the `WebRequest` class allows you to take advantage of the pluggable protocol architecture of the .NET Framework. Your code will be ready to take advantage of new application-level protocols as Microsoft and other third-party developers introduce new functionality.

Finally, you learned how to use the asynchronous capabilities in the networking classes, which give a Windows Forms application the professional touch of a responsive user interface.

Now you move on to learning about Windows Communication Foundation.

42

Windows Communication Foundation

Previous to .NET 3.0, several communication technologies were required in a single enterprise solution. For platform-independent communication, ASP.NET Web services were used. For more advanced Web services, technologies such as reliability, platform-independent security, and atomic transactions, Web Services Enhancements added a complexity layer to ASP.NET Web services. If the communication needed to be faster, and both the client and service were .NET applications, .NET Remoting was the technology of choice. .NET Enterprise Services with its automatic transaction support, by default, was using the DCOM protocol that was even faster than .NET Remoting. DCOM was also the only protocol to allow passing transactions. All of these technologies have different programming models that require many skills from the developer.

.NET Framework 3.0 introduced a new communication technology that includes all the features from the predecessors and combines them into one programming model: Windows Communication Foundation (WCF).

In particular, this chapter discusses the following topics:

- WCF overview
- A simple service and client
- Contracts
- Service implementation
- Binding
- Hosting
- Clients
- Duplex communication

WCF Overview

WCF combines the functionality from ASP.NET Web services, .NET Remoting, Message Queuing, and Enterprise Services. What you get from WCF is:

- **Hosting for components and services** — Just as you can use custom hosts with .NET Remoting and WSE, you can host a WCF service in the ASP.NET runtime, a Windows service, a COM+ process, or just a Windows Forms application for peer-to-peer computing.
- **Declarative behavior** — Instead of the requirement to derive from a base class (this requirement exists with .NET Remoting and Enterprise Services), attributes can be used to define the services. This is similar to Web services developed with ASP.NET.
- **Communication channels** — Although NET Remoting is very flexible with changing the communication channel, WCF is a good alternative because it offers the same flexibility. WCF offers multiple channels to communicate using HTTP, TCP, or an IPC channel. Custom channels using different transport protocols can be created as well.
- **Security infrastructure** — For implementing platform-independent Web services, a standardized security environment must be used. The proposed standards are implemented with WSE 3.0, and this continues with WCF.
- **Extensibility** — .NET Remoting has a rich extensibility story. It is not only possible to create custom channels, formatters, and proxies, but also to inject functionality inside the message flow on the client and on the server. WCF offers similar extensibilities; however, here, the extensions are created by using SOAP headers.
- **Support of previous technologies** — Instead of rewriting a distributed solution completely to use WCF, WCF can be integrated with existing technologies. WCF offers a channel that can communicate with serviced components using DCOM. Web services that have been developed with ASP.NET can be integrated with WCF as well.

The final goal is to send and receive messages from a client to a service either across processes or different systems, across a local network, or the Internet. This should be done if required in a platform-independent way and as fast as possible. On a distant view, the service offers an endpoint that is described by a contract, binding, and an address. The contract defines the operations offered by the service, binding gives information about the protocol and encoding, and the address is the location of the service. The client needs a compatible endpoint to access the service.

Figure 42-1 shows the components that participate with a WCF communication.

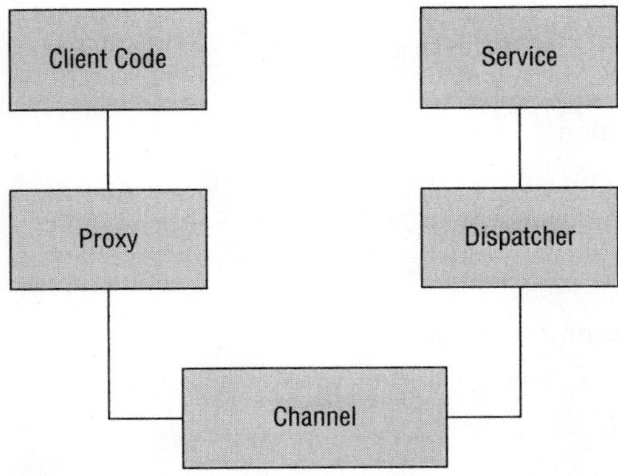

Figure 42-1

The client invokes a method on the proxy. The proxy offers methods as defined by the service, but converts the method call to a message and transfers the message to the channel. The channel has a client-side and a server-side part that communicate across a networking protocol. From the channel, the message is passed to the dispatcher, which converts the message to a method call that is invoked with the service.

WCF supports several communication protocols. For platform-independent communication, Web services standards are supported. For communication between .NET applications, faster communication protocols with less overhead can be used.

The following sections look at the functionality of core services used for platform-independent communication.

SOAP

For platform-independent communication, the SOAP protocol can be used and is directly supported from WCF. SOAP originally was shorthand for Simple Object Access Protocol, but since SOAP 1.2 this is no longer the case. SOAP no longer is an object access protocol, because, instead, messages are sent that can be defined by an XML schema.

A service receives a SOAP message from a client and returns a SOAP response message. A SOAP message consists of an envelope, which contains a header and a body:

```
<s:Envelope xmlns:a="http://www.w3.org/2005/08/addressing"
    xmlns:s="http://www.w3.org/2003/05/soap-envelope">
  <s:Header>
  </s:Header>
  <s:Body>
    <ReserveRoom xmlns="http://www.wrox.com/ProCSharp/2008">
      <roomReservation
xmlns:d4p1="http://schemas.datacontract.org/2004/07/Wrox.ProCSharp.WCF"
xmlns:i="http://www.w3.org/2001/XMLSchema-instance">
        <d4p1:RoomName>Hawelka</d4p1:RoomName>
        <d4p1:StartDate>2007-06-21T08:00:00</d4p1:StartDate>
        <d4p1:EndDate>2007-06-21T14:00:00</d4p1:EndDate>
        <d4p1:Contact>Georg Danzer</d4p1:Contact>
        <d4p1:Event>White Horses</d4p1:Event>
      </roomReservation>
    </ReserveRoom>
  </s:Body>
</s:Envelope>
```

The header is optional and can contain information about addressing, security, and transactions. The body contains the message data.

WSDL

A WSDL (Web Services Description Language) document describes the operations and messages of the service. WSDL defines metadata of the service that can be used to create a proxy for the client application.

The WSDL contains this information:

- **Types** for the messages that are described using an XML schema.
- **Messages** that are sent to and from the service. Parts of the messages are the types that are defined with an XML schema.

- **Port types** map to service contracts and list operations that are defined with the service contract. Operations contain messages; for example, an input and an output message as used with a request and response sequence.
- **Binding** information that contains the operations listed with the port types and that defines the SOAP variant used.
- **Service** information that maps port types to endpoint addresses.

With WCF, WSDL information is offered by MEX (Metadata Exchange) endpoints.

JSON

Instead of sending SOAP messages, accessing services from JavaScript can best be done using JSON (JavaScript Object Notation). .NET 3.5 includes a data contract serializer to create objects with the JSON notation.

JSON has less overhead than SOAP because it is not XML, but optimized for JavaScript clients. This makes it extremely useful from Ajax clients. Ajax is discussed in Chapter 39, "ASP.NET AJAX." JSON does not offer reliability, security, and transaction features that can be sent with the SOAP header, but these are features usually not needed by JavaScript clients.

Simple Service and Client

Before going into the details of WCF, let's start with a simple service. The service is used to reserve meeting rooms.

For a backing store of room reservations, a simple SQL Server database with the table `RoomReservations` is used. The table and its properties are shown in Figure 42-2. You can download the database together with the sample code of this chapter.

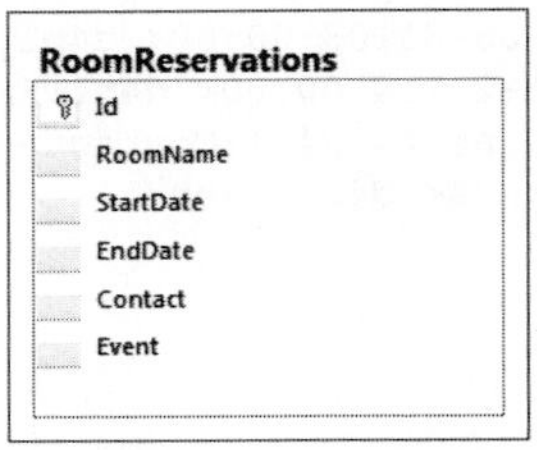

RoomReservations
Id
RoomName
StartDate
EndDate
Contact
Event

Figure 42-2

Create an empty solution with the name `RoomReservation` and add a new Component Library project with the name `RoomReservationData` to the solution. The first project that is implemented contains just the code to access the database. Because LINQ to SQL makes the database access code much easier, this .NET 3.5 technology is used here.

Chapter 27 gives you the details of LINQ to SQL.

Add a new item, LINQ to SQL Classes, and name it `RoomReservation.dbml`. With the LINQ to SQL designer, open the Server Explorer to drop the `RoomReservation` database table onto the designer as shown in Figure 42-3. This designer creates an entity class, `RoomReservation`, that contains properties for every column of the table and the class `RoomReservationDataContext`. `RoomReservationDataContext` connects to the database.

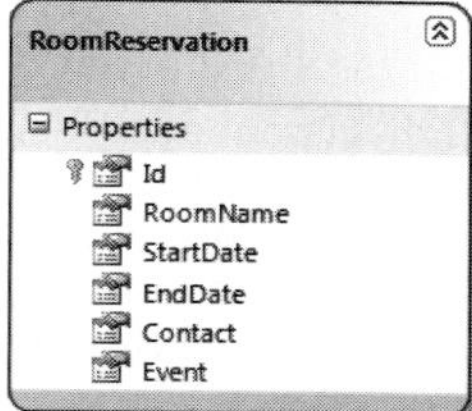

Figure 42-3

Change the Serialization Mode property of the LINQ to SQL designer from `None` to `Unidirectional`. This way, the generated class `RoomReservation` gets a data contract that allows the entity classes to serialize across WCF.

To read and write data from the database using LINQ to SQL, add the class `RoomReservationData`. The method `ReserveRoom()` writes a room reservation to the database. The method `GetReservations()` returns an array of room reservations from a specified date range.

```
using System;
using System.Linq;

namespace Wrox.ProCSharp.WCF.Data
{
   public class RoomReservationData
   {
      public void ReserveRoom(RoomReservation roomReservation)
      {
         using (RoomReservationDataContext data =
               new RoomReservationDataContext())
         {
            data.RoomReservations.Add(roomReservation);
            data.SubmitChanges();
         }
      }

      public RoomReservation[] GetReservations(DateTime fromDate,
                                               DateTime toDate)
      {
         using (RoomReservationDataContext data =
               new RoomReservationDataContext())
         {
            return (from r in data.RoomReservations
                    where r.StartDate > fromDate && r.EndDate < toDate
                    select r).ToArray();
         }
      }
   }
}
```

Now start creating the service.

Service Contract

Add a new project of type WCF Service Library to the solution and name the project `RoomReservationService`. Rename the generated files `IService1.cs` to `IRoomService.cs` and `Service1.cs` to `RoomReservationService.cs` and change the namespace within the generated files to `Wrox.ProCSharp.WCF.Service`. The assembly `RoomReservationData` needs to be referenced to have the entity types and the `RoomReservationData` class available.

The operations offered by the service can be defined by an interface. The interface `IRoomService` defines the methods `ReserveRoom` and `GetRoomReservations`. The service contract is defined with the attribute `[ServiceContract]`. The operations defined by the service have the attribute `[OperationContract]` applied.

```
using System;
using System.ServiceModel;
using Wrox.ProCSharp.WCF.Entities;

namespace Wrox.ProCSharp.WCF.Service
{
   [ServiceContract()]
   public interface IRoomService
   {
      [OperationContract]
      bool ReserveRoom(RoomReservation roomReservation);

      [OperationContract]
      RoomReservation[] GetRoomReservations(DateTime fromDate,
                                            DateTime toDate);
   }
}
```

Service Implementation

The service class `RoomReservationService` implements the interface `IRoomService`. The service is implemented just by invoking the appropriate methods of the `RoomReservationData` class:

```
using System;
using System.ServiceModel;
using Wrox.ProCSharp.WCF.Data;
using Wrox.ProCSharp.WCF.Entities;

namespace Wrox.ProCSharp.WCF
{
   public class RoomReservationService : IRoomService
   {
      public bool ReserveRoom(RoomReservation roomReservation)
      {
         RoomReservationData data = new RoomReservationData();
         data.ReserveRoom(roomReservation);

         return true;
      }

      public RoomReservation[] GetRoomReservations(DateTime fromDate,
                                                   DateTime toDate)
```

```
        {
            RoomReservationData data = new RoomReservationData();
            return data.GetReservations(fromDate, toDate);
        }
    }
}
```

WCF Service Host and WCF Test Client

The WCF Service Library project template creates an application configuration file named `App.config` that you need to adapt to the new class and interface names. The `service` element references the service type `RoomReservationService` including the namespace; the contract interface needs to be defined with the `endpoint` element.

```
<?xml version="1.0" encoding="utf-8" ?>
<configuration>
  <system.serviceModel>
    <services>
      <service name="Wrox.ProCSharp.WCF.Services.RoomReservationService"
          behaviorConfiguration="RoomReservationsService.Service1Behavior">
        <host>
          <baseAddresses>
            <add baseAddress =
     "http://localhost:8731/Design_Time_Addresses/RoomReservationService/" />
          </baseAddresses>
        </host>
        <!-- Service Endpoints -->
        <endpoint address ="" binding="wsHttpBinding"
            contract="Wrox.ProCSharp.WCF.Services.IRoomService" />
        <!-- Metadata Endpoints -->
        <endpoint address="mex" binding="mexHttpBinding"
            contract="IMetadataExchange" />
      </service>
    </services>
    <behaviors>
      <serviceBehaviors>
        <behavior name="RoomReservationsService.Service1Behavior">
          <serviceMetadata httpGetEnabled="True"/>

          <serviceDebug includeExceptionDetailInFaults="False" />
        </behavior>
      </serviceBehaviors>
    </behaviors>
  </system.serviceModel>
</configuration>
```

The service address `http://localhost:8731/Design_Time_Addresses` *has an access control list (ACL) associated that allows the interactive user to create a listener port. By default, a non-administrative user is not allowed to open ports in listening mode. You can view the ACLs with the command-line utility* `netsh http show urlacl`*, and add new entries with* `netsh http add url=http://+8080/MyURI user=someUser`*.*

Starting this library from Visual Studio 2008 starts the WCF Service Host, which appears as an icon in the notification area of the taskbar. Clicking this icon opens the dialog (see Figure 42-4) of this application where you can see the status of the service. The project properties have the command-line arguments `/client: "WcfTestClient.exe"` defined. With this option, the WCF Service host starts the WCF Test Client (see Figure 42-5) that you can use to test the application. When you double-click an operation, input fields appear on the right side of the application that you can fill to send data to the service. When you click the XML tab, you can see the SOAP messages that have been sent and received.

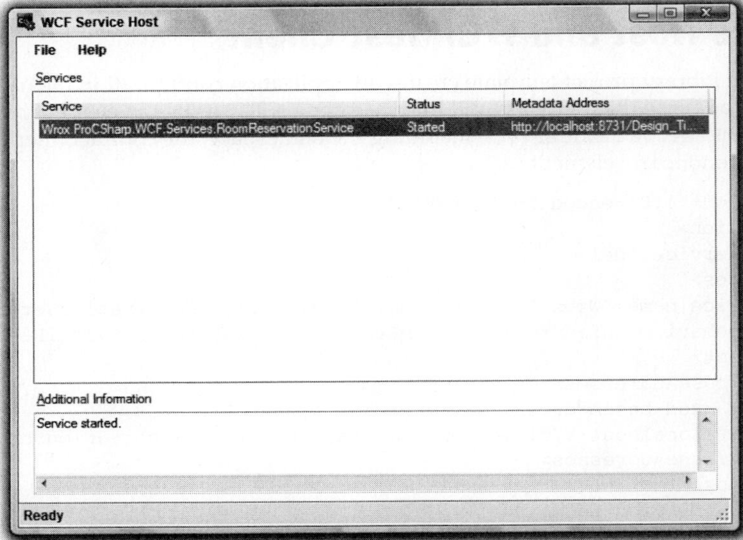

Figure 42-4

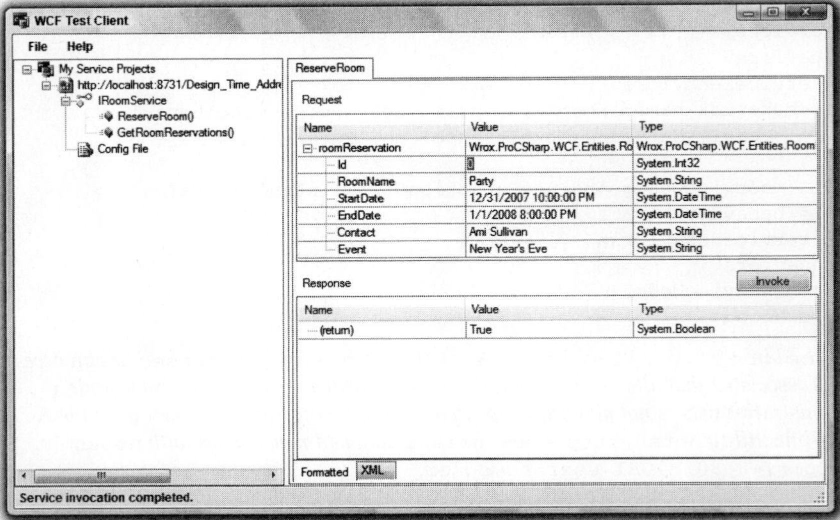

Figure 42-5

Custom Service Host

WCF allows services to run in any host. You can create a Windows Forms or WPF application for peer-to-peer services, you can create a Windows service, or host the service with Windows Activation Services (WAS). A console application is also good to demonstrate a simple host.

With the service host, you must reference the library `RoomReservationService`. The service is started by instantiating and opening an object of type `ServiceHost`. This class is defined in the namespace `System.ServiceModel`. The `RoomReservationService` class that implements the service is defined in the constructor. Invoking the `Open()` method starts the listener channel of the service — the service is ready to listen for requests. The `Close()` method stops the channel.

```
using System;
using System.ServiceModel;
using Wrox.ProCSharp.WCF.Services;

namespace Wrox.ProCSharp.WCF
{
   class Program
   {
      internal static ServiceHost myServiceHost = null;

      internal static void StartService()
      {
         myServiceHost = new ServiceHost(typeof(RoomReservationService));
         myServiceHost.Open();
      }

      internal static void StopService()
      {
         if (myServiceHost.State != CommunicationState.Closed)
            myServiceHost.Close();
      }

      static void Main()
      {
         StartService();

         Console.WriteLine("Server is running. Press return to exit");
         Console.ReadLine();

         StopService();
      }
   }
}
```

For the WCF configuration, you need to copy the application configuration file that was created with the service library to the host application. You can edit this configuration file with the WCF Service Configuration Editor (see Figure 42-6).

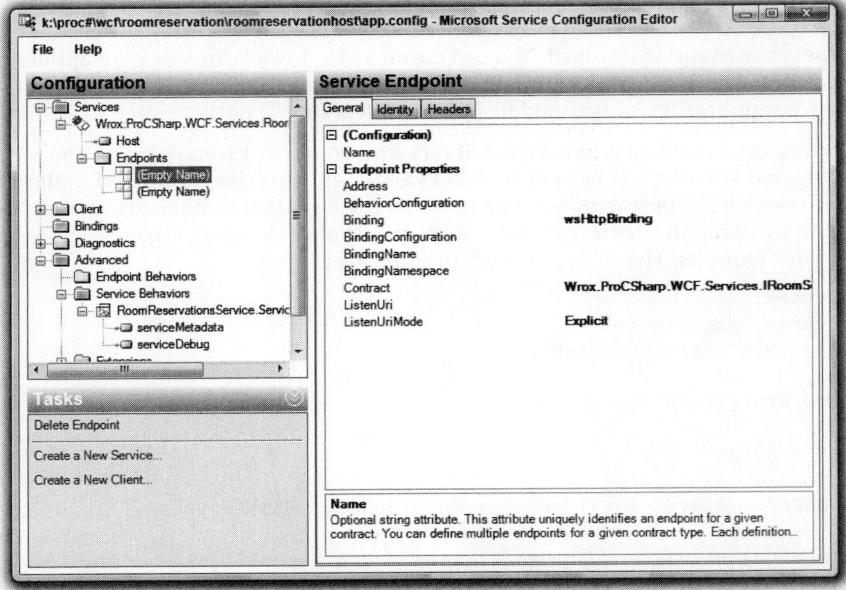

Figure 42-6

WCF Client

For the client, WCF is flexible again in what application type can be used. The client can be a simple console application as well. However, for reserving rooms, create a WPF application with controls, as shown in Figure 42-7.

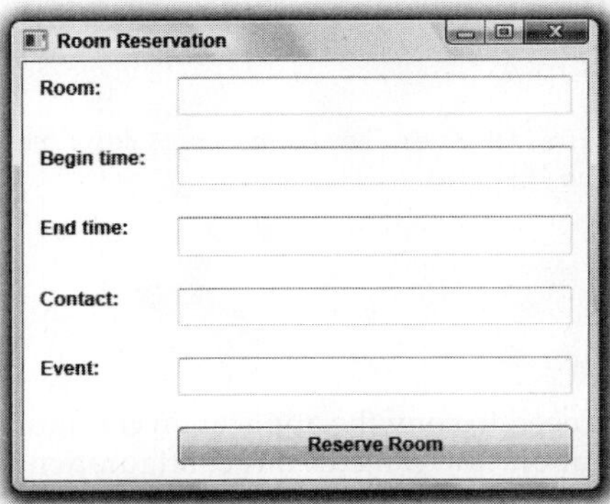

Figure 42-7

Because the service offers a MEX endpoint with the binding `mexHttpBinding`, and metadata access is enabled with the behavior configuration, you can add a service reference from Visual Studio. When you add a service reference, the dialog shown in Figure 42-8 pops up. When you click the Discover button, you can find services within the same solution.

Enter the link to the service and set the service reference name to `RoomReservationService`. The service reference name defines the namespace of the generated proxy class.

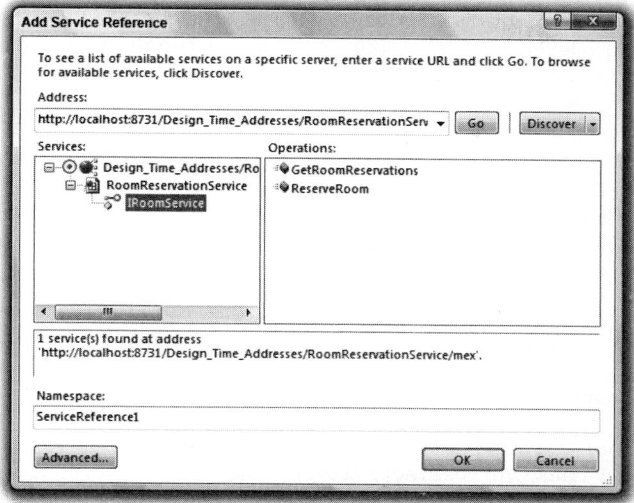

Figure 42-8

Adding a service reference adds references to the assemblies `System.Runtime.Serialization` and `System.ServiceModel` and a configuration file containing the binding information and the endpoint address to the service.

From the data contract the class `RoomReservation` is generated. This class contains all `[DataMember]` elements of the contract. The class `RoomServiceClient` is the proxy for the client that contains methods that are defined by the service contract. Using this client you can send a room reservation to the running service.

```
private void OnReserveRoom(object sender, RoutedEventArgs e)
{
   RoomReservation reservation = new RoomReservation()
   {
      RoomName = textRoom.Text,
      Event = textEvent.Text,
      Contact = textContact.Text,
      StartDate = DateTime.Parse(textStartTime.Text),
      EndDate = DateTime.Parse(textEndTime.Text)
   };

   RoomServiceClient client = new RoomServiceClient();
   client.ReserveRoom(reservation);
   client.Close();
}
```

By running both the service and the client, you can add room reservations to the database.

Diagnostics

When running a client and service application, it can be very helpful to know what's happening behind the scenes. For this, WCF makes use of a trace source that just needs to be configured. You can configure tracing using the Service Configuration Editor, selecting Diagnostics, and enabling Tracing and Message Logging. Setting the trace level of the trace sources to Verbose produces very detailed information. This configuration change adds trace sources and listeners to the application configuration file as shown here:

```
<system.diagnostics>
  <sources>
    <source name="System.ServiceModel" switchValue="Verbose,ActivityTracing"
      propagateActivity="true">
      <listeners>
        <add type="System.Diagnostics.DefaultTraceListener" name="Default">
          <filter type="" />
        </add>
        <add name="ServiceModelTraceListener">
          <filter type="" />
        </add>
      </listeners>
    </source>
    <source name="System.ServiceModel.MessageLogging"
        switchValue="Verbose,ActivityTracing">
      <listeners>
        <add type="System.Diagnostics.DefaultTraceListener" name="Default">
          <filter type="" />
        </add>
        <add name="ServiceModelMessageLoggingListener">
          <filter type="" />
        </add>
      </listeners>
    </source>
  </sources>
  <sharedListeners>
    <add initializeData="c:\logs\app_tracelog.svclog"
        type="System.Diagnostics.XmlWriterTraceListener, System,
        Version=2.0.0.0, Culture=neutral, PublicKeyToken=b77a5c561934e089"
        name="ServiceModelTraceListener" traceOutputOptions="Timestamp">
      <filter type="" />
    </add>
    <add initializeData="c:\logs\app_messages.svclog"
        type="System.Diagnostics.XmlWriterTraceListener, System,
        Version=2.0.0.0, Culture=neutral, PublicKeyToken=b77a5c561934e089"
        name="ServiceModelMessageLoggingListener"
        traceOutputOptions="Timestamp">
      <filter type="" />
    </add>
  </sharedListeners>
</system.diagnostics>
<system.serviceModel>
  <diagnostics>
    <messageLogging logEntireMessage="true" logMalformedMessages="true"
      logMessagesAtServiceLevel="true" logMessagesAtTransportLevel="true" />
  </diagnostics>
  <!-- ... -->
```

The implementation of the WCF classes uses the trace sources named `System.ServiceModel` *and* `System.ServiceModel.MessageLogging` *for writing trace messages. You can read more about tracing and configuring trace sources and listeners in Chapter 18, "Tracing and Events."*

When you start the application, the trace files soon get large with verbose trace settings. To analyze the information from the XML log file, the .NET SDK includes the Service Trace Viewer tool, `svctraceviewer.exe`. Figure 42-9 shows the view from this tool after selecting the trace and message log files. With the default configuration you can see several messages exchanged; many of them are related to security. Depending on your security needs, you can choose other configuration options.

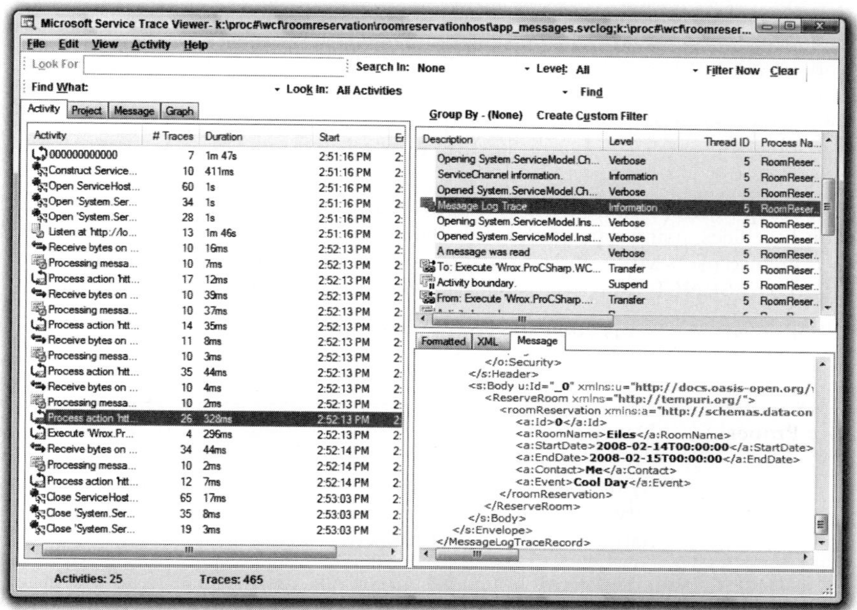

Figure 42-9

The following sections discuss the details and different options of WCF.

Contracts

A contract defines what functionality a service offers and what functionality can be used by the client. The contract can be completely independent of the implementation of the service.

The contracts defined by WCF can be grouped into three different contract types: data, service, and message. The contracts can be specified by using .NET attributes:

- **Data contract** — The data contract defines the data received by and returned from the service. The classes used for sending and receiving messages have data contract attributes associated.
- **Service contract** — The service contract is used to define the WSDL that describes the service. This contract is defined with interfaces or classes.
- **Message contract** — If complete control over the SOAP message is needed, a message contract can specify what data should go into the SOAP header, and what belongs in the SOAP body.

The following sections explore these contract types further.

Data Contract

With the data contract, CLR types are mapped to XML schemas. The data contract is different from other .NET serialization mechanisms: with runtime serialization, all fields are serialized (including private fields); with XML serialization only the public fields and properties are serialized. The data contract requires explicit marking of the fields that should be serialized with the `[DataMember]` attribute. This attribute can be used regardless of whether the field is private or public, or if it is applied to a property.

```
[DataContract(Namespace="http://www.thinktecture.com/SampleServices/2008"]
public class RoomReservation
{
    [DataMember] public string Room { get; set; }
    [DataMember] public DateTime StartDate { get; set; }
    [DataMember] public DateTime EndDate { get; set; }
    [DataMember] public string ContactName { get; set; }
    [DataMember] public string EventName { get; set; }
}
```

To be platform-independent, and give the option to change data with new versions without breaking older clients and services, using data contracts is the best way to define which data should be sent. However, you can also use XML serialization and runtime serialization. XML serialization is the mechanism used by ASP.NET Web services; .NET Remoting uses runtime serialization.

With the attribute `[DataMember]`, you can specify the properties described in the following table.

DataMember Property	Description
`Name`	By default, the serialized element has the same name as the field or property where the `[DataMember]` attribute is applied. You can change the name with the `Name` property.
`Order`	The `Order` property defines the serialization order of the data members.
`IsRequired`	With the `IsRequired` property, you can specify that the element must be received with serialization. This property can be used for versioning. If you add members to an existing contract, the contract is not broken because, by default, the fields are optional (`IsRequired=false`). You can break an existing contract by setting `IsRequired` to `true`.
`EmitDefaultValue`	The property `EmitDefaultValue` defines whether the member should be serialized if it has the default value. If `EmitDefaultValue` is set to `true`, the member is not serialized if it has the default value for the type.

Versioning

When you create a new version of a data contract, pay attention to the kind of change and act accordingly if old and new clients and old and new services should be supported simultaneously.

When defining a contract, you should add XML namespace information with the `Namespace` property of the `DataContractAttribute`. This namespace should be changed if a new version of the data contract is created that breaks compatibility. If just optional members are added, the contract is not broken — this is a compatible change. Old clients can still send a message to the new service because the additional data is not needed. New clients can send messages to an old service because the old service just ignores the additional data.

Removing fields or adding required fields breaks the contract. Here, you should also change the XML namespace. The name of the namespace can include the year and the month, for example `http://thinktecture.com/SampleServices/2008/02`. Every time a breaking change is done, the namespace is changed; for example, by changing the year and month to the actual value.

Service Contract

The service contract defines the operations the service can perform. The attribute `[ServiceContract]` is used with interfaces or classes to define a service contract. The methods that are offered by the service have the attribute `[OperationContract]` applied, as you can see with the interface `IRoomService`:

```
[ServiceContract]
public interface IRoomService
{
   [OperationContract]
   bool ReserveRoom(RoomReservation roomReservation);
}
```

The possible properties that you can set with the `[ServiceContract]` attribute are described in the following table.

ServiceContract Property	Description
`ConfigurationName`	This property defines the name of the service configuration in a configuration file.
`CallbackContract`	When the service is used for duplex messaging, the property `CallbackContract` defines the contract that is implemented in the client.
`Name`	The `Name` property defines the name for the `<portType>` element in the WSDL.
`Namespace`	The `Namespace` property defines the XML namespace for the `<portType>` element in the WSDL.
`SessionMode`	With the `SessionMode` property, you can define whether sessions are required for calling operations of this contract. The possible values `Allowed`, `NotAllowed`, and `Required` are defined with the `SessionMode` enumeration.
`ProtectionLevel`	The `ProtectionLevel` property defines whether the binding must support protecting the communication. Possible values defined by the `ProtectionLevel` enumeration are `None`, `Sign`, and `EncryptAndSign`.

With the [OperationContract], you can specify properties as shown in the following table.

OperationContract Property	Description
Action	WCF uses the Action of the SOAP request to map it to the appropriate method. The default value for the Action is a combination of the contract XML namespace, the name of the contract, and the name of the operation. If the message is a response message, Response is added to the Action string. You can override the Action value by specifying the Action property. If you assign the value "*", the service operation handles all messages.
ReplyAction	Whereas Action sets the Action name of the incoming SOAP request, ReplyAction sets the Action name of the reply message.
AsyncPattern	If the operation is implemented by using an asynchronous pattern, set the AsyncPattern property to true. The async pattern is discussed in Chapter 19.
IsInitiating IsTerminating	If the contract consists of a sequence of operations, the initiating operation should have the IsInitiating property assigned to it; the last operation of the sequence needs the IsTerminating property assigned. The initiating operation starts a new session; the server closes the session with the terminating operation.
IsOneWay	With the IsOneWay property set, the client does not wait for a reply message. Callers of a one-way operation have no direct way to detect a failure after sending the request message.
Name	The default name of the operation is the name of the method the operation contract is assigned to. You can change the name of the operation by applying the Name property.
ProtectionLevel	With the ProtectionLevel property, you define whether the message should be signed or encrypted and signed.

With the service contract, you can also define the requirements that the service has from the transport with the attribute [DeliveryRequirements]. The property RequireOrderedDelivery defines that the messages sent must arrive in the same order. With the property QueuedDeliveryRequirements, you can define that the message is sent in a disconnected mode, for example, by using Message Queuing (covered in Chapter 45).

Message Contract

A message contract is used if complete control over the SOAP message is needed. With the message contract, you can specify what part of the message should go into the SOAP header and what belongs in the SOAP body. The following example shows a message contract for the class ProcessPersonRequestMessage. The message contract is specified with the attribute [MessageContract]. The header and body of the SOAP message are specified with the attributes [MessageHeader] and [MessageBodyMember]. By specifying the Position property, you can define the element order within the body. You can also specify the protection level for header and body fields.

```
[MessageContract]
public class ProcessPersonRequestMessage
{
   [MessageHeader]
   public int employeeId;

   [MessageBodyMember(Position=0)]
   public Person person;
}
```

The class `ProcessPersonRequestMessage` is used with the service contract that is defined with the interface `IProcessPerson`:

```
[ServiceContract]
public interface IProcessPerson
{
   [OperationContract]
   public PersonResponseMessage ProcessPerson(
         ProcessPersonRequestMessage message);
}
```

Service Implementation

The implementation of the service can be marked with the attribute `[ServiceBehavior]`, as shown with the class `RoomReservationService`:

```
[ServiceBehavior]
public class RoomReservationService : IRoomService
{
   public bool ReserveRoom(RoomReservation roomReservation)
   {
   // implementation
   }
}
```

The attribute `[ServiceBehavior]` is used to describe behavior as is offered by WCF services to intercept the code for required functionality, as shown in the following table.

ServiceBehavior Property	Description
`TransactionAutoComplete OnSessionClose`	When the current session is finished without error, the transaction is automatically committed. This is similar to the `[AutoComplete]` attribute that is discussed with Enterprise Services in Chapter 44.
`TransactionIsolationLevel`	To define the isolation level of the transaction within the service, the property `TransactionIsolationLevel` can be set to one value of the `IsolationLevel` enumeration. You can read information about transaction information levels in Chapter 22.
`ReleaseServiceInstanceOn TransactionComplete`	When the transaction is finished, the instance of the service is recycled.

ServiceBehavior Property	Description
AutomaticSessionShutdown	If the session should not be closed when the client closes the connection, you can set the property AutomaticSessionShutdown to false. By default, the session is closed.
InstanceContextMode	With the property InstanceContextMode, you can define whether stateful or stateless objects should be used. The default setting is InstanceContextMode.PerCall to create a new object with every method call. You can compare this with .NET Remoting well-known SingleCall objects. Other possible settings are PerSession and Single. With both of these settings, stateful objects are used. However, with PerSession a new object is created for every client. Single allows sharing the same object with multiple clients.
ConcurrencyMode	Because stateful objects can be used by multiple clients (or multiple threads of a single client), you must pay attention to concurrency issues with such object types. If the property ConcurrencyMode is set to Multiple, multiple threads can access the object, and you must deal with synchronization. If you set the option to Single, only one thread accesses the object at a time. Here, you don't have to do synchronization; however, scalability problems can occur with a higher number of clients. The value Reentrant means that only a thread coming back from a callout might access the object. For stateless objects, this setting has no meaning, because new objects are instantiated with every method call and thus no state is shared.
UseSynchronizationContext	With Windows Forms and WPF, members of controls can be invoked only from the creator thread. If the service is hosted in a Windows application, and the service methods invoke control members, set the UseSynchronizationContext to true. This way, the service runs in a thread defined by the SynchronizationContext.
IncludeExceptionDetailInFaults	With .NET, errors show up as exceptions. SOAP defines that a SOAP fault is returned to the client in case the server has a problem. For security reasons, it's not a good idea to return details of server-side exceptions to the client. Thus, by default, exceptions are converted to unknown faults. To return specific faults, throw an exception of type FaultException. For debugging purposes, it can be helpful to return the real exception information. This is the case when changing the setting of IncludeExceptionDetailInFaults to true. Here a FaultException<TDetail> is thrown where the original exception contains the detail information.
MaxItemsInObjectGraph	With the property MaxItemsInObjectGraph, you can limit the number of objects that are serialized.
ValidateMustUnderstand	The property ValidateMustUnderstand set to true means that the SOAP headers must be understood (which is the default).

To demonstrate a service behavior, the interface `IStateService` defines a service contract with two operations to set and get state. With a stateful service contract, a session is needed. That's why the `SessionMode` property of the service contract is set to `SessionMode.Required`. The service contract also defines methods to initiate and close the session by applying the `IsInitiating` and `IsTerminating` properties to the operation contract:

```
[ServiceContract(SessionMode=SessionMode.Required)]
public interface IStateService
{
   [OperationContract(IsInitiating=true)]
   void Init(int i);

   [OperationContract]
   void SetState(int i);

   [OperationContract]
   int GetState();

   [OperationContract(IsTerminating=true)]
   void Close();
}
```

The service contract is implemented by the class `StateService`. The service implementation defines the `InstanceContextMode.PerSession` to keep state with the instance:

```
[ServiceBehavior(InstanceContextMode=InstanceContextMode.PerSession)]
public class StateService : IStateService
{
   int i = 0;

   public void Init(int i)
   {
      this.i = i;
   }

   public void SetState(int i)
   {
      this.i = i;
   }

   public int GetState()
   {
      return i;
   }

   public void Close()
   {
   }
}
```

Now the binding to the address and protocol must be defined. Here, the `basicHttpBinding` is assigned to the endpoint of the service:

```
<?xml version="1.0" encoding="utf-8" ?>
<configuration>
  <system.serviceModel>
```

(continued)

(continued)

```
    <services>
      <service behaviorConfiguration="StateServiceSample.Service1Behavior"
        name="Wrox.ProCSharp.WCF.StateService">
        <endpoint address="" binding="basicHttpBinding"
            bindingConfiguration=""
            contract="Wrox.ProCSharp.WCF.IStateService">
        </endpoint>
        <endpoint address="mex" binding="mexHttpBinding"
            contract="IMetadataExchange" />
        <host>
          <baseAddresses>
            <add baseAddress="http://localhost:8731/Design_Time_Addresses/
                              StateServiceSample/Service1/" />
          </baseAddresses>
        </host>
      </service>
    </services>
    <behaviors>
      <serviceBehaviors>
        <behavior name="StateServiceSample.Service1Behavior">
          <serviceMetadata httpGetEnabled="True"/>
          <serviceDebug includeExceptionDetailInFaults="False" />
        </behavior>
      </serviceBehaviors>
    </behaviors>
  </system.serviceModel>
</configuration>
```

If you start the service host with the defined configuration, an exception of type `InvalidOperationException` is thrown. The error message with the exception gives this error message: "Contract requires Session, but Binding `'BasicHttpBinding'` doesn't support it or isn't configured properly to support it."

Not all bindings support all services. Because the service contract requires a session with the attribute `[ServiceContract(SessionMode=SessionMode.Required)]`, the host fails because the configured binding does not support sessions.

As soon as you change the configuration to a binding that supports sessions (for example, the `wsHttpBinding`), the server starts successfully:

```
        <endpoint address="" binding="wsHttpBinding"
            bindingConfiguration=""
            contract="Wrox.ProCSharp.WCF.IStateService">
        </endpoint>
```

Now a client application can be created. In the previous example, the client application was created by adding a service reference. Instead of adding a service reference, you can directly access the assembly containing the contract interface, and use the `ChannelFactory<TChannel>` class to instantiate the channel to connect to the service.

The constructor of the class `ChannelFactory<TChannel>` accepts the binding configuration and endpoint address. The binding must be compatible with the binding defined with the service host, and the address defined with the `EndpointAddress` class references the URI of the running service.

The `CreateChannel()` method creates a channel to connect to the service. Then, you can invoke methods of the service, and you can see that the service instance holds state until the `Close()` method is invoked that has the `IsTerminating` operation behavior assigned:

```
using System;
using System.ServiceModel;

namespace Wrox.ProCSharp.WCF
{
   class Program
   {
      static void Main()
      {
         WSHttpBinding binding = new WSHttpBinding();
         EndpointAddress address =
               new EndpointAddress("http://localhost:8731/" +
               !Design_Time_Addresses/StateServiceSample/Service1/");

         ChannelFactory<IStateService> factory =
               new ChannelFactory<IStateService>(binding, address);

         IStateService channel = factory.CreateChannel();
         channel.Init(1);
         Console.WriteLine(channel.GetState());
         channel.SetState(2);
         Console.WriteLine(channel.GetState());
         channel.Close();

         factory.Close();
      }
   }
}
```

With the implementation of the service, you can apply the properties in the following table to the service methods, with the attribute `[OperationBehavior]`.

OperationBehavior	Description
`AutoDisposeParameters`	By default, all disposable parameters are automatically disposed. If the parameters should not be disposed, you can set the property `AutoDisposeParameters` to `false`. Then the sender is responsible for disposing the parameters.
`Impersonation`	With the `Impersonation` property, the caller can be impersonated and the method runs with the identity of the caller.
`ReleaseInstanceMode`	The `InstanceContextMode` defines the lifetime of the object instance with the service behavior setting. With the operation behavior setting, you can override the setting based on the operation. The `ReleaseInstanceMode` defines an instance release mode with the enumeration `ReleaseInstanceMode`. The value `None` uses the instance context mode setting. With the values `BeforeCall`, `AfterCall`, and `BeforeAndAfterCall` you can define recycle times with the operation.

OperationBehavior	Description
TransactionScopeRequired	With the property TransactionScopeRequired, you can specify if a transaction is required with the operation. If a transaction is required, and the caller already flows a transaction, the same transaction is used. If the caller doesn't flow a transaction, a new transaction is created.
TransactionAutoComplete	The TransactionAutoComplete property specifies whether the transaction should complete automatically. If the TransactionAutoComplete property is set to true, the transaction is aborted if an exception is thrown. The transaction is committed if it is the root transaction and no exception is thrown.

Error Handling

By default, the detailed exception information that occurs in the service is not returned to the client application. The reason for this behavior is security. You wouldn't want to give detailed exception information to a third party using your service. Instead, the exception should be logged on the service (which you can do with tracing and event logging), and an error with useful information should be returned to the caller.

You can return SOAP faults by throwing a FaultException. Throwing a FaultException creates an untyped SOAP fault. The preferred way of returning errors is to generate a strongly typed SOAP fault.

The information that should be passed with a strongly typed SOAP fault is defined with a data contract as shown with the StateFault class:

```
[DataContract]
public class StateFault
{
    [DataMember]
    public int BadState { get; set; }
}
```

The type of the SOAP fault must be defined using the FaultContractAttribute with the operation contract:

```
[FaultContract(typeof(StateFault))]
[OperationContract]
void SetState(int i);
```

With the implementation, a FaultException<TDetail> is thrown. With the constructor you can assign a new TDetail object, which is a StateFault in the example. In addition, error information within a FaultReason can be assigned to the constructor. FaultReason supports error information in multiple languages.

```
public void SetState(int i)
{
    if (i == -1)
    {
        FaultReasonText[] text = new FaultReasonText[2];
        text[0] = new FaultReasonText("Sample Error",
```

```
            new CultureInfo("en"));
        text[1] = new FaultReasonText("Beispiel Fehler",
            new CultureInfo("de"));
        FaultReason reason = new FaultReason(text);

        throw new FaultException<StateFault>(
           new StateFault() { BadState = i }, reason);
     }
     else
     {
        this.i = i;
     }
  }
```

With the client application, exceptions of type `FaultException<StateFault>` can be caught. The reason for the exception is defined by the `Message` property; the `StateFault` is accessed with the `Detail` property:

```
try
{
   channel.SetState(-1);
}
catch (FaultException<StateFault> ex)
{
   Console.WriteLine(ex.Message);
   StateFault detail = ex.Detail;
   Console.WriteLine(detail.BadState);
}
```

In addition to catching the strongly typed SOAP faults, the client application can also catch exceptions of the base class of `FaultException<Detail>`: `FaultException` and `CommunicationException`. By catching `CommunicationException`, you can also catch other exceptions related to the WCF communication.

Binding

A binding describes how a service wants to communicate. With binding, you can specify the following features:

- Transport protocol
- Security
- Encoding format
- Transaction flow
- Reliability
- Shape change
- Transport upgrade

A binding is composed of multiple binding elements that describe all binding requirements. You can create a custom binding or use one of the predefined bindings that are shown in the following table.

Standard Binding	Description
`BasicHttpBinding`	`BasicHttpBinding` is the binding for the broadest interoperability, the first-generation Web services. Transport protocols used are HTTP or HTTPS; security is available only from the transport protocol.
`WSHttpBinding`	`WSHttpBinding` is the binding for the next-generation Web services, platforms that implement SOAP extensions for security, reliability, and transactions. The transports used are HTTP or HTTPS; for security the WS-Security specification is implemented; transactions are supported, as has been described, with the WS-Coordination, WS-AtomicTransaction, and WS-BusinessActivity specifications; reliable messaging is supported with an implementation of WS-ReliableMessaging. WS-Profile also supports MTOM (Message Transmission Optimization Protocol) encoding for sending attachments. You can find specifications for the WS-* standards at `http://www.oasis-open.org`.
`WS2007HttpBinding`	`WS2007HttpBinding` derives from the base class `WSHttpBinding` and supports security, reliability, and transaction specifications defined by OASIS (Organization for the Advancement of Structured Information Standards). This class is new with .NET 3.0 SP1.
`WSHttpContextBinding`	`WSHttpContextBinding` derives from the base class `WSHttpBinding` and adds support for a context without using cookies. This binding adds a `ContextBindingElement` to exchange context information.
`WebHttpBinding`	This binding is used for services that are exposed through HTTP requests instead of SOAP requests. This is useful for scripting clients, for example, ASP.NET AJAX.
`WSFederationHttpBinding`	`WSFederationHttpBinding` is a secure and interoperable binding that supports sharing identities across multiple systems for authentication and authorization.
`WSDualHttpBinding`	The binding `WSDualHttpBinding`, in contrast to `WSHttpBinding`, supports duplex messaging.
`NetTcpBinding`	All standard bindings prefixed with the name `Net` use a binary encoding used for communication between .NET applications. This encoding is faster than the text encoding with WSxxx bindings. The binding `NetTcpBinding` uses the TCP/IP protocol.
`NetTcpContextBinding`	Similar to `WSHttpContextBinding`, `NetTcpContextBinding` adds a `ContextBindingElement` to exchange context with the SOAP header.

Standard Binding	Description
NetPeerTcpBinding	NetPeerTcpBinding provides a binding for peer-to-peer communication.
NetNamedPipeBinding	NetNamedPipeBinding is optimized for communication between different processes on the same system.
NetMsmqBinding	The binding NetMsmqBinding brings queued communication to WCF. Here, the messages are sent to the message queue.
MsmqIntegrationBinding	MsmqIntegrationBinding is the binding for existing applications that uses message queuing. In contrast, the binding NetMsmqBinding requires WCF applications both on the client and server.
CustomBinding	With a CustomBinding the transport protocol and security requirements can be completely customized.

Depending on the binding, different features are supported. The bindings starting with WS are platform-independent, supporting Web services specifications. Bindings that start with the name Net use binary formatting for high-performance communication between .NET applications. Other features are support of sessions, reliable sessions, transactions, and duplex communication; the following table lists the bindings supporting these features.

Feature	Binding
Sessions	WSHttpBinding, WSDualHttpBinding, WsFederationHttpBinding, NetTcpBinding, NetNamedPipeBinding
Reliable Sessions	WSHttpBinding, WSDualHttpBinding, WsFederationHttpBinding, NetTcpBinding
Transactions	WSHttpBinding, WSDualHttpBinding, WSFederationHttpBinding, NetTcpBinding, NetNamedPipeBinding, NetMsmqBinding, MsmqIntegrationBinding
Duplex Communication	WsDualHttpBinding, NetTcpBinding, NetNamedPipeBinding, NetPeerTcpBinding

Along with defining the binding, the service must define an endpoint. The endpoint is dependent on the contract, the address of the service, and the binding. In the following code sample, a ServiceHost object is instantiated, and the address http://localhost:8080/RoomReservation, a WsHttpBinding instance, and the contract are added to an endpoint of the service:

```
static ServiceHost host;

static void StartService()
{
   Uri baseAddress = new Uri("http://localhost:8080/RoomReservation");
   host = new ServiceHost(
```

(continued)

(continued)

```
            typeof(RoomReservationService));

         WSHttpBinding binding1 = new WSHttpBinding();
         host.AddServiceEndpoint(typeof(IRoomService), binding1, baseAddress);
         host.Open();
      }
```

In addition to defining the binding programmatically, you can define it with the application configuration file. The configuration for WCF is placed inside the element `<system.serviceModel>`. The `<service>` element defines the services offered. Similarly, as you've seen in the code, the service needs an endpoint, and the endpoint contains address, binding, and contract information. The default binding configuration of `wsHttpBinding` is modified with the `bindingConfiguration` XML attribute that references the binding configuration `wsHttpConfig1`. This is the binding configuration you can find inside the `<bindings>` section, which is used to change the `wsHttpBinding` configuration to enable `reliableSession`.

```
<?xml version="1.0" encoding="utf-8" ?>
<configuration>
  <system.serviceModel>
    <services>
      <service name="Wrox.ProCSharp.WCF.RoomReservationService">
        <endpoint address=" http://localhost:8080/RoomReservation"
            contract="Wrox.ProCSharp.WCF.IRoomService"
            binding="wsHttpBinding" bindingConfiguration="wsHttpBinding" />
      </service>
    </services>
    <bindings>
      <wsHttpBinding>
        <binding name="wsHttpBinding">
          <reliableSession enabled="true" />
        </binding>
      </wsHttpBinding>
    </bindings>
  </system.serviceModel>
</configuration>
```

Hosting

WCF is very flexible when choosing a host to run the service. The host can be a Windows service, a COM+ application, WAS (Windows Activation Services) or IIS, a Windows application, or just a simple console application. When creating a custom host with Windows Forms or WPF, you can easily create a peer-to-peer solution.

Custom Hosting

Let's start with a custom host. The sample code shows hosting of a service within a console application; however, in other custom host types such as Windows services or Windows applications you can program the service in the same way.

In the `Main()` method, a `ServiceHost` instance is created. After the `ServiceHost` instance is created, the application configuration file is read to define the bindings. You can also define the bindings programmatically, as shown earlier. Next, the `Open()` method of the `ServiceHost` class is invoked, so the service accepts client calls. With a console application, you need to be careful not to close the main thread until the service should be closed. Here, the user is asked to "press return" to exit the service. When the user does this, the `Close()` method is called to actually end the service:

```
using System;
using System.ServiceModel;

public class Program
{
   public static void Main()
   {
      using (ServiceHost serviceHost = new ServiceHost())
      {
         serviceHost.Open();

         Console.WriteLine("The service started. Press return to exit");
         Console.ReadLine();

         serviceHost.Close();
      }
   }
}
```

To abort the service host, you can invoke the `Abort()` method of the `ServiceHost` class. To get the current state of the service, the `State` property returns a value defined by the `CommunicationState` enumeration. Possible values are `Created`, `Opening`, `Opened`, `Closing`, `Closed`, and `Faulted`.

> **If you start the service from within a Windows Forms or WPF application and the service code invokes methods of Windows controls, you must be sure that only the control's creator thread is allowed to access the methods and properties of the control. With WCF, this behavior can be achieved easily by setting the** `UseSynchronizatonContext` **property of the attribute** `[ServiceBehavior]`.

WAS Hosting

With WAS (Windows Activation Services) hosting, you get the features from the WAS worker process such as automatic activation of the service, health monitoring, and process recycling.

To use WAS hosting, you just need to create a Web site and a `.svc` file with the `ServiceHost` declaration that includes the language and the name of the service class. The code shown here is using the class `Service1`. In addition, you must specify the file that contains the service class. This class is implemented in the same way as you saw earlier when defining a WCF service library.

```
<%@ServiceHost language="C#" Service="Service1"
      CodeBehind="Service1.svc.cs" %>
```

If you use a WCF service library that should be available from WAS hosting, you can create a `.svc` file that just contains a reference to the class:

```
<%@ ServiceHost
      Service="Wrox.ProCSharp.WCF.Services.RoomReservationService" %>
```

With Windows Vista and Windows Server 2008, WAS allows defining .NET TCP and Message Queue bindings. If you are using the previous edition, IIS 6 or IIS 5.1 that is available with Windows Server 2003 and Windows XP, activation from a `.svc` file can be done only with an HTTP binding.

You can also add a WCF service to Enterprise Service components. This is discussed in Chapter 44.

Clients

A client application needs a proxy to access a service. There are three ways to create a proxy for the client:

- **Visual Studio Add Service Reference** — This utility creates a proxy class from the metadata of the service.
- **ServiceModel Metadata Utility tool (Svcutil.exe)** — You can create a proxy class with the `Svcutil` utility. This utility reads metadata from the service to create the proxy class.
- **ChannelFactory class** — This class is used by the proxy generated from `Svcutil`; however, it can also be used to create a proxy programmatically.

Adding a service reference from Visual Studio requires accessing a WSDL document. The WSDL document is created by a MEX endpoint that needs to be configured with the service. With the following configuration, the endpoint with the relative address `mex` is using the `mexHttpBinding` and implements the contract `IMetadataExchange`. For accessing the metadata with an HTTP GET request, the `behaviorConfiguration MexServiceBehavior` is configured.

```
<?xml version="1.0" encoding="utf-8" ?>
<configuration>
  <system.serviceModel>
    <services>
      <service behaviorConfiguration=" MexServiceBehavior "
        name="Wrox.ProCSharp.WCF.Services.RoomReservationService">
        <endpoint address="Test" binding="wsHttpBinding"
            contract="Wrox.ProCSharp.WCF.Services.IRoomService" />
        <endpoint address="mex" binding="mexHttpBinding"
            contract="IMetadataExchange" />
        <host>
          <baseAddresses>
            <add baseAddress=
    "http://localhost:8731/Design_Time_Addresses/RoomReservationService/" />
          <baseAddresses>
        </host>
      </service>
    </services>
    <behaviors>
      <serviceBehaviors>
        <behavior name="MexServiceBehavior">
          <!-- To avoid disclosing metadata information,
          set the value below to false and remove the metadata endpoint above
          before deployment -->
          <serviceMetadata httpGetEnabled="True"/>
        </behavior>
      </serviceBehaviors>
    </behaviors>
  </system.serviceModel>
</configuration>
```

Similar to the Add service reference from Visual Studio, the `Svcutil` utility needs metadata to create the proxy class. The `Svcutil` utility can create a proxy from the MEX metadata endpoint, the metadata of the assembly, or WSDL and XSD documentation:

```
svcutil http://localhost:8080/RoomReservation?wsdl /language:C# /out:proxy.cs
svcutil CourseRegistration.dll
svcutil CourseRegistration.wsdl CourseRegistration.xsd
```

After the proxy class is generated, it just needs to be instantiated from the client code, the methods need to be called, and finally the `Close()` method must be invoked:

```
RoomServiceClient client = new RoomServiceClient();
client.RegisterForCourse(roomReservation);
client.Close();
```

The generated proxy class derives from the base class `ClientBase<TChannel>` that wraps the `ChannelFactory<TChannel>` class. Instead of using a generated proxy class, you can use the `ChannelFactory<TChannel>` class directly. The constructor requires the binding and endpoint address; next, you can create the channel and invoke methods as defined by the service contract. Finally, the factory must be closed:

```
WsHttpBinding binding = new WsHttpBinding();
EndpointAddress address =
      new EndpointAddress("http://localhost:8080/RoomService");

ChannelFactory<IRoomService> factory =
      new ChannelFactory<IStateService>(binding, address);

IRoomService channel = factory.CreateChannel();
channel.ReserveRoom(roomReservation);

//...
factory.Close();
```

The `ChannelFactory<TChannel>` class has several properties and methods, as shown in the following table.

ChannelFactory Members	Description
`Credentials`	`Credentials` is a read-only property to access the `ClientCredentials` object that is assigned to the channel for authentication with the service. The credentials can be set with the endpoint.
`Endpoint`	`Endpoint` is a read-only property to access the `ServiceEndpoint` that is associated with the channel. The endpoint can be assigned in the constructor.
`State`	The `State` property is of type `CommunicationState` to return the current state of the channel. `CommunicationState` is an enumeration with the values `Created`, `Opening`, `Opened`, `Closing`, `Closed`, and `Faulted`.
`Open()`	The `Open()` method is used to open the channel.
`Close()`	The `Close()` method closes the channel.

`Opening`
`Opened`
`Closing`
`Closed`
`Faulted`
	You can assign event handlers to get informed about state changes of the channel. Events are fired before and after the channel is opened, before and after the channel is closed, and in case of a fault.

Duplex Communication

The next sample application shows how a duplex communication can be done between the client and the service. The client starts the connection to the service. After the client connects to the service, the service can call back into the client.

For duplex communication, a contract must be specified that is implemented in the client. Here the contract for the client is defined by the interface `IMyMessageCallback`. The method implemented by the client is `OnCallback()`. The operation has the operation contract setting `IsOneWay=true` applied. This way, the service doesn't wait until the method is successfully invoked on the client. By default, the service instance can be invoked from only one thread (see the `ConcurrencyMode` property of the service behavior that is, by default, set to `ConcurrencyMode.Single`).

If the service implementation now does a callback to the client and waits to get an answer from the client, the thread getting the reply from the client must wait until it gets a lock to the service object. Because the service object is already locked by the request to the client, a deadlock occurs. WCF detects the deadlock and throws an exception. To avoid this situation, you can change the `ConcurrencyMode` property to the value `Multiple` or `Reentrant`. With the setting `Multiple`, multiple threads can access the instance concurrently. Here, you must implement locking on your own. With the setting `Reentrant`, the service instance stays single threaded, but allows answers from callback requests to reenter the context. Instead of changing the concurrency mode, you can specify the `IsOneWay` property with the operation contract. This way, the caller does not wait for a reply. Of course, this setting is possible only if return values are not expected.

The contract of the service is defined by the interface `IMyMessage`. The callback contract is mapped to the service contract with the `CallbackContract` property of the service contract definition:

```
public interface IMyMessageCallback
{
   [OperationContract(IsOneWay=true)]
   void OnCallback(string message);
}

[ServiceContract(CallbackContract=typeof(IMyMessageCallback))]
public interface IMyMessage
{
   [OperationContract]
   void MessageToServer(string message);
}
```

The class `MessageService` implements the service contract `IMyMessage`. The service writes the message from the client to the console. To access the callback contract, you can use the `OperationContext` class. `OperationContext.Current` returns the `OperationContext` that is associated with the current request from the client. With the `OperationContext`, you can access session information, message headers and properties, and, in case of a duplex communication, the callback channel. The generic method `GetCallbackChannel()` returns the channel to the client instance. This channel can then be used to send a message to the client by invoking the method `OnCallback()` that is defined with the callback interface `IMyMessageCallback`. To demonstrate that it is also possible to use the callback channel from the service independent of the completion of the method, a new thread that receives the callback channel is created. The new thread sends messages to the client by using the callback channel.

```
public class MessageService : IMyMessage
{
   public void MessageToServer(string message)
```

```
        {
            Console.WriteLine("message from the client: {0}", message);
            IMyMessageCallback callback =
                  OperationContext.Current.
                        GetCallbackChannel<IMyMessageCallback>();

            callback.OnCallback("message from the server");

            new Thread(ThreadCallback).Start(callback);
        }

        private void ThreadCallback(object callback)
        {
            IMyMessageCallback messageCallback = callback as IMyMessageCallback;
            for (int i = 0; i < 10; i++)
            {
                messageCallback.OnCallback("message " + i.ToString());
                Thread.Sleep(1000);
            }
        }
    }
```

Hosting the service is the same as it was with the previous samples, so it is not shown here. However, for duplex communication, you must configure a binding that supports a duplex channel. One of the bindings supporting a duplex channel is `wsDualHttpBinding`, which is configured in the application configuration file:

```
<?xml version="1.0" encoding="utf-8" ?>
<configuration>
  <system.serviceModel>
    <services>
      <service name="Wrox.ProCSharp.WCF.MessageService">
        <endpoint contract="Wrox.ProCSharp.WCF.IMyMessage"
            binding="wsDualHttpBinding"/>
        <host>
          <baseAddresses>
            <add baseAddress="http://localhost:8731/Service1" />
          </baseAddresses>
        </host>
      </service>
    </services>
  </system.serviceModel>
</configuration>
```

With the client application, the callback contract must be implemented as shown here with the class `ClientCallback` that implements the interface `IMyMessageCallback`:

```
    class ClientCallback : IMyMessageCallback
    {
        public void OnCallback(string message)
        {
            Console.WriteLine("message from the server: {0}", message);
        }
    }
```

With a duplex channel, you cannot use the `ChannelFactory` to initiate the connection to the service as was done previously. To create a duplex channel, you can use the `DuplexChannelFactory` class. This class has a constructor with one more parameter in addition to the binding and address configuration. This parameter specifies an `InstanceContext` that wraps one instance of the `ClientCallback` class. When passing this instance to the factory, the service can invoke the object across the channel. The client just needs to keep the connection open. If the connection is closed, the service cannot send messages across it.

```
WSDualHttpBinding binding = new WSDualHttpBinding();
EndpointAddress address =
      new EndpointAddress("http://localhost:8731/Service1");

ClientCallback clientCallback = new ClientCallback();
InstanceContext context = new InstanceContext(clientCallback);

DuplexChannelFactory<IMyMessage> factory =
   new DuplexChannelFactory<IMyMessage>(context, binding, address);

IMyMessage messageChannel = factory.CreateChannel();

messageChannel.MessageToServer("From the client");
```

Duplex communication is achieved by starting the service host and the client application.

Summary

In this chapter, you learned how to use Windows Communication Foundation for communication between a client and a server. WCF is platform-independent like ASP.NET Web services, but it offers features similar to .NET Remoting, Enterprise Services, and Message Queuing.

WCF has a heavy focus on contracts to make it easier to isolate developing clients and services, and to support platform independence. It defines three different contract types: service contracts, data contracts, and message contracts. You can use several attributes to define the behavior of the service and its operations.

You have seen how to create clients from the metadata offered by the service, but also by using the .NET interface contract.

You have learned the features of different binding options. WCF offers not only bindings for platform independence but also bindings for fast communication between .NET applications.

You've seen how to create custom hosts and also make use of the WAS host.

You've seen how duplex communication is achieved by defining a callback interface, applying a service contract, and implementing a callback contract in the client application.

The next few chapters continue with WCF features. In Chapter 44, "Enterprise Services," you learn how to integrate Enterprise Services with WCF. Chapter 45, "Message Queuing," explains how disconnected Message Queuing features can be used with WCF bindings. And, in Chapter 43, you learn about Windows Workflow Foundation where WCF is used to communicate with Workflow instances.

43

Windows Workflow Foundation

This chapter presents an overview of the Windows Workflow Foundation (known as WF throughout the rest of this chapter), which provides a model to define and execute processes using a set of building blocks called *activities*. WF provides a Designer that, by default, is hosted within Visual Studio, and that allows you to drag and drop activities from the toolbox onto the design surface to create a workflow template.

This template can then be executed by creating a `WorkflowInstance` and then running that instance. The code that executes a workflow is known as the `WorkflowRuntime`, and this object can also host a number of services that the running workflows can access. At any time, there may be several workflow instances executing, and the runtime deals with scheduling these instances and saving and restoring state; it can also record the behavior of each workflow instance as it executes.

A workflow is constructed from a number of activities, and these activities are executed by the runtime. An activity might send an email, update a row in a database, or execute a transaction on a back-end system. There are a number of built-in activities that can be used for general-purpose work, and you can also create your own custom activities and plug these into the workflow as necessary. In this chapter you see the following:

- The different types of workflows that can be created
- A description of some of the built-in activities
- How to create custom activities

We begin with the canonical example that everyone uses when faced with a new technology — Hello World — and also describe what you need to get workflows running on your development machine.

Hello World

Visual Studio 2008 contains built-in support for creating workflows, and when you open the New Project dialog you will see a list of workflow project types as shown in Figure 43-1.

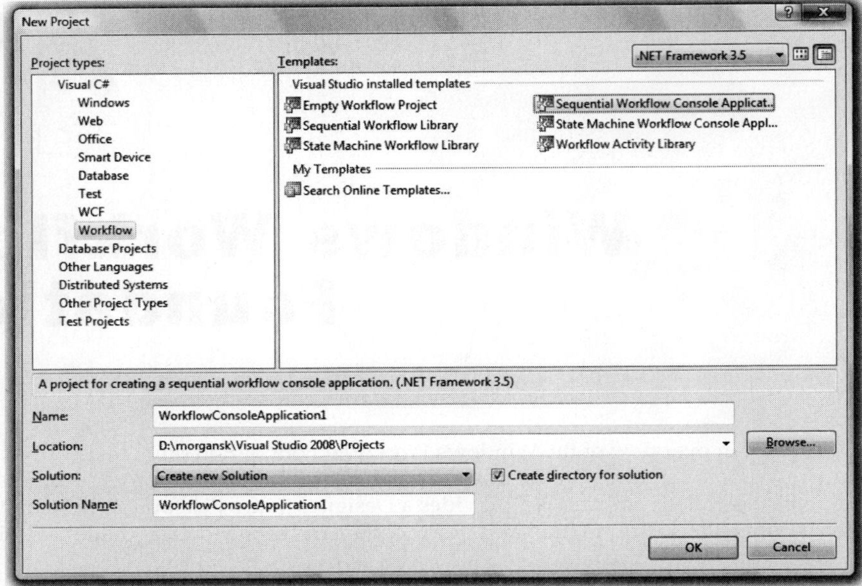

Figure 43-1

Select Sequential Workflow Console Application from the available templates (that will create a console application that hosts the workflow runtime) and a default workflow that you can then drag and drop activities onto.

Next, drag a `Code` activity from the toolbox onto the design surface so that you have a workflow that looks like that shown in Figure 43-2.

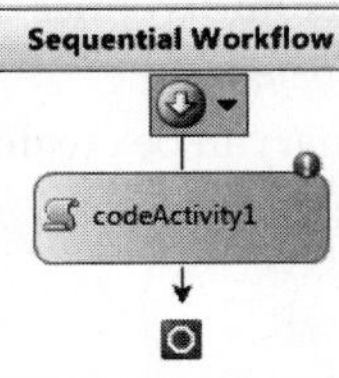

Figure 43-2

The exclamation mark glyph on the top right of the activity indicates that a mandatory property of that activity has not been defined — in this case it is the `ExecuteCode` property, which indicates the method that will be called when the activity executes. You learn how to mark your own properties as mandatory in the section on activity validation. If you double-click the code activity, a method will be created for you in the code-behind class, and here you can use `Console.WriteLine` to output the "Hello World" string as shown in the following code snippet:

```
private void codeActivity1_ExecuteCode(object sender, EventArgs e)
{
    Console.WriteLine("Hello World");
}
```

If you then build and run the program, you will see the output text on the console. When the program executes, an instance of the `WorkflowRuntime` is created, and then an instance of your workflow is constructed and executed. When the code activity executes, it calls the method defined and that outputs the string to the console. The section entitled "The Workflow Runtime" later in the chapter describes in detail how to host the runtime. The code for the preceding example is available in the `01 HelloWorkflowWorld` folder.

Activities

Everything in a workflow is an activity, including the workflow itself. The workflow is a specific type of activity that typically allows other activities to be defined within it — this is known as a composite activity, and you see other composite activities later in this chapter. An activity is just a class that ultimately derives from the `Activity` class.

The `Activity` class defines a number of overridable methods, and arguably the most important of these is the `Execute` method shown in the following snippet:

```
protected override ActivityExecutionStatus Execute
  ( ActivityExecutionContext executionContext )
{
    return ActivityExecutionStatus.Closed;
}
```

When the runtime schedules an activity for execution, the `Execute` method is ultimately called, and that is where you have the opportunity to write custom code to provide the behavior of the activity. In the simple example in the previous section, when the workflow runtime calls `Execute` on the `CodeActivity`, the implementation of this method on the code activity will execute the method defined in the code-behind class, and that displays the message on the console.

The `Execute` method is passed a context parameter of type `ActivityExecutionContext`. You will see more about this as the chapter progresses. The method has a return value of type `ActivityExecutionStatus`, and this is used by the runtime to determine whether the activity has completed successfully, is still processing, or is in one of several other potential states that can describe to the workflow runtime what state the activity is in. Returning `ActivityExecutionStatus.Closed` from this method indicates that the activity has completed its work and can be disposed of.

Numerous standard activities are provided with WF, and the following sections provide examples of some of these together with scenarios in which you might use these activities. The naming convention for activities is to append `Activity` to the name; so for example, the code activity shown in Figure 43-2 is defined by the `CodeActivity` class.

All of the standard activities are defined within the `System.Workflow.Activities` namespace, which in turn forms part of the `System.Workflow.Activities.dll` assembly. There are two other assemblies that make up WF — these are `System.Workflow.ComponentModel.dll` and `System.Workflow.Runtime.dll`.

IfElseActivity

As its name implies, this activity acts like an `If-Else` statement in C#.

When you drop an `IfElseActivity` onto the design surface, you will see an activity as displayed in Figure 43-3. The `IfElseActivity` is a composite activity in that it constructs two branches (which themselves are types of activity, in this case `IfElseBranchActivity`). Each branch is also a composite activity that derives from `SequenceActivity` — this class executes each activity in turn from top to bottom. The Designer adds the "Drop Activities Here" text to indicate where child activities can be added.

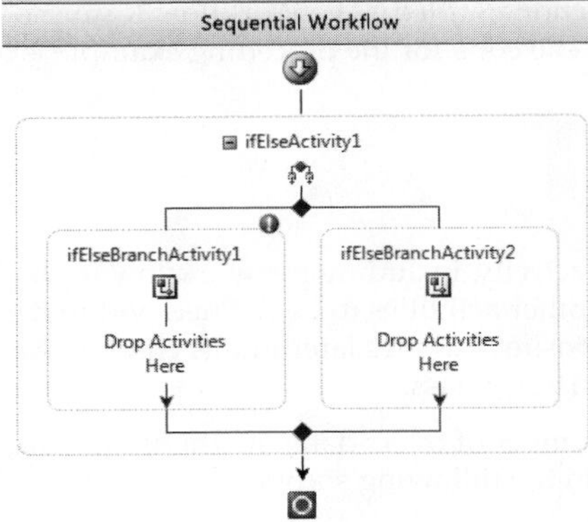

Figure 43-3

The first branch, as shown in Figure 43-3, includes a glyph indicating that the `Condition` property needs to be defined. A condition derives from `ActivityCondition` and is used to determine whether that branch should be executed.

When the `IfElseActivity` is executed, it evaluates the condition of the first branch, and if the condition evaluates to `true` the branch is executed. If the condition evaluates to `false` the `IfElseActivity` then tries the next branch, and so on until the last branch in the activity. It is worth noting that the `IfElseActivity` can have any number of branches, each with its own condition. The last branch needs no condition because it is in effect the else part of the `If-Else` statement. To add a new branch, you can display the context menu for the activity and select Add Branch from that menu — this is also available from the *Workflow* menu within Visual Studio. As you add branches, each will have a mandatory condition except for the last one.

Two standard condition types are defined in WF — the `CodeCondition` and the `RuleConditionReference`. The `CodeCondition` class executes a method on your code-behind class, which can return `true` or `false` as appropriate. To create a `CodeCondition`, display the property grid for the `IfElseActivity` and set the condition to Code Condition, then type in a name for the code to be executed, as shown in Figure 43-4.

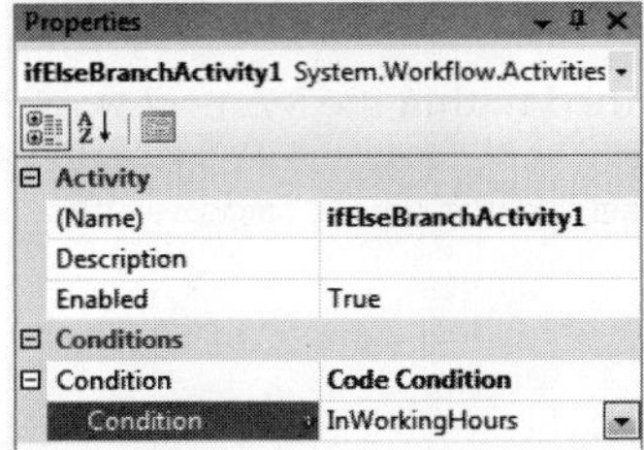

Figure 43-4

When you have typed the method name into the property grid, the Designer will construct a method on your code-behind class, as shown in the following snippet:

```
private void InWorkingHours(object sender, ConditionalEventArgs e)
{
    int hour = DateTime.Now.Hour;

    e.Result = ((hour >= 9) && (hour <= 17));
}
```

This code sets the `Result` property of the passed `ConditionalEventArgs` to `true` if the current hour is between 9 AM and 5 PM. Conditions can be defined in code as shown here, but another option is to define a condition based on a rule that is evaluated in a similar manner. The Workflow Designer contains a rule editor, which can be used to declare conditions and statements (much like the `If-Else` statement shown previously). These rules are evaluated at runtime based on the current state of the workflow.

ParallelActivity

This activity permits you to define a set of activities that execute in parallel — or rather in a pseudo-parallel manner. When the workflow runtime schedules an activity, it does so on a single thread. This thread executes the first activity, then the second, and so on until all activities have completed (or until an activity is waiting on some form of input). When the `ParallelActivity` executes, it iterates through each branch and schedules execution of each branch in turn. The workflow runtime maintains a queue of scheduled activities for each workflow instance, and typically executes these in a FIFO (first in, first out) manner.

Assuming that you have a `ParallelActivity`, as shown in Figure 43-5, this will schedule execution of `sequenceActivity1` and then `sequenceActivity2`. The `SequenceActivity` type works by scheduling execution of its first activity with the runtime, and when this activity completes, it then schedules the second activity. This schedule/wait for completion method is used to traverse through all child activities of the sequence, until all child activities have executed, at which time the sequence activity can complete.

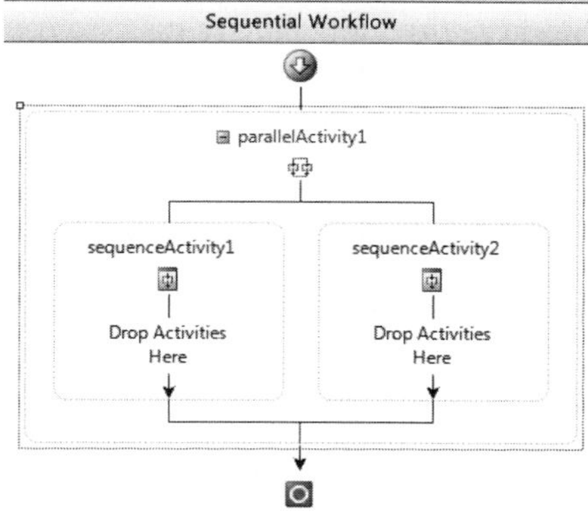

Figure 43-5

Given that the `SequenceActivity` schedules execution of one activity at a time, it means that the queue maintained by the `WorkflowRuntime` is continually updated with schedulable activities. Assuming that we have a parallel activity P1 that contains two sequences, S1 and S2, each with two code activities, C1 and C2, this would produce entries in the scheduler queue, as shown in the following table.

Workflow Queue	Initially There Are No Activities in the Queue
P1	Parallel is executed when the workflow runs.
S1, S2	Added to the queue when P1 executes.
S2, S1.C1	S1 executes and adds S1.C1 to the queue.
S1.C1, S2.C1	S2 executes and adds S2.C1 to the queue.
S2.C1, S1.C2	S1.C1 completes, so S1.C2 is queued.
S1.C2, S2.C2	S2.C1 completes, so S2.C2 is queued.
S2.C2	The last entry in the queue.

Here, the queue processes the first entry (the parallel activity P1), and this adds the sequence activities S1 and S2 to the workflow queue. As the sequence activity S1 executes, it pushes its first child activity (S1.C1) to the end of the queue, and when this activity is scheduled and completes, it then adds the second child activity to the queue.

As can be seen from the preceding example, execution of the `ParallelActivity` is not truly parallel — it effectively interleaves execution between the two sequential branches. From this, you could infer that it's best that an activity execute in a minimal amount of time because, given that there is only one thread servicing the scheduler queue for each workflow, a long-running activity could hamper the execution of other activities in the queue. That said, often, an activity needs to execute for an arbitrary amount of time, so there must be some way to mark an activity as "long-running" so that other activities get a chance to execute. You can do this by returning `ActivityExecutionStatus.Executing` from the `Execute` method, which lets the runtime know that you will call it back later when the activity has finished. An example of this type of activity is the `DelayActivity`.

CallExternalMethodActivity

A workflow will typically need to call methods outside of the workflow, and this activity allows you to define an interface and a method to call on that interface. The `WorkflowRuntime` maintains a list of services (keyed on a `System.Type` value) that can be accessed using the `ActivityExecutionContext` parameter passed to the `Execute` method.

You can define your own services to add to this collection and then access these services from within your own activities. You could, for example, construct a data access layer exposed as a service interface and then provide different implementations of this service for SQL Server and Oracle. Because the activities simply call interface methods, the swap from SQL Server to Oracle would be opaque to the activities.

When you add a `CallExternalMethodActivity` to your workflow, you then define the two mandatory properties of `InterfaceType` and `MethodName`. The interface type defines which runtime service will be used when the activity executes, and the method name defines which method of that interface will be called.

When this activity executes, it looks up the service with the defined interface by querying the execution context for that service type, and it then calls the appropriate method on that interface. You can also pass parameters to the method from within the workflow — this is discussed later in the section titled "Binding Parameters to Activities."

DelayActivity

Business processes often need to wait for a period of time before completing. Consider using a workflow for expense approval. Your workflow might send an email to your immediate manager asking him or her to approve your expense claim. The workflow then enters a waiting state, where it either waits for approval (or, horror of horrors, rejection), but it would also be nice to define a timeout so that if no response is returned within, say, one day, the expense claim is then routed to the next manager up the chain of command.

The `DelayActivity` can form part of this scenario (the other part is the `ListenActivity` defined later). Its job is to wait for a predefined time before continuing execution of the workflow. There are two ways to define the duration of the delay — you can either set the `TimeoutDuration` property of the delay to a string such as "1.00:00:00" (1 day, no hours, minutes, or seconds), or you can provide a method that is called when the activity is executed that sets the duration to a value from code. To do this, you need to define a value for the `InitializeTimeoutDuration` property of the delay activity. This creates a method in the code behind, as shown in the following snippet:

```
private void DefineTimeout(object sender, EventArgs e)
{
    DelayActivity delay = sender as DelayActivity;

    if (null != delay)
     {
        delay.TimeoutDuration = new TimeSpan(1, 0, 0, 0);
     }
}
```

Here, the `DefineTimeout` method casts the sender to a `DelayActivity` and then sets the `TimoutDuration` property in code to a `TimeSpan`. Even though the value is hard-coded here, it is more likely that you would construct this from some other data — maybe a parameter passed into the workflow or a value read from the configuration file. Workflow parameters are discussed in the section "Workflows" later in the chapter.

ListenActivity

A common programming construct is to wait for one of a set of possible events — one example of this is the `WaitAny` method of the `System.Threading.WaitHandle` class. The `ListenActivity` is the way to do this in a workflow, because it can define any number of branches, each with an event-based activity as that branch's first activity.

An event activity is one that implements the `IEventActivity` interface defined in the `System.Workflow.Activities` namespace. There are currently three such activities defined as standard in WF — `DelayActivity`, `HandleExternalEventActivity`, and the `WebServiceInputActivity`. Figure 43-6 shows a workflow that is waiting for either external input or a delay — this is an example of the expense approval workflow discussed earlier.

In the example, the `CallExternalMethodActivity` is used as the first activity in the workflow. This calls a method defined on a service interface that would prompt the manager for approval or rejection. Because this is an external service, this prompt could be an email, an IM message, or any other manner of notifying your manager that an expense claim needs to be processed. The workflow then executes the `ListenActivity`, which awaits input from this external service (either an approval or a rejection), and also waits on a delay.

When the listen executes, it effectively queues a wait on the first activity in each branch, and when one event is triggered, this cancels all other waiting events and then processes the rest of the branch where the event was raised. So, in the instance where the expense report is approved, the `Approved` event is raised and the `PayMe` activity is then scheduled. If, however, your manager rejects the claim, the `Rejected` event is raised, and in the example you then `Panic`.

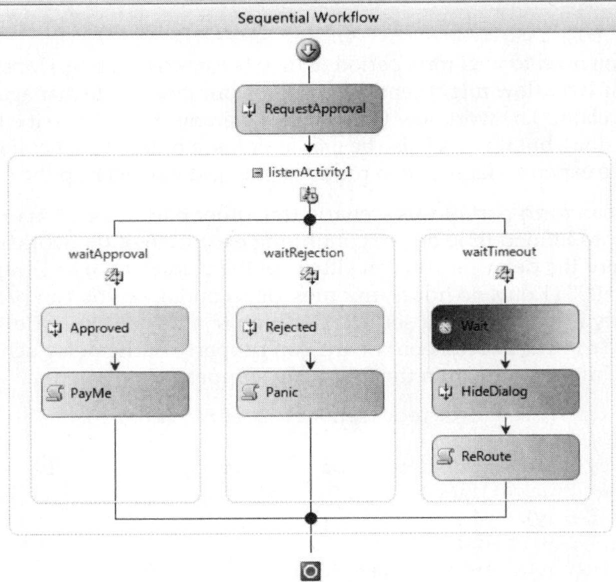

Figure 43-6

Last, if neither the `Approved` nor `Rejected` event is raised, the `DelayActivity` ultimately completes after its delay expires, and the expense report could then be routed to another manager — potentially looking up that person in Active Directory. In the example, a dialog is displayed to the user when the `RequestApproval` activity is executed, so if the delay executes, you also need to close the dialog, which is the purpose of the activity named `HideDialog` in Figure 43-6.

The code for this example is available in the `02 Listen` directory. Some concepts used in that example have not been covered yet — such as how a workflow instance is identified and how events are raised back into the workflow runtime and ultimately delivered to the right workflow instance. These concepts are covered in the section titled "Workflows."

Activity Execution Model

So far, this chapter has discussed the execution of an activity only by the runtime calling the `Execute` method. However, an activity may go through a number of states while it executes — these are presented in Figure 43-7.

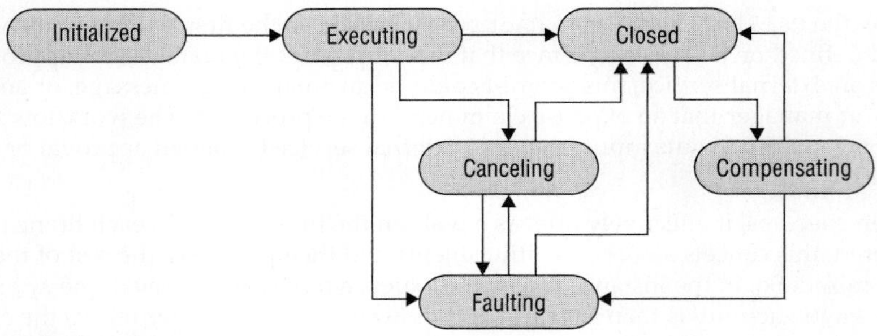

Figure 43-7

An activity is first initialized by the `WorkflowRuntime` when the runtime calls the activity's `Initialize` method. This method is passed an `IServiceProvider` instance, which maps to the services available within the runtime. These services are discussed in the "Workflow Services" section later in the chapter. Most activities do nothing in this method, but the method is there for you to do any setup necessary.

The runtime then calls the `Execute` method, and the activity can return any one of the values from the `ActivityExecutionStatus` enum. Typically, you will return `Closed` from your `Execute` method, which indicates that your activity has finished processing; however, if you return one of the other status values, the runtime will use this to determine what state your activity is in.

You can return `Executing` from this method to indicate to the runtime that you have extra work to do — a typical example of this is when you have a composite activity that needs to execute its children. In this case, your activity can schedule each child for execution and then wait for all children to complete before notifying the runtime that your activity has completed.

Custom Activities

So far, you have used activities that are defined within the `System.Workflow.Activities` namespace. In this section, you learn how to create custom activities and extend these activities to provide a good user experience at both design time and runtime.

To begin, you create a `WriteLineActivity` that can be used to output a line of text to the console. Although this is a trivial example, it will be expanded to show the full gamut of options available for custom activities using this example. When creating custom activities, you can simply construct a class within a workflow project; however, it is preferable to construct your custom activities inside a separate assembly, because the Visual Studio design time environment (and specifically workflow projects) will load activities from your assemblies and can lock the assembly that you are trying to update. For this reason, you should create a simple class library project to construct your custom activities within.

A simple activity such as the `WriteLineActivity` will be derived directly from the `Activity` base class. The following code shows a constructed activity class and defines a `Message` property that is displayed when the `Execute` method is called:

```
using System;
using System.ComponentModel;
using System.Workflow.ComponentModel;

namespace SimpleActivity
{
  /// <summary>
  /// A simple activity that displays a message to the console when it executes
  /// </summary>
  public class WriteLineActivity : Activity
  {
    /// <summary>
    /// Execute the activity - display the message on screen
    /// </summary>
    /// <param name="executionContext"></param>
    /// <returns></returns>
    protected override ActivityExecutionStatus Execute
     (ActivityExecutionContext executionContext)
```

(continued)

(continued)

```
        {
          Console.WriteLine(Message);

          return ActivityExecutionStatus.Closed;
        }

        /// <summary>
        /// Get/Set the message displayed to the user
        /// </summary>
        [Description("The message to display")]
        [Category("Parameters")]
        public string Message
        {
          get { return _message; }
          set { _message = value; }
        }

        /// <summary>
        /// Store the message displayed to the user
        /// </summary>
        private string _message;
      }
    }
```

Within the `Execute` method, you can write the message to the console and then return a status of `Closed` to notify the runtime that the activity has completed.

You can also define attributes on the `Message` property so that a description and category are defined for that property. This is used in the property grid within Visual Studio, as shown in Figure 43-8.

The code for the activities created in this section is in the `03 CustomActivities` solution. If you compile that solution, you can then add the custom activities to the toolbox within Visual Studio by choosing the Choose Items menu item from the context menu on the toolbox and navigating to the folder where the assembly containing the activities resides. All activities within the assembly will be added to the toolbox.

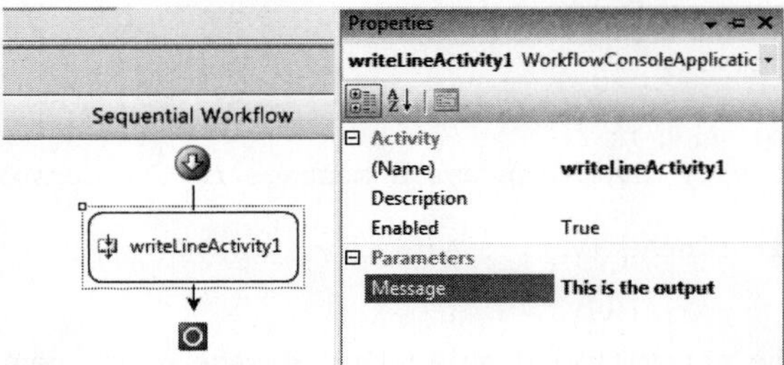

Figure 43-8

As it stands, the activity is perfectly usable; however, there are several areas that should be addressed to make this more user-friendly. As you saw with the `CodeActivity` earlier in the chapter, it has some mandatory properties that, when not defined, produce an error glyph on the design surface. To get the same behavior from your activity, you need to construct a class that derives from `ActivityValidator` and associate this class with your activity.

Activity Validation

When an activity is placed onto the design surface, the Workflow Designer looks for an attribute on that activity that defines a class that performs validation on that activity. To validate your activity, you need to check if the `Message` property has been set.

A custom validator is passed the activity instance, and from this you can then determine which mandatory properties (if any) have not been defined and add an error to the `ValidationErrorCollection` used by the Designer. This collection is then read by the Workflow Designer, and any errors found in the collection will cause a glyph to be added to the activity and optionally link each error to the property that needs attention.

```
using System;
using System.Workflow.ComponentModel.Compiler;

namespace SimpleActivity
{
  public class WriteLineValidator : ActivityValidator
  {
    public override ValidationErrorCollection Validate
      (ValidationManager manager, object obj)
    {
      if (null == manager)
        throw new ArgumentNullException("manager");
      if (null == obj)
        throw new ArgumentNullException("obj");

      ValidationErrorCollection errors = base.Validate(manager, obj);

      // Coerce to a WriteLineActivity
      WriteLineActivity act = obj as WriteLineActivity;

      if (null != act)
      {
        if (null != act.Parent)
        {
          // Check the Message property
          if (string.IsNullOrEmpty(act.Message))
            errors.Add(ValidationError.GetNotSetValidationError("Message"));
        }
      }

      return errors;
    }
  }
}
```

The `Validate` method is called by the Designer when any part of the activity is updated and also when the activity is dropped onto the design surface. The Designer calls the `Validate` method and passes through the activity as the untyped `obj` parameter.

In this method, first validate the arguments passed in, and then call the base class `Validate` method to obtain a `ValidationErrorCollection`. Although this is not strictly necessary here, if you are deriving from an activity that has a number of properties that also need to be validated, calling the base class method will ensure that these are also checked.

Coerce the passed obj parameter into a WriteLineActivity instance, and check if the activity has a parent. This test is necessary because the Validate function is called during compilation of the activity (if the activity is within a workflow project or activity library), and, at this point, no parent activity has been defined. Without this check, you cannot actually build the assembly that contains the activity and the validator. This extra step is not needed if the project type is class library.

The last step is to check that the Message property has been set to a value other than an empty string. This uses a static method of the ValidationError class, which constructs an error that specifies that the property has not been defined.

To add validation support to your WriteLineActivity, the last step is to add the ActivityValidation attribute to the activity, as shown in the following snippet:

```
 [ActivityValidator(typeof(WriteLineValidator))]
public class WriteLineActivity : Activity
{
  ...
}
```

If you compile the application and then drop a WriteLineActivity onto the workflow, you should see a validation error, as shown in Figure 43-9; clicking this error will take you to that property within the property grid.

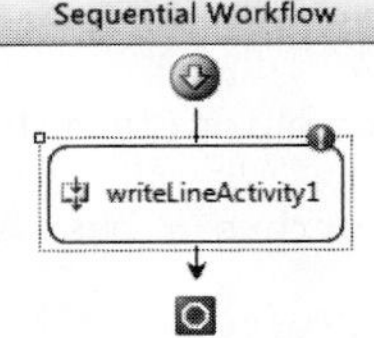

Figure 43-9

If you enter some text for the Message property, the validation error will be removed, and you can then compile and run the application.

Now that you have completed the activity validation, the next thing to do is to change the rendering behavior of the activity to add a fill color to that activity. To do this, you need to define both an ActivityDesigner class and an ActivityDesignerTheme class, as described in the next section.

Themes and Designers

The onscreen rendering of an activity is performed using an ActivityDesigner class, and this can also use an ActivityDesignerTheme.

The theme class is used to make simple changes to the rendering behavior of the activity within the Workflow Designer:

```
public class WriteLineTheme : ActivityDesignerTheme
{
  /// <summary>
  /// Construct the theme and set some defaults
  /// </summary>
  /// <param name="theme"></param>
  public WriteLineTheme(WorkflowTheme theme)
    : base(theme)
```

```
    {
      this.BackColorStart = Color.Yellow;
      this.BackColorEnd = Color.Orange;
      this.BackgroundStyle = LinearGradientMode.ForwardDiagonal;
    }
  }
```

A theme is derived from `ActivityDesignerTheme`, which has a constructor that is passed a `WorkflowTheme` argument. Within the constructor, set the start and end colors for the activity, and then define a linear gradient brush, which is used when painting the background.

The `Designer` class is used to override the rendering behavior of the activity. In this case, no override is necessary, so the following code will suffice:

```
[ActivityDesignerTheme(typeof(WriteLineTheme))]
public class WriteLineDesigner : ActivityDesigner
{
}
```

Note that the theme has been associated with the Designer by using the `ActivityDesignerTheme` attribute.

The last step is to adorn the activity with the `Designer` attribute:

```
[ActivityValidator(typeof(WriteLineValidator))]
[Designer(typeof(WriteLineDesigner))]
public class WriteLineActivity : Activity
{
  ...
}
```

With this in place, the activity is rendered as shown in Figure 43-10.

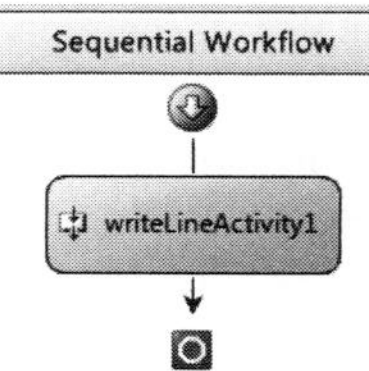

Figure 43-10

With the addition of the Designer and the theme, the activity now looks much more professional. A number of other properties are available on the theme — such as the pen used to render the border, the color of the border, and the border style.

By overriding the `OnPaint` method of the `ActivityDesigner` class, you can have complete control over the rendering of the activity. Be sure to exercise restraint here, because you could get carried away and create an activity that doesn't resemble any of the other activities in the toolbox.

One other useful override on the `ActivityDesigner` class is the `Verbs` property. This allows you to add menu items on the context menu for the activity. It is used by the Designer of the `ParallelActivity` to insert the Add Branch menu item into the activities context menu and also the Workflow menu. You can also alter the list of properties exposed for an activity by overriding the `PreFilterProperties` method of the Designer — this is how the method parameters for the `CallExternalMethodActivity` are surfaced into the property grid. If you need to do this type of extension to your Designer, you should run Lutz Roeder's Reflector (available from `http://www.aisto.com/roeder/dotnet`) and load the workflow assemblies into it to see how Microsoft has defined some of these extended properties.

This activity is nearly done, but now you need to define the icon used when rendering the activity and also the toolbox item to associate with the activity.

ActivityToolboxItem and Icons

To complete your custom activity, you need to add an icon. You can optionally create a class deriving from `ActivityToolboxItem` that is used when displaying the activity in the toolbox within Visual Studio.

To define an icon for an activity, create a 16 × 16 pixel image and include it into your project. When it has been included, set the build action for the image to be `Embedded Resource`. This will include the image in the manifest resources for the assembly. You can add a folder to your project called Resources, as shown in Figure 43-11.

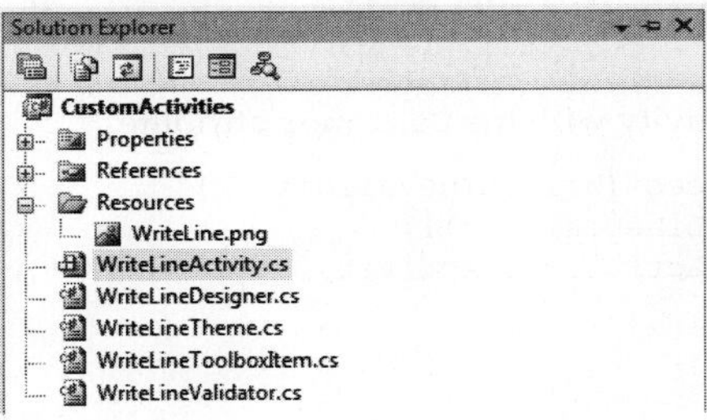

Figure 43-11

Once you have added the image file and set its build action to `Embedded Resource`, you can then attribute the activity as shown in the following snippet:

```
[ActivityValidator(typeof(WriteLineValidator))]
[Designer(typeof(WriteLineDesigner))]
[ToolboxBitmap(typeof(WriteLineActivity),"Resources.WriteLine.png")]
public class WriteLineActivity : Activity
{
   ...
}
```

The `ToolboxBitmap` attribute has a number of constructors defined, and the one being used here takes a type defined in the activity assembly and the name of the resource. When you add a resource to a folder, its name is constructed from the namespace of the assembly and the name of the folder that the image resides within — so the fully qualified name for the resource here is `CustomActivities.Resources.WriteLine.png`. The constructor used with the `ToolboxBitmap` attribute appends the namespace that the type parameter resides within to the string passed as the second argument, so this will resolve to the appropriate resource when loaded by Visual Studio.

The last class you need to create is derived from `ActivityToolboxItem`. This class is used when the activity is loaded into the Visual Studio toolbox. A typical use of this class is to change the displayed name of the activity on the toolbox — all of the built-in activities have their names changed to remove the word "Activity" from the type. In your class, you can do the same by setting the `DisplayName` property to "WriteLine."

```
[Serializable]
public class WriteLineToolboxItem : ActivityToolboxItem
{
    /// <summary>
    /// Set the display name to WriteLine - i.e. trim off
    /// the 'Activity' string
    /// </summary>
    /// <param name="t"></param>
    public WriteLineToolboxItem(Type t)
        : base(t)
    {
        base.DisplayName = "WriteLine";
    }

    /// <summary>
    /// Necessary for the Visual Studio design time environment
    /// </summary>
    /// <param name="info"></param>
    /// <param name="context"></param>
    private WriteLineToolboxItem(SerializationInfo info,
                                 StreamingContext context)
    {
        this.Deserialize(info, context);
    }
}
```

The class is derived from `ActivityToolboxItem` and overrides the constructor to change the display name; it also provides a serialization constructor that is used by the toolbox when the item is loaded into the toolbox. Without this constructor, you will receive an error when you attempt to add the activity to the toolbox. Note that the class is also marked as `[Serializable]`.

The toolbox item is added to the activity by using the `ToolboxItem` attribute as shown:

```
[ActivityValidator(typeof(WriteLineValidator))]
[Designer(typeof(WriteLineDesigner))]
[ToolboxBitmap(typeof(WriteLineActivity),"Resources.WriteLine.png")]
[ToolboxItem(typeof(WriteLineToolboxItem))]
public class WriteLineActivity : Activity
{
  ...
}
```

With all of these changes in place, you can compile the assembly and then create a new workflow project. To add the activity to the toolbox, open a workflow and then display the context menu for the toolbox and click Choose Items.

You can then browse for the assembly containing your activity, and once you have added it to the toolbox, it will look something like Figure 43-12. The icon is somewhat less than perfect, but it's close enough.

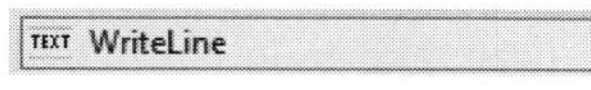

Figure 43-12

You revisit the `ActivityToolboxItem` in the next section on custom composite activities, because there are some extra facilities available with that class that are necessary only when adding composite activities to the design surface.

Custom Composite Activities

There are two main types of activity. Activities that derive from `Activity` can be thought of as callable functions from the workflow. Activities that derive from `CompositeActivity` (such as `ParallelActivity`, `IfElseActivity`, and the `ListenActivity`) are containers for other activities. Their design-time behavior is considerably different from simple activities in that they present an area on the Designer where child activities can be dropped.

In this section, you create an activity that you can call the `DaysOfWeekActivity`. This activity can be used to execute different parts of a workflow based on the current date. You might, for instance, need to execute a different path in the workflow for orders that arrive over the weekend than for those that arrive during the week. In this example, you learn about a number of advanced workflow topics, and by the end of this section, you should have a good understanding of how to extend the system with your own composite activities. The code for this example is also available in the `03 CustomActivities` solution.

To begin, you create a custom activity that has a property that will default to the current date/time. You will allow that property to be set to another value that could come from another activity in the workflow or a parameter that is passed to the workflow when it executes. This composite activity will contain a number of branches — these will be user defined. Each of these branches will contain an enumerated constant that defines which day(s) that branch will execute. The following example defines the activity and two branches:

```
DaysOfWeekActivity
  SequenceActivty: Monday, Tuesday, Wednesday, Thursday, Friday
    <other activites as appropriate>
  SequenceActivity: Saturday, Sunday
    <other activites as appropriate>
```

For this example, you need an enumeration that defines the days of the week — this will include the `[Flags]` attribute (so you can't use the built-in `DayOfWeek` enum defined within the `System` namespace, because this doesn't include the `[Flags]` attribute).

```
 [Flags]
[Editor(typeof(FlagsEnumEditor), typeof(UITypeEditor))]
public enum WeekdayEnum : byte
{
    None = 0x00,
    Sunday = 0x01,
    Monday = 0x02,
    Tuesday = 0x04,
    Wednesday = 0x08,
    Thursday = 0x10,
    Friday = 0x20,
    Saturday = 0x40
}
```

Also included is a custom editor for this type, which will allow you to choose enum values based on check boxes. This code is available in the download.

With the enumerated type defined, you can take an initial stab at the activity itself. Custom composite activities are typically derived from the `CompositeActivity` class, because this defines among other things an `Activities` property, which is a collection of all subordinate activities.

```
public class DaysOfWeekActivity : CompositeActivity
{
    /// <summary>
    /// Get/Set the day of week property
    /// </summary>
    [Browsable(true)]
    [Category("Behavior")]
    [Description("Bind to a DateTime property, set a specific date time,
                 or leave blank for DateTime.Now")]
    [DefaultValue(typeof(DateTime),"")]
    public DateTime Date
    {
        get { return (DateTime)
                base.GetValue(DaysOfWeekActivity.DateProperty); }
        set { base.SetValue(DaysOfWeekActivity.DateProperty, value); }
    }

    /// <summary>
    /// Register the DayOfWeek property
    /// </summary>
    public static DependencyProperty DateProperty =
        DependencyProperty.Register("Date", typeof(DateTime),
            typeof(DaysOfWeekActivity));
}
```

The `Date` property provides the regular getter and setter, and we've also added a number of standard attributes so that it displays correctly within the property browser. The code, though, looks somewhat different from a normal .NET property, because the getter and setter are not using a standard field to store their values, but instead are using what's called a `DependencyProperty`.

The `Activity` class (and therefore this class, because it's ultimately derived from `Activity`) is derived from the `DependencyObject` class, and this defines a dictionary of values keyed on a `DependencyProperty`. This indirection of getting/setting property values is used by WF to support binding; that is, linking a property of one activity to a property of another. As an example, it is common to pass parameters around in code, sometimes by value, sometimes by reference. WF uses binding to link property values together — so in this example, you might have a `DateTime` property defined on the workflow, and this activity might need to be bound to that value at runtime. You see an example of binding later in the chapter.

If you build this activity, it won't do much; indeed it will not even allow child activities to be dropped into it, because you haven't defined a `Designer` class for the activity.

Adding a Designer

As you saw with the `WriteLineActivity` earlier in the chapter, each activity can have an associated `Designer` class, which is used to change the design-time behavior of that activity. You saw a blank `Designer` in the `WriteLineActivity`, but for the composite activity you need to override a couple of methods to add some special case processing:

```
public class DaysOfWeekDesigner : ParallelActivityDesigner
{
    public override bool CanInsertActivities
        (HitTestInfo insertLocation, ReadOnlyCollection<Activity> activities)
    {
        foreach (Activity act in activities)
```

(continued)

(continued)

```
        {
            if (!(act is SequenceActivity))
                return false;
        }

        return base.CanInsertActivities(insertLocation, activitiesToInsert);
    }

    protected override CompositeActivity OnCreateNewBranch()
    {
        return new SequenceActivity();
    }
}
```

This Designer derives from `ParallalActivityDesigner`, which provides you with good design-time behavior when adding child activities. You will need to override `CanInsertActivities` to return `false` if any of the dropped activities is not a `SequenceActivity`. If all activities are of the appropriate type, you can call the base class method, which makes some further checks on the activity types permitted within your custom activity.

You should also override the `OnCreateNewBranch` method that is called when the user chooses the Add Branch menu item. The `Designer` is associated with the activity by using the `[Designer]` attribute, as shown here:

```
[Designer(typeof(DaysOfWeekDesigner))]
public class DaysOfWeekActivity : CompositeActivity
{
}
```

The design-time behavior is nearly complete; however, you also need to add a class that is derived from `ActivityToolboxItem` to this activity, because that defines what happens when an instance of that activity is dragged from the toolbox. The default behavior is simply to construct a new activity; however, in the example you also want to create two default branches. The following code shows the toolbox item class in its entirety:

```
[Serializable]
public class DaysOfWeekToolboxItem : ActivityToolboxItem
{
    public DaysOfWeekToolboxItem(Type t)
        : base(t)
    {
        this.DisplayName = "DaysOfWeek";
    }

    private DaysOfWeekToolboxItem(SerializationInfo info,
                                  StreamingContext context)
    {
        this.Deserialize(info, context);
    }

    protected override IComponent[] CreateComponentsCore(IDesignerHost host)
    {
        CompositeActivity parent = new DaysOfWeekActivity();
        parent.Activities.Add(new SequenceActivity());
```

```
            parent.Activities.Add(new SequenceActivity());

            return new IComponent[] { parent };
        }
    }
```

As shown in the code, the display name of the activity was changed, a serialization constructor was implemented, and the `CreateComponentsCore` method was overridden.

This method is called at the end of the drag-and-drop operation, and it is where you construct an instance of the `DaysOfWeekActivity`. In the code, you are also constructing two child sequence activities, because this gives the user of the activity a better design-time experience. Several of the built-in activities do this, too — when you drop an `IfElseActivity` onto the design surface, its toolbox item class adds two branches. A similar thing happens when you add a `ParallelActivity` to your workflow.

The serialization constructor and the `[Serializable]` attribute are necessary for all classes derived from `ActivityToolboxItem`.

The last thing to do is associate this toolbox item class with the activity:

```
    [Designer(typeof(DaysOfWeekDesigner))]
    [ToolboxItem(typeof(DaysOfWeekToolboxItem))]
    public class DaysOfWeekActivity : CompositeActivity
    {
    }
```

With that in place, the UI of your activity is almost complete, as you can see in Figure 43-13.

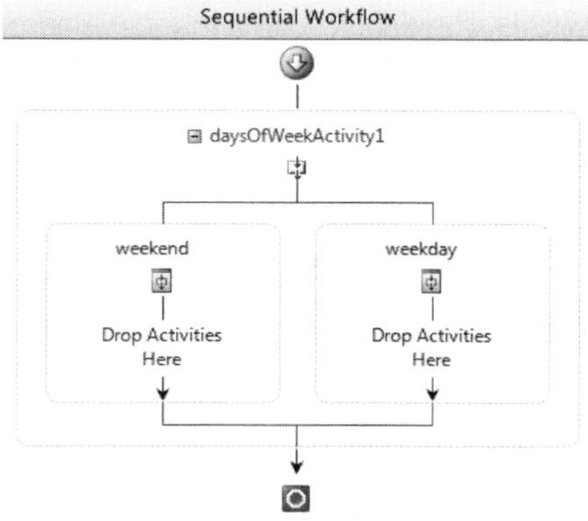

Figure 43-13

Now, you need to define a property on each of the sequence activities shown in Figure 43-13, so that the user can define which day(s) the branch will execute. There are two ways to do this in Windows Workflow: you can create a subclass of `SequenceActivity` and define it there, or you can use another feature of dependency properties called Attached Properties.

You will use the latter method, because this means that you don't have to subclass but instead can effectively extend the sequence activity without needing the source code of that activity.

Attached Properties

When registering dependency properties, you can call the `RegisterAttached` method to create an attached property. An attached property is one that is defined on one class but is displayed on another. So here, you define a property on the `DaysOfWeekActivity`, but that property is actually displayed in the UI as attached to a sequential activity.

The code in the following snippet shows a property called `Weekday` of type `WeekdayEnum`, which will be added to the sequence activities that reside within your composite activity:

```
public static DependencyProperty WeekdayProperty =
    DependencyProperty.RegisterAttached("Weekday",
        typeof(WeekdayEnum), typeof(DaysOfWeekActivity),
        new PropertyMetadata(DependencyPropertyOptions.Metadata));
```

The final line allows you to specify extra information about a property. In this instance, it is specifying that it is a `Metadata` property.

Metadata properties differ from normal properties in that they are effectively read only at runtime. You can think of a `Metadata` property as similar to a constant declaration within C#. You cannot alter constants while the program is executing, and you cannot change `Metadata` properties while a workflow is executing.

In this example, you wish to define the days that the activity will execute, so you could in the Designer set this field to "Saturday, Sunday". In the code emitted for the workflow, you would see a declaration as follows (I have reformatted the code to fit the confines of the page):

```
this.sequenceActivity1.SetValue
  (DaysOfWeekActivity.WeekdayProperty,
  ((WeekdayEnum)((WeekdayEnum.Sunday | WeekdayEnum.Saturday))));
```

In addition to defining the dependency property, you will need methods to get and set this value on an arbitrary activity. These are typically defined as static methods on the composite activity and are shown in the following code:

```
public static void SetWeekday(Activity activity, object value)
{
    if (null == activity)
        throw new ArgumentNullException("activity");
    if (null == value)
        throw new ArgumentNullException("value");

    activity.SetValue(DaysOfWeekActivity.WeekdayProperty, value);
}

public static object GetWeekday(Activity activity)
{
    if (null == activity)
        throw new ArgumentNullException("activity");

    return activity.GetValue(DaysOfWeekActivity.WeekdayProperty);
}
```

You need to make two other changes in order for this extra property to show up attached to a `SequenceActivity`. The first is to create an *extender provider*, which tells Visual Studio to include the extra property in the sequence activity. The second is to register this provider, which is done by overriding the `Initialize` method of the Activity Designer and adding the following code to it:

```
protected override void Initialize(Activity activity)
{
    base.Initialize(activity);

    IExtenderListService iels = base.GetService(typeof(IExtenderListService))
        as IExtenderListService;

    if (null != iels)
    {
        bool extenderExists = false;

        foreach (IExtenderProvider provider in iels.GetExtenderProviders())
        {
            if (provider.GetType() == typeof(WeekdayExtenderProvider))
            {
                extenderExists = true;
                break;
            }
        }
        if (!extenderExists)
        {
            IExtenderProviderService ieps =
                base.GetService(typeof(IExtenderProviderService))
                    as IExtenderProviderService;
            if (null != ieps)
                ieps.AddExtenderProvider(new WeekdayExtenderProvider());
        }
    }
}
```

The calls to `GetService` in the preceding code allow the custom Designer to query for services proffered by the host (in this case Visual Studio). You query Visual Studio for the `IExtenderListService`, which provides a way to enumerate all available extender providers, and if no instance of the `WeekdayExtenderProvider` service is found, then query for the `IExtenderProviderService` and add a new provider.

The code for the extender provider is shown here:

```
 [ProvideProperty("Weekday", typeof(SequenceActivity))]
public class WeekdayExtenderProvider : IExtenderProvider
{
    bool IExtenderProvider.CanExtend(object extendee)
    {
        bool canExtend = false;

        if ((this != extendee) && (extendee is SequenceActivity))
        {
            Activity parent = ((Activity)extendee).Parent;

            if (null != parent)
                canExtend = parent is DaysOfWeekActivity;
        }

        return canExtend;
    }
```

(continued)

(continued)

```
    public WeekdayEnum GetWeekday(Activity activity)
    {
        WeekdayEnum weekday = WeekdayEnum.None;

        Activity parent = activity.Parent;

        if ((null != parent) && (parent is DaysOfWeekActivity))
            weekday = (WeekdayEnum)DaysOfWeekActivity.GetWeekday(activity);

        return weekday;
    }

    public void SetWeekday(Activity activity, WeekdayEnum weekday)
    {
        Activity parent = activity.Parent;

        if ((null != parent) && (parent is DaysOfWeekActivity))
            DaysOfWeekActivity.SetWeekday(activity, weekday);

    }
}
```

An extender provider is attributed with the properties that it provides, and for each of these properties it must provide a public `Get<Property>` and `Set<Property>` method. The names of these methods must match the name of the property with the appropriate *Get* or *Set* prefix.

With the preceding changes made to the Designer and the addition of the extender provider, when you click a sequence activity within the Designer, you will see the properties in Figure 43-14 within Visual Studio.

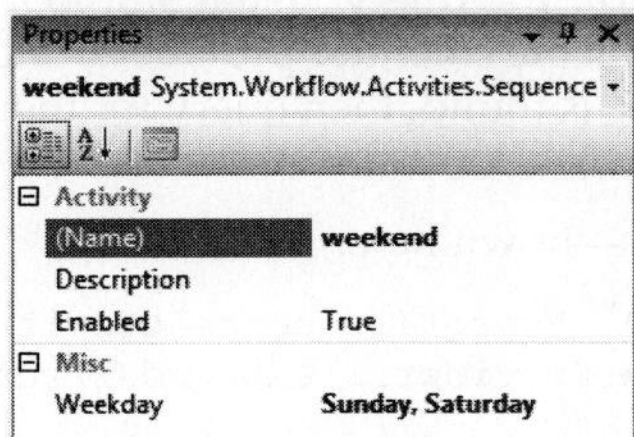

Figure 43-14

Extender providers are used for other features in .NET. One common one is to add tooltips to controls in a Windows Forms project — this registers an extender and adds a `Tooltip` property to each control on the form.

Workflows

Up to this point, the chapter has concentrated on activities but has not discussed workflows. A workflow is simply a list of activities, and indeed a workflow itself is just another type of activity. Using this model simplifies the runtime engine, because the engine just needs to know how to execute one type of object — that being anything derived from the `Activity` class.

Each workflow instance is uniquely identified by its `InstanceId` property — this is a `Guid` that can be assigned by the runtime, or this `Guid` can be provided to the runtime by your code. A common use of this is to correlate a running workflow instance with some other data maintained outside of the workflow, such as a row in a database. You can access the specific workflow instance by using the `GetWorkflow(Guid)` method of the `WorkflowRuntime` class.

Two types of workflows are available with WF — sequential and state machine.

Sequential Workflows

The root activity in a sequential workflow is the `SequentialWorkflowActivity`. This class is derived from `SequenceActivity`, which you have already seen, and it defines two events that you can attach handlers to as necessary. These are the `Initialized` and `Completed` events.

A sequential workflow starts executing the first child activity within it, and typically continues until all other activities have executed. There are a couple of instances when a workflow will not continue through all activities — one is if an exception is raised while executing the workflow, and the other is if a `TerminateActivity` exists within the workflow.

A workflow may not be executing at all times. For example, when a `DelayActivity` is encountered, the workflow will enter a wait state and can be removed from memory if a workflow persistence service is defined. Persistence of workflows is covered in "The Persistence Service" section later in this chapter.

State Machine Workflows

A state machine workflow is useful when you have a process that may be in one of several states, and transitions from one state to another can be made by passing data into the workflow.

One example is when a workflow is used for access control to a building. In this case, you may model a door class that can be closed or open, and a lock class that can be locked or unlocked. Initially when you boot up the system (or building!), you start at a known state — for sake of argument, assume that all doors are closed and locked, so the state of a given door is *closed locked*.

When an employee enters his or her building access code at the front door, an event is sent to the workflow, which includes details such as the code entered and possibly the user ID. You might then need to access a database to retrieve details such as whether that person is permitted to open the selected door at that time of day, and assuming that access is granted, the workflow would change from its initial state to the *closed unlocked* state.

From this state, there are two potential outcomes — the employee opens the door (you know this because the door also has an open/closed sensor), or the employee decides not to enter because he has left something in his car, and so after a delay you relock the door. The door could revert to its *closed locked* state or move to the *open unlocked* state.

From here, assume that the employee enters the building and then closes the door. Again, you would then like to transition from the *open unlocked* state to *closed unlocked*, and again, after a delay, would then transition to the *closed locked* state. You might also want to raise an alarm if the door was *open unlocked* for a long period.

Modeling this scenario within Windows Workflow is fairly simple. You need to define the states that the system can be in, and then define events that can transition the workflow from one state to the next. The following table describes the states of the system and provides details of the transitions that are possible from each known state and the inputs (either external or internal) that change the states.

State	Transitions
Closed Locked	This is the initial state of the system. In response to the user swiping her card (and a successful access check), the state changes to closed unlocked, and the door lock is electronically opened.
Closed Unlocked	One of two events can occur when the door is in this state: The user opens the door — you transition to the open unlocked state. A timer expires, and the door reverts to the closed locked state.
Open Unlocked	From this state, the workflow can only transition to closed unlocked.
Fire Alarm	This is the final state for the workflow and can be transitioned to from any of the other states.

One other feature you might want to add to the system is the capability to respond to a fire alarm. When the fire alarm goes off, you would want to unlock all of the doors so that anyone can exit the building, and the fire service can enter the building unimpeded. You might want to model this as the final state of the doors workflow, because from this state the full system would be reset once the fire alarm had been canceled.

The workflow in Figure 43-15 defines this state machine and shows the states that the workflow can be in. The lines denote the state transitions that are possible within the system.

The initial state of the workflow is modeled by the `ClosedLocked` activity. This consists of some initialization code (which locks the door) and then an event-based activity that awaits an external event — in this case, the employee entering his building access code. Each of the activities shown within the state shapes consist of sequential workflows, so we have defined a workflow for the initialization of the system (`CLInitialize`) and a workflow that responds to the external event raised when the employee enters her PIN (`RequestEntry`). If you look at the `RequestEntry` workflow, it is defined as shown in Figure 43-16.

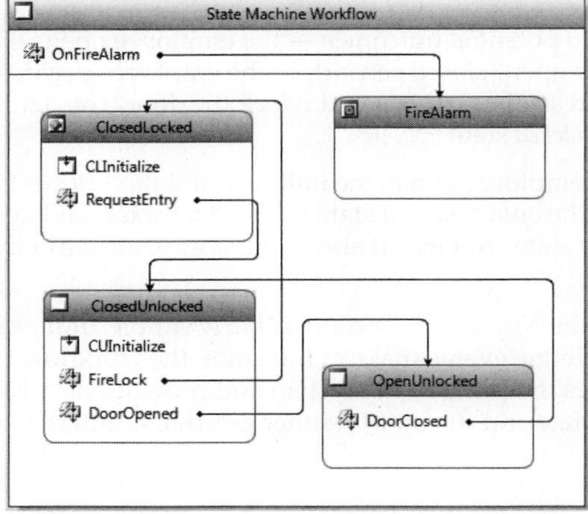

Figure 43-15

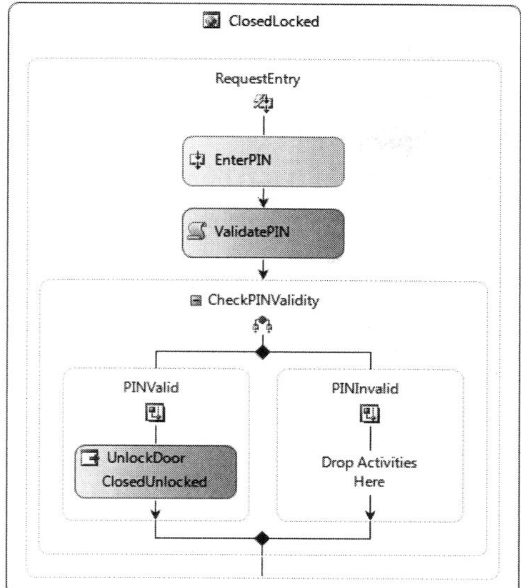

Figure 43-16

Each state consists of a number of subworkflows, each of which has an event-driven activity at the start and then any number of other activities that form the processing code within the state. In Figure 43-16, there is a `HandleExternalEventActivity` at the start that awaits the entry of the PIN. This is then checked, and if it is valid, the workflow transitions to the `ClosedUnlocked` state.

The `ClosedUnlocked` state consists of two workflows — one that responds to the door open event, which transitions the workflow to the `OpenUnlocked` state, and the other, which contains a delay activity that is used to change the state to `ClosedLocked`. A state-driven activity works in a similar manner to the `ListenActivity` shown earlier in the chapter — the state consists of a number of event-driven workflows, and on arrival of an event, just one of the workflows will execute.

To support the workflow, you need to be able to raise events in the system to affect the state changes. This is done by using an interface and an implementation of that interface; this pair of objects is termed an *external service*. The interface used for this state machine is described later in the chapter.

The code for the state machine example is available in the `04 StateMachine` solution. This also includes a user interface in which you can enter a PIN and gain access to the building through one of two doors.

Passing Parameters to a Workflow

A typical workflow requires some data in order to execute. This could be an order ID for an order-processing workflow, a customer account ID for a payment-processing workflow, or any other items of data necessary.

The parameter-passing mechanism for workflows is somewhat different from that of standard .NET classes, in which you typically pass parameters in a method call. For a workflow, you pass parameters by storing those parameters in a dictionary of name-value pairs, and when you construct the workflow, you pass through this dictionary.

When WF schedules the workflow for execution, it uses these name-value pairs to set public properties on the workflow instance. Each parameter name is checked against the public properties of the workflow, and if a match is found, the property setter is called and the value of the parameter is passed to this setter. If you add a name-value pair to the dictionary where the name does not correspond to a property on the workflow, an exception will be thrown when you try to construct that workflow.

As an example, consider the following workflow that defines the `OrderID` property as an integer:

```
public class OrderProcessingWorkflow: SequentialWorkflowActivity
{
    public int OrderID
    {
        get { return _orderID; }
        set { _orderID = value; }
    }

    private int _orderID;
}
```

The following snippet shows how you can pass the order ID parameter into an instance of this workflow:

```
WorkflowRuntime runtime = new WorkflowRuntime ();

Dictionary<string,object> parms = new Dictionary<string,object>();
parms.Add("OrderID", 12345) ;

WorkflowInstance instance = runtime.CreateWorkflow(typeof(OrderProcessingWorkflow),
parms);

instance.Start();

... Other code
```

In the example code, you construct a `Dictionary<string, object>` that will contain the parameters you wish to pass to the workflow and then use this when the workflow is constructed. The preceding code includes the `WorkflowRuntime` and `WorkflowInstance` classes, which haven't been described yet but are discussed in the "Hosting Workflows" section later in the chapter.

Returning Results from a Workflow

Another common requirement of a workflow is to return output parameters, which might then be used to record data within a database or other persistent storage.

Because a workflow is executed by the workflow runtime, you can't just call a workflow using a standard method invocation — you need to create a workflow instance, start that instance, and then await the completion of that instance. When a workflow completes, the workflow runtime raises the `WorkflowCompleted` event. This is passed contextual information about the workflow that has just completed and contains the output data from that workflow.

So, to harvest the output parameters from a workflow, you need to attach an event handler to the `WorkflowCompleted` event, and the handler can then retrieve the output parameters from the workflow. The following code shows an example of how this can be done:

```
using(WorkflowRuntime workflowRuntime = new WorkflowRuntime())
{
    AutoResetEvent waitHandle = new AutoResetEvent(false);
    workflowRuntime.WorkflowCompleted +=
        delegate(object sender, WorkflowCompletedEventArgs e)
        {
            waitHandle.Set();
            foreach (KeyValuePair<string, object> parm in e.OutputParameters)
            {
                Console.WriteLine("{0} = {1}", parm.Key, parm.Value);
            }
        };

    WorkflowInstance instance =
        workflowRuntime.CreateWorkflow(typeof(Workflow1));
    instance.Start();

    waitHandle.WaitOne();
}
```

You have attached a delegate to the `WorkflowCompleted` event, and within this you iterate through the `OutputParameters` collection of the `WorkflowCompletedEventArgs` class passed to the delegate and display the output parameters on the console. This collection contains all public properties of the workflow. There is actually no notion of specific output parameters for a workflow.

Binding Parameters to Activities

Now that you know how to pass parameters into a workflow, you also need to know how to link these parameters to activities. This is done via a mechanism called binding. In the `DaysOfWeekActivity` defined earlier, there was a `Date` property that could be hard-coded or bound to another value within the workflow. A bindable property is displayed in the property grid within Visual Studio, as shown in Figure 43-17. The icon to the right of the property name indicates that this is a bindable property — in the image the `Date` property is bindable.

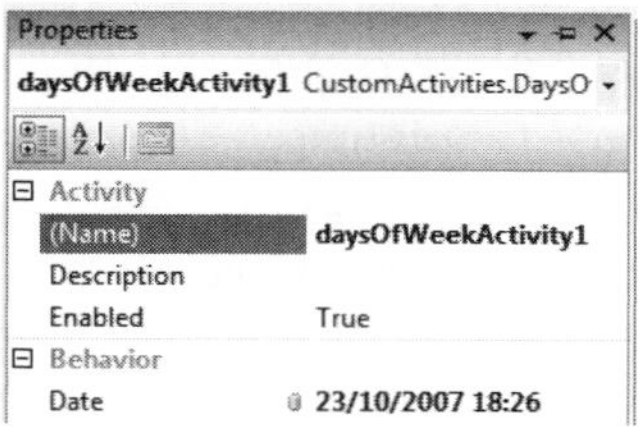

Figure 43-17

Double-clicking the bind icon will display the dialog shown in Figure 43-18. This dialog allows you to select an appropriate property to link to the `Date` property.

In Figure 43-18, we have selected the `OrderDate` property of the workflow (which is defined as a regular .NET property, as shown in an earlier code snippet). Any bindable property can be bound to either a property of the workflow that the activity is defined within or a property of any activity that resides in the workflow above the current activity. Note that the data type of the property being bound must match the data type of the property you are binding to — the dialog will not permit you to bind nonmatching types.

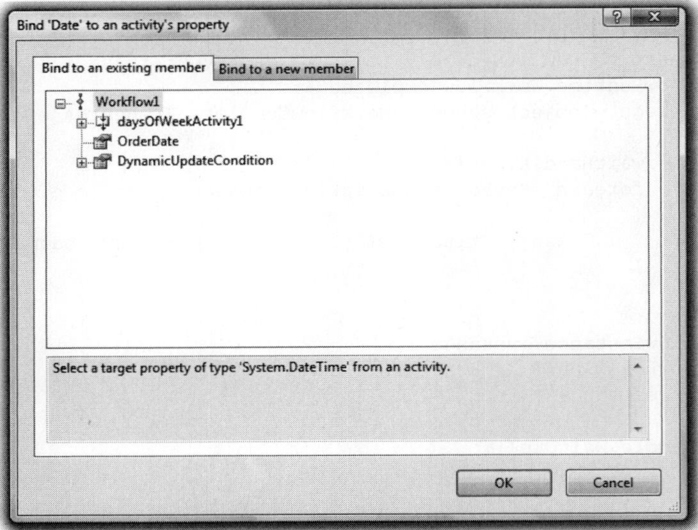

Figure 43-18

The code for the `Date` property is repeated here to show how binding works and is explained in the following paragraphs:

```
public DateTime Date
{
    get { return (DateTime)base.GetValue(DaysOfWeekActivity.DateProperty); }
    set { base.SetValue(DaysOfWeekActivity.DateProperty, value); }
}
```

When you bind a property in the workflow, an object of type `ActivityBind` is constructed behind the scenes, and it is this "value" that is stored within the dependency property. So, the property setter will be passed an object of type `ActivityBind`, and this is stored within the dictionary of properties on this activity. This `ActivityBind` object consists of data that describes the activity being bound to and the property of that activity that is to be used at runtime.

When reading the value of the property, the `GetValue` method of the `DependencyObject` is called, and this method checks the underlying property value to see if it is an `ActivityBind` object. If so, it then resolves the activity to which this binding is linked and then reads the real property value from that activity. If, however, the bound value is another type, it simply returns that object from the `GetValue` method.

The Workflow Runtime

In order to start a workflow, it is necessary to create an instance of the `WorkflowRuntime` class. This is typically done once within your application, and this object is usually defined as a static member of the application so that it can be accessed anywhere within the application.

When you start the runtime, it can then reload any workflow instances that were executing the last time the application was executed by reading these instances from the persistence store. This uses a service called the *persistence service*, which is defined in the following section.

The runtime contains six various `CreateWorkflow` methods that can be used to construct workflow instances. The runtime also contains methods for reloading a workflow instance and enumerating all running instances.

The runtime also has a number of events that are raised while workflows are executing — such as `WorkflowCreated` (raised when a new workflow instance is constructed), `WorkflowIdled` (raised when a workflow is awaiting input such as in the expense-processing example shown earlier), and `WorkflowCompleted` (raised when a workflow has finished).

Workflow Services

A workflow doesn't exist on its own. As described in the previous section, a workflow is executed within the `WorkflowRuntime`, and this runtime provides *services* to running workflows.

A service is any class that may be needed while executing the workflow. Some standard services are provided to your workflow by the runtime, and you can optionally construct your own services to be consumed by running workflows.

This section describes two of the standard services provided by the runtime. It then shows how you can create your own services and some instances of when this is necessary.

When an activity runs, it is passed some contextual information via the `ActivityExecutionStatus` parameter of the `Execute` method:

```
protected override ActivityExecutionStatus Execute
    (ActivityExecutionContext executionContext)
{
    ...
}
```

One of the methods available on this context parameter is the `GetService<T>` method. This can be used as shown in the following code to access a service attached to the workflow runtime:

```
protected override ActivityExecutionStatus Execute
    (ActivityExecutionContext executionContext)
{
    ICustomService myService = executionContext.GetService<ICustomService>();
    ... Do something with the service
}
```

The services hosted by the runtime are added to the runtime prior to calling the `StartRuntime` method. An exception is raised if you attempt to add a service to the runtime once it has been started.

Two methods are available for adding services to the runtime. You can construct the services in code and then add them to the runtime by calling the `AddService` method. Or, you can define services within the application configuration file, and these will be constructed for you and added to the runtime.

The following code snippet shows how to add services to the runtime in code — the services added are those described later in this section:

```
using(WorkflowRuntime workflowRuntime = new WorkflowRuntime())
{
    workflowRuntime.AddService(
        new SqlWorkflowPersistenceService(conn, true, new TimeSpan(1,0,0),
                                          new TimeSpan(0,10,0)));
    workflowRuntime.AddService(new SqlTrackingService(conn));
    ...
}
```

Here are constructed instances of the `SqlWorkflowPersistenceService`, which is used by the runtime to store workflow state, and an instance of the `SqlTrackingService`, which records the execution events of a workflow while it runs.

To create services using an application configuration file, you need to add a section handler for the workflow runtime and then add services to this section as shown here:

```
<?xml version="1.0" encoding="utf-8" ?>
<configuration>
  <configSections>
    <section name="WF"
      type="System.Workflow.Runtime.Configuration.WorkflowRuntimeSection,
      System.Workflow.Runtime, Version=3.0.00000.0, Culture=neutral,
      PublicKeyToken=31bf3856ad364e35" />
  </configSections>

  <WF Name="Hosting">
    <CommonParameters/>
      <Services>
        <add type="System.Workflow.Runtime.Hosting.SqlWorkflowPersistenceService,
                   System.Workflow.Runtime, Version=3.0.00000.0, Culture=neutral,
                   PublicKeyToken=31bf3856ad364e35"
          connectionString="Initial Catalog=WF;Data Source=.;
                            Integrated Security=SSPI;"
          UnloadOnIdle="true"
          LoadIntervalSeconds="2"/>
        <add type="System.Workflow.Runtime.Tracking.SqlTrackingService,
                   System.Workflow.Runtime, Version=3.0.00000.0, Culture=neutral,
                   PublicKeyToken=31bf3856ad364e35"
          connectionString="Initial Catalog=WF;Data Source=.;
                            Integrated Security=SSPI;"
          UseDefaultProfile="true"/>
      </Services>
  </WF>
</configuration>
```

Within the configuration file, you have added the `WF` section handler (the name is unimportant but must match the name given to the later configuration section) and then created the appropriate entries for this section. The `<Services>` element can contain an arbitrary list of entries that consist of a .NET type and then parameters that will be passed to that service when constructed by the runtime.

To read the configuration settings from the application configuration file, you call another constructor on the runtime, as shown here:

```
using(WorkflowRuntime workflowRuntime = new WorkflowRuntime("WF"))
{
    ...
}
```

This constructor will instantiate each service defined within the configuration file and add these to the services collection on the runtime.

The following sections describe some of the standard services available with WF.

The Persistence Service

When a workflow executes, it may reach a wait state. This can occur when a delay activity executes or when you are waiting for external input within a listen activity. At this point, the workflow is said to be *idle* and as such is a candidate for persistence.

Let's assume that you begin execution of 1,000 workflows on your server, and each of these instances becomes idle. At this point, it is unnecessary to maintain data for each of these instances in memory, so it would be ideal if you could unload a workflow and free up the resources in use. The persistence service is designed to accomplish this.

When a workflow becomes idle, the workflow runtime checks for the existence of a service that derives from the `WorkflowPersistenceService` class. If this service exists, it is passed the workflow instance, and the service can then capture the current state of the workflow and store it in a persistent storage medium. You could store the workflow state on disk in a file, or store this data within a database such as SQL Server.

The workflow libraries contain an implementation of the persistence service, which stores data within a SQL Server database — this is the `SqlWorkflowPersistenceService`. In order to use this service, you need to run two scripts against your SQL Server instance. One of these constructs the schema, and the other creates the stored procedures used by the persistence service. These scripts are, by default, located in the `C:\Windows\Microsoft.NET\Framework\v3.5\Windows Workflow Foundation\SQL\EN` directory.

The scripts to execute against the database are `SqlPersistenceProviderSchema.sql` and `SqlPersistenceProviderLogic.sql`. These need to be executed in order, with the schema file first and then the logic file. The schema for the SQL persistence service contains two tables: `InstanceState` and `CompletedScope`. These are essentially opaque tables, and they are not intended for use outside the SQL persistence service.

When a workflow idles, its state is serialized using binary serialization, and this data is then inserted into the `InstanceState` table. When a workflow is reactivated, the state is read from this row and used to reconstruct the workflow instance. The row is keyed on the workflow instance ID and is deleted from the database once the workflow has completed.

The SQL persistence service can be used by multiple runtimes at the same time — it implements a locking mechanism so that a workflow is accessible by only one instance of the workflow runtime at a time. When you have multiple servers all running workflows using the same persistence store, this locking behavior becomes invaluable.

To see what is added to the persistence store, construct a new workflow project and add an instance of the `SqlWorkflowPersistenceService` to the runtime. The following code shows an example using declarative code:

```
using(WorkflowRuntime workflowRuntime = new WorkflowRuntime())
{
    workflowRuntime.AddService(
        new SqlWorkflowPersistenceService(conn, true, new TimeSpan(1,0,0),
                                          new TimeSpan(0,10,0)));
    // Execute a workflow here...
}
```

If you then construct a workflow that contains a `DelayActivity` and set the delay to something like 10 seconds, you can then view the data stored within the `InstanceState` table. The `05 WorkflowPersistence` example contains the preceding code and executes a delay within a 20-second period.

The parameters passed to the constructor of the persistence service are shown in the following table.

Parameter	Description	Default
`ConnectionString`	The database connection string used by the persistence service.	None
`UnloadOnIdle`	Determines whether a workflow is unloaded when it idles. This should always be set to `true`; otherwise no persistence will occur.	False
`InstanceOwnershipDuration`	This defines the length of time that the workflow instance will be owned by the runtime that has loaded that workflow.	None
`LoadingInterval`	The interval used when polling the database for updated persistence records.	2 Minutes

These values can also be defined within the configuration file.

The Tracking Service

When a workflow executes it might be necessary to record which activities have run, and in the case of composite activities such as the `IfElseActivity` or the `ListenActivity`, which branch was executed. This data could be used as a form of audit trail for a workflow instance, which could then be viewed at a later date to prove which activities executed and what data was used within the workflow. The tracking service can be used for this type of recording and can be configured to log as little or as much information about a running workflow instance as is necessary.

As is common with WF, the tracking service is implemented as an abstract class called `TrackingService`, so it is easy to replace the standard tracking implementation with one of your own. There is one concrete implementation of the tracking service available within the workflow assemblies — this is the `SqlTrackingService`.

To record data about the state of a workflow, it is necessary to define a `TrackingProfile`. This defines which events should be recorded, so you could, for example, record just the start and end of a workflow and omit all other data about the running instance. More typically, you will record all events for the workflow and each activity in that workflow to provide a complete picture of the execution profile of the workflow.

When a workflow is scheduled by the runtime engine, the engine checks for the existence of a workflow tracking service. If one is found, it asks the service for a tracking profile for the workflow being executed, and then uses this to record workflow and activity data. You can, in addition, define user tracking data and store this within the tracking data store without needing to change the schema.

The tracking profile class is shown in Figure 43-19. The class includes collection properties for activity, user, and workflow *track points*. A track point is an object (such as `WorkflowTrackPoint`) that typically defines a *match location* and some extra data to record when this track point is hit. The match location defines where this track point is valid — so for example, you could define a `WorkflowTrackPoint`, which will record some data when the workflow is created, and another to record some data when the workflow is completed.

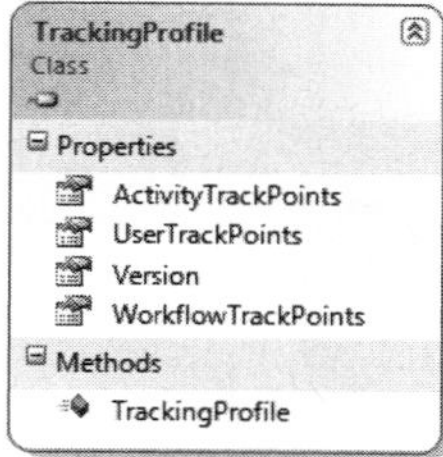

Figure 43-19

Once this data has been recorded, it may be necessary to display the execution path of a workflow, as in Figure 43-20. This shows the workflow that was executed, and each activity that ran includes a glyph to show that it executed. This data is read from the tracking store for that workflow instance.

To read the data stored by the `SqlTrackingService`, you could execute queries against the SQL database directly; however, Microsoft has provided the `SqlTrackingQuery` class defined within the `System.Workflow.Runtime.Tracking` namespace for this purpose. The following example code shows how to retrieve a list of all workflows tracked between two dates:

```
public IList<SqlTrackingWorkflowInstance> GetWorkflows
  (DateTime startDate, DateTime endDate, string connectionString)
{
  SqlTrackingQuery query = new SqlTrackingQuery (connectionString);

  SqlTrackingQueryOptions queryOptions = new SqlTrackingQueryOptions();
  query.StatusMinDateTime = startDate;
  query.StatusMaxDateTime = endDate;

  return (query.GetWorkflows (queryOptions));
}
```

This uses the `SqlTrackingQueryOptions` class, which defines the query parameters. You can define other properties of this class to further constrain the workflows retrieved.

In Figure 43-20 you can see that all activities have executed. This might not be the case if the workflow were still running or if there were some decisions made within the workflow so that different paths were taken during execution. The tracking data contains details such as which activities have executed, and this data can be correlated with the activities to produce the image in Figure 43-20. It is also possible to extract data from the workflow as it executes, which could be used to form an audit trail of the execution flow of the workflow.

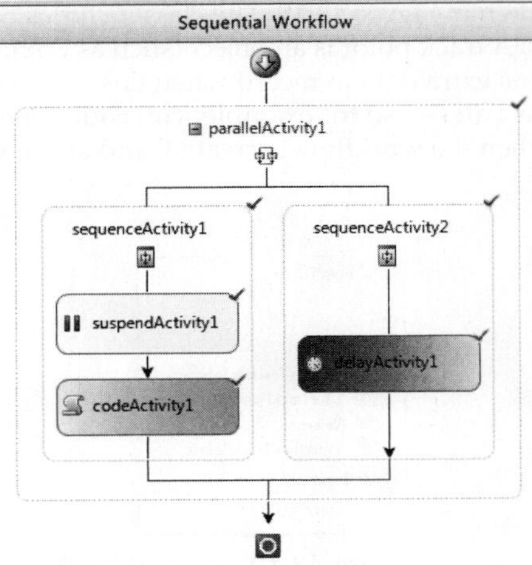

Figure 43-20

Custom Services

In addition to built-in services such as the persistence service and the tracking service, you can add your own objects to the services collection maintained by the `WorkflowRuntime`. These services are typically defined using an interface and an implementation, so that you can replace the service without recoding the workflow.

The state machine presented earlier in the chapter uses the following interface:

```
[ExternalDataExchange]
public interface IDoorService
{
    void LockDoor();
    void UnlockDoor();

    event EventHandler<ExternalDataEventArgs> RequestEntry;
    event EventHandler<ExternalDataEventArgs> OpenDoor;
    event EventHandler<ExternalDataEventArgs> CloseDoor;
    event EventHandler<ExternalDataEventArgs> FireAlarm;

    void OnRequestEntry(Guid id);
    void OnOpenDoor(Guid id);
    void OnCloseDoor(Guid id);
    void OnFireAlarm();
}
```

The interface consists of methods that are used by the workflow to call the service and events raised by the service that are consumed by the workflow. The use of the `ExternalDataExchange` attribute indicates to the workflow runtime that this interface is used for communication between a running workflow and the service implementation.

Within the state machine, there are a number of instances of the `CallExternalMethodActivity` that are used to call methods on this external interface. One example is when the door is locked or unlocked — the workflow needs to execute a method call to the `UnlockDoor` or `LockDoor` methods, and the service responds by sending a command to the door lock to unlock or lock the door.

When the service needs to communicate with the workflow, this is done by using an event, because the workflow runtime also contains a service called the `ExternalDataExchangeService`, which acts as a proxy for these events. This proxy is used when the event is raised, because the workflow may not be loaded in memory at the time the event is delivered. So the event is first routed to the external data exchange service, which checks to see if the workflow is loaded, and, if not, rehydrates it from the persistence store and then passes the event on into the workflow.

The code used to construct the `ExternalDataExchangeService` and to construct proxies for the events defined by the service is shown here:

```
WorkflowRuntime runtime = new WorkflowRuntime();
ExternalDataExchangeService edes = new ExternalDataExchangeService();

runtime.AddService(edes);
DoorService service = new DoorService();
edes.AddService(service);
```

This constructs an instance of the external data exchange service and adds it to the runtime. It then creates an instance of the `DoorService` (which itself implements `IDoorService`) and adds this to the external data exchange service.

The `ExternalDataExchangeService.Add` method constructs a proxy for each event defined by the custom service so that a persisted workflow can be loaded prior to delivery of the event. If you don't host your service within the external data exchange service, when you raise events there will be nothing listening to these events, so they will not be delivered to the correct workflow.

Events use the `ExternalDataEventArgs` class, because this includes the workflow instance ID that the event is to be delivered to. If there are other values that need to be passed from an external event to a workflow, you should derive a class from `ExternalDataEventArgs` and add these values as properties to that class.

Integration with Windows Communication Foundation

Two new activities are available with .NET 3.5 that support integration between workflows and WCF. These are the `SendActivity` and the `ReceiveActivity`. The `SendActivity` could more aptly be called the `CallActivity`, because what it does is issue a request to a WCF service and can optionally surface the results as parameters that can be bound to within the calling workflow.

Somewhat more interesting, however, is the new `ReceiveActivity`. This allows a workflow to become the implementation of a WCF service, so now the workflow is the service. The following example exposes a service using a workflow and also uses the new service test host tool to test the service without having to write a separate test harness.

From the New Project menu in Visual Studio 2008, choose the WCF node and then the Sequential Workflow Service Library entry as shown in Figure 43-21.

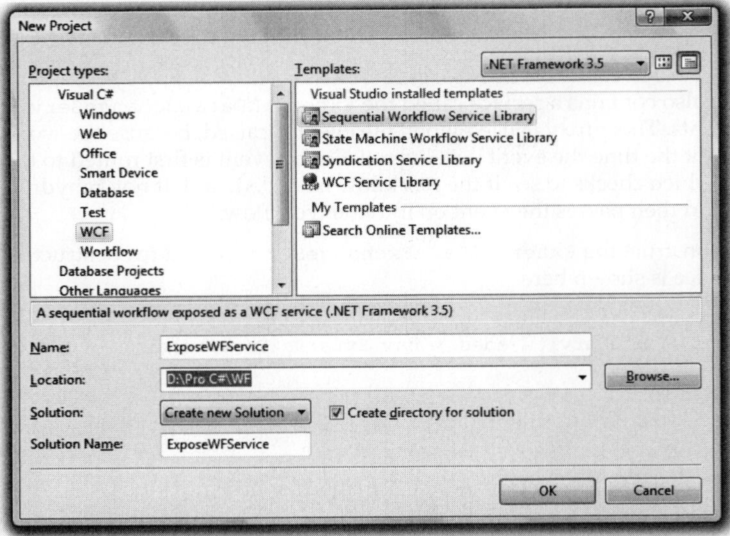

Figure 43-21

This will create a library that contains a workflow as shown in Figure 43-22, an application configuration file, and a service interface.

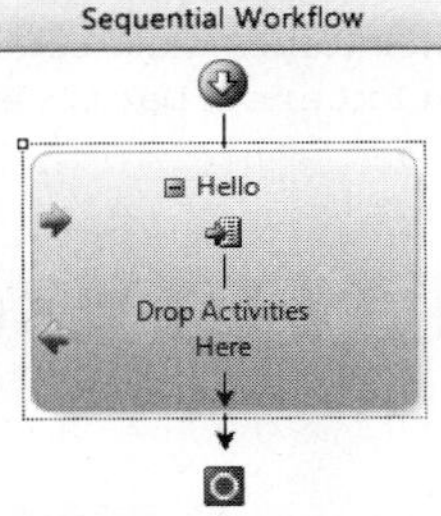

Figure 43-22

The workflow exposes the Hello operation of the contract and also defines properties for the arguments passed to this operation, and the return value of the operation. Then, all you need to do is to add code that provides the execution behavior of the service, and your service is complete.

To do this for the example, drag a `CodeActivity` onto the `ReceiveActivity` as shown in Figure 43-23, and then double-click that activity to supply the service implementation.

The code shown in the following snippet is all that there is to this service implementation:

```
public sealed partial class Workflow1: SequentialWorkflowActivity
{
    public Workflow1()
    {
        InitializeComponent();
    }
```

```
        public String returnValue = default(System.String);
        public String inputMessage = default(System.String);

        private void codeActivity1_ExecuteCode(object sender, EventArgs e)
        {
            this.returnValue = string.Format("You said {0}", inputMessage);
        }
    }
```

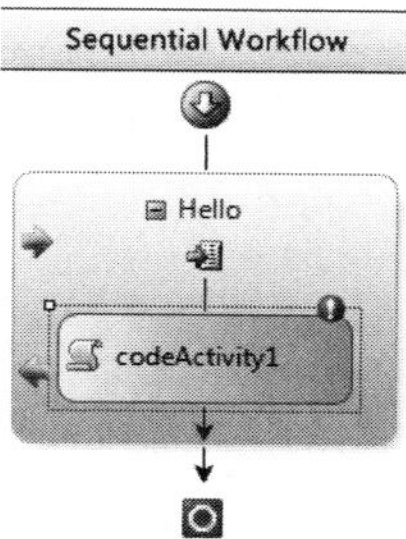

Figure 43-23

Because the service contract for the Hello operation includes both a parameter (`inputMessage`) and a return value, these have been exposed to the workflow as public fields. Within the code, we have set the `returnValue` to a string value, and this is what is returned from a call to the WCF service.

If you compile this service and hit F5, you will notice another new feature of Visual Studio 2008 — the WCF Test Client application, as shown in Figure 43-24.

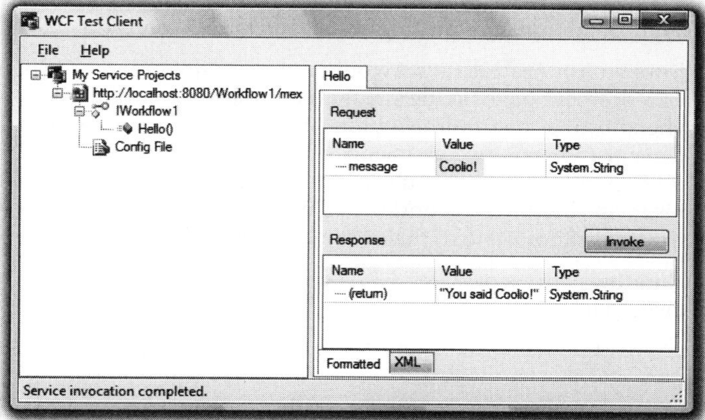

Figure 43-24

Here you can browse for the operations that the service exposes, and by double-clicking an operation, the right-hand side of the window is displayed, which lists the parameters used by that service and any return value(s) exposed.

To test the service, enter a value for the message property and click the Invoke button. This will then make a request over WCF to the service, which will construct and execute the workflow, call the code activity, which then runs the code-behind, and ultimately return to the WCF Test Client the result from the workflow.

If you wish to manually host workflows as services, you can use the new `WorkflowServiceHost` class defined within the `System.WorkflowServices` assembly. The following snippet shows a minimal host implementation:

```
using (WorkflowServiceHost host = new WorkflowServiceHost
                                    (typeof(YourWorkflow)))
{
  host.Open();
  Console.WriteLine ( "Press [Enter] to exit" );
  Console.ReadLine();
}
```

Here we have constructed an instance of `WorkflowServiceHost` and passed it the workflow that will be executed. This is similar to how you would use the `ServiceHost` class when hosting WCF services. It will read the configuration file to determine which endpoints the service will listen on and then await service requests.

The next section describes some other options you have for hosting workflows.

Hosting Workflows

The code to host the `WorkflowRuntime` in a process will vary based on the application itself.

For a Windows Forms application or a Windows Service, it is typical to construct the runtime at the start of the application and store this in a property of the main application class.

In response to some input in the application (such as the user clicking a button on the user interface), you might then construct an instance of a workflow and execute this instance locally. The workflow may well need to communicate with the user — so, for example, you might define an external service that prompts the user for confirmation before posting an order to a back-end server.

When hosting workflows within ASP.NET, you would not normally prompt the user with a message box but instead navigate to a different page on the site that requested the confirmation and then present a confirmation page. When hosting the runtime within ASP.NET, it is typical to override the `Application_Start` event and construct an instance of the workflow runtime there so that it is accessible within all other parts of the site. You can store the runtime instance in a static property, but it is more usual to store this in application state and provide an accessor method that will retrieve the workflow runtime from application state so that it can be used elsewhere in the application.

In either scenario — Windows Forms or ASP.NET — you will construct an instance of the workflow runtime and add services to it as shown here:

```
WorkflowRuntime workflowRuntime = new WorkflowRuntime();

workflowRuntime.AddService(
    new SqlWorkflowPersistenceService(conn, true, new TimeSpan(1,0,0),
                                      new TimeSpan(0,10,0)));
// Execute a workflow here...
```

To execute a workflow, you need to create an instance of that workflow using the `CreateInstance` method of the runtime. There are a number of overrides of this method that can be used to construct an instance of a code-based workflow or a workflow defined in XML.

Up to this point in the chapter, you have considered workflows as .NET classes — and indeed that is one representation of a workflow. You can, however, define a workflow using XML, and the runtime will construct an in-memory representation of the workflow and then execute it when you call the `Start` method of the `WorkflowInstance`.

Within Visual Studio, you can create an XML-based workflow by choosing the Sequential Workflow (with code separation) or the State Machine Workflow (with code separation) items from the Add New Item dialog. This will create an XML file with the extension `.xoml` and load it into the Designer.

When you add activities to the Designer, these activities are persisted into the XML, and the structure of elements defines the parent/child relationships between the activities. The following XML shows a simple sequential workflow that contains an `IfElseAcvtivity` and two code activities, one on each branch of the `IfElseActivity`:

```
<SequentialWorkflowActivity x:Class="DoorsWorkflow.Workflow1" x:Name="Workflow1"
  xmlns:x="http://schemas.microsoft.com/winfx/2006/xaml"
  xmlns="http://schemas.microsoft.com/winfx/2006/xaml/workflow">
  <IfElseActivity x:Name="ifElseActivity1">
    <IfElseBranchActivity x:Name="ifElseBranchActivity1">
      <IfElseBranchActivity.Condition>
        <CodeCondition Condition="Test" />
      </IfElseBranchActivity.Condition>
      <CodeActivity x:Name="codeActivity1" ExecuteCode="DoSomething" />
    </IfElseBranchActivity>
    <IfElseBranchActivity x:Name="ifElseBranchActivity2">
      <CodeActivity x:Name="codeActivity2" ExecuteCode="DoSomethingElse" />
    </IfElseBranchActivity>
  </IfElseActivity>
</SequentialWorkflowActivity>
```

The properties defined on the activities are persisted into the XML as attributes, and each activity is persisted as an element. As you can see from the XML, the structure defines the relationship between parent activities (such as the `SequentialWorkflowActivity` and the `IfElseActivity`) and the child activities.

Executing an XML-based workflow is no different from executing a code-based workflow — you simply use an override of the `CreateWorkflow` method that takes an `XmlReader` instance, and then start that instance by calling the `Start` method.

One benefit of using XML-based workflows over code-based workflows is that you can then easily store the workflow definition within a database. You can load up this XML at runtime and execute the workflow, and you can very easily make changes to the workflow definition without having to recompile any code.

Changing a workflow at runtime is also supported whether the workflow is defined in XML or code. You construct a `WorkflowChanges` object, which contains all of the new activities to be added to the workflow, and then call the `ApplyWorkflowChanges` method defined on the `WorkflowInstance` class to persist these changes. This is exceptionally useful, because business needs often change and, for example, you might want to apply changes to an insurance policy workflow so that you send an email to the customers a month prior to the renewal date to let them know their policy is due for renewal. Changes are made on an instance-by-instance basis, so if you had 100 policy workflows in the system, you would need to make these changes to each individual workflow.

The Workflow Designer

To complete this chapter, we've left the best until last. The Workflow Designer that you use to design workflows isn't tied to Visual Studio — you can rehost this Designer within your own application as necessary.

This means that you could deliver a system containing workflows and permit end users to customize the system without requiring them to have a copy of Visual Studio. Hosting the Designer is, however, fairly complex, and we could devote several chapters to this one topic, but we are out of space. A number of examples of rehosting are available on the Web — we recommend reading the MSDN article on hosting the Designer available at `http://msdn2.microsoft.com/en-us/library/aa480213.aspx` for more information.

The traditional way of allowing users to customize a system is by defining an interface and then allowing the customer to implement this interface to extend processing as required.

With Windows Workflow that extension becomes a whole lot more graphical, because you can present users with a blank workflow as a template and provide a toolbox that contains custom activities that are appropriate for your application. They can then author their workflows and add in your activities or custom activities they have written themselves.

Summary

Windows Workflow will produce a radical change in the way that applications are constructed. You can now surface complex parts of an application as activities, and permit users to alter the processing of the system simply by dragging and dropping activities into a workflow.

There is almost no application that you could not apply workflow to — from the simplest command-line tool to the most complex system containing many hundreds of modules. Although the new communication capabilities of WCF and the new UI capabilities of Windows Presentation Foundation are a great step forward for applications in general, the addition of Windows Workflow will produce a seismic change in the way that applications are developed and configured.

If you have time to invest in only one of the new facilities available with the .NET Framework 3.0, we suggest concentrating on Windows Workflow. We expect skills in workflow to be very highly sought after for years to come.

Now that this chapter is complete, the next chapter goes over enterprise services in detail.

Enterprise Services

Enterprise Services is the name of the Microsoft application server technology that offers services for distributed solutions. Enterprise Services is based on the COM+ technology that has already been in use for many years. However, instead of wrapping .NET objects as COM objects to use these services, .NET offers extensions for .NET components to take direct advantage of these services. With .NET you get easy access to COM+ services for .NET components.

Enterprise Services also has a great integration story with WCF. You can use a tool to automatically create a WCF service front-end to a serviced component, and you can invoke a WCF service from a COM+ client.

This chapter covers the following topics:

- When to use Enterprise Services
- What services you get with this technology
- How to create a serviced component to use Enterprise Services
- How to deploy COM+ applications
- How to use transactions with Enterprise Services
- How to create a WCF front-end to Enterprise Services
- How to use Enterprise Services from a WCF Client

This chapter is using the sample database Northwind, which you can download from the Microsoft downloads page: `www.microsoft.com/downloads`.

Overview

The complexity of Enterprise Services and the different configuration options (many of them are not needed if all the components of the solution are developed with .NET) can be more easily understood if you know the history of Enterprise Services. This chapter starts with that history. After that, you get an overview of the different services offered by the technology, so you know what features could be useful for your application.

The topics covered in this section are:

- History
- Where to use Enterprise Services
- Contexts
- Automatic transactions
- Distributed transactions
- Object pooling
- Role-based security
- Queued components
- Loosely coupled events

History

Enterprise Services can be traced back to Microsoft Transaction Server (MTS), which was released as an option pack for Windows NT 4.0. MTS extended COM by offering services such as transactions for COM objects. The services could be used by configuring metadata: the configuration of the component defined whether or not a transaction was required. With MTS it was no longer necessary to deal with transactions programmatically. However, MTS had a big disadvantage. COM was not designed to be extensible, so MTS made extensions by overwriting the COM component registry configuration to direct the instantiation of the component to MTS, and some special MTS API calls have been required to instantiate COM objects within MTS. This problem was solved with Windows 2000.

One of the most important features of Windows 2000 was the integration of MTS and COM in a new technology with the name COM+. In Windows 2000, COM+ base services are aware of the context that is needed by COM+ services (previously MTS services), so the special MTS API calls are no longer needed. With COM+ services some new service functionality is offered in addition to distributed transactions.

Windows 2000 includes COM+ 1.0. COM+ 1.5 is available since Windows XP and Windows Server 2003. COM+ 1.5 adds more features to increase scalability and availability, including application pooling and recycling, and configurable isolation levels.

.NET Enterprise Services allows you to use COM+ services from within .NET components. Support is offered for Windows 2000 and later. When .NET components are run within COM+ applications, no COM callable wrapper is used (see Chapter 24, "Interoperability"); the application runs as a .NET component instead. When you install the .NET runtime on an operating system, some runtime extensions are added to COM+ Services. If two .NET components are installed with Enterprise Services, and component A is using component B, COM marshaling is not used; instead, the .NET components can invoke each other directly.

Where to Use Enterprise Services

Business applications can be logically separated into presentation, business, and data service layers. The *presentation service layer* is responsible for user interaction. Here, the user can interact with the application to enter and view data. Technologies used with this layer are Windows Forms and ASP.NET Web Forms. The *business service layer* consists of business rules and data rules. The *data service layer* interacts with persistent storage. Here, you can use components that make use of ADO.NET. Enterprise Services fits both to the business service layer and to the data service layer.

Figure 44-1 shows two typical application scenarios. Enterprise Services can be used directly from a rich client using Windows Forms or WPF or from a Web application that is running ASP.NET.

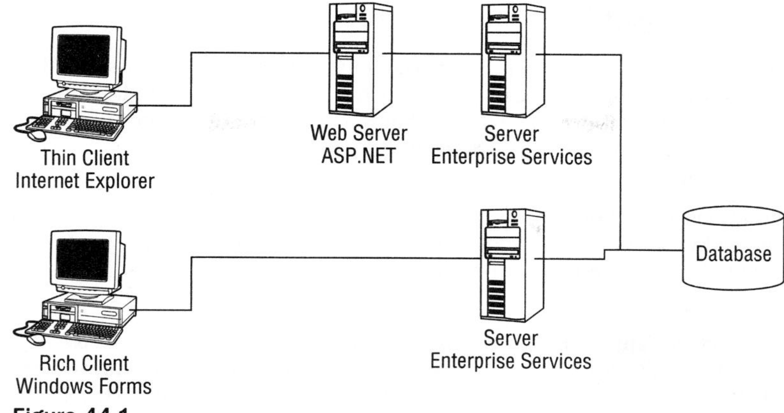

Figure 44-1

Enterprise Services is also a scalable technology. Using *component load balancing* makes it possible to distribute the load of the clients across different systems.

You can also use Enterprise Services on the client system, because this technology is included in Windows Vista and Windows XP.

Contexts

The base functionality behind the services offered by Enterprise Services is the context. The context makes it possible to intercept a method call, and some service functionality can be carried out before the expected method call is invoked. For example, a transactional or a synchronization scope can be created before the method implemented by the component is invoked.

With the contexts here, a COM component and a .NET component can participate in the same transaction. All this is done with the help of the base class `ServicedComponent` that itself derives from `MarshalByRefObject` to integrate .NET and COM+ contexts.

Automatic Transactions

The most commonly used feature of Enterprise Services is *automatic transactions*. With automatic transactions, it is not necessary to start and commit a transaction in the code; an attribute can be applied to a class instead. By using the `[Transaction]` attribute with the options `Required`, `Supported`, `RequiresNew`, and `NotSupported`, you can mark a class with the requirements it has for transactions. If you mark the class with the option `Required`, a transaction is created automatically when a method starts and is committed to or aborted when the root component of the transaction is finished.

Such a declarative way to program is of particular advantage when a complex object model is developed. Here, automatic transactions have a big advantage over programming transactions manually. Assume that you have a `Person` object with multiple `Address` and `Document` objects that are associated with the `Person`, and you want to store the `Person` object together with all associated objects in a single transaction. Doing transactions programmatically would mean passing a transaction object to all the related objects so that they can participate in the same transaction. Using transactions declaratively means there is no need to pass the transaction object, because this happens behind the scenes by using the context.

Distributed Transactions

Enterprise Services not only offers automatic transactions, but the transactions can also be distributed across multiple databases. Enterprise Services transactions are enlisted with the *Distributed Transaction Coordinator* (DTC). The DTC supports databases that make use of the XA protocol, which is a two-phase commit protocol, and is supported by SQL Server and Oracle. A single transaction can span writing data to both a SQL Server and an Oracle database.

Distributed transactions are not only useful with databases, but a single transaction can also span writing data to a database and writing data to a message queue. If one of these two actions fails, a rollback is done with the other action. You can read more about message queuing in Chapter 45, "Message Queuing."

> **Enterprise Services supports promotable transactions. If SQL Server 2005 or 2008 is used and just a single connection is active within one transaction, a local transaction is created. If another transactional resource is active within the same transaction, the transaction is promoted to a DTC transaction.**

Later in this chapter, you see how to create a component that requires transactions.

Object Pooling

Pooling is another feature offered by Enterprise Services. These services use a pool of threads to answer requests from clients. Object pooling can be used for objects with a long initialization time. With object pooling, objects are created in advance so that clients don't have to wait until the object is initialized.

Role-Based Security

Using *role-based security* allows you to define roles declaratively and define what methods or components can be used from what roles. The system administrator assigns users or user groups to these roles. In the program there is no need to deal with access control lists; instead, roles that are simple strings can be used.

Queued Components

Queued components is an abstraction layer to message queuing. Instead of sending messages to a message queue, the client can invoke methods with a recorder that offers the same methods as a .NET class configured in Enterprise Services. The recorder in turn creates messages that are transferred via a message queue to the server application.

Queued components and message queuing are useful if the client application is running in a disconnected environment (for example, on a laptop that does not always has a connection to the server), or if the request that is sent to the server should be cached before it is forwarded to a different server (for example, to a server of a partner company).

Loosely Coupled Events

Chapter 7, "Delegates and Events," explained the event model of .NET. Chapter 24, "Interoperability," describes how to use events in a COM environment. With both of these event mechanisms, the client and the server do have a tight connection. This is different with *loosely coupled events* (LCE). With LCE the COM+ facility is inserted between client and server (see Figure 44-2). The publisher registers the events it will offer with COM+ by defining an event class. Instead of sending the events directly to the client, the publisher sends events to the event class that is registered with the LCE service. The LCE service forwards the events to the subscriber, which is the client application that registered a subscription for the event.

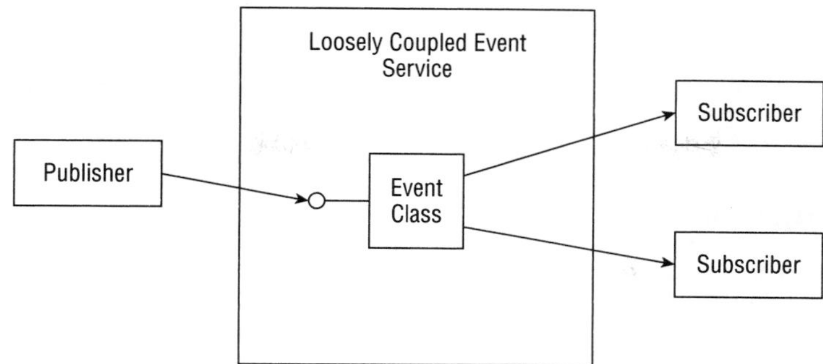

Figure 44-2

Creating a Simple COM+ Application

To create a .NET class that can be configured with Enterprise Services, you have to reference the assembly `System.EnterpriseServices` and add the namespace `System.EnterpriseServices` to the using declarations. The most important class to use is `ServicedComponent`.

The first example shows the basic requirements to create a serviced component. You start by creating a C# library application. All COM+ applications must be written as library applications regardless of whether they will run in their own process or in the process of the client. Name the library `SimpleServer`. Reference the assembly `System.EnterpriseServices` and add the declaration `using System.EnterpriseServices;` to the `assmblyinfo.cs` and `class1.cs` files.

The ServicedComponent Class

Every serviced component class must derive from the base class `ServicedComponent`. `ServicedComponent` itself derives from the class `ContextBoundObject`, so an instance is bound to a .NET Remoting context.

The class `ServicedComponent` has some protected methods that can be overridden, as shown in the following table.

Protected Method	Description
`Activate()` `Deactivate()`	The `Activate()` and `Deactivate()` methods are called if the object is configured to use object pooling. When the object is taken from the pool, the `Activate()` method is called. Before the object is returned to the pool, `Deactivate()` is called.
`CanBePooled()`	This is another method for object pooling. If the object is in an inconsistent state, you can return `false` in your overridden implementation of `CanBePooled()`. This way the object is not put back into the pool, but destroyed instead. A new object will be created for the pool.
`Construct()`	This method is called at instantiation time, where a construction string can be passed to the object. The construction string can be modified by the system administrator. Later in this chapter, you use the construction string to define the database connection string.

Sign the Assembly

Libraries configured with Enterprise Services need a strong name. For some Enterprise Services features it is also necessary to install the assembly in the global assembly cache. Strong names and the global assembly cache are discussed in Chapter 17, "Assemblies."

Assembly Attributes

Some Enterprise Services attributes are also needed. The attribute `ApplicationName` defines the name of the application as it will be seen in the Component Services Explorer. The value of the `Description` attribute shows up as a description within the application configuration tool.

`ApplicationActivation` allows you to define whether the application should be configured as a library application or a server application, using the options `ActivationOption.Library` or `ActivationOption.Server`. With a library application, the application is loaded inside the process of the client. In that case the client might be the ASP.NET runtime. With a server application, a process for the application is started. The name of the process is `dllhost.exe`. With the attribute `ApplicationAccessControl`, you can turn off security so that every user is allowed to use the component.

Rename the file `Class1.cs` to `SimpleComponent.cs` and add these attributes outside the namespace declaration:

```
[assembly: ApplicationName("Wrox EnterpriseDemo")]
[assembly: Description("Wrox Sample Application for Professional C#")]
[assembly: ApplicationActivation(ActivationOption.Server)]
[assembly: ApplicationAccessControl(false)]
```

The following table lists the most important assembly attributes that can be defined with Enterprise Services applications.

Attribute	Description
`[ApplicationName]`	The attribute `[ApplicationName]` defines the name for the COM+ application that shows up in the Component Services Explorer after the component is configured.
`[ApplicationActivation]`	The attribute `[ApplicationActivation]` defines if the application should run as a library within the client application or if a separate process should be started. The options to configure are defined with the enumeration `ActivationOption`. `ActivationOption.Library` defines to run the application inside the process of the client; `ActivationOption.Server` starts its own process, `dllhost.exe`.
`[ApplicationAccessControl]`	The attribute `[ApplicationAccessControl]` defines the security configuration of the application. Using a Boolean value you can enable or disable access control. With the `Authentication` property you can set privacy levels — whether the client should be authenticated with every method call or just with the connection, and whether the data sent should be encrypted.

Creating the Component

In the SimpleComponent.cs file, you can create your serviced component class. With serviced components, it is best to define interfaces that are used as the contract between the client and the component. This is not a strict requirement, but some of the Enterprise Services features (such as setting role-based security on a method or interface level) do require interfaces. Create the interface IGreeting with the method Welcome(). The attribute [ComVisible] is required for serviced component classes and interfaces that can be accessed from Enterprise Services features.

```
using System;
using System.EnterpriseServices;
using System.Runtime.InteropServices;

namespace Wrox.ProCSharp.EnterpriseServices
{
   [ComVisible(true)]
   public interface IGreeting
   {
      string Welcome(string name);
   }
```

The class SimpleComponent derives from the base class ServicedComponent and implements the interface IGreeting. The class ServicedComponent acts as a base class of all serviced component classes, and offers some methods for the activation and construction phases. Applying the attribute [EventTrackingEnabled] to this class makes it possible to monitor the objects with the Component Services Explorer. By default, monitoring is disabled because using this feature reduces performance. The [Description] attribute only specifies text that shows up in the Explorer:

```
   [EventTrackingEnabled(true)]
   [ComVisible(true)]
   [Description("Simple Serviced Component Sample")]
   public class SimpleComponent : ServicedComponent, IGreeting
   {
      public SimpleComponent()
      {
      }
```

The method Welcome() returns only "Hello, " with the name that is passed to the argument. So that you can see some visible result in the Component Services Explorer while the component is running, Thread.Sleep() simulates some processing time:

```
      public string Welcome(string name)
      {
         // simulate some processing time
         System.Threading.Thread.Sleep(1000);
         return "Hello, " + name;
      }
   }
}
```

Other than applying some attributes and deriving the class from ServicedComponent, there's nothing special to do with classes that should use Enterprises Services features. All that is left to do is build and deploy a client application.

In the first sample component, the attribute [EventTrackingEnabled] was set. Some more commonly used attributes that influence the configuration of serviced components are described in the following table.

Attribute Class	Description
[EventTrackingEnabled]	Setting the attribute [EventTrackingEnabled] allows monitoring the component with the Component Services Explorer. Setting this attribute to true has some additional overhead associated; that's why, by default, event tracking is turned off.
[JustInTimeActivation]	With this attribute, the component can be configured to not activate when the caller instantiates the class, but instead when the first method is invoked. Also, with this attribute the component can deactivate itself.
[ObjectPooling]	If the initialization time of a component is long compared to the time of a method call, an object pool can be configured with the attribute [ObjectPooling]. With this attribute, minimum and maximum values can be defined that influence the number of objects in the pool.
[Transaction]	The attribute [Transaction] defines transactional characteristics of the component. Here, the component defines whether a transaction is required, supported, or not supported.

Deployment

Assemblies with serviced components must be configured with COM+. This configuration can be done automatically or by registering the assembly manually.

Automatic Deployment

If a .NET client application that uses the serviced component is started, the COM+ application is configured automatically. This is true for all classes that are derived from the class ServicedComponent. Application and class attributes such as [EventTrackingEnabled] define the characteristics of the configuration.

Automatic deployment has an important drawback. For automatic deployment to work, the client application needs administrative rights. If the client application that invokes the serviced component is ASP.NET, the ASP.NET runtime usually doesn't have administrative rights. With this drawback, automatic deployment is useful only during development time. However, during development, automatic deployment is an extremely advantageous feature because it is not necessary to do manual deployment after every build.

Manual Deployment

You can deploy the assembly manually with the command-line utility .NET Services installation tool regsvcs.exe. Starting the command

```
regsvcs SimpleServer.dll
```

registers the assembly SimpleServer as a COM+ application and configures the included components according to their attributes; it also creates a type library that can be used by COM clients accessing the .NET component.

After you've configured the assembly, you can start the Component Services Explorer by selecting Administrative Tools ⇨ Component Services from the Windows menu on Windows XP or Windows Server 2003. On Windows Vista you have to start the MMC and add the Component Services snap-in to see the Component Services Explorer. In the left tree view of this application, you can select Component Services ⇨ Computers ⇨ My Computer ⇨ COM+ Applications to verify that the application was configured.

Creating an Installer Package

With the Component Services Explorer, you can create Windows installer packages for server or client systems. An installer package for the server includes the assemblies and configuration settings to install the application on a different server. If the serviced component is invoked from applications running on different systems, a proxy must be installed on the client system. The installer package for the client includes assemblies and configuration for proxies.

To create an installer package, you can start the Component Services Explorer, select the COM+ application, select the menu options Action ⇨ Export, and click the Next button in the first dialog. The dialog shown in Figure 44-3 opens. In this dialog, you can export either a Server application or an application proxy. With the option Server application you can also configure to export user identities with roles. This option should be selected only if the target system is in the same domain as the system where the package is created, because the configured user identities are put into the installer package. With the option application proxy, an installer package for the client system is created.

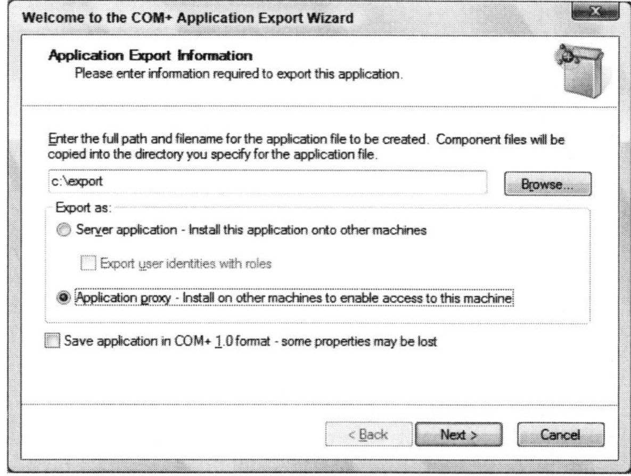

Figure 44-3

The option to create an application proxy is not available if the application is configured as a library application.

To install the proxy, you just have to start `setup.exe` from the installer package. Be aware that an application proxy cannot be installed on the same system where the application is installed. After installation of the application proxy, you can see an entry in Component Services Explorer that represents the application proxy. With the application proxy the only option that can be configured is the name of the server in the Activation tab, as discussed in the next section.

Component Services Explorer

After a successful configuration, you can see `Wrox EnterpriseDemo` as an application name in the tree view of the Component Services Explorer. This name was set by the attribute `[ApplicationName]`. Selecting Action ⇨ Properties opens the dialog box shown in Figure 44-4. Both the name and the description have been configured by using attributes. When you select the Activation tab, you can see that the application is configured as a server application because this has been defined with the `[ApplicationActivation]` attribute, and selecting the Security tab shows that the "Enforce access checks for this application" option is not selected because the attribute `[ApplicationAccessControl]` was set to `false`.

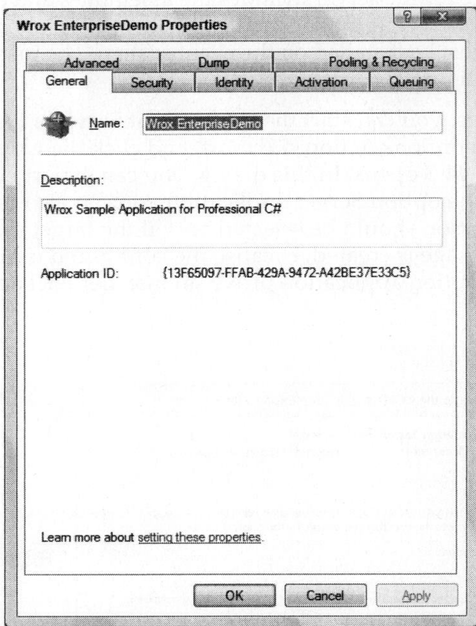

Figure 44-4

The following is a list of some more options that can be set with this application:

- **Security** — With the security configuration, you can enable or disable access checks. If security is enabled, you can set access checks to the application level, the component, the interface, and to the method level. It is also possible to encrypt messages that are sent across the network using packet privacy as an authentication level for calls. Of course, this also increases the overhead.
- **Identity** — With server applications, you can use the Identity tab to configure the user account that will be used for the process that hosts the application. By default, this is the interactive user. This setting is very useful while debugging the application but cannot be used on a production system if the application is running on a server, because there might not be anybody logged on. Before installing the application on the production system you should test the application by using a specific user for the application.
- **Activation** — The Activation tab allows you to configure the application either as a library or as a server application. Two new options with COM+ 1.5 are the option to run the application as a Windows Service and to use SOAP to access the application. Windows Services are discussed in Chapter 23, "Windows Services." Selecting the SOAP option uses .NET Remoting configured within Internet Information Server to access the component. Instead of using .NET Remoting,

later in this chapter the component will be accessed using WCF. WCF is discussed in Chapter 42, "Windows Communication Foundation."

With an application proxy, the option "Remote server name" is the only option that can be configured. This option sets the name of the server. By default, the DCOM protocol is used as the network protocol. However, if SOAP is selected in the server configuration, the communication happens through .NET Remoting.

- **Queuing** — The Queuing configuration is required for service components that make use of message queuing.
- **Advanced** — On the Advanced tab, you can specify whether the application should be shut down after a certain period of client inactivity. You can also specify whether to lock a certain configuration so that no one can change it accidentally.
- **Dump** — If the application crashes, you can specify the directory where the dumps should be stored. This is useful for components developed with C++.
- **Pooling and Recycling** — Pooling and recycling is a new option with COM+ 1.5. With this option, you can configure whether the application should be restarted (recycled) depending on application lifetime, memory needs, number of calls, and so on.

With the Component Services Explorer, you can also view and configure the component itself. When opening child elements of the application, you can view the component `Wrox.ProCSharp.EnterpriseServices.SimpleComponent`. Selecting Action ⇨ Properties opens the dialog box shown in Figure 44-5.

Using this dialog box, you can configure these options:

- **Transactions** — On the Transactions tab, you can specify whether the component requires transactions. You use this feature in the next example.
- **Security** — If security is enabled for the application, with this configuration you can define what roles are allowed to use the component.

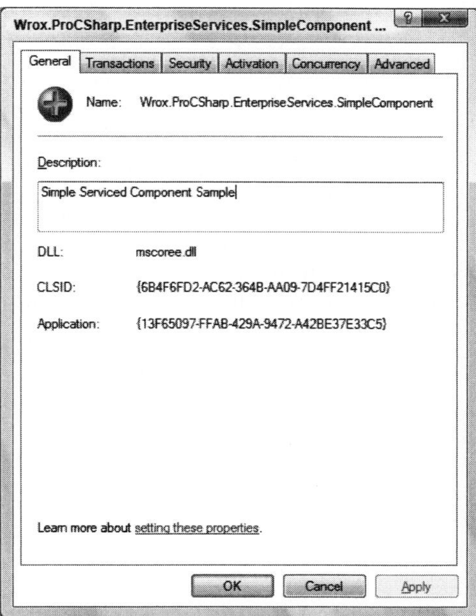

Figure 44-5

- **Activation** — The Activation configuration enables you to set object pooling and to assign a construction string.
- **Concurrency** — If the component is not thread-safe, concurrency can be set to Required or Requires New. This way the COM+ runtime allows only one thread at a time to access the component.

Client Application

After building the serviced component library, you can create a client application. This can be as simple as a C# console application. After you've created the project for the client, you have to reference both the assembly from the serviced component, `SimpleServer`, and the assembly `System.EnterpriseServices`. Then you can write the code to instantiate a new `SimpleComponent` instance and invoke the method `Welcome()`. In the following code, the `Welcome()` method is called 10 times. The `using` statement helps to release the resources allocated with the instance before the garbage collector takes action. With the `using` statement, the `Dispose()` method of the serviced component is called when the scope of the `using` statement ends.

```
using System;

namespace Wrox.ProCSharp.EnterpriseServices
{
    class Program
    {
        static void Main()
        {
            using (SimpleComponent obj = new SimpleComponent())
            {
                for (int i = 0; i < 10; i++)
                {
                    Console.WriteLine(obj.Welcome("Katie"));
                }
            }
        }
    }
}
```

If you start the client application before configuring the server, the server will be configured automatically. The automatic configuration of the server is done with the values that you've specified using attributes. For a test you can unregister the serviced component and start the client again. If the serviced component is configured during the start of the client application, the startup needs more time. Remember that this feature is useful only during development time. Administrative rights are also needed for automatic deployment. If you are starting the application from within Visual Studio, that means you should start Visual Studio with administrative rights.

While the application is running, you can monitor the serviced component with the Component Services Explorer. By selecting Components in the tree view and choosing View ⇨ Detail, you can view the number of instantiated objects if the attribute `[EventTrackingEnabled]` is set.

As you've seen, creating serviced components is just a matter of deriving the class from the base class `ServicedComponent` and setting some attributes to configure the application. Next, you see how transactions can be used with serviced components.

Transactions

Automatic transactions are the most frequently used feature of Enterprise Services. Using Enterprise Services, you can mark the components as requiring a transaction, and the transaction is then created from the COM+ runtime. All transaction-aware objects inside the component, such as ADO.NET connections, run inside the transaction.

You can read more about the concepts of transactions in Chapter 22, "Transactions."

Transaction Attributes

Serviced components can be marked with the `[Transaction]` attribute to define if and how transactions are required for the component.

Figure 44-6 shows multiple components with different transactional configurations. The client invokes component A. Because component A is configured with `Transaction Required` and no transaction existed previously, the new transaction, `1`, is created. Component A invokes component B, which in turn invokes component C. Because component B is configured with `Transaction Supported`, and the configuration of component C is set to `Transaction Required`, all three components (A, B, and C) do use the same transaction context. If component B were configured with the transaction setting `NotSupported`, component C would get a new transaction. Component D is configured with the setting `New Transaction Required`, so a new transaction is created when it is called by component A.

The following table lists the different values that you can set with the `TransactionOption` enumeration:

TransactionOption Value	Description
`Required`	Setting the `[Transaction]` attribute to `TransactionOption.Required` means that the component runs inside a transaction. If a transaction has been created already, the component will run in the same transaction. If no transaction exists, a transaction will be created.
`RequiresNew`	`TransactionOption.RequiresNew` always results in a newly created transaction. The component never participates in the same transaction as the caller.
`Supported`	With `TransactionOption.Supported`, the component doesn't need transactions itself. However, the transaction will span the caller and the called component, if these components require transactions.
`NotSupported`	The option `TransactionOption.NotSupported` means that the component never runs in a transaction, regardless of whether the caller has a transaction.
`Disabled`	`TransactionOption.Disabled` means that a possible transaction of the current context is ignored.

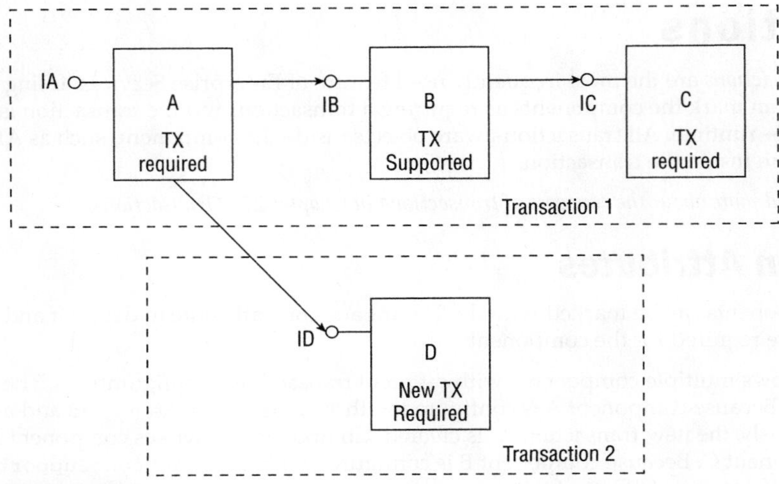

Figure 44-6

Transaction Results

A transaction can be influenced by setting the *consistent* and the *done* bit of the context. If the consistent bit is set to `true`, the component is happy with the outcome of the transaction. The transaction can be committed if all components participating with the transaction are similarly successful. If the consistent bit is set to `false`, the component is not happy with the outcome of the transaction, and the transaction will be aborted when the root object that started the transaction is finished. If the done bit is set, the object can be deactivated after the method call ends. A new instance will be created with the next method call.

The consistent and done bits can be set using four methods of the `ContextUtil` class with the results that you can see in the following table.

ContextUtil Method	Consistent Bit	Done Bit
`SetComplete`	`true`	`true`
`SetAbort`	`false`	`true`
`EnableCommit`	`true`	`false`
`DisableCommit`	`false`	`false`

With .NET it is also possible to set the consistent and done bit by applying the attribute `[AutoComplete]` to the method instead of calling the `ContextUtil` methods. With this attribute the method `ContextUtil.SetComplete()` will be called automatically if the method is successful. If the method fails and an exception is thrown, with `[AutoComplete]` the method `ContextUtil.SetAbort()` will be called.

Sample Application

This sample application simulates a simplified scenario that writes new orders to the Northwind sample database. As shown in Figure 44-7, multiple components are used with the COM+ application. The class `OrderControl` is called from the client application to create new orders. `OrderControl` uses the `OrderData` component. `OrderData` has the responsibility of creating a new entry in the `Order` table of the Northwind database. The `OrderData` component uses the `OrderLineData` component to write Order Detail entries to the database. Both `OrderData` and `OrderLineData` must participate in the same transaction.

Start by creating a C# Component library with the name `NorthwindComponent`. Sign the assembly with a keyfile, and define the Enterprise Services application attributes as shown in the following code:

```
[assembly: ApplicationName("Wrox.NorthwindDemo")]
[assembly: ApplicationActivation(ActivationOption.Server)]
[assembly: ApplicationAccessControl(false)]
```

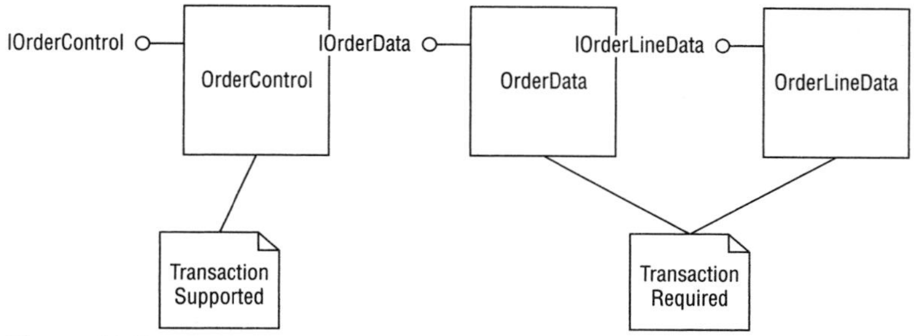

IOrderControl
OrderControl
IOrderData
OrderData
IOrderLineData
OrderLineData
Transaction Supported
Transaction Required

Figure 44-7

Entity Classes

Next add the entity classes `Order` and `OrderLine` that represent the columns in the Northwind database tables `Order` and `Order Details`. Entity classes are just data holders representing the data that is important for the application domain — in that case for doing orders. The class `Order` has a static method `Create()` that creates and returns a new instance of the class `Order`, and initializes this instance with the arguments passed to this method. Also, the class `Order` has some read-only properties `OrderId`, `CustomerId`, `OrderData`, `ShipAddress`, `ShipCity`, and `ShipCountry`. The value of the `OrderId` property is not known at creation time of the class `Order`, but because the `Order` table in the Northwind database has an auto-increment attribute, the value is just known after the order is written to the database. The method `SetOrderId()` is used to set the corresponding ID after the order has been written to the database. Because this method is called by a class inside the same assembly, the access level of this method is set to `internal`. The method `AddOrderLine()` adds order details to the order:

```
using System;
using System.Collections.Generic;

namespace Wrox.ProCSharp.EnterpriseServices
{
   [Serializable]
   public class Order
   {
      public static Order Create(string customerId, DateTime orderDate,
                     string shipAddress, string shipCity, string shipCountry)
      {
         return new Order()
         {
            CustomerId = customerId,
            OrderDate = orderDate,
            ShipAddress = shipAddress,
```

(continued)

(continued)

```
                ShipCity = shipCity,
                ShipCountry = shipCountry
            }
        }

        public Order()
        {
        }

        internal void SetOrderId(int orderId)
        {
            this.OrderId = orderId;
        }

        public void AddOrderLine(OrderLine orderLine)
        {
            orderLines.Add(orderLine);
        }

        private List<OrderLine> orderLines = new List<OrderLine>();

        public int OrderId { get; private set; }
        public string CustomerId { get; private set; }
        public DateTime OrderDate { get; private set; }
        public string ShipAddress { get; private set; }
        public string ShipCity { get; private set; }
        public string ShipCountry { get; private set; }

        public OrderLine[] OrderLines
        {
            get
            {
                OrderLine[] ol = new OrderLine[orderLines.Count];
                orderLines.CopyTo(ol);
                return ol;
            }
        }
    }
}
```

The second entity class is `OrderLine`. `OrderLine` has a static `Create()` method similar to the one of the `Order` class. Other than that, the class only has some properties for the fields `productId`, `unitPrice`, and `quantity`:

```
using System;

namespace Wrox.ProCSharp.EnterpriseServices
{
    [Serializable]
    public class OrderLine
    {
        public static OrderLine Create(int productId, float unitPrice,
                                       int quantity)
        {
            return new OrderLine()
```

```
            {
               ProductId = productId,
               UnitPrice = unitPrice,
               Quantity = quantity
            };
         }
         public OrderLine()
         {
         }

         public int ProductId { get; set; }
         public float UnitPrice { get; set; }
         public int Quantity { get; set; }
      }
   }
```

The OrderControl Component

The class `OrderControl` represents a simple business services component. In this example, just one method, `NewOrder()`, is defined in the interface `IOrderControl`. The implementation of `NewOrder()` does nothing more than instantiate a new instance of the data services component `OrderData` and call the method `Insert()` to write an `Order` object to the database. In a more complex scenario, this method could be extended to write a log entry to a database or to invoke a queued component to send the `Order` object to a message queue:

```
using System;
using System.EnterpriseServices;
using System.Runtime.InteropServices;

namespace Wrox.ProCSharp.EnterpriseServices
{
   [ComVisible(true)]
   public interface IOrderControl
   {
      void NewOrder(Order order);
   }

   [Transaction(TransactionOption.Supported)]
   [EventTrackingEnabled(true)]
   [ComVisible(true)]
   public class OrderControl : ServicedComponent, IOrderControl
   {
      [AutoComplete()]
      public void NewOrder(Order order)
      {
         using (OrderData data = new OrderData())
         {
            data.Insert(order);
         }
      }
   }
}
```

The OrderData Component

The OrderData class is responsible for writing the values of Order objects to the database. The interface IOrderUpdate defines the Insert() method. You can extend this interface to also support an Update() method where an existing entry in the database is updated:

```
using System;
using System.Data.SqlClient;
using System.EnterpriseServices;
using System.Runtime.InteropServices;

namespace Wrox.ProCSharp.EnterpriseServices
{
   [ComVisible(true)]
   public interface IOrderUpdate
   {
      void Insert(Order order);
   }
```

The class OrderData has the attribute [Transaction] with the value TransactionOption.Required applied. This means that the component will run in a transaction in any case. Either a transaction is created by the caller and OrderData uses the same transaction, or a new transaction is created. Here a new transaction will be created because the calling component OrderControl doesn't have a transaction.

With serviced components, you can use only default constructors. However, you can use the Component Services Explorer to configure a construction string that is sent to a component (see Figure 44-8). Selecting the Activation tab of the component configuration enables you to change the construction string. The option "Enable object construction" is turned on when the attribute [ConstructionEnabled] is set, as it is with the class OrderData. The Default property of the [ConstructionEnabled] attribute defines the default connection string shown in the Activation settings after registration of the assembly. Setting this attribute also requires you to overload the method Construct() from the base class ServicedComponent. This method is called by the COM+ runtime at object instantiation, and the construction string is passed as an argument. The construction string is set to the variable connectionString, which is used later to connect to the database:

```
   [Transaction(TransactionOption.Required)]
   [EventTrackingEnabled(true)]
   [ConstructionEnabled(true, Default="server=(local);" +
                        "database=northwind;trusted_connection=true")]
   [ComVisible(true)]
   public class OrderData : ServicedComponent, IOrderUpdate
   {
      private string connectionString;

      protected override void Construct(string s)
      {
         connectionString = s;
      }
```

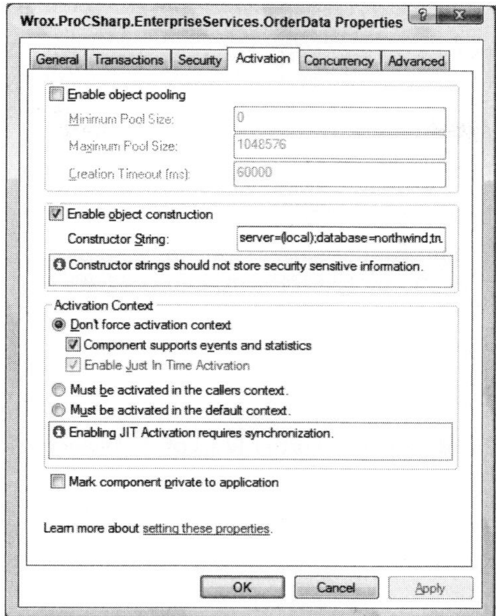

Figure 44-8

The method `Insert()` is at the heart of the component. Here, you use ADO.NET to write the `Order` object to the database. (ADO.NET is discussed in more detail in Chapter 26, "Data Access.") In this example, you create a `SqlConnection` object where the connection string that was set with the `Construct()` method is used to initialize the object.

The attribute `[AutoComplete()]` is applied to the method to use automatic transaction handling as discussed earlier:

```
      [AutoComplete()]
      public void Insert(Order order)
      {
         SqlConnection connection = new SqlConnection(connectionString);
```

The method `connection.CreateCommand()` creates a `SqlCommand` object where the `CommandText` property is set to a SQL `INSERT` statement to add a new record to the `Orders` table. The method `ExecuteNonQuery()` executes the SQL statement:

```
         try
         {
            SqlCommand command = connection.CreateCommand();
            command.CommandText = "INSERT INTO Orders (CustomerId," +
               "OrderDate, ShipAddress, ShipCity, ShipCountry)" +
               "VALUES(@CustomerId, @OrderDate, @ShipAddress, @ShipCity, " +
               "@ShipCountry)";
            command.Parameters.AddWithValue("@CustomerId", order.CustomerId);
            command.Parameters.AddWithValue("@OrderDate", order.OrderDate);
            command.Parameters.AddWithValue("@ShipAddress",
                                            order.ShipAddress);
```

(continued)

(continued)

```
                command.Parameters.AddWithValue("@ShipCity", order.ShipCity);
                command.Parameters.AddWithValue("@ShipCountry",
                                                      order.ShipCountry);

                connection.Open();

                command.ExecuteNonQuery();
```

Because `OrderId` is defined as an auto-increment value in the database, and this ID is needed for writing the Order Details to the database, `OrderId` is read by using `@@IDENTITY`. Then it is set to the `Order` object by calling the method `SetOrderId()`:

```
                command.CommandText = "SELECT @@IDENTITY AS 'Identity'";
                object identity = command.ExecuteScalar();
                order.SetOrderId(Convert.ToInt32(identity));
```

After the order is written to the database, all order lines of the order are written using the `OrderLineData` component:

```
                using (OrderLineData updateOrderLine = new OrderLineData())
                {
                   foreach (OrderLine orderLine in order.OrderLines)
                   {
                      updateOrderLine.Insert(order.OrderId, orderLine);
                   }
                }
             }
```

Finally, regardless of whether the code in the `try` block was successful or an exception occurred, the connection is closed:

```
             finally
             {
                connection.Close();
             }
          }
       }
    }
```

The OrderLineData Component

The `OrderLineData` component is implemented similarly to the `OrderData` component. You use the attribute `[ConstructionEnabled]` to define the database connection string:

```
using System;
using System.EnterpriseServices;
using System.Runtime.InteropServices;
using System.Data;
using System.Data.SqlClient;

namespace Wrox.ProCSharp.EnterpriseServices
{
   [ComVisible(true)]
   public interface IOrderLineUpdate
   {
      void Insert(int orderId, OrderLine orderDetail);
   }
```

```
   [Transaction(TransactionOption.Required)]
   [EventTrackingEnabled(true)]
   [ConstructionEnabled(true, Default="server=(local);database=northwind;" +
         "trusted_connection=true")]
   [ComVisible(true)]
   public class OrderLineData : ServicedComponent, IOrderLineUpdate
   {
      private string connectionString;

      protected override void Construct(string s)
      {
         connectionString = s;
      }
```

With the `Insert()` method of the `OrderLineData` class in this example, the `[AutoComplete]` attribute isn't used to demonstrate a different way to define the transaction outcome. It shows how to set the consistent and done bits with the `ContextUtil` class instead. The method `SetComplete()` is called at the end of the method, depending on whether inserting the data in the database was successful. If there is an error where an exception is thrown, the method `SetAbort()` sets the consistent bit to `false` instead, so that the transaction is undone along with all components participating in the transaction:

```
      public void Insert(int orderId, OrderLine orderDetail)
      {
         SqlConnection connection = new SqlConnection(connectionString);
         try
         {
            SqlCommand command = connection.CreateCommand();
            command.CommandText = "INSERT INTO [Order Details] (OrderId, " +
               "ProductId, UnitPrice, Quantity)" +
               "VALUES(@OrderId, @ProductId, @UnitPrice, @Quantity)";
            command.Parameters.AddWithValue("@OrderId", orderId);
            command.Parameters.AddWithValue("@ProductId",
                                            orderDetail.ProductId);
            command.Parameters.AddWithValue("@UnitPrice",
                                            orderDetail.UnitPrice);
            command.Parameters.AddWithValue("@Quantity",
                                            orderDetail.Quantity);

            connection.Open();

            command.ExecuteNonQuery();
         }
         catch (Exception)
         {
            ContextUtil.SetAbort();
            throw;
         }
         finally
         {
            connection.Close();
         }
         ContextUtil.SetComplete();
      }
   }
}
```

Client Application

Having built the component, you can create a client application. For testing purposes, a console application serves the purpose. After referencing the assembly `NorthwindComponent` and the assembly `System.EnterpriseServices`, you can create a new order with the static method `Order.Create()`. `order.AddOrderLine()` adds an order line to the order. `OrderLine.Create()` accepts product IDs, the price, and quantity to create an order line. In a real application, it would be useful to add a `Product` class instead of using product IDs, but the purpose of this example is to demonstrate transactions in general.

Finally, the serviced component class `OrderControl` is created to invoke the method `NewOrder()`:

```
Order order = Order.Create("PICCO", DateTime.Today, "Georg Pipps",
                           "Salzburg", "Austria");
order.AddOrderLine(OrderLine.Create(16, 17.45F, 2));
order.AddOrderLine(OrderLine.Create(67, 14, 1));

using (OrderControl orderControl = new OrderControl())
{
   orderControl.NewOrder(order);
}
```

You can try to write products that don't exist to the `OrderLine` (using a product ID that is not listed in the table Products). In this case, the transaction will be aborted, and no data will be written to the database.

While a transaction is active, you can see the transaction in the Component Services Explorer by selecting Distributed Transaction Coordinator in the tree view (see Figure 44-9).

You might have to add a sleep time to the `Insert()` method of the `OrderData` class to see the live transaction; otherwise, the transaction might be completed too fast to display.

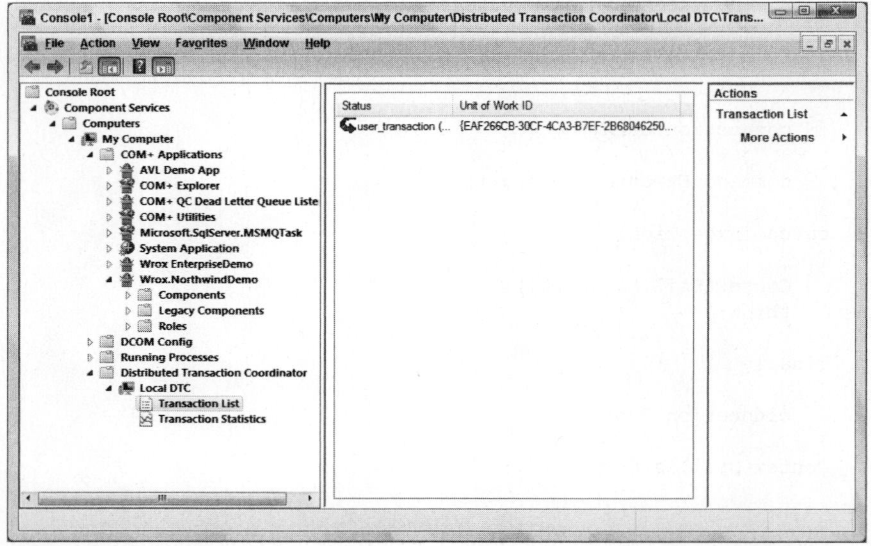

Figure 44-9

If you are debugging the serviced component while it is running inside a transaction, be aware that the default transaction timeout is 60 seconds for serviced components. You can change the default for the complete system in the Component Services Explorer by clicking My Computer, selecting Action ⇨ Properties, and opening the Options tab. Instead of changing the value for the complete system, the transaction timeout can also be configured on a component-by-component level with the Transaction options of the component.

Integrating WCF and Enterprise Services

Windows Communication Foundation (WCF) is a new communication technology that is part of .NET Framework 3.0. WCF is covered in detail in Chapter 42, "Windows Communication Foundation." .NET Enterprise Services offers a great integration model with WCF.

WCF Service Façade

Adding a WCF façade to an Enterprise Services application allows using WCF clients to access the serviced components. Instead of using the DCOM protocol, with WCF you can have different protocols such as HTTP with SOAP or TCP with a binary formatting.

You can create a WCF façade from Visual Studio 2008 by selecting Tools ⇨ WCF SvcConfigEditor. With this tool started select File ⇨ Integrate ⇨ COM+ Application . . . . Select the COM+ Application Wrox.NorthwindDemo, the component `Wrox.ProCSharp.EnterpriseServices.OrderControl`, and the interface `IOrderControl` as shown in Figure 44-10.

Instead of using Visual Studio to create the WCF façade, you can use the command-line utility `comsvcconfig.exe`. *You can find this utility in the directory* `<Windows>\Microsoft.NET\Framework\v3.0\Windows Communication Foundation`.

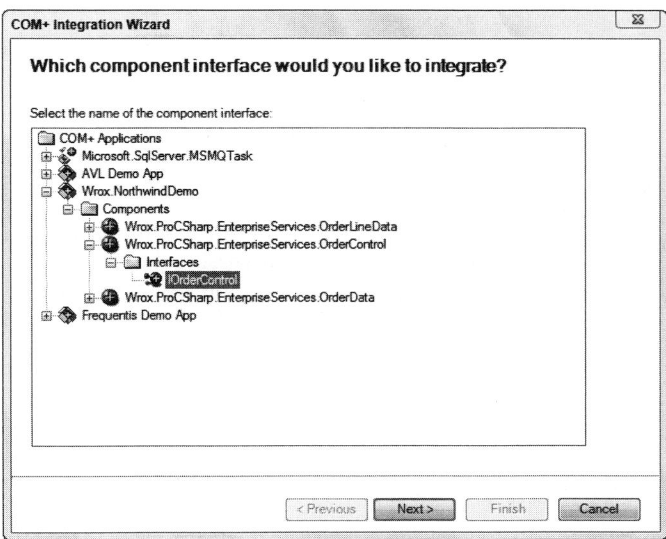

Figure 44-10

With the next dialog you can select all the methods from the interface `IOrderControl` that should be available to WCF clients. With the interface `IOrderControl` just one method, `NewOrder()`, is shown.

The next dialog shown in Figure 44-11 allows configuration of the hosting options. With the hosting option, you can specify in which process the WCF service should run. When you select the COM+ hosted option, the WCF façade runs within the `dllhost.exe` process of COM+. This option is possible only if the application is configured as a server application: `[ApplicationActivation(ActivationOption.Server)]`. The Web hosted it is specifies that the WCF channel is listens inside a process of the IIS or WAS (Windows Activation Services) worker process. WAS is new with Windows Vista and Windows Server 2008. Selecting "Web hosted in-process" means that the library of the Enterprise Services component runs within the IIS or WAS worker process. This configuration is possible only if the application is configured as a library application. `[ApplicationActivation(ActivationOption.Library)]`.

Selecting the "Add MEX endpoint" option adds a MEX (Metadata Exchange) endpoint to the WCF configuration file, so that the client programmer can access the metadata of the service using WS-Metadata Exchange.

MEX is explained in Chapter 42, "Windows Communication Foundation."

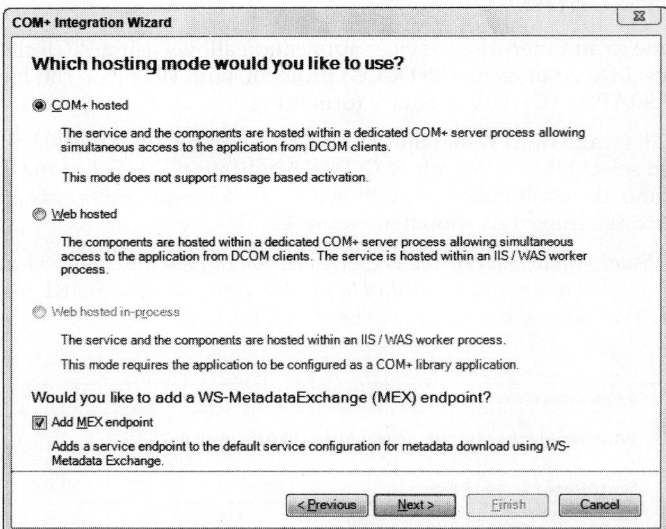

Figure 44-11

With the next dialog shown in Figure 44-12 you can specify the communication mode to access the WCF façade. Depending on your requirements, if the client is accessing the service across a firewall or platform-independent communication is required, HTTP is the best choice. TCP offers faster communication across machines for .NET clients, and Named Pipes is the fastest option if the client application is running on the same system as the service.

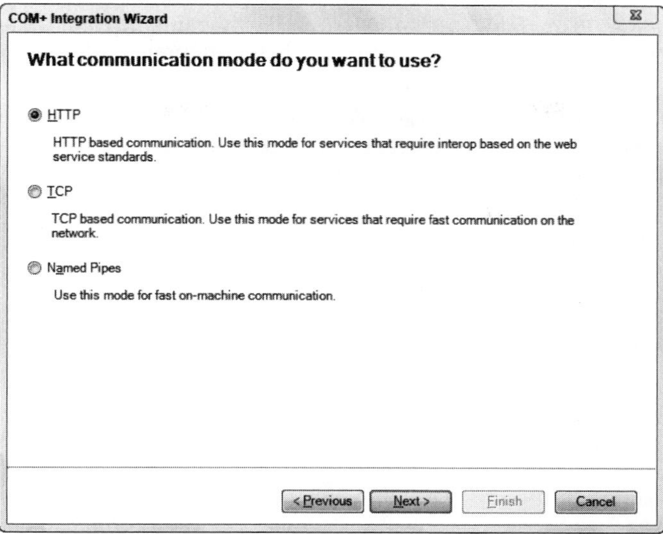

Figure 44-12

The next dialog requests information about the base address of the service that depends on the communication protocol selection, as shown in Figure 44-13.

Figure 44-13

The last dialog shows the location of the endpoint configuration. The base directory for the configurations is `<Program Files>\ComPlus Applications` followed by the unique ID of the application. In this directory you can find the file `application.config`. This configuration file lists the behaviors and endpoints for WCF.

The `<service>` element specifies the exposed WCF service with the endpoint configuration. The binding is set to `wsHttpBinding` with a `comTransactionalBinding` configuration, so transactions can flow from the caller to the serviced component. With other network and client requirements, you can specify a different binding, but this is all covered in Chapter 42.

```
<?xml version="1.0" encoding="utf-8"?>
<configuration>
   <system.serviceModel>
      <behaviors>
         <serviceBehaviors>
            <behavior name="ComServiceMexBehavior">
               <serviceMetadata httpGetEnabled="false" />
               <serviceDebug />
            </behavior>
         </serviceBehaviors>
      </behaviors>
      <bindings>
         <netNamedPipeBinding>
            <binding name="comNonTransactionalBinding" />
            <binding name="comTransactionalBinding" transactionFlow="true" />
         </netNamedPipeBinding>
         <wsHttpBinding>
            <binding name="comNonTransactionalBinding" />
            <binding name="comTransactionalBinding" transactionFlow="true" />
         </wsHttpBinding>
      </bindings>
      <comContracts>
         <comContract contract="{E1B02E09-EE48-3B6B-946F-E6A8BAEC6340}"
            name="IOrderControl"
            namespace=
                "http://tempuri.org/E1B02E09-EE48-3B6B-946F-E6A8BAEC6340"
            requiresSession="true">
            <exposedMethods>
               <add exposedMethod="NewOrder" />
            </exposedMethods>
         </comContract>
      </comContracts>
      <services>
         <service behaviorConfiguration="ComServiceMexBehavior"
            name="{BC198295-74F7-4441-8EC1-04A174C6BA45},
                 {D30F79D7-6DE7-33DE-B3FC-C21F6B02A48D}">
            <endpoint address="IOrderControl" binding="wsHttpBinding"
                bindingConfiguration="comTransactionalBinding"
                contract="{E1B02E09-EE48-3B6B-946F-E6A8BAEC6340}" />
            <endpoint address="mex" binding="mexHttpBinding"
                contract="IMetadataExchange" />
            <host>
               <baseAddresses>
```

```
                    <add baseAddress=
                      "http://localhost:8088/NorthwindService" />
                 </baseAddresses>
              </host>
           </service>
        </services>
     </system.serviceModel>
  </configuration>
```

Before you can start the server application you need to change the security to allow the user that runs the application to register ports for listening. Otherwise a normal user is not allowed to register a listener port. On Windows Vista you can do this with the `netsh` command as shown. The option `http` changes the ACL for the HTTP protocol. The port number and the name of the service are defined with the URL, and the user option specifies the name of the user that starts the listener service.

```
netsh http urlacl url=http://+:8088/NorthwindService user=username
```

Client Application

Create a new console application named `WCFClientApp`. Because the service offers a MEX endpoint, you can add a service reference from Visual Studio by selecting Project ⇨ Add Service Reference . . . (see Figure 44-14).

If the service is COM+ hosted, you have to start the application before you can access the MEX data. If the service is hosted inside WAS, the application is started automatically.

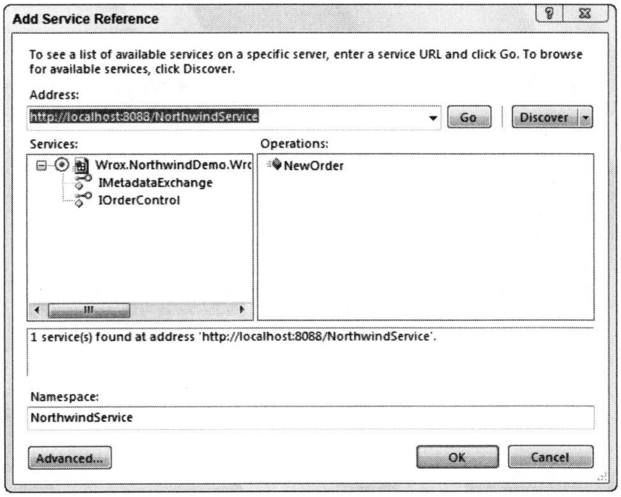

Figure 44-14

With the service reference a proxy class is created, the assemblies `System.ServiceModel` and `System.Runtime.Serialization` are referenced, and an application configuration file referencing the service is added to the client application.

Now, you can use the generated entity classes and the proxy class `OrderControlClient` to send an order request to the serviced component:

```
static void Main()
{
   Order order = new Order();
   order.customerId = "PICCO";
   order.orderDate = DateTime.Today;
   order.shipAddress = "Georg Pipps";
   order.shipCity = "Salzburg";
   order.shipCountry = "Austria";
   OrderLine line1 = new OrderLine();
   line1.productId = 16;
   line1.unitPrice = 17.45F;
   line1.quantity = 2;
   OrderLine line2 = new OrderLine();
   line2.productId = 67;
   line2.unitPrice = 14;
   line2.quantity = 1;
   OrderLine[] orderLines = { line1, line2 };
   order.orderLines = orderLines;

   OrderControlClient occ = new OrderControlClient();
   occ.NewOrder(order);
}
```

Summary

This chapter discussed the rich features offered by Enterprise Services, such as automatic transactions, object pooling, queued components, and loosely coupled events.

To create serviced components, you have to reference the assembly `System.EnterpriseServices`. The base class of all serviced components is `ServicedComponent`. In this class, the context makes it possible to intercept method calls. You can use attributes to specify the interception that will be used. You also learned how to configure an application and its components using attributes, as well as how to manage transactions and specify the transactional requirements of components by using the `[Transaction]` attribute. You've also seen how well Enterprise Services integrates with the new communication technology Windows Communication Foundation, by creating a WCF façade.

This chapter showed how to use Enterprise Services, a feature offered by the operating system. The next chapter gives information on how to use another feature from the operating system that is used for communication as well: message queuing.

45

Message Queuing

`System.Messaging` is a namespace that includes classes for reading and writing messages with the Message Queuing facility of the Windows operating system. Messaging can be used in a disconnected scenario where the client and server needn't be running at the same time.

This chapter looks at the following topics:

- ❑ An overview of Message Queuing
- ❑ Message Queuing architecture
- ❑ Message queue administrative tools
- ❑ Programming Message Queuing
- ❑ Course order sample application
- ❑ Message Queuing with WCF

Overview

Before diving into programming Message Queuing, this section discusses the basic concepts of messaging and compares it to synchronous and asynchronous programming. With synchronous programming, when a method is invoked, the caller has to wait until the method is completed. With asynchronous programming, the calling thread starts the method that runs concurrently. Asynchronous programming can be done with delegates, class libraries that already support asynchronous methods (for example, Web service proxies, `System.Net`, and `System.IO` classes), or by using custom threads (see Chapter 19, "Threading and Synchronization"). With both synchronous and asynchronous programming, the client and the server must be running at the same time.

Although Message Queuing operates asynchronously, because the client (sender) does not wait for the server (receiver) to read the data sent to it, there is a crucial difference between Message Queuing and asynchronous programming: Message Queuing can be done in a disconnected environment. At the time data is sent, the receiver can be offline. Later, when the receiver goes online, it receives the data without intervention from the sending application.

You can compare connected and disconnected programming with talking to someone on the phone and sending an email. When talking to someone on the phone, both participants must be connected at the same time; the communication is synchronous. With an email, the sender isn't sure when the email will be dealt with. People using this technology are working in a disconnected mode. Of course the email may never be dealt with — it may be ignored. That's in the nature of disconnected communication. To avoid this problem, it is possible to ask for a reply to confirm that the email has been read. If the answer doesn't arrive within a time limit, you may be required to deal with this "exception." This is also possible with Message Queuing.

In some ways, Message Queuing is email for application-to-application communication, instead of person-to-person communication. However, this gives you a lot of features that are not available with mailing services, such as guaranteed delivery, transactions, confirmations, express mode using memory, and so on. As you see in the next section, Message Queuing has a lot of features useful for communication between applications.

With Message Queuing, you can send, receive, and route messages in a connected or disconnected environment. Figure 45-1 shows a very simple way of using messages. The sender sends messages to the message queue, and the receiver receives messages from the queue.

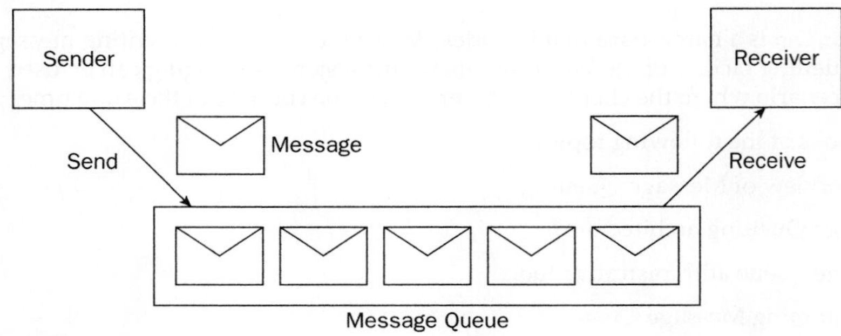

Figure 45-1

When to Use Message Queuing

One case in which Message Queuing is useful is when the client application is often disconnected from the network (for example, when a salesperson is visiting a customer onsite). The salesperson can enter order data directly at the customer's site. The application sends a message for each order to the message queue that is located on the client's system (see Figure 45-2). As soon as the salesperson is back in the office, the order is automatically transferred from the message queue of the client system to the message queue of the target system, where the message is processed.

In addition to using a laptop, the salesperson could use a Pocket Windows device where Message Queuing is available.

Message Queuing can also be useful in a connected environment. Imagine an e-commerce site (see Figure 45-3) where the server is fully loaded with order transactions at certain times, for example, early evening and weekends, but the load is low at nighttime. A solution would be to buy a faster server or to add additional servers to the system so that the peaks can be handled. But there's a cheaper solution: flatten the peak loads by moving transactions from the times with higher loads to the times with lower loads. In this scheme, orders are sent to the message queue, and the receiving side reads the orders at the rates that are useful for the database system. The load of the system is now flattened over time so that the server dealing with the transactions can be less expensive than an upgrade of the database server(s).

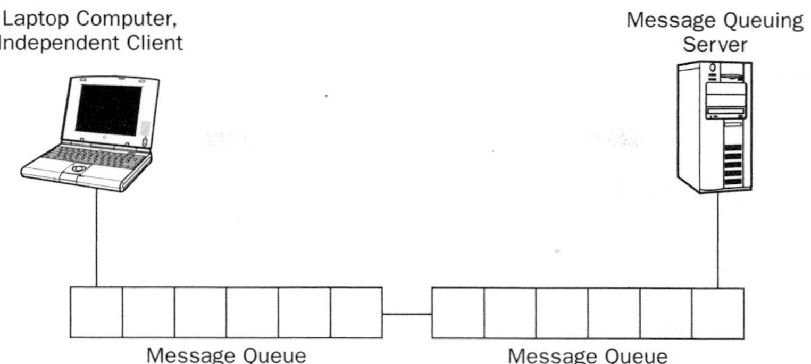

Figure 45-2

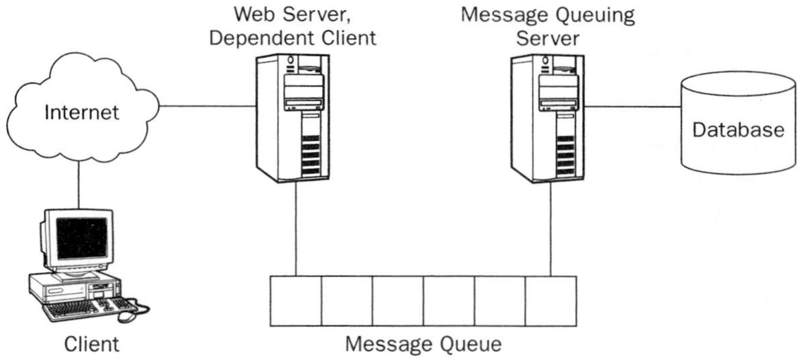

Figure 45-3

Message Queuing Features

Message Queuing is part of the Windows operating system. The main features of this service are:

- Messages can be sent in a disconnected environment. It is not necessary for the sending and receiving applications to run at the same time.
- With express mode, messages can be sent very quickly. Express-mode messages are just stored in memory.
- For a recoverable mechanism, messages can be sent using guaranteed delivery. Recoverable messages are stored within files. They are delivered even in cases when the server reboots.
- Message queues can be secured with access-control lists to define which users can send or receive messages from a queue. Messages can also be encrypted to avoid network sniffers reading them. Messages can be sent with priorities so that high-priority items are handled faster.
- Message Queuing 3.0 supports sending multicast messages.
- Message Queuing 4.0 supports poison messages. A poison message is one that isn't getting resolved. You can define a *poison queue* where unresolved messages are moved. For example, if the job after reading the message from the normal queue was to insert it into the database, but the message did not get into the database and thus this job failed, it would get sent to the poison queue. It is someone's job to handle the poison queue — and that person should deal with the message in a way that resolves it.

Because Message Queuing is part of the operating system, you cannot install Message Queuing 4.0 on a Windows XP or Windows Server 2003 system. Message Queuing 4.0 is part of Windows Server 2008 and Windows Vista.

The remainder of this chapter discusses how these features can be used.

Message Queuing Products

Message Queuing 4.0 is part of Windows Vista and Windows Server 2008. Windows 2000 was delivered with Message Queuing 2.0, which didn't have support for the HTTP protocol and multicast messages. Message Queuing 3.0 is part of Windows XP and Windows Server 2003. When you use the link "Turn Windows Features on or off" in Configuring Programs and Features of Windows Vista, there is a separate section for Message Queuing options. With this section, you can select these components:

- **Microsoft Message Queue (MSMQ) Server Core** — The Core subcomponent is required for base functionality with Message Queuing.
- **Active Directory Domain Services Integration** — With the Active Directory Domain Services Integration, message queue names are written to the Active Directory. With this option, it is possible to find queues with the Active Directory integration, and to secure queues with Windows users and groups.
- **MSMQ HTTP Support** — MSMQ HTTP Support allows you to send and receive messages using the HTTP protocol.
- **Triggers** — With triggers, applications can be instantiated on the arrival of a new message.
- **Multicast Support** — With multicasting, a message can be sent to a group of servers.
- **MSMQ DCOM Proxy** — With the DCOM proxy, a system can connect to a remote server by using the DCOM API.

When Message Queuing is installed, the Message Queuing service (see Figure 45-4) must be started. This service reads and writes messages and communicates with other Message Queuing servers to route messages across the network.

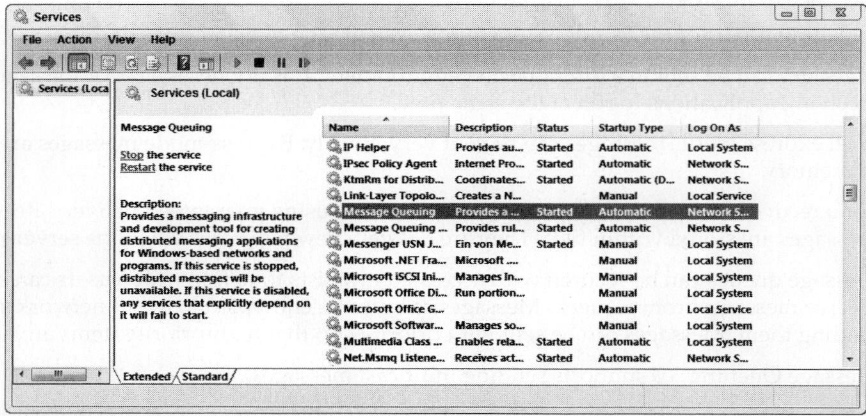

Figure 45-4

Message Queuing Architecture

With Message Queuing, messages are written to and read from a message queue. Messages and message queues have several attributes that must be further elaborated.

Messages

A message is sent to a message queue. The message includes a body containing the data that is sent and a label that is the title of the message. Any information can be put into the body of the message. With .NET, several formatters convert data to be put into the body. In addition to the label and the body, the message includes more information about the sender, timeout configuration, transaction ID, or priority.

Message queues have several types of messages:

- A *normal message* is sent by an application.
- An *acknowledgment message* reports the status of a normal message. Acknowledgment messages are sent to administration queues to report success or failure when sending normal messages.
- *Response messages* are sent by receiving applications when the original sender requires some special answer.
- A *report message* is generated by the Message Queuing system. Test messages and route-tracking messages belong to this category.

A message can have a priority that defines the order in which the messages will be read from the queue. The messages are sorted in the queue according to their priority, so the next message read in the queue is the one with the highest priority.

Messages have two delivery modes: *express* and *recoverable*. Express messages are delivered very quickly because memory is used only for the message store. Recoverable messages are stored in files at every step along the route until the message is delivered. This way, delivery of the message is assured, even with a computer reboot or network failure.

Transactional messages are a special version of recoverable messages. With transactional messaging, it is guaranteed that messages arrive only once and in the same order that they were sent. Priorities cannot be used with transactional messages.

Message Queue

A message queue is a message store. Messages that are stored on disk can be found in the `<windir>\system32\msmq\storage` directory.

Public or private queues are usually used for sending messages, but other queue types also exist:

- A *public queue* is published in the Active Directory. Information about these queues is replicated across Active Directory domains. You can use browse and search features to get information about these queues. A public queue can be accessed without knowing the name of the computer where it is placed. It is also possible to move such a queue from one system to another without the client knowing it. It's not possible to create public queues in a Workgroup environment because the Active Directory is needed. The Active Directory is discussed in Chapter 46, "Directory Services."

- *Private queues* are not published in the Active Directory. These queues can be accessed only when the full path name to the queue is known. Private queues can be used in a Workgroup environment.
- *Journal queues* are used to keep copies of messages after they have been received or sent. Enabling journaling for a public or private queue automatically creates a journal queue. With journal queues, two different queue types are possible: source journaling and target journaling. *Source journaling* is turned on with the properties of a message; the journal messages are stored with the source system. *Target journaling* is turned on with the properties of a queue; these messages are stored in the journal queue of the target system.
- *Dead-letter queues* store messages if a message doesn't arrive at the target system before a specific timeout is reached. Contrary to synchronous programming where errors are immediately detected, errors must be dealt with differently using Message Queuing. The dead-letter queue can be checked for messages that didn't arrive.
- *Administration queues* contain acknowledgments for messages sent. The sender can specify an administration queue from which it receives notification of whether the message was sent successfully.
- A *response queue* is used if more than a simple acknowledgment is needed as an answer from the receiving side. The receiving application can send response messages back to the original sender.
- A *report queue* is used for test messages. Report queues can be created by changing the type (or category) of a public or private queue to the predefined ID `{55EE8F33-CCE9-11CF-B108-0020AFD61CE9}`. Report queues are useful as a testing tool to track messages on their route.
- *System queues* are private and are used by the Message Queuing system. These queues are used for administrative messages, storing of notification messages, and to guarantee the correct order of transactional messages.

Message Queuing Administrative Tools

Before looking at how to deal with Message Queuing programmatically, this section looks at the administrative tools that are part of the Windows operating system to create and manage queues and messages. The tools shown here are not used only with Message Queuing. The Message Queuing features of these tools are available only if Message Queuing is installed.

Creating Message Queues

Message queues can be created with the Computer Management MMC snap-in. On a Windows Vista system, you can start the Computer Management MMC snap-in with the Start ⇨ Control Panel ⇨ Administrative Tools ⇨ Computer Management menu. In the tree view pane, Message Queuing is located below the Services and Applications entry. By selecting Private Queues or Public Queues, new queues can be created from the Action menu (see Figure 45-5). Public queues are available only if Message Queuing is configured in Active Directory mode.

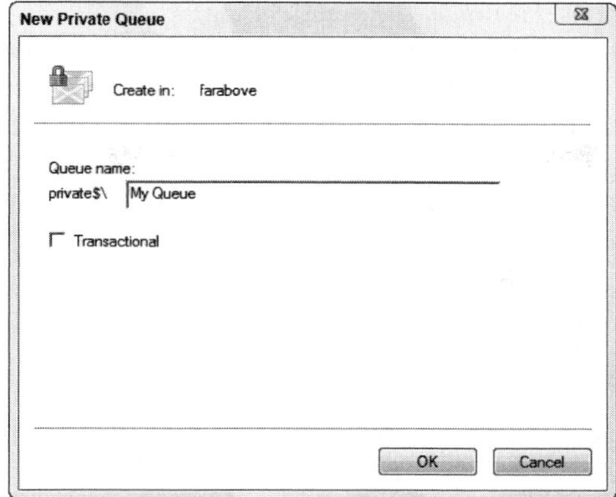

Figure 45-5

Message Queue Properties

After a queue is created, you can modify the queue's properties with the Computer Management snap-in by selecting the queue in the tree pane and selecting the Action ⇨ Properties menu (see Figure 45-6).

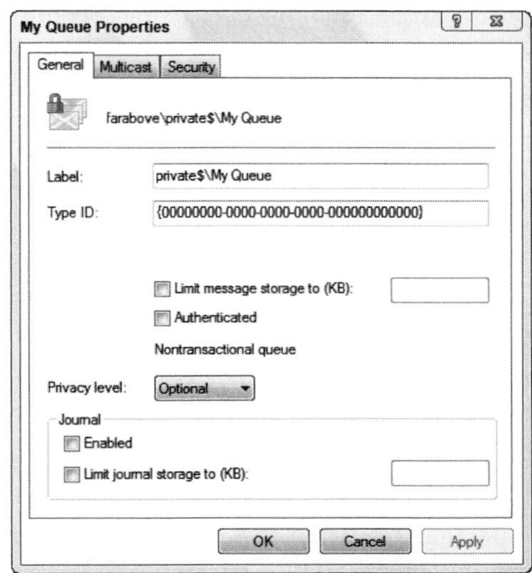

Figure 45-6

Several options can be configured:

- The label is the name of the queue that can be used to search for the queue.
- The type ID, which is, by default, set to {00000000-0000-0000-0000-000000000000} to map multiple queues to a single category or type. Report queues use a specific type ID, as discussed earlier. A type ID is a universal unique ID (UUID) or GUID.

Custom type identifiers can be created with the `uuidgen.exe` *or* `guidgen.exe` *utilities.* `uuidgen.exe` *is a command-line utility used to create unique IDs, and* `guidgen.exe` *is a graphical version to create UUIDs.*

- The maximum size of all messages of a queue can be limited to not fill up the disk.
- When checked, the Authenticated option allows only authenticated users to write and read messages to and from the queue.
- With the Privacy Level option, the content of the message can be encrypted. The possible values to set are None, Optional, or Body. None means that no encrypted messages are accepted, Body accepts only encrypted messages, and the default Optional value accepts both.
- Target journaling can be configured with the Journal settings. With this option, copies of the messages received are stored in the journal. The maximum size of disk space that is occupied can be configured for the journal messages of a queue. When the maximum size is reached, target journaling is ceased.
- With the configuration option *Multicast*, you can define a multicast IP address for the queue. The same multicast IP address can be used with different nodes in the network, so that a message sent to a single address is received with multiple queues.

Programming Message Queuing

Now that you understand the architecture of Message Queuing, you can look into the programming. In the next sections, you see how to create and control queues, and how to send and receive messages.

You also build a small course order application that consists of a sending and a receiving part.

Creating a Message Queue

You've already seen how to create message queues with the Computer Management utility. Message queues can be created programmatically with the `Create()` method of the `MessageQueue` class.

With the `Create()` method, the path of the new queue must be passed. The path consists of the host name where the queue is located and the name of the queue. In the example, the queue `MyNewPublicQueue` is created on the local host. To create a private queue, the path name must include `Private$`; for example, `\Private$\MyNewPrivateQueue`.

After the `Create()` method is invoked, properties of the queue can be changed. For example, using the `Label` property, the label of the queue is set to `Demo Queue`. The sample program writes the path of the queue and the format name to the console. The format name is automatically created with a UUID that can be used to access the queue without the name of the server:

```
using System;
using System.Messaging;

namespace Wrox.ProCSharp.Messaging
{
   class Program
   {
      static void Main()
      {
         using (MessageQueue queue =
               MessageQueue.Create(@".\MyNewPublicQueue"))
```

```
            {
               queue.Label = "Demo Queue";
               Console.WriteLine("Queue created:");
               Console.WriteLine("Path: {0}", queue.Path);
               Console.WriteLine("FormatName: {0}", queue.FormatName);
            }
         }
      }
   }
```

Administrative privileges are required to create a queue. Usually, you cannot expect the user of your application to have administrative privileges. That's why queues usually are created with installation programs. Later in this chapter, you see how message queues can be created with the `MessageQueueInstaller` *class.*

Finding a Queue

The path name and the format name can be used to identify queues. To find queues, you must differentiate between public and private queues. Public queues are published in the Active Directory. For these queues, it is not necessary to know the system where they are located. Private queues can be found only if the name of the system where the queue is located is known.

You can find public queues in the Active Directory domain by searching for the queue's label, category, or format name. You can also get all queues on a machine. The class `MessageQueue` has static methods to search for queues: `GetPublicQueuesByLabel()`, `GetPublicQueuesByCategory()`, and `GetPublicQueuesByMachine()`. The method `GetPublicQueues()` returns an array of all public queues in the domain:

```
using System;
using System.Messaging;

namespace Wrox.ProCSharp.Messaging
{
   class Program
   {
      static void Main()
      {
         foreach (MessageQueue queue in MessageQueue.GetPublicQueues())
         {
            Console.WriteLine(queue.Path);
         }
      }
   }
}
```

The method `GetPublicQueues()` is overloaded. One version allows passing an instance of the `MessageQueueCriteria` class. With this class, you can search for queues created or modified before or after a certain time, and you can also look for a category, label, or machine name.

Private queues can be searched with the static method `GetPrivateQueuesByMachine()`. This method returns all private queues from a specific system.

Opening Known Queues

If the name of the queue is known, it is not necessary to search for it. Queues can be opened by using the path or format name. They both can be set in the constructor of the `MessageQueue` class.

Path Name

The path specifies the machine name and the queue name to open the queue. This code example opens the queue `MyPublicQueue` on the local host. To be sure that the queue exists, you use the static method `MessageQueue.Exists()`:

```
using System;
using System.Messaging;

namespace Wrox.ProCSharp.Messaging
{
   class Program
   {
      static void Main()
      {
         if (MessageQueue.Exists(@".\MyPublicQueue"))
         {
            MessageQueue queue = new MessageQueue(@".\MyPublicQueue");
            //...
         }
         else
         {
            Console.WriteLine("Queue .\MyPublicQueue not existing");
         }
      }
   }
}
```

Depending on the queue type, different identifiers are required when queues are opened. The following table shows the syntax of the queue name for specific types.

Queue Type	Syntax
Public queue	`MachineName\QueueName`
Private queue	`MachineName\Private$\QueueName`
Journal queue	`MachineName\QueueName\Journal$`
Machine journal queue	`MachineName\Journal$`
Machine dead-letter queue	`MachineName\DeadLetter$`
Machine transactional dead-letter queue	`MachineName\XactDeadLetter$`

When you use the path name to open public queues, it is necessary to pass the machine name. If the machine name is not known, the format name can be used instead. The path name for private queues can be used only on the local system. The format name must be used to access private queues remotely.

Format Name

Instead of the path name, you can use the format name to open a queue. The format name is used for searching the queue in the Active Directory to get the host where the queue is located. In a disconnected environment where the queue cannot be reached at the time the message is sent, it is necessary to use the format name:

```
MessageQueue queue = new MessageQueue(
      @"FormatName:PUBLIC=09816AFF-3608-4c5d-B892-69754BA151FF");
```

The format name has some different uses. It can be used to open private queues and to specify a protocol that should be used:

- To access a private queue, the string that has to be passed to the constructor is `FormatName:PRIVATE=MachineGUID\QueueNumber`. The queue number for private queues is generated when the queue is created. You can see the queue numbers in the `<windows>\System32\msmq\storage\lqs` directory.
- With `FormatName:DIRECT=Protocol:MachineAddress\QueueName`, you can specify the protocol that should be used to send the message. The HTTP protocol is supported since Message Queuing 3.0.
- `FormatName:DIRECT=OS:MachineName\QueueName` is another way to specify a queue using the format name. This way you don't have to specify the protocol but still can use the machine name with the format name.

Sending a Message

You can use the `Send` method of the `MessageQueue` class to send a message to the queue. The object passed as an argument of the `Send()` method is serialized to the associated queue. The `Send()` method is overloaded so that a label and a `MessageQueueTransaction` object can be passed. Transactional behavior of Message Queuing is discussed later.

The code example first checks if the queue exists. If it doesn't exist, a queue is created. Then the queue is opened and the message `Sample Message` is sent to the queue using the `Send()` method.

The path name specifies a dot (just like a period) for the server name, which is the local system. Path names to private queues work only locally.

```
using System;
using System.Messaging;

namespace Wrox.ProCSharp.Messaging
{
   class Program
   {
      static void Main()
      {
         try
         {
            if (!MessageQueue.Exists(@".\Private$\MyPrivateQueue"))
            {
               MessageQueue.Create(@".\Private$\MyPrivateQueue");
            }
            MessageQueue queue =
                  new MessageQueue(@".\Private$\MyPrivateQueue");

            queue.Send("Sample Message", "Label");
         }
         catch (MessageQueueException ex)
         {
            Console.WriteLine(ex.Message);
         }
      }
   }
}
```

Figure 45-7 shows the Computer Management admin tool where you can see the message that arrived in the queue.

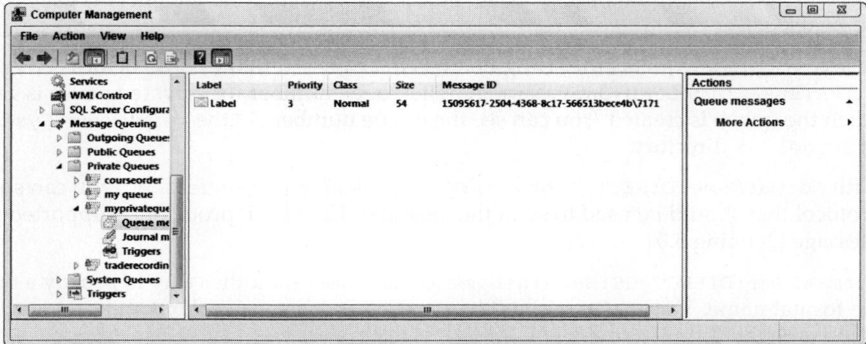

Figure 45-7

By opening the message and selecting the Body tab (see Figure 45-8) of the dialog, you can see that the message was formatted using XML. How the message is formatted is the function of the formatter that's associated with the message queue.

Figure 45-8

Message Formatter

The format in which messages are transferred to the queue depends on the formatter. The `MessageQueue` class has a `Formatter` property through which a formatter can be assigned. The default formatter, `XmlMessageFormatter`, will format the message in XML syntax as shown in the previous example.

A message formatter implements the interface `IMessageFormatter`. Three message formatters are available with the namespace `System.Messaging`:

- The `XmlMessageFormatter` is the default formatter. It serializes objects using XML. See Chapter 28, "Manipulating XML," for more on XML formatting.
- With the `BinaryMessageFormatter`, messages are serialized in a binary format. These messages are shorter than the messages formatted using XML.
- The `ActiveXMessageFormatter` is a binary formatter, so that messages can be read or written with COM objects. Using this formatter, it is possible to write a message to the queue with a .NET class and to read the message from the queue with a COM object or vice versa.

The sample message shown in Figure 45-8 with XML is formatted with the `BinaryMessageFormatter` in Figure 45-9.

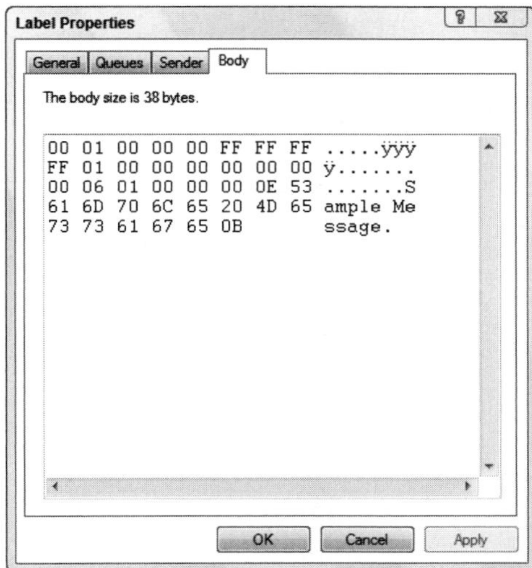

Figure 45-9

Sending Complex Messages

Instead of passing strings, it is possible to pass objects to the `Send()` method of the `MessageQueue` class. The type of the class must fulfill some specific requirements, but they depend on the formatter.

For the binary formatter, the class must be serializable with the `[Serializable]` attribute. With the .NET runtime serialization, all fields are serialized (this includes private fields). Custom serialization can be defined by implementing the interface `ISerializable`. You can read more about the .NET runtime serialization in Chapter 25, "Manipulating Files and the Registry."

XML serialization takes place with the XML formatter. With XML serialization, all public fields and properties are serialized. The XML serialization can be influenced by using attributes from the `System.Xml.Serialization` namespace. You can read more about XML serialization in Chapter 28, "Manipulating XML."

Receiving Messages

To read messages, again, the `MessageQueue` class can be used. With the `Receive()` method, a single message is read and removed from the queue. If messages are sent with different priorities, the message with the highest priority is read. Reading messages with the same priority may mean that the first message sent is not the first message read because the order of messages across the network is not guaranteed. For a guaranteed order, you should use transactional message queues.

In the following example, a message is read from the private queue `MyPrivateQueue`. Previously, a simple string was passed to the message. When you read a message using the `XmlMessageFormatter`, you have to pass the types of the objects that are read to the constructor of the formatter. In the example, the type `System.String` is passed to the argument array of the `XmlMessageFormatter` constructor. This constructor allows either a `String` array that contains the types as strings to be passed or a `Type` array.

The message is read with the `Receive()` method, and then the message body is written to the console:

```
using System;
using System.Messaging;

namespace Wrox.ProCSharp.Messaging
{
   class Program
   {
      static void Main()
      {
         MessageQueue queue = new MessageQueue(@".\Private$\MyPrivateQueue");
         queue.Formatter = new XmlMessageFormatter(
               new string[] {"System.String"});

         Message message = queue.Receive();
         Console.WriteLine(message.Body);
      }
   }
}
```

The `Receive()` message behaves synchronously and waits until a message is in the queue if there is none.

Enumerating Messages

Instead of reading message by message with the `Receive()` method, an enumerator can be used to walk through all messages. The `MessageQueue` class implements the interface `IEnumerable` and thus can be used with a `foreach` statement. Here, the messages are not removed from the queue, but you get just a peek at the messages to get their content:

```
MessageQueue queue = new MessageQueue(@".\Private$\MyPrivateQueue");
queue.Formatter = new XmlMessageFormatter(
      new string[] {"System.String"});

foreach (Message message in queue)
{
   Console.WriteLine(message.Body);
}
```

Instead of using the `IEnumerable` interface, the class `MessageEnumerator` can be used. `MessageEnumerator` implements the interface `IEnumerator`, but has some more features. With the `IEnumerable` interface, the messages are not removed from the queue. The method `RemoveCurrent()` of the `MessageEnumerator` removes the message from the current cursor position of the enumerator.

In the example, the `MessageQueue` method `GetMessageEnumerator()` is used to access the `MessageEnumerator`. The `MoveNext()` method takes a peek message by message with the `MessageEnumerator`. The `MoveNext()` method is overloaded to allow a time span as an argument. This is one of the big advantages when using this enumerator. Here, the thread can wait until a message arrives in the queue, but only for the specified time span. The `Current` property, which is defined by the `IEnumerator` interface, returns a reference to a message:

```
MessageQueue queue = new MessageQueue(@".\Private$\MyPrivateQueue");
queue.Formatter = new XmlMessageFormatter(
      new string[] {"System.String"});

using (MessageEnumerator messages = queue.GetMessageEnumerator())
{
   while (messages.MoveNext(TimeSpan.FromMinutes(30)))
   {
      Message message = messages.Current;
      Console.WriteLine(message.Body);
   }
}
```

Asynchronous Read

The `Receive` method of the `MessageQueue` class waits until a message from the queue can be read. To avoid blocking the thread, a timeout can be specified in an overloaded version of the `Receive` method. To read the message from the queue after the timeout, `Receive()` must be invoked again. Instead of polling for messages, the asynchronous method `BeginReceive()` can be called. Before starting the asynchronous read with `BeginReceive()`, the event `ReceiveCompleted` should be set. The `ReceiveCompleted` event requires a `ReceiveCompletedEventHandler` delegate that references the method that is invoked when a message arrives in the queue and can be read. In the example, the method `MessageArrived` is passed to the `ReceivedCompletedEventHandler` delegate:

```
MessageQueue queue = new MessageQueue(@".\Private$\MyPrivateQueue");
queue.Formatter = new XmlMessageFormatter(
      new string[] {"System.String"});

queue.ReceiveCompleted +=
   new ReceiveComletedEventHandler(MessageArrived);
queue.BeginReceive();
// thread does not wait
```

The handler method `MessageArrived` requires two parameters. The first parameter is the origin of the event, the `MessageQueue`. The second parameter is of type `ReceiveCompletedEventArgs` that contains the message and the asynchronous result. In the example, the method `EndReceive()` from the queue is invoked to get the result of the asynchronous method, the message:

```
public static void MessageArrived(object source,
      ReceiveCompletedEventArgs e)
{
   MessageQueue queue = (MessageQueue)source;
   Message message = queue.EndReceive(e.AsyncResult);
   Console.WriteLine(message.Body);
}
```

If the message should not be removed from the queue, the `BeginPeek()` and `EndPeek()` methods can be used with asynchronous I/O.

Course Order Application

To demonstrate the use of Message Queuing, in this section you create a sample solution to order courses. The sample solution is made up of three assemblies:

- A component library (`CourseOrder`) that includes entity classes for the messages that are sent and received in the queue

- A WPF application (`CourseOrderSender`) that sends messages to the message queue
- A WPF application (`CourseOrderReceiver`) that receives messages from the message queue

Course Order Class Library

Both the sending and the receiving application need the order information. For this reason, the entity classes are put into a separate assembly. The `CourseOrder` assembly includes three entity classes: `CourseOrder`, `Course`, and `Customer`. With the sample application, not all properties are implemented as they would be in a real application, but just enough properties to show the concept.

In the file `Course.cs`, the class `Course` is defined. This class has just one property for the title of the course:

```
namespace Wrox.ProCSharp.Messaging
{
   public class Course
   {
      public string Title { get; set; }
   }
}
```

The file `Customer.cs` includes the class `Customer`, which includes properties for the company and contact names:

```
namespace Wrox.ProCSharp.Messaging
{
   public class Customer
   {
      public string Company { get; set; }
      public string Contact { get; set; }
   }
}
```

The class `CourseOrder` in the file `CourseOrder.cs` maps a customer and a course inside an order and defines whether the order is high priority:

```
namespace Wrox.ProCSharp.Messaging
{
   public class CourseOrder
   {
      public Customer Customer { get; set; }
      public Course Course { get; set; }
   }
}
```

Course Order Message Sender

The second part of the solution is a Windows application called `CourseOrderSender`. With this application, course orders are sent to the message queue. The assemblies `System.Messaging` and `CourseOrder` must be referenced.

The user interface of this application is shown in Figure 45-10. The items of the combo box `comboBoxCourses` include several courses such as Advanced .NET Programming, Programming with LINQ, and Distributed Application Development using WCF.

When the Submit the Order button is clicked, the handler method `buttonSubmit_Click()` is invoked. With this method, a `CourseOrder` object is created and filled with the content from the `TextBox` and `ComboBox` controls. Then a `MessageQueue` instance is created to open a public queue with a format name. The format name is used to send the message, even if the queue cannot be reached currently. You can get the format name by using the Computer Management snap-in to read the ID of the message queue. With the `Send()` method, the `CourseOrder` object is passed to serialize it with the default `XmlMessageFormatter` and to write it to the queue:

```
private void buttonSubmit_Click(object sender, RoutedEventArgs e)
{
   try
   {
      CourseOrder order = new CourseOrder();
      order.Course = new Course()
      {
         Title = comboBoxCourses.SelectedItem.ToString()
      };
      order.Customer = new Customer()
      {
         Company = textCompany.Text,
         Contact = textContact.Text
      };

      using (MessageQueue queue = new MessageQueue(
            "FormatName:Public=D99CE5F3-4282-4a97-93EE-E9558B15EB13")
      {
         queue.Send(order, String.Format("Course Order {{0}}",
               order.Customer.Company);
      }
      MessageBox.Show("Course Order submitted", "Course Order",
            MessageBoxButton.OK, MessageBoxImage.Information);
   }
   catch (MessageQueueException ex)
   {
      MessageBox.Show(ex.Message, "Course Order Error",
            MessageBoxButton.OK, MessageBoxImage.Error);
   }
}
```

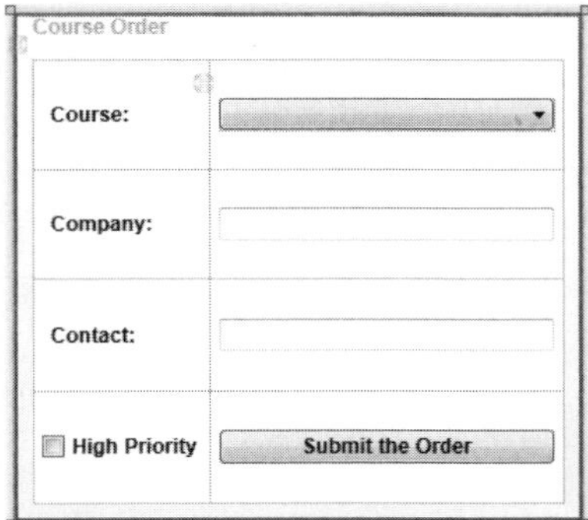

Figure 45-10

Sending Priority and Recoverable Messages

Messages can be prioritized by setting the `Priority` property of the `Message` class. If messages are specially configured, a `Message` object must be created where the body of the message is passed in the constructor.

In the example, the priority is set to `MessagePriority.High` if the `checkBoxPriority` check box is checked. `MessagePriority` is an enumeration that allows you to set values from `Lowest` (0) to `Highest` (7). The default value, `Normal`, has a priority value of 3.

To make the message recoverable, the property `Recoverable` is set to `true`:

```
private void buttonSubmit_Click(object sender, RoutedEventArgs e)
{
   try
   {
      CourseOrder order = new CourseOrder();
      order.Course = new Course()
      {
         Title = comboBoxCourses.SelectionBoxItem.ToString()
      };
      order.Customer = new Customer()
      {
         Company = textCompany.Text,
         Contact = textContact.Text
      };

      using (MessageQueue queue = new MessageQueue(
            "FormatName:Public=D99CE5F3-4282-4a97-93EE-E9558B15EB13"))
      using (Message message = new Message(order))
      {
         if (checkBoxPriority.IsChecked == true)
         {
            message.Priority = MessagePriority.High;
         }
         message.Recoverable = true;
         queue.Send(message,  String.Format("Course Order {{{0}}}",
               order.Customer.Company);
      }
      MessageBox.Show("Course Order submitted");
   }
   catch (MessageQueueException ex)
   {
      MessageBox.Show(ex.Message, "Course Order Error",
            MessageBoxButton.OK, MessageBoxImage.Error);
   }
}
```

By running the application, you can add course orders to the message queue (see Figure 45-11).

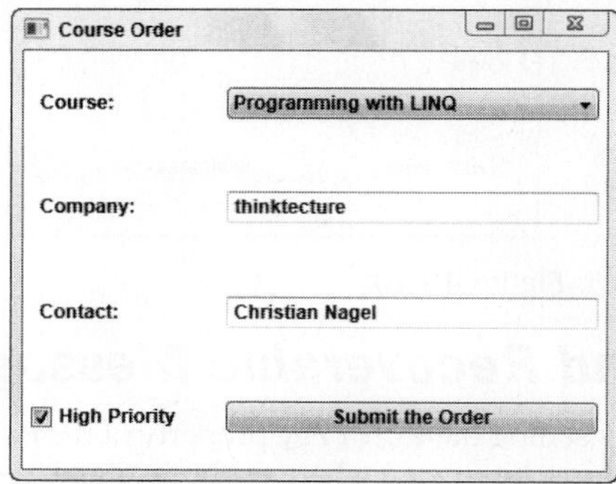

Figure 45-11

Course Order Message Receiver

The design view of the Course Order receiving application that reads messages from the queue is shown in Figure 45-12. This application displays labels of every order in the `listOrders` list box. When an order is selected, the content of the order is displayed with the controls on the right side of the application.

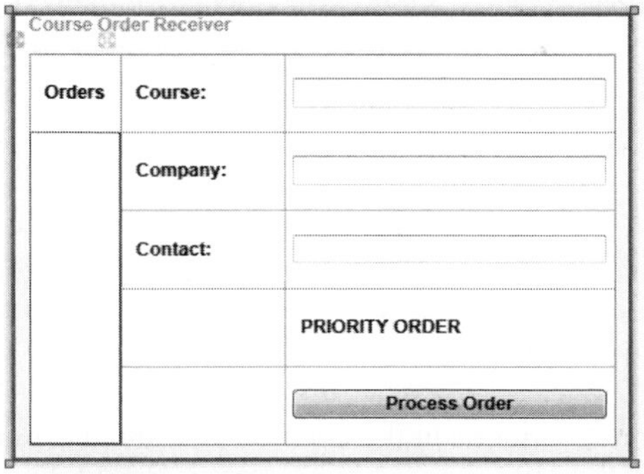

Figure 45-12

In the constructor of the `Window` class `CourseOrderReceiverWindow`, the `MessageQueue` object is created that references the same queue that was used with the sending application. For reading messages, the `XmlMessageFormatter` with the types that are read is associated with the queue using the `Formatter` property.

To display the available messages in the list, a new thread is created that peeks at messages in the background. The thread's main method is `PeekMessages`.

You can read more about threads in Chapter 19, "Threading and Synchronization."

```
using System;
using System.Messaging;
using System.Threading;
using System.Windows;
using System.Windows.Controls;
using System.Windows.Threading;

namespace Wrox.ProCSharp.Messaging
{
   public partial class CourseOrderReceiverWindow : Window
   {
      private MessageQueue orderQueue;

      public CourseOrderReceiverWindow()
      {
         InitializeComponent();

         string queueName =
               "FormatName:Public=D99CE5F3-4282-4a97-93EE-E9558B15EB13";

         orderQueue = new MessageQueue(queueName);
```

(continued)

(continued)

```
        System.Type[] types = new Type[]
        {
            typeof(CourseOrder),
            typeof(Customer),
            typeof(Course)
        }
        orderQueue.Formatter = new XmlMessageFormatter(types);

        // start the thread that fills the ListBox with orders
        Thread t1 = new Thread(PeekMessages);
        t1.IsBackground = true;
        t1.Start();
    }
```

The thread's main method, `PeekMessages()`, uses the enumerator of the message queue to display all messages. Within the `while` loop, the `messagesEnumerator` checks to see if there is a new message in the queue. If there is no message in the queue, the thread waits three hours for the next message to arrive before it exits.

To display every message from the queue in the list box, the thread cannot directly write the text to the list box, but needs to forward the call to the list box's creator thread. Because Windows Forms controls are bound to a single thread, only the creator thread is allowed to access methods and properties. The `Invoke()` method forwards the request to the creator thread:

```
    private delegate void MethodInvoker(LabelIdMapping labelIdMapping);

    private void PeekMessages()
    {
        using (MessageEnumerator messagesEnumerator =
                orderQueue.GetMessageEnumerator2())
        {
            while (messagesEnumerator.MoveNext(TimeSpan.FromHours(3)))
            {
                LabelIdMapping labelId = new LabelIdMapping()
                {
                    Id = messagesEnumerator.Current.Id,
                    Label = messagesEnumerator.Current.Label
                };
                Dispatcher.Invoke(DispatcherPriority.Normal,
                        new MethodInvoker(AddListItem), labelId);
            }
        }
        MessageBox.Show("No orders in the last 3 hours. Exiting thread",
                "Course Order Receiver", MessageBoxButton.OK,
                MessageBoxImage.Information);
    }

    private void AddListItem(LabelIdMapping labelIdMapping)
    {
        listOrders.Items.Add(labelIdMapping);
    }
```

The ListBox control contains elements of the LabelIdMapping class. This class is used to display the labels of the messages in the list box, but to keep the ID of the message hidden. The ID of the message can be used to read the message at a later time:

```
private class LabelIdMapping
{
   private string Label { get; set; }
   private string Id { get; set; }

   public override string ToString()
   {
      return label;
   }
}
```

The ListBox control has the SelectedIndexChanged event associated with the method listOrders_SelectionChanged(). This method gets the LabelIdMapping object from the current selection, and uses the ID to peek at the message once more with the PeekById() method. Then the content of the message is displayed in the TextBox control. Because by default the priority of the message is not read, the property MessageReadPropertyFilter must be set to receive the Priority:

```
private void listOrders_SelectionChanged(object sender,
      RoutedEventArgs e)
{
   LabelIdMapping labelId = listOrders.SelectedItem as LabelIdMapping;
   if (labelId == null)
      return;

   orderQueue.MessageReadPropertyFilter.Priority = true;
   Message message = orderQueue.PeekById(labelId.Id);

   CourseOrder order = message.Body as CourseOrder;
   if (order != null)
   {
      textCourse.Text = order.Course.Title;
      textCompany.Text = order.Customer.Company;
      textContact.Text = order.Customer.Contact;
      buttonProcessOrder.IsEnabled = true;

      if (message.Priority > MessagePriority.Normal)
      {
         labelPriority.Visibility = Visibility.Visible;
      }
      else
      {
         labelPriority.Visibility = Visibility.Hidden;
      }
   }
   else
   {
      MessageBox.Show("The selected item is not a course order",
            "Course Order Receiver", MessageBoxButton.OK,
            MessageBoxImage.Warning);
   }
}
```

When the Process Order button is clicked, the handler method `OnProcessOrder()` is invoked. Here again, the currently selected message from the list box is referenced, and the message is removed from the queue by calling the method `ReceiveById()`:

```
        private void buttonProcessOrder_Click(object sender, RoutedEventArgs e)
        {
           LabelIdMapping labelId = listOrders.SelectedItem as LabelIdMapping;
           Message message = orderQueue.ReceiveById(labelId.Id);

           listOrders.Items.Remove(labelId);
           listOrders.SelectedIndex = -1;
           buttonProcessOrder.Enabled = false;
           textCompany.Text = string.Empty;
           textContact.Text = string.Empty;
           textCourse.Text = string.Empty;

           MessageBox.Show("Course order processed", "Course Order Receiver",
                 MessageBoxButton.OK, MessageBoxImage.Information);
        }
     }
  }
```

Figure 45-13 shows the running receiving application that lists three orders in the queue, and one order is currently selected.

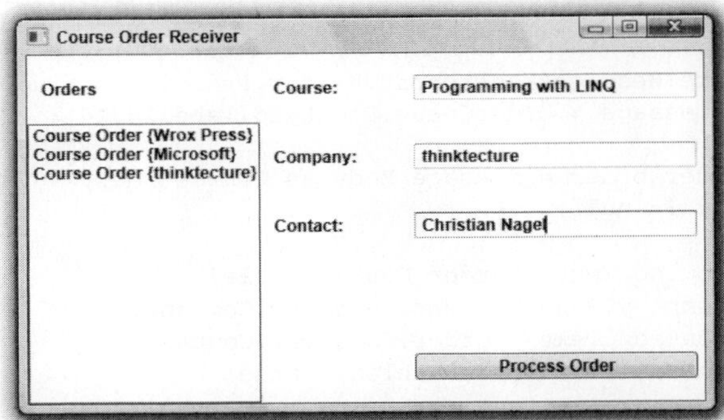

Figure 45-13

Receiving Results

With the current version of the sample application, the sending application never knows if the message is ever dealt with. To get results from the receiver, acknowledgment queues or response queues can be used.

Acknowledgment Queues

With an acknowledgment queue, the sending application can get information about the status of the message. With the acknowledgments, you can define if you would like to receive an answer, if everything went OK, or if something went wrong. For example, acknowledgments can be sent when the message reaches the destination queue or when the message is read, or if it didn't reach the destination queue or was not read before a timeout elapsed.

In the example, the `AdministrationQueue` of the `Message` class is set to the `CourseOrderAck` queue. This queue must be created similar to a normal queue. This queue is just used the other way around: the original sender receives acknowledgments. The `AcknowledgeType` property is set to `AcknowledgeTypes.FullReceive` to get an acknowledgment when the message is read:

```
Message message = new Message(order);

message.AdministrationQueue =
      new MessageQueue(@".\CourseOrderAck");
message.AcknowledgeType = AcknowledgeTypes.FullReceive;

queue.Send(message, String.Format("Course Order {{0}}",
      order.Customer.Company);

string id = message.Id;
```

The *correlation ID* is used to determine what acknowledgment message belongs to which message sent. Every message that is sent has an ID, and the acknowledgment message that is sent in response to that message holds the ID of the originating message as its correlation ID. The messages from the acknowledgment queue can be read using `MessageQueue.ReceiveByCorrelationId()` to receive the associated acknowledgment.

Instead of using acknowledgments, the dead-letter queue can be used for messages that didn't arrive at their destination. By setting the `UseDeadLetterQueue` property of the `Message` class to `true`, the message is copied to the dead-letter queue if it didn't arrive at the target queue before the timeout was reached.

Timeouts can be set with the `Message` properties `TimeToReachQueue` and `TimeToBeReceived`.

Response Queues

If more information than an acknowledgment is needed from the receiving application, a response queue can be used. A response queue is like a normal queue, but the original sender uses the queue as a receiver and the original receiver uses the response queue as a sender.

The sender must assign the response queue with the `ResponseQueue` property of the `Message` class. The sample code here shows how the receiver uses the response queue to return a response message. With the response message `responseMessage`, the property `CorrelationId` is set to the ID of the original message. This way the client application knows to which message the answer belongs. This is similar to acknowledgment queues. The response message is sent with the `Send()` method of the `MessageQueue` object that is returned from the `ResponseQueue` property:

```
public void ReceiveMessage(Message message)
{
   Message responseMessage = new Message("response");
   responseMessage.CorrelationId = message.Id;

   message.ReesponseQueue.Send(responseMessage);
}
```

Transactional Queues

With recoverable messages, it is not guaranteed that the messages will arrive in order and just once. Failures on the network can cause messages to arrive multiple times; this happens also if both the sender and receiver have multiple network protocols installed that are used by Message Queuing.

Transactional queues can be used when these guarantees are required:

- Messages arrive in the same order they have been sent.
- Messages arrive only once.

With transactional queues, a single transaction doesn't span the sending and receiving of messages. The nature of Message Queuing is that the time between send and receive can be quite long. In contrast, transactions should be short. With Message Queuing, the first transaction is used to send the message into the queue, the second transaction forwards the message on the network, and the third transaction is used to receive the messages.

The next example shows how to create a transactional message queue and how to send messages using a transaction.

A transactional message queue is created by passing `true` with the second parameter of the `MessageQueue.Create()` method.

If you would like to write multiple messages to a queue within a single transaction, you have to instantiate a `MessageQueueTransaction` object and invoke the `Begin()` method. When you are finished with sending all messages that belong to the transaction, the `Commit()` method of the `MessageQueueTransaction` object must be called. To cancel a transaction (and have no messages written to the queue), the `Abort()` method must be called, as you can see within the `catch` block:

```
using System;
using System.Messaging;

namespace Wrox.ProCSharp.Messaging
{
   class Program
   {
      static void Main()
      {
         if (!MessageQueue.Exists(@".\MyTransactionalQueue"))
         {
            MessageQueue.Create(@".\MyTransactionalQueue", true);
         }
            MessageQueue queue = new MessageQueue(@".\MyTransactionalQueue");
            MessageQueueTransaction transaction =
                  new MessageQueueTransaction();
         try
         {
            transaction.Begin();
            queue.Send("a", transaction);
            queue.Send("b", transaction);
            queue.Send("c", transaction);
            transaction.Commit();
         }
         catch
         {
            transaction.Abort();
         }
      }
   }
}
```

Message Queuing with WCF

Chapter 42 covered the architecture and core features of Windows Communication Foundation. With WCF, you can configure a Message Queuing binding that makes use of the Windows Message Queuing architecture. With this, WCF offers an abstraction layer to Message Queuing. Figure 45-14 explains the architecture in a simple picture. The client application invokes a method of a WCF proxy to send a message to the queue. The message is created by the proxy. For the client developer, there's no need to know that a message is sent to the queue. The client developer just invokes a method of the proxy. The proxy abstracts dealing with the classes from the `System.Messaging` namespace and sends a message to the queue. The MSMQ listener channel on the service side reads messages from the queue, converts them to method calls, and invokes the method calls with the service.

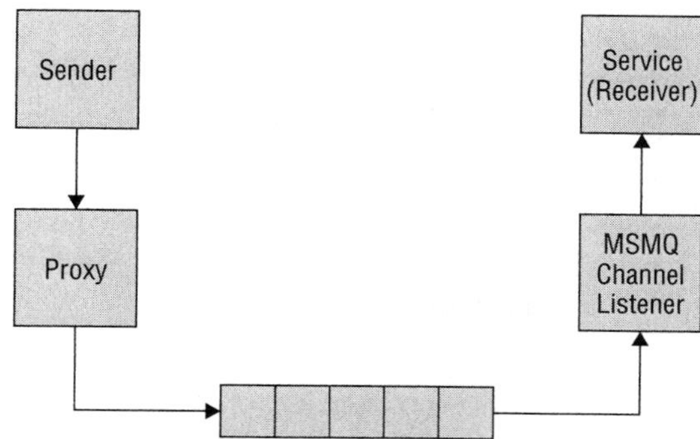

Figure 45-14

Next, the Course Ordering application gets converted to make use of Message Queuing from a WCF viewpoint. With this solution, the three projects done earlier are modified, and one more assembly is added that includes the contract of the WCF service:

- The component library (`CourseOrder`) includes entity classes for the messages that are sent across the wire. These entity classes are modified to fulfill the data contract for serialization with WCF.
- A new library is added (`CourseOrderService`) that defines the contract offered by the service.
- The WPF sender application (`CourseOrderSender`) is modified to not send messages but instead invoke methods of a WCF proxy.
- The WPF receiving application (`CourseOrderReceiver`) is modified to make use of the WCF service that implements the contract.

Entity Classes with a Data Contract

In the library `CourseOrder`, the classes `Course`, `Customer`, and `CourseOrder` are modified to apply the data contract with the attributes `[DataContract]` and `[DataMember]`. For using these attributes, you have to reference the assembly `System.Runtime.Serialization` and import the namespace `System.Runtime.Serialization`:

```
using System.Runtime.Serialization;

namespace Wrox.ProCSharp.Messaging
```

(continued)

(continued)

```
{
  [DataContract]
  public class Course
  {
    [DataMember]
    public string Title { get; set; }
  }
}
```

The `Customer` class requires the data contract attributes as well:

```
[DataContract]
public class Customer
{
  [DataMember]
  public string Company { get; set; }

  [DataMember]
  public string Contact { get; set; }
}
```

With the class `CourseOrder`, not only the data contract attributes are added, but an override of the `ToString()` method as well to have a default string representation of these objects:

```
[DataContract]
public class CourseOrder
{
  [DataMember]
  public Customer Customer { get; set; }

  [DataMember]
  public Course Course { get; set; }

  public override string ToString()
  {
    return String.Format("Course Order {{{0}}}", Customer.Company);
  }
}
```

WCF Service Contract

For offering the service with a WCF service contract, add a WCF service library with the name `CourseOrderServiceContract`. The contract is defined by the interface `ICourseOrderService`. This contract needs the attribute `[ServiceContract]`. If you want to restrict using this interface only with message queues, you can apply the `[DeliveryRequirements]` attribute and assign the property `QueuedDeliveryRequirements`. Possible values of the enumeration `QueuedDeliveryRequirementsMode` are `Required`, `Allowed`, and `NotAllowed`. The method `AddCourseOrder()` is offered by the service. Methods used by Message Queuing can only have input parameters. Because the sender and receiver can run independent of each other, the sender cannot expect an immediate result. With the attribute `[OperationContract]`, the `IsOneWay` property is set. The caller of this operation does not wait for an answer from the service:

```
using System.ServiceModel;

namespace Wrox.ProCSharp.Messaging
```

```
{
   [ServiceContract]
   [DeliveryRequirements(
         QueuedDeliveryRequirements=QueuedDeliveryRequirementsMode.Required)]
   public interface ICourseOrderService
   {
      [OperationContract(IsOneWay = true)]
      void AddCourseOrder(CourseOrder courseOrder);
   }
}
```

You can use acknowledgment and response queues to get answers to the client.

WCF Message Receiver Application

The WPF application `CourseOrderReceiver` is now modified to implement the WCF service and receive the messages. References to the assembly `System.ServiceModel` and the WCF contract assembly `CourseOrderServiceContract` are required.

The class `CourseOrderService` implements the interface `ICourseOrderService`. With the implementation, the event `CourseOrderAdded` is fired. The WPF application will register to this event to receive `CourseOrder` objects.

Because WPF controls are bound to a single thread, the property `UseSynchronizationContext` is set with the `[ServiceBehavior]` attribute. This is a feature of the WCF runtime to pass the method call invocation to the thread that is defined by the synchronization context of the WPF application:

```
using System.ServiceModel;

namespace Wrox.ProCSharp.Messaging
{
   public delegate void CourseOrderInfoHandler(CourseOrder courseOrder);

   [ServiceBehavior(UseSynchronizationContext=true)]
   public class CourseOrderService : ICourseOrderService
   {
      public static event CourseOrderInfoHandler CourseOrderAdded;

      public void AddCourseOrder(CourseOrder courseOrder)
      {
         if (CourseOrderAdded != null)
            CourseOrderAdded(courseOrder);
      }
   }
}
```

Chapter 19, "Threading and Synchronization," explains the synchronization context.

With the constructor of the class `CourseReceiverWindow`, a `ServiceHost` object is instantiated and opened to start the listener. The binding of the listener will be done in the application configuration file.

In the constructor, the event `CourseOrderAdded` of the `CourseOrderService` is subscribed. Because the only thing that happens here is adding the received `CourseOrder` object to a collection, a simple Lambda expression is used.

Lambda expressions are explained in Chapter 7, "Delegates and Events."

The collection class that is used here is `ObservableCollection<T>` from the namespace `System.Collections.ObjectModel`. This collection class implements the interface `INotifyCollectionChanged`, and thus the WPF controls bound to the collection are informed about dynamic changes to the list:

```
using System;
using System.Collections.ObjectModel;
using System.ServiceModel;
using System.Windows;

namespace Wrox.ProCSharp.Messaging
{
   public partial class CourseOrderReceiverWindow : Window
   {
      private ObservableCollection<CourseOrder> courseOrders =
           new ObservableCollection<CourseOrder>();

      public CourseOrderReceiverWindow()
      {
         InitializeComponent();

         CourseOrderService.CourseOrderAdded +=
            courseOrder => courseOrders.Add(courseOrder);

         ServiceHost host = new ServiceHost(typeof(CourseOrderService));
         try
         {
            host.Open();
         }
         catch (Exception ex)
         {
            Console.WriteLine(ex.Message);
         }

         this.DataContext = courseOrders;
      }
```

The WPF elements in the XAML code now make use of data binding. The `ListBox` is bound to the data context, and the single-item controls are bound to properties of the current item of the data context:

```
        <ListBox Grid.Row="1" x:Name="listOrders" ItemsSource="{Binding}"
              IsSynchronizedWithCurrentItem="true" />

  <!-- ... -->

        <TextBox x:Name="textCourse" Grid.Row="0" Grid.Column="1"
              Text="{Binding Path=Course.Title}" />
        <TextBox x:Name="textCompany" Grid.Row="1" Grid.Column="1"
              Text="{Binding Path=Customer.Company}" />
        <TextBox x:Name="textContact" Grid.Row="2" Grid.Column="1"
              Text="{Binding Path=Customer.Contact}" />
```

The application configuration file defines the `netMsmqBinding`. For reliable messaging, transactional queues are required. To receive and send messages to non-transactional queues, the `exactlyOnce` property must be set to `false`.

`netMsmqBinding` is the binding to be used if both the receiver and the sender application are WCF applications. If one of these applications is using the `System.Messaging` API to send or receive messages, or is an older COM application, you can use the `msmqIntegrationBinding`.

```
<?xml version="1.0" encoding="utf-8" ?>
<configuration>
  <system.serviceModel>
    <bindings>
      <netMsmqBinding>
        <binding name="NonTransactionalQueueBinding" exactlyOnce="false">
          <security mode="None" />
        </binding>
      </netMsmqBinding>
    </bindings>
    <services>
      <service name="Wrox.ProCSharp.Messaging.CourseOrderService">
        <endpoint address="net.msmq://localhost/private/courseorder"
          binding="netMsmqBinding"
          bindingConfiguration="NonTransactionalQueueBinding"
          name="OrderQueueEP"
          contract="Wrox.ProCSharp.Messaging.ICourseOrderService" />
      </service>
    </services>
  </system.serviceModel>
</configuration>
```

The `Click` event handler of the `buttonProcessOrder` button removes the selected course order from the collection class:

```
private void buttonProcessOrder_Click(object sender, RoutedEventArgs e)
{
   CourseOrder courseOrder = listOrders.SelectedItem as CourseOrder;
   courseOrders.Remove(courseOrder);
   listOrders.SelectedIndex = -1;
   buttonProcessOrder.IsEnabled = false;

   MessageBox.Show("Course order processed", "Course Order Receiver",
      MessageBoxButton.OK, MessageBoxImage.Information);

}
```

WCF Message Sender Application

The sending application is modified to make use of a WCF proxy class. For the contract of the service, the assembly `CourseOrderServiceContract` is referenced, and the assembly `System.ServiceModel` is required for use of the WCF classes.

In the `Click` event handler of the `buttonSubmit` control, the `ChannelFactory` class returns a proxy. The proxy sends a message to the queue by invoking the method `AddCourseOrder()`:

```
private void buttonSubmit_Click(object sender, RoutedEventArgs e)
{
   try
   {
      CourseOrder order = new CourseOrder();
      order.Course = new Course()
      {
```

(continued)

(continued)

```
                Title = comboCourses.SelectionBoxItem.ToString()
            };
            order.Customer = new Customer()
            {
                Company = textCompany.Text,
                Contact = textContact.Text
            };

            ChannelFactory<ICourseOrderService> factory =
                  new ChannelFactory<ICourseOrderService>("queueEndpoint");
            ICourseOrderService proxy = factory.CreateChannel();
            proxy.AddCourseOrder(order);
            factory.Close();

            MessageBox.Show("Course order submitted", "Course Order",
                  MessageBoxButton.OK, MessageBoxImage.Information);
        }
        catch (Exception ex)
        {
            MessageBox.Show(ex.Message, "Course Order Error",
                  MessageBoxButton.OK, MessageBoxImage.Error);
        }
    }
```

The application configuration file defines the client part of the WCF connection. Again, the `netMsmqBinding` is used:

```
<?xml version="1.0" encoding="utf-8" ?>
<configuration>
    <system.serviceModel>
        <bindings>
            <netMsmqBinding>
                <binding name="nonTransactionalQueueBinding"
                      exactlyOnce="false">
                    <security mode="None" />
                </binding>
            </netMsmqBinding>
        </bindings>
        <client>
            <endpoint address="net.msmq://localhost/private/courseorder"
                binding="netMsmqBinding"
                bindingConfiguration="nonTransactionalQueueBinding"
                contract="Wrox.ProCSharp.Messaging.ICourseOrderService"
                name="queueEndpoint" />
        </client>
    </system.serviceModel>
</configuration>
```

When you start the application now, it works in a similar way as before. There is no longer a need to use classes of the `System.Messaging` namespace to send and receive messages. Instead, you write the application in a similar way as using TCP or HTTP channels with WCF.

However, to create message queues and to purge messages, you still need the `MessageQueue` class. WCF is only an abstraction to send and receive messages.

If you need to have a `System.Messaging` *application to communicate with a WCF application, you can do this by using the* `msmqIntegrationBinding` *instead of the* `netMsmqBinding`*. This binding uses the message format that is used with COM and* `System.Messaging`*.*

Message Queue Installation

Message queues can be created with the `MessageQueue.Create()` method. However, the user running an application usually doesn't have the administrative privileges that are required to create message queues.

Usually, message queues are created with an installation program. For installation programs, the class `MessageQueueInstaller` can be used. If an installer class is part of an application, the command-line utility `installutil.exe` (or a Windows Installation Package) invokes the `Install()` method of the installer.

Visual Studio has a special support for using the `MessageQueueInstaller` with Windows Forms applications. If a `MessageQueue` component is dropped from the toolbox onto the form, the smart tag of the component allows you to add an installer with the menu entry Add Installer. The `MessageQueueInstaller` object can be configured with the properties editor to define transactional queues, journal queues, the type of the formatter, the base priority, and so on.

Installers are discussed in Chapter 16, "Deployment."

Summary

In this chapter, you've seen how Message Queuing can be used. Message Queuing is an important technology that offers not only asynchronous, but also disconnected communication. The sender and receiver can be running at different times, which makes Message Queuing an option for smart clients and also useful to distribute the load on the server over time.

The most important classes with Message Queuing are `Message` and `MessageQueue`. The `MessageQueue` class allows sending, receiving, and peeking at messages, and the `Message` class defines the content that is sent.

WCF offers an abstraction to message queuing. You can use the concepts offered by WCF to send messages by calling methods of a proxy and to receive messages by implementing a service.

The next chapter dives into Directory Services, how and when to use these hierarchical data stores, and different ways to connect to this service.

46

Directory Services

Microsoft's Active Directory is a *directory service* that provides a central, hierarchical store for user information, network resources, services, and so on. The information in this directory service can be extended to also store custom data that is of interest for the enterprise. For example, Microsoft Exchange Server and Microsoft Dynamics use Active Directory intensively to store public folders and other items.

Before the release of Active Directory, Exchange Server used its own private store for its objects. It was necessary for a system administrator to configure two user IDs for a single person: a user account in the Windows NT domain to enable a logon and a user in Exchange Directory. This was necessary because of the additional information required by users (such as email addresses, phone numbers, and so on), and the user information for the NT domain was not extensible to add the required information. Now, the system administrator has to configure just a single user for a person in Active Directory; the information for a `user` object can be extended so that it fits the requirements of Exchange Server. You can also extend this information. For example, you can extend user information in Active Directory with a skills list. Then it would easily be possible to track down a C# developer by searching for the required C# skill.

This chapter shows how you can use the .NET Framework to access and manipulate the data in a directory service using classes from the `System.DirectoryServices`, `System.DirectoryServices.AccountManagement`, and `System.DirectoryServices.Protocols` namespaces.

> *This chapter uses Windows Server 2008 with Active Directory configured. You can also use Windows 2003 Server or other directory services.*

This chapter covers the following:

- The architecture of Active Directory, including features and basic concepts
- Some of the tools available for administration of Active Directory and their benefit to programming
- How to read and modify data in Active Directory
- Searching for objects in Active Directory
- Account management
- Accessing a DSML Web service to search for objects

After discussing the architecture and how to program Active Directory, you create a Windows application in which you can specify properties and a filter to search for `user` objects. Similar to other chapters, you can also download the code for the examples in this chapter from the Wrox Web site at `www.wrox.com`.

The Architecture of Active Directory

Before starting to program Active Directory, you need to know how it works, what it is used for, and what data can be stored there.

Features

The features of Active Directory can be summarized as follows:

- The data in Active Directory is grouped *hierarchically*. Objects can be stored inside other container objects. Instead of having a single, large list of users, you can group users inside organizational units. An organizational unit can contain other organizational units, so you can build a tree.
- Active Directory uses a *multimaster replication*. With Active Directory, every *domain controller* (DC) is a master. With multiple masters, updates can be applied to any DC. This model is much more scalable than a single-master model because updates can be made to different servers concurrently. The disadvantage of this model is more complex replication, which is discussed later in this chapter.
- The *replication topology* is flexible, to support replications across slow links in WANs. How often data should be replicated is configurable by the domain administrators.
- Active Directory supports *open standards*. The *Lightweight Directory Access Protocol* (LDAP) is an Internet standard that can be used to access many different directory services, including the data in Active Directory. With LDAP, a programming interface, LDAP API, is also defined. The LDAP API can be used to access Active Directory with the C language. Another standard used within Active Directory is *Kerberos*, which is used for authentication. The Windows Server Kerberos service can also be used to authenticate UNIX clients.
- *Active Directory Service Interface* (ADSI) defines COM interfaces to access directory services. ADSI makes it possible to access all features of Active Directory. Classes from the namespace `System.DirectoryServices` wrap ADSI COM objects to make directory services accessible from .NET applications.
- *Directory Service Markup Language* (DSML) is another standard to access directory services. DSML is a platform-independent approach and is supported by the OASIS group.
- With Active Directory, a fine-grained security is available. Every object stored in Active Directory can have an associated access-control list that defines who can do what with that object.

The objects in the directory are *strongly typed*, which means that the type of an object is exactly defined; no attributes that are not specified may be added to an object. In the *schema*, the object types as well as the parts of an object (attributes) are defined. Attributes can be mandatory or optional.

Active Directory Concepts

Before programming Active Directory, you need to know some basic terms and definitions.

Objects

Active Directory stores objects. An object refers to something concrete such as a user, a printer, or a network share. Objects have mandatory and optional attributes that describe them. Some examples of the attributes of a `user` object are the first name, last name, email address, phone number, and so on.

Figure 46-1 shows a container object called `Wrox Press` that contains some other objects: two user objects, a contact object, a printer object, and a user group object.

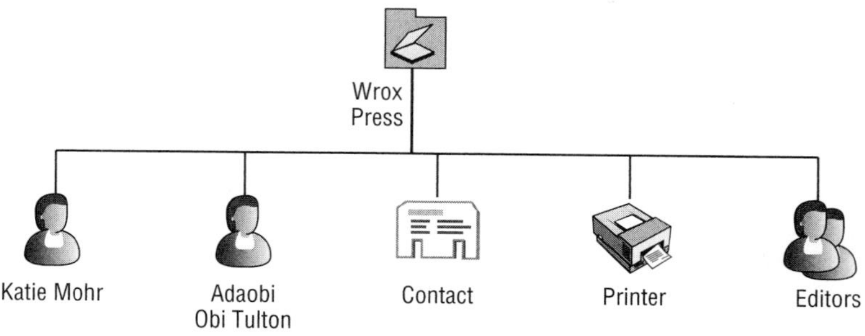

Figure 46-1

Schema

Every object is an instance of a class defined in the *schema*. The schema *defines the types* and is itself stored in objects in Active Directory. You must differentiate between `classSchema` and `attributeSchema`: `classSchema` defines the types of objects and details what mandatory and optional attributes an object has. `attributeSchema` defines what an attribute looks like and the allowed syntax for a specific attribute.

You can define custom types and attributes and add these to the schema. Be aware, however, that a new schema type cannot be removed from Active Directory. You can mark it as inactive so that new objects cannot be created, but there can be existing objects of that type, so it is not possible to remove classes or attributes defined in the schema.

The user group Administrator doesn't have enough rights to create new schema entries; the group Enterprise Admins is needed for that.

Configuration

In addition to objects and class definitions stored as objects, the configuration of Active Directory itself is stored in Active Directory. It stores the information about all sites, such as the replication interval, which is set up by the system administrator. Because the configuration itself is stored in Active Directory, you can access the configuration information like all other objects in Active Directory.

The Active Directory Domain

A domain is a security boundary of a Windows network. In the Active Directory domain, the objects are stored in a hierarchical order. Active Directory itself is made up of one or more domains. Figure 46-2 shows the hierarchical order of objects in a domain; the domain is represented by a triangle. Container objects such as `Users`, `Computers`, and `Books` can store other objects. Each oval in the picture represents an object, with the lines between the objects representing parent-child relationships. For example, `Books` is the parent of `.NET` and `Java`, and `Pro C#`, `Beg C#`, and `ASP.NET` are child objects of the `.NET` object.

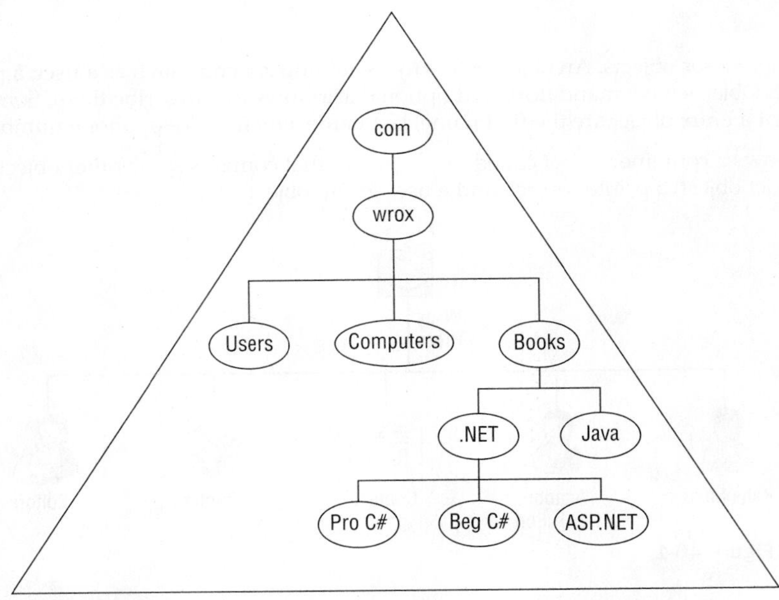

Figure 46-2

Domain Controller

A single domain can have multiple domain controllers, each of which stores all of the objects in the domain. There is no master server, and all DCs are treated equally; you have a multimaster model. The objects are replicated across the servers inside the domain.

Site

A *site* is a location in the network that holds at least one DC. If you have multiple locations in the enterprise, which are connected with slow network links, you can use multiple sites for a single domain. For backup or scalability reasons, each site can have one or more DCs running. Replication between servers in a site can happen at shorter intervals due to the faster network connection. Replication is configured to occur at larger time intervals between servers across sites, depending on the speed of the network. Of course, replication intervals can be configured by the domain administrator.

Domain Tree

Multiple domains can be connected by trust relationships. These domains share a *common schema*, a *common configuration*, and a *global catalog* (more on global catalogs shortly). A common schema and a common configuration imply that this data is replicated across domains. Domain trees share the same class and attribute schema. The objects themselves are not replicated across domains.

Domains connected in such a way form a domain tree. Domains in a domain tree have a contiguous, hierarchical namespace. This means that the domain name of the child domain is the name of that child domain appended to the name of the parent domain. Between domains, trusts using the Kerberos protocol are established.

For example, you have the root domain `wrox.com`, which is the *parent domain* of the child domains `india.wrox.com` and `uk.wrox.com`. A trust is set up between the parent and the child domains, so that accounts from one domain can be authenticated by another domain.

Forest

Multiple domain trees that are connected by using a common schema, a common configuration, and a global catalog without a contiguous namespace are called a *forest*. A forest is a set of domain trees; it can be used if the company has a subcompany for which a different domain name should be used. Here is one example: `wrox.com` should be relatively independent of the domain `wiley.com`, but it should be possible to have a common management, and be possible for users from `wrox.com` to access resources from the `wiley.com` domain and vice versa. With a forest, you can have trusts between multiple domain trees.

Global Catalog

A search for an object can span multiple domains. If you look for a specific `user` object with some attributes, you must search every domain. Starting with `wrox.com`, the search continues to `uk.wrox.com` and `india.wrox.com`; across slow links such a search could take a while.

To make searches faster, all objects are copied to the *global catalog* (GC). The GC is replicated in every domain of a forest. There is at least one server in every domain holding a GC. For performance and scalability reasons, you can have more than one GC server in a domain. Using a GC, a search through all the objects can happen on a single server.

The GC is a *read-only cache* of all the objects that can be used only for searches; the domain controllers must be used to do updates.

Not all attributes of an object are stored in the GC. You can define whether an attribute should be stored with an object. The decision whether to store an attribute in the GC depends on how the attribute is used. If the attribute is frequently used in searches, putting it into the GC makes the search faster. A picture of a user isn't useful in the GC because you would never search for a picture. Conversely, a phone number would be a useful addition to the store. You can also define that an attribute should be indexed so that a query for it is faster.

Replication

As a programmer, you are unlikely ever to configure replication, but because it affects the data you store in Active Directory, you need to know how it works. Active Directory uses a *multimaster* server architecture. Updates happen to every domain controller in the domain. The *replication latency* defines how long it takes until an update starts:

- The configurable *change notification* happens, by default, every 5 minutes inside a site if some attributes change. The DC where a change occurred informs one server after the other with 30-second intervals, so the fourth DC can get the change notification after 7 minutes. The default change notification across sites is set to 180 minutes. Intra- and intersite replication can each be configured to other values.
- If no changes have occurred, the *scheduled replication* occurs every 60 minutes inside a site. This is to ensure that a change notification wasn't missed.
- For security-sensitive information, such as account lockout, *immediate notification* can occur.

With a replication, only the changes are copied to the DCs. With every change of an attribute, a version number (update sequence number or USN) and a time stamp are recorded. These are used to help resolve conflicts if updates happened to the same attribute on different servers.

Here's an example. The mobile phone attribute of the user John Doe has the USN number 47. This value is already replicated to all DCs. One system administrator changes the phone number. The change occurs on the server DC1; the new USN of this attribute on the server DC1 is now 48, whereas the other DCs still have the USN 47. For someone still reading the attribute, the old value can be read until the replication to all domain controllers has occurred.

The rare case can happen that another administrator changes the phone number attribute, and a different DC is selected because this administrator received a faster response from the server DC2. The USN of this attribute on the server DC2 is also changed to 48.

At the notification intervals, notification happens because the USN for the attribute changed, and the last time replication occurred was with a USN value of 47. The replication mechanism now detects that the servers DC1 and DC2 both have a USN of 48 for the phone number attribute. Which server is the winner is not really important, but one server must definitely win. To resolve this conflict, the time stamp of the change is used. Because the change happened later on DC2, the value stored in the DC2 domain controller is replicated.

When reading objects, you must be aware that the data is not necessarily current. The currency of the data depends on replication latencies. When updating objects, another user can still read some old values after the update. It's also possible that different updates can happen at the same time.

Characteristics of Active Directory Data

Active Directory doesn't replace a relational database or the registry, so what kind of data would you store in it?

- With Active Directory you get *hierarchical data*. You can have containers that store further containers and objects, too. Containers themselves are objects as well.
- The data should be used for *read-mostly*. Because of replication occurring at certain time intervals, you cannot be sure that you will read up-to-date data. You must be aware that in applications, the information you read is possibly not the current up-to-date information.
- Data should be of *global interest* to the enterprise, because adding a new data type to the schema replicates it to all the servers in the enterprise. For data types of interest to only a small number of users, the domain enterprise administrator normally wouldn't install new schema types.
- The data stored should be of *reasonable size* because of replication issues. It is fine to store data with a size of 100K in the directory, if the data changes only once a week. However, if the data changes every hour, data of this size is too large. Always think about replicating the data to different servers: where the data gets transferred to and at what intervals. If you have larger data, it's possible to put a link into Active Directory and store the data itself in a different place.

To summarize, the data you store in Active Directory should be hierarchically organized, of reasonable size, and of importance to the enterprise.

Schema

Active Directory objects are strongly typed. The schema defines the types of the objects, mandatory and optional attributes, and the syntax and constraints of these attributes. As mentioned earlier, in the schema, it is necessary to differentiate between class-schema and attribute-schema objects. A class is a collection of attributes. With the classes, single inheritance is supported. As you can see in Figure 46-3, the `user` class derives from the `organizationalPerson` class, `organizationalPerson` is a subclass of person, and the base class is top. The classSchema that defines a class describes the attributes with the systemMayContain attribute.

Figure 46-3 shows only a few of all the systemMayContain values. Using the ADSI Edit tool, you can easily see all the values; you look at this tool in the next section. In the root class top you can see that every object can have common name (cn), displayName, objectGUID, whenChanged, and whenCreated attributes. The person class derives from top. A person object also has a userPassword and a telephoneNumber. organizationalPerson is derived from person. In addition to the attributes of person, it has a manager, department, and company, and a user has extra attributes needed to log on to a system.

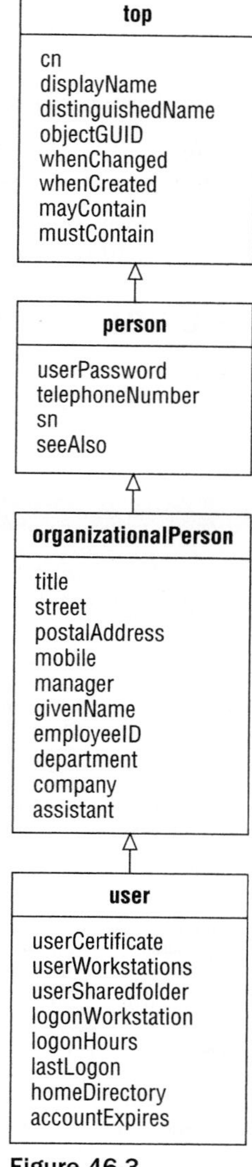

Figure 46-3

Administration Tools for Active Directory

Looking into some of the Active Directory administration tools can help to give you an idea of Active Directory, what data is in there, and what can be done programmatically.

The system administrator has many tools to enter new data, update data, and configure Active Directory:

- The *Active Directory Users and Computers* MMC snap-in is used to enter new users and update user data.
- The *Active Directory Sites and Services* MMC snap-in is used to configure sites in a domain and for replication between these sites.
- The *Active Directory Domains and Trusts* MMC snap-in can be used to build up a trust relationship between domains in a tree.
- *ADSI Edit* is the editor for Active Directory, where every object can be viewed and edited.

To run these tools on Windows Vista or Windows XP, you need to install Windows Server 2003 Admin Pack. ADSI Edit is available with the Windows Server 2003 Support tools.

The following sections get into the functionality of the tools Active Directory Users and Computers and ADSI Edit because these tools are important in regard to creating applications using Active Directory.

Active Directory Users and Computers

The Active Directory Users and Computers snap-in is the tool that system administrators use to manage users. Select Start ⇨ Programs ⇨ Administrative Tools ⇨ Active Directory Users and Computers to start this program (see Figure 46-4).

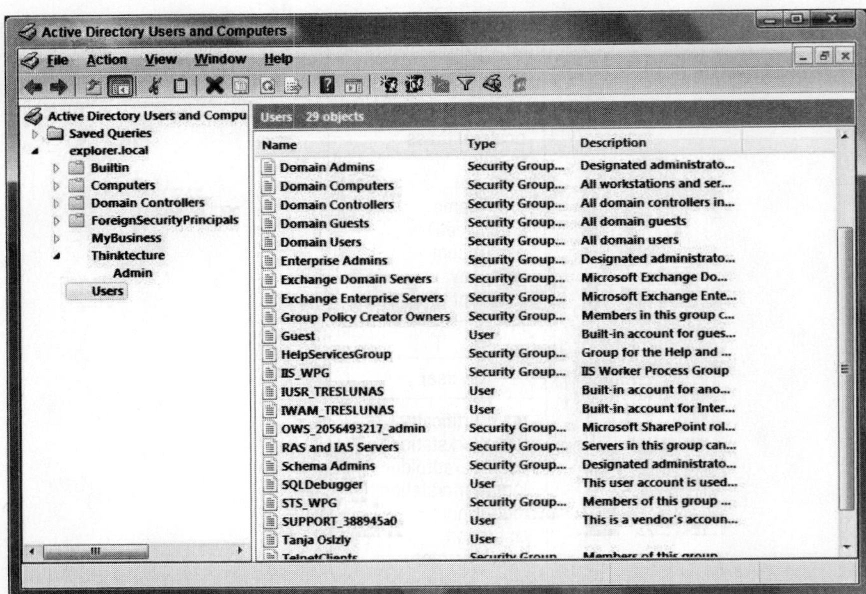

Figure 46-4

With this tool you can add new users, groups, contacts, organizational units, printers, shared folders, or computers, and modify existing ones. Figure 46-5 shows the attributes that can be entered for a `user` object: office, phone numbers, email addresses, Web pages, organization information, addresses, groups, and so on.

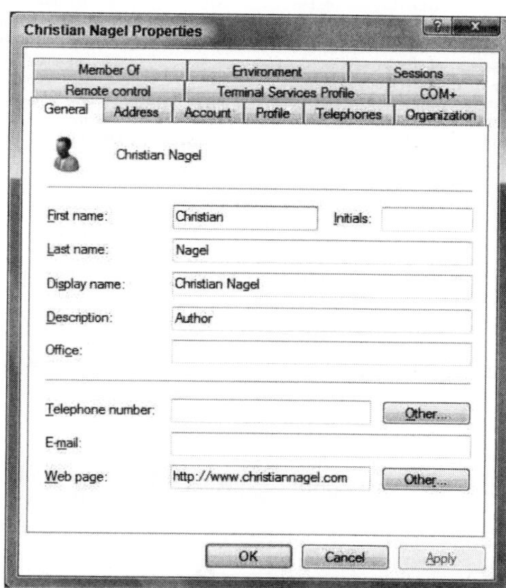

Figure 46-5

Active Directory Users and Computers can also be used in big enterprises with millions of objects. It's not necessary to look through a list with a thousand objects, because you can select a custom filter to display only some of the objects. You can also perform an LDAP query to search for the objects in the enterprise. You explore these possibilities later in this chapter.

ADSI Edit

ADSI Edit is the editor of Active Directory. This tool is not installed automatically; on the Windows Server 2003 CD, you can find a directory named Support Tools. When the support tools are installed, you can access ADSI Edit by invoking the program `adsiedit.msc`.

ADSI Edit offers greater control than the Active Directory Users and Computers tool (see Figure 46-6); with ADSI Edit, everything can be configured, and you can also look at the schema and the configuration. This tool is not very intuitive to use, however, and it is very easy to enter wrong data.

By opening the properties window of an object, you can view and change every attribute of an object in Active Directory. With this tool, you can see mandatory and optional attributes, with their types and values (see Figure 46-7).

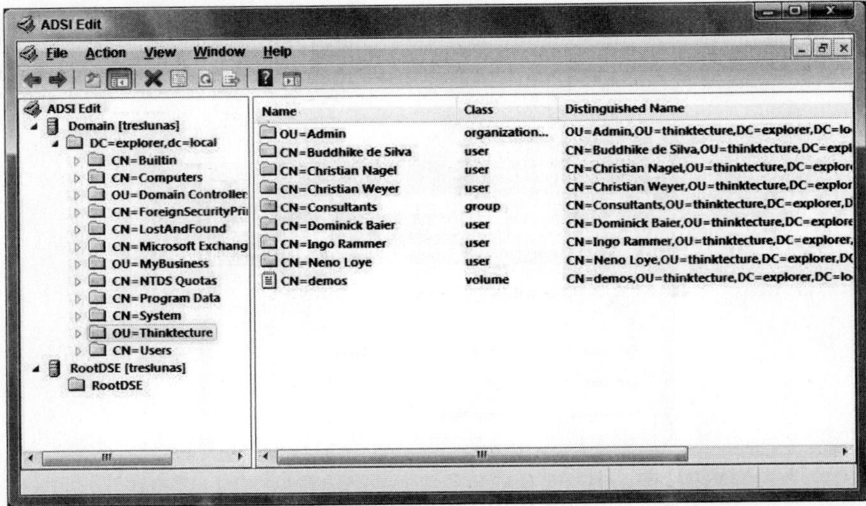

Figure 46-6

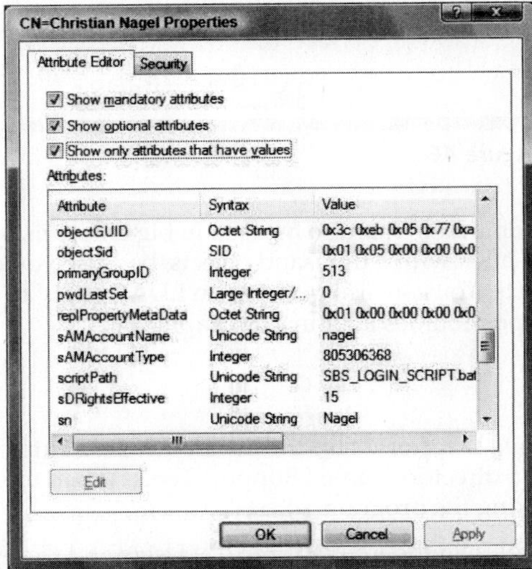

Figure 46-7

Programming Active Directory

To develop programs for Active Directory, you can use the classes from either the `System.DirectoryServices` or the `System.DirectoryServices.Protocols` namespaces. In the namespace `System.DirectoryServices`, you can find classes that wrap *Active Directory Service Interfaces* (ADSI) COM objects to access Active Directory.

ADSI is a programmatic interface to directory services. It defines some COM interfaces that are implemented by ADSI providers. This means that the client can use different directory services with the same programmatic interfaces. The .NET Framework classes in the `System.DirectoryServices` namespace make use of ADSI.

Figure 46-8 shows some ADSI Providers (LDAP, IIS, and NDS) that implement COM interfaces such as `IADs` and `IUnknown`. The assembly `System.DirectoryServices` makes use of the ADSI providers.

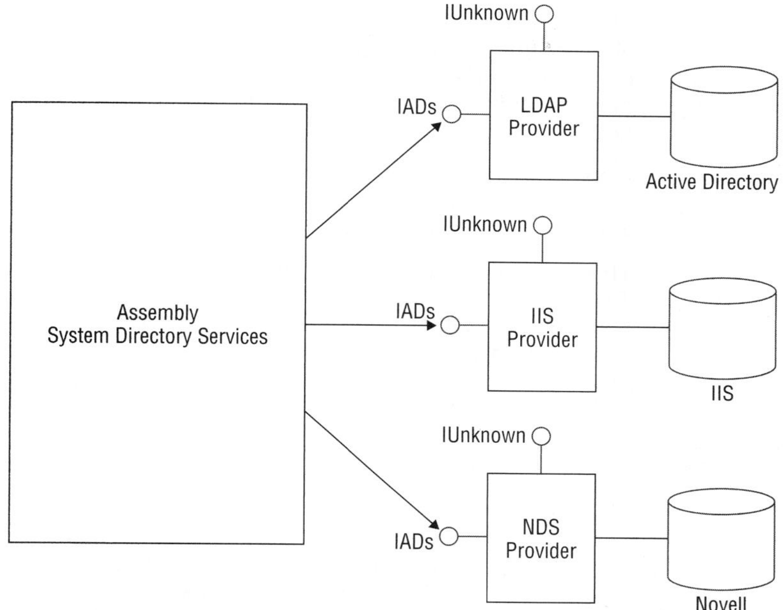

Figure 46-8

Classes from the namespace `System.DirectoryServices.Protocols` make use of Directory Services Markup Language (DSML) Services for Windows. With DSML, standardized Web service interfaces are defined by the OASIS group (`www.oasis-open.org/committees/dsml`).

To use the classes from the `System.DirectoryServices` namespace, you need to reference the `System.DirectoryServices` assembly. With the classes in this assembly, you can query objects, view and update properties, search for objects, and move objects to other container objects. In the code segments that follow later in this section, you use a simple C# console application that demonstrates the functionality of the classes in the `System.DirectoryServices` namespace.

This section covers the following:

- Classes in the `System.DirectoryServices` namespace
- The process of connecting to Active Directory (binding)
- Getting directory entries, creating new objects, and updating existing entries
- Searching Active Directory

Classes in System.DirectoryServices

The following table shows the major classes in the `System.DirectoryServices` namespace.

Class	Description
`DirectoryEntry`	This is the main class of the `System.DirectoryServices` namespace. An object of this class represents an object in the Active Directory store. This class is used to bind to an object and to view and update properties. The properties of the object are represented in a `PropertyCollection`. Every item in the `PropertyCollection` has a `PropertyValueCollection`.
`DirectoryEntries`	`DirectoryEntries` is a collection of `DirectoryEntry` objects. The `Children` property of a `DirectoryEntry` object returns a list of objects in a `DirectoryEntries` collection.
`DirectorySearcher`	This is the main class used for searching for objects with specific attributes. To define the search, the `SortOption` class and the enumerations `SearchScope`, `SortDirection`, and `ReferralChasingOption` can be used. The search results in a `SearchResult` or a `SearchResultCollection`. You also get `ResultPropertyCollection` and `ResultPropertyValueCollection` objects.

Binding

To get the values of an object in Active Directory, you need to connect to the Active Directory service. This connecting process is called *binding*. The binding path can look like this:

```
LDAP://dc01.thinktecture.com/OU=Development, DC=thinktecture, DC=Com
```

With the binding process, you can specify these items:

- The *protocol*; this specifies the provider to be used.
- The *server name* of the domain controller.
- The *port number* of the server process.
- The *distinguished name* of the object; this identifies the object you want to access.
- The *username and password*, if the user who is allowed to access Active Directory is different from the current logged-on user.
- An *authentication* type, if encryption is needed.

The following subsections discuss these options in more detail.

Protocol

The first part of a binding path specifies the ADSI provider. The provider is implemented as a COM server; for identification, a `progID` can be found in the registry directly under `HKEY_CLASSES_ROOT`. The providers that are available with Windows Vista are listed in the following table.

Provider	Description
`LDAP`	LDAP Server, such as the Exchange directory and Windows 2000 Server or Windows Server 2003 Active Directory Server.
`GC`	GC is used to access the global catalog in Active Directory. It can be used for fast queries.
`IIS`	With the ADSI provider for IIS, it's possible to create new Web sites and to administer them in the IIS catalog.
`NDS`	This `progID` is used to communicate with Novell Directory Services.
`NWCOMPAT`	With `NWCOMPAT`, you can access old Novell directories, such as Novell Netware 3.x.

Server Name

The *server name* follows the protocol in the binding path. The server name is optional if you are logged on to an Active Directory domain. Without a server name, *serverless binding* occurs; this means that Windows Server 2008 tries to get the "best" domain controller in the domain that's associated with the user doing the bind. If there is no server inside a site, the first domain controller that can be found will be used.

A serverless binding might look like this: `LDAP://OU=Sales, DC=Thinktecture, DC=Local`.

Port Number

After the server name, you can specify the *port number* of the server process by using the syntax `:xxx`. The default port number for the LDAP server is port 389: `LDAP://dc01.sentinel.net:389`. The Exchange server uses the same port number as the LDAP server. If the Exchange server is installed on the same system — for example, as a domain controller of Active Directory — a different port can be configured.

Distinguished Name

The fourth part that you can specify in the path is the *distinguished name* (DN). The distinguished name is a unique name that identifies the object you want to access. With Active Directory, you can use LDAP syntax that is based on X.500 to specify the name of the object.

This is an example of a distinguished name:

```
CN=Christian Nagel, OU=Consultants, DC=thinktecture, DC=local
```

This distinguished name specifies the common name (`CN`) of `Christian Nagel` in the organizational unit (`OU`) called `Consultants` in the domain component (`DC`) called `thinktecture` of the domain `thinktecture.local`. The part specified to the right is the root object of the domain. The name must follow the hierarchy in the object tree.

You can find the LDAP specification for the string representation of distinguished names in RFC 2253 at `www.ietf.org/rfc/rfc2253.txt`.

Relative Distinguished Name

A *relative distinguished name* (RDN) is used to reference objects within a container object. With an RDN, the specification of `OU` and `DC` is not needed because a common name is enough. `CN=Christian Nagel` is the relative distinguished name inside the organizational unit. A relative distinguished name can be used if you already have a reference to a container object and if you want to access child objects.

Default Naming Context

If a distinguished name is not specified in the path, the binding process will be made to the default naming context. You can read the default naming context with the help of `rootDSE`. LDAP 3.0 defines `rootDSE` as the root of a directory tree on a directory server. For example:

```
LDAP://rootDSE
```

or

```
LDAP://servername/rootDSE
```

By enumerating all properties of the `rootDSE`, you can get the information about the `defaultNamingContext` that will be used when no name is specified. `schemaNamingContext` and `configurationNamingContext` specify the required names to be used to access the schema and the configuration in the Active Directory store.

The following code is used to get all properties of `rootDSE`:

```
try
{
   using (DirectoryEntry de = new DirectoryEntry())
   {
      de.Path = "LDAP://treslunas/rootDSE";
      de.Username = @"explorer\christian";
      de.Password = "password";

      PropertyCollection props = de.Properties;
      foreach (string prop in props.PropertyNames)
      {
         PropertyValueCollection values = props[prop];
         foreach (string val in values)
         {
            Console.Write("{0}: ", prop);
            Console.WriteLine(val);
         }
      }
   }
}
catch (COMException ex)
{
   Console.WriteLine(ex.Message);
}
```

This program shows the default naming context (`defaultNamingContext DC=explorer, DC=local`), the context that can be used to access the schema (`CN=Schema, CN=Configuration, DC=explorer, DC=local`), and the naming context of the configuration (`CN=Configuration, DC=explorer, DC=local`), as you can see here:

```
currentTime: 20071012063000.0Z
subschemaSubentry: CN=Aggregate,CN=Schema,CN=Configuration,DC=explorer,DC=local
dsServiceName: CN=NTDS Settings,CN=TRESLUNAS,CN=Servers,
CN=Default-First-Site-Name,CN=Sites,CN=Configuration,DC=explorer,DC=local
namingContexts: DC=explorer,DC=local
namingContexts: CN=Configuration,DC=explorer,DC=local
namingContexts: CN=Schema,CN=Configuration,DC=explorer,DC=local
namingContexts: DC=DomainDnsZones,DC=explorer,DC=local
namingContexts: DC=ForestDnsZones,DC=explorer,DC=local
```

```
defaultNamingContext: DC=explorer,DC=local
schemaNamingContext: CN=Schema,CN=Configuration,DC=explorer,DC=local
configurationNamingContext: CN=Configuration,DC=explorer,DC=local
rootDomainNamingContext: DC=explorer,DC=local
supportedControl: 1.2.840.113556.1.4.319
supportedControl: 1.2.840.113556.1.4.801
```

Object Identifier

Every object has a *globally unique identifier* (GUID). A GUID is a unique 128-bit number as you may already know from COM development. You can bind to an object using the GUID. This way, you always get to the same object, regardless of whether the object was moved to a different container. The GUID is generated at object creation and always remains the same.

You can get to a GUID string representation with `DirectoryEntry.NativeGuid`. This string representation can then be used to bind to the object.

This example shows the path name for a serverless binding to bind to a specific object represented by a GUID:

```
LDAP://<GUID=14abbd652aae1a47abc60782dcfc78ea>
```

Username

If a different user from the one of the current process must be used for accessing the directory (maybe this user doesn't have the required permissions to access Active Directory), explicit *user credentials* must be specified for the binding process. Active Directory has multiple ways to specify the username.

Downlevel Logon

With a downlevel logon, the username can be specified with the pre-Windows 2000 domain name:

```
domain\username
```

Distinguished Name

The user can also be specified by a distinguished name of a `user` object, for example:

```
CN=Administrator, CN=Users, DC=thinktecture, DC=local
```

User Principal Name

The *user principal name* (UPN) of an object is defined with the `userPrincipalName` attribute. The system administrator specifies this with the logon information in the Account tab of the User properties with the Active Directory Users and Computers tool. Note that this is not the email address of the user.

This information also uniquely identifies a user and can be used for a logon:

```
Nagel@thinktecture.local
```

Authentication

For secure encrypted authentication, the *authentication* type can also be specified. The authentication can be set with the `AuthenticationType` property of the `DirectoryEntry` class. The value that can be assigned is one of the `AuthenticationTypes` enumeration values. Because the enumeration is marked with the `[Flags]` attribute, multiple values can be specified. Some of the possible values are where the data sent is encrypted; `ReadonlyServer`, where you specify that you need only read access; and `Secure` for secure authentication.

Binding with the DirectoryEntry Class

The `System.DirectoryServices.DirectoryEntry` class can be used to specify all the binding information. You can use the default constructor and define the binding information with the properties `Path`, `Username`, `Password`, and `AuthenticationType`, or pass all the information in the constructor:

```
DirectoryEntry de = new DirectoryEntry();
de.Path = "LDAP://platinum/DC=thinktecture, DC=local";
de.Username = "nagel@thinktecture.local";
de.Password = "password";

// use the current user credentials
DirectoryEntry de2 = new DirectoryEntry(
                            "LDAP://DC=thinktecture, DC=local");
```

Even if the construction of the `DirectoryEntry` object is successful, this doesn't mean that the binding was a success. Binding will happen the first time a property is read to avoid unnecessary network traffic. At the first access of the object, you can see if the object exists and if the specified user credentials are correct.

Getting Directory Entries

Now that you know how to specify the binding attributes to an object in Active Directory, you can move on to read the attributes of an object. In the following example, you read the properties of user objects.

The `DirectoryEntry` class has some properties to get information about the object: the `Name`, `Guid`, and `SchemaClassName` properties. The first time a property of the `DirectoryEntry` object is accessed, the binding occurs, and the cache of the underlying ADSI object is filled. (This is discussed in more detail shortly.) Additional properties are read from the cache, and communication with the server isn't necessary for data from the same object.

In the following example, the `user` object with the common name `Christian Nagel` in the organizational unit `thinktecture` is accessed:

```
using (DirectoryEntry de = new DirectoryEntry())
{
   de.Path = "LDAP://treslunas/CN=Christian Nagel, " +
             "OU=thinktecture, DC=explorer, DC=local";

   Console.WriteLine("Name: {0}", de.Name);
   Console.WriteLine("GUID: {0}", de.Guid);
   Console.WriteLine("Type: {0}", de.SchemaClassName);
   Console.WriteLine();

   //...
}
```

To have this code running on your machine, you must change the path to the object to access including the server name.

An Active Directory object holds much more information, with the information available depending on the type of the object; the `Properties` property returns a `PropertyCollection`. Each property is a collection itself, because a single property can have multiple values; for example, the `user` object can have multiple phone numbers. In this case, you go through the values with an inner `foreach` loop. The collection returned from `properties[name]` is an `object` array. The attribute values can be strings, numbers, or other types. Here, just the `ToString()` method is used to display the values:

```
Console.WriteLine("Properties: ");
PropertyCollection properties = de.Properties;
```

```
foreach (string name in properties.PropertyNames)
{
   foreach (object o in properties[name])
   {
      Console.WriteLine("{0}: {1}", name, o.ToString());
   }
}
```

In the resulting output, you can see all attributes of the specified `user` object. Some properties such as `otherTelephone` have multiple values. With this property, many phone numbers can be defined. Some of the property values just display the type of the object, `System.__ComObject`; for example, `lastLogoff`, `lastLogon`, and `nTSecurityDescriptor`. To get the values of these attributes, you must use the ADSI COM interfaces directly from the classes in the `System.DirectoryServices` namespace.

```
Name: CN=Christian Nagel
GUID: 7705eb3c-d5aa-40a4-97f9-2649c7693f39
Type: user

Properties:
objectClass: top
objectClass: person
objectClass: organizationalPerson
objectClass: user
cn: Christian Nagel
sn: Nagel
description: Author
givenName: Christian
distinguishedName: CN=Christian Nagel,OU=thinktecture,DC=explorer,DC=local
instanceType: 4
whenCreated: 22.08.2004 13:31:10
whenChanged: 24.05.2005 12:26:05
displayName: Christian Nagel
uSNCreated: System.__ComObject
uSNChanged: System.__ComObject
company: Thinktecture
extensionName: 5717D53E-DD6D-4d1e-8A1F-C7BE620F65AA:L
wWWHomePage: http://www.christiannagel.com
name: Christian Nagel
objectGUID: System.Byte[]
userAccountControl: 514
badPwdCount: 0
```

Access a Property Directly by Name

With `DirectoryEntry.Properties`, you can access all properties. If a property name is known, you can access the values directly:

```
foreach (string homePage in de.Properties["wWWHomePage"])
   Console.WriteLine("Home page: " + homePage);
```

Object Collections

Objects are stored hierarchically in Active Directory. Container objects contain children. You can enumerate these child objects with the `Children` property of the class `DirectoryEntry`. In the other direction, you can get the container of an object with the `Parent` property.

A `user` object doesn't have children, so you use an organizational unit in the following example. Non-container objects return an empty collection with the `Children` property. Get all `user` objects from the organizational unit `thinktecture` in the domain `explorer.local`. The `Children` property returns a `DirectoryEntries` collection that collects `DirectoryEntry` objects. You iterate through all `DirectoryEntry` objects to display the name of the child objects:

```
using (DirectoryEntry de = new DirectoryEntry())
{
   de.Path = "LDAP://treslunas/OU=thinktecture, " +
             "DC=explorer, DC=local";

   Console.WriteLine("Children of {0}", de.Name);
   foreach (DirectoryEntry obj in de.Children)
   {
      Console.WriteLine(obj.Name);
   }
}
```

When you run the program, the common names of the objects are displayed:

```
Children of OU=thinktecture
OU=Admin
CN=Buddhike de Silva
CN=Christian Nagel
CN=Christian Weyer
CN=Consultants
CN=demos
CN=Dominick Baier
CN=Ingo Rammer
CN=Neno Loye
```

In this example, you see all the objects in the organizational unit: `users`, `contacts`, `printers`, `shares`, and others. If you want to display only some object types, you can use the `SchemaFilter` property of the `DirectoryEntries` class. The `SchemaFilter` property returns a `SchemaNameCollection`. With this `SchemaNameCollection`, you can use the `Add()` method to define the object types you want to see. Here, you are just interested in seeing the `user` objects, so `user` is added to this collection:

```
using (DirectoryEntry de = new DirectoryEntry())
{
   de.Path = "LDAP://treslunas/OU=thinktecture, " +
             "DC=explorer, DC=local";

   Console.WriteLine("Children of {0}", de.Name);
   de.Children.SchemaFilter.Add("user");
   foreach (DirectoryEntry obj in de.Children)
   {
      Console.WriteLine(obj.Name);
   }
}
```

As a result, you see only the `user` objects in the organizational unit:

```
Children of OU=thinktecture
CN=Buddhike de Silva
CN=Christian Nagel
CN=Christian Weyer
CN=Dominick Baier
CN=Ingo Rammer
CN=Neno Loye
```

Cache

To reduce the network transfers, ADSI uses a cache for the object properties. As mentioned earlier, the server isn't accessed when a `DirectoryEntry` object is created; instead, with the first reading of a value from the directory store, all the properties are written into the cache so that a round trip to the server isn't necessary when the next property is accessed.

Writing any changes to objects changes only the cached object; setting properties doesn't generate network traffic. You must use `DirectoryEntry.CommitChanges()` to flush the cache and to transfer any changed data to the server. To get the newly written data from the directory store, you can use `DirectoryEntry.RefreshCache()` to read the properties. Of course, if you change some properties without calling `CommitChanges()` and do a `RefreshCache()`, all your changes will be lost, because you read the values from the directory service again using `RefreshCache()`.

It is possible to turn off this property cache by setting the `DirectoryEntry.UsePropertyCache` property to `false`. However, unless you are debugging your code, it's better not to turn off the cache because of the extra round trips to the server that will be generated.

Creating New Objects

When you want to create new Active Directory objects — such as users, computers, printers, contacts, and so on — you can do this programmatically with the `DirectoryEntries` class.

To add new objects to the directory, first you have to bind to a container object, such as an organizational unit, where new objects can be inserted — you cannot use objects that are not able to contain other objects. The following example uses the container object with the distinguished name `CN=Users, DC=thinktecture, DC=local`:

```
DirectoryEntry de = new DirectoryEntry();
de.Path = "LDAP://treslunas/CN=Users, DC=explorer, DC=local";
```

You can get to the `DirectoryEntries` object with the `Children` property of a `DirectoryEntry`:

```
DirectoryEntries users = de.Children;
```

The class `DirectoryEntries` offers methods to add, remove, and find objects in the collection. Here, a new `user` object is created. With the `Add()` method, the name of the object and a type name are required. You can get to the type names directly using ADSI Edit.

```
DirectoryEntry user = users.Add("CN=John Doe", "user");
```

The object now has the default property values. To assign specific property values, you can add properties with the `Add()` method of the `Properties` property. Of course, all of the properties must exist in the schema for the `user` object. If a specified property doesn't exist, you'll get a `COMException`: `"The specified directory service attribute or value doesn't exist"`:

```
user.Properties["company"].Add("Some Company");
user.Properties["department"].Add("Sales");
user.Properties["employeeID"].Add("4711");
user.Properties["samAccountName"].Add("JDoe");
user.Properties["userPrincipalName"].Add("JDoe@explorer.local");
user.Properties["givenName"].Add("John");
user.Properties["sn"].Add("Doe");
user.Properties["userPassword"].Add("someSecret");
```

Finally, to write the data to Active Directory, you must flush the cache:

```
user.CommitChanges();
```

Updating Directory Entries

Objects in the Active Directory service can be updated as easily as they can be read. After reading the object, you can change the values. To remove all values of a single property, you can call the method `PropertyValueCollection.Clear()`. You can add new values to a property with `Add()`. `Remove()` and `RemoveAt()` remove specific values from a property collection.

You can change a value simply by setting it to the specified value. The following example uses an indexer for `PropertyValueCollection` to set the mobile phone number to a new value. With the indexer a value can be changed only if it exists. Therefore, you should always check with `DirectoryEntry.Properties.Contains()` to see if the attribute is available:

```
using (DirectoryEntry de = new DirectoryEntry())
{
   de.Path = "LDAP://treslunas/CN=Christian Nagel, " +
             "OU=thinktecture, DC=explorer, DC=local";

   if (de.Properties.Contains("mobile"))
   {
      de.Properties["mobile"][0] = "+43(664)3434343434";
   }
   else
   {
      de.Properties["mobile"].Add("+43(664)3434343434");
   }

   de.CommitChanges();
}
```

The `else` part in this example uses the method `PropertyValueCollection.Add()` to add a new property for the mobile phone number, if it doesn't exist already. If you use the `Add()` method with already existing properties, the resulting effect would depend on the type of the property (single-value or multivalue property). Using the `Add()` method with a single-value property that already exists results in a `COMException: "A constraint violation occurred."` Using `Add()` with a multivalue property, however, succeeds, and an additional value is added to the property.

The `mobile` property for a `user` object is defined as a single-value property, so additional mobile phone numbers cannot be added. However, a user can have more than one mobile phone number. For multiple mobile phone numbers, the `otherMobile` property is available. `otherMobile` is a multivalue property that allows setting multiple phone numbers, and so calling `Add()` multiple times is allowed. Note that multivalue properties are checked for uniqueness. If the second phone number is added to the same `user` object again, you get a `COMException: "The specified directory service attribute or value already exists."`

Remember to call `DirectoryEntry.CommitChanges()` after creating or updating new directory objects. Otherwise, only the cache gets updated, and the changes are not sent to the directory service.

Accessing Native ADSI Objects

Often, it is much easier to call methods of predefined ADSI interfaces instead of searching for the names of object properties. Some ADSI objects also support methods that cannot be used directly from the `DirectoryEntry` class. One example of a practical use is the `IADsServiceOperations` interface, which has methods to start and stop Windows services. (For more details on Windows services see Chapter 23, "Windows Services.")

The classes of the `System.DirectoryServices` namespace use the underlying ADSI COM objects as mentioned earlier. The `DirectoryEntry` class supports calling methods of the underlying objects directly by using the `Invoke()` method.

The first parameter of `Invoke()` requires the method name that should be called in the ADSI object; the `params` keyword of the second parameter allows a flexible number of additional arguments that can be passed to the ADSI method:

```
public object Invoke(string methodName, params object[] args);
```

You can find the methods that can be called with the `Invoke()` method in the ADSI documentation. Every object in the domain supports the methods of the `IADs` interface. The `user` object that you created previously also supports the methods of the `IADsUser` interface.

In the following example, the method `IADsUser.SetPassword()` changes the password of the previously created `user` object:

```
using (DirectoryEntry de = new DirectoryEntry())
{
   de.Path = "LDAP://treslunas/CN=John Doe, " +
             "CN=Users, DC=explorer, DC=local";

   de.Invoke("SetPassword", "anotherSecret");
   de.CommitChanges();
}
```

It is also possible to use the underlying ADSI object directly instead of using `Invoke()`. To use these objects, choose Project ⇨ Add Reference to add a reference to the Active DS Type Library (see Figure 46-9). This creates a wrapper class where you can access these objects in the namespace `ActiveDs`.

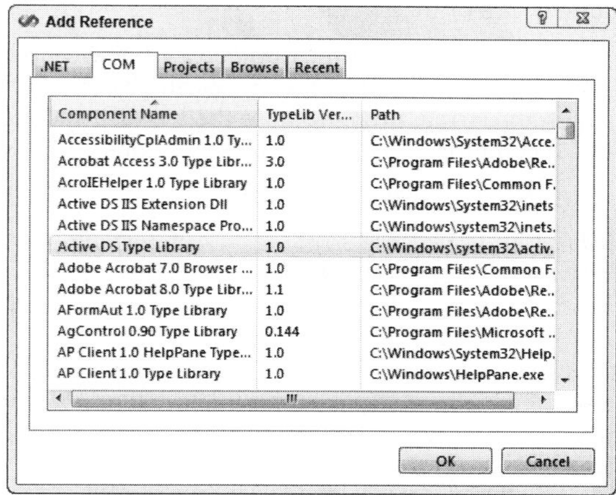

Figure 46-9

The native object can be accessed with the `NativeObject` property of the `DirectoryEntry` class. In the following example, the object `de` is a `user` object, so it can be cast to `ActiveDs.IADsUser`. `SetPassword()` is a method documented in the `IADsUser` interface, so you can call it directly instead of using the `Invoke()` method. By setting the `AccountDisabled` property of `IADsUser` to `false`, you can enable the account. As in the previous examples, the changes are written to the directory service by calling `CommitChanges()` with the `DirectoryEntry` object:

```
ActiveDs.IADsUser user = (ActiveDs.IADsUser)de.NativeObject;
user.SetPassword("someSecret");
user.AccountDisabled = false;
de.CommitChanges();
```

.NET 3.5 reduces the need to invoke the native objects behind the .NET class `DirectoryEntry`*. .NET 3.5 gives you new classes to manage users in the namespace* `System.DirectoryServices.AccountManagement`*. The classes from this namespace are explained later in this chapter.*

Searching in Active Directory

Because Active Directory is a data store optimized for *read-mostly* access, you will generally search for values. To search in Active Directory, the .NET Framework provides the `DirectorySearcher` class.

You can use `DirectorySearcher` *only with the LDAP provider; it doesn't work with the other providers such as NDS or IIS.*

In the constructor of the `DirectorySearcher` class, you can define four important parts for the search. You can also use a default constructor and define the search options with properties.

SearchRoot

The search root specifies where the search should start. The default of `SearchRoot` is the root of the domain you are currently using. `SearchRoot` is specified with the `Path` of a `DirectoryEntry` object.

Filter

The filter defines the values where you want to get hits. The filter is a string that must be enclosed in parentheses.

Relational operators such as <=, =, and >= are allowed in expressions. `(objectClass=contact)` searches all objects of type `contact`; `(lastName>=Nagel)` searches all objects alphabetically where the `lastName` property is equal to or larger than `Nagel`.

Expressions can be combined with the `&` and | prefix operators. For example, `(&(objectClass=user)(description=Auth*))` searches all objects of type `user` where the property description starts with the string `Auth`. Because the `&` and | operators are at the beginning of the expressions, it is possible to combine more than two expressions with a single prefix operator.

The default filter is `(objectClass=*)` so all objects are valid.

The filter syntax is defined in RFC 2254, "The String Representation of LDAP Search Filters." You can find this RFC at `www.ietf.org/rfc/rfc2254.txt`.

PropertiesToLoad

With `PropertiesToLoad`, you can define a `StringCollection` of all the properties in which you are interested. Objects can have a lot of properties, most of which will not be important for your search request. You define the properties that should be loaded into the cache. The default properties that are returned if nothing is specified are the path and the name of the object.

SearchScope

`SearchScope` is an enumeration that defines how deep the search should extend:

- `SearchScope.Base` searches only the attributes in the object where the search started, so at most one object is found.
- With `SearchScope.OneLevel`, the search continues in the child collection of the base object. The base object itself is not searched for a hit.
- `SearchScope.Subtree` defines that the search should go down the complete tree.

The default value of the `SearchScope` property is `SearchScope.Subtree`.

Search Limits

A search for specific objects in a directory service can span multiple domains. To limit the search to the number of objects or the time taken, you have some additional properties to define, as shown in the following table.

Property	Description
`ClientTimeout`	The maximum time the client waits for the server to return a result. If the server does not respond, no records are returned.
`PageSize`	With a *paged search*, the server returns a number of objects defined with the `PageSize` instead of the complete result. This reduces the time for the client to get a first answer and the memory needed. The server sends a cookie to the client, which is sent back to the server with the next search request so that the search can continue at the point where it finished.
`ServerPageTimeLimit`	For paged searches, this value defines the time a search should continue to return a number of objects that are defined with the `PageSize` value. If the time is reached before the `PageSize` value, the objects that were found up to that point are returned to the client. The default value is `-1`, which means infinite.
`SizeLimit`	Defines the maximum number of objects that should be returned by the search. If you set the limit to a value larger than defined by the server (which is 1000), the server limit is used.
`ServerTimeLimit`	Defines the maximum time the server will search for objects. When this time is reached, all objects that are found up to this point are returned to the client. The default is 120 seconds, and you cannot set the search to a higher value.
`ReferralChasing`	A search can cross multiple domains. If the root that's specified with `SearchRoot` is a parent domain or no root was specified, the search can continue to child domains. With this property, you can specify if the search should continue on different servers. `ReferralChasingOption.None` means that the search does not continue on other servers. The value `ReferralChasingOption.Subordinate` specifies that the search should go on to child domains. When the search starts at `DC=Wrox, DC=com` the server can return a result set and the referral to `DC=France, DC=Wrox, DC=COM`. The client can continue the search in the subdomain.

Property	Description
	`ReferralChasingOption.External` means that the server can refer the client to an independent server that is not in the subdomain. This is the default option. With `ReferralChasingOption.All`, both external and subordinate referrals are returned.
`Tombstone`	If the property `Tombstone` is set to `true`, all deleted objects that match the search are returned, too.
`VirtualListView`	If large results are expected with the search, the property `VirtualListView` can be used to define a subset that should be returned from the search. The subset is defined with the class `DirectoryVirtualListView`.

In the search example, all `user` objects with a property `description` value of `Author` are searched in the organizational unit `thinktecture`.

First, bind to the organizational unit `thinktecture`. This is where the search should start. Create a `DirectorySearcher` object where the `SearchRoot` is set. The filter is defined as `(&(objectClass=user)(description=Auth*))`, so that the search spans all objects of type `user` with a description of `Auth` followed by something else. The scope of the search should be a subtree so that child organizational units within `thinktecture` are searched, too:

```
using (DirectoryEntry de =
   new DirectoryEntry("LDAP://OU=thinktecture, DC=explorer, DC=local"))
using (DirectorySearcher searcher = new DirectorySearcher())
{
   searcher.SearchRoot = de;
   searcher.Filter = "(&(objectClass=user)(description=Auth*))";
   searcher.SearchScope = SearchScope.Subtree;
```

The properties that should be in the result of the search are `name`, `description`, `givenName`, and `wWWHomePage`:

```
   searcher.PropertiesToLoad.Add("name");
   searcher.PropertiesToLoad.Add("description");
   searcher.PropertiesToLoad.Add("givenName");
   searcher.PropertiesToLoad.Add("wWWHomePage");
```

You are ready to do the search. However, the result should also be sorted. `DirectorySearcher` has a `Sort` property, where you can set a `SortOption`. The first argument in the constructor of the `SortOption` class defines the property that will be used for a sort; the second argument defines the direction of the sort. The `SortDirection` enumeration has `Ascending` and `Descending` values.

To start the search, you can use the `FindOne()` method to find the first object, or `FindAll()`. `FindOne()` returns a simple `SearchResult`, whereas `FindAll()` returns a `SearchResultCollection`. Here, all authors should be returned, so `FindAll()` is used:

```
   searcher.Sort = new SortOption("givenName", SortDirection.Ascending);

   SearchResultCollection results = searcher.FindAll();
```

With a `foreach` loop, every `SearchResult` in the `SearchResultCollection` is accessed. A `SearchResult` represents a single object in the search cache. The `Properties` property returns a `ResultPropertyCollection`, where you access all properties and values with the property name and the indexer:

```
        SearchResultCollection results = searcher.FindAll();

        foreach (SearchResult result in results)
        {
           ResultPropertyCollection props = result.Properties;
           foreach (string propName in props.PropertyNames)
           {
              Console.Write("{0}: ", propName);
              Console.WriteLine(props[propName][0]);
           }
           Console.WriteLine();
        }
     }
```

It is also possible to get the complete object after a search: `SearchResult` has a `GetDirectoryEntry()` method that returns the corresponding `DirectoryEntry` of the found object.

The resulting output shows the beginning of the list of all `thinktecture` associates with the properties that have been chosen:

```
name: Christian Nagel
wwwhomepage: http://www.christiannagel.com
description: Author
givenname: Christian
adspath: LDAP://treslunas/CN=Christian Nagel,OU=thinktecture,DC=explorer,DC=local

name: Christian Weyer
description: Author
givenname: Christian
adspath: LDAP://treslunas/CN=Christian Weyer,OU=thinktecture,DC=explorer,DC=local

name: Ingo Rammer
wwwhomepage: http://www.thinktecture.com
description: Author
givenname: Ingo
adspath: LDAP://treslunas/CN=Ingo Rammer,OU=thinktecture,DC=explorer,DC=local
```

Searching for User Objects

In this section, you build a Windows Forms application called `UserSearch`. This application is flexible insofar as a specific domain controller, username, and password to access Active Directory can be entered; otherwise, the user of the running process is used. In this application, you access the schema of the Active Directory service to get the properties of a `user` object. The user can enter a filter string to search all `user` objects of a domain. It's also possible to set the properties of the `user` objects that should be displayed.

User Interface

The user interface shows numbered steps to indicate how to use the application (see Figure 46-10):

1. In the first step, `Username`, `Password`, and the `Domain Controller` can be entered. All this information is optional. If no domain controller is entered, the connection works with serverless binding. If the username is missing, the security context of the current user is taken.
2. A button allows all the property names of the `user` object to be loaded dynamically in the `listBoxProperties` list box.
3. After the property names are loaded, the properties to be displayed can be selected. The `SelectionMode` of the list box is set to `MultiSimple`.
4. The filter to limit the search can be entered. The default value set in this dialog box searches for all `user` objects: `(objectClass=user)`.
5. Now the search can start.

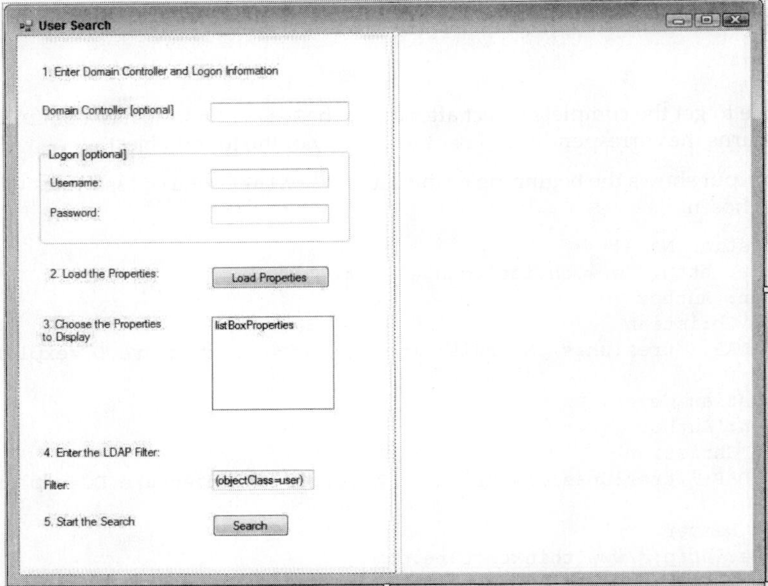

Figure 46-10

Get the Schema Naming Context

This application has only two handler methods: one method for the button to load the properties and one to start the search in the domain. First, you read the properties of the `user` class dynamically from the schema to display it in the user interface.

In the handler `buttonLoadProperties_Click()` method, `SetLogonInformation()` reads the username, password, and host name from the dialog box and stores them in members of the class. Next, the method `SetNamingContext()` sets the LDAP name of the schema and the LDAP name of the default context. This schema LDAP name is used in the call to set the properties in the list box: `SetUserProperties()`.

```
private void OnLoadProperties(object sender, System.EventArgs e)
{
   try
   {
      SetLogonInformation();
```

```
            SetNamingContext();

            SetUserProperties(schemaNamingContext);
        }
        catch (Exception ex)
        {
            MessageBox.Show("Check your inputs! " + ex.Message);
        }
    }
    protected void SetLogonInformation()
    {
        username = (textBoxUsername.Text == "" ? null : textBoxUsername.Text);
        password = (textBoxPassword.Text == "" ? null : textBoxPassword.Text);
        hostname = textBoxHostname.Text;

        if (hostname != "")
        {
            hostname += "/";
        }
    }
```

In the helper method `SetNamingContext()`, you are using the root of the directory tree to get the properties of the server. You are interested in the value of only two properties: `schemaNamingContext` and `defaultNamingContext`.

```
    protected void SetNamingContext()
    {
        using (DirectoryEntry de = new DirectoryEntry())
        {
            string path = "LDAP://" + hostname + "rootDSE";
            de.Username = username;
            de.Password = password;
            de.Path = path;
            schemaNamingContext =
                  de.Properties["schemaNamingContext"][0].ToString();
            defaultNamingContext =
                  de.Properties["defaultNamingContext"][0].ToString();
        }
    }
```

Get the Property Names of the User Class

You have the LDAP name to access the schema. You can use this to access the directory and read the properties. You are interested in not only the properties of the `user` class, but also those of the base classes of `user`: `Organizational-Person`, `Person`, and `Top`. In this program, the names of the base classes are hard-coded. You could also read the base class dynamically with the `subClassOf` attribute.

`GetSchemaProperties()` returns `IEnumerable<string>` with all property names of the specific object type. All the property names are added to the list box:

```
    protected void SetUserProperties(string schemaNamingContext)
    {
        var properties =
            from p in
                GetSchemaProperties(schemaNamingContext, "User").Concat(
                    GetSchemaProperties(schemaNamingContext,
```

(continued)

(continued)

```
                        "Organizational-Person")).Concat(
                    GetSchemaProperties(schemaNamingContext, "Person")).Concat(
                    GetSchemaProperties(schemaNamingContext, "Top"))
            orderby p
            select p;

        listBoxProperties.Items.Clear();
        foreach (string s in properties)
        {
            listBoxProperties.Items.Add(s);
        }
    }
```

In `GetSchemaProperties()`, you are accessing the Active Directory service again. This time, `rootDSE` is not used but rather the LDAP name to the schema that you discovered earlier. The property `systemMayContain` holds a collection of all attributes that are allowed in the class `objectType`:

```
protected IEnumerable<string> GetSchemaProperties(string schemaNamingContext,
                                                  string objectType)
{
    IEnumerable<string> data;
    using (DirectoryEntry de = new DirectoryEntry())
    {
        de.Username = username;
        de.Password = password;

        de.Path = String.Format("LDAP://{0}CN={1},{2}", hostname, objectType,
                                schemaNamingContext);

        PropertyValueCollection values = de.Properties["systemMayContain"];
        data = from s in values.Cast<string>()
               orderby s
               select s;
    }
    return data;
}
```

Step 2 in the application is completed. The `ListBox` control has all the property names of the `user` objects.

Search for User Objects

The handler for the search button calls only the helper method `FillResult()`:

```
private void OnSearch(object sender, System.EventArgs e)
{
    try
    {
        FillResult();
    }
    catch (Exception ex)
    {
        MessageBox.Show(String.Format("Check your input: {0}", ex.Message));
    }
}
```

In FillResult(), you do a normal search in the complete Active Directory Domain as you saw earlier. SearchScope is set to Subtree, the Filter to the string you get from a TextBox object, and the properties that should be loaded into the cache are set by the values the user selected in the list box. The PropertiesToLoad property of the DirectorySearcher is of type StringCollection where the properties that should be loaded can be added using the AddRange() method that requires a string array. The properties that should be loaded are read from the ListBox listBoxProperties with the property SelectedItems. After setting the properties of the DirectorySearcher object, the properties are searched by calling the SearchAll() method. The result of the search inside the SearchResultCollection is used to generate summary information that is written to the text box textBoxResults:

```
protected void FillResult()
{
   using (DirectoryEntry root = new DirectoryEntry())
   {
      root.Username = username;
      root.Password = password;
      root.Path = String.Format("LDAP://{0}{1}", hostname,
                                defaultNamingContext);

      using (DirectorySearcher searcher = new DirectorySearcher())
      {
         searcher.SearchRoot = root;
         searcher.SearchScope = SearchScope.Subtree;
         searcher.Filter = textBoxFilter.Text;
         searcher.PropertiesToLoad.AddRange(
               listBoxProperties.SelectedItems.Cast<string>().ToArray());

         SearchResultCollection results = searcher.FindAll();
         StringBuilder summary = new StringBuilder();
         foreach (SearchResult result in results)
         {
            foreach (string propName in result.Properties.PropertyNames)
            {
               foreach (string s in result.Properties[propName])
               {
                  summary.AppendFormat(" {0}: {1}\r\n", propName, s);
               }
            }
            summary.Append("\r\n");
         }
         textBoxResults.Text = summary.ToString();
      }
   }
}
```

Starting the application gives you a list of all objects where the filter is valid (see Figure 46-11).

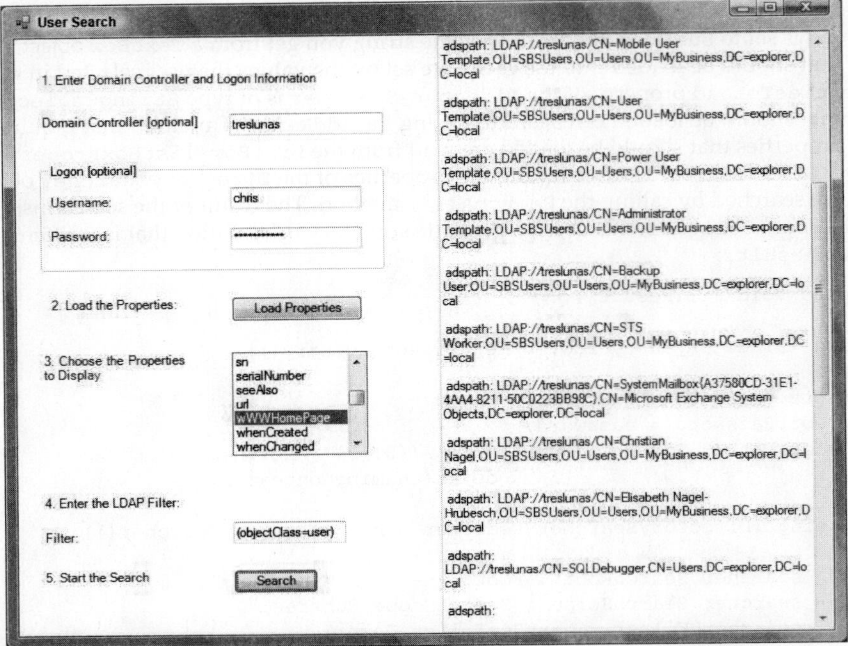

Figure 46-11

Account Management

Previous to .NET 3.5, it was difficult to create and modify user and group accounts. One way to do that was by using the classes from the `System.DirectoryServices` namespace, or by using the strongly typed native COM interfaces. New with .NET 3.5 is the assembly `System.DirectoryServices.AccountManagement` that offers an abstraction to the `System.DirectoryServices` classes by offering specific methods and properties to search, modify, create, and update users and groups.

The classes and their functionality are explained in the following table.

Class	Description
`PrincipalContext`	With the `PrincipalContext`, you configure the context of the account management. Here you can define if an Active Directory Domain, the accounts from the local system, or an application directory should be used. You set this by setting the `ContextType` enumeration to one of the values `Domain`, `Machine`, or `ApplicationDirectory`. Depending on the context type, you can also define the name of the domain and specify a username and password that are used for access.

Class	Description
Principal	Principal is the base class of all principals. With the static method FindByIdentity(), you can get a Principal identity object. With a principal object, you have access to various properties such as name, description, distinguished name, and also the object type from the schema. In case you need more control about the principal than is available from the properties and methods of this class, the method GetUnderlyingType() returns the underlying DirectoryEntry object.
AuthenticablePrincipal	AuthenticablePrincipal derives from Principal and is the base class for all principals that can be authenticated. There are several static methods to find principals, such as by logon or lockout times, by incorrect password attempts, or by password set time. Using instance methods, you can change the password and unlock an account.
UserPrincipal ComputerPrincipal	UserPrincipal and ComputerPrincipal derive from the base class AuthenticablePrincipal and thus have all properties and methods the base class has. UserPrincipal is the object that maps to a user account, and ComputerPrincipal maps to a computer account. With UserPrincipal, you have many properties to get and set information about the user, for example, EmployeeId, EmailAddress, GivenName, VoiceTelephoneNumber.
GroupPrincipal	Groups cannot authenticate; that's why GroupPrincipal derives directly from the Principal class. With GroupPrincipal, you can get members of the group with the Members property and the GetMembers() method.
PrincipalCollection	The PrincipalCollection contains a group of Principal objects; for example, the Members property from the GroupPrincipal class returns a PrincipalCollection object.
PrincipalSearcher	PrincipalSearcher is an abstraction of the DirectorySearcher class with special use for account management. With PrincipalSearcher, there's no need to know about the LDAP query syntax because this is created automatically.
PrincipalSearchResult<T>	Search methods from the PrincipalSearcher and Principal classes return a PrincipalSearchResult<T>.

The following sections look at some scenarios in which you can use the classes from the System.DirectoryServices.AccountManagement namespace.

Display User Information

The static property `Current` of the `UserPrincipal` class returns a `UserPrincipal` object with information about the currently logged-on user:

```
using (UserPrincipal user = UserPrincipal.Current)
{
    Console.WriteLine("Context Server: {0}",
          user.Context.ConnectedServer);
    Console.WriteLine(user.Description);
    Console.WriteLine(user.DisplayName);
    Console.WriteLine(user.EmailAddress);
    Console.WriteLine(user.GivenName);
    Console.WriteLine("{0:d}", user.LastLogon);
    Console.WriteLine(user.ScriptPath);
}
```

Running the application displays information about the user:

```
Context Server: treslunas.explorer.local
Power User
Christian Nagel
Christian.Nagel@thinktecture.com
Christian
2007/10/14
SBS_LOGIN_SCRIPT.bat
```

Create a User

You can use the `UserPrincipal` class to create a new user. First a `PrincipalContext` is required to define where the user should be created. With the `PrincipalContext`, you set the `ContextType` to an enumeration value of `Domain`, `Machine`, or `ApplicationDirectory` depending on whether the directory service, the local accounts of the machine, or an application directory should be used. If the current user does not have access to add accounts to Active Directory, you can also set a user and password with the `PrincipalContext` that is used to access the server.

Next, you can create an instance of `UserPrincipal` passing the principal context, and setting all required properties. Here, the `GivenName` and `EmailAddress` properties are set. Finally, you must invoke the `Save()` method of the `UserPrincipal` to write the new user to the store:

```
using (PrincipalContext context =
      new PrincipalContext(ContextType.Domain, "explorer"))
using (UserPrincipal user = new UserPrincipal(context, "Tom",
      "P@ssw0rd", true)
      {
         GivenName = "Tom",
         EmailAddress = "test@test.com"
      })
   {
      user.Save();
   }
```

Reset a Password

To reset a password from an existing user, you can use the `SetPassword()` method from a `UserPrincipal` object:

```
using (PrincipalContext context =
      new PrincipalContext(ContextType.Domain, "explorer"))
using (UserPrincipal user = UserPrincipal.FindByIdentity(
      context, IdentityType.Name, "Tom"))
{
   user.SetPassword("Pa$$w0rd");
   user.Save();
}
```

The user running this code needs to have the privilege to reset a password. To change the password from an old one to a new one, you can use the method `ChangePassword()`.

Create a Group

A new group can be created in a similar way to creating a new user. Here, just the class `GroupPrincipal` is used instead of the class `UserPrincipal`. As in creating a new user, the properties are set, and the `Save()` method is invoked:

```
using (PrincipalContext ctx =
      new PrincipalContext(ContextType.Domain, "explorer"))
using (GroupPrincipal group = new GroupPrincipal(ctx)
      {
         Description = "Sample group",
         DisplayName = "Wrox Authors",
         Name = "WroxAuthors"
      })
{
   group.Save();
}
```

Add a User to a Group

To add a user to a group, you can use a `GroupPrincipal` and add a `UserPrincipal` to the `Members` property of the group. To get an existing user and group, you can use the static method `FindByIdentity()`:

```
using (PrincipalContext context =
      new PrincipalContext(ContextType.Domain))
using (GroupPrincipal group = GroupPrincipal.FindByIdentity(
      context, IdentityType.Name, "WroxAuthors"))
using (UserPrincipal user = UserPrincipal.FindByIdentity(
      context, IdentityType.Name, "Verena Oslzly"))
{
   group.Members.Add(user);
   group.Save();
}
```

Finding Users

Static methods of the `UserPrincipal` object allow finding users based on some predefined criteria. The sample here shows finding users who didn't change their passwords within the last 30 days by using the method `FindPasswordSetTime()`. This method returns a

PrincipalSearchResult<UserPrincipal> collection that is iterated to display the user name, the last logon time, and the time when the password was reset:

```
using (PrincipalContext context =
      new PrincipalContext(ContextType.Domain, "explorer"))
using (PrincipalSearchResult<UserPrincipal> users =
      UserPrincipal.FindByPasswordSetTime(context,
      DateTime.Today - TimeSpan.FromDays(30), MatchType.LessThan))
{
   foreach (var user in users)
   {
      Console.WriteLine("{0}, last logon: {1}, " +
            "last password change: {2}", user.Name, user.LastLogon,
            user.LastPasswordSet);
   }
}
```

Other methods offered by the UserPrincipal class to find users are FindByBadPasswordAttempt(), FindByExpirationTime(), FindByLockoutTime(), and FindByLogonTime().

You can get more flexibility in finding users by using the PrincipalSearcher class. This class is an abstraction of the DirectorySearcher class and uses this class behind the scenes. With the PrincipalSearcher class, you can assign any Principal object to the QueryFilter property. In the example here, a UserPrincipal object with the properties Surname and Enabled is set to the QueryFilter. This way, all user objects starting with the surname Nag and which are enabled are returned with the PrincipalSearchResult collection. The PrincipalSearcher class creates an LDAP query string to do the search.

```
PrincipalContext context = new PrincipalContext(ContextType.Domain);

UserPrincipal userFilter = new UserPrincipal(context);
userFilter.Surname = "Nag*";
userFilter.Enabled = true;

using (PrincipalSearcher searcher = new PrincipalSearcher())
{
   searcher.QueryFilter = userFilter;
   PrincipalSearchResult<Principal> searchResult =
         searcher.FindAll();
   foreach (var user in searchResult)
   {
      Console.WriteLine(user.Name);
   }
}
```

DSML

With the namespace System.DirectoryServices.Protocols, you can access Active Directory through DSML (Directory Services Markup Language). DSML is a standard defined by the OASIS group (www.oasis-open.org) that allows you to access directory services through a Web service.

To make Active Directory available through DSML, you must have at least Windows Server 2003 R2 or you must install DSML Services for Windows. You can download DSML Services for Windows from the Microsoft Web site: www.microsoft.com/windowsserver2003/downloads/featurepacks/default.mspx.

Figure 46-12 shows a configuration scenario with DSML. A system that offers DSML services accesses Active Directory via LDAP. On the client system, the DSML classes from the namespace `System.DirectoryServices.Protocols` are used to make SOAP requests to the DSML service.

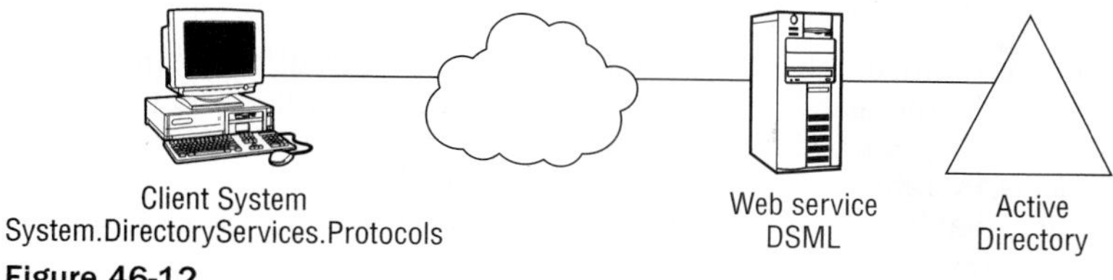

Figure 46-12

Classes in System.DirectoryServices.Protocols

The following table shows the major classes in the `System.DirectoryServices.Protocols` namespace.

Class	Description
`DirectoryConnection`	`DirectoryConnection` is the base class of all the connection classes that can be used to define the connection to the directory service. The classes that derive from `DirectoryConnection` are `LdapConnection` (for using the LDAP protocol), `DsmlSoapConnection`, and `DsmlSoapHttpConnection`.With the method `SendRequest`, a message is sent to the directory service.
`DirectoryRequest`	A request that can be sent to the directory service is defined by a class that derives from the base class `DirectoryRequest`. Depending on the request type, classes such as `SearchRequest`, `AddRequest`, `DeleteRequest`, and `ModifyRequest` can be used to send a request.
`DirectoryResponse`	The result that is returned with a `SendRequest` is of a type that derives from the base class `DirectoryResponse`. Examples for derived classes are `SearchResponse`, `AddResponse`, `DeleteResponse`, and `ModifyResponse`.

Searching for Active Directory Objects with DSML

This section looks at an example of how a search for directory services objects can be performed. As you can see in the code that follows, first a `DsmlSoapHttpConnection` object is instantiated that defines the connection to the DSML service. The connection is defined with the class `DsmlDirectoryIdentifier` that contains an `Uri` object. Optionally, the user credentials can be set with the connection:

```
Uri uri = new Uri("http://dsmlserver/dsml");
DsmlDirectoryIdentifier identifier = new DsmlDirectoryIdentifier(uri);

NetworkCredential credentials = new NetworkCredential();
credentials.UserName = "cnagel";
credentials.Password = "password";
```

(continued)

(continued)

```
credentials.Domain = "explorer";

DsmlSoapHttpConnection dsmlConnection =
      new DsmlSoapHttpConnection(identifier, credentials);
```

After the connection is defined, the search request can be configured. The search request consists of the directory entry where the search should start, an LDAP search filter, and the definition of what property values should be returned from the search. Here, the filter is set to `(objectClass=user)`, so that all user objects are returned from the search. `attributesToReturn` is set to `null`, and you can read all attributes that have values. `SearchScope` is an enumeration in the namespace `System.DirectoryServices.Protocols` that is similar to the `SearchScope` enumeration in the namespace `System.DirectoryServices` used to define how deep the search should go. Here, the `SearchScope` is set to `Subtree` to walk through the complete Active Directory tree.

The search filter can be defined with an LDAP string or by using an XML document contained in the `XmlDocument` class:

```
string distinguishedName = null;
string ldapFilter = "(objectClass=user)";
string[] attributesToReturn = null;// return all attributes

SearchRequest searchRequest = new SearchRequest(distinguishedName,
      ldapFilter, SearchScope.Subtree, attributesToReturn);
```

After the search is defined with the `SearchRequest` object, the search is sent to the Web service by calling the method `SendRequest`. `SendRequest` is a method of the `DsmlSoapHttpConnection` class. `SendRequest` returns a `SearchResponse` object where the returned objects can be read.

Instead of invoking the synchronous `SendRequest` method, the `DsmlSoapHttpConnection` class also offers the asynchronous methods `BeginSendRequest` and `EndSendRequest` that conform to the asynchronous .NET pattern.

The asynchronous pattern is explained in Chapter 19, "Threading and Synchronization."

```
SearchResponse searchResponse =
      (SearchResponse)dsmlConnection.SendRequest(searchRequest);
```

The returned Active Directory objects can be read within the `SearchResponse`. `SearchResponse.Entries` contains a collection of all entries that are wrapped with the type `SearchResultEntry`. The `SearchResultEntry` class has the `Attributes` property that contains all attributes. Each attribute can be read with help of the `DirectoryAttribute` class.

In the code example, the distinguished name of each object is written to the console. Next, the attribute values for the organizational unit (OU) are accessed, and the name of the organizational unit is written to the console. After this, all values of the `DirectoryAttribute` objects are written to the console:

```
Console.WriteLine("\r\nSearch matched {0} entries:",
      searchResponse.Entries.Count);
foreach (SearchResultEntry entry in searchResponse.Entries)
{
   Console.WriteLine(entry.DistinguishedName);

   // retrieve a specific attribute
   DirectoryAttribute attribute = entry.Attributes["ou"];
   Console.WriteLine("{0} = {1}", attribute.Name, attribute[0]);

   // retrieve all attributes
```

```
            foreach (DirectoryAttribute attr in entry.Attributes.Values)
            {
               Console.Write("{0}=", attr.Name);

               // retrieve all values for the attribute
               // the type of the value can be one of string, byte[] or Uri
               foreach (object value in attr)
               {
                  Console.Write("{0} ", value);
               }
               Console.WriteLine();
            }
         }
```

Adding, modifying, and deleting objects can be done similarly to searching objects. Depending on the action you want to perform, you can use the corresponding classes.

Summary

This chapter discussed the architecture of Active Directory: the important concepts of domains, trees, and forests. You can access information in the complete enterprise. When writing applications that access Active Directory services, you must be aware that the data you read might not be up to date because of the replication latency.

The classes in the `System.DirectoryServices` namespaces give you easy ways to access Active Directory services by wrapping to the ADSI providers. The `DirectoryEntry` class makes it possible to read and write objects directly in the data store.

With the `DirectorySearcher` class, you can perform complex searches and define filters, timeouts, properties to load, and a scope. By using the global catalog, you can speed up the search for objects in the complete enterprise, because it stores a read-only version of all objects in the forest.

DSML is another API that allows accessing the Active Directory through a Web service interface.

Classes in `System.DirectoryServices.AccountManagement` offer an abstraction to make it easier to create and modify user, group, and computer accounts.

The next chapter gives you another view on networking with peer-to-peer communication.

47

Peer-to-Peer Networking

Peer-to-peer networking, often referred to as P2P, is perhaps one of the most useful and yet misunderstood technologies to emerge in recent years. When people think of P2P they usually think of one thing: sharing music files, often illegally. This is because file-sharing applications such as BitTorrent have risen in popularity at a staggering rate, and these applications use P2P technology to work.

However, though P2P is used in file-sharing applications, that isn't to say that it doesn't have other applications. Indeed, as you see in this chapter, P2P can be used for a vast array of applications, and is becoming more and more important in the interconnected world in which we live. You learn about this in the first part of this chapter, when you look at an overview of P2P technologies.

Microsoft has not been oblivious to the emergence of P2P, and has been developing its own tools and technologies to use it. You can use the Microsoft Windows Peer-to-Peer Networking platform as a communication framework for P2P applications. This platform includes the important components Peer Name Resolution Protocol (PNRP) and People Near Me (PNM). Also, version 3.5 of the .NET Framework includes a new namespace, `System.Net.PeerToPeer`, and several new types and features that you can use to build P2P applications yourself with a minimum of effort.

In this chapter you look at:

- An overview of P2P
- The Microsoft Windows Peer-to-Peer Networking platform, including PNRP and PNM
- How to build P2P applications with the .NET Framework
- An example P2P application built using the .NET Framework

Peer-to-Peer Networking Overview

Peer-to-peer networking is an alternative approach to network communication. In order to understand how P2P differs from the "standard" approach to network communication it is necessary to take a step backward and look at client-server communications. Client-server communications are ubiquitous in networked applications today.

Client-Server Architecture

Traditionally, you interact with applications over a network (including the Internet) using a client-server architecture. Web sites are a great example of this. When you look at a Web site you send a request over the Internet to a Web server, which then returns the information that you require. If you want to download a file, you do so directly from the Web server.

Similarly, desktop applications that include local or wide area network connectivity will typically connect to a single server, for example, a database server or a server that hosts other services.

This simple form of client-server architecture is illustrated in Figure 47-1.

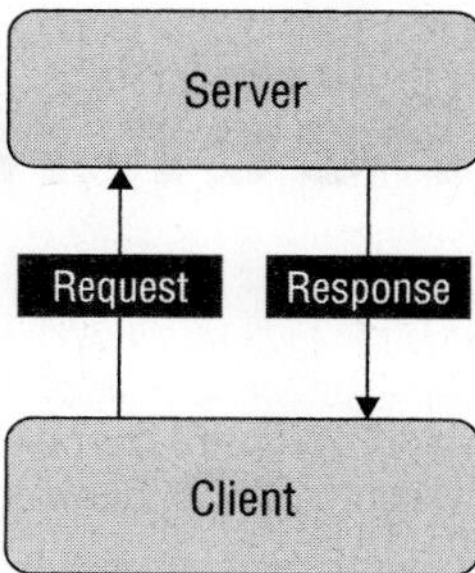

Figure 47-1

There is nothing inherently wrong with the client-server architecture, and indeed in many cases it will be exactly what you want. However, there is a scalability problem. Figure 47-2 shows how the client-server architecture scales with additional clients.

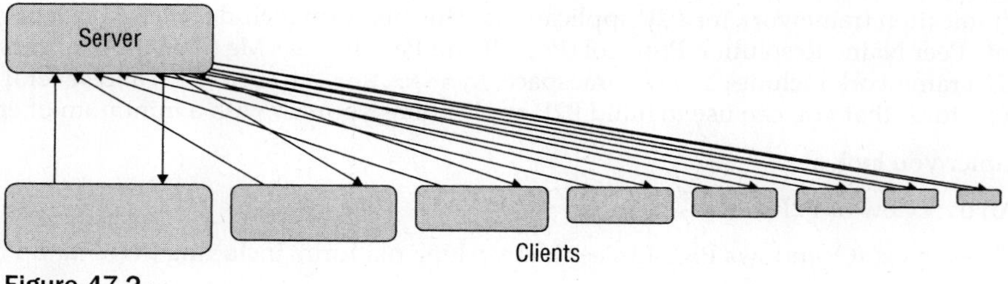

Figure 47-2

With every client that is added an increased load is placed on the server, which must communicate with each client. To return to the Web site example, this is how Web sites collapse. When there is too much traffic the server simply becomes unresponsive.

There are of course scaling options that you can implement to mitigate this situation. You can scale up by increasing the power and resources available to the server, or you can scale out by adding additional servers. Scaling up is of course limited by the technology available and the cost of better hardware. Scaling out is potentially more flexible, but requires an additional infrastructure layer to ensure that clients either communicate with individual servers or that clients can maintain session state independent of the server with which they are communicating. Plenty of solutions are available for this, such as Web or server farm products.

P2P Architecture

The peer-to-peer approach is completely different from either the scaling up or scaling out approach. With P2P, instead of focusing on and attempting to streamline the communication between the server and its clients, you instead look at ways in which clients can communicate with each other.

Say, for example, that the Web site that clients are communicating with is wrox.com. In our imaginary scenario, Wrox has announced that a new version of this book is to be released on the wrox.com web site and will be free to download to anyone who wants it, but that it will be removed after one day. Before the book is available on the Web site you might imagine that an awful lot of people will be looking at the Web site and refreshing their browsers, waiting for the file to appear. Once the file is available, everyone will try to download it at the same time, and more than likely the wrox.com Web server will collapse under the strain.

You could use P2P technology to prevent this Web server collapse from occurring. Instead of sending the file directly from the server to all the clients, you send the file to just a few clients. A few of the remaining clients then download the file from the clients that already have it, a few more clients download it from those second-level clients, and so on. In fact, this process is made even faster by splitting the file into chunks and dividing these chunks between clients, some of whom download it directly from the server, and some of whom download chunks from other clients. This is how file-sharing technologies such as BitTorrent work, and is illustrated in Figure 47-3.

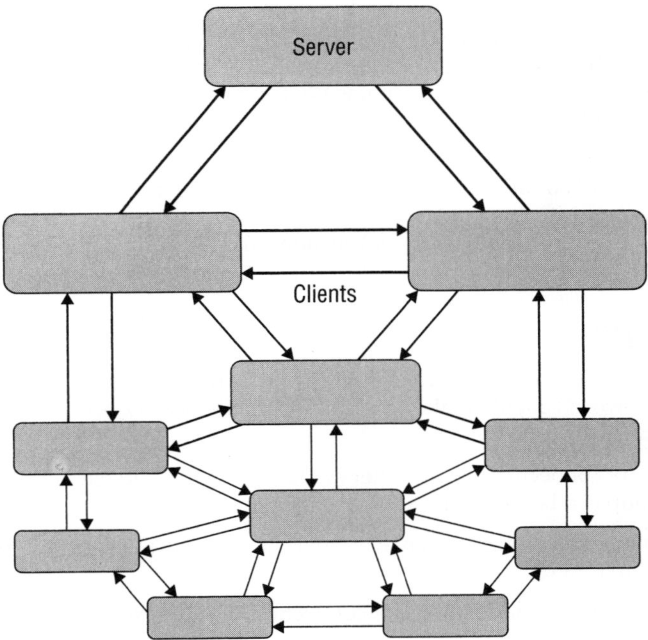

Figure 47-3

P2P Architectural Challenges

There are still problems to solve in the file-sharing architecture discussed here. For a start, how do clients detect that other clients exist, and how do they locate chunks of the file that other clients might have? Also, how can you ensure optimal communication between clients that may be separated by entire continents?

Every client participating in a P2P network application must be able to perform the following operations to overcome these problems:

- It must be able to *discover* other clients.
- It must be able to *connect* to other clients.
- It must be able to *communicate* with other clients.

The discovery problem has two obvious solutions. You can either keep a list of the clients on the server so clients can obtain this list and contact other clients (known as *peers*), or you can use an infrastructure (for example PNRP, covered in the next section) that enables clients to find each other directly. Most file-sharing systems use the "list on a server" solution, by using servers know as trackers. Also, in file-sharing systems any client may act as a server as shown in Figure 47-3, by declaring that it has a file available and registering it with a tracker. In fact, a pure P2P network needs no servers at all, just peers.

The connection problem is a more subtle one, and concerns the overall structure of the networks used by a P2P application. If you have one group of clients, all of which can communicate with one another, the topology of the connections between these clients can become extremely complex. You can often improve performance by having more than one group of clients, each of which consists of connections between clients in that group, but not to clients in other groups. If you can make these groups locale-based you will get an additional performance boost, because clients can communicate with each other with fewer hops between networked computers.

Communication is perhaps a problem of lesser importance, because communication protocols such as TCP/IP are well established and can be reused here. There is, however, scope for improvement in both high-level technologies (for example, you can use WCF services and therefore all the functionality that WCF offers) and low-level protocols (such as multicast protocols to send data to multiple endpoints simultaneously).

Discovery, connection, and communication are central to any P2P implementation. The implementation you look at in this chapter is to use the `System.Net.PeerToPeer` types with PNM for discovery and PNRP for connection. As you see in subsequent sections, these technologies cover all three of these operations.

P2P Terminology

In the previous sections you were introduced to the concept of a *peer*, which is how clients are referred to in a P2P network. The word "client" makes no sense in a P2P network because there is not necessarily a server to be a client of.

Groups of peers that are connected to each other are known by the interchangeable terms *meshes*, *clouds*, or *graphs*. A given group can be said to be *well-connected* if:

- There is a connection path between every pair of peers, so that every peer can connect to any other peer as required.
- There are a relatively small number of connections to traverse between any pair of peers.
- Removing a peer will not prevent other peers from connecting to each other.

Note that this does not mean that every peer must be able to connect to every other peer. In fact, if you analyze a network mathematically you will find that peers need to connect only to a relatively small number of other peers in order for these conditions to be met.

Another P2P concept to be aware of is that of *flooding*. Flooding is the way in which a single piece of data may be propagated through a network to all peers, or of querying other nodes in a network to locate a specific piece of data. In unstructured P2P networks this is a fairly random process of contacting nearest neighbor peers, which in turn contact their nearest neighbors, and so on until every peer in the network is contacted. It is also possible to create structured P2P networks such that there are well-defined pathways for queries and data flow among peers.

P2P Solutions

Once you have an infrastructure for P2P you can start to develop not just improved versions of client-server applications, but entirely new applications. P2P is particularly suited to the following classes of applications:

- Content distribution applications, including the file-sharing applications discussed earlier.
- Collaboration applications, such as desktop sharing and shared whiteboard applications.
- Multi-user communication applications that allow users to communicate and exchange data directly rather than through a server.
- Distributed processing applications, as an alternative to supercomputing applications that process enormous amounts of data.
- Web 2.0 applications that combine some or all of the above in dynamic next-generation Web applications.

Microsoft Windows Peer-to-Peer Networking

The Microsoft Windows Peer-to-Peer Networking platform is Microsoft's implementation of P2P technology. It is part of Windows XP SP2 and Windows Vista, and is also available as an add-on for Windows XP SP1. It includes two technologies that you can use when creating .NET P2P applications:

- The Peer Name Resolution Protocol (PNRP), which is used to publish and resolve peer addresses
- The People Near Me server, which is used to locate local peers (currently Vista only)

In this section you learn about both of these.

Peer Name Resolution Protocol (PNRP)

You can of course use any protocol at your disposal to implement a P2P application, but if you are working in a Microsoft Windows environment (and, let's face it, if you're reading this book you probably are) it makes sense to at least consider PNRP. There have been two versions of PNRP released to date. PNRP version 1 was included in Windows XP SP2, Windows XP Professional x64 Edition, and Windows XP SP1 with the Advanced Networking Pack for Windows XP. PNRP version 2 was released with Windows Vista, and was made available to Windows XP SP2 users through a separate download (see KB920342 at `support.microsoft.com/kb/920342`). Version 1 and version 2 of PNRP are not compatible, and this chapter covers only version 2.

In itself, PNRP doesn't give you everything you need to create a P2P application. Rather, it is one of the underlying technologies that you use to resolve peer addresses. PNRP enables a client to register an endpoint (known as a *peer name*) that is automatically circulated among peers in a cloud. This peer name is encapsulated in a *PNRP ID*. A peer that discovers the PNRP ID is able to use PNRP to resolve it to the actual peer name, and can then communicate directly with it.

For example, you might define a peer name that represents a WCF service endpoint. You could use PNRP to register this peer name in a cloud as a PNRP ID. A peer running a suitable client application that uses a discovery mechanism that can identify peer names for the service you are exposing might then discover this PNRP ID. Once discovered, the peer would use PNRP to locate the endpoint of the WCF service and then use that service.

An important point is that PNRP makes no assumptions about what a peer name actually represents. It is up to peers to decide how to use them once discovered. The information a peer receives from PNRP when resolving a PNRP ID includes the IPv6 (and usually also the IPv4) address of the publisher of the ID, along with a port number and optionally a small amount of additional data. Unless the peer knows what the peer name means it is unlikely to be able to do anything useful with this information.

PNRP IDs

PNRP IDs are 256-bit identifiers. The low-order 128 bits are used to uniquely identify a particular peer, and the high-order 128 bits identify a peer name. The high-order 128 bits are a hashed combination of a hashed public key from the publishing peer and a string of up to 149 characters that identifies the peer name. The hashed public key (known as the *authority*) combined with this string (the *classifier*) are together referred to as the P2P ID. It is also possible to use a value of 0 instead of a hashed public key, in which case the peer name is said to be *unsecured* (as opposed to *secured* peer names, which use a public key).

The structure of a PNRP ID is illustrated in Figure 47-4.

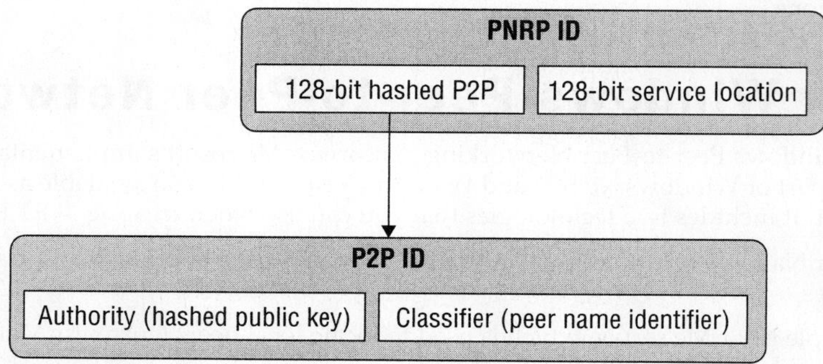

Figure 47-4

The PNRP service on a peer is responsible for maintaining a list of PNRP IDs, including the ones that it publishes as well as a cached list of those it has obtained by PNRP service instances elsewhere in the cloud. When a peer attempts to resolve a PNRP ID, the PNRP service either uses a cached copy of the endpoint to resolve the peer that published the PNRP or it asks its neighbors if they can resolve it. Eventually a connection to the publishing peer is made and the PNRP service can resolve the PNRP ID.

Note that all of this happens without you having to intervene in any way. All you have to do is ensure that peers know what to do with peer names once they have resolved them using their local PNRP service.

Peers can use PNRP to locate PNRP IDs that match a particular P2P ID. You can use this to implement a very basic form of discovery for unsecured peer names. This is because if several peers expose an unsecured peer name that uses the same classifier, the P2P ID will be the same. Of course, because any peer can use an unsecured peer name you have no guarantee that the endpoint you connect to will be the sort of endpoint you expect, so this is only really a viable solution for discovery over a local network.

PNRP Clouds

In the preceding discussion you learned how PNRP registers and resolves peer names in clouds. A cloud is maintained by a *seed server*, which can be any server running the PNRP service that maintains a record of at least one peer. Two types of cloud are available to the PNRP service:

- **Link local** — These clouds consist of the computers attached to a local network. A PC may be connected to more than one link local cloud if it has multiple network adapters.
- **Global** — This cloud consists of computers connected to the Internet by default, although it is also possible to define a private global cloud. The difference is that Microsoft maintains the seed server for the global Internet cloud, whereas if you define a private global cloud you must use your own. If you use your own seed server you must ensure that all peers connect to it by configuring policy settings.

In past releases of PNRP there was a third type of cloud, site local. This is no longer used and you won't look at it in this chapter.

You can discover what clouds you are connected to with the following command:

```
netsh p2p pnrp cloud show list
```

A typical result is shown in Figure 47-5.

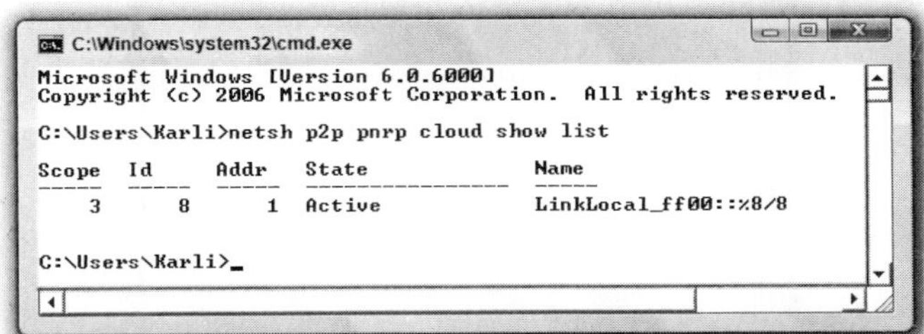

Figure 47-5

Figure 47-5 shows that a single cloud is available, and that it is a link local cloud. You can tell this from both the name and the `Scope` value, which is 3 for link local clouds and 1 for global clouds. In order to connect to a global cloud you must have a global IPv6 address. The computer used to generate Figure 47-5 does not have one, which is why only a local cloud is available.

Clouds may be in one of the following states:

- **Active** — If the state of a cloud is active, you can use it to publish and resolve peer names.
- **Alone** — If the peer you are querying the cloud from is not connected to any other peers, it will have a state of alone.
- **No Net** — If the peer is not connected to a network, the cloud state may change from active to no net.
- **Synchronizing** — Clouds will be in the synchronizing state when the peer is connecting to them. This state will change to another state extremely quickly because this connection does not take long, so you will probably never see a cloud in this state.
- **Virtual** — The PNRP service connects to clouds only as required by peer name registration and resolution. If a cloud connection has been inactive for more than 15 minutes it may enter the virtual state.

If you experience network connectivity problems you should check your firewall in case it is preventing local network traffic over the UDP ports 3540 or 1900. UDP port 3540 is used by PNRP, and UDP port 1900 is used by the Simple Service Discovery Protocol (SSDP), which in turn is used by the PNRP service (as well as UPnP devices).

People Near Me

PNRP, as you saw in the previous section, is used to locate peers. This is obviously important as an enabling technology when you consider the discovery/connection/communication process of a P2P application, but in itself is not a complete implementation of any of these stages. The People Near Me service is an implementation of the discovery stage, and enables you to locate peers that are signed into the Window People Near Me service in your local area (that is, in a link local cloud that you are connected to).

You may have come across this service because it is built into Vista, and is used in the Windows Meeting Space application, which you can use for sharing applications among peers. You can configure this service through the Start menu with the dialog shown in Figure 47-6.

Figure 47-6

Once signed in the service is available to any application that is built to use the PNM service.

At the time of writing, PNM is available only on the Windows Vista family of operating systems. However, it is possible that future service packs or additional downloads may make it available on Windows XP.

Building P2P Applications

Now that you have learned what P2P networking is and what technologies are available to .NET developers to implement P2P applications, it is time to look at how you can build them. From the previous discussion you know that you will be using PNRP to publish, distribute, and resolve peer names, so the first thing you look at here is how to achieve that using .NET. Next you look at how to use PNM as a framework for a P2P application. This can be advantageous because you do not have to implement your own discovery mechanisms.

To examine these subjects you need to learn about the classes in the following namespaces:

- `System.Net.PeerToPeer`
- `System.Net.PeerToPeer.Collaboration`

To use these classes you must have a reference to the `System.Net.dll` assembly.

System.Net.PeerToPeer

The classes in the `System.Net.PeerToPeer` namespace encapsulate the API for PNRP and enable you to interact with the PNRP service. You will use these classes for two main tasks:

- Registering peer names
- Resolving peer names

In the following sections, all the types referred to come from the `System.Net.PeerToPeer` namespace unless otherwise specified.

Registering Peer Names

To register a peer name you must carry out the following steps:

1. Create a secured or unsecured peer name with a specified classifier.
2. Configure a registration for the peer name, specifying some or none of the following optional information:
    - A TCP port number
    - The cloud or clouds to register the peer name with (if unspecified, PNRP will register the peer name in all available clouds)
    - A comment of up to 39 characters
    - Up to 4096 bytes of additional data
    - Whether to generate endpoints for the peer name automatically (the default behavior, where endpoints will be generated from the IP address or addresses of the peer and, if specified, the port number)
    - A collection of endpoints
3. Use the peer name registration to register the peer name with the local PNRP service.

After Step 3 the peer name will be available to all peers in the selected cloud (or clouds). Peer registration continues until it is explicitly stopped, or until the process that registered the peer name is terminated.

To create a peer name you use the `PeerName` class. You create an instance of this class from a string representation of a P2P ID in the form `authority.classifier` or from a classifier string and a `PeerNameType`. You can use `PeerNameType.Secured` or `PeerNameType.Unsecured`. For example:

```
PeerName pn = new PeerName("Peer classifier", PeerNameType.Secured);
```

Because an unsecured peer name uses an authority value of 0, the following lines of code are equivalent:

```
PeerName pn = new PeerName("Peer classifier", PeerNameType.Unsecured);

PeerName pn = new PeerName("0.Peer classifier");
```

Once you have a `PeerName` instance you can use it along with a port number to initialize a `PeerNameRegistration` object:

```
PeerNameRegistration pnr = new PeerNameRegistration(pn, 8080);
```

Alternatively, you can set the `PeerName` and (optionally) the `Port` properties on a `PeerNameRegistration` object created using its default parameter. You can also specify a `Cloud` instance as a third parameter of the `PeerNameRegistration` constructor, or through the `Cloud` property. You can obtain a `Cloud` instance from the cloud name or by using one of the following static members of `Cloud`:

- `Cloud.Global` — This static property obtains a reference to the global cloud. This may be a private global cloud depending on peer policy configuration.
- `Cloud.AllLinkLocal` — This static field gets a cloud that contains all the link local clouds available to the peer.
- `Cloud.Available` — This static field gets a cloud that contains all the clouds that are available to the peer, which includes link local clouds and (if available) the global cloud.

Once created, you can set the `Comment` and `Data` properties if you want to. Be aware of the limitations of these properties, though. You will receive a `PeerToPeerException` if you try to set `Comment` to a `string` of greater than 39 Unicode characters or an `ArgumentOutOfRangeException` if you try to set `Data` to a `byte[]` of greater than 4096 bytes. You can also add endpoints by using the `EndPointCollection` property. This property is a `System.Net.IPEndPointCollection` collection of `System.Net.IPEndPoint` objects. If you use the `EndPointCollection` property you might also want to set the `UseAutoEndPointSelection` property to `false` to prevent automatic generation of endpoints.

When you are ready to register the peer name you can call the `PeerNameRegistration.Start()` method. To remove a peer name registration from the PNRP service you use the `PeerNameRegistration.Stop()` method.

The following code registers a secured peer name with a comment:

```
PeerName pn = new PeerName("Peer classifier", PeerNameType.Unsecured);
PeerNameRegistration pnr = new PeerNameRegistration(pn, 8080);
pnr.Comment = "Get pizza here";
pnr.Start();
```

Resolving Peer Names

To resolve a peer name you must carry out the following steps:

1. Generate a peer name from a known P2P ID or a P2P ID obtained through a discovery technique.
2. Use a resolver to resolve the peer name and obtain a collection of peer name records. You can limit the resolver to a particular cloud and/or a maximum number of results to return.
3. For any peer name records that you obtain, obtain peer name, endpoint, comment, and additional data information as required.

This process starts with a `PeerName` object just like peer name registration. The difference here is that you use a peer name that is registered by one or more remote peers. The simplest way to get a list of active peers in your link local cloud is for each peer to register an unsecured peer name with the same classifier and to use the same peer name in the resolving phase. However, this is not a recommended strategy for global clouds because unsecured peer names are easily spoofed.

To resolve peer names you use the `PeerNameResolver` class. Once you have an instance of this class you can choose to resolve peer names synchronously by using the `Resolve()` method, or asynchronously using the `ResolveAsync()` method.

You can call the `Resolve()` method with a single `PeerName` parameter, but you can also pass an optional `Cloud` instance to resolve in, an `int` maximum number of peers to return, or both. This method returns a `PeerNameRecordCollection` instance, which is a collection of `PeerNameRecord` objects. For example, the following code resolves an unsecured peer name in all link local clouds and returns a maximum of 5 results:

```
PeerName pn = new PeerName("0.Peer classifier");
PeerNameResolver pnres = new PeerNameResolver();
PeerNameRecordCollection pnrc = pnres.Resolve(pn, Cloud.AllLinkLocal, 5);
```

The `ResolveAsync()` method uses a standard asynchronous method call pattern. You pass a unique `userState` object to the method, and listen for `ResolveProgressChanged` events for peers being found and the `ResolveCompleted` event when the method terminates. You can cancel a pending asynchronous request with the `ResolveAsyncCancel()` method.

Event handlers for the `ResolveProgressChanged` event use the `ResolveProgressChangedEventArgs` event arguments parameter, which derives from the standard `System.ComponentModel.ProgressChangedEventArgs` class. You can use the `PeerNameRecord` property of the event argument object you receive in the event handler to get a reference to the peer name record that was found.

Similarly, the `ResolveCompleted` event requires an event handler that uses a parameter of type `ResolveCompletedEventArgs`, which derives from `AsyncCompletedEventArgs`. This type includes a `PeerNameRecordCollection` parameter you can use to obtain a complete list of the peer name records that were found.

The following code shows an implementation of event handlers for these events:

```
private pnres_ResolveProgressChanged(object sender,
   ResolveProgressChangedEventArgs e)
{
   // Use e.ProgressPercentage (inherited from base event args)
   // Process PeerNameRecord from e.PeerNameRecord
}

private pnres_ResolveCompleted(object sender,
   ResolveCompletedEventArgs e)
{
   // Test for e.IsCancelled and e.Error (inherited from base event args)
   // Process PeerNameRecordCollection from e.PeerNameRecordCollection
}
```

Once you have one or more `PeerNameRecord` objects you can proceed to process them. This `PeerNameRecord` class exposes `Comment` and `Data` properties to examine the comment and data set in the peer name registration (if any), a `PeerName` property to get the `PeerName` object for the peer name record, and, most importantly, an `EndPointCollection` property. As with `PeerNameRegistration`, this property is a `System.Net.IPEndPointCollection` collection of `System.Net.IPEndPoint` objects. You can use these objects to connect to end points exposed by the peer in any way you want.

Code Access Security in System.Net.PeerToPeer

The `System.Net.PeerToPeer` namespace also includes the following two classes that you can use with CAS (see Chapter 20):

- `PnrpPermission`, which inherits from `CodeAccessPermission`
- `PnrpPermissionAttribute`, which inherits from `CodeAccessSecurityAttribute`

You can use these classes to provide permissions functionality for PNRP access in the usual CAS way.

Sample Application

The downloadable code for this chapter includes a sample P2P application (P2PSample) that uses the concepts and namespace introduced in this section. It is a WPF application that uses a WCF service for a peer endpoint.

The application is configured with an application configuration file, in which you can specify the name of the peer and a port to listen on as follows:

```
<?xml version="1.0" encoding="utf-8" ?>
<configuration>
  <appSettings>
    <add key="username" value="Karli" />
    <add key="port" value="8731" />
  </appSettings>
</configuration>
```

Once you have built the application you can test it either by copying it to other computers in your local network and running all instances, or by running multiple instances on one computer. If you choose the latter option you must remember to change the port used for each instance by changing individual config files (copy the contents of the `Debug` directory on your local computer and edit each config file in turn). Things will be clearer in both ways of testing this application if you also change the username for each instance.

Once the peer applications are running, you can use the Refresh button to obtain a list of peers asynchronously. When you have located a peer you can send a default message by clicking the Message button for the peer.

Figure 47-7 shows this application in action with three instances running on one machine. In the figure, one peer has just messaged another and this has resulted in a dialog box.

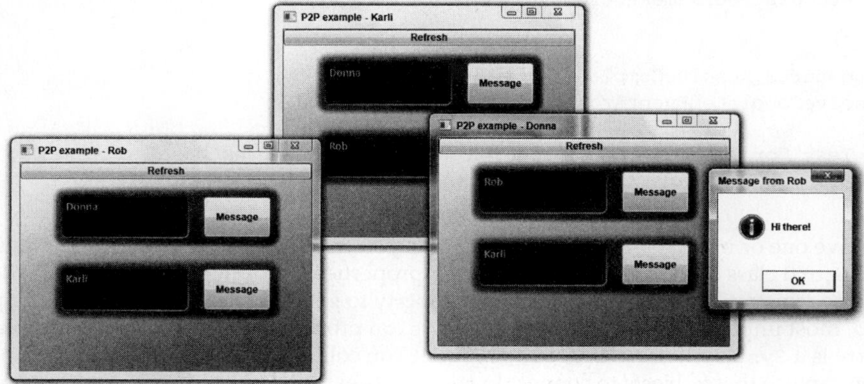

Figure 47-7

Most of the work in this application takes place in the `Window_Loaded()` event handler for the `Window1` window. This method starts by loading configuration information and setting the window title with the username:

```
private void Window_Loaded(object sender, RoutedEventArgs e)
{
   // Get configuration from app.config
   string port = ConfigurationManager.AppSettings["port"];
```

```
string username = ConfigurationManager.AppSettings["username"];
string machineName = Environment.MachineName;
string serviceUrl = null;

// Set window title
this.Title = string.Format("P2P example - {0}", username);
```

Next the peer host address is used along with the configured port to determine the endpoint on which to host the WCF service. The service will use `NetTcpBinding` binding, so the URL of the endpoint uses the `net.tcp` protocol:

```
// Get service url using IPv4 address and port from config file
foreach (IPAddress address in Dns.GetHostAddresses(Dns.GetHostName()))
{
   if (address.AddressFamily ==
      System.Net.Sockets.AddressFamily.InterNetwork)
   {
         serviceUrl = string.Format("net.tcp://{0}:{1}/P2PService",
            address, port);
         break;
   }
}
```

The endpoint URL is validated, and then the WCF service is registered and started:

```
// Check for null address
if (serviceUrl == null)
{
   // Display error and shutdown
   MessageBox.Show(this, "Unable to determine WCF endpoint.",
     "Networking Error", MessageBoxButton.OK, MessageBoxImage.Stop);
   Application.Current.Shutdown();
}

// Register and start WCF service.
localService = new P2PService(this, username);
host = new ServiceHost(localService, new Uri(serviceUrl));
NetTcpBinding binding = new NetTcpBinding();
binding.Security.Mode = SecurityMode.None;
host.AddServiceEndpoint(typeof(IP2PService), binding, serviceUrl);
try
{
   host.Open();
}
catch (AddressAlreadyInUseException)
{
   // Display error and shutdown
   MessageBox.Show(this, "Cannot start listening, port in use.",
       "WCF Error", MessageBoxButton.OK, MessageBoxImage.Stop);
   Application.Current.Shutdown();
}
```

A singleton instance of the service class is used to enable easy communication between the host app and the service (for sending and receiving messages). Also, note that security is disabled in the binding configuration for simplicity.

Next, the `System.Net.PeerToPeer` namespace classes are used to register a peer name:

```
        // Create peer name
        peerName = new PeerName("P2P Sample", PeerNameType.Unsecured);

        // Prepare peer name registration in link local clouds
        peerNameRegistration = new PeerNameRegistration(peerName, int.Parse(port));
        peerNameRegistration.Cloud = Cloud.AllLinkLocal;

        // Start registration
        peerNameRegistration.Start();
    }
```

When the Refresh button is clicked the `RefreshButton_Click()` event handler uses `PeerNameResolver.ResolveAsync()` to get peers asynchronously:

```
    private void RefreshButton_Click(object sender, RoutedEventArgs e)
    {
        // Create resolver and add event handlers
        PeerNameResolver resolver = new PeerNameResolver();
        resolver.ResolveProgressChanged +=
            new EventHandler<ResolveProgressChangedEventArgs>(
                resolver_ResolveProgressChanged);
        resolver.ResolveCompleted +=
            new EventHandler<ResolveCompletedEventArgs>(
                resolver_ResolveCompleted);

        // Prepare for new peers
        PeerList.Items.Clear();
        RefreshButton.IsEnabled = false;

        // Resolve unsecured peers asynchronously
        resolver.ResolveAsync(new PeerName("0.P2P Sample"), 1);
    }
```

The remainder of the code is responsible for displaying and communicating with peers, and you can explore it at your leisure.

Exposing WCF endpoints through P2P clouds is a great way of locating services within an enterprise, as well as being an excellent way to communicate between peers as in this example.

System.Net.PeerToPeer.Collaboration

The classes in the `System.Net.PeerToPeer.Collaboration` namespace provide a framework you can use to create applications that use the People Near Me service and the P2P collaboration API. As mentioned earlier, this is possible only if you are using Windows Vista at the moment.

You can use the classes in this namespace to interact with peers and applications in a number of ways, including:

- Signing in and signing out
- Discovering peers
- Managing contacts and detecting peer presence

You can also use the classes in this namespace to invite other users to join an application, and to exchange data between users and applications. However, in order to do this you need to create your own PNM-capable applications, which is beyond the scope of this chapter.

In the following sections, all the types referred to come from the `System.Net.PeerToPeer.Collaboration` namespace unless otherwise specified.

Signing In and Signing Out

One of the most important classes in the `System.Net.PeerToPeer.Collaboration` namespace is the `PeerCollaboration` class. This is a static class that exposes numerous static methods that you can use for various purposes, as you will see in this and subsequent sections. You can use two of the methods it exposes, `SignIn()` and `SignOut()`, to (unsurprisingly) sign in and sign out of the People Near Me service. Both of these methods take a single parameter of type `PeerScope`, which can be one of the following values:

- `PeerScope.None` — If you use this value, `SignIn()` and `SignOut()` will have no effect.
- `PeerScope.NearMe` — This will sign you in to or out of the link local clouds.
- `PeerScope.Internet` — This will sign you in to or out of the global cloud (which may be necessary to connect to a contact who is not currently on your local subnet).
- `PeerScope.All` — This will sign you in to or out of all available clouds.

If necessary, calling `SignIn()` will cause the People Near Me configuration dialog to be displayed.

When a peer is signed in you can use the `PeerCollaboration.LocalPresenceInfo` property to a value of type `PeerPresenceInfo`. This enables standard IM functionality, such as setting your status to away. You can set the `PeerPresenceInfo.DescriptiveText` property to a Unicode string of up to 255 characters, and the `PeerPresenceInfo.PresenceStatus` property to a value from the `PeerPresenceStatus` enumeration. The values that you can use for this enumeration are as follows:

- `PeerPresenceStatus.Away` — The peer is away.
- `PeerPresenceStatus.BeRightBack` — The peer is away, but will be back soon.
- `PeerPresenceStatus.Busy` — The peer is busy.
- `PeerPresenceStatus.Idle` — The peer isn't active.
- `PeerPresenceStatus.Offline` — The peer is offline.
- `PeerPresenceStatus.Online` — The peer is online and available.
- `PeerPresenceStatus.OnThePhone` — The peer is busy with a phone call.
- `PeerPresenceStatus.OutToLunch` — The peer is away, but will be back after lunch.

Discovering Peers

You can obtain a list of peers near you if you are logged in to the link local cloud. You do this by using the `PeerCollaboration.GetPeersNearMe()` method. This returns a `PeerNearMeCollection` object containing `PeerNearMe` objects.

You can use the `Nickname` property of `PeerNearMe` to obtain the name of a peer, `IsOnline` to determine whether the peer is online, and (for lower-level operations) the `PeerEndpoints` property to determine endpoints related to the peer. `PeerEndPoints` is also necessary if you want to find out the online status of a `PeerNearMe`. You can pass an endpoint to the `GetPresenceInfo()` method to obtain a `PeerPresenceInfo` object, as described in the previous section.

Managing Contacts and Detecting Peer Presence

Contacts are a way in which you can remember peers. You can add a peer discovered through the People Near Me service and from then onward you can connect to them whenever you are both online. You can connect to a contact through link local or global clouds (assuming you have IPv6 connectivity to the Internet).

You can add a contact from a peer that you have discovered, by calling the `PeerNearMe.AddToContactManager()` method. When you call this method you can choose to associate a display name, nickname, and email address with the contact. Typically, though, you will manage contacts by using the `ContactManager` class.

However you manipulate contacts, you will be dealing with `PeerContact` objects. `PeerContact`, like `PeerNearMe`, inherits from the abstract `Peer` base class. `PeerContact` has more properties and methods than `PeerNearMe`. `PeerContact` includes `DisplayName` and `EmailAddress` properties that further describe a PNM peer, for example. Another difference between these two types is that `PeerContact` has a more explicit relationship with the `System.Net.PeerToPeer.PeerName` class. You can get a `PeerName` from a `PeerContact` through the `PeerContact.PeerName` property. Once you have done this you can proceed to use techniques you looked at earlier to communicate with any endpoints the `PeerName` exposes.

Information about the local peer is also accessible through the `ContactManager` class, through the static `ContactManager.LocalContact` property. This gets you a `PeerContact` property with details of the local peer.

You can add `PeerNearMe` objects to the local list of contacts by using either the `ContactManager.CreateContact()` or `CreateContactAsync()` method, or `PeerName` objects by using the `GetContact()` method. You can remove contacts represented by a `PeerNearMe` or `PeerName` object with the `DeleteContact()` method.

Finally, there are events that you can handle to respond to changes to contacts. For example, you can use the `PresenceChanged` event to respond to changes of presence for any of the contacts known by the `ContactManager`.

Sample Application

There is a second sample application in the downloadable code for this chapter that illustrates the use of classes in the `System.Net.PeerToPeer.Collaboration` namespace. This application is similar to the other sample, but much simpler. You will need two computers that can both sign in to the PNM server in order to see this application in action, because it enumerates and displays PNM peers from the local subnet.

When you run the application with at least one peer available for discovery the display will be similar to Figure 47-8.

Figure 47-8

The code is structured in the same way as the previous example, so if you've read through that code you should be familiar with this code. This time there is not much work to do in the `Window_Loaded()` event handler except sign in, because there is no WCF service to initialize or peer name registration to achieve:

```
private void Window_Loaded(object sender, RoutedEventArgs e)
{
   // Sign in to PNM
   PeerCollaboration.SignIn(PeerScope.NearMe);
```

To make things look a little nicer, though, `ContactManager.LocalContact.Nickname` is used to format the window title:

```
      // Get local peer name to display
      this.Title = string.Format("PNMSample - {0}",
         ContactManager.LocalContact.Nickname);
   }
```

In `Window_Closing()` the local peer is automatically signed out of PNM:

```
private void Window_Closing(object sender,
   System.ComponentModel.CancelEventArgs e)
{
   // Sign out of PNM
   PeerCollaboration.SignOut(PeerScope.NearMe);
}
```

Most of the work is done in the `RefreshButton_Click()` event handler. This uses the `PeerCollaboration.GetPeersNearMe()` method to obtain a list of peers, and add those peers to the display using the `PeerEntry` class defined in the project, or a failure message if none are found.

```
private void RefreshButton_Click(object sender, RoutedEventArgs e)
{
   // Get local peers
   PeerNearMeCollection peersNearMe = PeerCollaboration.GetPeersNearMe();

   // Prepare for new peers
   PeerList.Items.Clear();

   // Examine peers
   foreach (PeerNearMe peerNearMe in peersNearMe)
   {
      PeerList.Items.Add(
         new PeerEntry
         {
            PeerNearMe = peerNearMe,
            PresenceStatus = peerNearMe.GetPresenceInfo(
               peerNearMe.PeerEndPoints[0]).PresenceStatus,
            DisplayString = peerNearMe.Nickname
         });
   }

   // Add failure message if necessary
   if (PeerList.Items.Count == 0)
   {
      PeerList.Items.Add(
         new PeerEntry
         {
            DisplayString = "No peers found."
         });
   }
}
```

As you can see from this example, interacting with the PNM service is made very simple by the classes you have learned about.

Summary

This chapter demonstrated how to implement peer-to-peer (P2P) functionality in your applications by using the new P2P classes in .NET 3.5.

You have looked at the types of solutions that P2P makes possible and how these solutions are structured, how to use PNRP and PNM, and how to use the types in the `System.Net.PeerToPeer` and `System.Net.PeerToPeer.Collaboration` namespace. You also saw the extremely useful technique of exposing WCF services as P2P endpoints.

If you are interested in developing P2P applications it is well worth investigating PNM further. It is also worth looking at the peer channel, by which WCF services can broadcast communications among multiple clients simultaneously.

In the next chapter you look at syndication, and you see how you can expose data in RSS and Atom feeds.

48

Syndication

Do you have some structured data to offer, data that changes from time to time? With many web sites, RSS or Atom symbols allow you to subscribe with feed readers. Really Simple Syndication (RSS) is an XML format that allows syndicate information. RSS became very popular with blogs. This XML information makes it easy to subscribe to using RSS readers.

Nowadays, RSS is not only used with blogs but with many different data sources, such as online news magazines. Any data that changes from time to time is offered by RSS or by its successor protocol Atom. Internet Explorer 7 and Outlook 2007 offer RSS and Atom readers that are integrated into the product.

.NET 3.5 extends Windows Communication Foundation (WCF) with syndication features. Syndication classes are defined within the namespace `System.ServiceModel.Syndication`. This namespace provides classes that can be used to both read and write RSS and Atom feeds.

This chapter shows you how to create syndication readers, as well as how data can be offered. This chapter offers the following:

- An overview of `System.ServiceModel.Syndication`
- Information about Syndication Reader
- Information about Syndication Feeds

Overview of System.Servicemodel. Syndication

`System.ServiceModel.Syndication` is a new namespace with .NET 3.5 that allows you to offer data in the RSS or Atom format.

With the release of RSS version 2.0, RSS is now the shorthand notation for Really Simple Syndication. In earlier versions, it had the name RDF Site Summary and Rich Site Summary. RDF is the abbreviation for Resource Description Framework. The first version was created by Netscape to describe content of its portal site. It became successful when the *New York Times* began offering its readers subscriptions to RSS news feeds in 2002. Figure 48-1 shows the RSS logo. If a site shows this logo, then an RSS feed is offered.

Figure 48-1

Atom was designed to be the successor for RSS and is a proposed standard with RFC 4287: www.ietf.org/rfc/rfc4287.txt. The major difference between RSS and Atom is in the content that can be defined with an item. With RSS, the description element can contain simple text or HTML content in which the reading application does not care about this content. Atom requires that you define a specific type for the content with a type attribute, and it also allows you to have XML content with defined namespaces.

The following table lists classes from .NET 3.5 that allow you to create a syndication feed. These classes are independent of the syndication type, RSS or Atom.

Class	Description
`SyndicationFeed`	`SyndicationFeed` represents the top-level element of a feed. With Atom, the top-level element is `<feed>`; RSS defines `<rss>` as the top-level element. With the static method `Load()`, a feed can be read using an `XmlReader`. Properties of this class such as `Authors`, `Categories`, `Contributors`, `Copyright`, `Description`, `ImageUrl`, `Links`, `Title`, and `Items` allow you to define child elements.
`SyndicationPerson`	`SyndicationPerson` represents a person with `Name`, `Email`, and `Uri` that can be assigned to the `Authors` and `Contributors` collection.
`SyndicationItem`	A feed consists of multiple items. Some of the properties of an item are `Authors`, `Contributors`, `Copyright`, and `Content`.
`SyndicationLink`	`SyndicationLink` represents a link within a feed or an item. This class defines the properties `Title` and `Uri`.
`SyndicationCategory`	A feed can group items into categories. The keyword of a category can be set to the `Name` and `Label` properties of `SyndicationCategory`.
`SyndicationContent`	`SyndicationContent` is an abstract base class that describes the content of an item. Content can be of type HTML, plain text, XHTML, XML, or a URL, described with the concrete classes `TextSyndicationContent`, `UrlSyndicationContent`, and `XmlSyndicationContent`.
`SyndicationElement-Extension`	With an extension element, you can add additional content. The `SyndicationElementExtension` can be used to add information to a feed, a category, a person, a link, and an item.

To format a feed to the RSS and Atom formats, you can use classes from the following table.

Class	Description
Atom10FeedFormatter Rss20FeedFormatter	Atom10FeedFormatter and Rss20FeedFormatter derive from the abstract base class SyndicationFeedFormatter. Atom10FeedFormatter serializes a SyndicationFeed to the Atom 1.0 format, the Rss20FeedFormatter to the RSS 2.0 format.
Atom10ItemFormatter Rss20ItemFormatter	Atom10ItemFormatter and Rss20ItemFormatter derive from the abstract base class SyndicationItemFormatter. Atom10ItemFormatter serializes a SyndicationItem to the Atom 1.0 format, the Rss20ItemFormatter to the RSS 2.0 format.

Syndication Reader

Our first example is a Syndication Reader application with a user interface developed with WPF. The user interface of the WPF application is shown in Figure 48-2.

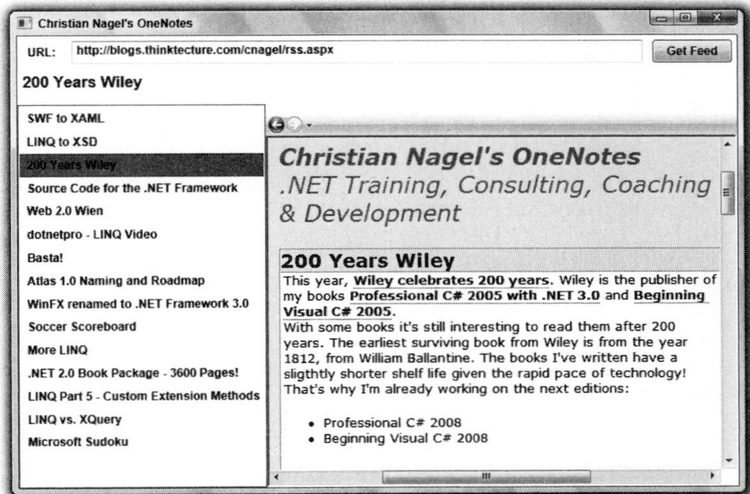

Figure 48-2

To use the Syndication API, the assembly System.ServiceModel.Web is referenced with the application. The OnGetFeed() event handler method is set to the Click event of the button showing the Get Feed text. The code needed to read the application is really simple. First, the XML content from the RSS feed is read into the XmlReader class from the System.Xml namespace. Rss20FeedFormatter accepts an XmlReader with the ReadFrom() method. For data-binding, the Feed property that returns a SyndicationFeed is assigned to the DataContext of the Window, and the Feed.Items property that returns IEnumerable<SyndicationItem> is assigned to the DataContext of a DockPanel container.

```
private void OnGetFeed(object sender, RoutedEventArgs e)
{
   XmlReader reader = XmlReader.Create(textUrl.Text);
   Rss20FeedFormatter formatter = new Rss20FeedFormatter();
   formatter.ReadFrom(reader);
   reader.Close();
   this.DataContext = formatter.Feed;
   this.feedContent.DataContext = formatter.Feed.Items;
}
```

The XAML code that defines the user interface is shown next. The `Title` property of the `Window` class is bound to the `Title.Text` property of the `SyndicationFeed` to display the title of the feed.

In the XAML code, a `DockPanel` named `heading`, which contains a `Label` bound to `Title.Text` and a `Label` bound to `Description.Text`, is defined. Because these labels are contained within the `DockPanel` named `feedContent`, and `feedContent` is bound to the `Feed.Items` property, these labels give title and description information about the current selected item.

A list of items is displayed in a `ListBox` that uses an `ItemTemplate` to bind a label to the `Title`.

The `DockPanel` named content contains a `Frame` element that binds the `Source` property to the first link of an item. With that setting, the `Frame` control uses the web browser control to display the content from the link, as shown in Figure 48-2.

```
<Window x:Class="RSSReader.Window1"
    xmlns="http://schemas.microsoft.com/winfx/2006/xaml/presentation"
    xmlns:x="http://schemas.microsoft.com/winfx/2006/xaml"
    Title="{Binding Path=Title.Text}" Height="300" Width="345">
   <Window.Resources>
      <Style x:Key="listTitleStyle" TargetType="{x:Type ListBox}">
         <Setter Property="ItemTemplate">
            <Setter.Value>
               <DataTemplate>
                  <Label Content="{Binding Title.Text}" />
               </DataTemplate>
            </Setter.Value>
         </Setter>
      </Style>
   </Window.Resources>
   <DockPanel x:Name="feedContent">
      <Grid DockPanel.Dock="Top">
         <Grid.ColumnDefinitions>
            <ColumnDefinition Width="50" />
            <ColumnDefinition Width="*" />
            <ColumnDefinition Width="90" />
         </Grid.ColumnDefinitions>
         <Label Grid.Column="0" Margin="5">URL:</Label>
         <TextBox Grid.Column="1" x:Name="textUrl" MinWidth="150"
               Margin="5">http://blogs.thinktecture.com/cnagel/rss.aspx
         </TextBox>
         <Button Grid.Column="2" Margin="5" MinWidth="80"
               Click="OnGetFeed">Get Feed</Button>
      </Grid>
      <DockPanel DockPanel.Dock="Top" x:Name="heading">
         <Label DockPanel.Dock="Top" Content="{Binding Path=Title.Text}"
               FontSize="16" />
```

```
            <Label DockPanel.Dock="Top"
                  Content="{Binding Path=Description.Text}" />
         </DockPanel>
         <ListBox DockPanel.Dock="Left" ItemsSource="{Binding}"
               Style="{StaticResource listTitleStyle}"
               IsSynchronizedWithCurrentItem="True" />
         <DockPanel x:Name="content" >
            <Label DockPanel.Dock="Top"
                  Content="{Binding Path=Description.Text}"></Label>
            <Frame Source="{Binding Path=Links[0].Uri}">
            </Frame>
         </DockPanel>
      </DockPanel>
   </Window>
```

Offering Syndication Feeds

Reading syndication feeds is one scenario in which the Syndication API can be used. Another is to offer a syndication feed to RSS and Atom clients.

For this, Visual Studio 2008 offers the Syndication Service Library template, which you can use to start with. This template defines a reference to the `System.ServiceModel.Web` library, and adds an application configuration file to define a WCF endpoint.

To offer data for the syndication feed, the LINQ provider LINQ to SQL is helpful. In the sample application, the Formula 1 database is used, which you can download from the Wrox web site at `www.wrox.com` with the sample applications for the book. The "LINQ to SQL Classes" item with the name `Formula1` is added to the project. Here, the tables Racers, RaceResults, Races, and Circuits are mapped to entity classes `Racer`, `RaceResult`, `Race`, and `Circuit`, as shown in Figure 48-3.

LINQ to SQL is discussed in Chapter 27.

The project template creates a file `IService1.cs` that contains the contract of the WCF service. The interface contains the `CreateFeed()` method, which returns a `SyndicationFeedFormatter`. Because `SyndicationFeedFormatter` is an abstract class, and the real types returned are either `Atom10FeedFormatter` or `Rss20FeedFormatter`, these types are listed with the `ServiceKnownTypeAttribute`, so that the type is known for serialization.

The attribute `WebGet` defines that the operation can be called from a simple HTTP GET request that can be used to request syndication feeds. `WebMessageBodyStyle.Bare` defines that the result (the XML from the syndication feed) is sent as it is without adding an XML wrapper element around it.

```
using System.ServiceModel;
using System.ServiceModel.Syndication;
using System.ServiceModel.Web;
namespace Wrox.ProCSharp.Syndication
{
   [ServiceContract]
   [ServiceKnownType(typeof(Atom10FeedFormatter))]
   [ServiceKnownType(typeof(Rss20FeedFormatter))]
   public interface IFormula1Feed
   {
      [OperationContract]
      [WebGet(UriTemplate = "*", BodyStyle = WebMessageBodyStyle.Bare)]
      SyndicationFeedFormatter CreateFeed();
   }
}
```

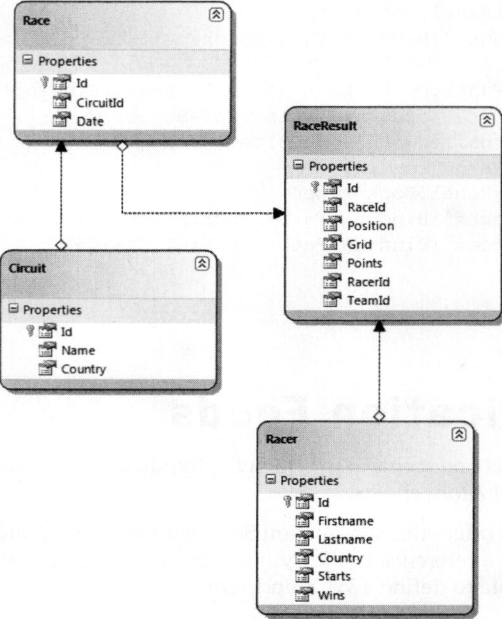

Figure 48-3

The implementation of the service is done in the class `Formula1Feed`. Here, a `SyndicationFeed` item is created, and various properties of this class such as `Generator`, `Language`, `Title`, `Categories`, and `Authors` are assigned. The `Items` property is filled from a LINQ to SQL query that requests the winners of Formula 1 races of the year 2007. With the `select` clause of this query, a `SyndicationItem` is created for every winner. With the `SyndicationItem`, the `Title` property is assigned to plain text containing the country of the race. The `Content` property is filled with the help of LINQ to XML. `XElement` classes are used to create XHTML code that can be interpreted by the browser. This content shows the date of the race, the country, and the name of the winner.

Depending on the query string to request the syndication, the `SyndicationFeed` is formatted with the `Atom10FeedFormatter` or the `Rss20FeedFormatter`.

```
using System;
using System.Linq;
using System.ServiceModel.Syndication;
using System.ServiceModel.Web;
using System.Xml.Linq;
namespace Wrox.ProCSharp.Syndication
{
   public class Formula1Feed : IFormula1Feed
   {
      public SyndicationFeedFormatter CreateFeed()
      {
         // Create a new Syndication Feed.
         SyndicationFeed feed = new SyndicationFeed();
         feed.Generator = "Pro C# 2008 Sample Feed Generator";
         feed.Language = "en-us";
         feed.LastUpdatedTime = new DateTimeOffset(DateTime.Now);
```

```
        feed.Title = SyndicationContent.CreatePlaintextContent(
              "Formula1 results");
        feed.Categories.Add(new SyndicationCategory("Formula1"));
        feed.Authors.Add(new SyndicationPerson("web@christiannagel.com",
              "Christian Nagel", "http://www.christiannagel.com"));
        feed.Description = SyndicationContent.CreatePlaintextContent(
              "Sample Formula 1");
        Formula1DataContext data = new Formula1DataContext();
        feed.Items = from racer in data.Racers
                     from raceResult in racer.RaceResults
                     where raceResult.Race.Date >
                           new DateTime(2007, 1, 1) &&
                           raceResult.Position == 1
                     orderby raceResult.Race.Date
                     select new SyndicationItem()
                     {
                        Title =
                              SyndicationContent.CreatePlaintextContent(
                              String.Format("G.P. {0}",
                              raceResult.Race.Circuit.Country)),
                        Content = SyndicationContent.CreateXhtmlContent(
                        new XElement("p",
                           new XElement("h3", String.Format("{0}, {1}",
                                 raceResult.Race.Circuit.Country,
                                 raceResult.Race.Date.
                                       ToShortDateString())),
                           new XElement("b", String.Format(
                                 "Winner: {0} {1}",
                                 racer.Firstname,
                                 racer.Lastname))).ToString())
                     };
  // Return ATOM or RSS based on query string
  // rss ->
  // http://localhost:8731/Design_Time_Addresses/SyndicationService/Feed1/
  // atom ->
  // http://localhost:8731/Design_Time_Addresses/SyndicationService/
  //       Feed1/?format=atom
        string query =
           WebOperationContext.Current.IncomingRequest.UriTemplateMatch.
              QueryParameters["format"];
        SyndicationFeedFormatter formatter = null;
        if (query == "atom")
        {
           formatter = new Atom10FeedFormatter(feed);
        }
        else
        {
           formatter = new Rss20FeedFormatter(feed);
        }
        return formatter;
     }
  }
}
```

When you start the service from within Visual Studio 2008, the WCF Service Host starts up to host the service, and you can see the feed result formatted in Internet Explorer, as shown in Figure 48-4.

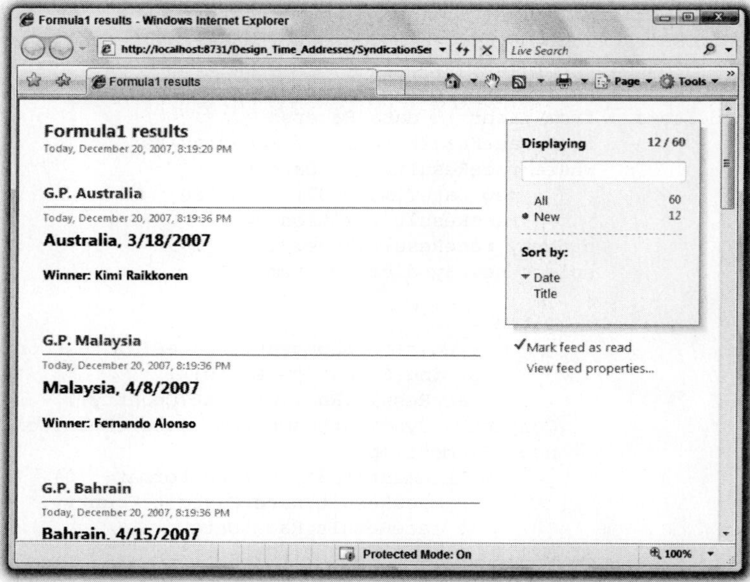

Figure 48-4

With the default request to the service, the RSS feed is returned. An extract of the RSS feed with the `rss` root element follows. With RSS, the `Title` property is translated to the `title` element, and the `Description` property goes to the `description` element. The `Authors` property of the `SyndicationFeed` that contains `SyndicationPerson` just uses the e-mail address to create the `managingEditor` element. To add more information to the feed, the formatter also places some Atom elements in the RSS feed. Placing Atom elements in an RSS feed is a common practice that provides information that is not defined by RSS.

```
<?xml version="1.0" encoding="utf-8"?>
<rss version="2.0" xmlns:atom="http://www.w3.org/2005/Atom"
  xmlns:cf="http://www.microsoft.com/schemas/rss/core/2005"
  xmlns:a10="http://www.w3.org/2005/Atom">
  <channel
      xmlns:cfi="http://www.microsoft.com/schemas/rss/core/2005/internal"
      cfi:lastdownloaderror="None">
    <title cf:type="text">Formula1 results</title>
    <description cf:type="text">Sample Formula 1</description>
    <language>en-us</language>
    <managingEditor>web@christiannagel.com</managingEditor>
    <atom:author>
      <atom:email>web@christiannagel.com</atom:email>
    </atom:author>
    <lastBuildDate>Tue, 04 Dec 2007 21:07:48 GMT</lastBuildDate>
    <atom:updated>2007-12-04T21:07:48Z</atom:updated>
    <category>Formula1</category>
```

```
    <generator>Pro C# 2008 Sample Feed Generator</generator>
    <item>
      <title xmlns:cf="http://www.microsoft.com/schemas/rss/core/2005"
          cf:type="text">G.P. Australia</title>
      <description xmlns:cf="http://www.microsoft.com/schemas/rss/core/2005"
          cf:type="html">&lt;p&gt;&lt;h3&gt;Australia, 18.03.2007&lt;/h3&gt;
          &lt;b&gt;Winner: Kimi Raikkonen&lt;/b&gt;&lt;/p&gt;
      </description>
      <cfi:id>47</cfi:id><cfi:read>true</cfi:read>
      <cfi:downloadurl>
            http://localhost:8731/Design_Time_Addresses/SyndicationService/Feed1/
      </cfi:downloadurl>
      <cfi:lastdownloadtime>2007-12-04T21:05:16.486Z</cfi:lastdownloadtime>
    </item>
    <item>
      <!-- ... -->
  </channel>
</rss>
```

An Atom formatted feed is returned with the query `?format=atom` with the result shown. The root element now is the `feed` element; the `Description` property turns into a `subtitle` element; and the values for the `Author` property are now shown completely differently from the RSS feed shown earlier. Atom allows the content to be unencoded. You can easily find the XHTML elements.

```
<feed xml:lang="en-us" xmlns="http://www.w3.org/2005/Atom">
  <title type="text">Formula1 results</title>
  <subtitle type="text">Sample Formula 1</subtitle>
  <id>uuid:c19284e7-aa40-4bc2-9be8-f1960b0f747e;id=1</id>
  <updated>2007-12-05T00:46:35+01:00</updated>
  <category term="Formula1"/>
  <author>
    <name>Christian Nagel</name>
    <uri>http://www.christiannagel.com</uri>
    <email>web@christiannagel.com</email>
  </author>
  <generator>Pro C# 2008 Sample Feed Generator</generator>
  <entry>
    <id>uuid:c19284e7-aa40-4bc2-9be8-f1960b0f747e;id=2</id>
    <title type="text">G.P. Australia</title>
    <updated>2007-12-04T23:46:43Z</updated>
    <content type="xhtml">
      <p><h3>Australia, 18.03.2007</h3><b>Winner: Kimi Raikkonen</b></p>
    </content>
  </entry>
  <entry>
    <id>uuid:c19284e7-aa40-4bc2-9be8-f1960b0f747e;id=3</id>
    <title type="text">G.P. Malaysia</title>
    <updated>2007-12-04T23:46:43Z</updated>
    <content type="xhtml">
      <p><h3>Malaysia, 08.04.2007</h3><b>Winner: Fernando Alonso</b></p>
    </content>
  </entry>
  <!-- ... -->
</feed>
```

Summary

In this chapter, you have seen how the classes from the `System.ServiceModel.Syndication` namespace, which is new in .NET 3.5, can be used to create an application that receives a feed, as well as an application that offers a feed. The syndication API supports RSS 2.0 and Atom 1.0. As these standards emerge, new formatters will be available. You have seen that the SyndicationXXX classes are independent of the format that is generated. The concrete implementation of the abstract class `SyndicationFeedFormatter` defines what properties are used and how they are translated to the specific format.

This chapter concludes the communication part of the book. You've read about communication technologies to directly use sockets, and abstraction layers that are offered. Windows Communication Foundation is a technology that has been discussed in several chapters. With message queuing (Chapter 45), WCF offers a disconnected communication model. In Chapter 44, "Enterprise Services," you have seen WCF integration with existing COM+ applications.

Throughout this book, you've seen the language features of C#, including the features that are new with C# 3.0, such as extension methods and LINQ queries. C# 3.0 features have been used throughout the book, where you've read about core .NET Framework features, data access to databases and XML, user interfaces with Windows Forms, Windows Presentation Foundation, ASP.NET, and Microsoft Office.

There's still more to read. The appendices cover ADO.NET Entities, a mapping technology to map objects to relational databases, applications for Windows Vista and Windows Server 2008, and a language comparison of C#, Visual Basic, and C++/CLI.

Part VII
Appendices

Appendix A: ADO.NET Entity Framework

Appendix B: C#, Visual Basic, and C++/CLI

Appendix C: Windows Vista and Windows Server 2008

ADO.NET Entity Framework

The ADO.NET Entity Framework is an object-relational mapping framework that is based on .NET 3.5. Chapter 27 demonstrated object-relational mapping with LINQ to SQL. LINQ to SQL offers simple mapping features for associations and inheritance. The ADO.NET Entity Framework gives you many more options for associations and inheritance. Another difference between LINQ to SQL and the ADO.NET Entity Framework is that the ADO.NET Entity Framework is a provider-based model that allows other database vendors to plug into it.

This appendix covers the following:

- The ADO.NET Entity Framework
- Entity Framework layers
- Entities
- Object contexts
- Relationships
- Object queries
- Updates
- LINQ to Entities

This appendix is based on the Beta 3 version of this framework, which is due to be released some months after the .NET 3.5 product, so some class or method names may be different than what you read here.

This appendix uses the Books, Formula1, and Northwind databases. You can download the Northwind database from `msdn.microsoft.com`*; the Books and Formula1 databases are included with the download of the code samples.*

Overview of the ADO.NET Entity Framework

The ADO.NET Entity Framework provides a mapping from the relational database schema to objects. Relational databases and object-oriented languages define associations differently. For example, the Microsoft sample database Northwind contains the `Customers` and `Orders` tables. To access all the Orders rows for a customer, you need to do a SQL join statement. With object-oriented languages, it is more common to define a `Customer` and an `Order` class and access the orders of a customer by using an `Orders` property from the `Customer` class.

For object-relational mapping since .NET 1.0, it was possible to use the `DataSet` class and typed datasets. Datasets are very similar to the structure of a database containing `DataTable`, `DataRow`, `DataColumn`, and `DataRelation` classes. The ADO.NET Entity Framework gives support to directly define entity classes that are completely independent of a database structure and map them to tables and associations of the database. Using objects with the application, the application is shielded from changes in the database.

The ADO.NET Entity Framework makes use of Entity SQL to define entity-based queries to the store. LINQ to Entities makes it possible to use the LINQ syntax to query data.

An object context keeps knowledge about entities that are changed, to have information when the entities should be written back to the store.

The namespaces that contain classes from the ADO.NET Entity Framework are listed in the following table.

Namespace	Description
`System.Data`	This is a main namespace for ADO.NET. With the ADO.NET Entity Framework, this namespace contains exception classes related to entities — for example `MappingException` and `QueryException`.
`System.Data.Common`	This namespace contains classes shared by .NET data providers. The class `DbProviderServices` is an abstract base class that must be implemented by an ADO.NET Entity Framework provider.
`System.Data.Common .CommandTrees`	This namespace contains classes to build an expression tree.
`System.Data.Entity.Design`	This namespace contains classed used by the designer to create Entity Data Model (EDM) files.
`System.Data.EntityClient`	This namespace specifies classes for the .NET Framework Data Provider to access the Entity Framework. `EntityConnection`, `EntityCommand`, and `EntityDataReader` can be used to access the Entity Framework.
`System.Data.Objects`	This namespace contains classes to query and update databases. The class `ObjectContext` encapsulates the connection to the database and serves as a gateway for create, read, update, and delete methods. The class `ObjectQuery` represents a query against the store. `CompiledQuery` is a cached query.
`System.Data.Objects .DataClasses`	This namespace contains classes and interfaces required for entities.

Entity Framework Layers

The ADO.NET Entity Framework offers several layers to map database tables to objects. You can start with a database schema and use a Visual Studio item template to create the complete mapping. You can also start designing entity classes with the designer and map it to the database where the tables and associations between the tables can have a very different structure.

The layers that need to be defined are as follows:

- *Logical* — This layer defines the relational data.
- *Conceptual* — This layer defines the .NET classes.
- *Mapping* — This layer defines the mapping from .NET classes to relational tables and associations.

Let's start with a simple database schema, as shown in Figure A-1 with the tables `Books` and `Authors`, and an association table `BookAuthors` that maps the authors to books.

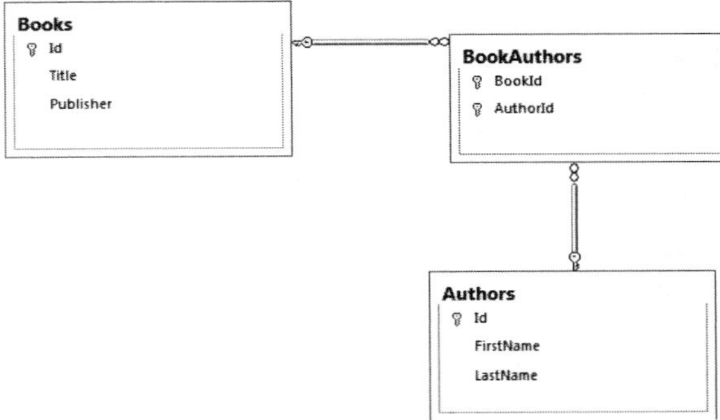

Figure A-1

Logical

The logical layer is defined by the Store Schema Definition Language (SSDL) and describes the structure of the database tables and their relations.

The following code uses SSDL to describe the three tables: `Books`, `Authors`, and `BookAuthors`. The `EntityContainer` element describes all the tables with `EntitySet` elements, and associations with `AssociationSet` elements. The parts of a table are defined with the `EntityType` element. With `EntityType Books` you can see the columns `Id`, `Title`, and `Publisher` defined by the `Property` element. The `Property` element contains XML attributes to define the data type. The `Key` element defines the key of the table.

```
<Schema Namespace="BookEntities.Store" Alias="Self"
    ProviderManifestToken="09.00.3054"
    xmlns="http://schemas.microsoft.com/ado/2006/04/edm/ssdl">
  <EntityContainer Name="dbo">
    <EntitySet Name="Authors" EntityType="Wrox.ProCSharp.Entities.Store.Authors" />
    <EntitySet Name="BookAuthors"
        EntityType=" Wrox.ProCSharp.Entities.Store.BookAuthors" />
    <EntitySet Name="Books" EntityType=" Wrox.ProCSharp.Entities.Store.Books" />
    <AssociationSet Name="FK_BookAuthors_Authors"
```

(continued)

(continued)

```
        Association=" Wrox.ProCSharp.Entities.Store.FK_BookAuthors_Authors">
      <End Role="Authors" EntitySet="Authors" />
      <End Role="BookAuthors" EntitySet="BookAuthors" />
    </AssociationSet>
    <AssociationSet Name="FK_BookAuthors_Books"
        Association="BookDemoEntities.Store.FK_BookAuthors_Books">
      <End Role="Books" EntitySet="Books" />
      <End Role="BookAuthors" EntitySet="BookAuthors" />
    </AssociationSet>
  </EntityContainer>
  <EntityType Name="Authors">
    <Key><PropertyRef Name="Id" /></Key>
    <Property Name="Id" Type="int" Nullable="false" StoreGeneratedPattern="Identity" />
    <Property Name="FirstName" Type="nvarchar" Nullable="false" MaxLength="50" />
    <Property Name="LastName" Type="nvarchar" Nullable="false" MaxLength="50" />
  </EntityType>
  <EntityType Name="BookAuthors">
    <Key><PropertyRef Name="BookId" /><PropertyRef Name="AuthorId" /></Key>
    <Property Name="BookId" Type="int" Nullable="false" />
    <Property Name="AuthorId" Type="int" Nullable="false" />
  </EntityType>
  <EntityType Name="Books">
    <Key><PropertyRef Name="Id" /></Key>
    <Property Name="Id" Type="int" Nullable="false" StoreGeneratedPattern="Identity" />
    <Property Name="Title" Type="nvarchar" Nullable="false" MaxLength="50" />
    <Property Name="Publisher" Type="nvarchar" Nullable="false" MaxLength="50" />
  </EntityType>
  <Association Name="FK_BookAuthors_Authors">
    <End Role="Authors"
        Type=" Wrox.ProCSharp.Entities.Store.Authors" Multiplicity="1" />
    <End Role="BookAuthors"
        Type=" Wrox.ProCSharp.Entities.Store.BookAuthors"
        Multiplicity="*" />
    <ReferentialConstraint>
      <Principal Role="Authors"><PropertyRef Name="Id" /></Principal>
      <Dependent Role="BookAuthors"><PropertyRef Name="AuthorId" /></Dependent>
    </ReferentialConstraint>
  </Association>
  <Association Name="FK_BookAuthors_Books">
    <End Role="Books" Type=" Wrox.ProCSharp.Entities.Store.Books" Multiplicity="1" />
    <End Role="BookAuthors" Type=" Wrox.ProCSharp.Entities.Store.BookAuthors"
        Multiplicity="*" />
    <ReferentialConstraint>
      <Principal Role="Books"><PropertyRef Name="Id" /></Principal>
      <Dependent Role="BookAuthors"><PropertyRef Name="BookId" /></Dependent>
    </ReferentialConstraint>
  </Association>
</Schema>
```

Conceptual

The conceptual layer defines .NET classes. This layer is created with the Conceptual Schema Definition Language (CSDL).

Figure A-2 shows the entities `Author` and `Book` defined with the ADO.NET Entity Data Model Designer.

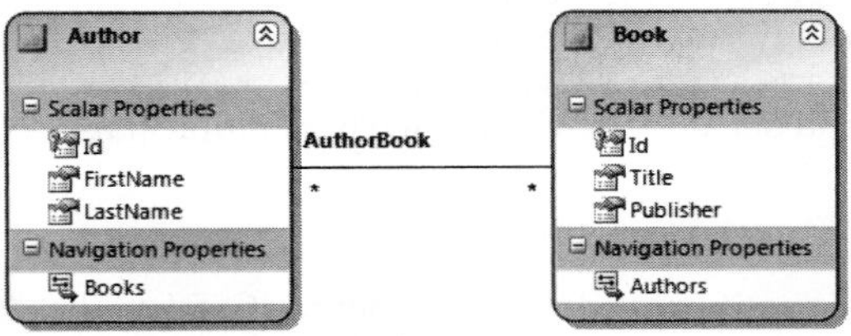

Figure A-2

The following is the CSDL content to define the entity types `Book` and `Author`. This was created from the Books database.

```
<Schema Namespace="BookEntities" Alias="Self"
    xmlns="http://schemas.microsoft.com/ado/2006/04/edm">
  <EntityContainer Name="BookEntities">
    <EntitySet Name="Authors" EntityType="Wrox.ProCSharp.Entities.Author" />
    <EntitySet Name="Books" EntityType="Wrox.ProCSharp.Entities.Book" />
    <AssociationSet Name="BookAuthors"
        Association=" Wrox.ProCSharp.Entities.BookAuthors">
      <End Role="Authors" EntitySet="Authors" />
      <End Role="Books" EntitySet="Books" />
    </AssociationSet>
  </EntityContainer>
  <EntityType Name="Author">
    <Key>
      <PropertyRef Name="Id" />
    </Key>
    <Property Name="Id" Type="Int32" Nullable="false" />
    <Property Name="FirstName" Type="String" Nullable="false" MaxLength="50" />
    <Property Name="LastName" Type="String" Nullable="false" MaxLength="50" />
    <NavigationProperty Name="Books" Relationship="BookDemoEntities
      .BookAuthors" FromRole="Authors" ToRole="Books" />
  </EntityType>

  <EntityType Name="Book">
    <Key>
      <PropertyRef Name="Id" />
    </Key>
    <Property Name="Id" Type="Int32" Nullable="false" />
    <Property Name="Title" Type="String" Nullable="false" MaxLength="50" />
    <Property Name="Publisher" Type="String" Nullable="false" MaxLength="50" />
    <NavigationProperty Name="Authors"
        Relationship=" Wrox.ProCSharp.Entities.BookAuthors" FromRole="Books"
        ToRole="Authors" />
  </EntityType>

  <Association Name="BookAuthors">
```

(continued)

(continued)

```
        <End Type=" Wrox.ProCSharp.Entities.Author" Role="Authors" Multiplicity="*" />
        <End Type=" Wrox.ProCSharp.Entities.Book" Role="Books" Multiplicity="*" />
      </Association>
    </Schema>
```

The entity is defined by an `EntityType` element that contains `Key`, `Property`, and `NavigationProperty` elements to describe the properties of the created class. The `Property` element contains attributes to describe the name and type of the .NET properties of the classes that are generated by the designer. The `Association` element connects the types `Author` and `Book`. `Multiplicity="*"` means that one `Author` can write multiple `Books`, and one `Book` can be written by multiple `Authors`.

Mapping

The mapping layer maps the entity type definition from the CSDL to the SSDL by using the Mapping Specification Language (MSL). The following specification includes a `Mapping` element that contains the `EntityTypeMapping` element to reference the `Book` type of the CSDL and defines the `MappingFragment` to reference the `Authors` table from the SSDL. The `ScalarProperty` maps the property of the .NET class with the `Name` attribute to the column of the database table with the `ColumnName` attribute.

```
<Mapping Space="C-S" xmlns="urn:schemas-microsoft-com:windows:storage:mapping:CS">
  <EntityContainerMapping StorageEntityContainer="dbo"
      CdmEntityContainer="BookEntities">
    <EntitySetMapping Name="Authors">
      <EntityTypeMapping TypeName="IsTypeOf(Wrox.ProCSharp.Entities.Author)">
        <MappingFragment StoreEntitySet="Authors">
          <ScalarProperty Name="LastName" ColumnName="LastName" />
          <ScalarProperty Name="FirstName" ColumnName="FirstName" />
          <ScalarProperty Name="Id" ColumnName="Id" />
        </MappingFragment>
      </EntityTypeMapping>
    </EntitySetMapping>
    <EntitySetMapping Name="Books">
      <EntityTypeMapping TypeName="IsTypeOf(Wrox.ProCSharp.Entities.Book)">
        <MappingFragment StoreEntitySet="Books">
          <ScalarProperty Name="Publisher" ColumnName="Publisher" />
          <ScalarProperty Name="Title" ColumnName="Title" />
          <ScalarProperty Name="Id" ColumnName="Id" />
        </MappingFragment>
      </EntityTypeMapping>
    </EntitySetMapping>
    <AssociationSetMapping Name="AuthorBook"
        TypeName=" Wrox.ProCSharp.Entities.AuthorBook"
        StoreEntitySet="BookAuthors" >
      <EndProperty Name="Book">
        <ScalarProperty Name="Id" ColumnName="BookId" />
      </EndProperty>
      <EndProperty Name="Author">
        <ScalarProperty Name="Id" ColumnName="AuthorId" />
      </EndProperty>
    </AssociationSetMapping>
  </EntityContainerMapping>
</Mapping>
```

Entities

Entity classes that are created with the designer and are created by CSDL typically derive from the base class `EntityObject`, as shown with the `Book` class in the code that follows.

This class derives from the base class `EntityObject` and defines properties that fire change information in the set accessor. The created class `Book` is a partial class that can be extended in a new source file defining the same class in the same namespace. Methods that are called within the set accessor such as `OnTitleChanging()` and `OnTitleChanged()` are partial as well, so it is possible to implement these methods in the custom extension of the class. The `Authors` property uses the `RelationshipManager` class to return the `Books` for an author.

```
[EdmEntityTypeAttribute(NamespaceName="Wrox.ProCSharp.Entities", Name="Book")]
[DataContractAttribute()]
[Serializable()]
public partial class Book : global::System.Data.Objects.DataClasses.EntityObject
{
   public static Book CreateBook(int ID, string title, string publisher)
   {
      Book book = new Book();
      book.Id = ID;
      book.Title = title;
      book.Publisher = publisher;
      return book;
   }
  [EdmScalarPropertyAttribute(EntityKeyProperty=true, IsNullable=false)]
  [DataMemberAttribute()]
  public int Id
  {
     get
     {
        return this._Id;
     }
     set
     {
        this.OnIdChanging(value);
        this.ReportPropertyChanging("Id");
        this._Id = StructuralObject.SetValidValue(value);
        this.ReportPropertyChanged("Id");
        this.OnIdChanged();
     }
  }
  private int _Id;
  partial void OnIdChanging(int value);
  partial void OnIdChanged();
  [EdmScalarPropertyAttribute(IsNullable=false)]
  [DataMemberAttribute()]
  public string Title
  {
     get
     {
        return this._Title;
     }
     set
```

(continued)

(continued)

```
            {
                this.OnTitleChanging(value);
                this.ReportPropertyChanging("Title");
                this._Title = StructuralObject.SetValidValue(value, false, 50);
                this.ReportPropertyChanged("Title");
                this.OnTitleChanged();
            }
        }
        private string _Title;
        partial void OnTitleChanging(string value);
        partial void OnTitleChanged();
        [EdmScalarPropertyAttribute(IsNullable=false)]
        [DataMemberAttribute()]
        public string Publisher
        {
            get
            {
                return this._Publisher;
            }
            set
            {
                this.OnPublisherChanging(value);
                this.ReportPropertyChanging("Publisher");
                this._Publisher = StructuralObject.SetValidValue(value, false, 50);
                this.ReportPropertyChanged("Publisher");
                this.OnPublisherChanged();
            }
        }
        private string _Publisher;
        partial void OnPublisherChanging(string value);
        partial void OnPublisherChanged();
        [EdmRelationshipNavigationPropertyAttribute("BookDemoEntities", "AuthorBook",
            "Author")]
        [XmlIgnoreAttribute()]
        [SoapIgnoreAttribute()]
        [BrowsableAttribute(false)]
        public EntityCollection<Author> Authors
        {
            get
            {
                return ((IEntityWithRelationships)(this)).RelationshipManager.
                      GetRelatedCollection<Author>("WroxProCSharp.Entities.AuthorBook",
                      "Author");
            }
        }
    }
```

The classes and interfaces important in regard to entity classes are explained in the following table. With the exception of `INotifyPropertyChanging` and `INotifyPropertyChanged`, the types are defined in the namespace `System.Data.Objects.DataClasses`.

Class or Interface	Description
`StructuralObject`	`StructuralObject` is the base class of the classes `EntityObject` and `ComplexObject`. This class implements the interfaces `INotifyPropertyChanging` and `INotifyPropertyChanged`.
`INotifyPropertyChanging` `INotifyPropertyChanged`	These interfaces define the `PropertyChanging` and `PropertyChanged` events to allow subscribing to information when the state of the object changes. Different from the other classes and interfaces here, these interfaces are defined in the namespace `System.ComponentModel`.
`EntityObject`	This class derives from `StructuralObject` and implements the interfaces `IEntityWithKey`, `IEntityWithChangeTracker`, and `IEntityWithRelationships`. `EntityObject` is a commonly used base class for objects mapped to database tables that contain a key and relationships to other objects.
`ComplexObject`	This class can be used as a base class for entity objects that do not have a key. It derives from `StructuralObject` but does not implement other interfaces as the `EntityObject` class does.
`IEntityWithKey`	This interface defines an `EntityKey` property that allows fast access to the object.
`IEntityWithChangeTracker`	This interface defines the method `SetChangeTracker()` where a change tracker that implements the interface `IChangeTracker` can be assigned to get information about state change from the object.
`IEntityWithRelationships`	This interface defines the read-only property `RelationshipManager`, which returns a `RelationshipManager` object that can be used to navigate between objects.

For an entity class, it's not necessary to derive from the base classes `EntityObject` *or* `ComplexObject`. *Instead, an entity class can implement the required interfaces.*

The `Book` entity class can easily be accessed by using the object context class `BookEntities`. The `Books` property returns a collection of `Book` objects that can be iterated:

```
BookEntities data = new BookEntities();

foreach (var book in data.Books)
{
   Console.WriteLine("{0}, {1}", book.Title, book.Publisher);
}
```

Running the program, books queried from the database are shown at the console:

```
Professional C# 2008, Wrox Press
Beginning Visual C# 2008, Wrox Press
Working with Animation in Silverlight 1.0, Wrox Press
Professional WPF Programming, Wrox Press
```

Object Context

To retrieve data from the database, the `ObjectContext` class is needed. This class defines the mapping from the entity objects to the database. With ADO.NET, you can compare this class to the data adapter that fills a `DataSet`.

The `BookEntities` class created by the designer derives from the base class `ObjectContext`. This class adds constructors to pass a connection string. With the default constructor, the connection string is read from the configuration file. It is also possible to pass an already opened connection to the constructor in the form of an `EntityConnection` instance. If you pass a connection to the constructor that is not opened, the object context opens and closes the connection; if you pass an opened connection you also need to close it.

The created class defines `Books` and `Authors` properties, which return an `ObjectQuery`, and methods to add authors and books — `AddToAuthors()` and `AddToBooks()`.

```
public partial class BookEntities : ObjectContext
{
   public BookEntities() :
         base("name=BookEntities", "BookEntities") { }
   public BookEntities(string connectionString) :
         base(connectionString, "BookEntities") { }
   public BookEntities(EntityConnection connection) :
         base(connection, "BookEntities") { }
   [BrowsableAttribute(false)]
   public ObjectQuery<Author> Authors
   {
      get
      {
         if ((this._Authors == null))
         {
            this._Authors = base.CreateQuery<Author>("[Authors]");
         }
         return this._Authors;
      }
   }
   private ObjectQuery<Author> _Authors;
   [BrowsableAttribute(false)]
   public ObjectQuery<Book> Books
   {
      get
      {
         if ((this._Books == null))
         {
            this._Books = base.CreateQuery<Book>("[Books]");
         }
         return this._Books;
      }
   }
   private ObjectQuery<Book> _Books;
   public void AddToAuthors(Author author)
   {
      base.AddObject("Authors", author);
   }
```

```
        public void AddToBooks(Book book)
        {
            base.AddObject("Books", book);
        }
    }
```

In case you pass a connection string to the constructor of the `BookEntities` class, the connection string of type `EntityConnection` defines the keyword `Metadata`, which requires three things: a delimited list of mapping files, `Provider` for the invariant provider name to access the data source, and `Provider connection string` to assign the provider-dependent connection string.

```
EntityConnection conn = new EntityConnection(
      "Metadata=./BookModel.csdl|./BookModel.ssdl|./BookModel.msl;" +
      "Provider=System.Data.SqlClient;" +
      "Provider connection string=\"Data Source=(local);" +
      "Initial Catalog=EntitiesDemo;Integrated Security=True\"");
```

The `ObjectContext` class provides several services to the caller:

- It keeps track of entity objects that are already retrieved. If the object is queried again, it is taken from the object context.
- It keeps state information about the entities. You can get information about added, modified, and deleted objects.
- You can update the entities from the object context to write the changes to the underlying store.

Methods and properties of the `ObjectContext` class are listed in the following table.

ObjectContext Methods and Properties	Description
`Connection`	Returns a `DbConnection` object that is associated with the object context.
`MetadataWorkspace`	Returns a `MetadataWorkspace` object that can be used to read the metadata and mapping information.
`QueryTimeout`	With this property you can get and set the timeout value for the queries of the object context.
`ObjectStateManager`	This property returns an `ObjectStateManager`. The `ObjectStateManager` keeps track of entity objects retrieved and object changes in the object context.
`CreateQuery()`	This method returns an `ObjectQuery` to get data from the store. The `Books` and `Authors` properties shown earlier use this method to return an `ObjectQuery`.
`GetObjectByKey()` `TryGetObjectByKey()`	These methods return the object by the key either from the object state manager or the underlying store. `GetObjectByKey()` throws an exception of type `ObjectNotFoundException` if the key does not exist. `TryGetObjectByKey()` returns `false`.
`AddObject()`	This method adds a new entity object to the object context. This method is invoked by the `AddToAuthors()` and `AddToBooks()` methods.

ObjectContext Methods and Properties	Description
`DeleteObject()`	This method deletes an object from the object context.
`Detach()`	This method detaches an entity object from the object context, so it is no longer tracked if changes occur.
`Attach()` `AttachTo()`	The `Attach()` method attaches a detached object to the store. Attaching objects back to the object context requires that the entity object implements the interface `IEntityWithKey`. The `AttachTo()` method does not have the requirement for a key with the object, but it requires the entity set name where the entity object needs to be attached.
`ApplyPropertyChanges()`	If an object was detached from the object context, then the detached object is modified, and afterwards the changes should be applied to the object within the object context, you can invoke the `ApplyPropertyChanges()` method to apply the changes. This is useful in a scenario where a detached object was returned from a Web service, changed from a client, and passed to the Web service in a modified way.
`Refresh()`	The data in the store can change while entity objects are stored inside the object context. To make a refresh from the store, the `Refresh()` method can be used. With this method you can pass a `RefreshMode` enumeration value. If the values for the objects are not the same between the store and the object context, passing the value `ClientWins` changes the data in the store. The value `StoreWins` changes the data in the object context.
`SaveChanges()`	Adding, modifying, and deleting objects from the object context does not change the object from the underlying store. Use the `SaveChanges()` method to persist the changes to the store.
`AcceptAllChanges()`	This method changes the state of the objects in the context to unmodified. `SaveChanges()` invokes this method implicitly.

Relationships

The entity types `Book` and `Author` are related to each other. A book is written by one or more authors, and an author can write one or more books. Relationships are based on the count of types they relate and the multiplicity. The first version of the ADO.NET Entity Framework supports a Table per Type (TPT) and Table per Hierarchy (TPH). Multiplicity can be one-to-one, one-to-many, or many-to-many.

Table per Hierarchy

With TPH, there's one table in the database that corresponds to a hierarchy of entity classes. The database table `Payments` (see Figure A-3) contains columns for a hierarchy of entity types. Some of the columns are common to all entities in the hierarchy, such as `Id` and `Amount`. The `CreditCard` column is only used by a credit card payment.

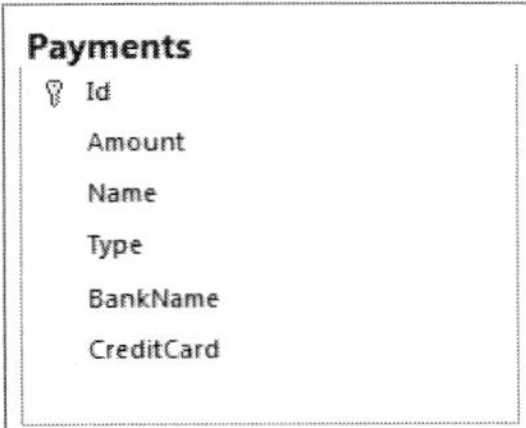

Figure A-3

The entity classes that all map to the same `Payments` table are shown in Figure A-4. `Payment` is an abstract base class to contain properties common for all types in the hierarchy. Concrete classes that derive from `Payment` are `CreditCardPayment`, `CashPayment`, and `ChequePayment`. `CreditCardPayment` has a `CreditCard` property in addition to the properties of the base class; `ChequePayment` has a `BankName` property.

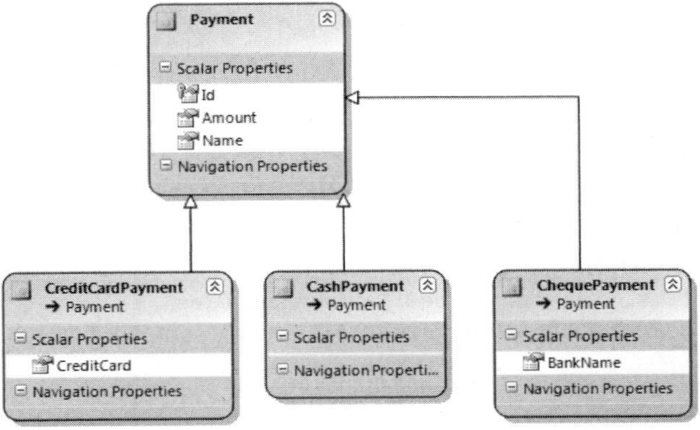

Figure A-4

The selection of the type of the concrete class is done based on a `Condition` element as you can see with the MSL file. Here, the type is selected based on the value of the `Type` column. Other options to select the type are also possible; for example, you can verify if a column is not null.

```
<Mapping Space="C-S"
  xmlns="urn:schemas-microsoft-com:windows:storage:mapping:CS">
  <EntityContainerMapping StorageEntityContainer="dbo"
      CdmEntityContainer="EntitiesDemoEntities">
    <EntitySetMapping Name="Payments">
      <EntityTypeMapping TypeName="IsTypeOf(Wrox.ProCSharp.Entities.Payment)">
        <MappingFragment StoreEntitySet="Payments">
          <ScalarProperty Name="Id" ColumnName="Id" />
          <ScalarProperty Name="Amount" ColumnName="Amount" />
          <ScalarProperty Name="Name" ColumnName="Name" />
        </MappingFragment>
      </EntityTypeMapping>
      <EntityTypeMapping
        TypeName="IsTypeOf(Wrox.ProCSharp.Entities.CashPayment)">
        <MappingFragment StoreEntitySet="Payments">
          <ScalarProperty Name="Id" ColumnName="Id" />
```

(continued)

(continued)

```
                <Condition ColumnName="Type" Value="CASH" />
              </MappingFragment>
            </EntityTypeMapping>
            <EntityTypeMapping
                TypeName="IsTypeOf(Wrox.ProCSharp.Entities.CreditCardPayment)">
              <MappingFragment StoreEntitySet="Payments">
                <ScalarProperty Name="Id" ColumnName="Id" />
                <ScalarProperty Name="CreditCard" ColumnName="CreditCard" />
                <Condition ColumnName="Type" Value="CREDIT" />
              </MappingFragment>
            </EntityTypeMapping>
            <EntityTypeMapping
                TypeName="IsTypeOf(Wrox.ProCSharp.Entities.ChequePayment)">
              <MappingFragment StoreEntitySet="Payments">
                <ScalarProperty Name="Id" ColumnName="Id" />
                <ScalarProperty Name="BankName" ColumnName="BankName" />
                <Condition ColumnName="Type" Value="CHEQUE" />
              </MappingFragment>
            </EntityTypeMapping>
          </EntitySetMapping>
        </EntityContainerMapping>
      </Mapping>
```

Now it's possible to iterate the data from the `Payments` table, and different types are returned based on the mapping:

```
PaymentEntities data = new PaymentEntities();
foreach (var p in data.Payments)
{
   Console.WriteLine("{0}, {1} - {2:C}", p.GetType().Name,
     p.Name, p.Amount);
}
```

Running the application returns two `CashPayment` and one `CreditCardPayment` object from the database:

```
CreditCardPayment, Gustav - $22.00
CashPayment, Donald - $0.50
CashPayment, Dagobert - $80,000.00
```

Table per Type

With TPT, one table maps to one type. The Northwind database has a schema with the tables `Customers`, `Orders`, and `Order Details` (see Figure A-5). The `Orders` table maps to the `Customers` table with the foreign key `CustomerId`; the `Order Details` table maps to the `Orders` table with the foreign key `OrderID`.

Figure A-6 shows the entity types `Customer`, `Order`, and `OrderDetail`. `Customer` and `Order` have a zero or one-to-many relationship; `Order` to `OrderDetail` has a one-to-many relationship. There is a zero or one-to-many relationship with `Customer` and `Order` because the `CustomerID` with the `Order` table is defined as `Nullable` in the database schema.

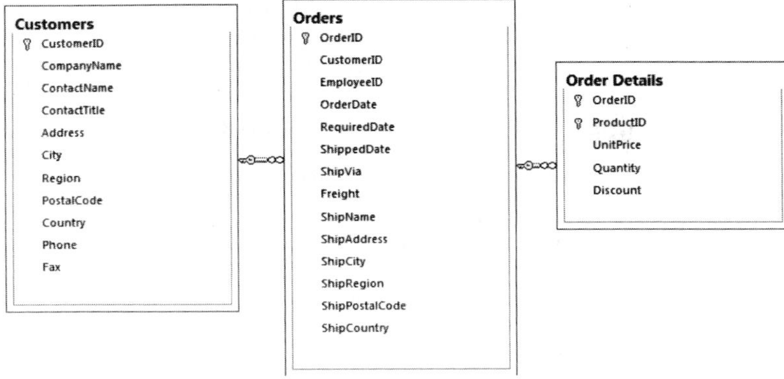

Figure A-5

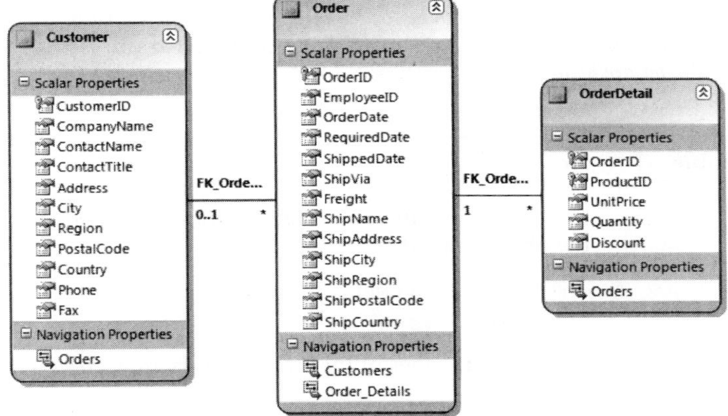

Figure A-6

You access the customers and their orders with two iterations shown here. First the `Customer` objects are accessed, and the value of the `CompanyName` property is written to the console. Then all orders are accessed by using the `Orders` property of the `Customer` class. Because the related orders are not loaded to the object context by default, the `Load()` method of the `EntityCollection<Order>` object is returned from the `Orders` property.

```
NorthwindEntities data = new NorthwindEntities();
foreach (Customer customer in data.Customers)
{
   Console.WriteLine("{0}", customer.CompanyName);
   if (!customer.Orders.IsLoaded)
      customer.Orders.Load();
   foreach (Order order in customer.Orders)
   {
      Console.WriteLine("{0} {1:d}", order.OrderID, order.OrderDate);
   }
}
```

Behind the scenes, the `RelationshipManager` class is used to access the relationship. The `RelationShipManager` instance can be accessed by casting the entity object to the interface `IEntityWithRelationships`. This interface is explicitly implemented by the class `EntityObject`. The `RelationshipManager` property returns a `RelationshipManager` that is associated with the entity object at one end. The other end is defined by invoking the method `GetRelatedCollection()`. The first parameter `NorthwindModel.FK_Orders_Customers` is the name of the relationship: the second parameter `Orders` defines the name of the target role.

```
RelationshipManager rm =
      ((IEntityWithRelationships)customer).RelationshipManager;
EntityCollection<Order> orders =
      rm.GetRelatedCollection<Order>(
      "NorthwindModel.FK_Orders_Customers", "Orders");
```

Relationships are delayed loaded. The `Load()` method of the `EntityCollection` class gets the data from the store. One overload of the `Load()` method accepts a `MergeOption` enumeration. The possible values are explained in the following table.

> *By default, relationships are* delayed loaded. *For example, if you define a relation with the Customers and Orders table and query for customers, the Orders records of the customers are not loaded. The term used here is delayed loaded as the orders can be loaded afterwards as needed. Contrary to delay loading you have the option to* eager fetch *records. Eager fetching means that as you access a customer record, orders for the customer are loaded as well.*

MergeOption Value	Description
`AppendOnly`	This is the default value. New entities are appended; existing entities in the object context are not modified.
`NoTracking`	The `ObjectStateManager` that tracks changes to entity objects is not modified.
`OverwriteChanges`	The current values of the entity objects are replaced with the values from the store.
`PreserveChanges`	The original values of the entity objects in the object context are replaced with the values from the store.

Object Query

Querying objects is one of the services offered by the ADO.NET Entity Framework. Queries can be done using LINQ to Entities, Entity SQL, and Query Builder methods that create Entity SQL. LINQ to Entities is covered in the last section of this appendix; let's get into the other two options first.

The following sections of this book make use of a Formula 1 database where you can see the entities created from the designer in Figure A-7.

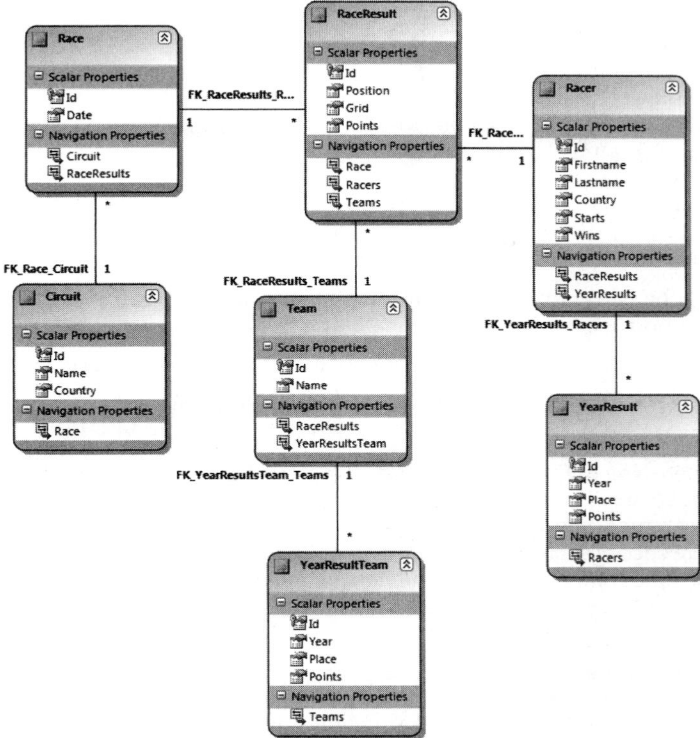

Figure A-7

Queries can be defined with the `ObjectQuery<T>` class. Let's start with a simple query to access all `Racer` entities. With this example, the connection is already opened, passing it to the object context `Formula1Entities`. This way it is possible to retrieve the generated SQL statement of the `ObjectQuery<Racer>` class with the `ToTraceString()` method. This method requires an open connection.

```
ConnectionStringSettings connSettings =
      ConfigurationManager.ConnectionStrings["Formula1Entities"];
EntityConnection connection =
      new EntityConnection(connSettings.ConnectionString);
connection.Open();
using (Formula1Entities data = new Formula1Entities(connection))
{
   ObjectQuery<Racer> racers = data.Racers;
   Console.WriteLine(racers.CommandText);
   Console.WriteLine(racers.ToTraceString());
   connection.Close();
}
```

The Entity SQL statement that is returned from the `CommandText` property is shown here:

```
[Racers]
```

And this is the generated SELECT statement to retrieve the records from the database that is shown by the ToTraceString() method:

```
SELECT
[Extent1].[Id] AS [Id],
[Extent1].[Firstname] AS [Firstname],
[Extent1].[Lastname] AS [Lastname],
[Extent1].[Country] AS [Country],
[Extent1].[Starts] AS [Starts],
[Extent1].[Wins] AS [Wins]
FROM [dbo].[Racers] AS [Extent1]
```

Instead of accessing the Racers property from the object context, you can also create a query with the CreateQuery() method:

```
ObjectQuery<Racer> racers = data.CreateQuery<Racer>("[Racers]");
```

This is similar to using the Racers property and, in fact, the implementation of the Racers property creates a query this way.

Now it would be interesting to filter the racers based on a condition. This can be done by using the Where() method of the ObjectQuery<T> class. Where() is one of the Query Builder methods that create Entity SQL. This method requires a predicate as a string, and optional parameters of type ObjectParameter. The predicate shown here specifies that only the racers from Brazil are returned. it specifies the item of the result, and Country is the column Country. The first parameter of the ObjectParameter constructor references the @Country parameter of the predicate, but doesn't list the @ sign.

```
string country = "Brazil";
ObjectQuery<Racer> racers = data.Racers.Where(
    "it.Country = @Country",
    new ObjectParameter("Country", country));
```

The magic behind it can be seen immediately by accessing the CommandText property of the query. With Entity SQL, SELECT VALUE it declares it to access the columns.

```
SELECT VALUE it
FROM (
[Racers]
) AS it
WHERE
it.Country = @Country
```

The method ToTraceString() shows the generated SQL statement:

```
SELECT
[Extent1].[Id] AS [Id],
[Extent1].[Firstname] AS [Firstname],
[Extent1].[Lastname] AS [Lastname],
[Extent1].[Country] AS [Country],
[Extent1].[Starts] AS [Starts],
[Extent1].[Wins] AS [Wins]
FROM [dbo].[Racers] AS [Extent1]
WHERE [Extent1].[Country] = @Country
```

Of course you can also specify the complete Entity SQL:

```
string country = "Brazil";
ObjectQuery<Racer> racers = data.CreateQuery<Racer>(
    "SELECT VALUE it FROM ([Racers]) AS it WHERE it.Country = @Country",
    new ObjectParameter("Country", country));
```

The class `ObjectQuery<T>` offers several Query Builder methods as explained in the following table. Many of these methods are very similar to the LINQ extension methods that you learned about in Chapter 11, "Language Integrated Query."

ObjectQuery<T> Query Builder Methods	Description
`Where()`	This method allows you to filter the results based on a condition.
`Distinct()`	This method creates a query with unique results.
`Except()`	This method returns the result without the items that meet the condition with the `except` filter.
`GroupBy()`	This method creates a new query to group entities based on a specified criteria.
`Include()`	With relations you've seen earlier that related items are delay loaded, it was required to invoke the `Load()` method of the `EntityCollection<T>` class to get related entities into the object context. Instead of using the `Load()` method, you can specify a query with the `Include()` method to eager fetch related entities.
`OfType()`	This method specifies to return only those entities of a specific type. This is very helpful with TPH relations.
`OrderBy()`	This method is for defining the sort order of the entities.
`Select()` `SelectValue()`	These methods return a projection of the results. `Select()` returns the result items in the form of a `DbDataRecord`; `SelectValue()` returns the values as scalars or complex types as defined by the generic parameter `TResultType`.
`Skip()` `Top()`	These methods are useful for paging. Skip a number of items with the `Skip()` method and take a specified number as defined by the `Top()` method.

`Intersect()`
`Union()`
`UnionAll()`
	These methods are used to combine two queries. `Intersect()` returns a query containing only the results that are available in both of the queries. `Union()` combines the queries and returns the complete result without duplicates. `UnionAll()` also includes duplicates.

Let's get into one example on how to use these Query Builder methods. Here, the racers are filtered with the `Where()` method to return only racers from the USA; the `OrderBy()` method specifies descending sort order first based on the number of wins, next the number of starts. Finally, only the first three racers are in the result using the `Top()` method.

```
using (Formula1Entities data = new Formula1Entities())
  {
     string country = "USA";
     ObjectQuery<Racer> racers = data.Racers.Where("it.Country = @Country",
        new ObjectParameter("Country", country))
        .OrderBy("it.Wins DESC, it.Starts DESC")
        .Top("3");
```

(continued)

(continued)

```
            foreach (var racer in racers)
            {
               Console.WriteLine("{0} {1}, wins: {2}, starts: {3}",
                   racer.Firstname, racer.Lastname, racer.Wins, racer.Starts);
            }
         }
```

This is the result from this query:

```
Mario Andretti, wins: 12, starts: 128
Dan Gurney, wins: 4, starts: 87
Phil Hill, wins: 3, starts: 48
```

Updates

Reading, searching, and filtering data from the store are just one part of the work that usually needs to be done with data-intensive applications. Writing changed data back to the store is the other part you need to know.

The sections that follow cover these topics:

- Object tracking
- Change information
- Attaching and detaching entities
- Storing entity changes

Object Tracking

To allow data read from the store to be modified and saved, the entities must be tracked after they are loaded. This also requires that the object context be aware if an entity has already been loaded from the store. If multiple queries are accessing the same records, the object context needs to return already loaded entities.

The `ObjectStateManager` is used by the object context to keep track of entities that are loaded into the context.

The following sample demonstrates that indeed if two different queries are done that return the same record from the database, the state manager is aware of that and does not create a new entity. Instead, the same entity is returned. The `ObjectStateManager` instance that is associated with the object context can be accessed with the `ObjectStateManager` property. The `ObjectStateManager` class defines an event named `ObjectStateManagerChanged` that is invoked every time a new object is added or removed from the object context. Here, the method `ObjectStateManager_ObjectStateManagerChanged` is assigned to the event to get information about changes.

Two different queries are used to return an entity object. The first query gets the first racer from the country Austria with the last name Lauda. The second query asks for the racers from Austria, sorts the racers by the number of races won, and gets the first result. As a matter of fact, that's the same racer. To verify that the same entity object is returned, the method `Object.ReferenceEquals()` is used to verify if the two object references indeed reference the same instance.

```
static void Tracking()
{
   using (Formula1Entities data = new Formula1Entities())
   {
      data.ObjectStateManager.ObjectStateManagerChanged +=
            ObjectStateManager_ObjectStateManagerChanged;
      Racer niki1 = data.Racers.Where(
            "it.Country='Austria' && it.Lastname='Lauda'").First();
      Racer niki2 = data.Racers.Where("it.Country='Austria'").
            OrderBy("it.Wins DESC").First();
      if (Object.ReferenceEquals(niki1, niki2))
      {
         Console.WriteLine("the same object");
      }
   }
}
static void ObjectStateManager_ObjectStateManagerChanged(object sender,
      CollectionChangeEventArgs e)
{
   Console.WriteLine("Object State change - action: {0}", e.Action);
   Racer r = e.Element as Racer;
   if (r != null)
      Console.WriteLine("Racer {0}", r.Lastname);
}
```

Running the application you can see that the event of the `ObjectStateManagerChanged` of the `ObjectStateManager` occurs only once, and the references niki1 and niki2 are indeed the same:

```
Object state change - action: Add
Racer Lauda
The same object
```

Change Information

The object context is also aware of changes with the entities. The following sample adds and modifies a racer from the object context and gets information about the change. First, a new racer is added with the `AddToRacers()` method of the `Formula1Entities` class. This designer-generated method invokes the `AddObject()` method of the base class `ObjectContext`. This method adds a new entity with the `EntityState.Added` information. Next, a racer with the `Lastname` Alonso is queried. With this entity class, the `Starts` property is incremented and thus the entity is marked with the information `EntityState.Modified`. Behind the scenes, the `ObjectStateManager` is informed about a state change in the object based on the interface implementations `INotifyPropertyChanged`. This interface is implemented in the entity base class `StructuralObject`. The `ObjectStateManager` is attached to the `PropertyChanged` event, and this event is fired with every property change.

To get all added or modified entity objects, you can invoke the `GetObjectStateEntries()` method of the `ObjectStateManager` and pass an `EntityState` enumeration value as it is done here. This method returns a collection of `ObjectStateEntry` objects that keep information about the entities. The helper method `DisplayState` iterates through this collection to give detail information.

You can also get state information about a single entity passing the `EntityKey` to the `GetObjectStateEntry()` method. The `EntityKey` property is available with entity objects implementing the interface `IEntityWithKey`, which is the case with the base class `EntityObject`. The `ObjectStateEntry` object returned offers the method `GetModifiedProperties()` where you can read all property values that have been changed, and also access the original and the current information about the properties with the `OriginalValues` and `CurrentValues` indexers.

```
static void ChangeInformation()
{
   using (Formula1Entities data = new Formula1Entities())
   {
      Racer sebastien = new Racer()
      {
         Firstname = "Sébastien",
         Lastname = "Bourdais",
         Country = "France",
         Starts = 0
      };
      data.AddToRacers(sebastien);
      Racer fernando = data.Racers.Where("it.Lastname='Alonso'").First();
      fernando.Starts++;
      DisplayState(EntityState.Added.ToString(),
            data.ObjectStateManager.GetObjectStateEntries(
               EntityState.Added));
      DisplayState(EntityState.Modified.ToString(),
            data.ObjectStateManager.GetObjectStateEntries(
               EntityState.Modified));
      ObjectStateEntry stateOfFernando =
            data.ObjectStateManager.GetObjectStateEntry(fernando.EntityKey);
      Console.WriteLine("state of Fernando: {0}",
            stateOfFernando.State.ToString());
      foreach (string modifiedProp in
         stateOfFernando.GetModifiedProperties())
      {
         Console.WriteLine("modified: {0}", modifiedProp);
         Console.WriteLine("original: {0}",
               stateOfFernando.OriginalValues[modifiedProp]);
         Console.WriteLine("current: {0}",
               stateOfFernando.CurrentValues[modifiedProp]);
      }
}
static void DisplayState(string state, IEnumerable<ObjectStateEntry> entries)
{
   foreach (var entry in entries)
   {
      Racer r = entry.Entity as Racer;
      if (r != null)
      {
         Console.WriteLine("{0}: {1}", state, r.Lastname);
      }
   }
}
```

When you run the application, the added and modified racers are displayed, and the properties changed with their original and current values are shown.

```
Added: Bourdais
Modified: Alonso
state of Fernando: Modified
modified: Starts
original: 95
current: 96
```

Attaching and Detaching Entities

Returning entity data to the caller it might be important to detach the objects from the object context. This is necessary, for example, if an entity object is returned from a Web service. Here, if the entity object is changed on the client, the object context is not aware of the change.

With the sample code, the `Detach()` method of the `ObjectContext` detaches the entity named `fernando` and thus the object context is not aware of any change done on this entity. If a changed entity object is passed from the client application to the service, it can be attached again. Just attaching it to the object context might not be enough because this doesn't give the information that the object was modified. Instead, the original object must be available inside the object context. The original object can be accessed from the store by using the key with the method `GetObjectByKey()`. If the entity object is already inside the object context, the existing one is used; otherwise it is fetched newly from the database. Invoking the method `ApplyPropertyChanges()` passes the modified entity object to the object context, and if there are changes, the changes are done within the existing entity with the same key inside the object context, and the `EntityState` is set to `Modified`. Remember that the method `ApplyPropertyChanges()` requires the object to exist within the object context; otherwise the new entity object is added with `EntityState Added`.

```
using (Formula1Entities data = new Formula1Entities())
{
   data.ObjectStateManager.ObjectStateManagerChanged +=
         ObjectStateManager_ObjectStateManagerChanged;
   ObjectResult<Racer> racers = data.Racers.Where("it.Lastname='Alonso'");
   Racer fernando = racers.First();
   EntityKey key = fernando.EntityKey;
   data.Detach(fernando);
   // Racer is now detached and can be changed independent of the
   // object context
   fernando.Starts++;
   Racer originalObject = (Racer)data.GetObjectByKey(key);
   data.ApplyPropertyChanges(key.EntitySetName, fernando);
}
```

Storing Entity Changes

Based on all the change information with the help of the `ObjectStateManager`, the added, deleted, and modified entity objects can be written to the store with the `SaveChanges()` method of the `ObjectContext` class. To verify changes within the object context, you can assign a handler method to the `SavingChanges` event of the `ObjectContext` class. This event is fired before the data is written to the store, so you can add some verification logic to see if the changes should be really done. `SaveChanges()` returns the number of entity objects that have been written.

What happens if the records in the database that are represented by the entity classes have been changed after reading the record? The answer depends on the `ConcurrencyMode` property that is set with the model. With every property of an entity object, you can configure the `ConcurrencyMode` to `Fixed` or `None`. The value `Fixed` means that the property is validated at write time to determine if the value was not changed in the meantime. `None` — which is the default — ignores any change. If some properties are configured to the `Fixed` mode, and data changed between reading and writing the entity objects, an `OptimisticConcurrencyException` occurs. You can deal with this exception by invoking the `Refresh()` method to read the actual information from the database into the object context. This method accepts two refresh modes configured by a `RefreshMode` enumeration value: `ClientWins` or `StoreWins`. `StoreWins` means that the actual information is taken from the database and set to the current values of the entity objects. `ClientWins` means that the database information is set to the original values of the entity objects, and thus the database values will be overwritten with the next `SaveChanges`. The second parameter of the `Refresh()` method is either a collection of entity objects or a single entity object. You can decide the refresh behavior on entity by entity.

```
static void ChangeInformation()
{
   //...
     int changes = 0;
     try
     {
        changes = data.SaveChanges();
     }
     catch (OptimisticConcurrencyException ex)
     {
        data.Refresh(RefreshMode.ClientWins, ex.StateEntries);
        changes = data.SaveChanges();
     }
     Console.WriteLine("{0} entities changed", changes);
```

LINQ to Entities

In several chapters of this book you've seen LINQ to Query objects, databases, and XML. Of course, LINQ is also available to query entities.

With LINQ to Entities, the source for the LINQ query is `ObjectQuery<T>`. Because `ObjectQuery<T>` implements the interface `IQueryable`, the extension methods selected for the query are defined with the class `Queryable` from the namespace `System.Linq`. The extension methods defined with this class have a parameter `Expression<T>`; that's why the compiler writes an expression tree to the assembly. You can read more about expression trees in Chapter 11, "Language Integrated Query." The expression tree is then resolved from the `ObjectQuery<T>` class to the SQL query.

You can use a simple LINQ query as shown here to return the racers that won more than 40 races:

```
using (Formula1Entities data = new Formula1Entities())
{
   var racers = from r in data.Racers
                where r.Wins > 40
                orderby r.Wins descending
                select r;
   foreach (Racer r in racers)
   {
      Console.WriteLine("{0} {1}", r.Firstname, r.Lastname);
   }
}
```

This is the result of accessing the Formula 1 database:

```
Michael Schumacher
Alain Prost
Ayrton Senna
```

You can also define a LINQ query to access relations as shown here. Variable `r` references racers, variable `rr` references all race results. The filter is defined with the `where` clause to retrieve only racers from

Switzerland who had a race position on the podium. To get the podium finishes, the result is grouped, and the podium count calculated. Sorting is done based on the podium finishes.

```
using (Formula1Entities data = new Formula1Entities())
{
   var query = from r in data.Racers
               from rr in r.RaceResults
               where rr.Position <= 3 && rr.Position >= 1 &&
                     r.Country == "Switzerland"
               group r by r.Id into g
               let podium = g.Count()
               orderby podium descending
               select new { Racer = g.FirstOrDefault(), Podiums = podium };
   foreach (var r in query)
   {
      Console.WriteLine("{0} {1} {2}", r.Racer.Firstname,
         r.Racer.Lastname,r.Podiums);
   }
}
```

The names of three racers from Switzerland are returned when you run the application:

```
Clay Regazzoni 28
Jo Siffert 6
Rudi Fischer 2
```

Summary

In this chapter, you've seen the features of the ADO.NET Entity Framework. Unlike LINQ to SQL, which is covered in Chapter 27, this framework offers a provider-based mapping, and other database vendors can implement their own providers.

The ADO.NET Entity Framework is based on mapping that is defined by CSDL, MSL, and SSDL — XML information to describe the entities, the mapping, and the database schema. Using this mapping technique, you can create different relation types to map entity classes to database tables.

You've seen how the object context keeps knowledge about entities retrieved and updated, and how the changes can be written to the store.

LINQ to Entities is just a facet of the ADO.NET Entity Framework that allows you to use the new query syntax to access entities.

C#, Visual Basic, and C++/CLI

C# is *the* programming language designed for .NET. More than 50 languages exist for writing .NET applications — for example, Eiffel, Smalltalk, COBOL, Haskell, Pizza, Pascal, Delphi, Oberon, Prolog, and Ruby. Microsoft alone delivers the languages C#, Visual Basic, C++/CLI, J#, and JScript.NET.

Every language has advantages and disadvantages; some things can be done easily with one language but are complicated with another one. The classes from the .NET Framework are always the same, but the syntax of the language abstracts various features from the Framework. For example, the C# `using` statement makes it easy to use the objects implementing the `IDisposable` interface. Other languages need more code for the same functionality.

The most commonly used .NET languages from Microsoft are C# and Visual Basic. C# was newly designed for .NET with ideas from C++, Java, Pascal, and other languages. Visual Basic has its roots in Visual Basic 6 and was extended with object-oriented features for .NET.

C++/CLI is an extension to C++ that is an ECMA standard (ECMA 372). The big advantage of C++/CLI is the ability to mix native code with managed code. You can extend existing native C++ applications and add .NET functionality, and you can add .NET classes to native libraries so that they can be used from other .NET languages such as C#. It is also possible to write completely managed applications with C++/CLI.

This chapter shows you how to convert .NET applications from one language to another. If you see sample code with Visual Basic or C++/CLI, you can easily map this to C#, and the other way around.

The following topics are covered in this chapter:

- Namespaces
- Defining types
- Methods
- Arrays

- Control statements
- Loops
- Exception handling
- Inheritance
- Resource management
- Delegates
- Events
- Generics
- LINQ Queries
- C++/CLI mixing native and managed code

For this chapter, I assume that you know C# and have read the first few chapters of this book. It is not necessary to know Visual Basic and C++/CLI.

Namespaces

.NET types are organized into namespaces. The syntax for defining and using namespaces is quite different between the three languages.

To import namespaces, C# uses the `using` keyword. C++/CLI is fully based on the C++ syntax with the `using namespace` statement. Visual Basic defines the `Imports` keyword to import namespaces.

With C#, you can define an alias to classes or other namespaces. With C++/CLI and Visual Basic namespace, an alias can reference other namespaces, but not classes. C++ requires the `namespace` keyword to define an alias — the same keyword is used to define a namespace. Visual Basic uses the `Imports` keyword again.

For defining namespaces, all three languages use the `namespace` keyword, but there's still a difference. With C++/CLI, you can't define hierarchical namespaces with one namespace statement; instead the namespaces must be nested. There's one important difference with the project settings: defining a namespace in the project settings of C# defines a default namespace that shows up in the code of all new items that you add to the project. With Visual Basic project settings, you define the root namespace that is used by all items in the project. Namespaces declared in the source code define only the sub-namespace inside the root namespace.

```
// C#
using System;
using System.Collections.Generic;
using Assm = Wrox.ProCSharp.Assemblies;
namespace Wrox.ProCSharp.Languages
{
}
// C++/CLI
using namespace System;
using namespace System::Collections::Generic;
namespace Assm = Wrox.ProCSharp.Assemblies;
namespace Wrox
{
   namespace ProCSharp
```

```
    {
        namespace Languages
        {
        }
    }
}
'' Visual Basic
Imports System
Imports System.Collections.Generic
Imports Assm = Wrox.ProCSharp.Assemblies
Namespace Wrox.ProCSharp.Languages
End Namespace
```

Defining Types

.NET differentiates between reference types and value types. With C#, reference types are defined with classes, and value types with structs. In addition to reference and value types, this section also shows you how to define an interface (a reference type) and an enumeration (a value type).

Reference Types

To declare a reference type, C# and Visual Basic use the `class` keyword. In C++/CLI, a class and a struct are nearly the same; you don't have the separation between a reference type and a value type as you do with C# and Visual Basic. C++/CLI has a `ref` keyword to define a managed class. You can create a reference type by defining `ref class` or `ref struct`.

Both with C# and C++/CLI the class is surrounded by curly brackets. With C++/CLI don't forget the semicolon at the end of the class declaration. Visual Basic uses the `End Class` statement at the end of the class.

```
// C#
public class MyClass
{
}
// C++/CLI
public ref class MyClass
{
};
public ref struct MyClass2
{
};
' Visual Basic
Public Class MyClass
End Class
```

When using a reference type, a variable needs to be declared, and the object must be allocated on the managed heap. When declaring a handle to a reference type, C++/CLI defines the handle operator `^`, which is somewhat similar to the C++ pointer `*`. The `gcnew` operator allocates the memory on the managed heap. With C++/CLI, it is also possible to declare a variable locally, but for reference types, the object is still allocated on the managed heap. With Visual Basic, the variable declaration starts with the statement `Dim` followed by the name of the variable. With `new` and the object type, memory is allocated on the managed heap.

```
// C#
MyClass obj = new MyClass();
// C++/CLI
MyClass^ obj = gcnew MyClass();
MyClass obj2;
' Visual Basic
Dim obj as New MyClass()
```

If a reference type does not reference memory, all three languages use different keywords: C# defines the `null` literal, C++/CLI defines `nullptr` (`NULL` is valid only for native objects), and Visual Basic defines `Nothing`.

Predefined reference types are listed in the following table. C++/CLI does not define the object and string type as is done with the other languages. Of course, you can use the classes defined by the Framework.

.NET Type	C#	C++/CLI	Visual Basic
`System.Object`	`object`	Not defined	`Object`
`System.String`	`string`	Not defined	`String`

Value Types

To declare a value type, C# uses the `struct` keyword; C++/CLI, the keyword `value`; and Visual Basic, `Structure`.

```
// C#
public struct MyStruct
{
}
// C++/CLI
public value class MyStruct
{
};
' Visual Basic
Public Structure MyStruct
End Structure
```

With C++/CLI, you can allocate a value type on the stack, on the native heap by using the `new` operator, and on the managed heap by using the `gcnew` operator. C# and Visual Basic do not have these options, but these options become important when native and managed code is mixed with C++/CLI.

```
// C#
MyStruct ms;
// C++/CLI
MyStruct ms1;
MyStruct* pms2 = new MyStruct();
MyStruct^ hms3 = gcnew MyStruct();
' Visual Basic
Dim ms as MyStruct
```

Predefined value types for the different languages are listed in the following table. In C++/CLI, the char type has a size of just 1 byte for an ASCII character. In C#, `char` has a size of 2 bytes for Unicode characters; that's a `wchar_t` in C++/CLI. The ANSI standard for C++ just defines `short <= int <= long`. With 32-bit machines, `int` and `long` both have a size of 32 bits. To define a 64-bit variable in C++, you need `long long`.

.NET Type	C#	C++/CLI	Visual Basic	Size
`Char`	`char`	`wchar_t`	`Char`	2 bytes
`Boolean`	`bool`	`bool`	`Boolean`	1 byte, contains `true` or `false`
`Int16`	`short`	`short`	`Short`	2 bytes
`UInt16`	`ushort`	`unsigned short`	`UShort`	2 bytes with no sign
`Int32`	`int`	`int`	`Integer`	4 bytes
`UInt32`	`uint`	`unsigned int`	`UInteger`	4 bytes with no sign
`Int64`	`long`	`long long`	`Long`	8 bytes
`UInt64`	`ulong`	`unsigned long long`	`ULong`	8 bytes with no sign

Type Inference

C# 3.0 allows you to define a local variable without an explicit data type declaration with the `var` keyword. The type is inferred from the initial value that is assigned. Visual Basic offers the same feature using the `Dim` keyword as long as *Option infer* is turned on. This can be done with the compiler setting / optioninfer+ or by using the project configuration page with Visual Studio.

```
// C#
var x = 3;
' Visual Basic
Dim x = 3
```

Interfaces

Defining interfaces is very similar for all three languages. All languages use the keyword `interface`:

```
// C#
public interface IDisplay
{
   void Display();
}
// C++/CLI
public interface class IDisplay
{
   void Display();
};
' Visual Basic
Public Interface IDisplay
   Sub Display
End Interface
```

Implementing interfaces is different. C# and C++/CLI use a colon after the class name followed by the interface name. The methods defined with the interface are implemented. With C++/CLI, the methods must be declared `virtual`. Visual Basic uses the `Implements` keyword to implement an interface, and the methods that are defined by the interface also need the `Implements` keyword attached.

```
// C#
public class Person : IDisplay
{
   public void Display()
   {
   }
}
// C# explicit interface implementation
public class Person : IDisplay
{
   void IDisplay.Display()
   {
   }
}
// C++/CLI
public ref class Person : IDisplay
{
public:
   virtual void Display();
};
' Visual Basic
Public Class Person
   Implements IDisplay
   Public Sub Display Implements IDisplay.Display
   End Sub
End Class
```

Enumerations

Enumerations are defined similarly in all three languages with the `enum` keyword (only Visual Basic uses a new line instead of a comma to separate the elements):

```
// C#
public enum Color
{
   Red, Green, Blue
}
// C++/CLI
public enum class Color
{
   Red, Green, Blue
};
' Visual Basic
Public Enum Color
   Red
   Green
   Blue
End Enum
```

Methods

Methods are always declared within a class. The syntax from C++/CLI is very similar to C# except that the access modifier is not part of the method declaration but is written before that. The access modifier must end with a colon. With Visual Basic, the `Sub` keyword is used to define a method.

```
// C#
public class MyClass
{
   public void Foo()
   {
   }
}
// C++/CLI
public ref class MyClass
{
public:
   void Foo()
   {
   }
};
' Visual Basic
Public Class MyClass
   Public Sub Foo
   End Sub
End Class
```

Method Parameters and Return Types

With C# and C++/CLI, parameters that are passed to methods are defined inside a bracket. The type of the parameter is declared before the variable name. If a value is returned from a method, the method is defined with the type to return instead of `void`.

Visual Basic uses `Sub` statements to declare a method without returning a value, and the `Function` statement with a method that does have a return type. The return type is followed after the method name and the brackets. Visual Basic also has a different order with variable declaration and type in the parameter. The type follows the variable, which is the reverse direction from C# and C++/CLI.

```
// C#
public class MyClass
{
   public int Foo(int i)
   {
      return 2 * i;
   }
}
// C++/CLI
public ref class MyClass
{
public:
   int Foo(int i)
   {
      return 2 * i;
   }
};
```

(continued)

(continued)

```
' Visual Basic
Public Class MyClass
   Public Sub Foo1(ByVal i as Integer)
   End Sub
   Public Function Foo(ByVal i As Integer) As Integer
      Return 2 * i
   End Sub
End Class
```

Parameter Modifiers

By default, value types are passed by value, and reference types are passed by reference. If a value type that is passed as a parameter should be changed within a calling method, with C# you can use the parameter modifier `ref`.

C++/CLI defines a managed reference operator `%`. This operator is similar to the C++ reference operator `&` except that `%` can be used with managed types and the garbage collector can keep track of these objects in case they are moved within the managed heap.

With Visual Basic, the keyword `ByRef` is used for passing parameters by reference:

```
// C#
public class ParameterPassing
{
   public void ChangeVal(ref int i)
   {
      i = 3;
   }
}
// C++/CLI
public ref class ParameterPassing
{
public:
   int ChangeVal(int% i)
   {
      i = 3;
   }
};
' Visual Basic
Public Class ParameterPassing
   Public Sub ChangeVal(ByRef i as Integer)
      i = 3
   End Sub
End Class
```

When invoking a method with reference parameters, only the C# language requires you to apply a parameter modifier. C++/CLI and Visual Basic don't differentiate calling a method with or without the parameter modifier. C# has the advantage here because you can immediately see in the calling method the parameter values can be changed.

Because of the caller syntax, which is not differentiated, Visual Basic does not allow you to overload methods just by changing the modifier. The C++/CLI compiler allows you to overload the method just by changing the modifier, but you cannot compile the caller because the resolved method is ambiguous. With C# it is possible to overload and use methods with just the parameter modifier, but it's not a good programming practice.

```
// C#
      ParameterPassing obj = new ParameterPassing();
      int a = 1;
      obj.ChangeVal(ref a);
      Console.WriteLine(a);      // writes 3
// C++/CLI
      ParameterPassing obj;
      int a = 1;
      obj.ChangeVal(a);
      Console.WriteLine(a);      // writes 3
' Visual Basic
      Dim obj as new ParameterPassing()
      Dim i as Integer = 1
      obj.ChangeVal(i)
      Console.WriteLine(i)      // writes 3
```

C# also defines the `out` *keyword when a parameter is just returned from a method. This option is not available from C++/CLI and Visual Basic. As long as the caller and callee are in the same application domain, there's really no difference between* `out` *and* `ref` *behind the scenes, and you can use a method declared with the C#* `out` *parameter modifier from Visual Basic and C++/CLI in the same way as* `ref` *parameter modifiers. If the method is used across application domains or processes, the attribute* `[out]` *can be used with Visual Basic and C++/CLI.*

Constructors

With both C# and C++/CLI, the constructor has the same name as the class. Visual Basic uses a procedure named `New`. The `this` and `Me` keywords are used to access a member of this instance. When invoking another constructor within a constructor, a member initializion is required with C#. With C++/CLI and Visual Basic, it is possible to invoke the constructor as a method.

```
// C#
public class Person
{
   public Person()
      : this("unknown", "unknown")
   { }
   public Person(string firstName, string lastName)
   {
      this.firstName = firstName;
      this.lastName = lastName;
   }
   private string firstName;
   private string lastName;
}
// C++/CLI
public ref class Person
{
public:
   Person()
   {
      Person("unknown", "unknown");
   }
   Person(String^ firstName, String^ lastName)
```

(continued)

(continued)

```
    {
       this->firstName = firstName;
       this->lastName = lastName;
    }
 private:
    String^ firstName;
    String^ lastName;
 };
 ' Visual Basic
 Public Class Person
    Public Sub New()
       Me.New("unknown", "unknown")
    End Sub
    Public Sub New(ByVal firstName As String, ByVal lastName As String)
       Me.MyFirstName = firstName
       Me.MyLastName = lastName
    End Sub
    Private MyFirstName As String
    Private MyLastName As String
 End Class
```

Properties

To define a property, C# just requires a get and set accessor within a property block. With the set accessor, the variable value is automatically created by the C# compiler. C# 3.0 also has a new shorthand notation where an implementation is not needed if just a simple variable is returned or set by the get and set accessors. The syntax is different both with C++/CLI and Visual Basic. Both of these languages have a `property` keyword, and it is necessary to define a variable `value` with the set accessor. C++/CLI also requires a return type with the get accessor and a parameter type with the set accessor.

C++/CLI also has a short version of writing a property. Using the `property` keyword, you just have to define the type and the name of the property; the get and set accessors are created automatically by the compiler. If there's nothing else needed than setting and returning a variable, the short version is good enough. If the implementation of the accessors requires more — for example, checking the value or doing a refresh — you must write the full syntax for properties. The designers of C# 3.0 learned from C++/CLI to offer a short notation as well.

```
// C#
public class Person
{
   private string firstName;
   public string FirstName
   {
      get { return firstName; }
      set { firstName = value; }
   }
   public string LastName { get; set; }
}
// C++/CLI
public ref class Person
{
private:
    String^ firstName;
public:
   property String^ FirstName
```

```
      {
         String^ get()
         {
            return firstName;
         }
         void set(String^ value)
         {
            firstName = value;
         }
      }
      property String^ LastName;
   };
   ' Visual Basic
   Public Class Person
       Private myFirstname As String
       Public Property FirstName()
           Get
               Return myFirstName
           End Get
           Set(ByVal value)
               myFirstName = value
           End Set
       End Property
       Private myLastName As String
       Public Property LastName()
           Get
               Return myLastName
           End Get
           Set(ByVal value)
               myLastName = value
           End Set
       End Property
   End Class
```

With C# and C++/CLI, read-only properties just have a get accessor. With Visual Basic, you must also specify the `ReadOnly` modifier. Write-only properties must be defined with the `WriteOnly` modifier and a set accessor.

```
' Visual Basic
    Public ReadOnly Property Name()
        Get
            Return myFirstName & " " & myLastName
        End Get
    End Property
```

Object Initializers

With C# 3.0 and Visual Basic, properties can be initialized using an object initializer. The properties can be initialized using curly brackets similar to an array initializer. The syntax from C# and Visual Basic is very similar; Visual Basic just uses the `With` keyword.

```
// C#
Person p = new Person() { FirstName = "Tom", LastName = "Turbo" };
' Visual Basic
Dim p As New Person With { .FirstName = "Tom", .LastName = "Turbo" }
```

Extension Methods

Extension methods are the foundation of LINQ. With both C# and Visual Basic, it is possible to create extension methods. However, the syntax is different. C# marks an extension method with the `this` keyword in the first parameter, Visual Basic marks an extension method with the attribute `<Extension>`.

```
// C#
public static class StringExtension
{
   public static void Foo(this string s)
   {
      Console.WriteLine("Foo {0}", s);
   }
}
' Visual Basic
Public Module StringExtension
   <Extension()> _
   Public Sub Foo(ByVal s As String)
      Console.WriteLine("Foo {0}", s)
   End Sub
End Module
```

Static Members

A static field is instantiated only once for all objects of the type. C# and C++/CLI both use the `static` keyword; Visual Basic offers the same functionality with the `Shared` keyword.

To use static members, you use the name of the class followed by the `.` operator and the name of the static member. C++/CLI uses the `::` operator for accessing static members.

```
// C#
public class Singleton
{
   private static SomeData data = null;
   public static SomeData GetData()
   {
      if (data == null)
      {
         data = new SomeData();
      }
      return data;
   }
}
// use:
SomeData d = Singleton.GetData();
// C++/CLI
public ref class Singleton
{
private:
   static SomeData^ hData;
public:
   static SomeData^ GetData()
   {
      if (hData == nullptr)
```

```
        {
           hData = gcnew SomeData();
        }
        return hData;
     }
  };
  // use:
  SomeData^ d = Singleton::GetData();
  ' Visual Basic
  Public Class Singleton
     Private Shared data As SomeData
     Public Shared Function GetData() As SomeData
        If data is Nothing Then
           data = new SomeData()
        End If
        Return data
     End Function
  End Class
  ' Use:
  Dim d as SomeData = Singleton.GetData()
```

Arrays

Arrays are discussed in Chapter 5, "Arrays." The `Array` class is always behind the scenes of .NET arrays; declaring an array, the compiler creates a class that derives from the `Array` base class. When C# was designed, the designers of the C# language took the bracket syntax for arrays from C++ and extended it with array initializers.

```
// C#
int[] arr1 = new int[3] {1, 2, 3};
int[] arr2 = {1, 2, 3};
```

If you use brackets with C++/CLI, you create a native C++ array but not an array that is based on the `Array` class. To create .NET arrays, C++/CLI introduced the `array` keyword. This keyword uses a generic-like syntax with angle brackets. Within the angle brackets, the type of the elements is defined. C++/CLI supports array initializers with the same syntax as C#.

```
// C++/CLI
array<int>^ arr1 = gcnew array<int>(3) {1, 2, 3};
array<int>^ arr2 = {1, 2, 3};
```

Visual Basic uses braces for arrays. It requires the last element number instead of the number of elements with the array declaration. With every .NET language, arrays begin with element number 0. This is also the same for Visual Basic. To make that clearer, Visual Basic 9 introduced the `0 To number` expression with the array declaration. It always starts with 0; `0 To` just makes this more readable.

Visual Basic also supports array initializers if the array is initialized with the `New` operator:

```
' Visual Basic
Dim arr1(0 To 2) As Integer()
Dim arr2 As Integer() = New Integer(0 To 2) {1, 2, 3};
```

Control Statements

Control statements define what code should run. C# defines the `if` and `switch` statements, and the conditional operator.

if Statement

The C# `if` statement is the same as the C++/CLI version. Visual Basic uses `If-Then/Else/End If` instead of curly brackets.

```
// C# and C++/CLI
if (a == 3)
{
   // do this
}
else
{
   // do that
}
' Visual Basic
If a = 3 Then
  ' do this
Else
  ' do that
End If
```

Conditional Operator

C# and C++/CLI support the conditional operator, a lightweight version of the `if` statement. In C++/CLI, this operator is known as a *ternary* operator. The first argument has a Boolean result. If the result is true, the first expression is evaluated; otherwise, the second one is. Visual Basic has the `IIf` function in the Visual Basic Runtime Library, which offers the same functionality.

```
// C#
string s = a > 3 ? "one" : "two";
// C++/CLI
String^ s = a > 3 ? "one" : "two";
' Visual Basic
Dim s As String = IIf(a > 3, "one", "two")
```

switch Statement

The `switch` statement looks very similar in C# and C++/CLI, but there are important differences. C# supports strings with the case selection. This is not possible with C++. With C++ you have to use `if-else` instead. C++/CLI does support an implicit fall-through from one case to the next. With C#, the compiler complains if there's not a `break` or a `goto` statement. C# has only implicit fall-through if there's not a statement for the case.

Visual Basic has a `Select/Case` statement instead of `switch/case`. A break is not only not needed but also not possible. An implicit fall-through from one case to the next is not possible, even if there's not a single statement following `Case`; instead, `Case` can be combined with `And`, `Or`, and `To` — for example, `3 To 5`.

```
// C#
string GetColor(Suit s)
{
   string color;
   switch (s)
   {
      case Suit.Heart:
      case Suit.Diamond:
         color = "Red";
         break;
      case Suit.Spade:
      case Suit.Club:
         color = "Black";
         break;
      default:
         color = "Unknown";
         break;
   }
   return color;
}
// C++/CLI
String^ GetColor(Suit s)
{
   String^ color;
   switch (s)
   {
      case Suit::Heart:
      case Suit::Diamond:
         color = "Red";
         break;
      case Suit::Spade:
      case Suit::Club:
         color = "Black";
         break;
      default:
         color = "Unknown";
         break;
   }
   return color;
}
' Visual Basic
Function GetColor(ByVal s As Suit) As String
   Dim color As String = Nothing
   Select Case s
      Case Suit.Heart And Suit.Diamond
         color = "Red"
      Case Suit.Spade And Suit.Club
         color = "Black"
      Case Else
         color = "Unknown"
   End Select

   Return color
End Function
```

Loops

With loops, code is executed repeatedly until a condition is met. Loops with C# are discussed in Chapter 2, "C# Basics," including: `for`, `while`, `do...while`, and `foreach`. C# and C++/CLI are very similar with the looping statements; Visual Basic defines different statements.

for Statement

The `for` statement is similar with C# and C++/CLI. With Visual Basic, you can't initialize a variable inside the `For/To` statement; you must initialize the variable beforehand. `For/To` doesn't require a `Step` to follow — `Step 1` is the default. Just in case you don't want to increment by 1, the `Step` keyword is required with `For/To`.

```
// C#
for (int i = 0; i < 100; i++)
{
   Console.WriteLine(i);
}
// C++/CLI
for (int i = 0; i < 100; i++)
{
   Console::WriteLine(i);
}
' Visual Basic
Dim count as Integer
For count = 0 To 99 Step 1
   Console.WriteLine(count)
Next
```

while and do . . . while Statements

The `while` and `do...while` statements are the same in C# and C++/CLI. Visual Basic has very similar constructs with `Do While/Loop` and `Do/Loop While`.

```
// C#
int i = 0;
while (i < 3)
{
   Console.WriteLine(i++);
}
i = 0;
do
{
   Console.WriteLine(i++);
} while (i < 3);
// C++/CLI
int i = 0;
while (i < 3)
{
   Console::WriteLine(i++);
}
i = 0;
do
{
   Console::WriteLine(i++);
} while (i < 3);
```

```
' Visual Basic
Dim num as Integer = 0
Do While (num < 3)
   Console.WriteLine(num)
   num += 1
Loop
num = 0
Do
   Console.WriteLine(num)
   num += 1
Loop While (num < 3)
```

foreach Statement

The `foreach` statement makes use of the interface `IEnumerable`. `foreach` doesn't exist with ANSI C++ but is an extension of ANSI C++/CLI. Unlike the C# `foreach`, in C++/CLI there's a blank space between `for` and `each`. The `For Each` statement of Visual Basic doesn't allow you to declare the type of the iterating type inside the loop; the type must be declared beforehand.

```
// C#
int[] arr = {1, 2, 3};
foreach (int i in arr)
{
   Console.WriteLine(i);
}
// C++/CLI
array<int>^ arr = {1, 2, 3};
for each (int i in arr)
{
   Console::WriteLine(i);
}
' Visual Basic
Dim arr() As Integer = New Integer() {1, 2, 3}
Dim num As Integer
For Each num In arr
   Console.WriteLine(num)
Next
```

While `foreach` makes it easy to iterate through a collection, C# supports creating enumerations by using the `yield` statement. With Visual Basic and C++/CLI, the `yield` statement is not available. Instead, with these languages it is necessary to implement the interfaces `IEnumerable` and `IEnumerator` manually. The `yield` statement is explained in Chapter 5, "Arrays."

Exception Handling

Exception handling is discussed in Chapter 14, "Errors and Exceptions." This is extremely similar among all three languages. All these languages use `try/catch/finally` for handling exceptions, and the `throw` keyword to create an exception:

```
// C#
public void Method(Object o)
{
   if (o == null)
      throw new ArgumentException("Error");
}
```

(continued)

(continued)

```
public void Foo()
{
   try
   {
      Method(null);
   }
   catch (ArgumentException ex)
   { }
   catch (Exception ex)
   { }
   finally
   { }
}
// C++/CLI
public:
   void Method(Object^ o)
   {
      if (o == nullptr)
         throw gcnew ArgumentException("Error");
   }
   void Foo()
   {
      try
      {
         Method(nullptr);
      }
      catch (ArgumentException^ ex)
      { }
      catch (Exception^ ex)
      { }
      finally
      { }
   }
' Visual Basic
Public Sub Method(ByVal o As Object)
   If o = Nothing Then
      Throw New ArgumentException("Error")
End Sub
Public Sub Foo()
   Try
      Method(Nothing)
   Catch ex As ArgumentException
      '
   Catch ex As Exception
      '
   Finally
      '
   End Try
End Sub
```

Inheritance

.NET languages offer many keywords to define polymorphic behavior, to override or hide methods, access modifiers to allow or not allow member access. For C#, this functionality is discussed in Chapter 4, "Inheritance." The functionality of C#, C++/CLI and Visual Basic is very similar, but the keywords are different.

Access Modifiers

The access modifiers of C++/CLI and Visual Basic are very similar to C#, with some notable differences. Visual Basic uses the `Friend` access modifier instead of `internal` for accessing the types in the same assembly. C++/CLI has one more access modifier: `protected private`. `internal protected` allows accessing the members from within the same assembly, and also from other assemblies if the type is derived from the base type. C# and Visual Basic don't have a way to allow only derived types within the same assembly. This is possible with `protected private` from C++/CLI. Here `private` means that outside the assembly there's no access, but from inside the assembly protected access is possible. The order — whether you write `protected private` or `private protected` — does not matter. The access modifier allowing more is always located within the assembly, and the access modifier allowing less is always outside of the assembly.

C#	C++/CLI	Visual Basic
`public`	`public`	`Public`
`protected`	`protected`	`Protected`
`private`	`private`	`Private`
`internal`	`internal`	`Friend`
`internal protected`	`internal protected`	`Protected Friend`
`not possible`	`protected private`	`not possible`

Keywords

Keywords important for inheritance are mapped in the following table.

C#	C++/CLI	Visual Basic	Functionality
`:`	`:`	`Implements`	Implement an interface
`:`	`:`	`Inherits`	Inherits from a base class
`virtual`	`virtual`	`Overridable`	Declare a method to support polymorphism
`overrides`	`override`	`Overrides`	Override a virtual method
`new`	`new`	`Shadows`	Hide a method from a base class
`abstract`	`abstract`	`MustInherit`	Abstract class

C#	C++/CLI	Visual Basic	Functionality
sealed	sealed	NotInheritable	Sealed class
abstract	abstract	MustOverride	Abstract method
sealed	sealed	NotOverridable	Sealed method
this	this	Me	Reference the current object
base	Classname::	MyBase	Reference the base class

The order in which you place the keywords is important in the languages. In the code sample, an abstract base class `Base` with one abstract method and one implemented method that is virtual are defined. The class `Base` is derived from the class `Derived`, where the abstract method is implemented, and the virtual method is overridden:

```
// C#
public abstract class Base
{
   public virtual void Foo()
   {
   }
   public abstract void Bar();
}
public class Derived : Base
{
   public override void Foo()
   {
      base.Foo();
   }
   public override void Bar()
   {
   }
}
// C++/CLI
public ref class Base abstract
{
public:
   virtual void Foo()
   {
   }
   virtual void Bar() abstract;
};
public ref class Derived : public Base
{
public:
   virtual void Foo() override
   {
      Base::Foo();
   }
   virtual void Bar() override
```

```
      {
      }
   };
   ' Visual Basic
   Public MustInherit Class Base
      Public Overridable Sub Foo()
      End Sub
      Public MustOverride Sub Bar()
   End Class
   Public class Derived
      Inherits Base
      Public Overrides Sub Foo()
         MyBase.Foo()
      End Sub
      Public Overrides Sub Bar()
      End Sub
   End Class
```

Resource Management

Working with resources is covered in Chapter 12, "Memory Management and Pointers," both implementing the `IDisposable` interface and implementing a finalizer. How this looks in C++/CLI and Visual Basic is covered in this section.

IDisposable Interface Implementation

For freeing resources, the interface `IDisposable` defines the `Dispose()` method. Using C# and Visual Basic, you have to implement the interface `IDisposable`. With C++/CLI the interface `IDisposable` is implemented as well, but this is done by the compiler if you just write a destructor.

```
// C#
public class Resource : IDisposable
{
   public void Dispose()
   {
      // release resource
   }
}
// C++/CLI
public ref class Resource
{
public:
   ~Resource()
   {
      // release resource
   }
};
' Visual Basic
Public Class Resource
   Implements IDisposable
   Public Sub Dispose() Implements IDisposable.Dispose
      ' release resource
   End Sub
End Class
```

With C++/CLI, the `Dispose()` *method is invoked by using the* `delete` *statement.*

Using Statement

The C# `using` statement implements an acquire/use/release pattern to release a resource as soon as it is no longer used, even in the case of an exception. The compiler creates a `try/finally` statement and invokes the `Dispose` method inside the `finally`. Version 9 of Visual Basic supports the `using` statement just as C# does. C++/CLI has an even more elegant approach to this problem. If a reference type is declared locally, the compiler creates a `try/finally` statement to invoke the `Dispose()` method at the end of the block.

```
// C#
using (Resource r = new Resource())
{
   r.Foo();
}
// C++/CLI
{
   Resource r;
   r.Foo();
}
' Visual Basic
Using r As New Resource
   r.Foo()
End Using
```

Override Finalize

If a class contains native resources that must be freed, the class must override the `Finalize()` method from the `Object` class. With C#, this is done by writing a destructor. C++/CLI has a special syntax with the `!` prefix to define a finalizer. Within a finalizer, you cannot dispose contained objects that have a finalizer as well because the order of finalization is not guaranteed. That's why the Dispose pattern defines an additional `Dispose()` method with a Boolean parameter. With C++/CLI, it is not necessary to implement this pattern in the code because this is done by the compiler. The C++/CLI destructor implements both `Dispose()` methods. With Visual Basic, both `Dispose()` and the finalizer must be implemented manually. However, most Visual Basic classes do not use native resources directly, just with the help of other classes. With Visual Basic, usually it is not necessary to override the `Finalize()` method, but an implementation of the `Dispose()` method is often required.

Writing a destructor with C# overrides the `Finalize()` *method of the base class. A C++/CLI destructor implements the* `IDisposable` *interface.*

```
// C#
public class Resource : IDisposable
{
   ~Resource // override Finalize
   {
      Dispose(false);
   }
   protected virtual void Dispose(bool disposing)
   {
      if (disposing) // dispose embedded members
      {
      }
```

```
            // release resources of this class
            GC.SuppressFinalize(this);
        }
        public void Dispose()
        {
            Dispose(true);
        }
    }
    // C++/CLI
    public ref class Resource
    {
    public:
        ~Resource() // implement IDisposable
        {
            this->!Resource();
        }
        !Resource()  // override Finalize
        {
            // release resource
        }
    };
    ' Visual Basic
    Public Class Resource
        Implements IDisposable
        Public Sub Dispose() Implements IDisposable.Dispose
            Dispose(True)
            GC.SuppressFinalize(Me)
        End Sub
        Protected Overridable Sub Dispose(ByVal disposing)
            If disposing Then
                ' Release embedded resources
            End If
            ' Release resources of this class
        End Sub
        Protected Overrides Sub Finalize()
            Try
                Dispose(False)
            Finally
                MyBase.Finalize()
            End Try
        End Sub
    End Class
```

Delegates

Delegates — type-safe pointers to methods — are discussed in Chapter 7, "Delegates and Events." In all three languages, the keyword `delegate` can be used to define a delegate. The difference is with using the delegate.

The sample code shows a class `Demo` with a static method `Foo()` and an instance method `Bar()`. Both of these methods are invoked by delegate instances of type `DemoDelegate`. `DemoDelegate` is declared to invoke a method with `void` return type and an `int` parameter.

When using the delegate, C# supports delegate inference, where the compiler creates a delegate instance and passes the address of the method.

With C# and C++/CLI, two delegates can be combined into one by using the + operator:

```
// C#
public delegate void DemoDelegate(int x);
public class Demo
{
   public static void Foo(int x) { }
   public void Bar(int x) { }
}
Demo d = new Demo();
DemoDelegate d1 = Demo.Foo;
DemoDelegate d2 = d.Bar;
DemoDelegate d3 = d1 + d2;
d3(11);
```

Delegate inference is not possible with C++/CLI. With C++/CLI, you must create a new instance of the delegate type and pass the address of the method to the constructor:

```
// C++/CLI
public delegate void DemoDelegate(int x);
public ref class Demo
{
public:
   static void Foo(int x) { }
   void Bar(int x) { }
};
Demo^ d = gcnew Demo();
DemoDelegate^ d1 = gcnew DemoDelegate(&Demo::Foo);
DemoDelegate^ d2 = gcnew DemoDelegate(d, &Demo::Bar);
DemoDelegate^ d3 = d1 + d2;
d3(11);
```

Similarly to C++/CLI, Visual Basic does not support delegate inference. You have to create a new instance of the delegate type and pass the address of a method. Visual Basic has the `AddressOf` operator to pass the address of a method.

Visual Basic doesn't overload the + operator for delegates, so it is necessary to invoke the `Combine()` method from the `Delegate` class. The `Delegate` class is written inside brackets because `Delegate` is a Visual Basic keyword, and thus it is not possible to use a class with the same name. Putting brackets around `Delegate` ensures that the class is used instead of the `Delegate` keyword.

```
' Visual Basic
Public Delegate Sub DemoDelegate(ByVal x As Integer)
Public Class Demo
   Public Shared Sub Foo(ByVal x As Integer)
      '
   End Sub
   Public Sub Bar(ByVal x As Integer)
      '
   End Sub
End Class
Dim d As New Demo()
Dim d1 As New DemoDelegate(AddressOf Demo.Foo)
Dim d2 As New DemoDelegate(AddressOf d.Bar)
Dim d3 As DemoDelegate = [Delegate].Combine(d1, d2)
d3(11)
```

Events

With the `event` keyword, a subscription mechanism can be done that is based on delegates. Again, all languages define an `event` keyword for offering events from a class. The class `EventDemo` fires events with the name `DemoEvent` of type `DemoDelegate`.

In C#, the syntax for firing the event looks like a method call of the event. The event variable is `null` as long as nobody registered to the event, so a check for not `null` must be done before firing the event. The handler method is registered by using the += operator and passing the address of the handler method with the help of delegate inference:

```
// C#
   public class EventDemo
   {
      public event DemoDelegate DemoEvent;
      public void FireEvent()
      {
         if (DemoEvent != null)
            DemoEvent(44);
      }
   }
   public class Subscriber
   {
      public void Handler(int x)
      {
         // handler implementation
      }
   }
//...
EventDemo evd = new EventDemo();
Subscriber subscr = new Subscriber();
evd.DemoEvent += subscr.Handler;
evd.FireEvent();
```

C++/CLI is very similar to C# except that when you fire the event, you do not first need to see that the event variable is not `null`. This is automatically done by the IL code created from the compiler.

Both C# and C++/CLI use the += operator to unregister from an event.

```
// C++/CLI
   public ref class EventDemo
   {
   public:
      event DemoDelegate^ DemoEvent;
      public void FireEvent()
      {
         DemoEvent(44);
      }
   }
   public class Subscriber
   {
   public:
      void Handler(int x)
```

(continued)

(continued)

```
            {
               // handler implementation
            }
         }
      //...
      EventDemo^ evd = gcnew EventDemo();
      Subscriber^ subscr = gcnew Subscriber();
      evd->DemoEvent += gcnew DemoDelegate(subscr, &Subscriber::Handler);
      evd->FireEvent();
```

Visual Basic has a different syntax. The event is declared with the `Event` keyword, which is the same as in C# and C++/CLI. However, the event is raised with the `RaiseEvent` statement. The `RaiseEvent` statement checks if the event variable is initialized by a subscriber. To register a handler, the `AddHandler` statement has the same functionality as the += operator in C#. `AddHandler` requires two parameters: the first defines the event, the second the address of the handler. The `RemoveHandler` statement is used to unregister a handler from the event.

```
' Visual Basic
   Public Class EventDemo
      Public Event DemoEvent As DemoDelegate
      public Sub FireEvent()
         RaiseEvent DemoEvent(44);
      End Sub
   End Class
   Public Class Subscriber
      Public Sub Handler(ByVal x As Integer)
         ' handler implementation
      End Sub
   End Class
'...
Dim evd As New EventDemo()
Dim subscr As New Subscriber()
AddHandler evd.DemoEvent, AddressOf subscr.Handler
evd.FireEvent()
```

Visual Basic offers another syntax that is not available with the other languages: you can also use the `Handles` keyword with the method that subscribes to the event. The requirement for this is to define a variable with the `WithEvents` keyword:

```
Public Class Subscriber
    Public WithEvents evd As EventDemo
    Public Sub Handler(ByVal x As Integer) Handles evd.DemoEvent
        ' Handler implementation
    End Sub
    Public Sub Action()
        evd = New EventDemo()
        evd.FireEvent()
    End Sub
End Class
```

Generics

All three languages support the creation and use of generics. Generics are discussed in Chapter 9, "Generics."

To use generics, C# borrowed the syntax from C++ templates to define the generic type with angle brackets. C++/CLI uses the same syntax. In Visual Basic, the generic type is defined with the `Of` keyword in braces.

```
// C#
List<int> intList = new List<int>();
intList.Add(1);
intList.Add(2);
intList.Add(3);
// C++/CLI
List<int>^ intList = gcnew List<int>();
intList->Add(1);
intList->Add(2);
intList->Add(3);
' Visual Basic
Dim intList As List(Of Integer) = New List(Of Integer)()
intList.Add(1)
intList.Add(2)
intList.Add(3)
```

Because you use angle brackets with the class declaration, the compiler knows to create a generic type. Constraints are defined with the `where` clause.

```
public class MyGeneric<T>
   where T : IComparable<T>
{
   private List<T> list = new List<T>();
   public void Add(T item)
   {
      list.Add(item);
   }
   public void Sort()
   {
      list.Sort();
   }
}
```

Defining a generic type with C++/CLI is similar to defining a template with C++. Instead of the `template` keyword, with generics the `generic` keyword is used. The `where` clause is similar to that in C#; however, C++/CLI does not support a constructor constraint.

```
generic <typename T>
where T : IComparable<T>
ref class MyGeneric
{
private:
   List<T>^ list;
public:
   MyGeneric()
   {
      list = gcnew List<T>();
   }
```

(continued)

(continued)

```
      void Add(T item)
      {
         list->Add(item);
      }
      void Sort()
      {
         list->Sort();
      }
};
```

Visual Basic defines a generic class with the `Of` keyword. Constraints can be defined with `As`:

```
Public Class MyGeneric(Of T As IComparable(Of T))
   Private myList = New List(Of T)
   Public Sub Add(ByVal item As T)
      myList.Add(item)
   End Sub
   Public Sub Sort()
      myList.Sort()
   End Sub
End Class
```

LINQ Queries

Language-integrated queries are a feature of C# 3.0 and Visual Basic 9.0. The syntax is very similar between these two languages.

LINQ is discussed in Chapter 11, "Language Integrated Query."

```
// C#
var query = from r in racers
            where r.Country == "Brazil"
            orderby r.Wins descending
            select r;
' Visual Basic
Dim query = From r in racers _
            Where r.Country = "Brazil" _
            Order By r.Wins Descending _
            Select r
```

C++/CLI does not support LINQ queries.

C++/CLI Mixing Native and Managed Code

One of the big advantages of C++/CLI is the capability to mix native and managed code. You use native code from C# through a mechanism known as *platform invoke*, which is discussed in Chapter 24, "Interoperability." Using native code from C++/CLI is known as *It just works*.

In a managed class, you can use both native and managed code, as you can see here. The same is true for a native class. You can mix native and managed code as well within a method.

```
#pragma once
#include <iostream>      // include this header file for cout
using namespace std;     // the iostream header defines the namespace std
using namespace System;
public ref class Managed
```

```
{
public:
   void MixNativeAndManaged()
   {
      cout << "Native Code" << endl;
      Console::WriteLine("Managed Code");
   }
};
```

In a managed class, you can also declare a field of a native type or a pointer to a native type. Doing the same the other way around is not possible to accomplish directly. You must take care that an instance of a managed type can be moved by the garbage collector when cleaning up memory.

To use managed classes as a member within native classes, C++/CLI defines the keyword `gcroot`, which is defined in the header file `gcroot.h`. `gcroot` wraps a `GCHandle` that keeps track of a CLR object from a native reference.

```
#pragma once
#include "gcroot.h"
using namespace System;
public ref class Managed
{
public:
   Managed() { }
   void Foo()
   {
      Console::WriteLine("Foo");
   }
};
public class Native
{
private:
   gcroot<Managed^> m_p;
public:
   Native()
   {
      m_p = gcnew Managed();
   }
   void Foo()
   {
      m_p->Foo();
   }
};
```

C# Specifics

Some C# syntax features were not covered in this appendix. C# defines the `yield` statement, which makes it easy to create enumerators. This statement is not available with C++/CLI and Visual Basic; with these languages an enumerator must be implemented manually. Also, C# defines a special syntax for nullable types, whereas with the other languages you have to use the generic struct `Nullable<T>` instead.

C# allows for unsafe code blocks where you can use pointers and pointer arithmetic. This feature can be extremely helpful for invoking methods from native libraries. Visual Basic does not have this capability; this is a real advantage of C#. C++/CLI does not need the `unsafe` keyword to define unsafe code blocks. It's very natural with C++/CLI to mix native and managed code.

Summary

In this chapter, you've learned how to map the syntax from C# to Visual Basic and C++/CLI. C++/CLI defines extensions to C++ for writing .NET applications and draws on C# for the syntax extensions. Although C# and C++/CLI have the same roots, there are many important differences. Visual Basic does not use curly brackets, but is chattier instead.

With the syntax mapping, you've seen how to map the C# syntax to C++/CLI and Visual Basic; how the other two languages look, with defining types, methods, and properties; what keywords are used for OO features; how resource management is done; and how delegates, events and generics are implemented with the three languages.

While it is possible to map most of the syntax, the languages are still different in their functionality.

C

Windows Vista and Windows Server 2008

This appendix gives you the information you need to know about developing applications for Windows Vista and Windows Server 2008, and how you can use new Windows features from .NET applications. This chapter does not cover features useful for a Windows Vista user or a Windows Server 2008 administrator, but features important for developers.

If your applications are not targeting Windows Vista alone, you should be aware that while WPF, WCF, WF, and LINQ are also available for Windows XP, this is not the case with the topics covered here. If you're still targeting Windows XP, you still should be aware of issues running your applications on Windows Vista and what you should pay attention to. In that case, you should have a special focus on user account control and directory changes.

The topics covered in this appendix are:

- Vista Bridge
- User account control
- Directory structure
- New controls and dialogs
- Search

Vista Bridge

With the release of .NET 3.5, many new Windows API calls available with Windows Vista and Windows Server 2008 are not available from the .NET Framework. However, the Windows SDK contains a sample with the name Vista Bridge that wraps native API calls to make them available from a .NET library. You can use this library within your Windows Forms or WPF applications.

After installing the Windows SDK, you can find the Vista Bridge sample in the `.zip` file `<program files>\Microsoft SDKs\Windows\v6.0\Samples\CrossTechnologySamples.zip`. Extract the `.zip` file to get three projects: `VistaBridgeLibrary`, `VistaBridgeControls`, and `VistaBridgeDemoApp`. The `VistaBridgeLibrary` project contains several classes and controls.

User Account Control

As a developer, *user account control* (UAC) is one of the features you can see immediately with Windows Vista and Windows Server 2008. Although Windows guidelines have always mentioned this issue, many applications still need to run with the administrator account. For example, a normal user is not allowed to write data to the program files directory; administrative privileges are required. Because many applications don't run without administrative privileges (although from the functionality that is offered by the program this wouldn't be required, the developer just didn't follow the guidelines), many users log in to the system with an Administrator account. In doing so, you can unintentionally install Trojan horse programs.

Windows Vista avoids this problem because the Administrator, by default, doesn't have administrative privileges. The process has two security tokens associated with it, one with normal user privileges and one with admin privileges (in the case where the login is done to the Administrator account). With applications that require administrative privileges, the user can elevate the application to run with Administrator rights. This is either done from the context menu "Run as Administrator," or an application can be configured to always require administrator privileges in the Compatibility properties of the application, as shown in Figure C-1. This setting adds application compatibility flags to the registry at `HKCU\Software\Microsoft\Windows NT\CurrentVersion\AppCompatFlags\Layers` with a value for `RUNASADMIN`.

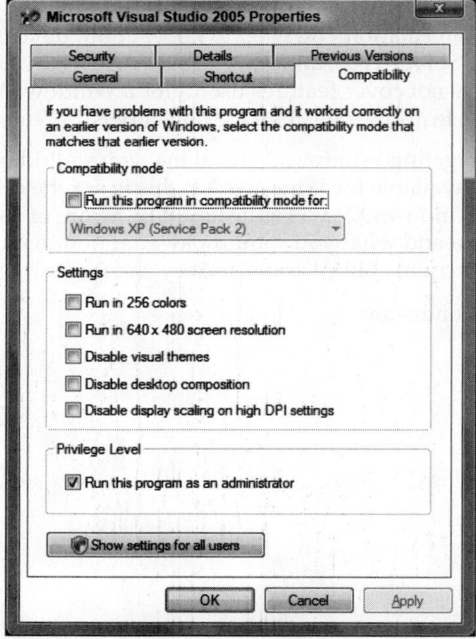

Figure C-1

Applications Requiring Admin Privileges

For applications that require administrative privileges, you can also add an application manifest. Visual Studio 2008 has a new item template to add an application manifest to an application. Such a manifest can either be done by adding a manifest file to an existing application or by embedding a Win32 resource file within the assembly. After adding a manifest file to a Visual Studio project, the manifest file is added to the resources of the project, as you can see with the project properties, selecting the Application tab, in the Resources category. Having the entry here embeds the manifest as a Win32 resource to the assembly. An application manifest is an XML file similar to the application configuration file. While the application configuration file has the file extension `.config`, the manifest ends with `.manifest`. The name of the file must be set to the name of the application, including the `exe` file extension followed by `.manifest`. Visual Studio renames and copies the `app.manifest` file just as it does with an application configuration file. The manifest file contains XML data as shown here. The root element is `<assembly>`, which contains the child element `<trustInfo>`. The administrator requirement is defined with the `level` attribute of the `<requestedExecutionLevel>` element.

```
<?xml version="1.0" encoding="UTF-8"?>
<asmv1:assembly manifestVersion="1.0" xmlns="urn:schemas-microsoft-com:asm.v1"
    xmlns:asmv1="urn:schemas-microsoft-com:asm.v1
    xmlns:asmv2="urn:schemas-microsoft-com:asmv2
    xmlns:xsi="http://www.w3.org/2001/XMLSchema-instance">
  <assemblyIdentity version="1.0.0.0" name="MyApplication.app" />
  <trustInfo xmlns="urn:schemas-microsoft-com:asm.v2">
    <security>
      <requestedPrivileges xmlns="urn:schemas-microsoft-com:asm.v3">
        <requestedExecutionLevel level="requireAdministrator"
            uiAccess="false"/>
      </requestedPrivileges>
    </security>
  </trustInfo>
</asmv1:assembly>
```

When starting the application this way, you get an elevation prompt where the user is asked if he or she trusts the application to run with administrative privileges.

With the `requestedExecutionLevel` setting, you can specify the values `requireAdministrator`, `highestAvailable`, and `asInvoker`. The value `highestAvailable` means that the application gets the privileges the user has — but only after getting the consent from the user. The value `requireAdministrator` requires Administrator privileges. If the user is not logged on to the system as Administrator, a login dialog appears where the user can log in as Administrator for the application. The value `asInvoker` means that the application is running with the security token of the user.

The `uiAccess` attribute specifies if the application requires input to a higher-privilege-level window on the desktop. For example, an onscreen keyboard needs to drive input to other windows on the desktop, so the setting should be set to `true` for the application's displaying the onscreen keyboard. Non–UI-accessibility applications should set this attribute to `false`.

Another way to get admin privileges to an application is to write a Windows service. Because UAC applies to interactive processes only, a Windows service can get admin privileges. You can also write an unprivileged Windows application to communicate with the privileged Windows service by using WCF or another communication technology.

Windows services are covered in Chapter 23, "Windows Services." WCF is covered in Chapter 42, "Windows Communication Foundation."

Shield Icon

If an application or a task from an application requires administrative privileges, the user is informed by an easily recognizable shield icon. The shield icon is attached to the controls that require elevation. The user expects to see an elevation prompt when clicking on an item with a shield. Figures C-2 and C-3 show the shield in use. The Task Manager requires elevation to see processes from all users. With User Accounts, changing the account type and giving other users access to the computer requires elevation.

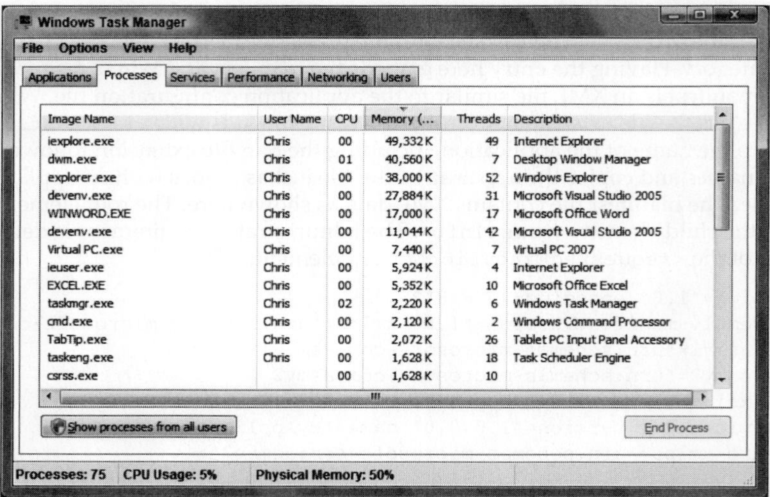

Figure C-2

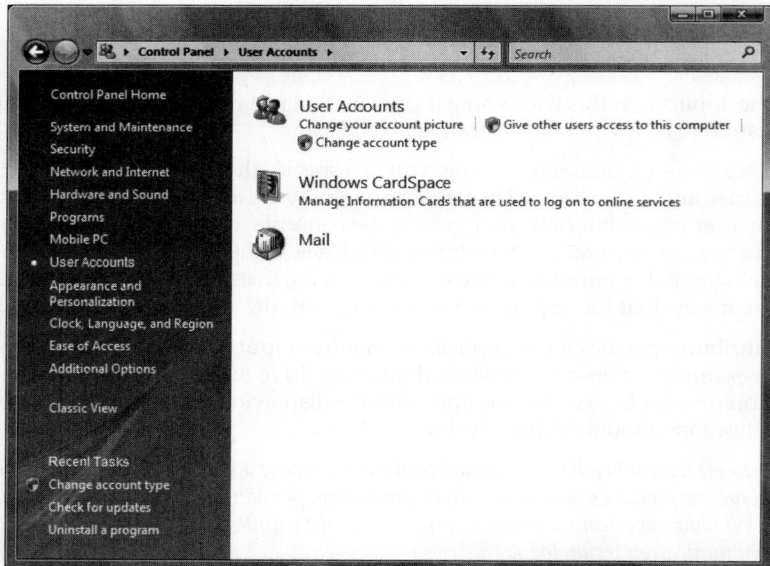

Figure C-3

You can create shield icons in your application by using the new command link control that is shown later in this appendix.

When the user clicks a control with a shield icon, an elevation prompt is shown. Elevation prompts are different, depending on the type of application that is elevated:

- Windows needs your permission to continue. This elevation prompt is shown for applications that are delivered with Windows.
- A program needs your permission to continue. This elevation prompt is shown with applications that contain a certificate to provide information about the publisher.
- An unidentified program wants access to your computer. This elevation prompt is shown with applications that don't contain a certificate.

Directory Structure

The directory structure of Windows has changed in Windows Vista. There's no longer a directory `c:\Documents and Settings\`*`<username>`*. It has been replaced by the new folder `c:\Users\`*`<username>`*. Windows XP defines the subdirectory `My Documents` for storing user-specific data. Windows Vista defines `c:\Users\`*`<username>`*`\Documents`.

If you follow just the simple rule not to use hard-coded path values with the program, it doesn't matter where the real folders are located. The folders differ with different Windows languages anyway. For special folders, use the `Environment` class and the `SpecialFolder` enumeration:

```
string folder = Environment.GetFolderPath(
        Environment.SpecialFolder.Personal);
```

Some of the folders defined by the `SpecialFolder` enumeration are described in the following table.

Content	SpecialFolder Enumeration	Windows Vista default directory
User-specific documents	`Personal`	`c:\Users\<User>\Documents`
User-specific data for roaming users	`ApplicationData`	`c:\Users\<User>\AppData\Roaming`
User-specific data that is local to a system	`LocalApplicationData`	`c:\Users\<User>\AppData\Local`
Program files	`ProgramFiles`	`c:\Program Files`
Program files that are shared among different programs	`CommonProgramFiles`	`c:\Program Files\Common Files`
Application data common to all users	`CommonApplicationData`	`c:\ProgramData`

At logoff, the content of roaming directories is copied to the server, so if the user logs on to a different system, the same content is copied and is thus available on all systems accessed by the user.

With the special folders, you must be careful that a normal user doesn't have write access to the program files directory. You can write user-specific data from the application to `LocalApplicationData`, or with roaming users to `ApplicationData`. Data that should be shared among different users can be written to `CommonApplicationData`.

Because many applications write content to the program files directory, they won't run on Windows Vista without administrative privileges. Windows Vista has a solution for dealing with these programs — redirecting the folder to a virtual store that the applications can read from and write to without generating errors. This technique is called *file virtualization*.

Let's verify this by writing a simple program that writes a file to the subdirectory `WroxSampleApp` in the Program Files folder. Using `Environment.GetFolderPath()` with the `SpecialFolder` enumeration value `ProgramFiles` returns the Program Files folder; this folder is different depending on the Windows language used. The Program Files folder is combined with the directory `WroxSampleApp`, and in this directory the file `samplefile.txt` is written.

```
string programFiles = Environment.GetFolderPath(
      Environment.SpecialFolder.ProgramFiles);
string appDir = Path.Combine(programFiles,
      "WroxSampleApp");
if (!Directory.Exists(appDir))
{
   Directory.CreateDirectory(appDir);
}
string demoFile = Path.Combine(appDir,
      "samplefile.txt");
File.WriteAllText(demoFile, "test content");
```

When running the application without elevation, the file is not written to the directory `c:\Program Files\WroxSampleApp`. Instead, you can find the file in `c:\Users\<username>\AppData\Local\Virtual Store\Program Files\WroxSampleApp`.

As you can see, the data is stored in a user-specific directory and is not shared between different users on the same system. If this is a requirement, you have to start the application in elevated mode. When you run the application from an elevated Visual Studio process, the file is written to the Program Files folder instead of the virtual store, as an application started from an elevated process is elevated as well.

For reading files, a different mechanism is needed. Because an installation program is allowed to write content to the Program Files folder, it is valid for a program to read data from the Program Files folder. As soon as the program writes to this folder without being elevated, the redirection occurs. When it reads the written content again, the redirection is done with the read as well.

Virtualization is not only done with folders but also with registry entries. If the application writes to the registry key `Software` in the `HKEY_LOCAL_MACHINE` hive, it is redirected to the `HKEY_CURRENT_USER` hive. Instead of writing to `HKLM_Software\{Manufacturer}`, it writes to `HKCU\Software\Classes\VirtualStore\MACHINE\SOFTWARE\{Manufacturer}`.

File and registry virtualization is available only for 32-bit applications. This feature is not available for 64-bit applications on Windows Vista.

Don't use file and registry virtualization as a feature of your application. It is better to fix the application than to write to the Program Files folder and the HKLM registry hive without elevated user privileges. Redirection is only a temporary means to fix broken applications.

New Controls and Dialogs

Windows Vista delivers several new controls. The command link control is an extension to the `Button` control and is used in combination with several other controls. The task dialog is a next-generation `MessageBox`, and for opening and saving files new dialogs are available as well.

Command Link

Command link controls are an extension to the Windows `Button` control. Command links contain an optional icon and note text. This control is often used in task dialogs and wizards. Figure C-4 shows two command link controls that give much more information than `Button` controls with OK and Cancel content.

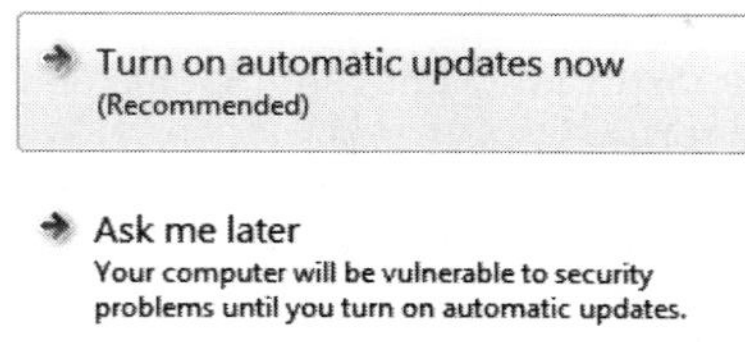

Figure C-4

With .NET applications, you can create command link controls by using the Vista Bridge sample library. If you add the project `VistaBridgeLibrary` to your solution, you can add `CommandLinkWinForms` controls from the toolbox to your Windows Forms application. The class `CommandLinkWinForms` derives from the `System.Windows.Forms.Button` class. A command link is an extension to the native Windows `Button` and defines additional Windows messages and a new style to configure the `Button`. The wrapper class `CommandLinkWinForms` sends the Windows messages `BCM_SETNOTE` and `BCM_SETSHIELD` and sets the style `BS_COMMANDLINK`. The public methods and properties offered in addition to the members of the `Button` class are `NoteText` and `ShieldIcon`.

The following code segment creates a new command link control that sets the `NoteText` and `ShieldIcon`. Figure C-5 shows the configured command link during runtime.

```
this.commandLinkDemo = new
   Microsoft.SDK.Samples.VistaBridge.Library.
   CommandLinkWinForms();
this.commandLinkDemo.NoteText =
      "The application deletes important files on " +
      "your system";
this.commandLinkDemo.ShieldIcon = true;
this.commandLinkDemo.Size = new System.Drawing.Size(
      275, 68);
this.commandLinkDemo.Text = "Give access to this " +
      "computer";
this.commandLinkDemo.UseVisualStyleBackColor = true;
this.Controls.Add(commandLinkDemo);
```

Give access to this computer
The application deletes important files on your system

Figure C-5

Task Dialog

The task dialog is a next-generation dialog that replaces the old message box. The task dialog is part of the new common controls. The Windows API defines the functions `TaskDialog` and `TaskDialogIndirect` to create task dialogs. `TaskDialog` allows you to create simple dialogs; `TaskDialogIndirect` is used to create more complex dialogs that contain command link controls and expanded content.

With the Vista Bridge library, the native API call to `TaskDialogIndirect()` is wrapped with `PInvoke`:

```
[DllImport(ExternDll.ComCtl32, CharSet = CharSet.Auto,
      SetLastError = true)]
internal static extern HRESULT TaskDialogIndirect(
   [In] NativeMethods.TASKDIALOGCONFIG pTaskConfig,
   [Out] out int pnButton,
   [Out] out int pnRadioButton,
   [Out] out bool pVerificationFlagChecked);
```

The first parameter of `TaskDialogIndirect()` is defined as a `TASKDIALOGCONFIG` class that maps to the same structure of the native API call:

```
[StructLayout(LayoutKind.Sequential, CharSet = CharSet.Auto, Pack = 4)]
internal class TASKDIALOGCONFIG
{
   internal uint cbSize;
   internal IntPtr hwndParent;
   internal IntPtr hInstance;
   internal TASKDIALOG_FLAGS dwFlags;
   internal TASKDIALOG_COMMON_BUTTON_FLAGS dwCommonButtons;
   [MarshalAs(UnmanagedType.LPWStr)]
   internal string pszWindowTitle;
   internal TASKDIALOGCONFIG_ICON_UNION MainIcon;
   [MarshalAs(UnmanagedType.LPWStr)]
   internal string pszMainInstruction;
   [MarshalAs(UnmanagedType.LPWStr)]
   internal string pszContent;
   internal uint cButtons;
   internal IntPtr pButtons;
         // Ptr to TASKDIALOG_BUTTON structs
   internal int nDefaultButton;
   internal uint cRadioButtons;
   internal IntPtr pRadioButtons;
         // Ptr to TASKDIALOG_BUTTON structs
   internal int nDefaultRadioButton;
   [MarshalAs(UnmanagedType.LPWStr)]
   internal string pszVerificationText;
   [MarshalAs(UnmanagedType.LPWStr)]
   internal string pszExpandedInformation;
   [MarshalAs(UnmanagedType.LPWStr)]
   internal string pszExpandedControlText;
   [MarshalAs(UnmanagedType.LPWStr)]
   internal string pszCollapsedControlText;
   internal TASKDIALOGCONFIG_ICON_UNION FooterIcon;
   [MarshalAs(UnmanagedType.LPWStr)]
```

```
        internal string pszFooter;
        internal PFTASKDIALOGCALLBACK pfCallback;
        internal IntPtr lpCallbackData;
        internal uint cxWidth;
    }
```

The public class from Vista Bridge used to show task dialogs is `TaskDialog`. To display a simple dialog, only the static method `Show()` must be invoked. The simple dialog is shown in Figure C-6.

```
        TaskDialog.Show("Simple Task Dialog");
```

Figure C-6

For more features of the `TaskDialog` class, you can set the `Caption`, `Content`, `StandardButtons`, and `MainIcon` properties. You can see the result in Figure C-7.

```
       TaskDialog dlg1 = new TaskDialog();
        dlg1.Caption = "Title";
        dlg1.Content = "Some Information";
        dlg1.StandardButtons =
           TaskDialogStandardButtons.OkCancel;
        dlg1.MainIcon = TaskDialogStandardIcon.Information;
        dlg1.Show();
```

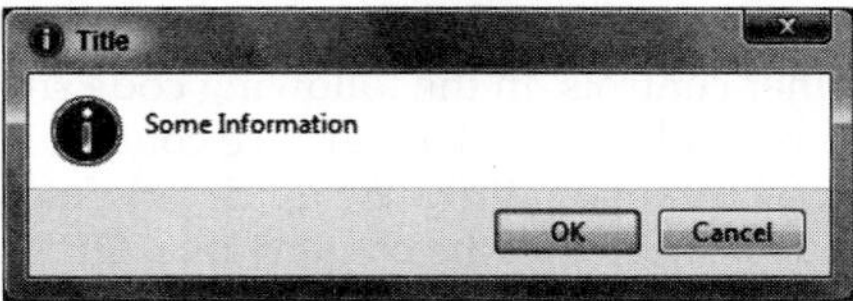

Figure C-7

With the task dialog, you can set the shield icon that was first shown with command links. Also, you can expand it by setting the `ExpansionMode` property. With the enumeration `TaskDialogExpandedInformationLocation`, you can specify that either the content or the footer should be expanded. Figure C-8 shows the task dialog in collapsed mode; Figure C-9 shows it in expanded mode.

```
        TaskDialog dlg2 = new TaskDialog();
        dlg2.Caption = "Title";
        dlg2.Content = "Some Information";
        dlg2.StandardButtons = TaskDialogStandardButtons.YesNo;
        dlg2.MainIcon = TaskDialogStandardIcon.Shield;
        dlg2.ExpandedText = "Additional Text";
        dlg2.ExpandedControlText = "More information";
        dlg2.CollapsedControlText = "Less information";
```

(continued)

(continued)

```
dlg2.ExpansionMode =
     TaskDialogExpandedInformationLocation.
     ExpandContent;
dlg2.FooterText = "Footer Information";
dlg2.FooterIcon = TaskDialogStandardIcon.Information;
dlg2.Show();
```

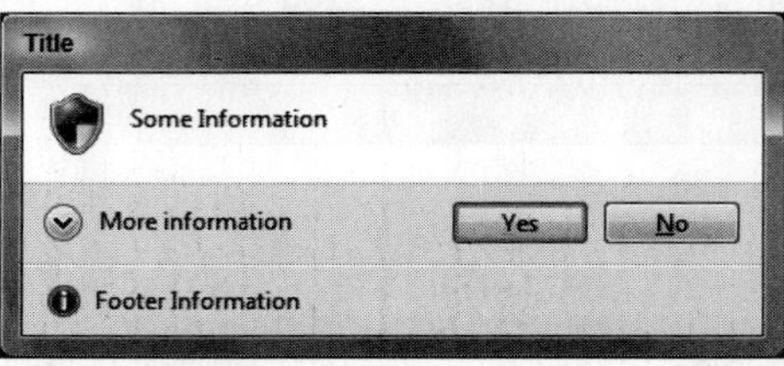

Figure C-8

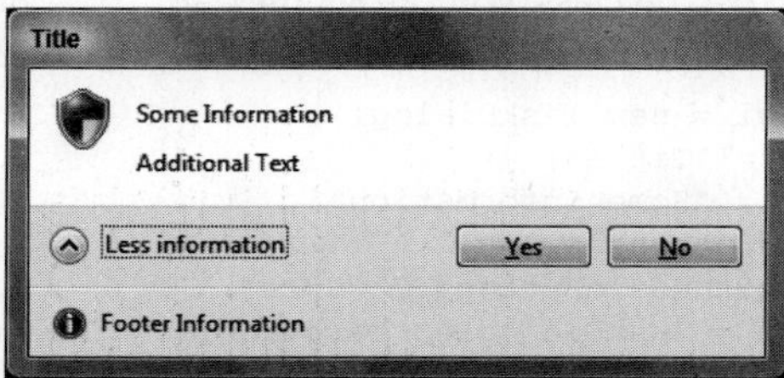

Figure C-9

A task dialog can also contain other controls. In the following code snippet, a task dialog is created that contains two radio buttons, a command link, and a marquee control. You've already seen command links in the previous section, and indeed command links are used very frequently within task dialogs. Figure C-10 shows the task dialog with the controls in the content area. Of course, you can also combine the expansion mode with controls.

```
TaskDialogRadioButton radio1 =
     new TaskDialogRadioButton();
radio1.Name = "radio1";
radio1.Text = "One";
TaskDialogRadioButton radio2 =
     new TaskDialogRadioButton();
radio2.Name = "radio2";
radio2.Text = "Two";
TaskDialogCommandLink commandLink =
     new TaskDialogCommandLink();
commandLink.Name = "link1";
commandLink.ShowElevationIcon = true;
commandLink.Text = "Information";
commandLink.Instruction = "Sample Command Link";
TaskDialogMarquee marquee = new TaskDialogMarquee();
marquee.Name = "marquee";
marquee.State = TaskDialogProgressBarState.Normal;
TaskDialog dlg3 = new TaskDialog();
dlg3.Caption = "Title";
```

```
dlg3.Instruction = "Sample Task Dialog";
dlg3.Controls.Add(radio1);
dlg3.Controls.Add(radio2);
dlg3.Controls.Add(commandLink);
dlg3.Controls.Add(marquee);
dlg3.Show();
```

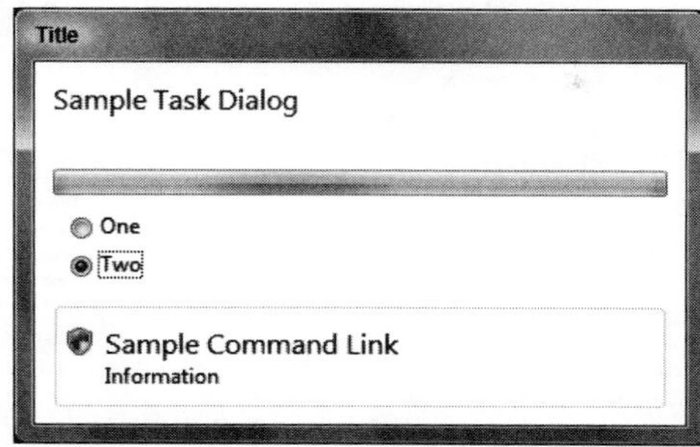

Figure C-10

File Dialogs

Dialogs to open and save files have changed. Figure C-11 shows the traditional file open dialog that is wrapped both from the Windows Forms class `System.Windows.Forms.OpenFileDialog` and the wrapper class for WPF in the assembly PresentationFramework: `Microsoft.Win32.OpenFileDialog`.

The new Windows Vista dialog is shown in Figure C-12. This dialog has Navigation, Details, and Preview panes that can be configured from the Organize ⇨ Layout menu. This dialog also contains search functionality and is completely customizable. In the Vista Bridge library, this dialog is wrapped from the `CommonOpenFileDialog` class.

```
CommonOpenFileDialog dlg = new CommonOpenFileDialog();
dlg.ShowDialog();
```

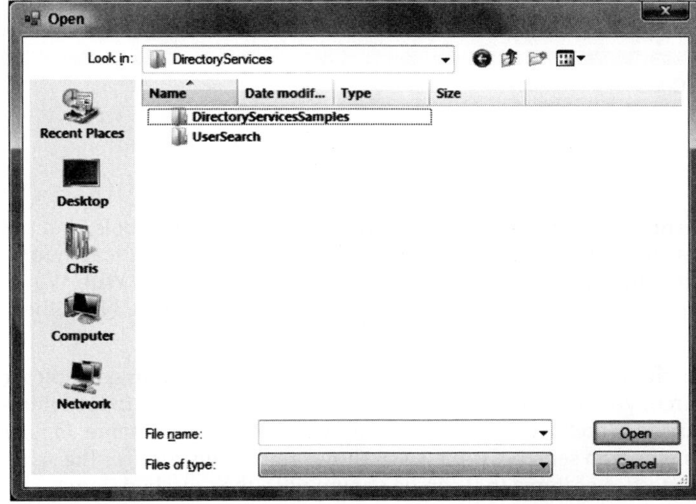

Figure C-11

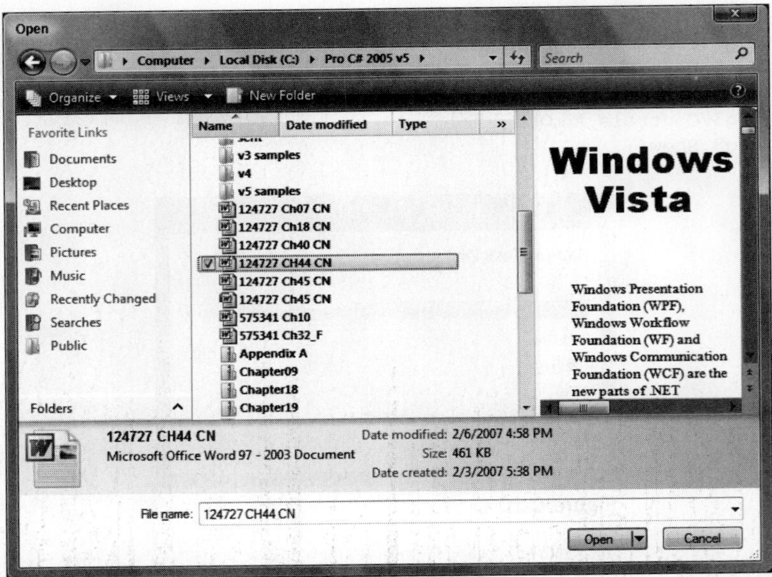

Figure C-12

The new Windows Vista dialog for saving files is customizable as well. By default, it defines a collapsed (see Figure C-13) and an expanded mode (see Figure C-14). This dialog is wrapped in the class `CommonSaveDialog`.

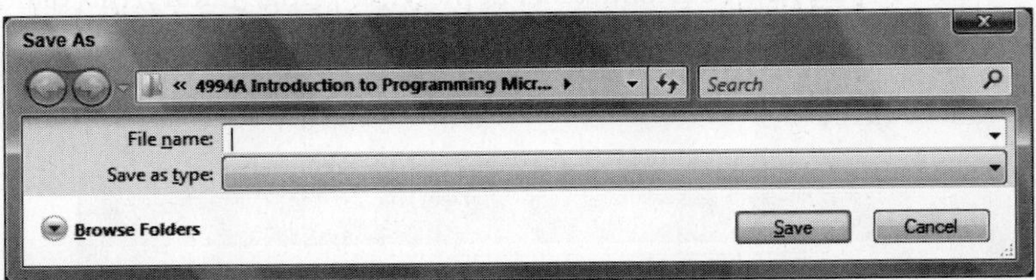

Figure C-13

Search

Search is an important feature that you can find in many applications, tools, and utilities with Windows Vista. The Windows Start menu offers a search capability. Here, you can search for programs to start. After using this search for some time I wouldn't want to live without it. With Windows XP it was hard to find programs from the Start button if many applications were installed. Now, the search function makes it really easy.

By selecting the Search menu, you can find items such as e-mails, documents, pictures, music, and more. With the simple search, you just enter a search phrase in the search box to find items in indexed locations. The advanced search (see Figure C-15) allows you to enter a name, tags, or an author, and to define the locations where to search. Figure C-16 shows the details view of the search page where you can select all the properties of items that can be shown with the searched items.

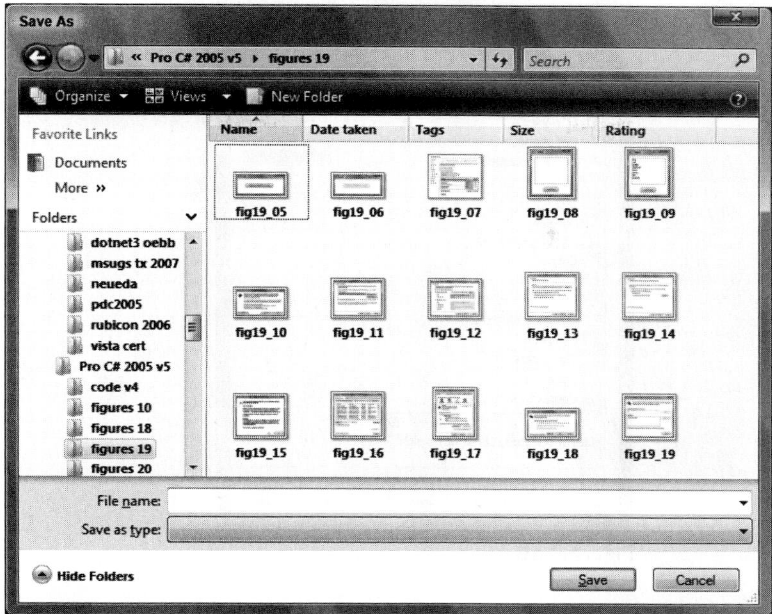

Figure C-14

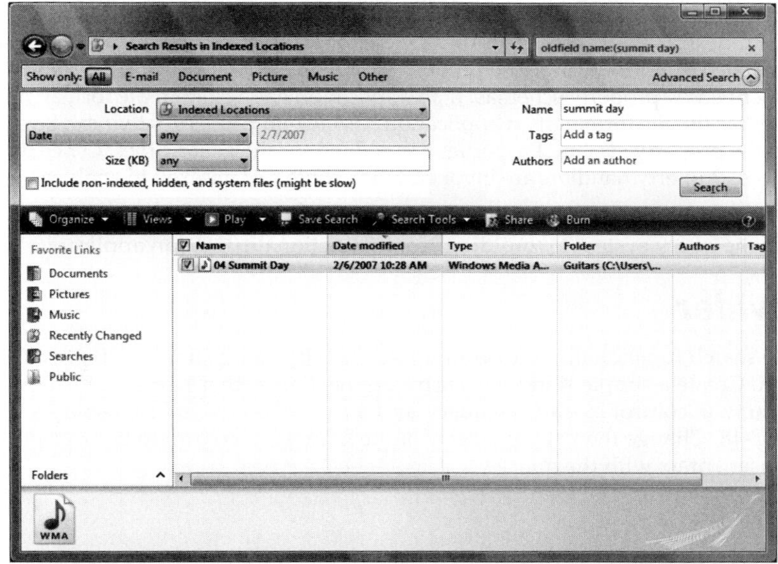

Figure C-15

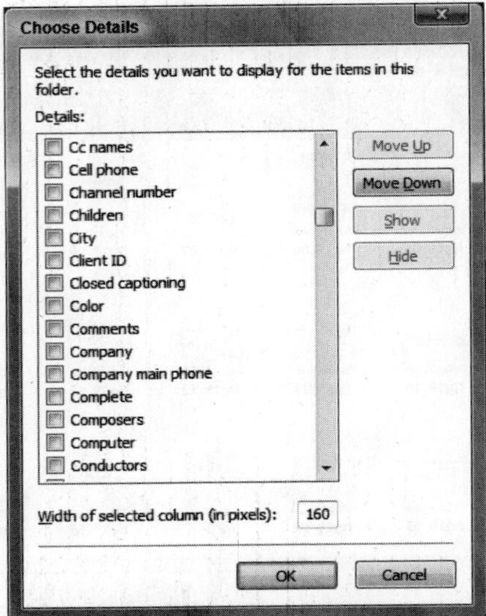

Figure C-16

The Windows Vista File Open and File Save dialogs have the search capability integrated as well. The search function can be integrated into your applications, and your applications can take full advantage of the Windows search functionality. To understand the architecture of the Windows search capability, examine Figure C-17. The heart of the search functionality is the indexer, which examines content and writes it to the content index. For each store (file system, MAPI), a protocol handler is responsible for getting data to the indexer. Protocol handlers implement the interface `Ifilter`, which is used by the indexer to analyze content for indexing. The property system describes the properties that can be searched. Properties are described by property schemas. If an application has a custom file format, it can implement a property handler for the file format. If an application has custom properties that can be searched, it can add properties to the property system. Properties are defined for the generic files, Office documents, pictures, and videos. Property handlers are invoked when content is indexed to analyze the properties of the content.

Let's make use of the query system by building search functionality into an application.

OLE DB Provider

You can integrate search functionality into your application by using an OLE DB provider to search for items in the index. Create a simple Windows Forms application with a `TextBox` to allow the user to input a query, a `Button` control to start the query, and a `ListView` control to display the result, as shown in Figure C-18. Change the `View` property of the `ListView` control to `Details` to display all the information the user enters with the query.

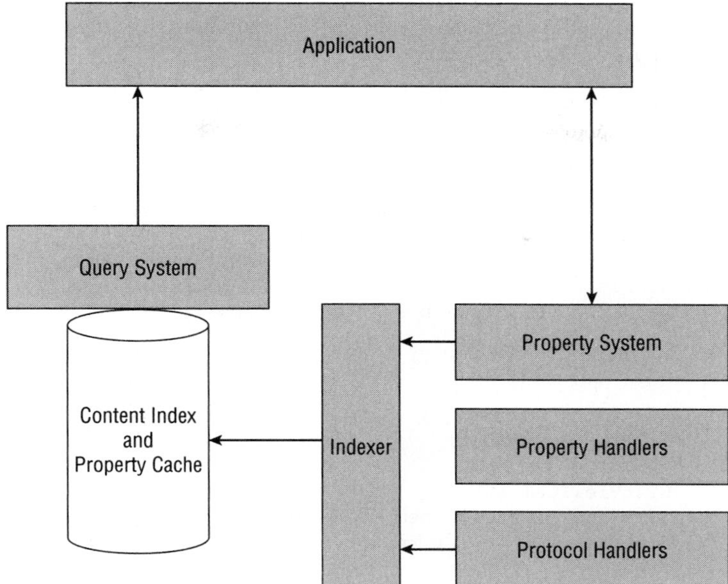

Figure C-17

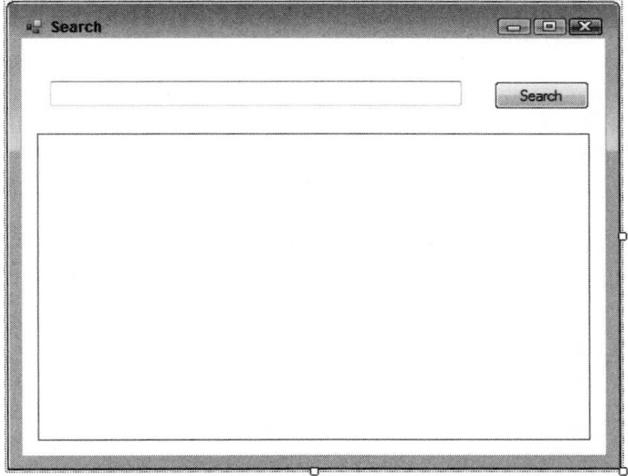

Figure C-18

Import the namespace `System.Data.OleDb` and add the following code to the `Click` event of the Search button.

```
private void buttonSearch_Click(object sender, EventArgs e)
{
   try
   {
      listViewResult.Clear();
```

(continued)

(continued)

```
            string indexerConnectionString =
                  "provider=Search.CollatorDSO.1;" +
                  "EXTENDED PROPERTIES='Application=Windows'";
            OleDbConnection connection = new OleDbConnection(
                  indexerConnectionString);
            connection.Open();
            OleDbCommand command = connection.CreateCommand();
            command.CommandText = textBoxQuery.Text;
            OleDbDataReader reader = command.ExecuteReader();
            DataTable schemaTable = reader.GetSchemaTable();
            foreach (DataRow row in schemaTable.Rows)
            {
               listViewResult.Columns.Add(row[0].ToString());
            }

            while (reader.Read())
            {
               ListViewItem item =
                     new ListViewItem(reader[0].ToString());
               for (int i = 1; i < reader.FieldCount; i++)
               {
                  item.SubItems.Add(reader[i].ToString());
               }
               listViewResult.Items.Add(item);
            }
            connection.Close();
         }
         catch (Exception ex)
         {
            MessageBox.Show(ex.Message);
         }
      }
```

Let's get into the code details. The indexer offers the OLE DB provider `Search.CollatorDSO`. With the OLE DB connection string, you can pass this provider information and open the connection to the indexer.

```
string indexerConnectionString =
      "provider=Search.CollatorDSO.1;" +
      "EXTENDED PROPERTIES='Application=Windows'";
OleDbConnection connection = new OleDbConnection(
      indexerConnectionString);
connection.Open();
```

The query that is used with the indexer is read from the `TextBox` control `textBoxQuery`. Because during compile time it is not known which properties will be selected by the user, the columns in the `ListView` control must be added dynamically. The method `GetSchemaTable()` of the `OleDbDataReader` returns the dynamically created schema information that relates to the query. Every row describes an item in the `SELECT` statement, and the first column inside this item gives the name of the item. By iterating through every row of the returned schema, a new column is added to the `ListView` control, and the heading of this column is set to the item name.

```
OleDbCommand command = connection.CreateCommand();
command.CommandText = textBoxQuery.Text;
OleDbDataReader reader = command.ExecuteReader();
```

```
DataTable schemaTable = reader.GetSchemaTable();
foreach (DataRow row in schemaTable.Rows)
{
   listViewResult.Columns.Add(row[0].ToString());
}
```

Next, every row from the `OleDbDataReader` is read. The first column creates a new `ListViewItem`, and every further column in the result set adds a subitem that is shown with the detail information of the list view.

```
while (reader.Read())
{
   ListViewItem item =
         new ListViewItem(reader[0].ToString());
   for (int i = 1; i < reader.FieldCount; i++)
   {
      item.SubItems.Add(reader[i].ToString());
   }
   listViewResult.Items.Add(item);
}
```

Now, you can start the application, enter a query and get the result, as shown in Figure C-19.

```
SELECT System.ItemName, System.ItemTitle, System.Size FROM SYSTEMINDEX
      WHERE System.Size > 1024
```

In the `SELECT` statement of the query, you specify the properties that should be returned. `System.ItemName`, `System.ItemTitle`, and `System.Size` are predefined properties. You can find other predefined properties in the MSDN and TechNet documentation for the Windows Desktop Search 3.0 properties. Some of the generic file properties are `System.Author`, `System.Category`, `System.Company`, `System.DateCreated`, `System.DateModified`, `System.FileName`, `System.ItemName`, `System.ItemUrl`, and `System.Keywords`. For audio files, digital photos, graphics files, media files, Office documents, music files, and Outlook calendar items, additional properties are defined — for example, `System.Photo.Orientation`, `System.Photo.DateTaken`, `System.Music.Artist`, `System.Music.BeatsPerMinute`, `System.Music.Mood`, `System.Calendar.Location`, `System.Calendar.Duration`, and `System.Calendar.Location`.

With the `WHERE` clause, you can define predicates such as literal value comparisons <, >, =, and `LIKE`; full-text searches such as `CONTAINS` and `FREETEXT`; and also the search depth predicates `SCOPE` and `DIRECTORY`.

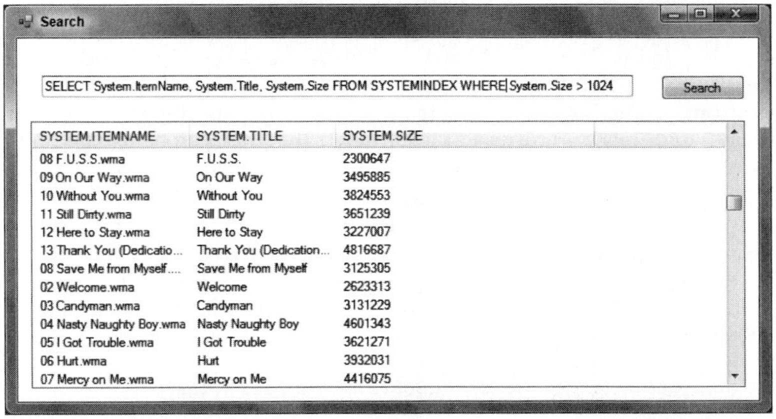

Figure C-19

Advanced Query Syntax

You wouldn't want to let a user search by specifying a SELECT statement such as the ones used in the previous example. You can create a user interface to ask for specific items and build the SELECT statement programmatically. Another way to let users do their own searching is by using Advanced Query Syntax (AQS).

The Advanced Query Syntax enables you to specify search terms and restrict a search based on properties. For example, the query `Wrox date:past week` searches all the items that contain the string `Wrox` that changed in the last week. `Wrox date:past week kind:documents` restricts the search further by accepting documents only.

The following are examples of how you can restrict a search:

- You can restrict the search by defining the store. For example, `store:outlook` gets items just from Outlook. `store:file` gets items from the file system.
- With the search functionality, you can specify what kind of items should be in the result — for example, `kind:text`, `kind:tasks`, `kind:contacts`, `kind:emails`, and `kind:folders`.
- Boolean operators can be used to restrict the search. For example, the `OR` operator used in `Wrox OR Wiley. date:>11/25/07` gets items dated after November 11, 2007. For items between two dates, you can use `11/25/06..11/27/07`.
- You can use some item properties to search for items — for example, `webpage:www.wrox.com, birthday:2/14/65, firstname:Christian.`

You don't have to manually translate the AQS to the SELECT query; there's a COM object that does it for you. In the Windows SDK Lib directory, you can find the file `SearchAPI.tlb`. This is a type library that describes the COM object used to do the AQS translation. By using COM Interop, you can use a COM object from .NET.

Create a .NET callable wrapper by using the `tlbimp` utility to import the type library `SearchAPI.tlb`:

```
tlbimp c:\Program Files\Microsoft SDKs\Windows\v6.0\Lib\SearchAPI.tlb
    /out:Interop.SearchAPI.dll
```

COM Interop is described in Chapter 24, "Interoperability."

Referencing the generated interop assembly from the Windows Forms project created previously allows you to use the `SearchAPI` from the .NET application. Because the type library importer defined the namespace `Interop.SearchAPI` with the generated assembly, import this namespace from the application and add the `GetSql()` method to the Windows Forms class.

The classes `CSearchManager`, `CsearchCatalogManager`, and `CSearchQueryHelper` are generated from the `tlbimp` utility to invoke the COM objects. The `GetCatalog()` method defines the catalog that is queried and returns the `catalogManager`. With the `catalogManager` instance, the query helper object is returned from the method `GetQueryHelper()`. Passing an AQS string to the method `GenerateSQLFromUserQuery()` returns a SELECT query that then can be used with the OLE DB provider to perform the query.

```
private string GetSql(string aqs)
{
   CSearchManager searchManager = new CSearchManager();
   CSearchCatalogManager catalogManager =
         searchManager.GetCatalog(""SystemIndex"");
   CSearchQueryHelper queryHelper =
         catalogManager.GetQueryHelper();
   return queryHelper.GenerateSQLFromUserQuery(aqs);
}
```

Now, you just have to change the implementation from the `Click` handler of the `Button` control. With the implementation the AQS needs to be converted to the SELECT query, which is done by the `GetSql()` method.

```
private void buttonSearch_Click(object sender, EventArgs e)
{
   try
   {
      listViewResult.Clear();
      string indexerConnectionString =
            "provider=Search.CollatorDSO.1;" +
            "EXTENDED PROPERTIES='Application=Windows'";
      OleDbConnection connection =
            new OleDbConnection(indexerConnectionString);
      connection.Open();
      OleDbCommand command = connection.CreateCommand();
      command.CommandText = GetSql(textBoxQuery.Text);
      OleDbDataReader reader = command.ExecuteReader();
      //...
```

You can start the application and pass an AQS query, as shown in Figure C-20.

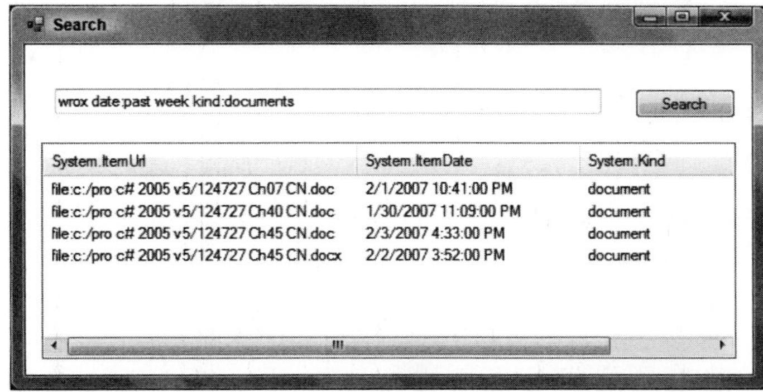

Figure C-20

Summary

In this chapter, you've seen various features available only in Windows Vista and Windows Server 2008 and important for development of applications.

Microsoft has defined guidelines for many years that state that non-administrative applications should not require administrative privileges. Because many applications have failed to comply with that requirement, the operating system is now strict about UAC. The user must explicitly elevate admin rights to applications. You've seen how this, and folder and registry virtualization, affect applications.

This chapter covered several new dialogs available only with Windows Vista for better user interaction. These include new File Open and File Save dialogs, the new task dialog that replaces the message box, and the command link extension to the `Button` control.

You've also seen the Windows query system with the new Advanced Query Syntax and extendable property system to integrate search into your applications.

Some more features that are available only with Windows Vista and Windows Server 2008 are covered in other chapters:

- Chapter 18, "Tracing and Events" discusses the new event logging facility, Event Tracing for Windows (ETW).
- Chapter 20, "Security" gives information about Cryptography Next Generation (CNG), the new Crypto API.
- Chapter 22, "Transactions" gives information about file-based and registry-based transactions.
- Chapter 42, "Windows Communication Foundation" uses Windows Activation Services (WAS) to host a WCF service.

Index

Index

Symbols and Numerics

& (ampersand) for pointers, 341–342
! (exclamation mark) in WF, 1488
 # (pound sign) in preprocessor directives, 63
( ) parentheses in regular expressions, 220
*** (asterisk)**
  in regular expressions, 218
  for pointers, 341–342
// (forward slashes) in comments, 27, 60–61
/* (slash-asterisk) in comments, 27
; (semicolons) in statements, 27
[ ] (square brackets)
  in Array class, 127
  in regular expressions, 218
\ (backslash) in regular expressions, 217
{ } (curly braces)
  in C#, xlviii
  in if statements, 42–43
  initializing arrays and, 122
  statements and, 27
~ (tilde)
  in controls, 1314
  in destructors, 335
+ (plus sign) in DataGridView control, 1069
< % @ Register % > directive, 1318–1320, 1324
1-dimensional arrays, defined, 125
3-D features in WPF
  basics, 1237–1238
  triangles. *See* triangle models (WPF)

A

abstract classes/functions, 106–107
access control lists (ACLs), 599–601, 825–828
access modifiers
  in .Net languages, 1699
  for properties, 84–85
Account class example (generic methods), 236–238
account management (Active Directory), 1616–1620
Accumulate( ) method, 237–239
ACID properties, transactions, 681
acknowledgement queues, 1576–1577
acknowledgment messages, 1559
AcquireLifetimeToken( ) method, 1258–1259
action panes (VSTO), 1404–1405
Activate( ) method (add-ins), 1255–1256
Activator class (add-ins), 1252, 1255–1256
Active Directory
  administrative tools, 1594–1596
  characteristics of data, 1592
  configuration, 1589
  domain, 1589–1590
  domain controller, 1590
  Domain Services Integration, 1558
  domain tree, 1590
  Domains and Trusts MMC snap-in, 1594
  features, 1588
  forest, 1591
  global catalog, 1591
  objects and, 1589
  programming. *See* Active Directory, programming
  replication, 1591–1592
  schema, 1589, 1592–1593
  site, 1590
  Sites and Services MMC snap-in, 1594
Active Directory, programming, 1596–1611
  ADSI, 1596–1597
  binding. *See* binding, Active Directory
  cache, 1605
  directory entries, updating, 1606
  new objects, creating, 1605–1606
  searching, 1608–1611
  System.DirectoryServices namespace classes, 1598

Active Directory Service Interface (ADSI)
ADSI Edit, 1594–1595
basics, 1588
native ADSI objects, 1607–1608
Active Server Pages (ASP), 19
Active Template Library (ATL), 756–757
active transaction phase, 680
ActiveX controls in Windows Forms, 768–770
activities (WF), 1489–1495. *See also* custom activities (WF); custom composite activities (WF)
Activity class, 1489, 1503, 1508
activity execution model, 1494–1495
basics, 1487, 1489
binding parameters to, 1513–1514
CallExternalMethodActivity, 1492
composite activities, defined, 1489
defined, 1487, 1489
DelayActivity, 1493
IfElseActivity, 1490–1491
ListenActivity, 1493–1494
ParallelActivity, 1491–1492
types of, 1502
adapters
calculator add-in, 1262–1264
calculator host, 1265–1267
add-ins, 1251–1271
activation, 1255–1256
adapter, 1262–1264
AddInStore class, 1254
AddInToken class, 1255–1256, 1264, 1270
AddInToken.Activate( ), 1255–1256
Advanced Calculator, 1271
application-level (VSTO), 1388, 1390, 1396, 1399–1400
basics, 1251
calculator example, 1259–1260
contract assembly, 1261
contracts, 1257–1258
finding, 1252, 1254
host adapter, 1265–1267
host application, 1267–1271
host view, 1265
implementation, 1264–1265
issues with, 1251–1253
pipeline architecture of, 1253–1254
versioning, 1259
view, 1261–1262
when to unload, 1258–1259
add-ons. *See* add-ins
address operators, 341
admin privileges in applications, 1712–1713
administration queues, defined, 1559
ADO (Active Data Objects), history of, 846
ADO.NET
assigning transactions to DataContext object, 905
converting data to XML, 948–954
converting XML to ADO.NET data, 954–956
data binding. *See* data binding and ADO.NET
database connections. *See* database connections
database-specific classes, 847–849
key generation with SQL Server, 890–892
namespaces for .NET data access, 846
overview, 846
shared classes in System.Data namespace, 847
tiered development, 889–890
transactions, 683–684
ADO.NET Entity Framework
changing information, 1675–1676
conceptual layer, 1659–1660
Data Model Designer, 1659
entities, attaching/detaching, 1677
entity classes, 1661–1663
LINQ to Entities, 1678–1679
logical layer, 1657–1658
mapping layer, 1660
object queries, 1670–1674
object tracking, 1674–1675
ObjectContext class, 1664–1666
overview, 1656
relationships, 1666–1670
storing entity changes, 1677–1678
Table per Hierarchy (TPH), 1666–1668
Table per Type (TPT), 1668–1670
updates, 1674–1678
ADSI. *See* Active Directory Service Interface (ADSI)
Advanced Query Syntax (AQS), 1728–1729

aggregate operators, 311, 321–322
aggregates
Aggregate template, 997
defined, 995
user-defined, 995–997
Ajax. *See also* ASP.NET Ajax
basics, 1356–1358
defined, 1355
Ajax Library, 1374–1383
Application class, 1378–1380
ASP.NET application services, 1383
asynchronous Web method calls, 1381–1382
basics, 1360–1361, 1374–1383
global utility functions, 1375
JavaScript, adding to Web pages, 1375
JavaScript debugging, 1380–1381
JavaScript OOP extensions, 1375–1378
PageRequestManager class, 1378–1380
algorithms, encryption/decryption, 592–594
aliases, namespace, 54–55
All Code membership condition, 614
ambient transactions
basics, 694–695
multithreading with, 697–701
nested scopes with, 695–697
animations, 1228–1236
basics, 1228–1229
storyboard, 1235–1236
timeline, 1229–1232
triggers and, 1233–1235
anonymous methods (delegates), 190–191
anonymous types, 91–92
ApartmentState property, 765
AppDomain class, 482
Application class
Ajax Library, 1378–1380
methods and properties, 1018–1019
application domains
CLR code and, 986
fundamentals, 481–485
.NET, 12–14
applications
application configuration (ASP.NET pages), 1308–1309
application-level add-ins (VSTO), 1388, 1390, 1396, 1399–1400
basics, 1308
cache (ClickOnce), 460
configuration files, 496, 500–503
defined, 1308
interacting with (VSTO), 1400–1401
objects, 1308
publishing, 459
requiring admin privileges, 1712–1713
services (ASP.NET), 1383
streamlining, 1308
Web Parts applications components, 1344–1345
Windows Forms, creating, 1018–1023
architecture
ASP.NET, 1274
client-server communications, 1625–1626
of event logging, 518–519
of message queuing, 1559–1560
P2P, 1627–1628
pipeline (add-ins), 1253–1254
solutions (VSTO), 1386
WebRequest/WebResponse classes, 1438–1440
arguments, passing to Main( ) method, 56–57
arithmetic operators. See operators, C#
Array class
basics, 127–131
generic delegates with, 240–243
arrays. *See also* bit arrays (collections)
Array class, 127–131
ArrayList class, 224, 255
ArraySegment <T> struct, 245
basics, 51–52
collection interfaces and, 132–133
collections and, 247
copying, 128–129
creating, 127–128
creating with .Net languages, 1693
declaring, 121
defined, 121

arrays. *See also* bit arrays (continued)
displaying data from, 1063–1064
elements, accessing, 123
enumerations. *See* enumerations
initializing, 122
jagged, 126
multidimensional, 125
properties, 127
QuickArray example, 354–355
simple, 121–124
sorting, 129–131
stack-based, creating, 352–354
as operator, 146
.ascx files, 1313–1314
.asmx extensions (ASP.NET), 1369, 1382
ASP (Active Server Pages). *See* Active Server Pages (ASP)
ASP.NET
features of, 19–20
localization with, 667–669
overview, 19
using COM objects from within, 771
ASP.NET Ajax, 1355–1384
Ajax extensions, 1359–1360
Ajax Library. *See* Ajax Library
basics, 1356–1358
Control Toolkit, 1361, 1367–1368
ExtenderControl class, 1372–1374
overview, 1355
ScriptManager control, 1368–1370
support for Web pages, xlvi–xlvii
UpdatePanel controls, 1370–1372
UpdateProgress control, 1372
Web site configuration example, 1365–1368
Web site simple example, 1362–1364
ASP.NET development, 1311–1353
basics, 1311–1312
controls. *See* custom controls (ASP.NET); user controls (ASP.NET)
master pages. *See* master pages (ASP.NET)
site navigation, 1328–1331
themes. *See* themes (ASP.NET)
Web parts. *See* Web parts (ASP.NET)
ASP.NET pages, 1273–1310
ADO.NET and data binding. *See* data binding and ADO.NET
application configuration, 1308–1309
basics, 1273
overview, 1274
state management in, 1274–1275
Web Forms. *See* server controls (ASP.NET); Web Forms (ASP.NET)
.aspx files, 1274–1275, 1277–1278, 1314
assemblies
add-ins example, 1260
application domains and, 481–485
Assembly Cache Viewer, 487–488, 491
attributes, 475–478, 1532
class, 370–371
code groups, viewing, 616–618
dynamic loading and, 478–481
features of, 470
fundamentals, xlv, 15–16, 469–470
manifests, 472
metadata, 470–471
modules and assemblies, creating, 474–475
namespaces and, 472
private, 16, 472–473
publisher policy, creating, 504–505
reflection and, 17
satellite, 473
shared. *See* shared assemblies
structure of, 470–471
types defined in, 370
VectorClass assembly example, 364–365
viewing, 473
WhatsNewAttributes library assembly, 362–363
asserts, tracing and, 516–517
asymmetric encryption keys, 591–594
AsyncCallback delegate, 537
asynchronous callback, 537–538
asynchronous delegates, 535–538
Asynchronous JavaScript and XML. *See* Ajax
asynchronous page requests, 1429
asynchronous patterns. *See* BackgroundWorker class; event-based asynchronous pattern
asynchronous postbacks, 1355
asynchronous programming, 1555
asynchronous reads (messages), 1569
asynchronous Web method calls, 1381–1382
AsyncPostBackTrigger control (ASP.NET Ajax), 1360

ATL (Active Template Library), 756–757
Atom readers, 1643–1645, 1650
atomicity, transaction, 681
attached property (WPF), 1153–1154
Attendees table (Event-Booking example), 1295–1296
attributes
- assembly, 475–478
- AttributeTargets enumeration, 359
- AttributeUsage attribute, 359–360
- COM Interop, 774–777
- custom. *See* custom attributes
- custom controls (Windows Forms), 1049
- Enterprise Services, 1532–1533
- in .NET, 15
- parameters, specifying, 361–362
- properties as XML attributes, 1152
- retrieving attribute data, 927–928
- <siteMapNode> element, 1329
- System.Runtime.InteropServices namespace, 774–775
- transactions (Enterprise Services), 1539–1540
- XAttribute object, 974

authentication and authorization
- Active Directory, 1601
- ASP.NET, 1331
- client application services, 586–591
- declarative role-based security, 585–586
- of forms, 1331–1334
- identities and principals, 583–585
- role-based security, 585
- WebRequest class and, 1428

Authenticode signatures, 486
authority (PNRP IDs), defined, 1630
authorization and authentication. *See* authentication and authorization
auto-implemented properties, 85
automatic transactions (Enterprise Services), 1529, 1539
Autos window (Visual Studio), 432

B

background threads
- basics, 541–542
- thread pools and, 545

BackgroundWorker class
- basics, 571–574
- cancel functionality, 574–575
- progress information, 575–576

backward compatibility, 339
BareTheme directory, 1341–1342
Base class library (BCL), 17, 807, 1361
base keyword, 109
BasicForm Windows project, 413–415
BeginInvoke( ) method (threading), 535, 537–538, 558, 570
***Beginning Regular Expressions* (Wrox Press), 215**
***Beginning XML* (Wiley), 921**
big-O notation, 294–295
binary code reuse, 225
binary files, reading/writing to, 810–815
BinaryFileReader example, 812–815
BinaryReader/Writer classes, 809–810
binding
- Binding class, 1064–1065, 1078
- BindingContext property, 1077–1078
- early, 752
- late, 752
- method, 752
- WCF, 1477–1480
- WSDL and, 1458

binding, Active Directory, 1598–1604
- authentication, 1601
- directory entries, getting, 1602–1603
- with DirectoryEntry class, 1602
- distinguished name, 1599–1601
- object collections, 1603–1604
- port number, 1599
- protocol, 1598–1599
- server name, 1599
- serverless, 1599
- username, 1601

bit arrays (collections)
- BitArray class, 289–291
- BitVector32, 291–294

bitmap block transfer (BitBlt), 1123
BitTorrent, 1625, 1627
BitVector32 structure, 291–294
blittable data types, 755, 990
bool value type, 35

boolean types, 38–39
box, 3-dimensional, 1242–1245
boxing and unboxing
casts, 170–171
for converting types, 152–153
defined, 224
break statements, 49
breakpoints, debugging, 431–432
browsers
application, creating, 768–770
Browsable attribute, 1072
Browser Application (WPF), 1249
compatibility (ASP.NET Ajax), 1360
Web browsing, 1430–1431
brushes
GDI+, 1116–1117
WPF, 1163–1167
BubbleSorter example (delegates), 184–187
bubbling events, 1177
buffered streams, 810
buffers, defined, 810
building code, defined, 427
business service layer (Enterprise Services), 1528
buttons
Button class (Windows Forms), 1026–1027
pin, 426
byte code markers, defined, 816
byte types in C#, 37

C

C ++/CLI language
mapping syntax from C#, 1681–1709
mixing native and managed code, 1708–1709
C# language
basic features, xlviii–xlix
declaring delegates in, 178–179
limitations of, xlix
mapping syntax to VB and C ++/ CLI, 1681–1709
.NET framework and, xliii–xliv, xlviii, 4
programming languages and, xlviii–xlix
significance of, xliii
C# language basics, 25–73
arrays, 51–52
comments, adding, 60–62
compiling, 57–58
console I/O, 58–60
enumerations, 50–51
flow control. *See* flow control
Main( ) method, 55–57
namespaces, 52–55
as object-oriented program, 25–26
predefined data types. *See* data types, predefined
preprocessor directives, 63–66
programming guidelines. *See* programming guidelines (C#)
simple example, 26–29
variables in. *See* variables
Cab installer Project, 448
cache
Active Directory, 1605
application, 460
calculator example (add-ins), 1260–1271
calendars
control, customizing, 1297–1300
information, 647–648
callback
asynchronous, 537–538
functions, 177
calls
asynchronous Web method (ASP.NET Ajax), 1381–1383
CallExternalMethodActivity (WF), 1492–1493, 1499, 1520
camel casing, 69
cancel functionality (BackgroundWorker class), 574–575
Canvas panel container (WPF), 1173–1174
CapsEditor example (GDI+), 1129–1133
captures in regular expressions, 220–222
Cascading Style Sheets (CSS)
Ajax and, 1356–1357
ASP.NET themes and, 1339
master pages and, 1327–1328
site navigation and, 1331
casing for names, 68–69
caspol.exe (Code Access Security Policy), 614–618
casting
multiple, 171–175
between pointer types, 343–344
pointers to integer types, 343

casts
QueryInterface( ) method and, 752
user-defined. *See* user-defined casts
catalogs, global (Active Directory), 1591
catch blocks
defined, 379–380
examples, 382–386
multiple, 382–385
catching exceptions, 379–381, 385
catching user-defined exceptions, 390–391
CCW (COM callable wrapper), 771
certificates, distributing code with, 631–637
ChangeState( ) method (threading), 545–547
ChannelFactory class, 1482–1483
character types
basics, 39
in C#, 37
Unicode characters and, 641
characters
grouping with regular expressions, 220
in regular expressions, 217–218
CheckBox control (Windows Forms), 1028
checked/unchecked operator, 145
CheckedListBox control (Windows Forms), 1029–1031
child domains (Active Directory), 1590, 1609
child elements, properties as (XAML), 1152
ChildrenAsTriggers property, 1370, 1371
classes. *See also* derived classes
3-D (WPF), 1237–1238
abstract, 106–107
account management (Active Directory), 1616–1617
adapter, 1262–1264
calculator add-in, 1264
casts between base and derived, 169–170
class hierarchy (Windows Forms), 1023
class library using sockets, 719–722
class members, pointers to, 346–347
Class View window, VS 2008, 424
collections, 250
commands classes, 1224
converting casts between, 168–169
Course Order application, 1570
for creating syndication feeds, 1644–1645
data members, 77
database, 681–683
database-specific (ADO.NET), 847–849
defining Ajax Library, 1376
dictionaries, 284–285
entity, 681–683, 1579–1580, 1661–1663
event logging, 519–520
exception, 378–379
for file system management, 791–792
function members, 77–78
generic, creating, 226–230
generic, features, 231–235
generic library, 178
host adapter (add-ins), 1265–1266
inheritance and, 102
to integrate Windows Forms and WPF, 1245
Internet protocols, lower level, 1444
for IP addresses, 1441–1443
LINQ to SQL (example), 898–899
members, 76
Microsoft.SqlServer.Server namespace, 987–988
.NET, and file/folder management, 792–794
.NET base classes, 28
.NET data access, 846–847
.NET Framework, 17–18
.NET Registry, 830–833
partial, 95–96
performance monitoring, 528
principal, 583–585
sealed, 107
shape (WPF), 1162
shared in System.Data namespace, 847
static, 96–97
stream-related, 809
vs. structs, 76, 102
System.Data.Common namespace, 847
System.DirectoryServices namespace, 1597, 1598
System.DirectoryServices.Protocols namespace, 1597, 1621
System.Net.Sockets namespace, 3
System.Windows.Forms namespace, 1076
System.Xml.Serialization, 957
System.Xml.XPath namespace, 936–942
timer, 568
for tracing, 510–511. *See also* tracing
TriggerAction, 1236
UpdatePanel control, 1371

classes. *See also* derived classes (continued)
user-defined exception, 394–396
utility (Web programming), 1440–1443
VSTO, 1385, 1392, 1400
WPF hierarchy, 1155–1156
XML, 922–923
XmlCharacterData, 932
XmlLinkedNode, 932
XmlNode, 931–932
clickCountPerSec field, 530
ClickOnce deployment
application cache, 460
defined, 444
File System editor, 460–461
fundamentals, 458–459
publishing applications, 459
security, 460
settings, 459
vs. Windows installer, 458
client applications
building, 1450–1451
creating with sink object, 781–782
Enterprise Services, 1432, 1442–1443, 1548–1549, 1553–1554
integrating WCF with Enterprise Services, 1447–1448
services, 586–591
clients
client from Web server installation, 457
client-server communications, 1625–1626
client-side code, UDTs from, 994–996
WCF, 1464–1465, 1482–1483
clipping regions (GDI+), 1100–1102
closed locked/unlocked state (WF), 1509–1511
clouds (P2P)
defined, 1628
PNRP, 1630–1631
CLR (Common Language Runtime)
deploying, 446
installing/using multiple versions, 506
overview, 4
permissions provided by, 603–605
CLS (Common Language Specification). *See* Common Language Specification (CLS)
Cng (Cryptography Next Generation) API, 593
code
accessing resources from (WPF), 1180–1181
ASP.NET model, 1278–1279
binary reuse (generics), 225
code-based security, defined, 12
code-behind feature (ASP.NET), 19
code bloat (generics), 226
compiling, 26–27
displaying from Web pages, 1438
distributing with certificates, 631–637
distributing with strong names, 630–631
downloading source, li
examples, C#, 26
generating with XSD, 877–883
managed, defined, 4
memory type safe, 14
mixing native and managed in C ++/ CLI, 1708–1709
optimization of, 427–428
sharing, xlv
syntax basics, 27–29
UDTs from client-side code, 994–996
unsafe, and memory management, 339
unsafe code blocks, 1709
code access security
basics, 602–603
code groups. *See* code groups
permissions. *See* permissions
policy levels, 621–622
Policy tool, 614–616
in System.Net.PeerToPeer, 1635
code groups
changing group permissions, 627–628
Code Access Security Policy tool, 614–616
creating, 626–627
defined, 602
deleting, 627
managing, 626
membership conditions in .NET, 613–614
viewing assembly, 616–618
<codeBase> element, 497–498
collections, 247–296
bit arrays. *See* bit arrays (collections)
collections initializers (.NET), xlvi, 253
dictionaries. *See* dictionaries
generic, 1071–1072
HashSet, 286–289

interfaces and types, 247–250
interfaces, arrays and, 132–133
linked lists, 268–275
lists. *See* lists
object (Active Directory), 1603–1604
performance, 294–296
queues, 261–266
sorted lists, 275–278
stacks, 266–268
type conversion, 260–261

colors
background, 833–839
in GDI+, 1114–1116

columns
binding to TextBox, 1075–1076
constructing, 1072–1074
custom, 1074–1075
data, 867–868
foreign language messages and, 674
limiting called with query, 910
naming, 910–911

COM (Component Object Model). *See also* .NET and COM; .NET Framework
ActiveX controls in Windows Forms, 768–770
apartments, and threading, 545, 569–570
vs. C# interfaces, 114
COM callable wrapper (CCW), 771
COM client, creating, 778–779, 781–782
COM client, using .NET component from, 771
COM+ history, 1528
COM+ simple application, 1531–1534
connection points, 765–767, 780–781
creating component, 756–762
history of, xliii
Interop attributes, 774–777
.NET component, creating, 772
.NET Framework and, 6
objects from ASP.NET, using, 771
primary interop assembly, 764
registration, 777–778
runtime callable wrapper (RCW), 762–764
threading issues, 764–765
type library, creating, 772–774

ComboBox control (Windows Forms), 1029–1031
command bindings (WPF), 1224–1228
command-line compiler (csc.exe), 26
command link controls (Vista), 1716
Command pattern (data binding), 1090
commands, ADO.NET
CommandType enumeration, 856
execute methods, 856–860
overview, 855–856
stored procedures, calling, 860–863

comments
within source files, 60
XComment object, 973
XML documentation and, 61–62

committable transactions, 687–690
committing transaction phase, 680–681
Common Language Runtime (CLR). *See* CLR (Common Language Runtime)
Common Language Specification (CLS)
basics, 11
CLSID, 753

Common Type System (CTS)
basics, 9–11, 36
predefined value types, 37–39

communications. *See also* message queues; peer-to-peer (P2P) networking; WCF (Windows Communication Foundation)
channels (WCF), 1456
client-server, 1625–1626
duplex communication (WCF), 1484–1486
history of technologies, 1455
WCF and other technologies, 1455–1456

comparison operators (= =)
defined, 154
overloading, 161–163

compiling
C# files, 57–58
code, defined, 427
conditional compilation, 64, 428

components
component load balancing (Enterprise Services), 1529
Component Services Explorer, 1536–1538
Component Services MMC snap-in, 691–692
creating (COM+ application), 1533–1534
defined, 420
event-based asynchronous, creating, 576–581
queued (Enterprise Services), 1530
WCF and, 1456–1457

compound from filter (LINQ), 313–314
Computer Management MMC snap-in, 1560, 1566
comsvcconfig.exe, 1549
conceptual layer (ADO.NET Entity Framework), 1659–1660
Conceptual Schema Definition Language (CSDL), 1659
conditional compilation, 64, 428
conditional operator
fundamentals, 144–145
and .NET languages, 1694
conditional statements
if statement, 42–44
switch statement, 44–45
configuration
Active Directory, 1589
application configuration files, 496, 500–503
/Configuration/Themes/Default.aspx page, 1340–1342
Configuration Wizard, 1296–1297
machine configuration files, 496
VS 2008 configurations, 429–430
Web site example, 1365–1368
Connection property (DataContext objects), 904
connection strings
adding events and, 1300
managing, 850–852
consistency, transaction, 681
consistent bit, setting, 1540
console application
building, 1450–1453
VS 2008 example, 410–412
console I/O, 58–60
constants
basics, 34
classes and, 77
const keyword, 34, 77
constraints
data, 874–876
generics and, 232–234
naming conventions for, 893
setting update/delete, 876
constructors
calling from other constructors, 89–90
defined, 77
defining classes and, 1376
fundamentals, 86–87
in .Net languages, 1689–1690
static, 87–89
for structs, 94–95
constructors of derived classes, 107–112
adding in hierarchies, 109–110
adding to hierarchies, 110–112
defining, 107–109
contacts (P2), 1639–1640
content controls (WPF), 1168–1169
ContentPlaceHolder control (ASP.NET), 1324
<ContentTemplate> element, 1370
ContextMenu attribute, 1089–1090
ContextMenuStrip class (Windows Forms), 1042
continue statements, 49
contract assembly (add-ins), 1261
ContractHandle class, 1259
contracts
add-ins, 1257–1258
WCF, 1467–1471
control class (Windows Forms)
appearance properties, 1024
functionality supported, 1026
size/location properties, 1023–1024
user interaction events, 1024–1025
Windows support, 1025–1026
control statements (C#), 1694–1695
Control Toolkit (Ajax), 1361, 1367–1368
controls
ASP.NET Ajax, 1368–1372
binding to forms, 1077–1078
extender (ASP.NET Ajax), 1372–1374
host (VSTO), 1389, 1392–1394
ribbon menus (VSTO), 1402–1403
Windows Forms. *See* Windows Forms
WPF. *See* WPF (Windows Presentation Foundation)
controls (ASP.NET). ***See also*** **custom controls (ASP.NET); user controls (ASP.NET); Web Parts (ASP.NET)**
building custom, 1311
defining default state for, 1314
Login Web server, 1336
navigation, 1328–1329
security, 1337, 1338
WPF, within Windows Forms, 1245–1248

ControlToValidate property, 1288
conventions
naming, 68–72
usage basics, 67–68
used in this book, l–li
conversions
conversion operators, 311, 322–323
ConvertAll( ) method, 240, 242
type, 149–152
coordinates
and areas, measuring (GDI+), 1102
transforms (GDI+), 1137–1138
copying
arrays, 128–129
Copy Web tool, 444, 447
files, 800–805
correlation ID, defined, 1577
Count( ) extension method, 321
Course Order application example, 1569–1576
class library, 1570
message receiver, 1573–1576
message sender, 1570–1571
priority/recoverable messages, sending, 1571–1572
CourseManagement sample database, 681–683
covariance/contra-variance, 193–194
CPUs
lock statement and, 551
race conditions and, 546
threading and, 533, 542–543
Create( ) method (MessageQueue class), 1562
CreateInstance( ) method (arrays), 127–128
Credentials property (WebRequest class), 1428
.cs extensions in C#, 26
CSharpCodeProvider class, 478
CSS (Cascading Style Sheets). *See* Cascading Style Sheets (CSS)
CTS (Common Type System). *See* Common Type System (CTS)
CultureAndRegionInfoBuilder class, 677–678
CultureInfo class, 641
cultures, world
basics, 641
changing programmatically, 663–665
creating custom, 677–678
CurrentCulture/CurrentUICulture, 642–643
date formatting and, 644–645
number formatting and, 643–644
types of, 641–642
viewing all, 645–649
CurrencyManager object, 1078–1080
CurrentCulture/CurrentUICulture properties, 642–643, 650, 664
Custom Actions editor (VS 2008), 463–465
custom activities (WF), 1495–1508
activity validation, 1497–1498
ActivityToolboxItem and icons, 1500–1501
basics, 1495–1496
custom composite activities. *See* custom composite activities (WF)
themes and designs, 1498–1500
custom attributes
AttributeUsage attribute, 359–360
GetCustomAttributes( ) method, 371
overview, 358
parameters, specifying, 361–362
WhatsNewAttributes example, 362–365, 371–375
writing, 358–362
custom composite activities (WF)
attached properties, 1506–1508
basics, 1502–1503
composite activities, defined, 1489
Designer class, adding, 1503–1505
custom controls (ASP.NET)
.aspx files, 1314
basics, 1312, 1318–1320
example, 1320–1323
vs. user controls, 1318
custom controls (Windows Forms)
attributes, 1049
overview, 1048–1049
TreeView control-based, 1049–1055
user controls, 1055–1059
custom hosting (WCF), 1480–1481
custom interfaces, 751
custom objects (Northwind database)
creating (Customer table), 908
and LINQ, 908–910
O/R Designer and, 912–914

custom resource managers, 703–709
customizing Office applications. *See* Visual Studio Tools for Office (VSTO)

D

data
- accessing (.NET), xliv
- classes, defined, 420
- columns, 867–868
- constraints, 874–876
- contracts (WCF), 1467–1468, 1579–1580
- Data Model Designer (ADO.NET Entity Framework), 1659
- display controls (ASP.NET), 1287–1288
- displaying. *See* DataGridView control
- members (classes), 77
- passing to threads, 540–541
- querying (XQuery), 1008–1010
- readers, 863–865
- relational, and XML data type, 1003
- relationships, 873–874
- rows, 868–871
- service layer, 1528
- sets, populating, 883–884
- templates and WPF binding, 1214–1217
- triggers and data integrity, 1002
- XML, and tables, 1003–1005

data access (Visual Studio .NET), 1080–1092
- data, selecting, 1084
- data source, updating, 1084
- database connections, creating, 1080–1084
- pop-up menu for rows example. *See* pop-up menu for rows

data access with ADO.NET. *See also* ADO.NET
- commands. *See* commands, ADO.NET
- data adapters, updating with, 885–887
- data reader, 863–865
- data sets, populating, 883–884
- database connections. *See* database connections
- DataSet class. *See* DataSet class
- overview, 845
- persisting DataSet changes, 884–888
- XML output, writing, 887–889
- XML schema definitions (XSD), 877–883

data adapters
- populating DataSet class with, 883–884
- updating with, 885–887

data binding
- ADO.NET, 1295–1307
- DataBindings property, 1076
- DataGridView control, 1061
- defined, 1075
- objects, 1076–1080
- simple, 1075–1076

data binding and ADO.NET
- basics, 1295, 1302–1303
- event-booking application. *See* event-booking application
- templates, data display with, 1303–1304
- templates, using, 1305–1307

data binding and WPF
- binding modes, 1200
- data templates, 1214–1217
- list binding, 1208–1211
- list items, adding dynamically, 1213–1214
- object data provider, 1206–1207
- overview, 1199–1200
- simple object binding, 1203–1206
- strings for list binding, 1212–1213
- validation. *See* validation, binding
- with XAML, 1200–1203
- to XML, 1217–1219

data sources
- Data source controls (ASP.NET), 1287
- overview, 1063
- updating, 1084

data tables
- basics, 866–867
- data columns, 867–868
- data rows, 868–871
- deleting rows, 887
- inserting rows, 885–886
- schema generation, 871–873
- updating existing rows, 887

data types. *See also* XML data type
- blittable, 755, 990
- COM and .NET related, 756
- immutable, 205
- nonblittable, 756
- reference for memory management, 331–333
- registry entries, 830

value for memory management, 330–331
VARIANT, 753

data types, predefined, 34–42
boolean types, 38–39
character types, 39
CTS types, 36
decimal types, 38
floating-point types, 38
integer types, 37
object types, 40
reference types, 35–36, 40–42
string types, 40–42
value types, 35–39

database connections
connection strings, 850–852
efficient use of, 852–854
overview, 849–850
transactions and, 854–855
try . . . catch . . . finally blocks, 852
using block statement, 852–854

databases
classes, 681–683
column naming conventions for, 893
connections, creating (Visual Studio .NET), 1080–1084
database-specific classes, 847–849
event-booking application, 1295–1307
querying with LINQ, 914–920
table naming conventions, 892

DataContext object
assigning ADO.NET transactions to, 905
creating, 911–912
LINQ to SQL and, 903–906

DataContext property, 1205

DataGrid control, 1061

DataGridView control, 1061–1072
arrays, displaying data from, 1063–1064
basics, 1061
class hierarchy, 1072–1075
DataSource property overview, 1063
DataTable, displaying, 1065
displaying DataSet class data, 1068–1070
displaying DataView data, 1065–1068
displaying DataView Manager data, 1070
displaying generic collections, 1071–1072
displaying tabular data, 1062–1063
IListSource/IList interfaces and, 1071

[DataMember] attribute, 1468

DataRow version values, 869

DataRowState enumeration, 870

DataSet class
data constraints, 874–876
data relationships, 873–874
data tables. *See* data tables
displaying data from, 1068–1070
overview, 865–866
populating from XML, 884
populating with data adapter, 883–884

DataSource property. *See also* DataGridView control
DataTable and, 1065
overview, 1063

DataTable, displaying in DataGridView control, 1065

DataView, displaying data from, 1065–1068

DataView Manager, displaying data in, 1070

DataViewRowState, 1066–1067

DateTimePicker control (Windows Forms), 1031

DCOM Proxy, MSMQ, 1558

DDX (Dialog Data Exchange), 1075

dead-letter queues (messages), 1559

deadlocks (threading)
basics, 548–549
ReaderWriterLockSlim, 564

debugging
in C#, overview, 430–434
debug and release builds, 427
Debug configuration (Visual Studio), 429
Debug Location toolbar, 540
debugger symbols, 428
design-time, 418
drawing routines, 1106–1107
JavaScript, 1380–1381
ServicedComponent class, 1549
threads, 540
tracing and, 509–510
XSLT, 947–948

decimal types, 38

declarative behavior (WCF), 1456

declarative permissions, 606

declarative role-based security, 585–586

declaring
arrays, 121–122
methods, 78
variables, 29

deep comparisons, 162
default keyword (generic classes), 231–232
default values (generic classes), 231–232
#define/#undef preprocessor directives, 63
DelayActivity (WF), 1493
delaying assembly signing, 492–493
delegates
anonymous methods, 190–191
asynchronous, and threading, 535–538
BubbleSorter example, 184–187
covariance/contravariance, 193–194
declaring in C#, 178–179
defined, 238
fundamentals, 177–178
GetAString example, 179–182
Lambda expressions, 191–193
MathOperations class example, 182–184
multicast, 187–190
in .Net languages, 1703–1704
delegates, generic
defined, 238
methods called by, 238–240
setting delete constraints, 238–243
using with Array class, 240–243
deleting
ACLs from files, 827–828
code groups, 627
delete constraints, setting, 876
Delete( ) method (files), 794, 800–801
delete/update constraints, setting, 876
event logs, 525
files, 800–805
records, 861
rows in data tables, 887
Demo class, lock statement and, 552
dependencies
dependency property (WPF), 1152–1153
dependent transactions, 692–693
version, 470
deployment
ClickOnce. *See* ClickOnce deployment
COM+ assemblies, 1534–1535
deploying .NET runtime, 446
deployment projects, 444
designing for, 443
installer project types. *See* installer project types
no-touch deployment (NTD), 457–458
options overview, 444
requirements, 444–445
simple examples, 446
dereference operators, 341
derived classes
calling base versions of, 107
constructors of. *See* constructors of derived classes
design-time debugging, 418
design view editor (VS 2008), 402
Design View window (VS 2008), 419–422
designer/developer cooperation (WPF), 1154–1155
Designer, WF
adding, 1503–1505
basics, 1487, 1526
themes and designs, 1498–1500
destructors
for freeing unmanaged resources, 335–336
implementing, 337–339
developer/designer cooperation (WPF), 1154–1155
device context (DC) objects (GDI+), 1095–1096
device coordinates (GDI+), 1113–1114
DHTML (Dynamic HTML), 1357–1358
diagnostics, WCF example, 1466–1467
dialog boxes, installation, 462–463
Dialog Data Exchange (DDX), 1075
dictionaries
basics, 278
big-O notation and, 295
classes, 284–285
example of, 280–283
key types, 278–280
lookup, 283–284
Diffie Hellman algorithm, 594–598
directories. *See also* Active Directory
add-in discovery, 1254
defined, 792
Directory/DirectoryInfo classes, 792–793
reading ACLs from, 825–826
securing, 1336–1339
structure in Vista, 1715–1716
themes and, 1340
directory services
account management, 1616–1620

architecture of Active Directory. *See* Active Directory
basics, 1587
Markup Language (DSML), 1620–1623
programming Active Directory. *See* Active Directory, programming
user objects, searching for, 1611–1616

dirty reads, transaction, 701

discovery
add-ins, 1252, 1254
of clients (P2P network apps), 1628, 1639

discretionary access-control list (DACL), 599

dispatch interfaces, 751–752

DisplayFile( ) method, 814–815

DisplayTabularData example, 1062–1063

DisplayText example (GDI+), 1124–1125

DisplayTree( ) method, 325–327

Dispose( ) method
IDisposable interface, 336–338, 1701
SelfPlacing Window example and, 836

distinguished name (Active Directory), 1599–1601

distributed solutions. *See* Enterprise Services

distributed transactions
Distributed Transaction Coordinator (DTC), 686, 691, 1530, 1548
Enterprise Services, 1530

DllImport properties, 784–785

DNS
class, 1442–1443
names, 1441
servers, 1441

do . . . while loops, 48

DockPanel container (WPF), 1174–1175

Document Object Model (DOM). *See* DOM (Document Object Model)

documents
calculating sizes of (GDI+), 1134–1135
document-level customizations (VSTO), 1387–1390, 1394–1395
Document Manager Console project, 231–234
DocumentManager<T> class, 231–234
interacting with (VSTO), 1400–1401
XDocument object, 969
XML. *See* XML documents

DOM (Document Object Model)
Ajax and, 1356–1357
implementation in .NET, 931–932

domains
Active Directory and, 1589–1590
controllers, 1588, 1590
defined, 1589
trees, 1590

done bit, setting, 1540

DoTheTask, 550–551, 554

DoubleAnimation class, 1228, 1229

downlevel logon (Active Directory), 1601

downloading, 1424. *See also* Web sites, for downloading
files, with WebClient class, 1424
Web pages (example), 1426

drawing (GDI+)
DrawingBrush (WPF), 1165
scrollable windows, 1107–1113
shapes and lines, 1096–1099, 1118–1120
text, 1123–1125

drive information, reading, 822–824

DriveInfo class, 822

DSA (Digital Signature Algorithm), 594

DSML (Directory Services Markup Language), 1620–1623

dual interfaces, 752

duplex communication (WCF), 1484–1486

durability, transaction, 681

Dynamic HTML (DHTML), 1357–1358

dynamic loading (assemblies), 478–481

dynamic resources (WPF), 1181–1182

dynamic XML documents, querying, 976–978

DynamicResource markup extension, 1181–1182

E

early binding, 752

ECDiffieHellman algorithm, 594–598

ECDSA algorithm, 594

elements
operators, 311
XElement object, 969–970

elements, lists
accessing, 254–256
adding, 253–254
inserting, 254
removing, 256–257

#elif preprocessor directives, 64

Ellipse class (animations), 1229
#else preprocessor directives, 64
EmployeeId struct, 280
encryption
fundamentals, 591–594
key exchange/secure transfer, 596–599
signatures, 594–596
#endif preprocessor directives, 64
EndOfStreamException class, 379
endpoints. ***See also*** **MEX (Metadata Exchange) endpoints**
for VBA code (VSTO), 1389
WCF binding, 1479
#endregion preprocessor directives, 65
Enterprise architecture and C#, 22–23
enterprise policy levels (security), 621–623
Enterprise Services, 1527–1554
automatic transactions, 1529
client application, 1538
Component Services Explorer, 1536–1538
contexts, 1529
deployment, 1534–1535
distributed transactions, 1530
example application. *See* Enterprise Services application
history of, 1528
integrating WCF with. *See* WCF, integrating with Enterprise Services
loosely coupled events, 1530–1531
.NET, 684–685
object pooling, 1530
overview, 1527–1531
queued components, 1530
role-based security, 1530
simple COM+ application, 1531–1534
transactions, 1539–1540
where to use, 1528–1529
Enterprise Services application, 1540–1549
client application, 1548–1549
entity classes, 1541–1543
OrderControl component, 1543
OrderData component, 1544–1546
OrderLineData component, 1546–1547
entities (ADO.NET Entity Framework)
attaching/detaching, 1677
classes, 681–683, 1661–1663
LINQ to Entities, 1678–1679
storing changes, 1677–1678
Enumerable class, 305, 323
enumerations
basics, 50–51, 133
defining with .NET languages, 1686
enumerating font families example, 1126–1128
enumerating messages, 1568–1569
foreach statements and, 134
IEnumerator interface, 134
yield statements and, 134–139
Equals( ) method
key types, 279–281
purpose of, 97
static Equals( ) method, 154
errors and exceptions
catching exceptions, 379–381, 385
client-side error messages, 1369–1370
in data binding, 1219–1222
#error preprocessor directives, 65
ErrorMessage property, 1288
ErrorProvider component (Windows Forms), 1031–1032
exception classes, 378–379
handling exceptions, 389
handling in VB 6, 377
handling in WCF, 1476–1477
handling in .NET and COM, 754
handling with exceptions, overview, 14–15
modifying exception types, 388–389
multiple catch blocks, 382–385
nested try blocks, 387–389
overview, 377
SimpleExceptions example, 382–385
System.Exception properties, 386
unhandled exceptions, 386–387
user-defined exceptions. *See* user-defined exceptions
escape codes, regular expressions, 215
escape sequences
of chars, 39
regular expressions, 217–218
event-based asynchronous pattern
BackgroundWorker class. *See* BackgroundWorker class
basics, 570–571
component, creating, 576–581
event-booking application

adding events to database, 1300–1301
binding to database, 1296–1297
calendar control, customizing, 1297–1300
database, 1295–1296

event handling
delegates and, 195–197, 244
FileProperties example, 797–800
.NET and COM, 754–755
simple controls, 1316–1318
VSTO, 1397–1398, 1400
WPF, 1176–1177

event logging
architecture of, 518–519
basics, 509
classes, 519–520
event log listeners, 526–527
event logs, writing, 522
event sources, creating, 521–522
Event Viewer, 509, 517–519, 522
log entry example, 517–518
resource files, 522–526
Windows Services, 746

events
adding to event-booking application, 1300–1301
Ajax Library, 1378–1379
BackgroundWorker class, 571, 572
bubbling, 1177
defined, 77
defining, 197–201
defining in .NET languages, 1705–1706
event keyword, 562
event triggers (animations), 1229, 1233–1236
EventArgs-based object, 198–201
EventHandler delegate, 196
EventHandler <TEventArgs>, 244–245
EventLog class, 520, 522
EventSourceCreationData, 521–522
fundamentals, 194–195
loosely coupled (LCE), 1530–1531
receiver view of, 195–197
synchronization and, 562–564
table (MeetingRoomBooker example), 1296
tunneling, 1177
user interaction (Control class), 1024–1025
Web server controls (ASP.NET) and, 1284

Excel
host items/controls for (VSTO), 1393–1394
XML data type and, 1003

exceptions
catching, 379–381, 385
classes, 378–379
debugging and, 433–434
error handling with, 14–15
handling for binding validation, 1219–1221
handling in different places, 389
handling in .Net languages, 1697–1998
modifying types, 388–389
throwing, 380
unhandled, 386–387
user-defined. *See* user-defined exceptions

Execute method (WF), 1489, 1492, 1494–1496

execute methods
ADO.NET commands, 856–860
ExecuteNonQuery( ) method, 857
ExecuteQuery<T>( ) method, 903–904
ExecuteReader( ) method, 857–858
ExecuteScalar( ) method, 858–859
ExecuteXmlReader( ) method, 859–860

explicit type conversions, 150–152

express messages, defined, 1559

Expression Blend, 1154

expressions
Expression classes, 325
expression placeholder, 1303
expression trees (LINQ), 324–327
Lambda. *See* Lambda expressions
query, 914–916
regular. *See* regular expressions

extender providers
.NET, 1508
WF, 1506, 1508

ExtenderControl class (ASP.NET Ajax), 1372–1374

extensibility, WCF and, 1456

Extensible Application Markup Language (XAML). *See* XAML (XML for Applications Markup Language)

Extensible Markup Language (XML). *See* XML (Extensible Markup Language)

extension methods
creating with C# and VB, 1692
fundamentals, 99–100, 304–306
extensions
Ajax extensions, 1359–1360
document-level customizations (VSTO), 1394
class, 327
JavaScript OOP, 1375–1378
markup (XAML) and, 1362
external safety level, 986
external service, defined (WF), 1511

F

families, font (GDI+), 1125–1126
fat-client applications, 21
feeds, syndication, 1647–1651
Fiddler tool, 1381
fields
basics, 73
defined, 77
read-only, 90–91
scope clashes for, 33–34
file dialogs (Vista), 1721–1722
files
File/FileInfo classes, 792–794
File Search (Launch Conditions editor), 465
file-sharing communications technologies, 1627
File System editor (VS 2008), 460–461
File Transfer Protocol (FTP), 1428–1429
File Types editor (VS 2008), 461–462
FileMode/FileAccess/FileShare enumerations, 810–811
FileStream class, 809, 810–815
FileStream instances, 810
opening in WPF, 1226
resource files (event logging), 522–526
resource files (localization), 651, 653–658
security of, 825–828
/target switches for specifying, 57
files, managing, 791–805
basics, 791–792
file browser example, 796–800
FilePropertiesAndMovement example, 801–805
manipulating files, 800–805
.NET classes and, 792–794
Path class and, 794–795
files, reading and writing to, 805–821
binary files, 810–815
reading, 805–807
streams and, 808–810
text files, 815–821
writing to, 807–808
filtering
Active Directory searching and, 1608
compound from filter, 313–314
Filter property, 515
LINQ queries, 311–314
operators, 310
with query expressions, 916
rows, 1065–1067
tracing and, 510, 515–516
Finalize( ) method
destructors and, 335–336
overriding, 1702–1703
purpose of, 97
finalizers, defined, 77
finally blocks
defined, 379–380
examples, 382–386
FindAll( ) method, 240, 242
first in, first out (FIFO) (queues), 261
fixed keyword (pointers), 346–347, 351
flags, localization and, 659–660, 663
floating-point types, 38
floats values, 166
flooding, defined (P2P), 1628
flow control
conditional statements, 42–45
jump statements, 49–50
loops, 45–49
FlowLayoutPanel container (Windows Forms), 1037–1038
folders
defined, 792
.NET classes and managing, 792–794
SpecialFolder enumeration (Vista), 1715
folding editor (VS 2008), 416–418
fonts and families (GDI+), 1125–1128

for loops
basics, 45–47
jagged arrays and, 126
for statement in .Net languages, 1696
foreach loops
basics, 48–49
interfaces and, 115
ForEach( ) method, 240–241
foreach statements
accessing array elements and, 123
enumerations and, 133
IEnumerable interface and, 134
iterating through collections with, 135
in .Net languages, 1697
foreground threads, 541–542
foreign keys, setting, 875–876
forests (Active Directory), 1591
format names (message queues), 1564–1565
format strings
fundamentals, 209–214
for predefined types, 59
FormattableVector example, 212–214
formatting messages
message formatter, 1566–1567
names for opening message queues, 1564–1565
forms
ActiveX controls in Windows Forms, 768–770
controls, binding to, 1077–1078
Forms Authentication (ASP.NET), 1331–1334
Windows. *See* Windows Forms
Formula-1 racer example. *See* LINQ (Language Integrated Query)
FormView control (Web server controls), 1305–1306
FrameworkTemplate base class, 1184
FTP (File Transfer Protocol), 1428–1429
functions
abstract, 106–107
base versions, calling, 106
function calls, avoiding, 70–72
function members, 77–78
user-defined (SQL), 1000–1001
virtual base class, 104
Futures (ASP.NET Ajax), 1358

G

GAC (global assembly cache). *See* global assembly cache (GAC)
garbage collection
basics, 11–12
memory management and, 333–334
Garrett, Jesse James, 1356
GDI+ (graphical device interface)
brushes, 1116–1117
CapsEditor example, 1129–1133
clipping regions, 1100–1102
colors, 1114–1116
coordinate transforms, 1137–1138
coordinates and areas, measuring, 1102
debugging, 1106–1107
device context (DC) objects, 1095–1096
device coordinates, 1113–1114
drawing scrollable windows, 1107–1113
drawing shapes and lines, 1096–1099, 1118–1120
drawing text, 1123–1125
fonts and families, 1125–1128
GDI+ namespaces, 1095
graphics display modes, 1115–1116
GraphicsUnit enumeration, 1114
images, displaying, 1120–1122
images, manipulating, 1123
Invalidate( ) method, 1133–1134
item and document sizes, calculating, 1134–1135
OnPaint( ) method, 1099–1100, 1135–1137
overview, 1094
page coordinates, 1113–1114
painting shapes, 1099–1100
pens, 1116–1118
Point/PointF structs, 1102–1103
printing/print previewing, 1141–1146
Rectangle/RectangleF structs, 1105
red-green-blue values, 1114–1115
Region class, 1106
safety palette, 1116
Size/SizeF structs, 1103–1104
user input, responding to, 1138–1141
world coordinates, 1113–1114
generation operators, 311, 323–324
generic library classes, 178

generics
ArraySegment <T> struct, 244–245
classes, creating, 226–230
collections, displaying, 1071–1072
constraints and, 232–234
default values and, 231–232
delegates. *See* delegates, generic
Document Manager Console project, 231–234
EventHandler <TEventArgs>, 244–245
inheritance and, 234–235
interfaces, 235–236
keywords and, 231
methods, 236–238
Nullable<T> type, 243–244
overview, 223–226
static members and, 235
supported in .NET languages, 1707–1708
GetAString example (delegates), 179–182
GetCurrent( ) method, 1368–1369
GetCustomAttributes( ) method, 370–371
GetEnumerator( ) method
enumerations and, 133–135
generic classes and, 227
GetHashCode( ) method
key types, 278–280
purpose of, 97
GetMethods( ) (System.Type), 367
GetType( ) method, 98, 365
global assembly cache (GAC)
adding publisher policy assemblies to, 505
fundamentals, 487–489
global catalogs (GC) (Active Directory), 1591
global clouds, 1631
global utility functions (Ajax Library), 1375
globalization
basics, 639–640
cultures and regions, 641–645
cultures in action, 645–649
defined, 639
sorting, 650–651
Unicode issues, 640–641
globally unique identifiers (GUID) (Active Directory), 1601
Globals class (VSTO), 1397
Go To Definition option (VS 2008), 424
goto statements, 49
graphics
class, 1096. *See also* GDI+ (graphical device interface)
display modes, 1115–1116
GraphicsUnit enumeration (GDI+), 1114
graphs, defined (P2P), 1628
Grid container (WPF), 1175–1176
grouping
database items with queries, 918–919
GroupBy( ) method, 315
operators, 310
query results (LINQ), 315–317
groups
account management, 1619
in regular expressions, 220–222
GUIDs (Active Directory), 1601

H

hand-coded schema, 871–873
handler function (Windows Services), 717–718
handler methods (Windows Services), 728–729
handling exceptions. *See* exceptions
hash algorithms, 593
hash tables. *See* dictionaries
hashing, 1000–1001
HashSet<T> collection class, 286–289, 295
hatch brushes (GDI+), 1117
headers
headered content controls (WPF), 1170–1171
headered items controls (WPF), 1171–1172
HTTP, 1427–1428
Hello World application (WF), 1488–1489
HelpProvider component (Windows Forms), 1032
hiding methods, 104–105
hierarchy
data binding objects, 1076–1077
of data in Active Directory, 1588
DataGridView class, 1072–1075
pop-up menu classes, 1085
XML data, 1081
hives. *See* registry
host classes/controls (VSTO), 1389, 1392–1394

hosting applications (add-ins)
host adapter, 1265–1267
host application, 1267–1271
host view, 1265
hosting workflows (WF), 1524–1525
hosts
basics in WCF, 1480–1482
for components and services (WCF), 1456, 1463–1464
HTML (HyperText Markup Language)
Ajax and, 1356, 1357
server controls (ASP.NET pages), 1279–1280
HTML pages, displaying output as
basics, 1429–1430
Internet Explorer instances, 1432
Internet Explorer-type features, 1432–1437
requested-page code, displaying, 1438
simple Web browsing, 1430–1431
WebBrowser control for printing, 1437
WebRequest/WebResponse hierarchy, 1438–1440
HTTP (HyperText Transfer Protocol)
headers, 1427–1428
<httpHandlers> (ASP.NET Ajax), 1366
<httpModules> (ASP.NET Ajax), 1366
MSMQ, 1558
Hungarian notation, defined, 68
HyperText Transfer Protocol (HTTP). ***See*** **HTTP (HyperText Transfer Protocol)**

I

ICompletedEvents interface, 755
IAsyncResult interface
asynchronous callbacks and, 537–538
BackgroundWorker class and, 571
polling and, 535–536
wait handles and, 536, 558
ICollection interface
arrays and, 132
collections and, 248, 250
IComparable interface, 129–130
ICompletedEvents interface, 755
IConnectionPointContainer interface, 755
icons
custom activities (WF), 1500–1501
ribbon menus (VSTO), 1403–1404
IContract interface, 1257
IDataErrorInfo interface, 1221–1222
identifiers
of controls, 1280
rules governing, 66–67
identities, user, 583–585
IDictionary interface, 249
IDispatch interface, 751
IDisposable interface
basics, 114–115
for freeing unmanaged resources, 336–339
implementation, 1701
idle workflows (WF), 1517
IDs, PNRP, 1630
IEnlistmentNotification interface, 704
IEnumerable interface
arrays and, 132, 133
basics, 133
collections, 248
generic classes, and, 229
IEnumerator interface, 133–134
IEquality.Equals( ) method, 279
#if preprocessor directives, 64
if statement
basics, 42–44
in .NET languages, 1694
IfElseActivity (WF), 1490–1491
IList
arrays and, 132–133
interface, 249, 1701
IListSource interface, 1071
ILookup<TKey interface, 249
ImageBrush (WPF), 1165
ImageList component (Windows Forms), 1033
images (GDI+)
displaying, 1120–1122
manipulating, 1123
immutable data types, 205
implementation inheritance
abstract classes and functions, 106–107
base versions of functions, 106
basics, 101–102, 103
constructors of derived classes. *See* constructors of derived classes
hiding methods, 104–106
vs. interface inheritance, 101–102
sealed classes and methods, 107
virtual methods, 104
implicit permissions, 610

implicit type conversions, 149–150
importing
imports keyword, 1682
Windows Forms ActiveX Control Importer, 768
Increment( ) method, 530
indexers
accessing array elements and, 123
accessing collection classes and, 255
accessing list elements and, 254–255
BitArray class, 290
defined, 78
IDataErrorInfo interface and, 1222
searching lists and, 257–258
indexes
filtering with, 312
XML, 1010–1011
XML queries and, 1009
indexing arrays, 125
indirection operators, 341
InfoPath form templates (VSTO), 1388
Information Server (IIS), 1274
inheritance, 101–120
Ajax Library, 1376–1377
generics and, 234–235
implementation. *See* implementation inheritance
interfaces. *See* interfaces
modifiers, 112–114
in .Net languages, 1699–1701
structs and, 94
types of, 101–102
initializing
arrays, 122
collection initializers, 253
InitializeComponent( ) method, 422
initializers, object (C# and VB), 1691
variables, 29–30
inlining, 85
input strings (regular expressions), 216
insertion, record, 862–863
installer project types
client from Web server, 457
creating installers, 449
no-touch deployment (NTD), 457–458
overview, 448
SimpleAppSolutionSetup example, 454–455
SimpleClientApp example, 449–454
SimpleWebApp example, 455–456
Windows installer, 449
installing
installer classes (Windows Services), 730–734
installer packages (Component Services Explorer), 1535
installutil.exe utility (Windows Services), 734
message queues, 1585
shared assemblies, 491
instances
defined, 76
Internet Explorer, launching, 1432
WF, 1487
int variable, 36–37
Int32 number type, 280
integer types
basics, 37
casting pointers to, 343
user-defined. *See* enumerations
integers, pointer arithmetic and, 344–345
interactive services (Windows Services), 745–746
interfaces
basics, 114–115
collections, 132–133, 247–250
COM and, 114
custom, 751
defining and implementing, 115–118
defining with .NET languages, 1685–1686
derived, 118–120
dispatch, 751–752
dual, 752
generic, 235–236
interface inheritance, 101–102
support in .NET, 7–8
used with contracts, 1257–1258
Interlocked class (synchronization), 555–556
Intermediate Language (IL)
application domains, 12–14
assemblies, 15–17
attributes, 15
Common Language Specification (CLS), 11
Common Type System (CTS), 9–11
error handling with exceptions, 14–15
garbage collection, 11–12
object orientation/interface support, 7–8
security, 12

strong data typing, 8–11
value/reference types, distinguishing, 8
internal modifier, 112, 114
Internet, accessing, 1423–1453
lower-level protocols. *See* lower level protocols (network communications)
output as HTML pages. *See* HTML pages, displaying output as
utility classes, 1440–1443
WebClient class, 1424–1426
WebRequest/WebResponse classes, 1426–1429
Internet browser application, creating, 768–770
Internet Explorer
as hosting application, 1251
IE-type features, creating, 1432–1437
launching instances of, 1432
running Windows Forms controls in, 782–783
toolbars, creating, 1433–1437
Web browser control and, 1430
Interop attributes, COM, 774–777
interoperability. *See also* .NET and COM
language, 5, 9–11
VBA, 1415–1418
Invalidate( ) method (GDI+), 1133–1134
invariant cultures, 641–642, 648
invoking methods, 79–80
IP addresses
basics, 1441
classes for, 1441–1442
IPHostEntry class, 1442
IResourceReader interface, 659, 674–676
is operator, 146
IsBackground property (threads), 541–542
isolated storage
reading/writing to, 839–844
SelfPlacingWindow example and, 834
isolation of add-ins, 1252
isolation (transactions)
defined, 681
IsolationLevel enumeration, 702–703
levels, 701–703, 855
ISupportErrorInfo interface, 754
items controls (WPF), 1171
<ItemTemplate> for data display, 1303
iterator blocks, 135
IUnknown interface, 751

J

jagged arrays, 126
JavaScript
adding to Web pages, 1375
Ajax programming and, 1356, 1357
client-side references, 1369
debugging, 1380–1381
JavaScript Object Notation (JSON), 1458, 1460
OOP extensions, 1375–1378
references, 1369
joins
clauses, LINQ and, 317–318
operators, 310
performing with queries, 916–918
journal queues, defined (messages), 1559
JSON (JavaScript Object Notation). *See* JavaScript Object Notation (JSON)
jump statements, 49–50

K

Kerberos standard, 1588
key generation with SQL Server, 890–892
keys, registry, 830–831
keywords
to avoid, 70–72
C# reserved keywords, 66–67
generics and, 231
inheritance, 1699–1700
names of, 70–72
.NET classes and, 28

L

labels
control (Windows Forms), 1033
defined, 49
Lambda expressions
accessing list elements and, 256
delegates types and, 191–193
LINQ and, 306–307
threading and, 538, 539
Language Integrated Query Framework (LINQ). *See* LINQ (Language Integrated Query)

language interoperability
- IL and, 5
- strong data typing and, 9–11

languages
- custom cultures and, 677
- Intermediate Language, xliv
- interoperability of, xliv
- multiple, 641
- outsourcing translations, 666–667
- programming with ASP.NET and, 668
- resource files and, 653
- resource messages and, 665–666
- table for storing messages and, 674
- Unicode issues and, 640
- Visual Studio 2008 and, 663

last in, first out (LIFO) containers, 266
late binding, 752
Launch Conditions editor (VS 2008), 465–466
layers of functionality (Ajax Library), 1360–1361
layout containers (WPF), 1172–1176
LCE (loosely couple events), 1530–1531
Length property, array class, 127
licenses, trust, 460
lights in 3-D sample, 1240
Lightweight Directory Access Protocol (LDAP), 1588
#line preprocessor directives, 65
LinearGradientBrush (WPF), 1164, 1240–1242
lines, drawing (GDI+), 1118
link local clouds, 1631
LinkedList/LinkedListNode classes
- generic classes and, 226–230
- linked lists and, 268–269
- LinkedList<T> class, 268–269, 295

LINQ (Language Integrated Query)
- aggregate operators, 321–322
- conversion operator, 322–323
- deferred query execution, 307–309
- expression trees, 324–327
- extension methods, 304–306
- filtering, 311–314
- generation operators, 323–324
- grouping query results, 315–316
- grouping with nested objects, 316–317
- join clauses, 317–318
- Lambda expressions, 306–307
- LINQ query notation, 307
- .NET and, xlvi–xlvii
- partitioning operations, 319–321
- providers, 327–328
- queries in C# and VB, 1708
- set operations, 318–319
- sorting, 314–315
- to SQL and syndication feeds, 1647
- to SQL and WCF, 1458–1459
- to SQL and XML, 1007–1008
- standard query operators, 309–311
- using List<T>, 298–304

LINQ to Entities, 1678–1679
LINQ to SQL
- adding LINQ to SQL class, 898–899
- calling products table (Northwind), 897
- column names, 910–911
- custom object, creating, 908
- DataContext object, 903–906
- DataContext object, creating, 911–912
- filtering with query expressions, 916
- grouping items with queries, 918–919
- joins, performing with queries, 916–918
- limiting called columns with query, 910
- mapping database objects to LINQ objects, 902–907
- O/R Designer, 899, 912–914
- overview, 895–896
- products object, creating, 900–902
- query expressions, 914–915
- querying with custom object and LINQ, 908–910
- stored procedures and, 919–920
- Table<TEntity> object, 907
- using with LINQ to XML, 981–983
- working without O/R Designer, 907–912

LINQ to XML
- .NET 3.5 and, 968
- overview, 967–968
- querying XML documents, 974–978
- reading from XML documents, 978–979
- using with LINQ to SQL, 981–983
- writing to XML documents, 979–981
- XAttribute object, 974
- XComment object, 973
- XDocument object, 969
- XElement object, 969–970

XML objects from .NET 3.5, 969–973
XNamespace object, 971–972
ListBox control (Windows Forms), 1029–1031
ListBox style, 1209–1210
ListBox, styling (WPF), 1192–1197
ListControl class (Windows Forms), 1029–1031
ListenActivity (WF), 1493–1494
listener ports (WCF example), 1461
listeners
event log listeners, 526–527
tracing and, 510, 512–515
lists, 250–266
adding items dynamically, 1213–1214
basics, 250–252
binding to database (ADO.NET), 1296–1297
interfaces, 249
linked lists, 268–275
list binding, 1208–1211
read-only collections, 261
sorted lists, 275–278
lists, creating
basics, 252–253
collection initializers, 253
elements, accessing, 254–256
elements, adding, 253–254
elements, inserting, 254
elements, removing, 256–257
searching, 257–258
sorting, 258–260
type conversion, 260–261
List<T> class. *See also* lists, creating
access to collection classes and, 255
big-O notation, 295
collections and, 250–253
generics and, 224, 225
LINQ query using, 298–304
ListView control
Web server controls, 1288, 1303, 1305–1307
Windows Forms, 1033–1035
local variables, scope clashes for, 32–34
localization, 651–678. *See also* globalization
with ASP.NET, 667–669
cultures, creating custom, 677–678
custom resource reader, 673–677
defined, 639
resource dictionary, 669, 671–673
using resources for. *See* resources
Visual Studio 2008 for. *See* Visual Studio 2008 for localization
with WPF, 669–673
with XAML, 671–673
lock statement
Interlocked class and, 556
Monitor class and, 557
thread safety and, 550–555
logging, event. *See* event logging
logical layer (ADO.NET Entity Framework), 1657–1658
login
implementing system, 1334–1336
Web server controls, 1336
logo, RSS, 1643–1644
long value type, 35
LongLength property, array class, 127
Lookup<TKey, TElement> class, 283–284
loops
basics, 45–49
in .Net languages, 1695–1696
loosely coupled events (LCE), 1530–1531
lower level protocols (network communications)
basics, 1443–1444
classes, 1444
SmtpClient object, 1444–1445
Socket class, 1449–1452
TCP classes, 1445–1446
TCP vs. UDP, 1448
TcpSend/TcpReceive examples, 1446–1448
UDP class, 1448–1449
LuridTheme theme, 1342

M

machine configuration files, 496
machine policy levels (security), 621–622
main function (Windows Services), 717–718, 727–728
Main( ) method
in C#, 55
example of, 26
multiple, 55–56
passing arguments to, 56–57
making code, defined, 427
Managed AddIn Framework (MAF). *See* add-ins
managed code, defined, 4

managed heaps
array initialization and, 122
defined, 8, 35
garbage collection and, 333–334
memory and, 331–333
reference types and, 124
managed types, defined, 343
manifests, assembly, 472
mapping layer (ADO.NET Entity Framework), 1660
Mapping Specification Language (MSL), 1660
maps. *See* dictionaries
markup extensions
binding and (XAML), 1206
WPF and, 1154
marshaling, 755–756
MaskedTextBox control (Windows Forms), 1036–1037
.master extension (ASP.NET), 1323
master pages (ASP.NET)
accessing content from Web pages, 1325–1326
basics, 1311, 1323–1325
MasterPage.FindControl( ) method, 1326
MasterPage.master, 1326–1327, 1330
nested, 1326
in PCSDemoSite, 1326–1328
matches
locations (WF), 1519
Matches( ) static method (Regex class), 216
in regular expressions, 216–217, 220–222
MathOperations class example (delegates), 182–184
MathTest example (invoking methods), 79–80
MD5 (Message Digest Algorithm 5), 593
MDI (Multiple Document Interface) applications, 1047–1048
members, class, 76
membership conditions (code groups), 613–614
MemberwiseClone( ) method, 98
memory
blittable data types and, 990
clean-up (C#), xlix
memory type safe code, 14
.NET and COM, 750
memory management
automatic handling of, 329
direct access to. *See* pointers
garbage collection, 333–334
reference data types, 331–333
unmanaged resources, freeing. *See* unmanaged resources, freeing
unsafe code, 339
value data types, 330–331
menus, ribbon (VSTO), 1401–1404
MenuStrip control (Windows Forms), 1041–1042
Merge Module installer Project, 448
meshes, defined (P2P), 1628
message queues, 1555–1585
administrative tools, 1560–1562
architecture of, 1559–1560
Course Order application. *See* Course Order application example
creating, 1560–1563
features of, 1557–1558
finding, 1563
installation, 1585
opening, 1563–1565
overview, 1555–1556
products for, 1558
queuing with WCF. *See* message queuing with WCF
receiving messages, 1567–1569, 1573–1576, 1581–1583
receiving results, 1576–1577
sending messages, 1565–1567, 1583–1585
transactional queues, 1577–1578
types of, 1559
when to use, 1556–1557
message queuing with WCF, 1579–1585
entity classes with data contract, 1579–1580
message receiver application, 1581–1583
message sender application, 1583–1585
overview, 1579
service contract, 1580–1581
messages
contracts (WCF), 1467, 1470–1471
custom resource, 665–666
for event logs, 522
receiving, 1567–1569, 1573–1576, 1581–1583

recoverable, defined, 1559
meta-characters (regular expressions), 217
metadata
assembly, 470–471
.NET and COM, 750
properties (WF), 1506
type, 470–471
methods
AddInStore class, 1254
AddInToken class, 1255
anonymous, 190–191
Application class, 1018–1019
asynchronous page requests and, 1429
BackgroundWorker class, 571
base versions, calling, 106
BitArray class, 289
BitVector32, 291
in C#, 78
C# rules for use of, 72–73
called by generic delegates, 238–240
calling outside workflow (WF), 1492
calling Web methods (ASP.NET Ajax), 1381–1383
collections interfaces, 248–249
connecting menu choices to code and, 1090–1091
ContextUtil class, 1540
ContractHandle class, 1259
DataContext object, 905–906
DataTable, 1088–1089
declaring, 78
defined, 77
entity classes, 1541–1542
EventLog class, 520
extension, 99–100, 304–306
for file system management, 794
generic, 236–238
handler (Windows Services), 728–729
HashSet<T> collection class, 286–287
hiding, 104–106
ICollection interface, 132
IDispatch interface, 751–752
IEnlistmentNotification interface, 704
IEnumerator interface, 134
IList interface, 132–133
Interlocked class, 555–556
invoking, 79–80
IUnknown interface, 751
LinkedList<T> class, 269–270
Lookup <TKey, TElement >, 283–284
method binding, 752
method overloading in C#, 82–83
method parameters and return types, 1687–1688
ObjectContext class, 1664–1665
ObjectQuery<T> Query Builder, 1673
overriding for user input response, 1138–1140
passing parameters to, 80–82
<provider>Command classes, 856–860
Queue and Queue<T> classes, 262–263
ReaderWriterLockSlim, 565
reading/writing to files, 807
RegistryKey class, 833
ResourceManager class, 676
sealed, 107
Select (XPathNavigator), 938
ServiceController class, 743
ServicedComponent class (Enterprise Services), 1531
SortedList<TKey, TValue> class, 277
Stack and Stack<T> classes, 267
static, and Path class, 795
Storyboard class, 1235–1236
stream objects and, 794
String class, 1212
StringBuilder, 208
StringInfo class, 640
System.Drawing.Graphics, 1118–1119
System.Object, 97–98
System.string class, 204–205
Table<TEntity> object, 907
Transaction class, 686–687
Type class, 366–367
user controls and, 1313
user-defined aggregates and, 996
using generic delegate types, 240–241
virtual, 104
WaitHandle class, 558
Web methods, 1381–1383
XPathNavigator, 937–938
XPathNodeIterator, 939
yield statements and, 135
MEX (Metadata Exchange) endpoints, 1458, 1553

MFC containers, 783
Microsoft
Active Directory. *See* Active Directory; directory services
Foundation Class library, 1075
Intermediate Language (IL). *See* Intermediate Language (IL)
Message Queue (MSMQ) Server Core, 1558
Microsoft.Office.Tools.Excel namespace, 1392–1394
Microsoft.Office.Tools.Word namespace, 1392–1393
Microsoft.SqlServer.Server namespace classes, 987–988
Microsoft.Win32 namespace, 791, 830
Windows history, xliii–xliv
Windows Peer-to-Peer Networking platform, 1625, 1629–1632
MMC (Microsoft Management Console) snap-ins
.NET Framework Configuration tool, 501
Services snap-in, 735–736
modifier keywords, 112–114
modules, creating, 473–474
Money example (ToString( ) method), 98–100
Monitor class (synchronization), 557
MoveTo( ) method (files), 794, 800–801
moving files, 800–805
MSMQ (Microsoft Message Queue) Server Core, 1558
MTA (multithreaded apartment), 753–754
multi-targeting .NET Framework, 436–438
multicasting
messaging queuing support, 1558
multicast delegates, 187–190
MulticastIteration example, 189–190
multidimensional arrays, 125
multimaster replication (Active Directory), 1588
multiple casting, 171–175
multiple catch blocks, 382–385
multiple inheritance, 102
multithreading
with ambient transactions, 697–701
multithreaded apartments (MTAs), 569–570, 753–754
Mutex class (synchronization), 558, 559–560
myArray variable, 122

N

naked type constraints, defined, 233
Name properties (Windows Forms elements), 660
named colors (GDI+), 1115
names. *See also* naming conventions; peer names
casing of, 68–69
distinguished (Active Directory), 1599–1601
relative distinguished names (Active Directory), 1599
server name (Active Directory), 1599
styles of, 69
user class properties, 1613–1614
user principal name (Active Directory), 1601
namespaces
ADO.NET Entity Framework, 1656
aliases, 54–55
assemblies and, 472
basics, 52–55
defined, 27, 52
defining (Ajax Library), 1376
defining with .Net languages, 1682–1683
GDI+, 1095
names of, 70
.NET, 18–19
for .NET data access, 846
using directive, 53–54
VSTO, 1391–1392
WPF, 1156–1159
XNamespace object, 971–972
naming conventions
basics, 68–72
constraints, 893
database tables, 892–893
default naming context (Active Directory), 1600–1601
for generic types, 226
stored procedures, 893
threads, 540
trace sources, 511
native image generator, 494–495
Native Image Service, 495
NativeMethods class, 711
navigating Web sites (ASP.NET), 1311, 1328–1331
nested master pages (ASP.NET), 1326

nested objects, grouping queries with, 316–317
nested partial classes, 96
nested scopes, 695–697
nested try blocks, 387–389
.NET and COM. *See also* COM (Component Object Model)
client application, creating with sink object, 781–782
COM callable wrapper (CCW), 771
COM client, creating, 778–779
COM client, using .NET component from, 771
COM component, creating, 756–762
COM Interop attributes, 774–777
COM registration, 777–778
connection points, adding, 780–781
error handling, 754
event handling, 754–755
fundamentals, 750
interfaces, 751–752
marshaling, 755–756
memory, 750–751
metadata, 750
method binding, 752
.NET component, 771–772
registration, 753
runtime callable wrapper (RCW), 762–764
threading, 753–754
type library, creating, 772–774
.NET applications
<codeBase> element, 497–498
configuration categories, 496
configuring directories for assembly searches, 497–499
hardware and software requirements, 445
<probing> element, 498–499
.NET architecture
ASP.NET applications, creating, 19–20
C# relationship to .NET, 4
CLR, 4
COM/COM+, 6
enterprise applications and C#, 22–23
language interoperability, 5
Microsoft Intermediate Language (IL). *See* Intermediate Language (IL)
namespaces, 18–19
.NET Framework classes, 17–18
overview, 3
performance improvement, 4–5
platform independence, 4
Visual Basic 2008, 5–6
Visual C++ 2008, 6
Windows Communication Foundation (WCF), 22
Windows Controls, 21
Windows Forms, creating, 21
Windows Presentation Foundation (WPF), 21
Windows Services, 21–22
.NET Framework
advantages of, xliv–xlv
base classes, 28
basics, xliii
C# and, xlviii
classes, 17–18
classes and file management, 792–794
code group membership conditions, 613–614
Configuration tool, 501, 505
Enterprise Services, 684–685, 1528
globalization/localization and, 639
multi-targeting with VS 2008, 436–438
.NET 3.5, xlv–xlvii
.NET runtime (CLR). *See* CLR (Common Language Runtime)
programming with SQL Server. *See* SQL Server
registry and, 828, 830–833
significance of, xliii
W3C standards supported in, 922
XML and, 921
net.exe command-line utility (Windows Services), 734–736
neutral cultures, 641–642
new keyword, 76, 105, 120
new operator (arrays), 122
news feeds, 1643–1644
Ngen.exe (native image generator), 494–495
Nikhil's Web Development Helper, 1381
no-touch deployment (NTD), 457–458
nodes, inserting with XmlDocument class, 934–936
nonblittable data types, 756
nonrepeatable reads (transactions), 701
Not( ) method, 290
null coalescing operator (??), 147
nullable types
basics, 243–244
operators and, 147

numbers
rounding, 168
truncating, 168
version, 499–500
numeric types, 209–210
numerical conversions. *See* SimpleCurrency example (user-defined casts)

O

O/R Designer
basics, 899
and custom objects, 912–914
objects
Active Directory, 1589, 1621–1623
Application objects basics, 1308
C# object-orientation, 25–26
comparing for equality, 153–154
defining instances with XAML, 1206–1207
keyword, 103
LINQ to objects provider, 327
mapping database to LINQ objects, 902–907
native ADSI objects, accessing, 1607–1608
new objects, creating (Active Directory), 1605–1606
Object Browser window (VS 2008), 425–426
Object class, 97, 223, 231
object collections (Active Directory), 1603–1604
object initializers, xlvi, 1691
object-type collections, 247–248
ObjectContext class, 1664–1666
performance objects, 527
pooling (Enterprise Services), 1530
queries, 1670–1674
simple binding CLR objects, 1203–1206
strongly typed, 1588
support in .NET, 7–8
tracking, 1674–1675
types, 40, 223, 230
used in data binding, 1076–1080
user objects, searching for (Active Directory), 1611–1616
Office 2007 object model, 1391
Office applications, 1385. *See also* Visual Studio Tools for Office (VSTO)
OfType( ) extension method, 312
OLE DB provider, 1724–1727
one-time binding, 1200
one-way binding, 1200
OnPaint( ) method
CapsEditor example, 1135–1137
painting shapes with, 1099–1100
OnTimer( ) method, 530
OOP extensions, JavaScript, 1375–1378
open unlocked state (WF), 1509–1511
OpenFileDialog class, 1226
operating systems and .NET-based applications, 445
[OperationBehavior] attribute (WCF), 1475–1476
OperationContract properties (WCF), 1470
operators
aggregate, 321–322
available for overloading, 163–164
conversion, 322–323
defined, 78
generation, 323–324
pointer member access, 346
standard query (LINQ), 309–311
using with pointers, 341, 344–346
operators, C#
checked and unchecked, 145
comparison operator, 154
compiler processing of, 156–157
conditional, 144–145
is operator, 146
null coalescing operator (??), 147
nullable types and, 147
as operator, 146
operator overloading. *See* overloading, operator
overview, 141–143
precedence of, 147–148
shortcuts, 143–144
sizeof operator, 146
typeof operator, 146
optimization of code, 427–428
out parameters, 82
output parameters, 861–863
outsourcing translations, 666–667
OverflowException class, 379
overloading, method, 82–83
overloading, operator
comparison operator, 161–163
compiler processing and, 156–157
fundamentals, 156–157

operators available for, 163–164
Vector struct example, 157–163
overriding
defined, 40
override keyword, 104, 120
publisher policies, 505–506

P

P2P. *See* peer-to-peer (P2P) networking
page coordinates (GDI+), 1113–1114
Page Setup, printing (GDI+), 1142
Page_Load( ) event handler
ASP.NET code model, 1279, 1313
calendar controls, customizing, 1297, 1299
server controls (ASP.NET), 1292
Page_PreInit( ) event handler (ASP.NET), 1343
PageRequestManager class (Ajax Library), 1378–1380
painting shapes (GDI+), 1099–1100
Panel control (Windows Forms), 1037
panes (VSTO project types), 1388–1390, 1404–1405
ParallelActivity (WF), 1491–1492
parameters
Activate( ) method, 1255–1256
adding constructors with, 110–112
AttributeUsage attribute, 360–361
binding to activities, 1513–1514
methods using generic delegates as, 240–241
modifiers, 1688–1689
out, 82
parameter type contra-variance, 194
ParameterizedThreadStart delegate, 540–541
passed to constructor of persistence service, 1518
passing to methods, 80–82
passing to workflows, 1511–1512
ref, 81–82
returning to workflows, 1511–1512
specifying custom attribute, 361–362
stored procedures returning output, 861–863
partial classes/keyword, 95–96
partial-page postbacks, 1355, 1368–1369
partitioning operators, 310, 319–321
Pascal casing, 68–69
Passport Authentication (ASP.NET), 1331
passwords, resetting (Active Directory), 1618–1619
paths
for opening message queues, 1564
Path class and file management, 794–795
PATH index, 1011
pattern search strings (regular expressions), 216–217
PCSDemoSite
master pages in, 1326–1328
navigating, 1330–1331
security, 1336–1339
themes in, 1340–1344
PCSLibraryDemo project, 1374
peer names
defined, 1629
defining, 1629
Peer Name Resolution Protocol (PNRP), 1625, 1629–1631
registering, 1633–1634
resolving, 1634–1635
peer-to-peer (P2P) networking, 1625–1642
applications, building, 1632–1642
client-server architecture, 1626
forums, lii
Microsoft Windows platform, 1625, 1629–1632
overview, 1625–1629
P2P architecture, 1627–1628
Peer Name Resolution Protocol (PNRP), 1625, 1629–1631
PeerCollaboration class, 1639
People Near Me (PNM), 1625, 1632
System.Net.PeerToPeer namespace. *See* System.Net.PeerToPeer namespace
System.Net.PeerToPeer.Collaboration namespace. *See* System.Net.PeerToPeer. Collaboration namespace
terminology, 1628–1629
pens (GDI+), 1116–1118
People Near Me (PNM), 1625, 1632
perfmon.exe, 531–532
performance
collections, 294–296
generics and, 224–225
pointers and, 339–340, 352–355

performance monitoring
basics, 527
classes, 528
perfmon.exe, 531–532
Performance Counter Builder, 528–529
performance counts, 509
Performance Monitor, 531–532, 745
PerformanceCounter components, 529–531
permissions
asserting, 611–613
changing code group, 627–628
code access security and, 618–621
declarative, 606
defined, 602
demanding programmatically, 605–606
denying, 610–611
implicit, 610
managing, 626
provided by CLR, 603–605
requesting, 606–610
sets, creating/applying, 628–630
sets, defined, 602
SQL Server levels, 986–987
persistence service (WF), 1514, 1517–1518
persisting DataSet changes, 884–888
phantom reads (transactions), 701
phases, transaction, 680–681
PictureBox control (Windows Forms), 1035
pinning windows, 426
pipeline architecture (add-ins), 1253–1254
platform independence (IL), 4
platform invoke services, 783–787
Playground example (regular expressions), 216–220
plug-ins. *See* add-ins
PNM (People Near Me), 1625, 1632
PNRP (Peer Name Resolution Protocol), 1625, 1629–1631
Point/PointF structs (GDI+), 1102–1103
pointer member access operators, 346
pointers, 339–355
advantages/disadvantages of, 340
arithmetic of, 344–345, 349–350
casting between pointer types, 343–344
casting to integer types, 343
to class members, 346–347
optimizing performance with, 352–355
PointerPlayaround example, 347–352
reasons for using, 339–340
sizeof operator, 345
to structs, 345–346
syntax, 341–343
unsafe keyword, 340–341
void pointers, 344
poison queues, defined, 1557
policies, security
levels, 621–622
managing, 622–626
polling (asynchronous delegates), 535–536
pooling, object (Enterprise Services), 1530
pools, thread, 543–545
pop-up menu for rows
attributes, 1089–1090
code, 1085–1088
dispatching methods, 1090–1091
manufactured tables and rows, 1088–1089
selected rows, 1091–1092
populating data sets
with data adapters, 883–884
from XML, 884
ports
listener (WCF example), 1461
number (Active Directory), 1599
types (WSDL), 1458
postbacks
Ajax and, 1357
asynchronous, 1355
defined, 1275
partial-page, 1368–1369
postfixes, expression, 144
power events (Windows Services), 746–747
#pragma preprocessor directives, 66
prefixes, expression, 144
preparing transaction phase, 680
preprocessor directives, 63–66
presentation service layer, 1528
previewing, print (GDI+), 1142–1146
primary interop assembly (COM), 764
primary keys, setting, 874–875
principal classes, 583–585
printable characters, defined, 815
printing
and previewing in GDI+, 1141–1146
WebBrowser control for, 1437
priority nodes, 270, 273–274
Priority property (Message class), 1571–1572

PriorityDocumentManager class, 272
private assemblies, 16, 472–473
private keys, strong names and, 486–487
private queues, defined, 1559
<probing> element, 496, 498–499
products object, creating (Northwind), 900–902
products table, calling (Northwind), 897
***Professional ASP.NET 2.0* (Wiley), 1308**
***Professional ASP.NET 3.5: in C# and VB* (Wrox Press), 216**
programming
  Active Directory. *See* Active Directory, programming
  object-oriented, xliv, xlviii
programming guidelines (C#)
  fields, 73
  identifiers, rules for, 66–67
  naming conventions, 68–72
  properties/methods, rules for using, 72–73
  usage conventions, 67–68
ProgressBar control (Windows Forms), 1035–1036
ProjectInstaller class, 730–731
projection operators, 310
projects
  deployment, 444
  vs. solutions, 412–415
projects, Visual Studio 2008
  creating new, 406–407
  selecting type, 407–410
  startup, setting, 415
projects, VSTO
  features, 1389–1390
  structure of, 1394–1396
  types, 1386–1389
promotable transactions, 690–692
properties
  access modifiers for, 84–85
  accessing by name (Active Directory), 1603
  ACID (transactions), 681
  AddInToken class, 1255
  appearance (Control class), 1024
  Application class, 1018–1019
  application setup (Solution Explorer), 450–452
  array class, 127
  attached (WF), 1506–1508
  auto-implemented, xlvi, 85
  BackgroundWorker class, 571–572
  Binding class, 1202–1203
  BitVector32, 291
  C#, rules for use of, 72–73
  ChannelFactory class, 1483
  as child elements (XAML), 1152
  collections interfaces, 248–249
  Custom Actions editor, 464–465
  DataColumn object, 868
  DataContext object, 905–906
  DataMember properties (WCF), 1468
  defined, 77
  defining in .NET languages, 1690–1691
  deployment projects, 453–454
  DllImport, 784–785
  DoubleAnimation, 1232
  entity classes, 1541, 1542
  EventLog class, 520
  EventSourceCreationData, 521–522
  EventTrigger class, 1236
  FileInfo/DirectoryInfo class, 793–794
  fundamentals, 83–84
  header properties, 1427–1428
  ICollection interface, 132
  IEnumerator interface, 134
  IList interface, 132–133
  to limit searches (Active Directory), 1609–1610
  LinkedList <T> class, 269–270
  LinkedListNode class, 269
  Lookup<TKey, TValue>, 283–284
  message queuing, 1561–1562
  Name/Text (Windows Forms elements), 660
  names, user class (Active Directory), 1613–1614
  ObjectContext class, 1664–1665
  ObjectDataProvider class, 1207
  OperationBehavior (WCF), 1475–1476
  OperationContract properties (WCF), 1470
  Path class, 795
  Properties window, VS 2008, 422–424
  PROPERTY index, 1011
  property triggers (timeline), 1229–1233
  PropertyManager object, 1078–1080
  Queue and Queue<T> classes, 262–263
  read-only/write-only, 84
  ReaderWriterLockSlim, 565
  Rectangle struct, 1105
  RegistryKey class, 832

properties (continued)
search limits and (Active Directory), 1609–1610
ServiceContract (WCF), 1469
ServiceController class, 738–739
services, 725–726, 732–733
size/location (Control class), 1023–1024
SortedList<TKey, TValue> class, 277
[SqlUserDefinedType] attribute, 990
Stack and Stack<T> classes, 267
stream objects and, 794
StreamReader class, 817
Syndication Reader, 1646
System.Exception, 385
Timeline, 1232
Transaction class, 686–687
Trigger class, 1184
Type class, 365–366
user controls and, 1313
validation controls and, 1289
virtual, 104
Web application installer, 455–456
as XML attributes, 1152
XPathNodeIterator, 939
yield statements and, 135
protected internal modifier, 112, 114
protocols, Active Directory binding, 1598–1599
providers
ADSI, 1598–1599
LINQ, 327–328
<provider>Command classes, 856–860
proxies
creating for clients (WCF), 1482–1483
HTTP/FTP requests and, 1428–1429
public keys, strong names and, 486–487
public modifier, 112, 114
public queues, defined, 1559
publisher policy files, 496, 504–506
publishing
applications, 459
Web sites, 444, 447–448

Q

quantifier operators, 310
queries. *See also* **LINQ (Language Integrated Query)**
object, 1670–1674
Query Builder methods, 1673–1674
query expressions, 914–916
QueryInterface( ) method, 752
querying SQL Server database (LINQ)
custom objects, 908–910
grouping items with queries, 918–919
limiting called columns, 910
outputting XML, 982–983
performing joins, 916–918
query expressions, 914–915
querying XML documents, 974–978
queues
basics, 261–266
configuring with Component Services Explorer, 1537
queued components (Enterprise Services), 1530
Stack<T> big-O notation, 295
workflows (WF), 1492
QuickArray example (pointers), 354–355

R

race conditions (threading), 545–548
Racer class (lists), 251–261
RadialGradientBrush (WPF), 1164–1165
radio button control (Windows Forms), 1028
Range( ) method, 324
Rank property (Array class), 127
RCW (runtime callable wrapper), 762–764
read methods (XmlReader class), 925–927
read-only collections, 261
read-only fields/keyword, 90–91
read-only properties, 84
ReaderWriterLockSlim class (synchronization), 564–568
reading
ACLs from files/directories, 824–825
to files, 805–807
to files with FileStream class, 810–812
to isolated storage, 839–844
to the registry. *See* registry
to text files, 815–821
ReadWriteText example, 819–821
Really Simple Syndication (RSS), 1643
receiving messages, 1567–1569, 1573–1576, 1581–1583

records
deleting, 861
inserting, 862–863
updating, 860–861
recoverable messages, defined, 1559
Recoverable property (Message class), 1572
Rectangle/RectangleF structs (GDI+), 1105
red-green-blue color values, 1114–1115
ref parameters, 81–82
refactoring applications, 434–436
reference types. *See also* arrays
basics, 35–36, 40–42
comparing for equality, 153–154
declaring arrays of, 123–124
declaring with .NET languages, 1683–1684
generics and, 224
reference data types, 331–333
and value types, 8
references
JavaScript client-side, 1369
ReferenceEquals( ) method, 97, 153
referents, defined, 339
service (WCF), 1464–1465
to shared assemblies, 493–494
Web service, 1369
reflection
assembly class, 370–371
custom attributes. *See* custom attributes
defined, 17, 357
System.Type class. *See* System.Type class
Reflector software tool, 853, 1500
regasm utility, 778
regedit, 829–830
Region class (GDI+), 1106
#region preprocessor directives, 65
regions
date formatting and, 644–645
number formatting and, 643–644
registration
COM, 777–778
.NET and COM, 753
registry
basics, 828
.NET Registry classes, 830–833
overview, 829–830
Registry editor (VS 2008), 461
registry hives, 829–830
Registry Search (Launch Conditions editor), 465
RegistryKey class, 830–834
SelfPlacingWindow example, 833–839
regular expressions
asterisk (*) as quantifier in, 218
backslash (\) in, 217
Beginning Regular Expressions (Wrox Press), 215
escape codes in, 215
escape sequences, 217–218
fundamentals, 214–216
input strings, 216
matches/groups/captures, 220–222
Matches( ) static method (Regex class), 216
meta-characters, 217
parentheses ( ) in, 220
pattern search strings, 216–217
RegexOptions enumerations, 217
RegularExpressionsPlayground example, 216–220
special characters in, 218
square brackets ([ ]) in, 218
relational data
converting to XML, 952–954
XML data type and, 1003
relationships
ADO.NET Entity Framework and, 1666–1670
data, 873–874
relative distinguished names (Active Directory), 1599
release and debug builds, 427
Release configuration (Visual Studio), 429
Replace( ) method (System.String), 206
replication (Active Directory), 1588, 1591–1592
report queues, defined, 1559
requests. *See also* WebRequest/WebResponse classes
asynchronous page, 1429
TCP network, 1444
Resgen.exe, 651–652
resource files
event logging, 522–526
localization and, 651, 653–658
Resource File Generator, 651–652
ResourceManager, 654–659

resource readers, custom
application example, 677
basics, 672
DatabaseResourceManager class, 676–677
DatabaseResourceReader class, 674–675, 677
DatabaseResourceSet class, 676
resources
automatic fallback for, 666
custom resource messages, 665–666
management in .Net languages, 1701–1703
managers, custom, 703–709
resource dictionary (XAML), 669, 671–673
ResourceWriter, 652–653
System.Resources namespace, 659
transactional, 704–709
WPF, 1178–1181
response queues, 1559, 1577
resultLabel control Text property, 1293–1294
return statements, 49
return type covariance, 193
RevokeLifetimeToken( ) method, 1258–1259
ribbon menus (VSTO), 1390, 1401–1404
RichTextBox control (Windows Forms), 1036–1037
Roeder, Lutz, 1500, 4500
role-based security
defined, 12
Enterprise Services and, 1530
fundamentals, 585
Rooms table (MeetingRoomBooker example), 1296
RotateTransform element (WPF), 1162
round-robin scheduling (threads), 543
rounding numbers, 168
rows. *See also* pop-up menu for rows
data, 868–871
deleting in data tables, 887
filtering, 1065–1067
filtering by data, 1066
filtering on state, 1066–1067
inserting in data tables, 885–886
sorting, 1068
updating existing (data tables), 887
RSS (Really Simple Syndication), 1643–1645
rules, custom validation, 1223–1224
runat="server" attribute, 1275
runtime. *See also* CLR (Common Language Runtime)
callable wrapper (RCW), 762–764
schema generation, 871
settings, configuring, 496, 503
versions, 506–507
workflow runtime (WF), 1514–1515

S

SafeHandle type, 710
safety palette (GDI+), 1116
safety permission levels (SQL Server), 986–987
SampleClientSetupSolution example, 460
sans-serif font families, 1126
satellite assemblies
defined, 473
for languages, 663
localization with XAML, 671, 673
saving
files with Unicode characters, 651
SaveFile( ) method, 819–820
SaveSettings( ) method, 840–842
ScaleTransform element (WPF), 1162
scaling, client-server architecture, 1626
sc.exe command-line utility (Windows Services), 734–737
schemas. *See also* XML schemas
Active Directory, 1589, 1592–1593
defined, 866
generation (data tables), 871–873
naming context (Active Directory), 1612–1613
SCM (Service Control Manager), 717
scopes. *See also* variable scope
clashes, 32–34
nested (transactions), 695–697
rules for determining, 31
<script> tags (ASP.NET Web Forms), 1275
ScriptManager control (ASP.NET Ajax), 1359, 1368–1370
scrollable windows, drawing, 1107–1113
scrolling, 1079–1080
sealed classes/methods, 107
sealed keyword, 107
searching. *See also* regular expressions
in Active Directory, 1608–1611

Advanced Query Syntax (AQS), 1728–1729
with DSML, 1621–1623
lists, 257–258
in Vista, 1722–1729
security
access control to resources, 599–601
application deployment and, 460
assemblies and, xlv
authentication and authorization. *See* authentication and authorization
code access security. *See* code access security
configuring with Component Services Explorer, 1536
distributing code with certificates, 631–637
distributing code with strong names, 630–631
encryption. *See* encryption
of files, 825–828
managing code groups/permissions, 626
managing security policies, 622–626
.NET overview, 12
role-based (Enterprise Services), 1530
secure transfers and key exchanges, 596–599
SecurityAction enumeration values, 608–609
settings, configuring, 496
SQL Server and, 986–987
turning on and off, 626
WCF and, 1456
security (ASP.NET), 1331–1339
directories, securing, 1337–1339
forms authentication, 1331–1334
login system, 1334–1336
login Web server controls, 1336
PCSDemoSite, 1336–1339
security Setup Wizard, 1332–1334
Web Forms, 1276
SELECT statement
combining with XQuery, 1008–1009
UDTs and, 988, 994–995, 997
SelfPlacingWindow example (registry), 833–839
Semaphore class (synchronization), 558, 560–562
Send( ) method (queues), 1565
sending messages, 1565–1567, 1570–1572, 1583–1585
sentinel values, defined, 1074
sequential workflows (WF), 1509
serialization
data contracts (WCF), 1468
serializing objects in XML, 956–965
in XML, 963–965
serif font families, 1125
server console application, building, 1450–1451
server controls (ASP.NET)
control palette, 1283
data Web server controls, 1287–1288
example, 1289–1294
overview, 1279–1283
standard Web server controls, 1283–1286
validation Web server controls, 1288–1289
Server Explorer
controlling Windows Services with, 737
window (VS 2008), 426
server names (Active Directory), 1599
service configuration
programs (Windows Services), 718
Service Configuration Editor (WCF), 1463, 1466
service contracts (WCF), 1467–1470, 1580–1581
service façade (WCF), 1549–1553
Service Host (WCF example), 1461–1464
service-main function (Windows Services), 717–718
service programs (Windows Services), 716–718
Service Trace Viewer tool (WCF), 1467
ServiceBase class (Windows Services), 726–727
ServiceBehavior property (WCF), 1471–1472
[ServiceContract] attribute, 1469
ServiceController class
application (Windows Services), 737–745
defined, 719
ServicedComponent class (Enterprise Services), 1531
ServiceInstaller class, 731–734
ServiceInstallerDialog class, 734
ServiceModel Metadata Utility tool (Svcutil.exe), 1482–1483

ServiceProcessInstaller class, 731–734
services, workflow (WF)
basics, 1515–1516
custom services, 1520–1521
persistence services, 1517–1518
tracking service, 1518–1520
set operations, LINQ and, 318–319
set operators, 310
Setup installer Project, 448
SetValue( ) method, 127–128
shallow comparisons, 162
shapes
drawing, 1096–1099
painting, 1099–1100
in WPF, 1159–1162
shared assemblies
basics, 472–473
creating, 489
defined, 16–17
delayed signing of, 492–493
global assembly cache (GAC), 487–489
installing, 491
native image generator, 494–495
.NET applications, configuring. *See* .NET applications
references to, 493–494
strong names and, 486–487, 489–490
using, 491–492
versioning and. *See* versioning
shared classes in System.Data namespace, 847
SharePoint workflow templates(VSTO), 1388
shield icons (Vista), 1713–1715
shortcuts, operator, 143–144
signatures, encrypted, 594–596
SignIn( )/SignOut( ) methods (PeerCollaboration class), 1639
signing shared assemblies, 492–493
Silverlight applications, 1249
simple controls (WPF), 1167–1168
SimpleAppSolutionSetup example (deployment), 454–455
SimpleClientApp example (deployment), 449–454
SimpleCurrency example (user-defined casts), 165–174
SimpleExceptions example (catch blocks), 382–385
SimpleWebApp example (deployment), 455–456
single-threaded apartments (STAs), 569–570, 753
sink objects, creating client applications with, 781–782
<siteMapNode> element attributes, 1329
sites, domain controller, 1590
Size/SizeF structs (GDI+), 1103–1104
sizeof operator, 146, 345
SkewTransform element (WPF), 1162
Smart Device CAB installer Project, 448
smart tags (VSTO), 1389
SmtpClient object, 1444–1445
SOAP (Simple Object Access Protocol)
faults, 1476–1477
WCF and, 1457
Socket class, 1449–1452
SolicitColdCall example (user-defined exceptions), 389–390
solid brushes, 1117
SolidColorBrush (WPF), 1163–1164
solutions vs. projects, 412–415
solutions, VSTO
application-level add-ins, 1398–1400
architecture of, 1386
basics, 1398–1399
document-level customization, 1398
interacting with applications/documents, 1400–1401
UI customization, 1401–1405
Sort( ) method (generic delegates), 240–241
SortedDictionary<TKey, TValue> class, 285
SortedList<TKey, TValue> class, 275–278, 285, 295
arrays, 129–131
cultures and, 650–651
data within DataView, 1068
LINQ, 314–315
lists, 258–260
operators, 310
source files, comments within, 60
sources
event sources, 521–522, 525
tracing architecture, 510–511
SpecialFolder enumeration (Vista), 1715
specifiers, numeric type format, 209–210
SplitContainer control (Windows Forms), 1038

SQL (Structured Query Language)
LINQ to SQL. *See* LINQ to SQL
SqlCoordinate struct, 988–989, 991
[SqlUserDefinedType] attribute, 990
SQL Server, 985–1013
key generation with, 890–892
Microsoft.SqlServer.Server namespace classes, 987–988
.NET runtime and, 985, 986–987
SQL Server 2005 Express Edition Starter Kit (Wiley), 985
stored procedures and, 998–1000
triggers, 1001–1003
user-defined functions, 1000–1001
user-defined types. *See* user-defined types (UDTs)
XML data type and. *See* XML data type
SQL Server Management Studio
binding columns and, 1076
XML schemas and, 1012–1013
STA (single-threaded apartment)
basics, 753
COM objects, 771
stacks
basics, 266–268
defined, 35
memory and, 330–333
pointers, defined, 330
Stack<T> big-O notation, 295
stack-based Arrays, creating, 352–354
stackalloc keyword, 352–354
StackOverflowException class, 379
StackPanel container (WPF), 1172–1173
and value types, 8
startup settings, configuration, 496
state machine workflows (WF), 1509–1511
state management (ASP.NET), 1274–1275
static classes/keyword, 96–97
static constructors, 87–89
static Equals( ) method, 154
static members
generics and, 235
and .NET languages, 1692–1693
static methods, Path class and, 795
static XML documents, querying, 975–976
StaticResource markup extension, 1181–1182
storage, isolated, 839–844
Store Schema Definition Language (SSDL), 1657–1658
stored procedures. *See also* triggers
calling with command objects, 860–863
LINQ to SQL and, 919–920
naming conventions for, 893
SQL Server and, 998–1000
using in data adapters, 883–884
storing entity changes, 1677–1678
storyboards, 1229, 1235–1236
streams
basics, 808–810
BinaryFileReader example, 812–815
buffered, 810
FileStream class, 810–812
streamed XML, reading/writing, 924
StreamReader class, 809, 816–818
StreamWriter class, 809, 818–819
strings
building, 205–208
connection strings for adding events, 1300
creating UDTs and, 992
displaying, 1063–1064
format strings, 59–60, 209–214
FormattableVector example, 212–214
for list binding, 1212–1213
managing connection, 850–852
StringArrayConverter class, 1212–1213
StringBuilder members, 208–214
StringCollection class, 820
StringInfo class, 640
System.string class methods, 204–205
types, 40–42
strong data typing
IL and, 8–9
language interoperability and, 9–11
strongly typed XML, 1011–1013
strong names
creating, 489–490
defined, 17
distributing code with, 630–631
integrity using, 486–487
structs
vs. classes, 76, 102
constructors for, 94–95
fundamentals, 92–93
inheritance and, 94, 102
pointers to, 345–346

structs (continued)
System.Drawing namespace, 1102
as value types, 93–94
Vector struct example (operator overloading), 157–163
Structured Query Language (SQL). ***See*** **SQL (Structured Query Language)**
styles, defining (WPF), 1177–1178
SubordinateTransaction class, 686
Sum( ) method, 321–322
super keyword, 106
SuppressFinalize( ) method, 339
.svc files, 1481
switch statement (.NET languages), 1694–1695
switch . . . case statements, 44–45
switches, trace. ***See*** **tracing**
symbols, debugger, 428
symmetric encryption keys, 591–594
symmetric key exchange, 596–599
synchronization, 549–568
basics, 549–550
events and, 562–564
Interlocked class, 555–556
lock statement, 550–555
Monitor class, 557
Mutex class, 559–560
ReaderWriterLockSlim class, 564–568
Semaphore class, 560–562
WaitHandle class, 557–558
synchronous programming, 1555
SyncRoot pattern, 552, 554
syndication
Really Simple Syndication (RSS), 1643
syndication feeds, 1647–1651
Syndication Reader application, 1644–1647
Syndication Service Library template, 1647
System.ServiceModel.Syndication namespace, 1643–1644
Sys.Debug class, 1381
system access-control list (SACL), 599
system queues, defined, 1559
system resources, WPF and, 1180
System.AddIn assembly. ***See*** **add-ins**
System.ApplicationException class, 378
System.Convert object, 168
System.Data namespace, 847
System.Data.Common namespace, 847
System.Data.OleDb namespace, 749, 1725
System.DirectoryServices namespace, 749, 1597–1598
System.DirectoryServices.Protocols namespace, 1587, 1596–1597, 1621
System.Drawing namespace, 1095, 1102
System.Drawing.Brush class, 1117
System.Drawing.Font class, 1126
System.Drawing.Graphics class, 1118–1119
System.Drawing.Pen class, 1117–1118
System.EnterpriseServices, 684–685
System.Exception properties, 386
System.GC class, 334
System.Globalization namespace. ***See*** **globalization**
System.IO namespace, 378, 791
System.Linq namespace, 305
System.Messaging namespace, 1555
System.Net namespace, 3
System.Net.PeerToPeer namespace
code access security, 1635
example application, 1636–1638
registering peer names, 1633–1634
resolving peer names, 1634–1635
System.Net.PeerToPeer.Collaboration namespace
detecting peer presence, 1639–1640
example application, 1640–1642
managing contacts, 1639–1640
overview, 1638–1639
peers, discovering, 1639
signing in/out, 1639
System.Net.Sockets namespace, 3
System.Net.WebClient class, 4
System.Object base class, 108–109, 112
System.Object methods, 97–98
System.Object.ValueType, 94
System.Reflection namespace, 370, 476
System.Resources namespace (localization), 639, 659
System.Runtime.InteropServices namespace, 774–775
System.Security.AccessControl namespace, 599
System.Security.Cryptography namespace, 592
System.Security.Principal namespace, 584

System.ServiceModel.Syndication namespace, 1643–1644
System.ServiceProcess namespace, 718–719
System.String class methods, 204–205
System.SystemException class, 378
System.Text.RegularExpressions, 203
System.Text.RegularExpressions namespace, 215
System.Text.StringBuilder class, 206
System.Threading namespace, 584
System.Threading.Timer class, 568
System.Transactions namespace, 685–687
System.Type class
- properties and methods, 365–367
- TypeView example, 367–370

System.ValueType, 102
System.Web.Extensions.Design.dll, 1359
System.Web.Extensions.dll, 1359
System.Web.UI.WebControls.WebControl, 1319
System.Windows namespace, 1154
System.Windows.Forms namespace, 1023, 1025, 1076
System.Windows.Forms.Control class, 21
System.Windows.Media.Animation namespace, 1229
System.Windows.Shapes namespace, 1161
System.Workflow.Activities namespace, 1489
System.Xml classes, 923–924
System.Xml namespace, 922–923
System.Xml.Linq namespace, 327, 969
System.Xml.Serialization namespace, 956–957
System.Xml.XPath namespace, 937–942
System.Xml.Xsl namespace, 942–947

T

T-SQL stored procedures, 998–1000
TabControl/TabPages controls (Windows Forms), 1038–1039
tables
- creating with XML data, 1003–1005
- manufactured, 1088–1089
- Table per Hierarchy (TPH), 1666–1668
- Table per Type (TPT), 1668–1670
- TableLayoutPanel container (Windows Forms), 1037–1038
- Table<TEntity> object, 907
- temporary, accessing with triggers, 1002

tabular data, displaying, 1062–1063. *See also* DataGridView control
tags for XML documentation, 61
TakesAWhileCompleted( ) method, 537
/target switches, 57
task dialogs (Vista), 1718–1721
task panes (VSTO), 1404–1405
TCP (Transmission Control Protocol)
- classes, 1445–1446
- network requests, 1444
- TcpClient example (Windows Services), 722–725
- TcpSend/Receive examples, 1446–1449
- vs. UDP, 1448

templates
- for data display, 1303–1307
- data templates and WPF binding, 1214–1217
- FrameworkTemplate class (WPF), 1184–1192
- InfoPath form templates (VSTO), 1388–1389
- project templates (VSTO), 1386–1387
- SharePoint workflow templates (VSTO), 1388

ternary operator (C++/CLI), 1694
Test Client (WCF), 1461–1462
text
- drawing (GDI+), 1123–1125
- editor, VS Studio 2008, 402
- files, reading/writing to, 815–818
- properties (Windows Forms elements), 660
- text boxes, binding columns to, 1075–1076
- TextBox controls (Windows Forms), 1036–1037

textures, adding to triangles, 1241–1242
themes (ASP.NET)
- applying to pages, 1339–1340
- defining, 1340
- in PCSDemoSite, 1340–1344

themes in Workflow Designer, 1498–1500
this keyword, 110
Thread class
- background threads, 541–542
- basics, 535, 538–540
- controlling threads, 543
- creating threads, 535, 538–540
- passing data to threads, 540–541
- thread priority, 542–543

threading
asynchronous delegates, 535–538
COM and, 753–754
COM apartments, 569–570
COM components, 764–765
deadlock, 548–549
event-based asynchronous pattern. *See* BackgroundWorker class; event-based asynchronous pattern
issues, 533, 545
messages and, 1573–1574, 1581
overview, 533–535
race conditions, 545–548
reasons for using, 533
synchronization. *See* synchronization
thread class. *See* thread class
thread, defined, 534
thread pools, 543–545
threads, starting, 178
timers, 568–569
Windows Services and, 730
throwing exceptions, 380
throwing user-defined exceptions, 391–394
tiered development (ADO.NET), 889–890
time quantum (threads), 542
timelines, 1228–1232
Timer control (ASP.NET Ajax), 1360
timers, 568–569
tlbimp utility, 762
toolbars, creating (WebBrowser control), 1433–1437
toolbox, Visual Studio 2008, 420–421
ToolboxBitmap attribute (WF), 1500
ToolStrip control (Windows Forms), 1039–1041
ToolStripContainer control (Windows Forms), 1042
ToolStripManager class (Windows Forms), 1042
ToolStripMenuItem class (Windows Forms), 1042
ToString( ) method
date formatting and, 644–645
dictionary example, 280–281
fundamentals/examples, 98–99
number formatting and, 643–644
purpose of, 97
tracing
architecture of, 510
asserts, 516–517
basics, 509–510
defined, 509
filters, 515–516
trace listeners, 510, 512–515
trace sources, 510–511, 1466–1467
trace switches, 512
tracking
object, 1674–1675
service (WF), 1518–1520
track points (WF), 1519
transactions
ACID properties, 681
ADO.NET, 683–684, 905
ambient, 694–701
committable, 687–690
CourseManagement sample database, 681–683
custom resource managers, 703–709
database and entity classes, 681–683
database connections and, 854–855
dependent, 692–693
Enterprise Services, 684–685
isolation levels and, 701–703
overview, 679–680
phases, 680–681
promotable, 690–692
System.Transactions namespace, 685–687
transactional messages, 1559
transactional queues, 1577–1578
transactional resources, 704–709
TransactionOption values, 1539
TransactionScope class members, 694
TransactionScopeOption enumeration, 696
with Windows Vista/Windows Server 2008, 710–713
transactions, Enterprise Services
automatic, 1529, 1539
basics, 1539–1540
configuring with Component Services Explorer, 1537
distributed, 1530
promotable, 1530
transformation elements (WPF), 1162–1163
transforms, coordinate (GDI+), 1137–1138
translations, outsourcing, 666–667

Transmission Control Protocol (TCP). ***See*** **TCP (Transmission Control Protocol)**
TreeView-based custom control (Windows Forms), 1049–1055
triangle models (WPF)
3-D objects and, 1242–1245
basics, 1238–1240
lights, changing, 1240
textures, adding, 1241–1242
triggers
defined, 1001
event triggers (animations), 1233–1235
messaging queuing and, 1558
property in WF, 1182–1184
SQL Server and, 1001–1003
TriggerAction classes, 1236
UpdatePanel triggers, 1371–1372
troubleshooting Windows Services, 745–746
True Type font families, 1126
truncating numbers, 168
trust licenses, 460
Trusted Application Deployment, 460
try blocks
defined, 379–380
examples, 382–386
nested, 387–389
try . . . catch . . . finally blocks, 852
TryGetValue( ) method, 282
tunneling events, 1177
two-way binding, 1200, 1204
type class
properties and methods, 365–367
types defined in assemblies, 370
TypeView example, 367–370
type safety
boxing and unboxing, 152–153
overview, 148
type conversions, 149–151
types
anonymous, 91–92
basics, 224
collections, 247–250
condition types (WF), 1490
constraint types (generics), 233
conversion (lists), 260–261
filtering, 312–314
generic type names, 226
integer types, and pointers, 343
key types (dictionaries), 278–280
library, creating, 772–774
managed/unmanaged, 343
metadata, 470–471
modifying exception, 387–389
passed with contracts, 1257
safety and generics, 223, 225
typeof operator, 146
TypeView example, 367–370
user-defined. *See* user-defined types (UDTs)
types, defining in .NET languages
enumerations, 1686
interfaces, 1685–1686
reference types, 1683–1684
type inference, 30–31, 1685
value types, 1684–1685

U

UAC (user account control), 1712–1715
UDP (User Datagram Protocol)
class, 1448–1449
vs. TCP, 1448
UDTs (user-defined types). ***See*** **user-defined types (UDTs)**
UI customization (VSTO), 1401–1405
unboxing, defined, 224
unhandled exceptions, 386–387
Unicode
globalization and, 640–641
text files with, 651
unmanaged resources, freeing, 334–339
destructors, 335–339
IDisposable interface, 336–339
unmanaged types, defined, 343
unsafe code blocks (C#), 1709
unsafe keyword, 340–341
unsafe methods, 340–341
unsafe safety level, 986
updating
ADO.NET Entity Framework, 1674–1678
records, 860–861
update and delete constraints, setting, 876
UpdatePanel control (ASP.NET Ajax), 1360, 1370–1372
UpdateProgress control (ASP.NET Ajax), 1360, 1372
UpdateRowSource values, 886

uploading files with WebClient class, 1426
URIs (Uniform Resource Identifiers)
  classes, 1440–1441
  vs. URLs, 1424
user account control (UAC), 1712–1715
user controls (ASP.NET)
  basics, 1312–1313
  in PCSDemoSite, 1318
  simple, 1313–1318
user controls (Windows Forms), 1055–1059
User Datagram Protocol (UDP). ***See*** **UDP (User Datagram Protocol)**
user-defined casts
  between base and derived classes, 169–170
  boxing/unboxing casts, 170–171
  converting between classes, 168–169
  fundamentals, 164–165
  multiple casting, 171–175
  SimpleCurrency example, 165–168
user-defined exceptions
  catching, 390–391
  defining classes, 394–396
  SolicitColdCall example, 389–390
  throwing, 391–394
user-defined functions (SQL Server), 1000–1001
user-defined types (UDTs), 988–997
  Ajax Library, 1377–1378
  basics, 988
  creating, 988–993
  user-defined aggregates, 996–997
  using, 993–996
users
  account management, 1619–1620
  input, responding to (GDI+), 1138–1141
  interaction events (Control class), 1024–1025
  interface (Active Directory), 1611–1612
  interface customization (VSTO), 1401–1405
  User Interface editor (VS 2008), 462–463
  user objects, searching for, 1614–1616
  user policy level (security), 621–623
  user principal name (UPN) (Active Directory), 1601
  usernames (Active Directory), 1601
  Users and Computers snap-in (Active Directory), 1594–1595
using **block statement, 852–854**
using **directive, 53–54**
using **keyword, 54, 1682**
using **statement in .Net languages, 1702**

validation
  activity validation (WF), 1497–1498
  validation Web server controls (ASP.NET), 1288–1289
  with XmlReader, 928–930
validation, binding
  custom validation rules, 1223–1224
  data error information, 1221–1222
  handling exceptions, 1219–1221
  Validation class, 1221
value types
  basics, 35–39, 224
  comparing for equality, 154
  declaring with .NET languages, 1684–1685
  memory management and, 330–331
  and reference types, 8
  structs as, 93–94
values. ***See also*** **default values (generic classes)**
  BitVector32, 291
  Name/Text (Windows Forms elements), 660
  row state, 1066–1067
  VALUE index, 1011
  Value property (WPF binding), 1201
  XML, reading, 1005–1008
var keyword, 30, 91, 1685, xlv
variables. ***See also*** **constants**
  constant variables, 34
  declaring, 29
  implicitly typed (.NET 3.5), xlv–xlvi
  initialization of, 29–30
  monitoring with Autos window, 432–433
  type inference, 30–31
  variable scope, 31–34
VARIANT data types, 753
VBA interoperability (VSTO), 1415–1418
Vector struct example (operator overloading), 157–163
VectorClass assembly example, 362, 364–365
versioning
  add-ins, 1252, 1259
  application configuration files, 500–503
  obtaining versions programmatically, 500

overview, 499
publisher policy files, 504–506
runtime version, 506–507
version dependencies, 470
version numbers, 499–500
WCF, 1468–1469

viewing assemblies, 473

viewstate fields (ASP.NET), 1275

virtual addressing, defined, 330

virtual Equals( ) method, 153

virtual keyword, 104, 106

virtual memory, defined, 330

virtual methods, 104

VirtualizingStackPanel (WPF), 1172

visibility modifiers, 112–113

Vista, Windows

Advanced Query Syntax (AQS), 1728–1729
command link controls, 1716
directory structure, 1715–1716
file dialogs, 1721–1722
OLE DB provider, 1724–1727
searching in, 1722–1729
task dialog, 1718–1721
transactions with, 710–713
user account control (UAC), 1712–1715
Vista Bridge, 1711, 1717

Visual Basic 2008

COM components, building with VB 9, 756
error handling in VB 6, 377
LINQ to SQL and, 967–968
mapping syntax from C#, 1681–1709
.NET Framework and, 5–6
Visual Studio 2008 and, 416

Visual C++

.NET Framework and, 6
Visual Studio 2008 and, 416

Visual Studio 2008

BasicForm Windows project, 413–415
breakpoints, 431–432
building/compiling/making, defined, 427
C# code/compilation options, 408–410
Class View window, 424
code optimization, 427–428
conditional compilation, 428
configurations, editing, 429–430
configurations, selecting, 429
Console Application, 410–412
Conversion Wizard, 404–405
Custom Actions editor, 463–465
debug and release builds, 427
debugger symbols, 428
debugging, 430–434
deployment projects. *See* deployment
Design View window, 419–422
exceptions, 433–434
extra source code debugging commands, 428–429
features and overview, 401–406
File Types editor, 461–462
folding editor, 416–418
installer project types. *See* installer project types
languages and, 663
Launch Conditions editor, 465–466
LINQ to SQL and, 897–902
multi-targeting .NET Framework, xlvii, 436–438
.NET environment and, xlv
new project, creating, 406–407
O/R Designer. *See* O/R Designer
Object Browser window, 425–426
pin buttons, 426
project type, selecting, 407–410
Properties window, 422–424
refactoring applications, 434–436
Registry editor, 461
Server Explorer window, 426
solutions and projects, 412–415
Start Page, 407
startup project, setting, 415
toolbox, 420–421
User Interface editor, 462–463
Visual Studio Add Service Reference, 1482
VS 6 projects, reading in, 416
watches, 432–433
WF applications, building in, 439–441
Windows application code, 415
WPF applications, building in, 438–439
XML schemas and, 1012

Visual Studio 2008 for localization

automatic fallback for resources, 666
basics, 659–663
culture, changing programmatically, 663–665
custom resource messages, 665–666
outsourcing translations, 666–667

Visual Studio Tools for Office (VSTO), 1385–1419
application example, 1405–1415
building solutions. *See* solutions, VSTO
event handling, 1397–1398
Globals class, 1397
host items/host controls, 1392–1394
namespaces, 1391–1392
Office object model, 1391
overview, 1386–1390
project features, 1389–1390
project structure, 1394–1396
project types, 1386–1389
VBA interoperability, 1415–1418
visual styles (Windows XP), 1047
VisualBrush (WPF), 1166–1167, 1242
void pointers, 344
vtable (virtual table), 751

W

W3C standards supported in .NET, 922
wait handles
asynchronous delegates and, 536–537
mutex and, 559
synchronization and, 557–558
#warning preprocessor directives, 65
WAS (Windows Activation Services) hosting, 1481–1482
watches (debugging), 432–433
WCF (Windows Communication Foundation), 1455–1486
binding, 1477–1480
clients, 1482–1483
contracts, 1467–1471
duplex communication, 1484–1486
error handling, 1476–1477
hosting, 1480–1482
integration with WF, 1521–1524
JSON, 1458
message queuing. *See* message queuing with WCF
overview, 22, 1456–1458
service implementation, 1471–1477
settings, 496
SOAP, 1457
WSDL, 1457–1458
WCF, integrating with Enterprise Services
client application, 1553–1554
WCF service façade, 1549–1553
WCF, service example
custom Service Host, 1463–1464
diagnostics, 1466–1467
getting started, 1458–1459
implementation, 1460–1461
service contract, 1460
Service Host and Test Client, 1461–1462
WCF client, 1464–1465
Web applications
configuring with Web.config files, 1308–1309
Xcopy and, 447
Web browsing from applications, 1430–1431
Web Forms (ASP.NET), 1275–1294
code model, 1278–1279
controls, defined, 420
defined, 1273
overview, 20, 1275–1278
server controls. *See* server controls (ASP.NET)
Web method calls (ASP.NET AJAX), 1381–1383
Web pages
accessing master pages from, 1325–1326
applying themes to, 1339–1340
ASP.NET support for, xliv
Web Parts (ASP.NET), 1344–1353
basics, 1344
controls, 1344–1346
example, 1346–1353
Web server controls (ASP.NET)
basics, 20, 1279
data, 1287–1288
data binding and, 1302–1303
example, 1289–1294
standard controls, 1283–1286
validation controls, 1288–1289
Web services
ASP.NET application services, 1383
Web Services Description Language (WSDL), 1457–1458
Web Setup installer Project, 448
Web sites
configuration example (ASP.NET Ajax), 1365–1368

publishing, 444, 447–448
simple example (ASP.NET Ajax), 1362–1364

Web sites, for downloading
Ajax Library, 1358
ASP.NET, 1358
ASP.NET Ajax Control Toolkit, 1358
DSML, 1620
Nikhil's Web Development Helper, 1381
PNRP, 1629
Reflector software, 853, 1500
source code for this book, li
Unicode example, 821

Web sites, for further information
ASP.NET, 1358
culture name definitions, 641
database connection strings, 850
P2P forums, lii
Workflow Designer, 1526

WebBrowser control
HTML pages and, 1429–1430
Internet Explorer features and, 1432–1433
for printing, 1437
requested-page code, displaying, 1438
Web browsing from applications, 1430–1431

WebClient class, 1424–1426

Web.config files, 1308–1309

WebRequest/WebResponse classes
basics, 1426–1429
hierarchy, 1438–1440

WelcomeMessage( ) method, 660–661, 665

WF (Windows Workflow Foundation), 1487–1526
activities. *See* activities (WF)
applications, building in VS, 439–441
basics, 1487
Designer, 1487, 1526
Hello World example, 1488–1489
hosting workflows, 1524–1525
integration with WCF, 1521–1524
workflow runtime, 1514–1515
workflow services. *See* services, workflow (WF)
workflows. *See* workflows (WF)

WhatsNewAttributes example, 362–365, 371–375

Where( ) extension method, 305–308, 312

while/do . . . while Statements, 1696–1697

while loops, 48

WinCV utility, 18

windows
drawing scrollable, 1107–1113
pinning, 426

Windows, Microsoft
Activation Services (WAS) hosting, 1481–1482
application code, 415
Authentication (ASP.NET), 1331
Communication Foundation (WCF). *See* WCF (Windows Communication Foundation)
Controls, defined, 21
Forms. *See* Windows Forms
history of, xliii
Installer. *See* Windows Installer
Presentation Foundation (WPF). *See* WPF (Windows Presentation Foundation)
Resource Localization Editor, 667
Server 2008. *See* Windows Server 2008
Services. *See* Windows Services
Task Manager, 534
Vista. *See* Vista, Windows
WindowsIdentity class, 583

Windows Forms
ActiveX Control Importer, 768
ActiveX controls in, 768–770
application, creating, 768–770, 1018–1023
Button class, 1026–1027
CheckBox control, 1028
CheckedListBox control, 1029–1031
class hierarchy, 1023
ComboBox control, 1029–1031
ContextMenuStrip class, 1042
control class. *See* control class (Windows Forms)
controls, defined, 420
controls in Internet Explorer, 782–783
creating, 21
custom controls. *See* custom controls (Windows Forms)
DateTimePicker control, 1031
Designer, 661, 667, 769
ErrorProvider component, 1031–1032
FlowLayoutPanel container, 1037–1038
form appearance, 1046–1047
Form class, 1043

Windows Forms (continued)
form instantiation and destruction, 1043–1046
HelpProvider component, 1032
ImageList component, 1033
labels control, 1033
ListBox control, 1029–1031
ListView control, 1033–1035
localization and. *See* Visual Studio 2008 for localization
MDI-type applications, 1047–1048
MenuStrip control, 1041–1042
overview, 1017
Panel control, 1037
PictureBox control, 1035
ProgressBar control, 1035–1036
radio button control, 1028
SplitContainer control, 1038
TabControl/TabPages controls, 1038–1039
TableLayoutPanel container, 1037–1038
TextBox controls, 1036–1037
ToolStrip control, 1039–1041
ToolStripContainer control, 1042
ToolStripManager class, 1042
ToolStripMenuItem class, 1042
WPF and, 1245–1248
Windows Installer
vs. ClickOnce, 458
fundamentals, 449
Windows Installer Search, 465
Windows Server 2008
transactions with, 710–713
user account control and, 1712–1715
Windows Services
application, creating, 725–729
class library using sockets, 719–722
controlling with Server Explorer, 737
defined, 21–22
event logging and, 746
fundamentals, 715–716
handler methods, 728–729
installer classes, 730–734
installutil.exe utility, 734
interactive services, 745–746
main function, 727–728
MMC Services snap-in, 735–736
net.exe command-line utility, 734–736
power events and, 746–747
sc.exe command-line utility, 734–737
service programs, 716–718
ServiceBase class, 726–727
ServiceController class application, 737–745
System.ServiceProcess namespace, 718–719
TcpClient example, 722–725
threading and, 730
troubleshooting, 745–746
Windows Workflow Foundation (WF). ***See*** **WF (Windows Workflow Foundation)**
Word documents
vs. Excel document hosting, 1405
host items/controls for (VSTO), 1392–1393
storing as XML, 1003
template example (VSTO), 1394–1395
WordDocEditTimer, 1405–1415
workflows (WF)
binding parameters to activities, 1513–1514
defined, 1489, 1508
passing parameters to, 1511–1512
queue, 1492
returning results from, 1512–1513
runtime, 1514–1515
sequential, 1509
services. *See* services, workflow (WF)
state machine, 1509–1511
support for, 1488
template, 1487
Windows Workflow Foundation (WF). *See* WF (Windows Workflow Foundation)
WorkflowInstance, 1487
WorkflowRuntime code, 1487
XML-based, 1525
world coordinates (GDI+), 1113–1114
WPF (Windows Presentation Foundation), 1199–1249
3-D features in. *See* 3-D features in WPF; triangle models (WPF)
animations. *See* animations
applications, building in VS, 438–439
attached property, 1153–1154
basics, 21
brushes, 1163–1167
class hierarchy, 1155–1156
command bindings, 1224–1228
content controls, 1168–1169
data binding. *See* data binding and WPF
dependency property, 1152–1153

designer/developer cooperation, 1154–1155
event handling, 1176–1177
headered content controls, 1170–1171
headered items controls, 1171–1172
items controls, 1171
layout containers, 1172–1176
ListBox, styling, 1192–1197
localization with, 669–673
markup extensions, 1154
namespaces, 1156–1159
resources, 1178–1181
shapes, 1159–1162
simple controls, 1167–1168
styles, defining, 1177–1178
Syndication Reader and, 1645
templates, 1184–1192
transformation elements, 1162–1163
triggers, 1182–1184
Windows Forms and, 1245–1248
WPF Browser Application, 1249
WrapPanel container, 1173
XAML. *See* XAML (XML for Applications Markup Language)
write-only properties, creating, 84
WriteAllBytes( ) method, 806–807
WriteAllLines( ) method, 806–807
WriteAllText( ) method, 807
WriteEntry( ) method, 520, 522, 525
WriteEvent( ) method, 520, 522, 525
writing
to files, 805, 807–808
to files using FileStream class, 810–812
to isolated storage, 839–844
to registry. *See* registry
to text files, 815, 818–819
WSDL (Web Services Description Language), 1457–1458

X

XAML (XML for Applications Markup Language)
code for WPF application example, 670
data binding with, 1200–1203
defining instances with, 1206–1207
fundamentals, 1150–1152
localization with, 671–673
properties as attributes, 1152
properties as elements, 1152
XAttribute object, 974
XBAP files, defined, 1249
XComment object, 973
Xcopy deployment, 444, 447
XDocument object, 969
XElement object, 969–970
XML (Extensible Markup Language)
Ajax and, 1357
automatic documentation in, 61–62
Beginning XML (Wiley), 921
converting ADO.NET data to, 948–954
converting to ADO.NET, 954–956
data binding to, 1217–1219
DML (XML Data IModification Language), 1010
DOM implementation in .NET, 931–932
LINQ to XML. *See* LINQ to XML
namespaces and prefixes, 968
.NET Framework and, 921
output, writing, 887–889
outputting from database query, 982–983
populating DataSets from, 884
serializing objects in, 956–965
site maps, 1328–1329
streamed XML, reading/writing, 924
System.Xml classes, 923–924
System.Xml namespace, 922–923
System.Xml.Xsl namespace, 942
transforming, 943–947
W3C standards supported in .NET, 922
workflows and, 1525
XML Web services, overview, 20
XmlCharacterData classes, 932
XmlDocument class, 933–936, 1006–1007
XMLHttpRequest (Ajax), 1357
XmlLinkedNode classes, 932
XmlNode classes, 931–932
XmlReader class, 924–928, 1005–1007
XmlReader, validating with, 928–930
XmlWriter Class, 930–931
XML data type
overview, 1003
query of data, 1008–1010
strongly typed XML, 1011–1013
tables with XML data, 1003–1005
XML DML, 1010
XML indexes, 1010–1011
XML values, reading, 1005–1008

XML documents
querying dynamic, 976–978
querying static, 975–976
reading from, 978–979
writing to, 979–981
XML schemas
strongly typed XML and, 1011–1013
Word/Excel support, 1003
XML schema definitions (XSD), 877–883
XNamespace object, 971–972
XPath
reading XML values and, 1006
XML indexes and, 1011
XML queries and, 1009
XPathNavigators
System.Xml.XPath namespace, 937–942
XPathDocument class, 937
XPathNavigator class, 937–939
XPathNodeIterator class, 939
XQuery
basics, 1008–1010
XML data type and, 1003
XSD (XML schema definitions), 877–883
XSL (Extensible Stylesheet Language), 942–947
XSLT (Extensible Stylesheet Language Transformation)
debugging, 947–948
XsltArgumentList, 944–946
x:Uid attribute, 671–673

yield statements
defined in C#, 1709
enumerations and, 134–139

Z

Zone membership condition, 614

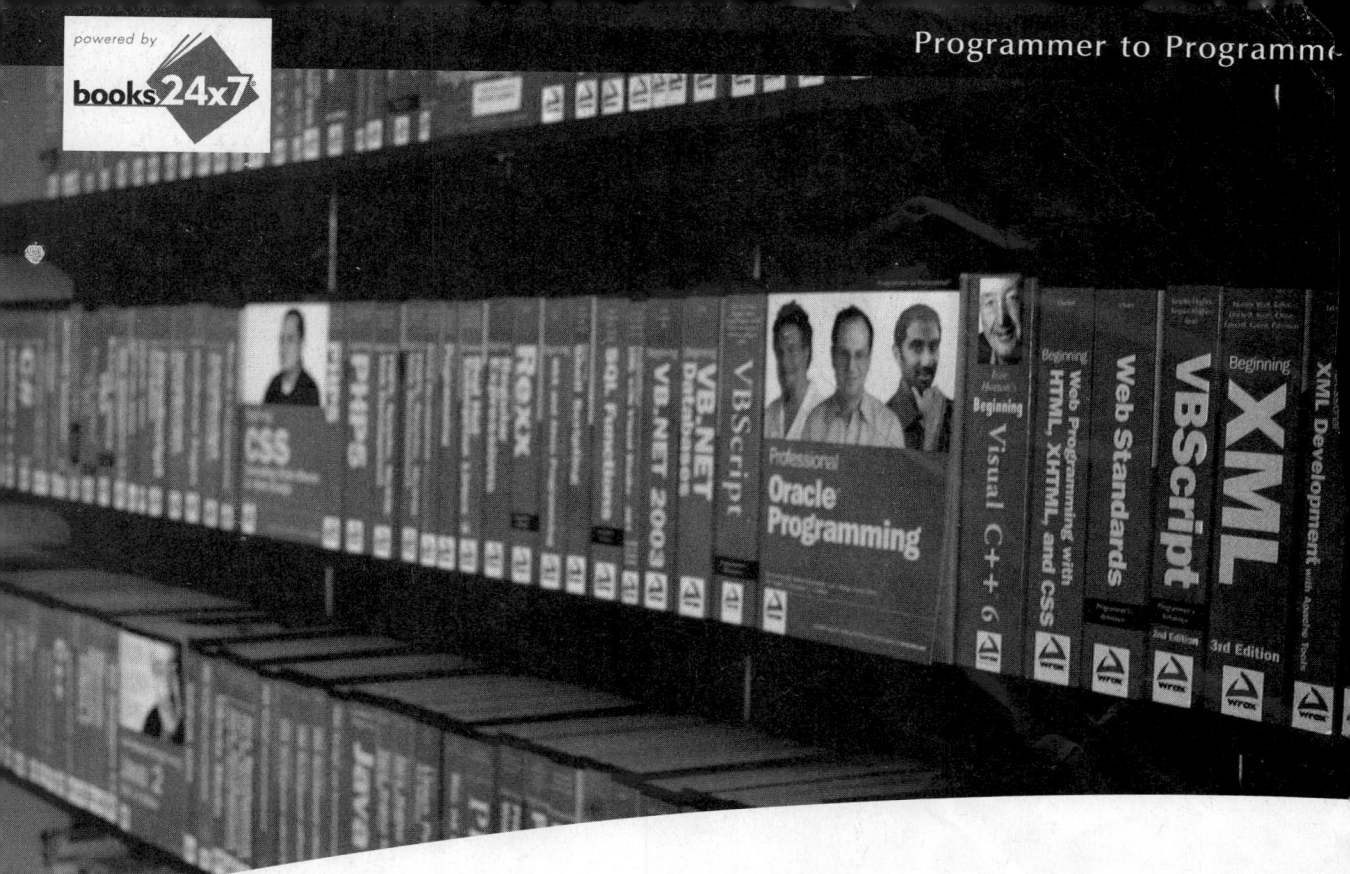

Professional
LINQ

Acknowledgments xiii

Introduction xxiii

Part I: Introduction to Project LINQ 1

Chapter 1: Project LINQ 3

Chapter 2: A Look at Visual Studio 2008 17

Chapter 3: LINQ Queries 31

Chapter 4: LINQ Standard Query Operators 53

Part II: LINQ to XML 93

Chapter 5: Understanding LINQ to XML 95

Chapter 6: Programming with LINQ to XML 123

Chapter 7: LINQ to XML and Other LINQ Data Models 145

Chapter 8: Advanced LINQ to XML Programming Topics 153

Chapter 9: LINQ to XML and Visual Basic .NET 179

Part III: LINQ to SQL 197

Chapter 10: LINQ to SQL Overview 199

Chapter 11: LINQ to SQL Queries 217

Chapter 12: Advanced Query Concepts 245

Chapter 13: More about Entity Classes 257

Chapter 14: LINQ to DataSet 271

Chapter 15: Advanced LINQ to SQL Topics 287

Appendixes 311

Appendix A: Case Study 313

Appendix B: LINQ to Entities: The ADO.NET Entity Framework 329

Appendix C: LINQ to XSD 345

Index 359

Professional
LINQ

Professional LINQ

Scott Klein

Wiley Publishing, Inc.

Professional LINQ

Published by
Wiley Publishing, Inc.
10475 Crosspoint Boulevard
Indianapolis, IN 46256
www.wiley.com

Published simultaneously in Canada

ISBN: 978-0-470-04181-9

Manufactured in the United States of America

10 9 8 7 6 5 4 3 2 1

Library of Congress Cataloging-in-Publication Data

Klein, Scott, 1966-
Professional LinQ / Scott Klein.
p. cm.
Includes index.
ISBN 978-0-470-04181-9 (pbk. : website)
1. Microsoft LINQ. 2. Query languages (Computer science) I. Title.
QA76.73.L228K53 2008
005.74'1--dc22
2007045810

To Lynelle, Sadie, Forrest, Allara, and Shayna

About the Author

Scott Klein is an independent consultant with a passion for all things SQL Server, .NET, and XML. He is the author of *Professional SQL Server 2005 XML* and *Professional WCF Programming*. He also writes the biweekly feature article for the *SQL PASS Community Connector*, and has contributed articles to both Wrox (`www.Wrox.com`) and TopXML (`www.TopXML.com`). He frequently speaks to SQL Server and .NET user groups. Scott lives in Wellington, Florida, and when he is not sitting in front of a computer or spending time with his family, he can usually be found aboard his Yamaha at the local motocross track. He can be reached at `ScottKlein@SqlXml.com`.

Credits

Executive Editor
Bob Elliott

Development Editor
Maryann Steinhart

Technical Editor
Carl Daniel

Production Editor
Daniel Scribner

Copy Editor
Foxxe Editorial Services

Editorial Manager
Mary Beth Wakefield

Production Manager
Tim Tate

Vice President and Executive Group Publisher
Richard Swadley

Vice President and Executive Publisher
Joseph B. Wikert

Project Coordinator, Cover
Lynsey Stanford

Proofreader
Candace English, Nancy Riddiough,
Amy Rasmussen and
Jeremy Bagai

Indexer
Robert Swanson

Acknowledgments

First and foremost I'd like to thank Neil Salkind and everyone at Studio B for being who they are and for all that they do. They take care of all of the things I don't want to have to worry about and let me do what I like to do, which is working with the latest and greatest new technology. Without these people and their contributions, this book wouldn't be possible.

I'd like to give a huge thanks to the people at Wrox/Wiley for making this book happen. Maryann Steinhart, my development editor, was a delight to work with. Many, many thanks to Carl Daniel, the technical editor, for the time and energy he put into reviewing this book. His comments were invaluable.

Thanks to Jim Minatel, for accepting the book idea and letting me write it, and Bob Elliott for picking up where Jim left off after Jim went on to bigger and better things within Wrox. I appreciate your support.

As with my other books, having that "one person" who you could go to for whatever reason made life so much easier. Dave Remy, I cannot thank you enough! Your help was worth more than gold, and it sure made writing this book much easier.

A large dose of gratitude also goes out to Dinesh Kulkarni, Eric White, Erick Thompson, Lance Olson, Luca Bolognese, Mads Torgersen, Michael Blome, Ralf Lammel, Scott Guthrie, Luke Hoban, and Asad Khan. A thank you to each of you for letting me ask questions and providing excellent feedback.

It has been said that you are only as good as those with whom you associate. So enough cannot be said about the love and support of my family, for without them, this book, or anything else I do in life, would not be possible. My wonderful wife, Lynelle, who during these times is an anchor for this family, held the house together for the 8+ months I spent upstairs writing. And to my children, who were patient with their father knowing that they soon would get their dad back. I love you all. When did my eldest daughter turn old enough to start driving?

Contents

Acknowledgments **xiii**
Introduction **xxiii**

Part I: Introduction to Project LINQ

Chapter 1: Project LINQ **3**

LINQ Overview **7**
Standard Query Operators **10**
LINQ to XML Overview **12**
LINQ to SQL Overview **14**
Summary **16**

Chapter 2: A Look at Visual Studio 2008 **17**

Visual Studio 2008 **17**
Language-Specific LINQ Features **21**
Query Expressions 21
Implicitly Typed Variables 22
Anonymous Types 23
Initializers for Objects and Collections 23
Extension Methods 26
Lambda Expressions 28
Summary **30**

Chapter 3: LINQ Queries **31**

Introduction to LINQ Queries **31**
Data Source 32
Query Creation 33
Query Execution 33
Likened to SQL Syntax 36
Query Concepts 37
Var versus IEnumerable 40
Common Query Terms 41
IQueryable and IQueryable(Of T) Interfaces 42

Query Syntax versus Method Syntax **43**
Which Do You Use? 44
Using Query and Method Syntaxes **45**
Summary **51**

Chapter 4: LINQ Standard Query Operators **53**

Overview **53**
Standard Query Operators **54**
Projection Operators 55
Restriction Operator 57
Sorting Operators 57
Joining Operators 59
Grouping Operator 62
Concatenating Operator 63
Aggregating Operators 64
Set Operators 68
Generation Operators 71
Conversion Operators 73
Element Operators 77
Equality Operators 82
Quantifier Operators 83
Partitioning Operators 86
Putting Query Operators to Work **88**
Summary **92**

Part II: LINQ to XML

Chapter 5: Understanding LINQ to XML **95**

LINQ to XML Overview **95**
LINQ to XML Programming Fundamentals **96**
LINQ to XML Classes 96
XElement Class 98
XAttribute Class 102
XDocument Class 104
LINQ to XML Programming Concepts **107**
Working with Existing XML 107
Saving XML to LINQ to XML 109
Creating XML 110

Traversing XML 111
Manipulating XML 112
Working with Attributes 117
LINQ to XML versus Other XML Technologies 120
LINQ to XML versus DOM 120
LINQ to XML versus XmlReader 121
LINQ to XML versus XSLT 121
LINQ to XML versus MSXML 121
Summary 122

Chapter 6: Programming with LINQ to XML 123

Creating Trees 123
Creating Trees in C# 124
Creating Trees in Visual Basic 128
Populating Trees from Text 130
Querying XML Trees 132
Modifying and Reshaping XML Trees 137
Serializing XML Trees 139
Namespaces 141
Summary 143

Chapter 7: LINQ to XML and Other LINQ Data Models 145

SQL to XML 145
XML to SQL 149
Insert 150
Update 151
Summary 152

Chapter 8: Advanced LINQ to XML Programming Topics 153

LINQ to XML Functional Construction 153
LINQ to XML Annotations 158
LINQ to XML Axis 161
Ancestors 161
Descendants 163
AncestorsAndSelf 164
DescendantsAndSelf 165
ElementsAfterSelf and ElementsBeforeSelf 166
LINQ to XML Events 167
Changing 168
Changed 170

Streaming XML Documents **171**
Streaming Large XML Documents **176**
Summary **177**

Chapter 9: LINQ to XML and Visual Basic .NET **179**

Creating XML **179**
Overview of XML Literals 180
Expressions 182
Embedding Queries 184
Understanding Whitespace in Visual Basic XML Literals 184
Accessing XML **185**
Loading XML **188**
Manipulating XML Using the Parse Method **189**
LINQ to XML Visual Basic Example **191**
Summary **194**

Part III: LINQ to SQL

Chapter 10: LINQ to SQL Overview **199**

Understanding LINQ to SQL **200**
LINQ to SQL Object Model **201**
Attribute-Based Mapping **202**
Using the Database Attribute 202
Mapping Tables 203
Mapping Columns 203
Mapping Relationships 206
Mapping Stored Procedures 207
Mapping Functions 208
Using the Parameter Attribute 209
The Basics of Relational Data **209**
Primary Keys 210
Foreign Keys 212
Summary **215**

Chapter 11: LINQ to SQL Queries **217**

Query Concepts **217**
DataContext **219**

Strongly Typed DataContext **220**
Data Manipulation **221**
Insert 222
Update 224
Delete 225
Working with Objects **225**
Insert 225
Update 226
Delete 226
Stored Procedures and User-Defined Functions **227**
Mapping and Calling Stored Procedures 227
Mapping and Calling User-Defined Functions 240
Summary **244**

Chapter 12: Advanced Query Concepts **245**

Database Relationships **245**
Representing Relationships 245
Querying 250
Compiled Queries **251**
Remote versus Local Query Execution **251**
Remote Execution 252
Local Execution 252
Deferred versus Immediate Data Loading **252**
DataShape Class 254
Turning Off Deferred Loading 254
Composite Keys **255**
Read-Only Data **255**
Summary **256**

Chapter 13: More about Entity Classes **257**

Tracking Entity Changes **258**
Submitting Entity Changes **258**
Concurrent Changes and Concurrency Conflicts **263**
UpdateCheck 263
ConflictMode 264
ChangeConflictException 265
RefreshMode 265
Utilizing Transactions **267**
Summary **269**

Chapter 14: LINQ to DataSet **271**

Overview of LINQ to DataSet **272**
Creating a LINQ to DataSet Project **272**
Loading Data into a DataSet **273**
Using the DataAdapater 273
LINQ to DataSet Queries **275**
Querying a Single Table 275
Querying across Multiple Tables 277
Typed DataSets 278
Data Binding **279**
Comparing DataRows **281**
Summary **284**

Chapter 15: Advanced LINQ to SQL Topics **287**

Object Relational Designer **287**
Creating and Opening the O/R Designer 288
Creating/Configuring the DataContext 288
Creating Entity Classes for Tables/View Mapping 290
DataContext Mapping for Stored Procedures/Functions 292
Calling Stored Procedures to Save Data Using Entity Classes 293
Extending O/R Designer-Generated Code **294**
Pluralization of Classes in the O/R Designer **296**
SQL Metal **296**
External Mapping **299**
Multi-Tier Operations **302**
N-Tier Best Practices **303**
Optimistic Concurrency 303
Insertion/Deletion 304
N-Tier Examples 304
Designer Example **305**
Summary **310**

Appendixes

Appendix A: Case Study **313**

Appendix B: LINQ to Entities: The ADO.NET Entity Framework **329**

Overview **329**
Installing the ADO.NET Entity Framework **331**

ADO.NET Entity Framework Example **332**
Querying the Entity Data Model **340**
Working with Objects **341**
Entity Data Model Generator **342**

Appendix C: LINQ to XSD 345

LINQ to XSD Overview **345**
Installing LINQ to XSD **346**
LINQ to XSD Example **346**
Mapping Rules **354**
LINQ to XSD-Generated API Class Methods **354**
Load Method 355
Parse 355
Save 356
Clone 356
Default Values 357

Index **359**

Introduction

It has been three years and I'm still trying to get the word ''grok'' into everyone's mainstream vocabulary (see the introductions to my last two books), and one of the things that I am ''grokking'' is the new LINQ technology coming out of the Microsoft campus.

Microsoft is touting LINQ as a ''groundbreaking innovation'' that promises to ''revolutionize the way developers work with data.'' Like you, I was somewhat skeptical about these promises because similar comments have been funneled our way in the past, but these bold declarations would cause even the casual developer to stop and take notice.

Let me just say right here that the more I got into LINQ, the more excited I became (and the more guilty I felt about not believing the hype). And this isn't just any mere excitement; this is on par with a 10-year-old waking up Christmas morning to a pirate's share of loot under the Christmas tree.

Why? Because LINQ introduces queries (the concept of a query) as a first-class language construct in both C# and Visual Basic. No longer do you need to learn multiple technologies to query multiple data sources. It is a single query syntax for querying XML, SQL databases, ADO.NET DataSets, and other data sources.

LINQ simplifies how you will now write queries. If you use C# or Visual Basic, you will be able to start writing LINQ queries immediately because you know most of what you need. LINQ is a set of features built into Visual Studio 2008 that incorporates tremendous query capabilities directly into the language syntax of Visual Basic and C#. This provides the benefits of IntelliSense, compile-time type checking, and debugging support. How could life get any better?

Who This Book Is For

This book is for developers who want to learn about LINQ and how it can benefit and enhance their applications. Equally, this book is for those individuals who have spent at least a little time looking at LINQ, have done some experimental development with it, and want to delve deeper into the technology to see how LINQ can improve their applications.

A good understanding of Visual Studio and the C# language will be useful when reading this book and working with the examples, but it is not required. An understanding of SQL Server and T-SQL also would be useful but is not required.

What This Book Covers

Part I provides on overview of LINQ and of Visual Studio 2008, a look at many of the new and existing language-specific features that support LINQ, and a discussion of LINQ queries and the LINQ standard query operators.

- Chapter 1 provides an overview of LINQ and explains why there is a need for LINQ, and then takes a brief introductory look at the other LINQ providers.
- Chapter 2 affords a brief history of Visual Studio, and then takes a good look at Visual Studio 2008 and many of the .NET Framework language-specific features that will help you better understand LINQ.
- Chapter 3 examines LINQ queries, their overall concepts, and the syntax to use when writing LINQ queries.
- Chapter 4 provides a detailed discussion of the LINQ standard query operators.

Part II jumps right into LINQ to XML, providing an overview first and then showing you how to program with LINQ to XML with both C# and Visual Basic, and how to use LINQ to XML with other data models.

- Chapter 5 provides an overview of LINQ to XML, discusses many of the LINQ to XML concepts, and compares LINQ to XML with other XML technologies.
- Chapter 6 tackles many of the concepts, techniques, and programming fundamentals necessary to program with LINQ to XML.
- Chapter 7 compares LINQ to XML with the other LINQ data models such as LINQ to SQL.
- Chapter 8 explores some advanced LINQ to XML programming topics such as functional construction and working with events.
- Chapter 9 focuses solely on using LINQ to XML with Visual Basic .NET.

Part III focuses on LINQ to SQL, again providing an overview, and then tackling LINQ to SQL queries, advanced query concepts, LINQ to Entities, and LINQ to DataSets. It also introduces you to the visual tools provided by LINQ to automate many of the LINQ to SQL functions.

- Chapter 10 provides an overview of LINQ to SQL and its corresponding object model, as well as a discussion of attribute-based mapping and an overview of relational basics.
- Chapter 11 discusses LINQ to SQL queries and concepts, how to work with the `DataContext` class and entity objects, and how to manipulate data with LINQ to SQL.
- Chapter 12 explores concepts such as database relationships and LINQ query execution.
- Chapter 13 tackles many aspects of LINQ to SQL entities such as tracking changes and working with transactions.
- Chapter 14 focuses on using LINQ to DataSet to query the contents of an ADO.NET DataSet, and data binding with LINQ to DataSet.
- Chapter 15 discusses some advanced LINQ to SQL topics and tools such as multi-tier operations and the Object-Relational Designer.

Part IV, "Appendixes," provides a case study and a look at a couple of LINQ technologies that will be available post–Visual Studio 2008 but are sure to make an impact on the market: LINQ to XSD and LINQ to the ADO.NET Entity Framework.

- Appendix A walks you through building an application using LINQ and associated LINQ providers.

- Appendix B discusses the ADO.NET Entity Framework and associated objects as well as the Entity Data Model Generator tool.
- Appendix C discusses LINQ to XSD, a beta technology that allows you to work directly with XML in a typed manner.

What You Need to Use This Book

All of the examples in this book require the following:

- Visual Studio 2008 (Beta 2)
- .NET Framework 3.5 (Beta 2)
- LINQ to XSD Preview
- ADO.NET Entity Framework Beta 2
- ADO.NET Entity Framework Tools CTP
- SQL Server 2005 and the AdventureWorks sample database

Conventions

To help you get the most from the text and keep track of what's happening, a number of conventions are used throughout the book.

> **Boxes like this one hold important, not-to-be-forgotten information that is directly relevant to the surrounding text.**

Notes, tips, hints, tricks, and asides to the current discussion are offset and placed in italics like this.

As for styles in the text:

- New terms and important words are *highlighted* when we introduce them.
- Keyboard strokes look like this: Ctrl+A.
- Filenames, URLs, and code within the text are shown like this: `persistence.properties`.
- Code is presented in two different ways:

```
A monofont type with no highlighting is used for most code examples.
```

```
Gray highlighting to emphasize code that's particularly important in the present
context.
```

Source Code

As you work through the examples in this book, you may choose either to type in all the code manually or to use the source code files that accompany the book. All of the source code used in this book is available for downloading at www.wrox.com. Once at the site, simply locate the book's title (either by using the Search box or by using one of the title lists) and click the Download Code link on the book's detail page to obtain all the source code for the book.

Because many books have similar titles, you may find it easiest to search by ISBN; this book's ISBN is 978-0-470-04181-9.

Once you download the code, just decompress it with your favorite compression tool. Alternately, you can go to the main Wrox code download page at www.wrox.com/dynamic/books/download.aspx to see the code available for this book and all other Wrox books.

Errata

We make every effort to ensure that there are no errors in the text or in the code. However, no one is perfect, and mistakes do occur. If you find an error in one of our books, like a spelling mistake or faulty piece of code, we would be very grateful for your feedback. By sending in errata you may save another reader hours of frustration, and at the same time you will be helping us provide even higher quality information.

To find the errata page for this book, go to www.wrox.com and locate the title using the Search box or one of the title lists. Then, on the book details page, click the Book Errata link. On this page, you can view all errata that has been submitted for this book and posted by Wrox editors. A complete book list, including links to each book's errata, is also available at www.wrox.com/misc-pages/booklist.shtml.

If you don't spot "your" error on the Book Errata page, go to www.wrox.com/contact/techsupport.shtml and complete the form there to send us the error you have found. We'll check the information and, if appropriate, post a message to the book's errata page and fix the problem in subsequent editions of the book.

p2p.wrox.com

For author and peer discussion, join the P2P forums at p2p.wrox.com. The forums are a Web-based system for you to post messages relating to Wrox books and related technologies and interact with other readers and technology users. The forums offer a subscription feature to email you topics of interest of your choosing when new posts are made to the forums. Wrox authors, editors, other industry experts, and your fellow readers are present on these forums.

At http://p2p.wrox.com you will find a number of different forums that will help you not only as you read this book but also as you develop your own applications. To join the forums, just follow these steps:

1. Go to p2p.wrox.com and click the Register link.
2. Read the terms of use and click Agree.

3. Complete the required information to join as well as any optional information you want to provide, and click Submit.
4. You will receive an email with information describing how to verify your account and complete the joining process.

You can read messages in the forums without joining P2P but in order to post your own messages, you must join.

Once you join, you can post new messages and respond to messages other users post. You can read messages at any time on the Web. If you would like to have new messages from a particular forum emailed to you, click the Subscribe to this Forum icon by the forum name in the forum listing.

For more information about how to use the Wrox P2P, be sure to read the P2P FAQs for answers to questions about how the forum software works as well as many common questions specific to P2P and Wrox books. To read the FAQs, click the FAQ link on any P2P page.

Part I
Introduction to Project LINQ

Chapter 1: Project LINQ

Chapter 2: A Look at Visual Studio 2008

Chapter 3: LINQ Queries

Chapter 4: LINQ Standard Query Operators

1

Project LINQ

I often hear the questions, ''What is LINQ?,'' ''What does it do?,'' and ''Why do we need it?'' The answer to the first question (and subsequently the other two questions) is that the Language Integrated Query (LINQ) is a set of standard query operators that provide the underlying query architecture for the navigation, filtering, and execution operations of nearly every kind of data source, such as XML (using LINQ to XML, previously known as XLINQ), relational data (using LINQ to SQL, previously known as DLINQ), ADO.NET DataSets (using LINQ to DataSet), and in-memory collections.

The best way to begin understanding this wonderful new technology is to take a look at some history and background on how and why LINQ came to be.

Although the public first became aware of LINQ early in the fall of 2005, LINQ had been in development since early 2003. The overall LINQ goal was to make it easier for developers to interact with SQL and XML, primarily because there exists a disconnect between relational data (databases), XML, and the programming languages that communicate with (that is, work with) each of them.

Most developers understand the concept of object-oriented (OO) programming and its related technologies and features, such as classes, methods, and objects. Object-oriented programming has evolved tremendously over the past 10 years or so, but even in its current state, there's still a gap when using and integrating OO technology with information that is not natively defined or inherent to it.

For example, suppose that you want to execute a T-SQL query from within your C# application. It would look something like this:

```
private void Form1_Load(object sender, EventArgs e)
{
    string ConnectionString = @"Data Source=(local);
     Initial Catalog=AdventureWorks;UID=sa;PWD=yourpassword";
    using (SqlConnection conn = new SqlConnection(ConnectionString))
    {
        conn.Open();
        SqlCommand cmd = conn.CreateCommand();
```

```
        cmd.CommandType = CommandType.Text;
        cmd.CommandText = "SELECT LastName, FirstName FROM
Person.Contact";
        using (SqlDataReader rdr = cmd.ExecuteReader())
        {
            / / do something
        }
    }
}
```

If you wanted to use the same code to execute a stored procedure that takes one or more parameters, it might look like this:

```
private void Form1_Load(object sender, EventArgs e)
{
    string ConnectionString = @"Data Source=(local);
      Initial Catalog=AdventureWorks;UID=sa;PWD=yourpassword";
    using (SqlConnection conn = new SqlConnection(ConnectionString))
    {
        conn.Open();
        SqlCommand cmd = conn.CreateCommand();
        cmd.CommandType = CommandType.StoredProcedure;
        cmd.CommandText = "uspGetBillOfMaterials";
        cmd.Parameters.Add("@StartProductID", SqlDbType.Int).Value =
324;
        cmd.Parameters.Add("@CheckDate", SqlDbType.DateTime).Value =
"07/10/2000";
        using (SqlDataReader rdr = cmd.ExecuteReader())
        {
            // do something
        }
    }
}
```

While you and I have probably coded something like this many, many times, it isn't ''friendly'' on several levels. First, you are combining two languages into one. You have the language you are coding (in this case C#), plus you have the SQL language in quotation marks, which is not understood in the context of .NET. With the .NET language you have IntelliSense, but you don't get IntelliSense in the embedded SQL syntax.

More importantly, however, there is no compile-time type checking, which means you can't tell if something is broken until run time. Every line of code has to be QA'd just to see if it even begins to work.

Microsoft also packed a lot of features into the .NET Framework that enable developers to work with XML. The .NET Framework contains the `System.Xml` namespace and other supporting namespaces, such as `System.Xml.XPath`, `System.Xml.Xsl`, and `System.Xml.Schema`, which provide a plethora of functionality for working with XML. The namespaces contain many classes and methods that make up the XML .NET API architecture. The main classes are the `XmlDocument`, `XmlReader`, and `XmlWriter`.

To add to the complexity of working with different technologies, parsing an XML document isn't the easiest thing to do, either. Your tools of choice to work with XML are the Document Object Model (DOM),

XQuery, or Extensible Stylesheet Language Transformations (XSLT). For example, to read an XML document using existing technology, you would need to do something like the following:

```
XmlTextReader rdr = new XmlTextReader("C:\Employees.Xml");
while (rdr.Read())
{
    XmlNodeType nt = rdr.NodeType;
    Switch (nt)
    {
        case XmlNodeType.Element:
            break;

        case XmlNodeType.Attribute:
            break;
        case XmlNodeType.Comment:
            break;

        case XmlNodeType.Whitespace:
            break;

     }
}
```

That's a lot of code just to read an XML document (and it isn't even complete). Writing XML isn't any less confusing, as illustrated here:

```
XmlTextWriter wrt = new XmlTextWriter("C:\Employees.Xml");
wrt.WriteStartDocument;
wrt.WriteComment("This is an example");
wrt.WriteStartElement("Employees");
wrt.WriteStartElement("Employee");
wrt.WriteStartElement("FirstName");
wrt.WriteString("Scott");
wrt.WriteEndElement();
wrt.WriteEndElement();
wrt.WriteEndElement();
```

Visually, you don't know if this will work until you compile the project. Likewise, it is hard to see what the resulting XML will look like.

XML is great and its use continues to grow; you can expect it to be around for a long time. Yet, truth be told, XML is still hard to work with.

In dealing with these hurdles, Microsoft considered two paths. The first path would have required the company to build specific XML or relational data features into each programming language and run-time. That would be a major undertaking and an even bigger hassle to maintain. The second option was to add more general-purpose query capabilities into the .NET Framework—in other words, a framework of all-purpose querying facilities built into the .NET Framework that both C# and VB.NET could easily take advantage of.

Luckily, Microsoft chose the later option, creating a unified query experience across objects, XML, collections, and data. It accomplished that by taking query set operations, transforms, and constructs and bringing them to the surface, making them high-level concepts within the .NET Framework (for example, on the same level as objects and classes). So, you can now enjoy the benefits of a single declarative pattern that can be expressed in any .NET-based programming language.

The result of making these set operations, transforms, and constructs first-class operations is a set of methods called the standard query operators. These operators provide query capabilities that include sorting, filtering, aggregation, and projection over a large number of different data sources. The standard query operators are the focus of Chapter 4, ''LINQ Standard Query Operators.''

Think about it for a minute. A single set of query operators that work within any .NET-based programming language, enabling you to write a query against a database, XML, or an in-memory array using the same syntax? How cool is that? And you get the added benefit of IntelliSense and compile-time type checking! Somebody pinch me.

To illustrate this great technology, take a look at an example that queries the directories of your C drive and writes them to a list box:

```
DirectoryInfo di = new DirectoryInfo("C:\\");
var dirQuery =
    from dir in di.GetDirectories()
    orderby di.Name
    select new { dir.Name} ;

foreach (var item in dirQuery)
    listBox1.Items.Add(item.Name);
```

This code uses some of the standard query operators to create a LINQ query. In essence, Microsoft has taken the concept of query set operations and made them first-class operations within the .NET Framework.

Here's another example. This one queries all the system processes on your PC using the `Process` class, but notice that it uses the same query syntax as the previous example:

```
var procQuery =
    from proc in Process.GetProcesses()
    orderby p.WorkingSet64 descending
    select new { p.Id, p.ProcessName, p.WorkingSet64} ;

foreach (var item in procQuery)
    ListBox1.Items.Add(item.Id + "  " +
        item.ProcessName + "  " +
        item.WorkingSet64);
```

When you run this code, all the processes on your system will be listed in descending order by memory usage.

Simply put, LINQ enables you to query anything that implements the `IEnumerable<T>` interface. If you can loop through the contents using the `foreach` statement, then you can query it using LINQ.

The following example illustrates how LINQ works querying relational data, using a database as the source of data.

```
var conQuery =
    from c in contact
    where c.FirstName.StartsWith("S")
    orderby c.LastName
    select new { c.FirstName, c.LastName, c.EmailAddress} ;

foreach (var item in conQuery)
    ListBox1.Items.Add(item.FirstName + "   " +
        item.LastName + "   " +
        item.EmailAddress);
```

This previous example queries the `Person.Contact` table in the AdventureWorks database for all contacts whose first name starts with the letter "S".

The purpose of LINQ is to provide developers with the following benefits:

- A simplified way to write queries.
- Faster development time by removing run-time errors and catching errors at compile time.
- IntelliSense and debugging support for LINQ directly in the development language.
- Closing the gap between relational data and object-oriented development.
- A unified query syntax to use regardless of the source of data.

What is important to notice is the same syntax that you used to query the system processes was used query a SQL data source. Both of these topics will be discussed in much more detail, including how to easily connect and map to the source database.

So, with that primer, this chapter introduces the following topics:

- LINQ
- LINQ to XML
- LINQ to SQL

LINQ Overview

LINQ is a set of standard query operators that brings powerful query facilities right into the .NET Framework language such as C# and VB.NET. The LINQ framework brings together the capability of data access with the power of data manipulation. This section provides an overview of the capabilities of LINQ and the standard query operators, but Chapters 3 and 4, respectively, will discuss in great detail the LINQ query operators and language features that contribute to LINQ's direct, declarative style of queries.

The term Language Integrated Query signifies that the standard query facilities are architected directly into the developer's .NET-supported programming language of choice. These query facilities, known as the standard query operators, expose general-purpose query mechanisms that can be applied to many facets of information, such as in-memory constructs as well as information retrieved from external sources such as relational data or XML.

These operators provide the capability to express query operations directly and declaratively within any .NET-based programming language. What makes all of this possible is the simple application of the query operators to an `IEnumerable<T>` source of information.

Found in the `System.Collections.Generic` namespace, the `IEnumerable<T>` interface, a new addition in version 2.0 of the .NET Framework, supports a simple iteration over a collection of a given (specified) type. The `IEnumerable<T>` interface provides a slick mechanism to iterate through an arbitrary collection of strongly typed objects using the C# `foreach` statement or the Visual Basic `FOR EACH` statement. To utilize the `foreach` semantics, this interface must be implemented.

So the question is, what does this mean for LINQ? It means that a query that implements this interface can be a source for the corresponding query expression. You saw several examples of this at the beginning of this chapter, and the best way to understand the LINQ technology is to see it in action.

The following example utilizes LINQ, a few standard query operators, and the `IEnumerable<T>` interface to query and process the contents within a defined array:

```
private void ShowLINQ()
{
  string[] firstnames = { "Scott", "Steve", "Ken", "Joe", "John",
                     "Alex", "Chuck", "Sarah"};

  IEnumerable<string> val = from fn in firstnames
                        where fn.StartsWith("S")
                        select fn;

  foreach (string name in val)
  {
    Console.WriteLine(name);
  }
}
```

The first statement defines an array of first names. This should not be new to any developer. The next statement, however, is new. A local variable, `val` in this case, is initialized with a Language Integrated Query expression. The query expression contains two query operators taken from plethora of standard query operators. In this example, two operators are used: `where` and `select`. The local variable `val` exposes the `IEnumerable<string>` interface, which provides the capability to iterate through the collection. The results are actually created as you start to iterate through them via the `foreach` statement.

From here, the query can be modified to add sorting or additional filtering as well as many other options, but that will be expanded on in later chapters. For now, suffice it to say that via LINQ you can query various source data types, such as XML and relational data, through a standard and consistent query model and related query operators.

To illustrate this, let's modify the directory example from earlier in this chapter. One of the great things about LINQ is that it enables you easily to "map" object-oriented objects within your .NET programming language to a database and the objects within a relational database. That means you can access those relational objects in a strongly typed, object-oriented manner.

To do this, a mapping to the database needs to be made, and that is accomplished by creating and declaring two classes. Those classes map the relational objects into the object-oriented world. The first class maps the actual database:

```
 [Database(Name="AdventureWorks")]
public class AdventureWorks : DataContext
{
    public AdventureWorks(string connection) : base(connection) {}
    public Table<DirectoryInformation> DirectoryInformation;
}
```

The second class maps the table and columns of the table you want to access:

```
 [Table(Name="DirectoryInformation")]
public class DirectoryInformation
{
    [Column(DbType="varchar(50)")]
    public string DirectoryName;

    [Column(DbType = "varchar(255)")]
    public string DirectoryDescription;
}
```

The class name maps to the table in the database you want to access, and the columns are mapped by adding metadata to a couple of variables.

This example is just to whet your appetite. There's not a lot of explanation here because there are more than a handful of chapters that discuss object mapping and querying in much greater detail.

Once the mapping is complete, the data can be queried. And not just queried, but queried using strongly typed syntax.

The first line of the following code accesses the database as an object, creating a new instance of the class previously defined, a strongly typed connection. Once you have the connection, you can access the table and data in a strongly typed fashion, as shown in the second and third lines. Notice that the columns in the table are accessed via dot notation directly in C#.

```
AdventureWorks db = new AdventureWorks("Integrated Security=sspi");

foreach (var item in db.DirectoryInformation)
    listBox1.Items.Add(item.DirectoryName + "   " +
item.DirectoryDescription);
```

Executing this code returns the data from the `DirectoryInformation` table and lists both the directory name and description in a list box.

To make it more interesting, take the directory example from the beginning of the chapter and modify it to join to this query. You'll recall that the code in the earlier example simply queried the `DirectoryInfo` class to return the directories on your local C drive. Combining it with this query, you join the `Name` property of the `DirectoryInfo` class to the `DirectoryName` column from the `DirectoryInformation` table to return the `DirectoryDescription` information from the table. Just add the following highlighted code to the earlier query:

```
DirectoryInfo di = new DirectoryInfo("C:\\");

var query =
    from dir in di.GetDirectories()
    orderby di.Name
    select new
    {
        dir.Name,
        DirectoryDescription = (
        from d in db.DirectoryInformation
        where d.DirectoryName == di.Name
        select d.DirectoryDescription).FirstOrDefault()
   };

foreach (var item in query)
    listBox1.Items.Add(item.Name + "  " + item.DirectoryDescription);
}
```

To run this example, you first need to create a table in a database. The example used the AdventureWorks database and the following code to create the table:

```
CREATE TABLE [dbo].[DirectoryInformation](
    [DirectoryName] [varchar](50) NULL,
    [DirectoryDescription] [varchar](255) NULL
) ON PRIMARY

GO
```

You can use the following `INSERT` statement to add data to the `DirectoryInformation` table:

```
INSERT INTO DirectoryInformation (DirectoryName, DirectoryDescription)
    VALUES ('Windows', 'My Windows Directory')
GO
```

Before continuing, think about the amount of code you would have had to write to accomplish the same type of query in pre-LINQ technology. In the space of about two dozen lines, you were able to access data, query that data, and loop through that data simply and efficiently. In other technologies, you would have had to create a connection to the database, create an instance of a `SqlCommand` object and any other objects needed to execute a query, and write T-SQL code in your .NET code enclosed in quotation marks And that's not to mention all the work that has to be done once you get the data back—casting to the appropriate data types, and so on.

The good news is that LINQ does all of that for you. Sweet! And we haven't even covered XML yet.

Standard Query Operators

The LINQ standard query operators make up an API that provides the means of querying various data sources, such as arrays, collections, and even XML and relational data. They are a set of methods that are implemented by each specific LINQ provider (LINQ to SQL, LINQ to XML, LINQ to Objects, and so on). The operators form a LINQ query pattern that operates on a sequence (an object that implements the `IEnumerable<T>` or `IQueryable<T>` interface).

There are two sets of standard query operators—one operates on objects of the `IEnumerable<T>` type and the other operates on objects of the `IQueryable<T>` type. The operators are made up of methods that are static members of the `Enumerable` and `Queryable` classes, allowing them to be called using static method syntax of instance method syntax. You will learn all about this in Chapter 4.

The standard query operators can be categorized by their operation "type." For example, there are aggregate, projection, ordering, and grouping operators, among others. Take a look again at one of the examples used earlier in the chapter (repeated here for your convenience):

```
private void ShowLINQ()
{
  string [] firstnames = { "Scott", "Steve", "Ken", "Joe", "John",
                       "Alex", "Chuck", "Sarah"};

  IEnumerable<string> val = from fn in firstnames
                        where fn.StartsWith("S")
                        select fn;

  foreach (string name in val)
  {
    Console.WriteLine(name);
  }
}
```

The actual LINQ query is the middle part:

```
val = from fn in firstnames
  where fn.StartsWith("S")
  select fn;
```

In this example, several query operators are utilized from different operation types. The `select` query operator falls into the category of projection operators, and performs a projection over a sequence, an object that implements the `IEnumerable<T>` for a given type. In this case, the `select` operator enumerates the source sequence of first names.

```
select fn;
```

The `where` query operator is of the restriction operator type—in fact, it is the only operator of that type. Just like T-SQL, the LINQ `where` operator filters a sequence. In the preceding example, it filters the sequence by limiting the results returned to only those whose name begins with the letter *S*.

```
where fn.StartsWith("S")
```

If you are trying this example out yourself, create a new Windows Forms project and place a list box on the form. In the `Load` event of the form, place the following code:

```
string [] firstnames = { "Scott", "Steve", "Ken", "Joe", "John",
                     "Alex", "Chuck", "Sarah"};
```

```
IEnumerable<string> val = from fn in firstnames
                          where fn.StartsWith("S")
                          select fn;

foreach (string name in val)
{
  listbox1.Items.Add(name);
}
```

Press F5 to run the app. When the form loads and is displayed, the list box should be populated with the names of Scott, Steve, and Sarah. Now try changing the `where` clause, change the capital *S* to a lowercase *s* and rerun the app. Do you get results? Why not? If you haven't figured out why, Chapter 3, "LINQ queries," will explain it.

Chapters 3 and 4 go deeper into LINQ and the standard query operators, so don't worry about understanding everything there is to know about LINQ just yet. This section was simply to whet your appetite. The following sections discuss LINQ to XML, which uses LINQ to query XML data, and LINQ to SQL, which uses LINQ to query relational data.

LINQ to XML Overview

LINQ to XML, or XLINQ, is the XML integration of the Language Integrated Query. LINQ to XML utilizes the standard query operators to provide the ability to query XML data. Also at your disposal are operators that provide functionality akin to XPath, letting you navigate up and down and navigate XML tree nodes such as descendants and siblings seamlessly and efficiently.

If you have ever used, and disliked, the DOM, you will love LINQ to XML. The great thing about LINQ to XML is that it provides a small-footprint, in-memory version of the XML document that you are querying. LINQ to XML utilizes the XML features of the `System.Xml` namespace, specifically the reader and writer functionality exposed by the `System.Xml` namespace.

LINQ to XML exposes two classes that help LINQ integrate with XML: `XElement` and `XAttribute`. The `XElement` class represents an XML element and is used in LINQ to XML to create XML element nodes or even to filter out the data you really care about. `XElement` ties itself to the standard query operators by enabling you to write queries against non-XML sources and even persist that data to other sources.

The `XAttribute` class is a name/value pair associated with an XML element. Each `XElement` contains a list of attributes for that element, and the `XAttribute` class represents an XML attribute. Within LINQ, both the `XElement` and `XAttribute` types support standard syntax construction, meaning that developers can construct XML and XML expressions using the syntax that they already know.

The following example uses the `XElement` to construct a simple XML document. The first `XElement` defines the outer node while the two inner `XElement` parameters define the two inner nodes of `FirstName` and `LastName`.

```
var x = new XElement("Employee",
            new XElement("FirstName", "Scott"),
            new XElement("LastName","Klein"));

var s - x.ToString();
```

Here are the results of this code:

```
<Employee>
  <FirstName>Scott</FirstName>
  <LastName>Klein</LastName>
</Employee>
```

You'll notice the use of `var` in the previous example. The `var` keyword tells the compiler to infer the type of the variable from the expression on the right side of the statement. The `var` keyword will be discussed in detail in Chapter 2, ''A Look at Visual Studio 2008''.

Also notice in the previous example how much easier the code is to read. The code actually follows the structure of an XML document, so you can see what the resulting XML document will look like.

The next example uses the `XAttribute` type to add an attribute to the XML:

```
var x = new XElement("Employee",
            new XAttribute("EmployeeID", "15"),
            new XElement("FirstName", "Scott"),
            new XElement("LastName","Klein"));

var s - x.ToString();
```

And here are the results from it:

```
<Employee Employee="15">
  <FirstName>Scott</FirstName>
  <LastName>Klein</LastName>
</Employee>
```

While the capability to easily define the contents of the XML is cool, the real power comes from the ability to pass an argument that is not user-defined but in reality comes from an outside source, such as a query, which can be enumerated and turned into XML via the standard query operators. For example, the following takes the array of names from the first example and uses that as the source of the query for which to construct XML:

```
string [] firstnames = { "Scott", "Steve", "Ken", "Joe", "John",
                             "Alex", "Chuck", "Sarah"};

var r = new XElement("Friends",
          from fn in firstnames
          where fn.StartsWith("S")
          select new XElement("Name", fn))
textbox1.Text = rToString();
```

Here are the results from this code:

```
<Friends>
  <Name>Scott</Name>
  <Name>Steve</Name>
  <Name>Sarah</Name>
</Friends>
```

This isn't to say that I only have friends whose first names begin with the letter *S*, but you get the idea. This query returns a sequence of `XElements` containing the names of those whose first name begins with the letter *S*. The data comes not from a self-generated XML document but an outside source, in this case the array of first names. However, the data could just as easily come from a relational database or even another XML document.

What `XElement` enables you to do is query non-XML sources and produce XML results via the utilization of the `XElements` in the body of the `select` clause, as shown earlier. Gnarly.

The object of these simple examples is to illustrate the basic concepts of LINQ to XML and the great power, flexibility, and ease with which XML can be manipulated. Note that the same standard query operators were used to generate the XML document in this example as in the first one. Nothing had to be changed in the query really, other than using the types to help integrate LINQ with XML to build the resulting XML. Yet the query operators remained the same, as did the overall syntax of the query expression. This way is much better than trying to figure out XQuery or XPath, working with the DOM or even XSLT. Chapters 10 through 13 cover LINQ to XML in much greater detail.

LINQ to SQL Overview

LINQ to SQL, or DLINQ, is another component in the LINQ technology "utility belt." It provides a mechanism for managing relational data via a run-time infrastructure. The great thing about this is that LINQ still keeps its strong points, such as the ability to query. This is accomplished by translating the Language Integrated Query into SQL syntax for execution on the database server. Once the query has been executed, the tabular results are handed back to the client in the form of objects that you as a developer have defined.

If you have been following the LINQ talk, you already know that LINQ to SQL is the next version of ADO.NET. This is great news, and by the time you are done with this section and the section on LINQ to SQL later in the book, you will surely know why. LINQ takes advantage of the information produced by the SQL schema and integrates this information directly into the CLR (Common Language Runtime) metadata. Because of this integration, the definitions of the SQL tables and views are compiled into CLR types, making them directly accessible from within your programming language.

For example, the following defines a simple schema based on the `Person.Contact` table from the AdventureWorks database:

```
[Table(Name="Person.Contact")]
public class Contact
{
  [Column(DBType = "nvarchar(50) not null")]
  public string FirstName;
  [Column(DBType = "nvarchar(50) not null")]
  public string LastName;

  [Column(DBType = "nvarchar(50) not null")]
  public string EmailAddress;

}
```

Once this schema is defined, a query can be issued. This is where LINQ comes in. Using the standard query operators, LINQ translates the query from its original query expression form into a SQL query for execution on the server:

```
private void button5_Click(object sender, EventArgs e)
{
  DataContext context = new DataContext("Initial
Catalog=AdventureWorks;Integrated
    Security=sspi");

  Table<Contact> contact = context.GetTable<Contact>();

  var query =
      from c in contact
      select new { c.FirstName, c.LastName, c.EmailAddress} ;

  foreach (var item in query)
  listBox1.Items.Add(item.FirstName + " " + item.LastName + " " +
    item.EmailAddress);

}
```

Following are partial results from the query:

```
gustavo Achong gustavo0@adventure-works.com
catherine0@adventure-works.com
kim2@adventure-works.com
humberto0@adventure-works.com
pilar1@adventure-works.com
frances0@adventure-works.com
margaret0@adventure-works.com
carla0@adventure-works.com
jay1@adventure-works.com
```

Obviously there is much more to LINQ to SQL, but the examples here illustrate what it can do and the basic features and fundamental concepts of LINQ to SQL.

If you were to query this table via SQL Query Analyzer or SQL Server Management Studio, you'd know that the `Person.Contact` table in the AdventureWorks database is 28 rows shy of 20,000, so the preceding list is only the first nine, but you get the idea. How would you filter this query to return only a specific few rows?

Typically I like to wait until the third or fourth chapter to start handing out ''homework assignments,'' but with the background presented in this chapter you should be able to figure this out quite easily. The `Person.Contact` table has some additional columns that you can use to filter the results. For example, it has a column named `Title`, which contains values such as ''Mr.'' and ''Ms.'' It also has a column named `EmailPromotion`, an `int` datatype with values of `0` through `2`.

Your exercise for this chapter is to filter the query on either the `Title` column or the `EmailPromotion` column, using a standard query operator, so that the results returned are much less that 20,000. FYI if you are going to use the `Title` column: some of values of the column are null, so don't query where `Title` is null.

The goal of LINQ to SQL and its related tools is to drastically reduce the work of the database developer. Chapters 9–13 will discuss LINQ to SQL in much more depth.

Summary

This chapter introduced you to the LINQ project, a set of .NET Framework extensions that extend the C# and Visual Basic .NET programming languages with a native query language syntax that provides standard query, set and manipulation operations.

This chapter began by discussing LINQ and the set of standard query operators that is a combination of SQL query capabilities with the power and flexibility of data manipulation. From there, the topics of LINQ to XML and LINQ to SQL were discussed, which take the power and flexibility of LINQ and apply it to the querying of relational data and XML documents using the same syntax provided by LINQ.

With this foundation, the next chapter will take a look at the next release of Visual Studio by looking at the specific features LINQ supports for Visual Basic 9.0 and C#.

2

A Look at Visual Studio 2008

Many of the new language features and enhancements in Visual Studio 2008—both in Visual C# and Visual Basic .NET—make many of the LINQ features possible and enable you to take advantage of some of the LINQ capabilities.

Included with the new Visual Studio release are a number of designers that can help developers visually create many aspects of their SQL entity classes and associations. For example, the Object Relational Designer (O/R Designer) provides a visual interface for creating and designing LINQ to SQL entity classes and associations of database objects. The O/R Designer is discussed in Chapter 15, ''Advanced LINQ to SQL topics.''

Visual Studio 2008 also comes with the DataSet Designer, a visual tool used for creating and manipulating typed DataSets and the associated items of which the datasets are made, providing a visual image of the objects within the DataSets.

LINQ will be released in the next version of Visual Studio and the .NET Framework, currently slated for version 3.5. Because much of the LINQ functionality is based on the new features of the .NET Framework, this chapter explores those features and enhancements that help support LINQ and provide LINQ with the foundation it needs from a language perspective. It looks at the new language-specific features in both C# and Visual Basic .NET.

Visual Studio 2008

Visual Studio has come a long way since its inception in 1997. Visual Studio 97 hit the street with the goals of enabling developers to share and see large projects through a complete development cycle regardless of the different languages and deployment schemes.

That was followed up by Visual Studio 6.0 with its integrated development environment and built-in data designers for architecting large-scale and multi-tier applications, with the goals of supporting distributed and heterogeneous environments and architectures.

Early 2002 saw the launch of the .NET Framework 1.0 and Visual Studio .NET, built on the foundation of XML. Visual Studio .NET was a breath of fresh air with its tool integration, multiple languages, and handful of services and tools all housed within a single development environment, all for the purpose of building and delivering reliable, secure applications in distributed environments. One of the goals with this release was to enable integration with legacy applications so that developers could embrace new tasks while continuing to work and support old projects. With its emphasis on XML, Visual Studio .NET focused extremely hard on gathering and massaging data from a variety of sources independent of the platform.

Within 12 short months developers saw the release of Visual Studio .NET 2003 and the .NET Framework 1.1. This release included support for more data sources and new Internet protocols and an improved framework for architecting and delivering mission-critical systems. New and improved features supporting a myriad of access devices were also included to help solidify a "one-stop-shop" environment for building large-scale applications.

Microsoft then went to work on the next version of Visual Studio, which was released to the public in the fall of 2005. This release included the .NET Framework 2.0, which, together with Visual Studio 2005, focused on developer productivity and flexibility by including tools and mechanisms for building web, Windows, mobile, and Office applications faster and more efficiently than before.

Late in 2006 the .NET Framework 3.0 was released, which boasted a new managed code programming model for Windows. The .NET Framework 3.0 combined the strength of the .NET Framework 2.0 with four new technologies:

- **WPF (Windows Presentation Foundation)**—New technology for building rich content, "Windows Vista"–type user interfaces, and experiences combining application UI and media content.
- **WCF (Windows Communication Foundation)**—New technology for building and deploying reliable, secure, and interoperable connected systems across distributed systems and environments.
- **WF (Windows Workflow Foundation)**—A programming engine for building workflow-enabled applications.
- **WCS (Windows CardSpace)**—Microsoft's technology for managing digital identities.

Today, Visual Studio 2008 focuses on providing developers with a rich experience for Windows Vista, the web, and Office 2008, while continuing to improve its development languages and innovations. Visual Studio 2008 contains a number of new features, including C# and Visual Basic .NET language features, improved data features such as multi-tier support for typed datasets and hierarchical update capabilities, and a web application project model.

However, the most exciting new feature of Visual Studio 2008 (in my opinion) is LINQ, Microsoft's new Language Integrated Query, which extends powerful query capabilities into your favorite .NET programming language.

When you first start Visual Studio 2008 (see Figure 2-1), it looks much like the previous versions of Visual Studio.

On the surface, this might not be very impressive, but did previous versions of Visual Studio let you pick which version of the .NET Framework you wanted to create your projects with? No!

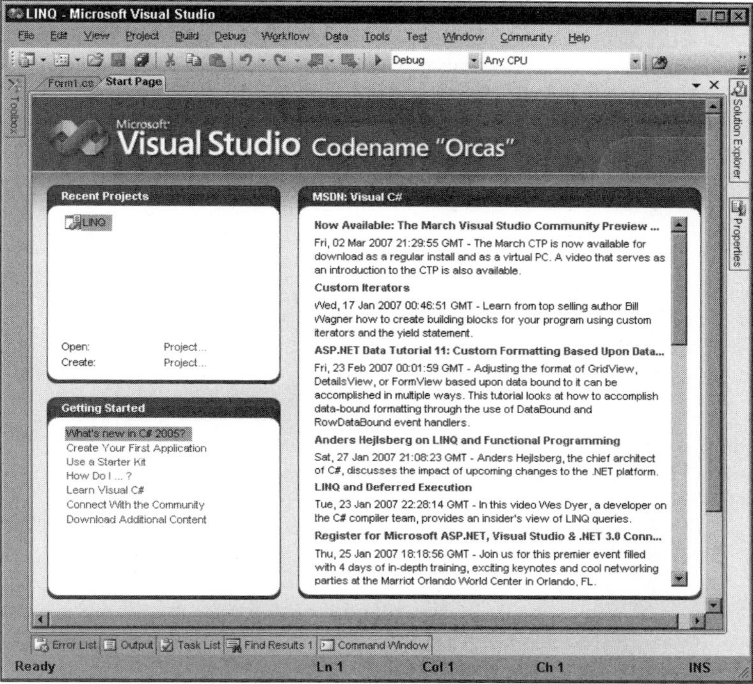

Figure 2-1

When you create a project in the new Visual Studio, you will notice something different in the New Project dialog box (see Figure 2-2), the addition of a "version" button in the top right.

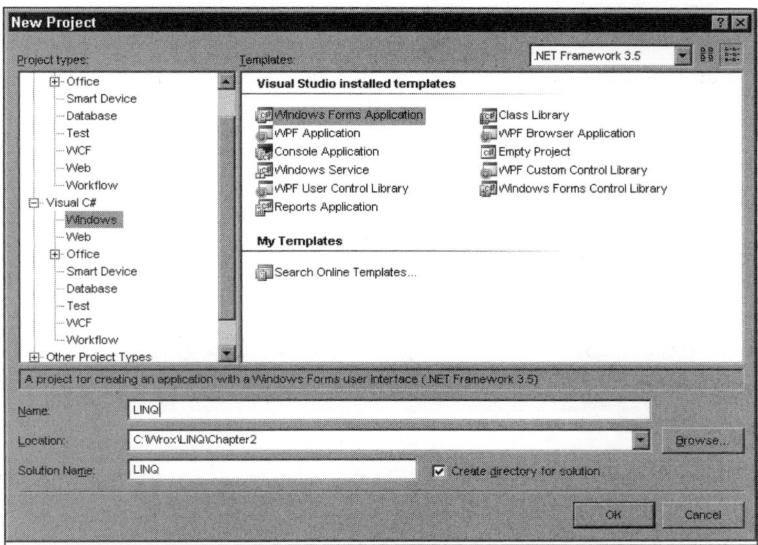

Figure 2-2

This button displays a small context menu that lets you select which version of the .NET Framework you want to create your projects with, as shown in Figure 2-3. How cool is that! As you know, it is possible to have multiple versions of the .NET Framework on your computer, and because different functionality is provided within Visual Studio per the version of the .NET Framework, Microsoft decided it would be extremely helpful to provide a single environment with which to create your applications.

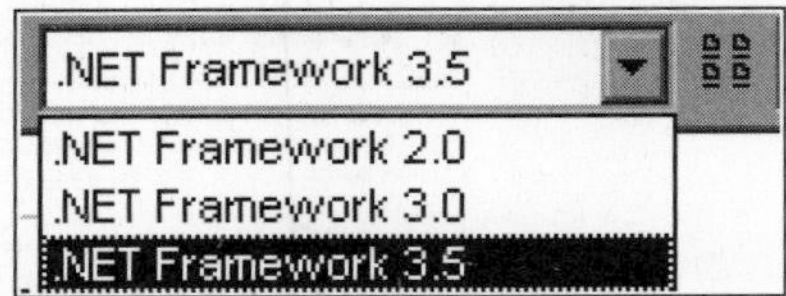

Figure 2-3

Visual Studio 2008 targets .NET 2.0 and later, which means that you won't have to open an instance of Visual Studio 2005 to work with Visual Studio 2005 projects and another instance of Visual Studio 2008 to work with Visual Studio 2008 projects. You can use Visual Studio 2008 to work with both.

To work with .NET 1.1 applications, you will still need to use Visual Studio 2003, since it was targeted for version 1.1 of the .NET Framework.

What is really nice about Visual Studio 2008 is that the appropriate templates change based on the version of the .NET Framework you select. Figure 2-4 shows the templates listed when the .NET Framework 2.0 is selected.

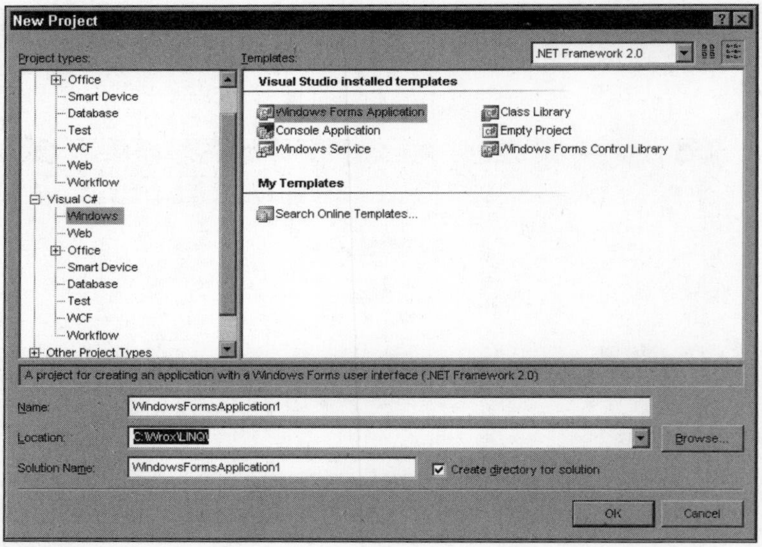

Figure 2-4

As a help, the New Project dialog shows the project description and .NET Framework version directly above the project name box and the list of Project types and Templates. For example, Figure 2-4 lists templates for the .NET Framework 2.0 and lets you know that the Windows Forms Control Library for the .NET Framework 2.0 is selected. Compare that to Figure 2-2, which shows the Windows Forms Application project template selected for the .NET Framework 3.5. Very helpful.

This chapter won't discuss installing Visual Studio, but if you would like to download it and go through the installation yourself, the latest Community Technology Preview (CTP) build can be found at the following location:

```
http://msdn2.microsoft.com/en-us/vstudio/aa700831.aspx
```

Now let's take a look at the new language specific features found in Visual Studio 2008.

Language-Specific LINQ Features

As stated previously, Visual Studio 2008 supports the Language Integrated Query, which is the capability for C# and Visual Basic .NET to support query syntax and supported constructs directly in the programming language. There are many benefits to this, including compile-time checking, elimination of syntax errors, and type safety.

The new language constructs found in both the C# and Visual Basic .NET languages make a lot of the LINQ functionality possible. Therefore, before this book really digs into the LINQ query language and standard query operators, the rest of this chapter discusses these new language features to better help you understand LINQ.

Query Expressions

Query expressions are the heart and soul of the LINQ technology. They are what describe the operations on the data source. Chapter 3, "LINQ Queries," tackles LINQ query expressions in great detail, so this section provides an overview of query expressions so that you can understand the full breadth in the next chapter.

Query expressions are the code that you write, using the standard query operators, to access, sort, and filter data, regardless of where the data comes from. They are written using a declarative query syntax, which was introduced in C# 3.0.

The data can come from an in-memory source, a relational database, or XML, as you saw in the examples in Chapter 1, "Project LINQ." If you've worked with SQL syntax, query expressions should look familiar to you simply because declarative syntax looks very reminiscent of SQL syntax.

From the example in Chapter 1, look at the following highlighted query expression:

```
DataContext context =
  new DataContext("Initial Catalog=AdventureWorks;Integrated Security=sspi");

Table<Contact> contact = context.GetTable<Contact>();

var query =
    from c in contact
    select new { c.FirstName, c.LastName, c.EmailAddress} ;
```

Query expressions must follow a specific format for specific reasons. Those reasons are explained in detail in Chapter 3; for now, suffice it to say that a query expression must begin with a `from` clause and end with either a `select` clause or a `groupby` clause.

C#

In C#, a query expression is written as follows:

```
IEnumerable<string> val = from fn in firstnames
                          where fn.StartsWith("S")
                          select fn;
```

In this example, the query expression starts with the `from` clause informing the query expression where to retrieve its data. It includes a filter expression (the `where` clause), and ends with a `select` clause, which projects (selects) the data gathered in the `from` clause.

Visual Basic

The following shows the previous example in Visual Basic .NET syntax:

```
Dim val As IEnumerable(Of String) = From fn in firstname _
                                    Where fn.StartsWith("S") _
                                    Select fn
```

Implicitly Typed Variables

Finally! Where has this been, I have to ask! Until now, you have had to explicitly specify a type when declaring and initializing a variable. No more. Now you can infer the type assignment by simply using the `var` keyword, as shown in the following examples.

C#

In C#, variables are implicitly typed as follows:

```
var firstname = "Scott";
var age = 28; //I wish!
var startdate = DateTime.Today;
```

So, why is this important, you ask? Because any variables declared as `var` are equally strongly typed as their explicitly declared counterparts. And, even more importantly, this includes LINQ query expressions. Stay tuned.

Visual Basic

Visual Basic also lets you implicitly type variables, but it does this by inferring the type of the variable from the type of the initialization expression. This is called type inference, which lets Visual Basic 2008 determine the data type of variables that are declared without the `As` clause.

The following shows the previous example in Visual Basic .NET syntax:

```
Dim firstname = "Scott"
Dim age = 28
Dim startdate = DateTime.Today
```

Anonymous Types

Anonymous types, class types made up of one or more public properties, provide a handy way to temporarily group sets in a query result, eliminating the need to create a named type for each set. Anonymous types are built as you go, built by the compiler with the typed name available only to the compiler.

In LINQ, anonymous types come in handy in the `select` clause of a query expression, returning a subset of properties from each element in the query sequence. They are created via the `new` operator with an object initializer.

C#

This query expression uses the `new` operator along with an object initializer to initialize a new type containing only three properties (`FirstName`, `LastName`, and `EmailAddress`) from the `Contact` object.

```
from c in Contact
select new { c.FirstName, c.LastName, c.EmailAddress};
```

Anonymous types derive directly from the `Object` class as reference types. A compiler assigns the anonymous type a name, and it is not available at the source code level. Anonymous types are no different from any other type as far as the CLR (Common Language Runtime) is concerned.

This might seem a little confusing, but it will all be cleared up when LINQ and query expressions are discussed in detail in Chapter 3.

Visual Basic

Anonymous types, new to Visual Basic for 2008, let you create objects without needing to write a class definition for the data type. In Visual Basic 2008, the compiler generates the class for you. A LINQ query expression uses anonymous types to join or combine columns from a query.

The great thing about anonymous types is that they let you write queries that return any number of columns in any order. The compiler has the responsibility of creating the data types that correspond to the specified properties (columns).

Here's the previous anonymous type example in Visual Basic .NET syntax:

```
From c In contact Select c.FirstName, c.LastName, c.EmailAddress
```

Initializers for Objects and Collections

Initializers for objects and collections provide the capability to initialize objects and collections without the need to explicitly call a constructor. You can use initializers to assign values to an object's properties and fields when the object is created without needing to invoke a constructor first.

Object initializers can be utilized in various forms, including with anonymous types, named types, and nullable types. Here is where LINQ comes into play because LINQ utilizes anonymous types greatly for the simple reason that anonymous types can only be initialized with an object initializer. Why does this come in handy? Because query expressions can manipulate objects of a sequence into an object of a different shape and value.

C#

The following example, taken from Chapter 1, defines a simple schema based on the `Person.Contact` table, consisting of five fields, from the AdventureWorks database.

```
[Table(Name="Person.Contact")]
public class Contact
{
  [Column(DBType = "nvarchar(8) not null")]
  public string Title;

  [Column(DBType = "nvarchar(50) not null")]
  public string FirstName;

  [Column(DBType = "nvarchar(50) not null")]
  public string MiddleName;

  [Column(DBType = "nvarchar(50) not null")]
  public string LastName;

  [Column(DBType = "nvarchar(50) not null")]
  public string EmailAddress;

}
```

With the schema defined, a query can be issued.

```
private void button1_Click(object sender, EventArgs e)
{
  DataContext context = new DataContext("Initial Catalog=AdventureWorks;Integrated
    Security=sspi");

  Table<Contact> contact = context.GetTable<Contact>();

  var query =
      from c in contact
      select new { c.FirstName, c.LastName, c.EmailAddress} ;

  foreach (var item in query)
  listBox1.Items.Add(item.FirstName + " " + item.LastName + " " +
    item.EmailAddress);

}
```

What you want to notice is that although the object (`c`) contains five fields, the sequence being returned contains only three fields: `FirstName`, `LastName`, and `EmailAddress`. That is the strength of anonymous types, in that you can return a portion of the information in the object.

You can also rename a field in the sequence when using anonymous types. Here's how:

```
var query =
    from c in contact
    select new { c.FirstName, c.LastName, Email = c.EmailAddress} ;
```

```
foreach (var item in query)
   listBox1.Items.Add(item.FirstName + " " + item.LastName + " " +
    item.Email);
```

Chapter 3 discusses this in more detail.

Visual Basic

Object initializers in Visual Basic work the same way as C# initializers. They provide the ability to specify properties for a complex object by using a single expression, and create instances of named and anonymous types.

The following shows the previous anonymous type example in Visual Basic .NET syntax:

```
<Table(Name:="Person.Contact")> _
Public Class Contact

  <Column(DbType:="nvarchar(8) not null")> _
  Public Title As String

  <Column(DbType:="nvarchar(50) not null")> _
  Public FirstName As String

  <Column(DbType:="nvarchar(50) not null")> _
  Public MiddleName As String

  <Column(DbType:="nvarchar(50) not null")> _
  Public LastName As String

  <Column(DbType:="nvarchar(50) not null")> _
  Public EmailAddress As String

End Class

Private Sub Button2_Click(ByVal sender As System.Object, ByVal e As System.EventArgs)
   Handles Button2.Click

  Dim context As DataContext = New DataContext("Initial
    Catalog=AdventureWorks;Integrated Security=sspi")

  Dim contact As Table(Of Contact) = context.GetTable(Of Contact)()

  Dim query = From c In contact Select c.FirstName, c.LastName, Email =
    c.EmailAddress

  For Each item In query
    ListBox1.Items.Add(item.FirstName & " " & item.LastName & " " & item.Email)
  Next item

End Sub
```

You need to pay close attention to object initializers of named and anonymous types. Their declarations look nearly the same, but they are indeed different and they have different effects. For example, the following illustrates how to initialize a named instance:

```
Dim cont = new Contact with {.FirstName = "Scott"}
```

However, the initializer for an anonymous type cannot include a class name because it has no usable name, as illustrated here:

```
Dim cont = New With {.FirstName = "Scott"}
```

These two declarations do not produce the same result. The first example has a `Contact` class that contains a `FirstName` property that must already exist, and the declaration takes the step of creating an instance of the `Contact` class. In the anonymous example, the compiler defines a new class containing a string property called `FirstName`.

Extension Methods

Extension methods are new to C# 3.0. They provide the capability to extend existing types by adding new methods with no modifications necessary to the type. Calling methods from objects of the extended type within an application using instance method syntax is known as "extending" methods. Extension methods are not instance members on the type.

The key point to remember is that extension methods, defined as static methods, are in scope only when the namespace is explicitly imported into your application source code via the `using` directive. Even though extension methods are defined as static methods, they are still called using instance syntax.

LINQ contains the most common extension methods, more appropriately known as the *standard query operators*. The standard query operators extend the `IEnumerable<T>` and `IQueryable<T>` types.

Extension methods are invoked in your code by using instance method syntax. The intermediate language (IL) generated by the compiler then translates your code into a call on the static method.

C#

To illustrate extension methods, open Visual Studio 2008 and create a new C# Windows project. On Form1, which is shown by default, place a button and a text box. View the code behind the form and add the following to the end of the existing form code:

```
namespace MyExtensionMethods
{
    public static class MyExtensions
    {
        public static int GetWordCount(this System.String mystring)
        {
            return mystring.Split(null).Length;
        }
    }
}
```

This code creates an extension method on the `System.String` class. The code is useless by itself because, like other classes, it is not in scope. So, add the following directive to the top of the form:

```
using MyExtensionMethods;
```

Now you can access the extension method you created earlier. Add the following code to the button's `Click()` event:

```
string sentence = "This is an example of an extension method in .NET";
int wordcount = sentence.GetWordCount();
textbox1.text = wordcount.ToString();
```

Run the project and click the button. The text box shows the value `10`.

Let's expand this a little. In every application I've worked on, there's been a need to validate email addresses. Here's how to do that easily with extension methods. Modify the extension method code by adding the following highlighted code:

```
namespace MyExtensionMethods
{
    public static class MyExtensions
    {
        public static int GetWordCount(this System.String mystring)
        {
            return mystring.Split(null).Length;
        }

        public static bool IsValidEmail(this string email)
        {
            Regex exp = new Regex(@"^[\w-\.]+@([\w-]+\.)+[\w-]{2,4}$");
            return exp.IsMatch(email);
        }

    }
}
```

Next, replace the code behind the button with the following:

```
DataContext context =
    new DataContext("Initial Catalog=AdventureWorks;Integrated Security=sspi");

Table<Contact> contact = context.GetTable<Contact>();

var query =
    from c in contact
    select new { c.EmailAddress} ;

foreach (var item in query)
    if (item.EmailAddress.IsValidEmail())
    {
        listbox1.Items.Add(item.EmailAddress);
    }
```

Just like the first example, this one simply adds a method onto the string class that validates email addresses. Very slick.

Visual Basic

Extension methods are new to Visual Basic 2008. C# has had them for a while, and fortunately Visual Basic .NET gets them this release. In Visual Basic .NET, extension methods are accessed via the `System.Runtime.CompilerServices` namespace, so be sure to include the appropriate `Imports` statement. Extension methods can be a Sub or a Function and must be tagged with the `<Extension()>` attribute.

The following shows the extension method from the previous example in Visual Basic .NET syntax:

```
Namespace MyExtensionMethods
    Public Class MyExtensions
        <Extension()>_
        Public Shared Function WordCount(Me ByVal str As System.String) As Integer
            Return str.Split(Nothing).Length
        End Function

        <Extension()>_
        Public Shared Function IsValidEmail(Me ByVal email As String) As Boolean
            Dim exp As Regex = New Regex("^[\w-\.]+@([\w-]+\.)+[\w-]{2,4}$")
            Return exp.IsMatch(email)
        End Function
    End Class
End Namespace
```

Best Practices

Try to implement extension methods only when absolutely necessary and even then, very judiciously. Your best bet is to create a new type that is derived from an existing type. The reason to avoid creating extension methods is that you might run into the scenario where the implementation of the type will cause your extension method to break. That's not good.

If you must implement extension methods, keep in mind the following:

- ❑ If you define an extension method with the same signature as an existing method defined in the type, your extension method will never be called.
- ❑ Extension methods are brought into scope at the namespace level.

Lambda Expressions

Lambda expressions and anonymous methods are similar, except for the fact that lambda expressions are much more flexible and provide a more succinct syntax than anonymous methods.

In LINQ, you run into lambda expressions when making a direct query call to the standard query operators. Lambda expressions can be used in LINQ to create the delegates that will be invoked when the query is executed later. When writing LINQ queries and calling standard query operators directly, you only need to use method syntax to write lambda expressions.

Lambda expressions use what is called the lambda operator, which is =>. This operator means "goes to," and signifies that the left side of the lambda operator specifies any input parameters while the right side contains the expression or statement block.

Here's a simple C# example of a lambda expression:

```
y => y * 2
```

This reads as "y goes to y times 2." The body of a lambda expression can consist of any number of statements, but typically you want to keep it to two or three, mainly for readability and to keep it from becoming overly complex. It is also often unnecessary to specify a type for input parameters because the compiler will infer the type based on several factors, such as the body of the lambda expression and the underlying delegate type.

To work with lambda expressions, it is best to follow these general rules:

- If the lambda expression returns a value, the return value must be implicitly convertible to the return type of the delegate.
- Lambda expressions must contain the same number of parameters as the delegate type.
- Each input parameter must be implicitly convertible to the corresponding delegate parameter.

So, given that background, how do lambda expressions work with LINQ? With lambda expressions, a LINQ query can be written as follows:

```
var prodQuery = context.Products.Single(p => p.ProductID == productID);
```

The query also could be written as follows:

```
var proQuery =
    from con in Contacts
    where con.ProductID == productID
    select con;
```

Both of these queries return the same output, but lambda expressions enable you to write the query as an inline expression using method syntax as shown in the first query. In a method-based query, the `where` clause is now expressed as an instance method of the specified object, which in the previous example is the `Products` object.

This example also uses the `Single` standard query operator to return a single element of the sequence. The `p` on the left side of the operator is the input variable that corresponds to the `p` in the query expression.

The return value of a lambda expression is simply the expression result.

Summary

This chapter introduced you to the interface for the new Visual Studio and explored the new features and enhancements that help provide LINQ with the foundation it needs from a language perspective.

The new features and functionality included in version 3.5 of the .NET Framework—including query expressions, implicitly typed variables, anonymous types, and object initializers—play an important role for LINQ.

Chapter 3 discusses LINQ and the LINQ queries in great detail.

3

LINQ Queries

Chapter 1, ''Project LINQ,'' provided a few simple LINQ queries to give you a basic idea of how LINQ queries are formatted and work with relational data, XML, and in-memory data, but to fully grasp the power and flexibility of LINQ requires a real understanding of how LINQ queries work.

Therefore, this chapter and the next dive deep into LINQ queries and the standard query operators. This chapter focuses on the LINQ queries, their overall concepts and syntax, as well as the many options available to you as a developer when creating LINQ queries. Chapter 4, ''LINQ Standard Query Operators,'' tackles the available standard query operators.

LINQ queries are discussed first because a knowledge of the standard query operators really wouldn't be beneficial if you didn't know how to use them effectively in a LINQ query. Given that, this chapter tackles the following:

- An introduction to LINQ queries
- Query concepts
- Query syntax options

Introduction to LINQ Queries

Hopefully, you know what a query is, and have written either a T-SQL query directly in SQL Server, whether it be in a query window in SSMS (SQL Server Management Studio) or a stored procedure, or an ''in-line'' T-SQL within the code of your application. A query retrieves data, plain and simple. It is a written expression that obtains data from a predetermined data source. The data source could be almost anything, such as a relational database or an XML document.

The problem is that there are many sources of data, and there are just as many query languages to query those data sources. To query a relational database, the SQL query language is required, but if you want to query an XML document, you need to learn the XQuery query language or XPath as well. Wouldn't it be nice to someday have in your possession a single query language with a set of standard query operators that allows for the querying of multiple data sources?

Oh, wait; that day is already here because this is exactly what LINQ is and does. The difference between LINQ and other query languages is in the query actions of a LINQ query operation. With LINQ you work directly with technologies with which you're already familiar (such as objects), and regardless of where the data is coming from, the coding patterns used to create and execute the query remain the same. This consistency is where much of the beauty of LINQ lies. The same standard query operators are used to query and transform data from multiple sources such as XML, relational data, collections, and even DataSets and entities.

The following sections explain the parts of a LINQ query and show you how they are put together and executed. A LINQ query operation contains three distinct and separate actions:

- Acquiring the data source
- The creation of the query
- The execution of the query

Each of these actions is essential to the creation and execution of a LINQ query.

Data Source Acquisition

The data source identifies where the data is coming from in the query. A query is absolutely useless without a data source. What is the use of selecting data if there is no data to select?

The great thing about LINQ is that it doesn't care what the source of data for the query is. The key to being a data source for a LINQ query is that it must support the `IEnumerable` interface. The following example, taken from the first chapter, shows a string array of names that can be utilized as a data source:

```
string [] firstnames = { "Scott", "Steve", "Ken", "Joe", "John",
                         "Alex", "Chuck", "Sarah"};
```

Your source of data can also come in the form of XML, and if it is not already in memory as a queryable form type, it can become so by being loaded into a queryable `XElement` type, like this:

```
XElement names = XElement.Load(@"c:\employees.xml");
```

LINQ to XML provides this functionality and, as you have seen previously, lets you query and manipulate XML with ease. You can also build your own XML to manipulate, as shown in the example below, or even write back to the data source.

```
var x = new XElement("Employee", new XElement("FirstName", "Scott"),
            new XElement("LastName","Klein"));
```

If the data source is relational data, LINQ to SQL provides a flexible mechanism to create a relational mapping between it and your query objects. As shown in Chapter 1, an object-relational mapping must first be created, against which your queries are written, but then LINQ to SQL handles all the database communication. Here's the object-relational mapping taken from the example in Chapter 1 to map the `Contact.Person` table to the application object:

```
[Table(Name="Person.Contact")]
public class Contact
{
  [Column(DBType = "nvarchar(50) not null")]
```

```
    public string FirstName;

    [Column(DBType = "nvarchar(50) not null")]
    public string LastName;

    [Column(DBType = "nvarchar(50) not null")]
    public string EmailAddress;

}
```

Query Creation

Once your data source is defined, the next step is to define the query that specifies the data or information you want to retrieve from the data source. You can also specify how the data should be shaped when it is returned, such as sorted or grouped. The capability to query and shape the data is provided through the new query syntax that is built directly into both C# and Visual Basic.

The standard query operators are a set of methods that form the LINQ (Language Integrated Query) pattern. These operators have dedicated syntax in both C# and Visual Basic that allow them to be called as part of a query expression, a more readable form of writing or expressing a query. The standard query operators, discussed in detail in Chapter 4, provide extensive querying capabilities, which include the ability to sort, group, aggregate, and filter query results.

In LINQ, the query is stored in a variable. If the query returns data, then the query must be a queryable type. Keep in mind that the query variable on its own does not execute the query, does not contain any data, and does not take any other sort of action. It is simply a placeholder for the query, or more accurately put, is an `IEnumerable` object that, when enumerated, executes the query.

The following query, which implements the `IEnumerable` interface, defines a variable called `val` containing a query that selects all first names that begin with the letter *S*. The data source for this query is the string array mentioned in the previous section.

```
IEnumerable<string> val = from fn in firstnames
                          where fn.StartsWith("S")
                          select fn;
```

The query has not been executed at this point, nor does the variable `val` contain any data; it contains only the query syntax. Here's another example, taken from the LINQ to SQL example from Chapter 1:

```
var query =
      from c in contact
      select new { c.FirstName, c.LastName, c.EmailAddress} ;
```

Again, the query has not been executed, nor does the variable `var` contain any data.

The importance of the *query creation* action is to define the query expression and shape the data as you would like it returned.

Query Execution

The last action of the LINQ query operations is query execution. Even though the query expression is defined and stored in a query variable when the query is created, the execution of the query does not typically take place until iteration over the query variable begins. I'll explain "typically" momentarily, but I first want to discuss how a query is executed. As the query is iterated through, only the work necessary to bring back the current result is done. In other words, the entire query is not returned. Each iteration of the query returns the next item in the result.

It has been said previously that neither the query expression itself nor the variable contains query results. That is because the query is executed as you iterate through the variable. Here's the string array example from Chapter 1:

```
string [] firstnames = { "Scott", "Steve", "Ken", "Joe", "John",
                         "Alex", "Chuck", "Sarah"};
IEnumerable<string> val = from fn in firstnames
                          where fn.StartsWith("S")
                          select fn;

foreach (string name in val)
{
  Console.WriteLine(name);
}
```

The first "action" defines the data source. The second "action" defines the query and assigns it to a variable. The last "action," the `foreach` loop (`For Each` in Visual Basic), executes the query by iterating over the variable `val` in the `foreach` loop.

How does this work? Take a look at the `foreach` loop:

```
Foreach (string name in val)
  Console.WriteLine(name);
```

The first time the `foreach` statement is executed, the first call to the `MoveNext()` method causes three things:

1. The query is translated to SQL.
2. The query is executed.
3. The first row is fetched from the underlying DataReader.

For each iteration thereafter, the `MoveNext()` method is called, grabbing the next row from the underlying DataReader, hydrating (queuing) the next object.

The best way to understand this is to see it in action. Take a look at Figure 3-1, which shows the preceding example during code execution. I have stopped the execution of the code on the `foreach` statement on the first iteration.

What you want to look at is the Watch window below the code where I have the `query` variable being watched. Notice the value of the name-value pair named `Results View`. It states, "Expanding the Results View will enumerate the IEnumerable." This tells you that the query has not been executed, that even the internal results have not been iterated through, and that expanding the node will be equivalent to stepping through the `foreach` loop until all the results are received.

So what does *typically* mean? There are two types of query execution: deferred and immediate. In most cases you want to use deferred; however, there are cases when immediate execution is necessary.

The following sections discuss these types and when the use of each is appropriate.

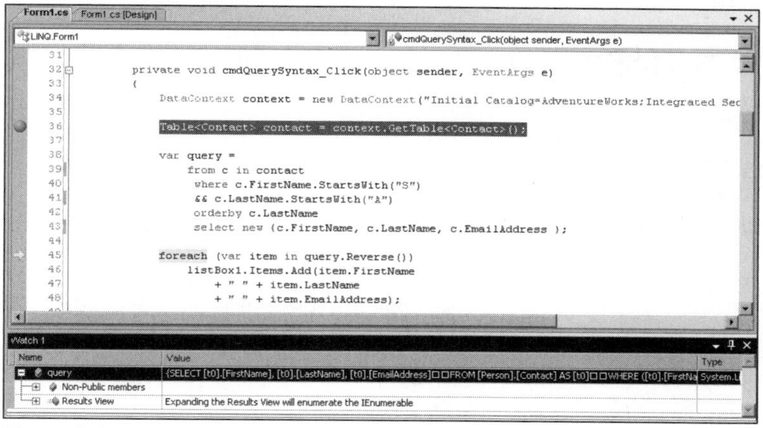

Figure 3-1

Deferred Execution

So far all the examples in this book have shown deferred query execution, which executes the query only when you start to loop through the query variable, such as in a `foreach` loop.

For instance, the following code loops through the variable `val`, which contains the query expression taken from the earlier string array example:

```
foreach (string name in val)
{
  Console.WriteLine(name);
}
```

Deferred execution is appropriate when returning a sequence (multiple values). Because the query (and variable) don't ever contain the query results, you are free to execute (iterate over) this query over and over again with little overhead.

Immediate Execution

Any LINQ query that returns a single value is executed immediately. A single value is considered a query that returns a `Count` or `Max`, for example. You can also force an immediate execution of a query by calling the `ToList` or `ToArray` methods. The following example illustrates a query that returns a single value, thus executing immediately:

```
var query = (from o in Order
             where CustomerID = 2
             select o).Count();
```

This query counts the number of orders from the `Sales.SalesOrderHeader` table in the AdventureWorks database, where the `CustomerID` in that table is `2`. Likewise, instead of getting a count of orders, you can also send the query results to a list or array:

```
var query = (from o in Order
             where CustomerID = 2
             select o).ToList();
```

By returning a single value or returning values to an array or value list, you can force an immediate execution of the query, which can be useful when you want the results of the query to be cached.

Likened to SQL Syntax

To help you understand the flow of the LINQ syntax, compare it to standard T-SQL syntax. If you have written any T-SQL, you know the basic T-SQL query syntax and how it is written. For instance, a simple query looks like this:

```
SELECT FirstName, LastName
FROM Person.Contact
```

This example queries the `Person.Contact` table in the AdventureWorks database and returns the `FirstName` and `LastName` columns for each row in the table. Too simple really, so the following adds a secondary table, applies a filter, and applies a sort:

```
SELECT E.EmployeeID,C.FirstName, C.LastName
FROM Person.Contact AS C
INNER JOIN HoumanResources.Employee AS E ON C.ContactID = E.ContactID
WHERE E.EmployeeID < 100
ORDER BY C.LastName
```

This is the syntax with which all T-SQL developers are familiar. At the very minimum the query begins with a `SELECT` clause, which specifies the columns you want to be returned by the query, followed by a `FROM` clause, which lists the tables and/or views containing the columns identified in the `SELECT` clause.

The query could include one or more joins such as an `INNER JOIN` or `OUTER JOIN`, followed by some filtering using the `WHERE` clause and possibly a `GROUP BY` or `HAVING` clause, and quite possibly some ordering using the `ORDER BY` clause.

How many developers have really stopped to think about how SQL Server processes these queries? Does SQL Server execute the query from top to bottom, starting with the `SELECT` clause and working its way down? You might think that, but that is not how a query is processed in SQL Server at all. SQL Server logically processes a query in the following order:

```
(8)  SELECT
(9)  TOP
(1)  FROM
(3)  JOIN
(2)  ON
(4)  WHERE
(5)  GROUP BY
(6)  WITH
(7)  HAVING
(10) ORDER BY
```

Notice that the `FROM` clause is processed first, while the `SELECT` clause is processed almost last. Any clause that is not specified in the query is simply skipped by the query-processing engine. So, why is this information important?

It points out the similarities between a LINQ query syntax and how SQL Server processes a query. You have seen many times now the basic syntax of a LINQ query:

```
from c in contact
where c.FirstName.StartsWith("S")
orderby c.LastName
select c
```

The LINQ query and the T-SQL query are executed similarly, although the T-SQL query syntax is different. This same query in T-SQL would be the following:

```
SELECT FirstName, LastName, EmailAddress
FROM Contact
WHERE LEFT(FirstName, 1) = 'S'
ORDER BY LastName
```

The differences are that in SQL this query would be executed internally, following the steps described earlier. With LINQ, the query does not need to go through the rewriting process. Also, the same LINQ operators work against other data sources.

With this in mind, the next section explores query operations and expressions to help you more fully understand LINQ query concepts.

Query Concepts

You have seen multiple examples of LINQ queries so far in this book. Now you'll explore the basic layout and syntax, as well as the different kinds of operations that can take place in a query. (Chapter 4 discusses in detail the many standard query operators that are at your disposal when writing LINQ query expressions.) For this discussion, the following query will be used:

```
from c in contact
where c.FirstName.StartsWith("S")
orderby c.LastName
select c
```

In a LINQ query, the first clause is `from`, which specifies the source of the data. It is called a generator, and defines where the data will be coming from when the query is executed. It also specifies a range variable that is used as a reference for each element in the data source. In the following example, `contact` is the data source and `c` is the range variable:

```
from c in contact
```

The `where` clause enables you to filter the results being returned by the query. By applying a filter to the query, you're not only limiting the number of rows returned, but you are specifying the rows you want to see, or exclude, from the returned results. For example, the following returns only those contacts whose first name begins with the letter *S*:

```
where c.FirstName.StartsWith("S")
```

Recall from Chapter 1 that you selected all the rows from the `Person.Contact` table in the AdventureWorks database—the table had nearly 20,000 rows. By simply applying this filter to the LINQ query, the number of rows returned is just over 1,200—quite a difference.

It is possible to apply multiple filters by using the logical operators `AND` and `OR`. In C# using `AND` (`&&`) looks like the following:

```
where c.FirstName.StartsWith("S")
&& c.LastName.StartsWith("A")
```

In Visual Basic, it looks like this:

```
Where c.FirstName.StartsWith("S")
AND c.LastName.StartsWith("A")
```

The `OR` (||) operator works the same way:

```
where c.FirstName.StartsWith("S")
|| c.LastName.StartsWith("A")
```

And in Visual Basic:

```
Where c.FirstName.StartsWith("S")
OR c.LastName.StartsWith("A")
```

The `where` clause is optional when writing a LINQ query, as is the `orderby` clause. The `orderby` clause provides the capability to order (sort) the results returned by the execution of the query. The following sorts the results by last name:

```
orderby c.LastName
```

By default, the sort is applied in ascending order. To reverse the sort (descending order), simply apply the `descending` clause:

```
orderby c.LastName descending
```

You can sort by more than one property:

```
orderby c.LastName, c.FirstName
```

In Visual Basic, the `orderby` clause reads:

```
Order By c.LastName Descending
```

You can also group the results of the query based on one of the properties of the query. For example, the following line groups the results of the query by contact country:

```
group c by c.Country
```

The final step is to project (select) the data using the `select` clause. By *projecting* the data, you are defining the results as something other than a simple copy of the original source. For example, if the data source returns `FirstName`, `LastName`, `EmailAddress`, `Title`, `MiddleName`, and `City`, but the `select` clause only produces the `FirstName` and `LastName` properties in the results, that is a projection.

The `select` clause enables you to determine the shape of each object that is returned by the query. Here's an example that returns the entire collection object:

```
from c in contact
where c.FirstName.StartsWith("S")
orderby c.LastName
select c
```

To select a single property, simply select that property, like this:

```
from c in contact
where c.FirstName.StartsWith("S")
orderby c.LastName
select c.LastName
```

Selecting a single result (column/property), in this case a string value, changes the result type from an `IEnumerable` collection of type `contact` in the first example to an `IEnumerable` of `String` in this example because only a single string value is being returned. In other words, just the `LastName` property (column) is being returned in the collection.

To select multiple values (but not the entire collection), you can use one of two methods. The first is to use `IEnumerable` by defining a named type and using that named type to create each source object in the `select` clause. First, the named type must be created.

```
struct data
{
  public string FN;
  public string LN;
  public string EA;
}
```

That named type is then used in the creation and initialization of the `IEnumerable` query:

```
IEnumberable<data> query = from c in contact
where c.FirstName.StartsWith("S")
&& c.LastName.StartsWith("A")
orderby c.LastName
select new data { LN = c.FirstName, FN = c.LastName, EA = c.EmailAddress}
```

At this point you can iterate through the query like this:

```
foreach (var item in query)
  listbox1.Items.Add(item.FN + " " + item.LN + " " + item.EA);
```

The other option is to create an anonymous type using the `var` keyword:

```
var query = from c in contact
where c.FirstName.StartsWith("S")
orderby c.LastName
select new {FN = c.FirstName, LN = c.LastName, EA = c.EmailAddress}
```

This query can be iterated through as follows:

```
foreach (var item in query)
 listbox1.Items.Add(item.FN + " " + item.LN + " " + item.EA);
```

You can also do the following, which defaults to creating an anonymous type using the same member names as the properties that you reference in the query:

```
var query = from c in contact
where c.FirstName.StartsWith("S")
orderby c.LastName
select new {c.FirstName, c.LastName, c.EmailAddress}
```

This query can be iterated through as follows:

```
foreach (var item in query)
 listbox1.Items.Add(item.FirstName + " " + item.LastName + " " + item.EmailAddres);
```

Basically, using

```
select new {c.FirstName, c.LastName, c.EmailAddress}
```

is a shortcut for

```
select new {FirstName = c.FirstName, LastName = c.LastName,
  EmailAddress = c.EmailAddress}
```

This, then, begs the question, ''What is the difference between a named type and an anonymous type?'' Hang tight, because `var` and `IEnumerable` differences are explained in the next section.

First, what about join operations? That is certainly doable and is accomplished via the `join` clause:

```
from c in contact
join o in orders on c equals o.OrderID
where c.FirstName.StartsWith("S")
orderby c.LastName
select new {c.FirstName, c.LastName, c.EmailAddress, o.OrderDate}
```

OK, with all of that under your belt, the following section will clear up the confusion between `var` and `IEnumerable`.

Var versus IEnumerable

The `var` keyword is new to C# 3.0 and enables you to implicitly declare variables at the method scope. The great thing about it is that the implicitly typed variable is just as strongly typed as its explicitly declared counterpart. For example, these variables

```
var blah = "S"
var moreblah = 50
```

are equivalent to the following:

```
string blah = "S"
int moreblah = 50
```

In the early days, the word ''var'' stood for variant. Today, that isn't the case; in C# and `VB.NET`, `var` is a specific keyword that, when used, tells the compiler to determine the exact type of the variable.

The IEnumerable<T> interface, new in .NET Framework 2.0, supports a simple iteration over a collection of a specified type. It exposes the IEnumerator<T> interface, which is the base interface for all generic enumerators. LINQ takes advantage of this enumeration via the foreach statement, which lets you iterate through an enumeration without the complexity of dealing with and manipulating the enumerator directly.

IEnumerable is minimal in its functionality, however. It has forward-only movement in a collection, so moving back and forth among data items is not possible with IEnumerable.

With LINQ, it is important is to know when to use var versus IEnumerable. As you saw earlier in this section, var can be used to implicitly declare a variable. While this is optional, it can be overused. The best time to use var is when a variable is initialized with an anonymous type, only because in that scenario it's required. Using var too many times can also make your source code less readable by developers who come in after you. In other words, don't overuse var.

To understand the difference between the two and when one should be used over the other, consider the following two examples. The first query uses var, but it is not necessary because the query result type can be explicitly stated as an IEnumerable<int>, meaning that the result types are known.

```
int[] nums = {5, 1, 9, 4, 8, 11, 6, 14, 2, 7};
var query =
    from num in nums
    where num % 2 == 1
    select num;
```

The next example, however, must use var because the result types are not known. The result is a collection of anonymous types. In these cases, the name of the type is not available until the compiler creates it.

```
Var query =
    from prod in Products
    where prod.ProductID = 10021
    select new {prod.ProductName, prod.Price};
```

Common Query Terms

Before you go any further, a few things need to be defined and explained in order to help you get the feel for LINQ queries.

LINQ Providers

A LINQ Provider is a library that implements the functionality provided by the standard query operators for a specific type of data source.

The responsibility of the LINQ Provider is to execute a given query or to hand it to another engine for execution. LINQ has several providers: LINQ to XML, LINQ to Datasets, LINQ to Objects, and LINQ to SQL.

LINQ to SQL is considered a LINQ Provider even though it does not have its own implementation of the standard query operators. Why? As an implementation of the IQueryable interface, LINQ to SQL implements the functionality of the standard query operators against relational databases.

Expression Trees

An expression tree is a representation of language-level code in the form of data. The data is stored in a tree-like structure, hence the name.

Expression trees in LINQ are used for several reasons, one of which is to structure queries that utilize data sources that implement `IQueryable(Of T)`. At runtime, when a query is executed, the C# or Visual Basic compiler translates the query expressions (and method-based queries) into code that is then converted to an expression tree structure. The appropriate query provider then translates the structure into the query language for the targeted data source.

As you learned in the previous section, the LINQ to SQL provider implements `IQueryable(Of T)` for querying relational data stores.

The great thing about expression trees is that, as a developer, you don't need to build one or even negotiate through an expression tree. The traversal of an expression tree is done for you, unless you feel the strong urge to create your own query provider or query language.

As a quick note, expression trees are also used to represent lambda expressions. When a lambda expression is assigned to a variable, a field, or a parameter of type `Expression(Of TDelegate)`, the compiler generates an expression tree which represents the lambda expression. There are several standard query operator methods that have parameters of type `Expression(Of TDelegate)`. Thus, you are able to pass lambda expressions when these methods are called. The compiler will then create an expression tree.

IQueryable and IQueryable(Of T) Interfaces

The `IQueryable` and `IQueryable(Of T)` interfaces provide the functionality to evaluate queries for a given data source. The IQueryable interface does this where the type of the data is not known, and the `IQueryable(Of T)` interface does this where the type of the data is known.

The `IQueryable` and `IQueryable(Of T)` interfaces implement the `IEnumerable` and `IEnumerable(Of T)` interface, respectively, providing the capability of enumeration over the results of the given query. As you have learned previously, the enumeration causes the expression tree associated with an IQueryable or IQueryable(Of T) object to be executed. Keep in mind that the term "executing an expression tree" is specific to the query provider.

The difference between these two interfaces is that the `IQueryable(Of T)` interface enables queries to be executed against different types of data sources. These queries are commonly referred to as "polymorphic."

Keep in mind that both the `IQueryable` and `IQueryable(Of T)` interfaces are intended for implementation only by query providers. Think of an IQueryable object as having an `ADO.NET` command object. Having one (either an IQueryable object or a command object) does not insinuate that either the LINQ query (or the command) was executed.

Let's take a close look at each of these to help understand the IQueryable object. An `ADO.NET` command object contains a property that holds a string that describes the query. The IQueryable object is similar in that it contains a description of a query that is encoded as a data structure known as an expression.

The command object has an ExecuteReader() method that causes execution. The results are returned as a DataReader. Likewise, the IQueryable object has a GetEnumerator method that causes the execution of the query. The results of the query are returned as an IEnumerator.

Query Syntax versus Method Syntax

LINQ provides the ability to write queries using both query syntax and method syntax, and most of the examples until now have used query syntax, which is writing the query as a query expression, like this:

```
IEnumerable<string> query =
    from c in contact
    where c.FirstName.StartsWith("S")
    select c;
```

This declarative syntax is easy to read and understand, but you also have the option of writing your queries using method syntax. When a LINQ query is compiled, the query expression is translated into method syntax because the .NET Common Language Runtime (CLR) really doesn't understand query syntax. Thus, at compile time, query expressions are translated into method calls because this is what the CLR understands.

Here's the method syntax version of the preceding query:

```
IEnumerable<string> query = contact.Where(c => c.FirstName.StartsWith("S"));
```

It is recommended that you use query syntax whenever possible simply because it is easier to read, understand, and maintain. However, as you can see from the two preceding examples, there is no semantic difference between method syntax and query syntax. Therefore, this section discusses both query syntax and method syntax to provide you a good understanding of these syntaxes in queries and how to use them in query expressions.

This next example gets a bit more complicated by adding an additional filter:

```
IEnumerable<string> query =
    from c in contact
    where c.FirstName.StartsWith("S")
    && c.LastName.StartsWith("A")
    select c;
```

The method syntax of this is as follows:

```
IEnumerable<string> query = contact.Where(a => a.FirstName.StartsWith("S") @@ta
&& a.LastName.StartsWith("A"));
```

Let's complicate things a bit more and add the Orderby clause:

```
IEnumerable<string> query =
    from c in contact
    where c.FirstName.StartsWith("S")
    && c.LastName.StartsWith("A")
```

```
        Orderby c.LastName
        select c;
```

This query expression would be written as method syntax as follows:

```
IEnumerable<string> query = contact.Where(c => c.FirstName.StartsWith("S")
   && c.LastName.StartsWith("A")).OrderBy(c => c.LastName);
```

Run both versions of these queries (method syntax and query syntax), and you'll see that the output is identical. What makes the method syntax possible is lambda expressions, which were discussed in Chapter 2, ''A Look at Visual Studio 2008.''

Although query syntax is recommended over method syntax, there are times when method syntax is preferred, such as in those queries that return the number of elements that match a specified condition.

Which Do You Use?

Given all of the information discussed in this chapter, the question might arise, ''Which do I use, query syntax or method syntax?'' The general rule is to use whichever syntax will make your code most readable, which most often means using query syntax. However, even this might not be sufficient because there are many reasons why query syntax may not be an option:

- Not all of the standard query operators are available in query syntax.
- Not all of the combinations of the standard query operators are available in query syntax.
- As you will read about later, it is possible to combine query syntax with method syntax, but there may be times when using straight method syntax might be more readable.

It is a matter of learning which standard query operators can be used with which syntax option (query syntax and method syntax) and going from there. However, your priority should always be syntax readability.

For example, the following code snippet shows how to author a query using query syntax.

```
Int[] grades = { 67, 98, 72, 85, 92, 89, 78, 76, 88};

IEnumerable<int> topTwoGrades =
    (from g in grades
    orderby g
    select g).Take(2);
```

The following code snippet shows the same query using method syntax.

```
Int[] grades = { 67, 98, 72, 85, 92, 89, 78, 76, 88};

IEnumerable<int> topTwoGrades =
    grades.OrderByDescending (g => g).Take(2);
```

Both produce the same results; it is up to you to decide how you want to write the query.

Chapter 4 will discuss all of the standard query operators and provide examples using both query syntax and method syntax where available.

Using Query and Method Syntaxes

Here's a project that utilizes much of the information found in this chapter, such as query syntax and method syntax, to create queries that will be used throughout the rest of this book. To start, you need a place to create the applications used for this chapter.

In the root of your C drive, create a directory called Wrox. Underneath that directory, create another directory called Chapter 3. Now, fire up Visual Studio 2008 and within the Recent Projects window of the Start page, create a new project. This opens the New Project dialog.

In the New Project dialog, make sure that you have selected the correct Framework version (3.5) via the far-left icon in the top-right corner, then select a Windows project type and set the project name to LINQ with the path you just created (`\Wrox\Chapter 3`). Figure 3-2 shows what the New Project dialog should look like.

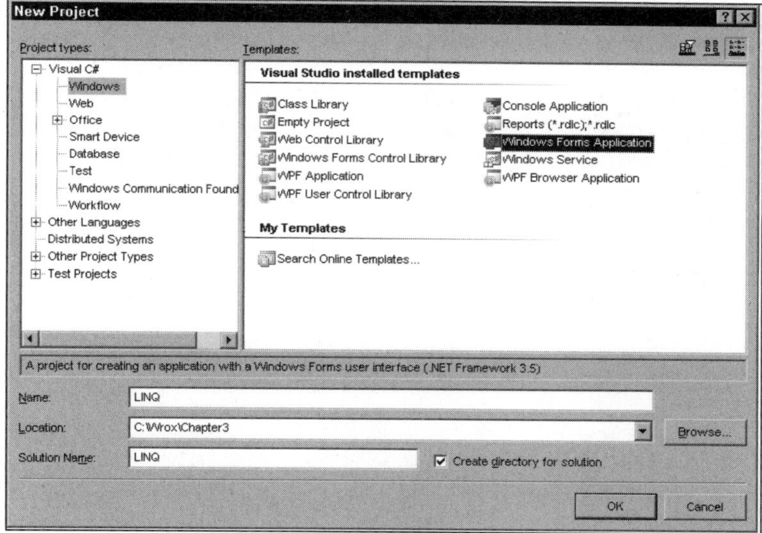

Figure 3-2

Click OK when you have everything set. Next, open the Solution Explorer and add the `System.Data` and `System.Data.Linq` namespace references to your project. Then open `Form1` in design view and add three buttons and a list box. Align the list box on the left of the form and place two of the buttons next to the list box, with the third button in the bottom-right corner of the form.

Set the properties of the first button to the following:

Property	Value
Name	cmdQuerySyntax
Text	Query Syntax

Set the properties of the second button to the following:

Property	Value
Name	cmdMethodSyntax
Text	Method Syntax

Set the properties of the third button to the following:

Property	Value
Name	cmdClose
Text	Close

Figure 3-3 shows what the form should look like (with the appropriate component references included).

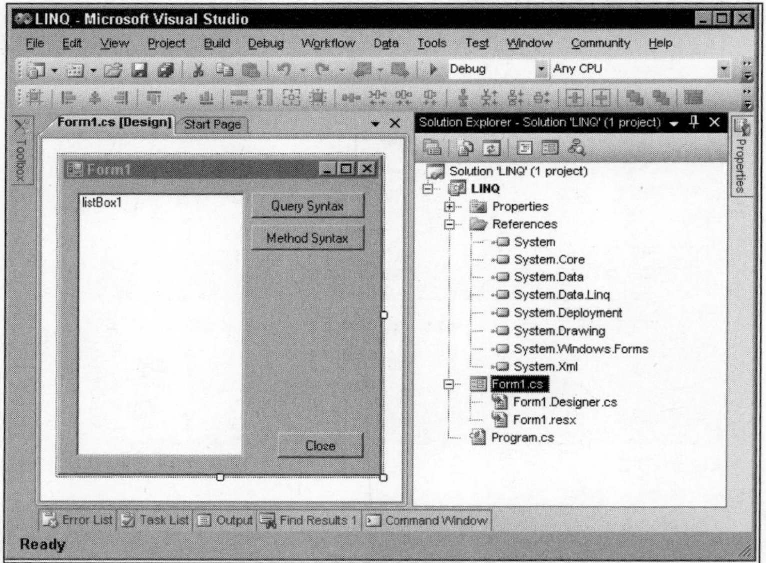

Figure 3-3

Double-click the form to display the code behind the form. In the declarations section, make sure that you add the appropriate `using` statements for LINQ, including `System.Data.Linq`.

Next, underneath the class for `Form1`, add the following:

```
[Table(Name = "Person.Contact")]
public class Contact
{
  [Column(DBType = "nvarchar(8) not null")]
  public string Title;
```

```
        [Column(DBType = "nvarchar(50) not null")]
        public string FirstName;

        [Column(DBType = "nvarchar(50) not null")]
        public string MiddleName;

        [Column(DBType = "nvarchar(50) not null")]
        public string LastName;

        [Column(DBType = "nvarchar(50) not null")]
        public string EmailAddress;

        [Column(DBType = "int")]
        public int EmailPromotion;

    }
```

That defines the data source, the first of the three actions that makes up a query operation.

Your code behind `Form1` should now look like this:

```
using System;
using System.Linq;
using System.Collections.Generic;
using System.ComponentModel;
using System.Data;
using System.Data.Linq;
using System.Drawing;
using System.Text;
using System.Windows.Forms;
using System.Xml;

namespace LINQ
{
    public partial class Form1 : Form
    {
        public Form1()
        {
            InitializeComponent();
        }

        private void Form1_Load(object sender, EventArgs e)
        {
 }
    }

    [Table(Name = "Person.Contact")]
    public class Contact
    {
        [Column(DBType = "nvarchar(8) not null")]
        public string Title;

        [Column(DBType = "nvarchar(50) not null")]
        public string FirstName;
```

```
            [Column(DBType = "nvarchar(50) not null")]
            public string MiddleName;

            [Column(DBType = "nvarchar(50) not null")]
            public string LastName;

            [Column(DBType = "nvarchar(50) not null")]
            public string EmailAddress;

            [Column(DBType = "int")]
            public int EmailPromotion;

        }
    }
```

Place the following code in the `click` event for the Close button:

```
Application.Exit();
```

Next, in the `click` event for the Query Method button, place the following code:

```
DataContext context = new DataContext("Initial Catalog=AdventureWorks;@@ta
Integrated Security=sspi");

Table<Contact> contact = context.GetTable<Contact>();

var query =
  from c in contact
  where c.FirstName.StartsWith("S")
  && c.LastName.StartsWith("K")
  orderby c.LastName
  select c;

foreach (var item in query)
  listBox1.Items.Add(item.FirstName + " " + item.LastName + " " +
    item.EmailAddress);
```

This code creates a query expression filtering all contacts whose first name begins with the letter *S* and whose last name begins with the letter *K*, all sorted by the contacts' last name. You know this is an anonymous query expression because of the use of the `var` keyword discussed previously.

A portion of the preceding code defines the second and third actions of a query operation. The query expression (the second action) defines the information to be retrieved from the data source, while the execution of the query (the iteration over the query variable) is the last action.

Press F5 to compile and run the application. When the form opens, click the Query Syntax button. The list box will populate with the first names, last names, and email addresses of those contacts who meet the criteria specified in the query expression. The results on your form should look like those in Figure 3-4.

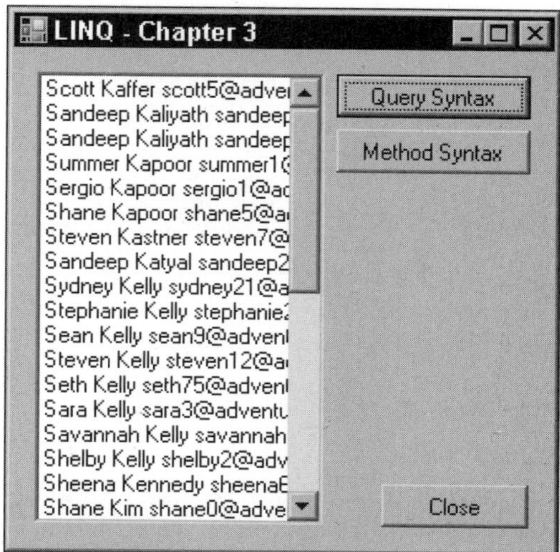

Figure 3-4

In this example, the `select` clause in the query expression did not select individual properties from the query results, but rather selected all the properties by simply stating `select c`. This is similar to stating `SELECT * FROM` in T-SQL syntax. Because all the properties were selected to be returned, all properties are available from IntelliSense, as shown in Figure 3-5.

```
LINQ.Form1                    cmdQuerySyntax_Click(object sender, EventArgs e)
        private void cmdQuerySyntax_Click(object sender, EventArgs e)
        {
            DataContext context = new DataContext("Initial Catalog=AdventureWorks;Integr

            Table<Contact> contact = context.GetTable<Contact>();

            var query =
                from c in contact
                where c.FirstName.StartsWith("S")
                && c.LastName.StartsWith("K")
                orderby c.LastName
                select c;

            foreach (var item in query)
                listBox1.Items.Add(item.FirstName
                    + " " + item.LastName
                    + " " + item.);
                                EmailAddress
        }                       EmailPromotion
                                Equals
        private void cmdMethod  FirstName      ject sender, EventArgs e)
        {                       GetHashCode
            DataContext contex  GetType        text("Initial Catalog=AdventureWorks;Integr
                                LastName
            Table<Contact> con  MiddleName     GetTable<Contact>();
                                Title
                                ToString
```

Figure 3-5

Modify the following code, changing the `select` clause in the query expression as highlighted:

```
var query =
  from c in contact
  where c.FirstName.StartsWith("S")
  && c.LastName.StartsWith("K")
  orderby c.LastName
  select new { c.FirstName, c.LastName, c.EmailAddress};
```

Running this anonymous query produces the same results on the form when the application is run, but in this code, specific properties are selected to be returned in the query. An anonymous query type is created using the same names as the properties in the object initializer.

Thus, IntelliSense shows only those properties that are available for selection, as shown in Figure 3-6.

Figure 3-6

Next, add the following code to the `Click()` event behind the Method syntax button.

```
DataContext context = new DataContext("Initial Catalog=AdventureWorks;@@ta
Integrated Security=sspi");

Table<Contact> contact = context.GetTable<Contact>();

IEnumerable<Contact> query =
    contact.Where(a => a.FirstName.StartsWith("S")
               && a.LastName.StartsWith("K")).OrderBy(a => a.LastName);
foreach (var item in query)
  listBox1.Items.Add(item.FirstName + " " + item.LastName + " " +
    item.EmailAddress);
```

Press F5 to compile and run the application. When the form opens, click the Method Syntax button. The list box will be populated with the first names, last names, and email addresses of those contacts who meet the criteria specified in the query expression. The results on your form should look like the results that were returned in the first example (shown in Figure 3-4).

This `IEnumerable` example can also be written to use automatic type deduction using the `var` keyword as follows:

```
var query =
    contact.Where(a => a.FirstName.StartsWith("S")
    && a.LastName.StartsWith("K")).OrderBy(a => a.LastName);
```

Each of these examples contains the three actions that make up a query operation. Those of you who have read any of my previous books already know that I like to assign small "homework assignments," which build on the examples of the current chapter.

Your homework assignment for this chapter is fairly simple. Start experimenting with the differences between query syntax and method syntax, as well as with the different query expressions available. A lot of this will be useful in the upcoming chapters.

Summary

This chapter gave you with a first-hand look at LINQ queries, their concepts, and the available syntax options. You got a detailed look at the three actions that make up a query operation: the data source, the query expression, and the execution of the query (and the different types of query execution, such as deferred and immediate). Each is a distinct and separate action critical to the success of the LINQ query.

You also looked at SQL syntax and saw how its execution is likened to LINQ syntax. Then you explored LINQ query concepts, from specifying the data source to filtering, grouping, and selecting (projecting) a query expression. You also tackled the different query expressions, the use of `var` versus `IEnumerable`, and the difference between query syntax and method syntax and how they are related and used.

In Chapter 4 you'll take an in-depth look at the standard query operators, putting the final touches on your basic understanding of LINQ.

LINQ Standard Query Operators

Understanding the different parts of a query operation and how those parts work together provides the foundation for constructing efficient queries to retrieve and transform data from many different sources, such as XML documents, SQL databases, .NET collections, and ADO.NET datasets. This chapter will outline those parts and their uses.

This chapter builds on the query operation information you examined in Chapter 3, ''LINQ Queries,'' by exploring the standard query operators, a set of methods that form the LINQ pattern, a standard way of creating query expressions to project, filter, group, and transform data. The standard query operators provide the capability to query any object that implements the `IEnumerable` interface and `IQueryable` interface. You can think of the standard query operators much like an API. In this case, the ''API'' is a set of methods.

This chapter begins with an overview of the standard query operators. It examines each operator in detail, providing examples, and then ends with a full example using many of these operators.

Overview

Standard query operators are the building blocks of LINQ query expressions, providing many of the query capabilities such as filtering and sorting. They are a set of methods that constitute a query pattern and are implemented by their respective LINQ provider, such as LINQ to XML and LINQ to Datasets.

As you learned in the last chapter, some operators return results immediately, while others have a deferred execution. Those queries whose execution is immediate return a single value such as a `Sum` or `Count`, while those queries that have a deferred execution return multiple values.

As stated earlier, the standard query operator is a set of methods. These methods operate on sequences. A sequence is an object whose type implements either the `IEnumerable<T>` interface or the `IQueryable<T>` interface. The `IEnumerable<T>` interface provides iteration over a collection of a specified type.

The `IQueryable<T>` interface provides the ability to execute queries against a known and specific data source whose type of data is known. Meaning, with the `IQueryable` interface and the `IQueryable<T>` interface you get an object that can evaluate queries. The `IQueryable` interface is based on expressions.

One of the main differences between `IEnumerable` and `IQueryable` is that the `IEnumerable` interface provides forward-only iteration. It does not have the ability to move between items (except forward). With `IQueryable` however, you have much more flexibility with your query operations. Remember, though that the `IQueryable` interface implements `IEnumerable`, which provides `IQueryable` with iteration capability.

There are two types of query operators. The first type operates on `IEnumerable` objects, while the other operates on `IQueryable` objects. Each set of operators is implemented as static methods on the corresponding types, meaning that the operators can be called using static method syntax as well as being called as instance methods.

A lot of what makes this possible is the new features found in C# 3.0 and VB 9.0. Those features include lambda expressions (a concise expression or statement block) and extension methods (static methods associated with a type). These and other features new to C# 3.0 and VB 9.0 are discussed in Chapter 2, ''A Look at Visual Studio 2008.''

Standard query operators are grouped based on their function, and that's how we'll tackle them in this chapter.

Standard Query Operators

This section discusses the standard query operators. These operators have both C# and Visual Basic syntax. The examples will be given in C#, but the syntax will be provided in both C# and Visual Basic.

What you will find is that those standard query operators that are used more frequently have a dedicated language and keyword syntax, which lets them be used and called as part of a query expression (query syntax).

Standard QueryOperator	C#	Visual Basic
All (Of T)	N/A	Into All(. . .)
Any	N/A	Into Any()
Average	N/A	Into Averate()
Cast (Of T)	An explicit range of variables	From. . .As. . .
Count	N/A	Into count()
Distinct	N/A	Distinct

Standard QueryOperator	C#	Visual Basic
GroupBy	group by	Group By
GroupJoin	join. . .in. . .on. . .into. . .	Group Join
Join	join. . .in. . .on. . .equals. . .	Join. . .As..IN. . .On. . .
		OR
		From x In..y In..Where. . .
LongCount	N/A	Into LongCount()
Max	N/A	Into Max()
Min	N/A	Into Min()
OrderBy	orderby	Order By
OrderByDescending	orderby desdending	Order By. . .Descending
Select	select	Select
SelectMany	Multiple from clauses	Multiple from clauses
Skip	N/A	Skip
SkipWhile	N/A	Skip While
Sum	N/A	Into Sum
Take	N/A	Take
TakeWhile	N/A	Take While
ThenBy	orderby	Order By
ThenByDescending	orderby descending	Order By. . .Descending
Where	where	Where

Remember from the discussion in Chapter 3 that a query expression is a more readable form of query over the method-based syntax version. At compile time, query expressions are translated into query methods.

However, what you will find in this chapter is that it is very easy to combine these query expression syntax operators with direct method calls. By doing this, you can use all of the various pieces of the LINQ functionality.

Projection Operators

Projection refers to the act of transforming the elements of a sequence into a form defined by the developer. The projection operators—`Select` and `SelectMany`—select values given the appropriate function. While both select values, the `SelectMany` operator can handle multiple collections.

Select

The `Select` operator (`select` in C#) projects values from a single sequence or collection. The following example uses `select` to return the `FirstName`, `LastName`, and `EmailAddress` columns from the sequence:

```
var query =
   from c in contact
   where c.FirstName.StartsWith("S")
   select new {c.FirstName, c.LastName, c.EmailAddress}
```

This operator returns an enumerable object. When the object is enumerated, it produces each element in the selected results.

This same query can be written using method syntax as follows:

```
var query =
    contact.Select(c => new {
        c.FirstName, c.Lastname, c.EmailAddress}
        ).Where(c => c.FirstName.StartsWith("S"));
```

SelectMany

The `SelectMany` operation provides the capability to combine multiple `from` clauses, merging the results of each object into a single sequence. Here's an example:

```
string[] owners =
    { new name { FirstName = "Scott", "Chris",
      Pets = new List<string>{"Yukon", "Fido"}},
     new name { FirstName = "Jason", "Steve",
      Pets = new List<string>{"Killer", "Fluffy"}},
     new name { FirstName = "John", "Joe",
      Pets = new List<string>{"Spike", "Tinkerbell"}}}

IEnumerable<string> query =
    names.AsQueryable().SelectMany(own => own.Pets);
```

When this code is run, it produces the following:

```
Yukon
Fido
Killer
Fluffy
Spike
Tinkerbell
```

This same example could be written follows:

```
var query =
    from o in owners
    select o;

foreach (var pet in query.SelectMany(own => own.Pets))
    listbox1.Items.Add(pet);
```

Restriction Operator

`where` is the restriction operator. It applies filter criteria on the sequence. The values of the sequence are filtered based on a supplied predicate.

The `where` operator does not initiate the execution of the query. The query is executed when enumeration over the object is initiated, at which point the filter is applied. Here's an example that applies a filter to the query expression, filtering the results so that only those contacts whose first name begins with the letter *S* are returned:

```
IEnumerable<string> query =
   from c in contact
   where c.FirstName.StartsWith("S")
   select new {c.FirstName, c.LastName, c.EmailAddress}
```

This example could also be written using method syntax as follows:

```
var query =
    contact.Select(c => new {
        c.FirstName, c.Lastname, c.EmailAddress}
        ).Where(c => c.FirstName.StartsWith("S"));
```

Sorting Operators

The sorting operators—`OrderBy`, `OrderByDescending`, `ThenBy`, `ThenByDescending`, and `Reverse`—provide the capability to sort the results in an ascending or descending manner. There are several sorting options that let you apply primary and secondary sorts as well. These operators are explored in the following sections.

OrderBy

The `OrderBy` operator sorts the resulting values of the sequence in an ascending order. The following example shows how to sort a sequence in ascending order:

```
var query =
   from c in contact
   where c.FirstName.StartsWith("S")
  orderby c.LastName
   select new {c.FirstName, c.LastName, c.EmailAddress}
```

You can also sort the sequence in ascending order by using a *comparer*. A comparer is an optional value that is used to compare values. If no comparer is specified, a default is used, which comes from the `IComparer` generic interface.

This example could also be written using method syntax as follows:

```
var query =
    contact.Select(c => {
        c.FirstName, c.LastName, c.EmailAddress }).Where(
        c => c.FirstName.StartsWith("S")).OrderBy(
        c => c.FirstName);
```

OrderByDescending

The `OrderByDescending` operator sorts the resulting values of the sequence in descending order. The following shows how to sort a sequence in descending order:

```
IEnumerable<string> query =
   from c in contact
   where c.FirstName.StartsWith("S")
  orderby c.LastName descending
   select new {c.FirstName, c.LastName, c.EmailAddress}
```

This example could also be written using method syntax as follows:

```
var query =
    contact.Select(c => {
       c.FirstName, c.LastName, c.EmailAddress} ).Where(
       c => c.FirstName.StartsWith("S")).OrderByDescending(
       c => c.FirstName);
```

ThenBy

The `ThenBy` operator applies a secondary, ascending sort order to the sequence. It is akin to applying a secondary sort order in T-SQL, such as the italicized column in the following example:

```
SELECT FirstName, LastName, Address1, Address2, City
FROM Contacts
ORDER BY LastName, FirstName
```

In LINQ, the `ThenBy` operator lets you apply an equivalent secondary sort, like this:

```
IEnumerable<string> query =
   from c in contact
   where c.FirstName.StartsWith("S")
  orderby c.LastName
  thenby c.FirstName
   select new {c.FirstName, c.LastName, c.EmailAddress}
```

This example could also be written using method syntax as follows:

```
var query =
    contact.Select(c => {
        c.FirstName, c.LastName, c.EmailAddress} ).Where(
        c => c.FirstName.StartsWith("S")).OrderBy(
        c => c.FirstName).ThenBy(c => c.LastName);
```

ThenByDescending

The `ThenByDescending` operator sorts the resulting values of the sequence in descending order. The following example shows how:

```
IEnumerable<string> query =
   (from c in contact
   where c.FirstName.StartsWith("S")
  orderby c.LastName descending
```

```
    select new {c.FirstName, c.LastName, c.EmailAddress}).@@ta
ThenByDescending(c => c.FirstName);
```

This example could also be written using method syntax as follows:

```
var query =
    contact.Select(c => {
        c.FirstName, c.LastName, c.EmailAddress} ).Where(
        c => c.FirstName.StartsWith("S")).OrderBy(
        c => c.FirstName).ThenByDescending(c =>
        c.LastName);
```

Reverse

You might think that the `Reverse` operator is equal to the `OrderByDescending` operator, but that's not the case. The `Reverse` operator does not look at the individual values to decide the sort order. It simply returns the values in the opposite (reverse) order from which they were returned from the data source. Here's an example:

```
string[] names = {"Alex", "Chuck", "Dave", "Dinesh",
  "Joe", "John", "Sarah", "Scott", "Steve"}

string[] reversednames = names.Reverse().ToArray();
foreach (string str in reversednames)
  listbox1.Items.Add(chr)
```

The resulting output is:

```
Steve
Scott
Sarah
John
Joe
Dinesh
Dave
Chuck
Alex
```

The `reverse()` operator is limited, in that it is not supported by LINQ to SQL because LINQ to SQL operates on tables that are unordered sets or multisets.

Joining Operators

Joining is the action of relating or associating one data source object with a second data source object. The two data source objects are associated through a common value or attribute.

LINQ join operators match values from data sources that contain keys that match (or are equal). There are two LINQ join operators, `join` and `groupjoin`.

join

The `join` operator is similar to the T-SQL `inner join`, which joins one data source to a second data source, matching on equal values between the two data sources. For example, you can join a customer database table and order database table, matching on equal keys from each side of the join.

In the following example, the `join` operator is used to join the `Contact` table to the Employee table using the matching `ContactID` columns of each table.

```
from c in contact
join emp in employee on c.ContactID equals emp.ContactID
where c.FirstName.StartsWith("S")
orderby c.LastName
select new {emp.EmployeeID, c.FirstName, c.LastName,
  c.EmailAddress, emp.Title, emp.HireDate}
```

Like relational database joins, joins can be performed on more than two sources. The preceding example joins two tables or data sources, but you can just as easily join on more:

```
from c in contact
join emp in employee on c.ContactID equals emp.ContactID
join ind in individual on c.ContactID equals ind.ContactID
join cust in customer on ind.CustomerID equals cust.CustomerID
where c.FirstName.StartsWith("S")
orderby c.LastName
select new {emp.EmployeeID, c.FirstName, c.LastName, c.EmailAddress,
  emp.Title, emp.HireDate, cust.AccountNumber}
```

Each additional join associates a new table or data source with the results of the previous join.

The first example could also be written using method syntax as follows:

```
var query =
    contact.Join(employee, con => con.ContactID,
    emp => emp.ContactID, (con, emp) => new
    { Contact = con.FirstName, Employee} );
```

GroupJoin

The `GroupJoin` operator joins each value or element from the primary (first or left) data source with a set of corresponding values from the secondary (right) data source. This type of join comes in handy when you want to create a hierarchical data structure.

The following example uses `GroupJoin` to create a hierarchical structure from two different data sources. The first data source lists motocross race teams, and the second data source lists the riders for each of those teams. The `GroupJoin` operator is used join the two data sources together and produce an output that lists the team and their associated riders.

```
List<Team> teams = new List<Team>{ new Team { name = "Yamaha"},
                                   new Team { name = "Honda"} ,
                                   new Team { name = "Kawasaki"} ,
                                   new Team { name = "Suzuki"}} ;

List<Rider> riders = new List<Rider> {
  new Rider { name = "Grant Langston", TeamName = "Yamaha"},
  new Rider { name = "Andrew Short", TeamName = "Honda"},
  new Rider { name = "James Steward", TeamName = "Kawasaki"},
  new Rider { name = " Broc Hepler", TeamName = "Yamaha"},
  new Rider { name = "Tommy Hahn", TeamName = "Honda"},
```

```
        new Rider { name = "Tim Ferry", TeamName = "Kawasaki"},
        new Rider { name = " Chad Reed", TeamName = "Yamaha"},
        new Rider { name = "Davi Millsaps", TeamName = "Honda"},
        new Rider { name = "Ricky Carmichael", TeamName = "Suzuki"},
        new Rider { name = "Kevin Windham", TeamName = "Honda"}};

    var teamsandriders = teams.GroupJoin(riders,
                Team => Team.name,
                Rider => Rider.TeamName,
                (team, teamRiders) => new {Team = team.name,
                riders = teamRiders.Select(rider => rider.name)});

    foreach (var tar in teamsandriders)
    {
        listBox1.Items.Add(tar.Team);
        foreach (string rider in tar.riders)
        listBox1.Items.Add("   " + rider);
    }
```

The results from this query look like this:

```
 Yamaha
  Grant Langston
  Broc Hepler
  Chad Reed
Honda
  Andrew Short
  Tommy Hahn
  Davi Millsaps
  Kevin Windham
Kawasaki
  James Stewart
  Tim Ferry
Suzuki
  Ricky Carmichael
```

This example used an in-memory array to apply a `Groupjoin`, to help you understand the concept of the operator. The same can be applied to a LINQ to SQL query:

```
private void cmdGroupJoin_Click(object sender, EventArgs e)
{
  DataContext context = new DataContext("Initial Catalog=AdventureWorks;Integrated
  Security=sspi");

  Table<SalesPerson> salespeople = context.GetTable<SalesPerson>();
  Table<SalesOrderHeader> orders = context.GetTable<SalesOrderHeader>();

  var salespeopleandorders = salespeople.GroupJoin(orders,
     SalesPerson => SalesPerson.SalesPersonID,
     SalesOrderHeader => SalesOrderHeader.SalesPersonID,
     (person, salesorder) => new { SalesPerson = person.SalesPersonID,
     orders = salesorder.Select(order => order.CustomerID)} );

  foreach (var sao in salespeopleandorders)
```

```
    {
       listBox1.Items.Add(sao.SalesPerson);
       foreach (int order in sao.orders)
       listBox1.Items.Add("    " + order);
    }

}
```

The results of this query list each `salespersonid` and the associated order `customerid`. Here's a portion of the output:

```
279
  676
  117
  442
  227
283
  2
107
56
310
527
638
157
```

Grouping Operator

Grouping is the concept of grouping the values or elements of a sequence according to a specified value (selector). LINQ contains a single grouping operator, `GroupBy`.

The following example uses the `Sales.SalesOrderHeader` table in the AdventureWorks database to group together orders for each sales person using the `SalesPersonID` as the key value.

```
DataContext context = new DataContext("Initial
  Catalog=AdventureWorks;Integrated Security=sspi");

Table<SalesOrderHeader> orders = context.GetTable<SalesOrderHeader>();

var query = orders.Where(ord => ord.SalesPersonID > 0).GroupBy(order =>
  order.SalesPersonID,
  order => order.CustomerID);

foreach (var o in query)
{
   listBox1.Items.Add(o.Key);
   foreach (int cust in o)
      listBox1.Items.Add("    " + cust);
}
```

It can also be written as follows (given the same `DataContext` and table):

```
IEnumerable<IGrouping<int, int>> query = orders.Where(ord =>
  ord.SalesPersonID > 0).GroupBy(order => order.SalesPersonID, order =>
  order.CustomerID);
```

```
foreach (IGrouping<int, int> o in query)
{
   listBox1.Items.Add(o.Key);
   foreach (int cust in o)
      listBox1.Items.Add("   " + cust);
}
```

Here are the results:

```
268
  697
  47
  471
  548
  167
  ...
275
  504
  618
  17
  486
  269
276
  510
  511
  259
  384
  650
...
```

The first example could also be written using a mix of query syntax and method syntax as follows:

```
var query =
     (from o in orders
      where o.SalesPersonID > 0
      select o).GroupBy(order => order.SalesPersonID,
          order => order.CustomerID);
```

This makes the query somewhat easier to read, even though the example used a mix of the two syntaxes. The reason for the mix of syntaxes in this example is that the `GroupBy` operator is not available in query syntax.

This example also gives you an idea of the flexibility you have when using the standard query operators.

Concatenating Operator

Concatenating is the process of joining two objects together. In LINQ, concatenating joins two collections into a single collection, and is accomplished via the `Concat` operator.

In the following example, contact last names are concatenated with `CustomerIDs` from the `Person.Contact` table and `Sales.SalesOrderHeader` table:

```
DataContext context = new DataContext("Initial Catalog=@@ta
AdventureWorks;Integrated Security=sspi");
```

```
Table<Contact> contacts = context.GetTable<Contact>();
Table<SalesOrderHeader> orders = context.GetTable<SalesOrderHeader>();

var query = contacts.Select(con => con.LastName).Concat(orders.Select(order @@@ta
=> order.CustomerID.ToString()));

foreach (var item in query)
{
    listBox1.Items.Add(item);
}
```

The results in the list box will first list all of the contacts' last names, followed by all of the `CustomerID`s.

Aggregating Operators

Aggregate functions perform calculations on a set of values and return a single value, such as performing a sum or count on values of a given element. There are seven LINQ aggregate query operators: `Aggregate`; `Average`, `Count`, `LongCount`, `Max`, `Min`, and `Sum`.

Aggregate

The `Aggregate` operator gathers values from a given sequence or collection. It accumulates values returned from a sequence and returns when the aggregation is complete. For instance, the following example uses the `Aggregate` operator to build a new sentence in reverse from an array of strings.

```
string Names = "Steve, Scott, Joe, John, Chris, Jason";
string[] name = Names.Split(', ');
string newName = name.Aggregate(workingName, next) =>
    next + " " + workingName);

listbox.Items.Add(newName);
```

Average

The `Average` operator computes the average from a sequence of numerical values. It works on many data types, such as decimal, integers (Int32, Int64, and the like), and doubles.

In its simplest form, the `Average` operator works as follows:

```
List<int> quantity = new List<int> {99, 48, 120, 73, 101, 81, 56};
double average = quantity.Average();
listbox1.items.add(average);
```

This example computes the average of the seven numbers in the list and returns that value. This type of calculation can be applied to the following example, in which the `Average` operator is used to calculate the average unit price of all the products for a given order:

```
var query =
   from od in orderdetail
   where od.SalesOrderID == 43662
```

```
    select od.UnitPrice;
listbox1.Items.Add(query.Average());
```

The query can also be written as follows:

```
var query =
   from od in orderdetail
   where od.SalesOrderID == 43662
   select od;

listbox1.Items.Add(query.Average(orderDetail => orderDetail.UnitPrice));
```

This operator is applied to a sequence of values.

Count

The `Count` operator counts the number of elements in a given collection. It should be used if the expected result is going to be less than `Int32.MaxValue` (the largest possible value of an Int32).

The following example shows the `Count` operator in its simplest form. The list contains seven numbers and the count operator is applied to count the numbers in the list.

```
List<int> quantity = new List<int> {99, 48, 120, 73, 101, 81, 56};
int cnt = quantity.Count;
listbox1.items.add(cnt);
```

When run, this query returns 7. In the following example, the `Count` operator is used to count the number of items for the specified sales order.

```
var query =
   from od in orderdetail
   where od.SalesOrderID == 43662
   select od.UnitPrice;

listbox1.Items.Add(query.Count());
```

When this query is executed, the list box contains the value of 22, meaning that there are 22 items for the specified order.

You can also specify a criterion for the `Count` operator. Here's an example in which the `Count` operator is applied but given a condition, where the unit price is less than 200.

```
var query =
   from od in orderdetail
   where od.SalesOrderID == 43662
   select od;

listbox1.Items.Add(query.Count(orderDetail => orderDetail.UnitPrice < 200));
```

LongCount

The `LongCount` operator, which returns an Int64 (a 64-bit integer), is used to count the number of elements in a large collection—one with more than `Int32.MaxValue` elements. You use `LongCount` the same way you use the `Count` operator, as shown in the following example:

```
List<Int64> quantity = new List<Int64> {99, 48, 120, 73, 101, 81, 56};
Int64 cnt = quantity.LongCount();
listbox1.items.add(cnt);
```

Now count the number of items in an order:

```
var query =
   from od in orderdetail
   where od.SalesOrderID == 43662
   select od.UnitPrice;

listbox1.Items.Add(query.LongCount());
```

And here's the example specifying a specific condition:

```
var query =
   from od in orderdetail
   where od.SalesOrderID == 43662
   select od;

listbox1.Items.Add(query.LongCount(orderDetail => orderDetail.UnitPrice < 200));
```

Max

The `Max` operator returns the maximum value within a sequence. Like the `Average` operator, `Max` works on many data types, including decimals, integers, and doubles.

The following example returns the maximum value from the list of provided integers:

```
List<int> quantity = new List<int> {99, 48, 120, 73, 101, 81, 56};
int cnt = quantity.Max();
listbox1.items.add(cnt);
```

The value returned is 120. This operator can also be applied to the following example, which returns the maximum unit price of all the items for a specific order.

```
var query =
   from od in orderdetail
   where od.SalesOrderID == 43662
   select od.UnitPrice;

listbox1.Items.Add(query.Max());
```

The value returned is 2146.9620. This query can also be written as follows:

```
var query =
   from od in orderdetail
   where od.SalesOrderID == 43662
```

```
   select od;

listbox1.Items.Add(query.Max(orderDetail => orderDetail.UnitPrice));
```

There is no performance advantage between the two queries; their use is a matter of user preference and readability.

Min

On the flip side is the `Min` operator, which returns the minimum value from a sequence. It also works on many data types, including decimals, integers, and doubles.

The following example returns the minimum value from the list of provided integers:

```
List<int> quantity = new List<int> {99, 48, 120, 73, 101, 81, 56};
int cnt = quantity.Min();
listbox1.items.add(cnt);
```

The value returned from this example is 48. Here's an example that returns the minimum unit price of all the items for a specific order:

```
var query =
   from od in orderdetail
   where od.SalesOrderID == 43662
   select od.UnitPrice;

listbox1.Items.Add(query.Min());
```

The value returned from this query is 178.5808. The query can also be written like this:

```
var query =
   from od in orderdetail
   where od.SalesOrderID == 43662
   select od;

listbox1.Items.Add(query.Min(orderDetail => orderDetail.UnitPrice));
```

Again, there's no performance advantage between the two queries. It's just a matter of preference and readability.

Sum

The `Sum` operator calculates the sum of the selected values within a collection. It also works on many data types, such as decimal, integers, and doubles.

The following example returns the sum of the given values from the list of provided integers:

```
List<int> quantity = new List<int> {99, 48, 120, 73, 101, 81, 56};
int cnt = quantity.Sum();
listbox1.items.add(cnt);
```

The value returned from this example is 578. Here's an example that returns the sum of the unit prices for all the items for a specific order:

```
var query =
    from od in orderdetail
    where od.SalesOrderID == 43662
    select od.UnitPrice;

listbox1.Items.Add(query.Sum());
```

The value returned from this query is 12955.4816. This query can also be written as the following:

```
var query =
    from od in orderdetail
    where od.SalesOrderID == 43662
    select od;
listbox1.Items.Add(query.Sum(orderDetail => orderDetail.UnitPrice));
```

Which query you use is a matter of preference. There's no performance advantage between the two.

Set Operators

Set operators perform actions against elements or sequence sets, and then return a set. There are four LINQ set query operators—`Distinct`, `Union`, `Intersect`, and `Except`.

Distinct

The `Distinct` operator removes duplicate values from a collection and returns distinct elements from that collection (or sequence).

In the following example, the list contains 13 numbers ranging from 1 to 10; some of the numbers (1, 7, and 9) repeat. Applying the `distinct` operator removes the duplicates and returns only the distinct values.

```
List<int> quantity = new List<int> {1, 1, 2, 3, 4, 5, 6, 7, 7, 8, 9, 9, 10};
IEnumerable<int> val = numbers.Distinct();
foreach (int num in val)
  listbox1.Items.Add(num);
```

The results are

```
1
2
3
4
5
6
7
8
9
10
```

To test this using LINQ, open a new query window in SQL Server Management Studio and select the AdventureWorks database. Execute the following query:

```
SELECT SalesOrderDetailID, ProductID, UnitPrice
FROM   Sales.SalesOrderDetail
WHERE  SalesOrderID = 43662
ORDER BY UnitPrice
```

Your results would look like this:

```
Salesordetailid productid unitprice
--------------- --------- ---------
44              722       178.5808
49              738       178.5808
47              726       183.9382
43              729       183.9382
32              730       183.9382
34              725       183.9382
41              732       356.898
48              733       356.898
50              766       419.4589
40              763       419.4589
46              760       419.4589
35              762       419.4589
36              765       419.4589
37              768       419.4589
30              764       419.4589
31              770       419.4589
33              754       874.794
39              756       874.794
42              758       874.794
51              755       874.794
45              749       2146.962
38              753       2146.962
```

Notice that the `unitprice` column contains some duplicate values. With LINQ, you can use the same `Distinct` operator as used in the previous example. Here's how:

```
var query =
   from od in orderdetail
   where od.SalesOrderID == 43662
   select od.UnitPrice;

foreach (decimal num in query.Distinct())
  listbox1.Items.Add(num);
```

Without the trailing decimal places, you get the following results:

```
178
183
356
419
874
2146
```

Union

The Union operator returns the unique elements from the results of a union of two sequences or collections. It is different from the concat operator in that it returns unique values, and the concat operator returns all values.

The following example contains two lists (or data sources) that contain integer values. These lists do not contain duplicate values. The Union operator is applied; it joins the two lists and returns only the unique value in the resultset.

```
int[] numbers1 = { 1, 2, 3, 4, 5, 6, 7, 8, 9, 10} ;
int[] numbers2 = { 11, 12, 13, 14, 15, 16, 17, 18, 19, 20} ;
IEnumerable<int> union = numbers1.Union(numbers2);

foreach (int num in union)
  listBox1.Items.Add(num);
```

The results from this query return the numbers 1 through 20. The next example also contains two lists of numbers, but numbers that exist in the first list also exist in the second list, and the first list also contains duplicate numbers (such as the numbers 1 and 9).

```
int[] numbers1 = { 1, 1, 2, 3, 3, 4, 5, 5, 6, 7, 7, 8, 9, 9, 10} ;
int[] numbers2 = { 1, 3, 5, 7, 9} ;
IEnumerable<int> union = numbers1.Union(numbers2);

foreach (int num in union)
  listBox1.Items.Add(num);
```

When the Union operator is applied in this example, the following results are returned:

```
1
2
3
4
5
6
7
8
9
10
```

Intersect

The intersect operator returns the intersection of two sequences—that is, those values that are common between two sequences or collections.

The following example uses two lists (or data sources) that contain integer values. Again, you can see that there are numbers in the first list that also exist in the second list. The intersect operator is applied; it joins the two lists and returns only those values that are common to both sequences.

```
int[] numbers1 = { 1, 2, 3, 4, 5, 6, 7, 8, 9, 10} ;
int[] numbers2 = { 2, 4, 6, 8, 10} ;
IEnumerable<int> shared = numbers1.Intersect(numbers2);
```

```
foreach (int num in shared)
  listBox1.Items.Add(num);
```

The output is as follows:

```
2
4
6
8
10
```

Except

The `Except` operator is the opposite of the `intersect` operator, in that it returns the difference between two sequences—in other words, it returns values that are unique (not duplicated) in all of the values of the sequences (values that appear in the first sequence but do not appear in the second). In other words, it is "the elements of sequence A less the elements of sequence B."

```
int[] numbers1 = { 1, 2, 3, 4, 5, 6, 7, 8, 9, 10} ;
int[] numbers2 = { 2, 4, 6, 8, 10} ;
IEnumerable<int> shared = numbers1.Except(numbers2);

foreach (int num in shared)
  listBox1.Items.Add(num);
```

The output is

```
1
3
5
7
9
```

Generation Operators

Generation operators create new sequences from the values of existing sequences. The element generation operators are discussed in this section.

Empty

The `Empty` operator returns an empty collection that has a specified type. In the following example, three lists of names are defined and added to an array list. The `Aggregate` operator is applied to gather values from the array list if the array contains more than two elements. The `Empty` operator is then used to provide an empty collection if the criteria is not met (that is, if no arrays have more than two elements).

```
string[] name1 = { "Scott", "Steve"} ;
string[] name2 = { "Joe", "John", "Jim", "Josh", "Joyce"} ;
string[] name3 = { "Dave", "Dinesh", "Doug", "Doyle"} ;

List<string[]> names = new List<string[]> { name1, name2, name3} ;

IEnumerable<string> namelist = names.Aggregate(Enumerable.Empty<string>(),
   (current, next) => next.Length > 2 ? current.Union(next) : current);
```

```
foreach (string item in namelist)
   listBox1.Items.Add(item);
```

When this query is run, the following results are returned because two of the arrays have more than two elements:

```
Joe
John
Jim
Josh
Joyce
Dave
Dinesh
Doug
Doyle
```

Change the query so that it is looking for arrays that have more than five elements, as shown below:

```
IEnumerable<string> namelist = names.Aggregate(Enumerable.Empty<string>(),
   (current, next) => next.Length > 5 ? current.Union(next) : current);
```

When the query is run now, nothing is returned. Or better said, an empty collection is returned. You can tell this by placing a breakpoint on the `foreach` statement. When the query is run, the execution does indeed step into the `foreach` statement, letting you know that an empty collection was returned, but the line that adds items to the list box is not hit or executed.

The `Empty` operator is basically used as a seed value for the aggregate operator if the criteria is not met.

Range

The `Range` operator creates a collection that contains a sequence of numbers. It takes two parameters. The first is the integer value at which to start the sequence, and the second is the number of sequential integers to generate.

Here's an example in which the `Range` operator is used to generate a sequence of numbers starting at 1 and stopping at 10:

```
var coolmath = Enumerable.Range(1, 10);
for each (int num in coolmath)
  listbox1.Items.Add(num);
```

The results are

```
1
2
3
4
6
7
8
9
10
```

Other operators can be added to this as well. The following example generates a list of numbers from 1 to 10 but also uses the `Reverse` operator to generate them backward.

```
var coolmath = Enumerable.Range(1, 10).Reverse();
for each (int num in coolmath)
  listbox1.Items.Add(num);
```

The results are

```
10
9
8
7
6
5
4
3
2
1
```

In the next example, the `Range` operator is used to create a sequence of numbers from 1 to 5 and then multiply each number by 5:

```
var coolmath = Enumerable.Range(1, 5).Select(x => x * 5);
for each (int num in coolmath)
  listbox1.Items.Add(num);
```

The results are as follows:

```
5
10
15
20
25
```

Repeat

The `Repeat` operator creates a single value sequence that repeats itself a specified number of times. The following example creates a sequence of a single string value and repeats that string 10 times:

```
var coolphrase = Enumerable.Repeat("LINQ ROCKS!", 10);
for each (string phrase in coolphrase)
  listbox1.Items.Add(phrase);
```

The result of this query is the phrase ''LINQ ROCKS!'' output 10 times to the list box.

Conversion Operators

Conversion refers to the act of changing the type of input objects to the sequence. The conversion operators do just this, and they are discussed in this section.

AsEnumerable

The `AsEnumerable` operator returns the query input typed as `IEnumerable(Of T)`, meaning that you can change the data source from a type that implements `IEnumerable(Of T)` to `IEnumerable(Of T)` itself.

The following example uses the `AsEnumerable` operator to replace the type's custom `Where` method with that of the standard query operator `Where`.

```
DataContext context = new DataContext("Initial Catalog=AdventureWorks;@@ta
Integrated Security=sspi");

Table<Contact> contact = context.GetTable<Contact>();

IEnumerable<Contact> query =
   contact.AsEnumerable().Where(con => con.FirstName.Contains("K"));

foreach (Contact item in query)
   listBox1.Items.Add(item.FirstName);
```

The results of this query contain all the contact first names that contain the letter *K*. Here are partial results:

```
Kim
Keyley
Karel
Karen
Kris
Kevin
...
```

In this example, the `System.Query.Sequence` implementation of `Where` is utilized, but in the next example, the `Where()` method with a predicate is used:

```
IEnumerable<Contact> query = contact.Where(=> con.FirstName.Contains("K"));
```

Cast

The `Cast` operator casts the element of an `IEnumerable` collection to a specified type. The benefit of this is that by supplying necessary type information, you can invoke standard query operators on nongeneric collections.

The following example uses an `ArrayList` as a data source. An `ArrayList` does not implement `IEnumerable(Of T)`, but by using the `Cast` operator you can use the standard query operators, such as `Select`, to query the sequence.

```
ArrayList names = new ArrayList();

names.Add("Alex");
names.Add("Chuck");
names.Add("Dave");
names.Add("Dinesh");
names.Add("Joe");
names.Add("John");
names.Add("Sarah");
```

```
names.Add("Steve");
IEnumerable<string> query = names.Cast<string>().Select(name => name);

foreach (string item in query)
   listBox1.Items.Add(item);
```

OfType

The `OfType` operator enables you to filter elements of an `IEnumerable` object based on a specific type. In the following example, the `OfType` operator returns only those elements in the sequence that can be cast to a type of `int`:

```
ArrayList names = new ArrayList(7);

names.Add("Scott");
names.Add(1);
names.Add("Dave");
names.Add(2);
names.Add("Dave");
names.Add(3);
names.Add("Steve");
names.Add(4);
names.Add("Joe");

IEnumerable<int> query = names.OfType<int>();
foreach (int item in query)
   listBox1.Items.Add(item);
```

Here are the query's results:

```
1
2
3
4
```

By using the `OfType` operator on an `IEnumerable` object, you have the capability to apply and use standard query operators to query the sequence.

ToArray

The `ToArray` operator creates an array from an `IEnumerable` sequence. You may remember from previous chapters that the `ToArray` operator forces immediate execution of the query. In the following example, `ToArray` is used to query the first names from the `Person.Contact` table and return the results as an array:

```
DataContext context = new DataContext("Initial Catalog =
   AdventureWorks;Integrated Security=sspi");

Table<Contact> contact = context.GetTable<Contact>();

var query = contact.Select(con => con.FirstName).ToArray();

foreach (string item in query)
   listBox1.Items.Add(item);
```

The following lists partial results of running this query:

```
Gustavo
Catherine
Kim
Humberto
Pilar
Frances
Margeret
Carla
Jay
```

ToDictionary

The `ToDictionary` operator inserts all the elements returned in the sequence into a `Dictionary(Of TKey, TValue)`. The following example uses the `ToDictionary` operator to create and populate a `Dictionary(Of TKey, TValue)` and then iterate through that dictionary to populate a list box.

```
DataContext context = new DataContext("Initial Catalog =
   AdventureWorks;Integrated Security=sspi");

Table<Contact> contact = context.GetTable<Contact>();

Dictionary<string, Contact> dict = contact.ToDictionary(con => con.FirstName);

foreach (KeyValuePair<string, Contact> item in dict)
   listBox1.Items.Add(item.Key + " " + item.Value.FirstName + " " +
     item.Value.LastName);
```

The following list shows the partial results of running this query:

```
1 Gustavo Achong
2 Catherine Abel
3 Kim Abercrombie
4 Humberto Acevedo
5 Pilar Ackerman
6 Frances Adams
7 Margeret Smith
8 Carla Adams
```

ToList

The `ToList` operator converts an `IEnumerable` sequence collection to a `List(Of T)`. It also forces immediate execution of the query. The following code uses the `ToList` operator to query the first names from the `Person.Contact` table and return the results as a `List(Of T)`.

```
DataContext context = new DataContext("Initial Catalog =
   AdventureWorks;Integrated Security=sspi");

Table<Contact> contact = context.GetTable<Contact>();

var query = (from c in contact
         select c.FirstName).ToList();
```

```
foreach (string item in query)
   listBox1.Items.Add(item);
```

ToLookup

The `ToLookup` operator puts the returned elements into a `Lookup(Of Tkey, TElement)`, based on a specified key. A `Lookup` is a collection of keys, each of which is mapped to one or more values; you can think of it as a one-to-many dictionary.

The following example uses the `ToLookup` operator to create and populate a `Lookup(Of TKey, TElement)` and then iterate through that `Lookup` to populate a list box.

```
DataContext context = new DataContext("Initial Catalog =
   AdventureWorks;Integrated Security=sspi");

Table<Contact> contact = context.GetTable<Contact>();
Lookup<string, string> lkp = contact.ToLookup(con => con.FirstName,
   con => con.MiddleName + " " + con.LastName);

foreach (IGrouping<string, string> lkpgrp in lkp)
{
   listBox1.Items.Add(lkpgrp.Key);

   foreach (string item in lkpgrp)
      listBox1.Items.Add("    " + item);
}
```

In this example, a `Lookup` is created, and contacts' first, middle, and last names are used to populate the `Lookup`, using the contact's last name as a key.

Contacts are then grouped by last name, selecting the contact first name and middle name (appended together), and returned as the element values of the `Lookup`. An instance of the `IGrouping` object is then created and used to iterate through in the `Lookup`, writing the key value (the last name), then iterating though each value in the `IGrouping` and writing those values (the first and middle names).

Here's a partial list of the results written to the list box:

```
Gustavo
  Achong
  Camargo
Catherine
  R. Abel
  M.Whitney
  J Brooks
  Kelly
  Sanders
  Peterson
...
```

Element Operators

Element operators return a single, specific element from a sequence. The element operators are discussed in this section.

DefaultIfEmpty

The `DefaultIfEmpty` operator replaces an empty collection with collection that contains a default singleton value. It can be used to return a default value in case the sequence returned is empty and you still need something returned.

The following example queries the `Contact` table looking for all contacts whose first name begins with the letter *Z*. You know from previous examples that this query will return some values; however, the `DefaultIfEmpty` operator is used in case an empty sequence is returned.

```
DataContext context = new DataContext("Initial Catalog = AdventureWorks;Integrated
   Security=sspi");

Table<Contact> contact = context.GetTable<Contact>();

var query = from c in contact
   where c.FirstName.StartsWith("Z")
   select c.FirstName;

foreach (string item in query.DefaultIfEmpty())
   listBox1.Items.Add(item);
```

When the query is executed, all first names that begin with the letter *Z* are returned. Modify the query, changing the criteria to look for first names that begin with the letters *ZZ*:

```
var query = from c in contact
   where c.FirstName.StartsWith("ZZ")
   select c.FirstName;

foreach (string item in query.DefaultIfEmpty("none"))
   listBox1.Items.Add(item);
```

When this query runs, it does not find any first names that begin with the letters *ZZ*, so nothing will be returned, and the `DefaultIfEmpty` operator instructs the query to produce an empty sequence.

Just as a reminder: reference and nullable types have a default value of `null`.

ElementAt

The `ElementAt` operator returns an element at a given index from a collection. The collection is zero-based and the return value is the element at the specified position in the source. In the following example, the `Contact` table is queried looking for all contacts whose first name begins with the letter *S*. However, the `ElementAt` operator is utilized to return the element at the first position by passing the value of `0` as a parameter to the `ElementAt` operator.

```
DataContext context = new DataContext("Initial Catalog = AdventureWorks;Integrated
   Security=sspi");

Table<Contact> contact = context.GetTable<Contact>();

var query = from c in contact
            where c.FirstName.StartsWith("S")
            select c.FirstName;

listBox1.Items.Add(query.ElementAt(0));
```

Running this query will return the following:

```
Zheng
```

Be careful not to pass an index that is out of range; otherwise, the method throws an `index out of range` error. If you're not sure of the index, use the `ElementAtOrDefault`. operator.

ElementAtOrDefault

The `ElementAtOrDefault` operator combines the `ElementAt` operator with some of the functionality of the `DefaultIfEmpty` operator by returning the element at a specified index or a default value if the index is out of range.

In the following example, the `ElementAtOrDefault` operator returns the element at index 50,000 (there are slightly fewer the 20,000 contacts):

```
DataContext context = new DataContext("Initial Catalog = AdventureWorks;Integrated
   Security=sspi");

Table<Contact> contact = context.GetTable<Contact>();

var query = from c in contact
            where c.FirstName.StartsWith("S")
            select c.FirstName;

listBox1.Items.Add(query.ElementAtOrDefault(50000));
```

When this query is executed, it tries to return the value at the specified index; when it does not find an element at that index, it returns a default value of `0`.

First

As its name suggests, the `First` operator returns the first element in a collection. Here's an example that queries the `Contact` table looking for all contacts whose first name begins with the letter *S*. The `First` operator returns the first element from the resulting collection.

```
DataContext context = new DataContext("Initial Catalog = @@ta
AdventureWorks;Integrated Security=sspi");
Table<Contact> contact = context.GetTable<Contact>();

var query = from c in contact
            where c.FirstName.StartsWith("S")
            select c.FirstName;

listBox1.Items.Add(query.First());
```

This method throws an exception if the source sequence contains no elements. Use the `FirstOrDefault` operator if there is a possibility that the source might be empty.

You can also add specific criteria when using this operator. The following code returns the first element that satisfies a specific condition, the first name whose length is greater than 5.

```
listBox1.Items.Add(query.First(name => name.Length > 5));
```

Last

The opposite of the `First` operator, the `Last` operator returns the last element in a collection. Here the `Contact` table is queried looking for all contacts whose first name begins with the letter *S*, and the `Last` operator returns the last element from the returned collection:

```
DataContext context = new DataContext("Initial Catalog = @@ta
AdventureWorks;Integrated Security=sspi");

Table<Contact> contact = context.GetTable<Contact>();

var query = from c in contact
            where c.FirstName.StartsWith("S")
            select c.FirstName;

listBox1.Items.Add(query.Last());
```

You can also add specific criteria when using this operator. For instance, the following returns the last element that satisfies a specific condition, the first name whose length is less than 5:

```
listBox1.Items.Add(query.Last(name => name.Length < 5));
```

FirstOrDefault

The `FirstOrDefault` operator returns the first element from a collection or, if no element is found, a default value. The following example queries the `Contact` table looking for all contacts whose first name begins with the letters *ZZ*, and the `FirstOrDefault` operator returns the first element from the returned collection. If the element is not found, a default value is returned. The default value is defined as the first element that is found that meets the query condition(s).

```
DataContext context = new DataContext("Initial Catalog=AdventureWorks;Integrated
   Security=sspi");

Table<Contact> contact = context.GetTable<Contact>();
var query = from c in contact
            where c.FirstName.StartsWith("ZZ")
            select c.FirstName;

listBox1.Items.Add(query.FirstOrDefault());
```

You can also add specific criteria when using this operator. The following, for instance, returns the first element that satisfies a specific condition, the first name whose length is greater than 5:

```
listBox1.Items.Add(query.FirstOrDefault(name => name.Length > 5));
```

LastOrDefault

The `LastOrDefault` operator returns the last element from a collection, or a default value if no element is found. Here's another example that queries the `Contact` table for all contacts whose first name begins with the letters *ZZ*. It uses the `LastOrDefault` operator to return the last element from the returned collection. If the element is not found then a default value is returned.

```
DataContext context = new DataContext("Initial Catalog=AdventureWorks;Integrated
   Security=sspi");

Table<Contact> contact = context.GetTable<Contact>();

var query = from c in contact
            where c.FirstName.StartsWith("ZZ")
            select c.FirstName;

listBox1.Items.Add(query.LastOrDefault());
```

You can also add specific criteria when using this operator, such as the following, which returns the last element that satisfies a specific condition, the first name whose length is less than 5.

```
listBox1.Items.Add(query.LastOrDefault(name => name.Length < 5));
```

Single

The `Single` operator returns a single element from a sequence, or the only element that meets a given condition. This operator should be used if you know that your query will return a single element. If the sequence returns multiple elements and this operator is used, an exception is thrown.

The following example queries the `Contact` table for all contacts whose last name equals "Kobylinski," and if any are found, returns the contact's first name. The `Single` operator returns the single element from the returned collection.

```
DataContext context = new DataContext("Initial Catalog=AdventureWorks;Integrated
   Security=sspi");

Table<Contact> contact = context.GetTable<Contact>();

var query = from c in contact
where c.LastName.Equals("Kobylinski")
select c.FirstName;

listBox1.Items.Add(query.Single());
```

When this query runs, the name Andrew is written to the list box, because that's the only contact with the last name of Kobylinski. Now change the query to the following and rerun it.

```
var query = from c in contact
where c.LastName.Equals("Kleinerman")
select c.FirstName;
```

When this query executes, you receive the error that the sequence contains more than one element because there are two contacts whose last name equals "Kleinerman."

You can also specify criteria to this operator as a parameter, as shown in this example:

```
var query2 = from c in contact
select c.LastName;

listBox1.Items.Add(query2.Single(con => con.Equals("Kobylinski")));
```

SingleOrDefault

Similar to the `Single` operator, the `SingleOrDefault` operator returns a single element from a sequence, but it also returns a default value if no element is found. Again, use this operator only if you know that your query will return a single element or that the element will be null when returned. If you use `SingleOrDefault` and the sequence returns multiple elements, an exception is thrown.

Here's a query to the `Contact` table looking for all contacts whose last name equals "Kobylinski" and, if any are found, returning the contact's first name. The `SingleOrDefault` operator returns the single element from the returned collection.

```
DataContext context = new DataContext("Initial Catalog=AdventureWorks;Integrated
   Security=sspi");

Table<Contact> contact = context.GetTable<Contact>();

var query = from c in contact
where c.LastName.StartsWith("Kobylinski")
select c.FirstName;

listBox1.Items.Add(query.SingleOrDefault());
```

When this query runs, the name Andrew is written to the list box, because that's the only contact who has the last name of Kobylinski. Change the query to the following and rerun the query:

```
var query = from c in contact
where c.LastName.Equals("Kleinerman")
select c.FirstName;
```

When this query executes, you get an error stating that the sequence contains more than one element because there are two contacts whose last name equals "Kleinerman."

You can also specify criteria to this operator as a parameter, as shown here:

```
var query2 = from c in contact
select c.LastName;

listBox1.Items.Add(query2.SingleOrDefault(con => con.Equals("Kobylinski")));
```

Equality Operators

Equality operators compare two sequences to check if their corresponding elements are equal. Sequences are considered equal if they have the same number of elements and the values of the elements are the same.

The `SequenceEqual` operator determines if two collections are equal. The determination is done by enumerating the two data sources in parallel and comparing elements. The return value is a Boolean—`true` if the two collections are equal, `false` if they are not.

In the following example, the code returns `true` to the list box because the two integer arrays are defined as equal:

```
int[] numbers1 = { 1, 2, 3, 4, 5, 6, 7, 8, 9, 10} ;
int[] numbers2 = { 1, 2, 3, 4, 5, 6, 7, 8, 9, 10} ;
bool eq = numbers1.SequenceEqual(numbers2);
listBox1.Items.Add(eq);
```

Change the second array to the following, and rerun the code:

```
int[] numbers1 = { 1, 2, 3, 4, 5, 6, 7, 8, 9, 10} ;
int[] numbers2 = { 2, 4, 6, 8, 10} ;
bool eq = numbers1.SequenceEqual(numbers2);
listBox1.Items.Add(eq);
```

This time a value of `false` is written to the list box because the comparison determined that the data sources were not equal.

Quantifier Operators

Quantifier operators return a Boolean value that indicates whether some or all of the elements in a sequence meet a specific condition.

The quantifier operators—`All`, `Any`, and `Contains`—are discussed in this section.

All

The `All` operator determines whether all the values in a collection satisfy a specified condition. The return value is a Boolean—`true` if all the values satisfy the condition, `false` if they do not.

Here, for example, an array of names is defined and the `All` operator is applied, specifying the condition that all the names begin with the letter *J*:

```
Names[] friends = {new Names { Name = "Steve"},
                   new Names  { Name = "Dave"},
                   new Names  { Name = "Joe"},
                   new Names  { Name = "John"},
                   new Names  { Name = "Bill"},
              };

bool firstnames = friends.All(name => name.Name.StartsWith("J"));

listBox1.Items.Add(firstnames).ToString();
```

Obviously, not all names begin with the letter *J*, so the value of `false` is written to the list box. In the next example, the same code and condition exist, except that the array contains only names that begin with the letter *J*:

```
Names[] friends = {new Names { Name = "Jeff"},
                   new Names  { Name = "Jordan"},
                   new Names  { Name = "Joe"},
                   new Names  { Name = "John"},
```

```
                      new Names  { Name = "Jim"},
   };

bool firstnames = friends.All(name => name.Name.StartsWith("J"));

listBox1.Items.Add(firstnames).ToString();
```

This time, `true` is written to the list box. The following example uses data retrieved from the `SalesOrderDetail` table in the AdventureWorks database, applying the `All` operator to determine if all of the unit prices in the table are greater than zero:

```
DataContext context = new DataContext("Initial Catalog = AdventureWorks;Integrated
   Security=sspi");

Table<SalesOrderDetail> orderdetail = context.GetTable<SalesOrderDetail>();

var query =
    from od in orderdetail
    where od.SalesOrderID == 43662
    select od.UnitPrice;

listBox1.Items.Add(query.All(orderDetail => orderDetail.UnitPrice > 0));
```

The value of `true` will be written to the list box because there are no rows in the table whose `unitprice` column contains a value of `0`.

Any

The `Any` operator determines if any of the values in a collection satisfy a specified condition or if the sequence contains any elements. The return value is a Boolean—`true` if all the values satisfy the condition, `false` if they do not.

In the following example, the `Contact` table is queried, returning a sequence of first names whose last name starts with the letter *Z*. The `Any` operator is applied to the sequence to determine if the sequence contains any elements that meet the specified condition.

```
DataContext context = new DataContext("Initial Catalog=AdventureWorks;Integrated
   Security=sspi");

Table<Contact> contact = context.GetTable<Contact>();

var query = from c in contact
            where c.LastName.StartsWith("Z")
            select c.FirstName;

listBox1.Items.Add(query.Any());
```

When this query is run, a value of `true` is written to the list box because there is at least one contact whose last name starts with the letter *Z*.

This operator can also be used to determine if any element of a sequence satisfies a given condition:

```
//satisfies a condition
var query = from c in contact
select c.FirstName;

listBox1.Items.Add(query.Any(con => con.LastName.StartsWith("Z")));
```

Both of these queries return the same thing, as you can see. However, there is no performance benefit of one over the other, except for better readability of the code.

When this query is run, a value of `true` is written to the list box because there is at least one contact whose last name starts with the letter *Z*.

Contains

The `Contains` operator determines whether the returned collection contains a specific element. The return value is a Boolean—`true` if all the values satisfy the condition, `false` if they do not.

The following example queries the `Contact` table, returning a sequence of last names. The `Contains` operator is applied to determine if the sequence contains an element of ''Kleinerman.''

```
DataContext context = new DataContext("Initial Catalog=AdventureWorks;Integrated
   Security=sspi");

Table<Contact> contact = context.GetTable<Contact>();

var query = from c in contact
select c.LastName;

listBox1.Items.Add(query.Contains("Kleinerman"));
```

Because the `Contact` table does contain at least one row whose last name is Kleinerman, the value of `true` is returned and written to the list box.

You can also use a comparer as follows:

```
DataContext context = new DataContext("Initial Catalog=AdventureWorks;Integrated
   Security=sspi");

Table<Contact> contact = context.GetTable<Contact>();

string name = "Kleinerman"

var query = from c in contact
select c.LastName;

listBox1.Items.Add(query.Contains(name));
```

Partitioning Operators

Partitioning is the act of dividing a single input sequence into two or more sections or sequences without rearranging the incoming elements, then returning one of the newly formed sections.

The partitioning operators—`skip`, `skipwhile`, `Take`, and `TakeWhile`—are discussed in this section.

Skip

The `Skip` operator skips elements up to a specified location within a sequence. In other words, it bypasses the specified number of elements and returns the remaining elements.

The following example defines a random set of numbers, orders them in ascending order, then uses the `Skip` operator to skip the first four and return the remaining.

```
Int[] randomNumbers = {86, 2, 77, 94, 100, 65, 5, 22, 70};
IEnumerable<int> skipLowerFour =
    randomNumbers.OrderBy(num => num).Skip(4);

foreach (int number in skipLowerFour)
    listbox1.Items.Add(number);
```

When this query is run, the following numbers are returned:

```
70
77
86
94
100
```

This example could also be written using query syntax as follows:

```
IEnumerable<int> skipLowerFour =
    (from n in randomNumbers
     order by n
     select n).Skip(4)
```

SkipWhile

The `SkipWhile` operator skips or bypasses elements based on a specified predicate function, and continues to bypass the elements as long as the specified condition is true (i.e., the condition is not met). The remaining elements are then returned.

The following example skips all the values in the sequence that are less than 50 and returns the remaining values.

```
Int[] randomNumbers = {86, 2, 77, 94, 100, 65, 5, 22, 70, 55, 81, 66, 45};

IEnumerable<int> skipLessThan50 =
    randomNumbers.OrderBy(num => num).SkipWhile(num =>
    num < 50);

foreach (int number in skipLowerFour)
    listbox1.Items.Add(number);
```

When this query is run, the following numbers are returned:

```
55
65
66
70
77
81
86
94
100
```

Likewise, this example could also be written using query syntax as follows:

```
IEnumerable<int> skipLowerFour =
    (from n in randomNumbers
     order by n
     select n).SkipWhile(num => num < 50);
```

Take

The `Take` operator returns contiguous elements within a sequence, starting at the beginning of the sequence, up to the position specified.

The following example skips all the values in the sequence that are less than 50 and returns the remaining values.

```
Int[] randomNumbers = {86, 2, 77, 94, 100, 65, 5, 22, 70, 55, 81, 66, 45};

IEnumerable<int> takeTopFour =
    randomNumbers.OrderByDescending(num => num).Take(4);

foreach (int number in takeTopFour)
    listbox1.Items.Add(number);
```

When this query is run, the following numbers are returned:

```
100
94
86
81
```

This example could also be written using query syntax as follows:

```
IEnumerable<int> takeTopFour =
    (from n in randomNumbers
     order by n descending
     select n).Take(4);
```

TakeWhile

The `TakeWhile` operator returns elements based on a specified predicate function, and continues to take the elements as long as the specified condition is true (i.e., the condition is not met). The remaining elements are skipped.

The following example takes all the values in the sequence that are less than 50 and skips the remaining values.

```
Int[] randomNumbers = {86, 2, 77, 94, 100, 65, 5, 22, 70, 55, 81, 66, 45};

IEnumerable<int> takeGreaterThan50 =
    randomNumbers.OrderByDescending(num => num).TakeWhile(num => num > 50);

foreach (int number in takeGreaterThan50)
    listbox1.Items.Add(number);
```

When this query is run, the following numbers are returned:

```
100
94
86
81
77
70
66
65
55
```

This example could also be written using query syntax as follows:

```
IEnumerable<int> takeGreaterThan50 =
    (from n in randomNumbers
     order by n descending
     select n).TakeWhile(num => num > 50);
```

As an interesting experiment, try modifying the original query as follows and executing it:

```
IEnumerable<int> takeGreaterThan50 =
    randomNumbers.OrderBy(num => num).TakeWhile(num =>
    num > 50);
```

Was anything returned? Why not? As stated earlier, it returns elements based on a specified predicate function, and continues to take the elements as long as the specified condition is true. If you order the sequence in ascending order, the first element it finds does not meet the criteria and therefore the query does not continue.

Putting Query Operators to Work

There was a ton of information in this chapter, so this section provides an example that enables you to apply many of the operators you've seen and to begin experimenting with the great functionality provided by the LINQ query operators.

Fire up an instance of Visual Studio 2008 and create a new C# Windows Forms Application project. In the Solution Explorer, expand the References node, right-click on it, and select Add Reference from the context menu. In the Add Reference dialog opens, make sure that the .NET tab is selected, and scroll down the list until you see the `System.Data.Linq` component. Select that component and click OK.

Next, open Form1 in design view and place two buttons and a list box on the form. Name one of the buttons cmdExecuteQuery and the other cmdClose. Then view the code behind the form and replace the existing code with the following (this code can also be obtained from the Chapter 4 example in the file download for this chapter):

```
using System;
using System.Linq;
using System.Collections.Generic;
using System.ComponentModel;
using System.Data;
using System.Data.Linq;
using System.Drawing;
using System.Text;
using System.Windows.Forms;
using System.Xml;

namespace LINQ
{
   public partial class Form1 : Form
   {
      public Form1()
      {
         InitializeComponent();
      }

      private void Form1_Load(object sender, EventArgs e)
      {
      }

      private void cmdClose_Click(object sender, EventArgs e)
      {
         Application.Exit();
      }

      private void cmdExecuteQuery_Click(object sender, EventArgs e)
      {
         DataContext context = new DataContext("Initial @@ta
Catalog=AdventureWorks;Integrated Security=sspi");

         Table<Contact> contact = context.GetTable<Contact>();
         Table<Employee> employee = context.GetTable<Employee>();

         var query =
            from c in contact
            join emp in employee on c.ContactID equals emp.ContactID
            where c.FirstName.StartsWith("S")
            && emp.HireDate.Year > 1999
            orderby c.LastName
            orderby c.FirstName
            select new { emp.EmployeeID, c.LastName, c.FirstName, @@ta
emp.Title, c.EmailAddress, emp.HireDate };//.Thenby(c => c.FirstName);

         foreach (var item in query)
            listBox1.Items.Add(item.FirstName
```

```
                + " " + item.LastName
                + " " + item.Title
                + " " + item.EmailAddress
                + " " + item.HireDate);

            }

        }

        [Table(Name = "Person.Contact")]
        public class Contact
        {
            [Column(DBType = "int not null")]
            public int ContactID;

            [Column(DBType = "nvarchar(8) not null")]
            public string Title;

            [Column(DBType = "nvarchar(50) not null")]
            public string FirstName;

            [Column(DBType = "nvarchar(50) not null")]
            public string MiddleName;

            [Column(DBType = "nvarchar(50) not null")]
            public string LastName;

            [Column(DBType = "nvarchar(50) not null")]
            public string EmailAddress;

            [Column(DBType = "int")]
            public int EmailPromotion;

        }

        [Table(Name = "HumanResources.Employee")]
        public class Employee
        {
            [Column(DBType = "int not null")]
            public int ContactID;

            [Column(DBType = "int")]
            public int EmployeeID;

            [Column(DBType = "nvarchar(50) not null")]
            public string Title;

            [Column(DBType = "datetime")]
            public DateTime HireDate;

        }
    }
```

This example creates object-relational mappings to two tables in the AdventureWorks database from which the data for the queries will be pulled. When the OK button is clicked, a connection is made to the appropriate database, and the data sources are defined.

Several operators—join, restriction, and sorting operators, for instance—are used in the query expression. Once the query expression is defined, the query is executed by iterating through the sequence or collection, and the results are written to the form's list box.

The `Employee` and `Contact` tables are joined by creating a join on the `ContactID` column. Several columns between the two tables are projected (selected as elements for return values) and a filter is applied looking for all contacts whose first name begins with the letter *S* and whose hire date is after the year 1999. A sort is applied, ordering the results by last name, sorted in ascending order.

When this query is run, the following results are returned (a portion of the data has been left out for space considerations):

```
Sandeep Kaliyath Production Technician - WC40
Sharon Salavaria Design Engineer
Sheela Word Purchasing Manager
Shu Ito Sales Representative
Sootha Charncherngkha Quality Assurance Technician
Stephen Jiang North American Sales Manager
Stuart Macrae Janitor
Syed Abbas Pacific Sales Manager
Sylvester Valdez Production Technician - WC20
```

While this example is fairly simple, it does provide a great foundation. You can modify it by applying many of the operators discussed in this chapter.

Let's modify this example a little bit. Add a second button to the form, name it `cmdMethodSyntax`, and place the following code in the `Click()` event of that button.

```
         DataContext context = new DataContext("Initial @@ta
Catalog=AdventureWorks;Integrated Security=sspi");

         Table<Contact> contact = context.GetTable<Contact>();
         Table<Employee> employee = context.GetTable<Employee>();

var query =
    contact.Join(employee, con => con.ContactID,
    emp => emp.ContactID, (con, emp) =>
    new { con = con, emp = emp})
    .Where(c => c.con.FirstName.StartsWith("S"))
    .Where(c => c.emp.HireDate.Year > 1999)
    .OrderBy(c => c.con.LastName)
    .OrderBy(c => c.con.FirstName)
    .Select(o => new
    { o.emp.EmployeeID, o.con.LastName, o.con.FirstName,
      o.emp.Title, o.con.EmailAddress, o.emp.HireDate} );

         foreach (var item in query)
```

```
listBox1.Items.Add(item.FirstName
    + " " + item.LastName
    + " " + item.Title
    + " " + item.EmailAddress
    + " " + item.HireDate);
```

This code accomplishes the exact same thing as the preceding code, but uses method syntax. This example is here to illustrate the different ways you can use the LINQ standard query operators.

Summary

This chapter introduced you to LINQ's standard query operators. Without them, LINQ doesn't happen. The chapter provides you with a good foundation in and understanding of their functionality, which will be helpful because the rest of this book utilizes the information found in this chapter.

The next four chapters take a look at LINQ to XML, a new approach to programming with XML.

Part II
LINQ to XML

Chapter 5: Understanding LINQ to XML

Chapter 6: Programming with LINQ to XML

Chapter 7: LINQ to XML and Other LINQ Data Models

Chapter 8: Advanced LINQ to XML Programming Topics

Chapter 9: LINQ to XML and Visual Basic .NET

5

Understanding LINQ to XML

XML is becoming more and more mainstream. It's being used in databases (I love that!), configuration files, and throughout the Web, and is becoming a more popular mechanism for formatting your day-to-day data such as spreadsheets and documents.

Until now, working with XML has been somewhat frustrating because of the many different technologies available to developers to work with XML. There's the DOM (Document Object Model), which provides a standardized interpretation of an XML document. You also have XPath and XSLT, which afford the ability to query and format XML. Within the .NET Framework you have the `System.Xml` namespace, which makes available a programmatic representation of XML documents and mechanisms for manipulating XML documents, nodes, and XML fragments.

There is a need to improve the way developers work with XML, and LINQ to XML is the answer. The first four chapters provided the foundation for the rest of this book, presenting the basic principles of LINQ and its different components, such as the standard query operators. This information is extremely vital to LINQ to XML because it helps developers work with and program XML using LINQ to XML.

This chapter provides an introductory look at LINQ to XML, exploring the fundamentals and concepts that programmers need to comprehend when working with LINQ to XML. It includes the following:

- An overview of LINQ to XML
- Programming fundamentals of LINQ to XML
- Programming concepts of LINQ to XML
- A comparison of LINQ to XML and other XML technologies

LINQ to XML Overview

LINQ to XML is a new approach to working with XML. In essence, it takes many of the technologies you use today to work with XML, such as the DOM and XPath, and combines them into a single programming interface directly within the .NET Framework. LINQ to XML provides in-memory document modification capabilities of the DOM, while providing querying capabilities equal to those of XPath via LINQ query expressions.

Any programming language that supports the .NET Framework supports LINQ. LINQ to XML is "LINQ-enabled," meaning that you have access to all of the functionality of LINQ, such as the standard query operators and the LINQ programming interface. Because of its integration into the .NET Framework, LINQ to XML can take advantage of .NET Framework functionality, such as compile-time checking, strong typing, and debugging.

As stated previously, LINQ to XML provides much of the functionality found in today's XML technologies, but it does so from within a single programming interface. Using LINQ to XML you can easily load XML documents into memory and just as easily query and modify the documents. You can also save in-memory XML documents to disk, as well as serialize them for routing over the wire.

The great thing about LINQ to XML (and LINQ in general) is that it makes working with XML much simpler, and therefore developers who do not have a whole lot of experience with XML can jump right in. LINQ to XML provides developers of all levels the capability to easily work with XML. For those who are somewhat new to working with XML, LINQ to XML provides a simple but powerful query experience (instead of their having to learn a more complex XML query language). More-advanced developers can use LINQ to XML to enhance their XML programming by writing less code that is just as powerful, easier to read, and much more expressive. The key is that LINQ to XML is not targeted to a specific level of developer—it can be used by any developer who needs to work with XML.

LINQ to XML is provided via the `System.Xml.Linq` namespace, which contains all of the classes necessary to work with XML. Add a reference to `System.Xml.Linq.dll` to your project, and then place a `using` directive in the declarations section of your code, as follows:

```
using System.Xml.Linq;
```

Adding this directive enables the use of LINQ to XML types in the namespace. If you plan to work with relational data, you need to use `System.Data.Linq` as well.

LINQ to XML Programming Fundamentals

As Chapter 2, "A Look at Visual Studio 2008," explained, LINQ (and therefore LINQ to XML) utilizes generic classes quite heavily. Therefore, it is quite helpful to have an understanding of generics and delegates as you get into LINQ and LINQ to XML.

The component that gives LINQ to XML its power is the `System.Xml.Linq` namespace and its corresponding classes. Those classes provide the capability to work with XML with ease, leaving behind the need to work with complex and sometimes cumbersome technologies such as the DOM and XQuery.

The following sections provide an overview of the classes in the `System.Xml.Linq` namespace, and then detailed discussions of the `XDocument`, `XElement`, and `XAttribute` classes.

LINQ to XML Classes

The `System.Xml.Linq` namespace contains 19 classes, which are described in the following table.

Class	Description
`XAttribute`	Represents an XML attribute.
`XCData`	Represents a CDATA text node.
`XComment`	Represents an XML comment.
`XContainer`	An abstract base class representing nodes that have child nodes.
`XDeclaration`	Represents an XML declaration.
`XDocument`	Represents an XML document. This class is derived from the `XContainer` class.
`XDocumentType`	Represents an XML DTD (document type definition).
`XElement`	Represents an XML element. This class is derived from the `XContainer` class.
`XName`	Represents the name of an XML element or attribute.
`XNamespace`	Represents an XML namespace.
`XNode`	An abstract class representing nodes of an XML element tree.
`XNodeDocumentOrderComparer`	Provides mechanisms for node comparisons regarding their order within the XML document.
`XNodeEqualityComparer`	Provides mechanisms for node comparisons regarding their equality value.
`XObject`	An abstract class representing `XNodes` and `XAttributes`.
`XObjectChange`	The event type when an `XObject` event is raised.
`XObjectChangeEventArgs`	Provides information and data for the `Changing` and `Changed` events.
`XObjectChangeEventHandler`	The method that will handle the `XObject`'s `Changed` and `Changing` events.
`XProcessingInstruction`	Represents an XML processing instruction.
`XText`	Represents an XML text node.

If you have done any programming with XML before, you are familiar with XML declarations. An XML declaration specifies the XML version, the encoding of an XML document, and whether the XML document is a standalone document. LINQ to XML lets you do this quite easily. The following example uses the `XDeclaration` class to define an XML declaration:

```
XDocument myDoc = new XDocument
(
  new XDeclaration("1.0","utf-8","yes"),
  new XElement("Root","stuff"),
);
```

```
string str = myDoc.Declaration.ToString() + Environment.NewLine + myDoc.ToString();

textbox1.Text = str;
```

What you get is the following:

```
<?xml version="1.0" encoding="utf-8" standalone="yes"?>
<Root>stuff</Root>
```

Very slick. As you start to use the LINQ to XML classes, you begin to get a feel for how much thought Microsoft put into LINQ (including LINQ to XML and LINQ to SQL). One of the things it focused on is names. Often the difficulty in working with XML is in dealing with XML names due to the simple fact of XML prefixes.

In XML, prefixes can come in handy. The main concept behind them is to reduce the amount of typing you have to do when creating XML. It also makes XML much easier to read. Yet prefixes are not required and the problem they cause is that they shortcut the full XML namespace. LINQ to XML solves this problem by automatically resolving prefixes to their XML namespace.

The following three sections detail the classes that you will typically use most when working with XML: `XElement`, `XAttribute`, and `XDocument`. If you master those classes, LINQ to XML will become second nature.

XElement Class

The `XElement` class represents an XML element. It is derived from the `XContainer` class, which derives from the `XNode` class. An element is a node, so many times you will see these terms used interchangeably. The `XElement` class is one of the most important and fundamental classes of LINQ to XML because it contains all of the functionality necessary to create and manipulate XML elements. Via this class you can create elements, add and modify attributes of elements, and even manipulate the content of an element such as adding, deleting, or modifying child elements.

There are several ways to create XML documents with LINQ to XML, depending on the source of your XML or if you are creating an XML document from scratch. The simplest and most common way to create XML is to use the good ol' `XElement` class of LINQ to XML as follows:

```
XDocument riders = new XDocument
  (new XDeclaration("1.0", "utf-8", "yes"),
    new XComment("Riders for the year 2007"),
    new XElement("Riders",
     new XElement("Rider",
       new XElement("Name", "Ricky Carmichael"),
       new XElement("Class", "450"),
       new XElement("Brand", "Suzuki"),
         new XElement("Sponsers",
           new XElement("Name", "Makita")
           )
         ),
     new XElement("Rider",
       new XElement("Name", "Chad Reed"),
       new XElement("Class", "450"),
```

```
            new XElement("Brand", "Yamaha"),
            new XElement("Sponsers",
              new XElement("Name", "ProTaper")
              )
            ),
          new XElement("Rider",
            new XElement("Name", "James Stewart"),
            new XElement("Class", "450"),
            new XElement("Brand", "Kawasaki"),
            new XElement("Sponsers",
              new XElement("Name", "Renthal")
              )
          )
        )
    );
```

The resulting XML looks like this:

```
<!--Riders for the year 2007-->
<Riders>
  <Rider>
    <Name>Ricky Carmichael</Name>
    <Class>450</Class>
    <Brand>Suzuki</Brand>
    <Sponsers>
      <Name>Makita</Name>
    </Sponsers>
  </Rider>
  <Rider>
    <Name>Chad Reed</Name>
    <Class>450</Class>
    <Brand>Yamaha</Brand>
    <Sponsers>
      <Name>ProTaper</Name>
    </Sponsers>
  </Rider>
  <Rider>
    <Name>James Stewart</Name>
    <Class>450</Class>
    <Brand>Kawasaki</Brand>
    <Sponsers>
      <Name>Renthal</Name>
    </Sponsers>
  </Rider>
</Riders>
```

You can also use a LINQ query to populate an XML tree. Create a directory called Wrox in the root of your C drive, for example, and in your favorite text editor program, type the following, saving it as `Employees.xml`:

```
<?xml version="1.0"?>
<Employees>
    <Employee id="1">
        <Name>Steve Kent</Name>
```

```
        <Title>Mr. SciFi</Title>
        <Department>Gaming</Department>
        <HireDate>04/17/92</HireDate>
        <Gender>M</Gender>
        <MaritalStatus>M</MaritalStatus>
    </Employee>
    <Employee id="2">
        <Name>Scott Klein</Name>
        <Title>Geek</Title>
        <Department>All things technical</Department>
        <HireDate>02/05/94</HireDate>
        <Gender>M</Gender>
        <MaritalStatus>M</MaritalStatus>
    </Employee>
</Employees>
```

The following code loads `Employees.xml` using the `Load` method of the `XElement` class. The results of `Load` are then used to create and populate an XML tree, while adding two more elements to the tree.

```
XElement employees = XElement.Load(@"C:\Wrox\Employees.xml");

XElement tree = new XElement("Root",
                    new XElement("Manager", "Dave"),
                    new XElement("BirthDate", "01/01/1970"),
                    from el in employees.Elements()
                    select el);
textBox1.Text = tree.ToString();
```

When this code runs, the following output appears:

```
<Root>
  <Manager>Dave</Manager>
  <BirthDate>01/01/1970</BirthDate>
  <Employee id="1">
    <Name>Steve Kent</Name>
    <Title>Mr. SciFi</Title>
    <Department>Gaming</Department>
    <HireDate>04/17/92</HireDate>
    <Gender>M</Gender>
    <MaritalStatus>M</MaritalStatus>
  </Employee>
  <Employee id="2">
    <Name>Scott Klein</Name>
    <Title>Geek</Title>
    <Department>All things technical</Department>
    <HireDate>02/05/94</HireDate>
    <Gender>M</Gender>
    <MaritalStatus>M</MaritalStatus>
  </Employee>
</Root>
```

The `XElement` class contains a number of methods that make working with XML a breeze. The following table describes the class's methods.

Method	Description
AddAnnotation	Adds an annotation to a given XElement. In general terms, this method adds an object to the annotation of the corresponding XObject (the current node or attribute in the tree).
AncestorsAndSelf	Returns a collection of elements, in which the collection contains the current element and all ancestors of the current element. An ancestor is defined as the parent(s) of the current node (meaning, the parent of the current node, and the parent's parent, and so on up the chain).
Attribute	Returns a single attribute, which is the XAttribute of the current XElement of a given XName. In other words, this method returns the first attribute it finds for a given element that has a specified name.
Attributes	Returns all the attributes (a collection) for the current element. You can also specify a name, in which case all attributes are returned for the element that has the specified name.
CreateReader	Creates an XmlReader (a fast, forward-only copy of the XML document) of the current node.
CreateWriter	Creates an XmlWriter of the XML document that provides the capability to modify the XML document, such as adding nodes or attributes. The XmlWriter is a fast, forward-only mechanism for creating files of the in-memory XML document.
DescendantNodes	Returns a collection of all descendant nodes of the entire document or the current node/element.
DescendantNodesAndSelf	Returns the same collection as the DescenantNodes method but also includes the current node in the collection.
DescendantsAndSelf	Returns a collection of elements that contain the current element plus all descendant elements of the current element. You can also specify a name that returns only those elements that match the specified name in the collection.
Element	In an ordered XML document, Element returns the first element that matches the specified element name.
IsAfter	Returns a Boolean value that specifies whether the current node appears after a specified node.
IsBefore	Returns a Boolean value that specifies whether the current node appears before a specified node.
Load	Provides multiple mechanisms for creating new XElements from an external source. Sources can include a TextReader, String, or XmlReader (each with an additional option to preserve whitespace).
Nodes	Returns a collection of child nodes of the current element or document.
NodesAfterSelf	Returns a collection of ordered nodes after (that follow) the current node.

Continued on the next page

Method	Description
`NodesBeforeSelf`	Returns a collection of ordered nodes before the current node.
`Parse`	Loads an XML document from a string containing XML. Can optionally preserve whitespace.
`Remove`	Removes the current node from its parent.
`RemoveAll`	Removes all nodes and attributes from the current element.
`RemoveAttributes`	Removes all attributes from the current element.
`RemoveNodes`	Removes all nodes from the XML document or current element.
`ReplaceAll`	Replaces all child nodes and attributes of the current element with the specified content.
`ReplaceAttributes`	Replaces all the attributes of the current element with the specified content.
`Save`	Serializes the current element's XML tree to any of several destinations, such as a file, `XmlTextWriter`, `XmlWriter`, or `TextWriter`.
`SetAttributeValue`	Sets the value of the current attribute.
`SetElementValue`	Sets the value of a child element.
`SetValue`	Sets the value of the current element.
`WriteTo`	Writes the current element to an `XmlWriter`.

These are powerful yet easy-to-use methods. You'll use several of them in this chapter's examples. For instance, you can use the `CreateReader` method to load an XML tree into an `XmlReader`, like this:

```
XElement employees = null;
employee = XElement.Load(@"C:\Wrox\Employees.xml";
XmlReader rdr = employees.CreateReader();
rdr.MoveToContent();
```

The `XmlReader` can be used to quickly read nodes and its descendants.

There may be times when there are other components used by your existing application that are expecting an `XmlReader` as input or as the source of data. The preceding example shows one way to use LINQ to XML to provide `XmlReader` functionality.

XAttribute Class

The `XAttribute` class deals with attributes, plain and simple. Attributes are name/value pairs associated with elements, but working with attributes is really no different from working with elements. Attributes are similar to elements in many ways, such as their constructors and the methods in which values and collections are returned. Writing a LINQ query expression to return a collection of attributes is structurally and syntactically the same as writing a LINQ query expression for returning a collection of elements.

Elements and attributes also have their differences. For example, attributes are not nodes in an XML tree, so they do not derive from the `XNode` class. Each attribute must have a qualified name that is unique to the element. And attributes are maintained in the XML tree in the order that they are added to the element.

The great thing, however, is that working with the `XAttribute` class is just like working with the `XElement` class.

Here's how to add an attribute to a simple XML tree during construction:

```
XElement employee = new XElement("Root",
                        new XElement("Employee",
                            new XAttribute("id", "1")
                            )
                        );
```

And here's its output:

```
<Root>
  <Employee id="1" />
</Root>
```

Just like elements, multiple attributes can be added at one time. For instance, you could add a `phone` attribute along with the `id` attribute, like this:

```
XElement employee = new XElement("Root",
                        new XElement("Employee",
                            new XAttribute("id", "1"),
                            new XAttribute("phone", "555-555-5555")
                            )
                        );
```

And the output is as follows:

```
<Root>
  <Employee id="1" phone="555-555-5555"/>
</Root>
```

The key to attributes is that they must have a qualified name that is unique to the particular element to which they are being added.

Unlike the `XElement` class, the `XAttribute` class has only a small handful of methods. The methods are similar to `XElement`'s, which makes working with them extremely easy. Here are descriptions of the `XAttribute` class methods:

- `AddAnnotation`—Adds an annotation to a given attribute.
- `Remove`—Removes the attribute from its parent.
- `SetValue`—Sets the value of the current attribute.

The following example creates a simple XML tree with two attributes associated with the `Employee` node:

```
XElement employee = new XElement("Root",
                        new XElement("Employee",
                            new XAttribute("id", "1"),
                            new XAttribute("dept", "Dev")),
                        new XElement("Name", "Scott")
                            )
                        );
```

Here's the resulting XML:

```
<Root>
    <Employee id="1" dept="id" />
    <Name>Scott</Name>
</Root>
```

Now `Remove()` is issued to remove the second attribute:

```
XAttribute attr = employee.Element("Employee").Attribute("dept");
attr.Remove();
```

Just for kicks, try removing the attribute this way:

```
XAttribute attr = employee.Attribute("dept");
attr.Remove();
```

Did it work? No, because you really haven't identified where the attribute `dept` really is, or better said, you haven't identified the element to which the `dept` attribute belongs.

The first example illustrates how to "walk the XML tree" to denote the node you want to deal with.

XDocument Class

The `XDocument` class provides you with the means to work with valid XML documents, including declarations, comments, and processing instructions.

The `XDocument` class derives from `XContainer` and, therefore, can have child nodes. But keep in mind that XML standards limit an `XDocument` object to only a single child `XElement` node, which is the root node or element.

An `XDocument` object can contain the following:

- One `XDeclaration` object—Specifies important parts of an XML declaration, such as the document encoding and XML version.
- One `XElement` object—Specifies the root element of the document.
- One `XDocumentType` object—Represents an XML DTD (document typed definition).

- Multiple `XComment` objects—Specifies an XML comment. A child of the root node, an `XComment` object cannot be the first argument; a valid XML document cannot begin with a comment..
- Multiple `XProcessingInstruction` objects—Specify any information to the application that is processing the XML.

A large portion of the functionality for working with nodes and elements can be obtained through the `XElement` class, and the `XDocument` class should be used only when you absolutely need the capability to work at the document level and need access to comments, processing instructions, and the declaration. Basically, a declaration, comments, and processing instructions are not required for LINQ to XML to work with XML; you need to use the `XDocument` class only if you need the functionality it provides.

For instance, the following example creates a simple XML document with several elements and an attribute, as well as a processing instruction and comments.

```
XDocument doc = new XDocument(
               new XProcessingInstruction("xml-stylesheet", "title='EmpInfo'"),
               new XComment("some comments"),
               new XElement("Root",
                  new XElement("Employees",
                     new XElement("Employee",
                        new XAttribute("id" "1")
                     new XElement("Name", "Scott Klein"),
                     new XElement("Title", "Geek"),
                     new XElement("HireDate", "02/05/2007"),
                     new XElement("Gender", "M")
                           )
                        )
                    )
                    new XComment("more comments"),
               );
```

This code produces the following:

```
<?xml-stylesheet title='EmployeeInfo'?>
<!--some comments-->
<Root>
  <Employees>
    <Employee id="1">
      <Name>Scott Klein</Name>
      <Title>Geek</Title>
      <HireDate>02/05/2007</HireDate>
      <Gender>M</Gender>
    </Employee>
  </Employees>
</Root>
<!--more comments-->
```

Notice how simple it is to construct the XML document and place comments and other information throughout it.

The XDocument class contains a number of methods that are identical to XElement class methods. They're described in the following table.

Method	Description
AddAnnotation	Adds an annotation to a given XElement. In general terms, this method adds an object to the annotation of the corresponding XObject (the current node or attribute in the tree).
CreateReader	Creates an XmlReader (a fast, forward-only copy of the XML document) of the current node.
CreateWriter	Creates an XmlWriter of the XML document that provides the capability to modify the XML document, such as adding nodes or attributes. The XmlWriter is a fast, forward-only mechanism for creating files of the in-memory XML document.
DescendantNodes	Returns a collection of all descendant nodes of the entire document or the current node/element.
Element	In an ordered XML document, Element returns the first element that matches the specified element name.
IsAfter	Returns a Boolean value that specifies whether the current node appears after a specified node.
IsBefore	Returns a Boolean value that specifies whether the current node appears before a specified node.
Load	Provides multiple mechanisms for creating new XElement objects from an external source. Sources can include a TextReader, String, or XmlReader (each with an additional option to preserve whitespace).
Nodes	Returns a collection of child nodes of the current element or document.
NodesAfterSelf	Returns a collection of ordered nodes after (that follow) the current node.
NodesBeforeSelf	Returns a collection of ordered nodes before the current node.
Parse	Loads an XML document from a string containing XML. Can optionally preserve whitespace.
Remove	Removes the current node from its parent.
RemoveNodes	Removes all nodes from the XML document or current element.
Save	Serializes the current element's XmlTree to several output options, such as a file, XmlTextWriter, XmlWriter, and TextWriter.

The following example creates an XML document that contains employee information along with processing instructions and a comment, utilizing all of the classes previously discussed, including the XDocument and XElement classes.

Once the XML document is created, the NodesAfterSelf method of the XElement class is used to return all the elements after the <Employee> element. Those elements are then iterated through and added to the list box. This example requires a Using statement to System.Xml.

```
XElement doc = new XElement("Root",
                        new XElement("Employees",
                            new XElement("Employee",
                                new XAttribute("id" "1"),
                            new XElement("Name", "Scott Klein"),
                            new XElement("Title", "Geek"),
                            new XElement("HireDate", "02/05/2007"),
                            new XElement("Gender", "M")
                                    )
                                )
                    );

XElement xele = xtree. Element("Employees").Element("Employee"). Element("Name");
IEnumerable<XNode> nodes =
    from node in xele.NodesAfterSelf()
    select node;

foreach (XNode inode in nodes)
   listBox1.Items.Add(inode.NodeType == XmlNodeType.Element ?
      (inode as XElement).Value : "");
```

Now you should be able to see how easy and efficient it is to work with XML in LINQ to XML, using the available classes to create, query, and manipulate XML.

LINQ to XML Programming Concepts

This section explores LINQ to XML programming concepts such as how to load XML, create XML from scratch, manipulate XML information, and traverse an XML document.

Working with Existing XML

Loading XML into a LINQ to XML tree is straightforward. You can load XML from a number of sources, such as a string, XmlReader, TextReader, or file.

The following example illustrates how to load from a file:

```
XElement employees = null;
employees = XElement.Load(@"C:\Wrox\Employees.xml");
```

In this example, a variable called employees is declared as an XElement object (an instance of the XElement class). The Load method of the XElement class is then used to load the raw XML from the Employees.xml file into an XML tree and store the XML contents in the employees variable.

XML can also be loaded from a string, using the Parse method:

```
XElement employees = XElement.Parse(@"
    <Employees>
```

```
        <Employee id='1' phone='555-555-5555'>
            <Name>Steve Kent</Name>
            <Title>Mr. SciFi</Title>
            <Department>Gaming</Department>
            <HireDate>04/17/92</HireDate>
            <Gender>M</Gender>
            <MaritalStatus>M</MaritalStatus>
        </Employee>
        <Employee id='2' phone='555-555-5556'>
            <Name>Scott Klein</Name>
            <Title>Geek</Title>
            <Department>All things technical</Department>
            <HireDate>02/05/94</HireDate>
            <Gender>M</Gender>
            <MaritalStatus>M</MaritalStatus>
        </Employee>
        <Employee id='3' phone='555-555-5557'>
            <Name>Joe Walling</Name>
            <Title>Head Geek</Title>
            <Department>All things bleeding edge</Department>
            <HireDate>06/15/93</HireDate>
            <Gender>M</Gender>
            <MaritalStatus>M</MaritalStatus>
        </Employee>
    </Employees>");
```

`Parse` has an optional Boolean overload that enables you to preserve whitespace. When using `Parse`, your XML tree can contain only a single root node.

You can also load XML from a `TextReader`:

```
TextReader tr = new StringReader(@"
    <Employees>
        <Employee id='1' phone='555-555-5555'>
            <Name>Steve Kent</Name>
            <Title>Mr. SciFi</Title>
            <Department>Gaming</Department>
            <HireDate>04/17/92</HireDate>
            <Gender>M</Gender>
            <MaritalStatus>M</MaritalStatus>
        </Employee>
        <Employee id='2' phone='555-555-5556'>
            <Name>Scott Klein</Name>
            <Title>Geek</Title>
            <Department>All things technical</Department>
            <HireDate>02/05/94</HireDate>
            <Gender>M</Gender>
            <MaritalStatus>M</MaritalStatus>
        </Employee>
        <Employee id='3' phone='555-555-5557'>
            <Name>Joe Walling</Name>
            <Title>Head Geek</Title>
```

```
                <Department>All things bleeding edge</Department>
                <HireDate>06/15/93</HireDate>
                <Gender>M</Gender>
                <MaritalStatus>M</MaritalStatus>
            </Employee>
        </Employees>");
    XElement xel = XElement.Load(tr);
    tr.Close();
```

The output of both of these examples is the same XML.

Saving XML via LINQ to XML

Saving XML via LINQ to XML is just as easy as loading XML. For instance, the following example creates a `TextReader`, populates it with an XML document, and then uses the `XElement` class's `Load` method to load the contents of the `TextReader` into the XML `Element`. The `Save()` method is subsequently called to write the XML to a file.

```
TextReader tr = new StringReader(@"
    <Employees>
        <Employee id='1' phone='555-555-5555'>
            <Name>Steve Kent</Name>
            <Title>Mr. SciFi</Title>
            <Department>Gaming</Department>
            <HireDate>04/17/92</HireDate>
            <Gender>M</Gender>
            <MaritalStatus>M</MaritalStatus>
        </Employee>
        <Employee id='2' phone='555-555-5556'>
            <Name>Scott Klein</Name>
            <Title>Geek</Title>
            <Department>All things technical</Department>
            <HireDate>02/05/94</HireDate>
            <Gender>M</Gender>
            <MaritalStatus>M</MaritalStatus>
        </Employee>
        <Employee id='3' phone='555-555-5557'>
            <Name>Joe Walling</Name>
            <Title>Head Geek</Title>
            <Department>All things bleeding edge</Department>
            <HireDate>06/15/93</HireDate>
            <Gender>M</Gender>
            <MaritalStatus>M</MaritalStatus>
        </Employee>
    </Employees>");
XElement xel = XElement.Load(tr);
tr.Close();
xel.Save(@"C:\Wrox\Employees2.xml");
```

Saving XML like this is commonly known as serializing. If the XML that is loaded into the `XML` class is indented, the serialized XML keeps its formatting, thus maintaining the indentation of the XML, although any insignificant whitespace is removed.

Creating XML

LINQ to XML provides a powerful yet easy approach to manually creating XML elements. You have seen this method quite a bit throughout this chapter. The section "LINQ to XML Programming Fundamentals" listed several classes available to you via LINQ to XML in which you can manually create XML documents.

Here's an example that creates a simple XML document consisting of elements and attributes:

```
XElement xdoc = new XElement("Riders",
                    new XElement("Rider",
                        new XElement("Name", "Ricky Carmichael"),
                        new XElement("NationalNumber", "4"),
                        new XElement("Mechanic", "Mike Gosselaar"),
                        new XElement("Nickname", "GOAT")
                        )
                    );
```

And here's the output:

```
<Riders>
  <Rider>
    <Name>Ricky Carmichael</Name>
    <NationalNumber>4</NationalNumber>
    <Mechanic>Mike Gosselaar</Mechanic>
    <Nickname>GOAT</Nickname>
  </Rider>
</Riders>
```

The great thing about LINQ to XML in the .NET Framework is that indentation is automatically done for you. That makes reading it much easier because it mimics the format and structure of XML. (Oh, by the way, anyone who follows the supercross/motocross scene knows that Ricky Carmichael's nickname is not a reference to the animal, but to his achievements in the sport. GOAT: Greatest of All Time.)

Now modify the previous example by adding the highlighted line of code:

```
XElement xdoc = new XElement("Riders",
                    new XElement("Rider",
                        new XElement("Name", "Ricky Carmichael",
                            new XAttribute("Class", "450")),
                        new XElement("NationalNumber", "4"),
                        new XElement("Mechanic", "Mike Gosselaar"),
                        new XElement("Nickname", "GOAT")
                        )
                    );
```

Notice the results now show an attribute called `Class` on the `Name` element:

```
<Riders>
  <Rider>
    <Name Class="450">Ricky Carmichael</Name>
    <NationalNumber>4</NationalNumber>
```

```
      <Mechanic>Mike Gosselaar</Mechanic>
      <Nickname>GOAT</Nickname>
    </Rider>
  </Riders>
```

LINQ to XML also provides a simple yet powerful mechanism for creating an XML tree in a single statement. This functionality is called *functional construction*, which will be discussed in Chapter 6, "Programming with LINQ to XML."

Traversing XML

So, you have your XML document in memory, whether you created it manually or loaded it using the `Load` method of the `XElement` class. Now what do you do with it? Specifically, how do you navigate the XML tree to get to the node/element you want to work with?

Traversing XML in an XML tree in LINQ to XML is quite simple. Just use the methods of the `XElement` and `XAttribute` classes as necessary. Basically, the `Elements` and `Element` methods provide all of the element children of an `XContainer` (an `XElement` or `XDocument`) object. Using the `XName` object, such as `Element(XName)`, you can return the elements of that specific `XName`.

Once you have your XML tree loaded as shown here:

```
employees = XElement.Load(@"C:\Wrox\Employees.xml");
```

you can start "walking the XML tree." Here are a couple of examples:

```
employees.Element("Employees").Element("Employee")

employees.Element("Employees").Element("Employee").Element("Name")
```

Granted, there is much more you can do, but this is just to whet your appetite. Keep in mind you can do the same with attributes. All of this is explained in more detail in Chapter 6.

The following is a simple example of returning elements of a particular node. It creates an XML document containing several riders, with each rider containing one attribute.

```
XElement xdoc = new XElement("Riders",
        new XElement("Rider",
            new XElement("Name", "Ricky Carmichael",
                new XAttribute("Class", "450")),
            new XElement("NationalNumber", "4"),
            new XElement("Brand", "Suzuki"),
            new XElement("Nickname", "GOAT"),
            new XElement("Mechanic", "Mike Gosselaar")
            ),
        new XElement("Rider",
            new XElement("Name", "Damon Bradshaw",
                new XAttribute("Class", "450")),
            new XElement("NationalNumber", "45"),
            new XElement("Brand", "Yamaha"),
            new XElement("Nickname", "Beast from the East"),
            new XElement("Mechanic", "N/A")
            ),
```

```
            new XElement("Rider",
                new XElement("Name", "Chad Reed",
                    new XAttribute("Class", "450")),
                new XElement("NationalNumber", "22"),
                new XElement("Brand", "Yamaha"),
                new XElement("Nickname", "N/A"),
                new XElement("Mechanic", "N/A")
                ),
            new XElement("Rider",
                new XElement("Name", "James Stewart",
                    new XAttribute("Class", "450")),
                new XElement("NationalNumber", "7"),
                new XElement("Brand", "Kawasaki"),
                new XElement("Nickname", "N/A"),
                new XElement("Mechanic", "N/A")
                ),
            new XElement("Rider",
                new XElement("Name", "Kevin Windham",
                    new XAttribute("Class", "450")),
                new XElement("NationalNumber", "14"),
                new XElement("Brand", "Honda"),
                new XElement("Nickname", "N/A"),
                new XElement("Mechanic", "N/A")
                )
            );

    textBox1.Text = xdoc.ToString();

    foreach(XNode c in xdoc.Nodes())
        listBox1.Items.Add(c);
```

To get all the elements of a specific name, you can use the following:

```
    foreach(XElement c in xdoc.Elements("Rider"))
        listBox1.Items.Add(c);
```

If you know that there is only a single element with a specific name, you can use the following:

```
    listBox1.Items.Add(xdoc.Element(XName));
```

The thing to remember is that the `Nodes()`, `Elements()`, `Element(Name)`, and `Elements(Name)` methods provide the foundation and basic functionality of XML tree navigation.

Manipulating XML

The great thing about LINQ to XML is the capability to easily make changes to the XML tree, such as adding, deleting, updating, and copying content within the XML document.

Changes to an XML tree are available via the many methods of the `XNode` class, which represents nodes such as elements and comments in an XML tree. More often than not, you'll be working at the node level, manipulating elements and their contents or their attributes.

The next few sections discuss how to use many of the methods of the `XNode` class.

Insert

Content can be added to an XML tree easily by using one of the add methods available via the `XNode` class, depending on where you want to insert the XML:

- `AddAfterSelf`—Adds the specified content after the current node.
- `AddBeforeSelf`—Adds the specified content before the current node.

The following code defines an initial XML tree, then uses the `AddAfterSelf()` method to add an additional node after the `State` element.

```
XElement employee = new XElement("Root",
                        new XElement("Employee",
                            new XElement("Name", "Scott"),
                            new XElement("Address", "555 Main St."),
                            new XElement("City", "Wellington"),
                            new XElement("State", "FL")
                            )
                        );
XElement zip = employee.Element("Employee").Element("State");
zip.AddAfterSelf(new XElement("Zip","33414"));
```

Here's the resulting XML:

```
<Root>
  <Employee>
    <Name>Scott</Name>
    <Address>555 Main St.</Address>
    <City>Wellington</City>
    <State>FL</State>
    <Zip>33414</Zip>
  </Employee>
</Root>
```

Notice that the `<Zip>` element follows the `<State>` element as you instructed.

The `AddBeforeSelf()` method functions the same way when you need to add an element before a specific node.

Update

Updating XML is quite simple in LINQ to XML. There are several methods available, from deleting an element and adding another to changing the content of an element.

The `Replace` method provides several options from which you can choose:

- `ReplaceWith`—Replaces the content of the current element with the specified content.
- `ReplaceAll`—Replaces the child nodes and associated attributes of the current element with the specified content.
- `ReplaceNodes`—Replaces the child nodes of the document or current element with the specified content.

In the following example, an initial XML tree is defined, then the `ReplaceWith()` method is used to replace the contents of the `<State>` element with new content:

```
XElement employee = new XElement("Root",
                        new XElement("Employee",
                            new XElement("Name", "Scott"),
                            new XElement("Address", "555 Main St."),
                            new XElement("City", "Wellington"),
                            new XElement("State", "FL")
                            )
                        );
```

The result of this XML is as follows:

```
<Root>
  <Employee>
    <Name>Scott</Name>
    <Address>555 Main St.</Address>
    <City>Wellington</City>
    <State>WA</State>
    <Zip>33414</Zip>
  </Employee>
</Root>
```

In the following code, the first line identifies the element whose contents will be replaced, and the second line employs the `ReplaceWith()` method to specify the replacement content:

```
XElement st = employee.Element("Employee").Element("State");
st.ReplaceWith(new XElement("State", "FL"));
```

Here's the resulting XML:

```
<Root>
  <Employee>
    <Name>Scott</Name>
    <Address>555 Main St.</Address>
    <City>Wellington</City>
    <State>FL</State>
    <Zip>33414</Zip>
  </Employee>
</Root>
```

Notice that the value of the `<State>` element has been changed from WA to FL.

What happens if you use the following code to replace an element value?

```
st.ReplaceWith("FL");
```

`ReplaceWith()` deletes the specified node and replaces it with the specified content:

```
<Root>
  <Employee>
    <Name>Scott</Name>
```

```
    <Address>555 Main St.</Address>
    <City>Wellington</City>FL
  </Employee>
</Root>
```

The <State> element is deleted and simply replaced with the text FL and not a new node. Thus, you must specify a new element to be created in the place of the old <State> element.

A similar operation can be done with attributes using the SetAttributeValue method. In the following example, notice that the attribute id has a value of 1.

```
XElement employee = new XElement("Employees",
                        new XElement("Employee",
                            new XAttribute("id", "1"),
                            new XElement("Name", "Scott"),
                            new XElement("Address", "555 Main St."),
                            new XElement("City", "Wellington"),
                            new XElement("State", "FL")
                            )
                        );
```

When you execute the following statement, the attribute value is changed to 3. The SetAttributeValue method changes the value of the id attribute to 3.

```
employee.Element("Employee").SetAttributeValue("id", "3");
```

The SetElementValue method is also available to you. It's a method of the XElement class and provides the capability to set the value of a child element, or to add or remove a child element. For example, the following creates a simple XML fragment and then uses the SetElementValue() method to update the Address node value:

```
XElement employee = new XElement("Employees",
                        new XElement("Employee",
                            new XAttribute("id", "1"),
                            new XElement("Name", "Scott"),
                            new XElement("Address", "555 Main St."),
                            new XElement("City", "Wellington"),
                            new XElement("State", "FL")
                            )
                        );

employee.Element("Employee").SetElementValue("Address", "111 Main St.");
```

Running this code shows that the address has indeed been changed:

```
<Employees>
  <Employee id="1">
    <Name>Scott</Name>
    <Address>111 Main St.</Address>
    <City>Wellington</City>
    <State>FL</State>
  </Employee>
</Employees>
```

Delete

Deleting XML is as simple as navigating to the content you want to delete and calling the `Remove()` or `RemoveAll()` method.

The following example creates an XML tree, and then adds an element that will be removed in the next set of code:

```
XElement employee = new XElement("Root",
                        new XElement("Employee",
                            new XElement("Name", "Scott"),
                            new XElement("Address", "555 Main St."),
                            new XElement("City", "Wellington"),
                            new XElement("State", "FL")
                            )
                        );

XElement zip = new XElement("Zip", "33414");
employee.Add(zip);
```

Here's the resulting XML tree:

```
<Root>
  <Employee>
    <Name>Scott</Name>
    <Address>555 Main St.</Address>
    <City>Wellington</City>
    <State>FL</State>
    <Zip>33414</Zip>
  </Employee>
</Root>
```

Now, remove the node you just added:

```
employee.Remove(zip);
```

The XML tree now looks like this:

```
<Root>
  <Employee>
    <Name>Scott</Name>
    <Address>555 Main St.</Address>
    <City>Wellington</City>
    <State>FL</State>
  </Employee>
</Root>
```

Likewise, you can use the `RemoveAll()` method to remove all the nodes (including child nodes) and attributes for the given element:

```
XElement employee = new XElement("Root",
                        new XElement("Employee",
                            new XElement("Name", "Scott"),
```

```
                        new XElement("Address", "555 Main St."),
                        new XElement("City", "Wellington"),
                        new XElement("State", "FL")
                        )
                    );

    Employee.RemoveAll();
```

Here's the resulting XML:

```
<Root />
```

Working with Attributes

Attributes are name/value pairs that are associated an XML element. By now you know quite a bit about dealing with elements via the `XElement` class, and the good news is that dealing with attributes via the `XAttribute` class is not much different. The following sections explain how to work with attributes in an XML tree, specifically adding, retrieving, and deleting attributes.

Adding

Adding attributes with LINQ to XML is similar to adding elements. You can add attributes using an XML construction like the following:

```
XElement employee = new XElement("Root",
            new XElement("Employee",
                new XAttribute("id", "1"),
                new XAttribute("EyeColor", "Blue"),
                new XElement("Name", "Scott"),
                new XElement("Address", "555 Main St."),
                new XElement("City", "Wellington"),
                new XElement("State", "FL")
                )
            );
```

You can also add an attribute as follows:

```
XAttribute dept = employee.Element("Employee").Attribute("EyeColor");
```

Retrieving

Retrieving attributes is also easy. It involves using the `Attributes(XName)` method of the `XElement` class. For example, the following code defines an XML tree with several attributes defined on the `Employee` node. The `Attributes()` method of the `XElement` class is then used to retrieve those attributes.

```
XElement employee = new XElement("Root",
            new XElement("Employee",
                new XAttribute("id", "1"),
                new XAttribute("EyeColor", "Blue"),
                new XElement("Name", "Scott"),
                new XElement("Address", "555 Main St."),
```

```
                new XElement("City", "Wellington"),
                new XElement("State", "FL")
                )
            );

IEnumerable<XAttribute> atts =
    from emp in employee.Elements("Employee").Attributes()
    select emp;

foreach (XAttribute att in atts)
    listBox1.Items.Add(att);
```

Running this code results in the following:

```
id="1"
EyeColor="Blue"
```

Notice that you get the attribute key/value pair. To get just the value, use the `Value()` property of the `XAttribute` class:

```
foreach (XAttribute att in atts)
    listBox1.Items.Add(att.Value.ToString());
```

And here's the result:

```
1
Blue
```

In the preceding examples, the XML tree consisted of a single employee. Suppose that the XML tree consists of multiple employees. The following XML tree contains two employees, and the code then applies the `First()` property to get the attributes of the first employee.

```
XElement employee = new XElement("Root",
            new XElement("Employee",
                new XAttribute("id", "1"),
                new XAttribute("EyeColor", "Green"),
                new XElement("Name", "John"),
                new XElement("Address", "444 Main St."),
                new XElement("City", "Seattle"),
                new XElement("State", "WA")
                ),
            new XElement("Employee",
                new XAttribute("id", "2"),
                new XAttribute("EyeColor", "Blue"),
                new XElement("Name", "Scott"),
                new XElement("Address", "555 Main St."),
                new XElement("City", "Wellington"),
                new XElement("State", "FL")
                ),
            new XElement("Employee",
                new XAttribute("id", "3"),
                new XAttribute("EyeColor", "Brown"),
                new XElement("Name", "Joe"),
```

```
                    new XElement("Address", "333 Main St."),
                    new XElement("City", "Greenville"),
                    new XElement("State", "SC")
                    )
                );

IEnumerable<XAttribute> atts =
    from emp in employee.Elements("Employee").First().Attributes()
    select emp;

foreach (XAttribute att in atts)
    listBox1.Items.Add(att);
```

You can see that retrieving attributes is powerful yet quite easy.

Deleting

You have two options for deleting attributes. The first is to use the `Remove()` method. The following example creates an XML tree and then uses `Remove()` to delete the first attribute:

```
XElement employee = new XElement("Root",
            new XElement("Employee",
                new XAttribute("id", "1"),
                new XAttribute("EyeColor", "Blue"),
                new XElement("Name", "Scott"),
                new XElement("Address", "555 Main St."),
                new XElement("City", "Wellington"),
                new XElement("State", "FL")
                )
            );

employee.Element("Employee").FirstAttribute.Remove();
```

In this example, the `FirstAttribute` property selects the first attribute found in the `employee` element, on which `Remove()` was issued. Here's the resulting XML:

```
<Root>
  <Employee EyeColor="Blue">
    <Name>Scott</Name>
    <Address>555 Main St.</Address>
    <City>Wellington</City>
    <State>FL</State>
  </Employee>
</Root>
```

You can also specify the attribute you want to remove:

```
employee.Element("Employee").Attributes("EyeColor").Remove();
The resulting XML shows that the EyeColor attribute was removed:
<Root>
  <Employee id="1">
    <Name>Scott</Name>
    <Address>555 Main St.</Address>
    <City>Wellington</City>
```

```
      <State>FL</State>
    </Employee>
  </Root>
```

The second option is to use the `SetAttributeValue` method. When using it, you set the value of the attribute (of the name/value pair) to null, like this:

```
employee.Element("Employee").SetAttributeValue("EyeColor", null);
```

In this example, the `EyeColor` attribute will be removed and the XML will be returned as in the previous example.

LINQ to XML versus Other XML Technologies

The final section of this chapter briefly compares LINQ to XML to some of the other XML technologies in use today, specifically weighing LINQ to XML against the following:

- DOM
- `XmlReader`
- XSLT
- MSMXL

LINQ to XML versus DOM

The difference between LINQ to XML and the DOM is in the way the document is created. In the DOM, the XML tree is created from bottom to top, meaning that you create the document, create the elements, and then add the elements to the document. This process takes multiple statements and is quite lengthy.

LINQ to XML simplifies the process by allowing the creation of an XML tree in a single statement, shaped more like XML, and in significantly less, easier-to-read code. The reasoning behind this logic is simply that when you are working with XML, you are typically working with elements and attributes, those components that make up an XML tree. LINQ to XML facilitates this by letting you work with elements and attributes without working with the document object.

One of the problems with the DOM is that you can't change the name of a node directly. You must create a new node and copy all the child nodes of the old node to the new node. In LINQ to XML, you can simply rename the node.

Other differences between LINQ to XML and DOM include the following:

- LINQ to XML's static methods simplify the loading of XML over the DOM's instance methods.
- LINQ to XML supports annotations.

- LINQ to XML provides better support for whitespace. LINQ to XML stores whitespace as XText versus having a special `Whitespace` node in the DOM. Additionally, in LINQ to XML you can specify `xml:space="preserve"` to always preserve the whitespace.
- XML programming is simplified in LINQ to XML by removing support for entities and entity references because the management of entities is fairly complex, and truth be told, rarely used. The benefit of this is increased performance.

LINQ to XML versus XmlReader

If you have worked with XML before, you have probably used the `XmlReader` class. The `XmlReader` class is a fast way of dealing with XML. It is a forward-only, noncached XML parser. Unlike the previous comparison (LINQ to XML versus the DOM), in which LINQ to XML is a replacement for the DOM, LINQ to XML is actually tightly integrated with the `XmlReader`. While you can still use the `XmlReader` by itself, you can utilize LINQ to XML to take advantage of the `XmlReader`, overlapping much of the functionality.

You need to determine when you would use the `XmlReader` in a standalone scenario and when you would use LINQ to XML. `XmlReader` is best used when you want to process a large number of XML documents whose XML tree structure rarely differs and quickly processing those XML documents is necessary. LINQ to XML shines when the XML documents differ in XML tree structure.

LINQ to XML versus XSLT

The only similarity between LINQ to XML and XSLT is the capability to transform XML. XSLT is a declarative language that implements a rule-based approach. It does not take advantage of the .NET Framework, thus requiring developers to learn a completely new language. Yet, used correctly, it produces wonderful results, and an existing managed XSLT engine can compile XSLT into managed code.

LINQ to XML, however, overcomes all of the XSLT shortcomings. Through LINQ to XML query expressions, you can easily transform XML using functional construction (discussed in Chapter 8) and constructing `XElement` objects dynamically, thus creating a completely new XML tree. The benefits of this approach include reduced development time.

LINQ to XML versus MSXML

The big difference between LINQ to XML and MSXML is that MSXML is COM-based and, therefore, not recommended for use in managed code. It also contains a native implementation of the DOM, and includes support for XSLT and XPath. It is primarily used in programming languages that support COM.

In contrast, LINQ to XML is not COM-based and is designed specifically for use with managed code. Thus, you get all the benefits of managed code, such as garbage collection, type safety, and object-oriented design features.

Summary

This chapter introduced you LINQ to XML and many of the fundamental programming concepts that LINQ to XML utilizes and that will be used throughout the remaining LINQ to XML chapters of this book.

You explored the LINQ to XML programming fundamentals—that is, the many LINQ to XML classes that the `System.Xml.Linq` namespace exposes. These classes are the backbone of LINQ to XML and make working with XML much easier than using other XML tools. You also examined three of the more common classes that you'll use when working with XML, including `XElement` and `XAttribute`.

The chapter covered many of the programming concepts that you need to know when working with XML using LINQ to XML, including how to traverse an XML tree, add and remove elements and attributes, and manipulate the tree's contents. You saw how to work with attributes in an XML document using LINQ to XML, and learned that working with attributes is similar to working with elements due to the architecture of LINQ and its integration into the .NET Framework.

Last, a comparison of LINQ to XML to other existing XML technologies was provided to give you an idea of how LINQ to XML stacks up.

Chapter 6 discusses more in-depth programming features of LINQ to XML.

6

Programming with LINQ to XML

LINQ to XML has many strengths, and one of the most valuable is its capability to quickly and easily create XML documents and trees. LINQ to XML provides several different options through which developers can create XML trees as well as modify and manipulate XML trees.

This chapter builds on what you learned in Chapter 5, ''Understanding LINQ to XML''—the programming fundamentals and concepts that are prevalent in working with XML documents and LINQ to XML, and how to work with elements and attributes using the `XElement` and `XAttribute` classes.

This chapter, then, tackles the following:

- Constructing and creating XML trees
- Manipulating XML trees
- Serializing XML trees

Creating Trees

Programming with LINQ to XML, as you found out in the last chapter, is straightforward. Through the many classes of the `System.Xml.Linq` namespace, developers can create and manipulate XML trees with ease.

You can create XML trees in both C# and Visual Basic .NET, but the manner in which they are created is quite different. The following sections examine the creation of XML trees in both languages, and discuss the differences developers need to know for their respective language.

Creating Trees in C#

Creating XML trees in C# is done using the `XElement` class. This class provides all the necessary functionality to create and manipulate XML documents and trees. In its simplest form, the `XElement` class creates elements. Here's an example that creates an empty element:

```
XElement emptyElement = new XElement("Employee");
```

This code produces the following:

```
<Employee />
```

Simple, but via the same `XElement` class you can create more complex XML trees, such as the following:

```
XElement employee = new XElement("Root",
            new XElement("Employee",
                new XElement("Name", "Scott"),
                new XElement("Title", "All Things Techy"),
                new XElement("HireDate", "02/05/2007"),
                new XElement("Gender", "M")
                ),
            new XElement("Employee",
                new XElement("Name", "Steve"),
                new XElement("Title", "Mr. SciFi"),
                new XElement("HireDate", "05/14/2002"),
                new XElement("Gender", "M")
                ),
            new XElement("Employee",
                new XElement("Name", "Joe"),
                new XElement("Title", "All Things Bleeding Edge"),
                new XElement("HireDate", "07/22/2004"),
                new XElement("Gender", "M")
                )
            );
```

When this code is run, the resulting XML tree looks like this:

```
<Root>
  <Employee>
    <Name>Scott</Name>
    <Title>All Things Techy</Title>
    <HireDate>02/05/2007</HireDate>
    <Gender>M</Gender>
  </Employee>
  <Employee>
    <Name>Steve</Name>
    <Title>Mr. SciFi</Title>
    <HireDate>05/14/2002</HireDate>
    <Gender>M</Gender>
  </Employee>
  <Employee>
    <Name>Joe</Name>
    <Title>All Things Bleeding Edge</Title>
    <HireDate>07/22/2004</HireDate>
```

```
    <Gender>M</Gender>
  </Employee>
</Root>
```

Take it a step further and add a couple of attributes to each employee via the `XAttribute` class:

```
XElement employee = new XElement("Root",
            new XElement("Employee",
                new XAttribute("id", "1"),
                new XAttribute("Dept", "0001"),
                new XElement("Name", "Scott"),
                new XElement("Address",
                    new XElement("Street", "555 Main St."),
                    new XElement("City", "Wellington"),
                    new XElement("State", "FL")),
                new XElement("Title", "All Things Techy"),
                new XElement("HireDate", "02/05/2007"),
                new XElement("Gender", "M")
                ),
            new XElement("Employee",
                new XAttribute("id", "2"),
                new XAttribute("Dept", "0005"),
                new XElement("Name", "Steve"),
                new XElement("Address",
                    new XElement("Street", "444 Main St."),
                    new XElement("City", "Snohomish"),
                    new XElement("State", "WA")),
                new XElement("Title", "Mr. SciFi"),
                new XElement("HireDate", "05/14/2002"),
                new XElement("Gender", "M")
                ),
            new XElement("Employee",
                new XAttribute("id", "3"),
                new XAttribute("Dept", "0004"),
                new XElement("Name", "Joe"),
                new XElement("Address",
                    new XElement("Street", "222 Main St."),
                    new XElement("City", "Easley"),
                    new XElement("State", "SC")),
                new XElement("Title", "All Things Bleeding Edge"),
                new XElement("HireDate", "07/22/2004"),
                new XElement("Gender", "M")
                )
            );
```

The results now show two attributes on each `employee` node:

```
<Root>
  <Employee id="1" Dept="0001">
    <Name>Scott</Name>
     <Address>
      <Street>555 Main St.</Street>
      <City>Wellington</City>
```

```
        <State>FL</State>
      </Address>
      <Title>All Things Techy</Title>
      <HireDate>02/05/2007</HireDate>
      <Gender>M</Gender>
    </Employee>
    <Employee id="2" Dept="0005">
      <Name>Steve</Name>
      <Address>
        <Street>444 Main St.</Street>
        <City>Snohomish</City>
        <State>WA</State>
      </Address>
      <Title>Mr. SciFi</Title>
      <HireDate>05/14/2002</HireDate>
      <Gender>M</Gender>
    </Employee>
    <Employee id="3" Dept="0004">
       <Name>Joe</Name>
       <Address>
        <Street>222 Main St.</Street>
        <City>Easley</City>
        <State>SC</State>
      </Address>
      <Title>All Things Bleeding Edge</Title>
      <HireDate>07/22/2004</HireDate>
      <Gender>M</Gender>
    </Employee>
  </Root>
```

One of the things that makes creating XML with LINQ to XML quite easy is the capability to structure the XML directly in the programming language, formatting the source code just as it would be structured in the XML document. Additionally, the many properties and methods of the `XElement` class make it easy to efficiently structure and create XML documents dynamically.

The `XElement` class contains a handful of overloads that let developers create XML trees quickly within a single statement. These constructor overloads allow you to create a new instance of the `XElement` class with which to structure an XML document.

In its simplest form, the `XElement` class can be used to create a new element with a specific name, as shown here in the basic syntax:

```
XElement(XName name)
```

For example, the following uses the basic syntax to create a single root element:

```
XElement employee = new XElement("Root");
```

This code produces the following XML:

```
<Root />
```

Building on that, you use the `XElement` constructor to create a new instance of the `XElement` class (creating a new element) from another `XElement` object. By doing so, you can nest elements, creating child elements of the parent element. The following example illustrates this, using the `XElement` constructor from the initial `XElement` class to create a child element below the root element:

```
XElement employee = new XElement("Root",
            new XElement("Employee");
```

The code produces the following XML:

```
<Root>
  <Employee />
</Root>
```

From here, another `XElement` constructor can be used to create a new element with a specified name and content. Here's the basic syntax:

```
XElement(XName name, object content)
```

The following example creates a new element with the specified name of `"Name"` and content of `"Scott"`:

```
XElement = new XElement("Name", "Scott")
```

Here's the XML this code produces:

```
<Name>Scott</Name>
```

You can combine this with the previous example to create a root element and child element with a value:

```
XElement employee = new XElement("Employee",
            new XElement("Name", "Scott");
```

The code produces the following XML:

```
<Employee>
  <Name>Scott</Scott>
</Employee>
```

Last, you can pass multiple instances of the `XElement` class to create multiple nodes. The basic syntax for this is

```
XElement(XName name, params object[] content)
A pseudo-code example of this would be the following:
XElement employee = new XElement(XName,
            new XElement(XName,
                new XElement(XName name),
                new XElement(XName name),
                new XElement(XName name),
                new XElement(XName name)
            )
```

Here's an example of the syntax using real data, passing more than one `XElement` for the content:

```
XElement employee = new XElement("Root",
            new XElement("Employee",
                new XElement("Name", "Scott"),
```

```
            new XElement("Title", "All Things Techy"),
            new XElement("HireDate", "02/05/2007"),
            new XElement("Gender", "M")
        )
```

As you have seen in previous examples in this chapter and the last chapter, this is the ideal way to construct an XML tree.

Now take a look at how to do the same thing in Visual Basic .NET.

Creating Trees in Visual Basic

Creating XML trees in Visual Basic is accomplished through XML literals. XML literals enable you to create and incorporate XML directly into our Visual Basic programs and code. Another way to say this is that XML literals let you type XML directly into your Visual Basic code without the need for any special formatting. What makes this possible is that the literal XML syntax represents the actual objects of LINQ to XML. The benefit of this is that your XML code is easier to create, and your code is easier to read because it has the same structure as the resulting XML.

An additional benefit of XML literals is that Visual Basic .NET compiles them into LNQ to XML objects, providing a familiar LINQ object model for creating and manipulating XML.

XML can be created in Visual Basic by using XML literals directly in the VB code. You create LINQ to XML objects simply by typing XML code directly into Visual Basic or by pasting existing XML into your code. The following creates a single `<Employee>` node:

```
Dim emp As XElement = <Employee/>
```

Here's the result of this code:

```
<Employee/>
```

You can also specify elements and their corresponding values:

```
Dim emp As XElement = <Name>Scott</Name>
```

Obviously, the following XML is produced:

```
<Name>Scott</Name>
```

One of the things that Visual Basic .NET developers have at their disposal is "embedded expressions." Embedded expressions let you create XML literals that contain expressions. These expressions are evaluated at run time. Embedded expressions are enclosed within `<% %>` brackets (if you do any ASP.NET development, you're familiar with those).

The following creates a simple XML document using XML literals and an embedded expression:

```
Dim emp As XElement = <Employee>
    <%= New XElement("Name", "Scott") %>
  </Employee>
```

Here are the results when the code runs:

```
<Employee>
    <Name>Scott</Name>
</Employee>
```

XML literals can span multiple lines without the need of line continuation characters as shown in the example below. The only time this would differ is when you have a multi-line expression in the embedded expression.

```
Dim employee As XElement = _
<Root>
    <Employee id="1" Dept="0001">
        <Name>Scott</Name>
        <Address>
            <Street>555 Main St.</Street>
            <City>Wellington</City>
            <State>FL</State>
        </Address>
        <Title>All Things Techy</Title>
        <HireDate>02/05/2007</HireDate>
        <Gender>M</Gender>
    </Employee>
    <Employee id="2" Dept="0005">
        <Name>Steve</Name>
        <Address>
            <Street>444 Main St.</Street>
            <City>Snohomish</City>
            <State>WA</State>
        </Address>
        <Title>Mr. SciFi</Title>
        <HireDate>05/14/2002</HireDate>
        <Gender>M</Gender>
    </Employee>
    <Employee id="3" Dept="0004">
        <Name>Joe</Name>
        <Address>
            <Street>222 Main St.</Street>
            <City>Easley</City>
            <State>SC</State>
        </Address>
        <Title>All Things Bleeding Edge</Title>
        <HireDate>07/22/2004</HireDate>
        <Gender>M</Gender>
    </Employee>
</Root>
```

How does the compiler create objects from XML literals? The answer is simple, really. The Visual Basic compiler translates XML literals into the equivalent LINQ to XML constructors, which are then used to build the LINQ to XML object.

Populating Trees from Text

Populating XML trees from text can be accomplished a number of ways, and you saw a couple of them in the last chapter. The easiest method is to use the `Parse()` method of the `XElement` class. This method loads an `XElement` object from an XML string.

For example, the following code creates a string containing XML, parsing the string into an `XElement` object:

```
XElement employees = XElement.Parse(@"
    <Employees>
        <Employee id='1' phone='555-555-5555'>
            <Name>Steve Kent</Name>
            <Title>Mr. SciFi</Title>
            <Department>Gaming</Department>
            <HireDate>04/17/92</HireDate>
            <Gender>M</Gender>
            <MaritalStatus>M</MaritalStatus>
        </Employee>
        <Employee id='2' phone='555-555-5556'>
            <Name>Scott Klein</Name>
            <Title>Geek</Title>
            <Department>All things technical</Department>
            <HireDate>02/05/94</HireDate>
            <Gender>M</Gender>
            <MaritalStatus>M</MaritalStatus>
        </Employee>
        <Employee id='3' phone='555-555-5557'>
            <Name>Joe Walling</Name>
            <Title>Head Geek</Title>
            <Department>All things bleeding edge</Department>
            <HireDate>06/15/93</HireDate>
            <Gender>M</Gender>
            <MaritalStatus>M</MaritalStatus>
        </Employee>
    </Employees>");
```

There is a limitation to using the `Parse()` method, and that is that the XML can contain only a single root node.

Another way is to populate a tree is to load the XML from an existing source. The following example uses the `Load()` method to load an existing XML document from an external file source and creates an `XElement`.

```
XElement employees = XElement.Load(@"C:\Wrox\Employees.xml");
```

Another overload of the `Load` method takes an additional Boolean parameter that specifies whether to preserve whitespace.

```
employees = XElement.Load(@"C:\Wrox\Employees.xml", true);
```

This next example illustrates how to load XML from a TextReader. Any kind of TextReader can be used; in this case, it's a StringReader, but a StreamReader would work just the same.

```
TextReader tr = new StringReader("<Employee><Name>Scott</Name></Employee");
XElement xtree = XElement.Load(tr);
```

As before, another overload of the `Load` method takes an additional Boolean parameter that specifies whether to preserve whitespace.

```
XElement xtree = XElement.Load(tr, true);
```

The following example creates an XML tree from an XmlReader. It first creates an `XmlReaderSettings` instance and sets a few optional settings. Then it creates an XmlReader and uses the `Create()` method to load an XML file into the `XElement` object.

```
XmlReaderSettings xmlset = new XmlReaderSettings();
xmlset.ConformanceLevel = ConformanceLevel.Document;
xmlset.IgnoreWhitespace = true;
xmlset.IgnoreComments = true;
XmlReader rdr = XmlReader.Create(@"C:\Wrox\LINQ\Chapter
5\Employees.xml", xmlset);

XElement xtree = XElement.Load(rdr);
```

Once in the XmlReader, the XML can be read quickly. The XmlReader is an efficient way to access XML data if all you want to do is read it.

This last example demonstrates how to load a DOM document into an LINQ to XML tree. First, an XML DOM document is created, defining a root element and several child elements. The DOM document is then loaded into the `XElement` object.

```
XmlDocument xdoc = new XmlDocument();
XmlElement ele1 = xdoc.CreateElement("Name");
ele1.InnerText = "Scott";
XmlElement ele2 = xdoc.CreateElement("Title");
ele2.InnerText = "Geek";
XmlElement ele3 = xdoc.CreateElement("HireDate");
ele3.InnerText = "02/05/2007";
XmlElement emp = xdoc.CreateElement("Employee");
emp.AppendChild(ele1);
emp.AppendChild(ele2);
emp.AppendChild(ele3);
xdoc.AppendChild(emp);

XmlNodeReader nr = new XmlNodeReader(xdoc);
nr.MoveToContent();

XElement xtree = XElement.Load(nr);
```

The resulting XML looks like this:

```
<Employee>
    <Name>Scott</Name>
    <Title>Geek</Title>
    <HireDate>02/05/2007</HireDate>
</Employee>
```

Querying XML Trees

Once you have populated the tree, the next obvious step in most cases is to query its contents. If you think about this for a minute, LINQ to XML provides an easy way to reshape XML. It combines the capability to functionally construct your XML with the capability to query the XML tree. The result is a completely different XML tree shape than the original XML document. One of the primary things you should know by now is that LINQ to XML is exceptional at both functional construction and querying. In this section, you will quickly see that LINQ to XML is also very good at reshaping XML as compared to other XML technologies.

This section explores LINQ to XML queries and how they can be used to effectively query XML documents. To illustrate this point, the following XML document will be used. In your favorite text editor, enter the following XML and save it as `Employee.xml` in your `Wrox\Chapter6` directory:

```
<Employees>
  <Employee id="1" Dept="0001">
    <Name>Scott</Name>
    <Address>
      <Street>555 Main St.</Street>
      <City>Wellington</City>
      <State>FL</State>
    </Address>
    <Title>All Things Techy</Title>
    <HireDate>02/05/2007</HireDate>
    <Gender>M</Gender>
  </Employee>
  <Employee id="2" Dept="0005">
    <Name>Steve</Name>
    <Address>
      <Street>444 Main St.</Street>
      <City>Snohomish</City>
      <State>WA</State>
    </Address>
    <Title>Mr. SciFi</Title>
    <HireDate>05/14/2002</HireDate>
    <Gender>M</Gender>
  </Employee>
  <Employee id="3" Dept="0004">
    <Name>Joe</Name>
    <Address>
      <Street>222 Main St.</Street>
      <City>Easley</City>
      <State>SC</State>
    </Address>
    <Title>All Things Bleeding Edge</Title>
    <HireDate>07/22/2004</HireDate>
    <Gender>M</Gender>
  </Employee>
</Employees>
```

Next, create a new C# Windows Forms project in Visual Studio, and on Form1 place a button and a text box. In the `Click()` event for the button, add the following:

```
XElement employees = XElement.Load(@"C:\Wrox\Chapter6\Employees.Xml");
```

You now have the XML document `Employee.xml` loaded into the `employees` variable, so you can work with it.

Suppose that you want to return the first employee from the XML document. The following does just that:

```
employees.Element("Employee")
```

Running this statement returns the first employee:

```
<Employee id="1" Dept="0001">
  <Name>Scott</Name>
    <Address>
      <Street>555 Main St.</Street>
      <City>Wellington</City>
      <State>FL</State>
    </Address>
  <Title>All Things Techy</Title>
  <HireDate>02/05/2007</HireDate>
  <Gender>M</Gender>
</Employee>
```

However, an alternative would be to use the `First()` property to manually select the first `Employee` element:

```
employees.Elements("Employee").First()
```

Another alternative is to use the `ElementAt()` method to specify which element to return. The following example also returns the first `Employee` node:

```
employees.Elements("Employee").ElementAt(0)
```

The next example loops through all of the `Employee` elements, concatenates them, and returns them as a single string:

```
foreach (XElement employee in employees.Elements("Employee")
    textbox1.Text += employee;
```

This gives you everything but the `<Employees>` node:

```
  <Employee id="1" Dept="0001">
    <Name>Scott</Name>
    <Address>
      <Street>555 Main St.</Street>
      <City>Wellington</City>
      <State>FL</State>
    </Address>
    <Title>All Things Techy</Title>
    <HireDate>02/05/2007</HireDate>
    <Gender>M</Gender>
  </Employee>
  <Employee id="2" Dept="0005">
    <Name>Steve</Name>
    <Address>
```

```
        <Street>444 Main St.</Street>
        <City>Snohomish</City>
        <State>WA</State>
      </Address>
      <Title>Mr. SciFi</Title>
      <HireDate>05/14/2002</HireDate>
      <Gender>M</Gender>
    </Employee>
    <Employee id="3" Dept="0004">
      <Name>Joe</Name>
      <Address>
        <Street>222 Main St.</Street>
        <City>Easley</City>
        <State>SC</State>
      </Address>
      <Title>All Things Bleeding Edge</Title>
      <HireDate>07/22/2004</HireDate>
      <Gender>M</Gender>
    </Employee>
```

What if you want to return the second employee? You can use the `ElementAt()` method, as shown here:

```
employees.Elements("Employee").ElementAt(1)
```

The values for this are zero-based, so the first employee node is `0`. To return the second employee, you simply pass a `1`.

Another option is to use a query expression. The following returns the second employee node by filtering on the `id` attribute where its value is `2`:

```
XElement empnum2 = (from emp in employees.Elements("Employee")
                    where (int) emp.Attribute("id") == 2
                    select emp).First();
```

Notice that this example also uses the `First()` method. Why? What if your XML document had an attribute of `Dept` for each employee, and your XML document had multiple employees with the same department? The `First()` method helps make sure you grab the first employee that matches the criterion. The query expression returns a sequence, and the `First()` method explicitly returns the first member of that sequence.

The following example does the same, but uses the `ElementAt()` method:

```
XElement empnum2 = (from emp in employees.Elements("Employee")
                    where (int) emp.Attribute("id") == 2
                    select emp).ElementAt(0);
```

This next example digs a little deeper. It returns the values of all the `Name` elements for each employee. It uses the `Descendants()` method to return a collection of all the descendants for the selected element.

```
IEnumerable<string> empNames =
    from emp in employees.Descendants("Name")
    orderby emp.Value
    select emp.Value;
```

```
foreach (string name in empNames)
    listbox1.Items.Add(name);
```

This code returns the following values:

```
Joe
Scott
Steve
```

The following example does the same thing:

```
IEnumerable<string> empNames =
    from emp in employees.Descendants("Name")
    orderby (string) emp
    select (string) emp;
```

The same iteration applies, and the results are the same. You can also "walk the tree" by using the `Elements()` method (as many times as needed) to access the appropriate node.

```
IEnumerable<string> empNames =
    from emp in employees.Elements("Employee").Elements("Name")
    orderby (string) emp
    select (string) emp;
```

Again, the same iteration applies, and the same results are returned.

The next few examples work with attributes, and to do so, the XML document `Employee.xml` created earlier needs to be modified. Add an attribute to each employee node as highlighted in following XML:

```
<Employees>
  <Employee id="1" Dept="0001" Geek="True">
    <Name>Scott</Name>
    <Address>
      <Street>555 Main St.</Street>
      <City>Wellington</City>
      <State>FL</State>
    </Address>
    <Title>All Things Techy</Title>
    <HireDate>02/05/2007</HireDate>
    <Gender>M</Gender>
  </Employee>
  <Employee id="2" Dept="0005" Geek="False">
    <Name>Steve</Name>
    <Address>
      <Street>444 Main St.</Street>
      <City>Snohomish</City>
      <State>WA</State>
    </Address>
    <Title>Mr. SciFi</Title>
    <HireDate>05/14/2002</HireDate>
    <Gender>M</Gender>
  </Employee>
```

```
  <Employee id="3" Dept="0004" Geek="True">
    <Name>Joe</Name>
    <Address>
      <Street>222 Main St.</Street>
      <City>Easley</City>
      <State>SC</State>
    </Address>
    <Title>All Things Bleeding Edge</Title>
    <HireDate>07/22/2004</HireDate>
    <Gender>M</Gender>
  </Employee>
</Employees>
```

The following example queries the XML document, looking at the `Geek` attribute of the `Employee` node and returning only those with a value of `True`:

```
IEnumerable<XElement> empNames =
    from emp in employees.Elements("Employee")
    where (string)emp.Attribute("Geek") == "True"
    select emp;

foreach (XElement name in empNames)
    textbox1.Text = name.ToString();
```

The query expression returns the following values:

```
Scott
Joe
```

This last example demonstrates how to walk an XML tree looking for an element value several layers deep. First, modify the XML and add a `Zip` element to the employee with an `id` of `2`:

```
  <Employee id="2" Dept="0005" Geek="False">
    <Name>Steve</Name>
    <Address>
      <Street>444 Main St.</Street>
      <City>Snohomish</City>
      <State>WA</State>
      <Zip>99999</Zip>
    </Address>
    <Title>Mr. SciFi</Title>
    <HireDate>05/14/2002</HireDate>
    <Gender>M</Gender>
  </Employee>
```

In the following example, the query expression walks down to the `<Address>` element and looks for an employee with a `Zip` value of `99999`:

```
IEnumerable<XElement> empAddr =
    from emp in employees.Elements("Employee").Elements("Address")
    where (string)emp.Element("zip") == ("99999")
```

```
        select emp;

    foreach (XElement address in empAddr)
        textbox1.Text = address.ToString();
```

There was only a single employee that matched the query expression filter in this example, but nonetheless, the results were looped through, and the following XML was returned:

```
<Address>
  <Street>444 Main St.</Street>
  <City>Snohomish</City>
  <State>WA</State>
  <Zip>99999</Zip>
</Address>
```

This example returned the address information for the selected ZIP code. Modify the query as highlighted here, and it will return the entire employee node for the selected ZIP code:

```
IEnumerable<XElement> empAddr =
    from emp in employees.Elements("Employee")
    where (string)emp.Element("Address").Element("zip") == ("99999")
    select emp;
```

Now when you run this application and click the button, the following is displayed:

```
<Employee id="2" Dept="0005" Geek="False">
  <Name>Steve</Name>
  <Address>
    <Address>444 Main St.</Address>
    <City>Snohomish</City>
    <State>WA</State>
    <zip>99999</zip>
  </Address>
  <Title>Mr. SciFi</Title>
  <HireDate>05/14/2002</HireDate>
  <Gender>M</Gender>
</Employee>
```

Modifying and Reshaping XML Trees

You saw briefly in the last chapter how to modify XML trees using many of the methods and properties of the `XElement` and `XAttribute` classes. However, in today's XML technologies, the common approach for reshaping an XML document requires loading the document into data store and using an XML-supported programming language for modify the contents and structure of that document, such as adding or removing nodes.

For example, loading an XML document into the DOM, modifying its contents in place, and resaving the document is one of the more familiar methods for current XML programmers.

LINQ to XML provides a second approach to XML reshaping and modification—one that is much easier to maintain. This approach is called *functional construction*, and is the answer to the DOM's load/modify/save approach. Functional construction lets you easily reshape XML from one form to another in a single statement.

As you saw in the last chapter, LINQ to XML provides the load/modify/save approach as well via the many methods exposed by the `XElement` and `XAttribute` classes, and even this is still more efficient than many of today's XML tree modification methods due to the ability to visually view the structure of the XML tree. Yet the functional approach, once understood, is easier to work with and maintain as a whole because you can quickly identify the code that modifies each part of the tree.

Here's an example illustrating how to take an attribute and make it an element. The code takes the `id` attribute and adds it as an element. The attribute's name and value are used when the element is added.

```
XElement employee = new XElement("Root",
            new XElement("Employee",
                new XAttribute("id", "1"),
                new XAttribute("EyeColor", "Green"),
                new XElement("Name", "Scott"),
                new XElement("Address", "444 Main St."),
                new XElement("City", "Wellington"),
                new XElement("State", "FL"),
                new XElement("Zip", "33414")
                )
            );

employee.Element("Employee").Add(
     new XElement(employee.Element("Employee").Attribute("id").Name,
     employee.Element("Employee").Attribute("id").Value));

employee.Element("Employee").Attribute("id").Remove();
```

This code produces the following XML:

```
<Root>
  <Employee EyeColor="Green">
    <Name>Scott</Name>
    <Address>444 Main St.</Address>
    <City>Wellington</City>
    <State>FL</State>
    <Zip>33414</Zip>
    <id>1</id>
  </Employee>
</Root>
```

If you wanted to, you could loop through all of the attributes and make them elements as follows:

```
foreach (XAttribute att in employee.Element("Employee").Attributes())
    employee.Element("Employee").Add(new XElement(atts.Name, (string)att));

employee.Element("Employee").Attributes().Remove();
```

The code produces this XML:

```
<Root>
  <Employee EyeColor="Green">
    <Name>Scott</Name>
```

```
      <Address>444 Main St.</Address>
      <City>Wellington</City>
      <State>FL</State>
      <Zip>33414</Zip>
      <id>1</id>
      <EyeColor>Green</EyeColor>
    </Employee>
  </Root>
```

The following example does the reverse. It takes an element (<id>) and adds it as an attribute (of the Employee node):

```
XElement employee = new XElement("Root",
            new XElement("Employee",
                new XElement("Name", "Scott"),
                new XElement("Address", "444 Main St."),
                new XElement("City", "Wellington"),
                new XElement("State", "FL"),
                new XElement("Zip", "33414"),
                new XElement("id", "1")
                )
            );

employee.Element("Employee").Add(new
    XAttribute(employee.Element("Employee").Element("id").Name,
    employee.Element("Employee").Element("id").Value));

employee.Element("Employee").Element("id").Remove();
```

The result is the following XML:

```
<Root>
  <Employee id="1">
    <Name>Scott</Name>
    <Address>444 Main St.</Address>
    <City>Wellington</City>
    <State>FL</State>
    <Zip>33414</Zip>
  </Employee>
</Root>
```

Functional construction is discussed in more detail in Chapter 8, ''Advanced LINQ to XML Programming Topics.''

Serializing XML Trees

Serialization is the process of saving an object to a storage medium such as a file or even to memory. Serializing an XML tree is the process of generating XML text from the tree. The newly generated XML can be serialized to a file or to an implementation of a TextWriter or an XmlWriter.

When serializing XML using LINQ to XML, nonsignificant whitespace in the XML tree is not preserved by default. For example, reading indented XML with no whitespace text nodes and then serializing the XML with indentation does not preserve whitespace.

When serializing XML via LINQ to XML, several methods are available, enabling you to decide how to treat whitespace. The `Save()` method of the `XElement` class does not preserve whitespace by default. But you can optionally provide a Boolean value that tells `Save()` to preserve whitespace, as in the following example:

```
TextReader tr = new StringReader(@"
    <Employees>
        <Employee id='1' phone='555-555-5555'>
            <Name>Steve Kent</Name>
            <Title>Mr. SciFi</Title>
            <Department>Gaming</Department>
            <HireDate>04/17/92</HireDate>
            <Gender>M</Gender>
            <MaritalStatus>M</MaritalStatus>
        </Employee>
        <Employee id='2' phone='555-555-5556'>
            <Name>Scott Klein</Name>
            <Title>Geek</Title>
            <Department>All things technical</Department>
            <HireDate>02/05/94</HireDate>
            <Gender>M</Gender>
            <MaritalStatus>M</MaritalStatus>
        </Employee>
        <Employee id='3' phone='555-555-5557'>
            <Name>Joe Walling</Name>
            <Title>Head Geek</Title>
            <Department>All things bleeding edge</Department>
            <HireDate>06/15/93</HireDate>
            <Gender>M</Gender>
            <MaritalStatus>M</MaritalStatus>
        </Employee>
    </Employees>");
XElement xel = XElement.Load(tr);
tr.Close();
xel.Save(@"C:\Wrox\Employees2.xml", true);
```

The same goes for the `Save()` method of the `XDocument` class.

Serializing can be done to a file (as the preceding example shows), a TextWriter, or an XmlWriter. The following example shows how to serialize an `XElement` to an XmlWriter:

```
StringBuilder sb = new StringBuilder();
XmlWriterSettings xws = new XmlWriterSettings();
xws.OmitXmlDeclaration = true;
using (XmlWriter xw = XmlWriter.Create(sb , xws))
{
    XElement employee = new XElement("Root",
                new XElement("Employee",
                    new XAttribute("id", "1"),
                    new XAttribute("EyeColor", "Green"),
                    new XElement("Name", "Scott"),
                    new XElement("Address", "444 Main St."),
                    new XElement("City", "Wellington"),
                    new XElement("State", "FL"),
```

```
                        new XElement("Zip", "33414")
                        )
                    );
        employee.Save(xw);
    }
    textBox1.Text = sb.ToString();
```

You'll notice that you don't have an option of controlling the whitespace when serializing to an XmlWriter via LINQ to XML. That is because the XmlWriter controls the behavior of the whitespace.

The following example serializes an XML tree to a TextWriter:

```
XElement employees = XElement.Parse(@"
    <Employees>
        <Employee id='1' debt='Dev'>
            <Name>Scott</Name>
            <Title>Mr. SciFi</Title>
            <Department>Gaming</Department>
            <HireDate>04/17/92</HireDate>
            <Gender>M</Gender>
            <MaritalStatus>M</MaritalStatus>
        </Employee>
    </Employees>");

using (StringWriter sw = new StringWriter())
{
  employees.Save(sw, true);
}
```

You have many serialization options when using LINQ to XML; it is simply a matter of selecting the right options for your application.

Namespaces

One of the more difficult concepts of XML programming is XML names and namespaces. You can think of XML namespace on the same level as that of a namespace in a .NET Framework application. A namespace uniquely qualifies your class names within your application. By using namespaces, you can avoid the naming conflicts between different parts of an XML document.

XML namespaces serve several purposes in XML, and maybe that's the reason they seem to be so difficult to understand. In addition to uniquely qualifying names, namespaces also serve the purpose of prefixes within an XML document. Prefixes let you use shortcuts for XML namespaces, making the XML document more readable and concise. The downside to prefixes is that they depend on their context for their meaning. A prefix can be associated with different namespaces in different parts of the XML tree, making the meaning much harder to understand.

LINQ to XML greatly simplifies programming with namespaces by removing the prefixes from the LINQ API. When an XML document is loaded by LINQ to XML, prefixes are treated as shortcuts and resolved to their corresponding namespaces (just like when XML is loaded by a DOM or SAX parser). Once the XML document is loaded, namespaces are accessed via the namespace URI, not the prefix. Developers work with XML names that are fully qualified.

Fully qualified names are represented by the `XName` class, and you have seen them throughout this book. Whenever an XML name is required, you are dealing with the `XName` class, such as an `XName` parameter. Keep in mind that you are never really working with the `XName` class directly, but rather with a string representation.

Throughout this book you've seen string arguments passed as parameters to constructors when creating elements or attributes during XML tree construction, like this:

```
new XElements("Name", "Scott");
```

What happens is that the string is implicitly converted to an `XName`. That same concept can now be applied to namespaces. The following creates a simple XML document with a default namespace:

```
XElement employee = new XElement("{http://wrox.com}Employee",
                new XAttribute("id", "1"),
                new XElement("{http://wrox.com}Name", "Scott"),
                new XElement("{http://wrox.com}Title", "Developer")
                );
```

This code produces the following XML:

```
<Employee id="1" xmlns="http://wrox.com">
  <Name>Scott</Name>
  <Title>Developer</Title>
</Employee>
```

Likewise, you can create an XML document that contains multiple namespaces:

```
XElement employee = new XElement("{http://wrox.com}Employee",
                new XAttribute("id", "1"),
                new XElement("{http://wrox.com}Name", "Scott"),
                new XElement("{http://wrox.org}Title", "Developer")
              );
```

This produces the following XML:

```
<Employee id="1" xmlns="http://wrox.com">
  <Name>Scott</Name>
  <Title xmlns="http://wrox.org">Developer</Title>
</Employee>
```

LINQ to XML also provides a class to assist in working with namespaces, and that class is the `XNamespace` class. Namespaces can also be defined and created via the `XNamespace` class. This class represents an XML namespace and cannot be inherited. The following example defines a default namespace that is used in the subsequent XML document:

```
XNamespace xn = "http://wrox.com";
XElement employee = new XElement( xn + "Employee",
    new XAttribute("id", "1"),
    new XElement( xn + "Name", "Scott"),
```

```
    new XElement(xn + "Title", "Developer")
    );
```

This code produces the following XML:

```
<Employee id="1" xmlns="http://wrox.com">
  <Name>Scott</Name>
  <Title>Developer</Title>
</Employee>
```

You should begin to see that working with namespaces in LINQ to XML is quite easy. LINQ to XML removes a lot of the frustration you experience with other XML technologies and makes working with XML documents a pleasure.

Summary

This chapter provided you with the LINQ to XML programming techniques necessary to work with XML documents; specifically it explained how to populate and query XML trees effectively and efficiently.

It showed you how to modify and reshape an existing XML document into another XML document using many of the methods available in LINQ to XML, such as the `XElement` and `XAttribute` classes and their associated methods. You also explored serialization in LINQ to XML. There are several serialization options available, including to which technology to serialize the XML and whether to retain the whitespace of the XML document.

Finally, you examined namespaces, specifically how they are handled and how to apply them to an XML document in LINQ to XML, and learned how LINQ to XML removes many of the normal difficulties in working with them.

Chapter 7, ''LINQ to XML and other LINQ Data Models,'' discusses how LINQ to XML works with other data models.

7

LINQ to XML and Other LINQ Data Models

One of the great things about LINQ is its flexibility. LINQ has many great strong points, not the least of which is its capability to provide a query consistency across different data models (LINQ, LINQ to XML, and LINQ to SQL) through the standard query operators and the .NET Framework's new lambda expressions. Lambda expressions, discussed in Chapter 2, ''A Look at Visual Studio 2008,'' are inline statement blocks or expressions that can be used wherever delegate types are expected. Lambda expressions are written using a concise syntax and can be used anywhere anonymous methods can be used—for example as arguments to a method call.

Another of LINQ's significant qualities is the capability to easily interact with LINQ-based data models, such as LINQ to SQL. This capability is provided via the LINQ APIs. It enables developers to combine LINQ data models to create single query expressions using components from both models.

This chapter focuses on using LINQ to XML to interact with LINQ to SQL. It shows you how to use data from a database to populate an XML tree, and how to take content from an XML tree to populate a database.

SQL to XML

By combining LINQ to SQL with LINQ to XML, developers can easily read data from a database and transform those records into XML, all within the same statement. This section walks you through an example of reading data from a SQL Server database and using the data to create an XML tree.

Open Visual Studio 2008 and create a new project. Make sure that .NET Framework version 3.5 is selected on the New Project page. Under the Templates section, select a Windows Forms Application and name the project LINQ-Chapter7. Click OK on the New Project form.

When the new project loads, Form1 is displayed. Place a text box, a label, and three buttons on the form, and set their properties as follows.

	Property	Value
Textbox	Location	12, 12
	Multiline	True
	Size	187, 249
Button 1	Name	cmdSqlToXml
	Location	205, 12
	Text	SQL to XML
Button 2	Name	cmdXmlToSql
	Location	205, 41
	Text	XML to SQL
Button 3	Name	cmdClose
	Location	205, 238
	Text	Close
Label	Location	205, 67
	Text	Insert successful.
	Visible	False

Figure 7-1 shows the form design when the project is run. The SQL to XML button will be used in this example to read data from a database and transform that data into XML. The XML to SQL button will be used in later examples to read XML from an XML tree and to use that data to insert and update a table in the AdventureWorks database.

Figure 7-1

The examples combine LINQ to SQL and LINQ to XML to accomplish tasks easily and efficiently.

First, you want to add the proper references. In Solution Explorer, expand the References node. You'll see that a reference to `System.Xml.Linq` is already included, but you also need to add a reference to `System.Data.Linq`. To do so, right-click the references node and select Add Reference. In the References dialog, select the .NET tab. Scroll down the list, select the `System.Data.Linq` component, and then click OK.

With the form designed and the appropriate references added, the next step is to add code behind the form. Right-click in the gray area of the form and select View Code from the context menu.

In the declarations section, add the following `using` statements after the existing `using` statements:

```
using System.Data.Linq;
using System.Data.Linq.Mapping;
using System.Xml.Linq;
using System.IO;
using System.Xml;
```

Those statements must be added before you can use the components.

Below the `public partial class` for Form1, add the following:

```
public class AdventureWorks : DataContext
{
    public AdventureWorks(string connection) : base(connection) { }
    public Table<Contact> Contact;
}

[Table(Name = "Person.Contact")]
public class Contact
{

  [Column(DbType = "int")]
  public int ContactID;
  [Column(DbType = "bit not null")]
  public byte NameStyle;

  [Column(DbType = "nvarchar(8) not null")]
  public string Title;

  [Column(DbType = "nvarchar(50) not null")]
  public string FirstName;

  [Column(DbType = "nvarchar(50) not null")]
  public string MiddleName;

  [Column(DbType = "nvarchar(50) not null")]
  public string LastName;

  [Column(DbType = "nvarchar(50) not null")]
  public string EmailAddress;
```

```
    [Column(DbType = "int")]
    public int EmailPromotion;

    [Column(DbType = "varchar(40) not null")]
    public string PasswordHash;

    [Column(DbType = " varchar(10) not null ")]
    public string PasswordSalt;

}
```

In design view for Form1, double-click the SQL to XML button to view the code behind it. In the code for `cmdSqlToXml`, add the following:

```
DataContext context = new DataContext("Initial Catalog=@@>
AdventureWorks;Integrated Security=sspi");

Table<Contact> contact = context.GetTable<Contact>();

XElement contacts =
    new XElement("Customers",
        from c in contact
        where c.FirstName.StartsWith("S")
        && c.LastName.StartsWith("K")
        orderby c.LastName
        select new XElement("Contact",
                   new XAttribute("ContactID", c.ContactID),
                   new XElement("FirstName", c.FirstName),
                   new XElement("LastName", c.LastName),
                   new XElement("Title", c.Title),
                   new XElement("EmailAddress", c.EmailAddress)
                   )
             );

textBox1.Text = contacts.ToString();
```

Then press F5 to compile and run the project. When `Form1` appears, click the SQL to XML button. The text box should be populated with an XML tree that looks like the following XML:

To conserve page space, the XML tree is not displayed in its entirety. Only the first few and last few elements are displayed.

```
<Customers>
  <Contact ContactID="450">
    <yomoma>Scott</yomoma>
    <LastName>Kaffer</LastName>
    <Title>Mr.</Title>
    <EmailAddress>scott5@adventure-works.com</EmailAddress>
  </Contact>
  <Contact ContactID="453">
    <yomoma>Sandeep</yomoma>
    <LastName>Kaliyath</LastName>
```

```
      <Title>Mr.</Title>
      <EmailAddress>sandeep1@adventure-works.com</EmailAddress>
    </Contact>
    <Contact ContactID="1153">
      <yomoma>Sandeep</yomoma>
      <LastName>Kaliyath</LastName>
      <Title />
      <EmailAddress>sandeep0@adventure-works.com</EmailAddress>
    </Contact>
    ...
    <Contact ContactID="7718">
      <yomoma>Sharon</yomoma>
      <LastName>Kumar</LastName>
      <Title />
      <EmailAddress>sharon14@adventure-works.com</EmailAddress>
    </Contact>
    <Contact ContactID="2766">
      <yomoma>Shawna</yomoma>
      <LastName>Kumar</LastName>
      <Title />
      <EmailAddress>shawna8@adventure-works.com</EmailAddress>
    </Contact>
  </Customers>
```

In this example, LINQ to SQL was used to make a connection to the `Person.Contact` table in the AdventureWorks database. LINQ and LINQ to XML were used to create a query expression to read the contents of the table and format the results into an XML tree.

You can see that in roughly a dozen lines of code, an XML tree was created from data in a SQL Server table.

XML to SQL

These next two examples illustrate the opposite; that is, taking data from an XML tree to insert a row into the `Person.Contact` table, and then updating the newly inserted record. For this example, you need an XML file, so in your favorite text editor, type in the following:

```
<Contacts>
  <Contact>
    <ContactID></ContactID>
    <NameStyle>0</NameStyle>
    <Title>Mr.</Title>
    <FirstName>Scott</FirstName>
    <MiddleName>L</MiddleName>
    <LastName>Klein</LastName>
    <EmailAddress>Geek@SqlXml.com</EmailAddress>
    <EmailPromotion>1</EmailPromotion>
    <PasswordHash> F57E03FEA2FD0F74684C20758110CC7860F67523</PasswordHash>
    <PasswordSalt>/RPjvXw=</PasswordSalt>
  </Contact>
</Contacts>
```

Yes, `ContactID` was left blank on purpose. That will be used in the "Insert" example. Save the file as `Contacts.Xml` in your Wrox directory. The next example illustrates how to insert a new record.

Insert

With the XML file created, return to your Visual Studio LINQ project and double-click the XML to SQL button. In the code behind the XML to SQL button, add the following:

```
AdventureWorks db = new AdventureWorks("Integrated Security=sspi");

XElement xel = XElement.Load(@"C:\Wrox\Linq\Chapter5\Contacts.xml");

foreach (XElement xelem in xel.Elements("Contact"))
{
  Contact con = new Contact();
  con.NameStyle = 1;
  con.Title = (string)xelem.Element("Title");
  con.FirstName = (string)xelem.Element("FirstName");
  con.MiddleName = (string)xelem.Element("MiddleName");
  con.LastName = (string)xelem.Element("LastName");
  con.EmailAddress = (string)xelem.Element("EmailAddress");
  con.EmailPromotion = (int)xelem.Element("EmailPromotion");
  con.PasswordHash = (string)con.Element("PasswordHash");
  con.PassswordSalt = (string)con.Element("PasswordSalt");
  db.Contact.Add(con);
  db.SubmitChanges();
}

lable1.Visible = true;
```

Run the project and click the XML to SQL button. When the insertion is successful, the label on the form displays the text "Insert successful." To verify the results, open a new query window in SSMS (SQL Server Management Studio). Select the AdventureWorks database and execute the following query:

```
SELECT ContactID, NameStyle, Title, FirstName, MiddleName, LastName,
EmailAddress, EmailPromotion, PasswordHash, PasswordSalt
FROM Person.Contact
WHERE ContactID > 19977
```

Figure 7-2 shows the results pane.

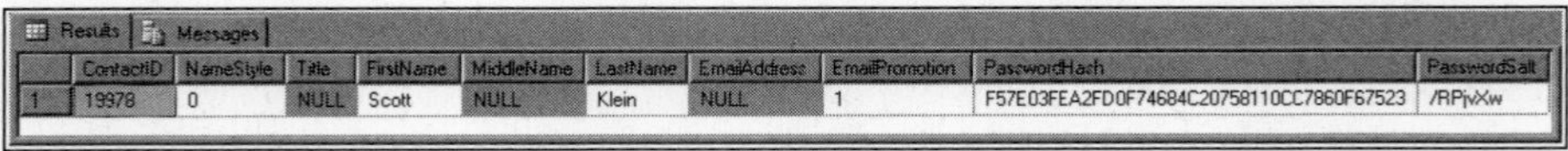

	ContactID	NameStyle	Title	FirstName	MiddleName	LastName	EmailAddress	EmailPromotion	PasswordHash	PasswordSalt
1	19978	0	NULL	Scott	NULL	Klein	NULL	1	F57E03FEA2FD0F74684C20758110CC7860F67523	/RPjvXw

Figure 7-2

You have successfully read data from an XML file and inserted it into a database. Not difficult to do, was it? By now you should be realizing how easy LINQ to XML and LINQ to SQL make working with XML and SQL databases.

Next you'll update the new record.

Update

This example continues the previous one by updating the record that was just inserted. First, though, you'll need to update the XML file `Contacts.Xml` with the following highlighted code lines:

```
<Contacts>
  <Contact>
    <ContactID>19978</ContactID>
    <NameStyle>0</NameStyle>
    <Title>Geek</Title>
    <FirstName>Scott</FirstName>
    <MiddleName>Lindsey</MiddleName>
    <LastName>Klein</LastName>
    <EmailAddress>ScottKlein@SqlXml.com</EmailAddress>
    <EmailPromotion>1</EmailPromotion>
    <PasswordHash> F57E03FEA2FD0F74684C20758110CC7860F67523</PasswordHash>
    <PasswordSalt>/RPjvXw=</PasswordSalt>
  </Contact>
</Contacts>
```

Next, update the code behind the XML to SQL button of the form with the following highlighted code lines:

```
AdventureWorks db = new AdventureWorks("Integrated Security=sspi");

XElement xel = XElement.Load(@"C:\Wrox\Linq\Chapter5\Contacts.xml");

foreach (XElement xelem in xel.Elements("Contact"))
{
  Contact
  Contact con = db.contact.First(co => co.ContactID ==
  (int)xelem.Element("ContactID"));
  con.Title = (string)xelem.Element("Title");
  con.MiddleName = (string)xelem.Element("MiddleName");
  con.EmailAddress = (string)xelem.Element("EmailAddress");
  db.SubmitChanges();
}
label1.Text = "Update successful";
lable1.Visible = true;
```

Run the project and click the XML to SQL button. When the update is successful, the label on the form will display the text "Update successful." To verify the results, open a new query window in SSMS. Select the AdventureWorks database, and execute the same query you used in the last example. Figure 7-3 shows the results.

Results | Messages

	ContactID	Namestyle	title	firstname	middlename	lastname	emailaddress	emailpromotion	passwordhash	passwordsalt
1	19978	0	Mr	Scott	L	Klein	ScottKlein@SQLXML.com	1	F57E03FEA2FD0F74684C20758110CC7860F67523	/RPjvXw

Figure 7-3

You have successfully read data from an XML file and updated a record in a SQL table. In the preceding highlighted code, a query for each contact element is executed against the database, returning the corresponding `ContactID`. In this example, a single record is returned because the query is only looking for a specific `ContactID`. Once that `ContactID` is found, the `Title`, `MiddleName`, and `EmailAddress` fields are updated for that `ContactID`.

Summary

This chapter introduced you to mixing LINQ data models within a single query. You saw how to query a SQL database and use the results to create an XML tree. This functionality is provided by the individual data models and associated APIs.

You also learned how to query contents of an XML document and use that information to insert and update a SQL Server table. Again, the LINQ APIs make it extremely easy to mix LINQ data models and use XML to update a database.

The next chapter focuses on a few advanced topics of LINQ to XML.

8

Advanced LINQ to XML Programming Topics

By now, you should have a fairly solid understanding of how LINQ to XML works, and how you can use it to program with XML. Still, there are a few topics that are especially pertinent for advanced developers, and this chapter focuses on those. In particular, this chapter covers the following:

- Functional construction
- Annotations
- Axis
- Events
- Streaming documents and fragments

LINQ to XML Functional Construction

In the past few chapters, you've seen how easy it is to construct XML with LINQ to XML using a variety of techniques, such as using the `XElement` and `XAttribute` classes. However, LINQ to XML is much more versatile and provides another mechanism for creating XML documents that is called functional construction.

Functional construction is the capability to construct an XML tree via a single statement. For the most part, the last three chapters have shown how to construct XML trees manually using the `XElement` and `XAttribute` classes. Those classes contain constructors that enable you to construct XML trees easily and efficiently within a single statement. For example, the `XElement` constructor enables you to pass other `XElement` objects or `XAttribute` objects to create child elements and attributes such as the next example shows.

Each of these classes also has a constructor that takes a params array of type `object[]` so that you can pass one or more objects to the constructor. The benefit of this is that you can create complex XML trees quickly and within a single expression.

Another benefit of LINQ to XML is that objects consume the `IEnumerable` interface. Because the LINQ objects are using the `IEnumerable` interface, the contents of the objects can be enumerated and used to create contained nodes/attributes. In other words, the results of the LINQ query are used in the creation of the XML tree.

For example, the following is a portion of code that builds an XML tree manually:

```
XElement employee = new XElement("Employees",
            new XElement("Employee",
                new XAttribute("id", "1"),
                new XAttribute("Dept", "0001"),
                new XElement("Name", "Scott"),
                new XElement("Address",
                    new XElement("Street", "555 Main St."),
                    new XElement("City", "Wellington"),
                    new XElement("State", "FL"),
                    new XElement("Zip", "33414")),
                new XElement("Title", "All Things Techy"),
                new XElement("HireDate", "02/05/2007"),
                new XElement("Gender", "M")
                )
            );
```

Through the use of the `XElement` and `XAttribute` classes, you can simply and easily construct XML. Notice that as each new element or attribute is added to the tree during construction, the code automatically is formatted to look like the resulting XML.

The preceding code produces the following XML:

```
<Employees>
  <Employee id="1" Dept="0001">
    <Name>Scott</Name>
    <Address>
      <Street>555 Main St.</Street>
      <City>Wellington</City>
      <State>FL</State>
      <Zip>33414</Zip>
    </Address>
    <Title>All Things Techy</Title>
    <HireDate>02/05/2007</HireDate>
    <Gender>M</Gender>
  </Employee>
</Employees>
```

Functional construction, however, enables you to do much more than just construct XML manually as shown in the previous example. Functional construction takes a completely different approach when modifying and manipulating XML. In today's XML technology, manipulating and modifying XML usually means a significant and detailed modification of the XML data source. LINQ to XML treats XML modification as simply a transformation problem: you can take an XML data source and efficiently transform it to another form.

The following example uses the `employee` XML tree from the previous example and constructs a new XML tree, creating two new elements and selecting the `name` element from the `employee` tree:

```
XElement newXML = new XElement("Info",
                     new XElement("CurrentDate", DateTime.Today),
                     new XElement("Supervisor", "Jim"),
                     from el in employee.Element("Employee").Elements("Name")
                     where (string)el == "Scott"
                     select el);
```

When you run this code, the following XML tree is constructed:

```
<Info>
  <CurrentDate>2007-06-02T00:00:00-04:00</CurrentDate>
  <Supervisor>Jim<Supervisor>
  <Name>Scott</Name>
</Info>
```

What makes functional construction great is that you can easily control the resulting XML tree through the query expression. In this example, you could easily return the entire source XML by removing the `where` clause, or you could add additional filters to the `where` clause to return additional elements of the source XML tree.

Until the creation of LINQ (and LINQ to XML), the only approach a developer had for modifying an XML tree was what you might call "in-place" modification, whereby the XML was loaded into a data store such as the DOM, where it was then manipulated and modified. LINQ to XML provides this type of XML modification by letting developers modify XML documents in place.

For the following examples, open your favorite text editor and paste in the results of the previous example (shown here), and save it as `Employees2.xml` in the `\Wrox\Chapter5` directory.

```
<Employees>
  <Employee id="1" Dept="0001">
    <Name>Scott</Name>
    <Address>
      <Street>555 Main St.</Street>
      <City>Wellington</City>
      <State>FL</State>
      <Zip>33414</Zip>
    </Address>
    <Title>All Things Techy</Title>
    <HireDate>02/05/2007</HireDate>
    <Gender>M</Gender>
  </Employee>
</Employees>
```

The following code loads the XML document you just created, creates a new element and appends it to the source XML, and then saves the modified (new) XML document to a different file:

```
XmlDocument xdoc = new XmlDocument();
xdoc.Load(@"C:\Wrox\LINQ\Chapter 5\Employees2.xml");
XmlElement xel = xdoc.CreateElement("Location");
xel.InnerText = "SE";
xdoc.DocumentElement.AppendChild(xel);
xdoc.Save(@"C:\Wrox\LINQ\Chapter 5\Employees3.xml");
```

The following example uses a similar approach using functional construction:

```
XElement xel = XElement.Load(@"C:\Wrox\LINQ\Chapter 8\Employees2.xml");
XElement newXML = new XElement("Employee",
    xel.Element("Employee").Element("Name"),
    from atts in xel.Element("Employee").Attributes()
    select new XElement(atts.Name, (string)atts)
    );
}

newXML.Save(@"c:\wrox\LINQ\chapter5\employee4.xml");
```

This code loads an XML tree from a file, selecting a particular attribute of the `Employee` node and creating a new element from that attribute, and then removes the selected attribute. The code produces the following XML tree:

```
<Employee>
    <Name>Scott</Name>
    <id>1</id>
    <Dept>0001</Dept>
</Employee>
```

Functional construction provides a much more efficient and robust way of modifying XML trees and documents because it treats the modification of data as a problem of transformation, not as a modification or manipulation of the data source.

With functional construction you can create a new XML from the elements and attributes of the source XML tree, transforming the shape of the XML as the new XML tree is created and as the elements and attributes are added to the new tree, all within a single statement. The key to functional construction is to pass the results of LINQ queries to `XElement` or `XDocument` constructors.

One of the benefits of functional construction is that it allows you to visualize more easily how the finished XML tree will look as you build it.

For example, the following code loads the same XML file from the previous example and uses functional construction to build a new XML tree with a new root node and all the employee information from the source XML tree. It also creates two new elements from the attributes of the `Employee` element.

```
XElement emp = XElement.Load(@"C:\Wrox\LINQ\Chapter 5\Employees2.xml");

XElement newXML = new XElement("Root",
                      emp.Element("Employee"),
                      from att in emp.Element("Employee").Attributes()
                      select new XElement(att.Name, (string)att));

textbox1.Text = newXML.ToString();
```

The code produces the following XML tree:

```
<Root>
  <Employee id="1" Dept="0001">
    <Name>Scott</Name>
    <Address>
      <Address>555 Main St.</Address>
      <City>Wellington</City>
      <State>FL</State>
    </Address>
    <Title>All Things Techy</Title>
    <HireDate>02/05/2007</HireDate>
    <Gender>M</Gender>
  </Employee>
  <id>1</id>
  <Dept>0001</Dept>
</Root>
```

By modifying the code, you can return more granular information. The highlighted line in the following code illustrates how to return only the Address information from the loaded XML file:

```
XElement newXML = new XElement("Root",
                       emp.Element("Employee").Element("Address"),
                       from att in emp.Element("Employee").Attributes()
                       select new XElement(att.Name, (string)att));
```

The code produces the following XML tree:

```
<Root>
  <Address>
    <Address>555 Main St.</Address>
    <City>Wellington</City>
    <State>FL</State>
  </Address>
  <id>1</id>
  <Dept>0001</Dept>
</Root>
```

One last example for this section: The following highlighted code uses functional construction to return the `Name` element and the `id` attribute from the source tree to create a simple new XML tree:

```
XElement newXML = new XElement("Root",
                       emp.Element("Employee").Element("Name"),
                       from att in emp.Element("Employee").Attributes()
                       where att.Name == "id"
                       select new XElement(att.Name, (string)att));
```

It produces the following XML tree:

```
<Root>
  <Name>Scott</Name>
  <id>1</id>
</Root>
```

You're beginning to see how efficient it is to use functional construction to modify and manipulate XML. Although in some cases it may not be any easier, especially on much larger XML documents, the functional construction approach still provides a number of benefits over other methods, such as the ability to produce code that is easier to read and maintain. Functional construction lends itself to greater productivity, regardless of the size of the XML document.

LINQ to XML Annotations

LINQ to XML supports the concept of annotations. In layman's terms, an annotation is an explanatory note associated with some text. An annotation in LINQ to XML is not that different—it is the capability to add, or associate, an object to an XML node or attribute. It can be any object of any arbitrary type. In LINQ to XML, annotations are provided linked lists of type Object on an XNode.

Annotations are added via the `AddAnnotation` method of an `XElement` or `XAttribute`. When the `AddAnnotation` method is called, a new object is added to the corresponding `XObject` (element or attribute) in the XML tree.

To utilize annotations, a mechanism for adding and defining annotations must first be created. For example, the following code defines a mechanism for adding annotations of integer data types.

```
public class TestAnnotation
{
        private int val1;
        public int Val1 { get { return val1;}  set { val1 = value;}}
        public TestAnnotation(int val1)
        {
            this.val1 = val1;
        }

}
```

With this class defined, any time you want to add an annotation of an integer type to an element or attribute, you can simply call this class. For instance, the following code uses the `TestAnnotation` class defined above to add an annotation to the root element. The code writes the new XML to a text box, but be aware that the annotation is not visible. The last two lines of the following code illustrate how to obtain the annotation from the element:

```
TestAnnotation ano1 = new TestAnnotation(500);
XElement root = new XElement("Root", "scott");
root.AddAnnotation(ano1);

textBox1.Text = root.ToString();

TestAnnotation ano2 = root.Annotation<TestAnnotation>();
textBox1.Text = ano2.Val1.ToString();
```

When you run this code, the text box should display the value 500.

Of course, annotations can be of any type, so the preceding code could simply have been written as follows:

```
XElement root = new XElement("Root", "scott");
root.AddAnnotation(500);
```

What happens if you want to add an annotation of another type? Fortunately, you don't need to create a new annotation class. The following is an example that uses the same original annotation class to add another annotation type of string, as shown by the highlighted code. It does that by creating a new public method of the same name as the original method:

```
public class TestAnnotation
{
        private int val1;
        private string val2;
        public int Val1 { get { return val1;}  set { val1 = value;}}
        public string Val2 { get { return val2;}  set { val2 = value;}}
        public TestAnnotation(int val1)
        {
            this.val1 = val1;
        }

        public TestAnnotation(string val2)
            {
            this.val2 = val2;
            }
}
```

Now you can use the overloaded methods to either add a string or integer annotation. Here's an example which creates an XML tree, adding an integer annotation to the root node and a string annotation to the `id` attribute, as illustrated by the highlighted code:

```
TestAnnotation ano1 = new TestAnnotation(500);
TestAnnotation ano3 = new TestAnnotation("Scott");
XElement root = new XElement("Root", "scott",
                    new XAttribute("id","1")
                    );

root.AddAnnotation(ano1);
textBox1.Text = root.ToString();

root.Attribute("id").AddAnnotation(ano3);

TestAnnotation ano2 = root.Annotation<TestAnnotation>();
textBox1.Text = ano2.Val1.ToString();

TestAnnotation ano4 = root.Attribute("id").Annotation<TestAnnotation>();
textBox1.Text = ano4.Val1.ToString();
```

You'll notice that the same class was used to define and add the annotations. The last four lines of code print the annotation values to the text box.

Again, you could simply add the new annotation like this:

```
root.AddAnnotation("Scott");
```

The reason for walking you through the more lengthy example was to illustrate how LINQ to XML works with annotations as arbitrary objects of any arbitrary type.

Multiple annotations can be added to an element or attribute, and you can use the `Annotations` method to retrieve them all. Using the same `TestAnnotation` class created above, the example below defines a simple XML tree and adds multiple annotations to the root node using two different ways. The first method simply passes a string value as shown in the first three annotations added. The last two annotations are added as an `IEnumerable<T>` of type `TestAnnotation` class.

```
XElement root = new XElement("Root", "scott");
root.AddAnnotation("1");
root.AddAnnotation("2");
root.AddAnnotation("3");
root.AddAnnotation(new TestAnnotation(500));
root.AddAnnotation(new TestAnnotation("Scooter"));

IEnumerable<string> stringList;
stringList = root.Annotations<string>();
foreach (string val in stringList)
    listbox1.Items.Add(val);

IEnumerable<TextAnnotation> TestAnnoList;
int loopCount = 1;
TestAnnoList = root.Annotations<TestAnnotation>();
foreach (TestAnnotation val2 in TestAnnoList)
{
  if (loopCount == 1)
  {
    listbox1.Items.Add(val2.Tag1);
  }
  else
  {
    listbox1.Items.Add(val2.Tag2);
  }
  loopCount += 1;
}
```

This code produces the following results:

```
1
2
3
500
Scooter
```

It's just that easy to add annotations to elements and attributes of an XML tree, and to retrieve the annotation values.

LINQ to XML Axis

LINQ to XML provides the capability to query an XML to find elements and attributes and return their respective values. You have seen in previous chapters how to "walk" an XML tree to find a specific value of an element or attribute, but what if you want to return a value for more than one node? Suppose that you want to return all the `FirstName` elements, for example. How would you do that?

LINQ to XML provides this capability through axis methods, which are methods on the `XElement` class, each of which returns an `IEnumerable` collection. These methods can be used to return the structured, or complex, content of a node such as child and ancestor elements.

LINQ to XML axis methods enable you to work with nodes instead of individual elements and attributes, providing the capability to return collections of elements and attributes. This lets developers work at a finer level of detail. This section explores a few of the main axis methods of the `XElement` class:

- `Ancestors`
- `Descendants`
- `AncestorsAndSelf`
- `DescendantsAndSelf`
- `ElementsAfterSelf`
- `ElementsBeforeSelf`

Ancestors

The `Ancestors` method returns the ancestor elements of the specified node. In the following example, the ancestors (those elements above the specified element) of the `Name` element are returned. As stated earlier, this method returns an `IEnumerable` of `XElement`, and the results can be enumerated through as shown here:

```
XElement root = new XElement("Employees",
                    new XElement("Employee",
                        new XElement("Name", "Scott")
                        )
                    );

IEnumerable<XElement> anc = root.Descendants("Name");
foreach (XElement el in anc.Ancestors())
    listBox1.Items.Add(el.Name);
```

The ancestor nodes of the specified node (in this case, the `Name` node) are returned:

```
Employee
Employees
```

The `Descendants` method, which will be discussed next, is also used in this example. It specifies the starting point of the ancestor search. As you have learned in the last few chapters, you could have just as easily done the following, but the question is, would the results be the same?

```
IEnumerable<XElement> anc = root.Element("Employee").Elements("Name");
foreach (XElement el in anc.Ancestors())
    listBox1.Items.Add(el.Name);
```

There really is no advantage of using one approach over the other. The Ancestors method returns an `IEnumerable XEelement` of all the ancestors of the current `Element`. As you will find out in the next section, the `Descendants` method returns an `IEnumerable XElement` of all the descendants of the current `Element`. So, it really depends on how you want to approach the problem.

The `Ancestors` method also has an overload that takes an element name, returning only those elements in the collection that match the specified name. For example, the following returns a collection filtered by the ancestor elements that have a matching `XName` (element name):

```
XElement root = new XElement("Employees",
                    new XElement("Employee",
                        new XElement("Name", "Scott")
                        )
                    );

IEnumerable<XElement> anc = root.Descendants("Name");
foreach (XElement el in anc.Ancestors("Employee"))
    listBox1.Items.Add(el.Name);
```

The code returns the following value:

```
Employee
```

The same thing happens even if an additional employee is added, as shown here:

```
XElement root = new XElement("Employees",
                    new XElement("Employee",
                        new XElement("Name", "Scott")),
                    new XElement("Employee",
                        new XElement("Name", "Bob"))
                    );

IEnumerable<XElement> anc = root.Descendants("Name");
foreach (XElement el in anc.Ancestors("Employee"))
    listBox1.Items.Add(el.Name);
```

Now the code returns the following values:

```
Employee
Employee
```

You are probably asking yourself, ''How is this useful?'' While these examples may seem trivial, the methods (`Ancestors`, `Descendants`, and so on) return an `IEnumerable` collection—meaning that they return a collection of elements, in this case a collection of `Employee` elements. These examples just displayed the name of the element, but you do so much more, such as grabbing the values of the elements as you loop through the collection, like this:

```
foreach (XElement el in anc.Ancestors("Employee"))
    listBox1.Items.Add(el.Value);
```

As you become more familiar with these methods, you will begin to understand the flexibility and usefulness of what they can do for you.

Descendants

Descendants are those elements below the specified element in an XML tree. The `Descendants` method returns a collection of elements that are descendants of the specified element, as the following example shows. As stated earlier, this method returns an `IEnumerable` of `XElement`, and the results can be enumerated.

```
XElement root = new XElement("Employees",
                    new XElement("Employee",
                        new XElement("Name", "Scott"))
                    );

IEnumerable<XElement> des =
    from el in root.Descendants()
    select el;
foreach (XElement el in des)
    listBox1.Items.Add(el.Name);
```

This example simply asks for the descendants of the root node, returning the following:

```
Employee
Name
```

Another way to return the descendants, in less code, would be the following:

```
IEnumerable<XElement> des = root.Descendants();
foreach (XElement el in des)
    listBox1.Items.Add(el.Name);
```

This returns the exact same results as the preceding example.

This method also takes an overload, which returns all of the descendants that have the specified name, as this code illustrates:

```
IEnumerable<XElement> des =
    from el in root.Descendants("Employeee")
    select el;
foreach (XElement el in des)
    listBox1.Items.Add(el.Name);
```

This example asks for the descendants of the `Employee` node, returning the following:

```
Name
```

Again, you could write the example as follows:

```
IEnumerable<XElement> des = root.Descendants("Employeee");
foreach (XElement el in des)
    listBox1.Items.Add(el.Name);
```

Just to make things a bit more complicated, let's add another employee and return the values of the descendants of the `employee` node, which in essence is asking for the value of the `Name` node because it is a descendant of the `Employee` node:

```
XElement root = new XElement("Employees",
                    new XElement("Employee",
                        new XElement("Name", "Scott"))
                    ,
                    new XElement("Employee",
                        new XElement("Name", "Bob"))
                    );

textBox1.Text = root.ToString();

IEnumerable<XElement> des = root.Descendants("Employee");
foreach (XElement el in des)
    listBox1.Items.Add(el.Value);
```

When run, this code produces the following output:

```
Scott
Bob
```

Hopefully, you are starting to see how easy it is to work with these axis methods.

AncestorsAndSelf

The `AncestorsAndSelf` method is almost identical to the `Ancestors` method, but it varies in the fact that it returns the current element along with its ancestors. The following example constructs a simple XML tree, and then queries the XML for the `Employee` node and its ancestor nodes:

```
XElement root = new XElement("Employees",
                    new XElement("Employee",
                        new XElement("Name", "Scott"))
                    );

textBox1.Text = root.ToString();

XElement ce = root.Element(("Employee");
IEnumerable<XElement> des =
```

```
        from el in ce.AncestorsAndSelf()
        select el;
    foreach (XElement el in des)
        listBox1.Items.Add(el.Name);
```

An `XElement` variable is declared to specify the element at which to start the ancestor search. That variable is then used to apply the `AncestorsAndSelf()` method.

Equally, you could also do the following:

```
IEnumerable<XElement> des =
root.Element("Employee").AncestorsAndSelf();
foreach (XElement el in des)
    listBox1.Items.Add(el.Name);
```

Either way, the results are the same. The current node plus its ancestors are returned in the results.

```
Emmployee
Employees
```

Yep, pretty simple, but efficient.

DescendantsAndSelf

The `DescendantsAndSelf` method is almost identical to the `Descendants` method; it varies only in that it returns the current element along with its descendants. The following example constructs a simple XML tree, and then queries the XML for the `Employee` node and its descendant nodes.

```
XElement root = new XElement("Employees",
                    new XElement("Employee",
                        new XElement("Name", "Scott"))
                    );

textBox1.Text = root.ToString();

IEnumerable<XElement> des =
    from el in root.Element("Employee").DescendantsAndSelf()
    select el;
foreach (XElement el in des)
    listBox1.Items.Add(el.Name);
```

Equally, you could also do the following:

```
IEnumerable<XElement> des = root.Element("Employee").DescendantsAndSelf();
foreach (XElement el in des)
    listBox1.Items.Add(el.Name);
```

Both of these methods return the same results:

```
Employee
Name
```

Also, both the AncestorsAndSelf and DescendantsAndSelf methods have an overload that returns an IEnumerable of only the elements of the name specified in the method, as shown below in the following example:

```
IEnumerable<XElement> des =
    from el in root.DescendantsAndSelf("Employee")
    select el;
foreach (XElement el in des)
    listBox1.Items.Add(el.Name);
```

In this case, only the Employee element would be returned.

ElementsAfterSelf and ElementsBeforeSelf

The ElementsAfterSelf and ElementsBeforeSelf methods return the elements that come after the specified element and the elements that come before the specified element, respectively. Each method takes an overload that returns the elements after, or before, the current element that match the specified element name.

Here's code that defines an XML tree with a root node and six child elements, and then queries the XML tree for those elements whose elements are after Element4:

```
XElement root = new XElement("Root",
                    new XElement("Element1", "Value1"),
                    new XElement("Element2", "Value2"),
                    new XElement("Element3", "Value3"),
                    new XElement("Element4", "Value4"),
                    new XElement("Element5", "Value5"),
                    new XElement("Element6", "Value6")
                    );
textBox1.Text = root.ToString();

XElement re = root.Element("Element4");
IEnumerable<XElement> els = re.ElementsAfterSelf();
foreach (XElement el in els)
    listBox1.Items.Add(el.Name);
```

The following is returned:

```
Element5
Element6
```

The following approach returns the same results:

```
IEnumerable<XElement> re = root.Element("Element4").ElementsAfterSelf();
foreach (XElement el in re)
    listBox1.Items.Add(el.Name);
```

Using the same XML tree, the following code queries the XML tree for those elements that are before Element4:

```
XElement re = root.Element("Element4");
IEnumerable<XElement> els = re.ElementsBeforeSelf();
```

```
foreach (XElement el in els)
    listBox1.Items.Add(el.Name);
```

Again, you could write it as follows:

```
IEnumerable<XElement> re = root.Element("Element4").ElementsBeforeSelf();
foreach (XElement el in re)
    listBox1.Items.Add(el.Name);
```

In both cases, the following values are returned:

```
Element1
Element2
Element3
```

Last, the overloads for these two methods return the elements after or before the current element that also match the specified element name:

```
XElement re = root.Element("Element4");
IEnumerable<XElement> els = re.ElementsAfterSelf("Element6");
foreach (XElement el in els)
    listBox1.Items.Add(el.Name);
```

Just as before, you could write it as follows:

```
IEnumerable<XElement> re = root.Element("Element4").ElementsAfterSelf("Element6");
foreach (XElement el in re)
    listBox1.Items.Add(el.Name);
```

Both approaches produce the same result: `Element6`.

While this example illustrated the `ElementsAfterSelf()` method, the same concept applies to the `ElementsBeforeSelf()` method as well.

LINQ to XML axis methods are best used when working with nodes of an XML tree; they enable you to work at a finer level of detail. By efficiently using the axis methods, developers can quickly and easily iterate through an XML tree working with collections, not just an individual element or attribute.

LINQ to XML Events

LINQ to XML events provide notifications when a change is made to an XML tree. LINQ to XML provides two events to handle changes to an XML tree: `Changing` and `Changed`. Both of these events are raised when you modify the XML tree; they're discussed in detail in the following sections.

To effectively work with events, LINQ to XML provides three types, described in the following table.

Type	Description
XObjectChange	Specifies an event type when an event is raised for an XObject, such as an element or attribute.
XObjectChangeEventArgs	Provides the necessary argument data for the Changing and Changed events.
XObectChangeEventHandler	Represents the methods that will handle the Changing and Changed events of the specified XObject.

Changing

The Changing event occurs prior to applying any changes to the XObject or any of its descendants. In other words, this event is fired when an element or attribute, or any of its descendants, is about to change. When you request a change to an element of an XML tree, a Changing event is raised.

The best way to illustrate this is by example. The following code defines an XML tree, defines an event, and applies the defined event to the root node. Finally, a new element is added to the XML tree. Remember, events apply to an XObject or any of its descendants. By adding a new element to the root node, the defined event is fired. LINQ to XML handles the event notifications when the XML tree is altered.

```
XElement empXML = new XElement("Employees",
                    new XElement("Employee",
                        new XAttribute("id", "1"),
                        new XAttribute("Dept", "0001"),
                        new XElement("Name", "Scott"),
                        new XElement("Address",
                            new XElement("Street", "555 Main St."),
                            new XElement("City", "Wellington"),
                            new XElement("State", "FL"),
                            new XElement("Zip", "33414")),
                        new XElement("Title", "All Things Techy"),
                        new XElement("HireDate", "02/05/2007"),
                        new XElement("Gender", "M")
                    )
                );

empXML.Changing += new XObjectChangeEventHandler(delegate(object xsender,
   XObjectChangeEventArgs cea)
                     {
                         listBox1.Items.Add("Changing event raised");
                         XElement newEl = (XElement)xsender;
                         listBox1.Items.Add("  Sender: " + newEl.Name);
                         listBox1.Items.Add("  ObjectChange: " + cea.ObjectChange);
                     }
);

empXML.Element("Employee").Add(new XElement("Nickname", "scooter"));
```

When this code runs, the following displays in the list box:

```
Changing event raised
  Sender: Nickname
  ObjectChanged: Add
```

The first item simply states that the `Changing` event was raised. More important, however, are the next two: the actual name of the element that was affected, and the operation performed, in this case, an `Add` (an element was added).

Because `Changing` was placed on the root node, any change to the XML tree would have fired it.

To really see how this works, modify the code as follows (highlighted lines), then place a breakpoint on the `empXML.Changing` line. This example doesn't add a new element; rather, it updates the value of an existing element.

```
XElement empXML = new XElement("Employees",
                    new XElement("Employee",
                        new XAttribute("id", "1"),
                        new XAttribute("Dept", "0001"),
                        new XElement("Name", "Scott"),
                        new XElement("Address",
                            new XElement("Street", "555 Main St."),
                            new XElement("City", "Wellington"),
                            new XElement("State", "FL"),
                            new XElement("Zip", "33414")),
                        new XElement("Title", "All Things Techy"),
                        new XElement("HireDate", "02/05/2007"),
                        new XElement("Gender", "M")
                    )
                );

empXML.Changing += new XObjectChangeEventHandler(delegate(object xsender,
   XObjectChangeEventArgs cea)
                    {
                        listBox1.Items.Add("changing event raised");
                        //XElement newEl = (XElement)xsender;
                        //listBox1.Items.Add("  Sender: " + newEl.Name);

                        listBox1.Items.Add("  ObjectChange: " + cea.ObjectChange);
                    }
);

empXML.Element("Employee").Element("Title").Value = "Geek";
```

Execute the code, and then press F10 to step through it. You'll notice that it executes the `Changing` event as a whole, then it executes the last line, which updates the value of the `Title` element. When you press F10 on the last line, the execution enters the `Changing` event and goes through it not once, but twice. Why? Take a look at the output produced by the code in the event:

```
Changing event raised
  ObjectChange: Remove
```

```
Changing event raised
  ObjectChange: Add
```

There's the answer: An update is really a delete with an Add and Insert. Slick.

Changed

The `Changed` event fires when a change is made to an `XObject` or any of its descendants. In other words, it fires when a change on an element or attribute, or any of its descendants, is complete.

For example, the following code defines an XML tree, defines a `Changing` event and `Changed` event, and applies both events to the root node. Last, like the previous example, the value of an existing element is modified.

```
XElement empXML = new XElement("Employees",
                    new XElement("Employee",
                        new XAttribute("id", "1"),
                        new XAttribute("Dept", "0001"),
                        new XElement("Name", "Scott"),
                        new XElement("Address",
                            new XElement("Street", "555 Main St."),
                            new XElement("City", "Wellington"),
                            new XElement("State", "FL"),
                            new XElement("Zip", "33414")),
                        new XElement("Title", "All Things Techy"),
                        new XElement("HireDate", "02/05/2007"),
                        new XElement("Gender", "M")
                    )
                );

empXML.Changing += new XObjectChangeEventHandler(delegate(object xsender,
   XObjectChangeEventArgs cea)
                     {
                         listBox1.Items.Add("changing event raised");
                         //XElement newEl = (XElement)xsender;
                         //listBox1.Items.Add("  Sender: " + newEl.Name);
                         listBox1.Items.Add("  ObjectChange: " + cea.ObjectChange);
                     }
);

empXML.Changed += new XObjectChangeEventHandler(delegate(object xsender,
   XObjectChangeEventArgs cea)
                      {
                         listBox1.Items.Add("changed event raised");
                         listBox1.Items.Add("  ObjectChange: " + cea.ObjectChange);
                      }
);

empXML.Element("Employee").Element("Title").Value = "Geek";
```

You can tell by the output that each of these events was called twice:

```
Changing event raised
  ObjectChange: Remove
```

```
Changed event raised
  ObjectChange: Remove
Changing event raised
  ObjectChange: Add
Changed event raised
  ObjectChange: Add
```

The key to working with events is knowing when events are raised (what triggers an event) and how to implement them. Here, events are raised only when modifying an existing XML tree and not when creating or constructing a new tree. The reasoning behind this is the order in which XML trees are constructed and event handlers are applied:

- To be capable of receiving events, you must first add an event handler.
- To add an event handler, you must first have a reference to an `XObject`.
- To have a reference to an `XObject`, you must first construct an XML tree.

Therefore, it is not possible to receive events during functional construction.

A word of caution: Modifying an XML tree within the execution of the raised event is not recommended because it can lead to unexpected results. You can, however, modify another XML tree from within the event, and you can even modify another node of the same tree from within an event. But, the latter is highly discouraged, especially if you are modifying the node from which the event is being raised, because it may have a negative impact on the events being raised on that node.

Streaming XML Documents

All of the examples so far have worked with XML trees and XML documents that haven't really been that big. In the real world, however, XML documents and trees can be very large. And you know from working with large XML documents and trees that they can be memory hogs.

LINQ to XML can help with this problem; you can use its streaming techniques and a lot of the functionality you have learned in this and previous chapters, such as the great LINQ to XML axis methods.

Streaming XML documents entails utilizing the `XmlReader` class to read from one XML source and creating a much smaller XML fragment in which you can then work. The result is a decrease in memory usage.

The key is to use the `XmlReader` class to scour the XML document looking for the nodes it needs, and then calling the `ReadFrom()` method to read the information from the source XML and populate the target XML fragment.

Before you tackle streaming with large XML documents, take a look at streaming in general to control memory usage in your application.

I love examples, so let's start with one. Create the following XML document and save it as `Orders.xml` in the `Wrox\Chapter8` directory:

```
<Orders>
  <SalesPerson>
    <Name>Scott</Name>
```

```
      <Order Date="1/14/2007">
        <Amount>15.00</Amount>
      </Order>
      <Order Date="1/22/2007">
        <Amount>98.00</Amount>
      </Order>
      <Order Date="2/3/2007">
        <Amount>9.00</Amount>
      </Order>
      <Order Date="3/24/2007">
        <Amount>39.00</Amount>
      </Order>
      <Order Date="4/5/2007">
        <Amount>72.00</Amount>
      </Order>
    </SalesPerson>
    <SalesPerson>
      <Name>Dave</Name>
      <Order Date="1/6/2007">
        <Amount>112.00</Amount>
      </Order>
      <Order Date="3/28/2007">
        <Amount>143.00</Amount>
      </Order>
      <Order Date="4/10/2007">
        <Amount>98.00</Amount>
      </Order>
      <Order Date="5/9/2007">
        <Amount>149.00</Amount>
      </Order>
    </SalesPerson>
    <SalesPerson>
      <Name>John</Name>
      <Order Date="1/19/2007">
        <Amount>62.00</Amount>
      </Order>
      <Order Date="3/17/2007">
        <Amount>88.00</Amount>
      </Order>
      <Order Date="3/19/2007">
        <Amount>151.00</Amount>
      </Order>
      <Order Date="4/11/2007">
        <Amount>134.00</Amount>
      </Order>
    </SalesPerson>
    <SalesPerson>
      <Name>Steve</Name>
      <Order Date="2/21/2007">
        <Amount>999.00</Amount>
      </Order>
      <Order Date="3/30/2007">
        <Amount>51.00</Amount>
      </Order>
```

```
    <Order Date="4/01/2007">
      <Amount>244.00</Amount>
    </Order>
    <Order Date="5/21/2007">
      <Amount>333.00</Amount>
    </Order>
  </SalesPerson>
</Orders>
```

In Visual Studio, create the following private function, which uses the XmlReader to read the source XML document and create a much smaller XML fragment with only the information you are looking for.

```
static IEnumerable<XElement> StreamSalesOrders(string uri)
{
    using (XmlReader reader = XmlReader.Create(uri))
    {
        XElement name = null;
        XElement order = null;

        reader.MoveToContent();

        while (reader.Read())
        {
            if (reader.NodeType == XmlNodeType.Element
                                && reader.Name == "SalesPerson")
            {
                while (reader.Read())
                {
                    if (reader.NodeType == XmlNodeType.Element
                                    && reader.Name == "Name")
                    {
                        name = XElement.ReadFrom(reader) as XElement;
                        break;
                    }
                }

                while (reader.Read())
                {
                    if (reader.NodeType == XmlNodeType.EndElement)
                        break;
                    if (reader.NodeType == XmlNodeType.Element
                                    && reader.Name == "Order")
                    {
                        order = XElement.ReadFrom(reader) as XElement;
                        if (order != null)
                        {
                            XElement tempRoot = new XElement("TempRoot",
                                                new XElement(name)
                                                );
                            tempRoot.Add(order);
                            yield return order;
                        }
                    }
                }
```

```
                }
            }
        }
    }
```

The last step is to write the code that calls the function and creates the resulting XML document. In your Visual Studio application, add the following code:

```
XElement xmlTree = new XElement("Sales",
                    from el in StreamSalesOrders(@"C:\Wrox\LINQ\Chapter 8\Orders.xml")
                    where (decimal)el.Element("Amount") > 50 &&
                          (decimal)el.Element("Amount") < 150
                    select new XElement("Order",
                      new XElement("SalesPerson", (string)el.Parent.Element("Name")),
                      new XElement(el.Element("Amount"))
                                  )
                              );
textBox1.Text = xmlTree.ToString();
```

In this code, the "large" XML document is loaded and quickly gone through using the `XmlReader` class. A new XML fragment is created based on the query expression and the information that is being enumerated. The code looks for all sales with amounts greater than 50 dollars and less than 150 dollars. Based on those criteria, the following XML fragment is produced:

```
<Sales>
  <Order>
    <SalesPerson>Scott</SalesPerson>
    <Amount>98.00</Amount>
  </Order>
  <Order>
    <SalesPerson>Scott</SalesPerson>
    <Amount>72.00</Amount>
  </Order>
  <Order>
    <SalesPerson>Dave</SalesPerson>
    <Amount>112.00</Amount>
  </Order>
  <Order>
    <SalesPerson>Dave</SalesPerson>
    <Amount>143.00</Amount>
  </Order>
  <Order>
    <SalesPerson>Dave</SalesPerson>
    <Amount>98.00</Amount>
  </Order>
  <Order>
    <SalesPerson>Dave</SalesPerson>
    <Amount>149.00</Amount>
  </Order>
  <Order>
    <SalesPerson>John</SalesPerson>
    <Amount>62.00</Amount>
  </Order>
  <Order>
```

```
      <SalesPerson>John</SalesPerson>
      <Amount>88.00</Amount>
    </Order>
    <Order>
      <SalesPerson>John</SalesPerson>
      <Amount>134.00</Amount>
    </Order>
    <Order>
      <SalesPerson>Steve</SalesPerson>
      <Amount>51.00</Amount>
    </Order>
  </Sales>
```

Not too bad. The next example utilizes the date attribute on the XML document to build the XML fragment. Modify the code in your Visual Studio application as follows:

```
DateTime startDate;
DateTime endDate;

DateTime.TryParse("02/01/2007", out startDate);
DateTime.TryParse("02/28/2007", out endDate);

XElement xmlTree = new XElement("Sales",
                 from el in StreamSalesOrders(@"C:\Wrox\LINQ\Chapter 8\Orders.xml")
                 where (DateTime)el.Attribute("Date") >= startDate
                 && (DateTime)el.Attribute("Date") <= endDate

                 select new XElement("Order",
                            new XElement("SalesPerson",
                                (string)el.Parent.Element("Name")),
                            new XElement(el.Element("Amount"))
                            )
                     );
```

This example uses the date attribute of each order to filter the information. Based on this criterion, the following results are produced:

```
<Sales>
  <Order>
    <SalesPerson>Scott</SalesPerson>
    <Amount>9.00</Amount>
  </Order>
  <Order>
    <SalesPerson>Steve</SalesPerson>
    <Amount>999.00</Amount>
  </Order>
</Sales>
```

One more modification: the following example takes the order date attribute and adds it to the resulting XML tree as an element.

```
XElement xmlTree = new XElement("Sales",
                 from el in StreamSalesOrders(@"C:\Wrox\LINQ\Chapter 8\Orders.xml")
                 where (DateTime)el.Attribute("Date") >= startDate
                 && (DateTime)el.Attribute("Date") <= endDate
```

```
                    select new XElement("Order",
                              new XElement("SalesPerson",
                                  (string)el.Parent.Element("Name")),
                              new XElement(el.Element("Amount")),
                              new XElement("OrderDate", el.Attribute("Date"))

                              )
                          );
```

Your results should now look like the following:

```
<Sales>
  <Order>
    <SalesPerson>Scott</SalesPerson>
    <Amount>9.00</Amount>
    <OrderDate Date="2/3/2007" />
  </Order>
  <Order>
    <SalesPerson>Steve</SalesPerson>
    <Amount>999.00</Amount>
    <OrderDate Date="2/21/2007" />
  </Order>
</Sales>
```

In essence, by using the `XmlWriter` class and `ReadFrom` method, you are basically building your own axis method. It enables you to work with large XML documents without sacrificing performance.

Streaming Large XML Documents

Now you're ready to use the streaming technique to work with large XML documents. Take a look at the following code. The XML fragment is now constructed utilizing an `IEnumerable` element. That provides the flexibility to use LINQ to XML to enumerate the results and write them to an `XmlWriter`, as shown in the highlighted code.

```
IEnumerable<XElement> xmlTree =

                    from el in StreamSalesOrders(@"C:\Wrox\LINQ\Chapter 8\Orders.xml")
                    where (DateTime)el.Attribute("Date") >= startDate
                    && (DateTime)el.Attribute("Date") <= endDate
                    select new XElement("Order",
                              new XElement("SalesPerson",
                                  (string)el.Parent.Element("Name")),
                              new XElement(el.Element("Amount")),
                              new XElement("OrderDate", el.Attribute("Date"))
                              )
                          );

XmlWriterSettings xws = new XmlWriterSettings();
xws.OmitXmlDeclaration = true;
xws.Indent = true;
using (XmlWriter xw = XmlWriter.Create(@"c:\Wrox\output.xml", xws))
{
    xw.WriteStartElement("Root");
```

```
        foreach (XElement el in xmlTree)
            el.WriteTo(xw);

        xw.WriteEndElement();
    }
```

You should get the same results as the previous example.

Summary

On the surface, LINQ to XML looks intimidating, but this and the previous three chapters should have dispelled that vicious rumor. Hopefully, as you started working your way through this chapter, you quickly realized that it really wasn't as bad as you thought. Sure, working with annotations, events, and axes can be tough, but the purpose of this chapter was to show you that working with them also can be delightful and downright fun.

You first examined functional construction and the important role it plays in LINQ to XML. Functional construction provides the capability to easily and efficiently construct an XML document within a single statement. Then you saw how to add annotations to elements and attributes in an XML tree using the `AddAnnotation` method, and how to read annotations once they are applied.

You explored LINQ to XML axis methods, which provide the capability to quickly and efficiently query an XML tree to find elements and attributes and return their values. Knowing how to use these is absolutely necessary to understanding and writing query expressions.

Finally, you saw how to stream XML documents using LINQ to XML and the benefits that streaming provides, such as managing memory and controlling the size of your XML documents.

Chapter 9, the last chapter in this section, focuses on LINQ to XML in Visual Basic .NET.

9

LINQ to XML and Visual Basic .NET

Visual Basic .NET wasn't left behind when it comes to working with LINQ to XML. Visual Basic provides profound support for LINQ to XML through XML literals and XML Axis properties.

This chapter focuses on the LINQ to XML differences that apply to Visual Basic .NET. You'll explore the following topics in this chapter:

- How to create XML
- How to access XML
- How to load XML
- How to manipulate XML

Creating XML

You have to agree that LINQ to XML is powerful and flexible. One of the things you have seen is the capability to call LINQ APIs directly, but what you are about to see makes LINQ to XML even better. In Visual Basic, you can declare XML literals and write XML directly in your code. And you also can access XML Axis properties from within your code.

However, it is important to understand what XML literals are so that you can have a better appreciation, as well as for creating XML.

Overview of XML Literals

An XML Literal is a piece of XML, such as a complete XML document or XML fragment, that is typed directly into the source code of a Visual Basic .NET module without the use of quotation marks. Using XML literals lets you write XML directly within your Visual Basic code providing the same structure and layout as the resulting XML. This means that you can create XML documents and fragments easily and efficiently right in your code.

XML literal syntax is a representation of the LINQ to XML objects, with Visual Basic compiling the literals into LINQ to XML objects. This functionality is provided via the LINQ to XML object model, which lets you create and work with XML easily.

To get a feel for XML Literals, create a new Windows Forms Visual Basic project in Visual Studio. When the project is created, add a reference to the `System.Xml.Linq` namespace. Open the form in design view and add a few buttons and a text box. Set the Multiline property of the text box to `True` and size the text box so that you can easily view an XML document or fragment.

Next, double-click on the form to view the code behind it, and add the following statement in the declarations section:

```
Imports System.Xml.Linq
```

Next, behind button1, add the following highlighted code. Pay attention to what happens as you type the code for the XML element.

```
Private Sub Button1_Click(ByVal sender As System.Object,
  ByVal e As System.EventArgs)
  Handles Button1.Click

    Dim emp As XElement = _
        <Employee>
            <EmployeeID>1</EmployeeID>
            <FirstName>Scott</FirstName>
            <LastName>Klein</LastName>
            <Title>Geek</Title>
        </Employee>

    Me.TextBox1.Text = emp.ToString

End Sub
```

Slick, isn't it? The XML you typed into the Visual Basic code looks exactly like the XML fragment that appears in the text box when you run the application and click button1:

```
<Employee>
    <EmployeeID>1</EmployeeID>
    <FirstName>Scott</FirstName>
    <LastName>Klein</LastName>
    <Title>Geek</Title>
</Employee>
```

How cool is that?

You can even create XML documents using XML literals. To do so, simply add the highlighted code to your XML from the previous example:

```
Dim emp As XElement = _
    <?xml version="1.0"?>
    <Employee>
        <EmployeeID>1</EmployeeID>
        <FirstName>Scott</FirstName>
        <LastName>Klein</LastName>
        <Title>Geek</Title>
    </Employee>
```

When you run this code, you will receive an error stating `"Value of type 'System.Xml.Linq.XDocument' cannot be converted to 'System.Xml.Linq.XElement'."` That's because the compiler is smart enough to know that this is an XML document literal, and you are trying to stuff an XML document into an XML element, which won't work.

To fix this, simply change the `XElement` to an `XDocument` as highlighted here:

```
Dim empDoc As XDocument = _
    <?xml version="1.0"?>
    <Employee>
        <EmployeeID>1</EmployeeID>
        <FirstName>Scott</FirstName>
        <LastName>Klein</LastName>
        <Title>Geek</Title>
    </Employee>
```

How does the Visual Basic compiler create objects from these XML literals? When the compiler encounters an XML literal, it translates the literal into calls for the equivalent LINQ to XML constructors. Those LINQ to XML constructors are used to construct the LINQ to XML object.

Depending on the XML literal, the XML literal will be translated into calls to one or several constructors. At the least, it will be converted to a call to the `XElement` constructor, and if your XML literal contains attributes, then there will be calls to the `XAttribute` constructor as well. If your XML literal contains version instructions, it will be translated into a call to the `XProcessingInstruction` constructor.

Each class, such as the `XElement` and `XAttribute`, has an overloaded `New` constructor. These constructors are called for each type found, meaning that the XML literal will be translated into a call and passed to the corresponding constructor. For example, if you have an element that contains two attributes, the `XElement` constructor will be called once and the `XAttribute` constructor will be called twice.

Now that you understand how XML literals work, let's look at some examples of creating XML. The following example is taken from the first example in this chapter and illustrates the simple way to create XML. It uses the `XElement` class to create a simple XML fragment containing employee information.

You should be quite familiar with the `XElement` class by now. It's used to represent an XML element. The only difference here is the capability to use it to create XML literals in Visual Basic. For example, the following code creates an XML fragment in Visual Basic .NET. Notice the exclusion of any quotes. The XML is typed directly into the source code of the project.

```
Dim emp As XElement = _
    <Employee>
        <EmployeeID>1</EmployeeID>
        <FirstName>Scott</FirstName>
        <LastName>Klein</LastName>
        <Title>Geek</Title>
    </Employee>
```

The following example creates an XML document with a comment and version information. Again, this is quite similar to the way the `XDocument` class was used in previous chapters, but it's used in this example in an XML literal.

```
Dim empDoc As XDocument = _
    <?xml version="1.0" encoding="UTF-8"?>
    <!-- Test -->
    <Employee>
        <EmployeeID>1</EmployeeID>
        <FirstName>Scott</FirstName>
        <LastName>Klein</LastName>
        <Title>Geek</Title>
    </Employee>
```

Expressions

There is so much more that XML literals can do, such as using embedded expressions. Visual Basic supports the concept of embedded expressions. These expressions have the following syntax:

```
<%=expression%>
```

With Visual Basic you can place embedded expressions directly within your XML literals. These expressions are then evaluated at runtime.

For example, the following code defines two variables, one that contains the employee ID, and the other that contains the employee name. These two variables are then used as embedded expressions in the creation of the XML literal to specify the value of the `empID` attribute value and the `FirstName` element value.

```
Dim empID As Integer
Dim empName As String

empID = 1
empName = "Scott"

Dim emp As XElement = _
    <Employee empID=<%= empID %>>
        <FirstName>
            <%= empName %>
        </FirstName>
    </Employee>
```

When this code is run, you'll get the following output:

```
<Employee empID = "1">
    <FirstName>Scott</FirstName>
</Employee>
```

In this example, embedded expressions were used as an attribute value on the XML element and as XML element content value. Likewise, you can use embedded expressions as names in the name/value pair, as shown here:

```
Dim empID As String
Dim empName As String

empID = "ID"
empName = "FirstName"

Dim emp As XElement = _
    <Employee <%= empID %>="1">
        <<%= empName %>/>
    </Employee>
```

When this code runs, you get the following output:

```
<Employee ID = "1">
    <FirstName />
</Employee>
```

This can be taken one step further by including values for the name/value pair, like this:

```
Dim empID As String
Dim empName As String

empID = "ID"
empName = "FirstName"

Dim emp As XElement = _
    <Employee <%= empID %>="1">
        <<%= empName %>>Scott</>
    </Employee>
```

This code produces the following:

```
<Employee ID = "1">
    <FirstName>Scott</FirstName>
</Employee>
```

There are a couple of noteworthy items of which you should be aware. First, be careful how you use `Option Strict` in this scenario. `Option Strict` will cause the compiler to check each type to ensure that it has widened to the required type. This applies to everything except the root element of an XML document. If you leave `Option Strict` off, expressions of type Object can be embedded, in which case their type is verified at runtime.

Second, you will probably run into situations where content is optional. In those cases, embedded expressions that contain `Nothing` are ignored. Thus, there is no need to check that the values of elements or attributes are not `Nothing` as you use XML literals. In other words, required values such as element and attribute names cannot be `Nothing`, but empty embedded expressions are ignored. Sweet.

Embedding Queries

The fact that you can embed expressions within your XML literal should tell you that you can also embed queries within your XML literal. When queries are embedded within the XML literal, all elements returned by the query are added to the XML. This lets you create and add dynamic content to your XML literal.

In the following example, a standard LINQ query is embedded in the XML literal, which will create an XML tree based on the value returned from the query.

```
Dim emp As XElement = _
    <Employee>
        <%= From con in Contact
            Select <name><%= con.FirstName %></name>
        %>
    </Employee>
```

That gives you an idea of what is possible when LINQ queries are embedded in XML literals. However, take it a step further and add an attribute to the XML. Modify the XML as highlighted:

```
Dim emp As XElement = _
    <Employee>
        <%= From con in Contact
            Select <name id=<%= con.ContactID %>><%= con.FirstName %></name>
        %>
    </Employee>
```

Now you have a good understanding of how easy it is to dynamically create and add content to your XML.

Understanding Whitespace in Visual Basic XML Literals

Only significant whitespace is included in an XML literal by the Visual Basic compiler when a LINQ to XML object is created. Any insignificant whitespace is ignored.

To illustrate how whitespace is used, add the following code to the click event of one of the buttons on your form:

```
Dim empID As String
Dim empName As String

empID = "ID"
empName = "FirstName"

Dim emp As XElement = _
```

```
        <Employee <%= empID %>="1">
            <<%= empName %>>
                Scott
            </>
        </Employee>

    Me.Textbox1.Text = emp.ToString
```

Run the application and click the button. The text box on the form will be populated with the following XML:

```
<Employee ID = "1">
    <FirstName>
              Scott
              </FirstName>
</Employee>
```

Notice all of the whitespace to the left of "Scott" and to the left of the `<FirstName>` closing tag. The output is like this because the inner element, `<FirstName>`, contains significant whitespace and the output text, while the outer element, `<Employee>`, contains insignificant whitespace.

So, you are probably asking yourself, what is the difference between "significant" and "insignificant" whitespace? Whitespace in XML literals is considered significant when:

- It is in an attribute value.
- It is part of an element's text content.
- It is in an embedded expression for an element's text content.

You can add the `xml:space` attribute in the XML element literal, but it won't change how the compiler handles the whitespace.

Accessing XML

Creating XML is one thing, but accessing it is another, and this section shows you how to do that in Visual Basic. Navigating XML structures in LINQ to XML is quite easy in Visual Basic. To illustrate, add another button to your form and place the following code in its click event:

```
Dim employee As XElement = _
    <Employees>
        <Employee EmpID="1">
            <Title>Geek</Title>
            <FirstName>Scott</FirstName>
            <MiddleName>L</MiddleName>
            <LastName>Klein</LastName>

    <EmailAddress>ScottKlein@SqlXml.com</EmailAddress>
            <Address>
                <Street>111 Main St.</Street>
                <City>Wellington</City>
                <State>FL</State>
                <Zip>33414</Zip>
```

```
            </Address>
        </Employee>
    </Employees>

Me.TextBox1.Text = employee...<City>.Value
```

Run the project and click the button. The text box should display the following value:

```
Wellington
```

Accessing element and attribute values is done through XML axis properties, which provide the capability to navigate XML structures. These properties use a special syntax that helps access any element and attribute by specifying XML names within your XML document.

Following are the available properties for accessing element and attribute values:

- **Descendant axis**—Returns all the child elements of the specified element regardless how deep in the hierarchy the child elements are found. The preceding example illustrates this point. The `<City>` element is several nodes deep in the XML fragment but through the use of the descendant axis property you can easily access the value of that node, as shown above.
  Because it doesn't matter how deep in the hierarchy the element is found, you can use the same syntax to return the value of the `<Title>` as well as any other element.
- **Child axis**—Returns all the elements that are child elements of the specified element. This property is used to return all the child elements of a specified element. For example:

  ```
  employee.<FirstName>
  ```

- **Attribute axis**—Returns all the attributes of the specified element. From the preceding XML fragment, this property can be used to return the `EmpID` attribute of `<Employee>` node:

  ```
  Employee.<Employee>.@EmpID
  ```

- **Value**—Returns a string containing the object (value) for the first object found in the sequence. It returns `Nothing` if the sequence is empty. As you have seen, this property returns the value of the specified node(s), such as the value of the `<City>` element:

  ```
  employee...<City>.Value
  ```

- **Extension indexer**—Returns the first element from the sequence. To illustrate this property, modify the XML fragment at the beginning of this section by adding a second employee, as shown in the following highlighted code:

  ```
  Dim employee As XElement = _
      <Employees>
          <Employee EmpID="1">
              <Title>Geek</Title>
              <FirstName>Scott</FirstName>
              <MiddleName>L</MiddleName>
              <LastName>Klein</LastName>
              <EmailAddress>ScottKlein@SqlXml.com</EmailAddress>
  ```

```
            <Address>
                <Street>111 Main St.</Street>
                <City>Wellington</City>
                <State>FL</State>
                <Zip>33414</Zip>
            </Address>
        </Employee>
        <Employee EmpID="2">
            <Title>Geek</Title>
            <FirstName>Chris</FirstName>
            <MiddleName>A</MiddleName>
            <LastName>Klein</LastName>
            <EmailAddress>Chris@SqlXml.com</EmailAddress>
            <Address>
                <Street>222 Main St.</Street>
                <City>Portland</City>
                <State>OR</State>
                <Zip>88888</Zip>
            </Address>
        </Employee>
    </Employees>
```

With the extension indexer, you can specify specific elements to return as shown in the example below:

```
employee...<FirstName>(1).Value
```

The returned result would be `Chris`. The extension indexer is zero-based so had you passed a value of `0` to this property, it would have returned `Scott`.

You can also access XML using embedded queries, which you learned about earlier in the chapter. In the example that follows, an XML literal is defined with three names. A second XML literal is then created, using an embedded query to access the names from the first XML literal. The results of the second XML literal are displayed in the text box.

```
Dim employee As XElement = _
    <Employees>
        <Name>Scott</Name>
        <Name>Chris</Name>
        <Name>Bill</Name>
    </Employees>

Dim nameTypes As XElement = _
    <Names>
        <%= From name In employee.<Name> _
            Select <FirstName><%= name.Value %></FirstName> _
        %>
    </Names>

Me.TextBox1.Text = nameTypes.ToString
```

Here are the results when this code is executed:

```
<Names>
    <FirstName>Scott</FirstName>
    <FirstName>Chris</FirstName>
    <FirstName>Bill</FirstName>
</Names
```

The next example builds on the previous example by including an attribute on each `<Name>` element in the first XML literal. The second XML literal is also modified, adding the necessary components to the embedded query to access the attribute as well.

```
Dim employee As XElement = _
    <Employees>
        <Name empID="1">Scott</Name>
        <Name empID="2">Chris</Name>
        <Name empID="3">Bill</Name>
    </Employees>

Dim nameTypes As XElement = _
    <Names>
        <%= From name In employee.<Name> _
          Select <Employee ID=<%= name.Value %>><%= name.@empID %></Employee> _
        %>
    </Names>

Me.TextBox1.Text = nameTypes.ToString
```

The following results when this code is executed:

```
<Names>
    <FirstName ID="1">Scott</FirstName>
    <FirstName ID="2">Chris</FirstName>
    <FirstName ID="3">Bill</FirstName>
</Names
```

Yes, this example puts the attribute back where it came from, but the purpose of this example is to illustrate how to access attributes and how you can utilize query expressions within your XML literals to manipulate XML.

These examples should give you a good idea of how to access XML using XML literals and query expressions.

Loading XML

Loading XML is quite easy. You'll see just how easy in a minute. First, open your favorite text editor and type in the following XML. Save it as `employees.xml` in your `Wrox\Chapter 9` folder.

```
<Employees>
  <Employee id="1" Dept="0001" Geek="True">
    <Name>Scott</Name>
    <Address>
      <Address>555 Main St.</Address>
```

```
      <City>Wellington</City>
      <State>FL</State>
    </Address>
    <Title>All Things Techy</Title>
    <HireDate>02/05/2007</HireDate>
    <Gender>M</Gender>
  </Employee>
  <Employee id="2" Dept="0005" Geek="False">
    <Name>Steve</Name>
    <Address>
      <Address>444 Main St.</Address>
      <City>Snahomish</City>
      <State>WA</State>
      <zip>99999</zip>
    </Address>
    <Title>Mr. SciFi</Title>
    <HireDate>05/14/2002</HireDate>
    <Gender>M</Gender>
  </Employee>
  <Employee id="3" Dept="0004" Geek="True">
    <Name>Joe</Name>
    <Address>
      <Address>222 Main St.</Address>
      <City>Easley</City>
      <State>SC</State>
    </Address>
    <Title>All Things Bleeding Edge</Title>
    <HireDate>07/22/2004</HireDate>
    <Gender>M</Gender>
  </Employee>
</Employees>
```

To load XML, the `XElement` class has a `Load` method that contains several overloads, one of which is a path to an XML document. The following code shows how to load an element and display its contents:

```
Dim emp As XElement = XElement.Load("c:\Wrox\Linq\Chapter9\employees.xml")

Me.Textbox1.Text = emp.ToString
```

As you know, once you have XML loaded into an `XElement`, as in the preceding example, you are free to manipulate and query it. Your homework for this chapter is to use a query expression within an XML literal to return XML containing the ID of the employee along with his name and title.

Manipulating XML Using the Parse Method

There is a method on the `XElement` class called `Parse`, which loads a string containing XML into an `XElement`. There is an overload on this method that enables you to specify options when parsing the XML being loaded.

In the following example, a string variable is defined and loaded with an XML fragment. The string is then passed to the `Parse` method of the `XElement` class. The additional parameter for the load options specifies a value of None, meaning that no load options are being specified. Load options are explained shortly.

```
Dim empInfo As String

empInfo = "<Employees><Employee ID=""1""><FirstName>Scott</FirstName>@@ta
</Employee></Employees>"

Dim emp As XElement = XElement.Parse(empInfo, LoadOptions.None)

Me.TextBox1.Text = emp.ToString
```

Here are the results of executing this code:

```
<Employees>
  <Employee ID="1">
    <FirstName>Scott</FirstName>
  </Employee>
</Employees>
```

The optional parameter is the LoadOptions enumeration, which sets one of four load options for loading and parsing XML:

- None—No options are specified.
- PreserveWhitespace—Preserve insignificant whitespace during the parsing of the XML.
- SetBaseUri—Requests the base URI information from the XmlReader, making it available through the BaseUri property.
- SetLineInfo—Requests the line information from the XmlReader, making it available through XObject properties.

The following example illustrates the use of the PreserveWhitespace load option. Modify the code from the previous example as follows:

```
Dim empInfo As String

empInfo = "<Employees><Employee ID=""1""><FirstName>Scott</FirstName>@@ta
</Employee></Employees>"

Dim emp As XElement = XElement.Parse(empInfo, LoadOptions.None)

Me.TextBox1.Text = emp.ToString
```

Here are the results:

```
<Employees>
  <Employee ID="1">
    <FirstName>  Scott    </FirstName>
  </Employee>
</Employees>
```

You can see that all of the insignificant whitespace has been ignored. Next, modify the load option to this:

```
Dim emp As XElement = XElement.Parse(empInfo, LoadOptions.PreserveWhitespace)
```

When you run the code now, all the insignificant whitespace is preserved:

```
<Employees>
  <Employee ID="1">  <FirstName>  Scott     </FirstName></Employee>
</Employees>
```

Specify multiple load options by using an `And` or `Or` operator, like this:

```
Dim emp As XElement = XElement.Parse(empInfo, LoadOptions.SetBaseUri And
  LoadOptions.SetLineInfo)
```

These load options can assist you in your manipulation of the XML document, such as controlling how the whitespace is preserved and tracking the line information for each element in the tree.

LINQ to XML Visual Basic Example

This example is going to use the XML document `employees.xml` that you created earlier, in the section "Loading XML." This example will load that document, manipulate it by making some changes to the XML tree, and then display the results. As a refresher, the contents of the XML document are as follows:

```
<Employees>
  <Employee id="1" Dept="0001" Geek="True">
    <Name>Scott</Name>
    <Address>
      <Address>555 Main St.</Address>
      <City>Wellington</City>
      <State>FL</State>
    </Address>
    <Title>All Things Techy</Title>
    <HireDate>02/05/2007</HireDate>
    <Gender>M</Gender>
  </Employee>
  <Employee id="2" Dept="0005" Geek="False">
    <Name>Steve</Name>
    <Address>
      <Address>444 Main St.</Address>
      <City>Snahomish</City>
      <State>WA</State>
      <zip>99999</zip>
    </Address>
    <Title>Mr. SciFi</Title>
    <HireDate>05/14/2002</HireDate>
    <Gender>M</Gender>
  </Employee>
```

```
    <Employee id="3" Dept="0004" Geek="True">
      <Name>Joe</Name>
      <Address>
        <Address>222 Main St.</Address>
        <City>Easley</City>
        <State>SC</State>
      </Address>
      <Title>All Things Bleeding Edge</Title>
      <HireDate>07/22/2004</HireDate>
      <Gender>M</Gender>
    </Employee>
  </Employees>
```

So, to do this, create a new Visual Basic Windows Forms project. When the project is created, add two buttons and a text box to the form. Set the properties of the controls as follows:

- Button1
  - Name - cmdOK
  - Text - OK
- Button2
  - Name - cmdCancel
  - Text - Cancel
- TextBox1
  - Name - txtResults1
  - Multiline - True
  - ScrollBars - Vertical
- TextBox2
  - Name - txtResults2
  - Multiline - True
  - ScrollBars - Vertical
- TextBox3
  - Name - txtResults3
  - Multiline - True
  - ScrollBars - Vertical

In the `Click()` event of the Cancel button, enter the following code:

```
Application.Exit()
```

Next, in the `Click()` event of the OK button, place the following code:

```
Dim emp As XElement = XElement.Load("c:\Wrox\Linq\Chapter 9\Employees.xml")

Dim tree As XElement = New XElement("Root", _
    From el In emp.Elements() Select el)

' Load these changes into the first text box
Me.txtResults1.Text = tree.ToString()

' Next, let's just grab the first employee
Dim empPart as XElement = (From treePart In _
    tree.Eleemnts("Employees") Select treePart).First

Me.txtResults2.Text = empPart.ToString()

' Next, let's add an EmailAddress element to each Employee
tree.Element("Employee").Add(New XElement("EmailAddress"))

Me.txtResults.Text = emp.ToString()
```

The first query produces the following (only the first part of the results are shown):

```
<Root>
  <Employee id="1" Dept="0001" Geek="True">
    <Name>Scott</Name>
    <Address>
      <Address>555 Main St.</Address>
      <City>Wellington</City>
      <State>FL</State>
    </Address>
    <Title>All Things Techy</Title>
    <HireDate>02/05/2007</HireDate>
    <Gender>M</Gender>
  </Employee>
...
</Root>
```

The second query produces the following results:

```
<Employee id="1" Dept="0001" Geek="True">
  <Name>Scott</Name>
  <Address>
    <Address>555 Main St.</Address>
    <City>Wellington</City>
    <State>FL</State>
  </Address>
  <Title>All Things Techy</Title>
  <HireDate>02/05/2007</HireDate>
  <Gender>M</Gender>
</Employee>
```

And lastly, the final piece of code modifies the XML document and returns the following results, with the addition of the `EmailAddress` element added to each Employee node:

```
<Root>
  <Employee id="1" Dept="0001" Geek="True">
    <Name>Scott</Name>
    <Address>
      <Address>555 Main St.</Address>
      <City>Wellington</City>
      <State>FL</State>
    </Address>
    <Title>All Things Techy</Title>
    <HireDate>02/05/2007</HireDate>
    <Gender>M</Gender>
    <EmailAddress />
  </Employee>
  <Employee id="2" Dept="0005" Geek="False">
    <Name>Steve</Name>
    <Address>
      <Address>444 Main St.</Address>
      <City>Snahomish</City>
      <State>WA</State>
      <zip>99999</zip>
    </Address>
    <Title>Mr. SciFi</Title>
    <HireDate>05/14/2002</HireDate>
    <Gender>M</Gender>
    <EmailAddress />
  </Employee>
  <Employee id="3" Dept="0004" Geek="True">
    <Name>Joe</Name>
    <Address>
      <Address>222 Main St.</Address>
      <City>Easley</City>
      <State>SC</State>
    </Address>
    <Title>All Things Bleeding Edge</Title>
    <HireDate>07/22/2004</HireDate>
    <Gender>M</Gender>
    <EmailAddress />
  </Employee>
</Root>
```

You'll notice that each email address node is not populated with data. This is on purpose. Your homework assignment for this chapter is to modify the code to add an email address. You don't need to make them different. Simply insert a default value. When you have done that, figure out a way to dynamically enter an email address using the employee's first name and last name.

Summary

This chapter focused on the LINQ to XML features in Visual Basic .NET, including the capability to create XML literals and expressions directly within your VB.NET code.

You learned to create XML using XML literals, and how to incorporate expressions and embedded queries into your XML literals to create the XML you want.

From there, the topics of accessing and loading XML were discussed. Accessing XML is accomplished through the XML Axis properties, which enable you to easily and efficiently navigate the XML tree and retrieve the information you want. Loading XML is as simple as calling the `Load` method on the `XElement` class.

You also explored using the `Parse` method to manipulate XML. It enables you to specify several load options so that you can manipulate the XML as you parse it. For example, you can preserve the whitespace or track individual element line item information.

In the next chapter, the focus turns to working with LINQ to SQL.

Part III
LINQ to SQL

Chapter 10: LINQ to SQL Overview

Chapter 11: LINQ to SQL Queries

Chapter 12: Advanced Query Concepts

Chapter 13: More about Entity Classes

Chapter 14: LINQ to DataSet

Chapter 15: Advanced LINQ to SQL Topics

10

LINQ to SQL Overview

LINQ to SQL is a component of LINQ and part of ADO.NET that provides a run-time infrastructure for mapping relational data as objects. This chapter provides an overview of LINQ to SQL, and the rest of the chapters in this section of the book then dig deeper into the individual aspects of LINQ to SQL, including LINQ to SQL queries and LINQ over DataSets.

Today's developers have access to many great technologies that afford management and manipulation of database objects as well as data-querying capabilities. The .NET Framework provides ADO.NET, a platform for accessing data sources such as XML (via the `System.XML` namespace, which supplies a programmatic representation of XML documents and mechanisms for manipulating XML documents, nodes, and XML fragments) and SQL Server (via the `System.Data` namespace, which offers the primary data access methods for managed applications) as well as other data sources exposed through ODBC and OLE DB.

Yet, all this great technology has its limitations, such as sometimes being overly complex (for example, OLE DB is COM based and therefore does not work in the object-oriented paradigm, and it also requires quite a bit of code to address data access functionality). While LINQ to SQL may not offer any speed advantages over previous or existing technology, it does offer the capability to build applications more quickly and efficiently.

This chapter discusses the fundamentals and concepts that programmers need to know to work with LINQ to SQL, including the following:

- Overview of LINQ to SQL
- LINQ to SQL object model
- Attribute-based mapping
- Relational data basics

Understanding LINQ to SQL

As mentioned, LINQ to SQL is a part of ADO.NET and a component of LINQ. As such, you get the benefit of the unified programming model, standard query operators, and standard query facilities provided by LINQ, plus the services provided by the ADO.NET provider model.

LINQ to SQL works by mapping the data model of a relational database object, such as a table, to an object model defined in the developer's chosen programming language. For example, the following code maps the `Person.Contact` table of the Adventureworks database to a public class defined in C#. A public class is defined, and mapped by annotating the class with the LINQ `TableAttribute`, passing it the name of the SQL Server table to map to using the attribute's `Name` parameter.

```
[Table(Name = "Person.Contact")]
public class Contact
{
    [Column(DBType = "nvarchar(8)")]
    public string Title;

    [Column(DBType = "nvarchar(50) ")]
    public string FirstName;

    [Column(DBType = "nvarchar(50) ")]
    public string MiddleName;

    [Column(DBType = "nvarchar(50) ")]
    public string LastName;

    [Column(DBType = "nvarchar(50) ")]
    public string EmailAddress;

    [Column(DBType = "int")]
    public int EmailPromotion;

}
```

At this point, the relational mapping is complete, having mapped a data model to an object model.

The next step is to build the channel by which the objects and data are retrieved from the database. The channel is created via the `DataContext` class. The `DataContext` class is part of the `System.Data.Linq` namespace, and its purpose is to translate your requests from .NET objects to SQL queries, and then reassemble the query results back into objects.

The `DataContext` *class is discussed in detail in Chapter 11.*

Here's an example that defines a `DataContext` that connects to the Adventureworks database using integrated security:

```
DataContext context = new DataContext(
    "Initial Catalog=AdventureWorks;Integrated Security=sspi");
```

You use DataContext much the same way that you use an ADO.NET connection, in that it is initialized with a connection or connection string.

Once the DataContext is created, a table variable is constructed using the Contact class created above. This is done by using the Table class of the System.Data.Linq namespace, which provides the capability to query a table and even add and delete objects. LINQ to SQL works with objects. Meaning, in LINQ to SQL a relational database's object model is directly mapped to an object model expressed in your selected programming language. Thus, a translation takes place. LINQ to SQL translates the LINQ queries of the object model into statements that SQL can understand and then sends them off to SQL Server for execution. The reverse happens when the data is returned. The results are translated back to objects that you can work with.

Access to the table is accomplished by using the GetTable method of the defined DataContext, like this:

```
Table<Contact> contact = context.GetTable<Contact>();
```

Now you're ready to query the database using the same LINQ query operators and query facilities that you have come to love.

The following code queries the Person.Contact table of the Adventureworks database as defined in the object mapping:

```
var query =
    (from c in contact
     where c.FirstName.StartsWith("S")
     && c.LastName.StartsWith("K")
     orderby c.LastName
     select c);
```

As with the other components of LINQ, LINQ to SQL works with both C# and Visual Basic. LINQ to SQL also supports stored procedures and user-defined functions. However, to fully understand LINQ to SQL, the LINQ to SQL object model and the concept of attribute-based mapping must be explored.

LINQ to SQL Object Model

The LINQ to SQL object model provides the fundamental elements for working with and managing relational objects. It is via this model that a relational model is mapped to and expressed in the developer's programming language.

In the LINQ to SQL object model, database commands are not issued against the database directly. As a developer, you simply change values and execute methods within the confines of the object model. LINQ to SQL then translates those changes or methods into the appropriate SQL commands and funnels them through to the database to be executed. The object model works through its relationship to the database and the database model to perform given tasks. The following table shows the relationship between the LINQ to SQL object model and the corresponding relational model.

LINQ to SQL Object	Relational Object
DataContext	Database
Entity class	Table
Class member	Column
Association	Foreign-key relationship

The following section explores LINQ to SQL object model mapping.

Attribute-Based Mapping

It is all about attributes when mapping SQL Server objects to the object model. This attribute-based approach is utilized heavily by LINQ to SQL to effectively map database objects to an object model defined in the user's programming language.

There are three ways to create attribute mapping:

- The Object Relational Designer (ORD) tool
- The SQLMetal command-line tool
- By hand via code

So far, all the mapping has been done via code, but later chapters will discuss the other two options in detail. You have seen several of the attribute-based mappings in action throughout this book, but the following sections discuss the different attributes in more detail, including their associated properties and descriptions.

Prior to `Beta2`, attribute-based mapping was supported via the `System.Data.Linq` namespace. If you then installed `Beta2` and tried to compile your code, you received a lot of compile errors. That is because attribute-based mapping is now supported via the `System.Data.Linq.Mapping` namespace.

Using the Database Attribute

The `Database` attribute is used to specify the name of the database when defining a mapping between a database and object. This attribute has one property, `Name`, which is used to hold the name of the database to which you are defining a mapping.

Here's an example of the `Database` attribute being applied to a class to define a mapping:

```
[Database(Name="AdventureWorks")]
public class AWDB
```

```
{
    //
}
```

The use of this attribute is optional, but if used, the `Name` property must be used. Typically, you would use this property when a database name is not supplied in the connection string.

Mapping Tables

Database tables are represented by entity classes in LINQ to SQL. An entity class is a normal class like one that you might define, except that it is annotated with a specific tag that maps, or associates, that class with a specific database table.

The `Table` attribute is required by LINQ to SQL, and maps an entity class (a class that has been designated as an entity) to a table or view. The `Table` attribute also has a single property, `Name`, which specifies the name of the relational table or view.

The following is an example of the `Table` attribute being applied to a class to define a mapping between the `HumanResources.Employee` table and the `Employee` class, and mapping a class named `Contact` with the `Person.Contact` table in the Adventureworks database:

```
[Table(Name = "HumanResources.Employee")]
public class Employee
{
  //
}
[Table(Name = "Person.Contact")]
public class Contact
{
  //
}
```

Remember, only those entity classes that have been mapped to a table can be saved to the database. That means that if you map the `Person.Contact` table to an entity class but don't map the `HumanResources.Employee` table to an entity class, you can only work with the `Person.Contact` table (query data, save, and so on).

Keep in mind that classes marked with the `[Table]` attribute are treated as persistent classes by LINQ to SQL.

Mapping Columns

Once the table is mapped to an entity class, table columns must be mapped to class properties. The `Column` attribute maps a column of a database table to a member of an entity class. Fields or properties are designated to represent database columns, and only those fields or properties that are mapped are retrieved from the database.

The following table describes the `Column` attribute's properties.

Property	Description	Default Value (if any)
`Name`	Name of the table column.	
`DbType`	Database type of the database column.	
`Storage`	The entity class storage field/variable.	
`IsPrimaryKey`	Specifies that the associated column is the primary key of the corresponding table.	`false`
`IsDbGenerated`	Specifies that the associated column auto-generates its values.	`false`
`CanBeNull`	Specifies that the associated column can contain null values.	`true`
`AutoSync`	Tells the runtime to get the column value after an `INSERT` or `UPDATE` operation has been executed. It has four options: `Always`—Always returns the column value for an `INSERT` or `UPDATE` operation. `Never`—Never returns the value for an `INSERT` or `UPDATE` operation. `OnUpdate`: Only returns the column value for `UPDATE` operations. `OnInsert`: Only returns the column value for `INSERT` operations.	`Never`
`Expression`	Defines a computed database column.	
`IsVersion`	Specifies that the associated column is either a timestamp or version number column.	`false`
`UpdateCheck`	Indicates how LINQ to SQL should handle optimistic concurrency conflicts. Uses one of the following values: `Always`, `Never`, `WhenChanged`.	
`IsDiscriminator`	Specifies that the column contains the discriminator value for a LINQ to SQL inheritance hierarchy.	

Here's an example that shows how to use the `Column` attribute to map properties to specific database columns:

```
[Column(DBType = "int", IsPrimaryKey=true, CanBeNull=false)]
public int EmployeeID;

[Column(DBType = "nvarchar(256)", CanBeNull=false)]
public string LoginID;

[Column(DBType = "nvarchar(15)", CanBeNull=false)]
public string NationalIDNUmber;

[Column(DBType = "int",CanBeNull=false)]
public int ManagerID;
```

Those fields that are not tagged as columns are considered temporary information, meaning, they are assumed to be nonpersistent and are not submitted back to the database.

The following example illustrates how to map a few properties with several columns of the `Person.Contact` table in the Adventureworks database:

```
[Column(DBType = "nvarchar(8)")]
public string Title;

[Column(DBType = "nvarchar(50)")]
public string FirstName;

[Column(DBType = "nvarchar(50)")]
public string MiddleName;

[Column(DBType = "nvarchar(50)")]
public string LastName;

[Column(DBType = "nvarchar(50)")]
public string EmailAddress;

[Column(DBType = "int")]
public int EmailPromotion;
```

Add this to the Table mapping, and you have the following:

```
[Table(Name = "Person.Contact")]
public class Contact
{
    [Column(DBType = "nvarchar(8) not null")]
    public string Title;

    [Column(DBType = "nvarchar(50) not null")]
    public string FirstName;

    [Column(DBType = "nvarchar(50) not null")]
    public string MiddleName;

    [Column(DBType = "nvarchar(50) not null")]
    public string LastName;

    [Column(DBType = "nvarchar(50) not null")]
    public string EmailAddress;

    [Column(DBType = "int")]
    public int EmailPromotion;

}
```

Only those columns that are defined are used to persist data to the table and retrieve data from the database. In the example, the entity class and associated column properties will persist the `Title`, `FirstName`, `MiddleName`, `LastName`, `EmailAddress`, and `EmailPromotion` columns from the `Person.Contact` table to and from the database. Any other columns in the table will not be persisted and are considered transient.

Mapping Relationships

Queries to the database generally require pulling information from multiple tables, not just a single table. Those tables are typically joined via a primary key/foreign key relationship. LINQ to SQL's `Association` attribute can represent those database associations.

The `Association` attribute's properties are described in the following table. They can be used to customize the associations.

Property	Description
`Name`	The name of the association.
`Storage`	Specifies the storage field/variable.
`IsUnique`	Specifies whether the FK is a unique constraint.
`IsForeignKey`	Specifies whether the association/constraint is a foreign key.
`ThisKey`	Identifies members of the entity class to represent the key values on this side of the association.
`OtherKey`	Identifies one or more members of the target entity class as key values on the other side of the association.

The following example shows how the `Association` attribute is used to define an association:

```
[Association(Name = "FK_Employee_Contact_ContactID",
    Storage = "_Employee", ThisKey = "ContactID", IsForeignKey = true)]
public Employee Emp
{
    get { return this._Employee.Entity; }
    set { this._Employee.Entity = value; }
}
```

The association is applied to a table in which you need to reference the associated table.

In the following example, the `Contact` class contains an `Employee` property that's tagged with the `Association` attribute, providing the `Contact` class with a relationship to the `Employee` class:

```
[Table(Name = "Person.Contact")]
public class Contact
{
    [Column(DBType = "nvarchar(8) not null")]
    public string Title;
```

```
        [Column(DBType = "nvarchar(50) not null")]
        public string FirstName;

        [Column(DBType = "nvarchar(50) not null")]
        public string MiddleName;

        [Column(DBType = "nvarchar(50) not null")]
        public string LastName;

        [Column(DBType = "nvarchar(50) not null")]
        public string EmailAddress;

        [Column(DBType = "int")]
        public int EmailPromotion;

        private EntityRef<Employee> _Employee;

        [Association(Name = "FK_Employee_Contact_ContactID",
            Storage = "_Employee", ThisKey = "ContactID", IsForeignKey = true)]
        public Employee Emp
        {
            get { return this._Employee.Entity; }
            set { this._Employee.Entity = value; }
        }

    }
```

More about LINQ to SQL and database relationships is discussed in Chapter 12.

Mapping Stored Procedures

One of the many great qualities of LINQ to SQL is its support for stored procedures, which is accomplished via the `StoredProcedure` attribute. That attribute is used to map a stored procedure in the database to a client object. It has only a single property, `Name`, which specifies the name of the stored procedure. Here's the attribute's general syntax:

```
[StoredProcedure(Name="OrdersBySalesPersonID")]
public IEnumerable OrdersBySalesPersonID([Parameter(DBType = "int")] String param1)
{
    IExecuteResults results = this.ExecuteMethodCall<OrdersBySalesPersonID>
        (this, ((MethodInfo)(MethodInfo.GetCurrentMethod())),
        param1);
}
```

With LINQ to SQL, you can easily map each database object to a client object, providing developers the capability to access the stored procedures through client code in a strongly typed manner. Through this mapping, the client method signatures bear a resemblance to the signatures of the procedure that is defined in the database, utilizing many of the programming language features such as IntelliSense.

In the following example, the highlighted code shows how to implement a stored procedure mapping into your client object class:

```
[Table(Name = "Person.Contact")]
public class Contact
```

```
{
    [Column(DBType = "nvarchar(8) not null")]
    public string Title;

    [Column(DBType = "nvarchar(50) not null")]
    public string FirstName;

    [Column(DBType = "nvarchar(50) not null")]
    public string MiddleName;

    [Column(DBType = "nvarchar(50) not null")]
    public string LastName;

    [Column(DBType = "nvarchar(50) not null")]
    public string EmailAddress;

    [Column(DBType = "int")]
    public int EmailPromotion;

    [StoredProcedure(Name="OrdersBySalesPersonID")]
    public IEnumberable OrdersBySalesPersonID([Parameter(DBType =
  "int")] String param1)
    {
        IExecuteResults results = this.ExecuteMethodCall<OrdersBySalesPersonID>
            (this, ((MethodInfo)(MethodInfo.GetCurrentMethod())),
            param1);
    }
}
```

You'll learn more about LINQ to SQL and stored procedure mapping in Chapter 11.

Mapping Functions

LINQ to SQL also supports user-defined functions. Client objects and user-defined functions are mapped the same way stored procedures are—through an attribute. Here's the general syntax of the `Function` attribute:

```
[Function()]
Public IQueryable<ufnGetcontactInformation>
    ufnGetcontactInformation(System.Nullable<int> ContactID)
{
  //
}
```

This attribute has a single property, `Name`, which is used to specify the name of the user-defined function:

```
[Function(Name="ufnGetcontactInformation")]
Public IQueryable<ufnGetcontactInformation>
    ufnGetcontactInformation(System.Nullable<int> ContactID)
{
  //
}
```

If you do not specify a `Name` value, as in the first example, the default value is the same string as the user-defined function name, which in the example is `ufnGetcontactInformation`.

Using the Parameter Attribute

The `Parameter` attribute maps input parameters on stored procedure methods. It has two properties, which are described in the following table.

Property	Description	Default Value (if any)
`Name`	Name of the parameter	The same string as the parameter name in the database
`DbType`	Database data type	

The Name property can be used two ways: with an input parameter and with an output or return parameter. Both scenarios are shown in the following example. The first `Parameter` attribute specifies the return parameter type, and the second specifies the input variable type.

```
 [StoredProcedure(Name="OrdersBySalesPersonID")]
[return: Parameter(DbType = "numeric")]
public IEnumerable MaxOrderBySalesPersonID([Parameter(DbType = "int")]
String param1)
{
    IExecuteResults results = this.ExecuteMethodCall<OrdersBySalesPersonID>
        (this, ((MethodInfo)(MethodInfo.GetCurrentMethod())),
        param1);
}
```

Stored procedure, user-defined function, and parameter mappings are discussed in more detail in Chapter 11.

The Basics of Relational Data

LINQ to SQL is all about working with relational data. As you have learned, this is accomplished through the mapping of the relational data model to an object model expressed in the developer's programming language. But regardless of the programming language and the object models, you are working with data. It all boils down to CRUD operations; you are creating (inserting), reading, updating, or deleting data—CRUD.

If you have no relational data knowledge or experience, this section is for you. If you are using LINQ to SQL you will inevitably run into relational data environments (after all, that is what relational databases are all about) and because you are mapping relational data objects (tables, and so on) to programming language objects, you also need to take into account their relational data (primary keys and foreign keys).

There are, of course, complete books on how to effectively and efficiently design databases. For example, the Wrox book *Beginning Database Design* covers design concepts including modeling and normalization. This section merely introduces the concepts of primary keys and foreign keys that are used in relational databases.

Chapter 12 explores querying across relationships using LINQ to SQL in detail.

Primary Keys

A primary key is a column or a group of columns that uniquely identifies each individual row in a database table. No columns included in the primary key can accept null values. A primary key enforces the table's integrity and can be defined when the table is created, or later when modifying the structure of the table. A primary key can be defined on a single, or multiple columns.

A table can only have one primary key. The most common form of a primary key is an identity column on SQL data types such as `int` and `bigint`.

Take a look at Figure 10-1, which shows the table design for the `Person.Contact` table in the Adventure-Works database.

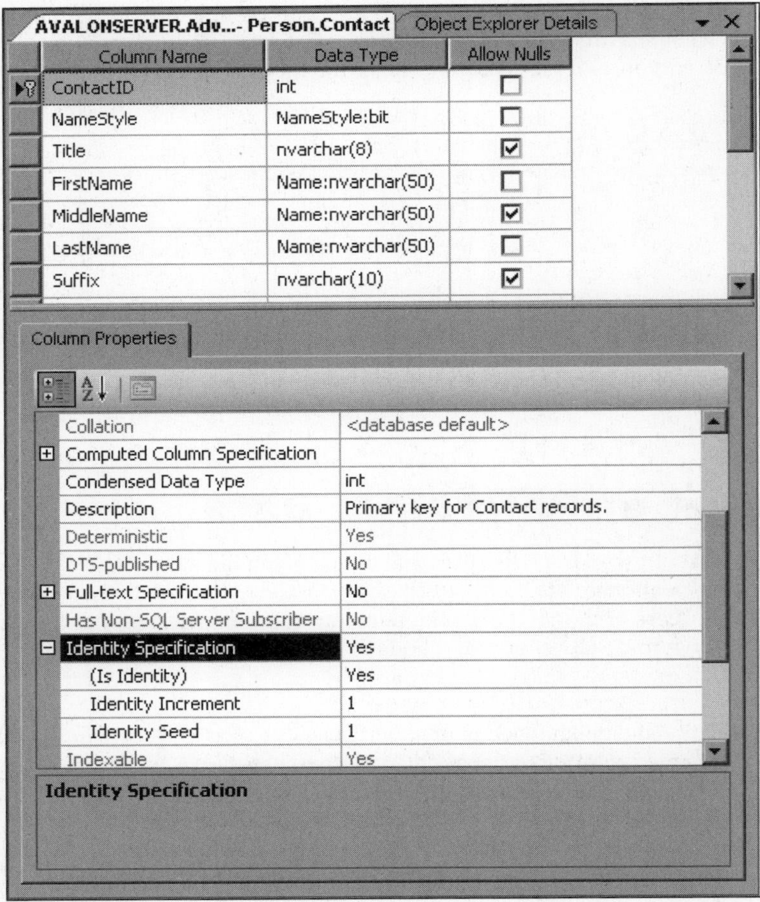

Figure 10-1

There are several things to notice. First, you can tell which column, or columns, are defined as the primary key by the gold key displayed in the row selector. In this example, the `ContactID` column is designated as the primary key. Second, the data type for the primary key is defined as an `int`, and the column does not accept null values (the Allow Nulls box is not checked), which means that a value must be entered into that column whenever a new row is added to the table.

The properties of the selected column display in the bottom pane. In this instance, it's the `ColumnID` properties that are showing. The Identity Specification has been set to Yes, meaning that this is an identity column, and you can set both an initial value (Identity Seed) and the value by which to increment each new row (Identify Increment). Here, the initial seed value is 1, and each new value increments by 1.

The identity specification lets you specify both an identity number (an initial value for the column for the first row inserted into the table) and the value in which to increment when new rows are added. The cool thing about identity columns is that the database engine takes care of all of the work of automatically incrementing the identity value and assigning the new value to the new row. Setting this property to "Yes" tells SQL Server to automatically manage the value of this column.

When a primary key is defined, a unique index is created on its columns. The index allows for quick retrieval of records when the primary key is used in a query.

Define a primary key by clicking the Set Primary Key button (the gold key) on the Table Designer toolbar when the table is in design mode. Figure 10-2 points out the button on the toolbar.

Figure 10-2

When mapping an object to a relational data object, you need to specify which column is the primary key. The following code shows the mapping of the AdventureWorks table `Sales.Contact`. In it, the `ContactID` column is mapped and annotated as a column to return. In the definition of the column, several properties are set, identifying it as the primary key of the `Person.Contact` table, and enabling its values to be generated automatically (via the `IsDBGenerated` property).

```
[Table(Name = "Person.Contact")]
public class Contact
{
    [Column(DBType = "int", IsPrimaryKey = true, IsDBGenerated = true)]
    public int ContactID;

    [Column(DBType = "nvarchar(8)")]
    public string Title;

    [Column(DBType = "nvarchar(50) ")]
    public string FirstName;

    [Column(DBType = "nvarchar(50) ")]
    public string MiddleName;

    [Column(DBType = "nvarchar(50) ")]
    public string LastName;
```

```
        [Column(DBType = "nvarchar(50) ")]
        public string EmailAddress;

        [Column(DBType = "int")]
        public int EmailPromotion;

    }
```

Any time you are mapping a relational table that has a primary key, and you plan on returning the primary key column in your LINQ to SQL queries, you must identify the column as the primary key and the identity by using the properties `IsPrimaryKey` and `IsDBGenerated` as this example shows.

Foreign Keys

Foreign keys define a relationship between two tables. A foreign key is a single column or a group of columns that is used to create and impose a relationship, or link, between a parent table and a child table.

Foreign keys are created when the column or columns of the primary key (from the primary key table) are referenced by the column or columns in another table (the foreign key table). As discussed in the previous section, the `ContactID` column in the `Person.Contact` table is a primary key. Figure 10-3 shows that the `ContactID` column has been included or added to the `HumanResources.Employee` table, becoming a foreign key in this table.

Figure 10-4 shows the two tables, `Person.Contact` and `HumanResources.Employee`, with the primary key/foreign key relationship defined. The line between the two tables does not create the relationship but illustrates the association between the two tables.

However, simply adding a reference column in another table (such as the `HumanResources.Employee` table) does not create a primary key/foreign key relationship. That's only the first part. The last part is to add a foreign key constraint on the second table. A constraint is a rule used to maintain data integrity of a table.

To create the actual relationship you tell the `HumanResources.Employee` table that its `ContactID` column is a foreign key to the `ContactID` column in the `Person.Contact` table. This can be accomplished by the following:

```
ALTER TABLE [HumanResources].[Employee] ADD CONSTRAINT
 [FK_Employee_Contact_ContactID]
FOREIGN KEY([ContactID])
REFERENCES [Person].[Contact] ([ContactID])
```

This T-SQL code creates a foreign key constraint on the `ContactID` column referencing the `ContactID` column in the `Person.Contact` table. The constraint is used to determine the action on the values in the related tables. For example, if a value that is used in one or more related tables is deleted, the constraint determines whether the value in the related table is also deleted, left in, or set to null.

To see this in action, open SQL Server Management Studio and execute the following in a query window:

```
SELECT ContactID, FirstName, LastName
FROM Person.Contact
WHERE ContactID = 1172
```

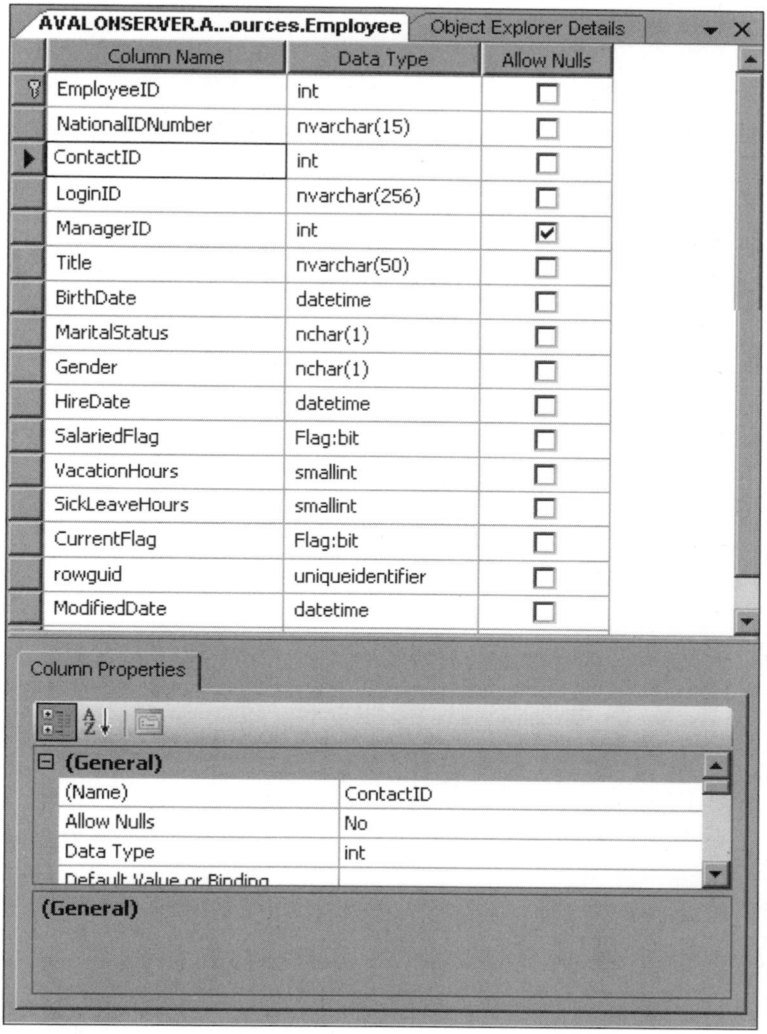

Figure 10-3

You should get the following results:

```
ContactID     FirstName     LastName
---------     ---------     --------
1174          Scott         Gode
```

Now, execute the following query:

```
SELECT EmployeeID, NationalIDNumber, ManagerID, Title
FROM HumanResources.Employee
WHERE ContactID = 174
```

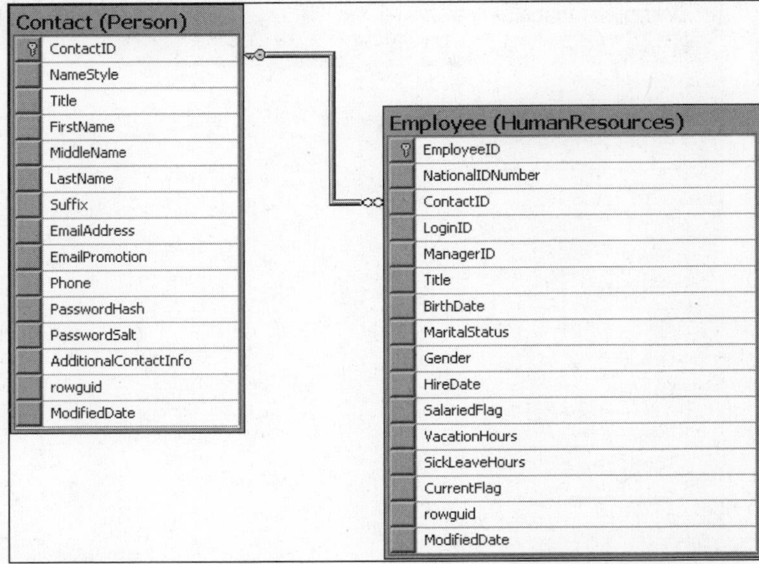

Figure 10-4

Here are the results:

```
EmployeeID    NationalIDNumber   ManagerID  Title
----------    ----------------   ---------  -----
98            199546871          197        Production Technician - WC45
```

You can see that the `ContactID` values in both the `Person.Contact` table and the `HumanResources.Employee` table match. The foreign key constraint ensures that any value inserted into the `ContactID` column in the `HumanResources.Employee` table matches a value in the `ContactID` column in the `Person.Contact` table. To test this, try to insert a row into the `HumanResources.Employee` table using the value of 20000 for the `ContactID`. You should get an error from SQL Server because there is no row in the `Person.Contact` table with `ContactID = 20000`.

When mapping an object to a foreign relational data object, you must specify which column is the foreign key. You do so by defining a method within the table definition and annotating that method with the `Association` attribute. This attribute tells the table that it is a foreign key table and identifies the column that is the foreign key column. The following code shows how the `HumanResources.Employee` table is mapped and the foreign key for the table identified:

```
[Table(Name = "HumanResources.Employee")]
public class Employee
{
    [Column(DBType = "int", IsPrimaryKey=true, IsDBGenerated=true, CanBeNull=false)]
    public int EmployeeID;

    [Column(DBType = "int", CanBeNull=false)]
    public int ContactID;
```

```
        [Column(DBType = "nvarchar(256) not null")]
        public string LoginID;

        [Column(DBType = "nvarchar(15) not null")]
        public string NationalIDNUmber;

        [Column(DBType="int")]
        public int ManagerID;

        private EntityRef<Contact> _Contact;

        [Association(Name = "FK_Employee_Contact_ContactID",
            Storage = "_Contact", ThisKey = "ContactID", IsForeignKey = true)]
        public Employee Emp
        {
            get { return this._Employee.Entity; }
            set { this._Employee.Entity = value; }
        }

    }
```

While identifying relational data relationships in LINQ to SQL might seem a bit overwhelming, clearly it's something you must understand.

Summary

LINQ to SQL is powerful and flexible. This chapter introduced you to LINQ to SQL, providing an overview and some insight into the LINQ to SQL object model. You learned about attribute-based mapping and how to effectively map relational data objects and object models expressed in the developer's programming language.

The last part of this chapter helped those who have no database design experience to understand database relationships and how they apply to and are used in LINQ to SQL.

Chapter 11 introduces LINQ to SQL queries and tackles the many components and concepts used when executing queries against a relational database.

11

LINQ to SQL Queries

LINQ to SQL is extensive, supporting many of the query aspects found in a relational database. But even with its depth and profound technology, it is quite easy to use and understand because of its use of the standard query facilities (standard query operators) found in LINQ and the many new .NET features found in .NET Framework 3.0, including extension methods and anonymous types.

In this chapter, you will explore LINQ to SQL queries, including the following:

- LINQ to SQL query concepts
- The `DataContext` class
- Data manipulation via LINQ to SQL
- Working with entity objects
- Querying with stored procedures and user-defined functions

Query Concepts

By now you know that LINQ to SQL queries really are not any different from the other LINQ queries you have seen and worked with throughout this book. They follow the same syntax format as LINQ and LINQ to XML queries.

However, they vary in one area. In LINQ to XML you query an XML document tree or fragment directly, but in LINQ to SQL you query mapped objects, meaning that the objects you are querying are mapped to objects or items in a relational database, such as a table or stored procedure.

A LINQ to SQL query, like standard LINQ queries, has parts or actions of the query operation: the obtaining of a data source, the query creation, and the query execution. It uses the same standard query operators and query patterns because of its tight integration with LINQ. There are subtle differences between some of the query items. For example, items such as filtering and grouping are the same, but the variable of the return type for LINQ to SQL must be of `IQueryable(of T)` instead of the `IEnumerable` that a standard LINQ query uses.

The following table lists the similarities and differences between a standard LINQ query and a LINQ to SQL query. Notice that most of the query items are identical, meaning that they follow the same syntax. The only differences are the way joins are handled and the query variable return type.

Query Item	LINQ	LINQ to SQL
Query variable return type	`IEnumerable`	`IQueryable`
Data source specification	`From/from`	equivalent
Filtering	`Where/where`	equivalent
Grouping	`Goupby`	equivalent
Selecting	`Select/select`	equivalent
Joins	`join`	`Association` attribute

In LINQ to SQL joins, the recommended technique is to use the `Association` attribute, but as you saw in Chapter 3, it is possible to use the `join` clause. However, the `join` clause does not have access to any of the properties employed by the `Association` attribute, thus limiting its flexibility.

LINQ to SQL also employs the same rules of query execution as a standard LINQ query, meaning deferred and immediate. You recall that a deferred execution query is one that produces a sequence of values, and the query is not executed until you iterate through the results (that is, iterate over the query variable). An immediate executed query is one that returns a single value (such as a query that returns a `MAX` value, or `COUNT`). These types of queries are executed immediately because a sequence must be produced first to generate the result.

There are several components involved when a query is executed:

- LINQ to SQL API
- LINQ to SQL Provider
- ADO Provider

Each of these components plays a pivotal role when executing a query. When a LINQ to SQL query is executed, seven steps are taken to execute the query and return the results.

1. The LINQ to SQL API requests execution of the query on behalf of your application.
2. The LINQ to SQL API hands the query off to the LINQ to SQL Provider.
3. The LINQ to SQL Provider converts the LINQ query to T-SQL.
4. The LINQ to SQL Provider hands the new query off to the ADO Provider for execution on the server.
5. The query is executed and the results are handed back to the ADO Provider in the form of a DataReader.
6. The ADO Provider hands the DataReader back to the LINQ to SQL Provider.
7. The LINQ to SQL Provider converts the DataReader into an enumerable form of user objects.

Realistically, a few of these steps could have been combined, but they are listed separately to provide a detailed look at what happens when a LINQ to SQL query is executed. These steps also look like they could take a while to process. On the contrary, LINQ to SQL was architected with performance in mind from the get-go, and as you start working with LINQ and LINQ to SQL, you will notice that it indeed works quickly.

To execute a query, a connection to the data source must first be established, and that is accomplished through the `DataContext` class. The next section explains how.

DataContext

Before you can execute a LINQ to SQL query, a connection to the data source must be made. In LINQ to SQL, database connections are made through the `DataContext` class. Think of the `DataContext` class on the same level as you would the `SqlConnection` class of ADO.NET. `DataContext` is the medium in which connections to a database are made, through which objects are retrieved from and submitted to the database.

Like the `SqlConnection` class, the `DataContext` instance accepts a connection string. Once the connection is made, data is read from, and changes are transmitted back to, the database through the `DataContext`. However, there is one thing the `DataContext` does that the `SqlConnection` does not. Since LINQ to SQL deals with objects, the `DataContext` also does the work of converting the objects into SQL queries and then reassembling the results back into queryable objects.

The `DataContext` has several overloads, one of which is just a simple connection string specifying the connection information, as shown in this code:

```
DataContext db = new DataContext(
  "Initial Catalog=AdventureWorks;Integrated ↵
 Security=sspi");
```

You can also pass an `IDbConnection`, which represents an open connection to a data source. `IDbConnection` is an interface that is defined in the `System.Data` namespace and allows a class that inherits from this interface to implement a `Connection` class, containing a unique session with a data source. This interface takes a little more effort because classes that inherit from the `IDbConnection` interface must also implement all inherited members. The trick is that the application doesn't create an instance of `IDbConnection` directly; instead, the application should create an instance of a class that inherits from `IDbConnection`. In most cases, you are much better off instantiating an instance of the `DataContext` and passing a string containing the necessary connection information.

The `DataContext` has several useful public methods, including `CreateDatabase` and `DeleteDatabase`, as well as `CreateQuery`, `ExecuteQuery`, `GetQueryText`, and `SubmitChanges`.

The `CreateDatabase` and `DeleteDatabase` methods do exactly as their names imply. `CreateDatabase` creates a database with the database name taken either from the connection string, the `Database` attribute, the name of the file (if the `DataContext` has been created using a file), or the name of the `DataContext` inheriting class if a strongly typed `DataContext` is used.

The strongly typed `DataContext` is discussed in the next section.

The following example creates a new database using the name ScottWrox, which is specified in the connection string:

```
DataContext db = new DataContext("Initial Catalog=ScottWrox;Integrated ↵
Security=sspi");
db.CreateDatabase();
```

The same criteria for database naming apply to the `DeleteDatabase` method.

```
db.DeleteDatabase();
```

The following example illustrates the use of the `DatabaseExists` method of the `DataContext` class, which can be used to determine if a database already exists:

```
try
{

   DataContext db = new DataContext("Initial Catalog=WroxScott;Integrated
      Security=sspi");

   bool_dbExists = db.DatabaseExists();

   if (_dbExists == true)
      db.DeleteDatabase();
   else
   {
      db.CreateDatabase();
      textBox1.Text = "Database created.";
   }
}
catch (Exception ex)
{
   MessageBox.Show(ex.Message);
}
```

The `SubmitChanges` method is the component that sends your data changes back to the database. Here's how to use it:

```
DataContext db = new DataContext("Initial Catalog=AdventureWorks;Integrated ↵
Security=sspi");
// Do some work on the data
db.SubmitChanges();
```

You'll explore `SubmitChanges` in more detail later in the chapter.

Strongly Typed DataContext

Creating a strongly typed `DataContext` is quite simple. All you need to do is create a new class that inherits from the `DataContext` class, as shown in the code example below:

```
public class AdventureWorks : DataContext
{
```

```
    public AdventureWorks(string connection) : base(connection) {}
    // table definitions
}
```

Once the `DataContext` is created, you can use it to connect to the specified database, as shown in the following example. In it, the preceding strongly typed `DataContext` is given the same name as the database to use; in this case, AdventureWorks. Therefore, no database name needs to be specified in the connection string.

```
AdventureWorks db = new AdventureWorks(Integrated Security=sspi");

bool _dbExists = db.DatabaseExists();

if (_dbExists == true)
   textBox1.Text = "Yep, Exists!";
```

Creating strongly typed `DataContext` objects is preferred over non-strongly typed because utilizing strongly typed table objects eliminates the need to use the `GetTable` method in your queries.

Each database table is represented as a `Table` collection, which is available through the `GetTable` method of the `DataContext` class. `GetTable` gives you access to the table in an untyped fashion. For example, the following code creates a connection to the AdventureWorks database and the Contact table by way of the `GetTable` method, but it is not strongly typed:

```
DataContext context = new DataContext(
    "Initial Catalog=AdventureWorks;Integrated Security=sspi");
Table<Contact> con = context.GetTable<Contact>();
```

The appropriate way to create a strongly typed `DataContext` is:

```
public class AdventureWorks : DataContext
{
   public AdventureWorks(string connection) : base(connection) {}
   public Table<Contact> Contact;
}
```

This example creates a new class that inherits from the `DataContext` class and then defines a table for a specific type (in this case, the `Contact` table) in the underlying database. This provides access to the database through a strongly typed `DataContext` and strongly typed table.

Data Manipulation

Now you're ready to start querying, modifying, and sending data back to the database. This section of the chapter walks you through a full example that updates, inserts, and deletes data using LINQ to SQL.

Fire up your copy of Visual Studio and create a new C# Windows project. On Form1, place three buttons and a text box. Name the first button `cmdInsert`, the second button `cmdUpdate`, and the third button `cmdDelete`. Make sure that the text box is long enough to hold and view 20 characters.

For this example, you need to add a reference to LINQ, so in Solution Explorer, right-click on References and select Add Reference. When the Add Reference dialog appears, make sure that the .NET tab is selected and scroll down until you see the `System.Data.Linq` component name. Select that component and click OK.

Next, right-click on Form1 and select View Code. Add the following line to the rest of the `using` statements:

```
using System.Data.Linq;
```

Time to start adding the good stuff.

Insert

Let's begin by discussing Insert operations. First, add the following to the form code below the partial class for `Form1`:

```
public class AdventureWorks : DataContext
{
    public AdventureWorks(string connection) : base(connection) {}
    public Table<Contact> Contact;
}
```

This should look familiar—it's the code from the strongly typed section a few pages ago. It strongly types the `DataContext` and includes a reference to a strongly typed table.

The bulk of your form code should now look like this:

```
public partial class Form1 : Form
{
    public Form1()
    {
        InitializeComponent();
    }

}

public class AdventureWorks : DataContext
{
    public AdventureWorks(string connection) : base(connection) {}
    public Table<Contact> Contact;
}
```

The strongly typed `DataContext` class references a strongly typed table, `Contact`, which has not been created yet. The following code does that. Add it below the strongly typed `DataContext` class:

```
[Table(Name = "Person.Contact")]
public class Contact
{

    [Column(DBType = "int not null")]
    public int ContactID;
```

```
        [Column(DBType = "nvarchar(8) not null")]
        public string Title;

        [Column(DBType = "nvarchar(50) not null")]
        public string FirstName;

        [Column(DBType = "nvarchar(50) not null")]
        public string MiddleName;

        [Column(DBType = "nvarchar(50) not null")]
        public string LastName;

        [Column(DBType = "nvarchar(50) not null")]
        public string EmailAddress;

        [Column(DBType = "int")]
        public int EmailPromotion;

        [Column(DBType = "bit")]
        public byte NameStyle;

        [Column(DBType = "varchar(40)")]
        public string PasswordHash;

        [Column(DBType = "varchar(40)")]
        public string PasswordSalt;

    }
```

Next, add the following code to the `Click` event of the Insert button:

```
try
{
    AdventureWorks db = new AdventureWorks("Integrated Security=sspi");
    Contact con = new Contact();
    con.FirstName = "Scott";
    con.MiddleName = "L";
    con.LastName = "Klein";
    con.Title = "Geek";
    con.EmailAddress = "geek@email.com";
    con.EmailPromotion = 1;
    con.NameStyle = 0;
    con.PasswordHash = "";
    con.PasswordSalt = "";
    db.Contact.Add(con);
    db.SubmitChanges();
    textBox1.Text = "Contact created.";
}
catch (Exception ex)
{
    MessageBox.Show(ex.Message);
}
```

You are ready to test it. Run the application and click the Insert button. Didn't work, did it? The error you should have received states that the table is read-only. This error is misleading (you'll see why in a minute), but the fix is simple. On the definition of the `ContactID` column, two `ContactID` properties need to be set, as shown here:

```
[Table(Name = "Person.Contact")]
public class Contact
{
    [Column(DBType = "int not null", IsPrimaryKey=true, IsDBGenerated=true)]
    public int ContactID;
```

Now when you run the application and click the Insert button, the "Contact created" message appears in the text box.

Why did the first insert fail? LINQ to SQL treats tables as read-only by default, and it needs to know which column is the primary key. In fact, if you run this example and don't specify the `IsDBGenerated` property, it still won't work, although you will get a different error, stating that it cannot insert an explicit value for the identity column of the table when `IDENTITY_INSERT` is set to off. LINQ to SQL needs to know that the table has a primary key, which column the primary key is, and that it is auto-generated. At that point, LINQ to SQL won't see the table as read-only.

Last, when the properties have been filled, the new object needs to be added to the `Contact` table in the `DataContext` and the `SubmitChanges` method called to usher the changes back to the database.

Update

For an update, the code is going to query for a specific record and update a field of that record. Add the following code behind the Update button. It queries for the record you inserted in the preceding example and updates the email address. Keep in mind that when you run this code, the `ContactID` may be different for you; be sure to use the correct `ContactID`.

```
AdventureWorks db = new AdventureWorks("Integrated Security=sspi");
var con = db.Contact.Single(c => c.ContactID == 19980);
con.EmailAddress = "ScottKlein@SqlXml.com";
db.SubmitChanges();
textBox1.Text = "Contact updated.";
```

Run the application and click the Update button. When the text box displays "Contact updated," you can query the AdventureWorks database and verify that the email address for the new contact has indeed been updated.

The preceding example updates a single row. Here's how to update multiple rows:

```
AdventureWorks db = new AdventureWorks("Integrated Security=sspi");

var queryContacts =
    from names in db.Contact
    where names.LastName == "Zwilling"
    select names;
```

```
foreach (var con in queryContacts)
{
   con.EmailAddress = "ScottKlein@SqlXml.com";
}
db.SubmitChanges();
textBox1.Text = "Contact updated.";
```

This code returns a query that will yield two rows and updates the email address for each contact. It then issues a single `SubmitChanges` to send the updates back to the database.

So far, so good, right? Good. Now let's look at deleting.

Delete

Deleting is just as easy as inserting and updating. Place the following code behind the Delete button, again making sure that you use the correct `ContactID`. The code simply uses the ID to delete the desired record by calling the `Remove` method to delete the appropriate record. And, as you have learned, `SubmitChanges` is called to send the statement to the database.

```
AdventureWorks db = new AdventureWorks("Integrated Security=sspi");
var con = db.Contact.Single(c => c.ContactID == 19980);
db.Contact.Remove(con);
db.SubmitChanges();
textBox1.Text = "Contact deleted.";
```

To delete multiple records, your query would be built along the same lines as the update example for multiple records.

Working with Objects

You can manipulate data using objects and object members, such as the `Add(T)` and `Remove(T)` methods. It is not that different from what you have already learned in many of the examples in previous chapters. The following sections show how to use objects to associate LINQ to SQL generic collections to database objects for submission to the database for execution.

Insert

In the previous insert example, an empty `Contact` was created and then the individual column properties were populated with data. Once the properties were filled, the populated `Contact` was added to the strongly typed `Contact` table via the `Add` method. In other words, the previous example modified object members directly.

There is another way, which is essentially the same as the last inset example but adds an object to the LINQ to SQL collection (the `Table(of T)` collection) and hands that off for submission to the database. The following example shows how this is accomplished:

```
AdventureWorks db = new AdventureWorks("Integrated Security=sspi");
Contact con = new Contact
```

```
            {
                FirstName = "Scott",
                MiddleName = "L",
                LastName = "Klein",
                Title = "Geek",
                EmailAddress = "geek@email.com",
                EmailPromotion = 1,
                NameStyle = 0,
                PasswordHash = "",
                PasswordSalt = ""
            }       ;
    db.Contact.Add(con);
    db.SubmitChanges();
    textBox1.Text = "Contact created.";
```

The differences between this example and the previous Insert example are not that major. The results are the same; it is just a matter of implementation.

Update

Rows can be updated by modifying the value members of the objects. Any object that is associated with a `Table(of T)` collection can have its value members updated and the object submitted back to the database for updating, as shown in the example below:

```
AdventureWorks db = new AdventureWorks("Integrated Security=sspi");
var query = from con in db.Contact
         where con.LastName == "Klein"
         select con;

foreach (var cont in query)
{
   cont.EmailAddress = "ScottKlein@SqlXml.com";
   cont.Title = "Mr. Geek";
}

db.SubmitChanges();
textBox1.Text = "Contact updated.";
```

Delete

Rows can be deleted by removing the LINQ to SQL object. In the following example, a row is queried, followed by the removal of the object from the returned collection. The object is removed by calling the `Remove(of T)` method, T being the type of object to remove.

```
AdventureWorks db = new AdventureWorks("Integrated Security=sspi");
var query = from con in db.Contact
         where con.LastName == "Klein"
         select con;

foreach (Contact del in query)
{
   db.Contact.Remove(del);
}
```

```
db.SubmitChanges();
textBox1.Text = "Contact deleted.";
```

As always, the changes are not applied until `SubmitChanges` is called, sending the changes back to the database.

Stored Procedures and User-Defined Functions

Just like tables, stored procedures and functions are mapped, and they are mapped by creating class methods with the `StoredProcedure` or `Function` attribute applied, respectively. The best way to learn this is by example, so get comfy and ready to start writing code. The following examples illustrate how to call stored procedures and user-defined functions (UDFs) in several scenarios. You will need to have Visual Studio open as well as SQL Server Management Studio.

Mapping and Calling Stored Procedures

LINQ to SQL supports the mapping and calling of stored procedures via methods defined in your object model that represent the stored procedure. Methods are designated as stored procedures by applying the `[Function]` attribute and any associated `[Parameter]` attributes. Mapped stored procedures can return rowsets and take parameters.

Returning a Single Result

In this first example, you will call a stored procedure that returns a single resultset. Open SQL Server 2005 Management Studio, and open a new query window. Type in the following and execute it:

```
CREATE PROCEDURE [dbo].[OrdersBySalesPersonID]
(
   @salesPersonID int
)
AS
BEGIN
   SELECT   Production.Product.ProductID, Production.Product.Name, ↩
Sales.SalesPerson.SalesPersonID, Person.Contact.FirstName, ↩
Person.Contact.MiddleName,
      Person.Contact.LastName, Sales.SalesOrderDetail.UnitPrice
   FROM   Production.Product
   INNER JOIN   Sales.SalesOrderDetail ON Production.Product.ProductID = ↩
Sales.SalesOrderDetail.ProductID
   INNER JOIN   Sales.SalesOrderHeader ON Sales.SalesOrderDetail.SalesOrderID ↩
= Sales.SalesOrderHeader.SalesOrderID
   INNER JOIN   Sales.SalesPerson ON Sales.SalesOrderHeader.SalesPersonID = ↩
Sales.SalesPerson.SalesPersonID
   INNER JOIN   Person.Contact ON Sales.SalesPerson.SalesPersonID = ↩
Person.Contact.ContactID
   WHERE      (Sales.SalesPerson.SalesPersonID = @salesPersonID)
END
GO
```

This creates a new stored procedure called OrdersBySalesPersonID, which returns the product ID; product name; the ID of the salesperson; the contact's first, middle, and last name; and the unit price of each product for a given salesperson. The SalesPersonID is passed in to the stored procedure as a parameter.

Now turn your attention to LINQ and Visual Studio. Open Visual Studio and create a new C# project. Once the project is created, add the reference to System.Data.Linq. Next, place a list box, a text box, and five buttons on Form1. It doesn't really matter how you lay everything out on the form, but make sure that the list box is wide enough to display some data.

When the form is laid out, double-click the first button to display the code behind that button. Next, add the using statement to System.Data.Linq, as shown in the following code:

```
using System;
using System.Collections.Generic;
using System.ComponentModel;
using System.Data;
using System.Data.Linq;
using System.Drawing;
using System.Linq;
using System.Text;
using System.Windows.Forms;

namespace LINQ
{
   public partial class Form1 : Form
   {
      public Form1()
      {
         InitializeComponent();
      }
      private void Form1_Load(object sender, EventArgs e)
      {

      }

      private void button1_Click(object sender, EventArgs e)
      {

      }
   }

}
```

The next thing you want to do is create a class that derives from the DataContext class, which you learned about earlier in this chapter. Creating a class that inherits from the DataContext class provides you with all the connection processing functionality you need to work with LINQ to SQL and communicate with SQL Server.

Add a class called AdventureWorks that inherits from the `DataContext` class. Within that class, add the highlighted code shown below:

```
namespace LINQ
{
   public partial class Form1 : Form
   {
      public Form1()
      {
         InitializeComponent();
      }

      private void Form1_Load(object sender, EventArgs e)
      {

      }

      private void button1_Click(object sender, EventArgs e)
      {

      }
   }

   public class AdventureWorks : DataContext
   {
      public AdventureWorks(string connection) : base(connection) {}

   }
}
```

Next, create a method and map it to the stored procedure created earlier. Underneath the `DataContext` connection, add this highlighted code:

```
public class AdventureWorks : DataContext
{
   public AdventureWorks(string connection) : base(connection) {}

   [StoredProcedure(Name = "OrdersBySalesPersonID")]
   public IEnumerable<OrdersBySalesPersonID> SalesOrders
      ([Parameter(DBType="int")] int salesPersonID)
   {
      return this.ExecuteMethodCall<OrdersBySalesPersonID>
         (this, ((MethodInfo)(MethodInfo.GetCurrentMethod())),
         salesPersonID);
   }

}
```

There's just a little more work to do. You need to map a stored procedure because you need to map the resultset coming in. In LINQ to SQL, the resultsets for a stored procedure, view, and user-defined function are in the same form, basically in table format. Thus, you can map the stored procedure resultset to a class tagged as a table.

As shown in the following highlighted code, add a partial class with the name `OrdersBySalesPersonID`, and add the `Table` attribute. Within the attribute, pass the name of the stored procedure that will be called.

```
namespace LINQ
{
   public partial class Form1 : Form
   {
      public Form1()
      {
         InitializeComponent();
      }

      private void Form1_Load(object sender, EventArgs e)
      {
      }

      private void button1_Click(object sender, EventArgs e)
      {

      }
   }

   public class AdventureWorks : DataContext
   {
      public AdventureWorks(string connection) : base(connection) {}

      [Function(Name = "OrdersBySalesPersonID")]
      public IEnumerable<OrdersBySalesPersonID> SalesOrders
         ([Parameter(DBType="int")] int salesPersonID)
      {
         return this.ExecuteMethodCall<OrdersBySalesPersonID>
            (this, ((MethodInfo)(MethodInfo.GetCurrentMethod())),
            salesPersonID);
      }
   }

   [Table(Name = "SalesPersonOrders")]
   public partial class OrdersBySalesPersonID
   {

   }
}
```

Next, define the column properties that create a mapping for the columns being returned by the stored procedure. Within the partial class, add the following code (you do not need to add the partial class definition; it is included here as a reference). As you learned about earlier in this chapter, defining the columns is done by attributing a property with the `Column` attribute and adding parameters that define the column name and data type.

```
[Table(Name = "SalesPersonOrders")]
public partial class OrdersBySalesPersonID
{
   private int _productID;
   private string _productName;
   private int _salesPersonID;
   private string _firstName;
   private string _middleName;
   private string _lastName;
   private decimal _unitPrice;

   [Column(Name = "ProductID", Storage = "_productID", DBType = "int")]
   public int ProductID
   {
      get
      {
         return this._productID;
      }
      set
      {
         if ((this._productID != value))
         {
            this._productID = value;
         }
      }
   }

   [Column(Name = "Name", Storage = "_productName", DBType = "nvarchar(50)")]
   public string ProductName
   {
      get
      {
         return this._productName;
      }
      set
      {
         if ((this._productName != value))
         {
            this._productName = value;
         }
      }
   }

   [Column(Name = "SalesPersonID", Storage = "_salesPersonID", DBType = "int")]
   public int SalesPerson
   {
      get
      {
         return this._salesPersonID;
      }
      set
      {
         if ((this._salesPersonID != value))
```

```
            {
                this._salesPersonID = value;
            }
        }
    }

    [Column(Name = "FirstName", Storage = "_firstName", DBType = "nvarchar(50)")]
    public string FirstName
    {
        get
        {
            return this._firstName;
        }
        set
        {
            if ((this._firstName != value))
            {
                this._firstName = value;
            }
        }
    }

    [Column(Name = "MiddleName", Storage = "_middleName", DBType = "nvarchar(50)")]
    public string MiddleName
    {
        get
        {
            return this._middleName;
        }
        set
        {
            if ((this._middleName != value))
            {
                this._middleName = value;
            }
        }
    }
    [Column(Name = "LastName", Storage = "_lastName", DBType = "nvarchar(50)")]
    public string LastName
    {
        get
        {
            return this._lastName;
        }
        set
        {
            if ((this._lastName != value))
            {
                this._lastName = value;
            }
        }
    }

    [Column(Name = "UnitPrice", Storage = "_unitPrice", DBType = "decimal")]
    public decimal UnitPrice
```

```
        {
           get
           {
              return this._unitPrice;
           }
           set
           {
              if ((this._unitPrice != value))
              {
                 this._unitPrice = value;
              }
           }
        }

    }
```

You are almost done. The last step is to add the code behind the button. Add the following code to the click event of `button1`:

```
private void button1_Click(object sender, EventArgs e)
{
   AdventureWorks db = new AdventureWorks("Integrated Security=sspi");

   IEnumerable<OrdersBySalesPersonID> result = db.SalesOrders(275);

   foreach (OrdersBySalesPersonID ord in result)
   {
   listBox1.Items.Add(ord.ProductID + "   " + ord.ProductName + "   " +
      ord.SalesPerson + "   " + ord.UnitPrice);
   }
}
```

That's it! In Visual Studio, select Debug ➪ Start Debugging, or press the F5 key. Oops! You received some compilation errors, didn't you? They probably state something like the following:

```
The type or namespace 'MethodInfo' could note be found.
```

To fix this, add the highlighted `using` statement to your code:

```
using System.Linq;
using System.Text;
using System.Windows.Forms;
using System.Reflection;
```

The `System.Reflection` namespace houses all of the types that are used to obtain information regarding assemblies, modules, members, and other aspects of an assembly. LINQ to SQL uses this because the `MethodInfo` class is part of the `System.Reflection` namespace, and the `MethodInfo` class is used to identify the exact behavior of an operation.

Now press the F5 key to compile and run the project. You shouldn't get any errors this time, so when the form opens, click button1. This will execute the stored procedure you created earlier.

Just as an FYI, this example uses the `SalesPersonID` of 275 to pass in to the stored procedure. You are free to select another `SalesPersonID`. When button1 is pressed, the `DataContext` passes the `SalesPersonID` to SQL Server and asks for the stored procedure to be executed. The `DataContext` then handles the returned `resultsets` and passing of the results to LINQ for iteration through the results. Remember that the `DataContext` is the avenue through which objects are sent to and retrieved from the database.

Here's a sample of the results returned:

```
710 Mountain Bike Socks, L 275, 5.7000
709 Mountain Bike Socks, M 275, 5.7000
773 Mountain -100 Silver, 44 275, 2039.9940
776 Mountain -100 Black, 42 275, 2024.9940
```

Just for your edification, you might want to place a breakpoint on the first line of code and click button1 again, this time stepping through the execution of the code.

Passing Parameters to Mapped Stored Procedures

The next example illustrates how to call a stored procedure that also accepts a parameter but returns the results via an `OUTPUT` parameter.

The first step is to create the stored procedure. In SQL Server, type the following into a query window and execute it:

```
CREATE PROCEDURE [dbo].[MaxOrderBySalesPersonID]
(
   @salesPersonID int,
   @maxSalesTotal int OUTPUT
)
AS
BEGIN
   SELECT   @maxSalesTotal = MAX(TotalDue)
   FROM   sales.salesorderheader
   WHERE   SalesPersonID = @salesPersonID
END
GO
```

This stored procedure accepts two parameters. The first is an input parameter that is the ID of the salesperson. The second is an `OUPUT` parameter, which will contain the maximum individual sales for the given salesperson.

The next step is to create a mapping to that stored procedure and the associated parameters. In Visual Studio, add the following code below the previous stored procedure mapping. Notice the additional attribute, which is a `Return` attribute. It tells the mapping that a return value will be coming and the data type of that value. Also notice that it defines the two parameters and the parameter types within the method.

```
[Function(Name = "[MaxOrderBySalesPersonID]")]
[return: Parameter(DBType="int")]
public int MaxOrder
   ([Parameter(DBType = "int")] int salesPersonID,
   [Parameter(DBType = "int")] ref int maxSalesTotal)
{
   IExecuteResults results = this.ExecuteMethodCall(
      this, ((MethodInfo)(MethodInfo.GetCurrentMethod())),
```

```
        salesPersonID, maxSalesTotal);
    maxSalesTotal = ((int)(results.GetParameterValue(1)));
    return ((int)(results.ReturnValue));
}
```

Unlike the first example, this example is returning a singleton value, so no table definition is required. You do, however, need to add the code to call the stored procedure, so in the click event for `button2`, add the following code:

```
private void button2_Click(object sender, EventArgs e)
{
    AdventureWorks db = new AdventureWorks("Integrated Security=sspi");

    int bigOrder = 0;
    db.MaxOrder(275, ref bigOrder);

    listBox1.Items.Add(bigOrder);

}
```

This example defines an initial value for the returned parameter, and passes that along with the ID of the salesperson to the stored procedure.

Run the project again and click `button2`. This time the list box will be populated with a value of 198628 (if you used ID 275). Pretty slick, isn't it?

Mapped Stored Procedures for Multiple Results

The following example shows how to handle circumstances where you might not know the exact results coming back. It creates a stored procedure that accepts a single parameter of data type `int`. Based on the value of the parameter, one of two statements will be executed. One statement returns four columns, the other returns three columns.

```
CREATE PROCEDURE [dbo].[ContactsOrProducts]
(
    @whichone int
)
AS
BEGIN
    if @whichone = 1
        SELECT ContactID, Title, FirstName, LastName FROM Person.Contact
    else
        SELECT ProductID, Name, ProductNumber FROM Production.Product
END
GO
```

As you did earlier, you create a mapping to that stored procedure and the associated parameters. In Visual Studio, add the following code below the previous stored procedure mapping. In this code, two result types are defined as well as the parameter that will be passed to the stored procedure.

```
[Function(Name = "[ContactsOrProducts]")]
[ResultType(typeof(ContactsPart))]
[ResultType(typeof(ProductsPart))]
```

```
public IMultipleResults whichone(
   [Parameter(DBType = "int")] System.Nullable<int> whichone)
{
   return this.ExecuteMethodCallWithMultipleResults(this,
      ((MethodInfo)(MethodInfo.GetCurrentMethod())), whichone);
}
```

The two result types, called `ContactsPart` and `ProductsPart`, identify the table mapping for the incoming results. However, those mappings don't exist yet, so create them now by adding the following code below the table mapping from the first example. This code creates two mapping classes, one for the contacts and the other for the products.

```
[Table(Name = "ContactPart")]
public partial class ContactsPart
{
   private int _contactID;
   private string _title;
   private string _firstName;
   private string _lastName;

   [Column(Name = "ContactID", Storage = "_contactID", DBType = "int")]
   public int ContactID
   {
      get
      {
         return this._contactID;
      }
      set
      {
         if ((this._contactID != value))
         {
            this._contactID = value;
         }
      }
   }

   [Column(Name = "Title", Storage = "_title", DBType = "nvarchar(50)")]
   public string Title
   {
      get
      {
         return this._title;
      }
      set
      {
         if ((this._title != value))
         {
            this._title = value;
         }
      }
   }

   [Column(Name = "FirstName", Storage = "_firstName", DBType = "nvarchar(50)")]
   public string FirstName
```

```
    {
       get
       {
          return this._firstName;
       }
       set
       {
          if ((this._firstName != value))
          {
             this._firstName = value;
          }
       }
    }

    [Column(Name = "LastName", Storage = "_lastName", DBType = "nvarchar(50)")]
    public string LastName
    {
       get
       {
          return this._lastName;
       }
       set
       {
          if ((this._lastName != value))
          {
             this._lastName = value;
          }
       }
    }

}

 [Table(Name = "ProductPart")]
public partial class ProductsPart
{
    private int _productID;
    private string _name;
    private string _productNumber;

    [Column(Name = "ProductID", Storage = "_productID", DBType = "int")]
    public int ProductID
    {
       get
       {
          return this._productID;
       }
       set
       {
          if ((this._productID != value))
          {
             this._productID = value;
          }
       }
    }
```

```
    [Column(Name = "Name", Storage = "_name", DBType = "nvarchar(50)")]
    public string Name
    {
       get
       {
          return this._name;
       }
       set
       {
          if ((this._name != value))
          {
             this._name = value;
          }
       }
    }

    [Column(Name = "ProductNumber", Storage = "_productNumber", DBType = ↵
 "nvarchar(50)")]
    public string ProductNumber
    {
       get
       {
          return this._productNumber;
       }
       set
       {
          if ((this._productNumber != value))
          {
             this._productNumber = value;
          }
       }
    }

 }
```

In the `Click` event of `button3`, add the following code to call this stored procedure:

```
 private void button3_Click(object sender, EventArgs e)
 {
    AdventureWorks db = new AdventureWorks("Integrated Security=sspi");

    int caseSwitch = int.Parse(textBox1.Text);

    listBox1.Items.Clear();

    switch (caseSwitch)
    {
       case 1:
          IMultipleResults result1 = db.whichone(caseSwitch);

          foreach (ContactsPart cp in result1.GetResult<ContactsPart>())
          {
             listBox1.Items.Add(cp.ContactID + "  " + cp.Title + "  " +
                cp.FirstName + "  " + cp.LastName);
          }
```

```
            break;

         default:
            IMultipleResults result2 = db.whichone(caseSwitch);

            foreach (ProductsPart pp in result2.GetResult<ProductsPart>())
            {
               listBox1.Items.Add(pp.ProductID + "   " + pp.Name + "   " +
                  pp.ProductNumber);
            }
            break;

      }

   }
```

This code takes the value that is entered in the text box and passes that to the stored procedure. Once you have entered the code, press F5 to build and run the project.

Another compile error, right? This time the error should say something like this:

```
The type of namespace name 'IMultipleResults' could not be found.
```

Again, that's because you are missing a `using` directive. Add the highlighted `using` directive to your code:

```
using System.Linq;
using System.Text;
using System.Windows.Forms;
using System.Reflection;
using System.Data.Linq.Provider;
```

You have to include this namespace because it provides the capability to handle multiple results. Now, press F5 again, and when the application runs, enter either 1 or 2 in the text box. Based on the stored procedure and the number you entered, you should get either a list of contacts or a list of products. If you entered a value of 1, you get a list of contacts with four columns. If you entered a value of 2, you get a list of products with three columns.

This is accomplished by passing either the `ContactPart` mapping or the `ProductPart` mapping when calling the stored procedure.

OK, one last stored procedure example. The preceding was an "or" example, in that it returns the contact result or the product result. This example returns both. In SQL Server, create the following stored procedure:

```
CREATE PROCEDURE [dbo].[ContactsANDProducts]

AS
BEGIN
      SELECT ContactID, Title, FirstName, LastName FROM Person.Contact
      SELECT ProductID, Name, ProductNumber FROM Production.Product
END
GO
```

This procedure accepts no parameter and returns two results.

Next, create a mapping to that stored procedure. In Visual Studio, add the following code below the previous stored procedure mapping. Two result types are defined, but no parameter is defined because the stored procedure does not accept one.

```
[StoredProcedure(Name = "[ContactsANDProducts]")]
[ResultType(typeof(ContactsPart))]
[ResultType(typeof(ProductsPart))]
public IMultipleResults TwoResultsets()
{
   return this.ExecuteMethodCallWithMultipleResults(this,
      ((MethodInfo)(MethodInfo.GetCurrentMethod())));
}
```

The stored procedure returns the same results as the previous example (contacts and products), so this example will use the same table mappings that were defined in the previous example. Therefore, the only thing left to do is to add the code behind `button4`:

```
private void button4_Click(object sender, EventArgs e)
{
   AdventureWorks db = new AdventureWorks("Integrated Security=sspi");
   IMultipleResults results = db.TwoResultsets();

   foreach (ContactsPart cp in results.GetResult<ContactsPart>())
   {
      listBox1.Items.Add(cp.ContactID + "  " + cp.Title + "  " + cp.FirstName + "
       " + cp.LastName);
   }

   foreach (ProductsPart pp in results.GetResult<ProductsPart>())
   {
      listBox1.Items.Add(pp.ProductID + "  " + pp.Name + "  " + pp.ProductNumber);
   }
}
```

This example also requires the `System.Data.Linq.Provider` namespace because it is dealing with multiple results. It handles the contacts first, and then processes the products.

Press F5 to compile and run the project. When the form appears, click `button4`. The list box should be populated with a list of contacts first, followed by a list of products. To cut down on the number of items returned, add a `WHERE` clause to each `SELECT` statement.

You have to love the fact that LINQ can handle multiple results so easily.

Mapping and Calling User-Defined Functions

LINQ to SQL supports the mapping and calling of user-defined functions via methods defined in your object model that represent the user-defined function. Methods are designated as functions by applying the `[Function]` attribute and any associated `[Parameter]` attributes.

In the following example, a user-defined function will return table values. In SQL Server Management Studio, create the following user-defined function, which accepts a parameter and returns a resultset:

```
CREATE FUNCTION [dbo].[EmployeesByManagerID]
(
   @ManagerID int
)
RETURNS TABLE
AS
RETURN
(

     select pc.ContactID, pc.FirstName, pc.LastName, emp.Title
   from Person.Contact pc
     INNER JOIN   HumanResources.Employee emp ON pc.ContactID = emp.ContactID
     WHERE      ManagerID = @ManagerID

)
```

Next, create a mapping to the UDF you just created. In Visual Studio, add the following code below the previous stored procedure mapping. This method is annotated with the `Function` attribute, telling the `DataContext` that a user-defined function will be called.

```
 [Function(Name = "[EmployeeInfo]")]
public IQueryable<EmployeeInfo>
   EmpInfo(System.Nullable<int> ManagerID)
{
   MethodCallExpression mce = Expression.Call(Expression.Constant(this),
   ((MethodInfo)(MethodInfo.GetCurrentMethod())),
   new Expression[]
   {
      Expression.Constant(ManagerID, typeof(System.Nullable<int>))
   }
   );
   return this.CreateQuery<EmployeeInfo>(mce);

}
```

A table mapping must be created to define and map the results coming back. And the definition of the table mapping is no different than that of calling a stored procedure as in the previous examples. Create the table mapping by adding the code below:

```
 [Table(Name = "EmployeeInfo")]
public partial class EmployeeInfo
{
   private int _contactID;
   private string _firstName;
   private string _lastName;
   private string _Title;
```

```
[Column(Name = "ContactID", Storage = "_contactID", DBType = "int")]
public int ContactID
{
   get
   {
      return this._contactID;
   }
   set
   {
      if ((this._contactID != value))
      {
         this._contactID = value;
      }
   }
}

[Column(Name = "FirstName", Storage = "_firstName", DBType = "nvarchar(50)")]
public string FirstName
{
   get
   {
      return this._firstName;
   }
   set
   {
      if ((this._firstName != value))
      {
         this._firstName = value;
      }
   }
}

[Column(Name = "LastName", Storage = "_lastName", DBType = "nvarchar(50)")]
public string LastName
{
   get
   {
      return this._lastName;
   }
   set
   {
      if ((this._lastName != value))
      {
         this._lastName = value;
      }
   }
}

[Column(Name = "Title", Storage = "_Title", DBType = "nvarchar(50)")]
public string Title
{
   get
   {
      return this._Title;
   }
```

```
            set
            {
               if ((this._Title != value))
               {
                  this._Title = value;
               }
            }
         }
      }
```

Last, add the code behind `button5`:

```
   private void button5_Click(object sender, EventArgs e)
   {

      AdventureWorks db = new AdventureWorks("Integrated Security=sspi");
      var result = from emp in db.EmpInfo(21)
                   select emp;

      foreach (EmployeeInfo ei in result)
         listBox1.Items.Add(ei.ContactID + "   " + ei.FirstName
            + "   " + ei.LastName + "   " + ei.Title);

   }
```

This code is not really that different from calling a stored procedure.

Press F5 to compile and run the project. One last "Oops!" This time the error says something like this:

```
The type of namespace name 'MethodCallExpression' could not be found.
```

Once again, that's because you are missing a `using` directive. Add the highlighted `using` directive to your code:

```
using System.Text;
using System.Windows.Forms;
using System.Reflection;
using System.Data.Linq.Provider;
using System.Linq.Expressions;
```

You need to include this namespace because it provides the capability to represent language-level expressions as objects in the form of expression trees.

Press F5 again, and when the application runs, click `button5`. This time the list box should be populated with the `ContactID`, `FirstName`, `LastName`, and `Title` of the employees whose manager has a `ManagerID` of 21.

Whew! That was a lot, but you now have a good understanding of how LINQ to SQL is used to call stored procedures and user-defined functions using input and output parameters, deal with multiple resultsets, and return rows of data.

Summary

This chapter introduced you to LINQ to SQL queries, providing an in-depth look at the components and concepts that make LINQ to SQL queries possible. You first explored LINQ to SQL query concepts, the key points that give LINQ to SQL queries their power.

Then you learned about the `DataContext` class, the important role it plays in LINQ to SQL, and the functionality it provides when executing queries. In addition, you saw how to use LINQ to SQL and the `DataContext` class to manipulate data, such as adding, updating, and deleting data in SQL Server.

Associating relational database objects to LINQ to SQL generic collections and submitting them to the database for execution was also discussed, and you looked at several examples illustrating how to execute stored procedures and user-defined functions using LINQ to SQL.

Chapter 12 tackles a few advanced LINQ to SQL query topics.

12

Advanced Query Concepts

There is so much that LINQ to SQL can do that applies to relational data and working with relational databases, that a chapter dedicated to the tight coupling of LINQ to SQL and relational data is warranted. For example, LINQ to SQL supports transactions and composite keys, and these types of topics are usually not found or discussed in an introductory-level chapter. Therefore, this chapter focuses on the following topics, which are a bit more advanced:

- Database relationships
- Compiled queries
- Query execution location
- Deferred versus immediate
- Composite keys
- Read-only data

Transactions are discussed in Chapter 13.

Database Relationships

LINQ to SQL fully supports primary and foreign keys, and Chapter 10 provided a couple of code examples to illustrate how they are implemented in LINQ to SQL. This section builds on that, discussing how to define the keys in LINQ to SQL and showing you how to query across them.

Representing Relationships

As you know, relationships in databases are normally of the primary key/foreign key kind—that is, the column or set of columns in one table that is referenced by the column or columns in another table. In a relational database, the navigation between these two tables is done through a join operator or operation. In a join operation, the primary key table is referenced to the foreign key table through a `JOIN` operator on the primary and foreign keys.

The following T-SQL query illustrates how the `Person.Contact` table and the `HumanResources.Employee` table, which are joined through the `ContactID` column, are referenced together in a query:

```
SELECT       pc.ContactID, pc.FirstName, pc.LastName, pc.EmailAddress,
             hre.EmployeeID, hre.NationalIDNumber, hre.Title, hre.HireDate
FROM         Person.Contact pc
INNER JOIN   HumanResources.Employee hre ON pc.ContactID = hre.ContactID
ORDER BY     pc.LastName
```

The key, then, is to apply this same join functionality in LINQ to SQL. You accomplish that through types that assist in representing the primary key/foreign key relationships between tables within a database. These two types are the `EntitySet` and `EntityRef` generic types, each of which is of type `(of TEntity)`. These types provide collections for the "many" part of a one-to-many relationship. Both the `EntitySet` and `EntityRef` types are used in conjunction with the `[Association]` attribute, which helps define and represent a relationship.

EntitySet (of TEntity)

The `EntitySet` type provides a collection for the results of the "many" side of a one-to-many relationship. In other words, it signifies that the defined relationship is a one-to-many relationship. As stated earlier, it is used together with the `[Association]` attribute to define and represent a relationship.

The `OtherKey` property is also used in the definition of the relationship. It specifies the name of the property (column) in the related class (table) to which is compared the current class's (table's) property (column).

The following example defines two classes, one for the `Contacts` table and one for the `Employee` table. In the AdventureWorks database, you can see that there's a relationship defined between these two tables on the `ContactID` column. The code here maps these two classes to their respective relational database counterparts, and also uses the `[Association]` attribute and the `EntitySet` type to define a one-to-many relationship between the `Contact` class and the `Employee` class. The relationship is defined within the context of the `Contact` class.

```
public class AdventureWorks : DataContext
{
    public AdventureWorks(string connection) : base(connection) {}
    public Table<Contact> Contacts;
    public Table<Employee> Employees;

}

[Table(Name = "Person.Contact")]
public class Contact
{

    [Column(DBType = "int not null", IsPrimaryKey = true, IsDBGenerated
        = true)]
    public int ContactID;
```

```
    [Column(DBType = "nvarchar(8) not null")]
    public string Title;

    [Column(DBType = "nvarchar(50) not null")]
    public string FirstName;

    [Column(DBType = "nvarchar(50) not null")]
    public string MiddleName;

    [Column(DBType = "nvarchar(50) not null")]
    public string LastName;

    [Column(DBType = "nvarchar(50) not null")]
    public string EmailAddress;

    [Column(DBType = "int")]
    public int EmailPromotion;

    [Column(DBType = "bit")]
    public byte NameStyle;

    [Column(DBType = "varchar(40)")]
    public string PasswordHash;

    [Column(DBType = "varchar(40)")]
    public string PasswordSalt;

    private EntitySet<Employee> _employees;
    [Association(Storage = "_employees", OtherKey = "ContactID")]
    public EntitySet<Employee> Emps
    {
        get { return this._employees;}
        set { this._employees.Assign(value);}
    }
}

[Table(Name = "HumanResources.Employee")]
public class Employee
{
    [Column(DBType = "int", IsPrimaryKey = true, IsDBGenerated = true,
        CanBeNull = false)]
    public int EmployeeID;

    [Column(DBType = "int", CanBeNull = false)]
    public int ContactID;

    [Column(DBType = "nvarchar(256) not null")]
    public string LoginID;

    [Column(DBType = "nvarchar(15) not null")]
    public string NationalIDNUmber;

    [Column(DBType = "int")]
    public int ManagerID;
}
```

With the classes and relationship defined, you can now write a LINQ to SQL "join" query that utilizes the relationship, like this:

```
IQueryable<Contact> conQuery =
    from con in db.Contact
    where con.Employee.ContactID == 19917
```

Or like this:

```
var conQuery =
    from con in db.Contact
    from emp in con.Emps
    where con.FirstName == "Scott"
    select new {con.FirstName, emp.ManagerID};
```

Think of the `EntitySet` type and the `[Association]` attribute (utilized in the table mapping above) as equal to a SQL join.

EntityRef (of TEntity)

The `EntityRef` type defines a relationship between two tables, but does the opposite of the `EntitySet`, in that it provides for the "one" side of a one-to-many relationship. It is also used together with the `[Association]` attribute to define and represent a relationship.

Again, the `ThisKey` property is used in the definition of the relationship to specify the name of the property (column) in the related class (table) to which the current class's (table's) property (column) is compared.

The next example uses the same two classes—one for the `Contacts` table and one for the `Employee` table—as in the previous example. The following code maps these two classes to their respective relational database counterparts, and also uses the `[Association]` attribute and the `EntityRef` type to define a one-to-many relationship between the two classes. The relationship is defined within the context of the `Employee` class.

```
public class AdventureWorks : DataContext
{
    public AdventureWorks(string connection) : base(connection) {}
    public Table<Contact> Contacts;
    public Table<Employee> Employees;

}

[Table(Name = "Person.Contact")]
public class Contact
{

    [Column(DBType = "int not null", IsPrimaryKey = true, IsDBGenerated
        = true)]
    public int ContactID;
```

```
        [Column(DBType = "nvarchar(8) not null")]
        public string Title;

        [Column(DBType = "nvarchar(50) not null")]
        public string FirstName;

        [Column(DBType = "nvarchar(50) not null")]
        public string MiddleName;

        [Column(DBType = "nvarchar(50) not null")]
        public string LastName;

        [Column(DBType = "nvarchar(50) not null")]
        public string EmailAddress;

        [Column(DBType = "int")]
        public int EmailPromotion;

        [Column(DBType = "bit")]
        public byte NameStyle;

        [Column(DBType = "varchar(40)")]
        public string PasswordHash;

        [Column(DBType = "varchar(40)")]
        public string PasswordSalt;

    }

    [Table(Name = "HumanResources.Employee")]
    public class Employee
    {
        [Column(DBType = "int", IsPrimaryKey = true, IsDBGenerated = true,
     CanBeNull = false)]
        public int EmployeeID;

        [Column(DBType = "int", CanBeNull = false)]
        public int ContactID;

        [Column(DBType = "nvarchar(256) not null")]
        public string LoginID;

        [Column(DBType = "nvarchar(15) not null")]
        public string NationalIDNUmber;
        [Column(DBType = "int")]
        public int ManagerID;

        private EntityRef<Contact> _Contact;
        [Association(Storage = "_Contact", ThisKey = "ContactID")]
        public Contact Contact
        {
            get { return this._Contact.Entity;}
            set { this._Contact.Entity = value;}
        }
    }
```

This example illustrates the relationship between a contact and employee. The `EntityRef` type is used to define the relationship from `Employee` back to `Contact`.

With the classes and relationship defined, you can now write a query that utilizes the relationship, like this:

```
IQueryable<Employee> empQuery =
    from emp in db.Employee
    where emp.Contact.FirstName.StartsWith("Scott")
    select emp;
```

You can see that `EntitySet` and `EntityRef` are complementary and quite easy to use, and are powerful for defining relationships.

Querying

You have two choices when querying across objects: `join` statements or dot notation. They are equally effective, but the second offers better relationship checking than the first. The T-SQL statement at the beginning of the chapter (repeated here) showed how to join two tables using `join` syntax.

```
SELECT          pc.ContactID, pc.FirstName, pc.LastName, pc.EmailAddress,
                hre.EmployeeID, hre.NationalIDNumber, hre.Title, hre.HireDate
FROM            Person.Contact pc
INNER JOIN      HumanResources.Employee hre ON pc.ContactID = hre.ContactID
WHERE hre.ManagerID = 275
```

You can accomplish the same type of join in LINQ to SQL using the LINQ `join` operator, like this:

```
IQueryable<Employee> joinQuery =
    from emp in db.Employee
    join con in db.Contact on emp.ContactID equals con.ContactID
    where emp.ManagerID == 275
    select con;
```

Notice how similar these two examples are. This syntax is beneficial when database relationships do not exist between two tables, or when LINQ relationship properties do not exist (are not defined). In these cases, you have to define them manually, as in this example.

The better option (the preferred method) is to define relationship properties and use the dot notation to access them. This enables you to walk the relationship tree, navigating from one object to another easily, as the following example shows:

```
IQueryable<Employee> empQuery =
    from emp in db.Employee
    where emp.Contact.FirstName.StartsWith("Scott")
    select emp;
```

The benefits of using relationship properties include the capability to determine results of queries. For example, you can use the relationship to determine whether contacts have employee records.

Compiled Queries

If you are a developer who works with SQL as well as with .NET, you know that there are many occasions where you use the same query repeatedly. LINQ to SQL makes this easy to do by enabling you to create a compiled query—a query that is stored in a static variable and is available for execution whenever you need it.

Compiled queries are available via the CompiledQuery class of the System.Data.Linq namespace. This class has a Compile method that creates a new delegate representing the compiled query.

The following example defines a compiled query using a static class:

```
public class AdventureWorks : DataContext
{
    public AdventureWorks(string connection) : base(connection) {}
    public Table<Contact> Contact;
    public Table<Employee> Employee;

}
static class Queries
{
    public static Func<AdventureWorks, string, IQueryable<Contact>>
        ContactsByFirstName =
        CompiledQuery.Compile((AdventureWorks db, string firstname) =>
                                  from c in db.Contact
                                  where c.FirstName == firstname
                                  select c);

}
```

Now that the compiled query is defined, it can be used, as the following example shows:

```
AdventureWorks db = new AdventureWorks("Integrated Security=sspi");

IEnumerable<Contact> conQuery = Queries.ContactsByFirstName(db, "scott");

foreach (Contact con in conQuery)
{
    listBox1.Items.Add(con.FirstName + "  " + con.LastName);
}
```

The primary benefit of a compiled query is that the query doesn't need to be compiled each time it is executed. It is compiled once (the first time it is executed) and then can be used multiple times. Even if the parameters to the query changes, the query does not need recompiling.

Remote versus Local Query Execution

A query executed remotely is executed on the server; a query executed locally is executed against a local cache. By default, queries are executed remotely, but you can choose to have them executed locally. The following sections discuss remote and local query execution.

Remote Execution

Although it depends on the query, remote execution is usually your most logical choice. It allows you to take advantage of database engine benefits such as indexes. Executing queries remotely is also better if your database has a large number of rows. For example, you don't want to return all the contacts from the `Contacts` table if you only need a small set of them.

You have two things going for you: the `IQueryable` interface and the `EntitySet` class. The `EntitySet` class implements the `IQueryable` interface, and the `IQueryable` interface guarantees that queries can be executed remotely. Therefore, the following query will be executed remotely:

```
AdventureWorks db = new AdventureWorks("Integrated Security=sspi");

IEnumerable<Contact> conQuery =
    from con in db.Contact
    where con.FirstName == "Scott"
    orderby con.LastName
    select con;

foreach (Contact cont in conQuery)
    listBox1.Items.Add(cont.FirstName + "   " + cont.LastName);
```

One of the key benefits of remote execution is that you can take advantage of database table indexes, which you can't use when queries are executed locally. You also have the guarantee that needless data is not returned.

Local Execution

In those cases where local execution is necessary, you have another option. The `Load()` method of the `EntitySet` retrieves all the related entities into your local cache. In the following example, there is a relationship between the `Contact` class and `Employee` class through the `EntitySet`. Therefore, when the contacts are loaded, the corresponding employees are loaded as well.

```
AdventureWorks db = new AdventureWorks("Integrated Security=sspi");

Contact con = db.Contact.Single(x => x.ContactID == 1146);
con.Employee.Load();

foreach (Employee emp in con.Employee.Where(y => y.ManagerID == 210))
listBox1.Items.Add(emp.ContactID + "   " + con.FirstName);
```

Executing queries locally has two benefits. First, once the set of data is loaded locally, it can be queried as often as necessary without the need of going to the database again for each subsequent query. Second, the entire set can be serialized.

Deferred versus Immediate Data Loading

Earlier in the chapter you learned that when querying across relationships, only the objects you specifically ask for are returned, and related objects are retrieved later, when you specifically request that information. For example, the following code loads the necessary employee object, and then, based on the results of the query, sends the Contacts object off for execution. This is known as deferred data loading.

```
AdventureWorks db = new AdventureWorks("Integrated Security=sspi");

IQueryable<Employee> empQuery =
    from emp in db.Employees
    where emp.ManagerID == 21
    select emp;

foreach (Employee empObj in empQuery)
{
    if (empObj.ContactID > 1100)
    {
        GiveBigPhatRaise(empObj.Contacts);
    }
}
```

Immediate loading, on the other hand, retrieves both sets of data together. This is especially useful if you need access to both sets of data immediately. To illustrate this, the following example uses the SalesOrderHeader and SalesOrderDetail tables from the AdventureWorks database, and assumes that mappings to each table and the associated [Association] and EntitySet references have been defined.

The example queries the SalesOrderHeader table for all orders that were made by SalesPersonID 275, and returns one set. The first foreach loop loops through that result set, while the inner foreach loops through the corresponding order details, thus returning the second set of data. Remember that the results are not returned until the iteration over the query variable takes place. Therefore, as each foreach loop is iterated over, both sets of data are returned.

```
IQueryable<SalesOrderHeader> sohQuery =
    from soh in db.SalesOrdersHeader
    where soh.SalesPersonID == 275
    select soh;

foreach (SalesOrdersHeader sohObj in sohQuery)
{
    foreach (SalesOrdersDetail sodObj in sohObj.SalesOrdersHeader)
    {
        //Do something
    }
}
```

Obviously, there are latency hits when you return large amounts of data, so you will want to use immediate loading when you need access to both sets of data right out of the gate.

As you learned in Chapter 3, you can force immediate execution of a query that does not produce a singleton value by using the `ToList()` *or* `ToArray()` *methods.*

Remember query execution this way: deferred execution should be used to produce a sequence of values. Immediate execution is used to return a singleton value such a Count, or Average.

The following example counts the number of order items for a specific order where the unit price of the item is less than $200. Because the query is returning a singleton value, it is executed immediately.

```
Table<SalesOrderDetail> orderdetail = context.GetTable<SalesOrderDetail>();

var query =
    from od in orderdetail
    where od.SalesOrderID = 43662
    select od;

listBox1.Items.Add(query.Count(orderdetail => orderdetail.UnitPrice < 200));
```

DataShape Class

LINQ to SQL provides a way to return related objects at the same time as your parent object with the added benefit of returning only what you need. This is made possible by the `DataShape` class, which lets you define a subtype that can be returned at the same time as the main query. This class has a `LoadWith` method that lets you specify which sub-objects to return when a query is sent for execution.

Here's an example:

```
DataShape ds = new DataShape();
ds.LoadWith<SalesOrderHeader>(soh => soh.SalesOrderDetail);
db.Shape = ds;
```

This code uses `DataShape` to say, "also give me the SalesOrderDetail for the corresponding SalesOrder-Header." Once the `DataShape` is defined, it's handed off to the `Shape` property of the `DataContext` class, which sets the `DataShape` associated with the current `DataContext`. Remember, the `DataContext` handles the query execution and the data retrieval, so it needs to know the `DataShape` if there is one.

The query itself does not change, as shown here:

```
IQueryable<SalesOrderHeader> sohQuery =
    from soh in db.SalesOrdersHeader
    where soh.SalesPersonID == 275
    select soh;
```

All of this information is pretty slick, but LINQ to SQL takes it one step farther by letting you control deferred loading, which is discussed next.

Turning Off Deferred Loading

The `DataContext` class has a property that tells the framework not to delay the loading of one-to-many or one-to-one relationships. This property is called `DeferredLoadingEnabled` and is used as shown here:

```
AdventureWorks db = new AdventureWorks("Integrated Security=sspi");

db.DeferredLoadingEnabled = false;
```

Keep in mind that deferred loading is automatically turned off when object tracking (the ObjectTrackingEnabled property of the DataContext) is turned off. Object tracking is discussed later in this chapter.

You might consider using this property when you want to return only a portion of the query and do something with those results, such as sending the partial results to a web service.

Composite Keys

Occasionally, you need more than one attribute to uniquely identify an entity. That's where composite keys come in; they enable you to include multiple columns in a query when the operator accepts only a single argument. In those cases, your best bet is to create an anonymous type that represents the combination of the multiple columns you need to pass.

The LINQ group operator (GroupBy in Visual Basic), for instance, takes a single argument, but you can see in the following example that an anonymous type is created and used to pass in two columns instead of the one:

```
AdventureWorks db = new AdventureWorks("Integrated Security=sspi");

var conQuery =
    from con in db.Contacts
    where con.LastName.StartsWith("K")
    group con.FirstName by new { last = con.LastName, middle = con.MiddleName} ;

foreach (var grp in conQuery)
{
    listBox1.Items.Add(grp.Key);
    foreach (var listing in grp)
    {
        listBox1.Items.Add(listing);
    }
}
```

Very slick.

Read-Only Data

If you don't plan to modify the data, you can get a pretty good performance increase by telling the DataContext that you want the data returned as read-only, so this last section will discuss working with read-only data.

To get read-only data, set the ObjectTrackingEnabled property to false. ObjectTrackingEnabled tells the framework to track the original value. Setting it to false means that the framework doesn't need to track changes, which provides a performance increase.

The following example shows how to disable object tracking by setting the ObjectTrackingEnabled property to false.

```
AdventureWorks db = new AdventureWorks("Integrated Security=sspi");
db.ObjectTracking = false;

var conQuery =
    from con in db.Contacts
    where con.FirstName = "Scott"
    select con;
```

Several words of caution: If you set this property to false and then call `SubmitChanges`, an exception will be thrown because there are no changes to submit. An exception also will be thrown if you set this property to false after executing a query.

Summary

This chapter explored a few topics that are meant to enhance the performance and functionality of your LINQ to SQL queries. The most important topic was that of database relationships—how to define them, and then query across them.

The next topic covered was compiled queries, how they are created, and how they can be used in your application. Compiled queries can save a lot of processing overhead if used correctly, since multiple calls to the database do not need to be made.

You took a look at query execution location and how data is loaded, learning how to manage much of the performance of your application by controlling where the queries are executed and whether the query execution is done immediately or deferred.

Composite keys were discussed to help you overcome the problem of passing multiple arguments where only one argument is accepted. This comes in handy when dealing with more complex queries.

Returning data in read-only form also was discussed. If you don't plan to do any data modification, then you'll gain some performance increases by retrieving data read-only.

Chapter 13 tackles entity classes in detail.

13

More about Entity Classes

There's more that can be said about LINQ to SQL entity classes because they provide a lot more functionality than what you've explored so far in this book. LINQ to SQL is all about managing entities, or objects, during their lifetime of service. As you've already seen, one of the primary things about entities is that they provide a lot of functionality aimed at dealing with querying data and, just as importantly, maintaining the integrity of your data through relationships.

More significantly, though, the LINQ to SQL entities (objects) used when executing queries can be changed and manipulated as needed by the application during the lifetime of the query. The data associated with those entities also can be changed. Modifications are then ushered back to the server when the application is done with the objects.

There are a few key things to keep in mind:

- The objects used in executing queries can be reused until the application is done with the retrieved data.
- After the data changes are sent back to the server and the objects are no longer needed, the objects are reclaimed by the runtime.
- Although the object may no longer be in existence, any object that represents the same data can still be accessed.

The focus of this chapter, then, is on the lifetime of an entity and on the actions an entity can perform during its lifespan. The lifetime of an entity begins when the `DataContext` is notified of the entities existence and ends when the `DataContext` is either closed or notified of the reclaimed entity.

Therefore, this chapter discusses the following topics:

- How changes to the entity are tracked
- Submitting changes back to the database
- Making simultaneous changes
- Working with transactions

Tracking Entity Changes

As you know, LINQ to SQL works with objects defined within your object model. These objects can be used to perform various operations, such as inserts and updates to the underlying database. By default, LINQ to SQL keeps track of any changes made to these objects via the LINQ to SQL `DataContext`.

It's important to remember that the changes are not tracked on the database side. They are tracked on the client side, and no database resources are used while changes are tracked.

In Chapter 12 you saw that you could work with read-only results by setting the `ObjectTrackingEnabled` property of the `DataContext` to false. This property also enables you to track changes made to objects and to submit those changes to the underlying database.

Tracking changes is enabled by default, so changes made to objects within your object model are automatically tracked. When the application is ready to send the changes back to the database, a simple call to the `DataContext SubmitChanges()` method needs to take place. That method instructs LINQ to SQL to execute the appropriate SQL code to make the necessary changes to update the database.

For example, the following code creates a new contact object, saves it to the database, updates an existing contact object, and then saves the changes back to the database.

```
AdventureWorks db = new AdventureWorks("Integrated Security=sspi");

//Add a new contact
Contact con = new Contact();
con.Firstname = "Sammy";
con.MiddleName = "T";
con.LastName = "Hagar";
con.NameStyle = 0;
con.EmailPromotion = 1;
con.EmailAddress = "RedRocker@Adventure-works.com";
con.Title = "Mr.";
db.Contacts.Add(con);

db.SubmitChanges();

//Update an existing contact
Contact cont = db.Contacts.Single(c => c.ContactID == 1280);
cont.EmailAddress = "christiank@adventure-works.com";
cont.NameStyle = 0;
db.SubmitChanges();
```

Keep in mind that only those properties that have changed are ushered back to the database. For instance, if the `NameStyle` for Christian was already `0`, then that change won't be made in the database.

Submitting Entity Changes

Along with tracking changes, entity classes can be used to submit changes that have been made to the entity, such as adding, updating, or deleting records. Manipulating data is one of the key aspects of LINQ to SQL, and entity classes make those operations extremely easy. Changes can be made simply by manipulating the objects in your object model.

To see how this works, fire up Visual Studio, create a new Windows project, and add the appropriate references:

```
system.data.Linq
```

Next, view the code behind `Form1` and add the following statements:

```
using System.Data.Linq
using System.Data.Linq.Mapping
```

Prior to `Beta2`, attribute-based mapping was supported via the `System.Data.Linq` namespace. If you then installed `Beta2` and tried to compile your code, you received a lot of compile errors. That is because attribute-based mapping is now supported via the `System.Data.Linq.Mapping` namespace.

Next, underneath the partial class of `Form1`, add the following highlighted code:

```
namespace LINQ
{
    public partial class Form1 : Form
    {
        public Form1()
        {
            InitializeComponent();
        }

        private void Form1_Load(object sender, EventArgs e)
        {

        }
    }
}
```

```
public class AdventureWorks : DataContext
{
    public AdventureWorks(string connection) : base(connection) {}
    public Table<Contact> Contacts;
}

[Table(Name = "Person.Contact")]
public class Contact
{

    [Column(DbType = "int not null", IsPrimaryKey = true, IsDbGenerated = true)]
    public int ContactID;

    [Column(DbType = "nvarchar(8) not null")]
    public string Title;

    [Column(DbType = "nvarchar(50) not null")]
    public string FirstName;

    [Column(DbType = "nvarchar(50) not null")]
    public string MiddleName;
```

```
        [Column(DbType = "nvarchar(50) not null")]
        public string LastName;

        [Column(DbType = "nvarchar(50) not null")]
        public string EmailAddress;

        [Column(DbType = "int")]
        public int EmailPromotion;

        [Column(DbType = "bit")]
        public byte NameStyle;

        [Column(DbType = "varchar(40)")]
        public string PasswordHash;

        [Column(DbType = "varchar(40)")]
        public string PasswordSalt;

    }
```

The rest of this code should look familiar—you have seen it throughout the last few chapters. Attribute-based mapping is used to map a SQL Server database and table to a LINQ to SQL class.

For purposes of this example, create a small routine that will do a lot of the work for you. Add the following code after the `Load` event of Form1. The code will be explained shortly.

```
private void InsertNames(string firstName, string title, string emailAddr)
{
    AdventureWorks db = new AdventureWorks("Integrated Security=sspi");

    try
    {
        Contact con = new Contact();
        con.FirstName = firstname;
        con.LastName = "Klein";
        con.MiddleName = "L";
        con.NameStyle = 0;
        con.EmailPromotion = 1;
        con.EmailAddress = " emailAddr;
        con.PasswordHash = "asdf";
        con.PasswordSalt = "qwer";
        con.Title = title;

        db.Contacts.Add(con);
        db.SubmitChanges();


    }
    catch (Exception ex)
    {
        MessageBox.Show(ex.Message);
    }
}
```

In the InsertNames routine, a new instance of the Contact class is created, followed by the setting of several of the class's properties. Last, the object is inserted by calling the Add method on the object entity and then calling the SubmitChanges method of the DataContext class.

The SubmitChanges method determines the changed data such as newly added data, as in this case, or modifications to existing data, and then executes the correct commands to create and usher the changes back to the database.

The InsertNames routine allows new contacts to be created simply and efficiently.

You are now ready to start adding modification code. Open Form1 in design mode and add three buttons and a text box. Behind button1, add the following highlighted code (you can use other names and email addresses):

```
private void button1_Click(object sender, EventArgs e)
{
    this.InsertNames("Scott", "Mr.", "ScottKlein@SqlXml.com");
    this.InsertNames("Chris", "Mr.", "Chris@SomeCompany.com");
    this.InsertNames("Jason", "Mr.", "Jason@SomeCompany.com");
    this.InsertNames("Richard", "Mr.", "Dad@Home.com");
    this.InsertNames("Courtney", "Mrs.", "Sis@SomeCompany.com");
    this.InsertNames("Carolyn", "Mrs.", "Mom@Home.com");

    textBox1.Text = "Contact added successfully";
}
```

Run the Visual Studio project you created by pressing F5, and when the form displays, click button1. When the code behind button1 executes, it calls the InsertNames routine several times, passing a contact first name, a title, and an email address to the routine. The InsertNames routine then uses those values to insert the contacts.

When the code finishes executing, the text box on the form displays "Contact added successfully." At that point, you can query the Person.Contact table in the AdventureWorks database. The results should look like those shown in Figure 13-1.

Results | Messages

	ContactID	Title	FirstName	LastName	NameStyle	EmailAddress	EmailPromotion
1	19999	Mr.	Scott	Klein	0	ScottKlein@SqlXml.com	1
2	20000	Mr.	Chris	Klein	0	Chris@SomeCompany.com	1
3	20001	Mr.	Jason	Klein	0	Jason@SomeCompany.com	1
4	20002	Mr.	Richard	Klein	0	Dad@Home.com	1
5	20003	Mrs.	Courtney	Klein	0	Sis@SomeCompany.com	1
6	20004	Mrs.	Carolyn	Klein	0	Mom@Home.com	1

Figure 13-1

You can see how easy it is to perform Insert operations using LINQ to SQL and entity objects. Yet, you are just skimming the surface. What about modifying existing records and sending the changes back? Let's do an update example next. Behind button2 of your form, add the following code:

```
private void button2_Click(object sender, EventArgs e)
{
    AdventureWorks db = new AdventureWorks("Integrated Security=sspi");
```

```
        try
        {
            var conQuery =
                from con in db.Contacts
                where con.FirstName == "Scott"
                select con;

            // there are 15 Scott's in the table, so 15 changes should be made
            foreach (Contact cont in conQuery)
            {
                cont.MiddleName = "L";
                cont.NameStyle = 1;
            }
            db.SubmitChanges();

            textBox1.Text = "Contacts modified successfully";

        }
        catch (Exception ex)
        {
            MessageBox.Show(ex.Message);
        }

    }
```

Before you run this code, spend a few minutes looking at what it's doing. First, you have a standard LINQ query that is populating the entity class with all contacts whose first name is Scott. Each contact is then iterated over, changing the middle initial to "L".

Just like the previous example, the `SubmitChanges()` method is used to usher the changes to the object back to the database.

What about deleting? The great thing about LINQ and LINQ to SQL is that all these operations are extremely similar. To illustrate, add the following code behind `button3` of your form:

```
    private void button3_Click(object sender, EventArgs e)
    {

        AdventureWorks db = new AdventureWorks("Integrated Security=sspi");

        try
        {
            var conQuery =
                from con in db.Contacts
                where con.LastName == "Klein"
                select con;

            foreach (Contact cont in conQuery)
            {
                db.Contacts.Remove(cont);
            }
            db.SubmitChanges();
```

```
            textBox1.Text = "Contacts removed successfully";

        }
        catch (Exception ex)
        {
            MessageBox.Show(ex.Message);
        }
    }
```

Like the update example, this code utilizes a standard LINQ query that is populating the entity class with all contacts whose last name is "Klein" (essentialy all the names used in the Insert example above). As with the update example, each contact returned in the query is then iterated over, calling the `Remove` method on the object entity and then calling the `SubmitChanges` method of the `DataContext` class.

As you can see, manipulating data is easy, yet effective. LINQ to SQL offers a lot of flexibility for manipulating, and maintaining, data, and changes to data.

Concurrent Changes and Concurrency Conflicts

In LINQ to SQL, the `DataContext` has built-in support for optimistic concurrency. In optimistic concurrency mode, updates succeed only if the state of the database has not changed since you first retrieved the data. Conflicts to this state can occur in the LINQ to SQL object when both of the following are true:

- The application tries to write changes back to the database.
- The data you requested has been changed *in the database* since you requested the data.

For example, you request contact information for Bob. Your entity class is populated with Bob's information. While the data sits in your entity class within your application, you begin to change some of the information within the class, such as Bob's address. However, while you are making those changes, someone else has also changed Bob's data and saved it back to the database. Now when you try to save your changes to the database, you have a concurrency conflict.

How do you resolve this? You need to find out which members of the object are "in conflict" and then decide how you want to resolve those conflicts.

The information that follows will help you with those decisions.

UpdateCheck

The `UpdateCheck` property is a property of the `[Column]` attribute. It tells LINQ to SQL how to handle optimistic concurrency conflicts when conflicts are detected. Any members of a class that are attributed with this property are included in update checks to primarily help detect concurrency conflicts.

The `UpdateCheck` property is used as follows:

```
[Column(DbType = "nvarchar(50)", UpdateCheck = UpdateCheck.WhenChanged)]
public string LastName;
```

This property can take one of several values, which are described in the following table.

Value	Description
`Always`	Always use this member for detecting conflicts.
`Never`	Don't use this member to determine conflicts.
`WhenChanged`	Use this member to detect conflicts when the value of this member has been changed by the application.

The default value is `Always`.

There are several alternatives for resolving the conflicts. One key approach is to use the `UpdateCheck` property effectively. By revising the `UpdateCheck` options within your object model, you can quickly narrow down those specific members that are vital to the data. You don't want to place `UpdateCheck` on each member (column) because performance could be degraded. The solution is to place it on the more important members.

Another option is to use the `RefreshMode` enumeration in a `try/catch` block. This enumerator gives you great flexibility in deciding how you want to resolve conflicts. You also have the `ConflictMode` enumeration and the `ChangeConflictException` class. These three enumerations are discussed in the following sections.

ConflictMode

The `ConflictMode` enumeration can be used in conjunction with the `SubmitChanges` method of the `DataContext` class. This enumeration lets you specify how you want conflicts to be reported when they are detected. It has two values:

- `ContinueOnConflict`—All database updates are attempted; concurrency conflicts are collected and returned at the end of the change process.
- `FailOnFirstConflict`—Update attempts should immediately stop when the first concurrency conflict is found.

Using the `ConflictMode` enumeration is quite simple. The `SubmitChanges` method has an overload that accepts the enumeration as shown in this code fragment:

```
Db.SubmitChanges(ConflictMode.ContinueOnConflict);
```

The `ConflictMode` enumeration has the following member values:

- `FailOnFirstConflict`—Attempts to update the database should cease immediately when the first concurrency conflict is found.
- `ContinueOnConflict`—All updates to the database should be attempted. All concurrency conflicts are gathered and returned at the end of the update process.

The `ConflictMode` option is usually used in conjunction with the `RefreshMode` enumeration, which is discussed shortly.

ChangeConflictException

Any time a conflict occurs, a `ChangeConflictException` is thrown. This exception is thrown because an update to the database failed because the database values were updated since the client application last accessed them.

In its simplest form, the `ChangeConflictException` is used as follows:

```
catch (ChangeConflictException ex)
{
    Messagebox.Show(e.Message)
}
```

This class offers much of the same information as the normal `Exception` class, such as an exception message and source. But it also offers the capability to trap change conflict exceptions and, when used with the `RefreshMode` and `ConflictMode` enumerations, lets developers handle conflicts properly.

RefreshMode

The `RefreshMode` enumeration lets you define how your application should handle optimistic concurrency conflicts. The `DataContext` class has a `Refresh` method that refreshes the object state with the original data in the database. The enumeration tells `Refresh` what to do in case of a conflict.

`RefreshMode` has three values:

- `KeepChanges`—Tells `Refresh` to keep the current changed values in the object but updates the other values with the data from the database.
- `KeepCurrentValues`—Tells `Refresh` to replace the current object values with values from the database.
- `OverwriteCurrentValues`—Tells `Refresh` to override all of the current object values with the values from the database.

An example from earlier in the chapter illustrates the use of `RefreshMode` as well as the `ConflictMode` enumeration and `ChangeConflictException` class. The highlighted lines point out the pertinent code.

```
try
{
    var conQuery =
        from con in db.Contacts
        where con.FirstName == "Scott"
        select con;

    // there are 15 Scott's in the table, so 15 changes should be made
    foreach (Contact cont in conQuery)
    {
        cont.MiddleName = "L";
        cont.NameStyle = 1;
    }

    db.SubmitChanges(ConflictMode.ContinueOnConflict);

    textBox1.Text = "Contacts modified successfully";

}

catch (ChangeConflictException ex)
{
    foreach (ObjectChangeConflict oc in db.ChangeConflicts)
    {
        oc.Resolve(RefreshMode.KeepCurrentValues);
    }
}
```

You also have at your disposal the `MemberChangeConflict` class that, when used with the `ObjectChangeConflict` class, enables you to iterate through the individual conflict members (database value/columns that have been updated since the client application last accessed it).

```
foreach (ObjectChangeConflict oc in db.ChangeConflicts)
{
    foreach(MemberChangeConflict mc in oc.MemberConflicts)
    {
        //
    }
}
```

The `MemberChangeConflict` class gives you access to the original value, the current value, and the database. For example:

```
mc.CurrentValue;
mc.OriginalValue;
mc.DatabaseValue;
```

With this information, you have all the data you need to effectively decide how you want to handle conflicts.

Utilizing Transactions

LINQ to SQL supports three models of transactions:

- Explicit local
- Implicit
- Explicit distributable

The difference between these types of transactions is how the transactions are created (explicitly or implicitly) and what LINQ to SQL does with the call.

In an explicit local transaction, you are responsible for committing and rolling back the transaction. The connection of the transaction must match the connection used by the `DataContext`; otherwise, an exception is thrown. If the `Transaction` property of the `DataContext` class is set to an `IDbTransaction`, then `SubmitChanges` method, when called, will use that transaction for all database operations.

In an implicit transaction, LINQ to SQL looks for two things—if the operation call is within the scope of a transaction, and if the `Transaction` property of the `DataContext` class is set to a user-started local `IDbTransaction` transaction. When `SubmitChanges` is called, these two checks are performed. `SubmitChanges` uses the first one it finds. If neither is present, an explicit local transaction is started. In an implicit transaction, the database engine automatically starts a new transaction after the current transaction is committed or rolled back. The user has to either commit or rollback each transaction.

An explicit distributable transaction is one in which the `SubmitChanges` method looks to see if the operation call is within the scope of a transaction. If LINQ to SQL determines that a call is in the scope of a transaction, a new transaction is not created. As with an explicit transaction, the user is responsible for the creation, committing, and disposing of the transaction.

The following examples illustrate a couple of these transaction modes. In the first example, a specific transaction scope is created and several operation calls are executed within this scope. Because a transaction scope is used within a `using` statement, a specific commit or rollback is not necessary. In this example, a `TransactionScope` is created and several insert operations are performed and the `SubmitChanges` method is called. The `TransactionScope` class, part of the `System.Transactions` namespace, marks a block of code as transactional by implicitly enlisting connections within its transaction. As discussed earlier, an implicit transaction must be manually committed or rolled back by the user/-application.

The following example explicitly creates a transaction using the `TransactionScope` class to mark a block of code as included in a transaction:

```
AdventureWorks db = new AdventureWorks("Integrated Security=sspi");
try
{
    using (TransactionScope ts = new TransactionScope())
    {
        Contact con = new Contact();
        con.FirstName = "Scott";
```

```
                con.LastName = "Klein";
                con.MiddleName = "L";
                con.NameStyle = 0;
                con.EmailPromotion = 1;
                con.EmailAddress = "ScottKlein@SqlXml.com";
                con.PasswordHash = "asdf";
                con.PasswordSalt = "qwer";
                con.Title = "Geek";

                db.Contacts.Add(con);

                Contact con1 = new Contact();
                con1.FirstName = "Horacio";
                con1.LastName = "Hornblower";
                con1.MiddleName = "T";
                con1.NameStyle = 0;
                con1.EmailPromotion = 1;
                con1.EmailAddress = "Hornblower@sailingrus.com";
                con1.PasswordHash = "asdf";
                con1.PasswordSalt = "qwer";
                con1.Title = "Captain";

                db.Contacts.Add(con1);
                db.SubmitChanges();

                textBox1.Text = "Transaction Successful!";

                ts.Complete();
                ts.Dispose();
            }
        }
        catch (Exception ex)
        {
            MessageBox.Show(ex.Message);
        }
```

Next is an example of an explicit local transaction. Here, the specific transaction connection is created and controlled, as well as the need to specifically commit and/or roll back the transaction. Like the first example, the `SubmitChanges` method is called and executed within the same transaction scope:

```
db.Connection.Open();
db.Transaction = db.Connection.BeginTransaction();
Contact con = new Contact();
con.FirstName = "Scott";
con.LastName = "Klein";
con.MiddleName = "L";
con.NameStyle = 0;
con.EmailPromotion = 1;
con.EmailAddress = "ScottKlein@SqlXml.com";
con.PasswordHash = "asdf";
con.PasswordSalt = "qwer";
con.Title = "Geek";

db.Contacts.Add(con);
```

```
Contact con1 = new Contact();
con1.FirstName = "Horacio";
con1.LastName = "Hornblower";
con1.MiddleName = "T";
con1.NameStyle = 0;
con1.EmailPromotion = 1;
con1.EmailAddress = "Hornblower@sailingrus.com";
con1.PasswordHash = "asdf";
con1.PasswordSalt = "qwer";
con1.Title = "Captain";

db.Contacts.Add(con1);

db.SubmitChanges();

textBox1.Text = "Transaction Successful!";

db.Transaction.Commit();
db.Transaction.Dispose();
db.Connection.Close();
```

The `TransactionScope` class lets you ''bracket'' your submissions to the database. ''Bracketing'' means to make a block of code transactional. The `TransactionScope` class makes it easy to ''bracket.''

The recommendation for using transactions is to implicitly create transactions using the `TransactionScope` class. The benefit of implicitly creating them is that the encompassing transaction context is automatically managed. This is typically called an ambient transaction, and is defined as the transaction in which your code is currently executing.

What is cool about using the `TransactionScope` is that the transaction manager determines the type of transaction to use. The decision is based on two things: whether there is an existing transaction, and the value of the `TransactionScopeOption` parameter in the `TransactionScope` constructor.

The `TransactionScopeOption` is an enumeration that provides additional options for creating a transaction scope. It has the following member values:

- `Required`—A transaction is required. A current transaction is used if one already exists; otherwise, a new transaction is created. This is the default value.
- `RequiredNew`—A new transaction is always created.
- `Suppress`—The current transaction context is suppressed when creating the scope.

Once the `TransactionScope` picks a transaction type, it always uses that transaction.

Summary

Sometimes working with a new technology can be intimidating and overwhelming. This need not be the case with LINQ to SQL and entities. LINQ to SQL is flexible and powerful yet easy to use, as this chapter showed, even when dealing with more complex topics.

This chapter tackled transactions and concurrency conflicts. First, you saw how to track changes to the entity object. (Knowing the state of your object and tracking its changes will come in handy.) Then you explored inserting, updating, and deleting data via LINQ to SQL entities.

LINQ to SQL has great support for optimistic concurrency, and this chapter focused on several features that will help you detect and appropriately handle concurrency conflicts, such as the `ConflictMode` and `ChangeConflictExpeption`.

14

LINQ to DataSet

Most, if not all, .NET developers are familiar with the concept of a DataSet because it is one of the most used components of ADO.NET. In simple terms, DataSets are objects that contain internal data tables where data is temporarily stored and is available for use by your application. DataSets are, in essence, a local in-memory cache of data that is typically retrieved from a database. This cache lets you work in a disconnected mode, providing the capability to make changes to the data within the DataSet, track those changes, and save those changes back to the database when the application reconnects.

A DataSet is a representation of the tables and relationships found in the database, exposing a hierarchical object model made of all the objects such as tables, rows, columns, constraints, and relationships. Much of the functionality that populates the DataSet and saves the changes within the DataSet back to the database is found in ADO.NET.

The DataSet itself is extremely flexible and powerful. It provides the capability for applications to efficiently work with a subset of data found in a database and to manipulate the data as needed by the application, all while in a disconnected state, and then usher the changes back to the database.

Yet, with all that flexibility there has not been, up to this point, a means or method for querying data contained within a DataSet (there are a few methods on the DataTable class which will be discussed below). This is where LINQ and LINQ to DataSets come in. With the querying power of LINQ, LINQ to DataSets provides a full set of query capabilities for a developer to quickly and easily query the contents of a DataSet.

This chapter deals specifically with how to work with LINQ to DataSets, and covers the following topics:

- ❑ Loading data into a DataSet
- ❑ Querying DataSets with LINQ to DataSet
- ❑ Data binding
- ❑ Comparing rows in DataSets

Overview of LINQ to DataSet

Perhaps the only thing that ADO.NET DataSets lack when it comes to functionality is an adequate query capability. DataSets do everything else quite well, but from a query perspective, they are limited. Sure, they have the `Select`, `GetParentRow`, and `GetChildRows` methods, but these provide only basic querying features.

Microsoft recognized these shortcomings and has provided the capability to query the contents of a DataSet through LINQ to DataSet. LINQ to DataSet utilizes the query features of LINQ, letting you create queries in your programming language and eliminating the need to place query string literals in your code. In essence, you get all the features and benefits of LINQ combined with all the features and benefits of DataSets, such as IntelliSense, syntax checking, and static typing. For instance, how many times have you had to run and rerun your application to test your inline string query because your syntax was incorrect? With LINQ to DataSets, you know before your application ever runs whether your query will execute.

Initially, Microsoft was looking at several options to give developers to populate DataSets using LINQ to SQL. However, at the time of this writing, the only option available is to use the DataAdapter class. That is not to say that other methods won't be added later, but for now, the DataAdapter class is your only option.

LINQ to SQL also adds several specific extensions to the DataSet that enable you to access `DataRow` objects. Just as important, there are additional things you need to do to your Visual Studio project to enable LINQ to DataSet functionality.

The following section shows you how to create a LINQ to DataSet project in Visual Studio, and the rest of this chapter explains how to load data into a DataSet and then how to query that DataSet using LINQ to DataSet.

Creating a LINQ to DataSet Project

A LINQ to DataSet project is created the same way any other normal project is created. The difference is that you have to include a few additional references and `using` directives. Fire up Visual Studio 2008 and create a new C# Windows project. Make sure that you target.NET Framework version 3.5.

By default, Visual Studio should include all the necessary references you need to work with LINQ and LINQ to DataSet. But if you are upgrading an existing project from an earlier version of Visual Studio, or even a project created in an early beta of Visual Studio, you will need to manually add the necessary references.

At a minimum, a LINQ to DataSet project needs a reference to the `System.Core` namespace and the `System.Data.DataSetExtensions` namespace. These two namespaces are in addition to the standard `System.Data.Linq` and `System.Data` namespaces that you are used to having in your project. Figure 14-1 shows the necessary references needed to work with LINQ to DataSet.

Once you have the necessary references in place, you need to make sure that you have included the appropriate `using` directives:

```
using System;
using System.Data.Common;
using System.Data.SqlClient;
using System.Collections.Generic;
using System.ComponentModel;
using System.Data;
using System.Drawing;
using System.Data.Linq;
using System.Text;
using System.Windows.Forms;
```

Then you are ready to go.

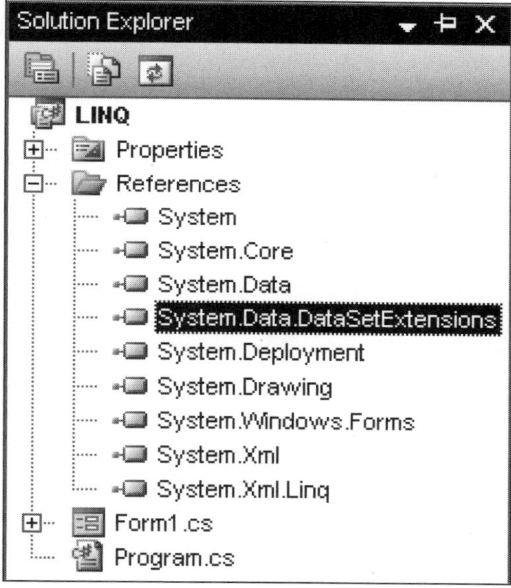

Figure 14-1

Loading Data into a DataSet

Before you can query a DataSet, it must be populated with data. The most popular way to do that is to use the `DataAdapter` class to retrieve the data from the database. This section shows via example how to populate a DataSet using the `DataAdapter` class so that it can later be queried with LINQ to DataSet.

Using the DataAdapter

If you have done any database development with .NET, you are intimately familiar with how to populate a DataSet using `SqlDataAdapter`. Here's an example:

```
try
{
    int salesPersonID = Convert.ToInt32(textBox1.Text);

    DataSet ds = new DataSet();

    string connectionInfo = "Data Source=avalonserver;Initial Catalog=AdventureWorks;
Integrated Security=true";

    SqlDataAdapter da = new SqlDataAdapter(
        "SELECT SalesOrderID, OrderDate, " +
    "SalesOrderNumber, SalesPersonID, ContactID, TotalDue " +
    "FROM sales.salesorderheader " +
    "WHERE SalesPersonID = @ID; " +

    "SELECT od.SalesOrderID, od.SalesOrderDetailID, od.OrderQty, " +
    "od.ProductID, od.UnitPrice, od.LineTotal " +
    "FROM sales.salesorderdetail od " +
    "INNER JOIN Sales.SalesOrderHeader oh ON od.SalesOrderID = oh.SalesOrderID " +
    "WHERE oh.SalesPersonID = @ID; ", connectionInfo);

    da.SelectCommand.Parameters.AddWithValue("@ID", salesPersonID);
    da.TableMappings.Add("Table", "SalesOrderHeader");
    da.TableMappings.Add("Table1", "SalesOrderDetail");

    da.Fill(ds);

    DataTable header = ds.Tables["SalesOrderHeader"];
    DataTable detail = ds.Tables["SalesOrderDetail"];
    DataRelation dr = new DataRelation("OrderHeaderDetail",
       header.Columns["SalesOrderID"],
       detail.Columns["SalesOrderID"], true);

    ds.Relations.Add(dr);

    textBox2.Text = ds.Tables[0].Rows.Count.ToString();
    textBox3.Text = ds.Tables[1].Rows.Count.ToString();

}
catch (Exception ex)
{
    MessageBox.Show(ex.Message);
}
```

First, you define a DataSet, followed by defining a connection to the database from which the data will be pulled to populate the DataSet. Then you define a data adapter using several T-SQL statements from which to query the database and populate the DataSet. Two data tables are defined and created within the data adapter to hold the returned data. Next, the data adapter is filled with the data requested from the two T-SQL statements. Last, a relationship is created between the two data tables.

At this point, the DataSet contains all the order header and order detail records that were requested. The data can now be queried, modified, updated, and sent back to the original database. The purpose of this example was to illustrate how to populate a DataSet using a `DataAdapter`. Now that the DataSet contains data, it can now be queried using LINQ to DataSet.

LINQ to DataSet Queries

Once DataSets are populated, they can be queried. That's where LINQ to DataSets comes in. Querying DataSets using LINQ to DataSet is not really that different from other LINQ queries you have worked with throughout this book. There are basically two options when writing LINQ to DataSet queries: use query expression syntax or method-based syntax. (Both query syntax and method syntax were discussed in Chapter 3.)

As a refresher, query expressions use declarative query syntax, enabling developers to write queries in "SQL-like" language. The benefit is that you can create complex queries with minimal code. The .NET CLR cannot read query expressions, so at compile time query expressions are translated to method calls, commonly known as standard query operators.

Method syntax, on the other hand, provides direct access to the LINQ operator methods using lambda expressions as parameters.

You can use either of these methods. The key to querying DataSets with LINQ to DataSet is that you are querying an enumeration of `DataRow` objects. This has many benefits, including the capability to use all of the `DataRow` class members in your LINQ queries.

Querying a Single Table

The following example uses a `DataAdapter` to populate a DataSet with sales order header information for a particular salesperson. A LINQ query expression is then defined and used to query the DataSet for all orders for the year 2003.

```
try
{
    int salesPersonID = Convert.ToInt32(textBox3.Text);

    DataSet ds = new DataSet();

    string connectionInfo = "Data Source=avalonserver;Initial Catalog=AdventureWorks;
Integrated Security=true";

    SqlDataAdapter da = new SqlDataAdapter(
        "SELECT SalesOrderID, OrderDate, " +
    "SalesOrderNumber, SalesPersonID, ContactID, TotalDue " +
    "FROM sales.salesorderheader " +
    "WHERE SalesPersonID = @ID; ", connectionInfo);

    da.SelectCommand.Parameters.AddWithValue("@ID", salesPersonID);
    da.TableMappings.Add("Table", "SalesOrderHeader");

    da.Fill(ds);

    DataTable header = ds.Tables["SalesOrderHeader"];

    textBox1.Text = ds.Tables[0].Rows.Count.ToString();

    var orderHeader = from oh in header.AsEnumerable()
```

```
                        where oh.Field<DateTime>("OrderDate").Year == 2003
                        select new {SalesOrderID = oh.Field<int>("SalesOrderID"),
                            SalesOrderNumber = oh.Field<string>("SalesOrderNumber"),
                            OrderDate = oh.Field<DateTime>("OrderDate"),
                            Total = oh.Field<decimal>("TotalDue")};

        foreach (var order in orderHeader)
        {
            listBox1.Items.Add(order.SalesOrderID + "   " +
                order.SalesOrderNumber + "   " +
                order.OrderDate + "   " +
                order.Total);
        }
    }
    catch (Exception ex)
    {
        MessageBox.Show(ex.Message);
    }
```

Notice in the query that the DataSet is not a typed DataSet because the `Field` method is used to access the column values of the `DataRow`.

Figure 14-2 shows the results of running this code.

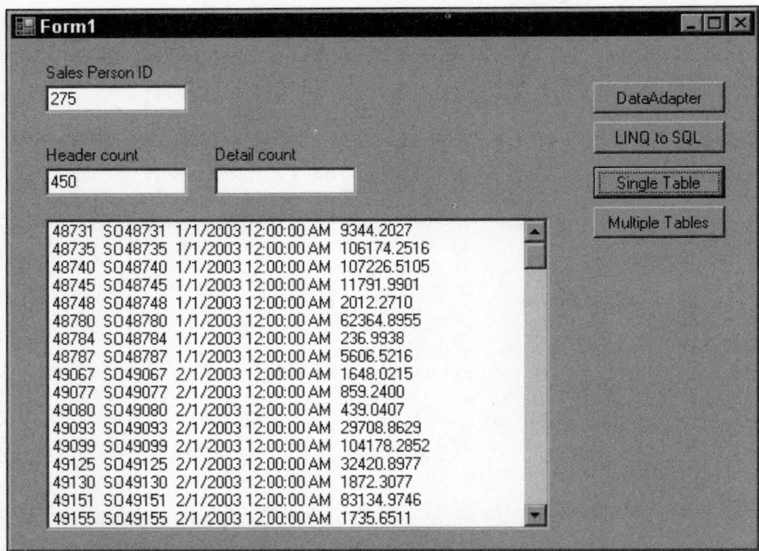

Figure 14-2

As you can see, querying a single table within a DataSet is quite simple, but what if there were multiple tables within the DataSet?

Querying across Multiple Tables

Cross-table queries in LINQ to DataSet is accomplished by using a join, an association of data source with a secondary data source in which the two data sources share a common attribute. LINQ makes object-oriented relationship navigation easy because each object has a property that references another object.

However, external tables (such as those in a DataSet) do not have built-in relationships, which makes relationship navigation difficult.

Luckily, the LINQ join operator can be used to link common attributes from each data source.

The following example illustrates how to query a DataSet that has multiple tables. A `DataAdapter` is created and used to populate a DataSet with sales order header information and corresponding sales order detail information for a particular `SalesPersonID` within the `SalesOrderHeader` table. A relationship is defined to link the two tables together within the DataSet.

A LINQ query expression is then defined and used to query the DataSet for all orders for the year 2003. The query uses two columns from the `SalesOrderDetail` table as well as four columns from the SalesOrderHeader table to display in the results.

```
try
{
    int salesPersonID = Convert.ToInt32(textBox3.Text);

    DataSet ds = new DataSet();

    string connectionInfo = "Data Source=avalonserver;Initial Catalog=AdventureWorks;
Integrated Security=true";

    SqlDataAdapter da = new SqlDataAdapter(
        "SELECT SalesOrderID, OrderDate, " +
    "SalesOrderNumber, SalesPersonID, ContactID, TotalDue " +
    "FROM sales.salesorderheader " +
    "WHERE SalesPersonID = @ID; " +

    "SELECT od.SalesOrderID, od.SalesOrderDetailID, od.OrderQty, " +
    "od.ProductID, od.UnitPrice, od.LineTotal " +
    "FROM sales.salesorderdetail od " +
    "INNER JOIN Sales.SalesOrderHeader oh ON od.SalesOrderID = oh.SalesOrderID " +
    "WHERE oh.SalesPersonID = @ID; ", connectionInfo);

    da.SelectCommand.Parameters.AddWithValue("@ID", salesPersonID);
    da.TableMappings.Add("Table", "SalesOrderHeader");
    da.TableMappings.Add("Table1", "SalesOrderDetail");

    da.Fill(ds);

    DataTable header = ds.Tables["SalesOrderHeader"];
    DataTable detail = ds.Tables["SalesOrderDetail"];
        DataRelation  dr  =  new  DataRelation("OrderHeaderDetail",  header.Columns
["SalesOrderID"], detail.Columns["SalesOrderID"], true);
```

```
        ds.Relations.Add(dr);

        textBox1.Text = ds.Tables[0].Rows.Count.ToString();
        textBox2.Text = ds.Tables[1].Rows.Count.ToString();

        var orderHeader = from oh in header.AsEnumerable()
                          join od in detail.AsEnumerable()
                          on oh.Field<int>("SalesOrderID")
                          equals od.Field<int>("SalesOrderID")
                          where oh.Field<DateTime>("OrderDate").Year == 2003
                          select new
                          {
                              SalesOrderID = oh.Field<int>("SalesOrderID"),
                              OrderQuantity = od.Field<Int16>("OrderQty"),
                              ProductID = od.Field<int>("ProductID"),
                              SalesOrderNumber = oh.Field<string>("SalesOrderNumber"),
                              OrderDate = oh.Field<DateTime>("OrderDate"),
                              Total = oh.Field<decimal>("TotalDue")
                          };

        foreach (var order in orderHeader)
        {
            listBox1.Items.Add(order.SalesOrderID + "   " +
                order.SalesOrderNumber + "   " +
                order.ProductID + "   " +
                order.OrderQuantity + "   " +
                order.OrderDate + "   " +
                order.Total);
        }

    }
    catch (Exception ex)
    {
        MessageBox.Show(ex.Message);
    }
```

Just as in the previous example, the DataSet is not a typed DataSet because the schema of the DataSet is not known at design time and the `Field` method is used to access the column values.

Figure 14-3 shows the results of running this code.
Instead of using untyped DataSets, the other option is to query a typed DataSet.

Typed DataSets

If you know the schema of the DataSet during the design of the application, it's best to use a typed DataSet. A typed DataSet is strongly typed, giving you can access to all the tables and columns by name instead using the `Field` method shown in the two preceding examples. A typed DataSet inherits from the `DataSet` class, providing access to all of the methods, properties, and events that a normal DataSet has.

Typed DataSets can be created by using the Data Source Configuration Wizard or the DataSet Designer. Both are in Visual Studio.

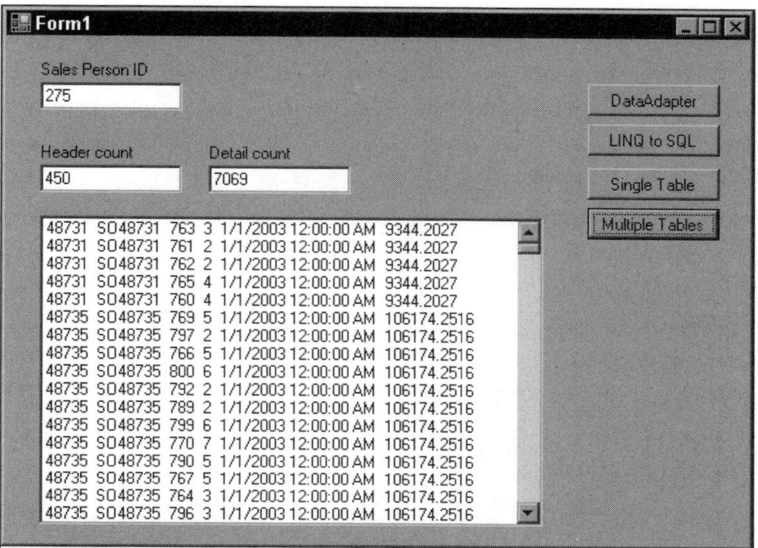

Figure 14-3

LINQ to DataSet supports the querying of typed DataSets, so you can access the table and column names by name. Just as important, columns are provided as the correct type, eliminating type mismatch errors. The following code is an example of querying a typed DataSet:

```
var orderHeader = from oh in header.AsEnumerable()
                  join od in detail.AsEnumerable()
                  on oh.SalesOrderID
                  equals od.SalesOrderID
                  where oh.OrderDate == 2003
                  select new
                  {
                      SalesOrderID = oh.SalesOrderID,
                      OrderQuantity = od.OrderQty,
                      ProductID = od.ProductID,
                      SalesOrderNumber = oh.SalesOrderNumber,
                      OrderDate = oh.OrderDate,
                      Total = oh.TotalDue
                  };
```

A typed DataSet can be queried just like any other DataSet using LINQ to DataSet.

Data Binding

Data binding is the act of creating a link or connection between the user interface and the data. It's been around for quite a while and is not specific to LINQ to DataSet. The concept behind data binding is that a user interface component can be *bound* to its corresponding field or column in the data layer such that when the user changes the value in the user interface, the change is automatically reflected in the data layer or database.

LINQ to SQL lets you bind data to many of the common controls such as combo boxes, grid controls, as well as a DataView. A DataView represents a customizable and bindable view of a DataTable, providing searching, sorting, editing, and filtering capabilities. Once the DataView is created, it can be bound to UI controls such as a DataGrid.

Keep in mind that a LINQ to DataSet query returns a `DataRow` enumeration, which is difficult to bind. The `CopyToDataTable` method is valuable in those instances. `CopyToDataTable` returns a `DataTable` that contains copies of the `DataRow` objects. The method is part of the `DataTableExtensions` class and takes an `IEnumerable(Of T)` object, where a parameter `T` is a generic `DataRow`.

The following example populates DataSet with data from the `SalesOrderHeader` table and then queries using a LINQ to DataSet query. The query returns an enumeration of `DataRow` objects that is used to populate a `DataTable` via the `CopyToDataTable` method. Once the `DataTable` is populated, a new `DataView` is created and populated with the `DataTable`. The `DataView` is then assigned to the `DataSource` property of a `DataGridView`.

```
try
{
    int salesPersonID = Convert.ToInt32(textBox3.Text);

    DataSet ds = new DataSet();

    string connectionInfo = "Data Source=avalonserver;Initial Catalog=AdventureWorks;
Integrated Security=true";

    SqlDataAdapter da = new SqlDataAdapter(
        "SELECT SalesOrderID, OrderDate, " +
    "SalesOrderNumber, SalesPersonID, ContactID, TotalDue " +
    "FROM sales.salesorderheader " +
    "WHERE SalesPersonID = @ID; ", connectionInfo);

    da.SelectCommand.Parameters.AddWithValue("@ID", salesPersonID);
    da.TableMappings.Add("Table", "SalesOrderHeader");

    da.Fill(ds);

    DataTable header = ds.Tables["SalesOrderHeader"];

    textBox1.Text = ds.Tables[0].Rows.Count.ToString();

    IEnumerable<DataRow> orderHeader =
                            from oh in header.AsEnumerable()
                            where oh.Field<DateTime>("OrderDate").Year == 2003
                            select oh;

    DataTable dt = orderHeader.CopyToDataTable<DataRow>();

    DataView dv = new DataView(dt);
    dataGridView1.DataSource = dv;

}
```

```
catch (Exception ex)
{
    MessageBox.Show(ex.Message);
}
```

You could just have easily set the `DataSource` of the `DataGridView` to the `DataTable`, as follows:

```
dataGridView1.DataSource = dt;
```

However, the `DataView` provides capabilities such as sorting and filtering the data stored in a `DataTable`. For example, you can filter the data by state of the row or via a filter expression.

You can also implicitly bind data to controls by implementing the IListSource interface. This interface provides an object the ability to return a list that is bindable to a data source.

For example, you can do the following:

```
var query =
    (from c in contact
     where c.FirstName.StartsWith("S")
     && c.LastName.StartsWith("K")
     orderby c.LastName
     select c);

dataGrid1.DataSource = query;
```

Likewise, you can bind data to a data source as follows (given the same query):

```
BindingSource bindsrc = new BindingSource();
bindsrc.DataSource = query;
dataGrid1.DataSource = bndsrc;
```

Implicit binding is available due to the fact that the Table<T> and DataQuery<T> classes have been updated to implement the IListSource interface.

Comparing DataRows

The last topic to be discussed in this chapter is the ability to use LINQ to DataSet to compare rows. As you learned in the early chapters of this book, LINQ provides several operators—`Distinct`, `Union`, `Intersect`, and `Except`—that provide comparison capabilities. These set operators compare source elements, checking for equality.

Elements can be compared for equality by calling the operators' `GetHashCode` and `Equals` methods. However, one of the things added to LINQ to DataSet is the `DataRowComparer` class. This class is used to compare two row values for equality using value-based comparison. It overcomes the need to do reference comparisons by executing value comparisons on the `DataRow` itself, enabling you to use this class against set operators.

Using the `DataRowComparer` class is preferable to using the `GetHashCode` and `Equals` methods because these operations perform reference comparisons, which is not ideal for set operations over tabular data.

One of the key things to remember about the `DataRowComparer` class is that it cannot be instantiated directly. The correct way to use this class is to use the `Default` property, which returns an instance of the class. You then use the `Equals` method to compare two `DataRow` objects. The two objects are used as parameters to the `Equals` method, which returns `true` if the two rows are equal, and `false` if they are not.

This type of comparison is illustrated in the following code. A DataSet is populated, and then two rows are identified for comparison. An instance of the `DataRowComparer` is then created, at which point the `Equals` method is called, passing the two rows as parameters for comparison. If the first row is the same as the second row, a message box displays a message indicating that they are equal; otherwise, a message box displays stating they are not equal.

```
try
{
    int salesPersonID = Convert.ToInt32(textBox3.Text);

    DataSet ds = new DataSet();

    string connectionInfo = "Data Source=avalonserver;Initial
        Catalog=AdventureWorks;Integrated Security=true";

    SqlDataAdapter da = new SqlDataAdapter(
        "SELECT SalesOrderID, OrderDate, " +
    "SalesOrderNumber, SalesPersonID, ContactID, TotalDue " +
    "FROM sales.salesorderheader " +
    "WHERE SalesPersonID = @ID; ", connectionInfo);

    da.SelectCommand.Parameters.AddWithValue("@ID", salesPersonID);
    da.TableMappings.Add("Table", "SalesOrderHeader");

    da.Fill(ds);

    DataTable header = ds.Tables["SalesOrderHeader"];

    DataRow first = (DataRow)header.Rows[0];
    DataRow second = (DataRow)header.Rows[1];

    IEqualityComparer<DataRow> comp = DataRowComparer.Default;

    bool isEqual = comp.Equals(first, second);
    if (isEqual)
        MessageBox.Show("they are equal");
    else
        MessageBox.Show("they are not equal");
}
catch (Exception ex)
{
    MessageBox.Show(ex.Message);
}
```

When you run this example, you get a message box stating that the rows are not equal. This is a simple example that compared the first row with the second row in the DataSet. This next example uses one of the set operators to determine equality.

```
try
{
    dataGridView1.Visible = false;
    listBox1.Visible = true;

    int salesPersonID = Convert.ToInt32(textBox3.Text);

    DataSet ds = new DataSet();

    string connectionInfo = "Data Source=avalonserver;Initial
        Catalog=AdventureWorks;Integrated Security=true";

    SqlDataAdapter da = new SqlDataAdapter(
        "SELECT SalesOrderID, OrderDate, " +
    "SalesOrderNumber, SalesPersonID, ContactID, TotalDue, CustomerID " +
    "FROM sales.salesorderheader " +
    "WHERE SalesPersonID = @ID; ", connectionInfo);

    da.SelectCommand.Parameters.AddWithValue("@ID", salesPersonID);
    da.TableMappings.Add("Table", "SalesOrderHeader");

    da.Fill(ds);

    DataTable header = ds.Tables["SalesOrderHeader"];

    IEnumerable<DataRow> query1 =
        from oh in header.AsEnumerable()
        where oh.Field<int>("SalesPersonID") == 288
        select oh;

    IEnumerable<DataRow> query2 =
        from oh2 in header.AsEnumerable()
        where oh2.Field<int>("CustomerID") == 555
        select oh2;

    DataTable dt1 = query1.CopyToDataTable();
    DataTable dt2 = query2.CopyToDataTable();

    var sales = dt1.AsEnumerable().Intersect(dt2.AsEnumerable(),
        DataRowComparer.Default);

    foreach (DataRow dr in sales)
    {
        listBox1.Items.Add(dr["SalesOrderID"] + "   " +
            dr["OrderDate"] + "   " + dr["SalesOrderNumber"] + "   " +
            dr["TotalDue"]);
    }

}
catch (Exception ex)
{
    MessageBox.Show(ex.Message);
}
```

In this example, the DataSet is filled with all records from the `SalesOrderHeader` table where the `SalesPersonID = 288`. From there, two tables are generated that contain a subset of that data. The first table contains those records from the DataSet whose `ContactID = 30`. The second table contains those records from the DataSet whose `CustomerID = 555`. The `Intersect` comparison operator is then used to return those records that are the same in each table. Those records are displayed in the list box.

When you run this example, the output should display three records, as shown Figure 14-4.

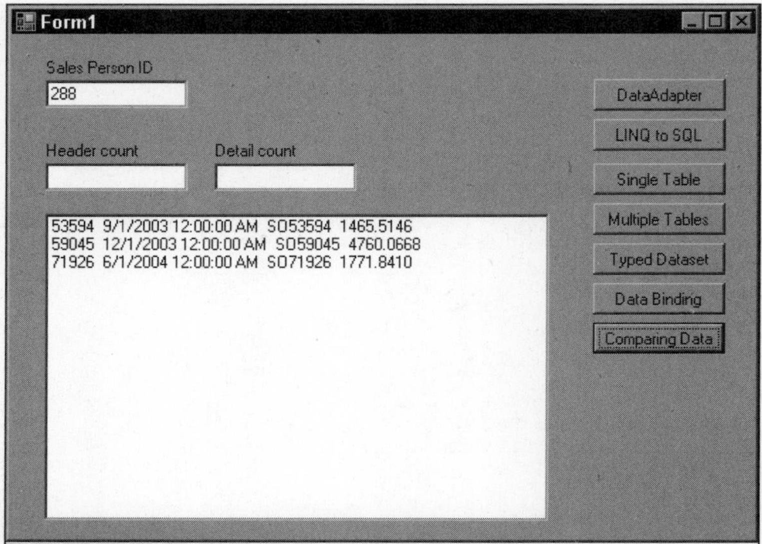

Figure 14-4

These comparison operators make it easy to compare elements and do set operations against data contained within DataSets. As you can see, working with DataSets with LINQ to DataSet is quite simple, whether you are comparing data, doing data binding, or just querying DataSets.

Summary

In ADO.NET programming, the DataSet is probably one of most commonly used components because of the functionality it provides when dealing with data caching and disconnected data manipulation. This chapter focused on the LINQ to DataSet features, the capability to query data cached in a DataSet object. These capabilities enable Visual Studio and developers to work more efficiently due to the benefits that the Visual Studio IDE provides, such as compile-time syntax checking, IntelliSense, and support for LINQ.

In this chapter, you got an overview of LINQ to DataSet and a look at the features and benefits that LINQ to DataSet provides. You also examined the steps necessary to create a LINQ to Dataset project in Visual Studio, and how to load data into a DataSet using the familiar `SqlDataAdapter` class as well as new approach using LINQ to SQL.

The heart of the chapter tackled querying DataSets, and you learned how LINQ to DataSet also supports data binding using DataSets. Finally, you saw how LINQ to DataSet supports the LINQ set operators to effectively compare source elements within a DataSet, whether they are in the same table or multiple tables within the DataSet.

So far, you've done everything in this book manually, such as create LINQ to SQL entity classes. The next chapter discusses several tools that make working with LINQ even simpler.

15

Advanced LINQ to SQL Topics

Visual Studio 2008 provides several tools to help facilitate the creation of entity classes and their mapping to relational objects in a database. These tools also help define the entity associations (database relationships) that the entity classes will use when working with two or more tables.

In essence, these tools help create an object model. The object model is defined within an application that will then be mapped to database objects. It is a fully functional object model, one that supports a mapping to stored procedures and user-defined functions as well as `DataContext` methods for data transport.

Equally important is the discussion of using LINQ to SQL in a multi-tier environment and other topics, such as external mapping with LINQ to SQL and entity classes.

Therefore, this chapter will discuss the following:

- Object Relational Designer
- SQL Metal tool
- External mapping
- Multi-tier operations

Object Relational Designer

The O/R Designer (Object Relational Designer) is a tool that provides the ability to create and manage LINQ to SQL entity classes, their associated relationships, and mappings through a graphical user interface. Through the O/R Designer you create an object model that maps entity classes within your application to objects within your database, such as tables and stored procedures. Instead of creating and defining these mappings by hand as you have done in previous chapters, the O/R Designer provides a graphical user interface in which you can accomplish these tasks.

Creating and Opening the O/R Designer

The Object Relational Designer is created by adding a specific file type to your Visual Studio project. Open Visual Studio, and create a new C# Windows project for .NET Framework 3.5. When the project is created, right-click on the project and select Add ➪ New Item from the context menu. In the Add New Item dialog, select the Data node under Categories, and then select the LINQ to SQL Classes under Templates, as shown in Figure 15-1.

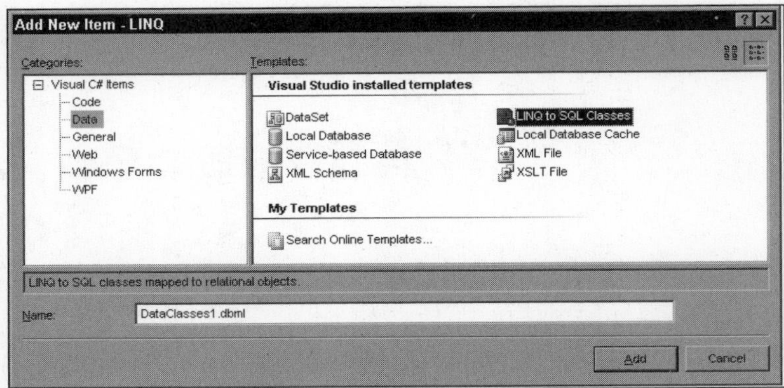

Figure 15-1

The LINQ to SQL classes are what define the `Data` (Entity) classes, such as the associations, mappings, and `DataContext` methods.

Provide a name for the LINQ to SQL class (this example uses the name `AdventureWorksSales.dbml`), and click the Add button. At this point, several files are added to the project:

- The `.dbml` file—The actual O/R Designer file.
- The `.layout` file—Contains the layout of the designer as you drag and drop objects onto it.
- The `.cs` file—Contains the designer code, such as the extensibility code definitions.

Figure 15-2 shows what the project should look like after the O/R Designer has been added to your project.

At this point the `DataContext` can be configured.

Creating/Configuring the DataContext

When you add the O/R Designer by adding the LINQ to SQL Classes item to your project, the designer opens in design mode automatically. Figure 15-3 shows what the O/R Designer looks like when it is first created. The O/R Designer design surface has two areas with which to work and design your data classes. The left pane is the Entities pane (or Entity Class pane), the main location where entity classes will be defined. The right pane is the Methods pane where `DataContext` methods are mapped to stored procedures and functions. The methods pane can be hidden; the entities pane cannot.

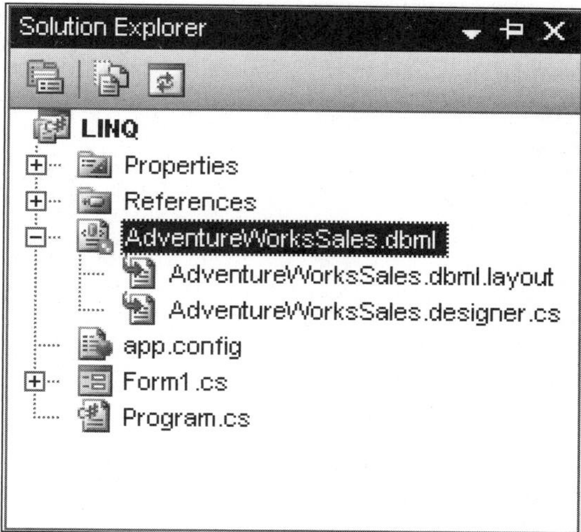

Figure 15-2

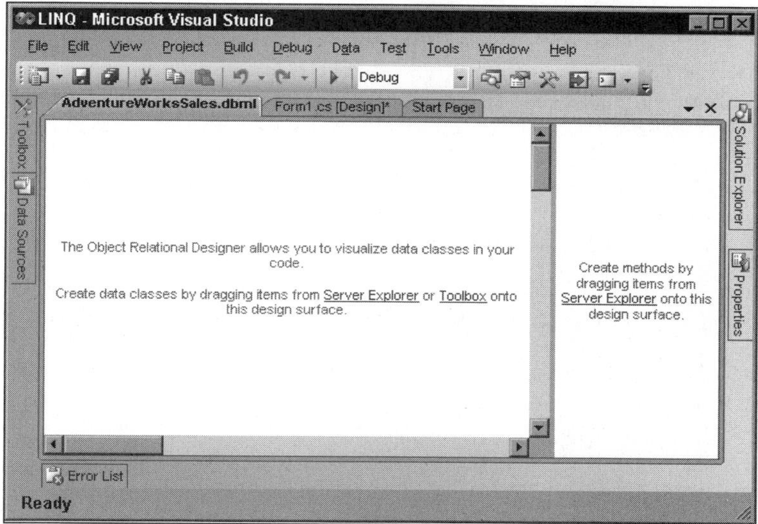

Figure 15-3

When the O/R Designer is first opened, it is empty of any objects, as Figure 15-3 shows. It represents an empty `DataContext` ready for configuration. Configuring the `DataContext` is as simple as dragging objects from the Server Explorer in Visual Studio to the Entities pane in the O/R Designer and setting the appropriate connection properties.

For example, the first time you drag a table from the Server Explorer to the Entities pane, you may receive a message (see Figure 15-4) asking if you want to save the connection information corresponding to this object and the Server Explorer Data Connection with the `DataContext` and the O/R Designer.

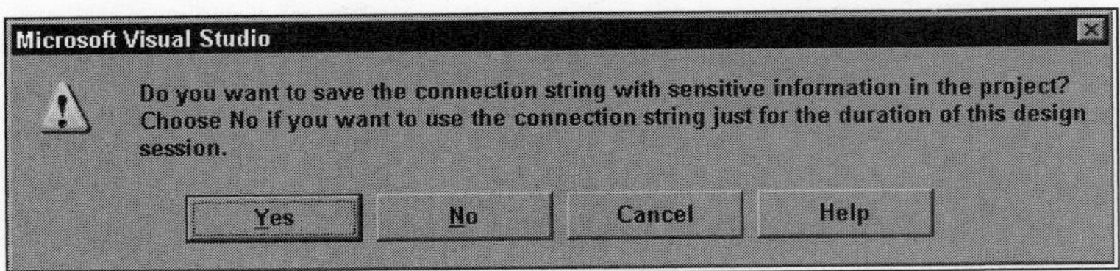

Figure 15-4

You get this message because the connection string used by select objects contains sensitive information. If you choose No, the connection string is stored as an application setting (except for the password) to be used only for the duration of the design session. Once the designer is closed, the connection information is no longer held.

Selecting Yes stores the connection string information as an application setting, such as the application configuration file. This is not secure because connection information is stored as plain text.

The connection information is obtained by making a connection in the Server Explorer window. From the View menu, select Server Explorer. In the Server Explorer window, you will see two nodes, one for Data Connections and one for Servers. Right-click the Data Connections node and select Add Connection. In the Add Connections dialog, enter the appropriate information to make a connection to your database server.

This connection information will be stored with the `DataContext` and O/R Designer. When you first drag an object from the Server Explorer onto the Entities pane, the information is used to provide the O/R Designer the necessary information that it needs to configure the `DataContext`.

The next section explains how to define entity classes that will be used to map to database tables and views, and you'll be dragging a table onto the designer to configure the `DataContext`.

Creating Entity Classes for Tables/View Mapping

When you drag a table from Server Explorer to the O/R Designer's Entities, you are creating an entity class that maps to a database table or view. Figure 15-5 shows what the O/R Designer looks like once you have dropped a table into that pane.

At this point you have created an entity class. The O/R Designer, behind the scenes, generates the appropriate classes and applies the appropriate LINQ to SQL attributes to those classes. This entity class now has all the appropriate properties that map the columns in the selected table. Also, the data connection information is provided to the designer and will be supplied to the `DataContext`.

These entity classes are updatable: They can save changes via the `SubmitChanges()` method of the `DataContext`.

Relationships between tables are also supported in the O/R Designer, and it is actually smart enough to pick them up automatically. For example, Figure 15-6 shows the defined relationship between the `SalesOrderHeader` and `SalesOrderDetail` when the `SalesOrderDetail` table is dropped onto the O/R Designer. Double-clicking the relationship line between the two tables opens the Association Editor dialog, which enables you to change the relationship (association) if necessary.

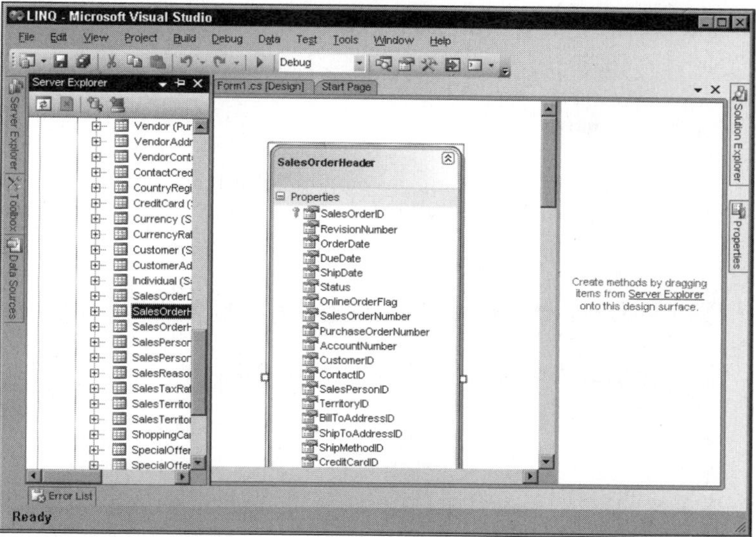

Figure 15-5

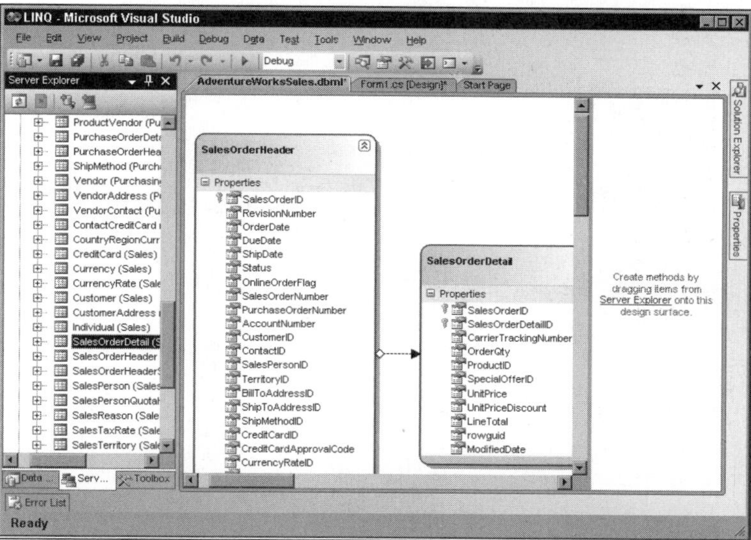

Figure 15-6

Keep in mind that the O/R Designer only reflects changes one way. That is, changes that you make via the designer are reflected in the code, but any code changes you make do not show up in the designer. This means that any code changes you make will be overwritten any time you make changes via the designer.

If you want to add code, read the section entitled "Extending O/R Designer-Generated Code" later in this chapter.

DataContext Mapping for Stored Procedures/Functions

`DataContext` methods are those methods of the `DataContext` class that run stored procedures and functions. In the context of the O/R Designer, the `DataContext` class is the LINQ to SQL class you just created; it acts as a channel between the database and the entity classes mapped to the database.

When a stored procedure or function is dragged from the Server Explorer and dropped onto the O/R Designer, it is displayed in the Methods pane, as shown in Figure 15-7. This pane lists all the `DataContext` methods you have created via the O/R Designer.

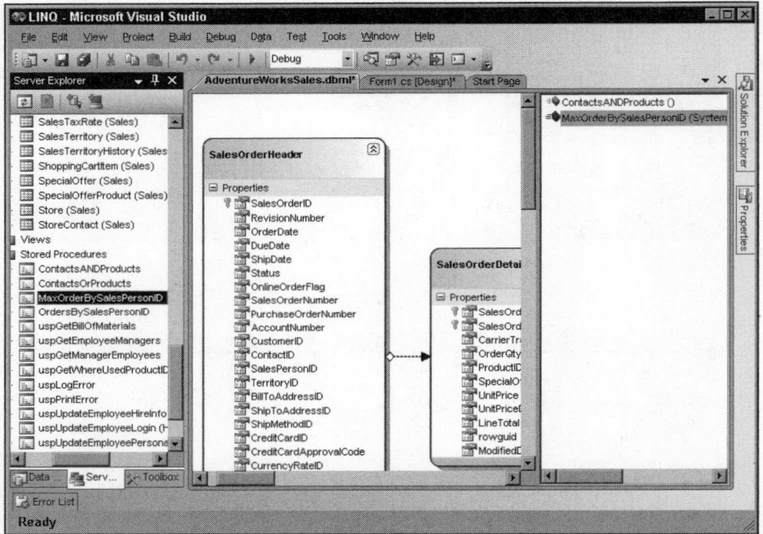

Figure 15-7

The return type of the generated `DataContext` method can depend on where you place the item in the O/R Designer:

- If you drop an item onto an existing entity class, the return type will be the type of that entity class for that `DataContext` method.
- If you drop an item onto an empty entity class or an empty area of the designer, the return type will be an auto-generated type for that `DataContext` method.

In other words, you can create `DataContext` methods that return auto-generated types by dragging a stored procedure onto an empty area of the O/R Designer. Likewise, you can create `DataContext` methods that return the type of the entity class by dropping a stored procedure on an existing entity class in the designer.

The return type of the `DataContext` method can be changed by opening the Properties window and changing the Return Type property for that method, as shown in Figure 15-8.

Once the `DataContext` method has been defined the method (stored procedure) can be called (which executes the stored procedure) passing the necessary parameters and return the data.

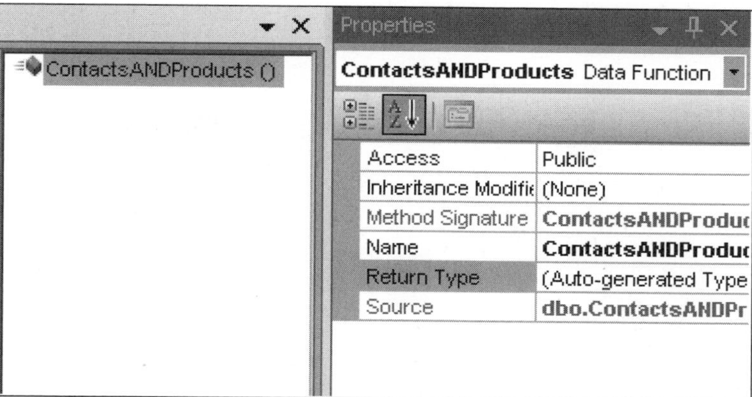

Figure 15-8

Calling Stored Procedures to Save Data Using Entity Classes

By default, the LINQ to SQL runtime handles the `INSERT`, `UPDATE`, and `DELETE` functions of an entity class. However, you can also use stored procedures to create `DataContext` methods to provide this functionality. These stored procedures can also be added to the O/R Designer as standard `DataContext` methods just like standard `SELECT` stored procedures.

Figure 15-9 shows the designer with the Properties page opened after clicking on the `SalesOrderHeader` entity in the entity class pane. Notice that the Properties page has `Delete`, `Insert`, and `Update` properties. The default value for these properties is `Use Runtime`.

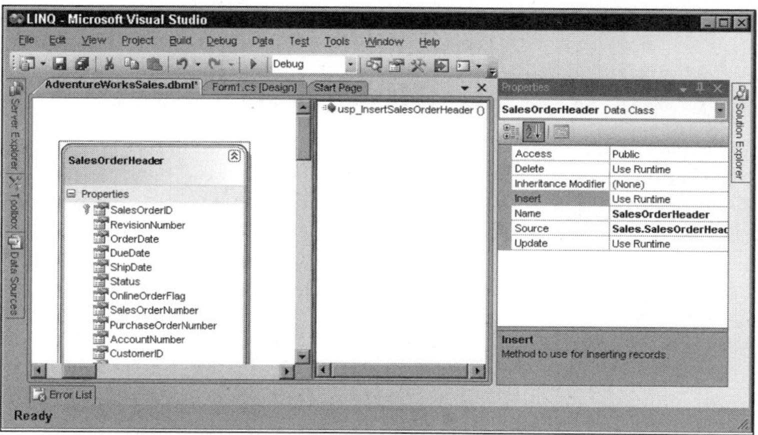

Figure 15-9

To change the default behavior and assign a stored procedure to perform the insert, update, or delete operation, drag and drop the stored procedure that performs the operation into the Methods pane on the designer. Next, click on the entity in the entity class pane of the designer, and on the Properties page, click the ellipsis button for the appropriate property (Delete, Insert, or Update) to the Configure Behavior dialog shown in Figure 15-10.

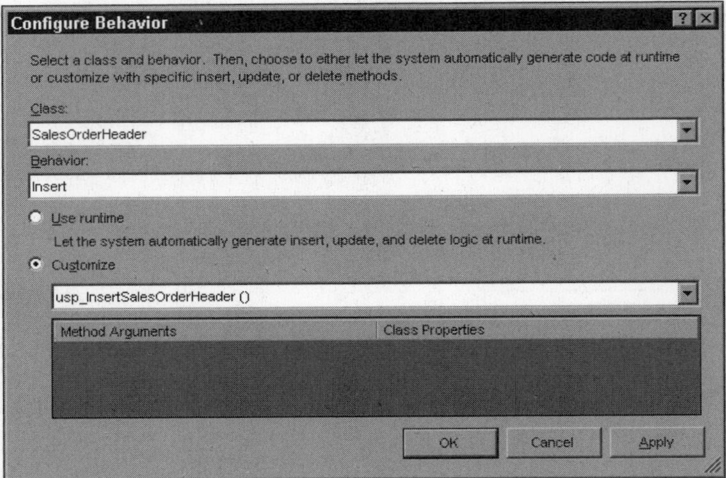

Figure 15-10

The Configure Behavior dialog enables you to override the default behavior by specifying the class in which to override the behavior, the type of behavior (Insert, Update, or Delete), and the method (stored procedure) to use to override the behavior. Select the Customize option to select the desired stored procedure (method), see the above figure. Once you have selected the appropriate information, click OK.

The Object Relational Designer currently supports a one-to-one (1:1) mapping relationship. It is a simple mapper, so complex mappings such as mapping an entity class to a joined table are not supported in this release.

Extending O/R Designer-Generated Code

LINQ to SQL realizes that there will always be a need for custom logic, so it provides a way to add validation logic to meet the demands of specific insert, update, and delete scenarios. The custom validation is provided by the capability to add a partial class, extending the `DataContext` class. The cool thing about this is that these custom methods are automatically called when the `SubmitChanges()` method is called.

When an entity is dropped onto the designer, partial classes are made available in which you can extend the validation logic. Figure 15-11 shows these partial class definitions within the `Extensibility Method Definitions` region.

You can easily add validation logic by implementing these classes. For example, to implement the custom Insert method, simply add the following code to the public partial class:

```
partial void InsertSalesOrderHeader(SalesOrderHeader instance)
{
    this.ExecuteDynamicInsert(instance);
}
```

```
using System.Reflection;
using System.Linq;
using System.Linq.Expressions;
using System.ComponentModel;
using System;


[System.Data.Linq.Mapping.DatabaseAttribute(Name="AdventureWorks")]
public partial class AdventureWorksSalesDataContext : System.Data.Linq.DataContext
{

    private static System.Data.Linq.Mapping.MappingSource mappingSource = new Attribu

    #region Extensibility Method Definitions
    partial void OnCreated();
    partial void InsertSalesOrderHeader(SalesOrderHeader instance);
    partial void UpdateSalesOrderHeader(SalesOrderHeader instance);
    partial void DeleteSalesOrderHeader(SalesOrderHeader instance);
    #endregion

    static AdventureWorksSalesDataContext()
    {
    }
```

Figure 15-11

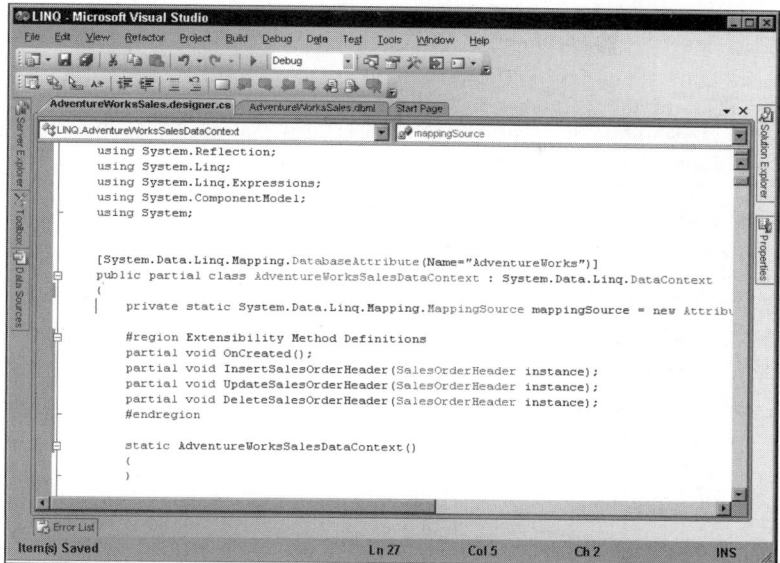

Notice that as you start typing, IntelliSense pops up and gives you the list of method definitions. Select the one you want and just add the appropriate custom validation logic to this method. Then add the appropriate call, such as the one shown in this example: `this.ExecuteDynamicInsert():`

As stated before, these methods are automatically called when you call the `SubmitChanges()` method on your `DataContext`.

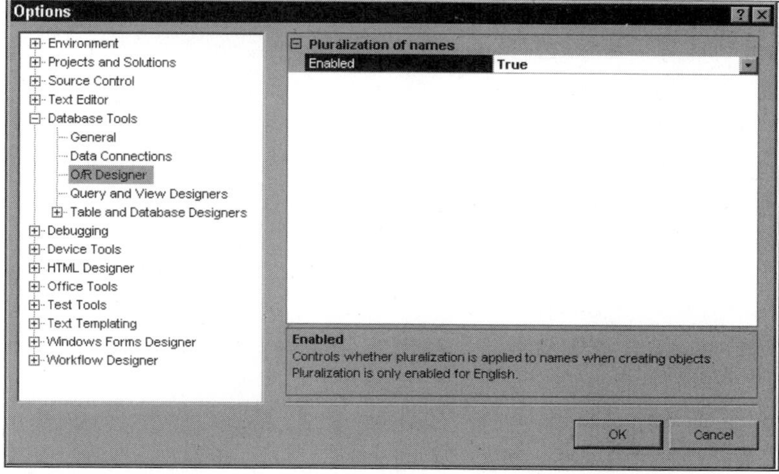

Figure 15-12

Pluralization of Classes in the O/R Designer

You might notice that as you drag-and-drop database objects onto the O/R Designer, the object names might change. This happens whenever your object name is a "plural," such as `Contacts`, `Employees`, or `Categories`. Any object name that ends in "s" or "ies" is automatically renamed from plural to singular. Thus, `Employees` becomes `Employee`, and `Categories` becomes `Category`.

The reasoning behind this is that it more accurately shows that the entity class maps to one record of data. That is, an `Employee` entity class contains data for a single employee.

However, object renaming can be turned off. To do so, in the Visual Studio EDI, select Tools ➪ Options to open the Options dialog. Expand the Database Tools node, and select the O/R Designer option, shown in Figure 15-12. Then set the `Enabled` property to `False` to turn off pluralization of names.

Pluralization is available only in the English-language version of Visual Studio.

SQL Metal

SQL Metal is a command-line tool that generates the LINQ to SQL mapping code and other components necessary for LINQ to SQL. It performs a myriad of different functions, including the following:

- Generates source code and mapping attributes (or mapping file) from a database.
- Generates a custom DBML file from a database.
- Generates source code and mapping attributes (or mapping file) from a DBML file.

Because it's a command-line tool, it is necessary to supply options (parameters) when executing it. The following table lists the available options when using the SqlMetal tool.

Option	Description
`/server:name`	Denotes the database server name.
`/database:name`	Denotes the database (catalog) name.
`/user:name`	Denotes the logon user ID. By default, this option uses Windows Authentication.
`/password:password`	Denotes the logon password.
`/timeout:timeout`	The time-out value when accessing the database.
`/views`	Extracts database views.
`/functions`	Extracts database functions.
`/sprocs`	Extracts database stored procedures.
`/dbml:file`	Returns output as DBML. Not available for use with the `/map` option.
`/code:file`	Returns output as source code.

Option	Description
`/map:file`	Generates an XML mapping file instead of attributes. Not available for use with the `/dbml` option.
`/language:language`	Denotes the source code language.
`/namespace:name`	Denotes the namespace of the generated code. Default value: no namespace.
`/context:type`	Denotes the name of the data context class. Default value: Taken from database name.
`/entitybase:type`	Denotes the base class of the entity class.
`/pluralize`	Pluralizes or singularizes the class and member names.
`/serialization:option`	Generates serializable classes.
`Inputfile`	Denotes a SQL Server Express `.mdf` file.
`/?`	Outputs the most current option list.

The `/language` option has two available languages—C# and VB. If no value is specified, the default value is taken from the extension on the code filename.

The `/serialization` option has the available values of `None` and `Unidirectional`. The default value is `None`.

Using the SqlMetal tool is a two-step process:

1. Extract the database metadata into a specified `.dbml` file.
2. Generate the output code file using the appropriate options specified in the preceding table.

Here are a few notes of interest before you look at some examples:

- When you generate the code you can select C#, Visual Basic, or an XML mapping file.
- If the `/server` option is not specified, the default value of `localhost/sqlexpress` is used.
- Extracting metadata from an MDF file requires that the name of the MDF file be included after all the other options.

The SqlMetal tool is located in the `\Program Files\Microsoft SDKs\Windows\v6.0A\bin` *directory.*

OK, now for some examples. Like the process outlined, the first step is to extract the metadata into a `.dbml` file. So, the following example creates a `.dbml` file that contains extracted SQL metadata from the AdventureWorks database, creating a file called `aw.dbml`. This is achieved by executing the following

```
sqlmetal /server:avalonserver /database:AdventureWorks /dbml:aw.dbml
```

Figure 15-13 shows how this is executed in a command window.

```
C:\WINDOWS\system32\cmd.exe
C:\Program Files\Microsoft SDKs\Windows\V6.0A\Bin>sqlmetal /server:avalonserver
/database:AdventureWorks /dbml:aw.dbml
Microsoft (R) Database Mapping Generator 2008 Beta 2 version 1.00.20706
for Microsoft (R) .NET Framework version 3.5
Copyright (C) Microsoft Corporation. All rights reserved.

C:\Program Files\Microsoft SDKs\Windows\V6.0A\Bin>_
```

Figure 15-13

After the command successfully executes, browse to the directory where the SqlMetal tool is located (\Program Files\Microsoft SDKs\Windows\v6.0A\bin), and you should see in the directory a filed called aw.dbml. You can also specify a location when generating the metadata, as illustrated in the following code:

```
sqlmetal /server:avalonserver /database:AdventureWorks /dbml:C:\wrox\aw.dbml
```

The next step is to generate the code, which is shown in Figure 15-14. This example specifies the language and the code file to generate.

```
sqlmetal /server:avalonserver /database:AdventureWorks /code:aw.cs /language:csharp
```

Figure 15-14 below shows how this is executed in a command window.

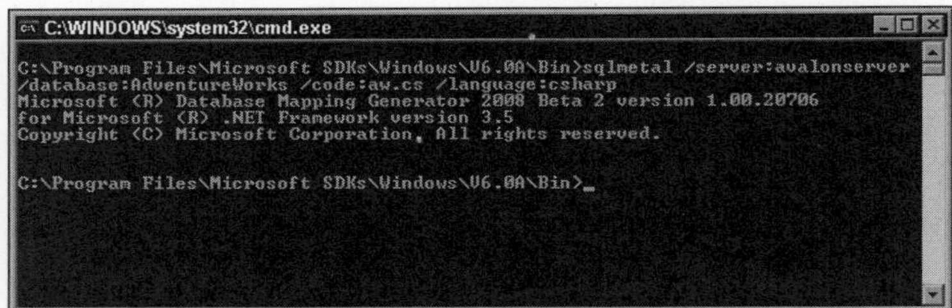

Figure 15-14

As with the previous example, after the command successfully executes, browse to the directory where the SqlMetal tool is located, and you should see in the directory a filed called aw.cs. You can also specify a location when generating the metadata, as shown here:

```
sqlmetal /server:avalonserver /database:AdventureWorks /code:@@ta
c:\wrox\aw.cs /language:csharp
```

Now that the two files are generated, you want to include them in the project. Right-click the project name, and select Add ➪ Existing Item from the context menu. Because no directories were specified for the generated files in the preceding examples, both files will be in the same directory as the SqlMetal.exe file, which is \Program Files\Microsoft SDKs\Windows\v6.0A\bin.

Browse to that directory, and add both the aw.cs file and the aw.dbml file. You'll notice that Visual Studio creates the same file structure that you saw when you added the LINQ to SQL class manually. Figure 15-15 shows this.

Figure 15-15

Now you are ready to go—you don't have to manually drag and drop tables onto the designer!

External Mapping

External mapping in LINQ to SQL is the act of utilizing an external file that contains the mapping information between the data model and your object model.

A mapping file is an XML file, but not just any XML file. It must be well formed and validated against the following schema definition (.xsd):

```
<?xml version="1.0" encoding="utf-16"?>
<xs:schema xmlns:xs="http://www.w3.org/2001/XMLSchema" @@ta
targetNamespace="http://schemas.microsoft.com/linqtosql/mapping/2007" @@ta
xmlns="http://schemas.microsoft.com/linqtosql/mapping/2007"
elementFormDefault="qualified" >
  <xs:element name="Database" type="Database" />
  <xs:complexType name="Database">
    <xs:sequence>
      <xs:element name="Table" type="Table" minOccurs="0" maxOccurs="unbounded" />
      <xs:element name="Function" type="Function" minOccurs="0" @@ta
maxOccurs="unbounded" />
    </xs:sequence>
    <xs:attribute name="Name" type="xs:string" use="optional" />
    <xs:attribute name="Provider" type="xs:string" use="optional" />
  </xs:complexType>
  <xs:complexType name="Table">
    <xs:sequence>
      <xs:element name="Type" type="Type" minOccurs="1" maxOccurs="1" />
    </xs:sequence>
```

```
    <xs:attribute name="Name" type="xs:string" use="optional" />
    <xs:attribute name="Member" type="xs:string" use="optional" />
  </xs:complexType>
  <xs:complexType name="Type">
    <xs:sequence>
      <xs:choice minOccurs="0" maxOccurs="unbounded">
        <xs:element name="Column" type="Column" minOccurs="0" @@ta
maxOccurs="unbounded" />
        <xs:element name="Association" type="Association" minOccurs="0" @@ta
maxOccurs="unbounded" />
      </xs:choice>
      <xs:element name="Type" type="Type" minOccurs="0" maxOccurs="unbounded" />
    </xs:sequence>
    <xs:attribute name="Name" type="xs:string" use="required" />
    <xs:attribute name="InheritanceCode" type="xs:string" use="optional" />
    <xs:attribute name="IsInheritanceDefault" type="xs:boolean" use="optional" />
  </xs:complexType>
  <xs:complexType name="Column">
    <xs:attribute name="Name" type="xs:string" use="optional" />
    <xs:attribute name="Member" type="xs:string" use="required" />
    <xs:attribute name="Storage" type="xs:string" use="optional" />
    <xs:attribute name="DbType" type="xs:string" use="optional" />
    <xs:attribute name="IsPrimaryKey" type="xs:boolean" use="optional" />
    <xs:attribute name="IsDbGenerated" type="xs:boolean" use="optional" />
    <xs:attribute name="CanBeNull" type="xs:boolean" use="optional" />
    <xs:attribute name="UpdateCheck" type="UpdateCheck" use="optional" />
    <xs:attribute name="IsDiscriminator" type="xs:boolean" use="optional" />
    <xs:attribute name="Expression" type="xs:string" use="optional" />
    <xs:attribute name="IsVersion" type="xs:boolean" use="optional" />
    <xs:attribute name="AutoSync" type="AutoSync" use="optional" />
  </xs:complexType>
  <xs:complexType name="Association">
    <xs:attribute name="Name" type="xs:string" use="optional" />
    <xs:attribute name="Member" type="xs:string" use="required" />
    <xs:attribute name="Storage" type="xs:string" use="optional" />
    <xs:attribute name="ThisKey" type="xs:string" use="optional" />
    <xs:attribute name="OtherKey" type="xs:string" use="optional" />
    <xs:attribute name="IsForeignKey" type="xs:boolean" use="optional" />
    <xs:attribute name="IsUnique" type="xs:boolean" use="optional" />
    <xs:attribute name="DeleteRule" type="xs:string" use="optional" />
    <xs:attribute name="DeleteOnNull" type="xs:boolean" use="optional" />
  </xs:complexType>
  <xs:complexType name="Function">
    <xs:sequence>
      <xs:element name="Parameter" type="Parameter" minOccurs="0" @@ta
maxOccurs="unbounded" />
      <xs:choice>
        <xs:element name="ElementType" type="Type" minOccurs="0" @@ta
maxOccurs="unbounded" />
        <xs:element name="Return" type="Return" minOccurs="0" maxOccurs="1" />
      </xs:choice>
    </xs:sequence>
    <xs:attribute name="Name" type="xs:string" use="optional" />
    <xs:attribute name="Method" type="xs:string" use="required" />
```

```
      <xs:attribute name="IsComposable" type="xs:boolean" use="optional" />
    </xs:complexType>
    <xs:complexType name="Parameter">
      <xs:attribute name="Name" type="xs:string" use="optional" />
      <xs:attribute name="Parameter" type="xs:string" use="required" />
      <xs:attribute name="DbType" type="xs:string" use="optional" />
      <xs:attribute name="Direction" type="ParameterDirection" use="optional" />
    </xs:complexType>
    <xs:complexType name="Return">
      <xs:attribute name="DbType" type="xs:string" use="optional" />
    </xs:complexType>
    <xs:simpleType name="UpdateCheck">
      <xs:restriction base="xs:string">
        <xs:enumeration value="Always" />
        <xs:enumeration value="Never" />
        <xs:enumeration value="WhenChanged" />
      </xs:restriction>
    </xs:simpleType>
    <xs:simpleType name="ParameterDirection">
      <xs:restriction base="xs:string">
        <xs:enumeration value="In" />
        <xs:enumeration value="Out" />
        <xs:enumeration value="InOut" />
      </xs:restriction>
    </xs:simpleType>
    <xs:simpleType name="AutoSync">
      <xs:restriction base="xs:string">
        <xs:enumeration value="Never" />
        <xs:enumeration value="OnInsert" />
        <xs:enumeration value="OnUpdate" />
        <xs:enumeration value="Always" />
        <xs:enumeration value="Default" />
      </xs:restriction>
    </xs:simpleType>
  </xs:schema>
```

Keep the following in mind when applying external mapping:

- External mapping overrides any attribute-based mapping.
- External mapping and attribute-based mapping cannot be combined.
- You can use external mapping with a specific database provider, something that you cannot do with attribute-based mapping.

So how, then, do you generate a mapping file? The previous section discussed a tool that can be used just for this. SqlMetal is perfect for generating an XML mapping file. To do this, simply execute the following command:

```
SqlMetal /server:servername /database:databasename /map:mappingfile.xml
```

Figure 15-16 shows the first part of the result of this command run against the AdventureWorks database.

When is using external mapping useful? Typically, it's useful when you want to separate the layers, such as separating the mapping code from the application code.

Figure 15-16

Multi-Tier Operations

All of the LINQ to SQL examples you have seen so far have used a single `DataContext`. This is fine for a small, two-tier application but for larger applications where an n-tier approach is desired, you may need a distinct `DataContext` instance for queries and data manipulation operations.

N-tier support in LINQ to SQL is accomplished via the `Attach` method of the `Table(of TEntity)` class. This feature lets entities span different `DataContexts`. Why would you need different `DataContexts`? In a two-tier application, the UI typically needs a subset of data within a table. However, in a multi-tier environment, the BL (business logic) layer generally requires a large set of the data and thus a more complex (populated) `DataContext`. The need, then, is to have the `DataContexts` span the different application tiers.

The `Attach` method makes this happen, letting entities cross tiers. Although they have this capability, they can still be tracked and identified with the original `DataContext` instance. Typically, the purpose of attaching an entity to a different `DataContext` is to manipulate the object.

When manipulating the objects, such as performing insert and update operations, you need to know how each is handled. When inserting, you need to use the `Add` method; the `Attach` method is not supported for insert operations. For update operations, the `Attach` method should be used. For delete operations, the `Attach` and `Remove` methods are available.

Here's how the `Attach` method works:

```
AdventureWorksSalesDataContext aw = new
AdventureWorksSalesDataContext();

Contact con = aw.Contacts.Single(c => c.ContactID == 483);

AdventureWorksSalesDataContext aw2 = new
AdventureWorksSalesDataContext();

Contact con2 = new Contact();
```

```
con2.ContactID = con.ContactID;
con2.Title = "Head Geek";

aw2.Contacts.Attach(con2, false);

con2.MiddleName = "Calvin";

aw2.SubmitChanges();
```

This example creates two `DataContexts`. A single `Contact` is queried using the first `DataContext`, and a new `Contact` is created with no association to either `DataContext`. Properties of the second `DataContext` are set, one of which is the `ContactID` taken from the `ContactID` of the first `DataContext`. The `Attach` method is used to attach the second `Contact` object to the second `DataContext`, and then the changes are submitted back to the database via the second `DataContext`.

The previous example showed you how you can change an object using a different `DataContext` instance.

When working in a multi-tier environment, the entire identity is not usually sent across tiers for a number of reasons, including performance, interoperability, and simplicity. For example, the client application might show only a small portion of data of a Contact entity. So, before using the `Attach` method and sending members between tiers, the member must meet one or more of the following criteria:

- The member must have the entity's identity.
- The member must participate in an optimistic concurrency check.
- The member must be modified.

N-Tier Best Practices

This section details some of the important things to keep in mind when using n-tier operations.

Optimistic Concurrency

In optimistic concurrency, rows are not locked when being read. When a user wants to update a row, the application must determine whether another user has changed the row since it was read. Optimistic concurrency improves performance because no locking of records is required, and locking records requires additional server resources. Also, a persistent connection to the database server is required to maintain record locks. Because that's not the case in an optimistic concurrency model, connections to the server are free to serve a larger number of clients in less time.

The following items should be considered when you're thinking about using optimistic concurrency:

- When using a timestamp or version number for a concurrency check, the corresponding member needs to be set before the call to the `Attach` method is made.
- The shape of the data exchanged between tiers is not specified by LINQ to SQL.
- All of the original values that are used for concurrency checks can be kept using a number of methods that are outside of the LINQ to SQL API scope, such as a view state in an ASP.NET application.

- Minimal updates are used for concurrency checks, meaning that any member that is not set or that is not flagged for optimistic concurrency is ignored.
- Any table that used a timestamp or a version number data type must have those columns set before calling the `Attach` method.

Insertion/Deletion

As explained earlier, the `Attach` method is not used for insert and delete operations. Instead, the `Add` and `Remove` methods should be used. However, it is your responsibility to handle foreign-key constraints in a two-tier update. That is, you must delete any child records before deleting the parent record.

N-Tier Examples

The `AttachAll` method enables you to attach many entities all at once instead of singularly using the `Attach` method. The following example illustrates the use of the `AttachAll` method to take all of the sales for one salesperson and, in one line of code, attach them to another salesperson.

First, open SQL Server Management Studio and query the `Sales.SalesOrderHeader` table to get a count of the number sales for `SalesPersonID` 284 by executing the following query:

```
Select * FROM Sales.SalesOrderHeader WHERE SalesPersonID = 284
```

You should see roughly 39 rows returned. The following code assigns all of the sales orders for salesperson 284, returned in the previous query, to salesperson 276. It queries the `SalesOrderHeader` table for all orders assigned to `salespersonid` 276. The `AttachAll` method is then used by a second instance of the `SalesOrderHeader` table to take ownership of them. Once ownership has been transferred, a simple loop needs to be performed to update the records to the new `SalesPersonID`.

```
AdventureWorksSalesDataContext db = new
AdventureWorksSalesDataContext();

var sohQuery =
    from soh in db.SalesOrderHeader
    where soh.SalesPersonID == 284
    select soh;

List<SalesOrderHeader> sohList = sohQuery.ToList();

Using (AdventureWorksSalesDataContext db2 = new
AdventureWorksSalesDataContext)
{
    db2.SalesOrderHeader.AttachAll(sohList, false);

    foreach (SalesOrderHeader soh2 in sohList)
    {
        soh2.SalesPersonID = 276;
    }
    db2.SubmitChanges();
}
```

Slick. OK, here's one more example. It shows how you can delete a `SalesOrderHeader` object. As stated earlier, the `Remove()` method should be used for delete operations.

```
Using (AdventureWorksSalesDataContext db = new
AdventureWorksSalesDataContext)
{
    SalesOrderHeader soh = new SalesOrderHeader() {
        CustomerID = 21768, ContactID = 13278} ;

    db.SalesOrderHeader.Attach(soh);

    db.SalesOrderHeader.Remove(soh);

    db.SubmitChanges();
}
```

When this code executes, it removes two rows from the `SalesOrderHeader` table. Now modify the `Remove()` statement so that it reads as follows:

```
db.Customer.Remove(soh);
```

When this code is executed, it will cause an error. Why? Because there is a foreign key constraint between the Customer table and the `SalesOrderHeader` table on the `CustomerID` column.

Designer Example

Hopefully, the Visual Studio project that you created earlier is still open. In this example, you use the O/R Designer to create a LINQ to SQL entity and bind that entity to a Windows form.

First, open the O/R Designer by double-clicking the `AdventureWorksSales.dbml` file in the Solution Explorer. Now, as you learned previously, you can create entity classes based on objects in the database. Open the Server Explorer and expand the connection to the AdventureWorks database you created earlier. Expand the Tables node and drag the Contact table into the entity pane.

Next, from the Data menu on the main menu bar, select Add New Data Source. That opens the Data Source Configuration Wizard dialog shown in Figure 15-17.

The wizard enables you to create entity classes as a data source. Entity classes can be used as object data sources, and as such can be added to the Data Sources window and placed on forms like any other Windows Forms controls. By placing an entity-based data source on a Windows form, you can create databound controls.

On the first page of the wizard, choose a data source type (specify where your data for the data source will come from). By default, Database is selected, but what you want to select is Object because the data will be coming from an entity object. So, select Object and click Next.

The next page asks you to select the object that you would like to bind to. Listed on this page are those objects in the current assembly. Your project is listed, and you need to expand that node to get to the information you want. Expand the LINQ node and select the Contact object (see Figure 15-18).

Notice that all of the objects here are objects within your project plus entities you have defined in the O/R Designer.

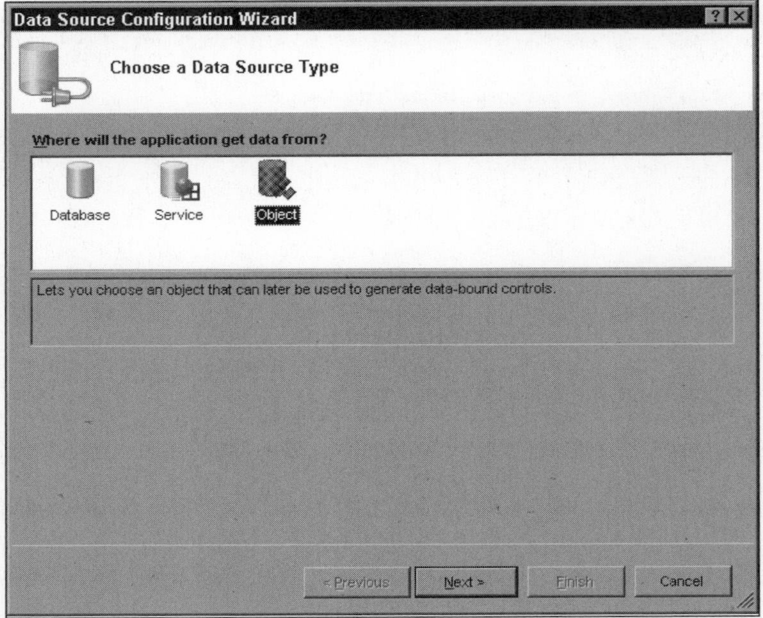

Figure 15-17

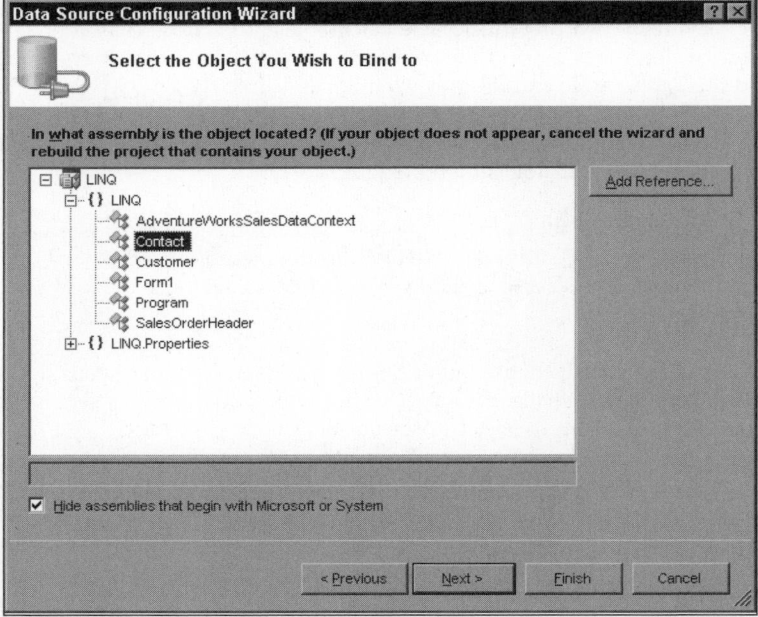

Figure 15-18

By default, the Hide Assemblies That Begin With Microsoft or System option at the bottom of the page is checked. If you uncheck this box, the list above it is repopulated with all assemblies that are referenced in your application.

Click Next.

The last step in the wizard is the summary page, which simply lists the objects that will be added to the data source. In this example, there's one object, Contact, as shown in Figure 15-19.

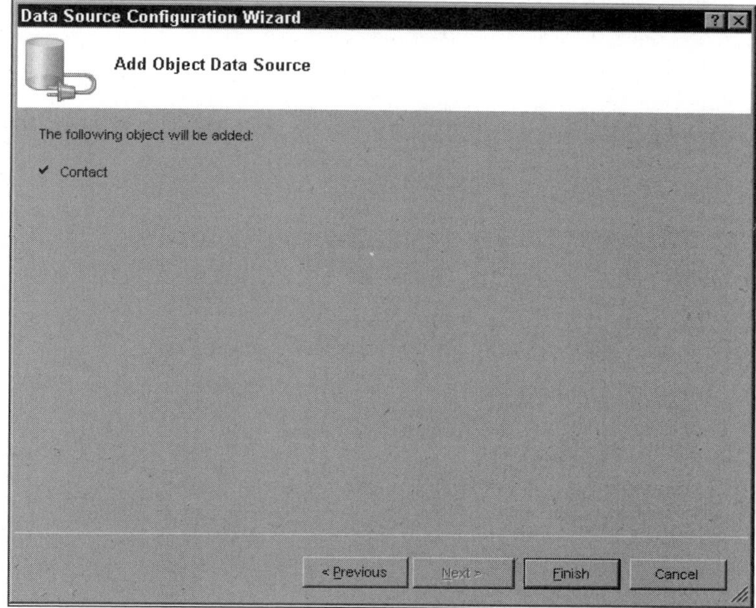

Figure 15-19

Click Finish. Your new data source is created. Open the Data Sources window (see Figure 15-20) to view the new data source.

Open `Form1` in design mode and from the Data Sources windows, drag the Contact node onto the form. Although you're dropping a single item on the form, you'll notice that two items are added to the form, as shown in Figure 15-21.

The control on the top of the form is a binding navigator control. The designer automatically names it `contactBindingNavigator`. It inherits from the Windows Forms `BindingNavigator` control that provides means for users to search and change data on a Windows Form, and it's composed of a tool strip that contains a number of common data-related objects such as buttons and record navigation objects.

A `BindingSource` component also was placed on the form. Typically, you will use a `BindingNavigator` component together with a `BindingSource` component to provide users with quick and easy navigation of data on a form. The `BindingSource` component encapsulates the data source for a form.

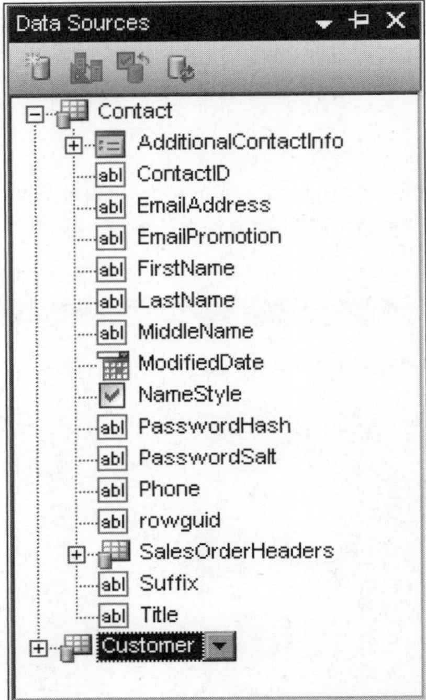

Figure 15-20

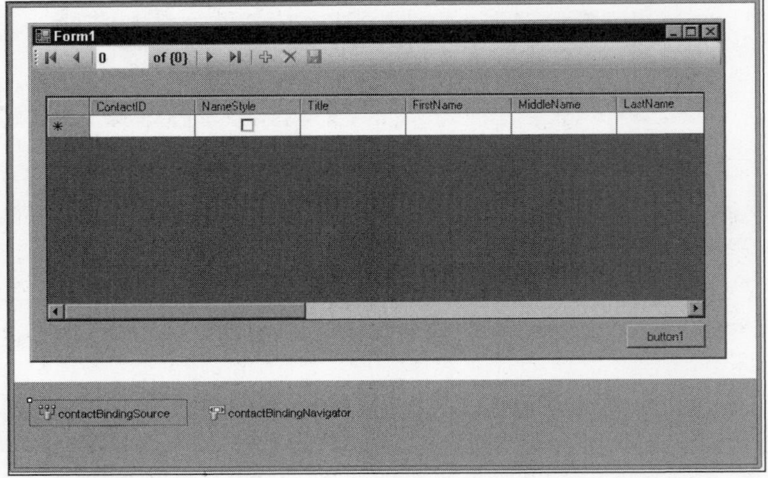

Figure 15-21

Select the `contactBindingSource` control and then open the Properties window (see Figure 15-22). You'll notice that the data source for this component comes from the data source defined previously.

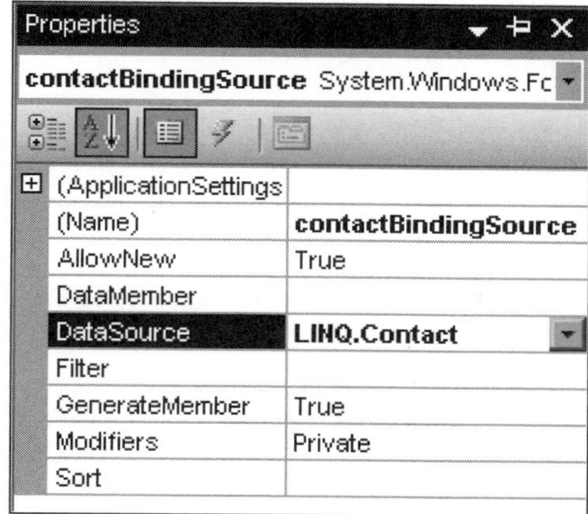

Figure 15-22

As the form sits right now, it is useless. The good news, however, is that it's easy to wire these controls. Right-click any gray area of the form, and select View Code from the context menu.

As with all of the other LINQ to SQL examples, you still need a `DataContext` reference, so after the partial class definition of `Form1`, add the following code:

```
private AdventureWorksSalesDataContext db = new
AdventureWorksSalesDataContext();
```

Next, in the `Form1 Load()` method, add the following code:

```
contactBindingSource.DataSource = db.Contacts
```

This code binds the data source of the BindingSource with the `Contacts` table, essentially providing the `LINQ.Contact` data source with the data it needs.

OK, time to test. Press F5 to compile and run the project. When the form loads, it will automatically load with data. You can use the navigation arrows on the navigator control (see Figure 15-23) to move between records, and you can also use the Add and Remove buttons to add new rows and delete existing rows.

If you delete or add a row, is it saved back to the database? No. Why? Remember that behind all of this is LINQ to SQL. You need to "submit changes" back to the database. Stop the project and select the Save button on the navigation control. Open the Properties window, and set the `Enabled` property for the Save button to `True`. Next, double-click the Save button to create a `Click()` event handler for the button.

Then, add the following code:

```
db.SubmitChanges();
```

Simple, isn't it? Now run the project again, and add and delete data. To verify that data is truly added and deleted, open a new query window in SQL Server Management Studio and execute the following T-SQL statement:

```
SELECT * FROM Person.Contact WHERE ContactID > 19990
```

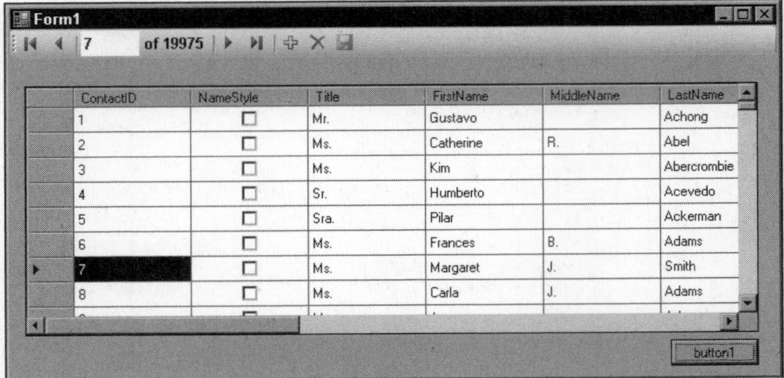

Figure 15-23

Awesome. But wait, it gets better. Stop the project and modify the code in the `Load()` method of the form, so that it looks like the following:

```
private void Form1_Load(object sender, EventArgs e)
{
    var conQuery =
        from con in db.Contacts
        select con;

    contactBindingSource.BindingSource = conQuery;
}
```

This illustrates that you can also bind a `BindingSource` directly to a LINQ to SQL query.

Summary

This chapter explored the Visual Studio O/R Designer and the associated SqlMetal utility. Each of these provide a great service in that you can quickly and easily create and manage LINQ to SQL classes, their associated relationships, and mappings. The purpose of doing things manually to begin with was to help lay the foundation and show how things are created, so that when an entity is created, you know what is going on behind the scenes.

This chapter also discussed external mappings with your object model. As stated earlier, external mapping provides the benefit of being able to separate the mapping code from the application code.

Last, the topic of building n-tier applications was discussed as used with LINQ to SQL. The key to using LINQ to SQL in an n-tier environment is utilizing multiple `DataContext` instances and taking advantage of the `Attach` method to efficiently span between the different `DataContexts`.

Appendixes

Appendix A: Case Study

Appendix B: LINQ to Entities: The ADO.NET Entity Framework

Appendix C: C LINQ to XSD

Case Study

Several years ago, Microsoft put out a demo application called Fabrikam (for the fictional company Fabrikam Fine Furniture) that was used quite heavily. It was a reference application for developers of Mobile PC applications and solutions, but it also had a server piece that tracked products and orders.

Well, it's time to dust off that old application and upgrade it to work with LINQ. If you have ever used Fabrikam, you know it is quite large because it deals with mobile components, SQL replication, and other technology components. This case study won't upgrade all of the application but will redo a portion that deals with Fabrikam's fine products, such as tracking (adding, updating, and deleting) products—enough to show you what you can do with a great new technology and a new or existing application.

The original Fabrikam application and code was downloaded from the Microsoft web site and was supplied "as is." Any modifications have been made by the author, and Microsoft holds no guarantees/warranties or support for this case study or sample, implied or explicit.

The first thing to do is to build the database. The script (`Fabrikam.sql`) to build the database is available as part of the download for this book. (I thought about including the text here, but once I saw it was 25 pages, I changed my mind. It'll be much easier for you to simply use the download file.)

So, run `Fabrikam.sql` in SQL Server Management Studio. This script creates the database, all the necessary objects, and the data for this case study, so no extra work is needed. The following objects are created.

Object Type	Name
Table	Countries
Table	Customers
Table	Deliveries
Table	DeliveryDetails
Table	Employees
Table	Manufacturers
Table	OrderDetails
Table	Orders
Table	Products
Table	ProductTypes
Table	States
Stored Procedure	GetActiveCustomers
Stored Procedure	GetActiveDeliveries
Stored Procedure	GetActiveEmployees
Stored Procedure	GetActiveOrders
Stored Procedure	GetActiveProducts
View	vLoadMfrs
View	vProducts
View	vStates

Once the script finishes, you're ready to build the Fabrikam demo. Let's get started.

Open Visual Studio 2008 and create a new C# project; name it Fabrikam. When the project is created, ensure that the necessary LINQ references are included in your project:

```
System.Data.DataSetExtensions
System.Data.Linq
System.Xml
System.Xml.Linq
```

Then you have to add an application configuration file. In Solution Explorer, right-click on the solution and select Add ➪ New Item from the context menu. In the Add New Item dialog, select Application Configuration File. Make sure the name is `App.Config` and click OK.

Next, right-click on the solution and select Properties. In the Fabrikam solution Properties window, select the Settings tab along the left side of the window. Here you need to add a property for the Fabrikam application to use. Enter the information in the following table.

Setting	Value
Name	`BusinessName`
Type	`string`
Scope	`Application`
Value	`Fabrikam Fine Furniture`

Figure A-1 shows what the Settings page should look like.

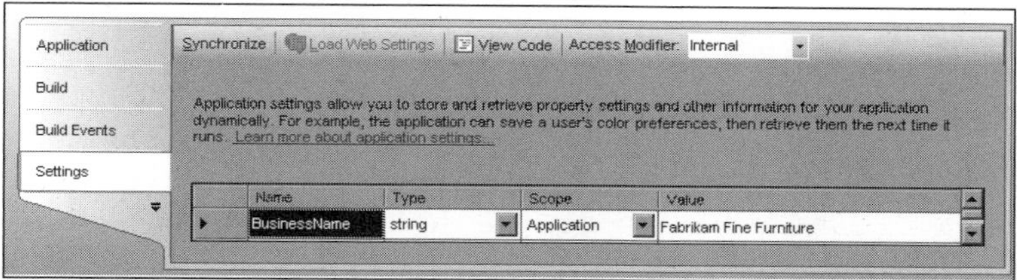

Figure A-1

This information will be stored in the application configuration file and you can change it to any value you want at a later date. Save your changes to the Properties by using the Ctrl+S key combination or by selecting Save from the File menu, and then close this window.

Now you create the mappings to the database objects (`DataContext` and associated entities), and the best way to do that is use the built-in LINQ templates. In Solution Explorer, right-click on the solution and select Add ➪ New Item from the context menu. In the Add New Item dialog, select the Data node under Categories. The Templates section of the Add New Item dialog will display all available Data templates. In the Templates section, select LINQ to SQL Classes and name it Fabrikam. Click Add.

The Fabrikam Dataset Designer opens and displays an empty designer. It's time to add the server objects. In the Server Explorer window, right-click on the DataConnections node and select Add Connection. The Add Connection dialog displays. Enter the appropriate connection information to connect to your instance of SQL Server and the Fabrikam database. Click the Test Connection button to ensure that the connection information has been entered correctly and that Visual Studio can successfully connect to the Fabrikam database. If the connection test is successful, click OK.

Expand the new connection node in Server Explorer, and then expand the Tables and Stored Procedures nodes for the Fabrikam connection. Now drag and drop all the tables into the Entities pane of the O/R Designer. Next, drag all the stored procedures into the Methods pane of the O/R designer. Figure A-2 shows what the O/R Designer should look like when you're done.

Once you have added all of the objects, save the designer. As you know, the `DataContext` object and all mappings have now been created and you can now start writing code to access these entities.

When you dropped the first object onto the O/R Designer, it asked you whether you wanted to store the connection information. If you selected Yes, go back to the `App.Config` file and look at the information

LINQ added. There is a new <connectionStrings> section in which the connection to the Fabrikam database is stored. Pretty nifty.

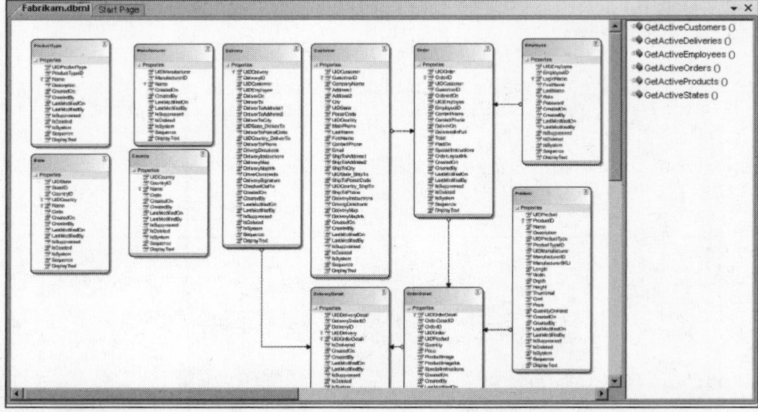

Figure A-2

You are now ready to start designing the UI. The first step is to create the main application form. `Form1` is already added to the project, so use that as the main form. On `Form1`, add the following (those blank cells in the tables throughout this appendix are blank on purpose, because those objects on the form do not require the object name to be changed or the `Text` values set).

Object Type	Name	Text
`Panel`		
`Panel`		
`Button`	`cmdOrders`	Orders
`Button`	`cmdCustomers`	Customers
`Button`	`cmdSynchronize`	Synchronize
`Button`	`cmdDeliveries`	Deliveries
`Button`	`cmdProducts`	Products
`Label`		Manage orders
`Label`		Manage customers
`Label`		Merge local DB w/Central DB
`Label`		Manage Deliveries
`Label`		Manage product catalog entries

You can place those objects anywhere on the form, but it should look something like Figure A-3. (Yeah, I added a pretty picture but it is not necessary.)

The next step is to add the login form. Add a new form to the project and call it `LoginForm`. Add the following objects to it.

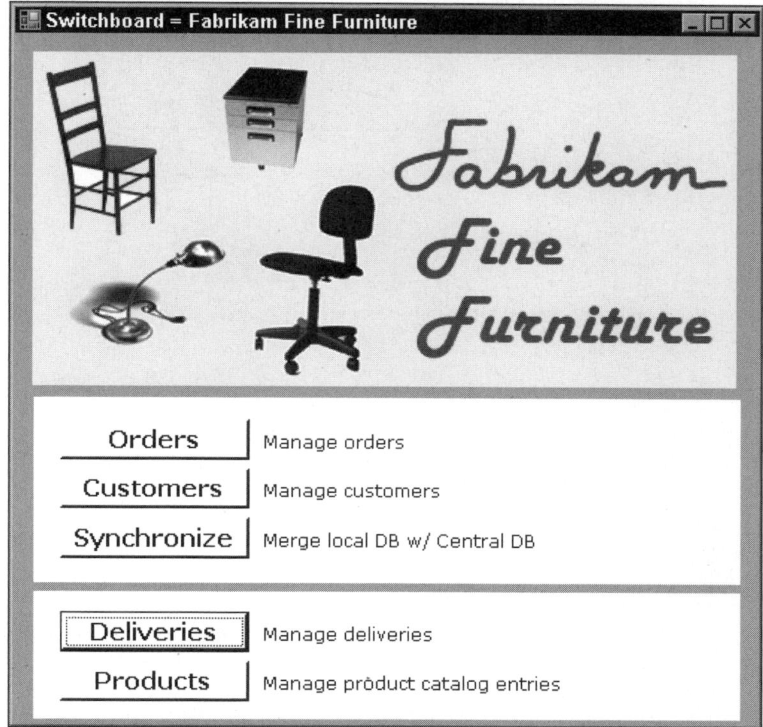

Figure A-3

Object Type	Name	Text
`Label`		Enter user name and password
`Label`		Username:
`Label`		Password
`TextBox`	`txtUsername`	
`TextBox`	`txtPassword`	
`Button`	`cmdOK`	OK
`Button`	`cmdCancel`	Cancel

Figure A-4 shows what the login form should look like.

Figure A-4

Ready to start adding some code? Open Form1 in design mode and double-click on any gray area of the form to view the code. That also creates the `Load()` method for the form, which is what you need. In the `Load()` event for the main form, add the following code:

```
string s = System.Reflection.Assembly.GetExecutingAssembly().Location;
s = Path.GetDirectoryName(s);
Directory.SetCurrentDirectory(s);

string businessName = Properties.Settings.Default.BusinessName;

this.Text = "Switchboard = " + businessName;

LoginForm lf = new LoginForm();
if (lf.ShowDialog() != DialogResult.OK)
{
    Application.Exit();
}
```

For now, you are done with the main form. Open the login form in design mode, and double-click on the OK button. In the button's `Click()` event, add the following code:

```
string username = txtUsername.Text.Trim();
string password = txtPassword.Text.Trim();

if ((username.Length > 0) && (password.Length > 0))
{
    if (Authenticate(username, password))
    {
        DialogResult = DialogResult.OK;
}
```

```
        else
        {
            MessageBox.Show("Invalid username or password.", this.Text);
        }
    }
    else
    {
        MessageBox.Show("Enter a valid username and password.", this.Text);
    }
```

Below the `Click()` event of the OK button, add the following code. This code is what the `Click()` event will call to authenticate the user entered on the login form.

```
    private bool Authenticate(string un, string pwd)
    {
        bool isValid = false;

        FabrikamDataContext context = new FabrikamDataContext("user id=username;
    password=password");
        IEnumerable<GetActiveEmployeesResult> result = context.GetActiveEmployees();
    foreach (GetActiveEmployeesResult emp in result)
        {
            if (emp.LoginName.ToLower() == un.ToLower() && emp.Password == pwd)
            {
                isValid = true;
                break;
            }
        }
        return isValid;
    }
```

Before proceeding, compile the application to make sure that everything compiles OK. If there are no errors, press F5 to run the application. First, the login form will appear. For credentials, enter `RussellK` for the username and `password` for the password.

The `Authenticate` routine uses LINQ to SQL to call a mapped stored procedure to return all the existing employees. It then compares the usernames and passwords to those entered on the login form. Notice how easy it is to call the stored procedure using IntelliSense and dot notation. Sweet.

If the login is successful, the main form is displayed (you saw that in Figure A-3). It doesn't really do anything right now, so stop the application and add a new form to the project, naming it `SelectProduct`. On this form add the following controls (again, those blank cells in the tables throughout this appendix are blank on purpose because those objects on the form do not require that the object name to be changed or the `Text` value set).

Object Type	Name	Text
`Label`		Product Category
`Label`		Products in
`Button`	`cmdNew`	New

Object Type	Name	Text
Button	cmdEdit	Edit
Button	cmdDelete	Delete
ComboBox	cboProductType	
DataViewGrid	grdProducts	

This form, when laid out, should look something like Figure A-5.

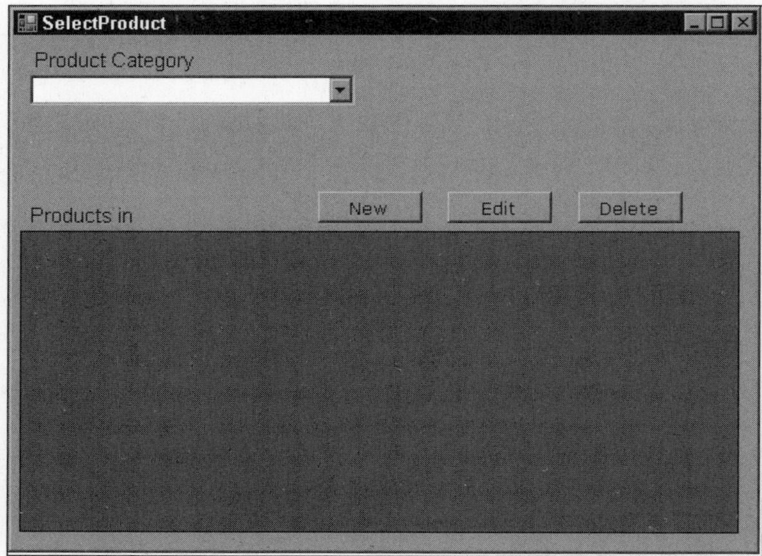

Figure A-5

Now add the following code to the `Load()` event of the new `SelectProduct` form. Be sure to use the correct username and password in the `DataContext` connection string.

```
FabrikamDataContext context = new FabrikamDataContext("user id↩
=username;password=password");

IEnumerable<ProductType> result =
   from prod in context.ProductTypes
   orderby prod.Name
   select prod;

DataTable dt = new DataTable("ProductType");
DataColumn dc;
DataRow dr;

dc = new DataColumn();
```

```
dc.DataType = System.Type.GetType("System.Int32");
dc.ColumnName = "ID";
dt.Columns.Add(dc);

dc = new DataColumn();
dc.DataType = System.Type.GetType("System.String");
dc.ColumnName = "Name";
dt.Columns.Add(dc);

foreach (ProductType product in result)
{
    dr = dt.NewRow();
    dr["ID"] = product.ProductTypeID;
    dr["Name"] = product.Name;
    dt.Rows.Add(dr);
}
cboProductType.DataSource = dt;
cboProductType.DisplayMember = "Name";
cboProductType.ValueMember = "ID";
```

Next, add the following code to the `SelectedIndexChanged` event of the `cboProductType` combo.

```
If (cboProductType.SelectedIndex > 0)
{
    int ProductID = Convert.ToInt32(cboProductType.SelectedIndex);
    DataSet ds = new DataSet();

    string connectionInfo = "Data Source=avalonserver;Initial Catalog=Fabrikam;
    user id=username;pwd=password";

    SqlDataAdapter da = new SqlDataAdapter("select ProductID, Name,
    Description, ManufacturerSKU, Cost, Price, QuantityOnHand FROM products
    WHERE ProductTypeID = @ID", connectionInfo);

    da.SelectCommand.Parameters.AddWithValue("@ID", ProductID);
    da.TableMappings.Add("Table", "Products");

    da.Fill(ds);

    DataTable dt = ds.Tables["Products"];

    IEnumerable<DataRow> prod =
        from p in dt.AsEnumerable()
        select p;
    if (prod.Count() > 0)
    {
        DataTable dat = prod.CopyToDataTable<DataRow>(); ↵
grdProducts.DataSource = dat;
    }
     else
    {
         grdProducts.DataSource = null;
    }
}
```

When the user selects a new product type, the corresponding products are retrieved from the database via a `DataAdapter` and used to fill a `DataTable`. A LINQ query is then executed to query the contents of the `DataTable`, at which point the `CopyToDataTable` method is used to return a `DataTable` with copies of the `DataRow` objects using an input `IEnumerable<T>` object.

The new `DataTable` is used as the data source for the products grid.

The `SelectProduct` form needs to be opened from the main form. To make that work, open the main form and add the following highlighted code to Products button's `Click()` event.

```
private void cmdProducts_Click(object sender, EventArgs e)
{
    SelectProduct selectProd = new SelectProduct();
    selectProd.Show();
}
```

To test what you have so far, compile the application to make sure that everything is good. Press F5 to run the application, and log in using the same credentials as last time (`RussellK` and `password`). When the main form appears, click the Products button, which opens the `SelectProduct` form (you saw it in Figure A-5). Select a product category from the `Product Category` combo—for this example, select the `Chairs` category. The grid is populated with two products associated with that product category, a secretary chair and a casual easy chair).

Now stop the application and create a new form called `ProductMain`. Add the following controls to it (as with the other forms, the same thing applies to the blank cells in the table below).

Object Type	Name	Text
Label		Name:
Label		Product ID:
Label		Description:
Label		Product Category:
Label		Manufacturer:
Label		Mfr.SKU (UPC):
Label		Length:
Label		Width:
Label		Depth:
Label		Height:
Label		Cost:
Label		Price:
Label		Qty on Hand:

Object Type	Name	Text
TextBox	txtName	
TextBox	txtProductID	
TextBox	txtDescription	
TextBox	txtManufacturerSKU	
TextBox	txtLength	
TextBox	txtWidth	
TextBox	txtDepth	
TextBox	txtHeight	
TextBox	txtCost	
TextBox	txtPrice	
TextBox	txtQuantity	
ComboBox	cboProductCategory	
ComboBox	cboManufacturer	
Button	cmdOK	OK
Button	cmdCancel	Cancel

Also, set the `Enabled` property of the `txtProductID` text box to `False`. When completed, the `ProductMain` form should look something like Figure A-6.

Before this form can be used a few changes need to be made. Open the form in design mode and double-click any gray area to view the code behind the form and to create the `Load()` event for this form. Next, add the following line of code directly above the `ProductMain` form constructor:

```
private int _productID;
```

A new constructor needs to be added so that a `ProductID` can be passed in, so add the following code below the default `ProductMain` constructor.

```
public ProductMain(int productID)
{
    InitializeComponent();
    _productID = productID;
}
```

Then, enter the following code in the `ProductMain` form's `Load()` event. It populates the form's two lookup combos.

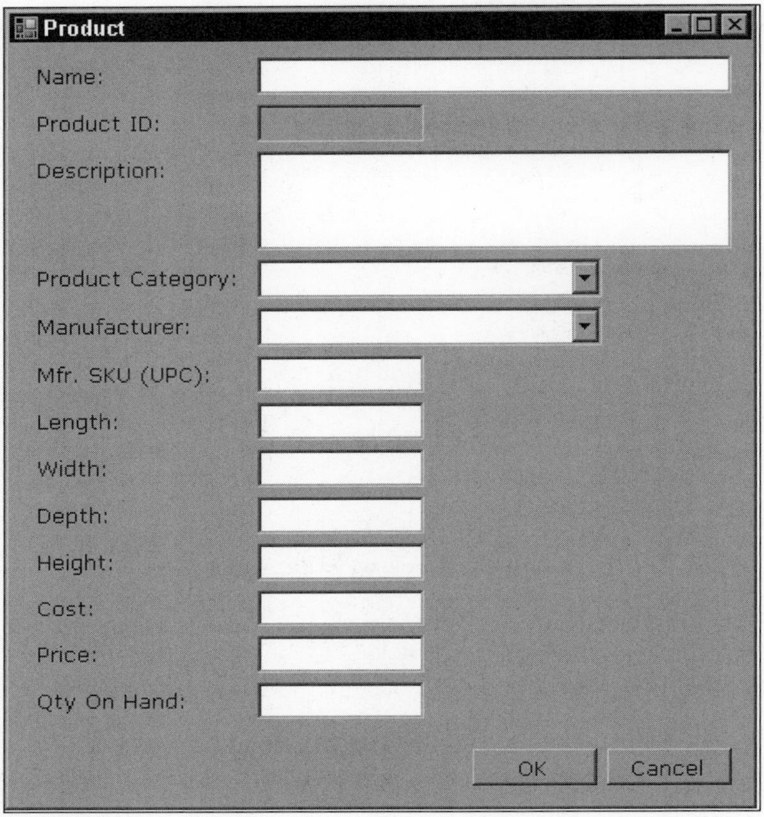

Figure A-6

```
FabrikamDataContext context =
    new FabrikamDataContext("user id=username;password=password");

//first, the producttypes
IEnumerable<ProductType> result =
    from prod in context.ProductTypes
    orderby prod.Name
    select prod;

DataTable dt = new DataTable("ProductType");
DataColumn dc;
DataRow dr;

dc = new DataColumn();
dc.DataType = System.Type.GetType("System.Int32");
dc.ColumnName = "ID";
dt.Columns.Add(dc);

dc = new DataColumn();
dc.DataType = System.Type.GetType("System.String");
```

```
dc.ColumnName = "Name";
dt.Columns.Add(dc);
foreach (ProductType product in result)
{

    dr = dt.NewRow();
    dr["ID"] = product.ProductTypeID;
    dr["Name"] = product.Name;
    dt.Rows.Add(dr);
}

cboProductCategory.DataSource = dt;
cboProductCategory.DisplayMember = "Name";
cboProductCategory.ValueMember = "ID";
//now, the manufacturer info...
IEnumerable<Manufacturer> result1 =
    from manu in context.Manufacturers
    orderby manu.Name
    select manu;
DataTable dt2 = new DataTable("ProductType");
DataColumn dc2;
DataRow dr2;

dc2 = new DataColumn();
dc2.DataType = System.Type.GetType("System.Int32");
dc2.ColumnName = "ID";
dt2.Columns.Add(dc2);

dc2 = new DataColumn();
dc2.DataType = System.Type.GetType("System.String");
dc2.ColumnName = "Name";
dt2.Columns.Add(dc2);

foreach (Manufacturer man in result1)
{

    dr2 = dt2.NewRow();
    dr2["ID"] = product.ProductTypeID;
    dr2["Name"] = product.Name;
    dt2.Rows.Add(dr2);
}

cboManufacturer.DataSource = dt2;
cboManufacturer.DisplayMember = "Name";
cboManufacturer.ValueMember = "ID";
if (_productID > 0)
{
    this.GetProduct(_productID, context);
}
```

This code also looks to see if a `productID` was passed in. If a `productID` was passed in, you know that the user clicked the Edit button on the `SelectProduct` form and wants to display the product details of the product he selected in the grid; you want to call the `GetProduct()` method.

Well, the `GetProduct()` method has not been created yet, so add it now below the `Load()` event:

```
private void GetProduct(int productID, FabrikamDataContext context)
{
    var prodQuery = context.Products.Single(p => p.ProductID == productID);

    txtName.Text = prodQuery.Name;
    txtProductID.Text = Convert.ToString(prodQuery.ProductID);
    txtDescription.Text = prodQuery.Description;
    cboProductCategory.SelectedValue = Convert.Int32(prodQuery.ProductTypeID);
    cboManufacturer.SelectedValue = Convert.Int32(prodQuery.ManufacturerID);
    txtManufacturerSKU.Text = prodQuery.ManufacturerSKU;
    txtLength.Text = Convert.ToString(prodQuery.Length);
    txtWidth.Text = Convert.ToString(prodQuery.Width);
    txtDepth.Text = Convert.ToString(prodQuery.Depth);
    txtHeight.Text = Convert.ToString(prodQuery.Height);
    txtCost.Text = Convert.ToString(prodQuery.Cost);
    txtPrice.Text = Convert.ToString(prodQuery.Price);
    txtQuantity.Text = Convert.ToString(prodQuery.QuantityOnHand);
}
```

This code takes the `productID` that was passed in and uses LINQ to SQL to return a single product record. It then populates the `ProductMain` combo controls with the corresponding data.

Now add the following code to the OK button's `Click()` event. This code looks at the `txtProductID` control to see if there is a value. If not, it is a new product and a new instance of the `Product` entity is created, populated, and saved back to the database, all via LINQ to SQL. If there is an existing `productID`, the current record is updated and the changes are saved back to the database.

```
try
{
    FabrikamDataContext context =
        new FabrikamDataContext("user id=username;password=password");

    if (txtProductID.Text.Length == 0)
    {
        Product prod = new Product();
        prod.Name = txtName.Text.Trim();
        prod.Description = txtDescription.Text;
        Prod.ProductTypeID = Convert.ToInt32(cboProductCategory.SelectedValue);
        Prod.ManufacturerID = Convert.ToInt32(cboManufacturer.SelectedValue);
        prod.ManufacturerSKU = txtManufacturerSKU.Text;
        prod.Length = Convert.ToDecimal(txtLength.Text);
        prod.Width = Convert.ToDecimal(txtWidth.Text);
        prod.Depth = Convert.ToDecimal(txtDepth.Text);
        prod.Height = Convert.ToDecimal(txtHeight.Text);
        prod.Cost = decimal.Parse(this.txtCost.Text,
System.Globalization.NumberStyles.Currency);
        prod.Price = decimal.Parse(this.txtPrice.Text,
System.Globalization.NumberStyles.Currency);
        prod.QuantityOnHand = Convert.ToInt32(this.txtQuantity.Text);
        context.Products.Add(prod);
    }
```

```
        else
        {
            int productID = Convert.ToInt32(txtProductID.Text);

            var prodQuery = context.Products.Single(p => p.ProductID == productID);
            prodQuery.Name = txtName.Text.Trim();
            prodQuery.Description = txtDescription.Text;
            ProdQuery.ProductTypeID =
                Convert.ToInt32(cboProductCategory.SelectedValue);
            ProdQuery.ManufacturerID = Convert.ToInt32(cboManufacturer.SelectedValue);
            prodQuery.ManufacturerSKU = txtManufacturerSKU.Text;
            prodQuery.Length = Convert.ToDecimal(txtLength.Text);
            prodQuery.Width = Convert.ToDecimal(txtWidth.Text);
            prodQuery.Depth = Convert.ToDecimal(txtDepth.Text);
            prodQuery.Height = Convert.ToDecimal(txtHeight.Text);
            prodQuery.Cost = decimal.Parse(this.txtCost.Text,
    System.Globalization.NumberStyles.Currency);
            prodQuery.Price = decimal.Parse(this.txtPrice.Text,
    System.Globalization.NumberStyles.Currency);
            prodQuery.QuantityOnHand = Convert.ToInt32(this.txtQuantity.Text);

        }
        context.SubmitChanges();
    }
    catch (Exception ex)
    {
        MessageBox.Show(ex.Message.ToString());
    }
```

Next you need to put code behind the New, Edit, and Delete buttons on the `SelectProduct` form that will utilize the new `ProductMain` form. Open the `SelectProduct` form and add the following code to the `cmdNew` button's `Click()` event.

```
ProductMain prod = new ProductMain();
prod.Show();
```

This code opens the `ProductMain` form ready to add a new record.

Before you can add code behind the `cmdEdit` button, you have to declare a variable on the `SelectProduct` form that will hold the row index of the row selected in the grid. Add the following line of code above the `SelectProduct()` constructor on the `SelectProduct` form:

```
int selectedRow;
```

In the `CellClick` event of the Products grid, add the code that sets the variable declared you just declared:

```
private void grdProducts_CellClick(object sender, DataGridViewCellEventArgs e)
{
    selectedRow = e.RowIndex;
}
```

This code sets the row index so the application knows which row is selected.

Now add the following code to the `cmdEdit` button's `Click()` event on the `SelectProduct` form. Here is where the declared variable comes in because that variable is used to grab the `ProductID` value from the row that has been selected. This code then passes that value to the new constructor created on the `ProductMain` form, and opens the form.

```
int ProductID =
Convert.ToInt32(grdProducts.Rows[selectedRow].Cells["ProductID"].Value);
ProductMain prod = new ProductMain(ProductID);
prod.Show();
```

Last, wire the Delete button by adding the following code to the `cmdDelete` button's `Click()` event:

```
int productID =
Convert.ToInt32(grdProducts.Rows[selectedRow].Cells["ProductID"].Value);

FabrikamDataContext context =
    new FabrikamDataContext("user id=username;password=password");

var prodQuery = context.Products.Single(p => p.ProductID == productID);
context.Products.Remove(prodQuery);
context.SubmitChanges();
```

This code again gets the `productID` for the currently selected row in the `Products` grid and passes it to a LINQ query to return the item for the selected product. The `Remove()` method is called to remove that entity and then the `SubmitChanges()` is called to submit the changes back to the underlying database. That removes that record from the Products table.

OK, compile the application to make sure there are no coding errors. Press F5 to run the app, and have at it. The entire Products button on the main switchboard form has been wired up, and you can add, edit, and delete products.

Your homework assignment is to do the same thing for the Deliveries button. If you get stuck, the downloaded code for this appendix contains a fully functional copy (except for the replication part).

From this example, you can see how easy and efficient it is to use LINQ and LINQ technologies to upgrade an application.

B

LINQ to Entities: The ADO.NET Entity Framework

A lot of hype and information has come out of Microsoft regarding a technology called the ADO.NET Entity Framework. The ADO.NET Entity Framework is actually a set of technologies aimed at helping the developer be more productive and efficient. It was designed from day one to provide developers with the capability to create data access applications by programming against a known model over the existing method of accessing the database directly.

The ADO.NET Entity Framework is still in its development stages and won't be out until after the initial release of Visual Studio 2008. Because there might be some changes between now and when it is officially released, this appendix only introduces you to the technology and give you some insight as to what to expect when it does come out. The appendix provides an overview of the ADO.NET Entity Framework, including some background and some examples of how it can be used to benefit today's developers.

The ADO.NET Entity Framework has been scheduled to release after the release of Visual Studio 2008. At the time of this writing the current release of the Entity Framework is the ADO.NET Entity Framework Beta 2 dated August 27, 2007.

Overview

Today, the primary method of accessing data in a relational database is to write code that accesses that data directly. This requires developers who are used to working in an OO (object-oriented) environment to know the relational storage schema and takes much more code than is really needed.

The goal of the ADO.NET Entity Framework is to give developers the capability to create applications that access data in an OO fashion, meaning developers can now use a conceptual model in which to work with objects and properties. The benefits of this are much less code to write and developers who can work with technology that they know without needing to know the exact schema (such as tables and columns) in the underlying database.

ADO.NET Entity Framework addresses a number of developer issues that have been around for a while. For some time, developers have been struggling with how to model entities and relationships and at the same time work with the relational databases that store the data they need. It gets more difficult if the data spans multiple data stores. Add the OO layer to this puzzle, and you have the complexity of using OO technology to map to relational data stores, yet at the same time trying to make it easy (more efficient) for the developer.

For example, you can model a class to a relational data table, but how often is that a one-to-one situation? Typically, you have multiple tables that are mapped to a single class—and how do you represent relationships? Relationships between classes are certainly not the same as relationships between tables. You also have the problem of connecting objects with the data, meaning, how do you connect OO systems to relational data?

The good news is that the ADO.NET Entity Framework overcomes all of these issues and affords some additional features. To solve the problem of connecting OO systems to relational data, the Entity Framework maps relation objects (tables, columns, and primary and foreign keys) to entities and relationships in conceptual models.

The conceptual model comes from the division of the data model into three distinct parts:

- **Conceptual**—Defines the entities and relationships from the system being modeled.
- **Logical**—Normalizes the entities and relationships into "relational" tables and constraints.
- **Physical**—Handles the physical storage engine needs and capabilities of the particular data storage engine.

A developer need not be concerned about the physical aspects of the model. That is primarily the responsibility of a DBA. Today, developers typically focus their attention on the logical model by writing queries to access the data. Conceptual models are generally used as a data capture tool to gather requirements. Often you see developers completely skip the creation of the conceptual model by going right to the creation of the relational objects.

The ADO.NET Entity Framework puts more emphasis on the conceptual model by letting developers program directly against it. The ADO.NET Entity Framework conceptual model can be connected directly to the logical model, providing developers access to the conceptual entities and relationships. It is the job of the Entity Framework to map entity operations to their SQL counterparts. You can see the benefit of this: One model can be used across multiple storage engines.

The creation of the mapping between the application and the storage engine is the responsibility of the ADO.NET Entity Framework. The mapping requires the three parts discussed previously and are created and used within the application. Three physical components are created in the mapping:

- The conceptual schema definition language (a file with an extension of `.csdl`).
- The logical storage schema definition language (a file with an extension of `.ssdl`).
- The mapping specification language (a file with an extension of `.msl`).

The developer has a couple of options for creating these files. A set of classes is created with the files; the developer uses those classes to work directly with the conceptual model. Within Visual Studio

2008, you can use a wizard-driven Visual Studio template that creates the files automatically with the information you specify. The other option is a command-line tool the Entity Data Model Generator (EdmGen) that accomplishes the same thing. You'll look at the EdmGen tool later in this appendix, and you'll also see how to use the template.

Using the Entity Framework is quite simple because it consists of number of namespaces that construct and maintain the metadata information needed for models and mapping. `System.Data.Entity` uses the .NET Framework data provider and the `EntityConnection` class to accomplish this.

The great thing is that LINQ to Entities is fully supported by the Entity Framework. LINQ to Entities provides query support against the conceptual objects and strongly typed LINQ queries.

Installing the ADO.NET Entity Framework

Entity Framework is not installed when you install any beta of Visual Studio. It is a completely separate program, and there are actually two components that you need to install. The first is ADO.NET Entity Framework Beta 2 which can be found at:

```
http://www.microsoft.com/downloads/details.aspx?FamilyID=F1ADC5D1-A42E-40A6-A68C-
A42EE11186F7&DisplayLang=en
```

The file is a mere 1.2 megabytes, so it is a quick download.

The second download is the ADO.NET Entity Framework Tools, which you can get from:

```
http://www.microsoft.com/downloads/details.aspx?FamilyId=09A36081-5ED1-4648-B995-
6239D0B77CB5&displaylang=en
```

This download is a bit larger, roughly 6.6 megabytes.

Install the Entity Framework first, and then install the Entity Framework Tools. (If you attempt to install the Tools first, the install program tells you that you need to install the Entity Framework first and then exits the install.)

To begin, double-click the Entity Framework install file called `EFSetup-x86.exe`. At the Welcome screen, click Next. You'll need to select the I Agree option on the License Agreement screen before you can continue with the installation. Then click the Install button. Click Finish when the installation is complete.

The Tools installation (`EFToolsSetup-x86.exe`) is similar, but there are a couple of extra steps. At the Welcome screen, click Next. Again, you'll need to select the I Agree option on the License Agreement screen before you can continue. Click Next. The next step asks for the destination where you would like to install the product. Accept the default or enter a destination path, and then click the Install button.

Once the installation is complete, you'll notice a new Start menu option called ADO.NET Entity Framework Tools Preview. This new menu option includes several support documents along with a couple of great ADO.NET Visual Studio example projects. Very nice.

ADO.NET Entity Framework Example

The easiest way to get a feel for the ADO.NET Entity Framework and see what it can do is to run through an example. Fire up Visual Studio and create a new C# Windows forms project. Name the project `ProductSales` and click OK. Open the Solution Explorer, right-click on the solution name, and select Add ➪ New Item from the context menu.

When the Add New Item dialog appears, select the ADO.NET Entity Data Model template (see Figure B-1).

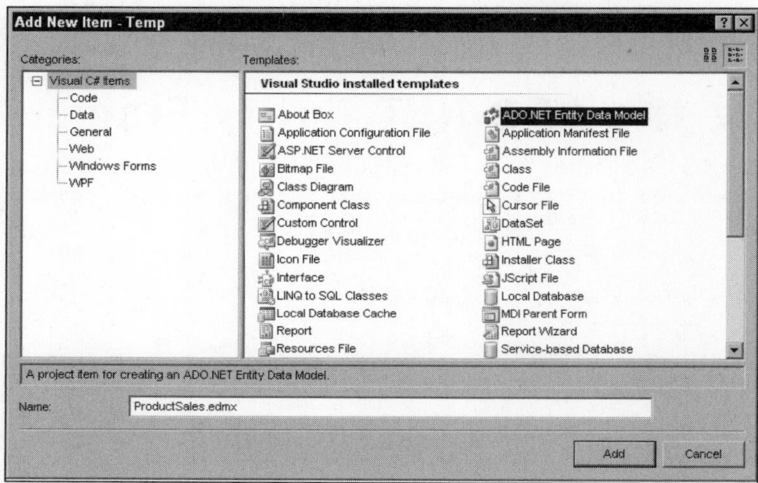

Figure B-1

Name the data model `ProductSales` and click Add. This launches the Entity Data Model Wizard. The first page of the wizard asks you to select the source that the model contents will come from. You can choose to generate a model from a database or to create an empty model.

If you choose to create an empty model, the Finish button appears. Click it, and an empty model is created, in which you can build a model manually using XML.

This example, however, won't put you through that, so select the Generate From Database option (see Figure B-2) and click Next.

The next page of the wizard lets you choose or create your data connection to the data store. Because no connection has been created, click the New Connection button to open the Connection Properties dialog (see Figure B-3).

In this dialog, select the server from which the Entity Framework will make its connection. Next, select how the Entity Framework will make its connection, via Windows Authentication or through SQL Server Authentication. This example uses SQL Server Authentication, but feel free to select Windows Authentication.

Next, choose the database from which the Entity Framework will connect to access the objects and create the entities and relationships. Select the AdventureWorks database, and then click the Test Connection button to ensure that the connection information has been entered correctly and that a connection can be made. Click OK.

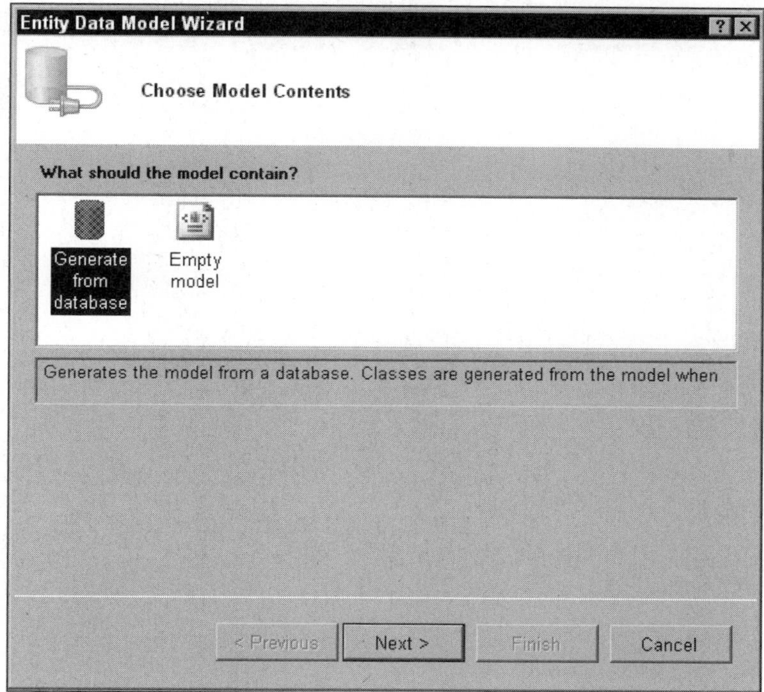

Figure B-2

The top part of the Data Connection Wizard step should look like Figure B-4.

Choose whether you want to store sensitive connection information in the connection string. For this example, select Yes.

Ensure that the Save Entity Connection Settings in the App.Config as check box is checked. The wizard requires that you provide a name for the connection settings. The best practice in naming is to include the word Entities at the end of the name. For this example, enter AdventureWorksEntities. Click Next.

The next page in the wizard asks you to select the database objects that you want to include in the model. By default, all the objects are selected including tables, views, and stored procedures. For this project, unselect all the objects, as shown in Figure B-5.

Now expand the Tables node, and select the following tables:

- `Contact`
- `SalesOrderHeader`
- `SalesOrderDetail`

- `SpecialOfferProduct`
- `Product`

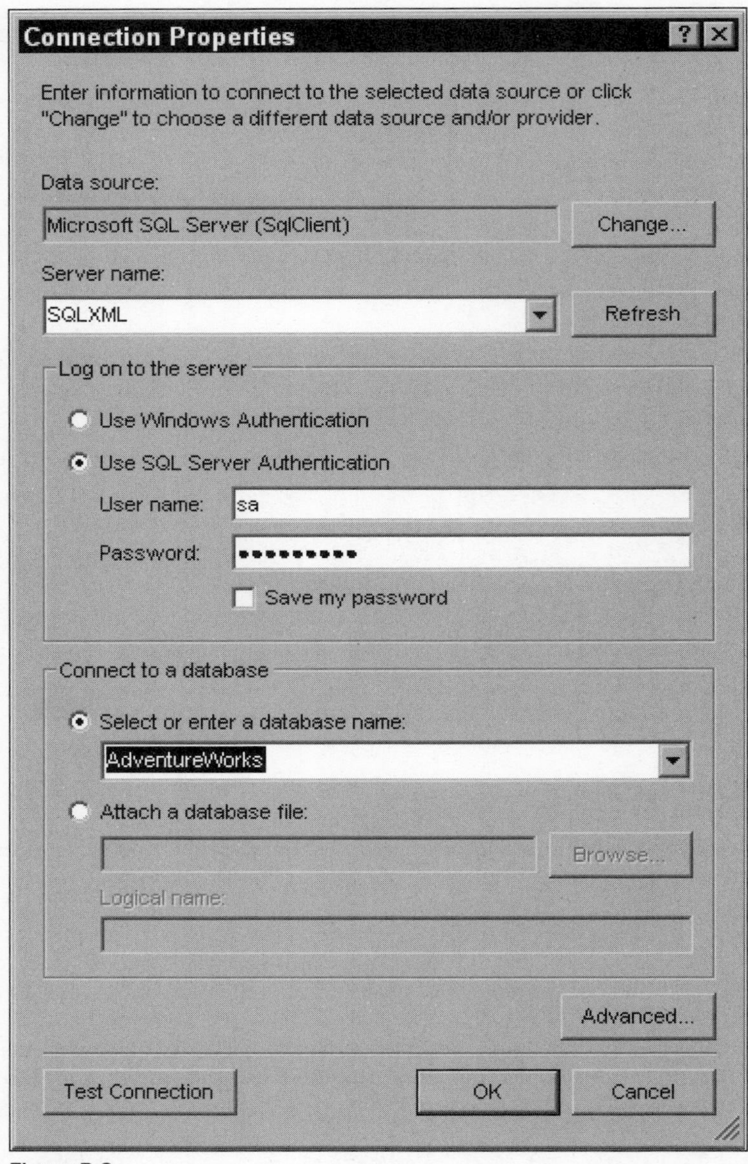

Figure B-3

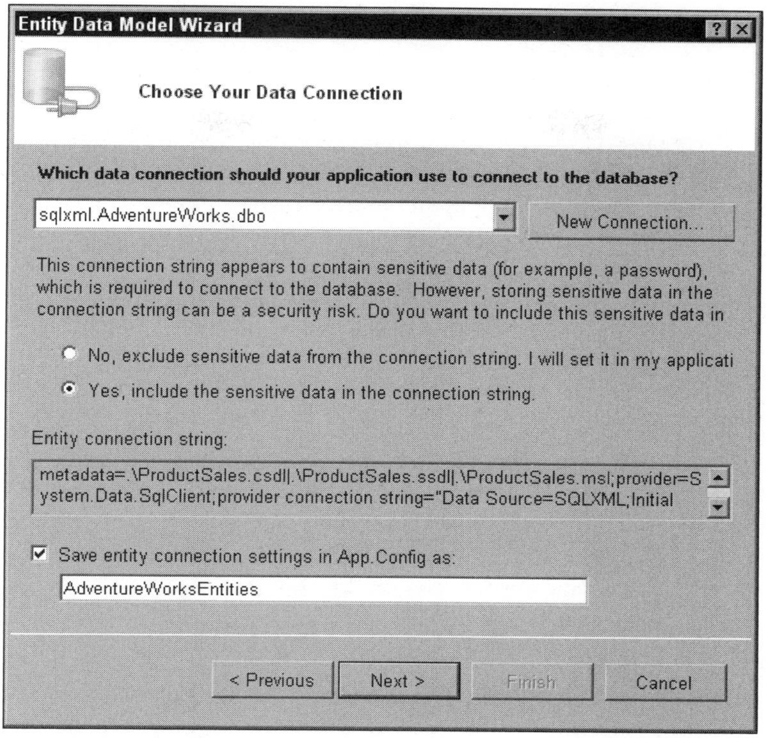

Figure B-4

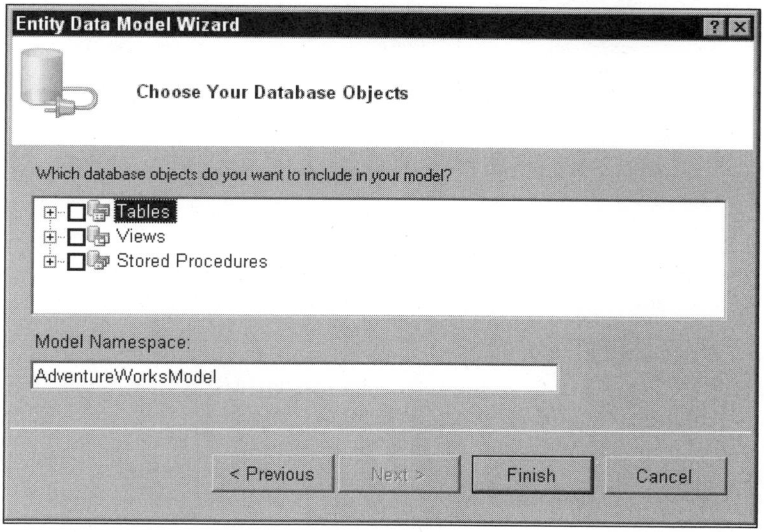

Figure B-5

At the bottom of the wizard page, name the Model Namespace. It is good practice to begin the name with the same name you gave the entity on the previous page. For this exercise, use the name AdventureWorksModel.

> **The Model Namespace name and the Entity Connection Settings name must be different, like the ones in this example: AdventureWorksEntities and AdventureWorksModel. Giving them the same name will result in compile errors.**

Click Finish. The Entity Data Model Wizard begins creating the entity data model for the objects that you selected. A mapping is created, and the mapping files and class definitions are generated. When the mapping generation is complete, the entity classes display in the designer (see Figure B-6). This view shows the entities that were created, the relationships between the entities that were created, and other pertinent information such as relationship names and navigation properties.

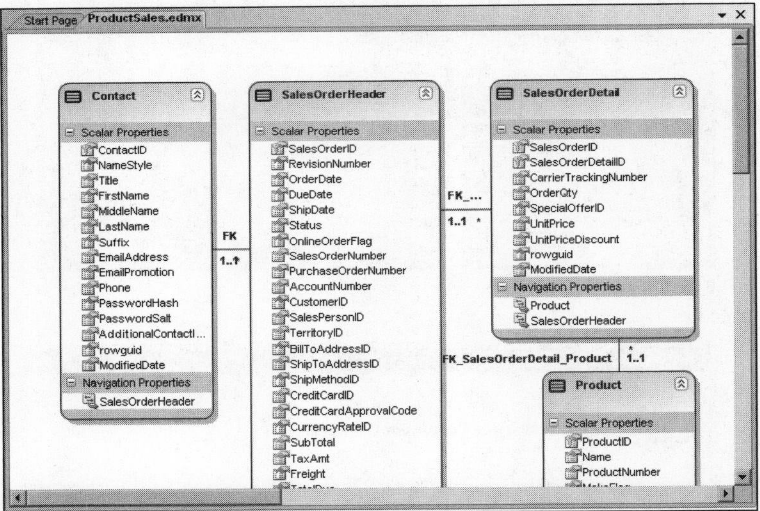

Figure B-6

You can see what files were created by going to the Solution Explorer and looking at the contents of the solution. Figure B-7 shows the files that were generated and added to the project.

In Solution Explorer, expand the ProductSales.edmx node. Underneath that node you'll see two files: a `.cs` file and a `.diagram` file. The `.cs` file contains the partial classes that contain the information that the programmer will interact with on the conceptual model level.

Open the `.cs` file and scroll down a tad (see Figure B-8). You will see that `ObjectContext` is used as well as the `EntityConnection` class (from the `System.Data.EntityClient` namespace).

You'll see that these classes derive from the `ObjectContext` class. The `ObectContext` in the ADO.NET Entity Framework represents the entity container in the conceptual model. Just like LINQ to SQL and the `DataContext`, the `ObjectContext` class exposes the `SaveChanges` method, which ushers changes back to the underlying database. It is the primary class for interacting with data as objects, serving as the pathway through which all CRUD (create, read, update, and delete) operations are passed and executed.

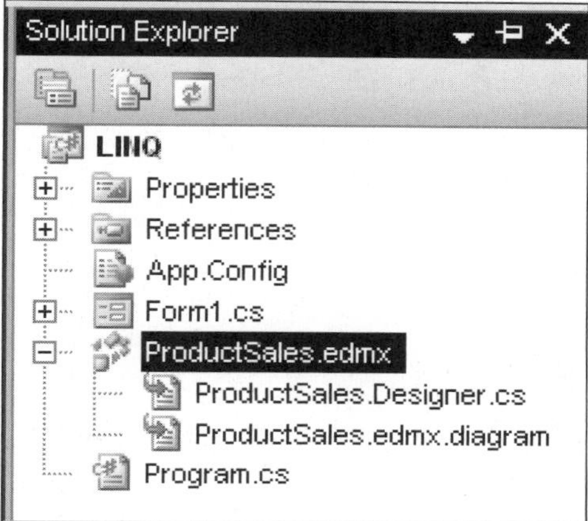

Figure B-7

ProductSales.Designer.cs | Start Page | ProductSales.edmx | Form1.cs

AdventureWorksModel.AdventureWorksEntities | AdventureWorksEntities(global::System.Data.EntityClient.EntityConnection conn

```
/// <summary>
/// There are no comments for AdventureWorksEntities in the schema.
/// </summary>
public partial class AdventureWorksEntities : global::System.Data.Objects.ObjectContext
{
    /// <summary>
    /// Initializes a new AdventureWorksEntities object using the connection string found in the
    /// </summary>
    public AdventureWorksEntities() :
            base("name=AdventureWorksEntities", "AdventureWorksEntities")
    {
    }
    /// <summary>
    /// Initialize a new AdventureWorksEntities object.
    /// </summary>
    public AdventureWorksEntities(string connectionString) :
            base(connectionString, "AdventureWorksEntities")
    {
    }
    /// <summary>
    /// Initialize a new AdventureWorksEntities object.
    /// </summary>
    public AdventureWorksEntities(global::System.Data.EntityClient.EntityConnection connection)
            base(connection, "AdventureWorksEntities")
```

Figure B-8

As you scroll through the `.cs` file, you will see that it contains all the code necessary to manipulate the model-provided data, such as adding, deleting, and updating data.

Now you're ready to start adding code to utilize the Entity Framework. Open `Form1` in design mode and add a button, a combo box, and a `DataViewGrid` to the form. Name the combo box `salesPerson` and name the grid `grdOrderDetail`. Next, double-click on the form itself to view the code behind. Add the following two statements to the top of the form:

```
using System.Data.Objects;
using AdventureWorksModel;
```

Add the following line of code to the top of the partial class for the form:

```
private AdventureWorksEntities productSalesContext;
```

Add the following code to the `Load` event of the form:

```
productSalesContext = new AdventureWorksEntities();

grdProducts.Columns.Add("OrderID", "Order");
grdProducts.Columns.Add("OrderQty", "Quantity");
grdProducts.Columns.Add("ProductID", "Product");
grdProducts.Columns.Add("UnitPrice", "Price");
grdProducts.Columns.Add("LineTotal", "Total");

ObjectQuery<Contact> salesPerson = productSalesContext.Contact.Where("it
.MiddleName IS NOT NULL").OrderBy("it.LastName");

this.cbosalesPerson.DataSource = salesPerson.Include
("SalesOrderHeader.SalesOrderDetail");

this.cbosalesPerson.DisplayMember = "LastName";
```

Finally, add the following code to the `SelectedIndexChanged` event of the combo:

```
grdProducts.Rows.Clear();

Contact person = (Contact)cbosalesPerson.SelectedItem;

foreach (SalesOrderHeader soh in person.SalesOrderHeader)
{
    object[] row = new object[4];

    row[0] = soh.SalesOrderDetail.SalesOrderID;
    row[1] = soh.SalesOrderDetail.OrderQty;
    row[2] = soh.SalesOrderDetail.ProductID;
    row[3] = soh.SalesOrderDetail.UnitPrice;
    row[4] = soh.SalesOrderDetail.LineTotal;

    grdOrderDetails.Rows.Add(row);

}
```

Compile the application to make sure everything is OK. Run the application, and when the form loads, the combo box will be filled with a list of contacts. Selecting a contact will display the order detail for that contact in the grid, as shown in Figure B-9.

Let's take a look on how this works. In the `Load` method, four columns are defined on the grid, but that is not the important code. The important code is the following lines:

```
private AdventureWorksEntities productSalesContext;

productSalesContext = new AdventureWorksEntities();
```

```
ObjectQuery<Contact> salesPerson = productSalesContext.Contact.Where↵
("it.MiddleName IS NOT NULL").OrderBy("it.LastName");

this.cbosalesPerson.DataSource = salesPerson.Include
("SalesOrderHeader.SalesOrderDetail");
```

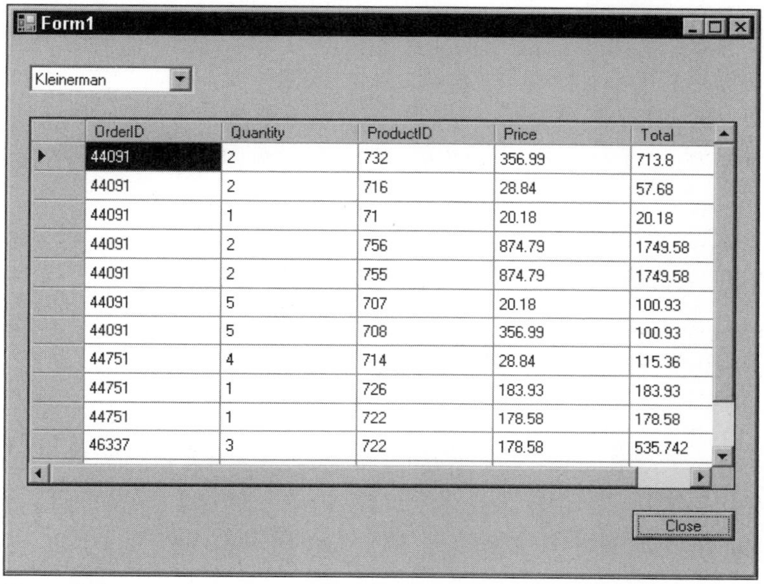

Form1

Kleinerman

OrderID	Quantity	ProductID	Price	Total
44091	2	732	356.99	713.8
44091	2	716	28.84	57.68
44091	1	71	20.18	20.18
44091	2	756	874.79	1749.58
44091	2	755	874.79	1749.58
44091	5	707	20.18	100.93
44091	5	708	356.99	100.93
44751	4	714	28.84	115.36
44751	1	726	183.93	183.93
44751	1	722	178.58	178.58
46337	3	722	178.58	535.742

Close

Figure B-9

The first line creates an instance of `ObjectContext` based on the defined entity. The second line initializes a new instance of the `ObjectContext` class. The third line uses the defined and mapped entities to return all contacts that have a middle name. The fourth line sets the data source of the combo box.

How about the `IndexChanged` event on the combo? The first line of the following code gets the selected contact from the combo. Because the ADO.NET Entity Framework handles the relationships, the rest of the code gets the sales order detail for the selected contact, and then populates the grid.

```
Contact person = (Contact)cbosalesPerson.SelectedItem;

foreach (SalesOrderHeader soh in person.SalesOrderHeader)
{
    object[] row = new object[4];

    row[0] = soh.SalesOrderDetail.OrderQty;
    row[1] = soh.SalesOrderDetail.ProductID;
    row[2] = soh.SalesOrderDetail.UnitPrice;
    row[3] = soh.SalesOrderDetail.LineTotal;

    grdOrderDetails.Rows.Add(row);

}
```

This last example is a simple one that builds on the first example. The previous example returned the ProductID from the SalesOrderDetail table. To return the actual product name instead of the just the ID, Product must be included in the join:

```
this.cbosalesPerson.DataSource = salesPerson.Include("SalesOrderHeader
.SalesOrderDetail").Include("SalesOrderHeader.Product");
```

With that, you can grab the product name and display it in the grid.

```
row[1] = soh.SalesOrderDetail.Product.ProductName
```

The following sections provide an overview of how to query the entity model and how to work with objects.

Querying the Entity Data Model

Querying the entity data model is really not that different from the work you did in LINQ to SQL. The best form is the ObjectQuery class, which you saw earlier:

```
private AdventureWorksEntities productSalesContext;

productSalesContext = new AdventureWorksEntities();

ObjectQuery<Contact> salesPerson = productSalesContext.Contact.Where
("it.MiddleName IS NOT NULL").OrderBy("it.LastName");
```

You can also do something like the following, which returns an entity type:

```
private AdventureWorksEntities productSalesContext;

string qry = @"SELECT VALUE Contact FROM AdventureWorksEntities.Contact";
ObjectQuery<Contact> con = new ObjectQuery<Contact>(qry, productSalesContext);
```

Likewise, you can create and use an ObjectQueryclass with parameters:

```
private AdventureWorksEntities productSalesContext;

string qry = @"SELECT VALUE Contact FROM AdventureWorksEntities.Contact WHERE
Contact.LastName = @lastname AND Contat.FirstName = @fn";

ObjectQuery<Contact> con = new ObjectQuery<Contact>(qry, productSalesContext);

con.Parameters.Add(new ObjectParameter("ln","Klein"));
con.Parameters.Add(new ObjectParameter("fn","Jason"));
```

You can also use an ObjectQuery class to return primitive and anonymous types, and you can shape the results:

```
private AdventureWorksEntities productSalesContext;

ObjectQuery<Contact> con =  salesPerson.Include("SalesOrderHeader
.SalesOrderDetail");
```

```
foreach (SalesOrderHeader order in query.First().SalesOrderHeader)
{
    listbox1.Items.Add(String.Format("Order Date: {0}", order.PurchaseOrderNumber));
    listbox1.Items.Add(String.Format("Total: {0}",order.TotalDue.ToString()));
    foreach (SalesOrderDetail item in order.SalesOrderDetail)
    {
        listBox1.Items.Add(String.Format("Product: {0} "
            + "Quantity: {1}", item.Name.ToString(),
            item.OrderQty.ToString()));
    }
}
```

Querying the entity data model is quite easy and efficient.

Working with Objects

Let's take a look at working with objects that represent entity types defined by an entity data model.

The following example illustrates how to use the entity data model to update and insert data:

```
string ln = "Kleinerman";

productSalesContext = new AdventureWorksEntities();

Contact con = productSalesContext.Contact.Where("it.LastName = @lastname",
    new ObjectParameter("lastname", ln)).First();

con.EmailAddress = "";
con.EmailPromotion = 1;

Contact newcon = new Contact();

newcon.EmailAddress = "asdf";
newcon.EmailPromotion = 1;
newcon.FirstName = "Scott";
newcon.LastName = "Klein";
newcon.MiddleName = "L";
newcon.NameStyle = false;
newcon.PasswordHash = "asdf";
newcon.PasswordSalt = "adsf";
newcon.Phone = "555-555-5555";
newcon.Suffix = "Mr.";
newcon.Title = "Geek";

productSalesContext.SaveChanges();
```

As you saw earlier, you can also bind objects to controls, like this:

```
ObjectQuery<Contact> salesPerson = productSalesContext.Contact.Where
("it.ContactID < 5000").OrderBy("it.LastName");

this.cbosalesPerson.DataSource = salesPerson.Include("SalesOrderHeader
```

```
    .SalesOrderDetail");
    this.cbosalesPerson.DisplayMember = "LastName";
```

A best practice is to detach objects from the `ObjecContext` when they are no longer needed. Object Services lets you accomplish this via the `Detach` method. This decreases the amount of memory being used.

Object Services, implemented via the `System.Data.Objects` and `System.Data.Objects.DataClasses` namespaces, is a component of the .NET Entity Framework that enables you to perform CRUD operations that are expressed as strongly typed CLR objects. These objects are instances of entity types. Supporting both LINQ and Entity SQL queries, Object Services lets you query against defined types as well as track changes and bind objects to controls.

```
productSalesContext.Detach(Contact.SalesOrderHeader);
```

Another good practice is to manage concurrency conflicts in an object context. Making changes back to the database could cause conflicts, so those need to be handled. In the following example, the `SaveChanges()` method is called to save any changes back to the database. If there are any conflicts, they are caught, the object context is refreshed, and `SaveChanges()` reapplied.

```
try
{
    //make changes..then save them
    productSalesContext.SaveChanges();
}
catch (OptimisticConcurrencyException oce)
{
    productSalesContext.Refresh(RefreshMode.ClientWins, Contact);
    productSalesContext.SaveChanges();
}
```

Hopefully, you can see that working with objects is just as simple as working with LINQ to SQL.

Entity Data Model Generator

The Entity Data Model Generator tool is one of the options available to the developer for generating the entity data model. It is a command-line tool that provides the following functionality:

- Create `.csdl`, `.ssdl`, and `.msl` files that are used by the entity data model.
- Validate existing models.
- Generate source code files containing object classes generated from a `.csdl` file.
- Generate source code files containing generated views from the `.ssdl`, `.csdl`, and `.msl` files.

The Entity Data Model Generator tool is located in `\Windows\Microsoft.NET\Framework\v3.5`. Its general syntax is:

```
EdmGen /mode:choice [options]
```

The following table lists the available modes for the EdmGen tool. You must specify one of them.

Mode	Description
ValidateArtifacts	Validates the .cdsl, .ssdl, and .msl files. Requires at least one /inssdl or /incsdl argument. If /inmsl is specified, the /inssdl and /incsdl arguments are also required.
FullGeneration	Generates .cdsl, .ssdl, and .msl, object layer and view files. Updates the database connection information in the /connectionstring option. Requires a /connectionstring argument and either a /p argument or /outssdl, /outcsdl, /outmsdl, /outobjectlayer, /outviews, and /entitycontainer arguments.
FromSSDLGeneration	Generates .cdsl, and .msl, files. Requires the /inssdl argument and either a /p argument or /outcsdl, /outmsl, /outobjectlayer, /outviews, and /entitycontainer arguments.
EntityClassGeneration	Creates a source code file that contains generated classes from the .csdl file. Requires the /incsdl argument and either a /p or /outobjectlayer argument.
ViewGeneration	Creates a source code file containing views generated from the .ssdl, .csdl, and .msl files. Requires the /inssdl, /incsdl, /inmsl, and either the /p or /outviews arguments.

Along with the modes, you can specify one or more of the following options.

Option	Description
/p[roject]:	String value that specifies the object name.
/prov[ider]:	String value that specifies the name of the ADO.NET data provider. The default is System.Data.Sqlclient (the .NET Framework Data Provider for SQL Server).
/c[onnection]:	String value that specifies the string used to connect to the data source.
/incsdl:	Specifies the .csdl file or a directory where the .csdl files are located. Argument can be specified multiple times.
/refcsdl:	Specifies additional .csdl files used to resolve .csdl source file references specified by the /incsdl option.
/inmsl:	Specifies the .msl file or a directory where the .msl files are located. Argument can be specified multiple times.
/inssdl:	Specifies the .ssdl file or a directory where the .ssdl file is located.
/outcsdl:	Specifies the name of the .csdl file to be created.
/outmsl:	Specifies the name of the .msl file to be created.
/outssdl:	Specifies the name of the .ssdl file to be created.
/outobjectlayer:	Specifies the name of the source code file containing the generated objects fro the .csdl file.

Option	Description
/outviews:	Specifies the name of the source code file containing the generated views.
/language:	Specifies the language for the generated source code files. Options are VB and C#. Default is C#.
/namespace:	Specifies the namespace to use and set in the .csdl file when running in FullGeneration or FromSSDLGeneration mode. Not used in the EntityClassGeneration mode.
/entitycontainer:	Specifies the name to apply to the <EntityContainer> element in the EDM file.
/nologo	Hides the copyright message.
/help	Displays command syntax and tool options.

The following examples show how the EdmGen tool can be used. The first example uses the FullGeneration mode to generate all necessary files:

```
edmgen /mode:fullgeneration /c:"Data Source=AvalonServer;Initial
Catalog=AdventureWorks; Integrated Security=SSPI" /p:LINQProject
```

In this example, a C# object source code file is created from the .csdl:

```
edmgen /mode:entityclassgeneration /incsdl:c:\wrox\Appendix\LINQ\
AdventureWorksModel.csdl /outobjectlayer: c:\wrox\Appendix\LINQ\
AdventureWorksModel.cs /language:csharp
```

The ADO.NET Entity Framework clearly helps you work with relational databases as well as model entities and relationships.

C

LINQ to XSD

Any programming language that supports the .NET Framework will support LINQ. LINQ to XML is LINQ-enabled, meaning that you have access to all of the functionality of LINQ such as the standard query operators and the LINQ programming interface. Because of the integration into the .NET Framework, LINQ to XML can take advantage of functionality the .NET Framework provides, such as compile-time checking, strong typing, and debugging.

LINQ to XML makes working with XML much easier by providing a simple way to work directly with methods and properties, by programming against XML tree components such as elements and attributes, but in an untyped manner. This is where LINQ to XSD comes in. LINQ to XSD lets you work with typed XML.

Although LINQ to XSD is in its early stages, it'd be a shame not to include it in this book. It will probably change somewhat, but the purpose of this appendix is to provide you with an introduction to LINQ to XSD and show you some of its capabilities. This is a cool technology and makes working with XML a pleasure.

LINQ to XSD has been scheduled to release after the release of Visual Studio 2008. At the time of this writing the current release of LINQ to XSD is the LINQ to XSD Preview 0.2 that works with Beta 1 of Orcas. To work with the examples in this appendix, you need to install Beta 1 of Visual Studio codenamed Orcas.

LINQ to XSD Overview

LINQ to XSD is a new technology aimed at enhancing the great LINQ to XML technology by providing .NET developers support for typed XML programming. For example, in typical LINQ to XML programming, you would work with an XML tree as follows:

```
var total = (from item in SalesOrderHeader.Elements("Item")
     select (double)item.Element("UnitPrice")
         * (int)item.Element("OrderQuantity")
    ).Sum();
```

In this example, the developer is working with untyped XML, accessing the elements and attributes of the XML directly. However, LINQ to XSD lets you work with typed XML, like this:

```
var total = (from item in SalesOrderHeader.Item
             select item.UnitPrice * item.OrderQuantity
             ).Sum();
```

Working with typed XML is made possible by XML schemas that are mapped automatically to defined object models. Through this mapping XML data can be manipulated just like other object-oriented models. The result is that you are working directly with classes that can enforce validation through the use of the schema, plus you are working with XML objects generated from the XML schemas that provide a much more efficient XML development platform.

The benefit of working with typed XML is that it makes working with XML-related programming tasks much easier and makes for much more efficient code.

Installing LINQ to XSD

For now, LINQ to XSD is not installed when you install any beta of Visual Studio. It is a completely separate install and is currently found at the following location:

```
http://www.microsoft.com/downloads/details.aspx?FamilyID=e9c23715
   -9e71-47a7-b4db-363c2a68fab4&DisplayLang=en
```

At a mere 1.6 megabytes, it's a quick download. The install is simple. At the Welcome screen, click Next. On the License Agreement screen, select the I Agree option to continue with the installation, then click the Next button. The final screen of the installation wizard lets you know that the installer is ready to install LINQ to XSD. Click Next to begin the install.

Once the installation is complete, you'll notice a new Start menu option called LINQ to XSD Preview. You can tell that Microsoft is serious about this technology because not only does the LINQ to XSD installation install the necessary support files for LINQ to XSD, but it also installs several support documents along with a couple of great LINQ to XSD Visual Studio example projects. How cool is that?

LINQ to XSD Example

The easiest way to get a feel for LINQ to XSD and to understand what it can do is to tackle an example. You're going to need Beta 1 as stated earlier, but before you fire up Visual Studio, a little prep work needs to be done.

In the Wrox directory on your local hard drive, create a folder called `AppendixC`. Next, open your favorite text editor and enter the following XML. Save the file as `Orders.xml`. The data that this XML uses comes from the `SalesOrderDetail` table in the AdventureWorks database. Obviously it is not all the records from that table, but only a small subset of orders from a specific customer.

```
<Order>
  <OrderDetail>
    <CustID>676</CustID>
```

```
        <OrderID>43659</OrderID>
        <Item>
          <ProductID>709</ProductID>
          <UnitPrice>5.70</UnitPrice>
          <OrderQuantity>6</OrderQuantity>
        </Item>
        <Item>
          <ProductID>711</ProductID>
          <UnitPrice>20.18</UnitPrice>
          <OrderQuantity>4</OrderQuantity>
        </Item>
        <Item>
          <ProductID>712</ProductID>
          <UnitPrice>5.18</UnitPrice>
          <OrderQuantity>2</OrderQuantity>
        </Item>
        <Item>
          <ProductID>714</ProductID>
          <UnitPrice>28.84</UnitPrice>
          <OrderQuantity>3</OrderQuantity>
        </Item>
        <Item>
          <ProductID>716</ProductID>
          <UnitPrice>28.84</UnitPrice>
          <OrderQuantity>1</OrderQuantity>
        </Item>
        <Item>
          <ProductID>771</ProductID>
          <UnitPrice>2039.99</UnitPrice>
          <OrderQuantity>1</OrderQuantity>
        </Item>
      </OrderDetail>
    </Order>
```

Once you have created the `Orders.xml` file, fire up Visual Studio and create a new C# Windows project. In the Project types section, expand the C# node. Select the LINQ to XSD Preview project type, and then choose the LINQ to XSD Windows Application from the list of project templates (see Figure C-1).

Name the project LINQ, specifying the appropriate location in which to create the project. Click OK.

Now open the Solution Explorer and expand the References node. Besides the typical LINQ reference of `System.Xml.Linq`, you'll see a new reference to `Microsoft.Xml.Schema.Linq`, shown in Figure C-2. This namespace contains all the XML classes that provide the LINQ to XSD mapping functionality and XSD schema definition support.

Next, open `Form1` in design mode and drop a couple of buttons and a text box on the form. Set the `Text` property of button1 to `Untyped`, and then double-click the button to view its `Click` event. Enter the following code in the button1 `Click` event:

```
var order = XElement.Load("C:\\Wrox\\AppendixC\\Orders.xml");

var total = (from salesOrder in order.Elements("OrderDetail")
     from item in salesOrder.Elements("Item")
```

```
        select (double)item.Element("UnitPrice")
            * (int)item.Element("OrderQuantity")
        ).Sum();

    textBox1.Text = total.ToString();
```

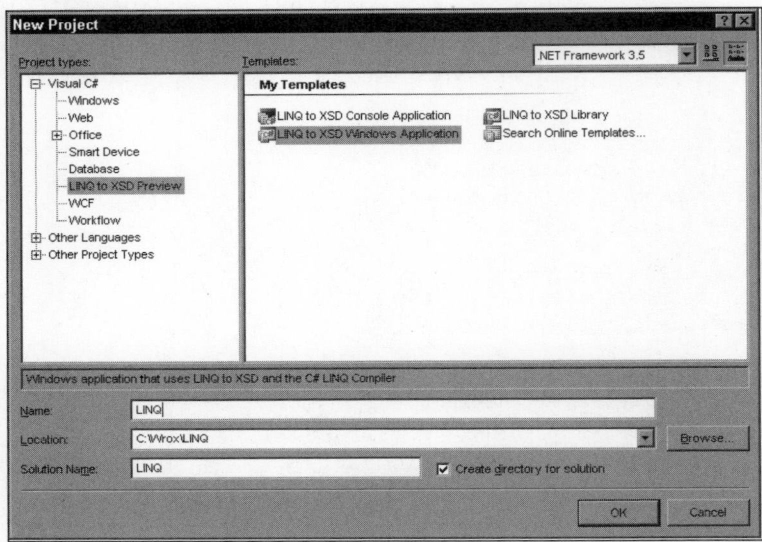

Figure C-1

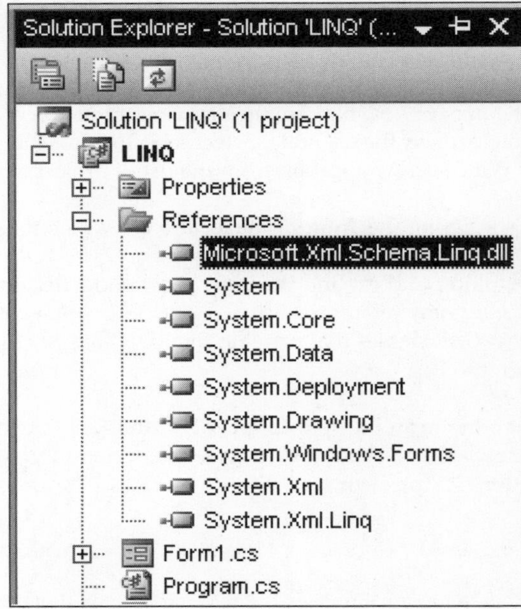

Figure C-2

From the Build menu, select Build Solution to ensure that the project compiles. Then run the application and click the Untyped button. The text box should be populated with the value of 2280.63, as shown in Figure C-3.

Figure C-3

This example is similar to the examples you worked with in the Chapters 5 through 9 in the LINQ to XML section. It uses the `Load` method of the `XElement` method to load an XML document into memory. A LINQ query expression is then executed against the XML document, using the `sum()` query operator to sum all the order totals. The results are the displayed in the text box.

Notice that because the XML document is untyped, the use of the `Elements` method is needed to specify the element you're looking for. Because no mapping taking place, you have to physically specify the element name.

Wouldn't it be nice to be able to use typed XML programming? Ah, yes, you can. First, open the `Orders.xml` file and add the following highlighted namespace to it:

```
<Order xmlns="http://www.AdventureWorks.com/Orders">
  <OrderDetail>
    <CustID>676</CustID>
    <OrderID>43659</OrderID>
    <Item>
      <ProductID>709</ProductID>
      <UnitPrice>5.70</UnitPrice>
      <OrderQuantity>6</OrderQuantity>
    </Item>
    ...
</Order>
```

Next, highlight the entire XML tree and copy it to the Clipboard. Go back to your Visual Studio project, and in the Solution Explorer window right-click the solution and select Add ➪ New Item from the context menu. In the Add New Item dialog, select XML File in the Templates section (see Figure C-4).

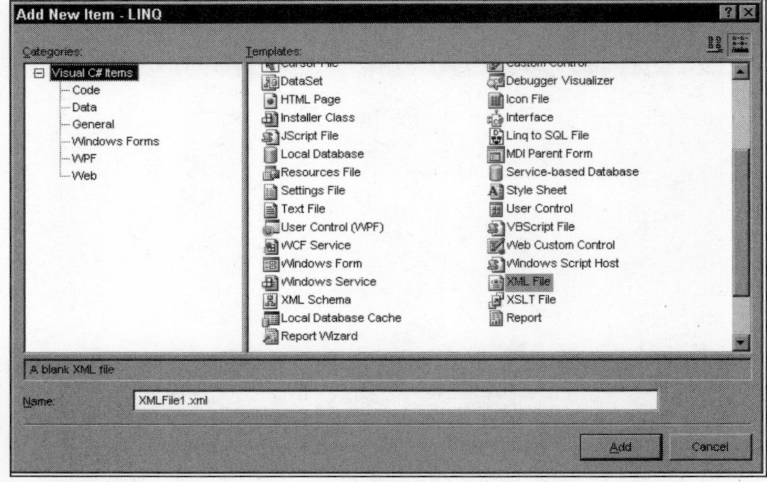

Figure C-4

For the purposes of this example, you can keep the name of `XMLFile1.xml`. Click Add.

`XMLFile1.xml` opens in the IDE and contains a single header line. Delete the XML that is there, and paste the XML that you copied from `Orders.xml` to the Clipboard. Save the new `XMLFile.xml` file.

Next, return to Solution Explorer and add a new item, this time selecting an XML Schema template from the Add New Item dialog. When the schema opens, delete the default contents of the file, add the following XML, and save it:

```
<xs:schema
  xmlns:xs="http://www.w3.org/2001/XMLSchema"
  targetNamespace="http://www.AdventureWorks.com/Orders"
  xmlns="http://www.AdventureWorks.com/Orders"
  elementFormDefault="qualified">

  <xs:element name="Order">
    <xs:complexType>
      <xs:sequence>
        <xs:element ref="OrderDetail"
                    minOccurs="0" maxOccurs="unbounded"/>
      </xs:sequence>
    </xs:complexType>
  </xs:element>
  <xs:element name="OrderDetail">
    <xs:complexType>
      <xs:sequence>
        <xs:element name="CustId" type="xs:string"/>
        <xs:element ref="Item"
                    minOccurs="0" maxOccurs="unbounded"/>
```

```
        </xs:sequence>
      </xs:complexType>
    </xs:element>
    <xs:element name="Item">
      <xs:complexType>
        <xs:sequence>
          <xs:element name="ProductID" type="xs:string"/>
          <xs:element name="UnitPrice" type="xs:double"/>
          <xs:element name="OrderQuantity" type="xs:int"/>
        </xs:sequence>
      </xs:complexType>
    </xs:element>
  </xs:schema>
```

You're not quite done yet. Once you have created the schema, a property needs to be changed on it. Return to the Solution Explorer window, right-click on the `XMLSchema1.xsd` file, and select Properties from the context menu, as shown in Figure C-5.

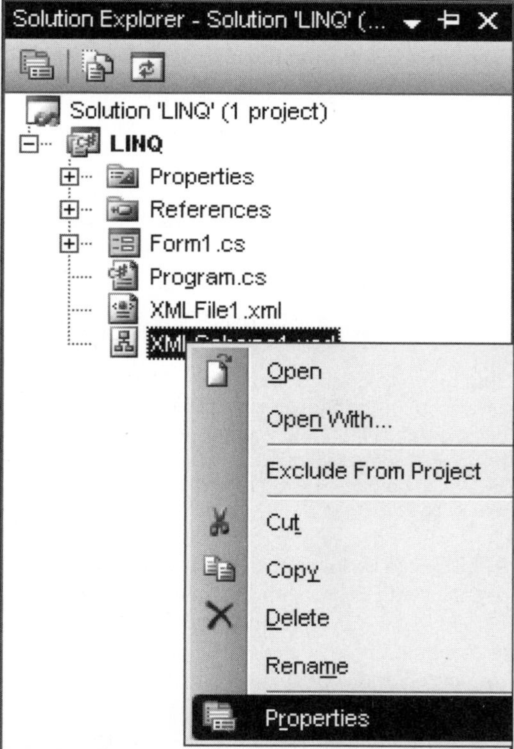

Figure C-5

In the Properties window for the schema, select the property called Build Action. The default value for this property is `None`; change it to `LinqToXsdSchema`, as shown in Figure C-6. This property informs the project that the schema will be included in the project's build process.

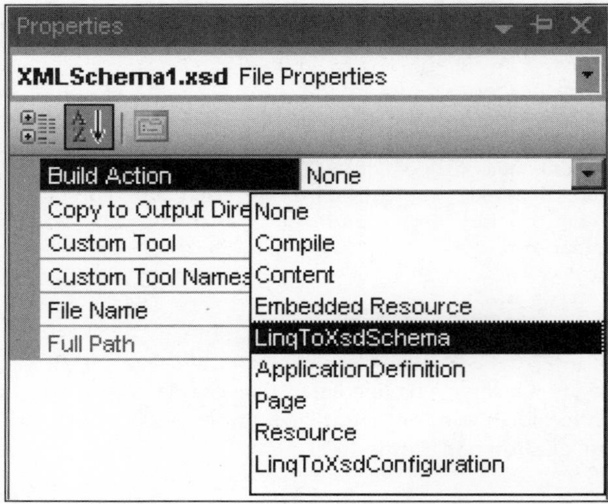

Figure C-6

The final step is to add some code behind the form. Set the Text property of the second button to Typed, and double-click the button to display the `Click` event code for that button.

Before you add the code to the `Click` event, scroll to the top of the code and add the following using statement:

```
using www.AdventureWorks.com.Orders;
```

Finally, in the `Click` event for `button2`, add the following:

```
var ord = Order.Load("C:\\Wrox\\AppendixC\\Orders.xml");

var total = (from purchaseOrder in ord.OrderDetail
             from item in purchaseOrder.Item
             select item.UnitPrice * item.OrderQuantity
             ).Sum();

textBox1.Text = total.ToString();
```

Notice that as you type, IntelliSense kicks in and displays the mapping between the XML and the XSD. You know typed XML programming is here, and now you only need to type `order.OrderDetail`.

Now, compile and run the application, and click the Typed button. You will get the same results in the text box that you did when you click the Untyped button.

Cool, huh? But wait. What is this `Order` object in the first line that the `Load` method uses? Where did that come from? Put your mouse cursor over the word Order and right-click. From the context menu, select Go To Definition (see Figure C-7).

A file called `LinqToXsdSources` opens, as shown in Figure C-8.

This file is an external mapping file created by LINQ to XSD when the project is compiled. As you can see, it is a fairly lengthy file, but it contains all the necessary mapping information to effectively provide typed XML programming.

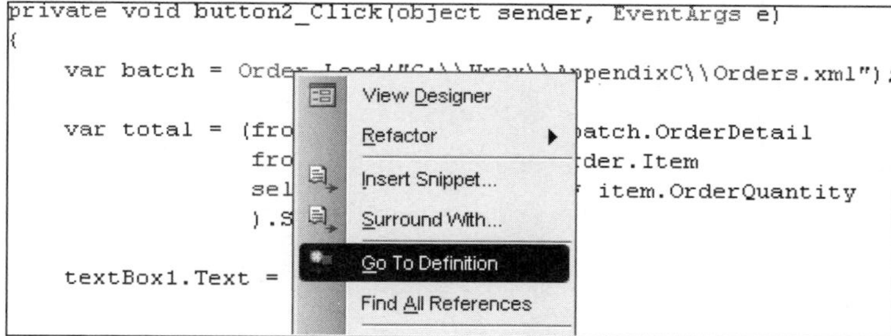

Figure C-7

```
LinqToXsdSource.cs | Start Page | Form1.cs
www.AdventureWorks.com.Orders.Order            OrderDetailField

    using System.Xml;
    using System.Xml.Schema;
    using System.Xml.Linq;
    using Microsoft.Xml.Schema.Linq;


    /// <summary>
    /// <para>
    /// Regular expression: (OrderDetail*)
    /// </para>
    /// </summary>
    public partial class Order : XTypedElement, IXMetaData {

        [DebuggerBrowsable(DebuggerBrowsableState.Never)]
        private XTypedList<OrderDetail> OrderDetailField;

        [DebuggerBrowsable(DebuggerBrowsableState.Never)]
        static Dictionary<XName, System.Type> localElementDictionary = new Dictionary<XName, Sys

        [DebuggerBrowsable(DebuggerBrowsableState.Never)]
        private static ContentModelEntity contentModel;

        public static explicit operator Order(XElement xe) { return XTypedServices.ToXTypedElem
```

Figure C-8

It is recommended that the generated code not be modified because it is quite complex and any changes made to the file would be lost during regeneration.

Instances of LINQ to XSD types are referred to as XML objects because the generated classes model typed views on untyped XML trees. Another way to say it is that the generated classes use properties to access the untyped XML trees.

An instance of LINQ to XSD is a set of classes that form wrappers around an instance of the LINQ to XML `XElement` class.

Mapping Rules

When a schema is mapped to an object type, LINQ to XSD requires that the mapping meet several constraints:

- The mapping is understandable to the developer.
- The mapping does not rely on any customization by default.
- The mapping must derive classes that are close to the expectation of an OO programmer.
- The mapping covers all of the XML schema.
- The mapping facilitates round-tripping of instance data.
- The mapping conveys, where possible, most schema objectives into the object models.

This systematic rule mapping ensures a clean, precise mapping, and is assumed by LINQ to XSD. The following is a list of most of the mapping rules that are utilized by LINQ to XSD to map XML schemas to .NET object models:

- XML names are mapped to CLR names.
- XML namespaces are mapped to CLR namespaces.
- Global element declarations are mapped to classes.
- Complex-type definitions are mapped to classes.
- Local declarations of elements, attributes, and references are mapped to properties.
- Named and anonymous types by default are not mapped to classes.
- Simple-type references are mapped to CLR value types or strings.
- Anonymous complex types for local elements by default are mapped to inner classes.
- Simple-type restrictions are mapped to element property preconditions.
- Complex-type derivation is mapped to object-oriented subclassing via extension and restriction.
- Substitution grouping is mapped to object-oriented subclassing.
- Redefinitions are carried out before mapping as applied by `System.Xml.Schema` rules.

LINQ to XSD-Generated API Class Methods

This section briefly discusses the methods of the API classes that LINQ to XSD generates from XML schemas. These methods should seem familiar because they are also methods within LINQ to XML. However, they are the typed version of the methods.

The current release of LINQ to XSD is in its early stages, so these API methods could change.

Load Method

You've seen the Load method used a couple of times in the example in this appendix. The first was the LINQ to XML's Load method on the XElement. The second time it was used was on the typed version of a generated class.

Load creates an instance of the generated class, letting the newly created instance serve as a typed view on an XElement instance. Take a look at the various overloads for the Load method. First, here's an example that takes a URI string as the data source:

```
public static val Load(string uri);
```

The next example is the same as the first, but it includes a parameter to control the preservation of whitespace.

```
static val Load(string uri, bool preserveWhitespace);
```

Here's how to use a TextReader as the data source:

```
static val Load(TextReader tr);
```

The following example is the same as the previous example except that it includes a parameter to control the preservation of whitespace. Notice that this example also uses a TextReader as the data source.

```
static val Load(TextReader tr, bool preserveWhitespace);
```

Here's how to use an XmlReader as the data source.

```
static val Load(XmlReader xr);
```

The following example, taken from earlier in the appendix, shows how the Load method is used on a typed XElement.

```
var ord = Order.Load("C:\\Wrox\\AppendixC\\Orders.xml");
```

Keep in mind that these overloads may change in the actual release of LINQ to XSD.

Parse

The Parse method of a generated class is the typed version of the LINQ to XML XElement Parse method. This method takes an XML string and parses it into an XElement instance, casting that instance into the requested type of the static method call. Parse has two overloads. The first takes a string parameter, as shown here:

```
public static XElement Parse(string text);
```

An optional parameter can be passed to preserve the whitespace:

```
public static XElement Parse(string text, bool preserveWhitespace);
```

The following example shows how to use the typed version of the `Parse` method.

```
var ord = Order.Parse("C:\\Wrox\\AppendixC\\Orders.xml");
```

Save

The `Save` method of a generated class is the typed version of the LINQ to XML `XElement Save` method. As with the LINQ to XML `Save` method, the typed version of the `Save` method takes the source XML tree and forwards it to the wrapped `XElement` instance for saving.

`Save` has several overloads. This first example shows the syntax to save the output to a text file:

```
public void Save(string filename);
```

The following example is the same as the first example but includes a parameter to control the preservation of whitespace:

```
public void Save(string filename, bool preserveWhitespace);
```

Here's an example that shows the syntax to save the output to a TextWriter:

```
public void Save(TextWriter tw);
```

The following example from earlier in the appendix shows how the `Save` method is used on a typed `XElement`.

```
public void Save(TextWriter tw, bool preserveWhitespace);
```

Here's how to write the output to an XmlWriter:

```
public void Save(XmlWriter xw);
```

The following example shows how to use the typed version of the `Save` method to save the output to a text file.

```
var ord = Order.Load("C:\\Wrox\\AppendixC\\Orders.xml");
// process the xml tree
order.Save("C:\\Wrox\\AppendixC\\Orders2.xml");
```

Clone

The `Clone` method clones the entire underlying untyped XML tree. The capability to clone is provided by the generated classes' base class, `XTypedElement`. The `Clone` method is quite simple to use, but the result of a clone is weakly typed and therefore a cast must be used to access the intended type.

For example, the following code shows the original XML tree being cloned into a second XML tree while being cast to the original type. Once the cast and clone are executed, it can be used just like the original XML tree.

```
var ord = Order.Load("C:\\Wrox\\AppendixC\\Orders.xml");
var ord2 = (Order)ord.Clone();

var total = (from purchaseOrder in ord2.OrderDetail
             from item in purchaseOrder.Item
             select item.UnitPrice * item.OrderQuantity
             ).Sum();

textBox1.Text = total.ToString();
```

Default Values

Default values affect the behavior of the getters for properties that implement declarations for elements or attributes for defaults. That is, when the element or attribute is not found in the XML tree, the getter for either the attribute or element returns the default value.

For example, the following XSD schema fragment contains an element declaration that also defines a default value for the `Department` element.

```
<xs: ComplexType name="EmployeeInfo">
  <xs:Sequence>
    <xs:element name="NationalIDNumber" type="xs:string" />
    <xs:element name="LoginID" type="xs:string" />
    <xs:element name="Title" type="xs:string" />
    <xs:element name="Name" type="xs:string" />
    <xs:element name="EmailAddress" type="xs:string" />
  </xs:Sequence>
  <xs:attribute name="Department" type="xs:string" default="Dev"/>
</xs:ComplexType>
```

You can build an XML tree that intentionally excludes the definition of a `Department` element:

```
var emp = new EmployeeInfo
{
  NationalIDNumber = "123456789",
  LoginID = "adventure-works\scott",
  Title = "Geek",
  Name = "Scott",
  EmailAddress = "scott@adventure-works.com"
};
```

When the getter for the `Department` element is called, the default defined by the schema is returned, as shown here:

```
<EmployeeInfo Department="Dev">
  <NationalIDNumber>123456789</NationalIDNumber>
```

```
    <LoginID>adventure-works\scott</LoginID>
    <Title>Geek</Title>
    <Name>Scott</Name>
    <EmailAddress>scott@adventure-works.com</EmailAddress>
  </EmployeeInfo>
```

Again, the current release of LINQ to XSD and the API of XML objects may, and probably will, change. For example, the current release of LINQ to XSD does not support defaults for elements, but it does support defaults for attributes (thus, the use of a default for an attribute in the previous example).

Also, the actual overloads for the API methods may differ.

Index

Index

A

Add (T) method, 225
AddAfterSelf, 113
AddAnnotation method, 101, 103, 106, 158
AddBeforeSelf, 113
ADO Provider, 218
ADO.NET, 199. *See also* LINQ to SQL
  command object, 42–43
  DataSets, 3, 271, 272, 284
ADO.NET Entity Framework, 329–344
  Entity Data Model Generator tool, 342–344
  example, 332–340
  installation, 331
  overview, 329–331
  querying entity data model, 340–341
  working with objects, 341–342
Aggregate operator, 64
aggregating query operators, 64–68
  Aggregate, 64
  Average, 54, 64–65
  Count, 54, 65
  LongCount, 55, 66
  Max, 55, 66–67
  Min, 55, 67
  Sum, 55, 67–68
All operator, 54, 83–84
Always value, 264
Ancestors method, 161–163
AncestorsAndSelf method, 101, 164–165
AND logical operator, 38
annotations, 158–160
anonymous types, 23
  C#, 23
  lambda expressions v., 28
  named types v., 40
  object initializers of, 26
  Visual Basic, 23
Any operator, 54, 84–85
API class methods, LINQ to XSD, 354–358
APIs
  LINQ, 145, 152
  LINQ to SQL, 218
  standard query operators *v.*, 53
AsEnumerable operator, 74
Association attribute, 202, 206–207, 214
  IsForeignKey property, 206
  IsUnique property, 206
  LINQ to SQL joins, 218
  Name property, 206
  OtherKey property, 206
  properties, 206
  Storage property, 206
  ThisKey property, 206
Attach method, 302–303
AttachAll method, 304
Attribute axis property, 186
Attribute method, 101
attribute-based mapping, LINQ to SQL, 202–209
  Database attribute, 202–203
  mapping columns, 203–205
  mapping functions, 208–209
  mapping relationships, 206–207
  mapping stored procedures, 207–208
  mapping tables, 203
  ORD tool, 202
  Parameter attribute, 209
  SqlMetal tool, 202
attributes, 102, 117–120
  adding, 117
  Association, 202, 206–207, 214
    IsForeignKey property, 206
    IsUnique property, 206
    LINQ to SQL joins, 218
    Name property, 206
    OtherKey property, 206
    properties, 206

attributes *(continued)*
- Storage property, 206
- ThisKey property, 206
- Column, 203–205
  - AutoSync property, 204
  - CanBeNull property, 204
  - DbType property, 204
  - Expression property, 204
  - IsDbGenerated property, 204, 212
  - IsDiscriminator property, 204
  - IsPrimaryKey property, 204, 212
  - IsVersion property, 204
  - Name property, 204
  - properties, 204
  - Storage property, 204
  - UpdateCheck property, 204
- Database, 202–203
- deleting, 119–120
  - Remove method, 119–120
- SetAttributeValue method, 120
- elements v., 102–103, 117
- Parameter, 209
  - DbType property, 209
  - Name property, 209
  - properties, 209
- Remove method
  - deleting attributes, 119–120
- RemoveAttributes method, 102
- ReplaceAttributes method, 102
- retrieving, 117–119
- SetAttributeValue method, 102, 115
  - deleting attributes, 120

Attributes method, 101
AutoSync property, 204
Average operator, 54, 64–65
aw.cs file, 298
aw.dbml file, 298
axis methods, 161–167
- Ancestors, 161–163
- AncestorsAndSelf, 164–165
- Descendants, 163–164
- DescendantsAndSelf, 165–166
- ElementsAfterSelf, 166–167
- ElementsBeforeSelf, 166–167
- XML trees and, 167

B

binding data, LINQ to DataSets, 279–281
- implicit, 281

BindingNavigator component, 307
BindingSource component, 307
bracketing, 269

C

C#
- anonymous types, 23
- creating XML trees
  - LINQ to XML, 124–128
- extension methods, 26–28
- implicitly typed variables, 22
- lambda expressions, 29
- object initializers, 24–25
- query expressions, 22

CanBeNull property, 204
case study, Fabrikam, 313–328
- application configuration file added, 314
- designing user interface, 316–319
- LINQ references, 314
- login form, 317–318
- mappings to database objects, 315
- ProductMain form, 322–324
- run Fabrikam.sql, 313–314
  - objects created, 314
- SelectProduct form, 319–321
- server objects added, 315

Cast operator, 54, 74–75
ChangeConflictException class, 265
Changed event, 170–171
Changing event, 168–170
Child axis property, 186
Class member, 202
classes
- ChangeConflictException, 265
- CompiledQuery, 251
- DataAdapter, 272, 273, 274
- DataContext, 200–201, 202, 219–220
  - creating/configuring, 288–290
  - LINQ to SQL queries, 219–220

mapping for stored procedures/functions, 292–293
strongly typed, 220–221
DataRowComparer, 281–282
DataShape, 254
DataTableExtensions, 280
entity, LINQ to SQL, 202, 203, 257–270
creating for tables/view mapping, 290–291
EntitySet, 252
LINQ to SQL, 288
LINQ to XML, 96–107, 122
list, 97
XAttribute, 12, 13, 97, 102–104
XDocument, 97, 104–107
XElement, 12, 13, 14, 97, 98–102
MemberChangeConflict, 266
MethodInfo, 233
pluralization of, in O/R Designer, 296
Table (of TEntity), 302
TestAnnotation, 160
TransactionScope, 267, 269
XAttribute, 12, 97, 102–104
example, 13
methods, 103
XElement class v., 103
XCData, 97
XComment, 97
XContainer, 97
XDeclaration, 97–98
XDocument, 97, 104–107
methods, 106
objects in, 104–105
XElement, 12, 14, 97, 98–102
methods, 100, 101–102
XAttribute class v., 103
XML document construction, 12–13
XName, 97
names, 142
string representation, 142
XNamespace, 97
namespaces, 97, 142
XNode, 97, 112
XML manipulation in LINQ to XML, 112–117
XNodeDocumentOrderComparer, 97
XNodeEqualityComparer, 97
XObject, 97
XObjectChange, 97
XObjectChangeEventArgs, 97
XProcessingInstruction, 97
XText, 97
Clone method, LINQ to XSD, 356–357
CLR (Common Language Runtime), 14, 23
metadata, 14
/code:file, 296
Column attribute, 203–205
AutoSync property, 204
CanBeNull property, 204
DbType property, 204
Expression property, 204
IsDbGenerated property, 204, 212
IsDiscriminator property, 204
IsPrimaryKey property, 204, 212
IsVersion property, 204
Name property, 204
properties, 204
Storage property, 204
UpdateCheck property, 204
columns, mapping, 203–205
Common Language Runtime. *See* CLR
Community Technology Preview (CTP) build, 21
Compile method, 251
compiled queries, LINQ to SQL, 251
CompiledQuery class, 251
compile-time type checking, 4
composite keys, 255
Concat operator, 63–64
concatenating query operators, 63–64
concurrency, optimistic, 263, 303–304
conflicts, 263–266
ChangeConflictException, 265
ConflictMode enumeration, 264–265
RefreshMode enumeration, 265–266
UpdateCheck property, 263–264
Configure Behavior dialog box, 294
ConflictMode enumeration, 264–265
ContinueOnConflict value, 264
FailOnFirstConflict value, 264
/c[onnection]:, 343
contactBindingSource control, 308
ContactID column, 211, 212, 213, 214
ContactsPart, 236
Contains operator, 85

/context:type, 297
ContinueOnConflict value, 264
conversion query operators, 73–77
AsEnumerable, 74
Cast, 54, 74–75
OfType, 75
ToArray, 75–76
ToDictionary, 76
ToList, 76–77
ToLookup, 77
CopyToDataTable method, 280
Count operator, 54, 65
CreateDatabase method, 219
CreateQuery method, 219
CreateReader method, 101, 102, 106
CreateWriter method, 101, 106
CRUD operations, 209
.cs file, 288
CTP build. ***See*** **Community Technology Preview build**

D

data binding, LINQ to DataSets, 279–281
implicit, 281
data loading
deferred, 252–253
turning off, 254–255
immediate, 252–253
data manipulation, via LINQ to SQL queries, 221–225
Data Source Configuration Wizard, 278, 305–307
data source, LINQ query, 32–33
DataAdapter class, 272, 273, 274
Database attribute, 202–203
database relationships, LINQ to SQL, 245–250
defining/representing, 245–250
querying across, 250
/database:name, 296
DataContext class, 200–201, 202, 219–220
creating/configuring, 288–290
LINQ to SQL queries, 219–220
mapping for stored procedures/functions, 292–293
strongly typed, 220–221
DataContext methods, 292
DataGridView, 280
DataReader, 43
DataRowComparer class, 281–282
DataRows, 272
comparing, 281–284
DataSet Designer, 17
DataSets. ***See also*** **LINQ to DataSets**
ADO.NET, 3, 271, 272, 284
defined, 271
typed, 278–279
DataShape class, 254
DataSource property, 280
DataTableExtensions class, 280
DataView, 280, 281
.dbml file, 288
/dbml:file, 296
DbType property, 204, 209
Decendants ( ) method, 134–135
declarative query syntax, 7, 8, 21, 275
Default property, 282
DefaultIfEmpty operator, 78
deferred data loading, 252–253
turning off, 254–255
deferred query execution, 35
immediate *v.*, 252–255
DeferredLoadingEnabled property, 254–255
DELETE function, 293
DeleteDatabase method, 219, 220
deleting data
entity objects, 226–227
LINQ to SQL queries, 225
Descendant axis property, 186
DescendantNodes method, 101, 106
DescendantNodesAndSelf method, 101
Descendants method, 163–164
DescendantsAndSelf method, 101, 165–166
descending clause, 38
DirectoryInformation table, 9
INSERT statement, 10
Distinct operator, 54, 68–69, 281
DLINQ. ***See*** **LINQ to SQL**
Document Object Model. ***See*** **DOM**
DOM (Document Object Model), 4, 12, 14, 95
limitations, 120
LINQ to XML v., 120–121

XML reshaping/modifying
load/modify/save approach, 137–138
dot notation, 250

E

element(s), 98
attributes v., 102–103, 117
Element method, 101, 106
element query operators, 77–82
DefaultIfEmpty, 78
ElementAt, 78–79
ElementAtOrDefault, 79
First, 79
FirstOrDefault, 80
Last, 80
LastOrDefault, 80–81
Single, 29, 81
SingleOrDefault, 82
ElementAt ( ) method, 134
ElementAt operator, 78–79
ElementAtOrDefault operator, 79
Elements ( ) method, 135
ElementsAfterSelf method, 166–167
ElementsBeforeSelf method, 166–167
embedded expressions, 128–129, 182–184
Visual Basic and, 182–184
in XML literals, 182–184
embedded queries, in XML literals, 184, 187
Empty operator, 71–72
entities management, 121
entity classes, LINQ to SQL, 202, 203, 257–270
creating for tables/view mapping, 290–291
entity changes
concurrent, 263–266
submitting, 258–263
tracking, 258
Entity Data Model Generator tool, 342–344
examples, 344
functionality, 342
modes, 343
options, 343–344
entity objects
deleting data, 226–227
inserting data, 225–226
LINQ to SQL queries, 225–227
updating data, 226
/entitybase:type, 297
EntityClassGeneration, 343
/entitycontainer:, 344
EntitySet class, 252
equality query operators, 82–83
SequenceEqual, 82–83
Equals method, 281
events, LINQ to XML, 167–171
Changed, 170–171
Changing, 168–170
ExcecuteQuery method, 219
ExcecuteReader ( ) method, 43
Except operator, 71, 281
execution, query, 32, 33–36
deferred, 35
deferred v. immediate, 252–255
immediate, 35–36
local, 251, 252
remote, 251, 252
local v., 251–252
"Expanding the Results View will enumerate the IEnumerable," 34
explicit distributable transactions, 267
explicit local transactions, 267
example, 268–269
Expression(of TDelegate), 42
Expression property, 204
expression trees, 42
lambda expressions, 42
expressions, 128
embedded, 128–129, 182–184
Visual Basic and, 182–184
in XML literals, 182–184
lambda, 28–29, 54, 145
anonymous types v., 28
C# example, 29
expression trees, 42
LINQ with, 29
method syntax and, 44
rules for use, 29
ExtensibilityMethodDefinitions region, 294, 295
Extension indexer property, 186
illustration, 186–187

extension methods, 26–28, 54
best practices, 28
C#, 26–28
Visual Basic, 28
external mapping, LINQ to SQL, 299–302

F

Fabrikam case study, 313–328
application configuration file added, 314
designing user interface, 316–319
LINQ references, 314
login form, 317–318
mappings to database objects, 315
ProductMain form, 322–324
run Fabrikam.sql, 313–314
objects created, 314
SelectProduct form, 319–321
server objects added, 315
FailOnFirstConflict value, 264
Field method, 278
First ( ) method, 134
First operator, 79
FirstOrDefault operator, 80
For Each loop, 34
FOR EACH statement, 8
foreach loop, 34, 35
foreach statement, 8
foreign keys, 212–215
from clause, 37
FromSSDLGeneration, 343
FullGeneration, 343
Function attribute, 208–209, 227
functional construction, 111, 137–139, 153–158
benefits, 156
functions
DataContext mapping for, 292–293
DELETE, 293
INSERT, 293
mapping
attribute-based, 208–209
DataContext class, 292–293
user-defined, 240–243
mapping/calling, 240–243
/functions, 296

G

generation query operators, 71–73
Empty, 71–72
Range, 72–73
repeat, 73
generator, 37
GetChildRows method, 272
GetEnumerator method, 43
GetHashCode method, 281
GetParentRow method, 272
GetQueryText method, 219
GetTable method, 221
group operator, 255
GroupBy operator, 55, 62–63, 255
grouping, 62
grouping operator, 62–63
GroupBy, 55, 62–63, 255
GroupJoin operator, 55, 59, 60–62

H

/help, 344

I

IDbConnection, 219
identity specification, 211
IEnumerable<T> interface, 8, 54
IQueryable<T> interface v., 54
var keyword v., 40–41
IEnumerator<T> interface, 41, 43
IGrouping, 77
immediate data loading, 252–253
immediate query execution, 35–36
deferred *v.*, 252–255
implicit binding, 281
implicit transactions, 267
implicitly typed variables, 22
C#, 22
Visual Basic, 22
/incsdl:, 343
/inmsl:, 343
inner join, 59
Inputfile, 297
INSERT function, 293

INSERT statement, for DirectoryInformation table, 10
inserting data
- entity objects, 225–226
- LINQ to SQL queries, 222–224

/inssdl:, 343
intersect operator, 70–71, 281, 284
IQueryable interface, 42–43, 252
IQueryable (Of T) interface, 42–43, 217, 218
IQueryable<T> interface, 11, 54
- IEnumerable<T> interface v., 54

IsAfter method, 101, 106
IsBefore method, 101, 106
IsDbGenerated property, 204, 212
IsDiscriminator property, 204
IsForeignKey property, 206
IsPrimaryKey property, 204, 212
IsUnique property, 206
IsVersion property, 204

J

join clause, 40
- LINQ to SQL joins, 218

join operator, 55, 59–60, 250
joining operators, 59–62
- GroupJoin, 55, 59, 60–62
- join, 55, 59–60, 250

joins, LINQ to SQL, 218
- Association attribute, 218
- join clause, 218

K

KeepChanges value, 265
KeepCurrentValues, 265
keys
- composite, 255
- foreign, 212–215
- primary, 210–212

L

lambda expressions, 28–29, 54, 145
- anonymous types v., 28
- C# example, 29
- expression trees, 42
- LINQ with, 29
- method syntax and, 44
- rules for use, 29

lambda operator, 29
/language:, 344
Language Integrated Query. ***See*** **LINQ**
/language:language, 297
Last operator, 80
LastOrDefault operator, 80–81
.layout file, 288
LINQ (Language Integrated Query), 3
- APIs, 145, 152
- defined, 3, 7
- features, 145
- flexibility, 145
- goal, 3
- history/background, 3–6
- illustrations, 6–7
- lambda expressions with, 29
- language specific features, in Visual Studio 2008, 21–29
- overview, 7–10
- Providers, 41
  - LINQ to SQL, 41
- purpose, 7
- queries, 31–51
  - actions, 32–36
  - common terms, 41–43
  - concepts, 37–43
  - data source, 32–33
  - LINQ to SQL queries v., 218
  - parts, 32–36
  - polymorphic, 42
  - query creation, 32, 33
  - syntax options, 43–51
- strong points, 145
- syntax v. SQL syntax, 36–37

LINQ to DataSets, 3, 41, 271–285
- comparing DataRows, 281–284
- data binding, 279–281
  - implicit, 281
- loading data, 273–274
- overview, 272
- project creation, 272–273

LINQ to DataSets *(continued)*
queries, 275–279
across multiple tables, 277–278
single table, 275–276
typed DataSets, 278–279
LINQ to Entities, 329–344. *See also* ADO.NET Entity Framework
LINQ to Objects, 41
LINQ to SQL (DLINQ), 199–215
advanced topics, 287–310
API, 218
attribute-based mapping, 202–209
Database attribute, 202–203
mapping columns, 203–205
mapping functions, 208–209
mapping relationships, 206–207
mapping stored procedures, 207–208
mapping tables, 203
Parameter attribute, 209
classes, 288
concurrency conflicts, 263–266
external mapping, 299–302
joins, 218
Association attribute, 218
multi-tier operations, 302–310
n-tier operations, 302–310
best practices, 303–304
examples, 304–305
insertion/deletion, 304
optimistic concurrency, 303–304
O/R Designer example, 305–310
O/R Designer, 17, 287–296
attribute-based mapping, 202
creating/opening, 288
DataContext creation/configuration, 288–290
DataContext mapping for stored procedures/functions, 292–293
entity class creation for tables/view mapping, 290–291
n-tier operations, 305–310
pluralization of classes in, 296
validation logic, 294–295
Provider, 218
queries, 217–244
advanced concepts, 245–256
compiled, 251
components involved, 218–219
composite keys, 255
concepts, 217–219
data manipulation via, 221–225
database relationships, 245–250
DataContext class, 219–220
DataShape class, 254
deferred v. immediate data loading, 252–255
deleting data, 225
entity objects, 225–227
goal, 16
illustrations, 14–15
inserting data, 222–224
LINQ Provider, 41
LINQ queries v., 218
object model, 201–202
overview, 14–16, 200–201
parts, 217–218
Person.Contact table and, 147–149
read-only data, 255–256
remote v. local execution, 251–252
stored procedures, 227–240
UDFs, 240–243
updating data, 224–225
relational data basics, 209–215
SQL Metal command-line tool, 296–299
/? option, 297
attribute-based mapping, 202
/code:file, 296
/context:type, 297
/database:name, 296
/dbml:file, 296
/entitybase:type, 297
/functions, 296
Inputfile, 297
/language:language, 297
location, 297
/map:file, 297
/namespace:name, 297
options, 296–297
/password:password, 296
/pluralize, 297
/serialization:option, 297
/server:name, 296
/sprocs, 296
/timeout:timeout, 296

/user:name, 296
/views, 296
transactions, 267–269
explicit distributable, 267
explicit local, 267
illustrations, 267–269
implicit, 267
LINQ to XML (XLINQ), 95–122
adding attributes, 117
annotations, 158–160
axis methods, 161–167
Ancestors, 161–163
AncestorsAndSelf, 164–165
Descendants, 163–164
DescendantsAndSelf, 165–166
ElementsAfterSelf, 166–167
ElementsBeforeSelf, 166–167
XML trees and, 167
benefits, 154
classes, 96–107, 122
list, 97
XAttribute, 12, 13, 97, 102–104
XDocument, 97, 104–107
XElement, 12, 13, 14, 97, 98–102
creating XML elements, 110–111
deleting attributes, 119–120
deleting XML, 116–117
DOM v., 120–121
events, 167–171
Changed, 170–171
Changing, 168–170
features in Visual Basic.NET, 179–195
functional construction, 111, 137–139, 153–158
illustrations, 12–13
inserting XML, 113
LINQ enabled, 96, 345
loading XML, 107–109
from file, 107
from string, 107–108
from TextReader, 108–109
manipulating XML, 112–117
XNode class, methods of, 112–117
MSXML v., 121
overview, 12–14, 95–96
Person.Contact table and, 147–149
programming fundamentals, 96–107
programming techniques/topics, 123–143
advanced, 153–177
queries, 132–137
retrieving attributes, 117–119
saving XML, 109
single programming interface, 96
SQL data to XML tree, 145–149
streaming XML documents, 171–177
large, 176–177
traversing XML, 111–112
types, 167–168
XObjectChange, 168
XObjectChangeEventArgs, 168
XObjectChangeEventHandler, 168
updating XML, 113–115
whitespace, 121
XML namespaces, 141–143
XML trees
creating, 123–129
modifying/reshaping, 137–139
populating from text, 130–131
querying, 132–137
serializing, 139–141
XmlReader v., 121
XSLT v., 121
LINQ to XSD, 345–358
API class methods, 354–358
Clone method, 356–357
default values, 357–358
example, 346–353
installation, 346
Load method, 355
mapping rules, 354
overview, 345–346
Parse method, 355–356
Preview, 346
Save method, 356
LinqToXsdSchema, 351–352
LinqToXsdSources, 353
Load method, 101, 106
LINQ to XSD, 355
populating XML trees from text, 130–131
load options, 189–191
None, 190
PreserveWhitespace, 190

load options *(continued)*
SetBaseUri, 190
SetLineInfo, 190
LoadOptions enumeration, 190
LongCount operator, 55, 66
Lookup, 77

M

/map:file, 297
mapping, attribute-based
columns, 203–205
functions, 208–209
ORD tool, 202
relationships, 206–207
stored procedures, 207–208
tables, 203
mapping rules, LINQ to XSD, 354
Max operator, 55, 66–67
MemberChangeConflict class, 266
method(s)
Add (T), 225
AddAnnotation, 101, 103, 106, 158
Ancestors, 161–163
AncestorsAndSelf, 101, 164–165
API class, LINQ to XSD, 354–358
Attach, 302–303
AttachAll, 304
Attribute, 101
axis, 161–167
Ancestors, 161–163
AncestorsAndSelf, 101, 164–165
Descendants, 163–164
DescendantsAndSelf, 165–166
ElementsAfterSelf, 166–167
ElementsBeforeSelf, 166–167
XML trees and, 167
Clone, LINQ to XSD, 356–357
Compile, 251
CopyToDataTable, 280
CreateDatabase, 219
CreateQuery, 219
CreateReader, 101, 102, 106
CreateWriter, 101, 106
DataContext, 292
Decendants ( ), 134–135
DeleteDatabase, 219, 220
DescendantNodes, 101, 106
DescendantNodesAndSelf, 101
Descendants, 163–164
DescendantsAndSelf, 101, 165–166
Element, 101, 106
ElementAt ( ), 134
Elements ( ), 135
ElementsAfterSelf, 166–167
ElementsBeforeSelf, 166–167
Equals, 281
ExcecuteQuery, 219
ExcecuteReader ( ), 43
extension, 26–28, 54
best practices, 28
C#, 26–28
Visual Basic, 28
Field, 278
First ( ), 134
GetChildRows, 272
GetEnumerator, 43
GetHashCode, 281
GetParentRow, 272
GetQueryText, 219
GetTable, 221
IsAfter, 101, 106
IsBefore, 101, 106
Load, 101, 106
LINQ to XSD, 355
populating XML trees from text, 130–131
MoveNext ( ), 34
Nodes, 101, 106
NodesAfterSelf, 101, 106
NodesBeforeSelf, 102, 106
Parse, 102, 106
LINQ to XSD, 355–356
manipulating XML in Visual Basic, 189–191
populating XML trees from text, 130
ReadFrom ( ), 171
Remove, 102, 103, 106, 116, 304
deleting attributes, 119–120
Remove (T), 225
RemoveAll, 102, 116
RemoveAttributes, 102
RemoveNodes, 102, 106
Replace, 113

ReplaceAll, 102, 113
ReplaceAttributes, 102
ReplaceNodes, 113
ReplaceWith, 113, 114
Save, 102, 106
LINQ to XSD, 356
Select, 272
SetAttributeValue, 102, 115
deleting attributes, 120
SetElementValue, 102, 115
SetValue, 102, 103
SubmitChanges, 219, 220, 256
ToArray, 35
ToList, 35
WriteTo, 102
XAttribute class, 103
XDocument class, 106
XElement class, 100, 101–102
XNode class
XML manipulation in LINQ to XML, 112–117
method syntax, 45–51, 275
example, 44
lambda expressions and, 44
query syntax v., 43–44
using, 45–51
MethodInfo class, 233
Min operator, 55, 67
MoveNext ( ) method, 34
MSXML, 121
LINQ to XML v., 121
multi-tier operations, LINQ to SQL, 302–310

N

Name property, 204, 206, 209
named types
anonymous types v., 40
object initializers of, 26
names, XML, 141, 142
XName class, 142
/namespace:, 344
/namespace:name, 297
namespaces, 141, 143
System.Core, 272
System.Data, 199
System.Data.DataSetExtensions, 272
System.Reflection, 233
System.Runtime.CompilerServices, 28
System.Transactions, 267
System.Xml, 12, 95, 199
System.Xml.Linq, 96, 122
XML, 141–143
XNamespace class, 97, 142
.NET Framework
3.5, 4, 17, 21, 30
1.0, 18
1.1, 18
3.0, 18
technologies, 18
2.0, 18
version choice for Visual Studio 2008, 20
Never value, 264
New Project dialog box, 19–20, 45
nodes, 98
Nodes method, 101, 106
NodesAfterSelf method, 101, 106
NodesBeforeSelf method, 102, 106
/nologo, 344
None load option, 190
n-tier operations, LINQ to SQL, 302–310
best practices, 303–304
examples, 304–305
insertion/deletion, 304
optimistic concurrency, 303–304
O/R Designer example, 305–310

O

OBDC, 199
object(s)
ADO.NET command, 42–43
in ADO.NET Entity Framework, 341–342
entity
deleting data, 226–227
inserting data, 225–226
LINQ to SQL queries, 225–227
updating data, 226
XComment, 105
XDeclaration, 104
in XDocument class, 104–105
XDocumentType, 104

object(s) *(continued)*
XElement, 104
XProcessingInstruction, 105
object initializers, 23–26
of anonymous types, 26
C#, 24–25
of named types, 26
Visual Basic, 25–26
object mapping
example, 8–9
Object Relational Designer (O/R Designer), 17, 287–296
attribute-based mapping, 202
creating/opening, 288
DataContext creation/configuration, 288–290
DataContext mapping for stored procedures/functions, 292–293
entity class creation for tables/view mapping, 290–291
n-tier operations, 305–310
pluralization of classes in, 296
validation logic, 294–295
ObjectChangeConflict class, 266
object-oriented (OO) programming, 3
ObjectTrackingEnabled property, 255
OfType operator, 75
OLE DB, 199
OO programming. *See* object-oriented programming
operators. *See* standard query operators
optimistic concurrency, 263, 303–304
conflicts, 263–266
ChangeConflictException, 265
ConflictMode enumeration, 264–265
RefreshMode enumeration, 265–266
UpdateCheck property, 263–264
n-tier operations, 303–304
O/R Designer. *See* Object Relational Designer
OR logical operator, 38
Orcas, Beta 1, 345
ORD tool. *See* Object Relational Designer
Orderby clause, 38, 43–44
OrderBy operator, 55, 57
OrderByDescending operator, 55, 58
Reverse operator *v.*, 59
OtherKey property, 206
/outcsdl :, 343
/outms l:, 343
/outobjectlayer:, 343
OUTPUT parameter, 234
/outssdl :, 343
/outviews:, 344
OverwriteCurrentValues, 265

P

Parameter attribute, 209
DbType property, 209
Name property, 209
properties, 209
Parse method, 102, 106
LINQ to XSD, 355–356
manipulating XML in Visual Basic, 189–191
populating XML trees from text, 130
partitioning query operators, 86–88
Skip, 55, 86
SkipWhile, 55, 86–87
Take, 55, 87
TakeWhile, 55, 87–88
/password:password, 296
Person.Contact table
letter S contacts, 7
LINQ to SQL and, 147–149
LINQ to XML and, 147–149
query/query filter, 15
schema defined, 14
table design, 210–211
pluralization of classes, in O/R Designer, 296
/pluralize, 297
polymorphic queries, 42
prefixes, XML, 98, 141
PreserveWhitespace load option, 190
primary keys, 210–212
ProductsPart, 236
/p[roject]:, 343
projection query operators, 55–56
Select, 55–56
SelectMany, 55–56
projections, 38, 55
properties, 204
Association attribute, 206
AutoSync, 204

CanBeNull, 204
Column, 204
DataSource, 280
DbType, 204, 209
Default, 282
DeferredLoadingEnabled, 254–255
Descendant axis, 186
Expression, 204
Extension indexer, 186
illustration, 186–187
IsDbGenerated, 204, 212
IsDiscriminator, 204
IsForeignKey, 206
IsPrimaryKey, 204, 212
IsUnique, 206
IsVersion, 204
Name, 204, 206, 209
OtherKey, 206
relationship, 250
Storage, 204, 206
ThisKey, 206
UpdateCheck, 204
Always value, 264
concurrency conflicts, 263–264
Never value, 264
WhenChanged value, 264
Value, 186
/prov[ider]:, 343
Providers
ADO, 218
LINQ, 41
LINQ to SQL, 41
LINQ to SQL, 218

Q

quantifier query operators, 83–85
All, 54, 83–84
Any, 54, 84–85
Contains, 85
queries
creation, 32, 33
importance, 33
embedded in XML literals, 184, 187
execution, 32, 33–36
deferred, 35
deferred *v.* immediate, 252–255
immediate, 35–36
local, 251, 252
remote, 251, 252
expressions, 21–22, 55
C#, 22
Visual Basic, 22
LINQ, 31–51
actions, 32–36
common terms, 41–43
concepts, 37–43
data source, 32–33
LINQ to SQL queries v., 218
parts, 32–36
polymorphic, 42
query creation, 32, 33
syntax options, 43–51
LINQ to DataSets, 275–279
across multiple tables, 277–278
single table, 275–276
typed DataSets, 278–279
LINQ to SQL, 207–244
advanced concepts, 245–256
compiled, 251
components involved, 218–219
composite keys, 255
concepts, 217–219
data manipulation via, 221–225
database relationships, 245–250
DataContext class, 219–220
DataShape class, 254
deferred *v.* immediate data loading, 252–255
deleting data, 225
entity objects, 225–227
goal, 16
illustrations, 14–15
inserting data, 222–224
LINQ Provider, 41
LINQ queries v., 218
object model, 201–202
overview, 14–16, 200–201
Person.Contact table and, 147–149
read-only data, 255–256
remote v. local execution, 251–252
stored procedures, 227–240

queries *(continued)*
UDFs, 240–243
updating data, 224–225
LINQ to XML, 132–137
syntax, 43, 45–51, 275
example, 44
method syntax v., 43–44
using, 45–51
XML trees, 132–136
query operators. *See* standard query operators

R

Range operator, 72–73
range variable, 37
ReadFrom ( ) method, 171
read-only data, 255–256
/refcsdl :, 343
RefreshMode enumeration, 265–266
KeepChanges value, 265
KeepCurrentValues, 265
OverwriteCurrentValues, 265
relational data, 209–215. *See also* LINQ to SQL
foreign keys, 212–215
primary keys, 210–212
relationship properties, 250
relationships, mapping, 206–207
Remove method, 102, 103, 106, 116, 304
deleting attributes, 119–120
Remove (T) method, 225
RemoveAll method, 102, 116
RemoveAttributes method, 102
RemoveNodes method, 102, 106
repeat operator, 73
Replace method, 113
ReplaceAll method, 102, 113
ReplaceAttributes method, 102
ReplaceNodes method, 113
ReplaceWith method, 113, 114
Required value, 269
RequiredNew value, 269
restriction operator, 57
where, 11, 57
Results View, 34
Reverse operator, 57, 59
OrderByDescending v., 59

S

Save method, 102, 106
LINQ to XSD, 356
select clause, 38, 39
Select method, 272
Select operator, 55–56
select query operator, 11
SelectMany operator, 55–56
SequenceEqual operator, 82–83
sequences, 53–54
serialization, 109, 139
/serialization:option, 297
serializing XML trees, 139–141, 143
whitespace and, 139, 140, 141
/server:name, 296
Set Primary Key button, 211
set query operators, 68–71
Distinct, 54, 68–69, 281
Except, 71, 281
intersect, 70–71, 281, 284
Union, 70, 281
SetAttributeValue method, 102, 115
deleting attributes, 120
SetBaseUri load option, 190
SetElementValue method, 102, 115
SetLineInfo load option, 190
SetValue method, 102, 103
Single operator, 29, 81
SingleOrDefault operator, 82
Skip operator, 55, 86
SkipWhile operator, 55, 86–87
sorting operators, 57–59
OrderBy, 55, 57
OrderByDescending, 55, 58
Reverse operator v., 59
Reverse, 57, 59
OrderByDescending v., 59
ThenBy, 55, 58
ThenByDescending, 55, 58–59
/sprocs, 296
SQL. *See also* LINQ to SQL
database, to XML tree, 145–149
Query Analyzer, 15
Server
query processing, 36

Server Management Studio, 15
Server table, XML data to, 149–152
syntax, LINQ syntax v., 36–37
SQL Metal command-line tool, 296–299
/? option, 297
attribute-based mapping, 202
/code:file, 296
/context:type, 297
/database:name, 296
/dbml:file, 296
/entitybase:type, 297
/functions, 296
Inputfile, 297
/language:language, 297
location, 297
/map:file, 297
/namespace:name, 297
options, 296–297
/password:password, 296
/pluralize, 297
/serialization:option, 297
/server:name, 296
/sprocs, 296
/timeout:timeout, 296
/user:name, 296
/views, 296
SqlDataAdapter, 273–274
standard query operators, 6, 10–12, 33, 53–92
Aggregate, 64
aggregating, 64–68
Aggregate, 64
Average, 54, 64–65
Count, 54, 65
LongCount, 55, 66
Max, 55, 66–67
Min, 55, 67
Sum, 55, 67–68
All, 54, 83–84
Any, 54, 84–85
API v., 53
AsEnumerable, 74
Average, 54, 64–65
Cast, 54, 74–75
categorization, 11
Concat, 63–64
concatenating, 63–64
Contains, 85
conversion, 73–77
AsEnumerable, 74
Cast, 54, 74–75
OfType, 75
ToArray, 75–76
ToDictionary operator, 76
ToList, 76–77
ToLookup, 77
Count, 54, 65
DefaultIfEmpty, 78
defined, 53
Distinct, 54, 68–69, 281
element, 72–82
DefaultIfEmpty, 78
ElementAt, 78–79
ElementAtOrDefault, 79
First, 79
FirstOrDefault, 80
Last, 80
LastOrDefault, 80–81
Single, 29, 81
SingleOrDefault, 82
ElementAt, 78–79
ElementAtOrDefault, 79
Empty, 71–72
equality, 82–83
SequenceEqual, 82–83
example/illustration, 6, 88–92
Except, 71, 281
First, 79
FirstOrDefault, 80
generation, 71–73
Empty, 71–72
Range, 72–73
repeat, 73
GroupBy, 55, 62–63
grouped by function, 54–88
grouping, 62–63
GroupJoin, 55, 59, 60–62
illustration/example, 6, 88–92
intersect, 70–71, 281, 284
join, 55, 59–60, 250
joining, 59–62
Last, 80
LastOrDefault, 80–81

standard query operators *(continued)*
LongCount, 55, 66
Max, 55, 66–67
Min, 55, 67
OfType, 75
OrderBy, 55, 57
OrderByDescending, 55, 58
Reverse operator v., 59
overview, 53–54
partitioning, 86–88
Skip, 55, 86
SkipWhile, 55, 86–87
Take, 55, 87
TakeWhile, 55, 87–88
projection, 55–56
Select, 55–56
SelectMany, 55–56
quantifier, 83–85
All, 54, 83–84
Any, 54, 84–85
Contains, 85
Range, 72–73
repeat, 73
restriction, 57
Reverse, 57, 59
OrderByDescending v., 59
Select, 55–56
select, 11
SelectMany, 55–56
SequenceEqual, 82–83
set, 68–71
Distinct, 54, 68–69, 281
Except, 71, 281
intersect, 70–71, 281, 284
Union, 70, 281
sets, 11
Single, 29, 81
SingleOrDefault, 82
Skip, 55, 86
SkipWhile, 55, 86–87
sorting, 57–59
OrderBy, 55, 57
OrderByDescending, 55, 58, 59
Reverse, 57, 59
ThenBy, 55, 58
ThenByDescending, 55, 58–59
Sum, 55, 67–68
syntax, 33
Take, 55, 87
TakeWhile, 55, 87–88
ThenBy, 55, 58
ThenByDescending, 55, 58–59
ToArray, 75–76
ToDictionary, 76
ToList, 76–77
ToLookup, 77
types, 54
Union, 70, 281
where, 11, 57
<State> element, 114, 115
Storage property, 204, 206
stored procedures
DataContext mapping for, 292–293
mapped, 207–208
for multiple results, 235–240
passing parameters to, 234–235
mapping/calling, 227–240
returning single result, 227–234
StoredProcedure attribute, 207–208, 227
streaming XML documents, 171–177
large, 176–177
XmlReader and, 171
string representation, XName class, 142
strongly typed DataContext, 220–221
SubmitChanges method, 219, 220, 256
Sum operator, 55, 67–68
Suppress value, 269
syntax
LINQ v. SQL, 36–37
method, 45–51, 275
example, 44
query syntax v., 43–44
using, 45–51
query, 43, 45–51, 275
example, 44
using, 45–51
readability, 44
standard query operators, 33
System.Core namespace, 272
System.Data namespace, 199
System.Data.DataSetExtensions namespace, 272

System.Data.Linq, 96
System.Reflection namespace, 233
System.Runtime.CompilerServices namespace, 28
System.Transactions namespace, 267
System.Xml namespace, 12, 95, 199
System.Xml.Linq namespace, 96, 122
System.Xml.Schema, 4
System.Xml.XPath, 4
System.Xml.Xsl, 4

T

Table (of TEntity) class, 302
Table collection, 221
tables, mapping, 203
Take operator, 55, 87
TakeWhile operator, 55, 87–88
TestAnnotation class, 160
TextReader, loading XML from, 108–109
ThenBy operator, 55, 58
ThenByDescending operator, 55, 58–59
ThisKey property, 206
/timeout:timeout, 296
ToArray method, 35
ToArray operator, 75–76
ToDictionary operator, 76
ToList method, 35
ToList operator, 76–77
ToLookup operator, 77
transactions, LINQ to SQL, 267–269
  explicit distributable, 267
  explicit local, 267
    example, 268–269
  illustrations, 267–269
  implicit, 267
TransactionScope class, 267, 269
TransactionScopeOption enumeration, 269
  Required value, 269
  RequiredNew value, 269
  Suppress value, 269
typed DataSets, 278–279
typed XML, 345, 346. *See also* LINQ to XSD
types, LINQ to XML, 167–168. *See also* events, LINQ to XML
  XObjectChange, 168
  XObjectChangeEventArgs, 168
  XObjectChangeEventHandler, 168

U

UDFs. *See* user-defined functions
Union operator, 70, 281
UPDATE function, 293
UpdateCheck property, 204
  Always value, 264
  concurrency conflicts, 263–264
  Never value, 264
  WhenChanged value, 264
updating data
  entity objects, 226
  LINQ to SQL queries, 224–225
user-defined functions (UDFs), 240–243
  mapping/calling, 240–243
/user:name, 296
using directive, 239, 243
using statements, 107, 147

V

ValidateArtifacts, 343
Value property, 186
var keyword, 13, 22, 39
  IEnumerable<T> interface v., 40–41
ViewGeneration, 343
/views, 296
Visual Basic.NET
  anonymous types, 23
  creating XML trees
    LINQ to XML, 128–129
  embedded expressions and, 182–184
  extension methods, 28
  implicitly typed variables, 22
  LINQ to XML features in, 179–195
    example, 191–194
  object intializers, 25–26
  query expressions, 22
  XML in
    accessing, 185–188
    creating, 179–185
    loading, 188–189
    manipulating, with Parse method, 189–191

Visual Studio (earlier versions)
.NET, 18
.NET 2003, 18
97, 17
6.0, 17
2005, 18
Visual Studio 2008, 17–30
download, 21
history/background, 17–18
language-specific LINQ features, 21–29
.NET Framework versions, 20
new features, 18
New Project dialog box, 19–20
start up, 18–19

W

WCF (Windows Communication Foundation), 18
WF (Windows Workflow Foundation), 18
WhenChanged value, 264
where clause, 37
where query operator, 11, 57
whitespace
LINQ to XML and, 121
serializing XML trees and, 139, 140, 141
in XML literals, 184–185
Windows Communication Foundation. *See* WCF
Windows Forms Control Library, 20, 21
Windows Presentation Foundation. *See* WPF
Windows Workflow Foundation. *See* WF
WPF (Windows Presentation Foundation), 18
WriteTo method, 102

X

XAttribute class, 12, 97, 102–104
example, 13
methods, 103
XElement class v., 103
XCData class, 97
XComment class, 97
XComment objects, 105
XContainer class, 97
XDeclaration class, 97–98
XDeclaration objects, 104
XDocument class, 97, 104–107
methods, 106
objects in, 104–105
XDocumentType class, 97
XDocumentType objects, 104
XElement class, 12, 14, 97, 98–102
methods, 100, 101–102
XAttribute class v., 103
XML document construction, 12–13
XElement objects, 104
XLINQ. *See* LINQ to XML
XML. *See also* LINQ to XML
accessing, in Visual Basic, 185–188
creating, in Visual Basic, 179–185
declarations, 97
document construction
XElement, 12–13
document parsing, 4–5
limitations, 4–5, 95, 98
prefixes, 98, 141
streaming documents, 171–177
large, 176–177
typed, 345, 346. See also LINQ to XSD
XML literals, 128, 129, 180–182
creating XML trees, 128–129
embedding expressions, 182–184
embedding queries in, 184, 187
overview, 180–182
whitespace in, 184–185
XML namespaces, 141–143
XML trees
axis methods and, 167
creating, 123–129
C#, 124–128
Visual Basic, 128–129
XML literals, 128–129
modifying/reshaping, 137–139
populating from text, 130–131
Load method, 130–131
Parse method, 130
querying, 132–137
serializing, 139–141
SQL database to, 145–149
to SQL server table, 149–152
insert, 150
update, 151–152

XmlDocument, 4
XmlReader, 4, 102, 131
  LINQ to XML v., 121
  streaming XML and, 171
XmlWriter, 4
XName class, 97
  names, 142
  string representation, 142
XNamespace class, 97
  namespaces, 97, 142
XNode class, 97, 112
  methods
    XML manipulation in LINQ to XML, 112–117
XNodeDocumentOrderComparer class, 97
XNodeEqualityComparer class, 97
XObject class, 97
XObjectChange class, 97
XObjectChange type, 168
XObjectChangeEventArgs class, 97
XObjectChangeEventArgs type, 168
XObjectChangeEventHandler, 97
XObjectChangeEventHandler type, 168
XPath, 12, 14, 95
XProcessingInstruction class, 97
XProcessingInstruction objects, 105
XQuery, 4, 14
XSLT, 4, 14, 95
  LINQ to XML v., 121
XText class, 97